Pronunciation – American English

This dictionary shows pronunciations used by most American speakers. Sometimes more than one pronunciation is shown. For example, many Americans say the first vowel in *data* as /eɪ/, while many others say this vowel as /æ/. We show *data* as /ˈdeɪt̬ə, ˈdæt̬ə/. This means that both pronunciations are possible and are commonly used by educated speakers. We have not, however, shown all possible American pronunciations. For example, *news* is shown only as /nuz/ even though a few Americans might pronounce this word as /nyuz/. The vowels /ɔ/ and /ɑ/ are both shown, but many speakers do not use the sound /ɔ/. These speakers say /ɑ/ in place of /ɔ/, so that *caught* and *cot* are both said as /kɑt/.

Use of the Hyphen

When more than one pronunciation is given for a word, we usually show only the part of the pronunciation that is different from the first pronunciation, replacing the parts that are the same with a hyphen: **economics** /ˌɛkəˈnɑmɪks, ˌikə-/. The hyphen is also used for showing the division between syllables when this might not be clear: **boyish** /ˈbɔɪ-ɪʃ/, **drawing** /ˈdrɔ-ɪŋ/, **clockwise** /ˈklɑk-waɪz/.

Symbols

The symbols used in this dictionary are based on the symbols of the International Phonetic Alphabet (IPA) with a few changes. The symbol /y/, which is closer to English spelling than the /j/ used in the IPA, is used for the first sound in *you* /yu/. Other changes are described in the paragraph **American English Sounds**.

Foreign Words

English pronunciations have been shown for foreign words, even though some speakers may use a pronunciation closer to that of the original language.

Abbreviations

No pronunciations are shown for most abbreviations. This is either because they are not spoken (and are defined as "written abbreviations"), or because they are pronounced by saying the names of the letters, with main stress on the last letter and secondary stress on the first: **VCR** /ˌvi si ˈɑr/. Pronunciations have been shown where an abbreviation is spoken like an ordinary word: **RAM** /ræm/.

W9-CSM-335

Words that are Forms of Main Words

A form of a main word that is a different part of speech may come at the end of the entry for that word. If the related word is pronounced by saying the main word and adding an ending, no separate pronunciation is given. If the addition of the ending causes a change in the pronunciation of the main word, the pronunciation for the related word is given. For example: **impossible** /ɪmˈpɑsəbəl/, **impossibility** /ɪmˌpɑsəˈbɪlət̬i/.

There are some pronunication changes that we do not show at these entries, because they follow regular patterns: (1) When a *-ly* or *-er* ending is added to a main word ending in /-bəl/, /-kəl/, /-pəl/, /-gəl/, or /-dəl/, the /ə/ is usually omitted. For example, **audible** is shown as /ˈɔdəbəl/. When *-ly* is added to it, it becomes **audibly** /ˈɔdəbli/. This difference is not shown. (2) When *-ly* or *-ity* is added to words ending in *-y* /i/, the /i/ becomes /ə/: **angry** /ˈæŋgri/ becomes **angrily** /ˈæŋgrəli/. This is not shown.

Stress

In English words of two or more syllables, at least one syllable is said with more force than the others. The sign /ˈ/ is put before the syllable with the most force. We say it has *main stress*: **person** /ˈpɚsən/, **percent** /pɚˈsɛnt/. Some words also have a stress on another syllable that is less strong than the main stress. We call this *secondary stress*, and the sign /ˌ/ is placed before such a syllable: **personality** /ˌpɚsəˈnælət̬i/, **personify** /ˌpɚˈsɑnəˌfaɪ/. Secondary stress is not usually shown in the second syllable of a two-syllable word, unless it is necessary to show that the second syllable must not be shortened, as in **starlit** /ˈstɑrˌlɪt/ compared to **starlet** /ˈstɑrlɪt/.

Unstressed Vowels

/ə/ and /ɪ/
Many unstressed syllables in American English are pronounced with a very short unclear vowel. This vowel is shown as /ə/ or /ɪ/; however, there is very little difference between them in normal connected speech. For example, the word *affect* /əˈfɛkt/ and *effect* /ɪˈfɛkt/ usually sound the same. The word *rabbit* is shown as /ˈræbɪt/, but it may also be pronounced /ˈræbət/.

/ə/ and /ʌ/
These sounds are very similar. The symbol /ə/ is used in unstressed syllables, and /ʌ/, which

is longer, is used in stressed and secondary stressed syllables. When people speak more quickly, secondary stressed syllables become unstressed so that /ʌ/ may be pronounced as /ə/. For example, *difficult* /ˈdɪfɪˌkʌlt/ and *coconut* /ˈkoʊkəˌnʌt/ may be pronounced as /ˈdɪfɪkəlt/ and /ˈkoʊkənət/. Only the pronunciation with /ʌ/ is shown.

Compound Words with a Space or Hyphen

Many compounds are written with either a space or a hyphen between the parts. When all parts of the compound appear in the dictionary as separate main words, the full pronunciation of the compound is not shown. Only its stress pattern is given. For example: **ˈbus stop**, **ˌtown ˈhall**.

Sometimes a compound contains a main word with an ending. If the main word is in the dictionary and the ending is a common one, only a stress pattern is shown. For example: **ˈwashing maˌchine**. *Washing* is not a main word in the Dictionary, but *wash* is; so only a stress pattern is shown because *-ing* is a common ending. But if any part is not a main word, the *full* pronunciation is given: **helter-skelter** /ˌhɛltɚˈskɛltɚ/.

Stress Shift

Some words may have a different stress pattern according to whether or not they are used directly before a noun. For example, the basic pronunciation of *independent* is /ˌɪndɪˈpɛndənt/, but directly before a noun the main stress may be lost and the earlier seondary stress then becomes the strongest syllable in the word, as in the phrase "an **ˌindependent ˈstate**". We show this possibility by adding the symbol /◂/ after the pronunciation: /ˌɪndɪˈpɛndənt◂/.

Syllabic Consonants

The sounds /n/ and /l/ can be *syllabic*. That is, they can themselves form a syllable, especially when they are at the end of a word (and follow particular consonants, especially /t/ and /d/). For example, in **sudden** /ˈsʌdn/ the /n/ is syllabic; there is no vowel between the /d/ and the /n/, so no vowel is shown. In the middle of a word, a hyphen or stress mark after /n/ or /l/ shows that it is syllabic: **finalist** /ˈfaɪnl-ɪst/ and **catalog** /ˈkæţlˌɔg/ are three-syllable words.

The sound *r* can be either a consonant, /r/, or a vowel, /ɚ/. When /ɚ/ is followed by an unstressed vowel, it may be pronounced as a sequence of two vowels, /ɚ/ plus the following vowel, or as /ə/ followed by a syllable beginning with /r/. For example, the word **coloring** may be pronounced as /ˈkʌlɚɪŋ/ instead of /ˈkʌlərɪŋ/. Only the pronunciation /ˈkʌlərɪŋ/ is shown.

LONGMAN
Advanced American Dictionary

PEARSON
Longman

NEW EDITION

Pearson Education Limited
Edinburgh Gate
Harlow
Essex CM20 2JE
England
and associated companies throughout the world

Visit our website:
http://www.longman.com/dictionaries

© Pearson Education Limited, 2000, 2005, 2007
All rights reserved; no part of this publication may be reproduced, stored in a retrieval system, or transmitted in any form or by any means, electronic, mechanical, photocopying, recording or otherwise, without the prior written permission of the Publishers.

First edition published 2000
Second edition published 2007

Words that the editor have reason to believe constitute trademarks have been described as such. However, neither the presence nor the absence of such a description should be regarded as affecting the legal status of any trademark.

ISBN 978 1 40582 0257 (Cased edition)

978 1 40582 0295 (Paper edition)
978 1 40582 9526 (Cased edition + CD-Rom)
978 1 40582 9540 (Paper edition + CD-Rom)

Set by Letterpart, U.K.
Printed in the U.S.

Contents

Acknowledgments

Director
Della Summers

Projects Director
Mike Mayor

Senior Publisher
Laurence Delacroix

Managing Editor
Stephen Bullon

Editors
Karen Cleveland Marwick
Stephen Handorf
Karen Stern

Lexicographer
Michael Murphy

Project Manager
Alan Savill

Senior Production Editor
Paola Rocchetti

Production Manager
David Gilmour

Corpus Development
Steve Crowdy
Kevin Fox
Duncan Pettigrew

Spoken Corpus Development
University of California at Santa Barbara:
Professor John Du Bois
Professor Wallace Chafe
Professor Sandra Thompson

Computational Linguists
Allan Orsnes
Andrew Roberts

Pronunciation Editors
Rebecca Dauer
Dinah Jackson

Design
Michael Harris

Illustrations
Chris Pavely

Proofreaders
Sandra Anderson
Pat Dunn
Isabel Griffiths
Wendy Lee
Ruth Noble
Daphne Trotter

Technical Support
Trevor Satchell
Kim Lee-Amies

Database Administrator
Denise McKeough

Keyboarder
Pauline Savill

Review of School Content Vocabulary by the following teachers and editors:
Kenneth Nealy, PhD, Linda Hudson, Michael Aleksius, Susan Jellis, Katherine Pate.

The publishers would like to express their gratitude to all the dedicated teachers who have attended focus groups and given their informed feedback on sample text: Christine Tierney, Ann Marie Schlender, Safa Motallebi, Nancy Pauliukoni, Alyce Slater Lentz, Beth Meetsma, Martin Jacobi, Mark Savitt, Steven Dominguez, Barbara Jackson, Robert Caren, Mark Yoffie, Frank Milano and his team, Carole Weisz and her team, Dr Laurie Moody, Liz Iannotti, Carrie Barnard, Suzy Doob, Jennifer Benichou, Peter Hoffman, Laurie Gluck, Sylvia Gonzales, Mary Nance-Tager.

The publishers would also like to thank Averil Coxhead for permission to highlight the Academic Wordlist (AWL, compiled in 2000) in this dictionary. Averil Coxhead is the author of the AWL and a lecturer in English for Academic Purposes at Massey University, New Zealand. For further information on the AWL, go to Averil's Website at: http://language.massey.ac.nz/staff/awl/index.shtm

---

The Publishers and editorial team would like to thank the people who have contributed to the first edition of this dictionary:
Daniel Baron, Elizabeth Beizai, Dileri Borunda Johnston, Rebecca Campbell, Rovert Clevenger, Korey Egge, Tammy Gales, Mark Hamer, Stephen Handorf, Alex Henderson, Wendalyn Nichols, Leslie Redick, Michael Rundell, Ruth Urbom

Reviews of the Dictionary

"The new *Longman Advanced American Dictionary* is a comprehensive yet highly practical resource. I appreciate the distinguishing features that make it so painless to navigate for teachers and students alike: the thoughtfully worded definitions, the illustrative example sentences that help provide a vibrant mental anchor, the Thesaurus boxes that guide developing writers in grasping the nuanced application of more precise, related words, the judicious use of color and bold face to help readers identify critical information, the word choice, grammar, thesaurus and spoken phrase boxes that prompt the self-directed student to engage in a brief, productive language tutorial, the rich and engaging references to North American contexts that help learners develop cultural and pragmatic knowledge.

I commend Longman for developing such a practical, gratifying vocabulary resource."

Dr Kate Kinsella, Teacher Trainer and School Consultant, San Francisco State University, Department of Secondary Education.

"Written specifically for second language learners, the *Longman Advanced American Dictionary* does not merely define words; it also contains a wealth of grammar and usage information. It is an excellent reference for students of English."

Betty Azar, Author of the Azar Grammar Series

"Whereas learners used to search, read, and leave, I believe that they will linger and learn using the new *LAAD*. The single strongest point to me as a language teacher and vocabulary researcher is language used in the definitions. The new *LAAD* excels here. In addition, this dictionary is outstanding in how it handles idioms. In conclusion, the words that come to mind when I think about this new dictionary are usable, accessible, and comprehensible."

Keith S. Folse, Ph.D., Coordinator, MA TESOL Program, University of Central Florida

"The *Longman Advanced American Dictionary* provides the kind of in-depth information a learner needs and the range of information is well organized and easy to use. The *Longman Advanced American Dictionary* takes the lead in two important ways. First, it makes a strong effort to cover not only individual words, but also the phraseology and collocations that research has found to be ever-present in language. Second, written discourse is lexically different from spoken in many ways, and the dictionary highlights many of the phrases particular to spoken discourse. The attached CD-ROM increases the value of this resource through introducing sound for pronunciation practice, and the numerous exercises provide a range of practice opportunities.

Norbert Schmitt, Reader in Applied Linguistics, Nottingham University
Diane Schmitt, Senior Lecturer in EFL/TESOL, Nottingham Trent University
Authors of *Focus on Vocabulary: Mastering the Academic Word List*, Longman.

"I am especially happy to see the enhancement of vocabulary building elements like the Thesaurus boxes and the expanded usage notes that will make it easier for students to locate and ultimately try new words. By making the information easier to find, students will reach for this dictionary more often because their searches will be shorter and more successful.

I will continue to recommend this dictionary enthusiastically."

Laurie Gluck, Department of Education and Language Acquisition, LaGuardia Community College

"I think the examples are excellent – this is what we go through in the classroom when we explain a lexical item. The Thesaurus boxes are fantastic. Labeling academic words is truly important for students, who need to be familiar with the distinction between academic words and casual language. The CD-ROM is an excellent tool. This edition seems even more useful to our students."

Elizabeth Iannotti, Academic Coordinator, The English Language Center, LaGuardia Community College

Key to the Dictionary

Dots show how words are divided into syllables.

af•fec•tion•ate /ə'fɛkʃənɪt/ *adj.* showing in a gentle way that you love someone: *an affectionate hug* | *affectionate children* | +**toward** *Jo is always very affectionate toward him.* —**affectionately** *adv.*

Pronunciation is shown in the International Phonetic Alphabet.

ar•got /'ɑrgət, -goʊ/ *n.* [C,U] ENG. LANG. ARTS expressions used by a particular group of people SYN **jargon**: *teenage argot*

Parts of speech – verb, noun, adjective, preposition etc. – are shown in italics.

am•ber /'æmbɚ/ *n.* [U] **1** a yellowish brown substance used to make jewelry **2** a yellowish brown color [**Origin:** 1300–1400 Old French, Medieval Latin *ambra*, from Arabic *anbar* **substance obtained from the body organs of whales**] —**amber** *adj.*

Words that are spelled the same but have different parts of speech are treated as homographs and have separate entries.

a•bode[1] /ə'boʊd/ *n.* [C] FORMAL or HUMOROUS someone's home

abode[2] *v.* a past tense of ABIDE

If a word has more than one meaning, each meaning is shown by a number in dark type.

annual[2] Ac *n.* [C] **1** BIOLOGY a plant that grows from a seed, has flowers, and dies all in one year → see also BIENNIAL **2** a YEARBOOK **3** a book, especially for children, that is produced once a year with the same title but different stories, pictures etc.

If a word can be spelled in two different ways, both spellings are shown.

ASAP, a.s.a.p. /ˌeɪ ɛs eɪ 'pi/ *n.* the abbreviation of "as soon as possible": *Call him ASAP.*

Meanings are explained in clear, simple language, using the 2000-word Longman Defining Vocabulary whenever possible.

a•bra•sive[1] /ə'breɪsɪv, -zɪv/ *adj.* **1** seeming rude or unkind in the way you behave toward people, especially because you say what you think very directly: *an abrasive personality* **2** having a rough surface, especially one that can be used to clean other surfaces by rubbing: *a dry abrasive cleaning pad* —**abrasively** *adv.*

Words that are not in the Defining Vocabulary are shown in small capital letters.

arch•er /'ɑrtʃɚ/ *n.* [C] someone who shoots ARROWS from a BOW

Useful, natural-sounding examples, are all based on information from the Longman Corpus Network.

Word origins tell you in which century a word entered the language, and which foreign language or languages it came from.

appeal[2] W3 *v.* **1** [I] to make a serious public request for help, money, information etc.: **appeal (to sb) for sth** *The police are appealing to the public for information.* | *The Pope appealed for an end to the violence.* | **appeal to sb to do sth** *The water company appealed to everyone to reduce the amount of water used.* **2** [I,T] to make a formal request to a court or someone in authority asking for a decision to be changed: *The defendant is planning to appeal.* | *They have the right to appeal the decision to a higher court.* **3 appeal to sb's common sense/better nature/sense of honor etc.** to try to persuade someone to do something by reminding them that it is a sensible, good, wise etc. thing to do [**Origin:** 1300–1400 Old French *apeler* **to accuse, appeal,** from Latin *appellere* **to drive to**]

appeal to sb *phr. v.* to seem attractive and interesting to someone: *The idea didn't appeal to me much.* | *The magazine is intended to appeal to working women in their 20s and 30s.*

Derived words are shown at the end of the entry when the meaning is clear from the definition of the main form.

am•biv•a•lent /æm'bɪvələnt/ *adj.* not sure whether you want or like something or not: +**about** *Many members were ambivalent about the protest.* [**Origin:** 1900–2000 *ambi-* + *-valent* **having a particular value**] —**ambivalence** *n.* [U] —**ambivalently** *adv.*

References to other words and phrases, and to pictures and Usage Notes, are given.

an•te[1] /'ænti/ *n.* **up/raise the ante** to increase your demands or try to get more things from a situation, even though this involves more risks: *Sanctions against the dictatorship upped the ante considerably in the crisis.* → see also PENNY ANTE

business for them: *I'm acting on behalf of my client, Mr. Harding.*
6 act as sth to do a particular job for a short time, for example while the usual person is absent: *DeConcini acted as host at the meeting.* → see also ACTING[1]
act sth ↔ **out** *phr. v.* **1** if a group of people act out a real or imaginary event, they show how it happened or could happen by pretending to be the people involved in it: *Computer games allow players to act out their fantasies.* **2** to express your feelings about something through your behavior or actions, especially when you have been feeling angry or nervous: *Children who act out violently have often been abused.* | *Teenagers can act out their anxieties in various aggressive ways.*
act up *phr. v.* INFORMAL **1** if children act up, they behave badly: *He's a tough kid who acts up a lot.* **2** if a machine or part of your body acts up, it does not work correctly: *The copy machine is acting up again.*

Phrasal verbs are listed in alphabetical order directly after the entry for their main verb. Separability of phrasal verbs is shown by the arrow. In the phrasal verb **act out**, the arrow means that you can say that you *act out* an event or *act* an event *out*. Note that if you use a pronoun, you can put the pronoun between the two parts of a phrasal verb (*act it out*), but you cannot put a pronoun after the second part of such a phrasal verb (~~*act out it*~~). There is no arrow shown in the entry for **act up**, which means that you cannot put anything between *act* and *up*.

'age ˌlimit *n.* [C] the youngest or oldest age at which you are allowed to do something: **raise/lower the age limit to 16/18/21 etc.** *They raised the age limit for buying tobacco to 18.*

Compound words are shown as headwords and their stress patterns are shown.

at·trib·ut·a·ble /ə'trɪbyət̬əbəl/ Ac *adj.* [not before noun] FORMAL **attributable to sth** likely to be caused by something: *deaths that are attributable to air pollution*

Grammatical information is shown in bold.

armchair[2] *adj.* **an armchair traveler/quarterback/critic etc.** someone who talks or reads about being a traveler, watches a lot of sports on television etc., but does not have any real experience of doing it

Phrases and idioms are shown and given their own definitions.

ar·gu·ment /'ɑrgyəmənt/ S2 W2 *n.* **1** [C] a situation in which two or more people disagree, often angrily: **+with** *I broke the vase during an argument with my husband.* | **+about/over** *an argument over who was at fault* | *Henning told the police she and her husband* ***had an argument*** *before he left.* | *I* ***got into an argument*** *with the other driver.* | *Shelton and the woman had a* ***heated argument*** (=very angry argument). **2** [C] a set of reasons that show that something is true or untrue, right or wrong etc.: *Rose presented a good argument.* | **+for/against** *a powerful argument against smoking* | *the* ***arguments in favor*** *of gun control* | **argument that** *the familiar argument that poverty breeds crime* **3** [U] the act of disagreeing or questioning something: *Nathan accepted the decision* ***without argument.*** | *I'm not sure that's an accurate description, but* ***for the sake of argument*** (=in order to discuss all the possibilities) *I'll accept it.*

The 3000 most frequent words in spoken and written English are highlighted in red. This shows you the important words you need to know. S1 S2 S3 show which are the most frequent 1000/2000/3000 words in spoken English. W1 W2 W3 show which are the most frequent 1000/2000/3000 words in written English.

Collocations – words that are often used together – are shown in bold in an example or followed by an explanation.

anchor[2] *v.*
1 BOAT [I,T] to lower the anchor on a ship or boat to hold it in one place: *Three tankers were anchored in the harbor.*
2 TV NEWS [T] to be the person who reads the news and introduces reports on TV: *The new hour-long program is anchored by Mark McEwen.*
3 FASTEN [T usually passive] to fasten something firmly so that it cannot move: *The panel was firmly anchored by two large bolts.*
4 SUPPORT [T] to provide a feeling of support, safety, or help for someone or an organization: *Stevens anchors the team's defense.*
5 be anchored in sth to be strongly related to a particular system, way of life etc.: *Her personal ideals were anchored in her Irish heritage.*

Signposts in longer entries help you to find the meaning that you need.

ap·pend /ə'pɛnd/ Ac *v.* [T] FORMAL to add something to a piece of writing [**Origin:** 1600–1700 French *appendre*, from Latin *appendere* **to weigh**]

Labels show the contexts or situations a word is typically used.

Words that have unpredictable spellings in plurals, across tenses, or in the comparative and superlative are shown in bold after the part of speech.

a·bet /ə'bɛt/ *v.* **abetted, abetting** [T] to help someone do something wrong or illegal → see also **aid and abet** at AID[2] (2)

an·a·pest /'ænə,pɛst/ *n.* [C] ENG. LANG. ARTS part of a line of poetry consisting of two short sounds then one long one

Words that have specialized meanings in specific subject areas are labeled.

,angular mo'mentum *n.* [C,U] PHYSICS the energy contained in an object that is turning in a circular movement around a central point, calculated by multiplying the object's mass by its angular velocity

The label Ac indicates that a word is included in the *Academic Word List*. These are important words which students need to be able to understand when reading English, and also to use when writing academic assignments.

a·nal·o·gy /ə'næləd͡ʒi/ Ac *n. plural* **analogies** [C,U] a comparison between two situations, processes etc. that seem similar, or the process of making this comparison: **+with/to/between** *analogies between human and animal behavior* | **draw/make an analogy** *Norma drew an analogy between childbirth and the creative process.* | *Dr. Wood explained the movement of light* ***by analogy with*** (=using an analogy of) *the movement of water.*

an·i·mus /'ænəməs/ *n.* [singular, U] FORMAL strong dislike or hatred SYN **hostility** SYN **animosity**

Words with similar meanings (synonyms) and words with opposite meanings (antonyms) are shown after the definition.

ac·cept·ance /ək'sɛptəns/ *n.* **1** [U] official agreement to take something that you have been offered OPP **refusal**: **+of** *Acceptance of economic aid from Western countries will speed up the country's recovery.* **2** [singular, U] the act of agreeing that an idea, explanation, activity etc. is right or true OPP **rejection**: **+of** *the growing acceptance of gay rights* | *Upper management's acceptance of the marketing plan is crucial.* | **gain/find acceptance** *Use of the drug has gained acceptance in the U.S.*

an·gry /'æŋgri/ S2 W2 *adj. comparative* **angrier**, *superlative* **angriest**

THESAURUS

annoyed a little angry: *I get annoyed with the kids when they don't listen.*
irritated feeling annoyed and not patient with people or things: *I was getting irritated by all the noise.*
furious/livid very angry: *I am furious at my father for refusing to let me go.*
mad INFORMAL very angry: *Mom was mad at me for not cleaning up.*
in a bad mood feeling a little angry for a period of time: *When I'm in a bad mood, I like to be on my own.*
outraged very angry and shocked, especially because you think something is unfair or wrong: *People were outraged when they raised parking fees by 25%.*
→ HAPPY, SAD

2 angry with/at yourself feeling strongly that you wish

Thesaurus Boxes explain the differences between words that are similar in meaning, or bring together words that belong to a particular topic.

an·swer[1] /'ænsɚ/ S1 W1 *v.*

THESAURUS

answer to say something to someone when he or she has asked you a question or spoken to you: *She reluctantly answered his question.*
reply to answer someone – used especially in written English: *"Nobody knows," Rosen replied.*
respond FORMAL to answer someone, especially in a detailed way: *Has anyone responded to your letter?*

2 TEST [I,T] to write or say the answer to a question in a

Longman Academic e-Tutor CD-ROM

The *Longman Academic e-Tutor CD-ROM* helps students prepare for exams such as SAT®, TOEFL® and TOEIC® with multiple-choice exam questions. Students can track their progress in the Self Assessment Center and choose their own personal Study Plan, helping them to improve their chances of exam success.

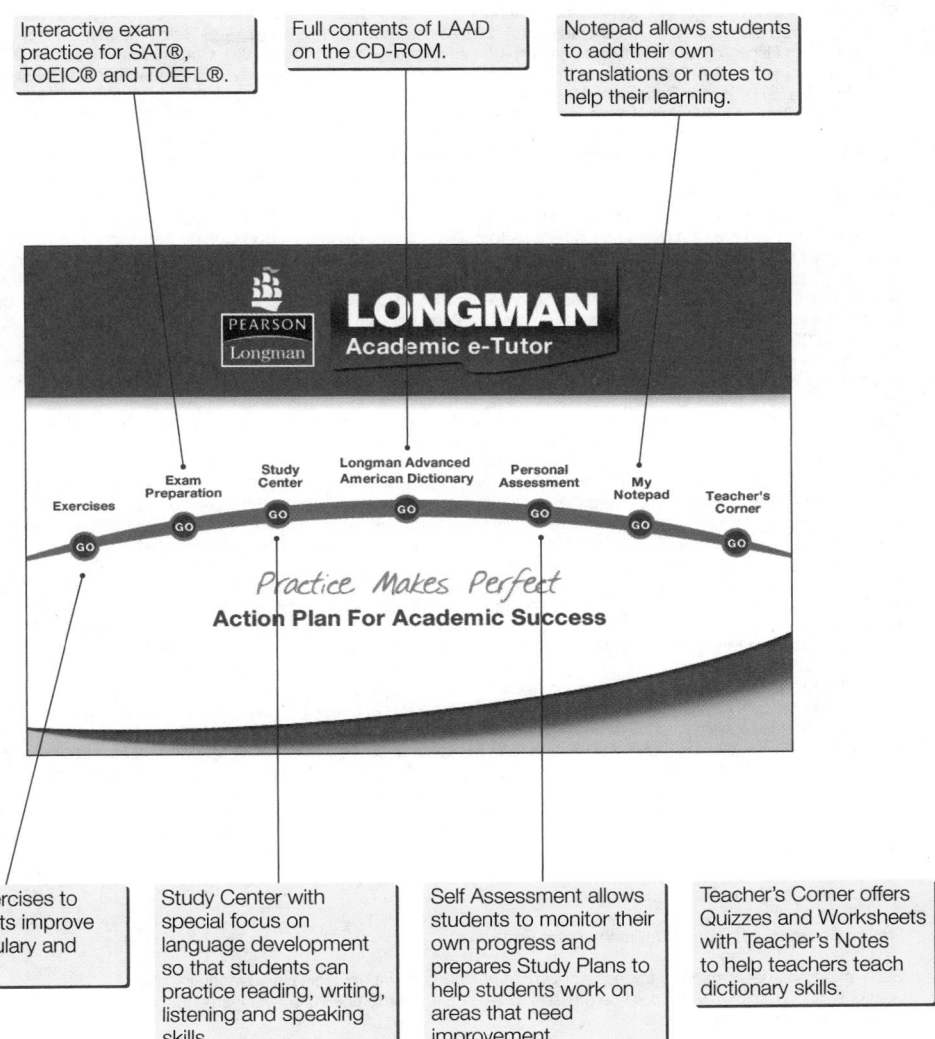

Interactive exam practice for SAT®, TOEIC® and TOEFL®.

Full contents of LAAD on the CD-ROM.

Notepad allows students to add their own translations or notes to help their learning.

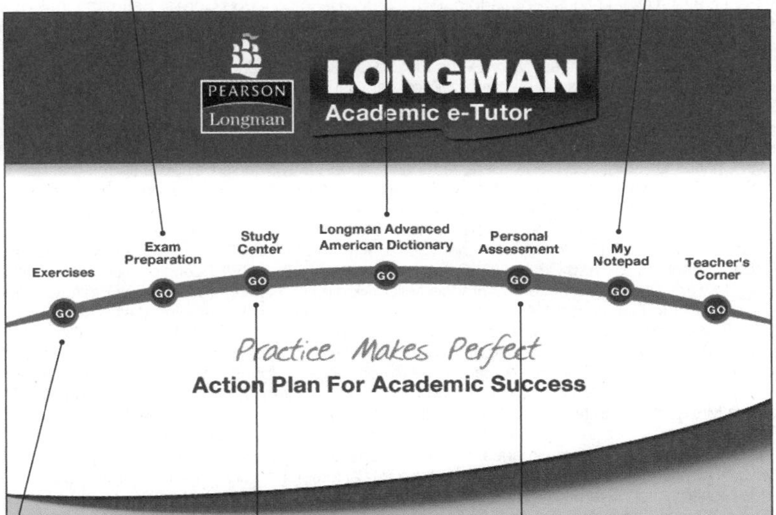

General exercises to help students improve their vocabulary and grammar.

Study Center with special focus on language development so that students can practice reading, writing, listening and speaking skills.

Self Assessment allows students to monitor their own progress and prepares Study Plans to help students work on areas that need improvement.

Teacher's Corner offers Quizzes and Worksheets with Teacher's Notes to help teachers teach dictionary skills.

Picture Credits

The publisher would like to thank the following for their kind permission to reproduce their photographs:

(Key: b-bottom; c-centre; l-left; r-right; t-top)

15 Corbis: (r). PunchStock: Blend Images (l). 40 Corbis: Bettmann. 42 Corbis: Corbis Sygma / Cardinale Stephane. 55 Corbis. 74 Getty Images: Hulton Archive / Stringer. 113 PunchStock: Digital Vision. 134 Getty Images: Time & Life Pictures / Alfred Eisenstaedt (t). Rex Features: (b). 201 Alamy Images: Nigel Hicks. 223 Getty Images: Time & Life Pictures / Ray Fisher (cl). 250 Getty Images: Time & Life Pictures / Ralph Crane. 301 Corbis: John Heseltine. 302 Corbis: Archivo Iconografico, S.A.. 307 Science Photo Library Ltd: Detlev Van Ravenswaay. 372 Ardea: Francois Gohier (tl). Corbis: Bettmann (br). 378 Corbis: Bettmann. 400 Alamy Images: Mary Evans Picture Library. 412 Getty Images: Hulton Archive / Stringer. 440 TopFoto: Topham Picturepoint. 499 Redferns Music Picture Library: Peter Still. 501 Corbis: Bettmann. 522 Rex Features. 608 Corbis. 637 Rex Features: Sipa Press (tr). 664 Alamy Images: Dinodia Images. 682 Corbis. 702 World Pictures / Photoshot Holdings. 755 Rex Features: Everett Collection (l); Marc Sharratt (r) 756 Alamy Images: Pictorial Press Ltd. 771 Rex Features: Everett Collection. 792 Alamy Images: Joern Sackermann. 829 Alamy Images: Mica. 865 Getty Images: Ezra Shaw. 872 Rex Features: Frederic Aranda (l). 875 Corbis: Bettmann. 876 Corbis: Bettmann (l). 879 Alamy Images: ImageState / Martin Ruegner. 881 Rex Features: Everett Collection. 921 Getty Images: Time & Life Pictures / Ray Fisher. 929 Alamy Images: Popperfoto. 942 Corbis: Bettmann. 969 Corbis: Bettmann (r). 973 Alamy Images: Oleg Shpak. 991 Corbis: Bettmann. 1071 Alamy Images: Visual Arts Library (London). 1072 Alamy Images: Andre Jenny (cr). 1136 Alamy Images: Mary Evans Picture Library. 1151 Corbis: Reuters / William Philpott. 1159 Alamy Images: Visual Arts Library (London). 1193 Alamy Images: Mary Evans Picture Library. 1219 Bridgeman Art Library Ltd: Silver over Black, White, Yellow and Red, 1948 (oil & enamel on paper laid on canvas) Pollock, Jackson (1912-56) / © ARS, NY and DACS, London 2007. 1376 Alamy Images: Popperfoto. 1389 Corbis: Richard T. Nowitz. 1396 Corbis: Bettmann. 1483 Corbis. 1504 Action Plus Sports Images: Steve Bardens. 1558 Corbis: Bettmann. 1708 Corbis. 1714 Corbis: Bettmann. 1838 Alamy Images: Jake Corke. A23 Corbis: MAPS.com. A24 Alamy Images: ImageState / Pictor International (Las Vegas); PCL (bc). Corbis: Charles O'Rear (steel plant); Gerald French (Silicon Valley); Louie Psihoyos (farm); Macduff Everton (tl); Reuters / Mike Segar (Stock Exchange). Getty Images: Hulton Archive / Bernard Gotfryd (br); Larry W. Smith (tr); NASA (bl). A25 Alamy Images: Popperfoto (Einstein) (br). Corbis: NASA / Roger Ressmeyer (John Glenn). Getty Images: Hulton Archive / Stringer (George Eastman) (bc) (bl); Hulton Archive / Stock Montage (tc). Rex Features: (tr). Science & Society Picture Library: Science Museum (Eli Whitney); Science Museum (tl). TopFoto: HIP / Ann Ronan Picture Library (Franklin); Topham Picturepoint (Henry Ford). A26 Corbis: (tl); Bettmann (Lindbergh) (br); DPA / Lennie Falcon (bc). Getty Images: Aurora / Todd Bigelow (tr); Time & Life Pictures / Francis Miller (Martin Luther King) (NATO). Rex Features: Sipa Press (Woodstock). Science Photo Library Ltd: NASA (moon) (bl). TopFoto: Topham Picturepoint (Wall Street Crash); Topham Picturepoint (tc). A27 akg-images Ltd: (J. S. Sargent). Bridgeman Art Library Ltd: Campbell's Soup Cans, 1965 (silkscreen on canvas) , Warhol, Andy (1930–87) / © Licensed by the Andy Warhol Foundation for the Visual Arts, Inc / ARS, New York and DACS, London 2007 (Andy Warhol); False Start, 1959 (oil on canvas), Johns, Jasper (b.1930) / © VAGA, New York / DACS, London 2007 (Jasper Johns). Corbis: © Bettmann / © Estate of Grant Wood / DACS, London / VAGA, New York 2007 (br); Brooklyn Museum / ARS, NY and DACS, London 2007 (tl); Burstein Collection / © ARS, NY and DACS, London 2007 (bl); © Christie's Images / © Kate Rothko Prizel & Christopher Rothko ARS, NY and DACS, London 2007 (Mark Rothko); Francis G. Mayer (tr). A28 Alamy Images: Stock Montage, Inc. / Tom Neiman (tl); SUNNYphotography.com (tr). Corbis: Buddy Mays (br); Charles Mauzy (bl); Nik Wheelere (Crazy Horse); Reuters / Mike Segar (tc). Getty Images: Christian Science Monitor / John Nordell (MBTA); Time & Life Pictures / George Skadding (Roosevelt). PunchStock: Stockbyte Platinum (Golden Gate). A29 Action Plus Sports Images: Leo Mason (bl); Mike Hewitt (paragliding); Zinou Guiri (kite surfing). Buzz Pictures: Dan Burton (tc); Neale Haynes (tr) (br). Rex Features: (tl); Image Source (snowboarding). A30 Alamy Images: Stock Connection Distribution / Steve Gottlieb (tc). Corbis: (thunderstorm); David Sailors (floods); Ed Kashi (fires); Galen Rowell (avalanche). Getty Images: John Barr (tr). PhotoEdit Inc.: Dennis MacDonald (tl); Mary Steinbacher (br). PunchStock: Digital Vision (hurricane). STILL Pictures The Whole Earth Photo Library: BIOS Gunther Michel (bl)

All other images © Hemera Photo Objects

Picture Research by: Sarah Purtill and Louise Edgeworth

Every effort has been made to trace the copyright holders and we apologise in advance for any unintentional omissions. We would be pleased to insert the appropriate acknowledgement in any subsequent edition of this publication.

A,a

A¹ /eɪ/ *n. plural* **A's** **1** also **a** *plural* **a's** **a)** the first letter of the English alphabet **b)** a sound represented by this letter **2** [C] the best GRADE that a student can get in a class or on a test: *an A on the test* | *He got* ***straight A's*** (=all A grades) *in high school.* **3** ENG. LANG. ARTS **a)** [C,U] the sixth note in the musical SCALE of C MAJOR **b)** [U] the musical KEY based on this note **4 an A student** someone who regularly gets the best GRADES possible for their work in school or college **5 from A to B** used to talk about getting from one place to another in the easiest or most basic way: *I just need a car to get me from A to B.* **6 (from) A to Z** describing, including, or knowing everything about a subject: *The book is an A to Z of French cooking.* **7** [U] a common type of blood

A² the written abbreviation of AMP

a /ə; *strong* eɪ/ S1 W1 also **an** *indefinite article, determiner* **1** used before a noun that names something or someone that has not been mentioned before, or that the person you are talking to does not know about → see also THE: *A new Star Trek movie is out.* | *We just bought a new sofa.* **2 a)** used before a noun that is one of a particular group or class of people or things: *She's an accountant.* **b)** used before someone's family name to show that they belong to that family: *He's a McGregor all right – look at his eyes!* **3 a)** one: *a thousand dollars* | *Do you want a piece of cake?* | *Wait a minute.* **b) a lot/a few/a little etc.** used before some words that express an amount of something: *A few people arrived late.* | *They've spent a great deal of money on the house.* **4 twice a week/$10 a day etc.** two times each week, $10 each day etc. SYN **per**: *"Time" magazine is delivered once a week.* | *The pay is $6.35 an hour.* **5** used before a noun to mean all things of that type: *A square has four sides* (=all squares have four sides). **6** used before two nouns that are mentioned together so often that they are thought of as one thing: *a needle and thread* | *a cup and saucer* **7 a)** used before singular nouns, especially words for actions, meaning one example of that action: *Can I have a look?* **b)** used before the -ing form of verbs when they are used as nouns: *a loud screeching of brakes* **c)** used before an UNCOUNTABLE noun when other information about the noun is added by an adjective or phrase: *There was a certain beauty to the scene.* | *a coarseness in his manner* **8** used before an UNCOUNTABLE noun to mean a type of it: *They make a delicious cheese that's worth trying.* **9** used before the name of a painter, artist etc. meaning a particular painting, SCULPTURE etc. by that person: *Is it a Monet?* **10** used before a name to mean having the same qualities as that person or thing: *He's like a modern Dickens.* **11 a)** used before someone's name when you do not know who they are: *A Mrs. Barnett is waiting for you.* **b)** used before names of days, events in the year etc. to mean a particular one: *It will certainly be a winter to remember.* **12** used after "such," "what," "rather," and "many" to emphasize what you are saying: *What a great idea!* | *She's such a cutie.*

a-¹ /ə/ *prefix* **1** in a particular condition or way: *alive* (=living) | *Read it aloud, please* (=in a voice that others can hear). **2** LITERARY or OLD-FASHIONED used to show that someone or something is in or on something, or at a place: *abed* (=in bed) | *afar* (=far away) | *atop* (=on top of something)

a-² /eɪ, æ/ *prefix* showing the opposite or the absence of something SYN **not** SYN **without**: *atypically* (=not typically) | *amoral* (=not moral)

A-1 /eɪ 'wʌn/ *adj.* OLD-FASHIONED very good or completely healthy, sometimes used in the names of companies: *He has an A-1 credit rating.* | *A-1 Window Cleaners*

AA /eɪ 'eɪ/ *n.* [C] **1 Associate of Arts** a college degree given after two years of study, usually at a COMMUNITY COLLEGE **2** ALCOHOLICS ANONYMOUS

AAA /ˌeɪ eɪ 'eɪ, ˌtrɪpəl 'eɪ/ **American Automobile Association** an organization for people who own cars

aah /ɑ/ *interjection* another spelling of AH

aard·vark /'ɑrdvɑrk/ *n.* [C] a large animal from southern Africa that has a very long nose and eats small insects [**Origin:** 1700–1800 Afrikaans **earth-pig**]

aargh /ɑrg, ɚ/ *interjection* INFORMAL used to show that you are angry, disappointed, annoyed etc.: *Aargh, this thing is so heavy!*

Aar·on /'ærən, 'ɛr-/, **Hank** /hæŋk/ (1934–) a U.S. baseball player famous for hitting more HOME RUNS than Babe Ruth

AARP /ˌeɪ eɪ ɑr 'pi/ → see AMERICAN ASSOCIATION OF RETIRED PERSONS

AB /eɪ 'bi/ *n.* [U] BIOLOGY a common type of blood

ABA /ˌeɪ bi 'eɪ/ → see AMERICAN BAR ASSOCIATION

a·back /ə'bæk/ *adv.* **be taken aback** to be very surprised or shocked by something: *Shulman was taken aback by the survey results.*

ab·a·cus /'æbəkəs, ə'bæ-/ *n.* [C] MATH a wooden frame with small BEADS used for COUNTING [**Origin:** 1300–1400 Latin, Greek *abax* **flat piece of stone**]

ab·a·lo·ne /ˌæbə'louni/ *n.* [C,U] a type of SHELLFISH that is used as food and whose shell contains MOTHER-OF-PEARL

a·ban·don¹ /ə'bændən/ Ac W2 *v.* [T] **1** to leave someone, especially someone you are responsible for: *The nine-year-old boy was abandoned by his alcoholic father.* **2** to go away from a place, vehicle etc., permanently, especially because the situation makes it impossible for you to stay: *The suspect abandoned the car in an alley.* | *The volcano eruption forced the U.S. to abandon Clark Air Force Base.* **3** to stop doing something because there are too many problems and it is impossible to continue: *They finally had to* ***abandon*** *their search* ***efforts.*** | **abandon a plan/project/program etc.** *Both countries were forced to abandon their plans to develop nuclear weapons.* **4** to stop having a particular idea, belief, or attitude: *Education leaders have abandoned their commitment to affordable college education.* | *Rescuers* ***abandoned*** *all* ***hope of*** *finding any more survivors of the crash.* **5 abandon yourself to sth** LITERARY to feel an emotion so strongly that you let it control you completely **6 abandon ship** to leave a ship because it is sinking [**Origin:** 1300–1400 Old French *abandoner* **to surrender**, from *a bandon* **into someone's power**] **—abandonment** *n.* [U]

abandon² Ac *n.* [U] **with reckless/wild abandon** in a careless or uncontrolled way, without thinking or caring about what you are doing: *Hamilton spent the company's money with reckless abandon.*

a·ban·doned /ə'bændənd/ Ac *adj.* **1** an abandoned building, car, boat etc. has been left completely by the people who owned it and is not used anymore: *an abandoned warehouse* | *The truck was later found, abandoned.* **2** someone who is abandoned has been left completely alone by the person who was taking care of them, who is not coming back: *an abused and abandoned child* **3** LITERARY behaving in a wild and uncontrolled way

a·base /ə'beɪs/ *v.* **abase yourself** to behave in a way that shows you accept that someone has complete power over you **—abasement** *n.* [U]

a·bashed /ə'bæʃt/ *adj.* [not before noun] embarrassed or ashamed because you have done something wrong or stupid: *Both girls looked down, abashed.*

a·bate /ə'beɪt/ *v.* [I,T] FORMAL to become less strong or decrease, or to make something do this: *Public anger does not appear to be abating.* **—abatement** *n.* [U]

ab·bess /'æbəs/ *n.* [C] a woman who is in charge of a CONVENT (=religious institution for women)

ab·bey /'æbi/ *n. plural* **abbeys** [C] a large church, especially one with buildings next to it where MONKS and NUNS live or used to live [**Origin:** 1200–1300 Old French *abaïe*, from Late Latin *abbas*, from Aramaic *abba* **father**]

ab·bot /ˈæbət/ *n.* [C] a man who is in charge of a MONASTERY (=place where a group of MONKS live)

abbr. also **abbrev.** the written abbreviation of "abbreviation"

ab·bre·vi·ate /əˈbriviˌeɪt/ *v.* [T] to make a word or expression shorter by not including letters or by using only the first letter of each word: *Extraterrestrial* ***is often abbreviated as*** *E.T.* [**Origin:** 1400–1500 Late Latin, past participle of *abbreviare*, from Latin *brevis* **short**]

ab·bre·vi·at·ed /əˈbriviˌeɪt̬ɪd/ *adj.* made shorter by not including letters or not including parts of a story, statement, event etc.: *an abbreviated version of the story*

ab·bre·vi·a·tion /əˌbriviˈeɪʃən/ *n.* **1** [C] a short form of a word or expression: **+of/for** *TV is the abbreviation of "television."* **2** [U] the act of abbreviating something

ABC /ˌeɪ bi ˈsi/ *n.* [U] **American Broadcasting Company** one of the national television companies in the U.S.

ABCs /ˌeɪ bi ˈsiz/ *n.* **1** [plural] the letters of the English alphabet as taught to children: *Do you know* ***your*** *ABCs?* **2 the ABCs of sth** the basic facts about a particular subject: *the ABCs of your computer*

ab·di·cate /ˈæbdɪˌkeɪt/ *v.* **1 abdicate responsibility/authority/leadership etc.** FORMAL to refuse to be responsible for something, be in control of something etc., when you should be or were before: *The federal government has abdicated its responsibility in dealing with housing needs.* **2** [I,T] to give up the position of being king or queen **3** [T] to officially give up an important government position or responsibility: **abdicate sth to sb/sth** *The city's elected officials seem to have abdicated their power to appointed staff.* [**Origin:** 1500–1600 Latin, past participle of *abdicare*, from *ab-* **away, off** + *dicare* **to say publicly**] —**abdication** /ˌæbdɪˈkeɪʃən/ *n.* [C,U]

ab·do·men /ˈæbdəmən/ *n.* [C] BIOLOGY **1** the part of your body between your chest and legs which contains your stomach **2** the back part of an insect's body, joined to the THORAX —**abdominal** /æbˈdɑmənl/ *adj.*: *abdominal cramps*

ab·duct /əbˈdʌkt, æb-/ *v.* [T] to take someone away by force SYN **kidnap**: **+from** *Lawson was abducted from her home.* [**Origin:** 1600–1700 Latin, past participle of *abducere*, from *ab-* **away** + *ducere* **to lead**] —**abduction** /əbˈdʌkʃən/ *n.* [C,U]

ab·duc·tee /ˌæbdʌkˈti, əbˌdʌkˈti/ *n.* [C] someone who has been abducted

ab·duc·tor /əbˈdʌktɚ/ *n.* [C] someone who abducts someone else

Ab·dul-Jab·bar /æbˌdʊl dʒəˈbɑr/**, Ka·reem** /kəˈrim/ (1947–) a U.S. basketball player, who is considered one of the best players ever

a·bed /əˈbɛd/ *adj.* [not before noun] OLD-FASHIONED in bed

Ab·e·lard /ˈæbəˌlɑrd/**, Peter** (1079–1142) a French PHILOSOPHER and THEOLOGIAN who used the methods of ancient Greek philosophers in his study of religion

ab·er·rant /ˈæbərənt, əˈbɛrənt/ *adj.* FORMAL not usual or normal SYN **abnormal**: *aberrant behavior*

a·ber·ra·tion /ˌæbəˈreɪʃən/ *n.* [C,U] **1** an action or event that is different from what usually happens or what someone usually does: *a temporary aberration in our foreign policy* | *a mental aberration* **2** a fault in the curved glass of a mirror or LENS, which produces an image that is not clear or has colors around the edges: *spherical aberration* | *chromatic aberrations* —**aberrational** *adj.*

a·bet /əˈbɛt/ *v.* **abetted, abetting** [T] to help someone do something wrong or illegal → see also **aid and abet** at AID[2] (2)

a·bey·ance /əˈbeɪəns/ *n.* **in abeyance** something such as a custom, rule, or system that is in abeyance is not being used at the present time: *The law is being* ***held in abeyance*** *until the court makes a decision about it.*

ab·hor /əbˈhɔr, æb-/ *v.* **abhorred** [T not in progressive] FORMAL to hate a type of behavior or way of thinking, especially because you think it is morally wrong: *I abhor discrimination of any kind.*

ab·hor·rence /əbˈhɔrəns, -ˈhɑr-/ *n.* [U] FORMAL a deep feeling of hatred toward something

ab·hor·rent /əbˈhɔrənt/ *adj.* FORMAL something that is abhorrent is completely unacceptable because it seems morally wrong SYN **repugnant**: **+to** *The practice of terrorism is abhorrent to the civilized world.*

a·bide /əˈbaɪd/ *v.* OLD-FASHIONED **1 sb can't abide sb/sth** used to say that someone dislikes someone or something very much because they are annoying: *I can't abide the idea of them getting married.* **2** [I always + adv./prep.] *past tense* **abode** /əˈboʊd/ to live somewhere

abide by sth *phr. v.* to accept and obey a decision, rule, agreement etc., even though you may not agree with it: *Tenants must abide by the rules of the mobile home park.*

a·bid·ing /əˈbaɪdɪŋ/ *adj.* an abiding feeling or belief continues for a long time and is not likely to change: *an abiding belief in the power of justice*

a·bil·i·ty /əˈbɪlət̬i/ S2 W1 *n. plural* **abilities** [C,U] **1** the state of being able to do something: *the gradual loss of physical ability* | **ability to do sth** *The goal is to improve the company's ability to compete.* | *Linda* ***has the ability to*** *absorb and understand large amounts of information quickly.*

THESAURUS

skill something that you do very well because you have learned and practiced it: *a class that will help you improve your writing skills*
talent a natural ability to do something well, that cannot be learned but that can be developed by practicing: *He has a remarkable musical talent.*
knack INFORMAL a natural ability to do something well: *Kate has a knack for decorating.*
flair/gift a natural ability to do something with a lot of skill and imagination: *He seems to have a flair for business.*

2 someone's level of skill at doing something: *The school teaches musicians of all abilities.* | *It takes hard work and* ***natural ability*** *to make it as a professional athlete.* | **athletic/artistic/musical etc. ability** *leadership ability* | *The test measures verbal and mathematical ability.* | **of high/low/average etc. ability** *students of average ability* **3 to the best of your ability** if you do something to the best of your ability, you do it as well as you can: *The men fought bravely and to the best of their ability.* [**Origin:** 1400–1500 Old French *habilité*, from Latin *habilis* **skillful**]

-ability /əbɪlət̬i/ *suffix* used with adjectives that end in -ABLE to form nouns: *availability* | *probability* → see also -IBILITY

a·bi·ot·ic /ˌeɪbaɪˈɑt̬ɪk/ *adj.* SCIENCE not containing or consisting of living things: *abiotic compounds* | *The abiotic environment consists of soil, rain, wind etc.* → see also BIOTIC

ˌabiotic ˈfactor *n.* [C] EARTH SCIENCE any of the physical things, not including living things, which form part of the environment or have an effect on it, such as water, soil, the weather, fire etc.

ab·ject /ˈæbdʒɛkt, əbˈdʒɛkt/ *adj.* **1 abject poverty/misery/failure etc.** the state of being extremely poor, unhappy, unsuccessful etc. **2** an abject action or expression shows that you feel very ashamed: *The manager was* ***abject in his apology.*** —**abjectly** *adv.* —**abjection** /æbˈdʒɛkʃən/ *n.* [U]

ab·jure /æbˈdʒʊr/ *v.* [T] FORMAL to state publicly that you will give up a particular belief or way of behaving SYN **renounce** —**abjuration** /ˌæbdʒʊˈreɪʃən/ *n.* [U]

a·blaze /əˈbleɪz/ *adj.* **1 be ablaze** to be burning with a lot of flames, often causing serious damage: *Dozens of* *homes were ablaze.* | *During the riot, a police car was* ***set ablaze*** (=made to start burning). **2** filled with a lot of bright light or color: **+with** *The hills were ablaze with fall colors.* **3 ablaze with anger/enthusiasm/excitement etc.** very angry, excited etc. about something → see also BLAZE[1]

a·ble /ˈeɪbəl/ S1 W1 *adj.* **1 be able to do sth a)** to have the skill, strength, knowledge etc. to do something: *Thomas is expected to be able to play again next weekend.* **b)** to have the chance to do something because the situation makes it possible for you to do it: *In 1944, we were able to return to Hawaii.* | *Ammiano still isn't able to make a living from acting.* **2** smart or good at doing something, especially at doing an important job SYN **competent**: *an able student*

-able /əbəl/ *suffix* [in adjectives] **1** used to form adjectives that show you can do something to a particular thing or person: *washable* (=it can be washed) | *lovable* (=easy to love) | *unbreakable* (=it cannot be broken) **2** used to show that someone or something has a particular quality or condition: *comfortable* | *knowledgeable* (=knowing a lot) [**Origin:** Old French, Latin *-abilis*, from *-bilis* **capable or worthy of**] —**-ably** *suffix* [in adverbs] *unbelievably* → see also -IBLE

ˌable-ˈbodied *adj.* physically strong and healthy, especially when compared with someone who is DISABLED: *Every able-bodied person should have the opportunity to work.*

a·bloom /əˈblum/ *adj.* [not before noun] LITERARY looking healthy and full of color: *a garden abloom with roses*

ab·lu·tions /əˈbluʃənz, æ-/ [plural] *n.* FORMAL or HUMOROUS the things that you do to make yourself clean, such as washing yourself, brushing your teeth etc.

a·bly /ˈeɪbli/ *adv.* intelligently, skillfully, or well: *He was ably defended by his lawyers.*

ab·ne·ga·tion /ˌæbnɪˈgeɪʃən/ *n.* [U] FORMAL the act of not allowing yourself to have or do something that you want

ab·nor·mal /æbˈnɔrməl/ Ac *adj.* very different from usual in a way that seems strange, worrying, wrong, or dangerous OPP **normal**: *an abnormal fear of being in open places* | *an abnormal heartbeat* | *My parents thought* ***it was abnormal*** *for a boy to be interested in ballet.*

ab·nor·mal·i·ty /ˌæbnɔrˈmæləṭi, -nɚ-/ *n. plural* **abnormalities** [C,U] an abnormal feature or CHARACTERISTIC, especially something that is wrong with part of someone's body: *a serious brain abnormality* | *genetic abnormalities*

ab·nor·mal·ly /æbˈnɔrməli/ Ac *adv.* **1 abnormally high/low/slow etc.** unusually high, low etc., especially in a way that could cause problems: *Abnormally dry weather is hurting crops.* **2** in an unusual and often worrying or dangerous way: *The child was acting abnormally.*

a·board[1] /əˈbɔrd/ *adv.* **1** on or onto a ship, airplane, or train: *The plane crashed, killing all 200 people aboard.* | *The boat swayed as he stepped aboard.* | *Reporters were not allowed to* ***go aboard***. **2 All aboard!** SPOKEN used to tell passengers of a ship, bus, or train that they must get on because it will leave soon

aboard[2] *prep.* on or onto a ship, airplane, or train: *Many passengers were already aboard the ship.*

a·bode[1] /əˈboʊd/ *n.* [C] FORMAL or HUMOROUS someone's home

abode[2] *v.* a past tense of ABIDE

a·bol·ish /əˈbɑlɪʃ/ *v.* [T] to officially end a law, system etc., especially one that has existed for a long time: *Welfare programs cannot be abolished quickly.* [**Origin:** 1400–1500 Old French *abolir*, from Latin *abolere*]

ab·o·li·tion /ˌæbəˈlɪʃən/ *n.* [U] **1** the official end of a law, system etc., especially one that has existed for a long time: **+of** *As a judge, Marshall worked for the abolition of the death penalty.* **2** also **Abolition** HISTORY the official ending of the system and practice of owning, buying, and selling SLAVES in the U.S.

ab·o·li·tion·ist /ˌæbəˈlɪʃənɪst/ *n.* [C] **1** someone who wants to end a system or law **2** HISTORY someone who took part in a series of actions intended to end the system and practice of owning, buying, or selling SLAVES in the U.S. during the 19th century

Aboˈlitionist ˌMovement, the HISTORY the group of people in the U.S. who worked together from the 1830s until 1870 to end SLAVERY and to set free all of the SLAVES living in North America. The Abolitionist Movement also tried to end the practices of keeping people of different races apart and of treating black men and women unfairly.

A-bomb /ˈeɪ bɑm/ *n.* [C] OLD-FASHIONED an ATOMIC BOMB

a·bom·i·na·ble /əˈbɑmənəbəl/ *adj.* extremely bad or of very bad quality: *an abominable crime* | *Their behavior was abominable.* —**abominably** *adv.*

aˌbominable ˈsnowman *n.* [C] a large creature like a human that is supposed to live in the Himalayas SYN **yeti**

a·bom·i·nate /əˈbɑməˌneɪt/ *v.* [T not in progressive] FORMAL to hate something very much SYN **abhor**

a·bom·i·na·tion /əˌbɑməˈneɪʃən/ *n.* [C] someone or something that is extremely offensive or unacceptable: *Forcing people to work overtime without paying them is an abomination.*

ab·o·rig·i·nal[1] /ˌæbəˈrɪdʒənəl/ *adj.* **1** FORMAL relating to the people or animals that have existed in a place or country from the earliest times SYN **indigenous** **2** relating to Australian aborigines

aboriginal[2] *n.* [C] an aborigine

ab·o·rig·i·ne /ˌæbəˈrɪdʒəni/ *n.* [C] a member of the group of people who have lived in Australia from the earliest times [**Origin:** 1500–1600 Latin *aborigines* (plural), from *ab origine* **from the beginning**]

a·bort /əˈbɔrt/ *v.* **1** [T] to stop an activity because it would be difficult or dangerous to continue it: *The rescue mission had to be aborted.* **2** [T] to deliberately end a PREGNANCY when the baby is still too young to live → see also MISCARRY: *The law allows women to abort an early-stage pregnancy.* **3** [I] if a PREGNANT woman or animal aborts, the baby is born too early and is dead when it is born: *The disease causes pregnant animals to abort.*

a·bor·tion /əˈbɔrʃən/ W2 *n.* [C,U] a medical operation to end a PREGNANCY so that the baby is not born alive: *The woman's doctor advised her to* ***have an abortion*** *for medical reasons.* | *Abortion has become a highly political issue.*

a·bor·tion·ist /əˈbɔrʃənɪst/ *n.* [C] **1** someone who does abortions, especially illegally **2** someone who supports laws that make abortion legal

a·bor·tive /əˈbɔrṭɪv/ *adj.* an abortive action is not successful: **an abortive attempt/effort** *an abortive attempt to ban junk food in schools* | *He was arrested for organizing the* ***abortive coup*** (=an attempt to take over a government that fails)

a·bound /əˈbaʊnd/ *v.* [I] FORMAL to exist in very large numbers or quantities: *Stories of illegal business dealings abounded.* | *Good restaurants abound in the area.*

abound with sth *phr. v.* if a place, situation etc. abounds with something, it contains a very large number or quantity of that thing: *Munich abounds with museums.*

a·bout[1] /əˈbaʊt/ S1 W1 *prep.* **1** on or dealing with a particular subject: *an article about the famine* | *They were talking about music.* | *Robert told her* ***all about*** *it* (=all the details of a particular subject).

THESAURUS

on if a book, lecture, conference etc. is **on** a particular subject, it relates to it. Do not use this to talk about invented stories: *a book on plants used in medicine*
concerning/regarding FORMAL about or relating to something: *The rules regarding safety issues are very clear.*

A

re used in business letters to introduce the subject that you are going to write about: *Re your letter of June 10...*

2 in the nature or character of a person or thing: *I'm not sure what it is about her, but guys really like her.* | *What did you like best about the book?* **3 what/how about** SPOKEN **a)** used to make a suggestion: *I think I'll have dessert. How about you?* **b)** used to ask for news or information about someone or something: *What about the people who were in the bus? Were they OK?* **4** SPOKEN used to introduce a subject that you want to talk about: *About this weekend – is everyone still going?* | *We have to talk – **it's about** your mom.* **5 do sth about** to do something to solve a problem or stop a bad situation: *What can be done about the increase in crime?* **6** if an organization, a job, an activity etc. is about something, that is its basic purpose: *Basically, the job's all about helping people get off welfare.* **7** in many different directions within a particular place, or in different parts of a place SYN **around**: *She began to walk restlessly about the room.* **8** LITERARY surrounding a person or thing: *There was death all about her* (=many people were dying near her).

about² S1 W1 *adv.* **1** more or less a particular number or amount SYN **approximately**: *Tim's about 25 years old.* | *Her music lesson is about 45 minutes long.*

THESAURUS

approximately a little more or a little less than a number, amount, distance, or time: *A kilo is approximately two pounds.*
around used when guessing a number, amount, time etc., without being exact: *Around 50 people came to the meeting.*
roughly a little more or a little less than a number, used when you are saying a number you know is not exact: *The company earned roughly $2 million last year.*
or so used when you cannot be exact about a number, amount, or period of time: *We have an informal reading group that meets every month or so.*

2 INFORMAL almost: *She's 11 months old and just about ready to start walking.* → see also **just about** at JUST¹ (4) **3 that's about it/all** INFORMAL **a)** used to tell someone that you have told them everything you know: *I've seen her at school a few times, but that's about it.* **b)** used to tell someone that there is nothing else available: *There's some ham in the fridge, and that's about it.* [**Origin:** from Old English *abutan*, from *a-* **on** + *butan* **outside**]

about³ S3 W2 *adj.* **1 be about to do sth** if someone is about to do something or if something is about to happen, they will do it or it will happen very soon: *Oh, I was just about to leave you a message.* **2 not be about to do sth** INFORMAL used to emphasize that you have no intention of doing something: *I wasn't about to let him pay for it.* → see also **out and about** at OUT¹ (45), **be up and about** at UP² (17)

aˌbout-'face *n.* [C usually singular] a complete change in the way someone thinks or behaves: *The president **did an about-face on** his promise of no new taxes.*

a•bove¹ /ə'bʌv/ S2 W2 *prep.* **1** in or to a higher position than something else OPP **below**: *He had a bruise above his eye.* | *a painting above the bed* | *the hills above the university* → see also OVER¹ **2** more than a particular number, amount, or level OPP **below**: *It was barely above freezing.* | *Tides rose six feet above their normal level.* **3 above all (else)** used to emphasize that something is more important than the other things you have already mentioned: *Above all, I want my daughter to be confident.* **4** louder or having a higher PITCH than other sounds: *You had to shout to be heard above the music.* **5 above suspicion/reproach/criticism etc.** so good that no one can doubt or criticize you: *Goodwin's work ethic is above reproach.* **6** to a greater degree than someone or something else: *Americans seem to value convenience above cost.* | *Sonsini has contributed **above and beyond** the ordinary call of duty.* **7** in a position of more importance: *Student athletes should not place athletics above academics.* **8** higher in rank, power, or authority OPP **below**: *She works hard, which pleases those above her.* **9 be above (doing) sth** to consider yourself so important that you do not have to do all the things that everyone else has to do: *She's not above helping the secretarial staff.* | *No one is **above the law** in this country.* → see also **over and above** at OVER¹ (20)

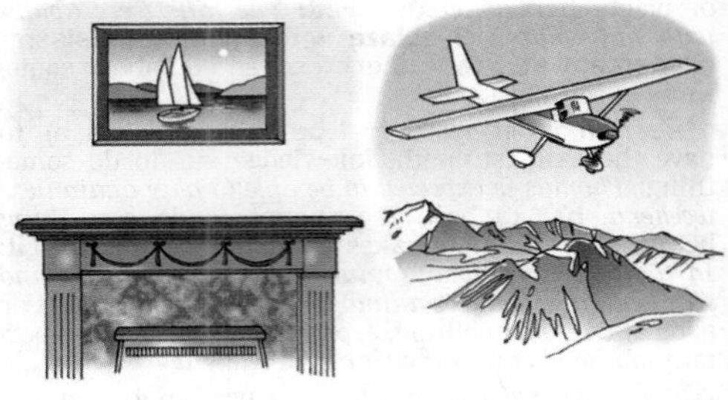

The picture is hanging above the fire place.

The plane is flying over the mountains.

above² S3 W3 *adv.* **1** in a higher place than something else: *The cereal goes in the cabinet above.* **2** more than a particular number, amount, or level: *Big-screen TVs are defined as 27 inches or above.* | *students of above-average ability* **3** higher in rank, power, or authority: *officers of the rank of Major and above* **4** FORMAL used in a book, article etc. to describe someone or something mentioned earlier in the same piece of writing: *See the rates listed above.* | *Christine Liddell, above, talks to Santa* (=there is a picture of Christine above the words). OPP **below**

above³ *adj.* [only before noun] used in a book, article etc. to describe someone or something mentioned earlier in the same piece of writing: *City offices in the above counties will be closed Wednesday.*

above⁴ *n.* **the above** FORMAL the person or thing mentioned before in the same piece of writing: *The correct answer was D: **none of the above*** (=none of the answers listed at A, B, or C). | *Better tasting than **all the above*** (=all the food mentioned before) *are the local chocolate cookies.*

a•bove•board /ə'bʌvˌbɔrd/ *adj.* [not before noun] honest and legal: *Tax experts say the practice is aboveboard.*

a'bove-ˌmentioned *adj.* FORMAL **1** [only before noun] mentioned on a previous page or higher up on the same page: *the above-mentioned authors* **2 the above-mentioned** people whose names have already been mentioned in a book, document etc.

ab•ra•ca•dab•ra /ˌæbrəkə'dæbrə/ *interjection* a word you say when you do a magic trick, which is supposed to make it successful

a•brade /ə'breɪd/ *v.* [I,T] TECHNICAL to rub something so hard that the surface becomes damaged

A•bra•ham /'eɪbrəˌhæm, -həm/ in the Bible, a religious leader who established the HEBREWS as a nation

ab•ra•sion /ə'breɪʒən/ *n.* TECHNICAL **1** [C] an area, especially on the surface of your skin, that has been damaged or injured by being rubbed too hard: *She was treated for cuts and abrasions.* **2** [U] the process of rubbing a surface very hard so that it becomes damaged or disappears

a•bra•sive¹ /ə'breɪsɪv, -zɪv/ *adj.* **1** seeming rude or unkind in the way you behave toward people, especially because you say what you think very directly: *an abrasive personality* **2** having a rough surface, especially one that can be used to clean other surfaces by rubbing: *a dry abrasive cleaning pad* —**abrasively** *adv.*

abrasive² *n.* [C] a rough substance that you use for cleaning other things by rubbing

a•breast /əˈbrɛst/ *adv.* **1 keep/stay abreast of sth** to make sure that you know all the most recent facts or information about a particular subject or situation: *The management has failed to keep abreast of changes in the market.* **2 walk/ride etc. abreast** to walk, ride etc. next to each other: *The training planes were flying **four abreast*** (=with four airplanes next to each other).

a•bridged /əˈbrɪdʒd/ *adj.* an abridged book, play etc. has been made shorter but keeps its basic structure and meaning —**abridge** *v.* [T] —**abridgment** *n.* [C,U]

a•broad /əˈbrɔd/ W3 *adv.* **1** in or to a foreign country: *young people **living abroad** | High school students may benefit from **going abroad** to study languages.* **2** FORMAL if a feeling, piece of news etc. is abroad, a lot of people feel it or know about it: *Corporations do not want their secrets spread abroad.*

ab•ro•gate /ˈæbrəˌgeɪt/ *v.* [T] FORMAL to officially end a law, legal agreement, practice etc.: *It was suggested that the treaty be abrogated.* —**abrogation** /ˌæbrəˈgeɪʃən/ *n.* [C,U]

a•brupt /əˈbrʌpt/ *adj.* **1** sudden and unexpected: *There may be an abrupt change in weather patterns.* | **an abrupt end/stop/halt etc.** *His resignation was an abrupt end to an impressive career.* **2** seeming rude and unfriendly, especially because you do not waste time in friendly conversation SYN **brusque**: *"Change it," he says in his usual abrupt style.* [**Origin:** 1500–1600 Latin, past participle of *abrumpere*, from *ab-* **away, off** + *rumpere* **to break**] —**abruptly** *adv.* —**abruptness** *n.* [U]

ABS /ˌeɪ bi ˈɛs/ *n.* [U] the abbreviation of ANTI-LOCK BRAKING SYSTEM

abs /æbz/ *n.* [plural] INFORMAL the muscles on your ABDOMEN

ab•scess /ˈæbsɛs/ *n.* [C] MEDICINE a painful swollen place in your skin or inside your body that has become infected and contains a yellow liquid [**Origin:** 1500–1600 Latin *abscessus* **act of going away, abscess**, from *abscedere*, from *abs-* **away** + *cedere* **to go**]

ab•scis•sion lay•er /æbˈsɪʒən ˌleɪɚ/ *n.* [C] BIOLOGY a layer of cells between the stem of a plant and a leaf, that can close off the flow of liquids from the plant into the leaf, allowing the leaf to fall off as part of a natural process

ab•scond /əbˈskɑnd, æb-/ *v.* [I] FORMAL **1** to suddenly leave the place where you work after having stolen money from it: +**with** *Royson absconded with money belonging to 40 clients.* **2** to escape from a place where you are being kept ►see THESAURUS box at **escape¹**

ab•sence /ˈæbsəns/ W3 *n.* **1** [C,U] the state of not being in the place where people expect someone or something to be, or the time someone or something is away: *She has come back to acting after an absence of 30 years.* | +**from** *Her absences from home have made it difficult for her family.* | **in/during sb's absence** (=while they are away) *In John's absence, Gina will manage the project.* **2** [U] the lack of something, or the fact that it does not exist: +**of** *a complete absence of confidence* | ***In the absence of** any evidence, the police had to let Myers go.* **3 absence makes the heart grow fonder** used to say that being away from someone makes you like them more → see also **conspicuous by your absence** at CONSPICUOUS (2), **leave of absence** at LEAVE²

ab•sent¹ /ˈæbsənt/ *adj.* **1** not at work, school, a meeting etc. because you are sick or decide not to go OPP **present**: +**from** *Two students were absent from class today.* **2 an absent look/expression etc.** a look etc. that shows you are not paying attention to or thinking about what is happening → see also ABSENTLY **3** FORMAL if someone or something is absent, they are missing or not in the place where they are expected to be: +**from** *Local women were conspicuously absent from the meeting.* | **absent father/parent/mother** *The agency reconnects absent fathers with their children.* [**Origin:** 1300–1400 Old French, Latin, present participle of *abesse*, from *ab-* **away** + *esse* **to be**]

ab•sent² /æbˈsɛnt/ *v.* [T] **absent yourself (from sth)** FORMAL to not go to a place or take part in an event where people expect you to be

ab•sen•tee /ˌæbsənˈtiː/ *n.* [C] someone who should be in a place or at an event but is not there

ˌabsentee ˈballot *n.* [C] a process by which people can vote by mail before an election because they will be away during the election

ab•sen•tee•ism /ˌæbsənˈtiːɪzəm/ *n.* [U] regular absence from work or school, usually without a good reason

ˌabsentee ˈlandlord *n.* [C] someone who lives a long way away from a house or apartment that they rent to other people, and who rarely or never visits it

ˌabsentee ˈvote *n.* [C] a vote that you send by mail in an election because you cannot be in the place where you usually vote

ˌabsentee ˈvoting *n.* [U] POLITICS arrangements that allow people to send a vote by mail in an election or to vote at a POLLING STATION in a place where they do not live

ab•sen•tia /æbˈsɛnʃə/ *n.* **in absentia** FORMAL when you are not at a court or an official meeting where a decision is made about you: *The court found Collins guilty in absentia.*

ab•sent•ly /ˈæbsəntˀli/ *adv.* in a way that shows that you are not paying attention to or thinking about what is happening: *"Thanks," she said absently.*

ˌabsent-ˈminded *adj.* likely to forget things, especially because you are thinking about something else: *Grandpa's been kind of absent-minded lately.* —**absent-mindedly** *adv.* —**absent-mindedness** *n.* [U]

ab•sinthe, absinth /ˈæbsɪnθ/ *n.* [U] a bitter green very strong alcoholic drink

ab•so•lute¹ /ˈæbsəˌlut, ˌæbsəˈlut/ S3 *adj.* **1** [only before noun] INFORMAL used to emphasize your opinion about something or someone, especially when you think they are very bad, stupid, unsuccessful etc.: *The show was an absolute disaster the first night.* | *His office is an absolute mess.* **2** complete or total: *No one can say with absolute certainty that the oil is there.* **3** definite and not likely to change: *April 10 is the absolute deadline.* **4** not restricted or limited: *absolute power* | *an absolute monarch* **5** not changing and true or correct in all situations: *an absolute standard of morality* **6 in absolute terms** measured by itself, not in comparison with other things: *In absolute terms, the experiment wasn't a complete failure.*

absolute² *n.* [C] something that is always true and does not change: *In business, there are very few absolutes.*

ˌabsolute adˈvantage *n.* [C] ECONOMICS an advantage one company or country has over another because it is able to produce a product for less money → see also COMPARATIVE ADVANTAGE

ˈabsolute ˌerror *n.* [C,U] MATH the difference between a measurement of a quantity and its true value, used in order to show how close two numbers are to being the same

ˌabsolute loˈcation *n.* [C] EARTH SCIENCE the exact place or position on the Earth of a country, city, river, mountain etc. On a map, this is shown by the degrees of LONGITUDE and LATITUDE.

ab•so•lute•ly /ˌæbsəˈlutli, ˈæbsəˌlutli/ S1 W3 *adv.* SPOKEN **1** completely and in every way: *The ride was absolutely amazing.* | *Are you absolutely sure?* | *It's absolutely the best museum in the country.* | *We had **absolutely no** warning.* | *Stacy knew **absolutely nothing** about the business when she started.* ►see THESAURUS box at **completely** **2 absolutely!** used to say that you completely agree with someone: *"It's the best restaurant in town." "Absolutely."* **3 absolutely not!** used when saying strongly that someone must not do something or when strongly disagreeing with someone: *"Can I go to the concert?" "Absolutely not!"*

A

ˌabsolute ˈmonarch *n.* [C] POLITICS a king or queen who rules a country without laws or a government controlling or limiting what he or she can do —**absolute monarchy** *n.* [C]

ˌabsolute ˈpower *n.* [U] POLITICS a situation in which a ruler has complete and unlimited control over a country, its government, and the people who live there

ˌabsolute ˈvalue *n.* [C] MATH the value of a number without considering if it is positive or negative, in other words, its distance from zero. For example, the absolute value of -3 is 3 and the absolute value of +3 is also 3.

ˌabsolute ˈvalue eˌquation *n.* [C] MATH an equation that contains absolute values, for which there are two possible solutions depending on whether the values are greater or less than zero

ˌabsolute ˈzero *n.* [U] PHYSICS the lowest temperature that is believed possible, at which the atoms within a substance almost completely stop moving. Absolute zero is measured as 0° KELVIN, which is equal to about -273° Celsius or -459° Fahrenheit.

ab·so·lu·tion /ˌæbsəˈluʃən/ *n.* [U] a process in the Christian religion by which someone is forgiven for the things they have done wrong

ab·so·lut·ism /ˈæbsəluˌtɪzəm/ *n.* [U] POLITICS a political system in which one ruler has complete power and authority —**absolutist** *n.* [C]

ab·solve /əbˈzɑlv, -ˈsɑlv/ *v.* [T] FORMAL **1** to say publicly that someone is not guilty or responsible for something: **absolve sb of sth** *Moving away will not absolve you of the responsibility for paying your debt.* **2** [often passive] if someone is absolved by the Christian Church or a priest for something they have done wrong, they are formally forgiven

ab·sorb /əbˈsɔrb, -ˈzɔrb/ W3 *v.* [T]
1 LIQUID/SUBSTANCE if something absorbs a liquid or other substance, it takes the substance into itself from the surface or space around it: *Simmer the rice until all the liquid is absorbed.* | **absorb sth into sth** *Lead that gets into your body is then absorbed into your bones.*
2 INTEREST to interest someone so much that they do not notice other things happening around them: *The movement and noise of the machines absorbed him completely.* | **be absorbed in sth** *He was absorbed in the conversation, and not paying much attention to his driving.*
3 INFORMATION to read or hear a large amount of new information and understand it: *Her ability to absorb information is amazing.*
4 BECOME PART OF to make a smaller country, company, or group become part of a larger place or group: *California absorbs many of the legal immigrants to the U.S.* | **be absorbed into sth** *Azerbaijan was absorbed into the Soviet Union in the 1920s.*
5 DEAL WITH BAD SITUATION to be able to deal with a problem, loss etc. without suffering too many other problems: *The university had to absorb a $14 million cut in funding.* | *The team managed to* ***absorb the loss of*** *three starting players.*
6 MONEY/TIME ETC. if something absorbs money, time etc. it uses a lot of it: *Defense spending absorbs almost 20% of the country's wealth.*
7 FORCE to reduce the effect of a sudden violent movement: *The lightweight padding is designed to* ***absorb shock.***
8 LIGHT/HEAT/ENERGY if a substance or object absorbs light, heat, or energy, it keeps it and does not REFLECT it (=send it back): *Darker colored surfaces absorb more heat than lighter ones.*
[**Origin:** 1400–1500 French *absorber*, from Latin *absorbere*, from *ab-* **away** + *sorbere* **to suck up**]

ab·sorb·ent /əbˈsɔrbənt, -ˈzɔr-/ *adj.* able to take in liquids easily: *absorbent diapers*

ab·sorb·ing /əbˈsɔrbɪŋ, -ˈzɔr-/ *adj.* enjoyable and interesting and holding your attention for a long time: *It's an absorbing and engaging show.*

ab·sorp·tion /əbˈsɔrpʃən, -ˈzɔrp-/ *n.* [U] **1** a process in which a material or object takes in liquid, gas, or heat: +**of** *the body's absorption of iron* **2** a process in which a country or organization makes a smaller country, organization, or group of people become part of itself: +**of** *the absorption of immigrants into the U.S. in the 19th century* **3** the fact of being very interested in something: +**with/in** *I don't understand James' absorption with military history.*

ab·stain /əbˈsteɪn/ *v.* [I] **1** POLITICS to say that you are not voting either for or against something in an election: *Three members of the committee abstained.* **2** FORMAL to not do something, especially something enjoyable, because you think it is bad for your health or morally wrong: +**from** *Teens are being urged to abstain from sex.* —**abstainer** *n.* [C]

ab·ste·mi·ous /æbˈstimiəs/ *adj.* FORMAL or HUMOROUS careful not to have too much food, drink etc. —**abstemiously** *adv.* —**abstemiousness** *n.* [U]

ab·sten·tion /əbˈstɛnʃən, æb-/ *n.* [C,U] POLITICS a vote in an election which is neither for nor against something or someone

ab·sti·nence /ˈæbstənəns/ *n.* [U] the practice of not doing something you enjoy, especially not drinking alcohol or having sex, or the length of time you do this —**abstinent** *adj.*

ab·stract[1] /əbˈstrækt, æb-, ˈæbstrækt/ Ac S3 *adj.* **1** based on general ideas or principles rather than specific examples or real events SYN **theoretical**: *By the age of seven, children are capable of thinking* ***in abstract terms*** (=about ideas rather than physical things or events). | *Human beings are the only creatures capable of* ***abstract thought*** (=thinking about ideas). | **abstract idea/concept** *the ability to translate abstract ideas into words* **2** existing only as an idea or quality rather than as something real that you can see or touch → see also CONCRETE: *the abstract nature of beauty* **3** ENG. LANG. ARTS abstract paintings, designs etc. consist of shapes and patterns that do not look like real people or things [**Origin:** 1300–1400 Latin, past participle of *abstrahere*, from *abs-* **away** + *trahere* **to pull**] → see also ABSTRACT NOUN, FIGURATIVE

abstract[2] /ˈæbstrækt, əbˈstrækt, æb-/ Ac *n.* [C] **1** ENG. LANG. ARTS a painting, design etc. that contains shapes or images that do not look like real things or people **2** ENG. LANG. ARTS a short written statement of the most important ideas in a speech, article etc. **3 in the abstract** considered in a general way rather than being based on specific details and examples: *In the abstract, democracy is wonderful, but a true democracy may not be possible.*

abstract[3] /əbˈstrækt, æb-, ˈæbstrækt/ Ac *v.* [T] **1** to use information from a speech, article etc. in a shorter piece of writing that contains the most important ideas **2** FORMAL to remove something from somewhere or from a place

ab·stract·ed /əbˈstræktɪd, æb-, ˈæbstræktɪd/ *adj.* not noticing anything around you because you are thinking carefully about something else —**abstractedly** *adv.*

ab·strac·tion /əbˈstrækʃən, æb-/ Ac *n.* **1** [C] a general idea about a type of situation, thing, or person, rather than a specific example from real life: *Until now, our generation only knew war as an abstraction.* **2** [U] a state in which you do not notice what is happening around you because you are thinking carefully about something else

ˌabstract ˈnoun *n.* [C] ENG. LANG. ARTS a noun that names a feeling, quality, or state rather than an object, animal, or person. For example, "hunger" and "beauty" are abstract nouns.

ab·struse /əbˈstrus, æb-/ *adj.* FORMAL difficult to understand in a way that seems unnecessarily complicated —**abstrusely** *adv.* —**abstruseness** *n.* [U]

ab·surd /əbˈsɝd, -ˈzɝd/ *adj.* completely stupid or unreasonable, especially in a silly way SYN **ridiculous**: *a TV show with an absurd plot* | *The idea seemed absurd.* [**Origin:** 1500–1600 French *absurde*, from Latin *absurdus*, from *ab-* **away** + *surdus* **deaf, stupid**] —**absurdity** *n.* [C,U]

ab•surd•ly /əbˈsɚdli/ *adv.* **absurdly cheap/difficult/easy etc.** so cheap, difficult etc. that it seems surprising, unusual, or even funny: *Interest rates have risen to absurdly high levels.*

Ab•u Dha•bi /ˌɑbu ˈdɑbi, ˌæ-/ **1** the largest EMIRATE of the United Arab Emirates **2** the capital city of the United Arab Emirates

A•bu•ja /ɑˈbudʒə/ the capital city of Nigeria

a•bun•dance /əˈbʌndəns/ *n.* [singular, U] a large quantity of something: +**of** *There is an abundance of fresh vegetables available.* | *Helium-3 is found **in abundance** on the moon.*

a•bun•dant /əˈbʌndənt/ *adj.* existing or available in large quantities so that there is more than enough SYN **plentiful**: *an abundant and cheap supply of oil*

a•bun•dant•ly /əˈbʌndəntli/ *adv.* **1** in large quantities: *Lavender grows abundantly here.* **2 abundantly clear** very easy to understand, so that anyone should be able to realize it: *It's abundantly clear why he's running for governor.* | *They **made it abundantly clear** that they wanted to be alone.*

a•buse¹ /əˈbyus/ W2 *n.* **1** [C,U] the use of something in a way that it should not be used: +**of** *Nixon was accused of the **abuse of** presidential **power**.* | *The environment cannot cope with our abuse of air, water, and land.* | **drug/alcohol etc. abuse** *the problem of drug abuse in our schools* | *The Medicare system is based on trust, so it is **open to abuse*** (=able or likely to be used in the wrong way). **2** [U] cruel or violent treatment of someone, especially by someone in a position of authority: *the abuse of the elderly* | *a case of **child abuse** at a daycare center* | *Women can escape **domestic abuse*** (=abuse by their husbands or boyfriends) *at the shelter.* | *An independent committee will look into alleged **human rights abuses**.* | **physical/sexual/racial etc. abuse** *Many children **suffer** racial **abuse** at school.* **3** [U] rude or offensive things that someone says to someone else: *the coach's **verbal abuse** of his players* | **shout/scream/hurl abuse (at sb)** *People on the street were shouting abuse at the soldiers.*

a•buse² /əˈbyuz/ *v.* [T] **1** to treat someone in a cruel and violent way, especially someone that you should take care of: *Some nursing home patients were neglected or abused.* | *She was **sexually abused** as a child.* **2** to use alcohol, drugs etc. too much or in the wrong way: *Many of the kids are abusing drugs.* → see also DRUG ABUSE **3** to deliberately use something such as power or authority for the wrong purpose: *Williams **abused** his **position** as Mayor to give jobs to his friends.* | *Most people on welfare do not **abuse the system**.* | *Morris **abused** the **trust** the company had in him.* **4** to say rude or offensive things to someone: *Some lawyers seem to enjoy **verbally abusing** witnesses.* **5** to treat something so badly that you start to destroy it: *athletes abusing their bodies with steroids* [**Origin:** 1400–1500 French *abuser*, from Latin past participle of *abuti*, from *ab-* **away** + *uti* **to use**]

a•bus•er /əˈbyuzɚ/ *n.* [C] **1** someone who is violent or cruel to someone else, especially someone in a position of authority or trust who hits someone: *a convicted child abuser* **2** someone who uses too much alcohol or drugs

a•bu•sive /əˈbyusɪv/ *adj.* using cruel words or physical violence: *her abusive parents* | *the use of abusive language* —**abusively** *adv.* —**abusiveness** *n.* [U]

a•but /əˈbʌt/ also **abut on** *v.* [T] TECHNICAL if one piece of land or a building abuts another, it is next to it or touches one side of it

a•but•ment /əˈbʌt˺mənt/ *n.* [C] a structure that supports each end of a bridge

a•buzz /əˈbʌz/ *adj.* [not before noun] having a lot of noise, activity, and excitement: +**with** *The classroom was abuzz with activity.*

a•bys•mal /əˈbɪzməl/ *adj.* very bad SYN **terrible**: *Living conditions were abysmal.* [**Origin:** 1600–1700 *abysm* **abyss** (14–20 centuries), from Old French *abisme*, from Late Latin *abyssus*] —**abysmally** *adv.*

a•byss /əˈbɪs/ *n.* [C] LITERARY **1** a very dangerous or frightening situation: +**of** *The country could **fall into the abyss of** economic ruin.* | *a country **on the edge of the abyss** of war* **2** a deep empty space, seen from a high point such as a mountain: *a deep rocky abyss* **3** a great difference which separates two people or groups: *There is an economic abyss in this city between the rich and the poor.*

AC /ˌeɪ ˈsi/ **1** the abbreviation of ALTERNATING CURRENT → see also D.C. **2** the abbreviation of AIR CONDITIONING → see also AC/DC

a•ca•cia /əˈkeɪʃə/ *n.* [C] a tree with small yellow or white flowers that grows in warm countries

ac•a•deme /ˈækəˌdim, ˌækəˈdim/ *n.* [U] ESPECIALLY HUMOROUS the activities that college or university PROFESSORS are involved in, such as writing articles, teaching classes etc.

ac•a•de•mi•a /ˌækəˈdimiə/ Ac *n.* [U] the area of activity and work relating to education in colleges and universities: *researchers working **in academia***

ac•a•dem•ic¹ /ˌækəˈdɛmɪk◂/ Ac S3 W3 *adj.* **1** [usually before noun] relating to education, especially in a college or university: *an academic institution* | *How is academic achievement to be measured?* → see also ACADEMIC YEAR **2** something that is academic seems important but cannot have any effect: *Talking about safety is academic unless we improve the condition of the building.* | *I knew the serial numbers of the stolen computers, but it turned out to be academic as they weren't insured.* **3** [usually before noun] relating to studying from books, as opposed to practical work: *an academic education* **4** good at studying and getting good grades at a school or college: *I'm not very academic, but I love to read.* —**academically** /-kli/ *adv.*

academic² Ac *n.* **1** [C] a teacher in a college or university **2 academics** [plural] subjects that students study in school: *Not all students can do well in academics.*

ac•a•dem•i•cian /ˌækədəˈmɪʃən, əˌkædə-/ *n.* [C] someone who teaches at a college or university and is well known for doing RESEARCH, writing books etc.

ˌacademic ˈyear *n.* [C usually singular] the period of the year during which there are school or college classes; school year

a•cad•e•my /əˈkædəmi/ Ac W3 *n. plural* **academies** [C] **1** a college where students are taught a particular subject or skill: *a military academy* | *the California Ballet Academy* **2** used in the names of some private schools: *St. Lawrence Academy* **3** an important official organization consisting of people interested in the development of literature, art, science etc.: *the American Academy of Arts and Letters* [**Origin:** 1500–1600 Latin *academia*, from Greek *Akademeia* school in Athens at which the ancient Greek thinker Plato taught]

AˌcademyˈAward *n.* [C] **1** an OSCAR: *The Academy Award for best actor went to Jamie Foxx.* **2 the Academy Awards** the ceremony in which the WINNERS of the OSCARS are announced

Aˌcademy of ˌMotion ˌPicture ˌArts and ˈSciences an organization that works to improve standards in movie making and gives the Academy Awards

a cap•pel•la /ˌɑkəˈpɛlə, ˌæ-/ *adj., adv.* sung or singing without any musical instruments: *She sang a capella.*

ac•cede /ækˈsid, ɪk-/ *v.*

accede to sth *phr. v.* FORMAL **1** to agree to a demand, proposal etc., especially after first disagreeing with it: *The House finally acceded to the President's request.* **2** to achieve a position of power or authority: *Henry IV acceded to the French throne at the end of the 16th century.*

ac•cel•er•an•do /ækˌsɛləˈrɑndoʊ, ɑˌtʃɛl-/ *adj., adv.* music getting gradually faster

ac•cel•er•ant /əkˈsɛlərənt, æk-/ *n.* [C] something, such as gasoline, that makes a fire begin burning more quickly

ac•cel•er•ate /əkˈsɛləˌreɪt/ *v.* **1** [I,T] if a process accelerates or if something accelerates it, it happens faster than usual or sooner than you expect: *measures to accelerate the rate of economic growth* **2** [I] if a vehicle or someone who is driving it accelerates, it starts to go faster: *The car can accelerate from 0 to 60 mph in 6.3 seconds.* ►see THESAURUS box at **drive**[1] OPP **decelerate**

ac,celerated depreci'ation *n.* [U] TECHNICAL the process of subtracting the largest amount of the cost of new machines or equipment from the profit made by a company or organization in the year in which they are bought, and smaller amounts in the following years, done in order to pay less tax

ac·cel·er·a·tion /əkˌsɛlə'reɪʃən/ *n.* **1** [singular, U] a process in which something happens more and more quickly: +**in** *the recent acceleration in inflation* | +**of** *the rapid acceleration of economic progress in Southeast Asia* **2** [U] the rate at which a car or other vehicle can go faster: *The car's acceleration and braking are excellent.* **3** [U] PHYSICS the rate at which the speed of an object increases over time: *the acceleration of objects caused by Earth's gravity*

ac·cel·er·a·tor /ək'sɛləˌreɪtɚ/ *n.* [C] **1** the part of a vehicle, especially a car, that you press to make it go faster SYN **gas pedal** **2** TECHNICAL a large machine used to make extremely small pieces of matter move at extremely high speeds

ac·cent[1] /'æksɛnt/ S2 *n.* [C] **1** the way someone pronounces the words of a language, showing which country or which part of a country they come from → see also DIALECT: *Alex spoke Portuguese with a Brazilian accent.* | *Vince has* ***a strong*** *New Jersey* ***accent***. ►see THESAURUS box at **language** **2 an accent on sth** if there is an accent on a particular quality, idea, feeling etc., that quality or feeling is emphasized: *At the Clover Bakery, there is an accent on tradition.* | ***The accent is on*** *chunky jewelry and big bold accessories this fall.* **3** the part of a word that you should emphasize when you say it: +**on** *In the word "corset," the accent is on the first syllable.* → see also STRESS[1] **4** a written mark used above certain letters in some languages to show how to pronounce that letter, such as â or é [**Origin:** 1500–1600 French, Latin *accentus*, from *ad-* **to** + *cantus* **song**]

ac·cent[2] /'æksɛnt, æk'sɛnt/ *v.* [T] **1** to emphasize a part of something, especially part of a word in speech **2** to make something more noticeable so that people will pay attention to it: *Skillful use of make-up can accent your cheekbones and hide small blemishes.* | *The side tables were accented by fresh flower arrangements.*

ac·cent·ed /'æksɛntɪd/ *adj.* spoken with an accent: *He spoke in* ***heavily accented*** (=with a strong accent) *English.*

ac·cen·tu·ate /ək'sɛntʃuˌeɪt, æk-/ *v.* [T] to emphasize something, especially the difference between two conditions, situations etc.: *The photograph seemed to accentuate his large nose.* | *Albright continued to* ***accentuate the positive***, *focusing on areas of agreement.* —**accentuation** /əkˌsɛntʃu'eɪʃən/ *n.* [C,U]

ac·cept /ək'sɛpt/ S2 W1 *v.*

1 GIFT/OFFER/INVITATION [I,T] to take something that someone offers you, or to agree to do something that someone asked you to do OPP **refuse**: *Alice accepted the job of sales manager.* | *Norton is in prison for accepting bribes.* | **accept sth from sb** *Will you accept a collect phone call from Beverly Hillman?* | *I'm always ready to* ***accept*** *a* ***challenge*** (=agree to do something difficult). | *Rick* ***accepted*** *her* ***offer*** *of coffee.* | *He* ***accepted*** *the* ***invitation*** *to stay with us.* | *They invited Taylor to sing the national anthem, and she* ***readily accepted*** (=quickly accepted).

> **THESAURUS**
>
> When someone asks you to do something, you **agree** to do it. Do not say "accept to do something": *The U.S. has agreed to provide aid.* You **accept** an invitation, a job, an offer etc.: *Schroeder accepted a job offer to teach at Princeton University.*

2 PLAN/SUGGESTION/ADVICE [T] to decide to do what someone advises or suggests OPP **reject**: *Yin's proposal was accepted by the committee.*

3 IDEA/STATEMENT/EXPLANATION [T] to agree that what someone says is right or true: *Owens refused to accept her explanation.* | **accept that** *The jury accepted that the DNA evidence was flawed.* ►see THESAURUS box at **admit**, **believe**

4 accept blame/responsibility to admit that you were responsible for something bad that happened: *The ship's owners are refusing to accept any responsibility for the accident.*

5 THINK SB/STH IS GOOD ENOUGH [T] to decide that someone has the necessary skill or intelligence for a particular job, course etc., or that a piece of work is good enough OPP **reject**: *The program accepts only the very best applicants.* | **be/get accepted to sth** *Bob's been accepted to Stanford!* | **accept sb/sth for sth** *Hsiu's article was accepted for publication in "Science" magazine.*

6 SITUATION/PROBLEM ETC. [T] to decide that there is nothing you can do to change a difficult and bad situation or fact and continue with your normal life: *Starting at a new school is hard, but you have to try and accept it.* | *I find it hard to* ***accept the fact that*** *she's left me.* ►see THESAURUS box at **tolerate**

7 ALLOW SB INTO A GROUP [T] to allow someone to become part of a group, society, or organization and to treat them in the same way as the other members OPP **reject**: **accept sb as sth** *The other kids gradually began to accept Jennifer as one of the family.* | **accept sb into sth** *It often takes years for immigrants to be accepted into the host community.*

8 AGREE TO TAKE/DEAL WITH STH [T] to agree to take or deal with something that someone gives you, or say that it is appropriate or good enough: *Do you accept travelers' checks here?* | *The office does not accept applications from nonresidents.* | *The president has* ***accepted*** *Lewis's* ***resignation***. | *Please* ***accept*** *my sincere* ***apologies***.

[**Origin:** 1300–1400 French *accepter*, from Latin *accipere* **to receive**, from *ad-* **to** + *capere* **to take**]

ac·cept·a·ble /ək'sɛptəbəl/ *adj.* **1** good enough to be used for a particular purpose or to be considered satisfactory: *a cheap and acceptable substitute for rubber* | +**to** *The dispute was settled in a way that was acceptable to both sides.* | **an acceptable level/amount of sth** (=one that is not too high or too low) ►see THESAURUS box at **satisfactory** **2** acceptable behavior is considered to be morally or socially good enough: *Lying is just not* ***acceptable behavior***. | *Smoking is no longer considered* ***socially acceptable*** *by many people.* | **acceptable (for sb) to do sth** *It is now considered acceptable for mothers to work outside the home.* | *It's* ***perfectly acceptable*** *to send a card instead of a gift.* —**acceptably** *adv.* —**acceptability** /əkˌsɛptə'bɪləṭi/ *n.* [U]

ac·cept·ance /ək'sɛptəns/ *n.* **1** [U] official agreement to take something that you have been offered OPP **refusal**: +**of** *Acceptance of economic aid from Western countries will speed up the country's recovery.* **2** [singular, U] the act of agreeing that an idea, explanation, activity etc. is right or true OPP **rejection**: +**of** *the growing acceptance of gay rights* | *Upper management's acceptance of the marketing plan is crucial.* | **gain/find acceptance** *Use of the drug has gained acceptance in the U.S.* **3** [U] the process of allowing someone to become part of a group or a society and of treating them in the same way as the other members OPP **rejection**: *Acceptance by their peer group is important to most youngsters.* | *A part of me still longs for my father's approval and acceptance.* **4** [U] the ability to accept a bad situation which cannot be changed, without getting angry or upset about it: *By the end of the story, Nicholas has moved toward acceptance of his fate.*

ac·cept·ed /ək'sɛptɪd/ *adj.* considered right or suitable by most people: *Legalized gambling continues to become more accepted.* | *Bribery is an* ***accepted practice*** *in many countries.* | **generally/commonly/widely accepted** *generally accepted principles of fairness and justice*

ac͵cepted ˈvalue *n.* [C] SCIENCE a standard quantity or measurement for something, that has been agreed on and accepted by a large number of scientists

ac·cess¹ /ˈæksɛs/ Ac S2 W2 *n.* [U] **1** how easy or difficult it is for people to enter a public building, reach a place, or talk to someone: +**to** *Many are jealous of Wright's political access to the President.* | +**for** *The hotel has rooms with access for wheelchairs.* | *Walkways allow* ***easy access*** *to the beach.* **2** the right to enter a place, use something, see something etc.: *Only selected employees* ***have access to*** *the safe.* | *All email accounts are protected by their own secret* ***access code****.* **3 have access to a phone/computer/car etc.** to have a telephone, computer etc. that you can use, even if you do not own it **4** the way by which you can enter a building or reach a place: +**to** *Access to the restrooms is through the foyer.* **5 gain/get access (to sth)** to succeed in entering a place or in seeing someone or something: *The police managed to gain access through an upstairs window.* [**Origin:** 1300–1400 Old French *acces* **arrival**, from Latin *accessus* **approach**]

access² Ac *v.* [T] **1** to find information, especially on a computer: *We don't want minors accessing pornography on the Internet.* **2** to enter or reach a place: *The balcony is accessed by a spiral staircase from the bar.*

ac·ces·si·ble /əkˈsɛsəbəl/ Ac *adj.* **1** easy to reach or get into OPP **inaccessible**: *All of the ski resorts are accessible from the hotel via free public transportation.* **2** easy to obtain or use: +**to** *Healthcare should be made accessible to everyone.* | *The Internet makes this kind of information* ***readily accessible*** *to parents.* **3** someone who is accessible is easy to meet and talk to, even if they are very important or powerful: *Griffey's fans say that he is very accessible and down-to-earth.* **4** easy to understand and enjoy: *Penn's artwork has gradually become more accessible.* —**accessibly** *adv.* —**accessibility** /əkˌsɛsəˈbɪləṭi/ *n.* [U]

ac·ces·sion /əkˈsɛʃən, æk-/ *n.* FORMAL **1** [U] a process in which someone becomes king, queen, president etc. → see also SUCCESSION: *Queen Elizabeth II's* ***accession to the throne*** (=the act of becoming queen) *occurred in 1952.* **2** [U] the act of agreeing to a demand **3** [C] an object or work of art that is added to a collection, especially in a MUSEUM

ac·ces·sor·ize /əkˈsɛsəˌraɪz/ *v.* [T usually passive] to add accessories to clothes, a room etc.: **accessorize sth with sth** *Sheila accessorized the outfit with a cross.*

ac·ces·so·ry /əkˈsɛsəri/ *n. plural* **accessories** [C] **1** [usually plural] something such as a bag, belt, jewelry etc. that you wear or carry because it is attractive: *fashion accessories* | *The store specializes in wedding gowns and accessories.* **2** [usually plural] something such as a piece of equipment or a decoration that is not necessary, but that makes a machine, car, room etc. more useful or more attractive: *cell phone accessories such as carrying cases and battery chargers* **3** LAW someone who helps a criminal, especially by helping them hide from the police: +**to** *Reece is charged with being an accessory to the robbery.* | **an accessory before/after the fact** (=someone who helps a criminal before or after the crime)

ˈaccess ͵road *n.* [C] a road that leads to a particular place

ˈaccess ͵time *n.* [C,U] COMPUTERS the time taken by a computer to find and use a piece of information in its memory

ac·ci·dent /ˈæksədənt, -ˌdɛnt/ S2 W2 *n.* [C] **1 by accident** in a way that is not planned or intended SYN **accidentally** OPP **on purpose** OPP **deliberately**: *The fire started by accident.* | *The pilot,* ***whether by accident or design*** (=whether it was planned or not planned)*, made the plane do a sharp turn.* | *She made the discovery* ***quite by accident****.* **2** a crash involving cars, trains etc.: **a car/traffic/boating etc. accident** *Rhoda's father was in a car accident last week.* | *a* ***serious*** *traffic* ***accident*** *on Interstate 5* | *The accident* ***happened*** *about 8:15 last night.* | *Jones was involved in a near* ***fatal accident*** *that left him paralyzed.*

THESAURUS

crash/collision an accident in which a vehicle hits something else
disaster something that happens which causes a lot of harm or suffering
catastrophe a very serious disaster
wreck an accident in which a car or train is badly damaged
pile-up an accident that involves several cars or trucks
mishap a small accident that does not have a very serious effect
fender-bender INFORMAL a car accident in which little damage is done

3 a situation in which someone is injured or something is damaged without anyone intending them to be: *Ken* ***had an accident*** *at work and had to go to the hospital.* **4** something, often something bad, that happens without anyone planning or intending it: *I'm really sorry about breaking your camera – it was an accident.* | ***It's no accident that*** *the top management positions are still held by men.* | **an accident of birth/geography/history etc.** (=an event or situation that happens without anyone planning it) *By an accident of history, Ft. Dearborn became an important trading post.* **5 an accident waiting to happen** used about a person, thing, or situation that is likely to cause an accident because no one is trying to prevent it: *That old machinery is an accident waiting to happen.* **6 have an accident** SPOKEN if someone, especially a child, has an accident, they URINATE in their clothes **7 accidents happen** SPOKEN used as an excuse for something bad that has happened: *It's too bad about the scratch, but accidents happen.* [**Origin:** 1300–1400 French, Latin *accidens* **additional quality, chance**, from *accidere* **to happen**, from *ad-* **to** + *cadere* **to fall**]

ac·ci·den·tal /ˌæksəˈdɛntl/ *adj.* happening without being planned or intended OPP **deliberate**: *Regulations are needed to limit accidental releases of these chemicals.*

ac·ci·den·tal·ly /ˌæksəˈdɛntl-i, -ˈdɛntˀli/ *adv.* **1** without intending to SYN **by accident** OPP **on purpose** OPP **deliberately**: *I accidentally locked myself out of the house.* **2 accidentally on purpose** HUMOROUS used to say that someone did something deliberately although they pretend they did not: *I think John lost his homework accidentally on purpose.*

ˈaccident-͵prone *adj.* tending to get hurt or break things easily

ac·claim¹ /əˈkleɪm/ *n.* [U] praise for a person or their achievements: *Her new album is receiving a great deal of* ***critical acclaim*** (=praise by people who are paid to give their opinion on art, music etc.). | **international/great/popular/public etc. acclaim** *Bonet has performed several times to great acclaim.* | *Gail's artwork has* ***won*** *her international* ***acclaim****.*

acclaim² *v.* [T] FORMAL to praise someone or something publicly OPP **laud**: *His work was acclaimed by art critics.*

ac·claimed /əˈkleɪmd/ *adj.* publicly praised by a lot of people: *Welles's* ***highly acclaimed*** *movie, "Citizen Kane"* | *a* ***critically acclaimed*** *novel* (=praised by people who are paid to give their opinion on art, music etc.)

ac·cla·ma·tion /ˌækləˈmeɪʃən/ *n.* FORMAL **1** [C,U] a strong expression of approval or welcome **2** [singular, U] the act of electing someone, using a spoken rather than written vote

ac·cli·mate /ˈækləˌmeɪt/ also **ac·cli·ma·tize** /əˈklaɪməˌtaɪz/ *v.* [I,T] to become used to a new place, situation, or type of weather, or to make someone become used to it: +**to** *Dogs take a while to acclimate to a new home.* | **acclimate yourself (to sth)** *Daniel is still acclimating himself to his new company.* | *At high altitudes, it takes your body several days to* ***get acclimated****.* —**acclimatization** /əˌklaɪməṭəˈzeɪʃən/ *n.* [U]

ac·co·lade /ˈækəˌleɪd/ *n.* [C usually plural] praise for someone who is greatly admired or a prize given to them for their work: *Already, the training program is **winning accolades**.* | *She received a Grammy Award, **the highest accolade** in the music business.* [**Origin:** 1600–1700 French *accoler* **to embrace**, from Vulgar Latin *accolare*, from Latin *collum* **neck**]

ac·com·mo·date /əˈkɑməˌdeɪt/ Ac *v.* **1** [T] to have or provide enough space for a particular number of people or things: *The hotel can only accommodate 200 people.* | *He bought a huge house to accommodate his library.* **2** [T] to accept someone's opinions or needs and try to do what they want, especially when their opinions or needs are different from yours: *We generally try to accommodate employees' requests for transfers.* **3** [T] to give someone a place to stay, live, or work: *Twenty cabins on the ship are designed to accommodate disabled passengers.* **4** [I,T] FORMAL to get used to a new situation, or make yourself do this: *Her eyes took a while to accommodate to the darkness.* [**Origin:** 1500–1600 Latin, past participle of *accommodare*, from *ad-* **to** + *commodare* **to make fit**, from *commodus* **suitable**]

ac·com·mo·dat·ing /əˈkɑməˌdeɪtɪŋ/ Ac *adj.* helpful and willing to do what someone else wants: *Most of the hotel staff was very accommodating.*

accommodation

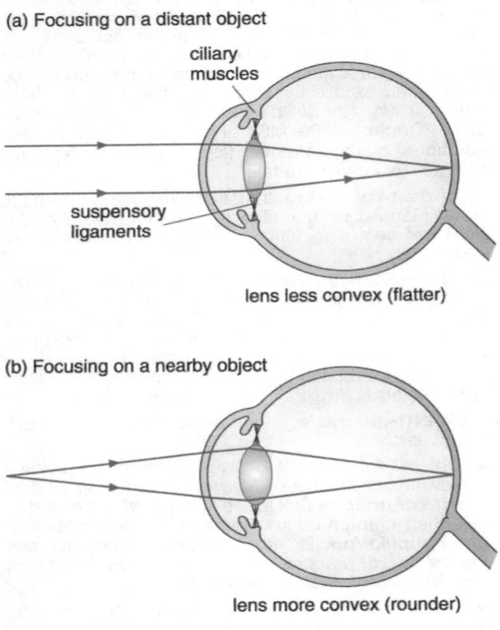

ac·com·mo·da·tion /əˌkɑməˈdeɪʃən/ Ac *n.* **1 accommodations** [plural] a room in a hotel or other place where you stay on vacation or when you are traveling: *Guest artists have to pay for their own **hotel accommodations** and meals.* | *The package includes **deluxe accommodations** and unlimited golf.* **2** [C,U] FORMAL an agreement or change in what is wanted or in the way things are done, in order to solve a problem or end an argument: *There needs to be more accommodation by both sides.* | *Accommodations must be made for students with learning disabilities.* | *Lawmakers are working hard to **reach an accommodation** on the budget issue.* **3** BIOLOGY the way in which the eye changes its shape slightly in order to be able to see things that are close or far away

ac·com·pa·ni·ment /əˈkʌmpənimənt/ Ac *n.* **1** [C,U] ENG. LANG. ARTS music that is played in the background together with another instrument or singer that plays or sings the main tune: *Bob's wife provided accompaniment on the piano.* | **musical/orchestral/instrumental/vocal accompaniment** *The musical accompaniment was jazzy and moody.* **2** [C] something that is provided or used with something else: **+to** *White wine makes an excellent accompaniment to fish.* **3 to the accompaniment of sth** ENG. LANG. ARTS while another musical instrument is being played or another sound can be heard: *They were exercising to the accompaniment of pop music.* **4** [C] FORMAL something that happens or exists at the same time as something else: **+of** *Depression is a very common accompaniment of Parkinson's disease.*

ac·com·pa·nist /əˈkʌmpənɪst/ *n.* [C] someone who plays a musical instrument while another person sings or plays the main tune

ac·com·pa·ny /əˈkʌmpəni/ Ac W2 *v.* **accompanies accompanied, accompanying** [T] **1** to go somewhere with someone: *John has decided to accompany me on my trip to India.* | *Children under 10 must be accompanied by an adult.* **2** ENG. LANG. ARTS to play a musical instrument while someone sings a song or plays the main tune: *Gary accompanied Jenna on the guitar.* **3** [usually passive] to happen or exist at the same time as something else: *Headaches due to viral infections may be accompanied by fever.* **4** if a book, document etc. accompanies something, it explains what it is about or how it works: *Your passport application should be accompanied by two recent photographs.* | *Please read the accompanying information before taking this medication.* [**Origin:** 1400–1500 Old French *acompaignier*, from *compaing* **companion**]

ac·com·pli /ˌɑkɑmˈpli, ˌæk-/ *adj.* → see FAIT ACCOMPLI

ac·com·plice /əˈkɑmplɪs/ *n.* [C] a person who helps someone such as a criminal to do something wrong

ac·com·plish /əˈkɑmplɪʃ/ W3 *v.* [T] to succeed in doing something, especially after trying very hard SYN **achieve**: *Amy's very proud of what she's accomplished.* | ***Mission accomplished** we have done what we intended to do.* [**Origin:** 1300–1400 Old French *acomplir*, from Latin *ad-* **to** + *complere* **to fill up**]

ac·com·plished /əˈkɑmplɪʃt/ *adj.* an accomplished writer, painter, singer etc. is very skillful: **highly accomplished** *a highly accomplished designer*

ac·com·plish·ment /əˈkɑmplɪʃmənt/ *n.* **1** [C] something successful or impressive that is achieved after a lot of effort and hard work SYN **achievement**: **a major/significant/great etc. accomplishment** *Our 15% increase in sales last year was a major accomplishment.* **2** [U] the act of finishing or achieving something good: *Setting short-term goals can help give you **a sense of accomplishment**.* | **+of** *the accomplishment of policy goals* **3** [C] an ability to do something well SYN **skill**: *Playing the piano is one of Joanna's many accomplishments.* **4** [U] skill in doing something: **+in** *He has an impressively high level of accomplishment in judo.*

ac·cord[1] /əˈkɔrd/ W3 *n.* **1 of sb's/sth's own accord** without being asked or forced to do something: *Nunn wasn't fired. He left of his own accord.* | *The door seemed to move of its own accord.* **2** [U] FORMAL a situation in which two people, ideas, or statements agree with each other: **be in accord with sb/sth** *These results are in accord with earlier research.* | **in perfect/complete accord** *All committee members were in complete accord.* **3** [C] a formal agreement between countries or groups: *the Helsinki Accord on human rights* | *Cohen directed the representatives to **reach** an **accord** by Wednesday.* **4 with one accord** OLD-FASHIONED, FORMAL if two or more people do something with one accord, they do it together

accord[2] *v.* FORMAL **1** [T] to give someone or something special attention or a particular type of treatment: **accord sth to sb/sth** *The law requires that racial minorities be accorded equal access to housing.* **2 accord with sth** to match or agree with something: *Some results had been changed to accord with the researchers' theory.*

ac·cord·ance /əˈkɔrdns/ *n.* **in accordance with sth** FORMAL according to a rule, system etc.: *The bank then* *invests the money* ***in accordance with*** *state* ***law.*** | *Warren was buried in his hometown,* ***in accordance with*** *his* ***wishes*** (=as he wanted).

ac•cord•ing•ly /əˈkɔrdɪŋli/ *adv.* **1** in a way that is appropriate for a particular situation or based on what someone has done or said: *Decide how much you can spend, and shop accordingly.* **2** [sentence adverb] FORMAL as a result of something SYN **therefore**: *There aren't many jobs available. Accordingly, companies receive hundreds of résumés for every opening.*

acˈcording to S2 W1 *prep.* **1** as shown by something or said by someone: *According to police, Miller was arrested at the scene of the robbery.* | *You still owe $235 according to our records.* **2** in a way that is directly affected or determined by something: *You will be paid according to the amount of work you do.* | *Everything at the dance* ***went according to plan*** (=happened as we planned it).

ac•cor•di•on[1] /əˈkɔrdiən/ *n.* [C] a musical instrument that you pull in and out to produce sounds while pushing buttons on one side to produce different notes —**accordionist** *n.* [C]

accordion

accordion[2] *adj.* [only before noun] having many folds like an accordion: *an accordion file*

ac•cost /əˈkɔst, əˈkɑst/ *v.* [T] to go toward someone you do not know and speak to them in an impolite or threatening way: *Two men accosted her in front of her apartment building.*

account[1] /əˈkaʊnt/ S2 W1 *n.*

1 DESCRIPTION [C] **a)** a written or spoken description which gives details of an event: **+of** *There were several different accounts of the story in the newspapers.* | *DeJong* ***gave an account*** *of the incident in his book.* | *Police have an* ***eyewitness account*** *of the robbery* (=description of events by someone who saw them). | *a fascinating* ***first-hand account*** (=description of events by someone who saw or took part in them) *of the Chinese Cultural Revolution* | *a* ***blow-by-blow account*** (=description of all the details of an event in the order that they happened) *of the trial* **b)** a detailed description of a process which explains how it happens and what makes it possible: **+of** *an account of how children learn language*

THESAURUS

story a description of how something happened, which may not be true
report a written or spoken description of a situation or event, giving people the information they need
version a particular person's description of an event, which is different from the description given by another person

2 AT A BANK [C] WRITTEN ABBREVIATION **acct.** an arrangement that you have with a bank to pay in or take out money: *I'd like to deposit this check into my account.* | *I just moved here and haven't* ***opened*** *a new* ***account*** *yet.* | *My husband and I have a* ***joint account*** (=one that is shared by two people). | *You can also check your* ***account balance*** (=amount of money that is in your account) *online.*

THESAURUS

Types of account
checking account one that you use regularly for making payments etc.
savings account one where you leave money for longer periods of time, and which pays you a higher rate of interest than a checking account
joint account one that is used by two people, usually a husband and wife

What you do with an account
open an account to start having an account
close an account to stop having an account
pay/put money into an account also **deposit money** FORMAL
take money out of an account also **withdraw money from an account**
balance the amount of money that you have in your account
have a credit balance to have money in your account
be overdrawn to owe the bank money because you have taken more money out of your account than you had in it
ATM/cash machine a machine that you can use to get money from your account
online banking the operation of an account using the Internet, so that you can make payments, check your balance etc. using your computer

3 **take account of sth** also **take sth into account** to consider or include particular facts or details when making a decision or judgment about something: *These figures do not take account of changes in the rate of inflation.*

4 WITH A STORE OR COMPANY [C] an arrangement that you have with a store or company, which allows you to buy goods or use a service and pay for them later or at regular times: *We charged the sofa to our Macy's account.* | *an email account* | *Make sure all your* ***account information*** *is up to date.*

5 **on account of sth** because of something else, especially because of a problem or difficulty SYN **because of**: *Games are often canceled on account of rain.*

6 **accounts** [plural] an exact record of the money that a company has received and the money it has spent: *The accounts for last year showed a profit of $2 million.* → see also ACCOUNTS PAYABLE, ACCOUNTS RECEIVABLE

7 BILL [C] a statement of money that you owe for things you have bought from a store SYN **bill**: **pay/settle your account** | *You must settle your account within 30 days.*

8 ARRANGEMENT TO SELL GOODS [C] an arrangement to sell goods and services to another company over a period of time: *Jack manages several accounts for the ad agency.*

9 **by/from all accounts** according to what a lot of people say: *By all accounts, Garcia was an excellent manager.*

10 **on sb's account** if you do something on someone's account, you do it because you think they want you to: *Don't go to any trouble on my account.*

11 **by sb's own account** according to what someone has said, especially when they have admitted doing something wrong: *By Danon's own account, he was driving too fast.*

12 **on no account** also **not on any account** used when saying that someone must not, for whatever reason, do something: *On no account are members allowed to discuss meetings with outsiders.*

13 **on your own account** by yourself or for yourself: *Carrie decided to do a little research on her own account.*

14 **on that/this account** because of a particular reason or situation: *I would not want the program canceled on that account.*

15 **bring/call sb to account** FORMAL to force someone who is responsible for a mistake or a crime to explain publicly why they did it and punish them for it if necessary: *The people responsible for the accident must be brought to account.*

16 **give a good/poor account of yourself** FORMAL to do something or perform very well or very badly: *Cooper gave a good account of himself in the fight.*

17 **of no/little account** FORMAL not important: *Geller's speech was of no account.*

18 **put/turn sth to good account** FORMAL to use something for a good purpose: *The extra time was turned to good account.*

account[2] W2 *v.* [T]

account for sth *phr. v.* **1** to make up a particular

amount or part of something: *The value of the land accounts for 30% of the house's price.* **2** to be the reason why something happens SYN **explain**: *Recent pressure at work may account for Steve's odd behavior.* **3** to give a satisfactory explanation of what happened or what you did SYN **explain**: *Can you account for your actions on July 12?* **4** to say where all the members of a group of people or things are, especially because you are worried that some of them may be lost: *All the stolen goods were later accounted for.* **5 there's no accounting for taste** FORMAL used when you find it difficult to understand why someone likes something or wants to do something

ac·count·a·ble /ə'kaʊntəbəl/ *adj.* [not before noun] responsible for the effects of your actions and willing to explain or be criticized for them: **+for** *We all must be accountable for our decisions.* | *The hospital should be **held accountable** (=considered responsible) for the quality of care it gives.* | **+to** *Corporate management is accountable to the company's shareholders.* —**accountability** /əˌkaʊntə'bɪləṭi/ *n.* [U] *There is strict accountability as to how the money is spent.*

ac·count·an·cy /ə'kaʊntənsi, ə'kaʊnt˺nsi/ *n.* [U] ACCOUNTING

ac·count·ant /ə'kaʊntənt, ə'kaʊnt˺nt/ *n.* [C] someone whose job is to keep and check financial accounts, prepare financial reports, calculate taxes etc.

ac·count·ing /ə'kaʊntɪŋ/ S3 *n.* [U] the profession or work of keeping or checking financial accounts, preparing financial reports, calculating taxes etc.

acˌcounts 'payable *n.* [U] TECHNICAL the amount of money that a company or organization owes for goods or services it has bought, or the department in a company or organization that deals with this

acˌcounts re'ceivable *n.* [U] TECHNICAL the amount of money that a company or organization should be paid for goods or services it has sold, or the department in a company or organization that deals with this

ac·cou·ter·ments, accoutrements /ə'kuṭəmənts, ə'kutrə-/ *n.* [plural] FORMAL or HUMOROUS small things, pieces of equipment etc. that you use or carry when doing a particular activity or that are related to a particular activity: *cell phones, laptops, and other accouterments of young professionals*

Ac·cra /ə'krɑ/ the capital city of Ghana

ac·cred·i·ta·tion /əˌkrɛdə'teɪʃən/ *n.* [U] official approval for a person or organization: *The school has gone through a lengthy accreditation process.*

ac·cred·it·ed /ə'krɛdɪṭɪd/ *adj.* **1** having official approval to do something, especially because of having reached an acceptable standard: *an accredited teacher* | *an accredited psychiatric hospital* **2 be accredited to sth** FORMAL if a government official is accredited to another country, they are sent to that country to officially represent their government there: *The Pope addressed diplomats who were accredited to the Vatican.* —**accredit** *v.* [T]

ac·cre·tion /ə'kriʃən/ *n.* **1** [C,U] TECHNICAL a layer of a substance which slowly forms on something **2** [U] FORMAL a gradual process by which new things are added and something gradually changes or gets bigger

ac·cru·al /ə'kruəl/ *n.* [C,U] TECHNICAL a gradual increase in the amount or value of something, especially money, or the process of doing this

ac·crue /ə'kru/ *v.* FORMAL **1** [I,T] if advantages accrue to you, or if you accrue them, you get those advantages in greater amounts over a period of time: *You can accrue up to five vacation days a year.* | *China continues to accrue influence in the world.* | **+to** *privileges that accrue to children of the wealthy* **2** [I,T] if money accrues or is accrued, it gradually increases over a period of time: *Interest will accrue until payment is made.*

acˌcrued 'benefit *n.* [C usually plural] TECHNICAL money that a company owes to one of its workers, especially money that has been saved for RETIREMENT

acct. the written abbreviation of ACCOUNT or ACCOUNTANT

ac·cul·tur·ate /ə'kʌltʃəˌreɪt/ *v.* [I,T] to become part of the society of a new country or area and learn to behave in a way that is appropriate there: **+into** *Young people can acculturate into new surroundings quite rapidly.* —**acculturation** /əˌkʌltʃə'reɪʃən/ *n.* [U]

ac·cu·mu·late /ə'kyumyəˌleɪt/ Ac *v.* **1** [T] to gradually get more and more money, possessions, knowledge etc. over a period of time: *Martin had accumulated $80,000 in debt.* **2** [I] to gradually increase in numbers or amount until there is a large quantity in one place: *Fat tends to accumulate around the hips and thighs.* —**accumulation** /əˌkyumyə'leɪʃən/ *n.* [C,U] *a large accumulation of snow*

acˌcumulated deˌpreci'ation *n.* [U] TECHNICAL the total amount of money that a company or organization can subtract from the value of a machine or piece of equipment as it becomes older

acˌcumulated 'dividend *n.* [C usually plural] TECHNICAL money that a company owes to someone who has bought STOCK in the company, but that has not yet been paid

acˌcumulated 'profit *n.* [C] TECHNICAL the money that a company or person has earned in previous years and that they have not used or not paid to people who bought STOCK

ac·cu·mu·la·tive /ə'kyumyələṭɪv, -ˌleɪṭɪv/ *adj.* FORMAL gradually increasing in amount or degree over a period of time SYN **cumulative** —**accumulatively** *adv.*

ac·cu·mu·la·tor /ə'kyumyəˌleɪṭə/ *n.* [C] COMPUTERS a part of a computer that calculates MATHEMATICAL problems and stores the results

ac·cu·ra·cy /'ækyərəsi/ Ac *n.* [U] **1** the ability to do something in an exact way without making a mistake **2** the quality of being correct or true: **+of** *There have been questions about the accuracy of the report.* OPP **inaccuracy**

ac·cu·rate /'ækyərɪt/ Ac W3 *adj.* **1** correct and true in every detail OPP **inaccurate**: *Tom was able to give the police an accurate description of the gunman.* | **fairly/reasonably accurate** *That's a fairly accurate assessment of the situation.* | **not strictly/entirely/completely accurate** *The evidence she gave to the court was not strictly accurate.* ▸see THESAURUS box at **right**[1] **2** measured, calculated, or recorded correctly OPP **inaccurate**: *Better equipment is needed to produce accurate results.* **3** a machine that is accurate is able to do something in an exact way without making a mistake: *The cutter is **accurate to within** 0.5 millimeter.* **4** an accurate shot, throw etc. succeeds in hitting or reaching the thing that it is intended to hit: *Rubens made an accurate throw to first base.* [**Origin:** 1500–1600 Latin, past participle of *accurare* **to take care of**, from *ad-* **to** + *cura* **care**] —**accurately** *adv.*: *It's impossible to predict the weather accurately.*

ac·cursed /ə'kəst, ə'kəsɪd/ *adj.* **1** [only before noun] LITERARY very annoying and causing you a lot of trouble **2** OLD-FASHIONED someone who is accursed has had a CURSE put on them

ac·cu·sa·tion /ˌækyə'zeɪʃən/ *n.* [C] a statement saying that you think that someone is guilty of a crime or of doing something wrong: *Pickens has denied the bribery accusations.* | **+of** *There are accusations of corruption within the agency.* | *He was forced to resign amid **accusations that** he had had an affair.* | *Mellor has **made** several serious **accusations against** the former governor.* | *Unfortunately, even **false accusations** have an effect.* | *The boy's parents **face accusations** (=are accused) of neglect and abuse.* | *The senator stated that the **accusations** were completely **unfounded**.* | *The main **accusation levelled against** him was that he tried to avoid military service.*

THESAURUS

allegation a statement that someone has done something illegal, which has not been proved: *He has denied the allegations of wrongdoing.*

charge an official statement by the police that someone may be guilty of a crime, or a statement by anyone that says that someone has done something illegal or bad: *The charges against her were dismissed.* | *He pointed out that the charge of noncooperation was not fair.*
indictment LAW an official written statement saying that someone may be guilty of a crime: *He is under indictment for credit card fraud.*

ac·cu·sa·tive /ə'kyuzət̬ɪv/ *n.* [C] ENG. LANG. ARTS a form of a noun in languages such as Latin or German, which shows that the noun is the DIRECT OBJECT of a verb —**accusative** *adj.*

ac·cu·sa·to·ry /ə'kyuzə,tɔri/ *adj.* FORMAL an accusatory remark, look etc. from someone shows that they think you have done something wrong

ac·cuse /ə'kyuz/ W2 *v.* [T] to say that you think someone is guilty of a crime or of doing something bad: **accuse sb of (doing) sth** *Are you accusing me of lying?* | *He's accused of murder.* | *The police* ***stand accused of*** (=are officially accused of) *inaction during the riots.* [**Origin:** 1400–1500 Old French *acuser*, from Latin *accusare* **to call someone to explain their actions**] —**accuser** *n.* [C]

THESAURUS

allege to say that someone has done something illegal or wrong, although this has not been proved: *He alleged that the man had attacked him first.*
charge to state officially that someone may be guilty of a crime: *She was charged with murder.*
indict LAW to officially make a written statement that says someone may be guilty of a crime: *He was indicted on charges of fraud.*

ac·cused[1] /ə'kyuzd/ *n.* **the accused** [singular or plural] the person or group of people who have been officially accused of a crime or offense in a court of law SYN **defendant**

accused[2] *adj.* [only before noun] **an accused murderer/rapist/bomber etc.** someone who has been officially CHARGED with committing a crime: *The accused terrorist appeared in court Thursday.*

ac·cus·ing /ə'kyuzɪŋ/ *adj.* an accusing look from someone shows that they think that you have done something wrong —**accusingly** *adv.*

ac·cus·tom /ə'kʌstəm/ *v.* [T] FORMAL to make yourself or another person become used to a situation or place: *It took a while for me to* ***accustom myself to*** *all the new rules and regulations.*

ac·cus·tomed /ə'kʌstəmd/ *adj.* **1 be accustomed to (doing) sth** to be used to something: *I'm not accustomed to getting up so early.* | *Steff was accustomed to a regular paycheck.* | **become/grow/get accustomed to sth** *Her eyes quickly became accustomed to the dark.* **2** [only before noun] FORMAL usual: *Mrs. Belton took her accustomed place at the head of the table.*

AC/DC /,eɪ si 'di si/ *adj.* SLANG sexually attracted to people of both sexes

ace[1] /eɪs/ *n.* [C] **1** a playing card with a single spot on it, which usually has the highest value in a game: *the ace of hearts* **2** someone who is extremely skillful at doing something: *a World War II flying ace* | *pitching ace Doug Jones* **3** a first shot in tennis or VOLLEYBALL which is hit so well that your opponent cannot reach the ball and you win the point **4 an ace in the hole** INFORMAL an advantage that you can use when you are in a difficult situation: *The letter from the president was his ace in the hole.* **5 have an ace up your sleeve** to have a secret advantage which could help you to win or be successful **6 hold all the aces** to have all the advantages in a situation so that you are sure to win **7 be/come within an ace of doing sth** to almost succeed in doing something [**Origin:** 1300–1400 Old French *as*, from Latin, **unit, a small coin**]

ace[2] *adj.* **an ace pilot/pitcher/skier etc.** someone who is a very skillful pilot, player etc.: *an ace detective* ▸see THESAURUS box at **good**[1]

ace[3] *v.* [T] **1** SPOKEN to do very well on a test, a piece of written work etc.: *I think I aced the history test.* **2** to hit your first shot in tennis or VOLLEYBALL so well that your opponent cannot reach the ball

a·cer·bic /ə'sɚbɪk/ *adj.* criticizing someone or something in an intelligent but fairly cruel way: *acerbic wit* —**acerbity** *n.* [U]

a·cet·a·min·o·phen /ə,sit̬ə'mɪnəfən, ,æsɪt̬ə-/ *n.* [U] a type of medicine that helps reduce pain, similar to ASPIRIN

ac·e·tate /'æsə,teɪt/ *n.* [U] **1** a smooth SYNTHETIC cloth used to make clothes **2** CHEMISTRY a chemical made from acetic acid

a·ce·tic ac·id /ə,sit̬ɪk 'æsɪd/ *n.* [U] the acid in VINEGAR

ac·e·tone /'æsə,toʊn/ *n.* [U] a liquid chemical that is used to remove paint or make it thinner, or to DISSOLVE other substances

a·ce·tyl·cho·line /ə,sit̬l'koʊlin/ *n.* [C] CHEMISTRY a chemical substance in your NERVOUS SYSTEM that helps to carry messages from one cell to another → see also NEUROTRANSMITTER

a·cet·y·lene /ə'sɛt̬l-ɪn, -,in/ *n.* [U] CHEMISTRY a gas which burns with a bright flame and is used in equipment for cutting and joining pieces of metal → see also OXYACETYLENE

ache[1] /eɪk/ *v.* [I] **1** if part of your body aches, you feel a continuous, but not very sharp, pain there: *Every inch of my body ached after skiing.* | *an aching back* ▸see THESAURUS box at **hurt**[1] **2 ache to do sth** also **ache for sth** to want to do or have something very much: *The children ached for attention.* **3** to have a strong unhappy feeling: **+with** *Sarah ached with sadness for her brother.* | *The sight of those children at their mother's funeral made my* ***heart ache.*** [**Origin:** Old English *acan*]

ache[2] *n.* [C] **1** a continuous pain that is not sharp, for example the pain you feel after you have used part of your body too much: *He complained of a* ***dull ache*** *in his right leg.* | *I have a few* ***aches and pains*** (=many small pains which you feel at the same time) *but no real health problems.* **2** a strong feeling of unhappiness or of wanting something: *the ache of his loneliness* → see also ACHY, BACKACHE, EARACHE, HEADACHE, HEARTACHE, STOMACHACHE, TOOTHACHE

a·chieve /ə'tʃiv/ Ac S3 W2 *v.* **1** [T] to succeed in doing something good or getting the result you wanted, after trying hard for a long time: *Women have yet to achieve full equality in the workplace.* | *The software division expects to achieve its sales targets this year.* **2** [I] to be successful in a particular kind of job or activity: *My parents constantly encouraged me to achieve.* [**Origin:** 1300–1400 Old French *achever*, from *chief* **end, head**] —**achievable** *adj.*

a·chieve·ment /ə'tʃivmənt/ Ac W3 *n.* **1** [C] something important that you succeed in doing by your own efforts: *Winning three gold medals is a* ***remarkable achievement.*** | *I'm very proud of my achievements as program director.* | *All students must pass an* ***achievement test*** (=test which measures how much they have learned in school) *to move on to the next grade.* | **+in** *a* ***major achievement*** *in the area of foreign policy* **2** [U] the act of achieving something: *We need to raise the level of academic achievement in public schools.* | *Teaching gave me a wonderful* ***sense of achievement*** (=a feeling or pride when you succeed in doing something difficult).

a·chiev·er /ə'tʃivɚ/ *n.* [C] someone who is successful because they are determined and work hard → see also OVERACHIEVER

A·chil·les /ə'kɪliz/ in ancient Greek stories the greatest Greek WARRIOR in the Trojan War

A,chilles' 'heel *n.* [C] a weak part of something, especially of someone's character, which is easy for other people to attack: *The team's offense is its Achilles' heel.* [**Origin:** 1800–1900 from the story that the ancient

Greek hero Achilles was dipped as a baby into the river Styx to protect him, but the part of his heel he was held by did not get wet, and so remained unprotected]

A,chilles 'tendon *n.* [C] BIOLOGY the part of your body that connects the muscles in the back of your foot with the muscles of your lower leg

a·choo /ə'tʃu/ *n.* [C] a word used to represent the sound you make when you SNEEZE

ach·y /'eɪki/ *adj.* if a part of your body feels achy, it is slightly painful, especially after you have used it too much: *an achy neck* → see also ACHE[1]

ac·id[1] /'æsɪd/ S3 *n.* **1** [C,U] CHEMISTRY a substance that forms a chemical SALT when combined with a BASE. Some acids can burn holes in things or damage your skin: *sulfuric acid* **2** [U] INFORMAL the illegal drug LSD

acid[2] *adj.* [only before noun] **1** having a very sour taste SYN **acidic** **2 an acid remark/comment/tone etc.** an acid remark etc. uses humor in a way that is not nice, in order to criticize someone **3** TECHNICAL an acid soil does not contain enough LIME [**Origin:** 1600–1700 French *acide*, from Latin *acere* **to be sour**] **—acidly** *adv.* **—acidity** /ə'sɪdəṭi/ *n.* [U] → see also ACID RAIN

a·cid·ic /ə'sɪdɪk/ *adj.* **1** very sour: *It tastes a little acidic.* **2** CHEMISTRY containing acid

a·cid·i·fy /ə'sɪdə,faɪ/ *v.* [I,T] CHEMISTRY to become an ACID or make something become an acid

,acid 'rain *n.* [U] EARTH SCIENCE rain that contains harmful substances such as NITRIC ACID and SULFURIC ACID, which can damage the environment and is caused by smoke from factories, waste gases from cars and trucks etc.

,acid 'test *n.* [C] a way of finding out whether something is as good as people say it is, whether it works, or whether it is true: *The acid test for the roof will be the next rainstorm.*

ac·knowl·edge /ək'nɑlɪdʒ/ Ac W2 *v.* [T]
1 ADMIT to admit or accept that something is true or that a situation exists: *Cooke acknowledges receiving gifts that could be seen as bribes.* | *Friends say he has privately acknowledged his wrongdoing.* | **acknowledge that** *An industry spokesman acknowledged that toxic chemicals had been released into the river.* ►see THESAURUS box at **admit**
2 RECOGNIZE SB'S/STH'S IMPORTANCE [usually passive] if a large number of people acknowledge someone or something, they recognize how good or important they are: **be acknowledged as sth** *Lasalle is widely acknowledged as the world's leading authority on Impressionist painting.* | **be widely/generally acknowledged to be something** *The mill produces what is widely acknowledged to be the finest wool in the world.*
3 ACCEPT SB'S AUTHORITY to officially accept that a government, court, leader etc. has legal or official authority: *Both defendants refused to acknowledge the authority of the court.* | **acknowledge sb as sth** *Many of the poor acknowledged him as their spiritual leader.*
4 LETTER/MESSAGE ETC. to tell someone that you have received their message, letter, package etc.: *The paper never even acknowledged my letter or printed a correction.*
5 SHOW THANKS to publicly announce that you are grateful for the help that someone has given you: *The author wishes to acknowledge the assistance of the Defense Department.*
6 SHOW YOU NOTICE SB to show someone that you have seen them or heard what they have said: *Callahan waved, acknowledging his fans.*

ac·knowl·edg·ement, acknowledgment /ək'nɑlɪdʒmənt/ Ac *n.* **1** [C,U] the act of admitting or accepting that something is true: *Simons resigned following his acknowledgment of illegal trading.* **2** [C,U] the act of publicly thanking someone for something they have done: *The award was given* ***in acknowledgement of*** *all Sylvia's hard work.* **3 acknowledgements** [plural] a short piece of writing at the beginning or end of a book in which the writer thanks all the people who have helped him or her **4** [C,U] a letter written to tell someone that you have received their letter, message etc.

ACLU /,eɪ si ɛl 'yu/ **American Civil Liberties Union** an organization that gives people advice and help about their CIVIL RIGHTS

ac·me /'ækmi/ *n.* **the acme of sth** FORMAL the best and highest level of something: *the acme of scientific knowledge*

ac·ne /'ækni/ *n.* [U] MEDICINE a skin problem that affects mainly young people and causes a lot of small red PIMPLES on the face and neck

a·coe·lo·mate /ə'silə,meɪt/ *n.* [C] BIOLOGY a living creature that does not have a COELOM (=hollow space within its body, between the inside surface of the skin and the organs inside the body) → see also COELOMATE

ac·o·lyte /'ækə,laɪt/ *n.* [C] **1** someone who serves an important person or believes in their ideas: *Freud and his acolytes* **2** someone who helps a priest at a religious ceremony

a·corn /'eɪkɔrn/ *n.* [C] the nut of the OAK tree

a·cous·tic /ə'kustɪk/ *adj.* **1** relating to sound and the way people hear things **2** an acoustic GUITAR or other musical instrument does not have its sound made louder electronically [**Origin:** 1700–1800 Greek *akoustikos* **of hearing**, from *akouein* **to hear**] **—acoustically** /-kli/ *adv.*

a·cous·tics /ə'kustɪks/ *n.* **1** [plural] the qualities of a room, such as its shape and size, which affect the way sound is heard in it: *The new auditorium has excellent acoustics.* **2** [U] the scientific study of sound

ac·quaint /ə'kweɪnt/ *v.*
acquaint sb with sth *phr. v.* FORMAL **1 acquaint yourself with sth** to deliberately find out about something: *Residents should acquaint themselves with earthquake safety rules.* **2** to give someone information about something: *The guidebook acquaints the traveler with the city's history and culture.* → see also ACQUAINTED

ac·quaint·ance /ə'kweɪnt⁻ns/ *n.* **1** [C] someone you know, but who is not a close friend: *Dottie is just a* ***casual acquaintance*** *from my college days.* | *Erik was introduced to his future wife by* ***a mutual acquaintance*** (=someone who knows both people). **2 make sb's acquaintance** also **make the acquaintance of sb** FORMAL to meet someone for the first time: *I'm pleased to make your acquaintance.* **3** [U] FORMAL knowledge of or experience with a particular subject: *John* ***had a personal acquaintance with*** *alcohol addiction.* **4 of sb's acquaintance** FORMAL a person of your acquaintance is someone that you know: *Ms. Nichols is a writer of my acquaintance.*

ac'quaintance ,rape *n.* [C,U] an attack in which someone is forced to have sex by someone they know → see also DATE RAPE

ac·quain·tance·ship /ə'kweɪnt⁻ns,ʃɪp/ *n.* [U] FORMAL the fact of knowing someone socially

ac·quaint·ed /ə'kweɪntɪd/ *adj.* [not before noun] **1 acquainted (with sb)** knowing someone, especially because you have met them only a few times: *I am acquainted with Tony Philips on a professional basis.* | *It was a chance for my stepdaughter and me to* ***get*** *better* ***acquainted*** (=learn more about someone you don't know well). **2 be acquainted with sth** FORMAL to know about something, because you have seen it, read it, used it etc.: *people who are acquainted with the problems of poverty* | *All our employees are* ***fully acquainted with*** *safety precautions.*

ac·qui·esce /,ækwi'ɛs/ *v.* [I] FORMAL to unwillingly agree to do what someone wants, or to let them do what they want, without arguing or complaining: **+in/to** *City officials eventually acquiesced to the protesters' demands.*

ac·qui·es·cence /,ækwi'ɛsəns/ *n.* [U] FORMAL the quality of being too ready to agree with someone or do what they want, without arguing or complaining **—acquiescent** *adj.* **—acquiescently** *adv.*

ac·quire /ə'kwaɪɚ/ Ac W2 *v.* [T] FORMAL **1** to buy or obtain something, especially something that is expensive or difficult to get: *AC Transit recently acquired 70* *new buses.* | *A major Hollywood studio has acquired the rights to the novel.* ►see THESAURUS box at **buy**[1], **get** **2** to get or gain knowledge, skills, qualities etc.: *Research helps us acquire new insight on the causes of diseases.* | *Many inner cities have acquired reputations for violent crime.* **3 acquire a taste for sth** to begin to like something: *She had acquired a taste for beer.* **4 an acquired taste** something that people only begin to like after they have tried, heard, seen etc. it a few times, and that some people may never begin to like: *For many people, opera is an acquired taste.* [**Origin:** 1400–1500 Old French *aquerre*, from Latin *acquirere*, from *ad-* **to** + *quaerere* **to look for, obtain**]

ac,quired im,mune de'ficiency ,syndrome *n.* [U] MEDICINE AIDS

ac·qui·si·tion /ˌækwəˈzɪʃən/ Ac *n.* **1** [U] the act of getting land, power, money etc.: +**of** *the acquisition of new sites for development* | *The government has approved the company's acquisition of its rival.* **2** [C] something that you have bought or obtained, especially a valuable object or something such as a company that costs a lot of money: *Funds will be used for new museum acquisitions.* | *In the past two years, the industry spent $70 billion in* ***mergers and acquisitions.*** **3** [U] the act of getting new knowledge, skills etc.: *second language acquisition*

ac·quis·i·tive /əˈkwɪzət̬ɪv/ *adj.* FORMAL showing too much desire to get new possessions —**acquisitiveness** *n.* [U]

ac·quit /əˈkwɪt/ *v.* **acquitted**, **acquitting** **1** [T usually passive] LAW to give a decision in a court of law that someone is not guilty of a crime OPP **convict**: *All the defendants were acquitted.* | **acquit sb of sth** *Bennett was acquitted of murder.* **2 acquit yourself well/honorably etc.** FORMAL to do something well, especially something difficult that you do for the first time in front of other people: *Although Perkins isn't known as a singer, he acquits himself admirably on this CD.* [**Origin:** 1200–1300 Old French *acquiter*, from *quite* **free of**]

ac·quit·tal /əˈkwɪtl/ *n.* [C,U] LAW an official statement in a court of law that someone is not guilty OPP **conviction**: *Few were surpised by Carver's acquittal.*

a·cre /ˈeɪkɚ/ S3 W3 *n.* [C] a unit for measuring areas of land, equal to 4,840 square yards (4,047 square meters): *They own 1,500 acres of farmland.* | *a 2,000-acre ranch*

a·cre·age /ˈeɪkərɪdʒ/ *n.* [U] the area of a piece of land measured in acres

ac·rid /ˈækrɪd/ *adj.* an acrid smell or taste is strong and bad and stings your nose or throat: *a cloud of acrid smoke*

ac·ri·mo·ni·ous /ˌækrəˈmoʊniəs◂/ *adj.* FORMAL an acrimonious meeting, argument etc. is full of angry remarks because people feel very strongly about something: *an acrimonious divorce* —**acrimoniously** *adv.* —**acrimoniousness** *n.* [U]

ac·ri·mo·ny /ˈækrəˌmoʊni/ *n.* [U] FORMAL angry feelings between people

acrobat

ac·ro·bat /ˈækrəˌbæt/ *n.* [C] someone who entertains people by doing difficult physical actions such as walking on their hands or balancing on a high rope, especially at a CIRCUS [**Origin:** 1800–1900 French *acrobate*, from Greek *akrobatos* **walking on the ends of the toes**]

ac·ro·bat·ic /ˌækrəˈbæt̬ɪk◂/ *adj.* acrobatic movements involve moving your body in a very skillful way, for example by jumping through the air or balancing on a rope: *an acrobatic catch* —**acrobatically** /-kli/ *adv.*

ac·ro·bat·ics /ˌækrəˈbæt̬ɪks/ *n.* [plural] acrobatic movements

ac·ro·nym /ˈækrəˌnɪm/ *n.* [C] ENG. LANG. ARTS a word made up from the first letters of the name of something such as an organization. For example, NASA is an acronym for the National Aeronautics and Space Administration. [**Origin:** 1900–2000 *acr-* **beginning, end** (from Greek *akr-*) + *-onym* (as in *homonym*)]

the Acropolis

a·crop·o·lis /əˈkrɑpəlɪs/ **1 the Acropolis** an ancient CITADEL (=a strong building defended by soldiers, where people could go if their city was being attacked) built on a hill in the center of Athens, Greece. There are many important historical religious buildings on the Acropolis. **2** [C] HISTORY in ancient Greek cities, a hill with walls or towers built on it, that could be defended if the city was being attacked

a·cross[1] /əˈkrɔs/ S1 W1 *prep.* **1** going, looking etc. from one side of a space, area, or line to the other side: *She took a ship across the Atlantic.* | *We gazed across the valley.* | *Would you like me to* ***help you across the street*** (=help you to cross it)? **2** reaching or spreading from one side of an area to the other: *Slowly a smile spread across her face.* | *Do you think this shirt is too tight across the shoulders?* | *There is a deep crack* ***all the way across*** *the ceiling.* **3** on or toward the opposite side of something: *My best friend lives across the street.* | *Jim yelled across the street to his son.* | **across sth from sth** *Across the street from where we're standing, you can see the old churchyard.* | *Hoboken is* ***right across*** *the river* (=directly opposite, on the other side) *from New York.* | *Miguel knew that* ***just across*** *the border lay freedom.* **4** in every part of a country, organization etc.: *The TV series became popular across five continents.* [**Origin:** 1200–1300 Anglo-French *an crois* **in cross**]

across[2] S2 W3 *adv.* **1** from one side of something to the other: *She came in the room, walked across, and opened the window.* **2** if you go, look, shout etc. across to someone, you go, look, or shout toward the other side of an area, to the place where they are: +**to/at** *I looked across at the other driver.* | *Tim shouted across to his friends.* **3 10 feet/20 miles etc. across** if something is 10 feet, 20 miles etc. across, that is how wide it is: *At its widest point, the river is two miles across.* **4 across from sb/sth** on the opposite side of a table, room, street etc. from someone or something: *I looked up at the woman sitting across from me on the subway.* → see Word Choice box at FRONT[1]

a,cross-the-'board *adj.* [only before noun] affecting everyone or everything in a situation or organization: *an across-the-board pay increase* —**across the board** *adv.*

A

a·cros·tic /ə'krɔstɪk, -'krɑs-/ *n.* [C] ENG. LANG. ARTS a poem or piece of writing in which the first or last letter of each line can be read from top to bottom to spell a word

a·cryl·ic¹ /ə'krɪlɪk/ *n.* **1** [U] a substance similar to plastic that is made from chemicals **2** [U] a type of cloth or YARN that is made from a particular chemical substance **3 acrylics** [plural] paints that contain a particular chemical substance [**Origin:** 1800–1900 *acrolein* **chemical compound** (19–21 centuries), from Greek *akr-* + Latin *olere* **to smell**]

acrylic² *adj.* acrylic paints, cloth, or other materials are made from a particular chemical substance

ACT /ˌeɪ si 'ti/ *n.* [C] TRADEMARK **American College Test** an examination taken by students in order to attend some universities

act¹ /ækt/ S2 W1 *n.* [C]

1 ACTION [C] one thing that someone does: *a criminal act* | **+of** *an act of senseless violence* | *Garcia was given the medal of honor for his acts of bravery.* | **in the act (of doing sth)** (=at the moment that you are doing something) *The photo shows her in the act of raising her gun to fire.* | *Bill was* ***caught in the act*** (=discovered while doing something bad or illegal). → see also SEX ACT ►see THESAURUS box at **action**

2 LAW [C] a law that has been officially accepted by Congress or a government: *the Civil Rights Act* | *an act of Congress*

3 PRETENDING [singular] insincere behavior in which you pretend to have a particular kind of feeling: *Tony tries to be so macho, but it's just an act.* | *Sally isn't just* ***putting on an act*** (=pretending to have a particular feeling), *she's really upset.*

4 PERFORMANCE [C] **a)** one of the several short performances in a theater or CIRCUS show: *a comedy act* | *The festival will feature a lot of different acts.* **b)** a performer, singer, group of musicians etc. who gives a performance: *Our next act is a young singer all the way from Dallas, Texas.*

5 THEATER [C] one of the main parts into which a stage play, OPERA etc. is divided: *In Act 2, Ross and Diane get married.* | *a one-act play*

6 get your act together INFORMAL to do something in a more organized way or use your abilities more effectively: *Angie would have a great future, if only she could get her act together.*

7 a hard/tough etc act to follow someone who does such an excellent job that it would be difficult for someone doing the same job after them to be as good: *John was an excellent manager and a hard act to follow.*

8 get in on the act INFORMAL to take part in an activity that someone else has started, especially in order to get a share of the advantages for yourself: *With so much money to be made, everyone is getting in on the act.*

9 an act of God an event that is caused by natural forces, such as a storm, flood, or fire, which you cannot prevent or control

10 balancing/juggling act the act of trying to do two or more things at once, especially when this is difficult: *For today's time-stressed parents, each day becomes a juggling act.*

11 an act of worship an occasion when people pray together and show their respect for God

[**Origin:** 1300–1400 Latin *actus* **doing, act** and *actum* **thing done, record**, from the past participle of *agere* **to drive, do**] → see also **clean up your act** at CLEAN UP (3)

WORD CHOICE act and action

Act is always countable, but **action** can be uncountable: *a thoughtful act* | *a series of quick actions* | *What we need now is quick action.* Use **act** in some set phrases when it means a particular type of action: *an act of kindness* | *She was caught in the act of* (NOT *in the action of*) *stealing the money.*

act² S1 W1 *v.*

1 DO SOMETHING a) [I] to do something to deal with an urgent problem, especially by using your official power or authority: *What will it take to get the president to act?* | **+on** *Congress must act soon before it is too late.* | **act to do sth** *The U.N. must act now to restore democracy.* **b)** [I always + adv./prep.] to do something in a particular way or for a particular reason: *Morgenstern claims he was acting in self-defense.* | *I acted more out of compassion than anything else.* | ***Acting on*** *a friend's* ***advice*** (=doing what his friend advised), *Schiller bought $5,000 worth of stock.* | *Police were* ***acting on information*** (=doing something because of information received) *from a member of the public.*

2 BEHAVE [I always + adv./prep./adj.] to behave in a particular way or pretend to have a particular feeling or quality: *The report says the officers acted professionally and responsibly.* | *Larry was acting really weird.* | **+like** *Bill always tries to act like such a tough guy.* | **+as if/though** *Gail acted as if she'd never seen me before.* | *For heaven's sake, Joe,* ***act your age*** (=stop behaving like a child)*!*

3 HAVE AN EFFECT [I] **a)** to have a particular effect or use: **+as** *The sugar in the fruit acts as a preservative.* | **+on** *Antibiotics act on the bacteria that cause the disease.* **b)** to start to have an effect: *It takes a couple of minutes for the drug to act.* | *a fast-acting decongestant*

4 PLAY/MOVIE ETC. [I,T] to perform in a play or movie: *I first started acting when I was 12 years old.* | *The picture has a good script and is wonderfully acted.*

5 act for sb also **act on sb's behalf** to represent someone, especially in a court of law or by doing business for them: *I'm acting on behalf of my client, Mr. Harding.*

6 act as sth to do a particular job for a short time, for example while the usual person is absent: *DeConcini acted as host at the meeting.* → see also ACTING¹

act sth ↔ **out** *phr. v.* **1** if a group of people act out a real or imaginary event, they show how it happened or could happen by pretending to be the people involved in it: *Computer games allow players to act out their fantasies.* **2** to express your feelings about something through your behavior or actions, especially when you have been feeling angry or nervous: *Children who act out violently have often been abused.* | *Teenagers can act out their anxieties in various aggressive ways.*

act up *phr. v.* INFORMAL **1** if children act up, they behave badly: *He's a tough kid who acts up a lot.* **2** if a machine or part of your body acts up, it does not work correctly: *The copy machine is acting up again.*

ac·tin /'æktɪn/ *n.* [U] BIOLOGY a PROTEIN found in cells that helps cells keep their shape and move around, and helps the muscles CONTRACT (=become shorter and tighter)

act·ing¹ /'æktɪŋ/ *adj.* **an acting manager/director etc.** someone who does an important job while the usual person is not there, or until a new person is chosen for the job

acting² *n.* [U] the job or skill of performing in plays, movies etc.

ac·tion /'ækʃən/ S2 W1 *n.*

1 DOING THINGS [U] the process of doing something in order to deal with a problem or difficult situation: *Some senators are urging military action.* | *The police were criticized for failing to* ***take action*** *during the riots.* | *One possible* ***course of action*** (=series of actions done to deal with something) *would be to raise taxes on tobacco.* | *They met to discuss a* ***plan of action.*** | *Business leaders demanded immediate and* ***decisive action*** *to end the dispute.* | **quick/swift/prompt action** *Ben's prompt action probably saved my life.* | **swing/spring into action** (=immediately begin doing something with a lot of energy)

2 SOMETHING DONE [C] something that someone does: *The child could not be held responsible for his actions.* | *He says he has documents to prove his actions were ordered by his superiors.*

THESAURUS

act a particular type of action: *people who commit acts of violence*
activities things that people do, especially for enjoyment or to achieve an aim: *The activities of volunteers keep many of these organizations going.*
behavior the things that a person or animal does:

Consistent rewards and punishments can help improve a child's behavior.
deed LITERARY an action, especially one that is very good or very bad: *his evil deeds*
exploits LITERARY exciting or brave actions: *his exploits searching for gold*
move something that you decide to do in order to achieve something: *His decision to give up his acting career had been a smart move.*
step one of a series of things that you do in order to deal with a problem or to succeed: *The mayor took immediate steps to stop the riots.*
measure an action, especially an official one, that is intended to deal with a particular problem: *increased security measures*

3 in action if you see someone or something in action, you see them doing the job or activity that they are trained or designed to do: *These photos show the ski jumpers in action.* | *It's a chance for students to see a TV station in action.*
4 put/call/bring sth into action to begin to use a plan or idea that you have, and to make it work: *If we had any good ideas, we would put them into action right away.*
5 out of action injured or broken, and therefore unable to move or work: *Miller will be out of action for six weeks due to his knee injury.* | *The earthquake* ***put a*** *number of freeways* ***out of action.***
6 COURT [C,U] the process of taking a case or a LAWSUIT against someone to a court of law: *Woods* ***filed an action*** *in the small claims court.* | *Payne threatened to* ***take legal action against*** *the magazine.* | *We may* ***bring an action against*** *the owners of the company.*
7 EXCITING EVENTS [U] **a)** INFORMAL exciting and important things that are happening: *There's never much action around here.* | *If you want to be* ***where the action is,*** *come to the Grand Rapids Speedway Friday night.* **b)** exciting scenes in movies or on TV, in which people fight, chase, and kill each other: *a movie with lots of action* | *Gibson got his start in* ***action movies.*** | *a TV* ***action hero***
8 FIGHTING [C,U] fighting or a battle during a war: *When the action ended, there were terrible losses on both sides.* | *The navy was sent* ***into action.*** | **missing/killed in action** *Their son was reported missing in action.* ▸see THESAURUS box at war
9 a piece/slice of the action INFORMAL a share of something, such as profits, a business etc.: *After five years in middle management, I'm ready for a real piece of the action.*
10 STORY the action the things that happen in a book, movie, or play: *In "Hamlet," the action takes place in Denmark.*
11 EFFECT [U] the way in which something such as a chemical or process has an effect on something else: *The rock had been worn away by the action of the falling water.* | **+on** *the action of alcohol on the liver*
12 MOVEMENT [C,U] the way something moves or works: *the horse's trotting action* | *a smooth braking action*
13 an action group/committee/project etc. a group formed to do something specific, especially to change a social or political situation: *a refugee action committee*
14 actions speak louder than words used to say that you are judged by what you do, rather than by what you say you will do
15 MOVIES action! used by a movie DIRECTOR to tell the actors and other movie workers to begin filming
16 MACHINERY [U] TECHNICAL the movement of the parts of a clock, gun, piano etc. → see Word Choice box at ACT¹

ac·tion·a·ble /ˈækʃənəbəl/ *adj.* **1** [usually before noun] FORMAL an actionable plan, piece of information etc. is one that can be done or used **2** LAW if something you say or do is actionable, it is so serious or damaging that a LAWSUIT could be FILED against you in a court of law because of it: *Lying to Congress is an* ***actionable offense.***

ˈaction ˌfigure *n.* [C] a child's toy that looks like a small person, especially someone from a movie or television show

ˈaction ˌforce *n.* [C] PHYSICS the first of a pair of forces described in NEWTON'S THIRD LAW that causes the second REACTION FORCE

ˌaction-ˈpacked *adj.* an action-packed story, movie, or show contains a lot of exciting events

ˈaction poˌtential *n.* [U] BIOLOGY a temporary increase in electrical activity in a nerve or muscle cell, that happens when an electrical signal travels along a nerve or muscle cell

ac·ti·vate /ˈæktəˌveɪt/ *v.* [T] **1** to make something, especially an electrical system, start working: *This button activates the car's alarm system.* **2** TECHNICAL to make a chemical action or natural process happen: *The manufacture of chlorophyll in plants is activated by sunlight.* **3** TECHNICAL to make something RADIOACTIVE **—activation** /ˌæktəˈveɪʃən/ *n.* [U]

ˌactivated ˈcomplex *n.* [C] CHEMISTRY a chemical structure formed for a short time during a chemical reaction between two or more substances when the atoms are in the process of combining and changing

actiˈvation ˌenergy *n.* [U] CHEMISTRY the smallest amount of energy needed to make the atoms in one substance combine with the atoms of another substance as part of a chemical reaction

ac·tive¹ /ˈæktɪv/ [S2] [W2] *adj.*
1 BUSY showing a lot of physical energy and the enjoyment of many different activities: *an active child* | *She was still very active, even when she was sick.* | **active life/lifestyle** *People over 65 often still have very active lifestyles.*
2 an active mind/imagination used when you are saying that someone is able to think intelligently or in way that shows a lot of imagination: *a child with a very active imagination*
3 INVOLVED involved in an organization, activity etc. and always busy doing things to help it: *an* ***active member*** *of St. Mark's Episcopal Church* | ***politically active*** *students* | *When my dad died, my uncle* ***took an active interest*** *in my future.* | **be active in (doing) sth** *Mark is active in the Republican Party.* | **take/play an active role/part in sth** *She has taken an active role in fundraising for the group.* | **active participation/involvement** *his active participation in various illegal activities*
4 DOING STH doing something regularly: *Most of the people who responded to the questionnaire were* ***sexually active.***
5 FUNCTIONING operating in a way that is normal or expected [OPP] inactive: *The virus is active even at low temperatures.*
6 ELECTRICAL SYSTEM TECHNICAL operating in the way it is supposed to: *The alarm becomes active when the switch is turned on.*
7 MILITARY active duty/service a) a soldier etc. who is on active duty is fighting or can be called to fight at any time: *There are 100,000 troops still on active duty in the region.* **b)** employment by the army etc., as opposed to being in the RESERVES: *He left active service to become reservist in 2002.*
8 STOCK MARKET active trading if there is active trading in a stock market, a large number of STOCKS and SHARES are being bought and sold
9 VOLCANO an active VOLCANO is likely to explode and pour out fire and LAVA (=hot liquid rock)
10 GRAMMAR ENG. LANG. ARTS if a verb or sentence is active, the person or thing doing the action is the SUBJECT. In "The boy kicked the ball," the verb "kick" is active. → see also PASSIVE
11 CHEMICAL CHEMISTRY producing a reaction in a substance or with another chemical **—actively** *adv.*: *The two sides are* ***actively engaged in*** *discussions.* | *My sister is* ***actively involved in*** *several local organizations.*

active² *n.* ENG. LANG. ARTS **the active** also **the active voice** the active form of a verb → see also PASSIVE

ˌactive imˈmunity *n.* [U] BIOLOGY protection from a disease that happens because your body is permanently able to produce ANTIBODIES to protect you. You have this protection either because you have had the disease or you have been given a VACCINE.

ˌactive 'site *n.* [C] CHEMISTRY the place on an ENZYME (=chemical substance that causes other substances to change) where the chemical reaction happens

ac·tiv·ist /'æktəvɪst/ W2 *n.* [C] someone who works hard to achieve social or political change, especially as an active member of a political organization: *environmental activists* —**activism** *n.* [U]

ac·tiv·i·ty /æk'tɪvət̬i/ S2 W1 *n. plural* **activities** **1** [U] a situation in which a lot of things are happening or people are doing things, moving around etc. OPP **inactivity**: *Police were aware of gang activity in the neighborhood.* | *The* ***level of activity*** *in the store increases dramatically at Christmas.* | **physical/mental activity** *Regular physical activity helps to control your weight.* **2** [C] something that you do for fun: *crafts and other activities for children* | *There are clubs and other* ***extracurricular activities*** (=sports, music, theater etc. that students can participate in after school) *at the school.* | **leisure/recreation/outdoor/cultural etc. activities** *The resort offers recreational activities such as swimming, windsurfing, and fishing.* **3** [C] things that people do in order to achieve a particular aim: **political/business etc. activity** *fundraising activities* | *The commission is investigating his business activities.* | **criminal/terrorist/illegal etc. activity** *organized criminal activity*

ac'tivity ˌseries *n.* [C] CHEMISTRY a list of chemical ELEMENTS in order from the one that is most likely to combine with other chemicals in a reaction to the one that is least likely to combine

ˌact of ad'mission *n.* [C] POLITICS an official action by the U.S. Congress allowing a new state to become part of the country

ˌAct of Tole'ration, the → see MARYLAND ACT OF TOLERATION

ac·tor /'æktɚ/ S2 W2 *n.* [C] someone who performs in a play, movie, or television program

ˌActors' 'Equity Associˌation the full name of the UNION Equity

ac·tress /'æktrɪs/ *n.* [C] a woman who performs in a play, movie, or television program

Acts /ækts/ also **The ˌActs of the A'postles** a book in the New Testament of the Christian Bible

ac·tu·al /'æktʃuəl, -ʃəl/ S1 W2 *adj.* [only before noun] **1** real, especially as compared with what is believed, expected, or intended: *It's a true story, based on actual events.* | *I'm not kidding. Those were his actual words!* **2 the actual sth** used to introduce the main part of what you are describing: *The cost will go up, but the actual amount is unknown.* [**Origin:** 1300–1400 Old French *actuel*, from Late Latin *actualis*, from Latin *actus* **doing, act**]

ac·tu·al·i·ty /ˌæktʃu'ælət̬i/ *n. plural* **actualities** FORMAL **1 in actuality** really SYN **in fact**: *Voters were promised that improvements would be made, but in actuality nothing has changed.* **2** [C usually plural] something that is real SYN **fact**: *the grim actualities of prison life* **3** [U] the state of being real SYN **existence**

ac·tu·al·ize /'æktʃuəˌlaɪz/ *v.* [T] to make something such as a dream or idea become real SYN **realize**: *a step toward actualizing your goals* —**actualization** /ˌæktʃuələ'zeɪʃən/ *n.* [U]

ac·tu·al·ly /'æktʃuəli, -tʃəli/ S1 W1 *adv.* **1** [sentence adverb] SPOKEN used when you are giving an opinion or adding new information to what you have just said: *I don't actually remember it all that well.* | *Actually, that was the best part of the whole trip.* | *Well, actually, you still owe me $200.* **2** used when you are telling or asking someone what the real and exact truth of a situation is, as opposed to what people may think: *He may look 30, but he's actually 45.* | *Unemployment has actually fallen for the past two months.* | *So, what actually happened?*

> **WORD CHOICE actually, currently, (right) now**
> **Actually** does not mean "now" or "at this time." Compare **currently** and **(right) now**: *Surprisingly, the population of Brown County actually fell during the 1980s* (=in fact). | *Currently/Right now, Steve Palmer is the assistant sales manager* (at this time).

'actual ˌyield *n.* [C,U] CHEMISTRY the amount of a chemical substance produced by a chemical reaction between two or more substances

ac·tu·ar·i·al /ˌæktʃu'ɛriəl/ *adj.* [only before noun] relating to CALCULATIONS of risks, especially in the insurance industry

ac·tu·ar·y /'æktʃuˌɛri/ *n. plural* **actuaries** [C] ECONOMICS someone who advises insurance companies on how much to charge for insurance, after calculating the various risks

ac·tu·ate /'æktʃuˌeɪt/ *v.* **1** [T] TECHNICAL to make a piece of machinery or electrical equipment start to operate **2 be actuated by sth** FORMAL to behave in a particular way because of a feeling or a quality in your character

a·cu·i·ty /ə'kyuət̬i/ *n.* [U] FORMAL the ability to think, see, or hear quickly and clearly: *mental acuity*

a·cu·men /ə'kyumən, 'ækyəmən/ *n.* [U] the ability to think quickly and make good judgments: *her impressive* ***business acumen***

ac·u·pres·sure /'ækyəˌprɛʃɚ/ *n.* [U] a method of stopping pain and curing disease by pressing on particular areas of the body

ac·u·punc·ture /'ækyəˌpʌŋktʃɚ/ *n.* [U] a medical treatment used to stop pain or cure an illness, that involves pushing special needles into the skin at particular points on the body where energy is believed to flow around your body —**acupuncturist** *n.* [C]

a·cute¹ /ə'kyut/ *adj.*
1 SERIOUS PROBLEM very serious or severe: *acute shortages of food* | *The loss of jobs was especially acute in inner-city areas.*
2 MEDICAL TECHNICAL **a)** an acute illness or disease quickly becomes dangerous → see also CHRONIC: *acute tuberculosis* **b) acute care** medical care for people with severe injuries or illnesses that need help urgently: *acute care hospitals*
3 PAIN very severe and sharp: *acute lower back pain*
4 INTELLIGENT showing the ability to notice things quickly and to think intelligently: *an acute analysis of the crisis* | *an acute observer of American life*
5 acute senses such as hearing, taste, touch etc. are very good and sensitive: *the animal's acute hearing* | *My father had* ***an acute sense of*** *smell.*
6 MATHEMATICS MATH an acute angle is one that is less than 90° → see picture at ANGLE¹
7 PRONUNCIATION MARK an acute ACCENT (=a mark used to show pronunciation) is the small mark put over a letter, such as in French → see also GRAVE
[**Origin:** 1300–1400 Latin, past participle of *acuere* **to sharpen**, from *acus* **needle**] —**acuteness** *n.* [U]

acute² *n.* [C] MATH an angle that is less than 90°

a·cute·ly /ə'kyutli/ *adv.* **1** feeling or noticing something very strongly: *He looked acutely embarrassed.* | *The president said he was* ***acutely aware*** *of the problem.* **2 acutely ill** very ill, so that you could easily die: *acutely ill patients*

aˌcute 'triangle *n.* [C] MATH a TRIANGLE whose three angles are each less than 90°

ad /æd/ S2 W2 *n.* [C] INFORMAL words, a picture, or a short movie that advertises a thing or service that is available or for sale SYN **advertisement**: *an ad campaign* | **+for** *Three hundred people responded to our ad for a secretary* (=one showing that you want someone to do the job of secretary). | **put/place an ad in sth** *The best way to sell your bike is to put an ad in the paper.* → see also CLASSIFIED AD, COMMERCIAL, WANT AD

A.D. /ˌeɪ 'di/ **Anno Domini** used to show that a date is a particular number of years after the birth of Jesus Christ: *The Mayan civilization ended around A.D. 830.* |

in the first/second/sixth etc. century A.D. *The bowl was made in the sixth century A.D.* → see also B.C.

ad·age /ˈædɪdʒ/ *n.* [C] ENG. LANG. ARTS a well-known phrase that says something wise about human experience SYN proverb

a·da·gio /əˈdɑdʒoʊ, -dʒioʊ/ *n.* [C] a piece of music to be played or sung slowly —**adagio** *adj., adv.*

Ad·am /ˈædəm/ **1** in the Bible, the first man **2 not know someone from Adam** INFORMAL to have no idea who someone is

ad·a·mant /ˈædəmənt/ *adj.* FORMAL determined not to change your opinion, decision etc.: +**about** *Newman is adamant about not using pesticides on his crops.* | +**that** *My mother was adamant that nothing would interfere with our education.* [**Origin:** 800–900 Old French, Latin *adamas* **hardest metal, diamond**, from Greek] —**adamantly** *adv.*: *We are* ***adamantly opposed*** *to the new version of the bill.*

Ad·ams, An·sel /ˈædəmz, ˈænsəl/ (1902–1984) a U.S. photographer famous for his photographs of the American West

Adams, John (1735–1826) the second President of the U.S. and Vice President under George Washington

Adams, John Quin·cy /dʒɑn ˈkwɪnsi/ (1767–1848) the sixth President of the U.S.

Adams, Samuel (1722–1803) an American politician and writer famous for protesting against British taxes before the American Revolution

ˈAdam's ˌapple *n.* [C] BIOLOGY the part at the front of a man's neck that sticks out slightly and moves up and down when you swallow

Adams O·nis Treat·y, the /ˌædəmz oʊˈnɪs ˌtriṭi/ also **ˌTransconti'nental ˌTreaty** HISTORY a TREATY (=official legal agreement) in 1819 between the U.S. and Spain that ended disagreements between the two countries over the borders of the U.S. and gave Florida to the U.S.

a·dapt /əˈdæpt/ Ac *v.* **1** [I,T] to gradually change your behavior and ideas to fit a new situation: **adapt to sth** *The kids adapted quickly to living in a small town.* | *The plants are* ***well adapted*** *to desert conditions.* | **adapt yourself/itself etc.** *How do these insects adapt themselves to new environments?* **2** [T] to change something so that it can be used in a different way or for a different purpose: **adapt sth to do sth** *Researchers adapted a blood test to look for early signs of the disease.* | **adapt sth for sb/sth** *The house has been adapted for wheelchair users.* ►see THESAURUS box at change[1] **3** [T] to change a book or play so that it can be made into a movie, television program etc.: *Her latest novel is soon to be adapted for television.* → see also ADJUST

a·dapt·a·ble /əˈdæptəbəl/ Ac *adj.* able to change in order to be appropriate or successful in new and different situations: *Red deer are adaptable animals.* | +**to** *The strategy is adaptable to the 21st century.* —**adaptability** /əˌdæptəˈbɪləṭi/ *n.* [U]

ad·ap·ta·tion /ˌædæpˈteɪʃən/ Ac *n.* **1** [C] a movie or play that was first written in a different form, for example as a book **2** [U] the process of changing something to make it suitable for a new situation: +**to** *adaptation to the environment* **3** [C] BIOLOGY a new and different physical feature that an animal, plant, or other living thing gets from its parents, that increases its chance of staying alive and reproducing (REPRODUCE)

a·dapt·er, adaptor /əˈdæptə/ *n.* [C] something used to connect two pieces of equipment, especially when they are of different sizes or use different levels of power

aˌdaptive radiˈation *n.* [U] BIOLOGY the process by which a group of animals or plants which are all similar and can breed together, gradually change and develop over a long period of time into different groups that are able to live in different environments

ADD /ˌeɪ di ˈdi/ *n.* [U] the abbreviation of ATTENTION DEFICIT DISORDER

add /æd/ S1 W1 *v.*

1 INCREASE/PUT WITH [I,T] to put something with another thing or group to increase the amount, size, or cost: *We are planning to add 500 jobs in the next 12 months.* | *Mix the egg and sugar, then add the flour.* | **add (sth) to sth** *Do you want to add your name to the list?* | *The new regulations will add to the cost of the project.* ►see THESAURUS box at cooking[1]

2 SAY MORE [T] to say more about something you have been talking about: *That's all I have to say. Is there anything you want to add?* | *"Hi I'm Carol," she said, and then added, "I'm a friend of Annie's."* | **add that** *Mike added that his father disagreed with his decision.* ►see THESAURUS box at say[1]

3 GIVE A QUALITY [T] to give something a particular quality: **add sth to sth** *We've* ***added value*** *to the information by organizing it.* | *Champagne always adds glamor to an occasion.*

4 COUNTING [I,T] MATH to put two numbers or amounts together and then calculate the total → see also SUBTRACT: *Add 6 and 6 and you get 12.* | *Do you know how to add?* | **add sth to sth** *Add $2.20 to the cost for shipping.*

5 add fuel to sth to make a bad situation even worse, especially by making someone more angry: *The report added fuel to complaints about government secrecy.* | *Threats will only* ***add fuel to the fire*** (=make the situation worse).

6 add insult to injury to do something that makes a situation even worse for someone, when they have already been badly or unfairly treated: *She didn't tell him she was married and,* ***to add insult to injury****, she let him pay for her dinner.*

[**Origin:** 1300–1400 Latin *addere*, from *ad-* **to** + *-dere* **to put**]

add sth ↔ **in** *phr. v.* to include something, especially in a total: *Wilson's salary is about $1.2 million when his stock options are added in.*

add sth ↔ **on** *phr. v.* **1** to increase the amount or cost of something by putting something more with it: *Labor costs could add on a further 25%.* | +**to** *They'd already added the tip on to the bill.* **2** to make a building larger by building another room: *We're thinking of adding on another bedroom.* | +**to** *The Lopezes recently added on to their kitchen.*

add to sth *phr. v.* **1** to increase something: *The new rules only added to the problem.* **2 add to this/that** used to introduce another fact, especially one that makes a situation seem even worse: *The script was poor. Add to that the sloppy acting and you have a disaster.*

add up *phr. v.* **1 add sth ↔ up** MATH to calculate the total of several numbers or amounts: *When you add the numbers up, you'll see how well we've done.* | *I can't get these figures to add up.* **2** INFORMAL to increase by small amounts until there is a large total: *The problems began to add up quickly.* | *Two or three bus passes at $15 each soon adds up.* | **it all adds up** (=used to say that lots of small amounts gradually make a large total) *There are five of us making long distance calls, so it all adds up.* **3 not add up** to not seem true or reasonable: *Jake's explanation* ***just didn't add up.***

add up to sth *phr. v.* to have a particular result: *Rising prison population and overcrowding add up to a real crisis.*

Ad·dams, Jane /ˈædəmz, dʒeɪn/ (1860–1935) a U.S. social REFORMER who worked to help poor people in cities and for peace and women's rights

add·ed /ˈædɪd/ *adj.* [only before noun] in addition to what is usual or expected SYN extra: *We now have the* ***added expense*** *of having two kids in college.* | **added advantage/bonus/benefit etc** *The system has the added advantage of recordable DVD drives.*

ad·den·dum /əˈdɛndəm/ *n. plural* **addenda** /-də/ [C] TECHNICAL something that is added to the end of a book, usually to give more information

ad·der /ˈædə/ *n.* [C] BIOLOGY **1** one of several types of snakes living in North America **2** a small poisonous snake living in northern Europe and northern Asia

A

[**Origin:** 1300–1400 *a nadder*, mistaken for *an adder*; *nadder* **adder** (11–17 centuries) from Old English *nædre*]

ad•dict /'ædɪkt/ *n.* [C] **1** someone who is unable to stop taking drugs: *Many addicts refuse to go to treatment centers.* | **a drug/heroin etc. addict** *Kevin is a recovering cocaine addict.* **2** someone who spends too much time doing something they like, but which may not be good or healthy for them: *a television addict* [**Origin:** 1500–1600 Latin, past participle of *addicere* **to give to formally or legally**, from *ad-* **to** + *dicere* **to say**]

ad•dict•ed /ə'dɪktɪd/ *adj.* [not before noun] **1** unable to stop taking a harmful substance, especially a drug: **+to** *One in seven people is addicted to alcohol or drugs.* **2** liking to have or do something, especially something that is not good or healthy, so much that you do not want to stop: **+to** *My kids are addicted to video games.*

ad•dic•tion /ə'dɪkʃən/ *n.* [C,U] **1** MEDICINE the need to take a harmful drug because you are addicted to it: *drug addiction* | **+to** *Her addiction to alcohol ruined her life.* **2** a strong desire to have or do something regularly, when this is difficult to stop: **+to** *my addiction to sweet foods*

ad•dic•tive /ə'dɪktɪv/ *adj.* **1** a substance or drug that is addictive makes you unable to stop taking it: *an addictive drug* | *Crack is a* ***highly addictive*** (=very addictive) *form of cocaine.* **2** also **addicting** INFORMAL a food or an activity that is addictive is so enjoyable that you do not want to stop: *Golf can be addictive and expensive.*

Ad•dis Ab•a•ba /ˌædɪs 'æbəbə/ the capital and largest city of Ethiopia

ad•di•tion /ə'dɪʃən/ S3 W1 *n.* **1 in addition** used in order to add information or show that something is more than what is usual or expected: *A new security system was installed. In addition, extra guards were hired.* | **+to** *You will be paid overtime in addition to your regular salary.* | *In addition to writing, I also enjoy rock climbing.*

THESAURUS

extra if something is **extra**, it is not included in the price of something and you have to pay more for it: *Dinner costs $15, but drinks are extra.*
on top of INFORMAL in addition to something: *On top of everything else, I have to work on Saturday.*

2 [U] the act of adding something to something else: **the addition of sth** *the addition of fertilizer to the soil* | **with the addition of sth** *With the addition of new prisoners comes the need for new space.* **3** [C] something that is added to something else, often in order to improve it: **+to** *The book would be a* ***welcome addition*** *to the library of any college student.* | **latest/new/recent addition** *Oakmont Elementary School is the most recent addition to the school district.*

THESAURUS

additive a substance that is added to food to make it taste or look better or to keep it fresh: *Additives help keep the color of the product from changing.*
supplement something that is added to something else to improve it: *vitamin supplements*

4 [C] a room or a part of a building that is added to the main building: *The Simpsons built a big addition onto the back of their house.* **5** [U] MATH the process of adding numbers or amounts to make a total → see also SUBTRACTION: *five-year-olds learning addition*

ad•di•tion•al /ə'dɪʃənəl/ S3 W2 *adj.* [usually before noun] more than what was agreed or expected SYN **extra**: *Additional troops may be sent to the region.* | *an additional cost of $180 million* | *Two additional factors need to be considered.*

ad•di•tion•al•ly /ə'dɪʃənəli/ *sentence adv.* in addition SYN **also**: *The group may be smuggling drugs. Additionally, they're suspected of several murders.*

ad•di•tive /'ædət̬ɪv/ *n.* [C] a substance, especially a chemical, that is added to something such as food, to preserve it, give it color, improve it etc.: *Our foods have no additives or preservatives.*

adˌditive 'inverse *n.* [C usually singular] MATH for any number, the additive inverse is the number you add to it to give the answer zero. For example, the additive inverse of 6 is -6. → see also MULTIPLICATIVE INVERSE

ad•dled /'ædld/ *adj.* ESPECIALLY HUMOROUS confused and unable to think clearly: *my addled brain* —**addle** *v.* [T]

'add-on *n.* [C] **1** a piece of equipment, service etc. that is sold or given separately from a product or service you are buying, and adds value to the product or service → see also PERIPHERAL: *add-ons such as modems and DVD drives* | *Most travel websites offer a variety of add-ons with every vacation package.* **2** something additional that is later added to a bill, plan, agreement etc.: **+to** *add-ons to the budget bill in the Senate*

ad•dress¹ /ə'drɛs, 'ædrɛs/ S1 W2 *n.* **1** [C] the number of the building and the name of the street and town etc. where someone lives or works → see also BILLING ADDRESS: *Write down your name, address, and phone number.* | *Keep us informed of any* ***change of address***. **2** the set of words that you type into a computer in order to send someone an email or look at a website: *Here is the site's address.* | **email/web address** *I'll give you my email address.* ▶see THESAURUS box at **Internet** **3** /ə'drɛs/ [C] a formal and important speech made to a group of people: **+to** *the President's* ***televised address*** (=shown on television) *to the nation* | **deliver/give an address** *Williams delivered* ***the keynote address*** (=the most important speech, when there are many) *at the convention.* | **an inaugural/a farewell/a commencement etc. address** *They have asked me to give the commencement address at the college* ▶see THESAURUS box at **speech** **4 a form/style/mode of address** the title or name that you use for someone when you are speaking to them: *What's the correct form of address for the governor of a state?*

ad•dress² S2 W2 /ə'drɛs/ *v.* [T] **1** to write on an envelope, package etc. the name and address of the person you are sending it to: **address sth to sb** *The letter was addressed to me.* | *Send us* ***a self-addressed, stamped envelope*** (=an envelope with your own address and a stamp on it) *to request an application.* **2** FORMAL if you address a problem, you start trying to solve it: **address a problem/question/issue etc.** *The report addresses the problems of malnutrition in the state.* | *He organized a meeting to address workers' complaints.* **3 address a meeting/crowd/conference etc.** to make a speech to a large group of people: *Dantley addressed a rally in Boston.* **4** to use a particular title or name when speaking or writing to someone: **address sb as sth** *You should address him as "Mr. President."* **5** FORMAL to speak directly to someone: *Suzanne turned to address the man asking the question.* **6** FORMAL if you address your comments, complaints etc. to someone, you say or write them directly to that person: **address sth to sb** *Please address any complaints to the main office.* [**Origin:** 1300–1400 Old French *adresser*, from *dresser* **to arrange**]

ad'dress book *n.* [C] **1** a book in which you write the addresses, phone numbers etc. of people you know **2** a place on your computer where you store names, addresses, phone numbers, email addresses etc. of people you know

ad•dress•ee /ˌædrɛ'si, əˌdrɛs'i/ *n.* [C] the person a letter, package etc. is addressed to → see also SENDER

ad•duce /ə'dus/ *v.* [T] FORMAL to give facts or reasons in order to prove that something is true

-ade /eɪd/ *suffix* [in U nouns] used in the names of drinks made from a particular fruit: *lemonade* (=drink made from lemons)

ad•e•noi•dal /ˌædn'ɔɪdl◂/ *adj.* an adenoidal voice sounds as if it is coming mainly through a person's nose

ad•e•noids /'ædnˌɔɪdz/ *n.* [plural] BIOLOGY the small soft pieces of flesh at the top of your throat, behind your nose, that sometimes become swollen → see also TONSIL

a·dept¹ /ə'dɛpt/ *adj.* good at doing something that needs care and skill SYN **skillful**: **adept at/in (doing) sth** *Holling soon became adept at sign language.* | *He was adept in spotting talented players.* —**adeptly** *adv.*

ad·ept² /'ædɛpt. ə'dɛpt/ *n.* [C] someone who is very skillful at doing something

ad·e·quate /'ædəkwɪt/ Ac *adj.* **1** enough in quantity or of a good enough quality for a particular purpose SYN **sufficient**: *Most people eat an adequate diet.* | *The company has not yet provided an adequate explanation for its actions.* | *His work is* ***barely adequate*** (=of such low quality that it is almost not good enough). | +**for** *The school's facilities are adequate for the students' needs.* | **adequate to do sth** *The lunch menu is* ***more than adequate*** *to satisfy the biggest appetite.* ►see THESAURUS box at **enough¹**, **satisfactory** **2** fairly good, but not excellent: *Redman's performance was adequate, but unoriginal.* [**Origin:** 1500–1600 Latin, past participle of *adaequare* **to make equal**, from *ad-* **to** + *aequare* **to equal**] —**adequately** *adv.*: *She wasn't adequately insured.* —**adequacy** *n.* [U]

THESAURUS

adequate FORMAL enough in amount or good enough in quality. Adequate sometimes seems negative, suggesting that the amount is just barely enough: *The pay was adequate.*
sufficient FORMAL enough in amount: *Is there sufficient evidence to charge him with the crime?*
enough as many or as much as is needed or wanted: *Are there enough eggs to make the cake?* | *The schools do not receive enough funding for music programs.*
satisfactory used when the quality of something is acceptable and enough: *Hansen's work was not satisfactory.*
good enough INFORMAL used when the quality of something is acceptable: *My Spanish was good enough to order a meal and get directions, but not much more.*
will/have to/should do SPOKEN used when something is acceptable, though it might not be perfect: *"Do we have enough Coke for the party?" "Six bottles should do, I think."* | *It's not very good, but it will have to do.*

ADHD /ˌeɪ di eɪtʃ 'di/ *n.* [U] the abbreviation of ATTENTION-DEFICIT HYPERACTIVITY DISORDER

ad·here /əd'hɪr/ *v.* [I] FORMAL to stick firmly to something: +**to** *The tape should adhere to any surface.*

adhere to sth *phr. v.* FORMAL to continue to behave according to a particular rule, agreement, or belief: **adhere to rules/guidelines/regulations etc.** *Few people* ***adhere strictly*** *to the guidelines* (=do exactly what the rules say).

ad·her·ence /əd'hɪrəns/ *n.* [U] the act of behaving according to a particular rule, belief, or principal: +**to** ***strict adherence*** *to democratic principles*

ad·her·ent /əd'hɪrənt/ *n.* [C] FORMAL someone who supports a particular idea, plan, political party etc.

ad·he·sion /əd'hiʒən/ *n.* **1** [C,U] BIOLOGY a piece of body TISSUE (=flesh) that has grown around a small injury or damaged area and has joined it to other tissue, or the process of joining two tissues together in this way **2** [U] the state of one thing sticking to another **3** [U] PHYSICS a force that makes the atoms of different substances join tightly together when the substances touch each other

ad·he·sive¹ /əd'hisɪv, -zɪv/ *n.* [C,U] a substance such as glue that can be used to make two things stick together firmly

adhesive² *adj.* adhesive material sticks firmly to surfaces: *adhesive tape*

ad hoc /ˌæd 'hɑk/ *adj.* [usually before noun] done or arranged only when the situation makes it necessary, and without any previous planning: *An ad hoc committee has been set up to deal with the problem.* | *Decisions were made* ***on an ad hoc basis*** (=according to what is needed at a particular time). —**ad hoc** *adv.*

ad·i·a·bat·ic /ˌædiə'bæṭɪk, ˌeɪdaɪə-/ *adj.* PHYSICS relating to a process that happens without a loss or gain of heat, used especially about currents of air that rise and fall without exchanging heat with the surrounding air

a·dieu /ə'du, ə'dyu/ *n.* *plural* **adieux** /ə'duz, ə'dyuz/ or **adieus** [C] LITERARY an act of saying goodbye: *He* ***bid*** *her a fond* ***adieu.*** [**Origin:** 1300–1400 French **to God**] —**adieu** *interjection*

ad in·fi·ni·tum /ˌæd ɪnfɪ'naɪṭəm/ *adv.* FORMAL continuing or repeated for a very long time, or without ever ending: *DNA can copy itself within a cell ad infinitum.*

ad·i·os /ɑdi'oʊs, æ-/ *interjection* goodbye [**Origin:** 1800–1900 Spanish **to God**]

ad·i·pose /'ædɪˌpoʊs/ *adj.* TECHNICAL consisting of or containing animal fat: *adipose tissue*

Ad·i·ron·dacks, the /ˌædə'rɑndæks/ also **the Adi'rondack ˌMountains** a range of mountains in New York State, in the northeastern U.S.

adj. the written abbreviation of "adjective"

ad·ja·cent /ə'dʒeɪsənt/ Ac *adj.* a room, building, piece of land etc. that is adjacent to something is next to it: *the sale of adjacent land* | +**to** *The fire started in the building adjacent to the library.* [**Origin:** 1400–1500 Latin, present participle of *adjacere* **to lie near**, from *ad-* **to** + *jacere* **to lie**]

adˌjacent 'angles *n.* [plural] MATH two angles that share one side and have the same VERTEX (=the point where the two lines of an angle meet) but do not share any other points → see picture at ANGLE¹

adˌjacent 'arcs *n.* [plural] MATH two ARCS (=curved lines) that are next to each other on the outside of the same circle and share only one point

ad·jec·ti·val /ˌædʒɪk'taɪvəl◂ / *adj.* **an adjectival phrase/clause etc.** ENG. LANG. ARTS a phrase etc. that is used as an adjective or that consists of adjectives. For example, "fully equipped" is an adjectival phrase. —**adjectivally** *adv.*

ad·jec·tive /'ædʒɪktɪv, 'ædʒətɪv/ *n.* [C] ENG. LANG. ARTS a word that describes a noun or PRONOUN, such as "black" in the sentence "She wore a black hat," or "happy" in the sentence "I'll try to make you happy." → see also ADVERB [**Origin:** 1300–1400 Old French *adjectif*, from Latin *adjectus*, past participle of *adjicere*, from *ad-* **to** + *jacere* **to throw**]

WORD CHOICE **bored, boring; interested in, interesting; frightened of, frightening etc.**
With pairs of adjectives like this, the one ending in **-ed** describes the person who has the feeling, and the one ending in **-ing** describes the thing or person that gives them that feeling: *Two weeks later, I got bored with the job.* | *The job got really boring.* | *Judy is really interested in art.* | *Judy thinks art is really interesting.* | *Thousands are frightened of losing their jobs.* | *Losing your job is a frightening experience.*

ad·join /ə'dʒɔɪn/ *v.* [T] if a room, building, or piece of land adjoins another one, it is next to it and joined to it: *A luxury hotel adjoins the convention center.* —**adjoining** *adj.* [only before noun] *adjoining hotel rooms*

ad·journ /ə'dʒən/ *v.* **1** [I,T] LAW if a meeting, law court, or Congress adjourns, or if the person in charge adjourns it, it stops for a short time: *The chairman can* ***adjourn the meeting*** *at any time.* | +**for/until** ***The trial*** *was* ***adjourned*** *for two weeks.* | *The committee adjourned until Tuesday.* **2 adjourn to sth** HUMOROUS to finish an activity and go somewhere: *We all adjourned to the bar to celebrate.* —**adjournment** *n.* [C,U]

ad·judge /ə'dʒʌdʒ/ *v.* [T] FORMAL to make a judgment about something or someone

ad·ju·di·cate /ə'dʒudɪˌkeɪt/ *v.* FORMAL **1** [I,T] to officially decide who is right in an argument between two groups or organizations: *An independent expert was* called in to adjudicate. | **adjudicate a case/claim/dispute etc.** *It took over two months for our case to be adjudicated.* **2** [I] to be the judge in a competition —**adjudicator** *n.* [C] —**adjudication** /əˌdʒudɪˈkeɪʃən/ *n.* [U]

ad·junct¹ /ˈædʒʌŋkt/ *n.* [C] FORMAL **1** something that is added or joined to something, but is not part of it: **+to** *Medication can be a useful adjunct to physical therapy.* **2** TECHNICAL an ADVERBIAL word or phrase that adds meaning to another part of a sentence, such as "on Sunday" in "They arrived on Sunday."

adjunct² *adj.* [only before noun] connected to something else, but not completely a part of it: *an adjunct power source* | *an adjunct professor* (=who works part-time at a college)

ad·jure /əˈdʒʊr/ *v.* [T] FORMAL to try very hard to persuade someone to do something

ad·just /əˈdʒʌst/ Ac S3 W3 *v.* **1** [I,T] to make small changes to something, especially to its position, in order to improve it, make it more effective etc.: *Adjust the heat so that the soup doesn't boil.* | *Seat belts* ***adjust to fit*** *short or tall drivers.* ►see THESAURUS box at change¹ **2** [I] to gradually get used to a new situation by making small changes to the way you do things: *It's amazing how quickly kids adjust.* | **+to** *It took a long time to adjust to the tropical heat.* | **adjust to doing sth** *My parents had trouble adjusting to living in an apartment.* **3** [T] if you adjust something you are wearing, you move it slightly so that it is neater, more comfortable etc.: *He adjusted his tie and knocked on the door.* [**Origin:** 1600–1700 French *ajuster*, from *juste* **exact, just**] → see also WELL-ADJUSTED

ad·just·a·ble /əˈdʒʌstəbəl/ *adj.* something that is adjustable can be changed in shape, size, or position to make it appropriate for a particular person or purpose: *an adjustable desk lamp*

ad·just·er /əˈdʒʌstɚ/ *n.* [C] someone who is employed by an insurance company to decide how much money to pay people who have had an accident, had something stolen etc.: *a claims adjuster*

ad·just·ment /əˈdʒʌstmənt/ Ac *n.* [C,U] **1** a small change to a machine, a system, a calculation, or to the way something looks: **+to** *We've had to* ***make*** *some* ***adjustments*** *to the schedule.* | **+for** *They should have made some adjustment for inflation.* | **a slight/minor adjustment** (=a small change) **2** a change that someone makes to the way they behave or think: *Moving to the city has been a difficult adjustment for us.* | *There is always an initial* ***period of adjustment***.

ad·ju·tant /ˈædʒətənt/ *n.* [C] an army officer responsible for office work

ad-lib /ˌæd ˈlɪb/ *v.* **ad-libbed, ad-libbing** [I,T] to say something in a speech, a performance of a play etc. without preparing or planning it: *I had to ad-lib the whole speech.* —**ad-lib** *n.* [C] —**ad-lib** *adj., adv.*

ad·man /ˈædmæn/ *n. plural* **admen** /-mɛn/ [C] INFORMAL a man who works in advertising

ad·min /ˈædmɪn/ *n.* [U] INFORMAL → see ADMINISTRATION

ad·min·is·ter /ədˈmɪnəstɚ/ *v.* [T] **1** to manage and organize the affairs of a company, government etc.: *Ms. O'Brien's office is in charge of administering welfare programs.* **2** to organize the way a test or punishment is given, or to organize the way laws are used: *It is the captain's job to administer punishment on the ship.* | *The test was administered fairly.* **3** FORMAL to give someone a medicine or drug to take: *Oxygen was being administered to the patient.* [**Origin:** 1300–1400 Old French *aministrer*, from Latin *administrare*, from *ad-* **to** + *ministrare* **to serve**]

ad·min·is·tra·tion /ədˌmɪnəˈstreɪʃən/ Ac S3 W1 *n.* **1** [C] POLITICS the government of a country at a particular time, especially the people and departments that approve decisions and are responsible for making laws work: *the Kennedy Administration* **2 the administration** the people who manage an institution or organization, especially a college or university: *conflicts between the faculty and the administration* **3** [U] all the activities that are involved in managing and organizing the affairs of a company, institution etc.: *We're looking for someone with experience in administration.* | *Some hospitals spend too much on administration and not enough on medical care.* **4** [U] the act of administering a test, law etc.: **+of** *the administration of justice*

ad·min·is·tra·tive /ədˈmɪnəˌstreɪt̬ɪv, -strə-/ Ac W3 *adj.* relating to the work of managing or organizing a company, institution etc.: *Phil's job is mainly administrative.* | *the department's* ***administrative costs*** | *I was given only* ***administrative duties.*** —**administratively** *adv.*

adˌministrative asˈsistant *n.* [C] someone who works in an office typing (TYPE) letters, keeping records, answering telephone calls, arranging meetings etc.

ad·min·is·tra·tor /ədˈmɪnəˌstreɪt̬ɚ/ Ac W3 *n.* [C] someone whose job is related to the management and organization of a company, institution etc.: *a hospital administrator*

ad·mi·ra·ble /ˈædmərəbəl/ *adj.* something that is admirable has many good qualities that you respect and admire: *an admirable achievement* —**admirably** *adv.*: *You all performed admirably.*

ad·mi·ral /ˈædmərəl/ *n.* [C] someone with a very high rank in the Navy [**Origin:** 1200–1300 Old French *amiral*, from Medieval Latin *admirallus*, from Arabic *amir-al-* **commander of the**]

ad·mi·ra·tion /ˌædməˈreɪʃən/ *n.* [U] a feeling of admiring something or someone: *Carlos has earned our respect and admiration.* | **+for** *She expressed her admiration for Albright's political abilities.*

ad·mire /ədˈmaɪɚ/ W3 *v.* [T not in progressive] **1** to have a very high opinion of someone because of a quality they have or because of something they have done: *We all admire the troops' bravery.* | **admire sb for sth** *Lewis was admired for his work in medieval literature.* | *I* ***admire the way*** *Miller handled the controversy.*

THESAURUS

respect to have a good opinion of someone because of his or her knowledge, skill, personal qualities etc.: *He is respected by his colleagues.*
look up to sb to admire and respect someone: *The other kids looked up to him.*
idolize to admire someone so much that you think she or he is perfect: *He's now on the same team as the player he idolized in high school.*

2 to look at something and think how beautiful or impressive it is: *We stopped halfway up the hill to* ***admire the view.*** **3 admire sb from afar** OLD-FASHIONED to be attracted to someone, without telling them how you feel [**Origin:** 1500–1600 French *admirer*, from Latin *admirari*, from *ad-* **to** + *mirari* **to wonder**] —**admiring** *adj.* —**admiringly** *adv.*

ad·mir·er /ədˈmaɪrɚ/ *n.* [C] **1** someone who admires another person or another person's work, especially when the other person is famous: *A crowd of admirers waved and cheered.* | **+of** *I'm* ***a real admirer of*** (=used in order to emphasize how much you admire someone) *Robert Frost's poetry.* **2** a man who is attracted to a particular woman: *Ellen had many admirers.* | *Yesterday, I got some flowers from* ***a secret admirer*** (=someone who likes you romantically, but has not told you).

ad·mis·si·ble /ədˈmɪsəbəl/ *adj.* FORMAL LAW admissible reasons, facts etc. are acceptable or allowed, especially in a court of law OPP **inadmissable**: *admissible evidence* —**admissibility** /ədˌmɪsəˈbɪlət̬i/ *n.* [U]

ad·mis·sion /ədˈmɪʃən/ W3 *n.* **1** [U] the cost of entrance to a concert, sports event etc.: *Admission is only $3.50.* **2** [C] a statement in which you admit that something is true or that you have done something wrong SYN **confession** OPP **denial**: **+that** *The Senator's admission that he had lied to Congress shocked many Americans.* | *Reese,* ***by his own admission*** (=used when someone is admitting something bad about themselves), *lacks the necessary experience.* | **admission of guilt/defeat/failure etc.** *an admission of guilt from the prisoner* **3** [U] permission given to someone to become a member of an organization, to enter a school or building etc.: *No admission after 10 p.m.* | **+to/into** *She was one of the first women ever to* ***gain admission to*** *the architectural profession.* | *He was* ***refused admission*** *to the university.* **4 admissions** [plural] the process of allowing people to enter a college, institution, hospital etc., or the number of people who can enter: *the college's admissions policy* | *They want to limit admissions to 500 students a year.* **5** [C,U] the process of taking someone into a hospital for treatment, tests, or care: *The number of emergency* ***hospital admissions*** *has risen dramatically.*

WORD CHOICE **admission, admittance, admissions**

- **Admission** is the usual word.
- **Admittance** is more formal and only used in the meaning of permission to go into a building, park etc., usually given by someone in authority. On a sign you might see: *Private Road: No Admittance.*
- **Admissions** is the word used by official organizations about the process of entering a college, school, hospital etc.: *the admissions department*

ad·mit /əd'mɪt/ S2 W2 *v.* **admitted, admitting**
1 ACCEPT TRUTH [I,T] to agree unwillingly that something is true or that someone else is right: *"I guess I was a little scared," he admitted.* | **admit (that)** *I admit that I didn't believe her at first.* | ***I have to admit*** *I was a little drunk* (=used when you are admitting something you do not want to say). | ***Admit it.*** *You really like those plastic reindeer on the roof at Christmas* (=used in order to try to make someone admit something). | **admit (to) doing sth** *He'd never admit to being embarrassed.* | **freely/openly admit sth** (=admit something without being ashamed)

THESAURUS

concede FORMAL to admit something: *He conceded that Harrison might be right.*
accept to agree that what someone says is right or true: *The measurement was accepted as accurate.*
acknowledge/recognize to admit or accept that something is true or that a situation exists: *The doctor was forced to acknowledge that his action had caused the patient's death.*
own up INFORMAL to admit that you have done something wrong: *He finally owned up to having lied to me.*
come clean INFORMAL to finally tell the truth about something you have been hiding: *It was time for him to come clean, to be honest with her about what he had done.*

2 STH WRONG/ILLEGAL [I,T] to say that you have done something wrong, especially something illegal SYN **confess** OPP **deny**: *The group has* ***admitted responsibility for*** *the bombing.* | **admit (to) doing sth** *A quarter of all workers admit to taking time off when they are not sick.* | **admit (to) sth** *After questioning, she admitted to the murder.*
3 ALLOW TO ENTER [T] to allow someone or something to enter a place: *Some countries refused to admit people with the disease.* | **admit sb to/into sth** *Only members will be admitted to the club for tonight's performance.*
4 ALLOW TO JOIN [T] to allow someone to join an organization, club, school etc.: **admit sb to/into sth** *Twenty-five students were admitted to the Honor Society yesterday.*
5 HOSPITAL ETC. [T usually passive] to take someone into the hospital, a NURSING HOME etc. for treatment and keep them there until they are well enough to leave: *What time was he admitted?* | **admit sb to sth** *Steve was admitted to the hospital Tuesday morning with stomach pains.*
6 admit defeat to stop trying to do something because you realize you cannot succeed: *Haskill refuses to admit defeat and sell the restaurant.*
7 admit (sth as) evidence to allow a particular piece of EVIDENCE to be used in a court of law: *The judge allowed the knife to be admitted as evidence.*

[**Origin:** 1300–1400 Latin *admittere*, from *ad-* **to** + *mittere* **to send**]

admit of sth *phr. v.* FORMAL to allow the possibility that something is correct or true: *The law admits of no exceptions.*

ad·mit·tance /əd'mɪt̚ns/ *n.* [U] FORMAL permission to enter a place: *Steven's grades weren't good enough to* ***gain admittance to*** (=get permission to enter) *Iowa State.* → see also ADMISSION → see Word Choice box at ADMISSION

ad·mit·ted·ly /əd'mɪt̬ɪdli/ *adv.* [sentence adverb] used when you are admitting that something is true: *The technique is painful, admittedly, but it benefits the patient greatly.*

ad·mix·ture /æd'mɪkstʃɚ/ *n.* [C + of] TECHNICAL a mixture, or a substance that is added to another substance in a mixture

ad·mon·ish /əd'mɑnɪʃ/ *v.* [T] FORMAL **1** to tell someone severely to change their behavior because they have done something wrong or unacceptable: **admonish sb for (doing) sth** *The witness was admonished for refusing to answer the question.* **2** to advise someone very strongly to do something or not to do something: **admonish sb to do sth** *Companies have been admonished to write documents in language the public can understand.* —**admonishment** *n.* [C]

ad·mo·ni·tion /ˌædmə'nɪʃən/ *n.* [C,U] FORMAL a warning or expression of disapproval about someone's behavior —**admonitory** /əd'mɑnəˌtɔri/ *adj.* FORMAL

ad nau·se·am /æd 'nɔziəm/ *adv.* if you say or do something ad nauseam, you say or do it so often that it becomes annoying to other people: *My mother used to repeat that saying ad nauseum.*

a·do /ə'du/ *n.* **without further ado/with no further ado** without delaying anymore, or wasting any more time: *So without further ado, I present Professor Barbara Davies.*

a·do·be /ə'doʊbi/ *n.* **1** [U] earth and STRAW that are made into bricks for building houses **2** [C] a house made using adobe [**Origin:** 1700–1800 Spanish, Arabic *at-tub* **the brick**, from Coptic *tobe* **brick**]

a·do·les·cence /ˌædl'ɛsəns/ *n.* [U] the time, usually between the ages of 12 and 18, when a young person is developing into an adult: ***During adolescence,*** *boys often lack self-confidence.* | **in early/late adolescence** (=in the first or later years of this time)

ad·o·les·cent[1] /ˌædl'ɛsənt/ *n.* [C] FORMAL a young person who is developing into an adult; a TEENAGER ▸see THESAURUS box at **child**

adolescent[2] *adj.* [usually before noun] relating to young people who are developing into adults: *adolescent girls* ▸see THESAURUS box at **young**[1]

a·dopt /ə'dɑpt/ S3 W2 *v.*
1 CHILD [I,T] to legally make another person's child part of your family so that he or she becomes one of your own children → see also FOSTER: *My mother was adopted when she was four.* | *The couple is still hoping to adopt.*
2 ACCEPT A SUGGESTION [T] to formally approve a proposal, especially by voting: *Congress finally adopted the law after a two-year debate.*
3 adopt an approach/strategy/policy etc. to start to use a particular method or plan for dealing with something: *California has adopted a tough approach to the problem.* | *The school recently adopted a new drug testing policy.*
4 HELP AN ORGANIZATION [T] to regularly help an organization, place etc. by giving it money, working for it etc.: *PTM Co. has adopted a neighborhood school, and employees often tutor students.*
5 STYLE/MANNER [T] to use a particular style of spea[k]ing, writing, or behaving, especially one that you [do] not usually use: *Kim adopts a different manner wh[en] she talks to men.*

A

6 adopt a name/country etc. to start to use or consider something as your own: *Stevens became a Muslim and adopted the name Yusuf Islam.*
[**Origin:** 1400–1500 French *adopter*, from Latin *adoptare*, from *ad-* **to** + *optare* **to choose**]

a·dopt·ed /əˈdɑptɪd/ *adj.* **1** an adopted child has been legally made part of a family that he or she was not born into → see also ADOPTIVE: *The Browns have one adopted son.* **2** your adopted country, religion, name etc. is one that you have chosen to use or consider as your own

a·dop·tee /əˌdɑpˈti/ *n.* [C] someone who has been adopted

a·dop·tion /əˈdɑpʃən/ *n.* **1** [C,U] the act or process of adopting a child: *Adoption is the obvious choice for couples who cannot have children.* | *Some adoptions take years.* **2** [U] the act of deciding to use a particular plan, method, law, way of speaking etc.: +**of** *the successful adoption of new technology*

a·dop·tive /əˈdɑptɪv/ *adj.* [only before noun] **1 an adoptive parent/father/mother** an adoptive parent, father, or mother is one who has adopted a child **2 an adoptive child** a child that has been adopted

a·dor·a·ble /əˈdɔrəbəl/ *adj.* someone or something that is adorable is so attractive that it fills you with feelings of love: *What an adorable baby!*

ad·o·ra·tion /ˌædəˈreɪʃən/ *n.* [U] **1** great love and admiration **2** LITERARY religious worship

a·dore /əˈdɔr/ *v.* [T not in progressive] **1** to love someone very much and feel very proud of them: *Betty adores her grandchildren.* **2** INFORMAL to like something very much: *As a child, I adored fairy tales.* [**Origin:** 1300–1400 French *adorer*, from Latin *adorare*, from *ad-* **to** + *orare* **to speak, pray**]

a·dor·ing /əˈdɔrɪŋ/ *adj.* [only before noun] liking and admiring someone very much: *Adoring fans crowded around the stage.* —**adoringly** *adv.*

a·dorn /əˈdɔrn/ *v.* [T usually passive] FORMAL to decorate something: **adorn sth with sth** *houses adorned with tiny white lights*

a·dorn·ment /əˈdɔrnmənt/ *n.* FORMAL **1** [C,U] something that you use to decorate something **2** [U] the act of adorning something

a·dren·a·line, adrenalin /əˈdrɛnl-ɪn/ *n.* [U] a chemical produced by your body when you are afraid, angry, or excited, which makes your heart beat faster so that you can move quickly: *Bungee jumping produces* ***an incredible adrenaline rush*** (=great feeling of excitement or fear). | ***My adrenaline was really pumping*** (=I felt very excited) *before the game.* —**adrenal** /əˈdrinl/ *adj.*: *adrenal glands*

A·dri·at·ic, the /ˌeɪdriˈæṭɪk◂/ also **the ˌAdriˈatic ˌSea** the part of the Mediterranean Sea between Italy, Slovenia, Croatia, Bosnia, Montenegro, and Albania

a·drift /əˈdrɪft/ *adj., adv.* [not before noun] **1** a boat that is adrift is not tied to anything or controlled by anyone: **set/cast a boat adrift** (=untie a boat) **2** someone who is adrift does not have anyone else helping them or leading them

a·droit /əˈdrɔɪt/ *adj.* smart and skillful, especially in the way you use words and arguments: *an adroit negotiator* —**adroitly** *adv.*: *He adroitly turned the conversation to a new topic.* —**adroitness** *n.* [U]

ad·u·la·tion /ˌædʒəˈleɪʃən/ *n.* [U] praise and admiration for someone that is more than they really deserve —**adulatory** /ˈædʒələˌtɔri/ *adj.* —**adulate** /ˈædʒəˌleɪt/ *v.* [T]

a·dult¹ /əˈdʌlt, ˈædʌlt/ Ac S3 W2 *n.* [C] **1** a fully grown person, or one who is old enough to be considered legally responsible for their actions: *Some children find it difficult to talk to adults.* | *Prosecutors are seeking to have the 15-year-old defendant* ***tried as an adult*** (=judged in court in the same way an adult would be). **2** a fully-grown animal: *The adults have white feathers.*

adult² Ac W3 *adj.* [only before noun] **1** fully grown or developed: *an adult lion* | *the adult population* | *The brothers lived most of their* ***adult lives*** (=the part of their lives when they were adults) *in Vermont.* **2** typical of an adult's behavior or of the things adults do: *dealing with problems in an adult way* **3 adult movies/magazines/bookstores etc.** movies, magazines etc. that relate to sex, show sexual acts etc. [**Origin:** 1500–1600 Latin, past participle of *adolescere* **to grow up**]

aˌdult eduˈcation also **aˌdult ˈed** SPOKEN *n.* [U] education provided for adults outside schools and universities, usually by means of classes that are held in the evening

a·dul·ter·ate /əˈdʌltəˌreɪt/ *v.* [T] to make food or drinks less pure by adding another substance of lower quality to it —**adulteration** /əˌdʌltəˈreɪʃən/ *n.* [C] → see also UNADULTERATED

a·dul·ter·er /əˈdʌltərɚ/ *n.* [C] OLD-FASHIONED a married person who has sex with someone who is not their wife or husband

a·dul·ter·ess /əˈdʌltrɪs/ *n.* [C] OLD-FASHIONED a married woman who has sex with a man who is not her husband

a·dul·ter·y /əˈdʌltəri/ *n.* [U] sex between a married person and someone who is not their wife or husband: *She had* ***committed adultery*** *on several occasions.* [**Origin:** 1400–1500 Old French *avoutrie*, from Latin *adulter* **adulterer**] —**adulterous** *adj.*

a·dult·hood /əˈdʌltˌhʊd/ Ac *n.* [U] the time when you are an adult

adv. the written abbreviation of ADVERB

ad·vance¹ /ədˈvæns/ W2 *v.*
1 MOVE [I] to move forward, especially in a slow and determined way OPP **retreat**: *A line of tanks was slowly advancing.* | +**across/through/toward etc.** *The army advanced across the plain.* | +**on** *Troops advanced on* (=moved forward to attack) *the city.*
2 DEVELOP [I,T] if something such as technical or scientific knowledge advances, or if something advances it, it develops and improves: *Computer technology is advancing rapidly.* | *The group's research has* ***advanced our knowledge of*** *the HIV virus.*
3 advance a cause/sb's interests/your career etc. to do something that will help you achieve an advantage or success: *Our main goal has to be to advance the nation's economic interests.*
4 MONEY [T] to give someone money before they have earned it: **advance sb sth** *The publishers advanced him $50,000 for his second novel.*
5 advance a plan/idea/proposal etc. FORMAL to suggest a plan etc. so that other people can consider it: *She spent her entire career advancing the theory.*
6 PRICE [I] TECHNICAL if the price or value of something advances, it increases OPP **decline**: *Oil stocks advanced today in heavy trading.*
7 MACHINE [I,T] FORMAL if you advance a clock, a musical recording, film in a camera etc., or if it advances, it goes forward → see also ADVANCED, ADVANCING

advance² S3 W3 *n.*
1 in advance before something happens or is expected to happen: *Much of the meal can be prepared in advance.* | *Buy your tickets* ***well in advance.*** | +**of** *Copies will be distributed in advance of the meeting.* | **days/weeks/months etc. in advance** *The tours are often booked months in advance.*
2 DEVELOPMENT/IMPROVEMENT [C] a change, discovery, or INVENTION that brings progress: +**in** *recent advances in biotechnology* | *The computer industry continues to* ***make major advances.*** | **a technological/scientific/medical etc. advance** *one of the great technological advances of the 20th century* | +**over** *a big advance over previous systems*
3 FORWARD MOVEMENT [C] forward movement or progress OPP **retreat**: *the army's advance on the capital*
4 MONEY [C usually singular] money that is paid to someone before the usual time: *She asked for a $200 advance.* | +**on** *an advance on your salary* → see also CASH ADVANCE
5 advances [plural] an attempt to start a sexual relation-

ship with someone: *Shaffer accused her boss of* ***making advances*** *to her.*
6 INCREASE [C] TECHNICAL an increase in the price or value of something, especially in the STOCK MARKET OPP **decline**: *a big advance in the price of gold*
[**Origin:** 1200–1300 Old French *avancier*, from Latin *abante* **before**]

advance³ *adj.* [only before noun] **1 advance planning/warning/notice etc.** planning etc. that is done before something else happens: *We received no advance warning of the storm.* **2 an advance copy** a copy of a book, CD etc. that has not yet been made available to the public **3 an advance payment** a payment made to a supplier, writer etc. before a product is delivered or before a piece of work is completed **4 an advance party/team** a group of people who are the first to go to a place where something will happen, in order to prepare for it

ad·vanced /əd'vænst/ S3 W3 *adj.* **1** using the most modern ideas, equipment, and methods: *advanced technology* | *a* ***highly advanced*** *weapons system* | **an advanced country/nation** (=a country or nation that has a lot of technology and industry) ►see THESAURUS box at **modern**

> **THESAURUS**
> **sophisticated** made or designed well, and often complicated: *sophisticated software*
> **high-tech** using the most modern machines and methods in industry, business etc.: *high-tech weapons*
> **state-of-the-art** using the newest methods, materials, or knowledge: *state-of-the-art digital technology*
> **cutting-edge** using the newest design or the most advanced way of doing something: *cutting-edge medical research*

2 studying or dealing with a school subject at a difficult level: *advanced students of English* | *advanced physics* **3** having reached a late point in time or development: *the advanced stages of the disease* **4** used to talk about the age of someone who is old: **sb's advanced age/years** *Despite his advanced years, he often traveled abroad alone.* | *Most of the members are fairly* ***advanced in years.***

Ad,vanced 'Placement ABBREVIATION **AP** *n.* [U] TRADEMARK a type of advanced course that can be taken by students who want to earn college CREDITS while they are still in high school

ad·vance·ment /əd'vænsmənt/ *n.* [C,U] FORMAL progress or development in your job, level of knowledge etc.: *career advancement* | +**in** *advancements in science*

ad·vanc·ing /əd'vænsɪŋ/ *adj.* **advancing years/age** the time when you are becoming very old: *Chances of developing cancer increase with advancing age.*

ad·van·tage /əd'væntɪdʒ/ S2 W2 *n.*
1 STH THAT HELPS YOU [C,U] something that helps you to be better or more successful than others OPP **disadvantage**: +**of** *the advantages of a college education* | *Jane will* ***have an advantage*** *if they need to run very far.* | +**over** *For certain types of work, wood has advantages over plastic.* | *The army's superior equipment definitely* ***gave*** *them* ***an advantage*** *over the enemy.* | *Her previous experience gives her* ***a big advantage*** *over the other applicants.* | *Government subsidies give these industries an* ***unfair advantage.*** | *Applicants with computer skills will* ***be at an advantage.*** | *Neither side seems to be* ***gaining an advantage.*** | **use/turn/put sth to your/good advantage** (=use something in a way that helps you succeed) *She knew how to use her family connections to her advantage.*
2 take advantage of sth to use a particular situation to do or get what you want: *Hundreds of people took advantage of the sale prices.* | *You'll want to* ***take full advantage of*** *the island's beautiful beaches.*
3 take advantage of sb/sth to treat someone unfairly to get what you want, especially someone who is generous or easily persuaded: *I felt that my friends were taking advantage of me as a free babysitter.* | **take advantage of sb's kindness/generosity/good nature** *Other people were always taking advantage of his good nature.*
4 STH GOOD [C,U] a good or useful quality or condition that something has OPP **disadvantage**: +**of/in** *the advantages and disadvantages of living in a big city* | *Is there really any advantage in getting there early?* | +**over** *the advantages of email over letters* | *Digital cameras* ***have*** *a number of* ***advantages*** *over conventional cameras.* | **a big/great/distinct etc. advantage** *The big advantage of this system is its speed.*
5 TENNIS advantage sb used to show that the person named has won the point after DEUCE: *Advantage Williams.*
6 show sb/sth off to (good/great) advantage to make the best features of someone or something very noticeable: *Her dress showed her figure to great advantage.*
[**Origin:** 1300–1400 Old French *avantage*, from *avant* **before**, from Latin *abante*]

ad·van·taged /əd'væntɪdʒd/ *adj.* FORMAL having more skill, success, money etc. than other people: **economically/culturally etc. advantaged** *She comes from a financially advantaged family.* → see also DISADVANTAGED

ad·van·ta·geous /,ædvæn'teɪdʒəs, -vən-/ *adj.* helpful and likely to make you successful: +**to** *The trade agreement is particularly advantageous to U.S. farmers.* —**advantageously** *adv.*

ad·vent /'ædvɛnt/ *n.* **1 the advent of sth** the time when something first begins to be widely used: *Many more people died of infections before the advent of penicillin.* **2 Advent** the period of four weeks before Christmas in the Christian religion

'Advent ,calendar *n.* [C] a picture with 25 small pictures or candies hidden in it, one of which is uncovered each day in December until Christmas Day

Ad·vent·ist /əd'vɛntɪst, æd-/ *n.* [C] a member of a Christian group that believes that Jesus Christ will soon come again to Earth —**Adventist** *adj.* → see also SEVENTH-DAY ADVENTIST

ad·ven·ture /əd'vɛntʃɚ/ W3 *n.* [C,U] **1** an exciting experience in which dangerous or unusual things happen: *a young man looking for adventure* | *He used to tell us about his adventures at sea.* | *an adventure story* **2 a sense/spirit of adventure** willingness to try new things, take risks etc. [**Origin:** 1200–1300 Old French *aventure*, from Latin *advenire* **to arrive**]

ad·ven·tur·er /əd'vɛntʃərɚ/ *n.* [C] **1** someone who enjoys adventure and often travels to places that are far away in order to have exciting experiences there **2** OLD-FASHIONED someone who tries to become rich or socially important using dishonest or immoral methods

ad·ven·tur·ism /əd'vɛntʃə,rɪzəm/ *n.* [U] involvement in risky activities that is used to gain an unfair advantage, especially in business or politics —**adventurist** *n.* [C]

ad·ven·tur·ous /əd'vɛntʃərəs/ also **ad·ven·ture·some** /əd'vɛntʃɚsəm/ *adj.* **1** eager to go to new places and do exciting or dangerous things: *adventurous travelers* ►see THESAURUS box at **brave¹** **2** not afraid of taking risks or trying new things: *Andy isn't a very adventurous cook.* **3** involving new and exciting things: *The sailors led an adventuresome life* —**adventurously** *adv.*

ad·verb /'ædvɚb/ *n.* [C] ENG. LANG. ARTS a word or group of words that describes or adds to the meaning of a verb, an adjective, another adverb, or a whole sentence, such as "slowly" in "He ran slowly," "very" in "It's very hot," or "naturally" in "Naturally, we want you to come." [**Origin:** 1400–1500 French *adverbe*, from Latin *adverbium*, from *ad-* **to** + *verbum* **word**] → see also ADJECTIVE

ad·ver·bi·al¹ /æd'vɚbiəl/ *adj.* ENG. LANG. ARTS used as an adverb: *an adverbial phrase*

A

adverbial² *n.* [C] ENG. LANG. ARTS a word or phrase used as an adverb

ad·ver·sar·i·al /ˌædvɚˈsɛriəl/ *adj.* involving two sides that oppose and attack each other: *an adversarial relationship*

ad·ver·sar·y /ˈædvɚˌsɛri/ *n. plural* **adversaries** [C] FORMAL a country or person you are fighting or competing against SYN **opponent**: *political adversaries*

ad·verse /ədˈvɚs, æd-, ˈædvɚs/ *adj.* [only before noun] not good or favorable OPP **favorable**: *adverse publicity* | **an adverse impact/effect** *The chemicals have an adverse effect on human health.* | **adverse conditions** (=conditions that make it difficult for something to happen or exist) *We had to abandon the climb because of adverse weather conditions.* [**Origin:** 1300–1400 Early French *advers*, from Latin *adversus*, past participle of *advertere*, from *ad-* **to** + *vertere* **to turn**] —**adversely** *adv.*: *The changes* ***adversely affected*** *their business.*

ad·ver·si·ty /ədˈvɚsəti, æd-/ *n. plural* **adversities** [C,U] a situation in which you have a lot of problems that seem to be caused by bad luck: *We've been through a lot of adversity as a team.*

ad·vert /ædˈvɚt/ *v.*

advert to sth *phr. v.* FORMAL to mention something

ad·ver·tise /ˈædvɚˌtaɪz/ *v.* **1** [I,T] to tell the public about a product, service, or job that is available or an event that is going to happen, to persuade people to buy or use it, go to the event etc.: *Businesses are spending more and more on advertising their products.* | *Posters all over town were advertising the concert.* | **+for** *Billtech is advertising for a marketing manager.* | **advertise sth on TV/in a newspaper etc.** *Why not advertise on the Internet?* | **be advertised as sth** *It was advertised as a toy gun.* | *In trying to attract the brightest students, colleges have found that* ***it pays to advertise*** (=advertising brings you good results).

THESAURUS

promote to advertise a product or event: *She's in Atlanta to promote her new book.*
market to try to persuade someone to buy something by advertising it in a particular way: *The clothes are marketed to active adults, such as climbers and hikers.*
hype to try to make people think something is good or important by advertising or talking about it a lot on television, the radio etc.: *The movie has been hyped as a possible award winner.*
plug to advertise a book, movie etc. by talking about it on a radio or television program: *The author was on the "Tonight" show to plug her new book.*

2 advertise the fact (that) [T] to show or tell people something about yourself: *Don't advertise the fact that you're looking for another job.* [**Origin:** 1400–1500 Early French *advertiss-*, stem of *advertir*, from Latin *advertere*, from *ad-* **to** + *vertere* **to turn**] —**advertiser** *n.* [C]

ad·ver·tise·ment /ˌædvɚˈtaɪzmənt/ *n.* [C] **1** a picture, set of words, a short movie etc. that is used to advertise a product or service that is available, an event that is going to happen etc. → see also COMMERCIAL SYN **ad**: *a job advertisement* | **+for** *an advertisement for laundry detergent* | **+in** *car advertisements in the Sunday paper* | **put/place an advertisement in sth** *How much does it cost to place an advertisement in the weekly bulletin?* | *The organization bought a* ***full-page advertisement*** *in the "New York Times".*

THESAURUS

commercial an advertisement on TV or radio
billboard a very large sign at the side of a road or on a building, used as an advertisement
poster an advertisement on a wall, often with a picture on it
want ads/classified ads short advertisements in a newspaper, in which people offer things for sale
flier a piece of paper with an advertisement on it, often given to you in the street
junk mail unwanted letters that you receive in the mail containing advertisements
spam unwanted emails containing advertisements

2 be an advertisement for sth to show the advantages of something: *Ben is a walking advertisement for the benefits of regular exercise.*

ad·ver·tis·ing /ˈædvɚˌtaɪzɪŋ/ S3 W2 *n.* [U] the activity or business of advertising things on television, in newspapers etc.: *advertising aimed at 18- to 25-year-olds*

ˈadvertising ˌagency also **ˈad ˌagency** *n.* [C] a company that designs and makes advertisements for other companies

ad·ver·tor·i·al /ˌædvɚˈtɔriəl/ *n.* [C] an advertisement in a newspaper or magazine that is made to look like a normal article

ad·vice /ədˈvaɪs/ S3 W2 *n.* [U] an opinion you give someone about what they should do: **+on/about** *a booklet with advice on car problems* | **ask (sb) for advice** *People were always asking him for advice.* | *They* ***gave*** *me some good* ***advice*** *about buying a house.* | **ask sb's advice** *I want to* ***ask*** *your* ***advice*** *about where to stay in Taipei.* | *Investors who* ***followed*** *Murphy's* ***advice*** (=did what he advised) *earned a big profit.* | *I* ***took*** *a friend's* ***advice*** (=did what he advised) *and tried acupuncture.* | *Let me give you* ***a piece of advice*** (=some advice) *– start looking for a new job.* | ***On*** *my doctor's* ***advice*** (=because the doctor advised me), *I'm taking some time off work.* | ***Against*** *his father's* ***advice*** (=not doing what his father said he should do), *he went to New York.* | **legal/financial/medical etc. advice** (=advice about the law, money etc.) | **professional/expert advice** (=advice from someone who knows a lot about a subject) [**Origin:** 1200–1300 Old French *avis* **opinion**]

THESAURUS

tip a helpful piece of advice: *useful tips on healthy eating*
recommendation advice about what to do, usually given by an expert or a group of people who have studied the issue: *one of the major recommendations of the safety report*
guidance helpful advice about work, education etc: *The center offers career guidance.*

adˈvice ˌcolumn *n.* [C] part of a newspaper or magazine in which someone gives advice to readers who have written letters about their personal problems —**advice columnist** *n.* [C]

ad·vis·a·ble /ədˈvaɪzəbəl/ *adj.* [not before noun] FORMAL something that is advisable should be done in order to avoid problems or risks: *For heavy smokers, regular medical checks are advisable.* | ***It is advisable to*** *disconnect the computer before you open it up.* —**advisability** /ədˌvaɪzəˈbɪləti/ *n.* [U]

ad·vise /ədˈvaɪz/ W3 *v.* **1** [I,T] to tell someone what you think they should do, especially when you know more than they do about something: **advise sb to do sth** *The doctor advised Lou to lose weight and exercise more.* | **advise sb on/about sth** *Your lawyer can advise you about the best course of action.* | **advise (sb) against doing sth** *We were advised against getting a cat because of Joey's allergies.* | *You are* ***strongly advised*** *to buy medical insurance when visiting China.* | **advise caution/patience/restraint etc.** advise someone to be careful, patient etc. *The manufacturers advise extreme caution when using this product.*

THESAURUS

recommend to advise someone to do something: *Doctors recommend eating five portions of fruit and vegetables each day.*
urge to strongly advise someone to do something: *I urged Frida to reconsider her decision to drop out of school.*

2 [I,T] to be employed to give advice on a subject about which you have special knowledge or skill: **advise (sb) on sth** *Young advises clients on stock investments.* **3** [T] FORMAL to inform someone about something [SYN] inform: **advise sb of sth** *We'll advise you of any changes in the delivery dates.* | ***Keep us advised of*** (=continue to inform us about) *the developments.* → see also ILL-ADVISED, WELL-ADVISED → see Grammar box at RECOMMEND

ad·vis·ed·ly /əd'vaɪzɪdli/ *adv.* after careful thought: *He behaved like a dictator, and **I use the word advisedly**.*

ad·vi·see /əd,vaɪ'zi/ *n.* [C] someone who gets advice from an adviser, especially at a school or college

ad·vise·ment /əd'vaɪzmənt/ *n.* **take sth under advisement** if a judge takes something under advisement, they take time outside the COURTROOM to consider something carefully

ad·vis·er, advisor /əd'vaɪzɚ/ [W3] *n.* [C] **1** someone whose job is to give advice because they know a lot about a subject, especially in business, law, or politics: *a financial adviser* | +**to** *an adviser to the president* **2** a teacher or PROFESSOR at a school or college who gives students advice on courses they should take, makes sure they are making good progress, and sometimes gives advice on personal problems

ad·vi·so·ry[1] /əd'vaɪzəri/ *adj.* having the purpose of giving advice: *the Environmental Protection Advisory Committee* | **an advisory role/capacity** *The army is acting only in an advisory capacity.*

advisory[2] *n. plural* **advisories** [C] an official warning or notice that gives information about a dangerous situation: *travel advisories*

ad·vo·ca·cy /'ædvəkəsi/ [Ac] *n.* [U] public support for a group of people, process, or way of doing things: *the group's strong advocacy of traditional values*

ad·vo·cate[1] /'ædvə,keɪt/ [Ac] *v.* [T] to publicly support a particular way of doing things: *The extremists **openly advocate** violence.*

ad·vo·cate[2] /'ædvəkət, -,keɪt/ [Ac] [W3] *n.* [C] **1** someone who publicly supports a particular way of doing things: +**of** *She is a passionate advocate of natural childbirth.* **2** someone who acts and speaks in support of someone else: +**for** *Volunteers serve as advocates for abused children.* **3** LAW a lawyer [**Origin:** 1300–1400 Old French *avocat*, from Latin, past participle of *advocare* **to summon**] → see also **play/be (the) devil's advocate** at DEVIL (10)

adze, adz /ædz/ *n.* [C] a sharp tool with the blade at a right angle to the handle, used in order to shape pieces of wood

Ae·ge·an Sea, the /ɪ'dʒiən ,si/ also **the Aegean** the part of the Mediterranean Sea between Greece and Turkey

ae·gis /'eɪdʒɪs, 'idʒɪs/ *n.* **under the aegis of sb/sth** FORMAL with the protection or support of a person or organization: *The refugee camp operates under the aegis of the U.N.*

Ae·o·li·an /i'oʊliən/ HISTORY one of the people from ancient Greece that settled on the coast of Turkey and the islands near it at the end of the twelfth century B.C.

aer·ate /'ɛreɪt/ *v.* [T] CHEMISTRY to put a gas or air into a liquid or solid under pressure —**aeration** /ɛr'eɪʃən/ *n.* [U]

aer·i·al /'ɛriəl/ *adj.* **1** from an airplane: *aerial photographs* **2** in or moving through the air

aer·i·al·ist /'ɛriəlɪst/ *n.* [C] someone who entertains people by doing difficult physical actions in the air, such as balancing on a high rope or swinging on a TRAPEZE → see also ACROBAT

aer·ie /'ɛri, 'iri/ *n.* [C] the NEST of a large bird, especially an EAGLE, that is usually built high up in rocks or trees

aero- /ɛroʊ, ɛrə/ *prefix* relating to the air or to aircraft: *aerodynamics* (=the science of how things move through air)

aer·o·bat·ics /,ɛrə'bætɪks/ *n.* [plural] tricks done in an airplane that involve making difficult or dangerous movements in the air —**aerobatic** *adj.*

ae·ro·bic /ə'roʊbɪk, ɛ-/ *adj.* **1** intended to strengthen the heart and lungs: *Examples of **aerobic exercise** are running, bicycling, and swimming.* **2** relating to aerobics: *aerobic shoes* (=shoes meant to be worn when doing aerobics) **3** BIOLOGY needing oxygen in order to live → see also ANAEROBIC

ae·ro·bics /ə'roʊbɪks, ɛ-/ *n.* [U] a very active type of physical exercise done to music, usually in a class

aer·o·dy·nam·ic /,ɛroʊdaɪ'næmɪk◂/ *adj.* **1** an aerodynamic car, design etc. uses the principles of aerodynamics to achieve high speed or low use of gasoline **2** TECHNICAL relating to or involving aerodynamics: *aerodynamic efficiency* —**aerodynamically** /-kli/ *adv.*

aer·o·dy·nam·ics /,ɛroʊdaɪ'næmɪks/ *n.* **1** [U] the scientific study of how objects move through the air **2** [plural] the qualities needed for something to move through the air, especially smoothly and quickly

aer·o·nau·tics /,ɛrə'nɔt̬ɪks, -'nɑ-/ *n.* [U] the science of designing and flying airplanes —**aeronautic** *adj.* —**aeronautical** *adj.*

aer·o·plane /'ɛrəpleɪn/ *n.* [C] the British spelling of airplane

aer·o·sol /'ɛrə,sɔl, -,sɑl/ *n.* [C] **1** a metal can containing a liquid and a gas under pressure, from which the liquid can be SPRAYED **2** TECHNICAL a group of very small pieces of a substance or amounts of a liquid in air —**aerosol** *adj.*: *an aerosol deodorant*

aer·o·space /'ɛroʊ,speɪs/ *n.* [U] the industry that designs and builds airplanes and space vehicles: **aerospace companies/engineers/workers etc.** *Employment in the aerospace industry has fallen in California.*

Aes·chy·lus /'ɛskələs, 'is-/ (525–456 B.C.) a writer in ancient Greece, famous for his plays

Ae·sop /'isɑp/ (?620–?560 B.C.) a writer in ancient Greece, famous for his FABLES

aes·thete, esthete /'ɛsθit/ *n.* [C] FORMAL someone who loves and understands beautiful things such as art and music

aes·thet·ic[1]**, esthetic** /ɛs'θɛt̬ɪk, ɪs-/ *adj.* **1** relating to beauty and the study of beauty: *The changes were made for purely aesthetic reasons.* **2** designed in a beautiful way: *factories that are aesthetic as well as functional* —**aesthetically** /-kli/ *adv.*: *aesthetically pleasing*

aesthetic[2]**, esthetic** *n.* [C] FORMAL a set of principles about beauty or art: *the simple aesthetic of Japanese architecture*

aes·the·ti·cian, esthetician /,ɛsθə'tɪʃən/ *n.* [C] someone whose job is to give people beauty treatments, especially to the face, hands, and feet

aes·thet·ics, esthetics /ɛs'θɛt̬ɪks/ *n.* [U] the study of beauty, especially beauty in art

AFAIK, afaik a written abbreviation of "as far as I know," used in email, on the Internet etc.

a·far /ə'fɑr/ *n.* **from afar** LITERARY from a long distance away: *I saw him from afar.*

AFC /,eɪ ɛf 'si/ *n.* **American Football Conference** a group of teams that is part of the NFL → see also NFC

AFDC /,eɪ ɛf di 'si/ **Aid to Families with Dependent Children** a U.S. government program that gives money to poor families

af·fa·ble /'æfəbəl/ *adj.* friendly and easy to talk to: *an affable guy* [**Origin:** 1400–1500 French, Latin *affabilis*, from *affari*, from *ad-* **to** + *fari* **to speak**] —**affably** *adv.* —**affability** /,æfə'bɪləti/ *n.* [U]

af·fair /ə'fɛr/ [W2] *n.* [C]
1 affairs [plural] **a)** public or political events and activities: **international/world affairs** *People know surprisingly little about world affairs.* | **internal/domestic affairs** (=political events and activities within a particular country) *They were accused of interfering in China's internal affairs.* | *She showed a strong interest*

A

in news and ***current affairs*** (=important public or political events that are happening now). | *Gedda has reported on **foreign affairs*** (=political events in other countries) *since 1968.* **b)** things relating to your personal life, your financial situation etc.: *She has always managed the family's **financial affairs**.* | **sb's private/personal affairs** *I'd rather not discuss my personal affairs at work.* | **get/set/put your affairs in order** (=to organize your affairs and deal with any problems) *He's spending more time with his family and trying to get his affairs in order.* → **a state of affairs** at STATE[1] (6)
2 EVENT a) an event or set of related events that people remember or are likely to remember, especially because it is impressive or shocking: *the Watergate affair* | *The reunion became an annual affair.* **b)** used when describing a particular type of event: *The party was a very grand affair.*
3 RELATIONSHIP a secret sexual relationship between two people, when at least one of them is married to someone else: *Her husband **had an affair with** her best friend.* → see also LOVE AFFAIR
4 THING INFORMAL, OLD-FASHIONED used when describing a particular type of object, machine etc.: *The computer was one of those little hand-held affairs.*
5 be sb's affair if something is your affair, it only concerns you and you do not want anyone else to get involved in it: *What I do in my free time is my affair and nobody else's.*
[**Origin:** 1100–1200 Old French *afaire*, from *à faire* **to do**]

af·fect /ə'fɛkt/ Ac S2 W2 *v.* [T] **1** to do something that produces an effect or change in someone or something: *The disease affects the central nervous system.* | *The new regulations won't affect us.* | *Citizens want more control over matters which **directly affect** their lives.* | *Many companies have been **adversely affected** by the recession.* **2** to make someone feel strong emotions: *At first, the news didn't really seem to affect her.* | *We were all **deeply affected** by the news of Sonia's death.* **3** to pretend to have a particular feeling, way of speaking etc., especially to appear impressive to others: *It is annoying when she tries to affect a British accent.* [**Origin:** (1, 2) 1300–1400 Latin, past participle of *afficere* **to influence**, from *ad-* **to** + *facere* **to do**]

WORD CHOICE **affect, effect**
• **Affect** is the usual verb and **effect** is the usual noun: *How do you think the changes will affect (v.) you?* | *What effect (n.) will the changes have on you?*
• The verb **effect** is fairly formal and is only used in particular meanings. For example, you might **effect** changes or a plan of action (=make them happen). It does not mean the same as **affect**.

af·fec·ta·tion /ˌæfɛk'teɪʃən/ *n.* [C,U] someone's behavior, attitude, or way of speaking that is not sincere or natural, especially because they are trying to appear impressive to others: *Calling everyone "darling" is just an affectation.*

af·fect·ed /ə'fɛktɪd/ Ac *adj.* not sincere or natural: *I hate that stupid affected laugh of hers.*

af·fect·ing /ə'fɛktɪŋ/ Ac *adj.* FORMAL producing strong emotions of sadness, pity etc.: *a deeply affecting story*

af·fec·tion /ə'fɛkʃən/ *n.* [C,U] **1** a gentle feeling of love and caring: +**for** *His affection for her was clear for everyone to see.* | **give/show/express affection** | *He finds it difficult to **show affection**.* | **sb's affections** *He felt the new baby was a rival for his parents' affections.* **2** FORMAL a feeling of liking something very much: +**for** *Since the age of eight, she's had an affection for music.*

af·fec·tion·ate /ə'fɛkʃənɪt/ *adj.* showing in a gentle way that you love someone: *an affectionate hug* | *affectionate children* | +**toward** *Jo is always very affectionate toward him.* —**affectionately** *adv.*

af·fec·tive /ə'fɛktɪv/ Ac *adj.* TECHNICAL relating to people's feelings and emotions → see also SEASONAL AFFECTIVE DISORDER

af·fi·anced /ə'faɪənst/ *adj.* OLD USE → see ENGAGED

af·fi·da·vit /ˌæfə'deɪvɪt/ *n.* [C] LAW a written statement made under OATH (=after promising to tell the truth), for use as proof in a court of law [**Origin:** 1500–1600 Medieval Latin **he or she has made a formal promise**, from *affidare*]

af·fil·i·ate¹ /ə'fɪliɪt, -ˌeɪt/ *n.* [C] a small company, organization etc. such as a television station that is related to or controlled by a larger one: *The firm has six affiliates across the country.* | +**of** *an affiliate of ABC* [**Origin:** 1700–1800 Medieval Latin, past participle of *affiliare* **to take over as a son**, from Latin *ad-* **to** + *filius* **son**]

af·fil·i·ate² /ə'fɪliˌeɪt/ *v.* **1 be affiliated with/to sth** if a group or organization is affiliated to a larger one, it is related to it or controlled by it: *The hospital is affiliated with Harvard Medical School.* **2** [I,T] to join or form a close relationship with a group, organization etc., or to make a person, group, or organization do this: +**with** *Several groups want to affiliate with the party.* | **affiliate sth with sth** *instructions on how to affiliate your team with the League* | **affiliate yourself with sth** *She affiliated herself with the Impressionist school of painting.*

af·fil·i·at·ed /ə'fɪliˌeɪt̬ɪd/ *adj.* having a close relationship with a larger group, organization etc.: *affiliated television stations* | +**with** *The group is not affiliated with any political party.*

af·fil·i·a·tion /əˌfɪli'eɪʃən/ *n.* **1** [C,U] involvement with a political or religious organization: *What are her political affiliations?* | +**with** *the organization's affiliation with the Catholic church* **2** [U] the act of a smaller group or organization joining a larger one

af·fin·i·ty /ə'fɪnət̬i/ *n. plural* **affinities** **1** [C usually singular, U] a strong feeling that you like something, or that you like and understand someone because you share the same ideas or interests: +**for** *Craig has a natural affinity for math.* | +**between** *There was a strong affinity between the two men.* | +**with** *Amanda's remarkable affinity with animals* **2** [C,U] a close similarity or relationship between two things because of qualities or features that they both have: +**between** *There is a surprising affinity between the two religions.* | +**with** *His work has affinities with recent Marxist writing.* **3** [C,U] PHYSICS a force or attraction between atoms, MOLECULES etc. that makes them combine [**Origin:** 1300–1400 Old French *afinité*, from Latin *affinis* **sharing a border, related by marriage**]

af'finity ˌcard also **afˌfinity 'credit ˌcard** *n.* [C] a CREDIT CARD that is connected with a particular company or CHARITY, so that each time it is used the company gives the user a special reward or the charity receives money

af·firm /ə'fɚm/ *v.* FORMAL **1** [T] to state publicly that something is true or correct SYN **confirm**: *The Supreme Court has affirmed the lower court's ruling.* | **affirm that** *The general affirmed that rumors of the attack were true.* **2** [T] to strengthen or support a feeling, belief, or idea: *He claims that modern physics affirms his Christian beliefs.* —**affirmation** /ˌæfɚ'meɪʃən/ *n.* [C,U]

af·firm·a·tive¹ /ə'fɚmət̬ɪv/ *adj.* FORMAL an affirmative word, sign etc. means "yes": *an affirmative nod* —**affirmatively** *adv.*

affirmative² *n.* **answer/reply in the affirmative** to say "yes" OPP **negative**

afˌfirmative 'action *n.* [U] the practice of choosing people for a job, college etc. who are usually treated unfairly because of their race, sex etc.: *an affirmative action program* → see also REVERSE DISCRIMINATION

af·fix¹ /ə'fɪks/ *v.* [T] FORMAL to fasten or stick something to something else

af·fix² /'æfɪks/ *n.* [C] ENG. LANG. ARTS a group of letters added to the beginning or end of a word to change its meaning or use, such as "un-," "mis-," "-ness," or "-ly" → see also PREFIX, SUFFIX

af·flict /ə'flɪkt/ *v.* [T often passive] FORMAL to make someone or something become seriously ill or experience serious problems: *This type of pneumonia frequently* *afflicts elderly people.* | **be afflicted by/with sth** *Several of her friends had been afflicted with Alzheimer's Disease.* | *a region afflicted by famine* [**Origin:** 1300–1400 Latin, past participle of *affligere* **to throw down**, from *ad-* **to** + *fligere* **to hit**]

af·flic·tion /ə'flɪkʃən/ *n.* [C,U] FORMAL something, usually a medical condition, that causes pain or unhappiness: *Smoking is a major cause of cancer and other afflictions.*

af·flu·ent /'æfluənt/ *adj.* having plenty of money, nice houses, expensive things etc.: *an affluent neighborhood* | *affluent families* [**Origin:** 1400–1500 Old French, Latin, present participle of *affluere* **to flow in large quantities**] —**affluence** *n.* [U]

af·ford /ə'fɔrd/ S2 W2 *v.* [T] **1 can afford a)** to have enough money to buy or pay for something: *I'm not sure I can afford $750 a month in rent.* | **can afford to do sth** *We can't afford to buy a new car.* **b)** to be able to do something without causing serious problems for yourself: **can afford to do sth** *We simply can't afford to offend such an important customer.* **c)** to have enough time to do something: *Helena doesn't feel she can afford any more time away from work.* **2** FORMAL to provide something or allow something to happen: *The window affords a beautiful view out over the city.* [**Origin:** Old English *geforthian* **to carry out**, from *forth*]

af·ford·a·ble /ə'fɔrdəbəl/ *adj.* not too expensive: *It's difficult to find child-care that's affordable.* | *affordable housing*

af·for·es·ta·tion /ə,fɔrɪ'steɪʃən, æ-, -,fɑr-/ *n.* [U] TECHNICAL the act of planting trees in order to make a forest OPP **deforestation** —**afforest** /æ'fɔrɪst/ *v.* [T]

af·fray /ə'freɪ/ *n.* [C] LAW a noisy fight or argument in a public place [**Origin:** 1300–1400 Old French *affreer* **to surprise and frighten**, from Vulgar Latin *exfridare*]

af·fri·cate /'æfrɪkɪt/ *n.* [C] ENG. LANG. ARTS a CONSONANT sound consisting of a PLOSIVE such as /t/ or /d/ that is immediately followed by a FRICATIVE pronounced in the same part of the mouth, such as /ʃ/ or /ʒ/. The word "church," for example, contains the affricate /tʃ/.

af·front[1] /ə'frʌnt/ *n.* [C usually singular] a remark or action that offends or insults someone: +**to** *The comments were an affront to his pride.* [**Origin:** 1300–1400 Old French *afronter*, from Vulgar Latin *affrontare* **to hit in the face**, from Latin *ad-* **to** + *frons* **forehead**]

affront[2] *v.* [T usually passive] LITERARY to offend or insult someone, especially by not showing respect

Af·ghan /'æfgæn/ *n.* [C] **1** someone who comes from Afghanistan **2** also **Afghan hound** BIOLOGY a tall thin dog with a pointed nose and very long silky hair —**Afghan** *adj.*

af·ghan /'æfgæn/ *n.* [C] a colorful BLANKET that is made of YARN in a pattern with many open spaces

Af·ghan·is·tan /æf'gænə,stæn/ a country in Asia that is west of Pakistan and east of Iran

a·fi·cio·na·do /ə,fɪʃə'nɑdoʊ/ *n. plural* **aficionados** [C] someone who is very interested in a particular activity or subject and knows a lot about it: *a movie aficionado* [**Origin:** 1800–1900 Spanish, past participle of *aficionar* **to cause to like**, from *afición* **affection**]

a·field /ə'fild/ *adv.* **far afield** far away, especially from home: *Artists from as far afield as Paris will show their works.*

a·fire /ə'faɪɚ/ *adj.* [not before noun] LITERARY **1** burning: *The oil tanker was afire.* **2** filled with strong emotions or excitement: +**with** *The country is afire with patriotism.* —**afire** *adv.*

a·flame /ə'fleɪm/ *adj.* [not before noun] LITERARY **1** burning **2** very bright with color or light: +**with** *The trees were aflame with autumn leaves.* **3** filled with strong emotions or excitement —**aflame** *adv.*

AFL-CIO /,eɪ ɛf ,ɛl si aɪ 'oʊ/ *n.* [singular] **the American Federation of Labor and Congress of Industrial Organizations** an association of American trade unions

a·float /ə'floʊt/ *adj.* [not before noun] **1** having enough money to operate or stay out of debt: *They're just hard-working people struggling to* ***stay afloat***. **2** floating on water **3** LITERARY on a ship —**afloat** *adv.*

AFN /,eɪ ɛf 'ɛn/ *n.* **Armed Forces Network** a radio station owned by the U.S. government that broadcasts American music and news all over the world

a·foot /ə'fʊt/ *adj.* [not before noun] **1** being planned or happening: *There were plans afoot for a second attack.* **2** OLD USE moving, especially walking

a·fore·men·tioned /'æfɚ,mɛnʃənd, ə'fɔr-/ also **a·fore·said** /ə'fɔrsɛd/ *adj.* **the aforementioned** [only before noun] FORMAL mentioned before in an earlier part of a document, article, book etc.: *The property belongs to the aforementioned Mr. Jones.* —**the aforementioned** *n.* [singular or plural]

a·fore·thought /ə'fɔrθɔt/ *adj.* → see **with malice aforethought** at MALICE (2)

a·foul /ə'faʊl/ *adv.* **run/fall afoul of sb/sth** FORMAL to cause problems by doing something that is against the rules or that goes against people's beliefs: *Quinn's company had run afoul of the law before.*

a·fraid /ə'freɪd/ S1 W2 *adj.* [not before noun]
1 FRIGHTENED frightened because you think that someone or something may hurt you or that something bad may happen SYN **scared** SYN **frightened**: *I could see she was afraid.* | +**of** *His brother is really afraid of dogs.* | *Everybody was afraid of him.* | **afraid of doing sth** *They were afraid of getting shot or killed.* | **afraid to do sth** *I'm still afraid to go back there.* | *When he came running at me, I was* ***afraid for my life*** (=frightened I might die). ▶see THESAURUS box at **frightened**
2 WORRIED very worried that something bad will happen: **afraid (that)** *Josh was afraid that the other kids would laugh at him.* | **afraid of doing sth** *I didn't tell Mom because I was afraid of upsetting her.* | +**of** *The producers were afraid of a negative public reaction.* | **afraid for sb/sth** (=very worried that something bad may happen to someone, or that something could be ruined) *Workers are afraid for their jobs.* | *We're all afraid for you – living on your own.*
3 I'm afraid SPOKEN used to politely tell someone something that may annoy them, upset them, or disappoint them: *I'm afraid you'll just have to wait.*
4 (I'm) afraid so SPOKEN used to say "yes" to something, especially when someone is likely to be disappointed by this: *"Do you have to work Christmas Day?" "I'm afraid so."*
5 (I'm) afraid not SPOKEN used to say "no" to something, especially when someone is likely to be disappointed by this: *"Are there any cookies left?" "****Afraid not****."*
6 DON'T MIND not afraid of (doing) sth, not afraid to do sth willing to do something difficult or unpleasant, or good at doing it: *Meg isn't afraid of hard work.* | *He's never been afraid to speak his mind.*
7 afraid of your own shadow INFORMAL easily frightened or always nervous
[**Origin:** 1300–1400 past participle of *affray* **to frighten** (14–19 centuries), from Old French *affreer*]

a·fresh /ə'frɛʃ/ *adv.* FORMAL if you do something afresh, you do it again from the beginning SYN **anew**: **start/begin afresh** *The family started afresh in America.*

Af·ri·ca /'æfrɪkə/ the CONTINENT that is south of the Mediterranean Sea

Af·ri·can[1] /'æfrɪkən/ *adj.* relating to or coming from Africa

African[2] *n.* [C] someone from Africa

,African A'merican *n.* [C] an American with dark brown skin, whose family originally came from the part of Africa south of the Sahara Desert —**African-American** *adj.*: *African-American businesses*

,African-A,merican 'Studies *n.* [U] a subject of study in colleges and universities which includes African-American history, politics, CULTURE etc.

,African 'Union, the ABBREVIATION **AU** POLITICS an organization begun by the members of the former Organization of African Unity in 2002 to help all African countries work together on social, economic, and political problems

Af·ri·kaans /ˌæfrɪˈkɑns/ *n.* [U] a language of South Africa that is similar to Dutch

Af·ri·ka·ner /ˌæfrɪˈkɑnɚ/ *n.* [C] a white South African whose family is related to the Dutch people who settled there in the 1600s

Af·ro /ˈæfroʊ/ *n. plural* **Afros** [C] a hair style popular with African Americans in the 1970s in which the hair is cut into a large round shape

Afro- /æfroʊ/ *prefix* relating to Africa SYN **African-**: *an Afro-American* (=an American whose family originally came from Africa) | *Afro-Cuban music* (=combining styles from Africa and Cuba)

ˌAfro-Aˈmerican *n.* [C] OLD-FASHIONED an AFRICAN AMERICAN —**Afro-American** *adj.*

Af·ro·cen·tric /ˌæfroʊˈsɛntrɪk◂/ *adj.* emphasizing African ideas, styles, values etc.: *NetNoir promotes and develops Afrocentric programming for the Internet.* —**Afrocentrism** *n.* [U]

AFT /ˌeɪ ɛf ˈti/ **American Federation of Teachers** a UNION of teachers in the U.S.

aft /æft/ *adj., adv.* TECHNICAL in or toward the back part of a boat OPP **fore**

af·ter¹ /ˈæftɚ/ S1 W1 *prep.*

1 WHEN STH IS FINISHED when a particular time or event has happened or is finished OPP **before**: *After the dance, a few of us went out for a drink.* | *I go swimming every day after work.* | *What's on after the 6 o'clock news?* | *Do you believe in life after death?* | **a month/3 weeks/4 years etc. after sth** *A year after the fire, they rebuilt the house.* | *We leave* ***the day after tomorrow****.* | **shortly/soon etc. after sth** *Not long after the wedding, his wife got pregnant.* | *Come home* ***right after*** (=immediately after) *school.*

2 LIST following someone or something else on a list or in a series, piece of writing, line of people etc. OPP **before**: *Whose name is after yours on the list?* | *The date should be written after the address.*

3 after 10 minutes/3 hours etc. when a particular amount of time has passed: *After 25 minutes, remove the cake from the oven.* | *After a while, things started to improve.* | *After months of arguments, they decided to get a divorce.*

4 TIME used when telling time to say how many minutes it is past the hour OPP **to**: *The movie starts at a quarter after seven.*

5 day after day/year after year etc. continuously, for a very long time: *I get bored doing the same exercises day after day.*

6 go/run/chase etc. after sb to follow someone in order to catch them: *Go after him and apologize.*

7 SECOND-BEST used when making a list of or naming things, to mean that you have not included a particular thing because that is the first or best one: *After dancing, going to the movies is my favorite weekend activity.*

8 BECAUSE OF because of something or as a result of something: *I'm not surprised he left her, after the way she treated him.* | *After your letter, I didn't think I'd ever see you again.*

9 after all a) used in order to say that something is true or is a fact, in spite of something that has happened: *He wrote to say they couldn't give me a job after all.* **b)** used in order to say that something you thought was true is not true: *Rita didn't have my pictures after all – Jake did.* **c)** used in order to say that something should be remembered or considered, because it helps to explain why something else is true or is a fact: *I don't know why you're so concerned; after all, it isn't your problem.*

10 after sb when someone has left a place, when someone is finished doing something etc.: *Remember to close the door after yourself.* | *I spend all day cleaning up after the kids.*

11 be after sb to be looking for someone and trying to catch them: *The FBI is after me for fraud.*

12 be after sth INFORMAL to want to have something that belongs to someone else: *I think Chris is after my job.*

13 IN SPITE OF in spite of something: *After all the trouble I had, Reese didn't even say thank you.*

14 call/shout/gaze etc. after sb to speak to or look toward someone as they move away from you: *"You have a nice day, now!" she called after us.*

15 one after another also **one after the other** if a series of events, actions etc. happen one after another, each one happens soon after the previous one: *Ever since we bought the house, it's been one problem after another.*

16 after you SPOKEN used to say politely that someone else can use or do something before you do: *"Do you need the copy machine?" "After you."*

17 ART MUSIC STYLE FORMAL in the same style as a particular painter, musician etc.: *a painting after Rembrandt*

[**Origin:** Old English *æfter*] → see also **a man/woman after my own heart** at HEART (22), TAKE AFTER

WORD CHOICE after (prep.), in, after (adv.), afterward, later

- You use **after** (prep.) to talk about something that happens at the end of a period of time when it is different from something that happens within that period: *After a few weeks, Jerry's strength returned* (=not until a few weeks had passed).
- You use **in** to talk about something that will happen in the future, after the time when you are speaking: *You'll feel better in a few days.* **After** (prep.) is more often used to talk about events in the past, and **in** about the future. *She left after an hour* (=after an hour had passed). | *She'll be leaving in an hour* (=after an hour has passed from now).
- With words that show length of time, **afterward** or **later** is more usual: *She arrived three days afterward/later* (NOT usually *three days after,* (though you could say *after that*). If you want to use a word with this meaning on its own, you would usually use **afterward**: *We went out to dinner and saw a movie afterward.* You would not usually begin a sentence with **after**, though: *Afterward/After that, we left* (NOT *after, we left*).

after² S1 W1 *conjunction* when a particular time or event has happened or is finished OPP **before**: *After you called the police, what did you do?* | *Walter changed his name after he left Germany.* | **two days/three weeks etc. after** *Ten years after I bought the painting, I discovered it was a fake.* | **shortly/soon etc. after** *Not long after we talked, I got the promotion.*

after³ S2 W3 *adv.* later than something that has already been mentioned SYN **afterward**: *Pat arrived on Monday, and I got here the day after.* | *Not long after, I heard that Mike had gotten married.* | *Having lost the final pages, we can only guess at what might come after* (=happen after something else).

THESAURUS

afterward after an event or time that has been mentioned: *He said afterward that it had been the scariest experience of his life.*
next immediately afterward: *What should we do next?*
later after the present time or a time you are talking about: *We can clean up later.*
subsequently after an event in the past: *Subsequently, the company filed for bankruptcy.*

after⁴ *adj.* [only before noun] **1 in after years** LITERARY in the years after the time that has been mentioned **2** TECHNICAL in the back part of a boat or an aircraft: *the after deck*

after- /æftɚ/ *prefix* coming or happening after something: *aftereffects* | *the afterlife* (=life after death)

af·ter·birth /ˈæftɚˌbɚθ/ *n.* [U] BIOLOGY the substance that comes out of female humans or animals just after they have had a baby SYN **placenta**

af·ter·burn·er /ˈæftɚˌbɚnɚ/ *n.* [C] a piece of equipment in a JET engine that gives it more power

af·ter·ef·fect /ˈæftɚəˌfɛkt/ *n.* [C usually plural] a bad effect that remains for a long time after the condition or event that caused it: *The town is still* ***suffering the aftereffects of*** *the plant closure.*

af·ter·glow /ˈæftɚˌgloʊ/ *n.* [C usually singular] **1** a good feeling that remains after a happy experience: *the afterglow of victory* **2** the light that remains in the western sky after the sun goes down

ˌafter-ˈhours *adj.* [only before noun] **1** an after-hours bar, club etc. is one that is legally allowed to stay open after the time the other bars etc. have to close **2** happening after the regular time when something happens or is done: *Stocks fell by 29% in after-hours trading.*

af·ter·im·age /ˈæftɚˌɪmɪdʒ/ *n.* [C] the image of something that you continue to see after you look away or close your eyes

af·ter·life /ˈæftɚˌlaɪf/ *n.* [singular] the life that some people believe people have after death

af·ter·mar·ket /ˈæftɚˌmɑrkɪt/ *n.* [C] TECHNICAL **1** the MARKET (=all the people who want to buy something) for additional parts, services, or pieces of equipment that people want to buy after they have bought a related product: *the computing aftermarket* **2** the STOCK EXCHANGES and other places where STOCK is bought and sold —**aftermarket** *adj.*

af·ter·math /ˈæftɚˌmæθ/ *n.* [singular] the period of time after something bad such as a war, storm, or accident has happened, when people are still dealing with the results: *Several people resigned* ***in the aftermath of*** *the scandal.* [**Origin:** 1600–1700 *aftermath* grass that grows after earlier grass has been cut (16–19 centuries), from *after* + *math* **mowing** (11–20 centuries)]

af·ter·noon /ˌæftɚˈnun◂ / [S1] [W2] *n.* [C,U] the period of time between 12 p.m. and the evening: *a hot summer afternoon* | *Our tickets are for the afternoon performance.* | **on Monday/Tuesday etc. afternoon** *We went swimming on Tuesday afternoon.* | **on Monday/Tuesday etc. afternoons** (=every Monday, Tuesday etc. afternoon) *I have piano lessons on Saturday afternoons.* | *Harry went to sleep* ***in the afternoon.*** | *Do you want to go shopping* ***tomorrow afternoon?*** | *Could you babysit for a few hours* ***this afternoon*** (=today in the afternoon)? → see also EVENING

af·ter·noons /ˌæftɚˈnunz/ *adv.* during the afternoon each day: *She only works afternoons.*

ˈafter-school *adj.* [only before noun] for children and happening in the afternoon after classes are finished: *after-school programs*

af·ter·shave /ˈæftɚˌʃeɪv/ *n.* [U] a liquid with a nice smell that a man puts on his face after he SHAVES

af·ter·shock /ˈæftɚˌʃɑk/ *n.* [C] **1** a small EARTHQUAKE, usually one in a series, that happens after a larger EARTHQUAKE **2** the effects of a shocking event: *the effects of the war and its aftershocks*

af·ter·taste /ˈæftɚˌteɪst/ *n.* [C usually singular] **1** a taste that stays in your mouth after you eat or drink something: *The wine has a bitter aftertaste.* **2** a bad feeling that stays in your mind as a result of an event or a bad experience: *The incident left a nasty aftertaste.*

af·ter·thought /ˈæftɚˌθɔt/ *n.* [C usually singular] something thought of, mentioned, or added later, especially something that was not part of the original plan: *Almost* ***as an afterthought,*** *he said that Melanie could come too.*

af·ter·ward /ˈæftɚwɚd/ [S2] also **afterwards** *adv.* after an event or time that has already been mentioned [SYN] **after**: *The ceremony lasts half an hour and afterward there's a meal.* | **five years/six months etc. afterward** *My parents met during college but didn't marry until five years afterward.* → see Word Choice box at AFTER[3]

af·ter·word /ˈæftɚˌwɚd/ *n.* [C] a short piece of writing at the end of a book, which gives more information about the person who wrote it or about events that have taken place since the book was written → see also FOREWORD

a·gain /əˈgɛn/ [S1] [W1] *adv.* **1** if something happens again, or someone does something again, it happens or they do it one more time: *Can you say that again?* | *I'll never go there again.* | *If it doesn't work, try again.* | ***Once again*** (=again, after happening several times) *the Allies pushed back the enemy troops.* | *I had to ask him for the book* ***yet again*** (=again, after asking many times before, especially when this is annoying). | *Come and see us again some time!* **2** back to the same condition or situation that you were in before: *Get some rest. You'll feel better again soon.* | *It's great to have you home again.* **3 all over again** used in order to say that you have to repeat something from the beginning, when this is annoying: *I had to explain it all over again.* **4 again and again** also **time and (time) again** or **over and over again** very often, making you or someone else annoyed: *I've told you again and again – no playing ball in the living room!* **5** SPOKEN used when you want someone to repeat information that they have already given you: *What did you say your name was again?* **6** used when making a statement that explains or emphasizes something you have just said: *And again, I want to thank you for taking the time to help us.* → see also **but then (again)** at THEN (6) **7 half/a third etc. again as much** one and a half, one and a third etc. times the original amount: *I earn about half again as much as I did last year.* [**Origin:** Old English *ongean* **opposite, back**] → see also **now and again** at NOW[1] (23)

a·gainst /əˈgɛnst/ [S1] [W1] *prep.*

1 DISAGREEING opposed to or disagreeing with an idea, belief, proposal etc.: *There were 10 votes for and 15 against the motion.* | *I'm against all forms of hunting.* | *Everyone was against closing the factory.* | *It's* ***against my principles*** *to borrow money* (=I don't believe it is right to borrow money). | **against sb's wishes/will** (=when someone does not want something to happen or be done) *He dropped out of college against his parents' wishes.* | *You can't do that! It's* ***against the law*** (=illegal).

2 FIGHT/COMPETE fighting or competing with another person, team, country etc.: *He was injured in the game against the Cowboys.* | *We'll be competing against some of the best companies in Europe.* | *the fight against terrorism*

3 DISADVANTAGE in a way that has a bad effect on someone or makes them have a disadvantage: *discrimination against women* | *Your lack of experience could* ***count against*** (=be a disadvantage to) *you.* | *The planning regulations tend to* ***work against*** (=be a disadvantage to) *smaller companies.*

4 HIT touching, hitting, or rubbing another surface: *The rain drummed against the window.* | *The cat rubbed her head against my legs.*

5 SUPPORT next to and touching an upright surface, especially for support: *a ladder propped up against the wall* | *The younger policeman was leaning against the desk.*

6 OPPOSITE DIRECTION in the opposite direction of something [OPP] **with**: *We had to sail against the wind.* | *swimming against the current*

7 be/come up against sth to have to deal with a difficult opponent or problem: *We were up against some tough competition, but we won.*

8 have sth against sb/sth to dislike or disapprove of someone or something: *I* ***have nothing against*** (=I do not disapprove of) *people making lots of money.* | *What have you got against cats?* (=why don't you like cats?)

9 SEEN TOGETHER seen or shown with something else behind or as a background: *The green looks great against the orange.*

10 OTHER EVENTS used to describe something in relation to other events that are happening at the same time: *The reforms were introduced against a background of social unrest.*

11 COMPARISON in comparison with someone or something: *She checked the contents of the box against the list.*

12 PROTECTION providing protection from harm or damage: *Eating good food is good insurance against sickness.*

A·ga·ma Ja·va /əˌgeɪmə ˈdʒɑvə/ *n.* [U] CULTURE a religion practiced by many Muslim people in Java (=an island that is part of Indonesia), that combines the

A

beliefs of Islam with some of the beliefs of Hinduism and Buddhism

A·ga·na /ə'gɑnyə/ the capital city of the U.S. TERRITORY of Guam

a·gape /ə'geɪp/ *adj., adv.* [only after noun] with your mouth wide open, especially because you are surprised or shocked: *She sat there with her mouth agape, staring at the ring.*

ag·ate /'ægɪt/ *n.* [C] a hard stone with bands of different colors, used in jewelry

a·ga·ve /ə'gɑvi/ also **'century plant** *n.* [C] a desert plant with long thin leaves at the base and a tall stem with flowers. The leaves can be used to make TEQUILA (=a type of strong alcohol).

age¹ /eɪdʒ/ S1 W1 *n.*
1 HOW OLD [C,U] the number of years someone has lived or something has existed: *Francis is the same age as I am.* | *Scientists had to guess at the age of the Earth.* | *He died **at the age of** 98.* | *The missing girl is 9 **years of age**.* | *Saul entered Yale **at age** 14.* | *She became a mother **at an early age*** (=very young). | *Anne's very tall **for her age*** (=compared with others of the same age). | ***At my age,*** (=emphasizing that someone is or feels old) *it gets harder to get up the stairs.* | **over/under the age of 5/18 etc.** *people over the age of 65* | *The children **range in age from** 6 to 17.* | *You need to start **acting your age*** (=behaving in a way that is appropriate for someone as old as you)*!*
2 LEGAL AGE [U] the age when you are legally old enough to do something: *What's the minimum age for getting a driver's license?* | *Jeff managed to buy the beer, even though he was obviously **under age*** (=too young). | *The usual **retirement age** is 65.*
3 PERIOD OF LIFE [C,U] one of the particular periods of someone's life: *He's at that **awkward age** when teenagers don't talk to their parents.* | *The show is sure to delight people **of all ages**.* | *women of **childbearing age*** → see also MIDDLE AGE, OLD AGE, TEENAGE
4 BEING OLD [U] the condition or fact of being old: *The newspapers were brown **with age*** (=because of being old). | *The furniture was **showing signs of age*** (=looking old).
5 PERIOD OF HISTORY [C usually singular] a particular period of history: *the Ice Age* | *We are living in the computer age.* → see also **in this day and age** at DAY (15), GOLDEN AGE
6 come of age a) reach the age when you are legally considered to be a responsible adult **b)** if something comes of age, it reaches a stage of development at which people accept is as being important, valuable etc.: *Movies really came of age in the 1940s.*
7 ages [plural] a long time: *Steve! I haven't seen you **for ages**!*
[**Origin:** 1200–1300 Old French *aage*, from Latin *aetas*, from *aevum* **lifetime, age**]

age² S3 W2 *v.* **1** [I,T] to look or seem older, or to make someone or something look older: *I was shocked to see how much she'd aged.* **2** [I] to become older: *As we age, we need less sleep.* **3** [I,T] if a food or alcohol ages or is aged, it is kept in controlled conditions to develop a better taste, smell etc.: *whiskey that is aged for ten years in oak barrels* **4 age well** if someone or something ages well, they do not look or seem old even though they are: *The film has aged well, and is now considered a classic.*

-age /ɪdʒ/ *suffix* [in nouns] **1** an activity, an action, or the result of doing something: *the passage of a bill through Congress* (=the activity of making it a law) | *I pay $49 a month for storage* (=the storing of my things in a particular place). | *Buy a larger size to allow for shrinkage* (=clothes getting smaller after they are washed). **2** a cost or amount: *Postage* (=the cost of sending something) *is extra.* | *a percentage of the profits* | *the voltage* (=how much electric power there is) *of your house wiring* **3** a particular situation or condition: *a ten-year marriage* (=the state of being married)

'age ˌbracket *n.* [C] the people between two particular ages, considered as a group: *people in the 40–50 age bracket*

aged¹ /eɪdʒd/ *adj.* **aged 5 to 10/16 to 18 etc.** between 5 and 10, 16 and 18 etc. years old: *The class is for children aged 12 **and over*** (=and older). | **+between** *a man aged between 30 and 35*

ag·ed² /'eɪdʒɪd/ *adj.* [only before noun] very old: *my aged parents* —**the aged** *n.* [plural]

'age discrimiˌnation *n.* [U] unfair treatment of old people, because of their age

'age grade *n.* [C] CULTURE a social class in some societies that is based on age and includes all the people who are the same age, and usually the same sex

'age group *n.* [C] all the people between two particular ages, considered as a group: *children in the 12–14 age group*

age·ism, agism /'eɪˌdʒɪzəm/ *n.* [U] AGE DISCRIMINATION

age·less /'eɪdʒlɪs/ *adj.* **1** never looking old or old-fashioned: *her ageless blue eyes* **2** LITERARY continuing for ever: *the ageless fascination of the ocean* —**agelessness** *n.* [U]

'age ˌlimit *n.* [C] the youngest or oldest age at which you are allowed to do something: **raise/lower the age limit to 16/18/21 etc.** *They raised the age limit for buying tobacco to 18.*

a·gen·cy /'eɪdʒənsi/ S3 W1 *n. plural* **agencies** [C] **1** POLITICS an organization or department, especially within a government, that does a specific job: *The UN agency is responsible for helping refugees.* **2** a business that provides information about other businesses and their products, or that provides a particular service: *a car rental agency* → see also NEWS AGENCY, TRAVEL AGENCY **3 by/through the agency of sb** FORMAL being done with or as the result of someone's help

a·gen·da /ə'dʒɛndə/ S3 W3 *n. plural* **agendas** [C] **1** plans for future political actions based on a set of political beliefs: *the Republicans' conservative agenda* **2** a set of problems or subjects that a government, organization etc. is planning to deal with: *Health-care reform was **high on the agenda*** (=one of the most important things to be dealt with) *in the President's second term.* **3** a list of the subjects to be discussed at a meeting: *What's the next item **on the agenda**?* [**Origin:** 1600–1700 Latin **things to be done**, from *agere* **to drive, lead, act, move, do**] → see also HIDDEN AGENDA

a·gent /'eɪdʒənt/ W1 *n.* [C]
1 BUSINESS a person or company that represents another person or company in business, in their legal problems etc.: *Our agent in Rio deals with all our Brazilian business.* | **+for** *We're **acting as agents** for Mr. Watson.* → see also REAL ESTATE AGENT, TRAVEL AGENT
2 ARTIST/ACTOR someone who is paid by actors, musicians etc. to find work for them, or who finds someone to publish a writer's work: *My agent sent me to an audition.* | *a **literary agent***
3 GOVERNMENT/POLICE someone who works for a government or police department, especially in order to get secret information about another country or organization: *an FBI agent* | *an **undercover*** (=secret) ***agent*** → see also DOUBLE AGENT, SECRET AGENT
4 CHEMICAL a chemical or substance that makes other substances change: *Soap is a cleansing agent.*
5 FORCE someone or something that affects or influences a situation: *Williams has been a major **agent of change*** (=someone who causes changes) *in the auto industry.*
[**Origin:** 1400–1500 Medieval Latin, from the present participle of Latin *agere* **to drive, lead, act, move, do**] → see also FREE AGENT

ˌAgent 'Orange *n.* [U] a chemical weapon used by U.S. soldiers during the Vietnam War to destroy forests

a·gent pro·vo·ca·teur /ˌɑʒɑn proʊvɑkə'tɚ, ˌeɪdʒənt-/ *n.* [C] LITERARY someone who is employed to encourage people who are working against a government to do something illegal so that they can be caught

ˌage of con'sent *n.* **the age of consent** the age when someone can legally get married or have a sexual relationship

ˌage-'old *adj.* [only before noun] having existed for a very long time: *the age-old hatred between the two groups*

ag·glom·er·ate /əˈglɑmərɪt/ *n.* [singular, U] EARTH SCIENCE a type of rock formed from pieces of material from a VOLCANO that have melted together

ag·glom·er·a·tion /əˌglɑməˈreɪʃən/ *n.* [C,U] a large collection of things that do not seem to belong together: +**of** *an agglomeration of laws and regulations* —**agglomerate** /əˈglɑməˌreɪt/ *v.* [I,T] —**agglomerate** /əˈglɑmərɪt/ *adj.*

ag·glu·ti·na·tion /əˌglutˈnˈeɪʃən/ *n.* [U] TECHNICAL **1** the state of being stuck together **2** ENG. LANG. ARTS the process of making new words by combining two or more words, such as combining "ship" and "yard" to make "shipyard"

ag·gran·dize·ment /əˈgrændɪzmənt, -daɪz-/ *n.* [U] FORMAL, DISAPPROVING an increase in power, size, or importance → see also SELF-AGGRANDIZEMENT

ag·gra·vate /ˈægrəˌveɪt/ *v.* [T] **1** to make a bad situation, an illness, or an injury worse [OPP] **improve**: *Their money problems were* ***further aggravated*** *by rising interest rates.* | *Building the new road will just* ***aggravate the situation.*** **2** to make someone angry or annoyed [SYN] **irritate**: *I know she says things just to aggravate me.* | ***It aggravates me*** *that he doesn't let me finish my sentences.* [**Origin:** 1500–1600 Latin, past participle of *aggravare* **to make heavier**, from *ad-* **to** + *gravare* **to make heavy**] —**aggravating** *adj.* —**aggravatingly** *adv.* —**aggravation** /ˌægrəˈveɪʃən/ *n.* [C,U]

ag·gra·vat·ed /ˈægrəˌveɪt̬ɪd/ *adj.* [only before noun] LAW an aggravated offense is one which the law considers to be especially serious, for example because the criminal uses violence: **aggravated assault/burglary etc.** *The men were charged with aggravated kidnapping.*

ag·gre·gate¹ /ˈægrɪgɪt/ [Ac] *n.* **1** [singular, U] the total after many different parts or figures have been added together: +**of** *The company will spend* ***an aggregate of*** *$2 million on the product.* | *The victims got back,* ***in the aggregate*** (=as a group in total)*, about 75% of medical costs.* **2** [U] TECHNICAL sand or small stones that are used in making CONCRETE

aggregate² [Ac] *adj.* [only before noun] TECHNICAL being the total amount of something, especially money: *aggregate income and investment*

ag·gre·gate³ /ˈægrɪˌgeɪt/ [Ac] *v.* FORMAL **1** [linking verb] to be a particular amount when added together: *Sheila's earnings from all sources aggregated $100,000.* **2** [I,T usually passive] to put things together in a group to form a total [SYN] **assemble**: *the aggregated data*

ˌaggregate deˈmand *n.* [U] ECONOMICS the total demand for goods and services in a country

ˌaggregate supˈply *n.* [U] ECONOMICS the total supply of goods and services available in a country

ag·gres·sion /əˈgrɛʃən/ *n.* [U] **1** angry or threatening behavior or feelings that often result in fighting: +**in** *Television violence seems to encourage aggression in children.* | +**toward** *Mr. Riley* ***showed*** *some* ***aggression*** *toward the doctor.* **2** the act of attacking a country, especially when that country has not attacked first: ***an*** *unprovoked* ***act of aggression*** | +**against** *aggression against peaceful nations* **3** BIOLOGY threatening behavior that one animal uses in order to get control over another animal [**Origin:** 1600–1700 Latin *aggressio*, from *aggredi* **to attack**]

ag·gres·sive /əˈgrɛsɪv/ [S3] [W3] *adj.* **1** behaving in an angry, threatening way, as if you want to fight or attack someone: *When I said "no," she became rude and aggressive.* | *an aggressive driver* **2** someone who is aggressive is very determined to succeed or get what they want: *A successful businessperson has to be aggressive.* **3** an aggressive action or plan uses strong or severe methods in order to be as effective and fast as possible: *an aggressive treatment for cancer* —**aggressively** *adv.* —**aggressiveness** *n.* [U]

ag·gres·sor /əˈgrɛsɚ/ *n.* [C] FORMAL a person or country that begins a fight or war with another person or country

ag·grieved /əˈgrivd/ *adj.* **1** feeling or showing anger and unhappiness because you think you have been treated unfairly: *an aggrieved tone of voice* **2** LAW having suffered as a result of the illegal actions of someone else: *the aggrieved parties*

a·ghast /əˈgæst/ *adj., adv.* [not before noun] feeling or looking shocked by something you have seen or just found out: +**at** *I was aghast at the violence I was witnessing.* [**Origin:** 1200–1300 the past participle of *aghast* **to frighten** (13–16 centuries), from Old English *gæstan*]

ag·ile /ˈædʒəl, ˈædʒaɪl/ *adj.* **1** able to move quickly and easily: *Harvey is very agile for a big man.* **2** someone who has an agile mind is intelligent and able to think very quickly —**agility** /əˈdʒɪləti/ *n.* [U]

ag·ing¹ /ˈeɪdʒɪŋ/ *adj.* [only before noun] becoming old: *aging movie stars* | *a fleet of aging aircraft* | *the country's* ***aging population*** (=with more old people than before)

aging² *n.* [U] the process of getting old: *Memory loss is often a part of aging.*

ag·i·tate /ˈædʒəˌteɪt/ *v.* **1** [I] POLITICS to argue strongly in public for something you want, especially a political or social change: +**for/against** *The unions are agitating for higher pay.* **2** [T] to make someone feel anxious, upset, and nervous: *He makes remarks on the show that are intended to agitate his viewers.* **3** [T] to shake or mix a liquid quickly

ag·i·tat·ed /ˈædʒəˌteɪt̬ɪd/ *adj.* so nervous or upset that you are unable to keep still or think calmly: *My mother was becoming increasingly agitated as we waited.*

ag·i·ta·tion /ˌædʒəˈteɪʃən/ *n.* **1** [U] feeling of being so anxious, nervous, or upset that you cannot keep still or think calmly: *Perry's agitation was so great he could hardly speak.* **2** [C,U] POLITICS a public argument or action for social or political change: +**for/against** *political agitation for a recount of the vote* **3** [U] the act of shaking or mixing a liquid

ag·i·ta·tor /ˈædʒəˌteɪt̬ɚ/ *n.* [C] **1** POLITICS someone who encourages people to work toward changing something in society: *a political agitator* **2** a part inside a washing machine that moves the clothes and water around

ag·it·prop /ˈædʒɪtˌprɑp/ *n.* [U] POLITICS music, literature, or art that tries to persuade people to follow a particular set of political ideas

a·glit·ter /əˈglɪt̬ɚ/ *adj.* [not before noun] LITERARY seeming to shine with flashing points of light: *Her green eyes were aglitter.*

a·glow /əˈgloʊ/ *adj.* **1** LITERARY bright and shining with warmth, light, or color: *The morning sun set the sky aglow.* **2** if someone's face or expression is aglow, they seem happy and excited: +**with** *Linda's face was aglow with happiness.*

Ag·new /ˈægnu/, **Spir·o** /ˈspɪroʊ/ (1918–1996) the Vice President of the U.S. under Richard Nixon

ag·nos·tic /ægˈnɑstɪk, əg-/ *n.* [C] someone who believes that people cannot know whether God exists or not [**Origin:** 1800–1900 Greek *agnostos* **unknown, unknowable**, from *a-* **not** + *gnostos* **known**] —**agnostic** *adj.* —**agnosticism** /ægˈnɑstɪˌsɪzəm/ *n.* [U] ▶see THESAURUS box at **religion** → see also ATHEIST

a·go /əˈgoʊ/ [S1] [W1] *adv.* used to show how far back in the past something happened: **5 minutes/an hour/two years etc. ago** *Her husband died 14 years ago.* | *I met my great aunt once,* ***a*** *very* ***long time ago.*** | *I had my keys* ***a minute ago****, and now I can't find them.* | *Tom got a letter from him just* ***a little while ago.*** | *They moved to Chicago* ***some time ago*** (=a fairly long time ago). | *I got a call from Dave* ***not that long ago*** (=fairly recently). [**Origin:** 1400–1500 the past participle of *ago* **to pass away** (11–17 centuries), from Old English *agan*,

A

from *gan* **to go**] see also FOR, SINCE² → see Word Choice box at SINCE²

a·gog /əˈgɑg/ *adj., adv.* [not before noun] LITERARY very interested, excited, and surprised, especially at something you are experiencing for the first time: **+at/over** *We stared agog at the massive fire.* [**Origin:** 1400–1500 Old French *en gogues* **in enjoyment, laughing**]

ag·o·nize /ˈægəˌnaɪz/ *v.* [I] to think about a difficult decision very carefully and with a lot of effort: **+over/about** *We agonized over whether to sell the house.* —**agonizing** *n.* [U]

ag·o·nized /ˈægəˌnaɪzd/ *adj.* [only before noun] expressing very severe pain: *an agonized scream*

ag·o·niz·ing /ˈægəˌnaɪzɪŋ/ *adj.* **1** extremely painful: *The pain was agonizing.* **2** involving a difficult choice or an uncertain situation that makes you very upset and worried: *an agonizing decision* | *Not knowing what was happening was agonizing.* —**agonizingly** *adv.*

ag·o·ny /ˈægəni/ *n. plural* **agonies** [C,U] **1** very severe pain: *the agony of arthritis* | *He was lying on the floor* ***in agony***. **2** a very sad or emotionally difficult situation: *It was agony not knowing where he was.* [**Origin:** 1300–1400 Late Latin *agonia*, from Greek, **trouble, great anxiety**, from *agon* **competition for a prize**]

ag·o·ra /ˈægərə/ *n.* [C] HISTORY an open place in an ancient Greek city where people met and goods were bought and sold

ag·o·ra·pho·bi·a /ˌægərəˈfoʊbiə/ *n.* [U] MEDICINE the fear of crowds and open spaces [**Origin:** 1800–1900 Greek *agora* **marketplace, place where people gather** + English *-phobia*] —**agoraphobic** *n.* [C] —**agoraphobic** *adj.* → see also CLAUSTROPHOBIA

a·grar·i·an /əˈgrɛriən/ *adj.* relating to farming or farmers: *an agrarian economy* (=an economy based on farming)

a·gree /əˈgri/ S1 W1 *v.*

1 SAME OPINION [I,T not in progressive] to have the same opinion about something as someone else OPP **disagree**: *Teenagers and their parents rarely agree.* | **+with** *I understand what he's saying, but I don't agree with it.* | **agree (that)** *Most scientists agree that global warming is a serious problem.* | **+on/about** *Mike and I don't agree on how to spend our money.*

2 SAY YES [I,T not in progressive] to say yes to an idea, plan, suggestion etc. OPP **refuse**: *I suggested we move to Chicago, and she agreed.* | **agree to do sth** *Bryan finally agreed to help us.* | **agree to sth** *My sister won't agree to selling the house.* ▸see THESAURUS box at **accept**

3 DECIDE TOGETHER [I,T not in progressive] to make a decision with someone after a discussion with them: **agree to do sth** *We agreed to meet again next Monday.* | **agree that** *The leaders agreed that missile production would be reduced.* | **+on** *It's a budget that the President and Congress can agree on.* | **+to** *Both sides have agreed to a ceasefire.*

4 BE THE SAME [I not in progressive] if two pieces of information agree, they say the same thing: **+with** *Your story doesn't agree with what the police told us.*

5 agree to disagree to accept that you do not have the same opinions as someone else and agree not to argue about it

[**Origin:** 1300–1400 Old French *agréer*, from *gré* **will, pleasure**, from Latin *gratus* **pleasing**]

agree with sb/sth *phr. v.* **1** to believe that a decision, action, or suggestion is correct or right: *I don't agree with hitting children.* **2 not agree with you** if a type of food does not agree with you, it makes you feel sick: *Green peppers don't agree with me.* **3** ENG. LANG. ARTS if an adjective, verb etc. agrees with a word, it matches that word by being plural if the subject is plural etc.

GRAMMAR

- If you have the same opinion as someone else, you **agree with** them. You can also **agree with** (=approve of) their attitude, ideas, plans, rules etc., or an activity or principle that you approve of: *Do you agree with gun control?*
- You **agree** with people **about** or **on** other matters: *I agree (with you) about Tom/on politics/about this issue* (NOT *I agree this issue*).
- If you and others decide on something after discussing it, you **agree on** it: *We finally agreed on a plan/a date/a solution/a deal.*
- If you accept something, you **agree to** it. *She agreed to the plan/the date/the solution/the deal* (NOT *She agreed the plan etc.*). You can also **agree to do** something: *They agreed to pay* (NOT *They accepted to pay*).

a·gree·a·ble /əˈgriəbəl/ *adj.* **1** FORMAL **agreeable to sb** acceptable and able to be agreed on: *an outcome that is agreeable to both countries* **2** WRITTEN or OLD-FASHIONED someone who is agreeable is very nice and is liked by other people OPP **disagreeable**: *an agreeable young man* **3** enjoyable: *an agreeable comedy* **4** FORMAL or HUMOROUS **be agreeable to sth** to be willing to do something or willing to allow something to be done: *I'm agreeable to trying something new.*

a·gree·a·bly /əˈgriəbli/ *adv.* intended to be nice or enjoyable: *He smiled agreeably.*

a·greed /əˈgrid/ *adj.* **1** [only before noun] an agreed plan, price, arrangement etc. is one that people have discussed and accepted: *an agreed price for the wheat* **2 be agreed** FORMAL if people are agreed, they have discussed something and agree about what to do: **+on** *All parties are now agreed on the plan.* | **+that** *We are all agreed that we have to try to save more money.* **3 Agreed** SPOKEN used in order to check if someone agrees, or to show that you agree: *"Let's forget it ever happened. Agreed?" "Agreed."*

a·gree·ment /əˈgrimənt/ S3 W1 *n.* **1** [C] an arrangement or promise to do something, made by two or more companies, governments, organizations etc.: *a trade agreement* | **+on** *an agreement on arms reduction* | **+with** *Gardner had an agreement with us to buy the farm.* | *Failure to* ***reach an agreement*** *will result in a strike.* | ***Under the agreement*** (=according to the agreement), *Hong Kong returned to Chinese rule in 1997.* | *The exact* ***terms of the agreement*** *are confidential.* | *They claimed the company* ***violated the agreement*** (=did not do what it had promised). | *They* ***had an agreement that*** *she could borrow his car when he wasn't using it.* **2** [U] a situation in which people have the same opinion as each other OPP **disagreement**: **+that** *There is agreement among doctors that pregnant women should not smoke.* | **+on** *Is there agreement on how much aid will be sent?* | *All members of the group were* ***in agreement***. | *It is easier for two groups to* ***reach agreement*** *than it is for three.* **3** [U] the act of saying "yes" to an idea, plan, or suggestion: **agreement to do sth** *his agreement to give her some money* | **+of** *These arrangements cannot be changed without the agreement of the bank.* **4** [C] LAW an official document that people sign to show that they accept something: *Please read the agreement and sign it.*

agri- /ægrɪ/ *prefix* relating to farming: *agriculture* → see also AGRO-

ag·ri·busi·ness /ˈægrɪˌbɪznɪs/ *n.* [C,U] the business of farming and producing and selling farm products on a large scale, or a company involved in this

ag·ri·cul·tur·al /ˌægrɪˈkʌltʃərəl/ *adj.* **1** related to farming: *agricultural exports* | *land used for agricultural purposes* **2** used for or involved in farming: *agricultural chemicals* | *agricultural societies*

Agriˌcultural Revoˈlution, the HISTORY **1** the period a long time ago when people first began to grow crops and raise farm animals on farms **2** the period of time in which there were many changes in methods of farming, which happened in England from the 16th to the 19th century. Farmers started growing new crops, farms became bigger and produced more crops for less money, and farmers started to use FERTILIZER (=substance that is put on the soil to help plants grow).

ag·ri·cul·ture /ˈæɡrɪˌkʌltʃɚ/ *n.* [U] the practice or science of farming: *More than 75% of the land is used for agriculture.* [**Origin:** 1400–1500 French, Latin *agricultura*, from *ager* **field** + *cultura* **use of land for crops**] —**agriculturalist** *n.* [C] → see also HORTICULTURE

agro- /æɡroʊ/ *prefix* relating to agriculture: *agroindustry* → see also AGRI-

a·gron·o·my /əˈɡrɑnəmi/ *n.* [U] the study of plants and the soil, and how to help farmers produce better crops —**agronomist** *n.* [C]

a·ground /əˈɡraʊnd/ *adv.* **run/go aground** if a ship runs aground, it becomes stuck in a place where the water is not deep enough

a·gue /ˈeɪɡyu/ *n.* [C,U] OLD-FASHIONED a fever that makes you shake and feel cold

ah /ɑ/ *interjection* used in order to show your surprise, anger, pain, happiness, agreement etc.: *Ah! There you are!*

a·ha /ɑˈhɑ/ *interjection* used in order to show that you understand or realize something: *Aha! I knew you were trying to trick me!* → see also HA

a·head /əˈhɛd/ S1 W1 *adv.*

1 IN FRONT OF SB/STH in front of someone or something by a short distance: *The road ahead was clear.* | +**of** *Tim pointed to a tree ahead of them.* | *We could see the lights of Las Vegas* ***up ahead*** (=in front of you, a little way in the distance).

2 FORWARD if someone or something moves, looks ahead etc., they move or look toward a place in front of them: *Let Tom walk ahead – he knows the way.* | +**of** *You can* ***go ahead of*** *me in line.* | *He was just staring* ***straight ahead*** (=not looking left or right).

3 BEFORE SB ELSE arriving, waiting, finishing etc. before other people: +**of** *There were four people ahead of me at the doctor's office.* | *She had* ***pulled ahead*** (=run, ridden, or driven ahead) *by the first turn.*

4 FUTURE in the future: *You have a long trip* ***ahead of you.*** | *We're not sure what difficulties* ***lie ahead*** (=are in the future). | **plan/look ahead** *Eddie never plans ahead.* | **in the days/weeks etc. ahead** *The decisions you make in the days ahead will affect your whole future.*

5 BEFORE AN EVENT before an event happens: +**of** *The stock market was down slightly, ahead of the long holiday weekend.*

6 ahead of time a) before an event happens: *Let me know ahead of time if you need money.* **b)** also **ahead of schedule** earlier than planned or arranged: *At this point we're ahead of schedule.*

7 PROGRESS/SUCCESS making progress and being successful in your job, education etc.: **get/keep/stay etc. ahead** *Getting ahead at work is the most important thing to Nita right now.*

8 WINNING winning in a competition or election: *His home run put the Dodgers ahead by two.*

9 go ahead SPOKEN **a)** used to tell someone they can do something: *"Can I borrow your book?" "Yeah, go ahead, I've read it."* **b)** used to say you are going to start doing something: *I'll go ahead and start the coffee.* **c)** to start doing something: *Frank will be late but we'll* ***go ahead with*** *the meeting anyway.* → see also GO-AHEAD[1]

10 ADVANCED ideas, achievements etc. that are ahead of others, have made more progress or are more developed: +**of** *VEMCO was years ahead of us in their research.* | *Her educational theories were way* ***ahead of their time*** (=so new that people did not like or understand them).

11 ahead of the game/curve INFORMAL in a position where you are in control of something, and more successful than your competitors: *Belmont city leaders are ahead of the curve in environmental matters.*

a·hem /mˈhm, əˈhɛm/ *interjection* a sound you make in your throat to attract someone's attention when you want to speak to them, warn them etc.

a·hold /əˈhoʊld/ *n.* [U] NONSTANDARD **1 get ahold of sb** to find or call someone and be able to talk to them, after being unable to find them for a period of time: *I finally got ahold of Nick last night.* **2 get ahold of sth** to find something that is difficult to find, in order to buy it or own it: *I've been trying to get ahold of that album for weeks.* **3 grab/get ahold of sth** to reach for something and hold it: *Lisa grabbed ahold of my arm and wouldn't let go.* **4 get ahold of yourself** to control your emotions after being unable to control them for a period of time: *You have to stop crying and try to get ahold of yourself.*

-aholic /əhɔlɪk, əhɑ-/ *suffix* [in nouns and adjectives] INFORMAL someone who wants or needs to do or use something all the time: *a chocaholic* (=someone who loves chocolate) | *a workaholic* (=someone who wants to work all the time)

a·hoy /əˈhɔɪ/ *interjection* OLD-FASHIONED used by SAILORS to get someone's attention or greet them

AI /ˌeɪ ˈaɪ/ *n.* [U] COMPUTERS the abbreviation of ARTIFICIAL INTELLIGENCE

aid[1] /eɪd/ Ac S3 W2 *n.* **1** [U] help, such as money or food, given by an organization to a country or to people who are in a difficult situation: *The Red Cross is delivering aid to the refugees.* | +**for** *federal* ***disaster aid*** *for the flood victims* | *a* ***humanitarian aid*** *mission* | **foreign/international/Western etc. aid** (=aid from other countries, Western countries etc.) → see also FINANCIAL AID ►see THESAURUS box at **help**[2] **2** [C,U] something such as a machine or tool that helps someone do something, or the help it gives you: *a hearing aid* | *The star can only be seen* ***with the aid of*** (=using) *a telescope.* **3** [U] help or advice given to someone who needs it: **come/go to sb's aid** *Several people came to the man's aid after he collapsed on the sidewalk.* **4** [C] another spelling of AIDE → see also FIRST AID ►see THESAURUS box at **help**[1]

aid[2] Ac *v.* [I,T] FORMAL **1** to help someone or something by making their situation or what they are doing easier: *Officers were aided in the search by drug-sniffing dogs.* | +**in** *Calcium* ***aids in the development of*** *strong bones.* | **aid sb with sth** *The local community aided us with our investigation.* ►see THESAURUS box at **help**[1] **2 aid and abet** LAW to help someone do something illegal [**Origin:** 1400–1500 French *aider*, from Latin *adjuvare*, from *ad-* **to** + *juvare* **to help**]

aide W2, **aid** /eɪd/ *n.* [C] someone whose job is to help someone in an important job: *a nurse's aide* | *White House aides denied the report.*

aide-de-camp /ˌeɪd dɪ ˈkæmp/ *n. plural* **aides-de-camp** /ˌeɪd dɪ-/ [C] a military officer who helps an officer of a higher rank to do his duties

AIDS /eɪdz/ *n.* [U] MEDICINE **Acquired Immune Deficiency Syndrome** a very serious disease caused by a VIRUS that makes your body unable to defend itself against infections: *The patient has now developed* ***full-blown AIDS*** (=shows signs of the disease, rather than just having the virus in his or her blood).

ˈaid ˌworker *n.* [C] someone working for an international organization who brings food and other supplies to people in danger from wars, floods etc.

Ai·ken /ˈeɪkən/, **Conrad** (1889–1973) a U.S. writer of poems and NOVELS

ail /eɪl/ *v.* **1 what ails sb/sth** the thing or things that cause difficulties for someone or something: *Bilingual education is not the answer to what ails our state's educational system.* **2** [I,T] OLD-FASHIONED to be sick, or to make someone feel sick or unhappy → see also AILING

ai·le·ron /ˈeɪləˌrɑn/ *n.* [C] TECHNICAL the back edge of the wing of an airplane which can be moved in order to keep the airplane level

Ai·ley /ˈeɪli/, **Al·vin** /ˈælvɪn/ (1931–1989) a U.S. dancer and CHOREOGRAPHER of modern dance

ail·ing /ˈeɪlɪŋ/ *adj.* [usually before noun] **1** an ailing company or ECONOMY is having a lot of problems and is not successful: *Action is needed to boost the country's ailing economy.* **2** FORMAL sick, weak, and unlikely to get better: *his ailing mother*

ail·ment /ˈeɪlmənt/ *n.* [C] an illness that is not very serious: *She suffered from a series of* ***minor ailments*** *that winter.*

aim[1] /eɪm/ W2 *v.* **1** [I] to try or intend to achieve something: **aim to do sth** *I'm aiming to lose ten* *pounds.* | **aim for sth** *We're not aiming for perfection.* | **be aimed at doing sth** *a campaign aimed at reducing street crime* **2** [I,T] to do or say something to a particular group or person, in order to influence them, annoy them etc.: **aim sth at sb** *Soft-drink commercials are aimed mainly at teenagers.* **3** [I,T] to choose the place, person etc. that you want to hit and carefully point your gun or other weapon toward them: *The man aimed his gun but did not shoot.* | **+at/for** *The rebels claim they only aim at military targets.* **4** [I,T] to try to make something reach or hit a particular place by throwing, kicking, or hitting it in that direction: **aim (sth) at sth** *I aimed the ball at the basket* | **aim for sth** *She aimed for the middle of the wall.* | **aim a blow/kick at sth** (=try and hit someone with a punch or a kick)

aim² W3 *n.* **1** [C] something you hope to achieve by a plan, action, or activity: **+of** *We **achieved** our **aim** of opening ten new stores in a year.* | **with the aim of** *Daniels proposed the bill with the aim of preserving local wetlands.* | **main/central/principal aim** *Our main aim is to educate the public about the issue.* ▶see THESAURUS box at **purpose¹** **2 take aim** to point a gun or weapon at someone or something you want to shoot: **+at** *Alan took aim at the target.* **3** [U] someone's ability to hit what they are aiming at when they throw or shoot something: *Valerie's **aim** was **perfect*** (=she hit exactly what she wanted to). **4 take aim at sb/sth a)** to try to stop something from happening, being used, or existing: *Environmentalists are taking aim at a dangerous chemical still used by farmers.* **b)** to criticize someone or something: *Critics took aim at the president's budget plan.* [**Origin:** 1300–1400 Old French *aesmer*, from Latin *aestimare* **to think important**]

aim·less /ˈeɪmlɪs/ *adj.* without a clear purpose or reason: *The dog was running around in aimless circles.* —**aimlessly** *adv.*: *He walked aimlessly through the streets.* —**aimlessness** *n.* [U]

ain't /eɪnt/ *v.* SPOKEN, NONSTANDARD a short form of "am not," "is not," "are not," "has not," or "have not"

air¹ /ɛr/ S1 W1 *n.*
1 GAS [U] the mixture of gases surrounding the Earth, that we breathe: *air pollution* | *There was a strong smell of burning **in the air**.* | *Let's go outside and get some **fresh air**.* → see also **a breath of fresh air** at BREATH (5)
2 SPACE ABOVE/BELOW the air the space above the ground or around things: *The balloon floated silently **through the air**.* | *She threw the ball high **into the air**.*
3 AIRPLANES/FLYING a) by air traveling by or using an airplane: *Do you want the package sent by air?* **b) air travel/crash/industry etc.** involving or relating to airplanes and flying: *Air travel is getting cheaper.* | *Our biggest priority is air safety.*
4 be on/off (the) air to be broadcasting on television or the radio right now, or to stop broadcasting: *We'll be on air in three minutes.*
5 be up in the air SPOKEN to not be decided, or not be certain to happen yet: *Our trip to Orlando is still up in the air.*
6 in the air a) if a particular emotion is in the air, a lot of people seem to feel it at the same time: *There was a sense of excitement in the air.* **b)** to be going to happen very soon: *Change is in the air.*
7 APPEARANCE [singular] if something or someone has an air of confidence, mystery etc., they seem confident, mysterious etc.: **an air of sth** *She had an air of quiet confidence.*
8 airs [plural] a way of behaving that shows someone thinks they are more important than other people: *Monica has been **putting on airs** ever since she got married.*
9 the air AIR CONDITIONING: *Could you turn on the air?*
10 get/catch some air SLANG to jump high off the ground, especially when playing basketball, SKIing, riding a SKATEBOARD
11 MUSIC [C] a simple piece of CLASSICAL music
[**Origin:** (1–7, 9) 1200–1300 Old French, Latin *aer*, from Greek] → see also **clear the air** at CLEAR² (13), **hot air** at HOT (26), ON-AIR, **thin air** at THIN¹ (14), **be walking on air** at WALK¹ (11)

air² *v.*
1 TV/RADIO [I,T] to broadcast a program on television or radio, or to be shown: *The network first aired the program in 1960.* | *The concert **airs live*** (=is shown as it happens, not recorded) *tonight at 7 p.m.*
2 air your views/opinions etc. to say publicly what you think about something important: *The meetings give citizens a chance to air their complaints.*
3 CLOTHES [I,T] also **air out** if you air a piece of clothing, a blanket etc. or if it airs, you hang it in the fresh air, especially outdoors, so that it smells fresh and clean: *I hung the sheets on the clothesline to air.*
4 ROOM [I,T] also **air out** if you air a room, or it airs, you let fresh air into it after it has been closed for a long time: *I opened the windows to air out the bedroom.* → see also AIRING

ˈair bag, airbag *n.* [C] a bag in a car that fills with air to protect the driver or passenger in a crash: *cars equipped with airbags*

air·ball, air ball /ˈɛrbɔl/ *n.* [C] a bad SHOT in basketball that does not even touch the basket

air·base /ˈɛrbeɪs/ *n.* [C] a place where military aircraft begin and end their flights, and where members of the military live

ˈair ˌbladder *n.* [C] BIOLOGY an organ inside the body of most fish, that can fill with air and allows the fish to float in water SYN **swim bladder**

air·borne /ˈɛrbɔrn/ *adj.* **1** flying or moving along through the air: *When the plane was airborne, the captain made an announcement.* | *infections passed by airborne particles* **2** airborne soldiers are trained to fight in areas that they get to by jumping out of an airplane

ˈair brake *n.* [C usually plural] a type of BRAKE that operates by using air pressure, especially in a truck

air·brush¹ /ˈɛrbrʌʃ/ *n.* [C] a piece of equipment that uses air to put paint onto a picture smoothly

airbrush² *v.* [T] to use an airbrush to make a picture more attractive, to cover certain parts of it etc.
airbrush sb/sth **out** *phr. v.* to remove someone or something from a photograph or picture by using an airbrush

ˈair conˌditioner *n.* [C] a piece of equipment that makes the air in a building or room cooler and drier

ˈair conˌditioning *n.* [U] a system that makes the air in a building, vehicle etc. cooler and drier —**air-conditioned** *adj.* → see also AC

ˈair ˌcover *n.* [U] TECHNICAL military aircraft that fly over an area where soldiers are fighting, in order to protect them from the enemy's aircraft

air·craft /ˈɛrkræft/ W3 *n. plural* **aircraft** [C] an airplane or other vehicle that can fly: *Several aircraft were lost in the battle.* | **military/civilian/commercial aircraft** *Commercial aircraft need thick concrete runways.* → see also LIGHT AIRCRAFT

ˈaircraft ˌcarrier *n.* [C] a type of military ship that has a large flat surface so that airplanes can fly from it and land on it

ˈair crew *n.* [C] the pilot and the people who are responsible for flying an airplane and serving the passengers

air·drop /ˈɛrdrɑp/ *n.* [C] an act of delivering supplies to people by dropping the supplies from an aircraft, when it is difficult or dangerous to use roads —**airdrop** *v.* [T]

ˈair-dry *v.* [I,T] to dry something or to let something dry naturally in the air, rather than by using a machine —**air-dried** *adj.*

ˈair fare, airfare *n.* [C] the price of a trip by airplane

air·field /ˈɛrfild/ *n.* [C] a place where airplanes can fly from, especially one used by the military

air·flow, air flow /ˈɛrfloʊ/ *n.* [U] the movement of air through or around something

air·foil /ˈɛrfɔɪl/ *n.* [C] TECHNICAL a surface or structure such as an airplane wing that helps aircraft to fly and be controlled

ˈair force *n.* [C usually singular] the part of a country's military forces that uses airplanes to fight → see also ARMY, MARINES, NAVY[1]

ˈair ˌfreshener *n.* [C,U] a substance or a small object used to make the air in a room or vehicle smell nice

ˈair guiˌtar *n.* [U] if someone plays air guitar, they pretend to play a GUITAR, usually while listening to ROCK music

ˈair gun *n.* [C] a gun that uses air pressure to shoot small round metal balls SYN **BB gun**

air•head /ˈɛrˌhɛd/ *n.* [C] SLANG someone who is stupid and behaves in a silly way SYN **ditz**

ˈair ˌhockey *n.* [U] a game in which two players try to hit a PUCK (=flat circular object) into opposite GOALS on a table that has air blowing through small holes in its surface to make the puck move more smoothly

air•i•ly /ˈɛrəli/ *adv.* without being serious or concerned: *"I don't really care," he said airily.*

air•ing /ˈɛrɪŋ/ *n.* **1** [singular] an occasion when an opinion, idea etc. is discussed: *The issue was **given an airing** at a public meeting.* **2** [C] an occasion when a program is broadcast on television or the radio: *the show's first airing on national TV*

ˈair kiss *n.* [C] HUMOROUS a way of greeting someone with a kiss that is near the side of their face, but that does not touch them

air•lane /ˈɛrleɪn/ *n.* [C] a path through the air that is regularly used by airplanes

air•less /ˈɛrlɪs/ *adj.* airless places or conditions are unpleasant because there is not enough fresh air: *a hot airless kitchen*

air•lift /ˈɛrlɪft/ *n.* [C] an act of taking people or things to an area by airplane, when it is difficult or dangerous to use roads —**airlift** *v.* [T]

air•line /ˈɛrlaɪn/ S3 W2 *n.* [C] a business that runs a regular service to take passengers and goods to different places by airplane: *The airline has a new service to Phoenix.* | **domestic/international airline** (=only flying to places within one country, or flying to places in more than one country)

air•lin•er /ˈɛrˌlaɪnɚ/ *n.* [C] FORMAL a large passenger airplane

air•lock /ˈɛrlɑk/ *n.* [C] a small room that connects two places that do not have the same air pressure, for example in a spacecraft

air•mail /ˈɛrmeɪl/ *n.* [U] letters, packages etc. that are sent somewhere on an airplane, or the system of doing this: *an airmail envelope* | *Do you want to **send this airmail** (=use airmail rather than another method)?*

air•man /ˈɛrmən/ *n. plural* **airmen** [C] /-mən/ a low rank in the U.S. Air Force, or someone who has this rank

ˈair ˌmarshal *n.* [C] another name for a SKY MARSHAL

air•park /ˈɛrpɑrk/ *n.* [C] a small airport, usually near an area of business or industry

air•plane /ˈɛrpleɪn/ S3 *n.* [C] a vehicle that flies by using wings and one or more engines SYN **plane**: *We **boarded the airplane** (=got on the airplane) at about two o'clock.* → see also **model airplane** at MODEL[2] (1)

air•play /ˈɛrpleɪ/ *n.* [U] the number of times that a particular song is played on the radio: *The new single is already **getting** lots of **airplay**.*

ˈair ˌpocket *n.* [C] a current of air that moves toward the ground and that makes an airplane suddenly drop down

air•port /ˈɛrpɔrt/ S2 W3 *n.* [C] a place where airplanes begin and stop flying, that has buildings for passengers to wait in: *Security **at the airport** was very tight.* | *Airport parking is expensive.*

THESAURUS

terminal a big building where people wait to get onto planes

airplane

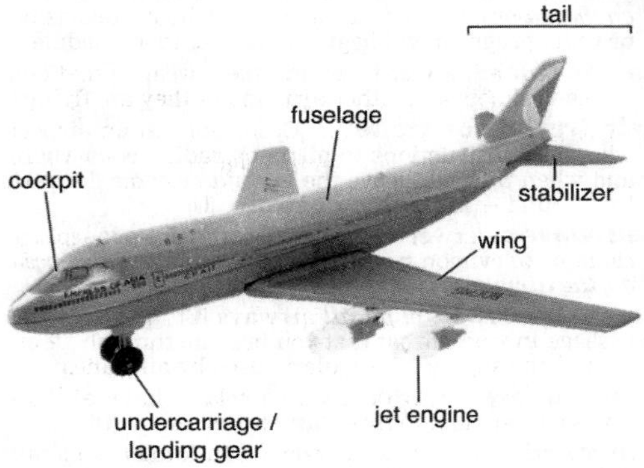

runway a long, specially prepared, hard surface like a road on which airplanes land and take off
check-in desk a place where you go when you first get to the airport to get your ticket checked and give your bags to the company you are flying with
departure lounge the place where you wait until your plane is ready to leave
departure gate the place you go through to get on your plane
baggage claim the place where you collect your suitcases and bags after a flight
immigration the place where officials check the documents of everyone entering the country
customs the place where your bags are checked for illegal goods when you enter a country

ˈair pump *n.* [C] a piece of equipment used to put air into something such as a TIRE

ˈair rage *n.* [U] violence and angry behavior by a passenger on a plane toward other passengers and the people who work on it

ˈair raid *n.* [C] an attack in which a lot of bombs are dropped on a place by military airplanes

ˈair ˌrifle *n.* [C] a gun that uses air pressure to fire a small round bullet

ˈair sac *n.* [C] BIOLOGY **1** an air-filled space inside a bird that reaches from the lungs into the bones, increasing the amount of air the bird can breathe and reducing the weight of its bones **2** an ALVEOLUS

air•ship /ˈɛrˌʃɪp/ *n.* [C] a large aircraft with no wings, that has an engine and is filled with gas to make it float

air•show /ˈɛrʃoʊ/ *n.* [C] an event at which people watch planes fly and do very complicated movements in the sky

air•sick /ˈɛrsɪk/ *adj.* feeling sick because of the movement of an airplane —**airsickness** *n.* [U]

air•space /ˈɛrspeɪs/ *n.* [U] the sky above a particular country that is legally controlled by that country: *Canadian airspace*

ˈair speed *n.* [singular, U] the speed at which an airplane travels

ˈair strike *n.* [C] an attack in which military aircraft drop bombs

air•strip /ˈɛrstrɪp/ *n.* [C] a long narrow piece of land that airplanes can fly from or land on, but which usually does not have airport TERMINALS for passengers

ˈair ˌterminal *n.* [C] a large building at an AIRPORT where passengers wait to get on airplanes SYN **terminal**

air•tight /ˈɛrˌtaɪt, ˌɛrˈtaɪt/ *adj.* **1** not allowing air to get in or out: *an airtight container* **2** planned or done carefully, so that nothing will cause any problems: *Security was airtight.* → see also WATERTIGHT

ˈair time, airtime *n.* [U] **1** the amount of time that a

A

radio or television station gives to a particular subject, advertisement etc.: *Advertisers have **bought air time** on the major networks.* **2** the time at which a television or radio program will begin, according to a schedule

ˌair-to-ˈair *adj.* **an air-to-air missile** a weapon that one airplane shoots at another airplane as they are flying

ˌair ˌtraffic conˈtroller *n.* [C] someone at an airport who gives instructions to pilots by radio about where and when they can leave the ground or come down to the ground —**air traffic control** *n.* [U]

air·waves /ˈɛrweɪvz/ *n.* INFORMAL **the airwaves** [plural] radio or television broadcasts: *The brothers have been **on the airwaves*** (=making broadcasts) *since 1976.*

air·way /ˈɛrweɪ/ *n. plural* **airways** [C] **1** BIOLOGY the passage in your throat that you breathe through **2** an area of the sky that is regularly used by airplanes

air·wor·thy /ˈɛrˌwɚði/ *adj.* an airplane that is airworthy is safe enough to fly —**airworthiness** *n.* [U]

air·y /ˈɛri/ *adj.* **1** an airy room or building has plenty of fresh air because it is large or has lots of windows: *a **light and airy** modern home* **2** cheerful, confident, and pleasant, even when you should be serious or worried: *"I'll deal with it," she said in an airy tone.* → see also AIRILY

aisle /aɪl/ *n.* [C] **1** a long passage between rows of seats in a theater, airplane, church etc., or between rows of shelves in a store: *supermarket aisles* | **up/down the aisle** *Your seat is farther down the aisle, on the left.* **2 go/walk down the aisle** INFORMAL to get married [**Origin:** 1300–1400 Old French *ele* **wing**, from Latin *ala*; influenced by English *isle* and French *aile* **wing**] → see also **be rolling in the aisles** at ROLL¹ (17)

ˈaisle seat *n.* [C] a seat next to the aisle on a bus, airplane etc., as opposed to a WINDOW SEAT

a·jar /əˈdʒɑr/ *adj.* [not before noun] a door that is ajar is slightly open [**Origin:** 1600–1700 *on char*, from *on* + *char* **turn, piece of work** (11–17 centuries) (from Old English *cierr*)]

AK the written abbreviation of ALASKA

a.k.a. /ˌeɪ keɪ ˈeɪ/ **also known as** used when giving someone's real name together with a different name they are known by: *Remember Mark Hamill, a.k.a Luke Skywalker from "Star Wars"?*

AKDT the written abbreviation of ALASKA DAYLIGHT TIME

Akhe·na·ton /ɑkˈnɑtˀn, ˌɑkə-/ (14th century B.C.) a king of Egypt who tried to start a new religion with the sun as its god

Akh·ma·to·va /ˌɑkməˈtoʊvə/**, An·na** /ˈænə/ (1888–1966) a Russian poet

A·ki·hi·to /ˌɑkiˈhitoʊ/ (1933–) the Emperor of Japan since 1989

a·kim·bo /əˈkɪmboʊ/ *adj.* **(with) arms akimbo** with your hands on your HIPS so that your elbows point away from your body [**Origin:** 1700–1800 *in kenbow*, *on kenbow* (15–17 centuries)]

a·kin /əˈkɪn/ *adj.* **akin to sth** very similar to something: *The flavor is akin to chicken.*

AKST the written abbreviation of ALASKA STANDARD TIME

AKT the written abbreviation of ALASKA TIME

AL **1** the written abbreviation of ALABAMA **2** /ˌeɪ ˈɛl/ the abbreviation of AMERICAN LEAGUE

-al /əl/ *suffix* **1** [in adjectives] relating to something, or being like something: *political* | *emotional* | *magical* → see also -IAL **2** [in nouns] the action of doing something: *her arrival* (=when she arrived) | *a refusal*

à la /ɑlə, ælə, ɑlɑ/ *prep.* in the style of: *The band has a heavy electric sound, à la Velvet Underground.*

Al·a·bam·a /ˌæləˈbæmə/ ABBREVIATION **AL** a state in the southeastern U.S.

al·a·bas·ter /ˈæləˌbæstɚ/ *n.* [U] a white stone, used for making STATUES or objects used in decoration

à la carte /ɑlə ˈkɑrt, ælə-, ˌɑlɑ-/ *adj., adv.* if food in a restaurant is à la carte, each dish has a separate price → see also PRIX FIXE: *the à la carte menu*

a·lack /əˈlæk/ *interjection* OLD USE used to express sorrow

a·lac·ri·ty /əˈlækrət̬i/ *n.* [U] FORMAL speed and eagerness: *He agreed **with alacrity**.*

A·lad·din /əˈlædn/ in THE ARABIAN NIGHTS, a young man who finds a lamp that makes a GENIE (=a magical spirit) appear and obey him

Al·a·mo, the /ˈæləmoʊ/ HISTORY a fort and former church in San Antonio, Texas, where 187 men fighting for Texas independence were killed by the Mexican army in 1836

à la mode /ˌɑlə ˈmoʊd, ˌælə-, ˌɑlɑ-/ *adj., adv.* **1** served with ICE CREAM: *apple pie à la mode* **2** OLD-FASHIONED according to the latest fashion

Al-A·non /ˈæl əˌnɑn/ an international organization for people who are related to ALCOHOLICS

a·larm¹ /əˈlɑrm/ S3 *n.* **1** [C] something such as a bell, loud noise etc. that warns people of danger: **a fire/burglar/security etc. alarm** *The fire alarm went off at 2 a.m.* | *There was a car **alarm going off*** (=making noises) *all night on our street.* | *Something has **set the alarm** system **off*** (=caused it to make a warning noise). **2** [C] an alarm clock: *I **set the alarm** for 6:00 a.m.* | *I didn't hear the **alarm go off*** (=make a noise). **3** [U] a feeling of fear or anxiety because something dangerous might happen: *We all looked up **in alarm** as someone screamed.* | *It is a normal side effect of the medicine, and there is no **cause for alarm**.* ►see THESAURUS box at fear¹ **4 sound/raise the alarm (about sth)** to warn everyone about something bad or dangerous that is already happening: *one of the first scientists to sound the alarm about the destruction of the rainforest* **5 sth sets off alarm bells** also **alarm bells ring** used in order to say that something makes you feel worried that something bad is happening: *The proposed merger is setting off alarm bells in local government.* [**Origin:** 1500–1600 French *alarme*, from Old Italian *all' arme* **to the weapon**] → see also FALSE ALARM

alarm² *v.* [T] to make people very worried about a possible danger: *The damage to the marsh has alarmed environmentalists.*

aˈlarm clock *n.* [C] a clock that will make a noise at a particular time to wake you up

a·larmed /əˈlɑrmd/ *adj.* **1** frightened and worried: *She became alarmed when she could not wake her husband.* | **+by/at/over** *Researchers are alarmed by an increase in AIDS infections among teenagers.* | **alarmed to see/hear/discover etc.** *Scientists were alarmed to find that several species of frog had disappeared.* **2** protected by an alarm system

a·larm·ing /əˈlɑrmɪŋ/ *adj.* worrying and frightening: *An alarming number of young girls are worried about their weight.* | *Sharks are being killed **at an alarming rate*** (=so quickly that it makes people worried). —**alarmingly** *adv.*: *an alarmingly large number of murders*

a·larm·ist /əˈlɑrmɪst/ *adj.* making people unnecessarily worried about dangers that do not exist: *alarmist publicity* —**alarmist** *n.* [C]

a·las¹ /əˈlæs/ *adv.* [sentence adverb] FORMAL unfortunately or sadly: *The promise, alas, was broken.*

alas² *interjection* LITERARY used to express sadness, shame, or fear [**Origin:** 1200–1300 Old French *a* **ah** + *las* **tired**]

A·las·ka /əˈlæskə/ ABBREVIATION **AK** the largest U.S. state, northwest of Canada —**Alaskan** *n., adj.*

Aˌlaska ˈDaylight Time ABBREVIATION **AKDT** *n.* [U] the time that is used in most of Alaska for over half the year, including the summer, when clocks are one hour ahead of Alaska Standard Time

Aˈlaska ˌRange a mountain RANGE in southern Alaska

Aˌlaska ˈStandard Time ABBREVIATION **AST** *n.* [U] the time that is used in most of Alaska for almost half the year, including the winter → see also ALASKA DAYLIGHT TIME

A'laska Time ABBREVIATION **AKT** *n.* [U] the time that is used in most of Alaska

Al-A·teen /'æl ə,tin/ an international organization for young people who are related to ALCOHOLICS

Al·ba·ni·a /æl'beɪniə, ɔl-/ a small country in the southeast of Europe next to the Adriatic Sea —**Albanian** *n., adj.*

Al·ba·ny /'ɔlbəni/ the capital city of the U.S. state of New York

al·ba·tross /'ælbə,trɔs, -,trɑs/ *n.* [C] **1** BIOLOGY a very large white sea bird **2 an albatross (around your neck)** something that causes problems for you and prevents you from succeeding [**Origin:** (2) from the dead albatross that brought bad luck to the sailor who killed it in the poem "The Ancient Mariner" (1798) by S. T. Coleridge]

Al·bee /'ɔlbi, 'ælbi/, **Ed·ward** /'ɛdwəd/ (1928–) a U.S. writer of DRAMATIC plays

al·be·it /ɔl'biɪt, æl-/ Ac *conjunction* FORMAL although; used to add information or details that are different from what you have already said: *The novel was made into a beautiful, albeit slow-paced, musical.*

Al·ber·ta /æl'bəṭə/ a PROVINCE in western Canada

al·bi·no /æl'baɪnoʊ/ *n. plural* **albinos** [C] MEDICINE a person or animal with a GENETIC condition that makes the skin and hair extremely pale or white [**Origin:** 1700–1800 Portuguese, Spanish, from *albo* **white**]

al·bum /'ælbəm/ S3 W2 *n.* [C] **1** a group of songs or pieces of music on a record, CD etc.: *an album of Disney songs* **2** a book in which you put photographs, stamps etc.: *a wedding album* [**Origin:** 1600–1700 Latin **unused surface for writing on**, from *albus* **white**]

al·bu·men /æl'byumɪn, 'ælbyʊ-/ *n.* [U] TECHNICAL the white or colorless part of the inside of an egg

Al·bu·quer·que /'ælbə,kəki/ a city in central New Mexico

Al·ca·traz /'ælkə,træz/ a former prison on an island in San Francisco Bay, which is now a museum

al·che·my /'ælkəmi/ *n.* [U] **1** a science studied in the Middle Ages that involved trying to change ordinary metals into gold **2** LITERARY magic: *financial alchemy* —**alchemist** *n.* [C]

al·co·hol /'ælkə,hɔl, -,hɑl/ S2 W2 *n.* **1** [U] drinks such as beer or wine that contain a substance that can make you drunk: *Ted doesn't drink alcohol anymore.* | ***alcohol abuse*** (=the habit of drinking too much alcohol) **2** [C,U] CHEMISTRY a chemical substance such as the one found in alcoholic drinks, which can make you drunk and which is also used in other products, such as cleaning products. Its chemical formula is C_2H_5OH. [**Origin:** 1500–1600 Medieval Latin **fine powder, liquid made by a purifying process**, from Old Spanish, from Arabic *al-kuhul* **the powdered antimony** (= a type of metal)]

al·co·hol·ic¹ /,ælkə'hɔlɪk◂, -'hɑ-/ *n.* [C] someone who regularly drinks too much alcohol and has difficulty stopping

alcoholic² *adj.* **1** relating to alcohol or containing alcohol OPP **nonalcoholic**: *alcoholic beverages* **2** suffering from alcoholism: *her alcoholic husband* **3** caused by drinking alcohol: *an alcoholic stupor*

,Alcoholics A'nonymous ABBREVIATION **AA** an international organization for ALCOHOLICS who want to stop drinking alcohol

al·co·hol·is·m /'ælkəhɔ,lɪzəm, -hɑ-/ *n.* [U] the medical condition of being an alcoholic

Al·cott /'ɔlkɑt, 'æl-, -kət/, **Lou·i·sa May** /lu'izə meɪ/ (1832–1888) a U.S. writer of NOVELS for children

al·cove /'ælkoʊv/ *n.* [C] a place in the wall of a room that is built further back than the rest of the wall [**Origin:** 1500–1600 French *alcôve*, from Spanish *alcoba*, from Arabic *al-qubbah* **the arch**]

Al·den /'ɔldən/, **John** (?1599–1687) one of the Pilgrim Fathers who came from England in the Mayflower to settle in the American colonies

al den·te /æl 'dɛnteɪ, ɑl-/ *adj.* food, especially PASTA, that is al dente is still firm after it has been cooked

al·der /'ɔldə/ *n.* [C,U] a tree that grows in northern countries, or the wood of this tree

al·der·man /'ɔldəmən/ *n.* [C] POLITICS an elected member of a town or city council in the U.S.

Al·drin /'ɔldrɪn/, **Ed·win (Buzz)** /'ɛdwɪn, bʌz/ (1930–) a U.S. ASTRONAUT who was the second man to step on the moon

ale /eɪl/ *n.* [U] **1** a type of beer with a slightly bitter taste **2** OLD-FASHIONED beer

al·eck /'ælɪk/ *n.* → see SMART ALECK

ale·house /'eɪlhaʊs/ *n.* [C] OLD-FASHIONED a place where people drink beer

a·lert¹ /ə'lət/ *adj.* **1** giving all your attention to what is happening, being said etc.: *The deer raised its head, suddenly alert.* | *When walking alone at night,* ***be alert to*** *your surroundings.* **2** able to think quickly and clearly: *Exercise helps keep me* ***mentally alert.*** | **stay/remain alert** *The medicine can make it difficult to remain alert.* **3 be alert to sth** to know about or understand something, especially a possible danger or problem: *The authorities should have been* ***alert to the possibility*** *of an attack.* [**Origin:** 1500–1600 French *alerte*, from Italian *all' erta* **on the watch**]

alert² *v.* [T] **1** to officially warn someone of a problem or danger, so that they can be ready to deal with it: *School officials alerted the police immediately.* **2** to make someone notice something important or dangerous: **alert sb to sth** *A large sign alerts drivers to bad road conditions.*

alert³ *n.* [C] **1** a warning to be ready for possible danger: *a smog alert* | *During a* ***security alert*** (=warning about an attack), *no planes can take off.* → see also RED ALERT **2 on (the) alert** ready to deal with a situation or problem: *Teachers are on the alert for signs of drug use.* | *All hospitals in the area were* ***put on alert*** (=warned so that they would be ready) *to receive casualties.* | **be on high/full alert** *Miami police were on high alert after a night of violence.*

A·leut /ə'lut/ a Native American tribe from Alaska

A·leu·tian Is·lands /ə,luʃən 'aɪləndz/ a group of islands off the southwest coast of Alaska

Al·ex·an·der the Great /ælɪg,zændə ðə 'greɪt/ (356–323 B.C.) a king of Macedonia who took control of Greece, Egypt, and most of the countries to the east of the Mediterranean Sea as far as India and established many cities including Alexandria in Egypt

al·fal·fa /æl'fælfə/ *n.* [U] a plant grown especially to feed farm animals

al'falfa sprout *n.* [C] a young alfalfa plant, eaten raw in SALADS

al·fres·co /æl'frɛskoʊ/ *adj., adv.* in the open air: *alfresco dining*

al·gae /'ældʒi/ *n.* [U] BIOLOGY a thing that looks similar to a plant without stems or leaves that grows in or near water

al·gal bloom /,ælgəl 'blum/ *n.* [U] BIOLOGY a sudden and great increase in the amount of algae growing on or near the surface of a body of fresh water, which uses up important supplies of oxygen in the water

al·ge·bra /'ældʒəbrə/ *n.* [U] MATH a type of mathematics that uses letters and other signs to represent numbers and values [**Origin:** 1500–1600 Medieval Latin, Arabic *al-jabr* **the reduction**] —**algebraic** /,ældʒə'breɪ-ɪk/ *adj.* —**algebraically** /-kli/ *adv.*

alge,braic ex'pression *n.* [C] MATH a mathematical statement containing numbers and letters representing numbers which are being multiplied, divided, added, or SUBTRACTED, and which does not include an equals sign

Al·ger /'ældʒə/, **Ho·ra·tio** /hə'reɪʃioʊ/ (1832–1899) a

U.S. writer, famous for his stories about boys who become rich

Al·ge·ri·a /æl'dʒɪriə/ a country in northwest Africa on the Mediterranean Sea —**Algerian** *n., adj.*

Al·giers /æl'dʒɪrz/ the capital and largest city of Algeria

Al·gon·quin /æl'gɑŋkwɪn/ a Native American tribe from eastern Canada

al·go·rithm /'ælgəˌrɪðəm/ *n.* [C] TECHNICAL a set of instructions that are followed in a particular order and used for solving a mathematical problem, making a computer program etc.

Muhammad Ali

A·li /a'li/, **Muhammad** (1942-) a U.S. BOXER who is considered one of the greatest boxers ever

a·li·as¹ /'eɪliəs, 'eɪlyəs/ *prep.* used when giving someone's real name together with another name they use: *Margaret Zelle, alias Mata Hari* [**Origin:** 1400–1500 Latin **otherwise**]

alias² *n.* [C] a false name, usually used by a criminal: *She checked into the hotel* ***under an alias*** (=using an alias).

al·i·bi /'æləˌbaɪ/ *n.* [C] **1** proof that someone was not where a crime happened and therefore could not have done it: **+for** *Enstrom* ***had an alibi*** *for the murder.* **2** an excuse for something you have failed to do or done wrong [**Origin:** 1600–1700 Latin **somewhere else**]

a·li·en¹ /'eɪliən, 'eɪlyən/ *adj.* **1** very different from what you are used to SYN **strange**: **+to** *a rural way of life that was alien to me* **2** [only before noun] relating to creatures from another world: *an alien spaceship* **3** belonging to another country or race SYN **foreign**: *alien cultures* [**Origin:** 1300–1400 Old French, Latin *alienus*, from *alius* **other**]

alien² *n.* [C] **1** TECHNICAL someone who lives or works in your country, but who comes from another country: *Under the amnesty law, many* ***illegal aliens*** *were given citizenship.* **2** a creature from another world: *an invasion of Earth by aliens*

ˌAlien and Se'dition Acts, the HISTORY laws passed by the U.S. Congress in 1798 that allowed the government to put people from other countries in prison or forced them to leave the country if they were considered dangerous or if they criticized the government too much

a·li·en·ate /'eɪliəˌneɪt, 'eɪlyə-/ *v.* [T] **1** to do something that makes someone unfriendly or unwilling to support you: *His comments alienated many baseball fans.* **2** to make someone feel that they do not belong in a particular group: **alienate sb from sb/sth** *His left-wing views alienated him from his family.* **3** LAW to give the legal right to a particular piece of land, property etc. to someone else

a·li·en·at·ed /'eɪliəˌneɪt̬ɪd/ *adj.* feeling separated from society or the group of people around you, and often unhappy: **+from** *voters who were alienated from the political process*

a·li·en·a·tion /ˌeɪliə'neɪʃən/ *n.* [U] **1** the feeling of not being part of society or a group: **+from** *his alienation from his homeland* **2** the state of being less friendly, understanding, or willing to give support as the result of something that is done: **+of** *the alienation of father from son*

a·light¹ /ə'laɪt/ *adj.* [not before noun] **1** burning: *Houses and cars were* ***set alight.*** **2** someone whose face or eyes are alight is excited and happy: **alight with excitement/pleasure etc.** *The girls' faces were alight with happiness.* **3** bright with light or color

alight² *v. past tense and past participle* **alit** /ə'lɪt/ or **alighted** [I] FORMAL **1** if a bird or insect alights on something, it stops flying to stand on a surface: **alight on/upon** *A large butterfly alighted on my arm.* **2 alight from sth** to step out of a vehicle at the end of a trip

a·lign /ə'laɪn/ *v.* **1** [I,T] to publicly support a political group, country, or person you agree with: **align (yourself) with sb/sth** *Church leaders aligned themselves with Conservatives.* **2** [I,T] to arrange things so that they form a line or are parallel to each other, or to be arranged in this way: *The desks were neatly aligned.* **3** [T] to organize or arrange something so that it has the right relationship with something else: **align sth with sth** *We have to align our budget with our goals.*

a·lign·ment /ə'laɪnmənt/ *n.* **1** [U] the state of being arranged in a line with or parallel to something: *the alignment of the sun, moon, and earth during an eclipse* | *The wheels are* ***out of alignment.*** **2** [C,U] if countries or groups form an alignment, they support each other: **+with** *the country's military alignment with the U.S.* **3** [U] the arrangement or organization of ideas, practices, or systems so that they work well together: *Are our educational programs* ***in alignment with*** *students' needs?* **4** [U] a way of arranging players in a sport to do a particular job

a·like¹ /ə'laɪk/ *adj.* [not before noun] very similar: *Do Jan and her sister look alike?* [**Origin:** Old English *onlic*, from *on + lic* **body**] ▸see THESAURUS box at **similar** → see also LOOK-ALIKE

alike² *adv.* **1** in a similar way: *You and I think alike.* **2** used in order to emphasize that you mean both people, groups, or things that you have just mentioned: *I learned a lot from teachers and students alike.*

al·i·men·tary ca·nal /æləˌmɛntri kə'næl/ *n.* [C] BIOLOGY the tube in your body that takes food through your body from your mouth to your ANUS

al·i·mo·ny /'æləˌmoʊni/ *n.* [U] money that a court orders someone to pay regularly to their former wife or husband after their marriage has ended

A-line /'eɪ laɪn/ *adj.* an A-line dress, skirt, or coat fits close to the body at the top and is wide at the bottom

a·lit /ə'lɪt/ *v.* a past tense and past participle of ALIGHT

a·live /ə'laɪv/ S2 W2 *adj.* [not before noun]

1 NOT DEAD still living and not dead: *We didn't know whether he was alive or dead.* | *He managed to* ***stay alive*** *throughout the war.* | *He's being* ***kept alive*** *by a feeding tube.* | *I have heard from my family, and they're* ***alive and well*** (=healthy).

2 STILL EXISTING continuing to exist: *Blues clubs like these help* ***keep*** *the music* ***alive.*** | *Unfortunately, discrimination against minorities is* ***alive and well*** (=exists in many places).

3 CHEERFUL active and happy: *I only really* ***feel alive*** *when I'm in the city.*

4 come alive a) if a situation or event comes alive, it becomes interesting and seems real: *Hodges' stories make history come alive.* **b)** if a town, city, place etc. comes alive, it becomes busy and full of activity: *The streets come alive after dark.* **c)** if people come alive, they start to have energy and be excited about what is happening: *In the second half, the team came alive and started winning.*

5 bring sth alive to make something seem interesting and real: *The way he describes the characters really brings them alive.*

6 be alive with sth to be full of something and seem busy or exciting: *The street was alive with music.* | *wooded canyons alive with birds*

7 be alive and kicking a) to be very healthy and active, especially when this is surprising: *At 98 she's still alive and kicking.* **b)** to continue to exist success-

fully, especially when this is surprising: *Despite financial problems, the firm is alive and kicking.* **8 be alive to sth** to realize that something is happening and that it is important: *Murphy is alive to the romance of his job.*
[**Origin:** Old English *on life* **in life**] → see also **skin sb alive** at SKIN² (3)

al•ka•li /ˈælkəˌlaɪ/ *n.* [C,U] CHEMISTRY a substance that forms a chemical salt when combined with an acid [**Origin:** 1300–1400 Medieval Latin, Arabic *al-qili* **the ashes (of a particular plant from which a type of alkali was obtained)**]

ˈalkali ˌmetal *n.* [C] CHEMISTRY any of the six soft white metal ELEMENTS that appear in group 1 of the PERIODIC TABLE. They are LITHIUM, SODIUM, POTASSIUM, RUBIDIUM, CESIUM, and FRANCIUM.

al•ka•line /ˈælkəlɪn, -ˌlaɪn/ *adj.* CHEMISTRY containing an alkali

ˌalkaline-ˈearth ˌmetal *n.* [C] CHEMISTRY any of the six metal ELEMENTS that appear in group 2 of the PERIODIC TABLE. They are BERYLLIUM, MAGNESIUM, CALCIUM, STRONTIUM, BARIUM, and RADIUM.

ˌalkaline soˈlution *n.* [C] CHEMISTRY a liquid containing an akali, which has a pH of more than 7 and will turn red LITMUS PAPER blue

al•kane /ˈælkeɪn/ *n.* [C] CHEMISTRY a chemical compound made of a chain of HYDROGEN and CARBON with only single BONDS between the atoms. Alkanes are SATURATED HYDROCARBONS, which means they contain the greatest amount of carbon that is possible. → see also ALKENE

al•kene /ˈælkin/ *n.* [C] CHEMISTRY a chemical compound made of a chain of HYDROGEN and CARBON with one or more double BONDS between the carbon atoms. Alkenes are UNSATURATED HYDROCARBONS, which means that they do not contain the greatest amount of carbon that is possible. → see also ALKANE

al•kyl ha•lide /ˌælkəl ˈheɪlaɪd/ *n.* [C] CHEMISTRY a chemical compound that is obtained by replacing one or more of the HYDROGEN atoms in an ALKANE with HALOGEN atoms

al•kyne /ˈælkaɪn/ *n.* [C] CHEMISTRY a chemical compound made of a chain of HYDROGEN and CARBON with three BONDS between the carbon atoms. Alkynes are UNSATURATED HYDROCARBONS, which means that they do not contain the greatest amount of carbon that is possible. → see also ALKANE

all¹ /ɔl/ S1 W1 *quantifier, pron.* **1** the complete amount or quantity of something; every one or every part of something: *He ate all the cake that was left.* | *Are you finished with all your chores?* | *They're all the same age.* | *I've heard it all before.* | **all of us/them/it etc.** *Put all of it in the garbage.* | **you/they/it all** *They all passed the test.* | *Bill talks about football* ***all the time*** (=a lot). → see Word Choice box at EACH¹ **2** used to emphasize the most basic or necessary facts or details about a situation: *All you need is a hammer and nails.* | *All I want is a few hours sleep.* **3 (not) at all** used in questions and negative statements to emphasize what you are saying: *Were they any help at all?* | *It's not at all uncommon.* | *I'm surprised the doctors said he could go at all.* | *"So you wouldn't mind if I came along?" "No, not at all!"* (=certainly not, please come) **4 all kinds/sorts of sth** very many different types of things, people, or places: *I met all kinds of people at the conference.* **5 most/least/best/first etc. of all** used in order to emphasize a superlative: *What do you want most of all?* | *First of all, I want to say "thank you" to everyone.* **6 in all** including every thing or person: *There were 215 candidates in all* **7 all in all** considering every part of a situation or thing: *It wasn't funny, but all in all it was a good movie.* **8 all of 40 seconds/$30 etc.** used to emphasize how small an amount actually is: *The whole interview lasted all of five minutes.* **9 for all sb knows/cares etc.** used in order to say that something could happen, especially something very bad or serious, and someone would not know or care about it: *Larry could be in prison for all I know.* **10 for all I know** used when you do not know anything about a subject, or when you do not know if anything about a situation has changed: *I opened the window, and for all I know it's still open.* **11 of all people/things/places etc.** used to show surprise or annoyance when mentioning a particular person, thing, or place: *You of all people should understand exactly what I'm talking about.* **12 ...and all** SPOKEN **a)** also **...and all that** the whole thing; including everything or everyone: *It's her birthday, so we'll be getting together for a party, presents and all that.* **b)** used at the end of a statement to emphasize that what you are talking about includes the unusual thing you have just mentioned: *He ate the whole fish, bones and all.* **13 for all...** in spite of a particular fact, quality, or situation: *For all his faults, he's a good father.* **14 sb was all...** SPOKEN used to report what someone said or did when telling a story: *He got in the car, and he was all, "I love this car!"* **15 all out** if you do something all out, you do it with a lot of energy and determination because you want to achieve something: *The team will have to* ***go all out*** *tonight.* → see also ALL-OUT **16 it's all or nothing** used to say that unless something is done completely or done in the exact way that you want, it is not acceptable: *The deal is all or nothing.* **17 when all is said and done** used in order to remind someone about an important point that needs to be considered: *When all is said and done, he's just a kid.* **18 it was all I could do to...** used to say that you just barely succeeded in doing something: *It was all I could do not to laugh.* **19 all innocence/smiles etc.** used to emphasize that someone or something has a particular quality of appearance: *Everyone was all smiles at the office.* → see also EACH¹, EVERY, **in all honesty** at HONESTY (3), **all and sundry** at SUNDRY (2)

GRAMMAR

All is used with a singular verb when it comes before an uncountable noun: *All the money is gone.* It is used with a plural verb when it comes before a plural noun: *All the kids are gone.*

all² S1 W1 *adv.* **1** [always + adj./adv./prep.] completely: *She was all alone in the house.* | *a woman dressed all in black* | *If he can turn the company around, I'm* ***all for*** *it* (=I strongly support it). **2** [always + adj.] very: *You're getting me all confused* | *I'm all excited now.* **3 all over a)** everywhere on an object or surface: *There are leaves all over the car.* | *She had flour all over her hands.* **b)** everywhere in a place: *People* ***from all over the world*** *come to visit Disneyland.* | *They're putting up new offices* ***all over the place.*** **c)** also **all done** finished: *I used to travel a lot, but that's all over.* **4 all at once a)** happening all together at the same time: *Should we send the packages all at once?* **b)** suddenly and unexpectedly: *All at once, she broke into a smile.* **5 all along** INFORMAL from the beginning and throughout a period of time: *I knew all along I wanted to live in the Santa Fe area.* **6 all of a sudden** in a very quick and surprising way: *All of a sudden I realized I didn't know where Jason was.* **7 not all that good/much/exciting etc.** SPOKEN not very good, much etc.: *The movie wasn't all that good.* | *I don't think it matters all that much.* **8 all the easier/healthier/more effectively etc.** used to emphasize how much more easy, healthy, effectively etc. something is than it would normally have been: *She likes her job, which makes leaving all the more difficult.* **9 all the same** SPOKEN in spite of something that you have just mentioned: *All the same, it would have been nice to go.* **10 one/four/ten etc. all** used when giving the points in a game in which both sides have made the same number of points: *At halftime, the teams were tied, 21 all.* **11 sb/sth is not all that** SLANG to be not very attractive or desirable: *I don't know why you like her – she's not all that.* **12 be all over sb** INFORMAL to be trying to kiss someone or touch them, especially in a sexual way **13 be all over sth** SPOKEN used humorously to emphasize that you are doing something confidently and with a lot of energy: *I was all over that history test today!* **14 it's all the same to sb** SPOKEN used to say that someone does not mind what decision is made, they would be pleased with any choice, or that they do not really care: *We can go out to eat if you want – it's all the same to me.* **15 all but** almost completely: *It is an old tradition that has all but disappeared.* **16 all too** much more than is desirable: *His career as a singer was all too short.* | ***All too often**, people do not have a will when they die.* **17 all told** counting or including everyone; all together: *All told, 28 people died.* **18 (not) all there** INFORMAL someone who is not all there cannot think in a clear normal way and seems slightly crazy: *I don't think he's all there.*

all³ *n.* **give your all** LITERARY to do everything possible to try to achieve something

all- /ɔl/ *prefix* **1** consisting of or made of only one type of thing: *an all-girl school* | *an all-wool dress* **2** continuing or operating during all of something: *an all-night party* (=continuing all night)

Al·lah /ˈælə, ˈɑlə/ *n.* the Muslim name for God [**Origin:** 1500–1600 Arabic]

ˌall-Aˈmerican *adj.* **1** having qualities that are considered to be typically American and that American people admire, such as being healthy and working hard: *Bennett is the all-American suburban mom.* **2** belonging to a group of players who have been chosen as the best in their sport at American universities: *an all-American player from Stanford*

ˌall-aˈround *adj.* [only before noun] good at doing many different things, especially sports: *a good all-around athlete*

al·lay /əˈleɪ/ *v.* [T] FORMAL **allay (sb's) fear/concern/suspicion etc.** to make someone feel less afraid, worried etc.: *The president tried to allay public anxiety.*

all-ˈclear *n.* **the all-clear a)** a signal such as a loud whistle that tells you that a dangerous situation has ended: *Residents stayed in shelters until **the all-clear sounded**.* **b)** official permission to begin doing something: **get/give the all-clear** *The book was finally given the all-clear for publication.*

ˌall ˈcomers *n.* [plural] **to all comers** to anyone who wants to take part in something: *The lessons are free and open to all comers.*

al·le·ga·tion /ˌæləˈgeɪʃən/ W3 *n.* [C] a statement that someone has done something wrong or illegal, which has not been proved: +**of** *allegations of sexual harassment* | **allegation that** *an allegation that a police officer punched the suspect* | *They shouldn't **make allegations** without knowing the facts.*

al·lege /əˈlɛdʒ/ *v.* [T] to say that something is true or that someone has done something wrong without showing proof: **allege (that)** *It is alleged that police officers were accepting bribes.* | **be alleged to be/do sth** *He's alleged to have killed two people.* [**Origin:** 1300–1400 Old French *alleguer*, from Latin *allegare* **to give reasons**]

al·leged /əˈlɛdʒd/ W3 *adj.* [only before noun] an alleged fact, quality etc. is supposed to be true, but has not been proven: *the alleged conspiracy to kill President Kennedy* | **alleged killer/victim etc.** *His alleged victim failed to appear in court.*

al·leg·ed·ly /əˈlɛdʒɪdli/ *adv.* [sentence adverb] used when reporting something that other people say is true, although it has not been proved: *He was arrested for allegedly stabbing his wife*

Al·le·ghe·ny Moun·tains, the /ˌæləgeɪni ˈmaʊntˀnz/ also **the Al·le·ghe·nies** /ˌæləˈgeɪniz/ a range of mountains which go from Virginia to Pennsylvania in the eastern U.S. and are part of the Appalachians

al·le·giance /əˈlidʒəns/ *n.* [C,U] loyalty to a person, country, belief etc. SYN **loyalty**: +**to** *the group's allegiance to values of democracy* | **swear/pledge allegiance** *I pledge allegiance to the flag of the United States of America.* | **shift/transfer allegiance** (=change your allegiance) [**Origin:** 1300–1400 Old French *ligeance*, from *lige* **person you owe loyal service to**, from Late Latin *laetus* **serf**]

al·le·go·ry /ˈæləˌgɔri/ *n. plural* **allegories** [C, U] a story, painting etc. in which the events and characters represent ideas or teach a moral lesson —**allegorical** /ˌæləˈgɔrɪkəl/ *adj.* —**allegorically** /-kli/ *adv.*

al·le·gro /əˈlɛgroʊ/ *n.* [C] a piece of music played or sung quickly —**allegro** *adj., adv.*

al·lele /əˈlil/ also **al·le·lo·morph** /əˈliləˌmɔrf/ *n.* [C] BIOLOGY one of a pair or series of GENES that have a specific position on a CHROMOSOME and that control which TRAITS (=features or qualities) that an animal or plant gets from its parents

al·le·lu·ia /ˌæləˈluyə/ *interjection* HALLELUJAH

ˌall-emˈbracing *adj.* including everyone or everything: *an all-embracing theory*

Al·len, E·than /ˈælən/, /ˈiθən/ (1738–1789) an American soldier who fought against the British in the American Revolutionary War

Woody Allen

Allen, Wood·y /ˈwʊdi/ (1935–) a U.S. movie DIRECTOR who makes humorous movies and also appears in them as an actor

ˈAllen wrench *n.* [C] a small tool you use to turn an Allen screw (=a type of screw with a hole that has six sides)

al·ler·gen /ˈælɚdʒən/ *n.* [C] TECHNICAL a substance that causes an allergy

al·ler·gic /əˈlɚdʒɪk/ *adj.* **1** MEDICINE having an allergy: **be allergic to sth** *My son is allergic to nuts.* **2 an allergic reaction/rash/response** MEDICINE an illness or a red painful area on your skin that some people get because of an allergy **3 be allergic to sth** INFORMAL, HUMOROUS to be always trying to avoid an activity or thing that you do not like

al·ler·gist /ˈælɚdʒɪst/ *n.* [C] a doctor who treats people who have allergies

al·ler·gy /ˈælɚdʒi/ *n. plural* **allergies** [C, U] BIOLOGY an extreme physical reaction to a substance that causes no problem to most other people: *She gets shots for her allergies.* | +**to** *an allergy to cow's milk* [**Origin:** 1900–2000 German *allergie*, from *all-* **all** + Greek *ergon* **work**] → see also ALLERGEN

al·le·vi·ate /əˈliviˌeɪt/ *v.* [T] to make something less bad, painful, severe, or difficult: *Heavy rains in March alleviated the drought conditions.* —**alleviation** /əˌliviˈeɪʃən/ *n.* [U]

al·ley /ˈæli/ *n. plural* **alleys** [C] **1** a narrow street between or behind buildings, that is used to get to parking areas, store GARBAGE etc., but is not used like a normal street that cars travel on: *A delivery truck blocked the alley.* **2 right up/down sb's alley** very appropriate for someone: *The job sounds right up your alley.* → see also BACK-ALLEY, BLIND ALLEY, BOWLING ALLEY, TIN PAN ALLEY

ˈalley cat *n.* [C] a cat that lives on the streets and does not belong to anyone

ˈalley ˌcropping *n.* [C] a method of planting crops in lines between rows of trees or bushes that help prevent the soil being blown away by the wind and that provide the crop with NITROGEN (=a chemical that helps plants grow well)

al·ley·way /ˈæliˌweɪ/ *n.* [C] an ALLEY

ˌall-ˈfired *adv.* SPOKEN a word meaning "completely" used before describing a quality that you think is extreme: *Why are you so all-fired impatient?*

ˌall ˈfours → see **on all fours** at FOUR (3)

ˌall get-ˈout *n.* **scared/violent/nervous etc. as all get-out** SPOKEN very afraid, violent etc.

al·li·ance /əˈlaɪəns/ W3 *n.* [C] **1** an arrangement in which two or more countries, groups, businesses etc. agree to work together to try to change or achieve something: +**between** *an alliance between farmers and environmentalists* | +**with** *Finnair once had an alliance* *with Swissair.* | *The three republics* ***formed an alliance.*** **2** a group that is formed when two or more countries, groups etc. work together: *the NATO alliance* **3 in alliance (with sb)** working together to achieve something: *Relief workers provide help in the area in alliance with local charities.* **4** FORMAL close relationship, especially a marriage, between people → see also **unholy alliance** at UNHOLY (1)

Al,liance for 'Progress, the HISTORY a plan started by President Kennedy in 1961 to help Latin American countries develop, so that there would be fewer poor people and more equality between people

al•lied /ə'laɪd, 'ælaɪd/ *adj.* **1 Allied** HISTORY belonging to or relating to the countries that fought together against Germany in World War I or II, or against Iraq in the Gulf War: *the Allied navies* | *the Allied commander in the Pacific* **2** allied things or groups are of a similar type, and are related because they share qualities and goals: **be allied to/with** *The group's ideals are closely allied to Christian beliefs.* | **allied industries/organizations/trades etc.** *agriculture and other allied industries* → see also RELATED **3** allied governments are joined by common political, military, or economic aims, and usually have an official agreement to work together: **+with** *a nation that is closely allied with Russia*

Al•lies /'ælaɪz/ *n.* HISTORY **1** the countries, including Britain, France, Russia, and the U.S., who fought together during World War I **2** the countries, including the U.S., the U.S.S.R., and the U.K., who fought together during World War II **3** the United Nations countries who fought together against Iraq during the Gulf War

al•li•ga•tor /'ælə,geɪṭɚ/ S3 *n.* **1** [C] BIOLOGY a large animal with a long mouth and sharp teeth that lives in the hot wet parts of the U.S. and China → see picture on page A31 **2** [U] the skin of this animal used as leather [**Origin:** 1500–1600 Spanish *el lagarto* **the lizard**, from Latin *lacerta*]

,all-in'clusive *adj.* including everything: *an all-inclusive vacation cruise* (=including food, entertainment, a place to sleep etc.)

al•lit•er•a•tion /ə,lɪṭə'reɪʃən/ *n.* [U] ENG. LANG. ARTS the use of several words close together that begin with the same CONSONANT (=any letter except "a," "e," "i," "o," "u," and "y"), used in order to produce a special effect in writing or poetry —**alliterative** /ə'lɪṭərəṭɪv, -,reɪṭɪv/ *adj.*

,all-'night *adj.* continuing or operating all through the night: *an all-night negotiating session*

,all-'nighter *n.* [C] INFORMAL an occasion when you spend the whole night studying or doing written work in college: *I* ***pulled an all-nighter*** (=studied all night) *last night.*

al•lo•cate /'ælə,keɪt/ Ac *v.* [T] [usually passive] to officially state that something must be used for a particular purpose or that a sum of money must be spent on a particular activity: **allocate sth for sth** *One million dollars has been allocated for disaster relief.* | **allocate sth to sb/sth** *the importance of* ***allocating resources*** *to local communities* [**Origin:** 1600–1700 Medieval Latin, past participle of *allocare*, from Latin *ad-* **to** + *locare* **to place**]

al•lo•ca•tion /,ælə'keɪʃən/ Ac *n.* **1** [C] the amount or share of something that has been allocated to a person or organization: *a new allocation of $80,000* **2** [U] the decision to allocate something, or the act of allocating something: *the allocation of funds to universities*

,all-or-'nothing *adj.* [only before noun] **an all-or-nothing situation/strategy/approach etc.** a situation etc. which involves either the whole of something or else none of it at all: *Avoid taking an all-or-nothing position.*

al•lot /ə'lɑt/ *v.* **allotted, allotting** [T] to decide officially to give something to someone or use something for a particular purpose: **allot sb sth** *Each speaker was allotted 30 minutes.* | **allot sth for sth** *Not enough funds are allotted for school lunches.* | **allot sth to sb/sth** *They are going to allot 30 minutes of radio time to Buck's show.*

al•lot•ment /ə'lɑt˺mənt/ *n.* [C,U] an amount or share of something such as money or time that is given to someone or something, or the process of doing this: *an allotment of two computers for each class* | **+of** *the allotment of scholarships to minorities*

al•lo•trope /'ælə,troʊp/ *n.* [C] CHEMISTRY one of the several different physical forms or structures of the same ELEMENT (=simple chemical substance with only one type of atom). For example, coal and DIAMONDS are allotropes of CARBON.

al•lot•ted /ə'lɑṭɪd/ *adj.* [only before noun] **allotted money/time/resources etc.** allotted money, time, resources etc. have been officially given to someone for a particular purpose: *the allotted budget for the year* | *I couldn't finish the test* ***in the allotted time.***

,all-'out *adj.* [only before noun] an all-out effort, attack, or war involves a lot of energy and determination, and all the people and equipment that are available: *an all-out fight against inflation* → see also **all out** at ALL[1] (15)

'all-over, allover *adj.* [only before noun] covering the whole surface of something: *an all-over suntan* → see also **all over** at ALL[2] (3)

al•low /ə'laʊ/ S1 W1 *v.* [T]
1 CAN DO STH to let someone do or have something, or let something happen SYN **permit** SYN **let**: *Our apartment complex does not allow pets.* | *We do not allow eating in the classrooms.* | **allow sb to do sth** *Do her parents really allow her to stay out all night?* | **allow sb in/out/up etc.** *I don't allow the cat in the bedroom.* | **be allowed (to do sth)** *"Can I smoke here?" "No, it's not allowed."* | *I'm allowed to stay out until 12 o'clock on weekends.* | **allow yourself (to do) sth** *I allowed myself to become lazy.*

THESAURUS

allow is used in both formal and informal English: *People in prison are not allowed to vote in elections.*
let is informal and is used a lot in spoken English. It is not used in the passive: *Will your Mom let you come to the party?*
permit is formal and is mainly used in written English: *Smoking is not permitted anywhere in the building.*

2 MAKE STH POSSIBLE to make it possible for something to happen or for someone to do something, especially something helpful or useful: **allow sb to do sth** *A 24-hour ceasefire allowed them to reach a solution to the conflict.* | **allow sb sth** *The new uniform allows greater freedom of movement.* | **allow for sth** *Our database allows for more efficient use of resources.*
3 HAVE ENOUGH to be sure that you have enough time, money, food etc. available for a particular purpose: **allow sb sth** *We allowed ourselves plenty of time to get to the airport.* | **allow sth for sth** *The schedule allows one hour for lunch.* | **allow for sth** *Leave enough time to allow for mistakes.*
4 CORRECT/PERMITTED FORMAL to accept or agree that something is correct or PERMITTED by the rules or the law: *The judge allowed the evidence.*
5 FORMAL to admit that something is true: **allow that** *I allow that there may have been a mistake.*
6 allow me! SPOKEN used as a polite way of offering to help someone do something: *"Allow me," the waiter said, helping her with her coat.*
[**Origin:** 1300–1400 Old French *allouer*, from Medieval Latin *allocare* **to place** and from Latin *adlaudare*, from *ad-* **to** + *laudare* **to praise**]

allow for sb/sth *phr. v.* to consider all the possible facts, problems, costs etc. involved in a plan or situation and make sure that you can deal successfully with them: *Allowing for inflation, the cost will be $2 million.* | *You have to* ***allow for the fact that*** *some people don't eat meat.*

allow of sth *phr. v.* FORMAL to show that something

A

exists or is possible: *The facts allow of only one interpretation.*

al·low·a·ble /əˈlaʊəbəl/ *adj.* acceptable according to rules or laws: ***The maximum allowable** speed is 90 mph.*

al·low·ance /əˈlaʊəns/ *n.* [C] **1** an amount of something that you are allowed, especially according to official rules: *The **baggage allowance** is 75 pounds per person.* | ***the recommended daily allowance of** Vitamin C* **2** an amount of money that you are given regularly or for a special reason: **a clothing/travel/housing etc. allowance** *my monthly travel allowance* **3** a small amount of money that a parent regularly gives to a child: *Do you get an allowance?* **4** something that you consider when making a decision, such as something unexpected that could happen: **+for** *an allowance for error* | *The budget **makes allowances for** additional staffing when needed.* **5 make allowances** to let someone behave in a way you would not normally approve of, because you know there are special reasons for their behavior: **+for** *We do make allowances for small children who don't know the rules.* **6** ECONOMICS an amount of money that you are allowed to earn without having to pay income tax on it: *the married person's allowance*

al·loy¹ /ˈælɔɪ/ *n. plural* **alloys** [C,U] a metal that is a mixture of two or more metals, or of a metal and a substance that is not metal: *an alloy of copper and zinc*

al·loy² /əˈlɔɪ, ˈælɔɪ/ *v.* **alloys alloyed, alloying** [T] **1** TECHNICAL to mix one metal with another **2** LITERARY to lower the value or quality of something by mixing it with something else

ˌall-ˈpowerful *adj.* having complete power or control: *the all-powerful Senate committees*

ˌall-ˈpurpose *adj.* [only before noun] able to be used in any situation: *an all-purpose cleaner*

all ˈright S1 W3 *adj., adv.* [not before noun] SPOKEN

1 GOOD a) satisfactory or acceptable, but not excellent SYN OK: *"What's the food like?" "It's all right."* | *"How's school going?" "Oh, all right, I guess."* **b)** good enough for a particular purpose; appropriate; correct SYN OK: *I'll see when Dr. Lopez is available. Is Thursday morning all right?*

2 YES a) used when agreeing with someone's suggestion or agreeing to do something SYN OK: *"Why don't we go to a movie?" "All right."* **b)** used when agreeing to do something or to allow something, even though you do not want to SYN OK: *"Can I play video games?" "Oh all right – but just for a little while."*

3 NO PROBLEMS not hurt, not sick, not upset, or not having any problems SYN OK: *Are you all right? What happened?* | *I'll go and make sure she's all right.* | *The kids seem to be doing all right in school.* | *Did everything **go all right*** (=happen without problems) *at the dentist?*

4 be doing all right (for yourself) to be successful in your job, life etc.

5 it's all right/that's all right a) used as a reply when someone thanks you: *"Thanks for all your help!" "That's all right. It's no problem."* **b)** used to tell someone that you are not angry when they say they are sorry for something: *"Sorry I'm late." "That's all right."*

6 it's all right used to make someone feel less afraid or worried: *It's all right. Mommy's here now.*

7 HAPPY SLANG said when you are happy because something good has happened: *"I got the job." "All right!"*

8 is it all right if... also **would it be all right if...** used when asking for permission do something: *Is it all right if I close the window?*

9 it's/that's all right by me used to agree with someone's suggestion: *"Let's stop there for today." "That's all right by me."*

10 CHECK UNDERSTANDING [sentence adverb] used to check that someone understands what you said, or to show that you understand SYN OK: *I'll leave the key with the neighbors, all right?* | *"No, I said turn left." "Oh, I see, all right."*

11 ANNOYED/ANGRY [sentence adverb] **a)** used when saying that you have heard and understood what someone has said, especially when you are annoyed: *"John, come downstairs right now!" "All right! I'm coming!"* **b)** used when asking what has happened or what someone means, especially in an angry or threatening way: *All right, who made this mess?*

12 INTRODUCE/CHANGE SUBJECT [sentence adverb] used to introduce a new subject or activity: *All right, folks, could everyone quiet down.*

13 EMPHASIZE [sentence adverb] used to emphasize that something is definitely true, will definitely happen etc.: *Sofia is the smart one in their family, all right.*

14 ADMIT STH IS TRUE [sentence adverb] used to admit that something is true, especially when saying that you also think that something else is not: *Wayne's experienced enough all right, but I don't know if he's right for this particular job.*

15 all right already! OLD-FASHIONED said in order to emphasize that you are annoyed by someone asking you to do something or the same question again and again: *"Cindy, come on!" "All right already! Stop rushing me!"*

ˈall-round *adj.* ALL-AROUND

all·spice /ˈɔlspaɪs/ *n.* [U] the dried fruit of a tropical American tree, crushed and used in cooking

ˈall-star *adj.* [only before noun] including many famous actors or sports players: *an all-star cast*

ˌall-terrain ˈvehicle *n.* [C] an ATV

ˈall-time *adj.* [only before noun] **1 all-time high/low/best etc.** the highest, lowest etc. level there has ever been: *Business confidence is **at an all-time** high.* **2 all-time record/classic etc.** the best thing of its type ever known: *the team's all-time leader in goals*

al·lude /əˈlud/ *v.* [**Origin:** 1500–1600 Latin *alludere*, from *ad-* **with** + *ludere* **to play**]

allude to sb/sth *phr. v.* FORMAL to mention something or someone in an indirect way: *She alluded to the Bible story of the three wise men.*

al·lure /əˈlʊr/ *n.* [singular, U] a mysterious, exciting, or desirable quality that is very attractive: **the allure of sth** *the allure of foreign travel* | **lose your/its allure** *At age 50, she has not lost her allure.*

al·lur·ing /əˈlʊrɪŋ/ *adj.* attractive and desirable: *a low alluring voice*

al·lu·sion /əˈluʒən/ *n.* [C,U] something that is said or written that brings attention to a particular subject in a way that is not direct: **+to** *allusions to famous works of literature* —**allusive** /əˈlusɪv/ *adj.*

al·lu·vi·al /əˈluviəl/ *adj.* EARTH SCIENCE made of soil left by rivers, lakes, floods etc.: *an alluvial plain*

al·lu·vi·um /əˈluviəm/ *n.* [U] EARTH SCIENCE soil left by rivers, lakes, floods etc.

ˌall-ˈweather *adj.* [only before noun] made to be used in all types of weather: *an all-weather coat*

al·ly¹ /ˈælaɪ/ W3 *n. plural* **allies** [C] **1** a country that makes an agreement to help or support another country, especially in a war: *a meeting of the European allies* → see also ALLIES **2** someone who helps and supports you in difficult situations: *She knew she had found an ally in Ted.* | **a staunch/close/loyal ally** *He was one of the president's closest allies.* | *a network of **political allies*** **3** something that helps you succeed in a difficult situation: *Exercise is an important ally in your campaign to lose weight.*

ally² /əˈlaɪ, ˈælaɪ/ *v.* **allies allied, allying** [I,T] to join with other people or countries to help and support each other: **ally yourself to/with sb** *The northern cities allied themselves with the emperor.* [**Origin:** 1300–1400 Old French *alier*, from Latin *alligare*, from *ad-* **to** + *ligare* **to tie**] → see also ALLIED

al·ma ma·ter /ˌælmə ˈmɑtə, ˌɑl-/ *n.* **1 sb's alma mater** the school or college that you used to attend **2** the song of a particular school or college [**Origin:** 1700–1800 a Latin phrase meaning **generous mother**]

al·ma·nac /ˈɔlməˌnæk/ *n.* [C] **1** a book that gives lists of information about a particular subject or activity, especially one that is printed every year: *the 2005 World Sports Almanac* **2** a book that gives information about the movements of the sun and moon, the times of the TIDES etc. for each day of a particular year

Al·ma·ty /ɑl'mɑṭi/ the capital and largest city of Kazakhstan

al·might·y /ɔl'maɪṭi/ *adj.* **1 Almighty God/Father** also **God/Lord Almighty** an expression used to talk about God when you want to emphasize His power **2 the Almighty** God **3 the almighty dollar/buck** INFORMAL an expression meaning "money," used when you think money is too important to someone: *He neglects his kids while going after the almighty dollar.*

al·mond /'ɑmənd, 'æm-/ *n.* [C] a flat pale nut with a slightly sweet taste, or the tree that produces these nuts → see picture at NUT

al·most /'ɔlmoʊst, ɔl'moʊst/ S1 W1 *adv.* very nearly but not completely: *I'm almost finished.* | *Are we almost there?* | *We stayed at Grandma's for almost a week.* | *It's an almost impossible task.* | *The wines are almost as expensive as champagne.* | *They sold* ***almost everything****.* | ***Almost all*** *the children here speak two languages.* | *The cause is* ***almost certainly*** *a virus.*

WORD CHOICE **almost, nearly, hardly, scarcely**
• Both **almost** and **nearly** can be used before words like *all, every,* and *everybody: Almost/nearly all of my friends came to the party* (NOT *Almost of my friends came...* or *Almost my friends came...*). Both can be used before negative verbs: *I almost/nearly didn't get up in time.* However, you do not use *not* with **hardly** or **scarcely**: *They hardly/scarcely have enough money to pay their bills.*
• **Almost** (NOT **nearly**) can be used before *any* and negative words like *no, nobody, never,* and *nothing: Almost no one came to the party* (NOT *Nearly no one...*). | *They can make almost any color of paint you want.*
• You can use *not* before **nearly**, but not before **almost**: *She's not nearly as pretty as her sister* (NOT *She's not almost as pretty...*). Both **nearly** and **almost** can be used with adjectives that have an extreme or absolute meaning: *nearly/almost perfect/frozen/dead/impossible*.

alms /ɑmz/ *n.* [plural] OLD-FASHIONED money, food, clothes etc. that are given to poor people

al·oe ver·a /ˌæloʊ 'vɛrə/ also **aloe** *n.* [U] **1** BIOLOGY a type of plant that has long thick pointed leaves **2** the juice from the leaves of an aloe plant used for making skin creams, medicine etc.

a·loft /ə'lɔft/ *adv.* [not before noun] FORMAL high up in the air: *The national flag was flying aloft.*

a·lo·ha /ə'loʊhɑ/ *interjection* used to say hello or goodbye in Hawaii

a·lone /ə'loʊn/ S1 W1 *adj., adv.* [not before noun]
1 NO OTHER PEOPLE without any other people: *Dorothy lives alone.* | *Get a babysitter – you need some time* ***alone with*** *your husband* (=with only him and no other people)*!* | *Suddenly they found themselves* ***alone together*** (=the only people there) *in the room.*
2 NO FRIENDS without any friends or people who you know, and feeling nervous or unhappy: *I was alone for the first time in my life.* | *Josie was* ***all alone*** *in a strange city.* | *He* ***felt*** *terribly* ***alone*** *when June left.*
3 NO HELP without help from anyone else: *He was forced to raise the children alone.*

THESAURUS
(all) on your own/(all) by yourself without help from anyone else: *Each child should work on the test on his own.* | *We need to resolve this problem by ourselves.*
unaided without the help of anyone or anything: *After treatment, he was able to go up and down stairs unaided.*
single-handedly used when something difficult or impressive is done by one person, without help from anyone else: *He almost single-handedly is responsible for the business's success.*
solo done alone, without anyone else helping you: *Lindbergh's solo flight across the Atlantic Ocean*
lone doing something alone: *A lone gunman killed five people in a supermarket.*

4 leave sb alone to stop annoying or interrupting someone: *Go away and leave me alone.*
5 leave sth alone to stop touching an object or changing something: *Leave that alone – you'll break it!*
6 EMPHASIZE [only after noun] **a)** used to emphasize that one particular thing or person is very important or has an effect on a situation: *The price alone was enough to make me change my mind.* **b)** used to say that someone or something is the only thing or person involved: *It's an expensive place – lunch alone was $20.* | *Stevenson alone is to blame.*
7 be alone in (doing) sth be the only person to do something: *You're not alone in wondering what's happening here.*
8 go it alone to start working or living on your own, especially after working or living with other people: *After years of working for a big company, I decided to go it alone.*
9 stand alone if an object or building stands alone, it is not near other buildings or objects: *The house stood alone at the end of the road.*
[**Origin:** 1200–1300 *all one* **wholly one**]

WORD CHOICE **alone, on your own, by yourself, lonely, lonesome, lone, solitary**
• If you are **alone**, or less formally, **on your own/by yourself**, it means that no one else is with you, and is neither good nor bad: *I spent the afternoon at home alone/by myself.*
• With verbs of action, **on your own** and **by yourself** often suggest that no one is helping you: *I want to swim alone* (=with no one else there). | *I want to swim on my own/by myself* (=either with nobody else there, or with other people there but not helping).
• If you are **lonely** or **lonesome**, you are unhappy because you are alone: *I felt lonely living away from my family.* | *a lonely old man.*
• Places can be **lonely** or **lonesome** if they make people feel lonely: *a lonesome farmhouse.* Things that you do can also be **lonely**: *a lonely drive/job/life etc.* **Lonely** is never an adverb but **alone** often is: *She traveled alone* (NOT *lonely*).
• In more formal English, a **lone** or **solitary** person or thing is the only one in a place: *a lone figure in the middle of the field* (=it is the only one there). Sometimes **solitary** can suggest that you choose to be alone: *She is a very solitary person.*

a·long¹ /ə'lɔŋ/ S2 W1 *prep.* **1** by the side of something, and from one part to another part of it: *We took a walk along the river.* **2** in a line next to or on something: *They put up a fence along the sidewalk.* | *Wild strawberries grew along the trail.* **3** at a particular place on or by the side of something, usually something long: *The Martins' house is somewhere along this road.* **4 along the way** during a process or period of time: *We had a few problems along the way.*

along² S1 W1 *adv.* **1** if someone or something moves along, they move forward: *I was driving along, listening to the radio.* | *He kept talking the whole time as we went along.* **2 go/come/be along** to go to, come to, or be in the place where something is happening: *We're going to Ben's – do you want to* ***come along****?* **3 take/bring sb along** to take or bring someone with you somewhere: *Mandy had brought some of her friends along.* **4 along with sb/sth** in addition to someone or something, and at the same time: *Add milk to the flour mixture, along with the melted butter.* **5 come/go/get along** to improve, develop, or make progress in a particular way: *"How's she doing after her operation?" "Oh, she's* ***coming along fine****."* | *The questions get harder* ***as you go along****.* [**Origin:** Old English *andlang*, from *and-* **against** + *lang* **long**]

A

a•long•side /əˌlɔŋˈsaɪd/ *adv., prep.* **1** next to or along the side of something: *We parked alongside the road.* | *Serve the sandwiches with a fresh salad alongside.* **2** if you do something alongside someone else, you do it together with them: *The Italians have been working alongside French NATO troops.* **3** if different types of things, ideas etc. are used or exist alongside each other, they are used together or exist at the same time: *CDs are sold alongside vegetables in supermarkets.* **4** used to say that one thing is being compared to another: *This achievement seems small alongside other recent advances.* | *Top Australian wines now* ***rank alongside*** (=are as good as) *the best French wines.*

a•loof /əˈluf/ *adj.* **1** not friendly, especially because you think you are better than other people: *She was polite but aloof.* **2 remain/stay/keep etc. aloof (from sb/sth)** to not become involved with something: *Ms. Morita has kept aloof from political activity.* [**Origin:** 1500–1600 *aloof* **to windward** (16–18 centuries), from *loof* **direction against the wind** (13–19 centuries), from Dutch *loef*] —**aloofly** *adv.* —**aloofness** *n.* [U]

a•loud /əˈlaʊd/ *adv.* **1** if you say something aloud, you say it in your normal voice: *The teacher read aloud to the class.* **2** LITERARY in a loud voice: *He cried aloud in pain.*

al•pac•a /ælˈpækə/ *n.* **1** [C] BIOLOGY an animal from South America that looks like a LLAMA **2** [U] the cloth made from the wool of an alpaca [**Origin:** 1700–1800 Spanish, Aymara *allpaca*]

al•pha /ˈælfə/ *n.* [C usually singular] **1** the first letter of the Greek alphabet **2 the alpha and omega (of sth)** the beginning and the end, or the most important part of something

al•pha•bet /ˈælfəˌbɛt/ *n.* [C] ENG. LANG. ARTS a set of letters, arranged in a particular order, used in writing language: *the Cyrillic alphabet* [**Origin:** 1500–1600 Late Latin *alphabetum*, from Greek, from *alpha* + *beta*]

al•pha•bet•i•cal /ˌælfəˈbɛt̬ɪkəl/ also **al•pha•bet•ic** /ˌælfəˈbɛt̬ɪk/ *adj.* ENG. LANG. ARTS relating to the alphabet: *The dictionary is arranged* ***in alphabetical order.*** —**alphabetically** /-kli/ *adv.*

ˌalphabetic ˈprinciple *n.* **the alphabetic principle** ENG. LANG. ARTS the principle on which an alphabet is based, which states that there is a specific letter or combination of letters to represent every sound that is spoken in a language

al•pha•bet•ize /ˈælfəbəˌtaɪz/ *v.* [T usually passive] to arrange things in the order of the letters of the alphabet: *The books are alphabetized by title.*

ˌalpha ˈmale *n.* [C usually singular] **1** TECHNICAL the highest-ranking male in a group of animals such as CHIMPANZEES **2** HUMOROUS the man who has the most power and influence and the highest social position in a particular group

al•pha•nu•mer•ic /ˌælfənuˈmɛrɪk◂/ *adj.* ENG. LANG. ARTS using letters and numbers: *an alphanumeric code*

ˈalpha ˌparticle *n.* [C] PHYSICS a PARTICLE (=a very small piece of matter) with a positive charge, that consists of two PROTONS and two NEUTRONS and is sent out by some RADIOACTIVE substances

ˈalpha ˌversion *n.* [C] TECHNICAL a new piece of SOFTWARE that is in its first stage of testing → see also BETA VERSION

al•pine /ˈælpaɪn/ *adj.* **1** also **Alpine** relating to the Alps **2** alpine plants grow near the top of a mountain where trees cannot grow **3** alpine SKIing involves going down mountains, rather than across flat land

Alps, the /ælps/ a range of mountains in Europe that runs through France, Switzerland, Italy, Germany, and Austria

al-Qae•da /ˌæl ˈkaɪdə, -ˈkeɪdə/ an ISLAMIC TERRORIST organization whose aim is to reduce Western influence on Islam and Islamic countries. The group has been responsible for many terrorist attacks, including the attacks on the World Trade Center and the Pentagon on September 11, 2001. → BIN LADEN, OSAMA

al•read•y /ɔlˈrɛdi, ɔˈrɛdi/ S1 W1 *adv.* **1** by or before now, or before a particular time: *"Do you want a cup of coffee?" "No thanks, I already have some."* | *"When are you going to do your homework?" "I already did it!"* | *It's too late – the letters have already been sent.* **2** used to say that something has happened too soon or before the expected time: *Are you leaving already?* | *I can't believe I already forgot his phone number!* | *Is it already 5 o'clock?* **3** used to say that a situation, especially a bad one, now exists and it might get worse, greater etc.: *The building's already costing us way too much money as it is.* [**Origin:** 1300–1400 *all ready* **completely ready**] → see also **enough already** at ENOUGH[2] (8) → see Word Choice box at JUST[1] → see Grammar box at STILL[1]

al•right /ɔlˈraɪt, ɔˈraɪt/ *adj., adv.* NONSTANDARD a spelling of ALL RIGHT which is usually considered incorrect

al•so /ˈɔlsoʊ, ˈɔsoʊ/ S1 W1 *adv.* **1** in addition to something else you have mentioned; as well as SYN too: *Six of Tom's friends were also arrested.* | *Nina runs a catering company. Also, she plans parties.* | *We talked to a counselor also.* | *The report has* ***not only*** *attracted much attention,* ***but also*** *some sharp criticism.* **2** used when saying that the same thing is true about another person or thing: *My girlfriend is also named Helen.* [**Origin:** Old English *eallswa*, from *eall* **completely** + *swa* **so**]

WORD CHOICE **also, too, as well, either, neither**

- When you want to say that something exists or happens in addition to something else, **too** and **also** are more common than **as well** in informal and spoken English. In a formal article you might see: *The company manufactures beauty products and markets pharmaceuticals as well.*
- If the verb is negative, you use **either**: *"I don't like liver." "I don't like it either."* (NOT *I don't like it too* or *I don't also like it.*)
- In informal English people usually say **not...either** rather than **neither**: *Lisa refused to help wash the dishes. She didn't do her homework either.* (If you said: *Lisa neither helped wash the dishes nor did her homework*, it would sound very formal.)

GRAMMAR **also, too, as well**

- **Also** usually comes before the main verb: *The college also has a new swimming pool* (NOT *The college has also a new swimming pool*). | *Brad can also play the guitar* (NOT usually *Brad also can play the guitar*). | *Many people were working full-time and also going to night school.* **Also** usually follows the verb *be* where it is used alone as a main verb: *Seattle is also a very nice city.*
- **Too** and **as well** are not used at the beginning of a sentence, but **also** may be used at the beginning of a sentence, especially in speech and informal writing.

ˈalso-ran *n.* [C] someone who has failed to win a competition or election, or someone who you think is unlikely to be successful

al•tar /ˈɔltɚ/ *n.* [C] **1** a table or raised surface that is the center of many religious ceremonies: *It was my job to light the candles on the altar.* **2** the part of a church, often at the front, where the priest or minister stands

ˈaltar boy *n.* [C] a boy who helps a Catholic priest during the church service

al•tar•piece /ˈɔltɚˌpis/ *n.* [C] a painting or SCULPTURE behind an altar

al•ter /ˈɔltɚ/ Ac W3 *v.* **1** [I,T] to change, or to make someone or something change SYN change: *Her face hadn't altered much over the years.* | **radically/significantly/fundamentally alter sth** *Having children has dramatically altered our lives.* | *The discovery* ***altered the course of*** *history.* ▶see THESAURUS box at change[1] **2** [T] to make a piece of clothing longer, wider etc. so that it fits better: *I* ***had*** *the dress* ***altered*** *for the wedding.* [**Origin:** 1300–1400 French *altérer*, from Latin *alter* **other**]

al·ter·a·tion /ˌɔltəˈreɪʃən/ Ac n. [C] **1** a small change that makes someone or something slightly different: *They're planning to **make a few alterations** to the house.* **2** a change in the shape or size of a piece of clothing to make it fit better

al·ter·ca·tion /ˌɔltɚˈkeɪʃən/ n. [C] FORMAL a short but noisy argument or fight, usually with someone you do not know

ˌalter ˈego n. [C] **sb's alter ego a)** another part of someone's character that is very different from their usual character **b)** a well-known character who is played by a particular actor **c)** FORMAL a person that someone trusts and who has similar attitudes and opinions

al·ter·nate¹ /ˈɔltɚnɪt/ Ac adj. [only before noun] **1** able to be used or chosen instead of another person or thing of the same type: *an alternate juror* | *an alternate method of payment* **2** two alternate actions, situations, or states happen one after the other in a repeated pattern SYN **alternating**: *alternate stripes of yellow and green* **3** happening or doing something on one of every two days, weeks etc.: *He works alternate days.* [**Origin:** 1500–1600 Latin, past participle of *alternare* **to alternate**, from *alternus* **alternate**]

al·ter·nate² /ˈɔltɚˌneɪt/ Ac v. [I,T] if two things alternate or you alternate them, they change from one to the other in a repeated pattern: +**between** *Her emotions alternated between outrage and sympathy.* | **alternate sth with sth** *Alternate alcoholic drinks with water to avoid drinking too much.* —**alternation** /ˌɔltɚˈneɪʃən/ n. [C,U]

al·ter·nate³ /ˈɔltɚnɪt/ Ac n. [C] someone who will do someone else's job if that person cannot do it: *Madsen is listed as an alternate for tonight's starting pitcher.*

ˌalternate ˈangles n. [plural] MATH two equal angles that are formed on opposite sides of a line that crosses two parallel lines: **alternate interior angles** (=the angles lying inside each of the parallel lines, where the other line crosses) | **alternate exterior angles** (=the angles lying outside each of the parallel lines, where the other line crosses) → see picture at ANGLE¹

ˌalternating ˈcurrent ABBREVIATION **AC** n. [U] PHYSICS a flow of electricity that regularly changes direction at a very fast rate → see also DIRECT CURRENT

al·ter·na·tive¹ /ɔlˈtɚnət̬ɪv/ Ac S3 W3 adj. **1** [only before noun] an alternative idea, plan etc. is one that can be used instead of another one SYN **alternate**: *Jones' book details alternative ways of coping with stress.* **2** [only before noun] an alternative system or solution is considered less damaging or more effective than the old one: *alternative sources of energy* **3** not based on or believing in traditional social or moral standards: *an alternative lifestyle* | *alternative music* —**alternatively** adv.

alternative² Ac W3 n. [C] something that you can choose to do or use instead of something else: *Which alternatives are likely to reduce traffic?* | +**to** *In this case, taking medication is a good alternative to surgery.* | ***I had no alternative but to*** (=I felt I had to) *report him to the police.* | *We don't want to move, but it seems to be **the only alternative**.* | **a viable/real/practical alternative** (=an alternative that is easy or sensible to use) *Cars damage the environment, but is public transportation a viable alternative?*

alˌternative ˈmedicine n. [U] one of the ways of treating illnesses that is not based on Western scientific methods

al·ter·na·tor /ˈɔltɚˌneɪt̬ɚ/ n. [C] PHYSICS an electric GENERATOR that produces an ALTERNATING CURRENT, used in motor vehicles

al·though /ɔlˈðoʊ, ɔˈðoʊ/ S1 W1 conjunction **1** used to introduce a statement that makes another statement seem surprising: *Although the car's old, it still runs well.* | *She continued to work although she was very sick.* **2** but SYN **however**: *You can look at my notes, although I'm not sure they're accurate.* [**Origin:** 1300–1400 *all* **even** + *though*] → see Word Choice box at DESPITE

al·ti·me·ter /ælˈtɪmət̬ɚ/ n. [C] an instrument used in aircraft that tells you how high you are

al·ti·pla·no /ˌɑltɪˈplɑnoʊ/ n. *plural* **altiplanos** [C] EARTH SCIENCE **1** a high PLATEAU (=area of high flat land) **2 the Altiplano** an area of high flat land in the Andes Mountains in South America

al·ti·tude /ˈæltəˌtud/ n. **1** [C] the height of an object or place above the surface of the ocean: *The plane normally flies at an altitude of 30,000 feet.* | **high/low altitude** *At high altitudes, it is difficult to get enough oxygen.* **2** MATH the distance from the VERTEX (=the point opposite the base) of a TRIANGLE to the base of the triangle, or to a line continuing from the base. The line measuring the height from the VERTEX to the base must meet the base at a RIGHT ANGLE.

ˈaltitude ˌsickness n. [U] a feeling of sickness that people get when they travel to places that are very high in the mountains, because there is not enough OXYGEN in the air

al·to /ˈæltoʊ/ n. *plural* **altos** [C] a woman with a low singing voice —**alto** adj.

al·to·geth·er¹ /ˌɔltəˈgɛðɚ, ˈɔltəˌgɛðɚ/ W3 adv. **1** a word meaning "completely" or "thoroughly," that is used to emphasize what you are saying: *It seems to have vanished altogether.* | *Eventually they chose an altogether different design.* | *How this is to be achieved is altogether a different matter.* **2** used when you are stating a total amount: *There were five people altogether who attended the presentation.* | *How much do I owe you altogether?* **3 not altogether** FORMAL used before an adjective, adverb, or verb to say that a situation is really closer to the opposite of that word: *The change is not altogether bad* (=it is fairly good). | *The boy was not altogether sure* (=he was fairly unsure) *the judge was talking to him.* **4** [sentence adverb] FORMAL used to make a final statement that gives the main idea of what you have been saying: *Sunshine, good food, and plenty of rest – altogether the perfect vacation!* [**Origin:** 1100–1200 *all* **everything, everyone** + *together*]

altogether² n. **in the altogether** HUMOROUS wearing no clothes SYN **nude** SYN **naked**

al·tru·ism /ˈæltruˌɪzəm/ n. [U] FORMAL the practice of thinking of the needs and desires of other people instead of your own [**Origin:** 1800–1900 French *altruisme*, from *autrui* **other people**] —**altruist** n. [C] —**altruistic** /ˌæltruˈɪstɪk◂/ adj. —**altruistically** /-kli/ adv.

a·lum /əˈlʌm/ n. [C] SPOKEN a former student of a school or college

a·lu·mi·num /əˈlumənəm/ n. [U] SYMBOL **Al** CHEMISTRY a silver-colored metal that is an ELEMENT and is light and easily made into different shapes

aˌluminum ˈfoil n. [U] a very thin sheet of shiny metal that you wrap around food to protect it

a·lum·na /əˈlʌmnə/ n. *plural* **alumnae** /-ni/ [C] FORMAL a woman who is a former student of a school or college

a·lum·ni /əˈlʌmnaɪ/ n. [plural] the former students of a school or college: *Berkeley alumni*

a·lum·nus /əˈlʌmnəs/ n. *plural* **alumni** /-naɪ/ [C] FORMAL a former student of a school or college

al·ve·o·lar /ælˈviəlɚ/ adj. ENG. LANG. ARTS relating to a sound such as /t/ or /d/ that is made by putting the end of the tongue at the top of the mouth behind the upper front teeth —**alveolar** n. [C]

al·ve·o·lus /ælˈviələs/ n. *plural* **alveoli** /-laɪ/ [C] BIOLOGY one of the very many small hollow spaces inside your lungs through which oxygen enters and CARBON DIOXIDE leaves → see picture at LUNG

al·ways /ˈɔlweɪz, -wiz, -wɪz, ˈɔwiz/ S1 W1 adv. **1** all the time, at all times, or each time: *Always lock your bicycle to something secure.* | *Grandma had always told us to be careful.* | *The wind is always blowing there.*

A

THESAURUS

permanently every time or at all times: *The door is permanently locked.*
all the time/the whole time continuously and often: *It rains here all the time.*

2 for as long as you can remember, or for a very long time: *I've always wanted to go to Paris.* | *He's always been very curious.*

THESAURUS

permanently forever or for a very long time: *His eyesight may be permanently damaged.*
forever for all time in the future: *I could stay here forever.*
for life for the rest of your life: *Marriage is supposed to be for life.*
for good used to say that a change is permanent: *I've given up smoking for good.*

3 if you say that you will always do something, you mean that you will do it forever: *I'll always remember that day.* **4** happening continuously or very often, especially in an annoying way: *My stupid car is always breaking down!* | *Jenna always talks too loud.* **5 you can/could always...** SPOKEN used to make a polite suggestion: *You could always take the test again next semester.* [**Origin:** 1300–1400 Old English *ealne weg* **all the way**]

GRAMMAR

Always usually comes after the first auxiliary or modal verb and before the main verb: *Sara always wanted a puppy* (NOT *Sara wanted always a puppy*). | *He had always lived there* (*had* is the auxiliary here). | *You should always be careful walking alone at night* (NOT *should be always careful*). **Always** usually follows the verb *be* where it is used alone as a main verb: *Ed is always tired* (NOT *Ed always is tired*).

USAGE

Remember it is **always** (NOT *allways* or *all ways*).

Alz·heim·er's Disease /ˈɑltshaɪmɚz dɪˌsiz, ˈɑltsaɪ-, ˈæl-/ also **Alzheimer's** *n.* [U] an illness that attacks and gradually destroys parts of the brain, especially in older people, so that they forget things and lose their ability to take care of themselves

AM /ˌeɪ ˈɛm◂ / *n.* [U] a system for broadcasting radio programs that is not as clear as FM

am /əm; *strong* æm/ *v.* the first person singular of the present tense of the verb to BE: *I am your new neighbor.* [**Origin:** Old English *eom*]

a.m., A.M. /ˌeɪ ˈɛm/ used when talking about times that are after MIDNIGHT but before NOON: *I start work at 9 a.m.* [**Origin:** 1700–1800 Latin *ante meridiem* **before noon**] → see also P.M.

A.M.A., the /ˌeɪ ɛm ˈeɪ/ **the American Medical Association** an organization for doctors and people who do medical RESEARCH

a·mal·gam /əˈmælgəm/ *n.* **1** [C] FORMAL a mixture or combination of different things or substances: **+of** *The band's songs are an interesting amalgam of different musical styles.* **2** [C,U] TECHNICAL a mixture of metals, used to fill holes in teeth

a·mal·gam·ate /əˈmælgəˌmeɪt/ *v.* [I,T] if two businesses or groups amalgamate, or if one business or group amalgamates with another, they join to form a bigger organization —**amalgamation** /əˌmælgəˈmeɪʃən/ *n.* [C,U]

am·a·ret·to /ˌæməˈrɛtoʊ, ˌɑ-/ *n.* [U] a type of strong alcohol made with the taste of ALMONDS (=a type of nut)

a·mass /əˈmæs/ *v.* [T] to gradually collect a large amount of money, knowledge, or information: *During the course of her lifetime, Mrs. Boone amassed over $5 million.*

am·a·teur¹ /ˈæmətʃɚ/ *adj.* **1** [only before noun] doing something only for pleasure or interest, not as a job: *an amateur golfer* | *an amateur orchestra* **2** amateurish: *The organization was woefully amateur in its methods and techniques.* [**Origin:** 1700–1800 French, Latin *amator* **lover**, from *amare* **to love**]

amateur² *n.* [C] **1** someone who plays a sport or does an activity for pleasure or interest, not as a job: *The cast was made up mostly of amateurs.* → see also PROFESSIONAL **2** someone who is not skillful at a particular activity: *Compared to those guys, I'm an amateur.*

am·a·teur·ish /ˌæməˈtʃʊrɪʃ/ *adj.* not skillfully done or made: *a surprisingly amateurish movie* —**amateurishly** *adv.* —**amateurishness** *n.* [U]

am·a·teur·ism /ˈæmətʃʊˌrɪzəm/ *n.* [U] **1** the belief that enjoying a sport or other activity is more important than earning money from it **2** lack of skill in doing an activity

am·a·to·ry /ˈæməˌtɔri/ *adj.* LITERARY expressing sexual or romantic love

a·maze /əˈmeɪz/ *v.* [T] to make someone very surprised: *Her skill amazed us all.* | **amaze sb by doing sth** *Dave amazed his friends by suddenly getting married.* | **amaze sb with sth** *Some kids will amaze you with what they can do.* | **it amazes sb that/how** *It amazes her that people consider these paintings beautiful.* | *The beauty of the area* ***never ceases to amaze me*** (=always surprises me). [**Origin:** Old English *amasian*, from an unrecorded *masian* **to confuse**]

a·mazed /əˈmeɪzd/ *adj.* [not before noun] extremely surprised: **+at** *We were amazed at his rapid recovery.* | **amazed (that)** *I was amazed that they'd show such a violent program on TV.* | **amazed to do sth** *Visitors are often amazed to discover how little the town has changed.*

a·maze·ment /əˈmeɪzmənt/ *n.* [U] a feeling of great surprise: *We looked at each other* ***in amazement*** *when we heard the news.* | ***To her amazement****, Sheila discovered she was pregnant.*

a·maz·ing /əˈmeɪzɪŋ/ S1 *adj.* **1** extremely good, especially in a surprising and unexpected way: *It's an amazing ride. You really feel like you're flying.* | *an amazing bargain* **2** so surprising that it is hard to believe: *amazing stories of UFOs* | **it's amazing that/how** *It's amazing how often you see drivers talking on cell phones.* ►see THESAURUS box at **surprising** —**amazingly** *adv.*: *an amazingly generous offer*

am·a·zon, Amazon /ˈæməˌzɑn/ *n.* [C] a tall strong woman with a forceful character, who may make men feel afraid —**amazonian, Amazonian** /ˌæməˈzoʊniən/ *adj.*

Am·a·zon, the /ˈæməˌzɑn/ a river in South America which is the second longest river in the world, and which flows through the largest area of RAIN FOREST in the world

ˌAmazon ˈRain ˌForest, the EARTH SCIENCE the large RAIN FOREST (=wet tropical forest) around the Amazon River in Brazil and other countries in northern South America

am·bas·sa·dor /æmˈbæsədɚ, əm-/ *n.* [C] **1** an important official who represents his or her government in a foreign country: **+to** *the U.S. ambassador to Spain* **2** someone who represents a particular sport, business etc. because they behave in a way that people admire: **+for** *He's a great ambassador for the film industry.* | *She's been appointed a* ***goodwill ambassador*** (=someone who is sent out to represent an organization and explain what it does) *for the U.N.'s children's fund.* [**Origin:** 1300–1400 French *ambassadeur*, from Latin *ambactus* **vassal**] —**ambassadorial** /æmˌbæsəˈdɔriəl/ *adj.* —**ambassadorship** /æmˈbæsədɚˌʃɪp/ *n.* [C,U]

am·ber /ˈæmbɚ/ *n.* [U] **1** a yellowish brown substance used to make jewelry **2** a yellowish brown color [**Origin:** 1300–1400 Old French, Medieval Latin *ambra*, from Arabic *anbar* **substance obtained from the body organs of whales**] —**amber** *adj.*

ambi- /æmbɪ/ *prefix* **1** used to say that something has

A

two parts or is done with two things: *ambidextrous* (=using either hand equally well) | *an ambiguous statement* (=one that could be understood in more than one way) **2** all around you: *ambient noise* (=noise that is all around you whenever you are in a place)

am·bi·ance /ˈæmbiəns, ˈɑmbiɑns/ *n.* [singular, U] another spelling of AMBIENCE

am·bi·dex·trous /ˌæmbɪˈdɛkstrəs/ *adj.* able to use either hand with equal skill for writing, playing sports etc.

am·bi·ence, ambiance /ˈæmbiəns, ˈɑmbiɑns/ *n.* [singular, U] FORMAL the qualities of a place that make you feel a particular way about it: *The restaurant's ambience is bright and inviting.*

am·bi·ent /ˈæmbiənt/ *adj.* **1 ambient temperature/pressure/noise etc.** TECHNICAL the temperature, pressure etc. of the surrounding area or room **2** ambient music is played on electronic instruments, has no strong beat, and is meant to make you feel relaxed

am·big·u·ous /æmˈbɪgyuəs/ Ac *adj.* **1** having more than one meaning, so that it is not clear which meaning is intended: *an ambiguous question* **2** difficult to understand, or not certain: *McClane's position in the company is ambiguous.* [**Origin:** 1500–1600 Latin *ambiguus*, from *ambigere* **to wander around**, from *ambi-* + *agere* **to drive**] —**ambiguously** *adv.* —**ambiguity** /ˌæmbɪˈgyuəṭi/ *n.* [C,U]

am·bit /ˈæmbɪt/ *n.* [singular] FORMAL the range or limit of someone's authority or influence: *These topics fell* ***within the ambit of*** *our research.*

am·bi·tion /æmˈbɪʃən/ *n.* **1** [U] determination to be successful, rich, powerful etc.: *What can you do with a kid who has no ambition?* | *She is young and full of ambition.* **2** [C] a strong desire to achieve something: *Kasich is thought to have grand political ambitions.* | **ambition to do sth** *It's been Bruce's lifelong ambition to climb Mt. Everest.* | **ambition of doing sth** *She fulfilled her ambition of breaking the world record.* [**Origin:** 1300–1400 Latin *ambitio*, from *ambire*, from *ambi-* + *ire* **to go**]

am·bi·tious /æmˈbɪʃəs/ *adj.* **1** determined to be successful, rich, powerful etc.: *Linda has always been an ambitious and hard-working manager.* **2** an ambitious plan, idea etc. shows a desire to do something good but difficult, involving a lot of work: *The Harbor Tunnel is an extremely ambitious project.* —**ambitiously** *adv.* —**ambitiousness** *n.* [U]

am·biv·a·lent /æmˈbɪvələnt/ *adj.* not sure whether you want or like something or not: +**about** *Many members were ambivalent about the protest.* [**Origin:** 1900–2000 *ambi-* + *-valent* **having a particular value**] —**ambivalence** *n.* [U] —**ambivalently** *adv.*

am·ble /ˈæmbəl/ *v.* [I always + adv./prep.] to walk in a slow relaxed way: +**along/across etc.** *Joe ambled over to say hello.* ►see THESAURUS box at **walk**[1] —**amble** *n.* [singular]

am·bro·sia /æmˈbroʊʒə/ *n.* [U] **1** food or drink that tastes or smells extremely good **2** the food eaten by gods in ancient Greek stories

am·bu·lance /ˈæmbyələns/ *n.* [C] a special vehicle used for taking people who are very sick or badly injured to the hospital [**Origin:** 1800–1900 French **place near a battle where wounds are treated**, from *ambulant* **walking**, from Latin *ambulare*]

ˈambulance ˌchaser *n.* [C] DISAPPROVING a lawyer who uses a lot of pressure to persuade people who have been hurt in accidents to SUE other people or companies in court, so that the lawyer will get part of the money if they win

am·bu·la·to·ry /ˈæmbyələˌtɔri/ *adj.* TECHNICAL able to walk or move around: *an ambulatory patient*

am·bush[1] /ˈæmbʊʃ/ *n.* [C] a sudden attack by people who have been waiting and hiding, or the place where this happens: *The three journalists were killed* ***in an ambush.*** [**Origin:** 1300–1400 Old French *embuschier*, from *en* **in** + *busche* **wood**] ►see THESAURUS box at **attack**[1]

ambush[2] *v.* [T] to attack someone from a place where you have been hiding

a·me·lio·rate /əˈmilyəˌreɪt/ *v.* [T] FORMAL to make something better: *Measures to ameliorate working conditions have little effect.* —**amelioration** /əˌmilyəˈreɪʃən/ *n.* [U]

a·men /ˌeɪˈmɛn, ˌɑ-/ *interjection* **1** used at the end of a prayer **2 amen (to that)!** used to show that you agree or approve: *"I think we can end the meeting now." "Amen to that!"* [**Origin:** 1000–1100 Late Latin, Greek, from Hebrew, **truth**]

a·me·na·ble /əˈminəbəl, -ˈmɛn-/ *adj.* **1** willing to listen or to do something: +**to** *The administration is amenable to a compromise.* **2** able to be changed or used in a particular way: +**to** *Not all jobs are amenable to flexible scheduling.* [**Origin:** 1500–1600 Old French *amener* **to lead up**, from *mener* **to lead**]

a·mend /əˈmɛnd/ Ac *v.* [T] to make small changes or improvements to a law or document [**Origin:** 1200–1300 Old French *amender*, from Latin *emendare*, from *menda* **something wrong, fault**]

a·mend·ment /əˈmɛndmənt/ Ac W2 *n.* [C,U] a written change or improvement to a law or official document, or the process of doing this: *a constitutional amendment* | +**to** *an amendment to the new banking bill*

aˈmendment ˌprocess *n.* [C] LAW a process by which changes to the U.S. Constitution are made

a·mends /əˈmɛndz/ Ac *n.* **make amends** to say you are sorry for something bad you did that harmed someone, and try to make things better

a·men·i·ty /əˈmɛnəṭi, əˈmi-/ *n. plural* **amenities** [C usually plural] something that makes a place comfortable and easier to live in: *The hotel has all the standard amenities, like air conditioning and a pool.* | *Many live in simple huts with only the most* ***basic amenities.*** [**Origin:** 1300–1400 Latin *amoenitas* **pleasantness**, from *amoenus* **pleasant**]

Am·er·a·sian /ˌæməˈreɪʒən/ *n.* [C] someone from Asia who has one American parent and one Asian parent → see also ASIAN-AMERICAN

A·mer·i·ca /əˈmɛrɪkə/ *n.* **1** the U.S.: *a trip across America* **2 the Americas** [plural] North, Central, and South America considered together as a whole

AˌmericaˈFirst Comˌmittee, the HISTORY a group of people who worked hard to try to stop the U.S. from becoming involved in World War II → see also ISOLATIONISM

A·mer·i·can[1] /əˈmɛrɪkən/ *adj.* **1** coming from or relating to the U.S.: *Most of the cars are American.* | *American forces led the attack.* **2** coming from or relating to the CONTINENTS of North and South America: *The frogs are a species found only in American rivers, especially in Brazil.*

American[2] *n.* [C] someone from the U.S.

A·mer·i·ca·na /əˌmɛrəˈkɑnə/ *n.* [U] objects, styles, people, stories etc. that are typical of the U.S.: *baseball cards and other pieces of Americana*

Aˌmerican Aˌcademy of ˌArts and ˈSciences, the an organization that helps scientists to work on particular problems and gives prizes for work in science and the arts

Aˌmerican Assoˌciation of Reˌtired ˈPersons, the ABBREVIATION **AARP** an organization for people who are 50 or older, especially people who have stopped working

Aˌmerican ˈBar Assoˌciation, the ABBREVIATION **ABA** a large national organization for lawyers

Aˌmerican ˈcheese *n.* [U] a type of yellowish-orange cheese that does not have a strong taste, is made in a factory, and is often bought in thin pieces wrapped in plastic

Aˌmerican ˌCivil ˈLiberties ˌUnion, the → see ACLU

Aˌmerican ˌCivil ˈWar, the → see CIVIL WAR

A

A,merican ,Council for the 'Arts, the an organization that helps artists, actors, and people who are teaching or learning about the arts

A,merican 'dream *n.* **the American Dream** the belief that everyone in the U.S. has the opportunity to become successful and rich if they work hard

A,merican Expe'ditionary ,Force, the ABBREVIATION **AEF** HISTORY the name given to the U.S. military forces who fought in Europe in World War I

A,merican 'Indian *n.* [C] another name for a NATIVE AMERICAN (=someone from one of the first groups of people who lived in America)

A,merican 'Indian ,Movement, the ABBREVIATION **AIM** HISTORY an organization whose aim is to protect the rights of Native Americans

A·mer·i·can·ism /ə'mɛrɪkə,nɪzəm/ *n.* [C] a word, phrase, or sound that is part of the English language as it is used in the U.S.

A·mer·i·can·ize /ə'mɛrɪkə,naɪz/ *v.* [T] to make something American in character, for example a way of speaking or writing, or the way something is organized —**Americanization** /ə,mɛrɪkənə'zeɪʃən/ *n.* [U]

A,merican 'League *n.* [singular] one of the two groups that professional baseball teams in the U.S. and Canada are divided into → see also NATIONAL LEAGUE

A,merican 'Legion, the a national organization for former members of the U.S. ARMED FORCES

American Sa·mo·a /ə,mɛrɪkən sə'moʊə/ a U.S. TERRITORY that consists of the eastern part of a group of islands in the South Pacific Ocean

A,mericans with Disa'bilities Act, the ABBREVIATION **ADA** POLITICS a U.S. law passed in 1990 that protects people with serious physical or mental problems from DISCRIMINATION at work and in other public situations

A'merican ,System, the HISTORY an idea developed in the early 19th century for encouraging the U.S. economy to grow and protecting its new businesses through government support and a National Banking system

A,merican 'way *n.* **the American way** a way of doing things that is considered typically American and obeys the principles of the U.S.: *I believe in the right to a trial by jury; it's the American way.*

Am·er·ind /'æmɚ,ɪnd/ also **Am·er·in·di·an** /,æmɚ'ɪndiən/ *adj.* TECHNICAL relating to American Indians or their languages —**Amerind** also **Amerindian** *n.* [C]

am·e·thyst /'æməθɪst/ *n.* **1** [C,U] a valuable purple stone used in jewelry **2** [U] a light purple color [**Origin:** 1200–1300 Old French *amatiste*, from Latin *amethystus*, from Greek, **preventer of drunkenness, amethyst**] —**amethyst** *adj.*

a·mi·a·ble /'eɪmiəbəl/ *adj.* friendly and easy to like: *She spoke in an amiable conversational tone.* —**amiably** *adv.* —**amiability** /,eɪmiə'bɪləṭi/ *n.* [U]

am·i·ca·ble /'æmɪkəbəl/ *adj.* FORMAL an amicable agreement, relationship etc. is one in which people feel friendly toward each other and do not want to argue: *amicable relations among employees* | **an amicable solution/agreement** *The parties have reached an amicable agreement.* [**Origin:** 1400–1500 Late Latin *amicabilis*, from *amicus* **friend**] —**amicably** *adv.* —**amicability** /,æmɪkə'bɪləṭi/ *n.* [U]

a·mid /ə'mɪd/ W3 *prep.* **1** while noisy, busy, or confused events are also happening: *The dollar fell in value amid rumors of weakness in the U.S. economy.* **2** among or surrounded by: *Old farm houses could be seen amid the trees.* [**Origin:** Old English *onmiddan* **in the middle**]

a·mid·ships /ə'mɪd,ʃɪps/ *adv.* TECHNICAL in the middle part of a ship

a·midst /ə'mɪdst/ *prep.* LITERARY amid

a·mi·go /ə'migoʊ/ *n. plural* **amigos** [C] SPOKEN a friend

a·mi·no ac·id /ə,minoʊ 'æsɪd/ *n.* [C] CHEMISTRY one of the substances that combine to form PROTEINS

A·mish /'ɑmɪʃ/ *n.* **the Amish** [plural] a Christian religious group that follows many strict rules, such as wearing plain traditional clothes and not using modern things such as telephones, cars, or televisions —**Amish** *adj.*

a·miss /ə'mɪs/ *adj.* if something is amiss, there is a problem: *Mr. McPherson insisted there was nothing amiss at his agency.*

am·i·ty /'æməṭi/ *n.* [U] FORMAL friendship, especially between countries: *a spirit of perfect amity*

Am·man /ɑ'mɑn/ the capital and largest city of Jordan

am·mo /'æmoʊ/ *n.* [U] INFORMAL AMMUNITION

am·mo·nia /ə'moʊnyə/ *n.* [U] **1** CHEMISTRY a clear liquid with a strong bad smell that is used for cleaning or in cleaning products **2** CHEMISTRY a poisonous gas with a strong bad smell that is used in making many chemicals, FERTILIZERS etc. [**Origin:** 1700–1800 Modern Latin, Latin *sal ammoniacus* **salt of Amon**, from *Amon* ancient Egyptian god near one of whose temples the substance was obtained]

am·mu·ni·tion /,æmyə'nɪʃən/ *n.* [U] **1** bullets, SHELLS etc. that are fired from guns **2** information that you can use to criticize someone or win an argument against them: *The oil spill **gave** environmentalists powerful new **ammunition against** the oil companies.*

am·ne·sia /æm'niʒə/ *n.* [U] MEDICINE the medical condition of not being able to remember anything [**Origin:** 1700–1800 Modern Latin, Greek, **forgetfulness**] —**amnesiac** /æm'niʒi,æk, -'nizi-/ *adj.* —**amnesiac** *n.* [C]

am·nes·ty /'æmnəsti/ *n. plural* **amnesties** **1** POLITICS **a)** [U] freedom from punishment that is officially given to prisoners or people who have done something illegal: *Congress is again considering **granting amnesty** to illegal aliens.* **b)** [C] an official order by a government that allows prisoners or people who have done something illegal to go free: *He was released after four years during a general amnesty.* **2** [C] a period of time when you can admit to doing something illegal without being punished: *an amnesty for people who handed in illegal guns* [**Origin:** 1500–1600 Greek *amnestia* **forgetfulness**, from *mnasthai* **to remember**]

,Amnesty Inter'national an organization that defends people's HUMAN RIGHTS

am·ni·o·cen·te·sis /,æmnioʊsɛn'tisɪs/ *n.* [C,U] a test to see if an unborn baby has any diseases or other problems, done by taking liquid from the mother's UTERUS

am·ni·ot·ic /,æmni'ɑṭɪk/ *adj.* BIOLOGY relating to the SAC surrounding an unborn baby in its mother's UTERUS

,amniotic 'egg *n.* [C] BIOLOGY an egg containing an unborn baby bird, MAMMAL, or REPTILE that has a hard shell surrounding a thin layer of skin with liquid inside it that protects the developing baby

a·moe·ba /ə'mibə/ *n. plural* **amoebas** or **amoebae** /-bi/ [C] BIOLOGY a very small creature that has only one cell and a changeable shape —**amoebic** *adj.*

a·mok /ə'mʌk, ə'mɑk/ also **a·muck** /ə'mʌk/ adv. **1 run amok a)** to suddenly behave in an uncontrolled way in which things are destroyed: *Drunken troops ran amok in the town.* **b)** to get out of control and cause a lot of problems: *an age in which global capitalism has run amok* **2 sth run amok** something that is completely uncontrolled and is causing a lot of destruction: *another example of medical bureaucracy run amok* [**Origin:** 1500–1600 Malay]

A·mon /'ɑmən/ in Egyptian MYTHOLOGY, the god of life

a·mong /ə'mʌŋ/ S3 W1 also **a·mongst** /ə'mʌŋst/ *prep.* **1** affecting many people in a particular group, or shared by many people in a particular group: *The problem is causing concern among parents.* | *His popularity has increased among older voters.* **2** through, between, or surrounded by: *We walked among the pines on the mountain slopes.* | *The letter is somewhere among* *these papers on her desk.* → see Word Choice box at BETWEEN[1] **3** included in a group of people or things: *We were among the first to arrive.* | *Innocent civilians were among the casualties.* | *He has a Matisse painting among his belongings.* | *She was selected* ***from among*** *500 candidates.* | **among friends/strangers/enemies etc.** *Jim relaxed, knowing he was among friends.* **4 among other things** used to say that you are only mentioning one or two things from a much larger group of things: *They discussed, among other things, recent events in the Middle East.* **5** if something is divided or shared among a group of people, each is given a part of it: *His money was shared among his three children.* **6 among ourselves/yourselves/themselves** with each other: *We talked among ourselves.* [**Origin:** Old English *on gemonge*, from *on* + *gemong* **crowd**]

a·mor·al /eɪˈmɔrəl, -ˈmɑr-/ *adj.* having no moral standards at all: *an amoral greedy businessman* —**amorality** /ˌeɪməˈræləṭi/ *n.* [U] → see also IMMORAL

am·o·rous /ˈæmərəs/ *adj.* involving or expressing sexual love: *The park is a favorite spot for amorous couples.* —**amorously** *adv.* —**amorousness** *n.* [U]

a·mor·phous /əˈmɔrfəs/ *adj.* FORMAL having no definite shape or features, or without clear DEFINITION: *an amorphous mass of twisted metal*

am·or·tize /ˈæmɚˌtaɪz/ *v.* [T] ECONOMICS to pay a debt by making regular payments —**amortizable** *adj.* —**amortization** /ˌæmɚṭəˈzeɪʃən/ *n.* [C,U]

a·mount[1] /əˈmaʊnt/ S1 W1 *n.* [C,U] **1** a quantity of something such as time, money, or a substance: +**of** *They spend equal amounts of time in California and New York.* | *Cook the vegetables in a small amount of water.* | *There was* ***a fair amount of*** (=a fairly large amount of) *traffic on Highway 10.* | **a large/considerable etc. amount** *The system can handle large amounts of data.* | *Please pay* ***the full amount*** *by the end of the month.* | *No specific* ***dollar amounts*** *were mentioned in Shaw's report.* **2** the level or degree to which a feeling, quality etc. is present: +**of** *Her case has attracted an enormous amount of public sympathy.* | *I felt* ***a certain amount of*** (=some) *embarrassment.* **3 no amount of sth will/can etc. do sth** used to say that something has no effect: *No amount of persuasion could make her change her mind.*

GRAMMAR

- **Amount** is usually used with uncountable nouns, and some people think this is the only correct use: *a large amount of money/food/electricity/hard work* (Note that you do not usually say a *high* or *big* amount.)
- With plural countable nouns it is best to use **number**: *a large number of mistakes/people.*

amount[2] *v.* [**Origin:** 1300–1400 Old French *amonter*, from *amont* **upward**, from *mont* **mountain**]

amount to sth *phr. v.* **1** if numbers amount to a particular total, they equal that total when they are added together: *Their share of the profits amounts to about $48 million.* **2** if an attitude, remark, situation etc. amounts to something, it has the same effect: *The court's decision amounts to a not-guilty verdict.* | *Ultimately, their opinions* ***amount to the same thing.*** **3 not amount to much/anything** also **not amount to a hill of beans** INFORMAL to not seem important, valuable, or successful: *Her academic achievements don't amount to much.* | *Jim's never going to amount to much.*

a·mour /əˈmʊr, ɑ-, æ-/ *n.* [C] LITERARY or HUMOROUS someone who you love and are having a sexual relationship with, often secretly

amp /æmp/ *n.* [C] **1** INFORMAL an AMPLIFIER **2** also **ampere** a unit for measuring electric current

am·per·age /ˈæmpərɪdʒ/ *n.* [singular, U] TECHNICAL the strength of an electrical current measured in amps

am·pere /ˈæmpɪr, -pɛr/ *n.* [C] TECHNICAL an AMP

am·per·sand /ˈæmpɚˌsænd/ *n.* [C] the sign "&" that means "and"

am·phet·a·mine /æmˈfɛṭəˌmin, -mɪn/ *n.* [C usually plural, U] a drug that gives you a feeling of excitement and a lot of energy

am·phib·i·an /æmˈfɪbiən/ *n.* [C] BIOLOGY an animal, such as a FROG, that lives in water for the first part of its life, but can live on land and breathe using lungs when it is an adult. Amphibians have wet skin and are COLD-BLOODED.

am·phib·i·ous /æmˈfɪbiəs/ *adj.* **1** BIOLOGY able to live on both land and water **2** an amphibious vehicle is able to move on land and water **3 an amphibious operation/force/assault etc.** a military action involving ships and land vehicles [**Origin:** 1600–1700 Greek *amphibios* **living a double life**, from *amphi-* **round, on both sides, both** + *bios* **way of life**]

am·phi·the·a·ter, amphitheatre /ˈæmfəˌθiəṭɚ/ *n.* [C] an outdoor theater with many rows of seats built in a half-circle shape

am·pho·ter·ic /ˌæmfəˈtɛrɪk/ *adj.* CHEMISTRY an amphoteric chemical substance can act as both an acid and a BASE: *amphoteric hydroxides*

am·ple /ˈæmpəl/ *adj.* [usually before noun] **1** more than enough: *You will have ample time to complete the test.* | *Every candidate will be given* ***ample opportunity*** *to be heard.* | *There is* ***ample evidence*** *that climate patterns are changing.* **2 an ample bosom/figure** used to refer to a woman's body, or a part of it, that is fairly large —**amply** *adv.*: *We were amply rewarded for our effort.*

am·pli·fi·er /ˈæmpləˌfaɪɚ/ *n.* [C] a piece of electrical equipment that makes sound louder SYN **amp**

am·pli·fy /ˈæmpləˌfaɪ/ *v.* **amplifies amplified, amplifying** [T] **1** to make a sound louder, especially musical sound: *The device amplifies the signal.* | *an amplified guitar* **2** FORMAL to explain something by giving more information about it: *Would you care to amplify your remarks?* **3** FORMAL to increase the effects or strength of something: *Critics say the Internet has amplified the problem of medical misinformation.* —**amplification** /ˌæmpləfəˈkeɪʃən/ *n.* [U]

am·pli·tude /ˈæmpləˌtud/ *n.* [U] **1** PHYSICS the distance between the middle and the top or bottom of a WAVE such as a SOUND WAVE **2** the large size, strength, or loudness of something: *The current warming of the Pacific Ocean is unequaled in amplitude.* **3** MATH the distance between the highest and the lowest values of a PERIODIC FUNCTION, divided by two → see also PERIOD OF FUNCTION

am·pule /ˈæmpyul, -pul/ *n.* [C] a small container for medicine that will be put into someone with a special needle

am·pu·tate /ˈæmpyəˌteɪt/ *v.* [I,T] to cut off someone's arm, leg, finger etc. during a medical operation: *Two toes had to be amputated because of frostbite.* [**Origin:** 1500–1600 Latin, past participle of *amputare*, from *amb-* **around** + *putare* **to cut**] —**amputation** /ˌæmpyəˈteɪʃən/ *n.* [C,U]

am·pu·tee /ˌæmpyəˈti/ *n.* [C] someone who has had an arm or a leg amputated

Am·ster·dam /ˈæmstɚˌdæm/ the capital city of the Netherlands

amu *n.* [U] the abbreviation of ATOMIC MASS UNIT

a·muck /əˈmʌk / *adv.* another spelling of AMOK

am·u·let /ˈæmyəlɪt/ *n.* [C] a small piece of jewelry worn to protect against bad luck, disease etc.

A·mund·sen /ˈɑmənsən/, **Ro·ald** /ˈroʊəld/ (1872–1928) a Norwegian EXPLORER who was the first person to reach the SOUTH POLE in 1911

a·muse /əˈmyuz/ *v.* [T] **1** to make someone laugh or smile: *He told jokes to amuse his sister.* **2** to make someone spend time in an enjoyable way, without getting bored SYN **entertain**: *We took plenty of toys to amuse the children during the flight.* | **amuse yourself** *We amused ourselves playing video games.* [**Origin:** 1400–1500 Old French *amuser*, from *muse* **mouth of an animal**]

a·mused /əˈmyuzd/ *adj.* **1** someone who is amused by something thinks it is funny, so that they smile or

A

laugh: *James watched with an amused smile.* | **+at/by** *Ellen seemed amused by the whole situation.* **2 keep sb amused** to entertain or interest someone for a long time so that they do not get bored: *Listening to the radio keeps me amused while I'm driving.* **3 sb is not amused** OFTEN HUMOROUS used to say that someone is angry about something: *When Dad saw the damage, he was not amused.*

a·muse·ment /əˈmyuzmənt/ *n.* **1** [U] the feeling you have when you think something is funny: *Sheila was hardly able to conceal her amusement.* | ***To everyone's amusement**, the dog ran off with the ball.* **2** [U] the process of getting or providing pleasure and enjoyment: *What do you do **for amusement** in this town?* **3** [C] something that entertains you and makes the time pass in an enjoyable way: *video games and other amusements*

aˈmusement ˌpark *n.* [C] a large area with many special machines that you can ride on, such as ROLLER COASTERS and MERRY-GO-ROUNDS

a·mus·ing /əˈmyuzɪŋ/ *adj.* funny and entertaining: *a charming and amusing book* —**amusingly** *adv.*

an /ən; *strong* æn/ S1 W1 *indefinite article, determiner* used instead of "a" when the following word begins with a vowel sound: *an orange* | *an X-ray* | *It's such an old house.* → see also A

-an /ən/ *suffix* **1** [in adjectives and nouns] someone or something from a place, or relating to a place: *an American* | *Appalachian* (=from Appalachia) *music* | *suburban housing* **2** [in adjectives and nouns] relating to the ideas of a particular person or group, or someone who follows these ideas: *Lutheran theology* (=relating to the teachings of Martin Luther) **3** [in adjectives] relating to or similar to a person, thing, or period of time: *the Roman Empire* → see also -EAN, -IAN

an- /ən, æn/ *prefix* showing the opposite or the absence of something, used instead of A- in a word beginning with a vowel sound SYN **not** SYN **without**: *anarchy* (=without government) | *anaerobic* (=without air or oxygen)

-ana /ɑnə, ænə/ *suffix* [in U nouns] a collection of objects, papers etc., relating to someone or something: *Americana* → see also -IANA

An·a·bap·tists /ˌænəˈbæptɪsts/ a group within the Christian religion in the 16th century who thought that only people who really believed the religion should be baptized (BAPTIZE)

an·a·bol·ic ster·oid /ˌænəbɑlɪk ˈstɛrɔɪd, ˈstɪr-/ *n.* [C] MEDICINE a drug that makes muscles grow quickly, sometimes used illegally in sports

a·nab·o·lism /əˈnæbəˌlɪzəm/ *n.* [U] CHEMISTRY a process by which living things combine simple substances to make more COMPLEX substances → see also CATABOLISM —**anabolic** /ˌænəˈbɑlɪk◂/ adj. TECHNICAL

a·nach·ro·nism /əˈnækrəˌnɪzəm/ *n.* [C] **1** someone or something that seems to belong to the past, not the present: *The mining law is simply an anachronism in this day and age.* **2** something in a play, movie etc. that seems wrong because it did not exist in the period of history in which the play etc. is set —**anachronistic** /əˌnækrəˈnɪstɪk/ *adj.* —**anachronistically** /-kli/ *adv.*

an·a·con·da /ˌænəˈkɑndə/ *n.* [C] a large South American snake

an·ae·robe /ˈænəˌroʊb/ *n.* [C] BIOLOGY a very small living thing that does not need oxygen in order to exist, for example a BACTERIUM → see also FACULTATIVE ANAEROBE

an·aer·o·bic /ˌænəˈroʊbɪk/ *adj.* BIOLOGY not needing oxygen in order to live

an·aes·the·sia /ˌænəsˈθiʒə/ *n.* [U] another spelling of ANESTHESIA

an·aes·thet·ic /ˌænəsˈθɛt̬ɪk/ *n.* [C,U] another spelling of ANESTHETIC

a·naes·the·tist /əˈnɛsθətɪst/ *n.* [C] another spelling of ANESTHETIST

a·naes·the·tize /əˈnɛsθəˌtaɪz/ *v.* [T] another spelling of ANESTHETIZE

an·a·gram /ˈænəˌgræm/ *n.* [C] ENG. LANG. ARTS a word or phrase that is made by changing the order of the letters in another word or phrase: **+of** *"Silent" is an anagram of "listen."*

a·nal /ˈeɪnl/ *adj.* **1** relating to the ANUS **2** also **anal retentive** INFORMAL showing too much concern with small details and keeping everything in order, especially in a way that annoys other people: *Stop being so anal!*

an·al·ge·si·a /ˌænlˈdʒiʒə, -ziə/ *n.* [U] MEDICINE the condition of being unable to feel pain while conscious

an·al·ge·sic /ˌænlˈdʒizɪk/ *n.* [C] MEDICINE a drug that reduces pain —**analgesic** *adj.*

an·a·log¹, analogue /ˈænlˌɑg, -ˌɔg/ *adj.* **1 an analog clock/watch/dial etc.** a clock, watch, or instrument that uses moving hands or a POINTER to show information, instead of using changing numbers **2** TECHNICAL analog technology uses changing physical quantities such as length, width, VOLTAGE etc. to send and store data → see also DIGITAL

analog², analogue *n.* [C] FORMAL something that is similar to something else in some way: **+to/of** *The Sierra Nevada mountains are the West Coast analog of the Appalachians.*

ˌanalog comˈputer *n.* [C] a computer that calculates things by measuring changing quantities such as VOLTAGE rather than using a BINARY system of counting

a·nal·o·gous /əˈnæləgəs/ Ac *adj.* FORMAL similar to another situation or thing so that a comparison can be made: **+to/with** *Scharf's findings are analogous with our own.* [**Origin:** 1600–1700 Latin *analogus*, from Greek *analogos*, from *ana-* **according to** + *logos* **reason, ratio**]

a·nal·o·gy /əˈnælədʒi/ Ac *n. plural* **analogies** [C,U] a comparison between two situations, processes etc. that seem similar, or the process of making this comparison: **+with/to/between** *analogies between human and animal behavior* | **draw/make an analogy** *Norma drew an analogy between childbirth and the creative process.* | *Dr. Wood explained the movement of light **by analogy with*** (=using an analogy of) *the movement of water.*

an·a·lyse /ˈænlˌaɪz/ Ac *v.* [T] the British spelling of ANALYZE

a·nal·y·sis /əˈnæləsɪs/ Ac S2 W2 *n. plural* **analyses** /-siz/ **1** [C,U] a careful examination of something in order to understand it better: **+of** *Further analysis of the data is needed.* | **do/carry out/conduct an analysis** *She did a careful analysis of all the exam results.* **2** [C,U] a careful scientific examination of something to see what it consists of: **+of** *Forensic experts are doing analyses of the samples.* | *The substance was sent to the lab **for analysis**.* **3** [C] a description or an opinion on something that is based on a careful examination of it: *Some people will disagree with this analysis.* | **+of** *a detailed analysis of the week's biggest news stories* **4 in the final/last analysis** used when giving the most basic or important facts about a situation: *In the final analysis, the project was a failure.* **5** [U] a process in which a doctor makes someone talk about their past experiences, relationships etc. in order to help them with mental or emotional problems SYN **psychoanalysis** [**Origin:** 1500–1600 Modern Latin, Greek, from *analyein* **to break up**]

an·a·lyst /ˈænl-ɪst/ Ac W1 *n.* [C] **1** someone who makes a careful examination of events or materials in order to make judgments about them: *a **stock market analyst*** | ***political analysts*** **2** someone such as a doctor who helps people who have mental or emotional problems by making them talk about their experiences and relationships SYN **psychoanalyst** → see also SYSTEMS ANALYST

an·a·lyt·ic /ˌænlˈɪt̬ɪk◂/ Ac also **an·a·lyt·i·cal** /ˌænlˈɪt̬ɪkəl/ *adj.* using methods that help you examine things carefully, especially by separating them into their different parts: *an analytic approach* | *analytical chemistry*

ˌanalytical 'chemistry *n.* [U] CHEMISTRY the scientific study of what chemicals materials are made of

an·al·yze /'ænlˌaɪz/ Ac W3 *v.* [T] **1** to carefully examine something using scientific methods and equipment to see what it consists of or what it means: *Researchers began **analyzing** the **data** as soon as the first signals came back from the space probe.* | *The **results** were **analyzed** and the findings published in a medical journal.* | *Experts are still analyzing the DNA evidence in the case.* **2** to think about something carefully and in great detail, in order to understand it: *You need to sit down and analyze why you feel so upset.* **3** to examine someone's mental or emotional problems by using analysis SYN **psychoanalyze**: *He analyzed his own as well as his patients' dreams.*

an·a·pest /'ænəˌpɛst/ *n.* [C] ENG. LANG. ARTS part of a line of poetry consisting of two short sounds then one long one

an·a·phase /'ænəˌfeɪz/ *n.* [U] BIOLOGY the third stage of the process that takes place when a cell divides, when pairs of CHROMOSOMES separate and move toward opposite ends of the cell → see also METAPHASE, PROPHASE, TELOPHASE

an·ar·chic /æ'nɑrkɪk/ *adj.* lacking any rules or order, or not following the moral rules of society: *a lawless anarchic city*

an·ar·chism /'ænɚˌkɪzəm/ *n.* [U] POLITICS the political belief that there should be no government and that ordinary people should work together to improve society

an·ar·chist /'ænɚˌkɪst/ *n.* [C] POLITICS someone who believes that governments, laws etc. are not necessary —**anarchistic** /ˌænɚ'kɪstɪk/ *adj.* —**anarchistically** /-kli/ *adv.*

an·ar·chy /'ænɚki/ *n.* [U] **1** a situation in which there is no order, and people are not obeying the rules: *There was a **state of** near **anarchy** in the classroom.* **2** a situation in which there is no effective government in a country: *The nation is in danger of **falling into anarchy**.* [**Origin:** 1500–1600 Medieval Latin *anarchia*, from Greek, from *anarchos* **having no ruler**]

A·na·sa·zi, the /ˌɑnə'sɑzi/ a Native American tribe who formerly lived in the southwest of the U.S.

a·nath·e·ma /ə'næθəmə/ *n.* **sth is anathema (to sb)** used to say that someone strongly dislikes something or disapproves of it: *Cutting government service is still anathema to liberals.* [**Origin:** 1500–1600 Late Latin, Greek, **thing given over to evil, curse**, from *anatithenai* **to set up, dedicate**]

an·a·tom·i·cal /ˌænə'tɑmɪkəl/ *adj.* BIOLOGY relating to the structure of human or animal bodies: *an anatomical model* —**anatomically** /-kli/ *adv.*: *an **anatomically correct** (=showing all the body parts) doll*

a·nat·o·mist /ə'nætˌəmɪst/ *n.* [C] someone who knows a lot about the anatomy of human or animal bodies

a·nat·o·my /ə'nætˌəmi/ *n. plural* **anatomies** **1** [U] BIOLOGY the scientific study of the structure of human or animal bodies: *human anatomy* **2** [C usually singular] MEDICINE the structure of a body, or of a part of a body: +**of** *the anatomy of the nervous system* **3 sb's anatomy** OFTEN HUMOROUS someone's body: *You could see a part of his anatomy that I'd rather not mention.* **4 the/an anatomy of sth a)** a study or examination of an organization, process etc. in order to understand and explain how it works: *Elkind's book is an anatomy of one man's discussion with his son about life.* **b)** the structure of an organization, process etc. or the way it works: *the anatomy of a secret government operation* [**Origin:** 1300–1400 Late Latin *anatomia* **cutting up a body**, from Greek *anatome*, from *anatemnein* **to cut up**]

An·ax·ag·o·ras /ˌænæk'sægərəs/ (500?–428 B.C.) a Greek PHILOSOPHER

-ance /əns/ *suffix* [in nouns] **1** used to make nouns from verbs, to show a state, a quality, or a fact: *a sudden appearance* (=someone appeared suddenly) | *We need more assistance* (=more help). | *There's a resemblance between the two children* (=they look like each other). **2** used to make nouns from adjectives ending in -ANT: *Picasso's brilliance* (=great intelligence, from BRILLIANT) → see also -ENCE

an·ces·tor /'ænˌsɛstɚ/ *n.* [C] **1** a member of your family who lived a long time ago: *Most of Luke's ancestors were Italian.* **2 the ancestor of sth** the form in which a modern machine, vehicle etc. first existed: *Babbage's invention was the ancestor of the modern computer.* [**Origin:** 1300–1400 Old French *ancestre*, from Latin *antecessor* **one who goes before**] → see also DESCENDANT —**ancestral** /æn'sɛstrəl/ *adj.*

'ancestor ˌworship *n.* [U] a religious practice in which people show great respect to the members of their family who lived a long time ago in the past, for example by praying to them or performing traditional religious ceremonies in their honor

an·ces·try /'ænˌsɛstri/ *n. plural* **ancestries** [C usually singular, U] the members of your family who lived a long time ago: *She traced her ancestry back to 17th-century England.* | **of French/Chinese/African etc. ancestry** *His mother is of Spanish ancestry.*

an·chor[1] /'æŋkɚ/ *n.* **1** [C] a piece of heavy metal that is lowered to the bottom of the ocean, a lake etc. to prevent a ship or boat from moving: *a rusty anchor* | **drop anchor** (=lower the anchor into the water when the ship is staying somewhere) | **weigh anchor** (=take the anchor out of the water when the ship is about to move again) **2** [C] someone who reads the news on TV and introduces news reports SYN **anchorperson**: *a local news anchor* **3** [C] someone or something that provides a feeling of support and safety: *These ancient trees are a spiritual anchor that our culture needs to hold on to.* **4** [C] someone on a sports team, usually the strongest member, who runs or competes last in a race or competition

anchor[2] *v.*
1 BOAT [I,T] to lower the anchor on a ship or boat to hold it in one place: *Three tankers were anchored in the harbor.*
2 TV NEWS [T] to be the person who reads the news and introduces reports on TV: *The new hour-long program is anchored by Mark McEwen.*
3 FASTEN [T usually passive] to fasten something firmly so that it cannot move: *The panel was firmly anchored by two large bolts.*
4 SUPPORT [T] to provide a feeling of support, safety, or help for someone or an organization: *Stevens anchors the team's defense.*
5 be anchored in sth to be strongly related to a particular system, way of life etc.: *Her personal ideals were anchored in her Irish heritage.*

An·chor·age /'æŋkərɪdʒ/ the largest city in the U.S. state of Alaska

an·chor·age /'æŋkərɪdʒ/ *n.* **1** [C] a place where ships can anchor **2** [C,U] TECHNICAL a place where something can be firmly fastened: *seat belt anchorages*

an·chor·man /'æŋkɚˌmæn/ *n. plural* **anchormen** /-ˌmɛn/ [C] a male ANCHOR

an·chor·per·son /'æŋkɚˌpɚsən/ *n. plural* **anchorpersons** or **anchorpeople** /-ˌpipəl/ [C] an ANCHOR

an·chor·wom·an /'æŋkɚˌwʊmən/ *plural* **anchorwomen** /-ˌwɪmɪn/ *n.* [C] a female ANCHOR

an·cho·vy /'ænˌtʃoʊvi, -tʃə-, æn'tʃoʊvi/ *n. plural* **anchovies** [C,U] BIOLOGY a very small fish that tastes very salty [**Origin:** 1500–1600 Spanish *anchova*]

an·cient[1] /'eɪnʃənt/ W2 *adj.* **1** [only before noun] belonging to a time thousands of years ago OPP **modern**: *the ancient civilizations of Asia* | **ancient Greece/Rome/Egypt etc.** *early democracy in ancient Greece* ►see THESAURUS box at **old** **2** having existed for a very long time: *an ancient tradition* **3** USUALLY HUMOROUS very old: *That hat makes me look ancient!* [**Origin:** 1300–1400 Old French *ancien*, from Latin *ante* **before**]

ancient[2] *n.* **the ancients** LITERARY people who lived thousands of years ago, especially the Greeks and

A

Romans: *The ancients believed that the sun and moon were planets.*

ˌancient ˈhistory *n.* [U] **1** the history of people and societies from thousands of years ago, especially in Greece and Rome **2** SPOKEN, HUMOROUS if you say that something is ancient history, you mean that it happened a long time ago and you do not want to talk about it anymore: *Will and I broke up a long time ago – that's ancient history now.*

an·cil·lar·y /ˈænsəˌlɛri/ *adj.* **1** FORMAL relating to or supporting something else, but less important than it: *Agreement was reached on several ancillary matters.* **2 ancillary workers/staff** workers who provide additional help and services for the people who do the main work in hospitals, schools etc. —**ancillary** *n.* [C]

-ancy /ənsi/ *suffix* [in nouns] **1** used to make nouns from adjectives and nouns, that mean the state or quality of being something: *pregnancy* (=state of being PREGNANT) | *There was hesitancy* (=quality of being unsure, from the adjective "hesitant") *in his voice.* **2** used to make nouns from verbs, meaning the state or quality of doing something: *a consultancy group* (=company that gives advice, from the verb "consult") | *occupancy* (=the state of occupying something) → see also -ENCY

and /ən, n, ənd; *strong* ænd/ [S1] [W1] *conjunction* **1** used to join two words, parts of sentences etc.: *Do you want a pen and some paper?* | *The movie starred Renée Zellweger and Colin Firth.* | *We've dealt with items one, two, and eleven.* | *Try to eat less and get more exercise.* | *You need to know what rights you have and how to use them.* **2** then [SYN] **afterward**: *Tara picked up the book and put it on the shelf.* | *He opened the door and went in.* | *You'll have to **wait and see** what happens.* **3** used to say that something is caused by something else: *I missed dinner and now I'm starving!* | *She took some medicine and threw up.* **4** used when adding numbers: *How much is fifteen and seven?* **5 come/go/try etc. and...** INFORMAL used instead of "to": *Let's go and have a cup of coffee.* | *I'll see if I can try and persuade her to come.* **6** SPOKEN used to introduce a statement, remark, question etc.: *And now I'd like to introduce our next speaker, Mrs. Thompson.* | *And where are you going on your vacation?* **7** used between repeated words to emphasize what you are saying: *More and more people are losing their jobs.* | *That was years and years ago.* | *We ran and ran.* **8 nice/good and...** SPOKEN used to emphasize a particular quality, or that something is exactly the way you want it: *The senator was good and mad.* | *Dennis, your steak is still nice and pink in the middle.* **9 three and three quarters, nineteen and a half etc.** used after the whole number and before the FRACTION or DECIMAL when saying numbers: *The baby is due in about two and a half months* (=2½ months). | *We had two and two tenths inches* (=2.2 inches) *of rain last week.* **10** used in descriptions of food and drink to mean "served with": *Do you want some cake and ice cream?* | *I'll have a gin and tonic.* | *a slice of **bread and butter*** (=bread with butter spread on it) **11 and?** SPOKEN used when you want someone to add something to what they have just said: *"I'm sorry." "And?" "And I promise it won't happen again."*

an·dan·te /ɑnˈdɑnteɪ/ *n.* [C] a piece of music played or sung at a speed that is neither very fast nor very slow —**andante** *adj., adv.*

An·der·sen /ˈændəsən/, **Hans Chris·tian** /hæns ˈkrɪstʃən/ (1805–1875) a Danish writer famous for his many FAIRY TALES

An·der·son /ˈændəsən/, **Sher·wood** /ˈʃəwʊd/ (1876–1941) a U.S. writer famous for his short stories (SHORT STORY)

An·des, the /ˈændiz/ a range of high mountains along the west coast of South America

and·i·ron /ˈændˌaɪən/ *n.* [C] one of a pair of iron objects that holds wood in a FIREPLACE

An·dor·ra /ænˈdɔrə/ a very small country in the Pyrenees between France and Spain —**Andorran** *n., adj.*

Andorra la Vel·la /ænˌdɔrə lɑ ˈvɛlə/ the capital city of Andorra

An·dret·ti /ænˈdrɛti/, **Ma·ri·o** /ˈmɑrioʊ/ (1940–) a U.S. race car driver

An·drew /ˈændru/, **Saint** (1st century A.D.) in the Bible, one of the 12 APOSTLES

and·ro·gyn·ous /ænˈdrɑdʒənəs/ *adj.* **1** someone who is androgynous looks both female and male **2** BIOLOGY having both male and female parts —**androgyny** *n.* [U]

an·droid /ˈændrɔɪd/ *n.* [C] a ROBOT that looks like a real person

An·dro·pov /ænˈdroʊpɔv, -ˈdrɑpɔf/, **Yu·ri** /ˈyʊri/ (1914–1984) the leader of the Communist Party of the former Soviet Union from 1982 to 1984

-andry /ændri/ *suffix* [in nouns] relating to males or men: *polyandry* (=having more than one husband at the same time)

an·ec·dot·al /ˌænɪkˈdoʊtl/ *adj.* consisting of short stories based on someone's personal experience: *The book is an anecdotal account of Kent's trip to Borneo.* | *The findings are based on **anecdotal evidence** rather than serious research.*

an·ec·dote /ˈænɪkˌdoʊt/ *n.* [C] a short story based on your personal experience [**Origin:** 1700–1800 French, Latin *anekdota* **things not published**, from Greek *ekdidonai* **to publish**]

a·ne·mi·a /əˈnimiə/ *n.* [U] a medical condition in which there are too few red cells in your blood

a·ne·mic /əˈnimɪk/ *adj.* **1** suffering from anemia **2** seeming weak and uninteresting: *It was an anemic disappointing performance.*

an·e·mom·e·ter /ˌænəˈmɑmət̬ə/ *n.* [C] SCIENCE an instrument for measuring the speed, power, and direction of the wind

a·nem·o·ne /əˈnɛməni/ *n.* [C] BIOLOGY **1** a SEA ANEMONE **2** a plant with red, white, or blue flowers

aneroid barometer

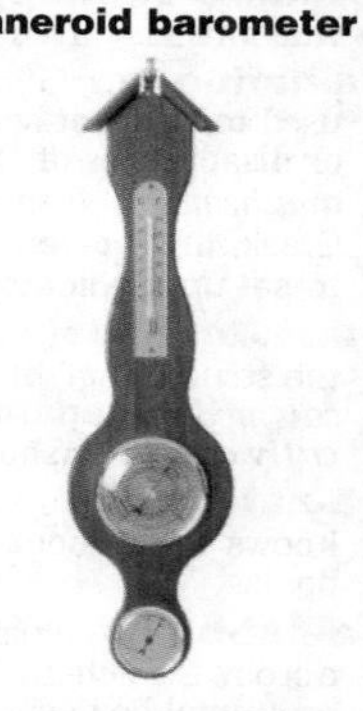

an·e·roid ba·rom·e·ter /ˌænərɔɪd bəˈrɑmət̬ə/ *n.* [C] a type of BAROMETER (=instrument for measuring changes in air pressure) with a round part at the front that has numbers and signs on it. You check the weather conditions by hitting the front part lightly with your finger.

an·es·the·sia, anaesthesia /ˌænəsˈθiʒə/ *n.* [U] **1** the use of anesthetics in medicine **2** the state of being unable to feel pain [**Origin:** 1700–1800 Modern Latin, Greek *anaisthesia*, from *aisthesis* **feeling**]

an·es·the·si·ol·o·gist, anaesthesiologist /ˌænəsˌθiziˈɑlədʒɪst/ *n.* [C] a doctor who gives anesthetics to a patient

an·es·thet·ic, anaesthetic /ˌænəsˈθɛt̬ɪk/ *n.* [C,U] a drug that stops you feeling pain: *Wisdom teeth are usually removed **under anesthetic**.* | *The surgery is done using **a local anesthetic*** (=one that only affects a particular area of your body). | *You will have to have **a general anesthetic*** (=one that affects your whole body and makes you unconscious) *for the surgery.*

a·nes·thet·ist, anaesthetist /əˈnɛsθətɪst/ *n.* [C] someone, such as a nurse, who is trained to give anesthetics

a·nes·the·tize, anaesthetize /əˈnɛsθəˌtaɪz/ *v.* [T] to give someone an anesthetic so that they do not feel pain

an·eu·rysm, aneurism /ˈænyəˌrɪzəm/ *n.* [C] a small place on the surface of a BLOOD VESSEL that is swollen and full of blood, and that can kill you if it breaks open

a·new /ə'nu/ *adv.* LITERARY **1** if you do something anew, you start doing it again: *Fighting began anew on May 15.* **2 start/begin anew** to begin a different job, start to live in a different place etc., especially after a difficult period in your life SYN **afresh**: *I wanted to start anew in California.*

an·gel /'eɪndʒəl/ S3 *n.* [C] **1** a spirit who is believed to live with God in heaven, often shown as a person dressed in white with wings **2** someone who is very kind, very good, or very beautiful: *That little girl of theirs is an angel.* | *Clark admits he **is no angel*** (=sometimes behaves badly). **3** SPOKEN someone who helps or supports you when you need it, and who you can depend on: *Bernie, you're an angel. What would I do without you?* **4** SPOKEN a way of speaking to a child or woman you love: *Goodnight, angel.* **5 (fools rush in) where angels fear to tread** used to say that it is not wise to do something too quickly without thinking carefully about it first [**Origin:** Old English *engel*, from Late Latin *angelus*, from Greek *angelos* **bringer of messages, angel**] → see also **fallen angel** at FALLEN[2] (3), GUARDIAN ANGEL

'angel ˌdust *n.* [U] SLANG the illegal drug PCP

An·gel Falls /ˌeɪndʒəl 'fɔlz/ a WATERFALL in southeast Venezuela that is the highest waterfall in the world

'angel food ˌcake *n.* [C,U] a type of light white cake that is made with the white part of eggs

an·gel·ic /æn'dʒɛlɪk/ *adj.* **1** looking good, kind, and gentle, or behaving in this way: *Timmy has such an angelic face.* **2** relating to angels: *angelic beings* —**angelically** /-kli/ *adv.*

an·gel·i·ca /æn'dʒɛlɪkə/ *n.* [U] a plant that smells sweet and is used in cooking

Maya Angelou

An·ge·lou /'ændʒəlu/, **May·a** /'maɪyə/ (1928–) an African-American writer and poet

an·ger[1] /'æŋgɚ/ *n.* [U] a strong feeling of wanting to harm, hurt, or criticize someone because they have done something unfair, cruel, offensive etc.: *She couldn't hide her anger.* | +**at** *His anger at his wife soon faded.* | *"It's a lie!" he shouted **in anger**.*

anger[2] *v.* [T] FORMAL to make someone angry: *The court's decision angered environmentalists.*

an·gi·na /æn'dʒaɪnə/ *n.* [U] MEDICINE a medical condition in which you have bad pains in your chest because your heart is weak [**Origin:** 1500–1600 Latin **sore throat**, from *angere* **to strangle**]

an·gi·o·plas·ty /'ændʒiəˌplæsti/ *n.* [C,U] a method of repairing or opening a closed or damaged BLOOD VESSEL, usually by putting a very small BALLOON filled with air into the BLOOD VESSEL to make it wider

an·gi·o·sperm /'ændʒiəˌspɚm/ *n.* [C] BIOLOGY a flowering plant that has the sex organs in the flower and produces seeds in a fruit → see also GYMNOSPERM

An·gle /'æŋgəl/ HISTORY one of the people from north Germany who settled in England in the fifth century A.D.

an·gle[1] /'æŋgəl/ S3 *n.* [C] **1** MATH the space between two straight lines or surfaces that touch or cross each other, measured in degrees: *a 45-degree angle* | +**of** *the angles of a triangle* | +**between** *the angle between walls and ceiling* → see also RIGHT ANGLE **2** a way of considering a problem or situation: *Try approaching the problem **from a** different **angle**.* **3 at an angle** leaning to one side and not straight or upright: *The portrait was hanging **at a slight angle**.* **4** a position from which you look at something or photograph it: *The photograph was taken **from an** unusual **angle**.* **5** the shape formed when two lines or surfaces join: *I bumped my knee on the angle of the coffee table.*

angle

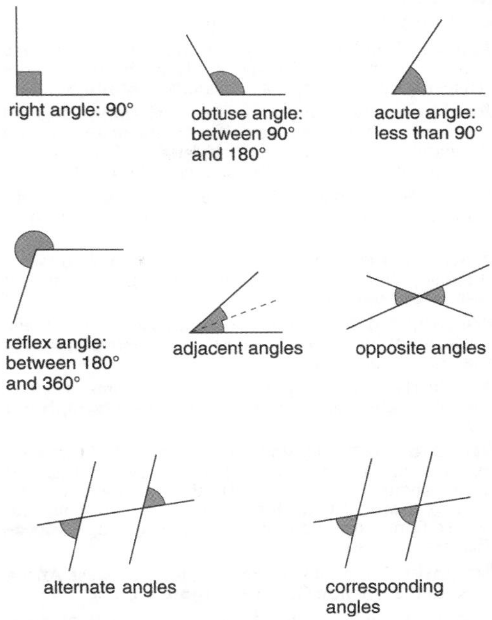

angle[2] *v.* **1** [T] if you angle something in a particular direction or if it angles in that direction, it is not upright or facing straight ahead: *The mirror was angled to reflect light from a window.* **2** [T usually passive] to present information from a particular point of view or for a specific group of people: *The book is angled towards a business audience.* **3 angle to do sth** to try to get something in an indirect and sometimes dishonest way: *He was angling to get a part in the movie.*

angle for sth *phr. v.* to try to get something by making suggestions and remarks instead of asking directly: *I think she's angling for an invitation to the party.*

ˌangle of de'pression *n.* [C usually singular] MATH an angle formed by a line going from a point on a HORIZONTAL line to a point below the line. The value of the angle depends on the position of the second point. If it is directly below the first point, the angle will be 90 degrees.

ˌangle of ele'vation *n.* [C usually singular] MATH an angle formed by a line going from a point on a HORIZONTAL line to a point above the line. The value of the angle depends on the position of the second point. If it is directly above the first point, the angle will be 90 degrees.

ˌangle of 'incidence *n.* [C] PHYSICS the angle between a beam of light that touches a surface and a line drawn at 90 degrees to the surface at the point where the beam of light touches

ˌangle of re'flection *n.* [C usually singular] PHYSICS the angle between a beam of light that is REFLECTED back from a surface and a line drawn at 90 degrees to the surface at the point where the the beam of light touches

an·gler /'æŋglɚ/ *n.* [C] OLD-FASHIONED someone who catches fish as a sport → see also FISHERMAN

An·gli·can /'æŋglɪkən/ *n.* [C] a Christian who is a member of the official church of England or related churches, such as the Episcopal church —**Anglican** *adj.* —**Anglicanism** *n.* [U]

an·gli·cism /'æŋgləˌsɪzəm/ *n.* [C] an English word or expression that is used in another language

A

an·gli·cize /ˈæŋgləˌsaɪz/ *v.* [T] to make someone or something more English

an·gling /ˈæŋglɪŋ/ *n.* [U] the sport of catching fish

An·glo /ˈæŋgloʊ/ *n. plural* **anglos** [C] INFORMAL **1** a white American who speaks English and is not Hispanic **2** CANADIAN an ANGLOPHONE —**Anglo** *adj.*

Anglo-, anglo- /æŋgloʊ/ *prefix* **1** relating to England or Great Britain: *an anglophile* (=someone who likes England and its culture very much) **2** English or British and something else: *an Anglo-Scottish family*

ˌAnglo-Aˈmerican *adj.* between or involving both England or the U.K. and the U.S.: *Anglo-American relations*

an·glo·phile /ˈæŋgləˌfaɪl/ *n.* [C] someone who is not English, but likes anything relating to England —**anglophilia** /ˌæŋgləˈfɪliə/ *n.* [U]

an·glo·phobe /ˈæŋgləˌfoʊb/ *n.* [C] someone who dislikes anything relating to England —**anglophobia** /ˌæŋgləˈfoʊbiə/ *n.* [U]

an·glo·phone /ˈæŋgləˌfoʊn/ *n.* [C] someone who speaks English as their first language —**anglophone** *adj.*

Anglo-Sax·on /ˌæŋgloʊ ˈsæksən◂/ *n.* **1** [C] HISTORY a member of the group of people who lived in England from about 600 A.D. **2** [U] the language of the Anglo-Saxons **3** [C] a white person, especially someone whose family originally came from England —**Anglo-Saxon** *adj.* → see also WASP

An·go·la /æŋˈgoʊlə/ a country in southwest Africa next to the Atlantic Ocean —**Angolan** *n., adj.*

an·go·ra /æŋˈgɔrə/ *n.* **1** [C] BIOLOGY a type of goat, rabbit, or cat with very long soft hair or fur **2** [U] wool or thread made from the fur of an angora goat or rabbit

an·gos·tur·a /ˌæŋgəˈstʊrə◂/ *n.* [U] a slightly bitter liquid used for adding taste to alcoholic drinks

an·gry /ˈæŋgri/ S2 W2 *adj. comparative* **angrier**, *superlative* **angriest** **1** feeling strong emotions which make you want to shout at someone or hurt them because they have behaved in an unfair, cruel, offensive etc. way, or because you think that a situation is unfair, unacceptable etc.: *I was stunned and angry when I found out.* | *an angry letter* | *Don't **get angry** – I said I was sorry.* | **+with/at** *She's still very angry with me for forgetting out anniversary.* | **+about/over** *My folks were really angry about my grades.* | *The book is sure to **make** a lot of women very **angry**.* | **+angry (that)** *Workers are angry that they still haven't been paid.*

THESAURUS

annoyed a little angry: *I get annoyed with the kids when they don't listen.*
irritated feeling annoyed and not patient with people or things: *I was getting irritated by all the noise.*
furious/livid very angry: *I am furious at my father for refusing to let me go.*
mad INFORMAL very angry: *Mom was mad at me for not cleaning up.*
in a bad mood feeling a little angry for a period of time: *When I'm in a bad mood, I like to be on my own.*
outraged very angry and shocked, especially because you think something is unfair or wrong: *People were outraged when they raised parking fees by 25%.*
→ HAPPY, SAD

2 angry with/at yourself feeling strongly that you wish you had done something or had not done something: *David was angry with himself for trusting Michael.* **3** an angry wound etc. is painful and red and looks infected **4** LITERARY an angry sky or cloud looks dark and stormy [**Origin:** 1200–1300 Old Norse *angr* **great sorrow**] —**angrily** *adv.*: *"You're an idiot," he said angrily.*

angst /ɑŋst, æŋst/ *n.* [U] strong feelings of anxiety and unhappiness because you are worried about your life or your future: *angst-filled poems*

an·guish /ˈæŋgwɪʃ/ *n.* [U] mental or physical suffering caused by extreme pain or worry: *the anguish of not knowing what had happened to her* [**Origin:** 1100–1200 Old French *angoisse*, from Latin *angustiae* **extreme upset**, from *angustus* **narrow**] —**anguished** *adj.*

an·gu·lar /ˈæŋgyələ/ *adj.* **1** thin and not having much flesh on your body, so that the shape of your bones can be seen: *a tall angular young man* **2** having sharp and definite corners: *angular patterns* **3** [only before noun] TECHNICAL having or forming an angle: *Mercury's angular distance from the sun*

ˌangular moˈmentum *n.* [C,U] PHYSICS the energy contained in an object that is turning in a circular movement around a central point, calculated by multiplying the object's mass by its angular velocity

ˌangular veˈlocity *n.* [C,U] PHYSICS the rate at which an object is moving around a central point

an·i·mal¹ /ˈænəməl/ S1 W1 *n.* [C] **1** BIOLOGY a living creature that is not a plant or a person: *farm animals* | *wild animals in the jungle* | *Beth is an **animal lover*** (=someone who likes animals). | *the enormous diversity of **the animal kingdom*** **2** BIOLOGY any living creature that is not a plant, including people: *Humans are highly intelligent animals.* **3** INFORMAL someone who behaves in a cruel, violent, or very rude way: *Get away from me, you animal!* **4 a (very/completely) different animal** something that is very different from the thing you have mentioned: *Writing email is a very different animal from other forms of written communication.* **5 a political/social etc. animal** INFORMAL someone who is interested in politics, in meeting other people etc. [**Origin:** 1300–1400 Latin *animalis* **having life**, from *anima* **soul**] → see also **party animal** at PARTY ANIMAL

animal² *adj.* [only before noun, no comparative] **1 animal urges/instincts etc.** human feelings, desires etc. that are related to sex, food, and other basic needs **2 animal products/fats/protein etc.** things that are made or come from animals

ˌanimal ˈhusbandry *n.* [U] farming that involves keeping animals and producing milk, meat etc.

an·i·ma·li·a /ˌænɪˈmeɪliə/ *n.* [U] BIOLOGY a name for all the living creatures in the world with more than one cell, whose cells do not have a cell wall, and who obtain the food they need in order to live and grow by eating other living things, rather than by producing food in their own body. The group includes all the animals in the world and many of the creatures that live in the ocean.

ˌanimal ˈrights *n.* [plural] the idea that people should treat animals well, and especially not use them in tests to develop medicines or other products: **animal-rights activists/protesters/groups etc.** (=people or groups who try to stop medical tests etc. involving animals)

an·i·mate¹ /ˈænəˌmeɪt/ *v.* [T] to give life or energy to something: *Laughter animated his face.* [**Origin:** 1300–1400 Latin, past participle of *animare* **to give life to**, from *anima* **soul**]

an·i·mate² /ˈænəmɪt/ *adj.* FORMAL living OPP **inanimate**: *animate beings*

an·i·mat·ed /ˈænəˌmeɪṭɪd/ *adj.* **1 an animated cartoon/movie/show etc.** a movie or program made by photographing a series of pictures, clay models etc. or by drawing a series of pictures with a computer **2** showing a lot of interest and energy: *We had a very animated discussion about women's rights.* —**animatedly** *adv.*

an·i·ma·tion /ˌænəˈmeɪʃən/ *n.* **1** [C,U] ENG. LANG. ARTS the process of making animated movies or television programs, or the movie or program itself: *They used a lot of **computer animation*** (=animation done by computer) *in the movie.* **2** [U] excitement: *Marco spoke with real passion and animation.*

an·i·ma·tor /ˈænəˌmeɪṭə/ *n.* [C] someone who makes animated movies or television programs

an·i·ma·tron·ics /ˌænəməˈtrɑnɪks/ *n.* [plural] the

method or process of making or using models that look and move like real animals or people, especially in movies —**animatronic** *adj.*

an·i·me /ˈænɪmeɪ, -mə/ *n.* [U] Japanese CARTOONS and computer ANIMATION (=pictures, movies etc. produced using a computer) → see also MANGA

an·i·mism /ˈænəˌmɪzəm/ *n.* [U] a religion in which all animals, plants, and objects in the world are believed to have spirits —**animist** *adj.* —**animist** *n.* [C]

an·i·mos·i·ty /ˌænəˈmɑsət̬i/ *n. plural* **animosities** [C,U] strong dislike or hatred SYN **hostility**: **+between** *There is a lot of animosity between Jerry and Frank.* [**Origin:** 1400–1500 Latin *animosus* **full of spirit**]

an·i·mus /ˈænəməs/ *n.* [singular, U] FORMAL strong dislike or hatred SYN **hostility** SYN **animosity**

an·i·on /ˈænˌaɪən/ *n.* [C] PHYSICS an ION (=atom or group of atoms with an electrical charge) with a negative electrical charge that is attracted to the ANODE inside a BATTERY, ELECTROLYTIC CELL etc. → see also CATION

an·ise /ˈænɪs/ also **an·i·seed** /ˈænɪsid/ *n.* [U] the strong-tasting seeds of a plant used in alcoholic drinks and in candy, especially LICORICE

An·ka·ra /ˈæŋkərə, ˈɑŋ-/ the capital city of Turkey

ankh /ɑŋk/ *n.* [C] a cross with a long tall circle at the top, used as a SYMBOL of life in ancient Egypt

an·kle /ˈæŋkəl/ S3 *n.* [C] **1** BIOLOGY the joint between your foot and your leg: **break/twist/sprain your ankle** *Janet slipped on the stairs and twisted her ankle.* **2 ankle socks/boots** short socks or boots that only come up to your ankle

an·klet /ˈæŋklɪt/ *n.* [C] **1** a ring or BRACELET worn around your ankle **2** a short sock worn by girls or women that only comes up to your ankle

an·nals /ˈænlz/ *n.* [plural] **1 in the annals of sth** FORMAL in the whole history of something: *one of the most unusual cases in the annals of crime* **2** used in the titles of official records of events or activities: *the Annals of Internal Medicine*

An·nap·o·lis /əˈnæpəlɪs/ the capital of the U.S. state of Maryland

an·neal /əˈnil/ *v.* [T] TECHNICAL to make metal or glass hard by heating it and then slowly letting it get cold

an·nex[1] /əˈnɛks, ˈænɛks/ *v.* [T] to take control of a country or area next to your own, especially by using force: *The Baltic republics were forcibly annexed by the Soviet Union in 1940.* —**annexation** /ˌænɛkˈseɪʃən/ *n.* [C,U]

an·nex[2] /ˈænɛks, -nɪks/ [C] **1** a separate building that has been added to a larger one **2** FORMAL a part that has been added to the end of a document, report etc. SYN **appendix**

an·ni·hi·late /əˈnaɪəˌleɪt/ *v.* [T] **1** to destroy something or someone completely: *Just one of these bombs could annihilate a city the size of New York.* **2** to defeat someone easily and completely in a game, competition, or election [**Origin:** 1500–1600 Late Latin, past participle of *annihilare* **to reduce to nothing**] —**annihilation** /əˌnaɪəˈleɪʃən/ *n.* [U]

an·ni·ver·sa·ry /ˌænəˈvɚsəri/ *n. plural* **anniversaries** [C] a date on which something special or important happened in a previous year, especially when someone was married: *our twentieth wedding anniversary* | **+of** *A huge parade is held each year on the anniversary of the 1959 revolution.* [**Origin:** 1200–1300 Latin *anniversarius* **returning each year**, from *annus* **year** + *vertere* **to turn**]

An·no Dom·i·ni /ˌænoʊ ˈdɑməni, -naɪ/ → see A.D.

an·no·tate /ˈænəˌteɪt/ *v.* [T usually passive] to add short notes to a book or piece of writing to explain parts of it: *The translation was annotated by W. H. Auden.* —**annotation** /ˌænəˈteɪʃən/ *n.* [C,U]

an·nounce /əˈnaʊns/ S3 W1 *v.* [T] **1** to officially tell people about a decision or something that will happen: *They announced plans to close 11 factories.* | **announce (that)** *Weaver announced that he would retire in June.* | **announce sth to sb** *The president announced his decision to Congress.* **2** to give information to people, especially using a LOUDSPEAKER or MICROPHONE in a public place: *A man's voice announced the departure of the L.A. bus.* **3** to say something in a loud and confident way, especially something that other people will not like: *"I'm not coming with you," she announced suddenly.* | **announce (that)** *He stood up and announced that he was ready to leave.* **4** to introduce a program, person, musical group etc. on television or radio: *It was his job to announce the guests.* **5 to be announced** used to say that a piece of information will be decided or given at a later time: *The meeting is in January, date and location to be announced.* [**Origin:** 1400–1500 French *annoncer*, from Latin *annuntiare*, from *ad-* **to** + *nuntiare* **to report**]

an·nounce·ment /əˈnaʊnsmənt/ S3 W3 *n.* **1** [C] an important or official statement: *The short written announcement gave no details.* | **+about/of/on** *They've produced several public service announcements about the risks of smoking.* | **announcement that** *The announcement that the athletes had taken drugs shocked the nation.* | *Dillon* ***made the announcement*** *at a news conference.* **2** [U] the act of telling people that something important is going to happen: *The announcement of the plan provoked demonstrations from the college's students.* **3** [C] a small advertisement or statement in a newspaper: **a wedding/birth/death announcement** *Their wedding announcement was in Sunday's paper.*

an·nounc·er /əˈnaʊnsɚ/ *n.* [C] someone who reads news or introduces people, musical groups etc., especially on television or radio

an·noy /əˈnɔɪ/ *v.* **annoys, annoyed, annoying** [T] to make someone feel slightly angry and unhappy about something: *The neighbor's kid walks across our lawn just to annoy us.* | *The way Brian talks to me really annoys me.* [**Origin:** 1200–1300 Old French *enuier*, from Latin *inodiare*, from *odium* **hate**]

an·noy·ance /əˈnɔɪəns/ *n.* **1** [U] a feeling of slight anger: *Her annoyance was obvious to everyone.* | *The meetings were held in secret,* ***much to the annoyance of*** *some members of Congress.* **2** [C] something that makes you slightly angry: *Smoking is a tremendous annoyance to non-smokers.*

an·noyed /əˈnɔɪd/ *adj.* slightly angry: **+at/with** *I was really annoyed at him that time.* | **+about/by** *Everyone is annoyed by the amount of traffic in the city.* | **annoyed (that)** *I'm annoyed that he didn't show up.* | *Rob* ***gets so annoyed*** *if you mix up his CDs.*

an·noy·ing /əˈnɔɪ-ɪŋ/ S3 *adj.* making you feel slightly angry: *Corey is the most annoying little kid I've ever met.* | *Computerized telephone sales calls are really annoying.* —**annoyingly** *adv.*

an·nu·al[1] /ˈænyuəl/ AC S3 W2 *adj.* **1** happening once a year: *the annual school homecoming dance* ▸see THESAURUS box at **regular**[1] **2** based on or calculated over a period of one year: *Her annual income is about $75,000.* [**Origin:** 1300–1400 Old French *annuel*, from Latin *annuus* **yearly** and *annalis* **yearly**, both from *annus* **year**] —**annually** *adv.*

annual[2] AC *n.* [C] **1** BIOLOGY a plant that grows from a seed, has flowers, and dies all in one year → see also BIENNIAL **2** a YEARBOOK **3** a book, especially for children, that is produced once a year with the same title but different stories, pictures etc.

an·nu·al·ize /ˈænyuəˌlaɪz/ *v.* [T] to calculate a number or amount in a way that shows a rate that is based on a period of one year —**annualized** *adj.*: *The FDA has estimated the annualized cost at $230 million a year over 15 years.*

ˌannual ˈmeeting *n.* [C] a meeting held once a year by a club, business, or organization

ˌannual perˈcentage rate *n.* [C usually singular] ECONOMICS APR

an·nu·i·ty /əˈnuət̬i/ *n. plural* **annuities** [C] ECONOMICS a particular amount of money that is paid each year to someone, usually until they die

an·nul /əˈnʌl/ *v.* **annulled, annulling** [T often passive]

TECHNICAL to officially end a marriage or legal agreement so that it is considered to have never existed —**annulment** *n.* [C,U]

an·ode /ˈænoʊd/ *n.* [C] PHYSICS the ELECTRODE through which ELECTRONS flow out of a BATTERY, ELECTROLYTIC CELL etc. and positive electric current seems to flow in. This is the electrode at which OXIDATION happens. → see also CATHODE

an·o·dyne[1] /ˈænəˌdaɪn/ *adj.* expressed in a way that is unlikely to offend anyone: *anodyne topics of conversation*

anodyne[2] *n.* [C] **1** TECHNICAL a medicine that reduces pain **2** FORMAL an activity or thing that comforts people

a·noint /əˈnɔɪnt/ *v.* [T] **1** to put oil or water on someone's head or body during a religious ceremony **2** to choose someone for an important job: *He still hasn't annointed his successor.* —**anointment** *n.* [C,U]

a·nom·a·lous /əˈnɑmələs/ *adj.* FORMAL different from what was expected, and therefore difficult to explain [**Origin:** 1600–1700 Late Latin *anomalus*, from Greek, **uneven, anomalous**, from *an-* **not** + *homalos* **even**] —**anomalously** *adv.*

a·nom·a·ly /əˈnɑməli/ *n. plural* **anomalies** [C,U] something that is noticeable because it is different from what is usual: *Pohnpei is an anomaly – it's a Pacific island without a beach.*

a·non /əˈnɑn/ *adv.* LITERARY soon

anon. the written abbreviation of ANONYMOUS

an·o·nym·i·ty /ˌænəˈnɪməṭi/ *n.* [U] **1** the state of not letting your name be known: *Laws protect the anonymity of the rape victim.* | *One official spoke* ***on condition of anonymity*** (=only if his or her name was not published). **2** the state of not showing who is involved in something: *the anonymity of the Internet* **3** the state of not having any unusual or interesting features: *the drab anonymity of the city*

a·non·y·mous /əˈnɑnəməs/ [S3] *adj.* **1** not known by name: *The paper cited two anonymous sources.* | *A member of the office staff, who asked to* ***remain anonymous****, gave us the information.* **2** done, sent, or given by someone who does not want their name to be known: *The college received an anonymous $5 million gift.* | **an anonymous letter/phone call etc.** *Police were led to the scene by an anonymous phone tip.* **3** without any interesting features or qualities: *an anonymous hotel room* [**Origin:** 1600–1700 Late Latin *anonymus*, from Greek, from *an-* **without** + *onyma* **name**] —**anonymously** *adv.* → see also ALCOHOLICS ANONYMOUS

a·noph·e·les /əˈnɑfəliz/ *n.* [C] a type of insect, known for spreading MALARIA to humans

an·o·rak /ˈænəˌræk/ *n.* [C] a short coat with a hood that keeps out the wind and rain [**Origin:** 1900–2000 Greenland Inuit *anoraq*]

an·o·rex·i·a /ˌænəˈrɛksiə/ also **anorexia ner·vo·sa** /-nɚˈvoʊsə/ *n.* [U] MEDICINE a mental illness that makes people, especially young women, stop eating because they believe they are fat and want to be thin [**Origin:** 1500–1600 Modern Latin, Greek, from *an-* **without** + *orexis* **desire to eat**]

an·o·rex·ic /ˌænəˈrɛksɪk/ *adj.* MEDICINE suffering from or relating to anorexia ►see THESAURUS box at **thin**[1] —**anorexic** *n.* [C]

an·oth·er /əˈnʌðɚ/ [S1] [W1] *determiner, pron.* **1** used to talk about one more person or thing of the same type: *Can I have another piece of cake?* | *I'll cancel that check and send you another.* | *The tape broke, so I'll have to make* ***another one****.* | **+of** *Mary, another of Christine's close friends, was shocked by the news.* | *The failure of the bill was* ***yet another*** (=the last in a series of) *setback for the Democrats.* | *He's had* ***one*** *problem* ***after another*** (=without much time between them) *this year.* ►see THESAURUS box at **more**[2] **2** a different person or thing, or some other type of person or thing: *They finally moved to another apartment.* | *Greg didn't like that dentist, so he went to another.* | *I'll see you another time.* | *Make sure you leave enough time to drive* ***from one*** *appointment* ***to another****.* | *Math will always be useful at some time* ***or another****.* | *There are a lot of people who,* ***for one reason or another****, can't have children.* | *They'll try to get the money* ***one way or another****.* **3** in addition to a particular amount, distance, period of time etc. [SYN] **further**: *She'll be ready to retire in another three years.* | *Another 13 residents were taken to safety by firefighters.* **4 one another** LITERARY used after a verb to show that two or more people or things do the same thing to each other: *We always call one another during the holidays.* **5 and another thing** SPOKEN used for adding a statement or question about something that you are annoyed about: *And another thing – she keeps stealing my pens.* **6 be another thing/matter (altogether)** used to suggest that something may not be true, possible, easy etc., after mentioning something that is: *The report is well written, but whether it is accurate is another thing altogether.* **7 not another... !** SPOKEN used when a series of bad or annoying things have happened and something of the same type seems to have just happened again: *Oh no! Not another accident!* **8 another Vietnam/another Babe Ruth etc.** used when talking about a situation or person that reminds you of another famous situation or person, especially because they have extremely good or extremely bad qualities

A·nou·ilh, **Jean** /ɑˈnui/, /ʒɑn/ (1910–1987) a French writer of plays

An·schluss /ˈɑnʃlʊs/ *n.* **the Anschluss** HISTORY the military action in which Germany, led by Adolf Hitler, took control of Austria in 1938. Many Austrian people supported the union with Germany, but many opponents were put into prison, and Jews living in Austria were treated very badly.

an·swer[1] /ˈænsɚ/ [S1] [W1] *v.*

1 REPLY [I,T] to say something to someone as a reply when they have asked you a question, made a suggestion etc. [SYN] **reply** [SYN] **respond**: *She thought for a moment before answering.* | *You still haven't* ***answered my question****.* | **answer (that)** *Hughes answered that he knew nothing about the robbery.* | **answer sb** *I answered him as honestly as I could.* | **answer yes/no** *When asked if he had ever taken drugs, he answered no.*

> **THESAURUS**
> **answer** to say something to someone when he or she has asked you a question or spoken to you: *She reluctantly answered his question.*
> **reply** to answer someone – used especially in written English: *"Nobody knows," Rosen replied.*
> **respond** FORMAL to answer someone, especially in a detailed way: *Has anyone responded to your letter?*

2 TEST [I,T] to write or say the answer to a question in a test, competition etc.: *Only one person* ***answered*** *all the* ***questions*** *correctly.*

3 answer the phone/the door/a call to pick up the telephone when it rings or open the door when someone knocks on it

4 LETTER [I,T] to send a reply to a letter, advertisement etc. [SYN] **reply** [SYN] **respond**: *Whitmore never answered any of my letters.*

5 answer criticism/charges/accusations etc. to explain why you did something when people are criticizing you: *Robinson appeared in court on Monday to answer the criminal charges against him.*

6 DO STH AS A REACTION [I,T] to do something as a reaction to criticism or attack [SYN] **respond** [SYN] **retaliate**: **answer by doing sth** *The army answered by firing into the crowd.*

7 DEAL WITH A PROBLEM [T] to be a way of dealing with or solving a problem: *Officials have made every effort to answer trade concerns.* | *Our transportation system is designed to* ***answer the needs*** *of the city's commuters.*

8 answer a description if someone answers a description, they match that description [SYN] **match**: *A hiker spotted a man answering the description given by police.*

[**Origin:** Old English *andswaru*]

GRAMMAR

• You **answer** (*v.*) a question, advertisement etc. (NOT *to/at* it). You also **answer** a person.
• If you **answer to** someone, they are the person directly responsible for you in an organization, at work etc., and you have to explain to them if anything goes wrong or if you are not doing something correctly.
• You give the **answer** (*n.*) **to** a question or criticism (NOT *of* it). You get an **answer** (*n.*) **from** someone (NOT *of* them).

answer back *phr. v.* **answer sb ↔ back** to reply in a rude way to someone that you are supposed to obey: *She's only three, and she's already answering back.*

answer for sth *phr. v.* **1** to explain to people in authority why you did something wrong or why something happened, and be punished if necessary: *The leaders will be made to answer for their actions.* **2 have a lot to answer for** INFORMAL to be responsible for causing a lot of trouble: *That sister of yours has an awful lot to answer for.* **3 I can't answer for sb** SPOKEN used to say that you cannot make a decision for someone who is not there, or give their opinion: *I'm sure John will help us – I can't really answer for the others.*

answer to sb/sth *phr. v.* **1** to give an explanation to someone or be responsible to someone, especially about something that you have done wrong: *We need small schools that can answer to the community.* **2 answer to the name of sth** to be called a particular name: *He's 6 foot 5, but he answers to the name of Shorty.*

answer² S1 W1 *n.*
1 REPLY [C,U] something you say when you reply to a question that someone has asked you SYN **reply** SYN **response**: *What was her answer?* | *There was a question and answer period after the lecture.* | *No one seemed able to* ***give an answer*** *on how the law would affect employers.* | *Every time I ask Jo about it,* ***I get a*** *different* ***answer***. | *I told you before,* ***the answer is no!*** | ***In answer to*** *the question, most employees said they were satisfied with their jobs.*
2 TEST/COMPETITION ETC. [C] something that you write or say in reply to a question in a test, competition etc.: +**to** *What was the answer to question 4?* | **a right/wrong/correct/incorrect answer** *Score one point for each correct answer.*
3 INVITATION/LETTER ETC. [C] a written reply to a letter, invitation, advertisement etc. SYN **reply** SYN **response**: +**to** *Did you ever get an answer to your letter?*
4 PROBLEM [C] a way of dealing with a problem SYN **solution**: *The obvious answer is to keep poisonous plants out of children's reach.* | *This may not* ***be the answer to*** *the problems of our health-care system.*
5 CALL/VISIT [singular, usually in questions and negatives] a reply when you telephone someone, knock on their door etc.: *I called him but* ***there was no answer*** *and he hasn't phoned me back.*
6 sb's answer to sth someone or something that is considered to be just as good as a more famous person or thing: *The Space Needle is Seattle's answer to the Eiffel Tower.*
7 sb knows/has all the answers INFORMAL used to say that someone seems to be very sure that they know everything about a situation, especially when they do not: *You act like you think you have all the answers.*
8 be the answer to (all) sb's prayers to be exactly what someone wants or needs most: *The job was the answer to all my prayers.* → see also **sb won't take no for an answer** at NO¹ (8)

an·swer·a·ble /ˈænsərəbəl/ *adj.* **1 be answerable to sb (for sth)** to have to explain your actions to someone in authority: *The agency is answerable to the governor.* **2** a question that is answerable can be answered OPP **unanswerable**

ˈanswering maˌchine S3 *n.* [C] a machine that records your telephone calls when you cannot answer them

ˈanswering ˌservice *n.* [C] a business that can receive your telephone calls when you are not able to do it yourself

ant /ænt/ *n.* [C] **1** BIOLOGY a small insect that lives in large groups **2 have ants in your pants** SPOKEN, HUMOROUS to be so excited or full of energy that you cannot stay still

A

-ant /ənt/ *suffix* **1** [in nouns] someone or something that does something: *an assistant* (=someone who helps someone else) | *a disinfectant* (=substance that kills GERMS) **2** [in adjectives] having a particular quality: *pleasant* (=pleasing to someone) | *expectant* (=expecting something) → see also -ENT

ant·ac·id /ˌæntˈæsɪd/ *n.* [C] a substance that gets rid of the burning feeling in your stomach when you have eaten too much, drunk too much alcohol etc.

an·tag·o·nism /ænˈtægəˌnɪzəm/ *n.* [U] **1** hatred between people or groups of people: +**between/to/toward** *The project aims to lessen the antagonism between racial groups.* ▶see THESAURUS box at **opposition** **2** opposition to an idea, plan etc.: +**to/toward** *There has been a lot of antagonism toward the new bridge building project.*

an·tag·o·nist /ænˈtægənɪst/ *n.* [C] your opponent in a competition, battle, argument etc. → see also PROTAGONIST

an·tag·o·nis·tic /ænˌtægəˈnɪstɪk/ **1** showing opposition to or hatred for an idea or group: *During the Cold War, the two countries were fiercely antagonistic.* | +**to/toward** *The older employees were antagonistic to new ideas.* **2** wanting to argue or disagree SYN **unfriendly**: *Michaels was described by witnesses as being drunk and antagonistic.* —**antagonistically** /-kli/ *adv.*

an·tag·o·nize /ænˈtægəˌnaɪz/ *v.* [T] to make someone feel angry with you by doing something that they do not like: *The White House is reluctant to antagonize its allies.* [**Origin:** 1600–1700 Greek *antagonizesthai*, from *anti-* + *agonizesthai* **to fight**]

An·ta·na·na·ri·vo /ˌæntəˌnænəˈrivoʊ/ the capital city of Madagascar

Ant·arc·tic /æntˈɑrktɪk, æntˈɑrt̮ɪk/ *n.* **the Antarctic** the very cold most southern part of the world

Ant·arc·ti·ca /æntˈɑrktɪkə, ænˈɑrt̮ɪkə/ the CONTINENT which is the most southern area of land on the Earth

Antˌarctic ˈCircle *n.* **the Antarctic Circle** an imaginary line drawn around the world at a particular distance from its most southern point (the South Pole) → see also ARCTIC CIRCLE → see picture at GLOBE

an·te¹ /ˈænti/ *n.* **up/raise the ante** to increase your demands or try to get more things from a situation, even though this involves more risks: *Sanctions against the dictatorship upped the ante considerably in the crisis.* → see also PENNY ANTE

ante² *v.* **anted** or **anteed**, **anteing**

ante up *phr. v.* **1 ante up sth** to pay an amount of money, especially when it seems large or unreasonable: *Small businesses that want to expand must ante up large legal fees.* **2** to pay the money you have bet, in a game such as cards

ante- /æntɪ/ *prefix* coming or happening before something: *to antedate* (=exist before something else) | *the antebellum South* (=before the Civil War) → see also POST

ant·eat·er /ˈæntit̮ɚ/ *n.* [C] an animal that has a very long nose and eats small insects

an·te·bel·lum /ˌæntɪˈbɛləm/ *adj.* existing before a war, especially the American Civil War: *antebellum Southern architecture*

an·te·ce·dent /ˌæntɪˈsidnt/ *n.* **1** [C] FORMAL an event, organization, or thing that is similar to the one you have mentioned, but that existed earlier: *historical antecedents of modern youth culture* **2 sb's antecedents** [plural] FORMAL the people in your family who lived a long time ago SYN **ancestors** **3** [C] ENG. LANG. ARTS a word, phrase, or sentence that is represented later by another word, for example a PRONOUN —**antecedent** *adj.*

A

an·te·cham·ber /ˈæntɪˌtʃeɪmbɚ/ *n.* [C] an ANTEROOM

an·te·date /ˈæntɪˌdeɪt, ˌæntɪˈdeɪt/ *v.* [T] FORMAL to come from an earlier time in history than something else: *The economic troubles antedate the current administration.* → see also BACKDATE, POSTDATE, PREDATE

an·te·di·lu·vi·an /ˌæntɪdəˈluviən/ *adj.* FORMAL or HUMOROUS very old-fashioned SYN **outdated**: *antediluvian attitudes about women*

an·te·lope /ˈæntlˌoʊp/ *n.* [C] an animal with long horns that can run very fast and is very graceful

an·te me·rid·i·em /ˌæntɪ məˈrɪdiəm/ A.M.

an·ten·na /ænˈtɛnə/ *n.* [C] **1** *plural* **antennas** a piece of equipment on a television, car, roof etc. for receiving or sending television or radio signals → see picture on page A35 **2** *plural* **antennae** /-ni/ BIOLOGY one of two long thin parts on an insect's head, that it uses to feel things [**Origin:** 1600–1700 Latin **pole holding up a sail**]

an·te·ri·or /ænˈtɪriɚ/ *adj.* [no comparative] **1** TECHNICAL at or toward the front OPP **posterior** **2** FORMAL happening or existing before something else

an·te·room /ˈæntɪˌrum/ *n.* [C] FORMAL a small room that is connected to a larger room, especially a small room where people wait to go into the larger room SYN **antechamber**

an·them /ˈænθəm/ *n.* [C] **1** a formal or religious song: *the Olympic anthem* → see also NATIONAL ANTHEM **2** a song that a particular group of people considers to be very important: *"Surf City" was more or less the anthem of the surfer boys and girls of the '60s.* [**Origin:** 900–1000 Late Latin *antiphona*, from Greek, from *antiphonos* **answering**]

an·ther /ˈænθɚ/ *n.* [C] BIOLOGY the part of a male flower that contains POLLEN → see also STAMEN → see picture at FLOWER[1]

ant·hill /ˈæntˌhɪl/ *n.* [C] a place in the ground where ANTS live

an·thol·o·gy /ænˈθɑlədʒi/ *n. plural* **anthologies** [C] ENG. LANG. ARTS a set of stories, poems, songs etc. by different people, collected together in one book: *an anthology of American literature* [**Origin:** 1600–1700 Modern Latin *anthologia*, from Greek, **gathering flowers**] —**anthologist** *n.* [C]

An·tho·ny, Su·san B. /ˈænθəni, ˈsuzən bi/ (1820–1906) a U.S. woman who helped women get the right to vote

an·thra·cite /ˈænθrəˌsaɪt/ *n.* [U] EARTH SCIENCE a very hard type of coal that burns slowly and produces a lot of heat

an·thrax /ˈænθræks/ *n.* [U] MEDICINE a serious disease of cattle and sheep, that also can cause death in people [**Origin:** 1300–1400 Latin, Greek, **coal, large red swelling on the skin**]

anthropo- /ænθrəpə, -poʊ/ *prefix* TECHNICAL like a human, or relating to humans: *anthropomorphic* (=having a human form or human qualities) | *anthropologist* (=someone who studies humans and their societies) [**Origin:** Latin, Greek, from *anthropos* **human being**]

an·thro·poid /ˈænθrəˌpɔɪd/ *adj.* BIOLOGY an anthropoid animal is one such as an APE, that is very much like a human —**anthropoid** *n.* [C]

an·thro·pol·o·gy /ˌænθrəˈpɑlədʒi/ *n.* [U] the scientific study of people, their societies, CULTURES etc.: *cultural anthropology* —**anthropologist** *n.* [U] —**anthropological** /ˌænθrəpəˈlɑdʒɪkəl/ *adj.* → see also ETHNOLOGY, SOCIOLOGY

an·thro·po·mor·phism /ˌænθrəpəˈmɔrˌfɪzəm/ *n.* [U] **1** writing or talking about animals or objects as if they have the same feelings and qualities as humans **2** TECHNICAL the belief that God can appear in a human or animal form —**anthropomorphic** *adj.*

anti- /æntɪ, æntaɪ, ænti/ *prefix* **1** opposed to something SYN **against**: *antinuclear* (=opposing the use of atomic weapons and power) | *anti-American feelings* **2** the opposite of something: *an anticlimax* (=unexciting ending instead of the CLIMAX you expect) **3** acting to prevent something: *antifreeze* (=liquid that prevents an engine from freezing) | *an antibiotic* (=medicine that stops an infection) [**Origin:** Old French, Latin, from Greek, from *anti* **opposite, against**] → see also ANTE-

an·ti·air·craft /ˌæntiˈɛrkræft/ *adj.* [only before noun] antiaircraft weapons are used against enemy aircraft: *antiaircraft missiles*

an·ti·bac·ter·i·al /ˌæntɪbækˈtɪriəl, ˌæntaɪ-/ *adj.* stopping the growth of or killing BACTERIA: *an antibacterial soap*

an·ti·bal·lis·tic mis·sile /ˌæntɪbəlɪstɪk ˈmɪsəl, ˌæntaɪ-/ ABBREVIATION **ABM** *n.* [C] a MISSILE that is used to destroy a BALLISTIC MISSILE while it is still in the air

an·ti·bi·ot·ic /ˌæntɪbaɪˈɑt̬ɪk◂, ˌæntaɪ-/ *n.* [C usually plural] MEDICINE a drug that is used to kill BACTERIA and cure infections

an·ti·bod·y /ˈæntɪˌbɑdi/ *n. plural* **antibodies** [C] BIOLOGY a PROTEIN that is produced in the body to combine with and destroy harmful substances as part of the system of fighting disease

an·ti·christ /ˈæntɪˌkraɪst, ˈæntaɪ-/ *n.* **the Antichrist** also **the antichrist** the great enemy of Jesus Christ who represents the power of evil and is expected to appear just before the end of the world

an·tic·i·pate /ænˈtɪsəˌpeɪt/ Ac W3 *v.* [T] **1** to expect an event or situation to happen SYN **expect**: *Schools anticipate an increase in student test scores.* | *Sales are better than anticipated.* | **anticipate that** *This year, we anticipate that our expenses will be 15% greater.* **2** to be ready and prepared for a question, request, need etc. before it happens: *A skilled waiter can anticipate a customer's needs.* | **anticipate doing sth** *I didn't anticipate having to do the cooking myself!* **3** to think about something that is going to happen, especially something pleasant: *Daniel was eagerly anticipating her arrival.* **4** to do something before someone else: *Copernicus anticipated several discoveries of the 17th and 18th centuries.* **5** FORMAL to use or consider something before you should [**Origin:** 1500–1600 Latin, past participle of *anticipare*, from *ante-* **before** + *capere* **to take**] —**anticipatory** /ænˈtɪsəpəˌtɔri/ *adj.*

an·tic·i·pa·tion /ænˌtɪsəˈpeɪʃən/ Ac *n.* [U] **1** a feeling of excitement because something good or fun is going to happen: *The crowd's mood was one of anticipation.* **2 do sth in anticipation of sth** to do something because you expect something to happen: *The workers have called off their strike in anticipation of a pay offer.*

an·ti·cler·i·cal /ˌæntɪˈklɛrɪkəl, ˌæntaɪ-/ *adj.* being opposed to priests having any political power or influence —**anticlericalism** *n.* [U]

an·ti·cli·max /ˌæntɪˈklaɪmæks/ *n.* [C,U] a situation or event that is not as exciting as you had expected, often because it happens after something that was more exciting: *After all the hype, the actual concert was something of an anticlimax.*

an·tics /ˈæntɪks/ *n.* [plural] behavior that seems strange, funny, silly, or annoying: *We're all getting tired of his childish antics.* [**Origin:** 1500–1600 *antic* **strange** (16–19 centuries), from Italian *antico* **ancient**, from Latin *antiquus*]

an·ti·cy·clone /ˌæntɪˈsaɪkloʊn/ *n.* [C] EARTH SCIENCE an area of high air pressure that causes calm weather in the place it is moving over → see also CYCLONE

an·ti·de·pres·sant /ˌæntɪdɪˈprɛsənt, ˌæntaɪ-/ *n.* [C] MEDICINE a drug used to treat DEPRESSION (=a mental illness that makes people very unhappy)

an·ti·dote /ˈæntɪˌdoʊt/ *n.* [C] **1** MEDICINE a substance that stops the effects of a poison: *a nerve gas antidote* | **+to/for** *an antidote for snake bites* **2** something that makes a bad situation better: **+to/for** *Laughter is a good antidote to stress.*

An·tie·tam /ænˈtit̬əm/ a place in the U.S. state of Maryland where a battle was fought in the American Civil War

ˌAnti-'Federalist, anti-Federalist *n.* [C] HISTORY one of a group of people who between 1787 and 1788 opposed signing the Constitution of the United States because they did not want America to have a strong central government, because they were afraid it would make laws that were not fair to everyone → see also FEDERALIST

an·ti·freeze /'æntɪˌfriz/ *n.* [U] a substance that is put in the water in car engines to stop it from freezing

an·ti·gen /'æntɪdʒən/ *n.* [C] BIOLOGY a substance that causes the production of antibodies (ANTIBODY)

An·ti·gua and Bar·bu·da /ænˌtigə, -gwə ənd bɑr'budə/ a country that consists of the islands of Antigua, Barbuda, and Redonda in the Caribbean Sea —**Antiguan** *n., adj.*

an·ti·her·o /'æntɪˌhɪroʊ, 'æntaɪ-/ *n.* [C] ENG. LANG. ARTS a main character in a book, play, or movie who is an ordinary or bad person and lacks the qualities that you expect a HERO to have

an·ti·his·ta·mine /ˌæntɪ'hɪstəmin, -mɪn/ *n.* [C] MEDICINE a drug that is used to treat an ALLERGY (=a bad reaction to particular foods, substances etc.)

An·til·les, the /æn'tɪliz/ the islands of the Caribbean Sea that form a curving line starting with Cuba near the east coast of Mexico and ending with Trinidad near the north coast of South America

ˌanti-lock 'brakes *n.* [plural] an anti-lock braking system

ˌanti-lock 'braking ˌsystem ABBREVIATION **ABS** *n.* [C] a piece of equipment that makes a vehicle easier to control when you have to stop very suddenly

an·ti·ma·cas·sar /ˌæntɪmə'kæsɚ/ *n.* [C] a piece of decorated cloth that is put on the back of a chair to protect it

an·ti·mat·ter /'æntɪˌmæt̬ɚ, 'æntaɪ-/ *n.* [U] PHYSICS a form of MATTER (=substance which the things in the universe are made of) consisting of antiparticles

an·ti·par·ti·cle /'æntɪˌpɑrtɪkəl, 'æntaɪ-/ *n.* [C] PHYSICS a piece of MATTER that is smaller than an atom and has the opposite electrical charge of the similar PARTICLE usually found in an atom

an·ti·pas·to /ˌæntɪ'pɑstoʊ, ˌɑn-/ *n.* [U] an Italian dish consisting of cold food that you eat before the main part of a meal

an·tip·a·thet·ic /ˌæntɪpə'θet̬ɪk/ *adj.* FORMAL having a very strong feeling of disliking or opposing someone or something

an·tip·a·thy /æn'tɪpəθi/ *n.* [U] FORMAL a feeling of strong dislike or opposition toward someone or something SYN **animosity**: **+to/toward** *a high level of antipathy toward lawyers* [**Origin:** 1500–1600 Latin *antipathia*, from Greek *antipathes* **of opposite feelings**]

an·ti·per·son·nel /ˌæntɪˌpɚsən'ɛl/ *adj.* [only before noun] an antipersonnel weapon is designed to hurt people rather than damage buildings, vehicles etc.

an·ti·per·spi·rant /ˌæntɪ'pɚspərənt/ *n.* [U] a substance that prevents you from SWEATing, especially under your arms → see also DEODORANT

An·tip·o·des /æn'tɪpədiz/ *n.* **the Antipodes** Australia and New Zealand [**Origin:** 1300–1400 Latin **people living on opposite sides of the world**, from Greek, from *antipous* **with feet opposite**] —**Antipodean** /ænˌtɪpə'diən/ *adj.*

an·ti·quar·i·an /ˌæntɪ'kwɛriən/ *adj.* [only before noun] an antiquarian store sells old valuable things such as books

an·ti·quat·ed /'æntɪˌkweɪt̬ɪd/ *adj.* old-fashioned and not suitable for modern needs or conditions SYN **outdated**: *antiquated laws*

an·tique¹ /ˌæn'tik◂/ *adj.* **1** antique furniture, jewelry etc. is old and often valuable: *an antique rosewood desk* ▸see THESAURUS box at **old** **2** LITERARY connected with ancient times, especially ancient Rome or Greece [**Origin:** 1400–1500 French, Latin *antiquus*, from *ante* **before**]

antique² *n.* [C] a piece of furniture, jewelry etc. that was made a long time ago and is therefore valuable: *The palace is full of priceless antiques.* | *an antiques dealer* | *an antique shop*

an·tiq·ui·ty /æn'tɪkwət̬i/ *n. plural* **antiquities** **1** [U] ancient times: *The common household fork was nearly unknown in antiquity.* **2** [U] the fact or condition of being very old: *the antiquity of Chinese culture* **3** [C usually plural] a building or object made in ancient times: *a collection of art and antiquities*

an·ti-Sem·ite /ˌænti'sɛmaɪt, ˌæntaɪ-/ *n.* [C] someone who hates Jewish people —**anti-Semitic** /ˌæntisə'mɪt̬ɪk, ˌæntaɪ-/ *adj.*

an·ti-Sem·i·tism /ˌænti'sɛməˌtɪzəm, ˌæntaɪ-/ *n.* [U] hatred of Jewish people

an·ti·sep·tic¹ /ˌæntə'sɛptɪk/ *n.* [C] a chemical substance that kills GERMS and helps stop wounds from becoming infected

antiseptic² *adj.* **1** helping to prevent infection: *antiseptic cream* **2** lacking emotion, interest, or excitement: *the antiseptic language of science*

an·ti·so·cial /ˌænti'soʊʃəl, ˌæntaɪ-/ *adj.* **1** violent and not behaving according to the normal moral rules of society: *The boy shows signs of* ***antisocial behavior***. **2** unwilling to meet people and talk to them, especially in a way that seems unfriendly or impolite: *Kip had always been shy, even antisocial.* ▸see THESAURUS box at **shy¹** **3** showing a lack of concern for other people: *Smoking cigarettes in public is increasingly considered antisocial.*

an·ti·tank /ˌænti'tæŋk, ˌæntaɪ-/ *adj.* [only before noun] an antitank weapon is designed to destroy enemy TANKS

an·tith·e·sis /æn'tɪθəsɪs/ *n.* **the antithesis of sth** FORMAL the exact opposite of something, or something that is completely different from something else: *Her style of writing is the antithesis of Dickens'.*

an·ti·thet·i·cal /ˌæntə'θɛt̬ɪkəl/ *adj.* FORMAL completely different from something, and often showing or resulting from opposing ideas, beliefs etc.: **+to** *The new law is clearly antithetical to the basic principles of free speech.*

an·ti·tox·in /ˌæntɪ'tɑksɪn/ *n.* BIOLOGY a substance produced by your body or put in a medicine to stop the effects of a poison

an·ti·trust /ˌæntɪ'trʌst, ˌæntaɪ-/ *adj.* [only before noun] ECONOMICS intended to prevent companies from unfairly controlling prices

ˌanti'trust laws *n.* [plural] ECONOMICS a set of laws that make it illegal for a company operating in the U.S. to restrict competition by controlling all or most of a business activity or by stopping another person from operating a business

ant·ler /'ænt˺lɚ/ *n.* [C usually plural] one of the two horns of a male DEER, MOOSE etc. → see picture at DEER [**Origin:** 1300–1400 Old French *antoillier*]

An·toi·nette /ˌɑntwɑ'nɛt,/, **Ma·rie** / mə'ri/ → see MARIE ANTOINETTE

an·to·nym /'æntəˌnɪm/ *n.* [C] ENG. LANG. ARTS a word that means the opposite of another word. For example, "good" is the antonym of "bad." [**Origin:** 1800–1900 French *antonyme*, from Greek *anti-* **against** + *onyma* **name**] —**antonymous** /æn'tɑnəməs/ *adj.* → see also SYNONYM

ant·sy /'æntsi/ *adj.* INFORMAL nervous and unable to keep still, because you want something to happen

a·nus /'eɪnəs/ *n.* [C usually singular] BIOLOGY the hole in your body through which solid waste leaves your BOWELS

an·vil /'ænvɪl/ *n.* [C] a heavy iron block on which pieces of metal are shaped using a hammer

anx·i·e·ty /æŋ'zaɪət̬i/ W3 *n. plural* **anxieties** **1** [C,U] the feeling of being very worried about something that may happen or may have happened, so that you think about it all the time: **+about/over** *People's anxiety about the economy is increasing.* | *Tom often has* ***anxi-***

A

ety attacks. **2** [C] something that makes you worry: *the anxieties of parenthood* **3** [U] a feeling of wanting to do something very much, but being worried that you will not succeed: **anxiety to do sth** *In her anxiety to help, Laurie tripped and broke several wine glasses.* [**Origin:** 1500–1600 Latin *anxietas*, from *anxius*]

anx·ious /ˈæŋkʃəs/ *adj.* **1** very worried about something that may happen or may have happened, so that you think about it all the time SYN **worried**: *Gail was feeling anxious and depressed.* | *anxious employees* | *an anxious glance* | +**about** *Most children feel anxious about returning to school.* | **anxious that** *Maria was anxious that he might say no.* ►see THESAURUS box at **worried** **2** an anxious time or situation is one in which you feel nervous or worried: *There were a few anxious moments near the end of the game.* **3** feeling strongly that you want to do something or want something to happen SYN **eager**: **anxious to do sth** *Both countries are anxious to establish a closer relationship to the West.* —**anxiously** *adv.*: *I waited anxiously by the phone.*

an·y[1] /ˈɛni/ S1 W1 *quantifier, pron.* **1** [with negatives and in questions] some or even the smallest amount: *Few of the students had any knowledge of classical music.* | *I didn't pay any attention to what he said.* | *She promised not to take any chances.* | *He had no friends and didn't deserve any.* | +**of** *I don't understand what any of this stuff means.* | *I tried, but it wasn't* ***any use*** (=it was not successful). | *I don't think there will be more than a dozen left,* ***if any*** (=it is likely that there will be none left at all). | *Brad was* ***not in any way*** *upset by his wife's decision.* | *If I can help you* ***in any way****, let me know.* **2** used to say that it does not matter which person or thing you choose from a group: *Any student caught cheating will be suspended.* | *There are bad things about any job.* | *Before you sign any written agreement, read it over carefully.* | *These tiles are an ideal choice for any bathroom.* | +**of** *Any of those will work okay.* | *Do any of you remember?* | *Are there* ***any other*** *comments?* **3** as much as possible: *We'll take any help we can get.* **4 in any case** also **at any rate** no matter what may happen SYN **at least**: *It wasn't a complete failure. At any rate, I learned something.* **5 just any** used to refer to something that is ordinary and not special: *You can't wear just any old clothes – you have to dress up.* **6 any day** used to emphasize that you think one thing is much better than another: *Champagne beats beer any day.*

any[2] S1 W3 *adv.* [with negatives and in questions] **1** [with comparatives] used especially in negative statements to mean "in the least" SYN **at all**: *I don't see how things could get any worse.* | *I can't walk any farther.* | *David could not stand it any longer.* | *Is Peggy feeling any better today?* **2** SPOKEN used to mean "at all" at the end of a sentence: *We tried talking to him, but that didn't help any.*

an·y·bod·y /ˈɛniˌbʊdi, -ˌbʌdi, -bədi/ S1 W2 *pron.* INFORMAL ANYONE: *Is anybody home?* | *I don't think anybody's going to come.*

an·y·hoo /ˈɛniˌhu/ *adv.* [sentence adverb] SPOKEN, HUMOROUS used in order to continue a story, change the subject of a conversation, or finish saying something without all the details SYN **anyhow**

an·y·how /ˈɛniˌhaʊ/ S3 *adv.* [sentence adverb] INFORMAL ANYWAY: *Well, that's what Jeb told me anyhow.* | *Anyhow, we have plenty of time to plan ahead.*

an·y·more /ˌɛniˈmɔr/ S1 W3 *adv.* **not... anymore** used to say that something does not happen or is not true now, although it used to happen or be true in the past SYN **no longer**: *Nick doesn't live here anymore.* | *I don't want to talk to you anymore.*

an·y·one /ˈɛniˌwʌn, -wən/ S1 W1 *pron.* **1** any person, when it is not important to say exactly who: *Anyone can learn to swim in just a few lessons.* | *Why would anyone want to do that?* | *You can choose anyone to be your partner.* | ***Anyone else*** (=any other person) *would have been embarrassed.* **2** [with negatives and in questions or statements expressing possibility] a person or people: *I don't want anyone to know.* | *Is anyone home?* | *If anyone asks, tell them I'll be back soon.* | *Do you know* ***anyone else*** (=a different person) *who wants a ticket?* → see also EVERYONE, SOMEONE[1]

an·y·place /ˈɛniˌpleɪs/ *adv.* INFORMAL anywhere: *Just set that down anyplace.* | *We didn't have anyplace else to go.*

an·y·thing /ˈɛniˌθɪŋ/ S1 W1 *pron.* **1** any thing, event, situation etc., when it does not matter exactly which: *If you believe that, you'll believe anything!* | *The cat will eat anything.* | *She doesn't want pizza, but* ***anything else*** (=any food that is not pizza) *will be fine.* **2** [with negatives and in questions or statements expressing possibility] nothing, or something: *You can't believe anything Kathy says.* | *Do you need anything from the store?* | *Have you heard anything about their new CD?* | *Don't do anything stupid.* | **anything to say/do etc.** *It was a great resort, but there wasn't really anything to do in the evening.* | *Would you like* ***anything else*** (=any addtional thing)*?* **3 anything but (clear/happy etc.)** used to emphasize that someone or something is not clear, happy etc.: *The bridge is anything but safe.* | *They told me she was stupid, but she's anything but.* **4 ...or anything** SPOKEN or something that is similar: *Do you want a Coke or anything?* | *It wasn't like we were going steady or anything.* **5 anything like sb/sth** INFORMAL similar in any way to something or someone else: *Does Brenda look anything like her mother?* **6 not anything like/near sth** INFORMAL used to emphasize that someone or something is not in a particular condition or state: *We don't have anything like enough money to buy a new car.* **7 anything goes** used to say that anything is possible or acceptable: *Don't worry about what to wear – anything goes at Ben's parties.* **8 for anything** INFORMAL if you will not do something for anything, you will definitely not do it: *After what happened last time, I wouldn't work for them again for anything.* **9 like anything** SPOKEN if you do something like anything, you do it a lot or to a great degree: *Tom only left last week and I already miss him like anything.*

an·y·time /ˈɛniˌtaɪm/ S3 *adv.* at any time: *Call me anytime – I'm always home.* | *The project won't be completed anytime soon.* | *They should arrive anytime between noon and 3 p.m.*

an·y·way /ˈɛniˌweɪ/ S1 W2 *adv.* [sentence adverb] **1** in spite of what has just been mentioned: *He said he didn't know much about computers, but that he'd try and help us anyway.* | *It's just a cold, but you should see the doctor anyway.* **2** SPOKEN used when adding a remark which shows that the fact just mentioned is not important: *They didn't offer me the job, but I really didn't want it anyway.* | *"Did you tell anyone?" "No. Who would believe me anyway?"* **3** SPOKEN used in order to return to an earlier subject or change the subject of a conversation: *Anyway, what was I saying?* | *I think she's around my age, but anyway, she's pregnant.* | *Anyway, how about getting some lunch?* **4** SPOKEN used when you are ignoring some details so you can talk about the most imporant part of something: *Anyway, after three months she made a full recovery.* **5** SPOKEN used when adding something that corrects or slightly changes what you have just said: *Let's think about it for a while, for a few days anyway.* | *There seems to have been a technical problem – anyway, that's what they told me.* **6** SPOKEN used in order to find out the real reason for something or what the real situation is: *So anyway, what were you doing in the park at two in the morning?* | *What is that thing for anyway?* **7** SPOKEN used when you want to end a conversation: *Anyway, I guess I'd better go now.*

an·y·ways /ˈɛniˌweɪz/ *adv.* [sentence adverb] SPOKEN, NONSTANDARD anyway

an·y·where /ˈɛniˌwɛr/ S1 W3 *adv.* **1** in or to any place, when it does not matter exactly where: *Sit anywhere – there are plenty of seats.* | *You can buy those jeans anywhere.* | +**in** *You can now call anywhere in the U.S. for 5 cents a minute.* | *I'd rather live* ***anywhere else*** *than here.* **2** [with negatives and in questions or statements expressing possibility] somewhere or nowhere: *I can't find my keys anywhere.* | *Do they need anywhere to stay for the night?* | *Did you go anywhere exciting on vacation* *this year?* | *These pictures are great – have you been* ***anywhere else*** (=any other place) *in Mexico?* **3 not anywhere near sth/sb** SPOKEN **a)** used to emphasize that someone or something is not near to another person or thing: *My car wasn't anywhere near yours. I couldn't have hit you.* **b)** used to emphasize that someone or something is not in a particular condition or state: *The money won't come anywhere near solving the school district's problems.* **4 not get anywhere** to not make any progress: *I'm trying to set up a meeting, but I don't seem to be getting anywhere.* **5 anywhere between/from one and ten etc.** used to mean any age, number, amount etc. between the numbers mentioned, when it is difficult to know exactly which age, number etc.: *She was one of those women who could be anywhere between 45 and 60.* **6 it won't get you anywhere** SPOKEN used to tell someone that they will not be able to change a situation: *You can try writing to complain, but I don't think it will get you anywhere.*

A-OK /ˌeɪ oʊˈkeɪ/ *adj.* INFORMAL in very good condition: *Everything's A-OK.* —**A-OK** *adv.*

a·or·ta /eɪˈɔrṭə/ *n.* [C] BIOLOGY the largest ARTERY (=tube for carrying blood) in the body, taking blood from the left side of the heart to all parts of the body except the lungs [**Origin:** 1500–1600 Modern Latin, Greek *aorte*, from *aeirein* **to lift**] → see picture at HEART

AP /ˌeɪ ˈpi/ **1** TRADEMARK the abbreviation of ADVANCED PLACEMENT **2** the abbreviation of ASSOCIATED PRESS

a·pace /əˈpeɪs/ *adv.* FORMAL quickly: **grow/continue etc. apace** *Overall activity in the construction sector continues to grow apace.*

A·pach·e /əˈpætʃi/ a Native American tribe from the western region of the U.S. —**Apache** *adj.*

a·part /əˈpɑrt/ S2 W2 *adj., adv.*

1 DISTANCE if things are apart, they have an amount of space between them: *The two towns are fifteen miles apart.* | +**from** *Families may be forced to sit apart from each other.*

2 TIME two hours/six weeks etc. apart if things are a particular time apart, they have that much time between them: *Our birthdays are only two days apart.* | *Carol's two daughters are three years apart* (=one was born three years after the other).

3 SEPARATE a) if you take or pull something apart, or something comes or falls apart, it is separated into many different parts or pieces: *The mechanics took the engine apart.* | *The upholstery had been ripped apart.* **b)** if you keep, pull, force etc. two things or people apart, you separate them: *Soldiers forced many families apart in the refugee camps.* | *We try to keep the cats apart as much as possible because they fight.*

4 CONDITION if something is coming apart, falling apart etc., it is in a very bad condition: *My purse is starting to come apart.* | *The old house is falling apart.*

5 apart from sb/sth a) except for; not including: *Apart from a couple of spelling mistakes, this looks fine.* **b)** in addition to SYN **besides**: *Apart from being used as a school, the building is used for weddings, parties, and meetings.*

6 NOT WITH SB ELSE in a different place from someone else: *The twins were adopted and raised apart.* | *They got back together after two years apart.*

7 COUNTRY/GROUP if something such as a country or group comes apart, it stops being whole or stops having a single organization: *Civil war has ripped the country apart.*

8 grow/drift apart if people or groups grow apart, their relationship slowly ends: *I think Dan and Tina just grew apart.*

9 be worlds/poles apart if people, beliefs, or ideas are worlds or poles apart, they are completely different from each other

10 quite apart from sth FORMAL without even considering something; completely separately from something: *Quite apart from being illegal, the activity is extremely dangerous.*

11 a sth apart FORMAL used to say that something is different in some way from other things of the same type: *We hope to find someone who will preserve the land as open space, a place apart.* | *Where I grew up, the lives of rich seemed* ***a world apart*** (=a completely different place or way of life).

[**Origin:** 1300–1400 Old French *a part* **to the side**] **fall apart** at FALL[1], **pull apart** at PULL[1], **set apart** at SET[1], **take apart** at TAKE[1], **tear apart** at TEAR[2]

a·part·heid /əˈpɑrtaɪt, -teɪt, -taɪd/ *n.* [U] HISTORY the former South African political and social system in which only white people had full political rights and people of other races, especially black people, were forced to go to separate schools, live in separate areas etc. [**Origin:** 1900–2000 Afrikaans **separateness**]

a·part·ment /əˈpɑrtˀmənt/ S1 W2 *n.* [C] **1** a set of rooms within a larger building, usually on one level, where someone lives: *a one-bedroom apartment* ►see THESAURUS box at **house**[1] **2** [usually plural] a large room with expensive furniture, decorations etc., used especially by an important person such as a president, prince etc.: *the presidential apartments* [**Origin:** 1600–1700 French *appartement*, from Italian *appartamento*, from *appartare* **to put aside, separate**]

aˈpartment ˌbuilding also **aˈpartment ˌhouse** *n.* [C] a large building containing many apartments

aˈpartment ˌcomplex *n.* [C] a group of apartment buildings built at the same time in the same area

ap·a·thet·ic /ˌæpəˈθeṭɪk◂/ *adj.* not excited and not caring about something, or not interested in anything and unwilling to make an effort to change and improve things: *Most people were just too apathetic to go out and vote.* —**apathetically** /-kli/ *adv.*

ap·a·thy /ˈæpəθi/ *n.* [U] the feeling of not being interested or not caring, either about a particular thing or about life: +**about** *widespread voter apathy about the elections* | +**among** *Bad management can lead to apathy among employees.* [**Origin:** 1600–1700 Greek *apatheia*, from *a-* **without** + *pathos* **feeling**]

ape[1] /eɪp/ *n.* [C] **1** BIOLOGY a large monkey without a tail, or with a very short tail, such as a GORILLA or a CHIMPANZEE **2 go ape** SLANG to suddenly become very angry or excited: *Joe went ape when he found out.* **3** OLD-FASHIONED a man who behaves in a stupid or annoying way

ape[2] *v.* [T] **1** to copy someone's way of doing something, so that what you do or produce is not good or original SYN **mimic**: *His music simply apes classical styles.* **2** to copy the way someone moves or speaks in order to make fun of them SYN **mimic** SYN **imitate**

Ap·en·nines, the /ˈæpəˌnaɪnz/ a RANGE of mountains down the middle of Italy, from the northwest to the south

a·per·i·tif, apéritif /əˌpɛrəˈtif, ɑ-/ *n.* [C] an alcoholic drink that is drunk before a meal

ap·er·ture /ˈæpəˑtʃəˑ/ *n.* [C] **1** the hole at the front of a camera or TELESCOPE, which can be changed to let more or less light in **2** TECHNICAL a small hole or space in something which is used for a particular purpose

a·pex /ˈeɪpɛks/ *n.* [C] **1** TECHNICAL the top or highest part of something **2** FORMAL the most successful part SYN **pinnacle**: +**of** *He reached the apex of his career before he was 40.*

a·phid /ˈeɪfɪd/ *n.* [C] a type of very small insect that drinks the juices of plants

aph·o·rism /ˈæfəˌrɪzəm/ *n.* [C] ENG. LANG. ARTS a short wise phrase —**aphoristic** /ˌæfəˈrɪstɪk◂/ *adj.*

a·pho·tic zone /eɪˈfoʊṭɪk ˌzoʊn/ *n.* **the aphotic zone** BIOLOGY the deep part of the ocean, where light from the sun does not reach and PHOTOSYNTHESIS does not happen → see also PHOTIC ZONE

aph·ro·dis·i·ac /ˌæfrəˈdiziˌæk, -ˈdɪz-/ *n.* [C] a food, drink, or drug that makes you want to have sex [**Origin:** 1700–1800 Greek *aphrodisiakos*, from *Aphrodite*, the ancient Greek goddess of love] —**aphrodisiac** *adj.*: *aphrodisiac properties*

Aph·ro·di·te /ˌæfrəˈdaɪṭi/ in Greek MYTHOLOGY, the goddess of love and beauty

A·pi·a /ə'piə/ the capital city of Western Samoa

a·pi·ar·y /'eɪpi,ɛri/ *n. plural* **apiaries** [C] TECHNICAL a place where BEES are kept

a·pic·al dom·i·nance /,eɪpɪkəl 'dɑmənəns/ *n.* [U] BIOLOGY the fact that the main stems and branches of a plant are stronger and more likely to live than the smaller ones growing off them

apical mer·i·stem /,eɪpɪkəl 'mɛrɪ,stɛm/ *n.* [U] BIOLOGY the area at the end of each shoot or root in a plant that forms new cells, producing new growth and increasing the size of the plant

a·piece /ə'pis/ *adv.* [only after number or noun] costing or having a particular amount each: *Oranges are 20 cents apiece.* | *I bought a dozen cookies, so you can take three apiece.*

a·plen·ty /ə'plɛnti/ *adj.* [only after noun] LITERARY in large amounts or numbers, especially more than you need: *There was food aplenty.*

a·plomb /ə'plɑm, ə'plʌm/ *n.* [U] **with aplomb** in a confident and skillful way, especially when you have to deal with difficult problems or a difficult situation: *Morgan handled the media attention with aplomb.* [**Origin:** 1800–1900 French **quality of being perpendicular**, from Old French *a plomb* **according to the plumb line**]

APO /,eɪ pi 'oʊ/ the abbreviation of "Army Post Office", used in writing addresses to people in the military

a·po·ca·lypse /ə'pɑkə,lɪps/ *n.* [C] **1 the apocalypse** the destruction and end of the world **2** a dangerous, frightening, and very serious situation causing death, harm, or destruction: *an environmental apocalypse* [**Origin:** 1200–1300 Late Latin *apocalypsis*, from Greek, from *apokalyptein* **to uncover**]

a·poc·a·lyp·tic /ə,pɑkə'lɪptɪk/ *adj.* **1** warning people about terrible events that will happen in the future: *an apocalyptic vision of the future* **2** relating to the final destruction and end of the world

a·poc·ry·phal /ə'pɑkrəfəl/ *adj.* an apocryphal story about a famous person or event is well known but probably not true

ap·o·gee /'æpədʒi/ *n.* [C] **1** FORMAL the most successful part of something SYN **apex**: +**of** *the apogee of her political career* **2** PHYSICS the point where the Moon, a SATELLITE, or other object that is traveling in a curved path through space around the Earth is farthest from the Earth OPP **perigee**

a·po·lit·i·cal /,eɪpə'lɪtɪkəl/ *adj.* not having any interest in or involvement with politics

A·pol·lo /ə'pɑloʊ/ in Greek and Roman MYTHOLOGY, the god of the sun, medicine, poetry, music, and PROPHECY

a·pol·o·get·ic /ə,pɑlə'dʒɛtɪk/ *adj.* showing or saying that you are sorry that something has happened, especially because you feel guilty or embarrassed about it: *an apologetic letter* | +**about** *Judi was very apologetic about forgetting my birthday.* —**apologetically** /-kli/ *adv.*: *"I know," she said apologetically.*

ap·o·lo·gi·a /,æpə'loʊdʒə/ *n.* [C] ENG. LANG. ARTS a statement in which you defend an idea that you believe in

a·pol·o·gist /ə'pɑlədʒɪst/ *n.* [C] LITERARY someone who tries to defend and explain an idea or system, especially one that is not popular: +**for** *an apologist for the current regime*

a·pol·o·gize /ə'pɑlə,dʒaɪz/ S3 *v.* [I] to tell someone that you are sorry that you have done something wrong: *The editors admitted the mistake and apologized.* | +**for** *The pilot apologized for the delay.* | *I* ***apologized profusely*** *for being late.* | +**to** *Marge should apologize to her daughter for reading her diary.*

a·pol·o·gy /ə'pɑlədʒi/ *n. plural* **apologies** [C] **1** something that you say or write to show that you are sorry for doing something wrong: +**for** *The police chief issued an apology for the officer's behavior.* | *Black residents are* ***demanding an apology*** *from the mayor.* | *It wasn't Angela's fault, and I* ***owe her an apology.*** | *Please* ***accept my apologies.*** | *The paper was forced to* ***make an apology.*** **2** LITERARY a statement in which you defend something you believe in after it has been criticized by other people [**Origin:** 1500–1600 Late Latin *apologia* **written or spoken defense**, from Greek, from *apo-* **away from, off** + *logos* **speech**]

ap·o·plec·tic /,æpə'plɛktɪk◂/ *adj.* **1** so angry or excited that your face becomes red: *The colonel was apoplectic with rage.* **2** MEDICINE relating to apoplexy

ap·o·plex·y /'æpə,plɛksi/ *n.* [U] OLD-FASHIONED MEDICINE an illness caused by a problem in your brain that can damage your ability to move, feel, or think SYN **stroke**

a·pos·ta·sy /ə'pɑstəsi/ *n.* [U] FORMAL the act of changing your beliefs so that you stop supporting a religion, political party etc.

a·pos·tate /ə'pɑsteɪt, -tɪt/ *n.* [C] FORMAL someone who has stopped believing in and supporting a religion or political party

a pos·te·ri·o·ri /,ɑ poʊstɪri'ɔri, ,eɪ pɑ-/ *adj.* FORMAL using facts or results to form a judgment about what must have happened before. For example, "The streets are wet, so it must have been raining," is an a posteriori statement. → see also A PRIORI

a·pos·tle /ə'pɑsəl/ *n.* [C] **1** one of the 12 men chosen by Jesus Christ to teach and spread the Christian religion **2** FORMAL someone who believes strongly in a new idea and tries to persuade other people: +**of** *an apostle of peace* [**Origin:** 900–1000 Late Latin *apostolus*, from Greek, **bringer of messages, apostle**]

ap·os·tol·ic /,æpə'stɑlɪk◂/ *adj.* **1** relating to the POPE (=leader of the Catholic Church) **2** relating to one of Jesus Christ's 12 apostles

a·pos·tro·phe /ə'pɑstrəfi/ *n.* [C] **1** ENG. LANG. ARTS the sign (') used in writing to show that numbers or letters have been left out, as in "don't" (=do not) and '06 (=2006) **2** the same sign used before or after the letter "s" to show that something belongs or is related to someone or something, as in "Joan's book," "Charles' mother," or "the boys' dog" **3** used before "s" to show the plural of letters and numbers, as in "Your r's look like v's." [**Origin:** 1500–1600 French, Late Latin *apostrophus*, from Greek, from *apostrephein* **to turn away**]

a·poth·e·car·y /ə'pɑθə,kɛri/ *n. plural* **apothecaries** [C] someone who mixed and sold medicines in past times

ap·o·them /'æpə,θɛm/ *n.* [singular] MATH the shortest distance from the center to the side of a POLYGON with equal sides and equal angles. The line drawn to measure this distance must meet the side at a RIGHT ANGLE.

a·poth·e·o·sis /ə,pɑθi'oʊsɪs, æ-/ *n.* **1 the apotheosis of sth** FORMAL the best and most perfect example of something: *the apotheosis of Gothic architecture* **2** [U] LITERARY the state of getting to the highest level of something such as honor, importance etc.

Ap·pa·la·chians, the /,æpə'leɪtʃənz, -'læ-/ also **the ,Appalachian 'Mountains** a long range of mountains in northeast America that go in a line southwest from Quebec in Canada to Alabama in the U.S.

ap·pall /ə'pɔl/ *v.* [T] to shock someone by being very bad or immoral: *The idea of killing animals for fur appalled her.* [**Origin:** 1500–1600 Old French *apalir*, from *palir* **to turn pale**]

ap·palled /ə'pɔld/ *adj.* very shocked by something very bad or immoral: *Appalled neighbors quickly called the police.* | +**at/by** *I was appalled by John's rude behavior.* | **be appalled to hear/see/discover etc.** *He was appalled to discover that his wife had been seeing another man.* | **appalled that** *I'm appalled that you would even think such a thing.*

ap·pall·ing /ə'pɔlɪŋ/ *adj.* **1** so bad or immoral that you are shocked: *apalling prison conditions* ▸see THESAURUS box at **bad**[1] **2** very bad: *The music kids listen to is appalling.* —**appallingly** *adv.*: *appallingly cruel treatment*

ap·pa·loo·sa /,æpə'lusə/ *n.* [C] a type of horse that is a pale color with dark spots

ap•pa•ra•tchik /ˌɑpəˈrɑtʃɪk/ *n.* [C] an official working for a government or other organization who obeys orders without thinking

ap•pa•rat•us /ˌæpəˈrætəs, -ˈreɪtəs/ *n. plural* **apparatus** or **apparatuses** [C,U] **1** a tool, machine, or set of equipment used especially for scientific, medical, or technical purposes SYN **equipment**: *The astronauts have special breathing apparatus.* **2** a system or process for doing something: *the government's security apparatus* [**Origin:** 1600–1700 Latin, past participle of *apparare* **to prepare**]

ap•par•el /əˈpærəl/ *n.* [U] a word meaning "clothing," used especially by stores or the clothing industry: *children's apparel* | *an athletic shoe and apparel company*

ap•par•ent /əˈpærənt/ Ac W3 *adj.* **1** easily noticed or understood SYN **clear**: +**to** *Her embarrassment was apparent to everyone.* | **it is apparent (that)** *It was apparent that the company would shut down.* | ***For no apparent reason,*** *our daughter has started refusing to go to school.* | *The difference in quality was* ***immediately apparent.*** → see also EVIDENT ►see THESAURUS box at **clear**[1] **2** seeming to be real or true, although it may not really be so: *an apparent contradiction between the men's stories* | *the committee's apparent inability to deal with the problem* [**Origin:** 1300–1400 Old French, Latin, present participle of *apparere* **to prepare**]

ap•par•ent•ly /əˈpærəntˀli/ Ac S1 W2 *adv.* **1** [sentence adverb] based on what you have heard is true, although you are not completely sure about it: *Nelson apparently committed suicide.* | *Apparently, it was a really good party.* **2** according to the way someone looks or a situation appears, although you cannot be sure: *Campaign funds have been used for apparently illegal activities.* → see also EVIDENTLY, OBVIOUSLY

ap•pa•ri•tion /ˌæpəˈrɪʃən/ *n.* [C] something that you imagine you can see, especially the spirit of a dead person: *a ghostly apparition*

ap•peal[1] /əˈpil/ W2 *n.*
1 REQUEST [C] an urgent request for something important such as money or help: +**for** *an urgent appeal for medical supplies* | +**to** *appeals to aid agencies for help* | **appeal to sb to do sth** *An appeal to the army not to use force was ignored.* | *Fowler went on the radio to* ***make an appeal*** *for law and order.*
2 ATTRACTIVENESS [U] a quality that makes you like someone or something, be interested in them, or want them: +**for** *The game has more appeal for older children.* | *Her music has* ***wide appeal*** (=liked by many people). | *He relies mainly on his* ***sex appeal*** (=the quality of being sexually attractive). | *Before long, the new job had* ***lost its appeal.***
3 REQUEST TO CHANGE COURT'S DECISION [C,U] a formal request to a court or to someone in authority asking for a decision to be changed: +**to** *an appeal to the Supreme Court* | *The decision was overturned* ***on appeal*** (=during the process of an appeal).
4 REQUEST FOR MONEY [C] an attempt to persuade people to give money in order to help people who need something: *The Cancer Society's appeal has raised more than $500,000.* | *The hospital has* ***launched an appeal*** *to raise money for new equipment.* → see also COURT OF APPEALS

appeal[2] W3 *v.* **1** [I] to make a serious public request for help, money, information etc.: **appeal (to sb) for sth** *The police are appealing to the public for information.* | *The Pope appealed for an end to the violence.* | **appeal to sb to do sth** *The water company appealed to everyone to reduce the amount of water used.* **2** [I,T] to make a formal request to a court or someone in authority asking for a decision to be changed: *The defendant is planning to appeal.* | *They have the right to appeal the decision to a higher court.* **3 appeal to sb's common sense/better nature/sense of honor etc.** to try to persuade someone to do something by reminding them that it is a sensible, good, wise etc. thing to do [**Origin:** 1300–1400 Old French *apeler* **to accuse, appeal,** from Latin *appellere* **to drive to**]

appeal to sb *phr. v.* to seem attractive and interesting to someone: *The idea didn't appeal to me much.* | *The magazine is intended to appeal to working women in their 20s and 30s.*

ap•peal•ing /əˈpilɪŋ/ *adj.* **1** attractive or interesting: *Davies' books are an appealing blend of wit and wisdom.* | +**to** *Why is the program so appealing to young women?* | *Some men seem to* ***find*** *these qualities* ***appealing*** *in women.* **2 an appealing look/voice etc.** FORMAL a look etc. that shows that someone wants help or sympathy: *She gave him an appealing look.* —**appealingly** *adv.*

apˈpeals ˌcourt *n.* [C usually singular] the COURT OF APPEALS

apˌpeal to auˈthority *n.* [C usually singular] an occasion when someone mentions what another person or book says about a subject in order to support or prove his or her own ideas

apˌpeal to eˈmotion *n.* [C usually singular] an occasion when someone tries to persuade other people to believe what he or she is saying, by saying or writing things that make people feel a strong emotion, rather than by using facts or information to support the idea

apˌpeal to ˈreason *n.* [C usually singular] an occasion when someone tries to persuade people to believe what he or she is saying by asking them to think clearly about whether or not the idea is reasonable

ap•pear /əˈpɪr/ S2 W1 *v.*
1 SEEM [linking verb, not in progressive] to seem: *Roger appeared very upset.* | *The city appeared calm after the previous night's fighting.* | **appear to be** *Karl appeared to be in his late twenties.* | **appear to do sth** *The gene appears to make people have a higher risk of developing cancer.* | *Police have found* ***what appear to be*** (=things that look like) *human remains.* | *The treatment* ***would appear to*** *be useful even in these cases* (=used when something is likely to be true, although you are not completely sure). | **it appears (that)** *It appears that the motive was robbery.* ►see THESAURUS box at **seem**
2 START TO BE SEEN [I] to start to be seen or to suddenly be seen: *An image appeared on the screen.* | *Cracks began appearing in the wall.* | *The dog* ***appeared out of nowhere*** (=suddenly appeared) *and began running alongside me.* | *A huge new housing development* ***appeared*** *practically* ***overnight*** (=appeared suddenly).
3 MOVIE/PLAY ETC. [I] to take part in a movie, play, concert, television program etc.: +**in/on** *Rogers appeared in 73 movies.* | *Hutchinson was not invited to appear on the show.* | +**at** *Once in a while, a big band like the Rolling Stones appears at the club.*
4 BE WRITTEN/SHOWN [I] to be written or shown on a list, in a book or newspaper, in a document etc.: +**in/on/at** *The story appeared in Thursday's paper.* | *Lauren's name appears at the front of the book.*
5 STH NEW [I] if a something such as a book, product, or idea appears, it becomes available or known about for the first time: *When the book finally* ***appeared on the shelves*** (=became available in bookstores), *it was a huge success.* | *Since Prozac* ***appeared on the scene,*** *research into similar drugs has increased dramatically.*
6 IN COURT ETC. [I] to be present in a court of law for a TRIAL that you are involved in, or to speak at a meeting of an official group: *Meeks is scheduled to appear in court February 5.* | +**before/in front of** *The senator appeared before the Ways and Means Committee.*
7 ARRIVE [I] to arrive, especially when people are not expecting you to: *Karen appeared at my house around nine o'clock.*
[**Origin:** 1200–1300 Old French *aparoir*, from Latin *apparere*, from *ad-* **to** + *parere* **to show yourself**]

ap•pear•ance /əˈpɪrəns/ W2 *n.*
1 WAY SB/STH LOOKS [C,U] the way someone or something looks or seems to other people: *O'Brien's article suggests ways to improve your appearance.* | +**of** *They've changed the appearance of the whole building.* | *Some of the Congressman's actions* ***gave the appearance of*** (=seemed) *being improper.* | *The sisters are very different* ***in appearance.*** | *She had an* ***outward appearance*** *of calm, but deep down she was really worried.* | *The* ***physical appearance*** *of the product is*

A

just as important as its function. | **by/from/to all appearances** *By all appearances, Craig has fully recovered from heart surgery.* | *The kids look interested, but* ***appearances can be deceiving*** (=they were not so interested as they looked).
2 ARRIVAL [C usually singular] the unexpected or sudden arrival of someone or something: **+of** *The sudden appearance of several reporters at the hospital caused a lot of confusion.*
3 STH NEW [singular] the point or time at which something new begins to exist or starts being used: **+of** *The industry has changed greatly with the appearance of new technologies.*
4 PLAY/MOVIE/GAME ETC. [C] the act of taking part in a movie, play, sports game etc.: *Thomas* ***made*** *his first* ***appearance*** *for Florida State in Friday's game.*
5 make an appearance also **put in an appearance** to go to an event for a short time, because you think you should: *Marc put in an appearance at the wedding, but didn't stay for the reception.*
6 IN PUBLIC [C] an occasion when a famous person is seen in public: *The new president* ***made*** *his first public* ***appearance***. | *He gets paid $5,000 for every* ***personal appearance***.
7 COURT/MEETING [C] the act of being present at a court of law or official meeting: *Ms. Lang* ***made a*** *brief* ***appearance*** *in court.*
8 keep up appearances to continue to do things in the way you used to do them even though your situation has changed a lot: *For now, I can keep up appearances and still go to the same restaurants as my friends.*
9 for the sake of appearance(s)/for appearances' sake if you do something for appearances' sake, you are trying to behave how people expect you to, especially to hide your true situation or feelings

ap·pease /ə'piz/ *v.* [T] to make someone less angry or stop them from attacking you by giving them what they want [**Origin:** 1300–1400 Old French *apaisier*, from *pais* **peace**]

ap·pease·ment /ə'pizmənt/ *n.* [C,U] FORMAL the act of trying to persuade someone not to attack you, or to make them less angry by giving them what they want, especially in politics

ap·pel·late court /ə,pɛlɪt˺ 'kɔrt/ *n.* [C] LAW a court in which people APPEAL against decisions made in other courts of law

ap,pellate juris'diction *n.* [U] LAW the official power that an appellate court has to consider and change a judgment made by a lower court

ap·pel·la·tion /,æpə'leɪʃən/ *n.* [C] LITERARY a name or title

ap·pend /ə'pɛnd/ [Ac] *v.* [T] FORMAL to add something to a piece of writing [**Origin:** 1600–1700 French *appendre*, from Latin *appendere* **to weigh**]

ap·pend·age /ə'pɛndɪdʒ/ *n.* [C] FORMAL **1** something that is connected to a larger or more important thing **2** BIOLOGY part of the body that extends beyond the main part, for example, an arm or a leg in humans, or an ANTENNA in insects

ap·pen·dec·to·my /,æpən'dɛktəmi/ *n. plural* **appendectomies** [C,U] a medical operation in which your APPENDIX is removed

ap·pen·di·ci·tis /ə,pɛndə'saɪtɪs/ *n.* [U] MEDICINE an illness in which your APPENDIX swells and causes pain

ap·pen·dix /ə'pɛndɪks/ [Ac] *n. plural* **appendixes** also **appendices** /-dɪsiz/ [C] **1** BIOLOGY a small part at the beginning of your large INTESTINE which has little or no use **2** a part at the end of a book containing additional information

ap·per·tain /,æpɚ'teɪn/ *v.* FORMAL
appertain to sth *phr. v.* to belong to or concern something

ap·pe·tite /'æpə,taɪt/ *n.* **1** [C,U] a desire for food: *Both of my kids have* ***a healthy appetite*** (=a desire to eat more than enough food). | *Watching open-heart surgery on TV made me* ***lose my appetite*** (=stop wanting to eat and feel slightly sick). | **spoil/ruin your appetite** *Don't eat that cake now – you'll spoil your appetite.* | *Walking all day, you can* ***work up an appetite*** (=get very hungry). **2** [C] a desire or liking for a particular activity: **+for** *an appetite for new experiences* | *County officials have shown* ***no appetite for*** *further negotiations.* | *People seem to have an* ***insatiable appetite*** *for any kind of gossip.* [**Origin:** 1300–1400 Old French *apetit*, from Latin, past participle of *appetere* **to try to get**] → see also **whet sb's appetite (for sth)** at WHET

ap·pe·tiz·er /'æpə,taɪzɚ/ *n.* [C] a small dish eaten at the beginning of a meal, before the main part

ap·pe·tiz·ing /'æpə,taɪzɪŋ/ *adj.* food that is appetizing smells or looks very good: *an appetizing aroma* —**appetizingly** *adv.*

ap·plaud /ə'plɔd/ *v.* **1** [I,T] to hit your open hands together to show that you have enjoyed a play, concert, speaker etc. [SYN] **clap**: *People laughed and applauded politely.* | *The president was applauded repeatedly during his 40-minute speech.* **2** to express strong approval of and praise for an idea, plan etc.: *We applaud the company's efforts to improve safety.*

ap·plause /ə'plɔz/ *n.* [U] **1** the sound of many people hitting their open hands together and shouting, to show that they have enjoyed something: *The audience* ***burst into applause*** *at Kramer's comments.* | *Let's* ***give*** *Ron* ***a*** *big* ***round of applause*** (=give someone a short period of applause)! **2** strong approval and praise for an idea, plan etc.: *Mowlam's statements and down-to-earth style have* ***won applause*** *among lawmakers in Washington.*

ap·ple /'æpəl/ [S1] [W2] *n.* [C,U] **1** BIOLOGY a hard round fruit that has red, light green, or yellow skin and is white inside: *apple pie* | *an apple treee* **2 be the apple of sb's eye** to be loved very much by someone: *Ben was always the apple of his father's eye.* **3 be as American as apple pie** to be typically or completely American: *The group's optimism is as American as apple pie.* **4 the apple doesn't fall far from the tree** used to say that children are usually similar to their parents, especially in a bad way [**Origin:** Old English *æppel*] → see also ADAM'S APPLE, **bob for apples** at BOB[1] (5), **a rotten apple** at ROTTEN[1] (6), **upset the apple cart** at UPSET[2] (6)

,apple-'cheeked *adj.* having pink cheeks and looking healthy

ap·ple·jack /'æpəl,dʒæk/ *n.* [U] a very strong alcoholic drink made from apples

'apple ,polisher *n.* [C] OLD-FASHIONED someone who tries to gain something, become popular etc. by praising or helping someone else without being sincere

ap·ple·sauce /'æpəl,sɔs/ *n.* [U] a food made from crushed cooked apples

Ap·ple·seed /'æpəl,sid/, **John·ny** /'dʒɑni/ (1774–1845) the popular name for John Chapman, who walked around the eastern U.S. planting apple trees

ap·plet /'æplɪt/ *n.* COMPUTERS a small computer program that is used within another program

ap·pli·ance /ə'plaɪəns/ *n.* [C] a piece of electrical equipment such as a STOVE or WASHING MACHINE, used in people's homes ▸see THESAURUS box at **machine**[1]

ap·pli·ca·ble /'æplɪkəbəl, ə'plɪkəbəl/ *adj.* affecting or relating to a particular person, group, or situation: **+to** *These tax laws are not applicable to foreign companies.* —**applicability** /,æplɪkə'bɪləṭi, ə,plɪkə-/ *n.* [U]

ap·pli·cant /'æplɪkənt/ *n.* [C] someone who has formally asked, usually in writing, to be considered for a job, an opportunity to study at a college, permission to do something etc.: **+for** *Applicants for immigrant visas must pay an additional $75 charge.*

ap·pli·ca·tion /,æplɪ'keɪʃən/ [S2] [W2] *n.*
1 WRITTEN REQUEST [C,U] a formal, usually written, request to be considered for something such as a job, an opportunity to study at a college, or permission to do something: *His application was rejected.* | **+for** *There were more than 2,000 applications for the grant.* | **+from** *The university welcomes applications from overseas students.* | *Please fill out the* ***application form*** *and*

return it. | **a job/loan/visa etc. application** *We received hundreds of job applications.*
2 COMPUTERS [C] a piece of SOFTWARE: *Students will learn how to use word-processing and spreadsheet applications.*
3 PRACTICAL USE [C,U] the practical purpose for which a machine, idea etc. can be used, or the act of using it for this: *The research has many practical applications.* | **+for** *software with applications for business* | **+to/in** *The article discusses the application of this theory to actual economic practice.*
4 PUT STH ON STH a) [C,U] the act of putting something such as paint, liquid, medicine etc. onto a surface: **+of** *The application of fertilizer increased the size of the plants.* **b)** [C] the amount of something that is put onto a surface at one time: *The larger bottle contains approximately 25 applications.*
5 EFFORT [U] attention or effort over a long period of time: *Making your new business successful requires luck, patience, and application.*

ap·pli·ca·tor /ˈæplɪˌkeɪtɚ/ *n.* [C] a special brush or tool used for putting paint, glue, medicine etc. on something

ap·plied /əˈplaɪd/ *adj.* [usually before noun] **applied science/physics/linguistics etc.** science, physics etc. that has a practical use OPP **theoretical** → see also PURE

ap·pli·qué /ˌæpləˈkeɪ/ *n.* [C,U] a piece of material that is sewn onto a piece of clothing etc. as a decoration, or the process of sewing pieces of material onto things —**appliqué** *v.* [T] —**appliquéd** *adj.*

ap·ply /əˈplaɪ/ S1 W1 *v.* **applies, applied, applying**
1 REQUEST FOR STH [I] to make a formal, usually written request to be considered for a job, an opportunity to study at a college, permission to do something etc.: **+to** *I applied to four colleges and was accepted by all of them.* | **+for** *Fletcher applied for the post of Eliot's secretary.* | *They applied for a permit to build an extension to their house.*
2 USE STH [T] to use something such as a method, idea, or law in a particular situation, activity, or process: *Some of the children seem unable to apply what they have learned.* | **apply sth to sth** *New technology is being applied to almost every industrial process.* | **apply force/pressure etc.** *The force applied to the walls is about 50 pounds per square foot.*
3 AFFECT SB/STH [I,T not in progressive] to have an effect on or to concern a person, group, or situation: *Many of the restrictions no longer apply.* | **+to** *The 20% discount only applies to club members.* | **apply when/where** *These tax laws apply when you borrow money to invest in a partnership.*
4 SPREAD PAINT/LIQUID ETC. [T] to put or spread something such as paint, liquid, or medicine onto a surface: *Apply the lotion evenly over the skin.*
5 MAKE STH WORK [T] to do something in order to make something such as a piece of equipment operate: *On wet or icy roads, apply the brakes gently.* | *The crystal vibrates when a small electric current is applied to it.*
6 apply yourself to work hard with a lot of attention for a long time: *I wish Sam would apply himself a little more in school.*
7 USE A WORD [I,T] to use a particular word or name to describe something or someone in an appropriate way: **+to/in** *The word "tragic" definitely applies in this situation.* | **apply sth to sth** *The term "mat" can be applied to any small rug.*
[**Origin:** 1300–1400 Old French *aplier*, from Latin *applicare*, from *ad-* **to** + *plicare* **to fold**]

ap·point /əˈpɔɪnt/ W3 *v.* [T] **1** to choose someone for a position or a job: *Pope John Paul II appointed several new bishops.* | **appoint (sb) as sth** *Lisa Lore was appointed as an associate athletic director at USC.* | **appoint sb sth** *The company appointed Koontz chief financial officer.* | **appoint sb to sth** *He's been appointed to the State Supreme Court in California.* | **appoint sb to do sth** *DeGenoa appointed a police commission to investigate the scandal.* **2** FORMAL to arrange or decide a time or place for something to happen: *Judge Bailey appointed a new time for the trial.*
[**Origin:** 1300–1400 Old French *apointier* **to arrange**, from *point*] —**appointed** *adj.*: *We met at the* ***appointed time*** (=the arranged time). → see also SELF-APPOINTED, WELL-APPOINTED

A

ap·point·ee /əˌpɔɪnˈti/ *n.* [C] FORMAL someone who is appointed to do a particular important job: *a presidential appointee*

ap·point·ment /əˈpɔɪntˀmənt/ S2 W3 *n.* **1** [C] an arrangement for a meeting at an agreed time and place, for some special purpose: *a doctor's appointment* | *a five o'clock appointment* | **+with** *Judy's appointment with the doctor is at 10:30.* | **an appointment to do sth** *Do we need an appointment to see the manager?* | *I* ***have an appointment*** *at the clinic tomorrow morning.* | *Call Mrs. Reynolds' secretary and* ***make an appointment.*** | *Dr. Sutton sees patients only* ***by appointment.*** **2** [C,U] the act of choosing of someone for an important position or job: **+of** *The president will make the appointment of a new Chief Justice this week.* | **+as** *They congratulated him on his appointment as chairman.* **3** [C] a job or position, usually involving some responsibility: *Barron recently received an appointment as vice chairman.*

apˈpointment ˌbook also **apˈpointment ˌcalendar** *n.* [C] a small book with a CALENDAR in it, in which you write the names of meetings, events, or other things you plan to do each day

Ap·po·mat·tox /ˌæpəˈmæt̬əks/ a town in the U.S. stage of Virginia, where General Robert E. Lee, the leader of the Confederate army, surrendered (SURRENDER) to General Ulysses S. Grant, the leader of the Union army, and ended the American Civil War

ap·por·tion /əˈpɔrʃən/ *v.* [T] to decide how something should be shared among various people: **apportion sth among/between** *Apportioning funds fairly among the schools in the district has been difficult.* | *It's not easy to* ***apportion blame*** (=say who deserves the blame) *when a marriage breaks up.* —**apportionment** *n.* [C,U] → see also REAPPORTIONMENT

ap·po·site /ˈæpəzɪt/ *adj.* FORMAL appropriate to what is happening or being discussed: *Ms. Emerson made a few brief but apposite remarks about the incident.*

ap·po·si·tion /ˌæpəˈzɪʃən/ *n.* [U] ENG. LANG. ARTS in grammar, an occasion in which a simple sentence contains two or more noun phrases that describe the same thing or person, appearing one after the other without a word such as "and" or "or" between them. For example, in the sentence "The defendant, a woman of thirty, denies kicking the policeman" the two phrases "the defendant" and "a woman of thirty" are in apposition.

ap·pos·i·tive /əˈpɑzəˌt̬ɪv/ *n.* [C] ENG. LANG. ARTS a noun phrase that is used with another noun phrase that gives information about the same person or thing

ap·prais·al /əˈpreɪzəl/ *n.* [C,U] a statement or opinion judging the worth, value, or condition of something: **+of** *an expert's appraisal of the antique clock* | *I took the necklace to a jewelry store* ***for appraisal.***

ap·praise /əˈpreɪz/ *v.* [T] to officially judge how successful, effective, or valuable someone or something is SYN **evaluate**: **appraise sth at sth** *The house was appraised at $450,000.* —**appraiser** *n.* [C]

ap·pre·cia·ble /əˈpriʃəbəl/ Ac *adj.* FORMAL large enough to be noticed or considered important: *Military leaders have seen no appreciable change in the situation.* —**appreciably** *adv.*: *Complaints of police abuse have increased appreciably.*

ap·pre·ci·ate /əˈpriʃiˌeɪt/ Ac S1 W3 *v.* **1** [T not in progressive] to be grateful for something someone has done: *Mom really appreciated the letter you sent.* | *I don't need any help, but I appreciate your offer.* **2** [T not in progressive] to understand or enjoy the good qualities or value of someone or something: *Jan's abilities are not fully appreciated by her employer.* | *All the bad weather here makes me appreciate home.* **3 I would appreciate it if...** SPOKEN used to ask for something politely: *I'd really appreciate it if you could babysit the kids Friday night.* **4** [T not in progressive] to understand how serious a situation or problem is or what some-

A

one's feelings are: *I don't think you appreciate the difficulties this delay will cause.* | **appreciate how/why etc.** *At first he didn't appreciate how cold the winters are in Iowa.* | *I didn't* ***fully appreciate*** *what he was saying at the time.* **5** [I] to gradually become more valuable over a period of time OPP **depreciate**: *Our house has appreciated over 20% in the last two years.* [**Origin:** 1600–1700 Late Latin, past participle of *appretiare*, from Latin *ad-* **to** + *pretium* **price**]

ap·pre·ci·a·tion /əˌprɪʃiˈeɪʃən, əˌpri-/ Ac *n.* **1** a feeling of being grateful to someone for something: *Theo, we'd like to invite you to dinner* ***in appreciation of*** *your hard work this week.* | **show/express my appreciation** *I'd like to express my appreciation for all your help.* **2** [C,U] an understanding of the importance or meaning of something: *Murphy teaches classes in art appreciation to young children.* | +**of** *Management does not have a realistic appreciation of the situation.* **3** [U] pleasure you feel when you realize something is good, useful, or well done: *As Lynn got older, her appreciation for her hometown grew.* **4** [singular, U] a rise in value, especially of land or possessions: *There has been an appreciation of 50% in property values.*

ap·pre·cia·tive /əˈpriʃət̬ɪv/ *adj.* feeling or showing admiration or thanks: *an appreciative audience* | +**of** *I'm very pleased and appreciative of the support and kindness you have given me.* —**appreciatively** *adv.*

ap·pre·hend /ˌæprɪˈhɛnd/ *v.* [T] **1** FORMAL if a criminal is apprehended, he or she is found and taken away by the police SYN **arrest**: *Agents at the Interstate 8 station apprehended more than 3,100 undocumented workers.* ▸see THESAURUS box at **catch**[1] **2** OLD USE to understand something [**Origin:** 1300–1400 Latin *apprehendere* **to take hold of**, from *ad-* **to** + *prehendere* **to seize**]

ap·pre·hen·sion /ˌæprɪˈhɛnʃən/ *n.* **1** [C,U] anxiety about the future, especially about dealing with something bad or unpleasant: *Dad has some apprehensions about having surgery.* | *Diplomats watched the events with growing apprehension.* **2** [C,U] FORMAL the act of apprehending someone SYN **arrest**: *a reward for information leading to apprehension of the killer* **3** [U] OLD USE understanding: *The discussion centered on our apprehension of the nature of God.*

ap·pre·hen·sive /ˌæprɪˈhɛnsɪv/ *adj.* worried or nervous about something that you are going to do, or about the future: +**about** *Dave's always a little apprehensive about flying.* —**apprehensively** *adv.*: *I waited apprehensively for his reply.*

ap·pren·tice[1] /əˈprɛntɪs/ *n.* [C] someone who agrees to work for an employer for a particular period of time in order to learn a particular skill or job: *an apprentice chef* [**Origin:** 1300–1400 Old French *aprentis*, from Latin *apprehendere* **to take hold of**] → see also INTERN

apprentice[2] *v.* **1** [T usually passive] to make someone an apprentice: **be apprenticed to sb** *He's apprenticed to a plumber.* **2** [I] to work as an apprentice: *Jones apprenticed with the architect Frank Lloyd Wright.*

ap·pren·tice·ship /əˈprɛntɪˌʃɪp/ *n.* [C,U] the job of being an apprentice, or the period of time in which you are an apprentice

ap·prise /əˈpraɪz/ *v.* [T] FORMAL to inform or tell someone about something: **apprise sb of sth** *The doctors will apprise you of your husband's progress.*

ap·proach[1] /əˈproʊtʃ/ Ac S3 W2 *v.*
1 MOVE TOWARD [I,T] to move toward or nearer to someone or something: *Three people approached me, asking for money.* | *When I approached, the deer immediately ran away.*
2 ASK [T] to ask someone for something, or ask them to do something, especially when you are not sure they will be interested: *Nash has already been approached by several pro football teams.* | **approach sb/sth about (doing) sth** *The company confirmed that it had been approached about a merger.* | **approach sb for sth** *Students should be able to approach teachers for advice.* → see also APPROACHABLE
3 FUTURE EVENT [I,T] if an event or a particular time approaches, or you approach it, it is coming nearer and will happen soon: *She was spending more time in the kitchen as Christmas approached.* | *Warren was in his late 50s and approaching retirement.* | *The end of the semester is* ***fast approaching***.
4 ALMOST REACH STH [I,T] to almost reach a particular high level or amount, or an extreme condition or state: *Temperatures could approach 100° today.*
5 DEAL WITH [T] to begin to deal with a difficult situation in a particular way or with a particular attitude: *Researchers are looking for new ways to approach the problem.*
[**Origin:** 1300–1400 Old French *aprochier*, from Late Latin *appropiare*, from Latin *ad-* **to** + *prope* **near**]

approach[2] Ac W1 *n.* **1** [C] a method of doing something or dealing with a problem: +**to** *a new approach to teaching languages* | *Higgins* ***took a diplomatic approach.*** **2** [C] a request from someone, asking you to do something for them: *Hanson made an approach regarding a company buyout.* **3** [C] a road, path etc. that leads to a place, and is the main way of reaching it: *The approach to the house was an old dirt road.* **4** [C,U] a movement toward or near something: *The plane was on its final approach to the airport when it crashed.* **5 the approach of sth** FORMAL the approach of a particular time or event is the fact that it is getting closer: *The plant usually dies with the approach of winter.*

ap·proach·a·ble /əˈproʊtʃəbəl/ Ac *adj.* friendly and easy to talk to: *An excellent manager must be very approachable.*

ap·pro·ba·tion /ˌæprəˈbeɪʃən/ *n.* [U] FORMAL official praise or approval

ap·pro·pri·ate[1] /əˈproʊpriɪt/ Ac S2 W2 *adj.* correct or right for a particular time, situation, or purpose OPP **inappropriate**: *We will take appropriate action once the investigation is over.* | +**for** *The movie is appropriate for children aged 12 and over.* | **it is appropriate (for sb) to do sth** *It is not appropriate to ask such personal questions in an interview.* | +**to** *They need to offer a salary appropriate to his experience and education.* | **an appropriate time/place** *I don't think this is the appropriate time to discuss this.* —**appropriately** *adv.*: *The police responded appropriately.* —**appropriateness** *n.* [U]

THESAURUS

appropriate used to talk about clothes or behavior that are right or acceptable for a particular situation: *an appropriate dress for the party*
suitable used to talk about something that has the right qualities for a particular person or purpose: *a suitable school for the children*
suited used to talk about someone who has the right qualities to do something: *He'd be well suited to the job.*

ap·pro·pri·ate[2] /əˈproʊpriˌeɪt/ Ac *v.* [T] **1** to take something for yourself, when you have no right to do this: *Carlin is suspected of appropriating company funds.* **2** to take something, especially money, to use for a particular purpose: **appropriate sth for sth** *Congress appropriated $11.7 billion for anti-drug campaigns.* [**Origin:** 1400–1500 Late Latin, past participle of *appropriare*, from Latin *ad-* **to** + *proprius* **own**] → see also MISAPPROPRIATE

ap·pro·pri·a·tion /əˌproʊpriˈeɪʃən/ *n.* [C,U] **1** ECONOMICS the process of saving or using money for a particular purpose, especially by a business or government: +**of** *the appropriation of $2 million for improving school buildings* **2** the act of taking control of something, usually without asking permission, and using it for your own purposes: *The exhibition focuses on Picasso's appropriation of photographs as the bases for his work.*

apˌpropriˈations bill *n.* [C] ECONOMICS a written proposal for a new law showing the planned spending on a particular FEDERAL or State government program, from money the government receives in tax. Each year, there are 13 appropriations bills which have to be approved by the Senate and the House of Representatives.

ap·prov·al /ə'pruvəl/ W3 *n.* **1** [C,U] official acceptance of a plan, proposal, or decision: *Approval of the plans for the new science lab is expected by next month.* | *We need parental approval before allowing students to go on field trips.* | *The FDA* ***granted approval*** *for 105 new drugs last year.* | *The bill has been sent to the House* ***for approval*** (=to be approved). | *The project has* ***won approval*** (=been approved) *from the planning commission.* | *The contract clearly says you must* ***seek approval*** *for any changes.* **2** [U] the fact or belief that someone or something is good or is doing the right things OPP **disapproval**: *The crowd of young Democratic supporters roared with approval.* | *Does the design* ***meet with*** *your* ***approval?*** | *Roger is still* ***seeking*** *his mother's* ***approval.*** | **nod/smile/clap etc. in approval** *The old women nodded their heads in approval.* **3 seal/stamp of approval** a statement or sign that someone has accepted something or believes that it is good: *The IMF has given its seal of approval to the government's economic strategy.* **4 on approval** if you take something home from a store on approval, you get permission to take it home without paying for it, in order to decide whether you like it well enough to buy it

ap·prove /ə'pruv/ S2 W2 *v.* **1** [T] to officially accept a plan, proposal etc.: *The Senate approved a plan for federal funding of local housing programs.*

THESAURUS

pass to officially accept a law or proposal, especially by voting: *Many anti-smoking laws have been passed.*
ratify to make a written agreement official by signing it: *The treaty was ratified by the Senate in 1988.*

2 [I] to think that someone or something is good or acceptable: *Some women do not join unions because their husbands do not approve.* | +**of** *Her parents didn't approve of the marriage.* [**Origin:** 1300–1400 Old French *aprover*, from Latin *approbare*, from *ad-* **to** + *probare* **to prove**]

ap·prov·ing /ə'pruvɪŋ/ *adj.* showing support or agreement for something: *an approving look* —**approvingly** *adv.*: *She smiled approvingly.*

ap·prox. the written abbreviation of APPROXIMATELY

ap·prox·i·mant /ə'prɑksəmənt/ *n.* [C] TECHNICAL a CONSONANT sound such as /w/ or /l/ made by air passing between the tongue or lip and another part of the mouth without any closing of the air passage

ap·prox·i·mate[1] /ə'prɑksəmɪt/ Ac *adj.* an approximate number, amount, or time is a little more or less than the exact number, amount etc.: *The approximate cost of materials for the class should be around $25.* [**Origin:** 1400–1500 Late Latin, past participle of *approximare* **to come near to**, from Latin *ad-* **to** + *proximare* **to come near**]

ap·prox·i·mate[2] /ə'prɑksəˌmeɪt/ Ac *v.* [T] FORMAL to be similar to something, but not exactly the same: *His snoring approximated the sound of a jet taking off.*

ap·prox·i·mate·ly /ə'prɑksəmɪtli/ Ac *adv.* a little more or less than an exact number, amount etc. SYN **about**: *The plane will be landing in approximately 20 minutes.* | *Approximately how far is it from here?*

ap·prox·i·ma·tion /əˌprɑksə'meɪʃən/ Ac *n.* [C,U] something that is similar to another thing, but not exactly the same: +**of/to** *The restaurant serves a close approximation of French cuisine.*

ap·pur·te·nance /ə'pɚt̚nəns/ *n.* [C usually plural] FORMAL something that you use or have with you when doing a particular activity

APR /ˌeɪ pi 'ɑr/ *n.* [C usually singular] ECONOMICS **Annual Percentage Rate** the rate of INTEREST that you must pay when you borrow money

après-ski /ˌæpreɪ 'ski, ˌɑ-/ *n.* [U] activities such as eating and drinking that you take part in after SKIING —**après-ski** *adj.* [only before noun] *après-ski clothes*

ap·ri·cot /'æprɪˌkɑt, 'eɪ-/ *n.* **1** [C] BIOLOGY a small round fruit that is orange or yellow and has a single large seed **2** [U] the color of this fruit —**apricot** *adj.*

A·pril /'eɪprəl/ WRITTEN ABBREVIATION **Apr.** *n.* [C,U] the fourth month of the year, between March and May: *This office opened* ***in April 2003.*** | *My new job starts* ***on April 3.*** | *Jenni got her hair cut really short* ***last April.*** | *I'm going to Africa* ***next April.*** | *We got married* ***April 12, 2003.*** [**Origin:** 1300–1400 Old French *avrill*, from Latin *Aprilis*] → see Grammar box at JANUARY

ˌApril 'fool *n.* [C] someone who is tricked on April Fools' Day, or the trick that is played on them

ˌApril 'Fools' Day *n.* [C,U] [singular] April 1, a day when people play tricks on each other

a pri·o·ri /ˌeɪ pri'ɔri, ˌɑ-, -praɪ-/ *adj., adv.* FORMAL using previous experiences or facts to decide what the likely result or effect of something will be. For example, "it is raining so the streets must be wet," is an a priori statement. → see also A POSTERIORI

a·pron /'eɪprən/ *n.* [C] **1** a piece of clothing that covers the front part of your clothes and is tied around your waist, worn to keep your clothes clean, especially while cooking **2 apron strings** INFORMAL the relationship between a child and its mother, especially in a relationship where the mother controls an adult son or daughter too much: *You're 25 years old, and you still haven't* ***cut the apron strings.*** | *It seems like Jeff is still* ***tied to*** *his mother's* ***apron strings.*** **3** the hard surface in an airport on which airplanes are turned around, loaded, unloaded etc. **4** ENG. LANG. ARTS the part of the stage in a theater that is in front of the curtain [**Origin:** 1500–1600 *a napron*, mistaken for *an apron*; *napron* (14–16 centuries) from Old French *naperon*, from *nape* **cloth**]

ap·ro·pos[1] /ˌæprə'poʊ, 'æprəˌpoʊ/ *adv.* FORMAL **apropos of sth** used to introduce a new subject that is related to something just mentioned: *She had nothing to say apropos of the latest developments.* | *He suddenly asked me* ***apropos of nothing*** (=not relating to anything previously mentioned), *if I liked cats.*

apropos[2] *adj.* [not before noun] appropriate for a particular situation: *Her remarks were very apropos.*

apse /æps/ *n.* [C] TECHNICAL the curved inside end of a building, especially the east end of a church

apt /æpt/ *adj.* **1 be apt to do sth** to have a tendency to do something: *Some of the employees are apt to arrive late on Mondays.* **2** exactly right for a particular situation or purpose: *"Intensive" is an apt description of the two-week course.* **3** FORMAL quick to learn and understand: *Paul was obviously an apt pupil.* [**Origin:** 1300–1400 Latin, past participle of *apere* **to fasten**] —**aptness** *n.* [U] → see also APTLY

apt. *n.* [C] the written abbreviation of APARTMENT

ap·ti·tude /'æptəˌtud/ *n.* [C,U] natural ability or skill, especially in learning: +**for/in** *Becky has a real aptitude for mathematics.*

'aptitude 'test *n.* [C] a test that measures your natural skills or abilities

apt·ly /'æptli/ *adv.* **aptly named/described/called etc.** named, described etc. in a way that seems very appropriate or right: *The hotel overlooking the ocean was aptly named The Lighthouse.*

aq·ua /'ɑkwɑ, 'æ-/ *n.* [U] a greenish-blue color —**aqua** *adj.*

aq·ua·cul·ture /'ɑkwəˌkʌltʃɚ, 'æk-/ *n.* the business of raising fish or SHELLFISH to sell as food

aq·ua·ma·rine /ˌɑkwəmə'rin, ˌæk-/ *n.* **1** [C,U] a greenish-blue jewel, or the type of stone it comes from **2** [U] a greenish-blue color —**aquamarine** *adj.*

a·quar·i·um /ə'kwɛriəm/ *n. plural* **aquariums** or **aquaria** /-riə/ [C] **1** a clear glass or plastic container for fish and other water animals **2** a building where people go to look at fish and other water animals

A·quar·i·us /ə'kwɛriəs/ *n.* **1** [U] the 11th sign of the ZODIAC, represented by a person pouring water and believed to affect the character and life of people born between January 20 and February 19 **2** [C] someone who was born between January 20 and February 19

a·quat·ic /ə'kwæṭɪk, ə'kwɑṭɪk/ *adj.* **1** BIOLOGY living or growing in water: *an aquatic plant* **2** involving or happening in water: *aquatic sports* [**Origin:** 1400–1500 French *aquatique*, from Latin *aqua* **water**] —**aquatically** /-kli/ *adv.*

aq·ua·tint /'ækwəˌtɪnt, 'ɑ-/ *n.* [C,U] a method of producing a picture using acid on a sheet of metal, or a picture printed using this method

aq·ue·duct /'ækwəˌdʌkt/ *n.* [C] a structure, especially one like a bridge, that carries water over a river or valley [**Origin:** 1500–1600 Latin *aquaeductus*, from *aquae* **of water** + *ductus* **act of leading**]

a·que·ous /'eɪkwiəs, 'ɑ-/ *adj.* TECHNICAL containing water or similar to water

ˌaqueous soˈlution *n.* [C] CHEMISTRY a liquid mixture of water and at least one other substance combined together

aq·ui·fer /'ækwəfɚ, 'ɑ-/ *n.* [C] EARTH SCIENCE a layer of stone or earth, under the surface of the ground, that contains water

aq·ui·line /'ækwəˌlaɪn, -lən/ *adj.* **1 aquiline nose** an aquiline nose has a curved shape like the beak of an EAGLE **2** LITERARY like an EAGLE

A·qui·nas /ə'kwaɪnəs/**, St. Thomas** (1225–1274) an Italian THEOLOGIAN and PHILOSOPHER whose ideas had an important influence on the Catholic part of the Christian religion

AR the written abbreviation of ARKANSAS

-ar /ɚ, ɑr/ *suffix* **1** [in adjectives] relating to something: *stellar* (=relating to stars) | *polar* (=relating to the North or South Pole) → see also -ULAR **2** [in nouns] someone who does something: *a beggar* (=who asks people for money) | *a liar* (=who tells lies)

Ar·ab /'ærəb/ *n.* [C] someone whose language is Arabic and whose family is originally from Arabia, the Middle East, or North Africa

ar·a·besque /ˌærə'bɛsk/ *n.* [C] ENG. LANG. ARTS **1** a position in BALLET, in which you stand on one foot with the other leg stretched out straight behind you **2** a decorative pattern of flowing lines

A·ra·bi·an¹ /ə'reɪbiən/ *adj.* coming from or relating to Arabia

Arabian² *n.* [C] a type of fast graceful horse

Ar·a·bic /'ærəbɪk/ *n.* [U] the language or writing of the Arabs, which is the main language of North Africa, the Middle East, and Arabia —**Arabic** *adj.*

ˌArabic ˈnumeral *n.* [C] MATH the sign 1, 2, 3, 4, 5, 6, 7, 8, 9, or 0, or a combination of these signs, used as a number → see also ROMAN NUMERAL

ar·a·ble /'ærəbəl/ *adj.* **arable land/soil** land or soil that is or can be used for growing crops [**Origin:** 1400–1500 Latin *arabilis*, from *arare* **to plow**]

a·rach·nid /ə'ræknɪd/ *n.* [C] BIOLOGY a small creature such as a SPIDER, that has eight legs and a body with two parts

a·rach·no·pho·bi·a /əˌræknə'foʊbiə/ *n.* [U] TECHNICAL a strong fear of SPIDERS

Ar·a·fat /'ærəfæt/**, Yas·ser** /'yæsɚ/ (1929–2004) the leader of the Palestinian Liberation Organization, from 1969 until 2004. He shared the Nobel Peace Prize in 1994 for helping to organize a peace plan between Israel and the Palestinians.

Ar·al Sea /ˌærəl 'si/ a sea that is surrounded by land, between Kazakhstan and Uzbekistan

A·rap·a·ho /ə'ræpəˌhoʊ/ a Native American tribe from the Great Plains region of the U.S. —**Arapaho** *adj.*

Ar·a·wak /'ærəˌwɑk, -ˌwæk/ a Native American tribe from the northwestern area of South America

ar·bi·ter /'ɑrbəṭɚ/ *n.* [C] **1** someone or something who influences society's opinions about what is stylish, socially acceptable etc.: **an arbiter of taste/fashion/culture etc.** *arbiters of style such as "Elle" magazine* | *He has long been considered one of society's moral arbiters.* **2** someone or something that settles an argument between two opposing sides: *The council is the* ***final arbiter*** *of the election process when there are disputes.*

ar·bi·trage /'ɑrbəˌtrɑʒ/ *n.* [U] ECONOMICS the process of buying something such as a COMMODITY or CURRENCY in one place and selling it in another place at the same time —**arbitrager** also **arbitrageur** /ˌɑrbətrɑ'ʒɚ/ *n.* [C]

ar·bi·trar·y /'ɑrbəˌtrɛri/ Ac *adj.* decided or arranged without any reason or plan, often unfairly: *arbitrary arrests and imprisonments* [**Origin:** 1400–1500 Latin *arbitrarius* **depending on the decision of a judge, uncertain**, from *arbiter*] —**arbitrariness** *n.* [U] —**arbitrarily** /ˌɑrbə'trɛrəli/ *adv.*

ar·bi·trate /'ɑrbəˌtreɪt/ *v.* [I,T] to officially judge how an argument between two opposing sides should be settled: *The commission has the power to arbitrate pay disputes.* | +**between** *A committee will arbitrate between management and unions.* —**arbitrator** *n.* [C]

ar·bi·tra·tion /ˌɑrbə'treɪʃən/ *n.* [U] the official process for settling a serious disagreement between two people or groups. The case is judged by an independent person or organization with the power to make decisions that both sides must accept and obey: *The dispute is* ***going to arbitration*** (=someone is being asked to arbitrate). | *The school district and teachers agreed to* ***binding arbitration*** (=judgments that must be accepted and followed by law).

ar·bor /'ɑrbɚ/ *n.* [C] a shelter in a park or yard made by making plants grow together on a frame shaped like an ARCH

ar·bo·re·al /ɑr'bɔriəl/ *adj.* BIOLOGY relating to trees, or living in trees

ar·bo·re·tum /ˌɑrbə'riṭəm/ *n.* [C] a place where trees are grown for scientific study

ar·bor·ist /'ɑrbərɪst/ *n.* [C] someone who studies and takes care of trees

arc¹ /ɑrk/ *n.* [C] **1** a curved shape: *The islands lie in an arc in the eastern Caribbean.* **2** MATH a smooth curved line that forms part of a circle or other curved shape **3** PHYSICS a flash of light formed by the flow of electricity between two points [**Origin:** 1300–1400 Old French, Latin *arcus* **bow, arch, arc**] → see also ARC LIGHT, ARC WELDING

arc² *v.* [I] **1** [always + adv./prep.] to move in a smooth curved line: *The Space Shuttle arced high above the Atlantic after takeoff.* **2** if electricity or electrical wires arc, they produce a flash of light because electricity jumps from one wire or object to another

ar·cade /ɑr'keɪd/ *n.* [C] **1** a special room or business where people go to play VIDEO GAMES **2** a passage or side of a building that has small stores next to it and is covered with an ARCHed roof **3** TECHNICAL a passage with an ARCHed roof supported by PILLARS [**Origin:** 1700–1800 French, Italian *arcata*, from *arca* **arch**]

Ar·ca·di·a /ɑr'keɪdiə/ *n.* [singular, U] LITERARY a place or scene of simple pleasant country life

ar·cane /ɑr'keɪn/ *adj.* LITERARY secret and known or understood by only a few people: *the arcane language of lawyers* [**Origin:** 1500–1600 Latin *arcanus* **secret**, from *arca* **box**]

arch¹ /ɑrtʃ/ *n.* [C] **1** a structure with a curved top and straight sides that supports the weight of a bridge or building **2** a curved structure above a door, window etc. **3** BIOLOGY a curved structure of bones in the middle of your foot **4** a shape with a curved top and straight sides [**Origin:** 1200–1300 Old French *arche*, from Latin *arcus* **bow, arch, arc**]

arch² *v.* [I,T] to form or make something form a curved shape: *Two rows of trees arched over the driveway.* | *The dog arched its back and showed its teeth.*

arch³ *adj.* showing that you are amused because you think you understand something better than other people —**archly** *adv.* → see also ARCH-

arch- /ɑrtʃ, ɑrk/ *prefix* belonging to the highest class or rank: *an archbishop* (=an important BISHOP) | *our archenemy* (=our worst enemy) | *the company's archrivals* (=main competitors) [**Origin:** Old French, Latin *arch-*, *archi-*, from Greek, from *archein* **to begin, rule**]

ar·chae·a /ɑr'kiə/ also **arch·ae·bac·te·ri·a** /ˌɑrkibæk'tɪriə/ *n.* [plural] BIOLOGY very small living things that consist of a single cell. They are similar in size and shape to BACTERIA.

ar·chae·ol·o·gy, **archeology** /ˌɑrki'ɑlədʒi/ *n.* [U] the study of ancient societies by examining what remains of their buildings, graves, tools etc. —**archaeological** /ˌɑrkiə'lɑdʒɪkəl/ *adj.*: *an archaeological dig* —**archaeologically** /-kli/ *adj.* —**archaeologist** /ˌɑrki'ɑlədʒɪst/ *n.* [C]

ar·cha·ic /ɑr'keɪ-ɪk/ *adj.* **1** old and not used anymore: *The text was full of archaic spellings.* **2** old-fashioned and needing to be replaced: *an archaic sound system* **3** from or relating to ancient times: *archaic civilizations* [**Origin:** 1800–1900 French *archaïque*, from Greek *archaikos* **ancient**]

ar·cha·ism /'ɑrkiˌɪzəm, -keɪ-/ *n.* [C] FORMAL ENG. LANG. ARTS an old word or phrase that is not used anymore

arch·an·gel /'ɑrkˌeɪndʒəl/ *n.* [C] one of the chief ANGELS in the Jewish, Christian, and Muslim religions

arch·bish·op /ˌɑrtʃ'bɪʃəp◂/ *n.* [C] a priest with a very high rank, who is in charge of all the churches in a particular area

arch·di·o·cese /ɑrtʃ'daɪəsɪs, -ˌsiz/ *n.* [C] the area that is governed by an archbishop

arch·duke /ˌɑrtʃ'duk◂/ *n.* [C] a prince who belonged to the royal family of Austria

ar·che·go·ni·um /ˌɑrkɪ'goʊniəm/ *n. plural* **archegonia** /-niə/ [C] BIOLOGY the female sex organ of some plants, such as MOSSES, FERNS, and CONIFERS

arch·en·e·my /ˌɑrtʃ'ɛnəmi/ *n. plural* **archenemies** [C] **1** someone's main enemy **2 the Archenemy** LITERARY the DEVIL

ar·che·o·cyte /'ɑrkiəˌsaɪt/ *n.* [C] BIOLOGY a type of cell found in SPONGES (=simple sea creatures) that is capable of developing into other types of cells

ar·che·ol·o·gy /ˌɑrki'ɑlədʒi/ *n.* [U] another spelling of ARCHAEOLOGY

arch·er /'ɑrtʃɚ/ *n.* [C] someone who shoots ARROWS from a BOW

arch·er·y /'ɑrtʃəri/ *n.* [U] the sport of shooting ARROWS from a BOW

ar·che·type /'ɑrkɪˌtaɪp/ *n.* [C] **1** [usually singular] a perfect example of something, because it has all the most important qualities of things that belong to that type: +**of** *France is seen as the archetype of the centralized nation-state.* **2** TECHNICAL a character in a story, movie etc. or a person who is very familiar to people and is considered a model for other characters etc.: *The biblical Mary is a powerful cultural archetype.* —**archetypal** /ˌɑrkɪ'taɪpəl◂/ *adj.* —**archetypical** /ˌɑrkɪ'tɪpɪkəl/ *adj.*

Ar·chi·me·des /ˌɑrkə'midiz/ (287–212 B.C.) a MATHEMATICIAN and inventor in ancient Greece

ˌArchimedes' ˌprinciple PHYSICS a scientific principle that says that an object placed in water will be affected by a force from below that is equal to the weight of the water moved by the object

ar·chi·pel·a·go /ˌɑrkə'pɛləˌgoʊ/ *n. plural* **archipelagos** [C] EARTH SCIENCE a group of small islands

ar·chi·tect /'ɑrkəˌtɛkt/ *n.* [C] **1** someone whose job is to design buildings and other large structures **2 the architect of sth** the person who originally thought of an important and successful idea: *the chief architect of Russia's economic reforms* [**Origin:** 1500–1600 French *architecte*, from Latin, from Greek *architekton* **chief builder**]

ar·chi·tec·ture /'ɑrkəˌtɛktʃɚ/ *n.* **1** [U] the style and design of a building or buildings: *modern architecture* | +**of** *the architecture of Venice* **2** [U] the art and business of planning and designing buildings **3** [U] the structure of something: *Minerals are understood in terms of their molecular architecture.* **4** [C,U] COMPUTERS the structure of a computer system and the way it works —**architectural** /ˌɑrkə'tɛktʃərəl/ *adj.*: *architectural features* —**architecturally** *adv.*: *The building plans were not architecturally appropriate for the neighborhood.*

ar·chive¹ /'ɑrkaɪv/ *n.* [C] **1** also **archives** [plural] a place where a large number of historical records are stored, or the records that are stored: *the National Archives in Washington, D.C.* | **archive photographs/recordings/tapes etc.** (=photographs etc. that are from an archive) **2** COMPUTERS copies of a computer's FILES that are stored on a DISK or in the computer's MEMORY in a way that uses less space than usual, so that the computer can keep them for a long time [**Origin:** 1600–1700 French, Latin *archivum*, from Greek *archeion* **government building**] —**archival** /ɑr'kaɪvəl/ *adj.*: *archival footage of the President's 1969 visit*

archive² *v.* [T] **1** to keep documents, books information etc. in an archive: *NOAA will analyze and archive data from satellites.* **2** COMPUTERS to save a computer FILE in a way that uses less space than usual, because you are not likely to use that FILE often but may need it in the future

ar·chi·vist /'ɑrkɪvɪst, -kaɪ-/ *n.* [C] someone who works in an archive

arch·ri·val /ˌɑrtʃ'raɪvəl/ *n.* [C] the person, team etc. who is your main competitor

arch·way /'ɑrtʃweɪ/ *n. plural* **archways** [C] a passage or entrance under an ARCH or ARCHES

-archy /ɚki, ɑrki/ *suffix* [in nouns] used to talk about a particular type of government: *anarchy* (=no government) | *monarchy* (=having a king or queen)

'arc light also **'arc lamp** *n.* [C] an electric light that produces a very bright light by passing electricity through a special gas

Arc·tic /'ɑrktɪk, 'ɑrṭɪk/ *n.* **the Arctic** the large area surrounding the North Pole

arc·tic /'ɑrktɪk, 'ɑrṭɪk/ *adj.* **1** also **Arctic** relating to or from the most northern part of the world **2** extremely cold: *arctic conditions* [**Origin:** 1300–1400 Latin *arcticus*, from Greek, from *arktos* **bear, Ursa Major** (= bear-shaped group of stars in the northern sky), north] ▸see THESAURUS box at **cold¹**

ˌArctic 'Circle *n.* **the Arctic Circle** an imaginary line drawn around the world at a particular distance from the most northern point (the North Pole) → see also ANTARCTIC CIRCLE → see picture at GLOBE

ˌArctic 'Ocean, the the ocean that surrounds the North Pole

ˌarc 'welding *n.* [U] a method or process of joining two pieces of metal together by heating them with a special tool

-ard /ɚd/ *suffix* [in nouns] someone who is usually or always in a particular state: *a drunkard*

ar·dent /'ɑrdnt/ *adj.* [usually before noun] **1** showing strong positive feelings about an activity and determination to succeed at it: *an ardent advocate of gun control* **2** LITERARY showing strong feelings of love: *an ardent lover* [**Origin:** 1300–1400 Old French, Latin, present participle of *ardere* **to burn**] —**ardently** *adv.*

ar·dor /'ɑrdɚ/ [U] **1** very strong admiration or excitement: *the revolutionary ardor of the reformers* **2** LITERARY strong feelings of love

ar·du·ous /'ɑrdʒuəs/ *adj.* involving a lot of strength and effort: *an arduous trip through the mountains* [**Origin:** 1500–1600 Latin *arduus* **high, steep, difficult**] —**arduously** *adv.* —**arduousness** *n.* [U]

are /ɚ; *strong* ɑr/ the present tense plural form of "be" [**Origin:** Old English *earun*]

A

ar·e·a /ˈɛriə/ Ac S1 W1 *n.* [C] **1** a particular part of a country, city etc.: *People from this area have traditionally worked in farming.* | **+of** *Many areas of Africa have suffered severe drought this year.* | **rural/urban/residential/coastal etc. areas** *There were over two inches of rain in coastal areas.* | *The police have searched the farm and* ***the surrounding area*** (=the area around a place). | *The fire* ***in the downtown area*** (=somewhere in or near downtown) *was quickly put out.* | ***Area residents*** (=people who live in a particular area) *complained about the noise.*

THESAURUS

region a large area of a country or the world: *the northwest region of Russia*
zone an area that is different in a particular way from the areas around it: *a no-parking zone*
district a particular area of a city or the country: *the financial district in Manhattan*
neighborhood an area of a town where people live: *a friendly neighborhood*
suburb an area outside the center of a city where people live: *a suburb of Boston*
slum an area of a city that is in very bad condition, where many poor people live: *one of the city's worst slums*
ghetto a very poor area of a city, usually where people of a particular race or class live: *the urban ghettos of Los Angeles*

2 a part of a house, office, yard etc. that is used for a particular purpose: *a no-smoking area* | *Each apartment has a storage area in the basement.* | *Their apartment has a large kitchen area.* **3** a part of the surface of something such as land, water, or skin: *The wreckage was spread over a wide area.* | **+of** *a small area of skin* **4** a particular subject, range of activities, or group of related subjects: *We're funding research in new areas like law enforcement technology.* | *The course covers three main* ***subject areas***. | **+of** *They have made some improvements in the area of human rights.* | *I'm afraid cooking is not my* ***area of expertise*** (=I cannot cook well). **5** MATH a measurement of the amount of space that a flat surface or shape covers: **+of** *Use this formula to calculate the area of a circle.* | *The lake has an area of 2,000 square miles.* [**Origin:** 1500–1600 Latin **piece of flat ground**] → see also **a gray area** at GRAY[1] (4)

ˈarea ˌcode *n.* [C] a group of three numbers you use before a telephone number when you want to call someone in a different area of the U.S. or Canada

ˈarea rug *n.* [C] a RUG that covers part of the floor in a room

a·re·na /əˈrinə/ *n.* [C] **1** a building with a large flat central area surrounded by seats, where sports or entertainments take place: *a new sports arena* **2** a particular area of activity such as politics, public life etc.: *He has made impressive achievements in this arena.* | **the political/public/international etc. arena** *Women are entering the political arena in larger numbers.* [**Origin:** 1600–1700 Latin **sand, sandy place**]

A·rendt /ˈɛrənt, ˈɑr-/, **Han·nah** /ˈhænə/ (1906–1975) a U.S. political PHILOSOPHER

aren't /ˈɑrənt/ *v.* **1** the short form of "are not": *They aren't here.* **2** the short form of "am not," used in questions: *I'm in big trouble, aren't I?*

Ar·es /ˈɑriz, ˈɛriz/ in Greek MYTHOLOGY, the god of war

Ar·gen·ti·na /ˌɑrdʒənˈtinə/ a large country in the southern part of South America —**Argentinean** /ˌɑrdʒənˈtɪniən/ *n., adj.*

ar·gon /ˈɑrgɑn/ *n.* [U] SYMBOL **Ar** CHEMISTRY a chemically inactive gas that is an ELEMENT and is found in the air and is sometimes used in electric lights [**Origin:** 1800–1900 Greek *argos* **lazy**; because it does not react chemically]

ar·got /ˈɑrgət, -goʊ/ *n.* [C,U] ENG. LANG. ARTS expressions used by a particular group of people SYN **jargon**: *teenage argot*

ar·gu·a·ble /ˈɑrgyuəbəl/ *adj.* **1** not certain, or not definitely true or correct, and therefore easy to doubt SYN **debatable**: *Whether or not Webb is the best person for the job is arguable.* **2 it is arguable that...** used in order to give good reasons why something might be true: *It is arguable that the changes have done more harm than good.*

ar·gu·a·bly /ˈɑrgyuəbli/ *adv.* used to say that there are good reasons why something might be true, although some people may disagree: **arguably the best/biggest/worst etc.** *Senna was arguably the greatest race car driver of all time.*

ar·gue /ˈɑrgyu/ S2 W1 *v.* **1** [I] to disagree with someone in words, often in an angry way SYN **fight** SYN **quarrel**: *We could hear the neighbors arguing.* | **+with** *He was sent off the court for arguing with a referee.* | **+about/over** *They were arguing about how to spend the money.* | *The kids were arguing over which TV program to watch.*

THESAURUS

argue or **have an argument**: *They started arguing over money.* | *We've had serious arguments before but never split up.*
fight or **have a fight**: *My mom and dad were always fighting.* | *The neighbors had a huge fight.*
quarrel or **have a quarrel** to have an angry argument: *They were quarreling about whose turn it was to wash the dishes.* | *She had a quarrel with her boyfriend.*
squabble/bicker to argue about unimportant things: *The kids were bickering over what program to watch.*

2 [I,T] to state, giving clear reasons, that something is true, should be done etc.: *a well-argued case* | **argue that** *They argued that a dam might actually increase the risk of flooding.* | **argue for/against doing sth** *He continues to argue against cutting the military budget.* | *Legal groups* ***argued the case for*** *changing the laws.* **3 sth argues for/against sth** used to say that something shows that something else is or isn't true or a good idea: *All the available evidence argues against continuing the program.* **4 you can't argue with that!** SPOKEN used to say that something sounds very good and impressive: *"You get three classes for only $20." "You can't argue with that."* [**Origin:** 1300–1400 Old French *arguer*, from Latin *arguere* **to make clear**]

ar·gu·ment /ˈɑrgyəmənt/ S2 W2 *n.* **1** [C] a situation in which two or more people disagree, often angrily: **+with** *I broke the vase during an argument with my husband.* | **+about/over** *an argument over who was at fault* | *Henning told the police she and her husband* ***had an argument*** *before he left.* | *I* ***got into an argument*** *with the other driver.* | *Shelton and the woman had a* ***heated argument*** (=very angry argument). **2** [C] a set of reasons that show that something is true or untrue, right or wrong etc.: *Rose presented a good argument.* | **+for/against** *a powerful argument against smoking* | *the* ***arguments in favor*** *of gun control* | **argument that** *the familiar argument that poverty breeds crime* **3** [U] the act of disagreeing or questioning something: *Nathan accepted the decision* ***without argument***. | *I'm not sure that's an accurate description, but* ***for the sake of argument*** (=in order to discuss all the possibilities) *I'll accept it.*

ar·gu·men·ta·tion /ˌɑrgyəmənˈteɪʃən/ *n.* [U] the way you organize your ideas and use language to support your views or to persuade people

ar·gu·men·ta·tive /ˌɑrgyəˈmɛntət̬ɪv/ *adj.* someone who is argumentative often argues or likes arguing: *an argumentative lawyer*

ar·gyle /ˈɑrgaɪl/ *n.* [U] a pattern of DIAMOND shapes and crossed lines, used especially on clothing

a·ri·a /ˈɑriə/ *n.* [C] a song that is sung by only one person in an OPERA or ORATORIO

-arian /ɛriən/ *suffix* **1** [in nouns] someone who believes in or does a particular thing: *a vegetarian* (=someone who does not eat meat) | *a librarian* (=someone who works in a library) → see also -GENARIAN **2** [in adjectives] for people who believe in or do a particular thing, or relating to them: *a vegetarian restaurant* | *an egalitarian society*

ar·id /ˈærɪd/ *adj.* **1** EARTH SCIENCE getting very little rain, and therefore very dry: *an arid climate* **2** an arid discussion, period of time etc. does not produce anything new —**aridity** /əˈrɪdəṭi/ *adj.*

Ar·ies /ˈɛriz/ *n.* **1** [U] the first sign of the ZODIAC, represented by a RAM (=male sheep), and believed to affect the character and life of people born between March 21 and April 20 **2** [C] someone who was born between March 21 and April 20

a·right /əˈraɪt/ *adv.* OLD-FASHIONED **1 set sth aright** to settle problems or difficulties: *Payne was helpful as the bank struggled to set itself aright.* **2** correctly

A·rik·a·ra /əˈrɪkərə/ a Native American tribe from the northern central area of the U.S.

a·rise /əˈraɪz/ W3 *v. past tense* **arose** /əˈroʊz/, *past participle* **arisen** /əˈrɪzən/ [I] **1** if something arises from or out of a situation, event etc., it is caused or started by that situation etc.: **+from/out of** *The civil war arose from the social injustices present in the country.* | *Several legal* ***questions arose*** *in the contract negotiations.* **2** if a problem or difficult situation arises, it begins to happen: *More problems are certain to arise.* **3 when/if the need arises** also **should the need arise** when or if it is necessary: *They are ready to fight if the need arises.* **4** LITERARY to get out of bed, or stand up: *Daniel arose at dawn.* **5** LITERARY if a group of people arise, they fight for or demand something they want [**Origin:** Old English *arisan*]

Ar·is·tide /ˌɑrɪˈstid/, **Jean-Ber·trand** /ʒɑn bɛrˈtrɑn/ (1953–) the former President of Haiti. He was first elected in 1990 but was forced by the army to leave the country in 1991. He was also President from 1994 to 1996, and again in 2001, but was forced to leave Haiti in 2004 after violent public protests against him.

ar·is·toc·ra·cy /ˌærəˈstɑkrəsi/ *n. plural* **aristocracies** **1** [C usually singular] the people in the highest social class, who traditionally have a lot of land, money, and power: *The nation's elite sends its children to boarding schools in the tradition of the British aristocracy.* **2** [U] POLITICS the system in which a country is governed by the people of the highest social class **3** [singular] HISTORY the group of rich and powerful men from a high social class who ruled the city states and controlled the government of ancient Greece [**Origin:** 1400–1500 French *aristocratie*, from Late Latin, from Greek *aristokratia*, from *aristos* **best** + *-kratia* **-cracy**] → see also DEMOCRACY

a·ris·to·crat /əˈrɪstəˌkræt/ *n.* [C] someone who belongs to the highest social class

a·ris·to·crat·ic /əˌrɪstəˈkræṭɪk/ *adj.* belonging to or typical of the aristocracy: *Pamela came from an aristocratic background.* | *his aristocratic manner*

Ar·is·toph·a·nes /ˌærɪˈstɑfəniz/ (?457–?385 B.C.) a writer from ancient Greece, famous for his humorous plays

a·rith·me·tic¹ /əˈrɪθməˌtɪk/ *n.* [U] MATH the science of numbers involving adding, multiplying etc. [**Origin:** 1200–1300 Old French *arismetique*, from Latin, from Greek, from *arithmein* **to count**] → see also MATHEMATICS

ar·ith·met·ic² /ˌærɪθˈmɛṭɪk◂/ also **ar·ith·met·i·cal** /ˌærɪθˈmɛṭɪkəl/ *adj.* MATH involving or related to arithmetic —**arithmetically** /-kli/ *adv.*

ˌarithmetic ˈmean *n.* [C] MATH the average of two or more numbers, amounts, or values, calculated by adding the numbers together and dividing the result by how many numbers there are. For example the arithmetic mean of 12 and 6 is 9: (12 + 6) ÷ 2 = 9.

ˌarithmetic proˈgression *n.* [C] MATH a set of numbers in order of value in which a particular number is added to each to produce the next (as in 2, 4, 6, 8...) → see also GEOMETRIC PROGRESSION

ˌarithmetic ˈsequence also **arithmetic progression** *n.* [C] MATH a list of related numbers formed by adding or SUBTRACTing one particular number to each of the numbers in the series. So, for example, 2, 4, 6, 8 is an arithmetic sequence in which the number 2 has been added to each number in the list. → see also GEOMETRIC SEQUENCE, NON-LINEAR PROGRESSION

ˌarithmetic ˈseries *n. plural* **arithmetic series** [C] MATH the sum of the numbers in an arithmetic sequence

Ar·i·zo·na /ˌærɪˈzoʊnə/ ABBREVIATION **AZ** a state in the southwestern U.S.

ark /ɑrk/ *n.* [C] **1 the Ark** in the Bible, the large boat built by Noah to save his family and the animals from a flood that covered the Earth **2** a large ship

Ar·kan·sas /ˈɑrkənˌsɔ/ ABBREVIATION **AR** a state in the southern central part of the U.S.

ˌArk of the ˈCovenant *n.* **the Ark of the Covenant** a box containing the laws of the Jewish religion that ancient Jews carried with them as they traveled through the desert

Ar·ling·ton Na·tion·al Cem·e·ter·y /ˌɑrlɪŋtən ˌnæʃənəl ˈsɛməˌtɛri/ a CEMETERY in Arlington, Virginia, where people who were in the U.S. army, navy, air force, or government are sometimes buried

arm¹ /ɑrm/ S1 W1 *n.* [C]

1 BODY BIOLOGY one of the two long parts of your body between your shoulders and your hands: *Dana broker her left arm.* | *He had a pile of books* ***in his arms.*** | *Pat was carrying a large box* ***under his arm.*** | *My mother* ***put*** *her* ***arms around*** *me.* | *a couple walking on the beach* ***arm in arm*** (=with their arms bent around each other's) | *She* ***took*** *him* ***by the arm*** (=led him by holding his arm) *and pushed him out of the door.* | *Jerry* ***took*** *Barbara* ***in his arms*** (=held her gently) *and kissed her.* | **cross/fold your arms** (=bend your arms so that they are resting on top of each other against your body, especially as a sign that you are angry)

2 WEAPONS arms [plural] weapons used for fighting wars SYN **weapons**: *sales of arms to terrorists* | *nuclear arms* | *the* ***arms trade*** | *Boys as young as 13 are* ***taking up arms*** (=getting weapons and fighting) *to defend the city.* | *He appealed for the rebels to* ***lay down their arms*** (=stop fighting). → see also SMALL ARMS

3 FURNITURE the part of a chair, SOFA etc. that you rest your arms on: *the arm of the couch*

4 CLOTHING the part of a piece of clothing that covers your arm SYN **sleeve**

5 be up in arms if a group of people is up in arms, they are angry and ready to argue: *Residents are up in arms about plans for a new road along the beach.*

6 with open arms if you do something with open arms, you show that you are happy to see someone or eager to accept something or someone: *My new in-laws welcomed me with open arms.*

7 sb would give their right arm to do sth used to say that someone would be willing to do anything to get or do something: *I would give my right arm to meet Bono.*

8 at arm's length if you hold something at arm's length, you hold it away from your body

9 keep/hold sb at arm's length to avoid developing a relationship with someone: *She had always kept men at arm's length to avoid getting hurt.*

10 as long as your arm INFORMAL a list or written document that is as long as your arm is very long

11 PART OF GROUP a part of a large group that is responsible for a particular type of activity: *the U.S. marketing arm of a Japanese company*

12 OBJECT/MACHINE a long part of an object or piece of equipment: *A 15-foot arm supports the antenna.*

13 on your arm OLD-FASHIONED if a man has a woman on his arm, she is walking beside him holding his arm

14 DESIGN arms [plural] a set of pictures or patterns, usually painted on a SHIELD, that is used as the special sign of a family, town, university etc. SYN **coat of arms**

[**Origin:** (1, 3, 4, 6–13) Old English *earm*] → see also **arms akimbo** at AKIMBO (1), **brothers in arms** at

BROTHER[1] (6), **cost an arm and a leg** at COST[2] (5), **fold sb in your arms** at FOLD[1] (8), **a shot in the arm** at SHOT[1] (14), **twist sb's arm** at TWIST[1] (10)

arm² *v.* [T] **1** to provide weapons for yourself, an army, a country etc. in order to prepare for a fight or a war: **arm sb with sth** *Local farmers have armed themselves with rifles and pistols.* → see also ARMED, UNARMED **2** to provide all the information, power etc. that are needed to deal with a difficult situation or argument: **arm sb with sth** *Arm yourself with all the documents you have to show you qualify for a loan.* [**Origin:** 1200–1300 Old French *armer*, from Latin *armare*, from *arma*]

ar·ma·da /ɑr'mɑdə/ *n.* [C] **1** a large group of ships traveling together, especially war ships **2 the Armada** HISTORY a large number of war ships sent by Spain in 1588 to take control of England. The ships were defeated by the English navy. [**Origin:** 1500–1600 Spanish, Medieval Latin *armata* **army, group of war ships**]

ar·ma·dil·lo /ˌɑrmə'dɪloʊ/ *n. plural* **armadillos** [C] a small animal that has a shell made of hard bone-like material, and lives in warm parts of North and South America [**Origin:** 1500–1600 Spanish *armado* **armed person**]

Ar·ma·ged·don /ˌɑrmə'gɛdn/ *n.* [singular, U] a terrible battle that will destroy the world: *a nuclear Armageddon* [**Origin:** 1800–1900 Greek, place of a great battle at the end of the world, described in the Bible]

ar·ma·ment /'ɑrməmənt/ *n.* **1** [C usually plural] the weapons and military equipment used in an army: *nuclear armaments* **2** [U] the process of preparing an army or country for war by giving it weapons → see also DISARMAMENT

ar·ma·ture /'ɑrmətʃə/ *n.* [C] **1** TECHNICAL a frame that you cover with clay or other soft material to make a model **2** PHYSICS the part of a GENERATOR, motor etc. that turns around to produce electricity, movement etc.

arm·band /'ɑrmbænd/ *n.* [C] a band of material that you wear around your arm to show that you have an official position, or to show that someone you love has died

arm·chair¹ /'ɑrmtʃɛr/ *n.* [C] a comfortable chair with sides that you can rest your arms on → see picture at CHAIR[1]

armchair² *adj.* **an armchair traveler/quarterback/critic etc.** someone who talks or reads about being a traveler, watches a lot of sports on television etc., but does not have any real experience of doing it

armed /ɑrmd/ W3 *adj.* **1** carrying weapons, especially a gun: *an* ***armed guard*** | **+with** *The suspect is armed with a shotgun.* | *She got ten years in prison for* ***armed robbery*** (=stealing using a gun). | *The President fears that* ***armed conflict*** (=a war) *is possible.* | *their* ***armed struggle*** (=a fight using weapons) *against the government* | *a* ***heavily armed*** *battleship* | *Many of the gangs are* ***armed to the teeth*** (=carrying a lot of weapons). **2 armed with sth** having the knowledge, skills, or equipment you need to do something: *She came to the meeting armed with all the facts and figures to prove us wrong.*

ˌarmed 'forces also **ˌarmed 'services** *n.* **the armed forces/services** [plural] a country's military organizations

Ar·me·ni·a /ɑr'miniə/ a country in western Asia, north of Iran —**Armenian** *n., adj.*

arm·ful /'ɑrmfʊl/ *n.* [C] the amount of something that you can hold in one or both arms: **+of** *an armful of books*

arm·hole /'ɑrmˌhoʊl/ *n.* [C] a hole in a shirt, dress, JACKET etc. that you put your arm through

ar·mi·stice /'ɑrməstɪs/ *n.* [C] an agreement to stop fighting, usually for a short time → see also CEASE-FIRE, TRUCE

arm·load /'ɑrmloʊd/ *n.* [C] the amount that you can carry in one or both arms SYN **armful**: **+of** *an armload of boxes*

ar·moire /ɑrm'wɑr/ *n.* [C] a large piece of furniture with doors, and sometimes shelves, that you hang clothes in

ar·mor /'ɑrmə/ *n.* [U] **1** metal or leather clothing that protects your body, worn by soldiers in battles in past times: *a suit of armor* **2** a strong metal layer that protects military vehicles **3** a strong layer or shell that protects some plants and animals → see also **a chink in sb's armor** at CHINK[1], **a knight in shining armor** at KNIGHT[1] (4)

ar·mored /'ɑrməd/ **1** armored vehicles have an outside layer made of metal to protect them from attack: *armored personnel carriers* **2** an armored car has special protection from bullets etc. and is used especially by important people **3** an armored army uses armored vehicles: *an armored division*

ar·mor·er /'ɑrmərə/ *n.* [C] someone who makes or repairs weapons and ARMOR

ˌarmor-'plated *adj.* something, especially a vehicle, that is armor-plated has an outer metal layer to protect it —**armor plating** *n.* [U] —**armor plate** *n.* [U]

ar·mor·y /'ɑrməri/ *n. plural* **armories** [C] **1** a place where weapons are stored **2** all the skills, information etc. someone has available to use in arguments, discussions etc.: *Make sure your résumé reflects all the skills* ***in your armory***.

arm·pit /'ɑrmˌpɪt/ *n.* [C] **1** BIOLOGY the hollow place under your arm where it joins your body **2 the armpit of sth** INFORMAL the ugliest or worst place in a particular area: *These four blocks are the armpit of the city.*

arm·rest /'ɑrmrɛst/ *n.* [C] a part of a chair that supports your arm

'arms conˌtrol *n.* [U] POLITICS the attempts by powerful countries to limit the number and type of war weapons that exist

'arms race *n.* [C usually singular] **1** the competition between different countries to produce and have a large number of powerful weapons **2 the Arms Race** HISTORY the competition between the U.S. and the Soviet Union to produce and have the greatest number of powerful weapons, especially NUCLEAR weapons. The Arms Race began at the end of World War II and continued until the late 1980s. → see also THE COLD WAR

Arm·strong /'ɑrmstrɔŋ/, **Lance** /læns/ (1971–) a U.S. professional bicycle RACER who won an important long race in France seven times, between 1999 and 2005, after being treated for CANCER

Louis Armstrong

Armstrong, Louis /'lui/ (1900–1971) a U.S. JAZZ musician and singer, who played the TRUMPET

Armstrong, Neil /nil/ (1930–) a U.S. ASTRONAUT who was the first man to step onto the moon, in 1969

ar·my /'ɑrmi/ S2 W1 *n. plural* **armies** **1 the army** the part of a country's military force that is trained to fight on land in a war: *The army is helping to clean up after the floods.* | *Both my sons are* ***in the army***. | *Neil* ***joined the army*** *when he was 17.*

THESAURUS

soldiers/troops members of the army
the armed forces/the military/the service used to talk in a general way about the army, navy, marines, and air force
enlist to join the army: *He enlisted in the navy when he finished high school.*
be drafted to be ordered to serve in the army by the government
conscription also **the draft** when people are ordered to serve in the army etc.

2 [C] a large organized group of people trained to fight on land in a war: *Rebel armies have taken control of the* *capital.* | *The government says it can* ***raise an army*** (=get enough people to fight) *of 20,000 men.* **3** [C] a large number of people or animals involved in the same activity: +**of** *an army of ants* [**Origin:** 1300–1400 Old French *armee*, from Medieval Latin *armata* **army, group of war ships**] → see also AIR FORCE, MARINES, NAVY[1]

Ar·no, the /ˈɑrnoʊ/ a river in central Italy that flows westward from the Apennines and through the city of Florence

Ar·nold /ˈɑrnəld/**, Ben·e·dict** /ˈbɛnədɪkt/ (1741–1801) an American military leader in the American Revolutionary War, known for changing to support the British

a·ro·ma /əˈroʊmə/ *n.* [C] a strong nice smell: *the aroma of fresh coffee* ►see THESAURUS box at **smell**[1]

a·ro·ma·ther·a·py /əˌroʊməˈθɛrəpi/ *n.* [U] a treatment in which your body is rubbed with nice-smelling natural oils to reduce pain and make you feel well —**aromatherapist** *n.* [C]

ar·o·mat·ic /ˌærəˈmæt̬ɪk◂/ *adj.* **1** having a strong nice smell: *aromatic oils* **2** CHEMISTRY aromatic chemical substances contain a ring of six CARBON atoms —**aromatically** /-kli/ *adv.*

a·rose /əˈroʊz/ *v.* the past tense of ARISE

a·round[1] /əˈraʊnd/ S1 W1 *prep.* **1** placed or arranged to surround something else: *We put a fence around the backyard.* | *The whole family was sitting around the dinner table talking.* | *She had a beautiful shawl wrapped around her shoulders.* **2** moving in a circular movement: *A few wolves were prowling around the cabin.* **3 around 200/5,000 etc.** used when you do not know an exact number or amount to give a number or amount that is close to it SYN **approximately**: *The stadium seats around 50,000 people.* | *Greg must have drunk around 10 beers.* ►see THESAURUS box at **about**[2] **4** in many places or parts of a particular area or place: *We took a walk around the park after breakfast.* | *Our company has branches around the world.* | *There were flowers* ***all around*** *the apartment.* **5** in or near a place: *I think Miguel lives somewhere around the high school.* | *Is there a bank around here?* **6** along or past the side of something, instead of through or over it: *We had to go around the lake.* **7** if something is organized around a particular person or thing, it is organized according to their needs, ideas, beliefs etc.: *a society built around the belief of reincarnation* **8 get around sth** to avoid or solve a particular problem or difficult situation: *How do we get around the new tax laws?*

around[2] S1 W1 *adv.* **1** placed or arranged surrounding something else: *Reporters crowded around as Jensen left the courtroom.* | *The prison had high walls* ***all around.*** **2** [only after verb] used to say that someone or something is moving in a circular movement: *The children were dancing around in a circle.* | *Kevin spun around to greet me.* | *The helicopter continued flying* ***around and around,*** *searching for survivors.* **3 sit/stand/lie etc. around** to sit, stand etc. without doing anything in particular, especially so that people think you are wasting time: *A bunch of kids were* ***hanging around*** (=standing in this way) *outside.* **4** [only after verb] in many places or in many different parts of a particular area: *Don't leave all your clothes lying around.* | *I traveled around for a while before I got my first job.* | *Let me show you around.* **5 a)** existing or available to use: *That joke's been around for years.* | *I think the B-52's were the best band around at the time.* **b)** if someone is around, they are in the same place as you: *It was 11:30 at night, and no one was around.* **6 fool/mess/play etc. around a)** used to mean that someone is wasting time by doing something stupid or dishonest: *Stop messing around! I know you hid my purse.* **b)** to have a secret sexual relationship with someone you should not have one with, for example someone's wife or husband: *I caught Jeff fooling around with my best friend.* **7 get around to (doing) sth** to finally do something that you have been intending to do for a long time: *I'll get around to painting the bedroom one of these days.* **8** toward or facing the opposite direction: *I turned the car around.* **9 two feet/100 cm etc. around** measuring a particular distance on the outside of a round object: *Redwood trees can measure 30 or 40 feet around.* **10 have been around** INFORMAL **a)** to have had experience of many different situations, so that you can deal with new situations confidently: *"How do you know all this?" "Oh, I've been around."* **b)** HUMOROUS to have had many sexual experiences

ˌaround-the-ˈclock *adj.* [only before noun] continuous through all hours of the day and night: *around-the-clock medical care*

a·rou·sal /əˈraʊzəl/ *n.* [U] excitement, especially sexual excitement

a·rouse /əˈraʊz/ *v.* [T] **1** to make someone have a particular feeling or reaction SYN **generate**: **arouse interest/expectations etc.** *Why didn't Ames' behavior arouse suspicions at the CIA?* | **arouse anger/fear/dislike etc.** *The speech aroused anger in many people.* **2** to make someone feel sexually excited: *She could see he was aroused.* **3** LITERARY to wake someone: +**from** *Anne had to be aroused from a deep sleep.*

ar·peg·gi·o /ɑrˈpɛdʒiˌoʊ, -dʒoʊ/ *n.* [C] the notes of a musical CHORD played separately rather than all at once [**Origin:** 1700–1800 Italian *arpeggiare* **to play on the harp**]

ˈarr. **1** the written abbreviation of "arranged by" **2** the written abbreviation of "arrives" or "arrival"

ar·raign /əˈreɪn/ *v.* [T] LAW to make someone come to court to hear what the court says their crime is: **arraign sb on sth** *Thompson was* ***arraigned on*** *three* ***charges of*** *murder.* [**Origin:** 1300–1400 Old French *araisner*, from *raisnier* **to speak**, from Latin *ratio* **reason**] —**arraignment** *n.* [C,U]

ar·range /əˈreɪndʒ/ S3 W2 *v.* **1** [I,T] to organize or make plans for something such as a meeting, party, or trip: *Efforts to arrange a ceasefire have failed.* | **arrange to do sth** *Jessica arranged to pick us up.* | **arrange for sth** *I arranged for a private meeting between Donovan and the President.* | **arrange for sb to do sth** *Peter arranged for a friend to drive him there.* | **arrange sth with sb** *Dixon called to arrange an interview with Mrs. Tracy.* | **arrange when/where/how etc.** *Did you arrange where to meet?* | *Matthew arrived at 2:00* ***as arranged*** (=in the way that was planned). **2** [T] to put a group of things or people in a particular order or position: *I arranged the flowers in a vase.* **3** [T] ENG. LANG. ARTS to write or change a piece of music so that it is suitable for particular instruments: +**for** *The symphony has been arranged for the piano.* [**Origin:** 1300–1400 Old French *arangier*, from *rengier* **to put in a row**]

arˌranged ˈmarriage *n.* [C,U] a marriage in which the parents choose a husband or wife for their child

ar·range·ment /əˈreɪndʒmənt/ W3 *n.* **1** [C usually plural] a plan or preparation that you must make to be ready for something: *childcare arrangements* | ***Special arrangements*** *can be made for passengers in wheelchairs.* | +**for** *arrangements for our 10-year high school reunion* | *The travel company* ***made arrangements*** *for our hotels and flights.* **2** [C,U] something that has been organized or agreed on SYN **agreement**: *We have an arrangement that works for all of us.* | +**between** *an arrangement between the neighbors* | +**with** *We have an arrangement with a local taxi company.* | *Pets are permitted at the resort* ***by prior arrangement.*** | *I'm sure we can* ***come to some kind of an arrangement*** (=make an arrangement that is suitable for both people). **3** [C usually plural] the way things have been organized: *the seating arrangement in the room* | *My parents didn't approve of my* ***living arrangements*** (=where or how I was living). | *What are the* ***sleeping arrangements*** *if the whole family comes to stay?* **4** [C,U] a group of things that have been arranged in an attractive or neat way, or the way in which they have been arranged: *a flower arrangement* | *the arrangement of the vegetables on the plate* **5** [C,U] ENG. LANG. ARTS a piece of music that has been written or

A

changed for a particular instrument: *a piano arrangement of an old folk song* ►see THESAURUS box at **music**

ar•rant /ˈærənt/ *adj.* [only before noun] FORMAL used to emphasize how bad something is: **arrant nonsense/hypocrisy/fool etc.** *The article accused him of being "an arrant racist."*

ar•ray¹ /əˈreɪ/ *n. plural* **arrays** **1** [C usually singular] a group or people or a collection of things that are related in some way: **+of** *a dazzling array of acting talent* | **a vast/wide array** *The museum has a vast array of Indian art.* **2** [C] a number of pieces of equipment of the same type connected together to do a particular job: **+of** *an array of computer screens* **3** [C] MATH a set of numbers or signs, or of computer memory units, arranged in lines across or down **4** [U] LITERARY beautiful or impressive clothing, especially for a special occasion

array² *v.* **arrays, arrayed, arraying** [T usually passive] **1** LITERARY to arrange something in an attractive way: *military medals arrayed on a cushion* **2 be arrayed against sb/sth** FORMAL if large amounts of information, facts etc., or large numbers of people, are arrayed against someone or something, they are ready to be used or to work against them: *the powerful forces arrayed against the reform plan* **3** FORMAL to put soldiers in position ready for battle

ar•rears /əˈrɪrz/ *n.* [plural] **1 be in arrears** if someone is in arrears or if their payments are in arrears, they are late in paying something that they should pay regularly, such as rent: *The rent is two months in arrears.* | *The family* ***fell into arrears*** (=became late with payments) *when Ben lost his job.* **2** money that you owe someone because regular payments such as rent have not been paid at the right time: *When will the U.S.* ***pay*** *its* ***arrears*** *to the U.N.?* [**Origin:** 1400–1500 *arrear* **backward, behind** (14–18 centuries), from Old French *arere*, from Vulgar Latin *ad retro* **to the back**]

ar•rest¹ /əˈrɛst/ W2 *v.* [T] **1** if the police arrest someone, they take that person away because they think he/she did something illegal: *Police arrested 26 demonstrators.* | **arrest sb for sth** *He was arrested for assault.* | *She* ***got arrested*** *for drunk driving.* | *Police* ***arrested*** *Fletcher* ***on charges of*** (=arrested for the specific crime of) *embezzlement.* | *Five men were* ***arrested in connection with*** *the attack.* ►see THESAURUS box at **catch¹** **2** FORMAL to stop something that is happening, or to make it happen more slowly: *drugs used to arrest the spread of the disease* | *Smoking at an early age is thought to arrest growth in children.* **3 sb can't get arrested** HUMOROUS used to say that someone who used to be famous or popular is now not famous or popular at all: *She's a big star in Paris, but she couldn't get arrested in New York.* [**Origin:** 1300–1400 Old French *arester* **to rest, arrest**, from Latin *ad-* **to** + *restare* **to remain, rest**]

arrest² W3 *n.* [C,U] the act of taking someone away and guarding them because they may have done something illegal: **+for** *her arrest for drunk driving in 2004* | *The police expect to* ***make an arrest*** *soon.* | *Dillman is* ***under arrest*** (=kept by police) *for his role in the robbery.* | **place/put sb under arrest** *He was put under arrest and taken to the station.* | *She was* ***placed under house arrest*** (=forced by the police or government to stay in her house) *in 1989.*

ar•riv•al /əˈraɪvəl/ W3 *n.* **1** [U] the act of arriving somewhere OPP **departure**: *Porter spoke to reporters shortly after his arrival.* | **+in** *our arrival in Los Angeles* | **+at** *his arrival at the courthouse* | **+from** *the arrival of Flight 227 from Moscow* | *Wyler was rushed to the hospital, but was dead* ***on arrival*** (=when he arrived). **2 the arrival of sth a)** the time when an important new idea, method, or product is first used or discovered: *the arrival of picture cellphones* **b)** the time when an event or period of time starts to happen: *the arrival of winter* **3** [C] someone who has just arrived in a particular place to live, work etc.: *Most of the* ***new arrivals*** *stay in urban areas.* | ***Late arrivals*** *were turned away from the class.* **4 arrivals** the place in an airport where people arrive when they get off a plane: *the arrivals building* **5** HUMOROUS a baby: *Congratulations on your* ***new arrival!***

ar•rive /əˈraɪv/ S3 W1 *v.* [I]
1 GET SOMEWHERE to reach a particular place where you are going: **+in/at/from** *What time does the plane arrive in New York?* | *The fire trucks* ***arrived on the scene*** (=arrived where something was happening) *too late.* | **arrive early/late** *We finally arrived at Carol's two hours late.*

THESAURUS

get to to reach a particular place: *What time will you get to Atlanta?*
reach to arrive at a particular place: *The climbers reached the top of Mt. Everest.*
come if someone comes, he or she arrives at the place where you are: *When are Grandma and Grandpa coming?*
turn up also **show up** to arrive somewhere, used especially when someone is waiting for you: *Lee turned up an hour late for the meeting.*
get in to arrive at a particular time or in a particular place: *The plane got in at 8:15.*
come in if an airplane, train, or ship comes in, it arrives in the place where you are: *I'll be there to pick you up when the train comes in.*
land to arrive somewhere in an airplane, boat etc.: *The first U.S. Marines landed in Vietnam in 1965.*

2 BE DELIVERED if something arrives, it is brought or delivered to you: *The packages arrived the day before Christmas.* | **+from** *The oranges just arrived from Florida.*
3 EVENT if an event or particular period of time arrives, it happens: *The day of the wedding finally arrived.*
4 STH NEW if a new idea, method, product etc. arrives, it begins to exist or starts being used: *Since Broadband arrived, more customers are online all the time.*
5 BIRTH to be born: *Sharon's baby arrived just after midnight.*
6 arrive at a conclusion/agreement/idea etc. to reach an agreement etc. after a lot of effort: *The jurors finally arrived at a verdict.*
7 sb has arrived used in order to say that someone has achieved success.: *When he saw his name on the door, he knew he'd arrived!*
[**Origin:** 1100–1200 Old French *ariver*, from Vulgar Latin *arripare* **to come to shore**] ►see THESAURUS box at **reach¹**

ar•ro•gance /ˈærəgəns/ *n.* [U] DISAPPROVING the quality of thinking that you are more important than other people, so that you behave in an impolite way: *I was astonished at his arrogance.*

ar•ro•gant /ˈærəgənt/ *adj.* so proud of your own abilities or qualities that you behave as if you are much more important than anyone else: *an arrogant selfish man* | *an arrogant smile* [**Origin:** 1300–1400 Latin, present participle of *arrogare*, from Latin *ad-* **to** + *rogare* **to ask**] —**arrogantly** *adv.*

ar•ro•gate /ˈærəˌgeɪt/ *v.* **arrogate (to yourself) sth** FORMAL to claim that you have a particular right, position etc. without having the legal right to it

ar•row /ˈæroʊ/ S3 *n.* [C] **1** a weapon like a thin straight stick with a point at one end that you shoot with a BOW: *They fought with* ***bows and arrows.*** **2** a sign in the shape of an arrow, used to show people which direction to go or look in: *Follow the red arrows to the X-ray department.* [**Origin:** Old English *arwe*] → see also STRAIGHT ARROW

ar•row•head /ˈæroʊˌhɛd/ *n.* [C] a sharp pointed piece of metal or stone attached to one end of an arrow

ar•row•root /ˈæroʊˌrut/ *n.* [U] a type of flour made from the root of a tropical American plant

ar•se•nal /ˈɑrsənl/ *n.* [C] **1** a large number of weapons: **+of** *an arsenal of 700 surface-to-air missiles* **2** the equipment, methods, or skills that you have to help you achieve something, for example in an argument: *We now have a new software package* ***in our arsenal.*** **3** a building where weapons are stored [**Origin:** 1500–1600

Italian *arsenale*, from Arabic *dar sina'ah* **house where things are made**]

ar·se·nic /ˈɑrsənɪk, ˈɑrsnɪk/ *n.* [U] SYMBOL **As** CHEMISTRY a very poisonous substance that is an ELEMENT and is sometimes used for killing rats and included in some chemicals used to kill insects or WEEDS

ar·son /ˈɑrsən/ *n.* [U] the crime of deliberately making something burn, especially a building: *an arson attack* —**arsonist** *n.* [C]

art¹ /ɑrt/ S1 W1 *n.* **1** [U] the use of painting, drawing, SCULPTURE etc. to represent things or express ideas: *The book studies cartoons as a form of art.* | *Picasso and other Cubists changed the course of* ***modern art***. | *He quickly became famous in* ***the art world*** (=the part of society that is made up of artists and people who are interested in art).

THESAURUS

Types of art
painting the art or skill of making a picture using paint
drawing the art or skill of making a picture using a pen or pencil
photography the art or skill of producing photographs
sculpture the art or skill of making objects out of stone, wood, or clay
ceramics/pottery the art or skill of making pots, plates, etc. from clay
→ see THESAURUS box at **artist**

2 [U] objects that are produced by art, such as paintings, drawings etc.: *an art exhibition* | *an art museum* | *the themes that run through his art* | *The exhibit features 175* ***works of art***. **3** [U] the skill of drawing or painting: *Ben was always good at art.* | *an art class* **4 the arts** [plural] art, music, theater, movies, literature etc. all considered together: *government funding for the arts* → see also **fine arts** at FINE ART (2), LIBERAL ARTS **5** [C,U] the ability or skill involved in doing or making something: *Phil has* ***turned*** *sandwich-making* ***into an art***. | **the art of (doing) sth** *Television is ruining the art of conversation.* | *I* ***have*** *the early morning routine* ***down to a fine art*** (=can do it extremely skillfully). [**Origin:** 1200–1300 Old French, Latin *ars*]

art² *v.* **thou art** OLD USE used to mean "you are" when talking to one person

art dec·o /ˌɑrt ˈdɛkoʊ/ *n.* [U] a style of art and decoration that uses simple shapes and was popular in the U.S. and Europe in the 1920s and 1930s

ˈart diˌrector *n.* [C] someone whose job is to decide on the total appearance of a magazine, advertisement, movie, television program etc.

ar·te·fact /ˈɑrt̬ɪˌfækt/ *n.* [C] another spelling of ARTIFACT

Ar·te·mis /ˈɑrt̬ɪmɪs/ in Greek MYTHOLOGY, the goddess of hunting and the moon

ar·te·ri·al /ɑrˈtɪriəl/ *adj.* [only before noun] **1** BIOLOGY involving the arteries: *arterial blood* **2 an arterial street/railroad etc.** a main road, railroad etc.

ar·te·ri·o·scle·ro·sis /ɑrˌtɪrioʊskləˈroʊsɪs/ *n.* [U] MEDICINE a disease in which your arteries become hard, which stops the blood from flowing through them smoothly

ar·ter·y /ˈɑrt̬əri/ *n. plural* **arteries** [C] **1** BIOLOGY one of the tubes that carries blood from the heart to the rest of the body → see also VEIN → see picture at HEART **2** a main road, railroad, river etc.

ar·te·sian well /ɑrˌtiʒən ˈwɛl/ *n.* [C] a WELL from which the water is forced up out of the ground by natural pressure

ˈart film also **ˈart ˌmovie** *n.* [C] a movie that tries to express ideas rather than only entertain people

art·ful /ˈɑrtfəl/ *adj.* FORMAL **1** showing or resulting from a lot of skill and artistic ability: *The script is an artful adaptation of a novel by Rosa Guy.* **2** skillful at deceiving people: *artful misrepresentations* —**artfully** *adj.*: *artfully concealed pockets* —**artfulness** *n.* [U]

ˈart ˌgallery *n.* [C] a building where important paintings are kept and shown to the public

ˈart house *n.* [C] a movie theater that shows mainly foreign movies, or movies made by small movie companies, or art films

ar·thri·tis /ɑrˈθraɪt̬ɪs/ *n.* [U] MEDICINE a disease that causes a lot of pain in the joints of your body [**Origin:** 1500–1600 Latin, Greek, from *arthron* **joint**] —**arthritic** /ɑrˈθrɪt̬ɪk/ *adj.*: *arthritic fingers*

Ar·thur /ˈɑrθɚ/ in old European stories, a king of Britain —**Arthurian** /ɑrˈθʊriən/ *adj.*

Arthur, Ches·ter /ˈtʃɛstɚ/ (1829–1886) the 21st President of the U.S.

ar·ti·choke /ˈɑrt̬ɪˌtʃoʊk/ *n.* [C] **1** also **globe artichoke** BIOLOGY a plant with thick pointed leaves that are eaten as a vegetable → see picture on page A35 **2** also **Jerusalem artichoke** BIOLOGY a plant that has a root like a potato that you can eat [**Origin:** 1500–1600 Italian dialect *articiocco*, from Arabic *al-khurshuf* **the artichoke**]

ar·ti·cle /ˈɑrt̬ɪkəl/ S1 W2 *n.* [C] **1** a piece of writing about a particular subject in a newspaper, magazine etc.: *a newspaper article* | **+about/on** *Mayer* ***wrote an article*** *about the Hubble telescope.* ▸see THESAURUS box at **newspaper** **2** a thing, especially one of a group of things: *The prisoners can keep a few personal articles.* | *She didn't take much with her, just a few* ***articles of clothing***. ▸see THESAURUS box at **thing** **3** LAW a part of a law or legal agreement, especially a numbered part: *Article 1 of the U.S. Constitution guarantees freedom of religion.* **4** ENG. LANG. ARTS a word used before a noun to show whether the noun refers to a particular example of something or to a general example of something. In English, "the" is the DEFINITE ARTICLE, and "a" or "an" are INDEFINITE ARTICLES. **5 an article of faith** FORMAL something that you feel very strongly about so that it affects how you think or behave, even though it has not been proven true: *A balanced budget has become an article of faith for the party.* [**Origin:** 1100–1200 Old French, Latin *articulus* **joint, division**, from *artus* **joint**]

ˌArticles of Confeˈderation, the also **the ˌArticles of Confedeˌration and Perˌpetual ˈUnion** HISTORY an agreement made in 1781 by the original American colonies (COLONY) which established a system of government and laws for the new country until it was replaced in 1789 by the Constitution of the United States

ˌarticles of ˈpartnership *n.* [plural] ECONOMICS a formal written agreement between two or more people who are partners together in a business, stating each partner's legal rights and duties

ar·tic·u·late¹ /ɑrˈtɪkyəlɪt/ *adj.* **1** able to talk easily, clearly, and effectively about things, especially difficult subjects OPP **inarticulate**: *bright articulate 17-year-olds* **2** writing or speech that is articulate is very clear and easy to understand even if the subject is difficult **3** BIOLOGY having joints: *articulate insects* [**Origin:** 1500–1600 Latin, past participle of *articulare* **to divide into joints, speak clearly**, from *articulus* **joint, division**] —**articulately** *adv.* —**articulateness** *n.* [U]

ar·tic·u·late² /ɑrˈtɪkyəˌleɪt/ *v.* [I] **1** to express what you are thinking or feeling very clearly: *It's hard to articulate exactly what I felt.* **2** to speak or pronounce your words clearly and carefully SYN **enunciate**: *Try to articulate the second syllable better.*

ar·tic·u·lat·ed /ɑrˈtɪkyəˌleɪt̬ɪd/ *adj.* TECHNICAL having two or more parts that are connected by a moving joint: *an articulated mechanical arm*

ar·tic·u·la·tion /ɑrˌtɪkyəˈleɪʃən/ *n.* **1** [U] the production of speech sounds SYN **enunciation**: *clear articulation* **2** [C,U] the expression of thoughts or feelings in words: *The document is an articulation of the agency's goals.* **3** [C] TECHNICAL a joint, especially in a plant

ar·ti·fact /ˈɑrt̬ɪˌfækt/ *n.* [C] an object that was made and used a long time ago, especially one that is studied by scientists: *ancient Egyptian artifacts*

A

ar·ti·fice /ˈɑrtɪfɪs/ *n.* FORMAL **1** [U] skillful tricks or insincerity, used to deceive someone: *He answered without artifice.* **2** [C] a skillful trick SYN **device**: *the artifices of stage productions*

ar·ti·fi·cial /ˌɑrtəˈfɪʃəl◂ / *adj.* [usually before noun] **1** not made of natural materials or substances, but made by people OPP **natural**: *artificial sweeteners for coffee* | *Our ice cream contains no artificial colors or flavors.* **2** not real or natural, but deliberately made to look real or natural OPP **natural**: *artificial Christmas trees* | *Glen uses an artificial leg.*

THESAURUS

synthetic made from artificial substances, not natural ones: *synthetic fabrics*
man-made used about materials and structures that are made by people rather than being natural: *man-made substances* | *a man-made lake*
fake made to look or seem like something else in order to deceive people: *fake identity cards*
simulated not real, but made to look, sound, or feel real: *a simulated space journey*
imitation something that looks real, but that is a copy: *imitation pearls*
false not real, but intended to seem real: *He was using a false name.*
virtual made, done, seen etc. on the Internet, rather than in the real world: *a virtual tour of the White House*
→ NATURAL[1]

3 artificial behavior is not natural or sincere because someone is pretending to be something they are not: *an artificial smile* **4** happening because someone has made it happen and not as part of a natural process: *artificial barriers to trade* [**Origin:** 1300–1400 Old French *artificiel*, from Latin *artificium* from *artifex* **skilled worker**] —**artificially** *adv.*: *artificially flavored drinks* | *Food prices are being kept artificially low.* —**artificiality** /ˌɑrtəfɪʃiˈæləti/ *n.* [U]

ˌartificial insemiˈnation *n.* [U] BIOLOGY the process of making a woman or female animal PREGNANT using a piece of equipment, rather than naturally

ˌartificial inˈtelligence ABBREVIATION **AI** *n.* [U] COMPUTERS the study of how to make computers do things that people can do, such as make decisions, see things etc.

ˌartificial respiˈration *n.* [U] a way of making someone breathe again when they have stopped, by blowing air into their mouth SYN **mouth-to-mouth resuscitation**

ˌartificial seˈlection *n.* [U] BIOLOGY the process of only breeding plants and animals with qualities or features that are considered useful or desirable in order to develop plants and animals with only these good qualities or features → see also NATURAL SELECTION

ar·til·ler·y /ɑrˈtɪləri/ *n.* [U] large guns, either on wheels or standing in a particular place

ar·ti·san /ˈɑrtəzən, -sən/ *n.* [C] someone who does skilled work with their hands SYN **craftsman** —**artisanal** *adj.*

art·ist /ˈɑrtɪst/ S2 W2 *n.* [C] **1** someone who produces art, especially paintings or drawings: *This is one of the artist's best works.*

THESAURUS

painter someone who paints pictures
photographer someone who takes photographs
sculptor someone who makes sculptures
potter someone who makes pots or other objects from clay
→ ART

2 a professional performer, especially in music, dance, or the theater: *Many of the artists in the show gave their fee to charity.* **3** INFORMAL someone who is extremely good at something: *She's an artist in the kitchen.*

ar·tiste /ɑrˈtist/ *n.* [C] a professional singer, dancer, actor etc. who performs in a show

ar·tis·tic /ɑrˈtɪstɪk/ *adj.* **1** relating to art or CULTURE: *members of the artistic community* | *artistic works* **2** showing skill or imagination in any of the arts: *She's very artistic.* | *a lack of artistic ability* **3** an artistic arrangement, design etc. looks attractive and has been done with skill and imagination: *the chef's artistic presentation of her food* —**artistically** /-kli/ *adv.*

art·ist·ry /ˈɑrtəstri/ *n.* [U] skill in a particular artistic activity: *Her performance was delivered with artistry and skill.*

art·less /ˈɑrtlɪs/ *adj.* LITERARY natural, honest, and sincere: *a naive artless young woman* —**artlessly** *adj.* —**artlessness** *n.* [U]

art nou·veau /ˌɑrt nuˈvoʊ/ *n.* [U] a style of art that used pictures of plants and flowers, popular in Europe and the U.S. at the end of the 19th century

art·sy /ˈɑrtsi/ *adj.* INFORMAL interested in art, seeming to know a lot about art, or showing qualities like those of art: *Celia's artsy friends* | *an artsy black-and-white movie*

art·sy-craft·sy /ˌɑrtsi ˈkræftsi/ *adj.* someone who is artsy-craftsy likes creating things in an artistic way, especially things to decorate their home

artsy-fart·sy /ˌɑrtsi ˈfɑrtsi/ *adj.* INFORMAL **1** someone who is artsy-fartsy tries too hard to show that they are interested in art, movies, theater, etc. SYN **pretentious** **2** likely to appeal to artsy-fartsy people SYN **pretentious**: *an artsy-fartsy movie*

art·work /ˈɑrtˀwɚk/ *n.* [C,U] **1** ENG. LANG. ARTS paintings, SCULPTURES etc. produced by artists **2** pictures that are made for a book or magazine, or for another product such as a computer program

art·y /ˈɑrti/ *adj.* ARTSY

a·ru·gu·la /əˈrugələ/ *n.* [U] a plant with leaves that are eaten in SALADS

-ary /ɛri, -əri/ *suffix* **1** [in adjectives] relating to something, or having a particular quality: *planetary bodies* (=that are PLANETS) | *customary* **2** someone who has a connection with something or who does something: *the beneficiaries of the will* (=people who get something from it) | *a functionary* (=someone with duties) **3** [in nouns] a thing or place relating to things of a particular kind, or containing these things: *a library* (=containing books) | *an ovary* (=containing eggs) → see also -ERY

Ar·y·an /ˈɛriən/ *n.* [C] someone from Northern Europe, especially someone with BLOND hair and blue eyes —**Aryan** *adj.*

as[1] /əz; *strong* æz/ S1 W1 *adv., prep.* **1** used when comparing things, or saying that they are like each other in some way: *These houses aren't* **as** *old* **as** *the ones downtown.* | *Jerry was* **as** *surprised* **as** *anyone when they offered him the job.* | *You can uses cherries instead of plums – they work* **just as** *well.* | *Could you have Carol call me* **as soon as possible** (=as soon as you can)? **2** used when describing what someone's job, duty, or position is: *In the past, women were mainly employed as secretaries or teachers.* | *The kids dressed up as animals for Halloween.* **3** used when describing the way something is being used or considered: *John used an old blanket as a tent.* | *Settlers saw the wilderness as dangerous rather than beautiful.* **4 as a result of sth** because of something: *Several businesses went under as a result of the recession.* **5 be regarded as sth** to be considered to be something: *"Novecento" is regarded by many as Bertolucci's best film.* → see also **as good as** at GOOD (1), **as/so long as** at LONG[2] (5), **as a matter of fact** at MATTER[1] (7), **as one** at ONE[2] (20), **such as** at SUCH[2] (2), **as well as** at WELL[1] (5)

as[2] S1 W1 *conjunction* **1** use when comparing things, or saying that they are like each other in some way: *I can't run nearly* **as** *fast* **as** *I used to.* | *Jim works in* **the same** *office* **as** *my sister does.* **2** in the way or manner mentioned: *Leave things as they are until the police arrive.* | *As I said earlier, this research has just started.* | *You'd better* **do as** *Mom* **says**. | *Roberta was late* **as usual**. **3** while or when something is happening: *I saw Peter as I was getting off the bus.* | *Be patient with your* *puppy as he adjusts to his new home.* | *The phone rang* ***just as** I was leaving.* **4 as if.../as though... a)** in a way that suggests that something is true SYN **like**: *You look as if you're having a good time.* | *It sounds as though she's been really sick.* | *Brian shook his head as if to say "don't trust her."* **b)** used to suggest a possible explanation for something, although you do not think that this is the actual explanation SYN **like**: *Joe always sounds as if he's drunk.* | *You make it seem as if you're being overworked.* **5 as to sth** concerning a particular subject or decision: *She offered no explanation* ***as to why*** *she'd left so suddenly.* | *I need some advice* ***as to which*** *college to choose.* | *The President asked for opinions as to the likelihood of war.* **6 as of today/December 15/next June etc.** starting from today, December 15 etc. and continuing: *The pay raise will come into effect as of January 1.* **7 as for sb/sth** concerning a person or subject that is related to what you were talking about before: *As for racism, much progress has been made, but there is still much to do.* | *As for you, young man, you're grounded.* **8 as it is a)** according to the situation that actually exists, especially when that situation is different from what you expected or need: *We were saving money to go to Hawaii, but as it is we can only afford to go on a camping trip.* **b)** already: *Just keep quiet – you're in enough trouble as it is.* **9** used to state why a particular situation exists or why someone does something SYN **since**: *James decided not to go out as he was still really tired.* **10 as (of) yet** [used in negatives] until and including the present time: *As of yet, we don't believe it was a drive-by shooting.* | *Local election results have not as yet been announced.* **11** though: *Unlikely as it might seem, I'm tired too.* | *Try as she might, Sue couldn't get the door open.* | *As smart as Jake is, he doesn't know how to manage people well.* **12 so cold/heavy/quick etc. as to...** or **such an idiot/a disaster etc. as to...** FORMAL used to show the reason that makes something happen or not happen: *The water was so cold as to make swimming impossible.* | *How could he have been such an idiot as to trust them in the first place?* **13 so as to do sth** with the purpose of doing something: *The little boy ran off so as not to be caught* (=so that he would not be caught). **14 it's not as if...** SPOKEN used to say that something is definitely not true, about a situation or someone's behavior: *I don't know why Sally's grades are so low. It's not as if she can't do the work.* **15 as if you would/as if you care/as if it matters** SPOKEN used to say that someone would definitely not do something, does not care etc. or that something does not matter at all: *Margaret told me she'd never speak to me again – as if I cared* (=I do not care at all). | *"I think Ken's deliberately ignoring us." "As if he would* (=he would not ignore us)*!"* **16 as is/was/does sb/sth** FORMAL in the same way as someone or something else is, does etc.: *Dawn's very quiet, as was her mother.* | *I voted Republican, as did my wife.* **17 as it were** SPOKEN FORMAL used when describing someone or something in a way that is not completely exact: *He became famous,* ***as it were****, for never having a hit record.* **18 as against sth** in comparison with something: *Profits this year are $2.5 million as against $4 million last year.* → see also **as/so long as** at LONG[2] (5), **as soon as** at SOON (2), **not as such** at SUCH[2] (6), **as well** at WELL[1] (6) → see Word Choice box at THAN[1]

ASAP, a.s.a.p. /ˌeɪ ɛs eɪ ˈpi/ *n.* the abbreviation of "as soon as possible": *Call him ASAP.*

as·bes·tos /æsˈbɛstəs, æz-, əs-, əz-/ *n.* [U] a gray mineral that does not burn easily, which was used as a building material or in protective clothing [**Origin:** 1600–1700 Latin, Greek from *asbestos* **that cannot be put out**, from *sbennynai* **to put out a fire**]

as·cend /əˈsɛnd/ *v.* FORMAL **1** [I] to move up through the air OPP **descend**: *The plane ascended rapidly.* **2** [T] to climb something or walk to a higher position, for example on a slope: *It was snowing as they ascended the final peak.* **3** [I,T] to move to a more important or responsible job, or to move higher in rank: **+to** *Thomas ascended to the Supreme Court.* | *Jordan's King Hussein* ***ascended the throne*** (=became King) *in 1953.* **4** [I,T] to lead or go up to a higher position: *Several ski lifts ascended the mountain.* **5 in ascending order** in order on a list so that each thing is higher, or greater in amount, than the one before it: *The scores are shown in ascending order.*

as·cen·dan·cy, ascendency /əˈsɛndənsi/ *n.* [U] a position of power, influence, or control: *The U.S.* ***gained ascendancy*** *after World War II.* —**ascendance** *n.* [U]

as·cen·dant[1] /əˈsɛndənt/ *adj.* FORMAL becoming more powerful or popular: *an ascendant politician*

ascendant[2] *n.* **be in the ascendant** to be or become powerful or popular: *During this period, liberal ideas were in the ascendant.*

as·cen·sion /əˈsɛnʃən/ *n.* [U] the act of moving up

As'cension ˌDay *n.* [U] a Christian holy day on the Thursday 40 days after Easter, when Christians remember when Jesus Christ went to heaven

as·cent /əˈsɛnt, ˈæsɛnt/ *n.* **1** [U] the process of becoming more important, powerful, or successful than before: **+to** *Putin's ascent to the presidency of Russia* **2** [C usually singular] the act of climbing something or moving toward the top of something: *The final ascent of Kilimanjaro began at 5:00 a.m.* **3** [C usually singular] a path or way up to the top of something, for example a mountain: *a rugged and steep ascent* OPP **descent**

as·cer·tain /ˌæsɚˈteɪn/ *v.* [I,T] FORMAL to find out something: *Read labels to ascertain the amount of fats in processed foods.* | **+how/when/why etc.** *We're still trying to ascertain who was driving the car.* [**Origin:** 1500–1600 Old French *acertainer*, from *certain*] —**ascertainable** *adv.*

as·cet·ic /əˈsɛt̬ɪk/ *adj.* living without any physical pleasures or comforts, especially for religious reasons: *an ascetic Jewish sect* —**ascetic** *n.* [C] —**ascetically** /-kli/ *adv.* —**asceticism** /əˈsɛt̬əˌsɪzəm/ *n.* [U]

ASCII /ˈæski/ *n.* [U] COMPUTERS **American Standard Code for Information Interchange** a system used in exchanging information between different computers by allowing them to recognize SYMBOLS, such as letters or numbers, in the same way

as·cot /ˈæskət, -kɑt/ *n.* [C] a wide piece of material worn by men loosely folded around their neck inside their collar

as·cribe /əˈskraɪb/ *v.*

ascribe sth **to** sb/sth *phr. v.* FORMAL **1** to be fairly sure about what the cause of something is, and claim that this is true: *Doctors ascribed his death to a virus.* **2** to believe something or someone has a particular quality: *The natives ascribe healing properties to this fruit.* **3** to claim that someone is the artist, writer etc. who produced a particular piece of work: *These writings have been ascribed to Orpheus.* —**ascribable** *adj.*

a·sep·tic /eɪˈsɛptɪk, ə-/ *adj.* MEDICINE a wound that is aseptic is completely clean without any harmful BACTERIA

a·sex·u·al /eɪˈsɛkʃuəl/ *adj.* **1** BIOLOGY not having sexual organs or not involving sex: *asexual reproduction* **2 a)** not seeming to have any sexual qualities **b)** not interested in sexual relations —**asexually** *adv.*

aˌsexual repro'duction *n.* [U] BIOLOGY a process by which some plants and some living creatures produce a new plant or creature without male and female sex cells joining together

ash /æʃ/ *n.* **1** [C,U] the soft gray powder that remains after something has been burned: *cigar ash* | *Investigators sifted through the ashes to find the cause of the fire.* → see picture at VOLCANO **2 ashes** [plural] the ash that remains when a dead person's body is burned: *McCrea wanted his ashes scattered at sea.* **3** [C,U] BIOLOGY a very hard wood, or the common type of forest tree that produces this wood → see also **rise from the ashes** at RISE[1] (14)

a·shamed /əˈʃeɪmd/ *adj.* [not before noun] **1** feeling embarrassed and guilty about something you have done: **+of/about** *I'm ashamed of the things I said.* | **ashamed to do sth** *Hassel was too ashamed to ask her family for help.* | **be ashamed that** *Later, I was ashamed that I hadn't helped.* | **be ashamed of doing sth** *He was ashamed of not being able to support his family.* | *Washington should be* ***ashamed of itself*** *for withholding economic aid.* | **be ashamed to admit/say (that)** *I'm ashamed to admit I haven't read your book.* | *Losing your job* ***is nothing to be ashamed of.*** ►see THESAURUS box at **guilty** **2** feeling uncomfortable or upset because someone does something that embarrasses you: **+of** *I'm ashamed of the actions of my government.* | **be ashamed to be/do sth** *His behavior makes me ashamed to be seen with him in public.* **guilty**

ash·can /ˈæʃkæn/ *n.* [C] OLD-FASHIONED a GARBAGE CAN

Ashe /æʃ/, **Arthur** (1943–1993) a U.S. tennis player famous for being the first African-American man to win the men's SINGLES competition at Wimbledon in 1975

ash·en /ˈæʃən/ *adj.* **1** very pale because of shock or fear: *Lisa's face had turned ashen.* **2** pale gray in color, like ash

Ash·er /ˈæʃɚ/ in the Bible, the head of one of the 12 tribes of Israel

Ash·ga·bat /ˈæʃkəˌbæt, -ˌbɑt/ the capital and largest city of Turkmenistan

a·shore /əˈʃɔr/ *adv.* on or toward the shore of a lake, river, or ocean: *Pieces of the boat* ***washed ashore*** (=were pushed ashore by waves). | *Two of the fisherman managed to* ***swim ashore.*** | **go/come ashore** (=leave a ship or boat for land)

ash·ram /ˈæʃrəm, -rɑm/ *n.* [C] a place where people who practice the Hindu religion live together, apart from other people [**Origin:** 1900–2000 Sanskrit *asrama*, from *a* **toward** + *srama* **religious exercise**]

ash·tray /ˈæʃtreɪ/ *n. plural* **ashtrays** [C] a small dish where you put cigarette ASHes and used cigarettes

ˌAsh ˈWednesday *n.* [C,U] the first day of Lent

ash·y /ˈæʃi/ *adj.* **1** having a light gray color **2** covered with ASHES

A·sia /ˈeɪʒə/ the world's largest CONTINENT, which includes the countries of the Middle East and countries such as India, China, Japan, and part of Russia

ˌAsia ˈMinor the historical name for the main part of Turkey

A·sian¹ /ˈeɪʒən/ *n.* someone from Asia, especially Japan, China, Korea etc.

Asian² *adj.* from Asia or relating to Asia

ˌAsian-Aˈmerican *n.* [C] an American citizen whose family was originally from Asia

ˌAsian ˈTigers, the the EAST ASIAN TIGERS

A·si·at·ic /ˌeɪʒiˈæṭɪk, -zi-/ *adj.* TECHNICAL from Asia or relating to Asia

a·side¹ /əˈsaɪd/ S3 W3 *adv.* **1 put/set/leave etc. sth aside (for sth) a)** to save an amount of money: *The company had set aside $140 million for bonus pay.* **b)** to keep something separate or not use it, especially because someone is going to buy or use it later: *Much of the forest was put aside for parkland.* **c)** to leave something to be considered or dealt with at another time: *During Thanksgiving, families try to put aside personal differences.* **d)** to stop using something and put it to one side: *Put grease in a baking pan and set it aside.* **2 step/stand/move etc. aside a)** to stop doing something so that someone else can have a chance: *Ms. Lawrence said she was stepping aside as chairman.* **b)** to move, step etc. to the side: *Jim stepped aside to let me pass.* **3 aside from sb/sth a)** except for: *Aside from coal, copper is the state's largest natural resource.* **b)** in addition to: *Aside from helpful tips, the book also contains a guide to the city's restaurants.* **4** used to show that something you have just said is not as important as what you are going to say next: *These problems aside, we think the plan should go ahead.* | **(all) kidding/joking aside** SPOKEN (=used when you have been joking, but you want to say something serious next) **5 take/pull/call etc. aside** to take someone a short distance to a more private place, so that you can talk to them: *A friend pulled him aside and told him to calm down.* **6 brush/sweep sth aside** to treat someone's idea or statement in a way that shows you do not think it is important: *The President brushed aside questions about this health.*

aside² *n.* [C] **1** a remark made in a low voice that you only intend particular people to hear **2** a remark or story that is not part of the main subject of a speech: *He noted as an aside that Mrs. Singer was also a member.* **3** ENG. LANG. ARTS words spoken by an actor to the people watching a play, that the other characters in the play do not hear

as·i·nine /ˈæsəˌnaɪn/ *adj.* extremely stupid or silly SYN **ridiculous**: *asinine questions*

ask /æsk/ S1 W1 *v.*

1 QUESTION [I,T] to say or write something in order to get an answer, a solution, or information: *"What's your name?" she asked.* | **ask (sb) who/what/where etc.** *She called and asked me what she should wear.* | **ask sb sth** *Don't ask me directions – I don't know where it is.* | **ask sb** *Why don't you just ask him?* | **ask (sb) if/whether** *Ask Jamie if she needs a ride home.* | *They* ***asked*** *a lot* ***of questions*** *about Medicare.* | **ask (sb) about** *Joe went and asked about getting a refund.* | *Everybody has a favorite restaurant, so* ***ask around*** (=ask a lot of people).

THESAURUS

order to ask for food or drinks in a restaurant: *He ordered a club sandwich.*
demand to ask for something in a firm or angry way: *She demanded to see the manager.*
request to ask for something in a polite or formal way: *I wrote to request information about the college.*
beg to ask for something that you want very much: *"Please can I have one?" she begged.* | *I begged her to stay.*
plead to ask for something important in an urgent way because you want it very much: *She pleaded with them to spare her son's life.*
nag/pester to keep asking for something, in an annoying way: *People were pestering him for his autograph.*
question/interrogate if the police question or interrogate someone, they ask them a lot of questions in order to get information: *The two men are being questioned by police about the robbery.*
inquire/enquire FORMAL to ask someone for information or facts about something: *Parents should inquire about how the school handles discipline problems.*
poll to officially ask a lot of people about something, for example to find out their opinion on something: *Over 1,000 people were polled for the report.*

2 FOR HELP/ADVICE ETC. [I,T] to make a request for help, advice, information etc.: *He just took a beer without asking.* | **ask sb to do sth** *She asked me to get her a cup of coffee.* | **ask to do sth** *Several employees asked to be given more time off.* | **+for** *Mrs. Costello asked for a copy.* | **ask sb for sth** *I'm going to ask her for a raise.* | **ask if you can do sth** *Ask your mom if you can come with us.* | **ask that sb do sth** FORMAL: *He asked that he be given more time.* ►see THESAURUS box at **request²**
3 INVITE [T] to invite someone to your home, to go out with you etc.: **ask sb to sth** *They've asked 200 people to the wedding.* | **ask sb to do sth** *A boy asked me to dance.* | *Did you* ***ask her out*** (=ask someone, especially someone of the opposite sex, to go to a movie, a restaurant etc. with you)? | *Why don't you* ***ask them over*** *for dinner* (=invite someone to come to your home)?
4 PRICE [T] to want a particular amount of money for something you are selling: **ask $30/$500 etc. for sth** *How much is he asking for it?*
5 DEMAND/EXPECT [T] if you ask something of someone,

you expect them to do it: *He* ***asks a lot*** *of his employees.* | *It's* ***asking too much*** *to expect a child to remember this.* | ***All I ask is*** (=the only thing I expect from you is) *that you get here on time.*

SPOKEN PHRASES

6 if you ask me used to emphasize your own opinion: *He's crazy if you ask me.*
7 sb is asking for it used to say that someone deserves something bad that happens to them: *The guy hit Dave hard, but Dave was asking for it.*
8 don't ask me used to say you do not know the answer to something: *"How does this thing work?" "Don't ask me!"*
9 don't ask used to say that something is too annoying or strange to explain: *"What did he want you to do?" "Oh, don't ask."*
10 I'm just asking used when you think someone was offended or annoyed by your question, to show that you did not mean to annoy or offend them: *"I can't do it right now!" "Okay, I was just asking."*
11 ask yourself to think carefully and honestly in order to find the answer to something: *And then I asked myself if what I was doing was really right.*
12 I ask you! OLD-FASHIONED used to express surprise at and disapproval of something stupid that someone has done

13 be asking for trouble to do something that is very likely to have a bad effect or result: *If you don't put new tires on, you're just asking for trouble.*
14 for the asking if you can have something for the asking, you only have to ask for it and you can have it: *This kind of information is usually available for the asking.*
[**Origin:** Old English *ascian*]

GRAMMAR

• Remember that you do not follow **ask** with a direct question, unless you are repeating the exact words: *Ask Ben what kind of ice cream he wants* (NOT *Ask what kind of ice cream does he want*). | *I asked Ben, "What kind of ice cream do you want?"* You **ask** people certain things without using *for* or *about*: *I asked her the way/her name/the price/the time/a favor* (NOT *asked her about the way*).
• You usually **ask for** or **about** most other things: *Should we stop and ask for directions?* | *Tom asked Sharon for a date* (NOT *Tom asked a date to Sharon*). | *Can I ask you about the grades on the test?* (NOT *...of the grades*)

a·skance /əˈskæns/ *adv.* **look askance (at sb/sth)** to look at or consider something in a way that shows you do not believe it or approve of it

a·skew /əˈskyu/ *adv.* not exactly straight or in the right position: *His hat was askew.*

ˈasking ˌprice *n.* [C] the price that someone wants to sell something for: *The asking price for the car is $11,500.*

ASL /ˌeɪ ɛs ˈɛl/ *n.* [U] **American Sign Language** a language that uses hand movements instead of spoken words, used in the U.S. by people who cannot hear

a·slant /əˈslænt/ *adv.* [not before noun] FORMAL not straight up or down, but across at an angle —**aslant** *adj.*

a·sleep /əˈslip/ S2 W3 *adj.* [not before noun] **1** sleeping: *Kelly was asleep on the sofa.* | **fast/sound asleep** (=sleeping very deeply) **2 fall asleep** to begin to sleep: *Her three-year-old daughter fell asleep while we talked.* **3** an arm or leg that is asleep has been in one position for too long, so you cannot feel it **4 half asleep** INFORMAL not paying attention to something because you are tired: *Sorry, what did you say? I'm half asleep.* **5 asleep at the switch/wheel** not paying attention to something, so that something bad happens: *If the management was asleep at the switch, then someone ought to be fired.* → see also **go to sleep** at SLEEP² (2)

As·ma·ra /æzˈmɑrə, -ˈmærə/ the capital and largest city of Eritrea

A

a·so·cial /eɪˈsoʊʃəl/ *adj.* TECHNICAL **1** unwilling to meet people and talk to them, especially in a way that seems unfriendly **2** asocial behavior shows a lack of concern for other people → see also ANTISOCIAL

asp /æsp/ *n.* [C] a small poisonous snake from North Africa

as·par·a·gus /əˈspærəgəs/ *n.* [U] a green vegetable shaped like a small stick with a point at one end → see picture on page A35

ASPCA, the /ˌeɪ ɛs ˌpi si ˈeɪ/ **American Society for the Prevention of Cruelty to Animals** a CHARITY organization that takes care of animals

as·pect /ˈæspɛkt/ Ac S2 W2 *n.* **1** [C] one part of a situation, idea, plan etc. that has many parts: *Cost is one aspect we haven't discussed yet.* | +**of** *She was active in many aspects of campus life.* | *Unemployment affects all aspects of family life.* ▶see THESAURUS box at characteristic¹ **2** [C] the direction in which a window, room, front of a building etc. faces: *a south-facing aspect* **3** [C,U] LITERARY the appearance of someone or something: *The storm gave the landscape a sinister aspect.* **4** [C,U] ENG. LANG. ARTS the form of a verb in grammar that shows whether an action is continuing, or if it happens always, again and again, or once. For example, "he dances" is different from "he is dancing" in aspect. [**Origin:** 1300–1400 Latin, past participle of *aspicere* **to look at**, from *ad-* **to** + *specere* **to look**]

as·pen /ˈæspən/ *n.* [C] a type of tree that grows in western North America, with leaves that make a pleasant noise in the wind

as·per·i·ty /æˈspɛrət̬i, ə-/ *n.* [C,U] FORMAL a way of speaking or behaving that is rough or severe

as·per·sion /əˈspɚʒən, -ʃən/ *n.* **cast aspersions on sb/sth** to make an unkind remark or an unfair judgment: *They cast aspersions on his professional conduct.* [**Origin:** 1500–1600 Latin *aspersio* **throwing drops of water on to someone in a religious ceremony**, from *aspergere*, from *ad-* **to** + *spargere* **to scatter**]

as·phalt /ˈæsfɔlt/ *n.* [U] a black sticky substance that becomes hard when it dries, used for making the surface of roads —**asphalt** *v.* [T]

as·phyx·i·a /əˈsfɪksiə, æ-/ *n.* [U] death caused by not being able to breathe [**Origin:** 1700–1800 Modern Latin, Greek, **stopping the flow of blood**, from *a-* **not** + *sphyzein* **to beat regularly, throb**]

as·phyx·i·ate /əˈsfɪksiˌeɪt, æ-/ *v.* [I,T] TECHNICAL to be unable to breathe or to make someone unable to breathe, often resulting in death SYN **suffocate** —**asphyxiation** /əˌsfɪksiˈeɪʃən/ *n.* [U]

as·pic /ˈæspɪk/ *n.* [U] a clear brownish JELLY made with juice from cooked meat, fish, or vegetables [**Origin:** 1700–1800 French **asp (= small snake)**]

as·pi·dis·tra /ˌæspəˈdɪstrə/ *n.* [C] a plant with broad green pointed leaves

as·pi·rant /ˈæspərənt/ *n.* [C] FORMAL someone who hopes to get a position of importance or honor

as·pi·rate¹ /ˈæspəˌreɪt/ *v.* **1** TECHNICAL [I,T] to breathe in, or to breathe something into your lungs by accident **2** [T] ENG. LANG. ARTS to make the sound of an "H" when speaking, or to blow out air when pronouncing some CONSONANTS

as·pi·rate² /ˈæspərɪt/ *n.* [C] ENG. LANG. ARTS the sound of the letter "H," or the letter itself

as·pi·ra·tion /ˌæspəˈreɪʃən/ *n.* **1** [C usually plural, U] a strong desire to have or achieve something: *The Senator has presidential aspirations* (=wants to be president). | +**to** *Cauther is a lawyer with aspirations to the bench* (=to become a judge). | +**of** *the aspirations of average Americans* **2** [U] ENG. LANG. ARTS the sound of air blowing out that happens when some CONSONANTS are pronounced, such as the /p/ in "pin"

as·pire /əˈspaɪɚ/ *v.* [I] to desire and work toward achieving something important: **aspire to do sth** *Johnson aspires to become the city's first woman mayor.* | +**to/after** *Kim aspires to a career as a travel*

A

agent. [**Origin:** 1300–1400 Old French *aspirer*, from Latin *aspirare* **to breathe on**]

as·pirin /ˈæsprɪn/ *n. plural* **aspirin** or **aspirins** [C,U] a medicine that reduces pain, INFLAMMATION, and fever [**Origin:** 1800–1900 German *acetylierte spirsäure* type of acid from which aspirin is obtained, from Modern Latin *spiraea* type of bush from which this acid is obtained]

ass /æs/ *n.* [C]
1 PART OF BODY VULGAR the part of your body that you sit on
2 kick/whip sb's ass also **kick (some) ass** VULGAR to beat someone easily in a fight, game, or sport
3 ANIMAL BIOLOGY a DONKEY
[**Origin:** (3) *assa* from Latin *asinus*]

as·sail /əˈseɪl/ *v.* [T] **1** [usually passive] LITERARY if a thought or feeling assails you, it worries or upsets you: *As soon as I'd finished the test, I was* ***assailed by doubts.*** **2** to criticize someone or something severely: **assail sb for sth** *Democrats have been assailing the President for ignoring the needs of the middle class.* **3** FORMAL to attack someone or something violently

as·sail·ant /əˈseɪlənt/ *n.* [C] FORMAL someone who attacks another person: *She tried to describe her assailant to police.*

as·sas·sin /əˈsæsən/ *n.* [C] someone who murders an important person: *a hired assassin* [**Origin:** 1500–1600 Medieval Latin *assassinus*, from Arabic *hashshashin* **one who smokes hashish (and then kills religious enemies)**]

as·sas·si·nate /əˈsæsəˌneɪt/ *v.* [T] to kill an important person: *Martin Luther King was assassinated in 1968.* → see also MURDER ►see THESAURUS box at **kill**[1]

as·sas·si·na·tion /əˌsæsəˈneɪʃən/ *n.* [C,U] the act of assassinating someone: *the assassination of Lincoln* | *Reagan was wounded in an* ***assassination attempt*** *in 1981.* → see also **character assassination** at CHARACTER (6), MURDER

as·sault[1] /əˈsɔlt/ *n.* [C,U] **1** the crime of physically attacking someone SYN **attack**: *She served three years in prison for assault.* | *an increase in* ***sexual assaults*** | **+on** *assaults on police officers* ►see THESAURUS box at **attack**[1], **crime** **2** a military attack to take control of a place controlled by the enemy SYN **attack**: **+on** *the assault on Midway Island* | **a military/air/ground etc. assault** *a massive aerial assault on the city* ►see THESAURUS box at **attack**[1] **3 assault on sth** an attempt to challenge or destroy someone else's ideas, plans etc. by making a strong spoken or written criticism of them: *Traditional family values are increasingly* ***under assault.*** | **+on** *the administration's assault on the welfare system* **4** an attempt to achieve something difficult, especially something physically difficult SYN **attempt**: **+on** *They made their assault on the south face of the glacier* (=an attempt to climb or cross it). **5** LAW the crime of threatening to physically hurt someone but not actually attacking them, or an act of doing this [**Origin:** 1200–1300 Old French *assaut*, from Latin *assaltus*, past participle of *assalire*, from *ad-* **to** + *salire* **to jump**]

assault[2] *v.* [T] **1** to attack someone in a violent way SYN **attack**: *A storekeeper was assaulted in an alley by eight teenagers.* | *The woman had been* ***sexually assaulted.*** **2** if a feeling assaults you, it affects you in a way that makes you uncomfortable or upset: *The noises and smells of the market assaulted her senses.*

asˌsault and ˈbattery *n.* [U] LAW the official name for a violent attack and the threats that the attacker makes before it

as·say /æˈseɪ, ˈæseɪ/ *v.* **assays, assayed, assaying** [T] to test a substance, especially a metal, in order to see how pure it is or what it is made of —**assay** /ˈæseɪ, æˈseɪ/ *n.* [C]

as·sem·blage /əˈsɛmblɪdʒ/ *n.* FORMAL **1** [C] a group of people or things that are together: *an assemblage of scholars* **2** [U] the act of putting parts together in order to make something

as·sem·ble /əˈsɛmbəl/ Ac *v.* **1** [I] if a group of people assemble in one place, they all go there together SYN **gather**: *Protesters started to assemble around 7 a.m.* ►see THESAURUS box at **meet**[1] **2** [T] to gather a large number of things or people together in one place or for one purpose: *He assembled a powerful team of lawyers.* **3** [T] to put all the parts of something together: *It was easy to assemble the bookcase myself.* ►see THESAURUS box at **build**[1] [**Origin:** 1200–1300 Old French *assembler*, from Latin *ad-* **to** + *simul* **together**]

Asˌsemblies of ˈGod a Pentecostal Christian church

as·sem·bly /əˈsɛmbli/ Ac W3 *n. plural* **assemblies** **1** [C] POLITICS a group of people who are elected to make laws for a particular country, area, or organization: *the U.N. General Assembly* **2** [C] a group of people who have gathered together for a particular purpose: **+of** *an assembly of leaders of Jewish community organizations* **3** [C,U] a meeting of all the teachers and students of a school **4** [U] the process of putting parts together in order to make something: *Some toy stores help with assembly.* **5 the right of assembly/freedom of assembly** LAW the right of any group to meet together in order to discuss things

asˈsembly ˌlanguage *n.* [C,U] COMPUTERS a computer language used in programs that are written to work with a specific kind of PROCESSOR

asˈsembly ˌline *n.* [C] a system for making things in a factory, in which the products move past a line of workers who each make or check one part

as·sem·bly·man /əˈsɛmblimən/ *n. plural* **assemblymen** [C] a male member of an ASSEMBLY

as·sem·bly·wom·an /əˈsɛmbliˌwʊmən/ *n. plural* **assemblywomen** [C] a female member of an ASSEMBLY

as·sent[1] /əˈsɛnt/ *n.* [U] FORMAL approval or agreement from someone who has authority SYN **approval**: *The court* ***gave its assent.*** → see also CONSENT[1], DISSENT[1]

assent[2] *v.* [I] FORMAL if someone who has authority assents, they agree to a suggestion, idea etc. after considering it carefully SYN **agree**

as·sert /əˈsɚt/ W3 *v.* [T] **1** to state firmly that something is true: *"It's a fairness issue," she asserted.* | **assert that** *He asserts that nuclear power is safe.* **2** to state or show very strongly that you have particular rights or powers: **assert your rights/independence/claim** *His sons both asserted their right to the money.* | **assert your power/control/authority** *Sometimes parents have to assert their authority.* **3 assert yourself** to say clearly what you think or want: *Don't be afraid to assert yourself in the interview.* **4 assert itself** if an idea, style, or belief asserts itself, it begins to influence something: *National pride began to assert itself.* [**Origin:** 1600–1700 Latin, past participle of *asserere*, from *ad-* **to** + *serere* **to join**]

as·ser·tion /əˈsɚʃən/ *n.* [C] something that you say or write that you strongly believe: **assertion that** *Bennet denied assertions that she was mentally unstable.*

as·ser·tive /əˈsɚṭɪv/ *adj.* behaving in a confident way so that people notice you: *an assertive ambitious woman* —**assertively** *adv.* —**assertiveness** *n.* [U]

as·sess /əˈsɛs/ Ac *v.* [T] **1** to make a judgment about a person or situation after thinking carefully about it: *Psychologists will assess the child's behavior.* | **assess what/how etc.** *It is difficult to assess how much has actually been done.* ►see THESAURUS box at **judge**[2] **2** to calculate the value or cost of something: *facilities with an* ***assessed value*** *of $95 million* | **assess sth at** *The house was assessed at $170,000.* [**Origin:** 1400–1500 Old French *assesser*, from Latin, past participle of *assidere* **to sit beside, help in making judgments**]

as·sess·ment /əˈsɛsmənt/ Ac W3 *n.* [C,U] **1** a process in which you make a judgment about a person or situation: **+of** *What's your assessment of the situation?* |

an assessment of the student's work **2** a calculation about the cost or value of something: *a tax assessment* **3** ECONOMICS an official judgment of the value of a property, made in order to calculate the amount of tax that must be paid: *property tax assessment* | *an assessment district*

as·ses·sor /ə'sɛsɚ/ *n.* [C] **1** someone whose job is to calculate the value of something or the amount of tax someone should pay: *a property assessor* **2** someone who knows a lot about a subject or activity and who advises a judge or an official committee

as·set /'æsɛt/ W2 *n.* [C] **1** [usually plural] ECONOMICS the things that a company or person owns, that can be sold to pay debts: *Currently, they have $6,230,000* ***in assets.*** | *Stocks, bonds, and bank deposits are* ***financial assets*** (=assets that are not things, but instead claims on something of value). **2** [usually singular] something or someone that is useful because they help you succeed or deal with problems: *A sense of humor is a big asset in this job.* | +**to** *Ronnie has been a real asset to the team.* [**Origin:** 1800–1900 *assets* (singular) **enough money to pay debts**, from Old French *assez* **enough**] → see also LIABILITY, LIQUID ASSETS

'asset ˌstripping *n.* [U] ECONOMICS the practice of buying a company cheaply and then selling all the things it owns to make a quick profit

as·sid·u·ous /ə'sɪdʒuəs/ *adj.* FORMAL very careful to make sure that something is done correctly or completely: *an assiduous study of Austen's writings* —**assiduously** *adv.* —**assiduousness** *n.* [U]

as·sign /ə'saɪn/ Ac S3 W3 *v.* [T] **1** to give someone a particular job or make them responsible for a particular person or thing: **assign sb to sb/sth** *a reporter assigned to the Middle East* | *Officer Crane was assigned to the vice squad.* | **assign sb to do sth** *Madison was assigned to investigate the accident.* | **assign sb the task/job/duty etc. of doing sth** *Troops have been assigned the task of securing the roads around the city.* **2** to give money, equipment etc. to someone or decide it should be used for a particular purpose: **be assigned sth** *She was assigned her own bodyguard.* | **assign sth to/for sth** *Part of the budget is assigned to research.* **3** to tell someone to go to a particular place as part of a system: **assign sb to sth** *Each of the children will be assigned to a classroom.* | *Patients were assigned to doctors hundreds of miles away.* **4** to give a particular value, place, number etc. to something: **assign sth to sth** *A code was assigned to each item.* | **be assigned sth** *Everyone is assigned a Social Security number at birth.*

as·sig·na·tion /ˌæsɪg'neɪʃən/ *n.* [C] LITERARY a secret meeting, especially with someone you are having a romantic relationship with

as·sign·ment /ə'saɪnmənt/ Ac S3 W3 *n.* **1** [C,U] a piece of work that is given to someone as part of their job: *Half the workers were given different assignments.* | *He was killed while* ***on assignment*** (=doing work) *in Italy.* **2** [C] work that a student is asked to do: *a* ***homework assignment*** | *Half of the students were* ***given a*** *different* ***assignment.*** | **a history/math/English etc. assignment** *The math assignment was hard.* ▸see THESAURUS box at **school**[1] **3** [C] something such as a place to sit, piece of equipment etc. that you are given to use for a particular purpose: *an airplane* ***seat assignment*** **4** [U] the act of giving someone something to use, for example a place to sit or piece of equipment: **the assignment of sth to sb** *the assignment of computer equipment to employees* **5** [U] the act of giving people particular jobs to do: *the assignment of chores*

as·sim·i·late /ə'sɪməˌleɪt/ *v.* **1** [I,T] if people assimilate or are assimilated into a country or group, they become part of it and are accepted by other people in it: +**into** *Many ethnic groups have been assimilated into American society.* **2 assimilate sth into sth** to include new or different things such as styles or beliefs in something that already exists, so that they become part of it: *Brubeck began to assimilate classical influences into his jazz performances.* **3** [I,T] FORMAL to completely understand and be able to use new ideas, information etc.: *It will take time to assimilate all the facts.* **4** [T] TECHNICAL if your body assimilates food, it takes it in and DIGESTS it

A

as·sim·i·la·tion /əˌsɪmə'leɪʃən/ *n.* [U] **1** the process of assimilating or being assimilated into a group: +**into** *the assimilation of women into the army* **2** the process of completely understanding and being able to use new information: +**of** *his rapid assimilation of new information* **3** ENG. LANG. ARTS the process in which a sound in a word changes because of the effect of another sound next to it, for example the "p" in "cupboard"

As·sin·i·boin /ə'sɪnəˌbɔɪn/ a Native American tribe from the northern U.S. and southern Canada

as·sist[1] /ə'sɪst/ Ac W3 *v.* FORMAL **1** [I,T] to help someone to do something,especially when they are doing the main part of the work and you are providing extra help SYN **help**: *She has three researchers who assist her.* | **assist (sb) with/in** *U.S. helicopters assisted in the rescue effort.* | *Ms. Allen assists immigrants with gaining citizenship.* ▸see THESAURUS box at **help**[1] **2** [T] FORMAL to make it easier for someone to do something SYN **help**: *Citizens have a duty to assist the police.* [**Origin:** 1400–1500 French *assister* **to be present, help**, from Latin *assistere*, from *ad-* **to** + *sistere* **to cause to stand**]

assist[2] Ac *n.* [C] an action that helps another player on your sports team to make a point

as·sist·ance /ə'sɪstəns/ Ac W3 *n.* [U] FORMAL help or support SYN **help** SYN **aid**: *financial assistance for students* | *Can I* ***be of*** *any* ***assistance*** (=can I help you)? | **offer/provide/give assistance** *The West can provide technical assistance to developing countries.* | *The research was conducted* ***with the assistance of*** *computer equipment.* | *I want to thank those who* ***came to my assistance*** (=helped me). ▸see THESAURUS box at **help**[2]

as·sist·ant[1] /ə'sɪstənt/ Ac W3 *adj.* **assistant manager/director/cook etc.** someone whose job is just below the level of manager, DIRECTOR etc.: *Mr. Wade is assistant manager at the store.* ▸see THESAURUS box at **position**[1], **rank**[1]

assistant[2] Ac S3 W3 *n.* [C] someone who helps someone else in their work, especially by doing the less important jobs: *a sales assistant* | +**to** *I was assistant to the general manager.*

asˌsistant pro'fessor, Assistant Professor *n.* [C] the lowest rank of PROFESSOR → see Word Choice box at PROFESSOR

asˌsisted 'suicide *n.* [U] a situation when someone who is dying from an illness kills themselves with the help of someone else, usually a doctor

assn. *n.* a written abbreviation of "association"

assoc. *n.* a written abbreviation of "association"

as·so·ci·ate[1] /ə'souʃiˌeɪt, -siˌeɪt/ S3 W2 *v.* **1 associate sb/sth with sth** to make a connection in your mind between one thing or person and another: *Ads try to associate drinking alcohol with fun.* **2 be associated (with sb/sth)** to be related with a particular subject, activity, group etc.: *the problems associated with cancer treatment* | *Poverty and crime are* ***closely associated*** (=there is a strong relationship between them). **3 associate with sb** to spend time with someone, especially a group whom other people disapprove of: *He is known to associate with criminals.* **4 associate yourself with sb/sth** to make a connection between yourself and someone or something, for example by saying you support them: *He did not want to associate himself with the prodemocracy movement.* [**Origin:** 1300–1400 Latin, past participle of *associare*, from *ad-* **to** + *sociare* **to join**]

as·so·ci·ate[2] /ə'souʃiɪt/ W3 *n.* [C] **1** someone with whom you work or do business with, or who you know through work: *He's a business associate of mine.* **2** an associate member of an organization: *a research associate at Harvard* **3** an ASSOCIATE OF ARTS degree

associate³ *adj.* **associate member/director/head etc.** someone who does not have all of the same rights or responsibilities as a member, DIRECTOR etc.: *the associate director of the museum*

as,sociated 'company *n.* [C] a company in which a different company owns 20 to 50 percent of the SHARES

As,sociated 'Press ABBREVIATION **AP** *n.* a company that employs REPORTERS in many different countries to send it news, so that it can sell these reports to many different newspapers

As,sociate of 'Arts also **as,sociate de'gree** *n.* [C] a degree given after two years of study at a COMMUNITY COLLEGE

as,sociate pro'fessor, Associate Professor *n.* [C] a PROFESSOR at a college or university whose job is above the rank of ASSISTANT PROFESSOR and below the rank of FULL PROFESSOR → see Word Choice box at PROFESSOR

as·so·ci·a·tion /əˌsoʊsiˈeɪʃən, -ʃiˈeɪ-/ W1 *n.* [C] **1** [C] an organization that consists of a group of people who have the same aims, do the same kind of work etc.: *the National Education Association* | *the college's alumni association* ►see THESAURUS box at **organization** **2** [C,U] a relationship with a particular person, organization, group etc.: **+with** *Franklin had a long association with Republican politics.* | *Lawyers said the charges were an attempt to prove guilt* ***by association*** (=to prove someone is guilty because their friends are guilty). **3** [C] a connection or relationship between two events, ideas, situations etc. SYN **link**: *an association between headaches and computer use* | *a word-association game* **4 in association with sb/sth** made or done together with another person, organization etc.: *concerts sponsored by the Arts Council in association with local businesses* **5** [C] a feeling or memory that is related to a particular place, event, word etc.: *This place has happy associations for me.* → see also FREE ASSOCIATION

as,sociative 'property *n.* [C] MATH the quality of particular types of operations in mathematics, such as addition or MULTIPLICATION, by which the result is the same no matter what order the calculations are done in, as in the examples $(3 + 5) + 2 = 3 + (5 + 2)$ and $(a \times b) \times c = a \times (b \times c)$

as·so·nance /ˈæsənəns/ *n.* [U] ENG. LANG. ARTS similarity in the vowel sounds of words that are close together in a poem, for example between the words "born" and "warm" [**Origin:** 1700–1800 French, Latin *assonare* **to answer with the same sound**, from *ad-* **to** + *sonare* **to sound**]

as·sort·ed /əˈsɔrt̬ɪd/ *adj.* of various different types: *a set of paintbrushes in assorted sizes* | *fruit and assorted cheeses* [**Origin:** 1700–1800 past participle of *assort* **to divide into types** (15–21 centuries), from Old French *assorter*, from *sorte* **sort**]

as·sort·ment /əˈsɔrtˀmənt/ *n.* [C] a mixture of different things or of various types of the same thing: **+of** *a wide assortment of merchandise*

asst. *n.* the written abbreviation of ASSISTANT

as·suage /əˈsweɪdʒ/ *v.* [T] LITERARY to make a bad feeling less painful or severe SYN **relieve**: *Debra tried to assuage my fears.* [**Origin:** 1200–1300 Old French *assouagier*, from Latin *ad-* **to** + *suavis* **sweet**]

as·sume /əˈsum/ Ac S1 W2 *v.* [T] **1** to think that something is true, although you have no proof of it SYN **presume**: **assume (that)** *I haven't heard from her, but I assume she's still going.* | *It is assumed that they will eventually join the EU.* | *I think* ***we can safely assume*** (=it is reasonable certain) *that this is legal unless we are told otherwise.* | ***Let's assume that*** (=used to talk about a possible fact or situation) *we can fire her. Should we do it?* **2** to start to do a job, especially an important one: **assume control/power/responsibility etc.** *When did Stalin assume control of the Soviet Union?* **3 assume a manner/air/expression etc.** FORMAL to behave in a way that does not show how you really feel, especially in order to seem more confident, cheerful etc. than you are SYN **put on**: *When walking alone at night, assume an air of confidence.* **4 assume costs/responsibility/debts etc.** to agree to pay for something: *Her mother assumed responsibility for her debts.* | *The agency agreed to assume all the building costs.* **5** to start to have a particular quality or appearance SYN **take on**: *Her family life assumed more importance after the accident.* **6** to be based on the idea that something else is correct SYN **presuppose**: *Coen's economic forecast assumes a 3.5 percent growth rate.* [**Origin:** 1500–1600 Latin *assumere*, from *ad-* **to** + *sumere* **to take**]

as,sumed 'name *adj.* a false name: *Davis applied for a loan* ***under an assumed name*** (=using one).

as·sump·tion /əˈsʌmpʃən/ Ac W3 *n.* **1** [C] something that you think is true although you have no proof: *Don't* ***make the assumption that*** *stream water is safe to drink.* | *The pricing is based* ***on the assumption that*** *sales will increase.* | *The* ***underlying assumption*** (=belief that is used to support a statement or idea) *is that women are inferior athletes.* **2** [U] FORMAL the act of starting to have control or power: **+of** *Castro's assumption of power in 1959*

as·sur·ance /əˈʃʊrəns/ Ac *n.* **1** [U] a feeling of calm confidence in your own abilities, especially because you have a lot of experience SYN **confidence** SYN **self-assurance**: *She began to sing with assurance, an old familiar song.* **2** [C,U] a promise that something will definitely happen or is definitely true, especially to make someone less worried: *jobs with little assurance of long-term employment* | **assurance that** *Despite assurances that everything was fine, Rob looked worried.*

as·sure /əˈʃʊr/ Ac W3 *v.* **1 assure sb** to tell someone that something will definitely happen or is definitely true, so that they are less worried: **+that** *Her doctors have assured us that she'll be fine.* | *It's a very good hotel,* ***I can assure you.*** | **assure sb of sth** *Their guarantee assures customers of fast delivery.* → see also **rest assured (that)** at REST² (4) **2** [T] to make something certain to happen or to be achieved: *Excellent reviews have assured the film's success.* | **assure sb of sth** *The team is assured of a spot in the finals.* [**Origin:** 1300–1400 Old French *assurer*, from Medieval Latin *assecurare*, from Latin *ad-* **to** + *securus* **safe**] → see Word Choice box at INSURE

as·sured /əˈʃʊrd/ Ac *adj.* **1** certain to happen or to be achieved: *Her victory looks assured.* **2** confident about your own abilities SYN **self-assured** SYN **confident**: *a calm and assured manner*

as·sur·ed·ly /əˈʃʊrɪdli/ Ac *adv.* FORMAL definitely or certainly: *Public reports on airline safety* ***most assuredly*** *influence their performance.*

As·syr·i·an /əˈsɪriən/ HISTORY one of the people that lived in northern Mesopotamia from the 25th century to the seventh century B.C.

A·staire /əˈstɛr/, **Fred** /frɛd/ (1889–1987) a U.S. dancer, singer, and actor who appeared in many movies

as·ta·tine /ˈæstəˌtin, -tɪn/ *n.* [U] a radioactive chemical element that is a member of the HALOGEN group

as·ter·isk /ˈæstərɪsk/ *n.* [C] a mark like a star (*), used especially to show something interesting or important in a document [**Origin:** 1300–1400 Late Latin *asteriscus*, from Greek, **little star**] ►see THESAURUS box at **punctuation mark** —**asterisk** *v.* [T]

a·stern /əˈstɚn/ *adv.* in or at the back of a ship

as·ter·oid /ˈæstəˌrɔɪd/ *n.* [C] PHYSICS one of the many small rocky objects that move around the sun, especially between Mars and Jupiter [**Origin:** 1800–1900 Greek *asteroeides* **like a star**, from *aster* **star**]

asth·ma /ˈæzmə/ *n.* [U] MEDICINE a medical condition that causes difficulties in breathing because the AIRWAYS become narrower, often caused by an ALLERGY [**Origin:** 1300–1400 Medieval Latin *asma*, from Greek *asthma*, from *azein* **to breathe hard**]

asth·mat·ic /æz'mætɪk/ *adj.* suffering from asthma: *asthmastic children* —**asthmatic** *n.* [C] —**asthmatically** /-kli/ *adv.*

a·stig·ma·tism /ə'stɪgməˌtɪzəm/ *n.* [U] MEDICINE difficulty in seeing clearly, caused by the inner shape of the eye not being correct [**Origin:** 1800–1900 A- **not** + Greek *stigma* **mark, point**; because there is no point at which light focuses] —**astigmatic** /ˌæstɪg'mætɪk◂ / *adj.*

a·stir /ə'stɚ/ *adj.* [not before noun] LITERARY **1** excited about something **2** awake and out of bed

as·ton·ish /ə'stɑnɪʃ/ *v.* [T] to surprise someone very much, especially because of being unusual or unexpected SYN **amaze**: *Einstein's work still astonishes physicists.* | *It astonished me that she had changed so little in 20 years.* [**Origin:** 1500–1600 *astone* **to astonish** (14–17 centuries) (from Old French *estoner*, from Latin *tonare* **to thunder**) + *-ish* (as in *abolish*)]

as·ton·ished /ə'stɑnɪʃt/ *adj.* very surprised about something, especially because it is unusual or unexpected SYN **amazed**: +**at/by** *We were astonished at some of the children's responses.* | **astonished that** *I'm astonished that you didn't tell me about it!* | **be astonished to hear/learn/find etc.** *I was astonished to learn that he'd already written three books.*

as·ton·ish·ing /ə'stɑnɪʃɪŋ/ *adj.* so surprising that it is difficult to believe SYN **amazing**: *Their album has sold an astonishing 11 million copies.* —**astonishingly** *adv.*

as·ton·ish·ment /ə'stɑnɪʃmənt/ *n.* [U] complete surprise: *The crowd gasped **in astonishment**.* | ***To everyone's astonishment**, 27 people volunteered.*

As·tor /'æstɚ/, **John Jacob** (1763–1848) a U.S. businessman who gave money for a public library in New York City

as·tound /ə'staʊnd/ *v.* [T] to make someone very surprised, shocked, or feel admiration SYN **astonish**: *The judge's decision to free him astounded everyone.*

a·stound·ed /ə'staʊndɪd/ *adj.* very surprised or shocked, especially because something is impressive SYN **astonished**: +**at/by** *I was astounded at the depth of understanding the children showed.*

as·tound·ing /ə'staʊndɪŋ/ *adj.* very surprising, especially because of being impressive SYN **astonishing**: *his astounding success as a painter* | *The difference between the two shows is astounding.* —**astoundingly** *adv.*

as·tra·khan /'æstrəkən, -ˌkɑn/ *n.* [U] black or gray fur used for making coats and hats

as·tral /'æstrəl/ *adj.* FORMAL relating to stars: *astral bodies*

a·stray /ə'streɪ/ *adv.* **1 go astray a)** to become lost: *Your letter must have gone astray.* **b)** to start behaving differently from how you should behave, especially by doing something bad, immoral, illegal: *teenagers who have gone astray* **c)** if a plan or action goes astray, it does not happen in the correct or planned way: *Things started to go astray soon after you left.* **2 lead sb astray a)** OFTEN HUMOROUS to encourage someone to do bad or immoral things that they would not normally do: *Pfeiffer plays a virtuous woman who is led astray.* **b)** to make someone believe something that is not true: *It's easy to be led astray by the news reports.*

a·stride /ə'straɪd/ *prep.* **1** having one leg on each side of something: *a woman sitting astride a horse* **2** FORMAL on both sides of something, such as a river, road etc.: *The village lay astride the main road to Verdun.*

as·trin·gent[1] /ə'strɪndʒənt/ *adj.* **1** criticizing someone very severely: *an astringent humorous novel* **2** TECHNICAL able to make your skin less oily or stop a wound from bleeding **3** having an acid taste like a LEMON [**Origin:** 1500–1600 Latin, present participle of *astringere* **to tie tightly**] —**astringency** *n.* [U]

astringent[2] *n.* [C,U] TECHNICAL a substance used to make your skin less oily or to stop a wound from bleeding

astro- /æstroʊ, -trə/ *prefix* relating to the stars, the PLANETS, or space: *an astronaut* (=someone who travels in space) | *astronomy* (=science of the stars) [**Origin:** Old French, Latin, from Greek, from *astron* **star**]

as·tro·labe /'æstrəˌleɪb/ *n.* [C] an instrument used in the past for measuring angles between stars in order to calculate the position of your ship. It was used until the development of the SEXTANT.

as·trol·o·ger /ə'strɑlədʒɚ/ *n.* [C] someone who uses astrology to tell people about their character, life, or future

as·trol·o·gy /ə'strɑlədʒi/ *n.* [U] the study of the relationship between the movements of the stars and PLANETS and their influence on people and events [**Origin:** 1300–1400 Old French *astrologie* **use of astronomy for human purposes**] —**astrological** /ˌæstrə'lɑdʒɪkəl/ *adj.* —**astrologically** /-kli/ *adv.* → see also HOROSCOPE, ZODIAC

as·tro·naut /'æstrəˌnɔt, -ˌnɑt/ *n.* [C] someone who travels and works in a SPACECRAFT

as·tron·o·mer /ə'strɑnəmɚ/ *n.* [C] a scientist who studies the stars and PLANETS

as·tro·nom·i·cal /ˌæstrə'nɑmɪkəl/ *adj.* **1** INFORMAL astronomical prices, costs etc. are extremely high: *The painting was sold at an astronomical price.* ▶see THESAURUS box at **expensive** **2** PHYSICS relating to the study of the stars: *an astronomical observatory* —**astronomically** /-kli/ *adv.*

as·tron·o·my /ə'strɑnəmi/ *n.* [U] PHYSICS the scientific study of the stars and PLANETS

as·tro·phys·ics /ˌæstroʊ'fɪzɪks/ *n.* [U] PHYSICS the scientific study of the chemical structure of the stars and the forces that influence them —**astrophysical** *adj.* —**astrophysicist** *n.* [C]

As·tro·Turf /'æstroʊˌtɚf/ *n.* [U] TRADEMARK an artificial surface like grass that people play sports on

as·tute /ə'stut/ *adj.* able to understand situations or behavior very well and very quickly, especially so that you can be successful: *astute management* | *an astute judge of talent* [**Origin:** 1600–1700 Latin *astutus*, from *astus* **skill**] —**astutely** *adv.* —**astuteness** *n.* [U]

A·sun·ción /ɑˌsunsi'oʊn/ the capital and largest city of Paraguay

a·sun·der /ə'sʌndɚ/ *adv.* **cast/tear/break etc. sth asunder** LITERARY to suddenly or violently separate something into pieces: *The family was torn asunder by war.*

As·wan High Dam /ˌæswɑn haɪ 'dæm/ a DAM built across the River Nile in southern Egypt

a·sy·lum /ə'saɪləm/ *n.* **1** [U] protection given to someone by a government because they have escaped from fighting or political trouble in their own country: *Thousands of refugees came to Europe **seeking asylum**.* | *The U.S. **granted** him **asylum**.* → see also POLITICAL ASYLUM **2** [C] OLD USE a hospital for people who are mentally ill **3** [C] OLD USE a home for children who have no parents [**Origin:** 1400–1500 Latin, Greek *asylon*, from *asylos* **not able to be seized**]

a·sym·met·ri·cal /ˌeɪsə'mɛtrɪkəl◂ / also **a·sym·met·ric** /ˌeɪsə'mɛtrɪk◂ / *adj.* **1** having two sides that are different in shape OPP **symmetrical**: *asymmetrical patterns* **2** FORMAL not equal or balanced: *an asymmetrical distribution of power* —**asymmetrically** /-kli/ *adv.*

a·symp·to·mat·ic /ˌeɪsɪmptə'mætɪk/ *adj.* MEDICINE if a person or the illness that they have is asymptomatic, there are no signs of the illness

as·ymp·tote /ˌæsɪm'toʊt/ *n.* [C] MATH a straight line on a GRAPH that a curved line continuously moves closer to but never touches

at /ət; *strong* æt/ S1 W1 *prep.* **1** used to show a point in space where someone or something is, or where an event is happening: *Meet me at my house.* | *They sat down at a corner table.* | *I saw your mother at the supermarket.* | *Pete is at Jane's right now* (=at Jane's house). **2 at a party/club/funeral etc.** at an event while it is taking place: *I met my wife at a dance.* | *They're all out at the movies.* **3 at school/work etc. a)** when you are in the place where you study, work etc.: *What did you do at school today?* **b)** in the place where you study, work etc.: *I'll be at work until 6:30.* **4 at lunch/dinner etc.** eating your LUNCH, dinner etc. in a place that is away from your office, CLASSROOM etc.: *She's at lunch; may I take a message?* **5** used to show a particular time: *The movie starts at 8 o'clock.* | *We're really busy* ***at the moment*** (=now). **6** used to show a particular period of time during which something happens: *Cliff works at night.* | *A lot of people get very lonely at Christmas.* **7** used to show the person or thing that an action is directed or aimed toward: *Those kids threw eggs at my car.* | *Look at that!* | *Stop shouting at me!* **8** used to show the person or thing that caused an action or feeling: *Nobody laughed at his jokes.* | *Andy, I'm surprised at you!* | *Dad got really mad at me for scratching the car.* **9** used to show the subject or activity that you are considering when making a judgment about someone's ability: *How's Kevin doing at his new job?* | **be good/bad etc. at sth** *Lisa's bad at saying she's sorry.* | *She's really good at sports.* **10** used to show a continuous state or activity: *The two nations are at war.* | *Many children are still at risk from the disease.* **11** used to show a price, rate, level, age, speed etc.: *Gas is selling at about $1.35 a gallon.* | *You should have more sense at your age.* | *The car was going at about 50 mph.* **12 at least/worst/most etc.** the least, worst etc. thing possible: *John practices for at least half an hour every day.* | *At most, 50% of the population could be affected.* | **at the very most/worst etc.** *I think his car's worth about $1,000 at the very most.* | **at sb's best/worst etc.** *This was Tom Brady at his best.* **13** used to show that you are trying to do something but are not succeeding or completing it: *I clutched at the rope but missed.* **14 at sb's invitation/command/request** because someone asks or orders you to do something: *She attended the dinner at the chairman's request.* **15 at that a)** also or besides: *She's pregnant, and having twins at that!* **b)** after something happens or as a result of it: *Tess called him a liar, and at that he stormed out of the room.* → see also **leave it at that** at LEAVE[1] (14) **16 at a time** at the same time: *She ran up the steps two at a time.* **17 where sb is at** SPOKEN **a)** NONSTANDARD used when saying where someone or something is: *I don't know where we're at – give me the map.* **b)** INFORMAL someone's opinion or situation: *Dan's not very happy were he's at.* **18 where it's at** OLD-FASHIONED used to describe a place or activity that is very popular, exciting, and fashionable: *The Hacienda Club is where it's at.* [**Origin:** Old English *æt*] → see also **(not) at all** at ALL[1] (3), **while you're at it** at WHILE[1] (5)

at·a·vis·tic /ˌæt̬əˈvɪstɪk◂/ *adj.* FORMAL atavistic feelings or behavior are like the feelings or ways of behaving that people have felt since humans have existed

ate /eɪt/ *v.* the past tense of EAT

-ate /ɪt, eɪt/ *suffix* **1** [in adjectives] full of a particular quality, or showing it: *very affectionate* (=showing love) **2** [in verbs] to make something have a particular quality: *to activate* (=make something start working) | *to regulate* (=control something or make it regular) **3** [in nouns] a group of people with particular duties: *the electorate* (=the voters) **4** TECHNICAL [in nouns] a chemical salt formed from a particular acid: *phosphate* **5** [in nouns] the job, rank, or degree of a particular type of person: *a doctorate* (=the degree of Doctor) —**-ately** /ɪtli/ *suffix* [in adverbs] *fortunately*

a·the·ist /ˈeɪθiɪst/ *n.* [C] someone who does not believe that God exists —**atheism** *n.* [U] —**atheistic** /ˌeɪθiˈɪstɪk◂/

A·the·na /əˈθinə/ also **A·the·ne** /əˈθini/ in Greek MYTHOLOGY the goddess of WISDOM and the arts

Ath·ens /ˈæθənz/ the capital city of Greece

ath·e·ro·scle·ro·sis /ˌæθəroʊskləˈroʊsɪs/ *n.* [U] BIOLOGY a medical condition in which fatty substances form on the inside surface of the tubes that carry blood from your heart to the rest of your body, limiting or blocking the flow of blood

ath·lete /ˈæθlit/ W3 *n.* [C] **1** someone who competes in sports competitions: *a professional athlete* **2** someone who is good at sports or who often does sports: *She's a natural athlete.* [**Origin:** 1400–1500 Latin *athleta*, from Greek *athletes*, from *athlon* **prize, competition**]

ˌathlete's ˈfoot *n.* [U] a medical condition in which the skin cracks and ITCHES on your foot and between your toes

ath·let·ic /æθˈlɛt̬ɪk/ *adj.* **1** physically strong and good at sports: *My sons are both athletic.* **2** relating to athletics: *the athletic department*

ath·let·ics /æθˈlɛt̬ɪks/ *n.* [U] physical activities such as sports and exercises

athˈletic supˌporter *n.* [C] FORMAL a JOCKSTRAP

-athon /əθɑn/ *suffix* INFORMAL [in nouns] an event in which a particular thing is done for a very long time, especially to collect money: *a swimathon* | *a walkathon*

a·thwart /əˈθwɔrt/ *prep.* LITERARY across

-ation /eɪʃən/ *suffix* [in nouns] the act, state, or result of doing something: *an examination of the contents* (=act of examining them) | *the combination of several factors*

-ative /ət̬ɪv/ *suffix* [in adjectives] tending to do something or to have a particular quality: *talkative* (=liking to talk a lot) | *argumentative* (=tending to argue) | *imaginative* (=showing imagination)

At·lan·ta /ətˈlæntə, æt-/ the capital and largest city of the U.S. state of Georgia

At·lan·tic Char·ter, the /ətˌlæntɪk ˈtʃɑrt̬ɚ/ HISTORY an agreement signed in 1941 by President Roosevelt of the U.S. and Prime Minister Churchill of Great Britain, which stated the purposes of the war against FASCISM. The United Nations is believed to have based its principles on the ideas contained in the Atlantic Charter.

AtˌlanticˈOcean, the the ocean between the east coast of North and South America and the west coast of Europe and Africa

at-ˈlarge *adj.* representing all of a country, area, or organization rather than a specific part of it: *the newspaper's editor-at-large* | *He was elected to an at-large seat on the board.* | **ambassador-/congressman- etc. at-large** *the ambassador-at-large for war crimes*

at·las /ˈætˀləs/ *n.* [C] a book of maps: *a world atlas* [**Origin:** 1500–1600 *Atlas* giant in an ancient Greek story who had to hold up the sky; because his name was used as the title of a 16th-century book of maps]

At·las Moun·tains, the /ˈætˀləs ˌmaʊntˀnz/ a system of mountain RANGES in northwest Africa, between the Mediterranean Sea and the Sahara Desert

ATM

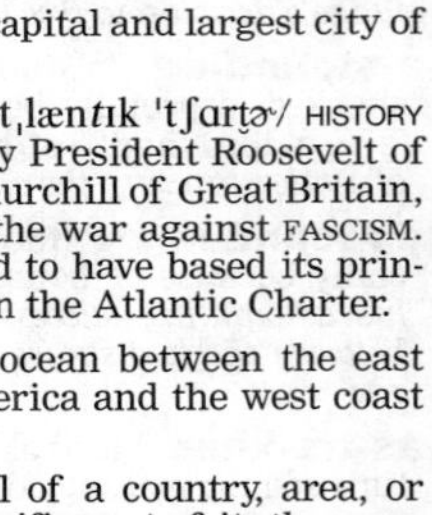

ATM /ˌeɪ ti ˈɛm/ *n.* [C] **Automated Teller Machine** a machine outside a bank that you use to get money from your account: *I lost my ATM card.*

at·man /ˈɑtmən/ *n.* [U] according to the Hindu religion, the most important and basic SPIRITUAL quality that is present in someone's soul and also in the UNIVERSE, that exists and continues always, without changing

at·mos·phere /ˈætˀməsˌfɪr/ S3 W2 *n.* **1** [C,U] the feeling that an event or place gives you: *The hotel has a* *very relaxed atmosphere.* | **+of** *an atmosphere of mistrust in the meetings* **2** [C] EARTH SCIENCE the mixture of gases that surrounds a planet: *Chunks of the comet slammed into Jupiter's atmosphere.* | *the amount of carbon dioxide in* ***the atmosphere*** (=Earth's atmosphere) **3** [U] if a place has atmosphere, it seems special and gives you a feeling of interest or excitement: *The old town was full of atmosphere.* **4** [C] the air inside a room: *a smoky atmosphere* **5** [C] also **standard atmosphere** WRITTEN ABBREVIATION **atm** PHYSICS a unit of pressure that is equal to the pressure needed to support a COLUMN of MERCURY 760 MILLIMETERS high at 0° Celsius at sea level [**Origin:** 1600–1700 Modern Latin *atmosphaera*, from Greek *atmos* **liquid in the air, vapor** + Latin *sphaera* **sphere**]

at·mos·pher·ic /ˌætˀməsˈfɪrɪk◂/ *adj.* **1** [only before noun] relating to the Earth's atmosphere **2** if a place, event, sound etc. is atmospheric, it gives you a particular feeling, especially a pleasant or mysterious one: *a writer of atmospheric novels*

ˌatmospheric ˈpressure *n.* [U] PHYSICS the pressure caused by the weight of the gases in the Earth's ATMOSPHERE pressing down on the surface of the Earth

at·mos·pher·ics /ˌætˀməsˈfɪrɪks/ *n.* [plural] **1** features, events, or statements that make you have a particular feeling **2** continuous cracking noises that sometimes interrupt radio broadcasts, or the unusual conditions in the Earth's atmosphere that produce them

at·oll /ˈætɔl, -tɑl/ *n.* [C] EARTH SCIENCE a CORAL island in the shape of a ring

atom

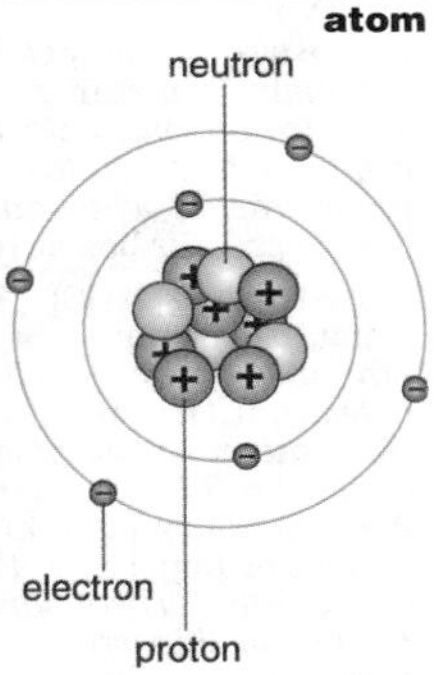

at·om /ˈæṭəm/ *n.* [C] **1** PHYSICS the smallest part of an ELEMENT that can exist alone or combine with other substances to form MOLECULES **2** a very small amount of something: *an atom of truth* [**Origin:** 1500–1600 Latin *atomus*, from Greek, from *atomos* **that cannot be divided**]

a·tom·ic /əˈtɑmɪk/ *adj.* PHYSICS **1** relating to the energy produced by splitting atoms or the weapons that use this energy: *atomic power* | *an atomic submarine* **2** relating to the atoms in a substance: *atomic weight*

aˌtomic ˈbomb also **ˈatom ˌbomb** *n.* [C] a NUCLEAR bomb that splits atoms to cause an extremely large explosion

aˌtomic ˈenergy *n.* [U] NUCLEAR ENERGY

aˌtomic ˈmass *n.* [U] PHYSICS the weight of an atom, usually given in atomic mass units

aˌtomic ˈmass ˌnumber also **aˌtomic ˈnumber** *n.* [C] PHYSICS the total number of PROTONS in the NUCLEUS (=central part) of an atom

aˌtomic ˈmass ˌunit *n.* [U] WRITTEN ABBREVIATION **amu** PHYSICS an amount used as a standard for representing the mass (=weight) of an atom, based on the weight of a CARBON-12 atom

aˌtomic ˈnumber *n.* [C] PHYSICS the total number of PROTONS in the NUCLEUS (=central part) of an atom

at·om·iz·er /ˈæṭəˌmaɪzɚ/ *n.* [C] a thing inside a bottle used to make a liquid such as PERFUME come out in very small drops like mist

a·to·nal /eɪˈtoʊnl/ *adj.* atonal music is not based on a particular KEY —**atonally** *adv.* —**atonality** /ˌeɪtoʊˈnæləṭi/ *n.* [U]

a·tone /əˈtoʊn/ *v.* [I + for] FORMAL a word meaning to do something good after you have done something wrong, in order to make a situation better, used especially about religious actions [**Origin:** 1500–1600 *at one* **in agreement**]

a·tone·ment /əˈtoʊnmənt/ *n.* [U] FORMAL something you do to make a bad situation better after you have done something wrong

a·top /əˈtɑp/ *prep.* LITERARY on top of something: *a hotel perched high atop a mountain*

-ator /eɪṭɚ/ *suffix* [in nouns] someone or something that does something: *a narrator* (=someone who tells a story) | *a generator* (=machine that produces electricity)

ˌat-ˈrisk *adj.* **at-risk children/patients etc.** people needing special care because they are in danger of being hurt or becoming sick: *at-risk kids in foster homes*

a·tri·um /ˈeɪtriəm/ *n. plural* **atriums** or **atria** /-triə/ [C] **1** a large open hall, usually in the middle of a large building, that reaches from the ground up several levels and often to a glass ceiling at the top of the building **2** BIOLOGY an AURICLE **3** BIOLOGY one of the two enclosed spaces in the top of your heart from which blood is sent into the VENTRICLES → see picture at HEART

a·tro·cious /əˈtroʊʃəs/ *adj.* extremely bad: *an atrocious crime* | *The traffic was atrocious.* [**Origin:** 1600–1700 Latin *atrox* **sad, cruel**, from *ater* **black** + *-ox* **looking, appearing**] —**atrociously** *adv.* —**atrociousness** *n.* [U]

a·troc·i·ty /əˈtrɑsəṭi/ *n. plural* **atrocities** [C usually plural, U] an extremely cruel and violent action, especially during a war: *wartime atrocities*

at·ro·phy /ˈætrəfi/ *v.* **atrophies, atrophied, atrophying** [I,T] to become weak, or make something become weak because of lack of use or lack of blood: *His muscles had atrophied after the surgery.* [**Origin:** 1600–1700 Late Latin *atrophia* **becoming smaller or weaker**, from Greek, from *atrophos* **badly fed**] —**atrophy** *n.* [U]

At·si·na /ætˈsɪnə/ a Native American tribe from the northern U.S. and southern Canada

at·ta /ˈæṭə/ **atta boy/girl!** SPOKEN used to tell a dog or a person that they have done something well: *You rolled double sixes again. Atta boy!*

at·tach /əˈtætʃ/ Ac S2 W3 *v.* **1** [T] to connect one object to another: **attach sth to sth** *Attach a recent photo to your application.* | **attach sth with sth** *The note was attached with tape.* | *a large house with an* ***attached garage*** ▶see THESAURUS box at **fasten** **2** [T] to connect a document or computer FILE to an email: *I'm attaching my resume here.* **3** [T] to believe that someone or something has a particular quality or feeling related to it SYN **attribute**: **attach sth to sth** *the shame attached to rape* | *Parry said he hadn't* ***attached*** *much* ***importance*** *to the decision.* | *No* ***blame*** *should be* ***attached*** *to my client for his actions* (=he should not be blamed). **4 be attached to sb/sth** to like someone or something very much, because you have known them or had them for a long time: *Regular babysitters can become deeply attached to the children they take care of.* **5 be attached to sth a)** to work for part of a particular organization, especially for a short period of time: *We have 352 people attached to the embassy in Moscow.* **b)** to be part of a bigger organization: *The computer department is attached to the consumer products division.* **6 attach yourself to sb** to spend a lot of time with someone, especially because you want people to think you are closely connected: *He succeeded by attaching himself to more powerful political figures.* **7 attach a condition to sth** to allow something, but only if someone agrees to do particular things: *Congress can attach conditions to its grants.* **8 attach a label to sth** to describe something in a particular way, especially when this is unfair or too general: *The group tried to get away from the "extremist" label that the media attached to it.* [**Origin:** 1300–1400 Old French *atachier, estachier*, from *estache* **sharp post**]

at·tach·é /ˌætæˈʃeɪ, ˌæṭə-/ *n.* [C] someone who works in an EMBASSY, and deals with a particular subject: *a military attaché*

A

atta'ché ˌcase *n.* [C] a thin hard container with a handle, used for carrying business documents

at·tach·ment /ə'tætʃmənt/ Ac *n.* **1** [C] COMPUTERS a document or FILE that is sent with an email message **2** [C,U] a feeling that you like or love someone or something and that you would be unhappy without them: *a romantic attachment* | **+to/for** *Children **form** very strong **attachments** to their dolls.* **3** [C] a part that you can put onto a machine to make it do different things: *an attachment for the vacuum cleaner* **4** [U] belief in and loyalty toward a particular idea: **+to/for** *their attachment to traditional customs* **5** [U] the act of fastening or connecting one thing to another: *Hooks on the ski boots make attachment easier.*

at·tack¹ /ə'tæk/ S3 W1 *n.*

1 IN A WAR [C,U] the act of using weapons against an enemy in a war: *Their home was damaged in the attack.* | **+on** *the attack on Pearl Harbor* | **be/come under attack** *The city is under attack again today.* | *Rebel forces **launched an attack*** (=started an attack) *late Sunday night.*

THESAURUS

invasion an occasion when an army enters a country and takes control of it
raid a short surprise military attack on a place
assault an attack by an army to take control of a place
ambush a sudden attack by people who have been waiting and hiding
counterattack an attack that you make against someone who has attacked you

2 VIOLENCE AGAINST SB [C] an act of deliberately using violence against someone: **+on** *Police are investigating a series of attacks on women.* | *a sudden increase in the number of **terrorist attacks*** | *Two young men were **the victims of a** knife **attack** last night.*

THESAURUS

rape the crime of forcing someone to have sex
mugging the crime of attacking and robbing someone in a public place
physical attack on a person
assault the crime of attacking someone
→ CRIME

3 CRITICISM [C,U] a statement that criticizes someone strongly: **+on** *recent scathing attacks on the government's welfare policy* | **be/come under attack** *Transportation cuts are under attack in the Senate.* | *a vicious **personal attack*** (=criticism of someone's personality or personal life rather than their policies) *on the Governor*

4 A SHORT PERIOD [C] **a)** a sudden short period of suffering from an illness, especially an illness that you have often: *an asthma attack* | *a massive **heart attack*** (=period when your heart stops working correctly or stops completely) **b)** a sudden short period when you have a strong feeling: **+of** *an attack of guilt* | **a panic/anxiety attack** (=a short period when you feel extremely frightened, anxious etc. and become unable to deal with the situation you are in)

5 ATTEMPT TO END STH an attack on sth a) actions intended to get rid of or stop something such as a system, a set of laws etc.: *the mayor's attack on organized crime* **b)** an attempt to end or harm something important, especially someone's rights, freedom etc.: *an attack on our basic human rights*

6 SPORTS [C,U] an attempt by a player or group of players to get points: *Brazil **went on the attack*** (=made an attempt to score) *and almost scored.* → see also HEART ATTACK

attack² S3 W2 *v.*

1 ATTACK SB [I,T] to deliberately use physical violence against someone: *Two men attacked him in the street.* | *A snake is unlikely to attack unless it feels threatened.* | **attack sb with sth** *He was arrested for attacking his brother with a knife.*

2 IN A WAR [I,T] to start using guns, bombs etc. against an enemy in a war: *Guerrillas attacked an army patrol.*

3 CRITICIZE [T] to criticize someone or something very strongly: *The bill has been attacked because it will put loggers out of work.* | **attack sb for (doing) sth** *Newspapers attacked the President for failing to cut taxes.* ►see THESAURUS box at **criticize**

4 DISEASE [T] to damage part of someone's body: *The virus attacks the body's immune system.*

5 BEGIN DOING STH [T] to begin doing a job or dealing with a problem with determination and eagerness: *There are several ways to **attack the problem** of rising rents.*

6 SPORTS [I,T] to move forward and try to get points: *The Canadian team began to attack more in the second half of the game.*

[**Origin:** 1600–1700 French *attaquer*, from Old Italian *attaccare* **to attach**, from *stacca* **sharp post**] —**attacker** *n.* [C]

at·tain /ə'teɪn/ Ac *v.* [T] FORMAL **1** to succeed in reaching a particular level or in getting something after trying for a long time: *She was 34 before she finally attained stardom.* | *India attained independence in 1947.* **2** to reach a high level: *The balloonists attained an altitude of 33,000 feet.* [**Origin:** 1200–1300 Old French *ataindre*, from Latin *attingere*, from *ad-* **to** + *tangere* **touch**] —**attainable** *adj.*: *an attainable goal*

at·tain·ment /ə'teɪnmənt/ Ac *n.* FORMAL **1** [U] success in getting something or reaching a particular level: *a low level of educational attainment* **2** [C] something that you have succeeded in getting or learning, such as a skill: *an article celebrating our cultural attainments*

at·tempt¹ /ə'tɛmpt/ W2 *v.* [T] to try to do something, especially something that is difficult: **attempt to do sth** *Two prisoners attempted to escape.* | *I attempted to explain why I had taken the money.* | **attempt sth** *The plane crashed while attempting an emergency landing.* ►see THESAURUS box at **try¹**

attempt² W2 *n.* [C] **1** an act of trying to do something, especially something difficult: **attempt to do sth** *an attempt to climb Mt. Everest* | **+at** ***failed attempts** at improving conditions for workers* | *Authorities **made no attempt** to stop the march.* | *The truck hit a guard rail **in an attempt to** avoid a child in the road.* **2** an act of trying to kill someone, especially someone famous or important: *There have been several **attempts on his life**.* | *There have been two **suicide attempts** in the prison this week.* | *He survived **an assassination attempt*** (=an attempt to kill an important person) *in 2004.* [**Origin:** 1300–1400 Latin *attemptare*, from *ad-* **to** + *temptare* **to touch, try**]

at·temp·ted /ə'tɛmptɪd/ *adj. only before noun* **attempted murder/assault/suicide etc.** used in order to describe the crime of trying to kill someone, injure someone etc.: *Hofmann was arrested for attempted murder.* | *the attempted coup*

at·tend /ə'tɛnd/ S3 W2 *v.* **1** [I,T] to go to an event such as a meeting or a class: *More than 1,000 people attended the conference.* | *Potential buyers were invited to attend.* **2** [I,T] to go regularly to a school, church etc.: *The law says you must attend school till you are 16.* **3** [T] if a doctor or nurse attends someone, they take care of them when they are sick: *the doctor who attended her* **4** [T] FORMAL to happen or exist at the same time as something: *Uncertainty attends the future of the industry.* [**Origin:** 1300–1400 Old French *atendre*, from Latin *attendere*, from *ad-* **to** + *tendere* **to stretch**]

attend to *phr. v.* **1 attend to sth** to deal with business or personal matters: *I have a few other things to attend to first.* **2 attend to sb** to take care of someone, especially because they are sick: *A nurse went to attend to the baby.* **3 attend to sb** to help a customer in a store or a restaurant to buy or order something **4 attend to sth** to pay attention to something, especially when you are listening to it: *I turned on the radio without really attending to it.*

at·tend·ance /ə'tɛndəns/ *n.* **1** [C,U] the number of people who attend a game, concert, meeting etc.: *an* *average attendance of 4,000 fans per game* | +**at** ***Attendance** at theme parks **was down*** (=was lower) *this year.* **2** [C,U] the act of going to a meeting, class etc. that is held regularly: +**at** *daily attendance at school* | *A student helped the teacher **take attendance*** (=count how many students are in class today). **3 be in attendance** FORMAL to be at a special or important event: *They had a private wedding with only a few close friends in attendance.* **4 be in attendance on sb** FORMAL to take care of someone or serve them

at·tend·ant¹ /ə'tɛndənt/ *n.* [C] **1** someone whose job is to help customers in a public place: *a gas station attendant* **2** someone who takes care of a very important person, such as a king or queen → see also FLIGHT ATTENDANT

attendant² *adj.* FORMAL **1** relating to something or caused by something: *the trial and all its attendant publicity* | +**on** *the political risks attendant on the program* **2** with someone in order to help them: *a prince and his attendant servants*

at·tend·ee /ə,tɛn'di, ,ætɛn-/ *n.* [C] someone who is at an event such as a meeting or a class

at·ten·tion /ə'tɛnʃən/ S1 W1 *n.*
1 WATCH/LISTEN/THINK CAREFULLY [U] careful thought you give to something that you are listening to, watching, or doing: *Sorry, I guess I wasn't **paying attention*** (=listening, watching, thinking, carefully about something). | *Stop talking and **pay attention to** your driving.* | **pay no attention/not pay attention** *The kids **weren't paying attention** in class.* | *Each letter was **given** special **attention.*** | **sb's attention is on sth** *My attention wasn't on the game.* | **close/serious attention** *It's important to pay close attention to your monthly bill.* | **undivided/full attention** *I need your undivided attention. This is very important.* | *The refinery explosion **focused attention on** safety issues.* | **hold/keep sb's attention** *These educational computer games kept our 5-year-old's attention for quite a while.* | *My **attention wandered*** (=I stopped paying attention) *as Jack's story continued.*
2 INTEREST [U] the special interest that people show in someone or something: *The media has **given** Stone's new movie a lot of **attention.*** | **get/receive/attract attention** *His drawings first attracted attention in the early '60s.* | *The Braves have been playing so well they **have** everyone's **attention.*** | *The press **turned** its **attention to*** (=started showing interest in) *the President's wife.* | *Rob always has to be **the center of attention*** (=the person who makes everyone notice them). | **public/press/media attention** *The new show is receiving a lot of attention from the press.* | **may/can I have your attention?** SPOKEN, FORMAL (=said when you want a group of people to listen to you)
3 NOTICE the fact that someone or something is noticed: **attract/catch/get sb's attention** *I tried to attract the waiter's attention.* | *We thought he was whining just to **get attention*** (=make people notice him because he felt people didn't notice him enough). | **draw/call sb's attention to sth** *It was Jenny who drew my attention to the hole in the ceiling.* | **draw/divert/turn attention away from sth** (=to make people stop being concerned about something such as a social problem) | *A student first **brought** the problem **to** his professor's **attention*** (=caused someone in authority to notice the problem). | *It **came to our attention*** (=we noticed or realized) *that many people were not paying for the service.* | **draw/call attention to yourself** (=to behave in an unusual way that makes people notice you)
4 CARE [U] things that you do to take care of or help someone or something: *My poor old bike **needs** some **attention*** (=it needs to be fixed, cleaned etc.). | *Snake bites require immediate **medical attention.***
5 stand at/to attention used to tell a soldier to stand up straight and stay still
6 Attention! used when ordering a group of soldiers to stand up straight → see also ATTENTIONS

at,tention 'deficit dis,order ABBREVIATION **ADD** *n.* [U] the former name of ATTENTION-DEFICIT HYPERACTIVITY DISORDER

at,tention-,deficit hyperac'tivity dis,order ABBREVIATION **ADHD** *n.* [U] a condition that affects especially children, causing them to be too active and not able to be quiet or pay attention for very long

at·ten·tions /ə'tɛnʃənz/ *n.* [plural] **sb's attentions** personal interest that shows that you care for someone, especially sexual or romantic interest: *She tried to make it clear that she didn't like his attentions.*

at'tention ,span *n.* [U] the amount of time that you are able to carefully listen or watch something that is happening: *a child with **a short attention span***

at·ten·tive /ə'tɛntɪv/ *adj.* **1** listening to or watching someone carefully because you are interested in them OPP **inattentive**: *an attentive father* | +**to** *Teachers are more attentive to good students.* **2** making sure someone has everything they need: *a very attentive waiter* | +**to** *a business that is attentive to its customers* —**attentively** *adv.* —**attentiveness** *n.* [U]

at·ten·u·at·ed /ə'tɛnyu,eɪtɪd/ *adj.* FORMAL made weaker or having less of an effect: *an attenuated form of the polio virus* —**attenuate** *v.* [T] —**attenuation** /ə,tɛnyu'eɪʃən/ *n.* [U]

at·test /ə'tɛst/ *v.* **1** [I,T] to show or prove that something is true: +**to** *Students attested to the value of the program.* | *She's an excellent cook, **as** her son **can attest.*** **2** [T] LAW to officially state that you believe something is true, especially in a court of law

at·tes·ta·tion /,ætɛ'steɪʃən/ *n.* [C,U] FORMAL a legal statement made by someone in which they say that something is definitely true

at·tic /'ætɪk/ *n.* [C] a space or room at the top of a house, often used for storing things: *The winter coats are **in the attic**.* [**Origin:** 1700–1800 French *attique* **of ancient Athens**, from Latin *Atticus*; from the use of an ancient Greek style in designing structures around the top of buildings]

At·til·a /ə'tɪlə, 'ætl-ə/ also **At,tila the 'Hun** (?406–453) a king of the Huns (=an ancient tribe from Asia) who attacked and took control of large parts of the Roman Empire

at·tire /ə'taɪə/ *n.* [U] FORMAL clothes: *business attire* [**Origin:** 1200–1300 *attire* (verb) Old French *atirier*, from *tire* **order, rank**]

at·tired /ə'taɪəd/ *adj.* [not before noun] FORMAL dressed in a particular way: *Sean was properly attired in coat and tie.*

at·ti·tude /'ætə,tud/ Ac S2 W2 *n.* **1** [C,U] the opinions and feelings that you usually have about something: *a macho attitude* | +**toward/about** *the French attitude toward food* ►see THESAURUS box at **opinion**
2 [C,U] the way that you behave toward someone or in a particular situation, especially when this shows how you feel: *The team came out for the second half with a different attitude.* | +**toward** *My boss **has** a patronizing **attitude** toward us.* | **the attitude that** *She begins every job with the attitude that failure is not an option.* | *Ben has a real **attitude problem*** (=he is not helpful or pleasant to be with). | **good/positive attitude** *Sarah's a good student with a positive attitude.* | **a bad/negative attitude** *If you have a bad attitude, you'll never win.* **3** [U] INFORMAL a style, behavior etc. that shows you have the confidence to do unusual and exciting things without caring what other people think: *This is great rock 'n' roll played **with attitude**.* [**Origin:** 1600–1700 French, Late Latin *aptitudo* **fitness**, from Latin *aptus*]

at·tor·ney /ə'tɚni/ W1 *n.* *plural* **attorneys** [C] LAW a word meaning a "lawyer," used in official letters and speech [**Origin:** 1300–1400 Old French *atorné*, past participle of *atorner* **to give a particular job or position to**]

at,torney 'general W3 *n.* [C] LAW the chief lawyer in a state or of the government in the U.S.

at·tract /ə'trækt/ S3 W2 *v.* **1** [T] to make someone interested in something, so that they want to take part in it, see it, support it etc.: *The industry needs to focus on*

A

what attracts customers. | **attract sb to sth** *What was it that attracted you to the sport?* | **attract attention/ interest** *Saturday's game attracted a lot of media interest.* | *a movement designed to **attract** wide **support*** (=make a lot of people want to support it) **2 be attracted to sb** to feel that you like someone and want to have a romantic or sexual relationship with them: *She was obviously attracted to him from the start.* **3** [T] to make someone like or admire something or have romantic feelings for someone: *Her smile was what first attracted me.* | **attract sb to sb** *What attracted you to her in the first place?* **4** [T] to make people or animals come to a place: *The seed mixture will attract a variety of wild songbirds.* | **attract sb/sth to sth** *These programs are designed to attract new business to the area.* **5** [T] PHYSICS if an object attracts another object, it makes that object move toward it: *Show the children how the magnet attracts paper clips, coins etc.* [**Origin:** 1400–1500 Latin, past participle of *attrahere*, from *ad-* **to** + *trahere* **to pull**]

at·trac·tion /ə'trækʃən/ *n.* **1** [C,U] a feeling of liking someone in a sexual way: *the **physical attraction** between us* | +**to** *his attraction to dark-haired women* **2** [C] something interesting or enjoyable to see or do: *"The Viper" is one of the theme park's most popular attractions.* | *the city's top **tourist attraction*** (=a place that many tourists visit) | *The beautiful beaches are the island's **main attraction*** (=most popular place, activity etc.). **3** [C,U] a feature or quality that makes something seem interesting or enjoyable: *The hills of Provence have a magical attraction for many.* | +**of** *Mexico's large labor force may have been the main attraction of the free trade agreement.* **4** [C,U] PHYSICS a force which makes things move together or stay together: *magnetic attraction*

at·trac·tive /ə'træktɪv/ S3 W3 *adj.* **1** someone who is attractive is good looking, especially in a way that makes you sexually interested in them: *an attractive young woman* | *Women seem to **find** him **attractive*** (=think he is attractive).

THESAURUS

good-looking/nice-looking used about anyone who is attractive
pretty used about a girl or woman who is attractive
beautiful used about a woman, girl, or baby who is extremely attractive
handsome used about a man or boy who is attractive
gorgeous/stunning used about anyone who is very attractive
cute used about a baby or young child who is attractive
cute used about someone you think is sexually attractive, especially someone under 25 years old
hot INFORMAL used about someone you think is sexually attractive
→ BEAUTIFUL

2 pleasant to look at: *an attractive outfit* **3** having qualities that make you want to accept something or be involved in it: *an attractive investment* | +**to** *Advertising campaigns make alcohol attractive to young people.* —**attractively** *adv.* —**attractiveness** *n.* [U]

at·trib·ut·a·ble /ə'trɪbyət̬əbəl/ Ac *adj.* [not before noun] FORMAL **attributable to sth** likely to be caused by something: *deaths that are attributable to air pollution*

at·trib·ute¹ /ə'trɪbyut/ Ac *v.*
attribute sth **to** sb/sth *phr. v.* **1** to say that a situation, state, or event is caused by something or someone: *Most airport delays are attributed to weather.* **2** to say that someone was responsible for saying or writing something, painting a famous picture etc., when you cannot be completely sure: *These paintings are attributed to Van Gogh.* **3** to say that someone or something has a particular quality: *It's a mistake to attribute human emotions to animals.* —**attribution** /ˌætrə'byuʃən/ *n.*

at·tri·bute² /'ætrəˌbyut/ Ac *n.* [C] a quality or feature, especially one that is considered to be good or useful: *Kindness is just one of her many attributes.* ▸see THESAURUS box at **characteristic¹**

at·trib·u·tive /ə'trɪbyət̬ɪv/ *adj.* ENG. LANG. ARTS describing and coming before a noun. For example, in the phrase "big city," "big" is an attributive adjective, and in the phrase "school bus," "school" is a noun in an attributive position. —**attributively** *adv.*

at·tri·tion /ə'trɪʃən/ *n.* [U] **1** the situation in which people who leave a company, course of study etc. are not replaced with more employees, students etc.: *a high rate of attrition* **2** the process of gradually destroying your enemy or making them weak by attacking them continuously: *a war of attrition* [**Origin:** 1400–1500 Latin *attritio*, from *atterere* **to rub against**]

at·tuned /ə'tund/ *adj.* [not before noun] **1** familiar with the way someone thinks or behaves so that you can react to them in an appropriate way: +**to** *City government needs to be more attuned to the public.* **2** if your senses are attuned to something, you can easily recognize it: +**to** *the need to be attuned to danger* —**attune** *v.* [T]

atty. *n.* a written abbreviation of ATTORNEY

ATV /ˌeɪ ti 'vi/ *n.* [C] **all-terrain vehicle** a motor vehicle with three or four wheels that you can drive on rough ground

a·twit·ter /ə'twɪt̬ɚ/ *adj.* [not before noun] LITERARY very excited or nervous about something: *Washington is all atwitter with the latest scandal.*

a·typ·i·cal /eɪ'tɪpɪkəl/ *adj.* not typical or usual: *This month's earnings were atypical.*

au·ber·gine /'oubɚʒin/ *n.* [U] a very dark purple color [**Origin:** 1800–1900 *aubergine* **eggplant** (18–21 centuries), from French, from Catalan *alberginia*, from Arabic *al-badhinjan* **the eggplant**] —**aubergine** *adj.*

au·burn /'ɔbɚn/ *adj.* auburn hair is a reddish brown color [**Origin:** 1400–1500 Old French *auborne* **blond**, from Medieval Latin *alburnus* **whitish**]

au cou·rant /ˌou ku'rɑnt/ *adj.* knowing a lot about recent events or fashions

auc·tion¹ /'ɔkʃən/ *n.* [C] a public meeting where land, buildings, paintings etc. are sold to the person who offers the most money for them: *The painting **sold at auction** for $6,500.* | *Items from Liberace's estate **went up for auction**.* | *It's the city's largest **auction house*** (=company that arranges auctions). [**Origin:** 1500–1600 Latin *auctio* **increase**, from *augere*; because the money offered increases]

auction² *v.* [T] to sell something at an auction: *Her possessions were auctioned off after her death.*

auc·tion·eer /ˌɔkʃə'nɪr/ *n.* [C] someone who controls an auction, selling the goods to the people who offer the most money

au·da·cious /ɔ'deɪʃəs/ *adj.* brave and shocking: *a brilliant audacious play* [**Origin:** 1500–1600 French *audacieux*, from *audace* **audacity**, from Latin *audax* **brave**] —**audaciously** *adv.*

au·dac·i·ty /ɔ'dæsət̬i/ *n.* [U] the quality of having enough courage to take risks or do things that are shocking or rude: *They **had the audacity to** use tax dollars to print this stuff.*

Au·den /'ɔdn/, **W. H.** (1907–1973) a British poet

au·di·ble /'ɔdəbəl/ *adj.* a sound that is audible is loud enough for you to hear it OPP **inaudible**: *There was an audible gasp from the audience.* | *She replied in a voice that was **barely audible**.* —**audibly** *adv.* —**audibility** /ˌɔdə'bɪlət̬i/ *n.* [U]

au·di·ence /'ɔdiəns/ S2 W2 *n.* [C] **1** a group of people who watch and listen to a concert, speech, movie etc.: *The audience clapped and swayed to the music.* ▸see THESAURUS box at **watch¹** **2** the number or type of people who regularly watch or listen to a particular program, read a particular magazine or book etc.: *The series was intended to **attract a** family* *audience.* | *She didn't expect her book to* ***reach*** *such a large* ***audience****.* | *MTV's* ***target audience*** (=the kind of people that a program, advertisement etc. is supposed to attract) *is young people between 14 and 30.* | *Advertisers have* ***a captive audience*** (=an audience that has no choice or nothing else to do but to listen or read) *on trains.* **3** a formal meeting with a very important person: *We were* ***granted an audience with*** (=given one with) *the Pope.* [**Origin:** 1300–1400 French, Latin *audientia* **hearing**, from *audire* **to listen**]

au·di·o /ˈɔdioʊ/ *n.* [U] sound, especially sound that is recorded, broadcast, or played on an electronic device: *audio equipment* | *The film was playing, but there was no audio.* [**Origin:** 1900–2000 *audio-* **of hearing**, from Latin *audire* **to listen**]

au·di·ol·o·gy /ˌɔdiˈɑlədʒi/ *n.* [U] the study of how people hear, especially the study of hearing problems —**audiologist** *n.* [C]

au·di·o·tape /ˈɔdioʊˌteɪp/ *n.* [C,U] TECHNICAL a long thin band of MAGNETIC material used to record sound, put into a small plastic case so that it can be played easily

au·di·o·vis·u·al /ˌɔdioʊˈvɪʒuəl/ *adj.* involving the use of pictures and recorded sound: *audiovisual equipment*

au·dit /ˈɔdɪt/ *v.* [T] **1** ECONOMICS to officially examine a company's financial records in order to check that they are correct: *The fund is audited annually by an accountant.* **2** to study a subject at college without getting a grade for it —**audit** *n.* [C]

au·di·tion[1] /ɔˈdɪʃən/ *n.* [C] a short performance by an actor, singer etc., which someone judges to decide if the person is good enough to act in a play, sing in a concert etc.: +**for** *an audition for the lead part* | *They are holding* ***open auditions*** (=auditions that anyone can go to without being invited) *for the part.*

audition[2] *v.* **1** [I] to perform in an audition: +**for** *Judy auditioned for a yogurt commercial.* **2** [T] to judge someone in an audition: **audition sb (for sth)** *We auditioned a lot of actors.*

au·di·tor /ˈɔdɪtɚ/ *n.* [C] ECONOMICS someone whose job is to officially examine a company's financial records

au·di·to·ri·um /ˌɔdɪˈtɔriəm/ *n.* [C] **1** a large room in a large building used for concerts or public meetings: *the school auditorium* **2** ENG. LANG. ARTS the part of a theater where people sit when watching a play, concert etc.

au·di·to·ry /ˈɔdɪˌtɔri/ *adj.* [only before noun] TECHNICAL relating to the ability to hear

Au·du·bon /ˈɔdəˌbɑn/**, John James** (1785–1851) a U.S. NATURALIST and painter of North American birds

ˈAudubon Soˌciety, the an organization that works to protect wild birds

Aug. *n.* the written abbreviation of AUGUST

au·ger /ˈɔgɚ/ *n.* [C] a tool used for making a hole in wood or in the ground [**Origin:** 1500–1600 *a nauger*, mistaken for *an auger*; *nauger* (11–17 centuries) from Old English *nafogar*, from *nafu* **center of a wheel, hub** + *gar* **spear**; because it was originally used to make the hole in the hub of a wheel]

aught /ɔt, ɑt/ *pron.* OLD USE anything

aug·ment /ɔgˈmɛnt/ *v.* [T] FORMAL to increase the value, amount, effectiveness etc. of something: *She teaches night school to augment her income.*

au gra·tin /oʊ ˈgrɑtˀn/ *adj.* au gratin potatoes or vegetables are covered in cheese, butter, and bread CRUMBS and then baked

au·gur /ˈɔgɚ/ *v.* **1** FORMAL to be a sign that something will be successful or unsuccessful: *Their attitudes do* ***not augur well for*** *the success of the peace talks.* **2** [I,T] LITERARY to use signs in order to say what will happen in the future [**Origin:** 1500–1600 *augur* **person who tells the future** (14–21 centuries), from Latin]

au·gu·ry /ˈɔgyəri, -gə-/ *n.* [C] LITERARY a sign of what will happen in the future, or the act of saying what will happen

Au·gust /ˈɔgəst/ WRITTEN ABBREVIATION **Aug.** *n.* [C,U] the eighth month of the year, between July and September [**Origin:** 1000–1100 Latin *Augustus*, from *Augustus* Caesar (63 B.C.–A.D. 14), Roman emperor] → see Grammar box at JANUARY

au·gust /ɔˈgʌst/ *adj.* LITERARY old, famous, and respected

Au·gus·ta /ɔˈgʌstə, ə-/ the capital city of the U.S. state of Maine

Au·gus·tine, St. /ˈɔgəˌstin/ also **St. ˌAugustine of ˈHippo** (354–430) a North African Christian leader, PHILOSOPHER, and writer whose books strongly influenced the development of Christianity

Au·gus·tus /ɔˈgʌstəs/ (63 B.C.–A.D. 14) the EMPEROR of Rome after Julius Caesar, and the first Roman emperor to be accepted by all the people and establish his power

au jus /oʊ ˈʒu, -ˈdʒus/ *adj.* served with a thin SAUCE made from the natural juices that come out of meat as it is cooking: *prime rib au jus*

auk /ɔk/ *n.* [C] BIOLOGY a black and white bird with short wings that lives on or near the ocean

au lait /oʊ ˈleɪ/ *adj.* with milk: *café au lait*

Auld Lang Syne /ˌoʊld læŋ ˈzaɪn/ a Scottish song that people sing when they celebrate the beginning of the new year at 12 o'clock MIDNIGHT on December 31

aunt /ænt, ɑnt/ S2 *n.* [C] **1** the sister of your father or mother, or the wife of your father's or mother's brother: *Aunt Mary* | *My aunt is coming over for dinner.* ►see THESAURUS box at **relative**[1] **2** INFORMAL a woman who is a friend of a small child's parents [**Origin:** 1200–1300 Old French *ante*, from Latin *amita*]

aunt·ie, aunty /ˈænti, ˈɑn-/ *n.* [C] INFORMAL aunt

au pair /oʊ ˈpɛr/ *n.* [C] a young woman who stays with a family in a foreign country to take care of their children [**Origin:** 1800–1900 French **on equal terms**]

au·ra /ˈɔrə/ [C] a quality or feeling that seems to surround or come from a person or a place: +**of** *The restaurant has taken on an aura of success.* [**Origin:** 1700–1800 Latin **air, light wind**, from Greek]

au·ral /ˈɔrəl/ *adj.* relating to the sense of hearing, or to someone's ability to understand a language —**aurally** *adj.*

au·re·ole /ˈɔriˌoʊl/ *n.* [C] LITERARY a bright circle of light SYN **halo**

au re·voir /ˌoʊ rəˈvwɑr/ *interjection* goodbye

au·ri·cle /ˈɔrɪkəl/ *n.* [C] BIOLOGY one of the two spaces inside the top of your heart that push blood into the VENTRICLES

au·ro·ra bo·re·al·is /əˌrɔrə bɔriˈælɪs/ *n.* [singular] SCIENCE bands of moving light that you can see in the night sky in the far north SYN **Northern Lights**

aus·pic·es /ˈɔspəsɪz, -ˌsiz/ *n.* **under the auspices of sb/sth** FORMAL with the help and support of a particular organization: *The negotiations will be held under the auspices of the U.N.* [**Origin:** 1700–1800 *auspice* **telling the future by watching the behavior of birds, good influence** (16–19 centuries), from Latin *auspicium*]

aus·pi·cious /ɔˈspɪʃəs/ *adj.* FORMAL showing that something is likely to be successful: *an auspicious beginning to her career*

Aus·sie /ˈɔsi, ˈɑsi/ *n.* [C] INFORMAL someone from Australia —**Aussie** *adj.*

Aus·ten /ˈɔstən/**, Jane** /dʒeɪn/ (1775–1817) a British writer of NOVELS

aus·tere /ɔˈstɪr/ *adj.* **1** deliberately plain and simple and without any decoration: *her austere way of dressing* **2** having very few things to make a place or situation comfortable or enjoyable: *an austere meal of bread and water* | *an austere way of life* **3** someone who is austere is very strict and looks very serious: *a cold austere woman* —**austerely** *adv.*

aus·ter·i·ty /ɔ'stɛrət̬i/ *n.* [U] **1** ECONOMICS bad economic conditions in which people do not have much money to spend: *years of great austerity* **2 austerity measures/policies/programs etc.** ECONOMICS plans or programs made by a government when it is trying to reduce the amount of money it spends: *an economic austerity package* **3** the quality of being austere: *the austerity of the room* | *his solemn austerity*

Aus·tin /'ɔstɪn, 'ɑ-/ the capital city of the U.S. state of Texas

Aus·tral·a·sia /ˌɔstrə'leɪʒə, ˌɑ-/ *n.* [U] Australia and the islands that are close to it

Aus·tral·a·sian /ˌɔstrə'leɪʒən, ˌɑ-/ *adj.* relating to Australasia

Aus·tra·lia /ɔ'streɪlyə, ɑ-/ a country between the Indian Ocean and the southern Pacific Ocean, which is also a CONTINENT —**Australian** *n., adj.*

Aus·tra·lian /ɔ'streɪlyən, ɑ-/ *n.* [C] someone from Australia: *He's an Australian.* —**Australian** *adj.*: *an Australian accent*

Aus·tri·a /'ɔstriə, 'ɑs-/ a country in central Europe, southeast of Germany —**Austrian** *n., adj.*

ˌAustria-'Hungary also **the ˌAustro-Hunˌgarian 'Empire** HISTORY a European country in the past that consisted of Austria and Hungary, and also parts of some other countries. It was established in 1867 by the Austrian EMPEROR Franz Joseph, and existed until 1918. During that time, Austria and Hungary had separate and independent governments, but the Austrian emperor was the head of both countries.

Aus·tri·an /'ɔstriən, 'ɑs-/ *n.* [C] someone who is from Austria —**Austrian** *adj.*

Austro- /ɔstroʊ, ɑ-, -strə/ *prefix* **1** Austrian and something else: *the Austro-Hungarian empire* **2** Australian and something else: *Austro-Malayan*

au·tar·chy /'ɔtɑrki/ *n.* [U] FORMAL POLITICS an AUTOCRACY

au·tar·ky /'ɔtɑrki/ *n.* TECHNICAL **1** [U] an economic system in which a country produces all the things it needs, as opposed to buying them from another country **2** [C] a country that has this economic system

au·then·tic /ɔ'θɛntɪk/ *adj.* **1** done or made in the traditional, correct, or original way SYN **genuine**: *an authentic Italian recipe for cannelloni* **2** used in order to describe a copy of something that is the same as or as good as the original SYN **genuine**: *These tiles look more authentic.* | *an authentic Texas Rangers uniform* **3** a painting, document, book etc. that is authentic has been proven to be the work of a particular person SYN **genuine**: *an authentic plaster statue by Michelangelo* **4** real or true in every way SYN **genuine**: *DiMaggio was an authentic folk hero.* [**Origin:** 1300–1400 Old French *autentique*, from Late Latin, from Greek *authentes* **person who did a particular thing**] —**authentically** /-kli/ *adv.*

au·then·ti·cate /ɔ'θɛntɪˌkeɪt/ *v.* [T] **1** to prove that something is real and not a copy: *a company that authenticates works of art* **2** to prove that something is true: *The Loch Ness Monster's existence has not been authenticated.* —**authentication** /ɔˌθɛntɪ'keɪʃən/ *n.* [U]

au·then·ti·ci·ty /ˌɔθən'tɪsət̬i/ *n.* [U] **1** the quality of being real or true and not a copy: *Art experts have questioned the painting's authenticity.* **2** the fact of being based on or reflecting real situations and people: *the authenticity of her fiction*

au·thor[1] /'ɔθɚ/ Ac W2 *n.* [C] **1** someone who writes a book, play, story etc.: *The author has signed the book on the title page.* | +**of** *a famous author of children's books* **2** FORMAL the person who develops a plan or idea: +**of** *Mr. Floyd was the author of the helmet law.* [**Origin:** 1300–1400 Old North French *auctour*, from Latin *auctor* **maker, writer**]

author[2] Ac *v.* [T] to be the writer of a book, report etc.

au·thor·i·tar·i·an /əˌθɔrə'tɛriən, əˌθɑr-/ *adj.* strictly forcing people to obey a set of rules or laws, especially ones that are often wrong or unfair: *an authoritarian government* | *His management style has been criticized as authoritarian.* —**authoritarian** *n.* [C] —**authoritarianism** *n.* [U]

au·thor·i·ta·tive /ə'θɔrəˌteɪt̬ɪv/ Ac *adj.* **1** an authoritative book, account etc. is respected because the person who wrote it knows a lot about the subject: *an authoritative biography of Theodore Roosevelt* **2** behaving or speaking in a confident and determined way that makes people respect and obey you: *an authoritative way of speaking* —**authoritatively** *adv.*

au·thor·i·ty /ə'θɔrət̬i/ Ac S3 W1 *n. plural* **authorities**

1 POWER [U] the power you have because of your official position or because people respect your knowledge and experience: **the authority to do sth** *Coach Harris* ***has the authority to*** *hire and fire players.* | +**over** *The generals were given authority over particular regions of the country.* | *Do women and men who are* ***in authority*** *control situations differently?* | *a culture where people do not* ***question authority*** (=express doubts about what someone in authority says)

2 ORGANIZATION [C] an official organization or a local government department which controls public affairs, provides public services etc.: *the Regional Water Authority*

3 the authorities the people or organizations that are in charge of a particular country or area: *Have you reported the incident to the authorities?* | **American/British/Chinese etc. authorities** *an agreement between the U.S. and Columbian authorities*

4 EXPERT [C] someone who knows a lot about a subject and whose knowledge and opinions are greatly respected: *an important religious authority in Egypt* | +**on** *Mr. Li is an authority on Chinese art.* | *a* ***leading authority*** (=one of the most knowledgeable and respected authorities) *in the field of linguistics* ►see THESAURUS box at **expert**[1]

5 I have it on good authority used to say that you are sure that something is true because you trust the person who told you about it: *I have it on good authority that the school board wants to fire the principal.*

6 PERMISSION [C,U] official permission to do something: *The attack was carried out* ***under*** *NATO's* ***authority***. [**Origin:** 1200–1300 Old French *auctorité*, from Latin *auctoritas* **opinion, decision, power**]

au'thority ˌfigure *n.* [C] someone who is or seems powerful: *The boy has no respect for authority figures.*

au·thor·i·za·tion /ˌɔθərə'zeɪʃən/ *n.* [C,U] official permission to do something, or the document giving this permission: **authorization to do sth** *You need to get special authorization to park here.* | +**for** *authorizations for the payment of expenses*

au·thor·ize /'ɔθəˌraɪz/ *v.* [T] to give official or legal permission for something: **authorize sb to do sth** *You are not authorized to enter this area.*

ˌauthorized 'capital *n.* [U] the largest amount of money a company is allowed to get by selling SHARES

'author's ˌchair *n.* [C usually singular, U] ENG. LANG. ARTS a CLASSROOM activity in which a student sits and reads a piece of writing to the other students in the class, usually a story that he or she has written. This expression is also used to talk about the chair a student sits in when doing this activity: *Author's Chair is an opportunity for the writer to receive positive feedback from their classmates.* | *advice for teachers on how to organize an author's chair*

au·thor·ship /'ɔθɚˌʃɪp/ Ac *n.* [U] **1** the fact that you have written a particular book, document etc.: *her authorship of the article* **2** the fact of being the person who thinks of and then makes a plan, piece of work, program etc. happen: *the authorship of the tax plan* **3** FORMAL the profession or process of writing books

au·tism /ˈɔˌtɪzəm/ *n.* [U] a severe mental illness that affects children and prevents them from communicating with other people —**autistic** /ɔˈtɪstɪk/ *adj.*: *an autistic child*

au·to /ˈɔt̬oʊ/ [W3] *adj.* relating to cars: *auto parts*

auto- /ɔt̬oʊ, -t̬ə/ *prefix* **1** working by itself: *an automobile* | *an automatic camera* **2** relating to yourself, or done by yourself: *an autobiography* (=a book about your life, written by yourself) [**Origin:** Greek *autos* **same, self**]

au·to·bahn /ˈɔt̬oʊˌbɑn, ˈɔt̬ə-/ *n.* [C] a wide road in Germany for very fast traffic

au·to·bi·og·ra·phy /ˌɔt̬əbaɪˈɑgrəfi/ *n. plural* **autobiographies** ENG. LANG. ARTS **1** [C] the story of your life, written by yourself ►see THESAURUS box at **book**[1] **2** [U] literature that is concerned with people writing about their own lives —**autobiographic** /ˌɔt̬əbaɪəˈgræfɪk/ *adj.* —**autobiographical** *adj.* —**autobiographically** /-kli/ *adv.* → see also BIOGRAPHY

au·toc·ra·cy /ɔˈtɑkrəsi/ *n. plural* **autocracies** POLITICS **1** [U] a system of government in which one person or group has unlimited power **2** [C] a country governed in this way

au·to·crat /ˈɔt̬əˌkræt/ *n.* [C] **1** POLITICS a ruler who has complete and unlimited power to govern a country **2** DISAPPROVING someone, especially a person with a high rank in an organization, who makes decisions and gives orders to people without ever asking other people for their opinion

au·to·crat·ic /ˌɔt̬əˈkræt̬ɪk◂/ *adj.* **1** making decisions and giving orders to people without asking them for their opinion: *an autocratic manager* **2** having unlimited power to govern a country: *an autocratic government* —**autocratically** /-kli/ *adv.*

au·to·graph[1] /ˈɔt̬əˌgræf/ *n.* [C] a famous person's name, written in their own writing: *Joe DiMaggio's autograph* | *She smiled and joked as she **signed autographs**.*

autograph[2] *v.* [T] if a famous person autographs a book, photograph etc., they write their name on it

ˌauto-imˈmune disˌease *n.* [U] MEDICINE a condition in which substances that normally prevent illness in the body attack and harm parts of it instead

au·to·mak·er /ˈɔt̬oʊˌmeɪkɚ/ *n.* [C] a word meaning a company that makes cars, used especially in newspapers or magazines

Au·to·mat /ˈɔt̬əˌmæt/ *n.* [C] TRADEMARK a type of restaurant in which you put money in machines to get food, that existed from about 1900 until 1990

au·to·mate /ˈɔt̬əˌmeɪt/ [Ac] *v.* [T] to change to a system in which jobs are done or goods are produced by machines instead of people

au·to·mat·ed /ˈɔt̬əˌmeɪt̬ɪd/ [Ac] *adj.* using machines to do a job or industrial process: *a highly automated factory*

au·to·mat·ic[1] /ˌɔt̬əˈmæt̬ɪk◂/ [Ac] [S3] *adj.* **1** an automatic machine, car etc. is designed to operate by itself after you start it, and can be operated using only a few controls: *an automatic weapon* | *a camera with automatic focus* | *Is the heating **on automatic**?* (=is it set to go on by itself) **2** done without thinking, especially because you have done the same thing many times before: *My automatic response to the question was, "No!".* | *Practice the breathing exercises until they become automatic.* **3** something that is automatic is certain to happen, especially because of a rule or law: *automatic yearly pay raises* [**Origin:** 1700–1800 Greek *automatos* **acting by itself**]

automatic[2] [Ac] *n.* [C] **1** a car with a system of GEARS that operate themselves without the driver needing to change them → see also STANDARD **2** a weapon that can fire bullets continuously

au·to·mat·i·cally /ˌɔt̬əˈmæt̬ɪkli/ [Ac] [S2] *adv.* **1** as the result of a situation: *Cancer is not automatically a death sentence.* **2** without thinking about what you are doing: *I automatically assumed she was right.* | *After a while, driving just **comes automatically**.* **3** by the action of a machine, without a person making it work: *The gates rise automatically during high tide.*

ˌautomatic ˈpilot *n.* [C] **1** a machine that flies an airplane by itself, without the need for a pilot to control it **2 be on automatic pilot** INFORMAL to be doing something without thinking about it at all, especially because you have done it many times before or are very tired: *I wasn't really asleep – I was just kind of running on automatic pilot.*

ˌautomatic transˈmission *n.* [U] a system that operates the GEARS of a car without the driver needing to change them

au·to·ma·tion /ˌɔt̬əˈmeɪʃən/ [Ac] *n.* [U] the use of machines instead of people to do a job or industrial process

au·tom·a·ton /ɔˈtɑməˌtɑn/ *n.* [C] **1** someone who seems to be unable to feel emotions **2** a machine, especially one in the shape of a human, that moves without anyone controlling it

au·to·mo·bile /ˌɔt̬əməˈbil, ˈɔt̬əməˌbil/ *n.* [C] a car: *the automobile industry*

au·to·mo·tive /ˌɔt̬əˈmoʊt̬ɪv◂/ *adj.* relating to cars: *automotive products*

au·ton·o·mous /ɔˈtɑnəməs/ *adj.* **1** POLITICS having the power to govern an area, country etc. without being controlled by anyone else: *an autonomous region* **2** FORMAL having the ability to work and make decisions by yourself without any help from anyone else [SYN] **independent** —**autonomously** *adv.*

auˌtonomous ˈregion *n.* [C] POLITICS a large area within a country that has the official right to be independent and govern itself

au·ton·o·my /ɔˈtɑnəmi/ *n.* [U] **1** POLITICS freedom to govern an area, country etc. without being controlled by anyone else: +**from** *Rebel forces are fighting for autonomy from the central government.* **2** the ability to make your own decisions without being influenced by anyone else [SYN] **independence**: *the autonomy of the individual*

au·to·pi·lot /ˈɔt̬oʊˌpaɪlət/ *n.* [C] AUTOMATIC PILOT

au·top·sy /ˈɔˌtɑpsi/ *n. plural* **autopsies** [C] an examination of a dead body to discover the cause of death: *Will they **perform an autopsy**?*

au·to·route /ˈɔt̬oʊˌrut/ *n.* [C] CANADIAN a HIGHWAY in Quebec

au·to·some /ˈɔt̬əˌsoʊm/ *n.* [C] BIOLOGY any CHROMOSOME that does not influence whether a person or animal is male or female —**autosomal** /ˌɔt̬əˈsoʊməl◂/ *adj.*: *autosomal chromosomes* —**autosomally** *adv.*: *Most genes are stored autosomally.*

au·to·sug·ges·tion /ˌɔt̬oʊsəgˈdʒɛstʃən/ *n.* [U] TECHNICAL the process of making someone believe or feel something, without them realizing that you are doing this

au·to·troph /ˈɔt̬əˌtrɑf, -ˌtroʊf/ *n.* [C] BIOLOGY a living thing that produces its own food from substances that do not contain living things, using the energy from the sun or from a chemical process. Most plants and creatures such as BACTERIA are autotrophs.

au·to·work·er /ˈɔt̬oʊˌwɚkɚ/ *n.* [C] someone who works in a factory making cars

au·tumn /ˈɔt̬əm/ *n.* [C,U] the season between summer and winter, when leaves change color and the weather becomes slightly colder [SYN] **Fall**

au·tum·nal /ɔˈtʌmnəl/ *adj.* relating to or typical of autumn: *autumnal colors*

A

aux. the written abbreviation of AUXILIARY, especially of AUXILIARY VERB

aux·il·ia·ry¹ /ɔgˈzɪləri, -ˈzɪlyəri/ *adj.* [only before noun] **1** providing additional help for someone: *auxiliary pilots* **2** an auxiliary motor, piece of equipment etc. is kept ready to be used if the main one stops working or if another one is needed: *the auxiliary generator* → see also AUXILIARY VERB

auxiliary² *n. plural* **auxiliaries** [C] **1** a person or group that provides additional help for someone: *the auxiliary for the Symphony* **2** ENG. LANG. ARTS an auxiliary verb: *a modal auxiliary*

auxˌiliary ˈverb *n.* [C] ENG. LANG. ARTS a verb that is used with another verb to show its tense, MOOD etc. In English the auxiliary verbs are "be", "do", and "have" (as in "I am running," "I didn't go," "they have gone") and all the MODALS

AV, A.V. an abbreviation of AUDIOVISUAL

a·vail¹ /əˈveɪl/ *n.* FORMAL **be to/of no avail** if something you do is to no avail, you do not succeed in achieving what you are trying to achieve: *We searched everywhere to no avail.*

avail² *v.* **avail yourself of sth** FORMAL to accept an offer or use an opportunity to do something: *Avail yourself of every opportunity to learn.*

a·vail·a·ble /əˈveɪləbəl/ Ac S2 W1 *adj.* **1** something that is available is able to be used or can easily be bought or found: *More money may become available later in the year.* | *We've used up all the available space.* | +**for** *The software is not yet available for sale.* | +**to** *The law* ***made*** *more loans* ***available to*** *small businesses.* | ***Every available*** (=all the ones that can be used) *ambulance rushed to the scene of the accident.* | **readily/freely available** (=easy to get) **2** [not before noun] someone who is available is not busy and has enough time to talk to you: *The mayor was* ***not available for comment*** (=not available to be interviewed by a reporter). **3** someone who is available does not have a wife, BOYFRIEND etc., and therefore may want to start a new romantic relationship with someone else —**availability** /əˌveɪləˈbɪləṭi/ *n.* [U] *the availability of health insurance to working families*

av·a·lanche /ˈævəˌlæntʃ, -ˌlɑntʃ/ *n.* [C] **1** EARTH SCIENCE a large amount of snow, ice, and rocks that falls down the side of a mountain **2 an avalanche of sth** a very large number of things such as letters, messages etc. that arrive suddenly at the same time [**Origin:** 1700–1800 French, French dialect *lavantse, avalantse*]

avalanche

Av·a·lon /ˈævəˌlɑn/ in old stories about King ARTHUR, a holy island where Arthur was buried

a·vant-garde /ˌævɑntˈgɑrd◂, ˌɑ-/ *adj.* ENG. LANG. ARTS **1** avant-garde music, literature etc. is extremely modern and often seems strange or slightly shocking **2 the avant-garde** the group of artists, writers, musicians etc. who produce avant-garde books, paintings etc.

av·a·rice /ˈævərɪs/ *n.* [U] FORMAL DISAPPROVING a strong desire to have a lot of money SYN **greed** —**avaricious** /ˌævəˈrɪʃəs◂/ *adj.* —**avariciously** *adv.*

av·a·tar /ˈævəˌtɑr/ *n.* [C] **1** a person who represents an idea, principle etc. completely: +**of** *an avatar of traditional family values* **2** COMPUTERS a picture of a person, animal, or other character that represents you on a computer screen, for example when you are playing computer games on the Internet or when you are in a CHAT ROOM **3** a person or animal which is really a god, especially the Hindu god Vishnu, in human or animal form

Ave. the written abbreviation of AVENUE: *6913 Broadway Ave.*

Av·e·don /ˈævəˌdɑn, -dən/, **Richard** (1923–2004) a U.S. fashion and art PHOTOGRAPHER

a·venge /əˈvɛndʒ/ *v.* [T] LITERARY to do something to hurt or punish someone because they have hurt or offended you: *He wanted to avenge his brother's death.* —**avenger** *n.* [C]

av·e·nue /ˈævəˌnu/ *n.* [C] **1** used in the names of streets in a town or city: *Fifth Avenue* | *Sherman Avenue* ▶see THESAURUS box at **road** **2** a possible way of achieving something: +**for/of** *Today, Yiddish still provides an avenue of communication.* [**Origin:** 1600–1700 French *avenir* **to come up to**, from Latin *advenire*]

a·ver /əˈvɚ/ *v.* [T] FORMAL to say something firmly and strongly because you are sure that it is true

av·erage¹ /ˈævrɪdʒ/ S2 W1 *adj.* **1** [only before noun] the average amount is the amount you get when you add together several quantities and divide this by the total number of quantities: *an average price of $9,000* | *What's the average rainfall in this area?* **2** an average amount or quantity is not unusually big or small: **of average height/size etc.** *I'd say he was* ***of average*** *height.* **3** having qualities that are typical of most people or things: *theories that the average person can understand* | *In an average week, I drive about 250 miles.* ▶see THESAURUS box at **normal¹** **4** INFORMAL neither very good nor very bad: *an average performance*

average² W3 ABBREVIATION **avg.** *n.* **1** [C] the amount calculated by adding together several quantities, and then dividing this amount by the total number of quantities: *The average of 2, 4, and 9 is 5.* | *Prices have risen by* ***an average of*** *1.5%.* | **the national/state/global etc. average** *The national average is a salary of about $20,000 per year.* **2 on average** based on a calculation about how many times something usually happens, how much money someone usually gets, how often people usually do something etc.: *On average, men are taller than women by several inches.* | *Japanese people, on average, live longer than Europeans.* **3** [C,U] the usual level or amount for most people or things in a group: **above/below average** (=better or worse than most other people's) *Paula's grades are well above average.* | **higher/lower than average** *higher than average levels of unemployment* [**Origin:** 1700–1800 *average* **(fair sharing out of costs resulting from) damage to or loss of a ship or the goods it carries** (15–20 centuries), from French *avarie*, from Arabic *'awariyah* **damaged goods**] → see also **law of averages** at LAW (11)

average³ *v.* [linking verb] **1** to usually do something, or usually happen a particular number of times, or usually be a particular size or amount: *I average about 25,000 miles a year in the car.* | *These fish average about two inches in length.* **2** to calculate the average of quantities

average out *phr. v.* **1** if a set of numbers averages out to a particular number, or you average them out, their average is calculated to be that number: *650,000 teachers have been hired over five years; that averages out to 130,000 a year.* **2 sth averages out** used to say that sometimes there is more of one thing, amount, activity etc. than at other times, but that there is a balance over a longer period of time: *Sometimes I pay for the food – sometimes she does. It all averages out.*

a·verse /əˈvɚs/ *adj.* **1 not be averse to (doing) sth** used to say that someone likes to do something sometimes, especially something that is slightly wrong or bad for them: *I don't drink much, but I'm not averse to the occasional glass of wine.* **2 be averse to (doing) sth** FORMAL to be unwilling to do something or to dislike something

a·ver·sion /əˈvɚʒən/ *n.* [singular, U] a strong dislike of something or someone: *These animals* ***have an aversion to*** *sunlight.*

a•vert /ə'vɚt/ *v.* [T] **1** to prevent something bad from happening: *A warning system could have averted the disaster.* **2 avert your eyes/gaze etc.** to look away from something that you do not want to see [**Origin:** 1300–1400 Old French *avertir*, from Latin *avertere*, from *ad-* **to** + *vertere* **to turn**]

avg. the written abbreviation of "average"

a•vi•an flu /ˌeɪviən 'flu/ also **ˌavian influ'enza** *n.* [U] another word for BIRD FLU

a•vi•ar•y /'eɪviˌɛri/ *n. plural* **aviaries** [C] a large CAGE or building where birds are kept

a•vi•a•tion /ˌeɪvi'eɪʃən/ *n.* [U] **1** the science or practice of flying in aircraft **2** the industry that makes aircraft [**Origin:** 1800–1900 French, Latin *avis* **bird**]

a•vi•a•tor /'eɪviˌeɪt̬ɚ/ *n.* [C] OLD-FASHIONED a pilot

Av•i•cen•na /ˌævə'sɛnə/ (980–1037) an Arab PHILOSOPHER

av•id /'ævɪd/ *adj.* **1** doing something as much as you can, because you enjoy it very much: **an avid reader/golfer/skier etc.** *an avid sailor* | *an avid supporter of the arts* | **an avid fan** (=someone who likes a particular activity, type of music etc. very much) **2 an avid interest/desire etc. (in sth)** a strong interest, desire etc.: *an avid interest in birds* [**Origin:** 1700–1800 French *avide*, from Latin *avidus*, from *avere* **to want to have**]

a•vi•on•ics /ˌeɪvi'ɑnɪks/ *n.* [U] TECHNICAL the science and development of the electronic systems used in aircraft

av•o•ca•do /ˌævə'kɑdoʊ, ˌɑ-/ *n. plural* **avocados** [C] BIOLOGY a fruit with a thick green or dark purple skin that is green inside and has a large seed in the middle [**Origin:** 1600–1700 Spanish *aguacate* **avocado**, from Nahuatl *ahuacatl* **testicle, avocado**; influenced by Spanish *avocado* **lawyer**]

av•o•ca•tion /ˌævə'keɪʃən/ *n.* [C] FORMAL an activity that someone does for pleasure; a HOBBY

A•vo•ga•dro's num•ber /ˌɑvə'gɑdroʊz ˌnʌmbɚ/ *n.* CHEMISTRY the number 6.0225×10^{23}, which is equal to the number of atoms in 12 grams of CARBON 12, and is used for calculating a MOLE of a substance

a•void /ə'vɔɪd/ [S3] [W1] *v.* [T] **1** to do something in order to prevent something bad from happening: *Children quickly learn how to avoid punishment.* | **avoid doing sth** *We want to avoid disappointing our customers* **2** to deliberately stay away from someone or something: *Have you been avoiding me?* | *She's at the age where she **avoids** boys **like the plague*** (=used to emphasize how much she does not like boys). **3** to succeed in not becoming involved in something that you do not want to be involved in, either deliberately or by accident: *I avoided the worst of the traffic.* | *Unlike his brother, he managed to avoid trouble with the law.* **4** to not do something deliberately, especially because it is dangerous, bad etc.: *We must avoid involvement in the war.* | **avoid doing sth** *Bill had done everything he could to avoid talking to me.* [**Origin:** 1300–1400 Old French *esvuidier*, from *vuidier* **to empty**] —**avoidable** *adj.*: *an easily avoidable mistake*

a•void•ance /ə'vɔɪdns/ *n.* [U] the act of avoiding someone or something: **+of** *the avoidance of punishment* | *his avoidance of the subject*

av•oir•du•pois /ˌævɚdu'pwɑ, -'pɔɪz/ *n.* [U] the system of weighing things that uses the standard measures of the OUNCE, POUND, and TON → see also METRIC SYSTEM

a•vow /ə'vaʊ/ *v.* [T] FORMAL to say or admit publicly something you believe promise —**avowal** *n.* [C,U]

a•vowed /ə'vaʊd/ *adj.* **1 an avowed Communist/atheist/nonsmoker etc.** someone who publicly shows or admits their belief in a particular idea or way of living **2 avowed goal/purpose/intention etc.** a goal, purpose etc. that someone has stated publicly: *Hitler's avowed intention to defeat the Soviet Union*

a•vun•cu•lar /ə'vʌŋkyəlɚ/ *adj.* LITERARY a man who is avuncular is kind to and concerned about someone who is younger or less experienced than himself

a•wait /ə'weɪt/ *v.* [T] FORMAL **1** to wait for something: *Two men are awaiting trial for the robbery.* **2** if a situation, event etc. awaits you, it is going to happen in the future: *We knew that blizzard conditions awaited us in Boston.* ▸see THESAURUS box at **wait**[1]

a•wake[1] /ə'weɪk/ [S2] *adj.* [not before noun] **1** not sleeping: *Are you awake?* | *I was **wide awake*** (=completely awake) *until 3 a.m.* | *The noise from the party **kept us awake*** (=stopped us from sleeping). | *I drank some coffee to try and **stay awake**.* | *My mother **lay awake** worrying all night.* **2 be awake to sth** to understand a situation and its possible effects: *Suddenly the world was awake to the dangers of nuclear weapons.*

awake[2] *v. past tense* **awoke** /ə'woʊk/, *past participle* **awoken** /ə'woʊkən/ [I,T] **1** FORMAL to wake up, or to make someone wake up: *I awoke, feeling that someone was nearby.* **2** LITERARY if something awakes an emotion or if an emotion awakes, you suddenly begin to feel that emotion

awake sb ↔ **to** sth *phr. v.* LITERARY to make someone understand a situation and its possible effects: *Artists finally awoke to the possibilities of photography.*

a•wak•en /ə'weɪkən/ *v.* FORMAL **1** [T] to make someone feel an emotion or begin to understand something: *The movie awakened a deeper understanding of Mexican culture in me.* **2** [I,T] to wake up or to make someone wake up: *He was awakened by the phone.*

awaken sb ↔ **to** sth *phr. v.* to make someone understand a situation and its possible effects: *People must be awakened to the danger to the environment.*

a•wak•en•ing /ə'weɪkənɪŋ/ *n.* [C] **1** an occasion when you suddenly realize that you understand something or feel something: *a teenager's sexual awakening* | *a spiritual awakening* | *The sudden fall in stock prices was a **rude awakening*** (=shocking moment when you realize the truth about something bad) *for new investors.* **2** the act of waking from sleep

a•ward[1] /ə'wɔrd/ [W3] *v.* [T] **1** to officially give someone something such as a prize or money as a reward for being brave, a high achievement etc.: **award sb sth** *Schultz was awarded a medal for bravery.* | **award sth to sb** *Prizes will be awarded to the top three runners.* ▸see THESAURUS box at **give**[1] **2** to officially decide that someone should receive a payment, a CONTRACT, or a particular legal decision: **award sb sth** *He was eventually awarded $750,000 in compensation by the jury.* | **award sth to sb** *The contract was awarded to a small architectural firm.*

award[2] [S2] [W2] *n.* [C] **1** something such as a prize or money given to someone to reward them for something they have done: *Paltrow won the "Best Actress" award.* **2** something, especially money, that is officially given to someone as a payment or because of a decision made in a court: *a $700 legal award* [**Origin:** 1300–1400 Old North French *eswarder*, from *warder* **to guard**]

a•ware /ə'wɛr/ [Ac] [S2] [W2] *adj.* [not before noun] **1** if you are aware that something such as a problem or a dangerous situation exists, you realize that it exists: **aware that** *Were you aware that your son was taking drugs?* | **+of** *Most people are aware of the dangers of drinking and driving.* | *Doctors want to **make** people **aware of** the risks.* | *"Does she have a boyfriend?" "**Not that I'm aware of.**"* | **well/acutely/fully aware** (=very aware) **2** if you are aware of something, you notice it, especially because you can see, hear, or smell it: **aware that** *She slowly became aware that the room was getting colder.* | **+of** *As it got light, I gradually became aware of where I was.* **3** understanding a lot about what is happening around you and paying attention to it, especially because you realize possible dangers and problems: **politically/environmentally/socially etc. aware** *environmentally aware teenagers* **4 as/so far as I am aware** SPOKEN used to emphasize that there may be things that you do not know about a situation: *As far as*

A

I'm aware, only the managers are going to the meeting. [**Origin:** Old English *gewær*, from *wær*]

a·ware·ness /ə'wɛrnɪs/ Ac *n.* [U] **1** knowledge or understanding of a particular subject or situation: *political awareness* | *We're trying to* ***raise awareness about*** (=make people think more seriously about) *domestic violence.* **2** the ability to notice something using your senses: +**of** *an artist's awareness of light and color*

a·wash /ə'wɑʃ, ə'wɔʃ/ *adj.* [not before noun] **1** containing too many things or people of a particular kind: +**with/in** *TV is awash with talk shows.* **2** covered with a liquid or light

a·way¹ /ə'weɪ/ S1 W1 *adv.* **1** to or at a distance from someone or something: *Go away!* | *The car quickly drove away.* | +**from** *Please keep children away from the glass objects.* | *Move away from the fire!* | *Joe* ***looked away*** (=turned his head in another direction), *trying to control his anger.* **2 3 miles/5 kilometers etc. away** at a distance of 3 miles, 5 kilometers etc. from someone or something: *It's a town about 50 miles away from here.* **3 2 days/3 weeks etc. away** if an event is 2 days, 3 weeks etc. away, it will happen after 2 days etc. have passed: *Christmas is only a month away.* **4** into a safe or enclosed place: *Put all your toys away now, please.* **5** if someone is away from school, work, or home they are not there: *I'm sorry, Mrs. Parker is away this week.* | +**from** *How long are you going to be away from home?* **6** so as to be gone or used up: *All the water had boiled away.* | *Ruben gave all his money away to charity.* | *Support for the Democrats has dropped away.* | *The young lovers danced the night away* (=danced all night). **7** used to emphasize a continuous action: *He's been working away on the deck all afternoon.* **8** if a team is away or is playing away, it is playing a game at its opponent's field, STADIUM etc.: *The Cubs are away in Los Angeles this week.* **9 away with sb/sth!** LITERARY used to tell someone to take someone or something away: *Away with the prisoner!* [**Origin:** Old English *onweg, aweg*, from *on* + *weg* **way**] → see also **far and away** at FAR¹ (4)

away² *adj.* [only before noun] an away game is played at your opponent's field, COURT etc. OPP **home**

awe¹ /ɔ/ *n.* [U] **1** a feeling of great respect and admiration for someone or something: *I felt enormous awe as I looked at the mountain.* | *He spoke* ***with awe*** *of the nuns who started the hospital.* **2 be/stand in awe of sb** to have great respect and admiration for and sometimes a slight fear of someone: *Gelb was clearly in awe of his older friend.*

awe² *v.* [T usually passive] if you are awed by someone or something, you feel great respect and admiration for them, and are often slightly afraid of them: *You can't help but be awed by the wonderful Alaskan scenery.* **—awed** *adj.* [only before noun] *an awed silence*

a·weigh /ə'weɪ/ *adj.* **anchors aweigh!** used to say that the ANCHOR of a ship has been lifted from the bottom of the ocean

'awe-in,spiring *adj.* extremely impressive in a way that makes you feel great respect and admiration: *an awe-inspiring ancient temple*

awe·some /'ɔsəm/ S2 *adj.* **1** extremely impressive, serious, or difficult, so that you feel great admiration, worry, or fear: *an awesome responsibility* | *The view was awesome.* **2** SLANG very good: *The food was totally awesome.* **—awesomely** *adv.*

awe·strick·en /'ɔ,strɪkən/ *adj.* awestruck

awe·struck /'ɔstrʌk/ *adj.* feeling extremely IMPRESSED by the importance, difficulty, or seriousness of someone or something: *She gazed awestruck at the jewels.*

aw·ful¹ /'ɔfəl/ S1 *adj.* **1** very bad, or not nice: *The weather was awful.* | *a really awful concert* | *I felt awful about not being able to help.* | *The soup tasted awful.* | *It sounds awful, but I just can't stand his parents.* ▸see THESAURUS box at **bad¹**, **horrible**, **horrible**, **taste¹** **2** [only before noun] SPOKEN used to emphasize how much or how good, bad etc. something is: *She used the van* ***an awful lot*** *last month.* **3 look/feel awful** to look or feel sick: *You look awful – what's wrong?* **4** LITERARY making you feel great admiration or fear: *an awful power* **—awfulness** *n.* [U]

awful² *adv.* [+ adj./adv.] SPOKEN, NONSTANDARD very: *an awful cute kid*

aw·fully /'ɔfli/ *adv.* SPOKEN very: *It's awfully noisy. Can we close the door?*

a·while /ə'waɪl/ S1 *adv.* for a short time: *Gil stood at the window awhile, watching boats.* → see also A WHILE

awk·ward /'ɔkwɚd/ *adj.* **1** making you feel so embarrassed that you are not sure what to do or say: *It was really awkward, because she and Rachel don't get along.* | *an awkward silence* | *Saul's demands* ***put*** *Mr. McGuire* ***in an awkward position*** (=made it difficult or embarrassing for him to do or say something). ▸see THESAURUS box at **embarrassed** **2** moving or behaving in a way that does not seem relaxed or comfortable SYN **clumsy**: *an awkward teenager* | *Seals are awkward on land, but graceful in the water.* ▸see THESAURUS box at **clumsy** **3** difficult to do, use, or handle: *Getting out of the car is awkward when you're pregnant.* | *The camera is awkward to use.* ▸see THESAURUS box at **difficult** **4** not smoothly done or not skillful: *the awkward wording of the letter* **5** not convenient: *I'm sorry, have I called at an awkward time?* **6** an awkward person is deliberately unhelpful [**Origin:** 1500–1600 *awk* **turned the wrong way** (15–17 centuries) (from Old Norse *öfugr*) + *-ward*] **—awkwardly** *adv.*: *"Excuse me, I mean, could you help me out?" she began awkwardly.* **—awkwardness** *n.* [U]

awl /ɔl/ *n.* [C] a pointed tool for making holes in leather

awn·ing /'ɔnɪŋ/ *n.* [C] a sheet of material hanging over a window, especially on a store, to keep off the sun or the rain

a·woke /ə'woʊk/ *v.* the past tense of AWAKE

a·wok·en /ə'woʊkən/ *v.* the past participle of AWAKE

AWOL /'eɪ,wɔl/ *adj.* **absent without leave** absent from your military group without permission: *Two soldiers had* ***gone AWOL*** *the night before.*

a·wry /ə'raɪ/ *adj.* **1 go awry** if something goes awry, it does not happen in the way that was planned: *Your best financial plans can sometimes go awry.* **2** not in the correct position

aw shucks /ɔ'ʃʌks/ *interjection* OLD-FASHIONED or HUMOROUS used in a joking way to show that you feel shy or embarrassed

aw-shucks /'ɔʃʌks/ *adj.* [only before noun] an aw-shucks attitude, smile etc. is one that shows that someone is shy or embarrassed

ax¹, axe /æks/ *n.* [C] **1** a tool with a heavy metal blade on the end of a long handle, used to cut down trees or split pieces of wood **2 get the ax** also **give sb the ax** INFORMAL **a)** to be dismissed from your job, or to dismiss someone from their job: *He had only been coaching for a year when he got the ax.* **b)** to get rid of something such as a system, service, program, position in a company etc., usually for financial reasons: *The management has not yet said which plants will get the ax.* **3 have an ax to grind** DISAPPROVING to have a personal reason for doing something: *I have no political ax to grind.*

ax², axe *v.* [T] INFORMAL **1** to suddenly dismiss someone from their job: *The nursing director says she was axed because the hospital couldn't afford her salary.* **2** to get rid of a system, service, program, position in a company etc., usually for financial reasons: *NBC axed the show after just three episodes.*

ax·i·om /'æksiəm/ *n.* [C] **1** FORMAL a rule or principle that is generally considered to be true **2** MATH something that is accepted as being true, and which is used as the basis for a THEORY or system in mathematics

ax·i·o·mat·ic /ˌæksiəˈmæt̬ɪk/ *adj.* FORMAL not needing to be proved because you can easily see that it is true SYN self-evident —**axiomatically** /-kli/ *adv.*

ax·is /ˈæksɪs/ *n. plural* **axes** /ˈæksiz/ [C] **1** EARTH SCIENCE the imaginary line around which a large round object, such as the Earth, turns → see picture at GLOBE **2** MATH a line drawn across the middle of a regular shape that divides it into two equal parts **3** MATH either of the two lines of a GRAPH, one going up and the other going across the page, along which the positions of points are marked → see also X-AXIS, Y-AXIS

ˌaxis of ˈsymmetry *n.* [C usually singular] MATH a line that divides a flat shape into two equal parts, where each side matches the other exactly

ˈAxis ˌPowers, the also **the Axis** *n.* HISTORY the countries, including Germany, Italy, and Japan, that fought together against the ALLIES (=countries that included the U.S., the U.K., and the U.S.S.R.) during World War II

ax·le /ˈæksəl/ *n.* [C] the bar connecting two wheels on a car or other vehicle → see picture at BICYCLE[1]

ax·on /ˈækˌsɑn/ *n.* [C] BIOLOGY a long thin part of part of a nerve cell, along which short electrical signals containing messages travel away from the cell toward other cells → see also DENDRITE

a·ya·tol·lah /ˌaɪyəˈtoʊlə, -ˈtɑ-/ *n.* [C] an important Shiite Muslim religious and political leader who has special knowledge of Islamic law, especially one living in Iran [**Origin:** 1900–2000 Persian, Arabic *ayatullah* **sign of god**]

aye /aɪ/ *adv.* SPOKEN, FORMAL used to say yes, especially when voting OPP **nay**: *All those in favor say aye.* —**aye** *n.* [C]: ***The ayes have it*** (=those who voted yes have won).

AZ a written abbreviation of ARIZONA

a·zal·ea /əˈzeɪlyə/ *n.* [C] a bush that produces bright-colored flowers

A·zer·bai·jan /ˌæzɚbaɪˈdʒɑn, ˌɑ-/ a country in western Asia, west of the Caspian Sea and north of Iran —**Azerbaijani** *n., adj.*

AZT /ˌeɪ zi ˈti/ TRADEMARK **azidothymidine** a drug used to treat AIDS

Az·tec /ˈæztɛk/ HISTORY one of the tribes who lived in and controlled Mexico from the 14th century until the 16th century —**Aztec** *adj.*: *Aztec jewelry*

az·ure /ˈæʒɚ/ *adj.* having a bright blue color like the sky —**azure** *n.* [U]

B,b

B

B /bi/ *plural* **B's** *n.* **1** also **b** *plural* **b's** [C] **a)** the second letter of the English alphabet **b)** the sound that is represented by this letter **2** ENG. LANG. ARTS **a)** [C,U] the seventh note in the musical SCALE of C MAJOR **b)** [U] the musical KEY based on this note **3** [C] a grade given to a student's work, to show that it is good but not excellent: *She earned mostly B's this semester.* **4** [U] a common type of blood → see also A → see also B-MOVIE, B-SIDE

b. the written abbreviation of BORN: *Andrew Lanham, b. 1885*

B & B /ˌbi ən ˈbi/ the abbreviation of BED AND BREAKFAST

B.A. /bi ˈeɪ/ *n.* [C] **Bachelor of Arts** the title of a first college degree in a subject such as literature, history etc.: *a B.A. in English Literature* → see also B.S.

baa /bɑ, bæ/ *v.* [I] to make a sound like a sheep —**baa** *n.* [C]

Baal Shem Tov /ˌbeɪl ʃɛm ˈtɔv/ (1700–1760) a Jewish religious leader who started Hasidism

Bab·bage /ˈbæbɪdʒ/, **Charles** (1792–1871) a British MATHEMATICIAN who designed a type of calculating machine which modern computers are based on

bab·ble¹ /ˈbæbəl/ *v.* **1** [I,T] to speak quickly in a way that is difficult to understand or sounds silly or has little meaning: *She* ***babbled on about*** *her children.* **2** [I] to make a sound like water moving over stones: *a babbling brook* —**babbler** *n.* [C]

babble² *n.* **1** the confused sound of many people talking at the same time: *the babble of a crowded party* **2** things that someone says that are silly or do not have any real meaning: *unscientific babble* **3** a sound like water moving over stones → see also PSYCHOBABBLE

babe /beɪb/ S3 *n.* **1** a way of speaking to someone you love, especially your wife or husband: *Hey, babe, how are you?* **2** APPROVING a word for an attractive young man or woman: *Brad's a total babe.* **3** a way of speaking to a young woman, often considered offensive **4** LITERARY a baby: *a woman with a* ***babe in arms*** (=a baby that has to be carried) **5 a babe in the woods** INFORMAL someone who can be easily deceived, because they do not know very much about life

ba·bel /ˈbæbəl, ˈbeɪ-/ *n.* [singular, U] LITERARY the confusing sound of many voices talking together [**Origin:** 1500–1600 Tower of *Babel*, (in the Bible) tower in ancient Babylon whose builders made God angry, so he made them unable to understand each other's speech]

ba·boon /bæˈbun/ *n.* [C] a large monkey that lives in Africa and South Asia [**Origin:** 1400–1500 French *babouin*, from *baboue* **ugly face**]

ba·bush·ka /bəˈbuʃkə/ *n.* [C] **1** a SCARF worn by women that covers the hair and is tied under the chin **2** INFORMAL an old Russian woman

ba·by¹ /ˈbeɪbi/ S1 W1 *n. plural* **babies** [C]
1 CHILD a very young child who has not yet learned to walk or talk: *A baby was crying upstairs.* | *They have a new baby girl.* | *baby food* | *My friend Joyce just* ***had a baby!*** | *Pam is* ***expecting a baby*** *in July* (=her baby will be born in July). | *a woman with her* ***newborn baby*** | *My wife and I have a little boy, and* ***a baby on the way.*** (=my wife is pregnant)

THESAURUS

A baby that has just been born is called a **newborn**. A very young baby who cannot walk or talk yet is called an **infant**. A baby who has learned how to walk is called a **toddler**.
→ CHILD

2 ANIMAL/PLANT a very young animal or plant: *baby birds*
3 baby carrots/corn/vegetables a special type of CARROT etc. that is smaller than normal
4 WOMAN SPOKEN **a)** a way of speaking to someone that you love: *Bye, baby, I'll be back by six.* **b)** a way of speaking to a young woman, often considered offensive
5 YOUNGEST a younger child in a family, especially the youngest: *I have three boys, but he's my baby.*
6 SILLY SPOKEN a word meaning someone who behaves in a stupid or silly way, used especially by children: *Don't be such a baby.*
7 RESPONSIBILITY INFORMAL something special that someone has developed or is responsible for: *The new chamber orchestra is Turner's baby.*
8 THING **this/that baby** SPOKEN a thing, especially a piece of equipment or a machine that you think is very good: *This baby will do 0–60 mph in 6 seconds.*
[**Origin:** 1300–1400 *babe*]

baby² *v.* **babies**, *past tense and past participle* **babied**, **babying** [T] INFORMAL to treat someone or something with special care: *You don't have to baby me! I'm 24 years old.*

ˌbaby ˈblues *n.* [plural] **1** INFORMAL a feeling of DEPRESSION that some women suffer from after they have had a baby SYN **postnatal depression** **2** eyes that are a light blue color: *Look at those beautiful baby blues.*

ˈbaby book *n.* [C] a book your parents make that has pictures of you and information about you when you were a baby

ˈbaby boom *n.* [C] a period when a lot of babies are born in a particular country, especially the period of 1946–1964 in the U.S.

ˈbaby ˌboomer *n.* [C] someone born during a period when a lot of babies were born, especially between 1946 and 1964 in the U.S.

ˈbaby ˌcarriage also **ˈbaby ˌbuggy** *n.* [C] a thing like a small bed with four wheels, used for taking a baby from one place to another when you are walking → see also STROLLER

ˈbaby-faced *adj.* a baby-faced person has a round or fat face like a child

ˈbaby fat *n.* [U] fat around a child's or young person's face that makes their face look round

ˌbaby ˈgrand *n.* [C] INFORMAL a small GRAND PIANO → see also CONCERT GRAND

ba·by·hood /ˈbeɪbiˌhʊd/ *n.* [U] the period of time when someone is a baby

ba·by·ish /ˈbeɪbiɪʃ/ *adj.* like a baby or appropriate for a baby or very young child: *She has a really babyish face.*

Bab·y·lon /ˈbæbɪˌlɑn/ an ancient city in the country that is now Iraq where the people were known for having lives full of wealth and pleasures of all kinds

ˌbaby's ˈbreath *n.* [C] small white flowers often used in arrangements of other flowers

ba·by·sit /ˈbeɪbiˌsɪt/ *v. past tense and past participle* **babysat** /-ˌsæt/, **babysitting** [I,T] to take care of children while their parents are not at home

ba·by·sit·ter /ˈbeɪbiˌsɪt̬ɚ/ *n.* [C] someone who takes care of children while their parents are not at home

ba·by·sit·ting /ˈbeɪbiˌsɪt̬ɪŋ/ *n.* [U] **1** the act of taking care of children in their home while their parents are not at home: *She earns some extra cash by babysitting.* | *a babysitting service* **2** the job of taking care of other people's children in your home while their parents are at work

ˈbaby ˌtalk *n.* [U] sounds or words that babies use when they are learning to talk

ˈbaby ˌtooth *n.* [C] *plural* **baby teeth** a tooth from the first set of teeth that young children have

ˈbaby ˌwalker *n.* [C] a frame on wheels that is used to support a baby while it is learning to walk

bac·ca·lau·re·ate /ˌbækəˈlɔriɪt, -ˈlɑr-/ *n.* [C] FORMAL a BACHELOR'S DEGREE

bac·ca·rat /ˈbɑkərɑ, ˈbæ-/ *n.* [U] a card game usually played for money

bac·cha·na·li·an /ˌbækəˈneɪliən, ˌbɑ-/ *adj.* LITERARY a bacchanalian party, celebration etc. involves alcohol, sex, and uncontrolled behavior

Bac·chus /ˈbækəs, ˈbɑ-/ the Roman name for the god DIONYSUS

Bach /bɑk/, **Jo·hann Se·bas·tian** /ˈyoʊhɑn səˈbæstʃən/ (1685–1750) a German musician, who wrote CLASSICAL music

bach·e·lor /ˈbætʃələ˞/ *n.* [C] a man who has never been married: *Morgan was* ***a confirmed bachelor*** (=a man who has chosen not to marry). | *The Crown Prince was Japan's most* ***eligible bachelor*** (=a rich young man who has not yet married). [**Origin:** 1200–1300 Old French *bacheler*]

ˈbachelor ˌparty *n.* [C] a party for men only, on the night before a man's wedding SYN stag party

ˈbachelor's deˌgree *n.* [C] the first level of college degree SYN B.A.

ba·cil·lus /bəˈsɪləs/ *n. plural* **bacilli** /-laɪ/ [C] BIOLOGY a long thin BACTERIUM, of which some types cause diseases

back¹ /bæk/ S1 W1 *adv.*

1 RETURN in or into the place or position where someone or something was before: *I should be back in time for dinner.* | *That's mine! Give it back!* | *We came back by bus.* | *We drove* ***there and back*** (=to a place and returning to where you started) *in a day.*

2 AS BEFORE in or into the condition that someone or something was in before: *I woke up at 4 a.m. and couldn't get back to sleep.* | *Do you think Ron and his wife will get back together?* | *If a starfish loses a leg, it grows back.* | *It's time I* ***got back to*** *work.* (=started working again) | *Once we sign the contract* ***there's no going back.*** (=we cannot change the situation to what it used to be)

3 REPLY as a reply or reaction to what someone has done: *Can you call me back later?* | *I'll have to get back to you on that.* | *I'll pay you back on Friday.*

4 NOT FORWARD in the direction that you have come from: *Michelle looked back at him over her shoulder and smiled.* | *He stepped back and fell.*

5 HOME/TOWN in or to a place where you or your family lived before: *She left home in 2000 and hasn't been back since.* | *Are you going* ***back home*** *for Christmas this year?* | **+in/at etc.** *Once he was back in New York, he found a job.*

6 AGAIN once again: *Play the tape back for me, okay?* | *I'll check back with you sometime next week.*

7 sit/lie/lean back to sit or lie in a comfortable, relaxed way: *Craig sighed and leaned back in his chair.*

8 THE PAST in or toward an earlier time: *I was making $15 an hour back at the hospital.* | **+in/on** *I had one of those VW Bugs back in high school.* | *This all happened about* ***three years back*** (=three years ago). | *Yeah, Jenny and I* ***go back*** *to sixth grade* (=we have known each other since sixth grade). | ***Looking back*** (=thinking about the past), *I see how hard it was for her.* | *a problem that* ***dates back to*** (=started in) *the 1970s*

9 AWAY FROM FRONT/SURFACE away from a surface, area, thing, or person: *Hold the curtains back from the window.* | *Her hair was pulled back in a ponytail.*

10 A DISTANCE AWAY located or kept at a distance from something: *The buildings are a long way back from the road.* | *Stay back from the edge of the cliff.*

11 back and forth if someone or something goes back and forth, they go in one direction then back to where they started from, and keep repeating this movement: *The chair squeaks when you rock back and forth.* | *Brach flies back and forth weekly, between New York and L.A.*

12 be back where you started to have failed to do what you have been trying to do: *If we lose tomorrow, we'll be back where we started.*

13 BOOK/MOVIE toward the beginning of a book or movie: *Turn back a page.*

14 FASHION used in order to say that something is fashionable again: *Styles from 30 years ago are coming back.*

15 pay/get sb back (for sth) to do something bad to someone because they have done something bad to you or someone you care about: *I'll get you back for this!*

16 go back on a promise/agreement etc. to do the opposite of what you promised to do: *Ken would never* ***go back on his word.*** → see also **set/put the clocks back** at CLOCK¹ (1)

back² S1 W1 *n.*

1 BODY [C] BIOLOGY **a)** the side of a person's or animal's body that is opposite the chest and goes from the neck to the top of the legs: *The cat wanted her back rubbed.* | *She had her hands tied behind her back.* | *Tom usually sleeps* ***on his back*** (=with his back on the bed). | *She carried the baby* ***on her back.*** | *She stood* ***with her back to*** *the camera.* | *Drexler fell* ***flat on his back*** *after bumping into me.* **b)** the bones that go from your neck to the top of your legs: *Megan has a* ***bad back*** (=a painful or injured back). | *I* ***threw my back out*** (=hurt my back) *moving the piano.*

2 BACK SIDE [C usually singular] the side of something that faces the opposite direction from its front or from the direction it moves in OPP front: **+of** *the back of the album* | *the hairs* ***on the back of*** *your neck*

3 BACK PART/AREA [singular, U] the part of a room, container, or other area that is farthest from the front OPP front: *We always sit* ***in the back of*** *the classroom.* | *Kids should always wear seatbelts, even* ***in back*** (=in the seats behind the driver).

4 AREA BEHIND [singular, U] the area behind a house or other building OPP front: *The pool is* ***in back of*** *the house.* | *There's a big garden* ***in the back.*** | *Tom's working on the car* ***out back*** (=behind a house or other building).

5 CHAIR [C] the part of a seat that you lean against when you are sitting: **+of** *Jack leaned against the back of the chair.*

6 BOOK/NEWSPAPER [C usually singular] the last pages of a book or newspaper: **+of** *Answers to the exercises are at the back of the book.*

7 behind sb's back if you do something behind someone's back, you do it without them knowing: *Are people talking about me behind my back?* | *She* ***went behind my back*** *and told my boss* (=told my boss without telling me first).

8 at/in the back of your mind a thought or feeling that is at the back of your mind is influencing you even though you are not thinking about it: *a feeling of fear at the back of his mind*

9 back to back a) happening one after the other: *We did three performances back to back that day.* **b)** with the backs toward each other: *Two rows of chairs were arranged back to back.* → see also BACK-TO-BACK

10 SPORTS [C] one of the defending players on a football, SOCCER, or HOCKEY team

11 get off my back SPOKEN said when you want someone to stop telling you to do something and you are annoyed about it: *I'll do it in a minute. Just get off my back!*

12 be on sb's back SPOKEN to keep telling someone to do something in a way that annoys them: *The boss has been on my back about that report.*

13 know somewhere like the back of your hand to know a place extremely well: *She knows the island like the back of her hand.*

14 have your back to the wall also **sb's back is against the wall** INFORMAL to be in a very difficult position with no choice about what to do: *The general has his back to the wall – he doesn't have enough troops to defend the city.*

15 when/while sb's back is turned if something is happening when your back is turned, it is happening when you are not able to see or know what someone is doing, and it might be something bad: *Do you know what your kids are doing when your back is turned?*

16 turn your back on sb/sth to refuse to help someone or be involved with something: *You're turning your back on a lot of money!*

17 be (flat) on your back to be so sick that you cannot get out of bed: *He's been flat on his back in the hospital for a week.*
18 on the back of sth as a result of something that already exists or something you have already done: *The company is getting new business on the back of existing contracts.*
19 I've/we've got your back INFORMAL used in order to tell someone that you are there to help them and support them if they are in trouble
20 at your back a) behind you: *The plane traveled with the wind at its back.* **b)** LITERARY supporting you: *Caesar marched into Rome with an army at his back.* → see also **at/in the back of your mind** at MIND[1] (33)

back[3] S2 W2 *v.*
1 MOVE SB [I always + adv./prep.,T always + adv./prep.] to move backward, or make someone else move backward: **back toward/across etc.** *Hardaway backed slowly toward the door.*
2 MOVE VEHICLE [I,T] to make a car move backward: **back (sth) into/out of etc.** *Marty backed into a parking space.* | *Teresa backed the car down the driveway.*
3 SUPPORT [T] to support someone or something, especially with money, power, or influence: *The crime bill is backed by the Democrats.* | *government-backed loans*
4 BACK SURFACE OF STH [T usually passive] to put something on the back surface of a flat piece of material: *a plastic-backed shower curtain*
5 MUSIC [T usually passive] ENG. LANG. ARTS if musicians back a singer or another musician, they play or sing the part of the music that is not the main part: *a singer backed by a jazz trio*
6 COMPETITION [T] to risk money on whether a horse, team etc. wins something: *Which team are you backing?*
7 BE BEHIND [T usually passive] to be at the back of something or behind it: *The stage was backed by a light blue curtain.*
8 WIND [I] TECHNICAL if the wind backs, it changes direction, moving around the COMPASS in the direction North-West-South-East

back away *phr. v.* **1** to move backward, away from something, especially because you are afraid, shocked etc.: **+from** *We slowly backed away from the rattlesnake.* **2** to stop supporting or being involved in something, or to decide not to do something you were planning to do: **+from** *The governor backed away from the controversial prison plan.*

back down *phr. v.* to admit that you were wrong or that you have lost an argument: *Anderson forced the company to back down and rehire her.*

back off *phr. v.* **1** to stop trying to force someone to do or think something: *Back off! I don't want your advice.* **2** to move backward, away from something: *Back off, you're too close.* **3** to stop supporting or being involved in something, or to decide not to do something you were planning to do: *The mayor backed off out of concern for public feelings.*

back onto sth *phr. v.* if a building backs onto something such as a river or field, its back faces it: *The houses back onto a busy road.*

back out *phr. v.* to decide not to do something that you had promised to do: *The potential buyer backed out.* | **+of** *The airline backed out of the deal.*

back up *phr. v.* **1 back sth ↔ up** if a vehicle backs up or you back it up, it goes backward: *The truck stopped and then backed up.* **2 back sth ↔ up** if traffic, work etc. backs up or something backs it up, it stops moving, flowing, or being done quickly: *The accident backed up traffic for three hours.* | *Usually traffic **is backed up** all the way to Fair Oaks Avenue by 7:30.* **3 back sth ↔ up** COMPUTERS to make a copy of the information on a computer PROGRAM or DISK **4 back sb/sth ↔ up** to say that what someone is saying is true or that what they are doing is correct: *Brown's statement was backed up by witnesses.* **5 back sb/sth ↔ up** to provide support or help for someone or something: *The police force was backed up by extra officers from nearby towns.* | **back sth up with sth** *The U.N. must back this plan up with action.* **6** to move backward: *Back up a little so that everyone can see.* **7** if a toilet, sink etc. backs up or is backed up, something is blocking it so that the water cannot flow out → see also BACKUP

back[4] S2 W2 *adj.* [only before noun] **1** at the back OPP **front**: *The kids should sit in the back seat.* | *the back entrance* | *the back wall of the factory* → see also BACK DOOR **2** behind something: *the back parking lot of the complex* **3** from the back: *a back view* | *I took the back way out of town.* **4 a back street/road etc.** a street, road etc. that is away from the main streets: *the back streets of Florence* **5 back rent/taxes/pay** money that someone owes from an earlier date **6 a back issue/copy/number** an old copy of a magazine or newspaper: *a pile of back copies of National Geographic* **7** ENG. LANG. ARTS a back vowel sound is made by raising your tongue at the back of your mouth OPP **front**

back·ache /ˈbækeɪk/ *n.* [C,U] a pain in your back

ˈback-ˌalley *adj.* [only before noun] a back-alley ABORTION is one that is done illegally

back·ba·con, back bacon /ˈbækˌbeɪkən/ *n.* [U] see CANADIAN BACON

back·bit·ing /ˈbækˌbaɪṭɪŋ/ *n.* [U] rude or cruel talk about someone who is not present —**backbiter** *n.* [C]

back·board /ˈbækbɔrd/ *n.* [C] the board behind the basket in the game of BASKETBALL

back·bone /ˈbækboʊn/ *n.* **1 the backbone of sth** the most important part of an organization, set of ideas etc.: *The cocoa industry is the backbone of Ghana's economy.* **2** [C] BIOLOGY the row of connected bones that go down the middle of your back SYN **spine** **3** [U] courage and determination: *Stuart doesn't have the backbone to be a good manager.*

back·break·ing /ˈbækˌbreɪkɪŋ/ *adj.* backbreaking work is physically very difficult and makes you very tired

ˈback ˌcountry *n.* [U] an area, especially in the mountains, away from roads and towns

back·court /ˈbækˌkɔrt/ *n.* [C] the area farthest from the GOAL or net in a sport such as basketball or tennis, or the players who play in that area

back·date /ˌbækˈdeɪt◂/ *v.* [T] **1** to write an earlier date on a document or check than the date when it was actually written **2** to make something have its effect from an earlier date: **backdate sth from/to sth** *The pay increase will be backdated to January.* → see also ANTEDATE, POSTDATE, PREDATE

ˌback ˈdoor *n.* [C] **1** a door at the back or side of a building **2** a way of doing something that is not the usual way, and that is secret or slightly dishonest: *The job can be a back door into the bank's training program.*

back·door /ˈbækdɔr/ *adj.* [only before noun] secret, or not publicly stated as your intention: *a backdoor diplomatic solution*

back·drop /ˈbækdrɑp/ *n.* [C] **1** LITERARY the SCENERY behind something that you are looking at: *The mountains made a wonderful backdrop for the concert.* **2** the conditions or situation in which something happens: *Their meeting will happen **against a backdrop of** increasing hardship for ordinary citizens.* **3** ENG. LANG. ARTS a painted cloth hung across the back of a stage

-backed /bækt/ *suffix* **low-backed/straight-backed/narrow-backed etc.** with a low, straight, narrow etc. back: *a high-backed chair*

back·er /ˈbækɚ/ *n.* [C] someone who supports a plan, especially by providing money: *backers of the local crime bill*

back·field /ˈbækfild/ *n.* **the backfield** the area behind the SCRIMMAGE line in football, or the group of players who play there

back·fire /ˈbækfaɪɚ/ *v.* [I] **1** if a plan or action backfires, it has a different and more negative effect than the one you intended: **+on** *This decision could easily backfire on the governor.* **2** if a car backfires, it makes a sudden loud noise because the engine is not working correctly

'back for,mation *n.* [C] ENG. LANG. ARTS a new word formed from an older word, for example "televise" formed from "television"

back·gam·mon /'bæk,gæmən/ *n.* [U] a game for two players, using flat round pieces and DICE on a special board

back·ground /'bækgraʊnd/ S2 W2 *n.* **1** [C] someone's family history, education, social class etc.: +**in** *Steve has a background in computer engineering.* | **ethnic/religious/cultural etc. background** *The men all have different religious backgrounds.* **2** [C,U] the events in the past that explain why something has happened in the way that it has: *Let me give you some background information before we start.* | +**of/to** *the* ***historical background*** *of the war* **3** [singular] the general situation in which something happens: *The elections took place* ***against a background of*** *high unemployment.* **4** [C] the pattern or color on top of which something has been drawn, printed etc.: *red letters* ***on a*** *white* ***background*** **5** [C,U] the sounds that you can hear, besides the main thing that you are listening to: *A television was on* ***in the background****.* | *There was a lot of* ***background noise*** *in the recording.* **6** [C, usually singular] the area that is behind the main thing that you are looking at, especially in a picture: *The background looks a little out of focus.* **7 keep/stay/remain in the background** to try not to be noticed: *Whitfield's mother stayed in the background as he talked to reporters.*

back·hand /'bækhænd/ *n.* [C usually singular] a hit in tennis and some other games in which the back of your hand is turned in the direction of the hit —**backhand** *adj.*

back·hand·ed /'bæk,hændɪd/ *adj.* **1** a backhanded remark or COMPLIMENT seems to express praise or admiration but in fact is insulting **2** a backhanded shot etc. is made with a backhand

back·hand·er /'bæk,hændɚ/ *n.* [C] a hit or shot made with the back of your hand

back·hoe /'bækhoʊ/ *n.* [C] a large digging machine used for making roads etc.

back·ing /'bækɪŋ/ *n.* **1** [U] support or help, especially with money: *The program* ***has*** *financial* ***backing of*** *the new government.* **2** [C] material that is used to make the back of an object **3** [C] ENG. LANG. ARTS the music that is played or sung with the main singer's voice —**backing** *adj.*

back·lash /'bæklæʃ/ *n.* [C] a strong but usually delayed reaction against recent events, especially against political or social developments: +**against** *a backlash against the women's movement* | +**from** *a backlash from angry voters*

back·less /'bæklɪs/ *adj.* a backless dress, SWIMSUIT etc. does not cover much or any of a woman's back

back·log /'bæklɔg, -lɑg/ *n.* [C usually singular] a large amount of work, especially work that should already have been completed: *a large backlog of orders* [**Origin:** 1900–2000 *backlog* **large piece of wood placed at the back of a fire** (17–21 centuries)]

back·lot /'bæklɑt/ *n.* [C] **1** land owned by a movie company, where movies or television programs are made **2** the area behind a company's main offices, where goods are stored

'back ,office *n.* [C] the department of a bank or other financial institution that managed or organizes the work of the institution, but that does not deal with customers

'back ,order *v.* [I,T] to make a request for a product to be delivered when it becomes available: *The product you have requested is back ordered.* —**back order** *n.* [C]

back·pack[1] /'bækpæk/ *n.* [C] a bag carried on your back, often supported by a light metal frame, used especially by climbers and HIKERS (=walkers) → see picture at BAG[1]

backpack[2] *v.* [I] to go walking and camping carrying a backpack: *We were backpacking on the Appalachian trail.* —**backpacker** *n.* [C]

back·ped·al /'bæk,pɛdl/ *v.* [I] **1** to start to change your opinion or actions about something that you had promised: *The government is backpedaling on some of the reforms.* **2** to PEDAL backward on a bicycle **3** to start running back toward a position you were in before

back·rest /'bækrɛst/ *n.* [C] the part of a chair, SOFA etc. that supports your back

back·room /'bækrum/ *adj.* backroom deals, politics etc. happen in a private or secret way, when they should happen in public

'back-,scratching, backscratching *n.* [U] the act of doing nice things for someone in order to get something in return, or to gain an advantage for yourself

'back seat *n.* **1** [C] a seat at the back of a car, behind where the driver sits **2 a back seat driver** INFORMAL **a)** a passenger in the back of a car who gives annoying and unwanted advice to the driver about how to drive **b)** someone in business or politics who tries to give advice and control things that they are not responsible for **3 take a back seat** to accept or be put in a less important position: *Women have often been forced to take a back seat in society.*

back·side /'bæksaɪd/ *n.* [C] INFORMAL the part of your body that you sit on

back·slap·ping /'bæk,slæpɪŋ/ *n.* [U] noisy cheerful behavior when people praise each other's achievements more than they deserve —**backslapper** *n.* [C]

back·slash /'bækslæʃ/ *n.* [C] a line (\) used in writing to separate words, numbers, or letters → FORWARD SLASH

back·slide /'bækslaɪd/ *v.* [I] to start doing the bad things that you used to do, after having improved your behavior for a while: +**into** *Many of the patients backslide into drug and alcohol abuse.* —**backslider** *n.* [C]

back·space /'bækspeɪs/ *n.* [usually singular] the part of a TYPEWRITER or computer KEYBOARD that you press to move backward toward the beginning of the line

back·spin /'bæk,spɪn/ *n.* [U] the turning movement of a ball that is spinning backward as it travels forward

back·splash /'bæksplæʃ/ *n.* [C] TECHNICAL the area of a bathroom or kitchen wall that is behind the FAUCET and covered with TILE to protect the wall

'back-,stab·bing, backstabbing *n.* [U] the act of secretly saying or doing unpleasant things to harm someone else's reputation, especially in order to gain an advantage —**backstabber** *n.* [C]

back·stage /,bæk'steɪdʒ◂/ *adv.* **1** behind the stage in a theater, especially in the actors' dressing rooms: *She invited us backstage.* **2** in private, especially within the secret parts of an organization: *The negotiating is done backstage.* —**backstage** *adj.*

back·stairs /'bækstɛrz/ *adj.* [only before noun] secret: *backstairs romantic encounters*

back·stop /'bækstɑp/ *n.* [C] **1** a fence or board at the edge of a playing area that prevents the ball from going outside the area **2** something that prevents a situation from getting worse

back·street /'bækstrit/ *adj.* backstreet activities are often illegal and done badly: *a backstreet abortion*

back·stretch, back stretch /'bækstrɛtʃ/ *n.* [singular] the straight part of a RACETRACK that is farthest away from the finish line: *Freeman took the lead* ***in the backstretch****.*

back·stroke /'bækstroʊk/ *n.* [U] a way of swimming on your back by moving first one arm upward and backward, then the other, while kicking your feet

back·talk /'bæktɔk/ *n.* [U] INFORMAL a rude reply to someone who is telling you what to do

,back-to-'back *adj.* [only before noun] happening one after another: *back-to-back victories*

back·track /'bæktræk/ *v.* [I] **1** to change your beliefs, statements etc. so that they are not as strong as they were earlier: +**on** *She eventually backtracked on her promise.* **2** to return by the same way that you came: *We had to backtrack about a mile.*

back·up /'bækʌp/ *n.* **1** [C] COMPUTERS a copy of computer information that you can use if the original information is lost or does not work: *a backup copy* | +**of** ***Make a backup of*** *any work you do.* **2** [C] something that you can use to replace something that is lost or does not work: *a backup generator* | *Take an extra flashlight* ***as a backup***. **3** something or someone used to provide support and help when it is needed: *Several police cars* ***provided backup*** *for the officers.* **4** [C] a player who plays on a sports team when another player is ill or injured

back·ward¹ /ˈbækwəd/ W3 also **backwards** *adv.* **1** in the direction that is behind you OPP **forward**: *Hannah took a step backward.* | *I moved slowly backwards.* **2** toward a time in the past OPP **forward**: *There's no point in looking backward.* **3** toward a worse state OPP **forward**: *It feels like the country is moving backward.* | *The new law is seen by some as* ***a major step backwards***. **4** starting from the end and going toward the beginning OPP **forward**: *He can say the alphabet backwards.* | *If you spell "madam" backward it's the same.* **5** with the back part in front → see also INSIDE OUT: *Your T-shirt* ***is on backward***. **6 backward and forward** first in one direction and then in the opposite direction, usually many times: *The trees blew backward and forward in the wind.* **7 bend/lean over backward (to do sth)** to try as hard as possible to help or please someone: *Officials bent over backward to help downtown businesses.*

backward² *adj.* **1** [only before noun] made in a direction toward what is behind you: *a backward glance* **2** developing slowly and less successfully than most others SYN **undeveloped** OPP **advanced**: *an economically backward region* | *The people there are a little bit backward.* → see also FORWARD —**backwardly** *adv.* —**backwardness** *n.* [U]

back·wash /ˈbækwɑʃ, -wɔʃ/ *n.* [U] **1** a backward flow of water, caused by an OAR, wave etc. **2** INFORMAL the SALIVA (=the liquid that is naturally in your mouth) and small pieces of food that sometimes go from your mouth into something you are drinking **3** the bad situation that remains after something bad has happened: *I don't want to be left in the backwash when the company goes bankrupt.*

back·wa·ter /ˈbækˌwɔṭə, -ˌwɑ-/ *n.* **1** a very quiet place not influenced by outside events or new ideas: *a sleepy little backwater* **2** a part of a river away from the main stream, where the water does not move

back·woods /ˌbækˈwʊdz◂ / *n.* [plural] an area in the forest that is far away from any towns

back·woods·man /ˌbækˈwʊdzmən/ *n.* [C] someone who lives in the backwoods

back·yard, back yard /ˌbækˈyɑrd◂ / *n.* **1** [C] an area of land behind a house, usually covered with grass: *kids playing* ***in the backyard*** **2 in sb's own back yard** INFORMAL used in order to talk about something bad that happens very near where someone lives, works etc.: *Our country would react differently to a war that was in our own back yard.* **3 not in my backyard** also **NIMBY** used to say that you do not want something to happen or be done near where you live: *the residents' "not in my backyard" attitude* —**backyard** *adj.* [only before noun]: *a backyard barbecue*

ba·con /ˈbeɪkən/ S3 *n.* [U] **1** salted or smoked meat from the back or sides of a pig, often served in narrow thin pieces: *I want bacon and eggs for breakfast.* ►see THESAURUS box at **meat** **2 bring home the bacon** INFORMAL to provide enough money to support your family [**Origin:** 1300–1400 Old French, from an ancient Germanic word meaning **back**] → see also **save sb's skin/bacon** at SAVE¹ (10)

Ba·con /ˈbeɪkən/, **Fran·cis** /ˈfrænsɪs/ (1909–1992) an Irish artist famous for painting people and animals in twisted shapes with dark, strong colors

Bacon, Sir Francis (1561–1626) an English politician, PHILOSOPHER, and writer

ˌBacon's Reˈbellion HISTORY in 1676 in the Virginia Colony, a period when a poor farmer led attacks on wealthy British owners of land in order to protest against high taxes, low prices for farm goods, and other problems. This was the first violent activity against British authority in the American colonies.

bac·te·ri·ol·o·gy /bækˌtɪriˈɑlədʒi/ *n.* [U] MEDICINE the scientific study of bacteria —**bacteriologist** *n.* [C] —**bacteriological** /bækˌtɪriəˈlɑdʒɪkəl/ *adj.*

bac·te·ri·o·phage /bækˈtɪriəˌfeɪdʒ/ *n.* [C] BIOLOGY a VIRUS (=small living thing that causes infectious illnesses) that infects and lives inside BACTERIA

bacterium

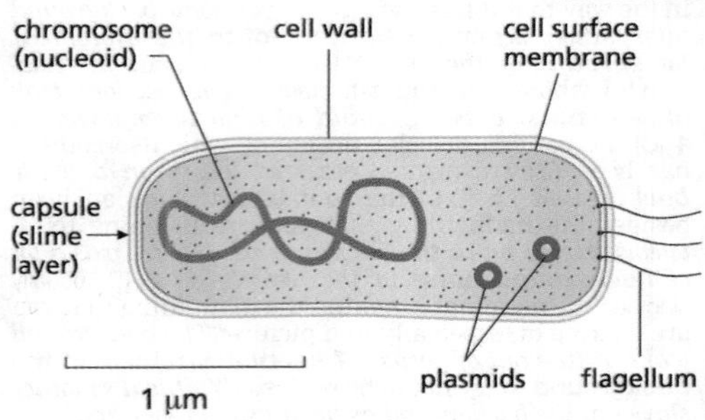

bac·te·ri·um /bækˈtɪriəm/ *n.* [C] *plural* **bacteria** /-riə/ BIOLOGY a tiny organism with a single cell. Some bacteria cause disease, but others are very important in natural processes such as FERMENTATION. → see also VIRUS —**bacterial** *adj.*: *a bacterial infection*

Bac·tri·an cam·el /ˌbæktriən ˈkæməl/ *n.* [C] a CAMEL from Asia with two HUMPS

bad¹ /bæd/ S1 W1 *adj. comparative* **worse**, *superlative* **worst**

1 NOT GOOD not good or not nice OPP **good**: *bad weather* | *a bad smell* | *Did you have a bad day at work?* | *I didn't think the situation could* ***get worse*** (=become worse).

THESAURUS

poor not as good as it could be or should be: *poor performance in school*
disappointing not as good as you hoped or expected: *The results have been disappointing.*
awful very bad or unpleasant: *The weather was awful.*
terrible extremely bad: *The whole experience was absolutely terrible.*
horrible very bad or upsetting: *What a horrible thing to say!*
lousy INFORMAL very bad in quality: *a lousy movie*
appalling/horrific FORMAL very bad and very shocking: *She suffered appalling injuries.* | *a horrific plane crash*
horrendous FORMAL very bad and very frightening or shocking: *The traffic that night was horrendous.* | *a horrendous crime*
atrocious FORMAL extremely bad and often very severe: *Her driving is atrocious.* | *atrocious weather conditions*
abysmal FORMAL very bad, used especially to describe the standard of something: *The quality of care at the hospital was abysmal.*
→ GOOD, HORRIBLE

2 LOW QUALITY low in quality or below an acceptable standard OPP **good**: *bad management* | *His handwriting is so bad!*
3 HARMFUL damaging or harmful OPP **good**: *a bad effect* | *Too much salt is* ***bad for you*** (=harmful to your health). | **be bad for sb/sth to do sth** *It's bad for you to be alone so much.*
4 SERIOUS serious or severe: *a bad cold* | *The pain was really bad.* | *The traffic was even worse today than yesterday.* | *Watch out. Mom's* ***in a*** *really* ***bad mood*** (=feeling very annoyed).
5 NOT APPROPRIATE not appropriate or right for a particular situation or action OPP **good**: *Borrowing more*

money is a bad idea. | *Her decision showed very* ***bad judgment.*** | **a bad time/moment** *Did I call at a bad time?*
6 NOT SKILLFUL having very little skill or ability in a particular activity OPP good: *a bad driver* | *the worst teacher I ever had* | **bad at math/tennis/drawing etc.** *I'm really bad at chess.* | **bad at doing sth** *Sam's really bad at saying "no."*
7 DANGEROUS a bad area or part of a city is dangerous to go to OPP good: *a bad neighborhood*
8 NOT MORALLY GOOD morally wrong or evil OPP good: *He plays one of the bad guys in the movie.* | *You had to tell him the truth. That doesn't make you a bad person.*

THESAURUS
evil/wicked used to describe a very bad person or his or her actions: *a fairy tale about a wicked witch* | *Were his intentions evil?*
immoral/wrong morally wrong, and not accepted by society: *It's wrong to steal.*
reprehensible reprehensible behavior is very bad and deserves criticism: *His conduct was reprehensible.*

9 FOOD food that is bad is not safe to eat because it has decayed: *bad apples* | *This fish has* ***gone bad.***
10 BODY PART a body part that is bad is permanently injured or does not work correctly: *My eyes are getting worse.* | **a bad heart/leg/back etc.** *The illness left him with a bad heart.*
11 SWEARING bad language is offensive and contains swearing or rude words: *Jacky said* ***a bad word*** (=a swear word)*!*
12 feel bad a) to feel ashamed or sorry about something: *I felt bad about lying to him.* **b)** to feel sick: *Are you still feeling bad?*
13 BEHAVIOR used in order to say that a child or animal is behaving in a way that they should not: *Katie was very bad today!* | **bad girl/boy/cat/dog! etc.** *Bad cat! Get off the table!*

SPOKEN PHRASES
14 too bad a) also **it's too bad** used to say that you are sorry that something bad has happened to someone: *It's too bad she had to give up teaching when she got sick.* **b)** also **that's too bad** used to say that you do not care that something bad happens to someone: *"I want to go out tonight." "Too bad, you have homework to do."*
15 not bad used to say that something is good or acceptable: *"How are you?" "Oh, not bad."* | *That's not a bad idea.*
16 not that bad also **not as bad as sth** used in order to say that something is not as bad as someone says it is: *Oh, come on. Three miles isn't that bad.*
17 not too/so bad used in order to say that something is not as bad as expected: *The roads weren't too bad.*
18 *comparative* **badder**, *superlative* **baddest** SLANG NONSTANDARD **a)** used when you think something is very good: *Now that's a bad car!* **b)** APPROVING someone who is bad is very determined and does not always obey rules

19 go from bad to worse to become even more difficult or lower in quality: *The schools have gone from bad to worse in this area.*
20 have/get a bad name also **give sth a bad name** to lose people's respect or trust: *Fighting gives hockey a bad name.*
21 not have a bad word to say about sb/sth if no one has a bad word to say about a particular person, everyone likes and respects that person: *Nobody who knew Jenny had a bad word to say about her.*
22 bad blood angry or bitter feeling between people SYN hostility: *There'd been some bad blood between the two men over a woman.*
23 bad news INFORMAL someone or something that always causes trouble: *Rich foods are bad news if you're on a diet.*
24 in bad faith if someone does something in bad faith they are behaving dishonestly and have no intention of keeping a promise: *We can't prove that the company was* ***acting in bad faith.***
25 sth can't be bad used to tell someone that something is good or worth doing: *The kids get a multicultural education, and that can't be bad.*
26 be in a bad way OLD-FASHIONED to be very sick, injured, or upset
27 a bad penny OLD-FASHIONED, INFORMAL someone or something that causes trouble and is difficult to avoid
it's bad enough at ENOUGH[1] (4) → see also BAD OFF
—**badness** *n.* [U]

bad[2] S3 *n.* **1 take the bad with the good** accept not only the good things in life but also the bad things **2 my bad!** SLANG used to say that you have made a mistake or that something is your fault

bad[3] S2 *adv.* SPOKEN, NONSTANDARD badly: *He needed a drink pretty bad.*

ˌbad 'debt *n.* [C] ECONOMICS a debt that is unlikely to be paid

bade /bæd, beɪd/ *v.* the past tense and past participle of BID

badge /bædʒ/ *n.* [C] **1** a small piece of metal, plastic etc. that you wear or carry to show people that you work for a particular organization, as for example a police officer: *The detective showed his badge and asked a few questions.* | *a security badge* **2** also **merit badge** a small piece of cloth with a picture on it, given to BOY SCOUTS or GIRL SCOUTS to show what skills they have learned: *a badge for photography* **3 a badge of honor/courage etc.** something that shows that you have a particular quality

badg·er[1] /ˈbædʒɚ/ *n.* [C] an animal which has black and white fur, lives in holes in the ground, and is active at night

badger[2] *v.* [T] to try to persuade someone by asking them something several times SYN pester: **badger sb to do sth/badger sb into doing sth** *Suppliers kept badgering the company to pay its bills.*

'bad guy *n.* [C] INFORMAL **1** someone who is bad, especially a character in a book or movie: *De Niro plays the bad guy.* **2** the person in a situation or relationship who always says "no" or says negative things: *I don't want to be the bad guy, but we can't afford a new car right now.*

bad·i·nage /ˌbædnˈɑʒ/ *n.* [U] FORMAL OR HUMOROUS playful joking conversation

bad·lands /ˈbædlændz/ *n.* [plural] GEOGRAPHY areas of land where no crops can grow and where there are rocky hills that have a strange shape

Bad·lands, the /ˈbædlændz/ an area of land in the northern central U.S. in the states of South Dakota and Nebraska that is very dry with strangely shaped rocks and hills

bad·ly /ˈbædli/ S3 W3 *adv. comparative* **worse**, *superlative* **worst 1** in an unsatisfactory or unsuccessful way: *a badly written story* | *Math is often taught very badly.* | *badly made furniture* | *The Warriors didn't* ***do too badly****, even without their star player.* **2** to a great or serious degree: *She wanted to go so badly.* | *Did you sprain it badly?* | *The refugees badly need food and clean water.* | *It was badly damaged in the storm.*

ˌbadly-'off *adj.* [not before noun] BAD OFF

bad·min·ton /ˈbædˌmɪntˀn/ *n.* [U] a game like tennis but played with a BIRDIE (=small feathered object) instead of a ball [**Origin:** 1800–1900 *Badminton* grand house in Gloucestershire, England where it was first played]

'bad-mouth *v.* [T] INFORMAL to criticize someone or something: *He's going around bad-mouthing me to my colleagues.*

ˌbad 'off *adj. comparative* **worse off**, *superlative* **worst off** [not before noun] INFORMAL **1** not having much money SYN poor: *We're not as bad off as some people we know.* **2** in a bad situation: *The state's water supply will be bad off without more rain.*

ˌbad-ˈtempered *adj.* easily annoyed or made angry

baf·fle[1] /ˈbæfəl/ *v.* [T] if something baffles someone, they cannot understand or explain it at all: *The disease has baffled doctors, who are unable to treat it.* —**bafflement** *n.* [U] —**baffling** *adj.*: *a baffling mystery*

baffle[2] *n.* [C] SCIENCE a board, sheet of metal etc. that controls the flow of air, water, or sound into or out of something

baf·fled /ˈbæfəld/ *adj.* unable to understand something at all: *Scientists are completely baffled by the results.*

bags

bag[1] /bæg/ [S1] [W2] *n.* [C]
1 CONTAINER a) a container made of paper, cloth etc., which usually opens at the top: *a paper bag* | *a garbage bag* **b)** a large bag used to carry your clothes, things etc. when you are traveling [SYN] **suitcase** → see also LUGGAGE, BAGGAGE: *We picked up our bags and went through Customs.* **c)** a PURSE [SYN] **handbag**: *She looked in her bag for her keys.* → see picture at CONTAINER
2 AMOUNT the amount that a bag will hold: +**of** *two bags of sugar*
3 SPORT one of the BASES in baseball
4 in the bag INFORMAL certain to be won or achieved: *They were ahead 6–2, and figured the game was in the bag.*
5 pack your bags INFORMAL to leave a place where you have been living, usually after an argument: *If he doesn't show me more respect, then he can pack his bags.*
6 EYES bags under your eyes dark circles or loose skin around your eyes, usually because of old age or being tired
7 sb's bag INFORMAL something that someone is very interested in or very good at: *Computers are **not** really **my bag**.*
8 a bag of bones INFORMAL a person or animal who is too thin
[**Origin:** 1200–1300 Old Norse *baggi*] → see also AIR BAG, **let the cat out of the bag** at CAT (2), **be left holding the bag** at HOLD[1] (30), **a mixed bag** at MIXED (6), SLEEPING BAG

bag[2] [S2] *v.* **bagged, bagging 1** [T] to put materials or objects into bags: *He got a job bagging groceries.* **2** SPOKEN to decide not to do something: *Let's bag this. I'm tired of waiting.* **3** [T] INFORMAL to manage to get something that a lot of people want, especially a prize or award: *Miller bagged the top songwriter's award.* **4** [T] INFORMAL to kill or catch animals or birds: *We bagged a rabbit.* **5** [I] also **bag out** INFORMAL if clothes or skin bags, it becomes stretched and hangs loosely [SYN] **sag**

bag·a·telle /ˌbægəˈtɛl/ *n.* **1** [U] a game played on a board with small balls that must be rolled into holes **2** [singular] something that is small and unimportant compared to everything else **3** [C] a short piece of CLASSICAL music

ba·gel /ˈbeɪgəl/ *n.* [C] a small ring-shaped type of bread: *a bagel with cream cheese* → see picture at BREAD[1] [**Origin:** 1900–2000 Yiddish *beygel*, from Old High German *boug* **ring**]

bag·ful /ˈbægfʊl/ *n.* [C] *plural* **bagfuls** or **bagsful** the amount a bag can hold

bag·gage /ˈbægɪdʒ/ *n.* [U] **1** the SUITCASES, bags, boxes etc. carried by someone who is traveling [SYN] **luggage**: *carry-on baggage* **2** INFORMAL past experiences that can cause emotional problems in the present: *She brought a lot of baggage to the marriage.* [**Origin:** 1400–1500 French *bagage*, from Old French *bague* **bundle**]

ˈbaggage ˌcar *n.* [C] the part of a train where boxes, bags etc. are carried

ˈbaggage ˌroom *n.* [C] a place, in a public building, where you can leave your bags and collect them later

Bag·gie /ˈbægi/ *n.* [C] TRADEMARK a small plastic bag used to keep food in

bag·gy /ˈbægi/ *adj.* baggy clothes hang in loose folds: *a baggy red sweater*

Bagh·dad /ˈbægdæd/ the capital and largest city of Iraq

ˈbag ˌlady *n.* [C] INFORMAL an impolite word for a woman without a home who carries all her possessions with her

bag·pipes /ˈbægpaɪps/ *n.* [plural] a musical instrument played especially in Scotland, in which air stored in a bag is forced out through pipes to produce the sound —**bagpipe** *adj.*

ba·guette /bæˈgɛt/ *n.* [C] a long thin LOAF of bread → see picture at BREAD[1]

bah /bɑ/ *interjection* used to show disapproval of something: *Bah! Christmas is too commercial.*

Ba·ha'i /bəˈhaɪ/ a member of the Baha'i Faith

Ba'ha'i Faith, the a religion started in 1863 and based on the belief that people should be peaceful and kind and respect all people, races, and religions

Ba·ha·mas, the /bəˈhɑməz/ a country that consists of a group of islands in the Atlantic Ocean, southeast of Florida —**Bahamian** /bəˈheɪmiən/ *n., adj.*

Ba·haul·lah /bɑˌhaʊˈlɑ/ (1817–1892) a Persian religious leader, originally called Mirza Huseyn Ali, who started the Baha'i Faith

Bah·rain, Bahrein /bɑˈreɪn/ a country consisting of a group of islands in the Persian Gulf, near the coast of Saudi Arabia —**Bahraini** *n., adj.*

baht /bɑt/ *n.* [C] the standard unit of money used in Thailand

Bai·kal, Lake /baɪˈkɑl/ a lake in southeast Russia that is the largest FRESHWATER lake in the Eurasian continent

bail[1] /beɪl/ *n.* [U] LAW money left with a court of law to prove that a prisoner will return when their TRIAL starts: *Harrell will be **released on bail*** (=let out of prison when bail is paid) *until his trial.* | *Carpenter **is free on bail** while he appeals his conviction.* | *She is being **held without bail*** (=staying in prison because bail is not allowed or cannot be paid) *after her arrest Thursday.* | **post/stand bail** (=pay the bail) | **jump/skip bail** (=to not return to trial as you promised) [**Origin:** 1300–1400 Old French **keeping someone as a prisoner**, from *baillier* **to deliver, keep as a prisoner**, from Medieval Latin *bajulare* **to control**]

bail[2] *v.* **1** [I,T] to remove water from the bottom of a boat **2** SLANG, DISAPPROVING also **bail on sb** to stop being involved in a situation because you do not want to be involved, especially when this leaves other people to finish something alone: *You totally bailed on us, man!*

bail out *phr. v.* **1 bail sb/sth ↔ out** to do something to help someone out of trouble, especially financial problems: *The state is bailing out the school districts* *by raising sales taxes.* **2** INFORMAL to escape from a situation that you do not want to be involved in anymore: *After ten years in the business, McArthur is bailing out.* **3 bail sb ↔ out** to leave a large sum of money with a court so that someone can be let out of prison while waiting for their TRIAL: *He called me to bail him out.* **4** to escape from an airplane, using a PARACHUTE **5 bail sth ↔ out** to remove water from the bottom of a boat

bai·ley /ˈbeɪli/ *n.* [C] an open area inside the outer wall of a castle

bail·iff /ˈbeɪlɪf/ *n.* [C] LAW an official of the legal system who watches prisoners and keeps order in a court of law

bail·i·wick /ˈbeɪliˌwɪk/ *n.* [C] FORMAL an area or subject that someone is interested in or responsible for

bail·out /ˈbeɪlaʊt/ *n.* [C] INFORMAL a situation in which financial help is given to a person or a company that is in difficulty: *a bailout by the government*

bait¹ /beɪt/ *n.* [singular, U] **1** food used to attract animals, especially fish, so that you can catch them: *The trout just weren't **taking the bait*** (=eating it and being caught). **2** something used to make someone do something, buy something etc., especially done in a way to deceive people: *Plenty of people **took the bait*** (=accepted what was offered) *and ended up losing their life savings.* **3 rise to the bait** to become angry when someone is deliberately trying to make you angry: *Sanders simply refused to rise to the bait.* **4 the (old) bait and switch** a situation in which a customer is attracted by a low price on a product, but pays much more for a different product [**Origin:** 1200–1300 Old Norse *beita* **food**]

bait² *v.* [T] **1** to put bait on a hook to catch fish or in a trap to catch animals **2** to deliberately try to make someone angry by criticizing them, using rude names etc.: *Goodman refused to be baited, and walked away.*

ˌbait and ˈswitch *n.* [U] ECONOMICS a dishonest and illegal method of attracting customers in which a company advertises a product for a very low price, and then persuades customers to buy a similar but more expensive product —**bait and switch** *adj.*: *consumers who have been subjected to bait and switch tactics*

baize /beɪz/ *n.* [U] thick cloth, usually green, used especially to cover tables on which games such as POOL are played

Ba·ja Cal·i·for·nia /ˌbɑhɑ kæləˈfɔrnyə/, also **Baja** a PENINSULA in Mexico that is south of the U.S. state of California

bake /beɪk/ S2 W3 *v.* **1** [I,T] if a cake, cookies etc. bakes or you bake them, you cook them using an OVEN: *Bake the mixture at 375 degrees for 20 minutes.* | *I smell cookies baking!* ►see THESAURUS box at **cook¹** **2** [I,T] to make something become hard by heating it, or to become hard in this way: *In former times, bricks were baked in the sun.* **3** [I] INFORMAL if a person, place, or thing bakes, they become too hot: *We were baking in the midday sun.* [**Origin:** Old English *bacan*] → see also HALF-BAKED

ˌbaked ˈbeans *n.* [plural] a food made with small white beans that have been cooked for a long time in a brown SAUCE, often sold in cans

Bake·lite /ˈbeɪklaɪt/ *n.* [U] TRADEMARK a hard plastic used especially in the 1930s and 1940s

bak·er /ˈbeɪkɚ/ *n.* [C] someone who bakes bread, cookies, cakes etc., especially to sell them in a store

ˌbaker's ˈdozen *n.* [singular] thirteen of something

bak·er·y /ˈbeɪkəri/ *n. plural* **bakeries** [C] a place where bread and cakes are baked, or a store where they are sold

ˈbake sale *n.* [C] an occasion when the members of a school group, church organization etc. make cookies, cakes etc. and sell them to make money for the organization

bak·ing /ˈbeɪkɪŋ/ *adj.* INFORMAL very hot: *a baking hot day*

ˈbaking ˌpowder *n.* [U] a powder used in baking cakes, cookies etc. to make them rise so that they are light

ˈbaking ˌsheet *n.* [C] a flat piece of metal that you bake food on

ˈbaking ˌsoda *n.* [U] a white powder used in baking to make cakes, cookies etc. lighter, and also used in cleaning things SYN **bicarbonate of soda**

ˈbaking tray *n.* [C] a BAKING SHEET

ba·kla·va /ˌbɑkləˈvɑ/ *n.* [U] a sweet food from the Middle East made from FILO DOUGH, nuts, and HONEY

bak·sheesh /bækˈʃiʃ, bɑk-/ *n.* [U] money that people in the Middle East give to poor people, to someone who has helped them, or as a BRIBE

Ba·ku /bɑˈku/ the capital and largest city of Azerbaijan

Ba·ku·nin /bəˈkunɪn/, **Mik·hail** /mɪˈkaɪl/ (1814–1876) a Russian REVOLUTIONARY who was an ANARCHIST and opposed Karl Marx

bal·a·lai·ka /ˌbæləˈlaɪkə/ *n.* [C] a musical instrument that has three strings, a long neck, and a TRIANGLE-shaped body, played especially in Russia

bal·ance¹ /ˈbæləns/ S2 W2 *n.*

1 STEADY [U] the state of keeping steady or ability to keep steady with an equal weight on each side of the body, so that you do not fall: *Riding a bike helps develop a child's **sense of balance**.* | *I leaned over and **lost** my **balance*** (=could not stay steady). | *One foot slipped, but she managed to **keep her balance*** (=stay steady and not fall). | *I was **off balance*** (=not steady) *when I threw the ball.* | **knock/push/throw sb off balance** (=hit, push, or suddenly move someone, making them fall) | **recover/regain your balance** (=stop yourself from falling after being unsteady)

2 EQUALITY [singular, U] a state in which very different things have the right amount of importance or influence in relation to each other OPP **imbalance**: **+between** *Try to keep a balance between work and play.* | **+of** *a nice balance of flavors* | *The car **strikes a balance*** (=makes sure two things have equal importance) *between safety and style.* | *His recreational activities help keep his life **in balance**.*

3 BANK [C] the amount of money that you have in your bank account or that you still have to pay: **+of** *a balance of $1,247* ►see THESAURUS box at **account¹**

4 off balance surprised or confused: *The question had **caught** him **off balance*** (=surprised him) *and he didn't know what to say.* | *Kelly's remarks **threw** Avery **off balance** for a second or two.* | *The offense managed to **keep** the other team **off balance*** (=keep them confused).

5 on balance if you think something on balance, you think it after considering all the facts: *On balance, it's a useful program, despite the problems.*

6 be/hang in the balance if the future or success of something hangs in the balance, you do not yet know whether the result will be bad or good: *The negotiations continue, with peace in the region hanging in the balance.*

7 tip/swing the balance to influence the result of an event: *Your letter of recommendation swung the balance in his favor.*

8 STH THAT IS LEFT OVER the balance the amount of something that remains after some has been used or spent: **+of** *Heinz will not serve the balance of his prison sentence.*

9 FOR WEIGHING [C] an instrument for weighing things by seeing whether the amounts in two hanging pans are equal

10 OPPOSITE FORCE/INFLUENCE [singular] a force or influence on one side which equals an opposite force or influence: **+to** *Her practicality **acts as a balance to** this wild inventiveness.*

11 the balance of evidence/probability etc. the most likely answer or result produced by gathered information, reasons etc.: *The balance of evidence suggests that there is likely to be life on other planets.*

B

[**Origin:** 1200–1300 Old French, Vulgar Latin *bilancia*, from Late Latin *bilanx* **having two pans**]

balance[2] S3 W3 *v.* **1** [I,T] to get into a steady position, without falling to one side or the other, or to put something into this position: **balance sth on sth** *She was balancing a plate of food on her knees.* | **+on** *I found him balancing on top of the ladder.* **2** [T] to compare and consider the importance of one thing in relation to another when making a choice or decision: **balance sth with sth** *It's not always easy to balance a career with a family.* | **balance sth against sth** *The courts must balance our civil liberties against our national security.* **3** [T] to have an opposite effect to something else, so that a good result is achieved: *You need enough sugar to balance the cranberries' tartness.* **4 balance the budget** if a government balances the budget, they make the amount of money that they spend equal to the amount of money available **5 balance the books** to show that the amount of money a business has received is equal to the amount spent

balance out *phr. v.* **1** if two or more things balance out, the final result is that they are equal in amount, importance, or effect: *Sometimes I do the housework – sometimes she does. It all balances out.* **2 balance sth ↔ out** to be equal in amount or effect to something that has the opposite effect, so that there is a satisfactory result: *The fall in domestic sales was balanced out by increased exports.*

ˈbalance ˌbeam *n.* [C] a long narrow wooden board on which a GYMNAST performs

bal•anced /ˈbælənst/ W3 *adj.* **1** giving equal attention to all sides or opinions SYN **fair**: *a balanced account of the events* ▸see THESAURUS box at **fair[1]** **2** arranged to include things or people of different kinds in the right amount: *a balanced approach to our transportation problems* | *It is very important for children to eat a* ***balanced diet*** (=containing a variety of good foods in the right amounts). **3** used to describe a situation in which one part is equal to or not greater than the other: *a* ***balanced budget*** (=when a government is not spending more money than it has available) | ***delicately balanced*** (=almost exactly even or equal) *plant and animal communities* **4** not giving too much importance to one thing: *He said he felt balanced and happy again.*

ˌbalanced eˈquation *n.* [C] CHEMISTRY a chemical EQUATION which has the same number of atoms on each side of the equals sign. For example, $2H_20 = 2H_2 + 0_2$ is a balanced equation.

ˌbalance of ˈpayments *n.* [singular] ECONOMICS the difference between what a country spends in order to buy goods and services abroad, and the money it earns selling goods and services abroad

ˌbalance of ˈpower *n.* [singular] POLITICS a situation in which political or military strength is shared evenly between different political groups or different countries: *The case could upset* ***the delicate balance of power between*** *the judicial and executive branches of government.*

ˌbalance of ˈtrade *n.* [singular] ECONOMICS the difference in value between the goods a country buys from abroad and the goods it sells abroad

ˈbalance sheet *n.* [C] ECONOMICS a statement of how much money a business has earned and how much money it has paid for goods and services: *the company's* ***strong balance sheet*** (=used to say that the company earns more than it spends)

Bal•an•chine /ˌbælənˈʃin/, **George** (1904–1983) a Russian-born U.S. CHOREOGRAPHER who helped to start the New York City Ballet

Bal•bo•a /bælˈbouə/, **Vas•co de** /ˈvɑskou də/ (1475–1519) a Spanish EXPLORER who crossed the Isthmus of Darien in Panama, the narrow piece of land that joins North and South America, saw the Pacific Ocean, and officially claimed that it belonged to Spain

bal•co•ny /ˈbælkəni/ *n.* *plural* **balconies** [C] **1** a structure you can stand on that sticks out from the upstairs wall of a building **2** ENG. LANG. ARTS the seats upstairs at a theater ▸see THESAURUS box at **theater**

balcony

bald /bɔld/ *adj.* **1** having little or no hair on your head: *his bald head* | *Dad has started* ***going bald*** (=losing his hair). **2** a bald tire is not safe anymore because its surface has become smooth **3** used to describe something that is stated without extra details in a direct way, without trying to be polite: **bald statement/language/truth etc.** *The bald truth is, he's lying.* —**baldness** *n.* [U]

ˈbald ˌeagle *n.* [C] BIOLOGY a large North American bird with a white head and neck, that is the national bird of the U.S. → see picture on page A34

bal•der•dash /ˈbɔldɚˌdæʃ/ *n.* [U] OLD-FASHIONED talk or writing that is stupid nonsense

ˌbald-ˈfaced *adj.* making no attempt to hide the fact that what you are doing or saying is wrong or untrue: *a bald-faced lie*

bald•ing /ˈbɔldɪŋ/ *adj.* a balding man is losing the hair on his head

bald•ly /ˈbɔldli/ *adv.* in a way that is true, gives few details, and makes no attempt to be polite → see also BALD

Bald•win /ˈbɔldwɪn/, **James** (1924–1987) an African-American writer of novels

bale[1] /beɪl/ *n.* [C] a large quantity of something such as paper or HAY that is tightly tied together, especially into a block: **+of** *a bale of hay*

bale[2] *v.* [T] to tie something such as paper or HAY into a large block

bale•ful /ˈbeɪlfəl/ *adj.* LITERARY expressing anger, hatred, or a wish to harm someone: *a baleful look* —**balefully** *adv.*

Ba•li /ˈbæli, ˈbɑli/ an island in Indonesia, to the east of Java

balk /bɔk/ *v.* **1** [I] to be unwilling to do, try, or accept something, because it seems difficult, unpleasant, or frightening: **+at** *Several of the managers balked at the decision.* **2** [I] if a horse balks, it stops suddenly and refuses to jump or cross something **3** [T] to stop someone or something from getting what they want: *an attempt to balk his scheme* [**Origin:** 1400–1500 *balk* **raised area that gets in the way of forward movement** (15–21 centuries), from Old English *balca* **pile of things on the ground**]

Bal•kan Moun•tains, the /ˌbɔlkən ˈmaʊntˀnz/ a RANGE of mountains in eastern Europe that runs from Serbia through Bulgaria, west of the Black Sea

Bal•kans, the /ˈbɔlkənz/ a large area in southeast Europe which includes Greece, Romania, Bulgaria, Albania, Slovenia, Croatia, Bosnia, and Serbia

balk•y /ˈbɔki/ *adj.* INFORMAL something or someone that is balky does not do what it is expected to do: *a balky air-conditioning system*

ball[1] /bɔl/ S1 W1 *n.* [C]

1 TO PLAY WITH a round object that is thrown, kicked, or hit in a game or sport: *Mommy, where's my ball?* | *a big beach ball* ▸see THESAURUS box at **dance[2]**

2 ROUND SHAPE something formed or rolled into a round shape: *a ball of string* | *Shape the dough into balls.*

3 on the ball INFORMAL thinking or acting quickly and intelligently: *If I'd been more on the ball, I would have noticed the problem.*

4 have a ball INFORMAL to have a very good time: *The kids had a ball building sandcastles.*

5 set/start the ball rolling to make a process or activity

start: *To start the ball rolling, you need to fill out a complaint form.*
6 BASEBALL a ball thrown in baseball that the hitter does not try to hit because it is not within the correct area
7 the movement of a ball when it is thrown, hit, or kicked in a game: *The next ball came high and fast.* | **a fast/curve/breaking etc. ball** (=a fast, curving, dropping etc. ball thrown in baseball)
8 the ball of the foot/hand/thumb the rounded part of the foot at the base of the toe, rounded part of the hand at the base of the thumb → see also EYEBALL[1] (1)
9 the ball is in your court it is your turn to take action or to reply: *We've made our proposal; the ball's in their court now.*
10 DANCE a large formal occasion at which people dance
11 the whole ball of wax INFORMAL the whole thing SYN **everything**: *Benton is in charge of marketing, personnel, sales – the whole ball of wax.*
12 a ball of fire someone who has a lot of energy and is active and successful
13 BULLET a round bullet fired from a type of gun that was used in past times
[**Origin:** (1–7, 9, 11–13) 1200–1300 Old Norse *böllr*] → see also **play ball** at PLAY[1] (13)

ball² *v.* [T] also **ball up** to form something into a small round shape so that it takes up less space

bal·lad /ˈbæləd/ *n.* [C] ENG. LANG. ARTS **1** a simple song, especially a popular love song **2** a short story in the form of a poem [**Origin:** 1400–1500 Old French *balade*, from Old Provençal *balada* **dance, song sung while dancing**, from Late Latin *ballare*]

bal·lad·eer /ˌbæləˈdɪr/ *n.* [C] someone who sings love songs

bal·last¹ /ˈbæləst/ *n.* [U] **1** heavy material that is carried by a ship to make it more steady in the water **2** material such as sand that is carried in a BALLOON and can be thrown out to make it rise **3** broken stones that are used as a surface under a road, railroad lines etc.

ballast² *v.* [T] to fill or supply something with ballast

ˌball ˈbearing *n.* [C] **1** an arrangement of small metal balls moving in a ring around a machine part so that the part turns more easily **2** one of these metal balls

ˈball boy *n.* [C] a boy who picks up tennis balls for people playing in important tennis matches

ball·club /ˈbɔlklʌb/ *n.* [C] a baseball team

ball·cock /ˈbɔlkɑk/ *n.* [C] a hollow floating ball on a stick that opens and closes a hole, to control water flowing into a container, for example in a TOILET

bal·le·ri·na /ˌbæləˈrinə/ *n.* [C] a woman who dances in ballets

bal·let /bæˈleɪ, ˈbæleɪ/ *n.* ENG. LANG. ARTS **1** [C] a performance in which a special style of dancing and music tell a story without any speaking: *"Swan Lake" is my favorite ballet.* ▸ see THESAURUS box at **theater** **2** [U] this type of dancing **3** [C] a group of BALLET dancers who work together: *the Bolshoi ballet* [**Origin:** 1600–1700 French, Italian *balletto*, from *ballo* **dance**, from *ballare*]

balˈlet ˌdancer *n.* [C] someone who dances in ballets

ˈball game *n.* INFORMAL **1** a game of baseball, football, or BASKETBALL: *Dad was watching the ball game on TV.* **2 a whole new ball game** also **a different ball game** a situation that is very different from the one you are used to: *I used to be a teacher, so working in an office is a whole new ball game.*

ˈball girl *n.* [C] a girl who picks up tennis balls for people playing in important tennis matches

bal·lis·tic /bəˈlɪstɪk/ *adj.* **go ballistic** SPOKEN to suddenly become very angry [**Origin:** 1900–2000 *ballistic* **of ballistics** (18–21 centuries), from Latin *ballista* **weapon for throwing large rocks**]

balˌlistic ˈmissile *n.* [C] a MISSILE that is guided up into the air and then falls freely

bal·lis·tics /bəˈlɪstɪks/ *n.* [U] PHYSICS the scientific study of the movement of objects that are thrown or fired through the air, such as bullets shot from a gun

bal·loon¹ /bəˈlun/ *n.* [C] **1** a small brightly colored rubber bag that can be filled with air and used as a toy or decoration for parties: *Could you **blow up the balloons** (=put air in them)?* **2** a very large bag of strong light cloth filled with gas or heated air so that it can float in the air, with a basket hanging below it for people to travel in SYN **hot-air balloon** **3** the circle drawn around the words spoken by the characters in a CARTOON **4 a balloon payment** money borrowed that must be paid back in one large sum after several smaller payments have been made **5 go down like a lead balloon** INFORMAL if a joke, remark etc. goes down like a lead balloon, people do not laugh or react as you expected [**Origin:** 1500–1600 French *ballon* **large football, balloon**, from Italian *ballone* **large football**] → see also TRIAL BALLOON

balloon² *v.* [I] **1** to become larger in amount: *The program's cost has ballooned to more than $1 billion.* **2** to gain weight suddenly: *He ballooned to 300 pounds after college.*

bal·loon·ing /bəˈlunɪŋ/ *n.* [U] the sport of flying in a balloon —**balloonist** *n.* [C]

bal·lot¹ /ˈbælət/ *n.* **1** [C,U] POLITICS a system of secret voting, or an occasion when you vote in this way: *a disappointing result in the ballot* | *There were 17 propositions **on the ballot** (=17 things to be voted on).* **2** [C] POLITICS a piece of paper on which you make a secret vote: *people waiting in line to **cast their ballots** (=vote)* **3** [C] POLITICS the number of votes recorded: *He won 45% of the ballot.* [**Origin:** 1500–1600 Italian *ballotta*, from *balla* **ball** because small balls were used for voting]

ballot² *v.* [I,T] to vote or to decide something by a vote

ˈballot box *n.* **1** [C] POLITICS a box that ballot papers are put in after voting **2 the ballot box** POLITICS the system or process of voting in an election: *The issue will be decided **at the ballot box** (=in an election).*

ball·park /ˈbɔlˌpɑrk/ *n.* **1** a field for playing baseball, with seats for watching the game ▸ see THESAURUS box at **sport¹** **2 in the (right) ball park** INFORMAL close to the amount, price etc. that you want or are thinking about: *The profit estimates are in the right ballpark.* **3 a ball park figure/estimate/amount** a number or amount that has not been calculated exactly

ball·play·er /ˈbɔlˌpleɪɚ/ *n.* [C] INFORMAL someone who plays baseball

ball·point /ˈbɔlpɔɪnt/ also **ˌballpoint ˈpen** *n.* [C] a pen with a ball at the end that rolls thick ink onto the paper

ball·room /ˈbɔlrum/ *n.* [C] a very large room used for dancing on formal occasions

ˌballroom ˈdancing *n.* [U] a type of dancing that is done with a partner and has different steps for particular types of music, such as the WALTZ

bal·ly·hoo /ˈbæliˌhu/ *n.* [U] INFORMAL a situation in which people publicly express a lot more excitement, anger etc. about something than is necessary or appropriate SYN **fuss**: *After all the ballyhoo, the film was a flop.* —**ballyhoo** *v.* [T] —**ballyhooed** *adj.*: *a much ballyhooed reunion concert*

balm /bɑm/ *n.* [C,U] **1** an oily liquid with a strong, pleasant smell that you rub into your skin, often to reduce pain: *lip balm* **2** LITERARY something that gives you comfort: *The performers were reassured by the balm of warm applause.*

balm·y /ˈbɑmi/ *adj.* *comparative* **balmier**, *superlative* **balmiest** balmy air, weather etc. is warm and pleasant: *a balmy summer night*

ba·lo·ney /bəˈlouni/ *n.* [U] **1** INFORMAL something that is silly or not true SYN **nonsense** **2** another spelling of BOLOGNA

bal·sa /ˈbɔlsə/ *n.* [C,U] a tropical American tree or the wood from this tree, which is very light

B

bal·sam /ˈbɔlsəm/ *n.* [C,U] BALM, or the tree that produces it

bal·sam·ic vin·e·gar /bɔlˌsæmɪk ˈvɪnəgɚ/ *n.* [U] an expensive kind of dark-colored VINEGAR used especially in SALADS and Italian dishes

Bal·tic, the /ˈbɔltɪk/ also **the ˌBaltic ˈSea** a sea that is part of the northern Atlantic Ocean and is surrounded by Denmark, Sweden, the Baltic States, and Poland

ˌBaltic ˈStates, the also **the Baltics** the countries of Estonia, Latvia, and Lithuania

Bal·ti·more /ˈbɔltɪˌmɔr/ the largest city in the U.S. state of Maryland

bal·us·trade /ˈbæləˌstreɪd/ *n.* [C] a row of upright pieces of stone or wood with a bar along the top, especially around a BALCONY [**Origin:** 1600–1700 French, Italian *balaustrata*, from *balaustro* **post supporting a handrail**, from *balaustra* **pomegranate flower**; because of the shape of the post]

Bal·zac /ˈbɔlzæk, ˈbæl-/, **Hon·o·ré de** /ˌɑnəˈreɪ də/ (1799–1850) a French writer of NOVELS

bam /bæm/ *interjection* **1** used to say that something happens quickly: *Just turn it on, and bam, you're ready to go.* **2** used to say that something has hit something else **3** used to make a sound like a gun

Ba·ma·ko /ˌbɑməˈkoʊ, ˌbæ-/ the capital and largest city of Mali

bam·boo /ˌbæmˈbu◂/ *n. plural* **bamboos** [C,U] a tall tropical plant with hollow stems, often used for making furniture [**Origin:** 1500–1600 Malay *bambu*]

bam·boo·zle /bæmˈbuzəl/ *v.* [T] INFORMAL to deceive, trick, or confuse someone

ban¹ /bæn/ W3 *n.* [C] an official order that forbids something from being used or done: +**on** *a ban on cigarette advertising* → see also TEST BAN

ban² W3 *v.* **banned, banning** [T] to say that something must not be done, seen, used etc.: *Elephant ivory is banned in the U.S.* | **ban sb from doing sth** *The military government banned private citizens from carrying guns.* [**Origin:** Old English *bannan* **to command people to come**] ►see THESAURUS box at **forbid** → see also BANNED

ba·nal /bəˈnæl, bəˈnɑl, ˈbeɪnl/ *adj.* ordinary and not interesting, because of a lack of new or different ideas: *a banal argument* [**Origin:** 1800–1900 French, Old French *ban* **military service that everyone must do, something common**] —**banality** /bəˈnæləṭi/ *n.* [C,U]

ba·nan·a /bəˈnænə/ S2 *n.* [C] BIOLOGY a long curved tropical fruit with a yellow skin [**Origin:** 1500–1600 Spanish, Portuguese, from Mande] → see also SECOND BANANA

baˈnana reˌpublic *n.* [C] DISAPPROVING a small poor country with a weak government that depends on financial help from other countries

ba·nan·as /bəˈnænəz/ *adj.* INFORMAL **1 go bananas** to become very angry or excited: *Dad will go bananas when he sees this.* **2** crazy or silly

baˈnana ˌsplit *n.* [C] a sweet dish with bananas and ICE CREAM

band¹ /bænd/ S1 W2 *n.* [C]

1 MUSICAL GROUP [C] ENG. LANG. ARTS a group of musicians, especially a group that plays popular music: *a rock band* | *The* ***band played*** *a few blues numbers.* | *She* ***joined the band*** *in 2001.* | ***I played in a band*** *in college.* | *an interview with* ***band members***

2 GROUP [C] a group of people formed because of a common belief or purpose SYN **group**: +**of** *a small band of rebels*

3 RING [C] a flat, narrow piece of material with one end joined to the other to form a circle: *an elastic band* | *a wide silk band*

4 NARROW AREA [C] a narrow area of light, color, land etc. that is different from the areas around it: *The snake has an orange band around its neck.* | +**of** *a thin band of clouds* ►see THESAURUS box at **line¹**

5 RADIO [C] a range of radio signals

6 MUSIC CLASS [U] a class in school in which students play WIND and BRASS instruments as part of a large group

[**Origin:** (1, 2, 6) 1400–1500 French *bande* **group of people**]

band² *v.* [T] to put a band of color or material on or around something

band together *phr. v.* to unite in order to achieve something: *Neighbors banded together to fight for a health clinic.*

ban·dage¹ /ˈbændɪdʒ/ *n.* [C] a narrow piece of cloth that you tie around a wound or around a part of the body that has been injured

bandage² *v.* [T] to tie or cover a part of the body with a bandage: *A paramedic bandaged his foot.*

Band-Aid /ˈbænd eɪd/ *n.* [C] TRADEMARK a piece of thin material that is stuck to the skin to cover cuts and other small wounds

ban·dan·na, bandana /bænˈdænə/ *n.* [C] a large brightly colored piece of cloth you wear around your head or neck [**Origin:** 1700–1800 Hindi *badhnu* **cloth tied and then colored**, from *badhna* **to tie**]

Ban·dar Se·ri Be·ga·wan /ˌbʌndɚ ˌsɛri bəˈgɑwən/ the capital city of Brunei

band·box /ˈbænd*b*ɑks/ *n.* [C] a box for keeping hats in

ban·dit /ˈbændɪt/ *n.* [C] someone who robs people, especially one of a group of people who attack travelers: *The bandits took jewelry and cash.* [**Origin:** 1500–1600 Italian *bandito*, from *bandire* **to banish**] → see also ONE-ARMED BANDIT —**banditry** *n.* [U]

band·mas·ter /ˈbænd*ˌ*mæstɚ/ *n.* [C] someone who CONDUCTS a military band, MARCHING BAND etc.

ban·do·lier /ˌbændəˈlɪr/ *n.* [C] a belt that goes over someone's shoulder and across their chest and is used to carry bullets

band·stand /ˈbænd*s*tænd/ *n.* [C] a small building in a park that has a roof but no walls and is used by a band playing music

band·wag·on /ˈbændˌwægən/ *n.* [C] an activity that a lot of people are doing: **jump/climb/get on the bandwagon** (=begin to do something that a lot of other people are doing) *Politicians are always quick to jump on the latest bandwagon.*

band·width /ˈbændˌwɪdθ/ *n.* [U] COMPUTERS the amount of information that can be carried through a telephone wire, computer connection etc. at one time

ban·dy¹ /ˈbændi/ *adj.* bandy legs curve out at the knees —**bandy-legged** *adj.*

bandy² *v.* **bandies, bandied, bandying bandy words (with sb)** OLD-FASHIONED to argue with someone

bandy sth **about** *phr. v.* to mention an idea, name, remark etc. several times, especially to appear impressive to someone: *A few names are being bandied about for the job.*

bane /beɪn/ *n.* [singular] something that causes trouble or makes people unhappy: **be the bane of sth** *Poison oak is the bane of campers.* | *This stupid computer has become* ***the bane of my existence*** (=a cause of continual trouble).

bane·ful /ˈbeɪnfəl/ *adj.* LITERARY evil or bad —**banefully** *adv.*

bang¹ /bæŋ/ *v.*

1 KNOCK/HIT STH [I,T] to hit something hard against something else, making a loud noise: *I banged the phone down.* | *They were banging drums and chanting.* | +**on** *Lara was banging on the wall and yelling.* ►see THESAURUS box at **hit¹**

2 CLOSE STH [I always + adv./prep.,T] to close something violently making a loud noise, or to make something close in this way: *He got out of the car and banged the door.* | *The screen door* ***banged shut.***

3 HIT STH [T] to hit a part of your body or something you are carrying against something, especially by accident; SYN **bump**: *I slipped and banged my knee.* | **bang sth**

on/against sth *I banged my toe on the door.* | *I accidentally banged the guitar against the door.* ▸see THESAURUS box at **hit**[1]
4 MAKE NOISE [I] to make a loud noise or noises: *The pipes bang when you turn the hot water on.*
5 bang your head against/on a (brick) wall INFORMAL to be wasting your efforts by doing something that does not produce any results: *Trying to teach that class is like banging your head against a brick wall.*

bang sth ↔ **out** *phr. v.* INFORMAL **1** to play a tune or song loudly and badly on a piano **2** to write something in a hurry, especially on a TYPEWRITER: *As a journalist, you have to bang out a column for each day.*

bang sb/sth ↔ **up** *phr. v.* INFORMAL to seriously damage something: *She banged up my car.*

bang[2] *n.* **1** [C] a sudden loud noise caused by something such as a gun or an object hitting a hard surface: *The front door slammed with a loud bang.* **2 bangs** [plural] hair cut straight across your FOREHEAD **3 get a bang out of sth** SPOKEN to enjoy something very much: *She got a real bang out of seeing the kids in the school play.* **4 with a bang** in a way that is very exciting or noticeable: *Brewster finished the season with a bang.* **5** [C] a hard knock or hit against something: *He walked away from the accident with only a slight bang on the head.* **6 more bang for the/your buck** a good effect or a lot of value for the effort or money you spend: *You get more bang for your buck when you buy used textbooks.*

bang[3] *adv.* **1** INFORMAL directly or exactly: *It starts at eight, bang on the dot.* **2** SPOKEN in a sudden, violent way: *I lost my balance and fell, bang, on my back on the ice.*

bang[4] *interjection* used to make a sound like a gun or explosion: *Then suddenly, bang! The engine just exploded.*

Bang·kok /ˈbæŋkɑk/ the capital and largest city of Thailand

Bang·la·desh /ˌbɑŋgləˈdɛʃ, ˌbæŋ-/ a country in Asia that is east of India —**Bangladeshi** *n., adj.*

ban·gle /ˈbæŋgəl/ *n.* [C] a solid band of gold, silver etc. that you wear loosely around your wrist as jewelry

Ban·gui /bɑŋˈgi/ the capital and largest city of the Central African Republic

ˈbang-up *adj.* INFORMAL very good: *They did **a bang-up job** on the display.*

ban·ish /ˈbænɪʃ/ *v.* [T] **1** to not allow someone or something to stay in a particular place: **banish sth from/to sth** *Smokers have been banished to an area outdoors.* **2** to send someone away permanently from their country or the area where they live, especially as an official punishment: **banish sb from/to sth** *Many Soviet dissidents were banished to Siberia.* **3** to prevent someone from doing something or something from happening: **banish sb from sth** *After the scandal, he was banished from baseball.* **4** to try to stop thinking about something, especially something that worries you: *The study should banish any doubts about women's ability to handle the pressures of business.* —**banishment** *n.* [U]

ban·is·ter /ˈbænəstɚ/ *n.* [C] a row of upright posts with a bar along the top, that stops you from falling over the edge of stairs

ban·jo /ˈbændʒoʊ/ *n. plural* **banjos** [C] a musical instrument with four or more strings, a long neck, and a round body used especially in COUNTRY AND WESTERN music

Ban·jul /ˈbɑndʒul/ the capital city of the Gambia

bank[1] /bæŋk/ [S1] [W1] *n.*
1 PLACE FOR MONEY [C] **a)** a business that keeps and lends money and provides other financial services: *The bill would force banks to lower credit card interest rates.* **b)** a local office of a bank: *I'll stop at the bank on the way home.*
2 RIVER/LAKE [C] land along the side of a river or lake: *the grassy banks of the river* ▸see THESAURUS box at **shore**[1]
3 a blood/sperm/organ etc. bank a place where human blood etc. is stored until someone needs it
4 PILE [C] a large pile of earth, sand, snow etc.: *He drove into a snow bank during the storm.*
5 a cloud/fog bank etc. [C] a large amount of clouds, mist etc.
6 a bank of televisions/elevators/computers etc. a large number of machines, television screens etc. arranged close together in a row
7 GAME [singular] the money in a GAMBLING game that people can win → see also **break the bank** at BREAK[1] (47), **it won't break the bank** at BREAK[1] (35)
8 ROAD [C] a slope made at a curve in a road or RACETRACK to make it safer for cars to go around
[**Origin:** (1, 3, 7) 1400–1500 Old French *banque*, from Old Italian *banca* **long seat, bank**] → see also FOOD BANK, MEMORY BANK

bank[2] [W2] *v.*
1 MONEY [T] to put or keep money in a bank: *She's managed to bank more than $300,000.*
2 A PARTICULAR BANK [I] to keep your money in a particular bank: **+with** *Who do you bank with?* | **+at** *They've always banked at Bank of America.*
3 TURN [I] to make an airplane, MOTORCYCLE, or car slope to one side when turning: *The enemy fighter banked left, then right.*
4 PILE/ROWS [T usually passive] to arrange something into a pile or into rows: *Dozens of candles were banked before the altar.*
5 CLOUD/MIST also **bank up** [I,T] to form a large amount of cloud, mist etc.: *Clouds were banking up in the morning sky.*
6 FIRE also **bank up** [T] to cover a fire with wood, coal etc. to keep it going for a long time: *Bank the hot coals on a grill.*
7 ROAD [T usually passive] to make a slope at a curve in a road or RACETRACK to make it safer for cars to go around

bank on sb/sth *phr. v.* to depend on something happening or someone doing something: *Branson is banking on the media attention to attract advertisers.* | **bank on doing sth** *I'd banked on being able to take that flight.*

bank·a·ble /ˈbæŋkəbəl/ *adj.* INFORMAL a bankable person or quality is likely to help you get money, success etc.: *one of Hollywood's most bankable stars*

ˈbank acˌcount *n.* [C] an arrangement between a bank and a customer that allows the customer to pay in and take out money

ˈbank ˌbalance *n.* [singular] the amount of money someone has in their bank account

ˈbank book *n.* [C] a book in which a record is kept of the money you put into and take out of your bank account [SYN] **passbook**

ˈbank ˌcard *n.* [C] a DEBIT CARD or CREDIT CARD provided by your bank

ˈbank draft also **ˈbanker's ˌdraft** *n.* [C] a check from one bank to another, especially a foreign bank, to pay a certain amount of money to a person or organization

bank·er /ˈbæŋkɚ/ [W3] *n.* [C] **1** someone who works in a bank in an important position **2** the player who is in charge of the money in some games

ˌbank ˈholding ˌcompany *n.* [C] ECONOMICS a company that completely or partly owns other banks, and often operates as a bank itself → see also HOLDING COMPANY

bank·ing /ˈbæŋkɪŋ/ *n.* [U] the business of a bank: *the international banking system*

ˈbank note *n.* [C] a piece of paper money of a particular value that you use to buy things [SYN] **bill**

ˈbank rate *n.* [C] ECONOMICS the rate of INTEREST decided by a country's main bank

bank·roll[1] /ˈbæŋkroʊl/ *n.* [C] a supply of money

bankroll[2] *v.* [T] INFORMAL to provide the money that someone needs for a business, a plan etc.: *The company is bankrolled by a Swiss investor.*

bank·rupt[1] /ˈbæŋkrʌpt/ *adj.* **1** ECONOMICS unable to pay your debts: *The state is virtually bankrupt.* | *a bankrupt steel manufacturer* | *The firm **went bankrupt***

B

(=became bankrupt) *before the building work was completed.* **2** completely lacking a particular good quality: *a **morally bankrupt** regime*

bankrupt² *v.* [T] ECONOMICS to make a person, business, or country bankrupt or very poor: *There are fears the new law could bankrupt some small businesses.*

B

bankrupt³ *n.* [C] ECONOMICS someone who has officially said in a court of law that they cannot pay their debts [**Origin:** 1500–1600 *bankrupt* **bankruptcy** (16–18 centuries), from French *banqueroute*, from Old Italian *bancarotta*, from *banca* **bank** + *rotta* **broken**]

bank·rupt·cy /ˈbæŋkˌrʌptsi/ *n. plural* **bankruptcies** **1** [U] ECONOMICS the legal state of being unable to pay your debts *School districts across the state are **declaring bankruptcy*** (=officially saying they cannot pay their debts). **2** ECONOMICS [C,U] legal action or a court case in which a person or business is judged to be unable to pay their debts, and any ASSETS they own are shared among the people or companies that they owe money to: *Last year, the financially troubled airline **filed for bankruptcy*** (=officially asked a court to make them bankrupt). | *an increase in corporate bankruptcies* | **bankruptcy proceedings/case** **3** [U] a total lack of a particular good quality: *the moral bankruptcy of this materialistic society*

Banks /bæŋks/, **Er·nie** /ˈɚni/ (1931–) a U.S. baseball player who was the first African-American member of the Chicago Cubs team.

ˈbank ˌstatement *n.* [C] a document sent regularly by a bank to a customer that lists the amounts of money taken out of and paid into their BANK ACCOUNT

ˈbank ˌteller *n.* [C] a TELLER

banned /bænd/ *adj.* not officially allowed to meet, exist, or be used: *Some fertilizers were found to contain the banned chemicals.*

ban·ner¹ /ˈbænɚ/ *n.* [C] **1** a long piece of cloth on which something is written, often carried between two poles: *The protesters were carrying anti-war banners.* **2 under the banner of sth a)** because of a particular principle or belief: *Civil rights groups have achieved a lot under the banner of equality.* **b)** as part of a particular group or organization: *He ran for office under the banner of the Liberal Party.* **3** LITERARY a flag

banner² *adj.* **a banner year/season/week etc.** an extremely good or successful period of time

ˈbanner ad *n.* [C] an advertisement that appears across the top of a page on the Internet —**banner advertising** *n.* [U]

ˌbanner ˈheadline *n.* [C] words printed in very large letters across the top of the first page of a newspaper

Ban·nis·ter /ˈbænɪstɚ/, **Sir Rog·er** /ˈrɑdʒɚ/ (1929–) a British runner who was the first person to run a mile in less than four minutes

Ban·nock /ˈbænək/ a Native American tribe from the northwestern area of the U.S.

ban·quet /ˈbæŋkwɪt/ *n.* [C] a formal dinner for many people on an important occasion [**Origin:** 1400–1500 French, Old Italian *banchetto*, from *banca* **long seat, bank**]

ˈbanquet room *n.* [C] a large room in which banquets take place

ban·shee /ˈbænʃi/ *n.* [C] **1** a spirit whose loud cry is believed to be heard when someone is going to die **2 scream/wail/howl etc. like a banshee** to make a loud unpleasant screaming sound [**Origin:** 1600–1700 Scottish Gaelic *bean-sith*]

ban·tam /ˈbæntəm/ *n.* [C] a type of small chicken [**Origin:** 1700–1800 *Bantam* place in Java from where the birds were thought to have been brought to Europe]

ban·tam·weight /ˈbæntəmˌweɪt/ *n.* [C] a BOXER who weighs between 112 and 118 pounds, or someone of a similar weight in other sports like WRESTLING

ban·ter¹ /ˈbæntɚ/ *n.* [U] conversation that has a lot of jokes and teasing (TEASE) remarks in it: *lighthearted and amusing banter*

banter² *v.* [I] to joke with and TEASE someone —**bantering** *adj.* —**banteringly** *adv.*

ban·yan /ˈbænyən/ *n.* [C] an Indian tree with large branches that spread out and form new roots

bap·tism /ˈbæpˌtɪzəm/ *n.* [C,U] **1** a Christian religious ceremony in which someone is touched with water or put completely in water to welcome them into a particular Christian faith, and sometimes to officially name them **2 a baptism of/by fire** a difficult or painful first experience of something: *The first night working in the hospital proved to be a baptism by fire.* —**baptismal** /bæpˈtɪzməl/ *adj.*

Bap·tist /ˈbæptɪst/ *n.* [C] a member of a Christian group that believes that members should be baptized when they are old enough to understand its meaning —**Baptist** *adj.*

bap·tize /ˈbæptaɪz, bæpˈtaɪz/ *v.* [T] **1** to perform the ceremony of baptism on someone **2** to accept someone as a member of a particular Christian church by a ceremony of baptism: *Both boys were baptized Catholic.* **3** to give a child a name in a baptism ceremony SYN **christen**: *Everyone calls her Amy, but she was baptized Amelia.* [**Origin:** 1200–1300 Old French *baptiser*, from Late Latin, from Greek *baptizein* **to dip, baptize**]

bar¹ /bɑr/ S1 W2 *n.* [C]

1 PLACE TO DRINK IN a place where alcoholic drinks are served: *We went to a bar to watch the game and have a few beers.*

2 PLACE TO BUY A DRINK the long table inside a bar where alcoholic drinks are served: *I found him sitting **at the bar**.*

3 BLOCK SHAPE something, especially something solid, that is longer than it is wide: *a candy bar* | +**of** *a bar of soap*

4 PIECE OF METAL/WOOD a length of metal or wood put across a door, window etc. to keep it shut or to prevent people going in or out: *A lot of houses had bars across the windows.*

5 a salad/coffee/sushi etc. bar a place where a particular kind of food or drink is served

6 LAWYERS LAW **the bar a)** lawyers considered as a group, or the profession of being a lawyer: *He was **admitted to the bar** last year.* **b)** also **the bar exam** the test that you must pass to become a lawyer: *Did she **pass the bar**?*

7 COMPUTER one of the long narrow areas of color at the top, bottom, or sides of a computer screen that you CLICK on to make the computer do something: *the scroll bar*

8 behind bars INFORMAL in prison

9 MUSIC ENG. LANG. ARTS a group of notes and RESTS, separated from other groups by VERTICAL lines, into which a line of written music is divided: *They played a few bars, then stopped.*

10 PILE OF SAND/STONES a long pile of sand or stones under the water at the entrance to a HARBOR: *One of the ships got stuck on a sand bar.*

11 a bar to (doing) sth something that prevents you from achieving something that you want: *Homosexuality is a bar to becoming a priest in many churches.*

12 COLOR/LIGHT a narrow band of color or light

13 ON UNIFORMS a narrow band of metal or cloth worn on a military uniform to show rank

[**Origin:** 1100–1200 Old French *barre*] → see also **raise the bar** at RAISE¹ (9), SALAD BAR, SNACK BAR

bar² *v.* **barred**, **barring** [T] **1** to officially prevent someone from entering a place or from doing something: **bar sb from sth** *Journalists are regularly barred from entering the country.* ►see THESAURUS box at **forbid** **2** to prevent people from going somewhere by placing something in their way: *She stood in the hall, **barring** my way.* **3** also **bar up** to shut a door or window using a bar or piece of wood so that people cannot get in or out: *They had barred the windows and doors.*

bar³ *prep.* **1 bar none** used to emphasize that someone is the best of a particular group: *They serve the best breakfast in town, bar none.* **2** FORMAL except: *No work's been done in the office today, bar a little typing.* → see also BARRING

Ba•ra•ka /bəˈrɑkə/, **A•mir•i** /əˈmɪri/ (1934-) a U.S. writer of poetry and plays about the situation of African-American people

barb /bɑrb/ *n.* [C] **1** the sharp curved point of a hook, ARROW etc. that prevents it from being easily pulled out **2** a remark that is smart and amusing, but also cruel → see also BARBED

Bar•ba•dos /bɑrˈbeɪdoʊs/ an island in the Caribbean Sea, which is an independent country —**Barbadian** *n., adj.*

bar•bar•i•an /bɑrˈbɛriən/ *n.* [C] **1** someone who does not behave correctly, or who does not show respect for education, art etc.: *She thought all wrestling fans were barbarians.* **2** someone who behaves in a cruel and violent way: *These attacks were the acts of barbarians.* **3** HISTORY in ancient times, someone from a different tribe or land, who people believe to be wild and violent and not CIVILIZED: *The barbarians conquered Rome.*

bar•bar•ic /bɑrˈbærɪk/ *adj.* very cruel, violent, and not CIVILIZED SYN **barbarous**: *the barbaric treatment of women prisoners*

bar•ba•rism /ˈbɑrbəˌrɪzəm/ *n.* **1** [U] cruel and violent behavior **2** [U] a state or condition in which people are not educated, behave violently etc.

bar•bar•i•ty /bɑrˈbærət̬i/ *n. plural* **barbarities** [C,U] a very cruel act, or cruel actions in general: *the barbarity of the Nazis*

bar•ba•rous /ˈbɑrbərəs/ *adj.* **1** extremely cruel in a way that is shocking SYN **barbaric** **2** wild and not CIVILIZED: *a savage, barbarous people* [**Origin:** 1400–1500 Latin *barbarus*, from Greek *barbaros* **foreign**] —**barbarously** *adv.*

bar•be•cue¹ /ˈbɑrbɪˌkyu/ S3 *n.* [C] **1** an outdoor party during which food is cooked and eaten outdoors: *The neighbors **had a barbecue** Saturday night.* ▸see THESAURUS box at **meal** **2** a metal frame for cooking food on outdoors [**Origin:** 1600–1700 American Spanish *barbacoa*]

barbecue² *v.* [T] to cook food on a metal frame over a fire outdoors ▸see THESAURUS box at **cook¹** —**barbecued** *adj.*: *barbecued chicken*

barbed /bɑrbd/ *adj.* **1** a barbed hook or ARROW has one or more sharp curved points **2** a barbed remark is unkind

ˌbarbed ˈwire *n.* [U] wire with short sharp points on it: *a high barbed-wire fence*

bar•bell /ˈbɑrbɛl/ *n.* [C] a metal bar with weights at each end, that you lift to make you stronger

bar•be•que /ˈbɑrbɪˌkyu/ another spelling of BARBECUE

bar•ber /ˈbɑrbɚ/ *n.* [C] a man whose job is to cut men's hair and sometimes to SHAVE them [**Origin:** 1200–1300 Old French *barbeor*, from *barbe* **barb, beard**]

bar•ber•shop, barber shop /ˈbɑrbɚˌʃɑp/ *n.* **1** [C] a store where men's hair is cut **2** [U] ENG. LANG. ARTS a style of singing popular songs in four parts in close HARMONY: *a barbershop quartet*

ˈbarber's ˌpole *n.* [C] a pole with red and white bands, used as a sign outside a barbershop

bar•bi•can /ˈbɑrbɪkən/ *n.* [C] a tower for defense at the gate or bridge of a castle

bar•bi•tu•rate /bɑrˈbɪtʃərɪt/ *n.* [C,U] MEDICINE a powerful drug that makes people calm and puts them to sleep [**Origin:** 1800–1900 *barbituric acid* type of acid (19–21 centuries), from German *barbitursäure*, from *Barbara* female name + *säure* **acid**]

ˈbar chart *n.* [C] MATH A BAR GRAPH

ˈbar code *n.* [C] a group of thin and thick lines from which a computer reads information about a product that is sold in a store

bard /bɑrd/ *n.* [C] **1** ENG. LANG. ARTS a poet **2 the Bard** INFORMAL William Shakespeare

Bar•deen /bɑrˈdin/, **John** (1908–1991) a U.S. scientist who worked on the development of an electronic TRANSISTOR and helped to develop the idea of SUPERCONDUCTIVITY

bare¹ /bɛr/ *adj.*
1 WITHOUT CLOTHES not covered by clothes: *bare feet* | *bare-chested men* ▸see THESAURUS box at **naked**
2 LAND/TREES not covered by trees or grass, or not having any leaves: *bare branches* | *bare and treeless hills*
3 NOT COVERED/EMPTY empty, not covered by anything, or not having any decorations: *Paint the bare wood with a primer.* | *a bare-looking room* ▸see THESAURUS box at **empty¹**
4 the bare facts/truth a statement that tells someone only what they need to know, with no additional details: *You only need to give the bare facts.*
5 SMALLEST AMOUNT NECESSARY [only before noun] the very least amount of something that you need to do something: *The measure passed by a bare majority of votes.* | *The refugees fled, taking only **the bare essentials**.* | *Try to keep administrative costs to a **bare minimum*** (=the smallest amount possible). → see also BARE BONES
6 lay bare also **lay sth bare a)** to uncover something that was previously hidden: *The excavation laid bare the streets of the ancient city.* **b)** to make known something that was secret: *Snyder's article lays bare the truth about the plot.*
7 with your bare hands without using a weapon or tool: *He killed a man with his bare hands.*
[**Origin:** Old English *bær*] —**bareness** *n.*

bare² *v.* [T] **1** to let something be seen, by removing something that is covering it: *The dog bared its teeth.* **2 bare your soul** to tell your most secret feelings to someone

bare•back /ˈbɛrbæk/ *adj., adv.* on the bare back of a horse, without a SADDLE: *Where did you learn to **ride bareback**?*

ˌbare ˈbones *n.* **the bare bones (of sth)** only the most basic or necessary parts of something: *She outlined the bare bones of the story.*

ˈbare-bones *adj.* INFORMAL having only the most basic things, information, qualities etc. that are needed: *We only have a bare-bones staff.*

bare•faced /ˈbɛrfeɪst/ *adj.* making no attempt to hide the fact that you are saying or doing something that is nasty or wrong SYN **bald-faced** SYN **blatant**: *barefaced lies*

bare•foot /ˈbɛrfʊt/ also **bare•foot•ed** /ˈbɛrˌfʊt̬ɪd/ *adj., adv.* without shoes on your feet: *As a kid, I loved **going barefoot**.*

bare•hand•ed /ˌbɛrˈhændɪd◂/ *adj., adv.* having no GLOVES on, or having no tools or weapons: *They fought barehanded.*

bare•head•ed /ˌbɛrˈhɛdɪd◂/ *adj., adv.* without a hat on your head: *These kids shouldn't be playing bareheaded in the snow.*

bare•leg•ged /ˈbɛrˌlɛgd, -ˌlɛgɪd/ *adj., adv.* with no clothing on your legs

bare•ly /ˈbɛrli/ S3 W2 *adv.* **1** in a way that almost does not happen, exist etc. SYN **just**: *They lost, but just barely.* | *Dave barely noticed my new dress.* | *She was barely eighteen, and pregnant with her second child.* **2** in a way that is simple, with no decorations or details: *The room was furnished barely.* **3** used to emphasize that something happens immediately after a previous action: *I'd barely gotten home when the phone rang.*

Bar•ents Sea, the /ˈbærənts si, ˈbɑr-/ a part of the Arctic Ocean that is northeast of Scandinavia

barf /bɑrf/ *v.* [I] INFORMAL to VOMIT —**barf** *n.* [U] —**barfy** *adj.*

bar•fly /ˈbɑrflaɪ/ *n. plural* **barflies** [C] INFORMAL someone who spends a lot of time in bars —**barfly** *adj.*

bar•gain¹ /ˈbɑrgən/ *n.* [C] **1** something bought cheaply or for less than its usual price: *The 10-ounce can is a better bargain than the 4-ounce one.* | *Airlines aren't making money on **bargain fares*** (=prices for plane travel that are very cheap). | *The car **was a***

B

B

***bargain** at $8,500.* | *The clothes were **a real bargain**.* | *Hundreds of people go **bargain-hunting** in the sales after Christmas.* ►see THESAURUS box at **cheap**[1] **2** an agreement, made between two people or groups, to do something in return for something else: *She had **made a bargain** and was now trying to back out of it.* | *The union representatives **drove a hard bargain** (=got an agreement favorable to them) in the talks.* | *They **struck a bargain** (=made an agreement) to marry and then divorce, in order to get him citizenship.* | *Negotiators are worried that the rebels will not **keep their side of the bargain** (=will not do what they promised in the agreement).* → see also PLEA BARGAIN **3 in the bargain** in addition to everything else: *It would be nice to get some exercise in the bargain.* **4 make the best of a bad bargain** to do the best you can under difficult conditions —**bargainer** *n.* [C]: *a wage bargainer*

bargain[2] *v.* [I] to discuss the conditions of a sale, agreement etc.: **+with** *The family refused to bargain with the kidnappers.* | **+for** *Oliver's bargaining for a raise.*

bargain for sth *phr. v.* to consider the possibility of something when you are making plans: *It turned out to be a **more** dangerous situation **than he'd bargained for*** (=more that he'd expected).

bargain on sth *phr. v.* to expect that something will happen and be ready for it: **bargain on (sb/sth) doing sth** *I hadn't bargained on it taking so long.*

ˌbargain 'basement *n.* [C] a part of a large store, usually in the floor below ground level, where goods are sold at reduced prices

bar·gain·ing /ˈbɑrɡənɪŋ/ *n.* [U] discussion aimed at reaching an agreement about a sale, contract etc, especially between an employer and an organization representing workers: *The 4% pay raise was the result of some **hard bargaining**.* | *the right to join a union and engage in **collective bargaining*** (=discussions between an employer and a LABOR UNION)

'bargaining ˌchip *n.* [C] something that one person or group in a business deal or political agreement has, that can be used to gain an advantage in the deal: *We are against the use of hostages as bargaining chips.*

'bargaining poˌsition *n.* [C] **a)** the fact of having bargaining power: **a good/strong bargaining position** *Most new artists and bands aren't in a strong bargaining position.* **b)** the opinions and demands that one person or group has when starting a discussion or agreement: *The group has not yet clearly stated its bargaining position.*

'bargaining ˌpower *n.* [U] the power that a person or group has in a discussion or agreement: *The new rules weaken the bargaining power of unions.*

barge[1] /bɑrdʒ/ *n.* **1** [C] a large low boat with a flat bottom used mainly for carrying heavy goods on a CANAL or river ►see THESAURUS box at **boat, ship**[1] **2** a large rowing boat used for an important ceremony [**Origin:** 1200–1300 Old French, Late Latin *barca*]

barge[2] *v.* [I always + adv./prep.] to move somewhere in an awkward way, often hitting against things: *A couple of kids barged past the guards at the door.* | *He **barged his way** through the room.*

barge in also **barge into** sth *phr. v.* to enter or rush in rudely: *The woman barged into the office and demanded to see the boss.*

barge in on sb/sth *phr. v.* to interrupt someone rudely, especially by coming in while they are doing something: *She just barged in on Duncan and Jessica.*

barge·man /ˈbɑrdʒmən/ *n.* [C] someone who drives or works on a barge

'barge pole *n.* [C] a long pole used to guide a barge

'bar graph also **'bar chart** *n.* [C] MATH a type of GRAPH with a series of boxes of different heights but equal widths, in which the height of each box represents a different amount, for example an amount of profit made in a particular month → see also HISTOGRAM → see picture at CHART[1]

bar·hop /ˈbɑrhɑp/ *v.* [I] INFORMAL to visit and drink at several bars, one after another

bar·i·tone /ˈbærəˌtoʊn/ *n.* [C] a male singing voice lower than a TENOR and higher than a BASS, or a male singer whose voice is in this range

bar·i·um /ˈbɛriəm, ˈbær-/ *n.* [U] **1** SYMBOL **Ba** CHEMISTRY a soft silvery-white metal that is an ELEMENT **2 a barium enema/swallow/meal** MEDICINE a substance containing barium that you swallow or that is put in your BOWELS before you have an X-RAY

bark[1] /bɑrk/ S2 *v.* **1** [I] to make the short loud sound that dogs and some other animals make: *Don't worry – he barks, but he doesn't bite.* | **+at** *Can you make the dog stop barking at the mailman?* **2** [T] also **bark out** to say something quickly in a loud voice: **+bark sth at sb** *The sergeant barked orders at us.* **3 be barking up the wrong tree** INFORMAL to have a wrong idea, especially about how to get a particular result: *You're barking up the wrong tree if you think Sam can help you.* **4 bark at the moon** INFORMAL to worry and complain about something that you cannot change, and that is not very important **5** [T] to rub the skin off your knee, elbow etc. by falling or knocking against something: *I barked my shin on the bed.* [**Origin:** Old English *beorcan*]

bark[2] *n.* [C,U] **1** the sharp loud sound made by a dog **2** BIOLOGY the hard outer covering of the stem and branches of a tree, that consists of dead cells **3** a loud sound or voice: *the bark of the guns* **4 sb's bark is worse than their bite** SPOKEN used to say that although someone talks in an angry way they would not behave violently **5** another spelling of BARQUE

bar·keep·er /ˈbɑrˌkipɚ/ also **bar·keep** /ˈbɑrkip/ *n.* [C] someone who serves drinks in a bar SYN **bartender**

bark·er /ˈbɑrkɚ/ *n.* [C] someone who stands outside a place at a CIRCUS, FAIR etc. shouting to people to come in

bar·ley /ˈbɑrli/ *n.* [U] a plant that produces a grain used for making food or alcohol

bar·maid /ˈbɑrmeɪd/ *n.* [C] OLD-FASHIONED a woman who serves drinks in a bar

bar·man /ˈbɑrmən/ *n.* [C] OLD-FASHIONED a BARTENDER

bar mitz·vah /ˌbɑr ˈmɪtsvə/ *n.* [C] **1** the religious ceremony held when a Jewish boy reaches the age of 13 and is considered an adult in his religion **2** a boy for whom this ceremony is held [**Origin:** 1800–1900 Hebrew *bar miswah* **son of (God's) law**] → see also BAT MITZVAH

barn /bɑrn/ *n.* [C] **1** a large farm building for storing crops, or for keeping animals in **2** INFORMAL a large plain building: *a huge barn of a house* **3 close the barn door after the horse has left/escaped/fled etc.** to try to prevent something when it is too late and harm has already been done [**Origin:** Old English *bereærn*, from *bere* **barley** + *ærn* **place**]

bar·na·cle /ˈbɑrnəkəl/ *n.* [C] a small sea animal with a hard shell that sticks firmly to rocks and the bottom of boats [**Origin:** 1500–1600 *barnacle* type of goose (12–21 centuries), from Medieval Latin *bernaca*; from the former belief that the goose was born from a barnacle]

Bar·nard /ˈbɑrnɑrd/, **Chris·ti·aan** /ˈkrɪstʃən/ (1922–2001) a South African doctor who in 1967 performed the first-ever heart TRANSPLANT

barn·storm /ˈbɑrnstɔrm/ *v.* [I] **1** to travel from place to place making short stops to give political speeches or theater performances **2** to perform tricks and difficult movements in the air in a small airplane to entertain people [**Origin:** 1800–1900 *barn* + *storm* **to attack**; from the performance of traveling actors in barns] —**barnstormer** *n.* [C] —**barnstorming** *n.* [U]

barn·yard /ˈbɑrnyɑrd/ *n.* [C] **1** a space surrounded by farm buildings: *barnyard animals* **2 barnyard humor** humor about sex and body waste

ba·rom·e·ter /bəˈrɑmət̬ɚ/ *n.* [C] **1** PHYSICS an instrument for measuring changes in the air pressure, used to look for weather patterns and to calculate height above sea level **2** something that shows or gives an idea of changes that are happening: *Applications for* *building permits are a barometer of future construction activity.* —**barometric** /ˌbærəˈmɛtrɪk◂/ *adj.* —**barometrically** /-kli/ *adv.*

bar·on /ˈbærən/ *n.* [C] **1** a businessman with a lot of power or influence: *media baron Rupert Murdoch* | *Colombian drug barons* **2** a man who is a member of the British NOBILITY or of a rank of European NOBILITY → see also ROBBER BARON

bar·on·ess /ˈbærənɪs, -ˌnɛs/ *n.* [C] **1** a woman who is a member of the British NOBILITY **2** the wife of a baron

bar·on·et /ˈbærənɪt/ *n.* [C] a British KNIGHT who is lower in rank than a baron, whose title passes on to his son when he dies

ba·ro·ni·al /bəˈroʊniəl/ *adj.* **1** a baronial room is very large and richly decorated **2** belonging to or involving a BARON

ba·roque, Baroque /bəˈroʊk/ *adj.* belonging to the very decorated style of art, music, buildings etc. that was common in Europe in the 17th century: *Baroque architecture* [**Origin:** 1700–1800 French **not regular, baroque**, from Portuguese *barroco* or Spanish *barrueco* **pearl not of a regular shape**] —**baroque** *n.* [singular]

barque, bark /bɑrk/ *n.* [C] a sailing ship with three, four, or five MASTS (=poles that the sails are attached to)

bar·racks /ˈbærəks/ *n.* [plural] a group of buildings in which soldiers live [**Origin:** 1600–1700 French *baraque* **small building**, from Catalan *barraca*]

bar·ra·cu·da /ˌbærəˈkudə/ *n.* [C] BIOLOGY a large tropical fish that eats flesh

barracuda

bar·rage¹ /bəˈrɑʒ/ *n.* **1** [C usually singular] the continuous firing of guns, especially large heavy guns, to protect soldiers as they move toward an enemy: *a barrage of anti-aircraft fire* **2** [singular] a lot of actions, sounds, questions etc. that happen at the same time or very quickly after each other: +**of** *a constant barrage of complaints*

bar·rage² /ˈbɑrɪdʒ/ *n.* [C] a wall of earth, stones etc. built across a river to provide water for farming or to prevent flooding

barˈrage balˌloon *n.* [C] a large bag that floats in the air to prevent enemy airplanes from flying near the ground

barred /bɑrd/ *adj.* **1** a barred window, gate etc. has bars across it **2** FORMAL having bands of different color: *red barred tail feathers* → see also BAR¹

bar·rel¹ /ˈbærəl/ *n.* [C] **1** a large curved container with a flat top and bottom, made of wood or metal: *a beer barrel* → see picture at CONTAINER **2** also **barrelful** the amount of liquid that a barrel contains, used especially as a measure of oil: *The area may contain up to 2 billion barrels of oil.* **3** the part of a gun that the bullets are fired through **4 have sb over a barrel** to put someone in a situation in which they are forced to accept or do what you want: *You've got him over a barrel, so tell him you want a raise or you'll quit.* **5 be a barrel of laughs** [often in negatives] to be very enjoyable: *It wasn't a barrel of laughs, but I learned a lot.* → see also **lock, stock, and barrel** at LOCK² (3), PORK BARREL, **scrape the bottom of the barrel** at SCRAPE¹ (4)

barrel² *v.* [I] INFORMAL to move very fast, especially in an uncontrolled way: *Smith barreled into him, knocking him over.*

ˌbarrel-ˈchested *adj.* a man who is barrel-chested has a round chest that sticks out

ˈbarrel ˌorgan *n.* [C] a musical instrument that you play by turning a handle, used especially in past times

bar·ren /ˈbærən/ *adj.* **1** GEOGRAPHY land or soil that is barren has no plants growing on it: *the barren hillsides after the fire* **2** a room or area that is barren has nothing in it: *a barren apartment in a poor area* **3** BIOLOGY a woman or a female animal who is barren cannot produce children or baby animals SYN **infertile** **4** BIOLOGY a tree or plant that is barren does not produce fruit or seeds **5** LITERARY without any useful results: *a pointless and barren discussion*

bar·rette /bəˈrɛt/ *n.* [C] a small metal or plastic object used for holding a woman or girl's hair in a particular position

bar·ri·cade¹ /ˈbærəˌkeɪd/ *n.* [C] a temporary wall or fence across a road, door etc. that prevents people from going through: *Soldiers fired over the barricades at the rioters.* [**Origin:** 1500–1600 French *barrique* **barrel**; because early barricades were made from barrels]

barricade² *v.* [T] to protect or close something by building a barricade: *Demonstrators barricaded the streets.* | **barricade yourself in/inside sth** *The gunman barricaded himself inside the building.*

Bar·rie /ˈbæri/, **J.M.** (1860–1937) a Scottish writer of plays and novels

bar·ri·er /ˈbæriɚ/ *n.* [C] **1** a rule, problem etc. that prevents people from doing something, or limits what they can do: *Their attempt to reduce trade barriers failed.* | +**to** *A lack of education is a barrier to many good jobs.* | +**between** | *Ballet is entertainment without* ***a language barrier*** (=problem caused by not speaking someone's language). **2** a type of fence or gate that prevents people from moving in a particular direction: *The police put up barriers to hold back the crowds.* **3** a physical object that keeps two areas, people etc. apart: *The mountains form* ***a natural barrier between*** *the two countries.* **4 the 10 second/40% etc. barrier** a level or amount of 10 seconds, 40% etc. that is seen as a limit which it is difficult to get beyond: *It may be possible to push the inflation rate below the 3% barrier.* → see also SOUND BARRIER

ˌbarrier ˈreef *n.* [C] EARTH SCIENCE a line of CORAL (=pink/white stone-like substance) separated from the shore by water

ˌbarrier to ˈentry *n.* [C] ECONOMICS something that prevents a company entering a business activity, such as strict government rules or the need to put a lot of money into the activity in order to make it financially successful

bar·ring /ˈbɑrɪŋ/ *prep.* unless something happens: *Barring power outages, the only use for candles is decorative.*

bar·ri·o /ˈbæriˌoʊ/ *n. plural* **barrios** [C] a part of an American town or city where many poor Spanish-speaking people live [**Origin:** 1800–1900 Spanish, Arabic *barri* **of the open country**]

bar·ris·ter /ˈbærɪstɚ/ *n.* [C] LAW a lawyer in the U.K. who can argue cases in the higher law courts → see also SOLICITOR

bar·room /ˈbɑrˌrum/ *n.* [C] INFORMAL a BAR

bar·row /ˈbæroʊ/ *n.* [C] **1** a WHEELBARROW **2** a small vehicle like a box on wheels, from which fruits, vegetables etc. used to be sold **3** HISTORY a large pile of earth like a small hill that was put over an important grave in ancient times

Bar·row /ˈbæroʊ/, **Clyde** /klaɪd/ (1909–1934) a young U.S. criminal who stole money from banks and businesses with Bonnie Parker

Bar·ry·more /ˈbærɪˌmɔr/ the family name of several U.S. actors who were famous in the late 19th and early 20th centuries. Ethel Barrymore (1879–1959) and John Barrymore (1882–1942) were famous for performing in plays and movies, and Lionel Barrymore (1878–1954) was famous for performing in movies.

bar·tend·er /ˈbɑrˌtɛndɚ/ *n.* [C] someone who makes, pours, and serves drinks in a bar or restaurant

bar·ter¹ /ˈbɑrt̬ɚ/ *v.* [I,T] to exchange goods, work, or services for other goods or services rather than for money: **barter (with sb) for sth** *We bartered with the local vendors for food in the bazaar.* | **barter sth for sth**

Pete barters plumbing or electrical work for groceries. [**Origin:** 1400–1500 French *barater* **to cheat, exchange, barter**]

barter² *n.* [U] **1** a system of exchanging goods and services for other goods and services rather than using money: *Most of the people get what they need by barter.* **2** goods or services that are exchanged in this kind of system: *Beads were used as barter in the early days of settlement.*

ˈbarter eˌconomy *n.* [C] ECONOMICS an economic system in which goods are exchanged for other goods or work is done in exchange for other work rather than for money

bar·ter·ing /ˈbɑrt̬ərɪŋ/ *n.* [U] ECONOMICS the activity of exchanging goods, work, or services for other goods or services rather than for money

Barth /bɑrt, bɑrθ/, **Karl** /kɑrl/ (1886–1968) a Swiss Protestant religious teacher and writer

Barthes /bɑrt/, **Ro·land** /ˈroʊlɑn/ (1915–1980) a French writer famous for developing STRUCTURALISM

Bar·thol·o·mew /bɑrˈθɑləˌmyu/ in the Bible, one of the 12 APOSTLES

Bar·tók /ˈbɑrtɑk/, **Bé·la** /ˈbeɪlə/ (1881–1945) a Hungarian musician who wrote CLASSICAL music

Bar·ton /ˈbɑrtˀn/, **Cla·ra** /ˈklærə/ (1821–1912) a U.S. nurse who started the American Red Cross in 1881

Bar·uch /bəˈruk/ a book in the Apocrypha of the Protestant Bible and in the Old Testament of the Catholic Bible

Baruch, Ber·nard /bəˈnɑrd/ (1870–1965) a U.S. FINANCIER and ECONOMIST who was a financial adviser to four U.S. presidents

Ba·rysh·ni·kov /bəˈrɪʃnɪˌkɔf/, **Mik·hail** /mɪˈkaɪl/ (1948–) a Russian BALLET dancer and CHOREOGRAPHER who left the Soviet Union and came to live in the U.S.

ba·salt /bəˈsɔlt, ˈbeɪsɔlt/ *n.* [U] EARTH SCIENCE a type of dark green-black rock

base¹ /beɪs/ [S2] [W1] *n.*
1 LOWEST PART [C usually singular] the lowest part of something, or the surface at the bottom of something [SYN] **bottom**: *a black vase with a round base* | **+of** *Pour the concrete around the base of the post.* | *He died of a blow to the base of the skull.* | *a lake at the base of the mountain*
2 KNOWLEDGE/IDEAS [U] the most important part of something, from which new ideas develop: *India has a good scientific research base.* | **+for** *Reading to your child provides a solid base for educational success.*
3 COMPANY/ORGANIZATION [C,U] the main place from which a group, company, or organization controls its activities: *Microsoft's base is in Redmond, Washington.* | **+for** *He used his home as the base for his printing business.*
4 MILITARY [C] a place where people in a military organization live and work: **military/naval/air etc. base** *Several military bases will be closed this year.*
5 PEOPLE/GROUPS [C usually singular] the people, money, groups etc. that form the main part of something: *They hope to attract new business and strengthen the city's* ***economic base*** (=things that produce jobs and money). | *The company's* ***customer base*** (=people who buy its goods) *is growing.* | *New jobs in the area will improve the city's* ***tax base*** (=the people who pay taxes). | *Volkswagen needed a* ***manufacturing base*** (=companies that make things) *in Asia to gain a share of the market.* → see also POWER BASE
6 off base INFORMAL completely wrong: *If he thinks there was any discrimination involved, he's way off base.*
7 touch base (with sb) to talk with someone in order to find out what is happening about something: *It's important to touch base with our allies in this issue.*
8 SPORTS [C] one of the four places that a player must touch in order to get a point in games such as baseball or SOFTBALL
9 cover/touch all the bases to prepare for or deal with a situation thoroughly: *The police have called in experts to make sure they've covered all the bases.*
10 SUBSTANCE/MIXTURE [singular, U] the main part of a substance to which something else is later added: *You should paint the outside walls with an oil base.* | **+for** *Onions form the base for many curries.* → see also BASE METAL
11 CHEMISTRY [C] CHEMISTRY a chemical substance that combines with an acid to form a SALT
12 NUMBERS [C usually singular] MATH the number in relation to which a number system or mathematical table is built up: *The decimal system uses a base of 10.*
13 SHAPE [C] MATH the lowest side or bottom face of a flat or solid GEOMETRIC shape: **+of** *the base of a cone*

base² [S2] [W1] *v.* [T usually in passive] to establish or use somewhere as the main place for your business or work: **be based in/at sth** *The toy company is based in Trenton, New Jersey.*
base sth **on/upon** sth *phr. v.* to use particular information or facts as a point from which to develop an idea, plan etc.: *What do you base your theory on?* | *The movie was based on a true story.*

base³ *adj.* **1 base pay/salary** the amount of money that someone receives as their regular pay, before any special payments or BENEFITS are added **2** LITERARY not having good moral principles: *base passions* [**Origin:** 1300–1400 Old French *bas*, from Medieval Latin *bassus* **short, low**]

ˈbase ˌangles *n.* [plural] MATH the two angles at the base of a flat shape such as a TRIANGLE or TRAPEZOID: *The base angles of an isoceles triangle are equal.*

base·ball /ˈbeɪsbɔl/ [S2] [W2] *n.* **1** [U] an outdoor game between two teams of nine players, in which players try to get points by hitting a ball and running around four bases **2** [C] the ball used in the game of baseball

ˈbaseball cap *n.* [C] a hat that fits closely around your head, with a stiff round part that sticks out at the front → see picture at HAT

base·board /ˈbeɪsbɔrd/ *n.* [C] a narrow board fastened to the bottom of indoor walls where they meet the floor

base·less /ˈbeɪslɪs/ *adj.* FORMAL not based on facts or good reasons: *baseless rumors*

base·line /ˈbeɪslaɪn/ *n.* **1** [C usually singular] TECHNICAL a standard measurement or fact to which other measurements or facts are compared, especially in medicine or science: *a baseline for measuring productivity* **2** the line at the back of the court in games such as tennis or VOLLEYBALL **3** the area that a player must run within, on a baseball field

base·man /ˈbeɪsmən/ *n.* [C] *plural* **basemen** /-mən/ **first/second/third baseman** the person who plays one of three positions near the BASES in baseball

base·ment /ˈbeɪsmənt/ [S2] *n.* [C] a room or area that is under the level of the ground

ˌbase ˈmetal *n.* [C,U] CHEMISTRY a metal that is not very valuable, such as iron or lead

bas·es /ˈbeɪsiz/ *n.* the plural of BASIS

bash¹ /bæʃ/ *v.* [I,T] INFORMAL **1** to hit someone or something hard, in a way that causes pain or damage: **bash sth on/against sth** *I bashed my toe on the bedpost.* | **+into/against** *He bashed into the car in front of him.* | **bash down/in/up etc. sth** (=destroy something by hitting it often) *They bashed in my locker and broke off the door.* ►see THESAURUS box at **hit¹**, **hit¹** **2** to criticize someone or something a lot: *The local newspaper has recently been bashing the city's court system.* → see also BASHING

bash² *n.* [C] INFORMAL a party or celebration: *a birthday bash* ►see THESAURUS box at **party¹**

bash·ful /ˈbæʃfəl/ *adj.* easily embarrassed in social situations [SYN] **shy**: *a bashful smile* | *Sheila was never bashful about asking a question.* —**bashfully** *adv.* —**bashfulness** *n.* [U]

bash·ing /ˈbæʃɪŋ/ *n.* **1 Congress-bashing/lawyer-bashing etc.** the act of criticizing a particular person or group: *There was a lot of Democrat-bashing in the last election.* **2 gay-bashing/Asian-bashing etc.** the act of physically attacking someone who belongs to a group of people the attacker dislikes

Ba•sho /ˈbɑʃoʊ/, **Mat•su•o** /mætˈsuoʊ/ (1644–1694) a Japanese poet famous as the first writer of HAIKU

Ba•sic /ˈbeɪsɪk/ *n.* [U] a commonly used computer language

ba•sic /ˈbeɪsɪk/ S2 W2 *adj.* **1** forming the main or most necessary part of something: *There are two basic problems here.* | *the basic principles of mathematics* | *Tax money pays for* ***basic services***.

THESAURUS

fundamental relating to the most basic and important parts of something: *The fundamental problem is a lack of resources.*
essential the essential parts, qualities, or features of something are the ones that are most important, typical, or easily noticed: *Religion is an essential part of their lives.*
central more important than anything else: *Pay is a central issue in these negotiations.*

2 at the simplest or least developed level: *You need at least a basic understanding of English.* | *His skills are very basic.* **3** [only before noun] basic desires, rights etc. are ones that everyone has: *basic human rights* **4 basic salary/pay etc.** the amount of money that you are paid before any special payments are added → see also BASICS

ba•si•cally /ˈbeɪsɪkli/ S1 W3 *adv.* **1** [sentence adverb] SPOKEN used when giving the most important reason or fact about something, or a simple explanation of something: *Basically, you just have to write what the teachers want.* | *Well, basically, she's just a lot of fun to work with.* **2** in the main or most important ways, without considering additional details or differences: *Norwegian and Danish are basically the same.* **3** in a very simple way, with only the things that are completely necessary: *The office was very basically equipped.*

ba•sics /ˈbeɪsɪks/ *n.* [plural] **1 the basics** the most important and necessary facts about something, from which other possibilities and ideas may develop: *You can do fancier things later on, after you've learned the basics.* | **+of** *the basics of French grammar* **2** things that everyone needs in order to live or to deal with a particular situation: *I went to the store to get a few basics.* **3 get/go back to basics** to return to teaching or doing the most important or the simplest part of something: *A lot of parents want the schools to get back to basics* (=to teach reading, writing, and mathematics thoroughly).

ˌbasic ˈtraining *n.* [U] the period when a new soldier learns military rules and does a lot of exercise

Ba•sie /ˈbeɪsi/, **Count** /kaʊnt/ (1904–1984) a U.S. JAZZ musician who played the piano and led a famous band

ba•sil /ˈbeɪzəl/ S3 *n.* [U] a sweet-smelling HERB used in cooking [**Origin:** 1400–1500 Old French *basile*, from Late Latin, from Greek *basilikos* **royal**]

ba•sil•i•ca /bəˈsɪlɪkə/ *n.* [C] **1** a large Christian church with long straight sides and one end that is shaped like half a circle **2** CULTURE an important Roman Catholic church that has been given special rights and advantages by the Pope: *the basilica of St. Peter's* [**Origin:** 1500–1600 Latin, Greek *basilike*, from *basilikos* **royal**, from *basileus* **king**]

bas•i•lisk /ˈbæsəˌlɪsk, ˈbæzə-/ *n.* [C] an imaginary animal in ancient stories, that is like a lizard and is supposed to be able to kill people by looking at them

ba•sin /ˈbeɪsən/ *n.* [C] **1** EARTH SCIENCE an area of land that is lower at the center than at the edges, especially

baseball

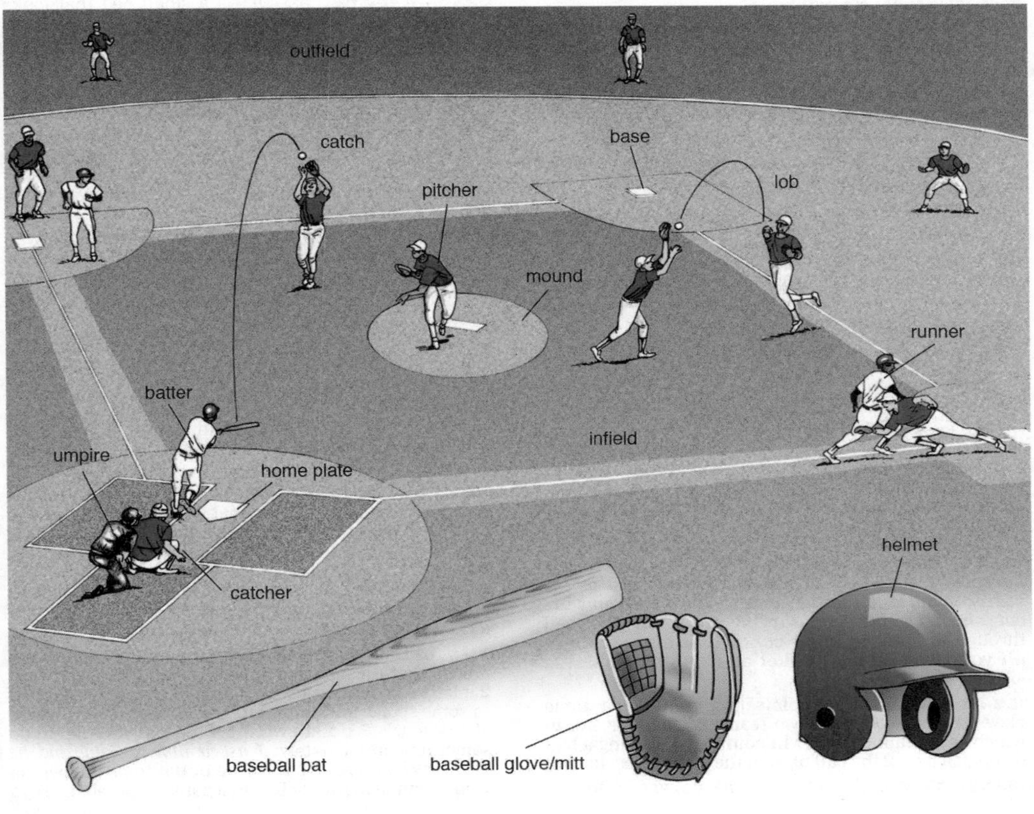

one from which water runs down into a river: *the Amazon Basin* **2** a large bowl, especially one for water, or the amount of liquid the bowl holds **3** a bowl-shaped area containing water: *Water splashed in the basin of the fountain.* **4** GEOGRAPHY a place where the Earth's surface is lower than in other areas: *the Pacific Basin* **5** a SINK [**Origin:** 1200–1300 Old French *bacin*, from Late Latin *bacchinon*]

'basin irri,gation *n.* [U] **1** GEOGRAPHY a method of supplying crops with water, in which the crops are planted in a level field and a raised bank of earth is built around the edge of the field, so that the water can build up on the surface before gradually sinking into the ground **2** GEOGRAPHY a similar system used in ancient Egypt for supplying crops grown by the side of the river Nile with water and natural chemicals

ba•sis S2 W2 *n. plural* **bases** /-siz/ [C] **1** the facts, ideas, or things from which something can be developed: **+for** *a basis for discussion* | *Bread **forms the basis of** their diet.* | **a firm/sound/solid etc. basis** *The course provides a sound basis in management theory.* | *His claims **have no basis in fact**.* **2** a way of organizing or doing something: *I'm saving money on a regular basis.* | **on a daily/weekly etc. basis** (=every day, week etc.) *Meetings are held on a monthly basis.* | **on a voluntary/part-time etc. basis** *Donna was hired on a freelance basis.* **3 on the basis of sth** because of a particular fact or situation: *discrimination on the basis of race or sex* [**Origin:** 1500–1600 Latin, Greek, **step, base**, from *bainein* **to go**]

bask /bæsk/ *v.* [I] **1** to enjoy the approval or attention that you are getting from other people: **+in** *Anderson basked in the glory of the victory.* | *Perry happily **basked in the reflected glory of*** (=shared the approval and praise that really belonged to) *his famous golf partner.* **2** to enjoy sitting or lying in the heat of the sun or a fire: **+in** *A lizard was basking in the heat of the afternoon sun.* [**Origin:** 1300–1400 Old Norse *bathask*, from *batha* **to take a bath**]

baskets

bas•ket /'bæskɪt/ S2 W3 *n.* [C] **1** a container made of thin pieces of plastic, wire, or wood woven together, used to carry things or put things in: *a shopping basket* | **+of** *a basket of fruit* **2** a net with a hole at the bottom hung from a metal ring, through which the ball is thrown in basketball **3** a point scored in basketball when the ball passes through the net: *Johnson **made a basket*** (=threw the ball into the basket) *just as the buzzer sounded to end the game.* | *Vic and Tommy are out **shooting baskets*** (=trying to throw the ball through the basket) *in the park.* → see also **put/have all your eggs in one basket** at EGG[1] (4), WASTEPAPER BASKET

bas•ket•ball /'bæskɪt,bɔl/ S2 W2 *n.* [U] **1** a game played indoors between two teams of five players, in which each team tries to win points by throwing a ball through a net **2** the ball used in the game of basketball

'basket case *n.* [C] INFORMAL someone who is so nervous or anxious that they cannot deal with simple situations: *Mom was a complete basket case at our wedding.*

bas•ket•ry /'bæskətri/ also **bas•ket•work** /'bæskɪt,wɚk/ *n.* [U] **1** baskets or other objects made by weaving together thin dried branches **2** the skill of making baskets

bas•ma•ti rice /bɑz,mɑṭi 'raɪs, bæs-/ *n.* [U] a type of high quality rice, often eaten with Indian food

basque /bæsk/ *n.* [C] a piece of underwear or part of a dress for a woman that covers her from under her arms to the top of her legs

bas-re•lief /,bɑ rɪ'lif/ *n.* [C,U] ENG. LANG. ARTS a style of art in which stone or wood is cut so that shapes are raised above the surrounding surface → see also HIGH RELIEF

bass[1] /beɪs/ *n.* **1** [C] a man whose singing or speaking voice is very low **2** [singular] ENG. LANG. ARTS the part of a piece of music that this person sings **3** [U] ENG. LANG. ARTS the lower half of the whole range of musical notes → see also TREBLE **4** [C] ENG. LANG. ARTS a BASS GUITAR: *The band features Willie Dixon **on bass*** (=playing the bass guitar). **5** [C] ENG. LANG. ARTS a DOUBLE BASS —**bass** *adj., adv.*

bass[2] /bæs/ *n. plural* **bass** or **bases** [C] BIOLOGY a fish that can be eaten and lives both in rivers and the ocean

bass clef /,beɪs 'klɛf/ *n.* [C] a sign (𝄢) at the beginning of a line of written music that shows that the top line of the STAVE is the A below MIDDLE C

bass drum /,beɪs 'drʌm/ *n.* [C] a type of large drum used for giving the main beat in a piece of music

bas•set /'bæsɪt/ also **'basset hound** *n.* [C] a dog with short legs and long ears, used for hunting

Basse•terre /bɑs'tɛr/ the capital city of St. Kitts and Nevis

bass gui•tar /,beɪs gɪ'tɑr/ *n.* [C] an electric musical instrument with four strings and a long neck, that plays low notes SYN bass —**bass guitarist** *n.* [C]

bas•si•net /,bæsɪ'nɛt/ *n.* [C] a small bed that looks like a basket, used for a very young baby

bass•ist /'beɪsɪst/ *n.* [C] someone who plays a BASS GUITAR or a DOUBLE BASS

bass line /'beɪs laɪn/ *n.* [C usually singular] a series of notes that make up the low sounds and RHYTHM of a piece of music, or its main tune

bas•soon /bə'sun, bæ-/ *n.* [C] a very long wooden musical instrument with a low sound, that is held upright and played by blowing into a thin curved metal pipe —**bassoonist** *n.* [C]

bas•tard /'bæstɚd/ *n.* [C] OLD-FASHIONED someone who was born to parents who were not married

bas•tard•ize /'bæstɚ,daɪz/ *v.* [T] to spoil something by changing its good parts: *a bastardized version of the play*

bas•tard•y /'bæstɚdi/ *n.* [U] OLD USE the situation of having parents who were not married to each other when you were born

baste /beɪst/ *v.* [I,T] **1** to pour liquid or melted fat over meat that is cooking **2** to fasten cloth with long loose stitches, in order to hold it together so that you can sew it correctly later

bas•tion /'bæstʃən/ *n.* [C] **1** something that protects a way of life, principle etc. that seems likely to change or disappear: **+of** *Hong Kong continued to be a bastion of free trade.* | *He described Hollywood as **the last bastion of** white supremacy in America.* **2** a place where a country or army has strong military defenses: *an American bastion in the Pacific* **3** TECHNICAL a part of a castle wall that sticks out from the rest

bat[1] /bæt/ S3 *n.* [C] **1** BIOLOGY a small animal like a mouse that flies around at night → see also FRUIT BAT **2** a long wooden stick with a special shape that is used in some sports and games: *a baseball bat* → see picture at BASEBALL **3 do sth right off the bat** INFORMAL to do something immediately: *I asked him to help, and he said yes right off the bat.* **4 be at bat** to be the person who is trying to hit the ball in a game of baseball **5 go**

to bat for sb INFORMAL to help and support someone: *Rene went to bat for me with the director, and I ended up getting the part.* **6 like a bat out of hell** INFORMAL very fast: *I drove like a bat out of hell to the hospital.* **7 old bat** SPOKEN an old woman who is not nice and is often in a bad mood **8 have bats in the belfry** OLD-FASHIONED to be slightly crazy [**Origin:** (1, 6–8) 1500–1600 *bat* (14–16 centuries)] → see also **as blind as a bat** at BLIND[1]

bat² *v.* **batted, batting 1** [I,T] to hit the ball with a bat in baseball **2** [I,T] to hit something lightly with your hand: +**at** *Our kittens had fun batting at balls of paper.* **3 not bat an eye/eyelid** INFORMAL to not seem to be shocked, surprised, or embarrassed: *He used to tell the worst lies without batting an eye.* **4 bat your eyes/eyelashes** if a woman bats her eyes, she opens and closes them quickly, especially in order to look attractive to men **5 bat a thousand** also **bat 1,000** INFORMAL to be very successful: *She's been batting a thousand ever since she got that new job.*

bat sth ↔ **around** *phr. v.* INFORMAL to discuss the good and bad parts of a plan, idea etc.

Ba·taan Death March, the /bəˌtæn ˈdeθ ˌmɑrtʃ/ HISTORY a time when American and Filipino soldiers fighting against the Japanese in World War II were taken prisoner and forced to march many miles to a prison camp, causing many of the soldiers to die. This was later treated as a war crime.

bat·boy /ˈbætˀbɔɪ/ *n.* [C] a boy whose job is to look after the equipment of a BASEBALL team

batch /bætʃ/ S3 *n.* [C] **1** a quantity of food, medicine etc. that is produced or prepared at the same time: *a batch of cookies* **2** a group of people or things that arrive or are dealt with together: *the latest batch of reports* [**Origin:** 1400–1500 from an unrecorded Old English *bæcce* **something baked**, from *bacan*]

ˈbatch ˌprocessing *n.* [U] COMPUTERS a type of computer system in which the computer does several jobs one after the other, without needing instructions between each job

bat·ed /ˈbeɪt̬ɪd/ *adj.* **with bated breath** feeling very anxious or excited: *The soldiers' families waited with bated breath for news.*

bath /bæθ/ S2 *n.* [C] **1** an act of washing your body in a bathtub: *Mom is **taking a bath**.* | *Dan, will you **give** the kids **a bath** tonight* (=wash them)*?* **2** water that you sit or lie in to wash yourself: *I love to soak in a hot bath.* | *Lisa **ran a bath** (=put water in a bathtub) for herself.* **3** a word meaning "bathroom," used in advertising for houses: *a three-bedroom, two-bath house* **4 take a bath** INFORMAL to lose money, especially in a business deal: *We really took a bath on that deal.* **5** a container full of liquid in which something is placed for a particular purpose: *a bath of black dye* **6 baths** a public building where people could go in past times to wash themselves: *the Roman baths* [**Origin:** Old English *bæth*] → see also BIRDBATH, BLOODBATH, BUBBLE BATH, **throw the baby out with the bath water** at THROW[1] (23), TURKISH BATH

bathe /beɪð/ *v.* **1** [I,T] to wash yourself or someone else in a bathtub: *Brenda bathed and changed the baby.* **2 be bathed in light/moonlight etc.** LITERARY an area or building that is bathed in light has light shining onto it in a way that makes it look pleasant or attractive: *The beach was bathed in bright sunlight.* **3** [T] to wash or cover part of your body with a liquid, especially as a medical treatment: *A nurse bathed her feet in medicine.* **4 be bathed in tears/sweat etc.** LITERARY to be covered in tears, SWEAT etc. → see also SUNBATHE

bath·er /ˈbeɪðɚ/ *n.* [C] **1** someone who is taking a bath **2** OLD-FASHIONED someone who is swimming

bathing suit /ˈbeɪðɪŋ ˌsut/ *n.* [C] a piece of clothing that you wear for swimming → see also SWIMMING TRUNKS, SWIMSUIT

ˈbath mat *n.* [C] a piece of thick cloth that you put on the floor next to the bathtub

ba·thos /ˈbeɪθɑs/ *n.* [U] LITERARY ENG. LANG. ARTS a sudden change from discussing something that is beautiful, moral, or serious to something that is ordinary, silly, or not important: *a drama that is full of bathos*

bath·robe /ˈbæθroʊb/ *n.* [C] a long loose piece of clothing shaped like a coat, that you wear especially before or after you take a SHOWER or bath

bath·room /ˈbæθrum/ S1 W3 *n.* **1** [C] a room in a house where there is a toilet, a SINK, and a bathtub or SHOWER ►see THESAURUS box at **toilet** **2** [C] a room where there is a toilet, especially in a public place SYN **restroom**: *Excuse me, where's the bathroom?* **3 go to the bathroom** to use a toilet: *Mommy, Mommy, I gotta go to the bathroom.*

ˈbath salts *n.* [plural] a substance that you put in bath water to make it smell nice

ˈbath ˌtowel *n.* [C] a large TOWEL (=piece of material for drying yourself)

bath·tub /ˈbæθtʌb/ *n.* [C] a long large container that you fill with water and sit or lie in to wash yourself

bath·y·sphere /ˈbæθɪˌsfɪr/ *n.* [C] TECHNICAL a strong container used for going deep under the ocean, especially to look at plants, animals etc.

ba·tik /bəˈtik, bæ-/ *n.* **1** [U] a way of printing colored patterns on cloth that involves putting WAX over some parts of the cloth **2** [C,U] cloth that has been colored in this way [**Origin:** 1800–1900 Malay, Javanese, **painted**]

bat mitz·vah /ˌbɑtˀ ˈmɪtsvə/ *n.* [C] **1** the religious ceremony held when a Jewish girl reaches the age of 13 and is considered an adult in her religion **2** a girl for whom this ceremony is held [**Origin:** 1900–2000 Hebrew *bath miswah* **daughter of (God's) law**] → see also BAR MITZVAH

ba·ton /bəˈtɑn/ *n.* [C] **1** a short thin stick used by a CONDUCTOR (=the leader of a group of musicians) to direct the music **2** a light metal stick that is spun and thrown into the air by someone marching with a band **3** a short thick stick used as a weapon by a police officer SYN **nightstick** **4** a short light stick that is passed from one person to another during a race

Bat·on Rouge /ˌbætˀn ˈruʒ/ the capital city of the U.S. state of Louisiana

bat·tal·ion /bəˈtælyən/ *n.* [C] a large group of soldiers consisting of several companies (COMPANY)

bat·ten¹ /ˈbætˀn/ *v.* **batten down the hatches a)** INFORMAL to prepare for a period of difficulty or trouble: *Businesses are focused on survival – everyone's battening down the hatches.* **b)** to firmly close the entrances to the lower part of a ship or SUBMARINE

batten² *n.* [C] a long narrow piece of wood that boards or SHINGLES are fastened to, or that is attached to other pieces of wood to keep them in place

bat·ter¹ /ˈbæt̬ɚ/ *n.* **1** [C,U] a mixture of flour, eggs, milk etc., used for making cakes, some types of bread etc.: *pancake batter* **2** [C] the person who is trying to hit the ball in baseball → see picture at BASEBALL

batter² *v.* [I always + adv./prep.,T] **1** to hit someone or something again and again, in a way that hurts someone or causes damage SYN **beat**: *Each year, perhaps 4 million women are battered by their husbands.* | **batter sth at/on/against etc.** *The storm battered the ship against the rocks.* **2** to make someone suffer from a loss, criticism etc.: *His campaign team was battered by a humiliating defeat in Iowa.* —**battering** *n.* [C,U]

bat·tered /ˈbæt̬ɚd/ *adj.* **1 a battered woman/spouse etc.** a woman, wife, husband etc. who has been violently treated by their husband, BOYFRIEND, wife etc.: *The agency helps battered women.* **2** old and in bad condition: *a battered 1969 Ford*

ˈbattering ˌram *n.* [C] a long heavy piece of wood or metal used to break through walls or doors

bat·ter·y /ˈbæt̬əri/ S1 *n. plural* **batteries** **1** [C] PHYSICS a set of connected electrical cells that produce an electric current by changing chemical energy into electrical energy: *Did you **change the batteries** in the flashlight?* | *I tried to start the car, but the **battery** was **dead*** (=stopped producing electricity). | **charge/**

recharge a battery *It takes an hour to recharge the batteries.* | **battery-powered/battery-operated** *a battery-powered radio* **2** [U] LAW the crime of hitting someone: *Ferguson was found guilty of battery.* → see also ASSAULT AND BATTERY **3 a battery of sth** a group of many things of the same type: *a battery of medical and psychological tests* **4** [C] several large guns used together: *He commands a battery of artillery.* **5 recharge your batteries** INFORMAL to rest or relax in order to get back your energy [**Origin:** (1) from the idea of a group of electricity-producing cells joined together]

bat·ting /ˈbæt̬ɪŋ/ *n.* [U] **1** the action or skill of hitting a ball in baseball **2** cotton or wool that is sewn between two pieces of cloth to make something soft or warm

bat·tle¹ /ˈbæt̬l/ S3 W2 *n.* [C]
1 BETWEEN ARMIES [C,U] a fight between opposing armies, groups of ships etc., especially one that is part of a larger war: *the Battle of Bunker Hill* | **+between** *a battle between government forces and rebels* | **+against/with** *a bloody battle against the invaders* | *The general has* ***fought*** *many* ***battles*** *in his career.* | **+for** *a battle for control of the city* | **win/lose a battle** *This was the first battle that the allies had lost.* | *Marks was killed* ***in battle*** *in 1943.* | *The vehicles are used to take troops* ***into battle.*** ▶see THESAURUS box at **war**
2 BETWEEN OPPONENTS [C] a situation in which opposing groups or people compete or argue with each other when trying to achieve success or control: *a long and costly legal battle* | **+for** *a battle for the league title* | **+between** *a political battle between Congress and the White House* | **+with** *a battle with Dawson for the mayor's job* | **+over** *a battle over the old man's estate* | *They're* ***fighting*** *a fierce* ***battle*** *for control of the agency.* | **win/lose a battle** *Democrats have lost the budget battle.* ▶see THESAURUS box at **fight²**
3 ATTEMPT [C usually singular] an attempt to solve a difficult problem or change a bad situation: **+against** *the battle against drug and alcohol abuse* | **+with** *a battle with allergies* | **win/lose a battle** *Williams finally lost his long battle with cancer.* | *You're* ***fighting a losing battle*** (=trying to do something that you won't succeed at) *trying to keep this house clean.*
4 be half the battle to be a difficult or important part of what you have to do: *Just getting an interview is half the battle.*
5 do battle (with sb) to argue with someone or fight against someone: *We are prepared to do battle with City Hall over this bill.*
6 a battle of wits a disagreement that opposing sides try to win by using their intelligence
7 the battle of the sexes the relationship between men and women when it is considered as a fight for power
8 the battle of the bulge INFORMAL, HUMOROUS the struggle to lose weight
[**Origin:** 1200–1300 Old French *bataille*, from Late Latin *battalia* **fighting**, from Latin *battuere* **to hit**]

battle² *v.* **1** [I,T] to try very hard to achieve something when this is very difficult: *Firefighters battled flames all night.* | **+against/with** *Minorities must still battle against discrimination.* | **+for** *Parents are battling for better schools.* | **battle to do sth** *Doctors battled to save his life.* | *The team* ***battled back*** (=worked hard to win from a losing position) *and won 57–51.* **2 battle it out** to keep fighting or opposing each other until one person or team wins: *The two teams are battling it out for the championship.* **3** [I,T] LITERARY to take part in a fight or war: *After the trial, rioters battled police.* | **+with** *Rival gangs battled with knives and chains.* | **+for** *The rebels claim to be battling for independence.*

ˈbattle ax, battle axe *n.* [C] **1** INFORMAL a woman who is unfriendly and not nice, and who tries to control other people **2** a large AX (=tool for cutting wood) used as a weapon in past times

ˈbattle ˌcruiser *n.* [C] a large fast ship used in war

ˈbattle cry *n.* [C usually singular] **1** a phrase used to encourage people, especially members of a political organization: *"Power to the people!" was their battle cry.* **2** a loud shout used in war to encourage your side and frighten the enemy

ˈbattle faˌtigue *n.* [U] a type of mental illness caused by the frightening experiences of war, in which someone feels very anxious and upset

bat·tle·field /ˈbæt̬lˌfild/ also **bat·tle·ground** /ˈbæt̬lˌgraʊnd/ *n.* [C] **1** a place where a battle is being fought or has been fought **2** a subject that people disagree or argue a lot about: *Prayer in schools has become a political battlefield.* **3** a place where an argument or disagreement happens, or where people are competing against each other: *a battleground state during the election*

bat·tle·front /ˈbæt̬lˌfrʌnt/ *n.* [singular] the place on a BATTLEFIELD where the opponents meet and start fighting

bat·tle·ground /ˈbæt̬lˌgraʊnd/ *n.* [C] a BATTLEFIELD

bat·tle·ments /ˈbæt̬lmənts/ *n.* [plural] HISTORY a low wall around the top of a castle, that has spaces to shoot guns or ARROWS through

ˌBattle of ˈBritain, the HISTORY the fighting between the German and British air forces, and the German bombing of Britain in 1940 during World War II

ˌBattle of Bull ˈRun, the also **the ˌBattle of Maˈnassas** HISTORY the first battle of the American Civil War, which was fought in 1861 in Virginia near Washington, D.C., and which the Confederate army won. A second battle was fought near the same place in 1862, and the Confederate army defeated the Union army again.

Battle of Bun·ker Hill, the /ˌbæt̬l əv ˌbʌŋkɚ ˈhɪl/ HISTORY the first important battle of the American Revolutionary War, fought on June 17, 1775, in Charlestown, Massachusetts, in which the British won the ground but lost about 1,000 soldiers, and the Americans lost only about 400

Battle of Chan·cel·lors·ville, the /ˌbæt̬l əv ˈtʃænsələzˌvɪl/ HISTORY an important battle in the American Civil War in 1863 in which the Confederate (southern) army won a battle against a much larger Union (northern) force

Battle of Cold Har·bor, the /ˌbæt̬l əv koʊld ˈhɑrbɚ/ HISTORY a very violent battle in 1864 during the American Civil War in which the Union (northern) troops lost many soldiers and did not win any ground

Battle of Fred·ericks·burg, the /ˌbæt̬l əv ˈfrɛdrɪksˌbɚg/ HISTORY an important battle in 1862 during the American Civil War which the Confederate (southern) army won, and the Union (northern) army lost large numbers of soldiers

ˌBattle of ˈGettysburg, the HISTORY an important battle in 1863 during the American Civil War which is considered to be the time when the Union (northern) army began to win the war

ˌBattle of ˌGuadalcaˈnal, the HISTORY an important battle in 1942–1943 during World War II, which was the first one in which U.S. ground forces took part in a battle in the Pacific region

Battle of I·wo Ji·ma, the /ˌbæt̬l əv ˌiwə ˈdʒimə/ HISTORY an important battle in 1945 during World War II on an island near Japan in which many American soldiers died

Battle of Lit·tle Big·horn, the /ˌbæt̬l əv ˌlɪt̬l ˈbɪghɔrn/ HISTORY a very famous battle between two Native American groups and the U.S. military in 1876 in which General George Custer and many U.S. soldiers died

Battle of Ma·nas·sas, the /ˌbæt̬l əv məˈnæsəs/ HISTORY the Southern name for the BATTLE OF BULL RUN

Battle of Mid·way, the /ˌbæt̬l əv ˈmɪdweɪ/ HISTORY an important sea battle in 1942 during World War II between the U.S. and Japan which gave the U.S. more power at sea than Japan and helped them win that part of the war

ˌBattle of New ˈOrleans, the HISTORY a battle in 1815 following the War of 1812 between the U.S. and Britain, which the U.S. won. The agreement to end the war had already been signed when the battle was fought, but the armies did not know it.

Battle of O·ki·na·wa, the /ˌbætl əv ˌoʊkɪˈnɑwə/ HISTORY in 1945, the last important battle of World War II between the U.S. and Japan

Battle of Sar·a·to·ga, the /ˌbætl əv ˌsærəˈtoʊgə/ HISTORY an important battle in 1777 during the American Revolutionary War, which is considered to be the point when the Americans began to win the war

ˌBattle of the ˈBulge, the HISTORY an important battle in 1944 during World War II between the Allies and Germany in which the Germans surprised the Allies and moved into the area that they had been holding

ˌBattle of the ˌCoral ˈSea, the HISTORY a battle in 1942 during World War II between the U.S. and the Japanese which was the first battle to be fought only by planes that took off from ships on the ocean

ˌBattle of the ˈWilderness, the HISTORY a battle in Virginia in 1864 during the American Civil War, which the Confederate (southern) Army won

Battle of Tip·pe·ca·noe, the /ˌbætl əv ˌtɪpikəˈnu/ HISTORY a battle in the Indiana Territory in 1811 between the U.S. military and the Native American people, the Shawnee, which led to the defeat of the Native Americans later

Battle of York·town, the /ˌbætl əv ˈyɔrktaʊn/ HISTORY the last battle, in 1781, of the American Revolutionary War in which the British SURRENDERED (=admitted they had lost the war)

bat·tle·ship /ˈbætlˌʃɪp/ *n.* [C] a very large ship used in war, with very big guns

Battles of Lex·ing·ton and Con·cord, the /ˌbætlz əv ˌlɛksɪŋtən ən ˈkɑŋkəd/ HISTORY the first battles of the American Revolutionary War fought on April 19, 1775 in Massachusetts

bat·ty /ˈbæti/ *adj.* INFORMAL crazy

bau·ble /ˈbɔbəl, ˈbɑ-/ *n.* [C] a cheap piece of jewelry

Baude·laire /boʊdˈlɛr/, **Charles** (1821–1867) a French poet

baud rate /ˈbɔd ˌreɪt/ *n.* [C] COMPUTERS a measurement of how fast information is sent to or from a computer, for example through a telephone line

Baum /bɑm/, **L. Frank** (1856–1919) a U.S. writer who wrote the book "The Wonderful Wizard of Oz"

baux·ite /ˈbɔksaɪt, ˈbɑk-/ *n.* [U] CHEMISTRY a soft substance that ALUMINUM (=a type of metal) is obtained from [**Origin:** 1800–1900 Les *Baux*, place in southern France where it was found]

Ba·var·i·a /bəˈvɛriə/ a state in southeast Germany —**Bavarian** *n., adj.*

bawd·y /ˈbɔdi/ *adj.* bawdy songs, jokes, stories etc. are about sex and are funny, enjoyable, and often noisy: *a bawdy new comedy* —**bawdily** *adv.* —**bawdiness** *n.* [U]

ˈbawdy house *n.* [C] OLD USE a BROTHEL

bawl /bɔl/ *v.* **1** [I] INFORMAL to cry loudly: *I couldn't help it, I just started bawling.* **2** [I,T] also **bawl out** to shout in a loud angry voice: *The captain stood at the front, bawling orders.*

bawl sb ↔ **out** *phr. v.* INFORMAL to speak angrily to someone because they have done something wrong: *The coach bawled us out for being late to practice.*

bay¹ /beɪ/ W2 *n. plural* **bays** [C]
1 OCEAN EARTH SCIENCE a part of the ocean that is enclosed by a curve in the land: *sailboats on the bay* | *the San Francisco Bay*
2 keep/hold sth at bay to prevent something dangerous or bad from happening or from coming too close: *Sandbags kept the floodwaters at bay.* | *The government hopes to keep inflation at bay.*
3 AREA an area within a building, airplane, ship etc. that is divided off and used for a special purpose: *the space shuttle's cargo bay*
4 FOR VEHICLES a place where a vehicle can park for a short time: *a loading bay*
5 TREE also **bay tree** BIOLOGY a tree that has leaves which smell sweet and are often used in cooking
6 HORSE BIOLOGY a horse that is a reddish brown color
7 BEND IN A WALL a part of a wall that is built farther back than the rest of the wall SYN alcove
8 SPACE FOR STH a space that is made for something to fit into: *a drive bay on a computer*
[**Origin:** (1) 1300–1400 Old French *baie*, from Old Spanish *bahia*]

B

bay² *v.* **bays, bayed, baying** [I] **1** if a dog bays, it makes a long high noise SYN howl: +**at** *In the distance, wolves were baying at the moon.* **2** to speak or behave in a way that reminds people of a noisy dog

bay³ *adj.* a bay horse is a reddish-brown color

ˈBay ˌArea, the the area of land around the San Francisco Bay in California, including cities such as San Francisco, Oakland, Berkeley, Palo Alto, and San José

ˈbay leaf *n.* [C] a leaf from the bay tree, used in cooking

ˌBay of ˈPigs inˌvasion, the HISTORY a failed attempt in 1961 to take over the Cuban government of Fidel Castro by a group of people who had been forced to leave Cuba and who were supported and trained by the U.S. government

bay·o·net¹ /ˈbeɪənɪt, -ˌnɛt, ˌbeɪəˈnɛt/ *n.* [C] a long knife that is attached to the end of a RIFLE (=long gun) [**Origin:** 1600–1700 French *baïonnette*, from *Bayonne* city in southwest France where it was first made]

bayonet² *v.* [T] to push the point of a bayonet into someone

bay·ou /ˈbaɪu, ˈbaɪoʊ/ *n.* [C] EARTH SCIENCE a large area of water in the southeast U.S. that moves very slowly and has many water plants [**Origin:** 1700–1800 Louisiana French, Choctaw *bayuk*]

ˌbay ˈwindow *n.* [C] a window that sticks out of the wall of a house, usually with glass on three sides

ba·zaar /bəˈzɑr/ *n.* [C] **1** a place, usually outdoors, where a lot of different things are sold, especially in India or the Middle East **2** an occasion when a lot of people sell different things to collect money for a good purpose: *a church bazaar* [**Origin:** 1500–1600 Persian *bazar*]

ba·zoo·ka /bəˈzukə/ *n.* [C] a long light gun that rests on your shoulder and is used especially for firing at TANKS

B-ball /ˈbi bɔl/ *n.* [U] INFORMAL basketball

BB gun /ˈbibi ˌgʌn/ *n.* [C] a gun that uses air pressure to shoot small round metal balls SYN air gun

BBQ /ˈbɑrbɪˌkyu/ *n.* [C] an abbreviation of BARBECUE

B.C. /ˌbi ˈsi/ *adv.* **Before Christ** used after a date to show that it was before the birth of Jesus Christ: *2600 B.C.* → see also A.D.

B.C.E. /ˌbi si ˈi/ **Before Common Era** used after a date to show that it is before the birth of Jesus Christ → see also C.E.

be¹ /bi/ S1 W1 *auxiliary verb* **1** used with a present participle to form the CONTINUOUS tenses of verbs: **be doing sth** *I'm still living with my parents.* | *Angela was reading when the phone rang.* | *They've been asking a lot of questions.* | *Bruce is always telling us stories.* | *You aren't leaving already, are you?* **2** used with past participles to form the PASSIVE: *Smoking is not permitted on this flight.* | *I was shown a copy of the contract.* | *The house is being painted.* | *His arrival may have been delayed by snow.* **3** used to show what is or was planned to happen: *I'll be leaving in about half an hour.* | **be to do sth** *Sam and Diane are to be married next June.* | *Talks were to have begun two weeks ago.* **4 be to do sth** FORMAL **a)** used to show what someone should do or what should happen: *What am I to tell her* (=what should I tell her?) *when she asks where he is?* | *He is more to be* (=should be more) *pitied than blamed.* **b)** used to give an order or to tell someone about a rule: *Fees are to be paid before classes begin.* | *The children are to go to bed by 8 o'clock.* **c)** used to show what had to happen or what did happen: *It was to be one of the most important judgments the court made.* **5 to be seen/found/heard etc.** LITERARY used to say that something can be seen, found, or heard somewhere: *Walker was nowhere to be found.* **6** used to make TAG QUESTIONS: *It's cold, isn't it?* | *You're not leaving, are you?* **7** used in CONDITIONAL sentences about a situation that does not or cannot exist: *If Biden were to run, would you vote for him?* | *I know what I'd do if he were my son.* **8** OLD USE used instead of "have" to form the PERFECT tenses of some verbs: *Christ is risen* (=has risen) *from the dead.*

B

be² S1 W1 *v.* **1** [linking verb] used to show that someone or something is the same as the subject of the sentence: *Hi, it's me.* | *These are Len's glasses.* | *Christie is my girlfriend.* | *The truth is, I don't have enough money.* | *The problem is how to get it done on time.* | *The goal is to raise about $200,000.* **2** [I always + adv./prep.] used to show position or time: *Where are the boys?* | *Jane's upstairs.* | *Mr. Smith's office is on the third floor.* | *How long has she been here?* | *The phone is in the hall.* | *When is the wedding?* **3** [linking verb] used to describe someone or something, or say what group or type they belong to: *Snow is white.* | *Horses are animals.* | *She wants to be a doctor when she grows up.* | *We were lost.* | *I'm not ready.* | *It's hot today.* | *A saw is for cutting wood.* **4 there is/are** [linking verb] used in order to say that something exists or happens: *There's a hole in your sweater.* | *There was a sudden loud bang.* **5** [linking verb] to behave in a particular way: *Be careful!* | *He was being really stupid.* **6** [linking verb] used in order to say how old someone is: *Andrew will be three in October.* | *How old are you?* **7** [linking verb] used in order to say who something belongs to: *Those are my books.* **8** [linking verb] used in order to talk about the price of something: *It was only $10!* ►see THESAURUS box at **cost²** **9** [linking verb] to be equal to a particular number or amount: *3 times 3 is 9.* **10 be yourself** to behave in a natural way, rather than trying to pretend to be different: *Don't try to impress him, just be yourself.* **11 be that as it may** FORMAL used to say that even though you accept that something is true it does not change a situation: *"Everyone knows it was your idea." "Be that as it may, we can present it together."* **12** [I] to exist: *That's just how it is.* **13 the be-all (and end-all)** the most important part of a situation or of someone's life: *Profit is important, but it is not the be-all and end-all.* [**Origin:** Old English *beon*] → see also **let sb/sth be** at LET (9)

be- /bɪ/ *prefix* **1** [in verbs] used to mean that someone or something becomes a particular thing or is treated in a particular way: *Don't belittle him* (=say he is unimportant). | *He befriended me* (=became my friend). **2** [in adjectives] LITERARY wearing or is covered by a particular thing: *a bespectacled boy* (=wearing glasses) | *a bejeweled woman* (=covered in jewels)

beach¹ /bitʃ/ S2 W2 *n.* [C] *plural* **beaches** an area of sand or small stones at the edge of an ocean or a lake: *a beautiful sandy beach* ►see THESAURUS box at **shore¹**

beach² *v.* [T] **1** if a WHALE or other sea animal beaches itself or is beached, it swims onto the shore and cannot get back in the water **2** to pull a boat onto the shore away from the water

ˈbeach ball *n.* [C] a large colored plastic ball that you blow air into and use for playing games on the beach

ˈbeach ˌbunny *n.* [C] INFORMAL a very attractive young woman at a beach, usually considered offensive by women

ˈbeach chair *n.* [C] a folding chair with a seat and back made of cloth or plastic, which is used outdoors, especially at the beach

beach·comb·er /ˈbitʃˌkoʊmɚ/ *n.* [C] someone who searches beaches for things that might be useful

beach·front /ˈbitʃfrʌnt/ *adj.* a beachfront building, piece of land etc. is on the edge of a beach: *beachfront hotels*

beach·head /ˈbitʃhɛd/ *n.* [C] an area of shore that has been taken from an enemy by force, and where soldiers can go onto the land from ships

beach·wear /ˈbitʃwɛr/ *n.* [U] clothes that you wear for swimming, lying on the beach etc.

bea·con /ˈbikən/ *n.* [C] **1** a light that is put somewhere to warn or guide people, vehicles, ships or aircraft **2** a radio or RADAR signal used by aircraft or boats to help them find their position and direction **3** a person, idea etc. that guides or encourages you: +**of** *The changes are a* ***beacon of hope*** *in this war-torn country.* **4** a fire on top of a hill, used in past times as a signal [**Origin:** Old English *beacen* **sign**]

bead /bid/ *n.* [C] **1** one of a set of small, usually round, pieces of glass, wood, plastic etc., that you can put on a string and wear as jewelry **2** a small drop of liquid such as water or blood: *Beads of sweat appeared on his forehead.* **3 draw a bead on sb/sth** to aim carefully before shooting a weapon [**Origin:** Old English *bed, gebed* **prayer**; because people counted beads while saying their prayers]

bead·ed /ˈbidɪd/ *adj.* **1** decorated with beads: *a beaded evening gown* **2 beaded with sweat/perspiration** having drops of SWEAT (=liquid produced by your body when you are hot) on your skin

bead·ing /ˈbidɪŋ/ *n.* [U] **1** a lot of beads sewn close together on clothes, leather etc. as decoration **2** long thin pieces of wood or stone that are used as a decoration on the edges of walls, furniture etc.

bead·y /ˈbidi/ *adj.* **1** beady eyes are small, round, and shiny, in a way that makes someone look dishonest or strange **2 have/keep your beady eye(s) on sb/sth** HUMOROUS to watch someone or something very carefully

bea·gle /ˈbigəl/ *n.* [C] a dog with short legs and smooth fur, sometimes used in hunting

beak /bik/ *n.* [C] **1** BIOLOGY the hard pointed mouth of a bird → see also BILL → see picture at BIRD **2** HUMOROUS a large pointed nose [**Origin:** 1200–1300 Old French *bec*, from Latin *beccus*]

beak·er /ˈbikɚ/ *n.* [C] CHEMISTRY a glass cup with straight sides that is used in chemistry for measuring and heating liquids

beam¹ /bim/ *n.* [C] **1 a)** a line of light shining from the sun, a lamp etc.: +**of** *the beam of the headlight* **b)** a line of light, energy etc. that you often cannot see: *a laser beam* | +**of** *a beam of electrons* **2** a long heavy piece of wood or metal used in building houses, bridges etc.: *a 55-ton concrete beam* **3** a BALANCE BEAM **4** TECHNICAL the widest part of a ship from side to side **5** a wide happy smile: +**of** *a beam of satisfaction*

beam² *v.* **1** [I] to smile very happily: *He looked at his son and beamed proudly.* | +**at** *His mother beamed at him.* | +**with** *Meg beamed with pleasure.* ►see THESAURUS box at **smile¹** **2** [T always + adv./prep.] to send a television or radio signal through the air, especially to somewhere very distant: *the TV programs beamed into our homes* **3** [I,T] to send out a line of light, heat, energy etc.: *The sun beamed down brightly.*

beam sb up/out *phr. v.* HUMOROUS an expression said when you want to leave a place because it is boring, strange etc., taken from the television program "Star Trek": *Beam me out of here!*

bean¹ /bin/ S2 *n.* [C] **1** BIOLOGY a seed or POD (=case containing seeds) that comes from a climbing plant and is cooked as food: *chicken and green beans* | *Soak the beans overnight.* | *kidney beans* **2** BIOLOGY a plant that produces beans **3** BIOLOGY a seed used in making some types or food or drinks: *coffee beans* | *cocoa beans* **4 not know/care beans (about) sb/sth** INFORMAL to not know anything or care at all about someone or something: *Sorry, I don't know beans about fixing radios.* [**Origin:** Old English] → see also **spill the beans** at SPILL¹ (4)

bean² *v.* [T] INFORMAL to hit someone on the head with an object: *Hughes got beaned by a wild pitch.*

ˈbean bag *n.* [C] **1** also **bean bag chair** a very large cloth or plastic bag that is filled with small balls of soft plastic and used as a chair **2** a small cloth bag filled with beans, used for throwing and catching in children's games

'bean ,counter, beancounter *n.* [C] INFORMAL DISAPPROVING someone whose job is to study financial figures [SYN] accountant

'bean curd *n.* [C] TOFU

bean•ie /'bini/ *n.* [C] a small round hat that fits close to your head

bean•pole /'binpoʊl/ *n.* [C] HUMOROUS a very tall thin person

'bean sprout *n.* [usually plural] a small stem that has just started growing from a bean seed, eaten as a vegetable

bear[1] /bɛr/ [S3] [W2] *v. past tense* **bore** /bɔr/, *past participle* **borne** /bɔrn/ [T]

1 BE RESPONSIBLE FOR FORMAL to be responsible for or accept something: **bear the cost/burden/expense etc.** *The company responsible for the oil spill should bear the expense of cleaning it up.* | **bear responsibility/the blame/the burden etc.** *U.N. agencies will bear the burden of resettling the refugees.* ►see THESAURUS box at carry[1]

2 DEAL WITH STH to bravely accept or deal with a painful, difficult, or upsetting situation [SYN] stand: *He bore the pain stoically.* | *They had borne untold suffering and hardship.* | *He wrote that he* ***could*** *hardly* ***bear*** *to be separated from her.* | *Make the water as hot as you* ***can bear***. | *His job requires long hours, and their marriage was unable to* ***bear the strain*** (=continue despite having to deal with difficult problems).

3 bear a resemblance/relation etc. to sb/sth to be similar to or related to someone or something else: *Ed bore little resemblance to the man she had described.* | *The final script bore absolutely no relation to the one I'd originally written.* | *The blaze bears several parallels to a previous fire last month.*

4 bear (sth) in mind to remember a fact or piece of information that is important or could be useful in the future [SYN] keep (sth) in mind: *Thanks, I'll bear that in mind.* | **+ (that)** *Tourists must bear in mind that they are visitors in another country.*

5 SIGN/MARK FORMAL to have or show a sign, mark, or particular appearance [SYN] have: *The stone marker bears the names of those killed in the riot.* | *Staff members wear T-shirts bearing the company's logo.* | *He had the disease as a child and still bears its scars.*

6 sb can't bear sb/sth a) to be so upset about something that you feel unable to accept it or let it happen [SYN] can't stand: *I can't bear violence toward another human being.* | *I* ***couldn't bear the thought of*** *having to start all over.* | **can't bear to do sth** *She was the kind of person who just couldn't bear to throw anything away.* **b)** to dislike something or someone so much that they make you very annoyed or impatient: *I really can't bear him.* | **can't bear doing sth** *I can't bear swimming in cold water.*

7 SUPPORT to be under something and support it [SYN] hold: *The ice wasn't thick enough to* ***bear*** *his* ***weight***. | *An oak table bore several photographs of the family.*

8 bear fruit a) if a plan, decision etc. bears fruit, it is successful, especially after a long period of time: *The project may not begin to bear fruit for at least two years.* **b)** if a tree bears fruit, it produces fruit

9 bear right/left to turn toward the right or left: *Bear left where the road divides.* | *The road bears to the right.*

10 BABY FORMAL to give birth to a baby: *Jean will never be able to bear children.* | **bear sb a son/daughter/child** *She bore him five children.*

11 BE AFFECTED BY STH to show physical or emotional signs of something that has happened to you: *He would* ***bear the scars*** *of his experience for the rest of his life* (=it will always affect him).

12 CARRY LITERARY to carry someone or something, especially something important [SYN] carry: *Several of the guests arrived bearing gifts.* | *the right to* ***bear arms*** (=carry a gun)

13 WIND/WATER/AIR LITERARY if wind, water, or air bears something, it carries it somewhere: *The seeds are borne long distances by the wind.*

14 bear (sb) a grudge to continue to feel annoyed about something that someone did a long time ago: *The suspect appears to have borne a grudge against his former colleagues.*

15 bring influence/pressure etc. to bear (on) to use your influence or power to get what you want: *More pressure is being brought to bear on the country to improve its human rights record.*

16 bear witness to sth FORMAL to show that something is true or exists: *Her latest book bears witness to her talent as a writer.*

17 sth doesn't bear thinking about used to say that something is so upsetting or shocking that you prefer not to think about it: *The reaction I'll get when my parents find out doesn't even bear thinking about.*

18 ABLE TO BE EXAMINED/COMPARED ETC. [often in negatives] to be appropriate or good enough to be tested, compared, repeated etc. without failing or being wrong: *We suspect that their statistics will not bear close inspection.* | *It is advice that* ***bears repeating***. | *His TV shows always* ***bear watching*** (=are always good to watch).

19 bear interest if a bank account, INVESTMENT etc. bears interest, the bank pays you a particular amount of money for keeping your money in the account

20 bear yourself FORMAL to walk, stand etc. in a particular way, especially when this shows your character: *Throughout the trial, she bore herself with great dignity.*

21 NAME/TITLE FORMAL to have a particular name: *She bears the title of "Executive Director."*

22 bear sb no malice/ill will etc. FORMAL to not feel angry toward someone

[**Origin:** Old English *beran*] → see also **bear the brunt** at BRUNT (1), **grin and bear it** at GRIN[1] (2)

bear down on sb/sth *phr. v.* **1 a)** to behave in a threatening way toward a person or group: *Federal regulators have been bearing down on campaign contributors.* **b)** to move quickly toward a person or place in a threatening way: *Sweeney tried to leap over the car when it bore down on him.* | *A strong Pacific storm system is bearing down on the West Coast.* **2** to use all your strength and effort to push or press down on something

bear on/upon sth *phr. v.* FORMAL to relate to and possibly influence something: *Luckily, the error didn't bear on the outcome of the game.*

bear sb/sth **out** *phr. v.* if facts or information bear out a claim, story, opinion etc., they help to prove that it is true: *Silberman said more people are carrying pistols, and gun sales bear him out.*

bear up *phr. v.* to show courage or determination during a difficult or upsetting time: *People who have hope bear up better in bad circumstances.*

bear with sb/sth *phr. v.* **1 bear with me** SPOKEN used to ask someone politely to wait while you find out information, finish what you are doing etc.: *Bear with me for a minute while I check our records.* **2 bear with sth** to be patient or continue to do something that is difficult or not fun: *It's boring at first, but bear with it because it gets better.*

bear[2] [S2] [W3] *n.* [C] **1** BIOLOGY a large strong animal with thick fur that eats flesh, fruit, and insects: *a mother bear and her cubs* → see also POLAR BEAR, TEDDY BEAR **2** INFORMAL something that is very difficult to do or to deal with: *The chemistry test was a real bear.* **3** INFORMAL a big man who behaves in a rough way or is in a bad mood **4** ECONOMICS someone who sells SHARES or goods when they expect the price to fall → see also BULL

bear•a•ble /'bɛrəbəl/ *adj.* something that is bearable is difficult or not nice, but you can deal with it [OPP] unbearable: *The breeze made the heat more bearable.* —**bearably** *adv.*

'bear claw *n.* [C] a PASTRY filled with fruit that has a row of long cuts across the top

beard /bɪrd/ *n.* [C] **1** hair that grows on a man's chin and JAW → see also MUSTACHE **2** something similar to a beard, such as hair growing on an animal's chin [**Origin:** Old English] —**bearded** *adj.*

B

bear·er /ˈbɛrɚ/ *n.* [C] **1** LAW the bearer of a legal document, for example a PASSPORT, is the person that it officially belongs to **2** someone who brings you information, a letter etc.: +**of** *I hated to be the bearer of bad news.* **3** FORMAL someone whose job is to carry something such as a flag or a STRETCHER (=light bed for a sick person) → see also PALLBEARER, STANDARD-BEARER

ˈbear hug *n.* [C] an action in which you put your arms around someone and hold them very tightly because you like them or are pleased to see them → see also HUG[2]

bear·ing /ˈbɛrɪŋ/ *n.* **1 have a/some/no bearing on sth** to have an effect or influence on something, or not to have any effect or influence: *Does this information have any bearing on the case?* **2 lose your bearings a)** to become confused about where you are or what you should do next: *We lost our bearings in the fog.* **b)** to become confused about what you should do next in order to be successful: *When Kelly left, the company began to lose its bearings.* **3 get your bearings a)** to find out exactly where you are: *I looked at the map to get our bearings.* **b)** to feel confident that you know what you should do next: *It will take a little time to get your bearings in your new job.* **4** [C] part of a machine that turns on another part, or in which a turning part is held **5** [C] a direction or angle that is shown by a COMPASS **6** [singular, U] FORMAL the way in which you move, stand, or behave, especially when this shows your character: *her dignified bearing*

bear·ish /ˈbɛrɪʃ/ *adj.* **1** ECONOMICS **a)** someone who is bearish expects the prices of SHARES to decrease: *Investors have **turned bearish on** Internet stocks.* **b)** a market that is bearish is one in which the prices of shares are decreasing OPP **bullish** **2** a man that is bearish is big and strong —**bearishly** *adv.* —**bearishness** *n.*

ˈbear ˌmarket *n.* [C] ECONOMICS a situation in which the value of STOCKS is decreasing

bear·skin /ˈbɛrˌskɪn/ *n.* [C,U] the skin of a bear: *a bearskin rug*

beast /bist/ *n.* [C] **1** an animal, especially a large or dangerous one **2** INFORMAL something of a particular type or that has a particular quality: *During the day it's full of office workers, but at night the city is a very **different beast**.* **3** OLD-FASHIONED someone who is cruel or in a very bad mood **4 the beast in sb** also **the beast within** the part of someone's character that makes them experience hatred, strong sexual feelings, violence etc. → see also **the nature of the beast** at NATURE (9)

beast·ly /ˈbistli/ *adj.* OLD-FASHIONED very bad or rude —**beastly** *adv.* —**beastliness** *n.* [U]

ˌbeast of ˈburden *n.* [C] OLD USE an animal that does heavy work

beat[1] /bit/ S1 W1 *v. past tense* **beat**, *past participle* **beaten** /ˈbitˀn/

1 COMPETITION/ELECTION/GAME ETC. [T] to get the most points, votes etc. in a game, race, or competition SYN **defeat**: *The Pacers were beaten 71–68 by the Bulls.* | **beat sb at sth** *He beat me at tennis.* | *She beat the pants off me last time we played.*

> **THESAURUS**
>
> **defeat** to win a victory over someone: *He defeated the Republican candidate in the mayor's race.*
> **trounce** to defeat someone completely: *The Bears trounced Nebraska 44–10.*
> **clobber/cream** INFORMAL to defeat someone easily: *We got creamed in the finals.*

2 HIT [I always + adv/prep,T] to hit someone or something many times, especially in order to make a noise: *A man was beating a drum.* | +**on/against/at etc.** *They were beating on the door.* | *Rain was beating on the windows.*
3 ATTACK [T] to deliberately hit a person or animal many times and hurt them: *He used to come home drunk and beat my mother.* | **beat sb to death/beat sb unconscious** (=hit someone until they die, become unconscious etc.) | *He was **beaten black and blue*** (=beaten until marks were made on his body) *by the crowd.* | **beat the living daylights out of sb** (=hit someone very hard) ▸see THESAURUS box at **hit[1]**
4 FOOD [I,T] to mix food together quickly with a fork or special kitchen tool: *Beat the eggs and pour in the milk.* | **beat sth in/beat in sth** *Gradually beat in the sugar.* | **beat sth together** *Beat together the brown sugar and shortening.* ▸see THESAURUS box at **cooking[1]**, **mix[1]**
5 DO BETTER [T] to do something better, faster etc. than what was best before or than what was expected: **beat a record/score etc.** *Hank Aaron beat the record for home runs set by Babe Ruth.* | *The company's profits this year beat expectations.*
6 HEART [I] BIOLOGY when your heart beats, it moves in a regular RHYTHM as it pumps your blood: *Her heart was beating fast.* | *Doctors rushed to try and save him after his heart stopped beating.*
7 CONTROL/DEAL WITH [T] to successfully deal with a problem you have been struggling with SYN **conquer**: *She beat breast cancer when she was in her thirties.* | *How can schools beat the problem of illegal drugs?*

> **SPOKEN PHRASES**
>
> **8 BE BETTER** [T not in progressive] to be much better and more enjoyable than something else: **it beats doing sth** *We got takeout – it beats cooking on a Friday night.* | ***Nothing beats** homemade cookies.* | ***You can't beat** the weather here.* | **you can't beat sth for sth** *For romance, you can't beat the Rainbow Lodge.* | *It's only ten bucks; you **can't beat that**.*
> **9 beats me** used to say that you do not know something or cannot understand or explain something: *"Who do you think is gonna win?" "Beats me."* | *Beats me why he'd want to cut his hair off.*
> **10 beat it!** used to tell someone to leave at once because they are annoying you or should not be there: *Go on, you kids! Beat it! Now!*
> **11 beat your brains out** to think about something very hard and for a long time
> **12 if you can't beat 'em, join 'em** used when you decide to take part in something although you disapprove of it, because everyone else is doing it and you cannot stop them
> **13 to beat the band** in large amounts or with great force: *It's raining to beat the band.*
> **14 can you beat that/it?** used to show that you are surprised or annoyed by something: *She made her bed without being asked. Can you beat that?*

15 beat around the bush INFORMAL to avoid or delay talking about something embarrassing or upsetting: *You'd better tell him how you feel and don't beat around the bush.*
16 DO BEFORE SB ELSE [T] INFORMAL to get or do something before someone else, especially if you are both trying to do it first: *Kerry beat me to a seat.* | *I was going to have that last piece of pie but somebody **beat** me **to it**.* | *Both companies spotted the opening in the market, but AT&T **beat** them **to the punch*** (=were successful first).
17 AVOID [T] INFORMAL to avoid situations in which a lot of people are trying to do something, usually by doing something early: *Shop now and **beat the** Christmas **rush**!* | *We left early to beat the traffic.*
18 beat a (hasty) retreat to leave somewhere or stop doing something very quickly, in order to avoid a bad situation
19 beat the clock to finish something very quickly, especially before a particular time: *Employees are working furiously to beat the clock.*
20 beat the system to find ways of avoiding or breaking the rules of an organization, system etc., in order to achieve what you want: *Accountants know a few ways to beat the system.*
21 beat the drum for sb/sth to speak eagerly in support of someone or something: *Goodman rushed back to L.A. to beat the drum for his new movie.*
22 beat sb like a drum to defeat an opponent by a lot of points in a game or sport: *Seles beat her like a drum.*
23 WINGS [I,T] if a bird beats its wings or its wings beat, they move up and down quickly and regularly

24 beat the rap INFORMAL to avoid being punished for something you have done: *He's been arrested three times and has beaten the rap every time.*
25 beat a path (to sb's door) also **beat down sb's door** if people beat a path to your door, they are interested in something you are selling, a service you are providing etc.: *People are going to beat a path from all over to play these golf courses.*
26 beat time to make regular movements or sounds to show the speed at which music should be played: *a conductor beating time with his baton*
27 beat the heat INFORMAL to make yourself cooler: *Strawberries in wine is a festive way to beat the heat.*
28 take some beating a) if an achievement or SCORE will take some beating, it will be difficult for anyone to do better: *Schumacher has a twelve-second lead, which will take some beating.* **b)** to be better, more enjoyable etc. than almost anything else of the same type: *As a great place for a vacation, Florida takes some beating.*
29 METAL [T] to hit metal with a hammer in order to shape it or make it thinner
30 HUNTING [I,T] to force wild birds and animals out of bushes, long grass etc. so that they can be shot for sport.
31 beat your breast LITERARY to show clearly that you are very upset or sorry about something
[**Origin:** Old English *beatan*] → see also BEATEN, BEATING, **beat/flog a dead horse** at DEAD[1] (11), **beat sb at their own game** at GAME[1] (13)

beat down *phr. v.* **1** if the sun beats down, it shines very brightly and the weather is hot **2** if the rain beats down, it is raining very hard **3 beat sb ↔ down** INFORMAL to make someone feel defeated: *A lot of people feel beaten down by the system.* **4 beat sth ↔ down** to hit something such as a door until it falls down

beat off *phr. v.* **beat sb/sth ↔ off** to succeed in defeating someone who is attacking or opposing you or competing against you: *McConnell beat off a challenge for his Senate seat.*

beat out *phr. v.* **1 beat sb ↔ out** to defeat someone in a competition: *Lockheed beat out a rival company to win the contract.* | **beat sb out for sth** *Michigan managed to beat out Penn State for the number one position in the country.* **2 beat sth out** if drums beat out a RHYTHM, or you beat out a rhythm on the drums, they make a continuous regular sound **3 beat sth out of sb** to force someone to tell you something by beating them: *I had the truth beaten out of me by my father.* **4 beat sth ↔ out** to put out a fire by hitting it with something such as a wet cloth

beat up *phr. v.* **1 beat sb ↔ up** to hurt someone badly by hitting them: *Her boyfriend got drunk and beat her up.* **2 beat up on sb** to hit someone and hurt them, especially someone younger or weaker than yourself: *I used to beat up on my brothers when we were kids.* **3 beat up on yourself** also **beat yourself up** INFORMAL to blame yourself too much for something: *Stop beating yourself up – you couldn't have prevented it.*

beat[2] *n.* **1** [C] one of a series of regular movements or hitting actions: *a heart rate of 80 beats per minute* **2** [C usually singular] a regular repeated noise SYN **rhythm**: +**of** *the slow beat of the drum* **3** [singular] ENG. LANG. ARTS the main RHYTHM that a piece of music or a poem has: *a song with a beat you can dance to* **4** [singular] a subject or an area of a city that someone is responsible for as their job: *journalists covering the political beat* | *police officers **on the beat*** (=working in their area) **5** [C] ENG. LANG. ARTS one of the notes in a piece of music that sounds stronger than the other notes

beat[3] *adj.* [not before noun] INFORMAL very tired SYN **exhausted**: *I'm beat.* ►see THESAURUS box at **tired**

beat·en /ˈbitˀn/ *adj.* [only before noun] **1 off the beaten path/track** not well known and far away from the places that people usually visit: *We stayed at a charming inn that's off the beaten path.* **2** a beaten path, track etc. has been made by many people walking the same way **3** beaten metal has been shaped with a hammer to make it thinner

beat·er /ˈbit̬ɚ/ *n.* [C] **1** an object that is designed to beat something: *Using clean beaters, whip the cream.* | *a rug beater* **2 a wife/child beater** someone who hits his wife or child, especially someone who does this often **3** INFORMAL an old car in bad condition → see also **fare beater** at FARE[1] (5), WORLD-BEATER

B

be·a·tif·ic /ˌbiəˈtɪfɪk◂/ *adj.* LITERARY a beatific look, smile etc. shows great peace and happiness —**beatifically** /-kli/ *adv.*

be·at·i·fy /biˈæt̬əˌfaɪ/ *v.* **beatifies, beatified, beatifying** [T] if the Catholic Church beatifies someone who has died, it says officially that they are a holy or special person —**beatification** /biˌæt̬əfəˈkeɪʃən/ *n.* [U]

beat·ing /ˈbit̬ɪŋ/ *n.* [C] **1** an act of hitting someone many times as a punishment or in a fight: *The cab driver died as a result of the beating.* **2 take a beating** to be defeated or criticized very badly: *The Mets took a real beating last Saturday.* → see also **take some beating** at BEAT[1] (28)

Beat·les, the /ˈbit̬lz/ a British popular music group who made their first record in 1962 and became one of the most famous groups ever. They had a great influence on the development of popular music. The members of the Beatles were George Harrison, John Lennon, Paul McCartney, and Ringo Starr.

beat·nik /ˈbitˀnɪk/ *n.* [C] one of a group of young people in the late 1950s and early 1960s, who did not accept the values of society and showed this by their choice of clothes and the way they lived

ˈbeat-up *adj.* INFORMAL a beat-up car, bicycle etc. is old and in bad condition SYN **battered**: *a beat-up old Chevy*

beau /boʊ/ *n.* [C] *plural* **beaux** /boʊz/ or **beaus** OLD-FASHIONED **1** a woman's close friend or lover SYN **boyfriend** **2** a fashionable well-dressed man

beau·coup /ˈboʊku/ *quantifier* [only before noun] SPOKEN a lot or many

Beau·jo·lais /ˌboʊʒəˈleɪ/ *n.* [C,U] a type of French red wine

beaut /byut/ *n.* [singular] SPOKEN something that is very good, attractive, or impressive: *The fish he caught was a real beaut.*

beau·te·ous /ˈbyut̬iəs/ *adj.* POETIC beautiful —**beauteously** *adv.*

beau·ti·cian /byuˈtɪʃən/ *n.* [C] OLD-FASHIONED someone whose job is to cut your hair, put MAKEUP on you, color your FINGERNAILS etc.

beau·ti·ful /ˈbyut̬əfəl/ S1 W2 *adj.* **1** someone or something that is beautiful is extremely attractive to look at OPP **ugly**: *a beautiful woman* | *The scenery was incredibly beautiful.* ►see THESAURUS box at **attractive** **2** very good or giving you great pleasure SYN **wonderful**: *beautiful music* | *He made a beautiful catch.* | *The weather was beautiful.* —**beautifully** *adv.*

THESAURUS
pretty used about a girl or woman who is attractive
attractive good to look at, especially in a way that makes you sexually interested
good-looking/nice-looking used about anyone who is good to look at
handsome used about a man or boy who is attractive
gorgeous/stunning used about anyone who is very attractive
cute used about a baby or young child who is attractive
cute used about someone you think is sexually attractive, especially someone under 25 years old
hot INFORMAL used about someone you think is sexually attractive
sexy used about someone you think is very sexually attractive

beau·ti·fy /ˈbyut̬əˌfaɪ/ *v.* **beautifies, beautified, beautifying** [T] FORMAL to make someone or something beautiful: *an effort to beautify the neighborhood*

beau·ty /ˈbyut̬i/ W2 *n. plural* **beauties**
1 APPEARANCE [U] a quality that things, places, or people have that makes them very attractive to look at SYN **attractive**: *her beauty and grace* | *beauty products* | *the **natural beauty** of America's national parks*
2 WOMAN [C] OLD-FASHIONED a woman who is very beautiful: *She was considered a beauty in her youth.*
3 POEM, SONG, EMOTION ETC. [U] a quality that something such as a poem, song, emotion etc. has, which gives you pleasure or makes you feel happy: **+ of** *the beauty of Handel's music*
4 EXAMPLE OF STH [C] SPOKEN an object that is a very good or impressive example of its type: *Eric's new car is a real beauty.*
5 the beauty of sth a particularly good quality that makes something especially appropriate or useful: *The beauty of this diet is that you never have to feel hungry.*
6 beauty is in the eye of the beholder used to say that different people have different opinions about what is beautiful
7 beauty is only skin deep used in order to say that someone's attractive appearance is not as important as having a good character
[**Origin:** 1200–1300 Old French *biauté*, from Latin *bellus* **pretty**]

ˈbeauty ˌcontest *n.* [C] a competition in which women are judged on how attractive they look SYN **pageant**

ˈbeauty mark *n.* [C] a small dark mark on a woman's skin, especially one on her face

ˈbeauty ˌpageant *n.* [C] a beauty contest

ˈbeauty ˌparlor *n.* [C] a beauty salon

ˈbeauty queen *n.* [C] OLD-FASHIONED the winner of a beauty contest

ˈbeauty saˌlon *n.* [C] a place in which you can receive treatments for your skin, get your hair cut etc., so that you look more attractive SYN **salon**

ˈbeauty shop *n.* [C] a beauty salon

ˈbeauty sleep *n.* [U] HUMOROUS enough sleep to keep you healthy and looking good

Beau·voir /boʊˈvwɑr/, **Si·mone de** /siˈmoʊn də/ (1908–1986) a French writer and FEMINIST famous for her book THE SECOND SEX

bea·ver /ˈbivɚ/ *n.* [C] a North American animal that has thick fur, a wide flat tail, and cuts down trees with its teeth → see also **eager beaver** at EAGER (3) → see picture on page A34

bea·ver·tail /ˈbivɚteɪl/ *n.* [C] a wide flat FRIED PASTRY eaten in Canada

be·bop /ˈbibɑp/ *n.* [U] a type of JAZZ music [**Origin:** 1900–2000 From the sound of the music, or the words sung to it]

be·calmed /bɪˈkɑmd/ *adj.* LITERARY a ship or boat that is becalmed cannot move because there is no wind

be·came /bɪˈkeɪm/ the past tense of BECOME

be·cause /bɪˈkɔz, -ˈkʌz/ S1 W1 *conjunction* **1** for the reason that: *Mark couldn't come because he had to work.* | *She's studying because she has a test tomorrow.* | *"Why can't I go?" "Because you're not old enough."* | *Sales went down, **partly because** there were distribution problems.* | *It doesn't make sense to hate someone **simply because** their skin is a different color.* | **largely/mainly because** *People eat more takeout meals, largely because they feel they don't have time to cook.* **2 because of sb/sth** used in order to say who or what causes something to happen or is the reason for something: *They're not playing today because of the rain.* | *I got interested in writing because of Denny* (=Denny influenced me). **3 just because...** SPOKEN used in order to say that although one thing is true, it does not mean that something else is true: *Pam seems to think that she can tell us what to do. Just because...* [**Origin:** 1300–1400 *by cause (that)*]

beck /bɛk/ *n.* **be at sb's beck and call** to always be ready to do what someone wants

Beck·et /ˈbɛkɪt/, **Saint Thomas** (1118–1170) an English priest who became the Archbishop of Canterbury. He had a serious argument with the king, Henry II, and was murdered by some of the king's soldiers.

Beck·ett /ˈbɛkɪt/, **Samuel** (1906–1989) an Irish writer of plays, novels, and poetry, famous for his play WAITING FOR GODOT

beck·on /ˈbɛkən/ *v.* [I,T] **1** to make a signal to someone with your hand or arm, to show that you want them to come toward you: **+to** *The woman beckoned to me to follow her.* | **beckon sb forward/to/toward etc.** *A guard beckoned the visitor onward.* **2** if something such as a place or an opportunity beckons, it seems very attractive and you want to have it: *The pool beckoned.* [**Origin:** Old English *biecnan*, from *beacen* **sign**]

be·come /bɪˈkʌm/ S1 W1 *v. past tense* **became** /bɪˈkeɪm/, *past participle* **become** **1** [linking verb] to begin to be something, or to develop in a particular way: *Baker became head coach.* | *The weather is becoming warmer.* | *These kinds of partnerships are becoming more common.* | *She started to become anxious about her son.* | *It is becoming harder to find decent housing in the city.*

THESAURUS

get ESPECIALLY SPOKEN used with most types of adjective to describe changes in people and things: *It gets dark early in December.* | *Your dinner's getting cold.*
turn used to say that something changes color, or with some changes in condition: *Jon turned pale when he heard the news.* | *Wait until the light turns green before you cross the street.* | *If the weather turns bad, we'll have the picnic another time.*
go used when someone's mind or body changes for the worse, or with some other changes in condition: *He went blind when he was twenty.* | *Everything went wrong.*

2 what will/has become of...? used especially in questions and negatives to talk about what has happened or what will happen to someone or something: *She used to have some of Grandma's pictures, but I don't know what became of them.* | *Do you ever wonder what became of that couple we met in Florida?* **3** [T not in progressive] FORMAL to look good on someone SYN **suit**: *I don't think that outfit really becomes you, Sheryl.* [**Origin:** Old English *becuman* **to come to, become**, from *cuman* **to come**]

GRAMMAR

Become is never followed by an infinitive with "to," though **come** can be followed by an infinitive with "to": *After a while, I came to like Chicago* (NOT *...became to like...*).

be·com·ing /bɪˈkʌmɪŋ/ *adj.* OLD-FASHIONED **1** making you look attractive SYN **flattering**: *Laura's new hairstyle is very becoming.* **2** words or actions that are becoming are appropriate for you or for the situation you are in: *Using bad language is not at all becoming.* —**becomingly** *adv.*

bec·que·rel /ˌbɛkəˈrɛl/ *n.* [C] TECHNICAL a unit of measurement of RADIOACTIVITY

bed¹ /bɛd/ S1 W1 *n.*
1 SLEEP [C,U] a piece of furniture for sleeping on: *an old brass bed* | *a double bed* (=for two people) | *I was lying **in bed** reading.* | *Kim usually **goes to bed** at about eleven.* | *She **got into bed** and turned off the light.* | *Have you **made your bed*** (=pulled the sheets, blankets etc. neatly into place)? | *I'll just **put** the kids **to bed**.* | *Come on Billy, it's **time for bed*** (=time to go to sleep). | *My wife **got me out of bed*** (=made me get up) *to take the dog for a walk.* | *I usually watch the news just **before bed*** (=before going to bed).
2 INVOLVED WITH STH/SB people or organizations that are in bed with each other have a close involvement

that gives them special advantages: *A lot of people believe Congress is in bed with big business.*
3 RIVER/LAKE/OCEAN [C] EARTH SCIENCE the flat ground at the bottom of a river, lake etc.: *the river bed* ►see THESAURUS box at **ground**[1]
4 GARDEN [C] an area of a garden, park etc. that has been prepared for plants to grow in: *rose beds*
5 BASE [C usually singular] a layer of something that forms a base that other things are put on top of: +**of** *pasta salad served on a bed of lettuce*
6 SEX [U] INFORMAL used in order to refer to having sex: *They never **went to bed** together until they were married.*
7 put sth to bed INFORMAL if you put something such as a piece of work or problem to bed, you finish it or solve it
8 get up on the wrong side of the bed SPOKEN to feel slightly angry or annoyed for no particular reason: *Ooh, looks like somebody got up on the wrong side of the bed today.*
9 oyster/coral etc. bed a place at the bottom of an area of water where there are a lot of OYSTERS etc.
10 ROCK [C] GEOGRAPHY a layer of rock → see also BEDROCK
11 a bed of roses a phrase meaning a happy, comfortable, or easy situation, used especially in negative sentences: *Brian's life hasn't exactly been a bed of roses.* (=he has had a very hard life)
12 you've made your bed and you have to lie in it SPOKEN used to say that you must accept the bad results of your actions
[**Origin:** Old English *bedd*]

bed[2] *v.* [T] **1** to put something firmly and deeply into something else: +**in** *The foundations were bedded in cement.* **2** also **bed out** to put plants into the ground so that they can grow
bed down *phr. v.* **1** to sleep somewhere that is not your bed and where you do not usually sleep: *About 65 homeless people bedded down in a school gymnasium.* **2 bed sb/sth down** to make a person or animal comfortable for the night

ˌbed and ˈbreakfast ABBREVIATION **B & B** *n.* [C] a private house or small hotel where you can sleep and have breakfast

be·daz·zled /bɪˈdæzəld/ *adj.* LITERARY if you are bedazzled by something, you think it is very impressive and feel surprised SYN **dazzled**

bed·bug /ˈbɛdbʌg/ *n.* [C] an insect that sucks blood and lives in houses, especially in beds

bed·cham·ber /ˈbɛdˌtʃeɪmbɚ/ *n.* [C] OLD USE a BEDROOM

bed·clothes /ˈbɛdklouz, -klouðz/ *n.* [plural] OLD-FASHIONED the sheets, covers etc. that you put on a bed

bed·ding /ˈbɛdɪŋ/ *n.* [U] **1** sheets, covers etc. that you put on a bed **2** something soft for animals to sleep on, such as dried grass or STRAW

be·deck /bɪˈdɛk/ *v.* [T usually passive] LITERARY to decorate something such as a building or street by hanging things all over it: *The ballroom was bedecked with flowers.*

be·dev·il /bɪˈdɛvəl/ *v.* [T usually passive] to cause a lot of problems and difficulties for someone or something over a period of time: *The senator has been bedeviled by allegations of corruption.* —**bedevilment** *n.* [U]

bed·fel·low /ˈbɛdˌfɛlou/ *n.* [C] **strange/odd/uneasy etc. bedfellows** two or more people, ideas etc. that are related or working together in an unexpected way: *Politics and religion often make very uneasy bedfellows.*

bed·lam /ˈbɛdləm/ *n.* [U] a wild noisy place or situation: *The classroom erupted into bedlam.* [**Origin:** 1600–1700 *bedlam* **mental hospital** (17–18 centuries), from *Bedlam* **Bethlehem** (10–17 centuries); from the Hospital of St. Mary of *Bethlehem* former London mental hospital]

ˈbed ˌlinen *n.* [U] the sheets and PILLOWCASES for a bed

Bed·ou·in /ˈbɛduɪn/ one of the Arab tribes living in North Africa and West Asia who traditionally live in tents and travel from place to place

bed·pan /ˈbɛdpæn/ *n.* [C] a low wide container used as a toilet by someone who has to stay in bed

bed·post /ˈbɛdpoust/ *n.* [C] one of the four main supports at the corners of an old-fashioned bed

be·drag·gled /bɪˈdrægəld/ *adj.* looking messy and dirty, especially because you have been out in the rain: *bedraggled refugees*

bed·rid·den /ˈbɛdˌrɪdn/ *adj.* unable to leave your bed, especially because you are old or very sick

bed·rock /ˈbɛdrɑk/ *n.* [U] **1** the basic ideas and principles of a belief, system, or set of ideas: *Facts are the bedrock of any trial.* **2** EARTH SCIENCE solid rock in the ground, below all the soil: *They excavated the sand until they reached bedrock.*

bed·roll /ˈbɛdroul/ *n.* [C] a special thick BLANKET or a number of BLANKETS rolled together and used for sleeping outdoors

bed·room[1] /ˈbɛdrum/ S1 W3 *n.* [C] **1** a room for sleeping in: *a house with four bedrooms* **2 have bedroom eyes** INFORMAL a look in your eyes that shows that you are sexually attracted to someone

bedroom[2] *adj.* **bedroom community/suburb** a place where people live but that does not have many businesses, so that people travel from there to work in a larger town every day

bed·side /ˈbɛdsaɪd/ *n.* [C] the area around your bed: *The doctor sat by his bedside.* | *the clock on her **bedside table*** | *a **bedside lamp***

ˈbedside ˌmanner *n.* [singular] a doctor's bedside manner is the way that he or she talks to the people that he or she is treating

bed·sore /ˈbɛdsɔr/ *n.* [C] a sore place on your skin caused by lying in bed in one position for a long time

bed·spread /ˈbɛdsprɛd/ *n.* [C] an attractive cover for a bed that goes on top of all the other covers

bed·stead /ˈbɛdstɛd/ *n.* [C] the wooden or metal frame of a bed

bed·time /ˈbɛdtaɪm/ *n.* [C,U] the time when you usually go to bed: *It's way past your bedtime!* | *a bedtime story*

ˈbed ˌwetting *n.* [U] the problem that some children have of passing URINE (=liquid waste from the body) while they are asleep —**bed-wetter** *n.* [C]

bee /bi/ S3 *n.* [C] **1** BIOLOGY a black and yellow flying insect with a round body that makes HONEY and can sting you: *a swarm of bees* → see also BUMBLEBEE, HONEYBEE **2 have a bee in your bonnet (about sth)** INFORMAL to think something is so important, so necessary etc. that you keep mentioning it or thinking about it, in a way that starts to annoy other people: *Dad has a bee in his bonnet about saving electricity.* **3 a sewing/quilting etc. bee** an occasion when people, usually women, meet in order to do a particular type of work **4 be the bee's knees** OLD-FASHIONED INFORMAL to be very good [**Origin:** Old English *beo*] → see also **the birds and the bees** at BIRD (3), **as busy as a bee** at BUSY[1] (6), SPELLING BEE

beech /bitʃ/ *n.* [C,U] a large tree with smooth gray BARK (=outer covering), or the wood from this tree

beef[1] /bif/ S2 *n.* **1** [U] the meat from a cow: *roast beef* ►see THESAURUS box at **meat** **2** [C] INFORMAL a complaint: *Some guy who **had a beef with** the manager came in.* **3 where's the beef?** SPOKEN used when you think someone's words and promises sound good, but you want to know what they actually plan to do: *"Where's the beef?" reporters asked Democratic leaders at a news conference.* [**Origin:** 1100–1200 Old French *buef*, from Latin *bos* **ox**] → see also CORNED BEEF, **ground beef** at GROUND[3] (1)

beef[2] *v.* [I] INFORMAL to complain a lot: +**about** *They're always beefing about something.*
beef sth ↔ **up** *phr. v.* INFORMAL to improve something, especially to make it stronger or more interesting: *Airport security has been beefed up.*

beef·cake /ˈbifkeɪk/ *n.* [C,U] INFORMAL a strong attractive man with large muscles, or men like this in general

beef·steak /ˈbifsteɪk/ *n.* [C,U] → STEAK (1)

B

beef·y /ˈbifi/ *adj. comparative* **beefier**, *superlative* **beefiest** INFORMAL a man who is beefy is big, strong, and often fat: *beefy football players*

bee·hive /ˈbihaɪv/ *n.* [C] **1** a structure where BEES are kept for producing HONEY **2** a way of arranging a woman's hair in a high pile on the top of her head, which was popular in the 1960s **3** a place with many people and a lot of activity: +**of** *The classroom was a beehive of activity.*

bee·keep·er /ˈbiˌkipɚ/ *n.* [C] someone who owns and takes care of BEES —**beekeeping** *n.* [U]

bee·line /ˈbilaɪn/ *n.* **make a beeline for sb/sth** INFORMAL to go quickly and directly toward someone or something

been /bɪn/ **1** the past participle of BE **2 have/has been** used to say that someone has gone to a place and come back: +**to** *I've never been to Japan.* | **have been to do sth** *Have you been to see Roger's new house?* **3 been there, done that** SPOKEN used to say that you are not interested in doing something, because you already have a lot of experience doing it

beep[1] /bip/ *v.* **1** [I] if a machine beeps, it makes a short high sound: *Why does the computer keep beeping?* **2** [I,T] if a car horn beeps or you make it beep, it makes a loud noise **3** [T] to telephone someone who has a beeper: *Beep Dr. Greene – he's needed in the ER.* [**Origin:** 1900–2000 From the sound]

beep[2] *n.* [C] **1** a short high sound made by an electronic machine: *Leave your message after the beep.* **2** the sound of a car horn **3** the action of telephoning someone who has a beeper

beep·er /ˈbipɚ/ *n.* [C] a small machine that you carry with you, that makes short high electronic sounds or moves slightly to tell you that you must telephone someone SYN **pager**

beer /bɪr/ S1 W2 *n.* **1** [U] an alcoholic drink made from MALT and HOPS: *a bottle of beer* **2** [C] a glass, bottle, or can of beer: *Want a beer, Pete?* [**Origin:** Old English *beor*] —**beery** *adj.*

ˈbeer ˌbelly also **ˈbeer gut** *n.* [C] an unattractive fat stomach caused by drinking too much beer

bees·wax /ˈbizwæks/ *n.* [U] **1** a substance produced by BEES, used especially for making furniture polish and CANDLES **2 none of your beeswax** SPOKEN used to tell someone rudely that what they have asked you is private or personal

beet /bit/ *n.* [C,U] **1** BIOLOGY a plant with a round dark red root that you cook and eat as a vegetable **2** also **sugar beet** BIOLOGY a vegetable that sugar is made from **3 red as a beet** INFORMAL having a red face, especially because you are embarrassed or sick

Beet·ho·ven /ˈbeɪˌtoʊvən/, **Lud·wig van** /ˈlʊdvɪg vɑn/ (1770–1827) a German musician who wrote CLASSICAL music

bee·tle /ˈbitl̬/ *n.* [C] an insect with a round hard back, which is usually black [**Origin:** Old English *bitula*, from *bitan*]

be·fall /bɪˈfɔl/ *v. past tense* **befell** /bɪˈfɛl/, *past participle* **befallen** /bɪˈfɔlən/ [T] FORMAL if something bad or dangerous befalls you, it happens to you: *A similar crisis could befall the nation's banks.*

be·fit /bɪˈfɪt/ *v.* **befitted**, **befitting** [T] FORMAL to be correct or appropriate for someone: *They gave him a funeral befitting a national hero.* —**befitting** *adj.* —**befittingly** *adv.*

be·fore[1] /bɪˈfɔr/ S1 W1 *prep.* **1** earlier than something or someone: *I visited them just before Christmas.* | *No cookies before dinner, Andy.* | *Denise got there before me.* | **before doing sth** *We lived in Ogden before moving to Salt Lake City.* | **five minutes/two hours etc. before sth** *Five minutes before the bell, the teacher collected our homework.* | *Larry got back from vacation* ***the day before yesterday*** (=two days ago).

THESAURUS

prior to sth before: *Please be at the gate at least 30 minutes prior to departure.*
earlier during the first part of a period of time, event, or process: *I saw Kim at the mall earlier today.*
previously before now, or before a particular time: *He had previously been arrested for drunken driving.*

2 ahead of someone or something else in a list or order SYN **ahead of** OPP **after**: *This lady was before you, sir.* | *Barnes comes before Barnett on the roll.* **3** FORMAL in front of someone or something SYN **in front of**: *The priest knelt before the altar.* | *The highway stretched out before them.* **4** if one quality or person comes before another, the first thing is more important than the second: *My son is most important – he comes before anyone.* | *Quality should come before quantity.* **5** if one place is before another place, the first place is nearer to you than the second, so that you will reach it first OPP **after**: *Turn left just before the traffic lights.* **6** if you do something before a person or group of people, you do it where they can watch you: *She gave a presentation before the board of directors.* **7** if something such as a report or EVIDENCE is put before a person or group of people, they must consider it and make a decision about it: *The proposal came before the city council a year ago.* **8** FORMAL if there is a job or situation before you, you have to do the job or face the situation soon SYN **ahead of**: *There are great challenges that* ***lie before us.*** | *She trembled before the prospect of meeting him again.* **9** FORMAL if a period of time is before you, it is about to start and you can do what you want during it SYN **ahead of**: *We had the whole summer before us.*

before[2] S1 W1 *conjunction* **1** earlier than a particular event or action: *Anthony wants to see you before you go.* | *It will be a few days before we know the full results.* | *Before you get angry, try and remember what it was like to be fifteen.* **2** used in order to say that something must happen in order for something else to be possible: *There's a lot to do before we can submit the proposal.* **3** used in order to say that something happens after a period of time: *It was several minutes before I realized what was going on.* **4** used in order to warn someone that something bad will happen if they do not do something: *Get out before I call the police.* | *You'd better lock up your bike before it gets stolen.* **5 before you know it** SPOKEN used in order to say that something will happen very soon: *Spring break will be here before you know it.* **6** used to emphasize that you do not want to do something: *I'd eat glue before I'd ever eat liver.* [**Origin:** Old English *beforan*, from *foran* **before**]

before[3] S1 W1 *adv.* **1** at an earlier time: *I know I've seen him somewhere before.* | *I've never been to this restaurant before.* | **the day/week/month etc. before** *Sales were up 14% from the year before.* | **as/like before** *I still get some fan letters, but not as many as before.* **2 before long** after not much time has passed: *Other stores will probably do the same thing before long.* **3** OLD USE ahead of someone or something else: *The king's guards walked before.*

be·fore·hand /bɪˈfɔrˌhænd/ *adv.* before something else happens or is done: *You should have told me beforehand that you might be late.* | *Almost all the food was prepared beforehand.*

be·foul /bɪˈfaʊl/ *v.* [T] FORMAL to make something very dirty

be·friend /bɪˈfrɛnd/ *v.* [T] FORMAL to behave in a friendly way toward someone, especially someone who is younger or needs help: *He was befriended by some neighborhood boys soon after his arrival.*

be·fud·dled /bɪˈfʌdld/ *adj.* completely confused [**Origin:** 1800–1900 *fuddle* **to drink alcohol, make drunk** (16–21 centuries)]

beg /bɛg/ S3 *v.* **begged, begging**
1 ASK [I,T] to ask for something in an anxious or urgent way, because you want it very much: **beg (sb) to do sth** *The boy begged to be left alone.* | *I begged him to stay, but he wouldn't.* | **beg (sb) for sth** *My daughter is begging me for a kitten.* | *On the tape you could hear him **begging for mercy**.* | *She ran to the nearest house and **begged for help**.* | *He **begged** his wife's **forgiveness**.* | *She **begged and pleaded** with them until they agreed.* ▸see THESAURUS box at **ask**
2 MONEY/FOOD [I,T] to ask people to give you food, money etc. because you are very poor: *Children were begging in the streets.* | **beg for sth** *They were reduced to begging for food.* | **beg from sb** *An old man begged from people who walked by.*
3 ANIMAL [I] if an animal such as a dog begs, it asks for food
4 I beg your pardon SPOKEN **a)** used in order to politely ask someone to repeat what they have just said: *"And the year of your birth?" "I beg your pardon?" "When were you born?"* **b)** used in order to politely say you are sorry when you have made a mistake, or have said something wrong or embarrassing: *Oh, I beg your pardon. Are you all right?* **c)** said to show that you strongly disagree with something that someone has said, or think it is unacceptable, often used humorously: *"East Coast people are kind of uptight, aren't they?" "I beg your pardon!"*
5 beg, borrow, or steal an expression meaning to do whatever you must in order to get what you want or to achieve something difficult, often used humorously: *The designers would beg, borrow, or steal in order to get the show ready.*
6 beg to differ FORMAL to firmly disagree with something that has been said: *Kreis begs to differ with the report on him printed in the Star.*
7 beg the question a) if something begs the question, it avoids dealing with the question or subject being discussed, and makes you want to ask that question: **+of** *The movie begs the question of how "real" a film can be if all the people in it know they are being filmed.* **b)** to argue or discuss something as though it were true or had been proved, when it may not be true: *The plan begs the question of whether the development is actually needed.*
[**Origin:** 1200–1300 Probably from Old English *bedecian*]
—**begging** *n.* [U]

be·get /bɪˈgɛt/ *v. past tense* **begot** /bɪˈgɑt/ or **begat** /bɪˈgæt/, *past participle* **begotten** /bɪˈgɑtˀn/ [T] **1** FORMAL to cause something or make it happen: *Poverty begets crime.* **2** OLD USE to become the father of a child

beg·gar¹ /ˈbɛgɚ/ *n.* [C] **1** someone who lives by asking people for food and money: *beggars on the streets* **2 beggars can't be choosers** SPOKEN used to say that when you have no money or no power to choose, you have to accept whatever you are given

beggar² *v.* [T] **1 beggar description/belief etc.** FORMAL to be impossible to describe, believe etc.: *Its immense beauty beggars description.* **2** FORMAL to make someone very poor

beg·gar·ly /ˈbɛgɚli/ *adj.* LITERARY a beggarly amount of money or something is much too small

beg·gar·y /ˈbɛgəri/ *n.* [U] OLD USE the state of being very poor

be·gin /bɪˈgɪn/ S1 W1 *past tense* **began** /bɪˈgæn/, *past participle* **begun** /bɪˈgʌn/, **beginning** *v.*
1 START DOING/FEELING [I,T] to start doing something or start feeling a particular way SYN **start** OPP **finish**: *All right, let's begin.* | **begin to do sth** *I began to realize I had been wrong.* | **begin sth** *Have you begun that new book yet?* | **begin doing sth** *I began working here in 1990.* | *He began feeling a little nervous.*
2 DO FIRST [I] to be the first thing you do in an activity, process etc. SYN **start** OPP **finish**: **+with** *Shall we begin with a prayer?* | **begin by doing sth** *Ms. Black began by asking him about his background.*
3 START HAPPENING [I,T] to start to happen or exist, especially from a particular time SYN **start** OPP **finish**: *Casting for the play will begin next week.* | *It was the coldest winter since records began.* | **+at** *The funeral service will begin at 3 p.m.* | **begin (sth) as** *He began his career in politics as a young adviser to the Defense Minister.*
4 to begin with a) used in order to introduce the first or most important point that you want to make: *To begin with, much of this new housing is not affordable.* **b)** used in order to say that something was already in a particular condition before something else happened: *It was broken to begin with; he didn't touch it.* **c)** during the first part of a process or activity: *The kids helped me to begin with, but they soon got bored.*
5 BOOK/WORD/MOVIE ETC. [I] if a movie, book, word etc. begins with something, it starts with a particular event, activity, letter etc. OPP **end**: **+with** *The book begins with a foreword by Professor Davies.*
6 SPEAKING [I] to start talking: *"Ladies and gentlemen," he began.*
7 I can't begin to understand/imagine etc. SPOKEN used to emphasize how difficult something is to understand etc.: *I can't even begin to imagine what it must be like to live under those conditions.*
[**Origin:** Old English *beginnan*] → see Word Choice box at COMMENCE

Be·gin /ˈbeɪgɪn/**, Me·na·chem** /məˈnɑkəm/ (1913–1992) an Israeli politician who was PRIME MINISTER from 1977 to 1983, and signed a peace TREATY with President Sadat of Egypt which is called the Camp David Agreement

be·gin·ner /bɪˈgɪnɚ/ *n.* [C] **1** someone who has just started to do or learn something: *Beginners need to ski on easier slopes.* **2 beginner's luck** unusual success that you have when you start doing something new

be·gin·ning /bɪˈgɪnɪŋ/ S1 W2 *n.* **1** [C usually singular] the start or first part of an event, story, period of time etc. SYN **start**: **+of** *the beginning of summer* | *He moved to a different school **at the beginning** of the school year.* | *This has been some of the worst fighting **since the beginning** of the war.* | *It's a good idea to set the rules **in the beginning**.* | *I liked her **from the beginning**.* | *There was something strange about the place **right from the beginning**.* | *We expected problems from **the very beginning**.* | **only/just the beginning** (=used in order to emphasize that something will continue or develop) *Judge Oster's decision is certain to be only the beginning of a long legal battle.* | *This painting **marked the beginning** of Homer's most productive period.* | *The novel is exciting **from beginning to end**.* **2 beginnings** [plural] the early part or early signs of something that later develops into something bigger or more important: *At age 11, Wharton showed her mother the beginnings of a novel.* | *The Web **had** its **beginnings** in the CERN physics lab in Switzerland.* | **from modest/humble etc. beginnings** *From humble beginnings in Dallas, the company has developed into one of the largest in America.* **3 the beginning of the end** the time when something starts to end or become less than it was before: *Mandela's release was the beginning of the end of apartheid.*

WORD CHOICE **at the beginning of, in the beginning**
• Something that happens at the very start of an event or period of time happens **at the beginning of** it: *At the beginning of the Civil War, Fort Sumter was attacked* (NOT *in the beginning of it*). | *There's a car chase at the beginning* (=at the start of the movie).
• If something happens **in the beginning** (not usually with *of*), it happens during a period of time near the start of an event or longer period of time: *In the beginning, the South had some success* (=during the early part of the Civil War). | *I was too shy to speak to her in the beginning* (=the first few times I saw her).

USAGE
Remember that there are two "n"s in the middle of **beginning.**

be·gone /bɪˈgɔn/ *interjection* OLD USE used to tell someone to go away

be·go·nia /bɪˈgoʊnyə/ *n.* [C] a plant with yellow, pink, red, or white flowers [**Origin:** 1700–1800 Modern Latin, from Michel *Bégon* (1638–1710), French governor of Santo Domingo, who discovered the plant]

B

be·got /bɪˈgɑt/ *v.* the past tense of BEGET

be·got·ten /bɪˈgɑt̚n/ *v.* the past participle of BEGET

be·grudge /bɪˈgrʌdʒ/ *v.* [T] **1** to feel JEALOUS of someone because they have something which you think they do not deserve: **begrudge sb sth** *We shouldn't begrudge her this success.* **2** to feel annoyed or unhappy that you have to pay something, give someone something etc.: **begrudge sb sth** *I pay my taxes; I don't begrudge the government its share.* | **begrudge doing sth** *Most people don't begrudge tipping the waiter.* —**begrudgingly** *adv.*

be·guile /bɪˈgaɪl/ *v.* [T] **1** to persuade or trick someone into doing something, especially by saying nice things to them: *a slick salesman who beguiles unwary investors* **2** to interest and attract someone: *He was beguiled by her beauty.* **3** LITERARY to do something that makes the time pass, especially in an enjoyable way

be·guil·ing /bɪˈgaɪlɪŋ/ *adj.* attractive and interesting, but often in a way that deceives you: *beguiling green eyes* —**beguilingly** *adv.*

be·gun /bɪˈgʌn/ *v.* the past participle of BEGIN

be·half /bɪˈhæf/ Ac *n.* **on behalf of sb/on sb's behalf** also **in behalf of sb/in sb's behalf a)** instead of someone, or as their representative: *Dante spoke on behalf of the Directors Guild of America.* **b)** because of someone: *Oh, don't go to any trouble on my behalf.* [**Origin:** 1300–1400 *by half* **on (someone's) side**]

be·have /bɪˈheɪv/ W3 *v.* [I] **1** [always + adv./prep.] to do things in a particular way SYN **act**: *You behaved bravely in a very difficult situation.* | *Many children behave differently when they're with friends rather than parents.* | **+like** *He's behaving like a complete jerk.* | **+in** *You need to show them that you can behave in a responsible way.* | **as if/though** *She's trying to behave as if nothing has changed.* **2** also **behave yourself** to behave in a way that people think is good or correct, by being polite and obeying people, not causing trouble etc. OPP **misbehave**: *Her kids just don't know how to behave.* | *They always behave so badly in the car!* | *If you behave yourself, I'll let you stay up to watch the movie.* | *a* ***well-behaved*** *young man* **3** [I] if something behaves in a particular way, it naturally does that thing: *Quantum mechanics is the study of the way atoms behave.* [**Origin:** 1400–1500 *have* **to hold or bear (yourself), behave** (14–16 centuries)]

be·hav·ior /bɪˈheɪvyɚ/ S2 W1 *n.* [U] **1** the things that a person or animal does: *the behavior of lions in the wild* | *Make it very clear what is acceptable behavior and what is not.* | **good/bad behavior** *Give the child a penalty for bad behavior.* | *the causes of* ***criminal behavior*** | *What is the effect of television on children's* ***social behavior****?* | *The dog has a few* ***behavior problems****.* | *Patients with diabetes need to change their* ***behavior patterns****.* | *It can be very hard to* ***change*** *your* ***behavior****.* | **+toward** *She complained about her boss's inappropriate behavior toward her.*

THESAURUS

conduct FORMAL the way someone behaves: *The chairman has denied any improper conduct.*
manner the way in which someone talks or behaves with other people: *His manner seemed strained and nervous.*
demeanor FORMAL the way someone behaves, dresses, speaks etc. that shows what his or her character is like: *her cheerful demeanor*

▸see THESAURUS box at **action** **2 be on your best behavior** to behave as well and politely as you can, especially in order to please someone: *Her son was on his best behavior.* **3** the things that an object, animal, substance etc. normally does: *a theory explaining the behavior of molecules in different substances* —**behavioral** *adj.*: *children with behavioral problems* —**behaviorally** *adv.*

be͵havioral isoˈlation *n.* [U] BIOLOGY a situation in which the romantic and sexual behavior of the people living in one particular place is very different to the behavior of people living in another place, so that people from the different groups do not enter into sexual relationships

be·hav·ior·ism /bɪˈheɪvyə͵rɪzəm/ *n.* [U] the belief that the scientific study of the mind should be based only on people's behavior, not on what they say about their thoughts and feelings —**behaviorist** *n.* [C]

be·hav·iour /bɪˈheɪvyɚ/ *n.* [U] the British and Canadian spelling of BEHAVIOR

be·head /bɪˈhɛd/ *v.* [T] to cut off someone's head as a punishment

be·he·moth /bɪˈhiməθ/ *n.* [C] LITERARY something that is very large [**Origin:** 1500–1600 *Behemoth* very large animal mentioned in the Bible (14–21 centuries), from Latin, from Hebrew]

be·hest /bɪˈhɛst/ *n.* [singular] **at the behest of sb** FORMAL because someone has asked for something or ordered something to happen: *The committee was formed at the behest of Governor Sinclair.*

be·hind¹ /bɪˈhaɪnd/ S1 W1 *prep.* **1** at or toward the back of something: *He sat behind me.* | *Is that your shoe behind the couch?* | *the mountains behind the city* | *I was driving behind a truck on the freeway.* | *I turned around and she was* ***right behind*** (=very close behind) *me.* **2** not as successful or not having made as much progress as someone or something else: *The Rams were 21 points behind the Falcons.* | *Mark's behind the rest of the class in his reading.* | *American manufacturers are* ***falling behind*** (=becoming less and less successful than) *their global competitors.* **3** late in doing something: *Interstate 880 opened Tuesday, three months* ***behind schedule****.* **4** supporting a person, idea etc.: *Congress appears to be firmly behind the president on this issue.* **5** responsible for a plan, idea etc. or for organizing something: *The police believe a local gang is behind the killings.* | *The Chamber of Commerce is behind this year's fund-raising dinner.* **6** if an experience or situation is behind you, you are not taking part in it anymore, or it does not upset you or affect your life anymore: *Ronstadt's days as a rock star are behind her, for now.* | *The victim wants to* ***put*** *this* ***behind*** *her and get on with her life.* **7** if a reason, experience, fact etc. is behind something, it is the reason why something exists or why it has happened: *It's interesting to learn the history behind the buildings.* | *What's behind Cooper's opposition to the changes?* | *The article examines the factors that* ***lie behind*** *the country's economic problems.* **8** if you have experience behind you, you have learned valuable skills or gotten important qualities that can be used: *Gutierrez has years of experience behind her.* **9** used when the real facts about a situation or someone's character are hidden by the way things seem or by the way a person behaves: *Behind his gruff exterior, she finds a sweet soul.* | *the truth behind the mystery* [**Origin:** Old English *behindan*, from *hindan* **from behind**] → see also **behind sb's back** at BACK² (7), **behind bars** at BAR¹ (8) → see Word Choice box at FRONT¹

behind² S2 W2 *adv.* **1** at or toward the back of something: *Anderson was in the lead, but several other runners followed* ***close behind****.* **2 be/get/fall behind a)** to be late or slow in doing something: *He's always been a little bit behind developmentally.* | **behind with sth** *We're already three months behind with the rent.* | **behind in sth** *Many U.N. member states are behind in their dues.* **b)** to be less successful than other people, or not make as much progress: *The Bruins fell behind in the first quarter.* | **behind in sth** *She has been falling further and further behind in school.* **3 stay/remain**

behind to stay in a place when other people have left it or gone somewhere else: *You go ahead – I'll stay behind and wait for Harry.* **4 leave sth behind** to leave something in a place where you were before or in a place after an event: *The beach was covered with litter left behind by the storm.* | *The movie is about a boy left behind by his family.*

behind³ *n.* [C] INFORMAL a word used to mean your BUTTOCKS when you want to be polite SYN **bottom**

be·hind·hand /bɪˈhaɪndˌhænd/ *adv.* FORMAL late or slow in doing something or paying a debt

be·hold /bɪˈhoʊld/ *v. past tense and past participle* **beheld** /bɪˈhɛld/ [T] LITERARY or OLD USE to see or to look at something SYN **see** —**beholder** *n.* [C] → see also **lo and behold** at LO

be·hold·en /bɪˈhoʊldən/ *adj.* **feel/be beholden to sb** to feel that you have a duty to someone because they have done something for you

be·hoove /bɪˈhuv/ *v.* **it behooves sb to do sth** FORMAL used to say that someone should do something because it is right or necessary, or because it will help them

beige /beɪʒ/ *n.* [U] a pale dull yellow-brown color —**beige** *adj.*

Bei·jing /ˌbeɪˈdʒɪŋ/ the capital city of the People's Republic of China

be·ing¹ /ˈbiɪŋ/ S3 W2 *n.* **1** [C] a living thing, especially a person: *a* ***human being*** | **an intelligent/rational being** *Are we the only intelligent beings in the universe?* | *a science fiction book about alien beings* **2 come into being/be brought into being** to begin to exist: *New democracies have come into being since the end of the Cold War.* **3** [U] LITERARY the most important quality or nature of something, especially of a person: **the core/roots/whole of sb's being** *Her religious faith is at the core of her being.* | *I regret my actions with every* ***fiber of my being*** (=I regret them completely).

being² *v.* [linking verb] **1** the present participle of BE **2** used in order to give a reason for something: *Being young and single, I wasn't really worried about what might happen.* | *I didn't expect them to sit still, kids being what they are.*

Bei·rut /beɪˈrut/ the capital and largest city of Lebanon

be·jew·eled /bɪˈdʒuəld/ *adj.* wearing jewels or decorated with jewels: *a bejeweled antique watch*

be·la·bor /bɪˈleɪbɚ/ *v.* [T] **1 belabor the point** to emphasize an idea or fact too strongly, especially by repeating it many times **2** OLD-FASHIONED to beat someone or something hard

Bel·a·rus /ˌbɛləˈrus/ a country in eastern Europe, east of Poland —**Belarussian** /ˌbɛləˈrʌʃən/ *n., adj.*

be·lat·ed /bɪˈleɪt̬ɪd/ *adj.* happening or arriving late: *a belated birthday card* —**belatedly** *adv.*

be·lay /bɪˈleɪ/ *v.* [I,T] **1** TECHNICAL to control a rope that a climber is attached to, in order to keep them safe while they climb **2** TECHNICAL to attach a rope to a ship by winding it under and over in the shape of a figure 8 on a special hook

belch /bɛltʃ/ *v.* **1** [I] to let air from your stomach come out loudly through your mouth SYN **burp** **2** [I,T] also **belch out** to send out large amounts of smoke, fire etc., or to come out of something in large amounts: *smokestacks belching black smoke into the air* —**belch** *n.* [C]

be·lea·guered /bɪˈligɚd/ *adj.* FORMAL **1** experiencing a lot of problems or criticism: *a beleaguered politician* **2** surrounded by an army: *a beleaguered city* [**Origin:** 1500–1600 Dutch *belegeren*, from *leger* **camp**]

Bel·fast /ˈbɛlfæst/ the capital city of Northern Ireland

bel·fry /ˈbɛlfri/ *n. plural* **belfries** [C] a tower for a bell, especially on a church → see also **have bats in the belfry** at BAT¹ (8)

ˌBelgian ˈendive *n.* [C] ENDIVE

Bel·gium /ˈbɛldʒəm/ a country in northwest Europe between France, Germany, Luxembourg, and the Netherlands —**Belgian** *n., adj.*

Bel·grade /ˈbɛlgreɪd/ the capital city of The Federal Republic of Yugoslavia

be·lie /bɪˈlaɪ/ *v.* [T] FORMAL **1** to give someone a false idea about something: *With a quickness that belied her age, she ran across the road.* **2** to show that something cannot be true or real: *Two large tears belied Rosalie's brave words.*

be·lief /bəˈlif/ W2 *n.* **1** [singular, U] the feeling that something is definitely true or definitely exists: +**in** *a* ***strong belief*** *in God* | +**that** *Several jurors expressed the belief that the two men were innocent.* | ***It is my belief that*** *we will find the cure to this disease within the next five years.* | *Most investors buy stocks* ***in the belief that*** *prices will rise in the long term.* | **deeply held/long-held belief** *a deeply held belief that stealing is wrong* | **a widely held/widespread belief** *There is a widespread belief that violence on TV is harmful to children.* | *They bought the house with the* ***mistaken belief*** *that it was well-built.* | *a* ***growing belief*** *that war was inevitable* | ***Contrary to popular belief*** (=unlike what most people believe) *pigs are actually very clean animals.* **2** [singular] the feeling that something is good and can be trusted: +**in** *a belief in the value of hard work* | *The judge's decision* ***shook*** *my* ***belief in*** *the legal system.* (=made me doubt that it is good or can be trusted) **3** [C] an idea that you believe to be true, especially one that forms part of a system of ideas: *their* ***religious beliefs*** | *Several members of the government still* ***hold*** *Marxist* ***beliefs***. ►see THESAURUS box at **faith** **4 beyond belief** used in order to emphasize that something is so extreme that it is difficult to believe: *Their incompetence is beyond belief.* → see also DISBELIEF, UNBELIEF

be·liev·a·ble /bəˈlivəbəl/ *adj.* something that is believable can be believed because it seems possible, likely, or real: *a story with believable characters* —**believably** *adv.*

be·lieve /bəˈliv/ S1 W1 *v.* [not in progressive]
1 BE SURE STH IS TRUE [T] to be sure that something is true or that someone is telling the truth: *You can't believe everything you read in the papers.* | *Students weren't sure who to believe.* | **believe (that)** *I can't believe that he really wanted to hurt her.* | **believe sb** *He made a promise, and I believed him.* | **truly/sincerely/honestly believe** *He truly believed he could make a difference.* | *She's charming and pretty, but you can't* ***believe a word*** *she says* (=you can't believe anything she says).

THESAURUS

accept to believe what someone says is true or right: *His wife accepted his explanation for why he was late.*
take sb's word to believe what someone says is true: *You don't have to take my word for it – go and see for yourself.*
swallow INFORMAL to believe a story or explanation that is not actually true: *Did he really think we'd swallow that story?*
fall for sth INFORMAL to be tricked into believing something that is not true: *I can't believe she fell for that old excuse!*
buy to believe an explanation or reason for something: *I don't buy it. He'd never make that kind of mistake.*

2 HAVE AN OPINION [T] to think that something is true, although you are not completely sure: **believe (that)** *Police believe that the victim knew her killer.* | *"Is your mother coming to the picnic?" "Yes, I* ***believe so.****"* (=think that it is true) | **be believed to be sth** *At 115, Mrs. Jackson is believed to be one of the oldest people in the world.* | *Customers* ***mistakenly believe*** *that software is included in the price.* | *The four men are* ***widely believed*** (=believed by a lot of people) *to have been killed by their captors.* | *We* ***have no reason to believe***

(that) (=have no proof) *he has left the country.* ▶see THESAURUS box at **think**

SPOKEN PHRASES

3 can't/don't believe sth said when you are very surprised or shocked by something: *When I saw the video, I was like, I don't believe it!* | *I can't believe you lied to me!*
4 it's difficult/hard to believe (that) used when you think that a fact is surprising: *It's hard to believe we've been married for 20 years.*
5 believe (you) me used to emphasize that something is definitely true: *No, it's too far to walk, believe me.*
6 would you believe it! or **I don't believe it!** said when you are surprised or angry about something: *Would you believe it, she actually remembered my birthday!*
7 believe it or not used when you are going to say something that is true but surprising: *Well, believe it or not, we're getting married.*
8 you'd better believe it! used to emphasize that something is true: *"Do they make money on them?" "You'd better believe it!"*
9 can't believe your eyes/ears to be very surprised by something you see or hear: *I couldn't believe my ears when she told me the cheapest flight was $1,100.*
10 don't you believe it! used to emphasize that something is definitely not true
11 if you believe that, you'll believe anything used to say that something is definitely not true, and that anyone who believes it must be stupid
12 seeing is believing or **I'll believe it when I see it** used to say that you will only believe that something happens or exists when you actually see it

13 RELIGION [I] to have a strong religious faith: *Only those who believe will go to heaven.*
[**Origin:** Old English *belefan*, from *lyfan*, *lefan* **to allow, believe**] → see also **make believe** at MAKE[1] (25)

believe in *phr. v.* **1 believe in sb** to be sure that someone exists: *She still believes in Santa Claus.* **2 believe in sth** to think that something is effective or right: *He believes in democracy.* | **believe in doing sth** *The school believes in maintaining small class sizes.* **3 believe in sb/sth** to think that someone is good or that they can be trusted: *You need to* ***believe in yourself*** *to succeed.* | *Many Americans no longer believe in their government.*

be·liev·er /bəˈlivɚ/ *n.* **1 be a great/firm believer in sth** to believe strongly that something is good and brings good results: *I'm a great believer in regular exercise.* **2** [C] someone who believes in a particular god, religion, or system of beliefs ▶see THESAURUS box at **religion**

be·lit·tle /bɪˈlɪtl̬/ *v.* [T] FORMAL to make someone or something seem small or unimportant: *She always belittled my efforts to speak French.*

Be·lize /bəˈliz/ a country in Central America on the Caribbean Sea

bell /bɛl/ S3 W3 *n.* [C] **1 a)** a hollow metal object shaped like an upside down cup, that makes a ringing sound when it is hit by a piece of metal that hangs down inside it: *church bells were ringing* **b)** a round ball of metal with another small ball inside it that makes a ringing sound: *a bell on the cat's collar* → see picture at BICYCLE[1] **2** a piece of equipment that makes a ringing sound, used as a signal or to get someone's attention: *Please* ***ring the bell*** *for assistance.* | **a bell rings/sounds/goes etc.** *The bell sounded to end the fight.* **3** the sound of a bell ringing as a signal or a warning: *When you hear the bell, stop writing.* **4 bells and whistles** INFORMAL special extra features you can have with something you buy: *The software has all the functions you need, plus a few bells and whistles.* **5 have/get your bell rung** INFORMAL to be hit on the head, sometimes hard enough to make you unconscious **6** something shaped like a bell: *Its flowers are tiny white bells.* **7 I'll be there with bells on** SPOKEN used to say that you will definitely be somewhere and eager and ready for what is going to happen [**Origin:** Old English *belle*] → see also **as clear as a bell** at CLEAR[1] (8), DIVING BELL, **ring a bell** at RING[2] (5)

Bell /bɛl/, **Al·ex·an·der Gra·ham** /ˈælɪgzændɚ ˈgreɪəm/ (1847–1922) a Scottish scientist and inventor who lived in the U.S. and is famous for inventing the telephone in 1876 → see picture on page A25

bel·la·don·na /ˌbɛləˈdɑnə/ *n.* [U] **1** BIOLOGY a poisonous plant SYN **deadly nightshade** **2** MEDICINE a substance from this plant, used as a drug [**Origin:** 1700–1800 Italian **beautiful lady**; because it was used in cosmetics]

ˈbell ˌbottoms *n.* [plural] a pair of pants with legs that become mcuh wider at the bottom → see also FLARES —**bell-bottomed** *adj.*

bell·boy /ˈbɛlbɔɪ/ *n. plural* **bellboys** [C] a bellhop

belle /bɛl/ *n.* [C] OLD-FASHIONED a beautiful girl or woman: *a Southern belle* | *Caroline was* ***the belle of the ball*** (=the most beautiful girl at a dance or party) *that night.*

belle é·poque /ˌbɛl eɪˈpɔk, -ˈpɑk/ *n.* [singular] a period of time in which art and CULTURE are very important, used especially about France in the early 20th century

belles let·tres /ˌbɛl ˈlɛtrə/ *n.* [U] literature or writings about subjects relating to literature

bell·hop /ˈbɛlhɑp/ *n.* [C] a young person who carries bags, takes messages etc. in a hotel

bel·li·cose /ˈbɛləkoʊs/ *adj.* LITERARY always wanting to fight or argue SYN **aggressive** —**bellicosity** /ˌbɛləˈkɑsət̬i/ *n.* [U]

-bellied /bɛlid/ [in adjectives] **black-bellied/fat-bellied/big-bellied** etc. having a black, fat etc. stomach: *a black-bellied duck*

bel·lig·er·ent /bəˈlɪdʒərənt/ *adj.* **1** very unfriendly and mean, and wanting to argue or fight: *George was drunk and belligerent.* **2** [only before noun] FORMAL a belligerent country is at war with another country —**belligerence** —**belligerency** *n.* [U]

bel·low[1] /ˈbɛloʊ/ *v.* **1** [I,T] to shout loudly, especially in a deep voice: *"He's guilty and I'll prove it!" Baines bellowed.* ▶see THESAURUS box at **shout**[1] **2** [I] to make the deep sound that a BULL makes

bellow[2] *n.* **1 bellows** [plural] **a)** an object that you use to blow air into a fire to make it burn better **b)** a part of a musical instrument that pushes air through pipes to produce sound, such as in an ORGAN **2** [C] the deep sound that a BULL makes

ˈbell ˌpepper *n.* [C] a hollow red, green, or yellow vegetable, often used to add flavor in cooking SYN **pepper**

ˈbell ˌringer *n.* [C] someone who rings a bell, especially in a church —**bell ringing** *n.* [U]

bell·weth·er /ˈbɛlˌwɛðɚ/ *n.* [C] FORMAL something, especially a company or STOCK, that people consider to be a sign of how an economic situation is changing: *General Motors stock, a bellwether, rose several points.*

bel·ly[1] /ˈbɛli/ *n. plural* **bellies** [C] INFORMAL **1 a)** BIOLOGY your stomach: *a full belly* **b)** the front part of your body between your chest and your legs: *She lay on her belly in the long grass.* → see also POTBELLY **2** BIOLOGY the middle part of an animal's body, near its stomach **3 go belly up** if a business goes belly up, it fails **4** a curved or rounded middle part of an object: *the belly of an airplane* [**Origin:** Old English *belg* **bag, skin**] → see also -BELLIED

belly[2] *v.* **bellies, bellied, bellying**

belly up to sth *phr. v.* INFORMAL **belly up to the bar/table etc.** to go and stand near a bar, table etc. to eat, drink, or take part in an activity that is going on there

bel·ly·ache[1] /ˈbɛliˌeɪk/ *n.* [C,U] a pain in your stomach

bellyache[2] *v.* [I] INFORMAL to complain a lot, especially about something that is not important: +**about** *He just kept bellyaching about the prices.*

'belly ˌbutton *n.* [C] INFORMAL the small hollow or raised place in the middle of your stomach SYN **navel**

'belly ˌdance *n.* [C] a dance from the Middle East performed by a woman using movements of her stomach and HIPS —**belly dancer** *n.* [C]

'belly flop *n.* [C] a way of jumping into water, in which the front of your body falls flat against the surface of the water —**belly flop** *v.* [I]

bel·ly·ful /'bɛliˌfʊl/ *n.* **have had a bellyful of sth** INFORMAL to be annoyed by something because you have heard or experienced too much of it: *Audiences have had a bellyful of gangster movies.*

'belly-ˌlanding *n.* [C] the act of landing an airplane without using the wheels —**belly-land** *v.* [I]

'belly laugh *n.* [C] INFORMAL a deep loud laugh

Bel·mo·pan /ˌbɛlmoʊ'pæn/ the capital city of Belize

be·long /bɪ'lɔŋ/ S2 W2 *v.* [I] **1** [always + adv./prep.] to be in the right place or situation: *Can you put that back where it belongs?* | +**in** *A violent man like that belongs in prison.* **2** to feel happy and comfortable in a place or situation, because you have the same interests and ideas as other people: *I loved the school. I felt I belonged there.* | +**in** *I taught in high schools, but I really belonged in the elementary schools.*

belong to **1 belong to sb/sth** to be the property of someone or of an organization: *Do the books belong to the school?* **2 belong to sth** to be a member of a group or organization: *They belong to the country club.* **3 belong to sth** to be related to something or be a part of something: *cars that belong to a different era* **4 belong to sb/sth** if a period of time belongs to someone, they are the most important or successful person, group or organization in it: *All the performances were good, but the evening belonged to a dance group from Moscow.* [**Origin:** 1300–1400 *long* **to be suitable** (12–19 centuries), from Old English *gelang* **dependent on**]

be·long·ings /bɪ'lɔŋɪŋz/ *n.* [plural] the things that you own, especially those that you can carry with you: *Soldiers searched through people's personal belongings.*

be·loved¹ /bɪ'lʌvd, bɪ'lʌvɪd/ *adj.* LITERARY OR HUMOROUS a beloved place, thing etc. is one that you love very much: *Tom's beloved car* | +**by/of** *The beaches are beloved by tourists and surfers alike.* → see also **dearly beloved** at DEARLY (3)

be·lov·ed² /bɪ'lʌvɪd/ *n.* LITERARY **my/her etc. beloved** LITERARY the person that someone loves most: *a visit from her beloved*

below

The boy is sitting under the boardwalk.
The sun is going down below the horizon.

be·low¹ /bɪ'loʊ/ S3 W2 *prep.* **1** in a lower place or position than something, or on a lower level than something OPP **above**: *a cut below his left eye* | *Print your name below your signature.* | *fish swimming just below the surface* **2** less than a particular number, amount, level etc. OPP **above**: *It was 20° below zero outside.* | *families living below the official poverty line* | *Thompson scored only eight points, 14 below his season average.* | **way/well below** (=very much lower than a particular number etc.) | *a **below average** (=not as good as the normal standard) student* | *Temperatures will remain **below freezing** (=lower than the temperature at which water freezes) for the rest of the week.* **3** in a lower less important job than someone else OPP **above**: *A captain is below a general.* [**Origin:** 1300–1400 from the adjective *low* Old Norse *lagr*] ▸see THESAURUS box at **under¹**

below² S3 W3 *adv.* **1** in a lower place or position, or on a lower level OPP **above**: *Water was dripping onto the ground below.* | *The colder water is **down below**, with the warmer water on top.* **2** mentioned or shown lower on the same page or on a later page OPP **above**: *Answer each of the questions below.* | *For more information, **see below**.* **3 10/15/20 below etc.** if a temperature is 10, 15, 20 below etc., it is that number of degrees lower than zero OPP **above** **4** less than a particular number, age, price etc. OPP **above**: *clothing offered at wholesale prices and below* **5** in a lower less important rank or job OPP **above**: *officers of the rank of captain and below* **6** on the lower level of a ship or boat: *Captain Parker **went below**, leaving Clooney in charge.* **7** LITERARY on Earth rather than in Heaven

belt¹ /bɛlt/ S2 W3 *n.* [C] **1** a band of leather, cloth etc. that you wear around your waist, especially to hold up your pants: *a black leather belt* | *I **tightened the belt** a notch.* **2** a circular band of a material such as rubber that connects or moves parts of a machine: *The pump belt was loose.* → see also CONVEYOR BELT, FAN BELT **3** a large area of land that has particular features: *the farm belt in the midwest* (=area where there are many farms) | *the sun belt states* (=states that have warm weather) **4 have/get sth under your belt** to have achieved something useful or important: *Skiing is fun, once you have a few lessons under your belt.* **5 below the belt** INFORMAL unfair or cruel: *Some say the ads **hit below the belt*** (=are unfair). **6** a hard hit usually with your hand: *She **gave him a belt across** the cheek.* **7** a drink of strong alcohol: *a belt of bourbon* → see also CHASTITY BELT, GARTER BELT, SEAT BELT, **tighten your belt** at TIGHTEN (6)

belt² *v.* INFORMAL [T] to hit someone or something hard: *Maggie turned around and belted him.*

belt sth ↔ **out** *phr. v.* INFORMAL to sing a song very loudly: *My colleagues belted out a chorus of "Happy Birthday."*

belt·ed /'bɛltɪd/ *adj.* fastened with a belt: *a belted jacket*

'belt-ˌtightening *n.* [U] the act or process of spending less money than before: *a period of belt-tightening*

belt·way /'bɛltˀweɪ/ *n.* **1** [C] a road that goes around a city to keep traffic away from the center **2 the Beltway** the U.S. government in Washington, D.C., and the politicians, lawyers, LOBBYISTS etc. who are involved in it: *The idea isn't popular **inside the Beltway**.*

be·lu·ga /bə'lugə/ *n.* **1** a type of WHALE **2** a type of expensive CAVIAR (=fish eggs) from a STURGEON

be·moan /bɪ'moʊn/ *v.* [T] to complain or say that you are disappointed about something: *an article bemoaning the lack of sports facilities in the area*

be·mused /bɪ'myuzd/ *adj.* someone who is bemused is slightly confused: *Carter looked bemused by the questions.*

bench¹ /bɛntʃ/ W3 *n.* **1** [C] a long seat for two or more people, used especially outdoors: *a long wooden bench* **2** [singular] **a)** a seat where members of a sports team sit when they are not playing: *We won the game, even with Brian **on the bench*** (=not playing). | *Hayden **came off the bench** (=he started playing) to score 14 points.* **b)** the players who do not usually play at the start of a game, but who may play later in the game when the stronger players stop playing: *a team with a strong bench* **3 the bench a)** LAW the job of being a judge in a court of law: *He was appointed to the bench in 1986.* | **serve/sit on the bench** (=to work as a judge) **b)** the seat where a judge sits in a court of law: *Smith* ***approached the bench*** (=spoke privately to the judge) *and asked for a delay.* **4** [C] a long heavy table used for working on with tools or equipment: *a carpenter's bench*

bench² *v.* [T] to not allow a sports player to play in a game, or to remove a player from a game: *Anderson was benched because of injuries.*

bench·mark /'bɛntʃmɑrk/ *n.* [C] **1** something that is used as a standard by which other things can be judged or measured: *The index rate is the benchmark used by lenders to set the mortgage rate.* **2** a mark made on a building, post etc. that shows its height above sea level, and is used to measure other heights and distances in a SURVEY

'bench ˌtrial *n.* [C] LAW a TRIAL in the U.S. that does not have a JURY, where a judge alone listens to the facts of a case and decides whether or not someone is guilty

bench·warm·er /'bɛntʃˌwɔrmɚ/ *n.* [C] INFORMAL, DISAPPROVING a sports player who does not often play in games

bend¹ /bɛnd/ S2 W3 *v. past tense and past participle* **bent** /bɛnt/

1 MOVE YOUR BODY [I always + adv./prep.,T] to move a part of your body so that it is not straight, or so that you are not standing upright anymore: *Bend your knees slightly.* | **+over/down** *Levy bent over to pick up the coins.* | **+forward/toward/across etc.** *Bending forward, he stroked the dog's head.* | **bend over sth** *She was bending over the desk.*

2 CURVE a) [T] to push or press something into a curved shape or fold it at an angle: *Heavy snow was bending the branches.* **b)** [I] to change to the shape of a curve, or to be in this shape: *Bamboo will bend without breaking.* | *The metal bar bends in the middle.*

3 ROAD [I] if a road bends, it changes direction to form a curve: *The road* ***bends sharply*** (=curves a lot) *to the left.*

4 bend over backward (to do sth) to try very hard to be helpful: *The hotel employees bent over backward to please us.*

5 bend the rules to allow someone to do something that is not normally allowed, or to do something that is not usually allowed: *a tough street cop who bends the rules*

6 bend sb's ear SPOKEN to talk to someone for a long time, in a way that is annoying to them

7 on bended knee a) trying very hard to persuade someone to do something: *The TV network begged her on bended knee to return to the program.* **b)** in a kneeling position: *George asked her to marry him on bended knee.*

8 bend your mind/efforts/thoughts etc. to sth FORMAL to give all your energy or attention to one activity, plan etc.

[**Origin:** Old English *bendan*]

bend² *n.* [C] **1** a curved part of something, especially a road or river: *The creek goes around a bend by the farm.* | **+in** *a* ***sharp bend*** (=one that curves a lot) *in the river* | **come/go around a bend** *The car came around the bend too fast.* **2** an action in which you bend a part of your body: *Start with a few knee bends.* **3 the bends** [plural] a very painful and serious condition that DIVERS get when they come up from under deep water too quickly

bend·a·ble /'bɛndəbəl/ *adj.* able to be bent: *bendable toys*

bend·er /'bɛndɚ/ *n.* [C] INFORMAL **go on a bender** to drink a lot of alcohol at one time

be·neath¹ /bɪ'niθ/ W3 *prep.* FORMAL **1** under something or covered by it SYN **under** SYN **underneath**: *the warm sand beneath her feet* | *The whale disappeared beneath the waves.* **2** if a particular action or activity is beneath someone, they refuse to do it because they do not think it is good enough for them: *She thinks it would be* ***beneath her*** *to apologize.* | *Too many doctors think family practice is* ***beneath*** *their* ***dignity*** (=think they are too important to do it). **3** a feeling or attitude that is beneath another feeling or attitude is covered or hidden by it SYN **behind** SYN **under** SYN **underneath**: *A strong personality* ***lies beneath*** *his shy manner.* | *racial tensions* ***beneath the surface of*** (=hidden by the outward appearance of) *our society* **4** in a lower less important rank or job than someone else SYN **under**: *He treats those beneath him very badly.* [**Origin:** Old English *beneothan*, from *neothan* **below**] ▸see THESAURUS box at **under¹**

beneath² *adv.* in or to a lower position: *The whales are black or gray on top, with white beneath.* | *He stood on the bridge, looking at the river beneath.*

Ben·e·dict /'bɛnəˌdɪkt/**, Saint** (?480–?547) an Italian religious leader who started the Benedictine group of Christian MONKS

Ben·e·dic·tine /ˌbɛnə'dɪktɪn, -tin/ *n.* [C] a member of a Christian religious order of MONKS —**Benedictine** *adj.*

ben·e·dic·tine /ˌbɛnə'dɪktɪn, -tin/ *n.* [C,U] a strong alcoholic drink that is a type of LIQUEUR

Ben·e·dic·tines /ˌbɛnə'dɪktɪnz, -tinz/ a Christian religious order of MONKS and NUNS —**Benedictine** *adj.*

ben·e·dic·tion /ˌbɛnə'dɪkʃən/ *n.* [C,U] a type of prayer in the Christian religion that asks God to protect and help someone [**Origin:** 1400–1500 Late Latin *benedictio*, from *benedicere* **to bless**]

Ben·e·dict XV /ˌbɛnədɪkt ðə fɪf'tinθ/**, Pope** (1854–1922) the POPE at the time of World War I

Benedict XVI, Pope /ˌbɛnədɪkt ðə sɪks'tinθ/ (1927–) a German priest who became POPE in 2005

ben·e·fac·tion /ˌbɛnə'fækʃən/ *n.* FORMAL **1** [U] the act of doing something good, especially by giving money to someone who needs it **2** [C] money given in this way

ben·e·fac·tor /'bɛnəˌfæktɚ/ *n.* [C] someone who gives money for a good purpose: *a $5 million donation from an unnamed benefactor*

ben·e·fac·tress /'bɛnəˌfæktrɪs/ *n.* [C] OLD-FASHIONED a woman who gives money for a good purpose

ben·e·fice /'bɛnəfɪs/ *n.* [C] the pay and position of the priest of a Christian PARISH

be·nef·i·cent /bɪ'nɛfəsənt/ *adj.* FORMAL doing things to help people SYN **generous** —**beneficence** *n.* [U] —**beneficently** *adv.*

ben·e·fi·cial /ˌbɛnə'fɪʃəl◂ / Ac *adj.* producing results that bring advantages OPP **detrimental**: *beneficial changes* | **+to** *an environmental program that is beneficial to all* | *The drug has* ***a beneficial effect*** *on the immune system.* | *a* ***mutually beneficial*** *relationship* (=one that helps both people or groups) —**beneficially** *adv.*

ben·e·fi·ci·ar·y /ˌbɛnə'fɪʃiˌɛri, -'fɪʃəri/ Ac *n. plural* **beneficiaries** [C] **1** someone who gets advantages from an action or change: **+of** *the beneficiary of U.S. aid* | **main/primary/principal etc. beneficiary** *Single mothers will be the chief beneficiaries of this new policy.* **2** LAW someone who receives money or property from someone else who has died: **+of** *He was the main beneficiary of his father's will.*

ben·e·fit¹ /'bɛnəfɪt/ Ac S2 W1 *n.* **1** [C,U] something that gives you advantages or improves your life in some way: *Young mothers* ***have the benefit of*** *day care on campus.* | *Liu Han translated what he had said* ***for my benefit*** (=in order to help me). | *Even older heavy smokers can* ***reap benefits*** (=gain advantages) *from quitting smoking.* | *a new drug that may* ***be of*** *clinical* ***benefit*** (=be useful or helpful) *for a life-threatening disease* | **with/without the benefit of sth** *The CD sold in huge numbers without the benefit of being played on the radio.* | **health/safety/economic etc. benefit** *the safety benefits of wearing bicycle helmets* **2** [C usually plural] the money or other advantages that you get as part of your job, or from something such as insurance or the government → see also PERK: *medical benefits* | *They offer a good salary and great benefits.* **3** [C] a concert, performance, dinner etc. arranged to make money for a CHARITY: *a benefit being held at a downtown hotel* | *a benefit concert for the Children's Hospital* **4 the benefit of the doubt** the act of accepting what someone tells you even though you think they may be lying: *I was willing to **give her the benefit of the doubt**.* [**Origin:** 1300–1400 Anglo-French *ben fet*, from Latin *bene factus* **well done**]

benefit² AC W2 *v.* **benefited, benefiting** also **benefitted, benefitting** **1** [I] to be helped by something: **+benefit from/by (doing) sth** *The whole nation benefits from having skilled and educated workers.* **2** [T] to bring advantages to someone or improve their lives in some way: *New regulations will greatly benefit the region's poorest residents.*

ˌbenefit in ˈkind *n.* [C] IN-KIND BENEFIT

Be·ne·lux /ˈbɛnlˌʌks/ *n.* the countries of Belgium, the Netherlands, and Luxembourg, considered as a group

Be·nét /bəˈneɪ/, **Ste·phen Vin·cent** /ˈstivən ˈvɪnsənt/ (1898–1943) a U.S. writer of poems and short stories

be·nev·o·lent /bəˈnɛvələnt/ *adj.* kind and generous: *a benevolent man* | *money for benevolent work* [**Origin:** 1400–1500 Latin *bene* **well** + *volens* (present participle of *velle* **to wish**)] —**benevolence** *n.* [U] —**benevolently** *adv.*

beˌnevolent ˈdespot *n.* [C] HISTORY another word for an ENLIGHTENED DESPOT

beˌnevolent ˈdictator *n.* [C] POLITICS a leader of a country who has complete political power, but who uses that power to help the people of the country, rather than to get anything for him or herself

Ben·ga·li¹ /bɛnˈgɔli/ *n.* **1** [U] the language of Bangladesh or West Bengal **2** [C] someone from Bengal

Bengali² *adj.* from or relating to Bengal

Ben-Gur·i·on /bɛn ˈgʊriən/, **Da·vid** /ˈdeɪvɪd/ (1886–1973) an Israeli politician born in Poland who is considered responsible for establishing the independent Jewish nation of Israel

be·night·ed /bɪˈnaɪt̬ɪd/ *adj.* FORMAL having no knowledge or understanding —**benightedly** *adv.*

be·nign /bɪˈnaɪn/ *adj.* **1** MEDICINE not caused by CANCER and not likely to be dangerous to your health OPP **malignant**: *a benign tumor* **2** FORMAL kind and unlikely to harm anyone OPP **malignant**: *the animal's benign nature* [**Origin:** 1300–1400 Old French *benigne*, from Latin *benignus*, from *bene* **well** + *gigni* **to be born**] —**benignly** *adv.* —**benignity** *n.* [U]

Be·nin /bəˈnin, bəˈnɪn, ˈbɛnɪn/, **the People's Republic of** a country in West Africa, between Togo and Nigeria

Ben·ja·min /ˈbɛndʒəmɪn/ in the Bible, the youngest son of Jacob and the head of one of the 12 tribes of Israel

bent¹ /bɛnt/ *v.* the past tense and past participle of BEND

bent² *adj.* **1 be bent on (doing) sth** to be completely determined to do something, especially something that could be harmful or wrong: *Our society seems bent on its own destruction.* | *Rudi seems bent on finding a new job.* **2** curved and not flat or straight anymore: *The nail is bent.*

THESAURUS

twisted bent in many directions or turned many times: *a cable made of twisted strands of wire*
curved bent in the shape of part of a circle, or having this shape: *The bird has a long curved bill.*
warped bent or twisted into the wrong shape: *The wood was warped from years in the sun and rain.*
crooked not straight, but bending sharply in one or more places: *the crooked streets in the old part of the city*
wavy used about something, especially hair, with a series of curved shapes: *She had wavy black hair.*

3 bent out of shape SPOKEN very angry or annoyed: *Hey, don't **get all bent out of shape**!*

bent³ *n.* [singular] a natural skill or ability: *Rebecca has an artistic bent.*

ben·thos /ˈbɛnθɑs/ *n.* [U] BIOLOGY all the animals and plants that live on, in, or near the bottom of the sea or a lake

be·numbed /bɪˈnʌmd/ *adj.* FORMAL **1** made NUMB (=unable to feel anything) by cold **2** not doing anything or not working, especially because you are shocked or upset

Benz /bɛnz/, **Karl** /kɑrl/ (1844–1929) a German engineer who built the first gasoline-driven car in 1885

ben·zene /ˈbɛnzin, bɛnˈzin/ *n.* [U] CHEMISTRY a liquid obtained from coal and used for making plastics

ben·zine /ˈbɛnzin, bɛnˈzin/ *n.* [U] CHEMISTRY a liquid obtained from PETROLEUM and used to clean clothes

be·queath /bɪˈkwiθ, bɪˈkwið/ *v.* [T] FORMAL **1** LAW to legally arrange for someone to have something that you own after your death: **bequeath sth to sb** *The letter was bequeathed to the museum by a collector.* | **bequeath sb sth** *His father bequeathed him his entire estate.* ▸see THESAURUS box at **give¹** **2** to pass knowledge, customs etc. to people who come after you or live after you: **bequeath sth to sb** *the problems bequeathed to us by our parents' generation* [**Origin:** Old English *becwethan*, from *cwethan* **to say**]

be·quest /bɪˈkwɛst/ *n.* [C] FORMAL LAW money or property that you bequeath to someone: *a bequest of $50,000*

be·rate /bəˈreɪt/ *v.* [T] FORMAL to speak angrily to someone because they have done something wrong: **berate sb for sth** *An angry father berated the school's principal for not acting soon enough.*

Ber·ber /ˈbɚbɚ/ one of the tribes from northwest Africa who live in Morocco, Algeria, Tunisia and Libya

be·reaved¹ /bəˈrivd/ *adj.* FORMAL **1** having lost a close friend or relative because they have recently died: *a bereaved mother* **2 the bereaved** [plural] the person or people whose close friend or relative has just died: *Our sympathies go to the bereaved.* [**Origin:** Old English *bereafian*, from *reafian* **to rob**]

be·reave·ment /bəˈrivmənt/ *n.* [C,U] FORMAL the fact or state of having lost a close friend or relative because they have died: *depression caused by bereavement or divorce*

be·reft /bəˈrɛft/ *adj.* FORMAL **1 bereft of hope/ideas/life etc.** completely without any hope, ideas etc.: *a city that is bereft of culture* **2** feeling very sad and lonely

be·ret /bəˈreɪ/ *n.* [C] a round hat with a tight band around the head and a soft loose top part → see picture at HAT

Berg·man /ˈbɚgmən/, **Ing·mar** /ˈɪŋmɑr/ (1918–) a Swedish movie DIRECTOR who is considered one of the most important directors ever

ber·i·ber·i /ˌbɛriˈbɛri/ *n.* [U] MEDICINE a disease of the nerves caused by lack of VITAMIN B [**Origin:** 1700–1800 Sinhalese *bæribæri* **weakness**]

Be·ring Sea, the /ˌbɛrɪŋ ˈsi/ a part of the northern Pacific Ocean that is between Siberia and Alaska

Bering Strait, the /ˌbɛrɪŋ ˈstreɪt/ a narrow passage of water between Asia and North America that connects the Bering Sea to the Arctic Ocean

Ber·lin /bɚˈlɪn/ the capital city of Germany

B

Ber·lin, Ir·ving /ˈɚvɪŋ/ (1888–1989) a U.S. SONGWRITER famous for his popular songs and MUSICALS

Irving Berlin

ˌBerlin ˈairlift, the *n.* [singular] HISTORY a time during 1948 and 1949 when British, French, and American aircraft brought food and supplies into western Berlin by aircraft because the Soviet Union had blocked all other ways into the area

ˌBerlin ˈWall, the *n.* [singular] HISTORY a huge wall built by the East German government in 1961 to stop people from Communist East Berlin traveling into West Berlin. The wall was torn down in 1989 ending the Cold War. → see also COLD WAR

Ber·li·oz /ˈbɚlioʊz/, **Hec·tor** /ˈhɛktɚ/ (1803–1869) a French musician who wrote CLASSICAL music

berm /bɚm/ *n.* [C] TECHNICAL **1** an area of ground beside a road that separates the road from other areas SYN shoulder **2** a long narrow pile of sand, dirt etc., built to separate one area from another in order to protect someone or something

Ber·mu·da /bɚˈmyudə/ a country that consists of a group of islands in the West Atlantic Ocean. Bermuda is a British COLONY, but has its own government.

Berˌmuda ˈshorts also **Bermudas** *n.* [plural] short pants that end at the knee and are made from thin cloth, often in very bright colors

Berˌmuda ˈTriangle, the an area in the Atlantic Ocean between Bermuda, Florida, and Puerto Rico where many ships and aircraft are believed to have strangely disappeared

Bern /bɚn, bɛrn/ the capital city of Switzerland

Ber·na·dette /ˌbɚnəˈdɛt/, **Saint** also **St. ˌBernadette of ˈLourdes** (1844–1879) a French girl who claimed to have seen the Virgin Mary at Lourdes, which made Lourdes a place of PILGRIMAGE, especially for the sick

Bern·hardt /ˈbɚnhɑrt/, **Sa·rah** /ˈsærə/ (1844–1923) a French actress who is considered one of the best actresses ever

Ber·ni·ni /bɚˈnini/, **Gio·van·ni Lo·ren·zo** /dʒoʊˈvɑni ləˈrɛnzoʊ/ (1598–1680) an Italian SCULPTOR, ARCHITECT, and PAINTER, famous for his work in the BAROQUE style

Bern·stein /ˈbɚnstaɪn, -stin/, **Leon·ard** /ˈlɛnɚd/ (1918–1990) a U.S. musician who wrote CLASSICAL music

Leonard Bernstein

ber·ry /ˈbɛri/ *n. plural* **berries** [C] a small soft fruit with small seeds: *ice cream served with fresh berries*

Ber·ry /ˈbɛri/, **Chuck** /tʃʌk/ (1926–) a U.S. musician and singer who was important in the development of ROCK 'N' ROLL

ber·serk /bɚˈsɚk, -ˈzɚk/ *adj.* **go berserk** to become very angry and violent [**Origin:** 1800–1900 Old Norse *berserkr* **wild fighter**, from *björn* **bear** + *serkr* **shirt**]

berth¹ /bɚθ/ *n.* [C] **1** a place for someone to sleep in a ship or on a train: *an upper berth* **2** a place where a ship can stop and be tied up **3** in sports, an opportunity to take part in a particular tournament or competition: *her first Olympic berth* → see also **give sb/sth a wide berth** at WIDE¹ (8)

berth² *v.* [I,T] to bring a ship into a berth or arrive at a berth

ber·yl /ˈbɛrəl/ *n.* [C] EARTH SCIENCE a valuable stone that is usually green or yellow

be·ryl·li·um /bəˈrɪliəm/ *n.* [U] SYMBOL **Be** CHEMISTRY a hard gray metal that is an ELEMENT. Beryllium is light and strong and is used especially as a building material or mixed with other metals to make ALLOYS.

Ber·ze·li·us /bɚˈziliəs/, **Jöns** /yɑns/ (1779–1848) a Swedish scientist who established the system of ATOMIC weights

be·seech /bɪˈsitʃ/ *v. past tense and past participle* **besought** /bɪˈsɔt/ or **beseeched** [T] LITERARY to eagerly and anxiously ask someone for something: **beseech sb to do sth** *He beseeched the judge to spare him from jail.*

be·set /bɪˈsɛt/ *v.* **beset, besetting** [T] FORMAL **1** [usually passive] to make someone experience serious problems or dangers: **+by/with** *families beset by financial difficulties* **2 besetting sin/weakness** OFTEN HUMOROUS a particular bad feature or habit

be·side /bɪˈsaɪd/ W3 *prep.* **1** next to or very close to someone or something: *Come sit beside me.* | *a cabin* ***right beside*** (=very close to) *the lake* **2** used to compare two people or things: *Our own troubles seem small beside this terrible disaster.* | *She looks huge beside her husband.* **3 be beside the point** to not be directly related to the main subject or problem that you are talking about: *The plot is unrealistic, but that's beside the point – it's just good entertainment.* **4 be beside yourself (with joy/anger/fear etc.)** to feel so much emotion that you find it difficult to control yourself: *I was beside myself with rage.* [**Origin:** Old English *be sidan* **at or to the side**]

be·sides¹ /bɪˈsaɪdz/ S3 W3 *adv.* **1** SPOKEN said when giving another reason for something after one that has just been mentioned: *I wanted to help her out. Besides, I needed the money.* **2** in addition to other things that you have mentioned: *We've bought everything on the list and a few other things besides.*

besides² S2 *prep.* in addition to a point, statement, person etc. that has just been mentioned: *Who's going to be there besides me?* | *Besides swimming twice a week, she walks everywhere.*

be·siege /bɪˈsidʒ/ *v.* [T] **1** [usually passive] if people, thoughts etc. besiege you, you are surrounded by them: **+by** *a movie star besieged by reporters and photographers* **2 be besieged with letters/demands/requests etc.** to receive a very large number of letters, requests etc.: *Her friends were besieged with calls.* **3** to surround a city, building etc. with a military force until the people inside let you take control: *Opposition forces besieged the parliament building.*

be·smirch /bɪˈsmɚtʃ/ *v.* [T] LITERARY **besmirch sb's honor/reputation** to spoil the good opinion that people have of someone [**Origin:** 1600–1700 *smirch* **to make dirty** (15–20 centuries)]

be·sot·ted /bɪˈsɑtɪd/ *adj.* loving someone or wanting something so much that you do not think or behave sensibly: **be besotted with/by** *a father besotted with his new daughter* [**Origin:** 1500–1600 *sot* **to cause to appear stupid** (14–17 centuries), from *sot* **stupid person** (11–18 centuries)]

be·sought /bɪˈsɔt/ *v.* the past tense and past participle of BESEECH

be·speak /bɪˈspik/ *v. past tense* **bespoke** /bɪˈspoʊk/, *past participle* **bespoken** /bɪˈspoʊkən/ [T] LITERARY to be a sign of an attitude or quality: *The crude furniture bespeaks a plain, uncomfortable lifestyle.*

be·spec·ta·cled /bɪˈspɛktɪkəld/ *adj.* wearing glasses

Bes·se·mer pro·cess, the /ˈbɛsəmɚ ˌprɑsɛs/ a successful and effective method for producing steel in large quantities from PIG IRON, invented by Henry Bessemer in 1855

best¹ /bɛst/ S1 W1 *adj.* [the superlative of "good"] **1** better than anything else or anyone else in quality, skill, effectiveness etc.: *Terry is the best player on our team.* | *What's the best way to get to El Paso?* | *Probably the best* *thing to do is to drop me off outside.* | *It's* ***one of the best*** *books I've ever read.* | *It's* ***easily*** *her* ***best*** *work in years.* | *Maui is* ***by far the best*** *base for whale watching.* | *Our pilots have* ***the very best*** *training.* | **be best to do sth** *It's best to have a bike shop check the bearings.* **2 best dress/shoes/clothes etc.** clothing that you only wear on special occasions: *Bobby was wearing his best shirt for the occasion.* **3 best friend** the friend that you know and like better than anyone else **4 best wishes a)** written in cards to say that you hope someone will be happy: **+for/on** *Best wishes for your marriage!* **b)** used to say goodbye at the end of a letter **5 best of all** used to introduce the one fact about a situation that is even better than the other good things: *The diet lets you lose five pounds a week, and best of all, you never feel hungry.* [**Origin:** Old English *betst*] → see also **be on your best behavior** at BEHAVIOR (2), **your best bet** at BET² (3), **the next best thing** at NEXT² (6), **the best/better part of sth** at PART¹ (7)

best² S2 W2 *adv.* [the superlative of "well"] **1** to the greatest degree SYN **most**: *You ask him – you know him best.* | *We liked the pumpkin pie from Gayle's Bakery best.* | **best-known/best-loved** *Country music's best-known singer* **2** in a way that is better than any other: *Try a few different skis to see what works best for you.* | *Our fashions have a look that can best be described as neat yet casual.* | *the best-dressed man in the office* **3 as best you can** SPOKEN as well as you can, even if this is not very good: *I'll deal with the problem as best I can.* **4 had best** FORMAL ought to: *They had best be careful.* **5 for reasons best known to herself/himself** used to say that you cannot understand why someone has done something: *For reasons best known to herself, she decided to quit her job.*

best³ S2 W3 *n.* **1 the best a)** [singular or plural] the person or thing that is better than any other: *The most expensive is not always the best.* | **+of** *Those two are the best of the new young writers.* | **+at** *Who's the best at chess?* **b)** [singular] the most successful, useful etc. situation or result that you can achieve: *All parents* ***want the best for*** *their children.* | *The acoustics in the auditorium* ***weren't the best*** (=were not very good). | *I'm sorry but* ***it's the best I can do*** (=used in order to apologize that something is not better). **2 bring out the best in sb** allow someone to show or use the qualities they have that are good: *a teacher who brings out the best in his students* **3 do the best you can** also **do your best** to try as hard as you can to do something: *I lost, but I feel like I did my best.* | *Doctors* ***did the best they could*** *to stop the bleeding.* **4 at best** used to emphasize that something is not very good by saying that your description of it is the best thing you can say about it: *At best, sales have been good but not great.* | *Public transportation is at best limited.* **5 at your/its best** performing as well or effectively as you are able to: *The music, at its best, is almost unbearably beautiful.* | *Some vegetables are at their best when eaten raw.* **6 make the best of sth** to accept an unsatisfactory situation, and do whatever you can to make it better: *It's not going to be fun, but we might as well make the best of it.* **7 not the best of sth** used in order to say that something is not very good or could be better: *He's not in the best of health.* **8 be for the best** used to say that a particular event may not be as bad as it seems: *Losing your job can be for the best if it forces you to change old habits.* **9 hope for the best** to hope that a bad or difficult situation will end in a way that is good: *We try to help the people who come in, and just hope for the best.* **10 to the best of your knowledge/recollection** used in order to say that you think a statement is true because it is based on what you know or remember: *To the best of my recollection, they never asked us for any money.* **11 to the best of your ability** used in order to say that someone does something as well as they can: *I'm sure she'll do the job to the best of her ability.* **12 the best of both worlds** a situation in which you have the advantages of two different things without any of the disadvantages: *Living in the country but close to the city, we have the best of both worlds.* **13 at the best of times** used in order to say that something is never very good or enjoyable, even when the things are generally good: *Even at the best of times the roads are dangerous.* **14 sb/sth is the best** SPOKEN used in order to say that you like someone or something very much: *Thanks, Dad. You're the best!* **15 Best of luck!** SPOKEN used in order to tell someone you hope they have good luck **16 all the best** used to express good wishes to someone for the future: *Tell him I said goodbye and wish him all the best.* **17 be the best of friends** if two people are the best of friends, they have a very close relationship

best⁴ *v.* [T] FORMAL to defeat someone

bes·tial /ˈbɛstʃəl, ˈbis-/ *adj.* FORMAL behaving like an animal, especially in a cruel way —**bestially** *adv.*

bes·ti·al·i·ty /ˌbɛstʃiˈæləṭi/ *n.* [U] **1** sexual relations between a person and an animal **2** FORMAL very cruel behavior

bes·ti·ar·y /ˈbɛstʃiˌɛri/ *n.* [C] an old book about strange animals, written in the Middle Ages

be·stir /bɪˈstɚ/ *v.* [T] **bestir yourself** FORMAL to start to do things, after relaxing or being lazy

ˌbest ˈman *n.* [singular] the man who stands beside and helps the BRIDEGROOM (=the man getting married) at a wedding ceremony

be·stow /bɪˈstoʊ/ *v.* [T] FORMAL to give someone something of great value or importance: **bestow sth on/upon sb** *The Gold Medal is the highest honor that Congress can bestow on anyone.*

be·stride /bɪˈstraɪd/ *v.* [T] LITERARY to sit or stand on or over something with one leg on each side of it

best·sell·er /ˌbɛstˈsɛlɚ/ *n.* [C] a very popular book which many people buy

ˈbest-ˌselling *adj.* [only before noun, no comparative] **1** a best-selling book, record etc. is one that is very popular and has been bought by a large number of people **2** a best-selling AUTHOR is one who has written a best-selling book

bet¹ /bɛt/ S1 W3 *v. past tense and past participle* **bet**, **betting** **1** [I,T] to risk money on the result of a race, game, competition, or other future event: **bet sth on sb/sth** *Todd bet $50 on the Bears to win.* | **+on** *In Oregon, it's legal to bet on sports games.* | **bet that** *A friend of mine bet that the Sharks would win 16 games this season.* | **bet sb $10/$50 etc. that** *I'll bet you ten bucks that Dan won't be there.* **2 I/I'll bet** SPOKEN **a)** [T] to be fairly sure that something is true, that something will happen etc., although you cannot prove this: *I'll bet that made her mad!* **b)** said to show that you understand or can imagine the situation that someone has just told you about: *"The vacation was great." "I'll bet."* | *"I'm tired." "I bet you are."* **c)** used when you are asking someone to guess something: *I bet you'll never guess who I saw this morning.* **d)** said to show that you do not believe what someone has just told you: *"I was really worried about you." "Yeah, I'll bet."* **3 you bet a)** SPOKEN said to emphasize that you agree with someone or to say that you are definitely going to do something: *"Are you taking the whole family?" "Sure, you bet."* | *Yeah, it helps to have a little more money – you bet it does.* **b)** SPOKEN used as a way of replying to someone when they thank you for something: *"All right, take care, thanks, Daphne." "You bet."* **4 (you) want to bet?** SPOKEN said when you disagree with someone and want to prove that you are right: *"You can't keep a secret." "Want to bet? I promise – I won't tell a soul."* **5 you can bet (your life) that** INFORMAL also **you can bet your bottom dollar that** used when you are sure that you know what someone will do or what will happen: *You can bet your life that she'll be late.* **6 bet the ranch/farm** INFORMAL to risk everything that you own: *Do we really want to bet the ranch on this deal?* → see also BETCHA, GAMBLE

bet on sth *phr. v.* **1** to hope and expect that something will happen: *Many experts are betting on a quick economic recovery.* **2 don't bet on it** SPOKEN also **I wouldn't bet on it** used to say that you do not think something is true or will happen: *Maybe he's really a nice guy, but I wouldn't bet on it.*

bet² S3 *n.* **1** [C] an agreement to risk money on the result of a race, game, competition etc.: *We **had a bet**, and he lost.* | +**on** *I had a bet on the Super Bowl.* | *People stood in line to **place a bet*** (=choose a horse, team etc. and bet on it). | **win/lose a bet** *If he scores now, I lose my bet.* **2** [C] money that you risk on a bet: *a $50 bet* **3 your best bet** SPOKEN said when giving someone advice about the best thing to do: *Your best bet would be to go back to Highway 218 and head north.* **4 a good/safe bet** an action, situation, or thing that is likely to have the effect or produce the results you want: *The earrings seemed like a good bet for a birthday present.* **5 it's a safe/sure bet (that)** SPOKEN used to say that something seems almost certain: *It's a pretty safe bet that the Wilsons will be at that party.* **6 my/your/his etc. bet is (that)** SPOKEN used when saying what you expect to happen in the future: *My bet is that he'll win the election easily.*

be·ta /ˈbeɪt̬ə/ *n.* [singular] the second letter of the Greek alphabet, or B

ˈbeta-ˌblocker *n.* [C] MEDICINE a drug that makes the heart beat more slowly, which is sometimes used to try and stop someone from having a HEART ATTACK

be·take /bɪˈteɪk/ *v. past tense* **betook** /bɪˈtʊk/, *past participle* **betaken** /bɪˈteɪkən/ **betake yourself to sth** LITERARY to go somewhere

ˈbeta ˌparticle *n.* [C] PHYSICS an ELECTRON given off by the NUCLEUS (=central part) of an atom when a NEUTRON breaks into a PROTON and an electron

ˈbeta ˌversion *n.* [C] COMPUTERS a new piece of SOFTWARE that is not ready to be sold because it may still contain some problems or small mistakes → see also ALPHA VERSION

bet·cha /ˈbɛtʃə/ SPOKEN, NONSTANDARD **1** a short way of saying of "I bet you": *Betcha I can run faster than you.* **2 you betcha** said when what someone has just said is correct: *"So you're going to be there tonight." "You betcha."*

be·tel /ˈbit̬l/ *n.* [U] an Asian plant, the leaves of which are chewed as a STIMULANT

ˈbetel nut *n.* [C] the seed of the betel plant that is wrapped in its leaves and chewed

bête noire /ˌbɛt ˈnwɑr/ *n.* [singular] LITERARY the person or thing that you dislike most

be·think /bɪˈθɪŋk/ *v. past tense and past participle* **bethought** /bɪˈθɔt/ OLD USE [T] to remember something or think about something

Beth·le·hem /ˈbɛθlɪˌhɛm, -həm/ a town on the West Bank of the River Jordan, near Jerusalem, thought to be where Jesus Christ was born

Be·thune /bəˈθun/**, Ma·ry Mc·Leod** /ˈmɛri məˈklaʊd/ (1875–1955) an African-American educator who started a college for African-American women and was an adviser to President Franklin D. Roosevelt

be·tide /bɪˈtaɪd/ *v.* → see **woe betide sb** at WOE (4)

be·times /bɪˈtaɪmz/ *adv.* OLD USE early or soon

be·to·ken /bɪˈtoʊkən/ *v.* [T] LITERARY to be a sign of something

be·tray /bɪˈtreɪ/ *v.* **betrays, betrayed, betraying** [T] **1** to be disloyal to someone who trusts you, so that you upset or hurt them: *Conservatives felt betrayed by the President's actions.* | *I trusted you with my money, and you **betrayed** that **trust**.* | **betray a confidence/secret** (=to tell a secret that someone trusted you not to tell) **2** to be disloyal to your country, especially by giving secret information to its enemies: *He was willing to betray his country for money.* **3** [not in progressive or passive] to reveal the truth or reveal sb's true feelings, especially when sb is trying to hide this SYN **reveal**: *If he felt any sadness, his voice didn't betray it.* | *His comments betrayed a deep ignorance of German history.* **4 betray your beliefs/principles/ideals etc.** to stop supporting your old beliefs and principles, especially in order to get power or avoid trouble [**Origin:** 1200–1300 *tray* **to betray** (13–16 centuries), from Latin *tradere* **hand over, deliver, betray**] —**betrayer** *n.* [C]

be·tray·al /bɪˈtreɪəl/ *n.* [C,U] an act of betraying your country, a friend, or someone who trusts you: *The policy is a betrayal of American principles.*

be·troth·al /bɪˈtroʊðəl/ *n.* [C] OLD USE an agreement that two people will be married SYN **engagement**

be·trothed¹ /bɪˈtroʊðd/ *adj.* OLD USE **be betrothed to sb** to have promised to marry someone —**betroth** *v.* [T]

betrothed² *n.* [singular] **sb's betrothed** the person that someone has agreed to marry

bet·ter¹ /ˈbɛt̬ɚ/ S1 W1 *adj.* [the comparative of "good"] **1** more satisfactory, more suitable, or of a higher standard OPP **worse**: *She bought a better car.* | *This one's better – try it.* | *You'll get a better deal online.* | *The team always **gets better** (=improves) as the season goes on.* | *A live performance is often **better than** a recording.* | **much better/far better/a lot better** *The restaurant across the street has much better food.* | *The more expensive shoes weren't a lot better than the cheaper ones.* | *The movie was boring, but **it was better than** sitting at home all evening.* **2** [the comparative of "well"] **a)** more healthy or less sick or painful than before OPP **worse**: *She's a little better than she was yesterday.* | *Do you **feel** any **better** than you did this morning?* | *You should exercise more – you'll **feel better for** (=feel better as a result of) it.* **b)** completely well again after being sick or injured: *I don't think you should go swimming until you're better.* | *I hope you **get better** (=become well again) soon.* ►see THESAURUS box at **healthy** **3 the sooner/bigger/later etc. the better** used to emphasize that you would prefer something to happen as soon as possible, be as big as possible etc.: *He needs counseling, and the sooner the better.* **4 the more-...the better** used to say that something is improved if something else happens a lot: *The more liquid you can squeeze out, the better.* **5 the less...the better** used to say that something is improved if something else does not happen very much: *The less a wine is handled, the better.* **6 so much the better** used to say that something would be even better or bring even more advantages: *If it makes illegal drug use even more difficult, so much the better.* **7 the better** used to mean the one that is better when you are comparing two similar people or things: +**of** *I don't particularly like him, but he's the better of the two candidates.* **8 be all the better for sb/sth** SPOKEN to be improved by a particular action, change etc.: *If we put more drug dealers in jail, all the better for the people of this state.*

SPOKEN PHRASES

9 that's better a) used to praise or encourage someone: *Straighten your arm when you hit the ball. That's better!* **b)** used when you are trying to make someone feel less upset: *Come on, give me a hug. There, that's better, isn't it?* **10 be better (to do sth)** used in order to give advice: *It's better if she doesn't stand for too long.* | *It'd be better to eat a good breakfast.* **11 is that better?** used in order to ask someone if they are happier with something after you have changed it: *Try it with more sugar. Is that better?* **12 better than nothing** used in order to say that something is not very good, but it is better than having or doing nothing: *Only two days at Disneyworld just isn't enough, but it's better than nothing.* **13 better luck next time** used to encourage someone who has done badly in a test, competition etc. **14 there's nothing better** used to say that something is perfect: *There's nothing better than reading a good book on a rainy day.*

15 have seen better days INFORMAL to be in a bad condition or to not be as skillful at something as you were in past times: *Our car has certainly seen better days.* **16 better still** used to say that something is even better than the first thing you mentioned: *She's someone who says what she means and, better still, does what she says she'll do.* **17 against your better judgment** if you do something against your better judgment, you do it even though you think it may not be sensible: *She asked if she could go, and Max, against his better judgment, said yes.* **18 be no better than**

sth to be almost as bad as something else: *The stock market is no better than a casino.* **19 better the devil you know (than the devil you don't)** it is better to deal with someone or something you know, even if you do not like them, than to deal with someone or something new that might be worse **20 sb's better nature** the part of someone's character that makes them want to be kind and generous, treat people well etc. [**Origin:** Old English *betera*] → see also **your better/other half** at HALF² (8), **best/better part of sth** at PART¹ (7)

better² S1 W1 *adv.* [the comparative of "well"] **1** to a higher degree SYN **more**: *I liked his last movie better.* | *Vidal is* ***better known*** *as a novelist.* | *Mel knows the area a lot* ***better than*** *I do.* **2** at a higher standard or quality than before OPP **worse**: *She looks* ***better than*** *she did in high school.* | *The car is running much better since I put in new spark plugs.* | *Hospitals are much better equipped now.* **3 do better** to perform better or reach a higher standard: *Some roses do better in different types of soil.* | *We did better than we expected.* **4 sb had better (do sth)** also **sb better (do sth)** SPOKEN, NONSTANDARD **a)** used to say what you or someone else should do: *"I'll call Randy right now." "Yeah, you'd better."* | *If a politician wants to be successful, he or she had better know how to use television.* | *Better wash your hands – it's dinnertime.* **b)** used to threaten someone: *You better shut up!* | *They'd* ***better not*** *be upstairs watching TV when I told them not to.* **5 go one better** INFORMAL to do something even more successfully than before, or more successfully than someone else who does it well: *The next year, he went one better and won the gold medal.* → see also BETTER OFF, **better late than never** at LATE² (7), **better safe than sorry** at SAFE¹ (8)

better³ S3 *n.* **1 get the better of sb a)** if your feelings or wishes get the better of you, you do not control them when you should: *Kramer's temper sometimes gets the better of him.* **b)** to defeat someone or make them fail: *Don't let stress get the better of you.* **2 for the better** in a way that improves the situation: *Anything they can do to improve children's health is for the better.* | *Smaller classes are definitely* ***a change for the better***. | *The relationship between the two countries has recently* ***taken a turn for the better***. (=improved) **3 for better or (for) worse a)** used to say that something must be accepted, whether the results will be good or bad, because it cannot be changed: *For better or for worse, this is a time of rapid change.* **b)** a phrase sometimes used in marriage ceremonies, in which people promise to stay together even in difficult times: *For better or for worse doesn't seem to mean much anymore.* **4** [C] another spelling of BETTOR **5 your betters** [plural] OLD-FASHIONED people who are more important than you or deserve more respect → see also WORSE

better⁴ *v.* [T] **1** to achieve a higher quality, amount, or standard than someone or something else: *His world record time is unlikely to be bettered for many years.* **2 better yourself** to improve your position in society by getting a better education or earning more money **3** FORMAL to improve something: *new laws aimed at bettering economic conditions*

ˌBetter ˈBusiness ˌBureau, the an organization for businesses and their customers, which helps customers who believe they have been treated unfairly by a company or have bought a bad product

bet·ter·ment /ˈbɛt̬ɚmənt/ *n.* [singular] FORMAL improvement, especially in someone's social and economic position

ˌbetter ˈoff *adj.* [no comparative] **1** richer than you were before → see also WELL-OFF: *Are you better off than you were four years ago?* **2** happier, improved, more successful etc.: *You're better off without him.* | **sb would be better off if** *We'd be better off if there were more women in government.* | **sb would be better off doing sth** *He'd be better off getting a job with his father.*

bet·tor, better /ˈbɛt̬ɚ/ *n.* [C] someone who bets on a game, sports event etc. SYN **gambler**

be·tween¹ /bɪˈtwin/ S1 W1 *prep.* **1** also **in between** in or into the space that separates two things or people: *the door between my room and Laura's room* | *I had corn stuck between my teeth.* | *Put a piece of waxed paper in between each layer.* | *a small town* ***halfway between*** *New York and Philadelphia* **2** also **in between** in the time that separates two events: *Are you taking any time off between now and Thanksgiving?* | *You can barely get to your locker in between classes.* **3** used to show a range of amounts, numbers, distances etc. often for when you cannot give an exact amount, number etc.: *She'll be here between seven and eight.* | *The project will cost between 10 and 12 million dollars.* **4** used to show the fact that something is divided or shared among two or more people, places, or things: *We had about two loads of laundry between us.* | *Linda and Dave split a milkshake between them.* | *Between the two of us, we used up all the stamps.* | **between doing sth** *Students alternated between writing notes and reading.* **5** used to show the relationship between two situations, things, people etc.: *Trade relations between the countries have improved.* | *What's* ***the difference between*** *the two computers?* (=How are they different?) **6** used to show a connection between two places: *We have eight flights daily between New York and Boston.* | *the highway between Fresno and Visalia* **7** SPOKEN used when it is difficult to give an exact description of something, or a name to something, so that you have to compare it to two things that are similar to it: *It tastes like* ***a cross between*** (=something that combines) *an apple and a pear.* | **something/somewhere between** *The sound was something between a scream and a roar.* **8 between you and me** SPOKEN said before telling someone something that you do not want them to tell anyone else: *Between you and me, I don't think she can do it.* **9 come between you/them etc.** if something comes between two people, it causes an argument or problems between them: *I hope you don't let money come between you.* [**Origin:** Old English *betweonum*]

WORD CHOICE between, among

- **Between** is usually used to talk about two people, things, or groups which are thought of separately or one after another: *a sense of cooperation between the two countries* | *We need to establish better communication between the sales and customer service departments* (NOT *among*). | *I had a piece of meat stuck between my teeth.*
- **Among** is used to talk about a group of three or more people or things together, especially using nouns that name groups: *Negotiations could reduce tensions among the nations involved.* | *Garcia's estate was divided equally among his four daughters.* | *I found this letter among Julia's papers* (*between the papers* would suggest that there were only two papers).

between² S3 *adv.* also **in between** **1** in or into the space that separates two things or people, or in the time that separates two events: *two yards with a fence between* | *We worked both weekends and all the time we had in between.* **2** greater than one extreme but less than another: **somewhere/something in between** *We're not the richest or the poorest. We're somewhere in between.* | **everyone/everything in between** *the young, the old and everyone in between*

be·twixt /bɪˈtwɪkst/ *prep.* **1** POETIC OR OLD USE between **2 betwixt and between** OLD-FASHIONED not completely belonging to one group or to another

bev·el /ˈbɛvəl/ *n.* [C] **1** a sloping edge or surface, usually along the edge of a piece of wood or glass **2** a tool for making this kind of edge or surface

bev·eled /ˈbɛvəld/ *adj.* with a sloping edge: *a mirror with beveled edges*

bev·er·age /ˈbɛvərɪdʒ/ *n.* [C] FORMAL a hot or cold drink: *alcoholic beverages* [**Origin:** 1300–1400 Old French *bevrage*, from *beivre* **to drink**, from Latin *bibere*]

bevy /ˈbɛvi/ *n. plural* **bevies** [C] a large group of people of the same type, especially girls or young women: **+of** *a bevy of teenagers*

be·wail /bɪˈweɪl/ *v.* [T] FORMAL to complain strongly and express sadness or disappointment about something

B

be·ware /bɪ'wɛr/ *v.* [I,T only in imperative and infinitive] used to warn someone to be careful because something is dangerous: +**of** *Beware of the dog!* | *The department warned consumers to beware.* [**Origin:** 1200–1300 *be* + *ware* **careful** (11–19 centuries) from Old English *wær*]

be·wigged /bɪ'wɪgd/ *adj.* FORMAL wearing a WIG

be·wil·der /bɪ'wɪldɚ/ *v.* [T] to confuse someone [**Origin:** 1600–1700 *wilder* **to lead the wrong way, confuse**]

be·wil·dered /bɪ'wɪldɚd/ *adj.* totally confused: *The kids seemed bewildered and scared after the accident.*

be·wil·der·ing /bɪ'wɪldərɪŋ/ *adj.* confusing, especially because there are too many choices or things happening at the same time: *a bewildering number of options*

be·wil·der·ment /bɪ'wɪldɚmənt/ *n.* [U] a feeling of being very confused

be·witch /bɪ'wɪtʃ/ *v.* [T] **1** to make someone extremely interested in or attracted to someone or something: *She was completely bewitched by the young trumpet player.* **2** to control someone with a magic SPELL —**bewitching** *adj.*: *a bewitching smile* —**bewitched** *adj.*

be·yond¹ /bɪ'yɑnd/ S2 W1 *prep.* **1** on or to the farther side of something: *The park is a couple of streets beyond the school.* **2** too difficult for someone to do or understand: *I liked science, but physics was completely beyond me.* | **beyond sb's abilities/capabilities** *Is the job beyond his capabilities?* **3** outside the range or limits of something: *That topic is beyond the scope of this discussion.* | *The events were* ***beyond*** *the committee's* ***control.*** | *Her efforts go way* ***beyond the call of duty.*** (=She has worked much harder than she was asked to) **4 beyond belief/doubt/recognition etc.** used to say that you cannot believe something, doubt something etc.: *In just six years, the town had changed beyond all recognition.* | *The car has been damaged beyond repair.* **5** more or greater than a particular amount, level, or limit: *The rate of inflation has risen beyond 5%.* | *Nobody wants to work beyond retirement age.* **6** later than a particular time, date etc.: *The ban on hunting these animals has been extended beyond 2001.* **7 it is beyond me why/what etc.** SPOKEN used to say that something seems completely stupid and you cannot understand the reason for it: *It's beyond me why they ever got married at all.* **8** used like "except" in negative sentences: *Santa Fe doesn't have much industry beyond tourism.* | *I can't tell you anything beyond what you know already.* [**Origin:** Old English *begeondan*, from *geondan* **beyond**]

beyond² *adv.* **1** on or to the farther side of something: *a view from the mountains with the plains beyond* | *A few yards beyond, some children were playing.* **2** later than a particular time, date etc.: *We're planning for the new year and beyond.*

beyond³ *n.* **the beyond** LITERARY whatever comes after this life

Bhu·tan /bu'tɑn, bu'tæn/ a country in the Himalayas, between India and China —**Bhutanese** /ˌbutˀn'iz◂, -'is◂/ *n., adj.*

bi- /baɪ/ *prefix* two SYN **twice**: *bilingual* (=speaking two languages) | *a biannual meeting* (=happening twice a year) → see also DI-, SEMI-, TRI-

BIA /ˌbi aɪ 'eɪ/ → see BUREAU OF INDIAN AFFAIRS, THE

bi·an·nu·al /baɪ'ænyuəl/ *adj.* happening twice each year → see also ANNUAL, BIENNIAL: *a biannual report*

bi·as¹ /'baɪəs/ Ac *n.* **1** [singular, U] DISAPPROVING an attitude that shows more support for one group, person, or belief than others, in a situation where fairness to all people and balanced treatment of all beliefs is important: +**against** *the newspaper's bias against women* | +**toward/in favor of** *The managment has shown a bias in favor of younger employees.* | **left-wing/right-wing/liberal etc. bias** *Conservatives say the press has a liberal bias.* (=shows too much support for liberal views) | **political/gender/racial etc. bias** (=a bias that shows someone prefers one political way of thinking, one group of people etc.) **2** [singular] a natural skill or interest in one particular area: *a strong artistic bias* **3 on the bias** in a DIAGONAL direction: *cloth cut on the bias*

bias² Ac *v.* [T] to unfairly influence attitudes, choices, or decisions

bi·ased /'baɪəst/ Ac *adj.* **1** DISAPPROVING unfairly showing support or preference for one person or group over another OPP **unbiased**: *Is your financial advisor giving you biased advice?* | *racially biased reporting* | +**against** *Jurors may be biased against the defendant because he comes from out of state.* | +**toward/in favor of** *The news reports were* ***heavily biased*** (=very biased) *toward the government.* **2** more interested in a particular thing than in another: +**toward** *The reading list is biased toward 19th century literature.*

'bias tape *n.* [U] cloth in the form of a narrow band, used when sewing edges

bi·ath·lon /baɪ'æθlɑn, -lən/ *n.* [C] a sports competition in which competitors SKI across country and then shoot a RIFLE —**biathlete** /baɪ'æθlit/ *n.* [C] → see also DECATHLON

bib /bɪb/ *n.* [C] **1** a piece of cloth or plastic tied under a baby's chin to keep food from falling on his or her clothes **2** the upper part of an APRON or pair of OVERALLS that is above the waist

bi·ble, Bible /'baɪbəl/ *n.* **1 the Bible** the holy book of the Christian religion, consisting of the OLD TESTAMENT and the NEW TESTAMENT **2** [C] a copy of the Bible **3** [singular] INFORMAL the most useful and important book on a particular subject: *the computer programmer's bible* [**Origin:** 1300–1400 Old French, Medieval Latin *biblia*, from Greek, plural of *biblion* **book**]

'Bible Belt, the an area in the south of the U.S. known for its very religious Christian people, who follow the teachings of the Bible very strictly

'Bible ˌthumper *n.* [C] DISAPPROVING someone who tries hard to make other people share their Christian beliefs by always talking about the Bible —**Bible-thumping** *adj.* [only before noun]

bib·li·cal, Biblical /'bɪblɪkəl/ *adj.* relating to the Bible

biblio- /bɪblioʊ, -liə/ *prefix* relating to books: *a bibliophile* (=someone who likes books)

bib·li·og·ra·phy /ˌbɪbli'ɑgrəfi/ *n. plural* **bibliographies** [C] **1** a list of all the books and articles used in preparing a piece of writing **2** a list of everything that has been written about a particular subject —**bibliographer** *n.* [C]

bib·li·o·phile /'bɪbliəˌfaɪl/ *n.* [C] FORMAL someone who likes books

bib·u·lous /'bɪbyələs/ *adj.* HUMOROUS or FORMAL liking to drink too much alcohol

bi·cam·er·al /baɪ'kæmərəl/ *adj.* [only before noun] POLITICS a bicameral LEGISLATURE (=part of the government that makes laws) consists of two parts, such as the Senate and the House of Representatives in the U.S. Congress → see also UNICAMERAL

bi·car·bon·ate of so·da /baɪˌkɑrbənɪt əv 'soʊdə/ also **bicarbonate** *n.* [U] TECHNICAL → see BAKING SODA

bi·cen·ten·ni·al /ˌbaɪsɛn'tɛniəl/ *n.* [C] the day or year exactly 200 years after an important event: *the bicentennial of the Declaration of Independence*

bi·cep /'baɪsɛp/ *n.* [C usually plural] BIOLOGY the large muscle on the front of your upper arm [**Origin:** 1600–1700 Modern Latin *biceps*, from Latin, **two-headed**, from *caput* **head**; because it is attached in two places]

bick·er /'bɪkɚ/ *v.* [I] to argue, especially about something very unimportant: *Stop bickering!* | +**about/over** *The kids were bickering about who would sleep in the top bunk.* [**Origin:** 1200–1300 Middle Dutch *bicken* **to attack**] —**bickering** *n.* [U]

bi·con·di·tion·al /ˌbaɪkən'dɪʃənəl/ *n.* [C] MATH a statement expressing two mathematical facts, one of which can only be true if the other one is true. It always contains the phrase "If and only if..." or the sign ↔. —**biconditional** *adj.*: *a biconditional proposition*

bi·cus·pid valve /baɪˈkʌspɪd ˌvælv/ *n* [C] BIOLOGY a small part on your heart between the left ATRIUM and the left VENTRICLE. It opens and closes to allow blood to flow from the atrium into the ventricle, and to prevent blood from flowing back into the atrium. → see picture at HEART

bi·cy·cle¹ /ˈbaɪsɪkəl/ S3 *n.* [C] a vehicle with two wheels that you sit on and make move by pushing its PEDALS with your feet SYN **bike**: *I was six when I learned to **ride a bicycle**.* [**Origin:** 1800–1900 French *bi-* + *-cycle* (as in *tricycle*)]

bicycle² *v.* [I always + adv./prep.] FORMAL to go somewhere on a bicycle SYN **ride** —**bicyclist** *n.* [C] —**bicycling** *n.* [U]

bid¹ /bɪd/ W3 *n.* [C] **1** an offer to do work or provide services for a specific price: **+for/on** *the lowest bid for the bridge-building project* **2** an attempt to achieve or obtain something: **+for** *Wilson's successful bid for the senate* | **bid to do sth** *a desperate bid to escape* **3** an offer to pay a particular price for something, especially at an AUCTION: **+for** *Walter **made a bid** for the painting.* **4** a statement of how many points you hope to win in a card game

bid² *v. past tense and past participle* **bid**, **bidding** **1** [I] to offer to do work or provide services for a specific price, in competition with other offers: **+for/on** *Four companies were invited to bid for the contract.* **2** [I,T] to offer to pay a particular price for goods, especially in an AUCTION: **bid (sb) sth for** *Jill bid $20,000 for an antique desk.* | **bid against sb** *The two men ended up bidding against each other* **3** [I,T] to say how many points you think you will win in a game of cards —**bidder** *n.* [C]

bid³ *v. past tense* **bade** /bæd, beɪd/ or **bid**, *past participle* **bid** or **bidden** /ˈbɪdn/, **bidding** OLD USE OR LITERARY **1 bid sb good afternoon/good morning etc.** to say good morning, good afternoon etc. to someone **2** [T] to order or tell someone what to do: **bid sb (to) do sth** *The queen bade us to enter.* **3 bid fair to do sth** to seem likely to do something

bid·ding /ˈbɪdɪŋ/ *n.* [U] **1** the activity of offering to do work or providing services for someone at a particular price: *The contract will be renewed with no bidding.* **2** the activity of bidding for goods, especially in an AUCTION: *The bidding was brisk and sales went well.* **3 do sb's bidding** LITERARY to obey someone's requests or orders **4 at sb's bidding** FORMAL because someone has told you to

bide /baɪd/ *v.* **1 bide your time** to wait until the right moment to do something: *Investors are biding their time, waiting for prices to drop.* **2** [I] OLD USE to wait or stay somewhere, often for a long time

bi·det /bɪˈdeɪ/ *n.* [C] a small low bathtub that you sit on to wash the lower part of your body [**Origin:** 1600–1700 French **small horse, bidet**]

bi·en·ni·al /baɪˈɛniəl/ *adj.* **1** a biennial event happens once every two years → see also ANNUAL, BIANNUAL **2** BIOLOGY a biennial plant lives for two years and produces its flowers and seeds in the second year → see also ANNUAL, PERENNIAL —**biennally** *adv.*

bier /bɪr/ *n.* [C] a frame like a table on which a dead body or COFFIN is placed

biff /bɪf/ *v.* [T] INFORMAL to hit someone hard with your FIST —**biff** *n.* [C]

bi·fo·cals /ˈbaɪˌfoʊkəlz, baɪˈfoʊkəlz/ *n.* [plural] special glasses with an upper part made for seeing things that are far away, and a lower part made for reading —**bifocal** *adj.*

bi·fur·cate /ˈbaɪfɚˌkeɪt/ *v.* [I] FORMAL if a road, river

bicycle

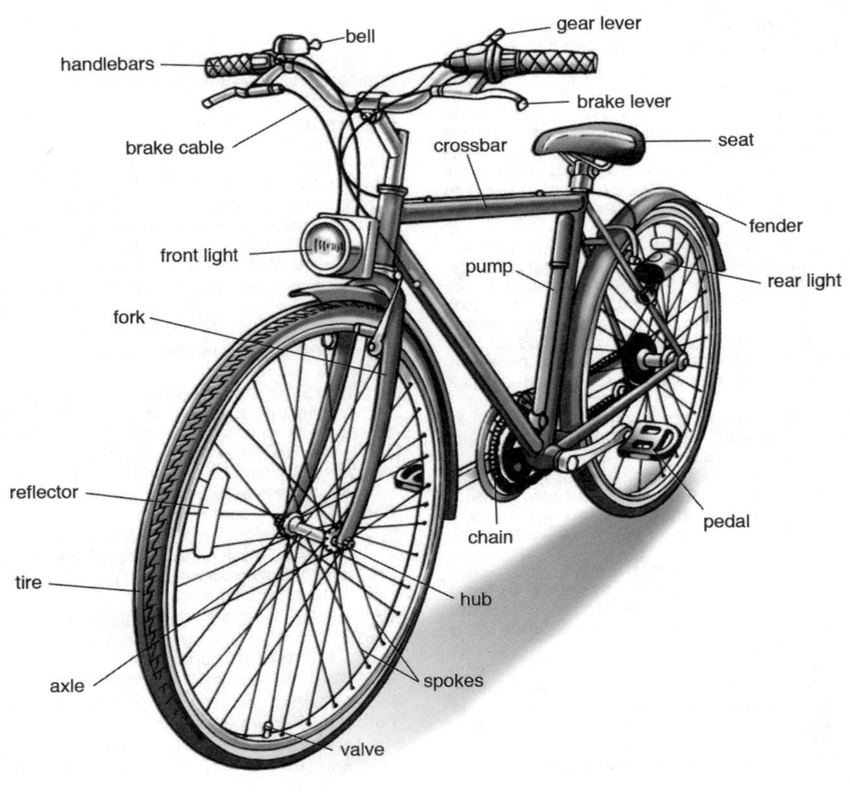

etc. bifurcates, it divides into two separate parts —**bifurcation** /ˌbaɪfɚˈkeɪʃən/ *n.* [C,U]

big /bɪɡ/ S1 W1 *adj. comparative* **bigger**, *superlative* **biggest**

B

1 SIZE a) of more than average size, amount, weight etc.: *a big tree* | *These jeans are too big.* | *The game works better if you have a bigger group.* | *a big difference in price* | *She's a cute baby with a big smile.* | *That boy* ***gets bigger*** *every time I see him.* | *Josie gave me a* ***great big*** (=very big) *hug.* **b)** used to show the size of something: ***How big*** *a piece of cake do you want?* | *It's about* ***as big as*** *a dime.* | *The bed is only* ***big enough*** *for one person.*

THESAURUS

large big or bigger than usual in physical size or amount: *the largest city in America* | *a large amount of money*
great used mainly to describe non-physical things or the degree of something: *a great advantage* | *He achieved great success.*
huge/enormous extremely big: *He died owing a huge sum of money.* | *an enormous tree*
vast extremely big: *The changes will affect vast numbers of people.*
gigantic extremely big or tall: *gigantic waves*
massive very big, solid, and heavy, or very large in amount: *a massive new office building* | *a massive increase in drug use*
immense extremely large or great: *We still have an immense amount of work to do.*
colossal very large: *The show was a colossal hit.*
substantial large in number or amount: *He earns a substantial amount of money.*
Big and **large** mean the same thing, but **large** is slightly more formal: *That's a big piece of cake!* | *It's the largest hotel in the city.*
Use **large**, not **big**, to describe amounts: *They have borrowed a large amount of money.*
Use **big**, not **large**, to describe something that is important: *a big opportunity* | *That's the big question.*

▸see THESAURUS box at **fat**[1]

2 IMPORTANT important or serious: *The big game is on Friday.* | *There will be some big changes in the way we work.* | *When is* ***the big day*** (=a day when an important event will happen)*?* | *There's* ***a big difference*** *between understanding something and explaining it to others.* → see also BIG CHEESE, BIG NAME, BIG SHOT, BIG TIME[1]

3 POPULAR/SUCCESSFUL INFORMAL successful or popular, especially in business or entertainment: *one of Hollywood's biggest stars* | **+in** *Microsoft is very big in the software business.* | *Cheerleading is big in Texas because football is big.* | *Can he* ***make it big*** (=become very successful) *in the NFL?* | *Small companies can still play with* ***the big boys*** (=the most powerful people or companies) *in the computer market.* ▸see THESAURUS box at **popular**

4 COMPANY a big company, organization, group etc. has a lot of people working for it: *one of the biggest companies in the insurance business*

5 MONEY involving or representing a lot of money: *She wrote us a big check.* | *These are the guys who get paid the big salaries.* | **big money/bucks** INFORMAL: *In 1979, Shearer moved to California "to make big bucks in the electronics industry."*

6 OLDER INFORMAL **a) big sister/brother** your older sister or brother: *My big sister goes to school.* **b)** used especially by children or when speaking to children to mean older: *The big kids won't let us play.* | *Sit up like a big girl and eat your dinner.*

7 LARGE DEGREE [only before noun] INFORMAL doing something to a very large degree: **big eater/drinker/gambler etc.** *Sandra is used to serving a family of big eaters.* | **a big fan/admirer** *I've never been a big jazz fan.* | *I'm a big admirer of your work.* | *When they lose, they lose* ***in a big way.*** (=used to emphasize that they lose badly)

8 BAD [only before noun] used to emphasize how bad something is: *It was a big mistake to invite Tom.* | *It's a simple repair that can prevent a big problem later.*

9 WITH ENERGY done with great energy and enthusiasm: *Let's* ***give a big hand to*** *the band!* (=hit your hands together with a lot of enthusiasm) | **a big hug/kiss** *He gave me a big kiss, right on the lips.*

SPOKEN PHRASES

10 be big on sth SPOKEN to like doing something very much or to be very interested in it: *I'm not big on foreign cars.*
11 what's the big idea? used when someone has done something annoying, especially when you want them to explain why they did it: *Hey, what's the big idea? Who said you could borrow my car?*
12 big mouth used in some expressions to mean that someone cannot keep a secret: *That girl* ***has a big mouth.*** | *I'm sorry. I shouldn't have* ***opened my big mouth.*** | **me and my big mouth** (=said when you wish you had not told someone a secret)
13 it is big of sb to do sth used to say that someone was very kind or generous to do something: *I think it was really big of Larry to admit he was wrong.*

14 have big ideas/plans to have impressive plans for the future: *Waller has big plans for her retirement.*

15 LETTERS INFORMAL a big letter is written in CAPITALS, for example G, R, A etc.

16 WORDS INFORMAL big words are long or unusual and are difficult to read or understand

17 have/carry/wield a big stick INFORMAL to threaten to use your power to get what you want

18 be/get too big for your boots INFORMAL to be too proud of yourself

19 the big enchilada HUMOROUS the most important person or thing in an organization or the most important part of a particular subject: *The big enchilada is the U.S. Supreme Court, and we're going to win our case there.* —**bigness** *n.* [U] → see also BIG DEAL, **think big** at THINK (16)

big·a·my /ˈbɪɡəmi/ *n.* [U] the crime of being married to two people at the same time —**bigamist** *n.* [C] —**bigamous** *adj.* → see also MONOGAMY, POLYGAMY

ˌBig ˈApple *n.* INFORMAL **the Big Apple** a name for New York City

ˌbig ˈband *n.* [C] a large musical band that plays JAZZ or dance music and has a leader who plays SOLOS. Big bands were especially popular in the 1940s and 1950s.: *Tommy Dorsey's big band* —**big-band** *adj.*

ˌBig ˈBang ˌtheory *n.* **the Big Bang theory** the idea that the universe began with a single large explosion (the "Big Bang"), and that the pieces are still flying apart → see also STEADY-STATE THEORY

ˈBig Board *n.* **the Big Board** the list of all the SHARE prices on the New York Stock Exchange: *Consolidated Aircraft's stock rose 50 cents to $12.625 on the Big Board.*

ˌbig-ˈboned *adj.* a big-boned person is large without being fat

ˌbig ˈbrother, Big Brother *n.* [singular, not with "the"] any person, organization, or system that seems to want to control people's lives and restrict their freedom: *With cameras on every street, it's like big brother is watching.* [**Origin:** 1900–2000 *Big Brother* powerful ruler who controlled everything in the book Nineteen Eighty-Four (1949) by George Orwell]

ˌBig ˈBrothers an organization that helps boys, especially boys who have family problems, by giving each boy someone who meets him regularly to give advice, listen to his problems etc.

ˌbig ˈbusiness *n.* [U] **1** very large companies, considered as a powerful group with a lot of influence **2** a product or type of activity that people spend a lot of money on: *Selling music to teenagers is big business.*

ˌbig ˈcat *n.* [C] NOT TECHNICAL a large animal of the cat family, such as a lion or tiger

ˌbig ˈcheese *n.* [C] INFORMAL, HUMOROUS an important and powerful person in an organization: *one of the big cheeses from NASA*

ˌbig ˈdeal S2 *n.* [singular] SPOKEN **1** said when you do not think something is as important as someone else thinks it is: *Anyway, he gave me a raise of 50 cents an hour. I mean, big deal.* | ***What's the big deal?*** *It's only a birthday, not the end of the world.* **2 no big deal a)** said in order to show that you are not upset or angry about something: *It's no big deal. Everybody forgets things sometimes.* **b)** said in order to show that something is not important: *The kids won't get as many presents this year, but that's no big deal.* **3** an important or exciting event or situation: *This audition is a big deal for Joey.* **4 make a big deal about/over sth** also **make a big deal out of sth** to get too excited or upset about something, or make something seem more important than it is: *I'm probably making a big deal out of nothing, but I'm worried about you.*

ˌBig ˈDipper *n.* **the Big Dipper** a group of seven bright stars in the shape of a bowl with a handle, seen only from northern parts of the world

Big·foot /ˈbɪgfʊt/ also **Sasquatch** an animal like a large hairy human, which some people claim to have seen in the northwest U.S., but which has never been proved to exist

ˌbig ˈgame *n.* [U] large wild animals, such as lions and ELEPHANTS, hunted as a sport: *a big game hunter*

big·gie /ˈbɪgi/ *n.* [C] **1** INFORMAL something very large, important, or successful: *The latest Disney movie is a biggie.* **2 no biggie** SPOKEN said when something is not important, or when you are not upset or angry about something: *"Oh, I'm sorry." "That's okay, no biggie."*

ˌbig ˈgovernment *n.* [U] DISAPPROVING POLITICS the behavior of government when people think it is controlling their lives too much: *We believe that big government is threatening American values.* **—big-government** *adj.* [only before noun]

ˌbig ˈgun *n.* [C] INFORMAL a person or company that has a lot of power or influence: *the big guns of the computing world such as IBM and Microsoft*

big·head·ed /ˈbɪgˌhɛdɪd/ *adj.* INFORMAL someone who is bigheaded thinks they are very important, smart etc.

ˈbig-ˌhearted *adj.* very kind and generous: *Larry's a big-hearted guy.*

Big·horn Moun·tains, the /ˈbɪghɔrn ˌmaʊntˀnz/ a RANGE of mountains in the northwestern U.S. that is part of the Rocky Mountains and is in the states of Wyoming and Montana

big·horn sheep /ˌbɪghɔrn ˈʃip/ *n.* [C] a wild sheep with long curved horns that lives in the mountains of western North America

bight /baɪt/ *n.* [C] **1** a slight bend or curve in a coast **2** a LOOP made in the middle of a rope when tying a knot

ˈbig-league *adj.* **1** also **big league** belonging or relating to the MAJOR LEAGUES **2** [no comparative] belonging or relating to an important company or group: *The Democrats are struggling to find a big-league presidential candidate.*

ˌBig Man on ˈCampus *n.* [C] INFORMAL an important and popular male student at a college or university, especially someone who is good at sports

ˌbig ˈmoney *n.* [U] INFORMAL a large amount of money: *Carter won big money in Vegas last year.* **—big-money** *adj.* [only before noun]

big·mouth /ˈbɪgmaʊθ/ *n.* [C] INFORMAL someone who cannot be trusted to keep secrets: *Who's the big mouth who told Carole about the party?* → see also **big mouth** at BIG (12)

ˌbig ˈname *n.* [C] a famous person or group, especially a musician, actor etc.: *None of the soloists are big names yet, but they will be one day.* **—big-name** *adj.* [only before noun]: *big-name entertainers*

big·ot /ˈbɪgət/ *n.* [C] DISAPPROVING someone who has such strong opinions about race, religion, or politics that they are unwilling to listen to anyone else's opinions **—bigoted** *adj.*

big·ot·ry /ˈbɪgətri/ *n.* [U] behavior or beliefs typical of bigots: *the mayor's blatant bigotry*

big ˈrig *n.* [C] INFORMAL an extremely large truck, used for carrying goods SYN semi

ˌbig ˈscreen *n.* **the big screen** the movies, rather than television or theater: *Several of his novels were adapted for the big screen.* **—big-screen** *adj.*

ˌbig-screen TˈV also **ˌbig-screen ˈtelevision** *n.* [C] a large television with a very large screen

ˈbig shot *n.* [C] INFORMAL someone who has a lot of power or importance in a company or an area of business: *a media big shot*

ˌBig ˈSisters an organization that helps girls, especially girls with family problems, by giving each girl someone who meets her regularly to give advice, listen to her problems etc.

ˈbig-ˌticket *adj.* [only before noun, no comparative] INFORMAL big-ticket items are expensive things, such as cars and houses

ˈbig time¹ *adv.* [no comparative] SPOKEN to a very large degree: *I lost, big time, on that investment.*

big time² *n.* INFORMAL **the big time** the position of being very famous or important, for example in the entertainment business or in politics: *He played in clubs for years before making it to the big time.*

ˈbig-time *adj.* [only before noun, no comparative] INFORMAL **1** belonging or relating to someone or something that is important and successful: *Fuller's a player with a chance to make it into big-time football.* **2** SPOKEN used to emphasize the extreme quality of something: *She's a big-time pain in the neck.*

ˌbig ˈtoe *n.* [C] the largest toe on your foot

ˌbig ˈtop *n.* [C] the very large tent in which a CIRCUS performance takes place

big·wig /ˈbɪgwɪg/ *n.* [C] INFORMAL an important person: *a corporate bigwig*

bike¹ /baɪk/ *n.* [C] INFORMAL **1** a bicycle: *The kids are outside **riding their bikes**.* | ***Let's go for a bike ride*** *before lunch.* **2** a MOTORCYCLE

bike² *v.* [I always + adv./prep.] to ride a bicycle: *She bikes to work every day.* ▶see THESAURUS box at **travel¹** **—biking** *n.* [U]: *I like biking and swimming.*

ˈbike ˌmessenger *n.* [C] someone whose job is taking documents from one company in a big city to another, riding a bicycle in order to get there quickly

bik·er /ˈbaɪkɚ/ *n.* [C] **1** someone who rides a MOTORCYCLE, especially as part of a group: *Most of the bikers rode Harley-Davidsons.* **2** someone who rides a bicycle: *trails for bikers and hikers*

bi·ki·ni /bɪˈkini/ *n.* [C] a piece of clothing in two separate parts that women wear for swimming [**Origin:** 1900–2000 French *Bikini* Atoll, after a nuclear bomb test was held there in 1946]

Bi·ki·ni At·oll /bɪˌkini ˈætɔl/ one of the Marshall Islands in the Pacific Ocean

biˈkini line *n.* [C] the place on a woman's legs where the hair around her sexual organs stops growing

bi·la·bi·al /baɪˈleɪbiəl/ *n.* [C] ENG. LANG. ARTS a CONSONANT sound such as /p/ or /b/ that is made using both lips → see also LABIAL **—bilabial** *adj.*

bi·lat·er·al /baɪˈlæṭərəl/ *adj.* POLITICS involving two groups or nations: *bilateral relations between the European Union and the U.S.* | **a bilateral agreement/arrangement/treaty etc.** (=an agreement, arrangement etc. between two countries or groups) → see also MULTILATERAL, UNILATERAL **—bilaterally** *adv.*

biˌlateral ˈsymmetry also **ˈplane ˌsymmetry** *n.* [U] BIOLOGY a quality that some animals, including humans, have, which means that they have two very similar sides. For example, humans have an arm and a leg on each side, an eye on each side, and so on.

bile /baɪl/ *n.* [U] **1** BIOLOGY a bitter green-brown liquid formed in the LIVER, which helps you to DIGEST fats **2** LITERARY anger and hate

bilge /bɪldʒ/ *n.* **1** [C] the curved part of a ship that joins the bottom to the sides **2** [U] INFORMAL nonsense

B

bi·lin·gual /baɪˈlɪŋgwəl/ *adj.* **1** able to speak two languages equally well: *Their kids are completely bilingual.* → see also MULTILINGUAL **2** written or spoken in two languages: *a bilingual dictionary* → see also MONOLINGUAL, MULTILINGUAL —**bilingual** *n.* [C]

bil·ious /ˈbɪlyəs/ *adj.* **1** feeling sick to your stomach **2** very ugly or disgusting: *a bilious green color* **3** in a bad mood —**biliousness** *n.*

bilk /bɪlk/ *v.*

bilk sb **out of** sth *phr. v.* INFORMAL to trick someone, especially by taking their money SYN **swindle**

bill¹ /bɪl/ S1 W1 *n.* [C]

1 PAYMENT a) a written list showing how much you have to pay for services you have received, work that has been done etc.: +**for** *The bill for the repairs came to $650.* | **gas/phone/electricity etc. bill** *Have you **paid** the phone **bill**?* **b)** a list showing how much you have to pay for food you have eaten in a restaurant SYN **check**: *Could we have the bill please?*

THESAURUS

check a bill that you are given in a restaurant: *Can I have the check, please?*
invoice a document that shows how much you owe for goods, work etc.: *Payment is due 10 days after receipt of the invoice.*
tab an amount of money that you owe for a meal or drinks you have had, but have not yet paid for: *People staying in the hotel can order food or drinks to be put on their tab.*

►see THESAURUS box at **restaurant**

2 LAW POLITICS a plan for a new law, that is written down for a government to decide on: *a new gun-control bill in Congress* | *The president is threatening to **veto the bill*** (=vote against it). | **pass/approve a bill** (=vote for it to become law)

3 MONEY a piece of paper money → see also COIN: *a five-dollar bill* ►see THESAURUS box at **money**

4 give sb/sth a clean bill of health to officially state that someone is in good health or that something is working correctly: *Maddox was given a clean bill of health by his doctor.*

5 fill the bill/fit the bill to be exactly what you need: *If you want a good collection of stories for children, this book will fit the bill.*

6 CONCERT/SHOW ETC. ENG. LANG. ARTS a program of entertainment at a theater, concert, the movies etc., with details of who is performing, what is being shown etc.: *We went to a **double-bill*** (=a performance, concert etc. in two parts) *of old Hitchcock movies.*

7 BIRD BIOLOGY a bird's beak

8 ADVERTISEMENT a printed notice advertising an event

9 PART OF A HAT the front part that sticks out on a hat such as a BASEBALL CAP

[**Origin:** (1–6, 8) 1300–1400 Medieval Latin *bille*, from Latin *bulla* **bubble, seal added to a document**]

bill² S2 W3 *v.* [T] **1** to send someone a bill: *Clients will be billed monthly.* | **bill sth to sb** *The calls will be billed to your home phone number.* | **bill sb for sth** *I was billed for products that I didn't order.* **2 bill sth as sth** to advertise or describe something in a particular way: *The boxing match was billed as "the fight of the century."*

bill·a·ble /ˈbɪləbəl/ *adj.* [no comparative] relating to time, costs etc. that your customers will pay for: *How many billable hours did you work this week?*

bill·board /ˈbɪlbɔrd/ *n.* [C] a large sign used for advertising

bil·let¹ /ˈbɪlɪt/ *n.* [C] a private house where soldiers live for a short time

billet² *v.* [T] to put soldiers in a private house to live there for a short time

bill·fold /ˈbɪlfoʊld/ *n.* [C] a small flat leather case, used for carrying paper money, CREDIT CARDS etc. in your pocket SYN **wallet**

bill·hook /ˈbɪlhʊk/ *n.* [C] a tool consisting of a curved blade with a handle, used for cutting off tree branches etc.

bil·liards /ˈbɪlyɚdz/ *n.* [U] a game played on a cloth-covered table in which balls are hit with a CUE (=a long stick) against each other and into pockets at the edge of the table → see also POOL: *a billiards table* [**Origin:** 1500–1600 French *billard* **(stick used in) billiards**, from *bille* **piece of wood, stick**]

bill·ing /ˈbɪlɪŋ/ *n.* **1 give sb top/star billing** to name a particular performer, actor etc. as being the most important person in a show, play etc. **2** the process of creating and sending bills to customers or CLIENTS so that they can pay you for goods or services you have provided

ˈbilling adˌdress *n.* [C] the address that your credit card company uses for you, which you have to give when you buy things on the Internet

bil·lion /ˈbɪlyən/ *plural* **billion** or **billions** NUMBER 1,000,000,000: *$7 billion* | **billions of dollars/pounds/yen etc.** *Billions of dollars have been spent.* | **a/one billion** *The final cost could be as much as a billion dollars.* → see Grammar box at HUNDRED¹ —**billionth** *adj., pron., n.*

bil·lion·aire /ˌbɪlyəˈnɛr, ˈbɪlyəˌnɛr/ *n.* [C] someone who has a billion or more than a billion dollars

bill of at·tain·der /ˌbɪl əv əˈteɪndɚ/ *n.* [C] LAW any law that says a person or a group of people is guilty of a crime and takes away their life, freedom, or property without first giving them a TRIAL. These kinds of laws are illegal according to the U.S. Constitution.

ˌbill of exˈchange *n.* [C] TECHNICAL a signed document ordering someone to pay someone else a particular amount of money

ˌbill of ˈfare *n.* [C] OLD-FASHIONED a list of the food that is served in a restaurant SYN **menu**

ˌbill of ˈlading *n.* [C] TECHNICAL a list of the goods being carried, especially on a ship

ˌbill of ˈrights *n.* [C] **1** POLITICS a written statement of the most important rights of the citizens of a country or of a particular group **2** HISTORY **the Bill of Rights a)** the first ten AMENDMENTS (=additions) to the U.S. Constitution that state the basic rights of U.S. citizens **b)** also **the English Bill of Rights** an official list of some of the rights of British citizens made by the British Parliament in 1689

ˌbill of ˈsale *n.* [C] a written document showing that someone has bought something

bil·low¹ /ˈbɪloʊ/ *v.* [I] **1** if something made of cloth billows, it moves in the wind, making a rounded shape: *Her long skirt billowed in the breeze.* **2** LITERARY if smoke billows, it rises or moves in large quantities in the shape of clouds: *Smoke billowed out of the chimney.*

billow² *n.* [C usually plural] **1** a moving cloud, or something such as smoke, moving in round shapes like clouds: *a billow of steam* **2** LITERARY a wave, especially a very large one

bil·ly club /ˈbɪli klʌb/ *n.* [C] a short stick carried by a police officer

ˈbilly goat *n.* [C] INFORMAL a word for a male goat, used especially by or to children → see also NANNY GOAT

bim·bo /ˈbɪmboʊ/ *n. plural* **bimbos** [C] OFFENSIVE an attractive but stupid young woman, especially one who you think has low moral standards [**Origin:** 1900–2000 Italian **baby**]

bi·me·tal·ic strip /ˌbaɪmətælɪk ˈstrɪp/ *n.* [C] PHYSICS a long narrow piece of metal, consisting of two different types of metal joined together, each of which bends at a different rate when heated. Bimetallic strips are used in equipment that controls or measures heat, for example a THERMOSTAT or a THERMOMETER.

bi·me·tal·lic stan·dard /ˌbaɪmətælɪk ˈstændɚd/ also **bi·met·al·ism** /baɪˈmɛtl̩ɪzəm/ *n.* HISTORY a system of money used in the 18th and 19th centuries based on gold and silver, with the RATIO between the two metals being fixed by law

bi·mo·dal /baɪˈmoʊdl/ *adj.* [usually before noun] MATH relating to a set of data that has two MODES (=two quantities or items that appear more often than any others in the data): *The bimodal frequency distribution graph has two peaks.*

bi·month·ly /baɪˈmʌnθli/ *adj.* appearing or happening every two months or twice each month: *a bimonthly magazine* —**bimonthly** *adv.*

bin /bɪn/ *n.* [C] a large container for storing things, such as goods in a store or substances in a factory

bi·na·ry /ˈbaɪˌnɛri, ˈbaɪnəri/ *adj.* TECHNICAL **1 the binary system** a system of counting, used in computers, in which only the numbers 0 and 1 are used **2** consisting of two parts SYN **double**: *a binary star system*

ˌbinary ˈcompound *n.* [C] CHEMISTRY a substance consisting of only two different chemical ELEMENTS (=types of atoms)

ˌbinary ˈfission *n.* [U] BIOLOGY a type of ASEXUAL REPRODUCTION in which a cell divides and forms into two new cells that are the same or almost the same

bind¹ /baɪnd/ W3 *v. past tense and past participle* **bound** /baʊnd/
1 KEEP A PROMISE [T] if an agreement, promise etc. binds people or groups, they must do what they have agreed or promised to do SYN **require**: *The monks are bound by vows of silence.* | **bind sb to do sth** *The treaty binds the two countries to reduce the number of nuclear weapons.*
2 TIE/FASTEN [T] FORMAL OR LITERARY **a)** to tie someone so that they cannot move or escape SYN **tie up**: *They found him bound to a chair, barely alive.* | **bound and gagged** (=tied up, and with cloth tied around your mouth) **b)** also **bind up** to tie things firmly together with cloth or string SYN **tie up**: *The newspapers were bound with string.*
3 STICK TOGETHER [I,T] to stick together in a MASS, or to make small parts or pieces of something stick together: *Use 2 tablespoons of water to bind the flour and butter mixture.* | **+with** *The hydrogen molecule binds with the oxygen molecule.*
4 FORM A CONNECTION [T] to form a strong emotional or economic connection between two people, countries etc. SYN **join**: **bind sb/sth together** *A common history binds people together.*
5 BOOK [T] to fasten the pages of a book together and put them in a cover
6 STITCH [T] to sew cloth over the edge of a piece of material, or stitch over it, to strengthen it: *The edges of the blanket were bound with ribbon.*
7 be bound over for trial to be forced by law to appear in a court of law
[**Origin:** Old English *bindan*] → see also BINDING¹, BOUND²

bind² *n.* an annoying or difficult situation: *When Robert quit, it really* ***put us in a bind.***

bind·er /ˈbaɪndɚ/ *n.* **1** [C] a removable cover for holding loose sheets of paper, magazines etc. **2** [C] a person or machine that fastens the parts of a book together **3** [C,U] a substance that makes things stick together **4** [C] TECHNICAL an agreement in which you pay something to show that you intend to buy some property

bind·ing¹ /ˈbaɪndɪŋ/ *adj.* **a binding contract/promise/agreement etc.** a promise, agreement etc. that legally forces someone to obey it

binding² *n.* **1** [C] a book cover **2** [C usually plural] the metal part on a SKI that you step on so that your ski boot fastens to the ski **3** [U] material sewn or stuck along the edge of a piece of cloth for strength or decoration

bind·weed /ˈbaɪndwid/ *n.* [U] a wild plant that winds itself around other plants

binge¹ /bɪndʒ/ *n.* [C] a short period when you do too much of something, especially drinking alcohol: *He died during a drug binge.* | **binge drinking/eating** *Binge drinking has increased among teenagers.* | *Consumers have gone* ***on a*** *spending* ***binge.*** [**Origin:** 1800–1900 English dialect *binge* **to make completely wet**]

binge² *v.* [I] INFORMAL to do too much of something, especially eating or drinking, in a short period of time: **+on** *I binge on chocolate.*

bin·go¹ /ˈbɪŋgoʊ/ *n.* [U] a game played for money or prizes in which numbers are chosen by chance and called out, and if you have the right numbers on your card you win

bingo² *interjection* said when you have just done something successfully or to tell someone that they have given the right answer: *Bingo! That's the one I've been looking for.* [**Origin:** 1900–2000 *bing* **sound of something being hit** (1900–2000)]

B

Bin La·den /bɪn ˈlɑdn/, **O·sa·ma** /oʊˈsɑmə/ (1957–) the man, born in Saudi Arabia, who began and led the TERRORIST organization AL-QAEDA, which was responsible for many attacks, including the attacks on the World Trade Center and the Pentagon

bin·oc·u·lars /bɪˈnɑkyələz, baɪ-/ *n.* [plural] a pair of special glasses that you hold up to your eyes in order to make distant objects look bigger or closer → see picture at OPTICAL [**Origin:** 1800–1900 *binocular* **using both eyes** (18–21 centuries), from Latin *bini* **two by two** + *oculus* **eye**]

biˌnocular ˈvision *n.* [U] BIOLOGY the ability to look at an object with two eyes and join the two separate images you see into one. This gives you the ability to judge distance and to see images as THREE-DIMENSIONAL.

bi·no·mi·al /baɪˈnoʊmiəl/ *n.* [C] MATH a mathematical expression that has two parts connected by the sign + or the sign –, for example 3x + 4y or x – 7 —**binomial** *adj.*

biˌnomial ˈnomenˌclature *n.* [singular, U] BIOLOGY a system of naming animals, plants, and other living things with a scientific word consisting of two separate parts. The first part of the word is the GENUS (=group of related animals, plants etc., which do not breed) and the second part is the SPECIES (=group of animals which breed and produce new animals, plants etc.).

bi·o /ˈbaɪoʊ/ *n. plural* **bios** [C] INFORMAL a biography

bio- /baɪoʊ, baɪə/ *prefix* relating to living things: *biomedical* [**Origin:** Greek *bios* **way of life**]

bi·o·chem·is·try /ˌbaɪoʊˈkɛmɪstri/ *n.* [U] CHEMISTRY the scientific study of the chemical processes that take place in living things —**biochemist** *n.* [C] —**biochemical** *adj.*

bi·o·de·grad·a·ble /ˌbaɪoʊdɪˈgreɪdəbəl/ *adj.* BIOLOGY materials, chemicals etc. that are biodegradable are changed naturally by BACTERIA into substances that do not harm the environment: *biodegradable plastics* —**biodegrade** *v.* [I]

bi·o·di·ver·sit·y /ˌbaɪoʊdɪˈvɚsəti, -daɪ-/ *n.* [U] BIOLOGY the number and variety of different plants, animals, and other living things in a particular place: *biodiversity of the Amazon rainforest*

bi·o·feed·back /ˌbaɪoʊˈfidbæk/ *n.* [U] a medical TECHNIQUE in which you measure, for example, the rate at which someone's heart beats, and then help that person learn to relax, so that he or she can see the heart beating slower. The technique is useful for reducing the number of headaches someone has, making his or her blood pressure lower etc.

bi·og·ra·pher /baɪˈɑgrəfɚ/ *n.* [C] someone who writes a book about someone else's life

bi·og·ra·phy /baɪˈɑgrəfi/ *n. plural* **biographies** ENG. LANG. ARTS **1** [C] a book that tells what has happened in someone's life, written by someone else SYN **life story**: *a new biography of John F. Kennedy* ▸see THESAURUS box at **book¹** **2** [U] the part of literature that consists of biographies —**biographical** /ˌbaɪəˈgræfɪkəl/ *adj.* —**biographically** /-kli/ *adv.* → see also AUTOBIOGRAPHY

bi·ol·o·gi·cal /ˌbaɪəˈlɑdʒɪkəl/ *adj.* **1** relating to the science of biology: *biological studies* **2** BIOLOGY relating to the natural processes performed by living things: *the effects of the disease on biological processes* **3 biological weapons/warfare/attack etc.** weapons, war etc. that involve the use of living things, including BACTERIA to harm other living things: *the fear that the country might use biological weapons* **4 sb's biological father/**

mother/parent a child's parent through birth, rather than a parent through ADOPTION [SYN] **natural father/mother/parent** → see also BIRTH FATHER, BIRTH MOTHER —**biologically** /-kli/ *adv.*

ˌbiological ˈclock *n.* [singular] **1** BIOLOGY the time system in plants and animals that controls when they sleep, eat, produce babies etc. [SYN] **body clock** **2** the idea that after a certain age women are too old have babies: *career women who hear the* ***biological clock ticking***

ˌbiological conˈtrol *n.* [U] BIOLOGY a method of controlling PESTS (=small insects that harm or destroy crops) by using other insects, birds, or animals to kill them

bioˌlogical magnifiˈcation *n.* [U] BIOLOGY a process by which the level of harmful chemicals in the bodies of animals increases in relation to their position in the FOOD CHAIN. For example, when a chemical gets into a river, it enters the bodies of fish and then appears in higher amounts in the bodies of animals that eat the fish.

bi·ol·o·gy /baɪˈɑlədʒi/ *n.* [U] **1** the scientific study of living things: *a degree in biology* **2** the scientific laws that control the life of a particular type of animal, plant etc.: +**of** *the biology of bacteria* —**biologist** *n.* [C]

bi·o·lu·mi·nes·cence /ˌbaɪoʊluməˈnɛsəns/ *n.* [U] BIOLOGY the production and sending out of light by some living creatures, for example GLOWWORMS and fish that live in the deepest parts of the ocean

bi·o·mass /ˈbaɪoʊˌmæs/ *n.* [U] BIOLOGY **1** the total number or weight of animals, plants, or other living things within a particular environment **2** plant and animal matter, especially waste from farming, that can be used to provide power or energy

bi·ome /ˈbaɪoʊm/ *n.* [C] SCIENCE all the plants, animals etc. that live in an area with its own particular type of weather or environment, for example the plants, animals etc. living in a rain forest, or a desert, or an ocean

bi·o·met·ric /ˌbaɪəˈmɛtrɪk◂/ *adj.* relating to machines that can be used to measure things such as people's eyes or FINGERPRINTS. These measurements can be kept on a computer and then used to check who someone is, for example when they show a passport at an airport.

bi·on·ic /baɪˈɑnɪk/ *adj.* INFORMAL HUMOROUS bionic arms, legs etc. are electronic and therefore stronger and faster than normal arms etc.

bi·o·phys·ics /ˌbaɪoʊˈfɪzɪks/ *n.* [U] the scientific study of how PHYSICS relates to biological processes

bi·o·pic /ˈbaɪoʊˌpɪk/ *n.* [C] INFORMAL a movie that tells the story of someone's life

bi·op·sy /ˈbaɪˌɑpsi/ *n. plural* **biopsies** [C] MEDICINE the removal of body TISSUE from someone who is sick, in order to find out what is wrong with them

bi·o·rhythms /ˈbaɪoʊˌrɪðəmz/ *n.* [plural] BIOLOGY regular changes in the speed at which physical processes happen in your body, which some people believe can affect the way you feel and behave

bi·o·sphere /ˈbaɪəˌsfɪr/ *n.* [singular] EARTH SCIENCE the parts of the Earth, including land, water, and the air, in which animals, plants etc. can live

bi·o·tech·nol·o·gy /ˌbaɪoʊtɛkˈnɑlədʒi/ also **bi·o·tech** /ˈbaɪoʊˌtɛk/ INFORMAL *n.* [U] BIOLOGY the use of living things such as cells and BACTERIA in science and industry, for example to make drugs, destroy waste matter, make bread etc. —**biotechnological** *adj.*

bi·o·tic /baɪˈɑt̬ɪk/ *adj.* SCIENCE relating to life and living things, especially the environment or how people, animal, plants etc. exist in a particular environment → see also ABIOTIC: *biotic change* | *biotic resources*

bi·par·ti·san /baɪˈpɑrt̬əzən/ *adj.* POLITICS involving two political parties, especially parties with opposing views: *The new bill has received bipartisan support.*

bi·par·tite /baɪˈpɑrtaɪt/ *adj.* **1** FORMAL shared by or agreed on by two different groups: *a bipartite treaty* **2** having two parts: *a bipartite leaf* → see also TRIPARTITE

bi·ped /ˈbaɪpɛd/ *n.* [C] BIOLOGY an animal with two legs, such as a human —**bipedal** /baɪˈpɛdl/ *adj.* → see also QUADRUPED

bi·plane /ˈbaɪpleɪn/ *n.* [C] an aircraft with two sets of wings, especially one built in the early 20th century → see also MONOPLANE

bi·po·lar /baɪˈpoʊlɚ/ *adj.* **1** consisting of or involving two opposite or clearly different ideas: *the bipolar world of the Cold War* **2** MEDICINE having bipolar disorder

biˌpolar disˈorder *n.* [U] MEDICINE MANIC DEPRESSION

bi·ra·cial /ˌbaɪˈreɪʃəl◂/ *adj.* representing or including people from two different races: *biracial families*

birch /bɚtʃ/ *n.* [C,U] a tree with smooth BARK (=outer covering) and thin branches, or the wood from this tree

bird /bɚd/ [S1] [W2] *n.* [C]

1 ANIMAL BIOLOGY an animal that can usually fly, with two legs, wings, and feathers. Many birds sing and build nests, and female birds lay eggs. → see also FOWL: *The tree was full of tiny, brightly colored birds.* | ***a flock of birds*** (=group of birds flying together)

2 sth is for the birds SPOKEN said when you think something is useless, stupid, boring etc.: *Working late is for the birds!*

3 the birds and the bees HUMOROUS the facts about sex, especially the things you tell children in order to explain sex to them

4 a bird in the hand (is worth two in the bush) used to say that it is better to keep what you have than to risk losing it by trying to get more

5 birds of a feather (flock together) used to say that two people or groups are very similar, do the same things etc.

6 a tough/strange/skinny old bird OLD-FASHIONED a person who has a particular quality [SYN] **character**: *He's a tough old bird.*

[**Origin:** Old English *bridd*] → see also **early bird** at EARLY[1] (10), **sb eats like a bird** at EAT (14), **kill two birds with one stone** at KILL[1] (12), **a little bird told me** at LITTLE[1] (8)

bird·bath /ˈbɚdbæθ/ *n.* [C] a stone bowl filled with water for birds to wash in

bird·brain /ˈbɚdbreɪn/ *adj.* INFORMAL someone who is silly or stupid —**birdbrained** *adj.*

ˈbird dog *n.* [C] a dog that is trained to find and bring back birds that have been shot

bird·er /ˈbɚdɚ/ *n.* [C] INFORMAL A BIRD WATCHER

ˈbird flu also **ˌavian ˈflu** *n.* [U] an infectious disease that spreads very quickly among birds and can sometimes kill them. People can also catch the disease from the birds.

bird·house /ˈbɚdhaʊs/ *n.* [C] a small wooden box put in the yard for birds to live in

bird·ie[1] /ˈbɚdi/ *n.* [C] **1** SPOKEN a word meaning "bird," used especially by or to children **2** in GOLF, when a player has put the ball in the hole using one STROKE less than PAR **3** the small object that you hit across the net in a game of BADMINTON [SYN] **shuttlecock**

birdie[2] *v.* [T] to hit the ball into the hole in GOLF with one STROKE less than PAR

ˌbird of ˈparadise *n.* [C] BIOLOGY a brightly colored bird from New Guinea

ˌbird of ˈpassage *n.* [C] **1** LITERARY someone who never stays in the same place for long **2** BIOLOGY a bird that flies from one area or country to another, according to the seasons

ˌbird of ˈprey *n.* [C] a bird that kills other birds or small animals for food

bird·seed /ˈbɚdsid/ *n.* [U] a mixture of seeds for feeding birds

ˌbird's-eye ˈview *n.* [singular] a view of something from high above it: *From the top, you get a bird's-eye view across the valley.*

bird•song /ˈbɚdsɔŋ/ *n.* [U] the musical noises made by birds: *The silence was broken only by birdsong.*

ˈbird ˌwatcher *n.* [C] someone who watches wild birds and tries to recognize different types SYN **ornithologist** —**bird-watching** *n.* [U]

bi•ret•ta /bəˈrɛt̬ə/ *n.* [C] a square cap worn by Catholic priests

Bir•ming•ham /ˈbɚmɪŋˌhæm/ a city in the U.S. state of Alabama

birth /bɚθ/ S2 W2 *n.* **1** [C,U] the time when a baby comes out of its mother's body: *Congratulations on the birth of your daughter!* | **birth date/date of birth** (=the date on which you were born) | *He only weighed three pounds **at birth**.* | *Women who smoke tend to have babies with a lower **birth weight**.* | *Please list your name and your **place of birth**.* | *Does **birth order*** (=whether someone is their parents' first, second etc. child) *affect children's personalities?* **2 give birth (to sb)** if a woman gives birth, she produces a baby from her body SYN **bear**: *At 9:40 Claudia gave birth to a nine-pound baby boy.* **3** [U] the time when something new starts to exist: +**of** *the birth of photography* | *the talented musicians who **gave birth to** rock and roll* **4** [U] the character, language, social position etc. that you have because of the family or country you come from: *She is French **by birth**.* | *A large portion of the population is **of** foreign **birth**.* [**Origin:** 1200–1300 Old Norse *byrth*]

ˈbirth cerˌtificate *n.* [C] an official document that shows when and where you were born

ˈbirth conˌtrol *n.* [U] the practice of controlling the number of children you have SYN **contraception**: *a safe method of birth control*

birth•day /ˈbɚθdeɪ/ S1 W3 *n. plural* **birthdays** [C] **1** a day that is an exact number of years after the day when you were born: *It's my 18th birthday next week.* | *My grandmother **celebrated** her 90th **birthday** in October.* | **Happy Birthday!** (=what you say to someone on their birthday) | **a birthday present/card/party etc.** *I met Anna at your birthday party last year.* | *a chocolate **birthday cake*** | **birthday boy/girl** (=the boy or girl whose birthday it is) **2 in your birthday suit** HUMOROUS not wearing any clothes

ˈbirth ˌdefect *n.* [C] a physical problem that a child is born with

ˈbirth ˌfather *n.* [C] a child's natural father, rather than the man who has become the child's father through ADOPTION SYN **biological father**

birth•mark /ˈbɚθmɑrk/ *n.* [C] a permanent red or brown mark on your skin that you have had since you were born

ˈbirth ˌmother *n.* [C] a child's natural mother, rather than the woman who has become the child's mother through ADOPTION SYN **biological mother**

birth•place /ˈbɚθpleɪs/ *n.* [C usually singular] **1** the place where someone was born, especially someone famous: *We visited Elvis' birthplace in Tupelo, Mississippi.* **2** the place where something first started to happen or exist: *New Orleans is the birthplace of jazz.*

birth•rate /ˈbɚθreɪt/ *n.* [C] the number of births for every 1,000 people in a particular year in a particular place → see also DEATH RATE

birth•right /ˈbɚθraɪt/ *n.* [C usually singular] **1** a basic right that you have because of the family or country you come from: *Freedom of speech is every American's birthright.* **2** property, money etc. that you have because it comes from your family

birth•stone /ˈbɚθstoʊn/ *n.* [C] a valuable stone that is used to represent the month of the year in which you were born: *Emerald is the birthstone of people born in May.*

Bis•cay, Bay of /ˈbɪskeɪ/ an area of the Atlantic Ocean between the west coast of France and the north coast of Spain

bis•cot•ti /bɪsˈkɑt̬i/ *n.* [U] a type of Italian cookie eaten with coffee

bis•cuit /ˈbɪskɪt/ *n.* **1** [C] a type of soft bread baked in small round pieces: *biscuits and gravy* **2** [U] a light yellowish-brown color **3** [C] BRITISH a cookie or a CRACKER [**Origin:** 1300–1400 Old French *bescuit*, from Latin *bis* **twice** + *coctus* **cooked**]

bi•sect /ˈbaɪsɛkt, baɪˈsɛkt/ *v.* [T] MATH to divide something, especially a line or angle, into two equal parts —**bisection** /ˈbaɪsɛkʃən, baɪˈsɛk-/ *n.* [U]

bi•sec•tor /ˈbaɪˌsɛktɚ/ *n.* [C] MATH a line that divides something into two equal parts: **an angle bisector** (=a line that divides an angle into two equal angles) → PERPENDICULAR BISECTOR

bi•sex•u•al /baɪˈsɛkʃuəl/ *adj.* **1** sexually attracted to both men and women → see also HETEROSEXUAL **2** having qualities or features of both sexes: *a bisexual plant* —**bisexual** *n.* [C] —**bisexuality** /ˌbaɪsɛkʃuˈæləti/ *n.* [U]

Bish•kek /bɪʃˈkɛk/ the capital and largest city of Kyrgyzstan

bish•op /ˈbɪʃəp/ *n.* [C] **1** a Christian priest with a high rank, who is the head of all the churches and priests in a large area **2** a piece in the game of CHESS that can be moved DIAGONALLY over any number of squares of the same color [**Origin:** Old English *bisceop*, from Late Latin *episcopus*, from Greek *episkopos* **person in charge, bishop**]

bish•op•ric /ˈbɪʃəprɪk/ *n.* [C] **1** the area that a bishop is in charge of SYN **diocese** **2** the position of being a bishop

Bis•marck /ˈbɪzmɑrk/ the capital city of the U.S. state of North Dakota

Bismarck, Ot•to von /ˈɑt̬oʊ vɑn/ (1815–1898) a German politician who was mainly responsible for joining all the separate German states together to form one country, and who them became CHANCELLOR of Germany

bis•muth /ˈbɪzməθ/ *n.* [U] SYMBOL **Bi** CHEMISTRY a gray-white metal that is an ELEMENT and is often used in medicine

bi•son /ˈbaɪsən/ *n. plural* **bison** or **bisons** [C] an animal like a large cow with long hair around the head and shoulders, which used to be common in western North America SYN **buffalo** → see picture on page A34

bisque /bɪsk/ *n.* [U] a thick creamy soup made from SHELLFISH: *lobster bisque*

Bis•sau /bɪˈsaʊ/ the capital city of Guinea-Bissau

bis•tro /ˈbistroʊ/ *n. plural* **bistros** [C] a small restaurant or bar

bit[1] /bɪt/ S2

1 SLIGHTLY/FAIRLY a bit INFORMAL slightly, but not very SYN **a little**: *I'm **a little bit** tired.* | *Let it warm up **a little bit**.* | *I'm feeling a bit better.* | *He looks **a bit like** Brad Pitt.* | *The movie is **a bit too** predictable.* | **a bit more/less** *This will make things a bit more difficult.*

2 TIME a bit a short amount of time SYN **a little**: *I'll come back to that point **in just a bit**.* | *I was a bit late.* | *It's better to be **a little bit** early if you can.*

3 AMOUNT a bit INFORMAL a small amount, especially of something that is not a physical object SYN **a little**: +**of** *All that's needed is a bit of imagination.* | *I like **a little bit** of half and half in my coffee.*

4 quite a bit a fairly large amount, or to a fairly large degree: *She said she learned quite a bit.* | *The other boy was quite a bit bigger than Tom.* | +**of** *He owes me quite a bit of money.*

5 a bit of a sth used to say that something has a particular quality, when you do not want to make it seem too important or strong: *Seeing him again, after so many years, was a bit of a shock.*

6 not a bit also **not the least bit** not at all: *"Did you regret not going to college?" "Not a bit."* | *He wasn't the least bit afraid.*

7 bit by bit gradually: *Bit by bit, our apartment started to look like a home.*

8 every bit as... just as much as: *She's every bit as pretty as her sister.*

B

bit² S1 W1 *n.* [C]
1 PIECE a small piece of something SYN **piece**: **+of** *The floor was covered with tiny bits of broken glass.* | **blow/tear/smash etc. sth to bits** *The aircraft was blown to bits.* | *He made a mosaic out of* ***bits and pieces*** *of old tiles.*
2 COMPUTER COMPUTERS the smallest unit of information that can be used by a computer → see also BYTE: *a 16-bit processor*
3 TOOL the sharp part of a tool for cutting or making holes: *a drill bit*
4 FOR A HORSE a metal bar that is put in the mouth of a horse and used for controlling its movements
5 MONEY OLD USE 12½ cents: *I wouldn't give you* ***two bits*** *for that old book.* → see also **two bits** at TWO (11)
6 do your bit INFORMAL to do part of something that needs to be done, especially to help other people: *We wanted to do our bit for the boys fighting in the war.*
[**Origin:** (1, 2–6) Old English *bita* piece bitten off, small piece of food] → see also BIT PART, **be chomping at the bit** at CHOMP (2)

bit³ the past tense of BITE

bitch /bɪtʃ/ *n.* [C] a female dog

bite¹ /baɪt/ S1 *v. past tense* **bit** /bɪt/, *past participle* **bitten** /ˈbɪtˀn/
1 WITH YOUR TEETH [I,T] to use your teeth to cut, crush, or chew something: *Even a friendly dog will bite if it's scared.* | *Taryn, stop* ***biting your nails!*** | **+into** *She stopped talking and bit into a cookie.* | **bite sth off** *His ear was bitten off in a fight.* | **bite your lip** (=gently bite your bottom lip because you are upset or not sure what to say)
2 INSECT/SNAKE [I,T] if an insect or snake bites you, it injures you by making a hole in your skin: *She was bitten by a rattlesnake.*
3 bite the bullet INFORMAL to start dealing with a bad or dangerous situation because you cannot avoid it any longer: *A lot of companies had to bite the bullet and lay off a lot of their employees.*
4 bite your tongue to stop yourself from saying what you really think, even though this is difficult: *I knew it would just make things worse, so I bit my tongue.*
5 bite sb's head off INFORMAL to answer someone or speak to them very angrily, especially when there is no good reason for doing this: *I never know if he's going to be in a good mood or if he's going to bite my head off.*
6 bite the hand that feeds you to harm someone who has helped or supported you
7 bite the dust INFORMAL **a)** to die, fail, or be defeated: *Half of all new restaurants bite the dust in the first year.* **b)** to stop working completely: *My old car's finally bitten the dust.*
8 bite off more than you can chew to try to do more than you are able to do: *Many kids who leave home to live alone find they have bitten off more than they can chew.*
9 FISH [I] if a fish bites, it takes food from a hook and so gets caught
10 BUY/BELIEVE [I] to buy a product or believe what someone is telling you, especially when someone is trying very hard to make you do this: *The product was withdrawn when consumers failed to bite.*
11 HAVE AN EFFECT [I] to have the effect that was intended, especially a negative or bad one: *The new tobacco taxes have begun to bite.*
12 he/she won't bite SPOKEN used to say that there is no need to be afraid of someone, especially someone in authority: *Well, go and ask him if he can help you – he won't bite!*
13 be bitten by the bug/fever etc. to develop a very strong interest in or desire for something: *Kinner was bitten by the flying bug in his twenties.*
14 PRESS INTO STH [I] if an object bites into a surface, it presses firmly into it and does not move or slip: **+into** *The ski's edge should bite into the snow.* | *The knotted rope bit into my skin.*
15 COLD/WIND [I] if cold weather or the wind bites, it makes you feel extremely cold
16 once bitten twice shy used to say that if you have failed or been hurt once, you will be very careful next time
17 sth bites (the big one) SLANG an impolite expression meaning that something is very bad in quality or that a situation is very bad: *Your mom won't let you go? That bites.*
[**Origin:** Old English *bitan*]
bite back *phr. v.* **1 bite sth ↔ back** to stop yourself from saying something or telling someone what you really feel: *Tamara bit back the insult that sprang to mind.* **2** to react strongly and angrily to something: *Shortly after the incident, Young bit back in court, filing a civil suit.*

bite² S2 *n.*
1 WHEN YOU EAT [C] the act of cutting or crushing something with your teeth: *party food that you can eat in one bite* | *"The chicken's dry," said Kim, after* ***taking a bite.*** | *Can I* ***have a bite of*** *your steak?*
2 ANIMAL/INSECT [C] a wound made when an animal or insect bites you: **snake/mosquito/spider etc. bite** *We came back from the walk covered in mosquito bites.* | **+of** *The bite of a black mamba snake can kill within minutes.*
3 a bite (to eat) SPOKEN a small meal: *We* ***had a bite to eat*** *before the movie.* | *I'll just* ***grab a bite*** *on the way to work.*
4 COLD [singular] a sharp feeling of coldness: **+of** *the bite of the November wind*
5 AMOUNT [singular] an amount of money that is taken from something, especially by the government: *The state will be* ***taking a bite*** *out of money earned from local traffic tickets.*
6 TASTE [U] a pleasantly strong, bitter, or sour taste: *The barbecue sauce lacked heat and bite.*
7 EFFECTIVENESS [U] a special quality in speech, writing, or a performance that makes arguments or criticisms effective and likely to persuade people: *a protest song with bite and wit*
8 FISH [C] an occasion when a fish takes the food from a hook: *Sometimes I sit for hours and never* ***get a bite.***
9 POSITION OF TEETH [C usually singular] the position of someone's upper teeth in relation to their lower teeth → see also SOUND BITE

ˈbite-size also **ˈbite-sized** *adj.* [only before noun]
1 small enough to fit into your mouth easily: *bite-size pieces of chicken* **2** small enough to understand or deal with quickly and easily: *bite-size chunks of information*

bit·ing /ˈbaɪt̬ɪŋ/ *adj.* **1** a biting wind feels very cold SYN **bitter** **2** a biting criticism or remark is very unkind: *biting sarcasm* —**bitingly** *adv.*

bit·map /ˈbɪtˀmæp/ WRITTEN ABBREVIATION **BMP** *n.* [C] COMPUTERS a computer image that is stored or printed as an arrangement of BITS: *bitmap fonts*

ˈbit part *n.* [C] a very small acting performance in a play or movie

bit·sy /ˈbɪtsi/ *adj.* INFORMAL very small → see also ITTY-BITTY

bit·ten /ˈbɪtˀn/ *v.* the past participle of BITE

bit·ter /ˈbɪt̬ɚ/ *adj.*
1 ANGRY/UPSET feeling angry, JEALOUS, and upset because bad things have happened to you or you have been treated unfairly: *a bitter and angry man* | *She shot a bitter glance in his direction.* | **+about** *Jensen admits that he is bitter about the experience.*
2 FULL OF HATE a bitter argument, attack, struggle etc. is one in which people oppose or criticize each other with strong feelings of hate and anger: *There has been bitter fighting in the capital.* | **bitter dispute/fight/battle/debate etc.** *a bitter legal battle over custody of the children*
3 CAUSING UNHAPPINESS [only before noun] making you feel very unhappy and upset: *Williams suffered a bitter defeat in the 1996 election and quit politics for good.* | *The news was a* ***bitter disappointment*** *to NASA employees.* | *We know* ***from bitter experience*** (=because of your own very bad experiences) *that guns in the home end up killing children.*
4 TASTE having a strong taste like black coffee without sugar, or very dark chocolate → see also SWEET: *The*

medicine tasted bitter. → SOUR[1] (1) ►see THESAURUS box at **taste**[1]
5 COLD extremely cold: *a bitter east wind* | *The children have to walk to school in the* ***bitter cold.***
6 bitter enemy/rival etc. two people or groups who are bitter enemies hate each other and have been fighting or arguing for a long time: *France and Germany, once bitter enemies, are now fast friends.*
7 to/until the bitter end continuing until the end, in spite of problems or difficulties: *We will* ***fight until the bitter end*** *to defend our land.*
8 a bitter pill (to swallow) something very bad that you have to accept: *Losing the business was a bitter pill to swallow.* → see also BITTERLY —**bitterness** *n.* [U]

bit·ter·ly /ˈbɪt̬ɚli/ *adv.* **1** in a way that produces or shows feelings of great sadness or anger: *The law was* ***bitterly opposed*** *by environmentalists.* | *It was a decision that she later bitterly regretted.* | *The children* ***complained bitterly*** *that no one would listen to them.* | *The nation is* ***bitterly divided*** *on the issue.* **2 bitterly cold** very cold

bit·tern /ˈbɪt̬ɚn/ *n.* [C] BIOLOGY a brown European bird with long legs that lives near water and makes a deep sound

bit·ters /ˈbɪt̬ɚz/ *n.* [U] a bitter liquid made from plants that is added to alcoholic drinks

bit·ter·sweet /ˌbɪt̬ɚˈswit◂/ *adj.* **1** feelings, memories, or experiences that are bittersweet are happy and sad at the same time: *bittersweet memories of childhood* **2** a taste or smell that is bittersweet is both sweet and bitter at the same time **3 bittersweet chocolate** chocolate that is not very sweet and that does not have a lot of milk in it

bit·ty /ˈbɪt̬i/ *adj.* INFORMAL very small: *a small house with a* ***little bitty*** *yard* → see also ITTY-BITTY

bi·tu·men /bɪˈtyumən, -ˈtu-, baɪ-/ *n.* [U] BLACKTOP —**bituminous** *adj.*

bi·valve /ˈbaɪvælv/ *n.* [C] BIOLOGY any sea animal that has two shells joined together, such as an OYSTER —**bivalved** *adj.*

bi·va·ri·ate /baɪˈvɛriɪt/ *adj.* MATH having two VARIABLES (=mathematical quantity that is not fixed and can be any of several amounts): *a bivariate analysis of the data* → see also MULTIVARIATE, UNIVARIATE

biv·ou·ac[1] /ˈbɪvuˌæk/ *n.* [C] a temporary camp built outside without any tents [**Origin:** 1700–1800 French, Low German *biwake*, from *bi* **at** + *wake* **guard**]

bivouac[2] *v. past tense and past participle* **bivouacked, bivouacking** [I] to spend the night outside without tents in a temporary camp: *The climbers bivouacked halfway up the mountain.*

bi·week·ly /baɪˈwikli/ *adj.* appearing or happening every two weeks or twice a week: *a biweekly magazine* —**biweekly** *adv.*

biz /bɪz/ *n.* [singular] INFORMAL a particular type of business, especially one relating to entertainment: *the music biz* → see also SHOWBIZ

bi·zarre /bɪˈzɑr/ S3 *adj.* very unusual or strange SYN **odd**: *Neighbors mentioned his bizarre behavior.* [**Origin:** 1600–1700 French, Italian *bizzarro* **always changing, unreasonable**, from Spanish *bizarro* **brave**] —**bizarrely** *adv.*

blab /blæb/ *v.* [I,T] INFORMAL to talk too much, often about something that should be secret: *A woman was blabbing on her cell phone.* | +**about** *Reporters can usually find someone willing to blab about a celebrity.* [**Origin:** 1500–1600 *blab* **person who talks too much, too much talk** (14–20 centuries)]

blab·ber·mouth /ˈblæbɚˌmaʊθ/ *n.* [C] INFORMAL someone who always talks too much and often says things that should be secret

black[1] /blæk/ S1 W1 *adj.*
1 COLOR having the darkest color, like coal or night: *a shiny black car* | *The letters were white on a black background.* | *She has* ***jet-black*** (=very dark black) *hair.* ►see THESAURUS box at **hair**
2 NO LIGHT very dark because there is no light: *The room was* ***pitch black*** (=completely dark).
3 PEOPLE also **Black a)** belonging to the race of people who originally came from Africa and who have dark brown skin: *Most of the students at Dorsey High are black.* **b)** [only before noun] relating to or concerning black people: *politics from a black perspective* | *contemporary Black music*
4 COFFEE black coffee does not have milk in it: *Do you take your coffee black?*
5 DIRTY very dirty: *My hands were black from working on the car.* | **black with soot/age/dirt** *firefighters whose faces are black with soot*
6 a black mark (against sb) if there is a black mark against you, someone has a bad opinion of you because of something you have done: *It is almost impossible to borrow money if you have any black marks against you.*
7 WITHOUT HOPE sad and without much hope for the future SYN **gloomy**: *Tony was in a black mood.* | *a black period in our history* | *It was a* ***black day*** (=when something very bad happens) *for the peace process.*
8 HUMOR making jokes about serious subjects, especially death: *The humor is as black as his shoes.* → BLACK COMEDY, BLACK HUMOR
9 ANGRY full of feelings of anger or hate: *Denise gave me a* ***black look.***
10 EVIL LITERARY very bad SYN **evil**: *black deeds*
[**Origin:** Old English *blæc*] → see also BLACKLY —**blackness** *n.* [C]

black[2] S3 W2 *n.* **1** [U] the dark color of night or coal: *Black is his favorite color.* | *You look good* ***in black*** (=wearing black clothes). **2** [C] also **Black** someone who belongs to the race of people who originally came from Africa and who have dark brown skin → see also WHITE: *The laws were used to discriminate against blacks.* **3 be in the black** to have more money than you owe OPP **be in the red** **4** [U] black paint, color, MAKEUP etc.: *Put some more black around your eyes.*

black[3] *v.*
black out *phr. v.* **1** to become unconscious SYN **faint** SYN **pass out**: *The clerk was hit on the head and blacked out.* **2 black sth ↔ out** to put a dark mark over something so that it cannot be seen: *The censors had blacked out several words.* **3 black sth ↔ out** to hide or turn off all the lights in a town or city, especially during war → see also BLACKOUT

ˌblack and ˈblue *adj.* skin that is black and blue has BRUISES (=dark marks) on it as a result of being hit

ˌblack and ˈwhite *adj.* **1** showing pictures or images only in black, white, and gray OPP **color**: *old black and white movies* **2** considering things in a very simple way, as if there are clear differences between good and bad, right and wrong etc.: *The situation is not black and white.* | *A lot of people* ***see things in black and white,*** *and don't understand how complex the issue is.* **3 in black and white** in written form, and therefore definite: *The rules are there in black and white for everyone to see.*

ˌblack ˈart *n.* [U] also **the black arts** [plural] BLACK MAGIC

black·ball /ˈblækbɔl/ *v.* [T] to make someone stop being part of a particular club, organization etc., especially by voting against them SYN **reject**

ˈblack bear *n.* [C] a North American bear with black or dark brown fur

ˈblack belt *n.* [C] **1** a high rank in sports such as JUDO and KARATE **2** someone who has this rank: +**in** *Sandy's a black belt in karate.*

Black·Ber·ry /ˈblækˌbɛri/ *n.* [C] TRADEMARK a piece of WIRELESS (=using electronic signals rather than wires) electronic equipment that you can hold in your hand. You can use it to store telephone numbers, addresses, and lists of meetings, to send and receive e-mails and TEXT MESSAGES, and to look at the Internet. You can also use it as a CELL PHONE.

black·ber·ry /ˈblækˌbɛri/ *n. plural* **blackberries** [C] a sweet black or dark purple BERRY

black·bird /ˈblækbɚd/ *n.* [C] BIOLOGY a common European and American bird, the male of which is completely black

black·board /ˈblækbɔrd/ *n.* [C] a board with a dark smooth surface, used in schools for writing on with CHALK → see also WHITEBOARD

B

ˌblack ˈbox *n.* [C] INFORMAL a piece of equipment on an airplane that records what happens during a flight, and that can be used to discover the cause of accidents SYN **flight recorder**

ˈblack codes *n.* [plural] HISTORY a set of laws, passed in 1865 by some southern states after the American Civil War, that severely restricted the freedom and rights of African-Americans who were former SLAVES. In 1866, the U.S. Congress passed the Civil Rights Act and later approved the Fourteenth Amendment in order to end these laws. → see also JIM CROW

ˌblack ˈcomedy *n.* [C,U] a play, story etc. that is funny, but also shows a side of life that is not very nice

ˌBlack ˈDeath *n.* **the Black Death** an illness that killed large numbers of people in Europe and Asia in the 14th century → see also BUBONIC PLAGUE, PLAGUE[1] (2)

ˌblack eˈconomy *n.* **the black economy** business activity that takes place secretly, especially in order to avoid tax → see also BLACK MARKET

black·en /ˈblækən/ *v.* **1** [I,T] to become black, or make something black: *A few people, their faces blackened by the smoke, ran out of the building.* **2 blacken sb's name/character/reputation etc.** to say things about someone that are not nice, in order to make other people have a bad opinion of them

ˌblack ˈEnglish *n.* [U] the variety of English spoken by some African-American people in the U.S. SYN **Ebonics**

ˌblack ˈeye *n.* [C] if you have a black eye, you have a dark area around your eye because you have been hit

ˌblack-eyed ˈpea *n.* [C] a small pale bean with a black spot on it

black-eyed Su·san /ˌblæk aɪd ˈsuzən/ *n.* [C] a yellow flower with a dark center that grows in North America

black·face /ˈblækfeɪs/ *n.* [U] someone who is in blackface has painted their face black, especially for a musical show popular in the early 1900s

Black·foot /ˈblækfʊt/ a Native American tribe from the northwest region of the U.S.

ˌBlack ˈForest, the an area of southwest Germany where there is a very large forest

ˌblack ˈgold *n.* [U] INFORMAL oil

black·guard /ˈblægɚd, ˈblækgɑrd/ *n.* [C] OLD USE a man who treats other people very badly SYN **scoundrel**

ˌBlack ˈHawk (1767–1838) a Sauk leader who fought against U.S. soldiers in 1832 in an attempt to get back his tribe's land

black·head /ˈblækhɛd/ *n.* [C] a small spot of dirt deep in someone's skin

ˌblack ˈhole *n.* [C] **1** PHYSICS an area in space where the force of GRAVITY is very strong, so light and other objects cannot escape from the area. A black hole sometimes forms when a star stops existing. ▶see THESAURUS box at space[1] **2** INFORMAL something that uses up a lot of money: *The downtown area is an economic black hole.*

black ˈhumor *n.* [U] jokes, funny stories etc. that deal with the parts of life that are not nice

ˌblack ˈice *n.* [U] a thin layer of ice that is very difficult to see: *black ice on the roads*

black·ing /ˈblækɪŋ/ *n.* [U] OLD-FASHIONED a very thick liquid or polish that is put on objects to make them black

black·jack /ˈblækdʒæk/ *n.* **1** [U] a card game, usually played for money, in which you try to get as close to 21 points as possible **2** [C] a weapon like a stick covered with leather, used to hit people

black ˈknight *n.* [C] INFORMAL a person or company that tries to take control of another company by buying most of the SHARES, when the owners do not want to sell them → see also WHITE KNIGHT

black·list[1] /ˈblækˌlɪst/ *n.* [C] a list of people, countries, products etc. that are disapproved of, and should therefore be avoided or punished: *They are on the blacklist of companies that pollute the environment.*

blacklist[2] *v.* [T] to put a person, country, product etc. on a blacklist: *More than 200 people in the movie industry were blacklisted during the McCarthy era.*

ˈblack ˌlung *n.* [U] a lung disease caused by breathing in coal dust over a long period of time, especially affecting MINERS

black·ly /ˈblækli/ *adv.* relating to something that shows the bad side of life or is about death in a humorous way: *The movie is blackly funny.*

ˌblack ˈmagic *n.* [U] magic that is believed to use the power of the Devil for evil purposes → see also WHITE MAGIC

black·mail[1] /ˈblækmeɪl/ *n.* [U] **1** the practice of getting money from someone or making them do what you want by threatening to tell secrets about them SYN **extortion** **2** an attempt to make someone do what you want by making threats or by making them feel guilty if they do not: *If I don't do overtime I'll lose my job – it's blackmail.* | *She'd already tried* ***emotional blackmail*** (=tried to make him feel bad) *to stop him leaving.* [**Origin:** 1500–1600 *black* + *mail* **payment** (11–20 centuries) from Old Norse *mal* **speech, agreement**]

blackmail[2] *v.* [T] to use blackmail against someone SYN **extort**: *He was sure they would use the videotape to blackmail him.* | **blackmail sb into (doing) sth** *Mr. Harris said he would not be blackmailed into making a hasty decision.* —**blackmailer** *n.* [C]

ˌblack ˈmarket *n.* [C] ECONOMICS the system by which people illegally buy and sell foreign money, goods that are difficult to obtain etc.: *black market cigarettes* | **+in** *a black market in weapons* | *Many foods were only available* ***on the black market.*** → see also BLACK ECONOMY

black mar·ket·eer /ˌblæk mɑrkɪˈtɪr/ *n.* [C] someone who sells things on the black market

ˌBlack ˈMountains a RANGE of mountains in the southeastern U.S. that is part of the Blue Ridge Mountains and is in the state of North Carolina

ˌBlack ˈMuslim *n.* [C] a member of a group of African-American people who believe in the religion of Islam

ˌBlack ˈNationalism *n.* [U] HISTORY a political and social MOVEMENT (=people working to achieve an aim) among African-Americans in the U.S. during the 1960s and 70s. It wanted African-Americans to be economically and politically independent from the rest of American society, and for them to be proud of being black. Some people in the movement also wanted to have a separate nation within the U.S. with only African-Americans living in it. —**Black Nationalist** *n.* [C]

black·out /ˈblækaʊt/ *n.* [C] **1** a period of darkness caused by a failure of the electricity supply SYN **power cut**: *There were blackouts throughout California.* **2** an occasion when you suddenly lose consciousness **3** also **news blackout** a situation in which particular pieces of news or information are not allowed to be reported: *Negotiators have* ***imposed a news blackout*** *on the talks.* **4** a period during a war when all the lights in a town, city etc. must be turned off

ˌblack ˈpepper *n.* [U] pepper made from crushed seeds from which the dark outer covering has not been removed

ˌBlack ˈPower *n.* [U] HISTORY a political MOVEMENT (=people working to achieve an aim) in the U.S. during the 1960s and 70s which tried to improve the rights of African-Americans and increase their political power

ˌBlack 'Sea, the a large sea to the northeast of the Mediterranean that is surrounded by land, and is between Turkey, Bulgaria, Romania, Ukraine, Russia, and Georgia

ˌblack 'sheep *n.* [C usually singular] someone who is regarded by other members of their family or group as a failure or embarrassment: *My sister's **the black sheep of the family**.*

Black·shirt, Black Shirt /'blækʃɚt/ *n.* [C] a member of a FASCIST organization that has a black shirt as part of its uniform

black·smith /'blæksmɪθ/ *n.* [C] someone who makes and repairs things made of iron, especially HORSESHOES

black·strap mo·las·ses /ˌblækstræp mə'læsɪz/ *n.* [U] the darkest thickest MOLASSES (=thick sweet liquid) produced when sugar is taken from sugar plants

'black-tie *adj.* a black-tie party or social occasion is one at which people wear special formal clothes, such as TUXEDOS for men: *a black-tie dinner* → see also WHITE-TIE

black·top /'blæktɑp/ *n.* **1** [U] a thick black sticky substance that becomes hard as it dries, used to cover roads **2 the blacktop** the surface of a road covered by this substance: *We left the blacktop and drove along a forest road.*

ˌBlack 'Tuesday HISTORY October 29, 1929; the day the U.S. stock market CRASHED (=lost a very large amount in value) and the Great Depression began

ˌblack water 'fever *n.* [U] a very severe form of the disease MALARIA

Black·well, Elizabeth /'blækwɛl/ (1821–1910) a U.S. doctor who was the first woman to QUALIFY officially as a doctor in the U.S.

ˌblack 'widow *n.* [C] a very poisonous type of SPIDER that is black with red marks

blad·der /'blædɚ/ *n.* [C] **1** BIOLOGY an organ of the body, that holds URINE (=waste liquid from the body) until it is passed out of the body **2** a bag of skin, leather, or rubber, for example inside a football, that can be filled with air or liquid → see also GALL BLADDER

blade¹ /bleɪd/ S2 *n.* [C] **1** the flat cutting part of a tool or weapon: *The blade should be kept sharp.* | *a **razor blade*** **2** BIOLOGY a long flat leaf of grass or a similar plant SYN **leaf**: *a blade of grass* **3** BIOLOGY the flat surface of the leaf of a plant, that receives sunlight **4** the flat wide part of an object that pushes against air or water: *a ceiling fan with wooden blades* **5** the metal part on the bottom of an ICE SKATE [**Origin:** Old English *blæd*] → see also SHOULDER BLADE

blade² *v.* [I] INFORMAL to SKATE using IN-LINE SKATES (=special boots with a row of wheels attached under them)

blad·er /'bleɪdɚ/ *n.* [C] INFORMAL someone who SKATES using IN-LINE SKATES

blah¹ /blɑ/ S3 *adj.* SPOKEN **1** not having an interesting taste, appearance, character etc.: *The chili was kind of blah.* **2** slightly sick or unhappy: *I feel really blah today.* [**Origin:** 1900–2000 From the sound of empty talk]

blah² *n.* [U] **blah, blah, blah** SPOKEN used when you do not need to complete what you are saying because it is boring or because the person you are talking to already knows it: *You know how Michelle talks: "Tommy did this, and Jesse did that, blah, blah, blah."*

blahs /blɑz/ *n.* INFORMAL **the blahs** a feeling of being sad and bored: *a case of the winter blahs*

blame¹ /bleɪm/ S2 W2 *v.* [T] **1** to say or think that someone or something is responsible for something bad SYN **hold sb responsible**: *Don't blame me – it's not my fault.* | **blame sb/sth for sth** *I used to blame my parents for messing up my life.* | *Dougan blamed the economy for weak Christmas sales.* | **blame sth on sb/sth** *The accident was blamed on pilot error.* | *Water levels have dropped, a situation **widely blamed** on global warming.* **2 sb is to blame for sth** used to say that someone is responsible for something bad that happened: *Officials believe that more than one person may be to blame for the fire.* | **partly/largely/solely to blame** *Alcohol or drugs may be partly to blame for the accident.* **3 don't blame me** SPOKEN used when you are advising someone not to do something, but you think they will do it anyway: *Go ahead, but don't blame me if it doesn't work.* **4 I don't blame you/them etc.** SPOKEN used to say that you think it was right or reasonable for someone to do what they did: *I don't blame her for being mad!* **5 only have yourself to blame** SPOKEN used to say that someone's problems are their own fault: *If they lose this game, they'll only have themselves to blame.* [**Origin:** 1100–1200 Old French *blamer*, from Late Latin *blasphemare*, from Greek *blasphemos* **speaking evil**]

B

blame² *n.* [U] responsibility for a mistake or for something bad: **+for** *Much of the blame for homelessness should go on the state's welfare system.* | *Nathalie is older, and she usually **gets the blame** when the kids fight.* | *Apparently, she **took the blame** for her husband, and spent time in jail.* | *Coaches and players must **share the blame**.* | *He was accused of trying to **shift the blame** onto his aides.* | **put/place/lay the blame on sb** (=say something is someone's fault) *Blame has to be laid on the parents.* | *In my opinion, the **blame lies** with our sick culture.* | **assign/apportion blame** (=say who is at fault)

blame·less /'bleɪmlɪs/ *adj.* FORMAL not guilty of anything bad SYN **innocent**: *In a divorce, no one is blameless.* | *a blameless life* —**blamelessly** *adv.*

blame·wor·thy /'bleɪmˌwɚði/ *adj.* FORMAL deserving blame or disapproval: *blameworthy conduct*

blanch /blæntʃ/ *v.* **1** [I] to become pale because you are frightened or shocked: **+at** *Most customers blanch at the thought of paying $150 for kids' shoes.* **2** [T] to put vegetables, fruit, or nuts into boiling water for a short time: *Blanch the spinach for 30 seconds.* **3** [T] to make a plant become pale by keeping it away from light

bland /blænd/ *adj.* **1** without any excitement, strong opinions, or special character SYN **dull**: *a bland suburban neighborhood* | *a few bland songs on the radio* **2** food that is bland has very little taste: *Tofu is a bland food made from soy beans.* ▸see THESAURUS box at **taste¹** —**blandly** *adv.* —**blandness** *n.* [U]

blan·dish·ments /'blændɪʃmənts/ *n.* [plural] FORMAL pleasant things you say that are intended to persuade or influence someone SYN **flattery**

blank¹ /blæŋk/ S3 *adj.* **1** [no comparative] without any writing, print, or recorded sound: *a blank sheet of paper* | *Are there any blank tapes?* | *She said she'd **left** her ballot paper **blank*** (=she had not written on it to vote). ▸see THESAURUS box at **empty¹** **2** showing no expression, understanding, or interest: **blank look/stare/expression etc.** *I said hello, and she gave me a blank look.* | *the blank faces of the students* **3 go blank a)** to be suddenly unable to remember something: *I just went blank and couldn't remember his name for a minute.* | *I worried that my **mind** might **go blank** on stage.* **b)** to stop showing any images, writing etc.: *Suddenly the screen went blank.* [**Origin:** 1200–1300 Old French *blanc* **white**] → see also BLANKLY, BLANK VERSE —**blankness** *n.* [U]

blank² *n.* [C] **1** an empty space on a piece of paper, where you are supposed to write a word or letter: ***Fill in the blanks** with your name and address* **2** a form with empty spaces on it: *the competition entry blank* **3** a CARTRIDGE (=container for a bullet in a gun) that contains an explosive but no bullet: *We didn't know the guns were **firing blanks**.* → see also **draw a blank** at DRAW¹ (14) —**blankness** *n.* [U]

blank³ *v.* **1** [T] INFORMAL to not allow your opponent or the opposing team to win points in a game or sport: *The Whalers blanked the Washington Capitals 2–0.* **2** [I] also **blank out** SPOKEN if your mind blanks, you are suddenly unable to remember something

blank sth ↔ **out** *phr. v.* INFORMAL **1** to cover something so that it cannot be seen, or to prevent something from being seen: *a picture with some of the names* *blanked out* **2** to completely forget something, especially deliberately: *I've just tried to blank out most of last year.*

ˌblank ˈcartridge *n.* [C] a CARTRIDGE in a gun that contains an explosive but no bullet

ˌblank ˈcheck *n.* [C] **1** a check that has been signed, but has not had the amount written on it **2 give sb a blank check** to give someone permission to do whatever they think is necessary in a particular situation: *Congress gave President Johnson a blank check to wage war in Vietnam.*

blan•ket¹ /ˈblæŋkɪt/ S3 *n.* **1** [C] a cover for a bed, often made of wool SYN **coverlet** **2** [singular] a thick covering or area of something: **+of** *The hills were covered with a* ***blanket of snow.*** | **blanket of fog/mist/smog etc.** [**Origin:** 1300–1400 *blanket* **white cloth** (13–15 centuries), from Old French *blankete*, from *blanc* **white**] → see also SECURITY BLANKET, WET BLANKET

blanket² *v.* [T usually passive] to cover something with a thick layer: **+in/with** *The mountains were blanketed in snow.*

blanket³ *adj.* [only before noun] **a blanket statement/rule/ban etc. (on sth)** a statement, rule etc. that affects everyone or includes all possible cases: *a blanket ban on ivory trading*

ˌblanket ˈprimary *n.* [C] POLITICS in the U.S., an election in which you do not need to be a member of a political party in order to vote, and you can vote for CANDIDATES from any political party → see also CLOSED PRIMARY

blank•e•ty-blank /ˌblæŋkəṭi ˈblæŋk◂/ *adj.* [only before noun] SPOKEN used to show annoyance when you want to avoid swearing: *The blankety-blank key is stuck!*

blank•ly /ˈblæŋkli/ *adv.* in a way that shows no expression, understanding, or interest: *Joe stared at her blankly.*

ˌblank ˈverse *n.* [U] ENG. LANG. ARTS poetry that has a particular RHYTHM but does not RHYME: *Shakespeare's blank verse* → see also FREE VERSE

blare /blɛr/ *v.* [I,T] also **blare out** to make a very loud unpleasant noise: *Sirens blared as firefighters raced to the scene.* | *The radio was blaring out the news.* —**blare** *n.* [singular]: *the blare of a horn*

blar•ney /ˈblɑrni/ *n.* [U] INFORMAL pleasant but untrue things that you say to someone in order to trick or persuade them [**Origin:** 1700–1800 *Blarney* Stone, large piece of stone in Blarney Castle, Ireland which is said to give skill in flattery to people who kiss it]

bla•sé /blɑˈzeɪ/ *adj.* not worried or excited about things that most people think are important, impressive etc.: *A trip to Disneyland excited even my blasé teenagers.* [**Origin:** 1800–1900 French, past participle of *blaser* **to make tired with too much of something**]

blas•pheme /blæsˈfim, ˈblæsfim/ *v.* [I] to speak in a way that insults God or people's religious beliefs, or to use the names of God and holy things when swearing SYN **curse** [**Origin:** 1300–1400 Late Latin *blasphemare*, from Greek, from *blasphemos* **speaking evil**] —**blasphemer** *n.* [C]

blas•phe•my /ˈblæsfəmi/ *n. plural* **blasphemies** [C,U] something you say or do that is insulting to God or people's religious beliefs —**blasphemous** *adj.*: *The book has been widely condemned as blasphemous.* —**blasphemously** *adv.*

blast¹ /blæst/ *n.*

1 AIR/WIND [C] a sudden strong movement of wind or air SYN **gust**: **+of** *A* ***blast of cold air*** *swept through the hut.*

2 EXPLOSION [C] an explosion, or the very strong movement of air that it causes: *The blast was heard three miles away.* | *Thirty-six people died* ***in the blast.*** | **bomb/nuclear/shotgun etc. blast** *a bomb blast in the subway*

3 FUN a blast INFORMAL an enjoyable and exciting experience: *The concert was a blast.* | *We* ***had a blast*** *at the fair.*

4 full blast as strongly, loudly, or fast as possible: *The heating was* ***on full blast.*** | **go/run full blast** *Air conditioners were going full blast.*

5 EMOTION a sudden strong expression of a powerful emotion, especially criticism or anger: **+at** *The article was a blast at Hollywood studios.*

6 a blast from the past INFORMAL something from the past that you remember, see, or hear again, that reminds you of that time in your life: *That's a blast from the past. No one's called me Janie in years.*

7 NOISE [C] a sudden very loud noise: *The referee gave a blast on his whistle and we were off.*

blast² *v.*

1 CRITICIZE [T] to criticize something very strongly SYN **criticize**: *Environmental groups blasted the plan for more logging in the area.* | **blast sb for (doing) sth** *He blasted Dillon for breaking his word.*

2 GUN/BOMB [T] to damage or destroy something, or to injure or kill someone, using a gun or a bomb: *Several Allied planes were blasted out of the sky.* | *The explosion* ***blasted a hole in*** *the county courthouse.*

3 MUSIC [I,T] also **blast out** to produce a lot of loud noise, especially music: *a radio blasting out music* | **+from** *Music blasted from the speakers in the living room.*

4 BREAK STH INTO PIECES [I,T] to break something into pieces using explosives, especially in order to build something such as a road: **+through** *Four tunnels were made by blasting through the canyon rock.* | **blast sth through/in sth** *Slowly they blasted a path through the mountains.* | **blast sth out of sth** *A huge statue is being blasted out of the rock.*

5 AIR/WATER [T] to direct air or water at something with great force: *A storm blasted the Florida coast with 75 m.p.h. winds.*

6 SPORTS to beat another team very badly: *The Seahawks were blasted 35–14 by the Broncos at the start of the season.*

7 HIT/KICK STH [T] to hit or kick something very hard, especially a ball in a sport: *Newman blasted one into left field in the second inning.*

8 blast sb's hopes LITERARY to destroy someone's hope of doing something

9 blast! also **blast her/it etc.** SPOKEN, OLD-FASHIONED said when you are very annoyed about something: *Oh blast! I've forgotten my key.*

blast away *phr. v.* to shoot at something or someone: *In the game, you ride a dragon and blast away at monsters.*

blast off *phr. v.* if a SPACECRAFT blasts off, it leaves the ground → see also BLAST-OFF

blast•ed /ˈblæstɪd/ *adj.* [only before noun] SPOKEN OLD-FASHIONED used to express annoyance: *I wish that blasted dog would stop barking!*

ˈblast ˌfurnace *n.* [C] a large industrial structure in which iron is separated from the rock that surrounds it

ˈblast-off *n.* [U] the moment when a SPACECRAFT leaves the ground: *10 seconds to blast-off*

blas•tu•la /ˈblæstʃələ/ *n.* [C] BIOLOGY an EMBRYO in the early stage of its development, when it is a hollow ball of cells

bla•tant /ˈbleɪtˀnt/ *adj.* an action that is blatant is obviously bad, but the person or people responsible for it are not embarrassed or ashamed SYN **flagrant**: *blatant discrimination* | *At first I tried ignoring his blatant sexual hints.* —**blatantly** *adv.* —**blatancy** *n.* [C]

blath•er /ˈblæðɚ/ *v.* [I] to talk for a long time about things that are not important —**blather** *n.* [U]

blaze¹ /bleɪz/ *v.* **1** [I] to burn very brightly and strongly: *A* ***fire*** *was* ***blazing*** *in the fireplace.* ►see THESAURUS box at **burn¹** **2** [I] to shine with a very bright light: *Lights blazed in every room in the house.* **3** [I] also **blaze away** to fire bullets rapidly and continuously: *An enemy plane roared past with its guns blazing.* **4 blaze a trail** also **blaze the trail of sth** to discover or develop something new, or do something important that no one has done before: *Poland blazed the trail of democratic reform in eastern Europe.* **5** if someone's eyes blaze, they show a very strong emotion, especially anger: +**with** *"Get out!" he screamed, his eyes blazing with hate.*

blaze² *n.*
1 FIRE a) [C] a word meaning a big dangerous fire, used especially in newspapers: *The blaze started near a campground.* | **fight/battle/tackle a blaze** *Six fire fighters were injured battling the blaze.* | *The **blaze spread** quickly.* **b)** [singular] the strong bright flames of a fire: *a cheerful blaze in the fireplace* ►see THESAURUS box at **fire¹**
2 LIGHT/COLOR [singular] very bright light or color: +**of** *a blaze of sunshine* | *In the fall, the trees are **a blaze of color**.*
3 GUNS [singular] the rapid continuous firing of a gun: +**of** *Six passengers were killed in a blaze of automatic gunfire.*
4 a blaze of glory/publicity etc. a lot of praise or public attention: *The movie opened at theaters **in a blaze of publicity**.*
5 a blaze of anger/hatred/passion etc. a sudden show of very strong emotion: *He was surprised by the sudden blaze of anger in her eyes.*
6 what the blazes/who the blazes etc. SPOKEN, OLD-FASHIONED used to emphasize a question when you are annoyed: *What the blazes is he trying to do?*
7 like blazes OLD-FASHIONED as fast, as much, or as strongly as possible: *We're going to have to work like blazes!*
8 MARK [C usually singular] a white mark, especially one down the front of a horse's face [**Origin:** (1–5) Old English *blaese* **torch**]

blaz·er /ˈbleɪzɚ/ *n.* [C] a suit JACKET (=piece of clothing like a short coat), without matching pants: *a blue wool blazer* [**Origin:** 1800–1900 *blaze*; from the originally bright colors of blazers]

blaz·ing /ˈbleɪzɪŋ/ *adj.* [only before noun, no comparative] **1** extremely hot: *We stood for hours in the **blazing sun**.* **2** extremely fast: *a runner with blazing speed on the track* **3** brightly colored: *the blazing reds and oranges of the flowers* **4** full of strong emotions, especially anger

bla·zon¹ /ˈbleɪzən/ *v.* [T] **be blazoned across/on sth** to be written or shown on something in a very noticeable way

blazon² *n.* [C] a COAT OF ARMS

bldg. the written abbreviation of BUILDING

bleach¹ /blitʃ/ *n.* [U] CHEMISTRY a chemical used to make things white or to kill GERMS

bleach² *v.* [T] to make something pale or white, especially by using chemicals or the sun: *I can't believe she **bleached** her **hair**.* | *The bones had been **bleached by the** desert **sun**.*

bleach·ers /ˈblitʃɚz/ *n.* [plural] long wooden BENCHES arranged in rows with no roof covering them, where you sit to watch a sport SYN **stands**

bleak /blik/ *adj.* **1** without anything to make you feel cheerful or hopeful SYN **hopeless**: *the bleakest year of the Depression* | *It looks pretty bleak for farmers here.* | **bleak future/prospect/outlook etc.** *Children in these camps face a bleak future.* **2** cold and without any pleasant or comfortable features: *a bleak January afternoon* | *The coast looked bleak and uninviting.* [**Origin:** 1300–1400 Old Norse *bleikr* **pale, white**] —**bleakly** *adv.* —**bleakness** *n.* [U]

blear·y /ˈblɪri/ also **ˌbleary-ˈeyed** *adj.* unable to see very clearly, because you are tired or have been crying: *A knock at the door woke the bleary-eyed Thompson at 3:00 a.m.* —**blearily** *adv.* —**bleariness** *n.* [U]

bleat /blit/ *v.* [I] to make the sound that a sheep or goat makes SYN **baa** —**bleat** *n.* [C]

bleed /blid/ S3 *v.* **bled** /blɛd/
1 BLOOD a) [I] MEDICINE to lose blood, especially because of an injury: *The cut on his cheek was still bleeding.* | **bleed profusely/heavily** *A deep cut on her wrist was bleeding profusely.* | *He **bled to death** after being shot in the stomach.* **b)** [T] to take some blood from someone's body, done in the past in order to treat a disease
2 MONEY [T] to make someone pay an unreasonable amount of money over a period of time: *Marcia bled him for every penny he had.* | *The ten-year war has **bled** the country **dry**.*
3 AIR/LIQUID [T] to remove air or liquid from a system in order to make it work correctly, for example from a heating system: *The brake line had to be bled.*
4 COLOR [I] to spread from one area of cloth or paper to another SYN **run**: *The dark blue bled into the white of the shirt.*
5 my heart bleeds (for sb) SPOKEN used to say that you feel a lot of sympathy for someone, but also often said in a joking way when you do not think someone deserves any sympathy: *My heart bleeds for those poor children.* | *You can't afford a third car? My heart bleeds!* [**Origin:** Old English *bledan*, from *blod* **blood**]

bleed·ing /ˈblidɪŋ/ *n.* [U] the condition of losing blood from your body: *Use pressure to control the bleeding.* | *He suffered a broken rib and internal bleeding.* | **serious/severe/massive/heavy bleeding** *One side effect of the drug can be severe bleeding.*

ˌbleeding ˈheart also **ˌbleeding heart ˈliberal** *n.* [C] INFORMAL someone who feels sympathy for poor people, criminals, people who have no education etc., in a way that you think is not practical or helpful

bleep¹ /blip/ *n.* [C] **1** a short high electronic sound: *the bleeps of a video game* **2** SPOKEN a word used instead of a swear word, especially in writing, when you do not want to offend people: *What the bleep is going on here?* [**Origin:** 1900–2000 From the sound]

bleep² *v.* **1** [T] also **bleep out** to prevent an offensive word being heard on television or the radio by covering it with a high electronic sound: *The TV network bleeped out the obscenities.* **2** [I] to make a high electronic sound SYN **beep**

blem·ish¹ /ˈblɛmɪʃ/ *n.* [C] a small mark, especially a mark on someone's skin or on the surface of an object, that spoils its appearance ►see THESAURUS box at **mark²**

blemish² *v.* [T often passive] to spoil the appearance, beauty, or PERFECTION of something [**Origin:** 1300–1400 Old French *blemir* **to make pale, injure**] —**blemished** *adj.* → see also UNBLEMISHED

blend¹ /blɛnd/ *v.* **1** [I,T] to mix together soft or liquid substances to form a single smooth substance SYN **mix**: *Blend the sugar, eggs, and flour.* | +**in** *Gradually blend in ½ cup of milk.* ►see THESAURUS box at **mix¹** **2** [I,T] to combine different things in a way that produces an effective or pleasant result, or to become combined in this way SYN **combine**: *The play blends fact and legend.* | +**with/together** *Rashad's sense of comedy blends well with Cosby's.* **3** [T usually passive] to produce tea, tobacco, WHISKEY etc. by mixing several different types together **4** [T] ENG. LANG. ARTS to combine parts of two words to make a new word: *Parts of "breakfast" and "lunch" are blended to produce "brunch."* **5** [T] ENG. LANG. ARTS to combine two or more sounds together in a word [**Origin:** 1300–1400 Old Norse *blanda*]

blend in *phr. v.* also **blend into sth** **1** if something blends in with the things around it, it looks similar to them in color or appearance: +**with** *The bird blended in with the gray-brown reeds growing in the water.* | *Planners want to ensure that the structure blends into the landscape.* **2** if someone blends in with a group of people, they easily become part of the group because they are similar to the people in it: +**with** *As much as I tried to blend in with my classmates, they knew my family was different.*

blend² *n.* [C] **1** a mixture of different qualities, foods, people etc. that combine together well: +**of** *Santos' music is a fiery blend of Cuban and Puerto Rican rhythms.* | *Curry powder is a blend of several spices.* ►see THESAURUS box at **mixture** **2** a product such as tea, tobacco, or WHISKEY that is a mixture of several different types **3** ENG. LANG. ARTS a combination of parts of two words to make a new word: *"Smog" is a blend of "smoke" and "fog."* **4** ENG. LANG. ARTS a combination of two or more sounds within a word: *The word "broil"* *contains the consonant blend "br" and the vowel blend "oi."*

ˌblended 'family *n.* [C] a family in which both parents have children from earlier relationships living with them

B

blend·er /'blɛndɚ/ *n.* [C] an electric machine that you use to mix liquids and soft foods together

bless /blɛs/ S2 *v.* [T] **1 (God) bless you!** SPOKEN **a)** what you say when someone SNEEZES **b)** used to thank someone for doing something for you: *God bless you for all the help you have given us.* **2** if God blesses someone or something, He helps and protects them: *May God bless you and keep you safe from harm.* **3** to ask God to protect and help someone or something: *Bless this house and all who live here.* **4** to receive something good, helpful, or useful: *Their friendship has blessed them both.* **5 be blessed with sth** to have a special ability, good quality etc.: *He's blessed with the ability to laugh at himself.* | *The city is blessed with an excellent location.* **6** to make something holy SYN **consecrate**: *Then the priest blesses the bread and wine.* **7 bless him/her etc.** SPOKEN used to show that you like someone, are amused by them, or are pleased by something they have done: *Bless him, he always helps when he can.* | *Joanie, **bless her heart**, brought me a card she'd made today.* **8 bless my soul!** also **I'll be blessed!** SPOKEN, OLD-FASHIONED used to express surprise [**Origin:** Old English *bletsian*, from *blod* **blood**; because blood was used in religious ceremonies]

bless·ed /'blɛsɪd/ *adj.* **1** holy: *Blessed are the peacemakers.* | *the Blessed Virgin* **2** protected or helped by God: *We are truly blessed.* **3** [only before noun] very enjoyable or desirable: *a few minutes of blessed silence* **4** [only before noun] SPOKEN used to emphasize something, especially when you are annoyed: *I couldn't remember a blessed thing.* —**blessedly** *adv.* —**blessedness** *n.* [U]

bless·ing /'blɛsɪŋ/ *n.*
1 APPROVAL [U] someone's approval or encouragement for a plan, activity, idea etc.: *The story was changed slightly for the movie, **with** the author's **blessing**.* | *The city has **given its blessing to** $60 million worth of new housing construction.* | *The project has **received the blessing** of the company's CEO.*
2 STH GOOD/HELPFUL [C] something that you have or something that happens which is good because it improves your life, helps you in some way, or makes you happy: *The store is a blessing for those on a budget.* | ***It's a blessing (that)** no one was badly hurt.*
3 a mixed blessing a situation that has both good and bad parts: *Finding information on the Internet can be a mixed blessing – it's easy to find, but there may be too much of it.*
4 FROM GOD [C,U] protection and help from God, or words spoken to ask for this SYN **benediction**: *The priest gave the blessing.*
5 a blessing in disguise something that seems to be bad or unlucky at first, but which you later realize is good or lucky: *The delay was a blessing in disguise, as we had a chance to practice more.*
6 count your blessings SPOKEN used to tell someone to remember how lucky they are, especially when they are complaining about something

blew /blu/ *v.* the past tense of BLOW

Bligh /blaɪ/, **Captain William** (1754–?1817) an officer in the British navy who was in command of the ship H.M.S. Bounty. Bligh was a very cruel leader, so the men on his ship attacked him and made him leave in a small boat.

blight¹ /blaɪt/ *n.* **1** [U] a plant disease in which parts of the plants dry up and die **2** [singular] something that makes people unhappy or that spoils their lives or the environment they live in: **+on** *Billboards are a blight on the community.* → see also URBAN BLIGHT

blight² *v.* [T] to spoil or damage something, especially by preventing people from doing what they want to do: *Litter blights our wilderness areas.* | *The country is blighted by poverty.* —**blighted** *adj.*: *a blighted childhood*

blimp /blɪmp/ *n.* [C] **1** an aircraft without wings that looks like a very large BALLOON **2** SPOKEN an impolite word for a very fat person

blind¹ /blaɪnd/ W3 *adj.*
1 CANNOT SEE a) unable to see SYN **visually impaired**: *a school for blind children* | **totally/completely/partially blind** *My grandmother is almost totally blind.* | *The accident left her **legally blind** in one eye.* | *In later stages of the disease, people often **go blind*** (=become blind). **b) the blind** [plural] people who are unable to see: *a library for the blind* **c) as blind as a bat** HUMOROUS not able to see well: *I'm as blind as a bat without my glasses.* → see also COLORBLIND ►see THESAURUS box at **see¹**
2 be blind to sth to completely fail to notice or realize something: *The White House seems blind to the struggles of the middle class.*
3 turn a blind eye (to sth) to deliberately ignore something that you know should not be happening: *Many landlords turn a blind eye to the fact that two families are sharing apartments.*
4 FEELINGS a) blind faith/loyalty/hate etc. strong feelings that you have without thinking about why you have them: *a blind loyalty to the Communist Party* **b) a blind panic/rage etc.** strong feelings that you cannot control: *Tyrell went into a blind rage, punching and kicking at everyone.*
5 a blind study/test/experiment etc. a study or test of something in which the people in the study are not given any information about the things being tested because it might influence them: *a blind taste test* → see also DOUBLE-BLIND
6 a blind corner/curve/driveway etc. a corner, curve, etc. that you cannot see beyond when you are driving
7 the blind leading the blind OFTEN HUMOROUS used to say that people who do not know much about what they are doing are helping or advising others who know nothing at all about it
8 blind flying/landing flying or landing an aircraft using only instruments because you cannot see through cloud, mist etc.
[**Origin:** Old English] —**blindness** *n.* [U] → see also BLINDLY

blind² *v.* [T] **1** to make it difficult for someone to see for a short time: *I was blinded by the truck's headlights.* **2** to make someone lose their good sense or judgment and be unable to see the truth about something: *Don't be blinded by emotion.* | **blind sb to sth** *His determination to succeed was blinding him to the needs of his family.* **3** to permanently destroy someone's ability to see: *Richards had been blinded in the war.* **4 blind sb with science** to confuse or trick someone by using complicated language

blind³ *n.* [C] **1** a piece of cloth or other material that can be UNROLLed from the top of a window to cover it SYN **window shade** → see also VENETIAN BLIND **2** a small shelter where you can watch birds or animals without being seen by them **3** a trick or excuse to stop someone from discovering the truth

blind⁴ *adv.* used to say that someone is driving or flying without being able to see anything because the conditions outside are very bad: *We were flying blind through thick cloud.*

ˌblind 'alley *n.* [C] **1** a small narrow street with no way out at one end **2** a course of action that seems as though it will have good results, but which in fact has no positive result at all: *False information led the police up a series of blind alleys.*

ˌblind 'date *n.* [C] an arranged meeting between a man and woman who have not met each other before

blind·ers /'blaɪndɚz/ *n.* [plural] **1** things fastened beside a horse's eyes to prevent it from seeing objects on either side **2** something that prevents you from noticing the truth about a situation: *You'd have to **have blinders on** not to notice the drug problem here.*

blind·fold¹ /'blaɪndfoʊld/ *n.* [C] a piece of cloth used to cover someone's eyes to prevent them from seeing anything

blindfold² *v.* [T] to cover someone's eyes with a piece of cloth: *Blindfold the prisoner!*

blind·fold·ed /ˈblaɪndfoʊldɪd/ *adj.* **1** with your eyes covered by a piece of cloth **2 sb can do sth blindfolded** INFORMAL used to say that it is very easy for someone to do something because they have done it so often: *Tomlinson could sail this boat blindfolded.*

blind·ing /ˈblaɪndɪŋ/ *adj.* **1** so bright or strong that you cannot see: *The sun shone on the blinding white sand.* | **blinding light/flash/glare etc.** *the blinding flash of an exploding bomb* | **blinding snow/rain** *Traffic was brought to a halt by a blinding snowstorm.* ►see THESAURUS box at **bright** **2 a blinding headache/pain etc.** a headache, pain etc. that is so strong that it makes you unable to think or behave normally **3** extreme: *He answered with* ***blinding speed.***

blind·ing·ly /ˈblaɪndɪŋli/ *adv.* very or extremely: *The computer is blindingly fast.*

blind·ly /ˈblaɪndli/ *adv.* **1** not thinking about something or trying to understand it: *Think first. Don't just blindly follow his advice.* **2** not seeing or noticing what is around you: *She ran blindly down the street, screaming.*

ˌblind man's ˈbluff *n.* [U] a children's game in which one player whose eyes are covered tries to catch the others

blind·side /ˈblaɪndsaɪd/ *v.* [T] INFORMAL **1** to hit the side of a car with your car in an accident: *Their car was blindsided by a bus at the intersection.* **2** to surprise someone so that they feel confused or upset: *I was blindsided by his suggestion.*

ˈblind spot *n.* [C] **1** something that you are unable or unwilling to understand: *Critics accuse him of having a blind spot on ethics.* **2** the part of the road that you cannot see when you are driving a car, even when you look in the mirrors or quickly look behind you: *The other car was right* ***in my blind spot.*** **3** BIOLOGY the point in your eye where the nerve enters, which is not sensitive to light

bling¹ /blɪŋ/ also **ˌbling-ˈbling** *adj.* SLANG relating to expensive and noticeable jewelry, clothes, etc., or relating to a way of life in which you like to own and show expensive things

bling² *n.* [U] SLANG expensive jewelry that is worn to be noticed

bli·ni /ˈblini/ *n.* [C] *plural* **blini** or **blinis** a small flat type of bread in the shape of a circle, often served with SALMON or CAVIAR on top

blink¹ /blɪŋk/ *v.* **1** [I,T] to close and open your eyes quickly: *He blinked as he walked out into the bright sunshine.* **2** [I] if lights blink, they go on and off continuously: *The neon lights on the theater blinked red and blue.* **3 blink back tears** to open and close your eyes to try to get rid of tears, as a way of trying to control your emotions: *Mrs. Wilson blinked back tears on the witness stand.* **4 not (even) blink (an eye)** to not seem at all surprised or concerned: *They didn't even blink when I told them the price.* [**Origin:** 1500–1600 Middle Dutch *blinken* **to shine**]

blink² *n.* **1 in/with the blink of an eye** very quickly: *Summer seemed to be over in the blink of an eye.* **2 on the blink** SPOKEN not working correctly: *The radio's on the blink again.* **3** [C] the action of quickly closing and opening your eyes

blink·er /ˈblɪŋkɚ/ *n.* [C] INFORMAL one of the small lights on a car that flash on and off to show which direction you are turning → see picture on page A36

blink·ered /ˈblɪŋkɚd/ *adj.* having a limited view of a subject, or refusing to accept or consider ideas that are new or different: *a brilliant but blinkered scientist*

blintz /blɪnts/ *n.* [C] a type of thin PANCAKE usually filled with a cheese mixture

blip /blɪp/ *n.* [C] **1** a flashing light on a RADAR screen **2** a sudden and temporary change from the way something typically happens, especially when a situation gets worse for a while before it improves again: *Except for the blip this month, unemployment has continued to fall this year.*

bliss¹ /blɪs/ *n.* [U] perfect happiness or enjoyment: *I didn't have to get up until 11 – it was* ***sheer bliss.*** | **wedded/domestic/marital bliss** (=happiness in marriage) [**Origin:** Old English *bliths*]

bliss² *v.*

bliss out *phr. v.* SPOKEN, INFORMAL to be completely happy and feel a lot of pleasure

bliss·ful /ˈblɪsfəl/ *adj.* **1** extremely happy or enjoyable: *blissful sunny days* **2 blissful ignorance** a situation in which you do not yet know about something bad or difficult —**blissfully** *adv.*: *blissfully happy*

blis·ter¹ /ˈblɪstɚ/ *n.* [C] **1** MEDICINE a swelling on your skin containing clear liquid, caused for example by a burn or continuous rubbing: *New shoes always give me blisters.* ►see THESAURUS box at **mark²** **2** a swelling on the surface of metal, rubber, painted wood etc. [**Origin:** 1300–1400 Old French *blestre*, *blostre* **swelling on the skin**, from *Middle Dutch bluyster* **blister**]

blister² *v.* **1** [I,T] to develop blisters or make blisters form: *The paint will blister in the heat.* **2** [T] to angrily criticize someone: *Brown blistered his players for their poor performance.* —**blistered** *adj.*: *blistered fingers*

blis·ter·ing /ˈblɪstərɪŋ/ *adj.* **1** extremely hot SYN **blazing**: *blistering summer days* **2 blistering attack/criticism etc.** very angry and disapproving remarks: *blistering attacks in the press* **3** used to describe something that happens very quickly: *The population has grown at a* ***blistering pace.*** —**blisteringly** *adv.*

ˈblister pack *n.* [C] a type of package in which each object is enclosed in clear plastic that fits closely around it, and is usually attached to a piece of CARDBOARD or plastic: *Each blister pack contains 12 aspirins.*

blithe /blaɪð, blaɪθ/ *adj.* **1** seeming not to think or worry about the effects of what you do: *Mary spoke with blithe certainty about her future.* **2** LITERARY cheerful and having no worries SYN **carefree**

blithe·ly /ˈblaɪðli/ *adv.* **1** in a way that shows that you are not thinking about or do not care about the effects of what you do: *My friend's mother blithely assumed that my family too celebrated Christmas.* **2** LITERARY happily and without worries

blith·er·ing /ˈblɪðərɪŋ/ *adj.* **blithering idiot** an insulting word for someone who behaves in a stupid way

blitz /blɪts/ *n.* [C usually singular] **1** a situation in football when several football players run at the QUARTERBACK to try to stop him from throwing the ball **2** a situation when you use a lot of effort to achieve something, usually in a short time: **media/advertising/marketing etc. blitz** *Both candidates ran a media blitz in the last few days of the campaign.* **3** a sudden military attack, especially from the air —**blitz** *v.* [T]

blitzed /blɪtst/ *adj.* SPOKEN very drunk

blitz·krieg /ˈblɪtskrig/ *n.* [U] a sudden and very powerful military attack that is intended to beat the enemy quickly using military forces both on the ground and in the air

bliz·zard /ˈblɪzɚd/ *n.* [C] **1** a severe storm with a lot of snow and wind: *blizzards on the East Coast* | *She got stuck in her car in a* ***raging blizzard.*** → see picture on page A30 ►see THESAURUS box at **snow¹** **2** INFORMAL a sudden large amount of something that you must deal with: *a blizzard of emails*

bloat·ed /ˈbloʊt̬ɪd/ *adj.* **1** much larger than usual because of being too full of water, gas, food etc. SYN **swollen**: *a bloated fish, floating in the river* **2** feeling bad because you have eaten too much: *I felt so bloated after Thanksgiving dinner.* **3** INFORMAL an organization, company etc. that is bloated is too big and does not work well or effectively: *the bloated government bureaucracy*

bloat·ing /ˈbloʊt̬ɪŋ/ *n.* [U] swelling in part of the body, because it has too much gas or liquid in it: *Symptoms include severe cramps and bloating.*

blob /blɑb/ *n.* **1** a small round MASS of liquid or sticky substance SYN **drop**: +**of** *a blob of oil* **2** something that is difficult to see clearly, especially because it is far away: *Without a telescope, the comet will look like a fuzzy blob.*

B

bloc /blɑk/ *n.* [C usually singular] POLITICS a large group of people or countries with the same political aims, working together SYN **alliance**: *the former Soviet bloc* → see also EN BLOC

block¹ /blɑk/ S2 W2 *n.* [C]
1 STREET/AREA a) the distance along a city street from where one street crosses it to the next: *My grandmother lived just three blocks away.* | *There's a good deli just* ***down the block*** *from my office.* **b)** a square area of houses or buildings formed by four streets: *Rob took the dog for a walk* ***around the block****.* | *There are quite a few families with small children living* ***on the block****.* | *The new building will cover an entire* ***city block****.* | **the 300/800/2000 block of sth** (=the area of houses on a particular road that have numbers between 300 and 399, 800 and 899 etc. in their addresses) *the 500 block of Stuart Street*
2 SOLID PIECE a solid piece of hard material such as wood or stone with straight sides: **concrete/cement block** *a wall made of concrete blocks* | +**of** *a block of ice* | *a block of wood* ►see THESAURUS box at **piece¹**
3 RELATED GROUP a group of things of the same kind, that are related in some way: +**of** *Each employee was given a block of shares in the company.* | *Jason says he can get a block of seats* (=seats next to each other) *for the concert.* | *The money is given to the state in the form of a block grant.*
4 a block of time a length of time that is not interrupted by anything: *Set aside a block of time to do your homework.*
5 a block of text written sentences on a page or computer screen, considered as a group: *Highlight a block of text, then press delete.*
6 TOYS [usually plural] a small piece of wood or plastic, often shaped like a CUBE, that children use to build things with: *Blocks are great for imaginative play.* | *a box full of colorful* ***building blocks***
7 UNABLE TO THINK [usually singular] the temporary loss of your normal ability to think, learn, write etc.: *Some perfectly intelligent people seem to have a* ***mental block*** *when it comes to computers.* | *After her first novel was published, she had* ***writer's block*** *for a year.*
8 on the block being sold, especially at an AUCTION
9 SPORTS a movement in sports that stops an opponent going forward or playing the ball forward
10 sb has been around the block (a few times) INFORMAL used to say that someone has experienced many different situations, and can deal with new situations confidently
11 LARGE BUILDING a large building divided into separate parts: *an apartment block*
12 block voting an arrangement that is made for a whole group to vote together
13 COMPUTER a physical unit of stored information on a MAGNETIC TAPE or computer DISK
14 PRINTING a piece of wood or metal with words or line drawings cut into it, for printing
15 the block a solid block of wood on which someone's head was cut off as a punishment, in past times: *He was prepared to go to the block for his beliefs.*
[**Origin:** 1300–1400 Old French *bloc*, from Middle Dutch *blok*] → see also BUILDING BLOCK, **be a chip off the old block** at CHIP¹ (7), CHOPPING BLOCK, CINDER BLOCK, **knock sb's block off** at KNOCK¹ (8), **the new kid on the block** at NEW (14), ROADBLOCK, STARTING BLOCK, STUMBLING BLOCK

block² S2 W2 *v.* [T] **1** also **block up** to prevent things from moving or flowing through a space by putting something across it or in it SYN **obstruct**: *The accident has blocked two lanes of traffic on the freeway.* | *The sink is blocked up again.* | *surgery to clear a blocked artery* **2** to prevent someone from moving to or toward a place: **block sb's way/path etc.** *I tried to get through, but there were too many people blocking my way.* **3** to stop something happening, developing, or succeeding: *The group has blocked efforts to restrict gun ownership.* | *The enzyme's activity can be blocked in cancer cells.* **4** also **block out** to prevent something from being seen or heard: *The chip blocks programs that you do not want your children to watch.* **5 block sb's view** to be in front of someone so that they cannot see something: *The view was blocked by two ugly high-rise apartment buildings.* **6** also **block out** to stop light reaching a place: *Could you move over? You're blocking my light.* **7** to prevent someone from making points, moving forward, or throwing or catching a ball in sports such as basketball, football, or HOCKEY **8** TECHNICAL to limit the use of a particular country's money: *a blocked currency*

block sth ↔ **off** *phr. v.* to completely close a road or path: *Exit 31 is blocked off due to an accident.*

block sth ↔ **out** *phr. v.* **1** to stop yourself from thinking about something or remembering it: *Carrie hears what she wants to hear and blocks out the rest.* **2** to prevent something from being seen or heard: *Heavy curtains blocked out the light.* | *Her face was blocked out of TV broadcasts by a large gray circle.* **3** to decide that you will use a particular time only for a particular purpose: *I try to block out two days a week for research.* **4** to make a drawing of something that is not exact: *Block out the design on the rug using stencils.*

block·ade¹ /blɑˈkeɪd/ *n.* [C] **1** [usually singular] the act of surrounding a place to stop people or supplies leaving or entering: *a naval blockade* | **lift/raise the blockade** (=to end a blockade) | *They've* ***imposed*** *an economic* ***blockade*** *on the country.* **2** something that is used to stop vehicles or people entering or leaving a place

blockade² *v.* [T] to put a blockade around a place: *Ships blockaded the port.*

block·age /ˈblɑkɪdʒ/ *n.* **1** [C] something that is stopping movement in a narrow place: *a blockage in the pipe* **2** [U] the state of being blocked or prevented

ˌblock and ˈtackle *n.* [C usually singular] a piece of equipment made with wheels and ropes, used for lifting heavy things

block·bust·er /ˈblɑkˌbʌstɚ/ *n.* [C] INFORMAL a book or movie that is very good or successful SYN **hit**: *a summer blockbuster*

ˈblock grant *n.* [C] ECONOMICS money given by central government to state governments in order to help pay for services such as the police, road building etc.

block·head /ˈblɑkhɛd/ *n.* [C] SPOKEN a very stupid person SYN **idiot**

block·house /ˈblɑkhaʊs/ *n.* [C] a small strong building used as a shelter from enemy guns

ˌblock ˈletters *n.* [plural] CAPITAL letters

ˈblock ˌparty *n.* [C] a party in the street for all the people living in the area near the street

blog /blɑg/ *n.* [C] COMPUTERS a Web page that is made up of information about a particular subject, in which the newest information is always at the top of the page. Readers of the blog can add their own opinions about what they read there. SYN **web log**: *The students each had to create a blog about their work for the class.* —**blogger** *n.* [C]

bloke /bloʊk/ *n.* [C] BRITISH INFORMAL a man

blond /blɑnd/ *adj.* **1** blond hair is pale or yellow in color **2** someone who is blond has pale or yellow hair → see also BRUNETTE

blonde¹ /blɑnd/ *adj.* **1** another spelling of blond, used when talking about a woman ►see THESAURUS box at **hair** **2 blonde bombshell** HUMOROUS an extremely attractive woman with light colored hair

blonde² *n.* [C] a woman with pale or yellow-colored hair

blood /blʌd/ S2 W1 *n.* [U]
1 IN YOUR BODY BIOLOGY the red liquid that your heart pumps around your body: *She* ***lost*** *a lot of* ***blood*** *in the accident.* | **give/donate blood** (=have blood taken from you and stored to be used when treating someone

else) | *There were* **drops of blood** *on his shoes.* | *The murder victim lay in a* **pool of blood**. | *Doctors took a* **blood sample** (=a little bit of blood for tests to be done) *from Schneider.* | *A small amount of aspirin can prevent the* **blood** *from* **clotting** (=from becoming thicker or more solid). | *After the bombing, dazed people in* **blood-soaked** *clothing wandered the streets.* | *a* **blood-stained** *t-shirt*
2 draw blood a) MEDICINE to take blood from someone, especially during medical treatment **b)** to make someone BLEED: *The dog bit me, but it didn't draw blood.*
3 new/fresh blood new members in a group or organization who bring new ideas and energy: *The firm desperately needs some new blood.*
4 in cold blood in a cruel and deliberate way: *He murdered the old man in cold blood.*
5 sweat blood to work extremely hard to achieve something: *Donald sweated blood to build up his business.*
6 have sb's blood on your hands to have caused someone's death
7 YOUR FAMILY/GROUP the family or group to which you belong from the time that you are born: *There's French blood on his mother's side.* → see also BLOOD RELATIVE
8 be in sb's blood also **have sth in your blood** if an ability or tendency is in someone's blood, it is natural to them and others in their family
9 get sth in your blood to begin to like something so much that you want to do it all the time and it seems very natural to you: *The acting business gets in your blood.*
10 make your blood boil to make you extremely angry
11 make your blood run cold to make you feel extremely frightened: *The sudden scream made my blood run cold.*
12 blood is thicker than water used to say that family relationships are more important than any other kind
13 blood, sweat, and tears extremely hard work
14 can't get/take blood from a stone used to say that you have no money to give someone
[**Origin:** Old English *blod*] → see also **bad blood** at BAD[1] (22), -BLOODED, **your own flesh and blood** at FLESH[1] (5), RED BLOOD CELL, WHITE BLOOD CELL, **young blood** at YOUNG[1] (6)

ˌblood-and-ˈguts *adj.* [no comparative] INFORMAL full of action or violence: *a blood-and-guts struggle between the two teams*

ˈblood bank *n.* [C] a place where human blood is kept to be used in hospital treatment

blood·bath /ˈblʌdbæθ/ *n.* [singular] the violent killing of many people at one time SYN massacre

ˈblood ˌbrother *n.* [C] a man who promises loyalty to another, often in a ceremony in which the men's blood is mixed together

ˈblood clot *n.* [C] a small amount of blood that has become thick so that it blocks one of the tubes that carry blood through the body

ˈblood count *n.* [C] **1** BIOLOGY the number of cells in someone's blood **2** MEDICINE a test of someone's blood to see how many cells it contains and of which type they are

blood·cur·dling /ˈblʌdˌkɚdl-ɪŋ/ *adj.* extremely frightening: *a bloodcurdling scream*

ˈblood ˌdonor *n.* [C] someone who gives their blood to be used in the medical treatment of other people

ˈblood drive *n.* [C] an event where people can go to give blood for the medical treatment of others

-blooded /blʌdɪd/ *suffix* having a particular type of blood: **warm-blooded/cold-blooded** *Fish are cold-blooded.* → see also HOT-BLOODED

ˈblood feud *n.* [C] an argument between people or families that continues for many years, in which each side murders or injures members of the other side

blood·hound /ˈblʌdhaʊnd/ *n.* [C] BIOLOGY a large dog with a very good sense of smell, often used for hunting

blood·less /ˈblʌdlɪs/ *adj.* **1** [no comparative] without killing or violence → see also BLOODY: *a bloodless invasion* **2** a bloodless part of your body is very pale: *His lips were thin and bloodless.* **3** lacking in human feeling SYN cold —**bloodlessly** *adv.*

blood·let·ting /ˈblʌdˌlɛt̬ɪŋ/ *n.* [U] **1** the act of killing people SYN bloodshed: *Troops are trying to stop the worst of the bloodletting in the capital.* **2** a situation in which a lot of people are forced to leave a company, political party etc.: *a major management bloodletting* **3** a medical treatment in past times which involved removing some of the sick person's blood

blood·line /ˈblʌdlaɪn/ *n.* [C] all the members of a family of people or animals over a period of time: *a royal bloodline*

ˈblood lust *n.* [U] a strong desire to be violent

blood·mo·bile /ˈblʌdmoʊˌbil/ *n.* [C] a special vehicle where people can go to give blood to be used in medical treatments

ˈblood ˌmoney *n.* [U] **1** money paid for murdering someone **2** money paid to the family of someone who has been murdered

ˈblood ˌorange *n.* [C] an orange with red flesh and juice

ˈblood ˌpoisoning *n.* [U] MEDICINE a serious medical condition in which an infection spreads through your blood

ˈblood ˌpressure *n.* [U] BIOLOGY the force with which blood travels through your body, that can be measured: **high/low blood pressure** (=when your blood pressure is higher or lower than normal) | **check/take sb's blood pressure** (=measure it) *A nurse will take your blood pressure.*

ˈblood-red *adj.* dark red, like blood: *blood-red lips*

ˈblood ˌrelative also **ˈblood reˌlation** *n.* [C] someone related to you by birth rather than by marriage

blood·shed /ˈblʌdʃɛd/ *n.* [U] the killing of people, usually in fighting or war: *Diplomats are working to stop the bloodshed.*

blood·shot /ˈblʌdʃɑt/ *adj.* if your eyes are bloodshot, the parts that are normally white have become red or pink

ˈblood sport *n.* [C] a sport that involves the killing of animals or birds SYN hunting

blood·stain /ˈblʌdsteɪn/ *n.* [C] a mark or spot of blood —**bloodstained** *adj.*: *a bloodstained shirt*

blood·stream /ˈblʌdstrim/ *n.* [singular] BIOLOGY blood as it flows around your body: *The drug is injected directly into the bloodstream.*

blood·suck·er /ˈblʌdˌsʌkɚ/ *n.* [C] **1** BIOLOGY a creature that sucks blood from the body of other animals **2** INFORMAL someone who tries to get a lot of money from someone else, especially by using BLACKMAIL

ˈblood test *n.* [C] a medical examination in which a small amount of blood is taken from someone so that it can be checked to see if the person has a disease, has taken drugs etc.

blood·thirst·y /ˈblʌdˌθɚsti/ *adj. comparative* **bloodthirstier**, *superlative* **bloodthirstiest** **1** eager to kill or wound, or enjoying seeing killing or violence: *a bloodthirsty monster* | *a bloodthirsty crowd* **2** describing or showing violence: *bloodthirsty speeches* —**bloodthirstiness** *n.* [U]

ˈblood transˌfusion *n.* [C] MEDICINE the process of putting blood into someone's body as a medical treatment

ˈblood type *n.* [C] BIOLOGY one of the types into which human blood can be separated, including A, B, AB, and O

ˈblood ˌvessel *n.* [C] BIOLOGY any of the tubes through which blood flows in your body → see also **burst a blood vessel** at BURST[1] (6)

blood·y[1] /ˈblʌdi/ *adj. comparative* **bloodier**, *superlative* **bloodiest** **1** covered in blood or BLEEDing: *a bloody nose* **2** with a lot of killing and injuries: *a bloody battle* **3 scream/yell bloody murder** INFORMAL **a)** to protest in

B

a loud and very angry way: *Fans are screaming bloody murder about ticket prices.* **b)** to scream very loudly

bloody² *v.* **bloodies, bloodied, bloodying** [T] **1** FORMAL to injure someone so that blood comes, or to cover something with blood: *The boy punched Jack and bloodied his nose.* **2 bloodied but unbowed** affected badly by an argument or difficult situation, but not defeated by it

ˌBloody 'Mary *n. plural* **Bloody Marys** [C] an alcoholic drink made by mixing VODKA, TOMATO juice, and SPICES

ˌBloody 'Sunday HISTORY January 22, 1905, when soldiers of Czar Nicholas II attacked and killed workers who were protesting peacefully in St. Petersburg, Russia

bloom¹ /blum/ *n.* **1** [C,U] BIOLOGY a flower, or a group of flowers: *beautiful red blooms* | *a mass of bloom on the apple trees* **2 in bloom** BIOLOGY a plant that is in bloom has flowers that are open: *The azaleas are **in full bloom**.* **3** LITERARY a good, happy, or successful time: *a boy in the full **bloom of youth***

bloom² *v.* [I] **1 a)** BIOLOGY if a plant blooms, it produces flowers **b)** if a flower blooms, it opens **2** to become happy and healthy, or successful: *The experiment bloomed into a $50 million business.*

bloom•ers /'bluməz/ *n.* [plural] **a)** underwear that women wore in past times, like loose pants that end at the knees **b)** short loose pants that end in a tight band at your knees, worn for sports by women in Europe and America in the late 19th century → see also **late bloomer/developer** at LATE¹ (8)

bloop /blup/ *v.* [T] to hit a ball in the air just past the INFIELD in a game of baseball —**bloop** *n., adj.*

bloop•er /'blupə/ *n.* [C] INFORMAL **1** an embarrassing mistake that you make in front of other people **2** a ball that is hit in the air just past the INFIELD in a game of baseball SYN **bloop** [**Origin:** 1900–2000 *bloop* **unpleasant sound** (1900–2000), from the sound]

blos•som¹ /'blɑsəm/ *n.* [C,U] **1** BIOLOGY a flower, or all the flowers on a tree or bush: *The tree was covered in pink blossoms.* | *orange blossom* **2 in blossom** BIOLOGY a bush or tree that is in blossom has flowers on it

blossom² *v.* [I] **1** BIOLOGY if a tree blossoms, it produces flowers SYN **bloom**: *The apple trees are just beginning to blossom.* **2** also **blossom out** to become happier, more beautiful, more successful etc.: *Pete has really blossomed in his new school.*

blot¹ /blɑt/ *v.* **blots, blotted, blotting** [T] to dry a wet surface by pressing soft paper or cloth on it

blot sth ↔ **out** *phr. v.* **1** to cover or hide something completely: *Gas and dust from the volcano blotted out the sun.* **2** to forget something, often deliberately: *She had blotted out all memory of the accident.*

blot sth ↔ **up** *phr. v.* to remove liquid from a surface by pressing a soft cloth, paper etc. onto it

blot² *n.* [C] **1** a mark or spot that spoils something or makes it dirty: ***ink blots*** **2** a building, structure etc. that is ugly and spoils the appearance of a place: **+on** *The oil rigs are a blot on the coastline.* **3** something that spoils the good opinion other people have of you: **+on** *The massacre is one of the great blots on our nation's history.*

blotch /blɑtʃ/ *n.* [C] an unattractive pink or red mark on the skin, or a colored mark on something: *a black cat with white blotches* —**blotchy** *adj.* —**blotched** *adj.*

blot•ter /'blɑtə/ *n.* **1** [C] a large piece of blotting paper kept on the top of a desk **2** [C] a book in which an official daily record is kept: *the police blotter*

'blotting ˌpaper *n.* [U] soft thick paper used for drying wet ink on a page after writing

blouse /blaʊs/ *n.* [C] a shirt for women: *a silk blouse*

blo•vi•ate /'bloʊviˌeɪt/ *v.* [I] INFORMAL to talk about something for a long time in a way that tries to make you seem important, which other people think is boring or annoying: *a reporter who bloviates about political issues on TV talk shows*

blow¹ /bloʊ/ S1 W2 *v. past tense* **blew** /blu/, *past participle* **blown** /bloʊn/

1 WIND **a)** [I] if the wind or a current of air blows, it moves: *A warm breeze was blowing from the south.* **b)** [I usually + adv./prep.,T] to move or move something, by the force of the wind or a current of air: *Her hair was blowing in the breeze.* | *The wind must have **blown the door shut**.*

2 FROM YOUR MOUTH [I,T] to send out a current of air from your mouth: *Blow on it, Danny, it's hot.* | *She blew smoke right in my face!*

3 EXPLODE/SHOOT [T] to damage or destroy something violently with an explosion or by shooting: **blow sth away/out/off** *His leg was blown off when he stepped on a landmine.* | **blow sth to pieces/bits/smithereens** *The missile hit the airplane and blew it to pieces.*

4 RUIN/LOSE OPPORTUNITY [T] INFORMAL to miss a good opportunity or ruin something, by making a mistake or by being careless: *We were winning, and I didn't want to **blow it**.* | *We've **blown** our **chance** of getting that contract.* | *One of the actors **blew** his **lines*** (=said the wrong thing).

5 blow your nose to clean your nose by forcing air through it into a cloth or a piece of soft paper

6 blow sb a kiss to kiss your hand and then pretend to blow the kiss toward someone: *Blow Grandma a kiss, Katie.*

7 MONEY [T] INFORMAL to spend all your money at one time in a careless way: *I blew it all on a trip to Hawaii.*

8 sth blows your mind SPOKEN to make you feel very surprised and excited by something: *Meeting her after so many years really blew my mind.* → see also MIND-BLOWING

9 blow your top/stack/cool also **blow a fuse** SPOKEN to become extremely angry quickly or suddenly: *My father blew his top when I told him I was quitting medical school.*

10 blow smoke INFORMAL to say things in order to confuse someone, in order to gain an advantage for yourself: *You have to tell them exactly what happened. You can't blow smoke at them.*

11 blow the whistle on sb INFORMAL to tell someone in authority about something wrong that is happening: *A few honest policemen were willing to blow the whistle on the captain.*

12 blow sb/sth out of the water to defeat or achieve much more than someone or something else you are competing with: *By then the Motown label had blown all the other record companies out of the water.*

13 blow sth (up) out of (all) proportion to make something seem much more serious or important than it is SYN **exaggerate**: *This issue has been blown up out of proportion.*

14 blow your own horn INFORMAL to talk a lot about your own achievements, usually in a way that other people disapprove of SYN **boast**: *He was never the type to blow his own horn.*

15 WHISTLE/HORN [I,T] if a horn or whistle blows or you blow it, it makes a sound when you pass air through it: *The whistle blew on the old steam engine.* | *The referee blew his whistle.*

16 MAKE/SHAPE STH [T] to make or shape something, such as a ring of smoke or a BUBBLE, by sending out a current of air from your mouth: *The kids were **blowing bubbles** in the backyard.* | **blow glass** (=shape glass by blowing into it when it is very hot and soft)

17 TIRE [I,T] if a tire blows, or if a car blows a tire, the tire bursts

18 ELECTRICITY [I,T] if an electrical FUSE blows, or if a piece of electrical equipment blows a FUSE, the electricity suddenly stops working because a thin wire has melted

19 STOP WORKING [I,T] also **blow out** if a piece of equipment blows or if something blows it, it suddenly stops working completely: *You're lucky you didn't blow out the whole engine.*

20 SECRET [T] to make known something that should be a secret: *Your coming here has blown the whole*

operation. | **blow sb's cover** (=make known what someone's real name or real job is)
21 blow chunks SLANG to bring food or drink up from your stomach, because you are sick [SYN] **vomit**
[**Origin:** Old English *blawan*]

blow sb ↔ **away** *phr. v.* SPOKEN **1** to make someone feel very surprised, often by something they like or admire: *It just blows me away, the way people are so friendly here.* **2** to kill someone by shooting them with a gun: *One move and I'll blow you away!* **3** to defeat someone completely, especially in a game: *Nancy blew away the rest of the skaters.*

blow sth ↔ **down** if the wind blows something down, or if something blows down, the wind makes it fall: *Hundreds of trees were blown down in the storm.*

blow in *phr. v.* also **blow into sth 1** if a storm or bad weather blows in, it arrives and begins to affect a particular area: *The first snowstorm blew in from the north.* **2** INFORMAL to arrive in a place, especially when you are only staying for a short time: *Jim blew in about an hour ago.* | *Westheimer* ***blew into town*** *on business.*

blow sb/sth **off** *phr. v.* **1** SPOKEN to treat someone or something as unimportant, for example by not meeting someone or not going to an event: *She never called back – she just blew me off.* | *I blew off my 8 a.m. class again.* **2 blow the lid off sth** INFORMAL to tell something that was secret, especially something involving important or famous people: *Her book blew the lid off the Reagan years.* **3 blow sb's head off** INFORMAL to kill someone with a gun **4 blow off steam** INFORMAL to get rid of anger or energy by doing something: *I went jogging to blow off some steam.*

blow out *phr. v.* **1 blow sth ↔ out** if you blow a flame or a fire out, or if it blows out, it stops burning: *Blow all the candles out.* | *The match blew out in the wind.* **2** if a tire blows out, it bursts **3 blow itself out** if a storm blows itself out, it ends **4 blow sb ↔ out** SPOKEN to easily defeat someone: *We blew them out, 28 – zero.* **5** if an oil or gas well blows out, oil or gas suddenly escapes **6 blow sb's/your brains out** to kill someone or yourself by a shot to the head **7 blow sth ↔ out** if you blow out your knee or another joint in your body, or if it blows out, you injure it badly

blow over *phr. v.* **1 blow sth ↔ over** if the wind blows something over, or it blows over, the wind makes it fall: *Our fence blew over in the storm.* | *The hurricane blew palm trees over.* **2** if an argument or bad situation blows over, it does not seem important anymore or is forgotten: *Many people expected the scandal to blow over in a few days.* **3** if a storm blows over, it comes to an end

blow up *phr. v.* **1 blow sth ↔ up** to destroy something, or to be destroyed, by an explosion [SYN] **explode**: *Police cleared the waterfront before the ship blew up.* | *Rebels attempted to blow up the bridge.* **2 blow sth ↔ up** to fill something with air or gas: *Ronnie was* ***blowing up balloons*** *for the party.* **3 blow sth ↔ up** if you blow up a photograph, you make it larger [SYN] **enlarge**: *I had the picture of Mom and Dad blown up.* **4** to become very angry with someone: **+at** *She blew up at me last Saturday for no reason.* **5** if a situation, argument etc. blows up, it suddenly becomes important or dangerous: *A crisis had blown up over the peace talks.* **6 blow up in sb's face** if something you have done or planned to do blows up in your face, it suddenly goes wrong: *As an inexperienced lawyer, he'd had at least one case blow up in his face.* **7** if bad weather blows up, it suddenly arrives

blow[2] [S3] *n.*
1 HARD HIT [C] a hard hit with the hand, a weapon, or a tool: **+to** *He was killed by a blow to the head.* | *three* ***heavy blows*** *from the hammer*
2 BAD EFFECT [C] an action or event that causes difficulty or sadness for someone: **+to** *Losing the job was a blow to her pride.* | **a major/serious/severe etc. blow** *This evidence is a major blow to the government's case.* | *Farmers coping with the drought have been* ***dealt*** *another* ***blow*** *– wind storms.* | *The action could deal a* ***final blow*** *to the peace negotiations.* | *It was a* ***knock-out blow*** *to his career.* (=it made him lose his career) | *Republicans in the Senate dealt a* ***fatal blow*** *to the bill.* | *The company* ***suffered a blow*** *when its biggest customer canceled their order.*
3 BLOWING AIR [C] an action of blowing air on something: *One blow and the candles were out.*
4 come to blows if two people come to blows, they get very angry and start hitting each other: *The police were called when their argument came to blows.*
5 a low blow SPOKEN something unkind you say to deliberately embarrass or upset someone
6 soften/cushion the blow to help someone accept something that is not nice or difficult to accept: *Some of the money will be used to soften the blow of budget cuts to education.*
7 WIND [singular] a strong wind or storm → see also BODY BLOW, **strike a blow to/at/against sth** at STRIKE[1] (19)

'blow-by-blow *adj.* [only before noun] **blow-by-blow account/description etc.** an account that includes all the details of an event exactly as they happened

'blow-dry *v.* **blow-dries, blow-dried, blow-drying** [T] to dry hair and give it shape by using a blow dryer —**blow-dry** *n.* [C]: *a cut and blow-dry*

'blow ˌdryer *n.* [C] a small electric machine that you hold and use to blow hot air onto your hair in order to dry it

blow·er /ˈbloʊɚ/ *n.* [C] a machine that blows out air: *a snow blower* → see also GLASSBLOWER

'blow-fly *n.* [C] a fly that lays its eggs on meat or wounds

blow·hard /ˈbloʊhɑrd/ *n.* [C] INFORMAL someone who talks too much and has very strong opinions

blow·hole /ˈbloʊhoʊl/ *n.* [C] **1** a hole in the top of the head of a WHALE, DOLPHIN etc. through which they breathe **2** a hole in the surface of ice to which water animals such as SEALS come to breathe

blown /bloʊn/ *v.* the past participle of BLOW

blow·out /ˈbloʊaʊt/ *n.* [C] **1** INFORMAL an easy victory over someone in a game: *a 60-point blowout* **2** also **blow-out** [usually singular] INFORMAL a big expensive meal or large social occasion: *We had a big blow-out for our twenty-fifth anniversary.* **3** a sudden bursting of a TIRE: *A blow-out at high speed can be really dangerous.* **4** a sudden uncontrolled escape of oil or gas from a well

blow·pipe /ˈbloʊpaɪp/ *n.* [C] a tube through which you can blow a small stone, a poisoned ARROW etc., used as a weapon

blow·sy /ˈblaʊzi/ *adj.* another spelling of BLOWZY

blow·torch /ˈbloʊˌtɔrtʃ/ *n.* [C] a piece of equipment that produces a small very hot flame, used especially for removing paint

'blow-up, blowup *n.* [C] **1** a photograph, or part of a photograph, that has been made larger **2** [C usually singular] a sudden noisy argument → see also **blow up** at BLOW[1]

blow·zy, blowsy /ˈblaʊzi/ *adj.* **1** a blowzy woman is fat and has a messy appearance **2** blowzy hair is messy

BLT /ˌbi ɛl ˈti/ *n.* [C] a SANDWICH made with BACON, LETTUCE, and TOMATO

blub·ber[1] /ˈblʌbɚ/ *v.* [I] to cry loudly, especially in a way that annoys people: *Quit blubbering!*

blubber[2] *n.* [U] **1** the fat of sea animals, especially WHALES **2** INFORMAL the fat on a person

blud·geon[1] /ˈblʌdʒən/ *v.* [T] **1** to hit someone several times with something heavy [SYN] **beat**: *Ruddock had been* ***bludgeoned to death.*** **2** to force someone to do something by making threats or arguing with them: **+into** *The kids had been* ***bludgeoned into submission*** (=threatened until they did what someone wanted).

bludgeon[2] *n.* [C] a heavy stick with a thick end, used as a weapon

blue[1] /blu/ [S1] [W1] *adj.* **1** having the color of the clear sky: *the blue waters of the lake* | **dark/light/bright/pale blue** *a dark blue sweater* **2** [not before noun] INFORMAL sad and without hope [SYN] **depressed**: *I've been* ***feeling***

B

kind of ***blue*** *lately.* **3 do sth till you're blue in the face** INFORMAL to do something a lot, without achieving what you want: *You can argue with her till you're blue in the face, but she won't change her mind.* **4** INFORMAL blue stories, jokes etc. are about sex, in a way that might offend some people: *blue language* → see also BLUE MOVIE, **once in a blue moon** at ONCE[1] (15), **talk a blue streak** at TALK[1] (36) **[Origin:** 1200–1300 Old French *blou*]

blue² S3 W3 *n.* **1** [C,U] the color of the sky on a clear day: *the rich blues and reds of the painting* | *Carolyn's the one dressed in blue.* **2 blues** also **the blues** [plural] ENG. LANG. ARTS a slow sad style of music that came from the African-American CULTURE in the southern U.S.: *a blues singer* → see also RHYTHM AND BLUES **3 the blues** [plural] INFORMAL feelings of sadness: *A lot of women* ***get the blues*** *after the baby is born.* **4 out of the blue** INFORMAL suddenly and without warning: *Symptoms of the disease often appear out of the blue.* → see also **a bolt from the blue** at BOLT[1] (4) **5 the blue** LITERARY the ocean or the sky → see also **the boys in blue** at BOY[1] (8)

'blue ˌbaby *n.* [C] a baby whose skin is slightly blue when it is born because it has problems with its heart or lungs

blue·bell /ˈblubɛl/ *n.* [C] a small plant with blue flowers that grows in woods

blue·ber·ry /ˈbluˌbɛri/ *n. plural* **blueberries** [C,U] BIOLOGY a small round blue fruit, or the bushy plant it grows on: *blueberry pie*

blue·bird /ˈblubɚd/ *n.* [C] BIOLOGY a small blue bird that lives in North America → see picture on page A34

'blue blood, blue-blood *n.* [C] someone who is born into a family that has a very high social position: *a spoiled blue blood* —**blue-blooded** also **blue-blood** *adj.*: *one of New York's blue-blooded families*

'blue book *n.* [C] **1** a book with a list of prices that you can expect to pay for any used car **2** a book with a blue cover that is used in colleges for writing answers to test questions

'blue cheese *n.* [C,U] a type of cheese with blue lines in it and a strong taste

'blue chip *adj.* [only before noun, no comparative] **1** a blue-chip company or INVESTMENT earns profits and is safe: *blue chip stocks and shares* **2 a blue-chip athlete** INFORMAL someone who is one of the best at playing a sport, especially someone who does not yet play for a PROFESSIONAL sports team **[Origin:** 1900–2000 *blue chip* **blue counter of high value used in gambling** (1900–2000)] —**blue chip** *n.* [C]

'blue-ˌcollar *adj.* [only before noun] blue-collar workers usually do physical work and are paid by the hour, rather than being paid a SALARY → see also PINK-COLLAR

blue·fish /ˈblufɪʃ/ *n.* [C] *plural* **bluefish** BIOLOGY a fish that lives in the Atlantic Ocean and is a bluish color

blue·grass /ˈblugræs/ *n.* [U] **1** ENG. LANG. ARTS a type of music from the southern and western U.S., played on instruments such as the GUITAR and VIOLIN **2** BIOLOGY a type of grass found in North America, especially in Kentucky

'blue gum *n.* [C] a tall Australian tree that is a type of EUCALYPTUS

'blue ˌhelmet *n.* [C] someone who works for the United Nations as part of the organization's effort to keep peace

blue·jay /ˈbludʒeɪ/ *n. plural* **bluejays** [C] BIOLOGY a common North American bird with blue feathers and feathers that form a point on its head → see picture on page A34

'blue jeans *n.* [plural] dark blue pants made of a heavy material SYN **jeans**

'blue law *n.* [C] LAW a law, used especially in the past in the U.S., that controls activities that were considered immoral, such as drinking alcohol or working on Sundays

'blue ˌmovie *n.* [C] OLD-FASHIONED a movie that shows a lot of sexual activity

blue·print /ˈbluˌprɪnt/ *n.* [C] **1** a plan for achieving something: + **for** *a blueprint for economic growth* **2** a plan for a building, machine etc. on special blue paper **3** BIOLOGY a pattern that all living cells contain, which decides how a person, animal, or plant develops and what it looks like: *the* ***genetic blueprint*** *of a caterpillar*

ˌblue 'ribbon *n.* [C] a small piece of blue material that is given to the winner of a competition

'blue-ribbon *adj.* [only before noun] **1** having won first prize in a competition: *a blue-ribbon recipe* **2 blue-ribbon committee/panel/commission etc.** a group of people chosen because they have special qualities that make them suitable to do something: *a blue-ribbon panel of 500 health care professionals*

ˌBlue Ridge 'Mountains, the also **the 'Blue Ridge** a range of mountains in the eastern U.S. that goes from southern Pennsylvania in the eastern U.S. to northern Georgia and is part of the Appalachians

'blue shift *n.* [U] PHYSICS a change in the WAVELENGTH of light and RADIATION from an object in space such as a star, in which the wavelength becomes shorter and appears more blue as the object is moving toward the person looking at it → see also RED SHIFT

'blue-sky *adj.* [only before noun] blue-sky tests, RESEARCH etc. are done to test ideas and not for any practical purpose

blues·y /ˈbluzi/ *adj.* relating to BLUES music: *a bluesy rhythm*

Blue·tooth /ˈblutuθ/ *n.* [U] TRADEMARK COMPUTERS a type of TECHNOLOGY that allows electronic equipment to communicate by using radio, so that, for example, a cell phone or a NOTEBOOK COMPUTER can work without having a wire connecting it to a system

bluff¹ /blʌf/ *v.* [I,T] **1** to pretend something, especially to get what you want when you are in a difficult or dangerous situation: *He's bluffing. He'll never do it.* | **bluff your way into/out of/through etc.** *He used a false I.D. to bluff his way onto the ship.* | **bluff sb into doing sth** *Giulio bluffed the guards into letting him in.* **2** to pretend you have better cards than you really do in a game of POKER

bluff² *n.* **1** [C,U] an attempt to deceive someone by making them think you will do something when you do not intend to do it: *Johnson said the threats were pure bluff.* **2 call sb's bluff** to tell someone to do what they threaten to do, because you do not believe they will really do it **3** [C] EARTH SCIENCE a very steep cliff or slope with a flat top

bluff³ *adj.* a bluff person, usually a man, behaves in a loud happy way but does not always consider how other people feel —**bluffly** *adv.* —**bluffness** *n.* [U]

Blu·ford /ˈblufɚd/, **Gui·on** /ˈgaɪən/ (1942–) the first African-American ASTRONAUT

blu·ish /ˈbluɪʃ/ *adj.* slightly blue: *The patient's lips were bluish.*

blun·der¹ /ˈblʌndɚ/ *n.* [C] a careless or stupid mistake: *a public relations blunder*

blunder² *v.* **1** [I always + adv./prep.] to enter a place or become involved in a difficult situation by mistake: +**into** *They blundered into a group of soldiers.* **2** [I] to make a big mistake, especially because you have been careless or stupid: *Police admitted that they blundered when they let Wylie go.* **3** [I always + adv./prep.] to move in an unsteady way, as if you cannot see well: +**into/around/about** *I blundered into a table in the dark.* —**blunderer** *n.* [C]

blun·der·buss /ˈblʌndɚˌbʌs/ *n.* [C] a type of gun used in past times

blun·der·ing /ˈblʌndərɪŋ/ *adj.* [only before noun] careless or stupid

blunt¹ /blʌnt/ *adj.* **1** not sharp or pointed OPP **sharp**: *a blunt knife* **2** speaking in an honest way even if this upsets people SYN **direct**: *blunt criticism* | *I'll* ***be blunt*** *– it's a very unrealistic plan.* ►see THESAURUS box at **honest** **3 blunt instrument a)** also **blunt object** a heavy object that is used to hit someone **b)** a method of doing something that does not work very well, because it has a lot of other effects that you do not want: *Economic sanctions against a country can be a blunt instrument.* → see also BLUNTLY —**bluntness** *n.* [U]

blunt² *v.* [T] **1** to make something less strong: *The latest bombing has blunted residents' hopes for peace.* **2** to make the point of a pencil or the edge of a knife less sharp

blunt·ly /ˈblʌntˀli/ *adv.* speaking in a direct honest way that sometimes upsets people: *Several people bluntly questioned his ability to do the job.* | ***To put it bluntly**, the situation has gotten much worse.*

blur¹ /blɚ/ *n.* **a)** **a blur** a shape that you cannot see clearly: *Everything's a blur without my glasses.* | +**of** *A blur of horses ran past.* **b)** something that you cannot remember clearly: *My wedding day is just a blur.*

blur² *v.* [I,T] **1** to make the difference between two ideas, subjects etc. less clear: **blur the line/distinction/boundary between sth and sth** *The show blurs the difference between information and entertainment.* **2** to become difficult to see or make something difficult to see, because the edges are not clear: *Problems with the mirrors blurred the telescope's view.* **3** [I,T] to make someone unable to see clearly, or to be unable to see clearly: *The headache made his **vision blur**.* → see also BLURRED —**blurry** *adj.*: *a blurry picture*

blurb /blɚb/ *n.* [C] a short description giving information about a book, new product etc. [**Origin:** 1900–2000 an invented word]

blurred /blɚd/ *adj.* **1** unclear in shape, or making it difficult to see shapes SYN **fuzzy**: *a blurred image* **2** difficult to remember or understand clearly: *blurred memories*

blurt /blɚt/ also **blurt sth ↔ out** *v.* [T] to say something suddenly and without thinking, usually because you are nervous or excited: *Jackie blurted out that she was pregnant.*

blush¹ /blʌʃ/ *v.* [I] **1** to become red in the face, usually because you are embarrassed SYN **flush**: *He looked at her and blushed.* **2 sth that would make sb blush** something you say or do that is so shocking that even someone who says or does similar things would be shocked by it: *language that would make a sailor blush* **3 the blushing bride** HUMOROUS a young woman on her wedding day **4** to feel ashamed or embarrassed about something: **blush to do sth** ***I blush to admit** I've never read any of her books.* [**Origin:** Old English *blyscan* **to become red**, from *blysa* **flame**] —**blushingly** *adv.*

blush² *n.* **1** [C] the red color on your face that appears when you are embarrassed, confused, or ashamed SYN **flush**: *Susan confessed with a blush that she'd been watching him.* **2** [C,U] cream or powder used for making your cheeks slightly red SYN **rouge** **3 at first blush** FORMAL when first thought of or considered: *At first blush, this discovery seems to confirm his theory.* **4** [C,U] BLUSH WINE

blush·er /ˈblʌʃɚ/ *n.* [U] another word for BLUSH

ˈblush wine *n.* [C,U] a wine with a slightly pink color

blus·ter¹ /ˈblʌstɚ/ *v.* [I] **1** to speak in a loud angry way and behave as if what you are doing is very important **2** if the wind blusters, it blows violently —**blustering** *adj.*: *blustering wintry weather*

bluster² *n.* [U] noisy proud talk

blus·ter·y /ˈblʌstəri/ *adj.* blustery weather is very windy: *a cold and blustery day*

blvd. the written abbreviation of BOULEVARD

Bly /blaɪ/, **Nel·lie** /ˈnɛli/ the PEN NAME of Elizabeth Cochrane Seaman (1867–1922), a U.S. JOURNALIST

BMI /ˌbi ɛm ˈaɪ/ *n.* [U] the abbreviation of BODY MASS INDEX

B-mov·ie /ˌbi ˈmuvi/ *n.* [C] a cheaply made movie of low quality, especially one made in the 1950s

B'nai B'rith /bəˌneɪ ˈbrɪθ/ an international organization of Jewish people that works to oppose ANTI-SEMITISM and helps Jewish people all over the world

B.O. /bi ˈoʊ/ *n.* [U] **body odor** a bad smell from someone's body caused by sweat

bo·a /ˈboʊə/ *n.* [C] **1** also **ˈboa conˌstrictor** BIOLOGY a large snake that is not poisonous, but kills animals by crushing them **2** a FEATHER BOA [**Origin:** 1300–1400 Latin, type of water snake]

boar /bɔr/ *n.* [C] **1** BIOLOGY a wild pig **2** BIOLOGY a male pig OPP **sow**

B

boards

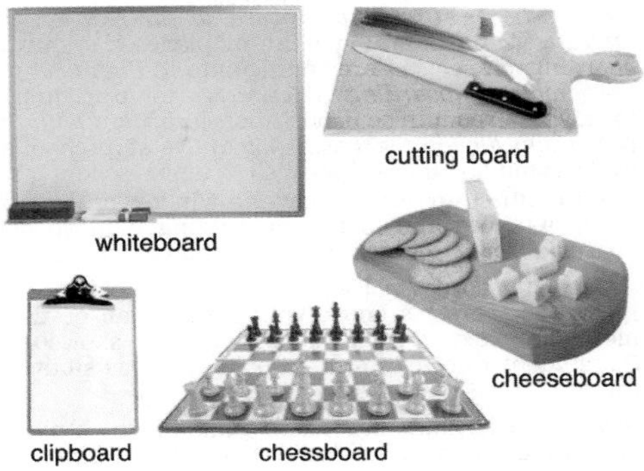

board¹ /bɔrd/ S1 W1 *n.*

1 GROUP OF PEOPLE [C] a group of people in an organization who make the rules and important decisions: *a board meeting* | *the local **school board*** | *There's only one woman on the **board of directors**.* | *an influential **board member*** | *Several politicians **sit on the** company's **board**.* | +**of** *the Los Angeles County Board of Supervisors*

2 INFORMATION [C] a flat wide piece of wood, plastic etc. that is fixed to a wall and is used to show information: *Your homework assignment is written **on the board**.* | *An announcement was posted on a board near the coffee machine.* → see also BLACKBOARD, BULLETIN BOARD, SCOREBOARD

3 FOR PUTTING THINGS ON [C] a flat piece of wood, plastic etc. that you use for a particular purpose such as cutting things on, or for playing indoor games: *Where's the chess board?* | *a cutting board* → see also BREADBOARD

4 FOR BUILDING [C] a long thin flat piece of wood used for making floors, walls, fences etc.: *cedar boards from an old fence* → see also FLOORBOARD (1)

5 on board a) on a ship or an airplane → see also ABOARD: *A light plane with four people on board crashed last night.* **b)** involved in something or working for an organization: *Since Morgan **came on board**, the band has given more concerts to school groups .* | *The change is aimed at **bringing** more House Democrats **on board**.*

6 across the board if something happens or is done across the board, it affects everyone in a particular group, place etc.: *They're cutting 10% of their staff across the board.*

7 college/medical boards examinations that you take when you APPLY to a college or medical school

8 SPORTS [C] INFORMAL a special board that you stand or lie on in sports such as SURFING, SKATEBOARDING etc. → see also BODY BOARD, SKATEBOARD, SNOWBOARD, SURFBOARD

9 the boards [plural] **a)** the low wooden wall around the area in which you play HOCKEY **b)** the stage in a theater → see also **tread the boards** at TREAD¹ (4)

10 BASKETBALL [C usually plural] INFORMAL **a)** the plastic or wooden object to which a BASKETBALL HOOP is attached **b)** an act of catching the ball after it has bounced back from the board

11 MEALS [U] the meals that are provided for you when you pay to stay somewhere: *Students pay for **room and board** each semester.*

12 go by the board/boards if a plan, idea, or way of behaving goes by the board, it is not possible anymore:

His Olympic dreams went by the board when he injured his ankle.
13 take sth on board to listen to and accept a suggestion, idea etc.: *Mr. Rice seemed to take our comments on board.*
14 ELECTRICITY a CIRCUIT BOARD
[**Origin:** Old English *bord*] → see also ABOVEBOARD, DIVING BOARD, DRAWING BOARD, IRONING BOARD

B

board² *v.* **1** [I,T] FORMAL to get on a bus, airplane, train etc. in order to travel somewhere: *They boarded a flight for Israel.* | **+at/to** *Please board to the rear of the aircraft.* **2 be boarding** if an airplane or a ship is boarding, passengers are getting onto it: *Flight 503 for Toronto is now boarding.* **3** [I always + adv./prep.] to pay to stay in a room in someone's house: *I board with the Nicholsons during the week.* **4** [I] to live at a school as well as studying there → see also BOARDING SCHOOL

board sth ↔ **up** *phr. v.* to cover a window or door, or all the windows and doors of a building, with wooden boards: *A lot of the store fronts were boarded up.*

board·er /ˈbɔrdɚ/ *n.* [C] **1** someone who pays to live in another person's house with some or all of their meals provided **2** someone who rides a SNOWBOARD **3** a student who lives at a school as well as studying there

ˈboard game *n.* [C] any indoor game in which pieces are moved around a specially designed board made of thick CARDBOARD or wood

board·ing /ˈbɔrdɪŋ/ *n.* [U] **1** the act of getting on a ship, an airplane etc. in order to travel somewhere: *Ladies and gentlemen, boarding will begin in just a few minutes.* **2** narrow pieces of wood that are fastened side by side, usually to cover a broken door or window

ˈboarding card *n.* a BOARDING PASS

ˈboarding house *n.* [C] a private house where you pay to sleep and eat

ˈboarding pass *n.* [C] an official piece of paper that you have to show before you get on an airplane

ˈboarding school *n.* [C] a school where students live as well as study

ˌboard of ˈgovernors *n.* [C] ECONOMICS **1 the Board of Governors** the group that makes decisions about how the Federal Reserve System (=U.S. money system) is run **2** a group that makes decisions about how a STOCK EXCHANGE or other organization is run

board·room /ˈbɔrdrum/ *n.* [C] a room where the members of the BOARD of a company or organization have meetings

board·walk /ˈbɔrdwɔk/ *n.* [C] a raised path made of wood, usually built next to the ocean → see also PIER

boast¹ /boʊst/ *v.* **1** [I,T] to talk too proudly about your abilities, achievements, or possessions, sometimes in a way that annoys other people SYN **brag**: *I don't want to boast, but I was the first woman ever to win the competition.* | *"I wouldn't be afraid," she boasted.* | **boast that** *The company boasts that its packaging is recyclable.* | **+about** *Scott was boasting about winning the game.* | **+of** *He boasted of having once sung with the Count Basie band.* | *They* ***like to boast*** *that their ad campaigns get noticed.* **2** [T] if a place, object, or organization boasts something, it has something that is very good: *The new athletic center boasts an Olympic-size swimming pool.* —**boaster** *n.* [C]

boast² *n.* [C] something you talk proudly about, sometimes so that it annoys other people: *His boast that he had cut taxes won him re-election.* | **sth is not an idle boast** (=something is true, not a boast)

boast·ful /ˈboʊstfəl/ *adj.* talking too proudly about yourself —**boastfully** *adv.* —**boastfulness** *n.* [U]

boat /boʊt/ S2 W2 *n.* [C] **1** a vehicle that travels across water: *a fishing boat* | *a motor boat* | *They set off down the river* ***in a*** *small* ***boat****.* | *There were three people* ***on the boat****.* | *Many Cubans fled the island* ***by boat****.*

THESAURUS
sailboat a small boat with a sail, used for pleasure
rowboat a small boat that you move through the water using oars (=long poles that are flat on the ends)
yacht a large boat with a sail, used for pleasure or sport
dinghy a small open boat used for pleasure, or for taking people between a ship and the shore
catamaran a sailing boat with two separate hulls (=the part that goes in the water)
barge a large low boat with a flat bottom, used for carrying heavy goods on a canal or river
→ SHIP

2 INFORMAL a ship, especially one that carries passengers **3 be in the same boat (as sb)** to be in the same bad situation as someone else: *We started talking to other customers, and eventually found there were 30 of us in the same boat.* [**Origin:** Old English *bat*] → see also GRAVY BOAT, **miss the boat** at MISS¹ (12), **rock the boat** at ROCK² (3)

boat·er /ˈboʊt̬ɚ/ *n.* [C] a hard STRAW hat with a flat top

ˈboat hook *n.* [C] a long pole with an iron hook at the end, used to pull or push a small boat

boat·house /ˈboʊthaʊs/ *n.* [C] a building that small boats are kept in when they are not being used

boat·ing /ˈboʊt̬ɪŋ/ *n.* [U] the activity of traveling in a small boat for pleasure: *There's boating on the lake on weekends.*

boat·load /ˈboʊtloʊd/ *n.* [C] the people or things that are or were on a boat: **+of** *a boatload of refugees*

boat·man /ˈboʊt˺mən/ *n.* [C] a man whom you pay to take you out in a boat or for the use of a boat

ˈboat ˌpeople *n.* [plural] people who leave their country in small boats to escape from a bad situation → see also REFUGEE

boat·swain /ˈboʊsən/ *n.* [C] an officer on a ship whose job is to organize the work and take care of the equipment SYN **bosun**

boat·yard /ˈboʊt˺yɑrd/ *n.* [C] an area where boats are built, repaired, or kept when they are not in the water

bob¹ /bɑb/ *v.*
1 MOVE IN WATER [I] to move up and down when floating on the surface of water: *Swimmers* ***bobbed up and down*** *in the waves.*
2 MOVE SOMEWHERE [I always + adv./prep.] to move quickly up or down in a particular direction: **+up/down/out etc.** *Her blonde ponytail bobbed up and down as she talked.*
3 HAIR [T] to cut a woman's or girl's hair in a bob
4 bob and weave a) to move your body up and down and around an area, in order to avoid something or avoid being hit: *The two boxers were bobbing and weaving in the ring.* **b)** to avoid directly answering a question: *Davidovich bobs and weaves through the questions reporters shout to him.*
5 bob for apples to play a game in which you try to pick up apples floating in water, using only your mouth
6 bob your head to move your head down quickly as a way of showing respect, greeting someone, or agreeing with them
7 bob (sb) a curtsy to make a quick small CURTSY to someone

bob² *n.* [C] **1** a way of cutting a woman's or girl's hair so that it hangs down to the level of her chin and is the same length all the way around: *a little girl with a short bob* → see picture at HAIRSTYLE **2** a quick up and down movement of your head or body, to show respect, agreement, greeting etc.: *The maid gave a little bob and left the room.* **3** a BOBSLED [**Origin:** (1) 1900–2000 *bob* **bunch (of hair)**]

bob·bin /ˈbɑbɪn/ *n.* [C] a small round object that you wind thread onto, especially for a SEWING MACHINE → see also SPOOL

bob·ble /ˈbɑbəl/ *v.* [T] to drop or hold a ball in an uncontrolled way SYN **fumble**: *The shortstop bobbled the ball and the runner ran home.*

bob·by /ˈbɑbi/ *n.* [C] OLD-FASHIONED, BRITISH a police officer

ˈbobby pin *n.* [C] a thin piece of metal bent into a narrow U shape that a woman uses to hold her hair in place

ˈbobby socks, bobby sox *n.* [plural] girls' short socks that have the tops turned over

bob·cat /ˈbɑbkæt/ *n.* [C] a large North American wild cat that has no tail SYN **lynx**

bob·sled /ˈbɑbslɛd/ *n.* **1** [C] a small vehicle with two long thin metal blades instead of wheels, that is used for racing down a special ice track **2** [U] a sports event in which people race against each other in bobsleds: *Sixteen teams took part in the 400m bobsled.* —**bobsledding** *n.* [U] —**bobsledder** *n.* [C] —**bobsled** *v.* [I]

bob·tail /ˈbɑbteɪl/ *n.* [C] **a)** a horse or dog whose tail has been cut short **b)** a tail that has been cut short

bob·white /ˌbɑbˈwaɪt/ *n.* [C] BIOLOGY a brown and white North American bird about the size of a chicken SYN **quail**

bod /bɑd/ *n.* [C] INFORMAL someone's body: *He has a gorgeous bod!*

bo·da·cious /boʊˈdeɪʃəs/ *adj.* SLANG **1** excellent: *a bodacious video* **2** brave and surprising or extreme: *Smith's bodacious promise*

bode /boʊd/ *v.* **1 bode well/ill (for sb/sth)** ESPECIALLY LITERARY to be a good or bad sign for the future: *The results of the opinion poll do not bode well for the Democrats.* **2** the past tense of BIDE

bo·de·ga /boʊˈdeɪgə/ *n.* [C] a small store that sells food

Bo·dhi·dhar·ma /ˌboʊdɪˈdɑrmə/ (6th century A.D.) an Indian Buddhist religious leader who taught in China and is believed to have started Zen Buddhism

bo·dhi·satt·va /ˌboʊdɪˈsʌtvə/ *n.* [C] a Buddhist who has become holy enough to enter NIRVANA but chooses to stay on earth and help other people

bod·ice /ˈbɑdɪs/ *n.* [C] **1** the part of a woman's dress above her waist **2** a tight woman's VEST worn over a BLOUSE in past times **3** OLD USE a CORSET

-bodied /bɑdid/ *suffix* **long-bodied/thick-bodied etc.** having a long thick etc. body: *They were thick-bodied men, used to hard labor.* → see also ABLE-BODIED, FULL-BODIED

bod·i·ly¹ /ˈbɑdl-i/ *adj.* [only before noun] relating to the human body: *bodily functions* | *the threat of death or serious bodily harm*

bodily² *adv.* by moving the whole of someone's body or by moving the whole of an object at once: *They lifted the child bodily aboard.*

bod·y /ˈbɑdi/ S1 W1 *n. plural* **bodies**
1 SB'S BODY [C] **a)** the physical structure of a person or animal: *a strong, healthy body* | *Many teenagers are self-conscious about their bodies.* | **body heat/temperature/weight etc.** *Babies rapidly increase their body weight during the first weeks.* | *The first* ***parts of the body*** *to get cold are feet and hands.* | **body image** (=the mental picture you have of your own body) **b)** the central part of a person or animal's body, not including the head, arms, legs, or wings SYN **torso**: *a man with a short body and long legs*

> **THESAURUS**
> Your **body** consists of your arms, legs, head etc., and may be healthy, skinny, dead etc.: *I had a fever and my body ached all over.* If you say that someone has a good/beautiful **body**, you mean that he or she is attractive.
> A woman's **figure** is the shape of her body: *She has a really nice figure.*
> **Build** can be used for the size and shape of both men and women: *a man with a heavy build* | *She has a very slight build.*

2 DEAD BODY [C] the dead body of a person or animal: *His body was flown home to be buried.* | *Laura had never seen a* ***dead body*** *before.*
3 GROUP OF PEOPLE [C] a group of people who work together to do a particular job or who are together for a particular purpose: **+of** *the body of believers in the church* | *the* ***governing body*** *of the university* (=people in the government of the university) | *the President of the* ***student body*** (=all the students in a school or college)
4 a/the body of sth **a)** a large amount or collection of something: **body of knowledge/evidence/opinion etc.** *the growing body of evidence in the case* | *Davies'* ***body of work*** *consists of eleven novels and various collections of stories and essays.* **b)** the main, central, or most important part of something: *the body of the report*
5 MAIN STRUCTURE [C] the main structure of something such as a vehicle or musical instrument that is made of one large part and other smaller parts: *The body of the plane broke in two.* | *The guitar is 16 inches wide across the body.*
6 HAIR [U] if your hair has body, it is thick and healthy
7 a body of water a large area of water such as a lake
8 TASTE [U] if food or an alcoholic drink has body, it has a strong FLAVOR (=taste): *Tomatoes will give the sauce more body.* | *a full-bodied wine* (=one with a strong taste)
9 SEPARATE OBJECT [C] TECHNICAL an object that is separate from other objects: *There is some kind of* ***foreign body*** (=object that is not part of something) *irritating his eye.*
10 body and soul **a)** completely: *She devoted herself body and soul to the fight for women's rights.* **b)** the whole of a person: *We work with all the strength of body and soul.*
11 keep body and soul together to continue to exist with only just enough food, money etc.
12 in a body if people do something in a body, they do it together in large numbers: *The demonstrators marched in a body to the main square.*
[**Origin:** Old English *bodig*] → see also -BODIED, **over my dead body** at DEAD¹ (18)

ˈbody ˌarmor *n.* [U] clothing worn by the police that protects them against bullets

ˈbody bag *n.* [C] a large bag used for removing a dead body from a place, used especially by the military: *the body bags coming home from the war*

ˈbody blow *n.* [C] **1** a serious loss, disappointment, or defeat: *The corporation* ***suffered a body blow*** *when Williams resigned last week.* **2** a hard hit between your neck and waist during a fight

ˈbody board, bodyboard *n.* [C] a BOOGIE BOARD —**body boarding** *n.* [U] —**bodyboarder** *n.* [C]

ˈbody building, bodybuilding *n.* [U] an activity in which you do hard physical exercise, especially lifting heavy weights, in order to develop big muscles —**body builder** *n.* [C]

ˈbody-check *v.* [T] to block an opponent in HOCKEY or LACROSSE by hitting them with your body —**body check** *n.* [C]

ˈbody clock *n.* [C] BIOLOGY the system in your body that controls types of behavior which happen at regular times, such as sleeping or eating SYN **biological clock**

ˈbody count *n.* [C] **1** the number of people or soldiers who are dead after a period of fighting or a serious accident: *a movie with a high body count* (=a large number of people killed in the story) **2** the process of counting dead bodies

ˈbody ˌdouble *n.* [C] someone whose body is used instead of an actor or actress's in a movie, especially in scenes in which they do not wear clothes

ˈbody ˌEnglish *n.* [U] the way someone's body moves or twists after they have thrown or hit a ball, as if they can influence the direction of the ball while it is in the air

bod·y·guard /ˈbɑdiˌgɑrd/ *n.* [C] **1** someone whose job is to protect an important person: *The agency provides bodyguards for movie and music stars.* **2** a group of people who work together to protect an important person

'body ˌlanguage *n.* [U] changes in your body position and movements that show what you are feeling or thinking: *You could see by her body language that she wanted to be left alone.*

B

'body mass ˌindex ABBREVIATION **BMI** *n.* [U] TECHNICAL the relationship between your height and your weight, used as a measure of whether you have too much fat on your body. It is measured by taking your weight in kilograms and dividing it by the square of your height in meters: *People with a body mass index of over 25 are considered to be overweight.*

'body ˌodor *n.* [C] a bad smell from someone's body caused by SWEAT SYN **B.O.**

'body ˌpiercing *n.* [C,U] the process of making a hole in a part of your body, so that you can wear jewelry there, or the hole itself

ˌbody 'politic *n.* [singular] POLITICS all the people in a nation forming a state that is under the control of a single government

'body search *n.* [C] a thorough search for drugs, weapons etc., that might be hidden on someone's body: *The reporter was subjected to a body search by presidential guards.* —**body-search** *v.* [T]

'body shop *n.* [C] a place where the main structure of a car is repaired, not including the engine, wheels etc. → see also GARAGE

'body ˌstocking *n.* [C] a close-fitting piece of clothing that covers the whole of your body

bod·y·suit, body suit /ˈbɑdisut/ *n.* [C] **1** a type of tight shirt worn by women that fastens between their legs **2** a piece of tight clothing that covers your whole body

bod·y·work /ˈbɑdiˌwɚk/ *n.* [U] **1** the metal frame of a vehicle, not including the engine, wheels etc.: *The bodywork is beginning to rust.* **2** work done to repair the frame of a vehicle, not including the engine, wheels etc.: *I know a garage that does good bodywork.*

Boer /bɔr, bʊr/ *n.* [C] someone from South Africa whose family came from the Netherlands [**Origin:** 1800–1900 Afrikaans, Dutch *boer* **farmer**] —**Boer** *adj.*

bof·fo /ˈbɑfoʊ/ *adj.* [only before noun, no comparative] INFORMAL a word meaning "successful" or "impressive," used especially about movies or performances: *The movie did boffo business in theaters.*

bog¹ /bɑg, bɔg/ *n.* [C,U] an area of low wet ground, sometimes containing bushes or grasses → see also MARSH

bog² *v.*

bog down *phr. v.* **1 bog sb/sth ↔ down** to delay something so that no progress is made, especially because too much detail is included or too much time is spent dealing with one particular thing: **+in/over** *The book gets bogged down in a lot of technical jargon.* **2** to become stuck in muddy ground and be unable to move: **+in** *The tanks had bogged down in mud.*

Bo·gart /ˈboʊgɑrt/**, Hum·phrey** /ˈhʌmfri/ (1899–1957) a U.S. movie actor

bo·gey /ˈboʊgi/ *n.* [C] **1** also **bogie, bogy** the action of hitting the ball one more time than PAR (=the usual number of shots) to get the ball into the hole in the game of GOLF → BIRDIE, EAGLE **2** a problem or difficult situation that makes you feel anxious: **+of** *the bogey of nuclear weapons in an unstable country* **3** a bogeyman [**Origin:** 1800–1900 *bogle* **evil spirit** (16–20 centuries), from *bug* **something causing great fear** (14–18 centuries)]

bo·gey·man /ˈbʊgiˌmæn/ *n.* [C] an evil spirit, especially in children's imaginations or stories

bog·gle /ˈbɑgəl/ *v.* **the mind boggles (at sth)** INFORMAL also **sth boggles the mind** if your mind etc. boggles when you think of something, it is difficult for you to imagine or accept it: **+at** *The mind boggles at the huge amounts of money involved.* → see also MIND-BOGGLING

bog·gy /ˈbɑgi/ *adj. comparative* **boggier**, *superlative* **boggiest** boggy ground is wet and muddy

bo·gie /ˈboʊgi/ *v.* [T] to use one more hit than PAR (=the usual number of strokes) to get the ball into the hole in GOLF —**bogie** *n.* [C]

Bo·go·tá /ˌboʊgəˈtɑ, ˈboʊgəˌtɑ/ the capital and largest city of Colombia

bo·gus /ˈboʊgəs/ *adj.* INFORMAL not true or real, although someone is trying to make you think it is SYN **fake**: *a bogus driver's license* [**Origin:** 1800–1900 *bogus* **machine for making illegal money** (1800–1900)]

bo·gy /ˈboʊgi/ *n.* [C] a BOGEY

bo·he·mi·an /boʊˈhimiən/ *adj.* living in a very informal or relaxed way and not accepting society's rules of behavior: *the bohemian lifestyles of the artists and musicians who lived there* [**Origin:** 1800–1900 *Bohemian* **of Bohemia, area and former country in the Czech Republic**; because of an association between Bohemia and traveling artists and gypsies] —**bohemian** *n.* [C]

Bohr /bɔr/**, Niels Hen·rik Da·vid** /nils ˈhɛnrɪk ˈdeɪvɪd/ (1885–1962) a Danish scientist who made important discoveries about the structure of atoms

boil¹ /bɔɪl/ S2 *v.* **1** [I,T] when a liquid boils, or you boil it, it becomes hot enough for BUBBLES to rise to the surface and for the liquid to change into gas → see also SIMMER: *Put the spaghetti into boiling, salted water.* | **+at** *Water boils at 100 degrees centigrade.* | *Boil the water before drinking it.* **2** [I,T] to cook something in boiling water: *Boil the vegetables for 10 minutes.* | *I've* ***put*** *the potatoes* ***on to boil.*** ►see THESAURUS box at **cook¹** **3** [I,T] if something containing liquid boils, the liquid inside is boiling: *The pot was boiling.* | *The pan had* ***boiled dry*** (=boiled until there was no liquid left). **4** [I] to be angry: *I didn't say anything, but I was boiling inside.* **5** [T] to clean something using boiling water: *Clothes had to be boiled to prevent the disease from spreading.* [**Origin:** 1200–1300 Old French *boillir*, from Latin *bullire*, from *bulla* **bubble**] → see also BOILING POINT, **make your blood boil** at BLOOD (10)

boil away *phr. v.* if a liquid boils away, it disappears because it has been heated too much

boil down *phr. v.* **1 boil down to sth** INFORMAL if a long statement, argument etc. boils down to something, that thing is the main reason or most basic part of it: *In the end, the case will boil down to whether the jury believes Smith or not.* **2 boil sth ↔ down** to make a list, piece of writing, television show etc. shorter by taking out anything that is not necessary or wanted: *The director boiled down 45 hours worth of film into the hour-long program.* **3 boil sth ↔ down** if a food or liquid boils down or you boil it down, the total amount of it becomes less after it is cooked: *Spinach tends to boil down a lot.*

boil over *phr. v.* **1** if a liquid boils over when it is heated, it rises and flows over the side of the container: *Turn down the heat so that the mixture does not boil over.* **2** if a situation or an emotion boils over, the people involved stop being calm: *Their rage and frustration finally boiled over.*

boil up *phr. v.* **1** if a situation or emotion boils up, bad feelings grow until they reach a dangerous level: *That summer, ethnic tensions boiled up again in the city.* **2 boil sth ↔ up** to heat food or a liquid until it begins to boil: *Boil the fruit up with sugar.*

boil² *n.* **1** [singular] the act or state of boiling: ***Bring*** *the sauce* ***to a boil*** *and cook for 5 minutes.* | *Heat the mixture until it* ***comes to a boil*** (=begins to boil). | **rolling boil** (=a boil in which there are a lot of bubbles constantly rising to the surface) **2** [C] MEDICINE a painful infected swelling under someone's skin

boil·er /ˈbɔɪlɚ/ *n.* [C] a container for storing or heating water, especially one in the heating system of a house or building → DOUBLE BOILER

boi·ler·plate /ˈbɔɪlɚˌpleɪt/ *n.* [C,U] a standard piece of writing or a design for something that can be easily used each time you need it, for example in business or legal documents: *a boilerplate for wills*

'boiler room *n.* [C] **1** a room in a large building where the building's boiler is **2** INFORMAL a room or office where people sell SHARES or services on the telephone, using unfair and sometimes dishonest methods

'boiler-room *adj.* [only before noun] relating to very direct methods of persuading people to buy something, especially on the telephone: *boiler-room sales techniques*

boil·ing /'bɔɪlɪŋ/ *adj.* SPOKEN very hot: *It was boiling this weekend.* | *His apartment is always* ***boiling hot*** *– I can't stand being in there.*

'boiling point *n.* [C usually singular] **1** CHEMISTRY the temperature at which a liquid boils. **2** a point when people cannot deal with a problem calmly anymore: *Relations between the two countries have almost* ***reached the boiling point.***

Boi·se /'bɔɪzi, -si/ the capital city of the U.S. state of Idaho

bois·ter·ous /'bɔɪstərəs/ *adj.* someone, especially a child, who is boisterous makes a lot of noise and has a lot of energy: *my boisterous nephews* [**Origin:** 1400–1500 *boistous* **rough** (14–16 centuries), from Old French *boistos*]

bok choy /ˌbɑk 'tʃɔɪ/ *n.* [U] a type of CABBAGE eaten especially in East Asia [**Origin:** 1900–2000 Chinese *paak ts'oi* **white vegetable**]

bold /boʊld/ *adj.*
1 ACTION/PERSON **a)** confident and not afraid of taking risks or making difficult decisions: *The speech began with a bold statement about racism.* | *a bold leader* | *The Governor felt he had to* ***make a bold move*** *to provoke progress.* | *We must* ***take bold steps*** *to protect the environment.* **b)** OLD-FASHIONED too confident or determined in a way that shocks people or is not considered polite: *a bold child* | *She just walked down the street in that skimpy outfit,* ***as bold as you please.*** | *He just asked me straight out,* ***as bold as brass.*** ►see THESAURUS box at brave[1]
2 COLORS/SHAPES/WRITING very clear and strong or bright, and therefore easy to notice: *wallpaper with bold stripes* | *The graphics are bold and colorful.*
3 in bold (type/print/letters) printed in letters that are darker and thicker than ordinary printed letters: *It said "Warning" on the top in bold letters.*
4 if I may be so bold SPOKEN FORMAL OLD-FASHIONED used when asking someone a question, to show that you are slightly annoyed with them: *And what, if I may be so bold, is the meaning of this note?*
5 be/make so bold as to do sth OLD-FASHIONED to do something that other people feel is rude or not acceptable
[**Origin:** Old English *beald*] —**boldly** *adv.* —**boldness** *n.* [U]

bold·face /'boʊldfeɪs/ *n.* [U] TECHNICAL a way of printing letters that makes them thicker and darker than normal —**boldface** *adj.* —**boldfaced** *adj.*

'bold-faced *adj.* BALD-FACED

bole /boʊl/ *n.* [C] LITERARY BIOLOGY the main part of a tree SYN **trunk**

bo·le·ro /bə'lɛroʊ/ *n. plural* **boleros** [C] **1** ENG. LANG. ARTS a type of Spanish dance, or the music for this dance **2** a short JACKET for a woman

bo·li·var /bə'livɑr/ *n.* [C] the standard unit of money used in Venezuela

Bo·li·var /bə'livɑr/, **Si·mon** /si'moʊn/, **the Liberator** (1783–1830) a South American soldier and political leader famous for fighting to win independence from Spain for Venezuela, Peru, Bolivia, Colombia, and Ecuador

Bo·liv·i·a /bə'lɪviə/ a country in the western part of South America, between Brazil and Peru —**Bolivian** *n., adj.*

boll /boʊl/ *n.* [C] the part of a cotton plant that contains the seeds

bol·lard /'bɑlərd/ *n.* [C] a thick metal or stone post used for tying ships to

boll 'weevil *n.* [C] an insect that eats and destroys cotton plants

bo·lo·gna /bə'loʊni/ *n.* a type of cooked meat often eaten in SANDWICHES

bo·lo tie /'boʊloʊ ˌtaɪ/ *n.* [C] a thick string that a man can wear around his neck and fasten with a decoration

Bol·she·vik /'boʊlʃəvɪk, 'bɑl-/ *n.* [C] **1** HISTORY someone who supported the COMMUNIST party at the time of the Russian Revolution in 1917 **2** an insulting word for someone who has LEFT-WING views [**Origin:** 1900–2000 Russian *bol'shevik*, from *bol'she* **larger**; because they formed the largest group in the Communist party] —**bolshevik** *adj.*

bol·ster[1] /'boʊlstər/ *v.* [T] **1** also **bolster sth ↔ up** to improve something by making it stronger or bigger: *Additional soldiers were sent to bolster the defenses at two naval bases.* **2** also **bolster sb/sth ↔ up** to help someone to feel better and more positive SYN **boost**: *The win bolstered Timman's confidence.*

bolster[2] *n.* [C] a long firm PILLOW, usually shaped like a tube

bolt[1] /boʊlt/ *n.* [C]
1 LOCK a metal bar that you slide across a door or window to lock it
2 SCREW a screw with a flat top and no point, for fastening two pieces of metal together
3 a bolt of lightning/a lightning bolt LIGHTNING that appears as a white line in the sky → see also THUNDERBOLT
4 a bolt from the blue/a bolt out of the blue something that happens very suddenly and without warning: *The attack on the airbase* ***came as a bolt from the blue.***
5 CLOTH a large long roll of cloth
6 GUN a short metal bar that you slide into the BARREL of a gun to load bullets and hold them in place
7 WEAPON a short heavy ARROW that is fired from a CROSSBOW
[**Origin:** Old English **short arrow**] → see also **the nuts and bolts of sth** at NUT (5)

bolt[2] *v.* **1** [I] to suddenly run somewhere very quickly, especially in order to escape or because you are frightened: *The dog bolted into the road.* ►see THESAURUS box at run[1] **2** [T] to lock a door or window by sliding a bolt across: *Jason bolted the door and closed all the curtains.* **3** [T] also **bolt down** to fasten two things together using a bolt: **bolt sth to sth** *A wrought-iron bench was bolted to the patio.* **4** [T] also **bolt down** to eat very quickly SYN **gobble**: *He bolted down his breakfast.* **5 bolt the party/team/country etc.** to leave a political party, team etc.

bolt[3] *adv.* **sit/stand bolt upright** to sit or stand with your back very straight, often because something has frightened you: *We found her sitting bolt upright in bed with all the lights on.*

'bolt-ˌaction *adj.* a bolt-action gun uses a bolt to load bullets and hold them in place

bomb[1] /bɑm/ S3 W2 *n.* [C]
1 WEAPON a weapon made of material that will explode: *A* ***bomb exploded*** *near the country's busiest airport before dawn today.* | *The* ***bomb went off*** *at 9:30 at night.* | *Warplanes began* ***dropping bombs*** *on the city.* | *No one claimed responsibility for* ***planting*** *the* ***bomb*** (=hiding it in order to destroy something). | *a* ***bomb attack*** *on American troops* | *a* ***bomb threat*** *against the county courthouse* | *The* ***bomb blast*** *killed two people and injured many more.* | *Children were playing outside when the* ***bomb detonated*** (=exploded). → see also ATOMIC BOMB, HYDROGEN BOMB, LETTER BOMB, NEUTRON BOMB, STINK BOMB, TIME BOMB
2 the bomb the ATOMIC BOMB or any NUCLEAR WEAPON: *What if the government decided to use the bomb?*
3 BAD PERFORMANCE/EVENT INFORMAL a play, movie, event etc. that is not successful: *The party was a bomb.*
4 CONTAINER a container in which insect poison, paint

etc. is kept under pressure: *a flea bomb* (=used for killing FLEAS)
5 FOOTBALL a throw of a football that goes a very long way: *Tolliver threw a 44-yard bomb into the end zone.*
6 be the bomb SLANG to be very good or exciting
[**Origin:** 1600–1700 French *bombe*, from Italian *bomba*] → see also **drop a bombshell/bomb** at DROP[1] (25)

bomb[2] W3 *v.* **1** [T] to attack a place by leaving a bomb there, or by dropping bombs on it from an airplane: *Military aircraft bombed a dozen towns.* **2** [I] INFORMAL if a play, movie, event etc. bombs, it is not successful: *His latest movie bombed at the box office.* **3** [I,T] SPOKEN to fail a test very badly: *I just bombed my midterm.* **4 bug-bomb/flea-bomb/paint-bomb etc.** to let insect poison, paint etc. out of a container where it has been kept under pressure, in order to fill or cover an area with that substance: *They had to bug-bomb the house yesterday, so we couldn't move in.*

bomb out *phr. v.* **1 be bombed out** if a building or the people who live there are bombed out, the building is completely destroyed by bombs: *The orphanage was bombed out in the war.* → see also BOMBED-OUT **2** to fail something so badly that you must leave: *He bombed out of college in his second year.*

bom·bard /bɑmˈbɑrd/ *v.* [T] **1** to attack a place for a long time using large weapons, bombs etc.: *Rockets bombarded residential areas of the capital.* **2** to do something too often or too much, for example criticizing someone or giving too much information: **bombard sb with sth** *The water department has been bombarded with complaints.*

bom·bar·dier /ˌbɑmbɚˈdɪr/ *n.* [C] the person on a military aircraft responsible for dropping bombs

bom·bard·ment /bɑmˈbɑrdmənt/ *n.* [U] a continuous attack on a place using large weapons, bombs etc.: **aerial/artillery/naval bombardment** (=attack from the air, land, or sea) *aerial bombardment on rebel positions* | **massive/heavy bombardment** *the massive bombardment of the city*

bom·bas·tic /bɑmˈbæstɪk/ *adj.* using long words that sound important but have no real meaning: *a politician noted for his bombastic style* —**bombast** /ˈbɑmbæst/ *n.* [U]

ˈbomb disˌposal *n.* [U] the job of dealing with bombs that have not exploded, and making them safe: **bomb disposal expert/squad/unit** (=person or group that makes bombs safe)

bombed /bɑmd/ *adj.* [not before noun] INFORMAL very drunk: *My dad used to get bombed every night.*

ˌbombed-ˈout *adj.* completely destroyed by bombs: *a bombed-out warehouse*

bomb·er /ˈbɑmɚ/ *n.* [C] **1** an airplane that carries and drops bombs ▸see THESAURUS box at **plane**[1] **2** someone who hides a bomb somewhere in order to destroy something

ˈbomber ˌjacket *n.* [C] a short JACKET which fits tightly around your waist

bomb·ing /ˈbɑmɪŋ/ *n.* [C,U] the use of bombs to attack a place: +**of** *the bombing of Dresden in World War II* | *Hundreds have been killed in the latest **wave of bombings*** (=series of attacks using bombs). | *a terrorist **bombing campaign*** (=many attacks using bombs) | *a **bombing raid** against rebel-held areas*

bomb·proof /ˈbɑmpruf/ *adj.* strong enough not to be damaged by a bomb attack: *a bombproof shelter*

ˈbomb scare *n.* [C] a situation in which people have to be moved out of a building or area because there may be a bomb there

bomb·shell /ˈbɑmʃɛl/ *n.* [C] INFORMAL an unexpected and very shocking piece of news: *Conley **dropped** a **bombshell** when she announced her resignation.* → see also **blonde bombshell** at BLONDE[1] (2)

ˈbomb ˌshelter *n.* [C] a room or building that is built to protect people from bomb attacks

ˈbomb site *n.* [C] a place where a bomb has destroyed one or more buildings in a town: *rescue workers at the bomb site*

ˈbomb squad *n.* [C] a group of people, usually police officers, who deal with bombs that have not exploded and make them safe

bo·na fide /ˈboʊnɚ ˌfaɪd, ˈbɑnə-/ *adj.* real, true, and not intended to deceive anyone: *a bona fide job offer*

bo·nan·za /bəˈnænzə, boʊ-/ *n.* [C] a lucky or successful situation in which people can make a lot of money, get a lot of attention etc.: *The story was a publicity bonanza for the company.* [**Origin:** 1800–1900 Spanish **good weather**, from Medieval Latin *bonacia*, changed from Latin *malacia* **calm at sea**]

Bo·na·parte /ˈboʊnəˌpɑrt/ → see NAPOLEON

bon ap·pe·tit /ˌboʊn æpeɪˈti, ɑpə-, ˌbɑn-/ *interjection* said to someone before they start eating a meal, to tell them you hope they enjoy their food

bon·bon /ˈbɑnbɑn/ *n.* [C] a round piece of soft candy that is usually covered in chocolate

bond[1] /bɑnd/ Ac W3 *n.*
1 RELATIONSHIP [C] something that unites two or more people or groups, such as love, or a shared interest or idea: +**with** *Marilyn's bond with her mother was very strong.* | *The United States has a special bond with Britain.* | +**between** *I felt that the troubles had strengthened the bond between us.* | **the bonds of friendship/marriage/family etc.** (=a special relationship that makes people loyal to each other) | *The English language is a **common bond** that helps hold our country together.*
2 MONEY [C] ECONOMICS an official document promising that a government or company will pay back money that it has borrowed, often with INTEREST: *U.S. **savings bonds*** | *the bond market* | *investments in **stocks and bonds***
3 IN A COURT [C,U] LAW money given to a court of law so that someone can be let out of prison while they wait for their TRIAL SYN **bail**: *Maxwell's lawyers **posted** the $100,000 **bond** and he was released.*
4 WITH GLUE [C] the way in which two surfaces become attached to each other using glue
5 ATOMS [C] CHEMISTRY the chemical force that holds atoms together in a MOLECULE
6 bonds [plural] LITERARY something that limits your freedom and prevents you from doing what you want to do: +**of** *the bonds of slavery*
7 WRITTEN AGREEMENT LAW a written agreement to do something, that makes you legally responsible for doing it SYN **contract**
8 bonds [plural] LITERARY chains, ropes etc. used for tying a prisoner
9 in bond also **out of bond** TECHNICAL in or out of a bonded warehouse
10 PAPER [U] BOND PAPER
11 PROMISE [C] LITERARY a serious promise or agreement: *My word is my bond.*
[**Origin:** 1200–1300 Old Norse *band*] → see also BOND ISSUE

bond[2] Ac *v.* **1** [I] to develop a special relationship with someone: +**with** *Fathers need time to bond with their children.* **2** [I] if two things bond, they become firmly stuck together, especially after they have been joined with glue: *It takes less than 10 minutes for the two surfaces to bond.* **3** [T] TECHNICAL to keep goods in a bonded warehouse

bond·age /ˈbɑndɪdʒ/ *n.* [U] **1** FORMAL the state of being a slave: *The men were accused of **selling** the 170 women and children **into bondage**.* **2** the practice of being tied up for sexual pleasure **3** FORMAL the state of having your freedom limited, or being prevented from doing what you want: +**of** *He was finally free of the bondage of fear.*

ˌbonded ˈwarehouse *n.* [C] ECONOMICS an official place to keep goods that have been brought into a country before tax has been paid on them

bond·hold·er /ˈbɑndˌhoʊldɚ/ *n.* [C] ECONOMICS someone who owns government or industrial BONDS

bond·ing /ˈbɑndɪŋ/ Ac *n.* [U] **1** a process in which a special relationship develops between two or more people: +**between** *the powerful bonding between mother and child* **2 male/female bonding** HUMOROUS the activity of doing things with other people of the same sex, so that you feel good about being a man or a woman: *Do a little female bonding – go shopping with a friend.* **3** CHEMISTRY the connection of atoms or of two surfaces that are glued together

ˈbond ˌissue *n.* [C] **1** an occasion when a government borrows public money to pay for something, which people must first approve of by voting for it: *The city government wants to get a bond issue passed so they can rebuild the bridge.* **2** an occasion when a company sells BONDS to pay for something

ˈbond ˌpaper *n.* [U] a type of thick writing paper with a lot of cotton in it

Bonds /bɑndz/, **Bar·ry** /ˈbæri/ (1964–) a baseball player who has the record for hitting the most HOME RUNS (73) in a single season

bone¹ /boʊn/ S2 W3 *n.*
1 BODY [C] BIOLOGY one of the hard parts that form the frame of a human or animal body: *The bone was broken in two places.* | *You shouldn't give chicken bones to a dog.* | **hip/cheek/leg etc. bone** *He broke his collar bone.* | **big-boned/small-boned/fine-boned etc.** (=with big etc. bones) *She was tall and big-boned.* | *Amy has inherited her mother's good* ***bone structure*** (=shape of face). | **thigh/arm/wrist etc. bone** *The boy's ankle bone had fractured.* → see picture at JOINT²
2 make no bones about (doing) sth to not feel nervous or ashamed about doing or saying something: *Mr. Stutzman makes no bones about his religious beliefs.*
3 be chilled/frozen to the bone to be extremely cold SYN be freezing
4 a bone of contention something that causes arguments between people: *Her drinking became a bone of contention between them.*
5 I have a bone to pick with you SPOKEN used to tell someone that you are annoyed with them and want to talk about it: *I have a bone to pick with you! Why didn't you tell me Sheila was coming over tonight?*
6 feel/know sth in your bones to be sure that something is true, even though you have no proof and cannot explain why you are sure: *I felt in my bones that he could not have done it.*
7 close to the bone close to the truth in a way that may offend or upset people: *His jokes were too close to the bone for most people.*
8 skin and bone very thin SYN emaciated: *The horses were skin and bone.*
9 throw/toss sb a bone INFORMAL to help someone in a small way because you feel sorry for them
[**Origin:** Old English *ban*] → see also **bag of bones** at BAG¹ (8), BARE BONES, BIG-BONED, **cut sth to the bone** at CUT¹ (23), **dry as a bone** at DRY¹ (1), SMALL-BONED, **work your fingers to the bone** at WORK¹ (25)

bone² *v.* [T] to remove the bones from fish or meat: *boned salmon*

bone up on sth *phr. v.* INFORMAL to learn a lot about a subject, especially before a test: *I've spent the last two weeks boning up on medieval history.*

ˌbone ˈchina *n.* [U] delicate and expensive cups, plates etc. that are made partly with crushed bone

ˌbone ˈdry, bone-dry *adj.* completely dry: *The soil is bone dry after three years of drought.*

bone·head /ˈboʊnhɛd/ *n.* [C] INFORMAL a stupid person

ˈbone ˌmarrow *n.* [U] BIOLOGY the soft TISSUE in the center of some large, flat bones, where red and white blood cells are produced SYN marrow: *a bone marrow transplant*

ˈbone meal *n.* [U] a substance made of crushed bones that is used to feed plants

bon·er /ˈboʊnɚ/ *n.* [singular] INFORMAL a stupid or embarrassing mistake

ˌbone-ˈtired *adj.* [not before noun] extremely tired

bon·fire /ˈbɑnˌfaɪɚ/ *n.* [C] a large outdoor fire, either for burning waste, or for a celebration [**Origin:** 1500–1600 *bonfire* **fire made from bones** (14–17 centuries)]

bong /bɑŋ/ *n.* **1** [C] an object used for smoking MARIJUANA in which the smoke goes through water to make it cool **2** [singular] a deep sound made by a large bell

bongos

bon·gos /ˈbɑŋgoʊz/ also **ˈbongo ˌdrums** *n.* [plural] a pair of small drums that you play with your hands [**Origin:** 1900–2000 American Spanish *bongó* (singular)]

Bon·hoef·fer /ˈbɑnˌhoʊfɚ/, **Die·trich** /ˈditrɪk/ (1906–1945) a German Protestant minister and religious teacher and writer, who opposed the Nazis

bon·ho·mie /ˌbɑnəˈmi, ˌboʊ-/ *n.* [U] LITERARY a friendly feeling among a group of people: *The atmosphere of bonhomie was suddenly gone.* [**Origin:** 1700–1800 French *bonhomme* **pleasant man**, from *bon* **good** + *homme* **man**]

bonk¹ /bɑŋk/ *v.* [T] INFORMAL to hit someone lightly on the head, or hit your head on something by mistake

bonk² *n.* [C] INFORMAL **1** the action of hitting someone lightly on the head, or hitting your head against something **2** a sudden short deep sound, for example, when something hits the ground

bon·kers /ˈbɑŋkɚz/ INFORMAL *adj.* **1 go bonkers** to become crazy or very excited: *The whole stadium went bonkers when the Giants finally scored.* **2 drive sb bonkers** to make someone feel crazy or annoyed: *The noise from the train tracks used to drive us bonkers.*

bon mot /boʊn ˈmoʊ, bɑn-/ *n.* [C] an intelligent remark

Bonn /bɑn/ a city in western Germany, which was the capital of West Germany

bon·net /ˈbɑnɪt/ *n.* [C] **1** a type of hat that ties under the chin, worn by babies, and by women in past times **2** BRITISH a HOOD → see also **have a bee in your bonnet** at BEE (2)

Bon·nie and Clyde /ˌbɑni ən ˈklaɪd/ two young U.S. criminals, Bonnie Parker (a woman) and Clyde Barrow (a man), who stole money from banks and businesses in the U.S. in the 1930s

bon·ny /ˈbɑni/ *adj.* OLD-FASHIONED pretty and healthy: *a bonny baby*

bonsai

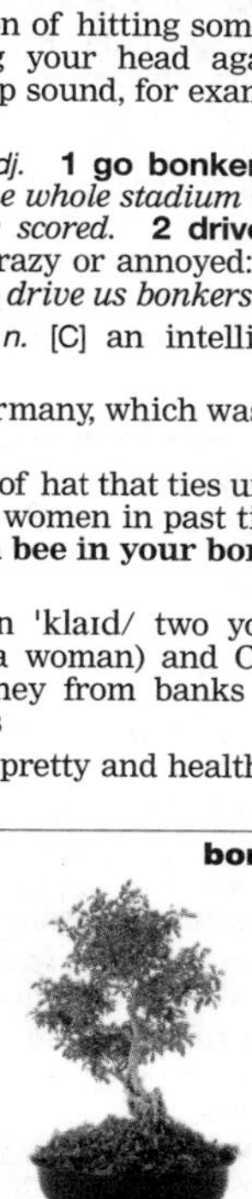

bon·sai /ˈbɑnsaɪ, -zaɪ/ *n.* [C,U] a tree that is grown so that it always stays very small, or the art of growing trees in this way [**Origin:** 1900–2000 Japanese **tray planting**] —**bonsai** *adj.*

bo·nus /ˈboʊnəs/ *n.* [C] **1** money added to someone's pay, especially as a reward for good work: *Did you get a bonus this year?* ►see THESAURUS box at pay² **2** something good that you get in addition to something else or in addition to what you expect: +**for** *The second win was a bonus for the team.* | *The fact that the house is so close to the school is* ***an added bonus****.* [**Origin:** 1700–1800 Latin **good**]

bon vi·vant /ˌboʊn viˈvɑnt, ˌbɑn-/ *n.* [C] LITERARY someone who enjoys good food and wine, and being with people

bon voy·age /ˌboʊn vɔɪˈɑʒ, ˌbɑn-/ *interjection* used to wish someone a good trip

bon·y /ˈboʊni/ *adj. comparative* **bonier**, *superlative* **boniest** **1** someone or part of their body that is bony is very thin: *bony fingers* **2** bony fish or meat contains a lot of small bones **3** a bony part of an animal consists mostly of bone

boo¹ /bu/ *v.* **boos, booed, booing** [I,T] to shout "boo" to show that you do not like a person, performance, idea etc. OPP cheer: *Some of the audience started booing.* |

Angry residents ***booed him off stage*** (=shouted "boo" until he left the stage) *at a political rally last month.*

boo² *n. plural* **boos** [C] a noise made by someone who does not like a person, performance, idea etc. OPP cheer: *Mitchell ignored the boos and hit another home run.*

boo³ *interjection* **1** a word you shout suddenly to someone as a joke, in order to frighten them **2** said loudly to show that you do not like a person, performance, idea etc. **3 not say boo** SPOKEN to not say anything at all in a situation when most people are talking: *He got to the party at eight, but didn't say boo all evening.*

boob /bub/ *n.* **1** [C usually plural] SPOKEN INFORMAL a woman's breast **2** [C] INFORMAL a stupid or silly person [**Origin:** (1) 1900–2000 *bubby* **breast**]

ˈboo-boo *n.* [C] SPOKEN **1** a word meaning a "silly mistake," often used when speaking to children: *Oh, I* ***made a boo-boo.*** **2** a word meaning a "small injury," used when speaking to children: *Do you have a boo-boo on your knee?*

ˈboob tube *n.* **the boob tube** OLD-FASHIONED television

boo·by /ˈbubi/ *n. plural* **boobies** [C] **1** INFORMAL a stupid or silly person **2** BIOLOGY a type of tropical SEA BIRD **3** [usually plural] SPOKEN, INFORMAL a word used by children to mean a woman's breast

ˈbooby hatch *n.* [singular] OLD-FASHIONED a mental hospital

ˈbooby prize *n.* [C] a prize given as a joke to the person who is last in a competition

ˈbooby trap *n.* [C] **1** a hidden bomb that explodes when you touch something else that is connected to it **2** a trap that you arrange for someone as a joke —**booby-trapped** *adj.*: *a booby-trapped car*

boog·er /ˈbʊgɚ/ *n.* [C] SPOKEN **1** a thick piece of MUCUS from your nose **2** someone who annoys you or causes trouble for you: *Ben took my magazine – the little booger!*

boog·ey·man /ˈbʊgiˌmæn/ *n.* [C] a BOGEYMAN

boog·ie¹ /ˈbʊgi/ *v.* [I] **1** INFORMAL to dance, especially to fast popular music: *Dance fans can boogie at Club Oasis and Paradise Beach.* **2** SLANG to go somewhere or do something quickly: *I've got to boogie – see you later.*

boogie² *n.* [U] BOOGIE WOOGIE

ˈboogie ˌboard *n.* [C] an object that you lie on to ride on ocean waves, that is half the length of a SURFBOARD —**boogie-boarder** *n.* [C] —**boogie-boarding** *n.* [U]

boogie woog·ie /ˌbʊgi ˈwʊgi/ *n.* [U] a type of music played on the piano with a strong fast RHYTHM

boo hoo /ˈbu hu/ *interjection* used especially in children's stories or as a joke to show that someone is crying

book¹ /bʊk/ S1 W1 *n.* [C]

1 PRINTED PAGES a set of printed pages that are held together in a cover so that you can read them: *Have you* ***read this book?*** | *It's* ***a*** *pretty* ***good book.*** | **+about/on** *a book about plants* | **+by** *a book by William Faulkner* | **+of** *a book of poems*

THESAURUS

Types of books
nonfiction books which describe real things or events
fiction books which describe imaginary events
literature fiction that people think is important
reference book a book such as a dictionary or encyclopedia that you look at to find specific information
textbook a book that is used in the classroom
hardcover/hardback a book which has a hard stiff cover
paperback a book which has a soft cover
novel a book about imaginary events
science fiction a book about imaginary events in the future or space travel
biography a book about a real person's life, written by another person
autobiography a book about someone's life, written by that person himself or herself

2 TO WRITE IN a set of sheets of paper held together in a cover so that you can write on them → see also NOTEBOOK: *an address book*

3 books [plural] **a)** written records of the financial accounts of a business or other organization: *The auditor is looking at the company's books.* | *For the past 6 months I've been working* ***off the books*** (=without the organization keeping written records, so you do not have to pay tax). **b) on sb's books** on a list of the names of people who use a company's services, or who are employed by a company: *We have more than 100 part-time employees on our books.* **c) on the books** a law that is on books of a particular city, area, or country, is part of the set of laws that are used to govern that place: *Canada has had gun control legislation on the books since 1978.*

4 SET OF THINGS a set of things such as stamps, matches, or tickets, held together inside a paper cover: *a book of matches*

5 by the book exactly according to rules or instructions: *Rules are not to be broken – Barb does everything by the book.*

6 be in sb's good/bad book(s) SPOKEN used to say that someone approves or disapproves of someone else, especially when they often change their opinion about people: *I think I'm back in Corinne's good books again.*

7 in my book SPOKEN said when giving your opinion: *Well, in my book, if you steal, you deserve to get caught.*

8 PART OF A BOOK one of the parts that a very large book such as the Bible is divided into: **+of** *the Book of Genesis*

9 bring sb to book (for sth) to punish someone for breaking laws or rules, especially when you have been trying to punish them for a long time: *The brothers were finally brought to book for running illegal dog fights.*

[**Origin:** Old English *boc*] → see also **cook the books** at COOK¹ (5), **one for the books** at ONE² (22), **read sb like a book** at READ¹ (9), **throw the book at sb** at THROW AT (2)

book² W3 *v.* **1** [I,T] to arrange to stay in a place, eat in a restaurant etc. at a particular time in the future, or buy a ticket for a flight, performance etc. in the future: *You'll have to book by tomorrow if you want the lower price.* | *I* ***booked a table*** (=at a restaurant) *for two at 8:00.* | *There are no tickets at the door – you have to* ***book in advance*** (=buy tickets before the event). | *I'm sorry sir, we're* ***fully booked*** (=there are no rooms, tables etc. available) *for the 14th.* | *a* ***heavily booked*** *flight* | *Classes are* ***booked solid*** (=completely full), *with many students unable to get the courses they need.* **2 be booked up a)** if a hotel, restaurant etc. is booked up, there are no more rooms or tables left **b)** if someone is booked up, they are extremely busy and do not have time to do anything new: *I'm all booked up this week, but I can see you on Monday.* **3** [T] to arrange for someone such as a speaker or singer to perform on a particular date: **book sb for sth** *Nelson was booked for a tour of Japan in August.* | **book sb to do sth** *She's been booked to speak at the conference.* **4** [T] LAW to put someone's name officially in police records, along with the charge made against them: *Dawkins was booked on suspicion of attempted murder.* | **book sb for sth** *They booked him for assault.* **5** [I] SPOKEN INFORMAL to go somewhere or do something fast: *Now, on Montana highways, you can really book.*

book sb **into** sth *phr. v.* to arrange for someone to stay at a hotel: *We've booked you into the Sheraton. Is that all right?*

book sb **on** sth *phr. v.* to arrange for someone to travel on a particular airplane, train etc.: *Could you book me on the next flight to Dallas?*

book·bind·ing /ˈbʊkˌbaɪndɪŋ/ *n.* [U] the art of fastening the pages of books inside a cover —**bookbinder** *n.* [C]

book•case /ˈbʊk-keɪs/ *n.* [C] a piece of furniture with shelves to hold books

ˈbook club *n.* [C] **1** a group of people who meet regularly to discuss books they have read **2** a club that offers books cheaply to its members

book•end¹ /ˈbʊkɛnd/ *n.* [C usually plural] one of a pair of objects that you put at each end of a row of books to prevent them from falling over

bookend² *v.* [T] if two similar things bookend something such as an event, performance, movie etc., they come at the beginning and the end of it: *The best parts are the two Reed songs that bookend the CD.*

book•ie /ˈbʊki/ *n.* [C] INFORMAL someone whose job is to collect money that people want to risk on the result of a race, competition etc., and who pays them if they guess correctly

book•ing /ˈbʊkɪŋ/ *n.* [C] **1** an arrangement in which a hotel, theater, AIRLINE etc. agrees to let you use a particular room, seat etc. at a particular time in the future: *a booking fee* | *We'll have to **make a booking** in the next few weeks.* | *We **canceled** our **booking** on the cruise and got a full refund.* | *This price is available only with a 21-day **advance booking*** (=a booking that is made 21 days ahead of time). | **online/telephone booking** *We offer a 10% discount for online bookings.* **2** an arrangement made by a performer to perform at a particular place and time in the future

book•ish /ˈbʊkɪʃ/ *adj.* **1** someone who is bookish is more interested in reading and studying than in sports or other activities **2** seeming to come from books rather than from real experience: *bookish language*

book•keep•ing /ˈbʊkˌkipɪŋ/ *n.* [U] the job or activity of recording the financial accounts of a company or organization —**bookkeeper** *n.* [C]

book•let /ˈbʊklɪt/ *n.* [C] a very short book that usually contains information: *a booklet on AIDS*

book•mak•er /ˈbʊkˌmeɪkɚ/ *n.* [C] a BOOKIE

book•mark /ˈbʊkmɑrk/ *n.* [C] **1** a piece of paper, leather etc. that you put in a book to show you the last page you have read **2** COMPUTERS a way of marking a website so that you can find it again quickly, by putting it on a list on your computer screen —**bookmark** *v.* [T]

book•mo•bile /ˈbʊkmoʊˌbil/ *n.* [C] a vehicle that contains a library and travels to different places so that people can use it

book•plate /ˈbʊkpleɪt/ *n.* [C] a decorated piece of paper with your name on it, that you stick in the front of your books

ˈbook reˌport *n.* [C] a report that children write for school, in which they describe a book they have read and give their opinion about it

book•rest /ˈbʊk-rɛst/ *n.* [C] a frame that holds a book upright so that you can read it without holding it in your hands

book•sell•er /ˈbʊkˌsɛlɚ/ *n.* [C] a person or company that sells books

book•shelf /ˈbʊkʃɛlf/ *n. plural* **bookshelves** /-ʃɛlvz/ [C] a shelf on a wall, or a piece of furniture with shelves, used for holding books

book•sign•ing /ˈbʊkˌsaɪnɪŋ/ *n.* [C] an event where the AUTHOR of a book agrees to sign copies of the book for people who buy it, especially as a way to sell more books

book•stall /ˈbʊkstɔl/ *n.* [C] a small store on a street that has an open front and sells books

book•store /ˈbʊkstɔr/ *n.* [C] a store that sells books → see also LIBRARY

ˈbook tour *n.* [C] a trip someone makes to advertise a book they have written

ˈbook ˌvalue *n.* [C] **1** the value of a business after you sell all of its ASSETS and pay all of its debts **2** how much something such as a car should be worth if it were sold → see also BLUE BOOK

book•worm /ˈbʊkwɚm/ *n.* [C] **1** someone who likes reading very much **2** BIOLOGY an insect that eats paper

boom¹ /bum/ S3 *n.*
1 INCREASE IN BUSINESS [singular] ECONOMICS a rapid increase of business activity: **+in** *a boom in new car sales* | **a construction/property/oil etc. boom** *the post-war property boom* | **boom times/years** (=when profits are being made) → see also BOOM TOWN
2 WHEN STH IS POPULAR [singular] a period when something suddenly becomes very popular or starts happening a lot: *The fitness boom started in the 1970s.* | **+in** *the boom in girls' soccer* | **baby/population boom** (=a time when a lot of babies are born)
3 SOUND [C] a deep loud sound that you can hear for several seconds after it begins, especially the sound of an explosion or a large gun: *Witnesses heard the first loud boom at 3:03 p.m.* | **+of** *the boom of thunder* → see also SONIC BOOM
4 LONG POLE [C] **a)** a long pole on a boat that is attached to a sail at the bottom **b)** a long pole used as part of a piece of equipment that loads and unloads things **c)** a long pole that has a camera or MICROPHONE on the end
5 ON A RIVER [C] something that is stretched across a river or a BAY to prevent things floating down or across it: *a log boom*

boom² *v.* **1** [I usually in progressive] if business, trade, or a particular area is booming, it is very successful SYN **flourish**: *We're happy to report that **business is booming** this year.* **2** [I usually in progressive] if interest in something is booming, it is quickly becoming more and more popular: *Interest in organic food is booming.* **3** [I] also **boom out** to make a loud deep sound: *Guns boomed in the distance.* **4** [T] also **boom (sth) out** to say something in a loud deep voice —**booming** *adj.*: *a booming economy*

ˈboom box *n.* [C] INFORMAL a large radio and CD PLAYER that you can carry around

boom•er /ˈbumɚ/ *n.* [C] INFORMAL **1** a BABY BOOMER **2** HISTORY one of the many people who in 1889 took part in officially organized races to claim land in Oklahoma that was formerly owned by Native Americans

boo•mer•ang¹ /ˈbuməˌræŋ/ *n.* [C] a curved stick that flies in a circle and comes back to you when you throw it

boomerang² *v.* [I] also **boomerang on sb** if something that you do boomerangs, it has a bad effect on you that you did not want or expect: *If your criticism is too severe, it can boomerang on you.*

ˈboom town, boomtown *n.* [C] INFORMAL a town or city that suddenly becomes very successful because there is a lot of new businesses or industry

boon /bun/ *n.* [C usually singular] something that is very useful and makes your life a lot easier or helps you make more money: **+to/for** *Internet shopping is a boon for busy people.*

ˌboon comˈpanion *n.* [C] LITERARY a very close friend

boon•docks /ˈbundɑks/ *n.* INFORMAL **the boondocks** a place that is a long way from the nearest town: *Myra lives way **out in the boondocks**.* [**Origin:** 1900–2000 Tagalog *bundok* **mountain**]

boon•dog•gle /ˈbunˌdɑgəl/ *n.* [singular] INFORMAL an official plan or activity that is very complicated and wastes a lot of time, money, and effort: *another government boondoggle*

Boone /bun/, **Daniel** (1734–1820) one of the first white Americans to go to Kentucky

boon•ies /ˈbuniz/ *n.* **the boonies** SPOKEN the BOONDOCKS

boor /bʊr/ *n.* [C] a man who behaves in a very rude way —**boorish** *adj.*: *boorish behavior* —**boorishly** *adv.*

boost¹ /bust/ *v.* **1** [T] to increase the amount or level of something, especially when it was lower than it should be: *Would year-round education really boost student performance?* | **boost sb's confidence/morale/ego** *Free phone calls to home can help to boost the troops' morale.* | **boost sales/earnings/profits** *The company plans to cut costs in order to boost profits.* **2** [I] to increase the popularity of someone or something: *His TV appearance boosted him in the opinion polls.* **3** [T] also **boost sb up** to help someone reach a higher place by lifting or pushing them: *I boosted the kid up so he could reach the branch.* **4** [I,T] SLANG to steal something. **5** [T] if a ROCKET or motor boosts a SPACECRAFT, it makes it go up into space or go in a particular direction

boost² *n.* [C usually singular] **1** something which increases or improves something: **+in** *a boost in oil prices* | **+for/to** *a major boost for the economy* | *These tax breaks have* ***given*** *the auto industry* ***a*** *tremendous* ***boost***. | **get/receive a boost** *The industry received a boost from the president's remarks.* **2** something that makes someone feel healthier, more positive, or more confident: *Some women may need an extra boost from vitamins.* | *Her compliments really* ***gave*** *me* ***a boost***. | **+for/to** *To win two games in a row is a big* ***ego boost*** *for this team* (=it helps them feel more confident). **3** a lift or push that helps someone reach a higher place: *I can't reach the top shelf – can you* ***give me a boost?*** **4** an increase in the amount of power available to a ROCKET, engine, etc.

boost·er /ˈbustɚ/ *n.* [C] **1** a small quantity of a drug that increases the effect of one that was given before, so that someone continues to be protected against a disease: *You will need a booster in six weeks' time* **2 confidence/ego/morale etc. booster** something that helps someone be more confident or less worried **3** someone who gives a lot of support to a person, organization, or an idea: *the Kennedy High School Booster Club* **4** a ROCKET that is used to provide additional power for a SPACECRAFT to leave the Earth

ˈbooster ˌseat *n.* [C] a special seat for a small child that lets them sit in a higher position in a car or at a table

boots

boot¹ /but/ S2 *n.* **1** [C] a type of shoe that covers your whole foot and the lower part of your leg: *a pair of hiking boots* **2 to boot** INFORMAL in addition to everything else you have mentioned: *The car is small, quick, and stylish to boot.* **3 get the boot** INFORMAL to be forced to leave your job **4 give sb the boot** INFORMAL to dismiss someone from their job SYN **fire** **5** [C] a DENVER BOOT **6** [C] BRITISH a TRUNK [**Origin:** (1) 1300–1400 Old French *bote*] → see also **be/get too big for your boots** at BIG (18), **lick sb's boots** at LICK¹ (6)

boot² *v.* **1** [I,T] also **boot up** COMPUTERS to start the PROGRAM that makes a computer ready to be used, before anything else can be done on the machine **2** [T] also **boot sb out** INFORMAL to force someone to leave a place, job, organization etc., especially because they have done something wrong: *As a result of that remark, the teacher booted him out of class.* | *The company has recently booted its CEO.* **3** [T] INFORMAL to kick someone or something hard: *Jaeger booted a 37-yard field goal.* **4** [T] to stop someone from moving their illegally parked vehicle by attaching a piece of equipment to one of its wheels [**Origin:** (1) 1900–2000 *bootstrap* **to boot up** (1900–2000)]

ˈboot camp *n.* [C] a training camp for people who have just joined the Army, Navy, or Marine Corps

ˈboot cut *adj.* boot cut pants are wide at the bottom so you can wear boots with them

booth /buθ/ S2 *n.* [C] **1** a small partly enclosed place where one person can do something privately, such as use the telephone or vote: *a phone booth* | *a ticket booth* **2** a partly enclosed place in a restaurant with a table between two long seats **3** a small enclosed structure where you can buy things, play games, or find out information, usually at a FAIR [**Origin:** 1100–1200 From a Scandinavian language]

Booth /buθ/**, John Wilkes** /dʒɑn wɪlks/ (1838–1865) the man who shot and killed U.S. President Abraham Lincoln

boo·tie, bootee /ˈbuṭi/ *n.* [C] a short thick sock that a baby wears instead of a shoe

boot·lace /ˈbutleɪs/ *n.* [C usually plural] a long piece of string that you use to fasten a boot

boot·leg¹ /ˈbutlɛg/ *adj.* [only before noun] bootleg products, such as alcohol or RECORDINGS, are made and sold illegally: *bootleg recordings of the concert*

bootleg² *n.* [C] an illegal recording of a music performance, piece of computer SOFTWARE etc.

boot·leg·ging /ˈbutˌlɛgɪŋ/ *n.* [U] illegally making or selling products such as alcohol or RECORDINGS —**bootlegger** *n.* [C] —**bootleg** *v.* [I,T]

boot·lick·ing /ˈbutˌlɪkɪŋ/ *n.* [U] INFORMAL behavior that is too friendly to someone in a position of authority, in order to get advantages for yourself —**bootlicker** *n.* [C] —**bootlicking** *adj.*

boot·straps /ˈbutstræps/ *n.* [plural] **pull yourself up by your bootstraps** to improve your situation in life by your own efforts, without help from other people: *He quit drugs and pulled himself up by his bootsraps.*

boo·ty /ˈbuṭi/ *n.* **1** [U] LITERARY valuable things that are stolen by people, especially by soldiers who have just won a war SYN **loot** SYN **plunder** **2** [C] SLANG the part of your body that you sit on SYN **butt** [**Origin:** 1400–1500 Old French *butin*, from Middle Low German *bute* **exchange**] → see also **shake your booty** at SHAKE¹ (14)

booze¹ /buz/ *n.* [U] INFORMAL alcoholic drink: *a bottle of cheap booze* [**Origin:** 1200–1300 Middle Dutch, Middle Flemish *busen*]

booze² *v.* [I] INFORMAL to drink alcohol, especially a lot of it: *The guys were out boozing after work.*

booz·er /ˈbuzɚ/ *n.* [C] INFORMAL someone who often drinks a lot of alcohol

booz·y /ˈbuzi/ *adj.* showing signs that someone has drunk too much alcohol: *boozy laughter*

bop¹ /bɑp/ *v.* **bopped, bopping** INFORMAL **1** [T] to hit someone without much force, or as a joke: *I just bopped her on the head with the umbrella.* **2** [I always + adv./prep.] SPOKEN INFORMAL to go somewhere: *We were bopping around town, doing some shopping.* **3** [I] to dance to popular music [**Origin:** (1) 1900–2000 From the sound of hitting]

bop² *n.* **1** [C] a gentle hit, often done as a joke **2** [singular] another word for BEBOP

bo·rax /ˈbɔræks/ *n.* [U] a mineral used for cleaning things

Bor·deaux /bɔrˈdoʊ/ a city in southwest France

bor·del·lo /bɔrˈdɛloʊ/ *n. plural* **bordellos** [C] LITERARY a BROTHEL

bor·der¹ /ˈbɔrdɚ/ S3 W2 *n.* [C] **1** POLITICS the official line that separates two countries, states, or areas, or the area close to this line SYN **frontier**: **+between** *the border between the U.S. and Canada* | **+with** *Chile's border with Peru* | *It's a national park* ***on the*** *Utah* ***border***. | *Refugees have been warned not to attempt to* ***cross the border***. | **across/over the border** *We drove* *across the border into Germany.* ►see THESAURUS box at **edge**[1] **2** a band along or around the edge of something, such as a picture or a piece of material: *a skirt with a red border* **3** a separation or difference between one situation, state, or person and another: *The music **crosses** cultural **borders**.* **4** an area of soil where you plant flowers or plants at the edge of an area of grass [**Origin:** 1300–1400 Old French *bordure*, from *border* **to border**, from *bort* **border**]

border[2] *v.* [T] **1** if one area borders another area, it is next to it and shares a border with it: *Azerbaijan borders the Caspian Sea.* **2** to form a border along the edge of something: *Willow trees bordered the river.*

border on sth *phr. v.* to be almost as extreme as a particular extreme quality: *He speaks with a confidence that borders on arrogance.*

'border ,crossing *n.* [C] a place where a road crosses a border between countries or states and where officials check vehicles, passports etc.

'border dis,pute *n.* [C] a disagreement between countries or states about where the border between them should be

bor·der·land /ˈbɔrdɚˌlænd/ *n.* [singular] **1** the land near the border between two areas **2** a BORDERLINE

bor·der·line[1] /ˈbɔrdɚˌlaɪn/ *adj.* **1** something that is borderline is very close to being unacceptable: *Caitlin's grades are borderline. She'll have to work harder.* **2** used to describe a person whose work or level of skill is almost bad enough to be unacceptable: *Most of the students are good, but there are a couple of **borderline cases**.* **3** [only before noun] used to say that something is almost good enough or bad enough to be described in a particular way: *Johnson's arguments range from ridiculous to borderline slander.* | **borderline anorexia/schizophrenia etc.** (=behavior with many or most of the signs of a particular psychological condition)

borderline[2] *n.* **1** [singular] the point at which one quality, condition, situation, emotion etc. ends and another begins: *the borderline between affection and love* | *We're **on the borderline** of having to ration water.* **2** [C] a BORDER

borderline[3] *adv.* [only before adjectives] INFORMAL almost SYN **practically**: *The new sitcom is rude, insulting to viewers, and borderline immoral.*

'border pa,trol *n.* [C] a group of soldiers or other officials whose job is to guard against people crossing borders illegally

'Border ,States, the HISTORY the U.S. states of Delaware, Maryland, Kentucky, and Missouri, which together formed a border between the North and the South during the American Civil War. The Border States did not vote to leave the Union, but many people living there did support the Confederacy.

bore[1] /bɔr/ *v.* **1** [T] to make someone feel bored: *Poetry bores me.* | *He was bored by the conversation.* | **bore sb with sth** *Angela's always boring us with her stories about her family.* | **bore sb to death/tears** (=make someone extremely bored) **2** [I,T] to make a deep round hole in a hard surface: **+through/into** *The drill is powerful enough to bore through solid rock.* | **bore sth through/in etc. sth** *They bored a tunnel underneath the village.* ►see THESAURUS box at **hole**[1], **pierce**

bore into sb *phr. v.* if someone's eyes bore into you, they look at you in a way that makes you feel uncomfortable

bore[2] *n.* **1** [C] someone who makes other people feel bored, especially because they talk too much about something: *She's such a bore!* | **a theater/photography/science etc. bore** (=someone who talks too much about a particular subject) **2** [singular] a situation or a job you have to do that is not interesting to you: *Washing the dishes is a bore.* **3** [singular] the size of the inside of a tube or something shaped like a tube, especially the barrel of a gun: *a 12-bore shotgun* **4** [C] a borehole

bore[3] *v.* the past tense of BEAR

bored /bɔrd/ S3 *adj.* tired and impatient because you do not think something is interesting, or because you have nothing to do: *Mom, I'm bored!* | **+with** *I quit because I was bored with my job.* | *Anna looks **bored to tears*** (=extremely bored). | *Can't we do something else? I'm **bored stiff*** (=extremely bored). → see Word Choice box at ADJECTIVE

bore·dom /ˈbɔrdəm/ *n.* [U] the feeling you have when you are bored: *I was going crazy with boredom* | *We played games to **relieve the boredom*** (=stop being bored).

bore·hole /ˈbɔrhoʊl/ *n.* [C] a deep hole made using special equipment, especially in order to get water or oil out of the ground

Bor·ges /ˈbɔrhɛs/, **Jor·ge Lu·is** /ˈhɔrheɪ luˈis/ (1899–1986) an Argentinian poet and writer of short stories

Bor·gias /ˈbɔrdʒəz/, **the** a powerful wealthy Italian family in the 15th and early 16th centuries, known for their cruel determination to gain political power, including Lucrezia Borgia (1480–1519) and her brother Cesare Borgia (1476–1507), who was a successful soldier and ruler, and the Prince in Machiavelli's book "The Prince" is based on him

Bor·glum /ˈbɔrgləm/, **Gut·zon** /ˈgʌtsən/ (1867-1941) a U.S. SCULPTOR famous for his very large SCULPTURE of the heads of four U.S. Presidents on Mount Rushmore in South Dakota

bor·ing /ˈbɔrɪŋ/ S2 *adj.* not interesting in any way OPP **interesting**: *The movie was boring.* | *He's one of the most boring people I've ever met.* → see Word Choice box at ADJECTIVE

> **THESAURUS**
> **dull** not interesting or exciting: *a dull lecture*
> **tedious** boring, and continuing for a long time: *Typing the report was a tedious job.*
> **not (very/that/all that) interesting**: *The book wasn't all that interesting.*
> **monotonous** boring and always the same: *Factory jobs can be monotonous.*
> → INTERESTING

born /bɔrn/ S1 W1 *adj.* **1 be born a)** when a person or animal is born, they come out of their mother's body or out of an egg: *Hey Mom, where were you born?* | **+in** *Neil was born in Brooklyn, right?* | *Melissa was born in 1968.* | **+at** *Were you born at home or in the hospital?* | **+on** *Their daughter was born on June 7.* | **+with** *Jenny was born with heart problems* (=she has had them since she was born). | **+to** *More babies are being born to older parents.* | *I was **born and raised** in Alabama* (=I grew up there). | **be born into wealth/poverty etc.** (=be born in a particular situation or type of family) | **be born blind/deaf etc.** (=be blind, deaf etc. when you were born) | **be born lucky/unlucky/free etc.** (=be lucky, unlucky etc. for your whole life) | **be born out of wedlock** (=be born to parents who are not married) **b)** when something is born, it starts to exist: *How a planet is born is a question that has only been partially answered.* **2 be born to do/be sth** to be very suitable for a particular job, activity etc.: *Jim was born to be a politician.* **3 a born leader/teacher/musician etc.** someone who has a strong natural ability to lead, teach etc.: *Lee is a born salesman.* **4 a born loser** someone who always seems to have bad things happen to them **5 sth is born (out) of sth** used to say that something exists as a result of a particular situation: *Labor unions were born out of a need for better working conditions.* **6 born and bred** born and having grown up in a particular place and having the typical qualities of someone from that place: *Meyer's a Texan, born and bred.* **7 be born with a silver spoon in your mouth** to be born into a rich family **8 be born under a lucky/unlucky star** to always have good or bad luck in your life

B

SPOKEN PHRASES

9 I wasn't born yesterday used to tell someone whom you think is lying to you that you are not stupid enough to believe them **10 there's one born every minute** used to say that someone has been very stupid or easily tricked **11 in all my born days** OLD-FASHIONED used to express surprise or annoyance at something that you have never heard about before: *I've never heard anything so stupid in all my born days.*

[**Origin:** Old English *boren*, past participle of *beran*]

-born /bɔrn/ [in adjectives] **Australian-born/Moroccan-born/Canadian-born etc.** born in a particular country: *an Egyptian-born businessman*

ˈborn-ˌagain *adj.* **1 a born-again Christian** someone who has chosen to become an EVANGELICAL Christian **2 a born-again non-smoker/vegetarian etc.** INFORMAL someone who has recently stopped smoking, eating meat etc., and who keeps encouraging other people to do the same

borne[1] /bɔrn/ *v.* the past participle of BEAR

borne[2] *adj.* **be borne in on/upon sb** LITERARY if a fact is borne in on someone, they realize that it is true

-borne /bɔrn/ *suffix* [in adjectives] **water-borne/air-borne/wind-borne etc.** carried by water, air etc.: *a blood-borne disease*

Bor·ne·o /ˈbɔrnioʊ/ the largest island of the Malay Archipelago in southeast Asia. Part of it belongs to Malaysia and part of it to Indonesia, and it also includes the Sultanate of Brunei.

bor·ough /ˈbɚoʊ, ˈbʌroʊ/ *n.* [C] a town or part of a large city that is responsible for managing its own schools, hospitals, roads etc.: *the borough of Brooklyn in New York City* [**Origin:** Old English *burg* **castle, town defended by a wall**]

bor·row /ˈbɑroʊ, ˈbɔroʊ/ S2 W3 *v.* **1** [T] to use something that belongs to someone else and give it back to them later → see also LEND: *Can I borrow your pen?* | **borrow sth from sb** *Did you borrow those tools from your dad?* → LOAN[2]

THESAURUS

lend to let someone use something that belongs to you, which he or she will give back to you later: *I can lend you the book if you want.*
loan INFORMAL to let someone borrow something of yours, especially money, which he or she will give back to you later: *I loaned him $20.* | *Mom and Dad will loan us their car for the weekend.*
rent to pay money to borrow something: *We rented a couple of DVDs on Saturday night.*
let sb use sth to allow someone to use something that belongs to you: *The neighbors let us use their pool sometimes.*

2 [I,T] to take money from a person or bank with the agreement that you will pay it back later: *Can I borrow $20?* | **borrow sth from sb** *Craig borrowed the money from his sister.* | *Many companies had* ***borrowed heavily*** (=borrowed a lot of money) *to cover their losses.* → see picture at LEND **3** to take or copy someone's ideas, words etc. and use them in your own work, language etc.: **borrow (sth) from sb/sth** *English borrows words from many languages.* **4 borrow trouble** INFORMAL to worry about something when it is not necessary to do this [**Origin:** Old English *borgian*] → see also **be living on borrowed time** at LIVE[1] (19)

bor·row·er /ˈbɑroʊɚ, ˈbɔr-/ *n.* [C] someone who has borrowed money from a bank → see also LENDER

bor·row·ing /ˈbɑroʊɪŋ/ *n.* **1** [plural,U] ECONOMICS the activity of borrowing money, or the total amount of money that is borrowed: *limits on federal borrowing* | *The Japanese company has invested its borrowings in bonds.* **2** [C usually plural] something such as a word, phrase, or idea that has been copied from another language, book etc.: *French borrowings* | **+from** *The music is full of borrowings from other composers.*

ˈborrowing ˌpowers *n.* [plural] ECONOMICS the amount of money that a company is allowed to borrow, according to its own rules

borscht /bɔrʃt/ *n.* [U] a soup made with BEETS, that you eat hot or cold

ˈborscht belt *n.* INFORMAL **the borscht belt** the vacation area in the Catskill Mountains with a lot of hotels that are used mainly by Jewish people

Bosch /bɑʃ/, **Hie·ron·y·mus** /ˌhaɪˈrɑnɪməs/ (1460–1516) a Flemish painter famous for his religious paintings showing strange and unnatural creatures and situations

bosh /bɑʃ/ *n.* [U] OLD-FASHIONED something that you do not believe or that does not make any sense [**Origin:** 1800–1900 Turkish *bos* **empty, useless**] **—bosh** *interjection*

Bos·ni·a /ˈbɑzniə/ also **Bosnia-Her·ze·go·vi·na** /-ˌhɛrtsəgəˈvinə/ a country in eastern Europe between Croatia and Serbia. It was formerly a part of Yugoslavia. **—Bosnian** *n., adj.*

bos·om /ˈbʊzəm/ *n.* **1** [C] OLD-FASHIONED a woman's breast or breasts **2 a bosom buddy/friend** a very close friend **3** [singular] LITERARY your chest, especially when you think of it as the place where your feelings are: *the bitterness and anger in his bosom* **4 the bosom of the family/Church etc.** a familiar situation in which you feel safe because you are with people who love and protect you

bos·om·y /ˈbʊzəmi/ *adj.* INFORMAL having large breasts

Bos·po·rus /ˈbɑspərəs/ also **the Bos·pho·rus** /ˈbɑsfərəs/ the narrow sea between the European and Asian parts of Turkey, connecting the Black Sea with the Sea of Marmara

boss[1] /bɔs/ S2 W3 *n.* [C] **1** the person who employs you or who is in charge of you at work: *Caroline asked her boss for the day off.* | *I've always wanted to* ***be my own boss*** (=work for myself rather than be employed by someone else). **2** INFORMAL someone with an important position in a company or other organization: **a party/political/union boss** *Party bosses no longer choose the candidates.* | **a crime/drug/mafia boss** (=a leader of a criminal group) **3** the person who is the strongest in a relationship, who controls a situation etc.: *Mom's the boss in this house.* | *With these kids, you just have to* ***let them know who's boss*** (=make sure you are in control). **4** a round decoration on the surface of something such as the ceiling of an old building [**Origin:** (1–3) 1800–1900 Dutch *baas* **man in charge**]

boss[2] *v.* [T] also **boss sb around** to tell people to do things, give them orders etc., especially when you have no authority to do it: *Stop bossing me around!*

boss[3] *adj.* SLANG very attractive or fashionable: *a totally boss leather jacket*

bos·sa no·va /ˌbɑsə ˈnoʊvə/ *n.* [C,U] a dance that comes from Brazil, or the music for this dance

boss·y /ˈbɔsi/ *adj. comparative* **bossier**, *superlative* **bossiest** always telling other people what to do in a way that is annoying: *Kevin's mother is really bossy.* **—bossily** *adv.* **—bossiness** *n.* [U]

Bos·ton /ˈbɔstən/ the capital city of the U.S. state of Massachusetts

ˌBoston ˈMassacre, the HISTORY an occasion in 1770 when British soldiers killed five people in Boston, which was one of the events that led to the beginning of the American Revolutionary War

ˌBoston ˈTea ˌParty, the HISTORY a protest against British taxes in 1773 during which people from Boston threw supplies of tea from British ships into the water. These actions helped start the American Revolution.

bo·sun /ˈboʊsən/ *n.* [C] another spelling of BOATSWAIN

Bos·well /ˈbɑzwɛl/, **James** (1740–1795) a Scottish writer, famous for his book about the life of Samuel Johnson

bo·tan·i·cal /bəˈtænɪkəl/ *adj.* [only before noun] BIOLOGY relating to plants or the scientific study of plants [**Origin:** 1600–1700 French *botanique*, from Greek *botanikos*, from *botane* **plant (that can be eaten)**] —**botanically** /-kli/ *adv.*

bo͵tanical 'garden *n.* [C] a large public garden where many different types of flowers and plants are grown for scientific study

bot·a·nist /'bɑt˺nɪst/ *n.* [C] BIOLOGY someone whose job is to make scientific studies of wild plants

bot·a·ny /'bɑt˺n-i/ *n.* [U] BIOLOGY the scientific study of plants

Bot·a·ny Bay /͵bɑt˺n-i 'beɪ/ a BAY on the southeast coast of Australia, close to Sydney

botch[1] /bɑtʃ/ *v.* [T] INFORMAL also **botch up** to do something badly, because you have been careless or because you do not have the skill to do it well: *The police are accused of botching the investigation.* —**botcher** *n.* [C]

botch[2] *n.* [C] INFORMAL **make a botch of sth** to do something badly because you are careless or because you lack skill

botched /bɑtʃt/ *adj.* [usually before noun] done very badly by someone who is careless or lacks skill: ***a badly botched** robbery **attempt***

both[1] /boʊθ/ S1 W1 *quantifier, pron.* **1** used to talk about two people, things, situations etc. together: *They both went to Harvard.* | *Hold it in both hands.* | *Both the girls play the piano.* | *I'd like to try a little of both.* | **+of** *Both of my grandfathers are farmers.* | **we/you/they both** *They can both swim.* | *We both went to Columbia.* | **us/you/them both** *I'd like to speak to you both.* **2 you can't have it both ways** SPOKEN used to say that you cannot have the advantages from both of two possible situations: *It's either me or her. You can't have it both ways!* → see also EITHER → see Word Choice box at EACH[1]

both[2] S3 W1 *conjunction* **both... and...** used to emphasize that not just one person, thing, situation etc. is included in a statement, but also another: *Donny plays both football and baseball.* | *Both he and his wife enjoy tennis.* | *Jane's kids are both rude and spoiled.*

both·er[1] /'bɑðɚ/ S1 W3 *v.*

1 ANNOY [T] to annoy someone, especially by interrupting them when they are trying to do something: *"Why didn't you ask me for help?" "I didn't want to bother you."* | *Don't bother Ellen while she's reading.* | ***Sorry to bother you, but*** (=used as a polite way of apologizing for interrupting someone) *could I use your phone?*

2 WORRY [I,T] to make someone feel slightly worried or upset: *Something's bothering him.* | **bother sb with sth** *I don't want to bother you with my problems.* | **it bothers sb that** *It bothers me that he hasn't been telling me the truth.*

3 MAKE AN EFFORT [I,T] to make the effort to do something: **not bother doing sth** *I'm not even going to bother studying.* | **not bother to do sth** *He didn't even bother to reply.* | **not bother with sth** *I don't think I'll bother with coffee right now.* | *"Do you want me to wait for you?" "No, please **don't bother**."* | *I tried to defend her, but **why bother**? There's no point.* | **+about** *U.S. officials no longer bother about diplomatic politeness.*

4 CAUSE PAIN [T] if a part of your body bothers you, it is painful or uncomfortable: *Actually, my back hasn't been bothering me.*

5 FRIGHTEN [T only in progressive] to upset or frighten someone by continuously trying to hurt them, touch them sexually etc.: *Excuse me, Miss, is that man bothering you?*

bother[2] *n.* **1** [C] something or someone that slightly annoys or upsets you because of the trouble or problems they cause: *I hate to **be a bother**, but could I use your phone?* **2** [U] used in some expressions instead of the word "trouble": **go to the bother of doing sth** (=make an effort to do something) | **sth is more bother than it's worth** (=something is too difficult to be worth doing) **3 (it's) no bother** SPOKEN used to say that you are not annoyed or that something does not cause you any problems: *"Sorry to interrupt you." "That's okay, no bother."*

both·ered /'bɑðɚd/ *adj.* [not before noun] worried or upset: **+that** *Nobody seemed bothered that Grandpa wasn't there.* → see also **be hot and bothered** at HOT (34)

both·er·some /'bɑðɚsəm/ *adj.* slightly annoying: *bothersome insects* | *a bothersome delay*

Bot·swa·na /bɑts'wɑnə/ a country in central southern Africa —**Botswanan** *adj.*

B

Bot·ti·cel·li /͵bɑt̬ɪ'tʃɛli/, **San·dro** /'sɑndroʊ/ (?1444–1510) an Italian PAINTER famous for his paintings based on Greek MYTHOLOGY

bot·tle[1] /'bɑt̬l/ S1 W3 *n.* [C] **1** a container with a narrow top for keeping liquids in, usually made of glass or plastic: *an empty wine bottle* | **+of** *a bottle of shampoo* **2** also **bottleful** the amount of liquid that a bottle contains: *I only want one glass, not a whole bottle.* **3** a container for babies to drink from, with a rubber part on top that they suck on: *Do you want me to give Kayla her bottle?* **4 the bottle** a word meaning "alcoholic drink," usually used when talking about the problems that drinking can cause: *Peter let the bottle ruin his life.* | *After his wife left, Judd **hit the bottle*** (=started drinking a lot of alcohol regularly) *pretty hard.* [**Origin:** 1300–1400 Old French *bouteille*, from Late Latin *buttis* **wooden container for liquid**] → see also **bring your own bottle** at BRING (21)

bottle[2] *v.* [T] to put a liquid, especially wine or beer, into a bottle after you have made it: *wine bottled in Oregon* → see also BOTTLER

bottle sth ↔ **up** *phr. v.* **1** to deliberately not allow yourself to show a strong feeling or emotion: *If you bottle up all that anger, you'll make yourself sick.* **2** to cause problems by delaying something: *The bill has been bottled up in Congress for months.*

'bottle cap *n.* [C] a small metal lid on a bottle

bottled /'bɑt̬ld/ *adj.* **bottled water/beer etc.** water, beer etc. that is sold in a bottle

'bottle-feed *v.* **bottle-fed** [T] to feed a baby with milk from a bottle rather than from the mother's breast —**bottle-feeding** *n.* [U] —**bottle-fed** *adj.*

'bottle ͵green *n.* [U] a very dark green color —**bottle green** *adj.*

bot·tle·neck /'bɑt̬l͵nɛk/ *n.* [C] **1** a place in a road where the traffic cannot pass easily, so that there are a lot of delays **2** a delay in one stage of a process that makes the whole process take longer: *Automatic packing machines should get rid of the bottlenecks.*

'bottle ͵opener *n.* [C] a small tool used for removing the metal lids from bottles

bot·tler /'bɑt̬l-ɚ, 'bɑtlɚ/ *n.* [C] a person or company that puts drinks into bottles or cans —**bottling** *n.* [U]

'bottle ͵rocket *n.* [C] a type of FIREWORKS that you shoot from a bottle

bot·tom[1] /'bɑt̬əm/ S1 W2 *n.*

1 LOWEST PART [C usually singular] the lowest part of something OPP **top**: **+of** *Hold the bottom of the ladder.* | *I was standing **at the bottom of** the stairs.* | *The answers are **on the bottom of** page 95.* | *My name is on **the very bottom** of the list* (=used to emphasize that you mean the lowest position).

2 LOWEST SIDE [C usually singular] the flat surface on the lowest side of an object OPP **top**: **+of** *Something's hanging from the bottom of your car.* | *What's that **on the bottom of** your shoe?* | *The stone was completely smooth **on the bottom**.*

3 LOWEST INNER PART [C usually singular] the lowest inner part of something such as a container OPP **top**: **+of** *the bottom of a well* | *Spread the tomato sauce **on the bottom of** a large dish.* | *Heavy objects should be packed **in the bottom of** your suitcase.*

4 LOWEST POSITION the bottom the lowest position in an organization or company OPP **top**: *The Giants are **at the bottom of** the league.* | *Watson is willing to **start at the bottom*** (=in a low position in a company) *and work his way up.* | **the bottom of the ladder/pile/barrel/heap** (=the lowest position in society, an organization etc.)

5 OCEAN/RIVER [C usually singular] the ground under an

ocean, river etc., or the flat land in a valley: +**of** *The bottom of the river is rocky.* | *Frogs can stay all winter* ***at the bottom of*** *a pond.* | **the ocean/lake/river etc. bottom** *fish living on the ocean bottom*
6 from the bottom up beginning by dealing with the most basic parts of something or with the people who have the least power: *We want to rebuild city government from the bottom up.*
7 BODY [C] a word meaning BUTTOCKS (=the part of your body that you sit on), used especially when speaking to children: *Did you fall on your bottom?*
8 CLOTHES [C usually plural] the part of a set of clothes that you wear on the lower part of your body OPP **top**: *pajama bottoms*
9 get to the bottom of sth INFORMAL to find out the cause of a problem or situation: *We're trying to get to the bottom of this, and see if she is lying.*
10 be/lie at the bottom of sth to be the basic cause of a problem or situation: *Lack of money is at the bottom of many family problems.*
11 be at the bottom of the list to not be at all important to someone: *Surprisingly, safety was at the bottom of the list for airline passengers.*
12 the bottom of the first/fifth/ninth etc. (inning) the second half of an INNING in baseball OPP **top**
13 from the bottom of your heart used to show that you are very sincere about what you are saying: *Thank you, from the bottom of my heart.*
14 the bottom drops out (of the market) used to say that people suddenly stop buying a particular product: *The copper mines stopped operating when the bottom dropped out of the market.*
15 bottoms up! SPOKEN used to tell someone to enjoy or finish their alcoholic drink
16 the bottom dropped out of sb's world/life used to say that something very bad suddenly happened to someone
17 SHIP [C] the part of a ship that is below water
[**Origin:** Old English *botm*] → see also **you can bet your bottom dollar** at BET[1] (5), -BOTTOMED, **knock the bottom out of sth** at KNOCK[1] (14), ROCK BOTTOM, **scrape the bottom of the barrel** at SCRAPE[1] (4), **(from) top to bottom** at TOP[1] (12)

bottom² S3 *adj.* [only before noun] **1** in the lowest place or position OPP **top**: *The book is on the bottom shelf.* | *You have some peanut butter on your bottom lip.* | *the bottom right-hand corner of the page* **2** the least important or successful OPP **top**: *Tim is in the bottom 10% of his class.*

bottom³ *v.*
bottom out *phr. v.* if a situation, price etc. bottoms out, it stops getting worse or lower, usually before improving again: *Housing prices appear to have bottomed out and are expected to rise.*

-bottomed /ˈbɑṭəmd/ [in adjectives] **big-bottomed/round-bottomed etc.** having a bottom or base that is big, round etc.

bot·tom·less /ˈbɑṭəmlɪs/ *adj.* **1** a bottomless hole or area of water is extremely deep: *the bottomless depths of the ocean* **2 a bottomless pit a)** a supply of something that seems so large that it can never be used up: *The U.S. is not a bottomless pit of aid money.* **b)** a system, situation, or activity that uses up all your money or other resources but never seems to improve or end: *Everything they earned was swallowed by their bottomless pit of debt.* **3 a bottomless cup** a cup of coffee or a SOFT DRINK you buy in a restaurant, that you pay for once and can fill as many times as you want

ˌbottom ˈline *n.* **1 the bottom line** a situation or fact that is basic, true, or most important, and that must be accepted even if you do not like it: *Wisconsin won the game, and that's the bottom line.* | *The bottom line is this: people don't really change.* **2** the profit or the amount of money that a business makes or loses: *Every business is worried about the bottom line.* **3 sb's bottom line** the lowest amount of money that someone is willing to pay or take for something: *I want at least $800 for the car. That's my bottom line.* —**bottom-line** *adj.*

bot·tom·most /ˈbɑṭəmˌmoʊst/ *adj.* [only before noun] in the lowest, farthest, or deepest position or place: *the bottommost rung of a ladder*

ˌbottom-ˈup *adj.* INFORMAL a bottom-up plan is one in which you decide on practical details before thinking about general principles → TOP-DOWN

bot·u·lism /ˈbɑtʃəˌlɪzəm/ *n.* [U] MEDICINE serious food poisoning caused by BACTERIA in preserved meat and vegetables [**Origin:** 1800–1900 German *botulismus*, from Latin *botulus* **sausage**; because the bacteria were first found in sausages and other cooked meats]

Bou·dic·ca, /buˈdɪkə/ also **Bo·a·di·ce·a** /ˌboʊədɪˈsiə/ (died A.D. 60) the Queen of the Iceni tribe of eastern Britain, who led them in battle against the Romans

bou·doir /ˈbudwɑr, buˈdwɑr/ *n.* [C] **1** the BEDROOM, especially considered as the place where people have sex: *secrets of the boudoir* **2** OLD USE a woman's BEDROOM or private sitting room [**Origin:** 1700–1800 French *bouder* **to pout**]

bouf·fant /buˈfɑnt/ *adj.* a bouffant hair style is brushed up and away from the head so that it stays high and looks thick

bou·gain·vil·lea /ˌbugənˈvɪlyə/ *n.* [C,U] a South American plant that has red or purple flowers and grows up walls

bough /baʊ/ *n.* [C] LITERARY a main branch on a tree [**Origin:** Old English *bog* **shoulder, bough**]

bought /bɔt/ *v.* the past tense and past participle of BUY

bouil·la·baisse /ˈbuyəˌbeɪs, ˌbuyəˈbeɪs/ *n.* [C,U] a strong-tasting soup or STEW made with fish

bouil·lon /ˈbulyɑn, ˈbʊlyən/ *n.* [C,U] a clear soup made by boiling meat and vegetables in water

ˈbouillon cube *n.* [C] a small square made of dried meats or vegetables, used to make soups and SAUCES taste better

Boul·der /ˈboʊldɚ/ a city in the U.S. state of Colorado

boul·der /ˈboʊldɚ/ *n.* [C] a large stone or piece of rock: *Two huge boulders blocked the road.*

bou·le·vard /ˈbʊləvɑrd, ˈbu-/ *n.* [C] **1** a wide road in a town or city, often with trees along the sides ►see THESAURUS box at **road** **2** a word used in the names of some roads: *Sunset Boulevard*

bounce¹ /baʊns/ S3 *v.*
1 FROM A SURFACE [I,T] if a ball or other object bounces, or if you bounce it, it immediately moves up or away from a surface after hitting it: *Two boys stood on the corner bouncing basketballs.* | **bounce off sth** *Both shots bounced off the rim of the basket.* | **bounce down/across etc. sth** *A rock bounced down the hill.*
2 MOVE UP AND DOWN [I always + adv./prep.] to move up and down, especially because you are jumping on a surface that is soft, has springs etc.: **bounce on sth** *The kids were bouncing on the sofa.* | *Dooley was* ***bouncing up and down*** *with excitement.*
3 MAKE STH MOVE [I,T] if someone or something bounces or something else bounces them, they move up and down or from side to side in an uncontrolled way: *Her hair bounced when she walked.* | **bounce (sb/sth) around** *We were bouncing around in the back of the bus.* | *Pack the hard disk well so it won't be bounced around.* | **bounce along/down etc.** *The plane bounced along the runway.*
4 CHANGE SITUATIONS [I,T] to move quickly from one situation, position, or place to another, or to make someone or something do this: *Doherty's case has bounced him from court to court.* | *Interest rates have* ***bounced up and down*** (=become larger or smaller in number) *throughout the year.*
5 CHANGE SUBJECTS [I] to change quickly from one subject, thought, idea etc. to another: *Grosso talks rapidly, bouncing from one thought to the next.*
6 CHECK [I,T] if a check bounces or a bank bounces a check, the bank will not pay any money because there is not enough money in the account of the person who wrote it: *If the check bounces, the bank charges a fee of $18.*

7 COMPUTER [I,T] also **bounce back** if an EMAIL message that you send bounces or is bounced, it is AUTOMATI-cally returned to you because of a technical problem **8 WALK** [I always + adv./prep.] to walk quickly and with a lot of energy: +**across/along/in etc.** *Laura came bouncing into the room with a smile on her face.* **9 LIGHT/SOUND** [I,T] also **bounce off** if light or sound bounces or bounces off something, it hits a surface and REFLECTS off it: *The radio signals are bounced off a satellite.* **10 MAKE SB LEAVE** [T] INFORMAL to force someone to leave a place, job, or organization, especially because they have done something wrong: **bounce sb from sth** *Sean has already been bounced from three schools.* **11 be bouncing off the walls** INFORMAL to be too excited or too full of energy: *The sugar goes straight into your bloodstream and you start bouncing off the walls.* **12 bounce sb on your knee/lap** to lift a child up and down while they are sitting on your knees [**Origin:** 1500–1600 *bounce* **to hit** (13–19 centuries)]

bounce around *phr. v.* **1** if someone bounces around, they move from one situation to another without any planning or control: *He's got a PhD, but he's been bouncing around between jobs.* | **bounce around sth** *After graduation I bounced around Europe for a few months.* **2 bounce ideas around** to discuss ideas with other people: *We sat down and bounced a few ideas around.* **3** if an object bounces around, something makes it keep moving in an uncontrolled way: *You don't want your stuff bouncing around in the back of the van, do you?*

bounce back *phr. v.* **1** to feel better quickly or become successful again, after having a lot of problems: *No matter what happens to Maria, she always bounces back.* | **bounce back from sth** *Farmers have bounced back from difficult times in the 1980s.* **2** if an email message bounces back or something bounces it back, it is sent back to you because it could not get to the person you sent it to

bounce sth **off** sb *phr. v.* to ask someone for their opinion about an idea, plan etc. before you make a decision: *Anytime I need to bounce ideas off someone, I give Debbie a call.*

bounce[2] *n.* **1** [C] an action in which something immediately moves up or away from a surface after hitting it: *I caught the ball on the first bounce.* **2** [U] energy and excitement: *Exercise is great. I feel like there's **a new bounce in my step*** (=I have more energy and feel more healthy). **3** [U] the ability to move up and down, or the ability of a surface to make something move up and down: *a basketball court with good bounce* **4** [U] hair that has bounce swings naturally and keeps its shape without looking stiff

bounc•er /ˈbaʊnsɚ/ *n.* [C] someone whose job is to stand at the door of a club, bar etc. and stop unwanted people from coming in, or make people leave if they are causing trouble

bounc•ing /ˈbaʊnsɪŋ/ *adj.* **a bouncing baby boy/girl** a very healthy baby

bounc•y /ˈbaʊnsi/ *adj. comparative* **bouncier**, *superlative* **bounciest** **1** happy and full of energy: *bouncy country music* **2** moving up and down on hard surfaces very easily or too easily: *a bouncy ride over rough roads* **3** a bouncy surface moves up and down easily when someone is on it: *I love these bouncy chairs. They're really comfortable.* **4** hair that is bouncy swings naturally and keeps its shape without looking stiff —**bounciness** *n.* [U]

bound[1] /baʊnd/ *adj.* [no comparative]
1 LIKELY be bound to do sth to be very likely to do something, to happen, to be true etc.: *Mom's bound to find out that you lied.* | **there is/are bound to be sth** *When two cultures are so different, there's bound to be conflict.*
2 LAW/AGREEMENT be bound (by sth) to have to do what a law, promise, agreement etc. says you must do: **be bound (by sth) to do sth** *The Foundation is bound by the treaty to help any nation that requests aid.* | *You are **legally bound to** report any change of address to the bank.*
3 bound for college/Houston/Mexico etc. also **college-bound/Houston-bound etc.** traveling toward a particular place, or intending to go there: *A plane bound for Peru crashed early Sunday morning.* | *After months of travel, we were at last **homeward bound**.* → see also EASTBOUND, NORTHBOUND, SOUTHBOUND, WESTBOUND
4 bound and determined very determined to do or achieve something, no matter how difficult it is: *Klein is bound and determined to win at least five races this year.*
5 be bound up in sth a) also **be bound up with sth** to be closely connected with a particular problem, situation etc.: *His problems are all bound up with his childhood experiences.* **b)** to be so involved in a difficult situation etc. that you cannot think about anything else: *Jim's too bound up in his own worries to be able to help us.*
6 be bound (together) by sth to feel a close relationship with somene because you share a particular feature or quality: *two nations bound together by a shared history*
7 BOOK a bound book or document is covered on the outside with paper, leather etc.: +**in** *a notebook bound in red velvet* | *a **leather-bound** world atlas*
8 be/feel bound to do sth to feel that you must do something: *We felt bound to tell her the truth.*
9 I'll be bound OLD-FASHIONED used when you are very sure that what you have just said is true
10 a bound form ENG. LANG. ARTS a part of a word that is always found in combination with another form, such as "un-" and "-er" in the words "unknown" and "speaker"

bound[2] *v.* the past tense and past participle of BIND

bound[3] *v.* **1** [I always + adv./prep.] to run with a lot of energy, because you are happy or excited: +**up/toward/across etc.** *George came bounding down the stairs.* **2 be bounded by sth** if a country or area of land is bounded by something such as a wall, river etc., it has the wall etc. at its edge: *The U.S. is bounded in the north by Canada.* [**Origin:** (1) 1500–1600 Old French *bondir*, from Vulgar Latin *bombitire* **to hum**, from Latin *bombus*]

bound[4] *n.*
1 LIMITS bounds [plural] **a)** limits or rules that are given by law or exist because of social custom: *We're here to make sure that the police operate **within the bounds** of the law.* | *The humor in the movie **goes beyond the bounds of** good taste* (=is outside the limits of what is acceptable). **b)** OLD-FASHIONED the edges of a town, city etc.
2 out of bounds a) outside the legal playing area in a sport such as football or basketball **b)** if a place or subject is out of bounds, you are not allowed to go there or to talk about it: +**to/for** *Those offices are out of bounds to non-management personnel.*
3 in bounds inside the legal playing area in a sport such as football or basketball
4 JUMP [C] LITERARY a long or high jump made with a lot of energy: *Superman can leap tall buildings in a single bound.* → see also **know no bounds** at KNOW[1] (23), **by leaps and bounds** at LEAP[2] (2)

-bound /baʊnd/ *suffix* [in adjectives] **1 snow-bound/fog-bound/wheelchair-bound etc.** limited by something, so that you cannot do what you want or go where you want: *a fog-bound airport* | *Sarah has been house-bound since the accident.* **2 duty-bound/tradition-bound etc.** doing something because it is your duty, it is traditional etc. even though it is not the best thing to do, or not what you want to do: *I am duty-bound to express the management's position on this issue.*

bound•a•ry /ˈbaʊndəri, -dri/ W3 *n. plural* **boundaries** **1** [C] a real or imaginary line that marks where one area of land is separate from other areas → see also BORDER: +**between** *The river forms a natural boundary between the states.* | *The property's **boundary line** is 25 feet from the back wall of the house.* | *In 1885, the state **drew the** southern **boundary*** (=decided where one area of land ends and another one starts) *for Linn County at the Lee River.* **2** [C usually plural] the limit of what can be included within something, or the limit of what is possible or acceptable within something: +**of** *We are limited only by the boundaries of our imagination.* | *Researchers are* ***pushing back the boundaries*** *of science* (=increasing knowledge about science by discovering new things). **3** [C] the point at which one feeling, quality etc. stops and another starts: *Concern for children's safety sometimes* ***crosses the boundary into*** (=goes beyond acceptable limits and becomes) *paranoia.* | +**between** *the boundary between lust and love*

B

bound·en /ˈbaʊndən/ *adj.* **your bounden duty** OLD-FASHIONED something that you should do because it is morally correct

bound·er /ˈbaʊndɚ/ *n.* [C] OLD-FASHIONED, DISAPPROVING a man who has behaved in a way that you think is morally wrong

bound·less /ˈbaʊndlɪs/ *adj.* used to emphasize that something seems to have no limit or end: *boundless enthusiasm* | *the boundless blue sky* —**boundlessly** *adv.* —**boundlessness** *n.* [U]

boun·te·ous /ˈbaʊntiəs/ *adj.* LITERARY very generous

boun·ti·ful /ˈbaʊntɪfəl/ *adj.* LITERARY **1** if something is bountiful, there is more than enough of it: *a bountiful harvest* **2** generous: *God is bountiful.*

boun·ty /ˈbaʊnti/ *n. plural* **bounties** **1** [C] an amount of money that is given to someone by the government as a reward for doing something, such as catching a criminal: +**on** *There was a $50 bounty on each wolf that was captured.* **2** [U] LITERARY a large amount of something, especially food: *the bounty of the harvest* **3** [U] LITERARY the quality of being generous [**Origin:** 1300–1400 Old French *bonté* **goodness**, from Latin *bonitas*, from *bonus* **good**]

ˈbounty ˌhunter *n.* [C] someone who catches criminals and brings them to the police in return for a reward

bou·quet /boʊˈkeɪ, bu-/ *n.* **1** [C] a bunch of flowers that you give to someone or carry on a formal occasion **2** [C,U] the smell of a wine: *It is a light wine with a clean bouquet.* [**Origin:** 1700–1800 French, Old North French *bosquet* **plants growing thickly together**, from Old French *bosc* **forest**]

Bour·bon /ˈbʊrbən/ the name of a family of French kings who ruled from 1589 to 1792

bour·bon /ˈbɚbən/ *n.* [U] a type of WHISKEY [**Origin:** 1800–1900 *Bourbon* county in Kentucky]

bour·geois[1] /bʊrˈʒwɑ, ˈbʊrʒwɑ/ *adj.* **1** belonging or relating to the MIDDLE CLASS especially the wealthy middle class **2** DISAPPROVING bourgeois attitudes are traditional and too interested in money and social positions **3** relating to the social class that is rich and owns property, factories etc. and makes money from the labor of the working class, according to MARXISM: *a bourgeois capitalist* [**Origin:** 1500–1600 French **person who lives in a town**, from Old French *borjois*, from *borc* **town**] → see also PETTY BOURGEOIS, PROLETARIAN

bourgeois[2] *n. plural* **bourgeois** [C] OLD-FASHIONED **1** a member of the MIDDLE CLASS **2** someone who belongs to the MIDDLE CLASS part of society and who is educated, owns land etc., according to MARXISM → see also PROLETARIAT

bour·geoi·sie /ˌbʊrʒwɑˈzi/ *n.* **the bourgeoisie a)** the MIDDLE CLASS people in a society who are educated, own land etc., according to MARXISM **b)** the MIDDLE CLASS

Bourke-White /bɚk ˈwaɪt/, **Mar·garet** /ˈmɑrgrɪt/ (1906–1971) a U.S. newspaper and magazine PHOTOGRAPHER

bout /baʊt/ *n.* [C] **1** a short period of time during which you suffer from a particular illness: +**of** *frequent bouts of depression* | +**with** *Miller died last week at 75 after a long bout with cancer.* **2** a BOXING or WRESTLING competition **3** a short period of time during which you do something a lot, especially something that is bad for you: +**of** *a bout of drinking* [**Origin:** 1500–1600 *bout* **one trip up the field and back in plowing** (16–19 centuries), from *bought* **bending** (14–17 centuries)]

'bout /baʊt/ *adv., prep.* SPOKEN NONSTANDARD a short form of "about": *I'm tired. How 'bout you?*

bou·tique /buˈtik/ *n.* [C] a small store that sells very fashionable clothes or other objects

bou·ton·niere /ˌbutˀnˈɪr, -ˈyɛr/ *n.* [C] a flower that a man wears in the LAPEL of his suit, especially at a wedding

bou·zou·ki /bʊˈzuki/ *n. plural* **bouzoukis** [C] a Greek musical instrument similar to a GUITAR

bo·vine /ˈboʊvaɪn/ *adj.* **1** TECHNICAL relating to cows: *bovine diseases* **2** slow and slightly stupid: *She smiled at us in a bovine sort of way.* [**Origin:** 1800–1900 Late Latin *bovinus*, from Latin *bos* **ox, cow**]

bow[1] /baʊ/ *v.* **1** [I] to bend the top part of your body forward, in order to show respect for someone important or as a way of thanking an AUDIENCE: *Archer bowed and left the stage.* | +**before/to etc.** *We bowed before the king.* **2 bow your head** to bend your neck so that you are looking at the ground, especially because you want to show respect for God or because you are embarrassed or upset: *I bowed my head and prayed.* | *Jerry stood there with his head bowed in shame.* **3** [I,T] to bend your body over something, especially in order to see it more closely: +**over** *Dr. Harris is usually in the lab, bowed over a microscope.* **4 bow and scrape** to show too much respect to someone in authority

bow down *phr. v.* **1** to bend forward from your waist, especially when you are already kneeling, in order to show respect: +**before/to etc.** *Old women bowed down before the statue of Mary.* **2 bow down to sb** LITERARY to let someone give you orders or tell you what to do

bow out *phr. v.* **1** to stop taking part in an activity, job etc., especially one that you have been doing for a long time: **bow out of sth** *Two more Republicans have bowed out of the presidential race.* **2** to not do something that you have promised or agreed to do: *Dreyfuss bowed out of the project at the last minute.*

bow to sb/sth *phr. v.* to finally agree to do something that people want you to, even though you do not want to do it: *He finally bowed to his parents' wishes.* | *The government has* ***bowed to*** *public* ***pressure*** *over tax increases.*

bow[2] /boʊ/ *n.* **1** [C] a knot of cloth or string with a curved part on each side, used especially for decoration: *She* ***wore her hair back in a bow*** (=pulled back and tied with a bow). **2** [C] a weapon used for shooting ARROWS, made of a long thin piece of wood held in a curve by a tight string **3** [C] ENG. LANG. ARTS a long thin piece of wood with tight strings fastened along it, used to play musical instruments that have strings, such as the VIOLIN **4 bow legs** legs that curve out at the knee → see also BOW-LEGGED

bow[3] /baʊ/ *n.* **1** [C] the act of bending the top part of your body forward to show respect for someone **2 take a bow** if someone takes a bow, they come on the stage at the end of a performance so that people can APPLAUD them **3** [C] the front part of a ship → see also STERN

bow[4] /boʊ/ *v.* **1** [I] to bend or curve **2 be bowed** someone who is bowed is bent slightly, for example because they are old or tired from carrying something heavy **3** [I,T] to play a piece of music on a musical instrument with a bow

bowd·ler·ize /ˈboʊdləˌraɪz/ *v.* [T] FORMAL ENG. LANG. ARTS to remove the parts of a book, play etc. that you think are offensive [**Origin:** 1800–1900 Thomas *Bowdler* (1754–1825), English editor who removed impolite words from Shakespeare's plays] —**bowdlerized** *adj.*: *a bowdlerized edition of "Tom Sawyer"*

bow·el /ˈbaʊəl/ *n.* **1 bowels** [plural] BIOLOGY the system of tubes inside your body in which food is made into solid waste material and through which it passes out of your body SYN **intestine**: **move/empty your bowels** (=get rid of solid waste from your body) **2** [singular] BIOLOGY one part of this system of tubes: *cancer of the* bowel **3 a bowel movement** FORMAL an act of getting rid of solid waste from your body **4 the bowels of sth** LITERARY the lowest or deepest part of something: *the bowels of the ship* [**Origin:** 1200–1300 Old French *boel*, from Medieval Latin *botellus*, from Latin *botulus* **sausage**]

bow·er /ˈbaʊɚ/ *n.* [C] LITERARY **1** a pleasant place in the shade under a tree, especially in a garden: *a rose-scented bower* **2** a woman's BEDROOM in a castle

Bow·ie /ˈboʊi, ˈbui/, **James** (1799–1836) a U.S. soldier who was one of the leaders at the battle of the Alamo, when the Texans were fighting to be independent of Mexico

bow·ie knife /ˈboʊi ˌnaɪf/ *n.* [C] a large heavy knife with a long blade that is sharp on one side, used especially for HUNTING

bow·ing /ˈboʊɪŋ/ *n.* [U] **1** the skill of using a BOW to play a musical instrument **2** the written markings that show what movements should be done with the BOW while playing a particular piece of music

bowl¹ /boʊl/ S2 W2 *n.* **1** [C] a wide round container that is open at the top, used to hold liquids, food etc.: *Mix the eggs and butter in a large bowl.* | **soup/salad/cereal etc. bowls** *a wooden salad bowl* **2** also **bowlful** [C] the amount that a bowl will hold: +**of** *a bowl of chili* **3** [C] the part of an object such as a spoon, pipe, toilet etc. that is shaped like a bowl: *the toilet bowl* **4** [C usually singular] a special game played by the best football teams after the normal playing season: *the Rose Bowl* **5** [C usually singular] a STADIUM shaped like a bowl, where people go to watch special events such as sports games or music CONCERTS: *the Hollywood Bowl* [**Origin:** Old English *bolla*]

bowl² S3 *v.* [I,T] to play the game of bowling [**Origin:** 1400–1500 *bowl* **ball used in bowling** (15–21 centuries), from Old French *boule*, from Latin *bulla* **bubble**]

bowl sb ↔ **over** *phr. v.* **1** to surprise, please, or excite someone very much: *I was bowled over by the hundreds of people who wrote to support me.* **2** to accidentally hit someone so that they fall down, because you are running too quickly: *Jackson bowls over linebackers like a runaway train.*

bow-leg·ged /ˈboʊˌlɛgɪd, -ˌlɛgd/ *adj.* having legs that curve out sideways at the knee

bowl·er /ˈboʊlɚ/ *n.* [C] **1** someone who plays the game of bowling **2** also **bowler hat** a DERBY

bowl·ing /ˈboʊlɪŋ/ *n.* [U] an indoor game in which you roll a large heavy ball along a wooden track in order to knock down a group of PINS (=wooden objects shaped like bottles): *The kids and I* ***went bowling*** (=went to a place to play this game) *yesterday.* → see also LAWN BOWLING

ˈbowling ˌalley *n.* [C] a building where you play the game of bowling

ˈbowling ball *n.* [C] the heavy ball you use in the game of bowling

ˈbowling green *n.* [C] an area of grass where you play the game of LAWN BOWLING

bow·man /ˈboʊmən/ *n.* [C] a soldier in past times who shot ARROWS with a BOW

bow·sprit /ˈbaʊsprɪt/ *n.* [C] a long pole on the front of a boat that the ropes from the sails are attached to

bow·string /ˈboʊstrɪŋ/ *n.* [C] the string on a BOW

bow tie /ˈboʊ taɪ/ *n.* [C] a short piece of cloth tied in the shape of a BOW that men wear around their neck

bow wave /ˈbaʊ weɪv/ *n.* [C] PHYSICS a V-shaped wave that is produced by an object traveling on liquid faster than the wave speed, for example the wave in front a boat as it travels through water

bow window /ˌboʊ ˈwɪndoʊ/ *n.* [C] a window that curves out from the wall

bow-wow, bowwow /ˈbaʊ waʊ/ *interjection* a word used to make the sound that a dog makes, used especially by children

boxes

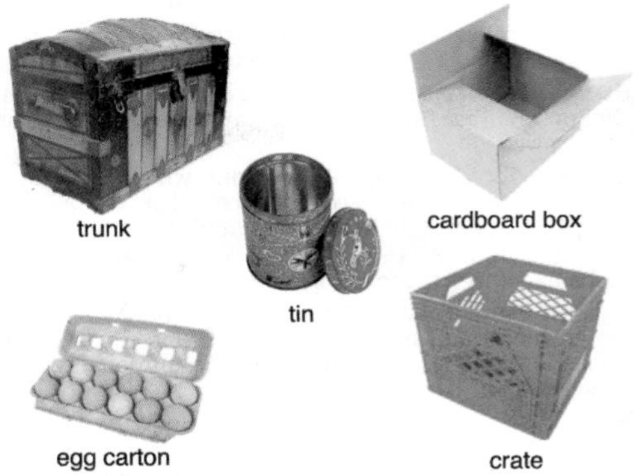

box¹ /bɑks/ S1 W1 *n.*
1 CONTAINER [C] a container for putting things in, especially one with four stiff straight sides: *a cardboard box* | *a cereal box* | *five wooden boxes* | **toolbox/shoebox/lunchbox etc.** (=a box used for keeping tools, shoes etc. in)
2 AMOUNT also **boxful** [C] the amount that a box can hold: +**of** *a box of chocolates*
3 SHAPE [C] **a)** a square on a page or website that people can write information in: *Write the total in the box below.* | ***Check this box*** (=put a check mark in the box) *if you would like more information.* **b)** a square or RECTANGLE on a page where information is given: *The box on the left gives a short history of the Alamo.*
4 IN A THEATER ETC. [C] a small area of seats in a theater, sports STADIUM etc. that is separate from where other people are sitting → see also SENTRY BOX
5 AT A POST OFFICE [C usually singular] a box with a number in a POST OFFICE, where you can have mail sent to instead of your own address: P.O. BOX
6 AREA OF A SPORTS FIELD [C] a special area of a sports field that is marked by lines and used for a particular purpose: *the penalty box* | *the batter's box*
7 SMALL BUILDING [C] a small building or structure used for a particular purpose SYN **booth**: *a sentry box* (=a small structure where a guard stands)
8 the box INFORMAL the television: *What's on the box tonight?*
9 in a box INFORMAL dead and in a COFFIN: *Too many soldiers were coming home in a box.*
[**Origin:** 900–1000 Latin *buxus*, from Greek *pyxis*, from *pyxos* type of tree, whose wood was used for making boxes] → see also BLACK BOX, **think outside the box** at THINK (21)

box² *v.* **1** [I,T] to fight someone as a sport by hitting them with your closed hands inside big leather GLOVES **2** also **box up** [T] to put things in boxes → see also BOXED **3** [T] to draw a box around something on a page **4 box sb's ears** OLD-FASHIONED to hit someone on the side of their head

box sb/sth **in** *phr. v.* **1** to surround someone or something so that they are unable to move freely: *My car was completely boxed in by two big trucks.* **2 box yourself in** to say or do something now that limits the way you can behave later: *He's boxing himself in by refusing to consult with his colleagues.* **3 feel boxed in a)** to feel that you are limited in what you can do because of a particular situation or what someone else wants: *Married for only six months, Dawn already felt boxed in.* **b)** to feel that you cannot move freely, because you are in a small space

box sth **off** *phr. v.* to separate a particular area from a larger one by putting walls around it: *We're going to box off that corner and make it a separate office.*

ˈbox ˌcanyon *n.* [C] EARTH SCIENCE a deep narrow valley with very straight sides and only one entrance

box·car /ˈbɑkskɑr/ *n.* [C] a railroad car with high sides and a roof, used for carrying goods

boxed /bɑkst/ *adj.* sold in a box or boxes: *a boxed set of CDs*

B

ˌbox end ˈwrench *n.* [C] a type of WRENCH with a hollow end that fits over a NUT that is being screwed or unscrewed

box·er /ˈbɑksɚ/ *n.* [C] **1** someone who BOXES, especially as a job: *a heavyweight boxer* **2** BIOLOGY a large dog with short light-brown hair and a flat nose [**Origin:** (2) 1900–2000 German, English *boxer* **fighter**; because of its flattened nose]

Box·er Re·bel·lion, the /ˈbɑksɚ rɪˌbɛlyən/ HISTORY an unsuccessful attempt by some Chinese in 1900 to make foreigners leave China and stop influencing Chinese culture

ˈboxer ˌshorts also **boxers** *n.* [plural] loose underwear like SHORTS for men

box·ing /ˈbɑksɪŋ/ *n.* [U] the sport of fighting with closed hands while wearing big leather GLOVES

ˈboxing ˌglove *n.* [C] a big leather GLOVE used for boxing → see picture at GLOVE

ˈboxing ˌring *n.* [C] a raised square floor with ropes around it that is used for boxing

ˈbox lunch *n.* [C] a LUNCH that you take to school or work with you in a LUNCHBOX

ˈbox ˌnumber *n.* [C] an address of a box at a POST OFFICE that people can use instead of their own address

ˈbox ˌoffice *n.* **1** [C] the place in a theater, concert hall etc. where tickets are sold ►see THESAURUS box at theater **2** [singular] used to describe how successful a movie, play, or actor is, by the number of people who pay to see them: **do well/badly/poorly etc. at the box office** (=be very successful or unsuccessful) | *The movie was* ***a huge box office hit*** (=it was very popular).

ˈbox spring *n.* [C usually plural] a set of metal springs inside a cloth cover that you put under a MATTRESS to make a bed

box·y /ˈbɑksi/ *adj. comparative* **boxier**, *superlative* **boxiest** something that is boxy is unattractive because it is too big and in the shape of a box: *a boxy car*

boy¹ /bɔɪ/ S1 W1 *n. plural* **boys**
1 CHILD [C] a male child or young man: *There are only five boys in the class.* | *a polite* ***little boy*** ►see THESAURUS box at man¹
2 SON [C] a son: *My two boys are still in college.* | *How old is your* ***little boy*** (=young son)*?*
3 **office/paper/delivery etc. boy** a young man who does a particular job, usually one that is not paid well
4 FROM A PLACE/GROUP INFORMAL a man from a particular place or group, or typical of a particular place or group: **country/city/farm etc. boy** *I'm just a country boy.* | **rich/college/frat etc. boy** *He hangs out with all the rich boys.* | **local/hometown boy** *a local boy who became a baseball superstar*
5 **the boys** INFORMAL a group of men who are friends and often go out together: *Ted's out playing cards with the boys.* | *I've always just wanted to be* ***one of the boys*** (=an ordinary man who is well liked).
6 ANIMAL [C] a way of addressing a male animal, especially a dog, cat, or horse: *Good boy, Rover!*
7 JOB **boys** INFORMAL **a)** a group of men who do the same job: *The press boys are going to love this story.* **b)** OLD-FASHIONED men in the army, navy etc., especially those who are fighting in a war: *our boys overseas*
8 **the boys in blue** OLD-FASHIONED the police
9 **boys will be boys** used to say that you should not be surprised when boys behave badly, are noisy etc.

boy² S1 *interjection* **1** also **oh boy** used when you are excited or pleased about something: *Boy, that chicken was good!* **2** **oh boy** used when you are slightly annoyed or disappointed about something: *Oh boy! My computer crashed again.*

bo·yar /boʊˈyɑr, ˈbɔɪɚ/ *n.* [C] HISTORY a person with a high social position in Russia. The boyars had a lot of political power until 1711.

boy·cott¹ /ˈbɔɪkɑt/ *v.* [T] to refuse to buy something, use something, or take part in something as a way of protesting about a situation, action etc.: *Six countries have threatened to boycott the Olympics.* ►see THESAURUS box at protest² [**Origin:** 1800–1900 Charles *Boycott* (1832-97), English official in Ireland who refused to reduce rents, so the local people refused to do any business with him]

boycott² *n.* [C] an act of boycotting something, or the period of time when it is boycotted: **+of/on/against** *a nationwide boycott of the drug company's products*

boy·friend /ˈbɔɪfrɛnd/ S2 *n.* [C] a man that you are having a romantic relationship with: *Is he your new boyfriend?* → see also GIRLFRIEND

boy·hood /ˈbɔɪhʊd/ *n.* [U] the time of a man's life when he is a boy: *I spent my boyhood on a farm in Indiana.* → see also GIRLHOOD

boy·ish /ˈbɔɪ-ɪʃ/ *adj.* **1** a man who is boyish looks or behaves like a boy in a way that is attractive: *his smooth boyish face* **2** a woman or girl who is boyish looks a little like a boy: *At 45, Nell still has a trim, boyish figure.* —**boyishly** *adv.* —**boyishness** *n.* [U]

Boyle /bɔɪl/, **Rob·ert** /ˈrɑbɚt/ (1627–1691) an Irish scientist famous for his new ideas that formed the beginning of modern chemistry

ˈBoyle's ˌlaw *n.* PHYSICS a scientific principle that states that the amount of space that a gas fills at a fixed temperature decreases as pressure increases and increases as pressure decreases

ˌBoys and ˌGirls Clubs of Aˈmerica an organization for young people in the U.S., that arranges activities and gives help with problems

ˈboy scout *n.* **1** **Boy Scout** [C] a member of the Boy Scouts → see also GIRL SCOUT **2** **the Boy Scouts** an organization for boys that teaches them practical skills and helps to develop their character **3** [C] a man or boy who you think is annoying because he always obeys rules and laws and always tries to do good things

ˌBoy Scouts of Aˈmerica, the an organization of SCOUTS in the U.S., for boys from age seven to age 18

boy·sen·ber·ry /ˈbɔɪzənˌbɛri/ *n. plural* **boysenberries** [C] a small dark red or black berry, similar to a RASPBERRY

ˌboy ˈwonder *n.* [C] a young man who is very successful: *At age 27, Williams was the boy wonder of banking.*

bo·zo /ˈboʊzoʊ/ *n. plural* **bozos** [C] INFORMAL someone who you think is silly or stupid

bps, BPS /ˌbi pi ˈɛs/ COMPUTERS the abbreviation of BITS per second; a measurement of how fast a computer or MODEM can send or receive information: *a 56,000 bps modem*

bra /brɑ/ S3 *n.* [C] a piece of underwear that a woman wears to support her breasts [**Origin:** 1900–2000 Early French *brassière* **top part of a dress**, from Old French *braciere* **arm protector**]

brace¹ /breɪs/ *v.* **1** [I,T] to prepare for something bad or difficult that is going to happen: **brace for sth** *Eastern Missouri braced for another foot of snow.* | *Castro told Cubans to* ***brace themselves for*** *widespread shortages of fuel.* **2** [I,T] to make your body or part of your body stiff in order to prepare to do something difficult, or to stop yourself from falling, being thrown forward etc.: *Stand with your back straight and your knees braced.* | *The pilot told passengers and crew to* ***brace themselves*** *for a crash landing.* **3** [T] to push part of your body against something solid in order to make yourself more steady: **brace sth against sth** *Terry braced his back against the wall and pushed.* **4** [T] to make something stronger by supporting it: *The building uses steel poles to brace the roof.*

brace² *n.* **1** [C] something that is used to strengthen, stiffen, or support something: *a neck brace* | *The steel beam serves as a brace for the ceiling.* **2** **braces** [plural] a connected set of wires that people, especially children, sometimes wear on their teeth to make them straight

3 [C usually plural] a metal support that someone with weak legs wears to help them walk **4** [C usually plural] one of a pair of signs { } used to show that information written between them should be considered together → see also BRACKET **5 a brace of sth** OLD-FASHIONED two of something [**Origin:** 1300–1400 Old French **two arms**, from Latin *bracchium* **arm**]

brace·let /ˈbreɪslɪt/ *n.* [C] a band or chain that you wear around your wrist or arm as a decoration

brac·er /ˈbreɪsɚ/ *n.* [C] INFORMAL a drink, especially one that contains alcohol, that makes you feel more active or able to think quickly and clearly

bra·ce·ro /brɑˈsɛroʊ/ *n.* [C] HISTORY someone from Mexico who came to the U.S. for a limited period of time to work on a farm. Mexican workers were legally allowed to do this between 1942 and 1964 under an agreement between the Mexican and U.S. governments called the Bracero Program.

brac·ing /ˈbreɪsɪŋ/ *adj.* **1** bracing air or weather is cold and makes you feel very awake and healthy: *a bracing ocean breeze* **2** exciting and interesting: *the bracing taste of ginger* | *a bracing musical experiment*

brack·en /ˈbrækən/ *n.* [U] a plant that often grows in forests and becomes reddish brown in the fall

brack·et¹ /ˈbrækɪt/ *n.* [C]
1 income/tax/age etc. bracket a particular range of incomes, taxes etc.: *children in the 6–12 age bracket* | *Peter's salary puts him in the highest tax bracket.*
2 PRINTED SIGN [usually plural] one of a pair of signs [ ] used to show that information written between them should be considered together → see also BRACE: *All grammar information is given* ***in brackets****.*
3 SUPPORT a piece of metal, wood, or plastic, often in the shape of the letter L, put in or on a wall to support something such as a shelf
[**Origin:** 1500–1600 French *braguette* **codpiece**, from *brague* **trousers**, from Latin *braca*; because of the way a bracket (3) sticks out]

bracket² *v.* [T] **1** to put brackets around a written word, piece of information etc., especially to show that the information given should be considered together: *Unpaid amounts have been bracketed.* **2** to consider two or more people or things as being similar or the same: **be bracketed together** *Subway, train, and bus services are bracketed together as "public transportation."* | **be bracketed with sb/sth** *Arizona has been bracketed with Iowa in the tournament.* **3** if two events bracket something, one happens before and the other after it: *The strong U.S. economy of the 1980s was bracketed by two recessions.*

brack·ish /ˈbrækɪʃ/ *adj.* brackish water is not pure because it is slightly salty

brad /bræd/ *n.* [C] **1** a small metal object like a button with two bendable straight parts that are put through several pieces of paper and folded down to hold the papers together **2** a small thin wire nail with either a small head or a part that sticks out to the side instead of a head

brad·awl /ˈbrædɔl/ *n.* [C] a small tool with a sharp point for making holes in wood for brads or screws

Brad·bur·y /ˈbrædbɛri/, **Ray** /reɪ/ (1920–) a U.S. writer of SCIENCE FICTION

Brad·ford /ˈbrædfɚd/, **William** (1590–1657) a leader of the Pilgrim Fathers who came from England in the Mayflower, who was elected GOVERNOR of the American COLONY of Plymouth 30 times

Brad·ley /ˈbrædli/, **Bill** /bɪl/ (1943–) a U.S. basketball player and politician who was a CANDIDATE for U.S. President in 2000

Bradley, O·mar /ˈoʊmɑr/ (1893–1981) a general in the U.S. Army during World War II

Bra·dy /ˈbreɪdi/, **James** also **Diamond Jim Brady** (1856–1917) a U.S. businessman who gave a lot of money to hospitals in Baltimore and New York City

Brady, Matthew B. (?1823–1896) a U.S. Civil War PHOTOGRAPHER

brag /bræg/ *v.* **bragged**, **bragging** [I,T] to talk too proudly about what you have done, what you own etc. SYN **boast**: **+about** *Grandparents were happily bragging about their grandkids.* | **+that** *A witness heard him bragging that he was responsible for all three murders.*

brag·ga·do·ci·o /ˌbrægəˈdoʊsioʊ, -tʃioʊ/ *n.* [U] ESPECIALLY LITERARY proud talk about something that you claim to own, to have done etc. [**Origin:** 1500–1600 *Braggadocchio*, proud-talking character in the poem The Faerie Queen (1590) by Edmund Spenser]

brag·gart /ˈbrægɚt/ *n.* [C] DISAPPROVING someone who is always talking too proudly about what they own or have done

Bra·he /ˈbrɑə, ˈbrɑhi/, **Ty·cho** /ˈtikoʊ, ˈtaɪkoʊ/ (1546–1601) a Danish ASTRONOMER who made many exact and important OBSERVATIONS

Brah·man /ˈbrɑmən/ *n.* [C] **1** also **Brahmin** someone belonging to the highest rank in the HINDU religion **2** also **Brahmin** according to the beliefs of the HINDU religion, the most important and basic religious force from which the universe and everything in it is made **3** also **Brahma** a cow developed in the southern U.S. that has a HUMP (=large raised part) on the front part of its back

Brah·man·i, Brahmanee /brɑˈmɑni/ *n.* [C] a woman belonging to the highest rank in the HINDU religion

Brah·man·ism /ˈbrɑməˌnɪzəm/ the earliest stage in the development of Hinduism

Brah·min /ˈbrɑmən/ *n.* [C] someone from New England, who is from a wealthy upper-class family: *a Boston Brahmin*

Brahms /brɑmz/, **Jo·han·nes** /yoʊˈhɑnɪs/ (1833–1897) a German musician who wrote CLASSICAL music

braid¹ /breɪd/ *n.* **1** [C] a length of hair that has been separated into three parts and then woven together: *Sally likes wearing her hair* ***in braids****.* → see also PLAIT → see picture at HAIRSTYLE **2** [U] a narrow band of material formed by twisting threads together, used to decorate the edges of clothes: *a blue jacket with gold braid*

braid² *v.* [T] to weave or twist together three pieces of hair or cloth to form one length —**braided** *adj.*

braille /breɪl/ *n.* [U] a form of printing with raised round marks that blind people can read by touching [**Origin:** 1800–1900 Louis *Braille*]

Braille /breɪl/, **Lou·is** /ˈlui/ (1809–1852) a French teacher who invented the BRAILLE form of printing that blind people can read by touch

brain¹ /breɪn/ S2 W2 *n.*
1 ORGAN [C] BIOLOGY the organ inside your head that controls how you think, feel, and move: *The doctors have found a tumor in his brain.* | *The brain has trillions of cells.*
2 INTELLIGENCE [singular] also **brains** [U] the ability to think clearly and learn quickly: *You need brains to do this job.* | *If you* ***used your brain*** (=tried to think in an intelligent way) *you could figure it out.* | *Ted's got more money than brains* (=he doesn't spend his money wisely).
3 PERSON [C] INFORMAL someone who is intelligent, with good ideas and useful skills: *Some of the best brains in the country are here tonight.* | *Louis was the brain in our class.* → see also BRAIN DRAIN
4 brain dead a) in a state where your brain has stopped working correctly, even though your heart may still be beating **b)** INFORMAL in a state in which you behave stupidly, especially because you are tired: *I was feeling completely brain dead when I wrote that email.*
5 be the brains behind/in sth to be the person who thought of and developed a particular plan, system, or organization, especially a successful one: *Silvetti is the brains behind the business.*
6 have sth on the brain INFORMAL to be unable to stop thinking about something: *You always have food on the brain.*
[**Origin:** Old English *brægen*] → see also **beat your**

brains out at BEAT[1] (11), BIRDBRAIN, FEATHER-BRAINED, HAREBRAINED, **pick sb's brain(s)** at PICK[1] (8), **wrack your brain(s)** at WRACK[1]

brain² *v.* [T] OLD-FASHIONED to hit someone very hard on the head

brain·child /ˈbreɪntʃaɪld/ *n.* [singular] INFORMAL **the brainchild of sb** also **sb's brainchild** an idea, plan, organization etc. that someone has thought of, often without any help from anyone else: *The world wide web was the brainchild of Tim Berners Lee.*

ˈbrain ˌdamage *n.* [U] damage to someone's brain caused by an accident or illness: *He suffered severe brain damage, caused by a single blow to the head.* —**brain-damaged** *adj.*

ˈbrain drain *n.* **the brain drain** the movement of highly skilled or professional people from their own country to a country where they can earn more money

brain·less /ˈbreɪnlɪs/ *adj.* INFORMAL stupid: *You brainless idiot!* —**brainlessly** *adv.*

ˈbrain stem, brainstem *n.* [C] BIOLOGY the part of the brain that connects the SPINAL CORD to the front and main parts of the brain

brain·storm¹ /ˈbreɪnstɔrm/ *n.* [singular] a sudden intelligent idea: *I **had a brainstorm** about the project last night.*

brainstorm² *v.* [I,T] to have a discussion or meeting, usually with other people at work, in order to come up with ideas relating to a specific project or problem: *We just sat down and started to brainstorm.* | *Get the team to brainstorm solutions to the problem.*

brain·storm·ing /ˈbreɪnˌstɔrmɪŋ/ *n.* [U] the act of trying to develop ideas and think of ways to solve problems, done with a group of people: *a brainstorming session to look at possible sources of funding*

ˈbrain ˌsurgery *n.* [U] **1** the process of performing operations on people's brains **2 sth is not brain surgery** SPOKEN used to emphasize that something is easy, or that you do not have to be very intelligent to do it: *Running the microwave isn't exactly brain surgery.* —**brain surgeon** *n.* [C]

brain·teas·er /ˈbreɪnˌtizɚ/ *n.* [C] a difficult problem that is fun to try to solve

ˈbrain trust *n.* [C] a group of very intelligent people who help a politician, company, team etc. make good decisions

brain·wash /ˈbreɪnwɑʃ/ *v.* [T] to make someone believe something that is not true, by using force, confusing them, or continuously repeating it over a long period of time: **brainwash sb into doing sth** *Consumers are being brainwashed into buying things they don't need.* —**brainwashing** *n.* [U]

ˈbrain wave, brainwave *n.* [C] an electrical force that is produced by the brain and that can be measured

brain·y /ˈbreɪni/ *adj.* *comparative* **brainier**, *superlative* **brainiest** INFORMAL able to learn quickly and think clearly: *My sister is the brainy one in our family.*

braise /breɪz/ *v.* [T] to cook meat or vegetables slowly in a small amount of liquid in a closed container —**braised** *adj.*

brake¹ /breɪk/ S3 *n.* [C] **1** a piece of equipment that makes a vehicle go more slowly or stop, usually operated by pressing on a bar with your foot or hand: *The back brake on my bike needs adjusting.* | ***Apply the brakes** gently.* | **put/slam on the brakes** *I managed to put on the brakes just in time.* | ***The brakes failed** and the car hit a tree.* → see also EMERGENCY BRAKE, HANDBRAKE, PARKING BRAKE → see picture at BICYCLE[1] → see picture on page A36 **2 put the brakes on sth** to stop something that is happening: *We need to put the brakes on unnecessary spending.* **3 act/serve as a brake on sth** to make something develop more slowly or be more difficult to do: *The chemical acts as a brake on the cell's growth.*

brake² *v.* [I] to make a vehicle or bicycle go more slowly or stop by using its brake: *She had to brake suddenly to avoid a dog.*

ˈbrake ˌfluid *n.* [U] a liquid, used in certain kinds of brakes, that is put under pressure in order to make them work

ˈbrake light *n.* [C] a light on the back of a vehicle that comes on when you use the brake → see picture on page A36

ˈbrake pad *n.* [C] a block that presses against the DISC of a DISC BRAKE

ˈbrake shoe *n.* [C] one of the two curved parts that press against the wheel of a vehicle in order to make it go more slowly or stop

bram·ble /ˈbræmbəl/ *n.* [C] a wild plant with THORNS and berries

brain

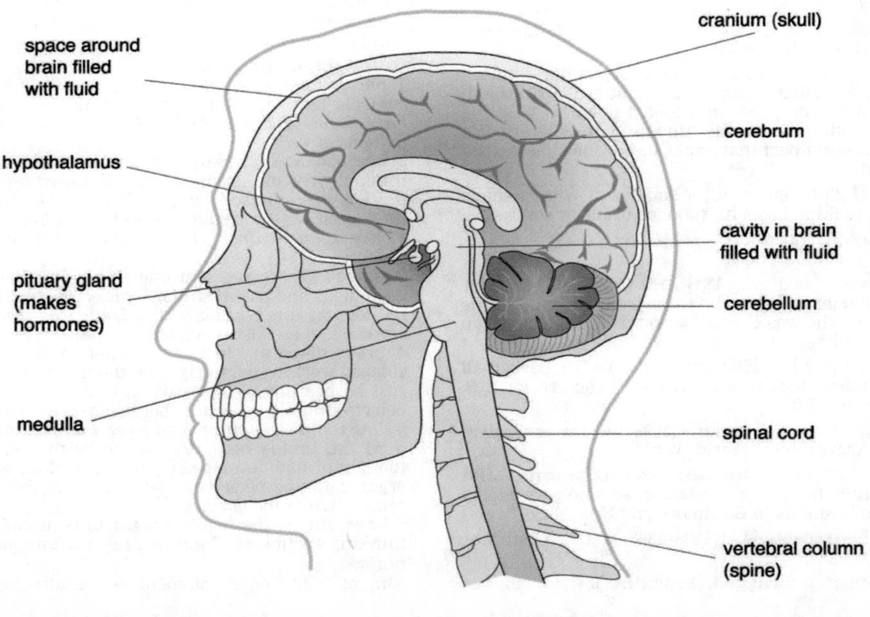

bran /bræn/ *n.* [U] the crushed outer skin of wheat or a similar grain, that is separated from the rest of the grain when making white flour

branch¹ /bræntʃ/ S3 W2 *n.* [C]
1 ON A TREE BIOLOGY the part of a tree that grows out from the TRUNK (=main stem) and has leaves, fruit, or smaller branches growing from it: *There were only a few leaves on the lower branches.* | **+of** *A swing hung from the branch of a tree.*
2 STORE/OFFICE a store, office etc. in a particular area that is part of a large company: *Her company has branches in Dallas and Chicago.* | **+of** *the local branch of the Boston library*
3 OF AN ORGANIZATION a part of a government or other organization that deals with one particular part of its work: **+of** *The President is in charge of the executive branch of our government.*
4 OF A SUBJECT one part of a large subject of study or knowledge: **+of** *the branch of international law that deals with war crimes*
5 SMALLER PART a smaller less important part of something such as a river, road, path etc. that leads away from the more important part of it: **+of** *a branch of the Missouri River*
6 OF A FAMILY a group of members of a family who all have the same grandparents or ANCESTORS: **+of** *the West Virginia branch of the family*
[**Origin:** 1200–1300 Old French *branche*, from Late Latin *branca* **animal's foot**]

branch² *v.* [I] **1** to divide into two or more smaller or less important parts: *Turn off where the road branches.* | **+into** *The tunnel branched into smaller passages.* **2** if a tree, bush, or plant branches, it grows new branches

branch into sth *phr. v.* to start doing something new or different in addition to what you usually do, especially in your work: *She and her husband branched into publishing last year.*

branch off *phr. v.* **1** if a story, conversation etc. or the person talking branches off, they change from one subject to another: **+into** *Then the conversation branched off into a discussion about movies.* **2** if a road, path, passage etc. branches off from another road etc., it separates from it and goes in a different direction: **+to/toward** | *The road branches off toward Springfield.*

branch out *phr. v.* to do something new in addition to what you usually do: *Some soybean farmers branched out by growing crops such as peanuts.* | **branch out into doing sth** *Foster has branched out into directing, as well as acting.*

brand¹ /brænd/ S3 W3 *n.* [C] **1** a type of product made by a particular company: **+of** *What brand of shampoo do you use?* | *It's been the* ***brand leader*** (=the brand that sells the most) *for the last two years.* | *I think there is less* ***brand loyalty*** (=the tendency to always buy a particular brand) *in computers than there was a few years ago.* | *The* ***store brand*** (=product made and sold by a particular store) *is usually cheaper than regular brands.* ▶see THESAURUS box at type¹ **2 sb's brand of humor/politics/religion etc.** a particular type of humor, politics etc.: *Grade-school boys love Elliott's brand of comedy.* | *Ethiopia's unique brand of Judaism* **3** a mark made or burned on an animal's skin that shows who it belongs to **4** LITERARY a piece of burning wood **5** POETIC a sword [**Origin:** Old English **torch, sword**]

brand² *v.* [T] **1** to describe someone or something as a very bad type of person or thing, often unfairly, so that it is difficult for them to change people's opinions: **brand sb (as) a sth** *Pete got branded as a troublemaker in school* ▶see THESAURUS box at call¹ **2 sth brands sb (as sth) for life** used to say that a single action gives people a bad opinion of you that will last for the rest of your life: *Stealing that money branded him for life.* **3** [usually passive] to make a mark on something such as an animal, especially by burning, in order to show who it belongs to

brand·ed /ˈbrændɪd/ *adj.* [only before noun] a branded product is made by a well-known company and has the company's name on it

Bran·deis /ˈbrændaɪs/, **Louis** (1856–1941) a judge on the U.S. Supreme Court

ˈbranding ˌiron *n.* [C] a piece of metal that is heated and used for burning marks on cattle or horses to show who they belong to

bran·dish /ˈbrændɪʃ/ *v.* [T] to wave something around in a dangerous or threatening way, especially a weapon: *The suspect was brandishing a knife.* [**Origin:** 1300–1400 Old French *brandir*, from *brand* **sword**]

ˈbrand ˌname *n.* [C] the name given to a product by the company that makes it: *Brand names such as Coca-Cola and Sony are recognized all over the world.* → see also NAME BRAND

brand-new /ˌbræn ˈnu◂/ S2 *adj.* new and never before used: *a brand-new motorcycle*

Bran·do /ˈbrændoʊ/, **Mar·lon** /ˈmɑrlən/ (1924–2004) a U.S. actor who is considered one of the best movie actors ever

ˌbrand-spanking-ˈnew *adj.* SPOKEN used to emphasize that something is new: *How can Ann afford a brand-spanking-new car like that?*

bran·dy /ˈbrændi/ *n. plural* **brandies** [C,U] a strong alcoholic drink made from wine, or a glass of this drink [**Origin:** 1600–1700 *brandywine* (1600–1700), from Dutch *brandewijn* **burnt wine, distilled wine**]

Braque /bræk, brɑk/, **Georges** /ʒɔrʒ/ (1882–1963) a French PAINTER famous for developing the style of CUBISM with Pablo Picasso

brash /bræʃ/ *adj.* **1** behaving in a way that is too confident and determined, and often speaking too loudly or behaving rudely: *a very brash young man* **2** a brash building, place, or object attracts attention by being very colorful, large, exciting etc., often in a way that people do not like: *The painting was bold, brash, and modern.* —**brashly** *adv.* —**brashness** *n.* [U]

Bra·si·lia /brəˈzɪlyə/ the capital city of Brazil

brass instruments

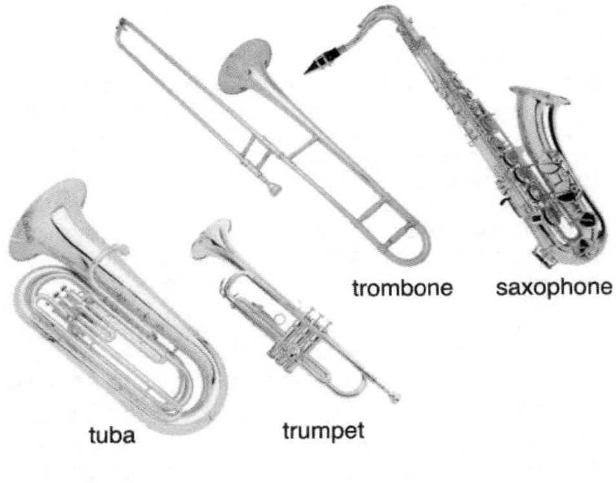

brass /bræs/ *n.*
1 METAL [U] a very hard bright yellow metal that is a mixture of COPPER and ZINC: *a brass bed*
2 the brass (section) the people in an ORCHESTRA or band who play musical instruments made of brass, such as the TRUMPET or horn
3 the (top) brass INFORMAL the people who hold the most important positions in a company, organization, the military etc.
4 get down to brass tacks INFORMAL to start talking about the most important details or facts
5 have the brass (to do sth) INFORMAL to have the self-confidence and lack of respect to do something that is rude: *He had the brass to tell me I was lazy!*
6 DECORATIONS [C,U] an object made of brass, usually with a design cut into it, or several brass objects

7 IN CHURCH [C] a picture and writing on brass, placed on the wall or floor of a church in memory of someone who died
[**Origin:** Old English *bræs*]

B

brass 'band *n.* [C] a band consisting mostly of brass musical instruments such as TRUMPETS or horns

bras·se·rie /ˌbræsə'ri/ *n.* [C] a cheap informal restaurant usually serving beer and other alcoholic drinks, and French food [**Origin:** 1800–1900 French *brasser* **to make beer**]

bras·siere /brə'zɪr/ *n.* [C] FORMAL a BRA

ˌbrass 'knuckles *n.* [plural] a set of connected metal rings worn over a person's fingers, used as a weapon

'brass ˌrubbing *n.* [C,U] the act of making a copy of a BRASS in a church by putting a piece of paper over it and rubbing it with a soft pencil, or a picture made in this way

brass·y /'bræsi/ *adj. comparative* **brassier**, *superlative* **brassiest** **1** like BRASS in color **2** a woman who is brassy is too loud, confident, or brightly dressed **3** a brassy sound is loud and unpleasant to listen to: *a brassy voice*

brat /bræt/ *n.* [C] INFORMAL a badly behaved child: *Stop acting like a **spoiled brat**.* —**bratty** *adj.*

Bra·ti·sla·va /ˌbrɑṭɪ'slɑvə/ the capital city of Slovakia

Brat·tain /'brætˀn/, **Wal·ter** /'wɔltɚ/ (1902–1987) an American scientist who worked on the development of an electronic TRANSISTOR

bra·va·do /brə'vɑdoʊ/ *n.* [U] behavior that is deliberately intended to show how brave and confident you are, but that is often unnecessary: *The new recruits were full of youthful bravado.*

brave¹ /breɪv/ *adj.* **1** dealing with danger, pain, or difficult situations with courage and confidence SYN **courageous**: *her brave fight against cancer* | *brave soldiers*

THESAURUS

courageous someone who is courageous behaves very bravely: *an honest and courageous leader*
daring willing to do dangerous things: *the daring young men who flew the first airplanes*
bold confident and willing to take risks: *Rebecca was a bold woman, willing to say what she thought.*
intrepid OFTEN HUMOROUS willing to do dangerous things or go to dangerous places: *the intrepid explorers who crossed the country to the Pacific coast*
adventurous used about someone who enjoys going to new places and doing new, possibly dangerous, things: *a trip that will appeal to the adventurous traveler*
fearless not afraid of anything or anyone: *a fearless campaigner for human rights*
heroic extremely brave or determined, and admired by many people: *the heroic work of the doctors*

2 put on a brave face to pretend that you are happy when you are really very upset: *My parents put on a brave face, but I knew they'd have to sell the house.* **3** very good: *It's a brave effort to compete with the big publishers.* **4 the brave** brave people: *Today we remember the brave who died defending our country.* [**Origin:** 1400–1500 French, Old Italian and Old Spanish *bravo* **brave, wild**, from Latin *barbarus*] —**bravely** *adv.*

brave² *v.* [T] to deal with a difficult, dangerous, or bad situation: *We decided to brave the city traffic.* | *Over 45,000 football fans **braved the elements** (=went out in bad weather) to watch Denver beat Miami.*

brave sth **out** *phr. v.* to deal bravely with something that is frightening or difficult

brave³ *n.* [C] a young fighting man from a Native American tribe

brav·er·y /'breɪvəri/ *n.* [U] actions, behavior, or an attitude that shows courage and confidence: *In 1944, he won the Military Cross for bravery.*

bra·vo /'brɑvoʊ, brɑ'voʊ/ *interjection* said to show your approval when someone, especially a performer, has done something very well

bra·vu·ra /brɑ'vyʊrə, -'vʊrə/ *n.* [U] great skill and confidence shown in the way you perform, write, paint etc, especially when you do something very difficult: *The orchestra played **with bravura**.*

brawl¹ /brɔl/ *n.* [C] a noisy fight among a group of people, especially in a public place: *a drunken brawl* ▶see THESAURUS box at **fight²** —**brawler** *n.* [C]

brawl² *v.* [I] to fight in a noisy way, especially in a public place: *Fans brawled outside the stadium.*

brawn /brɔn/ *n.* [U] physical strength, especially when compared with intelligence: *Football players are known more for their brawn than their brains.* [**Origin:** 1300–1400 Old French *braon* **muscle**]

brawn·y /'brɔni/ *adj. comparative* **brawnier**, *superlative* **brawniest** a person or part of their body that is brawny is very large and strong: *big brawny arms*

bray /breɪ/ *v.* **brays, brayed, braying** [I] **1** if a DONKEY brays, it makes a loud sound **2** if someone brays, they laugh or talk in a loud, slightly annoying way —**bray** *n.* [C] —**braying** *adj.*

bra·zen¹ /'breɪzən/ *adj.* **1** not embarrassed or ashamed about doing something or behaving in a way that most people consider wrong or immoral: *She was so brazen she even brought her lover to church.* | *She's just **a brazen hussy*** (=a woman who behaves this way, especially sexually). **2** a action or statement that is brazen is shocking because the person who does or says it is not ashamed of it: *a brazen lie* **3** LITERARY having a shiny yellow color

brazen² *v.*

brazen sth ↔ **out** *phr. v.* to deal with a situation that is difficult or embarrassing for you by appearing to be confident rather than ashamed

bra·zen·ly /'breɪzənli/ *adv.* without showing or feeling any shame: *She brazenly admitted she had spent the night with Greg.*

bra·zier /'breɪʒɚ/ *n.* [C] a metal container that holds a fire and is used for cooking or keeping a place warm

Bra·zil /brə'zɪl/ the largest country in South America —**Brazilian** *n., adj.*

Braz·za·ville /'bræzəˌvɪl, 'brɑ-/ the capital and largest city of the Republic of Congo

BRB, brb a written abbreviation of "be right back," used by people communicating in CHAT ROOMS on the Internet

breach¹ /britʃ/ *n.* **1** [C,U] an act of breaking a law, rule, or agreement between people, groups, or countries: +**of** *The U.N. says there have been grave breaches of human rights.* | *You are **in breach of** the rules.* | *If you try to get out of the deal, I'll sue you for **breach of contract**.* | *They committed no fraud or **breach of duty*** (=an action that is not allowed in the job that you do). **2** [C] a failure do do what you promised to do or are expected to do: **a breach of confidence/trust/etiquette etc.** *Showing this information to anyone outside the company would be a serious breach of trust.* **3 a breach of security** also **a security breach** a situation in which someone gets into a building or area without official permission, often in order to steal or cause damage: *a major breach of security at the embassy* **4** [C] a serious disagreement between people, groups, or countries, with the result that they do not have a good relationship anymore: *Britain could not risk a breach with the U.S. over the trade issue.* **5 step into the breach** to help by doing someone else's job or work when they are suddenly unable to do it **6** [C] a hole or broken place in a wall or similar structure, especially one made during a military attack

breach² *v.* [T] **1** to break a law, rule, agreement etc.: *The court ruled that he had breached the terms of the agreement.* **2** to break a hole in a wall or similar structure so that something can pass through: *On Friday, flood waters breached the river's banks.*

bread¹ /brɛd/ S1 W2 *n.* [U] **1** a common food made from flour, water, and YEAST: *Please pass the bread.* | *Could you pick up **a loaf of bread*** (=large piece of bread that can be cut into pieces) *on your way home?* | *four **slices of bread*** (=thin pieces of bread that you cut from a loaf) *with butter and jam* | **white/wheat/rye etc. bread** (=bread made with white, wheat etc. flour) → see also FRENCH BREAD **2** OLD-FASHIONED, SLANG money **3 sb's bread and butter** INFORMAL the thing that provides you with most of the money that you need in order to live or be successful: *Tourism is our bread and butter.* **4 know which side your bread is buttered on** INFORMAL to know who to be nice to in order to get advantages for yourself **5 sb's daily bread** OLD-FASHIONED, INFORMAL the money that you need in order to live [**Origin:** Old English]

bread² *v.* [T] to put BREADCRUMBS on the outside of meat or a vegetable before it is cooked

ˌbread-and-ˈbutter *adj.* [only before noun] **a bread-and-butter question/product/issue etc.** a question, product etc. that is concerned with the most important and basic things: *bread-and-butter issues like health care and education* → see also **sb's bread and butter** at BREAD¹ (3)

bread·bas·ket, **bread basket** /ˈbrɛdˌbæskɪt/ *n.* **1** [singular] INFORMAL the part of a country or other large area that provides most of its food: +**of** *The midwest is the breadbasket of America.* **2** [C] a basket for holding or serving bread

bread·board /ˈbrɛdbɔrd/ *n.* [C] **1** a wooden board on which you cut bread **2** a model of a CIRCUIT BOARD that is used to test the design before it is produced

bread·box /ˈbrɛdbɑks/ *n.* [C] a container for keeping bread in so that it stays fresh

bread·crumb, **bread crumb** /ˈbrɛdkrʌm/ *n.* [C usually plural] a very small piece of bread that is left after you have cut some bread, or very small pieces that are deliberately prepared this way to be used in cooking

bread·ed /ˈbrɛdɪd/ *adj.* covered in breadcrumbs: *breaded veal*

bread·fruit /ˈbrɛdfrut/ *n.* [C,U] BIOLOGY a large tropical fruit that looks like bread

bread·line /ˈbrɛdlaɪn/ *n.* [C] a line of poor people waiting to receive food from an organization or government: *On most days, the breadline begins to form by seven o'clock in the morning.*

breadth /brɛdθ, brɛtθ/ *n.* **1** [U] the fact or quality of having a wide variety or range of something, especially used about someone's knowledge or experience: +**of** *the breadth of her experience* | *the breadth of the training that the employees are given* | **breadth of vision/mind/outlook etc.** (=an ability to consider and understand a large range of ideas, attitudes, etc.) **2** [C,U] the distance from one side of something to the other → see also LENGTH SYN **width**: +**of** *His travels took him across the full breadth of the country.* | *The wall is two feet **in breadth**.* → see also BROAD¹, HAIR'S BREADTH

bread·win·ner /ˈbrɛdˌwɪnɚ/ *n.* [C] the member of a family who earns the money to support the others

break¹ /breɪk/ S1 W1 *v.* *past tense* **broke** /broʊk/, *past participle* **broken** /ˈbroʊkən/

1 IN PIECES [I,T] if something breaks or you break it, it separates into two or more pieces, for example because it has been hit, dropped, or bent: *Somebody broke the window and the car alarm went off.* | *Careful, those glasses break easily.* | +**off** *Part of it broke off when I touched it.* | **break (sth) in two/in half/into pieces etc.** *The force of the explosion had broken the door into pieces.*

THESAURUS

smash used when a plate, glass etc. breaks or is broken with a lot of force: *Angry crowds smashed windows downtown.*
shatter used when a plate, glass etc. breaks into a lot of small pieces: *The glass hit the floor, shattering everywhere.*
crack used when a plate, glass etc. is damaged so that there is a line between two parts of it: *One of the windows was cracked.*
tear used about paper or cloth: *I tore the letter to pieces.*
snap used about something that breaks into two pieces, making a loud noise: *The stick snapped in two.*
burst used when a pipe with liquid inside it breaks: *Our pipes had burst in the freezing weather.*
pop used when a bubble or balloon breaks: *The wind was so strong some of the balloons popped.*
split to break along a straight line: *The wood in the door had split.*

2 PART OF YOUR BODY [T] if you break your leg, arm etc. or break a bone, the bone splits into two or more pieces: *Tanya went skiing and broke her leg.*

3 NOT WORKING [I,T] to damage something such as a machine so that it does not work or cannot be used, or to become damaged in this way: *How did you manage to break the microwave?* | *I think the switch is broken.* | *I dropped the camera and it broke.*

4 break a law/rule to disobey a law or rule: *Smith was kicked off the team for breaking team rules.*

5 PROMISE/AGREEMENT to not do what you have promised to do or signed an agreement to do: **break a promise/your word** *She accused the senator of breaking his promise to support her.* | **break a contract/agreement** *You broke our agreement not to discuss the project publicly.*

6 END A SITUATION [T] to stop a bad or boring situation from continuing: *We took turns driving, in order to try and **break the monotony**.* | **break the deadlock/stalemate** (=end a situation in which an agreement or a solution cannot be found)

7 SURFACE/SKIN [I,T] if the surface of something breaks or if you break it, it splits or gets a hole in it: *Do not use this product if the seal has been broken.*

8 break a record to do something faster or better than it has ever been done before: *Collins retired after she **broke the world record**.* | *Sales of their new CD have **broken all records*** (=been much better or much more successful than anything before).

9 ACTIVITY [I] to stop working for a short time in order to eat or drink something: *We'll break in an hour.* | **break for lunch/coffee/dinner etc.** *What time do you want to break for lunch?*

10 break the news to sb to tell someone about something bad that has happened: *I couldn't break the news to Mom.*

11 NEWS [I,T] if news about an important event breaks, or if a newspaper, television station etc. breaks it, they make it known to everyone: *The next morning the news broke that the Senator was dead.* | *The Washington Post was the first to break the story.*

12 break a/the habit to stop doing something that you have regularly done for a long time, especially something that is bad for you: *I don't smoke anymore, but it was hard to break the habit.*

B

B

13 break even to neither make a profit nor lose money: *Thankfully, we broke even in our first year in business.*
14 break sb's heart to make someone very unhappy by ending a relationship with them or by doing something that they do not want you to do: *It really broke his heart when she told him it was over.* | *It'll break your father's heart if you tell him you're quitting the team.*
15 HOPE/DETERMINATION [I,T] if a person breaks, or if someone breaks them, they lose their hope, confidence, or determination, usually because of being under a lot of pressure: *He didn't break, even after several days of torture.* | *The years of pressure and criticism finally broke him.* | *Being kept away from her children for 15 years had not* ***broken her spirit****.*
16 DAY [I] if the day or the DAWN breaks, light begins to show in the sky as the sun rises
17 WAVE [I] if a wave breaks, the top part starts to fall down, usually because it is hitting or getting near the shore: *Waves broke against the rocks.*

SPOKEN PHRASES

18 break your neck to hurt yourself very badly, especially by falling onto the ground: *Careful here! I don't want you slipping and breaking your neck.*
19 you're/it's breaking my heart HUMOROUS used to show that you are not sad about something or do not have sympathy for someone, in a situation when you should: *"I've had it with you! I'm leaving!" "You're breaking my heart."*
20 break your back to work very hard to try and do something: *We've been breaking our backs trying to get this project done on time.*
21 break a leg! HUMOROUS used to wish someone good luck, especially someone who is acting in a play
22 break! used when telling BOXERS or WRESTLERS to stop fighting

23 break free a) to escape from an unpleasant situation or a situation that controls you in an unpleasant way: **+of/from** *India wanted to break free of the British Empire.* **b)** also **break loose** to escape from someone or somewhere by using force: *The cattle had broken loose during the night.*
24 break sb's fall to stop someone from falling straight onto the ground, so that they are not badly hurt: *Luckily some bushes at the bottom of the cliff broke his fall.*
25 break sb's concentration also **break sb's train of thought** to interrupt someone and stop them from being able to continue thinking or talking about something: *I never listen to music when I'm working – it breaks my concentration.*
26 break the back of sb/sth to defeat someone or something and destroy their chances of continued success: *The arrests could break the back of organized crime in the entire state.*
27 break a strike to force workers to end a STRIKE
28 break the silence/calm to end a period of silence or calm by talking or making a noise: *Rhonda's laugh broke the silence.*
29 break your silence to start talking about something in public after refusing to do so for a long time: *Fifteen years later, Rowland broke his silence about the murder.*
30 VOICE [I] **a)** if your voice breaks, it changes from one level to another suddenly, especially because of strong emotions: *Her voice breaks as she talks about her missing children.* **b)** when a boy's voice breaks, it changes and becomes lower, like a man's voice
31 break the surface (of the water) if something breaks the surface of water, it moves from below the surface to a position in which part of it is sticking out of the water: *The whale's back broke the surface for a moment.*
32 break the ice to do something or say something to make someone who you have just met be less nervous and more willing to talk, for example at a party or meeting: *I tried to break the ice by offering her a drink, but she said "no".* → see also ICEBREAKER (2)
33 break a sweat to begin SWEATing, especially because you are working or exercising hard
34 do sth without breaking a sweat also **do sth and not break a sweat** to do something easily: *She can disarm the most complicated security systems without breaking a sweat.*
35 it won't break the bank used to say that you can afford to buy something: *Well, I don't think it'll break the bank if we only go away for a weekend.*
36 break ranks to behave differently from the other members of a group, who are expecting you to support them: *Surprisingly, nine of the 31 Republicans in the Assembly broke ranks to vote with the Democrats.*
37 break fresh/new ground to do something completely new that no one has ever done before, or find out new information about a subject: *With this agreement, the agency is breaking new ground in dealing with sex discrimination.*
38 break your ties/connection/links etc. to end your connection or relationship with a person, group, organization etc.: *I broke all my ties with my father years ago.*
39 STORM [I] if a storm breaks, it suddenly begins: *The storm finally broke just as I was getting out of the car.*
40 WEATHER [I] if the weather breaks, it suddenly changes: *Farmers are anxious for the cold weather to break.*
41 CODE [T] to succeed in understanding what the letters or numbers in a secret CODE mean: *We've finally managed to break their secret code.*
42 break cover to move out of a place where you have been hiding so that you can be seen: *Suddenly, one of the elephants broke cover and charged straight at them.*
43 break camp to pack tents and other equipment and leave the place where you have been camping
44 break wind FORMAL to allow gas to escape from your BOWELS, making a noise and a bad smell SYN fart
45 break (sb's) serve to win a game in tennis when your opponent is serving (SERVE)
46 GAME [I] to begin a game of POOL, BILLIARDS etc. by being the first one to hit the ball: *I'll let you break next game.*
47 break the bank to win more money in a game of cards than a CASINO or a DEALER is able to pay you
[**Origin:** Old English *brecan*] → see also BREAKAWAY

break away *phr. v.* **1** to end your connection or relationship with a person, group, organization etc. because of a disagreement: **+from** *During that time, Portugal's colonies broke away from colonial rule.* **2** to escape from someone who is holding you: **+from** *He tried to break away from the policeman who was holding him.* **3** to escape from an unpleasant situation: *This was her chance to break away and find happiness.* **4** to move ahead of other people in a race or competition: *Radcliffe broke away 2 miles before the end of the race.* **5** to stop being attached to something: *Part of the plane's wing had broken away.*

break down

break down *phr. v.*
1 MACHINE if a large machine, especially a car, breaks down, it stops working: *My car broke down on the way to work.* | *The elevators in this building are always breaking down.*
2 FAIL if a discussion, system etc. breaks down, it fails or stops existing: *The talks broke down completely in June 1982.*

3 DOOR **break sth ↔ down** to hit something, such as a door, so hard that it breaks and falls to the ground
4 STOP REFUSING/OPPOSING **break (sb ↔) down** to stop opposing something or refusing to do something, or to force someone to stop doing this: *I finally broke down and ate the chocolate anyway.* | *They finally broke him down and made him talk.*
5 CHANGE CHEMICALLY **break sth ↔ down** if a substance breaks down or is broken down, it is reduced or changed, usually as a result of a chemical process: *Glycogen is broken down to glucose in the liver.*
6 CRY to be unable to stop yourself from crying, especially in public: *Margaret broke down several times during the funeral.*
7 CHANGE IDEAS **break sth ↔ down** to change bad feelings that prevent people from having a good relationship with each other: *No one has yet found a way to break down these prejudices.* | *We're trying to help* ***break down the barriers between*** *the ethnic groups.*
8 BECOME SICK to become mentally or physically ill: *If Tim keeps working this hard, he'll break down sooner or later.*
9 MAKE STH SIMPLE **break sth ↔ down** to divide something such as a job, report, plan etc. into parts in order to make it easier to deal with or understand: **break sth down into sth** *Try breaking the exam question down into three parts.*
10 SPORTS **break sb/sth ↔ down** to succeed in gaining points in a game in sports: *Seattle had no problem breaking down Dallas' defense.* → see also BREAKDOWN

break for sth *phr. v.* to go somewhere quickly, especially in order to escape from someone: *He suddenly broke for the door.*

break in *phr. v.* **1** to enter a building by using force, in order to steal something: *It looks like they broke in through that window.* → see also BREAK-IN, BREAKING AND ENTERING **2 break sb/sth ↔ in** to make a person or animal get used to a certain way of behaving or working: *They have a good training program for breaking in new employees.* **3** to interrupt a conversation or activity by saying or doing something: *The operator broke in, saying, "You need another 75¢ to continue the call."* | +**with** *TV news anchors periodically broke in with updates on the incident.* | +**on** *Sir, sorry to break in on your meeting, but your wife is outside.* **4 break sth ↔ in** if you break new shoes or boots in, or if they break in, they become less stiff and more comfortable because you have been wearing them

break into sth *phr. v.*
1 STEAL to enter a building by using force, in order to steal something: *Someone broke into our house while we were on vacation.*
2 break into a run/gallop/trot etc. to suddenly start running etc.: *The boy saw his father and broke into a run.*
3 NEW ACTIVITY to become involved in a new activity, especially a business activity: *We think this product will help us to break into the Eastern European market.*
4 break into tears/laughter/cheers etc. to suddenly start crying, laughing etc. → see also **break into a sweat** at SWEAT[2] (5)
5 INTERRUPT to interrupt an activity by saying or doing something: *Sorry to break into your lunch hour, but it's an emergency.*
6 MONEY to start to spend money that you did not want to spend: *I was hoping we wouldn't have to break into our savings.*

break sb **of** sth *phr. v.* to make someone stop having a bad habit: *a useful way of breaking your dog of barking at strangers* | *Try to* ***break yourself of the habit*** *of eating between meals.*

break off *phr. v.* **1 break sth ↔ off** to end a relationship, especially a political or romantic one: *The U.S. is threatening to break off diplomatic relations with the country's government.* | *Did you hear? They've broken off their engagement.* **2 break sth ↔ off** to break a piece from the main part of something, or to become broken from the main part of something: *I pulled the door and the handle broke off.* | *Can you break off a piece of that chocolate for me?* **3 break sth ↔ off** to suddenly stop talking or having a discussion: *She broke off, forgetting what she wanted to say.* | *Without explanation, management broke off contract negotiations.*

break out *phr. v.* **1** if something bad such as a fire, war, or disease breaks out, it begins to happen: *War broke out six months later.* **2 break out the...** INFORMAL to bring something out so that it is ready to be used: *If the Red Sox win tonight we'll break out the champagne.* **3 break out of sth** to change the way you live or behave, especially because you feel bored: *Once you break out of those old ways of thinking, you'll feel better.* | **break out of a rut/routine etc.** (=stop doing the same things all the time) **4** to begin to have red spots on your skin, especially on your face: *Chocolate makes me break out.* | *That soap made me* ***break out in a rash.*** **5** to escape from a prison or a similar place: +**of** *They were caught trying to break out of jail.* → see also BREAKOUT[1]

break through *phr. v.* **1 break through sth** to force a way through something: *Our troops finally managed to break through enemy lines.* **2 break through sth** to deal successfully with something, especially unreasonable behavior or bad feelings: *Somehow we managed to break through the racial prejudices and get people talking.* **3 break through sth** if the sun or light breaks through, you begin to see it through something such as clouds or mist **4** if a quality breaks through, it becomes noticeable: *Occasionally his humor breaks through.* → see also BREAKTHROUGH

break up *phr. v.*
1 MARRIAGE/GROUP to end a marriage or romantic relationship, or to stop being together as a group: *What year did the Beatles break up?* | *Their marriage broke up years ago.* | **break up with sb** *I broke up with Liz yesterday.* → see also BREAKUP
2 SEPARATE **break sth ↔ up** to separate something into several smaller parts or groups: *The state-owned gas company was broken up into six private companies.* | *I usually break the students up into pairs to work.*
3 BREAK INTO PIECES **break sth ↔ up** to break into many small pieces, or to make something do this: *Increased traffic of heavy trucks will break up local roads.* | *The drug causes blood clots to break up.*
4 FIGHT if a fight breaks up, or if someone breaks it up, the people stop fighting each other: *The police came and the fight broke up.* | *OK you guys,* ***break it up!***
5 CROWD **break sth ↔ up** if a crowd or meeting breaks up or someone breaks it up, people start to leave: *Force was used to break up the rally.*
6 MAKE SB LAUGH **break sb up** INFORMAL to say or do something that is so funny that people cannot stop laughing: *His comment about football players broke everyone up.*

break with sb/sth *phr. v.* **1** to leave a group of people or an organization, especially because you have had a disagreement with them: *Yugoslavia under Tito soon broke with Stalin's Russia.* **2 break with tradition** also **break with the past** to stop following old customs and do something in a completely different way

break² S1 W2 *n.*
1 A REST **a)** [C] a period of time when you stop what you are doing in order to rest, eat etc.: *a ten-minute break* | *I've been working since nine o'clock* ***without a break.*** | **coffee/lunch break** *When is your lunch break?* | *At 11, the band* ***took a break.*** **b)** [C] a short vacation: *We needed a break, so we went up to the mountains for a few days.* | **Thanksgiving/Spring/Christmas etc. break** (=the public or school holidays at Thanksgiving etc.) ▶see THESAURUS box at vacation[1]
2 A PAUSE IN STH [C] **a)** a period of time during which something stops, before continuing again: *There was a break of two years between his last book and this one.* | +**in** *Elaine took a six-month break in her studies.* | +**from** *We're having a break from our regular classroom work today.* **b)** a pause in a conversation or in what

someone is saying: +**in** *an awkward break in the conversation* **c)** also **commercial break** a pause for advertisements during a television or radio program: *We'll be right back after the break.*
3 give sb a break SPOKEN said when you want someone to stop annoying, criticizing, or being mean to you or someone else: *Give him a break, you guys. He's just learning.*
4 give me a break SPOKEN said when you do not believe something someone has just said or think that it was stupid: *"I think he's really sorry for what he said." "Oh, give me a break!"*
5 A CHANCE [C] INFORMAL a sudden or unexpected chance to do something, especially to be successful in your job: *young musicians looking for their first break* | **a big/lucky break** *The band's big break came when they sang on a local TV show.*
6 CHANGE [C usually singular] an occasion when one thing ends and something new or different begins: +**from** *a break from our company's usual manufacturing practices* | +**with** *a major break with the policies of the past 35 years* | *In* ***a break with tradition****, the city council decided not to have a parade.* | *Why argue about the terms of the divorce when both of you just want* ***a clean break*** (=a very clear and definite end to a relationship)*?*
7 a break in the weather a change in the weather, usually from bad to good weather: *We stayed in the tent, hoping for a break in the weather.*
8 A SPACE [C] a space between two things or between two parts of something: *a continuous line without any breaks* | +**in** *Occasionally you could see the moon through a break in the clouds.*
9 make a break for sth to suddenly start running toward something in order to escape from a place: *As soon as the guard turned around, they made a break for the door.* | *After the police fired tear gas, one hostage* ***made a break for it*** (=tried to escape).
10 BROKEN PLACE [C] the place where a bone in your body has broken: *The break has not healed correctly.*
11 TENNIS also **break of serve** [C] a situation in a game of tennis in which you win a game when your opponent is serving (SERVE) → see also BREAK POINT
12 the break of day LITERARY the time early in the morning when it starts getting light
13 a break in sb's voice an unsteady quality in someone's voice that shows they are upset
14 POINTS [C] the number of points won by a player when it is their turn to hit the ball in a game such as BILLIARDS

break·a·ble /ˈbreɪkəbəl/ *adj.* made of a material such as glass or clay that breaks easily

break·age /ˈbreɪkɪdʒ/ *n.* FORMAL **1** [U] the act of breaking **2 breakages** [plural] things that have been broken, especially things that belong to someone else that you must pay for: *You'll be required to pay for any breakages.*

break·a·way /ˈbreɪkəˌweɪ/ *adj.* **a breakaway group/party/movement etc.** a group, party etc. that has been formed by people who left another group because of a disagreement: *fighting in two of the breakaway republics* —**breakaway** *n.* [C]

break·dance /ˈbreɪkdæns/ *v.* [I] to do a type of dance involving ACROBATIC movements, for example spinning around on the ground —**breakdancing** *n.* [U] —**breakdancer** *n.* [C]

break·down /ˈbreɪkdaʊn/ *n.* **1** [C,U] the failure of a system or relationship: *marital breakdown* (=the failure of a marriage) | +**in** *a breakdown in the quality control system* | +**of** *the breakdown of the peace process* **2** [C] an occasion when a car or a piece of machinery stops working and must be fixed: *a mechanical breakdown* | +**in** *a breakdown in the cooling system* **3** [C] a written statement explaining the details of something such as a bill or the cost of a plan: +**of** *a breakdown of federal spending over the past year* | **a breakdown of sth by sth** *The report gave no breakdown of the figures by state or city.* **4** [singular] the process in which a natural material or substance separates into the parts or ELEMENTS that it is made of SYN **decomposition**: +**of** *the breakdown of glucose in the body* **5** [C] MEDICINE A NERVOUS BREAKDOWN

ˈbreakdown ˌlane also **eˈmergency ˌlane** *n.* [C] an area at the side of a road, especially a HIGHWAY or FREEWAY, where cars that have something wrong with them can wait safely until they can be fixed or pulled off the road

break·er /ˈbreɪkɚ/ *n.* [C] a large wave with a white top that rolls onto the shore → see also CIRCUIT BREAKER

break·e·ven /ˈbreɪkivən/ also **ˈbreakeven ˌpoint** *n* [U] relating to the level of business activity at which a company is not making a profit or a loss: *The company expects to* ***reach breakeven*** *this year.* —**breakeven** *adj.* → see also **break even** at BREAK[1]

break·fast /ˈbrɛkfəst/ S1 W3 *n.* [C,U] **1** the meal you have in the morning: ***At breakfast time****, I usually read the paper.* | *I* ***had*** *bacon and eggs* ***for breakfast****.* | **have/eat breakfast** *Did you eat breakfast this morning?* ►see THESAURUS box at **meal** **2 have/eat sb for breakfast** to deal with someone in a way that shows that you are much stronger, smarter, more effective etc than they are: *These are tough guys you're dealing with. They eat people like us for breakfast.* [**Origin:** 1400–1500 *break + fast*] —**breakfast** *v.* [I] → see also BED AND BREAKFAST, CONTINENTAL BREAKFAST

ˈbreak-in *n.* [C] an act of entering a building illegally and by using force, especially in order to steal things: *The break-in occurred between midnight and six a.m.*

ˌbreaking and ˈentering *n.* [U] LAW the crime of entering a building illegally and by using force

ˈbreaking point *n.* [singular] the point at which someone or something is not able to work well or deal with problems anymore: *As a therapist, I've seen many lawyers* ***at the breaking point****.* | *The fire department is* ***stretched to the breaking point*** (=they are doing as much as they can possibly do).

break·neck /ˈbreɪknɛk/ *adj.* **at breakneck speed/pace** extremely and often dangerously fast: *He was driving at breakneck speed.* | *Work on the project continues at breakneck pace.*

break·out[1] /ˈbreɪkaʊt/ *n.* [C] an escape from a prison, especially one involving a lot of prisoners → see also OUTBREAK

breakout[2] *adj.* **a breakout game/performance/show etc.** a game, performance etc. in which you perform very well, especially after a time in which you were not very successful: *The team is hoping for a breakout season.*

ˈbreak point *n.* [C,U] a situation in tennis when you only have to win one more point to win a game when your opponent is serving (SERVE)

break·through /ˈbreɪkθru/ *n.* [C] **1** an important new discovery in something you are studying, especially one made after trying for a long time: *Scientists have* ***made an*** *important* ***breakthrough*** *in the treatment of heart disease.* **2** a time when someone, especially a performer, begins to be successful at something: *Springsteen's breakthrough album*

break·up /ˈbreɪkʌp/ *n.* [C] **1** the act of ending a marriage or other relationship: +**of** *the breakup of their marriage* **2** the separation of a group, organization, or country into smaller parts, especially because it has become weaker or there are serious disagreements: +**of** *the breakup of the Soviet Union*

break·wa·ter /ˈbreɪkˌwɔṭɚ/ *n.* [C] a large strong wall built out into the ocean to protect the shore from the force of the waves

breast[1] /brɛst/ S3 W2 *n.*
1 WOMAN'S BODY [C] BIOLOGY one of the two round raised parts on a woman's chest that produce milk when she has a baby: *a bra designed for women with large breasts* | *breast cancer* | *breast milk*
2 MEAT [U] meat that comes from the front part of the body of a bird such as a chicken: *slices of turkey breast*
3 BIRD [C] BIOLOGY the front part of a bird's body,

between its neck and the stomach: *a robin with a red breast*
4 CHEST [C] BIOLOGY the part of your body between your neck and your stomach, especially the upper part of this area SYN **chest**: *His arms were folded across his breast.*
5 CLOTHES [singular] the part of a jacket or shirt the covers a person's chest +**of**: *He wore a row of medals on the breast of his uniform.*
6 EMOTIONS [C] LITERARY where your feelings of sadness, love, anger, fear etc. come from SYN **heart**: *Anger swelled the young man's breast.*
[**Origin:** Old English *breost*] → see also **beat your breast** at BEAT[1] (31), -BREASTED, **make a clean breast of it** at CLEAN[1] (16)

breast[2] *v.* [T] FORMAL **1** to reach the top of a hill or slope **2** to push against something with your chest

breast·bone /ˈbrɛstboʊn/ *n.* [C] BIOLOGY the long flat bone in the front of your chest to which the top seven pairs of RIBS are connected → see picture SKELETON[1]

-breasted /brɛstɪd/ *suffix* [in adjectives] **1 single-breasted/double-breasted** a coat, dress etc. that is single- or double-breasted has one or two rows of buttons down the front **2 small-breasted/bare-breasted etc.** having small breasts, no clothes over the breasts etc.

ˈbreast-feed *v.* **breast-fed** [I,T] if a woman breast-feeds, she feeds her baby with milk from her breast rather than from a bottle SYN **nurse** —**breast-fed** *adj.* [only before noun]: *a breast-fed baby* → see also SUCKLE

ˈbreast ˌimplant *n.* [C] a bag filled with a liquid or other substance that a doctor puts under the skin of a woman's chest, to make her breast bigger or to replace a breast that was removed

breast·plate /ˈbrɛstpleɪt/ *n.* [C] a leather or metal protective covering worn over the chest by soldiers during battles in past times

ˌbreast ˈpocket *n.* [C] a pocket on the outside of a shirt or JACKET, above the breast

breast·stroke /ˈbrɛststroʊk/ *n.* [U] **the breaststroke a)** a way of swimming in which you push your arms straight ahead and then bring them back in a circle toward your sides, while bending your knees toward your body and then kicking out: *I don't know how to* ***do the breaststroke***. **b)** a competition in which swimmers compete against each other swimming in this way

breath /brɛθ/ S2 W3 *n.*
1 AIR YOU BREATHE a) [U] the air that you send out of your lungs when you breathe: *I can smell alcohol on your breath.* | ***Let your breath out*** *slowly.* | *If someone has* ***bad breath*** (=breath that smells bad), *should you tell them?* **b)** [C,U] the air that you take into your lungs when you breathe: *Every time I* ***took a breath*** (=breathed air in) *of that foul air, I started coughing.* | *How long can you* ***hold your breath*** (=breathe in and not breathe out again) *under water?* | **a big/deep breath** (=an occasion when you breathe in a lot of air once) | *She heard his* ***sharp intake of breath*** (=a sudden breath, showing surprise or shock) *at the news.* **c)** [singular, U] an act or process of breathing in and out: *Her breath was coming more easily now.* | *Eric came running into the room,* ***out of breath*** (=having difficulty breathing because he had just been running). | *Do you ever find that you're* ***short of breath*** (=unable to breathe easily, especially because you are unhealthy) *after light exercise?* | *Mary had to stop to* ***get her breath back*** (=breathe normally again after running or making a lot of effort) *after walking up the hill.* | **gasp/fight for breath** *He collapsed on the ground gasping for breath.*
2 hold your breath to wait anxiously to see what is going to happen: *Pat held her breath, waiting for Lee's reply.*
3 don't hold your breath INFORMAL used to say that something is not going to happen soon: *They've promised that things will get better, but don't hold your breath.*
4 don't waste your breath also **save your breath** SPOKEN used to tell someone that what they want to say is not worth saying or will not change a situation: *Save your breath. He won't listen.*
5 a breath of fresh air a) something that is new and different in a way you think is exciting and enjoyable: *Moving to this big apartment was like a breath of fresh air.* **b)** also **a breath of air** the activity of going outside to breathe clean air in order to relax, especially because you are tired or hot: *I'm going outside for a breath of fresh air.*
6 take your breath away to be extremely beautiful or exciting: *The view from the overlook will take your breath away.*
7 under your breath in a very quiet voice: *"Oh no, not her," Bill muttered under his breath.*
8 in the same breath a) also **in the next breath** used to say that someone has said two things at once that are so different from each other they cannot both be true: *He seemed to be praising and criticizing us in the same breath.* **b)** if you mention two people or things in the same breath, you show that you think they are alike: *He's a performer who is frequently mentioned in the same breath as Mick Jagger.*
9 with your last/dying breath at the moment when you are dying: *With his last breath, he told me he would always love me.*
10 a breath of air/wind LITERARY a slight movement of air
[**Origin:** Old English *bræth*] → see also **with bated breath** at BATED, **catch your breath** at CATCH[1] (23)

breath·a·ble /ˈbriðəbəl/ *adj.* **1** clothing or cloth that is breathable allows air to pass through it easily: *a waterproof breathable jacket* **2** able to be breathed: *breathable air*

breath·a·lyze /ˈbrɛθəˌlaɪz/ *v.* [T] to make someone breathe into a special piece of equipment in order to see if they have drunk too much alcohol to be allowed to drive

Breath·a·lyz·er /ˈbrɛθəˌlaɪzɚ/ *n.* [C] TRADEMARK a piece of equipment used by the police to see if drivers have drunk too much alcohol

breathe /brið/ S2 W2 *v.*
1 AIR [I,T] to take air into your lungs and send it out again: *My eyes began to sting, and I couldn't breathe.* | *People are concerned about the quality of the air they breathe.* | *Relax and* ***breathe deeply*** (=take in a lot of air). | *She climbed the slope,* ***breathing hard*** (=with difficulty because she had been exercising). | *The boy was asleep,* ***breathing heavily*** (=loudly and with difficulty).

THESAURUS

pant to breathe quickly with short breaths, especially after exercising: *I ran to school and arrived sweaty and panting.*
wheeze to breathe with difficulty, making a noise in your throat and chest, usually because you are sick: *I woke up coughing and wheezing.*
snore to breathe noisily through your mouth and nose when asleep: *He snores and keeps me awake.*
be short of breath also **be out of breath** to have difficulty breathing, often after physical activity such as running, or because of sickness: *Patients quickly become short of breath and unable to stand.*
gasp for breath to breathe quickly and loudly, because you are having difficulty breathing either from exercising or because you are sick: *He was gasping for breath and his heart was pounding fiercely.*
gasp for air to breathe very deeply and loudly because there is not enough air: *He came up from under the water, gasping for air.*

2 BLOW [I,T] to blow air, smoke, or smells out of your mouth: +**on** *I breathed on my fingers to keep them warm.* | *It was cold, and everyone breathed clouds of vapor.*
3 breathe a sigh of relief to not be worried anymore about something that had been worrying or frighten-

ing you: *I breathed a sigh of relief that the boy had been found safe.*
4 be breathing down sb's neck INFORMAL to pay very close attention to what someone is doing, in a way that makes them feel nervous or annoyed: *I can't work with you breathing down my neck.*
5 not breathe a word to not tell anyone anything at all about something, because it is a secret: *You've got to promise not to breathe a word to anyone.*
6 breathe life/excitement/enthusiasm etc. into sth to change a situation so that people feel more excited or interested: *A few new teachers might breathe a little life into this school.*
7 breathe again/easy/easily to relax because something dangerous or frightening has finished: *With stocks going up, investors can breathe easily.*
8 WINE [I] if you let wine breathe, you open the bottle to let the air in before you drink it
9 CLOTHING/CLOTH [I] if a garment or a type of cloth breathes, air can pass through it so that your body feels pleasantly cool and dry
10 SAY STH QUIETLY [T] to say something very quietly, almost in a whisper: *"Come closer," he breathed.*
11 breathe your last (breath) LITERARY to die
12 breathe fire to behave and talk very angrily
[**Origin:** 1200–1300 *breath*] → see also **live and breathe sth** at LIVE[1] (18)

breathe in *phr. v.* **1** to take air into your lungs SYN **inhale**: *Ok, breathe in slowly.* **2 breathe sth ↔ in** to breathe air, smoke, a particular kind of smell etc. into your lungs: *We stood on the sand, breathing in the fresh ocean air.*

breathe out *phr. v.* **1** to send air out from your lungs SYN **exhale**: *OK, now breathe out slowly.* **2 breathe sth ↔ out** to send out air, oxygen, a particular kind of smell etc.: *Green plants breathe out oxygen in sunlight.*

breath·er /ˈbriðɚ/ *n.* INFORMAL to stop what you are doing for a short time in order to rest, especially when you are exercising SYN **break**: *Ok let's **take a** short **breather**.*

breath·ing /ˈbriðɪŋ/ *n.* [U] the process of breathing air in and out → see also **heavy breathing** at HEAVY[1] (16)

ˈbreathing room also **ˈbreathing space** *n.* [U] **1** a time when you stop doing something difficult, tiring etc., so that you have time to think more clearly about a situation or time to solve a problem: *This deal should **give** the company some extra **breathing room** before its loans are due.* **2** enough space to move or breathe easily and comfortably in: *Everyone move back and give him some breathing room.*

breath·less /ˈbrɛθlɪs/ *adj.* **1** having difficulty breathing, especially because you are very tired, excited, or frightened: *Walking up ten flights of stairs **left** him **breathless*** (=made him become breathless). **2** having or showing very strong feelings about something: *a look of **breathless admiration*** | **+with** *The kids were breathless with excitement as the parade approached.* **3** LITERARY too hot, with no fresh air or wind: *a breathless August night* **4** LITERARY very exciting or impressive, and often very fast: *They worked at a breathless pace.* —**breathlessly** *adv.* —**breathlessness** *n.* [U]

breath·tak·ing /ˈbrɛθˌteɪkɪŋ/ *adj.* very impressive, exciting, or surprising: *breathtaking scenery* | *The changes in the city have been breathtaking.* —**breathtakingly** *adv.*

ˈbreath test *n.* [C] a test in which the police make a car driver breathe into a special machine to see if he or she has drunk too much alcohol

breath·y /ˈbrɛθi/ *adj.* if someone's voice is breathy, you can hear their breath when they speak

Brecht /brɛkt/, **Ber·tolt** /ˈbɚtɔlt/ (1898–1956) a German writer of plays and poetry dealing with political ideas —**Brechtian** *adj.*

breathing

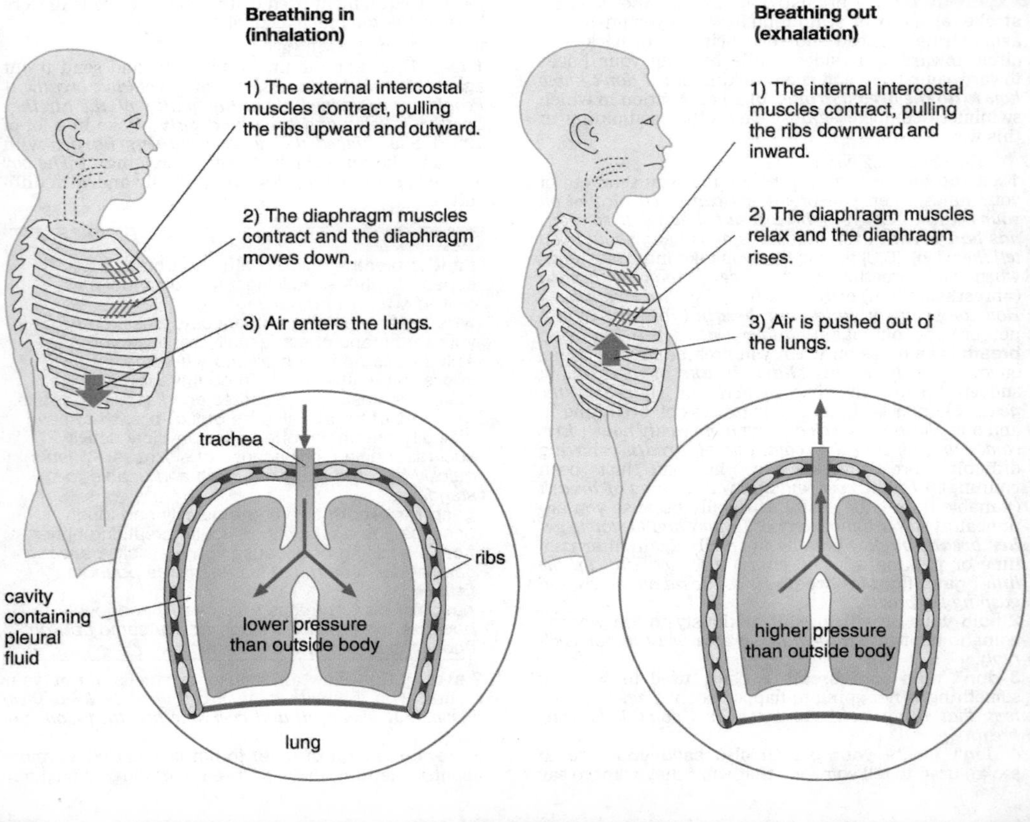

Breathing in (inhalation)
1) The external intercostal muscles contract, pulling the ribs upward and outward.
2) The diaphragm muscles contract and the diaphragm moves down.
3) Air enters the lungs.
trachea
ribs
cavity containing pleural fluid
lower pressure than outside body
lung
Breathing out (exhalation)
1) The internal intercostal muscles contract, pulling the ribs downward and inward.
2) The diaphragm muscles relax and the diaphragm rises.
3) Air is pushed out of the lungs.
higher pressure than outside body

bred /brɛd/ *v.* **1** the past tense and past participle of BREED **2 -bred** combined with names of places or areas to show where someone was born or where something comes from: *the young Georgia-bred singer* | *locally-bred small businesses* → see also PUREBRED, WELL-BRED

breech¹ /britʃ/ *adj.* if a baby is breech or is a breech delivery, the lower part of a baby's body comes out of its mother first when it is born

breech² *n.* [C] **1** the part of gun into which you put the bullets **2 breeches** [plural] **a)** short pants that fasten just below the knees: *riding breeches* **b)** OLD-FASHIONED long pants SYN **britches**

breed¹ /brid/ S3 *v.* **bred** /brɛd/ **1** [T] BIOLOGY to keep animals or plants in order to produce babies or new plants, or in order to develop animals or plants that have particular qualities: *Some of these animals were bred in zoos.* | **breed sth to do sth** *These trees are bred to resist pollution.* **2** [I] BIOLOGY if animals breed, they have babies: *a pond where ducks breed* **3** [T] to cause a particular feeling or condition: *Poor living conditions breed violence and despair.* **4** [T] if a place, situation, or thing breeds someone, it influences the way they think and behave: *Urban music from the 1980s bred a generation of fans.* [**Origin:** Old English *bredan*] → see also, **born and bred** at BORN, **-bred** at BRED, WELL-BRED

breed² S3 *n.* [C] **1** BIOLOGY a type of animal or plant, especially one that people have kept to breed, such as cats, dogs, and farm animals: +**of** *Spaniels are my favorite breed of dog.* **2** a particular kind of person or type of thing: *Real cowboys are* ***a dying breed*** (=not many exist anymore). | ***a new breed of*** *international criminal* | *He's one of the* ***rare breed*** (=there are not many of them) *of scientists who can explain his work to non-scientists.*

breed·er /ˈbridɚ/ *n.* [C] someone who breeds animals or plants as a job: *a dog breeder*

ˈbreeder reˌactor *n.* [C] PHYSICS a type of NUCLEAR REACTOR that produces PLUTONIUM (=a substance used to make nuclear power or nuclear weapons) as well as power

breed·ing /ˈbridɪŋ/ *n.* [U] **1** BIOLOGY the process of animals producing babies: *the birds'* ***breeding season*** (=time of the year when an animal has babies) **2** BIOLOGY the activity of keeping animals or plants in order to produce new or better types: *the breeding of pedigree dogs* | *the sale of* ***breeding stock*** (=animals you keep to breed from) **3** polite social behavior that someone learns from their family: *a woman of wealth and* ***good breeding***

ˈbreeding ground *n.* [C] **1** a place where animals go in order to breed **2** a place or situation where something bad or harmful grows and develops: +**for** *Overcrowded cities are breeding grounds for crime.*

breeze¹ /briz/ *n.* [C] **1** a gentle wind: *an ocean breeze* | *A cool Spring* ***breeze*** *was* ***blowing***. | *Flags waved* ***in the breeze***. ►see THESAURUS box at wind¹ **2 be a breeze** SPOKEN to be something that is very easy to do: *Installing the software is a breeze.* [**Origin:** 1500–1600 French *brise*] → see also **shoot the breeze** at SHOOT¹ (15)

breeze² *v.* [I always + adv./prep.] to walk somewhere in a calm confident way that other people think is not appropriate: +**in/into/out etc.** *Jenny breezed into the meeting thirty minutes late.*

breeze through sth *phr. v.* to achieve something very easily: *She breezed through all her exams.* | *The bill should breeze through the Senate.*

breez·y /ˈbrizi/ *adj.* **1** a breezy person, attitude, etc. is cheerful, confident, and relaxed: *her breezy charm* **2** breezy weather is when the wind blows strongly —**breezily** *adv.* —**breeziness** *n.* [U]

breth·ren /ˈbrɛðrən/ *n.* [plural] OLD-FASHIONED a way of addressing or talking about the members of an organization or association, especially a religious group

bre·vi·ar·y /ˈbriviˌɛri/ *n.* [C] a prayer book used in the Catholic Church

brev·i·ty /ˈbrɛvət̬i/ Ac *n.* [U] FORMAL **1** the quality of expressing something in very few words: *The article was edited for brevity and clarity.* **2** shortness of time: *the brevity of her visit*

brew¹ /bru/ *v.* **1** [T] to make beer **2** [I,T] if tea or coffee brews or you brew it, you pour boiling water over it to make it ready to drink **3** [I] if a bad situation is brewing, it will happen soon: *An argument is brewing over the tax cuts.* **4** [I] if a storm is brewing, it will happen soon

B

brew² *n.* [C,U] **1** SPOKEN beer, or a can or glass of beer **2** a drink that is brewed, such as coffee or tea → see also HOME BREW

brew·er /ˈbruɚ/ *n.* [C] a person or company that makes beer

brew·er·y /ˈbruəri/ *n. plural* **breweries** [C] a building where beer is made, or a company that makes beer

brew·ski /ˈbruski/ *n.* [C] SPOKEN a can or glass of beer

Brezh·nev /ˈbrɛʒnɛf/, **Le·o·nid** /ˈliəˌnid/ (1906–1982) the leader of the Soviet Union from 1977 to 1982

ˈBrezhnev ˌDoctrine, the HISTORY the idea, stated by Leonid Brezhnev in 1968 that the Soviet Union had the right to take action in other COMMUNIST countries to prevent them from changing their governments

bri·ar, brier /ˈbraɪɚ/ *n.* **1** [C,U] BIOLOGY a wild bush with branches that have small sharp points **2** [C] a tobacco pipe made from a briar

bribe¹ /braɪb/ *n.* [C] **1** money or gifts that you give someone to persuade them to do something, especially something dishonest: **take/accept bribes** *A local judge was charge with taking bribes.* | *He was* ***offered a bribe*** *to keep quiet.* **2** something special offered to someone, especially a child, in order to persuade them to do something: *Parents often use candy as a bribe.*

bribe² *v.* [T] **1** to illegally pay money or offer gifts to an official, in order to persuade them to do something for you: **bribe sb to do sth** *Jones bribed officials to get government contracts.* **2** to offer someone, especially a child, something special in order to persuade them to do something they do not want to do: **bribe sb with sth** *I had to bribe the kids with the promise of lunch at McDonalds.* [**Origin:** 1300–1400 Old French **bread given to a beggar**]

brib·er·y /ˈbraɪbəri/ *n.* [U] the act of taking or offering bribes: *The drug bosses used bribery to stay out of jail.* | *a bribery and sex scandal*

bric-a-brac /ˈbrɪk ə ˌbræk/ *n.* [U] small objects, especially things you have in your home, that are not worth very much money but are interesting or attractive

brick¹ /brɪk/ W3 *n.* **1** [C,U] a hard block of baked clay used for building walls, houses etc.: *a brick wall* | *Most of the houses were* ***built of brick***. **2** [C] INFORMAL an attempt to throw the ball through the BASKET in basketball that fails badly **3 you can't make bricks without straw** used to say you cannot do a job if you do not have the necessary materials [**Origin:** 1400–1500 French *brique*, from Middle Dutch *bricke*] → see also **bang your head against/on a (brick) wall** at BANG¹ (5), **hit a brick wall** at HIT¹ (30), **sth is like talking to a brick wall** at TALK¹ (20), **hit sb like a ton of bricks** at TON (4)

brick² *v.*

brick sth **off** *phr. v.* to separate an area from a larger area by building a wall of bricks

brick sth **up/in** *phr. v.* to fill or close a space using bricks

brick·bat /ˈbrɪkbæt/ *n.* [C] a severe criticism of something

brick·lay·er /ˈbrɪkˌleɪɚ/ *n.* [C] someone whose job is to build walls, buildings etc. with bricks —**bricklaying** *n.* [U]

brick·work /ˈbrɪkwɚk/ *n.* [U] **1** the way that bricks have been used to build something: *cracked brickwork* **2** the skill or work of building something with bricks

brick•yard /ˈbrɪkyɑrd/ *n.* [C] a place where bricks are made

bri•dal /ˈbraɪdl/ *adj.* relating to a wedding or the woman who is getting married: *a bridal gown*

ˈbridal ˌparty *n.* [C] a WEDDING PARTY

ˌbridal ˈregistry *n.* **a)** [C] a list of things from a particular store that a couple who are getting married would like to receive as gifts **b)** [C,U] the service, provided by the store, of arranging this list

ˌbridal ˈshower also **shower** *n.* [C] a party for a woman who is going to be married, given by her friends and family

bride /braɪd/ *n.* [C] a woman at the time she gets married or just after she is married: *You may kiss the bride.* [**Origin:** Old English *bryd*]

bride•groom /ˈbraɪdgrum/ *n.* [C] a GROOM

brides•maid /ˈbraɪdzmeɪd/ *n.* [C] a girl or woman who helps the bride on her wedding day and stands with her at the wedding

ˌbride-to-ˈbe *n.* [C] a woman who will soon be married: *Suzanne is Jonathan's bride-to-be.*

bridge[1] /brɪdʒ/ S2 W2 *n.*
1 OVER A RIVER/ROAD ETC. [C] a structure built over a river, road etc., that allows people or vehicles to cross from one side to the other: +**over/across** *the bridges across the Mississippi River* | *The vehicle was* ***crossing the bridge*** *when it was attacked.*
2 CONNECTION [C] something that provides a connection or relationship between two things: +**between** *He acts as a bridge between students and the college administration.* | *The mayor has been* ***building bridges*** (=making a better relationship) *between ordinary citizens and public officials.*
3 SHIP [C] the raised part of a ship from which the officers control it
4 CARD GAME [U] a card game for four players who play in pairs
5 PART OF NOSE [C usually singular] the upper part of your nose between your eyes: *He had a cut on* ***the bridge of his nose.***
6 PAIR OF GLASSES [C usually singular] the part of a pair of glasses that rests on the bridge of your nose
7 MUSICAL INSTRUMENT [C usually singular] a small piece of wood under the strings of a VIOLIN or GUITAR, used to keep them in a raised position
8 FOR TEETH [C] a small piece of metal that keeps false teeth in place by attaching them to your real teeth
[**Origin:** (1–3, 5–8) Old English *brycg*] → see also **burn your bridges** at BURN[1] (13), **cross that bridge when you come to it** at CROSS[1] (9), **be water under the bridge** at WATER[1] (6)

bridge[2] *v.* [T] **1** to reduce or get rid of the difference between two things: *Can we* ***bridge the differences between*** *the two cultures?* | **bridge the gap/gulf/chasm between** *our failure to bridge the gap between the rich and the poor* **2** to build or form a bridge over something: *A log bridged the stream.*

bridge•head /ˈbrɪdʒhɛd/ *n.* [C] a good position far forward in enemy land from which an army can go forward or attack

ˈbridge loan also **ˈbridging loan** *n.* [C] an amount of money that a bank lends you, to cover a short period of time before you receive a larger LOAN

Bridge•town /ˈbrɪdʒtaʊn/ the capital city of Barbados

bri•dle[1] /ˈbraɪdl/ *n.* [C] a set of leather bands put around a horse's head and used to control its movements

bridle[2] *v.* **1** [T] to put a bridle on a horse **2** [I,T] to become angry and offended about something: +**at** *Chris bridled at suggestions that he'd made mistakes.*

ˈbridle path *n.* [C] a path that you ride a horse on

Brie, brie /bri/ *n.* [U] a soft French cheese

brief[1] /brif/ Ac W2 *adj.*
1 TIME continuing for a short time: *a brief visit* | *Let's keep the meeting as brief as possible.* ▸see THESAURUS box at short[1]
2 SPEECH/LETTER using very few words or including few details: *a brief statement to the press* | *I'll* ***be brief*** (=say something using very few words) – *we've made lots of changes.*
3 in brief a) in as few words as possible: *In brief, the President plans to cut defense spending and lower taxes.* **b)** with very few details: *Here is the news in brief.*
4 be brief with sb to not say very much to someone in a way that seems impolite
5 CLOTHES clothes which are brief are short and cover only a small area of your body: *a very brief bikini*
[**Origin:** 1200–1300 Old French, Latin *brevis*]

brief[2] Ac *v.* [T] to give someone all the information about a situation that they will need: **brief sb on/about sth** *Colonel Roberts briefed the pilots about their mission.* → see also DEBRIEF

brief[3] Ac *n.* **1** [C] LAW a short spoken or written statement giving facts about a law case: *The ACLU* ***filed a brief*** (=gave one to the court) *opposing the decision.* **2** [C] a short report about something, especially information about something that has happened recently: *I've* ***prepared a brief*** *on the economic situation in China.* **3 briefs** [plural] men's underwear that fits tightly to the body and covers only the BUTTOCKS and sexual organs → see also BOXER SHORTS

brief•case /ˈbrifkeɪs/ *n.* [C] a flat suitcase with a handle, used especially by business people for carrying papers or documents → see picture at CASE[1]

brief•ing /ˈbrifɪŋ/ Ac *n.* [C,U] information or instructions that you get before you do something, or the meeting at which this is done

brief•ly /ˈbrifli/ Ac W3 *adv.* **1** for a short time: *He worked briefly for Walt Disney Studios.* **2** using as few words as possible: *Sonia explained briefly how the machine works.* | [sentence adverb] *Briefly, the problem was that I wanted a child and he didn't.*

bri•er /ˈbraɪɚ/ *n.* [C] a BRIAR

brig /brɪg/ *n.* [C] **1** a military prison, especially on a ship **2** a ship with two MASTS (=poles) and large square sails

bri•gade /brɪˈgeɪd/ *n.* [C] **1** a large group of soldiers forming part of an army **2** a group of people who are organized to do something: *In the Midwest, snowmobile brigades delivered food and medicine.* **3** INFORMAL, OFTEN HUMOROUS a group of people who have similar qualities and beliefs or wear similar clothes: *the back-to-nature brigade* [**Origin:** 1600–1700 French, Italian *brigata*, from *brigare* **to fight**] → see also FIRE BRIGADE

brig•a•dier /ˌbrɪgəˈdɪr◂/ *n.* [C] a high military rank, or someone holding this rank

ˌbrigadier-ˈgeneral *n.* [C] a high army rank, or someone holding this rank

brig•and /ˈbrɪgənd/ *n.* [C] LITERARY a thief, especially one of a group that attacks people in mountains or forests

brig•an•tine /ˈbrɪgənˌtin/ *n.* [C] a ship like a BRIG but with fewer sails

bright /braɪt/ S2 W2 *adj.*
1 LIGHT shining strongly or with plenty of light: *the bright afternoon sun* | *The light in here is not bright enough to read by.* | *a bright, airy room*

THESAURUS

strong a strong light is very bright: *Diana squinted in the strong sunlight.*
dazzling a dazzling light is so bright that you cannot see for a short time after you look at it: *Under the sun, the white of the snow is dazzling.*
blinding a blinding light is very bright and makes you unable to see for a short time: *Suddenly there was a blinding flash of lightning.*

▸see THESAURUS box at **sunshine**
2 COLORS bright colors are strong and easy to see: *a book with bright, bold illustrations* | *Many of the houses were painted bright colors.* | **bright red/blue/**

yellow etc. *a bright red T-shirt* ►see THESAURUS box at color[1]

3 INTELLIGENT intelligent and likely to be successful: *a bright eight-year-old girl | a bright idea | That wasn't a very bright thing to do.* ►see THESAURUS box at intelligent

4 FUTURE likely to be successful: *The outlook for the economy is not very bright. | Ruddock has **a** very **bright future** in the company.*

5 CHEERFUL cheerful, happy, or full of life: *a bright smile* | +**with** *Her eyes were bright with excitement.*

6 on the bright side relating to the good points in a situation that is bad in other ways: ***Look on the bright side** – at least you learned something from the experience.*

7 bright and early SPOKEN very early in the morning: *I'll be here bright and early to pick you up.*

8 the bright lights (of sth) the interesting exciting life that people are supposed to have in big cities: *He left home for the bright lights of New York*

9 bright spot an event or time that seems happy or good when everything else is upsetting or bad: *The one bright spot in the trip was our trip to the theater.*

10 as bright as a button smart and full of life

11 bright-eyed and bushy-tailed HUMOROUS completely awake and happy, even when it is very early in the morning: *Christie was there, bright-eyed and bushy-tailed, at 6:30 a.m.*

[**Origin:** Old English *beorht*] —**brightly** *adv.*: *The sun shone brightly.* —**brightness** *n.* [U]

bright·en /ˈbraɪt̚n/ *v.* **1** [T] also **brighten sth ↔ up** to make something more attractive by adding something colorful to it: *Fireworks brightened the sky. | New curtains would brighten up the room.* **2** [I,T] to become more successful or positive, or make something do this: *The political situation has brightened in recent months.* **3** [I,T] also **brighten sth ↔ up** to become happier or more excited, or make someone else feel like this: *Julie brightened up at the thought of visiting home. | Your letter really **brightened my day**.* **4** [I] to become brighter in color, or to shine with more light: *brighten the sky* **5** [I] also **brighten up** if the weather brightens or brightens up, the sun starts to shine a little and there are fewer clouds

brights /braɪts/ *n.* [plural] INFORMAL the HEADLIGHTS of a vehicle that shine more brightly than its regular HEADLIGHTS in order to help you see things far away → see also HIGH BEAM

bril·liance /ˈbrɪlyəns/ *n.* [U] **1** a very high level of intelligence or skill: *Jimi Hendrix's brilliance as a rock guitarist* **2** brightness of color

bril·liant[1] /ˈbrɪlyənt/ *adj.* **1** extremely intelligent or skillful: *a brilliant scientist | a brilliant idea* ►see THESAURUS box at intelligent **2** brilliant light or color is very bright and strong: *the brilliant lights of the stadium | brilliant red and yellow flowers* ►see THESAURUS box at color[1] **3** very successful: *a long and brilliant career* [**Origin:** 1600–1700 French, present participle of *briller* **to shine**, from Italian *brillare*] —**brilliantly** *adv.* —**brilliancy** *n.* [U]

brilliant[2] *n.* [C] TECHNICAL a valuable stone cut with a lot of surfaces that shine

Bril·lo pad /ˈbrɪloʊ ˌpæd/ *n.* [C] TRADEMARK a ball of wire filled with soap, used for cleaning pans

brim[1] /brɪm/ *n.* [C] **1** the bottom part of a hat that sticks out to protect you from sun and rain **2** the top of a container such as a glass or bowl: *The cup was **filled to the brim** with coffee.*

brim[2] *v.* **brimmed, brimming** [I] to be very full of something: +**with** *Andy's eyes brimmed with tears. | Her letter was brimming with happiness.*

brim over *phr. v.* **1** if a container is brimming over, it is so full of a liquid or substance that the liquid etc. comes out over the top edge: +**with** *The barrel was brimming over with water.* **2 brim over with confidence/excitement etc.** to be very confident, excited etc.: *The children were brimming over with excitement.*

brim·ful, brimfull /ˈbrɪmfʊl/ *adj.* **be brimful (of/with sth)** to be very full: *The bucket was brimful of oil.*

brim·stone /ˈbrɪmstoʊn/ *n.* [U] OLD USE SULFUR → see also **fire and brimstone** at FIRE[1] (10)

brin·dled /ˈbrɪndld/ *adj.* a brindled animal is brown with marks or bands of another color

brine /braɪn/ *n.* [U] **1** water that contains a lot of salt, used for preserving food **2 the brine** LITERARY ocean water

bring /brɪŋ/ S1 W1 *v.* past tense and past participle **brought** /brɔt/ [T]

1 HAVE SB/STH WITH YOU to take something or someone with you to the place where you are now, or to the place you are talking about: *Did you bring your coat? | Rick **brought** the kids **home**.* | **bring sb/sth to sb/sth** *Can I bring a friend to the party?* | **bring sb/sth with you** *Billy had brought a puppy with him.* | **bring sth for sb** *We brought some presents for the kids.*

> **THESAURUS**
>
> **take** to move something from one place to another, or help someone go from one place to another: *Don't forget to take your umbrella. | Who's taking you home?*
>
> **get** to go to another place and come back with something or someone: *I went upstairs to get my jacket.*

2 GET STH FOR SB to get something for someone and take it to them: **bring sb sth** *Could you bring me a glass of water?* | **bring sb/sth to sb/sth** *I brought the book to her.*

3 MAKE STH GOOD OR BAD HAPPEN to cause something good or bad to happen: *efforts to **bring peace** to the region* | **bring hope/happiness etc.** *Money does not bring happiness.* | **bring sb sth** *Four-leaf clovers are supposed to **bring** you **luck**.*

4 MAKE STH FINISH/STOP/CHANGE bring sb/sth to sth to cause someone or something to finish, stop, or reach a point of change in a state or situation: *Add the vegetables and **bring** the soup **to a boil**. | Many war criminals will never be **brought to justice**. | The U.S. helped **bring** his government **to power**. | Always bring the car to a complete stop at a stop sign.* | **bring to an end/close/halt** *Watson's speech brought the conference to an end.*

5 CAUSE A REACTION/FEELING to cause a particular reaction or emotional response SYN **draw**: *The article brought angry letters from readers. | The joke **brought a smile** to her face. | Their unexpected kindness **brought tears to** my **eyes**.*

6 LEGAL CASE if someone brings a legal action or charges against someone, they say officially that person has done something illegal: **bring sth against sb** *Ms. Burnett brought a libel suit against the newspaper. | The police did not have enough evidence to **bring charges**.*

7 MAKE STH AVAILABLE to make something available for people to use, have, enjoy etc.: *The hotel developments have brought jobs with them.* | **bring sth to sb/sth** *The tourist industry brings a lot of money to the area.*

8 TIME if a particular period of time brings an event or situation, it happens during that time: *Adolescence brings physical and emotional changes. | Who knows what the new year will bring?*

9 GO SOMEWHERE if something such as an event or situation brings people to a place, it makes them go there: *The discovery of gold brought thousands of people to California in 1849. | "Hello, Ben. **What brings you here?**"* (=why have you come)

10 MOVE STH to make something move to a place or position: *Bring your arms up level with your shoulder. | High winds brought the fence down.*

11 TV/RADIO sth is brought to you by sb if a television or radio program is brought to you by someone, they give money so that it can be broadcast, and advertisements for their product are shown during it: *This program is brought to you by Pepsi.*

12 bring sth to sb's attention/notice FORMAL to tell

someone about something: *Thank you for bringing the problem to our attention.*
13 bring the total/number/score etc. to sth used to say what a new total, number etc. is after an amount has been added or taken away: *More people have registered, bringing the total number of registered voters to 151 million.*
14 TALK ABOUT A SUBJECT SPOKEN used when saying that a particular subject is the next thing that you want to talk about: **bring sb to/onto sth** *They haven't won a game all season, which brings me to the question of why.* | ***This brings** me **to** the point of today's meeting.* | *This **brings** us **back to*** (=makes me start talking again about) *the important question of funding.*
15 not bring yourself to do sth if you cannot bring yourself to do something, you cannot make yourself do it, because it would upset you or someone else too much: *I couldn't bring myself to apologize to Stan.*
16 bring sth to bear FORMAL to use something, for example your power, authority, or knowledge, to have an effect on a situation: **+on/upon** ***Pressure** has been **brought to bear** on the governor by environmental groups.*
17 bring home the bacon INFORMAL to earn the money that your family needs to live
18 SELL [T] to be sold for a particular amount of money: *The painting brought $540,000 at the auction.*
19 bring a child into the world FORMAL **a)** if a woman brings a child into the world, she gives birth to it **b)** if a doctor brings a child into the world, he helps the mother give birth
20 sth brings with it sth used to say that a change, action etc. brings with it something such as a problem or advantage, the two things are connected and come together: *Every scientific advance brings with it its own risks.*
21 bring your own bottle ABBREVIATION **BYOB** used when you invite someone to an informal party to tell them that they should bring their own bottle of alcoholic drink
[**Origin:** Old English *bringan*] → see also **bring sth to a head** at HEAD[1] (11), **bring sb to heel** at HEEL[1] (8), **bring sth home to sb** at HOME[2] (4), **bring sb/sth to their knees** at KNEE[1] (5), **bring sb to their senses** at SENSE[1] (6)

bring sth ↔ **about** *phr. v.* to make something happen SYN **cause**: *Years of protest finally **brought about a change** in the law.*

bring sb/sth ↔ **along** *phr. v.* to take someone or something with you when you go somewhere: *I'd already finished the books I'd brought along.* | *Garvin brought a colleague along.*

bring sb/sth **around** *phr. v.* **1** to manage to persuade someone to do something or to agree with you: **+to** *He finally managed to bring his boss around to his point of view.* **2** to make someone become conscious again: *Paramedics eventually brought the man around.* **3 bring the conversation around to sth** to deliberately and gradually introduce a new subject into a conversation: *I'll try to bring the conversation around to the subject of money.* **4** to bring someone or something to someone's house: *I'll bring Jody around tomorrow so you can meet her.*

bring back *phr. v.* **1 bring sb/sth back** to take something or someone with you when you come back from somewhere: *I promised to bring the kids back for a visit.* | *I'll bring your books back on Wednesday.* | **bring sb back sth** *My dad brought me back a T-shirt from New York.* **2 bring sth ↔ back** to make you remember something: *Seeing the fire **brought back memories** of the day my own house burned down.* | *I found some of Sam's letters, and they **brought it all back** to me.* **3 bring sth ↔ back** to start to use something such as a law, method, or process that was used in the past: *Many states have voted to bring back the death penalty.*

bring sb/sth ↔ **down** *phr. v.* **1** to reduce something to a lower level: *new taxes to help bring down the deficit* | *The doctor gave me something to bring the fever down.* **2** to force the government or ruler to stop ruling a country: *a crisis that could bring down the country's government* **3** to move your arm or a weapon, tool etc. quickly toward the ground: *He brought down the ax with a thud.* **4** to shoot at an airplane, bird, or animal so that it falls to the ground: *A bomber was brought down by anti-aircraft fire.* **5 bring down the house** to perform so well that people APPLAUD (=hit their hands together to show they like something) a lot: *Fitzgerald brought down the house with her version of "Summertime."* **6** to fly an aircraft down to the ground and stop: *The pilot managed to bring the plane down safely.*

bring sth **down on/upon** sb *phr. v.* FORMAL to make something bad happen to someone, especially yourself: *What did I do to bring this down on myself?*

bring sth ↔ **forth** *phr. v.* LITERARY to produce something or make it appear SYN **cause**: *The smells from the kitchen brought forth happy memories of childhood.*

bring sth ↔ **forward** *phr. v.* **1** to change the date or time of an arrangement so that it happens sooner than was originally planned → see also PUT BACK: *The meeting's been brought forward to Thursday.* **2 bring forward legislation/plans/policies etc.** to introduce or suggest a new plan or idea: *Plans to restructure the department were brought forward.* **3** to move the total from one set of calculations onto the next page, so that more calculations can be done: *The balance brought forward is $21,765.*

bring in *phr. v.* **1 bring sth ↔ in** to earn a particular amount or produce a particular amount of profit: *The movie has brought in $30 million so far.* | *The resort brings tourist dollars into the area.* **2 bring sb ↔ in** to involve someone in a job, situation, activity, etc.: *D'Arezzo was brought in as the new marketing chief.* | **bring sb in to do sth** *The police brought in the FBI to help.* **3 bring sb ↔ in** to attract customers to a store or business: *To bring in customers, stores are offering great deals.* **4 bring in a verdict** when a court or JURY brings in a verdict, it says whether someone is guilty or not

bring into *phr. v.* **1 bring sth ↔ into sth** to cause something to exist or be in a particular situation: *The League of Nations was **brought into being*** (=made to start to exist) *after World War I.* **2 bring sb/sth ↔ into sth** to make someone become involved in something: *He wanted to bring Estonia into NATO.*

bring sth ↔ **off** *phr. v.* to succeed in doing something very difficult SYN **pull off**: *It's a complicated play, and the actors don't quite bring it off.*

bring sth ↔ **on** *phr. v.* **1** to make something bad happen SYN **cause**: *Abbot died of heatstroke brought on by the extremely high temperatures.* **2** used when you are excited about something or eager to do something: *Bring on the ice cream!* | *Am I ready for the game? Yeah, **bring it on**!*

bring sth **on/upon** sb *phr. v.* to make something bad happen to someone: *They've brought this problem on themselves.*

bring out *phr. v.* **1 bring sb/sth ↔ out** to make something easier to see, taste, notice etc.: *Add a little salt to bring out the flavor.* | *The Christmas holidays have a way of bringing out the child in us.* **2 bring out the best/worst in sb** to make someone behave in the best or worst way that they can: *Ingram always seems to bring out the best in his players.* **3 bring sth ↔ out** to produce and begin to sell a new product, book, record etc.: *His new album is being brought out next month.* **4 bring sth ↔ out** to take something out of a place: *Jenny brought out a couple of glasses.*

bring sb **through** (sth) *phr. v.* to help someone to successfully deal with a very difficult event or period of time: *My friends helped bring me through the divorce.*

bring sb ↔ **together** *phr. v.* **1** to introduce two people to each other, or to be the thing that does this: *They've been friends ever since a school project brought them together.* **2** to make a group of people have fun together or work well together: *It's a good game that brings people together.*

bring up *phr. v.* **1 bring sb/sth ↔ up** to mention a subject or start to talk about it SYN raise: *Several safety questions were brought up in the last meeting.* **2 bring sb up** to take care of and influence a child until they are grown up SYN raise: *He was born and brought up in Minneapolis.* | **be brought up to do sth** *All of our kids were brought up to respect other people.* | *I was brought up Lutheran* (=taught a particular religion as I grew up). **3 bring sth ↔ up** to make something appear on a computer screen: *He brought up the spreadsheet we were working on..* **4 bring sb up on charges** if the police, the courts etc. bring someone up on charges, they say officially that the person has done something illegal **5 bring up the rear** to be behind everyone else when you are going somewhere as a group: *Dad was bringing up the rear to make sure no one got lost.*

brink /brɪŋk/ *n.* **1 the brink (of sth)** a time or situation just before something happens, especially something bad SYN edge SYN verge: **on the brink (of sth)** *Hannah was on the brink of tears.* | *The company was* ***teetering on the brink*** *of bankruptcy.* | *a child* ***poised on the brink of*** *adulthood* | **to the brink (of sth)** *A series of bad decisions* ***pushed*** *the company* ***to the brink of*** *collapse.* | **back from the brink (of sth)** *They hope to* ***bring*** *the birds* ***back from the brink of*** *extinction.* **2 push/drive/shove etc. sb over the brink** to make someone start doing crazy or extreme things **3 the brink of sth** LITERARY the edge of a very high place such as a cliff SYN edge [**Origin:** 1200–1300 Old Norse *brekka* **slope**]

brink·man·ship /ˈbrɪŋkmənˌʃɪp/ also **brinks·man·ship** /ˈbrɪŋks-/ *n.* [U] **1** a way of gaining an advantage, especially in politics, by pretending that you are willing to do something very dangerous **2** used in 1956 by the then U.S. Secretary of State John Dulles to describe a political POLICY of risking war in order to protect a country's national interests

brin·y /ˈbraɪni/ *adj.* containing a lot of salt, or having a strong salty taste

bri·oche /briˈoʊʃ, -ˈɑʃ/ *n.* [C] a type of sweet bread made with flour, eggs, and butter

bri·quette /brɪˈkɛt/ *n.* [C] a block of pressed coal dust that is burned in a fire or BARBECUE

brisk /brɪsk/ *adj.* **1** quick and full of energy SYN fast: *a* ***brisk walk*** | *I took off at a* ***brisk pace.*** **2** trade or business that is brisk is very busy, with a lot of products being made and sold: *The store reported* ***brisk sales.*** | *The economy is keeping a* ***brisk pace.*** **3** weather that is brisk is cold and clear SYN crisp: *a brisk fall morning* **4** quick, practical, and showing that you want to get things done quickly —**briskly** *adv.* —**briskness** *n.* [U]

bris·ket /ˈbrɪskɪt/ *n.* [U] meat from an animal's chest, especially a cow

bris·tle¹ /ˈbrɪsəl/ *v.* [I] **1** to behave in a way that shows you are very angry or annoyed: +**with** *Joan was* ***bristling with rage.*** | +**at** *Teachers bristled at the criticism.* **2** if an animal's hair bristles, it stands up stiffly because the animal is afraid or angry

bristle with sth *phr. v.* to have a lot of something or be full of something: *a house that was bristling with TV antennas*

bristle² *n.* [C,U] **1** a short stiff hair, wire etc. that forms part of a brush → see picture at BRUSH¹ **2** short stiff hair that feels rough SYN whisker

bris·tly /ˈbrɪsəli, -sli/ *adj.* **1** bristly hair is short and stiff **2** a bristly part of your body has short stiff hairs on it: *a bristly chin*

Brit /brɪt/ *n.* [C] INFORMAL someone from Britain

britch·es /ˈbrɪtʃɪz/ *n.* [plural] OLD-FASHIONED **1** pants SYN trousers **2 be too big for your britches** INFORMAL to behave as though you are more important or better than you really are

Brit·ish /ˈbrɪt̬ɪʃ/ *adj.* **1** from or relating to Great Britain or the U.K.: *the British government* **2 the British** people from Great Britain or the U.K.

British Co·lum·bi·a /ˌbrɪt̬ɪʃ kəˈlʌmbiə/ ABBREVIATION **BC** a PROVINCE in western Canada, next to the Pacific Ocean

Brit·ish·er /ˈbrɪt̬ɪʃɚ/ *n.* [C] OLD-FASHIONED someone from Great Britain or the U.K.

ˌBritish ˈIsles *n.* the group of islands that includes Great Britain, Ireland, and the smaller islands around them

ˌBritish North Aˈmerica Act, the HISTORY an act of the British Parliament in 1867 that joined Ontario, Quebec, Nova Scotia, and New Brunswick into the country of Canada and allowed it to make its own laws

Brit·on /ˈbrɪtˀn/ *n.* [C] FORMAL someone from Great Britain or the U.K.: *the ancient Britons*

Brit·ten /ˈbrɪtˀn/, **Benjamin** (1913–1976) a British musician who wrote modern CLASSICAL music

brit·tle¹ /ˈbrɪt̬l/ *adj.* **1** easily broken into many small pieces SYN fragile: *The paper was old and brittle.* **2** a system, relationship etc. that is brittle is easily damaged or destroyed: *Relations between the two countries are still very brittle.* **3** if someone's laugh, expression, PERSONALITY etc. is brittle, they seem to force themselves to show happiness or politeness that they do not feel [**Origin:** 1300–1400 Old English *gebryttan* **to break into pieces**]

brittle² *n.* [U] PEANUT BRITTLE

bro /broʊ/ S3 *n.* [C] SLANG **1** your brother **2** used by boys or men as a way of greeting a male friend

broach /broʊtʃ/ *v.* [T] **1 broach the subject/question/matter etc.** to mention a subject that may be embarrassing or upsetting, or that may cause an argument SYN bring up: *Parents often find it difficult to broach the subject of sex with their children.* **2** to open a bottle or BARREL containing wine, beer etc. [**Origin:** 1400–1500 *broach* **to make a hole in, stab** (14–17 centuries), from *broach* **tool for making holes** (14–17 centuries), from French *broche*]

broad¹ /brɔd/ W2 *adj.*

1 WIDE a broad road, river, or part of someone's body etc. is wide: *Houston's broad streets* | *a tall, broad-shouldered man* → see also BREADTH, NARROW → see Word Choice box WIDE¹

2 INCLUDING A LOT including many different kinds of things or people OPP narrow: *The program is now attracting broader audiences.* | *recipes that have* ***broad appeal*** (=a lot of people like them) | **broad range/spectrum/array** *The committee will discuss a broad range of issues.* | *Successful business strategies fall into three* ***broad categories.*** | *The bill has a* ***broad base*** *of support in Congress.*

3 GENERAL concerning the main ideas or parts of something rather than all the details SYN general: *Military officials released a few broad statements.* | *The members were in* ***broad agreement.*** | *The White House issued only the* ***broad outlines*** *of the plan.*

4 LARGE AREA covering a large area of land or water: *a broad expanse of water*

5 a broad grin/smile a big smile which clearly shows that you are happy

6 in broad daylight if something such as a crime happens in broad daylight, it happens in the daytime when you would expect someone to prevent it: *The attack happened in broad daylight, in one of the busiest parts of town.*

7 paint sb/sth with a broad brush used when you describe something or have an opinion about something without considering details: *He has painted the Californian lifestyle with a broad brush.*

8 WAY OF SPEAKING a broad ACCENT clearly shows where you come from: *a broad Scottish accent*

9 broad humor/wit etc. humor that deals with sex

[**Origin:** Old English *brad*] → see also BREADTH

broad² *n.* [C] SPOKEN, OFFENSIVE a woman

broad·band /ˈbrɔdbænd/ *n.* [U] **1** COMPUTERS a system of connecting computers to the Internet and moving information, such as messages or pictures, at a very high speed ►see THESAURUS box at **Internet** **2** TECHNICAL a system of sending radio signals which allows several messages to be sent at the same time —**broadband** *adj.* [only before noun]

ˌbroad-ˈbased *adj.* [usually before noun] including many different types of things, people, or subjects: *a broad-based student group*

ˈbroad-brush *adj.* [only before noun] dealing only with the main parts of something, and not with the details: *a broad-brush look at the crisis* → see also **paint sb/sth with a broad brush** at BROAD[1] (7)

broad·cast[1] /ˈbrɔdkæst/ *n.* [C] a program on television or the radio: *a news broadcast* | *CNN's **live broadcast** of the trial* (=one that you see or hear at the same time as the events are happening)

broadcast[2] *v. past tense and past participle* **broadcast** **1** [I,T] to send out television or radio programs SYN **transmit**: *The interview was broadcast Sunday.* | *CBS will **broadcast** the game **live*** (=as it happens). **2** [T] to tell something to a lot of people: *Don't go broadcasting what I've told you all over the office.*

broad·cast·er /ˈbrɔdˌkæstɚ/ *n.* [C] **1** someone whose job is speaking on television or radio programs: *a well-known journalist and broadcaster* **2** a company which sends out television or radio programs: *a major broadcaster of children's programs*

broad·cast·ing /ˈbrɔdˌkæstɪŋ/ *n.* [U] the business of making television and radio programs: *a career in broadcasting*

broad·en /ˈbrɔdn/ *v.* **1** [T] to increase something such as your knowledge, experience, or range of activities SYN **widen**: *The class is meant to broaden people's understanding.* | *I traveled to Japan to **broaden my horizons*** (=learn, understand, and do new things). | *Travel **broadens the mind*** (=helps you understand and accept other people's cultures, beliefs etc.). **2** [T] to make something affect or include more people or things SYN **widen** OPP **narrow**: *Diplomats want to broaden the scope of the peace talks.* | *The Republican Party has tried to **broaden its appeal**.* **3** [I,T] to make something wider or to become wider SYN **widen** OPP **narrow**: *The road broadens a little further on.*

ˈbroad jump *n.* [U] LONG JUMP

broad·ly /ˈbrɔdli/ *adv.* **1** in a general way, covering the main facts rather than details SYN **generally**: *She knows broadly what to expect.* | ***Broadly speaking**, the cultures of the two countries are very similar.* | *Independent films, **broadly defined**, are movies that appeal to sophisticated audiences.* | *The two machines are **broadly similar**.* **2 smile/grin broadly** to have a big smile on your face which clearly shows that you are happy or amused **3** including many different kinds of things, people, or subjects SYN **widely**: *The company invests broadly to lessen the risk.* | *Support for the plan is **broadly based**.*

ˌbroad-ˈminded, **broadminded** *adj.* willing to respect opinions or behavior that are very different from your own OPP **narrow-minded**: *Her parents are very broadminded.* → see also SMALL-MINDED —**broad-mindedly** *adv.* —**broad-mindedness** *n.* [U]

broad·sheet /ˈbrɔdʃit/ *n.* [C] a newspaper printed on large sheets of paper → see also TABLOID

broad·side[1] /ˈbrɔdsaɪd/ *n.* [C] **1** a strong criticism of someone or something, especially a written one: *a broadside against abortion* **2** an attack in which all the guns on one side of a ship are fired at the same time

broad·side[2] /ˌbrɔdˈsaɪd◂/ *adv.* with the longest side facing something SYN **sideways**: *His van was hit broadside by a speeding car.*

broad·side[3] *v.* [T] **1** to crash into the side of another vehicle **2** to strongly criticize someone

broad·sword /ˈbrɔdsɔrd/ *n.* [C] a heavy sword with a broad flat blade

Broad·way /ˈbrɔdweɪ/ *n.* a street in New York where there are many theaters, known as the center of the American professional theater industry: *a Broadway musical* | *Miller's new play will soon open **on Broadway**.* → see also OFF-BROADWAY

Bro·ca /ˈbroʊkə/, **Paul** (1824–1880) a French doctor who discovered the part of the brain that produces speech

bro·cade /broʊˈkeɪd/ *n.* [U] thick heavy cloth which has a pattern of gold and silver threads [**Origin:** 1500–1600 Spanish *brocado*, from Italian *broccato*, from *broccare* **to set with large-headed nails**] —**brocaded** *adj.*

broc·co·li /ˈbrɑkəli/ *n.* [U] a green vegetable with thick groups of small dark-green flower-like parts at the top [**Origin:** 1600–1700 Italian, plural of *broccolo*, from *brocco* **small nail**, from Latin *broccus*]

bro·chure /broʊˈʃʊr/ S3 *n.* [C] a thin book giving information or advertising something: *a travel brochure* [**Origin:** 1700–1800 French *brocher* **to sew** because the pages are sewn together]

bro·gan /ˈbroʊgən/ *n.* [C] a heavy work shoe that covers the ANKLE

brogue /broʊg/ *n.* [C] **1** a thick strong leather shoe with a pattern in the leather **2** [usually singular] a strong ACCENT (=way of pronouncing words), especially an Irish or Scottish accent [**Origin:** (1) 1500–1600 Irish Gaelic and Scottish Gaelic *brog*, from Old Norse *brok* **leg-covering**]

broil /brɔɪl/ *v.* [I,T] **1** if you broil something, or if it broils, you cook it under or over direct heat, or over a flame on a BARBECUE SYN **grill**: *broiled chicken* ►see THESAURUS box at **cook**[1] **2** to become very hot: *We were broiling in the sun.* [**Origin:** 1300–1400 Old French *bruler* **to burn**]

broil·er /ˈbrɔɪlɚ/ *n.* [C] **1** a special area of a STOVE used for cooking food under direct heat **2** also **broiler chicken** a chicken that is intended to be cooked by broiling

broil·ing /ˈbrɔɪlɪŋ/ *adj.* broiling weather, sun etc. makes you feel extremely hot: *We worked all day in the broiling sun.*

broke[1] /broʊk/ *v.* the past tense of BREAK

broke[2] *adj.* [not before noun] **1** having no money: *I can't go – I'm broke.* | *Connie is **flat broke*** (=completely broke). ►see THESAURUS box at **poor** **2 go broke** if a company or business goes broke, it cannot operate any more because it has no money: *A lot of small businesses went broke during the recession.* **3 go for broke** INFORMAL to take big risks when you are trying to achieve something: *Jacobsen went for broke and won the tournament.*

bro·ken[1] /ˈbroʊkən/ the past participle of BREAK

broken[2] S3 W3 *adj.*

1 PIECE OF EQUIPMENT not working correctly: *The CD player's broken again.* | *How did the lawn mower **get broken*** (=become broken)?

2 OBJECT in small pieces because it has been hit, dropped etc. SYN **smashed**: *broken beer bottles* | *Pack the cookies carefully so they won't **get broken** in the mail.*

3 BONE cracked or split in more than one piece because you have had an accident: *The accident left her with three broken bones in her wrist.* | **a broken arm/leg/finger etc.** *a badly broken leg*

4 INTERRUPTED interrupted and not continuous: *a broken white line* | *New parents have months of broken sleep* (=interrupted sleep) *ahead of them.*

5 PERSON extremely mentally or physically weak because you have suffered a lot: *He returned from the war a broken man.*

6 a broken agreement/promise etc. an agreement, promise etc. in which someone did not do what they said they would do

7 broken English/French etc. English, French etc. that is spoken very slowly and with many mistakes by someone who knows only a little of the language

8 FAMILY/MARRIAGE a broken relationship, family etc. is one in which the husband and wife have separated: *a **broken marriage*** | *Kids from **broken homes** sometimes have more trouble in school.*

9 a broken heart a feeling of extreme sadness, especially because someone you love has died or left you

ˌbroken-ˈdown *adj.* broken, old, and needing a lot of repair: *a broken-down trailer*

ˌbroken-ˈhearted *adj.* extremely sad, especially because someone you love has died or left you —**broken-heartedly** *adv.*

bro•ker¹ /ˈbroʊkɚ/ *n.* [C] ECONOMICS someone whose job is to buy and sell property, insurance, STOCKS etc. for someone else SYN **agent**: *a real estate broker*

broker² *v.* [T] **broker a deal/settlement/treaty etc.** to help arrange the details of a deal etc. so that everyone can agree to it: *a settlement brokered by the U.N.*

bro•ker•age /ˈbroʊkərɪdʒ/ *n.* **1** [C] also **a brokerage house/firm** a company of brokers who buy and sell STOCKS, or the place where they work **2** [U] the business of being a broker **3** [U] the amount of money a broker charges

bro•mide /ˈbroʊmaɪd/ *n.* **1** [C,U] CHEMISTRY a chemical compound, sometimes used in medicine to make people feel calm **2** [C] FORMAL a statement which is intended to make someone less angry but which is not effective

bro•mine /ˈbroʊmin/ *n.* [U] a dark red liquid with an unpleasant smell that is a nonmetallic chemical element belonging to the HALOGEN group

bronc /brɑŋk/ *n.* [C] INFORMAL a BRONCO

bron•chi•al /ˈbrɑŋkiəl/ *adj.* BIOLOGY affecting the bronchial tubes: *a bronchial infection*

ˈbronchial tube *n.* [C usually plural] BIOLOGY one of the small tubes that take air into your lungs

bron•chi•ole /ˈbrɑŋkioʊl/ *n* [C] BIOLOGY a narrow tube that carries air into the lung from the BRONCHIAL TUBES (=the main air passages leading to the lungs) → see picture at LUNG

bron•chi•tis /brɑŋˈkaɪt̮ɪs/ *n.* [C] MEDICINE an illness which affects your bronchial tubes and makes you cough —**bronchitic** /brɑŋˈkɪt̮ɪk/ *adj.*

bron•hus /ˈbrɑŋkəs/ *n. plural* **bronchi** /-kaɪ/ [C] BIOLOGY one of two tubes that take air into your lungs from your TRACHEA → see picture at LUNG

bron•co /ˈbrɑŋkoʊ/ *n. plural* **broncos** [C] a wild horse from the western U.S. [**Origin:** 1800–1900 Mexican Spanish, Spanish, **rough, wild**]

bron•to•sau•rus /ˌbrɑnt̮əˈsɔrəs/ *n.* [C] a large DINOSAUR with a small head and a long neck [**Origin:** 1800–1900 Greek *bronte* **thunder** + *sauros* **lizard**]

Bron•të /ˈbrɑnti, -teɪ/ the family name of three English sisters who wrote some of the most famous English novels: Charlotte Brontë (1816–1865), Emily Brontë (1818–1858), and Anne Brontë (1820–1849)

Bronx, the /brɑŋks/ a COUNTY, and one of the five BOROUGHS of New York City

ˌBronx ˈcheer *n.* [C] INFORMAL a sound you make by putting your tongue between your lips and blowing, which is often considered rude SYN **raspberry**

bronze¹ /brɑnz/ *n.* **1** [U] a hard metal that is a mixture of COPPER and TIN **2** [U] the dark red-brown color of bronze **3** [C] ENG. LANG. ARTS a work of art such as a STATUE (=model of a person), made of bronze **4** [C] a BRONZE MEDAL [**Origin:** 1700–1800 French, Italian *bronzo*]

bronze² *adj.* **1** made of bronze: *a bronze statue* **2** having the red-brown color of bronze: *bronze skin*

ˈBronze Age *n.* [singular] **the Bronze Age** HISTORY the time, between about 6000 and 4000 years ago, when bronze was used for making tools, weapons etc. → see also IRON AGE, STONE AGE

bronzed /brɑnzd/ *adj.* having skin that is attractively brown because you have been in the sun SYN **tanned**

ˌbronze ˈmedal *n.* [C] a MEDAL made of bronze that is given to the person who comes third in a race or competition → see also GOLD MEDAL, SILVER MEDAL

ˌbronze ˈmedalist *n.* [C] someone who has won a bronze medal

brooch /broʊtʃ, brutʃ/ *n.* [C] a piece of jewelry that a woman fastens to her clothes SYN **pin** [**Origin:** 1200–1300 Old French *broche* **pointed tool, pin**, from Latin *broccus* **sticking out**]

brood¹ /brud/ *v.* [I] **1** to keep thinking about something that you are worried, angry, or upset about: **+over/about/on** *She's still brooding over the divorce.* **2** if a bird broods, it sits on its eggs to keep them warm until the young birds come out

brood² *n.* [C] **1** a family of young birds all born at the same time **2** HUMOROUS a lot of children in a family

brood³ *adj.* **brood mare/sow etc.** a horse, pig etc. that is kept for the purpose of producing babies

brood•ing /ˈbrudɪŋ/ *adj.* **1** worrying and thinking about something: *a silent, brooding man* **2** mysterious and threatening: *a brooding atmosphere* —**broodingly** *adv.*

brood•y /ˈbrudi/ *adj.* silent because you are thinking or worrying about something —**broodily** *adv.* —**broodiness** *n.* [U]

brook¹ /brʊk/ *n.* [C] a small stream SYN **creek**

brook² *v.* **brook no sth** FORMAL also **not brook sth** to not allow something to happen or exist: *Mrs. Madison brooks no nonsense in her class.*

Brook•lyn /ˈbrʊklən/ a BOROUGH and port area of New York City

broom /brum, brʊm/ *n.* **1** [C] a large brush with a long handle, used for sweeping floors **2** [U] BIOLOGY a large bush with small yellow flowers [**Origin:** Old English *brom* **broom plant**; (1) because broom branches were used for making brushes]

broom•stick /ˈbrumˌstɪk/ *n.* [C] **1** the long handle of a broom **2** a broom that a WITCH is supposed to fly on in children's stories

Bros. the written abbreviation of "Brothers", used in the names of companies: *Warner Bros.*

broth /brɔθ/ *n.* [U] soup made by cooking meat or vegetables in water and then removing them SYN **stock**: *chicken broth*

broth•el /ˈbrɑθəl, ˈbrɔ-, -ðəl/ *n.* [C] a house where men pay to have sex with PROSTITUTES SYN **bordello**

broth•er¹ /ˈbrʌðɚ/ S1 W1 *n.* [C] **1** a male who has the same parents as you: *I have two brothers, James and Karl.* | **little/younger/kid brother** *I have to take my little brother to school.* | **big/older/elder brother** *Michael's big brother plays on the basketball team.* | *His* ***twin brother*** *is in the class.* ►see THESAURUS box at **relative¹** **2** a member of a FRATERNITY (=a club of male university students) **3** SPOKEN a word meaning an African-American man, used especially by African-Americans **4** a male member of a group with the same interests, religion, profession etc. as you **5** *plural* **brothers** or **brethren** a male member of a religious group, especially a MONK **6 brothers in arms** soldiers who have fought together in a war [**Origin:** Old English *brothor*] → see also BIG BROTHER, BLOOD BROTHER

brother² *interjection* used to express annoyance or surprise: ***Oh, brother*** *– why is this happening now?*

broth•er•hood /ˈbrʌðɚˌhʊd/ *n.* **1** [U] a feeling of friendship between people SYN **fellowship**: *peace and brotherhood* **2** [C] an organization formed for a particular purpose, especially a religious one: *the Franciscan brotherhood* **3** [C] a union of workers in a particular trade **4** [U] the relationship between brothers

ˈbrother-in-law *n. plural* **brothers-in-law** [C] **1** the brother of your husband or wife **2** the husband of your sister **3** the husband of your husband's or wife's sister

broth•er•ly /ˈbrʌðɚli/ *adj.* showing the helpfulness, love, loyalty etc. that you would expect a brother to show: *brotherly love* —**brotherliness** *n.* [U]

brougham /brum, ˈbroʊəm/ *n.* [C] a light carriage

B

used in the past, which had four wheels and a roof and was pulled by a horse

brought /brɔt/ the past tense and past participle of BRING

B

brou·ha·ha /ˈbruhɑhɑ/ *n.* [singular, U] WRITTEN a lot of noise or angry protest about something SYN uproar: *the brouhaha over campaign funding*

brow /braʊ/ *n.* **1** [C] LITERARY the part of your face above your eyes and below your hair SYN forehead: **furrow/knit your brow** (=make lines appear on your brow because you are angry or worried) | **mop/wipe your brow** (=dry your forehead with your hand or a cloth because you are hot or nervous) **2** [C] an EYEBROW **3 the brow of the hill** LITERARY the top part of a slope or hill

brow·beat /ˈbraʊbit/ *v. past tense* **browbeat**, *past participle* **browbeaten** /ˈbraʊˌbitˀn/ [T] to make someone do something by continuously asking them to, especially in a threatening way: *Clausen has been known to browbeat witnesses.*

brown¹ /braʊn/ S2 W2 *adj.* **1** having the color of earth, wood, or coffee: *dark brown hair* | *a brown shirt* ►see THESAURUS box at hair **2** someone's skin that is brown has been turned brown by the sun: *Her skin gets really brown in the summer.* → see also TAN¹ (2) [**Origin:** Old English *brun*]

brown² *n.* [C,U] the color of earth, wood, or coffee: *the browns and greens of the landscape*

brown³ *v.* [I,T] **1** to heat food so that it turns brown or to become brown in this way by being heated: *Brown the meat in a frying pan.* **2** to become brown because of the sun's heat or to make something brown in this way: *The children's faces were browned by the sun.*

Brown /braʊn/, **John** (1800–1859) a U.S. citizen who tried to use violence to end SLAVERY

Brown, Robert /ˈrɑbɚt/ (1773–1858) a Scottish BOTANIST who made many important discoveries about the structure of plants

ˌbrown-and-ˈserve also **brown-n-serve** *adj.* [only before noun] brown-and-serve bread or SAUSAGES are partly cooked before you buy them, so that you only cook them for a short time before they are ready to eat

ˌbrown-ˈbag *v.* [I] **1** to bring your LUNCH to work, usually in a small brown paper bag: *I'm* ***brownbagging*** *it this week.* **2** to bring your own alcohol to a restaurant which does not serve alcohol —**brown-bagging** *n.* [U]

ˈbrown bread *n.* [U] bread made with WHOLE WHEAT

Brown·i·an mo·tion /ˌbraʊniən ˈmoʊʃən/ *n.* [U] CHEMISTRY irregular movement of the ATOMIC PARTICLES in a substance that is floating in a liquid or gas, caused by the particles being continuously hit by MOLECULES in the liquid or gas

brown·ie /ˈbraʊni/ *n.* **1** [C] a type of heavy flat chocolate cake **2 the Brownies** [plural] the part of the Girl Scouts organization that is for younger girls **3 Brownie** [C] a member of this organization **4 get/earn brownie points** INFORMAL to do something so that people in authority have a good opinion of you

Brown·ing /ˈbraʊnɪŋ/, **E·liz·a·beth Bar·rett** /ɪˈlɪzəbəθ ˈbærət/ (1806–1861) an English poet who married the poet Robert Browning

Browning, Rob·ert /ˈrɑbɚt/ (1812–1889) an English poet

ˈbrown-nose *v.* [I,T] INFORMAL to try to make someone with authority like you by being very nice to them, in a way that is annoying to other people —**brown-noser** *n.* [C] —**brown-nosing** *n.* [U]

brown·out /ˈbraʊnaʊt/ *n.* [C] a time when the electric power supplied to an area is reduced because of equipment failure or the use of too much electricity in the area

ˌbrown ˈrecluse also **ˌbrown ˌrecluse ˈspider** *n.* [C] a very poisonous brown SPIDER

ˌbrown ˈrice *n.* [U] rice that still has its outer layer

brown·stone /ˈbraʊnstoʊn/ *n.* **1** [U] a type of reddish-brown stone, often used for building in the eastern U.S. **2** [C] a house with a front made of this stone

ˈbrown ˌsugar *n.* [U] a type of sugar that contains MOLASSES

ˌBrown v. ˌBoard of Eduˈcation HISTORY a famous U.S. legal case (1954) which resulted in black students being allowed to attend the same schools and universities as white students

browse /braʊz/ *v.* **1** [I] to look through the pages of a book, magazine etc. and just read the most interesting parts SYN skim: +**through** *We browsed through a few travel books.* **2** [I] to look at the goods in a store without wanting to buy any particular thing: *I enjoy browsing in bookstores.* **3** [I,T] COMPUTERS to search for information on the Internet: *It's easy to spend hours just browsing the web.* **4** [I] if a goat, DEER etc. browses, it eats plants SYN graze —**browsing** *n.* [U]

brows·er /ˈbraʊzɚ/ *n.* [C] COMPUTERS a computer program that finds information on the Internet and shows it on your computer screen

brr /bɚ/ *interjection* said when you are cold

Brue·gel /ˈbrɔɪgəl, ˈbru-/, **Brueghel, Breughel, Pie·ter** /ˈpit̬ɚ/ **1 Bruegel the Elder** (?1525–1569) a Flemish PAINTER famous for his pictures of LANDSCAPES and ordinary people **2 Bruegel the Younger** (1564–1638) a Flemish PAINTER famous for his pictures of religious subjects

bruise¹ /bruz/ *n.* [C] **1** MEDICINE a purple or brown mark on your skin that you get because you have fallen, been hit etc.: *a few cuts and bruises* ►see THESAURUS box at injury, mark² **2** a mark on a piece of fruit that spoils its appearance

bruise² *v.* [I,T] **1** MEDICINE if part of your body bruises, or if you bruise it, a bruise appears because it has been hit: *Payton bruised his hip ten minutes into the game.* ►see THESAURUS box at hurt¹ **2** if a piece of fruit bruises, or if it is bruised, a bruise appears because it has been hit or dropped **3** if an experience bruises someone, they feel upset, unhappy, and less confident after it happens: **bruise sb's pride/ego** *Not getting the promotion really bruised his ego.* [**Origin:** Old English *brysan* **to press so as to break, bruise**, later influenced by Old French *brisier, bruisier* **to break**] —**bruised** *adj.*

bruis·er /ˈbruzɚ/ *n.* [C] INFORMAL a big strong man who likes fighting or arguing

bruis·ing /ˈbruzɪŋ/ *n.* [U] **1** purple or brown marks on your skin that you get because you have fallen, been hit etc. **2** marks on a piece of fruit that spoil its appearance → see also **be cruising for a bruising** at CRUISE¹ (6)

bruit /brut/ *v.*

bruit sth **about** *phr. v.* FORMAL to tell a lot of people about something

brunch /brʌntʃ/ *n.* [C,U] a meal eaten in the late morning, as a combination of breakfast and LUNCH

Bru·nei /bruˈnaɪ/ also **Brunei Da·rus·sa·lam** /-dəˌrusəˈlɑm/ a small country on the island of Borneo —**Bruneian** *n., adj.*

bru·nette, **brunet** /bruˈnɛt/ *n.* [C] a woman with dark brown hair

brunt /brʌnt/ *n.* **bear/take/suffer the brunt of sth** to receive the worst part of an attack, criticism, bad situation etc.: *The mayor took the brunt of the criticism.*

brush¹ /brʌʃ/ S3 *n.*

1 FOR HAIR [C] an object that you use to make your hair smooth and neat, consisting of thin pieces of plastic or BRISTLES attached to a handle SYN hairbrush

2 FOR CLEANING [C] an object that you use for cleaning, painting etc., made with a lot of hairs, BRISTLES, or thin pieces of plastic or wire attached to a handle: *Use a wire brush to remove the rust.* → see also PAINTBRUSH, TOOTHBRUSH

3 BUSHES/TREES [U] **a)** small bushes and trees covering an open area of land: *a brush fire* **b)** branches which have broken off bushes and trees

4 EXPERIENCE **brush with sth** a short, usually bad, experience SYN encounter: *People who wanted to meet*

the actor lined up for their brush with fame. | *He's had several* ***brushes with the law*** (=an occasion when you are stopped or questioned by the police). | *Her* ***brush with death*** (=she very nearly died) *has made her appreciate her life more.*
5 TOUCH [singular] a quick light touch, made by chance when two things or people pass each other: *I felt the brush of her sleeve as she walked past.*
6 TAIL [C] the tail of a FOX
[**Origin:** (1–3) 1300–1400 Early French *broisse*, from Old French *broce*]

brush² S2 *v.* **1** [T] to clean something or make something smooth and neat using a brush → see also SWEEP: *It's time to go brush your teeth.* **2** [I always + adv./prep.,T always + adv./prep.] to remove something with a brush or with your hand: **brush sth ↔ off/away etc.** *Helen brushed away a tear.* | *I got up and* ***brushed myself off.*** **3** [I always + adv./prep.,T] to put a liquid onto something using a brush: *Use small strokes to brush on the paint.* | **brush sth with sth** *Brush the dough with melted butter.* | **brush sth over/onto sth** *Brush the mixture evenly over the vegetables.* **4** [I always + adv./prep.,T] to touch someone or something lightly by chance when passing them: *Something brushed her shoulders.* | *He* ***brushed past*** *her and put the bag on the table.* | **brush (up) against sb/sth** *I brushed up against the man in front of me.* ▸see THESAURUS box at touch¹

brush sb/sth ↔ **aside** *phr. v.* to refuse to listen to or consider something SYN **dismiss**: *The idea was quickly brushed aside by upper management.*

brush sb/sth ↔ **off** *phr. v.* **1** to refuse to listen to someone or their ideas, especially by ignoring them or saying something rude: *Roberts just brushed off the neighbors' complaints.* **2** to clean something with a brush or with your hands

brush up (on) sth *phr. v.* to quickly practice and improve your skills or knowledge of something you learned in the past SYN **review**: *I need to brush up on my Spanish.*

brushed /brʌʃt/ *adj.* [only before noun] brushed cloth has been specially treated to make it feel much softer: *brushed cotton*

ˈbrush-off *n.* **give sb the brush-off** to ignore someone or make it clear that you do not want their friendship, invitations etc.

ˈbrush stroke *n.* [C] a line or mark that you make with a PAINTBRUSH, or the action of making this

brush·wood /ˈbrʌʃwʊd/ *n.* [U] small dead branches broken from trees or bushes

brush·work /ˈbrʌʃwɚk/ *n.* [U] the particular way in which someone puts paint on a picture using a brush

brusque /brʌsk/ *adj.* using very few words in a way that seems rude but is not intended to be SYN **abrupt**: *a brusque manner* [**Origin:** 1600–1700 French, Italian *brusco*, from Medieval Latin *bruscus* type of bush with sharp points] —**brusquely** *adv.* —**brusqueness** *n.* [U]

Brus·sels /ˈbrʌsəlz/ the capital city of Belgium and the city from which the business of the European Union and NATO is run

brus·sels sprout, **Brussel sprout** /ˈbrʌsəl ˌspraʊt/ *n.* [C] a small round green vegetable that has a slightly bitter taste [**Origin:** 1600–1700 *Brussels*, where it was first grown]

bru·tal /ˈbrut̬l/ *adj.* **1** very cruel and violent: *a brutal killer* | **brutal murder/attack/violence etc.** *Three men were charged with the brutal murder.* **2** honest, in way that seems unkind and not sensitive to people's feelings: *He replied with* ***brutal honesty.*** **3** unpleasant and extreme, and causing suffering or harm: *the* ***brutal realities*** *of life in prison* —**brutally** *adv.* —**brutality** /bruˈtæləṭi/ *n.* [C,U]

bru·tal·ize /ˈbrut̬lˌaɪz/ *v.* [T usually passive] **1** to treat someone in a cruel or violent way: *Many prisoners were brutalized by the guards.* **2** to affect someone so badly that they become cruel and violent: *Young men are often brutalized by their experiences in jail.* —**brutalization** /ˌbrut̬l-əˈzeɪʃən/ *n.* [U]

brute¹ /brut/ *n.* [C] **1** a man who is rough, cruel, and not sensitive **2** LITERARY an animal, especially a large or strong one SYN **beast**

brute² *adj.* [no comparative] **1 brute force/strength etc.** physical strength rather than thought or intelligence: *Brute force is used far too often by police.* **2** [only before noun] simple and not involving any other facts or qualities: *The brute fact is that the situation will not improve.*

brut·ish /ˈbrut̬ɪʃ/ *adj.* cruel and not sensitive to people's feelings —**brutishly** *adv.* —**brutishness** *n.* [U]

Bry·an /ˈbraɪən/**, Wil·liam Jen·nings** /ˈwɪlyəm ˈdʒɛnɪŋz/ (1860–1925) a U.S. lawyer and politician famous for his skill in public speaking

Bry·ant /ˈbraɪənt/**, Paul "Bear"** /pɔl bɛr/ (1913–1983) a U.S. college football COACH who set a record for winning the most games

Bryant, Wil·liam Cul·len /ˈwɪlyəm ˈkʌlən/ (1794–1878) a U.S. poet and JOURNALIST

Bryl·creem /ˈbrɪlkrim/ *n.* [U] TRADEMARK a substance used on men's hair to make it shiny and smooth

bry·o·phyte /ˈbraɪəˌfaɪt/ *n.* [C] BIOLOGY a plant such as MOSS that does not produce flowers or have tubes that carry liquid around its body

B.S. /ˌbi ˈɛs/ *n.* [C usually singular] **Bachelor of Science**; a first college degree in a science subject → see also B.A.: *a B.S. in Biology*

BSE /ˌbi ɛs ˈi/ *n.* [U] a serious brain disease that affects cows

B-side /ˈbi saɪd/ *n.* [C] **1** the side of a small record that has the less well-known song on it **2** the song on the back of this type of record

BTU /ˌbi ti ˈyu/ *n.* [C] **British Thermal Unit**; a unit used to measure how much heat something produces

BTW, **btw** a written abbreviation of "by the way," often used in EMAIL → see **by the way** at BY¹ (12)

bub /bʌb/ *n.* [C] OLD-FASHIONED, used to speak to a man you do not know, especially when you are angry

bub·ble¹ /ˈbʌbəl/ S3 *n.* [C] **1** a ball of air in liquid: *soap bubbles* | *Grandma was* ***blowing bubbles*** *with the kids.* **2** a small amount of air trapped in a solid substance: *Examine the glass carefully for bubbles.* **3** a successful or happy period of time, especially in business: *Japan's economic bubble in the 1980s* | *The real estate* ***bubble*** *finally* ***burst*** (=the successful period ended) *last year.* **4** also **cartoon/speech bubble** a circle around the words said by someone in a drawing or COMIC STRIP **5** a transparent structure that has a round shape: *The plastic bubble surrounds the patient, preventing infection.* → see also **burst the/sb's bubble** at BURST¹ (5)

bubble² *v.* **1** [I] to produce bubbles: *When the pancakes start to bubble, flip them over.* | +**up** *Oil was bubbling up to the surface.* **2** [I] to make the sound that water makes when it boils: +**away** *The water was bubbling away on the stove.* **3** [I] also **bubble over** to be full of a particular emotion, especially excitement: +**with** *Boyer bubbled with enthusiasm.* **4** also **bubble up** if a feeling or activity bubbles, it continues to exist and be noticed: *Their dislike of each other has been bubbling beneath the surface.*

B

'bubble bath *n.* **1** [U] a liquid soap that smells good and makes bubbles in your bath water **2** [C] a bath with this in the water

'bubble gum *n.* [U] a type of CHEWING GUM that you can blow into a BUBBLE

'bubble-gum *adj.* [only before noun] relating to music that is not serious and that only young people like

bub·bler /'bʌblɚ/ *n.* [C] INFORMAL a piece of equipment in a public place that produces a stream of water for you to drink from SYN **drinking fountain**

'bubble wrap also **'bubble pack** *n.* [U] a sheet of soft plastic covered with bubbles of air, used for wrapping and protecting things

bub·bly¹ /'bʌbli/ *adj.* **1** full of BUBBLES **2** always cheerful, friendly, and eager to do things: *a bubbly personality*

bubbly² *n.* [U] INFORMAL CHAMPAGNE

Bu·ber /'bubɚ/, **Mar·tin** /'mɑrt˺n/ (1878–1965) an Austrian Jewish religious writer and teacher

bu·bon·ic plague /buˌbɑnɪk 'pleɪg/ *n.* [U] MEDICINE a very serious disease spread by rats and FLEAS, that killed a lot of people in the 14th century → see also BLACK DEATH, PLAGUE¹ (2)

buc·ca·neer /ˌbʌkə'nɪr/ *n.* [C] **1** someone who attacks ships and steals from them SYN **pirate** **2** someone who is successful, especially in business, but may not be honest [**Origin:** 1600–1700 French *boucanier* **person living in the forest in the West Indies, buccaneer**, from *boucaner* **to dry meat in a wooden frame over a fire**]

Bu·chan·an /byu'kænən/, **James** (1791–1868) the 15th president of the U.S. (1857-61)

Bu·cha·rest /'bukəˌrɛst/ the capital and largest city of Romania

buck¹ /bʌk/ S1 *n.* [C]
1 MONEY INFORMAL a dollar: *Could I borrow ten bucks?* | *He's paying his lawyer* ***big bucks*** (=a lot of money). | *The new rule makes it tougher for companies to* ***make a buck*** (=earn money). | *Ellis will do anything to* ***make a fast buck*** (=make some money quickly, often dishonestly).
2 the buck stops here also **the buck stops with sb** used to say that a particular person is responsible for something: *It was my decision to close the hospital; the buck stops with me.*
3 ANIMAL BIOLOGY *plural* **buck** or **bucks** a male animal, such as a DEER or rabbit → see also DOE
4 feel/look like a million bucks INFORMAL to feel or look very healthy, happy, and beautiful
[**Origin:** (2) 1900–2000 *buck* object used in the card game of poker to mark the next person to play] → see also **more bang for the/your buck** at BANG² (6), **pass the buck** at PASS¹ (26)

buck² *v.*
1 HORSE [I] if a horse bucks, it kicks its back feet into the air, or jumps with all four feet off the ground
2 THROW SB [T] to throw a rider off by bucking
3 MOVE [I] if a car, plane etc. bucks, it moves suddenly up and down or forward and backward in an uncontrolled way
4 OPPOSE INFORMAL [T] to oppose something in a direct way SYN **resist**: *The school* ***bucked*** *a national* ***trend*** *when its students showed improved SAT scores.* | *A lot of women just don't feel confident enough to* ***buck the system*** (=avoid the usual rules).

buck for sth *phr. v.* to try very hard to get something, especially a good position at work: *Anne's bucking for a promotion.*

buck up *phr. v.* **1 buck sb up** to become more cheerful, or make someone more cheerful: *Buck up! Things aren't that bad.* **2 buck sth ↔ up** to improve, or to make something improve: *They've raised interest rates to buck up the peso.*

buck³ *adv.* **buck naked** wearing no clothes at all

Buck /bʌk/, **Pearl S.** /pɚl ɛs/ (1892–1973) a U.S. writer who wrote novels about China

buck·a·roo /ˌbʌkə'ru, 'bʌkəˌru/ *n.* [C] INFORMAL a COWBOY, used especially when speaking to children [**Origin:** 1800–1900 Spanish *vaquero* **cowboy**; influenced by *buck*]

buck·board /'bʌkbɔrd/ *n.* [C] a light vehicle which has four wheels and is pulled by a horse, used in the U.S. in the 19th century

buck·et /'bʌkɪt/ S3 *n.* [C] **1** an open container with a handle, used for carrying and holding things, especially liquids SYN **pail** **2** also **bucketful** the quantity of liquid that a bucket can hold: +**of** *four buckets of water* **3** INFORMAL an occasion when the ball goes through the basket in basketball **4** a part of a machine shaped like a large bucket and used for moving earth, water etc. **5 sweat/cry buckets** INFORMAL to SWEAT or cry a lot **6** INFORMAL a large amount of something: *He drinks beer* ***by the bucket.*** | +**of** *They made buckets of cash on the deal.* **7 in buckets** INFORMAL in large amounts: ***Rain*** *was* ***coming down in buckets.*** [**Origin:** 1200–1300 Anglo-French *buket*, from Old English *buc* **container for pouring liquid, belly**] → see also **sb can't carry a tune in a bucket** at CARRY¹ (29), **a drop in the bucket/ocean** at DROP² (7), **kick the bucket** at KICK¹ (10)

'bucket seat *n.* [C] a low car seat with a high back, for one person

buck·le¹ /'bʌkəl/ *v.* **1** [I,T] to fasten a buckle or be joined together with a buckle: *The strap buckles on the side.* **2** [I,T] to become bent or curved because of heat or pressure, or to make something bend or curve in this way: *The sidewalk was buckled from the earthquake.* **3** [I] if your knees or legs buckle, they become weak and bend SYN **give way** **4 buckle under pressure/strain etc.** to do something you do not want to do, because a difficult situation forces you to SYN **give in**: *Griffin buckled under pressure from investors to lay off workers.*

buckle down *phr. v.* to start working very hard: *It's time to buckle down and do your homework.*

buckle sth **↔ on** *phr. v.* to fasten a buckle: *Frank buckled on his safety harness.*

buckle under *phr. v.* to do something you do not want to do, because someone forces you to SYN **give in**: *They threatened a lawsuit, but he refused to buckle under.*

buckle up *phr. v.* **buckle sth ↔ up** to fasten your SEAT BELT in a car, plane etc.

buckle² *n.* [C] a piece of metal used for fastening the two ends of a belt, or for fastening a shoe, PURSE etc., or for decoration → see picture at FASTENER [**Origin:** 1300–1400 Old French *bocle* **buckle, raised part in the center of a shield**, from *buccola* **strap for a helmet**]

buck·shot /'bʌkʃɑt/ *n.* [U] a lot of small metal balls that you fire together from a gun

buck·skin /'bʌkˌskɪn/ *n.* [U] strong soft leather made from the skin of a DEER or goat

buck 'teeth *n.* [plural] teeth that stick forward out of your mouth —**buck-toothed** *adj.*

buck·wheat /'bʌkwit/ *n.* [U] a type of small grain used as food for chickens, and for making FLOUR [**Origin:** 1500–1600 Middle Dutch *boecweit*, from *boec* **beech** + *weit* **wheat**; because the grains are the same shape as beech-tree seeds]

bu·col·ic /byu'kɑlɪk/ *adj.* LITERARY relating to the land outside towns and cities [**Origin:** 1500–1600 Latin *bucolicus*, from Greek, from *boukolos* **person who looks after cows**] —**bucolically** /-kli/ *adv.*

bud¹ /bʌd/ *n.* [C] **1** BIOLOGY a young tightly rolled-up flower or leaf before it opens: *rose buds* **2** SPOKEN BUDDY → see also **nip sth in the bud** at NIP¹ (2)

bud² *v.* **budded, budding** [I] BIOLOGY to produce buds

Bu·da·pest /ˈbudəˌpɛst/ the capital and largest city of Hungary

Bud·dha /ˈbudə, ˈbʊ-/ **1 the Buddha** (?563–?483 B.C.) the title given to Gautama Siddhartha, a religious leader from India who taught the ideas on which the religion of Buddhism is based **2** [C] a STATUE or picture of the Buddha

Bud·dhis·m /ˈbudɪzəm, ˈbʊ-/ *n.* [U] a religion of east, south, and central Asia, based on the teachings of the Buddha that it is necessary to become free of human desires in order to escape from the suffering that is a part of life. Followers of Buddhism believe in REINCARNATION (=the idea that people are born again after they die, and that their next life depends on how they behaved in their previous life). → see also NIRVANA —**Buddhist** *adj., n.*: *a Buddhist monk* | *She became a Buddhist.*

bud·ding¹ /ˈbʌdɪŋ/ *adj.* **1 a budding singer/actor/writer etc.** someone who is just starting to sing, act etc. and will probably be successful at it **2** [only before noun] beginning to develop: *a budding romance*

budding² *n.* [U] **1** BIOLOGY the process by which a plant produces new BUDS **2** BIOLOGY a process by which YEAST produces more of itself and some simple living creatures produce new creatures, that happens when an existing part of the substance or creature becomes restricted and separates to form two new parts **3** BIOLOGY a method in which people produce a new variety of plant or tree by joining the BUD of one plant onto the stem of a different plant, used especially in order to produce a new fruit trees

bud·dy /ˈbʌdi/ S2 *n. plural* **buddies** [C] **1** INFORMAL a friend SYN **bud**: *We're good buddies.* **2** SPOKEN, INFORMAL used to speak to a man or boy, especially one you do not know SYN **bud**: *Hey, buddy! Is this your car?* **3** also **buddy boy** SPOKEN used to speak to a man or boy that you are angry or annoyed with: *It doesn't matter to me what you think, buddy boy.*

ˈbuddy-ˌbuddy *adj.* INFORMAL **be buddy-buddy (with sb)** to be very friendly with someone

ˈbuddy ˌsystem *n.* [C usually singular] a system in which people in a group are put in pairs to keep each other safe or to help each other

budge /bʌdʒ/ *v.* [usually in negatives] INFORMAL **1** [I,T] to move, or make someone or something move: *The car was stuck and we couldn't budge it.* | +**from** *Will hasn't budged from his room all day.* | *I couldn't get the window to **budge an inch**.* **2** [I] to change your opinion or accept something that is not exactly what you wanted, usually used in negative sentences: +**on** *They wouldn't budge on the price.* | +**from** *Democrats refused to budge from their opposition to the plan.*

Budge /bʌdʒ/, **Don** /dɑn/ (1915—2000) a U.S. tennis player

budg·et¹ /ˈbʌdʒɪt/ S2 W1 *n.* [C] ECONOMICS the money that is available to an organization or person, or the plan of how they will spend it: *the firm's annual budget* | **defense/athletic/advertising etc. budget** *More **cuts** in the defense **budget** are expected.* | +**of** *The organization has a budget of $35 million.* | +**for** *How much was the budget for the movie?* | *The state has a $14 billion **budget deficit*** (=a situation in which more money has been spent than is available). | *Several governors have tried, and failed, to **balance the budget*** (=make sure that they spend only the same amount of money as they receive). | **be over/under budget** (=to have spent more or less money than the amount allowed in the budget) | *The couple have to work within **a tight budget*** (=they do not have much money to spend). | *What can a family **on a budget*** (=without much money to spend) *do on their vacation?* [**Origin:** 1400–1500 Old French *bougette* **small leather bag**, from Latin *bulga*; from the idea of bringing your spending plan out of its bag]

budget² *v.* **1** [I,T] to carefully plan and control how much you spend: *The movie cost three times more than the studio had budgeted.* | +**for** *We budgeted $3,000 for the vacation.* **2** [I,T] to plan carefully how much of something will be needed: *You have two hours to answer four questions, so budget your time appropriately.*

budget³ *adj.* [only before noun, no comparative] **1** very low in price SYN **cheap**: *a budget flight* **2 low-budget/big-budget** used for saying whether a lot or only a little money was spent on doing something: *low-budget movies*

budg·et·ar·y /ˈbʌdʒəˌtɛri/ *adj.* relating to the way money is spent in a budget: *budgetary restrictions*

ˈbudget ˌdeficit *n.* [C] ECONOMICS the amount by which the money a government spends is more than it receives in tax or other income during a particular year

ˈbudget ˌsurplus also **ˌsurplus ˈbudget** *n.* [C] ECONOMICS money that a government still has available when it spends less money than it receives in taxes during a particular period

Bue·nos Ai·res /ˌbwɛnəs ˈæriz/ the capital and largest city of Argentina

buff¹ /bʌf/ *n.* **1** [C] **a movie/car/jazz etc. buff** someone who is very interested in movies, cars etc. and knows a lot about them SYN **fan** **2** [U] a pale yellow-brown color SYN **beige** **3 in the buff** INFORMAL having no clothes on SYN **naked** [**Origin:** (3) 1800–1900 *buff* **bare skin**]

buff² *v.* [T] to make a surface shine by polishing it with a dry cloth SYN **polish**

buff up *phr. v.* INFORMAL to exercise in order to make your muscles bigger

buff³ also **buffed** /bʌft/ *adj.* SPOKEN having a very attractive body, especially from doing exercise

Buf·fa·lo /ˈbʌfəˌloʊ/ a city in the U.S. state of New York

buf·fa·lo /ˈbʌfəˌloʊ/ *n. plural* **buffalos, buffaloes** or **buffalo** [C] **1** BIOLOGY a large animal like a cow with a very large head and thick hair on its neck and shoulders SYN **bison** **2** BIOLOGY an African animal similar to a large black cow with long curved horns → see also WATER BUFFALO

ˌBuffalo ˈBill → see CODY, WILLIAM

buff·er¹ /ˈbʌfɚ/ *n.* [C]

1 PROTECTION something that protects one thing or person from being harmed by another, especially by keeping them separate: +**against** *The trees act as a buffer against the freeway noise.* | +**between** *The U.N. forces will act as a buffer between the two sides.*

2 AREA also **buffer zone** an area between two armies, which is intended to separate them so that they do not fight

3 COUNTRY also **buffer state** POLITICS a smaller peaceful country between two larger countries, which makes war between them less likely

4 COMPUTER a place in a computer's memory for storing information for a short time

5 FOR POLISHING something used to polish a surface

6 CHEMICAL SUBSTANCE also **buffer solution** CHEMISTRY a substance that when added to an acid or a base does not cause a sudden or strong change in the PH (=the level of acid)

buffer² *v.* [T] **1** to reduce the bad effects of something: *Their savings helped to buffer the effects of the recession.* **2** COMPUTERS if a computer buffers information, it holds it for a short time before using it

buf·fet¹ /bəˈfeɪ, bʊ-/ *n.* [C] **1** a meal in which people serve themselves at a table and then move away to eat: *a meal served buffet-style* | *a **light buffet*** (=food of only a few types) *of cheese and cold meats* | *a party with a **full buffet*** (=hot food of all types) | **buffet breakfast/lunch/dinner** or **breakfast/lunch/dinner buffet** *The* *restaurant offers a fabulous buffet lunch.* **2** the table that a buffet meal is served from **3** a piece of furniture in which you keep the things you use to serve and eat a meal SYN sideboard

buf·fet² /ˈbʌfɪt/ *v.* [T usually passive] **1** if wind, rain, or the ocean buffets something, it hits it with a lot of force **2** to make someone have a lot of problems or bad experiences: *Local businesses have been buffeted by the troubled economy.* —**buffeting** *n.* [C]

buf·foon /bəˈfun/ *n.* [C] OLD-FASHIONED someone who does silly things that make you laugh SYN clown [**Origin:** 1500–1600 French *boufon*, from Old Italian *buffone*] —**buffoonery** *n.* [U]

bug¹ /bʌg/ S2 *n.* [C] **1** BIOLOGY a small insect **2** a sickness that people catch very easily from each other but is not very serious: **catch/get a bug** *I guess I caught a bug somewhere.* | *She missed school because of* ***a stomach bug*** (=sickness affecting her stomach). | *Jim's just getting over* (=recovering from) ***a flu bug.*** **3** COMPUTERS a small fault in the system of instructions that operates a computer → see also DEBUG ▸see THESAURUS box at defect¹, fault¹ **4** INFORMAL a sudden strong interest in doing something: **get/be bitten by/catch the bug** *Her brother started taking judo, and Marisa caught the bug.* | **the travel/acting etc. bug** *He got the rodeo bug at age 6.* **5** a small piece of electronic equipment for listening secretly to other people's conversations.

bug² S2 *v.* **bugged, bugging** [T] **1** INFORMAL to annoy someone: ***It really bugs*** *me when the car behind me drives too close.* **2** to put a BUG somewhere secretly in order to listen to conversations: *The FBI had bugged his apartment.*

bug off *phr. v.* INFORMAL used to tell someone to go away and stop annoying you

bug·a·boo /ˈbʌgəˌbu/ *n.* [C] INFORMAL something that makes people feel worried or afraid

bug·bear /ˈbʌgbɛr/ *n.* [C] a bugaboo

bug·eyed /ˈbʌgaɪd/ *adj.* having eyes that stick out

bug·ger /ˈbʌgɚ/ *n.* [C] SPOKEN a person or thing, especially one that is annoying

bug·gy /ˈbʌgi/ *n. plural* **buggies** [C] **1** a light carriage pulled by a horse **2** a thing like a small bed on wheels, that a baby lies in to be pushed around outside SYN baby carriage

bu·gle /ˈbyugəl/ *n.* [C] a musical instrument like a TRUMPET which is used in the army to call soldiers SYN horn [**Origin:** 1300–1400 *bugle horn* **instrument made from buffalo horn, bugle** (13–16 centuries), from *bugle* **buffalo**] —**bugler** *n.* [C]

build¹ /bɪld/ S1 W1 *v. past tense and past participle* **built** /bɪlt/

1 MAKE STH [I,T] to make something, especially a building or something large SYN construct: *Airport planners want to build another runway.* | *A small bird had built a nest in the tree.* | *We're planning to build near the lake.* | **build sb sth** *We'd like to build Katie a playhouse.*

THESAURUS

construct to build something large such as a building, bridge, etc: *There are plans to construct a new library.*
put up to build something such as a wall, fence, or building, or to put a statue somewhere: *The neighbors are putting up a new fence.*
erect FORMAL to build something: *plans to erect a memorial at the site of the World Trade Center*
assemble to put all the parts of something such as a machine or a piece of furniture together: *The bicycle is easy to assemble.*

2 MAKE STH DEVELOP [T] to make something develop or form SYN establish: *She built a successful career as a writer.* | *In six years, he has built a business that spans the globe.* | **build sth on sth** *His reputation was built on that one case.*
3 FEELING [I,T] also **build up** if a feeling builds, or if you build it, it increases gradually over a period of time SYN develop: *Tension is building between the two countries.* | *Success at the tasks builds self-esteem.*
4 be built of sth to be made using particular materials: *Many of the houses are built of brick.*
5 build bridges to try to establish a better relationship between people who do not like each other: *The group has been trying to build bridges between Cuba and the U.S.*
[**Origin:** Old English *byldan*] → see also -BUILT, BUILT-IN

build sth **around** sth *phr. v.* to base something on an idea or thing and develop it from there: *a meal built around healthy ingredients*

build sth ↔ **in** *phr. v.* to make something so that it is a permanent part of a wall, room etc.

build sth **into** sth *phr. v.* **1** to make something so that it is a permanent part of a wall, room etc.: *A secret cupboard was built into the wall.* **2** to make something a permanent part of a system, agreement etc.: *A strict completion date was built into the contract.*

build on *phr. v.* **1 build on sth** to use your achievements as a base for further development: *The project will build on successful anti-crime programs.* **2 build sth on sth** to base something on an idea or thing: *a relationship built on trust* **3 build sth ↔ on** to add another room to a building in order to have more space

build up *phr. v.*
1 INCREASE GRADUALLY build sth ↔ up if a substance, force, or activity builds up somewhere, or if you build it up, it gradually becomes bigger and stronger: *Both sides have built up huge stockpiles of arms.* | *Pressure was building up inside the engine..* → see also BUILD-UP
2 DEVELOP build sth ↔ up to make something develop or form: **+into** *He built up the family firm into a multinational company.*
3 FEELING build sth ↔ up if a feeling builds up, or if you build it up, it increases gradually over a period of time: *You have to build up the customers' trust.*
4 build up sb's hopes to unfairly encourage someone to think that they will get what they hope for
5 MAKE STRONGER build sb/sth ↔ up to make someone or something well and strong: *These exercises help build up strength in your legs.*
6 PRAISE build sb/sth ↔ up to praise someone or something so that other people think they are really good, even if they are not: *The media has built him up as the next world champion.*

build up to sth *phr. v.* to prepare for a particular moment or event: *I could tell my sister was building up to telling me something.*

build² *n.* [singular, U] the shape and size of someone's body: **slight/stocky/medium etc. build** *a small man with an athletic build* ▸see THESAURUS box at body

build·er /ˈbɪldɚ/ *n.* [C] **1** a person or a company that builds or repairs buildings or other things **2 consensus/coalition/bridge etc. builder** someone who tries to get people to understand or agree with each other

build·ing /ˈbɪldɪŋ/ S1 W3 *n.* **1** [C] a structure such as a house, church, or factory, that has a roof and walls: *The Sears Tower is one of the tallest buildings in the world.* | *an apartment building* **2** [U] the process or business of building things SYN construction: *the building of the State Capitol* | *building costs*

ˈbuilding block *n.* **1 building blocks** [plural] the pieces or parts which together make it possible for something big or important to exist: *Amino acids are the fundamental building blocks of protein.* **2** [C] a BLOCK

ˈbuilding code *n.* [C] an official rule giving the standards that must be followed in the structure and safety of new buildings or new parts within a building

ˈbuilding ˌcontractor *n.* [C] someone whose job is to organize the building of a house, office, factory etc.

ˈbuilding ˌsite *n.* [C] a place where a house, building etc. is being built

ˈbuild-up *n.* **1** [singular, U] an increase over a period of time: **+of** *a dangerous build-up of chemicals in the water* **2** [C] a description of someone or something in which you say they are very special or important, often when they are not: *The movie got a **big build-up** in the press.* → see also **build up** at BUILD[1]

built /bɪlt/ the past tense and past participle of BUILD

-built /bɪlt/ *suffix* [in adjectives] used for describing how large someone is, what something is made of, how it was built, or who built it: *a heavily-built man* | *a well-built house* | *a Soviet-built tank*

ˌbuilt-ˈin *adj.* forming a part of something that cannot be separated from it: *The camera has a built-in flash.*

ˌbuilt-ˈup *adj.* a built-up area has a lot of buildings and not many open spaces

Bu·jum·bu·ra /ˌbudʒəmˈbʊrə/ the capital and largest city of Burundi

bulb /bʌlb/ S3 *n.* [C] **1** the glass-covered part of an electric light, that the light shines from SYN **light bulb**: *a 100 watt bulb* **2** BIOLOGY a root shaped like a ball that grows into a flower or plant: *tulip bulbs* [**Origin:** 1500–1600 Latin *bulbus*, from Greek *bolbos* **plant with a bulb**]

bul·bous /ˈbʌlbəs/ *adj.* fat, round, and unattractive: *a bulbous nose*

Bul·finch /ˈbʊlfɪntʃ/, **Thomas** (1796–1867) a U.S. writer famous for his retelling of European MYTHS

Bul·gar·i·a /bəlˈgæriə, -ˈgɛr-/ a country in southeast Europe next to the Black Sea —**Bulgarian** *n., adj.*

bulge[1] /bʌldʒ/ *n.* [C] **1** a curved mass on the surface of something, usually caused by something under or inside it: *The gun made a bulge under his jacket.* **2** a sudden temporary increase in the amount or level of something: *a bulge in the birthrate* —**bulgy** *adj.* → see also **battle of the bulge** at BATTLE[1] (8)

bulge[2] *v.* [I] **1** also **bulge out** to stick out in a rounded shape, especially because something is very full or too tight: *a snake with bulging eyes* | +**with** *His pockets bulged with candy.* **2** INFORMAL +**with** to be very full of people or things

bul·gur /ˈbʌlgɚ/ *n.* [U] a type of wheat which has been dried and broken into pieces

bu·li·mi·a /bəˈlimiə, bu-/ *n.* [U] MEDICINE a mental illness in which a person cannot stop themselves from eating too much, and then VOMITS in order to control their weight [**Origin:** 1800–1900 Modern Latin, Greek *boulimia* **great hunger**, from *bous* **ox, cow** + *limos* **hunger**] —**bulimic** *adj.* —**bulimic** *n.* [C]

bulk[1] /bʌlk/ Ac *n.* **1 the bulk (of sth)** the main or largest part of something SYN **majority**: *The bulk of the book is about his experiences in Vietnam.* **2 in bulk** if you buy goods in bulk, you buy a large amount of something at one time **3** [U] the size of something or someone: *Let the dough rise until it is double in bulk.* **4** [U] the large size or shape of something: *For its bulk, the whale is a graceful swimmer.* [**Origin:** 1400–1500 Old Norse *bulki* **goods carried on a ship**]

bulk[2] Ac *adj.* **1** [only before noun] bulk goods are sold or moved in large quantities: *bulk coffee sold to restaurants* **2 bulk mail/rate** the sending of large amounts of mail for a smaller cost than usual **3 bulk buying** the buying of goods in large quantities at one time

bulk[3] Ac *v.* [I] to swell or increase in size

bulk up *phr. v.* INFORMAL **1 bulk yourself up** to deliberately gain weight or develop bigger muscles **2 bulk sth ↔ up** to make something look bigger, better, or more important by adding something: *Bulk up the sandwich by adding lettuce and tomatoes.*

bulk·head /ˈbʌlkhɛd/ *n.* [C] a wall which divides the structure of a ship or aircraft into separate parts

bulk·y /ˈbʌlki/ Ac *adj. comparative* **bulkier**, *superlative* **bulkiest** **1** something that is bulky is bigger than other things of its type and is difficult to carry: *a bulky package* **2** someone who is bulky is big and heavy —**bulkiness** *n.* [U]

bull /bʊl/ W3 *n.* [C]
1 ANIMAL a) BIOLOGY an adult male animal of the cattle family **b)** the male of some other large animals such as the ELEPHANT or WHALE
2 STH YOU SAY [U] SPOKEN INFORMAL something someone says that is completely untrue: *That's **a bunch of bull** – he wasn't even there.*
3 take the bull by the horns to bravely or confidently deal with a difficult or dangerous problem: *We decided to take the bull by the horns and go to court.*
4 BUSINESS ECONOMICS someone who buys SHARES because they expect prices to rise → see also BEAR
5 be like a bull in a china shop a) to behave in a way that is not sensitive to people's feelings or that shows you do not understand the rules or traditions in a situation **b)** to keep knocking things over, dropping things, breaking things etc. → see also PAPAL BULL, PIT BULL, **shoot the bull/breeze** at SHOOT[1] (15)

bull·dog /ˈbʊldɔg/ *n.* [C] a powerful dog with a large head, a short neck, and short thick legs

bull·doze /ˈbʊldouz/ *v.* [T] **1** to destroy buildings, structures etc. with a bulldozer **2** to push objects such as earth and rocks out of the way with a bulldozer **3** to force something to happen, or force someone to do something that they do not really want to do: *Congress is refusing to be bulldozed by the White House on the issue.*

bull·doz·er /ˈbʊlˌdouzɚ/ *n.* [C] a powerful vehicle with a broad metal blade, used for moving earth and rocks, destroying buildings etc.

bul·let /ˈbʊlɪt/ S3 W3 *n.* [C] **1** a small piece of metal that you fire from a gun: *He was killed by a single bullet.* | *She suffered a **bullet wound** in her leg.* | *There were **bullet holes** in the wall.* **2** also **bullet point** a small circle or square printed before each different piece of information in a list [**Origin:** 1500–1600 French *boulette* **small ball** and *boulet* **bullet**, from *boule* **ball**] → see also **bite the bullet** at BITE[1] (3), PLASTIC BULLET, RUBBER BULLET, SHELL, SHOT[1] (9)

bul·le·tin /ˈbʊlətˀn, ˈbʊlətɪn/ *n.* [C] **1** a letter or printed statement that a group or organization produces to tell people its news: *the church bulletin* **2** a short news report on television or radio **3** an official statement that is made to inform people about something important: *a police bulletin describing the suspect* [**Origin:** 1700–1800 French, Italian *bullettino*, from *bulla* **official announcement by the pope**]

ˈbulletin ˌboard *n.* [C] **1** a board on the wall that you put information or pictures on **2** also **electronic bulletin board** COMPUTERS a place in a computer information system where you can read or leave messages

bul·let·proof /ˈbʊlɪtˀˌpruf/ *adj.* designed to stop bullets from going through it: *a bulletproof vest*

ˈbullet train *n.* [C] a train that can go very fast, especially a train used in Japan

bull·fight /ˈbʊlfaɪt/ *n.* [C] a type of entertainment popular in Spain, in which a man fights and kills a BULL —**bullfighter** *n.* [C] —**bullfighting** *n.* [U]

bull·frog /ˈbʊlfrɑg/ *n.* [C] a type of large FROG that makes a loud noise

ˌbull-ˈheaded *adj.* unwilling to change your opinion or a decision, even when people think you are being unreasonable or stupid —**bullheadedly** *adv.* —**bullheadedness** *n.* [U]

bull·horn /ˈbʊlhɔrn/ *n.* [C] a piece of equipment that you hold up to your mouth to make your voice louder SYN **megaphone**

bul·lion /ˈbʊlyən/ *n.* [U] bars of gold or silver

bull·ish /ˈbʊlɪʃ/ *adj.* **1** [not before noun] feeling confident about the future: *We're very bullish about the company's prospects.* **2** ECONOMICS if a business market is bullish, the prices of STOCKS are rising or seem likely to rise —**bullishly** *adv.* —**bullishness** *n.* [U]

ˈbull ˌmarket *n.* [C] ECONOMICS a STOCK MARKET in which the price of STOCKS is going up and people are buying them, and prices are expected to continue rising

ˌBull ˈMoose ˌParty, the HISTORY an informal name for Theodore Roosevelt's Progressive Party

B

bull·necked /ˌbʊlˈnɛkt◂/ *adj.* having a short and very thick neck

bul·lock /ˈbʊlək/ *n.* [C] a young male cow, especially one that has had its sex organs removed

bull·pen /ˈbʊlpɛn/ *n.* [C usually singular] **1** the area on a baseball field in which PITCHERS practice throwing **2** the PITCHERS on a BASEBALL team, especially those who only play at the end of the game, when the starting pitcher becomes tired

bull·ring /ˈbʊlrɪŋ/ *n.* [C] the place where a BULLFIGHT is held

ˈBull ˌRun a place in the U.S. state of Virginia where there were two important battles in the American Civil War which the Union forces lost to Confederate forces

ˈbull ˌsession *n.* [C] INFORMAL an occasion when a group of people talk in a relaxed and friendly way

ˈbull's-eye *n.* [C] the center of a TARGET that you try to hit when shooting or in games like DARTS

ˌbull ˈterrier *n.* [C] a strong short-haired dog → see also PIT BULL

bull·whip /ˈbʊlwɪp/ *n.* [C] a large thick leather WHIP

bul·ly¹ /ˈbʊli/ *n. plural* **bullies** [C] someone who uses their strength or power to frighten or hurt someone who is weaker: *the school bully*

bully² *v.* **bullies, bullied, bullying** [T] to threaten to hurt someone or frighten them, especially someone smaller or weaker: *He used to bully the younger kids.* —**bullying** *n.* [U]

bul·rush /ˈbʊlrʌʃ/ *n.* [C] a tall plant that looks like grass and grows by water

bul·wark /ˈbʊlwɚk/ *n.* [C] **1** something that protects you from a bad situation: +**against** *Some people keep gold as a bulwark against financial disasters.* **2 bulwarks** [plural] the sides of a boat or ship above the DECK **3** a strong structure like a wall, built for defense

bum¹ /bʌm/ *n.* [C] INFORMAL **1** someone, especially a man, who is lazy: *Get out of bed, you **lazy bum**!* **2** OLD-FASHIONED someone, especially a man, who has no home or job, and who asks people for money SYN **homeless person** **3 a beach/ski etc. bum** someone who spends all their time on the beach, SKIING etc. **4 give sb the bum's rush** INFORMAL to make someone leave a place, especially a public place, quickly: *The protesters were given the bum's rush by the police.*

bum² *v.* **bummed, bumming** [T] SPOKEN to ask someone for something such as money, food, or cigarettes, without paying for them: *I bummed a ride from Sue.* | **bum sth from sb** *He bums money and cigarettes from all his friends.*

bum around sth *phr. v.* INFORMAL to travel around without any real plan, living very cheaply: *I spent some time bumming around Europe.*

bum sb **out** *phr. v.* SPOKEN to make someone feel sad or disappointed about something: *I don't want to bum you out, but we can't afford to go on vacation.* → see also BUMMED

bum³ *adj.* [only before noun, no comparative] **1 a bum ankle/leg/shoulder etc.** an ANKLE, leg etc. that is injured so that you cannot use it much **2** INFORMAL bad, useless, or unfair: *He **got a bum deal*** (=was treated unfairly) *when they changed his contract.* | *Someone **gave you a bum steer*** (=gave you bad advice). | *The downtown area has gotten **a bum rap*** (=been described unfairly) *in the press.*

bum·ble /ˈbʌmbəl/ *v.* [I always + adv./prep.] **1** to make a lot of mistakes when you do or say something: *Officials bumbled through their explanations of why the hospital had been bombed.* **2** to accidentally fall against things or knock things over when you walk —**bumbler** *n.* [C]

bum·ble·bee /ˈbʌmbəlˌbi/ *n.* [C] a large hairy BEE

bum·bling /ˈbʌmblɪŋ/ *adj.* [only before noun] making or tending to make a lot of mistakes, especially in a way that is slightly funny: *his bumbling attempts to organize the children*

bummed /bʌmd/ also **ˌbummed ˈout** *adj.* SPOKEN feeling sad or disappointed

bum·mer /ˈbʌmɚ/ *n.* [singular] SPOKEN a situation that is disappointing: *You can't go? **What a bummer!***

bump¹ /bʌmp/ S3 *v.* **1** [I always + adv./prep.,T] to hit or knock against something: +**against/into etc.** *We bumped into each other in the hallway.* | **bump sth on/against etc.** *I bumped my head coming down the stairs.* ►see THESAURUS box at **hit¹** **2** [T always + adv./prep.] INFORMAL to make someone change their place, position, rank etc.: **bump sb up/out of/from etc.** *The airline bumped me up to first class!* | *Tanner was bumped out of the number one spot in the semifinals.* **3** [I always + adv./prep.] to move up and down as you move forward in a vehicle, on a bicycle etc.: +**along/across etc.** *We bumped along in the old bus.* **4 bump and grind** INFORMAL to move your HIPS forward and back and around while dancing **5 bump heads (with sb)** INFORMAL to argue or compete with someone: *The movie's director and producer bumped heads about where to film.* [**Origin:** 1500–1600 From the sound]

bump into sb *phr. v.* to meet someone that you know when you were not expecting to SYN **run into**: *I bumped into Leo at the fair.*

bump sb **off** *phr. v.* INFORMAL to murder someone

bump sth **up** *phr. v.* INFORMAL to suddenly increase something by a large amount: *In the summer, they bump up the prices.*

bump² *n.* [C] **1** an area of skin that is raised up because you have hit it on something: *Pam got a lot of **bumps and bruises**, but she's okay.* ►see THESAURUS box at **injury** **2** a small raised area on a surface: *a bump in the road* **3** an occasion when something hits something else: *I was backing up when I felt a bump.* **4** the sound of something hitting a hard surface: *We heard a bump in the next room.* → see also GOOSEBUMPS, SPEED BUMP

bump·er¹ /ˈbʌmpɚ/ *n.* [C] the plastic or metal part on the front and back of a car, truck etc. that protects it if it hits anything

bumper² *adj.* **a bumper crop (of sth) a)** an unusually large amount of a grain, vegetable, etc. produced in a particular year **b)** INFORMAL an unusually large number of something: *a bumper crop of congressional candidates*

ˈbumper car *n.* [C] a small electric car that you drive in a special area at a FAIR and deliberately try to hit other cars with

ˈbumper ˌsticker *n.* [C] a small sign on the bumper of a car, with a humorous, political, or religious message

ˌbumper-to-ˈbumper *adj., adv.* with a lot of cars that are very close together and moving very slowly: *bumper-to-bumper traffic*

bump·kin /ˈbʌmpkɪn/ *n.* [C] INFORMAL someone from an area outside a city or town who is considered to be stupid: *My cousin in New York treats us like a bunch of **country bumpkins**.*

bump·tious /ˈbʌmpʃəs/ *adj.* too proud of your abilities in a way that annoys other people —**bumptiously** *adv.* —**bumptiousness** *n.* [U]

bump·y /ˈbʌmpi/ *adj. comparative* **bumpier**, *superlative* **bumpiest** **1** a bumpy surface is flat but has a lot of raised parts so it is difficult to walk or drive on it OPP **smooth**: *bumpy dirt roads* **2** a bumpy trip by car or airplane is uncomfortable because of bad road or weather conditions **3** having a lot of problems for a long time: *Teenage years are **a bumpy road*** (=a time when they have a lot of problems).

bun /bʌn/ *n.* [C] **1** a small round type of bread: *a hamburger bun* **2** a hairstyle in which a woman with long hair fastens it in a small round shape at the back of her head → see picture at HAIRSTYLE **3 buns** [plural] INFORMAL the part of your body that you sit on; BUTTOCKS

bunch¹ /bʌntʃ/ S1 *n.* [C] **1** [usually singular] a large number of similar things, or a large amount of something: *There are **a whole bunch of** good restaurants in the Square.* | *I lent him **a bunch of** money.* | *This wine is **the best of the bunch**.* **2** [usually singular] a group of people: ***a bunch of** kids hanging out at the beach* | *Reporters are generally a cynical bunch.* ►see THESAURUS box at **group**[1] **3** a group of similar things that are fastened or held together: ***a bunch of** bananas* | *The roses are $10 a bunch.* ►see THESAURUS box at **group**[1] → see also **thanks a bunch** at THANKS[1] (2)

bunch[2] also **bunch together/up** *v.* [I,T] **1** to stay close together in a group, or to move people or things together in a group: *The animals bunched up around the water hole.* **2** to pull material together tightly in folds: *The shorts were bunched at the waist.*

Bunche /bʌntʃ/, **Ralph** /rælf/ (1904–1971) a U.S. DIPLOMAT who was involved in starting the U.N. and was the first African-American person to win the Nobel Peace Prize

bun•co, bunko /ˈbʌŋkoʊ/ *n.* [U] INFORMAL dishonest ways of tricking someone into giving you or paying you money SYN **fraud**

bun•dle[1] /ˈbʌndl/ *n.* **1** [C] a group of things such as papers, clothes, or sticks that are fastened or tied together: *Stack the magazines in bundles.* | **+of** *a bundle of old letters* ►see THESAURUS box at **group**[1] **2** [C] computer SOFTWARE and sometimes other services or equipment that are included with a new computer at no additional cost **3 a bundle** [singular] a lot of money: *Hiring a chef will cost a bundle.* | *He **made a bundle** on the stock market.* **4** [C] a number of things that belong together or are dealt with together: *the best of a bundle of tax cuts* **5 not be a bundle of laughs/fun** used to emphasize that something is not enjoyable: *Working there wasn't a bundle of laughs.* **6 be a bundle of nerves** to be very nervous

bundle[2] *v.* **1** [T] to include computer SOFTWARE or other services with a new computer at no additional cost: *The computer **comes bundled with** all the basic software.* **2** [T always + adv/prep] to quickly push someone or something somewhere because you are in a hurry or you want to hide them: **bundle sb/sth into/out of etc.** *They bundled him into the car.* **3** [I always + adv/prep] to move somewhere quickly in a group: **bundle into/out of etc.** *We all bundled into a taxi.*

bundle sb **off** *phr. v.* to send someone somewhere quickly without asking them if they want to go: *Amy was bundled off to her grandmother's house.*

bundle sth ↔ **together** *phr. v.* **1** to put different things together so that they are dealt with at the same time: *The lawsuit bundles together several different claims.* **2** to put things together, especially computer software or equipment, so that they can be sold together: *Any three packages may be bundled together for $295.*

bundle up *phr. v.* **1 bundle sth ↔ up** to make a bundle by tying things together: *Can you bundle up the newspapers for recycling?* **2 bundle sb up** to put warm clothes on someone or yourself because it is cold: *Make sure to bundle up!* | **be bundled up in sth** *She was bundled up in a bright red sweater and scarf.*

Bundt cake /ˈbʌnt keɪk/ *n.* [C] TRADEMARK a type of heavy cake baked in a round pan with a hole in the middle

bung /bʌŋ/ *n.* [C] a round piece of rubber, wood etc. used to close the top of a container such as a BARREL [**Origin:** 1400–1500 Middle Dutch *bonghe*]

bun•ga•low /ˈbʌŋgəˌloʊ/ *n.* [C] a small house, usually with only one STORY (=level) [**Origin:** 1600–1700 Hindi *bangla* **(house) in the Bengal style**]

bung•ee cord /ˈbʌndʒi ˌkɔrd/ also **bungee** *n.* [C] **1** a short rope that stretches and has hooks on the ends, used to fasten things together **2** a rope that stretches, used in bungee jumping

bungee jum•ping /ˈbʌndʒi ˌdʒʌmpɪŋ/ *n.* [U] a sport in which you jump off something very high with a rope that stretches tied to your legs, so that you go up again without touching the ground —**bungee jump** *n.* [C] —**bungee jump** *v.* [I] —**bungee jumper** *n.* [C]

bun•gle /ˈbʌŋgəl/ *v.* [T] to be unsuccessful because you have made stupid mistakes: *Officers have bungled a number of recent criminal cases.* —**bungle** *n.* [C] —**bungler** *n.* [C] —**bungling** *n.* [U] —**bungled** *adj.*: *a bungled rescue attempt*

bun•gling /ˈbʌŋglɪŋ/ *adj.* [only before noun] unsuccessful as a result of making stupid mistakes: *a movie about three bungling thieves*

bun•ion /ˈbʌnyən/ *n.* [C] a painful red sore area on the first joint of your big toe

bunk[1] /bʌŋk/ *n.* **1** [C] one of two beds that are attached together, one on top of the other SYN **bunk bed**: *My brother sleeps in the top bunk.* **2** [C] a narrow bed that is fastened to the wall, for example on a train or ship **3** [U] also **bunkum** INFORMAL something someone says that is completely untrue

bunk[2] *v.* [I] INFORMAL to sleep somewhere, especially in someone else's house: *I bunked with friends in Washington.*

ˈbunk bed *n.* [C usually plural] one of two beds that are attached together, one on top of the other

bun•ker /ˈbʌŋkɚ/ *n.* [C] **1** a strongly built shelter for soldiers, usually under the ground **2** a place where you store coal, especially on a ship or outside a house

ˈbunker ˌbuster *n.* [C] INFORMAL a bomb that goes deep into the ground before it explodes, and which is used to destroy bunkers

bunk•house /ˈbʌŋkhaʊs/ *n.* [C] a building where workers sleep

bun•kum, buncombe /ˈbʌŋkəm/ *n.* [U] INFORMAL something someone says that is completely untrue SYN **bunk** [**Origin:** 1800–1900 *Buncombe* county in North Carolina, whose congressman in 1820 made a long pointless speech to impress the voters there]

bun•ny /ˈbʌni/ also **ˈbunny ˌrabbit** *n. plural* **bunnies** [C] a word for a rabbit, used especially by or to children → see also BEACH BUNNY, SNOW BUNNY

ˈbunny ˌslope *n.* [C] the area of a mountain where people learn to SKI

bunraku

bun•ra•ku /bʌnˈrɑku/ *n.* [U] traditional Japanese PUPPET theater in which plays are performed using large models of people or animals that are moved by pulling wires

bun•sen burn•er /ˈbʌnsən ˌbɚnɚ/ *n.* [C] a piece of equipment that produces a hot gas flame, for scientific EXPERIMENTS → see picture at LABORATORY

bunt /bʌnt/ *v.* [I] to deliberately hit the ball toward the ground in BASEBALL by holding the BAT a special way —**bunt** *n.* [C]

bunt•ing /ˈbʌntɪŋ/ *n.* [U] small paper or cloth flags on strings, used to decorate buildings and streets on special occasions

Bun•yan /ˈbʌnyən/, **John** (1628–1688) an English religious writer and PREACHER who wrote "The Pilgrim's Progress"

Bunyan, Paul in old American stories, a GIANT who changed the shape of the land as he traveled with his blue OX, Babe

bu•oy[1] /ˈbui, bɔɪ/ *n. plural* **buoys** [C] an object that floats on the ocean, a lake etc. to mark a safe or dangerous area

B

buoy² also **buoy up** *v.* [T] **1** to make someone feel happier or more confident: *Republicans were buoyed by election results.* **2** ECONOMICS to keep profits, prices etc. at a high level: *Easier credit would help buoy economic growth.* **3** to keep something floating [**Origin:** 1500–1600 Spanish *boyar* **to float**, from Latin *boia* **chain**]

buoy·an·cy /ˈbɔɪənsi/ *n.* [U] **1** PHYSICS the ability of an object to float: *the buoyancy of light wood* **2** PHYSICS the power of a liquid to make an object float: *Salt water has more buoyancy than fresh water.* **3** a feeling of happiness and a belief that you can deal with problems easily **4** ECONOMICS the ability of prices, a business etc. to quickly get back to a high level after a difficult period

buoy·ant /ˈbɔɪənt/ *adj.* **1** ECONOMICS buoyant prices, companies etc. tend to remain high or successful: *a buoyant economy* **2** able to float or keep things floating: *Cork is a very buoyant material.* **3** cheerful and confident: *her buoyant mood* —**buoyantly** *adv.*

bur /bɚ/ *n.* [C] another spelling of BURR

bur·ble /ˈbɚbəl/ *v.* **1** [I] to make a sound like a stream flowing over stones SYN **babble** **2** [I,T] to talk about something in a confused way that is difficult to understand SYN **babble** —**burble** *n.* [C]

burbs /bɚbz/ *n.* **the burbs** INFORMAL the SUBURBS (=areas around a city where people live)

bur·den¹ /ˈbɚdn/ W3 *n.* [C] **1** a situation or task that you are responsible for, which is very difficult or worrying: *Running the business alone has been a huge burden.* | *We need to reduce* ***the tax burden*** *of middle-income Americans.* | *I don't want to* ***be a burden on*** *my children when I'm old* (=don't want my children to have the responsibility of caring for me). | **carry/bear the burden** *Women still bear the main burden of childcare.* | **assume/shoulder a burden** *Why should the taxpayer shoulder the burden of this program?* | **ease/lighten/relieve the burden** *The new system will ease the burden on busy teachers.* **2** responsibility for paying a large amount of money: +**of** *countries struggling with a burden of debt* | **tax/debt/financial etc. burden** *ways of relieving the tax burden on new companies* **3 the burden of proof** LAW the duty to prove that something is true **4** [C] FORMAL something that is carried SYN **load** [**Origin:** Old English *byrthen*] → see also BEAST OF BURDEN

burden² *v.* **1** [T] to give someone a lot of problems or responsibility: **burden sb with sth** *I didn't want to burden her with my worries.* | **be burdened by/with sth** *The company is burdened by debt.* → see also UNBURDEN **2 be burdened with sth** to be carrying something heavy: *The man, burdened with grocery bags, had trouble walking up the steps.*

bur·den·some /ˈbɚdnsəm/ *adj.* causing problems or additional work: *burdensome responsibilities*

bu·reau /ˈbyʊroʊ/ W2 *n. plural* **bureaus** [C] **1** POLITICS a government department or a part of a government department: *the Federal Bureau of Investigation* **2** an office or organization that collects or provides information: *the visitor's information bureau* **3** an office of a company or organization that has its main office somewhere else: *the London bureau of the New York Times* **4** a piece of furniture with drawers, used for storing clothes SYN **dresser** [**Origin:** 1600–1700 French **desk, cloth covering for desks**, from Old French *burel* **woolen cloth**]

bu·reauc·ra·cy /byʊˈrɑkrəsi/ *n. plural* **bureaucracies** **1** [U] a complicated official system which is annoying or confusing because it has too many rules, processes etc. → see also RED TAPE: *There's too much bureaucracy in government departments.* **2 a)** [C] POLITICS a government organization that is divided into departments and operated by a large number of officials who are not elected: *a huge bureaucracy like the Department of Defense* **b)** [C] POLITICS a system in which the work of a government is done by departments operated by officials who are not elected **c)** [singular] POLITICS the officials who are employed rather than elected to do the work of a government, business etc.

bu·reau·crat /ˈbyʊrəˌkræt/ *n.* [C] someone who works in a bureaucracy and uses official rules very strictly

bu·reau·crat·ic /ˌbyʊrəˈkræt̬ɪk/ *adj.* involving a lot of complicated official rules and processes —**bureaucratically** /-kli/ *adv.*

ˌBureau of ˌAlcohol, Toˌbacco and ˈFirearms, the a U.S. government organization that is concerned with the rules about the sale and use of alcohol, tobacco, guns, and explosives

ˌBureau of ˌIndian Afˈfairs, the ABBREVIATION **BIA** *n.* a U.S. government organization which is concerned with the WELFARE and education of Native Americans and with other legal matters concerning RESERVATIONS

burg /bɚg/ *n.* [C] INFORMAL a small town

bur·geon /ˈbɚdʒən/ *v.* [I] FORMAL to grow or develop quickly

bur·geon·ing /ˈbɚdʒənɪŋ/ *adj.* [no comparative] increasing or developing very quickly: *Denver's burgeoning population*

burg·er /ˈbɚgɚ/ S3 *n.* [C] **1** GROUND BEEF in the shape of a circle, which is cooked and usually eaten with a BUN SYN **hamburger** **2** another meat or food that is cooked in a flat round shape, usually eaten with a BUN: *a veggie burger* [**Origin:** 1900–2000 *hamburger*] → see also **flip burgers** at FLIP¹ (3)

Bur·ger /ˈbɚgɚ/, **War·ren Earl** /ˈwɔrən ɚl/ (1907–1995) a CHIEF JUSTICE on the U.S. Supreme Court

bur·gess /ˈbɚdʒɪs/ *n.* [C] HISTORY a member of the government of Virginia or Maryland when the U.S. was under British rule

burgh·er /ˈbɚgɚ/ *n.* [C] OLD USE someone who lives in a particular town, especially someone who is rich

bur·glar /ˈbɚglɚ/ *n.* [C] someone who goes into houses to steal things → see also ROBBER [**Origin:** 1500–1600 Anglo-French *burgler*, from Medieval Latin *burgare* **to burgle**, from Latin *burgus* **defended place**] → see also CAT BURGLAR

ˈburglar aˌlarm *n.* [C] a piece of equipment that makes a loud noise when someone tries to get into a building or vehicle illegally SYN **thief**

bur·glar·ize /ˈbɚgləˌraɪz/ *v.* [T] to go into a building and steal things ▶see THESAURUS box at **steal¹**

bur·gla·ry /ˈbɚgləri/ *n. plural* **burglaries** [C,U] the crime of getting into a building to steal things: *Burglaries in the area have risen by 5%.*

bur·gun·dy /ˈbɚgəndi/ *n. plural* **burgundies** **1** [U] a dark red color **2** [C,U] also **Burgundy** red or white wine from the Burgundy area of France

bur·i·al /ˈbɛriəl/ *n.* [C,U] the act or ceremony of putting a dead body into a grave: *a private burial* | *a Native American burial site*

Bur·ki·na /bɚˈkinə/ a country in west Africa, to the north of Ghana —**Burkinese** /ˌbɚkɪˈniz◂/ *n., adj.*

bur·lap /ˈbɚlæp/ *n.* [U] a type of thick rough cloth

bur·lesque¹ /bɚˈlɛsk/ *n.* [C,U] ENG. LANG. ARTS **1** speech, acting, or writing in which a serious subject is made to seem silly or an unimportant subject is treated in a serious way **2** a performance involving a mixture of humor and STRIPTEASE, popular in America in the past [**Origin:** 1600–1700 French, Italian *burlesco*, from *burla* **joke**]

burlesque² *v.* [T] to make a serious subject seem silly to amuse people

bur·ly /ˈbɚli/ *adj.* a burly man is big and strong [**Origin:** 1300–1400 *burly* **noble, impressive** (13–17 centuries)] —**burliness** *n.* [U]

Bur·ma /ˈbɚmə/ the former name of Myanmar, a country in east Asia

Bur·mese¹ /ˌbɚˈmiz◂/ *n.* **1** [C] someone who is from Myanmar **2** [U] one of the main languages spoken in Myanmar

Burmese² *adj.* coming from or relating to Myanmar

burn[1] /bɚn/ S1 W2 *v.* *past tense and past participle* **burned** or **burnt** /bɚnt/

1 PRODUCE HEAT [I] to produce heat and flames: *The fire in the hills has been burning for a week.*

THESAURUS

be on fire/be alight also **be ablaze** ESPECIALLY WRITTEN to be burning
blaze to burn very brightly and strongly
smolder to burn slowly without a flame
catch fire to start burning
burst into flames to suddenly start to burn very strongly
light to make something such as a fire, cigarette, or candle start burning
set fire to something/set something on fire to make something start burning and being destroyed
ignite FORMAL to start burning, or to make something start burning
put something out also **extinguish** FORMAL to make something such as a fire, cigarette, or candle stop burning

2 DESTROY WITH FIRE [I,T] to be destroyed by fire, or to destroy something with fire: *I burned all his letters.* | *Over 35 houses* ***burned to the ground*** (=were completely burned) *in the wildfires.*
3 INJURE/KILL WITH HEAT [T] to hurt yourself or someone else with fire or something hot: *Marcus burned his hand on the stove.* | **be burned to death/be burned alive** (=to be killed in a fire)
4 FOOD [I,T] to spoil food by cooking until it is black and does not taste good, or to become spoiled in this way: *Oh no, I burned the toast!* | *The roast had* ***burned to a crisp.***
5 DAMAGE BY SUN [I,T] if the sun burns your skin, or if your skin burns, it becomes red and painful from the heat of the sun: *I burn easily* (=my skin burns easily in the sun). | *It looks like you* ***got burned*** *on the back of your neck.*
6 FAT/ENERGY [T] if you burn fat or calories, you use up energy stored in your body by being physically active: *exercises that help your body burn fat*
7 POWER/LIGHT/ENERGY ETC. [I,T] if you burn a FUEL, or if it burns, it is used to produce power, heat, light etc.: *The engine only burns diesel fuel.* | *Coal burns longer than wood.*
8 CD/DVD [T] if you burn a CD or DVD, you record music, images, or other information onto it
9 CHEMICALS [I,T] to damage or destroy something by a chemical action: *The acid burned through the metal.*
10 SHINE [I] if a light or lamp burns, it shines or produces light: *Christmas lights burned brightly all around town.*
11 be/get burned INFORMAL **a)** to be emotionally hurt by someone or something: *I like her, but I'm afraid of getting burned again.* **b)** to lose a lot of money, especially in a business deal: *A lot of people got burned buying junk bonds.*
12 FEEL HOT [I,T] to feel too hot and uncomfortable, or to make part of your body feel like this SYN **sting**: *My eyes were burning from the smoke.* | *Cheap liquor burns your throat.*
13 burn your bridges INFORMAL to do something that ends a situation, makes someone angry, etc. so that you cannot bring back the situation or relationship even if you want to: *Don't burn your bridges; you might want to work for them again.*
14 burn the candle at both ends INFORMAL to be very busy both at work and in your social life, so that you do not get much rest
15 burn the midnight oil INFORMAL to work or study until late at night: *students burning the midnight oil in the library*
16 burn a hole in your pocket INFORMAL if money is burning a hole in your pocket, you want to spend it as soon as you can
17 get your fingers burned INFORMAL to suffer the bad results of something that you have done: *The first time I played the stock market, I got my fingers burned.*
18 BE EMBARRASSED [I] if your face or cheeks are burning, they feel hot because you are embarrassed or upset
19 it burns me/her/him etc. that SPOKEN used to say that something makes someone feel angry or JEALOUS: *It really burns me that he treats her so badly.*
20 be burning to do sth to want to do something very much: *Hannah's burning to tell you her news.*
21 GO QUICKLY [I always + adv./prep.] to travel very quickly: **+along/through/up etc.** *In Germany, sports cars burn along the highway at speeds over 100 mph.*
22 be burning with rage/desire etc. to feel an emotion very strongly
23 burn rubber INFORMAL to start a car moving so quickly that the tires make a loud high noise
24 burn sb at the stake to kill someone by tying them to a post on top of a fire
[**Origin:** Old English *byrnan* **to burn** and *bærnan* **to cause to burn**] → see also **crash and burn** at CRASH[1] (6), **sb's ears are burning** at EAR (14)

burn away *phr. v.* if something burns away or is burned away, it is destroyed or reduced to something much smaller by fire

burn down *phr. v.* **1 burn sth ↔ down** if a building burns down, or if it is burned down, it is destroyed by fire: *The old school burned down thirty years ago.* | *Three teenagers are accused of burning down the store.* **2** if a fire burns down, the flames become weaker and it produces less heat

burn off *phr. v.* **1** if FOG or MIST burns off, it disappears when the day becomes warmer and the sun gets higher in the sky **2 burn sth ↔ off** to remove something by burning it: *The nuts are roasted to burn off the poisonous oil.* **3 burn sth ↔ off** to use energy or fat stored in your body by doing exercise: *a program to help you burn off excess fat*

burn out *phr. v.*
1 FIRE burn sth out if a fire burns out or burns itself out, it stops burning because there is no wood or FUEL left
2 FEEL TIRED to feel very tired and not interested in things anymore, because you are working too hard: *A lot of teachers are burning out and quitting.* → see also BURNED OUT
3 be burned out a) if something is burned out, the inside of it is destroyed by fire: *Many of the buildings were burned out.* **b)** if someone is burned out, they are very tired and no longer interested in things because they are working too hard
4 ENGINE burn sth ↔ out if an engine or electric wire burns out or is burned out, it stops working because it has been damaged by getting too hot
5 AIRCRAFT if a ROCKET or JET burns out, it stops operating because all its FUEL has been used → see also BURNOUT

burn up *phr. v.*
1 DESTROY burn sth ↔ up if something burns up or is burned up, it is completely destroyed by fire or great heat
2 BURN BRIGHTER if a fire burns up, it gets stronger and brighter
3 BE HOT SPOKEN if someone is burning up, they are very hot, especially because they have a fever
4 MAKE SB ANGRY burn sb up INFORMAL to make someone angry: *It burns me up that they can charge so much for doing absolutely nothing!*
5 GO QUICKLY burn up sth to run or dance very quickly, or travel very quickly in a car: *Matt and Jen were really burning up the dance floor.* | *cars burning up the race track*
6 burn up energy/fat/calories etc. to use energy etc. by doing physical exercise.

burn[2] *n.* **1** [C] an injury or mark caused by fire, heat, or chemicals: *She was treated for burns at the hospital.* | *cigarette burns in the carpet* | **minor/severe burns** (=injuries to the skin caused by fire or chemicals that are not serious/very serious) | ***burn marks*** *on the table* → see also FIRST-DEGREE, SECOND-DEGREE, THIRD-DEGREE **2** [C] red and painful skin caused by being out in the sun too long SYN **sunburn**: *I* ***got a bad burn****, sitting out on the deck.* **3** [C,U] a painful mark on the skin caused by it rubbing hard against something rough: *She wore gloves to protect herself from rope burn.* **4 the burn** INFORMAL a painful hot feeling in your muscles when you exercise a lot

B

burned /bɚnd/ also **burnt** *adj.* damaged or hurt by burning: *burned trees* | *The ground was burned and bare.*

ˌburned 'out also **ˌburnt 'out** *adj.* so tired and bored because of working hard that you are not interested in anything: *By that time, I was totally burned out and ready to quit.*

burn·er /ˈbɚnɚ/ *n.* [C] **1** the part of a STOVE that produces heat or a flame **2 put sth on the back burner** INFORMAL to delay doing something until a later time: *Congress has put the bill on the back burner for now.*

burn·ing¹ /ˈbɚnɪŋ/ *adj.* [only before noun] **1** being damaged or destroyed by flames: *The two boys were rescued from the burning apartment building.* **2** feeling very hot: *burning cheeks* **3 a burning question/issue** a very important question or problem: *The burning issue of this election is the economy.* **4** felt very strongly: *a burning desire to succeed* | *his* ***burning ambition*** *to be the champion*

burning² *adv.* **burning hot** very hot

bur·nish /ˈbɚnɪʃ/ *v.* [T] to polish metal until it shines —**burnished** *adj.*: *burnished copper*

bur·noose /bɚˈnus/ *n.* [C] a long loose dress or coat worn by Arab men and women

burn·out /ˈbɚnaʊt/ *n.* [C,U] **1** the feeling of always being very tired and uninterested in things, because you have been working too hard: *Nurses on these units have a high rate of burnout.* **2** the time when a ROCKET or JET has finished all of its FUEL and stops operating

Burns /bɚnz/, **Rob·ert** /ˈrɑbɚt/ (1759–96) a Scottish poet who wrote in the Scots dialect and is regarded as Scotland's national poet

burnt¹ /bɚnt/ a past tense and past participle of BURN

burnt² also **burned** *adj.* damaged or hurt by burning: *burnt toast*

burp /bɚp/ *v.* INFORMAL **1** [I] to pass gas loudly from your stomach out through your mouth SYN **belch** **2** [T] to help a baby to do this, especially by rubbing or gently hitting its back [**Origin:** 1900–2000 From the sound] —**burp** *n.* [C]

burr /bɚ/ *n.* [C] **1** a fairly quiet regular sound like something turning quickly SYN **whirr**: *the burr of a sewing machine* **2** a rough spot on a piece of metal after it has been made, cut, or DRILLED **3** also **bur** BIOLOGY a seed of some plants that is covered with PRICKLES that make it stick to things **4** a way of pronouncing English in which the tongue is used to make the /r/ sound very long, especially in Scottish ACCENTS → see also **roll your r's** at ROLL¹ (21)

Burr /bɚ/, **Aaron** (1756—1836) the Vice President of the U.S. under Thomas Jefferson

bur·ri·to /bəˈritoʊ/ *n. plural* **burritos** [C] a Mexican dish made with a TORTILLA (=flat thin bread) folded around meat or beans with cheese

bur·ro /ˈbɚoʊ, ˈbʊroʊ/ *n. plural* **burros** [C] a DONKEY, usually a small one [**Origin:** 1800–1900 Spanish *borrico*, from Late Latin *burricus* **small horse**]

bur·row¹ /ˈbɚoʊ, ˈbʌroʊ/ *v.* **1** [I always + adv./prep.,T] to make a hole or passage in the ground SYN **dig**: **+into/under etc.** *Turtles burrow into the sand to lay their eggs.* | *The worms burrow tunnels in the soil.* **2** [I,T always + adv./prep.] to press your body close to someone or under something because you want to get warm, feel safe etc.: **+into/under etc.** *We burrowed under the blankets for warmth.* **3** [I always + adv./prep.] to search for something that is hard to find, in a container or under other things: **+into/through etc.** *Helen burrowed in her purse for some change.*

burrow² *n.* [C] a passage in the ground made by a small animal such as a rabbit or FOX as a place to live

bur·sar /ˈbɚsɚ, -sɑr/ *n.* [C] someone at a college who is responsible for the money paid by students [**Origin:** 1200–1300 Medieval Latin *bursarius*, from *bursa* **bag (for money)**]

burst¹ /bɚst/ *v. past tense and past participle* **burst**
1 BREAK OPEN [I,T] if something bursts, or if you burst it, it breaks open or apart suddenly and violently because of pressure on it, so that the substance it contains comes out: *The kids were trying to burst the balloons by sitting on them.* | *A bag of flour had* ***burst open*** *in the cupboard.* | *After days of heavy rain, the dam finally burst.* ►see THESAURUS box at **break¹**
2 be bursting with sth INFORMAL to be filled with something, or have a lot of something: *The window boxes were bursting with flowers.* | *a story bursting with ideas* | **be bursting with pride/confidence/energy etc.** *Her parents watched, bursting with pride, as she walked on stage.* → see also **be bursting at the seams** at SEAM (4)
3 MOVE SUDDENLY [I always + adv./prep.] to move somewhere suddenly or quickly, especially into or out of a place: **+through/into/in etc.** *Four men burst into the store and tied up the clerks.* | *The door* ***burst open*** (=suddenly opened) *and the kids piled into the house.*
4 RIVER burst its banks if a river bursts its banks, water comes over the top of the river banks and goes onto the land around it
5 burst the/sb's bubble to make someone suddenly realize that something is not as good as they believed or hoped: *I hate to burst your bubble, but you look really dumb in that hat.*
6 burst a blood vessel SPOKEN to become extremely angry
7 be bursting to do sth INFORMAL to want to do something very much
[**Origin:** Old English *berstan*] → see also OUTBURST (1)

burst in on/upon sb/sth *phr. v.* to enter a room suddenly and interrupt something, in a way that embarrasses you or other people: *I burst in on them, thinking that the room was empty.*

burst into sth *phr. v.* **1** to suddenly begin to make a sound, especially to start singing, crying, or laughing: *The audience burst into wild applause.* | *As he worked he would often* ***burst into song****.* | *Ken's sister suddenly* ***burst into tears*** *while we were eating.* **2 burst into flames** to suddenly start to burn: *The aircraft burst into flames.*

burst out *phr. v.* **1 burst out laughing/crying etc.** to suddenly start to laugh, cry etc.: *Rubin burst out laughing as he read the letter.* **2** to suddenly say something in a forceful way: *"I don't believe you!" she burst out angrily.*

burst² *n.* [C] **1** a short sudden increase in effort or activity: *I try to work* ***in*** *short* ***bursts****.* | **+of** *The industry has seen a burst of activity recently.* | **a burst of speed/energy** *a burst of speed at the finish line* **2 a burst of sth a)** a short sudden and usually loud sound: *a burst of machine-gun fire* **b)** a sudden strong feeling or emotion: *a burst of anger* **3** the act of something bursting or the place where it has burst: *a burst in the pipe*

Bu·run·di /bʊˈrundi, -ˈrʊn-/ a country in east central Africa, west of Tanzania —**Burundian** *n., adj.*

bur·y /ˈbɛri/ S3 W3 *v.* **buries, buried, burying** [T]
1 PUT SB IN A GRAVE to put someone who has died in a grave: **bury sb in/at etc.** *Uncle Bill was buried in the Milk River cemetery.* | *Scottish Kings* ***lie buried*** *here.* | *The men were tortured and* ***buried alive*** (=killed by being buried while still alive).
2 PUT STH UNDER THE GROUND to put something under the ground, often in order to hide it: *The phone lines are buried beneath the streets.* | *The legend says that there is* ***buried treasure*** *on the island.*
3 COVER WITH STH [usually passive] to cover something with other things so that it is difficult to see it or find it: **bury sth under/beneath/in etc.** *His glasses were buried under a pile of papers.* | *cars buried in the snow*

4 **FEELING/MEMORY** to ignore a feeling or memory and pretend that it does not exist: *I had tried to bury those painful memories.*
5 **HIDE FACTS** to put a fact, report etc. in a place in a larger document where it is difficult to find, so that it is not likely to be read: *a story buried in the back of the paper*
6 **END** to make something end or stop: *The company hoped to bury any rumors of a takeover.*
7 **DEFEAT** INFORMAL to defeat someone easily in a competition, business situation etc.: *Tennessee buried Florida 45–3 in Saturday's game.*
8 **bury your face/head etc. (in sth)** to press your face etc. into something soft, usually to get comfort, to avoid someone, or to be able to smell something: *The girl buried her face in the fur of her dog's neck.*
9 **bury the hatchet** to agree to stop arguing about something and become friends again: *Two years later they agreed to bury the hatchet.*
10 **bury yourself in your work/studies etc.** to give all your attention to something: *After the divorce, she buried herself in her work.*
11 **bury your head in the sand** to ignore a bad situation and hope it will stop if you do not think about it: *If you bury your head in the sand now, you may lose your house.*
12 **PUSH STH INTO STH** to push something, especially something sharp, into something else with a lot of force: *The dog buried its teeth in my leg.*
13 **EXPERIENCE A DEATH** to experience the death of a member of your family: *At age 20, she had already had to bury two children.*
[**Origin:** Old English *byrgan*] → see also **dead and buried** at DEAD[1] (19)

bus[1] /bʌs/ S1 W2 *n.* *plural* **buses** also **busses** [C] a large road vehicle that can carry many people: *the bus to the airport* | *Traveling **by bus** is easy in the city.* | **take/ride the bus** *We took the bus downtown.* | *Show your ticket to the driver as you **get on the bus**.* | *I had to run to **catch the bus**.* | *Hurry or you'll **miss the bus*** (=be too late for the bus)*!* → see also **school bus** at SCHOOL[1] (1) [**Origin:** 1800–1900 *omnibus*]

bus[2] *v.* **bused, busing** also **bussed, bussing** [T] **1** to take a group of people somewhere in a bus: **bus sb to/into etc.** *Many children are bused to school.* **2** to take away dirty dishes from the tables in a restaurant: *I spent the summer **busing tables**.*

bus·boy /ˈbʌsbɔɪ/ *n.* [C] a young man who works in a restaurant whose job is to take away dirty dishes from the tables

bus·es /ˈbʌsɪz/ *n.* a plural of bus

bush /bʊʃ/ S3 *n.* **1** [C] BIOLOGY a low thick plant, smaller than a tree, and with a lot of thin branches growing close together: *a holly bush* **2 the bush** wild country that has not been cleared, especially in Australia or Africa [**Origin:** 1200–1300 Old French *bos, bosc* **wood**] → see also **beat around the bush** at BEAT[1] (15)

Bush /bʊʃ/, **George** (1924–) the 41st president of the U.S. and Vice President under Ronald Reagan

Bush, George W. (1946–) a U.S. POLITICIAN who was the GOVERNOR of Texas and became the 43rd president of the United States in 2000. He was elected again in 2004.

ˈbush ˌbaby *n.* [C] a small African animal that lives in trees and has large eyes and ears, and a long tail

bushed /bʊʃt/ *adj.* [not before noun] INFORMAL very tired

bush·el /ˈbʊʃəl/ *n.* [C] a unit for measuring grain or vegetables equal to 8 gallons or 36.4 liters

bush·i·do /ˈbʊʃɪdoʊ/ HISTORY a set of rules for living used by the Japanese SAMURAI (=a member of a powerful military class in Japan in past times)

ˈbush league[1] *adj.* INFORMAL not skillful, or not skillfully made or done SYN **amateurish**: *a bush league ad agency*

bush league[2] *n.* [C] INFORMAL a MINOR LEAGUE, usually in baseball

bush·man /ˈbʊʃmən/ *n.* [C] **1 Bushman** a member of a southern African tribe who live in the BUSH **2** someone who lives in the Australian BUSH

bush·whack /ˈbʊʃwæk/ *v.* **1** [T] to attack someone suddenly from a hidden place SYN **ambush** **2** [I,T] to push or cut your way through thick trees or bushes —**bushwhacker** *n.* [C]

bush·y /ˈbʊʃi/ *adj.* *comparative* **bushier**, *superlative* **bushiest** **1** bushy hair or fur is very thick: *a bushy tail* | *bushy eyebrows* **2** a bushy plant grows thickly —**bushiness** *n.* [U]

bus·i·ly /ˈbɪzəli/ *adv.* in a busy way: *He worked busily in the kitchen.* | **be busily doing sth** *The army is busily preparing for war.*

busi·ness /ˈbɪznɪs/ S1 W1 *n.*
1 **BUYING OR SELLING GOODS** [U] the activity of buying or selling goods and services, done by companies: *As an M.B.A. student, you study all aspects of business.* | *the **business community*** (=people who work in business) | *Williams was one of my **business partners**.* | *a list of the major U.S. companies that **do business in** Russia* | **the advertising/printing/shipping etc. business** *Paul's first job was in the movie business.* | *California's agricultural business* | *The firm **does** a lot of **business with** oil companies.* | *I'm thinking of **going into business** for myself* (=starting to run my own business). | *The company **went out of business** last year.* | *Most banks are **open for business** on Saturdays.* | *What **line of business** are you in* (=what type of work do you do)*?*

> **THESAURUS**
> **commerce** the buying and selling of goods and services: *laws that regulate commerce between nations*
> **industry** the production of goods, especially in factories: *The main industry in the area is car manufacturing.*
> **trade** the business of buying and selling things, especially between countries: *restrictions on trade*
> **private enterprise** the economic system in which private businesses can compete, and the government does not control industry

2 **WORK NOT PLEASURE** [U] things you do as part of your job rather than for pleasure: *Linda had to go to Chicago **on business*** (=because of her job). | **business trip/lunch/meeting etc.** *a business trip to Dallas*
3 **ORGANIZATION** [C] an organization that produces or sells goods or services: *She owns a **small business** with about 10 employees.* | *Taylor **runs** an office equipment **business**.* | *The bakery is an old **family business*** (=run by one family). ▸see THESAURUS box at **company**
4 **VALUE/AMOUNT** [U] the amount of work a company is doing or its value: *Defense contracts account for 60% of our business.* | ***Business** has been **slow** for retailers this Christmas* (=they are not selling very much). | **business is booming/brisk** (=a lot of things are being sold) | *Some people thought the war would **be good for business**.*
5 **IN A PARTICULAR JOB/TIME** [U] work that must be done in a particular job or during a period of time: *We discussed this week's business.* | **+of** *the routine business of government*
6 **your/sb's business** SPOKEN private information that concerns only a particular person and no one else: *His mother should stay home and **mind her own business**.* | *My personal life **is none of your business**.* | *"Are you going out with Kate tonight?" "**That's my business.**"*
7 **sb was (just) minding their own business** used to say that someone was not doing anything unusual or wrong at the time something unfair or bad happened to them: *I was just walking along, minding my own business, when this guy ran straight into me.*
8 **make it your business to do sth** to make a special effort to do something: *Ruth made it her business to get to know the customers.*
9 **SUBJECT/ACTIVITY** [singular] used to talk about a sub-

ject, event, situation, or activity, especially one that you have a particular opinion of: *What's this business about you getting into a fight at school?* | **a serious/strange/terrible etc. business** *For kids, playing is serious business.* | *the strange business of the missing necklace*
10 STH GENERAL [U] SPOKEN used to talk about something in general without giving details: *He handles the mail and all that business.*
11 business as usual used to say that, although there have been problems, things are happening the way they normally happen, especially at a business: *Despite the fire damage, it's business as usual at the barber shop.*
12 get down to business to start dealing with an important subject: *Okay, class, let's get down to business.*
13 be in business INFORMAL to have all that you need to start doing something: *I have finger paints and paper for the kids, so we're in business.*
14 go about your business to do the things that you normally do: *The street was filled with ordinary people going about their business.*
15 have no business doing sth also **have no business to do sth** to behave wrongly in doing something: *He was drunk – he had no business driving.*
16 not in the business of doing sth not planning to do something, because it is thought to be wrong: *This newspaper is not in the business of sensationalism.*
17 business is business used to say that profit is the most important thing to consider: *For these guys, business is business and worker safety is not important.*
18 the business end (of sth) INFORMAL the end of a tool or weapon that does the work or causes the damage: *the business end of a gun*
19 be all business to be serious about the work you are doing, and not do or talk about other things: *We'd fool around in practice, but during the games we were all business.*
20 any other business subjects to be discussed in a meeting after the main subjects have been dealt with: *Before we end the meeting, is there any other business?*
21 give sb the business OLD-FASHIONED to make jokes and laugh at someone for fun or to criticize them
[**Origin:** 1300–1400 *busy*] → see also BIG BUSINESS, **sb means business** at MEAN¹ (13), **monkey business** at MONKEY¹ (3), **like nobody's business** at NOBODY¹ (2), SHOW BUSINESS

'business associ,ation *n.* [C] ECONOMICS an organization that helps the businesses in a particular town, city, or state to develop and become more successful in order to increase business activity in the area

'business card *n.* [C] a card that shows a person's name, job, company, address, telephone number etc.

'business class *n.* [U] traveling conditions on an airplane that are more expensive than COACH but not as expensive as FIRST CLASS → see also ECONOMY CLASS

'business ,cycle *n.* [C] ECONOMICS a continuous and regular pattern of events, during which business activity increases, then decreases, and then increases again

'business ,franchise *n.* [C] ECONOMICS a FRANCHISE

'business hours *n.* [plural] the normal hours that stores and offices are open: *Our business hours are 8:00-6:00 Monday-Friday.*

'business ,license *n.* [C] ECONOMICS a legal document giving a company official permission to operate a business for a particular period of time

busi•ness•like /'bɪznɪsˌlaɪk/ *adj.* effective and practical in the way that you do things: *a businesslike manner*

busi•ness•man /'bɪznɪsˌmæn/ W3 *n. plural* **businessmen** /-ˌmɛn/ [C] a man who works in business

'business ,park *n.* [C] an area where many companies and businesses have buildings and offices

'business ,person *n. plural* **business people** [C] a person who works in business

'business ,plan *n.* [C] a document which explains what a company wants to do in the future, and how it plans to do it

'business suit *n.* [C] a suit that someone wears during the day at work, especially one that is CONSERVATIVE in style

busi•ness•wom•an /'bɪznɪsˌwʊmən/ *n. plural* **businesswomen** /-ˌwɪmɪn/ [C] a woman who works in business

bus•ing, bussing /'bʌsɪŋ/ *n.* [U] a system in the U.S. in which students ride buses to schools that are far from where they live, so that a school has students of different races

'bus lane *n.* [C] a part of a road that only buses are allowed to use

bus•load /'bʌsloʊd/ *n.* [C] the number of people on a bus that is full: **+of** *a busload of people*

bus•man's hol•i•day /ˌbʌsmənz 'hɑlədeɪ/ *n.* [singular] a vacation spent doing the same work as you do in your job

'bus pass *n.* [C] a ticket used for bus travel during a particular period of time such as a week or a month, which costs less than buying tickets for each trip

buss /bʌs/ *v.* [T] OLD-FASHIONED to kiss someone in a friendly rather than sexual way

bus•ses /'bʌsɪz/ a plural of the noun BUS, and a third person singular of the verb BUS

'bus ,shelter *n.* [C] a small structure with a roof that keeps people dry while they are waiting for a BUS

'bus ,station *n.* [C] a place where buses start and finish their trips

'bus stop *n.* [C] a place at the side of a road, marked with a sign, where buses stop for passengers

bust¹ /bʌst/ S3 *v.* [T] INFORMAL **1** [I,T] SPOKEN to break something, or be broken: *The window busted when the ball hit it.* | *You busted Dad's watch!* **2** [T] **a)** if the police bust someone, they charge them with a crime: **get/be busted (for sth)** *Her brother got busted for drunk driving* **b)** if the police bust a place, they go into it to catch people doing something illegal: *Federal agents busted several money-exchange businesses.* **3** [T] to use too much money, so that a business etc. must stop operating: *The trip to Spain will probably bust our budget.* **4 -busting** used with nouns to show that a situation is being ended or an activity is being stopped: *crime-busting laws* | *a drought-busting storm* **5 bust a gut** SPOKEN **a)** to try extremely hard to do something: *We busted a gut trying to get home on time.* **b)** to laugh a lot: *I busted a gut, watching him try to feed the baby.* **6 bust sb's chops** to criticize or deliberately annoy someone as a joke: *Don't worry – I'm just busting your chops!* **7 ...or bust!** used to say that you will try very hard to go somewhere or do something: *San Francisco or bust!*

bust out *phr. v.* **1** to escape from a place, especially prison **2 bust sb out** SPOKEN to strongly criticize someone: *I busted him out for forgetting to pay me back.*

bust up *phr. v.* **1 bust sb/sth ↔ up** SPOKEN to damage or break something, or to hit someone to injure them: *A bunch of bikers busted up the bar.* **2 bust sth ↔ up** SPOKEN to prevent an illegal activity or bad situation from continuing: *Last week the FBI busted up a big drug ring.* | *A couple of teachers tried to bust up the fight.* **3 bust sth ↔ up** to force a large company to separate into smaller companies: *A federal judge busted up AT&T in a decision on monopolies.* → see also BUST-UP

bust² *n.* [C] **1** INFORMAL a situation in which the police go into a place in order to catch people doing something illegal: *a drug bust* **2** a woman's breasts, or the measurement around her breasts and back: *a 30-inch bust* **3** ENG. LANG. ARTS a model of someone's head, shoulders and upper chest, made of stone or metal: **+of** *a bronze bust of Beethoven* [**Origin:** (2, 3) 1600–1700 French *buste*, from Latin *bustum* **place where a body is buried, statue put by such a place**]

bust³ *adj.* INFORMAL **go bust** a business that goes bust cannot continue operating: *Most of the steel factories around here went bust in the 1980s.*

bust•ed /'bʌstɪd/ *adj.* SPOKEN, INFORMAL **1** broken: *The*

TV's busted again. **2** caught doing something wrong and likely to be punished: *You guys are so busted!*

bust·er /ˈbʌstɚ/ *n.* **1** SPOKEN used when speaking to a man who is annoying you, or who you do not respect: *Keep your hands to yourself, buster!* **2** INFORMAL also **-buster** used with nouns to mean something that destroys or spoils something else: *The pilot of the plane, known as the tank buster, lost radio contact.* | *The Democrats' health-care bill has been called a budget-buster* (=something that will force the government to spend too much money). | **price-buster/deal-buster** (=a price you pay for a product that is better than any other price)

bus·ti·er /ˈbʌstiɚ/ *n.* [C] a piece of woman's clothing that fits her chest tightly and has no SLEEVES. It can be worn alone or under a JACKET or BLOUSE.

bus·tle¹ /ˈbʌsəl/ *v.* [I always + adv./prep.] to move around quickly, looking very busy: **+around/through etc.** *Grandma bustled around the kitchen.* → see also BUSTLING

bustle² *n.* **1** [U] busy and usually noisy activity: **+of** *the bustle of a big city* → see also **hustle and bustle** at HUSTLE² (1) **2** [C] a frame worn under women's skirts in the past to push out the back of the skirts

bus·tling /ˈbʌslɪŋ/ *adj.* a bustling place is very busy: *a small bustling Mexican restaurant*

ˈbust-up *n.* [C] INFORMAL the end of a relationship: *the bust-up of their marriage* → see also **bust up** at BUST¹

bust·y /ˈbʌsti/ *adj.* INFORMAL a busty woman has large breasts

bus·y¹ /ˈbɪzi/ S1 W3 *adj. comparative* **busier**, *superlative* **busiest**

1 PERSON someone who is busy has a lot of things to do and may not be free to do something else: *I'm kind of busy now, can I call you back?* | *a busy mother of four boys* | **+with** *I'm sorry, Mrs. Daniels is busy with a customer.* | **busy doing sth** *Sarah's busy studying for her final exams.* | *There are lots of activities to **keep** the kids **busy*** (=give them a lot of things to do).

2 TIME a busy time is full of work or other activities: *December is the busiest time of year for the mall.* | *You've had a busy day!*

3 PLACE a busy place is very full of people or vehicles and movement: *a busy freeway* | *the busiest airport in the world*

4 TELEPHONE if a telephone you are calling is busy, it makes a repeated sound to tell you the person you are calling is talking on their telephone: *It's busy. I'll call again later.* | *I called Mel, but **the line's busy**.* ►see THESAURUS box at **phone¹**

5 PATTERN a pattern or design that is busy has too many small details

6 as busy as a bee INFORMAL very busy doing something, especially something active

7 get busy SPOKEN, INFORMAL used to tell someone to start doing something: *There's a lot to do, so let's get busy.*

[**Origin:** Old English *bisig*] —**busily** *adv.*

busy² *v.* **busies, busied, busying** [T] to use your time by dealing with something: **busy yourself with sth** *I busied myself with preparations for the party.* | **busy yourself (by/with) doing sth** *She busied herself by cleaning the stove.*

bus·y·bod·y /ˈbɪziˌbɑdi, -ˌbʌdi/ *n. plural* **busybodies** [C] someone who annoys people by being too interested in other people's private activities

ˈbusy ˌsignal *n.* [C usually singular] the sound you hear on the telephone that tells you that the person you are trying to call is talking to someone else on their telephone

bus·y·work /ˈbɪziˌwɚk/ *n.* [U] work that gives someone something to do, but that is not really necessary

but¹ /bət; *strong* bʌt/ S1 W1 *conjunction* **1** used to connect two statements or phrases when the second one is different from the first: *It's an old car, but it's very reliable.* | *Cara's going to the concert, but I'm not.* | *Mom hated the movie, but Dad liked it.* | *It's an expensive but very useful book.* **2** used like "however" to give a reason why something did not happen or why you did not do something etc.: *Carla was supposed to come tonight, but her husband needed the car.* | *I'd like to go, but I'm too busy.*

SPOKEN PHRASES

3 but then (again) a) used before a statement that makes what you have just said seem less true, useful, or valuable: *You feel sorry for him, but then again it's hard to really like him.* **b)** used before a statement that may seem surprising, to say that it is not really surprising: *He doesn't have a strong French accent, but then he's lived here for twenty years.* **4** used to introduce a new subject in a conversation: *But now to the main issue.* | *That's why I've been so busy. But how are you, anyway?* **5** used after phrases such as "excuse me" and "I'm sorry": *I'm sorry, but you can't smoke in here.* | *Excuse me, but aren't you Julie's sister?*

6 used after a negative to emphasize that it is the second part of the sentence that it is true: *They aren't doing this to make money, but to help the church.* | *We had no alternative but to fire him.* **7 you cannot but.../you could not but...** FORMAL used to say that you have to do something or cannot stop yourself from doing it: *I could not but admire her.* **8 but for sb/sth** FORMAL without or except for: *But for my family, I'd be having real difficulties.* **9** used to emphasize a word or statement: *It'll be a great party – everyone, but everyone, is coming.* **10** [usually in negatives] LITERARY used to emphasize that a statement includes every single person or thing: *Not a day goes by but that I think of Jeff* (=I think of Jeff every day). [**Origin:** Old English *butan* **outside, without, except**]

WORD CHOICE **but, however**

- **But** is very frequent in spoken English, where it is often used at the beginning of a sentence: *I didn't like the opening act at the concert. But the main band was great.* **But** is also used in writing, though not usually at the beginning of a sentence.
- **However** is used especially in more formal writing, often with commas before and after it in the middle of a sentence: *The first act was somewhat amateurish. The second, however, was excellent.*

GRAMMAR

But or **however** is never used in a main clause next to another clause that contains **although**: *Although they're very busy, I think they enjoy it* (NOT ... but/however I think they enjoy it).

but² S1 W2 *prep.* except for: *There's no one here but me.* | *I could come any day but Thursday.* | *This car's been **nothing but** trouble* (=it has been a lot of trouble). | *The sales clerk was **anything but** helpful* (=the clerk was not helpful at all).

but³ *adv.* **1** ESPECIALLY LITERARY only: *You can but try.* **2** SPOKEN used to emphasize what you are saying: *They're rich, but I mean rich!*

but⁴ /bʌt/ *n.* **no buts (about it)** SPOKEN used to say that there is no doubt about something: *No buts, you are going to school today!*

bu·tane /ˈbyuteɪn/ *n.* [U] a gas stored in liquid form, used for cooking and heating

butch /bʊtʃ/ *adj.* INFORMAL **1** a woman who is butch looks or behaves in a way that is traditionally considered typical of men **2** a man who is butch seems big and strong, and typically male

butch·er¹ /ˈbʊtʃɚ/ *n.* [C] **1** someone who cuts and sells meat as a business **2** someone who has killed a lot of people cruelly and without reason [**Origin:** 1200–1300 Old French *bouchier*, from *bouc* **male goat**]

butcher² *v.* [T] **1** to kill animals and prepare them to be used as meat **2** to kill people cruelly or without reason, especially in large numbers: *They butchered hundreds of innocent people.* **3** INFORMAL to spoil something by working carelessly: *The hairdresser really butchered my hair!*

B

butch•er•y /ˈbʊtʃəri/ *n.* [U] **1** cruel and unnecessary killing: *the butchery of battle* **2** the preparation of meat for sale

but•ler /ˈbʌtlɚ/ *n.* [C] the main male servant of a house [**Origin:** 1200–1300 Old French *bouteillier* **bottle-carrier**]

butt¹ /bʌt/ S2 *n.* [C]

1 PART OF YOUR BODY INFORMAL the part of your body that you sit on: *I slipped and fell right on my butt.*

SPOKEN PHRASES

2 get your butt in/out/over etc. used to tell someone rudely to go somewhere or do something: *Get your butt out of that bathroom now.*

3 work/study etc. your butt off to work, study etc. very hard: *I worked my butt off in college.*

4 get off your butt used to tell someone rudely to start doing something when they have been lazy: *Get off your butt, and go mow the lawn.*

5 sit on your butt to not do anything important or useful: *I've just been sitting on my butt, watching TV all day.*

6 CIGARETTE the end of a cigarette after most of it has been smoked

7 be the butt of (sb's) jokes/humor to be the person or thing that other people often make jokes about: *Unfortunately for Ted, he's become the butt of jokes around the office.*

8 GUN the thick end of the handle of a gun: *a rifle butt*

9 HITTING WITH YOUR HEAD the act of hitting someone or something with your head SYN **headbutt**

butt² *v.* [I,T] **1** to hit or push against someone or something with your head **2** if an animal butts someone or something, it hits them with its horns

butt in *phr. v.* **1** to interrupt a conversation rudely: *Stop butting in!* **2** to become involved in a private situation that does not concern you: *I don't want you or anyone else butting in on my personal business.*

butt out *phr. v.* SPOKEN used to tell someone rudely that you do not want them to be involved in a conversation or situation: *Just butt out, OK? I don't want your advice.*

butte /byut/ *n.* [C] EARTH SCIENCE a very large rock with steep sides and a flat top, that sticks out of flat ground in the western U.S.

but•ter¹ /ˈbʌt̬ɚ/ S2 W3 *n.* [U] a solid yellow food made from milk or cream that you spread on bread or use in cooking: *Beat the butter and sugar together.* [**Origin:** Old English *butere*, from Latin *butyrum*, from Greek *boutyron*, from *bous* **cow** + *tyros* **cheese**] —**buttery** *adj.*

butter² *v.* [T] to spread butter on something: *buttered bread*

butter sb **up** *phr. v.* INFORMAL to say nice things to someone so that they will do what you want: *Don't try to butter me up.*

but•ter•ball /ˈbʌt̬ɚˌbɔl/ *n.* [C] INFORMAL someone who is fat

ˈbutter bean *n.* a large pale yellow bean

but•ter•cup /ˈbʌt̬ɚˌkʌp/ *n.* [C] a small shiny yellow wild flower

but•ter•fin•gers /ˈbʌt̬ɚˌfɪŋgɚz/ *n.* [singular] INFORMAL someone who often drops things they are carrying or trying to catch

but•ter•fly /ˈbʌt̬ɚˌflaɪ/ *n. plural* **butterflies** **1** [C] BIOLOGY a type of insect that has large wings, often with beautiful colors → see picture at METAMORPHOSIS **2 butterflies** [plural] INFORMAL a very nervous feeling you have before doing something: *It was the first performance, and I **had butterflies in my stomach**.* **3** [U] a way of swimming by lying on your front and moving your arms together in forward circles **4** [C] someone who usually moves on quickly from one activity or person to the next: *Gwen's **a** real **social butterfly**.*

ˈbutterfly kiss *n.* [C] the action of opening and closing your eye very close to someone's cheek, so that your EYELASHES touch it lightly; used as a way of showing love, especially to children

but•ter•milk /ˈbʌt̬ɚˌmɪlk/ *n.* [U] the liquid that remains after butter has been made, used in BAKING

but•ter•scotch /ˈbʌt̬ɚˌskɑtʃ/ *n.* [U] a type of candy made from butter and sugar boiled together

butt•in•ski /bəˈtɪnski/ *n. plural* **buttinskis** [C] INFORMAL someone who is annoying because they are too interested in other people's private activities

but•tock /ˈbʌt̬ək/ *n.* [C usually plural] one of the fleshy parts of your body that you sit on

but•ton¹ /ˈbʌtˀn/ S1 W3 *n.* **1** [C] a small circular flat object on your shirt, coat etc. that you put through a hole to fasten it: *a uniform with brass buttons* | *Why don't you **undo** your top **button**?* | *She was struggling to **button** all the tiny **buttons** (=fasten them) on her blouse.* → see picture at FASTENER **2** [C] a small part or area of a machine that you press to make it do something: **push/press a button** *Push the pause button.* **3** [C] an area on a computer screen that you CLICK on to make the computer do a specific thing: ***Click on the** OK **button**.* **4** a small metal or plastic pin with a message or picture on it: *They were wearing anti-war buttons.* **5 button nose/eyes** a nose or eyes that are small and round **6 (right) on the button** INFORMAL exactly correct, or at exactly the right time: *The weather forecast was right on the button.* | *She got to our house at two, on the button.* [**Origin:** 1300–1400 Old French *boton*, from *boter* **to push**] → see also **as bright as a button** at BRIGHT (10), HOT BUTTON, **at/with the push of a button** at PUSH² (6), **push sb's buttons** at PUSH¹ (14), PUSH-BUTTON

button² *v.* [I,T] **1** also **button up** to fasten clothes that have buttons, or to be fastened with buttons: *The pants button on the side.* | *Button up your coat, Nina – it's cold.* **2 button your lip/mouth** also **button up** SPOKEN used to tell someone in an impolite way to stop talking

ˈbutton-down *adj.* a button-down shirt or collar has the ends of the collar fastened to the shirt with buttons

ˌbuttoned-ˈup *adj.* INFORMAL someone who is buttoned-up is not able to express their feelings, especially sexual feelings

but•ton•hole /ˈbʌtˀnˌhoʊl/ *n.* [C] a hole for a button to be put through to fasten a shirt, coat etc.

but•tress¹ /ˈbʌtrɪs/ *n.* [C] a brick or stone structure built to support a wall

buttress² *v.* [T] to support a system, idea, argument etc.: *The professor gave statistics to buttress his argument.*

bux•om /ˈbʌksəm/ *adj.* a woman who is buxom is attractively large and healthy and has big breasts [**Origin:** 1500–1600 *buxom* **willing to obey, friendly** (11–17 centuries), from Old English *buhsum*, from *bugan* **to bend**]

buy¹ /baɪ/ S1 W1 *v. past tense and past participle* **bought** /bɔt/

1 WITH MONEY a) [I,T] to get something by paying money for it OPP **sell**: *We bought a house in Atlanta.* | *We decided to buy instead of rent.* | **buy sb sth** *Can I buy you a drink?* | **buy sth for sb/sth** *I bought a T-shirt for Craig.* | **buy sth from sb/sth** *Visitors can buy maps from the gift shop.* | *Members can **buy** tickets **for** $5 **each**.* **b)** [T] if a sum of money buys something, that is what you can get with it: *A dollar doesn't buy much these days.* | **buy sb sth** *$15 will easily buy us pizza and a drink.*

THESAURUS

purchase FORMAL to buy something: *They purchased 5,000 acres of land.*

acquire to buy a company or property: *Television companies were then allowed to acquire more stations.*

get to buy or obtain something: *I never know what to get Dad for his birthday.*

snap sth up to buy something immediately, especially because it is very cheap: *Real estate in the area is being snapped up by developers.*

pick sth up to buy something: *Could you pick up some milk on your way home?*
stock up to buy a lot of something that you intend to use later: *Before the blizzard, we stocked up on food.*

2 GAIN TIME to do something that allows you the extra time you need in order to do something else: *We tried to* ***buy time*** *by pretending our car wasn't working.*
3 BELIEVE [T] INFORMAL to believe an explanation or reason, especially one that is not very likely to be true: *She'll never buy that excuse.*
4 FOR ADVANTAGE a) [T usually passive] INFORMAL to pay money to someone, especially someone in an official position, in order to persuade them to do something dishonest that gives you an advantage SYN **bribe**: *They say the judge was bought.* **b)** [T] to use money to get something that is not a product or service, in order to get an advantage for yourself: *You can't buy respect.* | *They were accused of buying votes.*
5 GAIN STH IMPORTANT [T] to get something important or difficult to get by giving or losing something else: **buy sth with sth** *They bought our freedom with their lives.*
6 sb bought it also **sb bought the farm** SPOKEN to have been killed, especially in an accident or war: *I almost bought it twice in Vietnam.*
[**Origin:** Old English *bycgan*]

buy sth ↔ **back** *phr. v.* to get back something that you used to own by buying again: *We bought the house back ten years later.*

buy into sth *phr. v.* **1** INFORMAL to believe an idea: *A lot of women have bought into the idea that they have to be thin to be attractive.* **2** to buy SHARES in a company, industry, or in particular type of investments in order to make money: *He recommended buying into the wireless market.*

buy sb **off** *phr. v.* to pay someone money to stop them causing trouble or threatening you SYN **bribe**: *They are claiming that the Senator was bought off.*

buy out *phr. v.* **buy sb/sth out** to buy someone's SHARES of a business that you previously owned together, so that you have complete control → see also BUYOUT

buy up sth *phr. v.* to quickly buy as much as you can of something such as land, tickets, food etc.: *The park land is being bought up by two corporations.*

buy² S3 *n.* **be a good/bad buy** to be worth or to be not worth the price you paid: *The wine is a good buy at $6.49.*

buy·er /ˈbaɪɚ/ W3 *n.* [C] **1** someone who buys something expensive such as a house or car OPP **seller**: *Lower house prices should attract more buyers.* | *Are you* ***a first-time buyer?*** (=is this the first house you have bought?) ►see THESAURUS box at **customer** **2** someone whose job is to choose and buy the goods for a store or company

ˈbuyer's ˌmarket *n.* [singular] a situation in which there is plenty of something available so that buyers have a lot of choice and prices tend to be low OPP **seller's market**

buy·out /ˈbaɪaʊt/ *n.* [C] ECONOMICS a situation in which someone gains control of a company by buying all or most of its SHARES: *We are currently negotiating a buy-out of one of our rivals.*

buzz¹ /bʌz/ *v.*
1 MAKE A SOUND [I] to make a continuous sound, like the sound of a BEE: *I hear something buzzing in the engine.*
2 EXCITEMENT [I] if a group of people or a place buzzes, people are talking a lot and making a noise because they are excited: *Local people were buzzing about the murder.* | **+with** *The crowd buzzed with excitement.*
3 MOVE AROUND a) [I always + adv./prep.] to move around in the air making a continuous sound like a BEE: **+around/above etc.** *Dragonflies buzzed above the water.* **b)** to move quickly and in a busy way around a place: **+around/over etc.** *We were buzzing around town, trying to get the Christmas shopping done.*
4 CALL [I,T] to call someone or to make something happen, for example make a door open, by pushing a BUZZER: **buzz for sb** *I had to buzz for the stewardess to bring some napkins.* | **buzz sb in/out/through etc.** *The security guard buzzed me through the gate.*
5 EARS [I] if your ears or head are buzzing, you can hear a continuous annoying sound because you are not feeling well SYN **ring**
6 sb's head/mind is buzzing (with sth) if your head or mind is buzzing with thoughts, ideas etc., you cannot stop thinking about them
7 AIRCRAFT [T] INFORMAL to fly an aircraft low and fast over buildings, people etc.
8 buzz off! SPOKEN used to tell someone rudely to go away
[**Origin:** 1300–1400 from the sound]

buzz² *n.* **1** [C] a continuous noise like the sound of a BEE: *the buzz of helicopters overhead* **2** [singular] the sound of people talking a lot in an excited way: **+of** *the buzz of the crowd* **3** [singular] INFORMAL a strong feeling of excitement, pleasure, or success, or a similar feeling from drinking alcohol or taking drugs: *Playing well* ***gives me a buzz.*** | *Neil* ***gets a buzz*** *from drinking one beer.* **4 give sb a buzz** INFORMAL to call someone on the telephone **5 the buzz** INFORMAL unofficial news or information that is spread by people telling each other: ***The buzz is that*** *Jack is leaving.*

buz·zard /ˈbʌzɚd/ *n.* [C] **1** BIOLOGY a type of large bird that eats dead animals SYN **vulture** **2** BIOLOGY a type of large HAWK in Europe and Asia

buzz·cut /ˈbʌzkʌt/ *n.* [C] a very short HAIRCUT

buzz·er /ˈbʌzɚ/ *n.* [C] a small thing like a button that makes a buzzing sound when you push it, for example on a door: ***Push the buzzer*** *if you know the answer.* | **the buzzer sounds/goes** *The buzzer sounded for the end of the quarter.*

ˈbuzz saw *n.* [C] a SAW with a round blade that is spun around by a motor SYN **circular saw**

buzz·word /ˈbʌzwɚd/ *n.* [C] a word or phrase from one special area of knowledge that people suddenly think is very important: *The buzzword in website design is "content management".*

BWL, bwl a written abbreviation of "bursting with laughter," used by people communicating in CHAT ROOMS on the Internet

by¹ /baɪ/ S1 W1 *prep.* **1** used especially with a PASSIVE verb to show who or what did something or what caused something: *Jim was bitten by a dog.* | *The building was designed by Frank Gehry.* | *Everyone is worried by the rise in violent crime.* **2** using or doing a particular thing: *You can reserve the tickets by phone.* | *Send it by airmail.* | **by doing sth** *Caroline earns extra money by babysitting.* | **by car/train/plane/bus etc.** *We went from New York to Philadelphia by car.* **3** passing through or along a particular place: *It's quicker to go by the freeway.* | *Doris came in by the back door.* **4** beside or near something: *She stood by the window looking out over the fields.* | *Jane went and sat by Patrick.* **5 come/go/stop by sth** to visit or go to a place for a short time when you intend to go somewhere else after that: *Could you stop by the store and buy milk?* | *I'll come by your house before lunch.* **6** if you move or travel by someone or something, you go past them without stopping: *He walked by me without saying hello.* | *I go by John's place on my way to work; I can pick him up.* **7** used to show the name of someone who wrote a book, produced a movie, wrote a piece of music etc.: *the "Unfinished Symphony" by Schubert* | *"Hamlet" was written by Shakespeare.* **8** not later than a particular time, date etc.: *The report must be ready by next Friday.* | *I'll be home by 9:30.* **9** according to a particular rule, method, or way of doing things: *By law, cars cannot pass a school bus while it is stopped.* | *Profits were $6 million, but by their standards this is low.* **10** used to show the amount or degree of something: *The price of oil fell by a further $2 a barrel.* | *I was overcharged by $3.* | *Reading was* ***by far*** (=by a large amount or degree) *my favorite activity as a child.* **11** used when telling which part of a piece of equipment or of someone's body someone takes or holds: *I picked the pot up by the*

B

handle. | *She grabbed him by the arm.* **12 by the way** SPOKEN used to begin talking about a subject that is not related to the one you were talking about: *Oh, by the way, Vicky called while you were out.* **13** used between two numbers that you are multiplying or dividing: *What's 48 divided by 4?* **14** used when giving the measurements of a room, container etc.: *The living room is 10 feet by 13 feet.* **15** used to show a rate or quantity: *Most restaurant workers are paid by the hour.* | *You buy the wood by the square foot.* **16** SPOKEN used when expressing strong feelings or making serious promises: *By God, we actually did it!* **17 day by day/little by little etc.** used to show that something happens gradually or is done slowly and in small amounts: *Day by day he grew weaker.* | *Police searched the area house by house.* **18** used to show the situation or period of time during which you do something or something happens: *You'll ruin your eyes reading by flashlight.* | **by day/night** (=during the day or night) **19** used to show the relationship between one fact or thing and another: *Colette is French by birth.* | *It's fine by me if you want to go.* **20** as a result of an action or situation: *He brought over some of my mail that was delivered to his house* ***by accident.*** | *I deleted a whole afternoon's work on the computer* ***by mistake.*** **21** if a woman has children by a particular man, that man is the children's father: *Ann has two children by her ex-husband.* **22 (all) by yourself a)** completely alone: *Dave spent Christmas all by himself.* **b)** without any help: *Katherine made the cookies all by herself.* [**Origin:** Old English *be, bi*]

by² S1 W1 *adv.* **1** if someone or something moves or goes by, they go past: *Only two cars went by.* | *Three hours went by before she called.* | *James walked by without even looking in my direction.* **2 come/stop/go etc. by** to visit or go to a place for a short time when you intend to go somewhere else after that: *I'll drop by and have a look at your car this afternoon.* | *Come by* (=come to my house, office etc.) *any time tomorrow.* **3** beside or near someone or something: *A crowd of people were standing by, waiting for an announcement.* **4 by and large** used when talking generally about someone or something: *By and large, most of the people in the town work at the factory.* **5 by and by** ESPECIALLY LITERARY soon **6 by the by** SPOKEN, OLD-FASHIONED used when mentioning something that may be interesting but is not particularly important: *By the by, John might come over tonight.*

by-, bye- /baɪ/ *prefix* less important than the main part of something or the main event: *a byproduct* (=something that is also produced when the main product is made)

bye¹ /baɪ/ S1 also **bye-'bye** *interjection* SPOKEN goodbye

bye² *n.* [C] a situation in a sports competition or SEASON in which a player or a team does not have an opponent to play against and continues to the next part of the competition

'by-e,lection *n.* [C] POLITICS a special election that is held at a different time from usual to replace a politician who has left the government or died

by·gone /ˈbaɪgɔn, -gɑn/ *adj.* **bygone age/era/days etc.** a period of time in the past: *The buildings reflect the elegance of a bygone era.*

by·gones /ˈbaɪgɔnz/ *n.* **let bygones be bygones** to forget something bad that someone has done to you and forgive them

by·law /ˈbaɪlɔ/ *n.* LAW a rule made by an organization to control the people who belong to it

'by-line *n.* [C] a line at the beginning of an article in a newspaper or magazine giving the writer's name

BYOB /ˌbi waɪ oʊ ˈbi/ *adj.* **Bring Your Own Bottle/Beer/Booze** used when inviting someone to an informal party to tell them that they must bring their own bottle of alcoholic drink: *By the way, the party at Hank's is BYOB.*

by·pass¹ /ˈbaɪpæs/ *n.* [C] **1** also **heart bypass, bypass surgery** an operation to direct blood through new VEINS (=blood tubes) outside the heart **2** a road that goes around a town or other busy area rather than through it **3** TECHNICAL a tube that allows gas or liquid to flow around something rather than through it

bypass² *v.* [T] **1** to avoid a place or situation by going around it: *This highway bypasses the downtown area.* **2** to avoid obeying a rule, system, or someone in an official position: *There should be no way of bypassing the security measures on the computer.*

by·play /ˈbaɪpleɪ/ *n.* [U] something that is less important than the main action, especially in a play

by·prod·uct /ˈbaɪˌprɑdəkt/ *n.* [C] **1** something additional that is produced during a natural or industrial process: *milk byproducts* **2** an unplanned additional result of something that you do or something that happens: +**of** *Job losses are an unfortunate byproduct of the recession.* → see also END PRODUCT

Byrd /bɚd/, **Richard** (1888–1957) a U.S. EXPLORER who led five EXPEDITIONS to Antarctica

By·ron, Lord /ˈbaɪrən/ (1788–1824) an English poet

by·stand·er /ˈbaɪˌstændɚ/ *n.* [C] someone who watches what is happening without taking part SYN onlooker: *Two* ***innocent bystanders*** *were injured in the shooting.*

byte /baɪt/ *n.* [C] COMPUTERS a unit of computer information equal to eight BITS [**Origin:** 1900–2000 invented word based on *bit²* (5) and *bite*] → see also GIGABYTE, KILOBYTE, MEGABYTE

by·way /ˈbaɪˌweɪ/ *n.* [C] a small road that is not used very much

by·word /ˈbaɪwɚd/ *n.* **1 be/become a byword for sth** used to say that someone or something is so well known for a particular quality that they represent that quality: *For Americans, Benedict Arnold is a byword for treason.* **2** [usually singular] a word, phrase, or saying that is very well known: *Caution should be a byword for investors.*

Byz·an·tine /ˈbɪzənˌtin, -ˌtaɪn/ **1** one of the people that lived in the Greek city of Byzantium in northern Turkey from the seventh century B.C. to the second century A.D. **2** one of the people that lived in the Byzantine Empire from the fourth century to the fifteenth century A.D.

byz·an·tine, /ˈbɪzənˌtin, -ˌtaɪn/ *adj.* **1** complicated and difficult to understand: *byzantine tax laws* **2 Byzantine** relating to the Byzantines or the Byzantine Empire: *a 5th century Byzantine church*

ˌByzantine 'Empire, the HISTORY the eastern part of the Roman Empire, which controlled southeastern Europe, Turkey, and other areas from 330 to 1453

C,c

C¹ /si/ *n. plural* **C's** **1** also **c** *plural* **c's** [C] **a)** the third letter of the English alphabet **b)** a sound represented by this letter **2 a)** [C,U] ENG. LANG. ARTS the first note in the musical SCALE of C MAJOR **b)** [U] the musical KEY based on this note **3** [C] a grade given to a student's work to show that it is of average quality: *Terry got a C in algebra.*

C² **1** the number 100 in the system of ROMAN NUMERALS **2** PHYSICS the written abbreviation of CELSIUS **3** PHYSICS the written abbreviation of COULOMB

c **1** the written abbreviation of COPYRIGHT when printed inside a small circle: © **2** the written abbreviation of CUBIC

c. **1** a written abbreviation of "cent" **2** a written abbreviation of CIRCA (=about or approximately)

C&W *n.* [U] a written abbreviation of COUNTRY AND WESTERN music

CA a written abbreviation of CALIFORNIA

ca. a written abbreviation of CIRCA (=about or approximately)

cab /kæb/ *n.* [C] **1** a car in which you pay the driver to take you somewhere SYN **taxi**: *How much would it cost to **take a cab**? | Could you **call me a cab**, please?* (=telephone to get a cab to come to you) | *We spent ten minutes trying to **hail a cab*** (=attract the attention of a cab driver). **2** the part of a truck, bus, or train in which the driver sits **3** a carriage pulled by horses that was used like a taxi in past times

ca·bal /kəˈbɑl, -ˈbæl/ *n.* [C] a small group of people who make secret plans, especially in order to have political or economic power

ca·ban·a /kəˈbænə/ *n.* [C] a tent or small wooden structure used for changing clothes at a beach or pool [**Origin:** 1800–1900 Spanish *cabaña* **small wooden building**, from Medieval Latin *capanna*]

cab·a·ret /ˌkæbəˈreɪ/ *n.* **1** [C,U] ENG. LANG. ARTS entertainment, usually with music, songs, and dancing, performed in a restaurant or club while the customers eat and drink **2** [C] a restaurant or club where cabaret entertainment is performed [**Origin:** 1600–1700 French **drinking place, bar**]

cab·bage /ˈkæbɪdʒ/ *n.* [C,U] a large round vegetable with thick green or purple leaves [**Origin:** 1400–1500 French *caboche* **head**]

cab·bie, **cabby** /ˈkæbi/ *n.* [C] *plural* **cabbies** INFORMAL a cab driver

ˈcab driver, **cabdriver** *n.* [C] someone who drives a CAB as their job

ca·bil·do /kəˈbildoʊ/ *n.* [C] HISTORY a government council in Latin American towns that were under Spanish rule in the past

cab·in /ˈkæbɪn/ S3 W3 *n.* [C] **1** a small house, especially one made of wood, usually in a forest or the mountains: *a log cabin* **2** a small room on a ship in which you live or sleep **3** the area inside an airplane where the passengers or pilots sit [**Origin:** 1300–1400 Old French *cabane*, from Old Provençal *cabana* **small wooden building**]

ˈcabin boy *n.* [C] a young man who works as a servant on a ship

ˈcabin class *n.* [U] the rooms on a ship that are better than TOURIST CLASS but not as good as FIRST CLASS

ˈcabin crew *n.* [C] the group of people whose job is to take care of the passengers on a particular airplane

ˈcabin ˌcruiser *n.* [C] a large MOTORBOAT with one or more cabins for people to sleep in

cab·i·net /ˈkæbənɪt/ S3 W3 *n.* [C] **1** a piece of furniture with doors and shelves or drawers, used for storing or showing things → see also CUPBOARD: *kitchen cabinets | a display cabinet full of jewelry* → see also FILING CABINET **2** also **Cabinet** POLITICS an important group of politicians who make decisions or advise the leader of a government: *She was appointed to the Cabinet as secretary of commerce. | a Cabinet meeting* [**Origin:** 1500–1600 French **small room**, from Old North French *cabine* **room for gambling**]

cab·i·net·mak·er /ˈkæbənɪtˌmeɪkɚ/ *n.* [C] someone whose job is to make wooden furniture

ˈcabin ˌfever *n.* [U] INFORMAL a feeling of being upset and impatient, because you have not been outside for a long time

ca·ble¹ /ˈkeɪbəl/ S3 W2 *n.* **1** [U] a system of broadcasting television by using cables, that is paid for by the person watching it SYN **cable television**: *Do you have cable? | I saw the movie **on cable**. | a cable channel* **2** [C,U] a plastic or rubber tube containing wires that carry telephone messages, electronic signals, television pictures etc.: *They're **laying cable*** (=putting a cable under the ground) *for the telephone company.* **3** [C,U] a thick strong metal rope used on ships, to support bridges etc. **4** [C] OLD-FASHIONED a TELEGRAM [**Origin:** (1–3) 1200–1300 Old North French, Medieval Latin *capulum* **circle of rope for catching animals**, from Latin *capere* **to take**]

cable² *v.* [I,T] OLD-FASHIONED to send someone a TELEGRAM

ˈcable car *n.* [C] **1** a vehicle that is pulled along by a moving cable, used in cities to take people from one place to another **2** a vehicle that hangs from a cable and takes people to the top of mountains SYN **gondola**

ca·ble·cast /ˈkeɪbəlˌkæst/ *n.* [C] a show, movie, sports event etc. that is broadcast on a cable television station —**cablecast** *v.* [T]

ca·ble·gram /ˈkeɪbəlˌgræm/ *n.* [C] OLD-FASHIONED a TELEGRAM

ˈcable ˌrailway *n.* [C] a railroad on which vehicles are pulled up steep slopes by a moving CABLE

ˈcable stitch *n.* [C,U] a knotted pattern of stitches used in KNITTING

ˌcable ˈtelevision also **ˌcable TˈV** *n.* [U] a system of broadcasting television by using cables, that is paid for by the person watching it → see also SATELLITE TELEVISION

ca·boo·dle /kəˈbudl/ *n.* **the whole (kit and) caboodle** INFORMAL everything: *He bought the whole kit and caboodle – computer, printer, and monitor.*

ca·boose /kəˈbus/ *n.* [C] a small railroad car at the back of a train, usually where the official in charge of it travels

Cab·ot /ˈkæbət/, **John** (?1450–?1498) an Italian EXPLORER who reached the coast of North America in 1497

Ca·bri·ni /kəˈbrini/, **St. Fran·ces Xa·vi·er** /seɪnt ˈfrænsɪs ˈzeɪviɚ/ (1850–1917) also known as "Mother Cabrini"; a Catholic NUN who became the first U.S. citizen to be named a SAINT. Many churches and other institutions are named after her.

cab·ri·o·let /ˌkæbriəˈleɪ/ *n.* [C] a word used in the names of cars to show that they are CONVERTIBLES

cab·stand /ˈkæbstænd/ *n.* [C] a TAXI STAND

ca·cao /kəˈkaʊ/ *n.* [C] the seed from which chocolate and COCOA are made [**Origin:** 1500–1600 Spanish, Nahuatl *cacahuatl*]

cache¹ /kæʃ/ *n.* [C] **1** a number of things that have been hidden, or the place where they have been hidden: +**of** *Police found a cache of weapons in a warehouse.* **2** COMPUTERS a special section of MEMORY in a computer that helps it work faster by storing data for a short time [**Origin:** 1700–1800 French *cacher* **to press, hide**, from Vulgar Latin *coacticare* **to press together**]

cache² *v.* [T] to hide something in a secret place

ca·chet /kæ'ʃeɪ/ *n.* [singular, U] the quality of something that makes people think it is good or special: *It's a good university, but it lacks the cachet of Harvard.*

cack·le1 /'kækəl/ *v.* [I] **1** when a chicken cackles, it makes a loud high sound **2** to laugh in a loud way that does not sound nice, making short high sounds [**Origin:** 1100–1200 from the sound] ▶see THESAURUS box at laugh1

cackle2 *n.* [C,U] a short high laugh that does not sound nice: *loud cackles of amusement*

ca·coph·o·ny /kæ'kɑfəni/ *n.* [singular] a mixture of loud sounds together that are not pleasant to listen to: +**of** *a cacophony of car horns* [**Origin:** 1600–1700 Greek *kakophonia*, from *kakos* **bad** + *phone* **voice, sound**] —**cacophonous** *adj.*

cac·tus /'kæktəs/ *n. plural* **cacti** /-taɪ/ or **cactuses** [C] a desert plant with thick smooth stems and needles instead of leaves [**Origin:** 1700–1800 Latin, thistle-like plant, from Greek *kaktos*] → see picture on page A31

CAD /ˌsi eɪ 'di, kæd/ *n.* [U] COMPUTERS computer-aided design; the use of computer GRAPHICS to plan cars, aircraft, buildings etc.

cad /kæd/ *n.* [C] OLD-FASHIONED a man who cannot be trusted, especially one who treats women badly —**caddish** *adj.*

ca·dav·er /kə'dævɚ/ *n.* [C] TECHNICAL a dead human body

ca·dav·er·ous /kə'dævərəs/ *adj.* looking extremely pale, thin, and unhealthy: *a cadaverous face*

CAD/CAM /'kædkæm/ *n.* [U] computer-aided design and manufacture; the use of computers to plan and make industrial products

cad·dy1 /'kædi/ *n. plural* **caddies** [C] **1** also **caddie** someone who carries the GOLF CLUBS for someone who is playing GOLF **2** a small box for storing tea [**Origin:** (2) 1700–1800 Malay *kati* a unit of weight]

caddy2, **caddie** *v.* **caddies, caddied, caddying** [I + for] to carry GOLF CLUBS for someone who is playing GOLF

ca·dence /'keɪdns/ *n.* [C] ENG. LANG. ARTS **1** the way someone's voice rises and falls, especially when reading out loud: *She could imitate perfectly the cadence of my mother's voice.* **2** a regular repeated pattern of sounds or movements: *the cadence and rhythm of poetry* **3** a set of CHORDS at the end of a line or piece of music

ca·den·za /kə'dɛnzə/ *n.* [C] TECHNICAL a difficult part of a CONCERTO in which the performer plays without the ORCHESTRA to show his or her skill

ca·det /kə'dɛt/ *n.* [C] someone who is training to be an officer in the military or the police [**Origin:** 1600–1700 French, French dialect *capdet* **chief**, from Latin *caput* **head**]

cadge /kædʒ/ *v.* [I,T] INFORMAL to ask someone for something such as food or cigarettes, because you do not have any or do not want to pay SYN **mooch**

Cad·il·lac /'kædlˌæk/ *n.* [C] **1** TRADEMARK a type of very expensive and comfortable American car **2** INFORMAL something that is regarded as the highest quality example of a particular type of product: +**of** *the Cadillac of stereo systems*

cad·mi·um /'kædmiəm/ *n.* [U] SYMBOL **Cd** CHEMISTRY a type of metal that is an ELEMENT and is used in batteries (BATTERY)

ca·dre /'kædri, 'kɑ-, -dreɪ/ *n.* FORMAL [C] a small group of specially trained people in a profession, political party, or military force: *a cadre of highly trained scientists*

ca·du·ce·us /kə'duʃiəs/ *n.* [C] a sign consisting of two snakes around a stick that has wings at the top, used to represent a medical profession, especially that of doctors

Cae·sar /'sizɚ/, **Ju·li·us** /'dʒuliəs/ (100–44 B.C.) a Roman politician, military leader, and writer, who made himself the first Roman emperor

cae·sar·e·an /sɪ'zɛriən/ *n.* [C] another spelling of CESAREAN

cae·si·um /'siziəm/ *n.* [U] CHEMISTRY another spelling of CESIUM

cae·su·ra /sɪ'zʊrə, sɪ'ʒʊrə/ *n.* [C] ENG. LANG. ARTS a pause in the middle of a line of poetry

ca·fé /kæ'feɪ, kə-/ *n.* [C] a small restaurant where you can buy drinks and simple meals → see also INTERNET CAFÉ [**Origin:** 1800–1900 French **coffee, café**, from Turkish *kahve*]

caf·e·te·ri·a /ˌkæfə'tɪriə/ *n.* [C] a restaurant, often in a factory, school etc., where you choose from foods that have already been cooked and carry your own food to a table: *Students complained about the cafeteria food.* [**Origin:** 1800–1900 American Spanish **coffee shop**, from Spanish *café* **coffee**]

caf·e·to·ri·um /ˌkæfə'tɔriəm/ *n.* [C] a large room in a school that is used for activities such as preparing and eating food, exercising, and having meetings

caf·feine /kæ'fin, 'kæfin/ *n.* [U] a chemical substance in tea, coffee, and some other drinks that makes you feel more active: *Avoid caffeine before bedtime.* | ***caffeine-free*** (=without caffeine) *soft drinks* —**caffeinated** /'kæfəˌneɪt̬ɪd/ *adj.*

caf·tan, kaftan /'kæftæn/ *n.* [C] a long loose piece of clothing like a dress, usually made of silk or cotton and worn in the Middle East

cage1 /keɪdʒ/ S3 *n.* [C] a structure made of wires or bars in which birds or animals can be kept: *lions in a cage* [**Origin:** 1100–1200 Old French, Latin *cavea* **hollow place, cage**] → see also **rattle sb's cage** at RATTLE1 (4)

cage2 *v.* **1 feel caged in** to feel uncomfortable and annoyed because you cannot go outside or because a place is too small **2** [T] to put or keep an animal or bird in a cage

cag·ey /'keɪdʒi/ *adj.* INFORMAL unwilling to tell people definitely what your plans, intentions, or opinions are: +**about** *The White House is being very cagey about the contents of the report.* —**cagily** *adv.* —**caginess** *n.*

ca·hoots /kə'huts/ *n.* **be in cahoots (with sb)** INFORMAL to be working secretly with another person or group, especially in order to do something dishonest or illegal: *Rogers is accused of being in cahoots with the mafia.*

cai·man /'keɪmən/ *n.* [C] a type of small CROCODILE that lives in tropical areas of North, Central, and South America

Cain /keɪn/ in the Bible, Adam and Eve's first son, who killed his younger brother, Abel, and became the first murderer

cairn /kɛrn/ *n.* [C] a pile of stones, especially at the top of a mountain, to mark a place

Cai·ro /'kaɪroʊ/ the capital and largest city of Egypt

cais·son /'keɪsɑn, -sən/ *n.* [C] **1** a large box filled with air, that people go into to work under water **2** a large box with two wheels, used for carrying AMMUNITION

ca·jole /kə'dʒoʊl/ *v.* [I,T] to gradually persuade someone to do something by being nice to them or making promises to them: **cajole sb into doing sth** *Jacobs finally cajoled Beecher into taking the job.* [**Origin:** 1600–1700 French *cajoler* **to make noises like a bird in a cage, cajole**, from Old North French *gaiole* **birdcage**]

Ca·jun /'keɪdʒən/ *n.* a member of a group of people in southern Louisiana who had French-Canadian ANCESTORS [**Origin:** 1800–1900 *Acadian* **of Acadia** (18–21 centuries), from *Acadia* former French colony in eastern Canada] —**Cajun** *adj.*

cake1 /keɪk/ S1 W3 *n.* **1** [C,U] a soft sweet food made by baking a mixture of flour, butter, sugar, and eggs: *a birthday cake* | *Do you want a piece of cake?* | *Will you help me* ***bake the cake?*** **2** [C] a small piece of something, shaped into a block: +**of** *a cake of soap* **3 a fish/rice/potato etc. cake** fish, rice, potato etc. that has been formed into a flat round shape and then cooked **4 have your cake and eat it too** INFORMAL to have all the advantages of something without any of the disadvantages **5 take the cake** INFORMAL to be worse than anything else you can imagine: *You've done some pretty stupid things, but that really takes the cake!* [**Origin:** 1100–1200 Old Norse *kaka*] → see also **be selling/going like hotcakes** at HOTCAKE, PANCAKE, **be a piece of cake** at PIECE¹ (10)

cake² *v.* **1 be caked with/in sth** to be covered with a layer of something thick and hard: *Terry's elbow was caked with dried blood.* **2** [I] if a substance cakes, it forms a thick hard layer when it dries

'cake mix *n.* [C] a dry mixture that you buy and mix with eggs and milk to make a cake easily and quickly

'cake pan *n.* [C] a metal container in which you bake a cake

cake•walk /'keɪkwɔk/ *n.* [singular] INFORMAL a very easy thing to do, or a very easy victory: *Don't expect the game against Florida to be a cakewalk.* [**Origin:** 1800–1900 *cakewalk* **walking competition with a cake as first prize** (19–20 centuries)]

cal. an abbreviation of CALORIE

cal•a•bash /'kælə,bæʃ/ *n.* [C] BIOLOGY a large tropical fruit with a shell that can be dried and used as a bowl

cal•a•mine lo•tion /'kæləmaɪn ,loʊʃən/ *n.* [U] a pink liquid used to treat sore, ITCHY, or SUNBURNed skin

ca•lam•i•ty /kə'læməti/ *n. plural* **calamities** [C] a terrible and unexpected event that causes a lot of damage or suffering: *The hurricane was just the latest calamity to hit the state.* —**calamitous** *adj.* —**calamitously** *adv.*

cal•ci•fy /'kælsə,faɪ/ *v.* **calcifies, calcified, calcifying** [I,T] TECHNICAL CHEMISTRY to become hard, or make something hard, by adding LIME

cal•ci•um /'kælsiəm/ *n.* [U] SYMBOL **Ca** CHEMISTRY a silver-white metal that is an ELEMENT and that helps form teeth, bones, and CHALK

cal•cu•la•ble /'kælkyələbəl/ *adj.* [no comparative] something that is calculable can be measured by using numbers

cal•cu•late /'kælkyə,leɪt/ [W3] *v.* [T] **1** MATH to measure something or find out how much something will cost, how long something will take etc., by using numbers [SYN] **figure out**: *These instruments calculate distances precisely.* | **calculate (that)** *Scientists have calculated that the sample is over 100,000 years old.* | **calculate sth on sth** *Rates are calculated on an hourly basis.* | **calculate how much/many etc.** *Use the formula to calculate how much water is wasted.*

THESAURUS

figure out a less formal word for calculate: *Let's try to figure out how much this will cost.*
add sth and sth to put two or more numbers together to find the total: *Add seven and five to make twelve.*
subtract sth from sth also **take sth away from sth** to reduce one number by another number: *If you subtract twelve from fifteen, you get three.* | *Eight take away two is six.*
multiply to add a number to itself a particular number of times: *Four multiplied by ten is forty.*
divide to calculate how many times one number contains another number: *Ten divided by two equals five.*
plus used between numbers to show that you are adding them together: *Two plus two equals four.*
minus used between numbers to show that you are taking one away from the other: *Six minus five is one.*
times used between numbers to show that you are multiplying them together: *Six times three is eighteen.*

2 to guess something using as many facts as you can find: *It's difficult to calculate what effect the changes will have.* **3 be calculated to do sth** to be intended to have a particular effect: *The commercials are calculated to attract young single consumers.* [**Origin:** 1500–1600 Latin, past participle of *calculare*, from *calculus* **stone used in counting**]

calculate on sth *phr. v.* if you calculate on something, you are depending on it for your plans to succeed: **calculate on sb/sth doing sth** *Ken hadn't calculated on Williams refusing his offer.*

cal•cu•lat•ed /'kælkyə,leɪtɪd/ *adj.* [usually before noun] **1 a calculated risk/gamble** something risky that you do after thinking carefully about what might happen: *Police took a calculated risk in releasing him.* **2** a calculated crime or dishonest action is deliberately and carefully planned: *It was a calculated attempt to make the governor look foolish.* → see also CALCULATE

cal•cu•lat•ing /'kælkyə,leɪtɪŋ/ *adj.* [usually before noun] DISAPPROVING tending to make careful plans to get what you want, without caring about how it affects other people: *Yetter was a calculating troublemaker.*

cal•cu•la•tion /,kælkyə'leɪʃən/ *n.* [C usually plural,U] **1** MATH the act of adding, multiplying, dividing etc. numbers in order to find out an amount, price, or value: *Ellie looked at the report and **did** some quick **calculations**.* | ***By our calculations**, it will cost about $12 million to build.* **2** careful planning in order to get what you want: *clever political calculation*

cal•cu•la•tor /'kælkyə,leɪtər/ *n.* [C] a small electronic machine that can add, multiply, divide etc. numbers

cal•cu•lus /'kælkyələs/ *n.* [U] MATH the part of mathematics that deals with changing quantities, such as the speed of a falling stone or the slope of a curved line

Cal•cut•ta /kæl'kʌtə/ the capital and largest city of the state of West Bengal in India

Cal•der /'kɔldər/, **Alexander** (1898–1976) a U.S. SCULPTOR best known for his large outdoor works of art and his large MOBILES

cal•dron /'kɔldrən/ *n.* [C] another spelling of CAULDRON

cal•en•dar /'kæləndər/ [S2] *n.* [C] **1** a set of pages that show the days, weeks, and months of a particular year, that you usually hang on the wall: *a calendar for 2008* **2 a)** a book with separate spaces or pages for each day of the year, on which you write down the things you have to do [SYN] **appointment book** [SYN] **date- book** **b)** all the things you plan to do in the next days, months etc.: *My calendar is full for the rest of the week.* **3** a system that divides and measures time in a particular way, usually starting from a particular event: *the Jewish calendar* **4** all the events in a year that are important for a particular organization or activity: *The Tour de France is the biggest race in the cycling calendar.* [**Origin:** 1100–1200 Anglo-French *calender*, from Medieval Latin *kalendarium*, from Latin *kalendae* **first day of an ancient Roman month**]

,calendar 'month *n.* [C] **1** one of the 12 months of the year: *Salaries will be paid at the end of the calendar month.* **2** a period of time from a specific date in one month to the same date in the next month

,calendar 'year *n.* [C] the period of time from January 1 to December 31

calf /kæf/ [S3] *n. plural* **calves** /kævz/ **1** [C] BIOLOGY the part of the back of your leg between your knee and your foot **2** [C] BIOLOGY the baby of a cow, or of some other large animals such as the ELEPHANT **3** [U] CALFSKIN **4 be in calf** if a cow is in calf, it is going to give birth [**Origin:** (2–3) Old English *cealf*]

'calf-length *adj.* calf-length clothes cover your body to your calf: *a calf-length skirt* | *calf-length boots*

calf•skin /'kæf,skɪn/ *n.* [U] the skin of a calf, which has been preserved and is used for making shoes, bags etc.

Cal•houn /kæl'hun/, **John C.** (1782–1850) a U.S. politician who supported the states' right not to accept laws passed by the national government

cal•i•ber /'kæləbər/ *n.* **1** [singular, U] the level of quality or ability that someone or something has achieved: *He's a doctor **of the highest caliber**.* | *Where will we* *find another player* **of** *his* **caliber**? **2** [C] TECHNICAL **a)** the width of the inside of a gun or tube **b)** the width of a bullet [**Origin:** 1500–1600 French *calibre*, from Old Italian *calibro*, from Arabic *qalib* **block on which shoes are made**]

cal·i·brate /ˈkæləˌbreɪt/ *v.* [T] TECHNICAL **1** to check or slightly change an instrument or tool, so that it does something correctly **2** to mark an instrument or tool so that you can use it for measuring

C

cal·i·bra·tion /ˌkæləˈbreɪʃən/ *n.* [C,U] TECHNICAL **1** the process of checking or slightly changing an instrument or tool so that it does something correctly **2** a set of marks on an instrument or tool used for measuring, or the act of making these tools correct

cal·i·co /ˈkælɪˌkoʊ/ *n.* **1** [U] light cotton cloth with a small printed pattern **2** also **calico cat** a cat that has black, white, and brown fur

Cal·i·for·nia /ˌkælɪˈfɔrnyə/ ABBREVIATION **CA** a state on the west coast of the U.S. —**Californian** *n., adj.*

California, the Gulf of a part of the Pacific Ocean that is between the PENINSULA of Baja California in western Mexico and the Mexican MAINLAND

ˌCalifornia ˈGold Rush, the HISTORY the time after 1848, when gold was discovered in California, when large numbers of people went to California to find gold

Ca·lig·u·la /kəˈlɪgyələ/ (A.D. 12–41) a Roman emperor who was known for being extremely violent, cruel, and crazy

cal·i·pers /ˈkælɪpɚz/ *n.* [plural] a tool used for measuring thickness, the distance between two surfaces, or the DIAMETER (=inside width) of something

ca·liph /ˈkeɪlɪf, ˈkæ-/ *n.* [C] HISTORY a title of some MUSLIM rulers, especially in the past. A caliph's right to rule came from being related to the PROPHET Muhammad.

ca·liph·ate /ˈkæləˌfeɪt, ˈkeɪ-/ *n.* [C] the country a caliph rules, or the period of time when he rules it

cal·is·then·ics /ˌkælɪsˈθɛnɪks/ *n.* [U] a set of physical exercises that are intended to make you strong, healthy, and graceful

CALL /kɔl/ *n.* [U] COMPUTERS computer-assisted language learning; the use of computers to help people learn foreign languages

call¹ /kɔl/ S1 W1 *v.*

1 TELEPHONE [I,T] to talk to someone by telephone, or to attempt to do this SYN **phone**: *Patty called when you were out.* | *I called Sue yesterday.* ►see THESAURUS box at **phone²**

2 DESCRIBE [T] to use a particular word or phrase to describe someone or something that clearly shows what you think of them: **call sb/sth sth** *I would call the meeting a success.* | *Are you calling me a liar?* | *That's* ***what I call*** *good food!*

THESAURUS

describe to say what someone or something is like by giving details: *The suspect has been described as a young white man with brown hair.*
characterize to describe the character of someone or something in a particular way: *Psychologists characterized her as mentally unstable.*
label to use a particular word or phrase in order to describe someone: *He labeled their comments "ridiculous."*
brand to consider someone as a very bad type of person, often unfairly: *The defense lawyers tried to brand him as a racist cop.*
portray to describe or show someone or something in a particular way: *a politician who portrays himself as an environmentalist*

3 USE A NAME [T] to use a particular name or title for someone or something: *His name's actually Robert, but everyone just calls him Bob.* | **be called sth** *The arrow on the screen is called a cursor.* | *Do you want to be called Miss or Ms.?* | **be called by sth** *We always called him by his middle name.* | **What do you call...?** *What do you call that tool with the hook on the end?*

4 ASK/ORDER BY TELEPHONE [T] to ask someone to come to you by telephoning them: *Did somebody call a taxi?* | *Get out of here or I'll call the police!*

5 ASK/ORDER BY SPEAKING [T] to ask or order someone to come to you, either by speaking loudly or sending them a message: *Didn't you hear me calling you?* | **call sb into/over** *Later, the boss called Dan into her office.*

6 ARRANGE [T] to arrange for something to happen at a particular time: *A meeting has been called for 3 p.m. Wednesday.* | *Union leaders have called another strike.*

7 SAY/SHOUT [I,T] to say or shout something loudly because you want someone to hear you: *"Coming, Mom," I called.* | *I thought I heard someone call my name.* | +**through/down/up** *"Can you fetch me a towel," Claire called through the door.*

8 GIVE SB/STH A NAME [T] to give someone or something a name: **call sb/sth sth** *They've decided to call the baby Amanda.*

9 call sb names to insult someone by using words that are not nice to describe them: *The other kids always called him names.*

10 call yourself sth to claim that you are a particular type of person, although you do nothing to show this is true: *He calls himself a Christian, but he's not very nice to strangers.*

11 call the shots/tune INFORMAL to be in a position of authority so that you can give orders and make decisions: *Around here Randy calls the shots.*

12 call it a day INFORMAL to decide to stop working, especially because you have done enough or you are tired: *Come on, guys, let's call it a day.*

13 call it a night INFORMAL to decide that it is late and time to go to bed: *It's after midnight – I think I'm going to call it a night.*

14 call collect to make a telephone call that is paid for by the person who receives it

15 READ NAMES [T] to read names or numbers in a loud voice in order to get someone's attention SYN **call out**: *OK, when I call your name, raise your hand.*

16 GUESS [T] to make a guess or judgment about what will happen in the future: *I didn't think it would happen, but you called it.* | *The race is* ***too close to call*** (=the people in the competition are doing equally well and you cannot guess who will win).

17 SPORTS DECISION [T] to make an official decision about a particular shot or play in a sport: *The umpire called a foul.*

18 COURT [T usually passive] to tell someone that they must come to a law court or official committee: **call sb to do sth** *I've been called to testify at the trial.*

19 call sth into question to make people uncertain about whether something is right or true: *Bennett's ability as a leader has been called into question.*

20 be/feel called to do sth if you are called to do something, you feel strongly that it is your duty to do it or that you are the best person to do it: *Sandy felt called to do missionary work.*

21 call sb/sth to order FORMAL to tell people to obey the rules of a formal meeting: *I now call this meeting to order.*

22 call it $15/two hours etc. SPOKEN used to ask someone to agree to a particular price, amount of time, limit etc., especially in order to make things simpler: *"How much do I owe you?" "Oh, just call it $15."*

23 call it even SPOKEN used to say that someone who owes you something does not have to give you anything more than they have already given you: *Since you bought the movie tickets and I bought dinner, let's just call it even.*

24 call it a draw/tie if two opponents in a game call it a draw, they agree that neither of them has won

25 call sb's attention to sth to ask people to pay attention to a particular subject or problem: *May I call your attention to item seven on the agenda?*

26 call sth to mind a) to remind you of something: *Modesto is a city that calls to mind the words "hot" and "dry."* **b)** to remember something: *Can you call to mind when you last saw her?*

27 STOP A GAME [T] to decide that a sports game will not

be finished or take place SYN **call off** SYN **cancel**: *The game was called on account of rain.*
28 call a huddle INFORMAL to arrange for people to come together to have a meeting
29 TRAINS/SHIPS [I] OLD-FASHIONED if a train or ship calls at a place, it stops there for a short time: +**at** *This train will be calling briefly at Yonkers.*
30 COIN [I,T] to guess which side of a coin will land facing up after it is thrown in the air: *"OK, call it." "Heads."*
31 VISIT [I] OLD-FASHIONED to stop at a house or other place for a short time to see someone or do something: *Mr. Sweeney called while you were out.*
32 CARD GAME [I,T] to bet the same amount of money as the player who plays before you in a POKER game SYN **see**: *I'll call your dollar – what have you got?* → see also **draw/call attention to yourself** at ATTENTION (3), **call sb's bluff** at BLUFF² (2), **call it quits** at QUITS, SO-CALLED, **call a spade a spade** at SPADE (3)
[**Origin:** 1100–1200 Old Norse *kalla*]

call back *phr. v.* **call sb back** to telephone someone again, especially because one of you was not in or was busy: *Okay, I'll call back around three.* | *I'm sorry, Mr. Dunbar is in a meeting, can he call you back later?*

call sth ↔ **down on** sb/sth *phr. v.* LITERARY to pray loudly that something bad will happen to someone or something: *The old man called down curses on us.*

call for sb/sth *phr. v.* **1** to ask strongly and publicly for something to happen in order to change a situation: *Protesters are calling for an immediate end to the war.* | **call for sb/sth to do sth** *They're calling for volunteers to help rebuild the school.* **2** to demand or need a particular action, behavior, quality etc.: *This news calls for a celebration!* | *I don't really think comments like that are called for.* → see also UNCALLED FOR **3** to say that a particular kind of weather is likely to happen: *The weather forecast calls for more rain and high winds.* **4** OLD-FASHIONED to meet someone at their home in order to take them somewhere: *I'll call for you at seven o'clock.*

call sth ↔ **forth** *phr. v.* FORMAL to make something such as a quality appear so that you can use it SYN **summon**: *Calling forth all his strength, Arthur pulled the sword out of the stone.*

call in *phr. v.* **1 call sb/sth ↔ in** to ask or order a person or organization to help you with a difficult or dangerous situation: *The FBI has been called in to investigate.* **2** to telephone somewhere, especially the place where you work, to tell them where you are, what you are doing etc.: *Why don't you just **call in sick** (=telephone to say you are too sick to come to work)?* **3** to telephone a radio or television show to give your opinion or ask a question: *A number of people called in with good suggestions.* **4 call in a loan/favor** to ask someone to pay back money or to help you with something because you helped them earlier **5** OLD-FASHIONED to visit a person or place while you are on your way somewhere else: +**at/on** *Could you call in on Grandma on your way home?*

call off *phr. v.* **1 call sth ↔ off** to decide that a planned event will not take place SYN **cancel**: *The game was called off due to heavy rain.* **2 call sb/sth ↔ off** to order a dog or person to stop attacking someone: *Call off your dog!* **3 call off a strike/search etc.** to decide officially that something should be stopped after it has already started: *Rescuers have been forced to call off the search until the weather improves.*

call on/upon sb/sth *phr. v.* **1** to formally ask someone to do something: **call on sb to do sth** *Western countries have been called on to support the new government.* **2** to visit someone for a short time: *I spent most of the day calling on clients.*

call out *phr. v.* **1 call sth ↔ out** to say something loudly SYN **call**: *We'll call out your name when your order is ready.* | *I called out to you at the train station, but you didn't hear me.* **2 call sb/sth ↔ out** to ask or order a person or organization to help, especially with a difficult or dangerous situation: *Every fire engine in the city had been called out.*

call up *phr. v.* **1 call sb ↔ up** to telephone someone SYN **call**: *He called me up to tell me about it.* **2 call sth ↔ up** if you call up information on a computer, you make the computer show it to you **3 call sth ↔ up** to bring a memory into your mind SYN **bring up**: *The experience called up some painful memories.* **4 call sb/sth ↔ up** to make something appear or exist SYN **conjure up**: *The woman believes she can call up the spirits of the dead.* **5 call sb ↔ up** to move a baseball player from a MINOR LEAGUE team to a MAJOR LEAGUE team

call² S1 W1 *n.* [C]
1 TELEPHONE an attempt to speak to someone by telephone: *Have there been many calls?* | *I **got a call** from Pam yesterday.* | *Just **give** me **a call** when you arrive.* | *We always get so many **phone calls** at dinnertime.* | *Excuse me, I have to **make** an important phone **call**.* | *She never **returns my calls*** (=telephones me back). | *I'll **take the call*** (=answer a telephone call) *in my office.* | **a local/long-distance call** (=a phone call made within the city or area where you are, or one made to somewhere far away)
2 be on call if someone such as a doctor or engineer is on call, they are ready to go and help whenever they are needed as part of their job: *She's on call at the hospital every other night.*
3 SHOUT/CRY a) a shout or cry that you make to get someone's attention: +**for** *a call for help* **b)** the sound or cry that a bird or animal makes: +**of** *the distinctive call of the hyena*
4 REQUEST/ORDER a request or order for someone to do something or go somewhere: *Ambulances try to arrive within eight minutes of an emergency call.* | +**for** *They ignored the call for an end to the fighting.* | **a call for sb (to do sth)** *There have been calls for the chairman to resign.*
5 DECISION a) a decision made by a REFEREE (=judge) in a sports game: *the umpire's call* | **make good/bad calls** *The referee made several bad calls.* **b)** INFORMAL a decision: *"Where should we eat tonight?" "I don't know, **it's your call**."* | **a hard/easy call** (=a difficult or easy decision) *This is not an easy call.* | *Guilty or innocent? You **make the call*** (=decide).
6 good/bad call! SLANG used to say that you agree or disagree with someone's decision about something
7 there is no call for sth also **there is no call to do sth** SPOKEN used to tell someone that their behavior is wrong and unnecessary: *There was no call for him to do that.*
8 AIRPLANE an official message at an airport that an airplane for a particular place will soon leave: *This is **the last call for** flight 372 to Atlanta.*
9 VISIT OLD-FASHIONED a short visit, especially for a particular reason SYN **visit**: *We should **pay** Jerry **a call*** (=visit him) *since we're driving through Ohio.*
10 there isn't much call for sth used to say that something is not popular or is not needed: *There isn't much call for typewriters these days.*
11 the call of sth LITERARY the power that a place or way of life has to attract someone: *the call of the sea*
12 the call of nature INFORMAL a need to URINATE (=pass liquid from your body)
13 BANK [U] TECHNICAL a demand by a bank or other financial institution for money that has been borrowed to be paid back immediately → see also **be at sb's beck and call** at BECK, **judgment call** at JUDGMENT (4), PORT OF CALL, ROLL CALL

Cal·las /ˈkæləs/, **Ma·ri·a** /məˈriə/ (1923–1977) a U.S. OPERA singer who is considered one of the greatest opera singers of the 20th century

ˈcall box *n.* [C] a public telephone beside a street or FREEWAY, used to telephone for help

ˈcall ˌcenter *n.* [C] a place where a large number of people answer telephone calls from a company's customers, during which they try to sell things to customers or give them information

call·er /ˈkɔlɚ/ *n.* [C] **1** someone who is making a telephone call: *Didn't the caller say who she was?* **2** OLD-FASHIONED someone who visits your house

ˈcaller IˌD *n.* [U] a special service on your telephone that lets you know who is calling before you answer the telephone

ˈcall ˌforwarding *n.* [U] a telephone service that allows you to send your calls to a different telephone number, so that people who call your usual number can reach you at the other number

ˈcall girl *n.* [C] a PROSTITUTE who makes arrangements to meet men by telephone

C

cal·lig·ra·phy /kəˈlɪɡrəfi/ *n.* [U] the art of producing beautiful writing using special pens or brushes, or the writing produced this way —**calligrapher** *n.* [C]

ˈcall-in *adj.* [only before noun] used to describe a radio or television program in which people telephone to give their opinions —**call-in** *n.* [C]

call·ing /ˈkɔlɪŋ/ *n.* [C] **1** a strong desire or feeling of duty to do a particular kind of work, especially work that helps other people SYN **vocation**: *Helping the poor was her calling in life.* **2** FORMAL someone's profession or trade

ˈcalling card *n.* [C] a small card with a name and often an address printed on it, that people in the past used to give to people they visited

cal·li·o·pe /kəˈlaɪəpi/ *n.* [C] a large musical instrument like a piano, with large whistles that use steam to make sound, used especially in a CIRCUS

ˈcall ˌletters *n.* [plural] a name made up of letters and numbers, used by people operating communication radios to prove who they are

ˈcall ˌmoney *n.* [U] TECHNICAL the INTEREST rate that is charged on LOANS that a bank is asking to be paid back immediately

ˈcall ˌnumber *n.* [C] the numbers used on a library book to put it into a group with other books with the same subject, so that you can find it easily on the shelves

ˈcall ˌoption *n.* [C] ECONOMICS the right to buy a particular number of SHARES at a particular price within a particular period of time

cal·lous /ˈkæləs/ *adj.* unkind and not caring that other people are suffering: *a* ***callous disregard*** *for employee safety* —**callously** *adv.* —**callousness** *n.* [U]

cal·low /ˈkæloʊ/ *adj.* LITERARY young and without experience: *a callow youth*

ˈcall sign *n.* [C] CALL LETTERS

cal·lus /ˈkæləs/ *n.* [C] an area of thick hard skin, caused by the skin rubbing against something such as shoes, a tool etc. over a long period of time: *calluses on her feet*

cal·lused /ˈkæləst/ *adj.* covered in calluses: *His hands were rough and callused.*

ˌcall ˈwaiting *n.* [U] a telephone service that allows you to receive another call when you are already talking on the telephone, without ending the first call

calm¹ /kɑm/ *adj.* **1** relaxed and quiet, not angry, nervous, or upset: *His mother was a calm slow-speaking woman.* | **keep/stay/remain calm** *The breathing exercises help you to stay calm.*

THESAURUS

relaxed calm and not worried or angry: *He seemed relaxed and confident.*
laid-back relaxed and not seeming to worry about anything: *My dad's pretty laid-back, but my mother's always nagging.*
mellow friendly, relaxed, and calm: *She's a lot more mellow than she was when she was younger.*
cool INFORMAL calm, and not nervous or excited: *Try to stay cool during the interview.*

2 if a place, period of time, or situation is calm, there is less activity, trouble etc. than there sometimes is, or than there has been recently: *The streets are calm again after last night's disturbances.* ►see THESAURUS box at **quiet¹** **3** a calm ocean, lake etc. is smooth or has only gentle waves → see picture at CHOPPY **4** calm weather is not windy: *It was a calm, clear, beautiful day.* —**calmly** *adv.* —**calmness** *n.* [U]

calm² S3 also **calm down** *v.* [I,T] **1** to become quiet and relaxed, after you have been angry, excited, nervous, or upset, or to make someone become quiet and relaxed: *Calm down and tell me what happened.* | *He tried to calm the frightened children.* | *Awareness of polio was high, and the government tried to* ***calm*** *people's* ***fears****.* | **calm (yourself) down** *She lit a cigarette to calm herself down.* **2** if a situation calms down, it becomes easier to deal with because there are fewer problems and it is not as busy as it was before: *It took about six months for* ***things to calm down*** *after we had the baby.* [**Origin:** 1300–1400 Old French *calme*, from Late Latin *cauma* **heat**; because everything is quiet and still in the heat of the middle part of the day]

calm³ *n.* **1** [singular, U] a time that is quiet and peaceful: *We sat on the patio, enjoying the calm of the evening.* | *The last five years have seen a period of* ***relative calm****.* | *The president has* ***appealed for calm*** *and called for new elections.* **2 the calm before the storm** a calm peaceful situation just before a big argument, problem etc.

ca·lor·ic /kəˈlɔrɪk/ *adj.* relating to calories: *caloric intake*

cal·o·rie /ˈkæləri/ S3 *n.* [C] **1** a unit for measuring the amount of ENERGY a particular food will produce: *An average potato has about 90 calories.* | *A long walk will help you* ***burn off*** *a few* ***calories*** (=control your weight by using the energy from the food you have eaten). | *My wife finally convinced me to start* ***counting calories*** (=trying to control my weight by calculating the number of calories I eat). **2** also **small calorie** WRITTEN ABBREVIATION **cal** CHEMISTRY the amount of heat that is needed to raise the temperature of one gram of water by one degree Celsius **3** also **large calorie** WRITTEN ABBREVIATION **Cal** CHEMISTRY the amount of heat that is needed to raise the temperature of one kilogram of water by one degree Celsius SYN **kilocalorie** [**Origin:** 1800–1900 French, Latin *calor* **heat**]

cal·o·rif·ic /ˌkæləˈrɪfɪk◂/ *adj.* **1** calorific food tends to make you fat **2** PHYSICS producing heat

cal·o·rim·e·ter /ˌkæləˈrɪmət̬ɚ/ *n.* [C] CHEMISTRY an instrument for measuring heat in a chemical reaction or other process

ca·lum·ni·ate /kəˈlʌmniˌeɪt/ *v.* [T] FORMAL to say untrue and unfair things about someone SYN **slander**

cal·um·ny /ˈkæləmni/ *n. plural* **calumnies** FORMAL **1** [C] an untrue and unfair statement about someone that is intended to give people a bad opinion of them SYN **slander** **2** [U] the act of saying untrue and unfair things about someone SYN **slander**

cal·va·ry /ˈkælvəri/ *n. plural* **calvaries** [C] a model or STATUE that represents the death of Jesus Christ on the cross

calve /kæv/ *v.* [I] to give birth to a CALF (=baby cow)

calves /kævz/ *n.* the plural of CALF

Cal·vin /ˈkælvɪn/**, John** (1509–1564) a French-born Swiss religious leader, whose ideas had a strong influence on the beginnings of the Protestant religion → see also CALVINISM

Cal·vin·ism /ˈkælvəˌnɪzəm/ *n.* [U] the Christian religious teachings of John Calvin, which are based on the idea that events on Earth are controlled by God, and which led to the establishment of the PRESBYTERIAN church

Cal·vin·ist /ˈkælvənɪst/ *adj.* **1** following the teachings of Calvinism **2** also **Calvinistic** having strict moral standards and tending to disapprove of pleasure SYN **puritanical** —**Calvinist** *n.* [C]

ca·lyp·so /kəˈlɪpsoʊ/ *n. plural* **calypsos** [C] a type of Caribbean song based on subjects of interest in the news

ca·lyx /ˈkeɪlɪks/ *n. plural* **calyxes** or **calyces** /-lɪsiz/ [C] BIOLOGY the green outer part of a flower that protects it before it opens

cam /kæm/ *n.* [C] **1** a wheel or part of a wheel that is shaped to change circular movement into backward and forward movement **2** a WEBCAM

ca·ma·ra·der·ie /kæm'rɑdəri, kɑm-/ *n.* [U] a feeling of friendship that a group of people have, especially when they work together: *the soccer team's camaraderie*

cam·ber /'kæmbɚ/ *n.* [C,U] TECHNICAL a slight curve from the center to the side of a road or other surface that makes water run off to the side

Cam·bo·di·a /kæm'boʊdiə/ a country in Southeast Asia between Thailand and Vietnam —**Cambodian** *n., adj.*

cam·bric /'keɪmbrɪk/ *n.* [U] thin white cloth made of LINEN or cotton

cam·cord·er /'kæm,kɔrdɚ/ *n.* [C] a type of camera that you can hold in one hand to record pictures and sound onto VIDEOTAPE

came /keɪm/ *v.* the past tense of COME

cam·el /'kæməl/ *n.* [C] a large desert animal with a long neck and one or two HUMPS (=large raised parts) on its back [**Origin:** 900–1000 Latin *camelus*, from Greek *kamelos*] → see also **the straw that breaks the camel's back** at STRAW[1] (3)

cam·el·hair /'kæməl,hɛr/ *n.* [U] a thick yellowish brown cloth, usually used for making coats

ca·mel·lia /kə'milyə/ *n.* [C] a plant on which grow large sweet-smelling red, pink, or white flowers, or the flowers themselves [**Origin:** 1700–1800 Georg Josef *Kamel* (in Latin, *Camellus*) (1661-1706), priest and plant scientist]

Cam·e·lot /'kæmə,lɑt/ according to old stories about King Arthur, the place where Arthur and his KNIGHTS lived

cam·em·bert /'kæməm,bɛr/ *n.* [C,U] a soft French cheese, that is white outside and yellow inside

cam·e·o /'kæmioʊ/ *n. plural* **cameos** [C] **1** ENG. LANG. ARTS a small part in a movie or play acted by a well-known actor: *Danny DeVito made a cameo appearance as a lawyer.* **2** a small piece of jewelry that has a raised shape, usually of a person's face, on a dark flat background: *a cameo brooch* **3** ENG. LANG. ARTS a short piece of writing that gives a clear idea of a person, place, or event

cam·er·a /'kæmrə, -ərə/ S1 W2 *n.* [C] **1** a piece of equipment used for taking photographs: *smile at the camera*

THESAURUS

focus to change the camera controls slightly so that there is a clear image of a particular thing
flash a special bright light used especially when taking photographs indoors
load film (into a camera) to put film in a camera
have a film developed to use chemicals to make a film able to be looked at in the light and be used to print pictures
negative an image on a film that shows dark areas as light and light areas as dark, or shows the colors as opposites of each other, from which the final picture is printed
print a photograph on good quality paper
enlargement a photograph that has been printed again in a bigger size
digital camera a type of camera that does not use film, but stores pictures until you download them into a computer
download to move pictures from a digital camera to a computer

2 a piece of equipment used for making movies, videos, or television programs: *television cameras* | **on/off camera** *The crime was caught on camera by police.* **3 in camera** TECHNICAL a law case that is held in camera takes place secretly or privately [**Origin:** 1700–1800 *camera obscura* **box with a hole through which an image is made to appear on the inside of the box** (18–21 centuries), from Modern Latin, **dark room**]

cam·er·a·man /'kæmrə,mæn, -mən/ *n. plural* **cameramen** /-,mɛn, -mən/ [C] a man who operates a camera to film movies or television programs

'camera-,shy *adj.* not liking to have your photograph taken

cam·er·a·wo·man /'kæmrə,wʊmən/ *n. plural* **camerawomen** /-,wɪmɪn/ [C] a woman who operates a camera to film movies or television programs

Cam·e·roon, **Cameroun** /,kæmə'run, 'kæmə,run/ a country in west Africa, east of Nigeria —**Cameroonian** /,kæmə'runiən/ *n., adj.*

ca·mi·sole /'kæmɪ,soʊl/ *n.* [C] a light piece of women's underwear that reaches to the waist and has narrow bands that go over the shoulders [**Origin:** 1800–1900 French, Spanish *camisola*, from *camisa* **shirt**]

cam·o·mile /'kæmə,mil/ *n.* [C,U] another spelling of CHAMOMILE

camouflage

cam·ou·flage[1] /'kæmə,flɑʒ, -,flɑdʒ/ *n.* **1** [U] the way in which the color or shape of something makes it difficult to see in the place where it lives: *The stripes of the tiger provide important camouflage in its natural setting.* **2** [U] a way of hiding something, especially a military object, using branches, paint etc.: *We used leaves and sticks as camouflage.* **3** [U] the type of green and brown clothes, paint etc. that soldiers wear to make themselves more difficult to see: *The soldiers were dressed* ***in camouflage.*** | *camouflage pants* **4** [singular, U] behavior that is designed to hide something: *Aggression is often a camouflage for insecurity.* [**Origin:** 1900–2000 French *camoufler* **to change the appearance of**, from Italian *camuffare*]

camouflage[2] *v.* [T] to hide something by making it look the same as the things around it, or by making it seem like something else: *Entrances to the tunnels were carefully camouflaged.*

camp[1] /kæmp/ S2 W2 *n.* **1** [C,U] a place where people stay in temporary shelters, such as tents, especially for a short time and in mountains or forests: *a mining camp in the Yukon* | *Let's go back to camp.* | *We* ***set up camp*** *near the lake.* | *The soldiers* ***broke camp*** (=took down their tents, shelters etc.) *and left before dawn.* **2** [C,U] a place where children go to stay for a short time and take part in special activities, often as members of an organization: *scout camp* | *summer camp* | **basketball/football/tennis etc. camp** *The kids will be at tennis camp all day.* → see also DAY CAMP **3 a prison/refugee/labor etc. camp** a place where people are kept for a particular reason, when they do not want to be there → see also CONCENTRATION CAMP **4** [C] a permanent place where soldiers live or train: *Camp Pendleton* **5** [C] a group of people or organizations who have the same ideas or principles: *The party is split into two opposing camps.* **6** [U] a way of behaving in a silly, unnatural way and expressing too much emotion when you are acting in a movie, television program, or play: *If you like camp, you'll probably enjoy the movie.* [**Origin:** 1500–1600 French, Latin *campus* **field**] → see also BOOT CAMP, TRAINING CAMP

camp[2] S2 *v.* **1 a)** [I] to set up a tent or temporary shelter and stay there for a short time: *We camped by the river.* **b) be camped near/by/along etc. sth** to have set up a tent or temporary shelter in a particular place: *Troops were camped only a few miles from the city.* **2** [I] also **be camped outside/at etc. sth** to stay outside a place and refuse to go away: *Protesters camped outside the embassy.* → see also CAMPING

camp out *phr. v.* **1** to sleep outdoors, usually in a tent: *People camp out overnight to get a good place to*

C

see the parade. **2** to stay somewhere where you do not have all the usual things that you normally have at your house: *You can camp out in our living room until you find an apartment.* **3** also **be camped out** to stay outside a place and refuse to go away: *Reporters are camped out by the family's home.*

camp sth ↔ **up** *phr. v.* INFORMAL also **camp it up** to deliberately behave or act in a funny, unnatural way, with too much movement or expression

camp³ *adj.* INFORMAL **1** also **campy** clothes, decorations etc. that are camp are very strange, bright, or unusual: *That outfit is so camp.* **2** a man who is camp moves or speaks in the way that people used to think is typical of HOMOSEXUALS

cam·paign¹ /kæm'peɪn/ W1 *n.* [C] **1** a series of actions intended to achieve a particular result, especially in politics or business: *an election campaign* | *an advertising campaign* | *campaign funds* | +**for/against** *a campaign against the death penalty* | **launch/mount a campaign** (=plan and organize a campaign) *Police have launched a campaign to crack down on drug dealers.* ►see THESAURUS box at **fight²** **2** a series of battles, attacks etc. intended to achieve a particular result in a war: *a bombing campaign* [**Origin:** 1600–1700 French *campagne*, from Italian *campagna* **level country, campaign**, from Latin *campus*; because soldiers went out into the country for military exercises]

campaign² W3 *v.* [I] to lead or take part in a series of actions intended to achieve a particular result, especially in politics or business: +**for/against** *Women campaigned for equal rights throughout the 1960s and '70s.* —**campaigner** *n.* [C]

Cam·pa·nel·la /ˌkæmpə'nɛlə/, **Roy** /rɔɪ/ (1921–1993) a U.S. baseball player who was famous for his skill as a CATCHER, and was also one of the first African-American players in the Major Leagues

cam·pa·ni·le /ˌkæmpə'nili/ *n.* [C] a high bell tower that is usually separate from any other building

cam·pa·nol·o·gy /ˌkæmpə'nɑlədʒi/ *n.* [U] the skill of ringing bells —**campanologist** *n.* [C]

ˌcamp 'bed *n.* [C] a light bed that folds up

Camp·bell /'kæmbəl/, **Joseph** (1904–1987) an American writer famous for his books on MYTHOLOGY

Camp Da·vid /ˌkæmp 'deɪvɪd/ the country home of the U.S. President, where the President goes to relax

Camp ˌDavid Ac'cords, the HISTORY an agreement to work toward peace in the Middle East in 1978, signed in the U.S. by the leaders of Egypt and Israel

camp·er /'kæmpɚ/ *n.* [C] **1** someone who is staying in a tent or temporary shelter **2** a vehicle or special type of tent on wheels that has beds and cooking equipment in it so that you can stay in it while you are on vacation **3** a child who is taking part in special activities at a camp **4 a happy camper** SPOKEN, HUMOROUS someone who seems to be happy with their situation

cam·pe·si·no /ˌkæmpə'sinoʊ/ *n.* [C] a poor farmer or farm worker in South America who owns or rents a small amount of land

'Camp Fire an organization for girls and boys, which teaches them practical skills and helps them develop their character

camp·fire /'kæmpfaɪɚ/ *n.* [C] a fire made outdoors by people who are camping

'camp ˌfollower *n.* [C] **1** someone who supports an organization or a political party, but who is not actually a member of the main group **2** someone, especially a PROSTITUTE, who follows an army from place to place to provide services

camp·ground /'kæmpgraʊnd/ *n.* [C] an area where people can camp, that often has a water supply and toilets

cam·phor /'kæmfɚ/ *n.* [U] a white substance with a strong smell, that is used especially to keep insects away

camp·ing /'kæmpɪŋ/ *n.* [U] **1** the activity of sleeping in tents or other temporary shelters in the mountains, forests etc.: *Camping is one of my favorite things to do in the summer.* | *camping gear* **2 go camping** to take a vacation in which you sleep in tents or other temporary shelters in the mountains, forests etc.: *Scouts frequently go hiking and camping.*

'camp ˌmeeting *n.* [C] a religious meeting that often continues for more than one day, and that is usually held outside or in a very large tent

'camp-out *n.* [C] an occasion when you sleep outdoors, especially in a tent: *a camp-out in the backyard*

camp·site /'kæmpsaɪt/ *n.* [C] a place, usually within a CAMPGROUND, where one person or group can camp

cam·pus /'kæmpəs/ S1 W3 *n.* [C,U] **1** the land and buildings of a school, college, or university: *a college campus* | *Most first-year students live* ***on campus.*** **2** the land and buildings belonging to a large company

camp·y /'kæmpi/ *adj. comparative* **campier**, *superlative* **campiest** behaving or acting in a funny, unnatural way, with too much movement or expression: *a campy horror movie*

cam·shaft /'kæmʃæft/ *n.* [C] a metal bar that a CAM is attached to in an engine

Ca·mus /kæ'mu/, **Al·bert** /æl'bɛr/ (1913–1960) a French EXISTENTIALIST writer and PHILOSOPHER

can¹ /kən; *strong* kæn/ S1 W1 *modal verb past tense* **could** **1** to be able to do something: *Computers can store huge amounts of information.* | *She couldn't walk after the accident.* | *The police still haven't found her but they're doing all they can.* **2** to know how to do something: *Jean can speak French fluently.* | *I can't swim.* | *He could read when he was four.* **3** to have permission to do something or to be allowed to do something: *You can't go in there.* | *I told her she can watch TV till bedtime.* | *In soccer, you can't touch the ball with your hands* (=it is against the rules). **4** [in questions] SPOKEN used when asking someone to do something or give you something: *Can I have the check, please?* | *Can we turn the air conditioner on?* **5** [in questions] SPOKEN used when offering something: *Can I get you something to drink?* | *Can I help you?* **6** used to state a quality of something or a fact about how it is able to be used: *This knife can also be used as a can opener.* | *That kind of plastic can be molded into any shape.* **7** used to state what is possible or likely: *You can buy the dictionary in any bookstore.* | *The word "bill" can have several different meanings.* | *That can't be right.* | *There can be no doubt that he is guilty.* **8** SPOKEN used when making suggestions: *If you like, we can go fishing.* **9** used with the verbs "see," "hear," "feel," "smell," and "taste," and with verbs connected with thinking, to show that an action is happening: *Can you hear all right in the back row?* | *Oh, I can taste the lemon grass!* | *She couldn't understand why I was so upset.* **10** [usually in questions and negatives] used especially when you think there is only one possible answer to a question or one possible thing to do in a particular situation: *Sure she's mad, can you blame her?* | *That's really nice of you, but I really can't accept it.* **11** used for telling someone in an angry way to do something: *If you don't want to learn, you can leave right now.* **12** used especially in expressions of surprise: *You can't be serious!* | *Who can that be at the door?* | *They can't have left without me!* **13** used to show what sometimes happens or how someone sometimes behaves: *It can get pretty cold here at night.* | *He can be such a jerk sometimes.* **14 happy/nice/sweet etc. as can be** OLD-FASHIONED as happy, nice etc. as is possible: *She just sat there as pretty as could be.* **15 no can do** SPOKEN used to say that it is impossible for you to do something: *"Will you lend me the money?" "Sorry, no can do."* [**Origin:** Old English *cunnan*] → see also CAN-DO, CANNOT, COULD

can² /kæn/ S2 *n.* [C] **1** a metal container in which food or drinks are preserved without air, or the food contained in this: *soft drink cans* | +**of** *a can of tuna fish* → see picture at CONTAINER **2 a garbage/trash can** a large metal or plastic container for holding GARBAGE (=waste food, paper etc.) **3** a special metal container that keeps the liquid inside it under pressure, letting it out as a SPRAY when you press the button on the lid: *a can of hairspray* **4** a metal container with a lid that can be removed, used for holding liquid: *You'll need three large cans of paint.* **5 a (whole) can of worms** a very complicated situation that causes a lot of problems when you start to deal with it: *The investigations opened up a whole can of worms.* **6 the can** SLANG **a)** a toilet **b)** OLD-FASHIONED a prison **7 in the can** INFORMAL a movie that is in the can is complete and ready to be shown [**Origin:** Old English *canne*]

can³ *v.* **canned**, **canning** [T] **1** to preserve food by putting it into a closed container without air → see also CANNED **2** SPOKEN to dismiss someone from their job: *Did you hear that they canned Linda?* **3 can it!** SPOKEN used to tell someone in an impolite way to stop talking or making noise

Can·a·da /ˈkænədə/ a country in North America, north of the U.S. —**Canadian** /kəˈneɪdiən/ *n., adj.*

ˈCanada ˌDay *n.* [C,U] the Canadian national holiday, celebrated on July 1st

ˈCanada goose also **Caˈnadian goose** *n. plural* **Canada geese** [C] a common wild North American GOOSE, with gray feathers, a black head, and a white throat

Caˌnadian ˈbacon *n.* [U] meat from the back or sides of a pig, cut in thin pieces, and that tastes similar to HAM → see also BACON

canal

ca·nal /kəˈnæl/ *n.* [C] **1** long narrow passage dug into the ground and filled with water, either for ships or boats to travel along, or to take water to a place: *the Panama Canal* | *an irrigation canal* **2** a passage in the body of a person or animal → see also ALIMENTARY CANAL

caˈnal boat *n.* [C] a long narrow boat that is used on a canal

Ca·na·let·to /ˌkænlˈɛt̮oʊ/, **An·to·ni·o** /ænˈtoʊnioʊ/ (1697–1768) an Italian PAINTER famous for his paintings of Venice and of the Thames in London

can·a·lize /ˈkænlˌaɪz/ *v.* [T] to make a river deeper, straighter etc., especially in order to make a canal or prevent flooding —**canalization** /ˌkænl-əˈzeɪʃən/ *n.* [U]

Caˈnal ˌZone, the CULTURES a narrow area of land in Panama that contains the Panama Canal and was controlled by the U.S. until 1979

can·a·pé, **canape** /ˈkænəpi, -peɪ/ *n.* [C] a small piece of bread with cheese, meat, fish etc. on it, served with drinks at a party

ca·nard /kəˈnɑrd/ *n.* [C] a statement or piece of news that is deliberately false and told to harm someone

ca·nar·y /kəˈnɛri/ *n. plural* **canaries** [C] BIOLOGY a small yellow bird that sings and is often kept as a pet [**Origin:** 1500–1600 *Canary* Islands, islands in the Atlantic ocean where the bird comes from]

ca·nas·ta /kəˈnæstə/ *n.* [U] a card game in which two sets of cards are used [**Origin:** 1900–2000 Spanish **basket**]

Can·ber·ra /ˈkænbərə, -ˌbɛrə/ the capital city of Australia

can·can /ˈkænkæn/ *n.* [C] a fast dance from France, in which women kick their legs high into the air during a show

can·cel /ˈkænsəl/ S2 W3 *v.* **canceled**, **canceling**, also **cancelled**, **cancelling** [T] **1** to arrange that a planned activity or event will not happen: *Classes were canceled for the day.* **2** to end an agreement or arrangement that exists in law: *I called and canceled the order.* **3** to stamp or mark a CHECK, stamp, or ticket so that it cannot be used again: *a canceled check* [**Origin:** 1300–1400 French *canceller* **to cross out**, from Latin *cancellare* **to make like a frame of crossed bars**]

cancel sth **out** *phr. v.* to have an equal but opposite effect on something, so that a situation does not change: *Increased advertising costs have canceled out our sales gains.*

can·cel·la·tion /ˌkænsəˈleɪʃən/ *n.* [C,U] **1** a decision or statement that a planned or regular activity will not happen: *Bad weather led to the cancellation of most flights out of O'Hare.* **2** a decision to end an agreement or arrangement that you have with someone: *The hotel is booked, but we'll let you know of any cancellations.* | *a cancellation fee*

Can·cer /ˈkænsɚ/ *n.* **1** [U] the fourth sign of the ZODIAC represented by a CRAB, and believed to affect the character and life of people born between June 21 and July 22 **2** [C] someone who was born between June 21 and July 22

can·cer /ˈkænsɚ/ S2 W2 *n.* **1** [C,U] MEDICINE a very serious disease in which cells in a part of the body start to grow in an uncontrolled way that can cause death: *lung cancer* | *cancer of the liver* | *cancer cells* | *She was told that she* ***had cancer***. | *He* ***died of cancer*** *at the age of 63.* **2** [C] an activity that is increasing, and causes a lot of harm: *The mayor has called drug abuse "a cancer on our society."* [**Origin:** 1600–1700 Latin **crab, cancer**] —**cancerous** *adj.*: *a cancerous tumor*

can·del·a /kænˈdɛlə/ *n* [C] WRITTEN ABBREVIATION **CD** PHYSICS a standard unit which scientists use to measure the brightness of light

can·de·la·bra /ˌkændəˈlɑbrə/ also **can·de·la·brum** /-ˈlɑbrəm/ *n.* [C] a decorative holder for several CANDLES or lamps

can·did /ˈkændɪd/ *adj.* **1** directly truthful, even when the truth may be upsetting or embarrassing: *a candid biography of the author's parents.* ▶see THESAURUS box at **honest** **2** candid pictures or photographs are taken of someone who does not know that they are being photographed [**Origin:** 1600–1700 French *candide*, from Latin *candidus* **bright, white**] —**candidly** *adv.* → see also CANDOR

can·di·da /ˈkændədə/ *n.* [U] MEDICINE a YEAST INFECTION

can·di·da·cy /ˈkændədəsi/ *n. plural* **candidacies** [C,U] the position of being one of the people who are competing to be elected to a position, especially a political position: +**for** *Hammer's candidacy for the legislature*

can·di·date /ˈkændəˌdeɪt, -dɪt/ W1 *n.* [C] **1** someone who is being considered for a job or is competing to be elected: *a presidential candidate* | +**for** *There are only three candidates for the job.* **2** a person, group, or idea that is appropriate for something or likely to get something: +**for** *The school is an obvious candidate for extra funding.* | *The city is* ***a prime candidate*** *to host the next Olympics.* [**Origin:** 1600–1700 Latin *candidatus*, from *candidatus* **dressed in white**; because someone trying to get elected in ancient Rome wore white clothes]

can·died /ˈkændid/ *adj.* cooked in or covered with sugar: *candied fruit*

can·dle /ˈkændl/ S2 *n.* [C] **1** a round stick of WAX with a piece of string through the middle that you burn to produce light **2 can't hold a candle to sb/sth** INFORMAL to be not as good as someone or something else: *Today's singers can't hold a candle to her.* [**Origin:** 600–700 Latin *candela*, from *candere* **to shine**] → see also **burn the candle at both ends** at BURN[1] (14)

candle

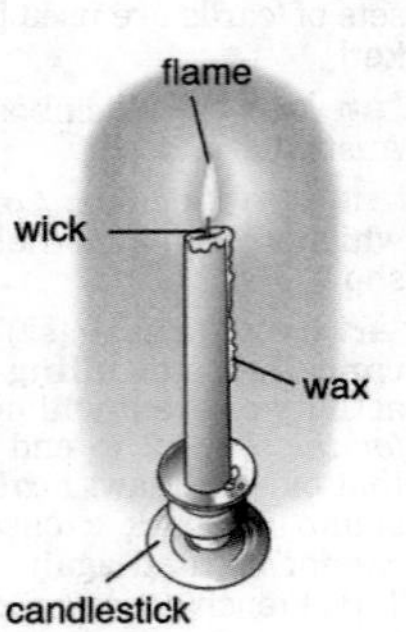

can·dle·light /ˈkændlˌlaɪt/ *n.* [U] the light produced when a candle burns: *We read* ***by candlelight.*** | *a candlelight dinner*

ˈcandle-lit *adj.* a candle-lit activity or place is one in which candles are used to produce light

can·dle·stick /ˈkændlˌstɪk/ *n.* [C] a specially shaped metal or wooden object used to hold a candle → see picture at CANDLE

ˌcan-ˈdo *adj.* [only before noun] INFORMAL willing to try anything and expecting that it will work: *Denver is a world-class city with a* ***can-do spirit.***

can·dor /ˈkændɚ/ *n.* [U] the quality of being honest and truthful: *She described her experiences with remarkable candor.* → see also CANDID

can·dy /ˈkændi/ S2 *n. plural* **candies** [C,U] **1** a sweet food made of sugar or chocolate, or a piece of this: *a piece of candy* | *chocolate candies* **2 mind/brain/eye etc. candy** INFORMAL something that is entertaining or pleasant to look at, but that does not make you think: *Most video games are just brain candy.* **3 like taking candy from a baby** INFORMAL very easy to do [**Origin:** 1200–1300 Old French *candi*, from Arabic *qandi* **covered with sugar**]

ˈcandy ˌapple *n.* [C] an apple covered with a sticky brown or red candy

ˈcandy bar *n.* [C] a long narrow bar of candy, usually covered with chocolate

ˈcandy cane *n.* [C] a stick of hard red and white sugar with a curved end

ˈcandy-ˌstriped *adj.* candy-striped cloth has narrow red or pink lines on a white background

candy strip·er /ˈkændi ˌstraɪpɚ/ *n.* [C] a young person, usually a girl, who does unpaid work as a nurse's helper in a hospital in order to learn about hospital work

cane[1] /keɪn/ *n.* **1** [C] a long thin stick with a curved handle, used to help someone walk: *He was walking slowly with a cane.* **2** [U] thin pieces of the stems of plants, some types of which are used for making furniture, baskets etc.: *a cane and wicker rocker* | *raspberry canes* **3** [C] a long, hard, yellow stem of BAMBOO, used for supporting other plants in the garden **4** [C, singular] a long thin stick used especially in past times by teachers to hit children with as a punishment, or the punishment of being hit with a cane **5** [U] SUGAR CANE [**Origin:** 1300–1400 Old French, Old Provençal *cana*, from Latin *canna*, from Greek *kanna*]

cane[2] *v.* [T] to punish someone, especially a child, by hitting them with a long thin stick

ˈcane ˌsugar *n.* [U] sugar that comes from SUGAR CANE

ca·nine[1] /ˈkeɪnaɪn/ *adj.* relating to dogs: *a police canine unit*

canine[2] *n.* [C] **1** also **canine tooth** one of four sharp pointed teeth in the front of the human mouth SYN **eye tooth** **2** BIOLOGY a dog

can·is·ter /ˈkænəstɚ/ *n.* [C] **1** a container with straight sides and a circular top, usually made of metal or plastic, in which you keep dry foods and some other types of objects: *a flour canister* | *canisters of film* **2** a round metal case that bursts when thrown or fired from a gun, scattering what is inside: *tear-gas canisters* **3** a round metal container that holds gas under pressure

can·ker /ˈkæŋkɚ/ *n.* **1** [C] also **canker sore** MEDICINE a painful sore inside your mouth **2** [C,U] an infected area on the wood of trees, or the disease that causes this —**cankerous** *adj.* —**cankered** *adj.*

can·na·bis /ˈkænəbɪs/ *n.* [U] TECHNICAL MARIJUANA

canned /kænd/ *adj.* [usually before noun] **1** canned food is preserved without air in a metal or glass container, and can be kept for a long time before it is opened: *canned peaches* **2 canned music/laughter/applause** music, laughter or applause that has been recorded and is used on television or in radio programs

can·nel·lo·ni /ˌkænəˈloʊni/ *n.* [U] small tubes of PASTA filled with meat or cheese, and covered in SAUCE

can·ner·y /ˈkænəri/ *n. plural* **canneries** [C] a factory where food is put into cans

can·ni·bal /ˈkænəbəl/ *n.* [C] **1** someone who eats human flesh **2** an animal that eats the flesh of other animals of the same kind [**Origin:** 1500–1600 Spanish *Canibal* member of the Carib people of the West Indies, who were said to eat human flesh] —**cannibalism** *n.* [U] —**cannibalistic** /ˌkænəbəˈlɪstɪk◂/ *adj.*

can·ni·bal·ize /ˈkænəbəˌlaɪz/ *v.* [T] to take something apart, especially a machine, so that you can use its parts to build something else

can·non /ˈkænən/ *n.* [C] a large, heavy, powerful gun, attached to the ground or on wheels, used in past times → see also **loose cannon** at LOOSE[1] (10)

can·non·ade /ˌkænəˈneɪd/ *n.* [C] a continuous heavy attack by large guns

can·non·ball /ˈkænənˌbɔl/ *n.* [C] a heavy iron ball fired from an old type of large gun

ˈcannon ˌfodder *n.* [U] INFORMAL ordinary members of the army, navy etc., whose lives are not considered to be very important

can·not /ˈkænɑt, kəˈnɑt, kæ-/ S1 W1 *modal verb* **1** a negative form of "can": *Many people cannot find affordable housing.* **2 cannot but do sth** FORMAL used to say that you feel you have to do something: *If we are attacked with violence, we cannot but respond with violence.*

can·ny /ˈkæni/ *adj. comparative* **cannier**, *superlative* **canniest** smart, careful, not easily deceived, and understanding a situation very well, especially in business or politics SYN **shrewd**: *canny marketing techniques* —**cannily** *adv.*

ca·noe[1] /kəˈnu/ *n.* [C] a long light narrow boat that is pointed at both ends, which you move along using a PADDLE [**Origin:** 1500–1600 French, Spanish *canoa*, from Arawakan] → see also KAYAK

canoe[2] *v.* [I] to travel by canoe —**canoeist** *n.* [C]

ca·no·la /kəˈnoʊlə/ *n.* [U] a plant with yellow flowers, grown as animal food and for its oil, which is used in cooking

can·on /ˈkænən/ *n.* [C] **1** FORMAL a generally accepted rule or standard on which an idea, subject, or way of behaving is based: *the canons of journalistic ethics* **2** an established law of the Christian church **3** ENG. LANG. ARTS **a)** a list of books or pieces of music that are officially recognized as being the work of a certain writer: *the 37 plays of the Shakespeare canon* **b)** all the books that are recognized as being the most important pieces of literature: *the literary canon* **4** ENG. LANG. ARTS a piece of music in which a tune is started by one singer or instrument and is copied by each of the others **5** a Christian priest who has special duties in a CATHEDRAL

ca·non·i·cal /kəˈnɑnɪkəl/ *adj.* according to CANON LAW

can·on·ize /ˈkænəˌnaɪz/ *v.* [T] to officially state that a dead person is a SAINT —**canonization** /ˌkænənəˈzeɪʃən/ *n.* [C,U]

ˌcanon 'law *n.* [U] the laws of the Christian church

ca·noo·dle /kə'nudl/ *v.* [I] OLD-FASHIONED if two people canoodle, they kiss and hold each other in a sexual way

'can ˌopener *n.* [C] a tool for opening a can of food

can·o·py /'kænəpi/ *n. plural* **canopies** [C] **1** a cover attached above a bed, seat etc. as a decoration or as a shelter: *a canopy over the patio* **2** the top branches and leaves of the tallest trees in a forest, which form a continuous cover over the forest **3** LITERARY something that spreads above you like a roof: *a canopy of twinkling stars* [**Origin:** 1300–1400 Medieval Latin *canopeum* **mosquito net**, from Greek *konops* **mosquito**] —**canopied** *adj.*

canst /kənst; *strong* kænst/ *v.* **thou canst** OLD USE used to mean "you can" when talking to one person

can't /kænt/ *modal verb* **1** the short form of "cannot": *Sorry, I can't help you.* **2** used to say that something is impossible or unlikely: *You can't miss it – it's a huge building.*

cant[1] /kænt/ *n.* **1** [U] FORMAL insincere talk about moral or religious principles by someone who is pretending to be better than they really are **2** [C,U] special words used by a particular group of people, especially in order to keep things secret SYN argot **3** [C] a sloping surface or angle

cant[2] *v.* [I,T] to lean, or make something lean

can·ta·loupe /'kæntlˌoʊp/ *n.* [C,U] a type of MELON with a hard green skin and sweet orange flesh [**Origin:** 1700–1800 *Cantelupo* former house of the pope near Rome in Italy, where it was grown]

can·tan·ker·ous /kæn'tæŋkərəs/ *adj.* someone who is cantankerous is easily annoyed, difficult to be friends with, and complains a lot: *a cantankerous old man* —**cantankerously** *adv.* —**cantankerousness** *n.* [U]

can·ta·ta /kən'tɑṭə/ *n.* [C] a piece of religious music sung by a CHOIR and single performers

can·teen /kæn'tin/ *n.* [C] **1** a small container for carrying water or other drinks, used especially by soldiers, HIKERS, or travelers **2** a store or place where people in the army, navy etc. can buy things or go to be entertained **3** a CAFETERIA [**Origin:** 1700–1800 French *cantine*, from Italian *cantina* **wine store**]

can·ter[1] /'kæntə/ *v.* [I,T] to ride or make a horse run fairly fast, but not as fast as possible [**Origin:** 1700–1800 *canterbury* **to canter** (1600–1700), from *Canterbury* city in southeast England; from the speed at which people rode when going to Canterbury on pilgrimage]

canter[2] *n.* **1** [singular] the movement of a horse when it is running fairly fast, but not as fast as possible **2** [C] a ride on a horse at this speed

can·ti·cle /'kæntɪkəl/ *n.* [C] a short religious song, usually using words from the Bible

can·ti·le·ver /'kænṭəˌlivə/ *n.* [C] a beam that sticks out from an upright post or wall and supports a shelf, the end of a bridge etc.

can·to /'kæntoʊ/ *n. plural* **cantos** [C] ENG. LANG. ARTS one of the parts into which a very long poem is divided

can·ton /'kæntɑn/ *n.* [C] POLITICS one of the areas with limited political powers that make up a country such as Switzerland

can·ton·ment /kæn'tɑnmənt/ *n.* [C] TECHNICAL a camp for soldiers

can·tor /'kæntə/ *n.* [C] **1** a man who leads the prayers and songs in a Jewish religious service **2** ENG. LANG. ARTS the leader of a CHOIR in some churches

Ca·nuck /kə'nʌk/ *n.* [C] INFORMAL a person from Canada

can·vas /'kænvəs/ *n.* **1** [U] a type of strong cloth used to make bags, tents, shoes etc.: *a canvas bag* **2** [C] ENG. LANG. ARTS a painting done with oil paints, or the piece of cloth it is painted on **3 a broader/wider/larger canvas** all of a situation, and not just part of it: *These questions must be considered on a broader canvas.* [**Origin:** 1300–1400 Old North French *canevas*, from Latin *cannabis* **hemp**]

can·vass /'kænvəs/ *v.* **1** [I,T] to try to get information about something or support for something, especially a political party, by going from place to place within an area and talking to people: *Police canvassed the neighborhood but didn't find anyone who knew the man.* **2** [T] to talk about a problem, suggestion etc. in detail: *The suggestion is being widely canvassed as a possible solution to the dispute.* —**canvass** *n.* [C] —**canvasser** *n.* [C]

can·yon /'kænyən/ *n.* [C] EARTH SCIENCE a deep valley with very steep sides of rock, that usually has a river running through it: *the Grand Canyon* [**Origin:** 1800–1900 American Spanish *cañón*, from Spanish, **tube, pipe**]

can·yon·ing /'kænyənɪŋ/ *n.* [U] the sport of swimming or floating along fast-flowing rivers in a CANYON

cap[1] /kæp/ S2 W3 *n.* [C]

1 HAT a) a type of soft flat hat that has a curved part sticking out at the front: *a baseball cap* **b)** a covering that fits very closely to your head and is worn for a particular purpose: *a shower cap* **c)** a special type of hat that is worn with a particular uniform or by a particular group of people: *a nurse's cap* → see also STOCKING CAP

2 TOP/COVERING a protective covering that you put on the end or top of an object: *the lens cap for a camera* | *a bottle cap* → see also ICE CAP, TOECAP ▶see THESAURUS box at cover[2]

3 LIMIT an upper limit that is put on the amount of money that someone can earn, spend, or borrow: *a spending cap*

4 TOOTH a hard cover that protects a damaged tooth or makes it look better

5 in (all) caps in capital letters

6 SMALL EXPLOSIVE a small paper container with explosive inside it, used especially in toy guns

[**Origin:** 900–1000 Late Latin *cappa* **covering for the head, cloak**] → see also **a feather in your cap** at FEATHER[1] (2), KNEECAP, **put on your thinking cap** at THINKING[1] (5), WHITECAPS

cap[2] *v.* **capped, capping** [T] **1 be capped by/with sth** to cover the top of something: *The mountain tops are capped with snow.* **2** to limit the amount of something, especially money, that can be used, allowed, or spent: *Some state colleges have capped enrollment.* **3** to be the last and usually best thing that happens in a game, situation etc.: *Payton capped the game with three baskets in the final minute.* **4** to cover a tooth with a special hard white surface **5 to cap it all (off)** SPOKEN used before describing the worst, best, funniest etc. part at the end of a story or description: *I had a terrible day at work, and to cap it all off I got a flat tire.*

cap. **1** also **caps.** the written abbreviation of "capital letter" **2** the written abbreviation of CAPACITY

Cap·a /'kæpə/, **Rob·ert** /'rɑbət/ (1913–1954) an American war PHOTOGRAPHER

ca·pa·bil·i·ty /ˌkeɪpə'bɪləṭi/ Ac *n. plural* **capabilities** [C] **1** the natural ability, skill, or power that makes a machine, person, or organization able to do something, especially something difficult: *The patrol plane has an infrared capability, so that searches can be made in the dark.* | **the capability to do sth** *The region had the capability to export two million barrels of oil per day.* | *I think the job was just* ***beyond*** *her* ***capabilities*** (=too difficult). **2** the ability that a country has to take a particular kind of military action: *The country is nearing the capability to produce nuclear weapons.*

ca·pa·ble /'keɪpəbəl/ Ac W3 *adj.* **1 capable of (doing) sth** having the skills, power, intelligence etc. needed to do something: *These computerized weapons are capable of hitting almost any target.* | *I'm* ***perfectly capable of*** *doing it myself.* **2** skillful and effective and able to do things well: *a strong, capable woman* | *Helen was put* ***in the capable hands*** *of hair stylist Daniel Herson.* [**Origin:** 1500–1600 French, Late Latin *capabilis*, from Latin *capere* **to take**] —**capably** *adv.*

ca·pa·cious /kə'peɪʃəs/ *adj.* FORMAL able to contain a lot: *a capacious theater* —**capaciousness** *n.* [U]

ca·pac·i·tor /kə'pæsəṭə/ *n.* [C] PHYSICS a piece of

equipment that collects and stores electricity for a short time

ca·pac·i·ty /kəˈpæsəṭi/ Ac W2 *n. plural* **capacities** **1** [singular, U] SCIENCE the space a container, room etc. has to hold things or people, or a measure of the amount that a space or container can hold: *The car's fold-down rear seat increases the trunk capacity.* | **+of** *The theater had a seating capacity of 1,400 people.* | ***Capacity crowds*** (=people filling all the seats in a room, hall etc.) *are expected at the festival.* | *All hotels were* ***filled to capacity*** (=completely full). **2** [C,U] someone's ability to do something: **+for** *a child's capacity for learning* | **capacity to do sth** *a capacity to think in an original way* **3** [singular] FORMAL someone's job, position, or duty SYN role: **in an official/a professional etc. capacity** *Rollins will be working in an advisory capacity on this project.* | **do sth in your capacity as sth** *Davis will continue to serve in his present capacity as treasurer.* **4** [singular, U] the amount of something that a factory, company, machine etc. can produce or deal with: *The company has the capacity to build seven million cars a year.* | *The reactor had been operating* ***at full capacity***. [**Origin:** 1400–1500 French *capacité*, from Latin *capacitas*]

C

ca·par·i·soned /kəˈpærəsənd/ *adj.* in MEDIEVAL times a caparisoned horse was one covered in a decorated cloth

cape /keɪp/ *n.* [C] **1** a long loose piece of clothing without SLEEVES, that fastens around your neck and hangs from your shoulders: *a long black cape* **2** EARTH SCIENCE a large piece of land surrounded on three sides by water: *Cape Cod*

Cape Ca·nav·er·al /ˌkeɪp kəˈnævrəl/ a CAPE in the U.S. state of Florida which is famous for the Kennedy Space Center, where U.S. SPACECRAFT are sent into space. Cape Canaveral was formerly called Cape Kennedy.

ˌCape ˈHorn a PENINSULA at the southern end of South America, where the Atlantic Ocean meets the Pacific Ocean

ˌCape of Good ˈHope, the a PENINSULA at the southwestern end of South Africa, where the Atlantic Ocean meets the Indian Ocean

ca·per[1] /ˈkeɪpɚ/ *n.* [C] **1** a small dark green part of a flower used in cooking to give a sour taste to food **2** behavior or an activity that is amusing or silly and not serious: *the comic capers of a cartoon cat and mouse* **3** a planned illegal activity, especially an illegal or dangerous one: *Stealing the statue was probably a student caper.* **4** a movie or story that is full of action, especially one about an activity that is illegal or dangerous: *an action caper starring Tom Cruise* **5** a short jumping or dancing movement

caper[2] *v.* [I always + adv./prep.] to jump around and play in a happy, excited way: *The dancers capered across the stage.*

Ca·pet /ˈkeɪpət, ˈkæ-, kæˈpeɪ/ the name of a family of French kings who ruled from 987 to 1328

Cape Verde /keɪp ˈvɚd/ a country that consists of a group of islands in the Atlantic Ocean, west of Senegal —**Cape Verdean** *n., adj.*

cap·il·lar·y /ˈkæpəˌleri/ *n. plural* **capillaries** [C] **1** BIOLOGY the smallest type of BLOOD VESSEL (=tube carrying blood) in the body → see also ARTERY, VEIN (1) **2** a very small tube as thin as a hair

ˌcapillary ˈaction also **ˌcapillary atˈtraction** *n.* [U] PHYSICS the way in which the surface of a liquid sticks to the surface of a solid, which makes the liquid rise or fall in a particular space, for example when a liquid rises up a narrow tube

cap·i·tal[1] /ˈkæpəṭl/ W2 *n.*
1 CITY [C] an important city where the main government of a country, state etc. is: **+of** *Albany is the capital of New York State.* | **state/regional/provincial etc. capital** *Austria's regional capitals*
2 MONEY [U] money or property, especially when it is used to start a business or to produce more wealth: *My dad started a grocery business in the 1930s with $1,000 in capital.* → see also VENTURE CAPITAL, WORKING CAPITAL
3 PEOPLE [U] ECONOMICS people's skills or the things people make that are needed in order to produce goods, provide services, or make wealth → see also CAPITAL GOODS: *a country that is beginning to invest heavily in* ***human capital*** (=the skills and knowledge that people have)
4 CENTER OF ACTIVITY [C usually singular] a place that is a center for an industry, business, or other activity: **+of** *Hollywood is the capital of the U.S. movie industry.*
5 LETTER [C] a letter of the alphabet written in its large form, for example at the beginning of a sentence or someone's name → see also LOWER CASE: *Please write your name and address in capitals.*
6 make capital out of sth to use a situation or event to help you get an advantage: *Johnson made* ***political capital out of*** *his military career.*
7 BUILDING TECHNICAL the top part of a COLUMN (=a long stone post used to support buildings)

capital[2] W2 *adj.* **1** relating to money or property that you use to start a business or to make more money: *The recycling industry is* ***making huge capital investments in*** *equipment.* **2** a capital letter is one that is written or printed in its large form, used for example at the beginning of a sentence or someone's name → see also LOWER CASE: *The company's logo is a large capital "B."* **3 a capital offense/crime etc.** an offense, crime etc. that may be punished by death **4** OLD-FASHIONED, SPOKEN excellent [**Origin:** 1100–1200 Latin *capitalis*, from *caput* head]

ˌcapital ˈassets *n.* [plural] TECHNICAL machines, buildings, and other property belonging to a company

ˌcapital ˈbudget *n.* [C] ECONOMICS a company's plan for spending on land, buildings, equipment etc., or the amount of money that will be spent

ˌcapital ˈdeepening *n.* [U] ECONOMICS an increase in the amount of money that a company or country spends on training people or improving their working methods etc., and on buying new equipment, in order to increase production and profit: *In the 1970s, 70% of growth in output per worker was attributable to capital deepening.*

ˌcapital ˈgain *n.* [C] ECONOMICS the financial profit made by a seller when selling something for more than it cost to buy: *The sale will result in a capital gain for Axa.* | *capital gains tax*

ˌcapital ˈgains *n.* [plural] profits that you make by selling STOCKS, property, or possessions

ˌcapital ˈgains tax *n.* [C] ECONOMICS a tax that you pay on the profit you make when selling property etc.

ˈcapital goods *n.* [plural] ECONOMICS goods such as machines or buildings that are made for the purpose of producing other goods → see also CONSUMER GOODS

ˌcapital-inˈtensive *adj.* a capital-intensive business, industry etc. needs a lot of money for it to operate well → see also LABOR-INTENSIVE

cap·i·tal·ism /ˈkæpəṭlˌɪzəm/ *n.* [U] POLITICS an economic and political system in which businesses belong mostly to private owners, not to the government → see also COMMUNISM → SOCIALISM

cap·i·tal·ist[1] /ˈkæpəṭl-ɪst/ *n.* [C] **1** someone who owns or controls a lot of money and lends it to businesses, banks etc. to produce more wealth → see also VENTURE CAPITAL **2** someone who supports capitalism: *the capitalists of the West* → see also COMMUNIST, SOCIALIST[2]

capitalist[2] also **cap·i·ta·lis·tic** /ˌkæpəṭlˈɪstɪk/ *adj.* POLITICS using or supporting capitalism: *the seven richest capitalist countries* | *the capitalist system*

cap·i·tal·ize /ˈkæpəṭlˌaɪz/ *v.* [T] **1** to write a letter of the alphabet using a CAPITAL letter: *You need to capitalize the names of rivers in English.* **2** [usually passive] ECONOMICS to supply a business with money so that it can operate: *highly capitalized industries* **3** [usually passive] ECONOMICS to calculate the value of a business based on the value of its STOCK or on the amount of money it makes: *The store's Japanese branches are* *capitalized at 2.8 million yen.* —**capitalization** /ˌkæpətl-əˈzeɪʃən/ *n.* [U]

capitalize on sth *phr. v.* to get as much advantage out of a situation, event etc. as you can: *The Bulls managed to capitalize on the mistakes Houston made.*

ˌcapital ˈloss *n.* [C] ECONOMICS a financial loss to a seller when something loses value or is sold for less than it cost to buy

ˈcapital ˌmarket *n.* [C] TECHNICAL ECONOMICS a financial market where businesses borrow money in the form of STOCKS or BONDS for periods of longer than one year

ˌcapital ˈpunishment *n.* [U] the punishment of legally killing someone for a crime after they have been found guilty in a court of law → see also DEATH PENALTY

cap·i·tol /ˈkæpət̬l/ *n.* **1 the Capitol** the building in Washington, D.C., where the U.S. Congress meets **2** [C] the building in each U.S. state where the people who make laws for that state meet

ˌCapitol ˈHill *n.* **1** POLITICS the U.S. Congress: *Capitol Hill has reacted slowly to the crisis.* **2** the hill in Washington, D.C., where the Capitol building stands

ca·pit·u·late /kəˈpɪtʃəˌleɪt/ *v.* [I] **1** to accept or agree to something that you have been opposing for a long time SYN **give in**: +**to** *Management finally capitulated to the union's demands.* **2** FORMAL to accept defeat by your enemies in a war SYN **surrender** —**capitulation** /kəˌpɪtʃəˈleɪʃən/ *n.* [C,U]

cap·let /ˈkæplɪt/ *n.* [C] a small smooth PILL (=solid piece of medicine) with a shape that is slightly longer and narrower than a TABLET

ca·pon /ˈkeɪpɑn/ *n.* [C] a male chicken that has had its sex organs removed to make it grow big and fat

Ca·pone /kəˈpoʊn/, **Al** /æl/ (1899–1947) a U.S. GANGSTER (=criminal who works in a violent group), who was the leader of ORGANIZED CRIME in Chicago

Truman Capote

Ca·po·te /kəˈpoʊt̬i/, **Tru·man** /ˈtrumən/ (1924–1984) a U.S. writer of novels and short stories

cap·puc·ci·no /ˌkæpəˈtʃinoʊ, ˌkɑ-/ *n. plural* **cappuccinos** [C,U] a drink made of ESPRESSO (=strong coffee) with hot milk on top, served in a small cup [**Origin:** 1900–2000 Italian **Capuchin** (= type of holy man who wears gray clothes, said to look like the coffee)]

Cap·ra /ˈkæprə/, **Frank** (1897–1991) a U.S. movie DIRECTOR

ca·price /kəˈpris/ *n.* LITERARY **1** [C] a sudden and unreasonable change in someone's opinion or behavior SYN **whim**: *the caprices of a spoiled child* **2** [U] the tendency to change your mind suddenly or behave in an unexpected way

ca·pri·cious /kəˈprɪʃəs/ *adj.* **1** FORMAL changing suddenly and without good reasons: *a capricious and difficult child* | *the capricious political situation in Somalia* **2** LITERARY changing quickly and suddenly: *a capricious wind* —**capriciously** *adv.*

Cap·ri·corn /ˈkæprɪˌkɔrn/ *n.* **1** [U] the tenth sign of the ZODIAC, represented by a goat and believed to affect the character and life of people born between December 22 and January 19 **2** [C] someone who was born between December 22 and January 19: *Greg's a Capricorn.*

cap·si·cum /ˈkæpsɪkəm/ *n.* [C,U] TECHNICAL a type of PEPPER (=a hollow green, red, or yellow vegetable)

cap·sid /ˈkæpsɪd / *n.* [C] BIOLOGY an outer layer of PROTEIN that surrounds the DNA and RNA of a VIRUS

cap·size /ˈkæpsaɪz, kæpˈsaɪz/ *v.* [I,T] if a boat capsizes or if you capsize it, it turns over in the water: *The ship capsized in seconds.* | *We all learned how to capsize our canoes safely.*

cap·stan /ˈkæpstən, -stæn/ *n.* [C] **1** a round machine shaped like a drum, used to wind up a rope that pulls or lifts heavy objects **2** a round part in a TAPE RECORDER that spins around to move the TAPE in a CASSETTE

capsize

cap·stone /ˈkæpstoʊn/ *n.* [C] **1** the last and usually best thing that someone achieves: *An appointment to the Supreme Court was* ***the capstone of his career.*** **2** a stone at the top of a building, wall etc.

cap·sule¹ /ˈkæpsəl/ *n.* [C] **1** a small closed tube with medicine inside that you swallow whole ▸see THESAURUS box at **medicine** **2** the part of a SPACECRAFT in which people live and work → see also TIME CAPSULE

capsule² *adj.* [only before noun] **1** a capsule description, account etc. is very short, including only the most important details: *capsule movie reviews* **2** very small SYN **compact**

Capt. the written abbreviation of CAPTAIN

cap·tain¹ /ˈkæptən/ W3 *n.* [C] **1** someone who commands a ship or aircraft ▸see THESAURUS box at **plane¹** **2** a military officer with a fairly high rank **3** someone who leads a team or other group of people: +**of** *the captain of the volleyball team* **4 a captain of industry** [usually plural] someone who owns an important company or has an important job at a large company [**Origin:** 1300–1400 French *capitain*, from Late Latin *capitaneus* **chief**, from Latin *caput* **head**]

captain² *v.* [T] **1** to lead a group or team of people: *She captained the school basketball team.* **2** to be in charge of a ship, aircraft etc.

cap·tain·cy /ˈkæptənsi/ also **cap·tain·ship** /ˈkæptənˌʃɪp/ *n.* [U] the position of being captain of a team, or the period during which someone is captain

cap·tion¹ /ˈkæpʃən/ *n.* [C] words printed above or below a picture in a book or newspaper or on a television screen to explain what the picture is showing [**Origin:** 1700–1800 *caption* **act of seizing or arresting, document allowing this** (14–19 centuries), from Latin *captio* **act of taking**]

caption² *v.* [T usually passive] to print words above or below a picture in a book or newspaper to explain what the picture is showing: *A photograph of the couple was captioned "rebuilding their romance."*

cap·tious /ˈkæpʃəs/ *adj.* LITERARY always criticizing unimportant things

cap·ti·vate /ˈkæptəˌveɪt/ *v.* [T] to attract or interest someone very much: *I was captivated by her smile.* | *The performance captivated the audience.*

cap·ti·vat·ing /ˈkæptəˌveɪt̬ɪŋ/ *adj.* very attractive or interesting: *a captivating smile* | *a captivating account of his childhood*

cap·tive¹ /ˈkæptɪv/ *adj.* **1** kept in a prison, or in a place that you are not allowed to leave: *captive soldiers* | *the breeding of captive animals* | *She was* ***taken captive*** (=made a prisoner) *by the rebel army.* | *The men were* ***held captive*** (=kept as prisoners) *for three days.* ▸see THESAURUS box at **prisoner** **2** captive animals live in zoos or similar places, and are not wild OPP **wild** **3 a captive audience** people who listen or watch someone or something because they have to, not because they are interested **4 be captive to sth** to be unable to think or speak freely because of being influenced too much by something: *The military is captive to events that it cannot control.* **5 captive market** a situation in which people cannot choose between different types of a product or service, especially because there is only one person or company selling it

captive² *n.* [C] **1** someone who is kept as a prisoner, especially in a war **2 a captive of sth** someone who is not able to think or speak freely because they are influenced too much by something: *Too many candidates are captives of the political establishment.*

C

cap·tiv·i·ty /kæpˈtɪvət̬i/ *n.* [U] the state of being kept as a prisoner or in a place you cannot escape from: *Wilson was* ***released from captivity*** *at the end of the war.* | *Elephants are never happy* ***in captivity*** (=when kept in a cage).

cap·tor /ˈkæptɚ/ *n.* [C] someone who is keeping another person prisoner: *Mann was finally freed by his captors.*

cap·ture¹ /ˈkæptʃɚ/ W3 *v.* [T]
1 PERSON to catch someone in order to make them a prisoner: *The rebels captured 417 government soldiers.* ▸see THESAURUS box at catch¹
2 PLACE to get control of a place that previously belonged to an enemy by fighting for it: *The town was captured after a siege lasting ten days.*
3 BUSINESS/POLITICS/SPORTS to get or win something or a share of something in a situation in which you are competing against other people, such as business, an election, or a sport: *Mayor Agnos captured 28.7% of the vote.* | *The Super Bowl always captures a large audience.* | *Cuba captured the first gold medal of the Olympic Games.*
4 ANIMAL to catch an animal after chasing or following it: *Many dolphins are accidentally captured in the nets of tuna fishermen.*
5 BOOK/PAINTING/MOVIE to succeed in showing or describing a situation or feeling using words or pictures, so that other people can see, understand, or experience it: *The article captures the political mood of the late 19th century.* | *The TV camera captured Dad waving as he left the airplane.*
6 capture sb's imagination/attention etc. to make someone feel very interested and attracted → see also CAPTIVATE: *Armstrong's landing on the moon captured the imagination of a generation.*
7 COMPUTERS to put something in a form that a computer can use: *The data is captured by an optical scanner.*
8 CHESS to remove one of your opponent's PIECES from the board in CHESS → see also **win/capture/steal sb's heart** at HEART (15)

capture² *n.* [U] **1** the act of catching a person in order to make them a prisoner: *The government offered $500,000 for information leading to his capture.* | **avoid/evade/elude capture** (=to avoid being captured) **2** the act of catching an animal: *Many countries ban the capture of seals.* **3 the capture of Rome/Jerusalem etc.** the act of getting control of a place that previously belonged to an enemy **4 the capture of sth** the act of getting control of something from someone you are competing with, especially in business, an election, or sport [**Origin:** 1500–1600 French, Latin *captura*, from *captus*] → see also DATA CAPTURE

car /kɑr/ S1 W1 *n.* [C] **1** a vehicle with four wheels and an engine, that you use to travel from one place to another: *a car parked on the side of the road* | *a car accident* | *You can* ***drive*** *my* ***car*** *today if you need to.* | *We decided to go* ***by car***.

THESAURUS

Types of car
hatchback a car with a door at the back that opens up
compact a small car, often with only two doors
sedan a large car with four doors, seats for at least four people, and a trunk
station wagon a large car with a door at the back and a lot of space for carrying things, usually used by families
minivan a large vehicle, used especially by families, with seats for six to eight people
sports car a low fast car, often with a roof that can be folded back
convertible a car with a roof that you can fold back or remove
limousine a very long, expensive car driven by someone who is paid to drive
SUV/sport-utility vehicle a type of vehicle that is bigger than a car and is made for traveling over rough ground
pickup/pick-up truck a vehicle with a large open part in the back that is used for carrying things
4x4/four-by-four, Jeep TRADEMARK a type of car made to travel over rough ground
→ DRIVE

2 one of the connected parts of a train that people sit in or that goods are carried in: *the dining car* **3** the part of an ELEVATOR in which people or goods are carried [**Origin:** 1800–1900 *car* **carriage** (14–19 centuries), from Anglo-French *carre*, from Latin *carrus*]

Ca·ra·cas /kəˈrɑkəs/ the capital and largest city of Venezuela

ca·rafe /kəˈræf/ *n.* [C] **1** a glass container with a wide neck, used for serving wine or water at meals **2** a glass coffee pot that is part of an electric coffee maker

ˈcar aˌlarm *n.* [C] a piece of equipment in a car that makes a loud noise if anyone tries to steal or damage the car

car·a·mel /ˈkærəməl, -ˌmɛl, ˈkɑrməl/ *n.* **1** [C,U] a brown candy made of sticky boiled sugar and milk or cream **2** [U] burned sugar, used for giving food a special taste and color [**Origin:** 1700–1800 French, Spanish *caramelo*]

car·a·mel·ize /ˈkærəməˌlaɪz, ˈkɑr-/ *v.* [I,T] if food caramelizes or is caramelized, the sugar in it burns slightly so that its color and taste change

car·a·pace /ˈkærəˌpeɪs/ *n.* [C] BIOLOGY a hard shell on the outside of some animals such as TURTLES or CRABS, that protects them

car·at /ˈkærət/ *n.* [C] a unit for measuring the weight of jewels, equal to 200 MILLIGRAMS [**Origin:** 1400–1500 French, Arabic *qirat* **bean pod, small weight**] → see also KARAT

Ca·ra·vag·gio /ˌkɑrəˈvɑdʒoʊ, -ˈvæ-/, **Mi·chel·an·ge·lo Me·ri·si da** /ˌmikəlˈændʒəloʊ mɛˈrisi də/ (1573–1610) an Italian PAINTER famous for his use of light and shadow in his paintings in the BAROQUE style

car·a·van·sa·ry /ˌkærəˈvænsəri/, **caravanserai** /-raɪ/ *n.* [C] LITERARY a hotel with a large open central area, used in the past in Middle Eastern countries by groups of people and animals traveling together

car·a·van /ˈkærəˌvæn/ *n.* [C] a group of people with animals or vehicles who are traveling together over a long distance, for example across a desert [**Origin:** 1500–1600 Italian *caravana*, from Persian *karwan*]

car·a·way /ˈkærəˌweɪ/ *n.* [U] a plant whose strong-tasting seeds are used to give a special taste to food

car·bine /ˈkɑrbaɪn/ *n.* [C] a short light RIFLE (=type of gun)

car·bo·hy·drate /ˌkɑrboʊˈhaɪdreɪt, -drɪt, -bə-/ *n.* **1** [C,U] CHEMISTRY one of several food substances such as sugar which consist of oxygen, HYDROGEN, and CARBON, and which provide the body of a person or animal with heat and energy **2 carbohydrates** [plural] foods such as rice, bread, and potatoes that contain carbohydrates

car·bol·ic a·cid /kɑrˌbɑlɪk ˈæsɪd/ *n.* [U] SCIENCE a liquid that kills BACTERIA, used for preventing the spread of disease or infection

ˈcar bomb *n.* [C] a bomb hidden inside a car or stuck underneath it

car·bon /ˈkɑrbən/ *n.* **1** [U] SYMBOL **C** CHEMISTRY a simple substance that is an ELEMENT and that exists in a pure form as DIAMONDS, GRAPHITE etc., or in an impure form as coal, gasoline etc. **2** [C,U] CARBON PAPER **3** [C] a CARBON COPY

car·bon·at·ed /ˈkɑrbəˌneɪt̬ɪd/ *adj.* carbonated drinks have a lot of small BUBBLEs in them: *carbonated spring water* —**carbonation** /ˌkɑrbəˈneɪʃən/ *n.* [U]

ˌcarbon ˈcopy *n. plural* **carbon copies** [C] **1** someone or something that is very similar to another person or thing: +**of** *The robbery is a carbon copy of one that happened last month.* **2** a copy, especially of something that has been made using CARBON PAPER

ˌcarbon ˈdating *n.* [U] SCIENCE a method used by scientists to find out the age of very old objects

carbon di·ox·ide /ˌkɑrbən daɪˈɑksaɪd/ *n.* [U] SYMBOL **CO_2** CHEMISTRY the gas produced when animals and people breathe out, when carbon is burned in air, or when substances decay

car·bon·if·er·ous /ˌkɑrbəˈnɪfərəs◂/ *adj.* EARTH SCIENCE producing or containing carbon or coal: *carboniferous rocks*

car·bon·ize /ˈkɑrbəˌnaɪz/ *v.* [I,T] CHEMISTRY to change or make something change into CARBON by burning without air —**carbonized** *adj.*

carbon mon·ox·ide /ˌkɑrbən məˈnɑksaɪd/ *n.* [U] SYMBOL **CO** CHEMISTRY a poisonous gas that is produced when CARBON, especially gasoline, burns in a small amount of air

ˈcarbon ˌpaper *n.* [C] thin paper, used in the past, with a blue or black substance on one side, that you put between sheets of paper when writing with a TYPEWRITER, in order to make copies

car·boy /ˈkɑrbɔɪ/ *n.* [C] TECHNICAL a large round bottle used for holding dangerous chemical liquids

carbs /kɑrbz/ *n.* [plural] SPOKEN INFORMAL foods such as rice, bread, and potatoes that contain CARBOHYDRATES: *Before a race, I make sure I eat plenty of carbs.*

car·bun·cle /ˈkɑrˌbʌŋkəl/ *n.* [C] **1** MEDICINE a large painful LUMP under someone's skin **2** LITERARY a red jewel, especially a GARNET

car·bu·re·tor /ˈkɑrbəˌreɪt̬ɚ/ *n.* [C] a part of a car engine that mixes the gasoline that burns in the engine with air to provide power

car·cass /ˈkɑrkəs/ *n.* [C] **1** the body of a dead animal, especially one that is ready to be cut up as meat **2** the main structure of a building, ship etc.: *The ferry's carcass lies 220 feet underwater.* **3 sb's carcass** SPOKEN someone's body, used especially when talking about someone who is tired or lazy: *Get your carcass out of my chair!*

car·cin·o·gen /kɑrˈsɪnədʒən/ *n.* [C] MEDICINE any substance that can cause CANCER

car·cin·o·gen·ic /ˌkɑrsɪnəˈdʒɛnɪk/ *adj.* MEDICINE likely to cause CANCER: *a* ***highly carcinogenic*** *substance*

car·ci·no·ma /ˌkɑrsəˈnoʊmə/ *n.* [C] MEDICINE an abnormal growth in the body caused by CANCER

card¹ /kɑrd/ [S1] [W1] *n.* [C]
1 INFORMATION a small piece of plastic or paper that shows who someone is, or shows that someone belongs to a particular organization, club etc.: *a library card* | *his party membership card* | *Employees must show their ID cards at the gate.* → see also GREEN CARD
2 MONEY a small piece of plastic that you get from your bank or from a store, that you use to pay for goods: *a VISA card* | *I gave the waiter my card.* | *Please enter your card number in the space below.* → see also CARDHOLDER, CHARGE CARD, CREDIT CARD
3 BIRTHDAY/CHRISTMAS ETC. a piece of folded thick stiff paper with a picture on the front, that you send to people on special occasions: *I got a Mother's Day card for Mom.* | **a birthday/Christmas/Valentine's etc. card** *Have you sent Jen a birthday card?* → see also GREETING CARD
4 GAMES one of a set of 52 small pieces of stiff paper with numbers or pictures on them, that are used for playing games: *We spent the entire evening* ***playing cards*** (=playing a game with cards) *and drinking.* | *a new* ***deck of cards*** (=set of cards)
5 FOR WRITING INFORMATION a small piece of thick stiff paper that information can be written or printed on: *a recipe card* | *She took notes on 3x5 cards* (=cards that are 3 inches high and 5 inches wide).
6 baseball/sports etc. card a small piece of thick stiff paper with a picture of and information about a baseball player etc., that is part of a set which people collect
7 BUSINESS a small piece of thick stiff paper that shows your name, job, and the company you work for [SYN] **business card**: *Mr. Kim gave me his card as I left.* → see also CALLING CARD
8 COMPUTER [C] COMPUTERS the thing inside a computer that the CHIPS are attached to, that allows the computer to perform specific actions
9 FROM VACATION a POSTCARD
10 SOCCER a small piece of red or yellow paper, shown by the referee to a player who has done something wrong in a game of soccer
11 be in the cards to seem likely to happen: *The increase in price has been in the cards for some time.*
12 put/lay your cards on the table to tell people what your plans and intentions are in a clear, honest way after keeping them secret for some time: *They're willing to put all their cards on the table and negotiate.*
13 your strong/strongest/best card something that gives you a big advantage in a particular situation: *The promise of tax cuts proved to be the Republicans' best card.* → see also **your trump card** at TRUMP¹ (3)
14 play/keep/hold your cards close to your chest also **play/keep/hold your cards close to your vest** to keep your plans, thoughts, or feelings secret: *The chairman is holding his cards close to his chest on the question of a merger.*
15 hold all the cards INFORMAL to have all the advantages in a particular situation so that you can control what happens: *In research, the larger well-financed firms hold all the cards.*
16 have a/another card up your sleeve to have an advantage that you have been keeping secret, that you can use to be successful in a particular situation
17 PERSON [usually singular] OLD-FASHIONED an amusing or unusual person: *Harold was always such a card!*
18 TOOL TECHNICAL a tool that is similar to a comb and is used for combing, cleaning and preparing wool or cotton for SPINNING
[**Origin:** 1400–1500 French *carte*, from Old Italian *carta* **sheet of paper**, from Latin *charta*] → see also **play your cards right** at PLAY¹ (21)

card² [S2] *v.* **1** [I,T] to ask someone to show a card proving that they are old enough to be in a particular place, especially a bar, or old enough to buy alcohol or cigarettes: *Clerks card everyone buying alcohol who looks under 30.* **2** [T] to comb, clean, and prepare wool or cotton, before making cloth

car·da·mom /ˈkɑrdəməm/ *n.* [U] BIOLOGY the seeds of an Asian fruit, used to give a special taste to Indian and Middle Eastern food

card·board¹ /ˈkɑrdbɔrd/ *n.* [U] a thick usually brown material like stiff paper, used especially for making boxes

cardboard² *adj.* **1** made from cardboard: *a cardboard box* → see picture at BOX¹ **2** [only before noun] seeming silly and not real: *the cardboard characters in romantic novels*

ˈcardboard ˌcutout *n.* [C] **1** a large photograph, usually of a person, cut out of cardboard and supported so that it stands by itself: *a life-sized cardboard cutout of Brad Pitt* **2** a person or character in a book, movie etc. who seems silly or unreal

ˈcard-ˌcarrying *adj.* **1 a card-carrying member/Republican/liberal etc.** someone who has paid money to an organization and is an involved member of it: *a card-carrying member of the ACLU* **2** USUALLY DISAPPROVING used to describe someone whose behavior or personality is strongly influenced by something they believe, do etc.: *a card-carrying computer geek*

ˈcard ˌcatalog *n.* [C] a box of cards that contain

information about something, especially about the books in a library, and are arranged in order

card·hold·er /ˈkɑrdˌhoʊldɚ/ *n.* [C] someone who has a CREDIT CARD

car·di·ac /ˈkɑrdiˌæk/ *adj.* [only before noun] MEDICINE connected with medical conditions relating to the heart: *cardiac surgery* | *cardiac patients*

ˌcardiac arˈrest *n.* [U] TECHNICAL a serious medical condition in which the heart stops beating SYN **heart attack**

C

Car·diff /ˈkɑrdɪf/ the capital and largest city of Wales

car·di·gan /ˈkɑrdəgən/ also **ˈcardigan ˌsweater** *n.* [C] a SWEATER that is fastened at the front with buttons [**Origin:** 1800–1900 Earl of *Cardigan* (1797–1868), British soldier]

car·di·nal¹ /ˈkɑrdn-əl, -nəl/ *n.* [C] **1** a priest of very high rank in the Catholic church **2** BIOLOGY a North American bird, the male of which is a bright red color → see picture on page A34 **3** MATH a CARDINAL NUMBER

cardinal² *adj.* [only before noun] very important or basic: *Having clean hands is one of the* ***cardinal rules*** *of food preparation.*

ˌcardinal diˈrection also **ˌcardinal ˈpoint** *n.* [C] EARTH SCIENCE any of the four main COMPASS points: north, south, east, and west

ˌcardinal ˈnumber *n.* [C] MATH a number such as 1, 2, or 3, that shows the quantity of something → see also ORDINAL NUMBER

ˌcardinal ˈsin *n.* [C] **1** a very bad or stupid action that you must avoid doing in a particular situation: *The mayor committed the cardinal sin of ignoring public opinion.* **2** TECHNICAL a serious SIN in the Christian religion

ˌcardinal ˈvirtue *n.* [C] FORMAL a moral quality that someone has which people greatly respect or value

car·di·o /ˈkɑrdioʊ/ *n.* [U] INFORMAL exercises that make your heart and lungs stronger: *I do weight training and cardio.*

cardio- /kɑrdioʊ, -diə/ *prefix* TECHNICAL concerning the heart: *a cardiograph* (=instrument that measures movements of the heart) [**Origin:** Greek *kardia* **heart**]

car·di·ol·o·gy /ˌkɑrdiˈɑlədʒi/ *n.* [U] the study or science of the heart —**cardiologist** *n.* [C]

car·di·o·pul·mo·nar·y /ˌkɑrdioʊˈpʊlməˌnɛri/ *adj.* [only before noun] TECHNICAL relating to the heart and the lungs

cardioˌpulmonary resusciˈtation *n.* [U] TECHNICAL → see CPR

car·di·o·vas·cu·lar /ˌkɑrdioʊˈvæskyələ/ *adj.* TECHNICAL BIOLOGY relating to the heart and the BLOOD VESSELS

ˈcard shark also **ˈcard sharp** *n.* [C] someone who cheats when playing cards in order to make money

ˈcard ˌtable *n.* [C] a small light table with legs that you can fold, used for playing cards

care¹ /kɛr/ S1 W1 *n.*

1 HELPING SB [U] the process of doing things for someone or something, especially because they are weak, sick, old etc. and unable to do things for themselves: *Your father will need constant medical care.* | **+of** *staff trained in the care of young children* | *The children had been left* ***in the care of*** *a babysitter.* | *Dr. Cook has 200 patients* ***under his care.*** → see also CHILD CARE, DAYCARE, HEALTH CARE, INTENSIVE CARE, **tender loving care** at TENDER¹ (5)

2 KEEPING STH IN GOOD CONDITION [U] the process of doing things to something so that it stays in good condition and works correctly: *skin care lotions* | **+of** *advice on the care of your new car*

3 CAREFULNESS [U] carefulness to avoid damage, mistakes etc.: *A lot of care goes into making the furniture.* | *The note on the box read, "Fragile – handle with care."*

4 take care of sb/sth a) to watch and help someone and be responsible for them: *My mother said she'd take care of Luisa next weekend.* **b)** to do things to keep something in good condition or working correctly: *The class teaches kids how to take care of their bikes.* **c)** to deal with all the work, arrangements etc. that are necessary for something to happen: *Her secretary will take care of the details.* **d)** an expression meaning "to pay for something," used when you want to avoid saying this directly: *Don't worry about the bill; it's taken care of.*

5 take care a) SPOKEN used when saying goodbye to family and friends **b)** to be careful: *It's very icy, so take care driving home.* | **+that** *Take care that the milk doesn't get too hot.* | **take care to do sth** *Hikers in the desert must take care to drink enough water.*

6 (in) care of sb ABBREVIATION **c/o** used when sending letters to someone at someone else's address: *Send me the package care of my cousins.*

7 PROBLEM/WORRY [C,U] LITERARY something that causes problems and makes you anxious or sad: *Movies set you free from your cares for a while.* | *Harry* ***doesn't have a care in the world*** (=does not have any problems or worries).

[**Origin:** Old English *caru*]

care² S1 W1 *v.* [I,T] **1** to feel that something is important, so that you are interested in it, worried about it etc.: **+about** *Children care about keeping the environment clean.* | **care who/what/whether etc.** *I don't care whether we win or lose.* | *I* ***care deeply*** (=care very much) *about what is happening in this town.* **2** to be concerned about what happens to someone, because you like or love them: *She felt that nobody cared.* | **+about** *Just listening to somebody shows you care about them.* → see also CARING **3 not care to do sth** to not like or want to do something: *It's not something I care to discuss.* **4 more/longer etc. than sb cares to admit/remember/mention etc.** used when something happens or is done more than you think is acceptable: *Mistakes happen more often than doctors would care to admit.* | *That bike's been in the basement for longer than I care to remember.*

SPOKEN PHRASES

5 who cares? used to say in an impolite or informal way that something does not worry or upset you, because you think it is not important: *So your house isn't perfectly clean. Who cares?* **6 I/he/they etc. couldn't care less** also **I/he etc. could care less** NONSTANDARD used to say in an impolite way that you do not care at all about something: *I couldn't care less about the Super Bowl.* **7 what do I/you/they etc. care?** used to say in an impolite way that someone does not care at all about something: *What does he care? He'll get his money whatever happens.* **8 for all sb cares** used to emphasize that something does not matter at all to someone: *"Dave's moving to Boston." "He can move to Timbuktu, for all I care."* **9 would you care to do sth?** FORMAL used to ask someone politely whether they want to do something: *Would you care to comment on that, Senator?*

care for *phr. v.* **1 care for sb** to help someone who is old, sick, weak etc. and not able to do things for themselves: *Angie cared for her mother after her stroke.* **2 care for sb** to love someone, but not in a romantic way: *Frequent visits are the best way to show your mother you care for her.* **3 care for sth** to do things to keep something in good condition or working correctly SYN **look after**: *It will rust if you don't care for it properly.* **4 not care for sb/sth** to not like someone or something: *I don't really care for Jeff's parents.* **5 would you care for sth?** FORMAL used to politely ask someone if they want something: *Would you care for a drink?*

ca·reen /kəˈrin/ *v.* [I always + adv./prep.] **1** to move quickly forward without control, making sudden sideways movements: **+down/over/around etc.** *The truck careened into a ditch.* **2** to keep changing in an uncontrolled way: **+from/toward** *Her emotions careened from hatred to pity and back again.*

ca·reer¹ /kəˈrɪr/ S3 W1 *n.* [C] **1** a job or profession that you have been trained for and intend to do for several years: *The win was the 250th in Anderson's* *coaching career.* | +**in** *a career in banking* | +**as** *I'm interested in a career as a doctor.* | *Noah plans to* ***pursue a career*** *in law* (=work as a lawyer). | *After 15 years in teaching, I'm ready for a* ***career change*** (=I want to start a different job). ▸see THESAURUS box at **job** **2** the period of time in your life that you spend doing a particular activity: *Will spent most of his long career as a lawyer.* | **sb's singing/professional/political etc. career** *The illness ended her singing career.* | **be at the height/peak of your career** (=be producing the best work of the time you have been doing a job) **3 make a career of doing sth** to do something again and again for a long time, so that you become well-known for doing this: *He made a career out of saying "no" to anyone who came to his organization for funding.* [**Origin:** 1500–1600 French *carrière*, from Old Provençal *carriera* **street**, from Latin *carrus*]

career² *adj.* **a career soldier/politician/diplomat etc.** someone who intends to be a soldier, politician etc. for most of their life, not just for a particular period of time

career³ *v.* [I always + adv./prep.] LITERARY to move forward very fast and often without control SYN **careen**

ca'reer ˌcounselor *n.* [C] someone whose job is to give people advice about what jobs and professional training might be appropriate for them —**career counseling** *n.* [U]

ca•reer•ist /kəˈrɪrɪst/ *n.* [C] DISAPPROVING someone whose career is more important to them than anything else —**careerist** *adj.* —**careerism** *n.* [U]

ca'reer ˌwoman *n.* [C] a woman whose career is very important to her, so that she may not want to get married or have children

care•free /ˈkɛrfri/ *adj.* having no worries or problems: *a carefree summer vacation* | *carefree and fun-loving youngsters*

care•ful /ˈkɛrfəl/ S1 W3 *adj.* **1** trying very hard to avoid causing something bad to happen, such as damaging or losing something or getting hurt SYN **cautious** OPP **careless**: *Deb's a very careful driver.* | ***Be careful!*** (=used to warn someone about danger) – *there's broken glass on the sidewalk.* | +**with** *Be careful with those scissors!* | +**about** *The press must be very careful about how information is presented.* | **be careful to do sth** *Sam was always careful to lock the door when he left.* | **be careful (that)** *We were careful that he didn't find out about the party.* | **careful who/what/how etc.** *Be careful who you let into your apartment.*

THESAURUS

methodical done in a careful and well-organized way, or always doing things this way: *a methodical approach to the problem*
thorough careful to do everything that you should and avoid mistakes: *The police have conducted a thorough investigation into her death.*
meticulous very careful about details, and always trying to do things correctly: *She keeps meticulous records.*
systematic organized carefully and done thoroughly: *The experiments must be done in a systematic way.*
painstaking very careful and thorough: *the painstaking work that has gone into this research*

2 paying a lot of attention to detail, so that something is done correctly and thoroughly: *her careful planning of the event* | **careful attention/consideration/thought** *They've given very careful attention to detail.* | +**about** *Kerry is careful about what she eats.* **3 if sb's not careful** used to say that something bad is likely to happen unless someone changes the way they behave: *You'll make yourself sick if you're not careful.* **4 you can't be too careful** used to say that you should do everything possible to avoid problems or danger: *You can't be too careful where computer viruses are concerned.* **5 careful with money** not spending more money than you need to SYN **thrifty**: *Napier hopes voters will remember that he's been careful with taxpayers' money.* —**carefulness** *n.* [U]

care•ful•ly /ˈkɛrfəli/ W2 *adv.* in a careful way: *The book must be handled carefully because of its age.* | **listen/look/think etc. carefully** *City officials need to listen carefully to citizens' views.* | **examine/consider sth carefully** *It's confusing, but you should consider your options carefully.* | **carefully chosen/planned/controlled etc.** *The study was conducted on a small, carefully selected group.*

care•giv•er /ˈkɛrˌgɪvɚ/ *n.* [C] someone who takes care of a child or sick person

'care ˌlabel *n.* [C] a small piece of cloth in a piece of clothing that tells you how to wash it

care•less /ˈkɛrlɪs/ *adj.* **1** not paying enough attention to what you are doing, so that you make mistakes, damage things etc.: *a fire started by careless campers* | *Keaton* ***got careless*** *and left fingerprints on the body.* | +**about** *He had become careless about taking his medication.* **2** done without much effort or attention to detail: *a careless mistake* **3** natural and not done with any deliberate effort or attention: *He ran a hand through his hair with a careless gesture.* **4 careless of sth** LITERARY deliberately ignoring something: *Careless of her own safety, she pulled the child out of the flames.* —**carelessly** *adv.* —**carelessness** *n.* [U]

'care ˌpackage *n.* [C] a package of food, magazines, and other interesting or useful items that is sent to someone living away from home, for example a soldier

ca•ress¹ /kəˈrɛs/ *v.* [T] **1** to gently touch someone in a way that shows you love them: *Stan lovingly caressed my cheek.* ▸see THESAURUS box at **touch¹** **2** POETIC to touch something gently, in a way that seems pleasant or romantic: *Waves caressed the shore.*

caress² *n.* [C] a gentle loving touch

car•et /ˈkærət/ *n.* [C] TECHNICAL the mark (‸) or (^) used in writing and printing to show where something is to be added

care•tak•er /ˈkɛrˌteɪkɚ/ *n.* [C] **1** someone who takes care of a house or land while the person who owns it is not there **2** someone who takes care of other people, especially a teacher, parent, nurse etc. **3 a caretaker administration/government etc.** a government etc. that has power only for a short period of time between the end of one government and the start of another

care•worn /ˈkɛrwɔrn/ *adj.* looking sad, worried, or anxious: *a careworn face*

car•fare /ˈkɑrfɛr/ *n.* [U] OLD-FASHIONED the amount of money that it costs to travel on a bus or STREETCAR

car•go /ˈkɑrgoʊ/ *n. plural* **cargoes** or **cargos** [C,U] the goods being carried in a ship, airplane, truck etc.: *The ship was carrying military cargo.* | *a cargo of oil-drilling equipment* | *a cargo plane* [**Origin:** 1600–1700 Spanish **load, charge**, from *cargar* **to load**, from Late Latin *carricare*]

car•hop /ˈkɑrhɑp/ *n.* [C] someone who carried food to people's cars at a DRIVE-IN restaurant, especially in past times

Car•ib /ˈkærɪb/ a Native American tribe from Central America and the northern area of South America

Car•ib•be•an /ˌkærɪˈbiən, kəˈrɪbiən/ *adj.* from or relating to the islands in the Caribbean Sea

ˌCaribbean 'Sea, the also **the Caribbean** the part of the western Atlantic Ocean between Central America, South America, and the Caribbean islands

ca•ri•bou /ˈkærəbu/ *n. plural* **caribou** or **caribous** [C] a North American REINDEER

caricature

C

car·i·ca·ture¹ /ˈkærəkətʃə, -ˌtʃʊr/ *n.* **1** [C] ENG. LANG. ARTS a funny drawing of someone that makes them look silly or stupid: *caricatures of politicians in the newspaper* ►see THESAURUS box at **picture**¹ **2** [C] ENG. LANG. ARTS a description of someone or something that emphasizes only some qualities, so that he, she, or it seems silly: *a caricature of the Californian way of life* **3** [C] someone or something that seems silly because they show very strongly the qualities that are considered to be typical of that type of person, thing, or group: *She is a caricature of an English upper-class lady.* **4** [U] ENG. LANG. ARTS the activity of making pictures of or writing about people in this way: *a cartoonist with a talent for caricature* [**Origin:** 1700–1800 French, Italian *caricatura*, from *caricare* **to load, make seem larger, worse etc.**, from Late Latin *carricare*]

caricature² *v.* [T] to draw or describe someone in a way that makes them seem silly or stupid: *Celebrities have been caricatured and hung on the restaurant's walls.*

car·i·ca·tur·ist /ˈkærɪkəˌtʃʊrɪst/ *n.* [C] someone who draws or writes caricatures

car·ies /ˈkɛriz/ *n.* [U] MEDICINE decay in someone's teeth

car·il·lon /ˈkærəˌlɑn, -lən/ *n.* [C] a set of bells in a tower that are controlled from a piano KEYBOARD, or a tune played on these bells

car·ing /ˈkɛrɪŋ/ *adj.* someone who is caring thinks about what other people need or would like, and tries to help them: *Roger's a warm and caring person.* | *a caring family*

car·jack·ing /ˈkɑrˌdʒækɪŋ/ *n.* [C,U] the crime of using a weapon to force the driver of a car to drive you somewhere or give your their car —**carjacker** *n.* [C] —**carjack** *v.* [T] → see also HIJACKING

car·load /ˈkɑrloʊd/ *n.* [C] the amount a car or a railroad car can hold: *a carload of kids* | *This year, the railroads carried 1.5 million carloads of chemicals.*

car·mak·er /ˈkɑrˌmeɪkə/ *n.* [C] a company that makes cars

Car·mel·ite /ˈkɑrməˌlaɪt/ **1** a member of a Christian group of FRIARS **2** a member of a Christian group of MONKS or NUNS

car·mine /ˈkɑrmaɪn/ *n.* [U] a deep purplish red color —**carmine** *adj.*

car·nage /ˈkɑrnɪdʒ/ *n.* [U] the killing and hurting of many people, especially in a war: *scenes of terrible carnage after the bombing* [**Origin:** 1600–1700 French, Medieval Latin *carnaticum* **meat, especially as given to a ruler**, from Latin *caro* **flesh**]

car·nal /ˈkɑrnl/ *adj.* **1** relating to the body or sex, used especially in religious language: *carnal desires* **2 carnal knowledge/relations** BIBLICAL or HUMOROUS sexual activity [**Origin:** 1400–1500 Late Latin *carnalis*, from Latin *caro* **flesh**] —**carnally** *adv.*

car·na·tion /kɑrˈneɪʃən/ *n.* [C] a white, pink, or red flower that smells sweet and is often worn as a decoration at formal ceremonies

Car·ne·gie /ˈkɑrnəgi, kɑrˈneɪgi/, **An·drew** /ˈændru/ (1835–1919) a U.S. BUSINESSMAN who gave money to start many public libraries in the U.S. and for building Carnegie Hall

car·nel·ian /kɑrˈniliən/ *n.* [C,U] a dark red or reddish-brown stone used in jewelry

car·ni·val /ˈkɑrnəvəl/ *n.* **1** [C] a noisy outdoor event at which you can ride on special machines and play games for prizes SYN **fair** **2** [C] an event held at a school in order to get money to pay for things at the school, in which students and other people play games for prizes SYN **fair** **3 Carnival** a celebration with dancing, drinking, and a PARADE through the streets, usually held just before the beginning of LENT (=a special period of time in the Christian calendar) → see also MARDI GRAS [**Origin:** 1500–1600 Italian *carnevale*, from *carne* **meat** + *levare* **to remove**; because after Carnival people stopped eating meat for a period]

car·ni·vore /ˈkɑrnəvɔr/ *n.* [C] **1** BIOLOGY an animal that eats other animals → see also HERBIVORE **2** HUMOROUS someone who eats meat → see also VEGETARIAN —**carnivorous** /kɑrˈnɪvərəs/ *adj.*

Car·not ef·fi·cien·cy /ˈkɑrnoʊ ɪˌfɪʃənsi/ *n.* [U] PHYSICS the greatest possible amount of energy that can be used in a heat engine to produce work effectively, without wasting energy

car·ny /ˈkɑrni/ *n. plural* **carnies** [C] INFORMAL someone who works in a CARNIVAL

car·ob /ˈkærəb/ *n.* [U] BIOLOGY the fruit of a Mediterranean tree, that tastes similar to chocolate and is sometimes eaten instead of chocolate

car·ol¹ /ˈkærəl/ also ˌ**Christmas** ˈ**carol** *n.* [C] a traditional Christmas song [**Origin:** 1500–1600 *carol* **circular dance with singing** (13–17 centuries), from Old French *carole*]

carol² *v.* [I] to sing carols or other songs in a cheerful way, often going around in a group to people's houses —**caroler** *n.* [C]

Car·o·lin·gian /ˌkærəˈlɪndʒən/ the name of a family of French kings who ruled from 751 to 987

car·om /ˈkærəm/ *v.* [I always +adv./prep.] if something caroms, it hits something and then quickly moves away from it: *The puck caromed off his skate and into the net.*

ca·rot·id ar·te·ry /kəˌrɑṭɪd ˈɑrṭəri/ *n.* [C] BIOLOGY one of the two arteries (ARTERY) in your neck, that supply blood to your head

ca·rouse /kəˈraʊz/ *v.* [I] LITERARY to drink a lot, be noisy, and have fun —**carousal** *n.* [C,U]

car·ou·sel, carrousel /ˌkærəˈsɛl/ *n.* [C] **1** a machine with painted wooden horses on it that turns around and around, which people can ride on for fun SYN **merry-go-round** **2** the circular moving belt that you get your bags and suitcases from at an airport **3** a circular piece of equipment that you put SLIDES into, in order to show them on a screen using a SLIDE PROJECTOR

carp¹ /kɑrp/ *n. plural* **carp** [C] BIOLOGY a large fish that lives in lakes and rivers and can be eaten

carp² *v.* [I usually in progressive] to complain about something or criticize someone all the time: **+about** *airplane passengers carping about the food* | **carp at sb** *The two men carped at each other throughout the meeting.*

car·pals /ˈkɑrpəlz/ *n* [plural] BIOLOGY the eight small bones that form the joint in the wrist → see picture at SKELETON¹

car·pal tun·nel syn·drome /ˌkɑrpəl ˈtʌnl ˌsɪndroʊm/ *n.* [U] MEDICINE a medical condition in which someone gets a lot of pain and weakness in their wrist

car·pe di·em /ˌkɑrpeɪ ˈdiəm/ *interjection* a Latin phrase meaning "seize the day," used to tell someone to do what they want to do, and not worry about the future

car·pel /ˈkɑrpəl/ *n.* [C] BIOLOGY the part of a flower where new seeds are formed → see picture at FLOWER

car·pen·ter /ˈkɑrpəntə/ *n.* [C] someone whose job is building wooden houses and making and repairing furniture and other wooden objects [**Origin:** 1100–1200

Old North French *carpentier*, from Latin *carpentarius* **carriage-maker**]

car·pen·try /'kɑrpəntri/ *n.* [U] the skill or work of a carpenter

car·pet[1] /'kɑrpɪt/ S2 *n.* **1** [C,U] heavy material for covering all of a floor or stairs, or a piece of this material → see also RUG **2 be/get called on the carpet** to be criticized by someone who has a higher rank than you, because you have done something wrong: *Danson got called on the carpet by the Board about his excessive spending.* **3 a carpet of leaves/flowers etc.** LITERARY a thick layer of leaves etc. [**Origin:** 1300–1400 Old French *carpite*, from Old Italian *carpita*, from *carpire* **to pull out**] → see also MAGIC CARPET, **sweep sth under the rug/carpet** at SWEEP[1] (14)

carpet[2] *v.* [T] **1** [usually passive] to cover a floor with carpet: *The hall was carpeted in a depressing shade of green.* **2 be carpeted with grass/flowers etc.** LITERARY to be covered with a thick layer of grass etc.

car·pet·bag /'kɑrpɪt¬ˌbæg/ *n.* [C] OLD-FASHIONED a bag used by someone when they are traveling, usually made of carpet

car·pet·bag·ger /'kɑrpɪt¬ˌbægə/ *n.* [C] **1** HISTORY someone from the Northern U.S. who went to the Southern U.S. after the Civil War of the 1860s in order to get rich, especially in a slightly dishonest or immoral way, without helping the people who lived there **2** POLITICS someone who moves to a different place in order to help their political CAREER

'carpet-bomb *v.* [T] to drop a lot of bombs over a small area to destroy everything in it. —**carpet bombing** *n.* [C]

car·pet·ing /'kɑrpət̬ɪŋ/ *n.* [U] a carpet or carpets in general, or heavy woven material used for making CARPETS

'carpet ˌsweeper *n.* [C] a simple machine that does not use electricity, used for sweeping CARPETS

car·pool[1], **car pool** /'kɑrpul/ *n.* [C] a group of people who travel together to work, school etc. in one car and share the costs

carpool[2], **car-pool** *v.* [I] if a group of people carpool, they travel together to work, school etc. in one car and share the costs

car·port /'kɑrpɔrt/ *n.* [C] a shelter for a car that has a roof but no door and sometimes no walls, usually built against the side of a house → see also GARAGE

car·rel /'kærəl/ *n.* [C] a small enclosed desk for one person to use in a library

car·riage /'kærɪdʒ/ *n.* **1** [C] a vehicle with wheels that is pulled by a horse, used in past times → see also BABY CARRIAGE **2** [C] the movable part of a machine that supports another part: +**of** *the carriage of a typewriter* **3** [C] something with wheels that is used to move a heavy object, especially a gun **4** [U] FORMAL the way someone walks and moves their head and body: *her upright carriage*

car·ri·er /'kæriə/ W3 *n.* [C] **1** a company that moves goods or passengers from one place to another, especially by airplane: *a carrier with routes to the eastern U.S.* **2** someone who carries something, especially as a job: *a newspaper carrier* | *We give a gift to the letter carrier* (=person who delivers mail) *at Christmas.* **3** a company that provides a service such as insurance or telephones: *Who's your long-distance carrier* (=for long-distance phone calls)*?* **4** a military vehicle or ship used to move soldiers, weapons etc. → see also AIRCRAFT CARRIER **5** MEDICINE someone who passes a disease or gene that causes a disease to other people without having the disease themselves

'carrier ˌpigeon *n.* [C] a PIGEON (=type of bird) that has been trained to carry messages

car·ri·on /'kæriən/ *n.* [U] dead flesh that is decaying

Car·roll /'kærəl/, **Lew·is** /'luis/ (1832–1898) a British writer who wrote two very famous children's stories: "Alice's Adventures in Wonderland" and "Through the Looking Glass"

car·rot /'kærət/ S3 *n.* [C] **1** BIOLOGY a plant with a long thick orange pointed root that you eat as a vegetable: *raw carrots* | *carrot soup* **2** something that is promised to someone in order to try and persuade them to work harder: *One of the carrots that Dad always dangled in front of me* (=promised me) *was that he was going to send me to college.* **3 a carrot-and-stick approach** a way of making someone do something that combines a promise of something good if they do it, and a threat of something bad if they do not do it: *a carrot-and-stick approach to punish and prevent corporate crime* [**Origin:** 1400–1500 French *carotte*, from Late Latin, from Greek *karoton*]

C

car·rou·sel /ˌkærə'sɛl/ *n.* [C] another spelling of CAROUSEL

car·ry[1] /'kæri/ S1 W1 *v.* **carries, carried, carrying**
1 LIFT AND TAKE [T] to take something somewhere by holding it in your hands or arms or supporting it as you move: *Would you carry my suitcase for me?* | *Five thousand people carried banners and signs in the protest march.* | **carry sth around/out/to etc.** *He carried the child up to bed.*

THESAURUS

tote INFORMAL to carry something: *guards toting machine guns*
lug INFORMAL to pull or carry something that is very heavy: *They lugged the mail in heavy canvas bags into the building.*
cart to carry or take something large and heavy somewhere: *Workers carted away several tons of trash.*
haul to carry or pull something heavy: *The company hauls furniture and household goods for people who are moving.*
schlep INFORMAL to carry or pull something heavy: *Marty schlepped the suitcases upstairs.*
bear FORMAL to bring or carry something: *They arrived bearing gifts.*

2 VEHICLE/SHIP/PLANE [T] to take people or things from one place to another: *We saw a lot of trucks carrying loads of grain.* | *The new plane can carry 555 passengers.*
3 PIPE/ROAD/WIRE [T] if a pipe, road, wire etc. carries something such as liquid or electricity, the liquid etc. flows along it or on it: *A single cable carries television and telephone signals.* | **carry sth down/through/across etc.** *Pipes carry the water across the desert.*
4 WATER/AIR [T always + adv./prep.] if a current of water or air carries something or someone, it takes them somewhere as it moves along: *Strong winds carried the poisonous gas for miles.*
5 HAVE WITH YOU [T] to have something with you in your pocket, on your belt, in your bag etc.: *I don't usually carry that much cash on me.* | *How many teenagers carry guns or knives to school these days?*
6 STORE [T] if a store carries goods, it has a supply of them for sale: *Any good hardware store will carry the bolts.* | *Discount stores carry name-brand merchandise at low prices.*
7 NEWSPAPER/BROADCAST [T] if a newspaper or a television or radio broadcast carries news, a program, an advertisement etc., it prints it or broadcasts it: *The paper carried the story on the front page.* | *The local cable station carries a broad variety of shows.*
8 LABEL/WRITING [T] if an object, container etc. carries information such as a warning, those words are written on it: *The card in his wallet carries details of his blood type.*
9 HAVE A QUALITY [T] to have a particular quality such as authority or confidence that makes people believe or not believe you: *Laura carries an unmistakable air of authority.* | *Greenspan's views usually* ***carry great weight*** (=have influence) *with members of Congress.* | *Matthew's voice did not* ***carry*** *much* ***conviction*** (=he did not seem very sure). | *Every treatment* ***carries a small risk.***
10 DISEASE [T] MEDICINE to have a disease and pass it to others, or to have a GENE that causes a disease: *Rats*

carry many diseases. | *a test to determine if a woman carries the breast cancer gene*
11 get/be carried away to be so excited, angry, interested etc. that you are not really in control of what you do or say anymore, or you forget everything else: *Norm tends to get carried away and talk too much.*
12 carry insurance to have insurance SYN **have**: *Most state employees carry some type of insurance.*
13 carry a guarantee/warranty to be sold with a GUARANTEE (=promise that a product you buy will be fixed without cost if it breaks within a particular time after you buy it): *All products carry a 12-month guarantee.*
14 CRIME/PUNISHMENT [T] if a crime carries a particular punishment, that is the usual punishment for the crime: *Murder carries a life sentence in this state.*
15 ELECTION [T] POLITICS if someone carries a state, COUNTY etc., they win an election in that area: *Reagan carried California in 1980.*
16 carry sth in your head/mind to remember information that you need, without writing it down: *The amount of knowledge Lee carries in her head is amazing.*
17 WEIGHT [T] to have a particular amount of weight on your body, especially when this is too much: *Mike carries 300 pounds on his 6-foot, 4-inch body.*
18 BUILDING [T] if a PILLAR, wall etc. carries something, it supports the weight of that thing: *These two columns carry the whole roof.*
19 PERSUADE [T] to persuade people to accept your suggestions or support you: *Stephanie's arguments carried the meeting.* | *Jackson's common-sense attitude* ***carried the day*** (=persuaded people to support his ideas).
20 carry yourself to stand and move in a particular way: *It was obvious by the way they carried themselves that they were soldiers.*
21 carry sth too far/to extremes/to excess to do or say too much about something: *OK, stop it – you've carried the joke too far.*
22 SOUND/SMELL [I] if a sound or smell carries to a particular place, it goes as far as that place: *The sounds of laughter carried as far as the lake.* | *Toni's high, thin voice did not carry well* (=it could not be heard very far away).
23 be carried if a suggestion, PROPOSAL etc. is carried, the people at a meeting approve it by voting: *The amendment to the bill was carried unanimously* (=everyone agreed to it). | *The motion was carried by 76 votes* (=76 more people voted for it than voted against it).
24 CHILD [T] if a woman is carrying a child, she is PREGNANT (=going to have a baby)
25 carry a (heavy) load/burden to have a lot of work to do or a lot of responsibility for something: *Moore carries most of the load for the team.*
26 carry sb (to victory/to the top etc.) to be the reason that a person or group is successful: *Democrats need a message that will carry them to victory.* | *Smith carried the team that night, scoring 35 points.*
27 carry the day to be the person or thing that is most successful or best liked: *In the end her argument carried the day.* | *The Republicans carried the day* (=won the election).
28 carry a tune to sing the notes of songs correctly: *As long as you can carry a tune, you're welcome to join the choir.*
29 sb can't carry a tune in a bucket HUMOROUS used to say that someone is completely unable to sing the notes of any song
30 as fast as his/her legs could carry him/her LITERARY as fast as possible: *She ran to her mother as fast as her legs could carry her.*
31 MATHEMATICS [T] to put a number into the next row to the left when you are adding numbers together: *Nine and three make twelve, put down the two and carry the one.*
32 carry a torch for sb to secretly love and admire someone who does not love you: *I think Seth is carrying a torch for Liz.*
33 carry the torch of sth to continue to support a belief or tradition when no one else wants to: *Ancient Greeks carried the torch of scientific study for many centuries.*
34 BALL [I] if a ball carries a particular distance, that is how far it travels when it is hit
[**Origin:** 1300–1400 Old North French *carier* **to take in a vehicle**, from *car* **vehicle**, from Latin *carrus*] → see also CARD-CARRYING, CARRIER

carry sth ↔ **forward** *phr. v.* **1** to move a total to the next page in order to add it to other numbers on that page **2** to continue something that had been started earlier: *I intend to carry forward the excellent work that you all have done.* **3** to make an amount of something such as money or vacation time available for use at a later time: *How many vacation days can be carried forward to next year?*

carry sth ↔ **off** *phr. v.* **1** to do something difficult successfully: *Rubens carried off several important diplomatic missions.* **2** to win a prize: *Bancroft carried off the Oscar for Best Actress.*

carry on *phr. v.* **1 carry on** to continue doing something SYN **go on**: *Wilde plans to carry on and finish writing the book.* | **carry on with sth** *I can't carry on with my life as though nothing has happened.* **2 carry on sth** to continue something that has been started by someone else: *June's daughters will carry on the family traditions.* **3 carry on a conversation** to talk to someone: *The people behind me were carrying on a conversation through the whole movie.* **4 carry sth ↔ on** to take luggage with you on an plane, rather than giving it to the AIRLINE to go with the other luggage **5** SPOKEN to behave or talk in a silly, excited, or anxious way that annoys other people: **+about** *He just kept carrying on about his new car.* **6 carry on with sb** OLD-FASHIONED to have a sexual relationship with someone, when you should not

carry sth ↔ **out** *phr. v.* **1** to do something that needs to be organized and planned: *an attack carried out by a group of 15 rebels* | *Teenagers carried out a survey on attitudes to drugs.* **2** to do something that you have said you will do or that someone has told you to do: *Will Congress carry out its promise to change the law?* | **carry out instructions/an order** *The soldiers claimed they were only carrying out orders.*

carry sth **over** *phr. v.* **1** if something is carried over into a new set of conditions, it continues to exist and influences the new conditions → see also CARRYOVER: **+into** *Worries at work often carry over into the home.* **2** to make an amount of something available to be used at a later time: *Only two days of vacation time can be carried over into next year.*

carry through *phr. v.* **1 carry sb through (sth)** to help someone to manage during an illness or a difficult period SYN **see sb through sth**: *Troy's sense of humor carried him through his cancer treatments.* **2 carry sth through** to complete or finish something successfully, in spite of difficulties SYN **see sth through**: *It's a good idea, and we'll try to carry it through.*

carry through on sth *phr. v.* to completely finish doing something that you said you would do SYN **follow through**: *They have not carried through on promised bank reforms.*

carry[2] *n.* [singular, U] TECHNICAL the distance a ball or bullet travels after it has been thrown, hit, or fired

car·ry·all /ˈkæri,ɔl/ *n.* [C] a large soft bag, usually made of cloth → see picture at BAG[1]

ˈcarrying caˌpacity *n.* [singular, U] BIOLOGY the total number of people or animals that can live in an area without damage to the environment

ˈcarrying charge *n.* [C] a charge added to the price of something you have bought by INSTALLMENT PLAN (=paying over several months)

ˈcarry-on *adj.* [only before noun] carry-on bags are ones that passengers are allowed to take onto an airplane with them —**carry-on** *n.* [C]

car·ry·out, carry-out /ˈkæri,aʊt/ *n.* [C] food that you can take away from a restaurant to eat somewhere else, or a restaurant that sells food like this SYN **takeout**

car·ry·o·ver /ˈkæri,oʊvɚ/ *n.* [C] **1** something that

affects an existing situation, but is the result of a past one: +**from** *Some of the problems are a carryover from the bitter presidential campaign.* **2** an amount of money that has not been used and is available to use later: +**of** *a carryover of funds to next year's budget* → see also **carry over**

ˈcar seat *n.* [C] a special seat for a baby or small child to hold them safely in a car

car·sick /ˈkɑrsɪk/ *adj.* feeling sick because you are traveling in a car —**carsickness** *n.* [U]

Car·son /ˈkɑrsən/, **Kit** /kɪt/ (1809–1868) a U.S. hunter and soldier who worked as a GUIDE for John C. Frémont on his trips through the western part of North America

Carson, Ra·chel /ˈreɪtʃəl/ (1907–1964) a U.S. scientist who was one of the first people to realize that PESTICIDES (=chemicals for protecting crops from insects) were damaging the environment

ˌCarson ˈCity the capital city of the U.S. state of Nevada

cart¹ /kɑrt/ *n.* [C] **1** a vehicle with two or four wheels that is pulled by a horse and used for carrying heavy things → see also HANDCART **2** also **shopping cart** a large wire basket on wheels that you use when shopping in a SUPERMARKET or some other large stores **3** a small table with wheels, used to move and serve food and drinks: *Then the waiter wheeled the dessert cart over to our table.* **4 put the cart before the horse** to do one thing before another thing that should have been done first [**Origin:** 1100–1200 Old Norse *kartr*] → see also GOLF CART, **upset the apple cart** at UPSET² (6)

cart² *v.* [T always + adv./prep.] INFORMAL to carry something somewhere, especially something that is awkward or heavy: *After years of carting my equipment around, it's nice to be working at home.* ▸see THESAURUS box at **carry¹**

cart away/off *phr. v.* INFORMAL **1 cart sb ↔ away/off** to take someone away by force, especially to prison: *The sheriff carted him off to prison.* **2 cart sth ↔ away/off** to carry something somewhere in a cart, truck etc.: *Workers carted away several tons of trash.*

carte blanche /ˌkɑrt ˈblɑnʃ/ *n.* [U] complete freedom to do whatever you like in a particular situation, especially to spend money: *The director was* ***given carte blanche*** *to make his epic movie.* [**Origin:** 1700–1800 a French phrase meaning **white card, document with no writing**]

car·tel /kɑrˈtɛl/ *n.* [C] ECONOMICS a group of companies who agree to sell something they produce for a particular price in order to limit competition and increase their own profits → see also MONOPOLY: *The* ***oil cartel****, OPEC, had just had its first major success in forcing up oil prices.* | *the Medellin* ***drug cartel*** (=a criminal group from Columbia, known especially for supplying the illegal drug cocaine)

Car·ter /ˈkɑrtɚ/, **James (Jim·my)** /dʒeɪmz, ˈdʒɪmi/ (1924–) the 39th President of the U.S.

cart·horse /ˈkɑrthɔrs/ *n.* [C] a large strong horse, often used for pulling heavy loads

Car·tier /kɑrˈtyeɪ/, **Jacques** /ʒɑk/ (1491–1557) a French EXPLORER who traveled up the St. Lawrence River in Canada and claimed officially that the area belonged to France

Cartier-Bres·son /kɑrˌtyeɪ brɛˈsoʊn/, **Hen·ri** /ɑnˈri/ (1908–2004) a French PHOTOGRAPHER

car·ti·lage /ˈkɑrtl̩-ɪdʒ/ *n.* [U] BIOLOGY a strong substance that can bend and stretch, that is around the joints in a person's or animal's body and in places such as the outer ear and the end of the nose → see picture at JOINT, LUNG

cart·load /ˈkɑrtloʊd/ *n.* [C] the amount that a CART can hold: +**of** *two cartloads of hay*

car·tog·ra·phy /kɑrˈtɑgrəfi/ *n.* [U] the activity of making maps —**cartographer** *n.* [C]

car·ton /ˈkɑrtˀn/ *n.* [C] **1** a box made of CARDBOARD (=stiff paper) that contains food or drinks: +**of** *a carton of eggs* | **a milk/egg/juice etc. carton** *an empty milk carton* → see picture at BOX¹ **2** a large container that holds many smaller containers of goods to be sold: +**of** *How many packs come in a carton of cigarettes?*

car·toon /kɑrˈtun/ [S3] *n.* [C] ENG. LANG. ARTS **1** a short movie that is made by photographing a series of drawings: *We always* ***watch cartoons*** *on Saturday mornings.* ▸see THESAURUS box at **television** **2** a funny drawing, especially a drawing about events in the news or politicians, that often includes a humorous remark ▸see THESAURUS box at **drawing, picture¹** **3** a set of small boxes with drawings that tell a funny story or a joke, usually printed in newspapers [SYN] **comic strip** **4** a drawing that is used as a model for a painting or other work of art [**Origin:** 1500–1600 Italian *cartone* **pasteboard, cartoon**, from *carta* **sheet of paper**]

car·toon·ish /kɑrˈtunɪʃ/ *adj.* like a cartoon in the way something is drawn or done: *Most action movies are full of cartoonish characters.*

car·toon·ist /kɑrˈtunɪst/ *n.* [C] someone who draws CARTOONS → see also ANIMATOR

car·tridge /ˈkɑrtrɪdʒ/ *n.* [C] **1** a small piece of equipment or a container that you put inside something to make it work: *a computer game cartridge* | *an ink cartridge* (=containing ink for a printer) **2** a tube containing explosive powder and a bullet that you use in a gun **3** the small part of a RECORD PLAYER containing the needle that takes sound signals from the record

cart·wheel /ˈkɑrtˀwil/ *n.* [C] a movement in which you throw your body sideways onto your hands while bringing your legs straight over your head and then stand back on your feet: **do/turn cartwheels** *A few players celebrated the goal by doing cartwheels.* —**cartwheel** *v.* [I]

carve /kɑrv/ *v.* **1** [T] ENG. LANG. ARTS to cut shapes out of solid wood or stone: *an elaborately carved staircase* | **carve sth out of/from sth** *Michelangelo carved the statue from a single block of marble.* | **carve sth into sth** *Luke plans to carve the wood into candlesticks.* **2** [T] to cut a pattern or letter on the surface of something: **carve sth on/in etc.** *Someone had carved their initials into the tree.* → see also **not be carved/etched in stone** at STONE¹ (7) **3** [T always + adv./prep.] to reduce the size of something by separating it into smaller parts or getting rid of part of it: **carve sth into sth/out of sth/from sth** *The land has been carved into 20-acre lots.* | *The company needs to carve $1 million from its annual budget.* **4** [I,T] to cut a large piece of cooked meat into smaller pieces using a big knife: *What's the best way to carve a turkey?* | **carve sth into sth** *Carve the roast into thin slices.* [**Origin:** Old English *ceorfan*] ▸see THESAURUS box at **cut¹** → see picture on page A32 —**carver** *n.* [C]

carve sth **↔ out** *phr. v.* **carve out a career/life/reputation etc.** to become successful and be respected: *Jenkins has carved out a successful career for herself as a photographer.* | *The company is trying to* ***carve out a niche*** *for itself in the casual clothing market* (=create a good position for itself in the market).

carve sth **↔ up** *phr. v.* to divide land or a company into smaller parts to be shared: *After World War I, the British and French carved up the Ottoman Empire.*

Car·ver /ˈkɑrvɚ/, **George Washington** (1860–1943) a U.S. scientist who studied farming and crops and was one of the first African-American scientists

carv·ing /ˈkɑrvɪŋ/ *n.* **1** [C] an object or pattern made by cutting a shape in wood or stone for decoration **2** [U] the activity or skill of carving

ˈcarving fork *n.* [C] a large fork used to hold cooked meat firmly while you are cutting it

ˈcarving knife *n.* [C] a large knife used for cutting cooked meat

ˈcar wash *n.* [C] a place where there is special equipment for washing cars

car·y·at·id /ˌkæriˈæt̬ɪd/ *n.* [C] TECHNICAL a PILLAR in the shape of a female figure

Cas•a•no•va /ˌkæsəˈnoʊvə/ *n.* [C] a man who has had a lot of sexual relationships: *Dave obviously thought he was a real Casanova.* [**Origin:** 1900–2000 Giacomo Girolamo *Casanova* (1725–1798), Italian famous for having many lovers]

cas•bah /ˈkæzbɑ, ˈkɑz-/ *n.* [C] an ancient Arab city, or the market in it

cas•cade¹ /kæˈskeɪd/ *n.* [C] **1** a small steep WATERFALL **2** something that hangs down in large quantities: **+of** *her cascade of dark curly hair* **3** a series of things that happen quickly one after the other, each one causing the next one: *a cascade of bad decisions that finally led to jail*

cascade² *v.* [I always + adv./prep.] to flow, fall, or hang down in large quantities: *Heavy rains caused mud to cascade down the hillside.*

ˈCascade Range, the also **the Cascades** /kæsˈkeɪdz/ a range of mountains in the west of the U.S. and Canada, that runs from British Columbia in the north down to northern California, where they join with the Sierra Nevada

cases

case¹ /keɪs/ S1 W1 *n.*

1 EXAMPLE [C] an example of a particular situation or of something happening, especially something bad: **+of** *Miller's actions were* ***a clear case of*** *sexual harassment.* | *Many southern cities are growing above the national average – Atlanta is* ***a case in point*** (=an example of this fact). | *This is* ***a classic case of*** (=a typical example of) *food poisoning.*

2 SITUATION [C usually singular] a situation that exists, especially when you consider how it affects a particular person or group: **in this/his/one etc. case** *In many cases, standards have greatly improved.* | *Many of the boys live in poverty, as in Mark's case.* | ***In the case of*** *these skeletons, 22 of 40 contained lead in dangerous amounts.* | *It may* ***be the case that*** *they just don't know what's going on.* | *I may be wrong,* ***in which case*** *I apologize.* | *You haven't done anything wrong, and* ***if that's*** *really* ***the case*** *then talk to the police.* ►see THESAURUS box at **situation**

3 LAW/CRIME [C] **a)** LAW a question or problem that will be dealt with by a court of law: *a court case* | **win/lose a case** *Watson won the discrimination case against her employer.* | **a civil/criminal case** (=a case relating to private legal matters or crime) | **hear a case** *The judge who heard the case was very good.* **b)** all the reasons that one side in a legal argument can give against the other side: ***the case against*** *the boy's accused killer* | *Ali's testimony* ***strengthened the case*** *for the prosecution* (=made them more likely to win). | *The District Attorney's office says it* ***has a*** *good* ***case*** *against Williams* (=they feel they are likely to win). **c)** an event or set of events that need to be dealt with by the police: **+of** *Detroit police are investigating the case of a man found strangled on Tuesday.* | *Luca is the investigator* ***on the case.***

4 (just) in case a) as a way of being safe from something that might happen or might be true: *There are spare batteries in there, in case you need them.* **b)** used to mean "if": *In case you missed the last program, here's a summary of the story.*

5 REASON/ARGUMENT [C,U] the facts, arguments, or reasons for doing something, supporting something etc.: **+for/against** *Smith* ***made a*** *good* ***case for*** *changing the way schools are run* (=he gave good reasons for it).

6 DISEASE/ILLNESS [C] an example of a disease or illness, or the person suffering this disease or illness: *The nurse treated several urgent cases.* | **+of** *Tara was treated for a slight case of frostbite.*

7 in any case used to say that a fact or part of a situation stays the same, even if other things change: *I've never been bitten, but in any case the spider's bite is not very poisonous.*

8 BOX/CONTAINER [C] **a)** a large box or container in which things can be stored or moved: *a packing case* | **+of** *a case of wine* **b)** a special box used as a container for holding or protecting something: *The exhibits were all in glass cases.* **c)** OLD-FASHIONED a SUITCASE → see also BOOKCASE, BRIEFCASE, PILLOWCASE

9 in case of sth used to describe what you should do in a particular situation, especially on official notices: *In case of fire, break the glass and push the alarm button.*

SPOKEN PHRASES

10 in that case used to describe what you will do, or what will happen, as a result of a particular situation or event: *"I'll be home late tonight." "Well, in that case, I won't cook dinner."*

11 be on sb's case to be criticizing someone continuously: *Dad's always on my case about getting a job.*

12 get off my case used to tell someone to stop criticizing you or complaining about you: *OK, OK, just get off my case, will you?*

13 make a (federal) case out of sth to complain or get very upset about something that has happened: *I just forgot! Don't make a federal case out of it.*

14 it is a case of sth used before describing a situation, especially when you use a familiar phrase to describe it: *Tim said that for him, it was a case of love at first sight.*

15 PERSON [C] someone who is being dealt with by a doctor, a SOCIAL WORKER, the police etc.

16 a case of the jitters/blahs/blues etc. INFORMAL an occasion when you feel a particular way: *He admitted he had a bad case of the jitters* (=he was nervous) *before the performance.*

17 GRAMMAR [C,U] ENG. LANG. ARTS the way in which the form of a word changes, showing its relationship to other words in a sentence: *case endings*

[**Origin:** (8) 1200–1300 Old French *cas*, from Latin *casus* **fall, chance**] → see also BASKET CASE, LOWER CASE, UPPER CASE

case² *v.* [T] **1 be cased in sth** to be completely surrounded by a material or substance: *a reactor cased in metal and concrete* → see also CASING **2 case the joint** HUMOROUS to look around a place that you intend to steal from, in order to find out information

case•book /ˈkeɪsbʊk/ *n.* [C] a detailed written record kept by a doctor, SOCIAL WORKER, or police officer of the cases they have dealt with

ˈcase ˌhistory *n. plural* **case histories** [C] a detailed record of someone's past illnesses, problems etc. that a doctor or SOCIAL WORKER studies

ˈcase law *n.* [U] LAW a type of law that is based on decisions made by judges in the past

case•load /ˈkeɪsloʊd/ *n.* [C usually singular] the number of people a doctor, SOCIAL WORKER etc. has to deal with

case•ment win•dow /ˈkeɪsmənt ˌwɪndoʊ/ also **casement** *n.* [C] a window that opens like a door with HINGES at one side

ˈcase ˌstudy *n.* [C] a detailed account of the development of a particular person, group, or situation that has been studied in a scientific way over a period of time, and a record of the decisions made

case·work /ˈkeɪswɚk/ *n.* [U] work that a SOCIAL WORKER does, which is concerned with the problems of a particular person or family that needs help —**caseworker** *n.* [C]

cash¹ /kæʃ/ S2 W2 *n.* [U] **1** money in the form of coins or bills rather than CREDIT CARDS etc.: *The burglar took cash and a notebook computer from the apartment.* | *He had about $150* ***in cash*** *in his wallet.* | *Is there a discount if I* ***pay cash?*** | *You can't use checks there – they only take payment in* ***hard cash*** (=bills and coins). ►see THESAURUS box at money **2** INFORMAL money in general: *The firm is so* ***short of cash*** (=has so little money) *that it may not survive.* | *I'm* ***strapped for cash*** (=have no money) *at the moment. I'll mail you a check next week.* **3 cash on delivery** C.O.D.; used when the customer must pay the person who delivers goods to them [**Origin:** 1500–1600 French *casse* **money box**, from Old Italian *cassa*, from Latin *capsa* **box, case**] → see also PETTY CASH

cash² *v.* [T] **cash a check/money order etc.** to exchange a check etc. for the amount of money it is worth: *The company cashed my check but hasn't sent my order.*

cash in *phr. v.* **1** to gain advantages from a situation: +**on** *Miller can cash in on her basketball talent by advertising athletic shoes.* **2 cash sth ↔ in** to exchange something such as an insurance POLICY or a BOND for its value in money **3 cash in your chips** HUMOROUS to die

cash out *phr. v.* **1** to add up the amount of money received in a store in a day so that it can be checked **2 cash sth ↔ out** to exchange something such as an insurance POLICY or a BOND for its value in money, especially before the date when you are supposed to do this

Cash /kæʃ/, **John·ny** /ˈdʒɑni/ (1932–2003) a singer and writer of COUNTRY AND WESTERN music

ˈcash adˌvance *n.* [C] money that you can get from a bank, using a CREDIT CARD

ˌcash and ˈcarry *n.* [U] a way of selling goods in which people can only pay using CASH (=paper money and coins) and have to take the goods away themselves —**cash-and-carry** *adj.*

ˈcash bar *n.* [C usually singular] a place at an event such as a company party, wedding etc. where you can buy alcoholic drinks

ˈcash box *n.* [C] a small metal box with a lock that you keep money in

ˈcash cow *n.* [C usually singular] the part of a business you can always depend on to make enough profits: *The magazine is a cash cow that sells 2.5 million copies a month.*

ˈcash crop *n.* [C] a crop grown in order to be sold, rather than to be used by the people growing it

ˌcash ˈdiscount *n.* [C] an amount by which a seller reduces a price if the buyer pays immediately in CASH or before a particular date

cash·ew /ˈkæʃu, kæˈʃu/ *n.* [C] **1** a small curved nut **2** BIOLOGY the tropical American tree that produces this nut [**Origin:** 1500–1600 Portuguese *cajú*, from Tupi *acajú*]

ˈcash flow *n.* [singular, U] ECONOMICS the movement of money into and out of a business or a person's accounts, which affects how much money they have available: *I've been* ***having a few cash flow problems*** (=have not had enough money) *lately.*

cash·ier¹ /kæˈʃɪr/ *n.* [C] someone whose job is to receive or pay out money in a store, office etc. ►see THESAURUS box at store¹

cashier² *v.* [T usually passive] TECHNICAL to force an officer to leave the military because he or she has done something wrong

caˈshier's check *n.* [C] a special type of check that will definitely be paid because it uses money taken from a bank's own account

cash·less /ˈkæʃlɪs/ *adj.* ECONOMICS done or working without using actual money: *a cashless transaction between two banks*

ˈcash maˌchine *n.* [C] a machine in or outside a bank from which you can obtain money with a special plastic card SYN ATM

cash·mere /ˈkæʒmɪr, ˈkæʃ-/ *n.* [U] a type of fine soft wool that comes from a particular type of goat: *a cashmere sweater* [**Origin:** 1600–1700 *Cashmere*, old spelling of *Kashmir* area on the border of India and Pakistan]

ˈcash price *n.* [C] the price that someone will sell something for if you pay for it immediately with money rather than with a CREDIT CARD

ˈcash ˌregister *n.* [C] a machine used in stores to keep the money in and show how much customers have to pay

ˈcash-strapped *adj.* not having enough money: *the cash-strapped school district*

ˈcash ˌtransfer *n.* **1 Cash Transfer** [C] ECONOMICS the payment of government money directly to people who are poor or in a difficult situation: *USAID's Cash Transfer program* | **Conditional Cash Transfer** (=a payment made on the condition that parents improve their children's chances of being successful in the future, for example by making sure that they attend school or receive regular health care) **2** also **money transfer** [C,U] the act of sending money from your bank account to someone who is in another place, or the money that is sent: *cash transfers through Western Union*

cas·ing /ˈkeɪsɪŋ/ *n.* [C] an outer layer that covers and protects something such as a wire, a bullet, or a SAUSAGE

ca·si·no /kəˈsinoʊ/ *n. plural* **casinos** [C] a place where people try to win money by playing card games or ROULETTE [**Origin:** 1700–1800 Italian *casa* **house**]

cask /kæsk/ *n.* [C] a round wooden container used for storing wine or other liquids, or the amount of liquid contained in this: +**of** *a cask of rum* [**Origin:** 1500–1600 French *casque* **helmet**, from Spanish *casco* **broken piece of a pot, skull, helmet**]

cas·ket /ˈkæskɪt/ *n.* [C] **1** a long box in which a dead person is buried or burned → COFFIN ►see THESAURUS box at funeral **2** OLD-FASHIONED a small decorated box in which you keep jewelry and other valuable objects

cas·pa·ri·an strip /kæsˌpɛriən ˈstrɪp/ *n.* [C] BIOLOGY a narrow band of material between cells in a plant that directs the flow of liquid to particular parts of the plant and stops it from reaching other parts

Cas·pi·an Sea, the /ˈkæspiən ˌsi/ the largest sea in the world that is surrounded by land, between southeast Europe and Asia. It is surrounded by Russia, Iran, Azerbaijan, Kazakhstan, and Turkmenistan.

Cas·satt /kəˈsæt/, **Mary** (1845–1926) a U.S. painter who worked mainly in France with the IMPRESSIONISTS

cas·sa·va /kəˈsɑvə/ *n.* [C,U] a tropical plant with thick roots that you can eat, or the flour made from these roots [**Origin:** 1500–1600 Spanish *cazabe* **cassava bread**, from Taino *caçabi*]

cas·se·role /ˈkæsəˌroʊl/ *n.* [C] **1** food that is cooked slowly in liquid in a covered dish in the OVEN: *a chicken casserole* **2** a deep covered dish used for cooking food in the OVEN [**Origin:** 1700–1800 French **cooking pan**, from *casse* **big spoon, pan**, from Greek *kyathos* **big spoon**]

cas·sette /kəˈsɛt/ also **casˈsette tape** *n.* [C] **1** a small flat plastic case containing MAGNETIC TAPE, that can be used for playing or recording sound or pictures SYN tape: **audio/video cassette** (=a cassette that records sound, or sound and pictures) **2** a closed container with photographic film in it, that can be put into a camera

casˈsette deck also **casˈsette ˌplayer** *n.* [C] a machine that plays cassettes

cas'sette re,corder *n.* [C] a machine used for recording sound or for playing cassettes SYN tape recorder

cas·sock /'kæsək/ *n.* [C] a long, usually black, piece of clothing worn by priests

cast[1] /kæst/ S3 W3 *v.* *past tense and past participle* **cast**

1 cast a vote also **cast a ballot** to vote in an election: *California residents will cast their votes today in the heated race for governor.*

2 cast doubt/blame/suspicion/aspersions on sb/sth to make people doubt someone, blame someone, think someone may have done something wrong etc.: *Barrett's lawyers tried to cast doubt on the FBI's evidence.* | *He denied responsibility and cast blame on another officer.* | *Experts cast suspicion on the reliability of the lie detector tests.* | *The article cast aspersions on his professional conduct* (=made people think he had not behaved correctly).

3 cast a shadow/cloud if something casts a shadow over an event, period of time etc., it makes people feel less happy or hopeful because they are worried about it: **+over** *At that time, the Cold War still cast a shadow over our children's future.*

4 LIGHT/SHADOW [T] LITERARY to make light or shadow appear somewhere: *Candles **cast** a romantic **light** in the restaurant's dining room.* | **+on/over/across etc.** *New York's skyscrapers **cast shadows** over the streets.*

5 ACTORS [T] ENG. LANG. ARTS to choose which people will act particular parts in a play, movie etc.: **cast sb in sth** *Before being cast in "Savannah," Luna attended cooking school.* | **cast sb as sb** *Coppola cast Gary Oldman as Dracula.*

6 LOOK [T] LITERARY to look quickly in a particular direction: **cast a look/glance** *Sandra cast a nervous glance over her shoulder.* | *The boys **cast their eyes** down as the charges were read.*

7 cast an eye over sth to examine or look at something quickly, especially in order to judge it: **+over/on** *Could you cast an eye over this letter before I mail it?*

8 DESCRIBE [T] to describe or represent something in a particular way: **cast sb as sth** *Supporters of the bill cast themselves as true defenders of liberty.* | *Barr refuses to be **cast in the role of** a victim of her childhood.*

9 cast (a) light on/onto sth to provide new information which makes something easier to understand: *Tobin's research could cast new light on the origin of the universe.*

10 cast a spell (on/over sb/sth) a) to use magic words or ceremonies to change someone or something: *The villagers accused her of being a witch who could cast evil spells.* **b)** to attract someone very strongly and keep their attention completely: *Sinatra's voice cast its usual spell on the audience.*

11 METAL [T usually passive] to make an object by pouring liquid metal, plastic etc. into a MOLD (=container with a special shape): *a statue of a horse cast in bronze*

12 be cast away LITERARY to be left alone on a shore or island, because the ship that you were on sank: *The story is about some sailors who were cast away on a desert island.*

13 FISHING [I,T] to throw a fishing line or net into the water: *Cast your line across the current and upstream.*

14 THROW [T always + adv./prep.] LITERARY to throw something somewhere SYN toss: *Sparks leaped as more wood was cast onto the fire.*

15 cast your net wide to consider or try as many things as possible in order to find what you want: *They're casting their net wide to find her replacement.*

16 cast your mind back LITERARY to try to remember something that happened a long time ago: **+to** *Cast your mind back to your first day at school.*

17 cast sb into prison/into a dungeon/into Hell etc. LITERARY to force someone to go somewhere bad: *Memet was cast into prison for life.*

18 cast a horoscope to prepare and write someone's HOROSCOPE

19 cast pearls before swine LITERARY to offer something that is very valuable or beautiful to someone who does not understand how valuable it is → see also **the die is cast** at DIE[2] (3), **cast your lot with sb** at LOT[2] (5)

cast around for sth *phr. v.* to try to think of something to do or say: *She cast around frantically for an excuse.*

cast sb/sth ↔ **aside** *phr. v.* to get rid of someone or something because you do not want or need them anymore: *They cast aside their differences to work for peace.*

cast off *phr. v.* **1 cast sb/sth ↔ off** LITERARY to get rid of something or someone that has been causing problems or difficulties SYN discard: *One by one, Eastern European countries cast off Communism in the late 20th century.* **2 cast sth ↔ off** to untie the rope that fastens your boat to the shore so that you can sail away **3 cast sth ↔ off** to finish a piece of KNITTING by taking the last stitches off the needle in a way that stops them from coming apart

cast on *phr. v.* **cast sth ↔ on** to start a piece of KNITTING by making the first stitches on the needle

cast sb/sth ↔ **out** *phr. v.* LITERARY to force someone or something to go away: *The saint is said to have cast out demons.*

cast[2] *n.* [C]

1 ACTORS [usually singular] ENG. LANG. ARTS all the people who act in a play, movie, or television program: **+of** *the cast of "Lord of the Rings"* | *an interview with three **cast members*** | *The movie has an excellent **supporting cast*** (=everyone except the main actors). | *the **all-star cast** of "Twelve Angry Men"*

2 cast of characters all the people in a story, movie etc., or all the people involved in an event: *Astor's biography has an enormous cast of characters.*

3 ON YOUR BODY MEDICINE a hard cover that is put over your arm, leg etc. because a bone is broken: *Mandy has to **have** her arm **in a cast** for six weeks.*

4 SHAPE a) a MOLD (=specially shaped container) into which you pour liquid metal, plastic etc. in order to make an object of a particular shape **b)** an object made in this way: *a plaster cast of the artist's face*

5 a cast of thousands HUMOROUS a very large number of people: *The President has a cast of thousands to remember facts for him.*

6 FISHING an act of throwing a fishing line or net into the water

7 COLOR a small amount of a particular color SYN hue: *The stone has a pinkish cast.*

8 sb's cast of mind LITERARY the way someone thinks or behaves: *He has an ironic cast of mind.*

cas·ta·nets /ˌkæstə'nɛts/ *n.* [plural] a musical instrument made of two small round pieces of wood or plastic that you knock together in your hand

cast·a·way /'kæstəˌweɪ/ *n. plural* **castaways** [C] someone who is left alone on an island after their ship has sunk

caste /kæst/ *n.* **1** [C,U] the system of social classes, which cannot be changed, into which Hindu people in India are born, or one of these classes **2** [C] a group of people who have a particular position in society **3** [C] BIOLOGY a group of insects that have a particular job in a COLONY of insects (=large group living together) for example "workers" or "soldiers" [**Origin:** 1500–1600 Portuguese *casta* **race**, from *casto* **pure**, from Latin *castus*]

cas·tel·lat·ed /'kæstəˌleɪṭɪd/ *adj.* TECHNICAL built to look like a castle

cast·er, **castor** /'kæstɚ/ *n.* [C] a small wheel attached to the bottom of a piece of furniture so that it can move in any direction

'caste ˌsystem *n.* [C] the Hindu system of social classes, which people are born into and cannot change

cas·ti·gate /'kæstəˌgeɪt/ *v.* [T] FORMAL to criticize or punish someone severely SYN chastise: **castigate sb for doing sth** *In his speech, he castigated the president for being soft on drugs.* —**castigation** /ˌkæstə'geɪʃən/ *n.* [U]

cast·ing /'kæstɪŋ/ *n.* **1** [U] the process of choosing the actors for a movie or play: *a casting director* **2** [C] an object made by pouring liquid metal, plastic etc. into a MOLD (=specially shaped container) **3 the casting couch** HUMOROUS a situation in which an actress is persuaded to have sex in return for a part in a movie, play etc.

ˈcast iron *n.* [U] a type of iron that is very hard but breaks easily, and that can be shaped in a MOLD

ˌcast-ˈiron *adj.* **1** made of cast iron: *a cast-iron skillet* **2 a cast-iron excuse/alibi/guarantee etc.** an excuse, alibi etc. that is very certain and cannot fail **3 a cast-iron stomach** someone with a cast-iron stomach can eat anything without feeling sick

cas·tle /ˈkæsəl/ *n.* [C] **1** a very large strong building, built in Europe in the past as a safe place that could be easily defended against attack **2** one of the pieces used in a game of CHESS SYN rook **3 build castles in the air** to make plans or imagine things that are unlikely ever to become real SYN daydream [**Origin:** 1000–1100 Old North French *castel*, from Latin *castellum* **building with a defensive wall**]

ˈcast-off *adj.* [only before noun] cast-off clothes or other goods are not wanted or have been thrown away

cast·off /ˈkæstɔf/ *n.* [C usually plural] clothes or other things that someone does not want anymore, and gives or throws away: *We furnished the house with castoffs from my parents' garage.*

cas·tor /ˈkæstɚ/ *n.* [C] another spelling of CASTER

ˈcastor oil *n.* [U] a thick oil made from the seeds of a plant, used in the past as a medicine to make the BOWELS empty

cas·trate /ˈkæstreɪt/ *v.* [T] to remove the sexual organs of a male animal or man —**castration** /kæˈstreɪʃən/ *n.* [U]

Cas·tries /ˈkæstriz, -tris/ the capital city of St. Lucia

Cas·tro /ˈkæstroʊ/, **Fi·del** /fiˈdɛl/ (1927–) a Cuban COMMUNIST leader who led the opposition to the DICTATOR Batista, and became Prime Minister of Cuba, and later its President

casual

casual clothes formal clothes

cas·u·al¹ /ˈkæʒuəl, -ʒəl/ *adj.*
1 CLOTHES/STYLE/EVENT not formal, or not for a formal situation OPP formal: *casual shoes* | *Are shorts appropriate at a casual party?* | *men's **casual clothing*** | *Many companies now allow employees to wear **casual dress*** (=informal clothes). | **casual day/Friday** (=a day when employees are allowed to wear informal clothes) ▸see THESAURUS box at clothes
2 RELAXED/NOT CARING relaxed and not worried, or seeming not to care about something SYN relaxed: *Thompson's management style is casual but organized.* | *Society seems to have an increasingly **casual attitude** toward violence.*
3 WITHOUT ATTENTION without any clear aim or serious interest: *Wayne took a casual glance at the newspaper.* | **casual observer/listener/viewer** (=someone who is not looking, listening etc. carefully) *To the casual observer, everything seemed normal.*
4 NOT PLANNED happening by chance, without being planned: *a casual encounter* | *She mentioned it in **casual conversation**.*
5 RELATIONSHIP knowing someone without having a close relationship with them OPP serious: *Did they have more than a **casual relationship**?* | *risky behavior such as drug taking and **casual sex*** (=sex between people who do not know each other well) | *A **casual acquaintance** told him about the fire.*
6 NOT REGULAR/OFTEN using or doing something only sometimes, not regularly or often SYN occasional OPP regular: *casual visitors to the museum* | *the casual use of marijuana*
7 casual worker/employment/labor etc. a worker, employment etc. that a company uses or offers only for a short period of time —**casually** *adv.*: *a casually dressed young man* —**casualness** *n.* [U]

C

casual² *n.* **1 casuals** [plural] informal clothes **2** [C] a worker who is not a regular EMPLOYEE at a company SYN temp

cas·u·al·ty /ˈkæʒuəlti, -ʒəlti/ *n. plural* **casualties** [C] **1** someone who is hurt or killed in an accident or battle: *More than 50 casualties were brought in to the hospital.* | *thousands of **civilian casualties*** (=people who are not soldiers who are hurt or killed) | **heavy/high casualties** (=a lot of people killed or injured) *There were heavy casualties in the first battle.* | *Army units are **suffering casualties** every day.* | **cause/inflict casualties** *Luckily, the rocket attack caused few casualties.* **2** someone or something that suffers as a result of a particular event or situation SYN victim: +**of** *The Safer City Project became a casualty of financial cutbacks.* [**Origin:** 1400–1500 Medieval Latin *casualitas* **chance, bad luck, loss**, from Late Latin *casualis*]

ca·su·ist·ry /ˈkæʒuəstri/ *n.* [U] FORMAL the use of intelligent but often false arguments to answer moral or legal questions SYN sophistry —**casuist** *n.* [C]

ca·sus bel·li /ˌkæsəs ˈbɛli, ˌkeɪsəs ˈbɛlaɪ/ *n.* [C] LAW an event or political action which directly causes a war

cat /kæt/ S1 W3 *n.* [C]
1 ANIMAL a) BIOLOGY a small furry animal with four legs that is often kept as a pet or used for catching mice → see also FELINE: *a black cat* | *a **tom cat*** (=male cat) | *an old **alley cat*** (=cat without a home) | *a **house cat*** (=pet that usually stays in the house) *playing with a ball of string* **b)** also **big cat** a large animal such as a lion or tiger
2 let the cat out of the bag to tell a secret, especially without intending to
3 cat and mouse also **a game of cat and mouse** a situation in which someone pretends to allow someone else to do or have what they want, and then stops that person from doing or having it: *The police **played** an elaborate **game of cat and mouse** in order to trap him.*
4 look like something the cat dragged in to look very sick, tired, or messy
5 like a cat on a hot tin roof so nervous or anxious that you cannot keep still or keep your attention on one thing
6 when the cat's away (the mice will play) used to say that people will not behave well when the person who has authority over them is not there
7 Cat got your tongue? SPOKEN used to ask someone, especially a child, why they are not talking
8 PERSON OLD-FASHIONED SLANG a person: *That Jefferson is one cool cat.*
9 look like the cat that ate the canary to show too much satisfaction with your own intelligence or success
[**Origin:** Old English *catt*] → see also CATTY, **fat cat** at FAT¹ (5), **it's raining cats and dogs** at RAIN² (4), **there's not enough room to swing a cat** at ROOM¹ (4)

ca·tab·o·lism /kəˈtæbəˌlɪzəm/ *n.* [U] BIOLOGY a process by which living things produce energy by breaking down more COMPLEX substances into simpler substances → see also ANABOLISM —**catabolic** /ˌkæt̬əˈbɑlɪk◂/ *adj.* TECHNICAL

cat·a·clysm /ˈkæt̬əˌklɪzəm/ *n.* [C] LITERARY a violent and sudden event or change, such as a serious flood or EARTHQUAKE SYN catastrophe

cat·a·clys·mic /ˌkæt̬əˈklɪzmɪk◂/ *adj.* FORMAL a cataclysmic event or change is one that has a very extreme, usually negative, effect SYN catastrophic: *the volcano's cataclysmic eruption*

cat·a·comb /ˈkæṭəˌkoʊm/ *n.* [C] **1** [usually plural] an area of passages and rooms below the ground where dead people are buried **2** a place that has many passages and small rooms which make it easy to get lost

cat·a·falque /ˈkæṭəˌfælk, -ˌfɔlk/ *n.* [C] FORMAL a decorated raised structure on which the dead body of an important person is placed before their funeral

Cat·a·lan /ˈkæṭəˌlæn, -ˌlɑn/ *n.* [U] a language spoken in the part of Spain around Barcelona

C

cat·a·log¹ S2, **catalogue** /ˈkæṭlˌɔg, -ˌɑg/ *n.* [C] **1** a book containing pictures and information about goods that you can buy: *a **mail-order catalog** | the department store's Christmas catalog* **2** a list of all the objects, paintings, books etc. in a place such as a MUSEUM or library → see also CARD CATALOG **3** a series of bad things that happen one after the other and never seem to stop: +**of** *a catalog of human rights abuses* **4** something that seems to include all the things that relate to a particular person, event, plan etc.: +**of** *The film is a catalog of special effects techniques.*

catalog², **catalogue** *v.* **catalogs** or **catalogues**, **cataloged** or **catalogued**, **cataloging** or **cataloguing** [T] **1** to make a complete list of all the things in a group, in a particular order: *The manuscripts have never been systematically catalogued.* **2** to list all the things that relate to a particular person, event, plan etc.: *The president catalogued his administration's successes.*

ca·tal·y·sis /kəˈtæləsɪs/ *n.* [U] TECHNICAL the process of making a chemical reaction quicker by adding a catalyst

cat·a·lyst /ˈkæṭl-ɪst/ *n.* [C] **1** something or someone that causes an important change or event to happen: +**for** *The women's movement acted as a catalyst for change in the workplace.* **2** CHEMISTRY a substance that makes a chemical reaction happen more quickly without being changed itself —**catalytic** /ˌkæṭlˈɪṭɪk◂ / *adj.*

ˌcatalytic conˈverter *n.* [C] SCIENCE a piece of equipment attached to the EXHAUST of a car, that reduces the amount of poisonous gases the engine sends out

cat·a·ma·ran /ˌkæṭəməˈræn, ˈkæṭəməˌræn/ *n.* [C] a sailing boat with two separate HULLS (=the part that goes in the water)

cat·a·pult¹ /ˈkæṭəˌpʌlt, -ˌpʊlt/ *n.* [C] **1** a large weapon used in past times to throw heavy stones, iron balls etc. **2** a piece of equipment used to send a military aircraft into the air from a ship

catapult² *v.* **1** [T always + adv./prep.] to push or throw something very hard so that it moves through the air very quickly: **catapult sb into/over/out etc.** *Two cars were catapulted into the air by the force of the blast.* **2 catapult sb to stardom/the top/fame etc.** to suddenly make someone very famous or successful: *Erickson's pitching has helped catapult the Twins to the top of the league.*

cat·a·ract /ˈkæṭəˌrækt/ *n.* [C] **1** MEDICINE a medical condition that causes the LENS in your eye to become white instead of clear, so that you cannot see well **2** LITERARY a large WATERFALL [**Origin:** (1) because a cataract blocks sight like a gate coming down]

ca·tas·tro·phe /kəˈtæstrəfi/ *n.* [C,U] **1** a terrible event in which there is a lot of destruction, suffering, or death SYN **disaster**: **environmental/economic/financial etc. catastrophe** *The oil spill will be an ecological catastrophe. | a **humanitarian catastrophe** (=a terrible event that makes people not have food, homes, medicine etc.) in the Sudan | Governments failed to **prevent the catastrophe** of World War II.* ▸see THESAURUS box at **accident** **2** an event or situation which is extremely bad for the people involved: *The economy seems to be moving toward catastrophe.* [**Origin:** 1500–1600 Greek *katastrephein* **to turn upside down**] —**catastrophic** /ˌkæṭəˈstrɑfɪk◂ / *adj.*: *a catastrophic fall in the price of stocks* —**catastrophically** /-kli/ *adv.*

cat·a·to·ni·a /ˌkæṭəˈtoʊniə/ *n.* [U] TECHNICAL a condition in which you cannot think, speak, or move any part of your body

cat·a·ton·ic /ˌkæṭəˈtɑnɪk◂ / *adj.* **1** MEDICINE caused or affected by a condition in which you cannot think, speak, or move any part of your body: *a catatonic patient* **2** NOT TECHNICAL not thinking or reacting to something: *The kids were almost catatonic with boredom.*

Ca·taw·ba /kəˈtɔbə/ a Native American tribe from the southeastern area of the U.S.

cat·bird seat /ˈkæt˺bɚd ˌsit/ *n.* INFORMAL **be (sitting) in the catbird seat** to be in a position where you have an advantage

ˈcat ˌburglar *n.* [C] a thief who gets into buildings by climbing up walls, pipes etc.

cat·call /ˈkæt˺kɔl/ *n.* [C usually plural] a loud whistle or shout expressing dislike or disapproval of a speech or performance: *The mayor was greeted by jeers and catcalls from the audience.* —**catcall** *v.* [I]

catch¹ /kætʃ/ S1 W1 *v. past tense and past participle* **caught** /kɔt/

1 TAKE AND HOLD a) [I,T] to get hold of and stop an object such as a ball that is moving through the air: *Denise caught the bride's bouquet. | "Can I borrow that pen?" "Sure, catch." | Taylor caught ten passes and ran for 180 yards.* **b)** [T] to suddenly take hold of someone or something: *Go on, jump. I'll catch you. | Rob **caught hold of** my sleeve and pulled me back.*

2 STOP/TRAP SB [T] **a)** to stop someone after you have been chasing them, and so prevent them from escaping SYN **capture**: *"You can't catch me!" she yelled. | soldiers who have been caught by the enemy* **b)** if the police catch a criminal, they find the criminal and stop him or her from escaping SYN **capture**: *State police have launched a massive operation to catch the murderer. | A lot of burglars never **get caught**.*

> **THESAURUS**
>
> **capture** to catch someone in order to keep him or her as a prisoner: *A French soldier was captured in the battle.*
> **arrest** if the police arrest someone, the person is taken away because the police think he or she has done something illegal: *He was arrested and charged with murder.*
> **apprehend** FORMAL if the police apprehend someone they think has done something illegal, they catch him or her: *The two men were later apprehended after robbing another store.*
> **corner** to move closer to a person or an animal so that he, she, or it cannot escape: *Most bears will only attack if they are cornered.*
> **trap** to catch someone by forcing them into a place from which they cannot escape: *Police have the man trapped inside the building.*

3 FIND SB DOING STH [T] to find or see someone while they are doing something illegal or something they did not want you to know they were doing: **catch sb doing sth** *If you get caught stealing you will lose your job. | Jean turned around and caught him looking at her intently. | Milian was **caught red-handed*** (=caught while doing something wrong) *attempting to break into a house. | Several graffiti artists were **caught in the act*** (=caught while doing something wrong) *on the Brown River bridge. | He'd tried to steal some money from the register, and got **caught at it**.*

4 ILLNESS [T] to get a disease or illness: *Dion caught a cold on vacation. | Many young people are still ignorant about how HIV is caught.* | **catch sth from sb** *The vet says you can't catch the disease from the cat.*

5 catch sb by surprise/catch sb off guard also **catch sb napping/unawares** to do something or to happen when someone is not expecting it, so that they are not ready to deal with it: *The demand for the book caught the publisher by surprise. | The public's reaction obviously caught the governor off guard.*

6 ANIMAL/FISH [T] to trap an animal or fish by using a trap, net, or hook, or by hunting it: *"We went fishing." "Did you catch anything?" | The cat caught a squirrel!*

7 catch a train/plane/bus to get on a train etc. in order to travel, or to arrive early enough to get on it before it leaves: *Kevin catches the bus home on Mondays and Wednesdays.* | *I should be able to catch the 12:05 train.* | *He **had a plane to catch** later that evening.* ►see USAGE NOTE box at **reach**[1]

8 NOT MISS SB/STH [T] to be early enough to see something, talk to someone, do something etc. OPP **miss**: *If you call around 8:30, you might catch Shirley.* | *This type of cancer is curable if it is caught early.* | *I only caught about the last 20 minutes of the movie.*

9 GET STUCK [I,T usually passive] if your hand, finger, clothing etc. catches or is caught in something, it becomes stuck or fastened there accidentally: *My pant leg caught on the fence and tore.* | *Steph's hair **got caught** in the machine, and they had to cut it.*

10 catch sb's attention/interest/imagination etc. if something catches your attention etc., you notice it or feel interested in it: *Rainey first caught Coach O'Malley's attention at a football camp.* | *It's a story that will catch the imagination of every child.*

SPOKEN PHRASES

11 HEAR/UNDERSTAND [T usually in questions or negatives] to hear or understand what someone says: *I didn't catch his first name.* | *It's a really funny play, but goes too fast to catch all the jokes.* | *Well, Jerry's not at Sue's apartment to play games, **if you catch my drift*** (=used when you are saying something indirectly, and want to check that someone understands this).

12 catch you later used to say goodbye: *Okay, Randy, catch you later.*

13 DO SOMETHING [T] to go somewhere to do something: *I caught their act* (=saw them perform) *at the Blue Note Jazz Club.* | *Would you like to go to dinner, maybe **catch a movie*** (=go to a movie)*?* | *Can I **catch a ride** with you* (=go in your car)*?* | *I'm gonna try and **catch some z's*** (=sleep).

14 you won't catch me doing sth used to say that you would never do something: *You won't catch me ironing his shirts!*

15 catch it to be punished very severely by a parent or teacher who discovers that you have done something bad: *Dylan's going to catch it when Mom gets home.*

16 NOTICE [T not in progressive] to see, smell, or notice something: *It was a really stupid mistake; I'm surprised Rachel didn't catch it.* | *Oh, you caught the sarcasm in my voice, huh?* | *Hundreds of fans were eagerly trying to **catch a glimpse of** their idol.* | *We suddenly **caught sight of** the ocean.* | *Ugh, did you **catch a whiff of*** (=notice the smell of) *his aftershave?*

17 DESCRIBE WELL [T] to accurately show or describe the character or quality of something in a picture, piece of writing, etc. SYN **capture**: *The novel catches the hardships of pioneer life.*

18 BURN a) catch fire if something catches fire, it starts to burn accidentally: *One of the engines caught fire.* **b)** [I] if a fire catches, it starts to burn: *For some reason the charcoal isn't catching.*

19 catch sb's eye a) to attract someone's attention and make them look at something: *All of a sudden, something red caught Barb's eye.* **b)** to look at someone at the same moment that they are looking at you: *I caught Ben's eye in the rear-view mirror and knew what he was thinking.*

20 catch yourself a) to suddenly realize that you are doing something: **catch yourself doing sth** *I caught myself watching everybody else instead of paying attention to the lecture.* **b)** to stop yourself from doing something quickly: *I was about to correct him, but I caught myself in time.*

21 HIT [T] to hit someone: *The branch sprang back, catching him in the face.* | *Tyson's punch **caught him on the chin**.*

22 IN A BAD SITUATION be caught in/without etc. also **get caught in/without etc.** to be in a situation that you cannot easily get out of, or in which you do not have what you need: *Jeff got caught in a snow storm.* | *You don't want to get caught without a diaper or a bottle of milk.*

23 catch your breath a) to pause for a moment after a lot of physical effort in order to breathe normally again: *Clark had to sit down to catch his breath.* **b)** to stop breathing for a moment because something has surprised, frightened, or shocked you **c)** to take some time to stop and think about what you will do next after having been very busy or active: *The students then have reading time, allowing the teacher to catch her breath.*

24 CONTAINER [T] if a container catches liquid, it is in a position where the liquid falls into it: *We had to put a bucket under the old sink to catch the dripping water.*

25 SHINE/LIGHT [T] if light catches something or if something catches the light, the light shines on it and makes it look bright: *The sunlight caught her hair and turned it to gold.*

26 WIND [T] if something catches the wind or the wind catches something, it blows on it: *Turn the boat so the sails catch the wind.*

[**Origin:** 1100–1200 Old North French *cachier* **to hunt**, from Latin *captare* **to try to catch**,]

catch at sth *phr. v.* LITERARY to try to take hold of something: *The old man caught at Jason's wrist.*

catch on *phr. v.* **1** to begin to understand or realize something: *Usually a couple of the children will catch on quickly and help the others.* | **+to** *The police finally caught on to what he was doing.* **2** to become popular and fashionable: *Mountain bikes caught on quickly and soon made up the bulk of bicycle sales.*

catch sb **out** *phr. v.* if something catches you out, you are not expecting it and so are not prepared for it: *We **got caught out** without our umbrellas.*

catch up *phr. v.* **1** to reach the same standard as other people in your class, group etc.: *I missed a lot of school, and it was really hard to catch up.* | **+with** *The U.S. spent a lot of money trying to catch up with the Soviet Union in space exploration.* **2** to come from behind and reach someone in front by going faster: *We had to run to catch up.* | **+with/to** *You go ahead. I'll catch up with you in a minute.* **3 be/get caught up in sth** to be or become involved in something, especially something bad: *We get caught up in the commercial aspects of Christmas.* **4** to spend time finding out what has been happening during the time you have not seen someone: **+with** *Spend some time catching up with your kids at the dinner table.*

catch up on sth *phr. v.* to do something that needs to be done, that you have not had time to do before: *I'll finally get a chance to catch up on some sleep.* | *It'll take a couple of days to **get caught up on** all this paperwork.*

catch up with sb *phr. v.* **1** to find someone who has been doing something illegal and punish them, after trying to find them for a long time: *The IRS finally caught up with him.* **2** if something bad catches up with you, you cannot avoid it anymore: *All that junk food will catch up with you someday* (=it will start affecting your health).

catch[2] *n.* **1** [C] the act of catching something that has been thrown or hit: *That was a great catch!* **2** [U] a game in which two or more people throw a ball to each other: *The boys are out back **playing catch**.* **3** [C] INFORMAL a hidden problem or difficulty: *The deal comes with a catch – you have to buy one before June.* | ***There is a catch** – you only get the bonus if sales go up.* | *The airfare is great, but **the catch is that** you have a four-hour stopover in St. Louis.* | *The whole thing almost sounds too simple. **What's the catch?*** **4** [C] a hook or something similar that fastens something and holds it closed: *The catch on my necklace is broken.* **5** [C] an amount of fish that has been caught **6 a catch in your voice/throat** a short pause you make while speaking, because you feel very upset or are beginning to cry: *With a catch in his voice, Dan told her how proud he was.* **7 be a good catch** OLD-FASHIONED if a man is a good catch, he is regarded as a very desirable husband, because he is rich and good-looking

Catch-22 /ˌkætʃ twɛntiˈtu/ *n.* [singular] a situation that you cannot solve, because you need to do one thing in order to do a second thing, but you cannot do the first thing until you have done the second thing: *It's a Catch-22 – without experience you can't get a job, and without a job you can't get experience.*

catch·all¹, catch-all /ˈkætʃɔl/ *adj.* [only before noun] intended to include all situations or possibilities: *"Activity toys" is a catchall term that includes blocks and outdoor games.*

catchall², catch-all *n.* [C] a drawer, cupboard etc. where you put any small objects

C

catch·er /ˈkætʃɚ/ *n.* [C] the baseball player who SQUATS behind the BATTER in order to catch missed balls → see picture at BASEBALL

catch·ing /ˈkætʃɪŋ/ *adj.* [not before noun] INFORMAL **1** a disease or illness that is catching is easily passed to other people SYN **contagious** **2** an emotion or feeling that is catching spreads quickly among people SYN **contagious**: *Julia's enthusiasm was catching.*

catch·ment /ˈkætʃmənt/ *n.* [C] a structure with an open top, used for collecting and storing water

ˈ**catch phrase, catchphrase** *n.* [C] a short phrase that is easy to remember and that has been made popular by an entertainer or politician

catch·word /ˈkætʃwɚd/ *n.* [C] a word or phrase that refers to a feature of a situation, product etc. that is considered important SYN **slogan**: *Globalization was the catchword of his administration.*

catch·y /ˈkætʃi/ *adj. comparative* **catchier**, *superlative* **catchiest** a catchy phrase or song is easy to remember and nice to listen to: *a catchy tune* | *stores with catchy names* | *a catchy advertising slogan* —**catchily** *adv.*

cat·e·chism /ˈkæt̬əˌkɪzəm/ *n.* [C] a set of questions and answers about the Christian religion that people learn in order to become full members of a church

cat·e·gor·i·cal /ˌkæt̬əˈgɔrɪkəl, -ˈgɑr-/ *adj.* a categorical statement is a clear statement that something is definitely true or false SYN **unequivocal**: *a categorical denial*

cateˌgorical ˈdata *n.* [U] MATH a set of data that can be divided into clearly separate groups according to type, for example, data for eye color, sex, animal breed etc. → see also CONTINUOUS DATA

cat·e·gor·i·cally /ˌkæt̬əˈgɔrɪkli/ *adv.* in such a sure and certain way that there is no doubt: *I am categorically opposed to animal testing.* | **categorically deny/reject/refuse etc.** *Ralston categorically denied cheating.* | **categorically false/untrue/wrong** *These allegations are categorically untrue.* | **say/state sth categorically** *Maris said categorically that he would not run for president.*

cat·e·go·rize /ˈkæt̬əgəˌraɪz/ *v.* [T] **1** to put people or things into groups according to what type they are SYN **classify**: *The population is* ***categorized according to*** *age, gender, and occupation.* | **categorize sb/sth by sth** *Programs are categorized by the age group that is expected to watch.* | **categorize sb/sth as sth** *The drug has been categorized as experimental.* **2** to describe someone or something in a particular way: **categorize sb/sth as sth** *His friends categorize him as a quiet person.* —**categorization** /ˌkæt̬əgərəˈzeɪʃən/ *n.* [C,U]

cat·e·go·ry /ˈkæt̬əˌgɔri/ Ac S2 W2 *n. plural* **categories** [C] a group of people or things that are all of the same type SYN **class**: +**of** *There are five categories of workers.* | **broad/narrow category** (=a category that includes many things or few things) *The service industry is a broad category that includes restaurant and hotel workers.* | **fall into/belong in/fit into a category** *Voters fall into three* ***main categories.*** [**Origin:** 1400–1500 Late Latin *categoria*, from Greek, from *kategorein* **to accuse, make a statement about**]

ˈ**category ˌkiller** *n.* [C] a large store that sells only one type of product, usually at very low prices

ca·ter /ˈkeɪt̬ɚ/ *v.* [I,T] to provide and serve food and drinks at a party, meeting etc., usually as a business: *a catered lunch* | +**for/at** *They cater food for an after-school program.* | **cater sth** *Who's catering your daughter's wedding?*

cater to/for sb/sth *phr. v.* to provide a particular group of people with something that they need or want: *Big software stores cater mostly to the business market.* | *programs such as Head Start that cater to the needs of children*

cat·er-cor·ner /ˈkæt̬iˌkɔrnɚ, ˈkæt̬ə-, ˈkɪt̬i-/ *adj.* another spelling of KITTY-CORNER

ca·ter·er /ˈkeɪt̬ərɚ/ *n.* [C] a person or company that is paid to provide and serve food and drinks at a party, meeting etc.

ca·ter·ing /ˈkeɪt̬ərɪŋ/ *n.* [U] the activity of providing and serving food and drinks at parties for money: *The restaurant also does take-out food and catering.*

cat·er·pil·lar /ˈkæt̬ɚˌpɪlɚ, ˈkæt̬ə-/ *n.* [C] a small creature with a rounded body and many legs, that eats leaves and that later develops into a BUTTERFLY or MOTH → see picture at METAMORPHOSIS [**Origin:** 1400–1500 Old North French *catepelose* **hairy cat, caterpillar**]

cat·er·waul /ˈkæt̬ɚˌwɔl/ *v.* [I] to make a loud high annoying noise like the sound a cat makes —**caterwaul** *n.* [singular]

cat·fight /ˈkætˀfaɪt/ *n.* [C] INFORMAL a word for a fight between two women, considered insulting by many women

cat·fish /ˈkætˀfɪʃ/ *n.* [C,U] BIOLOGY a common fish with long WHISKERS around its mouth, that lives mainly in rivers and lakes

cat·gut /ˈkætˀgʌt/ *n.* [U] strong thread made from the INTESTINES of animals and used for the strings of musical instruments

ca·thar·sis /kəˈθɑrsɪs/ *n.* [singular, U] FORMAL a way of dealing with bad or strong feelings and emotions, by expressing or experiencing them through writing, talking, DRAMA etc.

ca·thar·tic /kəˈθɑrt̬ɪk/ *adj.* helping you to deal with difficult emotions and get rid of them: *Talking to a counselor can be a cathartic experience.*

ca·the·dral /kəˈθidrəl/ *n.* [C] a large church, which is the main church of a particular area that a BISHOP is responsible for [**Origin:** 1500–1600 *cathedral church* **cathedral** (13–21 centuries); cathedral from Old French, from Latin *cathedra* **chair, bishop's chair**]

Cath·er /ˈkæðɚ/, **Wil·la** /ˈwɪlə/ (1876–1947) a U.S. writer who wrote about Nebraska at the time when Europeans first went to live there

Cath·erine II /ˌkæθrɪn ðə ˈsɛkənd/ also ˌ**Catherine the ˈGreat** (1729–1796) the EMPRESS of Russia from 1762 to 1796 who greatly increased the size of the Russian EMPIRE

cath·e·ter /ˈkæθət̬ɚ/ *n.* [C] a thin tube that is put into someone's body to take away liquids —**catheterize** *v.* [T]

cath·ode /ˈkæθoʊd/ *n.* [C] PHYSICS the ELECTRODE through which ELECTRONS flow into a BATTERY, ELECTROLYTIC CELL etc. and positive electric current seems to flow out. This is the electrode at which REDUCTION happens. → see also ANODE

ˌ**cathode ˈray tube** *n.* [C] PHYSICS a piece of equipment used in televisions and computers, in which negative ELECTRONS from the cathode produce an image on a screen

Cath·o·lic /ˈkæθlɪk, -θəlɪk/ *adj.* belonging or relating to the Roman Catholic Church: *a Catholic school* —**Catholic** *n.* [C] —**Catholicism** /kəˈθɑləˌsɪzəm/ *n.* [U]

cath·o·lic /ˈkæθlɪk, -θəlɪk/ *adj.* FORMAL including a very wide variety of things: *an artist with* ***catholic tastes*** [**Origin:** 1300–1400 French *catholique*, from Late Latin, from Greek *katholikos* **general, universal**] —**catholicity** /ˌkæθəˈlɪsət̬i/ *adj.*

cat·i·on /ˈkætˌaɪən/ *n.* [C] PHYSICS an ION (=atom or group of atoms with an electrical charge) with a positive electrical charge that is attracted to the CATHODE inside a BATTERY, ELECTROLYTIC CELL etc. → see also ANION

cat·kin /ˈkætˀkɪn/ *n.* [C] a soft flower that grows in long thin groups and hangs from the branches of trees such as the WILLOW or BIRCH [**Origin:** 1500–1600 Early Dutch *katteken* **kitten**; because it looks like a cat's tail]

Cat·lin /ˈkætlɪn/, **George** (1796–1872) a U.S. PAINTER famous for his pictures of Native Americans

ˈcat ˌlitter also **ˈkitty ˌlitter** *n.* [U] a substance like large grains of sand that people put into boxes for cats that live indoors, and which the cats use as a toilet

cat·nap /ˈkætˀnæp/ *n.* [C] INFORMAL a very short sleep: *New mothers learn to* ***take catnaps*** *while the baby is sleeping.* —**cat nap** *v.* [I]

cat·nip /ˈkætˀnɪp/ *n.* [U] a type of grass with a nice smell that cats are attracted to

cat-o'-nine-tails /ˌkæt ə ˈnaɪn ˌteɪlz/ *n.* [C] a whip made of nine strings with knots on the end, used in past times for punishing people

CAT scan /ˈkæt skæn/ also **CˈT scan** *n.* [C] **1** an image produced by a CAT scanner **2** the process of using a CAT scanner to produce an image of the inside of someone's body: *Todd underwent a CAT scan.*

CAT scan·ner /ˈkæt ˌskænɚ/ also **CˈT ˌscanner** *n.* [C] an electronic machine used in a hospital to produce an image of the inside of someone's body

ˌcat's ˈcradle *n.* [U] a game in which children wind string around their fingers and between their hands to make different patterns

Cats·kill Moun·tains, the /ˈkætskɪl ˌmaʊntˀnz/ also **The Catskills** a group of mountains in the southeast of New York state in the northeastern U.S. that is part of the Appalachians

cat·suit /ˈkætˀsut/ *n.* [C] a tight piece of women's clothing that covers all of the body and legs in one piece

cat·sup /ˈkɛtʃəp, ˈkæ-/ *n.* [U] another spelling of KETCHUP

Catt /kæt/, **Car·rie Chap·man** /ˈkæri ˈtʃæpmən/ (1859–1947) a U.S. woman who helped women get the right to vote

cat·tail /ˈkætˀteɪl/ *n.* [C] a plant that grows near water and has SAUSAGE-shaped groups of brown flowers and seeds

cat·tle /ˈkætl/ [S3] *n.* [plural] cows and BULLS kept on a farm for their meat or milk: *a* ***herd of cattle*** | *The ranch has enough land to graze 7,000* ***head of cattle*** (=7,000 cattle). | **beef/dairy cattle** *the farm where they raise dairy cattle* [**Origin:** 1200–1300 Old North French *catel* **personal property**, from Latin *capitalis*]

ˈcattle call *n.* [C] INFORMAL an event at which a large number of people give a short performance for the people who are in charge of the play or movie, in order to try to get a part in it [SYN] **audition**

ˈcattle guard *n.* [C] a set of bars placed over a hole in the road, so that animals cannot go across but cars can

cat·tle·man /ˈkætlmən/ *n. plural* **cattlemen** /-mən/ [C] someone who owns cattle

ˈcattle prod *n.* [C] a type of stick that gives an electric shock to cattle, to make them move along

cat·ty /ˈkæti/ *adj.* deliberately not nice in what you say about someone: *Joyce made a catty comment about Sonia's clothes.* —**cattiness** *n.* [U]

ˈcatty-ˌcorner *adv.* KITTY-CORNER

CATV /ˌsi eɪ ti ˈvi/ *n.* [U] community antenna television; a type of television service for areas that normally do not receive television broadcasts clearly

cat·walk /ˈkætˀwɔk/ *n.* [C] **1** a long raised path that MODELS walk on in a fashion show [SYN] **runway** **2** a narrow structure for people to walk on that is built along something such as a bridge or above a stage in a theater

Cau·ca·sian /kɔˈkeɪʒən/ *adj.* FORMAL someone who is Caucasian belongs to the race that has pale skin —**Caucasian** *n.* [C]

Cau·ca·sus, the /ˈkɔkəsəs/ also **Cau·ca·sia** /kɔˈkeɪʒə/ an area between the Black Sea and the Caspian Sea that includes part of Russia, Georgia, Azerbaijan, and Armenia and contains the Caucasus Mountains

ˌCaucasus ˈMountains, the a group of mountains in the Caucasus in southeast Europe

cau·cus /ˈkɔkəs/ *n. plural* **caucuses** [C] **1** POLITICS a local meeting of the members of a political party to choose people to represent them at a larger meeting, or to choose a CANDIDATE in an election → see also PARTY CAUCUS **2** an organized group of people who have similar aims or interests, especially political ones: *the chairman of the Congressional Hispanic Caucus*

cau·dil·lo /kɔˈdilyoʊ/ *n.* [C] CULTURES in Spanish-speaking countries, a military or political leader who has complete power over the country, especially one whose power has been gained by force and who rules strictly → see also DICTATOR

caught /kɔt/ *v.* the past tense and past participle of CATCH

caul·dron, **caldron** /ˈkɔldrən/ *n.* [C] **1** a large round metal pot for boiling liquids over a fire **2** a situation that is dangerous and that may produce war, violence etc.: +**of** *a cauldron of anti-immigrant feeling*

cau·li·flow·er /ˈkɔlɪˌflaʊɚ, ˈkɑ-/ *n.* [U] a vegetable with green leaves around a large firm white center made up of groups of flower-like parts [**Origin:** 1500–1600 Italian *cavolfiore*, from *cavolo* **cabbage** + *fiore* **flower**]

ˈcauliflower ˌear *n.* [C] an ear permanently swollen into a strange shape, especially as a result of an injury

caulk[1] /kɔk/ also **caulk·ing** /ˈkɔkɪŋ/ *n.* [U] a substance used to fill in holes, cracks, or other empty spaces between two things or two parts of something so that air or water cannot get through

caulk[2] *v.* [I,T] to fill in holes, cracks, or other empty spaces between two things or two parts of something with caulk

caus·al /ˈkɔzəl/ *adj.* **1** relating to the connection between two things, where one causes the other to happen or exist: **causal relationship/link/connection etc.** *Studies have not proven a causal relationship between violence on TV and violent crime.* **2** ENG. LANG. ARTS a causal CONJUNCTION, for example "because," introduces a statement about the cause of something —**causally** *adv.*

cau·sal·i·ty /kɔˈzæləti/ *n.* [U] FORMAL the relationship between a cause and the effect that it has

cau·sa·tion /kɔˈzeɪʃən/ *n.* [U] **1** FORMAL the action of causing something to happen or exist **2** FORMAL causality **3** MATH the relationship between two VARIABLES (=mathematical quantity that is not fixed and can be any of several amounts) in which a change in one produces a change in the other

caus·a·tive /ˈkɔzətɪv/ *adj.* **1** FORMAL acting as the cause of something: *Radon may be a causative factor in some cancer cases.* **2** TECHNICAL a causative verb expresses an action that causes something to happen or be —**causatively** *adv.*

cause[1] /kɔz/ [S1] [W1] *n.*

1 WHAT CAUSES STH [C] a person, event, or thing that makes something happen, especially something bad: +**of** *Officials are still trying to* ***determine the cause*** *of the crash.* | **a major/primary/chief cause** *Pollution is a major cause of the global rise in temperatures.* | **the root/underlying cause** (=the basic or main cause) | *The man's death was from* ***natural causes.*** | *High cholesterol is the* ***leading cause*** *of heart disease.* | *Heavy drinking may be both the* ***cause and effect*** *of personal problems.*

2 GOOD REASON [U] something that makes it right or fair for you to feel or behave in a particular way [SYN] **reason**: +**for** *FAA officials see no* ***cause for alarm*** *in safety procedures.* | *The decision is a* ***cause for celebration.*** | *There is* ***cause for concern*** (=a reason to be worried) *in the amount of time children spend on video games.* | *People are worried about the economy, and* ***with good cause.***

3 STH YOU SUPPORT [C] an organization, belief, or aim that a group of people support or fight for: **+of** *her devotion to the cause of women's rights* | **a worthy/good cause** (=one that aims to help people) *Twenty percent of the book's profit goes to a worthy cause.* | *a president who wants to **advance the cause** of democracy around the globe* | *I don't mind giving money **if it's for a good cause**.*
4 LAW [C] LAW a case that is brought to a court of law [**Origin:** 1200–1300 Old French, Latin *causa*] → see also **make common cause (with sb)** at COMMON[1] (11), **a lost cause** at LOST[1] (8), PROBABLE CAUSE

cause² S1 W1 *v.* [T] to make something happen, especially something bad: *Heavy traffic is causing long delays on the freeway.* | *The fire caused $500,000 in damage.* | **cause sb/sth to do sth** *Water flooded the ship in ten minutes, causing it to sink.* | *Local youths have been **causing trouble**.* | **cause sth for sb** *Striking bus drivers **caused problems** for commuters.* | **cause sb sth** *The tests have **caused** parents some **concern**.* | **cause concern/embarrassment/confusion etc.** *The animal's behavior was causing concern.*

THESAURUS
make to cause a particular state or situation to happen: *I'm sorry, I didn't mean to make you cry.*
be responsible for sth if you are responsible for something bad, it is your fault that it happened: *Was the teacher responsible for the injuries to the child, which happened during a P.E. class?*
bring about sth to make something happen: *The crisis brought about a change in government policy.*
result in sth if an action or event results in something, it makes that thing happen: *The fire resulted in the deaths of two children.*
lead to sth if one thing leads to something else, the first thing causes the second thing to happen or exist at a later time: *The information led to several arrests.*
trigger if one event triggers another, it makes the second event happen: *The incident triggered a wave of violence.*

'cause /kəz/ *conjunction* SPOKEN an informal way of saying BECAUSE: *"Why?" "'Cause I didn't want to."*

ˌcause and efˈfect *n.* [U] **1** ENG. LANG. ARTS a way of organizing a piece of written work in which you describe an event or a situation and explain the reasons why it happened and the effects that it has **2** the relationship between a cause and the effect that it has SYN **causality**

cause cé·lè·bre /ˌkɔz sɛˈlɛbrə, ˌkoʊz-/ *n.* [C] FORMAL an event or legal case that a lot of people become interested in, because it is an exciting subject to discuss or argue about: *Her comments were published and became a cause célèbre.*

cause·way /ˈkɔzweɪ/ *n.* [C] a raised road that goes across wet ground or an area of water

caus·tic /ˈkɔstɪk/ *adj.* **1** a caustic remark criticizes someone in a way that is unkind but often humorous: **caustic comment/humor/criticism etc.** *her caustic descriptions of her co-workers* **2** CHEMISTRY a caustic substance can burn through things by chemical action —**caustically** /-kli/ *adv.*

ˌcaustic ˈsoda *n.* [U] a very strong chemical substance that you can use for some difficult cleaning jobs SYN **lye**

cau·ter·ize /ˈkɔt̬əˌraɪz/ *v.* [T] TECHNICAL to treat a wound or a growth on your body by burning it with hot metal or a chemical to stop the blood or to prevent it from becoming infected

cau·tion¹ /ˈkɔʃən/ *n.* **1** [U] the quality of being very careful to avoid danger or risks: **with caution** *Beginners should **proceed with caution**.* | **treat/use etc. sth with caution** (=think carefully about something, because it might not be true) *The results of the survey must be treated with caution.* | *Senators from both parties **urged caution**.* | **extreme/great caution** *Travelers in the area should use extreme caution.* | *The FBI said anyone receiving such a package should **exercise** (=use) **caution** when opening it.* **2 a word/note of caution** a warning to be careful: *A word of caution: learn from an experienced surfer.* **3 throw/fling/cast caution to the wind(s)** LITERARY to stop worrying about danger and take a risk: *I decided to throw caution to the wind and say what I thought.* [**Origin:** 1500–1600 Latin *cautio*, from *cavere* **to be careful, be on guard**]

caution² *v.* [I,T] to warn someone that something might be dangerous, difficult etc. SYN **warn**: *"Hold on tight," she cautioned.* | **caution sb about/against sth** *Doctors were cautioned against using the new test until more research is done.* | **+against** *Officials cautioned against reading too much into the decision.* | **caution (sb) that** *A label cautions customers that the toy contains small parts.* | **caution sb to do sth** *He cautioned consumers not to make a decision on price alone.*

cau·tion·ar·y /ˈkɔʃəˌnɛri/ *adj.* giving a warning or advice: **cautionary note/reminder/lesson etc.** *The study sounds a cautionary note for users of cell phones.* | *a **cautionary tale*** (=a story that is used to warn people) *about how not to buy a computer*

cau·tious /ˈkɔʃəs/ *adj.* careful to avoid danger or risks SYN **careful**: *a cautious driver* | **+about** *Be cautious about giving out your phone number.* | *Both sides have expressed **cautious optimism** that an agreement will soon be reached* (=they are hoping for a good result, but are being careful not to expect too much). —**cautiously** *adv.*: *Sara opened the door cautiously.* —**cautiousness** *n.* [U]

cav·al·cade /ˌkævəlˈkeɪd, ˈkævəlˌkeɪd/ *n.* [C] **1** a line of people on horses or in cars moving along as part of a ceremony **2** a series of people or things: **+of** *a cavalcade of dances and songs*

cav·a·lier /ˌkævəˈlɪr/ *adj.* not caring enough about rules, principles, or people's feelings: *a **cavalier attitude** toward workers' safety*

cav·al·ry /ˈkævəlri/ *n.* [U] **1** the part of a modern army that uses TANKS **2** the part of an army that fights on horses, especially in past times

cav·al·ry·man /ˈkævəlrimən/ *n. plural* **cavalrymen** /-mən/ [C] a soldier who fights on a horse

cave¹ /keɪv/ *n.* [C] a large natural hole in the side of a cliff or hill, or under the ground [**Origin:** 1200–1300 Old French, Latin *cava*, from *cavus* **hollow**] → see picture on page 000

cave² *v.*
cave in *phr. v.* **1** to finally stop opposing something, especially because someone has persuaded or threatened you: **+to** *The department **caved in to pressure** from environmental groups.* **2** if the top or sides of something cave in, they fall down or toward the inside: *A section of the mine caved in.* —**ˈcave-in** *n.*

ca·ve·at /ˈkæviˌɑt/ *n.* [C] FORMAL a warning that you must pay attention to something before you make a decision or do something: *Bunk beds come with the caveat that children under six shouldn't sleep in the top bunk.*

caveat emp·tor /ˌkæviɑt ˈɛmptɚ, -tɔr/ *n.* [U] a phrase meaning "let the buyer beware," used to express the principle that when goods are sold, the buyer is responsible for checking the quality of the goods

cave·man /ˈkeɪvmæn/ *n. plural* **cavemen** /-men/ [C] **1** someone who lived in a CAVE many thousands of years ago **2** INFORMAL a man who behaves or thinks in a way that does not seem modern

cav·ern /ˈkævɚn/ *n.* [C] a large CAVE

cav·ern·ous /ˈkævɚnəs/ *adj.* a cavernous room, space, or hole is very large and deep —**cavernously** *adv.*

cav·i·ar, caviare /ˈkæviˌɑr/ *n.* [U] the salted eggs of various types of large fish, considered a special food, and usually expensive

cav·il /ˈkævəl/ *v.* [I + at] FORMAL to make unnecessary complaints about someone or something —**cavil** *n.* [C]

cav·ing /ˈkeɪvɪŋ/ *n.* [U] the activity or sport of going deep under the ground in CAVES SYN spelunking

cav·i·ty /ˈkævət̬i/ *n. plural* **cavities** [C] **1** a hole in a tooth made by decay **2** FORMAL a hole or space inside something: *The heart and lungs are located inside the chest cavity.*

ca·vort /kəˈvɔrt/ *v.* [I] to jump or dance around loudly in a playful or sexual way SYN frolic: *teenagers cavorting on the sand* | +**with** *pictures of him cavorting with an actress*

caw /kɔ/ *v.* [I] if a bird, especially a CROW, caws, it makes a loud sound —**caw** *n.* [C]

Cax·ton /ˈkækstən/, **William** (?1422–1491) an English printer, who was the first person in England to print books, after learning about printing in Germany

cay /ki, keɪ/ *n. plural* **cays** [C] EARTH SCIENCE a very small island formed from CORAL or sand

cay·enne pep·per /ˌkeɪɛn ˈpɛpɚ/ *n.* [U] red powder made from a PEPPER that has a very SPICY taste

cay·man /ˈkeɪmən/ *n.* [C] another spelling of CAIMAN

Ca·yu·ga /keɪˈyugə, kaɪ-/ a Native American tribe from the northeastern area of the U.S.

Cay·use /kaɪˈyus/ a Native American tribe from the northwestern area of the U.S.

CB /ˌsi ˈbi◂ / *n.* [U] **Citizens' Band** a radio on which people can talk to each other over short distances, especially when they are driving

CBO /ˌsi bi ˈoʊ/ ECONOMICS the abbreviation of CONGRESSIONAL BUDGET OFFICE

CBS /ˌsi bi ˈɛs/ *n.* **Columbia Broadcasting System** one of the national companies that broadcasts television and radio programs in the U.S.

CBT /ˌsi bi ˈti/ *n.* [U] **computer-based testing** a way of taking standard tests, such as the TOEFL or GRE, on a computer

cc **1** the abbreviation of "carbon copy"; used in a business letter or EMAIL to show that you are sending a copy to someone else: *To Neil Fry, cc: Andrea Baker, Matt Fox* **2** the abbreviation of CUBIC CENTIMETER: *an 800cc engine*

CD /ˌsi ˈdi◂ / S3 *n.* [C] **1** **compact disc** a small circular piece of hard plastic on which high quality recorded sound or large quantities of information can be stored: **on CD** *The album was recently reissued on CD.* → see also CD-ROM **2** TECHNICAL the abbreviation of CERTIFICATE OF DEPOSIT

CˈD ˌplayer *n.* [C] a piece of equipment used to play music CDs

CD-R /ˌsi di ˈɑr/ *n.* [C,U] **compact disc-recordable** COMPUTERS a type of CD onto which you can record music, images, or other information, using special equipment on your computer. You can record onto it only once.

CD-ROM /ˌsi di ˈrɑm/ *n.* [C,U] COMPUTERS **compact disc read-only memory** a CD on which large quantities of information can be stored to be used by a computer

CD-RW /ˌsi di ɑr ˈdʌbəlyu/ *n.* [C,U] **compact disc-rewritable** COMPUTERS a type of CD onto which you can record music, images, or other information, using special equipment on your computer. You can record onto it several times.

CDT the abbreviation of CENTRAL DAYLIGHT TIME

C.E. /ˌsi ˈi/ **Common Era** used after a date to show it was after the birth of Jesus Christ → see also B.C.E.

cease¹ /sis/ Ac *v.* [I,T] **1** FORMAL to stop doing something or stop happening SYN stop: *The newspaper has been forced to cease publication.* | *By noon the rain had ceased.* | **cease doing sth** *Hansen has ceased cooperating with the FBI investigation.* | **cease to do sth** *When the child's behavior ceases to be rewarding, the behavior will cease.* | *The Warsaw Pact has* ***ceased to exist.*** | *The quality of Walters' music* ***never ceases to amaze*** *me* (=it always surprises me). **2** **cease and desist** LAW to stop doing something [**Origin:** 1300–1400 Old French *cesser*, from Latin *cessare* **to delay**] → see also CEASE-FIRE, **wonders will never cease!** at WONDER² (5)

cease² Ac *n.* **without cease** FORMAL without stopping

cease·fire /ˈsisfaɪɚ/ *n.* [C] an agreement to stop fighting for a period of time, especially so that a more permanent agreement can be made → see also ARMISTICE

cease·less /ˈsislɪs/ Ac *adj.* FORMAL happening or existing for a long time without changing or stopping SYN incessant: *the ceaseless Arctic wind* —**ceaselessly** *adv.*

ce·dar /ˈsidɚ/ *n.* **1** [C] BIOLOGY a large EVERGREEN tree with leaves shaped like needles **2** also **cedarwood** [U] the hard reddish wood of this tree, which smells good

cede /sid/ *v.* [T] FORMAL to give something such as an area of land or a right to a country or person, especially when you are forced to SYN yield: **cede sth to sb** *The military has refused to cede power to elected officials.* → see also CESSION

ce·dil·la /sɪˈdɪlə/ *n.* [C] ENG. LANG. ARTS a mark put under the letter "c" in French and some other languages, to show that it is an "s" sound instead of a "k" sound. It is written "ç."

ceil·ing /ˈsilɪŋ/ S3 *n.* [C] **1** the inner surface of the top part of a room → see also ROOF: *a room with high ceilings* **2** the largest number or amount of something that is officially allowed: +**of** *a military-spending ceiling of $13 billion* | **raise/lower the ceiling (on sth)** *Congress may refuse to raise the* ***debt ceiling*** (=the amount of debt the government is allowed to have). | *Health care costs have* ***gone through the ceiling*** (=increased to very high levels). | +**on** *Gambling is allowed, but there is a $5 ceiling on bets.* **3** the height of the lowest layer of clouds over an area **4** TECHNICAL the greatest height at which an aircraft can fly or is allowed to fly [**Origin:** 1500–1600 *ceil* **to provide with a ceiling** (16–20 centuries)] → see also GLASS CEILING

ˈceiling ˌprice *n.* [C] ECONOMICS PRICE CEILING

cel·a·don /ˈsɛləˌdɑn/ *n.* [U] a pale or light green color —**celadon** *adj.*

ce·leb /səˈlɛb/ *n.* [C] INFORMAL a CELEBRITY

cel·e·brant /ˈsɛləbrənt/ *n.* [C] someone who performs or takes part in a religious ceremony

cel·e·brate /ˈsɛləˌbreɪt/ W3 *v.* **1** [I,T] to do something special because of a particular event or special occasion: *My folks are celebrating their 50th anniversary.* | *The graduation ceremony allows students to celebrate their achievements.* | *We're going out for a meal to celebrate.* | **celebrate Christmas/Thanksgiving etc.** *We'll be celebrating Christmas with Mark's family.* **2** [T] FORMAL to praise someone or something in speech, writing, or pictures: *His poems celebrate the joys of love.* **3** [T] to perform a religious ceremony, especially a Mass in the Catholic church [**Origin:** 1500–1600 Latin, past participle of *celebrare* **to visit often, celebrate**, from *celeber* **often visited, famous**]

cel·e·brat·ed /ˈsɛləˌbreɪt̬ɪd/ *adj.* famous or talked about a lot: *a celebrated professor* | +**for** *Chicago is celebrated for its architecture.*

cel·e·bra·tion /ˌsɛləˈbreɪʃən/ *n.* **1** [C] an occasion or party when you celebrate something: **birthday/anniversary/holiday etc. celebrations** *the New Year's celebrations in Times Square* | *Posadas is a nine-day celebration in Mexico before Christmas.* ►see THESAURUS box at party¹ **2** [U] the act of celebrating: *There will be a party* ***in celebration of*** *Joan and Dave's 40th anniversary.* | *The court's decision is a* ***cause for celebration.*** **3** [singular, U] something that praises someone or something in speech, writing, or pictures: +**of** *Her latest film is a celebration of motherhood.*

cel·e·bra·to·ry /ˈsɛləbrəˌtɔri/ *adj.* done in order to celebrate a particular event or occasion: *a celebratory dinner for their anniversary*

ce·leb·ri·ty /səˈlɛbrət̬i/ W3 *n. plural* **celebrities** **1** [C] a famous person, especially someone in the entertainment business SYN star: *a sports celebrity* | *magazines full of stories about celebrities* ►see THESAURUS box at **famous** **2** [U] FORMAL the state of being famous SYN **fame**

ce·ler·i·ty /səˈlɛrət̬i/ *n.* [U] FORMAL great speed

cel·er·y /ˈsɛləri/ *n.* [U] a vegetable with long firm pale green stems, often eaten raw: *a stalk of celery* [**Origin:** 1600–1700 Italian dialect *seleri*, from Late Latin *selinon* **parsley**, from Greek] → see picture on page A35

C

ce·les·tial /səˈlɛstʃəl/ *adj.* LITERARY **1** relating to the sky or heaven SYN **heavenly**: *Venus is the brightest* ***celestial body*** (=a star, moon, sun etc.) *after the moon.* **2** very beautiful: *celestial music*

cel·i·ba·cy /ˈsɛləbəsi/ *n.* [U] the state of not having sex, especially because of your religious beliefs: *a vow of celibacy* → see also ABSTINENCE

cel·i·bate /ˈsɛləbɪt/ *adj.* never having sex, especially because of your religious beliefs [**Origin:** 1800–1900 Latin *caelibatus*, from *caelebs* **unmarried**] —**celibate** *n.* [C]

cell /sɛl/ W2 *n.* [C] **1** BIOLOGY the smallest independent part of any living thing except a VIRUS. It consists of a NUCLEUS surrounded by CYTOPLASM inside a MEMBRANE: *cancer cells* | **blood/brain/muscle etc. cell** *red blood cells* **2** a small room in a police station or prison where prisoners are kept: **jail/prison/holding cell** *a shortage of jail cells* **3** INFORMAL a CELL PHONE **4** PHYSICS a piece of equipment that produces electricity from chemicals, heat, or light: *alkaline battery cells* | *cars powered by* ***fuel cells*** **5** a small group of people who are working secretly as part of a larger political organization: *a terrorist cell* **6** a small space that an insect or other small creature has made to live in or use: *the cells of a honeycomb* **7** a small room where someone sleeps in a MONASTERY or CONVENT [**Origin:** 1100–1200 Old French *celle*, from Latin *cella* **small room**]

cel·lar /ˈsɛlɚ/ *n.* [C] **1** a room under a house or other building, often used for storing things → see also BASEMENT **2** also **wine cellar** a large number of bottles of wine that belong to a person, restaurant etc. **3 the cellar** INFORMAL the last position in a sports LEAGUE, held by the team that has lost the most games: *The Braves managed to climb from the cellar to first place.*

ˈcell ˌbody *n.* [C] BIOLOGY the main part of a nerve cell, which contains the NUCLEUS and the parts that keep the cell alive → see also AXON

ˈcell ˌculture *n.* [C] BIOLOGY a group of cells grown in a special chemical solution from a single original cell

ˈcell ˌcycle *n.* [C] BIOLOGY a continuous series of related events in which a cell divides and forms two new cells

ˈcell diˌvision *n.* [U] BIOLOGY the process by which a cell divides to form two new cells

ˈcell fractionˌation *n.* [U] BIOLOGY a special process in which a scientist opens a cell and separates the different parts

Cel·li·ni /tʃəˈlini/, **Ben·ve·nu·to** /ˌbɛnvəˈnut̬oʊ/ (1500–1571) an Italian SCULPTOR famous for his work in gold and other metals

cel·list /ˈtʃɛlɪst/ *n.* [C] someone who plays the cello

cell·mate /ˈsɛlmeɪt/ *n.* [C] someone who shares a prison CELL with someone else

ˈcell ˌmembrane *n.* [C,U] BIOLOGY a thin layer of material that covers a cell, through which substances pass in and out SYN **plasma membrane**

cel·lo /ˈtʃɛloʊ/ *n. plural* **cellos** [C] a large wooden musical instrument, shaped like a VIOLIN, that you hold between your knees and play by pulling a BOW (=special stick) across wire strings

cel·lo·phane /ˈsɛləˌfeɪn/ *n.* [U] thin transparent material used for wrapping things

ˈcell phone S1 W2 *n.* [C] a telephone that you can carry with you, that works by using a network of radio stations to pass on signals SYN **cellular phone**

THESAURUS

voice mail messages that you can listen to on your cell phone

text message a message from someone that you can read on your cell phone

text to send a message to someone using the letter buttons on a cell phone

ˈcell respiˌration *n.* [U] BIOLOGY CELLULAR RESPIRATION

ˈcell specialiˌzation *n.* [U] BIOLOGY the fact that different cells in the body have different purposes and are involved in different activities or processes

cel·lu·lar /ˈsɛlyəlɚ/ *adj.* **1** BIOLOGY consisting of or relating to the cells of plants or animals: *cellular biology* **2** a cellular telephone system works by using a network of radio stations to pass on signals: *a cellular network*

ˌcellular ˈphone *n.* [C] FORMAL a cell phone

ˌcellular respiˈration *n.* [U] BIOLOGY the process in which a cell changes sugar and other substances into the energy it needs, usually by using oxygen

cel·lu·lite /ˈsɛlyəˌlaɪt/ *n.* [U] fat that is just below someone's skin and that makes the surface of their skin look uneven and unattractive

cel·lu·loid[1] /ˈsɛlyəˌlɔɪd/ *n.* [U] **1** the film used in past times to make movies: *Chaplin's comic genius is preserved* ***on celluloid***. **2** a substance like plastic, used in past times to make photographic film and other objects

celluloid[2] *adj.* relating to the movies, especially from the first half of the 20th century: *celluloid images of romance*

cel·lu·lose /ˈsɛlyəˌloʊs/ *n.* [U] **1** BIOLOGY the material that the cell walls of plants are made of, and that is used to make plastics, paper etc. **2** also **cellulose acetate** TECHNICAL a plastic that is used for many industrial purposes, especially making photographic film and explosives

ˌcell ˈwall *n.* [C] BIOLOGY the stiff outer part of the cells of plants and BACTERIA, which helps to support the growing plant or bacteria

Cel·si·us /ˈsɛlsiəs, -ʃəs/ ABBREVIATION **C** *n.* [U] a temperature scale in which water freezes at 0° and boils at 100° SYN **Centigrade** [**Origin:** 1800–1900 Anders *Celsius* (1701–44), Swedish scientist who invented the scale] —**Celsius** *adj.*: *a Celsius thermometer* | *12° Celsius*

Celt /kɛlt, sɛlt/ *n.* [C] **1** one of the people who lived in Britain and Ireland from about 400 B.C. before the arrival of the Romans in the first century B.C. **2** one of the people who lived in western Europe, especially in parts of France and Spain from about 1200 B.C. until the arrival of the Romans in the first century B.C.

Celt·ic /ˈkɛltɪk, ˈsɛltɪk/ *adj.* related to the Celts, an ancient European race, or to their languages

ce·ment[1] /sɪˈmɛnt/ *n.* [U] **1** a gray powder used in building things, that becomes hard when it is mixed with water and allowed to dry → see also CONCRETE: *a cement wall* **2** a thick sticky substance used for filling holes or as a glue **3** something that holds a relationship between people, countries etc. together or makes it strong: *Such deals were the cement of city politics.* [**Origin:** 1300–1400 Old French *ciment*, from Latin *caementum* **small pieces of stone used in making mortar**]

cement[2] *v.* [T] **1** also **cement over** to cover something with cement: *Some of the graves are cemented over.* **2** to make something stronger or more certain: *The film* ***cemented his reputation*** *as an innovative director.* | **cement a relationship/friendship/partnership etc.** *Cement your relationship with your kids by spending quality time with them.*

ceˈment ˌmixer *n.* [C] a machine with a round open container that turns around, into which you put cement, sand, and water to make CONCRETE SYN **concrete mixer**

cem·e·ter·y /ˈsɛməˌtɛri/ *n. plural* **cemeteries** [C] an area of land where dead people are buried [**Origin:** 1300–1400 Old French *cimitere*, from Late Latin *coemeterium*, from Greek *koimeterion* **sleeping room, burying place**] → see also GRAVEYARD

cen·o·taph /ˈsɛnəˌtæf/ *n.* [C] a MONUMENT built to remind people of soldiers, SAILORS etc. who were killed in a war and are buried somewhere else

Ce·no·zo·ic /ˌsinəˈzoʊɪk/ *n.* **the Cenozoic** EARTH SCIENCE the ERA (=long period of time in the history of the Earth) from about 65 million years ago until the present day → see also MESOZOIC —**Cenozoic** *adj.*: *the Cenozoic period*

cen·sor¹ /ˈsɛnsɚ/ *v.* [T] **1** to examine books, movies, letters etc. to remove anything that is offensive, morally harmful, or politically dangerous: *Prisoners' letters were always* ***heavily censored****.* **2 censor yourself** to not say or write something you think might offend, annoy, or hurt someone

censor² *n.* [C] someone whose job is to examine books, movies, letters etc. and remove anything that is offensive, morally harmful, or politically dangerous

cen·so·ri·ous /sɛnˈsɔriəs/ *adj.* FORMAL expressing criticism and disapproval: *His tone was censorious* —**censoriously** *adv.* —**censoriousness** *n.* [U]

cen·sor·ship /ˈsɛnsɚʃɪp/ *n.* [U] the practice or system of censoring something: *the censorship of school reading books*

cen·sure¹ /ˈsɛnʃɚ/ *n.* [U] FORMAL the act of officially expressing strong disapproval and criticism: *a vote of censure*

censure² *v.* [T] FORMAL to officially criticize someone for something they have done wrong: *Several senators called for Hayes to be censured for his conduct.*

cen·sus /ˈsɛnsəs/ *n. plural* **censuses** [C] an official count of all the people in a country, including information about their ages, jobs etc.: *When was the first U.S. census taken?* [**Origin:** 1600–1700 Latin *censere* **to make a judgment about, tax**]

cent /sɛnt/ S1 W2 *n.* [C] **1** WRITTEN ABBREVIATION **¢** a unit of money that is worth 1/100th of a dollar **2 put in your two cents' worth** INFORMAL to give your opinion about something, when other people do not want to hear it [**Origin:** 1300–1400 Old French **hundred**, from Latin *centum*] → see also **not one red cent** at RED¹ (6)

cen·taur /ˈsɛntɔr/ *n.* [C] a creature in ancient Greek stories that has the head, chest, and arms of a man and the body and legs of a horse

cen·te·nar·i·an /ˌsɛntəˈnɛriən/ *n.* [C] someone who is 100 years old or older

cen·ten·ni·al /sɛnˈtɛniəl/ also **cen·ten·a·ry** /sɛnˈtɛnəri, ˈsɛntˀnˌɛri/ *n.* [C] the day or year that is exactly 100 years after a particular event: *the centennial of Tchaikovsky's birth*

cen·ter¹ /ˈsɛntɚ/ S1 W1 *n.* [C]
1 MIDDLE the middle of a space, area, or object, especially the exact middle SYN **middle**: *a flower with yellow petals and a purple center* | **+of** *Draw a line through the center of the circle.* | *There was an enormous oak table* ***in the center of*** *the room.* → see Word Choice box at MIDDLE¹
2 BUILDING a building that is used for a particular purpose or activity: *the Fred Hutchinson Cancer Research Center* | *a huge shopping center* | *a new $3 million center for the elderly*
3 WHERE THINGS HAPPEN a place where there is a lot of a particular type of business, activity etc.: **business/commercial/financial etc. center** *a major banking center* | **+for** *a center for environmental policy* | **+of** *Nashville is still the center of the country music industry.*
4 INVOLVEMENT be at the center of sth to be involved in something more than other people or things are: *the businessman who is* ***at the center of the controversy***
5 be the center of attention to be the person everyone is giving attention to: *She's not happy unless she's the center of attention.*
6 center stage a position that attracts attention or importance: *The issue* ***took center stage*** *during the election.*
7 urban center also **center of population** an area where a large number of people live: *a major urban center*
8 POLITICS the center a MODERATE (=middle) position in politics which does not support extreme ideas: *Seymour appeals to the party's broad political center.* | **right/left of center** *Environmental and left of center groups attended the protest in large numbers.*
9 BASKETBALL the player on a basketball team who is usually the tallest and who usually plays nearest to the basket
10 FOOTBALL the player on a football team who starts the ball moving in each PLAY

center² *v.* [T] **1** to move something to a position at the center of something else: *The title wasn't centered on the page.* **2 be centered** to happen or be located mainly in a particular place: **+in** *Most of the fighting is centered in the southeast of the country.* | **+at** *The group of writers is centered at Vanderbilt University.*

center around sth *phr. v.* if your thoughts, activities etc. center around something, it is the main thing that you think is important: *The investigation centered around drug use within the armed forces.*

center on/upon sth *phr. v.* also **be centered on/upon sth** if an event or activity centers on something, that is the thing that people pay the most attention to: *The debate centered on the morality of abortion.*

ˈcenter diˌvider *n.* [C] a fence or raised area in the middle of a wide road, that separates cars going in opposite directions

cen·tered /ˈsɛntɚd/ *adj.* **1** having a particular person or thing as the most important part of something: *a child-centered approach to education* **2** feeling calm and in control of yourself: *Meditation can make you feel centered and healthy.* → see also SELF-CENTERED

ˈcenter field *n.* [C] the area in baseball in the center of the OUTFIELD —**center fielder** *n.* [C]

cen·ter·fold /ˈsɛntɚˌfoʊld/ *n.* [C] **1** a picture of a woman with no clothes on, that covers the two pages in the middle of a magazine **2** the two pages that face each other in the middle of a magazine or newspaper, and that often have a picture on them

ˌcenter of ˈgravity *n.* [singular] **1** the point on an object on which it can balance **2** the part of something that is most important or powerful, or that people pay the most attention to: *The Republicans' center of gravity has moved steadily to the right.*

ˌcenter of ˈmass *n.* [singular] PHYSICS the point on an object around which its weight seems to be centered

cen·ter·piece /ˈsɛntɚˌpis/ *n.* [C] **1** a decoration, especially an arrangement of flowers, in the middle of a table **2** the most important, noticeable, or attractive part of something: **+of** *Television is the centerpiece of many families' lives.*

centi- /sɛntə/ *prefix* also **cent-** **1** 100: *a centipede* (=a creature with 100 legs) **2** 100th part of a unit: *a centimeter* (=0.01 meters)

Cen·ti·grade /ˈsɛntəˌgreɪd/ *n.* [U] CELSIUS —**Centigrade** *adj.*

cen·ti·gram /ˈsɛntəˌgræm/ *n.* [C] a unit for measuring weight. There are 100 centigrams in one gram.

cent·i·li·ter /ˈsɛntəˌlitɚ/ *n.* [C] a unit for measuring liquid. There are 100 centiliters in one liter.

cen·time /ˈsɑntim/ *n.* [C] a unit of money that was worth 1/100 of a FRANC or some other types of money, or a coin worth this amount

cen·ti·me·ter /ˈsɛntəˌmitɚ/ WRITTEN ABBREVIATION **cm** *n.* [C] a unit for measuring length. There are 100 centimeters in one meter.

cen·ti·pede /ˈsɛntəˌpid/ *n.* [C] a very small creature with a long body and many legs

Cen·tral /ˈsɛntrəl/ *n.* a short form of Central Time

cen·tral /ˈsɛntrəl/ W1 *adj.* [no comparative] **1** [only before noun] in the middle of an object or an area: *the farming areas of central California* | *The roof is sup-*

ported by a central column. **2** [only before noun] used about the part of an organization, system etc. that controls the rest of it, or that controls its work: *the generals at central command* | *a house with central heating* | *central planning* **3** more important and having more influence than anything else: *the troubled central character of the novel* | **+to** *values which are central to our society* | **central issue/theme** *Crime was the central issue of the mayoral campaign.* | *Owen* ***played a central role*** *in the negotiations.* | *Ellington was a* ***central figure*** *in jazz history.* ►see THESAURUS box at basic, important **4** used to describe a place that is near the center of a town or area, and so is easy to get to: *a good hotel in a central location* **5 party/comedy etc. central** INFORMAL a place where something is happening a lot: *Tim's house became party central for the band and their friends.* —**centrally** *adv.*: *Our office is centrally located.* —**centrality** /sɛn'trælət̬i/ *n.* [C]

ˌCentral ˌAfrican Re'public, the a country in central Africa, that is north of Congo and west of Sudan

ˌcentral 'angle *n.* [C] MATH an angle in the center of a circle at the point where two lines going from the center to the edge of the circle meet

ˌcentral 'bank *n.* [C] ECONOMICS the official bank of a country, which is responsible for controlling the MONEY SUPPLY (=amount of money that exists in the country at a particular time), produces bank notes, and controls the country's banking system. A central bank can also lend money to the country's other banks.

ˌCentral 'Daylight Time WRITTEN ABBREVIATION **CDT** *n.* [U] the time that is used in the east-central part of the U.S. for over half the year, including the summer, when clocks are one hour ahead of Central Standard Time

ˌCentral 'Europe *n.* countries in the middle of Europe, such as Poland, the Czech Republic, and Hungary → see also EASTERN EUROPE

ˌCentral In'telligence ˌAgency *n.* the CIA

cen·tral·ism /'sɛntrəˌlɪzəm/ *n.* [U] POLITICS a way of governing a country or controlling an organization, in which one central group has power and tells people in other places what to do

cen·tral·ize /'sɛntrəˌlaɪz/ *v.* [T] POLITICS to organize the control of a country or organization so that everything is done or decided in one place or by one group of people: *Attempts to centralize the economy have failed.* —**centralized** *adj.*: *centralized planning* —**centralization** /ˌsɛntrələ'zeɪʃən/ *n.* [U] → see also DECENTRALIZE

ˌcentrally ˌplanned e'conomy *n.* [C] ECONOMICS the economic system in a country where the government makes most of the industrial and economic decisions

ˌcentral 'nervous ˌsystem *n.* [C] BIOLOGY the main part of your NERVOUS SYSTEM, consisting of your brain and your SPINAL CORD

ˌCentral 'Powers, the *n.* [plural] HISTORY a name for the countries of Germany and Austria-Hungary, and sometimes also Turkey and Bulgaria in World War I → see also ALLIES

ˌcentral 'processing ˌunit *n.* [C] COMPUTERS a CPU

ˌCentral 'Standard ˌTime WRITTEN ABBREVIATION **CST** *n.* [U] the time that is used in the east-central part of the U.S. for almost half the year, including the winter → see also CENTRAL DAYLIGHT TIME

ˌcentral 'tendency *n.* [U] MATH the degree to which STATISTICAL data groups around a particular point → see also MEASURE OF CENTRAL TENDENCY

'Central Time WRITTEN ABBREVIATION **CT** *n.* [U] the time that is used in the east-central part of the U.S.

cen·tre /'sɛntɚ/ the British and Canadian spelling of CENTER

cen·trif·u·gal force /sɛnˌtrɪfyəgəl 'fɔrs, -ˌtrɪfə-/ *n.* [U] PHYSICS a force that appears to make things move away from the center of something when they are moving or turning quickly around it

cen·tri·fuge /'sɛntrəˌfyudʒ/ *n.* [C] PHYSICS a machine used especially by scientists that spins a container around very quickly so that the heavier liquids and any solids are forced to the outer edge or bottom

cen·trip·e·tal force /sɛnˌtrɪpət̬l 'fɔrs/ *n.* [U] PHYSICS a force that makes things move toward the center of something when they are moving or turning quickly around it

cen·trist /'sɛntrɪst/ *adj.* POLITICS having political beliefs that are not extreme SYN **moderate** —**centrist** *n.* [C] —**centrism** *n.* [U]

cen·troid /'sɛntrɔɪd/ *n.* [C] MATH the point in the middle of a TRIANGLE where the MEDIANS (=lines drawn through the angles to the middle of the opposite sides of the triangle) cross

cen·tu·ri·on /sɛn'tʃʊriən/ *adj.* an army officer of ancient Rome, who was in charge of about 100 soldiers

cen·tu·ry /'sɛntʃəri/ S2 W1 *n. plural* **centuries** [C] **1** one of the 100-year periods measured from before or after the year of Jesus Christ's birth: **the 11th/18th/21st etc. century** *Cubism was one of the most significant art forms of* ***the 20th century*** (=the years 1900–1999). | *It was the worst air disaster* ***this century***. | **the next/last century** *one of the original settlers in the last century* | *The lake could be cleaned up by* ***the turn of the century*** (=the beginning of a century). **2** a period of time equal to 100 years: *Naismith invented basketball over a century ago.*

CEO /ˌsi i 'oʊ/ *n.* [C] **Chief Executive Officer** the person with the most authority in a large company

ce·phal·ic /sə'fælɪk/ *adj.* BIOLOGY relating to or affecting your head

ceph·a·li·za·tion /ˌsɛfələ'zeɪʃən/ *n.* [U] BIOLOGY the tendency for nerve cells and the parts of a person's or animal's body with which they see, smell, hear, taste, or feel something to be in the head or front of the body

ceph·a·lo·tho·rax /ˌsɛfələ'θɔræks/ *n. plural* **cephalothoraxes** or **cephalothoraces** /-rəsiz/ [C] BIOLOGY a body part that consists of a head joined to a THORAX. SPIDERS and some animals such as LOBSTERS and CRABS have a cephalothorax.

ce·ram·ic /sə'ræmɪk/ *n.* [U] hard baked clay that pots, bowls, TILES etc. are made of: *Most of the things in the store are made of ceramic.* —**ceramic** *adj.*: *ceramic tiles*

ce·ram·ics /sə'ræmɪks/ *n.* ENG. LANG. ARTS **1** [U] the art of making pots, bowls, TILES etc. by shaping pieces of clay and baking them until they are hard ►see THESAURUS box at art[1] **2** [plural] things that are made this way: *an exhibit of ceramics at the crafts museum*

ce·re·al /'sɪriəl/ S3 *n.* **1** [C,U] a breakfast food made from grain and usually eaten with milk: *a bowl of* ***breakfast cereal*** **2** [C] FORMAL a plant grown to produce grain, such as wheat, rice etc.: *cereal crops* [**Origin:** 1800–1900 French *céréale*, from Latin *cerealis* **of Ceres**, from *Ceres* ancient Roman goddess of grain and farming]

cer·e·bel·lum /ˌsɛrə'bɛləm/ *n. plural* **cerebellums** or **cerebella** /-lə/ [C] BIOLOGY the bottom part of the brain that controls the muscles → see also CEREBRUM → see picture at BRAIN[1]

ce·re·bral /sə'ribrəl, 'sɛrə-/ *adj.* **1** BIOLOGY relating to or affecting your brain: *a cerebral hemorrhage* (=bleeding in the brain) **2** thinking or explaining things in a very complicated way that takes a lot of effort to understand: *Winters' novel is cerebral, yet also scary and funny.*

ceˌrebral 'cortex *n.* [C] BIOLOGY the outer layer of the front part of your brain, where you think and receive signals from your senses

ceˌrebral 'palsy *n.* [U] MEDICINE a disease caused by damage to the brain before or during birth that makes it very difficult to speak or control your movements

cer·e·bra·tion /ˌsɛrə'breɪʃən/ *n.* [U] FORMAL the process of thinking

ce·re·bro·spin·al flu·id /səˌribroʊspaɪnl 'fluɪd/ *n.* [C,U] a liquid that fills the space between the bottom of the brain and the SPINAL CORD, protecting the brain and nerves from damage

cer·e·brum /səˈribrəm/ *n. plural* **cerebra** /-brə/ or **cerebrums** [C] BIOLOGY the front, larger part of the brain, where thought and decision-making processes happen, and which also controls movements of the body → see also CEREBELLUM → see picture at BRAIN[1]

cer·e·mo·ni·al[1] /ˌsɛrəˈmouniəl/ *adj.* used in a ceremony or done as part of a ceremony: *The Vice Mayor is a largely ceremonial position.* | *Native American ceremonial robes*

ceremonial[2] *n.* [C,U] FORMAL a special ceremony, or the practice of having ceremonies: *an occasion for public ceremonial*

cer·e·mo·ni·ous /ˌsɛrəˈmouniəs/ *adj.* paying great attention to formal correct behavior, as if you were in a ceremony —**ceremoniously** *adv.*: *The flag should be lowered ceremoniously.*

cer·e·mo·ny /ˈsɛrəˌmouni/ S3 W3 *n. plural* **ceremonies** **1** [C] an important social or religious event, when a traditional set of actions is performed in a formal way SYN **service**: *The wedding ceremony was held in the county park.* | *a graduation ceremony* **2** [U] the special actions and formal words traditionally used on particular occasions: *all the ceremony of the opening of Congress* **3 without ceremony** in a very informal way: *The bodies were buried without ceremony.* [**Origin:** 1300–1400 Old French *cerymonie*, from Latin *caerimonia*] → see also **not stand on ceremony** at STAND[1] (41)

Ce·res /ˈsɪriz/ the Roman name for the goddess Demeter

ce·rise /səˈris, -ˈriz/ *n.* [U] a bright pinkish red color —**cerise** *adj.*

cert. the written abbreviation of CERTIFICATE

cer·tain[1] /ˈsɚtˀn/ S1 W1 *determiner* **1** [only before noun] used to talk about a particular person, thing, group of things etc. without naming them or describing them exactly: *Some vegetables are only available at certain times of the year.* | *You have to be a certain height to go on some of the rides.* | *There are certain things I just can't talk to my mother about.* | **a certain kind/type** *She has trouble spelling certain types of words.* | **certain circumstances/situations** *Air bags in cars pose a danger to children in certain circumstances.* **2** some, but not a lot: *There is **a certain amount of** risk involved.* | *In certain ways Martha's good to work for, but she can be really tough.* **3 to a certain extent/degree** partly, but not completely: *To a certain extent, just about every business here is dependent on tourism.* | *Pollution can affect the acidity of water to a certain degree.* **4 a certain a)** enough of a particular quality to be noticed: *A baby was crying, and I felt a certain sympathy for it.* | *The restaurant has a certain charm.* **b)** FORMAL used to talk about someone you do not know, but whose name you have been told: *There's a certain Mrs. Myles on the telephone.* [**Origin:** 1200–1300 Old French, Vulgar Latin *certanus*, from Latin *certus* **decided, certain**]

certain[2] S3 W2 *adj.* **1** [not before noun] confident and sure, without any doubts that something is true SYN **sure** OPP **uncertain**: *She thought it was the same man, but she couldn't be certain.* | **certain (that)** *I'm almost certain that I passed the test.* | **certain who/what/how etc.** *Doctors are not certain what causes the disease.* | **+of/about** *Never eat a wild plant unless you are certain about what it is.* | *We are not certain of victory* (=not sure that we will win). **2 know/say/tell etc. for certain** to know, say etc. something without any doubt: *We may not know for certain until next year.* | *No one can say for certain what will happen.* **3 make certain a)** to do something in order to be sure that something is true or correct SYN **make sure**: **make certain (that)** *I went back into the house to make certain the stove was turned off.* **b)** to do something in order to be sure that something will happen SYN **make sure**: *I wanted to make certain that the kids would have a good time.* **4** if something is certain, it will definitely happen or is definitely true: *Her business faces certain bankruptcy.* | **it seems/is certain (that)** *It seems certain that several of the streets will be closed.* | **certain to do sth** *Beginning golfers are almost certain to get frustrated.* | **it is not certain who/what/how etc.** *It is not certain whether the fires were set deliberately* (=no one knows for sure). | **almost/fairly/virtually certain** *The case is almost certain to cause controversy.* **5 one thing is for certain** SPOKEN used when you are very sure about something, especially in a situation when you cannot be sure about other things: *One thing is for certain – we'll try our best.*

certain[3] *pron.* FORMAL **certain of sb/sth** several specific things or people in a group: *Certain of the documents were kept secret.*

cer·tain·ly /ˈsɚtˀnli/ S1 W1 *adv.* [sentence adverb] **1** without any doubt SYN **definitely**: *We're certainly a lot better off than we were five years ago.* | *Certainly, a backpacking trip in the high Sierras is not for everyone.* | *Hollis was **almost certainly** a Soviet spy.* | ***It is certainly** true that more could be done.*

> **THESAURUS**
>
> **certainly** used when you strongly feel or believe something, in spite of what others think, or when you are saying that one thing is true, but another thing is not: *I'm certainly not going to let him stay overnight.* | *Amy's certainly growing, but she's not gaining weight.*
> **surely** used to show that you believe something, and would be surprised if other people did not agree: *Surely you don't expect me to wait for you.*
> **sure** INFORMAL used before a verb to show that you strongly believe something and are surprised or annoyed by it: *Those kids sure eat a lot.*
> **definitely** used to show that you believe something so strongly that there is no doubt about it at all: *That movie is definitely not for small children.*
> **of course/naturally/obviously** used to show that you think something is true and not surprising: *She hasn't seen me since I was four, so of course she didn't recognize me.*

2 SPOKEN FORMAL used to agree or give your permission: *"Would you turn up the sound?" "Certainly."* | *"Are you going to go?" "**Certainly not!**"* (=I am not going to go)

cer·tain·ty /ˈsɚtˀnti/ *n. plural* **certainties** **1** [U] the state of being completely certain: *No one can say **with any certainty** how much oil is there.* | *Scientists may never be able to predict earthquakes with **absolute certainty**.* **2** [U] the fact that something is certain to happen: **certainty of (doing) sth** *Students face the certainty of owing a lot of money when they graduate.* | *There is no certainty of success.* | **certainty that** *the certainty that things will never be the same* **3** [C] something that is definitely true or that will definitely happen: *Further job cutbacks are a certainty.*

cer·ti·fi·a·ble /ˌsɚtəˈfaɪəbəl/ *adj.* **1** recognized as clearly true: *a certifiable fact* **2** OLD-FASHIONED crazy, especially in a way that is dangerous: *You'd have to be certifiable to do a bungee jump.* **3** good enough or correct enough to be officially approved: *grade A certifiable beef*

cer·tif·i·cate /sɚˈtɪfəkɪt/ S2 *n.* [C] **1** an official document that states that a fact or facts are true: **a birth/marriage/death certificate** *Send in your birth certificate with your passport application.* **2** an official document stating that you have the required education or training to do a particular job SYN **credential**: *a teaching certificate* ►see THESAURUS box at **qualification** **3** an official document stating that you have completed a short course of study: *a first aid certificate* **4** LAW a method used for asking the Supreme Court to examine a case that has already been heard in a lower court, and make a legal judgment on it [**Origin:** 1400–1500 French *certificat*, from Late Latin, past participle of *certificare*, from Latin *certus* **decided, certain**] → see also GIFT CERTIFICATE

C

cer·tif·i·cat·ed /sɚˈtɪfəˌkeɪtɪd/ *adj.* TECHNICAL having an official document that shows official facts, shows that something is of good quality etc.

cerˌtificate of deˈposit ABBREVIATION **CD** *n.* [C] a bank account that you must leave a particular amount of money in for a set amount of time in order to get INTEREST

cerˌtificate of incorpoˈration *n.* [C] ECONOMICS a legal document that a new company must obtain from the state government before it can operate as a business. The document contains the names of the company directors and the money or other things the company owns.

C

cer·ti·fi·ca·tion /ˌsɚt̬əfəˈkeɪʃən/ *n.* **1** [C,U] an official document that says that someone is allowed to do a certain job, that something is of good quality etc., or the state of having this document: *You must show proof of scuba certification before they will let you dive.* **2** [U] the process of giving someone or something an official document that says that they are allowed to do a certain job, that something is of good quality etc.: +**of** *the training and certification of healthcare workers*

cer·ti·fied /ˈsɚt̬əˌfaɪd/ S3 *adj.* **1** having successfully completed a training course for a particular profession: *a certified medical assistant* **2** something that is certified has been signed by someone in an official position to show that it is correct or official: *a certified copy of your birth certificate*

ˌcertified ˈcheck *n.* [C] TECHNICAL if you use a certified check to pay for something, the person receiving the check is certain to be paid, because you have already given the bank the money for the check

ˌcertified fiˌnancial ˈplanner *n.* someone whose job is to help people plan how they will save and spend their money, and who has successfully completed a course of training to do this

ˌcertified ˈmail *n.* [U] a method of sending mail in which the person who receives it must sign their name to prove they have received it

ˌcertified ˌpublic acˈcountant *n.* [C] a CPA

cer·ti·fy /ˈsɚt̬əˌfaɪ/ *v.* **certifies, certified, certifying** [T] **1** to officially state that something is correct or true: *documents certifying the value of the artwork* | **certify (that)** *Her job was to certify that the election had been free and fair.* | **certify sth as sth** *The green card shows that you are certified as a legal resident of the United States.* **2** to give an official paper to someone which states that they have completed a course of training for a profession: **certify sb as sth** *She was certified as a teacher in 1990.* **3** to officially state that someone is mentally ill

cer·ti·tude /ˈsɚt̬əˌtud/ *n.* [U] FORMAL the state of being or feeling certain about something

ce·ru·le·an /səˈruliən/ *n.* [U] TECHNICAL or LITERARY a deep blue color, like that of a clear sky —**cerulean** *adj.*

Cer·van·tes /sɚˈvɑntiz/**, Mi·guel de** /miˈgɛl deɪ/ (1547–1616) a Spanish writer, best known for his NOVEL "Don Quixote"

cer·vi·cal /ˈsɚvɪkəl/ *adj.* BIOLOGY **1** relating to the cervix: *cervical cancer* **2** relating to the neck: *cervical vertebrae* (=the bones in the back of your neck)

cer·vix /ˈsɚvɪks/ *plural* **cervices** /-vɪsiz, sɚˈvaɪsiz/ *n.* [C] BIOLOGY the narrow passage into a woman's UTERUS [**Origin:** 1400–1500 Latin **neck**]

ce·sar·e·an /sɪˈzɛriən/ also **ceˈsarean ˌsection** *n.* [C] an operation in which a woman's body is cut open to take a baby out [**Origin:** 1600–1700 Julius *Caesar* (100–44 BC), Roman soldier and political leader, who is said to have been born in this way]

ce·si·um, caesium /ˈsiziəm/ *n.* [U] SYMBOL **Cs** CHEMISTRY an extremely soft silver-gold metal that is an ELEMENT

ces·sa·tion /sɛˈseɪʃən/ *n.* [C,U] FORMAL a pause or stop: +**of** *a temporary cessation of nuclear tests*

ces·sion /ˈsɛʃən/ *n.* [C,U] FORMAL the act of giving up land, property, or rights, especially to another country after a war, or something that is given up in this way SYN **surrender**: +**of** *Red Cloud refused to give his signature for the cession of Indian lands.* → see also CEDE

cess·pool /ˈsɛspul/ *n.* [C] **1** a place or situation that is very dirty, or in which people behave in an immoral way: *The downtown area has become a cesspool of poverty and crime.* **2** also **cesspit** a large hole or container under the ground in which waste from a building, especially from the toilets, is collected

c'est la vie /ˌseɪ lɑ ˈvi/ *interjection* used to say that a situation is typical of life and cannot be changed: *Fads come and go – c'est la vie.*

ce·ta·cean /sɪˈteɪʃən/ *n.* [C] BIOLOGY a MAMMAL (=an animal which feeds its babies on milk) that lives in the ocean, such as a WHALE —**cetacean** *adj.*

ce·vi·che /səˈvitʃeɪ/ *n.* [U] a dish originally from Latin America, made from pieces of raw fish in LEMON or LIME juice, oil, and SPICES

Cey·lon /sɪˈlɑn, seɪ-/ the former name of Sri Lanka

Cé·zanne /seɪˈzæn/**, Paul** (1839–1906) a French PAINTER who influenced the development of CUBISM and ABSTRACT art

cf. used in writing to introduce something else that should be compared or considered

CFC /ˌsi ɛf ˈsi/ *n.* [C] also **chlorofluorocarbon** SCIENCE a gas used in REFRIGERATORS and AEROSOL cans and in making some plastics. The use of CFCs is believed to have damaged the OZONE LAYER.

CFO /ˌsi ɛf ˈoʊ/ *n.* [C] Chief Financial Officer; the person with the most financial authority in a large company

CGI /ˌsi dʒi ˈaɪ/ *n.* [U] **computer-generated imagery** a method of making ANIMATED movies using computers

ch. **1** the abbreviation of CHANNEL **2** the abbreviation of CHAPTER

cha-cha /ˈtʃɑ tʃɑ/ also **ˈcha-cha-cha** *n.* [C] a dance from South America with small, fast steps

Chad /tʃæd/ a country in north central Africa, west of Sudan —**Chadian** *n., adj.*

cha·dor /ˈtʃɑdɔr, -dɚ/ *n.* [C] a long, loose, usually black piece of clothing that covers the whole body including the head, worn by some Muslim women

chafe /tʃeɪf/ *v.* **1** [I] to be or become impatient or annoyed: +**at/under** *Smokers are chafing under the restrictions.* **2** [I,T] if a part of your body chafes or if something chafes it, it becomes sore because of something rubbing against it: *The boots have a soft lining to prevent your toes from chafing.* **3** [T] LITERARY to rub part of your body to make it warm [**Origin:** 1200–1300 Old French *chaufer* **to warm**, from Latin *calefacere*, from *calere* **to be warm** + *facere* **to make**]

chaff /tʃæf/ *n.* [U] **1** the outer seed covers that are removed from grain before it is used as food **2** dried grasses and plant stems that are used as food for farm animals → see also **separate the wheat from the chaff** at SEPARATE[2] (11)

ˈchafing dish *n.* [C] a container heated from below, that is used for cooking food or for keeping food warm at the table

Cha·gall /ʃəˈgɑl, -ˈgæl/**, Marc** /mɑrk/ (1887–1985) a Russian artist who lived in France and painted in bright colors

cha·grin[1] /ʃəˈgrɪn/ *n.* [U] FORMAL annoyance and sadness because something has not happened in the way you had hoped: ***To his chagrin** only a small crowd came to watch.*

chagrin[2] *v.* **be chagrined** FORMAL to feel annoyed and disappointed: *Lynch was chagrined at the delay.*

chain[1] /tʃeɪn/ S3 W2 *n.*
1 LINE OF RINGS [C,U] a series of rings, usually made of metal, connected together in a line, used as jewelry or for fastening things, supporting weights etc.: *a gold chain* | *a chain and a padlock* → see picture at BICYCLE[1]
2 STORES/HOTELS [C] a number of stores, hotels, restaurants etc. owned or managed by the same company or person: +**of** *a chain of health clubs* | **a hotel/**

restaurant/retail etc. chain *Leslie works for a major hotel chain.*
3 CONNECTED EVENTS/IDEAS [C] a connected series of events or actions, especially which lead to a final result: +**of** *a complicated chain of reasoning* | *the* ***chain of events*** *that led to World War I* | *The salesmen are just one* ***link in the chain*** (=part of a process) *of distribution.*
4 CONNECTED LINE [C] people or things which are connected or next to each other forming a line: *the Andean mountain chain* | *They quickly formed* ***a human chain*** (=a line of people who pass things from one person to the next) *to move the equipment.* | **a chain of atoms/molecules etc.** *a chain of amino acids*
5 the chains of sth LITERARY things such as rules or unfair treatment that limit your freedom: *the chains of colonialism*
6 PRISONERS [C usually plural] metal chains fastened to the legs and arms of prisoners, to prevent them from escaping: *He was led away* ***in chains.***
7 MEASURE [C] a measurement of length, used in past times → see also CHAIN OF COMMAND, FOOD CHAIN, KEY CHAIN
[**Origin:** 1200–1300 Old French *chaeine*, from Latin *catena*]

chain² *v.* **1** to fasten someone or something to something else using a chain, especially in order to prevent them from escaping or being stolen: *The gates were chained shut.* | **chain sb/sth to sth** *I chained my bicycle to a tree.* | **chain sb/sth up** *The hostages were chained up and kept in a dark room.* | **chain sb/sth together** *Protesters chained themselves together to block the trucks.* **2 be chained to something** to have your freedom restricted because of a responsibility you cannot escape: *With a sick husband, Sandy's chained to the house all day.*

ˈchain gang *n.* [C] a group of prisoners who are chained together to work outside their prison

ˈchain ˌletter *n.* [C] a letter sent to several people asking them to send copies of the letter to more people

ˌchain-link ˈfence *n.* [C] a type of fence made of metal wires twisted together to form DIAMOND shapes

ˈchain mail *n.* [U] protective clothing made by joining small metal rings together, worn by soldiers in past times

ˌchain of comˈmand *n.* [C usually singular] a system in an organization by which decisions are made and passed from people at the top of the organization to people lower down

ˌchain reˈaction *n.* [C] **1** CHEMISTRY a chemical or NUCLEAR reaction which produces energy and causes more reactions of the same kind **2** a series of related events, each of which causes the next: *A sudden drop on Wall Street can set off a chain reaction in other financial markets.*

chain·saw, chain saw /ˈtʃeɪnsɔ/ *n.* [C] a tool used for cutting wood, consisting of a circular chain with teeth, driven by a motor around the edge of a metal bar → see also CIRCULAR SAW

ˈchain-smoke *v.* [I,T] to smoke cigarettes continuously, one after another —**chain smoker** *n.* [C]

ˈchain stitch *n.* [C,U] a way of sewing in which each new stitch is pulled through the last one —**chain-stitch** *v.* [T]

ˈchain store *n.* [C] one of a group of stores, all of which are owned by one organization and which sell the same types of products → see also CHAIN¹

chair¹ /tʃɛr/ S1 W2 *n.* **1** [C] a piece of furniture for one person to sit on, which has a back, a seat, and legs: *He was sitting* ***in a chair.*** | *She sank exhausted* ***into a chair.*** **2** [C] someone who is in charge of a meeting, a committee, or a college department SYN **chairperson**: *Jones is the committee chair.* | +**of** *the chair of the board of governors* **3 the chair** the position of being in charge of a meeting or committee: *Republicans are set to* ***take the chair*** *of the committee.* **4 the chair** INFORMAL the punishment of death by electric shock given in an ELECTRIC CHAIR: *If he is found guilty, he could get the chair.* [**Origin:** 1200–1300 Old French *chaiere*, from Latin *cathedra*, from Greek, from *kata-* + *hedra* **seat**]

chairs

chair² *v.* [T] to be the CHAIRPERSON of a meeting, committee, or college department: *Biden chaired the Senate hearings.*

chair·lift, chair lift /ˈtʃɛrˌlɪft/ *n.* [C] a line of chairs hanging from a moving wire, used for carrying people up and down mountains, especially when they are SKIING

chair·man /ˈtʃɛrmən/ W1 *n. plural* **chairmen** /-mən/ [C] someone, especially a man, who is in charge of a meeting or directs the work of a committee, organization, or company: *the chairman of the board*

chair·man·ship /ˈtʃɛrmənˌʃɪp/ *n.* [U] the position of being a chairman, or the time when someone has this position: *Brown resigned the chairmanship in March.*

chair·per·son /ˈtʃɛrˌpɚsən/ *n. plural* **chairpersons** [C] someone who is in charge of a meeting or directs the work of a committee, organization, or company SYN **chair**

chair·wom·an /ˈtʃɛrˌwʊmən/ *n. plural* **chairwomen** /-ˌwɪmɪn/ [C] a woman who is a chairperson

chaise /ʃeɪz/ *n.* [C] **1** a chaise longue **2** a light carriage pulled by one horse, used in past times

chaise longue /ˌʃeɪz ˈlɔŋ/ also **ˌchaise ˈlounge** *n.* [C] **1** a long chair with a back that can be upright for sitting, or can lie flat for lying down, usually used outside **2** a long chair with an arm only on one end, on which you can sit and stretch your legs out

cha·let /ʃæˈleɪ, ˈʃæleɪ/ *n.* [C] a house with a steeply sloping roof, common in places with high mountains and snow, such as Switzerland

chal·ice /ˈtʃælɪs/ *n.* [C] a gold or silver decorated cup, often used to hold wine in Christian religious services → see also POISONED CHALICE

chalk¹ /tʃɔk/ *n.* **1** [C,U] small sticks of of a white or colored substance like soft rock, used for writing or drawing: *a piece of chalk* **2** [U] EARTH SCIENCE soft white or gray rock formed a long time ago from the shells of small animals that lived in the ocean: *chalk cliffs* [**Ori-**

gin: Old English *cealc*, from Latin *calx*, from Greek *chalix* **small stone**]

chalk² *v.* [T] to write, mark, or draw something with chalk

chalk sth ↔ **up** *phr. v.* INFORMAL **1** to succeed in getting or gaining something, especially points in a game: *The team chalked up another victory yesterday.* **2** to record or report what someone has done, how much money they owe etc.: *Tire manufacturers chalked up a 5.1% rise in sales.* **3** to give the reason or cause for something that has happened: **chalk sth up to sth** *Cain's success can be chalked up to his management style.* **4 chalk sth up to experience** to accept failure or disappointment calmly, and regard it as an experience that you can learn from **5 chalk one up for sb** INFORMAL used to say that someone has been successful at doing something: *Chalk one up for the consumers who worked to change the law.*

C

chalk·board /ˈtʃɔkbɔrd/ *n.* [C] a black or green smooth surface on the wall of a CLASSROOM that you write on with chalk → see also BLACKBOARD

ˈchalk talk *n.* [C] INFORMAL an occasion when a COACH (=person who trains a team in a sport) explains to a team what he or she wants them to do by drawing pictures on a chalkboard

chalk·y /ˈtʃɔki/ *adj.* similar to CHALK, or containing chalk: *This medicine tastes chalky.* —**chalkiness** *n.* [U]

chal·lah /ˈhɑlə/ *n.* [U] a type of bread that is made with eggs and twisted into a BRAIDed shape

chal·lenge¹ /ˈtʃæləndʒ/ Ac S3 W2 *n.*

1 STH DIFFICULT [C,U] something that tests your strength, skill, or ability, especially in a way that you find interesting: *My new job is quite a challenge.* | **the challenge of (doing) sth** *I like the challenge of learning new things.* | *Garvey now **faces the challenge of** improving the city's public transportation system.* | **meet a challenge/rise to a challenge** (=be ready to deal successfully with something difficult) | **intellectual/mental/physical challenge** *competitions with a series of mental and physical challenges*

2 QUESTION [C] an action or idea which shows that someone refuses to accept something or questions whether it is right, fair, or legal: **+to** *a challenge to traditional values* | *The company faces **a legal challenge** in Seattle.* | **pose/present/represent a challenge (to sb/sth)** *Strikes represent a serious challenge to management's authority.*

3 ATTEMPT TO WIN [C] an attempt to defeat someone in a fight, competition etc., or an invitation to someone to try to defeat you in a fight, competition etc.: *a leadership challenge* | *Holyfield accepted Lewis' challenge to fight for the title.* | **+from** *Government troops face a strong challenge from rebels.* | **+for** *a challenge for the Olympic gold medal*

4 ATTEMPT TO PERSUADE [C] a strong suggestion or invitation for someone to do something difficult, especially something that is also considered good or right: **a challenge (to sb) to do sth** *Collins issued a challenge to the group to donate all the money to charity.*

5 DIFFICULT PERSON [C usually singular] someone who is a challenge is difficult to talk to, work with, live with etc.: *Clint was a real challenge to all of his teachers.*

6 A DEMAND TO STOP [C] a demand from someone such as a guard to stop and give proof of who you are, and an explanation of what you are doing

7 IN LAW [C] LAW a statement made before the beginning of a court case that a JUROR is not acceptable: *Each lawyer may issue up to six challenges.*

challenge² Ac W2 *v.* [T]

1 QUESTION STH to question whether something is right, fair, or legal: *We went to court to challenge the decision.* | *Many have challenged the accuracy of his findings.* | **challenge sb on sth** *She never challenged him again on money matters.*

2 DEMAND THAT SB DO STH to demand that someone try to do something difficult, especially something that is also considered good or right → see also DARE: **challenge sb to do sth** *Civil rights activists have challenged the company to hire more minorities.* | *I challenge you to find anyone who wants to pay more taxes.*

3 INVITE SB TO COMPETE to invite someone to compete or fight against you → see also DARE: **challenge sb to a game/race/duel etc.** *She challenged him to a race and won.* | **challenge sb for sth** *Murray is again challenging him for the Wimbledon title.*

4 TEST SB/STH to test the skills or abilities of someone or something: *He's a good choir director – he really challenges us.* | **challenge sb to do sth** *Mrs. Eastman challenges her students to try new things.*

5 MAKE SB STOP to stop someone and demand proof of who they are, and an explanation of what they are doing: *Guards challenge anyone entering the building.*

6 MAKE A STATEMENT IN COURT LAW to state that a JUROR is not acceptable before a TRIAL begins

[**Origin:** 1200–1300 Old French *chalengier* **to accuse**, from Latin *calumniari* **to accuse falsely**] —**challenger** *n.* [C]

chal·lenged /ˈtʃæləndʒd/ Ac *adj.* **visually/mentally/physically etc. challenged** a phrase meaning that someone has difficulty seeing, thinking, doing things etc., used in order to be polite

chal·leng·ing /ˈtʃæləndʒɪŋ/ Ac *adj.* difficult in an interesting or enjoyable way: *Teaching is a challenging but rewarding job.* —**challengingly** *adv.*

cham·ber /ˈtʃeɪmbɚ/ W3 *n.*

1 ROOM [C] a room used for a special purpose, especially a purpose that is not nice: *a torture chamber* → see also GAS CHAMBER

2 chambers [plural] LAW an office or offices used by a judge

3 GUN [C] the place inside a gun where you put the bullet: *Always check to see if there is a bullet in the chamber.*

4 PEOPLE WHO MAKE LAWS [C] POLITICS a group or part of a group of people who make laws for a country, state etc. SYN **house**: *In Poland, the Sejm is the lower chamber of parliament.*

5 ENCLOSED SPACE [C] an enclosed space, especially in your body or inside a machine: *The heart has four chambers.*

6 MEETING ROOM [C] a large room in a public building used for important meetings: *The council chamber is on the third floor.*

7 PRIVATE ROOM [C] OLD USE a BEDROOM or private room

[**Origin:** 1100–1200 Old French *chambre*, from Late Latin *camera*, from Latin, **curved roof**, from Greek *kamara*]

cham·ber·lain /ˈtʃeɪmbɚlən/ *n.* [C] an important official who organizes things such as cooking, cleaning, buying food etc. in a king's or NOBLEMAN's court

Cham·ber·lain /ˈtʃeɪmbɚlən/, **Nev·ille** /ˈnɛvəl/ (1869–1940) The British Prime Minister at the beginning of World War II

Chamberlain, Wilt /wɪlt/ (1936–1999) a U.S. BASKETBALL player, known as "Wilt the Stilt" because of his height, who set several records for the number of points he won

cham·ber·maid /ˈtʃeɪmbɚˌmeɪd/ *n.* [C] a female servant or worker whose job is to clean rooms, especially in a hotel, or, in the past, for a rich person

ˈchamber ˌmusic *n.* [U] CLASSICAL MUSIC written for a small group of performers

ˌchamber of ˈcommerce, Chamber of Commerce *n.* [C] a group of business people in a particular town or city whose aim is to encourage business

ˈchamber ˌorchestra *n.* [C] a small group of musicians who play CLASSICAL MUSIC together

ˈchamber pot *n.* [C] a round container used in the past as a TOILET, kept in a BEDROOM under the bed

cham·bray /ʃæmˈbreɪ, ˈʃæmbreɪ/ *n.* [U] a type of cloth used especially for shirts, that is plain and made of a white and a colored thread woven together

cha·me·leon /kəˈmilyən, -liən/ *n.* [C] **1** BIOLOGY a LIZARD (=type of animal) that can change its color to match the colors around it **2** someone who changes their ideas, behavior etc. to fit different situations: *a Congressman with a reputation as a political chameleon*

cham•ois /ˈʃæmi/ *n. plural* **chamois** **1** also **chamois leather** [C,U] soft leather prepared from the skin of chamois, sheep, or goats and used for cleaning or polishing, or a piece of this leather **2** [C] BIOLOGY a wild animal like a small goat that lives in the mountains of Europe and southwest Asia

cham•o•mile, **camomile** /ˈkæməˌmil/ *n.* [C,U] a plant with small white and yellow flowers that are sometimes used to make tea

champ¹ /tʃæmp/ *n.* [C] INFORMAL a CHAMPION

champ² *v.* [I,T] **1** to bite food loudly SYN **chomp** **2 be champing at the bit** to be impatient to do something or for something to happen

cham•pagne /ʃæmˈpeɪn/ *n.* [U] a French white wine with a lot of BUBBLES, often drunk on special occasions [**Origin:** 1600–1700 French *Champagne* area of northeastern France]

cham•pi•on¹ /ˈtʃæmpiən/ *n.* **1** [C] a person, team etc. that has won a competition, especially in sports: *the national junior champion in ice skating* | *the* ***reigning*** *national soccer* ***champions*** (=the champions right now) ▸see THESAURUS box at **win¹** **2 a champion of sth** someone who publicly fights for and defends an aim or principle, such as the rights of a group of people: *Douglas has always been a champion of free speech.* [**Origin:** 1100–1200 Old French, Medieval Latin *campio*]

champion² *v.* [T] to publicly fight for and defend an aim or principle, such as the rights of a group of people: *Purcell championed social programs for the elderly.*

cham•pi•on•ship /ˈtʃæmpiənˌʃɪp/ W3 *n.* **1** [C] also **championships** [plural] a competition or series of competitions to find which player, team etc. is the best in a particular sport: *the sixth game of the chess championship* ▸see THESAURUS box at **competition** **2** [C] the position or period of being a champion: *Can she* ***win the championship*** *again this year?* **3** [U]+**of** the act of championing something or someone

Cham•plain /ʃæmˈpleɪn/, **Lake** a large lake in the northeastern U.S., on the border between the states of New York and Vermont and with its most northern part in Canada

Champlain, Sam•u•el de /ˈsæmuəl də/ (1567–1635) a French EXPLORER who discovered many places in Canada and started the city of Quebec

Cham•pol•lion /ʃɑmpɔlˈyoʊn/, **Jean** /ʒɑn/ (1790–1832) a French ARCHAEOLOGIST who discovered how to read ancient Egyptian writing

chance¹ /tʃæns/ S1 W1 *n.*

1 OPPORTUNITY [C] a time or situation that you can use to do something that you want to do SYN **opportunity**: *Here was the chance she'd been waiting for.* | **a chance (for sb) to do sth** *I took the class because it was a chance to learn more about computers.* | *She never even* ***gave me a chance*** *to say goodbye.* | *I'd like to* ***take this chance*** (=use this opportunity) *to say how much I have appreciated your help over the years.* | **have/get a chance to do sth** *I'm sorry I haven't had a chance to look at your essay yet.* | *Rachel* ***jumped at the chance*** (=eagerly and quickly used an opportunity) *to go to France for a year.* | *This is* ***your last chance*** *to prove you can be trusted.* | *Hey John,* ***now's your chance*** *to finally ask her for a date.* | ***Given half a chance*** (=if given even a small opportunity), *Rick could do really well.* | *Getting that job was definitely* ***the chance of a lifetime*** (=an opportunity you are not likely to get more than once). | **a second/another chance** (=another chance, in which you hope to do better after failing the first time)

2 POSSIBILITY [C,U] how possible or likely it is that something will happen or be true, especially something that you want: +**the chances of (doing) sth** *The chances of success are good.* | ***There's a chance that*** *she left her keys in the office.* | **sb's chances (of doing) sth** *What do you think our chances of getting that contract are?* | ***Chances are*** (=it is likely), *someone you know has been robbed.* | **a good/slight/fair chance** *There's a slight chance of showers this weekend.* | **some/no/little chance** *There seems to be little chance of a peaceful end to the conflict.* | *With the operation, he'll have* ***a fifty-fifty chance*** (=an equal chance of something happening or not happening) *of walking again.* | **a one in a million chance/a million to one chance** (=an extremely small chance)

3 stand/have a chance (of doing sth) if someone or something stands or has a chance of doing something, it is possible that they will succeed: *I think we* ***stand a*** *pretty* ***good chance*** (=are very likely to succeed) *of winning the World Series.* | *Polls show that Barton still* ***has a fighting chance*** (=has a small possibility of success) *in the election.*

4 take a chance also **take (my/your/any etc.) chances** to do something that involves risk: *She knew she was taking a chance, but she decided to buy the house anyway.* | +**on/with** *The record company decided to take a chance on the band.* | *Olympic officials were* ***taking no chances of*** *another terrorist attack.*

5 LUCK [U] the way some things happen without being planned or caused by people: *It was chance that brought us together.* | *He supervises every detail of the business and* ***leaves nothing to chance.*** | *A tourist had filmed the robbery* ***by chance*** (=without being planned or intended). | ***As chance would have it*** (=happening in a way that was not expected or intended), *we both got jobs at the same hospital.* | **pure/sheer/blind chance** *Solving the crime was pure chance.*

6 by any chance SPOKEN used to ask politely whether something is true: *Would you, by any chance, know where a pay phone is?*

7 fat chance! also **not a chance!** SPOKEN used to emphasize that you are sure something could never happen: *"Everybody will chip in a couple of dollars." "Fat chance!"*

8 on the off chance if you do something on the off chance, you do it hoping for a particular result, although you know it is not likely: *I keep all of my old clothes on the off chance that they might come back into fashion.*

9 any chance of...? SPOKEN used to ask whether you can have something or whether something is possible: *"Any chance of you two getting back together?" "I don't think so."*

[**Origin:** 1200–1300 Old French, Vulgar Latin *cadentia* **fall**, from Latin *cadere* **to fall**] → see also **a game of chance** at GAME¹ (1), **an outside chance** at OUTSIDE³ (5)

chance² *v.* [T] **1** INFORMAL to do something that you know involves a risk: *We could save money by hitchhiking, but why* ***chance it?*** **2** LITERARY to happen in an unexpected and unplanned way: **chance to do sth** *She ended up marrying a man who chanced to come by looking for a room.*

chance on/upon sb/sth *phr. v.* FORMAL to find something or meet someone when you are not expecting to: *We chanced on a beautiful little hotel just as it was getting dark.*

chance³ *adj.* [only before noun] not planned SYN **accidental**: **a chance meeting/encounter** (=an occasion when you meet someone by accident) | ***A chance remark*** *by one of his colleagues got him thinking.*

chan•cel /ˈtʃænsəl/ *n.* [C] the part of a church where the priests and the CHOIR (=singers) sit

chan•cel•ler•y /ˈtʃænsələri/ *n. plural* **chancelleries** [C] POLITICS **1** the building in which a chancellor has his office **2** the officials who work in a chancellor's office **3** the offices of an official representative of a foreign country SYN **chancery**

chan•cel•lor, Chancellor /ˈtʃænsələ/ *n.* [C] **1** the head of some universities: *the Chancellor of Indiana University* **2** POLITICS the head of the government in some countries: *the German Chancellor* [**Origin:** 1000–1100 Old French *chancelier*, from Late Latin *cancellarius* **doorkeeper, secretary**]

chan•cer•y /ˈtʃænsəri/ *n.* [singular] **1** LAW the part of the legal system that deals with situations where the existing laws may not provide a fair judgment: *the Delaware Court of Chancery* **2** POLITICS a government office that collects and stores official papers **3** POLITICS the offices of an official representative of a foreign country [SYN] **chancellery**

chanc·y /ˈtʃænsi/ *adj. comparative* **chancier**, *superlative* **chanciest** INFORMAL uncertain or involving a lot of risk: *Making financial forecasts can be a very chancy business.* —**chanciness** *n.* [U]

chan·de·lier /ˌʃændəˈlɪr/ *n.* [C] a large round structure that holds lights or CANDLEs, hangs from the ceiling, and is decorated with small pieces of glass

chan·dler /ˈtʃændlɚ/ *n.* [C] OLD USE someone who makes or sells CANDLES

Chan·dler, Ray·mond /ˈtʃændlɚ/, /ˈreɪmənd/ (1888–1959) an American writer of DETECTIVE stories whose best-known character is the PRIVATE DETECTIVE Philip Marlowe

Raymond Chandler

Chang, the /tʃɑŋ/ also **the Chang Jiang** /ˌtʃɑŋ ˈdʒyɑŋ/ the longest river in China, that flows eastward from Tibet to the China Sea. It is also called the Yangtze.

change¹ /tʃeɪndʒ/ [S1] [W1] *v.*

1 BECOME DIFFERENT [I,T] to become different: *Susan has changed a lot since I last saw her.* | *Things in Minnesota don't change very quickly.* | **change (from sth) to sth** *The water on the bridge had changed to ice during the night.* | **change into sth** *The hissing sound gradually changed into a low hum.* | *You can't expect society to* ***change overnight*** (=change very quickly). | **change for the better/worse** (=become better or worse) *His luck seemed to have changed for the worse.* | **change dramatically/drastically/radically** *Attitudes toward sex have changed dramatically.* | **changing conditions/circumstances/attitudes etc.** *Learning new skills helps workers adapt to changing economic conditions.*

2 MAKE SB/STH DIFFERENT [T] to make someone or something become different [SYN] **alter**: *How does the President plan to change the tax system?* | *Going to college really changed my life.* | **change sb/sth into sth** *A witch had changed him into a mouse.* | **change sth (from sth) to sth** *She changed the spelling of her name from Nancy to Nancie.* | *Why do leaves* ***change color*** *in the fall?* | **change sb/sth back** *At this point, it would be impossible to change the system back.*

THESAURUS

alter to change something, or to make something change: *Pressing the strings like this alters the sound.*
adapt/adjust/modify to change something slightly: *The group is pressuring Congress to modify the plan.* | *His doctor has adjusted the dosage of his medication.*
reform to change a system or organization, so that problems in it are no longer there: *plans to reform the health care system*
reorganize/restructure to change the way a system or organization is organized, so that it works better: *The company has reorganized the marketing department.*
revise to change something because of new information or ideas: *The rules of the game are constantly being revised.*
transform to change something completely: *They've completely transformed the downtown area.*
revolutionize to completely change the way people do something or think about something: *The discovery of penicillin revolutionized medicine.*
twist/distort/misrepresent to deliberately change facts, information, someone's words etc. in a way that is not completely true or correct: *He accused reporters of twisting his words.*

3 FROM ONE THING TO ANOTHER [I,T] to stop having or doing one thing and start having or doing something else instead [SYN] **switch**: **change (from sth) to sth** *The company has recently changed to a more powerful computer system.* | *Let's* ***change the subject*** (=talk about something else) *before someone gets upset.* | **change your name/phone number/address etc.** *Many women choose not to change their name when they marry.* | **change jobs/cars/boyfriends etc.** *An unhappy worker can change jobs.* | *It's quite rare for politicians to* ***change sides.*** | **change course/direction** (=start to do something very different from what you were doing before) *a willingness to experiment and change direction*

4 change your mind to change your decision, plan, or opinion about something: **+about/on** *The seller changed her mind about selling the house.*

5 CLOTHES a) [I,T] to take off your clothes and put on different ones: *I'm just going upstairs to change.* | *Why don't you go change that shirt?* | **change into sth/change out of sth** *We changed into our swimsuits and ran for the pool.* | *She has to* ***get changed*** (=put on different clothes) *before we go out.* **b)** [T] to put a clean DIAPER on a baby: *It's your turn to* ***change the baby.***

6 REPLACE STH [T] to put something new in place of something old, damaged, or broken: *When I lost my keys, we had to change all the locks.* | *Do you know how to change a tire?*

7 change the sheets to take SHEETS off a bed and put clean ones on it

8 EXCHANGE MONEY [T] **a)** to exchange a larger unit of money for smaller units that add up to the same value: *Can you change a $10 bill?* **b)** to exchange money from one country for money from another: **change sth into/for sth** *I want to change my dollars into pesos, please.*

9 AIRPLANES/TRAINS/BUSES [I,T] to get out of one airplane, train, or bus and into another one in order to continue your trip: **change planes/trains/buses** *We had to change trains twice.* | **+at/in** *All passengers bound for Boston should change at New Haven.*

10 change places (with sb) a) to give someone your place and take their place: *He immediately changed places so he could sit next to me.* **b)** to take someone else's social position or situation in life instead of yours: *Our lives are hard, but theirs are miserable. I would never change places.*

11 change hands to become someone else's property: *The theater recently changed hands.*

12 change your tune to start expressing a different attitude and reacting in a different way, after something has happened: *Newsome was originally against the plan, but later changed his tune.*

13 WIND [I] if the wind changes, it starts to blow in a different direction

14 GEARS [I,T] to put a bicycle or the engine of a vehicle into a higher or lower GEAR in order to go faster or slower [SYN] **shift**: *I* ***changed gear*** *as I approached the corner.* | **change into first/second etc. gear.** *You'll have to change into third gear to get up this hill.*

15 change your spots to change your character completely

[**Origin:** 1100–1200 Old French *changier*, from Latin *cambiare* **to exchange**]

change sth ↔ **around** *phr. v.* to move things into different positions: *I didn't really rewrite it – I just changed a few paragraphs around.*

change over *phr. v.* to stop doing or using one thing and start doing or using something different: **+to** *We hope to change over to the new software by next month.*

change² [S1] [W1] *n.*

1 THINGS BECOMING DIFFERENT [C] when someone or something becomes different: **+in** *a change in the weather* | *Management is planning to* ***make*** *several* ***changes.*** | **+to** *He hates making changes to his routine.* | *His artistic style has* ***undergone*** *many* ***changes.*** | **+of** *a change of attitude* | **a major/significant/dramatic etc. change** *Don't make any major changes just yet.* | *There has been* ***no change*** *in*

interest rates. | **a change for the better/worse** *There has been a change for the better in the patient's condition.* | *She had* ***a change of heart*** (=a change in attitude or decision), *and decided to stay.*
2 PROCESS [U] the process of becoming different: *Many people find it hard to accept change.* | *The 20th century was a time of change in every continent.* | **social/political/economic etc. change** *a general resistance to social change*
3 FROM ONE THING TO ANOTHER [C] a new or different thing or person used instead of something or someone else: *The car needs an oil change.* | **change (from sth) to sth** *The change from communism to democracy was very difficult.* | **+of** *There's been a change of plans – we can't leave until tomorrow.* | *Management has threatened to* ***make*** *sweeping* ***changes.*** | *I've sent out postcards telling everyone of our* ***change of address.***
4 PLEASANT NEW SITUATION [C usually singular] a situation or experience that is different from what happened before, and is usually interesting or enjoyable: **+from** *The rain was a welcome change from all the hot, dry weather.* | *Why don't you try being helpful* ***for a change?*** | *Painting with oils was* ***a change of pace*** *for me.* | ***A change of scenery*** (=a stay in a different place that is pleasant) *was just what I needed.*
5 MONEY [U] **a)** the money that you get back when you pay for something with more money than it costs: *Here is your change, sir.* | *I was* ***making change*** (=calculating the right amount of money that a customer should get back) *for a customer when the phone rang.* | *He told the waitress to* ***keep the change.*** **b)** money in the form of coins: *The clerk handed him $3* ***in change.*** | *I put my* ***spare change*** (=coins that I do not need) *in a charity bucket.* | *Matt emptied the* ***loose change*** (=coins, usually the coins in your pocket when there are not very many of them) *from his pockets.* **c)** coins or small bills that you give in exchange for the same amount of money in a larger unit: *Excuse me, do you have* ***change for $1?*** | *Can you* ***make change*** *for a $20 bill?* → see also CHUMP CHANGE, SMALL CHANGE → see Usage Note at MONEY ►see THESAURUS box at **money**
6 a change of clothes/underwear etc. an additional set of clothes that you have with you, for example when you are traveling: *You'd better bring a change of clothes since we're staying overnight.*
7 AIRPLANE/TRAIN/BUS [C] a situation in which you get off one airplane, train, or bus and get on another one in order to continue your trip

change·a·ble /ˈtʃeɪndʒəbəl/ *adj.* likely to change, or changing often: *We have very changeable weather here, especially in the winter.* —**changeableness** *n.* [U] —**changeably** *adv.* —**changeability** /ˌtʃeɪndʒəˈbɪləti/ *n.* [U]

changed /tʃeɪndʒd/ *adj.* **1 a changed man/woman** someone who has become very different from what they were before, as a result of a very important experience: *Since she stopped drinking, she's a changed woman.* **2 changed circumstances** a change in someone's financial situation

change·less /ˈtʃeɪndʒlɪs/ *adj.* LITERARY never seeming to change: *the changeless desert landscape* —**changelessly** *adv.*

change·ling /ˈtʃeɪndʒlɪŋ/ *n.* [C] LITERARY a baby that is said to have been secretly exchanged for another baby by fairies (FAIRY)

ˌchange of ˈlife *n.* **the change of life** MENOPAUSE

change·o·ver /ˈtʃeɪnˌdʒoʊvɚ/ *n.* [C] a change from one activity, system, or way of working to another: *the changeover from analog to digital television*

ˈchange purse *n.* [C] a small bag in which to keep coins

ˈchanging room *n.* [C] a room where people change their clothes when they play sports, go swimming, try on new clothes etc. SYN **locker room**

ˈchanging ˌtable *n.* [C] a special piece of furniture that you put a baby on while you take off its DIAPER and put a clean one on

chan·nel¹ /ˈtʃænl/ Ac S2 W2 *n.*
1 TELEVISION [C] a particular television station and all the programs broadcast by it: *What channel is the movie on?* | *the Channel 5 news* | **change/switch/flip channels** *A lot of people switch channels during the commercials.*
2 METHOD [C usually plural] a system or method that is used to send or obtain information, goods, permission etc.: *We need better distribution channels for our products.* | *New* ***channels of communication*** *have opened up between the two governments.*
3 OCEAN/RIVER [C] **a)** EARTH SCIENCE water that connects two larger areas of water: *the English Channel* **b)** the deepest part of a river, ocean etc., especially one that is deep enough to allow ships to sail in: *a shipping channel*
4 RADIO [C] PHYSICS a particular range of SOUND WAVES which can be used to send and receive radio messages
5 FOR WATER [C] a long passage dug into the ground that water or other liquids can flow along: *a channel for the water supply*
6 WAY TO EXPRESS STH [C] a way of expressing your thoughts, feelings, or physical energy SYN **outlet**: **+for** *Art provides a channel for children's creativity.*
7 IN A SURFACE [C] a deep line cut into a surface or a deep space between two edges SYN **groove**: *The sliding doors fit into these plastic channels.*
[**Origin:** 1300–1400 Old French *chanel*, from Latin *canalis* **pipe, channel**]

channel² Ac *v.* [T] **1** to control and direct energy, feelings, thoughts etc. toward a particular purpose SYN **direct**: **channel sth into sth** *I channeled all my anger into running.* **2** to control or direct people or things to a particular place, job, situation etc. using a route or system SYN **direct**: **channel sb/sth into sth** *Women were more likely to be channeled into the lower-paying jobs.* | **channel sth to sb/sth** *Profits are channeled to conservation groups.* | **channel sth through sth** *The famine relief money was channeled through the U.N.* **3** to send something such as water, air, light etc. through a passage: **channel sth to/into/through etc. sth** *These pipes will channel water to the settlement.* **4** to allow a spirit to come into your body and speak through you, or to tell people a message that you have received in this way **5** to cut a deep line or space into something

ˈchannel ˌhopping *n.* [U] CHANNEL SURFING

chan·nel·ing /ˈtʃænl-ɪŋ/ *n.* [U] a practice based on the belief that people can communicate with dead people by allowing a dead person's spirit to come into their body and speak through them —**channeler** *n.* [C]

ˈchannel ˌsurfing *n.* [U] the activity of continuously changing from one television program to another, watching only a very small amount of each program —**channel-surf** *v.* [I]

chant¹ /tʃænt/ *v.* [I,T] **1** to repeat a word or phrase again and again: *Supporters clapped and chanted his name.* **2** to sing or say a religious song or prayer in a way that involves using only one note or TONE: *A priest was chanting a prayer in Latin.*

chant² *n.* [C] **1** words or phrases that are repeated again and again: *Demonstrators blew whistles and screamed protest chants.* **2** a religious song or prayer with a regularly repeated tune, in which many words are sung or said using one note or TONE —**chanter** *n.* [C] → see also GREGORIAN CHANT

chan·tey, chanty /ˈʃænti, ˈtʃæn-/ *n. plural* **chanteys, chanties** [C] a song sung by SAILORS as they did their work in past times

chan·try /ˈtʃæntri/ also **ˈchantry ˌchapel** *n. plural* **chantries** [C] a small church or part of a church that is paid for by someone so that priests can pray for them there after they die

Cha·nu·kah /ˈhɑnəkə/ *n.* [U] another spelling of HANUKKAH

cha·os /ˈkeɪɑs/ *n.* [U] **1** a situation in which everything is happening in a confused way and nothing is organized or arranged in order: **complete/utter/absolute etc. chaos** *It's been total chaos since Helen left* *on vacation.* | *The country's economy is* ***in chaos*** (=in a state of chaos). **2** the state of the universe before there was any order [**Origin:** 1400–1500 Latin, Greek]

cha·ot·ic /keɪˈɑtɪk/ *adj.* a situation that is chaotic is very disorganized and confusing: *chaotic social and economic conditions*

chap¹ /tʃæp/ *n.* [C] BRITISH a man, especially a man you know and like → see also CHAPS

C

chap² *v.* **chapped, chapping** [I,T] if wind or cold chap your lips or hands or if they chap, they become dry, cracked, and sore

chap., Chap. *n.* a written abbreviation of CHAPTER

chap·ar·ral /ˌʃæpəˈræl/ *n.* [U] EARTH SCIENCE **1** land on which small trees and bushes grow close together in places that are hot and dry during the summer, especially land in the southwest of the U.S. **2** the small bushes and trees that grow on this type of land

chap·book /ˈtʃæpbʊk/ *n.* [C] a small printed book, usually consisting of writings about literature, poetry, or religion

chap·el /ˈtʃæpəl/ *n.* [C] a small church or a room in a hospital, prison, church etc. in which Christians pray and have religious services: *a wedding chapel* [**Origin:** 1100–1200 Old French *chapele*, from Medieval Latin *cappella*, from Late Latin *cappa* **cloak**; because the cloak of St. Martin of Tours was kept in such a building]

chap·er·on¹, chaperone /ˈʃæpəˌroʊn/ *n.* [C] **1** someone, usually a parent or teacher, who is responsible for young people on social occasions: *Thanks to the parent and teacher chaperons who accompanied the students for a week in Europe.* **2** LITERARY an older woman in past times who went out with a young unmarried woman on social occasions and was responsible for her behavior

chaperon², chaperone *v.* [T] to go somewhere with someone as their chaperon

chap·lain /ˈtʃæplɪn/ *n.* [C] a priest or minister who is responsible for the religious needs of a part of the army, a hospital etc.: *a prison chaplain* ►see THESAURUS box at **priest**

chap·lain·cy /ˈtʃæplənsi/ *n. plural* **chaplaincies** [C] the position of a chaplain, or the place where a chaplain works

chap·let /ˈtʃæplɪt/ *n.* [C] LITERARY a band of flowers worn on the head

Chap·lin /ˈtʃæplɪn/, **Char·lie** /ˈtʃɑrli/ (1889–1977) a British movie actor and DIRECTOR who worked mainly in the U.S. in humorous SILENT MOVIES (=movies made with no sound) during the 1920s

chapped /tʃæpt/ *adj.* chapped lips or hands are sore, dry, and cracked, especially as a result of cold weather or wind

chaps /tʃæps/ *n.* [plural] leather covers that fit over the sides of your pants, that protect your legs when you ride a horse through bushes, by fences etc. [**Origin:** 1800–1900 Mexican Spanish *chappareras*, from Spanish *chaparro*, type of small oak tree]

ˈChap Stick *n.* [U] TRADEMARK a stick of a WAX-like substance that you put on your lips to make them feel softer when they are chapped and to prevent them from becoming more chapped

chap·ter /ˈtʃæptɚ/ Ac S2 W1 *n.* [C] **1** one of the parts into which a book is divided: *Read Chapter 11 as your homework.* | *This chapter discusses power, and how people use it.* ►see THESAURUS box at **part¹** **2** a particular period or event in someone's life or in history: **+in** *an interesting chapter in American history* | **+of** *a new chapter of peace and cooperation* **3** the local members of a large organization such as a club: *the local chapter of the American Legion* **4** all the priests belonging to a particular church or organization, or a meeting of these priests **5 give/quote sb chapter and verse** to give someone exact and full details about something [**Origin:** 1100–1200 Old French *chapitre*, from Late Latin *capitulum*, from Latin *caput* **head**]

chap·ter·house /ˈtʃæptɚˌhaʊs/ *n.* [C] a building where the priests belonging to a particular church or organization meet

char /tʃɑr/ *v.* **charred, charring** [I,T] to burn something so that its outside becomes black: *The fire had charred most of the inside of the house.* → see also CHARRED

char·ac·ter /ˈkærɪktɚ/ S2 W1 *n.*

1 ALL SB'S QUALITIES [C,U] the particular combination of qualities that makes someone a particular kind of person: *interesting aspects of Ronald's character* | *That kind of sloppiness is completely* ***out of character*** *for Kris* (=not typical of how Kris usually behaves). | *It's perfectly* ***in character*** (=typical) *for Frederick to be rude.* | *The Civil War helped shape* ***the American national character*** (=qualities that are thought to be typical of people from a particular country). | *Kindness is one of Darla's most attractive* ***character traits.*** | **a character flaw/defect** (=an unpleasant part of someone's character) → see CHARACTERISTIC¹

2 QUALITIES OF STH [C,U] the particular combination of features and qualities that makes a thing or place different from all others: *Each neighborhood has its own unique character.* | **+of** *The character of the school has changed.* | *The discussions were political* ***in character.***

3 INTERESTING QUALITY [U] a quality that makes someone or something special and interesting: *an old house with lots of character* | *The town* ***lacks character*** (=is not interesting).

4 PERSON [C] **a)** ENG. LANG. ARTS a person in a book, play, movie etc.: *In the show, she plays the character Susan.* | *cartoon characters* | *I found it hard to like* ***the main character.*** **b) a character** an interesting and unusual person: *Max is quite a character!* **c)** a person of a particular kind SYN **type**: *He was a repulsive character.*

5 GOOD QUALITIES [U] a combination of qualities such as courage, loyalty, and honesty that are admired and regarded as valuable: *What you did showed real character.* | *a man of exceptional character* | *The club promotes* ***character building*** (=activity aimed at developing these qualities) *activities for young boys.* | *It* ***takes character*** *to admit you are wrong.* | *We admired her* ***strength of character.***

6 REPUTATION [U] the opinion that people have about whether you are a good person and can be trusted: *Release of the story will certainly damage his character.* | *The campaign was accused of* ***character assassination*** (=an unfair attack on someone's character) *because of the negative ads.* → see also CHARACTER REFERENCE, CHARACTER WITNESS

7 LETTER/SIGN [C] a letter, mark, or sign used in writing, printing, or on a computer: *the Chinese character for horse* | *The password should be at least six characters long.*

8 in character ENG. LANG. ARTS if actors do something in character, they do it in the way that the characters they are playing would do it, and not the way they would normally do it: *Do you* ***stay in character*** *all day on the set?*

[**Origin:** 1300–1400 Old French *caractere*, from Latin *character* **mark, particular quality**]

ˈcharacter ˌactor *n.* [C] an actor who typically plays unusual characters

char·ac·ter·is·tic¹ /ˌkærɪktəˈrɪstɪk/ *n.* [C usually plural] a special quality or feature of something or someone that is typical of them and easy to recognize: **+of** *the characteristics of a good manager* | *Can you describe the robber's* ***physical characteristics?***

THESAURUS

feature an important, interesting, or typical part of something: *An important feature of Van Gogh's paintings is their bright color.*

quality something that someone has as part of their character, especially good things: *A sense of humor was the quality most women wanted in their mates.*

property a natural quality of something: *an herb with healing properties*

attribute a good or useful quality: *What attributes should a good manager possess?*
aspect one part of a situation, activity etc. that has many parts: *She enjoys most aspects of her job.*
good points/bad points good qualities or features, or bad ones: *The seller will obviously emphasize the car's good points.*

characteristic² *adj.* very typical of a particular thing or of someone's character: *Naomi's characteristic optimism* | +**of** *The vase is characteristic of 16th century Chinese art.* | **a distinguishing/defining characteristic** (=one that makes it different from others of the same type) —**characteristically** /-kli/ *adv.*

char·ac·ter·i·za·tion /ˌkærɪktərəˈzeɪʃən/ *n.* **1** [U] the way in which the qualities of a real person or thing are described: **characterization of sb/sth as sth** *The characterization of him as weak is unfair.* **2** [C,U] ENG. LANG. ARTS the way in which a writer makes a person in a book, movie, or play seem like a real person: *The characterization is believable, but not great.*

char·ac·ter·ize /ˈkærɪktəˌraɪz/ W3 *v.* [T] **1** to describe the character of someone or something in a particular way: **characterize sb as sth** *Greenspan characterized the economy as "struggling."* ►see THESAURUS box at call¹ **2** to be typical of a person, place, or thing: *He has the confidence that characterizes successful businessmen.*

char·ac·ter·less /ˈkærɪktɚlɪs/ *adj.* not having any special or interesting qualities: *a characterless hotel*

ˈcharacter ˌreference *n.* [C] a REFERENCE

ˈcharacter ˌwitness *n.* [C] someone who says at a TRIAL that someone's character qualities and morals are good

cha·rade /ʃəˈreɪd/ *n.* **1** [C] a situation in which people pretend that something is true or serious and behave as if it were true or serious, when everyone knows it is not: *I suspect his "confession" was all a charade.* **2 charades** [U] a game in which one person uses only actions to show the meaning of a word or phrase, and other people have to guess what it is [**Origin:** 1700–1800 French, Provençal *charrado* **conversation**]

char·broil /ˈtʃɑrbrɔɪl/ *v.* [T] to cook food over a very hot charcoal fire —**charbroiled** *adj.*

char·coal /ˈtʃɑrkoʊl/ *n.* **1** [U] a black substance made of burned wood, used as FUEL: *Add charcoal to the grill as needed.* **2** [C,U] a black substance made of burned wood, or sticks of this substance, used for drawing: *colored charcoals* | *charcoal drawings*

chard /tʃɑrd/ *n.* [U] a vegetable with large leaves

charge¹ /tʃɑrdʒ/ S2 W1 *n.*
1 PRICE [C,U] the amount of money you have to pay for goods or services: *Interest charges on the loan totaled over $12,000.* | +**for** *There is a $15 charge for each visit to the doctor.* | *We deliver **free of charge*** (=at no cost). | *Each meal comes with a dessert **at no extra charge*** (=without having to pay more money). ►see THESAURUS box at cost¹
2 CONTROL a) in charge (of sth) controlling or responsible for a group of people or an activity: *Watterson is in charge of the business section of the paper.* | *The new position **puts** him **in charge*** (=gives him the responsibility) *of the whole department.* **b) take charge (of sth)** to take control of a situation, organization, or group of people: *Anderson took charge of the firm in August.*
3 CRIME [C] LAW an official statement made by the police saying that someone may be guilty of a crime: *Libel is a difficult charge to prove.* | +**against** *Harris's office was informed of the charges against him.* | +**of** *a charge of fraud* | **murder/drug/burglary etc. charges** *Police arrested him on three murder charges.* | *He's **facing charges*** (=going through the legal process that starts when the police say you may be guilty of a crime) *for the bombing.* | *Cathcart agreed to **drop charges*** (=say that someone will not have to go through the legal process) *against the restaurant.* | **press/bring charges (against sb/sth)** (=make official charges) *The store agreed not to press charges.* ►see THESAURUS box at accusation
4 BLAME [C] a written or spoken statement blaming someone for doing something bad or illegal SYN allegation: +**of** *charges of racism against the company* | **deny/counter charges** *Wallace denied charges that he lied to investigators.* | *The speech **laid** him **open to charges of*** (=made him likely to be blamed for) *political bias.*
5 get a charge out of sth SPOKEN to be excited by something and enjoy it very much: *I really get a charge out of watching the kids learn.*
6 be in/under sb's charge if someone or something is in your charge, you are responsible for taking care of them
7 BATTERY [C,U] PHYSICS electricity that is put into a piece of electrical equipment such as a BATTERY: *a positive electrical charge*
8 ELECTRICITY [U] PHYSICS positive or negative electrical force
9 EFFORT [C usually singular] a strong effort to do something: *Seymour **led the charge** against rent control for the real-estate industry.*
10 ATTACK [C] an attack in which soldiers, wild animals etc. move forward quickly
11 EXPLOSIVE [C] an explosive put into a gun or weapon
12 BASKETBALL [C] an act of running into an opposing player while you have the ball, which results in a FOUL and the other team being given the ball
13 SB YOU MUST TAKE CARE OF [C] FORMAL someone that you are responsible for taking care of: *Jill bought ice cream for her three young charges.*
14 STRENGTH OF FEELINGS [C] the power of strong feelings: *Cases of abuse have a strong emotional charge.*
15 AN ORDER TO DO STH [C] FORMAL an order to do something
16 ELECTRICITY IN MATTER [U] PHYSICS the electrical energy contained in all MATTER (=the material that everything in the universe is made of), which exists in a positive and negative form

charge² S1 W1 *v.*
1 MONEY a) [I,T] to have a fixed price for something you are selling: *The hotel charges $125 a night.* | **charge (sb) for sth** *They charged me $2 for this candy bar.* **b)** [T] to pay for something with a CREDIT CARD: *I charged the flights on American Express.* | *I didn't have the money, I had to **charge it**.* **c) charge sth to sb's account/room** to record the cost of something on someone's account, so that they can pay for it later: *Charge the dinner to Room 455, please.*
2 WITH A CRIME [T] LAW to state officially that someone may be guilty of a crime: **be charged with sth** *Her husband was charged with her murder.* ►see THESAURUS box at accuse
3 MOVE TO ATTACK [I,T] to deliberately rush quickly toward someone or something in order to attack them: *The mother bear turned and charged us.* | +**at/toward/into** *Police charged into the house.*
4 RUSH [I always + adv./prep.] to deliberately run or walk somewhere quickly: +**around/through/out etc.** *I could hear Willie and his friends charging down the stairs.* ►see THESAURUS box at rush¹
5 BLAME SB [T] FORMAL to say publicly that you think someone has done something wrong: **charge that** *Hundreds have charged that police used excessive force during the demonstration.*
6 ELECTRICITY also **charge up** [I,T] if a BATTERY charges or if you charge it, it takes in and stores electricity: *Did you charge the camcorder's batteries?* | *Leave it to charge overnight.*
7 ORDER SB [T] FORMAL to order someone to do something or make them responsible for it: **be charged with doing sth** *His staff is charged with organizing all the training programs.*
8 GUN [T] OLD USE to load a gun
[**Origin:** 1100–1200 Old French *chargier*, from Late Latin *carricare*, from Latin *carrus*]

charge·a·ble /ˈtʃɑrdʒəbəl/ *adj.* **1** chargeable costs must be paid: *chargeable expenses* **2** a chargeable offense is serious enough for the police to officially state that you may be guilty of it

'charge ac,count *n.* [C] an account you have at a store that allows you to take goods away with you now and pay for them later

'charge card *n.* [C] a plastic card that you can use to buy goods in a particular store and pay for them later

C

charged /tʃɑrdʒd/ *adj.* [usually before noun] a charged situation or subject makes people feel very angry, anxious, or excited, and is likely to cause arguments or violence: *the **charged atmosphere** surrounding the elections* | *a **highly charged** debate*

char·gé d'af·faires /ˌʃɑrʒeɪ dæ'fɛr/ *n.* [C] an official who represents a particular government during the absence of an AMBASSADOR or in a country where there is no ambassador

charg·er /'tʃɑrdʒɚ/ *n.* [C] **1** a piece of equipment used to put electricity into a BATTERY **2** LITERARY a horse that a soldier or KNIGHT rides in battle **3** a large dish that is not deep

'charge sheet *n.* [C] an official record kept in a police station of the crimes that the police say someone is guilty of

char·i·ot /'tʃæriət/ *n.* [C] a vehicle with two wheels, pulled by a horse, used in ancient times in battles and races

char·i·o·teer /ˌtʃæriə'tɪr/ *n.* [C] the driver of a chariot

cha·ris·ma /kə'rɪzmə/ *n.* [U] the natural ability to attract and interest other people and make them admire you: *She lacks charisma.* [**Origin:** 1600–1700 Greek **favor, gift**, from *charizesthai* **to favor**]

char·is·mat·ic¹ /ˌkærɪz'mæṭɪk◂/ *adj.* **1** able to attract and influence other people because of a powerful personal quality you have: *Jackson was one of the most charismatic figures in sports.* **2** believing that God gives people special abilities, such as healing people: *a charismatic church*

charismatic² *n.* [C] a Christian who believes that God gives people special abilities, such as curing people who have diseases

char·i·ta·ble /'tʃærəṭəbəl/ *adj.* **1** relating to money or gifts given to people who need help, or organizations that give this kind of help: *a charitable organization* **2** kind, generous, and sympathetic, especially in the way you judge people OPP **uncharitable**: *Let's be charitable – he probably didn't know what he was doing.* —**charitably** *adv.*

char·i·ty /'tʃærəṭi/ *n. plural* **charities** **1** [C] an organization that gives money, goods, or help to people who are poor, sick etc.: *Several charities sent aid to the flood victims.* | **a charity event/dinner/concert etc.** (=an event organized to collect money for a charity) **2** [U] charity organizations in general: *All profits **go to charity**.* | *He's **donated** over $200,000 **to charity**.* **3** [U] money or gifts given to help people who are poor, sick etc.: *Pride makes it difficult for even the poorest peasant to **accept charity** from strangers.* **4** [U] FORMAL kindness or sympathy that you show toward other people: *selfless acts of charity* **5 charity begins at home** a phrase meaning you should help your own family, country etc. before you help other people [**Origin:** 1100–1200 Old French *charité*, from Late Latin *caritas* **Christian love**]

char·la·tan /'ʃɑrlətən/ *n.* [C] DISAPPROVING someone who pretends to have special skills or knowledge: *I think the voters will see him as the charlatan he really is.*

Char·le·magne /'ʃɑrləˌmeɪn/ (742–814) the King of the Franks who gained control of most of western Europe in 800 by uniting its Christian countries, and who had a great influence on European civilizations by establishing a new legal system and encouraging art, literature, and education

Charles /tʃɑrlz/, **Prince** (1948–) the first son of the British Queen, Elizabeth II, who is expected to become the next British king. His official royal title is the Prince of Wales.

Charles' law also **Charles's law** /'tʃɑrlzɪz ˌlɔ/ *n.* PHYSICS a scientific principle that states that the amount of space a gas fills at a fixed pressure increases as the temperature increases and decreases as the temperature decreases

Charles·ton /'tʃɑrlstən/ *n.* **1** the capital city of the U.S. state of West Virginia **2** an old city in the U.S. state of South Carolina **3 the Charleston** a quick dance popular in the 1920s

char·ley horse /'tʃɑrli ˌhɔrs/ *n.* [C usually singular] INFORMAL a pain in a large muscle, especially in your upper leg, caused by the muscle becoming tight SYN **cramp**

Char·lotte /'ʃɑrlət/ the largest city in the U.S. state of North Carolina

Charlotte Am·a·lie /ˌʃɑrlət 'æməli/ the capital city of the U.S. TERRITORY of the Virgin Islands

Char·lotte·town /'ʃɑrlətˌtaʊn/ the capital and largest town of the Canadian PROVINCE of Prince Edward Island

charm¹ /tʃɑrm/ *n.* **1** [C,U] the special quality someone or something has that makes people like them, feel attracted to them, or be easily influenced by them: *Robert's boyish charm* | *He was unable to resist her charms.* | *Vanessa has both charm and talent.* | +**of** *the charm of a small New England town* | *Wayne certainly knows how to **turn on the charm*** (=use charm) *when he wants something out of you.* | *The room had no windows and **all the charm of** a prison cell* (=used to say that something has no charm). **2** [C] a very small object worn on a chain or BRACELET: *a necklace with an angel charm* | *That diamond horseshoe is her **lucky charm*** (=a charm that will bring good luck). **3 work like a charm** to work exactly as you had hoped: *Our new accounting system works like a charm.* **4** [C] a phrase or action believed to have special magic powers SYN **spell** [**Origin:** 1200–1300 Old French *charme*, from Latin *carmen* **song**, from *canere* **to sing**] ►see THESAURUS box at **magic¹**

charm² *v.* [T] **1** to please and interest someone: *It's a story that has charmed youngsters for generations.* **2** to attract someone and make them like you, especially so that you can easily influence them: *We were charmed by the friendliness of the local people.* **3** to gain power over someone or something by using magic

charmed /tʃɑrmd/ *adj.* always lucky, as if protected by magic: **lead/live/have a charmed life** *Cole admits he has led a charmed life.*

charm·er /'tʃɑrmɚ/ *n.* [C] someone who uses their charm to please or influence people → see also SNAKE CHARMER

charm·ing /'tʃɑrmɪŋ/ *adj.* very pleasing or attractive SYN **nice**: *It's a very charming restaurant.* | *Gabby's parents thought Bill was charming.* —**charmingly** *adv.*

'charm school *n.* [C] a school where young women were sometimes sent in the past to learn how to behave politely and gracefully

char·nel house /'tʃɑrnl ˌhaʊs/ *n.* [C] LITERARY a place where the bodies and bones of dead people are stored

charred /tʃɑrd/ *adj.* something that is charred has been burned until it is black: *the charred remains of the building*

chart¹ /tʃɑrt/ Ac S2 *n.* **1** [C] something such as a simple picture, set of figures, GRAPH etc., that shows information in an organized way that is easy to understand: *This chart shows last year's sales figures.* | *medical charts* **2 the charts** [plural] a weekly list of the most popular CDs or songs that have been DOWNLOADed from the Internet: *The song remains number one on the pop charts.* | *It was at the **top of the charts** for 11 weeks.* → see also CHART-TOPPING **3** [C] a detailed map, especially of an area of the ocean or of the stars [**Origin:** 1500–1600 French *charte*, from Latin *charta* **piece of papyrus, document**, from Greek *chartes*] → see also BAR CHART, FLOW CHART, PIE CHART

charts

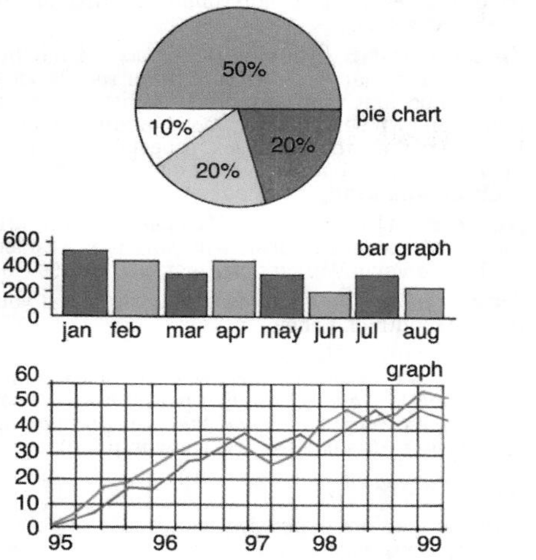

chart² Ac *v.* [T] **1** to record information about a situation or set of events over a period of time, in order to see how it changes or develops: *Lydell has spent years charting the movement of these asteroids.* **2** to make a plan of what should be done to achieve a particular result: *Moore has the task of* ***charting a course*** *of expansion for the company.* **3** to make a map of an area of land, ocean, or stars, or to draw lines on a map to show where you have traveled → see also UNCHARTED

char·ter¹ /ˈtʃɑrt̬ɚ/ *n.* **1** [C] a statement of the principles, duties, and purposes of an organization: *Donating money to political groups goes against the union's charter.* **2** [C,U] the practice of paying money to a company to use their boats, airplanes etc., or the airplane, boat etc. that is used in this way: *The airline is now primarily a charter service.* **3** [C] a signed statement from a government or ruler that allows a town, organization, or university to officially exist and have special rights **4** [C] HISTORY an official document signed in the past by a king or queen showing the special rights and advantages given to a particular town

charter² *v.* [T] **1** to pay a company for the use of their airplane, boat, train etc.: *I chartered a boat to take us to some of the smaller islands.* **2** to say officially that a town, organization, or university exists and has special rights

ˈcharter flight *n.* [C] an airplane trip that is arranged for a particular group or for a particular purpose

ˌcharter ˈmember *n.* [C] an original member of a club or organization

ˈcharter ˌschool *n.* [C] a school to which the state government has given money and special permission to operate, but that is operated by parents, companies etc. rather than by the public school system

char·treuse /ʃɑrˈtruz, -ˈtrus/ *n.* [U] a bright yellow-green color —**chartreuse** *adj.*

ˈchart-ˌtopping *adj.* **a chart-topping record/group/hit etc.** a record, group etc. that has sold the most records in a particular week

char·wom·an /ˈtʃɑrˌwʊmən/ *n. plural* **charwomen** [C] OLD-FASHIONED a woman who cleans people's houses or offices

char·y /ˈtʃɛri, ˈtʃæri/ *adj.* **be chary about/of doing sth** to be unwilling to risk doing something SYN **wary**: *The bank has become very chary about extending credit.*

chase¹ /tʃeɪs/ S3 *v.*
1 FOLLOW [I,T] to quickly follow someone or something in order to catch them: *Stop chasing your sister!* | **chase sb down/up/along etc. sth** *Police chased the suspect along Main Street.* | **+after** *Our cat often chases after birds.* | **chase sb/sth with sth** *She chased me with a stick.* ►see THESAURUS box at **follow**
2 MAKE SB/STH LEAVE [T] to make someone or something leave: **chase sb away/off** *An angry crowd chased reporters away.* | **chase sb/sth out of sth** *The boys chased the dog out of the yard.*
3 MAN/WOMAN [T] to try hard to make someone notice you and pay attention to you, because you want to have a romantic relationship with them: *He's been chasing the same girl for months.* | **+after** *It's embarrassing how she chases after men.*
4 TRY TO GET STH [I,T] to use a lot of time and effort trying to get something such as work or money: **+after** *Do we really need three reporters chasing after the same story?*
5 HURRY [I always + adv./prep.] to rush or hurry somewhere: *I chased around all day looking for a birthday present to give her.*
6 METAL [T] ENG. LANG. ARTS to decorate metal with a special tool: *chased silver*
[**Origin:** (1–5) 1200–1300 Old French *chacier*, from Vulgar Latin *captiare*]

chase sth ↔ **away** *phr. v.* to get rid of something unpleasant, especially a feeling: *She would sing to chase the blues away.*

chase sth ↔ **down** *phr. v.* **1** to run after someone or something and catch them: *Officers chased them down in the subway.* **2** to find something you have been looking for SYN **track down**: *Have you managed to chase down those contracts yet?*

chase² *n.* **1** [C] the act of following someone or something quickly in order to catch them: *a movie with a lot of* ***car chases*** | *He crashed during* ***a high-speed chase*** *with police.* **2** [singular] the activities involved in trying hard to get something you want: **+after/for** *society's chase after youth and beauty* **3 give chase** LITERARY to chase someone or something: *A patrol car spotted the vehicle and gave chase.* → see also **cut to the chase** at CUT¹ (24), PAPER CHASE, WILD GOOSE CHASE

Chase /tʃeɪs/, **Sal·mon** /ˈsæmən/ (1808–1873) a CHIEF JUSTICE on the U.S. Supreme Court

chas·er /ˈtʃeɪsɚ/ *n.* [C] a drink that you drink immediately after an alcoholic drink: *a shot of tequila and a beer chaser*

chasm /ˈkæzəm/ *n.* [C] **1** [usually singular] a big difference between the opinions, experience, ways of life etc. of different groups of people, especially when this means they cannot understand each other: **+between** *the chasm between rich and poor* **2** EARTH SCIENCE a very deep space between two high areas of rock or ice, especially one that is dangerous: *She died after her car plunged into the 40-foot chasm.*

chas·sis /ˈtʃæsi, ˈʃæ-/ *n. plural* **chassis** /-siz/ [C] **1** the frame on which the body, engine, wheels etc. of a vehicle are built **2** the landing equipment of an airplane **3** the frame in a radio, television, computer etc. that all of its electronic parts are attached to

chaste /tʃeɪst/ *adj.* **1** OLD-FASHIONED not having sex with anyone, or not with anyone except the person you are married to → see also CELIBATE: *Girls were expected to remain chaste until marriage.* → see also CHASTITY **2** not showing sexual feelings: *a* ***chaste kiss*** *on the cheek* **3** simple and plain in style, and not showing much of someone's body SYN **modest**: *a chaste white dress* —**chastely** *adv.*

chas·ten /ˈtʃeɪsən/ *v.* [T usually passive] FORMAL to make someone realize that their behavior is wrong or mistaken: *Military leaders, chastened by Vietnam, have learned to be cautious.*

chas·tise /tʃæˈstaɪz, ˈtʃæstaɪz/ *v.* [T] **1** FORMAL to criticize someone severely: *Coleman chastised the board for not taking action sooner.* **2** OLD-FASHIONED to physically punish someone —**chastisement** *n.* [C,U]

chas·ti·ty /ˈtʃæstət̬i/ *n.* [U] the principle or state of not having sex with anyone, or not with anyone except the person you are married to: *a* ***vow of chastity*** (=a promise to not have sex)

ˈchastity belt *n.* [C] a special belt with a lock, used in the past to prevent a woman from having sex

C

chas•u•ble /ˈtʃæzəbəl/ *n.* [C] a type of long loose coat without SLEEVES worn by a priest at a religious service

chat¹ /tʃæt/ *v.* **chatted**, **chatting** [I] **1** to talk in a friendly informal way, especially about things that are not important: *The two women chatted all evening.* | **+about** *We sat up late, chatting about life in the city.* | **+with/to** *Dad really enjoys chatting with people from other countries.* **2** to communicate with several people by computer, using a special Internet program that allows you to exchange written messages very quickly → see also CHAT ROOM

chat² *n.* [C,U] **1** a friendly informal conversation: *Mr. Reynolds wants to* ***have a chat with*** *me about my report.* **2** a conversation that you have with a person or group of people on the Internet, for example in a CHAT ROOM: *on-line chat* → see also CHIT-CHAT

châ•teau /ʃæˈtoʊ/ *n. plural* **châteaux** /-ˈtoʊz/ or **châteaus** [C] a castle or large house in the COUNTRYSIDE in France

chat•e•laine /ˈʃætl̩ˌeɪn/ *n.* [C] FORMAL the female owner, or wife of the owner, of a castle or large house in the COUNTRYSIDE in France

ˈchat line *n.* [C] a telephone service that people call to talk to other people who have called the same service

ˈchat room *n.* [C] a place on the Internet where you can write messages to other people and receive messages back from them immediately, so that you can have a conversation

chat•tel /ˈtʃætl̩/ *n.* [C,U] OLD-FASHIONED, LAW something that belongs to you, that you can move from one place to another

chat•ter¹ /ˈtʃætə˞/ *v.* [I] **1** to talk quickly in a friendly way without stopping, especially about things that are not serious or important: **+about** *What were you two chattering about?* **2** if birds or monkeys chatter, they make short high sounds **3** if your teeth are chattering, you are so cold or frightened that your teeth are knocking together [**Origin:** 1200–1300 from the sound]

chatter² *n.* [U] **1** a friendly informal conversation, especially about something that is not serious or important **2** a series of short high sounds made by some birds or monkeys **3** a hard quick repeated sound made by your teeth knocking together or by machines

chat•ter•box /ˈtʃætə˞ˌbɑks/ *n.* [C] INFORMAL someone, especially a child, who talks too much

chat•ty /ˈtʃæti/ *adj. comparative* **chattier**, *superlative* **chattiest** INFORMAL **1** liking to talk a lot in a friendly way: *a chatty energetic 75-year-old* **2** a chatty piece of writing has a friendly informal style: *a chatty letter*

Chau•cer /ˈtʃɔsə˞/, **Geof•frey** /ˈdʒɛfri/ (?1340–1400) an English writer known for his long poem "The Canterbury Tales," one of the most important works in English literature

chauf•feur¹ /ˈʃoʊfə˞, ʃoʊˈfə˞/ *n.* [C] someone whose job is to drive a car for someone else ►see THESAURUS box at **driver** [**Origin:** 1800–1900 French **person attending to the fire of a steam-driven vehicle, driver**, from *chauffer* **to heat**]

chauffeur² *v.* [T] **1** to drive a car for someone as your job **2** also **chauffeur sb around** to drive someone in your car, especially when you do not want to: *I've spent all day chauffeuring the kids around.*

chau•vin•ism /ˈʃoʊvəˌnɪzəm/ *n.* [U] **1** a belief that your own sex is better, more intelligent, or more important than the other sex, especially if you are a man: *There was strong evidence of male chauvinism in the military.* **2** a strong belief that your country or race is better or more important than any other: *national chauvinism* [**Origin:** 1800–1900 French *chauvinisme*, from Nicolas *Chauvin* early 19th-century French soldier who strongly expressed his love for France and Napoleon]

chau•vin•ist /ˈʃoʊvənɪst/ *n.* [C] **1** someone, especially a man, who believes that their own sex is better, more intelligent, or more important than the other sex **2** someone who strongly believes that their own country or race is better or more important than any other —**chauvinist** *adj.*

chau•vin•is•tic /ˌʃoʊvəˈnɪstɪk◂/ *adj.* **1** having the strong belief that your own country or race is better or more important than any other **2** having the belief that your own sex is better, more intelligent, or more important than the other sex, especially if you are a man: *a chauvinistic attitude toward women* —**chauvinistically** /-kli/ *adv.*

Cha•vez /ˈtʃavɛz, ˈʃa-/, **Ce•sar** /ˈseɪzɑr/ (1927–1993) a Mexican-American who was the president of the United Farm Workers of America from 1966 to 1993

chaw /tʃɔ/ *n.* [C] a large piece of tobacco that you put in your mouth and chew

cheap¹ /tʃip/ S1 W3 *adj.*

1 PRICE not expensive, or lower in price than you expected: *My flight to Reno was really cheap.* | *I bought the cheapest computer I could find.* | *Renting an apartment there is* ***dirt cheap*** (=very low in price).

THESAURUS

inexpensive not expensive and usually of good quality: *inexpensive clothes*
affordable cheap enough for people to be able to buy: *affordable housing*
good/great/excellent value worth at least the price you pay for it: *The stocks are currently good value.*
bargain, **good/great deal** something that is worth more money than you paid for it: *The apartment is a bargain; most units in this area rent for much more.* | *At this price, the car is a good deal.*
reasonable used about a price that is not too high and seems fair: *The restaurant serves good food at reasonable prices.*
competitive used about a price that is not more than that of other similar things: *goods for your home at competitive prices*
→ EXPENSIVE

2 CHARGING LESS charging a low price: *The outlet mall is a lot cheaper than stores downtown.*
3 BAD QUALITY low in price and quality, or not worth much: *cheap jewelry* | *I didn't want a substitute or a* ***cheap imitation****.*
4 NOT GENEROUS DISAPPROVING not liking to spend money: *She's too cheap to take a cab.*
5 CHEAP TO USE not costing much to use or to employ: *Small cars are cheaper to run.* | *The area's* ***cheap labor*** *has attracted many new businesses.*
6 UNKIND DISAPPROVING behaving in a way that is not kind, fair, or respectful to other people, especially people who cannot easily defend themselves: *I've had enough of his* ***cheap remarks*** (=unkind criticism). | *Burke's article was a* ***cheap shot*** (=unkind criticism) *at teenagers.* | *Pretending you would help him was a* ***cheap trick*** (=unkind action).
7 NOT DESERVING RESPECT DISAPPROVING behaving in a dishonest or immoral way that shows you do not respect or care about yourself, so that other people do not respect you: *That dress makes her look cheap.* | *The fight with Jenny left me* ***feeling cheap****.*
8 life is cheap used when talking about situations in which people can easily be killed: *These kids have seen the kind of money they can make selling drugs. What do they care? Life is cheap.*
9 on the cheap spending as little money as possible: *His new book tells how to visit New York on the cheap.*
10 a cheap thrill excitement that does not take much effort to get
[**Origin:** 1500–1600 *good cheap* **at a good price, cheaply**, from *cheap* **trade, price** (11–18 centuries), from Old English *ceap*] —**cheaply** *adv.*: *How do you feed a lot of people cheaply?* —**cheapness** *n.* [U]

cheap² *adv.* at a low price: *Old houses can sometimes be bought cheap and fixed up.* | *Comfort on this cruise ship* ***doesn't come cheap*** (=is expensive). | *Flights to Rio are* ***going cheap*** (=selling for a lower price than usual).

cheap•en /ˈtʃipən/ *v.* [T] **1** to make something or

someone seem to have lower moral standards than they had before: **cheapen yourself by doing sth** *Don't cheapen yourself by reacting to her insults.* **2** to make something seem to have less value or importance or to be less deserving of respect: *Using the national anthem as part of a comedy routine cheapens it.* **3** to become or make something become lower in price or value: *The dollar's rise in value has cheapened imports.*

cheap·o /ˈtʃipoʊ/ also **el cheapo** *adj.* [no comparative] SPOKEN, INFORMAL not of good quality and not costing very much: *I bought this cheapo camera during my vacation in Miami.*

cheap·skate /ˈtʃipskeɪt/ *n.* [C] INFORMAL, DISAPPROVING someone who does not like spending money and does not care if they behave in an unreasonable way to avoid spending it

cheat¹ /tʃit/ S2 *v.* **1** [I] to behave in a dishonest way in order to win or to get an advantage, especially in a competition, game, or test: *In the movie, she lies and cheats to get what she wants.* | **+on** *He got caught cheating on the test.* | **+at** *Mary always cheats at cards.* | *You can't look – **that's cheating**.*

THESAURUS

con to make someone believe your lies, especially in order to get something you want: *The press were conned into believing the attack had been a success.*
swindle to get money from someone by cheating them, especially in a clever way: *The scheme swindled hundreds of people out of their life savings.*
trick to deceive someone in order to get something from them or to make them do something: *He had tricked her into selling the car for less than it was worth.*
defraud FORMAL to get money from a person or organization by deceiving them: *He is facing trial for defrauding his business partner.*

2 [T] to trick or deceive someone who trusts you: *Are you trying to cheat me?* | **cheat sb (out) of sth** *He cheated clients out of thousands of dollars.* **3** [I] to be unfaithful to your husband, wife, or sexual partner by secretly having sex with someone else: **+on** *I would leave her if she ever cheated on me.* **4** [I] to do something that is not the usual or proper way of doing something, in order to do it more easily: *I cheated and bought the birthday cake from a store.* **5 feel cheated** to feel that you have been treated wrongly or unfairly and have not gotten what you deserve: *Many of the workers feel cheated by not getting their bonuses.* **6 cheat death/fate** to manage to avoid death or a very bad situation even though it seemed that you would not be able to [**Origin:** 1500–1600 *cheat* **legal removal of someone's property** (14–17 centuries), from *escheat*]

cheat² *n.* [C] **1** someone who is dishonest and cheats SYN **cheater**: *a liar and a cheat* **2** a set of instructions given to a computer that make it easier for someone who is playing a computer game to win

Chech·nya /ˈtʃɛtʃnyə, -niˌɑ/ a small area in Russia in the Caucasus Mountains, north of Georgia

check¹ /tʃɛk/ S1 W2 *v.*
1 EXAMINE [I,T] to look at something or do something to find out if it is correct, in good condition, or as it should be: *I always check my tires before a long trip.* | *A customs officer checked our passports.* | **check (sth) for sth** *Turn the water on and check for leaks.* | **+that** *Check that all the doors are locked securely.* | *Make sure you **double-check*** (=check something twice) *the spellings of these names.* | **check sth against sth** *Police checked his story against the girl's statement* (=compared them to see if they were the same). | *Perhaps next time you should **check your facts** more carefully.*

THESAURUS

make sure to find out if a fact, statement etc. is correct or true: *Make sure the door is locked, will you?*
double-check to check something again to find out if it is safe, ready, correct etc.: *Double-check your answers before turning the test in.*
confirm to say or prove that something is definitely true: *Anderson confirmed that he will step down at the end of this year.*
check out to make sure that something is actually true, correct, or acceptable: *The reporter called a few of his sources to check out the man's story.*
examine to look at something carefully and thoroughly because you want to find out something about it: *Examine the glass carefully for any flaws.*
go over something to examine something very carefully, for example to look for mistakes or faults: *Go over your work and correct any misspellings or other errors.*
inspect to examine something carefully or visit a place to check that everything is satisfactory: *The health department inspects restaurants for cleanliness and safety.*
test to examine or use something in order to find out its qualities or check that it is satisfactory: *The products are carefully tested before they are sold to the public.*
monitor to carefully watch or keep checking someone or something in order to see what changes take place over a period of time: *In intensive care, patients are monitored constantly.*

2 FIND OUT [I] to find out what the true or accurate situation is by looking at something, asking someone etc.: *"Is she here yet?" "I'll go and check."* | *He stopped and checked his watch.* | **+whether/how/who etc.** *I need to check when the letter arrived.* | **check with sb** *It's a good idea to check with your doctor before going on a diet.* | **check back (with sb)** *Check back in a week and see if anything has changed.* | **check (sth) to see if/whether/what etc.** *I want to check to see if my name is on the list.*
3 BAGS/COAT ETC. [T] to leave your bags, coat etc. at an official place, so they can be put on an airplane, train, bus etc. or so that they can be kept safe, or to take someone's bags in order to do this SYN **check in**: *Do you have any bags to check?*
4 MAKE A MARK [T] to make a mark (✔) next to something to show that you have chosen it, that it is correct, or that you have dealt with it: *Check the box that says "No."*
5 NOT DO STH [T] to suddenly stop yourself from saying or doing something because you realize it would be better not to: *I had to check the urge to laugh out loud.* | *I wanted to slap him, but managed to **check myself**.*
6 STOP STH [T] to stop something bad from getting worse or continuing to happen: *Doctors are trying to check the spread of the disease.*
7 SPORTS [T] to push another player very hard in HOCKEY

check in *phr. v.* **1** if someone checks you into a hotel, airport, or hospital or someone checks you in, you go to the desk and report that you have arrived: *Has Mr. Walker checked in yet?* → see also CHECK-IN **2 check sb ↔ in** if someone checks you in at a hotel, airport, or hospital, they officially record that you have arrived: *Airline employees were checking in passengers.* → see also CHECK-IN **3 check sth ↔ in** to leave your bags at an official place so they can be put on a plane, train etc. or to take someone's bags in order to do this: *Where can I check in my suitcase?* **4** to call someone to tell them that you are safe or where you are: *I wish he'd check in once in a while.*

check sth **↔ off** *phr. v.* to make a mark (✔) next to something to show that you have chosen it, that it is correct, or that you have dealt with it: *Good, now I can check that off the list.*

check on sb/sth *phr. v.* to make sure that someone or something is safe, has everything they need, or is doing what they are supposed to be doing: *Can you go up and check on the kids?* → see Thesaurus box at CONTROL¹

check out *phr. v.*
1 MAKE SURE check sth ↔ out INFORMAL to make sure that something is actually true, correct, or acceptable: *You should check that idea out with the boss first.*

C

2 **BE TRUE** if information checks out, it is proven to be true, correct, or acceptable: *We should see if his story checks out.*
3 **LOOK AT SB/STH check sb/sth ↔ out** SPOKEN to look at someone or something because they are interesting or attractive: *Wow, check out that girl in the striped pants.* | ***Check it out!*** *They're selling hamburgers for 99 cents.*
4 **HOTEL/HOSPITAL** to leave a hotel or hospital after paying the bill: *We have to check out by 1 p.m.*
5 **EXAMINE/TEST STH check sth ↔ out** to test something to find out if it works, how it works, whether it is appropriate for what you want etc.: *Have a mechanic check the car out before you buy it.*
6 **GET INFORMATION check sb ↔ out** INFORMAL to get information about someone, especially to find out if they are appropriate for something: *We'd better check him out before we offer him the job.*
7 **BUYING AT A STORE** to pay for your goods at a supermarket or other large store before leaving: *We can go as soon as I check out.* → see also CHECKOUT
8 **BOOKS check sth ↔ out** to borrow books or other materials from a library: *You can only check out three books at a time.*
9 **SELLING AT A STORE check sb ↔ out** to take the money that someone owes for goods at a supermarket or other large store

check over *phr. v.* **1 check sth ↔ over** to look closely at something to make sure it is correct or acceptable: *I'll have my lawyer check over the contract.* **2 check sb ↔ over** to examine someone to make sure they are healthy: *The doctor checked her over and couldn't find anything wrong.*

check up on sb/sth *phr. v.* to try and make sure that someone is doing what they said they would do or what you want them to do, or that something is correct: *Mom's always checking up on me to see if I'm eating right.*

check² S1 W2 *n.*
1 **FROM YOUR BANK** [C] a printed piece of paper that you sign and write an amount of money on in order to pay for things: +**for** *She gave the family a check for $2,450.* | *Can I* ***pay by check?*** | *I'll* ***write*** *you* ***a check*** *and put it in the mail today.* | *Have you* ***cashed the check*** (=asked a bank to give you the amount of money on a check) *yet?*
2 **FINDING OUT** [C] a process of finding out if something is safe, correct, true, or in the condition it should be: *a security check* | +**of** *a check of phone records* | *I want you to* ***run a check on*** (=do the things needed to find out about sth) *his credit history.* | +**for** *Ask the lab to* ***do a check for*** *any viruses.* | *a* ***background check*** (=check for a criminal record) *of new gun purchasers*
3 **IN A RESTAURANT** [C] a list that you are given in a restaurant that shows how much you must pay for what you have eaten SYN **bill**: *May I have the check, please?* ►see THESAURUS box at **bill¹**, **restaurant**
4 **A CONTROL ON STH** [usually singular] something that controls something else and stops it from getting worse or continuing to happen: +**on** *a check on the government's power* | *Higher interest rates will* ***act as a check on*** *public spending.*
5 **keep/hold sth in check** to keep someone or something under control: *The law is designed to keep rents in check.*
6 **keep a check (on sb/sth)** to watch or listen to someone or something regularly or continuously, in order to control something or gather information: *Keep a check on the engine temperature, so that it doesn't overheat.*
7 **MARK** [C] a mark (✓) that you put next to something to show that you chose it, that it is correct, or that you have dealt with it
8 **PATTERN** [C,U] a pattern of squares, especially on cloth: *a tablecloth with red and white checks* | **a check shirt/tie/jacket etc.** (=a shirt, tie etc. made with this pattern on it) → see also CHECKED
9 **checks and balances** a system of rules in government or business that keeps any one person or group from having too much power or control
10 **hat/coat check** a place in a restaurant, theater etc. where you can leave your coat, bag etc. to be guarded until you go home
11 **GAME** [U] the position of the KING (=most important piece) in a game of CHESS when it can be directly attacked by the opponent's pieces → see also CHECKMATE
12 **SPORTS** [C] an act of pushing another player very hard in HOCKEY
[**Origin:** (1–6, 9–11) 1300–1400 Old French *eschec* **check in chess**, from Arabic *shah*, from Persian, **king**]

check·book /ˈtʃɛkbʊk/ *n.* [C] a small book of checks that your bank gives you

ˈcheck card *n.* [C] a special plastic card that you can use to pay for things directly from your CHECKING ACCOUNT

checked /tʃɛkt/ *adj.* having a regular pattern of colored squares, usually of white and one other color: *a checked skirt* → see also CHECK²

check·er /ˈtʃɛkɚ/ *n.* **1** [C] someone who works at the CHECKOUT in a SUPERMARKET **2 spell/grammar checker** [C] a computer program that checks that the spelling of words or the grammar in a sentence is correct **3** [C] someone who makes sure that something is written or done correctly: *a fact-checker for a magazine* **4** [C] one of a set of round wood or plastic objects used in the game of CHECKERS **5 checkers** [U] a game for two players, using 12 flat round pieces each and a special board with 64 squares, in which the purpose is to take the other player's pieces by jumping over them with your pieces → see also CHINESE CHECKERS

check·er·board /ˈtʃɛkɚˌbɔrd/ *n.* [C] a board that you play checkers on, with 32 squares of one color and 32 squares of another color

check·ered /ˈtʃɛkɚd/ *adj.* **1** marked with squares of two different colors: *red and white checkered tiles* **2 a checkered history/past/career etc.** periods of failure as well as successful times in your past

ˌcheckered ˈflag *n.* [C] a flag covered with black and white squares that is waved at the end of a car or MOTORCYCLE race

ˈcheck-in *n.* **1** [U] the process of reporting your arrival at a hotel, airport, hospital etc.: *We're trying to make check-in easier.* **2** [C usually singular] a place where you report your arrival at a hotel, airport, hospital etc.: **a check-in counter/desk** *When we got to the check-in counter, he couldn't find his ticket.* → see also **check in** at CHECK¹

ˈchecking acˌcount *n.* [C] ECONOMICS a bank account that you can take money out of at any time, and for which you are given checks to use to pay for things → see also SAVINGS ACCOUNT

ˈcheck-ˌkiting *n.* [U] the crime of obtaining money using illegal CHECKS

check·list /ˈtʃɛkˌlɪst/ *n.* [C] a list that helps you by reminding you of the things you need to do or get for a particular job or activity: *She has a checklist she gives to the cleaning woman.*

check·mate¹ /ˈtʃɛkmeɪt/ *n.* [U] **1** the position of the KING (=most important piece) at the end of a game of CHESS when it is being directly attacked and cannot escape **2** a situation in which someone has been completely defeated

checkmate² *v.* [T] **1** to put someone in a position where they cannot avoid being defeated: *His rivals wanted to embarrass him and checkmate the scheme.* **2** to make a move in a game of CHESS which puts the other player's king in a position from which it cannot escape

check·out /ˈtʃɛk-aʊt/ *n.* **1** also **checkout counter/stand** [C] the place in a SUPERMARKET or other store where you pay for the goods you want to buy: *Luckily, there was no line at the checkout.* **2** [C,U] the time by which you must leave a hotel room: *Checkout is at noon.* → see also **check out** at CHECK¹

check·point /ˈtʃɛkpɔɪnt/ *n.* [C] a place, especially on a border, where an official person examines vehicles or people: *Tourist visas are issued at any border checkpoint.*

ˈcheck ˌregister *n.* [C] ECONOMICS a small book for keeping a record of the checks you have written, including details of who you paid them to and the amount spent

check·room /ˈtʃɛk-rum/ *n.* [C] a place in a restaurant, theater etc. where you can leave your coat, bags etc. to be guarded

ˈcheck stub *n.* [C] **1** the part of a PAYCHECK that tells you the amount of taxes and other amounts taken out of it **2** the part of a check that is left when you tear it out of a CHECKBOOK, used for recording the amount you have spent

check·up, **check-up** /ˈtʃɛk-ʌp/ *n.* [C] an occasion when a doctor or DENTIST examines you to see if you are healthy: *It's been a couple of years since I had my last checkup.*

ched·dar, **Cheddar** /ˈtʃɛdɚ/ *n.* [U] a firm smooth yellow or orange cheese [**Origin:** 1600–1700 *Cheddar* village in Somerset, southwest England, where the cheese was first made]

cheek /tʃik/ W3 *n.* **1** [C] the soft round part of your face below each of your eyes: *I kissed Mom on the cheek and said good night.* | *a little girl with pink cheeks* **2 cheek to cheek** if two people dance cheek to cheek, they dance very close to each other in a romantic way **3** [C] INFORMAL one of the two soft parts of your body that you sit on SYN **buttock** **4 turn the other cheek** to deliberately avoid reacting in an angry or violent way when someone has hurt or upset you: *It's hard to turn the other cheek when someone insults you.* **5 cheek by jowl** INFORMAL used to say that a group of people, things, or places are very close to each other: *Customers sat cheek by jowl along the counter of the bar.* **6** [singular, U] OLD-FASHIONED behavior that is rude or not respectful, especially toward someone in a position of authority SYN **nerve** [**Origin:** Old English *ceace*] → see also -CHEEKED, TONGUE-IN-CHEEK

cheek·bone /ˈtʃikboʊn/ *n.* [C usually plural] one of the two bones above your cheeks, just below your eyes: *She has **high cheekbones** (=cheekbones that stick out and are considered attractive) and full lips.*

-cheeked /tʃikt/ [in adjectives] **red-cheeked/hollow-cheeked/rosy-cheeked etc.** having red, hollow etc. cheeks on your face

cheek·y /ˈtʃiki/ *adj. comparative* **cheekier**, *superlative* **cheekiest** OLD-FASHIONED badly behaved or not respectful, sometimes in a way that is amusing rather than rude —**cheekily** *adv.* —**cheekiness** *n.* [U]

cheep /tʃip/ *v.* [I] if a young bird cheeps, it makes a weak, high noise —**cheep** *n.* [C]

cheer[1] /tʃɪr/ *v.* **1** [I,T] to shout as a way of showing happiness, praise, approval, or support of someone or something OPP **boo**: *Fans began to cheer as the teams entered the stadium.* | *The crowd cheered the soldiers as they got into the plane.* ►see THESAURUS box at **shout**[1] **2** [T usually passive] to make someone feel more hopeful when they are worried: *Investors were cheered by news of the merger.* [**Origin:** 1200–1300 Old French *chere* **(expression on) the face**] —**cheerer** *n.* [C]

cheer sb **on** *phr. v.* to shout encouragement at a person or team to help them do well in a race or competition: *All of my friends were here to cheer me on.*

cheer up *phr. v.* **1 cheer sb ↔ up** to become happier, or to make someone feel happier: *Pizza also cheers me up.* | *Billy cheered up when he saw her.* **2 cheer up!** SPOKEN used to tell someone not to be so sad: *Cheer up, it's not that bad!*

cheer[2] *n.* **1** [C] a shout of happiness, praise, approval, or encouragement OPP **boo**: *The audience filled the theater with cheers.* | *A deafening **cheer went up** from the crowd.* **2** [C] a special CHANT (=phrase that is repeated) that the crowd at a sports game shouts in order to encourage their team to win: *The cheer "Go Lions Go!" could be heard for over half a mile.* **3 three cheers for sb!** SPOKEN used to tell a group of people to shout three times as a way of showing support or praise for someone: *Three cheers for Coach Madison!* **4** [U] a feeling of happiness and confidence: *The rise in U.S. exports is certain to bring cheer to manufacturers.* | *She was full of health and **good cheer**.* | **festive/holiday/Christmas etc. cheer** (=happy feelings connected with Christmas) → see also CHEERS

cheer·ful /ˈtʃɪrfəl/ *adj.* **1** behaving in a way that shows you are happy, for example by smiling or being very friendly: *He arrived looking relaxed and cheerful.* | *a cheerful voice* ►see THESAURUS box at **happy** **2** something that is cheerful makes you feel happy because it is so bright or pleasant: *a bright, cheerful morning* | *a cheerful, spotlessly clean kitchen* **3** tending to be happy most of the time: *Mary Ellen is a cheerful and enthusiastic person.* **4** [only before noun] a cheerful attitude shows that you are willing to do whatever is necessary in a happy way: *a cheerful approach to the job* —**cheerfully** *adv.* —**cheerfulness** *n.* [U]

C

cheer·lead·er /ˈtʃɪrˌlidɚ/ *n.* [C] **1** a member of a team of people who encourage a crowd to cheer at sports games by shouting special words and dancing: *a high school cheerleader* **2** someone who encourages other people to do something: *Find a real estate agent who will be a cheerleader for your property.*

cheer·lead·ing /ˈtʃɪrˌlidɪŋ/ *n.* [U] **1** the activity of being a cheerleader **2** the act of supporting an organization, idea etc. and not being willing to listen to criticism of it

cheer·less /ˈtʃɪrlɪs/ *adj.* cheerless weather, places, or times make you feel sad, bored, or uncomfortable: *a cheerless winter sky* —**cheerlessly** *adv.* —**cheerlessness** *n.* [U]

cheers /tʃɪrz/ *interjection* used when you lift a glass of alcohol before drinking it, to say that you hope the people you are drinking with will be happy and have good health

cheer·y /ˈtʃɪri/ *adj. comparative* **cheerier**, *superlative* **cheeriest** cheerful, or making you feel happy: *A cheery fire burned in the fireplace.* —**cheerily** *adv.*

cheese /tʃiz/ S1 W3 *n.* [C,U] **1** a solid food made from milk, which is usually yellow or white and can be soft or hard: *half a pound of cheese* | *bagels and cream cheese* | *a tray of cheeses and cold meats* | **a piece/slice of cheese** *Do you want a slice of cheese on your sandwich?* | *Sprinkle the potatoes with **grated cheese**.* **2 say cheese** used to tell people to smile when you are going to take their photograph: *Come on everybody, say cheese!* [**Origin:** Old English *cese*] → see also BIG CHEESE

cheese·board /ˈtʃizbɔrd/ *n.* [C] **1** a board used to cut cheese on **2** a board used for serving a variety of cheeses → see picture at BOARD[1]

cheese·burg·er /ˈtʃizˌbɚgɚ/ *n.* [C] a HAMBURGER served with a piece of cheese on top of the meat

cheese·cake /ˈtʃizkeɪk/ *n.* **1** [C,U] a cake made from a mixture containing soft cheese: *a slice of cheesecake* **2** [U] OLD-FASHIONED photographs of pretty young women with few clothes on

cheese·cloth /ˈtʃizklɔθ/ *n.* [U] thin light cotton cloth used for wrapping some types of cheeses, and in cooking

chees·y /ˈtʃizi/ *adj. comparative* **cheesier**, *superlative* **cheesiest** **1** INFORMAL not having good style or quality, and slightly silly: *a cheesy soap opera* **2** tasting like cheese or containing cheese: *a cheesy sauce* **3** INFORMAL not sincere: *a cheesy grin* —**cheesily** *adv.*

chee·tah /ˈtʃiṭə/ *n.* [C] a member of the cat family that has long legs and black spots on its fur, and can run extremely fast [**Origin:** 1700–1800 Hindi *cita*, from Sanskrit *citrakaya* **tiger**, from *citra* **bright** + *kaya* **body**]

Chee·ver /ˈtʃivɚ/, **John** (1912–1982) a U.S. writer of short stories and NOVELS

chef /ʃɛf/ *n.* [C] a skilled cook, especially the main cook in a restaurant or hotel: *a pastry chef* [**Origin:** 1800–1900 French *chef de cuisine* **head of the kitchen**]

chef d'oeu·vre /ʃeɪ 'dʌvrə, -'dɚv/ *n.* [C] FORMAL the best piece of work by a painter, writer etc. SYN masterpiece

Chek·hov /'tʃɛkɔf, -kɑv/**, An·ton** /'æntɑn/ (1860–1904) a Russian writer of plays and short stories —**Chekhovian** /tʃɛ'koʊviən/ *adj.*

che·lic·er·a /kə'lɪsərə/ *n. plural* **chelicerae** /-ri/ [C] BIOLOGY one of a pair of sharp parts in the mouth of creatures such as SPIDERS and CRABS, which are used to catch and sometimes poison other creatures before eating them

C

chem·i·cal[1] /'kɛmɪkəl/ Ac W3 *n.* [C] **1** CHEMISTRY a substance that is used in or produced by a chemical process: *Farmers are moving away from the use of chemicals and pesticides.* | **toxic/hazardous/dangerous chemicals** *toxic chemicals in the groundwater* **2** a drug, especially an illegal one: *addiction to chemicals* | *chemical abuse*

chemical[2] Ac W3 *adj.* CHEMISTRY relating to or used in chemistry, or involving the changes that happen when two substances combine: *chemical engineering* | *a **chemical analysis of** the substance* | *the **chemical composition of** the atmosphere* | *The disease is caused by a **chemical imbalance** in the brain.* [**Origin:** 1500–1600 Modern Latin *chimicus* **alchemist**, from Medieval Latin *alchimicus*] —**chemically** /-kli/ *adv.*: *chemically treated water*

ˌchemical 'bond *n.* [C] CHEMISTRY a force holding together the atoms in a chemical compound

ˌchemical 'change *n.* [C,U] CHEMISTRY a process by which the chemical structure of something changes by combining with other chemicals or breaking apart into separate chemicals

ˌchemical e'quation *n.* [C] CHEMISTRY a written record of what happens when two or more chemicals are mixed together, with letters and numbers representing chemical substances

ˌchemical equi'librium *n.* [singular, U] CHEMISTRY a state in which a chemical reaction and its opposite reaction are balanced or happen at the same rate so that there is no change in the system as a whole

ˌchemical 'formula *n.* [C] CHEMISTRY a series of numbers and letters that represents the number and types of atoms in a chemical compound or reaction

ˌchemical 'property *n.* [C] CHEMISTRY the features or qualities of a substance that make it possible for its chemical structure to change

ˌchemical re'action *n.* [C,U] CHEMISTRY a chemical change that happens when two or more substances are mixed together, or the process in which this happens

ˌchemical 'symbol *n.* [C] CHEMISTRY the letter or letters that represent a chemical ELEMENT

ˌchemical 'warfare *n.* [U] methods of fighting a war using chemical weapons → see also BIOLOGICAL WARFARE

ˌchemical 'weapon *n.* [C] a poisonous substance, especially a gas, used as a weapon in war

ˌchemical 'weathering *n.* [U] EARTH SCIENCE the process by which the original chemical and physical structure of rock, MINERALS etc. is gradually changed by the effects of water and other chemicals, especially CARBON DIOXIDE

che·mise /ʃə'miz/ *n.* [C] **1** a simple dress that hangs straight from a woman's shoulders **2** a piece of loose women's underwear worn on the top half of her body

chem·ist /'kɛmɪst/ *n.* [C] a scientist who has special knowledge and training in chemistry

chem·is·try /'kɛməstri/ *n.* [U] **1** the science that studies the structure of substances and the way that they change or combine with each other **2** strong and exciting romantic feelings between two people: +**between** *There was a real chemistry between me and Sean.* **3** the way substances combine in a particular process, thing, person etc.: *The drug may cause changes in a person's body chemistry.* **4** a situation in which two or more people like, understand, and admire each other and work well together: *Teams with good chemistry win more often.*

'chemistry ˌset *n.* [C] a box containing equipment for children to do simple chemistry at home

chem·ist's /'kɛmɪsts/ *n.* [C] BRITISH A DRUGSTORE

che·mo /'kimoʊ/ *n.* [U] INFORMAL CHEMOTHERAPY

che·mo·syn·the·sis /ˌkimoʊ'sɪnθəsɪs/ *n.* [U] CHEMISTRY a process by which some living things, such as BACTERIA, make CARBOHYDRATES using energy from chemical reactions

che·mo·ther·a·py /ˌkimoʊ'θɛrəpi/ *n.* [U] MEDICINE the use of drugs to control and try to cure CANCER: *He **underwent chemotherapy** to remove the tumor.*

che·nille /ʃə'nil/ *n.* [U] twisted thread with a surface like a soft brush, or cloth made from this and used for clothes, decorations etc.

cheque /tʃɛk/ *n.* the British and Canadian spelling of CHECK

cher·ish /'tʃɛrɪʃ/ *v.* [T usually passive] **1** to feel that something is very important to you: *Sports has given me friendships that I cherish.* | *I still **cherish the memory** of that day.* | *The observance of Thanksgiving is a **cherished tradition** in the U.S.* **2** to love someone or something very much and take very good care of them: *All children should be loved and cherished.* | *They had to leave behind all their most **cherished possessions**.*

cher·no·zem /'tʃɛrnəˌzɛm/ *n.* [U] EARTH SCIENCE a rich black soil containing a lot of decayed plants, leaves, and chemicals that help plants grow, which forms the top layer of earth on the PRAIRIES in North America and Canada and the STEPPES in Russia

Cher·o·kee /'tʃɛrəˌki/ a Native American tribe from the U.S. states of North Carolina and Tennessee

che·root /ʃə'rut/ *n.* [C] a CIGAR with both ends cut straight

cher·ry /'tʃɛri/ S3 *n. plural* **cherries** **1** [C] BIOLOGY a small dark red round fruit with a long thin stem and a large seed: *a bunch of cherries* | *cherry pie* → see picture at FRUIT[1] **2 a)** also **cherry tree** [C] BIOLOGY the tree on which this fruit grows **b)** [U] the wood of this tree, used for making furniture **3** also **cherry red** [U] a bright red color **4 the cherry on (the) top** INFORMAL something additional that you did not expect, that is nice to have [**Origin:** 1300–1400 Old North French *cherise* (taken as plural), from Latin *cerasus* **cherry tree**, from Greek *kerasos*]

'cherry bomb *n.* [C] a round red FIRECRACKER that explodes with a loud bang

'cherry ˌbrandy *n.* [U] a sweet alcoholic drink that tastes like cherries

'cherry pick, cherry-pick *v.* [I,T] INFORMAL, DISAPPROVING to choose exactly the things or people you want from a group, in a way that is not fair to other people: *Firms can cherry pick skilled workers from anywhere in the world.*

'cherry ˌpicker *n.* [C] a vehicle which can raise and lower someone in a container like a bucket so that they can work high up, for example to fix a street lamp

'cherry toˌmato *n. plural* **cherry tomatoes** [C] a very small TOMATO

cher·ub /'tʃɛrəb/ *n.* [C] **1** an ANGEL shown in paintings, SCULPTURE etc. as a fat pretty child with small wings **2** INFORMAL a young pretty child who behaves very well **3** *plural* **cherubim** BIBLICAL one of the ANGELS that guard the seat where God sits —**cherubic** /tʃə'rubɪk/ *adj.*: *a cherubic-faced child*

cher·vil /'tʃɚvəl/ *n.* [U] a strong-smelling garden plant used as an HERB

Ches·a·peake Bay, the /ˌtʃɛsəpik 'beɪ/ a long narrow BAY of the Atlantic Ocean on the eastern coast of the U.S., in the states of Virginia and Maryland

chess /tʃɛs/ *n.* [U] a game for two players, who move their playing pieces according to particular rules across a special board to try to trap their opponent's

KING (=most important piece) [**Origin:** 1100–1200 Old French *esches*, plural of *escec*]

chess·board /ˈtʃɛsbɔrd/ *n.* [C] a square board with 64 black and white squares, on which you play chess → see picture at BOARD[1]

chess·man /ˈtʃɛsmæn, -mən/ also **chess·piece** /ˈtʃɛspis/ *n. plural* **chessmen** /-mɛn, -mən/ [C] one of the 16 black or 16 white playing pieces used in the game of chess

chest /tʃɛst/ S2 W3 *n.* [C] **1** BIOLOGY the front part of your body, between your neck and your stomach: *When doing sit-ups, keep your hands crossed on your chest.* | *Potter had pains in his chest.* | *He was admitted to the hospital after complaining of* ***chest pains***. → see also FLAT-CHESTED **2** a large strong box with a lid, that you use to store things in or to move your personal possessions from one place to another: *a toy chest* | *a chest for storing blankets in* → see also HOPE CHEST, ICE CHEST, MEDICINE CHEST, WAR CHEST **3 get something off your chest** to tell someone about something that has been worrying or annoying you for a long time, so that you feel better afterward: *Employees are able to get things off their chest in these meetings.* **4 chest-thumping/chest-pounding** the activity of telling other people how good you are or about the things you have done and are proud of: *Bryant's speech was just political chest-thumping.* [**Origin:** Old English *cest*, from Latin *cista* **box, basket**]

ches·ter·field /ˈtʃɛstɚˌfild/ *n.* [C] CANADIAN, BRITISH a large soft comfortable SOFA

chest·nut[1] /ˈtʃɛsnʌt/ *n.* **1** [C] BIOLOGY a smooth red-brown nut that you can eat **2** also **ˈchestnut tree** [C] BIOLOGY the tree on which this nut grows **3** [U] a reddish-brown color **4** [C] BIOLOGY a horse that is this color **5 an old chestnut** a joke or story that has been repeated many times → see also WATER CHESTNUT

chestnut[2] *adj.* red-brown in color: *a woman with thick chestnut hair*

ˌchest of ˈdrawers *n.* [C] a piece of furniture with drawers, used for storing clothes SYN **dresser**

chest·y /ˈtʃɛsti/ *adj.* **1** INFORMAL used to describe a woman with large breasts, when you want to avoid saying this directly **2** DISAPPROVING very proud of yourself or your achievements

che·val glass /ʃəˈvæl ˌglæs/ *n.* [C] a tall mirror in a frame that allows the mirror to be pointed up or down

chev·a·lier /ˌʃɛvəˈlɪr, ʃəˈvælˌyeɪ/ *n.* [C] **1** a title for someone who has a high rank in a special association in France **2** a member of the lowest rank of the French NOBILITY in past times

chev·ron /ˈʃɛvrən/ *n.* [C] **1** a pattern in a V shape **2** a piece of cloth in the shape of a V which soldiers have on their SLEEVES to show their rank

chew[1] /tʃu/ S2 *v.* **1** [I,T] to bite food several times before swallowing it: *You can just swallow oysters or you can chew them a little bit first.* **2** [T] if you chew gum or tobacco, you bite it repeatedly, moving it around your mouth, in order to taste it: *My worst habit is chewing gum.* **3** [I,T] to bite something, without trying to eat it: *She chewed her lip nervously.* | **+on/at** *I gave the baby my key ring to chew on.* **4 chew the fat** INFORMAL to have a long friendly conversation **5 chew the cud** if a cow or sheep chews the cud, it repeatedly bites food it has brought up from its stomach [**Origin:** Old English *ceowan*] → see also **bite off more than you can chew** at BITE[1] (8)

chew on sth *phr. v.* to think about something carefully for a period of time: *The new research has given scientists something to chew on.*

chew sb ↔ **out** *phr. v.* INFORMAL to talk angrily to someone in order to show them that you disapprove of what they have done: *I thought she was gonna chew me out for shrinking her sweater.*

chew sth **over** *phr. v.* to think about something carefully for a period of time: *Let me chew it over for a few days, and then I'll call you.*

chew sb/sth ↔ **up** *phr. v.* **1** to gradually break a piece of food or other object up, using the teeth: *Chew your meat up well.* | *The dog had completely chewed up the sofa.* **2** to damage or destroy someone or something by tearing it: *My résumé was chewed up by the copier.* **3** INFORMAL to use all of a supply of something: *The phone bill chewed up all but the last few dollars of my paycheck.*

chew[2] *n.* [C] **1** a piece of a special tobacco which you chew but do not swallow **2** something such as candy or cookies that you have to chew a lot: *a recipe for chocolate walnut chews*

ˈchewing gum also **gum** *n.* [U] a sweet sticky type of candy that you chew for a long time but do not swallow

chew·y /ˈtʃui/ *adj. comparative* **chewier**, *superlative* **chewiest** food that is chewy has to be chewed a lot to make it soft enough to swallow: *chewy candy* | *Steak becomes tough and chewy when it is cooked too long.*

Chey·enne /ʃaɪˈyæn, -ˈyɛn/ **1** a Native American tribe from the western region of the U.S. **2** the capital city of the U.S. state of Wyoming —**Cheyenne** *adj.*

Chiang Kai-shek /ˌtʃyɑŋ kaɪ ˈʃɛk/ (1887–1975) a Chinese soldier and politician, leader of the Chinese NATIONALIST Party, who was forced to move from mainland China to the island of Taiwan by the Communists in 1949, and ruled Taiwan as President until he died

chia·ro·scu·ro /ˌkyɑrəˈskyʊroʊ/ *n.* [U] the use of light and dark areas in a picture or painting

chic /ʃik/ *adj.* showing a good sense of what is attractive and good style: *a chic apartment* | *She is chic and witty.* —**chic** *n.* [U]

Chi·ca·go /ʃɪˈkɑgoʊ/ the largest city in the U.S. state of Illinois

Chi·ca·na /tʃɪˈkɑnə/ *n.* [C] a word for a woman who is a U.S. citizen but who was born in Mexico or whose family came from Mexico. Some Mexican Americans find this word offensive. → see also CHICANO

chi·can·er·y /ʃɪˈkeɪnəri/ *n.* [U] FORMAL the use of complicated plans or tricks to deceive people: *Many blacks were denied the right to vote through chicanery.*

Chi·ca·no /tʃɪˈkɑnoʊ/ *n.* [C] *plural* **Chicanos** a word for a U.S. citizen who was born in Mexico or whose family came from Mexico. Some Mexican Americans find this word offensive. [**Origin:** 1900–2000 Mexican Spanish, Spanish *mejicano* **Mexican man**] —**Chicano** *adj.*: *the Chicano community*

chi-chi /ˈʃi ʃi/ *adj.* INFORMAL, DISAPPROVING fashionable and expensive, and often very decorated: *a chi-chi Beverly Hills restaurant*

chick /tʃɪk/ S2 *n.* [C] **1** BIOLOGY a baby bird: *a hen and her chicks* **2** SPOKEN, INFORMAL a word for a young woman, sometimes considered offensive: *"Who is he talking to?" "Some chick named Melanie."*

chick·a·dee /ˈtʃɪkədi/ *n.* [C] BIOLOGY a North American bird with a black head

Chick·a·saw /ˈtʃɪkəˌsɔ/ a Native American tribe from the southeastern area of the U.S.

chick·en[1] /ˈtʃɪkən/ S1 W3 *n.*

1 BIRD [C] BIOLOGY a common farm bird that is kept for its meat and eggs: *We raise our own chickens.* → see also HEN, ROOSTER

2 MEAT [U] the meat from this bird, eaten as food: *fried chicken* | *Boy, that chicken smells good.*

3 LACKING COURAGE [C] INFORMAL someone who is not brave at all SYN **coward**: *I'm such a chicken when it comes to skiing.*

4 GAME [U] a game in which someone, especially a young person, must do something dangerous to show that they are brave

5 a chicken and egg situation/problem/thing etc. a situation in which it is impossible to decide which of two things happened first, or which action is the cause of the other: *That leaves the company in a chicken and egg dilemma.*

6 sb's chickens have come home to roost used to say that someone's bad or dishonest actions in the past have caused the problems that they have now

7 Which came first, the chicken or the egg? used to

say that it is difficult or impossible to decide which of two things happened first, or which action is the cause and which is the effect
[**Origin:** Old English *cicen* **young chicken**] → see also **don't count your chickens (before they've hatched)** at COUNT¹ (12), SPRING CHICKEN

chicken² *adj.* [not before noun] INFORMAL not brave enough to do something: *Dave's too chicken to ask her out.*

C

chicken³ *v.*
chicken out *phr. v.* INFORMAL to decide at the last moment not to do something, because you are afraid: *Margaret chickened out of starting her own business.*

ˈchicken ˌfeed *n.* [U] INFORMAL an amount of money that is too small to worry about: *$200 million is chicken feed to the military.*

ˌchicken-fried ˈsteak *n.* [C,U] a thin piece of BEEF covered in small pieces of bread and cooked in hot oil

ˈchicken-ˌlivered *adj.* not brave SYN cowardly

chick·en·pox /ˈtʃɪkənˌpɑks/ *n.* [U] an infectious disease that causes ITCHY spots on the skin and a slight fever, and that usually affects children

ˈchicken run *n.* [C] an area surrounded by a fence where you keep chickens

ˈchicken wire *n.* [U] a type of thin wire net, used especially for making fences

chick·pea, chick-pea /ˈtʃɪkpi/ *n.* [C] a large brown PEA that is cooked and eaten SYN garbanzo

chick·weed /ˈtʃɪkwid/ *n.* [U] a plant that is a WEED with small white flowers

chic·le /ˈtʃɪkəl, ˈtʃɪkli/ *n.* [U] the thick juice of a tropical American tree used for making CHEWING GUM

chic·o·ry /ˈtʃɪkəri/ *n.* [U] **1** BIOLOGY a European plant with blue flowers whose bitter leaves are eaten in SALADS **2** the roots of this plant, used in or instead of coffee

chide /tʃaɪd/ *v.* [I,T] LITERARY to tell someone in a gentle way that you disapprove or are angry about what they have done SYN scold: **chide sb for (doing) sth** *Harrell chides employees for not wearing their name tags.*

chief¹ /tʃif/ W1 *adj.* [only before noun] **1** most important SYN main SYN principal: *Safety is our chief concern.* | *the family's chief means of earning money* → see also CHIEFLY ►see THESAURUS box at important **2** highest in rank: *the chief medical officer* | *the Chief Justice of the Supreme Court* ►see THESAURUS box at position¹, rank¹ **3 chief cook and bottle washer** HUMOROUS someone who does a lot of different small jobs to make sure that something is successful

chief² S3 W2 *n.* [C] **1** the most important person in a company or organization: *the police chief* | *He was chief of SAS flight operations in Stockholm.* **2** the ruler of a tribe: *a Native American tribal chief* **3 the chief** INFORMAL the person in charge of the company or organization you work for [**Origin:** 1200–1300 Old French **head, chief**, from Latin *caput* **head**]

ˌChief ˈDiplomat *n.* **the Chief Diplomat** the President of the U.S., as the person who is officially responsible for the way the government deals with political events in foreign countries, and who represents the U.S. government when speaking to foreign government officials

ˌChief Exˈecutive *n.* **the Chief Executive** the President of the U.S., as the official leader of the U.S. government

ˌchief exˈecutive ˌofficer also **chief executive** *n.* [C] a CEO

ˌchief ˈjustice *n.* [C] LAW the most important judge in a court of law, especially of the U.S. SUPREME COURT or of state SUPREME COURTS

chief·ly /ˈtʃifli/ *adv.* mostly but not completely SYN mainly SYN largely: *Before 1849, travel was done chiefly on horseback.* | *I decided to come back to New York, chiefly to be near my parents.*

ˌchief of ˈstaff *n. plural* **chiefs of staff** [C] **1** an official of high rank who advises the man in charge of an organization or government: *the White House chief of staff* **2** an officer of high rank in the army, navy etc. who advises the officer in charge of a particular military group or operation

ˌChief of ˈState *n.* **the Chief of State** POLITICS the formal head of a government, as opposed to the leader of a government. In the U.S., the President is both Chief of State and the highest government official.

ˌChief ˈRabbi *n.* **the Chief Rabbi** the main leader of the JEWISH religion in a country

chief·tain /ˈtʃiftən/ *n.* [C] the leader of a tribe, group, or a Scottish CLAN —**chieftainship** *n.* [C,U]

chif·fon /ʃɪˈfɑn/ *n.* [U] a soft thin silk or NYLON material that you can see through: *a red chiffon gown* [**Origin:** 1700–1800 French **piece of thin cloth, chiffon**, from *chiffe* **old piece of dirty cloth**]

chif·fo·nier /ˌʃɪfəˈnɪr/ *n.* [C] a tall CHEST OF DRAWERS

chig·ger /ˈtʃɪgɚ/ *n.* [C] a very small insect that digs itself into your skin, causing severe ITCHing

chi·gnon /ˈʃinyɑn/ *n.* [C] hair that is tied in a smooth knot at the back of a woman's head

chi·hua·hua /tʃɪˈwɑwə/ *n.* [C] a very small dog with smooth short hair, originally from Mexico [**Origin:** 1800–1900 *Chihuahua* city in Mexico]

chil·blain /ˈtʃɪlbleɪn/ *n.* [C] a painful red area on your fingers or toes that is caused by cold weather

child /tʃaɪld/ S1 W1 *n. plural* **children** /ˈtʃɪldrən/ [C] **1 YOUNG PERSON** a young person who is not yet fully grown, especially someone younger than about 13 years old: *Admission is $5; children under 12 are free.* | *an attractive happy child* | *a child actor* | *He learned German* ***as a child*** (=when he was a child). | **young/small child** (=a very young child, usually under five years old)

THESAURUS
kid an informal word for "child"
teenager a child or young person between the ages of 13 and 19
adolescent a more formal word for "teenager"
youth a teenage boy, often used in newspapers and showing disapproval: *a gang of youths*
minor LAW someone who is not yet legally an adult
→ BABY

2 SON/DAUGHTER a son or daughter of any age: *How many children does Jane have?* | *Vic was an* ***only child*** (=he had no brothers or sisters). | **youngest/middle/oldest child** *Our youngest child still lives at home.* | *We have three* ***grown-up children.*** ►see THESAURUS box at relative¹
3 SB INFLUENCED BY AN IDEA someone who is very strongly influenced by the ideas and attitudes of a particular period of history: **+of** *a child of the '60s*
4 SB WHO IS LIKE A CHILD an adult who behaves in a silly or unreasonable way that is more typical of a child: *Don't be such a child!*
5 SB WITHOUT EXPERIENCE someone who has no experience or knowledge of something in a way that makes them seem very young: *He's still a child in matters of love.*
6 be with child OLD USE to be PREGNANT: **be heavy/great/big with child** (=to be almost ready to give birth)
[**Origin:** Old English *cild*] → see also CHILD'S PLAY

GRAMMAR
Remember the plural of **child** is **children**, never *childs* or *childrens*. But in the possessive form you write: *this child's education, these children's education.*

child·bear·ing /ˈtʃaɪldˌbɛrɪŋ/ *n.* [U] **1** BIOLOGY the process of being PREGNANT and giving birth to a baby **2 childbearing age/years** BIOLOGY the period of time during a woman's life when she is able to have babies

child·birth /ˈtʃaɪldbɚθ/ *n.* [U] the act of giving birth:

a class on natural childbirth and parenting | *His first wife died* ***in childbirth***.

ˈchild care, childcare *n.* [U] an arrangement in which someone, especially someone with special training, takes care of children while their parents are at work: *She pays $1,000 a month for childcare.* | *a child-care center*

child·hood /ˈtʃaɪldhʊd/ S3 W3 *n.* [C,U] the period of time when you are a child: *They've been friends since childhood.* | *Vince had a very unhappy childhood.* | *my childhood home* → see also SECOND CHILDHOOD

child·ish /ˈtʃaɪldɪʃ/ *adj.* **1** DISAPPROVING behaving in a silly way that makes you seem much younger than you really are SYN **immature**: *I wish politicians would stop this childish name-calling.* **2** relating to or typical of a child SYN **childlike**: *the childish joys of clowns and cotton candy* —**childishly** *adv.* —**childishness** *n.* [U]

child·less /ˈtʃaɪldlɪs/ *adj.* having no children: *a childless couple* —**childlessness** *n.* [U]

child·like /ˈtʃaɪldlaɪk/ *adj.* APPROVING having qualities that are typical of a child, especially qualities such as INNOCENCE, trust, and eagerness: *a childlike view of life* | *her childlike innocence* → see also CHILDISH

ˌchild ˈprodigy *n. plural* **child prodigies** [C] a child who is unusually skillful at doing something such as playing a musical instrument

child·proof /ˈtʃaɪldpruf/ *adj.* something that is childproof is designed to prevent a child from opening, damaging, or breaking it: *a childproof aspirin bottle*

chil·dren /ˈtʃɪldrən/ *n.* the plural of CHILD

ˈchild's play *n.* [U] INFORMAL something that is very easy to do: *Finding the answer is child's play with the Internet.*

ˈchild supˌport *n.* [U] money that someone pays regularly to their former wife or husband in order to support their children

Chil·e /ˈtʃɪli/ a country on the western coast of South America between the Pacific Ocean and the Andes mountains —**Chilean** *n., adj.*

chil·i /ˈtʃɪli/ S3 *n. plural* **chilies** **1** [C] also **chili pepper** a small type of PEPPER with a very strong SPICY taste **2** [U] a SPICY dish made with chilies or chili powder, tomatoes, beans, and often meat, originally from Mexico: *a bowl of chili* [**Origin:** 1600–1700 Spanish *chile*, from Nahuatl *chilli*] → see also CHILI POWDER

chil·i·dog /ˈtʃɪliˌdɔg/ *n.* [C] a HOT DOG (=meat in a tube-shape) with CHILI on it

ˈchili ˌpowder *n.* [U] a powder that contains a mixture of SPICES, including chili and CUMIN, used in cooking

chill[1] /tʃɪl/ *v.* **1** [I,T] if you chill something such as food or drink, or if it chills, it becomes very cold but does not freeze: *Chill the dough for at least an hour.* | *I think the wine should be chilled enough by now.* **2** [I] also **chill out** SPOKEN, INFORMAL used to tell someone to be calm instead of feeling angry or nervous: *Shelly, just chill out, okay?* **3** [I] also **chill out** SPOKEN, INFORMAL to relax without doing anything important: *A few of us were just chilling at my house.* **4** [T usually passive] to make someone very cold: *Chilled by the winds, people huddled under blankets.* **5** [T] LITERARY to frighten someone, especially by seeming very cruel or violent: *The look in her eye chilled me.*

chill[2] *n.* **1** [singular, U] a feeling of coldness: *There was* ***a chill in the air*** *that night.* | *A small heater keeps off the night chill.* **2** [C] a feeling of fear or shock caused by something that is very upsetting, violent, or cruel: *Her description of the murder* ***sent a chill through*** *the audience.* | ***A chill ran down my spine*** *when he said the word "cancer."* **3** [C] a feeling of being cold, caused by being sick: *Symptoms include fever, chills, and increased heart rate.* **4** [singular] a feeling that someone is not friendly, that you get from the way they behave or speak: *There was a definite chill in his voice when he answered.* **5** [singular] a situation in which something is not encouraged or is stopped: *The high price of oil* ***put a chill on*** *the auto industry.* → see also **send shivers/chills up (and down) your spine** at SEND (10)

chill[3] *adj.* **1 take a chill pill** SPOKEN used to tell someone to stop being excited, nervous, or angry **2** [only before noun] LITERARY very cold: *a chill wind*

chill·er /ˈtʃɪlɚ/ *n.* [C] INFORMAL a movie or book that is intended to frighten you: *the Stephen King chiller "The Shining"* → see also THRILLER

chil·ling /ˈtʃɪlɪŋ/ *adj.* **1** something that is chilling makes you feel frightened, especially because it is cruel, violent, or dangerous: *a chilling reminder of the war* **2** having a bad effect on what someone does: *Today's arrests should send a chilling message to anyone involved in insurance fraud.*

chill·y /ˈtʃɪli/ *adj. comparative* **chillier**, *superlative* **chilliest** **1** cold enough to make you feel uncomfortable: *a chilly evening* | *The room was chilly.* ▶see THESAURUS box at **cold**[1] **2** unfriendly: *a chilly smile* —**chilliness** *n.* [singular, U]

chime[1] /tʃaɪm/ *v.* **1** [I,T] if a bell or clock chimes, it makes a ringing sound, especially to tell you what time it is: *Church bells chimed to mark the occasion.* | *The big clock* ***chimed the hour*** (=rang to show which hour it was). **2** [I] to be the same as something else or to have the same effect: +**with** *Her views on art chime with my own.*

chime in *phr. v.* to say something in a conversation, especially to agree with what someone has just said: *"We'll miss you too!" the boys chimed in.*

chime[2] *n.* [C] **1 chimes** [plural] a set of bells or other objects that produce musical sounds → see also WIND CHIME **2** a ringing sound made by a bell or clock: *the chime of the doorbell*

chi·me·ra /kaɪˈmɪrə, -ˈmɛrə/ *n.* [C] **1** something, especially an idea or hope, that is not really possible and can never exist: *the chimera of a "universal language"* **2** an imaginary creature that breathes fire and has a lion's head, a goat's body, and a snake's tail

chi·mer·i·cal /kaɪˈmɛrɪkəl, -ˈmɪr-/ *adj.* LITERARY imaginary or not really possible

chim·ney /ˈtʃɪmni/ *n. plural* **chimneys** [C] **1** a pipe inside a building for smoke from a fire to go out through the roof: *Smoke drifted from a chimney.* **2** EARTH SCIENCE a narrow opening in tall rocks or cliffs that you can climb up **3** the glass cover that is put over the flame in an oil lamp [**Origin:** 1200–1300 Old French *cheminée*, from Latin *caminus* **fireplace**, from Greek *kaminos*]

ˈchimney sweep *n.* [C] someone whose job is to clean CHIMNEYS using special long brushes

chimp /tʃɪmp/ *n.* [C] INFORMAL a CHIMPANZEE

chim·pan·zee /ˌtʃɪmpænˈzi/ *n.* [C] an intelligent African animal with black or brown fur that is like a monkey without a tail [**Origin:** 1700–1800 Kongo *chimpenzi*]

chin /tʃɪn/ *n.* [C] **1** BIOLOGY the front part of your face below your mouth: *He smiled and rubbed his chin.* **2 (keep your) chin up!** SPOKEN used to tell someone to make an effort to stay cheerful when they are in a difficult situation: *Keep your chin up! We'll get through this together!* **3 take it on the chin** to be strongly criticized or put in a difficult situation and not complain about it: *I took it on the chin, but life goes on.* [**Origin:** Old English *cinn*]

Chi·na /ˈtʃaɪnə/ the largest country in eastern Asia

chi·na /ˈtʃaɪnə/ *n.* [U] **1** a hard white substance produced by baking a special type of clay at a high temperature: *a china tea cup* **2** also **chinaware** plates, cups etc. made of this substance: *We use our china only on special occasions.* [**Origin:** 1500–1600 Persian *chini* **Chinese**; because it was originally made in China]

ˌChina ˈSea, the the western part of the Pacific Ocean that goes along the coast of China and Vietnam

Chi·na·town /ˈtʃaɪnəˌtaʊn/ *n.* [C,U] an area in a city where there are Chinese restaurants, stores, and where a lot of Chinese people live

C

chin·chil·la /ˌtʃɪnˈtʃɪlə/ *n.* **1** [C] BIOLOGY a small South American animal bred for its fur **2** [U] the pale gray fur of the chinchilla: *a chinchilla coat* [**Origin:** 1600–1700 Spanish, Aymara or Quechua]

Chi·nese¹ /ˌtʃaɪˈniz◂, -ˈnis◂ / *n.* **1** [U] the language of China **2 the Chinese** [plural] people from China

Chinese² *adj.* from or relating to China

ˌChinese ˈcabbage *n.* [U] a type of CABBAGE with long leaves that have curly edges

C

ˌChinese ˈcheckers *n.* [U] a game in which you move small balls from hole to hole on a board that is shaped like a star

ˌChinese ˈlantern *n.* [C] a piece of folded colored paper that is put around a light for decoration

ˌChinese ˈmedicine *n.* [U] MEDICINE a type of medicine that uses special dried plants and ACUPUNCTURE

chink¹ /tʃɪŋk/ *n.* **1 a chink in sb's armor** a weakness in someone's character, argument etc. that you can use to attack them: *Opponents are looking for chinks in his political armor.* **2** [C] a narrow crack or hole in something that lets light or air through: *Through a chink in the shutter we could see Ralph.* **3** [C] a short high ringing sound made by metal or glass objects hitting each other: *the chink of knives and forks*

chink² *v.* [I,T] if glass or metal objects chink or you chink them, they make a short high sound when they knock together: *A few pennies chinked in my pocket.*

chi·no /ˈtʃinoʊ/ *n.* **1** [U] a strong material made of woven cotton, often light brown in color **2 chinos** [plural] loose pants made from this material: *Bruce was wearing his baggy old chinos.*

Chi·nook /ʃəˈnʊk, tʃə-/ a Native American tribe from the northwestern area of the U.S.

chin·strap /ˈtʃɪnstræp/ *n.* [C] a band of cloth that goes under your chin to keep a hat or HELMET in place

chintz /tʃɪnts/ *n.* [U] smooth cotton cloth that is printed with flowery patterns and used for making curtains, furniture covers etc.: *a chintz sofa*

chintz·y /ˈtʃɪntsi/ *adj. comparative* **chintzier**, *superlative* **chintziest** **1** INFORMAL cheap and badly made SYN **cheap**: *The car has chintzy uncomfortable seats.* **2** INFORMAL unwilling to give people things or spend money SYN **stingy** SYN **cheap**: *He's kind of chintzy with gifts.* **3** decorated or covered with chintz: *chintzy curtain materials*

ˈchin up, chinup *n.* [C] an exercise in which you hang on a bar and pull yourself up until your chin is above the bar

chip¹ /tʃɪp/ S2 W2 *n.*

1 FOOD [C usually plural] **a)** a thin dry flat piece of potato or TORTILLA cooked in very hot oil and eaten cold: *corn chips and guacamole* | *a bag of* ***potato chips*** **b)** BRITISH a FRENCH FRY: *fish and chips*

2 COMPUTER [C] **a)** COMPUTERS a small piece of SILICON that has a set of complicated electrical connections on it and is used to store and PROCESS information in computers **b)** the main MICROPROCESSOR of a computer

3 MARK [C] a small crack or mark on a plate, cup etc. where a piece has broken off: **+in** *The plate has a chip in it.*

4 PIECE [C] a small piece of wood, stone, metal etc., that has broken off something: *chips of plaster* | *wood chips*

5 have a chip on your shoulder to easily become offended or angry because you think you have been treated unfairly in the past: *Dave's had a chip on his shoulder since he didn't get promoted.*

6 GAME [C] a small flat colored piece of plastic used in games such as POKER and BLACKJACK to represent a particular amount of money

7 be a chip off the old block INFORMAL to be like one of your parents in the way you look or behave

8 when the chips are down SPOKEN in a serious or difficult situation, especially one in which you realize what is really true or important: *He knew how to be tough when the chips were down.*

9 let the chips fall (where they may) to not worry about what the results of a particular action will be: *I decided to tell her my opinion and let the chips fall where they may.*

10 SPORTS also **chip shot** [C] a hit or kick in GOLF or SOCCER that makes the ball go high into the air for a short distance

[**Origin:** Old English *cipp*, *cyp* **small piece of wood**, from Latin *cippus* **sharp post**] → see also BLUE CHIP, **cash in your chips** at CASH IN (3), CHOCOLATE CHIP, COW CHIP

chip² *v.* **chipped, chipping** **1** [I,T] if something such as a plate chips or if you chip it, a small piece of it breaks off accidentally: *The ball hit him in the face and chipped a tooth.* | **+off** *A tiny piece chipped off the tile, when I dropped the skillet.* **2** [T] to make a GOLF or SOCCER ball go high into the air for a short distance

chip sth ↔ **away** *phr. v.* to break small pieces off something hard, especially rock or a similar substance, by hitting it with a tool: *A drill was used to chip away the coal.* | **+at** *Archaeologists were carefully chipping away at the rock.*

chip away at sth *phr. v.* to gradually make something less effective or destroy it: *Howe continued to chip away at his opponent's popularity.*

chip in *phr. v.* **1** to give money, help, advice etc. to add to what other people are giving: *I was thinking we could all chip in $50 and buy Dad a new workbench.* | *Mercer chipped in with 16 points, giving the Eagles an easy win.* **2** to interrupt a conversation by saying something that adds more detail: *Then I chipped in and said I'd like to go, too.*

chip off *phr. v.* **1 chip sth ↔ off (sth)** to break small pieces off of something hard, especially rock or a similar substance, by hitting it with a tool: *She tried to chip the ice off the windshield.* **2 chip off (sth)** if a small piece of something chips off, it breaks off: *The paint was chipping off the wall.* | *A corner of the tile chipped off.*

chip·munk /ˈtʃɪpmʌŋk/ *n.* [C] a small American animal similar to a SQUIRREL that has black lines on its fur

chipped /tʃɪpt/ *adj.* something that is chipped has a small piece broken off the edge of it: *chipped plates*

ˌchipped ˈbeef *n.* [U] BEEF that has been dried and SMOKED and SLICED very thinly

Chip·pen·dale /ˈtʃɪpənˌdeɪl/, **Thomas** (1718–1779) an English furniture designer who had a great influence on the design of 18th-century furniture

chip·per /ˈtʃɪpɚ/ *adj.* INFORMAL cheerful and active: *You're looking very chipper this morning, Deborah.*

Chip·pe·wa, Ojibwa, Ojibway /ˈtʃɪpəˌwɔ, -ˌwɑ/ *n.* a Native American tribe from the state of Michigan in the U.S.

Chi·ri·co /ˈkɪriˌkoʊ/, **Gior·gio de** /ˈdʒɔrdʒoʊ deɪ/ (1888–1978) an Italian PAINTER whose paintings give the effect of dreams and influenced the development of SURREALISM in art

chi·ro·prac·tor /ˈkaɪrəˌpræktɚ/ *n.* [C] someone who treats physical problems by pressing on and moving the bones in your back —**chiropractic** *n.* [U]

chirp /tʃɚp/ also **chir·rup** /ˈtʃɪrəp/ *v.* [I] **1** if a bird or insect chirps, it makes short high sounds: *A bird sat chirping on a branch above.* **2** to speak in a cheerful, high voice: *"Good morning, Ricardo!" Judith chirped.* —**chirp** *n.* [C]

chis·el¹ /ˈtʃɪzəl/ *n.* [C] a metal tool with a sharp edge, used with a hammer to cut wood or stone [**Origin:** 1300–1400 Old North French]

chisel² *v.* **chiseled, chiseling,** or **chiselled, chiselling** [T] **1** to use a chisel to cut wood or stone, especially into a particular shape: **chisel sth into/in sth** *shapes chiseled into the huge rocks* | **chisel sth out of/from sth** *a huge figure chiseled out of granite* **2** OLD-FASHIONED to cheat or deceive someone —**chiseler** *n.* [C]

chis·eled /ˈtʃɪzəld/ *adj.* having a clear, sharp shape: *the chiseled features of his face*

Chis·holm /ˈtʃɪzəm/, **Shir·ley** /ˈʃɚli/ (1924–2005) a U.S. politician who was the first African-American woman to be elected as a member of Congress in 1969

ˈChisholm ˌTrail, the a path that was used for moving millions of cattle from Texas to Kansas during the 1800s

Chis·i·nau, Kishinev /ˌkiʃiˈnaʊ/ the capital city of Moldova

chit /tʃɪt/ *n.* [C] a note or small piece of paper with writing on it that you sign, especially to show you owe money for something

ˈchit-chat *n.* [U] INFORMAL conversation about things that are not very important: *chit-chat at the lunch table* **—chit-chat** *v.* [I]

chi·tin /ˈkaɪtɪn/ *n.* [U] BIOLOGY a strong substance that forms part of the cell walls of a FUNGUS and the outside body structure of creatures such as SPIDERS and CRABS

chit·ter·lings /ˈtʃɪtə·lɪŋz/ also **chit·lins** /ˈtʃɪtlɪnz/ *n.* [plural] the INTESTINE of a pig eaten as food, especially in the southern U.S.

chiv·al·rous /ˈʃɪvəlrəs/ *adj.* a man who is chivalrous behaves in a polite, kind, generous, and honorable way, especially toward women **—chivalrously** *adv.*

chiv·al·ry /ˈʃɪvəlri/ *n.* [U] **1** behavior that is honorable, kind, generous, and brave, especially a man's behavior toward women **2** HISTORY a system of religious beliefs and honorable behavior that KNIGHTS in the Middle Ages were expected to follow

chive /tʃaɪv/ *n.* [C usually plural] a long thin green plant that looks and tastes like an onion, and is used in cooking

chlo·ride /ˈklɔraɪd/ *n.* [C,U] CHEMISTRY a chemical compound that is a mixture of chlorine and another substance: *sodium chloride*

chlo·ri·nate /ˈklɔrəˌneɪt/ *v.* [T] CHEMISTRY to add chlorine to water to kill BACTERIA **—chlorinated** *adj.* **—chlorination** /ˌklɔrəˈneɪʃən/ *n.* [U] → see picture at PURIFICATION

chlo·rine /ˈklɔrin, klɔˈrin/ *n.* [U] SYMBOL **Cl** CHEMISTRY a greenish-yellow chemical ELEMENT, usually a gas, with a strong smell. It is used to keep the water in swimming pools clean.

chlo·ro·fluo·ro·car·bon /ˌklɔrəˌflʊroʊˈkɑrbən/ *n.* [C] SCIENCE a CFC

chlo·ro·form /ˈklɔrəˌfɔrm/ *n.* [U] a liquid that makes you become unconscious if you breathe it **—chloroform** *v.* [T]

chlo·ro·phyll /ˈklɔrəˌfɪl/ *n.* [U] CHEMISTRY a substance in plants that gives them their green color. It takes energy from sunlight and turns it into food for the plant. → see picture at PHOTOSYNTHESIS

chlo·ro·plast /ˈklɔrəˌplæst/ *n.* [C] BIOLOGY one of several parts of plant cells that contain CHLOROPHYLL (=a green-colored substance) which reacts with sunlight to produce the substance that the plant uses as food → see also PHOTOSYNTHESIS

choc·a·hol·ic /ˌtʃɑkəˈhɔlɪk, -ˈhɑ-/ *n.* [C] another spelling of CHOCOHOLIC

chock /tʃɑk/ *n.* [C] a block of wood or metal put in front of a wheel, door etc. to prevent it from moving: *He pulled the chocks out from under the airplane's wheels.* **—chock** *v.* [T]

chock-a-block /ˈtʃɑk ə ˌblɑk/ *adj.* completely full of people or things: **+with** *The shelves were chock-a-block with art books.* [**Origin:** 1800–1900 *chock-a-block* **with the wooden blocks of a tackle (= ropes for lifting) touching each other, so that no more can be lifted** (1800–1900), from *chock on block*; influenced by *chock-full*]

ˌchock-ˈfull *adj.* [not before noun] INFORMAL completely full: **+of** *bean soup, chock-full of smoked ham*

choc·o·hol·ic, chocaholic /ˌtʃɑkəˈhɔlɪk, -ˈhɑ-/ *n.* [C] INFORMAL someone who likes chocolate very much and eats it all the time

choco·late /ˈtʃɑklɪt/ S1 *n.* **1** [U] a sweet brown food made from COCOA that is eaten as candy, or used to give foods such as cakes a special sweet taste: *a chocolate bar* | *chocolate ice cream* | ***milk chocolate*** (=light brown chocolate that has milk added) | *I like **dark chocolate*** (=dark brown chocolate that tastes strong and slightly bitter). **2** [C] a small candy that consists of something such as a nut or CARAMEL covered with chocolate: *a box of chocolates* [**Origin:** 1600–1700 Spanish, Nahuatl *xocoatl*] → see also HOT CHOCOLATE

ˈchocolate chip *n.* [C] a small piece of chocolate put in foods such as cookies and cakes

ˌchocolate chip ˈcookie *n.* [C] a type of COOKIE containing small pieces of chocolate

choco·lat·y, chocolatey /ˈtʃɑkləţi/ *adj.* tasting or smelling like chocolate: *rich, chocolaty brownies*

Choc·taw /ˈtʃɑktɔ/ a Native American tribe from the southeastern region of the U.S. **—Choctaw** *adj.*

choice¹ /tʃɔɪs/ S2 W1 *n.*

1 ABILITY TO CHOOSE [singular] the right to choose or the chance to choose between two or more things: **have a/the choice** *I wouldn't ride my motorcycle without a helmet, but I think people should have a choice.* | **+between** *a choice between right and wrong* | **+of** *Dinner comes with bread and a choice of soup or salad.* | *freedom of choice* (=the right to choose what you want to do) | *I'll **give you a choice** – we can rent a movie or go out for a pizza.* | *With two seconds left, Stanford **had no choice** but to try for a 50-yard field goal* (=it was the only thing they could do). | *He **was left with no choice** but to resign.*

2 DECISION [C] a decision about which thing to have or do: *I think I **made** the right **choice**.* | **difficult/hard/painful choice** *the painful choice between raising taxes or cutting services* | *Many families were **faced with the choice of** stealing or starving.*

3 RANGE TO CHOOSE FROM [U] the range of people or things that you can choose from: *There's a bookstore in town, but it won't have much choice.* | **+of** *There's a choice of six colors.* | *restaurants with **a wide choice** of wines*

4 THING CHOSEN [C usually singular] the person or thing that someone has chosen: *The choices you make now will affect the rest of your life.* | **+of** *I didn't like her choice of dress.* | **first/second etc. choice** *My first choice would be to do track and field.* | **a good/wise choice** *Mexico is a good choice for a vacation.* | *I made a few **bad choices** when I was young.* | *Johnson was **the obvious choice** for the Democrats.*

5 of your choice chosen by you without anything limiting what you can choose from: *The prize includes dinner for two at the restaurant of your choice.*

6 by choice if you do something by choice, you do it because you want to do it and not because you are forced to do it: *She has no children by choice.*

7 the drug/treatment/newspaper etc. of choice the thing that a particular person or group prefers to use: *Beer is the drink of choice among sports fans.*

[**Origin:** 1200–1300 Old French *chois*, from *choisir* **to choose**] → see also CHOOSE

choice² *adj. comparative* **choicer**, *superlative* **choicest** **1** FORMAL of a very high quality or standard, used especially of food: *choice apples* | *Most of the choice summer jobs are already taken.* **2** choice meat, especially BEEF, is of a standard that is good but not the best → see also PRIME: *choice steak* **3 a few choice words/phrases** if you use a few choice words, your words show that you are angry: *Meyer had a few choice words for the lawyers who sent him to prison.*

choir /kwaɪə·/ *n.* **1** [C] ENG. LANG. ARTS a group of people who sing together, especially in a church or school: *the St. Joseph's Cathedral Choir* **2** [usually singular] in some churches, the part of the church where the choir sits [**Origin:** 1200–1300 Old French *cuer*, from Latin *chorus* **circular dance**]

choir·boy /ˈkwaɪə·bɔɪ/ *n. plural* **choirboys** [C] a young boy who sings in a church choir

ˈchoir ˌloft *n.* [C] the part of a church, usually at the front, in which the choir sits

choir·mas·ter /ˈkwaɪə·ˌmæstə·/ *n.* [C] someone who trains a choir SYN **director**

choke[1] /tʃoʊk/ S3 *v.*
1 STOP BREATHING [I,T] if something chokes you, or if you choke, you cannot breathe because something is blocking your throat or because there is not enough air: *Help him! He's choking!* | *The smoke was choking me.* | **choke on sth** *He choked on a piece of chicken.* | **choke to death** (=die by choking on something)
2 INJURE [T] to prevent someone from breathing by putting your hands around their throat and pressing on it: *Don't hold so tight! You're choking me.* | *The medical examiner concluded Perez had been* ***choked to death****.*
3 VOICE [I,T] if you choke with emotion, or if your voice chokes, you are so strongly affected by your feelings that you find it difficult to speak: **be choked with anger/emotion/grief etc.** *Deaton, choked with fury, banged the table.*
4 BLOCK [T] to fill an area or passage so that it is difficult to move through it: *Weeds were choking the stream* | **be choked with sth** *The roads were choked with traffic.*
5 SPORTS [I] INFORMAL to fail at doing something, especially a sport, because there is a lot of pressure on you: *I choked and missed an easy shot.*
6 PLANTS [I,T] also **choke out** to kill a plant by surrounding it with other plants that take away its light and room to grow: *Growth of the reed can choke out native water plants.*
7 enough sth to choke a horse SPOKEN if you have enough of something to choke a horse, you have a lot of it: *I have enough kitchen gadgets to choke a horse.*
8 SAY STH [T] also **choke out** to say something with difficulty because you are very upset or angry: *He began to sob, and choked out, "I have to go now."*
[**Origin:** 1300–1400 *achoke* **to choke** (11–14 centuries), from Old English *aceocian*]

choke sth ↔ **back** *phr. v.* to control your anger, sadness etc. so that you do not show it SYN **hold back**: *Kennedy paused, choking back tears.*

choke sth ↔ **down** *phr. v.* **1** to eat something quickly or with difficulty, especially because it tastes bad or because you are sick or in a hurry: *I was barely able to choke down her tuna casserole.* **2** to control your anger, sadness etc. so that you do not show it SYN **hold back**: *Margaret put her napkin to her mouth to choke down a sob.*

choke off sth *phr. v.* to prevent someone from doing something or stop something from happening SYN **cut off**: *an attempt to choke off the supply of cocaine to the U.S.*

choke up *phr. v.* **be/get choked up** to feel like you are going to cry because you are upset about something: *I get choked up every time I hear that song.*

choke[2] *n.* **1** [C] a piece of equipment in a vehicle that controls the amount of air going into the engine, and that is used to help the engine start **2** [U] the controlling of the amount of air going into an engine by using this piece of equipment: *Give it a bit more choke.* **3** [C] the act or sound of choking

choke·cher·ry /ˈtʃoʊkˌtʃɛri/ *n. plural* **chokecherries** [C] BIOLOGY a North American tree that produces small sour fruit

ˈchoke ˌcollar *n.* [C] a chain or band that is fastened around the neck of a dog in order to control it. The collar becomes tighter if the dog pulls against it.

chok·er /ˈtʃoʊkɚ/ *n.* [C] a piece of jewelry or narrow cloth that fits closely around your neck

chol·er /ˈkɑlɚ/ *n.* [U] LITERARY anger

chol·er·a /ˈkɑlərə/ *n.* [U] MEDICINE a serious disease of the stomach and BOWELS that is caused by infected water or food

chol·er·ic /ˈkɑlərɪk, kəˈlɛrɪk/ *adj.* LITERARY angry or in a bad mood: *He was impatient and choleric.*

cho·les·ter·ol /kəˈlɛstəˌrɔl, -ˌroʊl/ *n.* [U] BIOLOGY a chemical substance found in fat, blood, and other cells in your body, which can cause heart disease [**Origin:** 1800–1900 Greek *chole* **bile** + *stereos* **solid** + English *-ol* **chemical compound**]

chomp /tʃɑmp/ *v.* **1** [I] to bite food loudly: *Nick noisily chomped on his gum.* **2 be chomping at the bit** to be impatient to do something or for something to happen: *We were chomping at the bit to get started.*

Chom·sky /ˈtʃɑmski/, **Noam** /noʊm/ (1928–) a U.S. LINGUIST famous for his important ideas about language, including the idea that everyone is born with knowledge about grammar, and for his political ideas

choo-choo /ˈtʃu tʃu/ *n.* [C] SPOKEN a word meaning a "train," used by children or when talking to children

choose /tʃuz/ S1 W1 *v. past tense* **chose** /tʃoʊz/, *past participle* **chosen** /ˈtʃoʊzən/ [I,T] **1** to decide which one of a number of things, possibilities, people etc. that you want, because it is the best or most appropriate: *"Which movie do you want to watch tonight?" "You choose this time."* | *The city chose a new mayor on Tuesday.* | **choose to do sth** *She has chosen to carry on working after the baby is born.* | **choose sb to do sth** *I wonder who they'll choose to take over Rubin's job.* | **choose (sb/sth) from sth** *You can choose from over a thousand books.* | *Jurors are chosen from lists of people who have driver's licenses.* | **choose between sth and sth** *Many retired people have to choose between buying food and buying medicine.* | **choose which/when/what etc.** *You can choose when to make payments.* | **choose sb/sth as sth** *The company chose New York as its base.* | *We* ***chose*** *Chicago* ***for*** (=chose it because of) *its central location.* | *People should* ***be free to choose*** *their own doctor.* ►see THESAURUS box at **decide**

> **THESAURUS**
> **pick** to choose something or someone from a group of people or things: *Pick any number from one to ten.*
> **select** FORMAL to choose something or someone by thinking carefully about which is the best, most appropriate etc.: *Even as a young child, she enjoyed selecting special birthday gifts.*
> **opt for sth** to choose one thing instead of another: *Many of the students opt for the college preparatory classes.*
> **decide on sth** to choose one thing from many possible choices: *Have you decided on a name for the baby?*

2 to decide or prefer to do something: **choose to do sth** *Both departments have chosen to ignore the situation.* | *You can leave now,* ***if you choose****.* [**Origin:** Old English *ceosan*] → see also CHOICE[1]

choos·y /ˈtʃuzi/ *adj. comparative* **choosier**, *superlative* **choosiest** someone who is choosy will only accept someone or something that they consider to be very good SYN **picky**: *I get offered a lot of work now, so I can be a little choosy.* | +**about** *She's very choosy about the clothes she wears.*

chop[1] /tʃɑp/ S3 W3 *v.* **chopped**, **chopping** **1** [T] **chop sth up** to cut something such as food or wood into smaller pieces: **chop sth into pieces/chunks/cubes etc.** *Chop the carrots into bite-sized pieces.* | **finely/coarsely chopped** (=cut into small or large pieces) **2** [T] to reduce the number or amount of something, especially by a lot: *Over 200,000 jobs have been chopped this year.* | **chop sth off** *The university chopped off $22 million from the budget.* **3** [I always + adv./prep.] to swing a sharp heavy tool such as an AX in order to cut something: **chop (away) at sth** *Volunteers chopped away at the weeds covering the field.* | **chop through sth** *The rope was so thick we couldn't chop through it.* **4 chop wood** to cut trees into pieces using an AX, usually to be burned in a fire: *He's out back chopping wood.* **5** [T] to hit a ball in a quick downward way, using a BAT, RACKET etc.

chop sth ↔ **down** *phr. v.* to make a tree or large plant fall down by cutting it with a sharp tool such as an AX SYN **cut down**: *He chopped down the trees and built most of the house himself.*

chop sth **off** *phr. v.* to remove something by cutting it with a sharp tool so that it is not connected to something else anymore SYN **cut off**: *She chopped off all her hair.* | *Chop some of the lower branches off.*

chop[2] *n.* [C] **1** a small flat piece of meat on a bone, usually cut from a sheep or pig: *pork chops and applesauce* **2** a sudden downward movement with your hand: *a karate chop* **3 chops** [plural] INFORMAL the part of your face that includes your mouth and jaw: *The woman hit me right in the chops.* **4** the act of hitting something once with a sharp tool such as an AX → see also **lick your lips/chops** at LICK[1] (4)

ˌchop-ˈchop *interjection* an expression used when you want someone to hurry

Cho·pin /ˈʃoʊpæn/, **Fréd·é·ric** /ˈfrɛdərɪk/ (1810–1849) a Polish musician who wrote CLASSICAL music

Chopin, Kate /keɪt/ (1851–1904) a U.S. writer of short stories

chop·per /ˈtʃɑpɚ/ *n.* [C] **1** INFORMAL a HELICOPTER **2** a type of MOTORCYCLE on which the front wheel is in front of the HANDLEBARS instead of underneath them **3 choppers** [plural] SLANG teeth

ˈchopping block *n.* [C] **1** a large thick piece of wood that you cut food or wood on SYN **cutting board** **2 be on the chopping block** if someone's job is on the chopping block, they are about to lose their job: *About 800 positions were on the chopping block.*

choppy

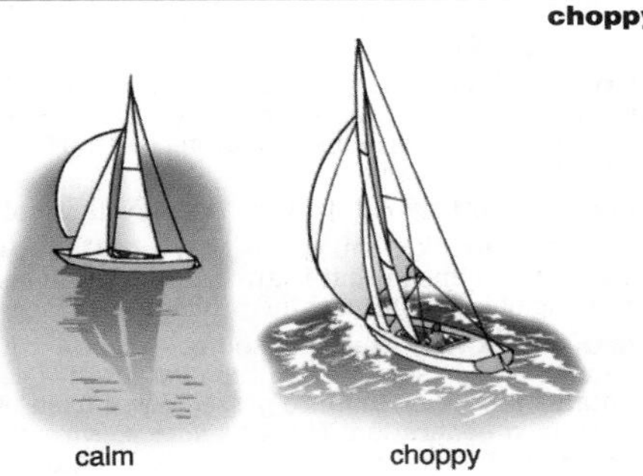

chop·py /ˈtʃɑpi/ *adj. comparative* **choppier**, *superlative* **choppiest** **1** choppy water has many small waves and is very rough to sail on **2** stopping and starting a lot: *music with a choppy rhythm* —**choppiness** *n.* [U]

chop·stick /ˈtʃɑpˌstɪk/ *n.* [C usually plural] one of the two thin sticks used for eating food, especially by people in Asia [**Origin:** 1600–1700 Pidgin English *chop* **fast** (from *Cantonese kap*) + English *stick*]

chop su·ey /ˌtʃɑp ˈsui/ *n.* [U] a Chinese dish made of BEAN SPROUTS and other vegetables and meat, served with rice

cho·ral /ˈkɔrəl/ *adj.* [only before noun] involving singing by a CHOIR (=group of people), or intended to be sung by a CHOIR: *Russian choral music* | *a choral symphony*

cho·rale /kəˈræl, -ˈrɑl/ *n.* [C] a piece of music praising God, usually sung by a CHOIR (=group of people): *a Bach chorale*

chord /kɔrd/ *n.* [C] **1** ENG. LANG. ARTS a combination of two or more musical notes played at the same time → see Usage note at CORD **2 strike/touch a chord** to do or say something that people feel is true or familiar to them and that will make them agree with you or understand you: *Many of the things she says will strike a chord with other young women.* **3** MATH a straight line joining two points on a curve

chore /tʃɔr/ *n.* [C] **1** a job that you have to do regularly, especially work that you do to keep a house clean: *household chores* | *He persuaded his sister to* ***do*** *his* ***chores*** *for him.* **2** something you have to do that is very boring or difficult: *Writing Christmas cards can be such a chore.* [**Origin:** 1700–1800 *chare* **work**]

cho·re·o·graph /ˈkɔriəˌgræf/ *v.* [T] to arrange how dancers should move during a performance

cho·re·og·ra·phy /ˌkɔriˈɑgrəfi/ *n.* [U] the art of arranging how dancers should move during a performance —**choreographer** *n.* [C]

cho·ris·ter /ˈkɔrɪstɚ, ˈkɑr-/ *n.* [C] a singer in a CHOIR, especially a boy in a church CHOIR

cho·ri·zo /tʃəˈrizoʊ/ *n.* [U] a type of SAUSAGE that is SPICY and is made from PORK (=the meat of a pig), used especially in Mexican and Spanish food

chor·tle /ˈtʃɔrtl̩/ *v.* [I] to laugh with a lot of pleasure SYN **chuckle** —**chortle** *n.* [C]

C

cho·rus[1] /ˈkɔrəs/ *n.* [C] ENG. LANG. ARTS
1 SONG the part of a song that is repeated after each VERSE
2 SINGERS a large group of people who sing together → see also CHOIR: *a 100-voice chorus*
3 a chorus of thanks/disapproval/protest etc. something expressed by many people at the same time: *A loud chorus of boos greeted the governor's statement.*
4 GROUP IN MUSICAL PLAY a group of singers, dancers, or actors who act together in a show but do not have the main parts: *the chorus of "West Side Story"*
5 MUSIC a piece of music written to be sung by a large group of people: *the "Hallelujah Chorus" in Handel's "Messiah"*
6 in chorus if people say something in chorus, they say the same thing at the same time: *"Mom!" the kids cried, in chorus.*
7 PLAY **a)** in ancient Greek plays, the group of actors who give explanations or opinions about the play **b)** in English plays of the early 1600s, a person who gives explanations or opinions about the play, especially at the beginning or the end

chorus[2] *v.* [T] if two or more people chorus something, they say it at the same time: *"What happened?" they chorused.*

ˈchorus girl *n.* [C] a woman who sings and dances in a group in a play or movie

ˈchorus line *n.* [C] a group of people who sing and dance together, especially while standing in a straight line, in a play or movie

chose /tʃoʊz/ *v.* the past tense of CHOOSE

cho·sen[1] /ˈtʃoʊzən/ *v.* the past participle of CHOOSE → see also WELL-CHOSEN

chosen[2] *adj.* [only before noun] **1** used for describing something that someone has decided to have or has decided to do: *his chosen profession* | *Mao's chosen successor* **2 the chosen few** the small number of important, special, or talented people who have been invited or SELECTED: *She became one of the chosen few to sing in a concert on the White House lawn.* **3 the chosen people** also **God's chosen people** a group of people with a particular religious faith who are believed to have been chosen by God because they are special in some way

chow[1] /tʃaʊ/ /tʃaʊ/ *v.*
chow down *phr. v.* INFORMAL to eat, especially in a noisy way or in a way that shows you are very hungry: *The children were chowing down on a pepperoni pizza.*

chow[2] *n.* **1** [U] SLANG food **2** also **chow chow** [C] BIOLOGY a dog with long thick fur and a dark-colored tongue, originally from China

chow·der /ˈtʃaʊdɚ/ *n.* [U] a thick soup made with milk, potatoes, onions, BACON, and another main ingredient, usually CLAMS or fish: *a bowl of clam chowder* | *corn chowder*

chow·der·head /ˈtʃaʊdɚˌhɛd/ *n.* [C usually singular] SLANG a stupid person

chow mein /ˌtʃaʊ ˈmeɪn/ *n.* [U] a Chinese dish made with meat, vegetables and NOODLES

Christ /kraɪst/ *n.* **1** also **Jesus Christ, Jesus** the man on whose life, death, and teaching Christianity is based, who Christians believe to be the son of God **2 the Christ** the title for the man predicted in the Old Testament of the Bible to save the Jews from suffering

chris·ten /ˈkrɪsən/ *v.* [T] **1** to be officially given your name at a Christian religious ceremony soon after you are born: **be christened sth** *She was christened Mildred Mary Petre on Nov. 10, 1895.* **2** to officially give a name to something such as a ship, a business etc.: *Former first lady Barbara Bush officially christened the ship.* **3** to invent a name for someone or something because it describes them well: *Derek christened his new sports car "Lightning."* **4** INFORMAL to use something for the first time: *We christened the new mugs that same night.*

C

Chris·ten·dom /ˈkrɪsəndəm/ *n.* [U] OLD-FASHIONED all the Christian people or countries in the world: *the largest church in Christendom*

chris·ten·ing /ˈkrɪsənɪŋ/ *n.* [C,U] a Christian religious ceremony at which someone is officially given their name and becomes a member of a Christian church

Chris·tian¹ /ˈkrɪstʃən, ˈkrɪʃtʃən/ *n.* [C] a person who believes in the ideas taught by Jesus Christ or belongs to a Christian church → see also BORN-AGAIN

Christian² *adj.* **1** believing the ideas taught by Jesus Christ, or belonging to a Christian church: *Christian ministers* **2** based on the ideas taught by Jesus Christ: *Christian doctrine* **3** also **christian** behaving in a good, kind way: *Laughing at his troubles wasn't a very christian act.* [**Origin:** 1200–1300 Latin *christianus*, from Greek, from *Christos* **Christ**, from *chriein* **to pour holy oil on**]

ˈChristian ˌera *n.* [singular] the period from the birth of Jesus Christ to the present

Chris·ti·an·i·ty /ˌkrɪstʃiˈænət̬i/ *n.* [U] the religion based on the life and teachings of Jesus Christ

ˈChristian name *n.* [C] someone's FIRST NAME, or the name someone is given when they are CHRISTENED

ˌChristian ˈScience *n.* [U] a religion which was started in the U.S. in 1866, whose members believe that they can cure their own illnesses using their minds rather than with medical help —**Christian Scientist** *n.* [C]

Chris·tie /ˈkrɪsti/, **Ag·a·tha** /ˈægəθə/ (1890–1976) a British writer known for her many popular novels about murders and the DETECTIVES who try to find out who committed them

Christ·mas /ˈkrɪsməs/ *n.* [C,U] **1** also **Christmas Day** December 25th, the day when Christians celebrate the birth of Jesus Christ: *Christmas presents* | *Christmas shopping* (=shopping for presents that you will give on Christmas Day) | *I **got** a new bike **for Christmas!*** | ***Merry Christmas*** (=used to wish someone a good Christmas) *and Happy New Year, everyone!* **2** the period before and after this day: *I always **spend Christmas** with my parents.* | *What are you doing **for Christmas*** (=where will you be over that period)*?* | *We'll see you **at Christmas**.* | *Julie and her boyfriend went snowboarding **over Christmas*** (=during Christmas). [**Origin:** Old English *Cristes mæsse* 'Christ's mass']

ˈChristmas card *n.* [C] a card that you send to friends and relatives at Christmas with your good wishes

ˌChristmas ˈcarol *n.* [C] a Christian song sung at Christmas SYN carol

ˈChristmas club *n.* [C] a bank account that you put money into regularly during the year so that you have money to spend at Christmas

ˌChristmas ˈcookie *n.* [C] a special COOKIE made before Christmas, especially one shaped like a tree, star, etc.

ˌChristmas ˈDay *n.* [C,U] December 25th, the day when Christians celebrate the birth of Jesus Christ: *She opened her gifts on Christmas Day*

ˌChristmas ˈdinner *n.* [C] a special meal eaten on Christmas Day

ˌChristmas ˈEve *n.* [C,U] December 24th, the day before Christmas Day: *an 11 p.m. church service on Christmas Eve*

ˌChristmas ˈstocking *n.* [C] a long sock that children leave out on Christmas Eve to be filled with small presents

Christ·mas·sy /ˈkrɪsməsi/ *adj.* INFORMAL typical of or relating to Christmas: *a nice Christmassy atmosphere*

Christ·mas·time /ˈkrɪsməsˌtaɪm/ *n.* [U] the period during Christmas when people celebrate

ˈChristmas tree *n.* [C] **1** a PINE or FIR tree that you put inside your house and decorate specially for Christmas **2** a plastic tree, made to look like a real Christmas tree

Chris·to·pher /ˈkrɪstəfɚ/, **Saint** (?A.D.–?250) a man who was supposed to have carried Jesus Christ across a river, and who, as a result, became the PATRON SAINT of travelers

chro·mat·ic /kroʊˈmæt̬ɪk, krə-/ *adj.* **1** relating to or containing bright colors **2** ENG. LANG. ARTS relating to the musical scale that consists of HALF TONES: *the chromatic scale*

chro·ma·tid /ˈkroʊmətɪd/ *n.* [C] BIOLOGY one of the two parts that a CHROMOSOME divides into during the process in which two new cells are formed from an original cell

chro·ma·tin /ˈkroʊmətɪn/ *n.* [C] BIOLOGY a substance that CHROMOSOMES are formed from, which consists of DNA, RNA, and PROTEINS

chrome /kroʊm/ *n.* [U] a hard ALLOY (=a combination of metals) of chromium and other metals, used for covering objects with a shiny protective surface: *a car with chrome bumpers*

ˌchrome ˈyellow *n.* [U] a very bright yellow color

chro·mi·um /ˈkroʊmiəm/ *n.* [U] SYMBOL **Cr** CHEMISTRY a blue or white metal that is an ELEMENT and is used for covering objects with a shiny protective surface

chro·mo·some /ˈkroʊməˌsoʊm, -ˌzoʊm/ *n.* [C] BIOLOGY a long, thin structure in the NUCLEUS of a cell that contains the genes that are passed down from parents to the next generation: *Humans have 46 chromosomes.* [**Origin:** 1800–1900 Greek *chroma* **skin, color** + *soma* **body**; because chromosomes easily take up coloring substances] → see picture at BACTERIUM

chron·ic /ˈkrɑnɪk/ *adj.* [usually before noun] **1** MEDICINE a chronic disease, illness, or condition is one that lasts for a very long time or is permanent → see also ACUTE: *chronic high blood pressure* **2** a problem or difficulty that you cannot get rid of or that keeps coming back: *chronic water shortages* | *chronic unemployment* **3 a chronic alcoholic/gambler etc.** someone who suffers from a particular problem or type of behavior for a long time and cannot stop [**Origin:** 1400–1500 French *chronique*, from Greek *chronikos* **of time**] —**chronically** /-kli/ *adj.*: *chronically ill*

chron·i·cle¹ /ˈkrɑnɪkəl/ *n.* [C] a written record of a series of events, especially historical events, written in the order in which they happened: +**of** *a detailed chronicle of the artist's last years*

chronicle² *v.* [T] to give an account of a series of events in the order in which they happened: *Baer's film chronicles our government's sad history of dealing with Native Americans.* —**chronicler** *n.* [C]

Chron·i·cles /ˈkrɑnɪkəlz/ **1 Chronicles, 2 Chronicles** two books in the Old Testament of the Christian Bible

chrono- /krɑnoʊ, -nə/ *prefix* relating to time: *a chronometer* (=instrument for measuring time very exactly)

chron·o·graph /ˈkrɑnəˌgræf/ *n.* [C] a scientific instrument for measuring and recording periods of time

chron·o·log·i·cal /ˌkrɑnlˈɑdʒɪkəl/ *adj.* arranged according to when something happened: *We had to memorize all the presidents **in chronological order**.* —**chronologically** /-kli/ *adv.*

chro·nol·o·gy /krəˈnɑlədʒi/ *n. plural* **chronologies** **1** [C] a list of events arranged according to when they happened: *a chronology of events in the Balkans* **2** [U] the science of giving times and dates to events

chro·nom·e·ter /krəˈnɑmət̬ɚ/ *n.* [C] a very exact clock for measuring time, used for scientific purposes

chrys·a·lis /ˈkrɪsəlɪs/ *n.* [C] BIOLOGY a MOTH or BUTTERFLY at the stage of development when it does not take in any food and has a hard outer shell, before becoming a LARVA and then an adult → see picture at METAMORPHOSIS

chry·san·the·mum /krɪˈsænθəməm/ *n.* [C] a garden plant with large round flowers that have many long thin PETALS

Chrys·ler /ˈkraɪslɚ/, **Wal·ter** /ˈwɔltɚ/ (1875–1940) a U.S. businessman who made cars and was the first President of the Chrysler Corporation

chub·by /ˈtʃʌbi/ *adj. comparative* **chubbier**, *superlative* **chubbiest** fat in a pleasant healthy-looking way: *He was this cute, chubby baby.* | *chubby cheeks* [**Origin:** 1500–1600 *chub* type of fish (15–21 centuries)] ▶see THESAURUS box at **fat** —**chubbiness** *n.* [U]

chuck¹ /tʃʌk/ *v.* [T] INFORMAL **1** to throw something in a careless or relaxed way: *Somebody chucked a bottle onto the field.* | **chuck sth in/into/on etc.** *I'll just chuck the shirt in the laundry basket.* ▶see THESAURUS box at **throw¹** **2** also **chuck out/away** to throw something away: *Just go ahead and chuck out the batteries.* **3** to stop doing something, especially something that is boring or annoying: *As much as I hate it, I'm not ready to chuck my job.* **4 chuck sb under the chin** to gently touch someone under their chin, especially a child

chuck sb/sth ↔ **out** *phr. v.* to make someone leave a place or a job: *They ended up chucking thousands of employees out into the street.*

chuck² *n.* **1** [C] part of a machine that holds something so that it does not move: *a drill chuck* **2** CHUCK STEAK: *ground chuck*

chuck·le /ˈtʃʌkəl/ *v.* [I] to laugh quietly: *Coulter chuckled and shook his head.* | **+at** *Kay chuckled at the idea.* ▶see THESAURUS box at **laugh¹** —**chuckle** *n.* [C]

chuck·le·head /ˈtʃʌkəlˌhɛd/ *n.* [C] INFORMAL a stupid person

ˈchuck steak *n.* [U] meat cut from the neck and shoulder area of a cow

ˈchuck ˌwagon *n.* [C] OLD-FASHIONED a vehicle that carries food for a group of people

chug /tʃʌg/ *v.* **chugged, chugging** **1** [I] if a car, train etc. chugs, it moves slowly making a repeated low sound: **+along/around/up etc.** *The ferry chugged across New York Harbor.* **2** [I] to make slow but steady progress: *Stocks chugged along today with no great gains or losses.* **3** [T] INFORMAL to drink all of something in a glass or bottle without stopping: *Ted sat back and chugged his beer.* —**chug** *n.* [C usually singular]

chum /tʃʌm/ *n.* **1** [C] OLD-FASHIONED a friend: *an old high school chum* **2** [U] small pieces of oily fish, used to catch other fish

Chu·mash /ˈtʃumæʃ/ a Native American tribe from the southwestern area of the U.S.

chum·my /ˈtʃʌmi/ *adj. comparative* **chummier**, *superlative* **chummiest** OLD-FASHIONED if two people are chummy, they have a close friendly relationship —**chummily** *adv.* —**chumminess** *n.* [U]

chump /tʃʌmp/ *n.* [C] INFORMAL someone who is silly or stupid, and who is easily tricked or deceived

ˈchump change *n.* [U] an expression meaning a small amount of money, often used in negative sentences: *They're offering $10,000 in prize money, which isn't chump change.*

chunk /tʃʌŋk/ [S3] *n.* [C] **1** a large piece of something that does not have an even shape: *pineapple chunks* | **+of** *a 40 million-year-old chunk of amber* ▶see THESAURUS box at **piece¹** **2** a large part or amount of something: *The rent takes a large chunk out of my monthly salary.* | **+of** *I deleted a chunk of text by mistake.* | *Dad risked* ***a*** *pretty big* ***chunk of*** *change* (=bet a large amount of money) *on the race.*

chunk·y /ˈtʃʌŋki/ *adj. comparative* **chunkier**, *superlative* **chunkiest** **1** chunky food has large pieces in it: *chunky peanut butter* **2** thick, solid, and heavy: *chunky silver jewelry* **3** someone who is chunky has a broad, heavy body

church /tʃɚtʃ/ [W1] *n.* **1** [C] a building where Christians go to WORSHIP in religious services: *There was a crowd outside the church.* | *a church service* ▶see THESAURUS box at **religion** **2** [U] the religious ceremonies in a church: *Come to our house for lunch after church.* | *Do you* ***go to church*** *every Sunday?* | *We didn't see you* ***at church*** *on Sunday.* | *Don't talk* ***in church*** (=during the service). **3 the church** the profession of the CLERGY (=priests and other people employed by the church) **4** [singular, U] the Christian religion, considered as a whole: *the church's attitude toward marriage*

> **THESAURUS**
>
> **denomination** a religious group that has slightly different beliefs from other groups who belong to the same religion: *Members of several Christian denominations work together at the InterFaith Council.*
>
> **sect** a group of people who have their own set of beliefs or religious habits, especially a group that has separated from a larger group: *He is a leader in the powerful Ansar Sunni Muslim sect.*
>
> **cult** an extreme religious group that is not part of an established religion: *Members of the cult all committed suicide on the same day.*

▶see THESAURUS box at **religion** **5** also **Church** [C] one of the separate groups within the Christian religion: *evangelical churches* | **the Catholic/Baptist/Methodist etc. Church** *I was brought up in the Catholic Church.* [**Origin:** Old English *cirice*, from Greek *kyriakos* **of the lord**]

church·go·er /ˈtʃɚtʃˌgoʊɚ/ *n.* [C] someone who goes to church regularly

Chur·chill /ˈtʃɚtʃɪl/, **Win·ston** /ˈwɪnstən/ (1874–1965) a British politician who was Prime Minister during most of World War II and again from 1951 to 1955

church·key /ˈtʃɚtʃki/ *n.* [C] INFORMAL a BOTTLE OPENER

church·man /ˈtʃɚtʃmən/ *n.* [C] *plural* **churchmen** /-mən/ a priest [SYN] **clergyman**

ˌChurch of ˌJesus ˌChrist of ˌLatter-Day ˈSaints, the → see MORMON

ˈchurch ˌschool *n.* [C] a private school that is supported by a particular religious group

church·yard /ˈtʃɚtʃyɑrd/ *n.* [C] a piece of land around a church, in which people were buried in past times

churl·ish /ˈtʃɚlɪʃ/ *adj.* not polite or friendly: *It seemed churlish to refuse his invitation.* [**Origin:** 1300–1400 Old English *ceorlic* **of a churl**, from *ceorl* **churl, person of low class**] —**churl** *n.* [C] —**churlishly** *adv.* —**churlishness** *n.* [U]

churn¹ /tʃɚn/ *v.* **1** [I] if your stomach churns, you feel sick because you are nervous or frightened: *My stomach was churning on the day of the exam* **2** [T] to make milk by using a churn **3** also **churn up** [I,T] if water churns or if it is churned, it moves around violently: *The winds were churning the waves.* | *The water churned around our little boat.*

churn sth ↔ **out** *phr. v.* to produce large quantities of something, especially without caring about the quality: *The factory churns out thousands of these toys every week.*

churn up *phr. v.* **1 churn sth ↔ up** to damage the surface of something, especially by walking on it or driving a vehicle over it: *The lawn had been churned up by the tractor* **2** to move water, mud, dust etc. around violently: *Ahead of us a truck was churning up clouds of dust.*

churn² *n.* [C] a container in which milk or cream is shaken until it becomes butter or ICE CREAM

chute /ʃut/ *n.* [C] **1** a long narrow structure that

C

slopes down, so that things or people can slide down it from one place to another: *a laundry chute* **2** INFORMAL a PARACHUTE **3** a long narrow structure that guides cattle, people etc. toward a particular place as they walk along it: *Cows were led down a chute to be branded.*

chut·ney /ˈtʃʌtni/ *n.* [U] a SAUCE, originally from India, made with a mixture of fruits, SPICES, and sugar, that is eaten with meat or cheese

C

chutz·pah /ˈhʊtspə/ *n.* [U] INFORMAL APPROVING a lot of confidence and courage, especially to do something that might involve being impolite to someone in authority SYN **nerve**: ***It took a lot of chutzpah** to quit your job like that.* [**Origin:** 1800–1900 Yiddish, Late Hebrew *huspah*]

chyme /kaɪm/ *n.* [U] BIOLOGY a thick liquid that passes from your stomach to your SMALL INTESTINE, consisting of partly eaten food and acids that break the food into smaller parts

CIA /ˌsi aɪ ˈeɪ/ *n.* **the CIA** the Central Intelligence Agency; the department of the U.S. government that collects information about other countries, especially secretly → see also FBI, THE

ciao /tʃaʊ/ *interjection* INFORMAL used to say goodbye [**Origin:** 1900–2000 Italian, Italian dialect, from *schiavo* **(I am your) slave**]

ci·ca·da /sɪˈkeɪdə/ *n.* [C] an insect that lives in hot areas, has large transparent wings, and makes a high singing noise

cic·a·trix /ˈsɪkəˌtrɪks/ also **cic·a·trice** /-ˌtrɪs/ *n.* [C] TECHNICAL or LITERARY a mark remaining from a wound SYN **scar**

Cic·e·ro /ˈsɪsəroʊ/, **Mar·cus Tul·li·us** /ˈmɑrkəs ˈtʌliəs/ (106–43 B.C.) a Roman politician and ORATOR who is considered one of the greatest Latin writers

-cide /saɪd/ *suffix* [in nouns] another form of the SUFFIX -ICIDE: *genocide* (=killing a whole race of people) | *suicide* (=act of killing yourself) **—-cidal** *suffix* [in adjectives] **—-cidally** *suffix* [in adverbs]

ci·der /ˈsaɪdɚ/ also **ˈapple ˌcider** *n.* [U] a drink made from pressed apples [**Origin:** 1200–1300 Old French *sidre*, from Late Latin *sicera* **alcoholic drink**, from Greek, from Hebrew *shekhar*]

ci·gar /sɪˈgɑr/ *n.* [C] a thick, tube-shaped thing that people smoke, that is made from tobacco leaves that have been rolled up → see also **close, but no cigar** at CLOSE² (15)

cig·a·rette /ˌsɪgəˈrɛt, ˈsɪgəˌrɛt/ S2 W2 *n.* [C] a thin tube-shaped thing that people smoke, that is made from finely cut tobacco leaves inside a tube of paper: *a pack of cigarettes* | *The ashtray was full of cigarette butts.* [**Origin:** 1800–1900 French *cigare* **cigar**, from Spanish *cigarro*]

cigaˈrette ˌholder *n.* [C] a long narrow tube that some people use to hold a cigarette while smoking it

cigaˈrette ˌlighter also **lighter** *n.* [C] a small object that produces a flame for lighting cigarettes, CIGARS etc.

cig·a·ril·lo /ˌsɪgəˈrɪloʊ/ *n.* [C] *plural* **cigarillos** a small thin cigar

ci·lan·tro /səˈlɑntroʊ, -ˈlæn-/ *n.* [U] the strong-tasting leaves of a small plant, used especially in Asian and Mexican cooking

cil·i·a·ry mus·cle /ˈsɪliˌɛri ˌmʌsəl/ *n* [C] MEDICAL BIOLOGY a muscle in your eye that controls the shape of the LENS → see picture at EYE¹

cil·i·um /ˈsɪliəm/ *n. plural* **cilia** /-liə/ [C] BIOLOGY one of many thin hair-like structures that grow from the surface of some cells and from some small living things, such as BACTERIA, that help move liquids past the cell or help the living thing move around

Ci·ma·bu·e /ˌtʃɪməˈbueɪ/, **Gio·van·ni** /dʒoʊˈvɑni/ (?1240–?1302) an Italian PAINTER who is sometimes called the father of Italian painting because he began to develop a new and more LIFELIKE style

C-in-C /ˌsi ɪn ˈsi/ *n.* an abbreviation of COMMANDER IN CHIEF

cinch¹ /sɪntʃ/ *n.* [singular] INFORMAL **1 sb/sth is a cinch to do sth** something that will definitely happen, or someone who will definitely do something: *He's a cinch to be champ.* **2** something that is very easy: *The test was a cinch.* | **be a cinch to do** *Good pie crust is a cinch to make.* **3 a cinch belt/strap etc.** a thin belt etc. made of a material that stretches, that you pull so that it is very tight [**Origin:** 1800–1900 Spanish *cincha* **leather band around a horse**, from Latin *cingula*]

cinch² *v.* [T] **1** to pull a belt, STRAP etc. tightly around something: *Her dress was cinched at the waist with a belt.* **2** to do something so that you can be sure something will happen: *Brown hopes to cinch the deal by Monday.*

Cin·cin·nat·i /ˌsɪnsɪˈnæṭi/ a city in the southwest of the U.S. state of Ohio

cin·der /ˈsɪndɚ/ *n.* [C usually plural] a very small piece of burned wood, coal etc.: *Burning cinders fell onto the roof.* | *The cake was* ***burned to a cinder*** (=completely burned).

ˈcinder block *n.* [C] a large gray brick used in building, made from CEMENT and cinders

Cin·der·el·la /ˌsɪndəˈrɛlə◂/ *n.* [C] **Cinderella team/city etc.** a team, city etc. that becomes successful or popular after a long period of being unsuccessful or unpopular: *basketball's latest Cinderella team*

cin·e·aste, **cinéaste** /ˈsɪneɪˌæst/ *n.* [C] FORMAL someone who is very interested in movies, especially ones with serious artistic value

cin·e·ma /ˈsɪnəmə/ *n.* **1** [U] ENG. LANG. ARTS the skill, industry, or art of making movies: *an important director in German cinema* **2** [C] OLD-FASHIONED a building in which movies are shown SYN **movie theater** [**Origin:** 1900–2000 *cinematograph* **movie camera, movie show** (19–20 centuries), from French *cinématographe*, from Greek *kinema* **movement** + French *-graphe* **recording instrument**]

cin·e·mat·ic /ˌsɪnəˈmæṭɪk◂/ *adj.* relating to movies: *early cinematic techniques that are still used today*

cin·e·ma·tog·ra·phy /ˌsɪnəməˈtɑgrəfi/ *n.* [U] the skill or art of movie photography: *Fellini had no formal training in cinematography.* **—cinematographer** *n.* [C]

ci·né·ma vé·ri·té, **cinema verite** /ˌsɪnəmə vɛriˈteɪ/ *n.* [U] a style of filming a movie or television program in which people or events are filmed in a natural way or as they happen

cin·na·bar /ˈsɪnəˌbɑr/ *n.* [U] a type of red-colored rock from which MERCURY (=a poisonous liquid metal) is taken

cin·na·mon¹ /ˈsɪnəmən/ *n.* [U] **1** a sweet-smelling brown SPICE that comes from the outer covering of a type of tree, used especially in the form of powder in baking cakes and cookies **2** a red-brown color

cinnamon² *adj.* having a red-brown color

CIO /ˌsi aɪ ˈoʊ/ Congress of Industrial Organizations; an organization of UNIONS that is now part of the AFL-CIO

ci·pher /ˈsaɪfɚ/ *n.* [C] **1** someone who is not important and has no power or influence: *At work she was just a cipher.* **2** FORMAL a system of secret writing SYN **code**: *the embassy's cipher equipment* **3** MATH the number 0 SYN **zero**

cir·ca /ˈsɚkə/ WRITTEN ABBREVIATION **ca.** *prep.* FORMAL used before a date to show that it is not the exact date when something happened: *The artifacts date from circa 1100 B.C.*

cir·ca·di·an /sɚˈkeɪdiən/ *adj.* [only before noun] TECHNICAL relating to a period of 24 hours, used especially when talking about changes in people's bodies: *the body's circadian cycle*

cirˌcadian ˈrhythm *n.* [C] BIOLOGY the regular pattern of changes that take place in your body at specific times during a 24-hour period, such as when you feel tired or hungry

cir·cle[1] /ˈsɚkəl/ S2 W2 *n.* [C]
1 SHAPE a) a completely round line with no end, like the letter O: *This circle is 4 inches in diameter.* | ***Draw a circle around** the right answer.* | *The birds flew **in circles*** (=they moved in the shape of circles) *over the lake.* **b)** a flat, completely round shape: *Cut the dough into several small circles.* ▶see THESAURUS box at **shape**[1] → see picture at SHAPE[1]
2 GROUP OF PEOPLE/THINGS a group of people or things forming a round shape: **+of** *a circle of chairs* | *The women sat **in a circle** among the trees.*
3 SOCIAL GROUP a group of people who know each other and meet regularly, or who have similar interests or jobs: **+of** *a large circle of friends* | **political/literary/scientific etc. circles** *The book has caused an uproar in Washington political circles.* | *Johnson was part of the president's **inner circle*** (=the small group of people who talk to the president a lot). | *He wanted his daughter to marry someone in their own **social circle**.*
4 come/go full circle to end in the same situation in which you began, even though there have been changes in the time in between: *Education has come full circle in its methods of teaching reading since the 1960s.*
5 go/run around in circles to think or talk about something a lot without deciding anything or making progress: *This conversation's going around in circles.* [**Origin:** 1000–1100 Old French *cercle*, from Latin *circulus*] → see also **square the circle** at SQUARE[3] (6), VICIOUS CIRCLE

circle[2] S3 *v.* **1** [T] to draw a circle around something: *Glenn circled the date on his calendar.* **2** [I,T] to move in a circle around something, especially in the air: *Helicopters circled overhead.* **3** [T] to make the shape of a circle around something: *Her arms circled his neck.*

cir·clet /ˈsɚklɪt/ *n.* [C] a narrow band of gold, silver, or jewels worn around someone's head or arm, especially in past times

cir·cuit /ˈsɚkɪt/ *n.* [C] **1** PHYSICS the complete path that an electric current travels round, usually including the source of electric energy: *an electrical circuit* **2** a series of places that are usually visited by someone who is regularly involved in a particular activity: **the tennis/lecture/college etc. circuit** *Vesey returned to the nightclub circuit as a singer.* **3** a trip around an area that forms a circle: *Gund did a circuit around the ice rink.* **4** LAW an area in which a judge travels around regularly, so that a court of law can meet in several different places [**Origin:** 1300–1400 Old French *circuite*, from Latin *circuitus*, past participle of *circumire*, *circuire* **to go around**] → see also CLOSED-CIRCUIT TELEVISION, PRINTED CIRCUIT, SHORT CIRCUIT

ˈcircuit board *n.* [C] PHYSICS a set of connections between points on a piece of electrical equipment which uses a thin line of metal to CONDUCT (=carry) the electricity SYN **printed circuit**

ˈcircuit ˌbreaker *n.* [C] PHYSICS a piece of equipment that stops an electric current if it becomes dangerous

ˈcircuit ˌcourt *n.* [C] LAW a court of law in a U.S. state that meets in different places within the area it is responsible for

cir·cu·i·tous /sɚˈkyuət̮əs/ *adj.* **1** going from one place to another in a way that is longer than the most direct way: *the river's circuitous course* **2** doing or achieving something in a way that is not very direct: *Lebeau took **a circuitous route** to academic life; he was a musician and a plumber first.* —**circuitously** *adv.*

cir·cuit·ry /ˈsɚkətri/ *n.* [U] PHYSICS a system of electric circuits

cir·cu·lar[1] /ˈsɚkyəlɚ/ *adj.* **1** shaped like a circle: *a circular table* ▶see THESAURUS box at **shape**[1] **2** a circular argument or way of thinking does not prove anything, because the series of statements or steps in the argument leads back to the original statement: *circular logic* **3** moving around in a circle or making a circle: *a satellite in circular orbit around the earth* —**circularity** /ˌsɚkyəˈlærət̮i/ *n.* [U]

circular[2] *n.* [C] a printed advertisement, announcement etc. that is sent to a lot of people at the same time

ˌcircular ˈflow ˌmodel *n.* [C] ECONOMICS a drawing showing how the economic activities of businesses, the government, and people who buy goods or services depend on and are affected by each other

ˌcircular ˈsaw *n.* [C] an electric tool with a round metal blade that has small sharp parts around the edge, used for cutting wood → see also CHAINSAW

cir·cu·late /ˈsɚkyəˌleɪt/ *v.* **1** [I,T] to move around within a system, or to make something do this: *Blood circulates around the body.* | *The vents circulate heat back into the room.* **2** [I] if information, facts, ideas etc. circulate, people tell them to other people: *Rumors have been circulating on the Internet.* | **+among** *The story circulated quickly among the student population.* **3** [T] to send something to all the people in a group, especially information: *We circulated a petition asking the city to change the system.* | **circulate sth to sb** *The report will be circulated to all members.* **4** [I] to talk to a lot of different people in a group, especially at a party: *Michael circulated among the guests.*

cir·cu·la·tion /ˌsɚkyəˈleɪʃən/ *n.* **1** [U] BIOLOGY the movement of blood around your body: *The bandage is **cutting off** my **circulation*** (=stopping the blood from flowing properly). | **good/poor circulation** *health problems related to poor circulation* **2** [U] the exchange of information, money etc. from one person to another in a group or society: *How many $100 bills are **in circulation*** (=currently being used by the public)? | *The library took the book **out of circulation*** (=stopped letting people borrow it). **3** [C usually singular] the average number of copies of a newspaper, magazine, or book that are usually sold over a particular period of time: **+of** *The newspaper has a daily circulation of 55,000.* **4** [C,U] the movement of liquid, air etc. in a system: *the circulation of fresh air* **5 out of circulation** INFORMAL not taking part in social activities for a period of time: *Joe's out of circulation until after his operation.*

cir·cu·la·tor·y /ˈsɚkyələˌtɔri/ *adj.* [usually before noun] BIOLOGY relating to the movement of blood through the body: *Diabetes can cause circulatory problems.*

circum- /sɚkəm/ *prefix* all the way around something: *to circumnavigate the world* (=travel around it) | *to circumvent* (=avoid something by finding a way around it)

cir·cum·cen·ter /ˈsɚkəmˌsɛnt̮ɚ/ *n.* [C] MATH a point in the middle of a TRIANGLE where PERPENDICULAR lines cross when they are drawn through the middle of each of the three sides

cir·cum·cir·cle /ˈsɚkəmˌsɚkəl/ *n.* [C] MATH a circle drawn through all the points of a flat regular shape such as a TRIANGLE. The center point of the circumcircle is the circumcenter.

cir·cum·cise /ˈsɚkəmˌsaɪz/ *v.* [T] **1** to cut off the skin around the end of the PENIS (=male sex organ) **2** to cut off a woman's CLITORIS (=part of her sex organs)

cir·cum·ci·sion /ˌsɚkəmˈsɪʒən/ *n.* [C,U] the act of circumcising someone, or an occasion when a baby is circumcised as part of a religious ceremony

cir·cum·ference /sɚˈkʌmfrəns/ *n.* [C,U] **1** MATH the distance measured around the outside of a circle or any round shape: *the circumference of the Earth* | *The cable is 1 meter **in circumference**.* **2** the measurement around the outside of any shape: *The island is only 9 miles in circumference.* —**circumferential** /sɚˌkʌmfəˈrɛnʃəl/ *adj.*

cir·cum·flex /ˈsɚkəmˌflɛks/ also **ˈcircumflex ˌaccent** *n.* [C] ENG. LANG. ARTS a mark placed above a vowel in some languages to show that it is pronounced in a particular way, for example ^ → see also GRAVE → ACUTE (7)

cir·cum·lo·cu·tion /ˌsɚkəmloʊˈkyuʃən/ *n.* [C,U] FORMAL the practice of using too many words to express an idea, instead of saying it directly —**circumlocutory** /ˌsɚkəmˈlɑkyəˌtɔri/ *adj.*

cir·cum·nav·i·gate /ˌsɚkəmˈnævəˌgeɪt/ *v.* [T] FORMAL to sail, fly, or travel completely around the

Earth, an island etc. **—circumnavigation** /ˌsɚkəmnævəˈgeɪʃən/ *n.* [C,U]

cir·cum·scribe /ˈsɚkəmˌskraɪb/ *v.* [T] **1** [often passive] FORMAL to limit power, rights, or abilities SYN **restrict**: *The church's role was tightly circumscribed by the new government.* **2** MATH to draw a shape so that it goes around and touches the outside points or edges of a square, a triangle, or other flat GEOMETRIC shape: *The drawing shows a circle that is circumscribed around triangle ABC.*

C

cir·cum·spect /ˈsɚkəmˌspɛkt/ *adj.* FORMAL **1** thinking carefully about things before doing them SYN **cautious**: +**in/about** *The new CEO was circumspect in discussing his plans.* **2** a circumspect action or answer is done or given only after careful thought SYN **cautious**: *a circumspect approach* **—circumspectly** *adv.* **—circumspection** /ˌsɚkəmˈspɛkʃən/ *n.* [U]

cir·cum·stance /ˈsɚkəmˌstæns/ Ac W2 *n.* **1** [C usually plural] the facts or conditions that affect a situation, action, event etc.: *changing political circumstances* | *Only in one particular circumstance could the court legally override the decision.* | *There are plenty of other people **in** similar **circumstances**.* | *The money will only be paid **under** certain **circumstances*** (=if particular conditions exist). | *Extensions on the loan can only be made **in extenuating circumstances*** (=in unusual situations). | *The woman was found dead **in suspicious circumstances*** (=in a way that makes you think something illegal happened). **2 under/given the circumstances** used to say that a particular situation makes an action, decision, statement etc. necessary, acceptable, or true when it would not normally be: *Under the circumstances, she did the best job she could.* **3 under no circumstances** used to emphasize that something must definitely not happen: +**verb/modal** *Under no circumstances should a baby be left alone in the house.* **4** [U] FORMAL the combination of facts, events etc. that influence your life, and that you cannot control: *His illness was a horrible accident of circumstance.* | *The workers who were laid off were purely **victims of circumstance**.* **5 circumstances** [plural] FORMAL the conditions in which you live, especially how much money you have: *The economic circumstances of the average family have changed.* | **family/personal circumstances** *He left school because of personal circumstances.* | **reduced/straightened circumstances** (=a situation in which you have much less money than you used to have) [**Origin:** 1100–1200 Old French, Latin *circumstantia*, from *circumstare* **to stand around**] → see also **pomp and circumstance** at POMP

cir·cum·stan·tial /ˌsɚkəmˈstænʃəl◂ / *adj.* LAW making something seem like it is true, because of the events relating to it, but not definitely proving that it is true: **circumstantial evidence/case** *The case against McCarthy is based largely on circumstantial evidence.* **—circumstantially** *adv.*

cir·cum·vent /ˌsɚkəmˈvɛnt, ˈsɚkəmˌvɛnt/ *v.* [T] FORMAL **1** to avoid something, especially a rule or law that restricts you, especially in a dishonest way: *I had no intention of circumventing Senate rules.* **2** to avoid something by changing the direction you are moving in **—circumvention** /ˌsɚkəmˈvɛnʃən/ *n.* [U]

cir·cus /ˈsɚkəs/ *n. plural* **circuses** [C] **1** a group of people and animals who travel to different places performing skillful tricks as entertainment, or a performance by these people and animals: *circus performers* | *Barnum and Bailey's **three-ring circus*** (=a circus that has three round areas where tricks are performed) **2** INFORMAL a meeting, group of people etc. that is very noisy and uncontrolled: *The media turned the trial into a circus.* **3** HISTORY a place in ancient Rome where fights, races etc. took place, with seats built in a circle [**Origin:** 1300–1400 Latin **circle, circus**]

cir·rho·sis /sɪˈroʊsɪs/ *n.* [U] MEDICINE a serious disease of the LIVER, often caused by drinking too much alcohol [**Origin:** 1800–1900 Modern Latin, Greek *kirrhos* **orange-colored**; from the appearance of the diseased liver]

cir·rus /ˈsɪrəs/ *n.* [U] EARTH SCIENCE a type of cloud that is light and shaped like feathers, high in the sky → see also CUMULUS → NIMBUS

CIS /ˌsi aɪ ˈɛs/ *n.* the Commonwealth of Independent States; the name given to a group of countries, the largest of which is Russia

cis·tern /ˈsɪstɚn/ *n.* [C] a large container that water is stored in

cit·a·del /ˈsɪṭədəl, -ˌdɛl/ *n.* [C] **1** a strong FORT built in past times as a place where people could go for safety if their city was attacked **2 the citadel of sth** LITERARY a place or situation in which an idea, principle, system etc. that you think is important is kept safe: *The U.S. is often seen as the citadel of capitalism.*

ci·ta·tion /saɪˈteɪʃən/ Ac *n.* [C] **1** an official order for someone to appear in court or pay a FINE for doing something illegal: +**for** *Turner was issued a traffic citation for reckless driving.* **2** a formal statement or piece of writing publicly praising someone's actions or achievements: +**for** *a citation for bravery* **3** ENG. LANG. ARTS a line taken from a book, speech etc. SYN **quotation**: *The Oxford English Dictionary's first citation for the word "garage" is from 1902.*

cite /saɪt/ Ac W2 *v.* [T] **1** to mention something as an example, especially one that supports, proves, or explains an idea or situation: *The judge cited a 1956 Supreme Court ruling in her decision.* | **cite sth as sth** *Wolfe cited several companies that are working to attract older customers.* ►see THESAURUS box at **mention**[1] **2** LAW to order someone to appear before a court of law or to pay a FINE, because they have done something wrong: **cite sb for sth** *Two protesters were cited for illegal camping.* **3** to give the exact words of something that has been written in order to support an opinion or prove an idea SYN **quote**: *The passage cited above is from a Robert Frost poem.* **4** FORMAL to mention someone because they deserve praise: **cite sb for sth** *The programs were cited for excellence by the committee.* [**Origin:** 1400–1500 French *citer*, from Latin *citare* **to cause to move, excite, order to come**]

cit·i·fied /ˈsɪṭɪˌfaɪd/ *adj.* DISAPPROVING relating to the city or the way people in cities live, dress, and behave: *three citified guys having a vacation on a ranch* → see also COUNTRIFIED

cit·i·zen /ˈsɪṭəzən/ W1 *n.* [C] **1** someone who lives in a particular town, country, or state: *some of the city's leading citizens* | +**of** *the citizens of San Francisco* **2** someone who legally belongs to a particular country and has rights and responsibilities there, whether they are living there or not → see also NATIONAL: *He became an American citizen in 1998.* | *We need to teach our children to be good citizens.* | *a group of **private citizens*** (=citizens who do not have jobs in the government) *who want to ban handguns* [**Origin:** 1200–1300 Anglo-French *citezein*, from Old French *citeien*, from *cité*] → see also **second-class citizen** at SECOND-CLASS (1), SENIOR CITIZEN

cit·i·zen·ry /ˈsɪṭəzənri/ *n.* [U] FORMAL all the citizens in a particular place

ˌcitizen's arˈrest *n.* [C] LAW the act of preventing someone from leaving a place until the police arrive, because you think that person has done something illegal

ˈcitizens ˌband, citizens' band, Citizens Band *n.* [U] → see CB

cit·i·zen·ship /ˈsɪṭəzənˌʃɪp/ *n.* [U] **1** the legal right of belonging to a particular country: *She has applied for citizenship.* | *Costas has **dual citizenship*** (=the legal right of being a citizen in two countries) *in the U.S. and the Philippines.* | **American/Canadian/French etc. citizenship** (=the state of being a citizen of the U.S., Canada etc.) **2** the quality of being a good citizen, for example being responsible and helping your COMMUNITY: *Scout groups help teach **good citizenship**.*

cit·ric ac·id /ˌsɪtrɪk ˈæsɪd/ *n.* [U] CHEMISTRY a weak acid found in some fruits, such as LEMONS

cit·ron /ˈsɪtrən/ *n.* [C] BIOLOGY a fruit that comes from India that is like a LEMON, but bigger and with thick skin

cit·ro·nel·la /ˌsɪtrəˈnɛlə/ *n.* [U] an oil used for keeping insects away

cit·rus /ˈsɪtrəs/ *n. plural* **citruses** [C] **1** also **ˈcitrus fruit** BIOLOGY a fruit with thick skin, such as an orange or LEMON **2** also **ˈcitrus tree** a type of tree that produces citrus fruits —**citrus** *adj.*

cit·y /ˈsɪt̬i/ S1 W1 *n. plural* **cities** [C] **1 a)** a large important town: *New York City* | *It's one of America's oldest cities.* | **a big/large/major city** *the problem of unemployment in our major cities* **b)** a town of any size that has definite borders and powers that were officially given by the state government: *The city of Parlier is in Fresno county.* **2** [usually singular] the people who live in a city: *Panic swept the city after the earthquake.* **3 the city** the government of a city: *The city is working to improve public transportation.* **4 ...city** SPOKEN used in order to say that there is a lot of something in a place or situation, or that a situation or place makes you feel something strongly: *It was sun city all weekend.* | *We biked all day, so it was like tired city.* [**Origin:** 1100–1200 Old French *cité*, from Latin *civitas* **citizenship, state, city of Rome**] → see also INNER CITY, SISTER CITY

ˌcity ˈcouncil *n.* [C] the group of elected officials who are responsible for governing a city and making its laws

ˈcity desk *n.* [C usually singular] a department of a newspaper that deals with local news

ˈcity ˌeditor *n.* [C] a newspaper EDITOR who is responsible for local news

ˌcity ˈfather *n.* [C usually plural] **1** a member of the group of people who govern a city **2** a man who helped start or develop a city

ˌcity ˈhall, City Hall *n.* **1** [U] POLITICS the government of a city: *The recycling program is a high priority at City Hall.* **2** [C usually singular] POLITICS the building a city government uses as its offices: *The library is near City Hall.*

ˌcity ˈplanning *n.* [U] the study of the way cities work best, so that streets, houses, services etc. can be provided effectively —**city planner** *n.* [C]

ˌcity ˈslicker *n.* [C] DISAPPROVING someone who lives and works in a city and has no experience of anything outside it

ˌcity-ˈstate *n.* [C] a city, especially in past times, that forms an independent country: *the city-state of Monaco*

cit·y·wide /ˌsɪt̬iˈwaɪd◂ / *adj.* involving all the areas of a city: *a citywide campaign to fight racism*

civ·et /ˈsɪvɪt/ *n.* **1** [C] also **ˈcivet cat** a small wild animal like a cat, that lives in Asia and Africa **2** [U] TECHNICAL a strong-smelling liquid from a civet cat, used to make PERFUME

civ·ic /ˈsɪvɪk/ *adj.* [only before noun] **1** relating to a town or city: *an important civic and business leader* **2** relating to the people who live in a town or city: *It is your* ***civic duty*** *to act as a juror.* | *The program is designed to boost* ***civic pride*** (=people's pride in their own city). [**Origin:** 1600–1700 Latin *civicus*, from *civis* **citizen**]

ˈcivic ˌcenter *n.* [C] a large public building where events such as sports games and concerts are held

civ·ics /ˈsɪvɪks/ *n.* [U] a school subject dealing with the rights and duties of citizens and the way government works

ˌcivic ˈvirtue *n.* [U] POLITICS a willingness to do things that will improve the country or town where you live, or that help other people living there: *Social studies teaches democratic principles and tries to inspire civic virtue in young people.*

civ·il /ˈsɪvəl/ Ac S3 W2 *adj.* **1** [only before noun] relating to the people who live in a country: **civil unrest/war/conflict etc.** (=fighting between different groups of people in the same country) → see also CIVIL LIBERTY, CIVIL RIGHTS **2** [only before noun] relating to the ordinary people or things in a country that are not part of military, government, or religious organizations: *They were married in a civil ceremony in May.* | *civil aviation* **3** [only before noun] LAW relating to the laws concerning the private affairs of citizens, such as laws about business or property, rather than laws about crime → see also CRIMINAL: *Many civil cases can be settled out of court.* → see also CIVIL LAW **4** polite, but not really very friendly: *I know you don't like Phil, but try to be civil.* ►see THESAURUS box at **polite** —**civilly** *adv.*

ˈcivil ˌcase *n.* [C] LAW a legal case concerning the private affairs of citizens, such as a disagreement about a business contract or the sale of a property, rather than a crime → see also CRIMINAL CASE

ˌcivil deˈfense *n.* [U] the organization of ordinary people to help defend their country from military attack

ˌcivil disoˈbedience *n.* [U] the action of not obeying a law in order to protest in a peaceful way against the government, especially when this is done by a large group of people

ˌcivil engiˈneering *n.* [U] the planning, building, and repair of roads, bridges, large buildings etc. —**civil engineer** *n.* [C]

ci·vil·ian /səˈvɪlyən/ *n.* [C] anyone who is not a member of the military forces or the police: *Many innocent civilians were killed during the war.* —**civilian** *adj.*: *Military rulers gave way to a civilian government 18 years ago.*

Ciˌvilian Conserˈvation ˌCorps, the abbreviation **CCC** *n.* HISTORY a 1933 U.S. government program, part of the series of programs called the New Deal, that gave young men jobs taking care of forests, parks, beaches etc.

ci·vil·i·ty /səˈvɪlət̬i/ *n. plural* **civilities** **1** [U] polite behavior that most people consider normal: *The debate began with calls for civility.* **2** [C usually plural] FORMAL something that you say or do in order to be polite: *We spent a few minutes exchanging civilities before getting down to business.*

civ·i·li·za·tion /ˌsɪvələˈzeɪʃən/ *n.* **1** [C,U] a society that is well organized and developed: *modern American civilization* | **+of** *the ancient civilizations of Greece and Rome* **2** [U] all the societies in the world considered as a whole: *The book looks at the relationship between religion and civilization.* **3** [U] HUMOROUS a place such as a city, where there is a lot to do or where you have things to make you feel clean and comfortable: *After a week in the mountains, all I wanted to do was get back to civilization.* **4** [U] the process in which societies become developed and organized: *the* ***dawn of civilization*** (=the beginning of civilization)

> WORD CHOICE **civilization, culture**
> • **Civilization** means societies that are advanced in their development, and that have a particular type of culture and way of life: *The Mayan civilization was at its height from 300 to 900 A.D.*
> • **Culture** is the art, music, literature etc. that a particular society has produced, and the way that society lives: *Singapore is influenced by both Western and Asian cultures.*

civ·i·lize /ˈsɪvəˌlaɪz/ *v.* [T] **1** to improve a society so that it is more organized and developed: *The Romans hoped to civilize all the tribes of Europe.* **2** to influence someone's behavior, by teaching them to act in ways acceptable to society: *Women's duty was to bear children and civilize them.*

civ·i·lized /ˈsɪvəˌlaɪzd/ *adj.* **1** well organized and developed socially, and having fair laws and customs: *Care for the disabled, old, and sick is essential in a* ***civilized society***. **2** HUMOROUS pleasant and comfortable: *The resort offers a very civilized vacation.* **3** behaving in a polite and sensible way: *I tried talking to her in a civilized manner, but she refused to listen.*

C

ˌcivil ˈlaw *n.* [U] LAW the area of law that deals with the affairs of private citizens, such as laws about business or property, rather than laws about crime

ˌcivil ˈliberty *n. plural* **civil liberties** [C usually plural,U] the right of all citizens to be free to do whatever they want while obeying the law and respecting the rights of other people

ˌcivil ˈpartnership *n.* [U] an official relationship between two people of the same sex, which gives them the same legal rights as two people who are married

C

ˌcivil ˈrights W3 *n.* [plural] the rights that every person should have, such as the right to vote or to be treated fairly by the law, whatever their sex, race, or religion: *In the 1960s, King and others struggled for civil rights.* | *an important civil rights leader*

Civil Rights Act of 1964, the /ˌsɪvəl ˈraɪts ækt əv ˌnaɪntin ˌsɪksti ˈfɔr/ HISTORY a law that made it illegal in the U.S. to DISCRIMINATE against someone (=treat them in a way that is unfair or not equal) because of their race, the color of their skin, their religion, or the country they came from

ˌCivil ˈRights ˌMovement, the HISTORY a political effort in the U.S. from 1954 until the present day to get equal rights for African-Americans and for people of any race and color, using protests, marches, and other actions but not by using violence

ˌcivil ˈservant *n.* [C] someone who works in the civil service

ˌcivil ˈservice *n.* [singular] the government departments that deal with all the work of the government, not including the military

ˌCivil ˈService Comˌmission, the HISTORY the U.S. government organization responsible for making sure that the employment rules for the civil service are fair and equal for everyone

ˌcivil ˈwar *n.* [C,U] **1** a war in which opposing groups of people from the same country fight each other in order to gain political control **2 the Civil War** HISTORY the war that was fought from 1861 to 1865 in the U.S. between the northern and southern states over whether it was right to own slaves

ˌCivil War Aˈmendments, the HISTORY the Thirteenth, Fourteenth, and Fifteenth AMENDMENTS which were added to the U.S. Constitution in 1865, 1868, and 1870 in order to protect the rights of African-American people in the period after the Civil War. The amendments ended SLAVERY, gave all citizens the same rights whatever their race or color, and gave all citizens the right to vote.

civ·vies /ˈsɪviz/ *n.* [plural] INFORMAL a word meaning ordinary clothes, not military uniforms, used mainly by people in the military

ck. the written abbreviation of CHECK

cl the written abbreviation of CENTILITER

clack /klæk/ *v.* [I,T] to make a short hard sound repeatedly: *The keys clacked as she typed.* —**clack** *n.* [C usually singular]

clad /klæd/ *adj.* LITERARY wearing a particular kind of clothing: **be clad in sth** *The model was clad in silk and lace.* | **warmly/poorly/scantily etc. clad** (=dressed in a particular way)

-clad /klæd/ [in adjectives] **snow-clad/ivy-clad etc.** LITERARY covered in a particular thing: *an armor-clad ship*

clad·ding /ˈklædɪŋ/ *n.* [U] a covering of hard material that protects the outside of a building, vehicle etc.

claim¹ /kleɪm/ S2 W1 *v.* [T] **1** to state that something is true, even though it has not been proven: **claim (that)** *A later report claimed that rebels had taken control of the capital.* | **claim to have done sth** *He claimed to have discovered the ruins of a lost city.* | **claim to be sth** *Tran claims to be the leader of the gang.* | **claim to do sth** *The education program claims to reach two million people nationwide.* | *The group* ***claimed responsibility*** (=said officially that they were responsible) *for the bombing.* **2** to officially demand or receive money from an organization because you have a right to it: *Congress intends to make welfare harder to claim.* | *Steiner filed a lawsuit* ***claiming damages*** *against her former employer.* **3** to state that you have a right to take or have something that legally belongs to you: *Kashmir is claimed by both India and Pakistan.* | *Lost items can be claimed between 10 a.m. and 4 p.m.* **4** WRITTEN if a war, accident etc. claims lives, people die because of it: *The 12-year-old civil war had claimed 1.5 million lives.* **5** if something claims your attention or time, you have to notice it or consider it [**Origin:** 1300–1400 Old French *clamer*, from Latin *clamare* **to cry out, shout**]

> **WORD CHOICE** **claim, demand**
>
> • Use **claim** when you are asking for money and think that there is an official reason why someone should give it to you: *Poor women with children may be able to claim food stamps.* | *You can claim certain deductions on your income tax return.*
>
> • Use **demand** when you are asking for something strongly, but there is no official reason why someone should give it to you: *He demanded a pay raise.* | *People are demanding stricter gun control laws.*

claim² S3 W2 *n.* [C]
1 MONEY a) an official request for money that you believe you have a right to: **+for** *claims for unemployment benefits* | *Ms. Byrd is* ***filing a claim*** *for unpaid child support.* | *You need to fill out a* ***claim form*** *first.* **b)** the sum of money you request when you make a claim: *They've paid out $30,000 in worker's compensation claims.*
2 STATEMENT OF TRUTH a statement that something is true, even though it has not been proved: *Companies will be allowed to* ***make*** *health* ***claims*** *for certain food products.* | **+that** *There were claims that he had acted irresponsibly.* | *They had made* ***false claims*** *about their weight-loss products.* | *Wentworth* ***makes no claim to*** *literary greatness* (=he does not pretend he is a good writer). | **dispute/deny/reject a claim** *A government spokesperson denied claims that the men were tortured.*
3 RIGHT TO OWN OR TAKE STH a right to have or get something such as land, a title etc. that belongs to you: **+to** *their claim to their ancestral lands* | **have a claim on/to** *Parents do not have a claim on their children's wages.* | *Both sides* ***lay claim to*** (=say they have a right to own) *the same land.* | **have a claim on sb's love/attention/time etc.** *Working mothers have many claims on their time.*
4 sb's/sth's claim to fame a place or person's claim to fame is the reason why they are known about: *In high school, my claim to fame was that I dated the entire basketball team.*
5 LAND a piece of land that contains valuable minerals: *a mining claim* → see also **jump a claim** at JUMP¹ (27), **stake (out) a claim** at STAKE² (2)

claim·ant /ˈkleɪmənt/ *n.* [C] LAW someone who officially asks for something that they think they have a right to: *a lawsuit representing 20 claimants* | *Claimants will receive their welfare checks early.*

clair·voy·ant /klɛrˈvɔɪənt/ *n.* [C] someone who says they can see what will happen in the future [**Origin:** 1800–1900 French *clair* **clear** + *voyant* **seeing**] —**clairvoyance** *n.* [U] —**clairvoyant** *adj.*

clam¹ /klæm/ *n.* [C] **1** a SHELLFISH that you can eat, which has a shell in two parts that open and close → see picture at SEAFOOD **2 as happy as a clam** INFORMAL very happy **3** INFORMAL someone who does not say what they are thinking or feeling **4** [usually plural] OLD-FASHIONED INFORMAL a dollar

clam² *v.* **clammed, clamming**
clam up *phr. v.* INFORMAL to suddenly stop talking, especially when you are nervous, shy, or unhappy: *A lot of men just clam up when they're having emotional problems.*

clam·bake /ˈklæmbeɪk/ *n.* [C] an informal party where clams are cooked and eaten outdoors, near the ocean

clam·ber /ˈklæmbɚ, ˈklæmɚ/ *v.* [I always + adv./prep.] to climb slowly, using your hands and feet: **+up/over/to etc.** *They clambered over the slippery rocks.*

'clam ˌchowder *n.* [U] a type of thick soup made with clams, potatoes, and milk

clam·my /'klæmi/ *adj.* *comparative* **clammier**, *superlative* **clammiest** feeling wet, cold, and sticky in a way that is not nice: *His hands were clammy.* —**clamminess** *n.* [U]

clam·or¹ /'klæmɚ/ *n.* [singular, U] **1** a very loud noise, often made by a large group of people or animals: *the clamor of factory machinery* **2** a complaint or a demand for something that is expressed by many people: +**for** *There has been a national clamor for better schools.* —**clamorous** *adj.*

clamor² *v.* [I] **1** to demand or complain about something loudly, as part of a group of people: +**for** *Kids clamored for an autograph.* | **clamor to do sth** *People are clamoring to get into the program.* **2** to talk or shout loudly, as part of a group of people: *We could hear children clamoring in the playground.*

clamp¹ /klæmp/ *n.* [C] a piece of equipment that can fasten or hold things together

clamp² *v.* [T always + adv./prep.] **1** to fasten or hold two things together using a clamp: **clamp sth together/onto/across etc.** *Clamp the boards together until the glue dries.* **2** to put or hold something firmly in a position where it does not move: **clamp sth over/between/around etc.** *His cigar was clamped firmly between his teeth.*

clamp down *phr. v.* to take firm action to stop a crime or other illegal activity from happening: +**on** *The police are clamping down on drunk drivers.*

clamp·down /'klæmpdaʊn/ *n.* [C usually singular] a sudden action by the government, the police etc. to stop a particular activity: +**on** *a clampdown on illegal immigration*

clan /klæn/ *n.* [C] **1** INFORMAL a large family, including aunts, cousins etc.: *The whole clan will be here for Thanksgiving.* **2** a large group of families who have the same ANCESTOR (=a member of your family who lived in past times), considered important in some societies [**Origin:** 1400–1500 Scottish Gaelic *clann* **family, race, clan**, from Old Irish *cland* **new growth on a plant, offspring**] —**clannish** *adj.*

clan·des·tine /klæn'dɛstɪn/ *adj.* clandestine activities or organizations are secret, and often illegal: *a clandestine meeting*

clang /klæŋ/ *v.* [I,T] if a metal object clangs or if you clang it, it makes a loud ringing sound —**clang** *n.* [C]

clan·gor /'klæŋɚ/ *n.* [U] a loud noise that continues for a long time

clank /klæŋk/ *v.* [I,T] if a metal object clanks or if you clank it, it makes a loud heavy sound —**clank** *n.* [C]

clans·man /'klænzmən/ *n.* *plural* **clansmen** [C] FORMAL a male member of a CLAN → see also KLANSMAN

clans·wom·an /'klænzˌwʊmən/ *n.* *plural* **clanswomen** [C] FORMAL a female member of a CLAN

clap¹ /klæp/ *v.* **clapped**, **clapping** **1** [I,T] **a)** if you clap, or if you clap your hands, you hit your hands together loudly and repeatedly to show that you have enjoyed something or that you approve of or agree with it → see also APPLAUD: *The audience clapped and cheered.* | *She clapped her hands in delight.* **b)** if you clap, or if you clap your hands, you hit your hands together one or two times to attract someone's attention or to stop them from doing something: *The teacher clapped her hands to get the class's attention.* **2 clap your hand on/over etc. sth** to put your hand somewhere quickly and suddenly: *She suddenly stopped speaking and clapped her hand over her mouth.* **3 clap sb on the back/shoulder** to hit someone lightly on their back or shoulder with your open hand in a friendly way **4 clap sb in jail** to put someone in prison: *He refused to pay taxes and was clapped in jail.* [**Origin:** Old English *clæppan*] —**clapping** *n.* [U]

clap² *n.* **1 a clap of thunder** a loud sound made by THUNDER **2 a clap on the back/shoulder** an act of hitting someone on the back or shoulder to show that you are friendly, amused, or approving **3** [C] a sudden loud sound that you make when you hit your hands together, especially to show that you enjoyed something or that you agree

clap·board /'klæbɚd, 'klæpbɔrd/ *n.* [C,U] a set of boards that cover the outside walls of a building, or one of these boards: *a clapboard house*

clap·per /'klæpɚ/ *n.* [C] the movable metal part inside a bell that hits the sides of the bell to make it ring

clap·trap /'klæptræp/ *n.* [U] INFORMAL things that people say that are stupid or show a lack of knowledge [**Origin:** 1800–1900 *claptrap* **something intended to make the people watching a show clap** (18–19 centuries)]

clar·et /'klærət/ *n.* [U] **1** red wine from the Bordeaux area of France **2** a dark red color —**claret** *adj.*

clar·i·fi·ca·tion /ˌklærəfə'keɪʃən/ Ac *n.* [C,U] the act of making something clearer or easier to understand, or an explanation that makes something clearer: +**of/on** *a clarification of his earlier statement* | **seek/ask for clarification** *I asked the department for clarification on the legal position.*

ˌclarified 'butter *n.* [U] butter that has been made clear and pure by heating it

clar·i·fy /'klærəˌfaɪ/ Ac *v.* **clarifies**, **clarified**, **clarifying** [T] to make something clearer and easier to understand by explaining it in more detail: *Illustrations help to clarify the written instructions.* | **clarify how/what etc.** *The rule clarifies what information can be given out.* | *Reporters asked him to* ***clarify his position*** *on welfare reform* (=say exactly what his beliefs are).

clar·i·net /ˌklærə'nɛt/ *n.* [C] a wooden musical instrument shaped like a long black tube, that you play by blowing into it and pressing KEYS to change the notes [**Origin:** 1700–1800 French *clarinette*] —**clarinetist** *n.* [C]

clar·i·on call /'klæriən ˌkɔl/ *n.* [C usually singular] FORMAL a strong and direct request for people to do something: *His speech was a clarion call to young people to vote.*

clar·i·ty /'klærəṭi/ Ac *n.* [singular, U] **1** the quality of expressing ideas or thoughts in a clear way: +**of** *the clarity of Irving's writing style* | *a lack of clarity in the law* **2** the ability to think, understand, or remember something clearly: *He remembered the performance* ***with great clarity.*** | *The war brought these countries together with* ***a clarity of purpose*** (=they had a clear reason for doing something). **3** the ability to be seen or heard clearly: *the clarity of the image on the screen*

Clark /klɑrk/, **William** (1770–1838) an American EXPLORER

clash¹ /klæʃ/ *v.* **1** [I] WRITTEN if two armies or groups of people clash, they suddenly start fighting each other: +**with** *More than 3,000 demonstrators clashed with police on Sunday.* **2** [I] WRITTEN if two people or groups of people clash, they argue because their opinions and beliefs are very different: +**with** *Humphrey has often clashed with Republican leaders.* | +**over** *The two lawyers clashed over the physical evidence.* **3** [I] if two colors or patterns clash, they look very bad together: +**with** *No, the red tie will clash with your shirt.* **4** [I,T] if two pieces of metal clash or if you clash them, they make a loud ringing sound: *The cymbals clashed.* [**Origin:** 1500–1600 From the sound of sharp blows]

clash² *n.* [C] **1** WRITTEN a short fight between two armies or groups of people: *There have been many border clashes.* | +**between** ***armed clashes*** *between police and gang members* | +**with** *Soldiers were involved in a* ***violent clash*** *with the rebels.* ▶see THESAURUS box at **war** **2** WRITTEN an argument between two people or groups of people, because they have different opinions or beliefs: +**between** *a clash between Democrats and Republicans in the Senate* | *a* ***personality clash*** *between the boy and his teacher* | *a* ***culture clash*** (=when people do not understand each other because their cultures are different) **3** a loud sound made by two metal objects being hit together: *the clash of* *swords* **4** a situation in which two events happen or are meant to happen at the same time in a way that is not possible or helpful: *a scheduling clash* **5** WRITTEN a sports competition that is expected to be very exciting: *Monday night's clash at the Sports Arena* **6** a combination of two colors, designs etc. that look bad together

clasp¹ /klæsp/ *n.* **1** [C] a small metal object that fastens a bag, belt, piece of jewelry etc. **2** [singular] a tight hold SYN **grip**: *the firm clasp of her hand*

C

clasp² *v.* [T] to hold someone or something tightly, closing your fingers or arms around them SYN **grip**: *A baby monkey clasps its mother's fur tightly.* | **clasp your hands/arms around/behind sth** *Lie down with your hands clasped behind your head.* | *Jill **clasped** the doll **to her chest*** (=held it tightly against her chest) *and ran to her mother.*

class¹ /klæs/ S1 W1 *n.*

1 GROUP OF STUDENTS [C] **a)** a group of students who are taught together: *a small class of ten people* | *We're **in the** same math **class**.* **b)** a group of students who finished college or HIGH SCHOOL in the same year: *a class reunion* | *a member of the **class of '89*** (=the group of students who finished in 1989)

2 TEACHING PERIOD [C,U] a period of time during which someone teaches a group of people, especially in a school: *When's your next class?* | *I **have class** until ten tonight.* | *I'm sure we read that article **in class*** (=during the class). | **English/history/math etc. class** *We had to read our stories out loud in English class.* ►see THESAURUS box at **school¹**

3 SUBJECT [C] a series of classes in which you study a particular subject: *a list of the classes offered this semester* | **+in** *a class in computer design* | **dance/aerobics/photography etc. class** *She's **taking a** ballet **class**.* ►see THESAURUS box at **university**

4 IN A SOCIETY a) [C] one of the groups in a society that different types of people are divided into according to their jobs, family, education etc.: *The Republicans are promising tax cuts for the middle class.* | *People were excluded from education based on their class and race.* → see also LOWER CLASS, MIDDLE CLASS, UPPER CLASS, WORKING CLASS **b)** [U] the system in which people are divided into such groups: *the class system in Britain*

5 SAME TYPE [C] a group into which people or things are divided according to their qualities, features, or abilities: *The car costs less than other cars in its class.* | **+of** *a new class of drugs* | **first/business/coach etc. class** (=one of the different standards of seats available on an airplane, train etc.) | *As a tennis player, he's **not in the same class*** (=not as good) *as Nadal.* | *Beene's designs are **in a class of their own*** (=are much better than other similar things). → see also BUSINESS CLASS, ECONOMY CLASS, FIRST CLASS, HIGH-CLASS, LOW-CLASS, SECOND CLASS, THIRD CLASS, TOURIST CLASS

6 STYLE [U] INFORMAL a high level of style or skill in the way you do something: *The players **showed** a lot of **class** under pressure.* | *Margaret's a person who really **has class**.* | *Harrison dealt with the problem **with class** and dignity.*

7 a class act INFORMAL someone or something that is very skillful, polite, attractive etc.: *Coach Williams is a real class act.*

8 BIOLOGY one of the groups into which scientists divide animals and plants. A class is larger than an ORDER, but smaller than a PHYLUM.

[**Origin:** 1500–1600 French *classe*, from Latin *classis* **class of citizens, social class**]

class² S1 *v.* [T often passive] FORMAL to decide that someone or something belongs in a particular group SYN **classify**: **class sb/sth as sth** *Stewart's books are classed as romantic mysteries.*

ˌclass 'action *n.* [C,U] LAW a LAWSUIT arranged by a group of people for themselves and other people with the same problem —**class-action** *adj.* [only before noun] *a class-action case*

'class-ˌconscious *adj.* believing that social class is important, and often judging other people according to their social class —**class-consciousness** *n.* [U]

clas·sic¹ /ˈklæsɪk/ Ac W3 *adj.* **1** [usually before noun] admired by many people, and having a value that continues for a long time: *classic novels such as "Jane Eyre"* | *the classic film "Citizen Kane"* | *the classic rock music of the '60s* | *a classic car* ►see THESAURUS box at **old** **2** having all the features that are typical or expected of a particular thing or situation: **classic example/case etc.** *This was a classic example of poisoning.* | *Lasagna is one of Italy's classic dishes.* **3** [usually before noun] a classic style of art or clothing is attractive in a simple or traditional way, and is not influenced very much by changing fashions: *a classic blue suit* **4 That's classic!** SPOKEN said when you think something is very funny

classic² Ac *n.* [C] **1** something such as a book, movie, or music that is considered very good and important, and that has a value that has continued for a long time: *a collection of literary classics* | **animated/modern/American etc. classic** *The play has become an American classic.* | **an instant classic** (=something new that is good and that people will admire for a long time) *a children's book that became an instant classic* **2** something that is very good and one of the best examples of its kind: *Tuesday night's game against the Clippers was a classic.* | **+of** *Barbecued ribs are one of the classics of Southern cuisine.*

clas·si·cal /ˈklæsɪkəl/ Ac *adj.* **1** belonging to a traditional style or set of ideas, especially in art or science: *classical physics, as opposed to quantum physics* | *The vase is modern, but made in a classical Chinese style.* **2** ENG. LANG. ARTS relating to classical music: *a classical CD* | **classical musician/composer etc.** *one of the top classical pianists* **3** ENG. LANG. ARTS relating to the language, literature etc. of ancient Greece and Rome: *classical architecture* | *a **classical education*** (=an education that includes studying Latin and Greek) —**classically** /-kli/ *adv.*

ˌclassical con'ditioning *n.* [U] BIOLOGY a learning process in which an animal makes a connection in its mind between something that makes them move or react and a reward or a punishment. After a period of time, the animal learns to move or react without the reward or punishment.

ˌclassical eco'nomics *n.* [U] ECONOMICS the economic ideas of a group of people who lived in the 18th and 19th century, including Adam Smith and John Stuart Mills. Some of the main ideas are that wealth increases when people follow their own interests, that competition encourages economic growth, and that an economic system will achieve a natural balance if nothing is done to control it.

ˌclassical 'music *n.* [U] a type of music that is considered to be important and serious and that has continuing artistic value, for example OPERAS and SYMPHONIES

clas·si·cism /ˈklæsəˌsɪzəm/ *n.* [U] a style of art that is simple, regular, and does not show too much emotion, based on the models of ancient Greece or Rome → see also REALISM, ROMANTICISM

clas·si·cist /ˈklæsəsɪst/ *n.* [C] someone who studies Classics

Clas·sics /ˈklæsɪks/ *n.* [U] the study of the languages, literature, and history of ancient Greece and Rome

clas·si·fi·ca·tion /ˌklæsəfəˈkeɪʃən/ *n.* **1** [C] a group that you put people or things into according to a set of rules: *job classifications* **2** [U] the process of putting something into the group or class it belongs to: *the classification of wines according to region*

clas·si·fied /ˈklæsəˌfaɪd/ *adj.* classified information or documents are ones that the government has ordered to be kept secret

ˌclassified 'ad *n.* [C] a small advertisement in a special part of a newspaper that contains many small advertisements for things that people want to buy or sell, or for jobs → see also WANT AD

clas·si·fieds /ˈklæsəˌfaɪdz/ *n.* [plural] INFORMAL **the classifieds** the part of a newspaper where the classified ads are

clas·si·fy /ˈklæsəˌfaɪ/ *v.* **classifies, classified, classifying** [T] **1** to decide what group something belongs to according to a system: **classify sth as sth** *Whales are classified as mammals rather than fish.* | **classify sth into sth** *Headaches can be classified into two major categories.* | **classify sth by/according to sth** *If children are classifying the beads by color, they ignore the shape.* **2** to make information or documents secret: *The military has classified the results of the weapons test.* —**classifiable** *adj.*

class·less /ˈklæslɪs/ *adj.* a classless society is one in which people are not divided into different social classes, so that no one has more advantages than other people —**classlessness** *n.* [U]

class·mate /ˈklæsmeɪt/ *n.* [C] someone who is in the same class as you in a school or college

ˈclass ring *n.* [C] a ring that shows which high school or college you went to and the year you GRADUATED

class·room /ˈklæsrum/ S2 W3 *n.* [C] **1** a room in a school where students are taught: *brightly decorated classrooms* | *classroom activities* **2 in the classroom** in schools or classes in general: *Computers are now common in the classroom.*

ˌclass ˈstruggle *n.* [singular, U] POLITICS the continuing struggle for political and economic power between workers and people who own businesses, according to Marxist ideas

class·work /ˈklæswɚk/ *n.* [U] school work that you do during class, rather than at home → see also HOMEWORK

class·y /ˈklæsi/ *adj. comparative* **classier**, *superlative* **classiest** INFORMAL **1** stylish and fashionable, and usually expensive: *classy restaurants* **2** having style or skill in the way you do something, that makes people notice and admire you: *a classy woman*

clat·ter /ˈklæṭɚ/ *v.* **1** [I,T] to make a loud noise by hitting hard objects together: **+to/onto/in etc.** *All the pots clattered to the floor.* **2** [I always + adv./prep.] to move quickly and with a lot of noise: **clatter over/down/along etc.** *A cable car clattered along the tracks.* —**clatter** *n.* [singular, U] *the clatter of dishes*

clause /klɔz/ Ac S3 *n.* [C] **1** LAW a part of a written law or legal document that deals with a particular subject, condition etc.: *A clause in the contract states when payment must be made.* **2** ENG. LANG. ARTS in grammar, a group of words that contains a subject and a verb, but which is usually only part of a sentence. In the sentence "Jim is the only one who knows the answer," "who knows the answer" is a clause. [**Origin:** 1200–1300 Old French, Medieval Latin *clausa* **end of a sentence**, from Latin *claudere*] → see also PHRASE

claus·tro·pho·bi·a /ˌklɔstrəˈfoubiə/ *n.* [U] a strong fear of being in a small enclosed space or among a crowd of people [**Origin:** 1800–1900 Modern Latin, Latin *claustrum* **bar keeping a door closed** + Modern Latin *phobia* **fear**] → see also AGORAPHOBIA

claus·tro·pho·bic /ˌklɔstrəˈfoubɪk◂/ *adj.* **1** feeling extremely anxious when you are in a small enclosed space: *I get claustrophobic in elevators.* **2** making you feel anxious and uncomfortable, because you are enclosed in a small space: *a small, claustrophobic apartment*

clav·i·chord /ˈklævɪˌkɔrd/ *n.* [C] a musical instrument like a piano that was played especially in past times

clav·i·cle /ˈklævɪkəl/ *n.* [C] BIOLOGY a COLLARBONE

claw[1] /klɔ/ *n.* [C] **1** BIOLOGY a sharp curved nail on the toe of an animal or bird → see picture at BIRD **2** [usually plural] BIOLOGY the part of the body of some insects and sea animals that is used for attacking and holding things: *a crab's claw* **3** a curved end of a tool or machine, used for pulling nails out of wood or lifting things: *a claw hammer* [**Origin:** Old English *clawu*]

claw[2] *v.* [I,T] **1** to tear or pull at something using claws: **+at** *The cat's been clawing at the furniture again.* **2** to pull or try to get hold of something: **+at** *Her toddler was clawing at her skirt.* **3 claw your way** to try very hard to reach a place or position, using a lot of effort and determination: **+up/along/back etc.** *He has managed to claw his way to the top.* | *Searchers clawed their way up the stony hillsides.*

claw back *phr. v.* **claw sth ↔ back** to get back something you had lost, by trying very hard: *The Rockets clawed back into the lead.*

clay /kleɪ/ *n.* [U] **1** a soft, usually gray or red sticky substance in soil that becomes hard when it is dry or baked, used for making pots, bricks etc. **2** a soft sticky substance that people can form into different shapes and make into figures etc.: *modeling clay* [**Origin:** Old English *clæg*] → see also **feet of clay** at FOOT[1] (24) —**clayey** *adj.*

Clay /kleɪ/, **Henry** (1777–1852) a U.S. politician who tried to establish an agreement between the states of the North and South before the American Civil War

Clay·ma·tion /kleɪˈmeɪʃən/ *n.* [U] TRADEMARK a process in which clay figures are filmed, moved, and filmed again repeatedly so that they look as though they move and talk

Clay·ton An·ti·trust Act, the /ˌkleɪtˀn æntɪˈtrʌst ˌækt/ HISTORY a law that was passed in 1914 as an AMENDMENT (=addition) to the Sherman Antitrust Act of 1890 in order to further limit the powers of big companies

clean[1] /klin/ S2 W2 *adj.*

1 WITHOUT DIRT/MESS not dirty or messy: *Are your hands clean?* | *a clean towel* | *I couldn't **get** the tiles any **cleaner**.* | *Make sure you **keep** the wound **clean**.* | *The house was **neat and clean**.* | **wash/wipe/sweep etc. sth clean** *The rain had washed the sidewalks clean.* | *a **spotlessly clean*** (=very clean) *kitchen* | *The whole house was **as clean as a whistle*** (=very clean).

THESAURUS

spotless completely clean
pristine completely clean and not damaged at all
immaculate used about rooms, clothes etc. that are very clean and neat
spick and span INFORMAL used about a room, house etc. that is completely clean and neat

2 AIR/WATER/POWER ETC. not containing or producing anything that is dirty or harmful, such as poisons: *The river is a lot cleaner than it used to be.* | **clean air/water/energy etc.** *Clean air and water are a necessity of life.* | *clean-burning natural gas* | *the **sparkling clean*** (=very clean and clear) *water of the lake*

3 DESIGN having a simple and attractive style or design: *the car's clean style* | *the clean lines of Morrison's drawings*

4 NO DRUGS/CRIME/WEAPONS ETC. INFORMAL [not before noun] **a)** not taking illegal drugs, especially when you did before: *Dave's been clean for over a year now.* | *She has remained **clean and sober** since then.* | *He's a **squeaky clean** kid — doesn't smoke, drink, do drugs, or anything.* | *She says **clean living*** (=not drinking alcohol, taking drugs, or behaving in an immoral way) *is the key to her long life.* **b)** not hiding any weapons or illegal drugs: *The police searched Romero, but he was clean.*

5 FAIR/LEGAL a) honest, fair, and not breaking any rules: *a clean fight* | *Everyone wants a clean and honest election.* | *The city's police department has always been seen as **squeaky clean*** (=very honest and fair). **b)** showing that you have followed the rules or the law: *Drivers with **clean** driving **records** pay less in insurance.*

6 come clean INFORMAL to finally tell the truth or admit that you have done something wrong: **+about** *Roberts finally came clean about his involvement in the scheme.*

7 NOT OFFENSIVE not offensive or not dealing with sex: *The resort offers **good, clean fun** for everyone.* | *The comedians were asked to **keep it clean*** (=asked not to use offensive language).

8 a clean bill of health a report that says you are healthy or that a machine or building is safe: *Doctors have **given** her **a clean bill of health**.*

9 a clean slate a situation in which you make a new start after doing everything wrong in the past: *They've*

paid all their debts and can ***start*** *the year* ***with a clean slate***.
10 a clean sweep a) a victory in all parts of a game or competition, especially by winning the first three places: *The three runners made a clean sweep for the U.S. in the 100 meters.* **b)** a complete change in a company or organization, made by getting rid of people
11 a clean break a) a complete and sudden separation from a person, organization, or situation: *The country is trying to* ***make a clean break*** *with its past.* **b)** a break in a bone or other object that is complete and has not left any small pieces
12 SMOOTH having a smooth edge: *Fortunately, the cut was clean and not jagged.* | *the car's clean lines*
13 PAPER a clean piece of paper has not been used yet SYN **fresh**
14 CLEAR PICTURES/WRITING looking clear and containing no mistakes: *The film produces clean, sharp images.* | *I need a* ***clean copy****; don't send a fax.*
15 MOVEMENT a clean movement is skillful and exact: *The dancing was clean and brilliantly fast.*
16 make a clean breast of sth SPOKEN to admit that you have done something wrong so that you do not feel guilty anymore
17 PEOPLE/ANIMALS behaving in a way that keeps things clean or having a clean appearance: *Cats are very clean animals.*
[**Origin:** Old English *clæne*] —**cleanness** *n.* [U] → see also CLEAN-CUT, CLEANLINESS, CLEANLY, **keep your nose clean** at NOSE[1] (12), **wipe the slate clean** at WIPE[1] (3)

clean² S1 *v.* **1** [I,T] to remove dirt from something by rubbing or washing: *I need to clean the bathtub.* | *She's busy cleaning.* | *Many working women still do most of the* ***cooking and cleaning***. | **clean sth off** *Use the hose to clean off your boots.* → see also DRY-CLEAN, SPRING-CLEANING

THESAURUS
wash to clean something with water
do/wash the dishes to wash plates and pans after a meal
scour/scrub to wash dirty pots and pans with a rough cloth
dry to dry plates, dishes etc. that have been washed
do the housework to clean the house
dust to clean the dust off of furniture
polish to make furniture, shoes etc. shiny by rubbing them
vacuum to clean carpets with a special machine
sweep (up) to clean the dirt from the floor or ground using a broom (=brush with a long handle)
scrub to clean the floor by rubbing it with a hard brush
wipe to clean a surface with a cloth, often a wet cloth
mop to clean the floor with water and a mop (=soft brush on a long handle)
do the laundry to wash clothes
handwash clothes/wash clothes by hand to wash clothes without using a machine
dry-clean clothes to clean clothes with chemicals instead of water

2 [T] also **clean off/up** to make something look neat by removing the things that make it look messy and putting things in their correct places: *Manion cleaned his desk before leaving for the day.* **3** [I,T] to clean a building or other people's houses as your job: *Anne comes in to clean twice a week.* **4** [T] to cut out the inside parts of an animal or bird that you are going to cook: *He cleaned the fish and cooked them over the fire.* **5 clean your plate** to eat all of the food that is on your plate **6 clean sb's clock** HUMOROUS to defeat or beat someone very severely

clean sb/sth **out** *phr. v.* **1 clean sth ↔ out** to make the inside of a room, house etc. clean and neat, especially by removing things from it: *I got rid of a lot of stuff when I was cleaning out my closets.* **2 clean sb/sth ↔ out** INFORMAL to steal everything from a place, or to steal all of someone's possessions: *One man held the gun, and the other cleaned out the cash register.* **3 clean sb out** INFORMAL to be forced to spend all of your money on something, so that you have none left: *The car repair bill cleaned us out.*

clean up *phr. v.* **1 clean sth ↔ up** to make something clean and neat, especially by removing the things that make it look messy: *We spent Saturday morning cleaning up.* | *They're working on a plan to clean up the bay.* | +**after** *I spend all my time cleaning up after the kids* (=making a place clean after the kids have used it). **2 clean sb ↔ up** to wash yourself after you have gotten very dirty, or to wash someone else: *Go upstairs, get cleaned up, and then we can go.* | *It takes an hour to clean up the kids after soccer practice.* **3 clean up your act** INFORMAL to start behaving in a responsible way: *Gwen finally told him to clean up his act or get out of her house.* **4** INFORMAL to win a lot of money or make a lot of money in a business deal: *Jack really cleaned up this time in Vegas.* **5 clean sth ↔ up** to improve moral standards in a place or organization: *He was voted in to clean up City Hall.* → see also CLEANUP

clean³ *adv.* INFORMAL used to emphasize the fact that an action or movement is complete or thorough: **clean away/through/past etc.** *The nail went clean through his finger.* | *Sorry, I* ***clean forgot*** (=completely forgot) *your birthday.*

ˌClean 'Air Act, the HISTORY a law passed in the U.S. in 1970 that aimed to control POLLUTION in the air and gave people the right to sue companies who did not obey the law

ˌclean-'cut *adj.* a clean-cut man or boy looks neat and clean, and appears to have a good moral character: *clean-cut college boys*

clean·er /ˈklinɚ/ *n.* [C] **1** a machine used for cleaning: *a vacuum cleaner* **2** a substance used for cleaning: *Keep household cleaners away from children.* **3 the cleaners** a DRY CLEANERS: *I need to pick my suit up from the cleaners.* **4 take sb to the cleaners** INFORMAL **a)** to get a lot of someone's money in a way that is not fair or not honest, especially in business or in a court of law: *She took her former husband to the cleaners.* **b)** to defeat someone completely: *The Lakers took the Bulls to the cleaners, winning 96–72.* **5** someone whose job is to clean other people's houses, offices etc.: *He'd worked as a pool cleaner.*

clean·ing /ˈklinɪŋ/ *n.* [U] the process of making something clean and neat: *Women still* ***do most of the cleaning*** *in the home.*

ˈcleaning ˌlady also **ˈcleaning ˌwoman** *n.* [C] a woman who cleans offices, houses etc. as her job

clean·li·ness /ˈklɛnlinɪs/ *n.* [U] **1** the practice of keeping yourself or the things around you clean **2 cleanliness is next to godliness** OLD-FASHIONED, SPOKEN used to say that keeping yourself and other things clean is a sign of good moral character

clean·ly /ˈklinli/ *adv.* **1** quickly and smoothly, in a neat way: *The branch snapped cleanly in two.* **2** if something burns cleanly, it does not produce any dirty or harmful substances as it burns

cleanse /klɛnz/ *v.* [T] **1** to make something completely clean: *Cleanse the wound with alcohol.* **2** LITERARY to remove everything that is immoral or bad from someone's character or from a place or organization: **cleanse sb/sth of sth** *The police force needed to be cleansed of corruption.* → see also **ethnic cleansing** at ETHNIC CLEANSING

cleans·er /ˈklɛnzɚ/ *n.* [C,U] **1** a chemical liquid or powder used for cleaning surfaces inside a house, office etc.: *household cleansers* **2** a liquid used for removing dirt or MAKEUP from your face

clean-shaven

John has a beard. Mike is clean-shaven.

ˌclean-ˈshaven *adj.* a man who is clean-shaven does not have hair on his face

clean·up, clean-up /ˈklinʌp/ *n.* [C usually singular] a process in which you get rid of dirt or waste from a place: *The cleanup of the oil spill took months.* | *The city must now pay millions of dollars in cleanup costs.*

ˌClean ˈWater Act, the HISTORY a law passed in 1972 in the U.S. that aimed to control POLLUTION in the country's rivers, lakes etc. and provided money for better SEWAGE systems (=for dealing with human waste)

clear[1] /klɪr/ S2 W1 *adj.*

1 EASY TO UNDERSTAND expressed in a simple and direct way so that people understand: *clear instructions* | *The test questions weren't very clear.* | **be clear about sth** *The school was very clear about its policy on student uniforms.* | **be clear about what/when/how etc.** *Be clear about what jobs need to be done, and by when.* | **be clear on sth** *I want to be very clear on this point.* | **be clear to sb** *It is clear to me that the company will have to make further job cuts.* | *Taylor's book* ***makes*** *the subject* ***clear*** *and even enjoyable.* | ***Make it clear that*** *you will not take sides.* | *Klein said that Martin had not* ***made himself clear*** (=had not expressed something well). | *Before asking for a raise, get* ***a clear idea*** (=a good understanding) *of what you plan to say.* | *He made his message* ***crystal clear*** (=very easy to understand).

2 IMPOSSIBLE TO DOUBT impossible to doubt, question, or make a mistake about: *clear evidence of his guilt* | *They won by a clear majority.* | **it is clear whether/why/how etc.** *It was not clear how we would be affected by the changes.* | *The tests* ***make it clear that*** *the drug is safe.* | ***It is clear that*** *the drug does benefit some patients.* | ***a clear case of*** *sexual discrimination*

THESAURUS

plain clear: *The effect is plain to see.*
noticeable easy to see: *a noticeable improvement in her behavior*
obvious extremely easy to recognize or understand: *I kept asking, despite her obvious irritation.*
evident/apparent ESPECIALLY WRITTEN easy to recognize or understand: *The pattern was readily apparent when the researchers looked at the data.*
blatant used about something bad that is very easy to see or recognize, and not hidden: *cases of blatant discrimination*

►see THESAURUS box at **noticeable**

3 SURE ABOUT STH feeling certain that you know or understand something: **+about/on** *There are a few points that I'm not really clear on.* | *Let me get this clear – you weren't even there at the time?* | ***a clear understanding*** *of the issues*

4 SEE THROUGH easy to see through, rather than colored or dirty SYN **transparent**: *clear glass bottles*

5 WATER/AIR clean and fresh: *a clear mountain lake* | *the* ***crystal clear*** *water in the river*

6 WEATHER without clouds, mist, smoke etc.: *a beautiful clear day*

7 EASY TO SEE having details, edges, lines etc. that are easy to see, or shapes that are easy to recognize: *Most of the photographs were sharp and clear.*

8 EASY TO HEAR easy to hear, and therefore easy to understand: *a clear speaking voice* | *The sound isn't very clear.* | *It's a good recording; the sound is* ***as clear as a bell*** (=very clear). ►see THESAURUS box at **hear**

9 NOT BLOCKED/COVERED not covered or blocked by anything that stops you from doing or seeing what you want: *The roads were fairly clear this morning.* | *We had a* ***clear view*** *of the ocean from our hotel room.* | **+of** *Landowners are required to keep their property clear of trash.*

10 EYES very pure in color and without any redness: *clear blue eyes*

11 SKIN smooth and without any red spots

12 THINKING able to think sensibly and quickly: *The drug prevents clear thinking.* | *I'll deal with it in the morning, when I have a* ***clear head.***

13 a clear conscience the knowledge that you have done the right thing: *She had done what she could and her conscience was clear.*

14 as clear as mud SPOKEN HUMOROUS used to say that something is very difficult to understand: *Joe's directions are as clear as mud.*

15 see your way clear (to doing sth) INFORMAL to have the necessary time or willingness to be able to do something: *If you can see your way clear, call this number to volunteer.*

16 NOT BUSY without any planned activities or events: *Next Monday is clear; how about 10 o'clock?*

17 be clear (of sth) to not be touching something, or to be past someone or something: *The curtains should be a couple of inches clear of the floor.* | *Wait until the street is clear of cars before you cross.*

18 AFTER TAXES a clear amount of profit, salary etc. is what is left after taxes have been paid on it SYN **net**: *Sullivan's company makes a clear $900,000 profit per year.*

[**Origin:** 1200–1300 Old French *cler*, from Latin *clarus* **clear, bright**] —**clearness** *n.* [U] → see also ALL-CLEAR, CLARITY, CLEARLY, **the coast is clear** at COAST[1] (2)

clear[2] S2 W2 *v.*

1 SURFACE/PLACE [T] to make a place neat or emptier by removing things from it: *Snowplows have been out clearing the roads.* | **clear sth of sth** *Volunteers were clearing the streets of rubble.* | *Barbara, it's your turn to* ***clear the table*** (=take off the used plates, forks etc. after you have eaten). | **clear sb/sth from sth** *Trucks have just finished clearing the wreck from the road.* | *He* ***cleared a space*** (=moved things to make room) *on his desk for the report.*

2 REMOVE PEOPLE [T] to make people, cars etc. leave a place: *Within minutes, police had cleared the area.* | **clear sb/sth from sth** *Crowds of demonstrators were cleared from the streets.*

3 CRIME/BLAME ETC. [T usually passive] to prove that someone is not guilty of something: *Rawlings was cleared after new evidence was produced.* | **clear sb of (doing) sth** *The jury cleared Johnson of the murder.* | *Tucker is determined to* ***clear*** *his father's* ***name*** (=show that he is not guilty of something).

4 WEATHER also **clear up** [I] if the weather, sky etc. clears, it becomes better or there is more sun: *The fog usually clears around noon.*

5 PERMISSION [T] **a)** to give or get official permission for something to be done: *The report was cleared by the State Department.* | **clear sth with sb** *I'll have to clear it with my boss first.* **b)** to give official permission for a person, ship, or aircraft to enter or leave a country: *Delta 7, you are cleared for takeoff.*

6 BANK [I,T] if a check clears or if a bank clears it, the bank allows the money to be paid into the account of the person who received the check

7 EARN [T] INFORMAL to earn a particular amount of money after taxes have been paid on it: *Wiley's business clears $300,000 a year.* ►see THESAURUS box at **earn**

8 clear a debt/loan to get rid of a debt by paying what you owe

9 GO OVER [T] to go over a fence, wall etc. without touching it: *The plane barely cleared the fence at the end of the runway.* | *Edwards cleared 18 feet in the pole vault.*

10 clear the way for sb/sth to make it possible for a

process to happen: *This agreement will clear the way for further talks.*
11 clear your throat to cough in order to be able to speak with a clear voice
12 clear your head/mind to stop worrying or thinking about something, or get rid of the effects of drinking too much alcohol: *I go for a long walk at lunchtime to clear my head.*
13 clear the air to do something in order to end an argument or bad situation: *The White House hopes that the investigation will clear the air.*
14 clear sth through customs also **clear customs** to be allowed to take things through CUSTOMS
15 SKIN also **clear up** [I] to not have marks or PIMPLES on your skin anymore
16 LIQUID also **clear up** [I] if a liquid clears, it becomes more transparent
17 clear the decks to do a lot of work that needs to be done before you can do other things: *We're trying to clear the decks before Christmas.*
18 FACE/EXPRESSION [I] if your face or expression clears, you stop looking worried or angry

clear sth ↔ away *phr. v.* to make a place look neat by removing things or putting things where they belong: *Homeowners are clearing away brush near their houses to prevent fires.* | *The train station will be closed until the wreckage is cleared away.*

clear out *phr. v.* **1 clear sth ↔ out** to make a place neat by removing things from it: *I need to clear out that closet.* **2** INFORMAL to leave a place or building quickly: *The gym cleared out quickly after the game.*

clear up *phr. v.* **1 clear sth ↔ up** to explain something or make it easier to understand: *There are a lot of questions about the case that still haven't been cleared up.* **2 clear sth ↔ up** to make a place look neat by putting things where they belong: *Come on, it's time to clear up this mess.* **3** if the weather clears up, it gets better: *I hope it clears up by the weekend.* **4** if an illness or infection clears up, it disappears

clear³ [S3] *adv.* **1** away from something, or out of the way: *Firefighters pulled the woman clear of the wreckage.* **2 steer/stay/keep clear (of sth)** to avoid someone or something because of possible danger or trouble: *Drivers should stay clear of the I-40 bridge because of ice.* **3 clear to/through/across etc. sth** INFORMAL used to emphasize a long distance: *You can see clear to the mountains today.* | *I had to walk clear across Oakland when my car broke down.* → see also **loud and clear** at LOUD¹ (4)

clear⁴ *n.* **in the clear a)** not guilty of something: *If Martin can prove he was at the office, then he's in the clear.* **b)** not having difficulties because of something: *The debt is being paid off, but we're not in the clear yet.* **c)** not having a particular illness or infection anymore, so that your health or life is not in danger

clear·ance /ˈklɪrəns/ *n.* **1** [C,U] official permission or approval for something: **get/receive/obtain clearance** *The movie crew got clearance to film in the park.* | **clearance to do sth** *He has received clearance to play from his doctor.* | +**for** *The pilot requested clearance for an emergency landing.* **2** [C,U] the amount of space around one object that is necessary for it to avoid touching another object: *We need 12 feet of overhead clearance for the truck.* **3** [C] a CLEARANCE SALE **4** [C,U] a SECURITY CLEARANCE **5** [C,U] a process by which a check goes from one bank to another **6** [C,U] the removal of unwanted things from a place: +**of** *the clearance of minefields* | **snow/forest/brush etc. clearance** *Brush clearance helps prevent fires spreading.*

ˈclearance sale *n.* [C] a sale in which goods are sold very cheaply in order to get rid of all of them

ˈclear-cut¹ *adj.* **1** easy to understand or be certain about [SYN] **definite**: *a clear-cut case of sexual harassment* **2** [only before noun] having a definite outer shape: *the clear-cut outline of the mountains*

clear-cut² *n.* [C] an area of forest in which all the trees have been cut down, or an act of cutting down all the trees in an area —**clear-cut** *v.* [T]

ˌclear-ˈheaded *adj.* able to think in a clear and sensible way —**clear-headedly** *adv.* —**clear-headedness** *n.* [U]

clear·ing /ˈklɪrɪŋ/ *n.* [C] a small area in the middle of a forest where there are no trees

clear·ing·house, clearing house /ˈklɪrɪŋˌhaʊs/ *n.* [C] **1** an office that receives goods or information from other organizations, and then gives them out or sells them: *a clearinghouse for airline ticket sales* **2** an office where banks exchange checks and other financial documents

clear·ly /ˈklɪrli/ [S2] [W1] *adv.* **1** [sentence adverb] without any doubt [SYN] **obviously**: *Clearly, racial problems in America have no easy answers.* **2** in a way that is easy to see, hear, or understand: *Please speak clearly.* | *The map clearly shows all the bike trails.* **3** in a way that is sensible: *It's late and I can't think clearly.*

ˌclear-ˈsighted *adj.* able to understand a problem or situation well: *a clear-sighted analysis of the market* —**clear-sightedly** *adv.* —**clear-sightedness** *n.* [U]

cleat /klit/ *n.* [C] **1 cleats** [plural] a pair of sports shoes that have short pieces of rubber, plastic, or metal attached to the bottom of them to prevent slipping **2** [usually plural] a short piece of rubber, plastic, or metal that is attached to the bottom of a sports shoe to prevent slipping **3** TECHNICAL a small bar with two short arms around which ropes can be tied, especially on a ship

cleav·age /ˈklivɪdʒ/ *n.* [C,U] **1** the space between a woman's breasts **2** FORMAL a difference between two people or things that often causes problems or arguments: *the cleavage between the country's rulers and the population*

cleave /kliv/ *v. past tense* **cleaved, clove** /kloʊv/, **cleft** /klɛft/, *past participle* **cleaved, cloven** /ˈkloʊvən/, **cleft** **1** [I always + adv./prep.,T always + adv./prep.] LITERARY to cut something into separate parts using a heavy tool: *The wooden door had been cleft in two.* **2 cleave the air/darkness etc.** LITERARY to move quickly through the air etc.: *His fist cleft the air.*

cleave to sb/sth *phr. v.* **1** FORMAL to be faithful to an idea, belief, or person: *John still cleaves to his romantic ideals.* **2** LITERARY to stick to someone or something, or to seem to surround them

clea·ver /ˈklivɚ/ *n.* [C] a heavy knife with a wide blade that is used for cutting up large pieces of meat

Clea·ver /ˈklivɚ/**, El·dridge** /ˈɛldrɪdʒ/ (1935–1998) a leader of the Black Panthers in the 1960s, who left the organization in 1975

clef /klɛf/ *n.* [C] a sign at the beginning of a line of written music to show the PITCH of the notes: *the treble clef* → see picture at MUSICAL¹

cleft¹ /klɛft/ *n.* [C] **1** a natural crack in the surface of rocks or the Earth: *a cleft in the granite cliff* **2** an area on the chin or lip that goes slightly inward, so that the chin or lip is not smooth and rounded

cleft² *adj.* **1** a cleft chin is one that is not smooth and rounded, but that has a small area that goes inward **2 a cleft lip/palate** a split in someone's upper lip or the top of the inside of their mouth that they are born with and that makes it difficult for them to speak clearly

cleft³ *v.* a past tense and past participle of CLEAVE

clem·a·tis /ˈklɛmət̬ɪs, klɪˈmæt̬ɪs/ *n.* [C,U] a plant with white or colored flowers that attaches itself to trees, buildings, fences etc. and covers them as it grows [**Origin:** 1500–1600 Latin, Greek *klematis* **small dead branches, clematis**, from *klema* **small branch**]

Cle·men·ceau /ˌklɛmənˈsoʊ/**, Georges** /ʒɔrʒ/ (1841–1929) the Prime Minister of France at the end of World War I

clem·en·cy /ˈklɛmənsi/ *n.* [U] FORMAL forgiveness and less severe punishment for a crime, usually given by someone in power such as a governor or president: **grant/give sb clemency** *She was granted clemency after serving ten years for killing her abusive husband.*

Clem•ens /ˈklɛmənz/, **Sam•u•el Lang•horne** /ˈsæmyuəl ˈlæŋhɔrn/ (1835–1910) the real name of Mark Twain

clem•ent /ˈklɛmənt/ *adj.* LITERARY clement weather is neither too hot nor too cold SYN mild OPP inclement —**clemently** *adv.*

clem•en•tine /ˈklɛmənˌtin, -ˌtaɪn/ *n.* [C] a type of small sweet orange

clench /klɛntʃ/ *v.* [T] **1 clench your fists/teeth/jaw etc.** to hold your hands, teeth etc. together tightly, especially because you feel angry or determined: *Jody paced the sidelines, her fists clenched.* **2** to hold something tightly in your hand or between your teeth: *Reese had a cigar clenched between his teeth.* —**clench** *n.* [C usually singular]

Cle•o•pat•ra /ˌkliəˈpætrə/ (69–30 B.C.) a queen of Egypt who became the lover of Julius Caesar and later of Mark Antony

clere•sto•ry /ˈklɪrˌstɔri/ *n. plural* **clerestories** [C] TECHNICAL the upper part of the wall of a large church, that has windows in it and rises above the lower roofs

cler•gy /ˈklɚdʒi/ *n.* **the clergy** [plural] the official leaders of religious activities in organized religions, such as priests, RABBIS, and MULLAHS: *members of the clergy* ►see THESAURUS box at **priest**

cler•gy•man /ˈklɚdʒimən/ *n. plural* **clergymen** /-mən/ [C] a male member of the clergy ►see THESAURUS box at **priest**

cler•gy•wom•an /ˈklɚdʒiˌwʊmən/ *n. plural* **clergywomen** /-ˌwɪmɪn/ [C] a female member of the clergy

cler•ic /ˈklɛrɪk/ *n.* [C] OLD-FASHIONED a member of the clergy

cler•i•cal /ˈklɛrɪkəl/ *adj.* **1** relating to office work: *a clerical error* | *The work you'll do is mainly clerical.* **2** relating to the clergy: *a clerical collar* (=a special black and white collar that priests wear)

clerk¹ /klɚk/ *n.* [C] **1** someone whose job is to help customers in a store: *a clerk at a convenience store* → see also SALESCLERK **2** someone whose job is to help people when they arrive at and leave a hotel: *Please return your keys to the* ***desk clerk****.* **3** a lawyer who works as an assistant to a judge in order to gain experience SYN **law clerk**: *a clerk for Judge Marshall* **4** somone who keeps records or accounts in an office: *a file clerk* **5** an official in charge of records in a court or for a government: *the county clerk* [**Origin:** 1000–1100 Old French *clerc* **man in a religious order, scholar, man who keeps records**, from Late Latin *clericus*]

clerk² *v.* [I] to work as a clerk, especially in a store or in a judge's or lawyer's office: +**for** *Rehnquist clerked for Justice Robert Jackson early in his career.*

Cler•mont, the /ˈklɛrmɑnt/ HISTORY a name for Robert Fulton's STEAMBOAT, which he built in 1807 and which was the first successful steamboat

Cleve•land /ˈklivlənd/ a city in the U.S. state of Ohio

Cleveland, Gro•ver /ˈgroʊvɚ/ (1837–1908) the 22nd and 24th President of the U.S., who was defeated in 1889 but elected again in 1893

clev•er /ˈklɛvɚ/ S3 *adj.* **1** done or made in an unusual or interesting way: *a clever device for chopping onions* | *a clever joke* **2** able to use your intelligence to do something, especially in a slightly dishonest way: *a clever lawyer* ►see THESAURUS box at **intelligent** **3** showing ability or skill, especially at making things or doing things: *her clever use of rhyme* **4** able to learn and understand things quickly SYN **smart**: *The main character in the story is a clever, beautiful girl.* —**cleverly** *adv.* —**cleverness** *n.* [U]

cli•ché, cliche /kliˈʃeɪ/ *n.* [C] DISAPPROVING ENG. LANG. ARTS an idea or phrase that has been used a lot in the past, so that it is not effective, not original, or does not have any meaning anymore: *The cliché that "truth is stranger than fiction" certainly applies here.* [**Origin:** 1800–1900 French, past participle of *clicher* **to print from a metal plate**] —**clichéd** *adj.*

click¹ /klɪk/ S3 *v.*

click

1 SHORT HARD SOUND [I,T] to make a short hard sound, or make something produce this sound: *Both men smiled as the cameras clicked.* | *The door* ***clicked shut****.* | **click into place/gear** *I heard the gears click into place.* | *Father* ***clicked his tongue*** (=made a short noise with his tongue) *in disapproval.* | *The dancers jumped up,* ***clicked their heels*** (=knocked the heels of their shoes together)*, and spun around.*
2 COMPUTER/EQUIPMENT [I,T] COMPUTERS to press a button on a computer MOUSE to choose something from the screen that you want the computer to do, or to press a button on something such as a REMOTE CONTROL: *We're used to* ***pointing and clicking*** *with the mouse.* | +**on** *Children can click on a sentence to hear it read aloud.* | **click sth** *Now click the "yes" button on the screen.* | *Click the button labeled "record."* → see also RIGHT-CLICK
3 HAPPEN [I] INFORMAL to happen in a good or successful way: *Everything clicked for the team all season long.*
4 UNDERSTAND [I] INFORMAL to suddenly understand or realize something: *I had a lot of trouble with algebra, but one day* ***it just clicked****.*
5 LIKE SB [I] INFORMAL if two people click, they like, understand, and agree with each other: *We just clicked from the moment we met.*

click² *n.* [C] **1** a short hard sound: *I heard a click, and the phone went dead.* **2** an action of pressing a button on a computer MOUSE: *A single* ***mouse click*** *will highlight the paragraph.* **3** CANADIAN, SPOKEN a KILOMETER or one kilometer per hour: *They live about five clicks out of town.* [**Origin:** 1500–1600 from the sound]

click•er /ˈklɪkɚ/ *n.* [C] SPOKEN a television REMOTE CONTROL

click•e•ty-clack /ˌklɪkəti ˈklæk/ also ˌ**clickety-ˈclick** *n.* [singular] a series of two different short hard sounds, especially the sound made by a moving train —**clickety-clack** *adv.*

ˈclick-fit *adj.* [only before noun] having a metal or plastic part that allows you to connect two pieces of equipment together without using tools

cli•ent /ˈklaɪənt/ S2 W2 *n.* [C] **1** someone who pays for services or advice from a professional person, company, or organization → see also CUSTOMER: *She was late for a meeting with an important client.* ►see THESAURUS box at **customer** **2** someone who receives money, food, or help from a government or other organization: *Social workers deal with as many as a dozen clients a day.* **3** COMPUTERS a computer on a network that receives information from a SERVER (=main computer that contains information that the others use) [**Origin:** 1300–1400 Old French, Latin *cliens*]

cli•en•tele /ˌklaɪənˈtɛl, ˌkliɑn-/ *n.* [C usually singular] **1** all the people who regularly go to a store, restaurant etc.: *restaurants that serve a young clientele* **2** the clients of a company, government organization etc.: *After the war, welfare began dealing with a different clientele.*

ˌ**client ˈstate** *n.* [C] POLITICS a country that is dependent on the support and protection of a more powerful country

cliff /klɪf/ *n.* [C] EARTH SCIENCE a high, steep side of a large area of rock or mountain: **sheer/steep/high cliffs** *the sheer cliffs at one side of the road* [**Origin:** Old English *clif*] → see picture on page A31

cliff•hang•er /ˈklɪfˌhæŋɚ/ *n.* [C] INFORMAL **1** a situation in a story or film that is very exciting because you do not know what will happen in the next part, and you will have to wait to find out: *the episode's cliffhanger ending* **2** a competition or fight whose result is in doubt until the very end: *cliffhanger election races* —**cliffhanging** *adj.*

C

cli•mac•tic /klaɪˈmæktɪk/ *adj.* forming a very exciting or important part of a story or event, especially near the end of it: *the climactic scene where the killer's name is revealed*

cli•mate /ˈklaɪmɪt/ *n.* [C] **1 a)** EARTH SCIENCE the average conditions of heat, rain or snow, and wind that produce the typical weather of a particular area: **a cool/dry/temperate etc. climate** *Los Angeles has a warm, dry climate.* **b)** an area with particular weather conditions: **a cold/warm/tropical etc. climate** *These flowers will not grow in cold climates.* **2** [usually singular] the general feeling or situation in a place at a particular time: **+of** *There is **a climate of** growing racial intolerance in the city.* | **economic/business/retailing climate** *Small businesses are finding it hard to survive in the present economic climate.* | **political/social/racial etc. climate** *The political climate has changed dramatically.* [**Origin:** 1300–1400 Old French *climat*, from Late Latin *clima*, from Greek *klima* **angle, latitude, climate**; because the weather depends on the angle of the sun to the earth]

C

cli•mat•ic /klaɪˈmæṭɪk/ *adj.* [only before noun] EARTH SCIENCE relating to the weather in a particular area: *harsh climatic conditions*

cli•max[1] /ˈklaɪmæks/ *n.* [C usually singular] **1** the most exciting or important part of a book, movie, situation etc., that usually happens at the end: **+of** *King's famous speech was the climax of the March on Washington.* | **+to** *the sensational climax to the trial* | *The crisis **reached a climax** last week, when two senators resigned.* **2** an ORGASM [**Origin:** 1500–1600 Latin, Greek *klimax* **ladder**, from *klinein* **to lean**]

climax[2] *v.* **1** [I,T] if a situation, process, or story climaxes, it reaches its most important or exciting part: **+with/in** *a concert that climaxes with a fireworks show* **2** [I] to have an ORGASM

climb[1] /klaɪm/ S2 W2 *v.*
1 MOVE UP/DOWN [I always + adv./prep.,T] to move up, down, or across something using your hands and feet, especially when this is difficult to do: *The kids love climbing trees.* | *Burglars climbed a high fence to gain access to the building.* | **+up/down/along etc.** *You have to climb down the cliff to get to the beach.* | *The wall is too high to climb over.*
2 TEMPERATURE/PRICES ETC. [I,T] to increase in number, amount, or level: *The temperature has climbed steadily since this morning.* | *Sales have climbed 11% this quarter.* | **+to** *Stock prices climbed to record levels on Friday.*
3 WALK UP [I always + adv./prep.,T] to walk up a steep slope or set of stairs: *Harry climbed the steps.* | *After climbing for hours, we reached the top.* | **climb up sth** *You have to climb up three flights of stairs.*
4 WITH DIFFICULTY [I always + adv./prep.] to get into or out of something, usually slowly and awkwardly: *The bus pulled in, and we climbed aboard.* | **+through/over/into etc.** *Ford climbed into a waiting limousine.* | *He climbed out of bed and got dressed.*
5 PATH/SUN/AIRPLANE ETC. [I,T] to move gradually to a higher position: *The roller coaster climbs 91 feet and reaches speeds of 45 miles per hour.* | **+to/into/up etc.** *The plane climbed to 10,000 feet before we leveled off.* | *The trail climbs high into the mountain pass.*
6 SPORT [I,T] to climb mountains or rocks as a sport: *the first man to climb Mount Everest* | *an active woman who loves to hike and climb* → see also CLIMBING
7 ON A LIST [I,T] to move higher on a list of teams, records etc. as you become more popular or successful: **+to** *Their new album has climbed to number two in the charts.*
8 PLANT [I] to grow up a wall or other structure: *Ivy climbed up the front of the building.*
9 IN YOUR JOB/LIFE [I,T] to move to a better position in your professional or social life: *Steve climbed rapidly through the sales division.* | *Women trying to **climb the corporate ladder*** (=become more successful) *still encounter discrimination.*
10 be climbing the walls SPOKEN to become extremely anxious, annoyed, or impatient: *If I drank another cup of coffee, I'd be climbing the walls.*
[**Origin:** Old English *climban*]

climb[2] *n.* [C usually singular]
1 MOVEMENT UPWARD a process in which you move up toward a place, especially while using a lot of effort: *It's a steep uphill climb all the way to the top.*
2 INCREASE an increase in value or amount: *The dollar continued its climb against the Japanese yen.* | **+in** *a steady climb in house prices*
3 IMPROVEMENT the process of improving something, especially your professional or social position: *Economists are predicting a slow climb out of the recession.* | **+to** *Dreyer's climb to power in city government was swift.*
4 LIST/COMPETITION a process in which someone or something gets a higher position on a list or in a competition because of being popular or successful: *The team's climb from the bottom of the league to first place surprised everyone.* | *the song's **climb up the charts***
5 ROCK/MOUNTAIN a steep rock, cliff, or mountain that you climb up: *Mount Rainier is a tough climb.*

climb•er /ˈklaɪmɚ/ *n.* [C] **1** someone who climbs as a sport: *a mountain climber* **2** a person or animal that can climb easily: *Monkeys are good climbers.* **3** a plant that grows up a wall or other structure → see also SOCIAL CLIMBER

climb•ing /ˈklaɪmɪŋ/ *n.* [U] the sport of climbing mountains or rocks: *climbing equipment* | **rock/mountain climbing** *the basic techniques of rock climbing* | *She and her husband **go climbing** every weekend.*

ˈclimbing wall *n.* [C] a special wall inside a building that rock climbers use for practice

clime /klaɪm/ *n.* [C usually plural] LITERARY an area that has a particular type of CLIMATE: *the warmer climes of Florida*

clinch[1] /klɪntʃ/ *v.* **1** [T] to finally win, achieve, or agree on something by doing a final thing that makes it certain: *A last-minute touchdown clinched the game for the Saints.* | *He flew to Paris to **clinch the deal**.* **2 clinch it** INFORMAL if an event, situation, process etc. clinches it, it makes someone finally decide to do something that they were already thinking of doing: *We'd talked about moving, but the job offer clinched it.* **3** [I] if two people clinch, they hold each other's arms tightly, especially when they are fighting **4** [T] to fasten a nail firmly by bending the point over

clinch[2] *n.* [C] **1** a situation in which two people hold each other's arms tightly, especially when they are fighting **2** a situation in which two people who love each other hold each other tightly

clinch•er /ˈklɪntʃɚ/ *n.* [C] INFORMAL a fact, action, or argument that finally persuades someone to do something, or that ends an argument or competition: *Johnson's home run was the clincher for the Twins.*

cline /klaɪn/ *n.* [C] TECHNICAL a range of very small differences in a group of things of the same kind SYN **continuum**

Cline /klaɪn/, **Pat•sy** /ˈpætsi/ (1932–1963) a U.S. singer of COUNTRY AND WESTERN music

cling[1] /klɪŋ/ *v. past tense and past participle* **clung** /klʌŋ/ [I] **1** [always + adv./prep.] to hold someone or something tightly, especially because you do not feel safe: **+to/on/at etc.** *Passengers clung desperately to the lifeboats.* **2** [always + adv./prep.] to stick to someone or something or seem to surround them: **+to/around etc.** *His wet shirt clung to his body.* | *The smell of smoke clung to her clothes.* **3** to stay close to someone all the time because you are too dependent on them or do not feel safe: *Some children cling during their first weeks in school.*

cling to sth *phr. v.* to continue to believe or do something, even though it may not be true or useful anymore: *They still cling to their traditions.* | **cling to a belief/idea/illusion etc.** *We cling to the notion that love at first sight is possible.*

cling² *n.* → see STATIC CLING

cling·y /ˈklɪŋi/ *adj. comparative* **clingier**, *superlative* **clingiest** **1** someone who is clingy is too dependent on another person: *a shy, clingy child* **2** clingy clothing or material sticks tightly to your body and shows its shape

clin·ic /ˈklɪnɪk/ W3 *n.* [C] **1** a place where medical treatment is given to people who do not need to stay in a hospital: *a dental clinic* | *the health clinic on campus* ▶see THESAURUS box at **hospital** **2** a place where medical treatment is given at a low cost: *the doctors who volunteer at an inner-city clinic* **3** a group of doctors who work together and share the same offices **4** a meeting at which a professional person gives help or advice to people: *a marriage clinic* | *a free clinic on caring for roses* [**Origin:** 1800–1900 French *clinique*, from Greek *klinike* **medical practice by the bed**]

clin·i·cal /ˈklɪnɪkəl/ *adj.* **1** [only before noun] relating to treating or testing people who are sick: *young doctors gaining clinical experience* | *The drug has undergone a number of* ***clinical trials*** (=tests to see if it is effective in treating people). | *a treatment that helps people with clinical depression* (=a strong feeling of sadness for which people need medical help) **2** MEDICINE relating to a hospital or clinic: *Music is often used in clinical settings to calm patients.* **3** considering only the facts and not influenced by emotions: *A formal marriage agreement sounds clinical, but it is a good idea.* **4** a clinical building or room is very plain and clean, but not attractive or comfortable: *The walls were painted a clinical white.* **5** INFORMAL done in a very exact and skillful way, especially in sports: *Klinsmann was absolutely clinical in scoring that goal.* —**clinically** /-kli/ *adv.*: *clinically-tested treatment methods*

cli·ni·cian /klɪˈnɪʃən/ *n.* [C] FORMAL a doctor who treats and examines people, rather than one who does RESEARCH

clink¹ /klɪŋk/ *v.* [I,T] if two glass or metal objects clink or if you clink them, they make a short ringing sound because they have been hit together: *The two men clinked their glasses in celebration.* [**Origin:** 1300–1400 fFrom the sound]

clink² *n.* **1** [C usually singular] the short ringing sound made by metal or glass objects hitting each other **2 the clink** SLANG prison

clink·er /ˈklɪŋkɚ/ *n.* **1** [C] INFORMAL something or someone that is a total failure: *Most of the songs are good, but there are a few clinkers.* **2** [C] INFORMAL a wrong note in a musical performance: *She hit a real clinker in the last verse.* **3** [U] the hard material like rocks which is left after coal has been burned

Clin·ton /ˈklɪntˀn/, **Hil·la·ry Rod·ham** /ˈhɪləri ˈrɑdəm/ (1946–) a U.S. politician who is a member of the U.S. Senate and the wife of former President Bill Clinton

Clinton, William (Bill) (1946–) the 42nd President of the U.S.

clip¹ /klɪp/ S3 *n.*
1 FOR FASTENING [C] a small metal or plastic object that holds or fastens things together: *a paper clip* | *Fasten the microphone clip to your shirt.*
2 MOVIE [C] a short part of a movie or television program that is shown by itself, especially as an advertisement: *clips from Mel Gibson's new movie*
3 GUN [C] a container for bullets which passes them rapidly into the gun so that they can be fired
4 at a good/rapid/fast etc. clip quickly: *The car was going at a pretty good clip when it hit the tree.*
5 NEWSPAPER [C] an article that is cut from a newspaper or magazine for a particular reason SYN **clipping**: *a clip of a cake recipe*
6 50 cents/$100 etc. a clip INFORMAL if things cost 50 cents, $100 etc. a clip, they cost that amount of money each

clip² *v.* **clipped**, **clipping**
1 FASTEN [I always + adv./prep.,T] to fasten something together or to be fastened together using a CLIP: **clip sth to/onto/together etc.** *She'd clipped a business card to her letter.* | **+on/to etc.** *The keys just clip onto your belt, like this.* ▶see THESAURUS box at **fasten**
2 CUT [T] to cut small amounts of something in order to make it neater: *Clip some of the bottom branches from the Christmas tree.* ▶see THESAURUS box at **cut¹**
3 CUT FROM NEWSPAPER [T] to cut an article or picture from a newspaper, magazine etc.: **clip sth out of/from sth** *a cartoon clipped from the paper*
4 HIT [T] to hit something quickly at an angle, often by accident: *A truck swerved and clipped a parked car.*
5 REDUCE [T] WRITTEN to slightly reduce an amount, quantity etc.: **clip sth off/from sth** *Lewis clipped a second off the world record.*
6 clip sb's wings to restrict someone's freedom, activities, or power → see also CLIPPED

clip·board /ˈklɪpbɔrd/ *n.* [C] **1** a small flat board with a CLIP on top that holds paper so that you can write on it **2** COMPUTERS an area of computer MEMORY that holds information when you are moving it from one document to another or to a different part of the same document

ˈclip-ˌclop *n.* [C usually singular] the sound made by a horse as it walks on a hard surface —**clip-clop** *v.* [I]

ˈclip joint *n.* [C] OLD-FASHIONED, SLANG a restaurant or NIGHTCLUB that charges too much for food, drinks etc.

ˈclip-on *adj.* [only before noun] fastened to something with a CLIP: *clip-on earrings* —**clip-on** *n.* [C]

clipped /klɪpt/ *adj.* **1** cut so that it is short and neat: *a clipped green lawn* **2** a clipped voice is quick and clear but not very friendly

clip·per /ˈklɪpɚ/ *n.* [C] a fast sailing ship used in past times

clip·pers /ˈklɪpɚz/ *n.* [plural] a special tool with two blades for cutting small pieces from something: *nail clippers*

clip·ping /ˈklɪpɪŋ/ *n.* [C] **1** an article or picture that has been cut out of a newspaper or magazine: *a few press clippings of the trial* **2** [usually plural] a small piece cut from something bigger: *grass clippings*

clique /klik, klɪk/ *n.* [C] DISAPPROVING a small group of people who think they are special and do not want other people to join their group [**Origin:** 1700–1800 French *cliquer* **to make a noise**]

cliqu·ish /ˈklikɪʃ/ also **cliquey** /ˈkliki/ *adj.* DISAPPROVING a cliquish organization, club etc. has a lot of cliques or is controlled by them

clit·o·ris /ˈklɪt̬ərɪs/ *n.* [C] BIOLOGY a small part of a woman's outer sexual organs, where she can feel sexual pleasure —**clitoral** *adj.*

clo·a·ca /kloʊˈeɪkə/ *n. plural* **cloacae** /kloʊˈeɪsi/ [C] BIOLOGY the area that the INTESTINE, URINARY tube, and GENITAL tube empties into in fish, birds, AMPHIBIANS, REPTILES, and some animals without a backbone

cloak¹ /kloʊk/ *n.* **1** [C] a warm piece of clothing like a coat that hangs loosely from your shoulders and does not have SLEEVES, worn mainly in past times **2** [singular] an organization, activity, or way of behaving that deliberately protects someone or keeps something secret: **+of** *A* ***cloak of secrecy*** *surrounds their decision-making process.* | *They hid their prejudice* ***under the cloak of*** *patriotism.* [**Origin:** 1200–1300 Old North French *cloque* **bell, cloak**, from Medieval Latin *clocca* **bell**; because of its shape]

cloak² *v.* [T usually passive] **1** to deliberately hide facts, feelings etc. so that people do not see or understand them: *Almost all military operations at the time were* ***cloaked in secrecy***. **2 be cloaked in darkness/rust/snow etc.** LITERARY covered in darkness, snow etc.: *hills cloaked in mist*

ˌcloak-and-ˈdagger *adj.* [only before noun] very secret and mysterious, and usually involving the work of spies (SPY): *a cloak-and-dagger operation*

cloak·room /ˈkloʊk-rum/ *n.* [C] a small room where you can leave your coat SYN **coatroom**

clob·ber /ˈklɑbɚ/ *v.* [T] INFORMAL **1** to hit someone very hard: *He got clobbered by a kid on the playground.* **2** to defeat someone very easily in a way that is embarrassing for the person or group that loses: *The Lakers clobbered the Jazz, 83 to 66.* ►see THESAURUS box at **beat**[1] **3** to affect someone or something badly, especially by making them lose money: *We got clobbered last year by rising production costs.*

cloche /kloʊʃ/ *n.* [C] a hat shaped like a bell, worn by women in the 1920s

C

clock[1] /klɑk/ S2 W3 *n.* [C] **1** an instrument that shows what time it is, in a room or on a building → see also WATCH: *The **clock** on the bank **said** six.* | *Mary **set** her **clock for** 6:30 a.m.* (=made sure it would ring at 6:30). | *Just as we left, **the clock struck** two.* | *It was so quiet I could hear the **clock ticking**.* | **set the clock(s) back/ahead/forward** (=change the time shown on the clock to one hour earlier or later, when the time officially changes) | **the clock is slow/fast** (=the clock shows a time that is earlier or later than the actual time) → see also ALARM CLOCK, CUCKOO CLOCK, GRANDFATHER CLOCK, O'CLOCK **2** an instrument that shows how much time is left in a game or sport that has a time limit: *With 15 seconds left **on the clock**, the score was 61–59.* | **stop/start the clock** (=stop or start measuring how much time is left) *The clock is stopped when a player runs out of bounds with the ball.* | **run out the clock/kill the clock** (=try to keep the ball for the rest of the game, so your opponents cannot get any points) **3 put/turn/set the clock back a)** to go back to the way things were done before, rather than trying new ideas or methods: *Women's groups warned that the law would turn the clock back 50 years.* **b)** to return to a good situation that you experienced in the past: *This is a team that would like to turn the clock back five years.* **4 around the clock** all day and all night without stopping: *The emergency telephone lines operate around the clock.* → see also ROUND-THE-CLOCK **5 against the clock a)** to work quickly in order to finish something before a particular time: *Doctors are **racing against the clock** to find a cure.* **b)** if you run, swim etc. against the clock, you run or swim a particular distance while your speed is measured **6 the 24-hour clock** a system for measuring time in which the hours of the day and night have numbers from 0 to 23 [**Origin:** 1300–1400 Middle Dutch *clocke* **bell, clock**, from Medieval Latin *clocca* **bell**] → see also BIOLOGICAL CLOCK, BODY CLOCK, **clean sb's clock** at CLEAN[2] (6), TIME CLOCK, **watch the clock** at WATCH[1] (6)

clock[2] S3 *v.* [T] **1** to measure or record the speed at which someone or something is moving: **clock sb/sth at sth** *The police clocked her at 42 mph in a 35 mph zone.* | *Ryan's fastball was officially clocked at 100.9 mph.* **2** to travel a certain distance in a particular time: *The runner from Lynbrook clocked the fastest time on the mile run.* **3** also **clock up** to reach or achieve a particular number or amount: *The average kid has clocked 19,000 hours watching TV by age 18.* | **clock in at sth** *One song clocked in at seven minutes.* **4** INFORMAL to hit someone in the head

clock in *phr. v.* to record on a special card the time you arrive at or begin work SYN **punch in**: *He clocked in at 8:30.*

clock out *phr. v.* to record on a special card the time you stop or leave work SYN **punch out**: *Hansen clocked out early today.*

clock up sth *phr. v.* to reach or achieve a particular number or amount: *The Dodgers have clocked up six wins in a row.* | *I clocked up 90,000 miles in my old Ford.*

ˈclock ˌradio *n.* [C] a clock that turns on a radio to wake you up

ˈclock speed *n.* [C] COMPUTERS a measurement of how quickly a computer's CPU (=main controlling part) can deal with instructions

clock·wise /ˈklɑk-waɪz/ *adv.* moving in the same direction in which the HANDS (=parts that point to the time) of a clock move OPP **counterclockwise**: *Turn the dial clockwise.* —**clockwise** *adj.*

clock·work /ˈklɑk-wɚk/ *n.* [U] **1 like clockwork a)** if something happens like clockwork, it happens in exactly the way you planned and without any problems: *The whole event **ran like clockwork**.* **b)** also **regular as clockwork** happening at the same time and in the same way every time: *At 6:30 every evening, like clockwork, Dan went out to milk the cows.* **2 with clockwork precision/accuracy** in an extremely exact way **3** a system of springs inside a toy or other object that makes the toy move or work when you turn a key or handle: *an old clockwork train*

clod /klɑd/ *n.* [C] **1** a lump of mud or earth **2** INFORMAL someone who is not graceful and behaves in a stupid way

clod·hop·per /ˈklɑdˌhɑpɚ/ *n.* **clodhoppers** [plural] HUMOROUS heavy strong shoes

clog[1] /klɑg/ also **clog up** *v.* **clogged, clogging 1** [I,T] to physically block something, or become blocked in this way, especially so that a movement or flow of something is stopped: *The sink has clogged again.* | **clog sth with sth** *The freeways were clogged with traffic.* **2** [T] to slow down or stop a process or system, because there is too much work, too few people to do the work, etc.: *An increased number of arrests has clogged the court system.* | **clog sth with sth** *The hospital waiting rooms were clogging up with patients.* [**Origin:** 1500–1600 *clog* **to prevent an animal from moving by tying a wooden block to it** (14–19 centuries)] —**clogged** *adj.*: *a clogged drain*

clog[2] *n.* [C usually plural] a shoe made of wood or with a wooden bottom → see picture at SHOE[1]

cloi·son·né /ˌklɔɪzəˈneɪ, ˌklwɑ-/ *n.* [U] a method of decorating something in which different colors of ENAMEL are put on the object and separated by thin metal bars —**cloisonné** *adj.*: *cloisonné earrings*

clois·ter[1] /ˈklɔɪstɚ/ *n.* [C] **1** a building where MONKS or NUNS live, that is meant to be quiet and away from the public **2** [usually plural] a covered passage that surrounds one side of a square garden or area of grass near a church, MONASTERY etc.

cloister[2] *v.* **cloister yourself** FORMAL to spend a lot of time alone in a room or building, especially because you need to study or work

clois·tered /ˈklɔɪstɚd/ *adj.* **1** protected from the difficulties and demands of ordinary life: *the cloistered world of the university* **2** a cloistered building contains cloisters **3** living in a cloister as a NUN or MONK, and having little or no communication with the world outside

clone[1] /kloʊn/ *n.* [C] **1** BIOLOGY an exact copy of an animal or plant that has the same DNA as the original animal or plant, because it was produced from one cell of that animal or plant **2** a computer that is built as an exact copy of a more famous BRAND of computer → see also COMPATIBLE: *an IBM clone* **3** INFORMAL someone or something that looks or seems extremely similar to someone or something else, especially someone famous: *Three Britney Spears clones walked past me.* [**Origin:** 1900–2000 Greek *klon* **small branch**]

clone[2] *v.* [T] **1** BIOLOGY to make an exact copy of a plant or animal by taking a cell from it and developing it artificially **2** to copy the number of a CELLULAR PHONE and then use that number on a different telephone, so that the owner receives the telephone bill **3** to copy the information from the strip on a CREDIT CARD or DEBIT CARD and use it to make an illegal copy of the card

clonk /klɑŋk/ *n.* [C] the sound made when a heavy object falls to the ground or hits another heavy object —**clonk** *v.* [I,T]

clop /klɑp/ *v.* **clopped, clopping** [I] if a horse clops, its hooves (HOOF) make a loud sound as they touch the ground —**clop** *n.* [C,U]

close[1] /kloʊz/ S1 W1 *v.*
1 SHUT [I,T] to shut something, or become shut in order to cover an opening SYN **shut** OPP **open**: *The door closed silently behind us.* | *Close the curtains – it's getting dark.* | *Okay, close your eyes and make a wish.*
2 BOOK/UMBRELLA [T] to move together the parts of

something so that there is no longer a space between them SYN **shut** OPP **open**: *Ann closed her book and stood up.*

3 FOR A PERIOD OF TIME [I,T] if a store or building closes, or if someone closes it, it stops being open to the public for a period of time, for example for the night or a holiday OPP **open**: *What time does the mall close tonight?* | *We close the hotel during the winter.* | **close for sth** *The shop closes for lunch at 12:30.*

4 STOP OPERATING also **close down** [I,T] if a company, store etc. closes or you close it, it stops operating permanently SYN **shut down** OPP **open**: *Hundreds of timber mills have been closed since World War II.* | *After 85 years, the local newspaper closed down last month.* | *The museum **closed its doors** to the public in 1977.*

5 COMPUTER [T] if you close a program or a window on a computer, you deliberately make it disappear from the screen OPP **open**: *Close all applications before shutting down your computer.*

6 ROAD/BORDER [T] to stop people or vehicles from entering or leaving a place OPP **open**: *The government closed the borders during the election.* | **close sth to sth** *Larkin Street is closed to traffic.*

7 BOOK/SPEECH ETC. [I,T always + adv./prep.] if a book, play, speech etc. closes or someone closes it, it ends in a particular way SYN **end** OPP **open**: *The novel closes when the family reunites in Prague.* | **close sth with/by** *Professor Schmidt closed his speech with a quote from Tolstoy.* | *In his **closing remarks*** (=the last part of a speech), *Merrill praised his staff.*

8 BECOME UNAVAILABLE [I,T] to be no longer happening or available after a particular date or time, or to cause something to no longer happen or be available OPP **open**: *Our special offer closes on June 3.* | *The producers decided to close the show after only three weeks on Broadway.*

9 close an account to stop having an account with a bank or stop having a CREDIT CARD account OPP **open**

10 FINANCIAL/ECONOMIC [I always + adv./prep.] ECONOMICS if a CURRENCY or business STOCK closes at a particular price, it is worth that amount at the end of a day's trading on the STOCK MARKET: *WalMart shares closed only 4 cents down.*

11 close a deal/sale/contract etc. to successfully arrange a business deal, sale etc.: *We met at the attorney's office to close the sale.*

12 OFFER/PROCESS [I] to finish on a particular date: *The special offer for tickets closes June 3.*

13 DISTANCE/DIFFERENCE [I,T] if a distance or difference between two things closes, or if you close it, the distance or difference becomes smaller: *Society needs to **close the gap** between rich and poor.* | *The distance between the two cars was closing fast.*

14 NOT AVAILABLE ANYMORE [T] to make an activity or opportunity unavailable: *The legislation closes a lot of loopholes in the tax law.*

15 HOLD STH [I,T always + adv./prep.] if your hands, arms etc. close around something, or if you close them around something, you hold it firmly: *She closed her fingers around the handle of the knife.* | **+around/over etc.** *The baby's tiny hand closed over Ken's finger.*

16 WOUND also **close up** [I,T] if a wound closes or you close it, it grows back together and becomes healthy, or you sew it together for it to become healthy: *The cut should close up within a few days.*

17 close ranks a) if people close ranks, they join together to protect each other, especially because their group, organization etc. is being criticized: *The Democrats closed ranks and refused to vote for the President's proposal.* **b)** if soldiers close ranks, they stand closer together

18 close the book(s) on sth to stop working on something, especially a police case, because you cannot continue: *Vallejo police closed the books on the case for lack of evidence.*

19 ELECTRICAL CIRCUIT to make a connection in an electrical circuit: *The switch opens and closes the circuit.*

[**Origin:** 1200–1300 Old French *clos*, past participle of *clore* **to close**, from Latin *claudere*] → see also CLOSED, CLOSING DATE, **shut/close the door on sth** at DOOR (3), **close/shut your eyes to sth** at EYE[1] (13)

close down *phr. v.* **close sth ↔ down** if a company, store etc. closes down or is closed down, it permanently stops operating SYN **shut down**: *Health department officials ordered the restaurant to be closed down.*

close in *phr. v.* **1** to move closer to someone or something, especially in order to attack them SYN **move in**: *The lion closed in for the kill.* | **close in on/around/upon etc.** *Warplanes and tanks closed in on the eastern cities.* **2** if night or darkness closes in, it begins to become dark: *It was 5:00 and darkness was closing in.* **3** if the weather closes in, it starts to become worse: *We wanted to get to shore before the weather closed in.* **4** if something closes in, it makes you feel strong emotions that are hard to control, especially unhappiness, fear, loneliness etc.: **close in on/around/upon etc.** *The silence closed in around her, and she felt totally alone.*

close sth **↔ off** *phr. v.* to separate an area, room etc. from the area around it so that people cannot go there or use it: *One of the lanes is closed off for repairs.* | **close sth off to sb** *This area is closed off to the general public.*

close on sb/sth *phr. v.* **1** to get nearer to someone or something that is ahead of you in a race, competition, election etc.: *The other car was closing on us fast.* | *New polls show that Marshall is closing on his opponent in the Senate race.* **2** to successfully arrange a LOAN, especially in order to buy a house: *After we closed on the house, we celebrated with a bottle of champagne.*

close sth **↔ out** *phr. v.* **1** to finish something in a particular way or by doing something: *The 49ers closed out the season with a win against the Bears.* **2** to sell a particular type of goods cheaply in order to get rid of them, because they will not be sold anymore: *The store is closing out this line of swimwear.* **3** to prevent light or noise from reaching a place by closing windows, curtains etc. SYN **shut out** SYN **block out**: *He shut the windows, closing out the noise from the street below.* **4** if you or the bank close out a bank account, you take all the money out of it and make it unavailable for use SYN **close**

close up *phr. v.* **1 close sth ↔ up** if someone closes up a house, store, or other building, they shut it and lock it and leave it: *He was mugged as he was closing up the store.* **2** to stop being open to the public for a period of time: *The public swimming pool closes up after August.* **3 close up shop** to stop doing something for a period of time or permanently: *Some of the big ad agencies close up shop early for the holidays.* **4 close sth ↔ up** if a wound closes up or if someone or something closes it up, it grows together or is sewn together and becomes healthy again **5** to deliberately not talk about your true emotions or thoughts SYN **clam up**: *Every time I ask Jenny about it, she just closes up.* **6 close sth ↔ up** if a group of people close up or something closes them up, they move nearer together

close with sb/sth *phr. v.* LITERARY to get closer to someone or something in order to do something such as attack them, watch them carefully etc.: *Marines planned to close with the enemy and destroy them.*

close² /klous/ S1 W1 *adj.*

1 NEAR IN SPACE not far: *The closest store is about a mile away.* | **+to** *Amy's house is close to the school.* | *The victim was shot **at close range*** (=from very near). | *Scientists could observe the whales **at close quarters*** (=from a short distance). | *Our office is **in close proximity to*** (=very near) *the airport.* ►see THESAURUS box at near[3]

2 NEAR IN TIME near to something in time: *Our birthdays are close together.* | **+to** *By the time we left, it was close to midnight.*

3 LIKE/LOVE if two people are close, they like or love each other very much: *Mom and I have always been close.* | **+to** *I'm not very close to my brothers.* | *We were pretty **close friends** in high school.*

4 CAREFUL looking at, thinking about, or watching

something very carefully: ***Take a closer look** at the statistics, before you make a judgment.* | *Scientists are **keeping a close watch on** the volcano.* | *The school district **keeps a close eye on** students with poor attendance records.* | *The Justice Department has **paid close attention to** the merger.*
5 NUMBER/AMOUNT almost the same amount or almost at the same level: +**to** *Inflation is now close to 6%.*
6 SIMILAR if two things are close, they are not exactly the same but are very similar: *The colors aren't a perfect match, but they're close.* | +**to** *I felt something close to jealousy.* | *The island was **the closest thing to** paradise I can imagine.*
7 LIKELY TO HAPPEN seeming likely to happen or to do something soon: *We haven't finished painting the kitchen yet, but we're close.* | **close to doing sth** *The two countries are close to signing a peace agreement.* | **close to tears/death/despair etc.** *Barnes was close to death.*
8 COMPETITION/ELECTIONS ETC. a close competition or election is one where both sides are almost equal: *It's always frustrating to lose a **close game**.* | *She is running **a close second** to Agnos in the polls* (=Agnos is in first place and she is behind Agnos by a very small amount). | *At this point, the game is **too close to call*** (=no one can say who the winner will be).
9 RELATIVE a close relative is a member of your family such as your brothers, sisters, parents, grandparents etc. OPP **distant**: *The wedding was attended only by close family members.* | **close relative/relation** *She had no children and no close relatives.*
10 ALMOST BAD INFORMAL used when you just manage to avoid something bad, dangerous, or embarrassing: ***That was close!** You almost hit that man!* | *We managed to rescue them, but it was a **close call*** (=a situation in which something bad almost happened).
11 keep in close contact/touch also **stay in close contact/touch** if two people keep in close contact, they see, talk to, or write to each other regularly
12 WORK/TALK TOGETHER if a relationship, association etc. is close, the people in it work or talk together a lot: *close cooperation between the departments* | **close links/ties/relations** *countries with close ties to China* | +**to** *White House aides close to the President*
13 close/you're close/that's close SPOKEN used to tell someone that they have almost guessed or answered something correctly: *"Is it a hundred miles?" "Close – it's 120 miles to Las Vegas."*
14 too close for comfort INFORMAL if something that happens is too close for comfort, it frightens you or makes you nervous: *We convinced the police we weren't lying, but the whole thing was too close for comfort.*
15 close, but no cigar INFORMAL used when something someone does or says is almost correct or successful
16 a close shave a) a process in which someone's hair is cut very close to the skin **b)** INFORMAL a situation in which you escape from something that is bad or dangerous
17 close work a process or activity which involves looking at or handling things in a very skillful and careful way: *Embroidery is very close work.*
18 be close with money FORMAL to not be generous SYN **stingy** —**closeness** *n.* [U] → see also CLOSELY

close³ /kloʊs/ S1 W1 *adv.* **1** not far away SYN **near**: *She was holding her baby close.* | *The girls were sitting **close together** on the bench.* | *I couldn't **get close** enough to see what was happening.* | *Her parents live **close by**.* | *The police were following **close behind** in an unmarked car.* | **close up/up close** *When I saw her close up, I realized she wasn't Jane.* ►see THESAURUS box at near³ **2** only a short time away: *Your birthday's **getting close**.* **3 close to sth** almost a particular amount, number, level etc.: *There were close to 200,000 people at the rally.* **4 come close to (doing) sth** to almost do something: *Carey came very close to victory.* | *I was so angry, I came close to hitting her.* **5 come close (to sb/sth)** to be almost as good as someone or something else: *It's not as good as his last album, but it comes close.* **6 hit/strike close to home a)** if a remark or criticism about someone hits close to home, it makes them feel embarrassed because they know it is true: *Jokes aren't funny when they strike too close to home.* **b)** if something bad happens close to home, you are directly affected by it: *The tragedy of the fire hit close to home.* **7 come close on the heels of sth** to happen very soon after something else: *Another bad snowstorm came close on the heels of the weekend blizzard.* **8** near to the surface of something: *An electric razor doesn't really shave as close as a blade.* → see also **play/keep your cards close to your chest** at CARD¹ (14)

close⁴ /kloʊz/ *n.* [singular] FORMAL the end of an activity or of a period of time SYN **end**: +**of** *The Mayor will speak at the close of the conference.* | **at/after/by etc. the close of sth** *At the close of trading, stock prices had risen 1.2%.* | *Millions of people were homeless as the war **drew to a close*** (=came to an end). | *A fireworks display will **bring** the festivities **to a close*** (=they will end the celebration). | *As four days of talks **came to a close*** (=ended), *the opposing sides were still unable to agree.*

close-cropped /ˌkloʊs ˈkrɑpt◂/ *adj.* close-cropped grass or hair is cut very short

closed /kloʊzd/ S1 *adj.*
1 DOOR/WINDOW/EYES ETC. not open SYN **shut** OPP **open**: *The windows were all closed.* | *Make sure the lid is closed.* | *She kept her eyes **tightly closed**.*
2 STORE/BUILDING [not before noun] if a store, public building, area etc. is closed, it is not open and people cannot enter or use it OPP **open**: *The store was already closed.* | **closed to the public/to visitors etc.** *The castle is closed to visitors in winter.* | *This area is closed to mountain bikes.*
3 MEETING restricted to a particular group of people, vehicles, activities etc.: *a closed meeting of the city council* | *The judges met **in closed session*** (=in a private meeting).
4 SUBJECT if a particular subject or matter is closed, you do not want or need to discuss it anymore: *You are not going, and that's final! The subject is closed.*
5 MIND not willing to discuss or think about new ideas: *We don't want members of the jury to have **closed minds**.*
6 a closed society/world a society or group of people who are not willing to accept new ideas or influences
7 behind closed doors something that takes place behind closed doors happens secretly: *The vote took place behind closed doors.*

ˌclosed ˈcaptioned *adj.* if a television program is closed captioned, the words that are being said can also be seen in written form on the screen —**closed captioning** *n.* [U] —**closed caption** *n.* [C usually plural]

ˌclosed-circuit ˈtelevision also **ˌCCTˈV** *n.* [U] a system of TV cameras in public places or within buildings, for example in order to deter crime

ˌclosed ˈcirculatory ˌsystem *n.* [C] BIOLOGY a system in which blood flows around the body contained in blood VESSELS, without directly flowing over the surrounding TISSUES → see also OPEN CIRCULATORY SYSTEM

ˌclosed-ˈdoor *adj.* [only before noun] closed-door meetings or discussions take place secretly

close·down /ˈkloʊzdaʊn/ *n.* [C] a situation in which work in a company, factory etc. is stopped, either for a short time or permanently

ˌclosed ˈprimary *n.* [C] POLITICS in the U.S., a PRIMARY election in which only members of a political party can vote, and they can vote only for CANDIDATES from that party → see also BLANKET PRIMARY

ˌclosed ˈshop *n.* [C] a company, factory etc. where all workers must belong to a particular UNION

close-fit·ting /ˌkloʊs ˈfɪtɪŋ◂/ *adj.* close-fitting clothes are tight and show the shape of your body

close-knit /ˌkloʊs ˈnɪt◂/ also **ˌclosely-ˈknit** *adj.* a close-knit group of people have good relationships with each other and support each other: *a close-knit family*

close·ly /ˈkloʊsli/ W2 *adv.* **1** if you look at or study something closely, you look at it in detail: *The detective watched him closely.* | *Voters should closely examine all the issues.* **2** near to other things in space or time: *The flash of lightning was closely followed by thunder.* | *The* houses were grouped closely together. **3** in a way that is similar to something or someone else or has a clear connection with them: *Choose a color that closely matches your natural hair color.* | **closely related/linked/associated etc.** *These two issues are closely linked.* | *The plot **closely resembles** one of his earlier novels.* **4** in a way that involves the continuous sharing of ideas, knowledge, or feelings: *a project that I am closely involved with* | *The two leaders **worked closely** to improve relations between their countries.*

ˌclosely held corpoˈration *n.* [C] ECONOMICS a CORPORATION (=large company or group of companies operating together) that sells its STOCK to only a few people, often only to family members

close-mouthed /ˌkloʊs ˈmaʊðd◂ ,-ˈmaʊθt◂/ also **ˌclosed-ˈmouthed** *adj.* not willing to say much because you are trying to keep a secret

close·out /ˈkloʊzaʊt/ *adj.* **a closeout sale/price etc.** a sale to get rid of goods cheaply, or something that is sold cheaply —**closeout** *n.* [C]

close-set /ˌkloʊs ˈsɛt◂/ *adj.* close-set eyes are very near to each other

clos·et[1] /ˈklɑzɪt/ *n.* [C] **1** an area that you keep clothes and other things in, built behind the wall of a room with a door on the front: *a closet full of clothes* | *The master bedroom has a **walk-in closet*** (=a closet like a small room). **2 come out of the closet** also **come out** INFORMAL to tell people that you are HOMOSEXUAL (=sexually attracted to people who are the same sex as you) after keeping that a secret **3 bring sth out of the closet** to cause an issue that has been kept secret to be discussed in public: *The trial brought the issue of sexual harassment out of the closet.* **4 be in the closet** INFORMAL to not tell people that you are HOMOSEXUAL → see also **a skeleton in the closet** at SKELETON[1] (5), WATER CLOSET

closet[2] *adj.* **a closet homosexual/liberal/alcoholic etc.** someone who is a HOMOSEXUAL, LIBERAL etc. but who does not admit in public what they think or do in private

closet[3] *v.* [T usually passive] to keep someone in a room away from other people in order to be alone or to discuss something private: **be closeted with sb/together** *All morning he'd been closeted with various officials.* | **closet yourself (away) somewhere** *She closets herself away in her room.*

close-up /ˈkloʊs ʌp/ *n.* [C,U] a photograph that someone takes from very near: *a close-up of the children's faces* | *Much of the movie is shot **in close-up*** (=from very near).

clos·ing /ˈkloʊzɪŋ/ *adj.* [only before noun] happening or done at the end of a period of time or event: *the closing stages of World War II* | *In her **closing remarks*** (=remarks at the end of a speech or event), *she emphasized the need for more research.*

ˈclosing ˌdate *n.* [C] the last official date on which it is possible to do something: *the closing date on the deal*

clo·sure /ˈkloʊʒɚ/ *n.* **1** [C,U] the act of closing a building, factory, school etc., either permanently or for a short time: *Officials announced the planned closure of two military bases in the region.* | *There are some school closures because of snow.* **2** a process in which a road, bridge etc. is blocked for a short time so that people cannot use it: *road closures in the area* **3** [U] the act of bringing an event or a period of time to an end, or the feeling that something has been completely dealt with: *Funerals help give people a sense of closure.*

clot[1] /klɑt/ *v.* **clotted, clotting** [I,T] if a liquid such as blood or milk clots or something clots it, it becomes thicker and more solid

clot[2] *n.* [C] a thick, almost solid mass formed when blood, milk, or some other liquids dry: *a blood clot*

cloth /klɔθ/ S3 *n.* **1** [U] material that is made from cotton, wool etc. and used for making things such as clothes: *beautiful cotton cloth* | *cloth napkins* **2** [C] a piece of cloth used for drying, cleaning, covering things etc.: *I dried the dishes with a clean cloth.* → see also DISHCLOTH, TABLECLOTH **3 a man of the cloth** FORMAL or HUMOROUS a Christian priest or minister [**Origin:** Old English *clath* **cloth, piece of clothing**] → see also CLOTHES

WORD CHOICE cloth, fabric, material

- Use **cloth** as an uncountable noun to talk about the cotton, wool etc. that is used for making clothes: *She bought some red cloth to make a dress.*
- **Fabric** can be countable or uncountable, and can be used about clothes and things other than clothes: *The sheets were made of a silky fabric.* | *fine Italian fabrics.*
- When **material** is an uncountable noun, it means the same as **fabric**: *There isn't enough material to make curtains.*

clothe /kloʊð/ S3 *v.* [T usually passive] FORMAL **1** to dress someone or be dressed in a particular way SYN **dress**: *He fell into the lake **fully clothed*** (=wearing all his clothes). **2** to provide clothes for someone: *They could barely keep the family fed and clothed.* **3 be clothed in sth** LITERARY to be completely covered by something: *mountains clothed in snow*

clothes /kloʊz, kloʊðz/ S1 W2 *n.* [plural] the things that people wear to cover their bodies or to keep warm: *My mother told me to **put on** my best **clothes**.* | *Pete **took his clothes off** and went to bed.* | *I still have to **change my clothes*** (=put on different ones) *before we leave.* | *She always **wears** such beautiful **clothes**.* | *He came down the stairs **with no clothes on*** (=not wearing any clothes). | **work/school/play clothes** (=clothes that are appropriate for work, school etc.) → see also **a change of clothes/underwear** at CHANGE[2] (6), CLOTHING

THESAURUS

clothing a more formal word than "clothes," often used to refer to a particular type of clothes: *Bring warm clothing with you.*
wear/dress used after a noun or adjective to refer to clothes worn by particular people or worn for a particular activity: *bridal wear* | *swim wear* | *casual dress*

Words used to describe clothes
tight
loose/baggy
skimpy not covering much of the body
fashionable/trendy
casual informal and comfortable
scruffy dirty and messy

clothes·horse /ˈkloʊzhɔrs/ *n.* [C] **1** a wooden or metal frame on which you hang wet clothes so that they can dry indoors **2** INFORMAL someone who is too interested in clothes and who likes to have many different clothes

clothes·line /ˈkloʊzlaɪn/ *n.* [C] a rope on which you hang clothes outside to dry

clothes·pin /ˈkloʊzpɪn/ *n.* [C] a small wooden or plastic object that you use to fasten wet clothes to a clothesline

cloth·ier /ˈkloʊðyɚ/ *n.* [C] OLD-FASHIONED someone who makes or sells men's clothes or material for clothes

cloth·ing /ˈkloʊðɪŋ/ S3 W3 *n.* [U] clothes in general, as opposed to a particular person's clothes: *blankets and clothing for homeless children* | *an expensive clothing store* | *Lab workers wear protective clothing.* | **piece/item/article of clothing** *Bring several warm pieces of clothing.*

clo·ture /ˈkloʊtʃɚ/ *n.* [C] POLITICS a way of ending an argument over a BILL in the U.S. government and forcing a vote on it

cloud[1] /klaʊd/ S3 W3 *n.*
1 IN THE SKY [C,U] a white or gray mass in the sky that consists of very small drops of water: *Dark clouds gathered overhead.* | **heavy/thick/dense cloud(s)** *The plane flew into dense cloud.* | *The sun was hidden by **low cloud**.*
2 IN THE AIR [C] a mass of something in the air, or a large number of things moving together in the air: +**of**

C

a cloud of flies | **a cloud of dust/smoke/gas etc.** *The volcano shot clouds of smoke and ash into the air.*
3 PROBLEM [C] a situation that causes problems and makes you feel afraid, unhappy, or worried: +**of** *the cloud of impending war* | *Budget problems mean there are* ***clouds on the horizon*** (=problems that are likely to happen). | *Several players are injured, and this has* ***cast a cloud over*** (=caused problems for) *the rest of the season.*
4 under a cloud (of sth) INFORMAL if someone is under a cloud, people have a bad opinion of them because they did something wrong: *Rylan resigned under a cloud of suspicion.*
5 be on cloud nine INFORMAL to be very happy about something
6 every cloud has a silver lining used to say that there is something good even in a situation that seems very sad or difficult
[**Origin:** Old English *clud* **rock, hill**; because some clouds look like rocks] → see also **have your head in the clouds** at HEAD[1] (33)

cloud[2] *v.*
1 THOUGHTS/MEMORIES [T] to make someone less able to think clearly or remember things: *Alcohol had clouded his judgment.* | *Doubt* ***clouded*** *my* ***mind.***
2 SPOIL STH [T] to make something less pleasant or more difficult than it should have been: *The team's victory was clouded by the tragedy in their hometown.*
3 CONFUSE cloud the issue/picture to make something difficult to understand, especially by introducing ideas or information that are not related to it: *The Supreme Court's latest decision has only clouded the issue.*
4 FACE also **cloud over** [I,T] LITERARY if someone's expression clouds or if something clouds it, they start to look angry or sad: **cloud with sth** *His face clouded with anger when he saw her.*
5 GLASS/LIQUID also **cloud over/up** [T] if something clouds a transparent material such as glass or a liquid, it makes the material more difficult to see through: *The display cases were clouded with dust.*
6 COVER WITH CLOUDS [T] to cover something with clouds: *Thick mist clouded the mountaintops.*
cloud over *phr. v.* **1** if the sky clouds over, it becomes dark and full of clouds **2** if someone's expression clouds over, they start to look angry or sad: *Anne's face clouded over as she remembered.*
cloud up *phr. v.* **1** if a transparent material such as glass or a liquid clouds up or if something clouds it up, it becomes less clear and more difficult to see through **2** if the sky clouds up, it becomes dark and full of clouds

cloud·burst /ˈklaʊdbɚst/ *n.* [C] a sudden short rain storm

cloud·ed /ˈklaʊdɪd/ *adj.* **1** not clear, so that you cannot see through it easily: *clouded glass* **2** a clouded face or expression shows that someone is unhappy or angry

cloud·less /ˈklaʊdlɪs/ *adj.* a cloudless sky is clear and bright

cloud·y /ˈklaʊdi/ *adj. comparative* **cloudier**, *superlative* **cloudiest** **1** cloudy weather is dark because the sky is full of clouds: *a cloudy day* ▸see THESAURUS box at sunshine **2** cloudy liquids are not clear or transparent **3** cloudy thoughts, memories etc. are not very clear or exact

clout[1] /klaʊt/ *n.* [U] INFORMAL the power to influence other people's decisions: **political/economic clout** *Conservative Christian groups have been gaining political clout in Washington.*

clout[2] *v.* [T] INFORMAL to hit someone or something hard

clove[1] /kloʊv/ *n.* **1** [C] one of the separate pieces that a BULB of GARLIC is divided into **2** [C,U] BIOLOGY a dried flower BUD with a strong sweet smell that is used as a SPICE

clove[2] *v.* a past tense of CLEAVE

clo·ven /ˈkloʊvən/ *v.* a past participle of CLEAVE

ˌcloven ˈhoof *n.* [C] a HOOF that is divided into two parts, which animals such as goats or sheep have

clo·ver /ˈkloʊvɚ/ *n.* [U] **1** BIOLOGY a small plant with three round leaves on each stem **2 a four-leaf clover** a clover plant that has four round leaves and is thought to bring good luck to the person who finds it **3 be in clover** INFORMAL to be living comfortably because you have plenty of money

clo·ver·leaf /ˈkloʊvɚˌlif/ *n.* [C] **1** a network of curved roads that connect two main roads where they cross, so that someone can drive from one road to the other without stopping **2** BIOLOGY the leaf of a clover plant

clown[1] /klaʊn/ *n.* [C] **1** a performer who wears funny clothes and tries to make people laugh, especially at a CIRCUS **2** someone who often makes jokes or behaves in a funny or silly way: *Doug was* ***the class clown*** (=someone at school who always behaves in a funny or silly way) *when he was younger.* **3** INFORMAL a stupid or annoying person: *Some clown cut me off on the freeway this morning.*

clown[2] also **clown around** *v.* [I] to behave in a silly or funny way: *Stop clowning around and get back to work.*

clown·ish /ˈklaʊnɪʃ/ *adj.* silly or stupid —**clownishly** *adv.* —**clownishness** *n.* [U]

cloy·ing /ˈklɔɪ-ɪŋ/ *adj.* **1** a cloying attitude or quality annoys you because it is too nice and seems false: *The plot was sort of okay, but the dialogue was just too cloying.* **2** cloying food or smells are too sweet and make you feel sick: *the cloying smell of cheap perfume*

cloze /kloʊz/ *adj.* **a cloze test/exercise/drill etc.** a test, exercise etc. in which students have to write the correct words into the spaces that have been left empty in a short piece of writing

club[1] /klʌb/ S1 W2 *n.* [C]
1 FOR AN ACTIVITY/SPORT an organization for people who share a particular interest or enjoy similar activities, or the place where this organization meets: *The school has started a chess club.* | *There's a health club across the street.* | *I decided to* ***join*** *the ski* ***club*** *in college.* | *She* ***belongs to*** *a health* ***club.*** ▸see THESAURUS box at organization
2 FOR DANCING/MUSIC a place where people go to dance, listen to music, and meet socially, or where they go to listen to COMEDIANS: *a jazz club* | *a comedy club* | *They're going out for dinner and then to a club.* ▸see THESAURUS box at dance[2]
3 PROFESSIONAL SPORT INFORMAL a professional organization including the players, managers, and owners of a sports team: *There are a number of clubs interested in getting a new quarterback.* | *The Red Sox are a hot* ***ball club*** (=baseball team) *this season.*
4 FOR HITTING A BALL one of the sticks used in GOLF to hit the ball SYN golf club
5 a book/record etc. club an organization that people join in order to buy books, records etc. cheaply: *the Book-of-the-Month Club*
6 WEAPON a thick heavy stick used to hit people or things
7 IN CARD GAMES a) a black shape with three round leaves, printed on cards for games **b) clubs** [plural] the SUIT (=group of cards) that has this shape printed on all its cards: *the ace of clubs*
8 FOR MEN an organization, usually for men only, that they pay to become members of so that they can relax and enjoy social activities, or the building where this club is
9 join the club also **welcome to the club** SPOKEN used after someone has described a bad situation that they are in, to tell them that you are in the same situation: *"He never listens to my ideas." "Join the club."* → see also COUNTRY CLUB, FAN CLUB
[**Origin:** 1100–1200 Old Norse *klubba* **heavy stick**]

club[2] *v.* **clubbed**, **clubbing** [T] to hit someone hard with a thick heavy object: *A soldier was* ***clubbed to death.***

club·bing /ˈklʌbɪŋ/ *n.* **1 go clubbing** INFORMAL to go to clubs where you can dance to popular music: *We always* ***go clubbing*** *when we're in New York.* **2** [U] the action of hitting someone or something with a CLUB —**clubber** *n.* [C]

ˌ**club 'foot** *n.* [C,U] a foot that has been badly twisted since birth and that prevents someone from walking correctly, or the medical condition of having this

club·house /ˈklʌbhaʊs/ *n.* [C] **1** a DRESSING ROOM for a sports team at a STADIUM or sports field **2** a building used by a club **3** a building at a GOLF COURSE that usually has a small restaurant and a store where you can buy equipment

ˌ**club 'sandwich** *n.* [C] a large SANDWICH consisting of three pieces of bread with meat and cheese between them

ˌ**club 'soda** *n.* [C,U] water filled with BUBBLES that is often mixed with other drinks

cluck[1] /klʌk/ *v.* **1** [I] to make a noise like a HEN (=female chicken) **2** [I,T] to express sympathy, approval, or disapproval by saying something, or by making a short low noise with your tongue: +**over/around/about** *The older relatives were clucking over the new baby.* —**clucking** *adj.*

cluck[2] *n.* **1** [C] a low short noise made by a HEN (=female chicken) **2** [C] a sound made with your tongue, used to show disapproval or sympathy: *Mrs. Newman shook her head with a disapproving cluck.* **3 dumb/stupid cluck** INFORMAL a stupid person

clue[1] /klu/ S2 *n.* [C] **1** an object, piece of information, reason etc. that helps you explain something or solve a crime: *Hayward police continued* ***searching for clues*** *in the death of a 43-year-old man.* | +**to/about** *Unexplained weight loss may be an early clue to a health problem.* | *Scientists examine fossils for clues about how dinosaurs lived and died.* | +**as to** *clues as to the cause of the car crash* | **provide/yield clues** *The analysis will provide clues about the author's true identity.* **2 not have a clue** also **have no clue** INFORMAL to not have any idea about the answer to a question, how to do something, how something works etc.: *Until I got there, I had no clue what I was going to say.* | +**about** *He doesn't have a clue about the business.* **3** a piece of information that helps you solve a PUZZLE, answer a question etc.: *I'll* ***give you a clue*** *– it's a kind of bird.* **4** a question that you must solve in order to find the answer to a CROSSWORD PUZZLE or other game [**Origin:** 1500–1600 *clew* **ball of string** (11–19 centuries), from Old English *cliewen*; from the use of a ball of string for finding the way out of a network of passages]

clue[2] *v.*

clue sb **in** *phr. v.* INFORMAL to give someone information about something: +**on** *Somebody must have clued him in on our sales strategy.*

ˌ**clued-'in** *adj.* INFORMAL knowing a lot about something

clue·less /ˈklulɪs/ *adj.* INFORMAL having no understanding or knowledge of something: *Joe's totally clueless.* | +**about** *Many teachers are clueless about the needs of immigrant students.*

clump[1] /klʌmp/ *n.* **1** [C] a group of trees, bushes, or other plants growing very close together: +**of** *a clump of daffodils* **2** [C + of] a small mass of something such as earth or mud **3** [U] the sound of someone walking with heavy steps —**clumpy** *adj.*

clump[2] *v.* **1** also **clump together** [I,T] to form a group or mass, or to arrange things so that they form a mass or group: *Humidity causes sugar to clump.* | *The plants grow best when they are clumped together.* **2** [I always + adv./prep.] to walk with slow noisy steps: +**up/down/along etc.** *The kids clumped up the stairs in their snowboots.*

clum·sy /ˈklʌmzi/ *adj. comparative* **clumsier**, *superlative* **clumsiest** **1** moving in an awkward way and tending to break things: *a shy, clumsy boy* | *my clumsy attempt to catch the ball*

THESAURUS

awkward moving or behaving in a way that does not seem relaxed or comfortable: *an awkward hug*
gawky awkward in the way you move: *a gawky teenager*
inelegant FORMAL not graceful or well done: *an inelegant style of writing*
klutzy INFORMAL very clumsy and likely to drop things or bump into things: *I've always been klutzy and broken things.*
accident-prone tending to get hurt or break things: *As a young boy he was very accident-prone. He broke his arm four times!*

2 done carelessly or badly, without enough thought: *His writing is clumsy and unconvincing.* | *The show is a clumsy blend of news and entertainment.* **3** a clumsy object is not easy to use and is often large and heavy: *a clumsy camera* —**clumsily** *adv.* —**clumsiness** *n.* [U]

clung /klʌŋ/ *v.* the past tense and past participle of CLING

clunk /klʌŋk/ *n.* [singular] a loud sound made when two heavy objects hit each other —**clunk** *v.* [I,T]

clunk·er /ˈklʌŋkɚ/ *n.* [C] INFORMAL **1** an old car or other machine that does not work very well **2** something that is completely unsuccessful

clunk·y /ˈklʌŋki/ *adj. comparative* **clunkier**, *superlative* **clunkiest** heavy and awkward to wear or use: *a pair of clunky old boots*

clus·ter[1] /ˈklʌstɚ/ *n.* [C] **1** a group of things of the same kind that are very close together: +**of** *a cluster of office buildings* | *The flowers grow* ***in clusters.*** **2** a group of people all in the same place: +**of** *A cluster of children stood around the ice cream van.* | *People stood around* ***in clusters*** *talking.* **3** TECHNICAL an unusually high number of events or cases of illness in the same place or at the same time: +**of** *clusters of cancer cases*

cluster[2] *v.* [I always + adv./prep.,T always + adv./prep.] to come together or be together in a group, or to be put together in a group: +**around/together etc.** *Reporters clustered together outside Fitzroy's office.*

ˈ**cluster ˌbomb** *n.* [C] a bomb that sends out a lot of smaller bombs when it explodes —**cluster-bomb** *v.* [T]

clutch[1] /klʌtʃ/ *v.* [T] to hold something tightly because you do not want to lose it or are afraid to let go SYN **grip**: *tourists clutching their pocket dictionaries* | *She was clutching her knee in pain.* ►see THESAURUS box at **hold**[1] → see also **be grasping/clutching at straws** at STRAW[1] (4)

clutch at sth *phr. v.* to try to hold something tightly because you are in danger or pain SYN **grab at**: *He clutched at the rail as he fell.* | *Paxton screamed, clutching at his chest.*

clutch[2] *n.*

1 VEHICLE [C] the PEDAL or LEVER in a vehicle that you press before you change GEARS, or the part that the pedal or lever controls: **push in/step on/put in the clutch** (=start to use the clutch) | **let out the clutch/release the clutch** *Put the car in first gear and slowly release the clutch.* → see picture on page A36

2 in the/a clutch INFORMAL in an important or difficult situation: *They need a player who can score consistently in the clutch.* | *Count on Tom to* ***come through in the clutch*** (=succeed in a difficult situation).

3 sb's clutches also **the clutches of sb** HUMOROUS the power, influence, or control that someone has over you: *Sam joined the Navy to escape from his mother's clutches.*

4 a clutch of sb/sth a small group of similar things or people: *a clutch of young football players*

5 sb's clutch [singular] a tight hold that someone has on something

6 EGGS [C] the number of eggs a chicken produces at one time

clutch[3] *adj.* [only before noun] **1** done well during a difficult situation: *a clutch kick through the goal posts* **2** able to perform well in a difficult situation: *Jordan's a good clutch player.*

ˈ**clutch bag** *n.* [C] a small PURSE that women carry in their hand, used especially on formal social occasions

clut·ter[1] /ˈklʌt̬ɚ/ also **clutter up** *v.* [T] to make something messy by filling or covering it with things: *Piles of books and papers cluttered his desk.* | **be cluttered**

(up) with sth *Their apartment was cluttered with photographs and books.* —**cluttered** *adj.*

clutter² *n.* [U] a lot of things that are scattered in a messy way: *I try to keep my desk free of clutter.*

cm the written abbreviation of CENTIMETER

Cmdr. the written abbreviation of COMMANDER

CNN /ˌsi ɛn ˈɛn/ *n.* Cable News Network; an organization that broadcasts television news programs all over the world

C-note /ˈsi nout/ *n.* [C] SLANG a 100 dollar bill

CO *n.* the written abbreviation of Colorado

C.O. /ˌsi ˈou◂ / *n.* [C] **Commanding Officer** an officer who commands a military unit

Co. **1** the written abbreviation of "company": *E.F. Hutton & Co.* **2** the written abbreviation of COUNTY

c/o the written abbreviation of "in care of," used when you are sending a letter for someone to another person who will keep it for them: *Send the letter to me c/o Anne Miller.*

co- /kou/ *prefix* **1** together with someone or something else: *to coexist* (=exist together or at the same time) | *a coeducational school* (=with boys and girls together) **2** doing something with someone else: *my co-author* (=someone who wrote the book with me) | *the copilot* (=someone who helps a pilot)

coach¹ /koutʃ/ S3 W1 *n.* **1** [C] someone who trains a person or team in a sport: *a basketball coach* | **+of** *the coach of the volleyball team* ►see THESAURUS box at **teacher** **2** [U] the cheapest type of seats on an airplane or a train: *All our employees fly coach.* **3** someone who gives private lessons in singing, acting etc.: *a drama coach* **4** [C] a large vehicle for people, pulled by horses and used in past times **5** [C] FORMAL a bus with space for bags under the seating area, used for trips between cities [**Origin:** 1500–1600 French *coche*, from German *kutsche*]

coach² W3 *v.* **1** [I,T] to train a person or team in a sport: *James used to coach high school football.* **2** [T] to give someone private lessons in singing, acting etc. **3** [T] to give someone instruction in what they should say or do in a particular situation, used especially when you disapprove of this: **coach sb on sth** *Kellogg coached the mayor on handling the questions from the press.* **4** [T] to give someone special help in preparing for a test

coach·ing /ˈkoutʃɪŋ/ *n.* [U] **1** the process or job of training a person or team in a sport: *The difference between the two teams is the quality of the coaching.* **2** the process of helping someone prepare for an important test or other event: *Coaching may raise some students' SAT scores.*

coach·man /ˈkoutʃmən/ *n. plural* **coachmen** /-mən/ [C] someone who drove a COACH pulled by horses in past times

co·ag·u·late /kouˈægyəˌleɪt/ *v.* [I,T] to change or be changed from a liquid into a thick substance or a solid: *The drug helps the blood to coagulate.* —**coagulation** /kouˌægyəˈleɪʃən/ *n.* [U]

coal /koul/ W3 *n.* **1** [U] EARTH SCIENCE a black mineral that is dug from the earth and burned for heat: *coal miners* **2** [C usually plural] a small piece of something such as wood or CHARCOAL that is GLOWING because it is burning or has been burned: *Grill the steaks over medium-hot coals for 5-7 minutes on each side.* [**Origin:** Old English *col*] → see also **rake sb over the coals** at RAKE² (4)

co·a·lesce /ˌkouəˈlɛs/ *v.* [I] FORMAL to grow together or combine to form one single group: *Several groups are coalescing to protest against the bill.* —**coalescence** *n.* [U]

coal

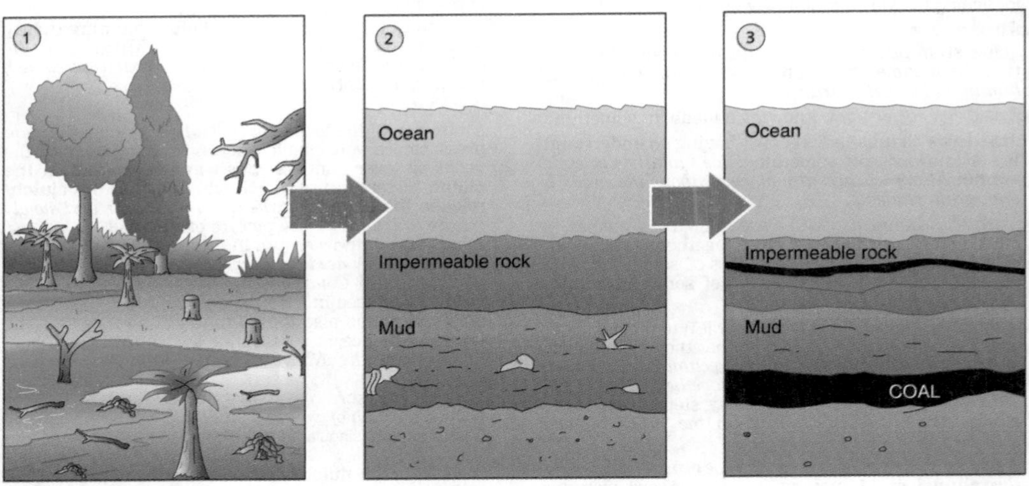

1) Millions of years ago when plants died they became buried in mud, which stopped them from rotting away completely.

2) Trapped in mud, these plants were transformed into fossils. More layers of mud then formed over the top, compressing the fossils.

3) This compression, together with the heat from inside the Earth, turned the mud into rock and the plant fossils into coal. Coal is called a fossil fuel.

coal·field /ˈkoʊlfild/ *n.* [C] EARTH SCIENCE an area where there is coal under the ground

ˈcoal gas *n.* [U] gas produced by burning coal, used especially for electricity and heating → see also NATURAL GAS

co·a·li·tion /ˌkoʊəˈlɪʃən/ W3 *n.* **1** [C] a group made up of people from many different groups who join together to achieve a particular purpose: *the California Coalition for Immigrant Rights* | *Community leaders hope to* ***form a*** *health-care reform* ***coalition***. **2** [C] POLITICS a union of separate political parties that allows them to form a government or fight an election together: *a three-party coalition* | *Italy's* ***coalition government*** (=a government of several different political parties working together) **3** [U] a process in which two or more political parties or groups join together [**Origin:** 1600–1700 French, Latin *coalitus*, past participle of *coalescere*, from *co-* + *alescere* **to grow**]

ˈcoal mine, coalmine [C] a mine from which coal is dug —**coal miner** *n.* [C]

ˈcoal tar *n.* [U] a thick black sticky liquid made by heating coal without air, from which many medicines and chemical products are made

coarse /kɔrs/ *adj.* **1** having a rough surface that feels slightly hard SYN **rough** OPP **smooth**: *a thick, coarse cloth* **2** consisting of thick or large pieces OPP **fine**: *a patch of coarse grass* | *coarse sand* **3** impolite and offensive, especially concerning sex SYN **crude**: *coarse humor* —**coarsely** *adv.* —**coarseness** *n.* [U]

coars·en /ˈkɔrsən/ *v.* [I,T] FORMAL **1** to become thicker or rougher, or to make something thicker or rougher: *Hard work had coarsened his hands.* **2** to become or to make someone become less polite in the way they talk or behave: *The political process has become coarsened.*

coast[1] /koʊst/ S3 W3 *n.* **1** [C] the area where the land meets the ocean → see also SHORE: *a road along the Pacific coast* | *the beaches* ***on the coast*** (=on the land near the ocean) *of North Carolina* | *a small island* ***off the coast*** (=in the ocean near the land) *of Scotland* | *The business has spread* ***from coast to coast*** (=across the whole country). | *a deserted* ***stretch of coast*** (=part of a coast) ►see THESAURUS box at **shore**[1] **2 the coast is clear** INFORMAL used to say that it is safe for you to do something without risking being seen or caught: *We raced out the door as soon as the coast was clear.* [**Origin:** 1300–1400 Old French *coste*, from Latin *costa* **rib, side**]

coast[2] *v.* [I] **1** [always + adv./prep.] to keep moving in a car or on a bicycle without using more power: +**down/around/along etc.** *Bev coasted downhill on her bicycle.* **2** to do something without using much effort: *Andy just coasted through High School.* | +**to/through** *Wilson coasted to victory in the election.* **3** TECHNICAL to sail in a boat along the coast while staying close to land

coast·al /ˈkoʊstl/ *adj.* [only before noun] EARTH SCIENCE in the ocean or on the land near the coast: *the coastal waters of Florida*

ˌcoastal ˈocean *n.* [C] EARTH SCIENCE the part of an ocean which is near to the coast of a CONTINENT, and which includes the part of the ocean by the shore to the part by the CONTINENTAL SHELF (=place where the edge of a continent slopes steeply down to the bottom of the ocean)

coast·er /ˈkoʊstɚ/ *n.* [C] **1** a small thin object you put under a glass or cup, to protect a table from heat or liquids **2** a ship that sails from port to port along a coast, but does not go further out into the ocean → see also ROLLER COASTER

ˈcoaster brake *n.* [C] a BRAKE on some types of bicycles that works when you move the PEDALS backward

ˈCoast Guard *n.* **the Coast Guard** the part of the military that is in charge of watching for ships in danger and preventing illegal activities in the ocean → see also MARINES, NAVY[1] (1)

coast·line /ˈkoʊstlaɪn/ *n.* [C] EARTH SCIENCE the land on the edge of the coast: *a rocky coastline*

coat[1] /koʊt/ S2 W3 *n.* [C] **1** a piece of clothing with long SLEEVES that you wear over your clothes to protect them or to keep warm: *her heavy winter coat* | *Billy!* ***Put your coat on*** *– it's cold outside!* | *The kids* ***took off their coats*** *and threw them on the floor.* **2** the fur, wool, or hair that covers an animal's body: *Huskies have a nice thick coat.* **3** a thin layer of something that covers a surface: +**of** *a coat of paint* **4** a JACKET that you wear as part of a suit SYN **jacket** [**Origin:** 1300–1400 Old French *cote*] → see also -COATED, COATING

coat[2] *v.* [T] to cover a surface with a thin layer of something: *Dust coated all of the furniture.* | **coat sth with/in sth** *Next, coat the fish with breadcrumbs.* → see also -COATED, SUGAR-COATED

ˈcoat check *n.* [C] a room in a public building where you can leave your coat, hat etc. while you are in the building SYN **cloakroom** —**coat checker** *n.* [C]

-coated /koʊt̬ɪd/ *suffix* **1 metal-coated/plastic-coated etc.** covered with a thin layer of metal etc. → see also SUGAR-COATED **2 white-coated/fur-coated/winter-coated etc.** wearing a white, fur etc. coat

ˈcoat ˌhanger *n.* [C] a HANGER

coat·ing /ˈkoʊt̬ɪŋ/ *n.* [C] a thin layer of something that covers a surface: *Rub a thin coating of oil onto the peppers, and grill them.*

ˌcoat of ˈarms *n. plural* **coats of arms** [C] a set of pictures or patterns painted on a SHIELD and used as the special sign of a family, town, university etc.

ˌcoat of ˈmail *n. plural* **coats of mail** [C] a coat made of metal rings that was worn to protect the top part of a soldier's body in the Middle Ages

ˈcoat rack *n.* [C] a board or pole with hooks on it that you hang coats on

coat·room /ˈkoʊt˺rum/ *n.* [C] a CLOAKROOM

ˈcoat stand *n.* [C] a tall pole with hooks at the top that you hang coats on

coat·tails /ˈkoʊt-teɪlz/ *n.* [plural] **1 on sb's coattails** if you achieve something on someone's coattails, you achieve it because of the other person's power or success: *He rose to power on the Prime Minister's coattails.* **2** the cloth at the back of a TAILCOAT that is divided into two pieces

coax /koʊks/ *v.* **1** [I,T] to persuade someone to do something that they do not want to do by talking to them in a kind, gentle, and patient way: *"How about letting me borrow your car?" Santos coaxed.* | **coax sb into (doing) sth** *Julie tried to coax her two children into smiling for a photo with Santa.* | **coax sb to do sth** *Scott coaxed him to give the new baby a kiss.* | **coax sb out/down/back etc.** *Members of the SWAT team coaxed Faustino out of his home.* ►see THESAURUS box at **persuade** **2** [T] to make something do something by dealing with it in a slow, patient, and careful way: *Many bulbs can be coaxed into bloom early.* | *He managed to coax a few sweet notes out of the old violin.* [**Origin:** 1500–1600 *cokes* **stupid person** (16–17 centuries)] —**coaxing** *n.* [U] —**coaxingly** *adv.*

coax sth **out of** sb *phr. v.* also **coax sth from sb** to persuade someone to tell you something or give you something: *Detectives coaxed a confession out of him.*

cob /kɑb/ *n.* [C] **1** the long hard middle part of an EAR of corn: *We had hot dogs, hamburgers, and* ***corn on the cob***. **2** BIOLOGY a male SWAN **3** BIOLOGY a type of horse that is strong and has short legs

co·balt /ˈkoʊbɔlt/ *n.* [U] **1** SYMBOL, **Co** CHEMISTRY a shiny silver-white metal that is a chemical ELEMENT, and that is used to make some metals and to give a blue color to some substances **2** a deep blue color, or a bright blue-green color [**Origin:** 1600–1700 German *kobalt*, from *kobold* **goblin**; because goblins were thought to mix it in with silver found in the ground] —**cobalt** *adj.*

Cobb /kɑb/, **Ty** /taɪ/ (1886–1961) a U.S. baseball player, known for being the first person to score 4,000 BASE HITS

cob·ble[1] /ˈkɑbəl/ *v.* [T] **1** OLD-FASHIONED to repair or make shoes **2** to put COBBLESTONES on a street

C

cobble sth ↔ **together** *phr. v.* INFORMAL to quickly make something that is useful but not perfect: *Several officials worked late trying to cobble together an agreement.* | *They managed to cobble together a home-made radio.*

cobble² *n.* [C] a COBBLESTONE

cob·bled /'kɑbəld/ *adj.* a cobbled street is covered with COBBLESTONES

cob·bler /'kɑblɚ/ *n.* [C] **1** cooked fruit covered with a sweet bread-like mixture: *warm peach cobbler* **2** OLD-FASHIONED someone who makes and repairs shoes

cob·ble·stone /'kɑbəl,stoʊn/ *n.* [C] a small round stone set in the ground, especially in past times, to make a hard surface for a road

co·bra /'koʊbrə/ *n.* [C] BIOLOGY a poisonous African or Asian snake that can spread the skin of its neck to make itself look bigger [**Origin:** 1800–1900 Portuguese *cobra (de capello)* **snake with a hood**, from Latin *colubra* **snake**]

co-brand·ing /'koʊ,brændɪŋ/ *n.* [U] the activity of two companies helping each other to do business or sell products by using both company names, for example having a particular bank inside a particular store

cob·web /'kɑbwɛb/ *n.* [C] **1** a very fine network of sticky threads made by a SPIDER to catch insects, that is covered in dust and makes a room look dirty → see also SPIDERWEB **2 blow/brush/clear etc. the cobwebs** to do something, especially go outside, in order to help yourself to think more clearly and have more energy: +**off/away** *I went for a walk to clear away the cobwebs.* [**Origin:** 1300–1400 *cop* **spider** (14–15 centuries) (from Old English *atorcoppe* **spider**) + *web*] —**cobwebbed** *adj.* —**cobwebby** *adj.*

co·ca /'koʊkə/ *n.* [U] a South American bush whose leaves are used to make cocaine

Co·ca-Co·la /,koʊkə 'koʊlə/ *n.* [C,U] TRADEMARK a sweet brown SOFT DRINK, or a glass of this drink SYN **Coke**

co·caine /koʊ'keɪn, 'koʊkeɪn/ *n.* [U] a drug, usually in the form of a white powder, that is taken illegally for pleasure or used in some medical situations to prevent pain [**Origin:** 1800–1900 *coca*] → see also CRACK²

coc·cyx /'kɑksɪks/ *n. plural* **coccyxes** or **coccyges** /'kɑksɪdʒiz, kɑk'saɪdʒiz/ [C] BIOLOGY the small bone at the bottom of your SPINE SYN **tailbone**

coch·i·neal /'kɑtʃə,nil, 'koʊ-/ *n.* [U] a red substance used to give food a red color [**Origin:** 1500–1600 French *cochenille*, from Old Spanish *cochinilla* **small insect from which cochineal is obtained**]

Co·chise /koʊ'tʃis, -'tʃiz/ (?1812–1874) a Native American chief of the Apaches who fought against U.S. soldiers from 1861 to 1872 in order to prevent them from taking land from his people

coch·le·a /'kɑkliə, 'koʊ-/ *n. plural* **cochleas** or **cochleae** /-li-i, -liaɪ/ [C] BIOLOGY a tube in the inner ear that is filled with liquid. It sends information about sound to the brain.

cock¹ /kɑk/ *n.*
1 CHICKEN [C] BIOLOGY a ROOSTER: *A cock crowed from the barn.* → see also COCK-A-DOODLE-DOO
2 cock and bull story a story or excuse that is silly and not likely but is told as if it were true: *He **gave me a cock and bull story** about the car just sliding off the road.*
3 MALE BIRD [C] BIOLOGY an adult male bird of any kind
4 CONTROL FLOW [C] something that controls the flow of liquid or gas out of a pipe → see also BALLCOCK, STOPCOCK
5 cock of the walk OLD-FASHIONED someone who behaves as if they were better or more important than other people → see also HALF-COCKED

cock² *v.* [T] **1** to lift a part of your body so that it is upright, or hold a part of your body at an angle: *She stood with her head **cocked to one side** and her hands on her hips.* | *Hardin cocked an eyebrow.* **2** to pull back the HAMMER of a gun so that it is ready to be fired: *The soldiers cocked their pistols.* **3** to put your hat on at an angle **4 keep an ear cocked** INFORMAL to pay close attention because you want to be sure you hear something you expect or think may happen

cock·ade /kɑ'keɪd/ *n.* [C] a small piece of cloth used as a decoration on a hat to show rank, membership of a club etc.

cock-a-doo·dle-doo /,kɑk ə ,dudl 'du/ *n.* [C] the loud sound made by a ROOSTER (=adult male chicken)

cock·a·ma·mie /'kɑkə,meɪmi/ *adj.* INFORMAL a cockamamie story, excuse, or idea is not believable or does not make sense: *a cockamamie story about the end of the world*

cock·a·too /'kɑkə,tu/ *n.* [C] an Australian PARROT with a lot of feathers on the top of its head

cock·crow /'kɑk-kroʊ/ *n.* [U] LITERARY the time in the early morning when the sun rises SYN **dawn**

,cocked 'hat *n.* [C] a hat with the edges turned up on three sides, worn in past times

cock·er·el /'kɑkərəl/ *n.* [C] a young male chicken

cock·er span·iel /,kɑkɚ 'spænyəl/ *n.* [C] a dog with long ears and long soft fur

cock·eyed /'kɑkaɪd/ *adj.* INFORMAL **1** an idea, situation, plan etc. that is cockeyed is strange and not practical: *a cockeyed theory* **2** not straight or level: *a cockeyed grin*

cock·fight /'kɑkfaɪt/ *n.* [C] a sport, illegal in many countries, in which two male chickens are made to fight each other —**cockfighting** *n.* [U]

cock·le /'kɑkəl/ *n.* [C] **1** a common European SHELLFISH that is often used for food **2 warm the cockles of sb's heart** OLD-FASHIONED to make someone feel happy and full of good feelings toward other people

cock·le·shell /'kɑkəl,ʃɛl/ *n.* [C] **1** the shell of the cockle, that is shaped like a heart **2** LITERARY a small light boat

cock·ney, Cockney /'kɑkni/ *n.* **1** [C] someone, especially a WORKING CLASS person, who comes from the eastern area of London **2** [U] a way of speaking English that is typical of someone from this area —**cockney** *adj.*

cock·pit /'kɑk,pɪt/ *n.* [C] **1** the part of an airplane, racing car, or small boat in which the pilot or driver sits **2** a small, usually enclosed area where COCKFIGHTS take place

cock·roach /'kɑk-roʊtʃ/ *n.* [C] a large black or brown insect that often lives where food is kept SYN **roach** [**Origin:** 1600–1700 Spanish *cucaracha*, from *cuca* **caterpillar**]

cocks·comb, coxcomb /'kɑks-koʊm/ *n.* [C] **1** BIOLOGY the red flesh that grows from the top of a male chicken's head **2** the cap worn by a JESTER (=someone employed to amuse a king in past times)

cock·sure /,kɑk'ʃʊr/ *adj.* INFORMAL too confident of your abilities or knowledge, in a way that is annoying to other people: *She sounds confident, but not cocksure.* [**Origin:** 1500–1600 *cock* word used to avoid saying **God** (14–19 centuries) + *sure*]

cock·tail /'kɑkteɪl/ *n.* [C] **1** an alcoholic drink made from a mixture of LIQUOR and other drinks **2 seafood/shrimp/lobster cocktail** a mixture of small pieces of fish, SHRIMP, or LOBSTER, served cold with a special sauce and eaten at the beginning of a meal **3** a mixture of dangerous substances, especially one that you eat or drink: *a deadly cocktail of alcohol and tranquilizers* → see also FRUIT COCKTAIL, MOLOTOV COCKTAIL

'cocktail ,bar *n.* [C] a place where people can buy cocktails as well as beer and wine

'cocktail ,dress *n.* [C] a formal dress that reaches just above or below your knees, for wearing to parties or other evening social events

'cocktail ,lounge *n.* [C] a public room in a hotel, restaurant etc., where alcoholic drinks may be bought

'cocktail ,party *n.* [C] a party at which alcoholic

drinks are served and for which people usually dress formally

ˈcocktail ˌshaker *n.* [C] a container in which COCKTAILS are mixed

ˈcocktail stick *n.* [C] a short pointed stick on which small pieces of food are served

ˈcocktail ˌwaitress *n.* [C] a woman who serves drinks to people sitting at tables in a BAR

cock·y /ˈkɑki/ *adj. comparative* **cockier**, *superlative* **cockiest** INFORMAL too confident about yourself and your abilities, especially in a way that annoys other people: *a cocky 15-year-old boy* —**cockily** *adv.* —**cockiness** *n.* [U]

co·coa /ˈkoʊkoʊ/ *n.* [U] **1** a brown powder made from cocoa beans, used to make chocolate and in cooking to make cakes, cookies etc. **2** a sweet hot drink made with this powder, sugar, and milk or water: *a cup of cocoa*

ˈcocoa bean *n.* [C] the small seed of a tropical tree, that is used to make cocoa

ˈcocoa ˌbutter *n.* [U] a fat obtained from the seeds of a tropical tree, used in making some COSMETICS

co·coa·nut /ˈkoʊkəˌnʌt/ *n.* [C,U] another spelling of coconut

ˈcocoa ˌpowder *n.* [U] COCOA

co·co·nut, **cocoanut** /ˈkoʊkəˌnʌt/ *n.* **1** [C] BIOLOGY the large brown seed of a tropical tree, which has a hard shell containing liquid that you can drink and a white part that you can eat **2** [U] the white part of this seed, often used in cooking: *shredded coconut* [**Origin:** 1600–1700 *coco* **coconut** (16–18 centuries) (from Portuguese, **grinning face**; because the bottom of a coconut, with its three spots, looks like a face) + *nut*]

ˈcoconut ˌmilk *n.* [U] the liquid inside a coconut

co·coon[1] /kəˈkun/ *n.* [C] **1** BIOLOGY a bag of silky threads that young MOTHS and some other insects make to cover and protect themselves while they are growing **2** a place where you feel comfortable and safe: *Her security staff formed a cocoon around her.* | +**of** *the cocoon of family life* **3** something that wraps around you completely, especially to protect you: +**of** *The baby looked out from a cocoon of blankets.* [**Origin:** 1600–1700 French *cocon*, from Provençal, from *coco* **shell**]

cocoon[2] *v.* [T] to protect or surround someone or something completely, especially so that they feel safe: *Experts say you shouldn't cocoon your children too much.* —**cocooned** *adj.*

co·coon·ing /kəˈkunɪŋ/ *n.* [U] INFORMAL the activity of spending a lot of time in your own home because you feel comfortable and safe there: *The trend toward cocooning leads to profits for home improvement stores.*

Coc·teau /kɑkˈtoʊ/, **Jean** /ʒɑn/ (1889–1963) a French writer and movie DIRECTOR, who was an important member of the SURREALIST movement

C.O.D. /ˌsi oʊ ˈdi/ *adv.* cash on delivery; a system in which you pay for something when it is delivered to you: *Send the equipment C.O.D.*

cod /kɑd/ *n.* **1** [C] BIOLOGY a large ocean fish that lives in the North Atlantic **2** [U] the white meat from this fish: *baked cod*

co·da /ˈkoʊdə/ *n.* [C] ENG. LANG. ARTS **1** an additional part at the end of a piece of music that is separate from the main part **2** a separate piece of writing at the end of a work of literature or a speech

cod·dle /ˈkɑdl/ *v.* [T] to treat someone in a way that is too kind and gentle and that protects them from pain or difficulty: *He believes society is coddling young criminals.*

code[1] /koʊd/ Ac S1 W2 *n.*

1 RULES/LAWS/PRINCIPLES [C] a set of rules, laws, or principles that tell people how to behave or how something should be done: *Building codes have been strengthened following the earthquake.* | *Churches help to teach children a strong* ***moral code.*** | *The school has a strict* ***dress code*** (=rules about what clothes students can and cannot wear). | **code of conduct/ethics/behavior** *He had ignored the legal profession's code of conduct.* | *The association has* ***a code of practice*** (=set of rules that people in a particular business or profession agree to obey) *for its members.* | **the criminal/penal code** (=the set of laws used in a country or area)

2 SECRET MESSAGE [C,U] a system of words, letters, or signs that you use instead of ordinary writing to send a message that only other people who know the system can understand: *The code was used by the Japanese Navy during World War II.* | *All government messages were to be sent* ***in code.*** | **break/crack a code** (=manage to understand a secret code)

3 SIGNS GIVING INFORMATION [C] a set of numbers, letters, or other marks that show what something is or that give information about it: *The code "ZZ35" on the CD means it was imported from Europe.*

4 a code of silence an unwritten rule, known to members of a group, that does not allow people in the group to tell anyone about wrong or illegal actions that other members of the group have done: *He claims there is a code of silence over reporting cases of corruption in the police force.*

5 COMPUTERS [C,U] COMPUTERS a set of instructions that tell a computer what to do: *Some programmers write code for more than 12 hours straight.* → see also MACHINE CODE, SOURCE CODE

6 SOUNDS/SIGNALS [C] a system of sounds or signals that represent words or letters when they are sent by machine: *a telegraphic code*

[**Origin:** 1500–1600 French, Latin *codex* **main part of a tree, piece of wood for writing on, book**] → see also AREA CODE, BAR CODE, DRESS CODE, GENETIC CODE, MORSE CODE, ZIP CODE

code[2] Ac S3 *v.* [T] **1** to put a set of numbers, letters, or signs on something to show what it is or give information about it: *Security badges are coded to show which buildings each person may enter.* **2** to put a message into a code so that it is secret **3 color code** to mark a group of things with different colors so that you can tell the difference between them: *color coded wires* —**coded** *adj.*: *a coded message*

co·deine /ˈkoʊdin/ *n.* [U] MEDICINE a strong drug used to stop pain

ˈcode name *n.* [C] a name that is used instead of someone's or something's real name in order to keep it a secret, or to keep secret the aims, facts etc. of a plan —**code name** *v.* [T]

ˌco-deˈpendent, **codependent** *adj.* someone who is co-dependent thinks that they cannot be happy or successful without someone else, and so tries to keep that person happy without taking care of their own needs, in a way that seems unhealthy —**co-dependence** —**codependency** *n.* [U]

ˈcode-ˌsharing *n.* [U] a system in which two AIRLINE companies sell tickets for the same journey, and the flight has two different flight numbers

ˈcode word *n.* [C] **1** a word or phrase that has a different meaning than what it seems to mean, used to communicate something secretly **2** a word or expression that you use instead of a more direct one, used when you want to avoid shocking or upsetting someone: +**for** *The fact is, "Japan bashing" is a phrase that's become a code word for racism.*

co·dex /ˈkoʊdɛks/ *n. plural* **codices** /-dɪsiz/ [C] TECHNICAL an ancient book written by hand: *a sixth-century codex*

cod·fish /ˈkɑdˌfɪʃ/ *n.* [C] a COD

codg·er /ˈkɑdʒɚ/ *n.* [C] INFORMAL **old codger** a phrase meaning an "old man," used when you are not being respectful

cod·i·cil /ˈkɑdɪsɪl/ *n.* [C] LAW a document stating any changes or additions to a WILL (=legal document that says who you want your money and property to be given to after you die)

cod·i·fy /ˈkɑdəˌfaɪ, ˈkoʊ-/ *v.* **codifies**, **codified**, **codifying** [T] to arrange laws, principles, facts etc. in a system: *The agreement must still be codified by federal legislation.* —**codification** /ˌkɑdəfəˈkeɪʃən/ *n.* [C,U]

C

ˌcod-liver ˈoil *n.* [U] a yellow oil from a codfish that contains many substances that are important for good health

co·dom·i·nance /koʊˈdɑmənəns/ *n.* [U] BIOLOGY a situation in which both ALLELES (=pair of GENES) are present to an equal degree on a CHROMOSOME, and both have an equal influence on a person's or animal's physical appearance and the type of blood they have —**codominant** *adj.*: *In individuals with an AB blood type, A and B alleles are codominant.*

cod·piece /ˈkɑdpis/ *n.* [C] a piece of colored cloth worn by men in the 15th and 16th centuries to cover the opening in the front of their pants

Co·dy /ˈkoʊdi/, **William** (1846–1917) a U.S. soldier and hunter, known as Buffalo Bill, who organized a famous Wild West show, in which people showed their skill at shooting and riding horses and tried to show what life was like in the American West

co·ed[1], **co-ed** /ˌkoʊˈɛd◂/ *adj.* using a system in which students of both sexes study or live together OPP **single-sex**: *coed exercise classes | The college* ***went coed*** (=started using this system) *in the 1990s.*

coed[2], **co-ed** *n.* [C] OLD-FASHIONED a woman student at a college or university

co·ed·u·ca·tion, co-education /ˌkoʊɛdʒəˈkeɪʃən/ *n.* [U] a system in which students of both sexes study or live together —**coeducational** *adj.* FORMAL

co·ef·fi·cient /ˌkoʊəˈfɪʃənt/ *n.* [C] MATH the number that does not change in a mathematical expression that has a VARIABLE: *In 8pq, the coefficient of pq is 8.*

ˌcoefˈficient ˌmatrix *n.* [C] MATH a MATRIX that is made up of the coefficients of a set of EQUATIONS

coe·lom /ˈsiləm/ *n.* [C] BIOLOGY a hollow space within the body of many animals, between the inside surface of the skin and the organs inside the body

coe·lo·mate /ˈsiləˌmeɪt/ *n.* [C] BIOLOGY a living creature that has a COELOM → see also ACOELOMATE

co·en·zyme /koʊˈɛnzaɪm/ *n.* [C] BIOLOGY a substance, often a VITAMIN or a mineral, that forms part of an ENZYME, and that must combine with a PROTEIN to make the enzyme work

co·e·qual /ˌkoʊˈikwəl◂/ *adj.* FORMAL if people or groups are coequal, they have the same rank, ability, importance etc.: *coequal members of a partnership* —**coequally** *adv.*

co·erce /koʊˈɚs/ *v.* [T] to make someone do something they do not want to do by threatening them SYN **force**: **coerce sb into doing sth** *Don't coerce a child into wearing something he or she doesn't like.* [**Origin:** 1400–1500 Latin *coercere*, from *co-* + *arcere* **to enclose**]

co·er·cion /koʊˈɚʃən, -ʒən/ *n.* [U] the use of threats or orders to make someone do something they do not want to do SYN **force**: *Coercion should not be used when questioning suspects.*

co·er·cive /koʊˈɚsɪv/ *adj.* using threats or orders to make someone do something they do not want to do: *coercive tactics used by the police* —**coercively** *adv.*

co·e·val /koʊˈivəl/ *adj.* FORMAL having the same age or having started at the same time or on the same date: +**with** *He suggests that law is coeval with society.*

co·ev·o·lu·tion /ˌkoʊɛvəˈluʃən/ *n.* [U] BIOLOGY a situation in which two different SPECIES of animals, plants, insects etc. both gradually change and develop in relation to each other over a long period of time, so that a change in one produces a change in the other. The relationship between insects and flowers or between an animal that is hunted and an animal that hunts are examples of coevolution.

co·ex·ist /ˌkoʊɪgˈzɪst/ *v.* [I] FORMAL to exist at the same time or in the same place, especially peacefully: *Can the two countries ever coexist peacefully?* | +**with** *Capitalism can coexist with environmentalism if the right laws are in place.*

co·ex·is·tence /ˌkoʊɪgˈzɪstəns/ *n.* [U] FORMAL **1** if two or more countries or people have a coexistence, they live close to each other without fighting: *The two countries signed an accord calling for* ***peaceful coexistence****.* **2** the state of existing together at the same time or in the same place —**coexistent** *adj.*

cof·fee /ˈkɔfi, ˈkɑ-/ S1 W2 *n.* **1** [U] a hot, dark brown drink that has a slightly bitter taste: *Do you want* ***a cup of coffee****? | She gave me a cup of strong* ***black coffee*** (=coffee with no milk added). **2** [U] coffee beans, or the brown powder that is made by crushing coffee beans, used to make coffee: *a pound of coffee | Sorry, all I have is* ***instant coffee*** (=a powder used to make coffee quickly). **3** [C] a cup of this drink: *That's four coffees and two pieces of apple pie, right?* **4** [C] a type of coffee that has a particular taste: *A variety of gourmet coffees are on sale.* **5** [U] a light brown color [**Origin:** 1500–1600 Italian *caffè*, from Turkish *kahve*, from Arabic *qahwa*] → see also **wake up and smell the coffee** at WAKE UP (3)

ˈcoffee bar *n.* [C] **1** a place where people can buy coffee beans, cups of coffee, and sweet foods which they can eat and drink there or take away with them **2** a COFFEE HOUSE → see also COFFEE SHOP

ˈcoffee bean *n.* [C] the seed of a tropical tree that is used to make coffee

ˈcoffee break *n.* [C] a short time when you stop working to relax and drink something, and sometimes eat a little bit of food

ˈcoffee ˌcake *n.* [C,U] a sweet heavy cake, usually eaten along with coffee

ˈcoffee ˌgrinder *n.* [C] a small machine that crushes coffee beans

ˈcoffee house *n.* [C] a small restaurant where people go to talk and drink coffee, eat desserts, etc. → see also COFFEE BAR

coffee klatch /ˈkɔfi ˌklætʃ/ *n.* [C] an informal social situation when people drink coffee and talk

ˈcoffee maˌchine *n.* [C] a machine that gives you a cup of coffee, tea etc. when you put money into it

ˈcoffee ˌmaker *n.* [C] an electric machine that makes a pot of coffee

ˈcoffee mill *n.* [C] a COFFEE GRINDER

ˈcoffee pot *n.* [C] a container for making or serving coffee

ˈcoffee shop *n.* [C] a restaurant that serves cheap meals SYN **diner** → see also COFFEE BAR → COFFEE HOUSE

ˈcoffee ˌtable *n.* [C] a small low table in a LIVING ROOM for putting drinks and magazines on

ˈcoffee table ˌbook *n.* [C] a large expensive book that usually has a lot of pictures in it

cof·fer /ˈkɔfɚ, ˈkɑ-/ *n.* [C] **1 coffers** [plural] the money that an organization, government etc. has available to spend: **state/government/city etc. coffers** *The monthly market adds about $500,000 to Pasadena's city coffers annually.* **2** a large strong box often decorated with jewels, silver, gold etc., and used to hold valuable or religious objects

cof·fer·dam /ˈkɔfɚˌdæm, ˈkɑ-/ *n.* [C] a large box filled with air that allows people to work under water

cof·fin /ˈkɔfɪn/ *n.* [C] a long box in which a dead person is buried SYN **casket** [**Origin:** 1300–1400 Old French *cophin*, from Latin *cophinus* **basket**] → see also **a nail in sb's/sth's coffin** at NAIL[1] (3)

cog /kɑg/ *n.* [C] **1** a wheel with small parts shaped like teeth sticking out around the edge, which fit together with the teeth of another wheel as they turn around in a machine **2 a cog in the machine/wheel** someone who is not important or powerful, who only has a small job or part in a large business or organization **3** one of the small teeth that stick out on a cog

co·gent /ˈkoʊdʒənt/ *adj.* FORMAL something such as an argument that is cogent is reasonable, so that people are persuaded that it is correct: *Clear, cogent evidence must be presented to the court.* —**cogently** *adv.* —**cogency** *n.* [U]

cog·i·tate /ˈkɑdʒəˌteɪt/ *v.* [I] FORMAL to think carefully and seriously about something —**cogitation** /ˌkɑdʒəˈteɪʃən/ *n.* [U]

co•gnac /ˈkɑnyæk, ˈkɔn-, ˈkoʊn-/ *n.* [C,U] a type of BRANDY (=alcoholic drink) made in France, or a glass of this drink [**Origin:** 1700–1800 French *Cognac* town in western France]

cog•nate[1] /ˈkɑgneɪt/ *adj.* ENG. LANG. ARTS cognate words or languages have the same origin

cognate[2] *n.* [C] ENG. LANG. ARTS a word in one language that has the same origin as a word in another language, or different words in the same language that have the same origin: *"Classic," "classical," and "class" are cognates.*

cog•ni•tion /kɑgˈnɪʃən/ *n.* [U] **1** TECHNICAL the way that your brain processes information that comes to it through the senses, experience, and thought: *Brain damage can affect cognition.* **2** FORMAL understanding: *Political cognition rises with education.*

cog•ni•tive /ˈkɑgnət̬ɪv/ *adj.* FORMAL or TECHNICAL relating to the process of knowing, understanding, and learning something: *cognitive psychology* —**cognitively** *adv.*

cog•ni•zance /ˈkɑgnəzəns/ *n.* [U] FORMAL **1 take cognizance of sth** to understand something and consider it when you do something or make a decision **2** knowledge or understanding of something: *He* ***has full cognizance*** (=understands completely) *of the risks involved.* **3** TECHNICAL responsibility for a particular area of knowledge, action etc.: *a program developed under the cognizance of the Defense Department*

cog•ni•zant /ˈkɑgnəzənt/ *adj.* **cognizant of sth** having knowledge or information about something: *The court is* ***cognizant of the fact that*** *your client has tried to pay the debt.*

cog•no•men /kɑgˈnoʊmən, ˈkɑgnə-/ *n.* [C] **1** FORMAL a name used instead of someone's real name, or a description added to someone's name, for example "the Great" in "Alexander the Great" **2** TECHNICAL a SURNAME (=last name or family name), especially in ancient Rome

co•gno•scen•ti /ˌkɑnyəˈʃɛnti, ˌkɑgnə-/ *n.* **the cognoscenti** people who have special knowledge about a particular subject, especially art, literature, or food

cog•wheel /ˈkɑg-wil/ *n.* [C] SCIENCE a COG

co•hab•it /ˌkoʊˈhæbɪt/ *v.* [I] if two unmarried people cohabit, they live together as though they are married —**cohabitation** /ˌkoʊhæbəˈteɪʃən/ *n.* [U]

co•here /koʊˈhɪr/ *v.* [I] FORMAL **1** if the ideas or arguments in a piece of writing cohere, they are connected in a clear and reasonable way **2** if two objects cohere, they stick together SYN **stick** → see also ADHERE

co•her•ence /koʊˈhɪrəns/ Ac *n.* [U] **1** ENG. LANG. ARTS the quality of having ideas or parts that relate to each other in a way that is clear, reasonable, and easy to understand, especially in a piece of writing: *Writing down your central idea will help give your arguments coherence.* **2** the quality that a group has when its members are connected or united because they share common aims, qualities, or beliefs: *By 1924, the party had lost all discipline and coherence.*

co•her•ent /koʊˈhɪrənt/ Ac *adj.* **1** if a piece of writing, set of ideas, plan etc. is coherent, it is easy to understand because it is clear and reasonable and the parts relate well to each other: *a coherent argument* | *The company needs a coherent strategy.* | *They tried to link the three programs into* ***a coherent whole*** (=a single unit made from several parts that work well together). **2** if someone is coherent, they are talking in a way that is clear and easy to understand OPP **incoherent**: *I was so angry, I'm sure I was* ***barely coherent*** (=talking in a way that is almost impossible to understand). **3** if a group of people is coherent, its members work together well as a unit, because they have the same aims, qualities, or beliefs: *They were never a coherent group.* **4** PHYSICS relating to light waves that have the same FREQUENCY and travel in the same direction OPP **incoherent**: *A laser produces coherent light.* —**coherently** *adv.*

co•he•sion /koʊˈhiʒən/ *n.* [U] **1** the quality a group of people, a set of ideas etc. has when all the parts or members of it are connected or related in a reasonable way to form a whole: *the lack of cohesion within the committee* **2** TECHNICAL a close relationship, based on grammar or meaning, between two parts of a sentence or the parts of a larger piece of writing **3** BIOLOGY a physical force that makes MOLECULES pull toward each other, keeping atoms of the same substance together —**cohesive** /koʊˈhisɪv, -zɪv/ *adj.* —**cohesively** *adv.* —**cohesiveness** *n.* [U]

C

co•hort /ˈkoʊhɔrt/ *n.* [C] **1** a group of people who do the same activity, are friends, or are similar in some way, often used when you disapprove of them: *Hawk and his cohorts cheated Jack out of a fortune.* **2** TECHNICAL a member of a particular age group, social class etc., or the group itself: *"Baby boomers" are the largest cohort of Americans living today.*

coif•fure /kwɑˈfyʊr/ *n.* [C] FORMAL the way someone's hair is arranged SYN **hairdo** —**coiffured** *adj.*

coil[1] /kɔɪl/ *v.* [I,T] also **coil up** to wind or twist into a round shape, or to wind or twist something in this way: *The 12-foot python was found coiled in a corner of the room.* | *Coil the rope tightly around the bar.* [**Origin:** 1500–1600 Old French *coillir* **to gather**] —**coiled** *adj.*

coil[2] *n.* [C] **1** a continuous series of circular rings into which something such as wire or rope has been wound or twisted: +**of** *high walls topped with coils of barbed wire* **2** PHYSICS a wire or a metal tube in a continuous circular shape that produces light or heat when electricity is passed through it: *a heating coil* **3** TECHNICAL the part of a car engine that sends electricity to the SPARK PLUGS

coin[1] /kɔɪn/ *n.* **1** [C] a piece of metal, usually flat and round, that is used as money → see also BILL: *I had a few coins in my pocket.* ►see THESAURUS box at **money** **2 toss/flip a coin** to choose or decide something by throwing a coin into the air and guessing which side of it will show when it falls: *We flipped a coin to decide which movie to rent.* **3** [U] money in the form of metal coins [**Origin:** 1300–1400 Old French **three-sided piece, corner**, from Latin *cuneus* **wedge**] → see also COIN TOSS, **the other side of the coin** at SIDE[1] (32), **two sides of the same coin** at SIDE[1] (33)

coin[2] *v.* **1** [T] to invent a new word or expression, especially one that many people start to use: *Freed was the disk jockey who coined the term "rock 'n' roll."* **2 to coin a phrase** said in a joking way when you use a very familiar expression that people often use too much, to show that you know it is used a lot: *Miller was trying to help his career and, to coin a phrase, snatch victory from the jaws of defeat.* **3** [T] to make coins from metal

coin•age /ˈkɔɪnɪdʒ/ *n.* **1** [C] a word or phrase that has been recently invented: *Many coinages, such as "blog," have arisen from the Internet.* **2** [U] the system of money used in a country: *the coinage used in 16th-century Italy* **3** [U] the use or making of new words or phrases **4** [U] the making of coins

co•in•cide /ˌkoʊɪnˈsaɪd/ Ac *v.* [I] **1** to happen at the same time as something else: **coincide with sth** *The attacks coincided with local people's growing worries about security in the area.* | **planned/timed to coincide** *The Senator's remarks were timed to coincide with the President's inauguration.* **2** [not in progressive] if two people's ideas, opinions etc. coincide, they are the same: *We work together when our needs coincide.* | +**with** *Their views do not coincide with ours.* [**Origin:** 1700–1800 Medieval Latin *coincidere*, from Latin *co-* + *incidere* **to fall into**]

co•in•ci•dence /koʊˈɪnsədəns/ Ac *n.* **1** [C,U] a surprising and unexpected situation in which two things that are related happen at the same time, in the same place, or to the same people: *It was a coincidence that we were in Paris at the same time.* | ***By coincidence****, it turned out that he had decorated my sister's house too.* |

*"I'm going to Concord tomorrow." "**What a coincidence!** I'm going out there too."* | ***It's no coincidence*** (=it is not by chance, so there must be a reason) *that all the students have complained about the principal.* | **be sheer/pure coincidence** (=happen completely by chance) **2** [singular] FORMAL an occasion when two ideas, opinions etc. are the same: +**of** *a coincidence of opinion among the board members*

co·in·ci·dent /koʊˈɪnsədənt/ Ac *adj.* FORMAL existing or happening at the same place or time

co·in·ci·den·tal /koʊˌɪnsəˈdɛntl/ Ac *adj.* happening completely by chance without being planned: *Was their meeting coincidental?* | **purely/entirely coincidental** *Any similarities between real events and this film are purely coincidental.* | +**that** *It wasn't coincidental that she arrived exactly at the same time.* —**coincidentally** *adv.* [sentence adverb] *Coincidentally, we were on the same plane.*

co·in·sur·ance /ˌkoʊɪnˈʃʊrəns/ *n.* [U] **1** a type of insurance in which the payment is split between two people, especially between an employer and a worker: *health coinsurance* **2** insurance that will only pay for part of the value or cost of something

co·in·sure /ˌkoʊɪnˈʃʊr/ *v.* [T] ECONOMICS to buy or provide insurance in which the payment is split between two people, or insurance that will only pay for part of the value or cost of something

ˈcoin toss *n.* [C usually singular] an occasion when someone throws a coin into the air to see which side it falls on, in order to decide something: *Our team won the coin toss and went first.*

coir /kɔɪɚ/ *n.* [U] the rough material that covers the shell of a COCONUT, used for making MATS, ropes etc.

co·i·tus /ˈkɔɪṭəs, ˈkoʊəṭəs/ *n.* [U] TECHNICAL the act of having sex

Coke /koʊk/ *n.* [C,U] TRADEMARK the drink COCA-COLA, or a bottle, can, or glass of this drink: *Regular fries and a large Coke, please.*

coke /koʊk/ *n.* [U] **1** INFORMAL the drug COCAINE **2** a solid black substance produced from coal and burned to provide heat

col /kɑl/ *n.* [C] EARTH SCIENCE a low point between two high places in a mountain range

Col. *n.* the written abbreviation of COLONEL

col. the written abbreviation of COLUMN

col- /kəl, kɑl/ *prefix* used instead of CON- before the letter "l"; with: *to collaborate* (=work together)

COLA /ˈkoʊlə/ *n.* [singular] **Cost of Living Adjustment** an increase in salary or SOCIAL SECURITY payments that is equal to the amount that prices, rents etc. have increased

co·la /ˈkoʊlə/ *n.* [C,U] a sweet brown SOFT DRINK, or a bottle, can, or glass of this drink

col·an·der /ˈkɑləndɚ, ˈkʌ-/ *n.* [C] a metal or plastic bowl with a lot of small holes in the bottom and sides, used to separate liquid from food

cold¹ /koʊld/ S1 W1 *adj.*
1 OBJECTS/LIQUIDS/PLACES ETC. having a low temperature: *My car doesn't run very well when the engine's cold.* | *How about a nice cold beer?* | *The office always **feels** so **cold** first thing on Monday morning.* | *Come sit down – your coffee's **getting cold**.* | **ice/stone/freezing cold** (=extremely cold)

THESAURUS

cool cold in a pleasant way, especially after it has been hot: *It's very hot during the day, but cooler at night.*
chilly cold, but not very cold: *a chilly fall day*
frosty very cold, with the ground covered in frost (=ice that is white and powdery and covers things when the temperature is very cold): *a bright frosty morning*
freezing (cold) extremely cold, so that water outside becomes ice: *It was freezing cold last night.*
icy (cold) extremely cold: *an icy wind*
bitter (cold) very cold in a way that feels very unpleasant: *a bitter cold night*
arctic extremely cold: *arctic winds*
→ HOT¹, WEATHER¹

2 WEATHER when the weather is cold, the temperature of the air is very low: *a cold, clear night* | *They say it's the coldest winter for over 50 years.* | **it's cold out/outside** *I'd wear a hat – it's cold out.* | **get/turn/grow cold** *It's going to get cold this weekend.* | **freezing/bitterly cold** (=extremely cold, in an unpleasant way)
3 be/feel/look/get cold if you are cold, your body is at a low temperature: *Aren't you cold?* | *Come inside before you get cold.* | *Your hands are **as cold as ice!*** (=extremely cold)
4 FOOD cold food has been cooked, but is not eaten while it is warm: *a selection of cold meats* | **eat/serve sth cold** *You can eat this dish hot or cold.* → see also COLD CUTS
5 LACKING FEELING unfriendly or lacking normal human feelings such as sympathy, pity, humor etc. OPP **warm**: *"I don't care," was her cold reply.* | *a cold, pragmatic decision* ►see THESAURUS box at **matter-of-fact**
6 leave sb cold INFORMAL to not feel interested in or affected by something at all: *Ballet just leaves me cold.*
7 get/have cold feet INFORMAL to suddenly feel that you are not brave enough to do something you planned to do: *They got cold feet and canceled the order.*
8 give sb/sth the cold shoulder INFORMAL to deliberately ignore someone or something, especially because you are upset or offended: *Haley is well-known for giving reporters the cold shoulder.*
9 pour cold water on sth to criticize an idea or plan a lot, so that other people no longer feel excited or enthusiastic about it: *I said I wanted to be an actor, but my parents poured cold water on the idea.*
10 cold (hard) cash INFORMAL money in the form of paper money and coins rather than checks or CREDIT CARDS
11 sb's trail/scent goes cold used to say that someone, especially the police, cannot find someone because it has been too long since they passed through or lived in a particular place: *They kept up the search for weeks, but the trail had gone cold.*
12 a cold fish DISAPPROVING a person who seems unfriendly and does not show their emotions
13 CHILDREN'S GAME SPOKEN used in a children's game to say that someone is far away from the hidden object they are trying to find OPP **warm**: *No, you're getting colder.*
14 COLOR/LIGHT a cold color or light reminds you of things that are cold: *Pouring in from outside windows is cold, blue light.*
15 in the cold light of day in the morning, when you can think or understand things clearly
16 cold steel LITERARY a weapon such as a knife or sword —**coldness** *n.* [U]
[**Origin:** Old English *ceald, cald*] → see also **in cold blood** at BLOOD (4), **cold/small comfort** at COMFORT¹ (7), **pour cold water over/on sth** at POUR (7), **a (cold) sweat** at SWEAT² (2)

cold² S2 *n.* **1** [C] MEDICINE a common illness that makes it difficult to breathe through your nose and often makes your throat hurt: *He's **had** so many **colds** this winter.* | *I had fun skiing, but I **caught a cold*** (=got one). → see also COMMON COLD **2 the cold** a low temperature or cold weather: *Nobody wanted to go out in the cold.* | *The cold affects the functioning of the engine.* **3 leave sb out in the cold** INFORMAL to not include someone in an activity, group, process etc.: *These trade negotiations have left farmers out in the cold.* **4 come in from the cold** to become officially accepted by a group of people or countries, after not being accepted by them

cold³ S3 *adv.* **1** suddenly and completely: *Judy stopped cold, realizing they were laughing at her.* **2 out cold** unconscious, especially because you have been hit on the head: *He was lying on the floor, out cold.* **3** without preparation: *I can't just get up there and make a speech cold!*

ˌcold-ˈblooded *adj.* **1** not showing any emotions or any pity for other people's suffering: *a cold-blooded murderer* **2** BIOLOGY a cold-blooded animal, such as a snake, has a body temperature that changes with the temperature of the air or ground around it → see also WARM-BLOODED —**cold-bloodedly** *adv.* —**cold-bloodedness** *n.* [U]

ˌcold ˈcall *n.* [C] a visit or telephone call you make to someone you have never met to try to sell something to them

ˈcold cream *n.* [U] a thick white oily cream used for cleaning your face and making it softer

ˈcold cuts *n.* [plural] thinly cut pieces of cold cooked meat

ˈcold front *n.* [C] EARTH SCIENCE the front edge of a mass of cold air that is moving toward a place → see also WARM FRONT

ˌcold-ˈhearted *adj.* behaving in a way that shows no pity or sympathy: *a cold-hearted businessman* —**cold-heartedly** *adj.* —**cold-heartedness** *n.* [U]

cold•ly /ˈkoʊldli/ *adv.* without friendly feelings: *"No autographs," he said coldly.*

ˈcold snap *n.* [C] a sudden short period of very cold weather

ˈcold sore *n.* [C] a painful spot on your lip or inside your mouth that you may get when you are sick

ˈcold spell *n.* [C] a period of several days or weeks of very cold weather

ˌcold ˈstorage *n.* [U] **1** a special cold container, room, building etc. where things such as food are stored so that they stay fresh **2 put sth in cold storage** to not do something about a plan or idea until later in the future: *Patton's plan to defend Hawaii was put in cold storage in 1940.*

ˌcold ˈturkey *n.* [U] INFORMAL **quit/go/stop cold turkey** to suddenly stop smoking cigarettes or stop taking a drug

ˌcold ˈwar *n.* **1** [singular, U] POLITICS an unfriendly political relationship between two countries who do not actually fight with each other **2 the Cold War** HISTORY this type of relationship between the U.S. and the Soviet Union, after World War II

Cole /koʊl/**, Thomas** (1801–1848) a U.S. PAINTER famous for his paintings of the American LANDSCAPE

Co•le•ridge /ˈkoʊlərɪdʒ/**, Sam•u•el Tay•lor** /ˈsæmyuəl ˈteɪlɚ/ (1772–1834) a British poet

cole slaw, coleslaw /ˈkoʊl slɔ/ *n.* [U] a SALAD made with thinly cut raw CABBAGE

Co•lette /kɔˈlɛt/ (1873–1954) a French writer of NOVELS

Col•gate /ˈkɔlgeɪt/**, William** (1783–1857) an American businessman who made soap and started the Colgate Palmolive Peet company

col•ic /ˈkɑlɪk/ *n.* [U] severe pain in the stomach and BOWELS, especially in babies —**colicky** *adj.*

col•i•se•um /ˌkɑləˈsiəm/ *n.* [C] a large structure with seats that has no roof, or a large building used for public events such as sports games, CONCERTS etc.

co•li•tis /kəˈlaɪt̬ɪs/ *n.* [U] MEDICINE an illness in which part of your COLON swells, causing pain

col•lab•o•rate /kəˈlæbəˌreɪt/ *v.* [I] **1** to work together with another person or group in order to achieve something, especially in science or art: **collaborate on sth** *We have* ***collaborated closely*** *with teachers on the new curriculum.* | **collaborarte with sb** *Ella Fitzgerald collaborated with some of the greatest musicians in jazz.* | **collaborate to do sth** *Six journalists have collaborated to produce a book on the history of southern Africa.* | **collaborate in (doing) sth** *Two biotech companies collaborated in the experiment.* **2** to help a country that your country is at war with, or one that has taken control of your country: **collaborate with sb** *After the war, he stood trial for* ***collaborating with the enemy.*** [**Origin:** 1800–1900 Late Latin, past participle of *collaborare*, from Latin *com-* + *laborare* **to work**]

col•lab•o•ra•tion /kəˌlæbəˈreɪʃən/ *n.* **1** [C,U] the act of working together with another person or group to achieve something, especially in science or art, or something produced in this way: +**between** *closer collaboration between the marketing and editorial departments* | +**with** *The film was the actor's first collaboration with director Roberto Rossellini.* | *Researchers conducted the tests* ***in collaboration with*** (=working together with) *a hospital in Stockholm.* **2** [U] help given to a country that your country is at war with, or one that has taken control of your country: +**with** *Nine people were jailed, suspected of collaboration with the enemy.*

C

col•lab•ora•tive /kəˈlæbrət̬ɪv/ *adj.* **collaborative project/effort/work etc.** a piece of work involving two or more people or groups working together to achieve something, especially in science or art

col•lab•o•ra•tor /kəˈlæbəˌreɪt̬ɚ/ *n.* [C] **1** someone who helps their country's enemies, for example by giving them information, when the enemy has taken control of their country: *a convicted collaborator* **2 sb's collaborator** someone who works with other people or groups in order to achieve something, especially in science or art: +**on** *He was her collaborator on a number of research projects.*

col•lage /kəˈlɑʒ, koʊ-/ *n.* **1** [C] ENG. LANG. ARTS a picture made by sticking other pictures, photographs, cloth etc. onto a surface **2** [U] the art of making pictures in this way [**Origin:** 1900–2000 French *coller* **to glue**, from *colle* **glue**, from Greek *kolla*]

col•la•gen /ˈkɑlədʒən/ *n.* [U] a PROTEIN substance, sometimes put into women's face creams

col•lapse[1] /kəˈlæps/ Ac *v.*

1 STRUCTURE [I] if a building, wall, piece of furniture etc. collapses, it suddenly falls down, usually because it is weak or damaged: *Part of the wall collapsed as a result of water damage.* | +**under** *Ted's chair collapsed under his weight.*

2 ILLNESS/INJURY [I] to suddenly fall down or become unconscious because you are sick or injured: *He collapsed and died from a heart attack.*

3 FAIL [I] if a system, idea, or organization collapses, it suddenly fails or becomes too weak to continue: *The economy seems close to collapsing.* | **collapse under the pressure/strain etc.** *The government collapsed under the pressure of internal disagreements.*

4 PRICES [I] if prices collapse, or if a market collapses, prices suddenly become much lower: *There were fears that property prices would collapse.*

5 SIT/LIE [I] to suddenly sit or lie down, especially because you are very tired: *I got home and collapsed on the sofa.*

6 MAKE STH SMALLER [I,T] if something collapses or you collapse it, you can fold it so that it becomes smaller: *The table collapses and can be stored in a closet.*

7 MEDICAL [I] MEDICINE if a lung or a BLOOD VESSEL collapses, it suddenly becomes flat because it does not have any air or blood in it anymore

[**Origin:** 1700–1800 Latin *collapsus*, past participle of *collabi*, from *com-* + *labi* **to fall, slide**]

collapse[2] Ac *n.* **1** [singular, U] a sudden failure in the way something works, so that it cannot continue: *the collapse of Communism in Eastern Europe* | **financial/economic collapse** *the country's virtual financial collapse* | **on the brink/verge/point of collapse** *The company is on the verge of collapse.* **2** [U] the act of suddenly falling down or in, because of a weakness in something's structure or because something has hit it violently: *The collapse of a wall left seven people injured.* | *The church roof is* ***in danger of collapse.*** **3** [singular] an occasion when someone falls down or becomes unconscious because of a sudden illness or injury: *The president is recovering from last week's collapse.* | *She seemed to be* ***on the point of collapse*** *after the race.* **4** [singular] a sudden decrease in the value of something: *the stock market collapse* | +**in** *a collapse in the value of pensions*

col·laps·i·ble /kə'læpsəbəl/ [Ac] *adj.* able to be folded up into a smaller size: *collapsible chairs*

col·lar¹ /'kɑlɚ/ [S3] *n.* [C]
1 CLOTHING the part of a shirt, dress, coat etc. that fits around your neck: *a blue dress with a white collar*
2 ANIMAL a narrow band of leather or plastic that is fastened around an animal's neck: *a stray dog with no collar*
3 MEDICAL a thick piece of stiff cloth that doctors give you to wear around your neck to support it when you have hurt it
4 PRIEST a special stiff round white collar that a priest wears
5 COLORED FUR/FEATHERS a band of fur, feathers, or skin around an animal's neck that is a different color from the rest of the animal
6 WORK ANIMAL a thick leather ring put over the shoulders of a work animal to help it pull machinery or a vehicle
7 MACHINE a ring that goes round a pipe to make it stronger, especially where two pieces of the pipe join together
8 POLICE SLANG if the police make a collar, they catch a criminal
[**Origin:** 1300–1400 Old French *coler*, from Latin *collare*, from *collum* **neck**] → see also BLUE-COLLAR, -COLLARED, DOG COLLAR, **hot under the collar** at HOT (29), WHITE-COLLAR

collar² *v.* [T] **1** INFORMAL to catch someone and hold them so that they cannot escape: *The police collared two suspects less than 20 minutes after the robbery.* **2** INFORMAL to find someone so that you can talk to them: *Hugh was quickly collared by a salesperson.* **3** to put a special collar on an animal, especially so that you know where it is, for scientific reasons: *Seventeen Florida panthers have been collared.*

col·lar·bone /'kɑlɚ,boʊn/ *n.* [C] BIOLOGY one of the pair of bones in your chest that go from the base of your neck to your shoulders

col·lard greens /'kɑlɚd ,grinz/ *n.* a vegetable with large green leaves, usually eaten cooked

-collared /kɑlɚd/ [in adjectives] **high-collared/blue-collared/open-collared etc.** having a particular type of collar: *a high-collared blouse*

'collar stud *n.* [C] an object like a button, used to fasten old-fashioned collars to shirts

col·late /kə'leɪt, kɑ-, 'koʊleɪt, 'kɑ-/ *v.* [T] **1** to arrange sheets of paper in the correct order before they are put in a book, report etc.: *Please collate and staple ten copies of the report for the meeting.* **2** FORMAL to gather information together, examine it carefully, and compare it with other information to find any differences

col·lat·er·al¹ /kə'lætərəl/ *n.* [U] ECONOMICS property or other goods that you promise to give to someone if you cannot pay back the money they lent you [SYN] security: *They **put up** their house **as collateral** for the loan.* —**collateralize** *v.* [T]

collateral² *adj.* FORMAL **1** relating to something or happening as a result of it, but not as important: *There may be collateral benefits to the plan.* **2** collateral relatives are members of your family who are not closely related to you

col,lateral 'damage *n.* [U] people who are hurt or property that is damaged as a result of war, although they are not the main TARGET, used especially by the Army, Navy etc.

col·la·tion /kə'leɪʃən/ *n.* **1** [U] the examination and comparing of information **2** [U] the arranging of sheets of paper in the correct order **3** [C] FORMAL a small, usually cold, meal

col·league /'kɑlig/ [Ac] [W2] *n.* [C] a word meaning someone you work with, used especially by professional people or managers: *friends and business colleagues* | **+at/in/from** *my colleagues at the university*
[**Origin:** 1500–1600 French *collègue*, from Latin *collega*, from *com-* + *legare* **to choose for a particular job**]

THESAURUS
coworker/co-worker someone whom you work with
employee someone who works for a company or organization
staff all the people who work for an organization

col·lect¹ /kə'lɛkt/ [S2] [W2] *v.*
1 BRING TOGETHER [T] to get things of the same type from different places and bring them together: *We collected samples of water from 15 different rivers.* | *He's been collecting voter signatures to get the measure on the ballot.* | **collect information/data/evidence etc.** *He spent five years collecting data for his book.*
2 KEEP OBJECTS [T] to get and keep objects because you think they are attractive or interesting: *Arlene collects teddy bears.* ►see THESAURUS box at **keep¹**
3 MONEY THAT IS OWED [T] to get money from people when they owe it to you: *Rent is collected once a month.* | *Some companies employ people to collect their debts for them.*
4 MONEY ETC. TO HELP PEOPLE [I,T] to ask people to give you money, goods etc. for a particular purpose: *Volunteers are collecting food and clothes to help earthquake victims.* | **collect (sth) for sb/sth** *Some kids came by, collecting for UNICEF.*
5 INCREASE IN AMOUNT [I,T] if something collects in a place, or if something collects it there, it gradually increases in amount: *The building uses solar panels for collecting the sun's heat.* | *I didn't know what to do with it, so it just sat there, **collecting dust**.*
6 **collect yourself** also **collect your thoughts** to make an effort to remain calm and think clearly and carefully about something: *I needed a few minutes to collect my thoughts.*
7 OBTAIN/WIN STH [T] to obtain or win something: *The team will soon collect its second NCAA title in three years.*
8 REMOVE [T] to come and take something away [SYN] **take away**: *They collect the trash once a week.*
9 CROWD [I] FORMAL to come together gradually to form a group of people [SYN] **gather**: *A crowd had collected outside the building.*
10 TAKE SB/STH FROM A PLACE [T] FORMAL to go and get someone or something from somewhere when they are ready or available for you [SYN] **pick up**: *I've come to collect Mr. Weinstein's order.*
[**Origin:** 1500–1600 Latin, past participle of *colligere*, from *com-* + *legere* **to gather**]

collect² *adv.* **call/phone sb collect** when you telephone someone collect, the person who receives the call pays for it

col·lect³ /'kɑlɪkt, -lɛkt/ *n.* [C] a short prayer in some Christian services

col'lect call *adj.* a telephone call that is paid for by the person who receives it

col·lect·ed /kə'lɛktɪd/ *adj.* **1** in control of yourself and your thoughts, feelings etc.: *She wanted to arrive feeling **cool, calm, and collected**.* **2** [only before noun] put together in one book or as a collection: *the collected works of Shakespeare*

col·lect·i·ble /kə'lɛktəbəl/ *adj.* something that is collectible is likely to be bought and kept as part of a group of similar things, especially because it might increase in value: *a selection of collectible cars* —**collectible** *n.* [C]

col·lec·tion /kə'lɛkʃən/ [S2] [W2] *n.*
1 SET/GROUP [C] **a)** a set of similar things that are kept or brought together because they are attractive or interesting: *a coin collection* | *the Permanent Collection at the Whitney Museum* | **+of** *a collection of antique vases* | **a large/an extensive/a vast etc. collection** *The museum has an extensive collection of books.* **b)** a group of things that are put together in the same place: *There was a collection of old newspapers on the table.*
2 BRINGING TOGETHER [U] the act of bringing together things of the same type from different places to form a

group: *Data collection takes time.* | +**of** *the collection of population statistics*
3 BOOKS/MUSIC [C] several stories, poems, pieces of music etc. that are in one book or on one recording: +**of** *a collection of love poems*
4 MONEY a) [C] the act of asking for money from people for a particular purpose: *Most Alcoholics Anonymous groups **take up a collection** at meetings to cover expenses.* | +**for** *We're organizing a collection for the local hospital.* **b)** [U] the act of obtaining money that is owed to you: *debt collection*
5 TAKING STH AWAY [C,U] the act of taking something from a place, especially when this is done regularly: *Christmas trees can be picked up with regular trash collection.*
6 CLOTHES [C] a number of different pieces of clothing designed by someone for a particular time of year: *Armani's summer collection*
7 PEOPLE [C usually singular] a group of people, especially people you think are strange or unusual in some way: +**of** *They're a real collection of misfits.*

col'lection ˌagency *n.* [C] a company that finds people who owe money to other businesses and forces them to pay it

col'lection ˌbox *n.* [C] a container with a small opening in the top into which people put money for CHARITY

col'lection ˌplate *n.* [C] a large, almost flat dish in which you put money during some religious services

col·lec·tive¹ /kəˈlɛktɪv/ *adj.* [only before noun] **1** shared or made by all the members of a group together: *collective ownership* | *It was a collective decision.* **2** [only before noun] owned by the government and controlled by a group of workers: *a collective farm*

collective² *n.* [C] **1** a group of people who work together to run something such as a business or farm: *A women's collective runs the small café across the street.* **2** ECONOMICS a business or farm that is run by a group of workers who rent it from the government

colˌlective 'bargaining *n.* [U] the discussions between employers and unions about pay, working conditions etc.

col·lec·tive·ly /kəˈlɛktɪvli/ *adv.* as a group: *Committee members are collectively responsible for their decisions.*

colˌlective 'noun *n.* [C] ENG. LANG. ARTS in grammar, a noun such as "committee" or "family" that is the name of a group of people or things considered as a unit

colˌlective se'curity *n.* [U] HISTORY an arrangement between two or more countries to give each other military protection if one of them is attacked

col·lec·tiv·ism /kəˈlɛktɪˌvɪzəm/ *n.* [U] POLITICS a political system in which all businesses, farms etc. are owned by the government —**collectivist** *adj.*

col·lec·tiv·i·za·tion /kəˌlɛktɪvəˈzeɪʃən/ *n.* [U] the act of combining together several farms into one large farm that is owned by all the people who work there or by the state. This happened especially in the past in some COMMUNIST countries: *The collectivization of farmland was one of Stalin's prize projects.* —**collectivize** /kəˈlɛktɪˌvaɪz/ *v.* [T] *The uprising was an attempt to get rid of the landowners and collectivize the estates.*

col·lec·tor /kəˈlɛktɚ/ *n.* [C] **1** someone whose job is to collect things such as taxes, tickets, debts etc. from people **2** someone who collects things that are interesting or attractive: *a stamp collector* **3 a collectors' item** something that a collector would like to have: *Some of those bikes were collectors' items, probably worth a lot of money.*

col·lege /ˈkɑlɪdʒ/ S1 W1 *n.*
1 ADVANCED EDUCATION [C,U] **a)** a large school where you can study after HIGH SCHOOL and get a BACHELOR'S DEGREE → see also UNIVERSITY: *He teaches at the college.* | *After college, he became a teacher.* | *a college degree* | *It's a project for some **college students**.* | *Fran just finished her freshman year **in college*** (=is a student at a college). | *Older people are **going back to college** to get a diploma.* | *Recent **college graduates** have had trouble finding jobs.* → see also COMMUNITY COLLEGE, JUNIOR COLLEGE **b)** a school for advanced education, especially in a particular subject or skill: *Tim's at business college to learn computer accounting.* ►see THESAURUS box at **university**
2 PART OF UNIVERSITY [C] **a)** the part of a university that teaches a particular subject: *the College of Engineering* **b)** one of the groups of students that some universities are officially divided into, which usually has a particular character and particular classes the students must take: *Revell College at UC San Diego*
3 STUDENTS AND TEACHERS [C] the students and teachers of a college: *Half of the college must've been at the demonstration.*
4 PROFESSIONAL ORGANIZATION [C] a group of people who have special rights and duties within a profession or organization: *the American College of Surgeons* → see also ELECTORAL COLLEGE
5 give sth the (old) college try to try very hard to achieve a GOAL with your group or team, especially when it seems very difficult
[**Origin:** 1300–1400 Old French, Latin *collegium* **society**]

ˌCollege 'Boards *n.* [plural] TRADEMARK a set of tests taken by students in order to attend some universities

col·le·giate /kəˈlidʒət/ *adj.* **1** relating to college or a college: *collegiate sports* **2** organized into COLLEGES: *a collegiate university*

col·lide /kəˈlaɪd/ *v.* [I] **1** to crash violently into something or someone: *The two players collided and Jordan fell to the floor.* | +**with** *His motorcycle collided with a car.* | *Both drivers were killed when the pickup truck **collided head-on** with a car* (=it hit a car moving directly toward it). ►see THESAURUS box at **hit¹** **2** to oppose a person or group, especially on a particular subject: +**over/with** *The groups have collided over plans for a new cemetery.* **3** if two very different ideas, ways of thinking etc. collide, they come together and conflict with each other: *a part of the world where East and West collide* [**Origin:** 1600–1700 Latin *collidere*, from *com-* + *laedere* **to injure by hitting**]

col·lie /ˈkɑli/ *n.* [C] a middle-sized dog with long hair, kept as a pet or trained to take care of sheep

col·lier /ˈkɑlyɚ/ *n.* [C] someone who works in a coal mine

col·lier·y /ˈkɑlyəri/ *n. plural* **collieries** [C] a coal mine and the buildings and machinery relating to it

col·lin·e·ar points /kəˌlɪniɚ ˈpɔɪnts/ *n.* [plural] MATH two or more points that lie on the same straight line

col·li·sion /kəˈlɪʒən/ *n.* [C,U] **1** a violent crash in which two or more vehicles or people hit each other: +**with** *Mike had a collision with another skier.* | *She was killed in a **head-on collision*** (=between two vehicles moving directly toward each other) *on Highway 218.* ►see THESAURUS box at **accident** **2** a strong disagreement between two people or groups: +**between** *a collision between police and demonstrators* **3 be on a collision course a)** to be likely to have serious trouble because your aims are very different from someone else's: *The two nations are on a collision course that could lead to war.* **b)** to be moving in a direction in which you will hit another person or vehicle

col·lo·cate /ˈkɑləˌkeɪt/ *v.* [I] ENG. LANG. ARTS when words collocate with each other, they are often used together and sound natural together —**collocate** /ˈkɑləkɪt/ *n.* [C]

col·lo·ca·tion /ˌkɑləˈkeɪʃən/ *n.* [C,U] ENG. LANG. ARTS the way in which some words are often used together, or a particular combination of words used in this way: *"Commit a crime" is a typical collocation in English.*

col·loid /ˈkɑlɔɪd/ *n.* [C] CHEMISTRY a mixture of substances in which small amounts of one substance are SUSPENDED (=floating) in the other → see also SUSPENSION

col·lo·qui·al /kəˈloʊkwiəl/ *adj.* ENG. LANG. ARTS colloquial language or words are used mainly in informal conversations rather than in writing or formal speech: *a colloquial expression* —**colloquially** *adv.*

col·lo·qui·al·ism /kəˈloʊkwiəˌlɪzəm/ *n.* [C] an expression or word used mainly in informal conversation

col·lo·qui·um /kəˈloʊkwiəm/ *n. plural* **colloquiums** or **colloquia** /-kwiə/ [C] an event at which someone such as a PROFESSOR gives a talk on a particular subject to a group of people

col·lo·quy /ˈkɑləkwi/ *n.* [C] FORMAL a conversation → see also SOLILOQUY

C

col·lude /kəˈlud/ *v.* [I] FORMAL to work with someone secretly, especially in order to do something dishonest or illegal: +**with** *Officials were accused of colluding with drug traffickers.*

col·lu·sion /kəˈluʒən/ *n.* [U] FORMAL LAW the act of agreeing secretly with someone else to do something dishonest or illegal

co·logne /kəˈloʊn/ *n.* [U] a liquid that smells good, which you put on your neck or wrists → see also PERFUME

Co·lom·bi·a /kəˈlʌmbiə/ a country in northern South America —**Colombian** *n., adj.*

Co·lom·bo /kəˈlʌmboʊ/ the capital and largest city of Sri Lanka

co·lon /ˈkoʊlən/ *n.* [C] **1** BIOLOGY the lower part of the INTESTINES, in which food is changed into waste matter → see picture at DIGESTIVE SYSTEM **2** ENG. LANG. ARTS the mark (:) used in writing and printing to introduce an explanation, example, list, QUOTATION etc. [**Origin:** (2) 1500–1600 Latin **part of a poem**, from Greek *kolon* **arm or leg, part of a poem**] → see also SEMICOLON ▶see THESAURUS box at **punctuation mark**

col·o·nel, **Colonel** /ˈkɚnl/ *n.* [C] a high rank in the Army, Marines, or Air Force, or someone who has this rank [**Origin:** 1500–1600 *coronal* **colonel** (16–17 centuries), from French *coronnel*, from Old Italian *colonnello* **column of soldiers, colonel**]

co·lo·ni·al¹ /kəˈloʊniəl/ *adj.* **1** POLITICS relating to the control of a country by a more powerful country, usually one that is far away: *The goal of the uprising was to overthrow the colonial government.* | *a country under* ***colonial rule*** **2** also **Colonial** made in a style that was common in the U.S. in the 18th century: *a Colonial-style brick house* **3** HISTORY relating to the U.S. when it was under British rule: *The town was first established in colonial times.* → see also COLONY

colonial² *n.* [C] **1** a house built in a style that was common in the 18th century **2** someone who lives in a COLONY but who is a citizen of the country that rules the colony

co·lo·ni·al·ism /kəˈloʊniəˌlɪzəm/ *n.* [U] POLITICS the principle or practice in which a powerful country rules a weaker one and establishes its own trade and society there → see also IMPERIALISM

co·lo·ni·al·ist /kəˈloʊniəlɪst/ *n.* [C] POLITICS a supporter of colonialism —**colonialist** *adj.*

col·o·nist /ˈkɑlənɪst/ *n.* [C] someone who settles in a new COLONY: *In 1638, Swedish colonists settled in present-day Delaware.*

col·o·nize /ˈkɑləˌnaɪz/ *v.* [I,T] to establish political control over an area or over another country, and send your citizens there to settle —**colonizer** *n.* [C] —**colonization** /ˌkɑlənəˈzeɪʃən/ *n.* [U]

col·on·nade /ˌkɑləˈneɪd/ *n.* [C] a row of upright stone posts that usually support a roof or row of ARCHES —**colonnaded** *adj.*

col·o·ny /ˈkɑləni/ *n. plural* **colonies** [C] **1** POLITICS a country or area that is ruled by a more powerful country, usually one that is far away: *Algeria was formerly a French colony.* → see also DOMINION (3), PROTECTORATE **2** HISTORY one of the 13 areas of land on the east coast of North America that later became the United States: *Many people who came to the colonies were escaping religious persecution.* **3** a group of a particular type of people or the place where they live: *an artists' colony* | *a nudist colony* **4** BIOLOGY a group of animals or plants of the same type that are living or growing together: *an ant colony* **5** a group of people or their DESCENDANTS who have left their home country to live in a colony [**Origin:** 1300–1400 Old French *colonie*, from Latin *colonia*, from *colonus* **farmer, someone who develops a new place**]

col·or¹ /ˈkʌlɚ/ S1 W1 *n.*

1 RED/BLUE ETC. [C,U] red, blue, yellow, green, brown, purple etc.: *Red is her favorite color.* | *Is it available in other colors?* | *a yellowish color* | **a bright/bold/strong color** *She usually wears bright colors.* | **a pale/light/pastel color** *I'd prefer a lighter color, please.* | *The sky was* ***changing color***. | ***What color are*** *his eyes?* | *The birds are golden* ***in color***. | *We pedaled through Vermont, which was ablaze with* ***fall colors*** (=the colors of the leaves on the trees during the fall).

THESAURUS

shade also **hue** LITERARY a particular type of a color such as red, green, blue etc.: *a pale shade of blue*
tint a small amount of a color: *The brown grass showed a faint tint of green.*
dark/deep used about a color that is strong and fairly close to black: *dark green*
rich used about a color that is fairly dark in an attractive way
light/pale/soft/pastel used about a color that has a lot of white in it
bright used about a color that is strong and easy to see
brilliant/vivid very bright
colorful having bright colors or many different colors
multicolored having many different colors
gaudy/garish too brightly colored

2 COLOR IN GENERAL [U] the bright appearance of something, or the fact that it has a lot of different colors: *There's not enough color in the design.* | *Summer flowers* ***add color to*** *a backyard.* | **a blaze/riot of color** (=a lot of different bright colors)
3 SUBSTANCE [C,U] a substance such as paint or DYE that makes something red, blue, yellow etc.: *food with artificial colors* | *Wash jeans separately, because the color may run.* | **lip/nail/hair color** *a new range of lip colors*
4 SB'S RACE [C,U] how dark or light someone's skin is, which shows which race they belong to: *people of all colors* | *There must be no discrimination based on skin color in this school.* → see also COLORED²
5 a person/woman/man of color someone who is not white: *I'm the only person of color in my class.*
6 SB'S FACE/SKIN [U] the general appearance and color of someone's skin, especially when this shows the state of their health or emotions: *A walk will put some color in your cheeks.* | *Slowly* ***the color drained from*** *her* ***face*** (=she became pale). | *At the mention of her name,* ***the color rose in*** *his* ***cheeks*** (=his face became red).
7 in color a television program, movie, or photograph that is in color contains colors such as red, green, and blue, rather than just black and white: *Is the movie in color or in black and white?* | *illustrations* ***in full color*** (=using all the colors) | *Footage of the war was broadcast* ***in living color*** (=in colors rather than black and white).
8 colors [plural] the colors that are used as a sign to represent a team, school, club etc.: *a shirt with the team colors*
9 STH INTERESTING [U] interesting and exciting details or qualities that a place or person has: *The old town is full of color.* | *A few personal stories can help* ***add color to*** *your writing* (=make it more interesting). | **a color analyst/commentator** (=someone who gives interesting details about players, games in the past etc. while telling you about a sports game you are watching or listening to)
10 sb's colors colors that someone likes or that make them look good when they wear them: *Pink and gray are my colors.* | *I'm* ***having*** *my* ***colors done*** (=a professional will tell me which colors look good on me) *tomorrow.*
11 see the color of sb's money SPOKEN to have definite proof that someone has enough money to pay for some-

thing: *I wouldn't give him the books until I saw the color of his money.* → see also **with flying colors** at FLYING[1] (2), OFF-COLOR, **show your true colors** at SHOW[1] (17)

color[2] S2 *v.* **1** [T] to make something change color, especially by using DYE: *Does she color her hair?* | *Our wool is colored with natural dyes.* | **color sth red/blue etc.** *Sunset colored the sky red.* **2** [I,T] also **color in** to put color onto a drawing or picture, or to draw a picture using colored pencils, CRAYONS etc.: *Give Grandma the picture you colored, Jenny.* | *Kids love to color.* | *He drew a fish and colored it in.* **3** [T] to influence the way someone thinks about something, especially so that they become less fair or reasonable: *Critics say the plan is colored by party politics.* | **color sb's judgment/opinions/attitudes etc.** *Don't let your personal feelings color your judgment.* **4** [I] FORMAL when someone colors, their face becomes redder because they are embarrassed → see also **color code** at CODE[2] (3)

color[3] *adj.* **a color television/photograph/movie etc.** a television, photograph etc. that produces or shows pictures in color rather than in black, white, and gray OPP black and white OPP monochrome

Col·o·ra·do /ˌkɑləˈrɑdoʊ◂, -ˈræ-/ ABBREVIATION **CO** a state in the western central part of the U.S.

ˌColorado ˈRiver a long river in the western U.S., that flows southwest through the U.S. states of Colorado, Utah, and Arizona, and into Mexico

ˈcolor ˌanalyst also **ˈcolor ˌcommentator** *n.* [C] someone who gives information about players, teams etc. during a sports broadcast, usually between descriptions of what is happening during the game

col·or·ant /ˈkʌlərənt/ *n.* [C] TECHNICAL a substance used to color something

col·or·a·tion /ˌkʌləˈreɪʃən/ *n.* [U] the way something is colored or the pattern these colors make SYN coloring

col·or·a·tu·ra /ˌkʌlərəˈtʊrə, ˌkɑ-/ *n.* **1** [U] ENG. LANG. ARTS a difficult piece of music that is meant to be sung fast **2** [C] ENG. LANG. ARTS a woman, especially a SOPRANO, who sings this type of music

col·or·blind, color-blind /ˈkʌlɚˌblaɪnd/ *adj.* **1** not able to see the difference between particular colors **2** treating people from different races equally and fairly: *In this court, justice is colorblind.* —**colorblindness** *n.* [U]

ˌcolor-coˈordinated *adj.* color-coordinated clothes or decorations have colors that look good together —**ˌcolor-coordiˈnation** *n.* [U]

col·ored[1] /ˈkʌlɚd/ *adj.* **1** having a color such as red, blue, yellow etc. rather than being black, white, or plain: *brightly colored bows and ribbons* | *cream-colored paper* **2** OLD-FASHIONED a word used to describe people who have dark or black skin, now considered offensive **3** colored hair has been DYED

colored[2] *n.* [C] OLD-FASHIONED a word for someone who has dark or black skin, now considered offensive

ˌcolored ˈpencil *n.* [C] a pencil that writes in a particular color, rather than black

color·fast /ˈkʌlɚˌfæst/ *adj.* colorfast cloth will not lose its color when it is washed —**colorfastness** *n.* [U]

col·or·ful /ˈkʌlɚfəl/ *adj.* **1** having a lot of bright colors or a lot of different colors: *American Indian dancers in colorful costumes* ▸see THESAURUS box at color[1] **2** interesting, exciting, and full of variety: *a lecture full of colorful stories* | *Mr. Watson is one of the most* ***colorful characters*** (=interesting and unusual people) *I've ever met.* | **a colorful history/past/life etc.** *The islands have a long and colorful history.* **3** colorful language, speech etc. uses a lot of swearing —**colorfully** *adv.*

col·or·ing /ˈkʌlərɪŋ/ *n.* **1** a substance used to give a particular color to food: *They use caramel coloring in colas.* **2** [U] the activity of putting colors into drawings, or of drawing using CRAYONS, colored pencils etc.: *a coloring contest for children* **3** [U] the color of someone's skin, hair, and eyes: *People with light coloring tend to sunburn easily.* **4** [U] the colors of an animal, bird, or plant: *fish with deep red coloring* → see also FOOD COLORING

ˈcoloring book *n.* [C] a book full of pictures that are drawn without color so that children can color them in

col·or·ize /ˈkʌləˌraɪz/ *v.* [T] to add color to a black-and-white picture or movie —**colorization** /ˌkʌlərəˈzeɪʃən/ *n.* [U]

col·or·less /ˈkʌlɚlɪs/ *adj.* **1** having no color: *a colorless gas* **2** not interesting or exciting SYN boring: *She gave a colorless performance as Hamlet's mother.* —**colorlessly** *adv.* —**colorlessness** *n.* [U]

ˈcolor line *n.* **the color line** a set of laws and customs in the past that did not let black people do the same things or go to the same places as white people: **cross/break etc. the color line** (=to do something that goes against these laws or customs)

ˈcolor scheme *n.* [C] the combination of colors that someone chooses for a room, painting etc.

ˈcolor wheel *n.* [C] a way of showing the range of colors in a circle, with similar colors next to each other and COMPLEMENTARY COLORS opposite each other

co·los·sal /kəˈlɑsəl/ *adj.* **1** extremely large in degree or amount: *a colossal waste of time* ▸see THESAURUS box at big **2** extremely large in size: *colossal statues* —**colossally** *adv.*

the Colosseum

Col·os·se·um, the /ˌkɑləˈsiəm/ *n.* HISTORY a large outdoor area with seats for many people that was built in Rome in the 1st century A.D. for people to watch competitions and fights, sometimes between people and animals

Co·los·sians /kəˈlɑʃənz/ a book in the New Testament of the Christian Bible

co·los·sus /kəˈlɑsəs/ *n.* [C] **1** someone or something that is very large or very important **2** HISTORY a very large STATUE (=person or animal made out of stone)

col·our /ˈkʌlɚ/ the British and Canadian spelling of COLOR, also used in other words that begin "color" in U.S. spelling

Colt /koʊlt/ *n.* [C] TRADEMARK a type of PISTOL: *a Colt .45*

colt /koʊlt/ *n.* [C] a young male horse → see also FILLY

colt·ish /ˈkoʊltɪʃ/ *adj.* **1** a coltish young person or animal has a lot of energy but moves in an awkward way **2** coltish arms or legs are long and thin

Col·trane /ˈkoʊltreɪn/, **John** (1926–1967) an American JAZZ musician who played the SAXOPHONE and had a great influence on the development of modern jazz

Co·lum·bi·a[1] /kəˈlʌmbiə/ the capital city of the U.S. state of South Carolina

Columbia[2] → see DISTRICT OF COLUMBIA

Coˌlumbian Exˈchange, the *n.* [singular] HISTORY the trade of goods and ideas between Europe, the Americas, Africa, and Asia that began in 1492 after Christopher Columbus made his first trip to North America

Coˌlumbia ˈRiver a river that flows south from the Rocky Mountains in southeastern Canada and through the U.S. state of Washington to the Pacific Ocean

col•um•bine /ˈkɑləmˌbaɪn/ *n.* [C] a garden plant with delicate leaves and bright flowers that hang down

Co•lum•bus /kəˈlʌmbəs/ the capital city of the U.S. state of Ohio

Columbus, Christopher (1451–1506) an Italian sailor and EXPLORER who is traditionally thought of as the first European to discover America, in 1492. Most people now think that America was first discovered about 500 years earlier, by the Norwegian Leif Ericsson.

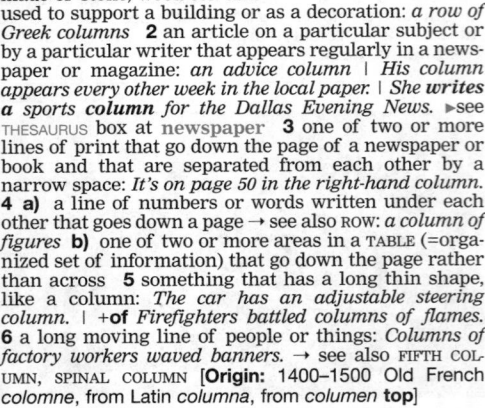

C. Columbus

Coˈlumbus ˌDay *n.* [C] a holiday on the second Monday in October in the U.S. to celebrate the discovery of the New World in 1492 by Christopher Columbus

col•umn /ˈkɑləm/ S2 W2 *n.* [C] **1** a tall solid upright post made of stone, wood etc. and used to support a building or as a decoration: *a row of Greek columns* **2** an article on a particular subject or by a particular writer that appears regularly in a newspaper or magazine: *an advice column* | *His column appears every other week in the local paper.* | *She **writes a** sports **column** for the Dallas Evening News.* ▸see THESAURUS box at **newspaper** **3** one of two or more lines of print that go down the page of a newspaper or book and that are separated from each other by a narrow space: *It's on page 50 in the right-hand column.* **4 a)** a line of numbers or words written under each other that goes down a page → see also ROW: *a column of figures* **b)** one of two or more areas in a TABLE (=organized set of information) that go down the page rather than across **5** something that has a long thin shape, like a column: *The car has an adjustable steering column.* | **+of** *Firefighters battled columns of flames.* **6** a long moving line of people or things: *Columns of factory workers waved banners.* → see also FIFTH COLUMN, SPINAL COLUMN [**Origin:** 1400–1500 Old French *colomne*, from Latin *columna*, from *columen* **top**]

co•lum•nar rock /kəˌlʌmnɚ ˈrɑk/ *n.* [U] EARTH SCIENCE a tall COLUMN (=upright structure) of rock formed by LAVA (=hot liquid rock) that has flowed from a VOLCANO and become cold

col•um•nist /ˈkɑləmnɪst, ˈkɑləmɪst/ *n.* [C] someone who writes articles, especially about a particular subject, that appear regularly in a newspaper or magazine: *a syndicated gossip columnist*

com /kɑm/ abbreviation of commercial organization; used in Internet addresses: *www.longman.com*

com- /kəm, kɑm/ *prefix* with or together; used instead of CON- before the letters "b," "m," or "p": *companion* (=someone you spend time with)

co•ma /ˈkoʊmə/ *n.* [C] MEDICINE a state in which someone is not conscious for a long time, usually after a serious accident or illness: *He's been **in a coma** since last week.* [**Origin:** 1600–1700 Modern Latin, Greek *koma* **deep sleep**]

Co•man•che /kəˈmæntʃi/ *n.* a Native American tribe from the southwestern region of the U.S. —**Comanche** *adj.*

Co•ma•neci /ˌkoʊməˈnitʃ/, **Na•di•a** /ˈnɑdiə/ (1961–) a Romanian GYMNAST famous for winning three GOLD MEDALS in the 1976 Olympic Games and for getting the first perfect mark of 10

co•ma•tose /ˈkoʊməˌtoʊs, ˈkɑ-/ *adj.* **1** TECHNICAL in a coma **2** INFORMAL so tired that you cannot think clearly: *We just sat comatose in front of the TV.*

comb¹ /koʊm/ *n.* [C] **1** a flat piece of plastic, metal etc. with a row of thin things like small sticks on one side, used to make your hair look neat **2** a small flat piece of plastic, metal etc. with a row of thin things like small sticks on one side, used for keeping your hair back or for decoration **3** BIOLOGY the red piece of flesh that grows on top of a male chicken's head **4** a HONEYCOMB [**Origin:** Old English *camb*] → see also FINE-TOOTHED COMB

comb² *v.* [T] **1** to make your hair look neat with a comb: *Comb your hair before you go out.* **2** to search a place thoroughly: *Volunteers combed the area until the body was found.* | **comb sth for sb/sth** *Police combed the forest for clues.*

comb sth ↔ **out** *phr. v.* to make messy hair look neat and smooth using a comb: *The worst thing about having long hair is combing out the tangles.*

comb through *phr. v.* to search through a lot of objects or information in order to find a specific thing or piece of information: *We spent weeks combing through old documents.*

com•bat¹ /ˈkɑmbæt/ *n.* **1** [U] organized fighting, especially in a war: *There were three days of fierce combat.* | *Over 120,000 soldiers were killed **in combat**.* | **see combat** (=be involved in fighting in a war) | **combat vehicle/jacket/boots etc.** (=one that is used when fighting a war) ▸see THESAURUS box at **war** **2** [C] a fight, argument, or battle: **+between/against** *It seemed like my life was one long combat against my father.* | *The soldiers are trained in **hand-to-hand combat*** (=fighting between people that involves physical contact). | *We observed a pair of lions, **locked in mortal combat*** (=fighting until one of the opponents dies). —**combat** *adj.*

com•bat² /kəmˈbæt, ˈkɑmbæt/ *v.* **combated, combating** [T] FORMAL **1** to try to stop something bad from happening or getting worse: *The government has introduced new measures to combat organized crime.* **2** to fight against an enemy or opponent in order to try and defeat them, especially in a war [**Origin:** 1500–1600 French *combattre*, from Latin *com-* + *battuere* **to hit**]

com•bat•ant /kəmˈbætˀnt/ *n.* [C] someone who fights in a war OPP **noncombatant**

ˈcombat faˌtigue *n.* [U] TECHNICAL BATTLE FATIGUE

com•ba•tive /kəmˈbæt̬ɪv/ *adj.* showing eagerness to fight or argue: *Political opponents dislike his combative style.* —**combatively** *adv.* —**combativeness** *n.* [U]

com•bi•na•tion /ˌkɑmbəˈneɪʃən/ S2 W2 *n.* **1** [C,U] two or more different things, qualities, substances etc. that are used or put together, or the process of putting them together: *I'll have the shrimp and chicken combination, please.* | **+of** *The design was a combination of Victorian and Tudor styles.* | *A **combination of factors** led to the program's failure.* | *Drinking and driving can be a **lethal combination**.* | *Use of the drug **in combination with** diet changes will help you lose weight.* | **a winning combination** (=a mixture of different people or things that work successfully together) ▸see THESAURUS box at **mixture** **2** [C] the series of numbers or letters you need to open a combination lock: *I forgot the combination again.* **3** [U] used before a noun in some phrases to mean that something does more than one job or uses more than one method: *a combination copier, fax, scanner, and printer* | *combination drug therapy*

combiˈnation lock *n.* [C] a lock that is opened by using a special series of numbers or letters

combiˈnation ˌplate *n.* [C] a plate with several different types of food on it, served to one person at a restaurant

combiˈnation reˌaction *n.* [C,U] CHEMISTRY a chemical change that happens when two or more substances mix together to form a new substance

com•bine¹ /kəmˈbaɪn/ W2 *v.* **1** [I,T] if you combine two or more different things, ideas, or qualities, or if they combine, they begin to exist or work together: *Modern and traditional teaching methods are combined at the school.* | **combine sth with sth** *You have to combine diet with exercise.* | **combine to do sth** *Art, history, and landscape combine to make Rome unique.* | *Poor service **combined with** high prices kept customers away.* **2** [I,T] if two or more different substances combine or if you combine them, they mix together to produce a new substance: *Combine the rest of the ingredients in a small saucepan.* | **combine to do sth** *Carbon combines with oxygen to form carbon dioxide.* | **combine sth with sth** *Steel is produced by combining iron with carbon.* ►see THESAURUS box at **mix**[1] **3** [T] to do two different activities at the same time: **combine sth with/and sth** *It's hard to combine family life with a career.* **4** [T] to add several numbers or amounts together to form a larger amount: *The banks plan to merge and combine their assets.* **5** [I,T] if two or more groups, organizations etc. combine, or if you combine them, they join or work together in order to do something SYN **merge**: *The coach combined the best players from the two teams.* | **+with** *We're combining with another local college so we can offer students a wider range of courses.* | **combine to do sth** *The two car makers combined to form a new company.* [**Origin:** 1400–1500 French *combiner*, from Late Latin *combinare*, from Latin *com-* + *bini* **two by two**]

com·bine² /ˈkɑmbaɪn/ *n.* [C] **1** a large machine used on a farm to cut a crop and separate the grain at the same time **2** a group of people, businesses etc. that work together

com·bined /kəmˈbaɪnd/ *adj.* **1** [only before noun] done, made, or achieved by several people or groups working together: *Changes were brought about by* ***the combined efforts of*** *dozens of local patients' groups.* | *The* ***combined effect*** *of these policies has been an increase in unemployment.* **2** calculated by adding several amounts or numbers together: *Our combined salaries were enough to afford the house we wanted.* | *They got more votes than* ***all the other*** *parties* ***combined.*** **3** involving two different things at the same time: *Ann felt a combined relief and sadness.*

com·bo /ˈkɑmboʊ/ *n. plural* **combos** [C] INFORMAL **1** ENG. LANG. ARTS a small group of musicians who play dance music **2** a combination of things, especially different foods at a restaurant: *I'll have the fish combo and a beer.*

com·bust /kəmˈbʌst/ *v.* [I] to start burning: *Oil-soaked rags sometimes* ***spontaneously combust*** (=start burning without being set on fire).

com·bus·ti·ble /kəmˈbʌstəbəl/ *adj.* able to begin burning easily: *Gasoline is* ***highly combustible.***

com·bus·tion /kəmˈbʌstʃən/ *n.* [U] **1** the process of burning **2** CHEMISTRY chemical activity that uses oxygen to produce light and heat → see also INTERNAL-COMBUSTION ENGINE

com'bustion ˌchamber *n.* [C] an enclosed space in which combustion happens in an engine

com'bustion reˌaction *n.* [C,U] CHEMISTRY a chemical change that happens when a substance reacts with oxygen to produce energy in the form of heat and light

come /kʌm/ S1 W1 *v. past tense* **came** /keɪm/, *present participle* **come** [I]

1 MOVE TO to move to or toward a person who is speaking or to the place where they were or will be: *Come a little closer.* | *Sarah's coming later on.* | **+to/toward/back/down etc.** *When are you coming back?* | *My boss didn't come to work today.* | **+for** *What day are your parents coming for dinner?* | **come and do sth** *Come and look at this.* | **come to do sth** *I've come to apologize.* | *Charlie,* ***come here,*** *quick.* | **come running/flying/speeding etc.** *Jesse came flying around the corner and banged right into me.*

2 VISIT to visit a place, especially someone's house, or go to an event: *We come here every summer.* | *Who else is coming tonight?* | **+for** *We have friends coming for the weekend.* | **+to** *Only ten people came to his lecture.* | **+down/over/up** *Why don't you come up to Vermont for the weekend?* | *Would you like to* ***come to dinner*** *sometime?* | *He* ***came to see*** *me in the hospital.* | *She* ***came*** *to the party* ***as*** (=dressed in a particular costume) *Little Red Riding Hood.*

3 ARRIVE to arrive: *Has the mail come yet?* | *Sarah came late.* | *Christianity came to Russia in 988.* | *Her mother* ***came home*** *from vacation a day early.*

4 MOVE WITH SB to move to a particular place with the person who is speaking: *Can Billy come too?* | **+with** *Why don't you come to the concert with me?* | *Brittany can* ***come along*** *too, if she wants.*

5 TRAVEL to travel in a particular way or for a particular distance or time in order to get somewhere: *How far have you come today?* | **+by/on/with etc.** *We came by train.*

6 HAPPEN if a time or event comes, it arrives or happens: *Winter came early that year.* | **+before/after** *The vote came after three hours of heated debate.* | *Just learn the basics now – the details will* ***come later.*** | ***The time has come for*** *some radical changes.* | *Economists say the worst is* ***yet to come*** (=will happen in the future).

7 BE AVAILABLE/EXIST [always + adv./prep.] **a)** to be produced, available, or sold: **+with** *The camera comes complete with battery and memory card.* | **+in** *These shoes don't come in size 11.* | *Houses like that* ***don't come cheap.*** | *A new version of the software is* ***coming soon*** (=used especially in advertisements). **b)** to exist: **+in** *Cats come in many shapes and sizes.* | **+with** *Parenthood comes with a lot of responsibility.*

8 LIST/ORDER [always + adv./prep.] to have a particular position in the order of something: **+before/after** *P comes before Q in the alphabet.* | **come first/second/next etc.** *Who comes third in the batting order?*

9 IMPORTANCE [always + adv./prep.] to be considered more important or less important with relation to other things: *I enjoy my work, but my family* ***comes first.*** | **+before/after** *Your health should come before your career.*

10 come as a surprise/relief/shock etc. (to sb) to make someone feel surprised, RELIEVED etc.: *It came as kind of a shock to me.* | *The food was excellent, which should* ***come as no surprise*** (=be expected) *to those who know the chef's reputation.*

11 come to think of/believe/feel etc. sth to begin to think or feel a particular way gradually or after a long time: *We've come to cherish those memories.* | *That's the kind of behavior we've* ***come to expect*** *from Bryant.*

12 LENGTH/HEIGHT [always + adv./prep.] to reach a particular height or length: **+to** *The grass came to my knees.* | **+up to/down to etc.** *Carrie's hair comes down to her waist.*

13 come open/undone/loose etc. to become open, loose etc.: *Your shoelace just came untied.* | *The bottle came open in my backpack!*

14 have come a long way to have made a lot of progress: *Computer technology has come a long way since the 1970s.*

15 years/weeks/days etc. to come used to emphasize that something is still in the future or will continue into the future: *We'll laugh about this* ***in the years to come.*** | *Nuclear waste will remain hazardous* ***for years to come.*** → see also COMING[1]

16 have it coming to deserve to be punished or to have something bad happen to you: *I don't feel sorry for Brad – he had it coming.*

17 as big/heavy/good etc. as they come also **as big/heavy etc. as it comes** having as much of a particular quality as is possible: *He's as smart as they come.*

18 LIGHT [always + adv./prep.] if light comes in or through something, you can see it in a particular place: *The morning sun came through the doorway.*

19 come easily/naturally (to sb) to be easy for someone to do, say etc.: *Acting has always come naturally to her.* | *Change doesn't always come easily.*

20 come of age a) to reach an age, usually 18 or 21, when you are considered by law to be an adult **b)** if an artist, style, organization etc. comes of age, they reach their best, most successful period of time: *Mozart's music came of age when the baroque style was at its height.*

21 come to pass BIBLICAL to happen after a period of time: ***It came to pass that*** *they had a son.*

22 come to be doing sth also **sth comes to be done** used for asking or saying how or why a situation exists: *How did you come to be working here?*

23 come what may whatever happens, even if things become difficult: *We decided to stay, come what may.*

24 come sb's way if something comes your way, you

get or experience it, especially if you were not expecting it: *We're determined to take every opportunity that comes our way.*

25 come calling **a)** to give someone a lot of attention because you want to offer them something or get something from them: *Major companies came calling with job offers.* **b)** OLD-FASHIONED to visit someone: *Rudy did not come calling the next day.*

26 not know whether you are coming or going INFORMAL to feel confused, especially because you have a lot of things to think about: *I'm so busy I don't know whether I'm coming or going.*

SPOKEN PHRASES

27 how come? used to ask someone why something has happened or how it was possible: *How come Tyler's still here?* | *"She's moving to Alaska." "How come?"*

28 here comes sb/sth said when you can see that someone or something is about to arrive at the place where you are: *Here comes Lori now.*

29 come to think of it said when you have just realized or remembered something: *Come to think of it, Cooper did mention it to me.*

30 take sth as it comes to accept something exactly as it happens or is given to you, without trying to change it or plan ahead: *I'll just take each day as it comes.* | *Don't fight the situation – just* ***take it as it comes.***

31 come July/next year/2010 etc. at a particular time in the future: *Come Monday, we'll be in our new house.*

32 come again? used to ask someone to repeat what they just said: *"She's a paleontologist." "Come again?"*

33 come now also **come, come** OLD-FASHIONED said to comfort or gently encourage someone, or to tell them you do not like what they are doing: *Come now, Sarah, don't cry.*

→ see also **come clean** at CLEAN[1], **come to grips with sth** at GRIP[1] (3), **come to life** at LIFE (13), **come/spring/leap to mind** at MIND, **come into play** at PLAY → see Grammar note at BECOME

come about *phr. v.* to happen or develop: *The opportunity came about by chance.* | ***How did*** *this change* ***come about?***

come across *phr. v.* **1 come across sb/sth** to meet someone or find or discover something by chance: *I came across these old photos in my desk.* | *He's the strangest person I've ever come across.* **2** to make someone have a particular opinion of you: *Some candidates simply do not come across well on screen.* | **come across as (being) sth** *Sometimes you come across as being kind of rude.* **3** if an idea comes across to someone, they understand it clearly: *Your point really came across at the meeting.*

come after sb *phr. v.* to look for someone so you can hurt them, punish them, or get something from them: *If I don't pay back the money, they're going to come after me.*

come along *phr. v.* **1** to happen or arrive, especially at a time you do not know or expect: *Jobs like this don't come along very often!* **2 be coming along** INFORMAL to be developing or improving: *The corn crop is really coming along.* | **+with** *How is Aaron coming along with his reading skills?*

come apart *phr. v.* **1** to split or break into pieces, without anyone using force: *The book just came apart in my hands.* **2** if an object comes apart, it is designed so that you can separate it into pieces: *The pump comes apart so you can clean it.* **3** if a situation comes apart, bad things start happening: *My marriage came apart that summer.* | *The lawsuit began* ***coming apart at the seams.***

come around *phr. v.* **1 come around sth** to visit someone: *She doesn't come around much anymore.* | *I don't want him coming around the apartment.* **2** to decide to agree with someone, after disagreeing with them: *It took some persuading, but he finally came around.* | **+to** *They eventually came around to the idea.* **3** if a regular event comes around, it happens as usual: *Christmas seems to come around so fast.* **4** to become conscious again: *It was 15 minutes before she came around.*

come at sb/sth *phr. v.* **1** to move toward someone in a threatening way: *The man came at me with a hammer.* **2** if information, work, people etc. come at you, they all have to be dealt with at once, so that you feel confused or anxious: *At work, things keep coming at you all the time.* **3** INFORMAL to consider or deal with a problem: *We need to come at the problem from a different angle.*

come away *phr. v.* **1** to become separated from something: **+from** *Cook the tamales until they come away easily from the cornhusk.* **2** to leave a place or situation with a particular feeling or thought: **+from** *I came away from the interview feeling really good.* | **come away with an idea/impression etc.** *She came away with the impression that the company was well run.*

come back *phr. v.* **1** to return from a place: *I won't be coming back tonight.* **2** to appear or exist again: *The pain suddenly came back.* **3** SPOKEN to be remembered, especially suddenly: *Memories came flooding back.* | **+to** *I can't remember her name, but it'll come back to me.* **4** to become fashionable or popular again: *The styles of the '80s are coming back.* **5** to reply to something that someone said with a quick funny remark: **+with** *I couldn't think of a clever remark to come back with.* → see also COMEBACK

come before sb *phr. v.* FORMAL to be given or shown to someone in authority in order to be considered or judged: *Briggs' case may come before a jury within the next month.*

come between sb *phr. v.* **1** to cause trouble between two or more people: *He never thought anything would come between us.* **2** to prevent someone from giving enough attention to something: **come between sb and sth** *I don't let anything come between me and my work.*

come by *phr. v.* **1 come by sth** to visit someone or go to someone's house for a short time before going somewhere else: *I'll come by later to pick up Katrina.* | *Do you want to come by our place later?* **2 come by sth** to get something that is difficult to find: *How on earth did you come by these tickets?* | *Jobs like this* ***are hard to come by*** (=are hard to find).

come down *phr. v.*

1 BECOME LOWER a) if a price, level etc. comes down, it becomes lower: *Wait until interest rates come down before you buy a house.* **b)** to offer or accept a lower price: **+on** *They refused to come down on the price.* | **+to** *The price of oil came down to $27 a barrel last week.*

2 BUILDING if a building comes down, it is destroyed by being pulled down: *A few barns came down in the storm.*

3 DRUGS INFORMAL to stop being affected by a powerful illegal drug such as HEROIN or LSD that you have taken

4 FEEL NORMAL INFORMAL to start to feel normal again after you have been feeling very happy and excited

5 come down in sb's opinion/estimation to do something that makes someone respect you less: *John really came down in my opinion after that.*

6 come (back) down to earth to begin dealing with ordinary practical problems in a practical way, after ignoring them for a time: *After first proposing huge raises, the union came down to earth.*

7 come down in the world to become poorer or less successful than you used to be. → see also COMEDOWN

come down on sb/sth *phr. v.* **1** to punish someone or something or criticize them severely: *The first time the boss came down on Pete, he quit.* | **come down on sb for doing sth** *My parents really came down on me for being out so late.* | *I thought the movie was okay, but the critics* ***came down hard on*** *it.* **2 come down on the side of sth** to decide to support something: *The court came down on the side of the boy's father.*

come down to sth *phr. v.* **1** if a difficult or confusing situation comes down to one thing, that thing is the most important or basic part of it: ***It came down to** a choice between cutting wages or cutting staff.* | ***When it comes down to it*** (=used to say that you are referring to the most important or basic part of a situation), *she doesn't really love him.* **2** if a document, object, idea etc. comes down to someone, it has continued to exist from a long time ago until the present: *The text which has come down to us is only a fragment of the original.*

come down with sth *phr. v.* INFORMAL to become infected with a particular illness: *I think I'm coming down with a cold.*

come for sb/sth *phr. v.* **1** to arrive to take someone or something away: *Did the guy come for the washing machine yet?* **2** to try to harm someone or take them away where they do not want to go: *An angry crowd came for the two men.*

come forward *phr. v.* to offer help or information in an official way or to someone in authority: *One of the boys came forward and confessed.* | +**with** *Several witnesses came forward with information.* | **come forward to do sth** *Local people came forward to help with the cleaning up.*

come from sb/sth *phr. v.* **1** to have been born in a particular place or into a particular family: *She comes from Texas.* | *He came from a very musical family.* **2** to have first existed, been made, or been produced in a particular place, thing, or time: *Milk comes from cows.* | *These words come from a novel by Dickens.* **3** if a sound comes from a particular place, it begins there: *Where's that music coming from?* **4** to be the result of something: *The mistakes came from lack of concentration.* | **come from doing sth** *Her disappointment comes from expecting too much.* **5 where sb's coming from** INFORMAL the opinions, feelings, intentions etc. that someone has: *I knew exactly where she was coming from.* **6 coming from sb** SPOKEN used to say that someone should not criticize another person for doing something because they have done the same thing themselves: *You think I'm selfish? That's ironic coming from you!*

come in *phr. v.*
1 ENTER to enter a room or house SYN **enter**: *I thought I recognized him when he came in.*
2 ARRIVE to arrive somewhere: *What time does Kelly's plane come in?*
3 BE RECEIVED to be received or earned: *Reports are coming in of a severe earthquake in Mexico.* | *How much money do you have coming in each month?*
4 BE INVOLVED to be involved in a plan, deal etc.: *I need somebody to help, and that's **where you come in**.* | +**on** *Jeanine might like to come in on the gift* (=buy it together) *with us.*
5 come in first/second etc. to finish first, second etc. in a race or competition: *Jones came in fifth in the 100-meter dash.*
6 come in useful/handy to be useful: *My Swiss Army knife came in handy on our trip around Europe.*
7 OCEAN when the TIDE (=level of the ocean) comes in, it rises OPP **go out**
8 BECOME FASHIONABLE to become fashionable or popular to use OPP **go out**: *Platform shoes came in again in the 1990s.* → see also **come in from the cold** at COLD[2]

come in for sth *phr. v.* **come in for criticism/blame/scrutiny** to be criticized, blamed etc. for something: *Thompson came in for sharp criticism from women's groups.*

come into sth *phr. v.*
1 come into effect/force/operation if a new law, system, rule etc. comes into effect, it begins to be used or to have an effect: *Government regulations came into effect this year that specify how much advertising can be shown during children's TV programs.*
2 come into sight/view to start being able to be seen: *As we turned the corner, the town came into view.*
3 come into being/existence to begin to exist: *Before the specialized units came into being, polio patients were treated in general hospitals.*
4 BE INVOLVED to be involved in something or to influence it: *John came into the business as an equal partner.* | *I don't think money comes into it.*
5 BEGIN TO BE CONSIDERED to begin to be considered or understood in a particular way: *The extent of the financial crisis is just now **coming into focus*** (=becoming clearly understood). | *Many of his claims have **come into question*** (=have begun to be doubted).
6 come into your own to become very good, useful, or important in a particular situation: *This season Brooks has really come into his own as a goal scorer.*
7 come into fashion/vogue to become a popular thing to wear or do: *A-line skirts are coming into fashion again.*
8 RECEIVE MONEY to receive money, land etc. after someone has died SYN **inherit**: *Last year they came into a large sum of money when their Uncle Harry died.*

come of sth *phr. v.* to result from something: ***Nothing** ever **came of** our discussion.*

come off *phr. v.*
1 NOT ON/ATTACHED **come off sth** to stop being on something, connected to it, or fastened to it: *A button came off my coat yesterday.* | *I can't get the lid to come off.* | +**onto/on** *Some wet paint came off onto her hands.*
2 ATTITUDE/QUALITY to seem like you have a particular attitude or quality because of something you say or do: +**as** *I tried not to come off as too critical.* | **come off looking/sounding like sth** *Marty came off looking like a hero.*
3 HAPPEN to happen, especially in a particular way: *The wedding came off as planned.*
4 FINISH **come off sth** if someone or something comes off something, they have just finished it before beginning something else: *The team is coming off a 10-point defeat to their Boston rivals.*
5 SUCCEED to be successful or have the intended effect: *The joke just didn't come off very well.*
6 come off it! SPOKEN said when you think someone is being stupid or unreasonable, or when you do not believe something they have just said: *Oh, come off it, George. Sheila wouldn't do that.*
7 DRUGS/MEDICINE **come off sth** to stop taking drugs or medicine, or stop eating or drinking something that you have been eating or drinking for a long time: *He's tried to come off the drugs several times.*

come on *phr. v.*
1 come on! SPOKEN **a)** used to tell a person or animal to hurry, or to come with you: *Come on! We're already late!* **b)** said in order to encourage someone to do something: *Come on, guys, you can do it!* **c)** said when you do not believe what someone has just said: *Oh come on, don't lie to me!* **d)** used when you think what someone has said or done is stupid or unreasonable: *Well, what was he supposed to do? Shoot him? Come on!* | *Come on, you know what I mean.*
2 come on in/back/down etc. used to tell someone to come to a particular place: *Joe! It's good to see you – come on in* (=come in to the room, office etc.). | *Come on down to Sky Ford, where the prices are unbeatable.*
3 LIGHT/MACHINE if a light or machine comes on, it starts working: *You clap your hands and the light comes on.*
4 TV/RADIO SHOW if a television or radio program comes on, it starts: *The news comes on at ten.*
5 ILLNESS if an illness comes on, you start to have it: *Julie could feel an asthma attack coming on.*
6 DEVELOP to improve, develop, or progress: *Last year, Chloe didn't play well, but this year she's **coming on strong*** (=improving a lot).
7 BEGIN if winter, spring, darkness etc. comes on, it begins: *The country is facing food shortages as winter comes on.*
8 come on strong/fast INFORMAL to make it very clear to someone that you think they are sexually attractive

come on to sb *phr. v.* INFORMAL if someone comes on to another person, they make it very clear that they are sexually interested in them: *A woman at the office started coming on to my husband.*

come out *phr. v.*

1 BECOME KNOWN to become publicly known, especially after being hidden: *Several weeks passed before the truth came out.* | *It eventually **came out that** she had lied.*

2 BE SOLD if a book, record etc. comes out, people are able to buy it: *When does her new book come out?*

3 SAY PUBLICLY to say something publicly or directly: **+for/against etc.** *Senator Peters came out strongly against abortion.* | *They want grandchildren, but they won't just **come right out and say** it.*

4 DIRT if dirt or a mark comes out of cloth, it can be washed out: *Will this ink come out?* | **+of** *This wine will never come out of my dress.*

5 BE SAID to be said, and then usually understood in a particular way: *The words just came out before I could stop myself.* | *That didn't come out the way I meant it to.* | *When I try to explain, it **comes out all wrong*** (=you do not say it in the way you intended), *and she gets mad.*

6 come out well/badly/right etc. if something comes out in a particular way, that is what it is like when it has been produced: *I can never get cakes to come out right.* | *Some of the wedding photos didn't come out very well.*

7 come out ahead also **come out on top** to be in a better position at the end of a series of events: *I figure I'll come out about $400 ahead every month with this new job.*

8 HOMOSEXUAL if someone comes out, they say openly that they are HOMOSEXUAL: **+to** *Has he come out to his parents?*

9 SUN/MOON if the sun, moon, or stars come out, they appear in the sky

10 FLOWER if a flower comes out, it opens: *The cherry blossoms are coming out.*

11 GIRL OLD-FASHIONED if a young woman comes out, she is formally introduced to upper-class members of society, usually at a dance

come out of sth *phr. v.* **1** to stop being in a bad situation SYN **emerge**: *We are beginning to come out of the crisis.* **2** to be in a particular situation at the end of a series of events: *She came out of the divorce quite well.* **3** to be the result of something: *Some great ideas came out of the meeting.* **4 come out of yourself** to start to behave more confidently after spending some time being very sad and having no confidence

come out with sth *phr. v.* **1** if a company comes out with a new product, they have made or developed it and are now making it available to be bought: *Chrysler has come out with a new line of minivans.* **2** SPOKEN to say something that is unexpected and funny or shocking: *Children are always coming out with funny things.*

come over *phr. v.* **1** to come or go to someone's house: *Come over to my place for drinks.* **2** to travel or move from another country to the place where you are now by crossing an ocean: *Thousands of tourists come over every year.* | **+to/from** *Her dad came over from Italy when he was in his twenties.* **3 come over sb** if a strong feeling comes over someone, they suddenly experience it: *A wave of sleepiness came over me.* | *I don't usually swear – **I don't know what came over me!*** (=I cannot explain why I behaved in a bad or strange way)

come through *phr. v.* **1 come through sth** to continue to live, exist, be strong, or succeed after a difficult or dangerous time: *Bill came through the operation all right.* | *Their house came through the storm without much damage.* **2** if something such as a LOAN (=money you borrow from a bank) comes through, it arrives or is approved by someone: *I can't get a work-study job until my financial aid comes through.* | *It may take up to a month for your visa to come through.* **3** to help or do something for someone, especially something you have promised to do: *Mike said he could get us tickets, so hopefully he'll come through.* | **+with** *There is pressure on the West to come through with more aid.* **4** if information, news etc. comes through, it becomes known or heard: *News of the coup came through late Tuesday night.*

come to *phr. v.* **1** to become conscious again after having been unconscious: *He came to a few minutes later.* **2 come to sth** to have a particular result, usually a bad result: *I never thought it would come to this.* **3 come to sb** if an idea, thought, or memory comes to you, you suddenly realize or remember it: *The solution came to him in a dream.* | *I've forgotten her name, but maybe it'll come to me later.* **4 come to a decision/an agreement/a conclusion** to make a decision or reach an agreement or a conclusion: *Have you come to a decision yet?* **5 come to a halt/stop a)** to stop moving: *The train suddenly came to a halt.* **b)** also **come to an end** to stop existing or stop being provided: *The relationship had come to an end.* **6 come to $20/$3 etc.** to add up to a total of $20, $3 etc.: *That comes to $24.67, ma'am.* | *How much did the meal come to?* **7 come to power** to start having political control of a country or government: *The Communists came to power in China in 1949.* **8 what is the world/country etc. coming to?** SPOKEN used to say that the world, the country etc. is in a very bad situation **9 come to nothing** also **not come to anything/much** to achieve no success or very little success: *In the end, all our efforts came to nothing.* **10 when it comes to sth** INFORMAL relating to a particular subject: *When it comes to relationships, everyone makes mistakes.*

come together *phr. v.* **1** if something comes together, it becomes good or successful, especially because different parts are working well together: *The production is starting to come together.* **2** when people come together, they meet or try to do something together: *We need to come together to solve the problem.*

come under sth *phr. v.* **1 come under attack/fire/pressure etc.** to experience something bad such as an attack, criticism etc.: *The future of the orchestra has come under threat.* **2** to be governed, controlled, or influenced by something: *Moldova came under Soviet control in 1940.* **3** to say what type of thing something is, or put it or list it in a particular group: *The proposals come under three main headings.* → see also **come/go under the hammer** at HAMMER[1] (2)

come up *phr. v.*

1 MOVE NEAR to move near someone or something, especially by walking SYN **approach**: *George came up and introduced himself to us.* | **+to/behind etc.** *Come up to the front of the room so everyone can see you.*

2 BE MENTIONED to be mentioned or suggested: *A lot of questions came up at the meeting.* | *Parson's name has come up for the position of head coach.*

3 HAPPEN if something, especially a problem, comes up, it suddenly happens SYN **occur** SYN **crop up**: *You should try to deal with each problem as it comes up.* | ***Something's come up**, so I won't be able to go with you.*

4 be coming up to be happening soon: *Alison's birthday is coming up.*

5 SUN/MOON when the sun or moon comes up, it rises: *The sun came up around 5:30.*

6 JOB/OPPORTUNITY if a job or opportunity comes up, it becomes available: *I've been out of work before, but something always comes up.*

7 APPEAR to appear or be shown, especially by chance: *If my lotto numbers come up, I'll be a millionaire!* | *Click twice, and the image will come up on screen.*

8 PLANTS when a plant comes up, you can see it start growing above the ground: *The tulips usually start coming up in late March.*

9 LAW COURT if your case comes up in a court of law, the court starts to deal with it

10 VOMIT if food that you have eaten comes up, you VOMIT

11 come up empty/empty-handed to not be able to find something or to not be successful in something

you are trying to do: *Even the FBI has come up empty in its search for Weiss.*
12 coming (right) up! SPOKEN used to say that something, especially food or drink, will be ready very soon: *"Two martinis, please." "Coming right up!"*
13 come up in the world to become richer or more successful in society: *She looks like she's come up in the world.*

come up against sth/sb *phr. v.* to have to deal with difficult problems or people: *We came up against some very strong competition.*

come up for sth *phr. v.* **1** if someone or something comes up for a particular treatment, the time comes for them to be treated in that way: **come up for review/renewal/discussion etc.** *The contract comes up for renewal next year.* | *The bill will **come up for a vote*** (=be voted on) *in September.* | *Four board members are **coming up for reelection** this spring.* **2 come up for sale** to become available to be sold: *The house came up for sale last summer.*

come up on sth *phr. v.* **be coming up on sth** INFORMAL to be getting closer to a time, date, event etc.: *We're coming up on Labor Day.*

come upon sb/sth *phr. v.* LITERARY to find or discover someone or something by chance: *Suddenly we came upon two bears in a clearing in the forest.*

come up to sth *phr. v.* to reach a particular standard or to be as good as you expected: *The resort failed to come up to expectations.*

come up with sth *phr. v.* **1** to think of an idea, plan, reply etc.: *Can you help me come up with some ideas for my presentation?* **2** to be able to get a particular amount of money: *We have to come up with $1,500 to get the car fixed.*

come with *phr. v.* **1 come with sth** to develop naturally as a result of something: *Experience comes with age.* **2** SPOKEN, INFORMAL to go somewhere along with someone else: *Danny and I are going to the Galleria. Do you want to come with?*

come·back /ˈkʌmbæk/ *n.* [C usually singular] **1** a return to being powerful, popular, or famous again after being unpopular or unknown for a long time: **make/stage a comeback** *Miniskirts are making a comeback.* **2** a situation in a sports competition in which a person or team begins playing better after playing badly: *The A's **made a comeback** in the eighth inning.* **3** a quick reply that is smart or funny SYN **retort**: *I can never think of a comeback when I need one.* → see also **come back** at COME

co·me·di·an /kəˈmidiən/ *n.* [C] **1** ENG. LANG. ARTS someone whose job is to tell jokes and make people laugh SYN **comic** **2** INFORMAL someone who is amusing: *Dan was always trying to be the class comedian.*

co·me·dic /kəˈmidɪk/ *adj.* [usually before noun] FORMAL relating to comedy: *a comedic role*

co·me·di·enne /kəˌmidiˈɛn/ *n.* [C] a female comedian

come·down /ˈkʌmdaʊn/ *n.* [C usually singular] a situation that is not as good, important, interesting etc. as the one you had previously → see also **come down** at COME

com·e·dy /ˈkɑmədi/ W3 *n. plural* **comedies** **1** [C,U] ENG. LANG. ARTS a funny movie, television program, play etc. that makes people laugh, or this type of entertainment → see also DRAMA: *a successful TV comedy* | *Capurro has been doing **stand-up comedy*** (=telling jokes in front of people as a job) *for about a year.* ►see THESAURUS box at **funny**, **movie** **2** [U] the quality in something that makes you laugh SYN **humor**: *Luckily, he could see the comedy in the situation.* **3 a comedy of errors** a situation in which a lot of things do not happen the way they should: *When the caterer canceled, the wedding turned into a comedy of errors.* **4 a comedy of manners** a comedy that shows how silly people's behavior is or can be [**Origin:** 1300–1400 French *comédie*, from Latin, from Greek *komoidia*, from *komos* **having fun, partying** + *aeidein* **to sing**] → see also BLACK COMEDY, SITUATION COMEDY

ˌcome-ˈhither *adj.* OLD-FASHIONED **come-hither look/eyes** a way of looking at someone that shows you think they are sexually attractive

come·ly /ˈkʌmli/ *adj.* LITERARY a comely woman has an attractive appearance —**comeliness** *n.* [U]

ˈcome-on *n.* [C] INFORMAL **1** something that someone does to try to make someone else sexually interested in them: *Rick's the kind of guy who thinks every smile is a come-on.* **2** an attempt to get people to buy something, by using an advertisement or giving something away free SYN **inducement** → see also **come on** at COME

com·er /ˈkʌmɚ/ *n.* **1 all comers** INFORMAL anyone who is interested, especially anyone who wants to take part in a competition: *The contest is open to all comers.* **2** [C usually plural] INFORMAL someone who is likely to be successful in a particular job: *These two young artists have been picked by critics as genuine comers.* → see also LATECOMER, NEWCOMER, UP-AND-COMER

co·mes·ti·bles /kəˈmɛstəbəlz/ *n.* [plural] FORMAL food

com·et /ˈkɑmɪt/ *n.* [C] SCIENCE an object in space like a bright ball with a tail, that moves around the sun [**Origin:** 1100–1200 Latin *cometa*, from Greek *kometes* **long-haired, comet**; because of its long tail]

comet

come·up·pance /kʌmˈʌpəns/ *n.* [singular] INFORMAL a punishment or something bad that happens to you because you have done something bad: *The play is about a greedy man who **gets his comeuppance**.*

com·fort¹ /ˈkʌmfɚt/ W3 *n.*
1 PHYSICAL [U] a feeling of being physically relaxed and satisfied, so that you are not feeling any pain or feeling too hot or cold: *He was enjoying the warmth and comfort of a real bed.* | *You can watch your favorite movies **in the comfort of your own home**.* | *Guests can relax **in comfort** in the pool and sauna.* | **be designed/made/crafted for comfort** *The chairs are designed for comfort and style.*
2 EMOTIONAL [U] a feeling of being calm or hopeful after you have been worried or sad: *Emilia goes to a women's group **for comfort** and emotional support.* | **take/find comfort in sth** *You can take some comfort in the fact that you did your best.* | **give/bring/offer (sb) comfort** *Her faith gave her comfort during a very difficult time.* | **take/draw/derive comfort from sth** *She draws great comfort from the support of friends.* | ***If it's any comfort**, I got lost the first time I drove in Chicago too.*
3 MONEY/POSSESSIONS [U] a way of living in which you have everything you need to be happy: *She grew up **in comfort** in a suburb of Los Angeles.*
4 SB/STH THAT HELPS [C] someone or something that helps you feel happier or calmer when you have been worried or unhappy: **+to/for** *The familiar surroundings were a comfort to the frightened children.* | ***It's a comfort** to know there's someone you can call on if you're sick.*
5 too close for comfort something bad that is too close for comfort makes you feel worried or upset, because it is too close in distance or time: *Cars were whizzing past us much too close for comfort.*
6 comforts [plural] the things that make your life nicer and more comfortable, but that are not necessary: *The beach cabin has **all the comforts of home**.* | *The cars are fast, but lack **creature comforts*** (=things that make them comfortable for people to sit in).
7 cold/small comfort a small piece of good news that does not make you feel better about a bad situation: *The company won't close, but that's cold comfort to the people who lost their jobs.* —**comfortless** *adj.* → see also COMFORT FOOD

comfort² *v.* [T] to make someone feel less worried or unhappy by being kind to them: *She held him and tried to comfort him.* | **comfort yourself** *She comforted her-*

self with the thought that it would soon be spring. [**Origin:** 1100–1200 Old French *conforter*, from Late Latin *confortare* **to strengthen**] —**comforting** *adj.*: *It's comforting to know I can call my parents anytime.* —**comfortingly** *adv.*

com·fort·a·ble /ˈkʌmftəˑbəl, ˈkʌmfəˑt̬əbəl/ S1 W2 *adj.*
1 FEELING PHYSICALLY COMFORTABLE feeling physically relaxed and satisfied, without feeling any pain or being too hot, cold etc. OPP **uncomfortable**: *I was comfortable and warm in bed.* | *Come in and **make yourself comfortable**.* | *My shoulder was hurting and I couldn't **get comfortable**.*
2 CLOTHES/FURNITURE/PLACES ETC. making you feel physically relaxed and satisfied OPP **uncomfortable**: *comfortable shoes* | *a comfortable apartment* | **comfortable to wear/sit on/use etc.** *Our new sofa is really comfortable to sit on.*
3 CONFIDENT if you are comfortable with an idea, person, or activity, you are confident that you can manage successfully OPP **uncomfortable**: **comfortable doing sth** *Are you comfortable using this software?* | **+with** *Japanese is the language he's most comfortable with.*
4 MONEY having enough money to live on without worrying about paying for things: *The Austins aren't rich, but they're comfortable.* | **comfortable retirement/life etc.** *They're looking forward to a comfortable retirement.*
5 SICK/INJURED if someone who is sick or injured is comfortable, they are not in too much pain
6 RACE/COMPETITION if you have a comfortable lead or have a comfortable win, you lead or win by a large number of points or a large distance: *The Nuggets had a **comfortable lead** in the third quarter.* | *The bill should pass in the House by a **comfortable margin**.*

com·fort·a·bly /ˈkʌmftəˑbli, -fəˑt̬əbli/ *adv.*
1 FURNITURE/PLACES/CLOTHES in a way that feels physically relaxed, without any pain or being too hot, cold etc.: *The backpack will comfortably fit children up to 4'6" tall.*
2 PHYSICALLY RELAXED feeling physically relaxed, without any pain or without being too hot, cold etc.: *He settled comfortably into a chair.*
3 WIN/ACHIEVEMENT easily and without problems: **+ahead** *Polls show him comfortably ahead in the campaign.* | *The Lakers **won comfortably**, 97-74.*
4 MONEY with enough money to live well, without worrying about how to pay for things: *White worked hard and saved enough to **live comfortably**.* | *Mrs. Jenkins is **comfortably off*** (=fairly rich).
5 be resting comfortably to not be in too much pain after an accident or illness: *The patient was resting comfortably last night.*
6 CONFIDENT in a confident, relaxed way: *They were soon talking comfortably.*

com·fort·er /ˈkʌmfəˑt̬əˑ/ *n.* [C] **1** a thick cover for a bed SYN **quilt** **2** someone who comforts you

ˈcomfort ˌfood *n.* [U] simple food that makes you feel relaxed and happy, especially because it is similar to the food your mother cooked when you were a child

ˈcomfort ˌstation *n.* [C] FORMAL a room where there are toilets for the public to use

com·fy /ˈkʌmfi/ *adj. comparative* **comfier**, *superlative* **comfiest** SPOKEN comfortable: *a comfy chair*

com·ic¹ /ˈkɑmɪk/ *adj.* **1** funny or amusing SYN **humorous** OPP **tragic**: *a comic novel* | **comic actor/talent/performer etc.** *a gifted comic actress* **2 comic relief** a funny part of a serious movie, book, situation etc.: *Every horror picture needs a little comic relief.*

comic² *n.* [C] **1** someone whose job is to tell jokes and make people laugh SYN **comedian**: *a stand-up comic* **2** a COMIC BOOK

com·i·cal /ˈkɑmɪkəl/ *adj.* funny, especially in a strange or unexpected way SYN **funny**: *a comical look at the fashion industry* —**comically** /-kli/ *adv.*

ˈcomic book *n.* [C] a magazine that tells a story using pictures that are drawn like comic strips

ˌcomic ˈopera *n.* [C,U] an OPERA in which the singers speak as well as sing, and that has an amusing story

com·ics /ˈkɑmɪks/ *n.* [plural] **the comics** the part of a newspaper that has comic strips SYN **the funnies**

ˈcomic strip *n.* [C] a series of pictures that tell a story, with each picture drawn inside a box → see also CARTOON

com·ing¹ /ˈkʌmɪŋ/ *n.* **1 the coming of sb/sth** the time when someone or something new arrives or begins SYN **advent**: *With the coming of the railroad, the population in the West grew quickly.* **2 comings and goings** INFORMAL the movements of people as they arrive at and leave places: **+of** *Cameras record the comings and goings of the bank's customers.*

coming² *adj.* [only before noun] FORMAL happening soon SYN **approaching**: *The Pilgrims prepared for the coming winter.* → see also UP-AND-COMING

ˌcoming of ˈage *n.* [singular] **1** the time in someone's life when society begins to consider them an adult: *a book about a young woman's coming of age during the 1960s* **2** the time when something develops enough to be considered successful: *The invention of email signaled the coming of age of the computer.*

Co·mis·key /kəˈmɪski/, **Charles** (1858–1931) an American baseball player, manager and team owner who helped to organize the American League

com·i·ty /ˈkɑməṭi/ *n.* [U] FORMAL behavior that is correct, respectful, and friendly

comm. **1** the written abbreviation of COMMISSION or COMMISSIONER **2** the written abbreviation of COMMITTEE **3** the written abbreviation of COMMUNICATION or COMMUNICATIONS

com·ma /ˈkɑmə/ S3 *n.* [C] ENG. LANG. ARTS the mark (,) used in writing to show a short pause, to separate single things in a list, or to separate parts of a sentence [**Origin:** 1500–1600 Latin **part of a sentence**, from Greek *komma* **part, clause**, from *koptein* **to cut**] → see also COMMA SPLICE

com·mand¹ /kəˈmænd/ S3 W3 *n.*
1 CONTROL [U] the control of a group of people or a situation: *The captain was drunk while **in command** of the ship.* | *The company has thrived **under** McCormack's **command**.* | *Janet **took command** of the situation.* | *Each congressman has a large staff **at his command*** (=available to be used). | *Sergeant Lynch was **relieved of his command*** (=his control over a group of people was taken away).
2 ORDER [C] an order that must be obeyed: *Fire when I **give the command**.*
3 COMPUTER [C] an instruction to a computer to do something
4 MILITARY [C] **a)** a part of an army, navy etc. that is controlled separately and has a particular job: *pilots from the Southern Air Command* **b)** a group of officers or officials who give orders: *the Army High Command* **c)** the group of soldiers that an officer is in control of
5 command of sth knowledge of something, especially a language, or the ability to use something: **good/basic/poor etc. command of sth** *a basic command of arithmetic* | *Fujiko **has** a good **command of** English.*
6 at your command if you have a particular skill at your command, you are able to use that skill well and easily: *a carpenter with years of experience at his command*
7 be in command of yourself to be able to control your emotions and thoughts: *Kathleen is in total command of herself.*

command² *v.*
1 ORDER [I,T] to tell someone officially to do something, especially if you are a military leader, a king etc. SYN **order**: **command sb to do sth** *Captain Richardson commanded the crew to report to the main deck.* ▸see THESAURUS box at **tell**
2 LEAD THE MILITARY [I,T] to be responsible for giving orders to a group of people in the Army, Navy etc.: *Lee commanded the 101st Airborne division in World War II.*

3 DESERVE AND GET [T] to get attention, respect etc. because you do something well or are important or popular: **command attention/respect/support etc.** *His presence on the stage commanded attention.* | *Dr. Young commands a great deal of respect as a surgeon.* | **command a high price/fee/wage etc.** *His paintings started commanding higher prices after his death.*
4 CONTROL [T] to control something: *Ford Motor Co. commands 16% of the market.*
5 VIEW [T] if a place commands a view, you can see something clearly from it: *His office commands a magnificent view of the Capitol Dome.*
[**Origin:** 1200–1300 Old French *comander*, from Vulgar Latin *commandare*, from Latin *commendare*] → see Word Choice box at ORDER[2]

com·man·dant /'kɑmən,dɑnt/ *n.* [C] the chief officer in charge of a military organization: *the commandant of a prison camp*

com'mand e,conomy *n.* [C] ECONOMICS an economic system in which the government of a country owns most of the industry and makes all the important economic decisions → see also FREE MARKET

com·man·deer /,kɑmən'dɪr/ *v.* [T] to take someone else's property for your own use SYN **seize**: *Two gunmen commandeered a car to escape in.*

com·mand·er /kə'mændɚ/ W3 *n.* [C] **1** an officer who is in charge of a group of soldiers, a particular military activity, a group of police officers etc.: *Burnside was later replaced as commander of the army.* | *Commander, here are the reports you asked for.* **2** an officer who has a middle rank in the Navy

com,mander in 'chief *n.* [C usually singular] **1** someone of high rank who is in control of all the military organizations in a country or of a specific military activity **2 Commander in Chief** a title for the U.S. president in his position as the official head of the military

com·mand·ing /kə'mændɪŋ/ *adj.* [usually before noun] **1** having the authority or position that allows you to give orders: *a commanding officer* **2** APPROVING having the confidence to make people respect and obey you: *She is a **commanding presence** on the stage.* **3** a commanding view or position is one from which you can see a long way: *The apartment offers a commanding view of the bay.* **4** being in a position from which you are likely to win a race or competition easily: *Polls have shown Isaacs to have a **commanding lead**.*

com·mand·ment /kə'mændmənt/ *n.* [C] **1** one of the ten rules given by God in the Bible that tell people how they should behave **2** LITERARY a command

com'mand ,module *n.* [C] the part of a space vehicle from which its activities are controlled

com·man·do /kə'mændoʊ/ *n. plural* **commandos** or **commandoes** **1** [C] a group of soldiers who are specially trained to make quick attacks into enemy areas: *a commando raid* **2** [C] a soldier who is a member of this group **3 go commando** INFORMAL to wear no underwear

com,mand per'formance *n.* [C] a special performance at a theater that is given at the request of a president, king etc.

com'mand post *n.* [C] the place from which military leaders and their officers control activities

'comma splice *n.* [C] TECHNICAL a sentence with two or more main CLAUSES joined using only a comma, such as "I'm tired, I want to go home." This is considered incorrect in English.

com·mem·o·rate /kə'mɛmə,reɪt/ *v.* [T] to remember a person or an event by having a special ceremony, or by making or building something special SYN **memorialize**: *a statue that commemorates Civil War soldiers* [**Origin:** 1600–1700 Latin, past participle of *commemorare*, from *com-* + *memorare* **to remind of**] —**commemorative** /kə'mɛmrət̬ɪv/ *adj.*

com·mem·o·ra·tion /kə,mɛmə'reɪʃən/ *n.* [C,U] a special action, ceremony, object etc. that makes you remember someone important or an important event in the past: *There will be a commemoration of the first flight across the Atlantic.* | *The monument was built **in commemoration of** those who died in the Vietnam war.*

com·mence /kə'mɛns/ Ac *v.* [I,T] FORMAL to start something SYN **begin** OPP **stop**: *Work will commence immediately.* | *They will commence production in April.* | **+with** *The tradition of lighting a torch commenced with the 1936 Olympic games.* | **commence doing sth** *The planes commenced bombing on Wednesday.* [**Origin:** 1300–1400 Old French *comencer*, from Vulgar Latin *cominitiare*, from Latin + *initiare* **to begin**]

WORD CHOICE commence, start, begin
Commence is a very formal word that is used more in written language than in spoken. In spoken language, it is more common to use **start**, which can also be used in written language, but **begin** is the most common word to choose in written language.

com·mence·ment /kə'mɛnsmənt/ Ac *n.* FORMAL **1** [U] the beginning of something SYN **start**: **+of** *the commencement of the trial* **2** [C,U] a ceremony at which college or high school students receive their DIPLOMAS SYN **graduation**: **commencement address/speech** *The mayor gave the commencement address.* | **commencement exercises/ceremony** *She was the only student speaker at the commencement exercises.*

com·mend /kə'mɛnd/ *v.* [T] FORMAL **1** to praise someone or something, especially in public SYN **praise**: *The principal commended his honesty.* | **commend sb for sth** *Judge Fein commended the two sides for reaching a fair settlement.* | *Bartholomew's work has been **highly commended**.* | *Her approach to the problem **is to be commended*** (=deserves praise). **2** FORMAL to tell someone that something is good or deserves attention SYN **recommend**: *The committee has commended achievement tests every four years.* | **commend sth to sb** *I commend the book to all students of the subject.* | **have much/little to commend it** (=something is very good or not very good) *The movie has little to commend it.* **3** LITERARY to give someone to someone else to take care of: *The priest commended the man's soul to God.*

com·mend·a·ble /kə'mɛndəbəl/ *adj.* FORMAL deserving praise SYN **laudable**: *commendable honesty* | *The team's recent record is **highly commendable**.* —**commendably** *adv.*

com·men·da·tion /,kɑmən'deɪʃən/ *n.* [C,U] FORMAL an honor or prize given to someone for being brave or successful

com·men·sal·ism /kə'mɛnsə,lɪzəm/ *n.* [U] BIOLOGY a relationship between two different kinds of ORGANISMS that live together, which helps one but neither helps nor hurts the other in any way

com·men·su·rate /kə'mɛnsərɪt, -ʃərɪt/ *adj.* FORMAL matching something in size, quality, or length of time SYN **corresponding**: **+with** *The punishment should be commensurate with their actions.*

com·ment[1] /'kɑmɛnt/ Ac S2 W2 *n.* **1** [C,U] an opinion that you express about someone or something SYN **remark**: *Are there any questions or comments?* | **+about/on** *The company has issued no public comment on the investigation.* | *He responded with a crude, sexist comment.* | *The president **made** his **comments** at a press conference.* **2** [U] criticism or discussion of something that someone has said or done: *The jurors were not available for comment after the trial.* **3 No comment** SPOKEN said when you do not want to answer a question, especially in public or during an INTERVIEW **4 be a comment on sth** to be a sign of the bad quality of something: *The number of adults who cannot read is a sad comment on the quality of our schools.* [**Origin:** 1300–1400 Late Latin *commentum*, from Latin, **invention**, from *comminisci* **to invent**]

comment[2] Ac S3 W3 *v.* [I,T] to give an opinion about someone or something: **+on** *The police have refused to comment on the investigation.* | **comment that** *Critics have commented that the movie is unnecessarily violent.*

com·men·tar·y /'kɑmən,tɛri/ Ac *n. plural* **commentaries** [C,U] **1** a description of an event, given while the event is happening, that is broadcast on the television or radio: **do/provide/give a commentary** *Schuler will do the World Series commentary.* | **+on** *the commentary on the parade* | **color commentary** (=descriptions of players, game plans etc. rather than just saying what happens in the game) | *The tour guide gave us a* ***running commentary*** (=continuous description) *as we walked round the museum.* **2** something such as a book or article that explains or discusses something, or the explanation itself: *political commentary* | **+on** *a commentary on the 2004 presidential election* **3 be a sad/tragic etc. commentary on sth** to be a sign of how bad a particular situation is: *It's a sad commentary on our culture that we need constant entertainment.*

C

com·men·tate /ˈkɑmənˌteɪt/ *v.* [I + on] to describe an event such as a sports game on television or radio

com·men·ta·tor /ˈkɑmənˌteɪt̬ɚ/ Ac *n.* [C] **1** someone who knows a lot about a particular subject, and who writes about it or discusses it on the television or radio: *a political commentator* **2** someone who describes an event as it is happening on television or radio: *a college basketball commentator*

com·merce /ˈkɑmɚs/ W2 *n.* [U] **1** the buying and selling of goods and services SYN **trade**: *interstate commerce* (=among U.S. states) ►see THESAURUS box at **business** **2** OLD-FASHIONED relationships and communication between people [**Origin:** 1500–1600 French, Latin *commercium*, from *com-* + *merx* **things to be sold**] → see also CHAMBER OF COMMERCE

ˈCommerce ˌClause *n.* **the Commerce Clause** HISTORY a CLAUSE in the U.S. Constitution that gives Congress the power to control trade between different states and between the U.S. and foreign countries

ˈcommerce ˌpower *n.* **the commerce power** ECONOMICS the official power the U.S. government has to control trade between different states and between the U.S. and foreign countries

com·mer·cial[1] /kəˈmɚʃəl/ S3 W2 *adj.* **1** relating to business and the buying and selling of goods and services: *commercial growth* | *Several commercial properties are vacant.* **2** a commercial business or activity produces goods and services to be sold: *a large commercial fish farm* | *a freelance commercial artist* **3** relating to the ability of a product or business to make a profit: *The designer insists her clothing styles are commercial.* | *The movie was a huge* ***commercial success.*** **4 commercial TV/radio/broadcasting etc.** television or radio broadcasts that are produced by companies that earn money through advertising → see also PUBLIC TELEVISION **5** [only before noun] a commercial product is sold to the public rather than to businesses: *All commercial milk is pasteurized.* **6** DISAPPROVING more concerned with money than with quality: *I used to like their music, but they've become very commercial.*

commercial[2] S2 *n.* [C] an advertisement on television or the radio: **car/beer/toy etc. commercial** *There are more toy commercials just before Christmas.* | **run/air a commercial** *The commercial will be aired during the Super Bowl.* ►see THESAURUS box at **advertisement** → see also AD

WORD CHOICE **commercial/advertisement**

- **Commercial** is used only about advertisements on the television and the radio.
- For advertisements in newspapers or magazines, or on signs, use **advertisement**.

comˈmercial ˌbank *n.* [C] TECHNICAL the kind of bank that most people use, that provides services both for ordinary people and for businesses

comˌmercial ˈbreak *n.* [C] a time when advertisements are shown during a television or radio program

comˌmercial ˈfarming *n.* [U] the practice of raising crops and animals in order to sell them —**commercial farmer** *n.* [C]

com·mer·cial·is·m /kəˈmɚʃəˌlɪzəm/ *n.* [U] DISAPPROVING the practice of being more concerned with making money than with the quality of what you sell or make SYN **commercialization**: *the increasing commercialism of modern culture*

com·mer·cial·ize /kəˈmɚʃəˌlaɪz/ *v.* [T] **1** [usually passive] DISAPPROVING to be more concerned with making money from something than about its quality: *Christmas is getting so commercialized.* **2** to make a profit from something, especially by selling something that would not usually be sold: *Some space launches will be commercialized in order to help pay for more research.* —**commercialization** /kəˌmɚʃələˈzeɪʃən/ *n.* [U]

com·mer·cial·ly /kəˈmɚʃəli/ *adv.* **1** considering whether a business or product is making a profit: *a* ***commercially successful*** *rock band* | *The project wasn't* ***commercially viable*** (=wasn't going to make a profit). [sentence adverb] *Commercially, the movie was a flop.* **2** produced or used in large quantities as a business: *commercially farmed land* **3 commercially available** a product that is commercially available can be bought in stores

com·mie /ˈkɑmi/ *n.* [C] SPOKEN **1** an insulting word for a COMMUNIST **2** an insulting word for someone who does not support traditional American beliefs, especially a belief in CAPITALISM

com·min·gle /kəˈmɪŋgəl, kɑ-/ *v.* FORMAL **1** [I,T] to mix together, or to make different things do this SYN **mix**: *Recyclable items can be commingled for collection.* **2** [T] if a financial organization commingles money, it mixes its own money with the money that belongs to one of its customers or to another part of the business, usually in an illegal way

com·mis·e·rate /kəˈmɪzəˌreɪt/ *v.* [I] FORMAL to express your sympathy for someone who is unhappy about something SYN **sympathize**

com·mis·er·a·tion /kəˌmɪzəˈreɪʃən/ *n.* FORMAL [U, plural] a feeling of sympathy for someone when something bad has happened to them: *a letter of commiseration* → see also CONDOLENCE

com·mis·sar /ˈkɑməˌsɑr/ *n.* [C] a Communist Party official whose job is to teach people about COMMUNISM and help them be loyal to it

com·mis·sar·y /ˈkɑməˌsɛri/ *n. plural* **commissaries** [C] **1** a store that supplies food and other goods in a military camp **2** a place where you can eat in a large organization such as a movie STUDIO, factory etc. SYN **cafeteria**

com·mis·sion[1] /kəˈmɪʃən/ Ac S3 W2 *n.*

1 PEOPLE [C] a group of people who have been given the official job of finding out about something or controlling something: *the California State Lottery Commission* | **+on** *a White House advisory commission on U.S.–Asia trade*

2 MONEY [C,U] an amount of money paid to someone for selling something, according to the value of the goods they have sold: *Each dealer* ***makes a 20% commission*** *on his sales* (=receives 20% of the price of what he sells). | *Jamil sells cars* ***on commission.***

3 JOB [C] **a)** a request for an artist, musician etc. to make a piece of art or music, for which they are paid: **get/receive a commission** *She has received a commission from the bank for a sculpture.* **b)** FORMAL a duty or job that you ask someone to do

4 out of commission a) not working or not able to be used: *I had to take the train as the car's out of commission.* **b)** INFORMAL sick or injured, and unable to go to work, play sports etc.: *My knee injury put me out of commission for two weeks.*

5 in commission if a military ship is in commission, it is still being used by the Navy

6 ARMY/NAVY ETC. [C] the position and authority given to an officer in the Army, Navy etc.: *Haley was asked to resign his commission.*

7 CRIME [U] FORMAL the commission of a crime is the act of doing it

[**Origin:** 1300–1400 Old French, Latin *commissio*, from *commissus*, past participle of *committere*]

commission[2] Ac *v.* [T] **1** to formally ask someone to do something for you, such as write an official report, produce a work of art etc.: *The orchestra is commission-*

ing new works from 14 composers. | **commission sb/sth to do sth** *City Hall has commissioned a study to examine using fluoride in the drinking water.* **2 be commissioned** be given an officer's rank in the Army, Navy etc.

com,missioned 'officer *n.* [C] a military officer who has a commission

com·mis·sion·er /kə'mɪʃənɚ/ Ac *n.* [C] **1** someone who is officially in charge of a police department, sports organization, government department etc.: *the commissioner of the National Football League* **2** a member of a COMMISSION

com·mit /kə'mɪt/ Ac S2 W2 *v.* **committed, committing**

1 CRIME [T] to do something wrong or illegal: *Women* ***commit*** *fewer* ***crimes*** *than men.* | **commit murder/fraud/a felony etc.** *Brady committed a series of brutal murders.* | *His brother* ***committed suicide*** (=killed himself deliberately). | *Both of them admitted* ***committing adultery*** (=having sex with someone who is not your husband or wife).

2 SAY YOU WILL DO STH [I,T] to say that you will definitely do something or that you must do something: **commit sb to doing sth** *The scholarship commits students to teaching in public schools.* | **commit sb to sth** *The speech did not commit the rebels to a ceasefire.* | *People often live together before* ***committing themselves*** *to marriage.*

3 RELATIONSHIP [I,T] to decide to have a long permanent relationship with someone: *Rick says he's not ready to commit.* | **commit yourself (to sb/sth)** *She didn't feel ready to commit herself to a relationship.*

4 MONEY/TIME [T] to decide to use money, time, people etc. for a particular purpose: *The state will commit $58 million for a new research facility.* | **commit sth to sth** *They are unwilling to commit that many soldiers to the U.N.*

5 PRISON/HOSPITAL [T] to order someone to be put in a hospital or prison SYN **institutionalize**: **commit sb to sth** *At age 26, she was committed to a mental institution.*

6 commit sth to memory to learn something so that you remember it SYN **memorize**

7 commit sth to paper FORMAL to write something down

[**Origin:** 1300–1400 Latin *committere*, from *com-* + *mittere* **to send**]

com·mit·ment /kə'mɪtˀmənt/ Ac S3 W2 *n.* **1** [C] a promise to do something or to behave in a particular way: *Marriage should be a lifelong commitment.* | **+to** *a commitment to equal pay and opportunities* | **commitment to do sth** *There is a growing commitment to fight poverty.* | *Volunteers must be able to* ***make a commitment*** *of four hours a week.* **2** [U] the hard work and loyalty that someone gives to an organization, activity etc.: *the energy and commitment shown by the players* | **+to** *a* ***strong commitment*** *to her work* **3** [U] someone's decision to have a permanent relationship with another person, especially a decision to get married: *Her parents' divorce left her with a fear of commitment.* **4** [C] something that you have promised you will do or that you have to do: *Many parents feel they have too many commitments.* | *We don't go out much because of* ***family commitments.*** | *I had a lot of* ***financial commitments*** (=money that I had to pay regularly). **5** [C,U] the use of money, time, people etc. for a particular purpose: *commitments of food and medical aid* | *The class is a big time commitment.*

com·mit·tal /kə'mɪtl/ *n.* [C,U] **1** the process in which a court sends someone to a mental hospital or prison **2** FORMAL the burying or burning of a dead person's body → see also NONCOMMITTAL

com·mit·ted /kə'mɪtɪd/ Ac *adj.* willing to work very hard at something: *John is a very committed student.* | **+to** *Residents are committed to solving their neighborhood's problems.*

com·mit·tee /kə'mɪti/ S2 W1 *n.* [C] a group of people chosen to do a particular job, make decisions etc.: *the school's fund-raising committee* | *a committee meeting* | **+on** *the Senate Select Committee on Intelligence* | *She's* ***on*** *the finance* ***committee.***

com·mode /kə'moʊd/ *n.* [C] **1** a word meaning "toilet," used by people who do not like saying the word "toilet" **2** a chair with a bowl under the seat that can be used as a toilet by old or sick people **3** an old-fashioned piece of furniture with drawers or shelves

com·mo·di·ous /kə'moʊdiəs/ *adj.* FORMAL a house or room that is commodious is very big SYN **spacious** —**commodiously** *adv.*

com·mod·i·ty /kə'mɑdəti/ Ac *n. plural* **commodities** [C] **1** ECONOMICS a product that is bought and sold and that is the same no matter who produces it, such as oil, metal, and farm products: *agricultural commodities* **2** FORMAL a useful quality: *Time is a precious commodity.*

com'modity ,money *n.* [U] ECONOMICS an object that has value, and which can be used as money or to buy other goods. Examples of commodity money include things such as gold and other valuable metals, DIAMONDS and other valuable stones, and cigarettes.

com·mo·dore /'kɑmə,dɔr/ *n.* [C] **1** a high rank in the Navy, or someone who has this rank **2** the CAPTAIN in charge of a group of ships that are carrying goods

com·mon¹ /'kɑmən/ S2 W1 *adj.*

1 A LOT existing in large numbers OPP **rare**: *Olson is a common last name in Minnesota.* | *Foxes are very common around here.*

2 HAPPENING OFTEN happening often and to many people, or in many places OPP **rare**: *Thunderstorms are common in August.* | *This is a common experience.* | **+among** *Bone disease is common among older women.* | **it is common for sb to do sth** *It's common for new fathers to feel jealous of the baby.* | *Heart disease is the most* ***common cause*** *of death.*

3 SHARED BY EVERYONE [usually before noun, no comparative] belonging to or shared by two or more people or things: *The Allies worked to defeat a common enemy.* | **+to** *These problems are common to all big cities.* | *Students and faculty are working toward a common goal.* | ***By common consent*** (=with everyone's agreement), *Joe was chosen as captain.* | *Crew members lacked a* ***common language*** (=they did not speak the same language).

4 ORDINARY [only before noun, no comparative] ordinary and not special in any way: *common salt* | *The song is a tribute to* ***the common man*** (=ordinary people).

5 common ground facts, opinions, and beliefs that very different people or groups can agree on: *Democrats and Republicans did find some common ground in the debates about privacy.*

6 the common good what is best for everyone in a society: *The government creates laws for the common good.*

7 common knowledge something that everyone knows: *It is common knowledge that cigarettes are a health risk.*

8 common practice a usual or accepted way of doing things: *Today, it is common practice to encourage children to choose their own writing topics.*

9 common courtesy/decency a polite way of behaving that you expect from people: *It's common courtesy to ask before lighting a cigarette in someone's home.*

10 common touch the ability of someone in a position of power or authority to talk to and understand ordinary people: *a politician with the common touch*

11 make common cause (with sb) FORMAL to join with other people or groups for a particular purpose: *In the 1940s, the U.S. made common cause with the Soviet Union against Nazi Germany.*

[**Origin:** 1200–1300 Old French *commun*, from Latin *communis*] → see also COMMON DENOMINATOR

common² *n.* **1 have sth in common (with sb)** to have the same interests, attitudes, qualities etc. as another person or group: *Terry and I* ***have a lot in common.*** | *I did* ***not have much in common with*** *the other kids in high school.* | *Although they were cousins, the boys seemed to* ***have little in common.*** | *four women with almost* ***nothing in common*** **2 have sth in com-**

C

mon (with sth) if objects or ideas have something in common, they share the same features: *His music **has more in common** with jazz than rock.* | *Favorite vacation spots **have one thing in common**: they're in warm places.* | *These paintings **have little in common with** traditional Chinese art.* | *The two games **have much in common**.* **3 in common with sb/sth** in the same way as someone or something else: *In common with a lot of other countries, we're in a recession.* **4** [C] a large area of open land in a town, that people can walk on or play sports on: *Boston Common* —**commonality** /ˌkɑməˈnæləṭi/ *n.* [C]

C

WORD CHOICE **common, general**

- When you have the same interests, attitudes, experiences etc. as someone else, you say that you have a lot **in common**: *As new parents, we have a lot in common.*
- When you mean that something happens or is true in most situations, use **in general**: *In general, new parents do not get enough sleep.*

ˌcommon ˈcold *n.* [C usually singular] a slight sickness in which it is difficult to breathe normally, and your throat and head hurt SYN **cold**

ˌcommon deˈnominator *n.* [C usually singular] **1** an attitude or quality that all the different members of a group have: *A common denominator is that all the men had graduated from Yale.* **2** MATH a number that can be divided exactly by all the DENOMINATORS (=bottom number) in a set of FRACTIONS **3 the lowest common denominator** the least attractive or least intelligent people or features in a situation: *trashy TV programs that appeal to the lowest common denominator*

ˌcommon desˈcent *n.* [U] BIOLOGY the belief that all the animals, plants, or other living things on Earth have developed from a single living thing or set of GENES that existed a very long time ago

ˌcommon ˈdifference *n.* [singular] MATH in an ARITHMETIC SEQUENCE (=series of related numbers), the difference between each number and the number that follows it. For example, the common difference in the series of numbers 1, 4, 7, and 10 is 3.

ˌcommon diˈvisor *n.* [C] MATH a number by which two or more other numbers can be divided exactly. For example, 3 is a common divisor of 6, 12, and 18.

com·mon·er /ˈkɑmənɚ/ *n.* [C] someone who is not a member of the NOBILITY

ˌcommon ˈfactor *n.* [C] MATH a number that divides exactly into each of a set of two or more other numbers. For example, 3 is a common factor of 6, 12, and 18.

ˌcommon ˈfraction *n.* [C] MATH a FRACTION that is shown by a number above and a number below a line, such as ½, rather than as a DECIMAL

ˌcommon ˈion *n.* [C] CHEMISTRY an ION (=atom or group of atoms with an electric charge) that is present in each of two or more chemical salts in a solution. For example, AgCl and NaCl have a common ion of Cl^-.

ˌcommon ˈion efˌfect *n.* [singular] CHEMISTRY the decrease in a salt's ability to DISSOLVE in a liquid when another salt with a common ion is added

ˌcommon ˈlaw *n.* [U] LAW the system of laws that are based on past decisions by courts of law

ˈcommon-law *adj.* [only before noun] **1 a common-law marriage/husband/wife** a relationship that is considered in law to be a marriage because the man and woman have lived together for a long time **2** LAW relating to or based on rules of law that developed over time through court decisions: *the common-law principle that protects your conversations with your lawyer*

ˌcommon ˈlogarithm *n.* [C] MATH a LOGARITHM which has ten as its base number (=ten must be multiplied by itself a specific number of times to equal another number)

com·mon·ly /ˈkɑmənli/ *adv.* **1** usually or by most people SYN **widely** SYN **usually**: *Sodium chloride is more **commonly known** as salt.* | *Durum wheat is commonly used for making pasta.* **2** often, in many places, or in large numbers SYN **widely** SYN **frequently**: *some commonly asked questions* | *This bird is commonly found in Malaysia.*

ˌcommon ˈnoun *n.* [C] ENG. LANG. ARTS any noun that is not the name of a particular person, place, or thing, for example "book" or "sugar" → see also PROPER NOUN → see also NOUN

com·mon·place¹ /ˈkɑmənˌpleɪs/ *adj.* happening or existing in many places, and therefore not special or unusual: *Equipment failures are commonplace.*

commonplace² *n.* **1** [C usually singular] something that happens or exists often or in many places, so that it is not considered unusual: *One-parent families are now a commonplace in our society.* **2** [C] something that has been said so often that it is no longer interesting or original SYN **cliché**

ˌcommon ˈratio *n.* [C] MATH in a GEOMETRIC SEQUENCE (=series of related numbers), the RATIO between each number and the number that follows it. For example, the common ratio between the series of numbers 3, 6, 12, 24, and 48 is 2 because you multiply each number by 2 to get the next number in the sequence

common ref·er·ent /ˌkɑmən ˈrɛfərənt, -rɪˈfɚənt/ *n.* [C] MATH any object or thing that can be used as an example of a particular measurement, for example the length of a football field as an example of what 100 yards looks like

ˌcommon ˈsense *n.* [U] the ability to behave in a sensible way and make practical decisions: ***Use your common sense** when deciding when children should go to bed.* —**common-sense** *adj.*: *a common-sense solution*

ˌcommon ˈstock *n* [C,U] ECONOMICS the most commonly sold type of STOCK, on which a DIVIDEND (=share of the profits in the company) is paid only after it has been paid on other types of stock, or which may not pay be paid at all if the company is doing badly → see also PREFERRED STOCK

com·mon·wealth /ˈkɑmənˌwɛlθ/ *n.* [C] **1** the official legal title of some U.S. states: *the Commonwealth of Massachusetts* **2** POLITICS a group of countries that are related politically or economically: *the Commonwealth of Independent States* **3** POLITICS an organization of about 50 countries that were once part of the British EMPIRE **4** POLITICS the official legal title of some places that are governed by the U.S. but are not states, such as Puerto Rico

ˌCommonwealth of ˈNations, the a social and economic ASSOCIATION (=type of organization) of countries that used to be part of the British Empire SYN **Commonwealth**

com·mo·tion /kəˈmoʊʃən/ *n.* [singular, U] sudden noisy activity or arguing: *I heard a commotion outside.* | *Everyone looked to see what was **causing the commotion**.* [**Origin:** 1300–1400 Old French, Latin *commotio*, from *commovere* **to move violently**]

com·mu·nal /kəˈmyunl/ *adj.* **1** shared by a group, especially a group of people who live together: *a communal bathroom* **2** relating or belonging to all the people in a particular community: *The pasture is located on communal land.* **3** relating to a commune: *children who are raised in communal situations* **4** involving people from different races, religions, or language groups: *outbreaks of communal violence*

com·mune¹ /ˈkɑmyun/ *n.* [C] **1** a group of people who live together and who share the work and their possessions: *a religious commune* **2** a group of people in a Communist country who work as a team, especially on a farm, and give what they produce to the government

com·mune² /kəˈmyun/ *v.*

commune with sb/sth *phr. v.* **1 commune with nature/the ocean etc.** to spend time outside in a natural place, enjoying it in a quiet, peaceful way **2** to communicate with a person, god, or animal, without using words, in a mysterious, SPIRITUAL way: *She claims to commune with the spirits of the dead.*

3 FORMAL to try to communicate your thoughts and feelings to someone: *It's a place where you feel free to commune with other women.*

com·mu·ni·ca·ble /kə'myunɪkəbəl/ Ac *adj.* **1** a communicable sickness can be passed on to other people SYN **contagious**: *AIDS is not communicable by food or drink.* | *Measles is a dangerous **communicable disease**.* **2** FORMAL able to be communicated: *Her ideas were not easily communicable.*

com·mu·ni·cant /kə'myunɪkənt/ *n.* [C] **1** someone who receives COMMUNION regularly in the Christian church **2** TECHNICAL someone who is communicating with someone else

com·mu·ni·cate /kə'myunə,keɪt/ Ac S3 W3 *v.*
1 EXCHANGE INFORMATION [I,T] to exchange information or conversation with other people, using words, signs, letters etc.: *We mostly communicate by email.* | **+with** *They communicate with each other using sign language.* | **communicate sth to sb** *We established a policy and communicated it to everyone involved.*
2 EXPRESS [T] to express your thoughts and feelings clearly, so that other people understand them: *A baby communicates its needs by crying.* | *A doctor's ability to **communicate effectively** is very important.* | **communicate sth to sb** *Without meaning to, she communicated her anxiety to her son.*
3 UNDERSTAND [I] if two people communicate, they are able to talk about and understand each other's thoughts and feelings: *Jack and I just aren't communicating anymore.* | **+with** *Parents sometimes find it difficult to communicate with their teenage children.*
4 DISEASE [T usually passive] MEDICINE to pass a disease from one person or animal to another: *Doctors are doing research into how the virus is communicated.*
[**Origin:** 1500–1600 Latin, past participle of *communicare* **to give information, take part**, from *communis*]

com·mu·ni·ca·tion /kə,myunə'keɪʃən/ Ac S2 W2 *n.* **1** [U] the process of speaking, writing etc., by which people exchange information: *Good communication is vital in a large organization.* | **+between** *regular communication between workers and management* | *Radio was the pilot's only **means of communication**.* **2** [U] the way people express their thoughts and feelings or share information: *a workshop called "Better Communication for Couples"* | *Some autistic children have limited **communication skills*** (=ways of expressing themselves clearly). **3 communications a)** [plural] ways of sending information, such as using radio, telephone, or computers: *Modern communications allow more people to work from home.* **b)** [U] the study of using radio, television, and movies to communicate: *a degree in communications* **c)** [U] the process of providing information about a company or other organization: *the office of corporate communications* **4** [C] FORMAL a letter, message, or telephone call: *a communication from the IRS* **5 be in communication with sb** FORMAL to talk or write to someone regularly **6** [C,U] BIOLOGY the process in which information is passed from one living creature, cell, or MOLECULE to another, for example through behavior or chemical signals: *prey to predator communication such as warning coloration*

com,muni'cations ,satellite *n.* [C] a SATELLITE that is used to send radio, television, and telephone signals around the world

com·mu·ni·ca·tive /kə'myunɪkəṭɪv, -,keɪṭɪv/ Ac *adj.* **1** willing or able to talk or give information: *Managers need to be communicative and flexible.* **2** relating to the ability to communicate, especially in a foreign language: *students' communicative skills*

com·mun·ion /kə'myunyən/ *n.* **1 Communion** also **Holy Communion** [U] the Christian ceremony in which people eat a small piece of bread and drink a small amount of wine as signs of Jesus Christ's body and blood: *She went to the church service, but didn't **take Communion**.* **2** [U] FORMAL a special relationship with someone or something which makes you feel that you understand them very well: **+between/with** *In the mountains, I feel in communion with nature.* **3** [C] FORMAL a group of people or organizations that share the same religious beliefs SYN **denomination**: *He belongs to the Anglican communion.*

com·mu·ni·qué /kə'myunə,keɪ, -,myunə'keɪ/ *n.* [C] an official report or announcement: *A military communiqué reported six soldiers killed.*

com·mu·nism, Communism /'kɑmyə,nɪzəm/ *n.* [U] **1** POLITICS a political system in which the government controls the production of all food and goods, and there is no privately owned property **2** the belief in this political system → see also CAPITALISM

com·mu·nist[1] /'kɑmyənɪst/ *n.* [C] **1** POLITICS someone who is a member of a political party that supports communism or who believes in communism → see also CAPITALIST **2** SPOKEN an insulting word for someone who expresses ideas that do not support traditional American beliefs, especially CAPITALISM

communist[2] W2, **Communist** *adj.* POLITICS relating to communism: *Communist countries* | *a communist regime*

,Communist 'bloc *n.* [singular] the group of countries, mostly in Eastern Europe, that had Communist governments and were controlled by the Soviet Union

com·mu·ni·ty /kə'myunəṭi/ Ac S2 W1 *n. plural* **communities**
1 PEOPLE [C] the people who live in the same area, town etc.: *An arts center will benefit the whole community.* | *Community leaders met to discuss the proposed golf course.* | *Part of her job is **community relations*** (=talking to people in the community to try and get them to cooperate).
2 TOWN [C] a town, area etc. that a group of people live in: *Borrego Springs is a desert community south of Los Angeles.* → see also **bedroom community/suburb** at BEDROOM[2]
3 PARTICULAR GROUP [C] a group of people who have the same interests, religion, race etc.: *Miami has a large Cuban exile community.* | *voters in **minority communities*** | **the gay/black/Hispanic etc. community** | **the business/academic/scientific etc. community** *The issue has divided the medical community.*
4 the community society and the people in it: *The police department wants to get officers out into the community.* | ***The international community*** (=all the countries of the world) *has responded generously to the disaster.*
5 sense of community the feeling that you belong to a particular community because people work together to help each other and improve the community
6 PLANTS/ANIMALS [C] BIOLOGY a group of ORGANISMS of different types that live together in the same place
[**Origin:** 1300–1400 Old French *comuneté*, from Latin *communitas*, from *communis*]

com'munity ,center *n.* [C] a place where people from the same area can go for social events, classes etc.

com'munity ,chest *n.* [C] OLD-FASHIONED money that is collected by the people and businesses in an area to help poor people

com'munity ,college *n.* [C] a college that people can go to, usually for two years, in order to learn a skill or to prepare to go to another college or university SYN **junior college**

com'munity ,property *n.* [U] LAW property that is considered to be owned equally by both a husband and wife

com,munity 'service *n.* [U] work that someone does to help other people without being paid, especially as punishment for a crime

com·mu·ta·tion /,kɑmyə'teɪʃən/ *n.* **1** [C,U] LAW a reduction in how severe a punishment is **2** [U] FORMAL the act of commuting: *The bridge is a major commutation route.*

com·mu·ta·tive /kə'myuṭəṭɪv, 'kɑmyə,teɪṭɪv/ *adj.* MATH a mathematical operation that is commutative can be done in any order

com·mute[1] /kə'myut/ *v.* **1** [I] to regularly travel a

C

long distance to get to work: +**to/from/between** *Jim commutes from Weehawken to Manhattan every day.* **2** [T] to change the punishment given to a criminal to one that is less severe: *His 20-year* ***sentence was*** *later* ***commuted to*** *three years.* [**Origin:** 1400–1500 Latin *commutare* **to exchange, change**]

commute² *n.* [C usually singular] the trip made to work and back every day: *My* ***morning commute*** *takes 45 minutes.* | *Traffic caused his commute time to double.* | +**to/from** *a long commute to work* ►see THESAURUS box at **trip¹**

C

com·mut·er /kəˈmyuṭɚ/ *n.* [C] someone who travels a long distance to work every day

Com·o·ros /ˈkɑməˌroʊs/ a country consisting of several islands in the Indian Ocean, east of Mozambique —**Comoran** *n., adj.*

comp¹ /kɑmp/ *n.* [C] **1** INFORMAL a ticket for a play, sports game etc. that is given away free **2** SPOKEN a short way of saying COMPENSATION → see also COMP TIME, WORKERS' COMPENSATION

comp² *v.* [T] SPOKEN to give someone something such as a ticket free: *We comped tickets for some of the volunteers.*

com·pact¹ /ˈkɑmpækt, kəmˈpækt/ *adj.* **1** small, but arranged so that everything fits neatly into the available space: *The dormitory rooms are very compact, with a desk, bed, and closet built in.* | *a compact car* **2** packed or put together firmly and closely: *a small bush with a compact shape* **3** small but solid and strong: *a short, compact-looking man* **4** expressing things clearly in only a few words [**Origin:** 1300–1400 Latin *compactus*, past participle of *compingere* **to put together**] —**compactly** *adv.* —**compactness** *n.* [U]

com·pact² /ˈkɑmpækt/ *n.* [C] **1** a small car: *a two-door compact* ►see THESAURUS box at **car** **2** a small flat container with a mirror, containing powder for a woman's face **3** LAW an agreement between two or more people, countries etc. with laws or rules that they must obey: *The state and Indian tribes signed a compact to restrict the building of new casinos.* → see also MAYFLOWER COMPACT

com·pact³ /kəmˈpækt/ *v.* [T] to press something together, so that it becomes smaller or more solid: *The dirt trail has been compacted from years of use.* —**compacted** *adj.*

compact disc /ˌkɑmpækt ˈdɪsk/ *n.* [C] a CD

com·pac·tor /kəmˈpæktɚ/ *n.* [C] a machine that presses something together, so that it becomes smaller or more solid: **a trash/garbage compactor**

com·pa·dre /kəmˈpɑdreɪ/ *n.* [C] INFORMAL a friend, or someone you spend a lot of time with

com·pan·ion /kəmˈpænyən/ *n.* [C] **1** someone you spend a lot of time with, especially a friend: *McCarthy came in first, followed by his three companions.* | *Sandy's doll is her* ***constant companion*** (=the doll is always with her). | *My* ***traveling companion*** *was asleep.* | **a lunch/dinner/dining companion** *an interesting dinner companion* **2** one of a pair of things that go together or can be used together: +**to** *The book is a companion to the TV series that aired last month.* | **companion volume/study/piece etc.** *a companion volume to "Traveling in Mexico"* **3** used in the title of books that explain something about a particular subject: *the Fisherman's Companion* **4** someone, especially a woman, who is paid to live or travel with an older person [**Origin:** 1200–1300 Old French *compagnon*, from Late Latin *companio*, from Latin *com-* + *panis* **bread, food**]

com·pan·ion·a·ble /kəmˈpænyənəbəl/ *adj.* nice and friendly: *They sat in companionable silence.* —**companionably** *adv.*

com·pan·ion·ship /kəmˈpænyənˌʃɪp/ *n.* [U] a friendly relationship in which you spend a lot of time with someone and talk, enjoy yourselves together etc.: *Older people often keep a dog for companionship and security.*

com·pa·ny /ˈkʌmpəni/ S1 W1 *n. plural* **companies**
1 BUSINESS [C] an organization that makes or sells goods or services SYN **business** SYN **firm**: *What company do you work for?* | *It's not company policy to exchange goods without a receipt.* | **the phone/electric/water etc. company** *I called the cable company about the bill.* | *She* ***started*** *her own media* ***company*** *last year.* | *Steve* ***joined the company*** (=became an employee) *straight out of high school.* | *Hutton* ***runs*** *his own* ***company***. → see also PUBLIC COMPANY

THESAURUS

firm a company that usually provides a service rather than producing goods: *a law firm*
business a company that often employs only a small number of people: *She set up her own catering business.* | *small businesses*
corporation a large company that often includes several smaller companies
multinational a very large company with offices in many different countries
subsidiary a company that is owned by a larger company

2 OTHER PEOPLE [U] the state of being with someone, so that you have someone to talk to or do not feel lonely: *Come over for dinner – I* ***could use the company*** (=I would like to be with people). | *Rita's husband is away, so I thought I'd go over and* ***keep*** *her* ***company***. | *Owen* ***is good company*** (=he is fun to talk to). | *Bessie was glad to have the dog* ***as company***. | ***I wasn't much company*** *for Aunt Margaret tonight* (=I did not feel like talking).
3 GROUP [U] a group of people who are together in the same place, often for a particular purpose or for social reasons: *Children need to learn how to behave* ***in company*** (=with other people). | *Some jokes are just not appropriate to tell* ***in mixed company*** (=in a group of both men and women). | *Catherine traveled there* ***in the company of*** *her two nieces and their mother.*
4 GUESTS [U] people who are visiting you in your home SYN **guests**: *It looks like the Hammills* ***have company***. | *We're* ***expecting company*** *tonight.*
5 FRIENDS [U] the group of people that you are friends with or spend time with: *People do tend to judge you by* ***the company you keep*** (=your friends). | *He's basically a nice guy who fell into some* ***bad company*** (=people who do things you disapprove of, especially illegal things).
6 PERFORMERS [C] ENG. LANG. ARTS a group of actors, dancers, or singers who work together: *the Kirov Ballet company* | *a* ***theater company***
7 be in good company used to tell someone who has made a mistake that they should not be embarrassed, because other people have made the same mistake: *If you can't program your VCR, you're in good company.*
8 sb and company INFORMAL used after a person's name to mean that person and their friends: *a magazine launched by Andy Warhol and company years ago*
9 ARMY [C] a group of about 120 soldiers, who are usually part of a larger group
10 two's company, three's a crowd INFORMAL used to suggest that two people would rather be alone together than have other people with them
11 in company with sth FORMAL if something happens in company with something else, both things happen at the same time: *Democracy progressed in company with the emancipation of women.*
[**Origin:** 1200–1300 Old French *compagnie*, from *compain* **companion**, from Late Latin *companio*] → see also **part company** at PART² (5), **present company excepted** at PRESENT¹ (5)

ˌcompany ˈcar *n.* [C] a car that your employer gives you to use while you work for them

ˈcompany town *n.* [C] a town or city whose ECONOMY is dependent on one particular company or factory, because a large number of its people work there

ˌcompany ˈunion *n.* [C] POLITICS a LABOR UNION made up of workers from one company and usually controlled by the people who are in charge of a company, not by elected representatives of the workers

com·pa·ra·ble /ˈkɑmpərəbəl/ *adj.* **1** similar to something else in size, number, quality etc., so that you can make a comparison: *Prices of comparable homes in New York State are much higher.* | **+with/to** *Is the pay rate comparable to that of other companies?* | *The planet Pluto is* ***comparable in size*** *to the moon.* **2** being equally important, good, bad etc.: **+with/to** *His poetry is hardly comparable with Shakespeare's.* —**comparability** /ˌkɑmpərəˈbɪləṭi/ *n.* [U]

com·pa·ra·bly /ˈkɑmpərəbli/ *adv.* in a similar way or to a similar degree: *comparably priced computers*

com·par·a·tive¹ /kəmˈpærəṭɪv/ *adj.* **1** when something or someone is measured or judged against something or someone else, or against what the situation was before SYN **relative**: *After a lifetime of poverty, his last few years were spent in comparative comfort.* | *a period of comparative calm* | *We've lived here five years, but we're still comparative newcomers.* **2 comparative study/analysis etc.** a study etc. that involves comparing something to something else that is similar: *The agent prepared a comparative market analysis.* **3** similar and able to be used when comparing things: *Comparative figures for last year were not available.* **4** ENG. LANG. ARTS the comparative form of an adjective or adverb shows an increase in size, quality, degree etc. For example, "bigger" is the comparative form of "big," and "more comfortable" is the comparative form of "comfortable." → see also SUPERLATIVE

comparative² *n.* **the comparative** ENG. LANG. ARTS the form of an adjective or adverb that shows an increase in size, quality, degree etc. For example, "bigger" is the comparative of "big," and "more comfortable" is the comparative of "comfortable."

comˌparative adˈvantage *n.* [C] ECONOMICS an advantage that one company or country has over another because it is better at making a particular product → see also ABSOLUTE ADVANTAGE

comˌparative ˈliterature *n.* [U] the study of literature from more than one country, which involves making comparisons between the writing from different countries

com·par·a·tive·ly /kəmˈpærəṭɪvli/ *adv.* as compared to something else or to a previous state SYN **relatively**: *The kids were comparatively well-behaved today.* | **comparatively small/low/few/high etc.** *the area's comparatively small population* | ***Comparatively speaking****, this part of the coast is still unspoiled.*

com·pare¹ /kəmˈpɛr/ S2 W1 *v.* **1** [T] to examine or judge two or more things in order to show how they are similar to or different from each other: *The report compares different types of home computers.* | **compare sth to/with sth** *The police compared the suspect's fingerprints with those found at the crime scene.* | ***Compare and contrast*** (=describe the similarities and differences of) *the main characters of these two novels.* **2 compared to/with sth** used when considering the size, quality, or amount of something in relation to something similar: *Compared to Los Angeles, Santa Barbara almost seems rural.* | *a 20% reduction in burglary compared with last year* **3** [T] to say that something or someone is like someone or something else, or that it is equally good, large etc.: **compare sb/sth to sb/sth** *Davies' writing style has been compared to Dickens'.* | **compare sb/sth with sb/sth** *Teachers are always comparing her with her brother.* | **sth doesn't/can't compare with sth** *It just can't compare with Disneyland* (=it is not as good as Disneyland). | *The imported fabric is 30% cheaper and* ***compares favorably*** (=is as good) *in quality.* **4 compare notes (with sb)** INFORMAL to talk to someone in order to find out if their experience of something is the same as yours: *The New Moms group allows us to compare notes.* [**Origin:** 1400–1500 French *comparer*, from Latin *comparare*, from *compar* **like**, from *com-* + *par* **equal**]

compare² *n.* **beyond/without compare** LITERARY a quality that is beyond compare is the best of its kind: *a beauty beyond compare*

com·par·i·son /kəmˈpærəsən/ W3 *n.*
1 COMPARING [U] the process of comparing two or more people or things: **+with** *Comparison with the director's earlier movies seems inevitable.* | **in comparison to/with** *In comparison to other games, this one is boring.* | *After living on the farm, town life seemed hectic* ***by comparison****.* | *The sales figures for 1996 were not available* ***for comparison*** (=for the purposes of comparing them). | *Her paintings* ***invite comparison with*** *those of the early Impressionists* (=they remind you of them). | *Irving's work* ***bears comparison*** *with the best of the modern writers.*
2 JUDGMENT [C] a statement or examination of how similar or different two people, places, things etc. are: **+of** *a comparison of smog levels in various cities* | **+between** *The article* ***makes a comparison*** *between the two novels.*
3 BE LIKE STH [C] a statement that someone or something is like someone or something else: **+to** *The comparison of the mall to a zoo seemed appropriate.* | **+between** *You can't* ***make a comparison*** *between American and Japanese schools – they're too different.* | *The writer* ***draws comparisons*** (=shows the similarities of) *between the two presidents.*
4 there's no comparison SPOKEN used when you think that someone or something is much better than someone or something else: **+between** *There's just no comparison between canned vegetables and fresh ones.*
5 GRAMMAR [U] ENG. LANG. ARTS a word used in grammar meaning the way an adverb or adjective changes its form to show whether it is COMPARATIVE or SUPERLATIVE

comˌparison and ˈcontrast *n.* [U] ENG. LANG. ARTS a way of organizing a piece of writing in which you describe the ways in which two or more things are similar and the ways in which they are different

comˈparison-ˌshop *v.* [I] to go to different stores in order to compare the prices of things, so that you can buy things for the cheapest possible price —**comparison shopping** *n.* [U]

com·part·ment /kəmˈpɑrt¬mənt/ *n.* [C] **1** a smaller enclosed space inside something larger: *the plane's baggage compartment* **2** one of the separate areas into which some trains are divided [**Origin:** 1500–1600 French *compartiment*, from Italian, from *compartire* **to mark out into parts**] → see also GLOVE COMPARTMENT

com·part·men·tal·ize /kəmˌpɑrt¬ˈmɛntl̩ˌaɪz/ *v.* [T] to divide something into separate parts or to divide things into separate groups, especially according to what type of things they are: *The brain does not neatly compartmentalize the areas used for language.* —**compartmentalized** *adj.* —**compartmentalization** /kəmˌpɑrt¬mɛntl̩-əˈzeɪʃən/ *n.* [U]

com·pass /ˈkʌmpəs/ *n.* **1** [C] an instrument that shows directions and has a needle that always points north: *a map and compass* **2** [C] MATH a V-shaped instrument with one sharp point and a pen or pencil at the other end, used for drawing circles and ARCS (=parts of circles), and for measuring distances on maps **3** [U] FORMAL the area or range of subjects that someone is responsible for or that is discussed in a book: **+of** *Within the brief compass of a single page, the author covers most of the major points.* [**Origin:** 1300–1400 Old French *compas* **measure, circle, compass**, from *compasser* **to measure**]

com·pas·sion /kəmˈpæʃən/ *n.* [U] a strong feeling of sympathy for people who are suffering, and a desire to help them SYN **sympathy**: **+for** *compassion for the sick* | **show/have/feel compassion** *The government needs to show more compassion for the poor.* | *Lieberman explores this sensitive topic* ***with compassion****.* [**Origin:** 1300–1400 Old French, Late Latin *compassio*, from *compati* **to feel sympathy**]

com·pas·sion·ate /kəmˈpæʃənɪt/ *adj.* feeling sympathy for people who are suffering SYN **sympathetic**: *a caring, compassionate man* —**compassionately** *adv.*

comˌpassionate ˈleave *n.* [U] special permission to have time away from work because one of your relatives has died or is very sick

ˈcompass ˌrose *n.* [C] a drawing that looks like a COMPASS, printed on a map and showing the directions north, south, east, and west etc.

compass rose

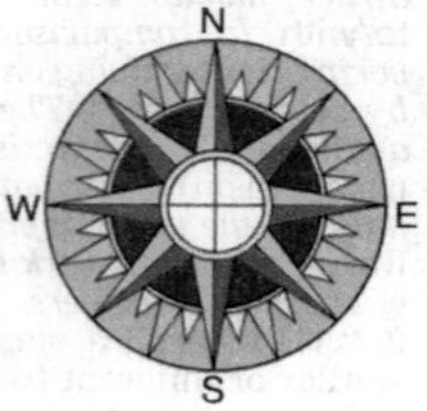

com·pat·i·bil·i·ty /kəmˌpæt̬əˈbɪlət̬i/ Ac *n.* [U] **1** the ability of one piece of computer equipment to be used with another one, especially when they are made by different companies **2** the ability to exist or be used together without causing problems **3** the ability to have a good relationship with someone, because you have similar interests, ideas etc.

com·pat·i·ble¹ /kəmˈpæt̬əbəl/ Ac *adj.* **1** if two pieces of computer equipment or software are compatible, they can be used together, even when they are made by different companies: *Windows® compatible products* **2** able to exist or be used together without causing problems: **+with** *The project is not compatible with the company's long-term aims.* **3** two people that are compatible are able to have a good relationship, because they have similar interests, ideas etc. [**Origin:** 1500–1600 French, Medieval Latin *compatibilis*, from Late Latin *compati* **to feel sympathy**]

compatible² Ac *n.* [C] a piece of computer equipment that can be used with another piece, especially one made by a different company

comˌpatible ˈnumber *n.* [C] MATH a number that is used in a calculation instead of a more exact value because it is easier to use and will give a result that is nearly correct. For example, to calculate 409 ÷ 79, you might use the compatible numbers 400 and 80, to easily get the result 5, which is close to the actual value 5.18.

com·pa·tri·ot /kəmˈpeɪtriət/ *n.* [C] **sb's compatriot** someone who was born in or is a citizen of the same country as someone else

com·pel /kəmˈpɛl/ *v.* **compelled**, **compelling** [T] **1** to force someone to do something: **compel sb to do sth** *The law will compel employers to provide health insurance.* | *Harris **felt compelled to** resign.* ▶see THESAURUS box at **force²** **2** FORMAL to make people have a particular feeling or attitude: *His performance **compels attention**.* → see also IMPEL

com·pel·ling /kəmˈpɛlɪŋ/ *adj.* **1** so interesting or exciting that you have to pay attention: *a compelling story* ▶see THESAURUS box at **interesting** **2 a compelling argument/reason/case etc.** an argument, reason etc. that makes you feel it is true or that you must do something about it: *Garcia presented a compelling case to the court.* **3 a compelling need/urge/desire etc.** a strong feeling that you need to do something: *Suddenly I had a compelling urge to see him.* —**compellingly** *adv.*

com·pen·di·um /kəmˈpɛndiəm/ *n. plural* **compendiums** or **compendia** /-diə/ [C] FORMAL a book that contains a complete collection of facts, drawings etc. on a particular subject: *a compendium of 19th century photographs*

com·pen·sate /ˈkɑmpənˌseɪt/ Ac *v.* **1** [I] to reduce or balance the bad effect of something: **+for** *Her intelligence compensates for her lack of experience.* **2** [I,T] to pay someone money because they have suffered injury, loss, or damage: *The fund will compensate victims of smoking-related diseases.* | **compensate sb for sth** *The firm was ordered to compensate clients for their losses.* [**Origin:** 1600–1700 Latin, past participle of *compensare*, from *compendere* **to weigh together**]

com·pen·sa·tion /ˌkɑmpənˈseɪʃən/ Ac *n.* **1** [U] money paid to someone because they have suffered injury or loss, or because something they own was damaged: **+for** *The fishermen have demanded compensation for the damage.* | *The jury awarded Tyler $1.7 million **in compensation**.* | *The parents are **seeking compensation** for the birth defects caused by the drug.* | *People who are wrongly arrested may be **paid compensation**.* | *The court **awarded** Jamieson $30,000 **compensation**.* **2** [C,U] something that makes a bad situation better: **+of** *One of the few compensations of losing my job was seeing more of my family.* **3** [U] the money someone is paid to do their job: *Board members will receive compensation in the form of stock options, as well as a salary.* | *a compensation package worth $16 million* **4** [singular, U] actions, behavior etc. that replace or balance something that is lacking or bad: **+for** *For some people, overeating can be a compensation for stress.*

com·pen·sa·to·ry /kəmˈpɛnsəˌtɔri/ Ac *adj.* [usually before noun] **1** compensatory payments are paid to someone who has been harmed or hurt in some way: *The Court awarded Mitchell $650,000 in **compensatory damages**.* **2** intended to reduce the bad effects of something: *Officers can earn compensatory time off.* **3** compensatory education is for children from poor backgrounds

comˌpensatory ˈnumber *n.* [C] MATH a number that is used to make a correction to a calculation that uses COMPATIBLE NUMBERS

com·pete /kəmˈpit/ S3 W2 *v.* [I]
1 BUSINESS to try to be more successful and sell more than another business: *The company has to compete in the international marketplace.* | **+with/against** *Fruit juice drinks do not compete directly with alcoholic drinks.* | **+for** *The downtown stores compete for customers during the Christmas season.* | **compete to do sth** *Several advertising agencies are competing to get the contract.* | *Small, independent bookstores simply **can't compete** (=are unable to be more successful) with the big national chains.*
2 PERSON to try to gain something, or to be better or more successful than someone else: **+for** *Sarah and Hannah are always competing for attention.* | **+against/with** *I had to compete against 19 other people for the job.* | *Melinda knew she **couldn't compete** (=couldn't be as successful) with her sister when it came to boys.*
3 IN A COMPETITION to take part in a competition or sports event: **+in/at** *How many runners are competing in the Boston Marathon?* | **+against** *Hodge will be competing against some of the world's best swimmers.* | **+for** *Blair is competing for the starting quarterback position.*
4 SOUND/SMELL if a sound or smell competes with another sound or smell, you can hear or smell both at the same time: **+with** *The songs of the birds competed with the sound of the church bells.*
[**Origin:** 1600–1700 Late Latin *competere* **to try (with others) to get**, from Latin, **to come together, agree, be suitable**]

com·pe·tence /ˈkɑmpət̬əns/ also **com·pe·ten·cy** /-pət̬ənsi/ *n.* **1** [U] the ability and skill to do what is needed OPP **incompetence**: *Players are judged by their competence on the field.* **2** [U] LAW normal mental abilities: *The judge questioned her **mental competence**.* **3** [U] LAW the legal power of a court of law to hear and judge something in court, or of a government to do something: *In the U.S., many legal issues are **within the competence of** the states rather than the federal government.* **4** [U] a special area of knowledge: *It is not **within my competence** to make such judgments.* **5** [C] FORMAL a skill needed to do a particular job: *Typing is considered by most employers to be a basic competence.*

com·pe·tent /ˈkɑmpət̬ənt/ *adj.* **1** having enough skill or knowledge to do something to a satisfactory standard OPP **incompetent**: *A competent mechanic should be able to fix the problem quickly.* | **competent to do sth** *I don't feel competent to answer that question.* | **+in** *New students are expected to be competent in math.* | *a **highly competent** surgeon* **2** satisfactory, but not especially good: *His work is competent, but not outstanding.* **3** LAW having normal mental abilities: *We believe the patient was not mentally competent.* | *A psychiatrist said McKibben was **competent to stand trial**.* **4** [not before noun] LAW having the legal power to deal with something in a court of law: **be competent to do sth** *This court is not competent to hear your case.*

[**Origin:** 1300–1400 Old French, Latin, present participle of *competere* **to be suitable**] —**competently** *adv.*

com·pet·ing /kəm'piṭɪŋ/ *adj.* [only before noun] **1 competing claims/ideas/interests etc.** two or more claims, ideas etc. that cannont all be right or accepted at the same time: *Several people gave competing accounts of the accident.* **2** competing companies or products are all trying to be more successful than each other: *competing soft drink brands*

com·pe·ti·tion /ˌkɑmpə'tɪʃən/ S3 W2 *n.* **1** [U] a situation in which people or organizations compete with each other: **+between/among** *competition between brothers* | *Competition among suppliers has brought the price down.* | **+for** *Competition for the job was intense.* | **stiff/intense/fierce etc. competition** *There is stiff competition among the three leading soap manufacturers.* | *Bookstores are **facing** increasingly fierce **competition** from online book sellers.* | **+in** *competition in the automobile industry* **2** [U] the people or groups that are competing against you, especially in business or in a sport: *What makes your company different from **the competition**?* | *Lewis is bound to win the race – there's just **no competition*** (=no one who is likely to be better). | *Farmers say they are being hurt by **foreign competition*** (=competition from companies in foreign countries). **3** [C] an organized event in which people or teams compete against each other: *a photography competition* | **a competition to do sth** *a competition to find a designer for the new airport* | *Who **won the competition** last year?* | *Teams from all over the state have **entered the competition**.* | *The **competition** will be **held** in Copenhagen next year.*

THESAURUS

championship a competition to find the best player or team in a particular sport: *The high school football team won the championship.*
tournament a competition in which many players or teams compete against each other until there is one winner: *a local volleyball tournament at Sunset Park*
contest a competition in which a judge or group of judges decides the winner: *Her recipe for chocolate cookies won first prize in the contest!*
playoff a game or series of games played by the best teams or players in a sports competition, in order to decide the final winner: *The Yankees make the playoffs nearly every year.* | *a playoff game against the Knicks*
round one of the parts of a competition that you have to finish or win before you can go on to the next part: *the first round of the contest*
heat one of a number of races or competitions whose winners then compete against each other: *Two of the runners in this race will go on to the next heat.*

com·pet·i·tive /kəm'pɛṭəṭɪv/ W3 *adj.* **1** able to be more successful than other people or businesses: *Some U.S. industries are not as competitive as they have been in the past.* | *The merger will give the company a **competitive edge*** (=a better ability to compete) *in the market.* **2** a competitive market or industry has a lot of businesses that are all trying hard to be more successful than the others: **highly/fiercely/intensely etc. competitive** *The market for airline companies is highly competitive.* **3** [only before noun] competitive sports involve teams or players competing against each other: *Competitive sports encourage children to work together as a team.* **4** competitive prices, salaries etc. are as good as or slightly better than prices or salaries in other stores or companies: *Long distance phone companies offer very competitive rates.* ►see THESAURUS box at **cheap**[1] **5** someone who is competitive is determined to win or to be more successful than other people: *I hate playing tennis with Stephen – he's too competitive.* —**competitively** *adv.*

comˌpetitive exˈclusion ˌprinciple *n.* [singular] BIOLOGY a scientific idea which states that two SPECIES of animal or plant that need exactly the same type of food, environment etc. in order to live cannot exist together in the same place at the same time because one SPECIES will naturally be more successful than the other

com·pet·i·tive·ness /kəm'pɛṭəṭɪvnɪs/ *n.* [U] **1** the desire to be more successful than other people: *Laura's competitiveness has rubbed off on the rest of the sales team.* **2** the ability of a company or a product to compete with others: *increases in the company's productivity and competitiveness*

com·pet·i·tor /kəm'pɛṭəṭɚ/ W3 *n.* [C] **1** a person, company, or product that is competing for business with another: *Last year they sold twice as many computers as their competitors.* **2** someone who takes part in a competition: *Two of the competitors failed to show up for the race.*

com·pi·la·tion /ˌkɑmpə'leɪʃən/ Ac *n.* **1** [C] a book, list, record etc. that puts together many different pieces of information, songs etc.: *a compilation of love songs* **2** [U] the process of compiling something: *the compilation of financial data*

com·pile /kəm'paɪl/ Ac *v.* [T] **1** to make a book, list, record etc. using different pieces of information, music etc.: *It took months to compile the list.* | **compile sth from sth** *The report was compiled from a survey of 5,000 households.* **2** COMPUTERS to put a set of instructions into a computer in a form that you can understand and use [**Origin:** 1300–1400 Old French *compiler*, from Latin *compilare* **to seize together, steal**]

com·pil·er /kəm'paɪlɚ/ *n.* [C] **1** someone who collects different pieces of information or facts to be used in a book, report, or list **2** COMPUTERS a set of instructions in a computer that changes a computer language known to the computer user into the form needed by the computer

com·pla·cen·cy /kəm'pleɪsənsi/ also **com·pla·cence** /-'pleɪsəns/ *n.* [U] a feeling of satisfaction with a situation or with what you have achieved, so that you stop trying to improve or change things: *Doctors have warned against complacency in fighting common diseases.*

com·pla·cent /kəm'pleɪsənt/ *adj.* pleased with a situation, especially something you have achieved, so that you stop trying to improve or change things: *We've been winning, but we're not going to get complacent.* | **+about** *The nation cannot become complacent about the quality of our schools.* [**Origin:** 1600–1700 Latin, present participle of *complacere* **to please greatly**] —**complacently** *adv.*

com·plain /kəm'pleɪn/ S2 W2 *v.* **1** [I,T not in passive] to say that you are annoyed, not satisfied, or unhappy about something or someone: *Residents are complaining because traffic in the area has increased.* | **+about** *Eventually we called the police to complain about the noise.* | **+of** *Several women have complained of sexual harassment.* | **complain (that)** *He complained that he hadn't been paid.* | **complain to sb** *I complained to the landlord about the leak.* | *Some employees have **complained bitterly** about the layoffs.*

THESAURUS

make a complaint to formally complain about something to someone in authority: *Some parents had made a formal complaint about conditions at the school.*
protest to complain about something that you think is wrong, especially publicly: *I took part in demonstrations to protest against the war.*
object to say that you oppose or disapprove of something: *Several people objected to the religious statue being displayed in a public place.*
grumble to keep complaining in an unhappy or bad-tempered way: *He grumbled about the length of the line he had to wait in.*
→ PROTEST

2 (I) can't complain SPOKEN said when you think a situation is satisfactory, even though there may be a few problems: *"How's life?" "Can't complain."* [**Ori-**

gin: 1300–1400 Old French *complaindre*, from Vulgar Latin *complangere*]

complain of sth *phr. v.* FORMAL to say that you feel sick or have a pain in a part of your body: *She went to the hospital complaining of chest pains.*

com·plain·ant /kəm'pleɪnənt/ *n.* [C] LAW someone who makes a formal complaint in a court of law SYN **plaintiff**

C

com·plaint /kəm'pleɪnt/ S3 W2 *n.* **1** [C,U] a statement in which someone complains about something: *Complaints are dealt with by the customer services department.* | **+about** *complaints about the quality of his work* | **+against** *complaints against the car company* | **+from** *complaints from residents about the pigeons* | **complaint that** *There have been complaints that the department is inefficient.* | *Amy and her friends* ***made*** *several* ***complaints*** (=complained formally) *to the school administrators.* | **lodge/file/submit a complaint** *She went to the city council and lodged a formal complaint.* | *The commission received over 10,000* ***letters of complaint.*** | **a customer/consumer complaint** *a decrease in customer complaints* **2** [C] something that you complain about: *My only complaint is that the price was too high.* **3** [C] MEDICINE a sickness that affects a particular part of your body: *He is having treatment for a minor skin complaint.* **4** LAW a legal document that states that someone has caused harm or is guilty of a crime: *The defendants were charged Monday in a federal criminal complaint.*

com·plai·sance /kəm'pleɪsəns, -zəns/ *n.* [U] FORMAL willingness to do what pleases other people —**complaisant** *adj.* —**complaisantly** *adv.*

-complected /kəmplɛktɪd/ [in adjectives] **fair-complected/light-complected/dark-complected** having light or dark skin: *a dark-complected man*

com·ple·ment¹ /'kɑmpləmənt/ Ac *n.* [C] **1** someone or something that emphasizes the good qualities of another person or thing: **+to** *White wine makes an excellent complement to fish.* **2** the number or quantity needed to make a group complete: *The submarines are equipped with a* ***full complement of*** *24 missiles.* **3** ENG. LANG. ARTS in grammar, a word or phrase that follows a verb and describes the subject of the verb, or that follows a verb and makes a sentence complete, or that follows the object of a verb and describes it. In the sentence "You look angry," "angry" is the complement. In "I want to go," "to go" is the complement. In "They elected John chairman," "chairman" is the complement. **4** MATH an angle that together with another angle already mentioned makes 90° → see also COMPLIMENT

comp·le·ment² /'kɑmplə,mɛnt/ Ac *v.* [T] to emphasize the good qualities of another person or thing, especially by adding something that was needed: *Buy a scarf that complements your dress.* → see also COMPLIMENT

com·ple·men·ta·ry /,kɑmplə'mɛntri◂, -'mɛntəri◂/ Ac *adj.* **1** emphasizing the good qualities of someone or something, or adding qualities that the other person or thing lacks: *Bain and McCaskill have complementary skills – she is creative while he is highly organized.* **2** MATH two complementary angles combine to form an angle of 90° → see also SUPPLEMENTARY

,complementary 'color *n.* [C usually plural] **1** PHYSICS one of a pair of colored lights or colors which, when you mix them together, produce white light or a gray color **2** a color on the opposite side of the COLOR WHEEL from another color, which makes the other color seem brighter when it is next to it. Pairs of complementary colors are red and green, blue and orange, and yellow and purple.

com·plete¹ /kəm'plit/ S2 W2 *adj.* **1** including all parts, details, facts etc., with nothing missing OPP **incomplete**: *a complete set of china plates* | *The list below is not complete.* | *We gave Vicki* ***the complete works of*** *Plato* (=a book containing all of Plato's writings) *as a present.* ▸see THESAURUS box at **done²** **2** [only before noun, no comparative] INFORMAL a word meaning "in every way," used in order to emphasize what you are saying SYN **total**: *The meeting was a complete waste of time.* | *a complete stranger* | *The police were* ***in complete control*** *of the situation.* | *He showed a* ***complete lack of*** *interest in the job.* | *I made a* ***complete and utter*** *fool of myself.* **3** [not before noun] finished OPP **incomplete**: *Work on the new building is nearly complete.* **4 complete with sth** having equipment or features: *The house comes complete with swimming pool and sauna.* [**Origin:** 1300–1400 Old French *complet*, from Latin, past participle of *complere* **to fill up**] —**completeness** *n.* [U]

complete² S2 W2 *v.* [T] **1** to finish doing or making something, especially when it has taken a long time SYN **finish**: *The book took five years to complete.* | *The students have just completed their program.* **2** to make something whole or perfect by adding what is missing: *I need one more stamp to complete my collection.* | *Complete the following sentences.* **3** to write the information that is needed on a form SYN **fill out**: *More than 650 people completed the questionnaire.*

com·plet·ed /kəm'plit̬ɪd/ *adj.* containing all the necessary parts or answers needed to finish something: *Be sure to mail your completed tax form by April 15.* | **recently/newly completed** *a newly completed research study*

com·plete·ly /kəm'plitli/ S1 W2 *adv.* **1** in every way or to the greatest degree possible SYN **totally**: *The carpet is completely ruined.* | *I completely forgot that it was his birthday yesterday.* | *Muscle cells and fat cells are completely different kinds of tissue.* | *His knee is not completely healed.*

THESAURUS

absolutely used especially to emphasize something, or to show that you strongly agree with something: *I was absolutely exhausted.* | *He's absolutely right.*
totally used especially to show that you are annoyed about something or strongly disagree with something: *She totally ignored me.* | *It was totally impossible to work with all the noise.*
entirely used especially in negative sentences or after "almost": *I'm not entirely sure.* | *The city is almost entirely Republican.*
utterly FORMAL used to emphasize something, especially a negative quality: *The situation was utterly bewildering.*

2 if something is done completely, every part of it is done: *Cover the seeds completely with soil.*

com,plete meta'morphosis *n.* [U] BIOLOGY the process in which some insects, such as butterflies (BUTTERFLY) and BEETLES, change completely as they go through four different stages of their development, from egg to LARVA to PUPA and finally into fully grown adult

com,pleting the 'square *n.* [U] MATH a method for changing the form of a QUADRATIC EQUATION (=one that contains numbers or quantities multiplied by itself two times) so that it is easier to solve

com·ple·tion /kəm'pliʃən/ *n.* [U] **1** the state of being finished: *Repair work is scheduled for completion in August.* **2** the act of finishing something: **+of** *The vote will take place two days after the completion of the hearings.* | *Participants' criminal records are erased* ***upon completion of*** *the program* (=when they have completed the program).

com·plex¹ /kɑm'plɛks, kəm-, 'kɑmplɛks/ Ac W2 *adj.* **1** consisting of many different parts or details and often difficult to understand SYN **complicated** OPP **simple**: *a complex mathematical formula* | *a complex personality* | *A complex network of roads connects the two cities.* | *The issue is very complex.* **2** ENG. LANG. ARTS a complex word or sentence contains a main part and one or more other parts. For example, the word "disadvantaged" is a complex word. The sentence "The picnic was canceled because of the rain" is a complex sentence. [**Origin:** 1600–1700 Latin *complexus*, past participle of *complecti* **to include (many different things)**]

com·plex² /ˈkɑmplɛks/ Ac *n.* [C] **1** a group of buildings or one large building with many parts used for a particular purpose: *an apartment complex* | *a six-screen movie complex* **2** an emotional problem in which someone is too anxious about something or thinks too much about something: *Jack **has a complex about** being short.* → see also ELECTRA COMPLEX, INFERIORITY COMPLEX, OEDIPUS COMPLEX

com·plex con·ju·gate /kɑmˌplɛks ˈkɑndʒəgɪt/ also **ˌconjugate comˌplex ˈnumber** *n.* [C] MATH either of a pair of complex numbers that have the same REAL NUMBER parts but opposite IMAGINARY NUMBER parts. For example, a + bi is the complex conjugate of a – bi.

comˌplex ˈfraction *n.* [C] MATH a FRACTION (=number such as ½ or ⅓) in which either the number above the line or the number below the line is a fraction, or the numbers above and below the line are both fractions

com·plex·ion /kəmˈplɛkʃən/ *n.* **1** [C,U] the natural color or appearance of the skin on your face: *Too much sun is bad for your complexion.* | *Alice is lighter in complexion than her mother.* | **a dark/ruddy/pale etc. complexion** *She had a long oval face with an olive complexion.* **2 the complexion of sth** the general character or nature of something: *The recent elections changed the complexion of the state assembly.* → see also -COMPLECTED, -COMPLEXIONED

-complexioned /kəmplɛkʃənd/ [in adjectives] **light-complexioned/dark-complexioned etc.** having light or dark skin: *a chubby, dark-complexioned woman*

com·plex·i·ty /kəmˈplɛksət̬i/ Ac *n.* plural **complexities** **1** [U] the state or quality of being complicated and detailed: **+of** *Many people struggle with the complexity of the tax forms.* **2** [C usually plural] the details and problems that make something difficult to understand or deal with: *The article attempts to explain the affair's legal and political complexities.*

comˌplex ˈnumber *n.* [C] MATH any number that can be written in the form a + bi, where a and b are REAL NUMBERS and i is the SQUARE ROOT of –1 → see also IMAGINARY NUMBER

comˌplex ˈplane also **comˌplex ˈnumber ˌplane** *n.* [C] MATH a PLANE that is made up of complex numbers. For example, the REAL NUMBER part of the complex number can be shown along the HORIZONTAL (=line going across) AXIS and the IMAGINARY NUMBER part can be shown along the VERTICAL (=line going up) AXIS.

com·pli·ance /kəmˈplaɪəns/ *n.* [U] **1** the act or fact of obeying a rule, agreement, or law: **+with** *compliance with the law* | ***In compliance with** Mrs. Kornfeld's wishes, she was buried next to her husband.* **2** the tendency to agree too willingly to someone else's wishes or demands → see also COMPLY

com·pli·ant /kəmˈplaɪənt/ *adj.* **1** willing to obey or agree to other people's wishes and demands: *Some patients are more compliant than others in the hospital.* **2** made, used, or done according to particular rules or standards: *All waste treatment facilities must be **fully compliant with** federal regulations.* | *a standards-compliant Web browser* —**compliantly** *adv.* → see also COMPLY

com·pli·cate /ˈkɑmpləˌkeɪt/ *v.* [T] **1** to make something more difficult to understand or deal with, especially by adding details to it: *The continued fighting has complicated the peace negotiations.* | ***To complicate matters**, they keep changing the system.* **2** [usually passive] to make a sickness worse: *His heart condition was complicated by pneumonia.* [**Origin:** 1600–1700 Latin, past participle of *complicare*, from *com-* + *plicare* **to fold**]

com·pli·cat·ed /ˈkɑmpləˌkeɪt̬ɪd/ S2 W3 *adj.* **1** difficult to understand or deal with, because of the many details or parts involved SYN **complex** OPP **simple**: *The new law is complicated and confusing.* | *a complicated set of instructions* **2** consisting of many closely related or connected parts: *The human brain is an incredibly complicated organ.*

com·pli·ca·tion /ˌkɑmpləˈkeɪʃən/ *n.* **1** [C usually plural] MEDICINE an additional medical problem or sickness that happens while someone is already sick: *She died of complications following surgery.* **2** [C,U] a problem or situation that makes something more difficult to understand or deal with: *The lack of money added further complications to the situation.*

com·plic·i·ty /kəmˈplɪsət̬i/ *n.* [U] FORMAL **1** the act of being involved in a crime with other people: **+in** *He denied complicity in the murder.* **2** involvement in or knowledge of a situation, especially one that is morally wrong or dishonest: *She was ashamed of her complicity in the deception.* —**complicit** *adj.*

com·pli·ment¹ /ˈkɑmpləmənt/ *n.* **1** [C] a remark that expresses admiration for someone or something: *"You look great!" "Thanks for the compliment."* | **+on** *Paula got a lot of compliments on her dress.* | *He's always **paying** her **compliments*** (=telling her she looks nice, did something well etc.) *and buying her flowers.* | *Mandy's always **fishing for compliments*** (=trying to get people to say something nice about her). **2 take sth as a compliment** if you take something as a compliment, you are pleased with what someone has said even though it really was not very nice: *I said he was a workaholic, and he seemed to take it as a compliment.* **3 pay sb the compliment of doing sth** to do something that shows you trust someone else and have a good opinion of them: *They paid me the compliment of electing me as their representative.* **4 compliments** [plural] praise, admiration, or good wishes: *Please give my compliments to the chef – the food was excellent.* **5 (with the) compliments of sb** also **with sb's compliments** used by a person or company when they send or give something to you: *Please accept these tickets with our compliments.* **6 a backhanded compliment** also **a left-handed compliment** something that someone says to you which is nice and not nice at the same time: *She's always giving backhanded compliments like "You don't look nearly as fat as you used to."* **7 return the compliment** to behave toward someone in the same way that they have behaved toward you: *They never even said hello to me, and I returned the compliment by ignoring them.* [**Origin:** 1600–1700 French, Italian, from Spanish *cumplimiento*, from *cumplir* **to complete, do what is needed, be polite**] → see also COMPLEMENT

comp·li·ment² /ˈkɑmpləˌmɛnt/ *v.* [T] to say something nice to someone in order to praise them: **compliment sb on sth** *All of us complimented Joe on his cooking.* | **compliment sb for sth** *Health officials were complimented for their fast action.* → see also COMPLEMENT

com·pli·men·ta·ry /ˌkɑmpləˈmɛntri◂, -ˈmɛntəri◂/ *adj.* **1** given free to people SYN **free**: *complimentary tickets to a Dodgers game* **2** expressing admiration, praise, or respect OPP **derogatory**: *Bell had only complimentary things to say about the organization.* | **+about** *She was very complimentary about your work.*

com·ply /kəmˈplaɪ/ *v.* **complies**, **complied**, **complying** [I] FORMAL to do what you must do or are asked to do: **+with** *Gas stations that fail to comply with the law will be fined.* [**Origin:** 1500–1600 Italian *complire*, from Spanish *cumplir* **to complete, do what is needed, be polite**] → see also COMPLIANCE

com·po·nent /kəmˈpoʊnənt/ Ac W3 *n.* [C] one of several parts that make up a whole machine or system: *stereo components* | *Exercise is one of the **key components** of a healthy lifestyle.* [**Origin:** 1500–1600 Latin, present participle of *componere*] → see also CONSTITUENT

com·port /kəmˈpɔrt/ *v.* FORMAL **comport yourself** to behave yourself in a particular way: *Leo comported himself very professionally.*

comport with sth *phr. v.* FORMAL to follow or be in agreement with an idea, belief, rule etc.: *These practices do not comport with the principle of providing fair trials.*

com·port·ment /kəmˈpɔrtˀmənt/ *n.* [U] FORMAL someone's behavior and the way they stand, walk etc.

com·pose /kəmˈpoʊz/ *v.* **1 be composed of sth** to be formed from a group of substances or parts → see also COMPRISE: *The jury was composed of six men and*

C

six women. | **be composed mainly/largely/entirely of sth** *The region is composed mainly of forest and mountains.* **2** [T not in progressive] to combine together with other things or people to form something: *The menu includes more than 60 small dishes from which you can compose a meal.* **3** [I,T] ENG. LANG. ARTS to write a piece of music, especially CLASSICAL or serious music: *Mozart composed his first symphony when he was still a child.* **4 compose a letter/poem/speech etc.** to write a letter, poem etc., thinking very carefully about it as you write it: *The class assignment was to compose a poem or short story.* **5** [T] to make yourself feel or look calm: *I needed a quiet place to **compose my thoughts**.* | **compose yourself** *She took a few minutes to compose herself before she answered the question.* **6** [T] ENG. LANG. ARTS to put colors, shapes, or images together in a particular way to form a piece of art: *Olsen knows how to compose a visually interesting scene.*

com·posed /kəmˈpoʊzd/ *adj.* **1** calm, rather than upset or angry: *The witness was composed and sure of her story.* **2** a composed SALAD is arranged carefully on a plate, rather than mixed together

com·pos·er /kəmˈpoʊzɚ/ *n.* [C] someone who writes music, especially CLASSICAL or serious music

com·pos·ite¹ /kəmˈpɑzɪt/ *adj.* [only before noun] **1** made up of different parts or materials: *The plane was made of fiber glass, foam and composite materials.* **2 a composite sketch/drawing** a drawing made by police from descriptions given by a witness

composite² *n.* [C] **1** something made up of different parts or materials: **+of** *a composite of three different metals* **2** a drawing of a possible criminal made by police from descriptions given by a WITNESS: *Several witnesses identified the man in the composite.*

com·po·si·tion /ˌkɑmpəˈzɪʃən/ *n.*
1 MAKING A WHOLE [U] **a)** the way in which something is made up of different parts, things, members etc., or the different parts, things, members themselves: **+of** *Both sides disagree over the composition of a temporary government.* **b)** CHEMISTRY the chemicals or other substances that make up something else: *the material's chemical composition*
2 MUSIC/ART/WRITING a) [C] ENG. LANG. ARTS a piece of music or art, or a poem: *a mixture of traditional songs and original compositions* **b)** [U] the art or process of writing pieces of music, poems, ESSAYS etc.: *Karina studied composition and music theory at the Juilliard School.* ►see THESAURUS box at **music**
3 PHOTOGRAPH/PICTURE [U] ENG. LANG. ARTS the way in which the different parts that make up a photograph or picture are arranged, or the different parts themselves: *The paintings of each series differ in terms of color and composition.*
4 SCHOOL SUBJECT [C,U] ENG. LANG. ARTS a short piece of writing about a particular subject that is done especially at school, or the art of writing about things: *We had to write a composition about our summer vacations.* | *a course in advanced composition*
5 PRINTING [U] TECHNICAL the process of arranging words, pictures etc. on a page before they are printed

com·pos·i·tor /kəmˈpɑzət̬ɚ/ *n.* [C] someone who arranges letters, pictures etc. on a page before they are printed

com·post¹ /ˈkɑmpoʊst/ *n.* [U] a mixture of decayed plants, leaves etc. used to improve the quality of soil: *Last year I started a **compost pile** (=a place where leaves etc. are left to decay) with leaves and grass cuttings.*

compost² *v.* [T] **1** to make plants, leaves etc. into compost **2** to put compost onto soil

com·po·sure /kəmˈpoʊʒɚ/ *n.* [U] a calm feeling that you have when you feel confident about dealing with a situation: *The judge allowed the witness a few minutes to **regain her composure**.* | *He's a player who **loses** his **composure*** (=becomes angry, anxious, or upset) *under pressure.* | **keep/maintain your composure** (=stay calm)

com·pote /ˈkɑmpoʊt/ *n.* [U] fruit that has been cooked in sugar and water and is eaten cold

com·pound¹ /ˈkɑmpaʊnd/ Ac *n.* **1** [C] an area that contains a group of buildings and is surrounded by a fence or wall: *a prison compound* | *the U.S. Embassy compound* **2** [C] CHEMISTRY a substance containing atoms from two or more ELEMENTS that together make a different substance. There has to be a fixed quantity of atoms. For example, water is made up of two atoms of HYDROGEN for every one atom of OXYGEN: *an organic compound* | **+of** *Sulfur dioxide is a compound of sulfur and oxygen.* ►see THESAURUS box at **mixture** **3 a compound of sth** a combination of two or more qualities or parts: *Communication ability is a compound of several different skills.* **4** [C,U] something that consists of a combination of two or more substances: *a rubber compound* **5** [C] ENG. LANG. ARTS in grammar, a noun, adjective, or verb made up of two or more words. For example, the noun "ice cream" is a compound.

com·pound² /kəmˈpaʊnd/ Ac *v.* [T] **1** to make a difficult situation worse by adding more problems: *The country's economic woes were compounded by a seven-year civil war.* **2** ECONOMICS to calculate INTEREST on both the sum of money and the interest that was paid or still owed before: *My bank compounds interest quarterly.* **3** to make something by mixing different parts or substances together: *Scientists often compound substances to produce new drugs.* [**Origin:** 1500–1600 Old French *compondre*, from Latin *componere*, from *com-* + *ponere* **to put**]

com·pound³ /ˈkɑmpaʊnd, kɑmˈpaʊnd/ Ac *adj.* **1 compound noun/adjective/verb** ENG. LANG. ARTS a noun, adjective, or verb that is made up of two or more words. For example, "ice cream" is a compound noun. **2 compound sentence** ENG. LANG. ARTS a sentence made up of at least two INDEPENDENT CLAUSES. For example, "The door opened and Charlie walked in" is a compound sentence. **3 a compound eye/leaf etc.** BIOLOGY a single eye, leaf etc. that is made up of two or more parts or substances

ˌcompound ˈfracture *n.* [C] MEDICINE a broken bone that cuts through someone's skin

ˌcompound ˈinterest *n.* [U] ECONOMICS INTEREST on a bank account or LOAN that is calculated on both the sum of money already lent or borrowed and on the unpaid interest already earned or charged → see also SIMPLE INTEREST

com·pre·hend /ˌkɑmprɪˈhɛnd/ *v.* [I,T not in progressive] FORMAL to understand something that is complicated or difficult SYN **understand**: *Even scientists do not comprehend these phenomena.* | **comprehend how/why/what** *It is difficult to comprehend how someone could harm a child.* | *Families are bound together in ways that cannot be **fully comprehended**.* [**Origin:** 1300–1400 Latin *comprehendere* **to take hold of completely**]

com·pre·hen·si·ble /ˌkɑmprɪˈhɛnsəbəl/ *adj.* easy to understand OPP **incomprehensible**: *comprehensible instructions* | **+to** *Most avant-garde music is not comprehensible to the average concertgoer.* —**comprehensibly** *adv.* —**comprehensibility** /ˌkɑmprɪˌhɛnsəˈbɪlət̬i/ *n.* [U]

com·pre·hen·sion /ˌkɑmprɪˈhɛnʃən/ *n.* [U] the ability to understand something, or knowledge of something: *a test of reading comprehension* | *Some politicians seem to **have no comprehension of** what it's like to be poor.* | *The complexities of these systems are almost **beyond comprehension*** (=impossible to understand).

WORD CHOICE **comprehension, understanding**
• **Comprehension** means the ability to understand the meaning of something, especially something spoken or written: *He showed little comprehension of the judge's statements.*
• Don't use **comprehension** about someone's ability to understand other people's feelings, attitudes, or culture/ Instead, use **understanding**: *Rhodes hoped the scholarships would contribute to world understanding and peace.*

com•pre•hen•sive¹ /ˌkɑmprɪˈhɛnsɪv/ Ac *adj.* **1** including everything that is necessary: *a comprehensive plan for dealing with a disaster* | *We want to make the policy clearer and more comprehensive.* **2** [only before noun] relating to comprehensive insurance: *a comprehensive policy* —**comprehensively** *adv.* —**comprehensiveness** *n.* [U]

comprehensive² Ac *n.* [C usually plural] a test of everything you have studied for your MAJOR, that you take at the end of your course of study at a university

compreˌhensive inˈsurance *n.* [U] a type of car insurance that pays to repair or replace your car if it is damaged or lost for some reason other than running into something else

com•press¹ /kəmˈprɛs/ *v.* **1** [I,T] to press something or make it smaller so that it takes up less space, or to become smaller: *Some computer file types compress more easily than others.* | **compress sth into sth** *The garlic is dried and then compressed into a pill.* **2** [T usually passive] to reduce the amount of time that it takes for something to happen or be done: **compress sth into sth** *Three years of training were compressed into 18 months.* **3** [T] to write or express something using fewer words: *The play has been compressed from a huge book.* [**Origin:** 1300–1400 Late Latin *compressare* **to press hard**, from Latin *comprimere* **to compress**] —**compressible** *adj.*

com•press² /ˈkɑmprɛs/ *n.* [C] a small thick piece of material that you put on part of someone's body to stop blood flowing out or to make it less painful: *Apply a* ***cold compress*** *to the injury.*

com•pres•si•bil•i•ty /kəmˌprɛsəˈbɪləti/ *n.* [U] PHYSICS a measure of how much less space MATTER fills under pressure

com•pres•sion /kəmˈprɛʃən/ *n.* [U] **1** PHYSICS the process of reducing the mass of a substance or the amount of space it fills under pressure, or the state of being reduced in this way: **+of** *the compression of matter* **2** PHYSICS in an engine that produces power by burning GASOLINE, the stage during which a combination of gasoline and air is compressed in a CYLINDER before it starts to burn **3** COMPUTERS a way of reducing the number of BITS needed to represent information on a computer in order to make the size of computer FILES smaller

com•pres•sor /kəmˈprɛsɚ/ *n.* [C] SCIENCE a machine or part of a machine that compresses air or gas

com•prise /kəmˈpraɪz/ Ac *v.* [T not in progressive] FORMAL **1** to consist of particular parts, groups etc.: *The Sea Grant Program comprises over 300 colleges nationwide.* | **be comprised of sth** *The council is comprised of members of the nine tribes in the Hanford region.*

THESAURUS

Comprise, **be composed of**, and **consist of** can each be used in order to talk about the parts that things are made of, or the things that something contains. **Comprise** is the more formal word. Each of the following sentences means the same thing, but the patterns are different: *The United States comprises 50 states.* | *The United States is composed of 50 states.* | *The United States consists of 50 states.*

2 [T] to form part of a larger group → see also COMPOSE SYN **make up** SYN **constitute**: *Hindus comprise 82% of India's population.* → see also CONSTITUTE

com•pro•mise¹ /ˈkɑmprəˌmaɪz/ *n.* [C,U] an agreement that is achieved after everyone involved accepts less than they wanted at first, or the act of making this agreement: *Compromise is an inevitable part of any relationship.* | **+between** *The bill is the result of a compromise between Democrats and Republicans.* | *Talks are continuing in the hope that the two factions will* ***reach a compromise***. | *I'm willing to* ***make compromises****, but you'll have to keep your side of the bargain.* [**Origin:** 1400–1500 French *compromis*, from Latin *compromissum* **joint promise**, from *compromittere*]

compromise² *v.* **1** [I] to end an argument by making an agreement in which everyone involved accepts less than what they wanted at first: *She admitted that she was unable to compromise.* | **+on** *You need to be willing to compromise on the price.* | **+with** *Bikers have been forced to compromise with city traffic officials.* **2** [T] to harm or damage something in some way, for example by behaving in a way that does not match a legal or moral standard: *We need to increase profits without compromising employees' safety.* | *Martha's immune system has been compromised by cancer treatments.* | *Watson has* ***compromised herself*** (=done something dishonest or embarrassing) *by accepting lobbyists' money for her election campaign.*

com•pro•mis•ing /ˈkɑmprəˌmaɪzɪŋ/ *adj.* likely to prove or make people think that you have done something morally wrong: **compromising documents/materials/photos etc.** *Investigators found compromising documents in the files.* | *Brown claims to possess photographs showing Wilson in* ***compromising*** (=embarrassing) ***positions***.

comp time /ˈkɑmp ˌtaɪm/ *n.* [U] vacation time that you are given instead of money, because you have worked more hours than you were REQUIRED to work

comp•trol•ler /kənˈtroʊlɚ, kəmp-/ *n.* [C] FORMAL ECONOMICS a CONTROLLER

com•pul•sion /kəmˈpʌlʃən/ *n.* **1** [C] a strong and unreasonable desire to do something: *The patient had a compulsion that led him to wash his hands 20 or 30 times a day.* | **a compulsion to do sth** *He felt a sudden compulsion to laugh out loud.* **2** [U] the act of forcing or influencing someone to do something they do not want to do, or the situation of being forced or influenced: *Compulsion is not the answer to get kids to perform better in school.* | *Remember, you are* ***under no compulsion to*** *sign the agreement.* → see also COMPEL

com•pul•sive /kəmˈpʌlsɪv/ *adj.* **1** compulsive behavior is very difficult for the person who is doing it to stop or control, and is often a sign of a mental problem: *Compulsive spending is often a symptom of deep unhappiness.* **2 a compulsive liar/gambler/drinker etc.** someone who has such a strong desire to lie etc. that they are unable to control it: *Not all compulsive eaters are overweight.* —**compulsively** *adv.* —**compulsiveness** *n.* [U]

com•pul•so•ry /kəmˈpʌlsəri/ *adj.* FORMAL REQUIRED to be done because of a rule or law SYN **mandatory**: *compulsory military service* | *Attendance at the meeting is compulsory.* | **+for** *English classes are compulsory for all students.* —**compulsorily** *adv.* → see also VOLUNTARY

com•punc•tion /kəmˈpʌŋkʃən/ *n.* [U] FORMAL **have/feel no compunction about (doing) sth** to not feel guilty or sorry about something, although other people may think that it is wrong: *He apparently felt no compunction about lying to us.*

com•pu•ta•tion /ˌkɑmpyəˈteɪʃən/ Ac *n.* [C,U] FORMAL MATH the process of calculating: *a series of complex computations* —**computational** *adj.*

com•pute /kəmˈpyut/ Ac *v.* [I,T] FORMAL **1** MATH to calculate a total, answer, result etc.: *The machine can compute the time it takes a sound wave to bounce back.* **2** SPOKEN [usually in negatives] if facts, ideas etc. do not compute, they do not seem sensible or correct: *His ideas just don't compute.* [**Origin:** 1600–1700 Latin *computare*, from *com-* + *putare* **to think**]

com•put•er /kəmˈpyutɚ/ Ac S1 W1 *n.* [C] an electronic machine that stores information and uses programs to help you find, organize, or change the information: *a desktop computer* | *computer software* | *colorful computer graphics* | *a computer monitor* | **be stored/kept/held on (a) computer** *The information is stored on computer.* | *Shoppers send in their orders* ***by computer***. | *Dr. Fonseca's office now keeps all the patients' details* ***on computer***. → see also LAPTOP, PERSONAL COMPUTER

C

THESAURUS

mouse a small object near your computer which you move and press to give instructions to the computer
menu a list of things on a computer screen which you can ask the computer to do
icon a small sign or picture on a computer screen that is used to start a particular program
cursor a mark that can be moved around a computer screen to show where you are working
scroll bar a line on the side or bottom of a computer screen that you can use in order to move up and down or from side to side to see more information in a document

Actions when using a computer
start up/boot up a computer to make it start working
log on/in to start using a computer system by typing your name and password
click on something to press a button on a computer mouse to choose a program, file etc. from the screen
install software to add new software to a computer so that the software is ready to be used
download information to move information, pictures, or music from the Internet onto your computer
upload information to move information, pictures, or music from your computer to a different computer across the Internet
open a file/program to make a file or program ready to use
scroll up/down to move information on a computer screen up or down so that you can read it
enter information to type information into a computer
delete information/a file to remove information from a computer
cut and paste information to remove information from one place and put it in another place
save a file to make a computer keep the work that you have done on it
close a file/program to stop having a file or program ready to use
log off/out to stop using a computer system by giving it particular instructions
shut down a computer to make it stop working
reboot/restart a computer to make it start working again

com,puter-aided de'sign *n.* [U] COMPUTERS CAD

com·put·er·ize /kəmˈpyuṭəˌraɪz/ *v.* [T] COMPUTERS to use a computer to control the way something is done, to store information etc.: *They've computerized all the patient records.* —**computerization** /kəmˌpyuṭərəˈzeɪʃən/ *n.* [U]

com'puter ,jockey also **com'puter ,jock** *n.* [C] INFORMAL someone who is very good at writing computer PROGRAMS

com,puter-'literate *adj.* able to use a computer —**computer literacy** *n.* [U]

com'puter ,modeling *n.* [U] the representation of a problem, situation, or real object on a computer in a form which lets you see it from all angles

com,puter 'science *n.* [U] the study of computers and what they can do

com,puter 'virus *n.* [C] a VIRUS

com·put·ing /kəmˈpyuṭɪŋ/ Ac *n.* [U] COMPUTERS the use of computers as a job, in a business etc.: *home computing*

com·rade /ˈkɑmræd/ *n.* [C] **1** FORMAL a friend, especially someone who shares difficult work or danger: *Two of his comrades were killed in action.* **2** a title used by members of a Communist or Socialist Party when talking or writing to each other: *Comrades, please support this motion.* [**Origin:** 1500–1600 French *camarade*, from Old Spanish *camarada* **group of people sleeping in one room, friend**]

,comrade in 'arms *n.* [C] FORMAL someone who has worked or fought with you to achieve particular GOALS

com·rade·ship /ˈkɑmrædˌʃɪp/ *n.* [U] FORMAL friendship and loyalty among people who work together, fight together etc.

Comte /kɔnt/, **Au·guste** /ɔˈgust/ (1798–1857) a French PHILOSOPHER

con¹ /kɑn/ *v.* **conned, conning** [T] INFORMAL **1** to trick someone in order to get their money or get them to do something: **con sb out of sth** *He tried to con me out of $20.* | **con sb into doing sth** *Tyrell conned several millionaires into investing in his business.* ►see THESAURUS box at **cheat¹** **2 con yourself** to try to make yourself believe something that is not true: *If you think she'll take you back after this, you're just conning yourself.*

con² *n.* [C] **1** a trick to get someone's money or make them do something: *If I'd known it was a con, I wouldn't have given him any money.* **2** SLANG a prisoner SYN **convict** → see also EX-CON **3** something that is a disadvantage → see also **the pros and cons (of sth)** at PRO¹ (3)

con- /kən, kɑn/ *prefix* together or with: *to conspire* (=plan together) | *a confederation* (=a group of people

computer

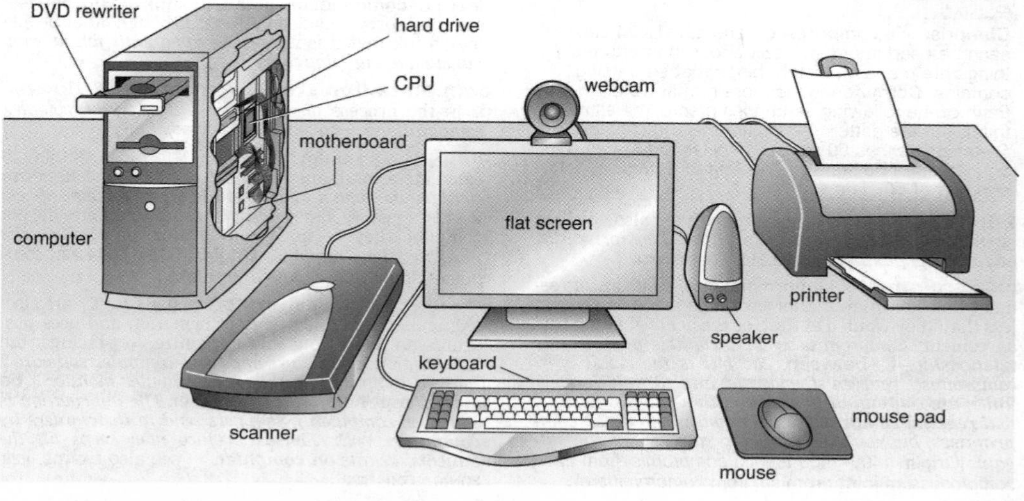

or organizations working together) → see also COL-, COM-, COR-

Con·a·kry /'kɑnəkri/ the capital and largest city of Guinea

Conan Doyle → see DOYLE, SIR ARTHUR CONAN

'con ˌartist *n.* [C] INFORMAL someone who tricks or deceives people in order to get money from them SYN con man

con·cat·e·na·tion /kənˌkætˀn'eɪʃən, -ˌkæţə'neɪ-/ *n.* [C,U + of] FORMAL a series of events or things joined together one after another

con·cave /ˌkɑn'keɪv◂ / *adj.* SCIENCE a concave surface is curved down or toward the inside in the middle OPP convex: *a concave mirror* —**concavity** /kɑn'kævəţi/ *n.* [C,U]

con·ceal /kən'sil/ *v.* [T] FORMAL **1** to hide someone or something carefully SYN hide: *The bomb was concealed in a portable radio.* | **conceal yourself** *The children made no effort to conceal themselves.* ►see THESAURUS box at hide[1] **2** to hide your real feelings or the truth SYN hide OPP reveal: *Cal could barely conceal his disappointment.* | **conceal sth from sb** *Dana concealed her pregnancy from her family and friends.* **3** to make something difficult to see by being in front of it or over it SYN hide: *A hat concealed her graying hair.* [**Origin:** 1200–1300 Old French *conceler*, from Latin *concelare*, from *com-* + *celare* **to hide**] —**concealed** *adj.*: *a concealed weapon* —**concealment** *n.* [U]

con·cede /kən'sid/ W3 *v.* **1** [T] to admit that something is true or correct, although you wish that it were not true SYN admit: *"My sister can be rude," I conceded.* | **concede (that)** *Eventually he conceded that he had been wrong.* | *She stubbornly refused to* ***concede the point.*** ►see THESAURUS box at admit **2** [I,T] to admit that you are not going to win a game, argument, battle etc.: *After three years of civil war, the rebels finally conceded.* | *Kavner* ***conceded defeat*** *after 75% of the vote had been counted.* ►see THESAURUS box at surrender[1] **3** [T] to give something to someone unwillingly: *How much will the president concede in order to reach a budget agreement?* | **concede sth to sb** *The king refused to concede any territory to neighboring countries.* **4 concede a goal/point etc.** to not be able to stop your opponent from getting a GOAL, point etc. during a game: *The Lakers conceded 12 points in a row to the Suns.* **5** [T] to give something to someone as a right or PRIVILEGE: **concede sth to sb** *The richer nations will never concede equal status to the poorer countries.* [**Origin:** 1400–1500 French *concéder*, from Latin *concedere*] → see also CONCESSION

con·ceit /kən'sit/ *n.* **1** [U] DISAPPROVING an attitude that shows you have too much pride in your own abilities, appearance etc. OPP modesty **2** [C] ENG. LANG. ARTS a clever and unusual way of showing or describing something in a play, movie, work of art etc.: *The movie's design conceit uses color for the dream, and black and white for the real world.* [**Origin:** 1600–1700 *conceit* **thought, opinion** (14–19 centuries), from *conceive*, on the model of *deceive*, *deceit*]

con·ceit·ed /kən'siţɪd/ *adj.* DISAPPROVING behaving in a way that shows too much pride in your abilities, appearance etc. OPP modest: *I don't want to sound conceited, but we are the experts here.* —**conceitedly** *adv.* —**conceitedness** *n.* [U]

con·ceiv·a·ble /kən'sivəbəl/ Ac *adj.* able to be believed or imagined OPP inconceivable: **it is conceivable (that)** *It is conceivable that the two jobs could be combined to save money.* | *The Olympic Games organizers are trying to prepare for* ***every conceivable*** *emergency.* —**conceivably** *adv.*

con·ceive /kən'siv/ Ac *v.* **1** [T] FORMAL to imagine a situation or what something is like: *No one could have conceived a more romantic first meeting.* | **conceive what/why/how etc.** *Many people find it hard to conceive what outer space is like.* | **conceive of (doing) sth** *I can't conceive of voting for anyone else.* | **conceive that** *It is difficult to conceive that our children might die before us.* **2** [T] to think of a new idea or plan: *Hastings is the man who conceived the show.* | **conceive of sth** *A large part of his time is spent conceiving of new ways to increase production.* | **first/originally conceived** *The atomic bomb was first conceived in the 1930s.* **3** [I,T] BIOLOGY to become PREGNANT: *The clinic offers treatment for women who have had difficulty conceiving.* [**Origin:** 1200–1300 Old French *conceivre*, from Latin *concipere* **to take in, conceive**] → see also CONCEPT, CONCEPTION

con·cen·trate[1] /'kɑnsənˌtreɪt/ Ac S3 W3 *v.* **1** [I] to think very carefully about something you are doing: *Okay, I'll stop talking so you can concentrate.* | +**on** *I can't concentrate on my homework with all that noise.* **2** [I,T] to be present in large numbers or amounts in a particular place, or to put a large number of people and things in one place: *Police are not saying where they are concentrating their activities.* | +**in/on/at etc.** *The radioactive particles tend to concentrate in the lungs.* | **be concentrated in/on/at etc.** *New Zealand's population is concentrated on the North Island.* **3** [T] to make a substance or liquid stronger by removing most of the water from it OPP dilute **4 concentrate sb's/the mind** FORMAL if something concentrates the mind, it makes you think very clearly [**Origin:** 1600–1700 *con-* + Latin *centrum* **center**]

concentrate on *phr. v.* **1 concentrate on sth** to think about or work on a particular subject, group etc., especially because you think it is more important than others: *I concentrated on getting a better grade in biology.* **2 concentrate sth on sth** to spend your time, effort, thought etc. considering or working on a particular subject, group etc., especially because you think it is more important than others: *The agency has concentrated its efforts on a new health education program.*

concentrate[2] Ac *n.* [C,U] a substance or liquid that has been made stronger by removing most of the water from it: *orange juice concentrate*

con·cen·trat·ed /'kɑnsənˌtreɪţɪd/ Ac *adj.* **1** a concentrated substance or liquid is stronger than usual because it has had most of the water removed from it: *a concentrated detergent* **2** [only before noun] showing a lot of determination or effort: *Solutions to these problems will take time and* ***concentrated effort.*** **3** containing a lot of a particular type of people or things in comparison to other places or situations: *Disease spread because of poor hygiene in a concentrated population.*

con·cen·tra·tion /ˌkɑnsən'treɪʃən/ Ac W3 *n.* **1** [U] the ability to think very carefully about something for a long time: *A good night's sleep will improve your concentration.* | *When you're playing chess, it's important not to* ***lose your concentration.*** **2** [singular, U] a process in which you put a lot of attention, energy etc. into a particular activity: +**on** *We need to increase our concentration on health and safety issues.* **3** [C,U] a large amount or number of people or things in a particular place: +**of** *the concentration of greenhouse gases in the atmosphere* | *areas of the state with* ***high*** *immigrant population* ***concentrations*** **4** [C] CHEMISTRY the amount of a substance contained in a liquid: +**of** *Tests show* ***high concentrations of*** *chemicals in the water.*

ˌconcen'tration ˌcamp *n.* [C] a prison where political prisoners and other people who are not soldiers are kept in very bad conditions without enough food, especially during a war

con·cen·tric /kən'sɛntrɪk/ *adj.* MATH concentric circles have their centers at the same point → see also ECCENTRIC

con·cept /'kɑnsɛpt/ Ac S2 W2 *n.* [C] an idea of how something is, or how something should be done: *The idea of a soul is a religious concept.* | +**of** *There are basic concepts of decent human behavior that we all share.* | **concept that** *The country is committed to the concept that the law is separate from politics.* | *Most young children* ***have no concept of*** *time.* | *It's difficult to* ***grasp the concept*** *of infinite space.* → see also CONCEIVE, CONCEPTION

con·cep·tion /kən'sɛpʃən/ Ac *n.* **1** [C,U] an idea

about what something is like, or a basic understanding of something: +**of** *changing conceptions of the world* | **have little/no conception of sth** *You have no conception of what I really want!* **2** [C,U] BIOLOGY the process by which a woman or female animal becomes PREGNANT, or the time when this happens: *the moment of conception* **3** [U] a process in which someone forms a plan or idea: *Sellers is responsible for the conception of the show and for most of its scripts.* → see also CONCEIVE, CONCEPT

C

con·cep·tu·al /kənˈsɛptʃuəl/ Ac *adj.* FORMAL dealing with ideas, or based on them, and not real yet: *The designs are still in the conceptual stage.* —**conceptually** *adv.*

con,ceptual 'art *n.* [U] TECHNICAL art in which the main aim of the artist is to show an idea, rather than to represent actual things or people

con·cep·tu·al·ize /kənˈsɛptʃuəˌlaɪz/ *v.* [I,T] to form an idea about what something is like or how it should be: *How do we as a nation conceptualize racial equality?* —**conceptualization** /kənˌsɛptʃuələˈzeɪʃən/ *n.* [C,U]

con·cern¹ /kənˈsɚn/ S3 W1 *n.*
1 WORRY a) [U] a feeling of worry about something important: *Local officials showed a surprising lack of concern.* | +**about/over** *public concern about the environment* | +**for** *Concern for human rights is basic to our foreign policy.* | **concern (that)** *There is concern that the gasoline additive will actually increase pollution.* | *Our principal* ***expressed concern*** *that there would not be enough classrooms.* | *The depletion of the ozone layer is* ***causing concern*** *among scientists.* | *The state of the economy remains a* ***cause for concern.*** **b)** [C] something that worries you: *My main concern is that we won't finish on time.* | +**about/over** *The new software raises concerns about users' privacy.* | +**for** *Owen's biggest concerns were for his wife and family.* | **concern that** *There are concerns that the two men may not receive fair trials.* | **express/voice concerns** *Several employees expressed concerns that jobs would be lost.* | *The incident* ***raised concerns*** *about the teachers' training.*
2 STH IMPORTANT [C,U] something that is important to you or that involves you: *Your immediate concern should be to find a job.* | +**for** *Development of parkland is a major concern for the voters in this area.* | *topics* ***of concern to*** *teenagers and young adults* | **main/primary/major concern** *Mark's main concern is his family.*
3 FEELING FOR SB [U] a feeling of wanting someone to be happy, safe, and healthy: *We thanked them for their concern.* | +**for** *Coach O'Brien was praised for his concern for students' well-being.*
4 BUSINESS [C] a business or company: *an engineering concern* | *There is doubt about the company's ability to continue as* ***a going concern*** (=a business that is making money).
5 not sb's concern also **none of sb's concern** FORMAL if something is not your concern, you do not need to worry about it or be involved with it: *How you spend your money is not my concern.*

concern² *v.* [T] **1** [not in passive] if an activity, situation, rule etc. concerns you, it affects you or involves you: *How I vote doesn't concern you.* **2** to make someone feel worried or upset: *Kate's behavior is starting to concern her parents.* | **it concerns sb that** *It concerns us that some students are regularly skipping classes.* **3** [not in passive] if a story, book, report etc. concerns someone or something, it is about them: *The report concerns drug use in schools.* **4 concern yourself with/about sth** to become involved in something that interests or worries you: *Our country's leaders must concern themselves with environmental protection.* **5 to whom it may concern** used at the beginning of a formal letter when you do not know the name of the person you are writing to [**Origin:** 1300–1400 French *concerner*, from Late Latin *concernere* **to mix together**] → see also CONCERNED

con·cerned /kənˈsɚnd/ S2 W2 *adj.*
1 WORRIED worried about something important: *Brian didn't seem concerned at all.* | *Concerned parents were calling the school.* | +**about** *Zoo officials are concerned about the mother elephant.* | +**for** *Rescuers are concerned for the safety of two men.* | **concerned that** *The police are concerned that the protests may lead to violence.* ►see THESAURUS box at **worried**
2 INVOLVED [not before noun] involved in something or affected by it: *Divorce is very painful, especially when children are concerned.* | +**in** *Everyone concerned in the incident was questioned by the police.* | +**with** *Businesses concerned with the oil industry do not support solar energy research.* | *The company's closure was a shock to* ***all concerned.***
3 THINK STH IS IMPORTANT [not before noun] believing that something is important: +**with** *They are more concerned with tourism than with preservation of the ruins.* | +**about** *These days, more people are concerned about good nutrition.*
4 as far as sb is concerned SPOKEN used to show what someone's opinion on a subject is or how it affects them: *It's a good deal, as far as I'm concerned.*
5 as far as sth is concerned also **where sth is concerned** SPOKEN used to show which subject or thing you are talking about: *Where taxes are concerned, savings bonds are better than CDs.*
6 LOVE/CARE caring about someone and whether they are happy and healthy: +**for/about** *The management has never been concerned about our happiness.*
7 be concerned with sb/sth if a book, story etc. is concerned with a person, subject etc., it is about that subject: *This story is concerned with a Russian family in the 19th century.*

con·cern·ing /kənˈsɚnɪŋ/ *prep.* FORMAL about or relating to: *We have several questions concerning the report.* | *information concerning the suspect's whereabouts*

con·cert /ˈkɑnsɚt/ S2 W3 *n.* **1** [C] ENG. LANG. ARTS a performance given by musicians or singers: *a rock concert* | +**of** *a concert of 20th-century American music* | *I'm* ***going to a concert*** *Sunday night.* ►see THESAURUS box at **theater** **2 in concert (with sb) a)** FORMAL people who do something in concert do it together after having agreed on it: *The government is working in concert with other Western states.* **b)** playing or singing at a concert: *I went to see Pavarotti in concert in Rome.* [**Origin:** 1500–1600 French, Italian *concerto*, from *concertare*, from Latin, **to fight, compete**]

con·cert·ed /kənˈsɚtɪd/ *adj.* [only before noun] **a concerted effort/attempt/action etc.** something that is done by people working together in a carefully planned and very determined way: *County officials have* ***made a concerted effort*** *to raise the standard of education.* [**Origin:** 1700–1800 *concert* **to do together or by agreement** (16–21 centuries), from French *concerter*] —**concertedly** *adv.*

con·cert·go·er /ˈkɑnsɚtˌgoʊɚ/ *n.* [C] someone who often goes to concerts, or someone who is at a particular concert

ˌconcert 'grand *n.* [C] a large GRAND PIANO that is used for concerts → see also BABY GRAND

'concert hall *n.* [C] a large public building where concerts are performed

con·cer·ti·na /ˌkɑnsɚˈtinə/ *n.* [C] a small musical instrument like an ACCORDION that you hold in your hands and play by pressing in from each side

ˌconcer'tina wire *n.* [U] RAZOR WIRE

con·cert·mas·ter /ˈkɑnsɚtˌmæstɚ/ *n.* [C] the most important VIOLIN player in an ORCHESTRA

con·cer·to /kənˈtʃɛrtoʊ/ *n. plural* **concertos** [C] a piece of CLASSICAL MUSIC, usually for one instrument and an ORCHESTRA: *a piano concerto*

con·ces·sion /kənˈsɛʃən/ *n.* **1** [C] something that you admit or that you allow someone to have in order to end an argument: +**to** *Employers agreed to a wide range of concessions.* | *Neither side is willing to* ***make concessions.*** | +**on** *The Republicans made a few concessions on spending cuts.* | +**to** *We will make no concessions to terrorists.* → see also CONCEDE **2** [C] **a)** the right to have a business in a particular place, especially in a place owned by someone else: *The company owns valuable logging and mining concessions.* **b)** a small business that sells things in a larger place owned by someone else: *Joe runs a hamburger concession in the mall.* **3 concessions** [plural] the food, drinks etc. sold at a small business that sells things in a larger place owned by someone else: *Concessions are always really expensive at baseball games.* **4** [C,U] HISTORY a special right to have a piece of land that is given to someone by the government, an employer etc. in exchange for using the land in a particular way

con·ces·sion·aire /kənˌsɛʃəˈnɛr/ *n.* [C] someone who has been given a CONCESSION, especially to run a business

con·ces·sion·ar·y /kənˈsɛʃəˌnɛri/ *adj.* given as a concession: *a concessionary agreement*

con'cession ˌstand *n.* [C] a small business that sells food, drinks, or other things at sports events, theaters etc.

conch /kɑŋk, kɑntʃ/ *n.* [C] the large twisted shell of a tropical sea animal that looks like a SNAIL

con·cierge /kɔnˈsyɛrʒ/ *n.* [C] someone in a hotel whose job is to help guests with problems, give them advice about local places to go etc. [**Origin:** 1500–1600 French, Latin *conservus* **fellow slave**]

con·cil·i·ate /kənˈsɪliˌeɪt/ *v.* [I,T] FORMAL to do something to make people more likely to stop arguing, especially by giving them something they want: *Who will conciliate in disputes over property?* —**conciliator** *n.* [C]

con·cil·i·a·tion /kənˌsɪliˈeɪʃən/ *n.* [U] the process of trying to get people to stop arguing and agree on something: *As a sign of conciliation, troops were withdrawn from the area.* → see also RECONCILIATION

con·cil·i·a·to·ry /kənˈsɪliəˌtɔri/ *adj.* doing something that is intended to make someone stop arguing with you: *We need to take a more* ***conciliatory approach*** *in the negotiations.* | *The government has made a series of* ***conciliatory gestures*** *toward its neighbors.*

con·cise /kənˈsaɪs/ *adj.* **1** short, with no unnecessary words: *clear, concise instructions* **2** shorter than the original book on which something is based: *a concise dictionary* [**Origin:** 1500–1600 Latin *concisus*, from the past participle of *concidere* **to cut up**] —**concisely** *adv.* —**conciseness** also **concision** /kənˈsɪʒən/ *n.* [U] FORMAL

con·clave /ˈkɑŋkleɪv/ *n.* [C] **1** a private or secret meeting, or the people at the meeting: *A small conclave had gathered in the professor's study.* **2** a meeting at which a group of CARDINALS chooses a new POPE

con·clude /kənˈklud/ Ac W2 *v.* **1** [T] to decide that something is true after considering all the information you have: **conclude that** *The jury concluded that the man was guilty.* | **conclude from sth that** *We can conclude from accident reports that the speed limit should be lowered.* **2** [T] to complete something that you have been doing, especially after a long time SYN **finish**: **conclude your work/investigation/research etc.** *The police hope to conclude the murder investigation soon.* **3** [I always + adv./prep.,T] if something such as a meeting or a speech concludes, or if you conclude it, you end it, often by doing or saying one final thing SYN **end**: *The sales convention will conclude on Sunday.* | *The Giants conclude the three-game series tonight.* | **concluded (sth) with sth** *Each chapter concludes with a short summary.* | *We conclude each meeting with an informal discussion.* | **conclude (sth) by doing sth** *She concluded by thanking everyone for coming.* **4** [T] used to report the last thing that someone says or writes: *"And that's really all I can say," he concluded firmly.* **5 conclude an agreement/treaty/contract etc.** to finish arranging an agreement etc. successfully: *The United States and Japan concluded a new trade agreement this month.* [**Origin:** 1200–1300 Latin *concludere* **to shut up, end, decide**]

con·clud·ing /kənˈkludɪŋ/ Ac *adj.* **a concluding sentence/remark/stage etc.** the last sentence, stage etc. in an event or piece of writing: *the chapter's concluding paragraph*

con·clu·sion /kənˈkluʒən/ Ac W2 *n.* **1** [C] something you decide after considering all the information you have: *the report's main conclusions* | *Becky* ***came to the conclusion that*** *Tim must have forgotten about their date.* | *The survey samples are too small for anyone to* ***draw conclusions****.* | *All the evidence* ***pointed to the conclusion that*** *he was guilty.* | *Don't* ***jump to conclusions*** (=make a decision too quickly) – *just because they're late doesn't mean they've had an accident!* **2** [C] the end or final part of something SYN **end**: *The process of reform is nearing its conclusion.* | +**of** *Lucy was given a standing ovation at the conclusion of her speech.* **3 in conclusion** used in a piece of writing or a speech to show that you are about to finish what you are saying: *In conclusion, I'd like to say how much I've enjoyed this opportunity to speak to you.* **4** [singular] the final arrangement of an agreement, a business deal etc.: *the successful conclusion of the deal* **5** [C] ENG. LANG. ARTS the part of a CONDITIONAL sentence that does not begin with "if" or "unless" and sometimes begins with "then": *In the sentence "if x > 2, then y must be positive," "then y must be positive" is the conclusion.* → see also FOREGONE CONCLUSION

con·clu·sive /kənˈklusɪv/ Ac *adj.* showing without any doubt that something is true OPP **inconclusive**: *There is no* ***conclusive evidence*** *to support the theory.* —**conclusively** *adv.*

con·coct /kənˈkɑkt/ *v.* [T] **1** to invent a story, excuse, or plan, especially in order to deceive someone: *John had concocted an elaborate excuse for being late.* **2** to make something such as a food or drink by mixing different things, especially things that are not usually combined: *Debbie started the business by concocting recipes in her kitchen.* [**Origin:** 1500–1600 Latin, past participle of *concoquere* **to cook together**]

con·coc·tion /kənˈkɑkʃən/ *n.* [C] something such as a food or drink made by mixing different things, especially things that are not usually combined: *He tasted the pink concoction cautiously.*

con·com·i·tant¹ /kənˈkɑmətənt/ *adj.* [only before noun] FORMAL existing or happening together, especially as a result of something: *members' concomitant rights and responsibilities* —**concomitantly** *adv.*

concomitant² *n.* [C] FORMAL something that often or naturally happens with something else: +**of** *Deafness is a frequent concomitant of aging.*

Con·cord /ˈkɑŋkɚd/ the capital city of the U.S. state of New Hampshire

con·cord /ˈkɑŋkɔrd/ *n.* [U] **1** FORMAL the state of having a friendly relationship, so that you agree on things and live in peace SYN **harmony** OPP **discord**: *international concord* **2** ENG. LANG. ARTS in grammar, concord between words happens when they match correctly, for example when a plural noun has a plural verb following it SYN **agreement**

con·cor·dance /kənˈkɔrdəns/ *n.* **1** [C] ENG. LANG. ARTS an alphabetical list of the words used in a book or set of books, with information about where they can be found and usually about how they are used **2** [U] FORMAL the state of being similar to something else or in agreement with it OPP **discord**: *There is apparent concordance between both parties.*

con·cor·dant /kənˈkɔrdənt/ *adj.* FORMAL being in agreement or having the same regular pattern OPP **discordant**: *concordant opinions*

con·course /ˈkɑŋkɔrs/ *n.* [C] a large hall or open place in a building such as an airport or train station: *Our sales office is on the lower concourse.* [**Origin:** 1800–1900 *concourse* **coming together of people, crowd** (14–21 centuries), from French *concours*, from Latin *concursus*]

con·crete¹ /ˈkɑŋkrit/ *n.* [U] a hard substance used for building things, made by mixing CEMENT, sand, small stones, and water

con·crete² /kɑnˈkrit, ˈkɑŋkrit/ *adj.* **1** [only before noun] made of concrete: *a concrete floor* **2** definite, specific, and clearly based on fact, rather than general and based on beliefs or guesses → see also ABSTRACT: *a concrete example* | *Just tell him what you want* ***in*** *clear and* ***concrete terms***. [**Origin:** 1300–1400 Latin *concretus*, past participle of *concrescere* **to grow together**] —**concretely** *adv.*

con,crete 'image *n.* [C] ENG. LANG. ARTS a written description that uses words that produce a strong image in a reader's mind about what something smells, tastes, feels, looks, or sounds like

,concrete 'jungle *n.* [C usually singular] INFORMAL an unpleasant area in a city that is full of tall buildings, with no open spaces

'concrete ,mixer *n.* [C] a CEMENT MIXER

con·cu·bine /ˈkɑŋkyəˌbaɪn/ *n.* [C] a woman in the past who lived with a man that she was not married to, especially when he already had a wife or wives —**concubinage** /kɑnˈkyubənɪdʒ/ *n.* [U]

con·cur /kənˈkɚ/ *v.* **concurred, concurring** [I] FORMAL **1** to agree with someone or have the same opinion as them: *"I think we should sell the building." "I concur."* | **+with** *The board members concurred with the recommendations.* | **+that** *We all concur that reading is a positive activity.* **2** to happen at the same time SYN **coincide**: *Everything concurred to produce the desired effect.* [**Origin:** 1300–1400 Latin *concurrere*, from *com-* + *currere* **to run**]

con·cur·rence /kənˈkɚəns, -ˈkʌr-/ *n.* FORMAL **1** [U] agreement: **+of** *Any final decision must have the concurrence of the White House.* **2** [C] an occasion when several things happen at the same time: **+of** *a strange concurrence of events*

con·cur·rent /kənˈkɚənt, -ˈkʌrənt/ Ac *adj.* **1** existing or happening at the same time: *He served concurrent prison sentences for the two robberies.* **2** FORMAL in agreement: *concurrent opinions* —**concurrently** *adv.*: *The two exhibits are running concurrently.*

con,current juris'diction *n.* [U] POLITICS the right of two different courts, for example a FEDERAL court and a state court, to make legal decisions in the same legal case

con,current 'lines *n.* [plural] MATH two or more lines that pass through the same single point

con,current 'powers *n.* [plural] POLITICS powers shared by both the FEDERAL and state governments

con,current reso'lution *n.* [C] POLITICS a formal decision agreed on and voted for by the House of Representatives and the Senate, which does not have the power of a law, and which does not have to be signed by the President

con,curring o'pinion *n.* [C] POLITICS a written document giving the opinions of a judge who supports the official decision reached in a court, which adds or emphasizes a point that was not made in the official judgment

con·cus·sion /kənˈkʌʃən/ *n.* [C] **1** MEDICINE an injury to the brain that makes you lose consciousness or feel sick for a short time, usually caused by something hitting your head: *Tom* ***suffered a mild concussion***. | *The man has a broken leg and a* ***serious concussion***. **2** FORMAL a violent shaking movement, caused by something such as an explosion: *The concussion shattered the window.* [**Origin:** 1500–1600 Latin *concussio*, from *concutere* **to shake violently**] —**concuss** /kənˈkʌs/ *v.* [T] —**concussed** *adj.*

con·demn /kənˈdɛm/ *v.* [T] **1** to say very strongly that you do not approve of something or someone, especially because you think it is morally wrong: *Politicians were quick to condemn the bombing.* | **condemn sb/sth for (doing) sth** *Ginny knew that society would condemn her for leaving her children.* | *The TV show was widely condemned for its violence.* | **condemn sb/sth as sth** *Other leaders have condemned Rev. Abernathy's story as false.* ►see THESAURUS box at **criticize** **2** to give someone a severe punishment after deciding they are guilty of a crime SYN **sentence**: **be condemned to 20 years/life imprisonment etc.** *Lewis has been condemned to ten years in prison.* | *He was convicted of first degree murder and* ***condemned to death***. **3** if a particular situation condemns someone to do something, it forces them to live in a bad way or to do something bad: **condemn sb to (do) sth** *If you don't learn from the past, you're condemned to repeat its mistakes.* | *The new laws will condemn many to a life of poverty.* **4** to state officially that a building is not safe enough to be used: *Inspectors condemned the three buildings after the fire.* [**Origin:** 1300–1400 Old French *condemner*, from Latin *condemnare*]

con·dem·na·tion /ˌkɑndəmˈneɪʃən/ *n.* [C,U] an expression of very strong disapproval of someone or something: **+of** *There was widespread condemnation of the attacks.*

con·dem·na·to·ry /kənˈdɛmnəˌtɔri/ *adj.* FORMAL expressing strong disapproval: *a condemnatory attitude*

con·demned /kənˈdɛmd/ *adj.* **1** a condemned person is going to be punished by being killed: *a condemned man* **2** a condemned building is officially not safe to live in or use

con·den·sa·tion /ˌkɑndənˈseɪʃən/ *n.* **1** [U] small drops of water that are formed when gas changes to liquid: *There was a lot of condensation on the windows.* **2** [U] CHEMISTRY the process of changing from gas to liquid, usually caused by the temperature becoming lower: *the condensation of steam into water* **3** [C,U] FORMAL the act of making something shorter, or the thing that has been made shorter: *the condensation of 150 years of history into a hundred pages*

con·dense /kənˈdɛns/ *v.* **1** [I,T] if gas condenses or is condensed, it becomes a liquid as it becomes cooler: *Within a second the vapor cools and condenses.* | *The steam is condensed as it enters the cylinder.* | **+into** *In the morning the mist condenses into drops on leaves.* **2** [T usually passive] to make a liquid thicker by removing some of the water: *The liquid is condensed and stored.* | *condensed soup* **3** [T] **a)** to make something shorter or smaller: *How could he condense his life into one short speech?* **b)** to make something that is spoken or written shorter, by removing some of the words or details: *The article was condensed in Sunday's paper.*

con'densed milk *n.* [U] milk which has been made thicker by removing some of the water, and has sugar added to it → see also EVAPORATED MILK

con·dens·er /kənˈdɛnsɚ/ *n.* [C] **1** a piece of equipment that makes a gas change into liquid → see picture at LABORATORY **2** a piece of equipment, for example in a car, that stores an electrical CHARGE for a short time SYN **capacitor**

con·de·scend /ˌkɑndɪˈsɛnd/ *v.* [I] **1** to behave as if you think other people are not as good, intelligent, or important as you are: **+to** *Be careful not to condescend to your readers.* **2** to do something in a way that shows you think it is below your social or professional position: **condescend to do sth** *Do you think the CEO would ever condescend to have lunch with us?* —**condescension** /ˌkɑndɪˈsɛnʃən/ *n.* [U]

con·de·scend·ing /ˌkɑndɪˈsɛndɪŋ◂/ *adj.* behaving as though you think other people are not as good, intelligent, or important as you are: *My philosophy professor is extremely condescending.* | *a condescending tone of voice* —**condescendingly** *adv.*

con·di·ment /ˈkɑndəmənt/ *n.* [C] FORMAL something such as KETCHUP, MUSTARD, or another SAUCE, that you add to food when you eat it to make it taste better [**Origin:** 1400–1500 French, Latin *condimentum*, from *condire* **to pickle**]

con·di·tion[1] /kənˈdɪʃən/ S2 W1 *n.*
1 STATE [singular, U] the particular state that someone or something is in, usually how good or bad it is: *We cannot guarantee the condition of the product after shipment.* | **in good/poor/satisfactory etc. condition** *The car has been well maintained and is in excellent condition.* | *What kind of condition is the house in?*
2 SITUATION **conditions** [plural] **a)** the situation in which people live or work, especially the physical things such as pay or food that affect the quality of

their lives: *Conditions in the prison were appalling.* | *The government promised improved* ***living conditions****.* | *a demonstration for better pay and* ***working conditions*** **b)** all the things that affect the way something happens: *difficult economic conditions* | **under certain/normal/different etc. conditions** *Under normal conditions, people will usually do whatever requires the least effort.*
3 AGREEMENT/CONTRACT [C usually plural,U] something that is stated in a contract or agreement that must be done or provided: **+of** *the conditions of participation in the program* | **+for** *The bank sets strict conditions for new loans.* | ***Under the conditions of*** *the agreement, the work must be completed by the end of the month.* | *Two employees agreed to speak to us* ***on condition that*** *they would not be named.* | *I'll talk to him, but only* ***on one condition****.* | *Senator Dodd is leading a campaign to* ***impose*** *strict* ***conditions on*** *U.S. military aid.* | *the* ***terms and conditions*** *of your employment* | **meet/satisfy a condition** (=obey what is demanded by a condition) *Applicant countries must satisfy all the conditions before joining the European Union.*
4 WEATHER **conditions** [plural] the weather at a particular time, especially when you are considering how this will affect you: *Travelers are advised not to fly because of severe weather conditions.* | **cold/windy/freezing etc. conditions** *Up to 10 inches of snow fell in blizzard conditions.*
5 NECESSARY SITUATION [C] something that must happen first before something else can happen: **+for/of** *Our goal is to create the conditions for a lasting peace.*
6 ILLNESS [C] MEDICINE an illness or health problem that affects you permanently or for a very long time: *a medical condition* | *Some people who have HIV show no outward signs of the condition.* | **a heart/lung/skin etc. condition** (=one that affects a particular organ) ►see THESAURUS box at **illness**
7 STATE OF HEALTH [singular, U] MEDICINE a person or animal's state of health: *an improvement in the patient's condition* | *She was taken to hospital and is* ***in a critical condition*** (=dangerously sick or very badly injured).
8 be in no condition to do sth to be too sick, drunk, or upset to be able to do something: *I was in no condition to drive home after the party.*
[**Origin:** 1200–1300 Old French, Latin *conditio*, from *condicere* **to agree**]

condition² *v.* **1** [T usually passive] to make a person or an animal think or behave in a particular way by influencing or training them over a period of time: **be conditioned to (do) sth** *The American public has been conditioned to think that this is just the way things are.* → see also CONDITIONING **2** [I,T] to keep hair or skin healthy by putting a special liquid on it: *This shampoo conditions your hair and makes it smell great.* → see also CONDITIONER **3** [T usually passive] FORMAL to make something depend on other facts being true or something else happening SYN **determine**: *What I buy is conditioned by the amount I earn.*

con·di·tion·al¹ /kən'dɪʃənəl/ *adj.* **1** if an offer, agreement etc. is conditional, it will only be done if something else happens OPP **unconditional**: *a conditional contract* | **+on/upon** *The deal is conditional on approval by the authorities.* **2** in grammar, a conditional sentence is one that includes "if" or "unless" and expresses something that must be true or that happens before something else can be true or happen —**conditionally** *adv.*

conditional² *n.* [C] ENG. LANG. ARTS **1 the conditional** in grammar, the form of the verb that expresses something that must be true or that happens before something else can be true or happen **2** ENG. LANG. ARTS a conditional sentence or CLAUSE

con,ditional proba'bility *n.* [singular] MATH the degree to which an event can reasonably be expected to happen when another event has already happened. For example, if someone has already picked two kings from a pack of cards, how likely is it that he will pick another king.

con·di·tion·er /kən'dɪʃənɚ/ *n.* [C,U] a liquid that you put on your hair after washing it to make it softer

con·di·tion·ing /kən'dɪʃənɪŋ/ *n.* [U] **1** the process by which people or animals are trained to behave in a particular way when particular things happen: *Social conditioning makes crying difficult for men.* **2** the process of making your body used to a particular level or type of activity or exercise: *physical conditioning* → see also AIR CONDITIONING

con·do /'kɑndoʊ/ *n. plural* **condos** [C] INFORMAL a CONDOMINIUM

con·do·lence /kən'doʊləns/ *n.* [C usually plural,U] sympathy for someone that something bad has happened to, especially when someone has died: *a message of condolence* | ***Please accept my condolences*** *on the loss of your mother.* | **send/offer/extend your condolences** (=to formally express your sympathy when someone has died) [**Origin:** 1600–1700 Late Latin *condolere* **to express sympathy**, from Latin *com-* + *dolere* **to feel pain**] → see also COMMISERATION

con·dom /'kɑndəm/ *n.* [C] a thin rubber bag that a man wears over his PENIS (=sex organ) during sex, to prevent a woman from having a baby, or to protect against sexual diseases

con·do·min·i·um /ˌkɑndə'mɪniəm/ *n.* [C] **1** one apartment in a building with several apartments, each of which is owned by the people living in it ►see THESAURUS box at **house¹** **2** a building containing several of these apartments [**Origin:** 1700–1800 Modern Latin, Latin *com-* + *dominium* **area ruled**]

con·done /kən'doʊn/ *v.* [T] to accept or forgive behavior that most people think is morally wrong: *I'm not condoning his behavior, but I can understand it.* [**Origin:** 1800–1900 Latin *condonare* **to forgive**]

con·dor /'kɑndɔr, -dɚ/ *n.* [C] a very large Californian or South American VULTURE (=bird that eats dead animals) [**Origin:** 1600–1700 Spanish *cóndor*, from Quechua *kuntur*]

con·duce /kən'dus/ *v.*
conduce to/toward sth *phr. v.* FORMAL to help to produce a particular quality or state

con·du·cive /kən'dusɪv/ *adj.* **be conducive to sth** FORMAL to provide conditions that make it easier to do something: *We want to create an environment that is conducive to learning.*

con·duct¹ /kən'dʌkt/ Ac *v.*
1 DO STH TO GET INFORMATION [T] to do something, especially in order to get information or prove facts: *A memorial service will be conducted for the crash victims.* | **conduct a survey/an investigation/a poll etc.** *The survey was conducted last fall.* | **conduct a test/an experiment** *The experiments were conducted with three of the zoo's monkeys.* | **conduct a meeting/an interview/a class** *Advanced classes are conducted entirely in the foreign language.*
2 MUSIC [I,T] ENG. LANG. ARTS to stand in front of a group of musicians and direct their playing: *Who will be conducting tonight?* | **conduct an orchestra/a band/a choir** *The orchestra is conducted by John Williams.* → see also CONDUCTOR
3 conduct yourself FORMAL to behave in a particular way, especially in a situation where people judge your behavior: *He conducted himself with extraordinary dignity.*
4 ELECTRICITY/HEAT [T] PHYSICS if something conducts electricity or heat, it allows the electricity or heat to travel along or through it: *Aluminum readily conducts heat.*
5 SHOW SB STH [T always + adv./prep.] to show someone a place or building by leading them around in it: **conduct sb through/around/to sth** *A guide will conduct us through the museum.*
[**Origin:** 1400–1500 Latin *conductus*, past participle of *conducere*]

con·duct² /'kɑndʌkt, -dəkt/ Ac *n.* [U] FORMAL **1** the way someone behaves, especially in public, in their job etc.: *an inquiry into the conduct of the police* | *Prisoners' release dates depend on continued* ***good conduct*** *while* *in custody.* | *The man was fined for* ***disorderly conduct*** (=the crime of causing trouble in public). ►see THESAURUS box at **behavior** **2** the way a business, activity etc. is organized: *complaints about the conduct of the elections*

con·duc·tion /kən'dʌkʃən/ *n.* [U] PHYSICS the process by which energy, in the form of heat, sound, or electricity, passes through a substance or object without movement in the substance or object, for example heat passing through metal: *electrical conduction* → see also CONVECTION

C

con·duc·tive /kən'dʌktɪv/ *adj.* PHYSICS able to conduct electricity, heat etc.: *Copper is a very conductive metal.* —**conductivity** /ˌkɑndʌk'tɪvəṭi/ *n.* [U]

conductor

con·duc·tor /kən'dʌktɚ/ *n.* [C] **1** ENG. LANG. ARTS someone who stands in front of a group of musicians or singers and directs their playing or singing ►see THESAURUS box at **orchestra** **2** someone who is in charge of a train and collects payments from passengers or checks their tickets **3** PHYSICS something that allows electricity or heat to travel along it or through it: *Wood is a poor conductor of heat.*

con·du·it /'kɑnduɪt/ *n.* [C] **1** a pipe or passage through which water, gas, electric wires etc. pass **2** a connection that allows people to pass ideas, news, money, weapons etc. from one place to another: **+for** *The Internet is a tremendous conduit for information.*

cone /koʊn/ *n.* [C] **1** MATH a solid or hollow shape with a round base whose sloping sides join in a point at the top, or something with this shape: *a volcanic cone* | *He rolled the newspaper into a cone.* → see picture at SHAPE[1] **2** a piece of thin cooked cake, shaped like a cone, that you put ICE CREAM in → see also ICE CREAM CONE, SNOW CONE **3** BIOLOGY the fruit of a PINE or FIR tree: *a pine cone* → see also CONIFER **4** an object shaped like a large cone, usually bright orange in color, that is put on a road to prevent cars from going somewhere or to warn drivers about something [SYN] **traffic cone** [SYN] **pylon** → see also NOSECONE **5** BIOLOGY a CELL in your eye that is shaped like a cone, that helps you see light and color → see also ROD

Co·ney Is·land /ˌkoʊni 'aɪlənd/ an area of Brooklyn, New York, famous for its AMUSEMENT PARK and beach

con·fab /'kɑnfæb, kən'fæb/ *n.* [C] INFORMAL a friendly, usually private conversation or meeting: *We'll have a quick confab about the party.*

con·fab·u·la·tion /kənˌfæbyə'leɪʃən/ *n.* [C] FORMAL a private conversation or meeting —**confabulate** /kən'fæbyəˌleɪt/ *v.* [I]

con·fec·tion /kən'fɛkʃən/ *n.* [C] FORMAL **1** something sweet, such as candy, cake, or cookies: *a chocolate confection* **2** a piece of clothing that is very delicate and complicated, or has a lot of decoration: **+of** *a dreamy confection of pink beads and satin* **3** something such as a movie or a song that is entertaining and not serious at all: *The movie is a pretty light-hearted confection.*

con·fec·tion·er /kən'fɛkʃənɚ/ *n.* [C] someone who makes or sells candy and other similar sweet things

con'fectioners' ˌsugar *n.* [U] POWDERED sugar

con·fec·tion·er·y /kən'fɛkʃəˌnɛri/ *n. plural* **confectioneries** **1** [U] candy and other similar sweet things **2** [C] OLD-FASHIONED a store that sells candy and other similar sweet things

con·fed·er·a·cy /kən'fɛdərəsi/ *n. plural* **confederacies** **1 the Confederacy** also **the Confederate States** HISTORY the southern states that fought against the northern states in the U.S. Civil War **2** [C] POLITICS a CONFEDERATION

con·fed·er·ate[1] /kən'fɛdərɪt/ *n.* [C] **1** someone who helps someone else do something, especially something secret or illegal: *The young woman was one of his confederates.* **2 Confederate** HISTORY a soldier from the southern states in the U.S. Civil War **3** POLITICS a member of a CONFEDERATION (=united group of people, political parties, or organizations) —**confederate**, **Confederate** *adj.*

con·fed·er·ate[2] /kən'fɛdəˌreɪt/ *v.* [I,T] FORMAL if groups, areas etc. confederate, or you confederate them, they join to become a confederation: **+with** *In 1949, Newfoundland confederated with Canada.*

Conˌfederate ˌStates of A'merica, the also **the Confederacy** abbreviation **the C.S.A.** *n.* [singular] HISTORY the group of 11 southern U.S. states that SECEDED from (=said they did not want to be a part of) the U.S. in 1860 and 1861, which led to the Civil War

con·fed·e·ra·tion /kənˌfɛdə'reɪʃən/ *n.* [C] **1** POLITICS a group of people, political parties, or organizations that have united for political purposes or trade **2** the act of forming a confederation, or the state of being a confederation

con·fer /kən'fɚ/ [Ac] *v.* **conferred, conferring** FORMAL **1** [I] to discuss something with other people, so that everyone can express their opinions and decide on something: **+with** *Franklin leaned over and conferred with his attorneys.* **2** [T] to officially give someone an award, a degree, a right etc.: **confer sth on/upon sb** *The university conferred an honorary doctorate on the actor.* [**Origin:** 1400–1500 Latin *conferre* **to bring together**] —**conferment** *n.* [C,U]

con·ference /'kɑnfrəns/ [Ac] [S2] [W2] *n.* [C] **1** a large formal meeting where a lot of people discuss important matters such as business, science, or politics, especially for several days: *a conference center* | **+on** *an international conference on AIDS* | *Dan went to Boston to* ***attend a conference.*** | *The teachers' union is* ***holding*** *its annual* ***conference*** *next week.* → see also NEWS CONFERENCE, PRESS CONFERENCE ►see THESAURUS box at **discussion** **2** a private meeting for a few people to discuss a particular subject: **+with** *After a brief conference with his aides, the senator left for the airport.* | **have/hold a conference** *They're having parent-teacher conferences at my kids' school this week.* | *The meeting will be held in the second floor* ***conference room.*** **3** a group of sports teams that play against each other to see who is best: *the most talented team in the conference* | *the conference championships*

'conference ˌcall *n.* [C] a telephone call in which several people in different places can all talk to each other at the same time

'conference comˌmittee *n.* [C] POLITICS a temporary committee, consisting of members of the House of Representatives and the Senate, whose job is to reach an agreement on a bill that has been passed in two different forms by each house

con·ferenc·ing /'kɑnfrənsɪŋ/ *n.* [U] **video/telephone/computer etc. conferencing** the use of VIDEO, telephone, computer etc. equipment to make it possible for several people in different places to talk to each other at the same time

con·fess /kən'fɛs/ *v.* [I,T] **1** to admit that you have done something wrong or illegal, especially to the police: *Woods was released from jail after the real murderers confessed.* | **confess to (doing) sth** *Holmes confessed to taking the money.* | **+that** *Her husband confessed he'd been having an affair.* **2** to admit something that you feel embarrassed about: **+that** *Marsha confessed that she didn't really know how to work the computer.* | **confess to doing sth** *Ralph confessed to spending the weekend watching TV.* | ***I must confess*** *I'm not very excited at the thought of dinner with the Martins.* **3** to tell a priest or God about the wrong things you have done so that you can be forgiven: *Gary felt better after* ***confessing his sins*** *to one of the priests.* [**Origin:** 1300–1400 Old French *confesser*, from Latin *confiteri* **to confess**]

con·fessed /kən'fɛst/ *adj.* [only before noun] having admitted publicly that you have done something: *a confessed killer* → see also SELF-CONFESSED —**confessedly** /kən'fɛsɪdli/ *adv.*

con·fes·sion /kən'fɛʃən/ *n.* **1** [C] a formal statement that you have done something wrong or illegal: *Sanchez's confession was read out to the court.* | +**of** *a confession of murder* | *At 3 a.m. Higgins broke down and* ***made a full confession****.* **2** [C] an act of saying that you have done something embarrassing or something that you are ashamed of: **confess that** *Carol overheard Mason's confession that he was drinking again.* | +**of** *a confession of weakness* | ***I have a confession to make*** *– I was actually home when you called.* **3** [C,U] a private statement to a priest or to God about the bad things that you have done: *Rita* ***goes to confession*** *at least once a month.* **4** [C] FORMAL a statement of what your religious beliefs are: +**of** *a confession of faith*

con·fes·sion·al[1] /kən'fɛʃənl/ *n.* [C] a place in a Catholic church, usually a small enclosed room, where a priest hears people make their confessions

confessional[2] *adj.* confessional speech or writing contains private thoughts or facts that you normally want to keep secret, especially private information about things you have done that were wrong

con·fes·sor /kən'fɛsɚ/ *n.* [C] FORMAL the priest to whom someone regularly makes their confession

con·fet·ti /kən'fɛt̬i/ *n.* [U] small pieces of colored paper that you throw at events such as parties, PARADES etc. [**Origin:** 1800–1900 Italian, plural of *confetto* **candy**, from Latin *conficere*; because candy was thrown at Italian street celebrations]

con·fi·dant /'kɑnfəˌdɑnt/ *n.* [C] someone you tell your secrets to or who you talk to about personal things: *Steve's* ***closest confidant*** *is his brother Phil.*

con·fi·dante /'kɑnfəˌdɑnt/ *n.* [C] a woman you tell your secrets to or who you talk to about personal things: *They were best friends and confidantes.*

con·fide /kən'faɪd/ *v.* [T] **1** to tell someone you trust about personal things that you do not want other people to know: **confide sth to sb** *Stella confided the truth to her best friend.* | **confide (that)** *Ted confided that he was having a relationship with someone from work.* | **confide to sb (that)** *Connie had confided to Michele that her marriage was in trouble.* **2** LITERARY to give something you value to someone you trust so they take care of it for you: **confide sth to sb** *Walter confided the money to his brother's safekeeping during the war.* [**Origin:** 1400–1500 Latin *confidere*, from *com-* + *fidere* **to trust**]

confide in sb *phr. v.* to tell someone about something very private or secret, especially a personal problem, because you feel you can trust them: *Marian never really felt able to confide in her sister Amelia.* | **confide in sb that** *Val confided in me that she was pregnant.*

con·fi·dence /'kɑnfədəns/ S3 W2 *n.*
1 FEELING SB/STH IS GOOD [U] the feeling that you can trust someone or something to be good, work well, or produce good results: +**in** *We must maintain the customer's confidence in our product.* | *Opinion polls show that voters have* ***lost confidence in*** *the mayor.* | **gain/win sb's confidence** *She quickly gained her teammates' confidence.* | *At first, we didn't* ***have*** *any* ***confidence that*** *Tony's methods were going to work.* | *Gail can now drive a truck* ***with confidence****.* | *The actions failed to* ***restore confidence in*** *the government.*
2 BELIEF IN YOURSELF [U] the belief that you have the ability to do things well or deal with situations successfully: *You need patience and confidence to be a good teacher.* | +**in** *I didn't have any confidence in myself.* | *Tom's a good student, but he* ***lacks confidence****.* | *Living in a foreign country* ***gave*** *Jessica* ***a lot of confidence****.* | **the confidence to do sth** *She soon developed the confidence to work alone.* | *She enrolled in karate to help* ***restore*** *her* ***confidence*** *after the mugging.* | *Being fired really* ***shook*** *his* ***confidence****.*
3 FEELING STH IS TRUE [U] the feeling that something is definite or true: *How can anyone say* ***with confidence*** *that the worst is over?* | *At that time he* ***had*** *little* ***confidence that*** *God existed.*
4 FEELING OF TRUST [U] a feeling of trust in someone, so that you can tell them something and be sure they will not tell other people: **earn/gain/win sb's confidence** *I only ask that you give me a chance to earn your confidence again.* | *I'm giving you this information* ***in the strictest confidence****.* | *Elsa* ***took*** *me* ***into*** *her* ***confidence*** *and told me about some of the problems she was facing.*
5 A SECRET [C] LITERARY a secret or a piece of information that is private or personal: *We spent the evening drinking wine and exchanging confidences.* → see also CONSUMER CONFIDENCE, VOTE OF CONFIDENCE, VOTE OF NO CONFIDENCE

'confidence-ˌbuilding *adj.* a confidence-building event, activity etc. increases your confidence: *confidence-building activities for youngsters*

'confidence trick also **'confidence ˌgame** *n.* [C] FORMAL a CON GAME

con·fi·dent /'kɑnfədənt/ W3 *adj.* **1** sure that you can do something or deal with a situation successfully: *Sandy gave her a confident smile.* | +**about** *I feel very confident about this game.* **2** [not before noun] sure that something will happen in the way that you want or expect: **confident (that)** *Doctors are confident that he'll make a full recovery.* | +**of** *He seems confident of victory in this year's Senate race.* | +**about** *Investors are less confident about the economic situation.* **3** sure that something is true: **confident (that)** *We are confident we have done nothing wrong.* [**Origin:** 1500–1600 Latin, present participle of *confidere*] → see also SELF-CONFIDENT —**confidently** *adv.*

con·fi·den·tial /ˌkɑnfə'dɛnʃəl◂ / *adj.* **1** spoken or written in secret, and intended to be kept secret: *A confidential government report was leaked to the press.* | *Both sides agreed to* ***keep*** *their financial agreement* ***confidential****.* | *What I'm telling you is* ***strictly confidential****.* ►see THESAURUS box at **secret**[1] **2** a confidential way of speaking or behaving shows that you do not want other people to know what you are saying: *His voice lowered to a confidential whisper.* **3** a confidential secretary is one who is trusted with secret information —**confidentially** *adv.*

con·fi·den·ti·al·i·ty /ˌkɑnfəˌdɛnʃi'æləṭi/ *n.* [U] a situation in which you trust someone not to tell secret or private information to anyone else: *The relationship between attorneys and their clients is based on confidentiality.* | *It is a* ***breach of confidentiality*** *for a priest to reveal what someone has confessed.* | *There was a* ***confidentiality clause*** *in his contract that prevented him from writing about his experiences later.*

con·fid·ing /kən'faɪdɪŋ/ *adj.* behaving in a way that shows you want to tell someone about something that is private or secret: *Her tone was suddenly confiding.* —**confidingly** *adv.*: *Maggie put her hand confidingly in his.*

con·fig·u·ra·tion /kənˌfɪgyə'reɪʃən/ *n.* [C,U] **1** FORMAL OR TECHNICAL the shape or arrangement of the parts of something SYN **layout**: +**of** *the configuration of the planets* **2** COMPUTERS the combination of equipment needed to run a computer system: +**of** *the configuration of a hard drive*

con·fig·ure /kən'fɪgyɚ/ *v.* [T] COMPUTERS to arrange something, especially computer equipment, so that it works with other equipment

con·fine /kən'faɪn/ AC *v.* [T]
1 KEEP SB IN A PLACE to keep someone in a place that they cannot leave, such as a prison: **confine sb to sth** *The area was placed under curfew, confining all residents to their homes.* | **be confined in sth** *The hostages were confined in a dark basement with the doors and windows barred.*
2 LIMIT to keep someone or something within the limits of a particular activity or subject SYN **restrict**: **be confined to (doing) sth** *The young officer's duties were*

confined to answering the telephone. | **confine yourself to sth** *We confined our study to ten cases.*
3 STOP STH SPREADING to stop something bad from spreading to another place: **confine sth to sth** *Firefighters managed to confine the blaze to one room.*
4 STAY IN ONE PLACE [usually passive] to have to stay in a place, especially because you are sick: *I had the flu and was* ***confined to bed.*** | *Scott's been* ***confined to a wheelchair*** *since the car crash.*
5 be confined to sb/sth to affect or happen to only one group of people, or in only one place or time: *My theory is not confined to political events.*
[**Origin:** 1500–1600 French *confiner*, from Latin *confinis*, from *confine* **border**]

C

con·fined /kən'faɪnd/ Ac *adj.* a confined space or area is one that is very small: *It wasn't easy to sleep in such a confined space.*

con·fine·ment /kən'faɪnmənt/ *n.* **1** [U] the act of putting someone in a room, prison etc., or the state of being there: *During his confinement, Wen taught himself how to read.* | *She was sentenced to 15 days' confinement for violating a direct order.* → see also SOLITARY CONFINEMENT **2** [C,U] OLD-FASHIONED the period of time before and during which a woman gives birth to a baby

con·fines /'kɑnfaɪnz/ Ac *n.* [plural] limits or borders: *The movie was filmed mostly* ***within the confines of*** *a studio.*

con·firm /kən'fɚm/ Ac S3 W2 *v.* [T] **1** to show that something is definitely true, especially by providing more proof: *New evidence has confirmed his story.* | **confirm that** *Research has confirmed that the risk is higher for women.* | **confirm what** *The study confirms what many experts have been saying for years.* ▸see THESAURUS box at **check**[1] **2** to say that something is definitely true: *U.S. officials said they could not confirm the report.* | **confirm that** *Tina called to confirm that you're working on Saturday.* | **confirm what** *My brother will confirm what I have told you.* | *Spokesmen for the agency would* ***neither confirm nor deny*** *reports that they were conducting an investigation.* **3** to tell someone that a possible arrangement, date, or time is now definite: *Could you confirm the dates we discussed?* | *I'll call the hotel and confirm our reservations.* **4** to make an idea or feeling stronger or more definite: *The test results confirmed his worst fears.* | **confirm sb in their belief/opinion/view etc. (that)** *The expression on his face confirmed me in my suspicions.* **5 be confirmed** to be made a full member of a Christian church in a special ceremony [**Origin:** 1200–1300 Old French *confirmer*, from Latin *confirmare*]

con·fir·ma·tion /ˌkɑnfɚ'meɪʃən/ Ac *n.* [C,U] **1** a statement or letter that says that something is definitely true, or the act of stating this: +**of** *No independent confirmation of the report was available.* | **confirmation that** *He just wanted confirmation that she still loved him.* **2** a letter, message etc. that tells you that a possible arrangement, date, or time is now definite: *written confirmation of your booking* **3** a religious ceremony in which someone is made a full member of the Christian church

con·firmed /kən'fɚmd/ Ac *adj.* **1 a confirmed bachelor/alcoholic/vegetarian etc.** someone who seems unlikely to change the way of life they have chosen **2 a confirmed case/diagnosis/report/sighting** proved and therefore known to be true or real: *three confirmed cases of the disease*

con·fis·cate /'kɑnfəˌskeɪt/ *v.* [T] to officially take someone's property away from them, usually as a punishment: *An increasing number of guns have been confiscated recently.* —**confiscation** /ˌkɑnfə'skeɪʃən/ *n.* [C,U] *the confiscation of private property* —**confiscatory** /kən'fɪskəˌtɔri/ *adj.*

con·fla·gra·tion /ˌkɑnflə'greɪʃən/ *n.* [C] FORMAL **1** a very large fire over a large area that destroys a lot of buildings, forests etc.: *One spark could start a conflagration.* **2** a violent situation or war: *The conflict has the potential to become a major conflagration.*

con·flate /kən'fleɪt/ *v.* [T] FORMAL to combine two or more things to form a single new thing, whether it is correct or not: *The public often conflates fame with merit.* —**conflation** /kən'fleɪʃən/ *n.* [C,U]

con·flict[1] /'kɑnˌflɪkt/ Ac S3 W2 *n.* **1** [C,U] a state of disagreement or argument between people, groups, countries etc.: *serious political conflict* | *With so many people around there are bound to be some conflicts.* | +**between** *the conflict between tradition and innovation* | +**with** *A school counselor helped Jason resolve a conflict with one of his teachers.* | +**over** *conflicts over wages* | *Nina seems to be permanently* ***in conflict with*** *her superiors.* | *Andy's management style has* ***brought*** *him* ***into conflict with*** *colleagues.* | *The medical community often* ***comes into conflict with*** *politicians.* | **political/social/industrial conflict** *the social and political conflict of the 1930s* **2** [C,U] a situation in which you have to choose between two or more opposing things: +**of** *a conflict of loyalties* | +**between** *conflict between the demands of work and family* | *The principles of democracy are sometimes* ***in conflict with*** *political reality.* **3** [C] something that you have to do at the same time that someone wants you to do something different: *Sorry, I* ***have a conflict*** *on Friday. Can we move the meeting to Monday?* **4** [C,U] fighting or a war: *Will this peace settlement bring an end to years of conflict?* | **armed/military/violent conflict** *Armed conflict may be unavoidable.* ▸see THESAURUS box at **war**
5 [C,U] a situation in which you have two opposite feelings about something: *an* ***inner conflict*** *between his religious beliefs and his drinking* **6** [C] ENG. LANG. ARTS a situation in a book, play, movie etc. in which different characters or forces oppose each other in a way that causes or influences the action of the story: *The central conflict in the story is between the boy and his father.*
[**Origin:** 1400–1500 Latin *conflictus*, from the past participle of *confligere* **to strike together**]

con·flict[2] /kən'flɪkt/ Ac *v.* [I] **1** if two ideas, beliefs, opinions etc. conflict, they cannot exist together or both be true: +**with** *If two laws conflict with each other, the court has a difficult task.* **2** if two events or activities conflict, they happen at the same time so you cannot do both: +**with** *The conference conflicts with my vacation plans.*

con·flict·ed /kən'flɪktɪd/ Ac *adj.* **be/feel conflicted** to be confused about what choice to make, especially when the decision involves strong beliefs or opinions: *She was deeply conflicted about reporting her brother's criminal activity.*

con·flict·ing /kən'flɪktɪŋ/ Ac *adj.* [only before noun] conflicting ideas, information, stories etc. are different and it does not seem possible that both can be true or right: *conflicting opinions* | *People keep giving me conflicting advice.*

ˌconflict of 'interest *n. plural* **conflicts of interest** [C] a situation in which you cannot do your job fairly because your position or influence can affect another business that you have connections with: *There is a growing conflict of interest between her political role and her business activities.*

con·flu·ence /'kɑnfluəns/ *n.* [singular] **1** GEOGRAPHY the place where two or more rivers flow together: +**of** *the confluence of the Missouri and Yellowstone rivers* **2** a situation in which two or more things happen or exist at the same time: *a confluence of unhappy events* —**confluent** *adj.*

con·form /kən'fɔrm/ Ac *v.* [I] **1** to behave in the way that most other people in your group or society behave OPP **rebel**: *There's a lot of pressure on schoolkids to conform.* | +**to/with** *You'll find that not everyone here conforms to traditional standards of behavior.* **2** to obey a rule or law: +**to/with** *All buildings must conform to a local eight-story limit.* | *Zach refuses to conform with school rules.* **3** to be similar to what people expect or think is usual: **conform to a pattern/model/ideal etc.** *Joseph does not conform to the stereotype of a policeman.* → see also CONFORMIST —**conformer** *n.* [C] —**conformance** *n.* [U]

conˌformal 'map *n.* [C] a flat map showing the actual

shape of a country or area but not real distances or sizes

con·for·ma·tion /ˌkɑnfɔrˈmeɪʃən, -fə-/ Ac *n.* [C,U] TECHNICAL the shape of something or the way in which it is formed: +**of** *the conformation of the earth*

con·form·ist /kənˈfɔrmɪst/ Ac *adj.* thinking and behaving like everyone else, because you do not want to be different, or forcing people to think or behave in this way OPP **nonconformist**: *views outside the conformist political mainstream* —**conformist** *n.* [C]

con·form·i·ty /kənˈfɔrməṭi/ Ac *n.* [U] **1** behavior that obeys the accepted rules of society or a group, and is the same as that of most other people: *Greg continued to resist conformity, later becoming a vegetarian.* **2 in conformity with sth** FORMAL in a way that obeys rules, customs etc.: *We must act in conformity with local regulations.*

con·found /kənˈfaʊnd/ *v.* [T] FORMAL **1** to confuse and surprise people by being unexpected: *Dan's speedy recovery confounded the medical experts.* **2** to prove someone or something wrong: **confound the critics/pundits/experts etc.** *She confounded the critics by turning the company around.* **3** if a problem, question etc. confounds you, you cannot understand it or explain it SYN **baffle**: *Even travel agents are confounded by the logic of airline ticket pricing.* **4** LITERARY to defeat an enemy, plan etc. **5 confound it/him/them etc.** OLD-FASHIONED used to show that you are annoyed

con·found·ed /kənˈfaʊndɪd, ˈkɑnˌfaʊn-/ *adj.* [only before noun] OLD-FASHIONED used to show that the thing you are talking about is annoying

con·fra·ter·ni·ty /ˌkɑnfrəˈtəːnəṭi/ *n. plural* **confraternities** [C] FORMAL a group of people, especially religious people who are not priests, who work together for some good purpose

con·frère, confrere /ˈkɑnfrɛr, kɑnˈfrɛr/ *n.* [C] FORMAL someone you work with or who belongs to the same organization as you

con·front /kənˈfrʌnt/ W3 *v.* [T] **1** [usually passive] if a problem, difficulty etc. confronts you, it needs to be dealt with: *Many pressing problems confront the new administration.* | **be confronted with sth** *Customers are confronted with a bewildering number of choices.* **2** [usually passive] to behave in a threatening way toward someone, as though you are going to attack them: *They were confronted by a man with a gun.* **3** to ACCUSE someone of doing something by showing them the proof: *The play is about a woman who confronts the man who tortured her in prison.* | **confront sb about/with sth** *I'm afraid to confront Vivian about her drinking.* **4** to deal with something very difficult or bad in a brave and determined way: *We try to help people confront their problems.* [**Origin:** 1500–1600 French *confronter* **to have a border with, confront**, from Latin]

con·fron·ta·tion /ˌkɑnfrənˈteɪʃən/ *n.* [C,U] **1** a situation in which there is a lot of angry disagreement between two people or groups with different opinions: *Julia prefers to avoid any confrontation.* | +**with/between** *an angry confrontation between two of the commissioners* **2** a fight or battle: *Two people were killed and several wounded in the confrontation.* | +**with/between** *a violent confrontation with police*

con·fron·ta·tion·al /ˌkɑnfrənˈteɪʃənl/ *adj.* likely to cause arguments or make people angry: *a radio talk show host with a confrontational style*

Con·fu·cian·ism /kənˈfyuʃəˌnɪzəm/ *n.* [U] a Chinese way of thought which teaches that one should be loyal to one's family, friends, and rulers and treat others as one would like to be treated. Confucianism was developed from the ideas of Confucius. —**Confucian** *adj.*

Con·fu·cius /kənˈfyuʃəs/ (551–479 B.C.) a Chinese PHILOSOPHER who taught social and moral principles that had a great influence on Chinese society and on the way the Chinese people think → see also CONFUCIANISM

con·fuse /kənˈfyuz/ *v.* [T] **1** to make someone feel that they cannot think clearly or do not understand something: *I hope my explanation didn't confuse anybody.* | *The instructions just confused me more.* **2** to think wrongly that one person, thing, or idea is someone or something else: *Try not to confuse "your" and "you're."* | **confuse sb/sth with sb/sth** *I always confuse you with your sister.* **3 confuse the issue/situation** also **confuse matters/things** to make it even more difficult to think clearly about or deal with a situation or problem: *John kept asking unnecessary questions, which just confused the issue.*

con·fused /kənˈfyuzd/ S2 *adj.* **1** unable to understand clearly what someone is saying or what is happening: *Now I'm totally confused. Can you say that again?* | +**about** *We're confused about what we're supposed to be doing.* | *Every time someone tries to explain the game to me, I* ***get more confused***. **2** not clear, or not easy to understand: *a lot of confused ideas* | *confused political thinking* **3** unable to remember things or think clearly: *a confused old man* [**Origin:** 1300–1400 Old French *confus*, from Latin *confusus*, past participle of *confundere* **to pour together, confuse**] —**confusedly** /kənˈfyuzɪdli/ *adv.*

con·fus·ing /kənˈfyuzɪŋ/ S3 *adj.* unclear and difficult to understand: *a confusing message* | *French wine labels can be very confusing.* | +**to/for** *The system can be confusing for new students.* —**confusingly** *adv.*

con·fu·sion /kənˈfyuʒən/ *n.* [U] **1** a state of not understanding what is happening or what something means because it is not clear: *I hope the meeting will clear up people's confusion.* | +**about/over/as to** *There was some confusion over how much we owe.* | **create/lead to/cause confusion** *Having three teachers called Wilson in the same school led to considerable confusion.* **2** a situation in which someone wrongly thinks that one person, thing, or idea is someone or something else: *To avoid confusion, the teams wore different colors.* | +**with/in** *The seminar was supposed to begin at 7:00, but there was some confusion with the scheduling.* | +**between** *a confusion between the two men's names* **3** a feeling of not being able to think clearly about what you should say or do, especially in an embarrassing situation: *Jake's confusion at meeting Sherri there was obvious.* | *Matt stared at her* ***in confusion***. **4** a very confusing situation, usually with a lot of noise and action: *With all the confusion, nobody noticed the two boys leave.*

con·ga /ˈkɑŋgə/ *n.* [C,U] ENG. LANG. ARTS **1** a Latin American dance in which people hold onto each other and dance in a line, or the music for this **2** also **conga drum** a tall drum that is usually played by hitting it with your hands [**Origin:** 1900–2000 American Spanish, Spanish, from *congo* **of the Congo (= area of central Africa)**]

ˈcon game *n.* [C] a dishonest trick played on someone in order to get their money SYN **con**

con·geal /kənˈdʒil/ *v.* [I] if a liquid such as blood congeals, it becomes thick or solid: *a puddle of congealed grease* [**Origin:** 1300–1400 Old French *congeler*, from Latin *congelare*, from *com-* + *gelare* **to freeze**]

con·ge·nial /kənˈdʒinyəl/ *adj.* **1** nice, in a way that makes you feel comfortable and relaxed SYN **friendly**: *a congenial atmosphere* | *Everyone there was very congenial* **2** appropriate for something: *The department provides a very congenial environment for research students.* —**congenially** *adv.* —**congeniality** /kənˌdʒiniˈæləṭi/ *n.* [U]

con·gen·i·tal /kənˈdʒɛnəṭl/ *adj.* **1** MEDICINE a congenital medical condition or disease affects someone from the time they are born: *a congenital birth defect* **2** existing as a part of your character and unlikely to change: *The city seems to have a congenital inferiority complex.* | *Brian is* ***a congenital liar***. —**congenitally** *adv.*

con·gest·ed /kənˈdʒɛstɪd/ *adj.* **1** a congested street, city etc. is very full of people or traffic: *congested airports* | *The roads were heavily congested.* **2** a congested nose, chest etc. is filled with thick liquid that does not flow easily, especially because you have a cold

C

C

—**congestion** /kən'dʒɛstʃən, -'dʒɛʃ-/ *n.* [U] *traffic congestion* | *nasal congestion*

con·glom·er·ate /kən'glɑmərɪt/ *n.* **1** [C] ECONOMICS a large business organization consisting of several different and unrelated companies that have joined together: *a large farming and food conglomerate* **2** [C,U] EARTH SCIENCE a type of rock consisting of different sizes of stones held together by clay **3** [C] a group of different things or people gathered together SYN **conglomeration**: **+of** *The country is an awkward conglomerate of very different regions.*

con·glom·er·a·tion /kən,glɑmə'reɪʃən/ *n.* **1** [C] a group of many different things gathered together: **+of** *The downtown is a conglomeration of loud bars, souvenir shops, and art galleries.* **2** [U] the process of forming business conglomerates

Con·go, the /'kɑŋgoʊ/ a long river in central Africa that flows toward the Atlantic Ocean through both the Republic of Congo and the Democratic Republic of Congo

Congo, the Democratic Republic of a very large country in central Africa, which was called Zaïre between 1971 and 1997, and before that was called the Belgian Congo —**Congolese** /,kɑŋgə'liz◂, -'lis◂/ *n., adj.*

Congo, the Republic of a country on the Equator in the western part of central Africa, to the west of the Democratic Republic of Congo —**Congolese** *n., adj.*

con·grats /kən'græts/ *interjection* INFORMAL a short form of CONGRATULATIONS

con·grat·u·late /kən'grætʃə,leɪt/ *v.* [T] **1** to tell someone that you are happy because they have achieved something or because something good has happened to them: *I'd like to congratulate all the prizewinners.* | **congratulate sb on (doing) sth** *She congratulated me warmly on my promotion.* | **congratulate sb for (doing) sth** *He congratulated her for being so perceptive.* | *All three* ***are to be congratulated*** *for doing so well.* ►see THESAURUS box at **praise**[1] **2 congratulate yourself** to feel pleased and proud of yourself because you have achieved something or something good has happened to you: **+on/for** *The resort is congratulating itself for installing new snow-making equipment in time for this season.* [**Origin:** 1500–1600 Latin, past participle of *congratulari* **to wish happiness**] —**congratulatory** /kən'grætʃələ,tɔri/ *adj.*

con·grat·u·la·tion /kən,grætʃə'leɪʃən/ *n.* **1 congratulations** [plural] words and expressions that you use to say that you are happy that someone has achieved something: *Sidney sent his congratulations.* | *I hear that* ***congratulations are in order*** (=something good has happened to you). **2 congratulations!** SPOKEN an expression used when you want to congratulate someone: *"I passed my driving test!" "Congratulations!"* | **+on** *Congratulations on a superb performance!* **3** [U] the act of expressing your happiness that someone has achieved something: *a letter of congratulation*

con·gre·gant /'kɑŋgrɪgənt/ *n.* [C] FORMAL one of a group of people who come together, especially in a church, for religious WORSHIP

con·gre·gate /'kɑŋgrə,geɪt/ *v.* [I] to come together in a group: *Insects tend to congregate on the underside of leaves.* [**Origin:** 1400–1500 Latin, past participle of *congregare*, from *com-* + *grex* **crowd**]

con·gre·ga·tion /,kɑŋgrə'geɪʃən/ *n.* [C] **1** a group of people gathered together in a church: *When the prayer ended, the entire congregation sat down.* **2** the people who usually go to a particular church: *Several members of the congregation organized a bake sale.* —**congregational** *adj.*

Con·gre·ga·tion·al /,kɑŋgrə'geɪʃənl/ *adj.* relating to a Protestant church in which each congregation is responsible for making its own decisions —**Congregationalism** *n.* [U] —**Congregationalist** *n.* [C]

con·gress /'kɑŋgrɪs/ W1 *n.* **1 Congress** POLITICS the group of people elected to make laws in the U.S., consisting of the Senate and the House of Representatives: *The President has lost the support of Congress.* | *an act of Congress* | *members of Congress* **2** [C,U] a formal meeting of the members of a group, especially a political party, to discuss ideas, exchange information etc. SYN **conference**: *an international congress of archaeologists* **3** [C] POLITICS the group of people chosen or elected to make the laws in some countries: *Brazil's congress* → see also SEXUAL CONGRESS [**Origin:** 1400–1500 Latin *congressus* **meeting**, from the past participle of *congredi* **to come together**]

con·gres·sion·al, Congressional /kəŋ'grɛʃənl/ W2 *adj.* [only before noun] relating to a congress, especially the U.S. House of Representatives: *a congressional subcommittee*

Con,gressional 'Budget ,Office, the ABBREVIATION **CBO** *n.* ECONOMICS a U.S. government department that provides the government with general economic information and information about the cost of government spending

con,gressional 'district *n.* [C] POLITICS an area of a U.S. state that has an elected representative in the U.S. House of Representatives

con·gress·man, Congressman /'kɑŋgrɪsmən/ *n.* *plural* **congressmen** [C] POLITICS a man who is a member of a congress, especially the U.S. House of Representatives

,Congress of ,Racial E'quality, the ABBREVIATION **CORE** *n.* [singular] POLITICS an organization started in 1942 to work for equality between the races using methods that were not violent. The organization later became more interested in helping African-Americans help themselves to live better lives.

con·gress·wom·an, Congresswoman /'kɑŋgrɪs,wʊmən/ *n.* *plural* **congresswomen** [C] POLITICS a woman who is a member of a congress, especially the U.S. House of Representatives

con·gru·ent /kəŋ'gruənt, 'kɑŋgruənt/ *adj.* **1** FORMAL fitting together well: **+with** *All of those societies had political systems that were congruent with their economic realities.* **2** MATH congruent shapes are the same size and shape as each other: *congruent triangles* —**congruence** *n.* [U] —**congruently** *adv.*

con·gru·ous /'kɑŋgruəs/ *adj.* FORMAL [+ with] fitting together well OPP **incongruous** —**congruity** /kəŋ'gruəṭi/ *n.* [C,U]

con·ic /'kɑnɪk/ *adj.* MATH relating to or shaped like a CONE

con·i·cal /'kɑnɪkəl/ *adj.* MATH shaped like a CONE: *a conical roof*

,conical 'flask *n* [C] SCIENCE a glass container with a wide flat base and a long narrow neck, used in science LABORATORIES → see picture at LABORATORY

,conic 'section *n.* [C] MATH a curved shape formed by a PLANE (=flat surface) going through a CONE. The conic section is either a circle, an ELLIPSE, a HYPERBOLA, or a PARABOLA, depending on the angle at which the flat surface meets and goes through the cone

con·i·fer /'kɑnəfɚ/ *n.* [C] BIOLOGY a tree, such as a PINE tree, that has needle-shaped leaves that stay on it during the winter, and produces brown CONES that contain its seeds —**coniferous** /kə'nɪfərəs, koʊ-/ *adj.*

conj. the written abbreviation of CONJUNCTION

con·jec·ture[1] /kən'dʒɛktʃɚ/ *n.* FORMAL **1** [U] the act of guessing about things when you do not have enough information: *There has been some conjecture about a possible merger.* | *What she said was* ***pure conjecture.*** **2** [C] an idea or opinion formed by guessing SYN **guess**: *My results show that this conjecture was, in fact, correct.* **3** [C] MATH a fact that you think is true as a result of DEDUCTIVE REASONING —**conjectural** *adj.*

conjecture[2] *v.* [I,T] FORMAL to form an idea or opinion without having much information to base it on SYN **guess** SYN **hypothesize**: *"Maybe Burt is jealous," Isabelle conjectured.* | **+that** *Sam conjectured that what happened to Dave might happen to him.*

con·join /kən'dʒɔɪn/ *v.* [I,T] FORMAL to join together, or to make things or people do this

con,joined 'twins *n.* [plural] TECHNICAL SIAMESE TWINS

con·ju·gal /'kɑndʒəgəl/ *adj.* [only before noun] FORMAL **1** relating to marriage or married people: *conjugal love* **2 a conjugal visit** a meeting between a married COUPLE, usually a prisoner and his wife or her husband, during which they are allowed to have sex

con·ju·gate¹ /'kɑndʒə,geɪt/ *v.* [T] ENG. LANG. ARTS to give the different grammatical forms of a verb in a particular order: *We have to conjugate these verbs in Latin.*

con·ju·gate² /'kɑndʒəgɪt/ *n.* [C] MATH a COMPLEX CONJUGATE

,conjugate com,plex 'number *n.* [C] MATH a COMPLEX CONJUGATE

con·ju·ga·tion /,kɑndʒə'geɪʃən/ *n.* [C] ENG. LANG. ARTS **1** the way that a particular verb conjugates **2** a set of verbs in languages such as Latin that are conjugated in the same way

con·junct /'kɑndʒʌŋkt/ *n.* [C] ENG. LANG. ARTS a CONJUNCTIVE —**conjunct** *adj.*

con·junc·tion /kən'dʒʌŋkʃən/ *n.* **1 in conjunction with sb/sth** FORMAL working, happening, or being used with someone or something else: *The worksheets should be used in conjunction with the course books.* **2** [C] ENG. LANG. ARTS a word such as "but," "and," or "while" that connects parts of sentences, phrases, or CLAUSES **3** [C usually singular] a combination of different things that have come together by chance

con·junc·tive /kən'dʒʌŋktɪv/ *n.* [C] TECHNICAL a word that joins phrases together —**conjunctive** *adj.*: *a conjunctive adverb*

con·junc·ti·vi·tis /kən,dʒʌŋktɪ'vaɪt̬ɪs/ *n.* [U] MEDICINE an infectious disease of the eyes that makes them red and makes the EYELIDS stick together SYN **pinkeye**

con·junc·ture /kən'dʒʌŋktʃə/ *n.* [C] FORMAL a combination of events or situations, especially one that causes problems: *the historic conjuncture from which Marxism arose*

con·jure /'kɑndʒə/ *v.* **1** [I,T] to perform tricks in which you seem to make things appear, disappear, or change as if by magic: *The magician conjured a rabbit out of his hat.* **2 conjure an image/thought/memory etc.** to bring a particular image, thought etc. to someone's mind SYN **conjure up**: *For me, Thanksgiving conjures images of Pilgrims and turkeys.* **3** [T] FORMAL to make something appear or happen in a way which is not expected: *He has conjured victories from worse situations than this.* [**Origin:** 1200–1300 Old French *conjurer*, from Latin, from *com-* + *jurare* **to swear**] —**conjuring** *n.* [U]

conjure sth ↔ **up** *phr. v.* **1** to bring a thought, picture, idea, or memory to someone's mind: *The music always conjures up happy memories of my teenage years.* **2** to make something appear or happen in a sudden or unexpected way: *Somehow the president managed to conjure up enough votes to get the proposal passed.* **3** to make the spirit of a dead person appear by saying special magic words

con·jur·er, conjuror /'kɑndʒərə/ *n.* [C] someone who entertains people by performing tricks in which things appear, disappear, or change as if by magic

conk /kɑŋk/ *v.* [T] INFORMAL to hit someone hard, especially on the head

conk out *phr. v.* INFORMAL **1** if a machine or car conks out, it suddenly stops working: *I was driving along on Highway 5 when my car conked out.* **2** if someone conks out, they fall asleep because they are very tired: *He just rolled over and conked out.*

'con man *n.* [C] someone who tricks or deceives people in order to get money from them SYN **con artist**

con·nect /kə'nɛkt/ W2 *v.*

1 JOIN [T] to join two or more things together SYN **link**: *I don't know how to connect these wires.* | *The highway connects Nepal and Tibet.* | **connect sth to/with sth** *Connect the speakers to the CD player.* | *two rooms with a* ***connecting door*** (=a door between the rooms)

2 RELATIONSHIP [T] to realize that two facts, events, or people are related to each other SYN **link**: *She did not connect the two events in her mind.* | **connect sb/sth with sth** *There is little evidence to connect them with the attack.* | **connect sb/sth to sth** *I'd seen him around, but I'd never connected the name to his face.*

3 ELECTRICITY/GAS ETC. [I,T] also **connect up** to join something to the main supply of electricity, gas, or water, or to the telephone network OPP **disconnect**: *Has the phone been connected yet?* | **connect (sth) to sth** *Click here to connect to the Internet.* | *Most homes are connected to the public water supply.*

4 AIRPLANE/TRAIN ETC. [I] if one airplane, bus etc. connects with another, it arrives just before the other one leaves so that you can continue your trip: **+with** *This train connects with the one in Rochester.* | *I missed the* ***connecting flight.***

5 TELEPHONE [T] to join two telephone lines so that two people can speak OPP **disconnect**: *Please hold. I'll try to connect you.*

6 UNDERSTAND PEOPLE [I] if people connect, they feel that they like each other and understand each other: *I talked to her for a while, but we just didn't connect.* | **+with** *They valued Deanna's ability to empathize and connect with others.*

7 HIT STH [I] to succeed in hitting someone or something: *He swung at the ball, but didn't connect.*

8 connect the dots a) an activity for children in which they make a picture by drawing lines between small points that are laid out on a piece of paper **b)** to put many pieces of information together to understand or show what the real connections between people and things are: *It's not hard to connect the dots between substance abuse and child abuse.*

[**Origin:** 1400–1500 Latin *connectere*, from + *nectere* **to tie**]

con·nect·ed /kə'nɛktɪd/ S3 *adj.* **1** if two facts, events etc. are connected, they affect each other or are related to each other: *Police are investigating whether the three shootings are connected.* | **+to** *The incident did not appear to be connected to any political group.* | **+with** *problems connected with drug abuse* | *The two issues are* ***closely connected.*** **2** if two things are connected, they are joined together: *The two continents were once connected.* | **+to** *Is this computer connected to the Internet?* **3** having a social or professional relationship with someone: *a politically connected businessman* | **+with** *Aren't they connected with his father's business in some way?* **4 well connected** having important or powerful friends or relatives

con·nect·ed·ness /kə'nɛktɪdnɪs/ *n.* [U] the feeling of understanding and liking someone: *Each of us has a need for human connectedness.*

Con·nect·i·cut /kə'nɛt̬ɪkət/ ABBREVIATION **CT** a state in the northeastern U.S.

con·nec·tion /kə'nɛkʃən/ S2 W3 *n.*

1 STH THAT CONNECTS THINGS [C,U] a relationship in which two or more facts, events, people etc. are related to each other, and one is affected or caused by the other: **+between** *the connection between smoking and cancer* | **+with** *He had no known connection with terrorist activity.* | **+to** *They denied any connection to the organization.* | *The evidence was there in the file, but no one* ***made the connection*** (=realized there was a connection). | *Students often* ***see*** *little* ***connection*** *between school and the rest of their lives.* | *the* ***close connection*** *between social conditions and health* | *Police have yet to* ***establish a connection*** *between the two murders.* | **a causal connection** (=a connection in which one thing causes the other)

2 ELECTRICAL WIRE [C] a wire or piece of metal joining two parts of a machine or electrical system: *Your computer screen must have* ***a loose connection*** *somewhere.*

3 PEOPLE YOU KNOW [plural] people whom you know who can help you by giving you money, finding you a job etc.: *She used her connections to get a better job.*

4 in connection with sth concerning or relating to something: *Two men have been arrested in connection with the attack.*

C

5 TELEPHONE/COMPUTER [C] the way in which phones or computers are connected to each other: *We have high-speed Internet connection now.* | *I didn't hear what you said – we must **have a bad connection**.*
6 AIRPLANE/TRAIN ETC. [C] an airplane, train, or bus that can be used by passengers from an earlier airplane, train, or bus who are continuing their trip: +**to** *The flight was late and we missed our connection.*
7 JOINING THINGS TOGETHER [U] the process or result of joining two or more things together: *fees for Internet connection* | +**to** *the connection of the building to the water supply*
8 ROAD/RAILROAD ETC. [C] a road, railroad etc. that joins two places and allows people to travel between them: *There are good rail connections between the major cities.*
9 FRIENDLY FEELING [C] a situation in which two people understand and like each other: *I felt an immediate connection with Luisa when I met her.*
10 FAMILY [plural] people who are related to you, but not very closely: *I believe Joe's family has Spanish connections.*

C

con·nec·tive¹ /kə'nɛktɪv/ *adj.* [only before noun] joining two or more things together

connective² *n.* [C] ENG. LANG. ARTS a word that joins phrases, parts of sentences etc.

con'nective ˌtissue *n.* [U, plural] BIOLOGY parts of the body such as fat or bone that support or join organs and other body parts together

'conning ˌtower *n.* [C] TECHNICAL the structure on top of a SUBMARINE (=ship that goes under water)

con·nip·tion /kə'nɪpʃən/ also **con'niption ˌfit** *n.* [C] INFORMAL **have/throw a conniption (fit)** to become very upset because you disagree with something or do not want to do something: *Mom had a conniption about Dan taking her car.*

con·nive /kə'naɪv/ *v.* **1 connive (with sb) to do sth** to work together secretly to achieve something, especially something wrong SYN **conspire**: *The two connived to drive Diana and Mark apart.* **2** [I] to allow something wrong to happen without trying to stop it, even though you know it is wrong: +**at** *Corrupt officials had connived at the importation of heroin.* [**Origin:** 1600–1700 French *conniver*, from Latin *connivere* **to close the eyes, connive**] —**connivance** *n.* [C]

con·niv·ing /kə'naɪvɪŋ/ *adj.* behaving in a way that does not prevent something wrong from happening, or actively helps it to happen: *She is a heartless conniving woman.*

con·nois·seur /ˌkɑnə'sɚ, -'sʊɚ/ *n.* [C] someone who knows a lot about something such as art, food, music etc.: *a wine connoisseur*

Con·nol·ly /'kɑnəli/, **Mau·reen** /mɔ'rin/ (1934–1969) a U.S. tennis player famous as the first woman to win the tennis GRAND SLAM

con·no·ta·tion /ˌkɑnə'teɪʃən/ *n.* [C] ENG. LANG. ARTS a feeling or an idea that a word makes you think of: *The word "liberal" has taken on **negative connotations**.* → see also DENOTATION —**connotative** /'kɑnəˌteɪtɪv/ *adj.*

con·note /kə'noʊt/ *v.* [T] FORMAL if a word connotes something, it makes you think of particular feelings and ideas: *The car's name is meant to connote luxury and quality.* → see also DENOTE

con·nu·bi·al /kə'nubiəl/ *adj.* FORMAL relating to marriage: ***connubial bliss*** (=being happily married)

con·quer /'kɑŋkɚ/ *v.* **1** [I,T] to defeat and take control of an area, country, or group of people by fighting a war: *Hernán Cortés led Spanish troops to conquer the Aztecs.* | *Alexander the Great **conquered the world**, but died at 33.* | *a **conquering hero*** → see also **divide and conquer** at DIVIDE¹ (7) **2** [T] to gain control over a feeling, or successfully deal with something that is difficult or dangerous SYN **overcome**: *He conquered his drinking problem and found a new career.* | *They're developing new drugs to conquer the disease.* | *The moral of the story is that **love conquers all*** (=love helps to solve any problem). **3** [T] to become very successful in a particular activity: *In the last few years, the company has succeeded in conquering the overseas markets.* | **conquer sb's heart** (=make someone love you) **4** [T] to succeed in climbing to the top of a mountain when no one has ever climbed it before: *Hillary and Tenzing conquered Mount Everest in 1953.* [**Origin:** 1200–1300 Old French *conquerre*, from Latin *conquirere* **to look for, collect**] —**conqueror** *n.* [C]

con·quest /'kɑŋkwɛst/ *n.* **1** [C,U] the act of defeating an army or taking land by fighting: *military conquests* | +**of** *the Roman conquest of Greece* **2** [C] land that is won in a war: *Spanish conquests in Latin America* **3** [C] someone whom you have persuaded to love you or to have sex with you, although you do not love or respect them: *I didn't want to be just another one of his conquests.* **4** [U] the act of gaining control of or dealing successfully with something that is difficult or dangerous: +**of** *the conquest of space*

con·quis·ta·dor /kɑn'kistəˌdɔr/ *n. plural* **conquistadors** or **conquistadores** /kɑnˌkistə'dɔreɪz/ [C] HISTORY one of the Spanish conquerors of Mexico, Central and South America in the 16th century

Con·rad /'kɑnræd/, **Joseph** (1857–1924) a British writer of novels, born in Poland, who is considered one of the greatest writers in English of the early 20th century

con·san·guin·i·ty /ˌkɑnsæŋ'gwɪnət̬i/ *n.* [U] LITERARY the state of being members of the same family

con·science /'kɑnʃəns/ *n.* **1** [C usually singular] the part of your mind that tells you whether the things you do are morally right or wrong: *I have to do what my conscience tells me.* | *It was his **guilty conscience*** (=knowledge that he had done something wrong) *that made him offer to help.* | *Smith says he has a **clear conscience*** (=knowledge that you have done nothing wrong) *about what happened.* | *If anything happens to Emily, I'll always **have it on** my **conscience*** (=feel guilty about it). | *She has a highly developed **social conscience*** (=a moral sense of how society should be). | *He refused to agree, as **a matter of conscience**, and was dismissed.* ►see THESAURUS box at **guilt¹** **2** [U] a feeling of GUILT because you did something wrong: *Parker displayed a remarkable lack of conscience about what he had done.* | *She felt a **pang of conscience** at lying to him.* **3 in good conscience** FORMAL if you do something in good conscience, you do it because you think it is the right thing to do: *I could not, in good conscience, agree with his decision.* [**Origin:** 1200–1300 Old French, Latin *conscientia*, from *conscire* **to be conscious (of being guilty)**] → see also PRISONER OF CONSCIENCE

con·sci·en·tious /ˌkɑnʃi'ɛnʃəs◂/ *adj.* showing a lot of care and attention: *We have made a very conscientious effort to reduce spending.* | *a conscientious worker* —**conscientiously** *adv.* —**conscientiousness** *n.* [U]

ˌconscientious ob'jector *n.* [C] someone who refuses to become a soldier because of their moral or religious beliefs → see also DRAFT DODGER

con·scious /'kɑnʃəs/ S2 *adj.* **1** [not before noun] noticing or realizing something SYN **aware**: +**of** *I was very conscious of the fact that I had to make a good impression.* | +**that** *Stanley was conscious that Mrs. Olenska was looking at him.* **2** awake and able to understand what is happening around you OPP **unconscious**: *The driver was still conscious when the ambulance arrived.* **3** thinking a lot about something that is important or that you are worried about: +**of** *He was very conscious of his responsibilities.* | *I try not to be overly conscious of my weight.* | **socially/environmentally/politically etc. conscious** *environmentally conscious consumers* **4 a conscious effort/decision/attempt etc. (to do sth)** an effort, decision etc. that is deliberate and intended SYN **deliberate**: *Vivien made a conscious effort to be friendly.* **5** conscious thoughts, memories etc. are ones which you know about → see also SUBCONSCIOUS: *the conscious mind* —**consciously** *adv.* → see also SELF-CONSCIOUS

-conscious /kɑnʃəs/ [in adjectives] **health-conscious/fashion-conscious etc.** thinking a lot about something such as health, fashion etc., and letting it influence the way you live or behave: *fashion-conscious teenagers*

con·scious·ness /ˈkɑnʃəsnɪs/ S2 W3 *n.* [U] **1** the condition of being awake and able to understand what is happening around you: *David* ***lost consciousness*** (=became unconscious) *and had to be taken to the hospital.* | **regain consciousness** (=wake up after being sick and unconscious) **2** your mind and your thoughts: *The painful memories eventually faded from her consciousness.* **3** someone's ideas, feelings, or opinions about politics, life etc.: *The experience helped to change her political consciousness.* **4** the state of knowing that something exists or is true SYN **awareness**: *The march is intended to* ***raise*** *people's* ***consciousness*** *about women's health issues.* → see also STREAM OF CONSCIOUSNESS

ˈconsciousness ˌraising *n.* [U] the process of making people understand and care more about a moral, social, or political problem —**consciousness-raising** *adj.* [only before noun]

con·script¹ /kənˈskrɪpt/ *v.* [T] FORMAL **1** to make someone join the military SYN **draft**: **+conscript sb into sth** *Many young men were forcibly conscripted into the military.* → see also RECRUIT **2** to make someone become a member of a group or take part in a particular activity: *She had conscripted him into helping her distribute the pamphlets.* [**Origin:** 1800–1900 Latin *conscriptus*, past participle of *conscribere* **to make a member of something**]

con·script² /ˈkɑnskrɪpt/ *n.* [C] FORMAL someone who has been made to join the military SYN **draftee** → see also RECRUIT

con·scrip·tion /kənˈskrɪpʃən/ *n.* [U] FORMAL the practice of making people join the military → see also DRAFT¹(3)

con·se·crate /ˈkɑnsəˌkreɪt/ *v.* [T] **1** to officially state in a special religious ceremony that something such as a place or building is holy and can be used for religious purposes: *The chapel was consecrated in 1475.* **2** to officially state in a special religious ceremony that someone is now a priest, BISHOP etc. —**consecrated** *adj.*: *consecrated ground* —**consecration** /ˌkɑnsəˈkreɪʃən/ *n.* [U]

con·sec·u·tive /kənˈsɛkyət̬ɪv/ *adj.* [only before noun] consecutive numbers, periods of time, or events follow one after the other without any interruptions: *It had rained for four consecutive days.* | *The Sharks have lost ten consecutive games.* —**consecutively** *adv.*: *Number the pages consecutively.*

conˌsecutive ˈangles *n.* [plural] MATH angles of a POLYGON (=flat shape with three or more sides) that share one of their sides with each other

conˌsecutive ˈintegers *n.* [plural] MATH two or more whole numbers that follow one after the other, such as the numbers 3, 4, and 5

con·sen·su·al /kənˈsɛnʃuəl/ *adj.* giving your permission for something, or agreeing to do something: *The jury must decide whether it was* ***consensual sex*** *or rape.*

con·sen·sus /kənˈsɛnsəs/ Ac *n.* [singular, U] an opinion that everyone in a group will agree with or accept: *the current consensus of opinion* | **+on/about** *There was a clear consensus on the need for change.* | *The group's task is to* ***reach a consensus*** *on the following questions.* | *Whenever possible decisions will be made* ***by consensus.***

conˈsensus ˌbuilder *n.* someone, especially a politician, who is good at helping people or groups reach agreements —**consensus building** *n.* [U]

con·sent¹ /kənˈsɛnt/ Ac S2 *n.* [U] **1** permission to do something, especially from someone in authority or from someone who is responsible for something SYN **permission**: *I want to read the form before I* ***give*** *my consent.* | *He took the car* ***without*** *the owner's* ***consent.*** | **written/verbal consent** *We have to get written consent from each participant.* → see also AGE OF CONSENT **2** agreement about something: *The wedding was canceled* ***by mutual consent*** (=by agreement between both people involved). → see also ASSENT¹, DISSENT¹

consent² Ac *v.* [I] to give your permission for something or agree to do something: **+to** *Wendy's father reluctantly consented to the marriage.* | **consent to do sth** *She rarely consents to give interviews.* [**Origin:** 1200–1300 Latin *consentire*, from *com-* + *sentire* **to feel**]

conˌsenting aˈdult *n.* [C] LAW someone who is considered legally an adult and chooses to have sex with someone else

con·se·quence /ˈkɑnsəˌkwɛns, -kwəns/ Ac W2 *n.* **1** [C usually plural] something that happens as a result of a particular action or situation: *Ignoring safety procedures can have potentially tragic consequences.* | **+of** *The economic consequences of vandalism are enormous.* | *You should be aware of the consequences of your actions.* | **suffer/face the consequences** (=to accept and deal with bad results of something you did) *He broke the law, and now he must face the consequences.* **2 as a consequence (of sth)** as a result of something: *Tyler rarely paid for anything and, as a consequence, had no idea what things cost.* **3 of little/no/any consequence** without much importance or value: *Your opinion is of little consequence to me.*

con·se·quent /ˈkɑnsəkwənt/ Ac *adj.* [only before noun] FORMAL happening as a result of a particular event or situation: *a drought and consequent famine* [**Origin:** 1400–1500 French, Latin, present participle of *consequi*, from *com-* + *sequi* **to follow**] → see also SUBSEQUENT

con·se·quen·tial /ˌkɑnsəˈkwɛnʃəl/ *adj.* FORMAL **1** important SYN **significant** OPP **inconsequential**: *The agency has taken a consequential role in the planning.* **2** happening as a direct result of a particular event or situation: *consequential effects of the policies* —**consequentially** *adv.*

con·se·quent·ly /ˈkɑnsəˌkwɛntli, -kwənt-/ Ac *adv.* [sentence adverb] as a result: *The book has no narrator or main character. Consequently, it lacks a traditional plot.* | *There was no fighting and consequently no casualties.* ►see THESAURUS box at **thus**

con·ser·van·cy /kənˈsɚvənsi/ *n. plural* **conservancies** [C] a group of people who work to protect an area of land, a river etc.: *the Santa Monica Mountains Conservancy*

con·ser·va·tion /ˌkɑnsɚˈveɪʃən/ *n.* [U] **1** the protection of natural things such as animals, plants, forests etc., to prevent them being damaged, or destroyed: *wildlife conservation* | *The organization promotes conservation of forest resources.* **2** the activity of keeping things in good condition and preventing them from being spoiled or damaged: *The museum has a staff of six people working on textile conservation.*

ˌconserˈvation ˌarea *n.* [C] EARTH SCIENCE an area where animals and plants are protected from being destroyed

con·ser·va·tion·ist /ˌkɑnsɚˈveɪʃənɪst/ *n.* [C] SCIENCE someone who works to protect animals, plants etc. —**conservationism** *n.* [U]

conserˌvation of ˈcharge *n.* [U] PHYSICS a scientific principle that says that the total electric charge of a system remains the same in spite of any changes that happen inside the system

con·serv·a·tism /kənˈsɚvəˌtɪzəm/ *n.* [U] **1** an attitude of not trusting change and new ideas: *the Pope's policy of conservatism on religious doctrine* **2** POLITICS conservative opinions and principles, especially on social and political subjects → see also LIBERALISM

con·serv·a·tive¹ /kənˈsɚvət̬ɪv/ W2 *adj.* **1** preferring to continue doing things the way they are being done or have been proven to work, rather than risking changes → see also LIBERAL: *a conservative rural community* | *Her views on the role of women are very conservative.* **2** POLITICS supporting political ideas that include less involvement by the government in business and people's lives, for example by encouraging everyone to work and earn their own money, and having strong ideas about moral behavior → see also LIBERAL: *conservative economic policies* | *a conservative newspaper columnist* **3** not very modern or fashionable in style, taste etc. SYN **traditional**: *a dark, conservative suit* | *Despite his conservative appearance, he has quite a sense of humor.* **4 a conservative estimate/guess** a guess which is likely to be lower than the real amount: *Conservative estimates indicate at least 150 people were killed.* —**conservatively** *adv.*

C

conservative² W3 *n.* [C] POLITICS someone with conservative opinions or principles: *According to a recent poll, the governor has lost support among conservatives.* → see also LIBERAL

con·serv·a·tor /kən'sɚvət̬ɚ/ *n.* [C] **1** LAW someone who is legally responsible for another person and their property because that person is not able to do it on their own **2** someone whose job is to preserve valuable things at a MUSEUM, library etc.

con·serv·a·to·ry /kən'sɚvəˌtɔri/ *n. plural* **conservatories** [C] **1** ENG. LANG. ARTS a college where people are trained in music or acting: *the National Conservatory of Music* **2** a building made mostly of glass, where plants are kept for people to come and look at them

con·serve¹ /kən'sɚv/ *v.* [T] **1** to use as little water, energy etc. as possible so that it is not wasted: *Try and rest frequently to conserve your energy.* | *Everyone needs to make efforts to conserve water.* **2** to protect something and prevent it from changing or being damaged: *We have to conserve our forests for future generations.*
[**Origin:** 1300–1400 Old French *conserver*, from Latin *conservare*, from *com-* + *servare* **to keep, guard**]

con·serve² /'kɑnsɚv/ *n.* [C,U] a sweet food made of pieces of fruit that are preserved by being cooked with sugar, usually eaten on bread → see also JAM → PRESERVE² (3)

con·served /kən'sɚvd/ *adj.* PHYSICS a conserved quantity of energy, electricity etc. remains the same before and after a particular reaction

con·sid·er /kən'sɪdɚ/ S1 W1 *v.* [T]
1 THINK ABOUT to think about something, especially about whether to accept something or do something: *We are considering a number of options.* | **consider doing sth** *I seriously considered resigning.* | *John was* ***considering the possibility of*** *moving to Japan.* | **consider whether/how/when etc.** *The union is still considering whether to go on strike.* ▸see THESAURUS box at **think**
2 HAVE AN OPINION to think of someone or something in a particular way: **consider sb/sth (to be) sth** *What do you consider your greatest achievement?* | *This film is not considered appropriate for children.* | *I consider myself to be a reasonable person.* | **consider it necessary/important etc. to do sth** *I did not consider it necessary to report the incident.*
3 REMEMBER TO THINK ABOUT to remember to think carefully about something before making a judgment or a decision: *Before you resign, you should consider the effect it will have on your family.* | **consider that** *Her work is impressive, especially when you consider that she's only 16.* | **consider what/how/who etc.** *We have to consider what's best for the students.*
4 DISCUSS FORMALLY to discuss something such as a report or problem, so that you can make a decision about it: *The committee will consider the report at their next meeting.* | **be considered for sth** *Stewart is being considered for promotion.*
5 all things considered SPOKEN used when giving your opinion or judgment after thinking about all the facts: *All things considered, I'm sure we made the right decision.*
6 PEOPLE'S FEELINGS to think about someone or their feelings etc. and try to avoid upsetting or hurting them: *The mayor needs to consider local residents when she decides where to put the new stadium.*
7 consider yourself lucky/fortunate SPOKEN used to tell someone they should be glad that something is true or happened as it did: *Consider yourself lucky you weren't in the car at the time.*
8 consider it done SPOKEN used to say "yes" very willingly when someone asks you to do something for them: *"Would you ask him to call me this afternoon?" "Consider it done."*
9 LOOK AT FORMAL to look at someone or something carefully SYN **look at**: *Henry considered the sculpture with an expert eye.*
[**Origin:** 1300–1400 Old French *considerer*, from Latin *considerare* **to look at the stars, look at closely, examine**]

con·sid·er·a·ble /kən'sɪdərəbəl/ Ac W3 *adj.* large enough to be noticeable or to have noticeable effects: *Attracting tourists to the area is going to take considerable effort.* | *The difference between the two descriptions is considerable.* | **a considerable amount/number of sth** *A considerable number of students suffer from stress.* → see also INCONSIDERABLE

con·sid·er·a·bly /kən'sɪdərəbli/ Ac *adv.* in a noticeable or important way: *The sea turtle's natural habitat has been considerably reduced.* | **considerably more/larger/faster etc.** *A few of the paintings sold for considerably more than we had predicted.*

con·sid·er·ate /kən'sɪdərɪt/ *adj.* always thinking of what other people need or want, and being careful not to upset them OPP **inconsiderate**: *considerate drivers* | **+of** *It was very considerate of you to let us know you were going to be late.* —**considerately** *adv.* —**considerateness** *n.* [U]

con·sid·er·a·tion /kənˌsɪdə'reɪʃən/ W3 *n.*
1 THOUGHT [U] FORMAL careful thought and attention: *He presented a list of requests* ***for consideration.*** | **serious/careful consideration** *After careful consideration I decided to resign.* | *I hope you'll* ***give*** *my offer serious* ***consideration.*** | *Several proposals are currently* ***under consideration*** (=being thought about). | **full/due consideration** *The company promises to give due consideration to the results of the vote.*
2 take sth into consideration to remember to think about something important when you are making a decision or judgment: *Class participation is taken into consideration in the student's final grade.*
3 STH THAT AFFECTS A DECISION [C] something that you must think about when you are planning to do something, which affects what you decide to do: *practical considerations* | *Political rather than economic considerations determined the location of the new factory.* | *Cost should not be your main consideration.*
4 KINDNESS [U] the quality of thinking about other people's feelings or situation and taking care not to upset them: **+for** *Jeff never shows any consideration for other people's feelings.* | *The number of outdoor concerts has been reduced,* ***out of consideration for*** *the neighbors.*
5 DISCUSSION [U] the act of thinking about or discussing something, especially in order to make a decision about it: *The Senate will return to its consideration of illegal immigration Monday.*
6 in consideration of/for sth FORMAL as a reward for something: *The payment was in consideration for their services.*
7 MONEY [singular] FORMAL a payment for a service: *I might be able to help you,* ***for a small consideration.***

con·sid·ered /kən'sɪdɚd/ *adj.* **sb's considered opinion/judgment** FORMAL an opinion, decision etc. based on careful thought: *It is my considered opinion that you should now resign.*

con·sid·er·ing¹ /kən'sɪdərɪŋ/ *prep., conjunction* used when describing a situation, before stating a fact that you know has had an effect on that situation: *Considering the weather and everything, the game wasn't that bad.* | **considering (that)** *You did well, considering it was your first attempt.* | **considering who/how etc.** *The service was pretty bad, considering how much we paid.*

considering² *adv.* SPOKEN used after you make a statement or give an opinion, to say that something is true in spite of another fact: *The office was busy, but it wasn't too bad, considering.*

con•sign /kən'saɪn/ *v.* [T] FORMAL **1** to make someone or something be in a particular situation, especially a bad one: **consign sb/sth to sth** *After being voted out of office, he was consigned to political obscurity.* **2** to put someone or something somewhere, especially in order to get rid of them: **consign sb/sth to sth** *She consigned the letter to the trash.* **3** to send or deliver something to someone who has bought it

con•sign•ee /ˌkɑnsaɪ'ni, -sə-, kənˌsaɪ'ni/ *n.* [C] TECHNICAL the person that something is delivered to

con•sign•ment /kən'saɪnmənt/ *n.* **1** [C] a quantity of goods that is sent to someone at the same time, especially in order to be sold: **+of** *a consignment of 5,000 tons of rice* **2 on consignment** goods that are on consignment are being sold by a store for someone else, for a share of the profit **3** [U] the act of delivering things

con'signment ˌshop *n.* [C] a store where goods, especially used clothes and furniture, are sold by the store for someone else, for a share of the profit

con•sig•nor /kənˌsaɪ'nɔr, kən'saɪnɚ/ *n.* [C] TECHNICAL the person who sends goods to someone else

con•sist /kən'sɪst/ Ac *v.* [**Origin:** 1500–1600 Latin *consistere* **to stand still or firm, exist**]

consist in sth *phr. v.* FORMAL to be based on or depend on something: *The error consisted in the fact that we confused cause and consequence.* | **consist in doing sth** *Happiness does not consist in having what you want, but in wanting what you have.*

consist of sth *phr. v.* to be made of or contain a number of different parts or things SYN **be made up of**: *Your password should consist of at least five characters.* | **consist mainly/largely/mostly of sb/sth** *The land consists largely of mountains and forests.* | **consist entirely/solely of sb/sth** *His diet consists entirely of fast food.* ▸see THESAURUS box at **comprise**

con•sist•en•cy /kən'sɪstənsi/ Ac *n. plural* **consistencies** **1** [U] the quality of always being the same, always being good, or always behaving in an expected way OPP **inconsistency**: *Her consistency helps the whole team.* | **+in** *The child also needs consistency in his care and love.* | **+between/among** *a lack of consistency between the two stories* **2** [C,U] how firm or thick a substance is: **+of** *Stir until the mixture thickens to the consistency of whipping cream.*

con•sist•ent /kən'sɪstənt/ Ac W3 *adj.* **1** always having the same beliefs, behavior, attitudes, quality etc. OPP **inconsistent**: *one of our most consistent players* | *Teaching by example has been a consistent theme in his work.* | **+in** *We need to be consistent in our approach.* **2** continuing to develop in the same way OPP **inconsistent**: *We've seen a consistent improvement in the team's performance.* | *consistent growth year after year* **3 be consistent with sth** to say the same thing or follow the same principles as something else OPP **inconsistent**: *Her injuries are consistent with having fallen from the building.* **4** consistent ideas, arguments etc. do not have any part that disagrees with another part OPP **inconsistent**: *a consistent argument* | *The results of the different studies are remarkably consistent.* —**consistently** *adv.*

con•so•la•tion /ˌkɑnsə'leɪʃən/ *n.* [C,U] **1** someone or something that makes you feel better when you are sad or disappointed: **+of** *He had the consolation of knowing that he had done his best.* | **+for/to** *The life sentence will offer some consolation to the victim's family.* | ***If it's any consolation**, you played better than you did last time.* | *His family **took consolation in** the fact that his short life made a difference for other cancer sufferers.* | **little/small/no consolation** *The recovery of some of the money was small consolation.* **2 a consolation game/semifinal etc.** a sports game played by two teams or players who lost in the early stages of a competition

ˌconso'lation prize *n.* [C] a prize that is given to someone who has not won a competition, to make them feel better

con•so•la•to•ry /kən'soʊləˌtɔri, -'sɑ-/ *adj.* FORMAL intended to make someone feel better

con•sole¹ /kən'soʊl/ *v.* [T] to make someone feel better when they are feeling sad or disappointed: *I wanted to console my mother, but I didn't know how.* | **console sb with sth** *Archer consoles himself with the thought that at least he tried hard.*

con•sole² /'kɑnsoʊl/ *n.* [C] **1** COMPUTERS a flat board that contains the controls for a machine, piece of electrical equipment, computer etc.: *a video game console* **2** a special cabinet in which a television, computer etc. is fitted [**Origin:** 1800–1900 *console* **bracket** (18–20 centuries), from French]

con•sol•i•date /kən'sɑləˌdeɪt/ *v.* **1** [I,T] to join together a group of companies, organizations etc., or to become joined together: *The mayor has promised to consolidate several city departments.* **2** [T] to combine two or more things such as jobs, duties, or large amounts of money, especially to form a single thing that is more effective or easier to deal with: *Why not consolidate your debts with a single loan?* **3** [T] to make your position of power stronger and more likely to continue: *Successful marketing has consolidated our position as market leader.* —**consolidated** *adj.* —**consolidation** /kənˌsɑlə'deɪʃən/ *n.* [C,U]

con•som•mé /ˌkɑnsə'meɪ/ *n.* [U] a thin clear soup made from meat or vegetables

con•so•nance /'kɑnsənəns/ *n.* **1 in consonance with sth** FORMAL agreeing with something or existing together without any problems **2** [C,U] TECHNICAL a combination of musical notes that sounds pleasant SYN **harmony** OPP **dissonance** **3** [U] ENG. LANG. ARTS the action of repeating the same CONSONANT sound or sounds, especially at the end of words, in a piece of writing or speech → see also ASSONANCE: *"Long string" is an example of consonance.*

con•so•nant¹ /'kɑnsənənt/ *n.* [C] ENG. LANG. ARTS **1** a speech sound made by partly or completely stopping the flow of air through the mouth **2** a letter of the English alphabet that represents one of these sounds. The letters "a," "e," "i," "o," and "u" represent vowels, and all the other letters are consonants.

consonant² *adj.* **1 be consonant with sth** FORMAL not seeming to show that a statement or belief is wrong SYN **consistent**: *The scholarship program is consonant with our mission to promote research.* **2** ENG. LANG. ARTS relating to a combination of musical notes that sounds pleasant OPP **dissonant** [**Origin:** 1300–1400 Old French, Latin, present participle of *consonare* **to sound together, agree**]

con•sort¹ /kən'sɔrt/ *v.*

consort with sb *phr. v.* FORMAL to spend time with someone, especially someone that other people do not approve of: *Williams was accused of consorting with drug dealers.*

con•sort² /'kɑnsɔrt/ *n.* [C] FORMAL **1 do sth in consort with sb** to do something together with someone else: *Our lawyers are acting in consort with the management of Central Hospital.* **2** the wife or husband of a ruler **3** ENG. LANG. ARTS a group of people who play music from past times or the group of old-fashioned instruments they use

con•sor•ti•um /kən'sɔrʃiəm, -ṭiəm/ *n. plural* **consortiums** or **consortia** /-ʃiə, -ṭiə/ [C] a combination of several companies, organizations etc. working together to buy something, build something etc.: *a consortium of oil companies*

con•spic•u•ous /kən'spɪkyuəs/ *adj.* **1** very easy to notice, especially because of being different from everything or everyone else OPP **inconspicuous**: *I felt very conspicuous in my red coat.* ▸see THESAURUS box at **noticeable** **2 conspicuous by sb's/sth's absence** used to say that people noticed that someone or something was not in the place they expected them to be in **3** unusually good, bad, skillful etc.: *The award is given for conspicuous achievement in science.* [**Origin:** 1500–1600 Latin *conspicuus*, from *conspicere* **to get to see**] —**conspicuously** *adv.* —**conspicuousness** *n.* [U]

conˌspicuous con'sumption *n.* [U] the act of buying a lot of things, especially expensive things that are not necessary, in a way that people notice

con·spir·a·cy /kən'spɪrəsi/ *n. plural* **conspiracies** [C,U] a secret plan made by two or more people to do something that is harmful or illegal: **conspiracy to do sth** *Police have arrested six people for conspiracy to distribute drugs.* | **+against** *a conspiracy against the government* | *There has been a* ***conspiracy of silence*** (=an agreement to keep quiet about something that should not be a secret) *about violations of regulations.* | *The book explores a new* ***conspiracy theory*** (=the idea that an event was caused by a conspiracy) *about Kennedy's assassination.*

con·spir·a·tor /kən'spɪrət̬ɚ/ *n.* [C] someone who is involved in a secret plan to do something harmful or illegal

con·spir·a·to·ri·al /kən,spɪrə'tɔriəl/ *adj.* **1** relating to a secret plan to do something harmful or illegal **2 a conspiratorial smile/giggle/wink etc.** a smile, giggle etc. shared by two people who know a secret —**conspiratorially** *adv.*

con·spire /kən'spaɪɚ/ *v.* [I] **1** to secretly plan with other people to do something harmful or illegal: **conspire (with sb) to do sth** *The company was accused of conspiring with local stores to fix prices.* | **conspire against sb** *He believed that his colleagues were conspiring against him.* **2** FORMAL if events conspire to make something happen, they happen at the same time and make something bad happen: **conspire to do sth** *Events conspired to ensure his defeat in the election.* [**Origin:** 1300–1400 Old French *conspirer*, from Latin *conspirare* **to breathe together, agree, conspire**]

con·sta·ble /'kɑnstəbəl/ *n.* [C] **1** another name for a POLICE OFFICER, especially in Canada, the U.K., and Australia **2** a person who has some, but not all, of the powers of a police officer and who can officially give or send legal documents that order people to do something or not do something

Con·sta·ble /'kɑnstəbəl/**, John** (1776–1837) a British painter known for his paintings and drawings of the English countryside

con·stab·u·lar·y /kən'stæbyə,lɛri/ *n. plural* **constabularies** [C] the POLICE FORCE of a particular area or country, especially in Canada, Britain, and Australia

con·stan·cy /'kɑnstənsi/ Ac *n.* [U] FORMAL **1** the quality of staying the same even though other things change: *The secret of success is patience and constancy of purpose.* **2** loyalty and faithfulness to a particular person

con·stant[1] /'kɑnstənt/ Ac W3 *adj.* **1** happening regularly or all the time: *He is in constant pain.* | *The winds are constant in winter.* **2** staying the same for a period of time: *You save more gas if you drive at a constant speed.* **3** LITERARY loyal and faithful: *a constant friend* [**Origin:** 1300–1400 Old French, Latin, present participle of *constare* **to stand firm, be constant, cost**]

constant[2] Ac *n.* [C] **1** MATH a number or quantity that never changes **2** FORMAL something that stays the same even though other things change → see also VARIABLE

Con·stan·tine /'kɑnstən,tin, -,taɪn/ HISTORY the EMPEROR of Rome from A.D. 312 to 337 who helped to spread Christianity

Con·stan·ti·no·ple /,kɑnstæntə'noʊpəl/ *n.* HISTORY the former name of the city of Istanbul in Turkey. In ancient times it was the capital of the eastern Roman Empire and of the Byzantine Empire.

con·stant·ly /'kɑnstəntli/ Ac S2 W3 *adv.* always, or very often: *That girl is on the phone constantly.* | *The English language is* ***constantly changing.***

,constant 'matrix *n.* [C] MATH a MATRIX that is made up of the set of CONSTANTS (=numbers that do not change) of a set of EQUATIONS

,constant of vari'ation *n.* [singular] MATH in EQUATIONS written y = kx or xy = k, the quantity represented by the letter k, whose value remains the same in both equations

,constant 'variable *n.* [C] BIOLOGY a CONTROLLED VARIABLE

con·stel·la·tion /,kɑnstə'leɪʃən/ *n.* [C] **1** PHYSICS a group of stars that forms a particular pattern and has a name ▸see THESAURUS box at space[1] **2 a constellation of sth** LITERARY a group of people or things that are similar: *Before him was a constellation of dials and switches.*

con·ster·na·tion /,kɑnstɚ'neɪʃən/ *n.* [U] a feeling of shock or worry that makes it difficult to decide what to do: *The attack has* ***caused consternation*** *among Western leaders.* | *A new power station is being built,* ***much to the consternation of*** *environmental groups.*

con·sti·pa·tion /,kɑnstə'peɪʃən/ *n.* [U] the condition of having difficulty emptying your BOWELS [**Origin:** 1500–1600 Medieval Latin *constipatio*, from Latin *constipare* **to crowd together**] —**constipated** /'kɑnstə,peɪt̬ɪd/ *adj.* —**constipate** *v.* [T]

con·stit·u·en·cy /kən'stɪtʃuənsi/ Ac *n. plural* **constituencies** [C] POLITICS **1** an area of a country that has one or more elected officials or representatives: *a rural constituency* | *a key constituency in the next election* **2** the people who live and vote in a constituency: *The speech was designed to appeal to the younger members of his constituency.* **3** any group that supports or is likely to support a politician or a political party: *Working families have always been his core constituency.*

con·stit·u·ent[1] /kən'stɪtʃuənt/ Ac *n.* [C] **1** POLITICS someone who votes and lives in a particular area represented by one or more elected officials: *He has lost the confidence of his constituents.* **2** FORMAL one of the parts that combine to form something → see also COMPONENT: *Sodium is one of the constituents of salt.*

constituent[2] Ac *adj.* [only before noun] being one of the parts that makes a whole: *the EU and its constituent members*

con·sti·tute /'kɑnstə,tut/ Ac W3 *v.* FORMAL **1** [linking verb, not in progressive] to be considered to be something: *The rise in crime constitutes a threat to society.* | *The company's action constituted fraud.* **2** [T not in progressive] if several parts constitute something, they form it together: *We may need to redefine what constitutes a family.* | **be constituted of** *Everything that exists is constituted of matter and form.* **3** [T usually passive] to officially form a group or organization: *The federation was constituted in 1949.* [**Origin:** 1400–1500 Latin, past participle of *constituere* **to set up, constitute**] → see also COMPRISE

con·sti·tu·tion /,kɑnstə'tuʃən/ Ac W2 *n.* [C] **1** also **Constitution** POLITICS a set of basic laws and principles that a DEMOCRATIC country is governed by, which cannot easily be changed by the political party in power: *The right to free speech is guaranteed in the U.S. Constitution.* | **+of** *the constitution of the European Union* **2** [usually singular] your natural and physical condition, and the ability of your body to fight disease and illness: **a strong/weak constitution** *She attributes her good health to her strong constitution.* **3** a set of rules and principles that an organization is governed by **4** FORMAL the way something is formed and how it is organized: **+of** *the chemical constitution of the dye*

con·sti·tu·tion·al[1] /,kɑnstə'tuʃənl/ Ac *adj.* **1** POLITICS officially allowed or restricted by the set of rules a government or organization has in a constitution OPP unconstitutional: *We have a* ***constitutional right*** *to keep weapons for self-defense.* | *Great Britain is* ***a constitutional monarchy*** (=a country ruled by a king or queen whose power is restricted by a constitution). **2** POLITICS relating to the constitution of a country or organization: *The Senate is voting on a proposed* ***constitutional amendment*** (=change to the original set of laws in a constitution). **3** relating to someone's health and their ability to fight illness → see also CONSTITUTIONALLY

constitutional[2] Ac *n.* [C] OLD-FASHIONED a walk you take or physical activity you do because it is good for your health

con·sti·tu·tion·al·ism /ˌkɑnstəˈtuʃənəˌlɪzəm/ *n.* [U] POLITICS the belief that a government should be based on a constitution —**constitutionalist** *n.* [C]

con·sti·tu·tion·al·i·ty /ˌkɑnstəˌtuʃəˈnæləṭi/ *n.* [U] POLITICS the quality of being acceptable according to the constitution

con·sti·tu·tion·al·ly /ˌkɑnstəˈtuʃənəli/ Ac *adv.* **1** in a way that obeys the rules of a country that has a constitution: *constitutionally protected forms of protest* **2** in a way that is related to someone's character or health and physical ability

ˌconstitutional ˈmonarchy *n.* POLITICS **1** [U] a political system in which a country is ruled by a king or queen whose powers are limited by law **2** [C] a country that is ruled by a king or queen whose powers are limited by law

con·strain /kənˈstreɪn/ Ac *v.* [T] **1** to stop someone from doing what they want to do SYN restrict: **constrain sb from doing sth** *Financial factors should not constrain doctors from offering the best treatment to patients.* **2** to prevent something from developing and improving SYN restrict: *Poor economies abroad may constrain demand for U.S. exports.* **3 constrain sb to do sth** to force someone to do something that they do not want to do: *The world around us constrains us to act in particular ways.* [**Origin:** 1300–1400 Old French *constraindre*, from Latin *constringere* **to constrict, constrain**]

con·strained /kənˈstreɪnd/ Ac *adj.* **1** prevented from developing, improving, or doing what you really want: *The Judge is constrained by an earlier decision of the court.* **2 be/feel constrained to do sth** to feel very strongly that you must do something: *I feel constrained to tell the truth.* **3** a constrained smile, manner etc. seems too controlled and is not natural —**constrainedly** /kənˈstreɪnɪdli/ *adv.*

con·straint /kənˈstreɪnt/ Ac *n.* **1** [C] something that limits your freedom to do what you want SYN restriction: **+on** *Constraints on spending have forced the company to rethink its plans.* | **financial/legal/environmental etc. constraints** *environmental constraints on the construction of new homes* | **time/budget constraints** *The program had to be postponed because of budget constraints.* **2** [U] control over the way people are allowed to behave, so that they cannot do what they want: *They have called on the military to show constraint.* **3 under constraint** being controlled or being forced to do something

con·strict /kənˈstrɪkt/ *v.* **1** [T] to make something smaller, narrower, or tighter: *Avoid clothing that constricts the blood circulation in your legs.* **2** [I] if a part of your body constricts, it becomes smaller, narrower, or tighter: *Linda felt her throat constrict, and she started to cry.* **3** [T] to limit someone's freedom to do what they want: *The law constricts people's choices about how to educate their children.* —**constricted** *adj.* —**constriction** /kənˈstrɪkʃən/ *n.* [C,U] —**constrictive** /-tɪv/ *adj.*

con·struct[1] /kənˈstrʌkt/ Ac W3 *v.* [T] **1** to build something large such as a building, bridge, or road SYN build: *The city plans to construct another runway at the airport.* | **construct sth of/from/in sth** *The mansion was constructed of wood with a brick facade.* ►see THESAURUS box at build[1] **2** to form something such as a sentence, argument, or system by joining words, ideas etc. together: *Boyce has constructed a new theory of management.* **3** TECHNICAL to draw a mathematical shape: *Construct a square with 2-inch-long sides.* [**Origin:** 1400–1500 Latin, past participle of *construere*, from *com-* + *struere* **to build**]

con·struct[2] /ˈkɑnstrʌkt/ Ac *n.* [C] **1** an idea formed by combining pieces of knowledge: *Our social constructs determine our relations to each other.* **2** FORMAL something that is built or made

con·struc·tion /kənˈstrʌkʃən/ Ac S3 W2 *n.* **1** BUILDINGS/ROADS ETC. [U] the process or method of building something large such as a building, bridge, or road: **+of** *Construction of the new highway will begin soon.* | ***construction workers*** | *Protective clothing must be worn by everyone visiting the* ***construction site*** (=the place where something is being built). | *A new water treatment plant is now* ***under construction*** (=being built).
2 MAKING STH USING MANY PARTS [U] the process or method of building or making something using many parts: *Read the instructions carefully before beginning construction of the model.*
3 PHRASE [C] ENG. LANG. ARTS the order in which words are put together in a sentence, phrase etc.: *complex grammatical constructions*
4 IDEAS/KNOWLEDGE [U] the method or process of forming something from knowledge or ideas: *the construction of sociological theory*
5 of simple/strong/wooden etc. construction FORMAL built in a simple way, built to be strong, built of wood etc.: *The natives live in wooden huts of simple construction.*
6 STH BUILT [C] FORMAL something that has been built: *a strange construction of metal and glass*
7 put a construction on sth FORMAL to think that a statement has a particular meaning or that something was done for a particular reason: *The judge put an entirely different construction on the man's remarks.*
8 MATHEMATICS [C] the process or result of drawing a GEOMETRIC FIGURE (=angle, shape etc.) using only a STRAIGHTEDGE and a COMPASS —**constructional** *adj.*

conˈstruction ˌpaper *n.* [U] a thick colored paper that is used especially by children at school

con·struc·tive /kənˈstrʌktɪv/ Ac *adj.* intended to be helpful, or likely to produce good results: *The meeting was very constructive.* | *Mrs. King says she welcomes* ***constructive criticism*** (=criticism that is intended to help her improve). —**constructively** *adv.* —**constructiveness** *n.* [U]

conˌstructive interˈference *n.* [U] TECHNICAL PHYSICS the addition of two or more WAVES of energy that are in PHASE to form a single wave with greater AMPLITUDE than the separate waves → see also DESTRUCTIVE INTERFERENCE

con·struc·tor /kənˈstrʌktɚ/ *n.* [C] a company or person that builds things

con·strue /kənˈstru/ *v.* **1 construe sth as sth** to understand a remark or action in a particular way OPP misconstrue: *Winston acknowledged that his comments could be construed as racist.* **2** [I,T] FORMAL to translate each word in a piece of writing, especially one in Greek or Latin

con·sub·stan·ti·a·tion /ˌkɑnsəbˌstænʃiˈeɪʃən/ *n.* [U] TECHNICAL the belief that the real body and blood of Jesus Christ exist together with the bread and wine offered by the priest at a Christian religious service → see also TRANSUBSTANTIATION

con·sul, Consul /ˈkɑnsəl/ *n.* [C] **1** a government official who lives in a foreign country and whose job is to help and protect citizens of their own country who also live or work there → see also AMBASSADOR: *the U.S. Consul in Munich, Germany* **2** one of the two chief public officials of the ancient Roman REPUBLIC, each elected for one year —**consular** *adj.*: *consular services* —**consulship** *n.* [C,U]

con·sul·ate, Consulate /ˈkɑnsəlɪt/ *n.* [C] the official building where a consul lives and works

con·sult /kənˈsʌlt/ Ac W3 *v.* [I,T] **1** to ask for information or advice from someone because it is their job to have the answers: *If your symptoms do not improve, consult your physician.* | **consult sb about sth** *She consulted an independent financial adviser about a pension plan.* | **+with** *I need to consult with my lawyer.* **2** to discuss something with someone so that you can make a decision together: *I can't believe you sold the car without consulting me.* | **+with** *The administration is consulting with allies on possible responses.* **3** to look for information in a book, map, list etc.: *The reporter took a moment to consult his notes.* [**Origin:** 1500–1600 French *consulter*, from Latin *consultare*, from *consulere* **to discuss, consult**]

C

con·sul·tan·cy /kən'sʌltənsi/ Ac *n. plural* **consultancies** [C] a company that gives advice and training in a particular area to people in other companies

con·sult·ant /kən'sʌltənt/ Ac W2 *n.* [C] someone with a lot of experience in a particular area whose job is to give advice about it: *He's working as a computer consultant.*

con·sul·ta·tion /ˌkɑnsəl'teɪʃən/ Ac *n.* **1** [C,U] a discussion in which people who are affected by a decision can say what they think should be done: +**with** *The principal took the decision after consultation with parents and teachers.* | *The plan was worked out* ***in consultation with*** (=with the agreement and help of) *the World Bank.* **2** [C] a meeting with a professional person, especially a doctor, for advice or treatment: *Lois took her daughter to the Mayo Clinic for a consultation.* **3** [U] advice given by a professional person: *Trained experts are available for consultation by phone.* **4** [U] the act of looking for information or help in a book

con·sul·ta·tive /kən'sʌltətɪv, 'kɑnsəlˌteɪtɪv/ Ac *adj.* providing advice and suggesting solutions to problems: *a consultative committee*

con·sult·ing /kən'sʌltɪŋ/ Ac *n.* [U] the service of providing information, advice, and training to companies

con'sulting firm *n.* [C] an organization that provides information, advice, and training in a particular area to people in other companies

con·sume /kən'sum/ Ac *v.* [T] **1** to completely use time, energy, goods etc.: *Smaller vehicles generally consume less fuel.* | *Medical expenses consumed about an eighth of my salary last year.* **2** FORMAL to eat or drink something: *Alcohol may not be consumed in the building.* **3 be consumed with guilt/passion/rage etc.** to have a very strong feeling that changes the way you behave and what you think about: *After the accident Joe was consumed with guilt.* → see also CONSUMING **4** FORMAL if fire consumes something, it destroys it completely: *All of her possessions had been consumed by the fire.* [**Origin:** 1300–1400 Old French *consumer*, from Latin *consumere*, from *com-* + *sumere* **to take up, take**] → see also CONSUMPTION, TIME-CONSUMING

con·sum·er /kən'sumɚ/ Ac W1 *n.* **1** [C] ECONOMICS someone who buys and uses products and services: *Consumers will soon be paying higher airfares.* ▶see THESAURUS box at **customer** **2** [singular] ECONOMICS all the people who buy goods and services, considered as a group: *The travel agents' group want more protection for* ***the consumer****.* | *Consumer spending rose 0.7 percent in November.* **3** [C] BIOLOGY a HETEROTROPH → see also CUSTOMER, PRODUCER (1) ▶see THESAURUS box at **customer**

conˌsumer 'confidence *n.* [U] ECONOMICS a measure of how satisfied people are with the present economic situation, as shown by how much money they spend: *Consumer confidence reached an all-time low in September.*

con'sumer coˌoperative *n.* [C] ECONOMICS a store that is owned and operated by the people who buy goods at the store

con'sumer ˌdocument *n.* [C] a document with useful information on it for the buyer of a product or service, such as a bill, GUARANTEE, or book of instructions about how to use a product → see also FUNCTIONAL DOCUMENT

conˌsumer e'conomy *n.* [C] ECONOMICS an economic system that depends on ordinary people buying products and services regularly in order to be successful

con'sumer goods *n.* [plural] ECONOMICS goods such as food, clothes, and equipment that people buy, especially to use in the home → see also CAPITAL GOODS

con'sumer group *n.* [C] an organization that makes sure that consumers are treated fairly and that products are safe

con·sum·er·is·m /kən'suməˌrɪzəm/ *n.* [U] **1** DISAPPROVING the belief that it is good to buy and use a lot of goods and services: *Consumerism works by convincing people that they actually "need" nonessential products.* **2** actions to protect people from unfair prices, advertising that is not true etc.

conˌsumer 'price ˌindex *n.* [C] ECONOMICS a list of the prices of particular products that is made to show how much prices have increased during a particular period of time

con'sumer soˌciety *n.* [C] a society in which the buying of products and services is considered extremely important

conˌsumer 'sovereignty *n.* [U] ECONOMICS the power that people have in controlling the amount, quality, type etc. of products and services that companies provide, because they buy and use these products and services. This idea is based on the belief that products and services are produced in order to supply the demand for them.

con·sum·ing /kən'sumɪŋ/ Ac *adj.* [only before noun] a consuming feeling is so strong that it controls you and often has a bad effect on your life: *She was possessed by a consuming rage.* | **a consuming passion/interest** *a consuming interest in baseball* | *an* ***all-consuming*** *obsession*

con·sum·mate¹ /'kɑnsəmɪt/ *adj.* FORMAL **1** very skillful: *Johnson was a consummate politician.* **2** complete and perfect in every way: *one of the consummate masterpieces of German opera* **3** used to emphasize how bad someone or something is: *consummate arrogance* —**consummately** *adv.*

con·sum·mate² /'kɑnsəˌmeɪt/ *v.* [T] FORMAL **1** to make a marriage or a relationship complete by having sex **2** to make something such as an agreement complete: *A trustee was appointed to consummate the sale.*

con·sum·ma·tion /ˌkɑnsə'meɪʃən/ *n.* [U] FORMAL **1** the point at which something is complete or perfect: *They filed suit to prevent the deal's consummation.* **2** the act of making a marriage or relationship complete by having sex

con·sump·tion /kən'sʌmpʃən/ Ac *n.* [U] **1** the amount of oil, electricity, gas etc. that is used: *Fuel consumption is predicted to rise.* **2** FORMAL the act of eating or drinking, or the amount of food or drink that is eaten or drunk: *The doctor recommended I reduce my alcohol consumption.* | +**of** *We need to increase our consumption of fresh fruit and vegetables.* | **fit/unfit for human consumption** (=safe or not safe for people to eat) **3** ECONOMICS the act of buying and using products: *an increase in the consumption of electrical products* | *The true meaning of Christmas has been overshadowed by* ***conspicuous consumption*** (=buying expensive goods in order to show other people how rich you are). **4 for public/general/popular etc. consumption** intended to be heard or read by anyone: *Senator McDonald's comments were not meant for public consumption.* **5** MEDICINE the lung disease TUBERCULOSIS

con·sump·tive /kən'sʌmptɪv/ *adj.* OLD USE someone who has the lung disease TUBERCULOSIS —**consumptive** *n.* [C]

cont. the written abbreviation of CONTAINING, CONTENTS, CONTINENT, and CONTINUED

con·tact¹ /'kɑntækt/ Ac S2 W2 *n.*

1 COMMUNICATION [U] communication or meetings with a person, organization, country etc., or the occasion on which the communication takes place: +**with** *The village is cut off from contact with the outside world.* | *We don't* ***have*** *much* ***contact with*** *the Australian division of the company.* | +**between** *There is very little contact between the two brothers.* | **get/keep/stay in contact with sb** *Have you managed to stay in contact with any of the kids from the old neighborhood?* | *We're afraid we'll* ***lose contact with*** *our granddaughters after our son's divorce.* | *She* ***put*** *me* ***in contact with*** (=gave me the name or telephone number of) *one of her colleagues.* | *I've* ***made contact with*** (=communicated with) *most of the people on the list.* | **close/social/personal/regular etc. contact** *Staff who have direct contact with customers must dress professionally.*

2 TOUCH [U] the state of touching or being close to someone or something: *The disease cannot be spread*

through casual contact. | +**with** *Children need close contact with a caring adult.* | +**between** *Football involves a lot of physical contact between players.* | *For a second his hand was* ***in contact with*** *mine.* | *Health care workers who* ***come in contact with*** *flu victims should wash their hands frequently.* | *These bombs explode* ***on contact*** (=at the moment of touching something). | **contact points/areas/surfaces etc.** *Scrape the contact surfaces with a knife, then reattach the cables.*
3 PERSON WHO CAN HELP [C] a person you know who may be able to help you or give you advice about something: *business contacts* | *I've* ***made*** *a few* ***contacts*** *in the industry.*
4 EXPERIENCE [U] the action of meeting someone or experiencing a particular kind of thing: *Dickens worked in a factory, which* ***brought*** *him* ***into contact with*** *the poor conditions of the working classes.* | *Everyone who* ***came into contact with*** *Anna felt better for knowing her.*
5 EYES [C] a contact lens
6 contacts [plural] a situation or relationship in which you communicate easily with another group, country etc.: *The two countries are determined to maintain diplomatic contacts.* | +**with** *We have good contacts with the local community.*
7 ELECTRICAL PART [C] PHYSICS an electrical part that completes a CIRCUIT when it touches another part
8 point of contact a) a place that you go to or a person that you meet when dealing with an organization or trying to get something: *The new service center will serve as the single point of contact for general customer inquiries.* **b)** a way in which two very different things are related or connected: *It's difficult to find a point of contact between theory and practice.* **c)** the part of something where another thing touches it → see also **eye contact** at EYE[1] (5)
[**Origin:** 1600–1700 French, Latin *contactus*, from the past participle of *contigere*]

contact² Ac S2 *v.* [T] to telephone or write to someone: *School officials immediately contacted the police.*

contact³ Ac *adj.* [only before noun] **1** a contact number or address is a telephone number or address where someone can be found if necessary: *Did Mr. Warren leave a contact number?* **2** contact explosives or chemicals become active when they touch something: *contact weedkillers*

'contact lens *n.* [C] a small round piece of plastic you put on your eye to help you see clearly

con·ta·gion /kən'teɪdʒən/ *n.* **1** [U] MEDICINE a situation in which a disease is spread by people touching each other or touching something that can infect them: *a serious risk of contagion* **2** [C] MEDICINE a disease that can be passed from person to person by touch **3** [U] FORMAL a feeling or attitude that spreads quickly from person to person

con·ta·gious /kən'teɪdʒəs/ *adj.* **1** MEDICINE a contagious disease can be passed from person to person by touch: *Chickenpox is a highly contagious disease.* **2** MEDICINE a contagious person has a disease that can be passed to another person by touch: *People with measles are highly contagious.* **3** a contagious feeling, attitude, or action is quickly felt or done by other people: *Hardy has a booming voice and a contagious enthusiasm.* —**contagiousness** *n.* [U] —**contagiously** *adv.*

con·tain /kən'teɪn/ W1 *v.* [T]
1 CONTAINER/PLACE to have something inside: *The box contained photographs and old letters.*
2 WRITING/MOVIE/SPEECH ETC. if a document, book, movie, speech etc. contains something, that thing is included in it: *Her report contained some interesting suggestions.* | *This film contains violence and nudity.*
3 SUBSTANCE if a substance contains something, that thing is part of it: *This product may contain nuts.*
4 CONTROL FEELINGS to keep a strong feeling or emotion under control: *I found it more and more difficult to contain my anger.* | **contain yourself** *Shaw was so excited he could hardly contain himself.*
5 STOP/LIMIT STH to stop something from spreading, escaping, increasing etc.: *Doctors are struggling to contain the epidemic.* | *Board members will discuss how to contain costs in the future.* → see also SELF-CONTAINED
6 MATH FORMAL to surround an area or an angle: *How big is the angle contained by these two sides?* → see also CONTENT[1]
[**Origin:** 1200–1300 Old French *contenir*, from Latin *continere* **to hold together, hold in, contain**]

con·tain·er /kən'teɪnɚ/ S3 *n.* [C] **1** something such as a box, bowl, or bottle that can be filled with something: *a small container of cottage cheese* | *a container with a tight lid* **2** a very large metal box in which goods are packed to make it easy to lift or move them onto a ship or vehicle: *cargo containers*

con·tain·ment /kən'teɪnmənt/ *n.* [U] **1** the act of keeping something under control: *cost containment* **2** the use of political actions to prevent an unfriendly country from becoming more powerful, especially the U.S.'s use of these types of actions against the former Soviet Union: *the Cold War policy of containment*

con·tam·i·nant /kən'tæmənənt/ *n.* [C] TECHNICAL a dangerous or poisonous substance that makes something impure

con·tam·i·nate /kən'tæmə,neɪt/ *v.* [T] **1** to spoil a place or substance by adding a dangerous or poisonous substance to it: *Lead in plumbing can contaminate drinking water.* **2** to influence someone or something in a way that has a bad effect: *Publicity before the trial can contaminate a jury.* [**Origin:** 1400–1500 Latin, past participle of *contaminare*, from *contamen* **contact**] —**contamination** /kən,tæmə'neɪʃən/ *n.* [U]

con·tam·i·nat·ed /kən'tæmə,neɪtɪd/ *adj.* **1** water, food etc. that is contaminated has dangerous or harmful things in it, such as chemicals or poison: *Contaminated water leaked from the nuclear reactor.* ►see THESAURUS box at **dirty¹** **2** influenced in a way that produces a bad effect

contd. a written abbreviation of CONTINUED

con·tem·plate /'kɑntəm,pleɪt/ *v.* **1** [T] to think about something that you intend to do in the future: *A spokeswoman denied that layoffs were being contemplated.* | **contemplate doing sth** *Have you ever contemplated committing suicide?* **2** [T] to accept the possibility that something is true: **too terrible/horrible etc. to contemplate** *The thought that she might be dead was just too awful to contemplate.* **3** [I,T] to think seriously about something for a long time, especially in order to understand it better: *I spend a lot of time sitting on my porch, just contemplating.* **4** [I] LITERARY to look at someone or something for a period of time in a way that shows you are thinking about them [**Origin:** 1500–1600 Latin, past participle of *contemplari*]

con·tem·pla·tion /,kɑntəm'pleɪʃən/ *n.* [U] quiet serious thinking about something, especially in order to understand it better: *The monks spend an hour in contemplation each morning.*

con·tem·pla·tive¹ /kən'tɛmplət̬ɪv/ *adj.* spending a lot of time thinking seriously and quietly: *a contemplative life* —**contemplatively** *adv.*

contemplative² *n.* [C] FORMAL someone who spends their life thinking deeply about religious ideas

con·tem·po·ra·ne·ous /kən,tɛmpə'reɪniəs/ *adj.* FORMAL happening or existing in the same period of time SYN **contemporary**: +**with** *The bones are contemporaneous with some of the earliest human fossils.* —**contemporaneously** *adv.* —**contemporaneity** /kən,tɛmpərə'niət̬i, -'neɪət̬i/ *n.* [U]

con·tem·po·rar·y¹ /kən'tɛmpə,rɛri/ Ac *adj.* **1** belonging to the present time SYN **modern**: *The café's decor is clean and contemporary.* | **contemporary art/music/dance etc.** *a contemporary opera by John Adams* **2** happening or existing in the same period of time: *The two manuscripts are thought to be contemporary.*

contemporary² Ac *n. plural* **contemporaries** [C] someone who lives in the same period of time or in the same place as a particular person or event: *Atkins is* *still working, long after many of his contemporaries have retired.* | **+of** *Aristotle was a contemporary of Plato.*

con·tempt /kən'tɛmpt/ *n.* [U] **1** a feeling that someone or something is not important and deserves no respect: **+for** *Jimmy has nothing but contempt for his boss.* | *The homeless are treated* ***with contempt*** *by the authorities.* | *He* ***held*** *all other artists of his day* ***in contempt*** (=felt contempt for them). | *Leaving litter in the wilderness is* ***beneath contempt*** (=so unacceptable that you have no respect for the person involved). **2** LAW failure to obey or show respect toward a court of law: **find/hold sb in contempt (of court)** *She was found in contempt for not appearing on the day of the trial.* | *Morgan was jailed* ***for contempt of court.*** **3 contempt for fear/danger/risk** complete lack of fear about something [**Origin:** 1300–1400 Latin *contemptus*, from *contemnere* **to think of with contempt**]

con·tempt·i·ble /kən'tɛmptəbəl/ *adj.* so unacceptable that you have no respect for the person involved: *The group's tactics were contemptible.* —**contemptibly** *adv.*

con·temp·tu·ous /kən'tɛmptʃuəs/ *adj.* **1** showing that you feel that someone or something deserves no respect: *a contemptuous attitude* | **+of** *He was contemptuous of anyone who had not gone to college.* **2 contemptuous of fear/danger/risk** not feeling any fear in a dangerous situation —**contemptuously** *adv.*

con·tend /kən'tɛnd/ W3 *v.* **1** [I] to compete against someone in order to gain something: **+for** *Ten teams are contending for the title.* **2** [T] to argue or state that something is true SYN **maintain**: **contend (that)** *The government contended that most of the refugees were fleeing poverty, not persecution.* [**Origin:** 1400–1500 Old French *contendre*, from Latin *contendere*, from *com-* + *tendere* **to stretch**] → see also CONTENTION

contend with sth *phr. v.* **have to contend with sth** also **have sth to contend with** to have to deal with something difficult or bad: *Rescuers also had bad weather to contend with.*

con·tend·er /kən'tɛndɚ/ *n.* [C] someone who is involved in a competition or a situation in which they have to compete with other people: *a middleweight boxing contender* | **+for** *a contender for the Democratic nomination*

con·tent¹ /'kɑntɛnt/ W3 *n.* **1 contents** [plural] **a)** the things that are in a box, bag, room etc.: *The jewelry box and its contents are priceless.* | **+of** *The contents of the safe had been removed.* **b)** the words or ideas that are written in a letter, book etc.: *He quickly outlined the report's contents.* | **+of** *She kept the contents of the letter a secret.* | *a* ***table of contents*** (=list at the beginning of a book, which shows the different parts into which the book is divided) **2** [singular] the amount of a substance that something contains: *Chestnuts have a high water content.* **3** [U] the ideas, facts, opinions, or information that are contained in a speech, book, movie, WEBSITE etc.: *The site's graphics are great, but the content is no good.* | *Many of the paintings are political* ***in content.*** → see also CONTAIN

con·tent² /kən'tɛnt/ S3 *adj.* [not before noun] **1** happy and satisfied: **content to do sth** *We were content to just sit and listen.* | **+with** *Carla seems pretty much content with her life.* ►see THESAURUS box at **happy** **2 not content with sth** thinking that something is not good enough and wanting to do more: *Not content with past creations, Leiber is always introducing new designs.*

content³ *v.* [T] **1 content yourself with sth** to do or have something that is not what you really want, but is still satisfactory: *Some companies will have to content*

containers

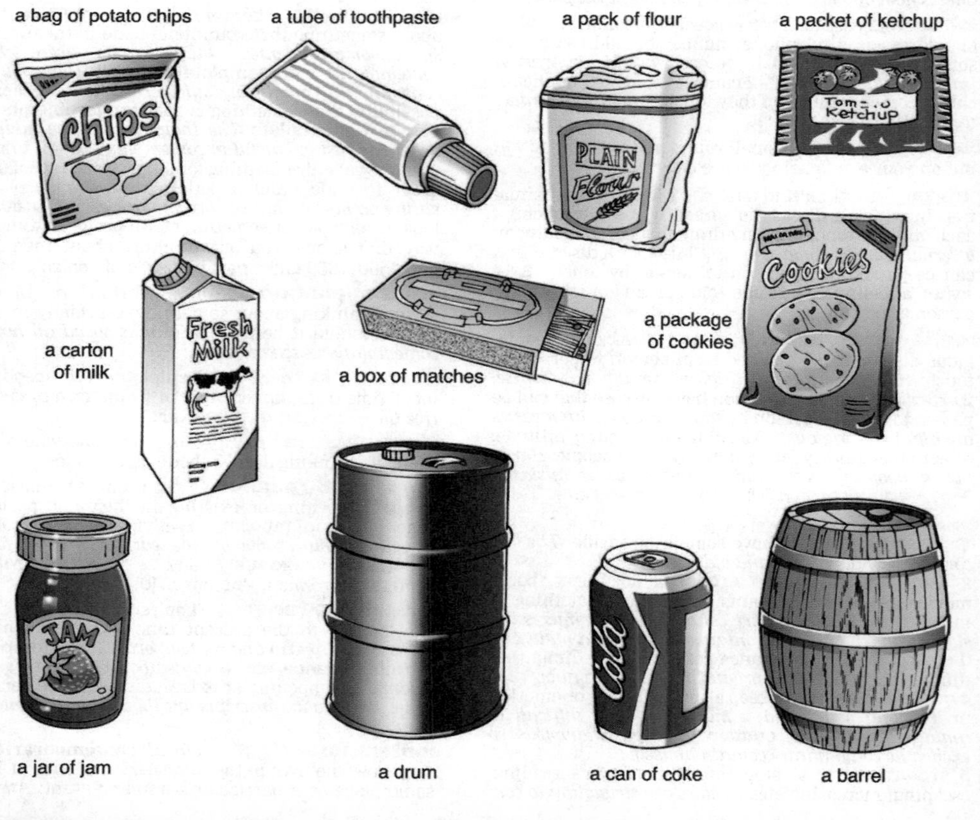

themselves with lower sales this year. **2** to make someone feel happy and satisfied: *I was no longer satisfied with the life that had once contented me.*

content⁴ *n.* [U] **1 do sth to your heart's content** to do something as much as you want: *I was able to browse through the bookstore to my heart's content.* **2** LITERARY a feeling of quiet happiness and satisfaction SYN **contentment** OPP **discontent**

con·tent·ed /kən'tɛntɪd/ *adj.* happy and satisfied because your life is good OPP **discontented**: *I'm pretty contented now.* | *a purring, contented cat* —**contentedly** *adv.*

con·ten·tion /kən'tɛnʃən/ *n.* **1** [C] FORMAL a belief or opinion that someone expresses: **contention that** *It is my contention that bicycle helmets should be required at all times.* | *Her main contention was that the doctor should have done more.* **2** [U] a situation in which people or groups are competing: *There are still six teams* ***in contention for*** *the playoffs.* | *Injury has put him* ***out of contention.*** **3** [U] FORMAL arguments and disagreement between people: *A key area of contention is the call for the wilderness to be opened to oil and gas drilling.* | *One of the issues* ***in contention*** (=being argued about) *is barriers to trade.* → see also **bone of contention** at BONE¹ (4) → CONTEND

con·ten·tious /kən'tɛnʃəs/ *adj.* **1** likely to cause a lot of argument and disagreement between people: *Logging on public lands is a contentious issue.* **2** someone who is contentious often argues with people —**contentiously** *adv.* —**contentiousness** *n.* [U]

con·tent·ment /kən'tɛnt˺mənt/ *n.* [U] the state of being happy and satisfied OPP **discontent**: *The people here seem to live in peace and contentment.*

con·test¹ /'kɑntɛst/ S3 W3 *n.* [C] **1** a competition, usually a small one: *The essay contest is open to all teenagers.* | *They* ***have a*** *children's talent* ***contest*** *every year.* | *I only* ***entered the contest*** *for fun.* ►see THESAURUS box at **competition** **2** a situation in which two or more people or groups are competing with each other: +**for** *the contest for the party's nomination* | *a* ***close contest*** *for the mayor's job* | +**between** *a contest between two great champions* **3 no contest** INFORMAL **a)** used to say that someone or something is clearly better than all the others: *I think you're the best rider here, no contest.* **b)** used to say that a choice or a victory is not difficult at all: *In the end, it was no contest and we beat them 9-2.* **4 plead no contest** LAW to say that you will not give any defense in a court of law for something you have done wrong: *He pleaded no contest to driving without a license.*

contest² /kən'tɛst/ *v.* [T] **1** LAW to say formally that you do not accept something or do not agree with it: *His brothers are contesting the will.* **2** to compete for something or try to win it: *The ruling party will contest 158 seats in Algeria's elections.* [**Origin:** 1500–1600 French *contester*, from Latin *contestari* **to call a witness, bring a legal case**] —**contested** *adj.*: *a* ***hotly contested*** *mayoral election*

con·test·ant /kən'tɛstənt/ *n.* [C] someone who competes in a contest: *Contestants for the game show go through a tough selection process.*

con·text /'kɑntɛkst/ Ac S2 W3 *n.* [C,U] **1** the situation, events, or information that are related to something, and that help you to understand it better: *To appreciate what these changes will mean, it is necessary to look at them* ***in context.*** | **political/social/historical etc. context** *The book explains economics in a historical context.* | *Urban poverty can only be understood* ***in the context of*** *politics and society as a whole.* | **put/place/keep sth in context** (=consider something together with the related situation, events etc.) **2** ENG. LANG. ARTS the words and sentences that come before and after a particular word, and that help you to understand the meaning of the word: *English words can have several meanings depending on context.* **3 take/quote sth out of context** to repeat a sentence or statement without describing the situation in which it was said, so that its meaning is not clear: *Jennings accused the program of quoting him out of context.* [**Origin:** 1400–1500 Latin *contextus* **connection of words**, from *contexere* **to weave together**]

'context ˌclue *n.* [C] ENG. LANG. ARTS information that helps you understand the meaning of a particular word or phrase, which you obtain from the surrounding words or from the situation or events etc. being described

con·tex·tu·al /kən'tɛkstʃuəl/ Ac *adj.* relating to a particular context: *contextual information* —**contextually** *adv.*

con·tex·tu·al·ize /kən'tɛkstʃuəˌlaɪz/ Ac *v.* [T] to consider something together with the situation, events, or information that relate to it, rather than alone —**contextualization** /kənˌtɛkstʃuələ'zeɪʃən/ *n.* [U]

con·tig·u·ous /kən'tɪgyuəs/ *adj.* FORMAL next to something, or near something in time or order: *the 48 contiguous states* (=the U.S. states that are next to each other) —**contiguously** *adv.* —**contiguity** /ˌkɑntə'gyuəṭi/ *n.* [U]

con·ti·nence /'kɑntənəns, 'kɑnt˺n-əns/ *n.* [U] **1** the ability to control your BLADDER and BOWELS OPP **incontinence** **2** OLD USE the practice of controlling your desire for sex

con·ti·nent¹ /'kɑntənənt, 'kɑnt˺n-ənt/ *n.* [C] GEOGRAPHY one of the main masses of land on the earth: *the continents of North and South America* [**Origin:** 1500–1600 Latin *continens* **continuous area of land**, from *continere*]

continent² *adj.* **1** able to control your BLADDER and BOWELS OPP **incontinent** **2** OLD USE controlling your desire to have sex OPP **incontinent**

con·ti·nen·tal /ˌkɑntən'ɛntl◂, ˌkɑnt˺n-/ *adj.* **1 the continental U.S./United States** all the states of the U.S. except for Alaska and Hawaii: *Housing prices here are the highest in the continental United States.* **2 continental Europe/Asia etc.** the part of Europe, Asia etc. that is not on islands: *The store is trying to expand into continental Europe.* **3** EARTH SCIENCE relating to a CONTINENT (=large mass of land): *shifting continental plates* **4** GEOGRAPHY typical of the warmer countries in Western Europe: *a continental-style café*

ˌContinental 'Army, the HISTORY the American army during the Revolutionary War

ˌcontinental 'breakfast *n.* [C] a breakfast consisting of coffee, juice, and a sweet ROLL (=type of bread)

ˌContinental Di'vide, the EARTH SCIENCE the long range of high mountains in North America that goes from Alaska down to New Mexico, and which separates the rivers and streams that flow west toward the Pacific Ocean and those that flow east toward the Atlantic Ocean. The Rocky Mountains are part of the Continental Divide.

ˌcontinental 'drift *n.* [U] EARTH SCIENCE the very slow movement of the CONTINENTS across the surface of the earth

ˌcontinental 'shelf *n. plural* **continental shelves** [C] EARTH SCIENCE the part of a CONTINENT that slopes down steeply to the bottom of the ocean

con·tin·gen·cy /kən'tɪndʒənsi/ *n. plural* **contingencies** [C] **1** an event or situation that might happen in the future, especially one that might cause problems: *a* ***contingency plan*** (=a plan that you make to deal with a problem that might happen) *for dealing with a dangerous flu epidemic* | *A will should allow for contingencies.* **2 a contingency fee** an amount of money that a lawyer will be paid only if the person they are advising wins in court

con·tin·gent¹ /kən'tɪndʒənt/ *adj.* FORMAL depending on something that may or may not happen in the future SYN **conditional**: +**on/upon** *Her promotion at work was contingent upon finishing a university degree.* —**contingently** *adv.*

contingent² *n.* [C] **1** a group of people who have something in common, and who are part of a larger group: +**of** *A sizable contingent of my family attended* *the wedding.* **2** a group of soldiers sent to help a larger group: **+of** *a large contingent of paratroopers*

con,tingent em'ployment *n.* [U] ECONOMICS the condition of being employed in a temporary job or having a job in which you work only part of each day or week

con·tin·u·al /kən'tɪnyuəl/ *adj.* **1** repeated many times, often in an annoying or harmful way: *the continual buzz of planes overhead* **2** continuing for a long time without stopping SYN **uninterrupted**: *They had endured seven days of almost continual fighting.* —**continually** *adv.*

C

THESAURUS

Continual and **continuous** can both be used to describe something that does not stop: *a continual/continuous process*
Continual is also used when something happens many times, especially something annoying: *There were continual interruptions all day.*
Continuous is used to emphasize that there is no pause or break between things: *six continuous hours of meetings*

con·tin·u·ance /kən'tɪnyuəns/ *n.* **1** [C usually singular] LAW the act of allowing the events in a court of law to stop for a period of time, usually so a lawyer can find more facts about the case **2** [singular, U] the state of continuing for a long period of time: *The election saw a continuance in power of the country's socialist party.*

con·tin·u·a·tion /kən,tɪnyu'eɪʃən/ *n.* **1** [singular, U] a situation in which something continues after a break: **+of** *the continuation of the peace talks* **2** [singular, U] a situation in which something continues without stopping or changing: *The new policy is a continuation of the old one.* | **+of** *the continuation of family traditions* **3** [C] something that is joined to something else as if it were part of it: **+of** *The Gulf of Mexico is a continuation of the Caribbean Sea.*

continu'ation ,school *n.* [C] a school for children who are not allowed to study at a high school because of bad behavior or other problems

con·tin·ue /kən'tɪnyu/ S2 W1 *v.* **1** [I,T] to keep happening, existing, or doing something without stopping: *Dry weather will continue through the weekend.* | *It's important to continue your education.* | **continue to do sth** *The population is continuing to grow rapidly.* | **+with** *Despite his illness, he will continue with his normal work schedule.* | **continue doing sth** *We continued talking and laughing until after midnight.* | **continue unabated/apace** (=continue without becoming any less) *The fighting has continued unabated.* **2** [I,T] to start doing something again after a pause SYN **resume**: *The concert will continue after a brief intermission.* | *Rescue teams will continue the search tomorrow.* | **continue doing sth** *He picked up his book and continued reading.* **3** [I] to go further in the same direction: **+on/down/in/after etc.** *Route 66 continues on to Texas from here.* **4** [I,T] to say something else after you have been interrupted: *"And so," he continued, "we will put more effort into reaching these students."* **5** [I] to stay in the same job, situation etc.: **+as** *Morris will continue as director of marketing.* **6 to be continued** used at the end of a television program to tell people that the story will not finish until a later program → see also CONTINUAL, DISCONTINUE [**Origin:** 1300–1400 French *continuer*, from Latin *continuare*, from *continuus*]

con·tin·ued /kən'tɪnyud/ *adj.* [only before noun] continuing to happen for a long time, or happening many times: *the continued failure of the negotiations*

con,tinuing edu'cation *n.* [U] education for adults, usually in classes that are held in the evening and are not part of the formal education system

con·ti·nu·i·ty /,kɑntə'nuəṭi/ *n.* [U] **1** the state of continuing over a long period of time, without being interrupted or changing: **+of** *Long-term employees provide a continuity of service.* **2** ENG. LANG. ARTS the organization of a movie or television program to make it seem that the action happens without pauses or interruptions

con·tin·u·o /kən'tɪnyu,oʊ/ *n.* [C] TECHNICAL a musical part consisting of a line of low notes with figures showing the higher notes that are to be played with them

con·tin·u·ous[1] /kən'tɪnyuəs/ *adj.* **1** continuing to happen or exist without stopping or without being interrupted: *continuous news coverage* | *a continuous improvement in customer service* ►see THESAURUS box at **continual** **2** something such as a line that is continuous does not have any spaces or holes in it SYN **unbroken**: *a continuous trail along the ridge* **3** ENG. LANG. ARTS the continuous form of a verb shows that an action is continuing. In English, this is formed by the verb "be," followed by a PRESENT PARTICIPLE, as in "I was walking to school." —**continuously** *adv.*

continuous[2] *n.* **the continuous** ENG. LANG. ARTS in grammar, the form of a verb that shows that an action or activity is continuing to happen. In English, this is formed by the verb "be" followed by a PRESENT PARTICIPLE. In the sentence "She is watching TV," "is watching" is in the continuous.

con,tinuous 'data *n.* [U] TECHNICAL MATH data that can represent any value on a scale, for example, data for size, weight, age etc. → see also CATEGORICAL DATA

con·tin·u·um /kən'tɪnyuəm/ *n. plural* **continuums** or **continua** /-nyuə/ [C] FORMAL ECONOMICS a range or series of related things, in which each thing is only slightly different from the one before or after, so that there are no clear dividing points SYN **cline**: *Mental development follows a set course along a continuum.*

con·tort /kən'tɔrt/ *v.* [I,T] if you contort something, especially your face or body, or if it contorts, it twists so that it does not have its normal shape and looks strange or unattractive SYN **twist**: **+with/in** *The boy's face was contorted with pain.*

con·tor·tion /kən'tɔrʃən/ *n.* **1** [C] a twisted position or movement that looks strange: *the contortions of some yoga positions* **2** [C] something difficult and complicated that you have to do in order to achieve something: *I had to* **go through** *bureaucratic* **contortions** *to get a work permit.* **3** [U] the act or fact of being twisted and looking strange or unattractive: *the involuntary contortion of muscles*

con·tor·tion·ist /kən'tɔrʃənɪst/ *n.* [C] someone who entertains people by twisting their body into strange and unnatural shapes and positions

con·tour /'kɑntʊr/ *n.* [C] **1** the shape of the outer edges of something, such as an area of land or someone's body: **+of** *the contours of the hillside* | *the contours of her face* **2** also **contour line** a line on a map that connects points of equal height above sea level, so that you can see where hills, valleys etc. are [**Origin:** 1600–1700 French, Italian *contorno*, from *contornare* **to round off, draw**, from Latin]

con·toured /'kɑntʊrd/ *adj.* **1** shaped so that something, especially your body, fits closely next to it: *The jacket is slightly contoured.* **2** having soft curves that give an attractive appearance: *a smoothly contoured golf course*

Con·tra, **contra** /'kɑntrə/ *n.* [C] a member of the military organization which fought the Communist Nicaraguan government in the 1980s

contra- /kɑntrə/ *prefix* **1** acting against something: *contraceptive devices* (=that prevent PREGNANCY) | *to contravene something* (=do something that is not allowed by a law or rule) **2** opposite to something: *plants in contradistinction to animals* [**Origin:** Latin *contra* **against, opposite**]

con·tra·band /'kɑntrə,bænd/ *n.* [U] **1** goods that are brought into or taken out of a country illegally, especially to avoid tax: *boats carrying contraband* **2** also **contraband of war** HISTORY goods that are illegal to supply to either side in a war —**contraband** *adj.*: *contraband cigarettes*

con·tra·bass /'kɑntrə,beɪs/ *n.* [C] a DOUBLE BASS

con·tra·cep·tion /,kɑntrə'sɛpʃən/ *n.* [U] the practice of making it possible for a woman to have sex without having a baby, or the methods for doing this SYN **birth control**: *an effective method of contraception*

con·tra·cep·tive /ˌkɑntrəˈsɛptɪv/ *n.* [C] a drug, object, or method used so that a woman can have sex without having a baby —**contraceptive** *adj.* [only before noun]

con·tract¹ /ˈkɑntrækt/ Ac S2 W1 *n.* [C] **1** a legal written agreement between two or more people, companies etc. which says what each side will do: *My contract guarantees me a pay raise every year.* | **+with** *a three-year contract with the Chicago White Sox* | **+between** *the contract between the school board and the teachers* | *You should never* ***sign a contract*** *without getting legal advice first.* | *He was paid what he was owed* ***under the contract*** (=according to what the contract said). | *The* ***terms of the contract*** (=the things you agree to do) *cannot be changed after it has been signed.* | *The company decided not to* ***renew*** *the advertising* ***contract***. | *Employees who refused to work on weekends were sued for* ***breach of contract*** (=for doing something that is not allowed by the contract). **2** a particular job that a person or company is employed to do: *The company* ***won*** *four* ***contracts*** *to build roads.* | **contract to do sth** *a contract to teach for three years* | *The city* ***awarded*** *them the construction* ***contract*** (=it chose them to do the construction). **3** INFORMAL an agreement to kill someone for money: *The mob* ***put a contract out on*** *him.*

con·tract² /kənˈtrækt, ˈkɑntrækt/ Ac S3 W3 *v.* **1** [T] to get an illness SYN **catch**: *Two-thirds of the adult population there has contracted AIDS.* **2** [I] to become smaller, narrower, or tighter OPP **expand**: *Metal contracts as it becomes cool.* | *The economy has contracted by 2.5% in the last three years.* **3** [I] if a muscle contracts, it becomes tighter, usually when you use it: *The muscles behind the knee begin to contract.* **4** [I,T] to sign a contract in which you agree formally that you will do something: **contract (with) sb for sth** *The interior building work is not yet contracted for.* | **contract to do sth** *I'm contracted to work 35 hours a week.* **5 contract a marriage/alliance etc.** FORMAL to agree formally that you will marry someone or have a particular kind of relationship with them [**Origin:** 1500–1600 Latin *contractus*, past participle of *contrahere* **to pull together, make a contract, make smaller**]

contract sth ↔ **out** *phr. v.* to arrange to have a job done by a person or company outside your own organization: *The city has contracted its garbage collection out to an independent company.*

ˌcontract ˈbridge *n.* [U] a form of the card game BRIDGE, in which one of the two pairs say how many TRICKS they will try to win

con·trac·tion /kənˈtrækʃən/ *n.* **1** [C] BIOLOGY a movement in which a muscle becomes tight, used especially when the muscles around the UTERUS suddenly and painfully become tight when a woman is going to give birth **2** [U] the process of becoming smaller or narrower OPP **expansion**: *a contraction in economic activity* | *the contraction of metal as it cools* **3** [C] ENG. LANG. ARTS a short form of a word or words, such as "don't" for "do not"

conˌtractionary ˈpolicy *n.* [C] ECONOMICS government actions, such as raising INTEREST rates, increasing taxes, and decreasing government spending, that are intended to reduce or slow down economic growth

con·trac·tor /ˈkɑnˌtræktɚ, kənˈtræk-/ Ac S3 *n.* [C] a person or company that agrees to do work or provide goods for another company: *a building contractor*

con·trac·tu·al /kənˈtræktʃuəl/ *adj.* agreed in a contract: *a contractual commitment* —**contractually** *adv.*

con·tra·dict /ˌkɑntrəˈdɪkt/ Ac *v.* **1** [T] if one statement, story etc. contradicts another one, the facts in it are different so that both statements cannot be true: *The witnesses' statements* ***contradict each other***, *and the facts remain unclear.* | **directly/flatly contradict** *This information flatly contradicts North's testimony.* **2** [I,T] to say that what someone else has said is wrong or not true, especially by saying that the opposite is true: *Dad couldn't stand being contradicted.* | **contradict sb** *She contradicted him, saying that it happened in 1972, not 1962.* **3 contradict yourself** to say something that is the opposite of what you said before: *During questioning, Robinson contradicted himself several times.* **4** [T] if one situation or event contradicts another, they cannot both happen at the same time or be true at the same time: *Heating the water to 150° F kills bacteria but contradicts efforts to save energy.*

con·tra·dic·tion /ˌkɑntrəˈdɪkʃən/ Ac *n.* **1** [C] a difference between two statements, beliefs, or ideas that means they cannot both be true: *His speech was full of lies and contradictions.* | **+between** *Republicans were quick to point out contradictions between the President's words and his actions.* | *How do you explain the* ***apparent contradictions*** (=things that seem to be contradictions, but may not be) *in his testimony?* **2** [C,U] an event, person, or situation that contains parts that are so different from one another that they seem strange or impossible together: *Gage is a man of contradictions: a vegetarian who owns a cattle ranch.* | *America is a society rich in contradiction.* **3 a contradiction in terms** a combination of words that mean opposite things, so that they describe something that cannot therefore be true: *the old joke that "military intelligence" is a contradiction in terms* **4 in (direct) contradiction to sth** in a way that is opposite to a belief or statement: *Hatred is in contradiction to Christian values.* **5** [U] the act of saying that someone else's opinion, statement etc. is wrong or not true

con·tra·dic·to·ry /ˌkɑntrəˈdɪktəri/ Ac *adj.* contradictory statements, beliefs etc. are so different from each other that they cannot all be true: *The witnesses gave contradictory answers.* → see also SELF-CONTRADICTORY

con·tra·dis·tinc·tion /ˌkɑntrədɪˈstɪŋkʃən/ *n.* [C] **in contradistinction to sth** FORMAL as opposed to something

con·trail /ˈkɑntreɪl/ *n.* [C] FORMAL a line of white steam made in the sky by an airplane

con·tral·to /kənˈtræltoʊ/ *n.* [C] the lowest female singing voice, or a woman who has this voice

con·tra·pos·i·tive /ˌkɑntrəˈpɑzət̬ɪv/ *n.* [C] a CONDITIONAL statement that follows in a reasonable way from another statement of truth, but expresses the statement in the opposite way. For example, for the statement "if x=2, then y=4," the contrapositive is "if y=4, then x=2."

con·trap·tion /kənˈtræpʃən/ *n.* [C] INFORMAL a strange-looking piece of equipment or machinery, especially one that you think is unlikely to work well [**Origin:** 1800–1900 perhaps from *contrivance* + *trap* + *invention*]

con·trar·i·wise /ˈkɑntrɛriˌwaɪz, kənˈtrɛr-/ *adv.* OLD-FASHIONED in the opposite way or direction SYN **conversely**

con·trar·y¹ /ˈkɑnˌtrɛri/ Ac *adj.* **1** contrary ideas, opinions, or actions are completely different from and opposed to each other: *contrary views on the issue* | **+to** *The lawyer had acted contrary to his client's best interests.* | *Contrary to his testimony, he was involved in the crime.* **2 contrary to popular belief/opinion** used to say that something is true even though people believe the opposite: *Contrary to popular belief, a desert can be very cold.* **3** someone who is contrary deliberately does things differently from the way that other people do them, or from the way that people expect SYN **perverse**: *a contrary old lady* **4** EARTH SCIENCE contrary weather conditions are ones that cause difficulties: *Contrary weather prevented the climb.* —**contrarily** *adv.* —**contrariness** *n.* [U]

contrary² Ac *n.* FORMAL **1 on the contrary** used to show that the opposite of what has just been said is actually true: *Interfering did not help. On the contrary, it made things much worse.* **2 to the contrary** showing that the opposite is true: *In spite of rumors to the*

C

contrary, I have no intention of resigning. **3 the contrary** the opposite of what has been said or suggested SYN **opposite**: *"Do you think the children are too young to see this movie?" "* ***Quite the contrary.*** *"*

con·trast[1] /ˈkɑntræst/ Ac W2 *n.* **1** [C,U] a difference between people, ideas, situations etc. that are being compared: *There are similarities between the two countries, but there are also great contrasts.* | **+between** *the economic and social contrasts between the poor and the rich* | **+with** *The smooth marble makes a pleasing contrast with the rough stone around it.* | **a sharp/stark/marked contrast** (=a great contrast) *The spirited mood on Friday was a sharp contrast to the tense atmosphere last year.* **2 in/by contrast** used when you are comparing objects or situations and saying that they are completely different from each other: *About one in four Hispanic Americans are poor. By contrast, about one in ten white Americans are below the poverty line.* | **+with** *The stock lost 60 cents a share, in contrast with last year, when it gained 21 cents.* | **+to** *The birth rate for older women has declined, in contrast to the rate for teenage girls, which has increased.* | **in sharp/marked/stark etc. contrast to** *This year's record profits stand in sharp contrast to last year's $2 million loss.* **3** [C] something that is very different from something else: **+to** *He wore a dark suit and tie, a contrast to the brightly colored shirts he usually wears.* **4** [U] ENG. LANG. ARTS the differences in color, or in light and darkness, on photographs or paintings: *an artist known for his use of contrast* **5** [U] the degree of difference between the light and dark parts of a television picture, X-RAY, PHOTOCOPY etc.

C

con·trast[2] /kənˈtræst/ Ac *v.* **1** [I] if two things contrast, the difference between them is very easy to see and is sometimes surprising: **+with** *The sharpness of the vinegar contrasts with the sweetness of the nuts.* | *The German view* ***contrasted sharply with*** *American opinion.* **2** [T] to compare two objects, ideas, people etc. to show how different they are from each other: *a book* ***comparing and contrasting*** *the two prison systems* | **contrast sth with sth** *The documentary contrasts the reality of war with its romanticized image.* [**Origin:** 1600–1700 French *contraster*, from Italian *contrastare* **to stand out against, fight against**]

con·trast·ing /kənˈtræstɪŋ/ Ac *adj.* two or more things that are contrasting are different from each other, especially in a way that is interesting or attractive: *a blue shirt with a contrasting collar*

con·tra·vene /ˌkɑntrəˈvin/ *v.* [T] FORMAL LAW to do something that is not allowed according to a law or rule SYN **violate**: *The proposal would contravene the First Amendment to the Constitution.*

con·tra·ven·tion /ˌkɑntrəˈvɛnʃən/ *n.* [C,U] FORMAL LAW the act of doing something that is not allowed by a law or rule SYN **violation**: **in contravention of sth** (=in a way not allowed by a rule or law) *The weapons had been shipped to the country in contravention of U.N. sanctions.*

con·tre·temps /ˈkɑntrəˌtɑn/ *n. plural* **contretemps** /-ˌtɑnz/ [C] LITERARY OR HUMOROUS **1** an argument that is not serious **2** an unlucky and unexpected event, especially an embarrassing one [**Origin:** 1600–1700 French **against time**]

con·trib·ute /kənˈtrɪbyut, -yət/ Ac W2 *v.* **1** [I,T] to give money, help, ideas etc. to something that a lot of other people are also involved in: *You can contribute by donating goods to sell.* | **contribute sth to/toward sth** *Three businessmen each contributed $100,000 to the fund.* | **+to** *Japan contributed to the cost of the research.* **2 contribute to sth** to be one of the causes or features of something: *Alcohol contributes to over 100,000 deaths a year in America.* **3** [I,T] to write articles, stories, poems etc. for a newspaper or magazine: *Several hundred people contributed articles, photographs, and cartoons.* **4** [I,T] to say something or express an idea or opinion during a conversation, meeting etc.: *Does anyone else have anything to contribute?* | **contribute (sth) to sth** *Many important writers have contributed to this debate.* [**Origin:** 1500–1600 Latin, past participle of *contribuere*]

con·tri·bu·tion /ˌkɑntrəˈbyuʃən/ Ac W2 *n.* **1** [C] something that you give or do in order to help something be successful: **+to/toward** *The ships are Portugal's contribution to the multinational force.* | *Schools must prepare students to* ***make a contribution*** *to society.* | **important/significant/substantial etc. contribution** *Wolko made outstanding contributions to children's medicine.* **2** [C] an amount of money that you give in order to help pay for something: *a campaign contribution* | **+to/toward** *Contributions to charities are tax deductible.* | **+of** *a contribution of $25* | ***Contributions will be made to*** *the Muscular Dystrophy Association.* **3** [C] a regular payment that you make to your employer or to the government in addition to what they pay for BENEFITS that you will receive: *health-care insurance contributions* **4** [C] a story, poem, or piece of writing that you write and that is printed in a magazine or newspaper: *a journal with contributions from well-known writers* **5** [U] the act of giving money, time, help etc.

con·trib·u·tor /kənˈtrɪbyət̬ɚ/ Ac *n.* [C] **1** someone who gives money, help, ideas etc. to something that a lot of other people are also involved in: *Seventeen of the guests were campaign contributors.* | **+to** *Harris has been a major contributor to the Republican Party.* **2** FORMAL someone or something that helps to cause something: **+to** *Carbon dioxide is the primary contributor to the greenhouse effect.* **3** someone who writes a story, article etc. that is printed in a magazine or newspaper: **+to** *a regular contributor to the magazine*

con·trib·u·to·ry /kənˈtrɪbyəˌtɔri/ *adj.* **1** [only before noun] helping to cause something: *Smoking is a contributory factor in the disease.* **2** a contributory RETIREMENT or insurance plan is one that is paid for by the workers as well as by the company

conˌtributory ˈnegligence *n.* [U] LAW failure to take enough care to avoid or prevent an accident, so that you are partly responsible for any loss or damage caused

ˈcon trick *n.* [C] a CONFIDENCE TRICK

con·trite /kənˈtraɪt/ *adj.* feeling guilty and sorry for something bad that you have done, or showing that you feel this way SYN **penitent**: *a contrite apology* [**Origin:** 1200–1300 Old French *contrit*, from Latin, past participle of *conterere* **to rub together, bruise**] —**contritely** *adv.* —**contrition** /kənˈtrɪʃən/ *n.* [U]

con·tri·vance /kənˈtraɪvəns/ *n.* FORMAL **1** [C] a contrivance in a story or movie is something that seems artificial or not natural, but that makes something happen: *a plot contrivance* **2** [C] a machine or piece of equipment that has been made or invented for a special purpose SYN **device**: *a contrivance used in 19th-century clothing factories* **3** [C,U] a plan or trick to make something happen or to get something, or the practice of doing this SYN **scheme**: *Harriet's matchmaking contrivances*

con·trive /kənˈtraɪv/ *v.* [T] **1** FORMAL to succeed in doing something in spite of difficulties: **contrive to do sth** *The chef contrives to keep the fresh taste of the vegetables.* **2** to arrange an event or situation secretly or by deceiving people: *Oil companies were accused of contriving a gasoline shortage to push up prices.* **3** to make or invent something in a skillful way, especially because you need it suddenly SYN **devise**: *Richter contrived a scale to measure the force of an earthquake.*

con·trived /kənˈtraɪvd/ *adj.* seeming false and not natural: *The script is contrived and unbelievable.*

con·trol[1] /kənˈtroʊl/ S1 W1 *n.*

1 MAKE SB/STH DO WHAT YOU WANT [U] the ability or power to make someone or something do what you want, or to make something happen in the way you want: *The disease robs you of muscle control.* | **+of/over** *Babies are born with very little control over their movements.* | *The device allows handicapped people to* ***have*** *more* ***control over*** *their lives.* | *Teachers must be* ***in control of*** *their classrooms.* | *Strong winds sent the boat* ***out of control*** (=it could not be controlled). | *His*

behavior was ***getting out of control*** (=becoming impossible to control). | *They must not be blamed for problems that are* ***beyond their control*** (=not possible for them to control). | *"Do you need any help?" "I have it* ***under control****, thanks."* | *She was driving too fast, and* ***lost control of*** (=was not able to control it any longer) *the car.* | *Captain Fisher was unable to* ***regain control of*** *the plane.*
2 POWER [U] the power to make the decisions about how a country, place, company etc. is organized or what it does: *The press was freed from political control.* | **+of/over** *Rebels battled for control of the city.* | *Sommers is firmly* ***in control of*** *the board.* | *Deng* ***gained control of*** *the Chinese Communist Party in 1978.* | *You have to* ***take control of*** *your own life.* | *Natural resources will remain* ***under*** *state* ***control*** (=being controlled by the state). | *Most of the area was* ***under the control of*** (=being controlled by) *the Khmer Rouge.* | *He* ***has*** *editorial* ***control*** *of the publication.* | *It is feared that the troops may* ***lose control of*** (=not be able to control a place any longer) *the area.* | *The Republicans* ***regained control*** *of the House and Senate.*

THESAURUS
be in charge (of sth/sb) to have control over or responsibility for an activity, thing, or group of people: *the nurse in charge of this area*
be in control (of sth) to have the power to make the decisions about how a country, company, organization etc. is organized or what it does: *At that time the Communists were in control of the country.*
be in power to have political control of a country: *the period when Stalin was in power*
run to organize or be in charge of a company, organization, country, or activity: *She runs a Girl Scout troop in her spare time.*
manage to be in charge of the work of a business or department: *The sales department is managed by Mrs. Williams.*
head/head up to be in charge of a team, government, organization etc.: *Miller will be heading up this project.*
direct to be in charge of something that people are doing: *the woman who directed the project*

3 WAY OF LIMITING STH [C,U] an action, method, or law that limits the amount or growth of something, especially something dangerous: *pest control on farms* | **+of** *the control of inflation* | **+on** *controls on pollution from cars and industry* | *Inflation appears to be* ***out of control*** (=it is not being limited). | **be/have/bring/keep sth under control** *The company must bring costs under control* (=not allow costs to increase). | *Firefighters had the blaze under control by 7:30 a.m.* | *an* ***arms control*** (=a limit on the number of weapons a country has) *treaty* | *Extra security people will assist with* ***crowd control****.* | **tight/rigid/strict controls on sth** *Senator Landers favors tight controls on handguns.* | **rent/price/gun etc. control** *the city's rent control laws*
4 ABILITY TO STAY CALM [U] the ability to remain calm even when you feel very angry, upset, or excited: **fight/struggle for control** *With tears in his eyes he paused, fighting for control.* | *I felt calm and* ***in control****.* | *He* ***lost control*** (=became unable to control his behavior) *and shouted at us.* | *Most five-year-olds don't have a lot of* ***self-control****.* | *Her rage was barely* ***under control*** (=being controlled). | *At first he panicked, but managed to* ***regain control*** (=succeeded in behaving calmly again).
5 COMPUTER also **control key** [usually singular] COMPUTERS a particular button on a computer that allows you to do certain operations: *Press control and F2 to exit.*
6 SPORTS [U] the ability to make points or win a game: *Hendricks* ***took control*** *of the ball and scored six straight points.* | *The Nuggets* ***had control*** *in the third quarter.* | *St. Louis* ***regained control*** *of the game when Cavallini scored.* | *A basket by Basey put Logan High* ***in control****.*
7 MACHINE/VEHICLE [C] the thing that you press or turn to make a machine, vehicle, television etc. work: *a car with manual controls* | *the TV control* | *Test pilot Chris Sanders was* ***at the controls*** (=controlling it). → see also REMOTE CONTROL
8 AIRCRAFT the people who give instructions to an airplane or SPACECRAFT: *air traffic control* | *The astronauts contacted mission control.*
9 SCIENTIFIC TEST [C] TECHNICAL a group used as a comparison to check if the results of an EXPERIMENT with another similar group are happening by chance or not → see also CONTROLLED EXPERIMENT
10 CHECKING STH [U] the process of checking that something is correct, or the place where this is done: *Please stop at passport control.* → see also BIOLOGICAL CONTROL, BIRTH CONTROL, QUALITY CONTROL

C

control² S2 W1 *v.* **controlled, controlling** [T]
1 POWER to have the power to make the decisions about how a country, place, company etc. is organized or what it does: *Many U.S. corporations are controlled by foreign companies.* | *Republicans now control the Senate.*
2 MACHINE/PROCESS/SYSTEM to make a machine, process, or system work in a particular way: *a radio-controlled car* | **control which/what/how etc.** *These switches control which track the trains are allowed to run on.*
3 LIMIT/KEEP AT CORRECT LEVEL to limit the amount or growth of something, or keep it at the correct level: *She exercises to control her weight.* | *an economic plan to control inflation* | *Insulin controls blood sugar levels in the body.*
4 EMOTION to behave in a calm and sensible way, even if you feel angry, upset, or excited: *He controlled the urge to laugh.* | *If you can't* ***control your temper****, you don't belong in this line of work.* | *She fought to* ***control herself*** (=tried to stop crying, stop being angry etc.) *as she told me what they had gone through.* | **control your voice/face/expression** (=make your voice, face etc. seem normal and not show your emotions)
5 SPORTS to be winning in a game, or to have the ball so that you can make points: *Washington State* ***controlled the ball*** *for almost the whole game.*
6 MAKE SB/STH DO WHAT YOU WANT to make someone or something do what you want, or make something happen in the way that you want: *If you can't control your dog, you should put it on a leash.* | *The police were called in to control the crowds.*
7 CHECK STH to make sure that something is done correctly: *The company strictly controls the quality of its products.*
[**Origin:** 1400–1500 Anglo-French *contreroller* **to keep a copy of an official document in rolled-up form**, from Medieval Latin *contrarotulare*]

con'trol ˌfreak *n.* [C] INFORMAL DISAPPROVING someone who is very concerned about controlling all the details in every situation they are involved in

con'trol ˌkey *n.* [C] COMPUTERS a special button on a computer that allows you to do certain operations

con·trol·la·ble /kən'troʊləbəl/ *adj.* able to be controlled: *Diabetes is a serious but controllable disease.*

con·trolled /kən'troʊld/ *adj.* **1** calm and not showing emotion, even if you feel angry, afraid etc.: *She seemed calm and controlled.* **2** deliberately done in a particular way, or made to have particular qualities: *the smooth and controlled movements of a dancer* | *a controlled explosion* **3** limited by a law or rule: **tightly/strictly/closely controlled** *Access to the site is strictly controlled.*

conˌtrolled 'drug *n.* [C] LAW a CONTROLLED SUBSTANCE

conˌtrolled e'conomy *n.* [C] an economic system in which the government controls all businesses

conˌtrolled ex'periment *n.* [C] BIOLOGY a scientific test in which you change only one single condition of the test and do not change any of the other conditions that might affect the test → see also CONTROLLED VARIABLE, DEPENDENT VARIABLE, MANIPULATED VARIABLE

conˌtrolled 'substance *n.* [C] LAW a drug that it is illegal to have or use

conˌtrolled 'variable *n.* [C] BIOLOGY in a scientific EXPERIMENT (=test), one of the conditions that you do not change so that its effect on other things in the experiment is always the same SYN **constant variable** → see also DEPENDENT VARIABLE → MANIPULATED VARIABLE

con·trol·ler /kən'troʊlɚ/ *n.* [C] **1** also **comptroller** ECONOMICS someone who is in charge of the money received or paid out by a company or government department: *the state controller* **2** someone who is in charge of a particular system or of part of an organization: *air traffic controllers*

C

con,trolling 'interest *n.* [C usually singular] ECONOMICS if you have a controlling interest in a company, you own enough SHARES to be able to make decisions about what happens to the company

con'trol room *n.* [C] the room from which a process, service, event etc. is controlled: *the submarine's control room*

con'trol ,tower *n.* [C] a tall building at an airport from which people direct the movement of airplanes on the ground and in the air

con·tro·ver·sial /ˌkɑntrə'vɚʃəl/ Ac W3 *adj.* causing a lot of disagreement, because many people have strong opinions about the subject being discussed: *a controversial drug that is used to treat depression* | **a controversial plan/decision/issue etc.** *In June, he made a controversial decision to increase the sales tax.* | *the* ***highly controversial*** *issue of abortion* | *He soon became a* ***controversial figure*** (=someone who does things some people disapprove of) *in the world of big business.* —**controversially** *adv.*

con·tro·ver·sy /'kɑntrəˌvɚsi/ Ac W3 *n. plural* **controversies** [C,U] a serious, public disagreement about an important issue, often over a long period of time: *He resigned Tuesday after months of controversy.* | **+over/about** *Controversy over the drug's safety still continues.* | *There's been a lot of* ***controversy surrounding*** *these experiments.* | **the subject/center of (a) controversy** *The matter continues to be a subject of controversy.* [**Origin:** 1300–1400 Latin *controversia*, from *controversus* **disagreed about**]

con·tu·sion /kən'tuʒən/ *n.* [C] MEDICINE a BRUISE —**contused** *adj.*

co·nun·drum /kə'nʌndrəm/ *n.* [C] **1** a confusing and difficult problem: *a moral conundrum* **2** a person or situation that is strange or confusing SYN **enigma**: *King remains a conundrum, a man of both major strengths and serious character flaws.* **3** a trick question asked for fun SYN **riddle**

con·ur·ba·tion /ˌkɑnɚ'beɪʃən/ *n.* [C] SOCIAL SCIENCE a group of towns that have grown and joined together to form an area with a high population, often with a large city as its center

con·va·lesce /ˌkɑnvə'lɛs/ *v.* [I] to spend time getting well after an illness or operation SYN **recuperate**: *He will need about a week to convalesce after the operation.*

con·va·les·cence /ˌkɑnvə'lɛsəns/ *n.* [singular, U] the process of getting well after an illness or operation SYN **recuperation**: *Mrs. Gwynn will continue her convalescence at home.*

con·va·les·cent[1] /ˌkɑnvə'lɛsənt/ *adj.* **a convalescent home/hospital etc.** a place where people stay when they need care from doctors and nurses but are not sick enough to be in a hospital → see also NURSING HOME

convalescent[2] *n.* [C] someone who is getting well after a serious illness or operation

con·vect /kən'vɛkt/ *v.* [I] PHYSICS to move heat by convection

con·vec·tion /kən'vɛkʃən/ *n.* [U] **1** PHYSICS the circular movement in a gas or liquid caused by an outside force such as GRAVITY **2** PHYSICS the transfer of heat through a liquid, caused by the movement of MOLECULES → see also CONDUCTION

con'vection ,oven *n.* [C] a special OVEN that makes hot air move around inside it so that all the parts of the food get the same amount of heat

con·vene /kən'vin/ Ac *v.* [I,T] if a group of people convene, or someone convenes them, they meet together, especially for a formal meeting SYN **convoke**: *A board was convened to judge the design competition.*

con·ven·ience /kən'vinyəns/ *n.* **1** [U] the quality of being appropriate or useful for a particular purpose, especially because it makes something easier or saves you time: *The convenience of a car means many of us do not use public transit.* | **the convenience of doing sth** *Online catalogs give you the convenience of shopping at home.* | ***For convenience****, the cheese is sold ready-sliced.* **2** [C] something that is useful because it saves you time or means that you have less work to do: *Being able to pay bills over the Internet is a real convenience.* **3** [U] what is easiest and best for someone: *I'd like to arrange a meeting* ***at your convenience.*** | ***For your convenience****, the bank stays open until 7 p.m.* **4 at your earliest convenience** FORMAL as soon as possible → MARRIAGE OF CONVENIENCE

con'venience ,food *n.* [C,U] food that is partly or completely prepared already, and that is sold frozen or in cans, packages etc., so that it can be prepared quickly and easily: *Many convenience foods are high in fat and sugar.*

con'venience ,store *n.* [C] a store where you can buy food, alcohol, magazines etc., that is often open 24 hours each day

con·ven·ient /kən'vinyənt/ S3 *adj.* **1** useful to you because it saves you time, or does not spoil your plans or cause you problems OPP **inconvenient**: *Is there a more convenient time to meet?* | *Walking is usually a convenient way to exercise.* | **convenient (for sb) to do sth** *The idea is to make it convenient for people to give blood.* | *This is a safe and convenient way to dispose of chemicals.* | **+for** *Is Friday convenient for you?* **2** close and easy to reach: *The bus stop around the corner is probably the most convenient.* | **+to** *The airport is convenient to the city's downtown area.* [**Origin:** 1300–1400 Latin, present participle of *convenire* **to come together, be suitable**]

con·ven·ient·ly /kən'vinyəntli/ *adv.* **1** in a way that is useful to you because it saves you time or does not spoil your plans or cause you problems: *Each property is conveniently listed by location and price.* **2** in a place that is close or easily reached: *The hotel is conveniently located near the airport.* **3** if someone has conveniently forgotten, ignored, or lost something, they deliberately do this because it helps them to avoid a problem or difficult situation: *People conveniently forget things that might be embarrassing to them.*

con·vent /'kɑnvɛnt, -vənt/ *n.* [C] a building or group of buildings where NUNS live [**Origin:** 1200–1300 Old French *covent*, from Latin *conventus* **group of people who have come together**, from *convenire*] → see also CONVENT SCHOOL

con·ven·tion /kən'vɛnʃən/ Ac W2 *n.* **1** [C] a large formal meeting of people who belong to the same profession, organization etc., or who have the same interests: *the Republican Convention* | *a convention for Star Trek fans* | *The issue will be voted on at the* ***annual convention.*** | *the city's new* ***convention center*** **2** [C,U] behavior and attitudes that most people in a society consider to be normal and right SYN **custom**: *The handshake is a* ***social convention.*** | *Sand refused to follow the conventions of her day.* | ***By convention****, the bride's father walks her down the aisle at her wedding.* → see HABIT ►see THESAURUS box at **habit** **3** [C] a formal agreement, especially between countries, about particular rules or behavior: **+on** *the European Convention on Human Rights* → see also PACT, TREATY **4** [C] ENG. LANG. ARTS a method or style often used in literature, art, the theater etc. to achieve a particular effect: *the conventions of the 19th-century novel* [**Origin:** 1400–1500 French, Latin *conventio*, from *convenire* **to come together, be suitable**]

con·ven·tion·al /kən'vɛnʃənl/ Ac W3 *adj.* **1** [only before noun] a conventional method, product, practice etc. is one that has been used for a long time and is considered the usual type: *These light bulbs last longer* *and use less energy than conventional ones.* **2** always following the behavior and attitudes that most people in a society consider to be normal, right, and socially acceptable, so that you seem slightly boring OPP **unconventional**: *a belief in conventional values* | **+in** *John is fairly conventional in his musical taste.* **3** [only before noun] conventional weapons, wars, and armies do not use NUCLEAR explosives or weapons: *At that time, the Soviet Union had far more* ***conventional forces*** (=they had more ordinary troops and weapons). **4 (the) conventional wisdom** the opinion that most people consider to be normal and right, but that is sometimes shown to be wrong: *Conventional wisdom says that countries with high education rates have lower birth rates.* **5 conventional medicine** the usual form of medicine practiced in the U.S., Canada, and most European countries SYN **western medicine** —**conventionally** *adv.* —**conventionality** /kən,venʃəˈnæləṭi/ *n.* [U]

con'ventional ,oven *n.* [C] an ordinary OVEN, not a MICROWAVE

'convent ,school *n.* [C] a school for girls that is run by Catholic NUNS

con·verge /kənˈvɚdʒ/ *v.* [I] **1** if groups of people converge in a particular place, they come there from many different places and meet together to form a large crowd: **+on** *Reporters quickly converged on the scene.* **2** to come from different directions and meet at the same point to become one thing SYN **merge** OPP **diverge**: *The rivers converge south of Pittsburgh.* **3** if different ideas or aims converge, they become the same OPP **diverge**: **+with** *This is one area where popular opinion converges with government policy.* **4** MATH if a series of numbers converge toward a number, they come closer and closer to that number as they reach the upper limit of the series

con'vergence ,zone *n.* [C] EARTH SCIENCE an area in Earth's ATMOSPHERE where two different flows of air continuously meet, with the result that particular types of weather patterns, storms etc. often happen there

con·ver·gent /kənˈvɚdʒənt/ *adj.* coming together at a point: *convergent lines* —**convergence** *n.* [C,U]

con,vergent evo'lution *n.* [U] BIOLOGY the natural way in which different SPECIES of animals, plants etc. living in different areas with a similar type of environment have developed similar physical features as they have changed gradually over a long period of time

con'verging ,lens *n.* [C] PHYSICS a piece of glass or plastic which changes the direction of beams of light passing through it so that they meet at a single point → see also DIVERGING LENS

con·ver·sant /kənˈvɚsənt/ *adj.* [not before noun] **1** FORMAL having knowledge or experience of something SYN **familiar**: **+with** *Are you fully conversant with the facts of the case?* **2** able to have a conversation in a foreign language, but not able to speak it perfectly: **+in** *Eban is conversant in ten languages.*

con·ver·sa·tion /,kɑnvɚˈseɪʃən/ S2 W2 *n.* [C,U] an informal talk in which people exchange news, feelings, and thoughts: *a telephone conversation* | *The buzz of conversation filled the hall.* | **+with** *a short conversation with the teacher* | **+about** *a long conversation about family and friends* | **have/hold a conversation** *They had a short conversation in Spanish.* | *It's impossible to* ***carry on a conversation*** *with all this noise.* | *Sophia and her sisters tried to* ***engage*** *him* ***in conversation.*** | *I* ***struck up a conversation*** (=started one) *with a fellow passenger.* | *"Did you have a good trip?" he asked, trying to* ***make conversation*** (=talk to someone in order to be polite). | *Naturally, the* ***conversation turned*** (=people started to talk about something different) *to work and the problems at work.* | *I found Annie* ***deep in conversation*** *with her sister.* [**Origin:** 1300–1400 Old French, Latin *conversatio*, from *conversari* **to live with, be with**]

con·ver·sa·tion·al /,kɑnvɚˈseɪʃənl, -ʃnəl/ *adj.* **1** a conversational style, phrase etc. is informal and commonly used in conversation: *McGovern lectures in a conversational style.* **2** relating to conversation: *a class in conversational Spanish.* —**conversationally** *adv.*

con·ver·sa·tion·al·ist /,kɑnvɚˈseɪʃənə,lɪst/ *n.* [C] someone whose conversation is intelligent, amusing, and interesting: *He's a good conversationalist.*

,conver'sation ,piece *n.* [C] something that provides a subject for conversation, often used in a joking way to describe objects that are very strange or unusual

con·verse¹ /kənˈvɚs/ Ac *v.* [I] FORMAL to have a conversation with someone SYN **talk**: **+with** *She enjoyed the chance to converse with someone who spoke her native language.* ▸see THESAURUS box at **talk¹**

con·verse² /ˈkɑnvɚs/ Ac *n.* **1 the converse** FORMAL the converse of a fact, word, statement etc. is the opposite of it SYN **opposite**: *If the project is successful, he'll get the credit, but the converse is also true: he'll get the blame if it fails.* **2** [singular, U] ALGEBRA a mathematical or LOGICAL statement in which the subject and the claim about the subject have been REVERSED. For example, the converse of "All X is Y" is "All Y is X"; the converse of the CONDITIONAL sentence "If p, then q" is "If q, then p." → see also INVERSE

con·verse³ /kənˈvɚs, ˈkɑnvɚs/ Ac *adj.* FORMAL opposite: *a converse opinion*

con·verse·ly /kənˈvɚsli, ˈkɑnvɚsli/ Ac *adv.* FORMAL used when one situation is the opposite of another: *Children who have strong verbal skills may, conversely, have trouble learning physical skills.*

con·ver·sion /kənˈvɚʒən, -ʃən/ Ac *n.* **1** [C,U] the act or process of changing something from one form, purpose, or system to a different one: **+to** *a conversion to the metric system* | **conversion of sth into/to sth** *the conversion of an old warehouse into apartments* **2** [C,U] an act of changing from one religion or belief to a different one: **+to** *her conversion to Catholicism* **3** [C] a way of getting more points after making a TOUCHDOWN in football: *a two-point conversion*

con'version ,factor *n.* [C] CHEMISTRY a fixed quantity which you can multiply or divide with another number to change one type of measurement into a different type of measurement, for example miles into kilometers

con·vert¹ /kənˈvɚt/ Ac S3 W3 *v.* **1** [I,T] to change into a different form, or change into something that can be used for a different purpose or in a different way, or to make something do this: **convert sth into sth** *They converted the spare room into an office.* | **+to** *Thousands of miles of old railroad lines have been converted to trails.* | *The screen converts to a color TV.* | **+into** *The seats convert into beds.* **2** [I,T] to change your opinions or habits, or to persuade someone else to do this: **+to** *Young Japanese people are converting from tea to coffee.* | **convert sb to sth** *Jones was converted from an opponent to a supporter during the meeting.* **3** [I,T] to change from one religion or belief to another, or to persuade someone to do this: **+to** *Ron converted to Judaism.* | **+convert sb to sth** *Missionaries converted thousands to Christianity.* **4** [I,T] to make a conversion in football [**Origin:** 1200–1300 Old French *convertir*, from Latin *convertere* **to turn around, convert**]

con·vert² /ˈkɑnvɚt/ Ac *n.* [C] someone who has been persuaded to change their beliefs and accept a particular religion or opinion: *a convert to Buddhism*

con·vert·er, convertor /kənˈvɚṭɚ/ *n.* [C] a piece of equipment that changes the form of something, especially so that it can be more easily used: *Cable TV subscribers get a converter that unscrambles the pictures.* → see also CATALYTIC CONVERTER

con·vert·i·ble¹ /kənˈvɚṭəbəl/ *n.* [C] a car with a roof that you can fold back or remove ▸see THESAURUS box at **car** → see also HARDTOP

convertible² Ac *adj.* **1** an object that is convertible can be folded or arranged in a different way so that it can be used as something else: *a convertible sofa bed* **2** ECONOMICS money that is convertible can be exchanged for the money of another country **3** ECONOMICS a financial document such as an insurance arrangement or BOND that is convertible can be exchanged for money, STOCKS etc. —**convertibility** /kən,vɚṭəˈbɪləṭi/ *n.* [U]

C

con·ver·tor /kən'vɝt̬ɚ/ *n.* [C] another spelling of CONVERTER

con·vex /ˌkɑn'vɛks◂ , kən-/ *adj.* curved outward, like the surface of the eye OPP **concave**: *a convex lens* | *a convex mirror* —**convexly** *adv.* —**convexity** /kən'vɛksət̬i/ *n.* [C,U] → see picture at ACCOMMODATION

con·vey /kən'veɪ/ *v.* **conveys, conveyed, conveying** [T] **1** to communicate a message or information, with or without using words: *All this information can be conveyed in a simple diagram.* | *Even silence can convey meaning.* | **convey to sb that** *I want to convey to children that reading is one of life's greatest treats.* | *Ads* ***convey the message*** *that thin is beautiful.* | **convey a sense/an impression/an idea etc.** *He somehow conveyed the impression that he didn't know what was going on.* **2** FORMAL to take or carry something from one place to another: *The guard was charged with conveying drugs to a prison inmate.* **3** LAW to legally change the possession of property from one person to another [**Origin:** 1300–1400 Old French *conveier* **to go with someone to a place**, from Vulgar Latin *conviare*]

con·vey·ance /kən'veɪəns/ *n.* **1** [C] FORMAL a vehicle: *No wheeled conveyances of any kind are allowed in the park.* **2** [U] FORMAL the act of taking something from one place to another: *the conveyance of goods* **3** [U] the act of communicating or expressing something, with or without using words: *Facial expressions are part of the conveyance of meaning.* **4** [U] LAW the act of changing the ownership of land, property etc. from one person to another

con·vey·or, conveyer /kən'veɪɚ/ *n.* [C] a conveyor belt or a machine that has a conveyor belt: *She put her groceries onto the conveyor.*

con'veyor belt *n.* [C] a long continuous moving band of rubber, cloth, or metal, used in a place such as a factory or airport to move things from one place to another: *Baggage is placed on the conveyor belt to go through the X-ray machine.*

con·vict[1] /kən'vɪkt/ W3 *v.* [T] LAW to prove or officially announce that someone is guilty of a crime after a TRIAL in a court of law OPP **acquit**: **convict sb of sth** *Smith was convicted of armed robbery.* | **convict sb on sth** *The three men were* ***convicted on*** *weapons* ***charges.*** | *a convicted murderer* [**Origin:** 1300–1400 Latin, past participle of *convincere* **to prove untrue, convict, prove**]

con·vict[2] /'kɑnvɪkt/ *n.* [C] someone who has been proven to be guilty of a crime and sent to prison: *an escaped convict* → see also EX-CON

con·vic·tion /kən'vɪkʃən/ W3 *n.* **1** [C] a very strong belief or opinion: **conviction that** *Americans held the conviction that anyone could become rich if they worked hard.* | **a deep/strong/firm conviction** *They have a deep conviction that marriage is for life.* | **religious/political convictions** *Religious convictions have a strong influence on people's behavior.* **2** [C] LAW a decision in a court of law that someone is guilty of a crime, or the process of proving that someone is guilty OPP **acquittal**: *He had no prior convictions.* | *Employers check that new workers have no* ***criminal convictions.*** | **+for** *a conviction for driving while drunk* | *the trial and conviction of Jimmy Malone* **3** [U] the feeling of being sure about something and having no doubts: **with/without conviction** (=feeling or not feeling sure) *"No," she said, but without conviction.* | *"We're going to win," he said, but his voice didn't* ***carry conviction*** (=it showed that he did not feel sure about what he was saying). → see also **have the courage of your (own) convictions** at COURAGE (2)

con·vince /kən'vɪns/ Ac S2 W3 *v.* [T] **1** to make someone feel certain that something is true SYN **persuade**: *His reasons didn't convince everyone.* | **convince sb (that)** *Bell's evidence convinced us that the reports were true.* | *It will be hard to convince voters he's a serious candidate.* | **convince sb of sth** *He'll try to convince you of Mitchell's innocence.* **2** to persuade someone to do something SYN **persuade**: **convince sb to do sth** *Kevin convinced her to go to the dance with him.* ▶see THESAURUS box at **persuade** [**Origin:** 1500–1600 Latin *convincere* **to prove untrue, convict, prove**]

con·vinced /kən'vɪnst/ Ac W3 *adj.* [not before noun] feeling certain that something is true: *Sue agreed, but she didn't sound very convinced.* | **+(that)** *I am convinced that sooner or later the Rilles will be caught by the police.* | *She was convinced she was doing the right thing.* | **be convinced of sth** *We are convinced of the safety of these products.* | *I am* ***fully convinced*** *that this is necessary.*

con·vinc·ing /kən'vɪnsɪŋ/ Ac *adj.* **1** making you believe that something is true or right: *No one could give me a convincing answer.* | ***convincing evidence*** *of his guilt* | *He gave a convincing performance as Lear.* **2 a convincing victory/win** an occasion when a person or team wins a game or competition by a lot of points —**convincingly** *adv.*

con·viv·i·al /kən'vɪviəl/ *adj.* friendly and pleasantly cheerful: *convivial conversation* —**convivially** *adv.* —**conviviality** /kənˌvɪvi'ælət̬i/ *n.* [U]

con·vo·ca·tion /ˌkɑnvə'keɪʃən/ *n.* FORMAL **1** [C usually singular] a large formal meeting of a group of people, especially church officials: *a convocation of priests* **2** [C usually singular] the ceremony held when students have finished their studies and are leaving a college or university SYN **graduation**: *Who's going to be the speaker at the convocation?* **3** [U] FORMAL the process of arranging for a large meeting to be held

con·voke /kən'voʊk/ *v.* [T] FORMAL to tell people that they must come together for a formal meeting SYN **convene**: *A conference was convoked to discuss the situation.*

con·vo·lut·ed /'kɑnvəˌlut̬ɪd/ *adj.* **1** complicated and difficult to understand: *The convoluted language of the report made it difficult to read.* | *The loan approval process is very convoluted.* **2** FORMAL having many twists and bends: *a convoluted freeway interchange* —**convolutedly** *adv.*

con·vo·lu·tion /ˌkɑnvə'luʃən/ *n.* [C usually plural] FORMAL **1** the complicated details of a story, explanation etc., which make it difficult to understand: **+of** *the endless convolutions of the plot* **2** a fold or twist in something which has many of them: *the many convolutions of the brain*

con·voy /'kɑnvɔɪ/ *n.* [C] a group of vehicles or ships without weapons traveling together, sometimes in order to protect one another: *Submarines sank all but one of the ships in the convoy.* | **+of** *a convoy of military trucks* —**convoy** *v.* [T]

con·vulse /kən'vʌls/ *v.* **1** [T] if something such as a war convulses a country, it causes a lot of problems and anxiety: *The city was convulsed by rioting and demonstrations.* **2 be convulsed with laughter** to be laughing so much that you shake and are not able to stop yourself **3** [I] if your body or a part of it convulses, it moves violently and you are not able to control it: *Suddenly the girl began to convulse.*

con·vul·sion /kən'vʌlʃən/ *n.* **1** [C usually plural] MEDICINE violent shaking movements of someone's body that they cannot control, because they are sick SYN **seizure**: *His temperature was very high and he* ***went into convulsions.*** **2** [C] a great change that affects a country: *the economic and political convulsions in Europe during the 1930s and 1940s* **3 be in convulsions (of laughter)** INFORMAL to be laughing a lot: *By the end of the first act, we were in convulsions.*

con·vul·sive /kən'vʌlsɪv/ *adj.* a convulsive movement or action is sudden, violent, and impossible to control: *He gave a convulsive shudder.* —**convulsively** *adv.*

co·ny, coney /'koʊni/ *n. plural* **conies, coneys** [C,U] OLD USE a rabbit or rabbit fur used in making coats

coo /ku/ *v.* [I] **1** to make the low soft cry of a DOVE or PIGEON **2** to make soft quiet sounds, or to speak in a soft quiet way: *The women began to coo at the baby.* —**coo** *n.* [C]

cook[1] /kʊk/ S1 W2 *v.* **1** [I,T] to prepare food for eating by using heat: *Mom taught me to cook.* | *It's important to cook the meat thoroughly.* | *Turn the chicken over, and cook for another five minutes.* | **cook sb sth** *He decided to cook his parents a special meal for their wedding anniversary.* | **cook (sth) for sb** *She cooks for her family of seven.* | *I'll cook something special for you while you're here.* | **cook dinner/supper/a meal etc.** *Dad cooks breakfast on weekends.* | **cook (sth) until** *Cook until the onion is softened.*

THESAURUS

bake to cook food such as bread or cookies in the oven
roast to cook meat or vegetables in an oven
fry to cook food in oil on the top part of the stove
sauté to fry vegetables for a short time in a small amount of oil
broil to cook food by placing it near to strong heat from above
grill to cook food over strong heat, especially over flames
boil to cook vegetables in very hot water on the top part of the oven
steam to cook vegetables by placing them in a container over very hot water, so that the steam from the hot water cooks them
poach to cook food gently in hot water
deep fry to fry food in a pan containing a lot of hot oil
microwave to cook food in a microwave oven
barbecue to cook food on a metal frame over a fire outdoors
toast to cook the outside surfaces of bread

THESAURUS

cook to make food ready to eat, using heat: *I cooked the potatoes for the salad yesterday.*
make to make food ready to eat, with or without using heat: *I made a sandwich for lunch.* | *Do you want to help me make cookies?*
fix INFORMAL to make food ready to eat, with or without using heat: *I'll fix you some cereal.* | *I have to be back by six to fix dinner.*
prepare FORMAL to make food ready to eat, especially when the food is difficult or complicated to make: *the time it takes to prepare Thanksgiving dinner*

2 [I] to be prepared for eating by being heated: *Cover and simmer until the chicken finishes cooking.* **3 be cooking** INFORMAL to be happening, especially in a secret way: *Hey, guys! What's cooking?* **4 be cooking (with gas)** SPOKEN used to say someone is doing something very well: *The band's really cooking tonight!* **5 cook the books** to dishonestly change official records and figures in order to steal money or give people false information: *Officials at the bank were found to have cooked the books.* → see also COOKING[1]

cook sth ↔ **up** *phr. v.* **1** to prepare food, especially quickly: *Dad's cooking up some steaks on the barbecue.* **2** INFORMAL to invent an excuse, reason, plan etc., especially one that is slightly dishonest or unlikely to work: *He cooked up some story to explain why they hadn't been there.* **3 cook up a storm** to cook a lot of food during a short time period

cook[2] S2 *n.* [C] **1** someone who prepares and cooks food as their job → see also CHEF: *She'd worked as a cook during college.* **2 be a good/bad/great etc. cook** to be good or bad at preparing or cooking food, when you cook for enjoyment, your family etc. rather than as a job: *My husband is a fabulous cook.* **3 too many cooks (spoil the broth)** used when you think there are too many people trying to do the same job at the same time, so that the job is not done well [**Origin:** Old English *coc*, from Latin *coquus*, from *coquere* **to cook**] → see also **chief cook and bottle-washer** at CHIEF[1] (3)

Cook /kʊk/, **Captain James** (1728–1779) a British sailor and EXPLORER who sailed to Australia and New Zealand, and was the first European to discover several islands in the Pacific Ocean, including Hawaii

cook·book /ˈkʊkbʊk/ *n.* [C] a book that tells you how to prepare and cook food: *a vegetarian cookbook*

cooked /kʊkt/ *adj.* cooked food is not raw and is ready for eating: *a pound of cooked ham*

cook·er /ˈkʊkɚ/ *n.* [C] a piece of equipment that you cook food in: *a rice cooker* → see also PRESSURE COOKER (1)

cook·er·y /ˈkʊkəri/ *n.* [U] the art or skill of cooking: *French cookery*

cook·house /ˈkʊkhaʊs/ *n.* [C] OLD-FASHIONED an outdoor kitchen where you cook food, especially in a military camp

cook·ie /ˈkʊki/ S1 *n.* [C] **1** a small flat sweet cake: *a glass of milk and a cookie* | *chocolate chip cookies* **2** COMPUTERS information that a website leaves in your computer so that the website will recognize you when you use it again: *You can set your browser to accept or refuse cookies.* **3 tough/smart cookie** INFORMAL someone who is smart and successful, and knows how to get what they want: *She was a smart cookie who knew what she wanted.* **4 that's the way the cookie crumbles** SPOKEN, INFORMAL said when something bad has happened and you must accept things the way they are, even though you do not want to **5** OLD-FASHIONED an attractive young woman [**Origin:** 1700–1800 Dutch *koekje*, from *koek* **cake**]

ˈcookie ˌcutter *n.* [C] a tool that cuts cookies into special shapes before you bake them

ˈcookie-cutter *adj.* [only before noun] almost exactly the same as other things of the same type, and not very interesting: *a street full of cookie-cutter houses*

ˈcookie sheet *n.* [C] a flat piece of metal that you bake cookies and some other foods on

cook·ing[1] /ˈkʊkɪŋ/ *n.* [U] **1** the act of making food and cooking it: *Do you do a lot of cooking?*

THESAURUS

Ways of preparing food
grate to make cheese, a carrot etc. into small pieces by rubbing it against a special tool
crush to use a lot of force to break something such as seeds into very small pieces or into a powder
melt to make butter, chocolate etc. become liquid
add to put a food into other food that you already have
season to add salt, pepper etc. to food
sift to put flour or other powders through a sifter (=tool containing a net made of wire)
mix to combine different foods together
stir to turn food around with a spoon
beat/whisk to mix food together quickly with a fork, electric mixer, or other tool
knead to press dough (a mixture of flour and water) many times with your hands when you are making bread
serve to put different foods together as part of a meal: *Serve with rice and a salad.*
→ COOK, CUT

2 food made in a particular way or by a particular person: *Gail's cooking is always good.* | **Southern/French/Cajun etc. cooking** *Fried chicken is typical of Southern cooking.* | *I miss my mother's* ***home cooking*** (=ordinary good food).

cooking[2] *adj.* [only before noun] relating to cooking, appropriate for cooking, or used in cooking: *Add the tomatoes and some of the cooking water.* | *The cooking time depends on the weight of the chicken.*

ˈcooking ˌapple *n.* [C] a type of apple used in cooking that is not very sweet → see also EATING APPLE

ˈcooking oil *n.* [U] oil from plants, such as SUNFLOWERS or OLIVES

cook·out /ˈkʊk-aʊt/ *n.* [C] a party or occasion when a meal is cooked and eaten outdoors: *We're* ***having a cookout*** *on Memorial Day.* → see also BARBECUE

cook·ware /ˈkʊk˺wɛr/ *n.* [U] containers and equipment used for cooking: *ceramic cookware*

cool¹ /kul/ [S1] [W3] *adj.*
1 TEMPERATURE low in temperature, but not cold, often in a way that feels nice: *a nice cool drink* | *Store the seeds in a cool, dry place.* | *It was a lot cooler and windier than earlier in the week.* → see COLD¹ ►see THESAURUS box at **cold¹**
2 APPROVAL INFORMAL said to show approval, especially of someone or something that is fashionable, interesting, attractive, or relaxed: *It's a really cool book.* | *Those are the coolest shoes.* | *Oh, look at you, you* ***look*** *so* ***cool.*** | *"Did you meet Nancy?" "Yeah, she's* ***pretty cool.***" | *I love these things. They are* ***so cool.*** | *Oh, look at all the kites,* ***that's*** *so* ***cool.*** | *"At the end they opened the cages and let all the doves fly out." "****Cool.****"* | *I really liked her. I thought she was* ***way cool*** (=very cool).
3 AGREEMENT SPOKEN said to show that you agree with something, that you understand it, or that it does not annoy you: *"Okay, all done." "****Cool.****"* | *Pizza, yeah, that would be cool* (=that is a good idea). | *Lisa wants to come, so I said okay,* ***that's cool.*** | *"Sorry, I have to go." "It's okay,* ***it's cool*** (=it does not upset me)." | **be cool with sb** *Would Friday be cool with you guys?* | **sb is cool with sth** *I had to tell them I'd be late, but they were cool with that.*
4 CALM calm and not nervous, upset, or excited [SYN] **composed**: *She felt cool and in control until they called out her name.* | **stay/keep cool** *It can be hard to stay cool while listening to angry complaints.* | ***Cooler heads*** *prevailed, and the fight broke up before it started* (=calm people were able to persuade angry people not to fight). | *The witness seemed* ***cool, calm, and collected.*** | *He's one* ***cool customer*** (=always behaves calmly). ►see THESAURUS box at **calm¹**
5 CLOTHES clothing that is cool is made of thin material so that you do not become too hot: *a cool cotton dress*
6 NOT FRIENDLY behaving in a way that is not as friendly or interested as you expect: *Her gaze was decidedly cool.* | **+toward** *Foley was cool toward the idea.* | *The proposal got a* ***cool reception*** *in Congress.*
7 COLOR a cool color is one such as blue or green that makes you think of cool things
8 a cool million/$200,000 etc. INFORMAL a surprisingly large amount of money that someone easily pays, earns etc.: *His new house cost a cool million.*
[Origin: Old English *col*] —**coolness** *n.* [U] —**coolly** *adv.*

cool² [S2] *v.* **1** [I,T] also **cool down** to make something slightly colder, or to become slightly colder: *Allow the cake to cool before removing it from the pan.* | *He blew on his soup to cool it.* | *a drink that will cool you down on a hot summer day* **2** [I] if a feeling, emotion, or relationship cools, it becomes less strong: *Interest in the toys is finally cooling.* | *When tempers had cooled, he apologized.* **3 cool it** SPOKEN **a)** to stop putting as much effort into something, or pressure on someone, as you have been: *You're kind of young to have a boyfriend, so it'd be better to cool it for now.* **b)** used to tell someone to stop being angry, violent etc.: *Cool it, guys. Just play the game.* **4 cool your heels** to be forced to wait: *Even though they had a reservation, they'd been cooling their heels for half an hour waiting for a table.*

cool down *phr. v.* **1** to become calm after being angry: *You need to give him some time to cool down.* **2 cool sb/sth ↔ down** to make something slightly colder, or to become slightly colder: *The air had cooled down a little.* | *Here, this will cool you down.*

cool off *phr. v.* **1** to return to a normal temperature after being hot: *It's just as hot at night – it hardly cools off at all.* | *Your body sweats to cool off.* **2** to become calm after being angry: *I took a walk to cool off.* **3** if sales, prices etc. cool off, they decrease

cool³ *n.* **1 keep your cool** to remain calm in a frightening or difficult situation: *The waitress was really busy, but she kept her cool.* **2 lose your cool** to stop being calm in a frightening or difficult situation: *Sam was the kind of guy who never lost his cool.* **3 the cool** a temperature that is pleasantly cold: **+of** *We went for a walk in the cool of the evening.*

cool⁴ *adv.* **play it cool** to behave in a calm way because you do not want someone to know that you are really nervous, angry etc.: *She was upset, but tried to play it cool.*

cool·ant /ˈkulənt/ *n.* [C,U] TECHNICAL a liquid or gas used to cool something, especially an engine

cool·er /ˈkulɚ/ [S3] *n.* [C] **1** a container in which you can keep food or drinks cold, especially so that you can keep them cold outdoors: *a cooler full of beer and soft drinks* **2** a WATER COOLER **3 the cooler** SLANG prison **4** an AIR CONDITIONER, especially one that only cools one room → see also WINE COOLER (1)

ˌcool-ˈheaded *adj.* not easily excited or upset: *a cool-headed and professional manager*

Coo·lidge /ˈkulɪdʒ/, **Calvin** (1872–1933) the 30th President of the U.S. and Vice President under Warren Harding

coo·lie /ˈkuli/ *n.* [C] OLD-FASHIONED an unskilled worker who is paid very little money, especially in parts of Asia

ˌcooling-ˈoff ˌperiod *n.* [C] **1** a period of time when two people or groups who are arguing about something can go away and think about how to improve the situation: *The governor hoped a 60-day cooling-off period would avoid a strike.* **2** a period of time that you must wait after you have bought a gun, before you can receive the gun from the store

ˈcooling ˌsystem *n.* [C] a system for keeping the temperature in a machine, engine etc. low: *the car's cooling system*

ˈcooling ˌtower *n.* [C] a large, round, tall building, used in industry for making water cool

coon /kun/ *n.* [C] INFORMAL a RACCOON

coon·skin /ˈkunˌskɪn/ *adj.* made from the skin of a RACCOON: *a coonskin cap*

coop /kup/ *n.* [C] a building for small animals, especially chickens → see also **fly the coop** at FLY¹ (22)

co-op /ˈkouap/ *n.* [C] a COOPERATIVE

ˌcooped ˈup *adj.* [not before noun] having to stay indoors or in a place that is too small for a period of time: **+in** *We spent half our vacation cooped up in a car.*

coo·per /ˈkupɚ/ *n.* [C] someone who makes BARRELS

Cooper /ˈkupɚ/, **James Fen·i·more** /dʒeɪmz ˈfɛnɪˌmɔr/ (1789–1851) a U.S. writer of novels about Native Americans and life on the American FRONTIER

co·op·er·ate /kouˈapəˌreɪt/ [Ac] *v.* [I] **1** to work with someone else to achieve something that you both want: *The event was the result of many organizations cooperating and working together.* | **+with** *Many companies cooperate with environmental groups to encourage recycling.* | **cooperate to do sth** *Countries are cooperating to fight terrorism.* | **+in/on** *The two governments are* ***cooperating closely*** *on this issue.* **2** to do what someone wants you to do: *It's pretty hard to get a kid dressed if he's not cooperating.* | *We'll be all right if the weather cooperates* (=if the weather remains good). | **+with** *A spokesman said the office was* ***cooperating fully*** *with the police investigation.*

co·op·er·a·tion /kouˌapəˈreɪʃən/ [Ac] [W3] *n.* [U] **1** the act of working with someone else to achieve something that you both want: **+between** *Cooperation between American and Canadian environmental groups has been effective.* | *The movie was produced* ***in cooperation with*** *an Australian studio.* | *They worked in* ***close cooperation*** *throughout the war.* | **+in/on** *public and private cooperation in development programs* | **+with** *the groups in Russia that favor cooperation with the West* **2** willingness to work with other people, or to do what they ask you to do: *Thank you for your cooperation.* | **full/complete cooperation** *We expect full cooperation from everyone concerned.*

co·op·era·tive¹ /kouˈaprət̬ɪv/ [Ac] *adj.* **1** willing to cooperate [SYN] **helpful** [OPP] **uncooperative**: *a cooperative witness* | *Most of the landowners have been very cooperative.* **2** made, done, or owned by people working together: *Car companies have started several cooperative ventures.*

cooperative² also **co-op** [Ac] *n.* [C] **1** a business or organization owned equally by all the people working there: *a potato farm cooperative* **2 a)** a building owned by a company that sells SHARES in the company to people who can then live in one of the building's apartments → see also CONDOMINIUM: *a Park Avenue co-op* **b)** an apartment in this building

co-opt /koʊ'ɑpt/ *v.* [T] DISAPPROVING to use something that was not originally yours to help you do something, or to persuade someone to help you: *Bloom tried to co-opt her by offering her a better contract.* | *Most designers do nothing more than co-opt street fashion.*

co•or•di•nate¹ /koʊ'ɔrdn,eɪt/ [Ac] *v.* **1** [T] to organize an activity so that the people involved in it work together and do the right things at the right times: *The Red Cross is coordinating relief aid to the refugees.* | **+with** *The department has been coordinating with the Park Service to buy the land for the trail.* **2** [T] to make the parts of your body move and work together well: *Her movements on the balance beam were perfectly coordinated.* **3** [I,T] if clothes, decorations etc. coordinate, or you coordinate them, they look good together because they have similar colors and styles: *Don't be afraid to mix colors, as long as they coordinate.*

co•or•di•nate² /koʊ'ɔrdn-ɪt/ [Ac] *n.* **1** [C] MATH a set of numbers showing the exact position of a point on a line, on a surface, or in a space, for example on a map or a GRAPH: *The teacher gave the children coordinates to locate on the globe.* **2 coordinates** [plural] things such as women's clothes that can be worn or used together because their colors match or their styles are similar

coordinate³ [Ac] *adj.* **1** ENG. LANG. ARTS equal in importance or rank in a sentence → see also SUBORDINATE: *coordinate clauses joined by "and"* **2** MATH involving the use of coordinates

co'ordinate ,plane *n.* [C] MATH a PLANE formed when two straight lines go across each other at right angles. Points on the plane can be described using COORDINATES

co,ordinating con'junction *n.* [C] ENG. LANG. ARTS a word such as "and" or "but," which joins two clauses of the same type

co•or•di•na•tion /koʊ,ɔrdn'eɪʃən/ [Ac] *n.* [U] **1** BIOLOGY the way in which your muscles move together when you perform a movement: *Drinking alcohol affects your coordination.* | *It takes good* ***hand-eye coordination*** (=the way your hands and eyes work together) *to play tennis.* **2** the organization of people or things so that they work together well: **+of** *the coordination of sales and marketing activities* | **+between** *There is a need for more coordination between countries to combat terrorism.* | *A project director works* ***in coordination with*** *the school district.*

co•or•di•na•tor /koʊ'ɔrdn,eɪtɚ/ [Ac] *n.* [C] someone who organizes the way people work together in a particular activity: *the hospital's nursing coordinator*

coot /kut/ *n.* [C] **1** BIOLOGY a small black and white water bird with a short beak **2 old coot** INFORMAL an old man who you think is strange or mean: *He's a crazy old coot.*

coo•ties /'kutiz/ *n.* [plural] SPOKEN a word meaning lice (LOUSE), used by children as an insult when they do not want to play with or sit with another child: *I don't want to go with him – boys* ***have cooties.***

cop¹ /kɑp/ [S2] [W3] *n.* INFORMAL **1** [C] a police officer: *a motorcycle cop* | *There are more criminals out there than cops to chase them.* ►see THESAURUS box at **police¹** **2 the cops** [plural] the police: *He called the cops as soon as he heard the shots.* [**Origin:** 1800–1900 *copper* **police officer** (19–21 centuries), from *cop* **to arrest** (19–20 centuries)]

cop² *v.* **copped, copping** [T] SPOKEN **1 cop a plea** to agree to say you are guilty of a crime in order to receive a less severe punishment: *Duckett copped a plea to avoid going to jail.* **2** to get or take something, often when it surprises people that you get it: *She copped the grand prize this year with her new novel.* **3 cop an attitude** to behave in a way that is not nice, especially by showing that you think you are better or more intelligent than other people **4 cop a feel** to touch someone in a sexual way when that person does not want you to

cop out *phr. v.* SLANG to not do something that you are supposed to do: *I was going to tell him myself, but I copped out.* → see also COP-OUT

cop to sth *phr. v.* SPOKEN to admit that you have done something, or that something is happening: *He copped to feeling "scared and nervous."*

co•pa•cet•ic /,koʊpə'sɛṭɪk/ *adj.* OLD-FASHIONED SLANG excellent

co•pay•ment /koʊ'peɪmənt/ *n.* [C] ECONOMICS a fixed amount that someone with medical insurance has to pay for using particular medical services, for example visits to the doctor: *copayments for outpatient visits*

cope¹ /koʊp/ *v.* [I] **1** to succeed in dealing with a difficult problem, situation, or job: *It's a lot of work, and sometimes I find it hard to cope.* | **+with** *advice on how to cope with stress* | *The children are struggling to cope with their mother's illness.* **2** if a machine or system copes with a particular type or amount of work, it does it [SYN] **handle**: **+with** *Computers can cope with a huge amount of data.* [**Origin:** 1600–1700 *cope* **to fight, keep fighting without giving up** (14–19 centuries), from Old French *couper* **to hit, cut**] → COPING¹

cope² *n.* [C] a long loose piece of clothing worn by priests on special occasions

Co•pen•ha•gen /'koʊpən,heɪgən, -,hɑ-/ the capital and largest city of Denmark

Co•per•ni•cus /kə'pɚnɪkəs, koʊ-/, **Nich•o•las** /'nɪkələs/ (1473–1543) a Polish ASTRONOMER who was the first person to suggest the idea that the Earth and the other PLANETS all travel in circles around the sun —**Copernican** *adj.*

cop•i•er /'kɑpiɚ/ *n.* [C] a machine that quickly copies documents onto paper by photographing them [SYN] **photocopier**

co•pi•lot /'koʊ,paɪlət/ *n.* [C] a pilot who helps the main pilot fly an airplane

cop•ing¹ /'koʊpɪŋ/ *adj.* [only before noun] coping skills, methods etc. are the things people do to help them deal with difficult situations or feelings

coping² *n.* [C,U] a layer of rounded stones or bricks at the top of a wall or roof

co•pi•ous /'koʊpiəs/ *adj.* existing or being produced in large quantities: *Officer Gomez took copious notes.* [**Origin:** 1300–1400 Latin *copiosus*, from *copia* **large amounts**, from *co-* + *ops* **wealth**] —**copiously** *adv.*: *She wept copiously.*

co•pla•nar /koʊ'pleɪnɚ/ *n.* [C] MATH coplanar lines or points lie in the same plane as each other

Cop•land /'koʊplənd/, **Aaron** (1900–1990) a U.S. musician who wrote modern CLASSICAL music

'cop-out *n.* [C] SLANG something you do or say in order to avoid doing or accepting something: *Blaming your parents for your problems is a cop-out.*

cop•per /'kɑpɚ/ *n.* **1** [U] SYMBOL **Cu** CHEMISTRY a reddish-brown metal that is an ELEMENT and that allows electricity and heat to pass through it easily. It is used for making wire, pipes etc. **2** [U] a reddish-brown color: *copper lipstick* [**Origin:** Old English *coper*, from Late Latin *cuprum*, from Latin *(aes) Cyprium* **metal of Cyprus, copper**]

,copper 'beech *n.* [C] a large tree with purple-brown leaves

cop•per•head /'kɑpɚ,hɛd/ *n.* [C] **1** BIOLOGY a poisonous yellow and brown North American snake **2 Copperhead** HISTORY a person from the North who supported the South in the American Civil War

cop•ra /'kɑprə/ *n.* [U] BIOLOGY the dried white inside part of a COCONUT, from which oil can be taken

copse /kɑps/ also **cop•pice** /'kɑpɪs/ *n.* [C] a group of

C

trees or bushes growing close together: +**of** *a copse of pine trees*

ˈcop shop *n.* [C] INFORMAL a POLICE STATION

cop·ter /ˈkaptɚ/ *n.* [C] INFORMAL a HELICOPTER

cop·u·la /ˈkapyələ/ *n.* [C] ENG. LANG. ARTS a type of verb that connects the subject of a sentence to its COMPLEMENT. For example, in the sentence "The house seems big," "seems" is the copula. SYN **linking verb**

C

cop·u·late /ˈkapyəˌleɪt/ *v.* [I] TECHNICAL to have sex —**copulation** /ˌkapyəˈleɪʃən/ *n.* [U]

cop·u·la·tive /ˈkapyələt̬ɪv, -ˌleɪt̬ɪv/ *n.* [C] ENG. LANG. ARTS a word or word group that connects other word groups —**copulative** *adj.*

cop·y[1] /ˈkapi/ S1 W2 *n. plural* **copies** **1** [C] something that is made to be exactly like another thing: *The application was sent in June, and this is a copy.* | +**of** *The chair is a copy of an original design.* | ***Make a copy*** *of the check for your records.* | *an* ***exact copy*** *of the original painting* | *Keep a* ***back-up copy*** *on disk.* **2** [C] one of many books, magazines, records etc. that are all exactly the same: *For a free copy, call 555-9121.* | +**of** *an illegal copy of the software program* | *The album sold more than a million copies.* **3** [U] TECHNICAL something written in order to be printed in a newspaper, magazine, advertisement etc.: *All copy must be on my desk by Monday morning.* | *The murder* ***made good copy*** (=was an interesting subject) *for the local newspaper.* [**Origin:** 1300–1400 Old French *copie*, from Latin *copia* **large amounts**] → see also HARD COPY

copy[2] S2 *v.* **copies, copied, copying** **1** [T] to deliberately make something exactly like another thing: *Copy the file onto a disk to save it.* | *Can you get the letter copied right away?* | **copy (sth) from sth** *a recipe copied from the newspaper*

> **THESAURUS**
>
> **photocopy** also **Xerox** TRADEMARK to copy a piece of paper with writing or pictures on it, using a special machine
> **forge** to illegally copy something written or printed: *He forged my signature.* | *a forged passport*
> **pirate** to illegally copy and sell a film, book, CD, or DVD that was made by another company: *pirated videos*

2 [T] to do something that someone else has done, or to behave like someone else: *Children often try to copy what they see on TV.* **3** [I,T] to cheat on a test, school work etc. by looking at someone else's work and writing the same thing that they have: *Several honors students were caught copying each other's answers.* | +**from/off** *He'd copied from the girl sitting next to him.*

copy sth ↔ **down** *phr. v.* to write something down exactly as it was said or written: *He copied down the facts onto an index card.*

copy sb **in** *phr. v.* to send someone a copy of an EMAIL message you are sending to someone else: +**on** *Can you copy me in on the memo you're sending to Chris?*

copy sth ↔ **out** *phr. v.* to write something again exactly as it is written in the document that you are looking at: *He copied out the number in his notebook.*

cop·y·cat /ˈkapiˌkæt/ *n.* [C] **1** INFORMAL a word used by children to criticize someone who copies other people's clothes, behavior, work etc. **2 a copycat crime/killing etc.** a crime, murder etc. that is similar to a famous crime done by another person: *Police fear there will be copycat killings.*

ˈcopy ˌeditor *n.* [C] someone whose job is to be sure that the words in a book, newspaper etc. are correct and ready to be printed —**copy-edit** *v.* [I,T]

cop·y·ist /ˈkapiɪst/ *n.* [C] someone who made written copies of documents, books etc. in past times

ˈcopy maˌchine *n.* [C] a COPIER

cop·y·right /ˈkapiˌraɪt/ *n.* [C,U] LAW the legal right to be the only maker or seller of a book, play, movie, or record for a specific length of time: *Mitchell's family* ***owns the copyright*** *to her book.* —**copyright** *adj.*: *a violation of copyright laws* —**copyright** *v.* [T]

cop·y·writ·er /ˈkapiˌraɪt̬ɚ/ *n.* [C] someone who writes the words for advertisements

coq au vin /ˌkoʊk oʊ ˈvæn, ˌkak-/ *n.* [U] a dish of chicken cooked in red wine

co·quet·ry /ˈkoʊkətri, koʊˈkɛtri/ *n. plural* **coquetries** [C,U] LITERARY behavior that is typical of a coquette

co·quette /koʊˈkɛt/ *n.* [C] LITERARY a woman who tries to attract the attention of men without having sincere feelings for them SYN **flirt** —**coquettish** *adj.* —**coquettishly** *adv.*

cor- /kɚ, kɔr, kar/ *prefix* used instead of CON- before the letter "r": *to correlate* (=connect ideas together)

cor·a·cle /ˈkɔrəkəl, ˈkar-/ *n.* [C] a small round boat that you move with a PADDLE

cor·al[1] /ˈkɔrəl, ˈkarəl/ *n.* [C,U] a hard red, white, or pink substance formed from the bones of very small ocean creatures that live in warm water, that is often used to make jewelry: *Searching for oil here would be harmful to the coral.* | *a coral necklace*

coral[2] *adj.* pink or reddish orange in color

ˌcoral ˈisland *n.* [C] EARTH SCIENCE an island formed from coral covered in sand and other natural substances

ˌcoral ˈreef *n.* [C] EARTH SCIENCE a long hard structure in warm ocean water that is not very deep, formed of coral

Cor·bett /ˈkɔrbɪt/, **James (Gentleman Jim)** (1866–1933) a U.S. BOXER who was world CHAMPION from 1892 to 1897

cord /kɔrd/ S3 *n.* **1** [C,U] an electrical wire or wires with a protective covering, usually for connecting electrical equipment to the supply of electricity: *The phone cord is all tangled.* | *I'll need an* ***extension cord*** *for the Christmas tree lights.* **2 cords** [plural] INFORMAL pants made from CORDUROY **3** [C,U] a piece of thick string or thin rope: *Her glasses hung around her neck on a cord.* **4** [C] a specific quantity of wood cut for burning in a fire: *Three cords of wood should last us all winter.* [**Origin:** 1200–1300 Old French *corde*, from Latin *chorda* **string**, from Greek *chorde*] → see also CORDLESS, **cut the cord** at CUT[1] (40), SPINAL CORD, UMBILICAL CORD, VOCAL CORDS

> **USAGE** **SPELLING: cord, chord**
>
> These two words are pronounced the same way but they have different meanings.
> • Use **cord** to talk about the electrical wire for connecting electrical equipment, such as televisions and telephones: *the black cord that goes to the DVD player.* **Cord** is also used to talk about a thick string or thin rope: *The cords for the blinds are all tangled.*
> • **Chord** is used to talk about a combination of musical notes that are played at the same time: *How can you be in a band if you can only play one chord?*

cord·age /ˈkɔrdɪdʒ/ *n.* [U] rope or cord in general, especially on a ship

cor·dial[1] /ˈkɔrdʒəl/ *n.* [C, U] a strong sweet alcoholic drink SYN **liqueur**: *an after-dinner cordial*

cordial[2] *adj.* friendly, but formal and polite: *a cordial thank-you note* ▸see THESAURUS box at **friendly** [**Origin:** 1300–1400 Medieval Latin *cordialis*, from Latin *cor* **heart**] —**cordiality** /ˌkɔrdʒiˈæləti/ *n.* [U]

cor·dial·ly /ˈkɔrdʒəli/ *adv.* in a friendly but polite and formal way: *You are cordially invited to our wedding on May 9.*

cord·ite /ˈkɔrdaɪt/ *n.* [U] a smokeless explosive used in bullets and bombs

cord·less /ˈkɔrdlɪs/ *adj.* a piece of equipment that is cordless is not connected to its power supply by wires: *a cordless phone*

cor·don[1] /ˈkɔrdn/ *n.* [C] a line of police officers, soldiers, or vehicles put around an area to stop people going there: *Rock-throwing protesters broke through the police cordon.* [**Origin:** 1700–1800 *cordon* **strip of cloth**

or decorative cord (16–21 centuries), from French, from *corde*]

cordon² *v.*

cordon sth ↔ **off** *phr. v.* to surround and protect an area with police officers, soldiers, or vehicles: *Police cordoned off the area.*

cor·don bleu /ˌkɔrdoʊn 'blu◂ , -dɑn-/ *adj.* [only before noun] relating to cooking of very high quality: *a cordon bleu chef*

cor·du·roy /'kɔrdəˌrɔɪ/ *n.* **1** [U] a thick strong cotton cloth with raised lines on it, used for making clothes: *a corduroy jacket* **2 corduroys** [plural] INFORMAL a pair of corduroy pants

core¹ /kɔr/ Ac S3 W2 *n.* [C]
1 FRUIT BIOLOGY the hard central part of fruit such as an apple: *Remove the cores, and bake the apples for 40 minutes.*
2 IMPORTANT PART the most important or central part of something: **+of** *Math, science, English, and history form the core of a high school education.* | **+at the core (of sth)** *Debt is at the core of the problem.*
3 PEOPLE a number of people who form a strong group which is very important to an organization: *MTV's core audience is 18- to 24-year-olds.* | **+of** *a core of dedicated volunteers*
4 core values/beliefs/concerns etc. the values, beliefs etc. that are most important to someone: *the core values of a large company*
5 to the core extremely or completely: *He's a military man to the core.* | *The financial system is* ***rotten to the core*** (=very bad). | **shaken/shocked to the core** *When I heard the news, I was shaken to the core.*
6 PLANETS EARTH SCIENCE the central part of the Earth or any other PLANET → see picture at GLOBE
7 NUCLEAR REACTOR PHYSICS the central part of a NUCLEAR REACTOR → see also HARDCORE

core² Ac *v.* [T] to take the center from a piece of fruit: *Core the apple and cut into ¼-inch slices.*

C.O.R.E. /ˌsi oʊ ɑr 'i/ *n.* POLITICS the abbreviation of CONGRESS OF RACIAL EQUALITY

ˌcore curˈriculum *n.* [U] the basic subjects that someone must study in school

ˌcore inˈflation ˌrate *n.* [U] ECONOMICS the rate at which goods continue to increase in price over a particular period of time, that does not include changes to certain goods that increase in price a lot, such as food and energy

cor·er /'kɔrɚ/ *n.* [C] a specially shaped knife for taking the hard centers out of fruit

ˈcore time *n.* [U] the period during the day when all employees are expected to be working, in a company or other place of work that allows people to come in or leave at different times

cor·gi /'kɔrgi/ *n. plural* **corgis** [C] a small dog with short legs and a pointed nose

co·ri·an·der /'kɔriˌændɚ/ *n.* [U] a plant used to give a special taste to food, especially in Asian and Mexican cooking SYN **cilantro**

Co·rin·thi·an /kə'rɪnθiən/ *adj.* of a style of Greek ARCHITECTURE that uses decorations of leaves cut into stone: *a Corinthian column*

Co·rin·thi·ans /kə'rɪnθiənz/ **1 Corinthians, 2 Corinthians** two books in the New Testament of the Christian Bible

cork¹ /kɔrk/ *n.* **1** [U] the BARK (=outer part) of a tree that grows in southern Europe and North Africa, used to make things: *a cork bulletin board* **2** [C] a long round piece of cork that is put into the top of a bottle, especially a wine bottle, to keep liquid inside

cork² *v.* [T] to close a bottle by blocking the hole at the top tightly with a long round piece of cork OPP **uncork**

cork·age /'kɔrkɪdʒ/ *n.* [U] the charge made by a hotel or restaurant for allowing people to drink alcoholic drinks which they bought somewhere else

cork cam·bi·um /'kɔrk ˌkæmbiəm/ *n.* [U] BIOLOGY a layer of cells in the woody part of a plant that produces cork

corked /kɔrkt/ *adj.* corked wine tastes bad because a decaying CORK has allowed air into the bottle

cork·screw¹ /'kɔrkskru/ *n.* [C] a tool made of twisted metal that you use to pull a CORK out of a bottle

corkscrew² *adj.* [only before noun] twisted or curly SYN **spiral**: *corkscrew curls*

cor·mo·rant /'kɔrmərənt, -ˌrænt/ *n.* [C] BIOLOGY a large black sea bird that has a long neck and eats fish

corn /kɔrn/ S2 *n.* **1** [U] BIOLOGY **a)** a tall plant with large yellow seeds that grow together on a COB (=long hard part). The seeds are cooked and eaten as a vegetable or fed to animals: ***an ear of corn*** (=the top part of the plant where the yellow seeds grow) **b)** the seeds of this plant: *The chickens are fed corn.* | *Do you want* ***corn on the cob*** (=the seeds cooked while still on the cob) *or green beans?* → see also INDIAN CORN **2** [C] MEDICINE a painful area of thick hard skin on your foot **3** [U] INFORMAL things such as songs, jokes, movies etc. which are old-fashioned, SENTIMENTAL, or silly [**Origin:** (1,2) Old English]

corn·ball /'kɔrnbɔl/ *adj.* [only before noun] INFORMAL cornball humor is too simple, old-fashioned, unoriginal, and silly: *His stories always have such cornball jokes in them.*

ˈCorn belt *n.* **the Corn Belt** the MIDWESTern part of the U.S., where there are a lot of farms

corn·bread , **corn bread** /'kɔrnbrɛd/ *n.* [U] bread made from CORNMEAL

ˈcorn chip *n.* [C] crushed corn formed into a small flat shape, cooked in oil and eaten cold, and sold in bags as a SNACK

corn·cob /'kɔrnkɑb/ also **cob** *n.* [C] the hard part of a corn plant on which the yellow seeds grow: *a corncob pipe* (=made from a dried corncob)

ˈcorn dog *n.* [C] a WIENER that is covered in CORN BREAD, fried (FRY), and eaten off a stick

cor·ne·a /'kɔrniə/ *n.* [C] BIOLOGY the transparent protective covering on the outer surface of your eye [**Origin:** 1300–1400 Medieval Latin, Latin, **horny**, from *cornu* **horn**; because its structure is like a horn] —**corneal** *adj.*

corned beef /ˌkɔrn 'bif◂ / *n.* [U] BEEF that has been covered in salt water and SPICES to preserve it: *a corned beef sandwich*

Cor·neille /kɔr'neɪ/, **Pierre** /pyɛr/ (1606–1684) a French writer of plays

Cor·nell /kɔr'nɛl/, **Ez·ra** /'ɛzrə/ (1807–1874) a U.S. businessman who developed TELEGRAPH systems in the U.S. and started Cornell University

cor·ner¹ /'kɔrnɚ/ S1 W2 *n.*
1 WHERE TWO LINES/EDGES MEET [C] the point at which two lines, surfaces, or edges meet: *She picked the tablecloth up by the corners and folded it neatly.* | **+of** *Gold tassels were sewn to the corners of the pillows.* | *The station's logo appears* ***in the corner*** *of the TV screen.* | *Jessie sat* ***on the corner*** *of her bed.*
2 STREETS the point where two streets, roads, or paths meet: **+of** *The hotel is* ***on the corner of*** *Thornton and Sycamore.* | *Several women were standing* ***at the corner***, *talking to two men.* | *kids hanging out on the* ***street corners*** | **corner store/bar/gas station etc.** *He bought a newspaper at the corner store.* | *Marnie's apartment is* ***just around the corner*** *from here.* | *The driver* ***took the corner*** (=went around it) *way too fast.*
3 CORNER OF A ROOM/BOX [C often singular] the place inside a room or box where two walls or sides meet: *A Christmas tree stood* ***in the corner*** *of the living room.* | **corner table/booth etc.** *They sat in a corner booth and drank coffee.* | **corner office** (=an office that has two outside walls at the corner of a building)
4 MOUTH/EYE [C] the side of your mouth or eye: *She rubbed a tear from the corner of her eye.*
5 DISTANT PLACE [C] a distant place in another part of the world: **+of** *He sent a postcard from some remote*

corner of Alaska. | **the far/four corners of the world/earth/globe** *Spaniards traveled to the far corners of the globe in search of new lands.*
6 DIFFICULT SITUATION [singular] a situation that is difficult to escape from: **back/force sb into a corner** *Interest payments and debts have backed the company into a corner.* | *With funding being cut, the music program is in a* ***tight corner.*** | *He's* ***painted himself into a corner*** *by issuing these threats.*
7 (just) around the corner likely to happen soon: *Economic recovery is just around the corner.*
8 see sth out of the corner of your eye to notice something by chance, without turning your head toward it or looking for it: *Out of the corner of her eye, she saw a man running out of the store.*
9 cut corners to do things too quickly, and not as carefully as you should, especially to save money or time: *The agency accused the airline of cutting corners on safety.*
10 SPORTS [C] **a)** a kick in SOCCER that one team is allowed to take from one of the corners of their opponent's end of the field **b)** any of the four corners of the area in which the competitors fight in BOXING or WRESTLING
11 have a corner on sth to be the only company, organization etc. that has a particular product, ability, advantage etc.: *We no longer have a corner on knowledge or technology.* | *The company has a* ***corner on the*** *soybean* ***market*** (=controls the supply of the product).
12 cut a corner to go across the corner of something, especially a road, instead of keeping to the edges: *If we cut the corner too tight, the trailer will hit the fence.*
[**Origin:** 1200–1300 Old French *cornere*, from *corne* **horn, corner**, from Latin *cornu* **horn, point**] → see also KITTY-CORNER

corner[2] *v.* **1** [T] to force a person or animal into a position from which they cannot easily escape, sometimes in order to ask or tell them something: *Hill cornered her at a party just before she left Washington.* ▸see THESAURUS box at **catch**[1] **2 corner the market** to gain control of the whole supply of a particular kind of goods: *The company has cornered 98% of the fried chicken market.* **3** [I] if a car corners, it goes around a corner or curve in the road: *The new Audis corner very well.*

cor·ner·stone /ˈkɔrnɚˌstoʊn/ *n.* [C] **1** something that is extremely important because everything else depends on it: **+of** *The magazine became the cornerstone of MacFadden's publishing empire.* **2** a stone set at one of the bottom corners of a building, often put in place at a special ceremony: *The* ***cornerstone*** *was* ***laid*** *in 1848.* → see also FOUNDATION STONE

cor·net /kɔrˈnɛt/ *n.* [C] a musical instrument like a small TRUMPET

ˈcorn-fed *adj.* having qualities that are considered typical of people who come from the central part of the U.S., such as being tall, strong, and healthy-looking, and having good moral values, but not knowing a lot about the world: *a corn-fed Kansas doctor*

corn·flakes /ˈkɔrnfleɪks/ *n.* [plural] small flat pieces of crushed corn, usually eaten for breakfast with milk

corn·flow·er /ˈkɔrnflaʊɚ/ *n.* [C] a wild plant with blue flowers

cor·nice /ˈkɔrnɪs/ *n.* [C] a decorative piece of wood or PLASTER along the top edge of a wall or door: *A carved cornice ran around the high-ceilinged room.*

cor·niche /kɔrˈniʃ/ *n.* [C] a road built along a coast

ˈcorn ˌliquor *n.* [U] CORN WHISKEY

corn·meal /ˈkɔrnmil/ *n.* [U] a rough type of flour made from crushed dried corn

ˌcorn on the ˈcob *n.* [U] the top part of a corn plant, cooked and eaten as a vegetable → see picture on page A35

corn pone /ˈkɔrn poʊn/ *n.* [U] a type of bread made from cornmeal, made especially in the southern U.S.

ˈcorn-pone *adj.* silly and funny in a CORNY way: *corn-pone jokes*

corn·rows /ˈkɔrnroʊz/ *n.* [plural] a way of arranging hair in which it is put into small tight BRAIDS along the head

corn·starch /ˈkɔrnstɑrtʃ/ *n.* [U] a fine white flour made from corn, used in cooking to make soups, SAUCES etc. thicker

ˌcorn ˈsyrup *n.* [U] a very sweet thick liquid made from corn, used in cooking

cor·nu·co·pi·a /ˌkɔrnəˈkoʊpiə/ *n.* **1** [C] a container in the shape of an animal's horn, full of fruit and flowers, used to represent ABUNDANCE (=a lot of food, good things etc.) **2** [singular] a lot of something: **+of** *a cornucopia of talent*

ˌcorn ˈwhiskey also **ˌcorn ˈliquor** *n.* [U] a strong alcoholic drink made from corn

corn·y /ˈkɔrni/ *adj. comparative* **cornier**, *superlative* **corniest** INFORMAL something that is corny tries to affect people's emotions or be funny in a way that is not very original and is slightly silly or old-fashioned: *a corny Hollywood romance* | *It may sound corny, but I enjoy helping people.* —**cornily** *adv.* —**corniness** *n.* [U]

cor·ol·lar·y /ˈkɔrəˌlɛri, ˈkɑr-/ *n. plural* **corollaries** [C] FORMAL **1** something that is the direct result of something else: *Surprisingly, environmental improvement has been a corollary to economic growth.* **2** MATH a statement that is true as a direct result of a THEOREM

co·ro·na /kəˈroʊnə/ *n.* [C] SCIENCE the shining circle of light seen around the sun when the moon passes in front of it in an ECLIPSE

Co·ro·na·do /ˌkɔrəˈnɑdoʊ/, **Fran·cis·co de** /frɑnˈsiskoʊ deɪ/ (1510–1554) a Spanish EXPLORER who traveled in Arizona and New Mexico

cor·o·na·ry[1] /ˈkɔrəˌnɛri/ *adj.* BIOLOGY relating to the heart: *coronary disease*

coronary[2] *n. plural* **coronaries** [C] a HEART ATTACK

cor·o·na·tion /ˌkɔrəˈneɪʃən, ˌkɑr-/ *n.* [C] the ceremony at which someone is officially made king or queen

cor·o·ner /ˈkɔrənɚ/ *n.* [C] an official whose job is to discover the cause of someone's death, especially if they died in a sudden or unusual way: *The San Francisco coroner's office said the dead woman was in her 40s.*

cor·o·net /ˌkɔrəˈnɛt, ˌkɑr-/ *n.* [C] **1** a small CROWN worn by princes or other members of a royal family, especially on formal occasions **2** anything that you wear on your head that looks like a CROWN: *a coronet of flowers*

Corp. /kɔrp, kɔr/ **1** the abbreviation of CORPORATION: *Toyota Motors Corp.* **2** the abbreviation of CORPORAL

cor·po·ra /ˈkɔrpərə/ *n.* the plural of CORPUS

cor·po·ral[1] /ˈkɔrpərəl/ *n.* [C] a low rank in the Army or Marines [**Origin:** 1500–1600 French *caporal*, from Old Italian *caporale*, from *capo* **head**]

corporal[2] *adj.* FORMAL relating to the body: *corporal injury*

ˌcorporal ˈpunishment *n.* [U] a way of officially punishing someone by hitting them, especially in schools and prisons: *In 1987, California prohibited corporal punishment in schools.*

cor·po·rate /ˈkɔrpərɪt/ Ac W1 *adj.* [only before noun] **1** belonging or relating to a corporation: *corporate profits* | *The company's moving its corporate headquarters* (=main offices) *from St. Louis to Atlanta.* | *the vice-president of corporate communications* | *They had a* ***corporate culture*** (=the way people in a corporation think and behave) *that was helpful to women.* | *The boat can be rented for* ***corporate hospitality*** (=entertainment provided by companies for their customers). **2** shared by or involving all the members of a group: *corporate responsibility* | *a huge corporate farm* **3** a number of organizations that form a single group: *a new corporate entity* —**corporately** *adv.*

ˌcorporate ˈbond *n.* [C] ECONOMICS a BOND that a CORPORATION gives out in order to develop its business

ˌ**corporate 'raider** *n.* [C] a person or an organization that tries to gain control of another company by buying most of that company's SHARES

ˌ**corporate 'tax** *n.* [C,U] ECONOMICS a tax on the profits made by a company

cor·po·ra·tion /ˌkɔrpə'reɪʃən/ Ac W2 *n.* [C] **1** ECONOMICS a big company, or a group of companies acting together as a single organization: *a multinational corporation* | **a large/big/major corporation** *all the resources of a major corporation* ▶see THESAURUS box at company **2** an organization or group of organizations that work together for a particular purpose, and that are officially recognized: *a development corporation created by the city*

cor·po·re·al /kɔr'pɔriəl/ *adj.* FORMAL **1** relating to the body as opposed to the mind, feelings, or spirit: *corporeal desires* **2** able to be touched: *his corporeal presence*

corps /kɔr/ W3 *n. plural* **corps** /kɔrz/ [C usually singular] **1** a group in the military with special duties: *the medical corps* **2** a group of people who work together to do a particular job: *the President's press corps* **3** TECHNICAL a trained army unit made of two or more DIVISIONS (=group of soldiers)

corpse /kɔrps/ *n.* [C] the dead body of a person

corps·man /'kɔrzmən/ *n. plural* **corpsmen** /-mən/ [C] someone in the military who is trained to give medical treatment to soldiers who are hurt

cor·pu·lent /'kɔrpyələnt/ *adj.* FORMAL very fat and large —**corpulence** *n.* [U]

cor·pus /'kɔrpəs/ *n. plural* **corpora** /-pərə/ or **corpuses** [C] ENG. LANG. ARTS **1** a collection of all the writing of a particular kind or by a particular person: *the entire corpus of Shakespeare's works* **2** a large collection of written or spoken language, held on a computer, and used for studying language [**Origin:** 1700–1800 Latin **body**] → see also HABEAS CORPUS

cor·pus·cle /'kɔrˌpʌsəl/ *n.* [C] BIOLOGY one of the red or white cells in the blood

cor·ral¹ /kə'ræl/ *n.* [C] a fairly small enclosed area where cattle, horses etc. are kept [**Origin:** 1500–1600 Spanish, Vulgar Latin *currale* **enclosed place for vehicles**, from Latin *currus* **wheeled vehicle**]

corral² *v.* **corrals, corralled, corralling** [T] **1** to make animals move into a corral: *They corralled the cattle before loading them onto the truck.* **2** to make people move into a particular area, especially to control them or in order to talk to them: *Keep the kids corralled safely in the backyard.*

cor·rect¹ /kə'rɛkt/ S2 W3 *adj.* **1** without any mistakes SYN **right** OPP **incorrect**: *If my calculations are correct, we're 10 miles from Westport.* | *Score one point for each* ***correct answer****.* | **correct in doing sth** *Am I correct in thinking that you two are brothers?* | **factually/grammatically/anatomically etc. correct** *The sentence is very long, but it's grammatically correct.* | *You're* ***absolutely correct*** *– we need to make some changes.* ▶see THESAURUS box at right¹ **2** appropriate and right for a particular situation SYN **right**: *We are convinced our decision was correct.* | *Make sure the switch is in the correct position.* | **correct in doing sth** *You were correct in insisting on a written reply.* | **it is correct to do sth** *I felt it was correct to keep the information private.* → see also POLITICALLY CORRECT **3** formal and polite SYN **proper**: *He was always very correct when dealing with customers.* [**Origin:** 1300–1400 Latin, past participle of *corrigere*, from *com-* + *regere* **to lead straight**] —**correctly** *adv.* —**correctness** *n.* [U]

correct² S2 *v.* [T] **1** to make something better or make it work the way it should: *I corrected a few spelling mistakes.* | *Some eyesight problems are relatively easy to correct.* **2** to tell someone that something is wrong and what is right: *Correct my pronunciation if it's wrong.* | *Hilda corrected her sister very sharply.* | **correct yourself** *He called her "Sara" and then quickly corrected himself.* **3** if a teacher corrects students' work, he or she makes marks on it to show the mistakes in it: *She spent all night correcting her students' math tests.* **4 correct sth for sth** to change calculations or measurements so that they are more accurate, by considering a particular fact SYN **adjust**: *These figures have been corrected for inflation.* **5 correct me if I'm wrong** SPOKEN used when you are not sure that what you are going to say is true or not: *Correct me if I'm wrong, but didn't you say you'd never met him before?* **6 I stand corrected** SPOKEN used to admit that something you have said is wrong after someone has told you it is wrong: *"It's a moose, not an elephant, Dad!" "Well, I stand corrected."*

cor·rec·tion /kə'rɛkʃən/ *n.* **1** [C] a change made in something in order to make it right or better: *Could I* ***make*** *one small* ***correction****?* | +**to** *a few corrections to the report* **2** [U] the act of changing something in order to make it right or better: *Please hand in your papers for correction.* | +**of** *correction of errors* **3** [C] SPOKEN used to say that what you have just said is wrong, and that you are about to say the correct thing: *That will basically cover 50... correction, 80% of all charges.* **4** [C,U] a fall in prices on a STOCK MARKET after a period when prices were high **5** [C,U] FORMAL punishment for people who have done something wrong or illegal: *the Department of Corrections*

cor·rec·tion·al /kə'rɛkʃənl/ *adj.* [only before noun] **1 a correctional facility/institution** a prison **2** relating to the punishment of criminals

cor'rection ˌfluid *n.* [U] FORMAL a special white liquid used for covering mistakes you make when writing or typing (TYPE) something

cor·rec·ti·tude /kə'rɛktɪˌtud/ *n.* [U] FORMAL correctness of behavior

cor·rec·tive¹ /kə'rɛktɪv/ *adj.* FORMAL intended to make something right or better again: *corrective surgery* | **corrective actions/measures** *The plan is a good start, but more corrective measures are needed.* —**correctively** *adv.*

corrective² *n.* [C] FORMAL something that is intended to make something right or better: +**to** *The success of his company is a useful corrective to the myth that new technology leads to job losses.*

cor·re·late¹ /'kɔrəˌleɪt, 'kɑr-/ *v.* [I,T] if two or more facts, ideas etc. correlate, or are correlated, they are closely related or one causes another: +**correlate (sth) with sth** *Stress is known to correlate with health problems.*

cor·re·late² /'kɔrəlɪt, 'kɑr-/ *n.* [C] either of two things that correlate with each other

cor·re·la·tion /ˌkɔrə'leɪʃən, ˌkɑr-/ *n.* **1** [C,U] a relationship between two ideas, facts etc., especially when one may be the cause of the other: +**between** *a correlation between athletic success and academic achievement* | **a strong/high/direct correlation** *There's a direct correlation between house prices and good schools.* **2** [C,U] SCIENCE a relationship between two sets of data: *A positive correlation means that two sets of data vary in the same direction; a negative or inverse correlation means they vary in opposite directions.* **3** [U] the process of correlating two or more things

corre'lation coefˌficient *n.* [C] MATH a number between +1 and −1 which is used to represent the relationship between quantities that increase or decrease in direct relation to one another

cor·rel·a·tive¹ /kə'rɛlət̬ɪv/ *adj.* **1** correlative facts, ideas etc. are closely related or dependent on each other: *Profits are* ***directly correlative*** *to the popularity of the product.* **2** TECHNICAL correlative words are frequently used together, but not usually next to each other. For example, "either" and "or" are correlative conjunctions.

correlative² *n.* [C] FORMAL one of two or more facts, ideas etc. that are closely related or that depend on each other

cor·re·spond /ˌkɔrə'spɑnd, ˌkɑr-/ Ac *v.* [I] **1** if two things or ideas correspond, the parts or information in one relate to the parts or information in the other: +**to/with** *The numbers correspond to points on the map.* **2** to be very similar or the same as something else:

C

These two accounts of what happened do not seem to correspond. | **+to** *Is there a word in English that corresponds to the Russian word "toska"?* **3** if two people correspond, they write letters to each other: *For the next three years they corresponded regularly.* | **+with** *He hasn't seen or corresponded with his children in six years.* [**Origin:** 1500–1600 French *correspondre*, from Medieval Latin, from Latin]

C

cor·re·spond·ence /ˌkɔrəˈspɑndəns, ˌkɑr-/ Ac *n.* [U] **1** letters exchanged between people, especially official or business letters: *I start my day by reading correspondence and writing replies.* **2** the process of sending and receiving letters: *They kept up a correspondence for over 20 years.* | *We had been **in correspondence** for several years before we finally met.* **3** a relationship or connection between two or more ideas or facts: **+between** *the lack of correspondence between his account and historical fact* | *There is rarely a **one-to-one correspondence** between words when translating a phrase into another language.*

corre'spondence ˌcourse *n.* [C] a course of lessons that students receive by mail and do at home, and then send completed work to their teacher by mail

cor·re·spond·ent¹ /ˌkɔrəˈspɑndənt, ˌkɑr-/ *n.* [C] **1** someone whose job is to report news from a distant area or about a particular subject for a newspaper or for television: *a White House correspondent* | *a **foreign correspondent** for the New York Times in Warsaw* ▸see THESAURUS box at **newspaper** **2** someone who writes letters

correspondent² *adj.* FORMAL appropriate for a particular situation: **+with** *The result was correspondent with the government's intentions.*

cor·re·spond·ing /ˌkɔrəˈspɑndɪŋ◂, ˌkɑr-/ Ac *adj.* [only before noun] **1** caused by or dependent on something you have already mentioned: *Rising real estate prices have had a corresponding effect on the area's rents.* **2** having similar qualities or a similar position to something you have already mentioned: *The corresponding chromosome in the other parent was found to be defective.* —**correspondingly** *adv.*

ˌcorresponding 'angles *n.* [plural] MATH a pair of angles formed when two parallel lines are crossed by another line. The crossing line makes eight angles, and the corresponding angles are on the same side of the two parallel lines and on the same side of the single line crossing them. → see picture at ANGLE¹

cor·ri·dor /ˈkɔrədɚ, -ˌdɔr, ˈkɑr-/ *n.* [C] **1** a long narrow passage in a building or on a train SYN **hallway**: *We had to wait **in the corridor** until our names were called.* | **down/along a corridor** *She hurried down the corridor.* **2** EARTH SCIENCE a narrow area of land between cities or countries that has different qualities or features from the land around it: *the Northeast corridor from Washington to Boston* **3 corridors of power** the places where important government decisions are made: *The message of the voters has been clearly heard in the corridors of power.* [**Origin:** 1500–1600 French, Old Italian *corridore*, from *correre* **to run**]

cor·rob·o·rate /kəˈrɑbəˌreɪt/ *v.* [T] FORMAL to provide information that supports or helps to prove someone else's statement, idea etc.: *Her statements were corroborated by the doctor's testimony.* —**corroboration** /kəˌrɑbəˈreɪʃən/ *n.* [U] —**corroborative** /kəˈrɑbəˌreɪt̬ɪv, -rət̬ɪv/ *adj.*

cor·rode /kəˈroʊd/ *v.* [I,T] CHEMISTRY to destroy something slowly, or to be destroyed slowly, especially by chemicals: *Acid rain has corroded the statue.* [**Origin:** 1300–1400 Latin *corrodere* **to eat away**]

cor·ro·sion /kəˈroʊʒən/ *n.* [U] **1** CHEMISTRY the process of something being destroyed slowly, especially by chemicals: *The leak is probably caused by corrosion of the pipes.* **2** a substance such as RUST (=weak red metal) that is produced by the process of corrosion

cor·ro·sive /kəˈroʊsɪv/ *adj.* **1** CHEMISTRY a corrosive substance such as an acid can destroy metal, plastic etc.: *a highly corrosive acid* **2** gradually making something weaker, and possibly destroying it: *We must fight the corrosive effect of discrimination.*

cor·ru·gat·ed /ˈkɔrəˌgeɪt̬ɪd, ˈkɑr-/ *adj.* shaped in rows of folds that look like waves, or made like this in order to give something strength: *The shed is made of **corrugated metal**.* —**corrugation** /ˌkɔrəˈgeɪʃən/ *n.* [C]

cor·rupt¹ /kəˈrʌpt/ *adj.* **1** using personal power in a dishonest or illegal way in order to get an advantage or money: *Corrupt judges have taken millions of dollars in bribes.* **2** very bad morally: *a corrupt society* | *corrupt practices* **3** corrupt computer software, equipment, or information is damaged: *a corrupt file* [**Origin:** 1300–1400 Latin *corruptus*, past participle of *corrumpere*, from *com-* + *rumpere* **to break**] —**corruptly** *adv.* —**corruptness** *n.* [U] → see also INCORRUPTIBLE

corrupt² *v.* [T] **1** to encourage someone to start behaving in an immoral or dishonest way: *Young prisoners are being corrupted by older, long-term offenders.* **2** to change the traditional form of something, such as a language, so that it becomes worse than it was: *The culture has been corrupted by Western influences.* **3** COMPUTERS to change the information in a computer, so that the computer does not work correctly anymore: *The virus corrupts the data on your hard drive.* —**corruptible** *adj.* —**corruptibility** /kəˌrʌptəˈbɪlət̬i/ *n.* [U]

cor·rup·tion /kəˈrʌpʃən/ W3 *n.* **1** [U] dishonest, illegal, or immoral behavior, especially from someone with power: *The government has been accused of corruption and abuse of power.* | *The investigation uncovered **widespread corruption**.* **2** [U] the act or process of making someone dishonest or immoral: *the corruption of the young and innocent* **3** [C,U] damage to computer software, equipment, or information: *The error is due to a corruption of the file.* **4** [C usually singular] a changed form of something, for example a word: *The word Thursday is a corruption of Thor's Day.*

cor·sage /kɔrˈsɑʒ/ *n.* [C] a group of small flowers that a woman fastens to her clothes or wrist on a special occasion, such as a wedding

cor·sair /ˈkɔrsɛr/ *n.* [C] OLD USE a North African PIRATE, or their ship

corse /kɔrs/ *n.* [C] OLD USE or POETIC a CORPSE

cor·set /ˈkɔrsɪt/ *n.* [C] **1** a tightly fitting piece of underwear that women wore in past times to make them look thinner **2** a strong, tightly fitting piece of clothing that supports your back when it is injured —**corseted** *adj.*

Cor·si·ca /ˈkɔrsɪkə/ a large island to the south of France in the Mediterranean Sea

cor·tege /kɔrˈtɛʒ/ *n.* [C] a line of people, cars etc. that move along slowly in a funeral

Cor·tés /kɔrˈtɛz/, **Her·nán** /hɚˈnɑn/ or **Her·nan·do** /hɚˈnɑndoʊ/ (1485–1547) a Spanish soldier who defeated the Aztecs in 1521 and took control of Mexico for Spain

cor·tex /ˈkɔrtɛks/ *n. plural* **cortices** /-t̬ɪsiz/ [C] BIOLOGY **1** the outer layer of an organ, such as your brain or your KIDNEY: *the visual cortex in the brain* **2** a layer of soft material between the EPIDERMIS (=outside layer) and the hard central part of a plant's root or stem —**cortical** /ˈkɔrt̬ɪkəl/ *adj.*

cor·ti·sone /ˈkɔrt̬ɪˌsoʊn, -ˌzoʊn/ *n.* [U] MEDICINE a HORMONE that is used especially in the treatment of diseases such as ARTHRITIS

cor·us·cat·ing /ˈkɔrəˌskeɪt̬ɪŋ, ˈkɑr-/ *adj.* FORMAL **1** a coruscating speech, piece of writing etc. is intelligent, quick, and impressive **2** flashing with light: *coruscating jewels*

cos /kɑs, koʊs/ *n.* the abbreviation of COSINE

co·sign /ˈkoʊsaɪn/ *v.* [T] to sign a paper that has already been signed by someone else, especially a legal document: *I cosigned the loan for my brother-in-law.* —**cosigner** *n.* [C]

co·sig·na·to·ry /koʊˈsɪgnəˌtɔri/ *n.* [C] FORMAL LAW one of a group of people who sign a legal document for their organization, country etc.: *We will need both cosignatories to sign the check.*

co·sine /ˈkoʊsaɪn/ *n.* [C] MATH a number relating to an ACUTE angle in a RIGHT TRIANGLE that is calculated by dividing the length of the side next to the angle by the length of the HYPOTENUSE (=longest side) → see also SINE

cos·met·ic /kɑzˈmɛt̬ɪk/ *adj.* [only before noun] **1** intended to make your skin or body look more attractive: *cosmetic products* | *She had the surgery for cosmetic reasons.* **2** dealing with the outside appearance rather than the important part of something SYN **superficial**: *The house needs no structural work, just a few cosmetic repairs.* **3** [only before noun] relating to COSMETICS: *a cosmetic bag* [**Origin:** 1600–1700 Greek *kosmetikos* **skilled in decoration**, from *kosmein* **to arrange, decorate**] → see also COSMETICS, COSMETIC SURGERY

cos·me·ti·cian /ˌkɑzməˈtɪʃən/ *n.* [C] someone who is professionally trained to put cosmetics on other people

cos·met·ics /kɑzˈmɛt̬ɪks/ *n.* [plural] **1** creams, powders etc. that you use on your face and body in order to look more attractive: *a range of cosmetics and perfumes* | *the cosmetics industry* **2** things that relate to the outside appearance rather than the important part of something

cosˌmetic ˈsurgery *n.* [U] medical operations that improve your appearance after you have been injured, or because you want to look more attractive → see also PLASTIC SURGERY

cos·me·tol·o·gy /ˌkɑzməˈtɑlədʒi/ *n.* [U] the art or skill of treating the face or body with cosmetics in order to make them more attractive —**cosmetologist** *n.* [C]

cos·mic /ˈkɑzmɪk/ *adj.* **1** PHYSICS relating to space or the universe: *cosmic radiation* **2** extremely large or important: *a scandal of cosmic proportions* —**cosmically** /-kli/ *adv.*

ˌcosmic ˈray *n.* [C usually plural] SCIENCE a stream of RADIATION reaching the Earth from space

cos·mo /ˈkɑzmoʊ/ *n.* [C] a COSMOPOLITAN

cos·mog·o·ny /kɑzˈmɑgəni/ *n. plural* **cosmogonies** [C,U] the origin of the universe, or a set of ideas about this

cos·mol·o·gy /kɑzˈmɑlədʒi/ *n.* [U] SCIENCE the science of the origin and structure of the universe, especially as studied in ASTRONOMY

cos·mo·naut /ˈkɑzməˌnɔt, -ˌnɑt/ *n.* [C] an ASTRONAUT from Russia or the former Soviet Union

cos·mo·pol·i·tan¹ /ˌkɑzməˈpɑlət˺n/ *adj.* **1** a cosmopolitan place has people from many different parts of the world in it: *a vibrant cosmopolitan city* **2** a cosmopolitan person, belief, opinion etc. shows a wide experience with different people and places: *a group of sophisticated cosmopolitan friends*

cosmopolitan² *n.* [C] someone who has traveled a lot and feels at home in any part of the world

cos·mos /ˈkɑzmoʊs, -məs/ *n.* **the cosmos** the whole universe, especially when you think of it as a system: *the mystery of the origin of the cosmos* [**Origin:** 1200–1300 Greek **order, universe**]

cos·set /ˈkɑsɪt/ *v.* **cossets, cosseted, cosseting** [T] to give someone as much care and attention as you can, especially when it is too much: *She enjoyed being pampered and cosseted.*

cost¹ /kɔst/ S1 W1 *n.* **1** [C,U] the amount of money that you have to pay in order to buy, do, or produce something: *Medical care costs keep rising.* | **the cost of (doing) sth** *The cost of repairing the damage is higher than we expected.* | **+to** *If you want figures for welfare, the cost to state taxpayers is over $5 billion.* | *Tenants pay a deposit to* ***cover the cost of*** *cleanup.* | *The bridge was constructed* ***at a cost of*** *$400,000.* | **high/low cost** *the high cost of real estate* | *Travel insurance is included* ***at no extra cost*** *to you.*

THESAURUS

expense a very large amount of money that you spend on something: *the expense of buying a computer*
price the amount of money you must pay for something: *Car prices have gone down.* | *the price of oil*
charge the amount that you have to pay for a particular service or to use something: *There is a small charge for using the lockers.* | *telephone charges*
fee the amount you have to pay to enter or join something, or that you pay to a lawyer, doctor etc.: *There is no entrance fee to the museum.* | *The membership fee is $125 a year.* | *legal fees*
fare the amount you have to pay to travel somewhere by bus, airplane, train etc.: *How much was the air fare to Houston?*
rent the amount you have to pay to live in or use a place that you do not own: *My rent is $900 a month.*
rate a charge or payment that is set according to a standard scale: *Most TV stations offer special rates to local advertisers.*

2 costs [plural] **a)** the money that you must regularly spend in a business, or on your home, car etc.: *The graph shows housing costs for all states.* | *We have to* ***cut costs*** (=spend less money) *to remain competitive.* | *The change may dramatically* ***increase*** *transportation* ***costs.*** | *The company* ***incurred costs*** *of over $20 million* (=had to pay over $20 million) *when they relocated to the West Coast.* | *We worry about having enough money to* ***cover our costs.*** **b)** the money that you must pay to lawyers if you are involved in a legal case: *Bellisario won the case and was awarded costs* (=the lawyers had to be paid by the people who lost the case). **3** [C,U] something that you lose, give away, damage etc. in order to achieve something: *War is never worth its cost in human life.* | **+to** *You should do what's right, despite the cost to yourself and your family.* | *He intends to hold onto power,* ***whatever the cost.*** | **at the cost of (doing) sth** *The profits were achieved at the cost of thousands of jobs.* | *They succeeded, but* ***at what cost?*** | **social/environmental/human etc. cost** *the environmental costs of burning coal* | *They need to weigh up the* ***costs and benefits*** (=disadvantages and advantages) *of increased regulation.* **4 at all costs/at any cost** whatever happens, or whatever effort is needed: *Margaret wants to have justice at all costs.* **5 at cost** for the same price that you paid to buy or make something: *Most of the materials were bought at cost from local suppliers.* → see also COST OF LIVING

cost² S1 W2 *v. past tense and past participle* **cost** [T] **1** if something costs a particular amount of money, you have to spend that much in order to pay for it: *Cable TV service costs $19.95 a month.* | **cost sb sth** *The coat cost me $150.* | **cost sth to do sth** *How much will it cost to repair the damage?* | ***It costs*** *$38 per adult, round trip.* | *Michelle's college bills are* ***costing*** *us* ***a fortune*** (=they are very expensive).

THESAURUS

be ESPECIALLY SPOKEN to cost a particular amount: *It's only $2.50.*
be priced at something to have a particular price
sell/go for something used to say what people pay for something: *The stock was selling for $3 a share.*
fetch used to say what people pay for something, especially at a public sale: *His paintings now fetch up to $40,000 each.*
set somebody back something INFORMAL to cost someone a lot of money: *It's an expensive book – it will set you back $70.*

2 to cause someone to lose something good or valuable: *Missing the field goal cost us the game.* | **cost sb their job/life/marriage etc.** *That mistake cost Joe his promotion* (=he did not get promoted in his job because of the

C

mistake). **3 it'll cost you** SPOKEN used to say that something will be expensive: *Sure, tickets are still available, but they'll cost you.* **4 sth costs money** SPOKEN used to remind or warn someone that they should be careful because something is expensive: *The kids need clothes, and they cost money.* **5 cost an arm and a leg** also **cost a pretty penny** INFORMAL to be extremely expensive: *Good childcare costs an arm and a leg.* **6 cost sb dearly** to do something that causes you a lot of trouble or makes you suffer: *Delays at the factory have cost us dearly.* **7 sth won't cost sb a penny/cent** used to say that someone will not have to pay for something: *The advice is free – it won't cost you a penny.* [**Origin:** 1300–1400 Old French *coster*, from Latin *constare* **to stand firm, cost**]

cost³ S1 W2 *v. past tense and past participle* **costed** [T usually passive] to calculate the price to be charged for a job, the time someone spends working on something etc.: *The options are being costed and analyzed.*

co·star¹, co-star /ˈkoʊ stɑr/ *n.* [C] one of two or more main actors that work together in a movie, play, or television program: *Who was Julia Roberts' costar in her last movie?*

co·star², co-star *v.* [I] to be one of the main actors that work in a movie, play, or television program: **+with** *Uma Thurman costars with John Travolta in the film.*

Cos·ta Ri·ca /ˌkɑstə ˈrikə, ˌkoʊ-/ a country in Central America between Nicaragua and Panama —**Costa Rican** *n., adj.*

ˌcost-ˈbenefit aˌnalysis *n.* [C] ECONOMICS a way of calculating the business methods or plans that will bring you the most profits or advantages for the smallest cost

ˈcost-efˌfective *adj.* bringing the best possible profits or advantages for the lowest possible costs: *a cost-effective way to reduce pollution* —**cost-effectively** *adv.* —**cost-effectiveness** *n.* [U]

cost·ing /ˈkɔstɪŋ/ *n.* [C,U] the process of calculating the cost of a future business activity, product etc., or the act of calculating this

cost·ly /ˈkɔstli/ *adj. comparative* **costlier**, *superlative* **costliest** **1** costing a lot of money, or too much money: *A lawsuit would be very costly.* **2** causing a lot of problems or trouble: *a costly mistake* —**costliness** *n.* [U]

ˌcost of ˈliving *n.* [singular] the average amount that people spend to buy food, pay bills, own a home etc. in a particular area: **high/low cost of living** *The Bay Area is known for its high cost of living.*

ˌcost-ˈplus *adj.* ECONOMICS a cost-plus contract gives someone who is selling something or who is providing a service all of their costs, along with a specific PERCENTAGE as a profit

ˈcost-push ˌtheory *n.* [U] ECONOMICS the idea that INFLATION is caused by companies increasing the cost of their goods or services to pay for increases in the cost of wages or materials

cos·tume /ˈkɑstum/ S3 *n.* **1** [C] an unusual set of clothes that you wear to an event such as a party, that makes you look like an animal, a character from a story, a GHOST etc.: *a Halloween costume* | *a costume party* (=a party where everyone has to wear a costume) **2** [C,U] a set of clothes that an actor wears when appearing in a movie, play etc.: *The costumes in the show were amazing.* | *The actor was still* ***in costume*** *when I interviewed him.* | *She makes three* ***costume changes*** *during the show.* **3** [C,U] a set of clothes that is typical of a particular place or historical period of time: *The museum guide was dressed in Pilgrim costume.* [**Origin:** 1700–1800 French, Italian, **custom, dress**, from Latin *consuetudo*]

ˈcostume ˌdrama *n.* [C] a play, movie, television program etc. that is about a particular time in history, and in which people wear costumes from that time

ˈcostume ˌjewelry *n.* [U] cheap jewelry that is designed to look expensive

co·sy /ˈkoʊzi/ *adj. comparative* **cosier**, *superlative* **cosiest** the British spelling of COZY

cot /kɑt/ *n.* [C] a light narrow bed that can be folded and stored: *Cots were set up in the local high school for flood victims.* [**Origin:** 1600–1700 Hindi *khat* **hammock, bed**]

co·tan·gent /koʊˈtændʒənt, ˈkoʊtæn-/ *n.* [C] MATH a number relating to an angle in a RIGHT TRIANGLE that is calculated by dividing the length of the side next to the angle by the length of the side across from it → see also TANGENT

Côte d'I·voire /ˌkoʊt diˈvwɑr/ → see IVORY COAST

co·ter·ie /ˈkoʊt̬əri/ *n.* [C] a small group of people who enjoy doing the same things together, and do not like including others in their group: *a coterie of loyal fans*

co·til·lion /kəˈtɪlyən, koʊ-/ *n.* [C] a formal occasion when people dance SYN **ball**

cot·tage /ˈkɑt̬ɪdʒ/ *n.* [C] a small house, especially in the country: *a cottage near the lake* [**Origin:** 1300–1400 Anglo-French *cotage*, from English *cot* **cottage**, from Old English]

ˈcottage cheese *n.* [U] a type of soft wet white cheese made from milk that has little fat in it

ˌcottage ˈindustry *n.* [C] a business that consists of people who produce things in their homes

cot·ton¹ /ˈkɑtˀn/ *n.* [U] **1** cloth or thread made from the soft white FIBERS that surround the seeds of a cotton plant: *The towels are 100% cotton.* | *a white cotton shirt* **2** a soft mass of FIBERS from a cotton plant that you use especially for cleaning and protecting wounds, or for removing makeup: *a ball of cotton* **3** BIOLOGY the plant that produces these FIBERS: *fields of cotton* [**Origin:** 1300–1400 Old French *coton*, from Arabic *qutn*]

cotton² *v.*

cotton on *phr. v.* INFORMAL to begin to understand something: **+to** *It took a while to cotton on to what she was suggesting.*

cotton to *phr. v.* INFORMAL **cotton to sth** to like someone or something that is new to you: *I didn't cotton to her at first, but she's really nice.*

ˈcotton ball *n.* [C] a small soft ball made from cotton, used for cleaning your skin, especially your face

ˈCotton Belt, the *n.* [singular] an area in the southeastern U.S., including South Carolina, Georgia, Alabama, and Mississippi, where cotton is or was the main crop grown

ˈcotton ˌcandy *n.* [U] a type of sticky pink candy that looks like cotton, often sold at FAIRS

ˈcotton gin *n.* [C] a machine that separates the seeds of a cotton plant from the cotton

ˈcotton ˌpicking *adj.* [only before noun] OLD-FASHIONED, SPOKEN used to emphasize that you are annoyed or surprised: *Just a cotton-picking minute!*

cot·ton·tail /ˈkɑtˀnˌteɪl/ *n.* [C] a small rabbit with a white tail

cot·ton·wood /ˈkɑtˀnˌwʊd/ *n.* [C,U] a North American tree with seeds that look like white cotton

cot·y·le·don /ˌkɑt̬əˈlidn, ˌkɑt̬lˈidn/ *n.* [C] BIOLOGY the first leaf that grows from a seed

couch¹ /kaʊtʃ/ S2 *n.* [C] **1** a comfortable piece of furniture, usually with a back and arms, on which more than one person can sit SYN **sofa**: *Mandy curled up* ***on the couch*** *to watch television.* **2** a long low piece of furniture that you lie down on during PSYCHOANALYSIS: *After 20 years* ***on the couch*** (=being treated), *Richard is finally giving up therapy.* [**Origin:** 1300–1400 French *couche*, from *coucher* **to lie**, from Latin *collocare* **to put in place**]

couch² *v.* [I] FORMAL to express something in a particular way in order to be polite or not offend someone: **couch sth in sth** *The offer was couched in legal jargon.*

ˈcouch poˌtato *n.* [C] INFORMAL someone who spends a lot of time sitting and watching television: *A lot of kids today are overweight couch potatoes.*

cou·gar /ˈkugɚ/ *n.* [C] a large brown wild cat from the mountains of western North America and South

America SYN **mountain lion** [**Origin:** 1700–1800 French *couguar*, from Modern Latin *cuguacuarana*, from Tupi *suasuarana*, from *suasu* **deer** + *rana* **false**] → see picture on page A34

cough¹ /kɔf/ S3 *v.* [I] **1** to push air out of your throat with a sudden rough sound, especially because you are sick: *I keep coughing and sneezing.* **2** to make a sound like a cough: *The engine coughed and sputtered.* [**Origin:** 1300–1400 from an unrecorded Old English *cohhian*]

cough up *phr. v.* **1 cough sth ↔ up** INFORMAL to unwillingly give someone money, information etc.: *Taxpayers may have to cough up an additional $10 billion.* **2 cough up sth** to get something out of your throat or lungs by coughing: *The woman was coughing up blood and was rushed to the hospital.*

cough² *n.* **1** [C] the action or sound of coughing: *Disease can be spread by coughs.* | *He gave a short cough.* **2** [singular, U] MEDICINE a medical condition that makes you cough a lot: *Jake's father had a* ***smoker's cough*** (=a cough caused by smoking). | *a* ***hacking cough*** (=a repeated, loud cough). | *a dry cough*

'cough drop *n.* [C] a type of medicine like a piece of candy that you suck to help you stop coughing

'cough ˌsyrup *n.* [U] a thick liquid medicine that you take to help you stop coughing

could /kəd; *strong* kʊd/ S1 W1 *modal verb third person singular* **could** *negative short form* **couldn't** **1** used to say what someone was able to do: *Could you sleep last night with all that noise outside?* | *Eleanor couldn't come to the party last weekend.* | *I knew we couldn't win the game.* **2** used to say that something might be possible or might happen: *I'm sure Francis could find out for you.* | *You could hurt yourself if you're not careful.* | *I don't think I could live with someone like that.* | *One small spark* ***could easily*** *cause an explosion.* | **could have done/been sth** *Do you think he could have forgotten?* | *I couldn't have been away for more than ten minutes.* **3** used instead of "can" when reporting what someone else said: *Dad said we could go swimming after lunch.* **4 could have done/been** used to say that something was a possibility in the past, but did not actually happen: *You could have been killed.* | *She could have come with us if she'd wanted.* **5** used to politely ask someone to do something: *Could you have her call me back when she gets home, please?* | *Could you drop off the kids on your way to work?* **6** used to say that something seems to be true although it is not true: *It's so hot, it could be the middle of summer.*

SPOKEN PHRASES

7 used to politely ask for permission to do something: *Could I have a drink of water?* | *What about Sam? Could he come along, too?* **8** used to suggest doing something: *Maybe we could meet for lunch.* | *We* ***could always*** *use plastic cups instead.* **9 I couldn't care less** used to say that you are not interested at all in something: *I couldn't care less what happens to you and Peter.* **10** said when you are annoyed because you think someone should have done something: *You could have told me you were going to be late!* | *You* ***could at least*** *apologize!* **11 couldn't be better/worse etc.** said to emphasize how good, bad etc. something is: *"How are you feeling?" "Fine. Couldn't be better!"* | *The system couldn't be simpler.* **12 sb/sth could do with sth** used to say that someone wants or needs something very much, or that something would be useful for something else: *You look like you could do with a drink.* **13 I could have strangled/hit/killed etc. sb** used to emphasize that you were very angry with someone: *Brent forgot our anniversary again! I could have killed him!*

[**Origin:** Old English *cuthe*, past tense of *cunnan*; influenced by *should* and *would*]

couldst /kʊdst/ *v.* OLD USE **thou couldst** an old form of "you could," used when talking to one person whom you know well

cou·lee /'kuli/ *n.* [C] a small valley with steep sides

cou·lomb /'kulɑm/ *n.* [C] PHYSICS a unit for measuring electric current, equal to the amount produced by one AMP in one second

Cou·lomb's law /ˌkulɑmz 'lɔ/ *n.* [singular] PHYSICS a scientific rule about the relationship between the strength of the force that makes PARTICLES with positive and negative electrical energy move toward or away from each other, the combined power of the positive and negative energy, and the distance between them

coun·cil /'kaʊnsəl/ W2 *n.* [C] **1** POLITICS a group of people who are elected as part of a town or city government: *the Los Angeles city council* | *a council meeting* **2** a group of people who make decisions for large organizations or groups, or who give advice: *the U.N. Security Council* | *Stuart is* ***on*** *the Regional Arts* ***Council.*** [**Origin:** 1100–1200 Old French *concile*, from Latin *concilium*, from *com-* + *calare* **to call**] → see also STUDENT COUNCIL

coun·cil·man /'kaʊnsəlmən/ *n. plural* **councilmen** /-mən/ [C] a man who is elected to be part of a town or city council

'council-ˌmanager ˌgovernment *n.* [C,U] POLITICS a system of local government in many U.S. cities, towns etc., that consists of an elected council, an elected MAYOR who has no independent official powers, and a manager who is chosen by the council and paid by them to run the city, town etc.

ˌCouncil of Ecoˌnomic Ad'visers, the ABBREVIATION **CEA** POLITICS a group of three ECONOMISTS who give the U.S. president advice about the ECONOMY

ˌcouncil of 'governments also **ˌregional 'council** *n. plural* **councils of governments** [C] POLITICS in the U.S., a group of government officials from several towns or cities in one area who get together to make decisions affecting the whole area

coun·cil·or /'kaʊnsələ/ *n.* [C] a member of a council

coun·cil·wom·an /'kaʊnsəlˌwʊmən/ *n. plural* **councilwomen** /-ˌwɪmɪn/ [C] a woman who is elected to be part of a town or city council

coun·sel¹ /'kaʊnsəl/ W3 *n.* **1** [U] LAW a lawyer or a group of lawyers who represent someone in a court of law, or who give legal advice: *The counsel for the defense gave her opening statement.* **2 keep your own counsel** to not talk about your private thoughts and opinions: *I was about to speak, but decided to keep my own counsel.* **3** [U] FORMAL advice: *I'll miss her because I value her counsel.* [**Origin:** 1100–1200 Old French *conseil*, from Latin *consilium*, from *consulere*]

counsel² *v.* **counseled** or **counselled**, **counseling** or **counselling** [T] **1** to listen to someone and give them support and advice about their personal problems: *Carvalho counsels cancer patients at the hospital.* **2** to advise a course of action SYN **advise**: **counsel sb to do sth** *She counseled them not to accept the settlement.*

coun·sel·ing /'kaʊnsəlɪŋ/ S3 *n.* [U] advice given to people about their personal problems or difficult decisions: *marriage and family counseling*

coun·sel·or /'kaʊnsələ/ S3 *n.* [C] **1** someone whose job is to help and support people with personal problems: *a counselor at a drug and alcohol treatment center* **2** someone, especially a young man or woman, who takes care of younger children at a summer CAMP

count¹ /kaʊnt/ S1 W2 *v.*

1 FIND THE TOTAL [T] to calculate the total number of people or things in a group SYN **count up**: *All the votes have been counted.* | *I counted 14 motorcycles on my way in to work.*

2 SAY NUMBERS [I] to say numbers in order, one by one or in groups: *The game teaches children to count in Spanish.* | **+from/to** *Take a deep breath, and then count to ten.*

3 BE ALLOWED [I,T usually passive] to be allowed or accepted according to a standard, set of ideas, or set of rules, or to allow something in this way: *If the ball is caught for the third out, the run* ***doesn't count.*** | **count (sth) as sth** *This money does not count as taxable*

income. | *Today's session will be counted as overtime.* | **+toward** *The course counts toward your final degree.*
4 INCLUDE [T] to include someone or something in a total: *Counting the helpers, about 60 people turned up.* | *If you don't count the teachers, there were 40 of us on the bus.*
5 CONSIDER STH [T] to consider someone or something in a particular way [SYN] **consider**: **count sb/sth as sth** *I think Mexico should be counted as part of Central America.* | *You should* ***count yourself lucky*** *that you weren't hurt.*
6 IMPORTANT [I] to be important or valuable: *First impressions do count, so look your best at the interview.* | **count for something/anything/nothing etc.** *His promises don't count for much.* | *We have to* ***make*** *our votes* ***count.***
7 ...and counting used after a number or amount of time to say that it is continuing to increase: *Total cost is $2.5 million and counting.*
8 count the days/hours/minutes etc. to wait for something to happen, especially when you know when it will happen but you are impatient for it to happen: *My daughter is already counting the days until Christmas.*
9 count the cost (of sth) to realize what you have lost as a result of something: *Across the region farmers are counting the cost of the floods.*
10 who's counting? SPOKEN used to say that you are not worried about the number of times something happens or how long something takes etc.
11 I/you can count sth on one hand SPOKEN used to emphasize how small the number of something is: *Ten years ago, you could count on one hand the number of people we knew with email.*
12 don't count your chickens (before they're hatched) SPOKEN used to say that you should not make plans that depend on something good happening, because it might not: *You'll probably get the job, but don't count your chickens just yet.*
13 count sheep to imagine a line of sheep jumping over a fence, one at a time, and count them as a way of making yourself go to sleep
[**Origin:** 1300–1400 Old French *conter*, from Latin *computare*] → see also **count your blessings** at BLESSING (6)

count against *phr. v.* **1 count against sb** to be a disadvantage to someone in a particular situation: *Will my lack of experience count against me?* **2 count against sth** to reduce a total amount: *Your days off sick do not count against your vacation allowance.*

count sth ↔ **down** *phr. v.* to count the number of days, minutes etc. left until a particular moment or event: *Robin is anxiously counting down the days until Jonathan arrives.* → see also COUNTDOWN

count sb **in** *phr. v.* INFORMAL to include someone in an activity: *If you're going rock climbing this weekend, you can count me in.*

count on sb/sth *phr. v.* **1** to depend on someone or something, especially in a difficult situation: *I knew I could count on Maggie.* | **count on doing sth** *We're all counting on winning this contract* | **count on sb to do sth** *You can count on me to take care of her.* | *You might make money, but* ***don't count on it.*** **2** to expect someone to do something, or expect something to happen: *He hadn't counted on the fog.* | **count on sb/sth doing sth** *We didn't count on so many people being on vacation.*

count out *phr. v.* **1 count sb out** INFORMAL to not include someone in an activity: *Well, you can count me out!* **2 count sb out** to decide that someone or something is not important or worth considering: *They're the most improved team in the league – I wouldn't count them out.* **3 count sth ↔ out** to put things down one by one as you count them: *Can you help me count out the ballots?*

count sth ↔ **up** *phr. v.* to calculate the total number of people or things in a group: *Count up how many people checked "yes."*

count² [S2] [W3] *n.* [C]
1 TOTAL the process of counting, or the total that you get when you count things: *The final count may exceed 2,000.* | **+of** *an exact count of the injured* | ***At the last count*** (=the last and most recent time you counted), *there were 82 people living on the island.*
2 MEASUREMENT a measurement that shows how much of a substance is present in a place, area etc. that is being examined: *My cholesterol count was high.*
3 lose count to forget a number you were calculating or a total you were trying to count: *Be quiet – you made me lose count!* | *I lost count after a hundred.*
4 keep count to keep a record of the changing total of something over a period of time: *Are you keeping count of how many people you've invited?*
5 SAYING NUMBERS the process of saying numbers starting from one and going up to a particular number: *Hold your breath for a count of ten.*
6 on all/several/both etc. counts in every way or about everything, in several ways or about several things etc.: *He proved many people in Washington wrong on several counts.*
7 LAW one of the crimes that someone is charged with: *Henderson pleaded guilty on one count of drunken driving.* | *Davis was found not guilty* ***on all counts.***
8 be out/down for the count a) to be defeated: *Many people felt he was down for the count and was considering bankruptcy.* **b)** to be in a deep sleep **c)** if a BOXER is out for the count, he or she has been knocked down for ten seconds or more
9 RANK/TITLE a European NOBLEMAN with a high rank: *the Count of Monte Cristo*

count·a·ble /ˈkaʊntəbəl/ *adj.* ENG. LANG. ARTS a countable noun is a noun such as "table," that has a singular and a plural form [OPP] **uncountable** → see also COUNT NOUN

count·down /ˈkaʊntˈdaʊn/ *n.* [C] the act of counting backward to zero before something happens, especially before a space vehicle is sent into the sky

coun·te·nance¹ /ˈkaʊntənəns/ *n.* FORMAL [C] your face or your expression

countenance² *v.* [T] FORMAL to accept, support, or approve of something: *In no way will we countenance terrorism to advance our cause.*

coun·ter¹ /ˈkaʊntɚ/ [S2] *n.* [C] **1** also **countertop** a flat surface in the kitchen where you work, prepare food etc.: *Just leave the dishes on the counter.* | *a countertop appliance* (=one that sits on top of a counter) **2** the place, usually a flat narrow surface, where you pay or are served in a store, bank, restaurant etc.: *The local supermarket has a good deli counter.* | *The cashier stood behind the counter.* **3 over the counter** over the counter medicines and drugs can be bought without a PRESCRIPTION from a doctor **4 under the counter** if you buy something under the counter, you buy it secretly and usually illegally **5** a piece of electrical equipment that counts something: *Set the video counter to zero before you press play.* → see also GEIGER COUNTER **6** a small object that you use in some games to mark a place on a board **7** a computer program that counts the number of people that have visited a WEBSITE and shows the number on the screen [**Origin:** (1, 2) 1300–1400 Old French *comptour*, from Medieval Latin *computatorium* **counting place**, from Latin *computare*]

counter² *v.* **1** [I,T] to react to a statement, criticism, argument, action etc. by saying or doing something that will prove that the statement is not true or that will have an opposite effect: *He was determined to counter the bribery allegations.* **2** [T] to do something in order to reduce the bad effects of something, or to defend yourself against them: *There are steps you can take to counter the effects of stress.*

counter³ *adj., adv.* **be/run counter to sth** to be the opposite of something or not be allowed by it: *Sending troops abroad would run counter to Japan's constitution.*

counter- /kaʊntɚ/ *prefix* **1** the opposite of something: *counterproductive* (=producing the opposite of what you want) **2** done or given as a reaction to something, especially to oppose it: *proposals and counterproposals* **3** matching something: *my counterpart in the Korean company* (=someone who has the same type of job that I have)

coun·ter·act /ˌkaʊntɚˈækt/ *v.* [T] to reduce or prevent the bad effect of something, by doing something that has the opposite effect: *Add some sugar to counteract the tartness of the lemon.* —**counteraction** /ˌkaʊntɚˈækʃən/ *n.* [C,U]

coun·ter·ar·gu·ment /ˈkaʊntɚˌɑrgyəmənt/ *n.* [C] ENG. LANG. ARTS a fact, opinion, set of reasons etc. that shows that the ideas or reasons someone is using in an argument may be wrong or not good enough: *The U.S. argued that this was a European problem, so Europe must deal with it. The Europeans' counterargument was that the problem could not be solved without help from the U.S.*

coun·ter·at·tack /ˈkaʊntɚəˌtæk/ *n.* [C] an attack against someone who has attacked you, in a war, sport, or an argument: *Government forces have launched a counterattack against the guerrillas.* ►see THESAURUS box at attack[1] —**counterattack** *v.* [I,T] —**counterattacker** *n.* [C]

coun·ter·bal·ance /ˌkaʊnt̬ɚˈbæləns, ˈkaʊnt̬ɚˌbæləns/ *v.* [T] to have an effect that is the opposite of the effect of something else: *Russia favored stronger ties with China as a counterbalance to the U.S.* —**counterbalance** /ˈkaʊntɚˌbæləns/ *n.* [C]

coun·ter·charge /ˌkaʊntɚˈtʃɑrdʒ/ *n.* [C] a statement that says someone else has done something wrong, made after they have said you have done something wrong: *a series of charges, countercharges, and lawsuits*

coun·ter·clock·wise /ˌkaʊntɚˈklɑk-waɪz/ *adv.* moving in the opposite direction to the hands on a clock OPP clockwise: *To remove the lid, turn it counterclockwise.*

coun·ter·cul·ture /ˈkaʊntɚˌkʌltʃɚ/ *n.* [U] the beliefs, behavior, and way of living of people, especially young people, who are against the usual or accepted beliefs, behavior etc. of society: *The counterculture of the 1960s was also called the hippie movement.*

coun·ter·es·pi·o·nage /ˌkaʊntɚˈɛspiəˌnɑʒ/ *n.* [U] the process of trying to prevent someone from SPYING on your country

coun·ter·ex·am·ple /ˈkaʊntɚɪgˌzæmpəl/ *n.* [C] ENG. LANG. ARTS a fact or opinion proving that the opposite of an existing fact or opinion is true, used to question whether someone's argument is reasonable or correct

coun·ter·feit[1] /ˈkaʊntɚfɪt/ *adj.* made to look exactly like something else, in order to deceive people SYN fake: *a counterfeit $20 bill* [**Origin:** 1300–1400 Old French, past participle of *contrefaire* **to copy**] ►see THESAURUS box at fake[2] —**counterfeit** *n.* [C]

counterfeit[2] *v.* [T] to copy something exactly in order to deceive people: *Twenty-dollar bills are the most likely to be counterfeited.* —**counterfeiter** *n.* [C]

coun·ter·foil /ˈkaʊntɚˌfɔɪl/ *n.* [C] FORMAL the part of something such as a check or ticket that you keep as a record

coun·ter·in·sur·gen·cy /ˌkaʊntɚɪnˈsɚdʒənsi/ *n.* [U] military action against people who are fighting against their own country's government

coun·ter·in·tel·li·gence /ˌkaʊntɚɪnˈtɛlədʒəns/ *n.* [U] action that a country takes in order to stop other countries from discovering its secrets

coun·ter·mand /ˈkaʊntɚˌmænd/ *v.* [T] to officially tell people to ignore an order, especially by giving them a different one

coun·ter·mea·sure /ˈkaʊntɚˌmɛʒɚ/ *n.* [C usually plural] an action taken to prevent another action from having a harmful effect: *new countermeasures against terrorism*

coun·ter·of·fen·sive /ˈkaʊntɚəˌfɛnsɪv/ *n.* [C] **1** a military attack on someone who has attacked you: *a counteroffensive against the rebels* **2** action that you take to oppose or defeat someone who has opposed, criticized, or harmed you in some way

coun·ter·pane /ˈkaʊntɚˌpeɪn/ *n.* [C] OLD-FASHIONED a BEDSPREAD

coun·ter·part /ˈkaʊntɚˌpɑrt/ *n.* [C] someone or something that has the same job or purpose as someone or something else in a different place: *Mexican officials are discussing a new trade agreement with their Brazilian counterparts.*

coun·ter·point /ˈkaʊntɚˌpɔɪnt/ *n.* **1** [C,U] ENG. LANG. ARTS a way of writing music so that two or more tunes can be played together at the same time, or a piece of music like this **2** [C] something that shows a clear difference when compared to something else

coun·ter·pro·duc·tive /ˌkaʊntɚprəˈdʌktɪv/ *adj.* achieving the opposite result to the one that you want: *A confrontation is really going to be counterproductive for everyone.*

coun·ter·rev·o·lu·tion /ˌkaʊntɚrɛvəˈluʃən/ *n.* [C,U] political or military actions taken to get rid of a government that is in power because of a previous REVOLUTION —**counterrevolutionary** *adj.*

coun·ter·rev·o·lu·tion·a·ry /ˌkaʊntɚrɛvəˈluʃəˌnɛri/ *n. plural* **counterrevolutionaries** [C] someone who is involved in a counterrevolution

coun·ter·sign /ˈkaʊntɚˌsaɪn/ *v.* [T] to sign a paper that has already been signed by someone else

coun·ter·ten·or /ˈkaʊntɚˌtɛnɚ/ *n.* [C] a man who is trained to sing with a very high voice

coun·ter·ter·ror·ist /ˌkaʊntɚˈtɛrərɪst◂/ *adj.* **a counterterrorist operation/squad etc.** a plan or group that tries to prevent the violent activities of political groups who use force —**counterterrorist** *n.* [C]

coun·ter·vail·ing /ˌkaʊntɚˈveɪlɪŋ◂/ *adj.* FORMAL with an equally strong but opposite effect: *countervailing forces within the church*

count·ess /ˈkaʊntɪs/ *n.* [C] a woman with the same rank as an EARL or a COUNT

ˈcounting house *n.* [C] an office where accounts and money were kept in the past

count·less /ˈkaʊntlɪs/ *adj.* too many to be counted: *She spent countless hours knitting by the fire.*

ˈcount noun *n.* [C] ENG. LANG. ARTS a COUNTABLE noun → see also UNCOUNT NOUN

coun·tri·fied /ˈkʌntrɪˌfaɪd/ *adj.* typical in appearance or behavior of the people or things that live outside towns and cities, or made to seem typical of this type of area: *This corner of America is known for its countrified ways.* → see also CITIFIED

coun·try[1] /ˈkʌntri/ S1 W1 *n. plural* **countries** **1** [C] a nation or state with its land and people: *Ukraine is a big country.* | *How many **foreign countries** have you been to?* | **across/over/throughout the country** *Letters came in from across the country.* → see also MOTHER COUNTRY → see Word Choice box at NATION

THESAURUS

nation a country and its people, used especially when considering its political and economic structures: *the major industrialized nations*
state a country and its people, used especially when considering its political and economic structures: *the leaders of former Communist states*
power a country that is very strong and important: *Germany is a major industrial power in Europe.*
land LITERARY a country or place: *a visit to her native land*

2 the country land that is outside towns and cities, including land used for farming SYN the countryside: *I've always wanted to live **in the country**.*

THESAURUS

countryside used when talking about the existence or appearance of land outside towns and cities, which has fields, forests etc.: *the green fertile countryside*
landscape used when talking about the appearance of an area of countryside or land of a particular type: *the seemingly flat landscape of the prairies*

scenery the natural features of a particular part of a country that you can see, such as mountains, forests, deserts etc.: *the beautiful scenery in the Rockies*
wilderness a large area of land that has never been developed or farmed: *areas of wilderness in Alaska*

3 the country all the people who live in a particular country: *The tragedy shocked the whole country.* **4** [U] COUNTRY MUSIC: *I'm a big fan of country.* **5 farm/Amish etc. country** an area of land that is appropriate for a particular activity, or where a particular type of people live: *We're now entering wine country.* [**Origin:** 1200–1300 Old French *contrée*, from Medieval Latin *contrata* **(land) which lies opposite**, from Latin *contra*]

C

country² *adj.* [only before noun] **1** in or relating to the area outside cities or towns: *twisting country roads* **2** relating to country and western music: *country music singer Dwight Yoakam*

ˌcountry and ˈwestern *n.* [U] COUNTRY MUSIC

country bump·kin /ˌkʌntri ˈbʌmpkɪn/ *n.* [C] someone who is considered to be stupid because they are from an area outside towns and cities

ˈcountry ˌclub *n.* [C] a sports and social club, especially one for rich people

ˌcountry ˈcousin *n.* [C] someone who does not have a lot of experience and who is confused by busy city life

ˌcountry ˈdancing *n.* [U] a traditional form of dance in which pairs of dancers move in rows and circles

coun·try·man /ˈkʌntrimən/ *n. plural* **countrymen** /-mən/ [C] someone from your own country

ˈcountry ˌmusic *n.* [U] a type of popular music from the southern and western U.S.

coun·try·side /ˈkʌntriˌsaɪd/ *n.* [U] a word meaning the area outside cities and towns, used especially when you are talking about its beauty: *the peacefulness of the Carolina countryside*

ˌcountry-ˈwestern *adj.* COUNTRY MUSIC **—country-western** *adj.* [only before noun] *a country-western singer*

coun·try·wom·an /ˈkʌntriˌwʊmən/ *n. plural* **countrywomen** /-ˌwɪmɪn/ [C] a woman who is from your own country

coun·ty /ˈkaʊnti/ S2 W2 *n. plural* **counties** [C] POLITICS a large area of land within a state or country, that has its own government to deal with local matters: *Cedric County, Kansas* | *county elections* [**Origin:** 1200–1300 Old French *conté* **area ruled by a count**, from Medieval Latin *comitatus*, from Latin *comes*]

ˌcounty ˈcourt *n.* [C] LAW in some states, a court that has authority in a county and deals with less important cases

ˌcounty ˈfair *n.* [C] an event that happens each year in a particular county, with games, competitions for the best farm animals, for the best cooking etc.

ˈcounty seat *n.* [C] the town in a COUNTY where its government is

coup /ku/ *n.* [C] **1** an action in which citizens or the army suddenly take control of the government by using violence or force SYN **coup d'état**: *a military coup* ►see THESAURUS box at **revolution** **2** something you do that is successful and impressive, especially because you would not normally do it: *Getting the band to play at the event was quite a coup.*

coup de grâce /ˌku də ˈgrɑs/ *n.* [singular] **1** an action or event that ends or destroys something that has gradually been getting weaker **2** a hit or shot that kills someone or something

coup d'é·tat /ˌku deɪˈtɑ/ *n. plural* **coups d'état** (same pronunciation) [C] a COUP

coupe /kup/ *n.* [C] a type of car with two doors, which is shorter than a SEDAN

Cou·pe·rin /ˌkupəˈræn/, **Fran·çois** /frɑnˈswɑ/ (1668–1733) a French musician who wrote CLASSICAL music

cou·ple¹ /ˈkʌpəl/ Ac S1 W1 *n.* **1 a couple (of) sth a)** a small number of things: *Let's wait a couple more minutes.* | *I've run into Darryl a couple of times this summer.* **b)** two people or things of the same kind: *I'll have a couple of tacos, please.* | *There are a couple of girls waiting for you.* **2** [C] two people who are married or having a sexual or romantic relationship: *A young couple lives next door.* | *a **married couple** with two children* [**Origin:** 1200–1300 Old French *cople*, from Latin *copula* **something that joins**]

WORD CHOICE **couple, pair**
• Use **couple** to talk about any two things of the same kind: *I haven't seen her for a couple of days.* Use **pair** to talk about something that has two main parts that are joined together: *a pair of shorts* | *a pair of glasses*
Pair can also be used to talk about two things that are used together as a set: *a new pair of shoes*

GRAMMAR
When you use **couple** to talk about two people, use a singular noun if you are considering them together: *A new couple is moving in next door,* or use a plural noun if you are considering them as two people: *A young couple were arguing at the next table.*

couple² Ac *v.* **1** [T] to join or fasten two things together, especially two vehicles: *Two processors are coupled together.* **2** [I] LITERARY to have sex

couple sth **with** sth *phr. v.* if one thing is coupled with another, the two things happen or are used together and produce a particular result: *Lack of rain coupled with high temperatures caused the crops to fail.*

cou·plet /ˈkʌplɪt/ *n.* [C] ENG. LANG. ARTS two lines of poetry, one following the other, that are the same length

cou·pling /ˈkʌplɪŋ/ Ac *n.* [C] **1** something that connects two things together, especially two vehicles or pipes **2** a combination of two things **3** LITERARY an act of having sex

cou·pon /ˈkupɑn, ˈkyu-/ S2 *n.* [C] **1** a small piece of printed paper that gives you the right to pay less for something or get something free: *This coupon is for 15 cents off paper towels.* **2** a printed form used when you order something, enter a competition etc. **3** TECHNICAL **a)** the rate of INTEREST paid on BONDS: *a two-year bond with a 10% coupon* **b)** a piece of paper attached to some types of BONDS that you tear off and give to a bank or the seller of the bond in order to receive the INTEREST [**Origin:** 1800–1900 French, Old French, **piece**, from *couper* **to cut**]

ˈcoupon rate *n.* [C] ECONOMICS the rate of INTEREST paid on BONDS and other securities (SECURITY)

cour·age /ˈkəɪdʒ, ˈkʌr-/ *n.* [U] **1** the quality of being brave when you are in danger, in pain, in a difficult situation etc.: *The men fought with great courage.* | *I just never **had the courage to** ask Lisa for a date.* | *It **takes a lot of courage** to go into combat, but that's my job.*

THESAURUS
bravery brave behavior in a dangerous or frightening situation: *Troops on both sides fought with bravery.*
guts INFORMAL the courage and determination that you need to do something difficult, dangerous, or unpleasant: *He didn't even have the guts to tell me himself.*
nerve INFORMAL the ability to stay calm in a dangerous, difficult, or frightening situation: *It takes a lot of nerve to give a speech in front of a crowd of people.*

2 the courage of your (own) convictions the quality of being brave enough to say or do what you think is right, even though other people may not agree or approve: *Larry showed the courage of his convictions by saying no.* [**Origin:** 1200–1300 Old French *corage*, from *cuer* **heart**, from Latin *cor*]

cou·ra·geous /kəˈreɪdʒəs/ *adj.* brave: *a courageous leader* | *The judge's decision was courageous.* **—courageously** *adv.* **—courageousness** *n.* [U]

Cour·bet /kʊrˈbeɪ/, **Gus·tave** /guˈstɑv/ (1819–1877) a French PAINTER famous for painting ordinary scenes in a style that made them look real

cou·ri·er[1] /ˈkʊriɚ, ˈkɚ-/ *n.* [C] someone who is employed to take a package, documents etc. somewhere: *The invitations were sent out* ***by courier***. ▶see THESAURUS box at **mail**[1]

courier[2] *v.* [T] to send something somewhere by using a courier: *I'll courier the contracts out to you this afternoon.*

course[1] /kɔrs/ S1 W1 *n.*

1 of course a) used when what you or someone else is saying is not surprising, because it is expected or already known: *We'll be spending more money, of course.* | *Of course, there are exceptions to every rule.* | *"His mother paid for the whole thing again." "Oh, of course."* **b)** also **course** SPOKEN used to agree with someone, or to give permission to someone: *"Can I have a word with you?" "Of course."* **c)** also **course** SPOKEN used to emphasize that you are saying yes to something, or that what you are saying is true or correct: *"He'll do it, won't he?" "Of course he will!"* → see Thesaurus box at CERTAINLY

2 (of) course not SPOKEN used to emphasize that you are saying no to something, or that something is not true or correct: *"Do you mind if I come a little late?" "Of course not!"*

3 CLASS [C] a class in a particular subject SYN **class**: *a writing course* | **+in/on** *a basic course in computers* | *Paul is* ***taking a course*** *on Spanish literature.* → see also CORRESPONDENCE COURSE, CRASH COURSE, REFRESHER COURSE

4 in the course of (doing) sth, **during/throughout/over the course of sth** FORMAL during a process or period of time: *If the card is used six times in the course of a year, there is no annual fee.*

5 ACTIONS [C] an action or series of actions that you could take in order to deal with a particular situation: *a future course for peace* | *What would be the best* ***course of action****?*

6 WAY STH DEVELOPS [C] the usual or natural way that something happens, develops, or is done: **+of** *the course of the epidemic* | *The coup* ***changed the course of*** *the nation's history.* | *Just relax and* ***let nature take its course*** (=allow something to happen in the usual way). | *The recession is expected to* ***run its course*** *by the end of the year.*

7 DIRECTION [C,U] the direction in which someone or something moves: *The plane had to* ***change course*** *to avoid the storm.* | *We had to paddle hard to keep the canoes* ***on course*** (=keep them going in the right direction). | *The ship was blown* ***off course*** (=the wind made it go in the wrong direction).

8 PLANS [singular, U] the general plans someone has to achieve something, or the general way something is happening: *Recent events have forced the administration to* ***change course***. | **on/off course** *He had the feeling that U.S. foreign policy had drifted off course.*

9 PART OF A MEAL [C] one of the separate parts of a meal: *The* ***main course*** *consists of chicken and peppers.* | **a three-/five-course meal** *A three-course meal here costs only $20.*

10 on course likely to achieve something, especially because you have already had some success: *Western leaders put the trade talks back on course.* | **on course to do sth** *The party is on course to return to power.*

11 SPORTS [C] an area of land or water on which some types of races are held or some sports are played: *a golf course* | *a cross-country ski course* → see also OBSTACLE COURSE

12 MEDICAL TREATMENT [C] an amount of medicine or medical treatment that you have regularly for a specific period of time: **a course of drugs/treatment/injections etc.** *Finish the entire course of antibiotics.*

13 RIVER [C] the direction a river moves in: *They changed the course of the stream.*

14 BRICKS/STONE [C] a layer of bricks, stone etc. → see also **in due time/course** at DUE[1] (6), **as a matter of course/routine** at MATTER[1] (4), **be par for the course** at PAR (4), **stay the course** at STAY[1] (6)

course[2] *v.* **1** [I always + adv./prep.] LITERARY if a liquid or electricity courses somewhere, it flows rapidly there: **+down/along/through etc.** *Tears coursed down Nicole's cheeks.* **2** [I always + adv./prep.] LITERARY if a feeling or thought courses through your body or mind, you feel it very strongly, or think it quickly: **+down/through** *Fear coursed through Paul.* **3** [I] to move through something very quickly: *The storm system coursed through Georgia and Alabama.* **4** [I,T] to chase a rabbit with dogs as a sport

court[1] /kɔrt/ S2 W1 *n.*

1 LAW [C,U] a building or room where all the information concerning a crime is given so that it can be judged: *A group of reporters gathered outside the court.* | *a court case* | *No cameras are allowed* ***in court***. | *My landlord is threatening to* ***take me to court*** (=have the case dealt with in a court). | *Our manager doesn't want this thing to* ***go to court***. | *O'Toole's case was* ***settled out of court*** (=dealt with without going to a court).

THESAURUS

In a court
defendant the person who is on trial for a crime
the defense the lawyers who are working for the defendant
the prosecution the lawyers who are trying to prove that the defendant is guilty
judge the official in charge of a court who decides how criminals should be punished
jury a group of people, usually 12 people, who listen to the facts and decide whether the defendant is guilty or not guilty
witness someone who describes in a court of law what he or she knows about a crime
testimony a formal statement made in a court of law about a particular situation or action
verdict the decision of the jury as to whether the defendant is guilty or not guilty

2 the court the judges, lawyers, and JURY who officially decide whether someone is guilty of a crime and what the punishment should be: *Please tell the court in your own words what happened.*

3 SPORT [C,U] an area that has been specially made for playing games such as tennis, basketball etc.: *a volleyball court* | *The players are due* ***on the court*** *in an hour.* ▶see THESAURUS box at **sport**[1]

4 KING/QUEEN ETC. [C] **a)** the official place where a king or queen lives and works: **+of** *the court of Versailles* **b)** the royal family and the people who work for them or advise them: *a court official*

5 hold court to speak in an interesting and amusing way so that people gather to listen to you: *Jeff was holding court upstairs to a group of fans.*

6 pay court to sb OLD-FASHIONED to give a lot of your attention to someone in order to seem attractive or impressive to them

7 CASTLE/LARGE HOUSE [C] a COURTYARD

[**Origin:** 1200–1300 Old French, Latin *cohors* **enclosed place, people in an enclosure, unit of soldiers in the ancient Roman army**] → see also **the ball is in your court** at BALL[1] (9), FOOD COURT, **be laughed out of court** at LAUGH[1] (7)

court[2] *v.* **1** [T] to try to get something you want from other people, by doing something to please them: *Politicians are courting voters before the elections.* **2 court disaster/danger etc.** to behave in a way that makes danger etc. more likely: *People may be courting disaster by using over-the-counter pain relievers.* **3 be courting (sb)** OLD-FASHIONED if a man and a woman are courting, they are having a romantic relationship and may get married **4** [T] OLD-FASHIONED if a man courts a woman, he visits her, takes her out etc. because he hopes she will love him SYN **woo**

cour·te·ous /ˈkɚt̬iəs/ *adj.* having good manners (MANNER) and respect for other people OPP **discourteous**: *The officers were very courteous.* | *courteous service* —**courteously** *adv.* —**courteousness** *n.* [U]

C

cour·te·san /ˈkɔrṭəzən, -ˌzɑn/ *n.* [C] a woman in past times who had sex with rich or important men for money

cour·te·sy /ˈkəṭəsi/ *n. plural* **courtesies** **1** [U] polite behavior that shows that you have respect for other people OPP discourtesy: *All our clients should be treated with courtesy.* | *Even after midnight, they don't* ***have the courtesy*** *to turn the volume down.* | *It's a matter of* ***common courtesy*** *to acknowledge letters.* **2** [C] something you do or say in order to be polite: ***As a courtesy to*** *other diners, we ask that all cell phones be left at the door.* **3 courtesy of sb/sth** by the permission or kindness of someone rather than by paying them: *Everyone on the flight was put up in a fancy hotel, all courtesy of the airline.*

ˈcourtesy bus *n.* [C] a bus provided by a hotel near an airport that their guests can use to travel to and from the airport

ˈcourtesy call *n.* [C] a visit to someone that you make to be polite or to show your respect for them

ˈcourtesy car *n.* [C] a car that a garage, hotel etc. lends to its customers while they are having their own car fixed, are staying at the hotel etc.

ˈcourtesy phone *n.* [C] a telephone in an airport, hotel etc. that you can use to talk to someone in the building without paying

court·house /ˈkɔrthaʊs/ *n.* [C] a building containing courts of law and government offices

court·i·er /ˈkɔrṭiə/ *n.* [C] someone in past times who had an important position in a king or queen's COURT

court·ly /ˈkɔrtli/ *adj. comparative* **courtlier**, *superlative* **courtliest** polite in a formal, old-fashioned way: *courtly manners* —**courtliness** *n.* [U]

ˈcourt-ˌmartial[1] *n. plural* **courts-martial** or **court-martials** [C] LAW **1** a military court that deals with people who break military laws **2** an occasion on which someone is judged by one of these courts

court-martial[2] *v.* **court-martialed** [T] LAW to hear and judge someone's case in a military court: *The Army decided against court-martialing him as a deserter.*

ˌCourt of Apˈpeals *n.* **the Court of Appeals** LAW one of 12 law courts in the U.S. that deals with cases when people are not satisfied with the judgment given by a lower court → see also APPELLATE COURT

ˌcourt of ˈlaw *n.* [C] FORMAL LAW a place where law cases are judged SYN court

ˌcourt ˈorder *n.* [C] LAW an order given by a court of law that someone must do or must not do something: *His computer was seized under a court order.*

ˌcourt reˈporter *n.* [C] someone who works in a court and records everything that is said during a case, on a special machine similar to a TYPEWRITER

court·room /ˈkɔrtˀrum/ *n.* [C] the room where a case is judged by a court of law

court·ship /ˈkɔrtˀʃɪp/ *n.* **1** [C,U] the period of time during which a man and woman have a romantic relationship before getting married: *My parents got married after a two-week courtship.* **2** [U] BIOLOGY special behavior used by animals to attract each other for sex

court·yard /ˈkɔrtˀyɑrd/ *n.* [C] an open space that is completely or partly surrounded by walls or buildings: *Our hotel room faced out on the courtyard.*

cous·cous /ˈkuskus/ *n.* [U] a North African dish made of grains of crushed wheat

cous·in /ˈkʌzən/ S2 W3 *n.* [C] **1** the child of your UNCLE or AUNT SYN first cousin → see also KISSING COUSIN, SECOND COUSIN ►see THESAURUS box at relative[1] **2** a person who is in your family but is not closely related to you: *I recently tracked down a* ***distant cousin*** *in Maine.* **3** someone or something who is connected or similar to something or someone else because they have the same or similar origins: +**of** *The plantain is a larger cousin of the banana.* | *Apes may be* ***distant cousins*** *of humans.* [**Origin:** 1200–1300 Old French *cosin*, from Latin *consobrinus*, from *com-* + *sobrinus* **cousin on the mother's side**]

Cous·teau /kuˈstoʊ/**, Jacques** /ʒɑk/ (1910–1997) a French underwater EXPLORER, famous for making movies about plants and animals that live in the ocean

cou·ture /kuˈtʊr/ *n.* [U] very expensive and fashionable clothes

co·va·lent /koʊˈveɪlənt/ *adj.* [only before noun] SCIENCE relating to the force that joins and holds two or more different chemical substances together: *The hydrogen atoms and the oxygen atom which make up the water molecule form strong covalent bonds.*

coˌvalent ˈbond *n.* [C] CHEMISTRY a chemical BOND between two atoms that forms when the atoms share one or more ELECTRONS

co·var·i·ant /koʊˈvɛriənt/ *adj.* MATH changing in direct relation to another number or quantity, so that the relationship between the two values always remains the same

cove /koʊv/ *n.* [C] EARTH SCIENCE a small area on a coast that is partly surrounded by land, so that it is protected from the wind: *a secluded cove* → see picture on page A31

cov·en /ˈkʌvən/ *n.* [C] a group or meeting of 13 WITCHES

cov·e·nant /ˈkʌvənənt/ *n.* [C] **1** a formal or legal agreement between two or more people: +**of** *the covenant of marriage* **2** in the Bible, a promise made between God and the Israelites in which God promised to help them if they did not worship other gods —**covenant** *v.* [T]

cov·er[1] /ˈkʌvə/ S1 W1 *v.* [T]

1 PUT STH OVER STH also **cover up** to put something over the top of something in order to hide, protect, or close it: *Cover the pot and bake for an hour.* | *You should cover the furniture before you start to paint.* | **cover sth with sth** *Dan covered his face with his hands.*

2 BE PUT ON STH to be on top of something in order to hide, protect, or close it: *A brightly colored scarf covered her head.* | *The makeup didn't cover her bruises very well.* | **be covered with sth** *The table was covered with a white cloth.*

3 FORM LAYER to be spread over a surface and form a layer on top of it: *Much of the country is covered by snow.* | **be covered with/in sth** *When they got home, their shoes were covered in mud.* | *The floor of the basement was covered with ants.*

4 DEAL WITH/INCLUDE to include or deal with something: *The book covers all aspects of business and law.* | *Certain areas are not covered by the treaty.* | *We* ***covered a lot of ground*** (=dealt with a lot of things) *during the meeting.*

5 INSURANCE if an insurance agreement covers someone or something, it states that money will be given to the person if they are injured, if something is damaged etc.: *Most health insurers don't cover cosmetic surgery.* | **cover sb against/for sth** *Are we covered for theft?*

6 NEWS to report the details of an event for a newspaper, television, or radio: *He now covers foreign affairs from Washington.*

7 PAY FOR STH money that covers a cost is enough to pay for it: *$100 should cover the hotel bill.* | *Airlines are raising fares to* ***cover the cost*** *of fuel.*

8 DISTANCE to travel a particular distance: *They were hoping to cover 300 miles yesterday.* | *Donna drove 400 miles in one day – she really* ***covered a lot of ground*** (=traveled a long way).

9 AN AREA to spread over an area: *The city covers 25 square miles.*

10 GUNS a) to protect someone by being ready to shoot anyone who attacks them: *We'll cover you while you run for the door.* **b)** to aim a gun at a person, or the door of a building with people in it, so that they cannot escape: *Police officers covered the back entrance.*

11 SPORTS to stay close to a member of the opposing team or a part of the field in a game, in order to prevent your opponents from gaining points SYN guard: *Porter, who was covering Rice, was called for a foul.*

12 cover all (the) bases INFORMAL to make sure that you

can deal with any situation or problem, so that nothing bad happens and no one can criticize you: *I want to make sure we cover all the bases in the new employee training class.*
13 MUSIC ENG. LANG. ARTS to perform or record a song that was originally recorded by another artist: *The Beatles' "Yesterday" has been covered more times than any other song.*
14 cover your back also **cover yourself** INFORMAL to do something now to avoid criticism or blame if something goes wrong in the future: *Take detailed notes of what you do for the client, in order to cover yourself.*
[**Origin:** 1200–1300 Old French *covrir*, from Latin *cooperire*, from *co-* + *operire* **to close, cover**] → see also **cover/hide a multitude of sins** at MULTITUDE (3), **cover/hide your tracks** at TRACK[1] (15)

cover for sb *phr. v.* **1** to do the work that someone else usually does, because they are sick or not present: *Who's going to cover for you while you're on vacation?* **2** to prevent someone from getting into trouble by lying about where they are or what they are doing: *Cindy refused to cover for him when his boss called.*

cover sth ↔ **over** *phr. v.* to put something on top of something else so that it is completely hidden: *The female lays a single egg and covers it over.*

cover up *phr. v.* **1 cover sb/sth ↔ up** to put something over someone or something else so that they cannot be seen: *She always wears a lot of makeup to cover her pimples up.* **2 cover sb/sth ↔ up** if something covers something else, it goes on top of it and hides it: *The clouds came along and covered up the sun.* **3 cover sth ↔ up** to prevent people from discovering mistakes or unpleasant facts: *Mom's worried, but she covers it up by joking.* → see also COVER-UP **4 cover yourself up** to put clothes on in order to keep warm or to prevent people from seeing your body: *Cover up, or stay out of the sun.*

cover up for sth *phr. v.* to protect someone by hiding unfavorable facts about them: *High-ranking military men were covering up for the murderers.*

cover² S2 W2 *n.*
1 STH THAT PROTECTS STH [C] something that is put over or onto something to protect it, keep dirt out etc.: *a plastic cover* | *a cushion cover* | *I need to buy a large casserole dish with a cover.*

THESAURUS
lid a cover for a container
top/cap the lid or cover for a container or a pen
wrapper paper or plastic that is around something you buy
wrapping cloth, paper etc. that is put around something to protect it

2 BOOKS [C] the outer front or back page of a magazine, book etc.: *His picture is on the cover of "Newsweek."* | **the front/back cover (of sth)** *There's a description on the back cover.* | *I* ***read*** *the magazine* ***from cover to cover*** (=read everything in it) *but I didn't see any coupons.*
3 the covers [plural] the sheets, BLANKETS etc. on a bed: *You're always stealing the covers!*
4 SHELTER/PROTECTION [U] shelter or protection from bad weather or attack SYN **shelter**: *The soldiers* ***ran for cover*** *when the shooting began.* | *We were forced to* ***take cover*** *under a tree.*
5 STH THAT HIDES STH BAD [U] something that hides something or keeps it secret, especially by seeming to be something else: **+for** *The gang used the shop as a cover for drug deals.*
6 WAR [U] military protection and support given to soldiers, aircraft, ships etc. that are likely to be attacked: *air cover*
7 under cover pretending to be someone else in order to do something without being noticed: *Cobb worked on the case under cover for the FBI.* → see also UNDERCOVER
8 MUSIC also **cover version** [C] ENG. LANG. ARTS a performance or recording of a song that was originally recorded by someone else: *a cover of an old Elvis song*
9 COVER CHARGE [C] a cover charge: *There's $5 cover because there's a band playing tonight.*
10 under cover of darkness/night LITERARY hidden by darkness: *Most attacks take place under cover of darkness.*
11 under separate cover if a letter, check etc. is sent under separate cover it is in a separate envelope: *A $300 refund will be sent under separate cover.*

cov·er·age /ˈkʌvərɪdʒ/ W3 *n.* [U] **1** the way in which a subject or event is reported on television or radio, or in newspapers: *continuous live coverage of the Senate hearings* **2** the amount of protection given to you by an insurance agreement: *Millions of people have no formal health care coverage.*

cov·er·alls /ˈkʌvɚˌɔlz/ *n.* [plural] a piece of clothing that you wear over all your clothes to protect them → see also OVERALLS

ˈcover charge *n.* [C] money that you have to pay in a bar or CLUB in addition to the cost of the food and drinks, especially to go dancing or to hear a band: *a $5 cover charge*

ˌcovered ˈwagon *n.* [C] a large vehicle with a curved cloth top that is pulled by horses, used in past times in North America

ˈcover girl *n.* [C] a young attractive woman whose photograph is on the front cover of a magazine

cov·er·ing /ˈkʌvərɪŋ/ *n.* **1** [singular] something that covers or hides something: *a tough protective covering* | **+of** *a light covering of snow* **2** [C] a layer of something such as paper, wood, or cloth used to cover walls, floors etc.: *floor coverings*

cov·er·let /ˈkʌvɚlɪt/ *n.* [C] a cloth cover for a bed SYN **bedspread**

ˈcover ˌletter *n.* [C] a letter that you send with documents or a package explaining what it is or giving additional information: *Make sure to send a cover letter along with your résumé.*

ˈcover ˌstory *n.* [C] the story that goes with a picture on the cover of a magazine

co·vert¹ /ˈkoʊvɚt, ˈkʌ-, koʊˈvɚt/ *adj.* secret or hidden OPP **overt**: *covert operations against the government* ►see THESAURUS box at **secret¹** —**covertly** *adv.*

covert² *n.* [C] a group of small bushes growing close together in which animals can hide

ˈcover-up *n.* [C] an attempt to prevent the public from discovering the truth about something: *People would suspect a cover-up if public hearings aren't held.* → see also **cover up** at COVER¹

cov·et /ˈkʌvɪt/ *v.* [T] FORMAL to have a very strong desire to have something that someone else has → see also ENVY: *Gatlin covets my job, which he has been in line for twice before.*

cov·et·ed /ˈkʌvət̬ɪd/ *adj.* something that is coveted is something that many people want but that few people can get: *the highly coveted Pulitzer Prize*

cov·et·ous /ˈkʌvət̬əs/ *adj.* FORMAL DISAPPROVING having a very strong desire to have something that someone else has, especially wealth SYN **envious**: *They began to cast covetous eyes on their neighbors' fields.* —**covetously** *adv.* —**covetousness** *n.* [U]

cov·ey /ˈkʌvi/ *n.* [C] **1** a small group of birds **2** INFORMAL a small group of people or things: **+of** *a covey of young girls*

cow¹ /kaʊ/ S2 W3 *n.* [C] **1 a)** BIOLOGY an adult female animal that is large and is kept on farms for the milk it produces and for meat → see also BULL: *cow's milk* **b)** a male or female animal of this type: *a herd of cows* **2** BIOLOGY the female of some large land and sea animals, such as the ELEPHANT or the WHALE → see also BULL **3 have a cow** SPOKEN to be very angry or surprised about something: *Pat had a cow because you didn't tell her about the party.* **4 till the cows come home** INFORMAL for a very long time, or forever: *They stay up and play cards till the cows come home.* [**Origin:** Old English *cu*]

cow² *v.* [T usually passive] to make someone afraid, or to control them by using violence or threats SYN **intimidate**: **be cowed into submission/silence** *Dissidents were cowed into silence by the army.*

cow·ard /ˈkaʊɚd/ *n.* [C] someone who is not brave at all: *He called me a coward because I wouldn't fight.* [**Origin:** 1200–1300 Old French *coart*, from *coe* **tail**]

Cow·ard /ˈkaʊɚd/**, No·ël** /ˈnoʊəl/ (1899–1973) a British actor, singer, and writer of songs and plays

.C

cow·ard·ice /ˈkaʊɚdɪs/ also **cow·ard·li·ness** /ˈkaʊɚdlinɪs/ *n.* [U] lack of courage: *It would be an act of cowardice to avoid the debate.*

cow·ard·ly /ˈkaʊɚdli/ *adj.* behaving in a way that shows that you are not brave: *a cowardly attack on an unarmed man*

cow·bell /ˈkaʊbel/ *n.* [C] a large bell that is put around a cow's neck so that it can be found easily

cow·boy /ˈkaʊbɔɪ/ *n.* **1** [C] a man whose job is to take care of cattle: *He'd been working as a cowboy on a Utah ranch.* **2 cowboys and Indians** a game played by children who pretend to be cowboys and Native Americans, fighting each other

ˈcowboy ˌboot *n.* [C] a type of leather boot with a raised HEEL and pointed toe

ˈcowboy ˌhat *n.* [C] a hat with a wide circular edge and a tall, stiff top, worn by cowboys → see picture at HAT

cow·catch·er /ˈkaʊˌkætʃɚ/ *n.* [C] a piece of metal on the front of a train used to push things off the track

ˈcow chip *n.* [C] a round flat mass of dry solid waste from a cow

cow·er /ˈkaʊɚ/ *v.* [I] to bend low and move back, especially because you are frightened: *The children were cowering in the corner.*

cow·girl /ˈkaʊgɚl/ *n.* [C] a woman whose job is to take care of cattle

cow·hand /ˈkaʊhænd/ *n.* [C] someone whose job is to take care of cattle

cow·hide /ˈkaʊhaɪd/ *n.* [C,U] the skin of a cow or the leather that is made from this

cowl /kaʊl/ *n.* [C] **1** a very large HOOD that covers your head and shoulders, especially worn by MONKS **2** a cover for a CHIMNEY that protects it from wind and rain

cow·lick /ˈkaʊˌlɪk/ *n.* [C] hair that sticks up on top of your head: *I can never get this cowlick to lie down.* [**Origin:** 1500–1600 because it looks as if it had been licked by a cow]

cowl·ing /ˈkaʊlɪŋ/ *n.* [C] a metal cover for an aircraft engine

ˌcowl ˈneck *n.* [C] the neck on a piece of clothing that falls in folds at the front: *a cowl neck sweater*

co·work·er, co-worker /ˈkoʊˌwɚkɚ/ *n.* [C] someone who works with you and has a similar position → see also COLLEAGUE: *Jeff's coworkers took him out for his birthday.*

ˌcow ˈpie *n.* [C] a COW CHIP

cow·poke /ˈkaʊpoʊk/ *n.* [C] OLD-FASHIONED INFORMAL a COWBOY

cow·pox /ˈkaʊpɑks/ *n.* [U] a disease that cows suffer from, from which a VACCINE can be made and given to humans to protect them from SMALLPOX

cow·punch·er /ˈkaʊˌpʌntʃɚ/ *n.* [C] OLD-FASHIONED INFORMAL a COWBOY

cow·rie /ˈkaʊri/ *n.* [C] a shiny brightly-colored tropical shell, used in past times as money in parts of Africa and Asia

cow·shed /ˈkaʊʃed/ *n.* [C] a building where cows live in the winter, or where their milk is taken from them

cow·slip /ˈkaʊˌslɪp/ *n.* [U] a small European wild plant with sweet smelling yellow flowers [**Origin:** Old English *cuslyppe* **cow dung, cowslip**]

ˈcow town *n.* [C] INFORMAL a small town in the U.S. in an area where cattle are raised

cox·comb /ˈkɑkskoʊm/ *n.* [C] another spelling of COCKSCOMB

cox·swain /ˈkɑksən, -sweɪn/ also **cox** /kɑks/ *n.* [C] someone who controls the direction of a rowing boat, especially in races [**Origin:** 1300–1400 *cock* **small boat** (14–18 centuries) (from Old French *coque*) + *swain* **boy, servant**]

coy /kɔɪ/ *adj.* **1** pretending to be shy in order to attract interest, or to avoid dealing with something difficult: *Leah gave him a coy smile.* **2** unwilling to give information about something, especially because you want to keep an advantage: **+about** *Gonzalez was coy about precisely where he's moving.* [**Origin:** 1300–1400 Old French *coi* **calm**, from Latin *quietus* **quiet**] **—coyly** *adv.* **—coyness** *n.* [U]

coy·o·te /kaɪˈoʊti, ˈkaɪ-oʊt/ *n.* [C] a wild animal like a dog that lives in western North America and Mexico: *At night you can hear coyotes howling.* [**Origin:** 1700–1800 Mexican Spanish, Nahuatl *coyotl*] → see picture on page A34

coz /kʌz/ *n.* INFORMAL used when speaking to your COUSIN

coz·en /ˈkʌzən/ *v.* [T] OLD USE to trick or deceive someone

co·zy /ˈkoʊzi/ *adj.* *comparative* **cozier**, *superlative* **coziest** **1** cozy places or clothes are comfortable and warm, and often small or soft: *The living room was warm and cozy.* | *a cozy bathrobe* **2** relaxed and friendly: *You and Mike looked pretty cozy at the party.* | *a cozy family gathering* **3** DISAPPROVING having a close connection or relationship, especially one you do not approve of: *a cozy relationship with local government officials* **—cozily** *adv.* **—coziness** *n.* [U]

CPA /ˌsi pi ˈeɪ/ *n.* [C] **certified public accountant** an ACCOUNTANT who has passed all his or her examinations

CPCTC /ˌsi pi ˌsi ti ˈsi/ **congruent parts of congruent triangles are congruent** MATH used to say that when two TRIANGLES are the same size and shape, the parts of each triangle are also the same shape and size

CPR /ˌsi pi ˈɑr/ *n.* [U] **cardiopulmonary resuscitation** MEDICINE the act of breathing into someone's mouth and pressing on their chest to make them breathe again and to make their heart start beating again

Cpt. *n.* the written abbreviation of CAPTAIN

CPU /ˌsi pi ˈyu/ *n.* [C] **central processing unit** COMPUTERS the part of a computer that controls and organizes what the computer does

crab¹ /kræb/ S3 *n.* **1** [C,U] BIOLOGY a sea animal with a round flat shell and two large CLAWS on its front legs, or the meat from this animal: *Alaskan king crabs* | *I'll have the crab cakes, please.* **2** [usually singular] INFORMAL someone who easily becomes annoyed about unimportant things: *She's such a crab.* **3 crabs** [plural] a medical condition in which a type of LOUSE is in the hair around the sexual organs

crab² *v.* **crabbed, crabbing** [I] **1** to catch crabs **2** INFORMAL to complain about something

ˈcrab ˌapple *n.* [C] a small apple that tastes sour, or the tree that it grows on

crab·bed /ˈkræbɪd/ *adj.* **1** crabbed writing is small and hard to understand: *tiny crabbed handwriting* **2** OLD-FASHIONED easily annoyed SYN **crabby**: *Mr. Archer was crabbed and unpleasant.*

crab·by /ˈkræbi/ *adj.* *comparative* **crabbier**, *superlative* **crabbiest** INFORMAL someone who is crabby easily becomes annoyed about unimportant things: *He's very crabby right now because he has a toothache.*

crab·grass /ˈkræbgræs/ *n.* [U] a type of thick, rough grass

crack¹ /kræk/ S2 W3 *v.*

1 BREAK/DAMAGE [I,T] to damage something so that it gets one or more lines on its surface and may eventually break into pieces, or to become damaged in this way: *Don't put boiling water in the glass or it will crack.* | *He fell while skiing and cracked a rib.* ▶see THESAURUS box at **break¹**

2 LOUD SOUND [I,T] to make a sudden quick sound like the sound of something breaking, or to make something do this: *Her stiff joints cracked as she got out of her easy chair.* | *Cowboys cracked their whips as they herded the cattle.*
3 HIT STH [T] **a)** to accidentally hit a part of your body hard, especially your head: **crack sth on/against sth** *Jim cracked his head on the bottom of the bunkbed.* **b)** to hit someone hard on the head with an object: *She* ***cracked*** *him* ***over the head with*** *a hammer.*
4 VOICE [I] if your voice cracks, it changes from one level to another suddenly because of strong emotions: *His voice cracked slightly as he tried to explain.*
5 EGG/NUT [T] to break the outside part of something, such as an egg or a nut, in order to get what is inside it: *He cracked a couple of eggs into a pan.*
6 crack a joke INFORMAL to tell a joke: *He was relaxed and cracking jokes, despite his ordeal.*
7 LOSE CONTROL [I] to lose control of your emotions, become unable to think clearly or behave normally, or tell a secret, because you are very tired, worried, busy etc.: *If I don't get some time off soon, I'll be so stressed I'll crack up.* | *He finally cracked and confessed to the police.* | **crack under the pressure/strain/burden etc.** *Some students crack under the strain.*
8 crack a window to open a window, especially one in a car, a small amount
9 STOP WORKING WELL [I] to be unable to continue doing something or working well because of a serious problem SYN **crack up**: *The Social Security system is cracking.*
10 BECOME SUCCESSFUL [T] to pass a particular level or measure of success in business or a sport: *It's the first time the Spartans have cracked the top 20 in the rankings.*
11 SOLVE [T] to find the answer to a problem or manage to understand something that is difficult to understand SYN **solve**: **crack a problem/code/case** *It took nearly two months to crack the code.* | *This new evidence could help detectives to crack the case.*
12 STOP A GROUP [T] to stop a group of people from doing illegal activities: *Police have* ***cracked*** *a drug* ***ring*** *that was operating in the nightclub.*
13 crack a smile INFORMAL to smile when you have been serious, sad, or angry: *The security guard did not crack a smile.*
14 crack a book also **crack the books** to read or study: *The test is tomorrow and he hasn't even cracked a book yet.*
15 get cracking (on sth) INFORMAL to start doing something or going somewhere as quickly as possible: *I'm going to the library – I've got to get cracking on this paper.*
16 crack (open) a bottle/the champagne etc. INFORMAL to open a bottle of alcohol for drinking: *Let's crack open a bottle to celebrate!*
17 STEAL [T] to open a SAFE illegally, in order to steal what is inside
18 COMPUTER COMPUTERS to illegally copy computer software by finding out how to avoid the protections that are intended to keep you from doing this
19 crack the whip INFORMAL to make people you have control over work very hard: *As editor, Dorothy likes to crack the whip.*

crack down *phr. v.* to become more strict in dealing with a problem and punishing the people involved: **+on** *We have to crack down on software pirates.*
[**Origin:** Old English *cracian*] → see also CRACKDOWN, HACK

crack into sth *phr. v.* to secretly enter someone else's computer system, especially in order to damage the system or steal the information stored on it: *A teenager was accused of cracking into the company's network.*

crack up *phr. v.* INFORMAL **1 crack sb up** to laugh a lot at something, or to make someone laugh a lot: *She tried to keep a straight face, but she kept cracking up.* | *That joke still cracks me up.* → see also CRACKUP **2** INFORMAL to suddenly become mentally ill and unable to continue your normal life: *If I don't get some time off soon, I'll crack up.* **3 sth's not all it's cracked up to be** INFORMAL used to say that something is not as good as people say it is: *The movie was OK, but it's not all it's cracked up to be.* **4** to be unable to continue doing something or working well because of a serious problem: *The whole transit system is cracking up.*

crack[2] S3 *n.*
1 THIN SPACE [C] a very narrow space between two things or two parts of something: **+in** *Weeds grew from every crack in the sidewalk.* | **+between** *a crack between two rocks* | *I crossed the room and* ***opened*** *the door* ***a crack.*** ►see THESAURUS box at **hole**[1]
2 BREAK [C] a thin line on the surface of something when it is broken but has not actually come apart: *The wall was full of cracks.* | **+in** *The cup had a crack in it.*
3 PROBLEM [C] a weakness or fault in an idea, system, organization, relationship etc.: *Cracks began to appear in the facade of their perfect family.* | **+in** *Disagreements over such issues could cause cracks in the coalition.*
4 SOUND [C] a sudden loud very sharp sound like the sound of a stick being broken: *The branch broke with a sudden crack.* | **+of** *a loud crack of thunder*
5 JOKE/REMARK [C] INFORMAL a cruel joke or remark: *Roger* ***made a crack about*** *his girlfriend's weight.*
6 CHANCE TO DO STH [C] INFORMAL an opportunity or attempt to do something, especially for the first time: **+at** *This is Hearst's first crack at painting.* | *You should* ***take another crack at*** *that Camus book.*
7 DRUG also **crack cocaine** [U] a very pure form of the illegal drug COCAINE, that some people smoke for pleasure
8 at the crack of dawn very early in the morning: *They both had to get up at the crack of dawn the next morning.*
9 fall/slip through the cracks if someone or something falls or slips through the cracks, they are not caught or helped by the system that is supposed to catch or help them: *Some kids will slip through the cracks of the educational system.*
10 HIT [singular] a hard hit on a part of the body, especially the head or face: **+on** *a crack on the head*
11 a crack in sb's voice a sudden change in the level of someone's voice, especially because they are very upset: *He noticed the crack in her voice as she tried to continue.*
12 sb's crack SLANG the space in the middle of someone's BUTTOCKS

crack[3] *adj.* [only before noun] having a lot of skill: *She's a* ***crack shot*** (=good at shooting).

'crack ˌbaby *n.* [C] a baby that is born with medical and mental problems because its mother smoked the illegal drug CRACK before the baby was born

crack•down /ˈkrækdaʊn/ *n.* [C usually singular] action that is taken in order to deal more strictly with a problem: **+on** *a major crackdown on drunk driving* → see also **crack down** at CRACK[1]

cracked /krækt/ *adj.* **1** something that is cracked has one or more thin lines on its surface because it has been damaged but not completely broken: *a cracked mirror* | *He suffered cracked ribs and bruising.* **2** someone's voice that is cracked sounds rough and uncontrolled because they are upset **3** [only before noun] cracked pepper, wheat etc. is broken into small pieces

crack•er /ˈkrækɚ/ S2 *n.* [C] **1** a type of hard dry bread that is thin and flat: *cheese and crackers* **2** a FIRECRACKER

crack•er•jack /ˈkrækɚˌdʒæk/ *adj.* having very good qualities or abilities: *a crackerjack police investigator*

crack•head /ˈkrækhɛd/ *n.* [C] SLANG someone who uses the illegal drug CRACK

'crack house *n.* [C] a place where the illegal drug CRACK is sold, bought, and smoked

crack•le /ˈkrækəl/ *v.* [I] to make a repeated short sharp sound like something burning in a fire: *The fire crackled in the fireplace.* | *A voice crackled over the intercom.* —**crackle** *n.* [singular]

crack•ling /ˈkræklɪŋ/ *n.* **1** [singular] the sound made by something when it crackles: *the crackling of paper as someone opened a candy wrapper* **2 cracklings** [plural] pieces of pig skin that have been cooked in oil and are eaten cold SYN **pork rinds**

crack·pot /ˈkrækpɑt/ *adj.* slightly crazy or strange: *one of his crackpot ideas* —**crackpot** *n.* [C]

crack·up, crack-up /ˈkræk-ʌp/ *n.* [C] INFORMAL **1** an accident involving one or more vehicles: *Brian's had a couple of crackups on his motorcycle.* **2** a NERVOUS BREAKDOWN → see also **crack up** at CRACK¹

C

-cracy /krəsi/ *suffix* [in nouns] **1** government by a particular type of people or according to a particular principle: *democracy* (=government by the people) | *bureaucracy* (=government by officials who are not elected) **2** a society or country that is governed in this way, or in which a particular group of people have power: *a theocracy* (=government according to religious laws) **3** the group or type of people who have power in a particular society: *the aristocracy* (=people in the highest social rank) [**Origin:** Old French *-cracie*, from Late Latin *-cratia*, from Greek, from *kratos* **strength, power**] → see also -OCRACY

cra·dle¹ /ˈkreɪdl/ *n.* **1** [C] a small bed for a baby that you can ROCK (=move gently from side to side): *The baby rested peacefully in his cradle.* **2 the cradle of sth** the place where something important began: *Athens is considered the cradle of democracy.* **3 from (the) cradle to (the) grave** all through your life: *He was a Dodgers fan virtually from cradle to grave.* **4** [C] the part of a telephone where you put the RECEIVER (=the part you hold to your ear) when it is not being used **5** [singular] the beginning of something: *He accused critics of trying to strangle the peace plan in its cradle.* | *She'd learned Chinese from the cradle* (=from the time when she was very young). **6** [C] a structure that is used to lift or support something heavy → see also CAT'S CRADLE, **rob the cradle** at ROB (3)

cradle² *v.* [T] **1** to gently hold someone or something in your hands or arms, as if to protect it: *a newborn baby cradled in her mother's arms* | *His arm was cradled in a sling.* **2** to hold a telephone RECEIVER by putting it between your ear and your shoulder

ˈcradle-ˌrobber *n.* [C] someone who has a romantic relationship with someone much younger than they are —**cradle-rob** *v.* [I]

craft¹ /kræft/ *n.* **1** [C] *plural* **crafts** a job or activity in which you make things with your hands, and that you need skill to do: *traditional rural crafts* | *I got these earrings at a craft fair.* | +**of** *the craft of weaving* **2** [singular] the skills needed for a particular profession: *A musician spends years perfecting his craft.* | +**of** *his thoughts on the craft of writing* **3** [C] *plural* **craft** a boat, ship, or airplane: *Search and rescue craft were at the scene of the crash.* **4** [U] skill in deceiving people: *Craft and cunning are necessary for the scheme to work.* → see also LANDING CRAFT [**Origin:** Old English *cræft* **strength, skill**]

craft² *v.* [T usually passive] to make something using a special skill, especially with your hands: *Each bowl is crafted individually.* | *a **hand-crafted** Fabergé egg*

-craft /kræft/ *suffix* [in nouns] **1** a vehicle of a particular kind: *a spacecraft* | *a hovercraft* | *several aircraft* **2** skill of a particular kind: *witchcraft* (=ability to use magic) | *stagecraft* (=skill in acting or directing plays)

crafts·man /ˈkræftsmən/ *n. plural* **craftsmen** /-mən/ [C] someone who is very skilled at a particular craft SYN **artisan**

crafts·man·ship /ˈkræftsmənˌʃɪp/ *n.* [U] **1** very detailed work that has been done using a lot of skill, so that the result is beautiful: *They make jewelry that is famous for its intricate craftsmanship.* **2** the special skill that someone uses to make something beautiful with their hands: *The design is inspired by Russian folk art and craftsmanship.*

crafts·wom·an /ˈkræftsˌwʊmən/ *n. plural* **craftswomen** /-ˌwɪmɪn/ [C] a woman who is very skilled at a particular craft

ˈcraft ˌunion *n.* [C] a LABOR UNION for people who do the same skilled job with their hands

craft·y /ˈkræfti/ *adj. comparative* **craftier**, *superlative* **craftiest** good at getting what you want by planning what to do and secretly deceiving people SYN **cunning** SYN **sly**: *a crafty criminal lawyer* —**craftily** *adv.* —**craftiness** *n.* [U]

crag /kræg/ *n.* [C] EARTH SCIENCE a high and very steep rough rock or mass of rocks

crag·gy /ˈkrægi/ *adj. comparative* **craggier**, *superlative* **craggiest** **1** a mountain that is craggy is very steep and covered in rough rocks: *the craggy peaks of the Sierra Madre* **2** having a face with many deep lines on it: *craggy good looks*

cram /kræm/ *v.* **crammed, cramming** **1** [T always + adv./prep.] to force something into a small space SYN **stuff**: **cram sth into/onto etc.** *I managed to cram all my stuff into the closet.* | **cram sth with sth** *Cars crammed with belongings left the disaster area.* ▸see THESAURUS box at **shove¹** **2** [I,T often passive] if a lot of people cram a place, they go into it and fill it SYN **jam**: *Thousands of people crammed the mall.* | +**into/onto/in** *Two families are crammed into one tiny apartment.* | *We all crammed into Jill's car.* **3** [I] to prepare yourself for a test by learning a lot of information very quickly: *I have a lot of cramming to do.* | **cram for sth** *She's cramming for a chemistry test.*

crammed /kræmd/ *adj.* completely full of things or people SYN **packed**: *crammed classrooms* | *Each kid has a room **crammed full** of toys.* | +**with** *Store aisles were crammed with Christmas shoppers.*

cramp¹ /kræmp/ *n.* **1** [C] MEDICINE a severe pain that you get in part of your body when a muscle becomes too tight, making it difficult for you to move that part of your body: *muscle cramps* | **have/get a cramp** *Johnson got a cramp in his calf.* → see also WRITER'S CRAMP **2 cramps** [plural] MEDICINE severe pains in the stomach, especially the ones that women get during MENSTRUATION [**Origin:** 1300–1400 Old French *crampe*]

cramp² *v.* **1** [I,T] also **cramp up** to get a cramp in a muscle: *His muscles cramped so severely he had to stop playing.* **2** [T] to prevent the development of someone or something SYN **hinder** SYN **restrict**: *Federal guidelines are cramping the state's ability to adjust its own budget.* **3 cramp sb's style** to prevent someone from behaving in the way they want to: *I don't want to take my sister along; she cramps my style.* —**cramping** *n.* [U]

cramped /kræmpt/ *adj.* **1** a cramped room, building etc. does not have enough space for the people in it: *I couldn't sleep on the plane – it was too cramped.* | *a cramped office* | *She grew up in **cramped quarters** in Harlem.* ▸see THESAURUS box at **small¹** **2** also **cramped up** unable to move much and uncomfortable because there is not enough space: *We all felt stiff from having been cramped up in the back of the car for so long.* **3** writing that is cramped is very small and difficult to read

cram·pon /ˈkræmpɑn/ *n.* [C usually plural] a piece of metal with sharp points on the bottom that you fasten onto your boots to help in mountain climbing in the snow

cran·ber·ry /ˈkrænˌbɛri/ *n. plural* **cranberries** [C] BIOLOGY a small red sour fruit: *cranberry sauce* [**Origin:** 1600–1700 Low German *kraanbere*, from *kraan* **crane** + *bere* **berry**; because a part of the flower looks like a crane's beak]

crane¹ /kreɪn/ *n.* [C] **1** a large tall machine used by builders for lifting heavy things **2** BIOLOGY a tall water bird with very long legs

crane² *v.* [I always + adv./prep.,T] to look around or over something by stretching or leaning: +**forward/over etc.** *Curious passengers craned forward to see what was happening.* | **crane your neck** *Parents and children craned their necks to see the parade.*

Crane /kreɪn/, **Hart** /hɑrt/ (1899–1932) a U.S. poet

Crane, Ste·phen /ˈstivən/ (1871–1900) a U.S. writer of NOVELS

cra·ni·um /ˈkreɪniəm/ *n. plural* **craniums** or **crania** /-niə/ [C] BIOLOGY the part of your head that is made of bone and covers your brain —**cranial** *adj.* → see picture at BRAIN[1], SKELETON[1]

crank[1] /kræŋk/ *n.* [C] **1** a handle on a piece of equipment, that you turn in order to move something **2** INFORMAL someone who easily gets angry or annoyed with people SYN **grouch** **3** INFORMAL someone who has unusual ideas and behaves strangely SYN **eccentric**: *It wasn't only cranks who were interested in this idea.*

crank[2] also **crank up** *v.* [T] SPOKEN **1** to make something move by turning a crank: *He cranked the engines, which sprang into life.* **2** to increase the level of sound, heat, cold etc. produced by a machine: *They had it cranked up pretty loud.* | *Don cranked the thermostat to 80.*

crank sth ↔ **out** *phr. v.* INFORMAL to produce a lot of something very quickly SYN **churn out**: *He cranks out two novels a year.*

ˈcrank call *n.* [C] a telephone call intended as a joke or made in order to frighten, annoy, or upset someone

crank·case /ˈkræŋk-keɪs/ *n.* [C] the container that encloses the crankshaft and other parts connected to the crankshaft

crank·shaft /ˈkræŋkʃæft/ *n.* [C] a long piece of metal in a vehicle that is connected to the engine and helps to turn the wheels

crank·y /ˈkræŋki/ *adj. comparative* **crankier**, *superlative* **crankiest** very easily annoyed, especially because you are tired SYN **crabby** SYN **grumpy** SYN **grouchy**: *I was feeling tired and cranky.* | *a cranky old man* [**Origin:** 1700–1800 partly from Old English *cranc*; partly from *crank* **loose, not working properly**] —**crankiness** *n.* [U]

Cran·mer /ˈkrænmɚ/, **Thomas** (1489–1556) an English priest who was the Archbishop of Canterbury and one of the leaders of the REFORMATION (=the start of the Protestant religion) in England

cran·ny /ˈkræni/ *n. plural* **crannies** [C] a small narrow hole in a wall or rock → see also **nook and cranny** at NOOK (2) —**crannied** *adj.*

crash[1] /kræʃ/ S3 *v.*

1 CAR/PLANE ETC. [I,T] to have an accident in a car, airplane etc. by violently hitting another vehicle or something such as a wall or tree: *Witnesses say the jet crashed shortly after takeoff.* | **crash a car/bus/plane etc.** *The tire blew, causing him to crash the car.* | **+into/onto etc.** *Their car hit ice on a bridge and crashed into the side rail.*

2 HIT SB/STH HARD [I always + adv./prep.,T always + adv./prep.] to hit someone or something extremely hard while moving, in a way that causes a lot of damage or makes a lot of noise: **+into/through etc.** *Suddenly, a baseball crashed through our window.* | *The plates* ***went crashing*** *to the floor.* | *A large branch* ***came crashing down.***

3 COMPUTER [I,T] COMPUTERS if a computer crashes or if someone or something crashes it, it suddenly stops working: *The system crashed and I lost three hours' worth of work.*

4 FINANCIAL [I] ECONOMICS if a STOCK MARKET crashes, the STOCKS suddenly lose a lot of value

5 SLEEP [I] SPOKEN **a)** to stay at someone's house for the night, especially when you have not planned to: *You can crash at our place if you can't get a ride home.* **b)** also **crash out** to go to bed, or to go to sleep very quickly, because you are very tired: *I crashed out on the sofa this afternoon.*

6 crash and burn INFORMAL to suddenly fail badly: *Her movie career crashed and burned in the late '90s.*

7 PARTY INFORMAL [T] to go to a party that you have not been invited to: *We crashed Stella's party last Friday.*

8 MAKE A LOUD NOISE [I] to make a sudden, loud noise: *The cymbals crashed, and the symphony came to an end.*

crash down *phr. v.* **come crashing down a)** if someone's hopes, plans etc. come crashing down, they fail in a sudden way: *If he doesn't do well in this primary election, his presidential campaign will come crashing down.* **b)** if a system or organization comes crashing down, it fails suddenly and completely: *He believed Stalin wanted the European economy to come crashing down.*

crash[2] W3 *n.* [C] **1** a very bad accident involving cars, airplanes etc. that have hit something SYN **collision**: *Both drivers were injured in the crash.* | **a plane/car/bus etc. crash** *a serious plane crash killing 350 people* | *a* ***fatal crash*** *during the race* | **crash victim/scene/investigation etc.** *Crash victims were taken to local hospitals.* ►see THESAURUS box at **accident** **2** COMPUTERS an occasion when a computer or computer system suddenly stops working **3** ECONOMICS an occasion on which the STOCKS in a STOCK MARKET suddenly lose a lot of value: *the stock-market crash of 1987* ►see THESAURUS box at **recession** **4** a sudden loud noise made by something falling, breaking etc.: *The pile of books came down* ***with a crash.*** | **+of** *a crash of thunder*

ˈcrash course *n.* [C] a course in which you learn the most important things about a particular subject in a very short period of time: **+in** *a crash course in Japanese*

ˈcrash ˌdiet *n.* [C] an attempt to lose a lot of weight quickly by strictly limiting how much you eat

ˈcrash ˌhelmet *n.* [C] a hard hat that covers and protects your head, worn by race car drivers, people on MOTORCYCLES etc.

ˌcrash ˈlanding *n.* [C] an occasion when a pilot has to fly an airplane down to the ground in a rougher and more dangerous way than usual because the plane has a problem: *He was forced to* ***make a crash landing*** *in the middle of the desert.*

crass /kræs/ *adj.* crass behavior or things are stupid and offensive, because they show that someone does not care about other people's feelings or does not know what is truly important SYN **crude**: *a crass remark* | *the crass commercialism of many hit movies* [**Origin:** 1400–1500 Latin *crassus* **thick, fat, coarse**] —**crassly** *adv.*

-crat /kræt/ *suffix* [in nouns] **1** a believer in a particular type or principle of government: *a democrat* (=who believes in government by the people) **2** a member of a powerful or governing social class or group: *an aristocrat* (=member of the highest social class) → see also -OCRAT

crate[1] /kreɪt/ *n.* [C] **1** a large wooden or plastic box used for moving things from one place to another or for storing them SYN **box**: *a big plastic crate for storing toys* | **+of** *a crate of beer* → see picture at BOX[1] **2** OLD-FASHIONED a very old car or airplane that does not work very well [**Origin:** 1300–1400 Latin *cratis* **framework of thin woven branches**]

crate[2] also **crate up** *v.* [T] to pack things into a crate

cra·ter /ˈkreɪt̬ɚ/ *n.* [C] **1** a round hole in the ground made by something that has fallen on it or exploded on it: *craters on the moon's surface* | *bomb craters* ►see THESAURUS box at **hole[1]** **2** EARTH SCIENCE the round open top of a VOLCANO [**Origin:** 1600–1700 Latin **bowl for mixing things, crater**, from Greek *krater*, from *kerannynai* **to mix**]

ˈcrater lake *n.* [C] EARTH SCIENCE a large area of water that forms inside the round open top of a VOLCANO that has not ERUPTed for a very long time → see picture on p. 372

cra·vat /krəˈvæt/ *n.* [C] **1** FORMAL a TIE **2** a wide piece of loosely folded material that men wear around their necks SYN **ascot** [**Origin:** 1600–1700 French *cravate*, from *Cravate* **Croatian**; from the scarves worn by 17th-century Croatian soldiers]

crave /kreɪv/ *v.* [T] to have an extremely strong desire for something: *Most little kids crave attention.*

cra·ven /ˈkreɪvən/ *adj.* FORMAL completely lacking courage SYN **cowardly** —**cravenly** *adv.* —**cravenness** *n.* [U]

crav·ing /ˈkreɪvɪŋ/ *n.* [C] an extremely strong desire for something: **+for** *a craving for chocolate*

craw /krɔ/ *n.* [C] → see **stick in sb's craw** at STICK[1] (8)

C

crater lake

craw·dad /ˈkrɔdæd/ also **craw·fish** /ˈkrɔˌfɪʃ/ *n.* [C] INFORMAL a CRAYFISH

crawl¹ /krɔl/ S2 *v.* [I] **1** to move along on your hands and knees or with your body close to the ground: *When did Sam start crawling?* | **+along/through/across etc.** *We had to crawl through a short tunnel to get to the cave.* **2** if an insect crawls, it moves using its legs: **+over/up etc.** *There's an ant crawling up your leg!* **3** if a vehicle crawls, it moves forward very slowly: **+along/by etc.** *The car crawled along the rutted dirt roads.* **4 crawl into/out of bed** to get into or out of bed slowly, because you are very tired: *Mark finally crawled into bed at two in the morning.* **5 be crawling with sth** to be completely covered with insects, people etc.: *The apartments were crawling with rats and fleas.* **6 crawl the Net/Web** if a computer program crawls the Internet, it quickly searches the Internet to find the particular information you need → SPIDER **7 come crawling (back to sb)** INFORMAL to admit that you were wrong and ask for something that you refused to accept in the past: *In a few months, he'll come crawling back, wanting his old job.* [**Origin:** 1300–1400 Old Norse *krafla*] → see also **make sb's skin crawl** at SKIN¹ (9)

crawl² *n.* **1** [singular] a very slow speed: *Traffic has slowed to a crawl.* **2 the crawl** a way of swimming in which you lie on your stomach and move one arm and then the other over your head

cray·fish /ˈkreɪˌfɪʃ/ *n. plural* **crayfish** [C,U] a small animal like a LOBSTER that lives in rivers and streams, or the meat from this animal → see picture at CRUSTACEAN

cray·on /ˈkreɪɑn, -ən/ *n.* [C] a stick of colored WAX that children use to draw pictures [**Origin:** 1600–1700 French *craie* **chalk**]

craze /kreɪz/ *n.* [C] a fashion, game, type of music etc. that becomes very popular for a short amount of time: *a new dance craze* | **+for** *the craze for dying your hair red*

crazed /kreɪzd/ *adj.* [no comparative] behaving in a wild and uncontrolled way, like someone who is mentally ill: *a crazed gunman* | **+with** *He was crazed with fear and pain.* [**Origin:** 1500–1600 *craze* **to make crazy** (15–19 centuries), from *craze* **to crack, crush** (14–20 centuries), from a Scandinavian language]

-crazed /kreɪzd/ [in adjectives] **sex-crazed/sports-crazed/drug-crazed etc.** too interested in sex, sports etc.: *fashion-crazed young women*

cra·zy¹ /ˈkreɪzi/ S1 W2 *adj. comparative* **crazier**, *superlative* **craziest** INFORMAL

1 STRANGE very strange or not sensible SYN **nuts**: *You must think I'm crazy.* | *a couple of crazy kids* | *Whose crazy idea was this?* | **be crazy to do sth** *It'd be crazy to try to drive home in this weather.* | *his* ***wild and crazy*** *college years* | *He often works 12 hours a day –* ***it's crazy.***

2 be crazy about sb/sth to like someone very much, or to be very interested in something: *My sister's crazy about scuba diving.*

3 ANGRY angry or annoyed SYN **nuts**: *Be quiet! You're* ***driving me crazy!*** (=really annoying me) | *Dad's going to* ***go crazy*** (=be very angry) *when he hears about this.*

4 like crazy very much or very quickly: *These mosquito bites are itching like crazy.* | *We ran like crazy to the bus stop.*

5 go crazy to do something too much, in a way that is not usual or not sensible, especially because you are excited: *Don't go crazy and spend it all at once.*

6 MENTALLY ILL mentally ill SYN **insane**: *I feel so alone, sometimes I wonder if I'm* ***going crazy.*** | *She was* ***acting crazy,*** *and we were worried.*

THESAURUS

mentally ill having an illness of the mind that affects the way you behave: *a hospital for people who are mentally ill and cannot care for themselves*
insane permanently and seriously mentally ill: *He was judged to be insane at the time he committed the murders.*
disturbed not behaving in a normal way because of mental or emotional problems: *emotionally disturbed children*
nuts INFORMAL crazy: *He looked at me like I was nuts.*
loony INFORMAL crazy: *De Niro plays a loony baseball fan stalking his favorite player.*
psychotic having a serious mental illness: *psychotic behavior*
unstable if someone is unstable, their emotional state often changes very suddenly: *Her mother was mentally unstable.*

7 boy/girl crazy a phrase meaning too interested in having romantic relationships with boys or girls, usually used about young people: *Stacy is 16 and completely boy crazy.*

8 crazy as a loon very strange and possibly mentally ill —**crazily** *adv.* —**craziness** *n.* [U]

crazy² *n. plural* **crazies** [C] INFORMAL someone who is crazy

ˈCrazy ˌHorse (?1849–1877) a Native American chief of the Sioux tribe, famous for helping Sitting Bull to win a victory over General Custer's army at the Little Bighorn

Crazy Horse

ˌcrazy ˈquilt *n.* [C] **1** a cover for a bed made from small pieces of cloth of different shapes and colors that have been sewn together **2 a crazy quilt of sth a)** several different kinds of things that form an unusual pattern together: *The fields formed a crazy quilt of green and brown.* **b)** several different methods, styles, laws etc. that are used together or exist together, especially in a confusing way: *What we have now is a crazy quilt of state insurance regulations.*

creak /krik/ *v.* [I] if something such as a door, wooden floor etc. creaks, it makes a long high noise when someone opens it, walks on it, sits on it etc.: *The floorboards creaked as she walked.* [**Origin:** 1300–1400 from the sound] —**creak** *n.* [C]

creak·y /ˈkriki/ *adj. comparative* **creakier**, *superlative* **creakiest 1** something such as a door, floor, or bed that is creaky creaks when you open it, walk on it, sit on it etc., especially because it is old and not in good condition **2** an organization, company etc. that is creaky uses old-fashioned methods or ideas and does not work very well: *a creaky national telephone system* —**creakily** *adv.* —**creakiness** *n.* [U]

cream¹ /krim/ S2 *n.* **1** [U] a thick yellow-white liquid that rises to the top of milk: *cream in your coffee* → see also SOUR CREAM, WHIPPED CREAM **2** [U] a pale yellow-white color **3** [C,U] used in the names of foods containing cream or something similar to it: *cream of chicken soup* | *banana cream pie* **4** [C,U] a thick smooth substance that you put on your skin to make it feel soft, treat a medical condition etc. SYN **lotion**: *cream for a rash* **5 the cream of the crop** the best people or things in a particular group: *These students represent the cream of the academic crop.* [**Origin:** 1300–1400 Old French *craime, cresme*, from Latin *cramum*]

cream² S3 *v.* [T] **1** INFORMAL to hit someone very hard or easily defeat someone in a game, competition etc.: *The Cougars creamed us last Saturday.* | *We **got creamed** 45-6.* ▶see THESAURUS box at **beat¹** **2** to mix foods together until they become a thick smooth mixture: *Next, cream the butter and sugar.* **3** to take cream from the surface of milk

cream sb/sth ↔ **off** *phr. v.* to choose the best people or things from a group, especially so that you can use them for your own advantage: *Most of the best students are creamed off by the large companies.*

ˈcream cheese *n.* [U] a type of soft white smooth cheese

ˈcream-ˌcolored *adj.* yellow-white in color

cream•er /ˈkrimɚ/ *n.* **1** [U] a white liquid or powder that you can use instead of milk or cream in coffee or tea **2** [C] a small container for holding cream

cream•er•y /ˈkriməri/ *n. plural* **creameries** [C] OLD-FASHIONED a place where milk, butter, cream, and cheese are produced or sold SYN **dairy**

ˌcream of ˈtartar *n.* [U] a white powder used in baking and in medicine

ˈcream puff *n.* [C] a light small sweet cake with WHIPPED cream inside

cream•y /ˈkrimi/ *adj. comparative* **creamier**, *superlative* **creamiest** **1** thick and smooth like cream: *creamy peanut butter* **2** containing cream: *fresh creamy milk* **3** yellow-white in color

crease¹ /kris/ *n.* [C] **1** a line on a piece of cloth, paper etc. where it has been folded, crushed, or pressed SYN **wrinkle**: *a crease in your skirt* **2** a fold in someone's skin SYN **wrinkle**

crease² *v.* [I,T] to become marked with a line or lines, or to make a line appear on cloth, paper etc. by folding or crushing it SYN **wrinkle**: *Linen creases easily.* | *A frown creased her forehead.*

cre•ate /kriˈeɪt/ Ac S1 W1 *v.* [T] **1** to make something exist that did not exist before: *Some people believe the universe was created by a big explosion.* | *The development should create 300 jobs.* | *It may create more problems than it solves.* ▶see THESAURUS box at **make¹** **2** to invent or design something: *The software makes it easy to create colorful charts and graphs.* | *The pen pal program was created by teacher Cindy Lee.* [**Origin:** 1300–1400 Latin, past participle of *creare*] ▶see THESAURUS box at **invent**

cre•a•tion /kriˈeɪʃən/ Ac W3 *n.* **1** [U] the act of creating something: +**of** *the creation of the committee to study the issue* | *a **job creation** program* **2** [U] the whole universe and all living things: *Are we the only thinking species in creation?* **3** [C] something new that has been made or invented: *his latest fashion creation* **4 the Creation** the act by God of making the universe and everything in it, according to the Bible

cre•a•tion•ism /kriˈeɪʃəˌnɪzəm/ *n.* [C] the belief that God created the universe in the way that is described in the Bible —**creationist** *n.* [C] —**creationist** *adj.*

creˈation ˌscience *n.* [U] a subject taught in some schools that is based on the idea that creationism can be proven scientifically

cre•a•tive¹ /kriˈeɪtɪv/ Ac S3 W3 *adj.* **1** involving the use of imagination to produce new ideas or things: *I enjoy my job, but I'd like to do something more creative.* | *creative architectural designs* | *a **creative writing** course* | *Failure is part of the **creative process**.* | *a **creative solution** to the problem* **2** someone who is creative is very good at using their imagination and skills to make things SYN **inventive**: *a creative young writer* **3 creative accounting** the act of changing business accounts to achieve the result you want in a way that hides the truth, but is not illegal —**creatively** *adv.* —**creativeness** *n.* [U]

creative² Ac *n.* [C] SLANG someone such as a writer or artist who uses their imagination or skills to make things

cre•a•tiv•i•ty /ˌkrieɪˈtɪvəṭi/ Ac *n.* [U] the ability to use your imagination to produce or use new ideas, make things etc.: *Companies need to encourage creativity and innovation.*

cre•a•tor /kriˈeɪṭɚ/ Ac *n.* **1** [C] someone who made or invented a particular thing: +**of** *Walt Disney was the creator of Mickey Mouse.* **2 the Creator** God

crea•ture /ˈkritʃɚ/ S3 W3 *n.*

1 LIVING THING [C] BIOLOGY anything that is living, such as an animal, fish, or insect, but not a plant: *a fossil of a small, sparrow-like creature* | *creatures of the deep* (=animals and fish that live in the ocean) | *Native Americans believe that all **living creatures** should be respected.*

2 IMAGINARY OR STRANGE [C] an imaginary animal or person, or one that is very strange and sometimes frightening: *creatures from outer space*

3 a creature of sth someone who is a creature of something is influenced by it a lot, controlled by it, or has a quality produced by it: *Mimi is a creature of Hollywood, an aspiring actress.*

4 STH MADE OR INVENTED [C] something, especially something bad, that has been made or invented by a particular person or organization: **a creature of sth** *The Housing Board was a creature of the mayor's design.* | *a creature of his imagination*

5 KIND OF PERSON someone who has a particular character or quality: **stupid/adorable/horrid etc. creature** *Get away from me, you horrid creature!* | *We are **creatures of habit*** (=someone who always does things in the same way or at the same time) *who are suspicious of change.*

[**Origin:** 1200–1300 Old French, Late Latin *creatura*, from Latin *creare*]

ˌcreature ˈcomforts *n.* [plural] all the things that people need to feel comfortable, such as good food, a warm house, and comfortable furniture

crèche /krɛʃ/ *n.* [C] a model of the scene of Jesus Christ's birth, often placed in churches and homes at Christmas [**Origin:** 1700–1800 French **bed for a baby**]

cre•dence /ˈkridns/ *n.* [U] FORMAL the acceptance of something as true: *His ideas quickly **gained credence*** (=started to be believed) *among economists.* | *I don't **give** any **credence*** (=believe or accept something as true) *to these rumors.* | *The DNA results **lend credence*** (=make something more believable) *to his claim of innocence.*

cre•den•tial /krɪˈdɛnʃəl/ *n.* [C] **1** something, especially a document, that shows you have earned a particular position or are legally allowed to do a particular job: *a teaching credential* **2 credentials** [plural] **a)** someone's education, achievements, experience etc., that prove that they have the ability to do something: *His **academic credentials** include a Ph.D. from MIT.* | +**as** *her credentials as a political activist* | +**for** *He had excellent credentials for the presidency.* **b)** a letter or other document that proves your good character or your right to have a particular position: *The commissioner presented his credentials to the State Department.* | *His **press credentials** were pinned to his coat.*

cre•den•za /krəˈdɛnzə/ *n.* [C] a piece of furniture like a long low set of shelves with doors on the front, used for storing things, especially in offices

cred•i•bil•i•ty /ˌkrɛdəˈbɪləṭi/ *n.* [U] **1** the quality of deserving to be believed and trusted: +**as** *The scandal ruined his credibility as a leader.* | +**of** *There are questions about the credibility of these reports.* | **gain/lose credibility** *Harris has lost credibility among his colleagues.* **2 a/the credibility gap** the difference between what someone, especially a politician, says and what people can believe

cred•i•ble /ˈkrɛdəbəl/ *adj.* deserving or able to be believed or trusted SYN **believable**: *Is she a credible*

C

witness? | *a credible threat of sanctions against the country* —**credibly** *adv.*

cred·it¹ /ˈkrɛdɪt/ Ac S1 W2 *n.*
1 DELAYED PAYMENT [U] ECONOMICS an arrangement with a store, bank etc. that allows you to buy something and pay for it later: *We bought a new stove* ***on credit*** (=using credit). | *One store offers six months of* ***interest-free credit*** (=credit with no INTEREST charges). | *a company with a* ***credit line*** (=the amount of credit they are allowed to have) *of $250,000*
2 AMOUNT OF MONEY [C] an amount of money that is put into someone's bank account or added to another amount → see also DEBIT: *Customers who were charged too much will get a credit.* | *a* ***tax credit*** *for research and development*
3 PRAISE [U] approval or praise for doing something good: +**for** *The* ***credit*** *for the team's winning season* ***goes to*** *the coach.* | *They never* ***give*** *Gene any* ***credit*** *for all the extra work he does.* | *If the economy improves, the White House will* ***take credit*** *for it.* | ***To*** *Navarro's* ***credit***, *he remained calm.* | *The kids themselves* ***deserve*** *a lot of* ***credit*** *for the success of the program.*
4 in credit to have money in your bank account
5 the credits [plural] a list of all the people involved in making a television program or movie, usually shown at the end of it
6 be a credit to sb/sth also **do sb/sth credit** to be so successful or good that everyone who is connected with you can be proud of you: *Jo's a credit to her profession.*
7 UNIVERSITY [C] a unit that shows you have successfully completed part of your studies at a school or college: *I don't have enough credits to graduate.* | *a four-credit class*
8 RESPONSIBILITY FOR DOING STH [U] the responsibility for achieving or doing something good: *She already* ***has*** *two best-selling novels* ***to her credit***. | *Two companies have* ***claimed credit*** *for inventing the microprocessor.*
9 TRUE/CORRECT [U] the belief that something is true or correct: *The witness's story* ***gained credit*** *with the jury.*
10 a credit report/statement a document that gives details of whether someone has been responsible about paying for anything they have bought using credit
[**Origin:** 1500–1600 French *crédit*, from Italian, from Latin *creditum* **something given to someone to keep safe, loan**]

credit² Ac *v.* [T not in progressive] **1** to add money to a bank account: +**with** *For some reason, my account's been credited with an extra $76.* | +**to** *The check has been credited to your account.* → see also DEBIT **2 credit sb with sth** to believe or admit that someone has a particular quality, or has done something good: *I wouldn't have credited him with that much intelligence.* **3 be credited to sb/sth** if something is credited to someone or something, they have achieved it or are the reason for it: *The new drug is widely credited to Kessler.* **4** FORMAL to believe that something is true: *His statements are* ***hard to credit***.

cred·it·a·ble /ˈkrɛdɪtəbəl/ *adj.* [only before noun] deserving praise or approval: *a creditable job* —**creditably** *adv.*

ˈcredit ˌbureau *n.* [C] ECONOMICS an organization that collects and sells information about the money people have borrowed and whether they have paid it back. Credit bureaus sell this information to banks and other financial institutions that lend money.

ˈcredit card S2 *n.* [C] a small plastic card that you use to buy goods or services and pay for them later: *We accept all major credit cards.* → see also DEBIT CARD

ˈcredit ˌhistory *n.* [C] someone's credit history says whether they have made regular payments for things they have bought using credit

ˈcredit ˌlimit *n.* [C] the amount of money that you are allowed to borrow or spend using your credit card

cred·i·tor /ˈkrɛdətə/ Ac *n.* [C] ECONOMICS a person, bank, or company that you owe money to → see also DEBTOR

ˈcreditor ˌnation *n.* [C] TECHNICAL a country that has INVESTED in or lent more money to other countries than other countries have INVESTED in or lent to it → see also DEBTOR NATION

ˈcredit ˌrating *n.* [C] ECONOMICS a judgment made by a bank or other company about how likely a person or business is to pay their debts

ˈcredit ˌunion *n.* [C] a business similar to a bank that is owned by the people who save money in it, and that also lends money to them for things such as cars or houses

cred·it·wor·thy /ˈkrɛdɪtˌwəði/ *adj.* ECONOMICS considered to be able to pay debts —**creditworthiness** *n.* [U]

cre·do /ˈkridoʊ/ *n. plural* **credos** [C] a short formal statement of the beliefs of a particular person, group, religion etc.

cre·du·li·ty /krɪˈduləti/ *n.* [U] FORMAL willingness or ability to believe that something is true: **stretch/strain credulity** (=seem very hard to believe) *Some parts of his testimony stretch credulity.*

cred·u·lous /ˈkrɛdʒələs/ *adj.* FORMAL always believing what you are told, and therefore easily deceived SYN **gullible**: *Quinn charmed credulous investors out of millions of dollars.* —**credulously** *adv.* —**credulousness** *n.* [U]

Cree /kri/ *n.* a Native American tribe from the northern region of the U.S. and from Canada

creed /krid/ *n.* [C] **1** a set of beliefs or principles, especially religious ones: *There were people* ***of every creed*** (=of all different religious beliefs) *and color.* ►see THESAURUS box at **faith**, **religion** **2 the Creed** a formal statement of belief spoken in some Christian churches

Creek /krik/ *n.* a Native American tribe from the southeastern region of the U.S.

creek /krik, krɪk/ *n.* [C] **1** a small narrow stream or river **2 be up the creek (without a paddle)** SPOKEN to be in a very difficult situation: *I'll really be up the creek if I don't get paid this week.*

creel /kril/ *n.* [C] a FISHERMAN's basket for carrying fish

creep¹ /krip/ *v. past tense and past participle* **crept** /krɛpt/ [I always + adv./prep.]
1 MOVE QUIETLY to move in a quiet, careful way, especially to avoid attracting attention: +**into/over/around etc.** *John crept up the stairs.*
2 MOVE SLOWLY if something such as an insect, small animal, or car creeps, it moves slowly and quietly: +**down/along/away etc.** *We crept along at 25 mph.*
3 CHANGE SLOWLY if prices, rates, levels etc. creep up or down, they slowly change from one price etc. to another: +**up/down** *The unemployment rate crept up to 5.7% in May.*
4 GRADUALLY OCCUR to gradually begin to appear or happen in something and change it: +**in/into/over etc.** *Bitterness crept into his voice.* | *Some English words have crept into Italian.*
5 PLANTS if a plant creeps, it grows or climbs up or along a particular place: +**up/over/around etc.** *All of the buildings have ivy creeping up their walls.*
6 MIST/CLOUDS ETC. LITERARY if mist, clouds etc. creep, they gradually fill or cover a place: +**into/over etc.** *Fog was creeping into the valley.*
7 make sb's flesh creep to make someone feel strong dislike or fear: *His touch made my flesh creep.*

creep up on sb/sth *phr. v.* **1** to surprise someone by walking up behind them silently: *Don't creep up on me like that!* **2** if something creeps up on you, it gradually increases without you noticing it for a long time: *Tiredness can creep up on you when you're stressed.* **3** to seem to come sooner than you expect: *Old age was creeping up on me.*

creep² *n.* SPOKEN **1** [C] someone you dislike a lot: *Get lost, you little creep!* **2 give sb the creeps** if a person or place gives you the creeps, they make you feel nervous and a little frightened, especially because they are strange: *Tony gives me the creeps.*

creep·er /ˈkripə/ *n.* [U] a plant that grows up trees or walls, or along the ground

creep·y /ˈkripi/ *adj.* *comparative* **creepier**, *superlative* **creepiest** making you feel nervous and a little frightened: *There's something creepy about the building.*

ˌcreepy ˈcrawly *n. plural* **creepy crawlies** [C] SPOKEN a word meaning an "insect," especially one that you are frightened of, used especially by children

cre·mains /krɪˈmeɪnz/ *n.* [plural] what is left of a dead person's body after it has been CREMATED (=burned)

cre·mate /ˈkrimeɪt, krɪˈmeɪt/ *v.* [T] to burn the body of a dead person after a funeral —**cremation** /krɪˈmeɪʃən/ *n.* [C,U]

cre·ma·to·ri·um /ˌkriməˈtɔriəm/ also **cre·ma·to·ry** /ˈkriməˌtɔri, ˈkrɛm-/ *n. plural* **crematoriums** or **crematoria** /-riə/ [C] a building in which the bodies of dead people are burned after a funeral

crème de la crème, **creme de la creme** /ˌkrɛm də lɑ ˈkrɛm, -lə-/ *n.* [singular] the very best of a type of thing or group of people: *Tokyo University is the crème de la crème of Japanese universities.*

crème de menthe /ˌkrɛm də ˈmɛnθ/ *n.* [U] a strong sweet green alcoholic drink

cren·e·lat·ed /ˈkrɛnlˌeɪtɪd/ *adj.* TECHNICAL a wall or tower that is crenelated has BATTLEMENTS

Cre·ole /ˈkrioʊl/ *n.* **1** [C,U] a language that is a combination of a European language and one or more other languages → see also PIDGIN **2 a)** someone who has some ANCESTORS (=early family members) who came from France or Spain and some who came from Africa **b)** someone living in the southern states around the Gulf of Mexico whose ANCESTORS were either French or Spanish **c)** someone living in the West Indies or Spanish-speaking America whose ANCESTORS were European

cre·ole /ˈkrioʊl/ *adj.* **1** relating to Creoles or their languages **2** creole food is prepared in the SPICY strong-tasting style of the states in the south on the coast of the Gulf of Mexico, especially Louisiana: *shrimp creole* [**Origin:** 1700–1800 French *créole*, from Spanish, from Portuguese *crioulo* **black person born in Brazil, home-born slave**, from *criar* **to breed**]

cre·o·sote /ˈkriəˌsoʊt/ *n.* [U] a thick, brown, oily liquid used for preserving wood [**Origin:** 1800–1900 German *kreosot*, from Greek *kreas* **flesh** + *soter* **preserver**; because it was used as an antiseptic] —**creosote** *v.* [T]

crepe, **crêpe** /kreɪp/ *n.* **1** [U] a type of light soft thin cloth with very small folded lines on its surface, made from cotton, silk, wool, etc. **2** [C] a very thin PANCAKE **3** [U] tightly pressed rubber used especially for making the bottoms of shoes

ˈcrepe ˌpaper *n.* [U] thin brightly colored paper with very small folded lines on its surface, used especially as a decoration at parties

crept /krɛpt/ *v.* [I always + adv./prep.] the past tense and past participle of CREEP

cre·scen·do /krəˈʃɛndoʊ/ *n. plural* **crescendos** [C] **1** ENG. LANG. ARTS if a sound or a piece of music rises to a crescendo, it gradually becomes louder OPP **diminuendo**: *The violins had* ***reached a crescendo****.* | *The shouting* ***rose to a crescendo****.* **2** LITERARY if an activity or feeling reaches a crescendo, it gradually becomes stronger until it is very strong: *a crescendo of excitement* —**crescendo** *adj.*

cres·cent /ˈkrɛsənt/ *n.* [C] **1** a curved shape that is wider in the middle and pointed on the ends: *a crescent moon* **2** this curved shape as a sign of the Muslim religion [**Origin:** 1300–1400 Old French *creissant*, from *creistre* **to grow, increase**, from Latin *crescere*]

cress /krɛs/ *n.* [U] a small plant with round green leaves that can be eaten and has a slightly SPICY taste

crest[1] /krɛst/ *n.* **1** [C usually singular] the top or highest point of something such as a hill or a wave: *the Pacific Crest Trail* | +**of** *the foam on the crest of the waves* **2 be on/riding the crest of sth** to be very successful, happy etc., especially for a limited period of time: *Minnesota is riding the crest of a six-game winning streak.* | *The President is* ***on the crest of a wave of*** *popularity.* **3** [C] BIOLOGY a pointed group of feathers on top of a bird's head **4** [C] a special picture used as a sign of a family, town, school etc.: *writing paper with the family crest* **5** [C] a decoration of bright feathers, worn, especially in past times, on top of soldiers' HELMETS

crest[2] *v.* **1** [I] if a wave, flood etc. crests, it reaches its highest point before it falls **2** [T] FORMAL to reach the top of a hill, mountain etc.

crest·ed /ˈkrɛstɪd/ *adj.* [only before noun] **1** BIOLOGY having a crest: *a red-crested cockatoo* **2** marked by a crest: *a crested navy blue jacket*

C

crest·fall·en /ˈkrɛstˌfɔlən/ *adj.* disappointed and sad, especially because you have failed to do something SYN **dejected**: *He came back looking crestfallen.*

cre·ta·ceous /krɪˈteɪʃəs/ *adj.* TECHNICAL **1** similar to CHALK or containing CHALK **2 the Cretaceous period** the time when rocks containing CHALK were formed

Crete /krit/ the largest island belonging to Greece, in the southeast Mediterranean Sea

cre·tin /ˈkritˀn/ *n.* [C] OFFENSIVE someone who is extremely stupid

cre·vasse /krəˈvæs/ *n.* [C] EARTH SCIENCE a deep wide crack, especially in thick ice

crev·ice /ˈkrɛvɪs/ *n.* [C] EARTH SCIENCE a narrow crack, especially in rock

crew[1] /kru/ S2 W2 *n.* **1** [C] all the people that work together on a ship, airplane etc.: *the crew of the space shuttle* ►see THESAURUS box at **group**[1] **2** [C] all the people, except the most important officers, who work on a ship, airplane etc., especially a military one: *I'd like to thank you on behalf of the officers and crew.* **3** [C] a group of people with special skills who work together on something: *the movie's cast and crew* → see also GROUND CREW **4** [singular] a group of people: *a happy crew of foreign students* → see also **a motley crew/bunch/crowd etc.** at MOTLEY (1) **5** [C] a team of people who compete in ROWING races: *the Boston College crew* **6** [U] the sport of rowing a boat in races: *He tried out for crew.* **7** [C] a group of musicians, especially in GARAGE music [**Origin:** 1500–1600 *crew* **additional soldiers, reinforcements** (15–16 centuries), from Old French *creue* **increase**, from *creistre*]

crew[2] *v.* [I,T] to be part of the crew on a boat: *a boat crewed by women*

ˈcrew cut *n.* [C] a very short hair style for men → see picture at HAIRSTYLE

crew·man /ˈkrumən/ *n. plural* **crewmen** /-mən/ [C] a member, especially a male member, of a CREW

ˈcrew ˌmember *n.* [C] a member of a CREW

ˈcrew neck *n.* [C] a plain round neck on a SWEATER → see also V-NECK

ˈcrew sock *n.* [C usually plural] a type of sock that is short, thick, and is RIBBED (=having a pattern of raised lines) above the ankle

crib[1] /krɪb/ *n.* [C] **1** a bed for a baby or young child, with bars on the sides to keep the baby from falling out **2** SLANG the place where someone lives **3** an open box or wooden frame holding food for animals SYN **manger**

crib[2] *v.* **cribbed**, **cribbing** [I,T] to copy something from someone else, sometimes dishonestly SYN **copy**: **crib sth from sb** *a phrase cribbed from Thomas Jefferson* [**Origin:** 1700–1800 *crib* **to steal from a basket**]

crib·bage /ˈkrɪbɪdʒ/ *n.* [U] a card game in which points are shown by putting small pieces of wood in holes in a small board

ˈcrib death *n.* [C] the sudden and unexpected death of a baby while it is asleep SYN **Sudden Infant Death Syndrome**

ˈcrib note also **ˈcrib sheet** *n.* [C] INFORMAL something on which answers to questions are written, usually used in order to cheat on a test

crick[1] /krɪk/ *n.* [C] a sudden painful stiffening of the muscles, especially in the back or the neck: +**in** *I woke up with a crick in my neck.*

crick² *v.* [T] to do something that produces a crick in your back or neck

Crick /krɪk/, **Fran·cis** /'frænsɪs/ (1916–2004) a British scientist who worked with James Watson, and discovered the structure of DNA, the substance that carries GENETIC information in the cells of plants, animals, and humans

C

crick·et /'krɪkɪt/ *n.* **1** [C] BIOLOGY a small brown jumping insect that makes a short loud noise by rubbing its wings together **2** [U] an outdoor game between two teams of 11 players, in which players try to get points by hitting a ball and running between two sets of special sticks [**Origin:** (2) 1500–1600 Old French *criquet*, **stick at which a ball is thrown**]

crime /kraɪm/ W1 *n.*
1 CRIME IN GENERAL [U] illegal activity in general: *Cedar Rapids has very little crime.* | *a fast-growing* ***crime rate*** (=the amount of crime in a society) | *Older people* ***commit*** *less* ***crime.*** | ***Violent crime*** *is increasing.* | *Police are cracking down on* ***juvenile crime*** (=crime caused by young people). | *his ideas for* ***fighting crime*** (=preventing or stopping it) | *the recent* ***crime wave*** (=a sudden increase in the amount of crime) | **soft/tough on crime** (=punishing or not punishing crime severely) *The Republican candidate accused his opponent of being soft on crime.* | *Kids in poor neighborhoods often* ***turn to crime*** (=start doing illegal things). → see also **(a) petty crime** at PETTY (3)

THESAURUS

Crimes that involve stealing things
theft the crime of stealing things: *car theft*
robbery the crime of stealing money or valuable things from a bank, store etc.
burglary the crime of going into someone's home in order to steal money or valuable things
larceny a formal word referring to the crime of stealing something
shoplifting the crime of taking things from a store without paying for them
Crimes that involve attacking people
assault a crime in which someone is physically attacked
mugging a crime in which someone is attacked and robbed in a public place
rape a crime in which someone is forced to have sex
murder a crime in which someone is deliberately killed
homicide a formal and legal word for "murder"
Crimes that involve deceiving people
fraud deceiving people in order to get money or things
forgery illegally copying official documents, money etc.
Crimes that involve harming property
vandalism deliberately damaging things, especially public property
arson deliberately making something burn, especially a building
→ ATTACK, CRIMINAL, STEAL

2 A PARTICULAR CRIME [C] a dishonest, violent, or immoral action that can be punished by law: +**against** *crimes against the elderly* | *Paulson* ***committed*** *a number of* ***crimes.*** | *Rape is a very* ***serious crime.*** | *kids who have been charged with* ***violent crimes*** | *The Texas law* ***made*** *abortion* ***a crime.*** | *Today, the jury was taken to the* ***crime scene*** (=place where a particular crime happened).
3 it's a crime SPOKEN said when you think something is completely wrong: *It's a crime to throw away all that food.*
4 crimes against humanity crimes of cruelty against a lot of ordinary people, especially during a war
5 a life of crime a way of living in which you get money by stealing or doing other illegal things
6 a crime of passion a crime, usually murder, caused by someone's sexual JEALOUSY
7 the perfect crime a crime in which the criminal can never be discovered
8 crime doesn't pay used to say that it is wrong to think that being involved in crime will bring you any advantage, because you will be caught and punished
[**Origin:** 1200–1300 Latin *crimen* **judgment, accusation, crime**] → see also HATE CRIME, ORGANIZED CRIME, **partner in crime** at PARTNER¹ (6), WAR CRIME, **white-collar crime** at WHITE-COLLAR (2)

crim·i·nal¹ /'krɪmənl/ W2 *adj.* **1** LAW relating to crime: *Some of the money came from* ***criminal activity.*** | **criminal act/offense** (=a crime) *Drinking and driving is a criminal offense.* | *None of his neighbors knew he had* ***a criminal background*** (=a history of doing illegal things). | *Ray got mixed up with the local* ***criminal element*** (=people within a particular group or area who do illegal things). **2** [no comparative] LAW relating to the part of the legal system that is concerned with crime → see also CIVIL: *a lawyer on a* ***criminal case*** | *the treatment of children in the* ***criminal justice system*** | *The company may face* ***criminal charges*** (=official statements saying that someone has done something illegal). | *The case will be tried in a* ***criminal court.*** **3** INFORMAL wrong, dishonest, and unacceptable, but not illegal: *It's criminal to charge so much for popcorn at the movies!* —**criminally** *adv.*

criminal² *n.* [C] someone who is involved in illegal activities or has been proven guilty of a crime: *a violent criminal* | *tougher punishments for* ***convicted criminals*** (=criminals who have been found guilty in a court) | *a prison full of* ***hardened criminals*** (=people who have been involved in crime for a long time) | *Society sees them as* ***common criminals*** (=ordinary criminals), *but they think they're revolutionaries.*

THESAURUS

offender a word meaning "criminal" that is used especially by the police, politicians etc.
thief someone who steals things
robber someone who steals money or valuable things from a bank, store etc.
burglar someone who goes into people's homes in order to steal
shoplifter someone who takes things from stores without paying for them
pickpocket someone who steals things from people's pockets, especially in a crowd
conman/fraudster someone who deceives people in order to get money or things
forger someone who illegally copies official documents, money etc.
mugger someone who attacks and robs people in public places
murderer someone who deliberately kills someone else
rapist someone who forces someone else to have sex
sex offender someone who is guilty of a crime related to sex
vandal someone who deliberately damages things, especially public property
arsonist someone who deliberately makes something burn, especially a building
→ ATTACK, STEAL

'criminal ˌcase *n.* [C] LAW a legal case in which a PROSECUTOR (=government lawyer) officially charges someone with a crime. The case may then be taken to court.

crim·i·nal·ize /'krɪmənlˌaɪz/ *v.* [T] LAW to make something illegal: *In 1937, the U.S. government criminalized the use of marijuana.*

ˌcriminal 'law *n.* [U] LAW laws or the study of laws relating to crimes and their punishments → see also CANON LAW, CIVIL LAW, COMMON LAW

ˌcriminal ˈrecord *n.* [C] an official record kept by the police of any crimes a person has done SYN **record**

crim•i•nol•o•gy /ˌkrɪməˈnɑlədʒi/ *n.* [U] the scientific study of crime and criminals —**criminologist** *n.* [C]

crimp¹ /krɪmp/ *n.* **put a crimp in/on sth** to reduce or restrict something so that it is difficult to do something: *Falling wheat prices have put a crimp on farm incomes.*

crimp² *v.* [T] **1** to restrict the development, use, or growth of something: *The lack of effective advertising has crimped sales.* **2** to press something, especially cloth, paper etc., into small regular folds **3** to make your hair slightly curly by using a special heated tool

crim•son¹ /ˈkrɪmzən/ *n.* [U] a dark slightly purple red color —**crimson** *adj.*

crimson² *v.* [I] FORMAL if your face crimsons, it becomes red because you are embarrassed

cringe /krɪndʒ/ *v.* [I] **1** to feel embarrassed by something that seems silly or stupid, which you or someone else has done: *It still **makes me cringe** when I remember it.* | +**at** *Paul **cringed at the thought** of having to sing in public.* **2** to move back or away from someone or something, especially because you are afraid or in pain SYN **cower**: *She cringed in terror.* | *The dog cringed at every new howl of the wind.* —**cringe** *n.* [C]

crin•kle¹ /ˈkrɪŋkəl/ *v.* [I,T] also **crinkle up** to become covered with small folds, or to make something do this: *Mandy crinkled up her nose in disgust.* —**crinkled** *adj.* → see also WRINKLE

crinkle² *n.* [C usually singular] a thin fold, especially in your skin or on cloth, paper etc. → see also WRINKLE

crin•kly /ˈkrɪŋkli/ *adj.* **1** having many thin folds: *The leaves turned brown and crinkly.* **2** hair that is crinkly is stiff and curly —**crinkliness** *n.* [U]

crin•o•line /ˈkrɪnl-ɪn/ *n.* **1** [U] a stiff rough material used as a support on the inside of hats and other pieces of clothing **2** [C] a round frame worn under a woman's skirt in past times to support it and give it shape

cripes /kraɪps/ *interjection* OLD-FASHIONED said to express surprise or annoyance: *Oh, cripes! My mom'll kill me if she sees this!*

crip•ple¹ /ˈkrɪpəl/ *v.* [T] **1** to hurt or wound someone so badly that they cannot walk or move their body correctly SYN **disable**: *The accident crippled her for life.* **2** to seriously damage something so that it no longer works or is no longer effective: *Asia's economy has been crippled by inflation.* —**crippled** *adj.* —**crippling** *adj.*

cripple² *n.* [C] **1** OFFENSIVE someone who cannot use their arms or legs correctly, especially someone who is physically unable to walk → see also DISABLED **2 emotional cripple** someone who is not able to deal with their own or other people's feelings: *Losing my family left me an emotional cripple.*

cri•sis /ˈkraɪsɪs/ W2 *n. plural* **crises** /-siz/ [C,U] **1** a very bad or dangerous situation that might get worse, especially in politics or economics: *a book about the Cuban missile crisis* | **economic/financial/political etc. crisis** *the long economic crisis of the 1930s* | **resolve/solve a crisis** *He urged the country's leaders to resolve the crisis peacefully.* | *Is the Social Security program **facing a crisis**?* | +**in** *the crisis in American education* | *Is the car industry **in crisis**?* **2** a time when an emotional problem or illness is at its worst: *In **times of crisis** you find out who your real friends are.* | *The book's young hero is in the midst of an **identity crisis*** (=feeling uncertain about what he wants to be). | *Her family helped her **through the crisis**.* **3 a crisis of/in confidence** a situation in which people do not believe that a government, ECONOMY, system etc. is working in the way that it should, so that they will not support it or work with it anymore: +**in** *The disaster led to a crisis of confidence in NASA's leadership.* **4 crisis management** the skill or process of dealing with unusually dangerous or difficult situations [**Origin:** 1400–1500 Latin, Greek *krisis* **decision**, from *krinein* **to judge, decide**] → see also MIDLIFE CRISIS

crisp¹ /krɪsp/ *adj.* **1** something that is crisp is hard, and makes a pleasant sound when you break or crush it: *His feet broke through the crisp outer layer of snow.* | *the crisp leaves on the lawn* **2** food that is crisp is pleasantly hard or firm when you bite it: *a crisp apple* | *a crisp salad* | *a crisp piece of bacon* ►see THESAURUS box at **hard¹** **3** paper or cloth that is crisp is fresh, clean, and new: *She handed me a crisp $20 bill.* **4** weather that is crisp is cold and dry OPP **humid**: *It was a crisp winter morning.* **5** if someone behaves or speaks in a crisp way, they are confident, polite, and firm, but not very friendly: *Her tone was crisp and businesslike.* **6** a picture or sound that is crisp is clear SYN **sharp** —**crisply** *adv.* —**crispness** *n.* [U]

crisp² *v.* [T] to make something become crisp, especially by cooking or heating it [**Origin:** 1500–1600 *crisp* **curly** (10–20 centuries), from Latin *crispus*]

crisp³ *n.* [U] a type of DESSERT in which fruit is baked with a mixture of sugar, butter, flour, and sometimes OATS on top: *apple crisp*

crisp•y /ˈkrɪspi/ *adj. comparative* **crispier**, *superlative* **crispiest** crisp and good to eat: *crispy fresh lettuce*

criss•cross¹ /ˈkrɪskrɔs/ *v.* [I,T] **1** to travel many times from one side of an area to the other: *They spent a year crisscrossing the country by bus.* **2** to make a pattern of straight lines that cross over each other

crisscross² *n.* [C] a pattern made up of a lot of straight lines that cross each other —**crisscross** *adj.*: *a crisscross pattern*

cri•te•ri•on /kraɪˈtɪriən/ Ac *n. plural* **criteria** /-riə/ [C usually plural] a standard that you use to judge something or make a decision about something: +**for** *What are the main criteria for awarding the prize?* | *To qualify, companies must **meet** the following **criteria**.* | *College admissions are not solely **based on** academic **criteria**.* | **a set/list of criteria** *a set of criteria for determining whether someone has the condition* [**Origin:** 1600–1700 Greek *kriterion*, from *krinein* **to judge, decide**]

> **GRAMMAR** **criterion, criteria**
> **Criterion** is singular and **criteria** is plural. However, many people use the word **criteria** when they are speaking about a single reason for something.

crit•ic /ˈkrɪt̬ɪk/ W2 *n.* [C] **1** someone whose job is to judge whether a movie, book etc. is good or bad: **music/art/movie etc. critic** *a food critic for the local paper* **2** someone who expresses strong disapproval or dislike of a person, idea, organization etc.: +**of** *an **outspoken critic** of the plan* [**Origin:** 1500–1600 Latin *criticus*, from Greek *kritikos*, from *krinein* **to judge, decide**] → see also **an armchair traveler/critic etc.** at ARMCHAIR² (1)

crit•i•cal /ˈkrɪt̬ɪkəl/ S3 W2 *adj.*
1 MAKING SEVERE JUDGMENTS if you are critical of something, you strongly criticize it: +**of** *Dillard is critical of the plan to reorganize the company.* | **sharply/highly/extremely critical** *He was sharply critical of the President's economic plans.*
2 IMPORTANT very important, because what happens in the future depends on it SYN **crucial**: *a decision on this critical issue* | +**to** *This next phase is critical to the project's success.* | +**for** *The win is critical for the team if they want to stay in the competition.* | *Foreign trade is **of critical importance** to the economy.* | *It is **absolutely critical** that we know the truth.*
3 DANGEROUS/UNCERTAIN a critical time or situation is very serious, worrying, or dangerous, because it might suddenly get worse: *The talks have reached a critical stage.* | *a critical shortage of medical equipment*
4 MAKING FAIR JUDGMENTS making careful and fair judgments about whether someone or something is good or bad: *a critical analysis of Faulkner's novels* | *The class teaches critical thinking.* | *He looks at the culture **with a critical eye**.*
5 ART/MOVIES/BOOKS ETC. ENG. LANG. ARTS according to critics who give judgments about art, movies, books etc.: *The play was **a critical success*** (=liked by the

critics). | *The book was published **to great critical acclaim*** (=critics said it was good).
6 in critical condition so sick that you could die: *The patient underwent surgery and was **listed in critical condition** Friday.*

ˌcritical ˈangle *n.* [C] PHYSICS the angle at which a beam of light needs to be traveling toward a surface in order for all of the light to be sent back from the surface → see also ANGLE OF INCIDENCE

C

crit·i·cally /ˈkrɪt̬ɪkli/ *adv.* **1 critically ill/injured etc.** so sick or so badly injured that you might die [SYN] fatally: *Ten people were critically injured in the accident.* **2** in a way that is very important or serious: *a **critically important** meeting* | *Food supplies are critically low in the region.* **3** in a way that shows you are criticizing someone or something: *Polly looked at me critically.* **4** in a way that shows you have thought about the good and bad qualities of something: *Students need to learn to **think critically** about what they read.* **5** done by or according to people who are paid to give their opinion on art, music etc.: *a **critically acclaimed*** (=praised by critics) *drama*

ˌcritical ˈmass *n.* [C,U] PHYSICS the amount of a substance necessary for an ATOMIC CHAIN REACTION to start

ˌcritical ˌpath aˈnalysis *n. plural* **critical path analyses** [C] TECHNICAL a method of planning a large piece of work so that there will be few delays and the cost will be as low as possible

crit·i·cism /ˈkrɪt̬əˌsɪzəm/ [W3] *n.* [C,U] **1** the act of saying what you think is bad about someone or something, or the written or spoken statements in which you do this: +**of** *There is growing criticism of the President's decision.* | **sharp/harsh/severe etc. criticism** *The action **drew** sharp **criticism** from environmentalists.* | *Graham's criticisms have no basis in fact.* | *Kathy doesn't **take criticism*** (=accept criticism) *very well.* | *The first lady **came under** heavy **criticism** for her statements.* | *I'm always willing to hear **constructive criticism*** (=advice that is intended to help someone or something improve). | **storm/torrent/barrage of criticism** (=a lot of criticism) *There was a storm of criticism from parents.* **2** the activity of forming judgments about the good or bad qualities of books, movies, music etc., or a piece of writing in which you do this: *literary criticism*

crit·i·cize /ˈkrɪt̬əˌsaɪz/ [W3] *v.* **1** [I,T] to express your disapproval of someone or something, or to talk about their faults [OPP] praise: *Ron does nothing but criticize and complain.* | **criticize sb for (doing) sth** *Fowler has been criticized for his decision.* | **sharply/harshly/roundly etc. criticize** *Some scientists have strongly criticized the study.* | *The new law has been **widely criticized**.*

THESAURUS

attack to criticize someone or something very strongly
lay into somebody/tear into somebody INFORMAL to criticize someone very strongly
pan to strongly criticize a movie, play etc. in a newspaper, on television, or on radio
be pilloried to be publicly criticized by a lot of people, especially in newspapers, on television etc.
condemn to say very strongly that you do not approve of something or someone, especially because you think what has been done is morally wrong

2 [T] to judge whether something is good or bad: *We look at each other's work and criticize it.*

cri·tique¹ /krɪˈtik/ *n.* [C,U] a detailed explanation of the good and bad qualities of something such as political ideas, a piece of writing etc.: +**of** *a critique of Updike's novel*

critique² *v.* [I,T] to say how good and bad something is: *Students critique each other's work.*

crit·ter /ˈkrɪt̬ɚ/ *n.* [C] INFORMAL an animal, fish, or insect [SYN] creature

croak¹ /kroʊk/ *v.* **1** [I] to make a deep low sound like the sound a FROG makes **2** [I] INFORMAL to die **3** [I,T] to speak in a low rough voice, as if you have a sore throat: *"I don't feel very well," he croaked.* [**Origin:** 1500–1600 from the sound]

croak² *n.* [C] **1** the sound a FROG makes **2** a low sound made in an animal's or person's throat

Cro·a·tia /kroʊˈeɪʃə/ a country in eastern Europe between Hungary and the Adriatic Sea —**Croatian** *n., adj.*

cro·chet /kroʊˈʃeɪ/ *v.* [I,T] to make clothes, hats etc. from YARN, using a special needle with a hook at one end —**crochet** *n.* [U] —**crotcheting** *n.* [U] → see also KNIT

crock /krɑk/ *n.* [C] OLD-FASHIONED a clay pot

crocked /krɑkt/ *adj.* [not before noun] SPOKEN drunk

crock·er·y /ˈkrɑkəri/ *n.* [U] dishes made from clay

Davy Crockett

Crock·ett /ˈkrɑkɪt/, **Da·vy** /ˈdeɪvi/ (1786–1836) a famous American who lived on the FRONTIER and who became a member of the U.S. Congress and was later killed trying to defend the Alamo (=a church in Texas)

ˈCrock-Pot *n.* [C] TRADEMARK a large electric pot that cooks foods very slowly

croc·o·dile /ˈkrɑkəˌdaɪl/ *n.* **1** [C] BIOLOGY a large REPTILE that has a long body and a long mouth with sharp teeth, and lives in hot wet areas **2** [U] the skin of this animal, used for making things such as shoes **3 crocodile tears** if someone cries crocodile tears, they seem sad, sorry, or upset, but they do not really feel this way: *Democrats accused Republicans of **shedding crocodile tears** over the failure of the bill.* [**Origin:** 1200–1300 Old French *cocodrille*, from Latin *crocodilus*, from Greek, **lizard, crocodile**, from *kroke* **small stone** + *drilos* **worm**]

cro·cus /ˈkroʊkəs/ *n.* [C] a small purple, yellow, or white flower that appears in early spring

crois·sant /krwɑˈsɑnt/ *n.* [C] a piece of bread, shaped in a curve and usually eaten for breakfast

Crom·well /ˈkrɑmwɛl/, **Ol·i·ver** /ˈɑlɪvɚ/ (1599–1658) an English military and political leader who led the army of Parliament against King Charles I in the English Civil War, defeated the King, and ruled until his death

crone /kroʊn/ *n.* [C] OLD-FASHIONED an ugly or mean old woman

Cro·nus, Kronos /ˈkroʊnəs/ in Greek MYTHOLOGY, a god, son of Uranus and one of the Titans, who became ruler of the universe until he was defeated by Zeus

cro·ny /ˈkroʊni/ *n. plural* **cronies** [C usually plural] one of a group of people who spend a lot of time with each other, and who will usually help each other even if it involves doing things that are not honest or fair: *the senator's political cronies*

cron·y·ism /ˈkroʊniˌɪzəm/ *n.* [U] the practice of unfairly giving the best jobs to your friends when you are in a position of power → see also NEPOTISM

crook¹ /krʊk/ *n.* [C] **1** INFORMAL a dishonest person or a criminal: *a petty crook* **2 the crook of your arm** the inside part of your arm where it bends, at the elbow **3** a bend in something: *a cat with a crook in its tail* **4** a long stick with a curved end, used by people who take care of sheep → see also **by hook or by crook** at HOOK¹ (7)

crook² *v.* [T] if you crook your finger or your arm, you bend it

crook·ed /ˈkrʊkɪd/ *adj.* **1** bent, twisted, or not in a straight line: *The picture's crooked.* | *crooked teeth* | *She gave a little **crooked smile**.* ▸see THESAURUS box at bent²

2 dishonest: *a crooked cop* —**crookedly** *adv.* —**crookedness** *n.* [U]

croon /krun/ *v.* [I,T] to sing or speak in a soft gentle voice, especially about love: *She lifted the baby, crooning to it.* —**crooner** *n.* [C]

crop¹ /krɑp/ *n.* [C] **1** BIOLOGY a plant such as corn, wheat, rice etc. that is grown by a farmer and used as food: *The main crops are wheat and barley.* | *Most of the land is used for growing crops.* **2** the amount of corn, wheat, rice etc. that is produced in a single season: *the apple crop* | *The cotton fields yielded* ***bumper crops*** (=large amounts). | +**of** *this summer's crop of vegetables* **3 a crop of sb/sth** a group of people or things who are similar or do similar things: *the* ***current crop*** *of young authors* | *a new crop of luxury cars* **4** a short whip used in horse riding **5** a very short HAIRSTYLE **6 a crop of hair/curls etc.** hair that is short, thick, and attractive **7** BIOLOGY the part under a bird's throat where food is stored before it goes into its stomach or is given to its babies **8** BIOLOGY a part of the DIGESTIVE SYSTEM of EARTHWORMS and some insects where the food they have eaten is stored before being changed into a form that their bodies can use [**Origin:** Old English *cropp* **bird's crop, top part of a plant**]

crop² *v.* **cropped, cropping** [T] **1** to cut someone's hair short: *a boy with* ***closely cropped*** *hair* **2** to cut a part off a photograph or picture so that it is a particular size or shape **3** if an animal crops grass or other plants, it makes them shorter by eating the top part

crop up *phr. v.* **1** if something, especially a problem, crops up, it happens or appears suddenly and in an unexpected way SYN **arise**: *Cases of the disease have cropped up in both the U.S. and Europe.* **2** if something such as a name or a subject crops up, it appears in something you read or hear SYN **come up**: *Your name kept cropping up in conversation.*

'crop-ˌdusting *n.* [U] the practice of using airplanes to spread chemicals that kill insects on crops

'crop roˌtation *n.* [U] the practice of changing the crops that you grow in a field each year to preserve the good qualities in the soil

cro·quet /kroʊ'keɪ/ *n.* [U] an outdoor game in which you hit balls under curved wires using a wooden MALLET (=hammer with a long handle) [**Origin:** 1800–1900 French dialect **hockey stick**, from Old North French, **tool with a hook**]

cro·quette /kroʊ'kɛt/ *n.* [C] a piece of crushed meat, fish, potato etc. that is made into a small round piece, covered in BREADCRUMBS, fried (FRY) and eaten

cross¹ /krɔs/ S2 W2 *v.*

1 GO FROM ONE SIDE TO ANOTHER [I,T] to go or stretch from one side of a road, river, room etc. to the other side: *Look both ways before crossing the street.* | *Ships took four or five days to cross the Atlantic.* | *An old wooden bridge crosses the river.* | +**over** *We crossed over to the beach.*

2 TWO ROADS/LINES ETC. [T] if two or more roads, lines etc. cross, they go across each other SYN **intersect**: *There's a post office where Oakland Road crosses 32nd Street.*

3 CROSS A LINE ETC. [T] if you cross a line, track etc., you go over and beyond it: *Johnson crossed the finish line in first place.*

4 LEGS/ARMS/ANKLES [T] if you cross your legs, arms, or ANKLES, you put one on top of the other: *Doris sat down and crossed her legs.*

5 cross your mind if an idea, thought etc. crosses your mind, you begin to think about it: *It* ***never crossed my mind*** *that she might be sick.* | *"You could fly to Boston to visit him."* ***"The thought has crossed my mind."*** (=used to tell someone you have thought of the thing they are suggesting)

6 BREED OF PLANT/ANIMAL [T] BIOLOGY to mix two or more different breeds of animal or plant to form a new breed SYN **crossbreed**: *Some species of plants can be crossed very easily.* | **cross sth with sth** *If you cross a horse with a donkey, you get a mule.* → see also CROSS²

7 sb's paths cross also **cross sb's path** if two people's paths cross or if they cross paths, they meet without expecting it: *Our paths did not cross again until 1941.*

8 cross sb's face if an expression crosses someone's face, it appears on their face: *A look of horror crossed Ken's face.*

9 cross that bridge when you come to it SPOKEN used to say that you will not think or worry about something until it actually happens

10 cross my heart (and hope to die) SPOKEN used to say that you promise that you will do something, or that what you are saying is true: *I didn't take it, cross my heart!*

11 cross your fingers a) used to say that you hope something will happen in the way you want: *Keep your fingers crossed for me.* **b)** if someone crosses their fingers while they tell you something, what they are saying is not true: *A memo said that doctors were told "with crossed fingers" that the company was doing safety studies.*

12 cross swords (with sb) to argue with someone: *The two countries have crossed swords on a number of trade issues.*

13 cross your eyes to look toward your nose with both of your eyes

14 MAKE SB ANGRY [T] to make someone angry by opposing their plans or orders: *I wouldn't cross her if I were you.*

15 cross yourself to move your hand in the shape of a cross across your chest and head, as Christians do in some churches, for example the Catholic Church → see also **dot the i's and cross the t's** at DOT² (5), **keep your fingers crossed** at FINGER¹ (2), **cross the Rubicon** at RUBICON

cross off *phr. v.* **cross sth ↔ off** to draw a line through one or more things on a list because you have dealt with them or they are not needed anymore: *Cross off their names as they arrive.*

cross sth ↔ **out** *phr. v.* to draw a line or lines through something you have written or drawn, usually because it is wrong: *The salesman crossed out $222 and wrote $225.*

cross over *phr. v.* **1** if a performer crosses over from one area of entertainment to another, they become successful in the second area as well as the first → see also CROSSOVER¹ **2** OLD USE to die

cross² S3 W3 *n.* [C]

1 CHRISTIAN SIGN a) an upright wooden post with another post crossing it near the top, that people were nailed to and left to die on as a punishment in ancient times: *Christians believe that Jesus died on a cross for our sins.* **b)** an object or picture in the shape of a cross, used as a sign of the Christian faith: *a tiny gold cross on a necklace*

2 MIXTURE OF THINGS a mixture of two or more things, breeds, qualities etc.: +**between** *My dog is a cross between a whippet and a retriever.* | *Her expression was a cross between pain and bewilderment.*

3 A MARK ON PAPER a mark (x or +) used on paper to represent where something is, or where something should be: *I've put a cross on the map to mark where our house is.*

4 MILITARY AWARD a decoration in the shape of a cross that is worn as an honor, especially for performing military actions that show courage: *Jones was awarded the Distinguished Service Cross.*

5 WAY OF HITTING a way of hitting someone in the sport of BOXING,in which your arm goes over theirs as they try to hit you: *Roberts was knocked out by* ***a right cross*** (=a hit using his right hand) *from Chavez.*

6 a (heavy) cross to bear a problem that makes you very unhappy or worried, often one that continues for a long time: *His mother's illness has been a very heavy cross to bear.*

[**Origin:** 900–1000 Old Norse *kross*, from an unrecorded Old Irish *cross*, from Latin *crux*] → see also **the sign of the cross** at SIGN¹ (8)

cross³ *adj.* OLD-FASHIONED angry or annoyed: *I'm sorry for* ***getting*** *so* ***cross with*** *you.*

cross- /krɔs/ *prefix* **1** going from one side of something to the other SYN **across**: *cross-country skiing*

(=across fields) **2** going between two things and joining them: *cross-cultural influences*

cross·bar /ˈkrɔsbɑr/ *n.* [C] **1** a bar that joins two upright posts, especially two GOALPOSTS **2** the metal bar between the seat and the HANDLEBARS on a man's bicycle → see picture at BICYCLE[1]

cross·bones /ˈkrɔsbounz/ *n.* [plural] → see SKULL AND CROSSBONES

ˈcross-ˌborder *adj.* [only before noun] involving two countries that are next to each other: *cross-border trade*

cross·bow /ˈkrɔsbou/ *n.* [C] a weapon like a small BOW attached to the end of a longer piece of wood, used for shooting ARROWS with a lot of force

cross·breed[1] /ˈkrɔsbrid/ *v. past tense and past participle* **crossbred** /ˈkrɔsbrɛd/ [I,T] BIOLOGY if one breed or plant or animal crossbreeds with another, or if you crossbreed them, they breed, producing a new type of plant or animal —**crossbred** /ˈkrɔsbrɛd/ *adj.*

crossbreed[2] *n.* [C] BIOLOGY an animal or plant that is a mixture of breeds → see also INTERBREED

cross·check /ˈkrɔsˌtʃɛk/ *v.* [T] to make sure that something is correct by using a different method to examine it again —**cross-check** *n.* [C]

ˈcross-ˌcountry[1] *adj.* **1** across fields and not along roads: *cross-country running* **2** from one side of a country to the other side: *a cross-country flight* —**cross-country** *adv.*: *I went traveling cross-country with my uncle.*

cross-country[2] *n.* **1** [U] a sport in which you run across fields and not along roads or a track **2** [C] a race in which you run this way

ˌcross-country ˈskiing *n.* [U] the sport of moving across fields, through woods etc. on SKIS → see also DOWNHILL SKIING

ˌcross-ˈcultural *adj.* belonging to or involving two or more different societies, countries, or CULTURES: *cross-cultural communication*

cross·cur·rent /ˈkrɔsˌkɚənt/ *n.* [C] **1** an idea or attitude that is opposed to another one: *the area's complex crosscurrents of racial and religious conflict* **2** a current in the ocean, a river etc. that moves across the general direction of the main current

crossed /krɔst/ *adj.* if a telephone line is crossed, it is connected by mistake to two or more telephones, so that you can hear other people's conversations → see also **get your wires crossed** at WIRE[1] (4)

ˌcross-exˈamine *v.* [T] LAW to ask someone questions about something they have just said to see if they are telling the truth, especially in a court of law —**cross-examiner** *n.* [C] —**ˌcross-examiˈnation** *n.* [C,U]

ˌcross-ˈeyed *adj.* having eyes that look in toward the nose

ˌcross-ˈfertilize *v.* [T] **1** BIOLOGY to combine the male sex cells from one type of plant with female sex cells from another **2** to influence someone or something with ideas from other areas: *an area where workers can mingle and cross-fertilize ideas* —**ˌcross-fertiliˈzation** *n.* [U]

cross·fire /ˈkrɔsfaɪɚ/ *n.* [U] **1** bullets from two or more different directions that pass through the same area: *A bystander was killed when she was* ***caught in the crossfire.*** **2** a situation in which people are arguing: *During a divorce, kids often get* ***caught in the crossfire.***

ˌcross-ˈgrained *adj.* wood that is cross-grained has lines that go across it instead of along it

cross ˈhairs *n.* [plural] two very thin wires that cross in the middle, that help you to aim when you look through something such as a gun

ˈcross-ˌhatching *n.* [U] lines drawn across part of a picture, DIAGRAM etc. to show that something is made of different material, or to produce the effect of shade

cross·ing /ˈkrɔsɪŋ/ *n.* [C] **1** a place where two lines, roads, tracks etc. cross: *A train hit a car at the crossing.* **2** a place where people can cross a border, or the act of crossing the border: *the officials at an Arizona border crossing* | *There are 300,000 illegal crossings each year.* **3** a trip across the ocean: *The crossing took over two weeks.* ►see THESAURUS box at **trip**[1] **4** a place where you can safely cross a road, railroad, river etc. → see also CROSSWALK

cross-leg·ged /ˈkrɔs ˌlɛgɪd, -ˌlɛgd/ *adv.* in a sitting position with your knees wide apart and your feet crossed: *children* ***sitting cross-legged*** *on the floor* —**cross-legged** *adj.*

cross-legged

cross·o·ver[1] /ˈkrɔsˌouvɚ/ *n.* **1** [C] ENG. LANG. ARTS the change a performer makes from working in one area of entertainment to another: **+from** *Few actors have made a successful crossover from TV to movies.* **2** [C,U] the fact of liking, using, or supporting different types of things or groups: *There is not much crossover among readers of romance and readers of science fiction.* → see also **cross over** at CROSS[1]

crossover[2] *adj.* [only before noun] moving or changing from one type of group, music, style etc. to another: *The band's crossover album became an instant bestseller.*

cross·patch /ˈkrɔspætʃ/ *n.* [C] OLD-FASHIONED someone who is easily annoyed or is in a bad mood

cross·piece /ˈkrɔspis/ *n.* [C] something that lies across another thing, especially in a building, railroad track etc.

ˌcross-ˈpurposes *n.* **at cross-purposes** if people or plans are at cross-purposes, they are trying to talk about or achieve different things, but fail to realize this: *Officials insist the two policies are not at cross-purposes.*

ˌcross-reˈfer *v.* **cross-referred, cross-referring** [I,T] to tell a reader of a book to look in another place in the book they are reading for more information

ˈcross-ˌreference *n.* [C] a note that tells the reader of a book to look in another place in the book for more information

cross·roads /ˈkrɔsroudz/ *n. plural* **crossroads** [C] **1** a place where two roads meet and cross each other → see also INTERSECTION **2** a time in your life when you have to make a very important decision that will affect your future: *Warren's career was* ***at a crossroads.***

ˈcross ˌsection, cross-section *n.* [C] **1** something that has been cut into two separate pieces so that you can look at the inside, or a drawing of this: *a cross section of the brain* **2** a group of people or things that is typical of a much larger group: *managers from a cross section of industries*

ˈcross stitch, cross-stitch *n.* [C,U] a stitch in the shape of the letter "x," used in sewing —**cross stitch** *v.* [I,T]

ˈcross street *n.* [C] a street that crosses another street: *The nearest cross street is Ellis Boulevard.*

cross·town /ˌkrɔsˈtaun◂ / *adj.* [only before noun] moving in a direction across a town or city: *the crosstown bus*

ˌcross-ˈtrainer *n.* [C usually plural] a type of shoe that can be worn for playing different types of sports

ˌcross-ˈtraining *n.* [U] **1** an exercise program that includes many different types of exercise, so that all your muscles are used **2** the activity of learning about other people's jobs within a company, so that you understand each other and work together better —**cross-train** *v.* [I,T]

cross·walk /ˈkrɔswɔk/ *n.* [C] a specially marked place for people to walk across a street

cross·wind /ˈkrɔsˌwɪnd/ *n.* [C] a wind that blows across the direction that you are moving in

cross·wise /ˈkrɔsˌwaɪz/ *adv.* **1 cut/slice etc. sth crosswise** to cut etc. something from one of its corners to the opposite corner **2** two things that are placed crosswise are arranged to form the shape of an "x" → see also LENGTHWISE

cross·word /ˈkrɔsˌwɚd/ also **ˈcrossword ˌpuzzle** *n.* [C] a game in which you write the words that are the answers to questions in a special pattern of numbered squares

crotch /krɑtʃ/ *n.* [C] the part of your body between the tops of your legs, or the part of a piece of clothing that covers this

crotch·et·y /ˈkrɑtʃəṭi/ *adj.* INFORMAL easily annoyed or made slightly angry SYN **crabby**: *a crotchety old man* [**Origin:** 1800–1900 *crotchet* **small hook, strange idea** (15–20 centuries), from French *crochet*]

crouch /kraʊtʃ/ *v.* [I] also **crouch down** **1** if a person or animal crouches, they lower their body close to the ground by bending their knees and back: +**behind/beside/in/on etc.** *I crouched behind a bush.* | *A black cat crouched in the corner.* **2** to bend your head and shoulders over something so that you are very near to it: +**over** *Chris crouched over the map.*

croup /krup/ *n.* [U] MEDICINE an illness in children which makes them cough and have difficulty breathing

crou·pi·er /ˈkrupiɚ/ *n.* [C] someone whose job is to collect and pay out money when people play cards, ROULETTE etc. for money [**Origin:** 1700–1800 French **person who rides on the back end of a horse, person who stands behind a player and gives advice, croupier**, from Old French *croupe* **back end of an animal**]

crou·ton /ˈkrutɑn/ *n.* [C] a small square piece of CRISP bread that is served with soup or on SALAD

Crow /kroʊ/ *n.* a Native American tribe from the northern region of the U.S. —**Crow** *adj.*

crow¹ /kroʊ/ *n.* **1** [C] BIOLOGY a large shiny black bird that makes a loud sound **2** [singular] the loud sound a ROOSTER makes **3 as the crow flies** measured in a straight line: *It's ten miles from here as the crow flies.* → see also **eat crow** at EAT (8)

crow² *v.* [I] **1** if a ROOSTER crows, it makes a loud high sound **2** DISAPPROVING to talk about what you have done in a very proud way, especially when other people have been less successful: +**over/about** *He was crowing over winning the bet.* **3** WRITTEN if someone, especially a baby, crows, they say something or make a noise to show pleasure: *The baby crowed with delight.*

crow·bar /ˈkroʊbɑr/ *n.* [C] a heavy iron bar used to lift or open things

crowd¹ /kraʊd/ S3 W1 *n.* **1** [C] a large group of people in a public place: *The crowd cheered.* | *An enormous* ***crowd gathered*** *to watch the parade.* | +**of** *She was surrounded by a crowd of children.* | *The streets were filled with* ***crowds of*** (=a very large number of) *angry people.* | *The event* ***drew a*** *large* ***crowd.*** | **a sellout/capacity crowd** (=a lot of people who fill every seat in a place) *a sellout crowd at the championship game* ►see THESAURUS box at **group¹** **2** [singular] INFORMAL a group of people who know each other, work together etc.: *I guess the usual crowd will be at the party.* **3 the crowd** ordinary people: *a child who just wants to* ***be one of the crowd*** (=do what everyone else does, so that you are not different) | *We want to hire someone who* ***stands out from the crowd*** (=is better than others).

crowd² S3 *v.* **1** [I,T] if people crowd somewhere, they gather together in large numbers, filling a particular place: *Angry protesters crowded the courthouse steps.* | +**around** *Everyone crowded around to listen.* | +**into** *Three families were crowded into one tiny apartment.* **2** [T] if thoughts or ideas crowd your brain, mind, head etc., they fill it: *A jumble of confused thoughts crowded my brain.* **3** [T] **a)** to make someone angry by moving too close to them: *Stop crowding me! There's plenty of room.* **b)** to make someone angry or upset by making too many unfair demands on them: *Don't crowd me! I need time to make this decision.* [**Origin:** Old English *crudan* **to press close**]

crowd sb/sth ↔ **out** *phr. v.* to force someone or something out of a place or situation: *Supermarket chains have crowded out small grocery stores.*

crowd·ed /ˈkraʊdɪd/ *adj.* too full of people or things: *a crowded room* | +**with** *The bus was crowded with schoolchildren.*

ˌcrowding-ˈout efˌfect *n.* [C] ECONOMICS a situation in which high government borrowing leads to high interest rates, making it difficult for private companies to borrow the money they need in order to make a business activity successful

ˈcrowd-pleaser, crowd pleaser *n.* [C] someone or something that large groups of people enjoy very much: *A chocolate dessert is a sure crowd-pleaser.* —**crowd-pleasing** *adj.*

crown¹ /kraʊn/ *n.*

1 HAT FOR KING/QUEEN [C] **a)** a circle made of gold and decorated with jewels, worn by kings and queens on their heads **b)** a circle, sometimes made of things such as leaves or flowers, worn by someone who has won a special honor

2 TOOTH [C] an artificial top for a damaged tooth

3 SPORTS [C] INFORMAL the position you have if you have won an important sports competition: *The high school team has won its first state soccer crown.*

4 KING/QUEEN the crown a) the position of being king or queen: *Prince Charles is next in line to the crown.* **b)** the government of a country such as Britain that is officially led by a king or queen: *The islands are possessions of the Crown.*

5 TOP PART [C usually singular] the top part of a hat, head, hill etc.: *a hat with a high crown*

6 MONEY [C] a unit of money in several European countries: *Norwegian crowns*

7 PICTURE [C] a mark, sign, BADGE etc. in the shape of a crown, used especially to show rank or quality

[**Origin:** 1100–1200 Old French *corone*, from Latin *corona* **circle of leaves put on someone's head, crown**, from Greek *korone*]

crown² *v.* [T] **1** to place a crown on someone's head, so that they officially become king or queen: *She was crowned at the age of eight.* | **crown sb king/queen etc.** *He was crowned emperor by the Pope.* **2** to say that someone has won a competition, and often to show this by putting a crown on their head: **be crowned sth** *She was crowned Miss America.* **3** to make something perfect by doing or getting the last and best thing SYN **cap**: *Winning the gold medal crowned a glittering career.* **4 be crowned with/by sth** LITERARY to have something on top SYN **cap**: *The mountains are crowned with snow.* **5** OLD-FASHIONED to hit someone on the head

ˌcrowned ˈhead *n.* [C usually plural] a king or queen

crown·ing /ˈkraʊnɪŋ/ *adj.* [only before noun] used to describe something that is the best and usually last of a series of things, or that is the best feature of something: *The championship was the* ***crowning achievement*** *of his career.* | *It was the* ***crowning glory*** *to a wonderful day.*

ˌcrown ˈjewel *n.* **1** [C] the best, prettiest, or most valuable thing that a person or place has: *Innsbruck's crown jewel is the old town center.* **2 the crown jewels** the crown, sword, jewels etc. worn by a king or queen for special ceremonies

ˌcrown ˈprince *n.* [C] the son of a king or queen, who is expected to become the next king

ˌcrown ˈprincess *n.* [C] the daughter of a king or queen, who is expected to become the next queen

ˈcrow's feet *n.* [plural] very small lines in the skin near your eyes

ˈcrow's nest *n.* [C] a small box at the top of a ship's MAST from which someone can watch for danger, land etc.

CRT /ˌsi ɑr ˈti/ *n.* [C] **1** the abbreviation of CATHODE RAY

TUBE **2** INFORMAL a computer screen that uses a CATHODE RAY TUBE

cru·cial /ˈkruʃəl/ Ac W3 *adj.* something that is crucial is extremely important, because everything else depends on it: *Teamwork was a crucial factor in their success.* | *Conservation is **of crucial importance**.* | *Teachers **play a crucial role in** the community.* [**Origin:** 1700–1800 French **cross-shaped**, from Latin *crux*] —**crucially** *adv.*

C

cru·ci·ble /ˈkrusəbəl/ *n.* [C] **1** CHEMISTRY a container in which substances are heated to very high temperatures **2** a situation that is very difficult, but that often produces something new or good

cru·ci·fix /ˈkrusəˌfɪks/ *n.* [C] a cross with a figure of Jesus Christ on it

cru·ci·fix·ion /ˌkrusəˈfɪkʃən/ *n.* **1** [C,U] in past times, the act of killing someone by fastening them to a cross and leaving them to die **2 the Crucifixion** the death of Jesus Christ in this way **3** also **Crucifixion** [C] a picture or other object representing Jesus Christ on the cross

cru·ci·form /ˈkrusəˌfɔrm/ *adj.* shaped like a cross

cru·ci·fy /ˈkrusəˌfaɪ/ *v.* **crucifies, crucified, crucifying** [T] **1** to kill someone by fastening them to a cross **2** to criticize someone severely and cruelly for something they have done, especially in public: *If the newspapers find out, you'll be crucified.*

crud /krʌd/ *n.* [U] INFORMAL something that is very bad or disgusting to look at, taste, smell etc.

crud·dy /ˈkrʌdi/ *adj. comparative* **cruddier**, *superlative* **cruddiest** INFORMAL bad, dirty, or of poor quality

crude[1] /krud/ *adj.* **1** DISAPPROVING offensive or rude, especially in a sexual way SYN **vulgar**: *crude jokes* | *Rudy was loud-mouthed and crude.* **2** not developed to a high standard, or made with little skill: *a crude homemade bomb* **3** done without attention to detail, but generally correct and useful SYN **rough**: *a crude estimate* | *Private morality, **in crude terms**, is not the law's business.* **4** [only before noun] crude oil, rubber etc. is in its natural or raw condition before it is treated with chemicals [**Origin:** 1300–1400 Latin *crudus* **raw, rough, cruel**] —**crudely** *adv.*: *crudely built shacks* —**crudity** also **crudeness** *n.* [C,U]

crude[2] also ˈ**crude oil** *n.* [U] EARTH SCIENCE oil that is in its natural condition, as it comes out of an OIL WELL, and before it has been treated with chemicals

cru·di·tés /ˌkrudɪˈteɪ/ *n.* [plural] pieces of raw vegetable served before a meal

cru·el /ˈkruəl/ *adj.* **1** deliberately hurting people or animals: *Killing animals just for their skins seems cruel.* | +**to** *Her mother could be cruel to her at times.* | *He was the victim of a **cruel joke**.* ►see THESAURUS box at **mean**[3], **unkind** **2** making someone suffer or feel unhappy: *Life can be very cruel.* | *a long cruel winter* | *Her death was a **cruel blow**.* | ***Cruel and unusual punishment** is banned by the Constitution.* **3 be cruel to be kind** to do something that will make someone upset or unhappy, in order to help them [**Origin:** 1200–1300 Old French, Latin *crudelis*, from *crudus* **raw, rough, cruel**] —**cruelly** *adv.*

cru·el·ty /ˈkruəlti/ *n. plural* **cruelties** **1** [U] behavior that deliberately causes pain to people or animals: *The children had suffered cruelty and neglect.* | +**to** *Cruelty to animals is punishable by law.* **2** [U] a willingness or desire to make people or animals suffer: *There was an edge of cruelty to their jokes.* **3** [C] a cruel action: *the cruelties of Stalin's regime*

cru·et /ˈkruət/ *n.* [C] a small bottle that holds oil, VINEGAR etc. on a table

cruise[1] /kruz/ *v.* **1** [I,T] to sail along slowly, especially for pleasure: *We spent the afternoon cruising on his yacht.* **2** [I] to move at a steady speed in a car, airplane etc.: *We were cruising along at 70 miles per hour.* **3** [I,T] to drive a car slowly through a place with no particular purpose: *Teenagers cruise Main Street on weekend nights.* **4** INFORMAL to do something well or successfully, without too much effort: +**to/into/through** *The Jayhawks cruised to a 7-0 victory over the Eagles.* **5** [I,T] SLANG to look for a sexual partner in a public place: *Let's go cruise some chicks* (=girls). **6 be cruising for a bruising** SPOKEN used to say that someone is being so annoying or stupid that they are very likely to get into trouble, a fight, an argument etc. [**Origin:** 1600–1700 Dutch *kruisen* **to make a cross, cruise**]

cruise[2] S3 *n.* [C] **1** a vacation in which you travel on a large ship: *a Caribbean cruise* **2** a trip by boat for pleasure

ˈ**cruise conˌtrol** *n.* [C] a piece of equipment in a car that makes it go at a steady speed, without you having to press with your foot on the ACCELERATOR

ˈ**cruise ˌliner** *n.* [C] a CRUISE SHIP

ˌ**cruise ˈmissile** *n.* [C] a large explosive weapon that flies close to the ground and can be aimed at an exact point hundreds of miles away

cruis·er /ˈkruzɚ/ *n.* [C] **1** a large fast ship used by a navy: *a battle cruiser* ►see THESAURUS box at **ship**[1] **2** a boat used for pleasure **3** a police car

ˈ**cruise ship** *n.* [C] a large ship with restaurants, bars etc. that people travel on for a vacation SYN **cruise liner**

cruis·ing /ˈkruzɪŋ/ *n.* [U] **1** the activity of driving a car slowly with no particular purpose **2** the activity of going on a vacation on a large ship **3** the activity of walking or driving around public places, looking for a sexual partner

crul·ler /ˈkrʌlɚ/ *n.* [C] a DONUT (=type of sweet bread) with a twisted shape

crumb /krʌm/ *n.* [C] **1** a very small piece of dry food, especially bread or cake: *bread crumbs* | *There were crumbs all over the carpet.* ►see THESAURUS box at **piece**[1] **2** a very small amount of something: +**of** *The children were anxious for any crumb of affection from their father.* **3** OLD-FASHIONED a person who is not nice, or not fun to be with

crum·ble /ˈkrʌmbəl/ *v.* **1** [I,T] to break apart into little pieces, or make something do this: *Crumble the cheese and set aside.* | *The leaves crumbled in my fingers.* **2** [I] if something made of rock or stone is crumbling, small pieces are breaking off it SYN **crumble away**: *Rangoon's old buildings are crumbling from neglect.* **3** [I] to lose power, become weak, or fail: *They are worried that American society is crumbling.*

crum·bly /ˈkrʌmbli/ *adj.* something such as food or soil that is crumbly breaks easily into small pieces: *The cookies were dry and crumbly.*

crum·my /ˈkrʌmi/ *adj. comparative* **crummier**, *superlative* **crummiest** **1** INFORMAL not pleasant, or of bad quality: *The weather is still pretty crummy.* **2** INFORMAL unkind: *That was a crummy thing to do.* **3** SPOKEN used to show that you are angry or annoyed, or to emphasize what you are saying: *I didn't want your crummy toy anyway!*

crum·pet /ˈkrʌmpɪt/ *n.* [C] a small round type of bread with holes in one side, that is eaten hot with butter

crum·ple /ˈkrʌmpəl/ *v.* **1** [I,T] also **crumple up** to crush something so that it becomes smaller and bent, or to be crushed in this way: *He crumpled up his shirt and threw it into the corner.* | *The whole front of the car crumpled on impact.* **2** [I] if your body crumples, you fall in an uncontrolled way because you are unconscious, drunk etc.: *As the bullet tore through his leg, he crumpled to the ground.* **3** [I] if your face crumples, you suddenly look sad or disappointed, as if you might cry: *Her face crumpled and she burst into tears.*

crum·pled /ˈkrʌmpəld/ *adj.* **1** also **crumpled up** crushed into a smaller bent shape: *a crumpled piece of paper* **2** clothes that are crumpled have a lot of lines or folds in them **3** someone who is crumpled is lying still in a strange position after they have fallen: *They found the boy crumpled on the pavement.*

ˈ**crumple zone** *n.* [C] a part of a car that crumples easily in an accident to protect the people inside

crunch¹ /krʌntʃ/ *n.* **1** [singular] a noise like the sound of something being crushed: +**of** *the crunch of footsteps on gravel* **2** [singular] a difficult situation caused by a lack of something, especially money or time: **a budget/cash/financial crunch** *We'll have to wait till the budget crunch is over to hire new workers.* | *Arrests have increased so much that courts are* ***feeling the crunch.*** **3** also **crunch time** [singular] a period of time when you have to make the most effort to make sure you achieve something: *The crunch came when my bank asked for my credit card back.* **4** [C] an exercise in which you lie on your back and lift your head and shoulders off the ground to make your stomach muscles strong SYN sit-up

crunch² *v.* **1** [I] to make a sound like something being crushed: *Broken window glass crunched under foot.* **2** [I always + adv./prep.,T] to eat hard food in a way that makes a noise: +**on** *The dog was crunching on a bone.* **3 crunch (the) numbers** INFORMAL to calculate a lot of numbers together: *We'll have to sit down and crunch the numbers.* → see also NUMBER CRUNCHER, NUMBER CRUNCHING

crunch·y /ˈkrʌntʃi/ *adj.* *comparative* **crunchier**, *superlative* **crunchiest** food that is crunchy is hard and makes a noise when you bite it: *crunchy celery sticks* —**crunchiness** *n.* [U]

cru·sade¹ /kruˈseɪd/ *n.* [C] **1** a determined attempt to change something, because you think you are morally right: +**to/for** *a crusade for gun control* | +**against** *He led a successful crusade against a major tobacco company.* **2** one of a series of wars fought in the 11th, 12th, and 13th centuries by Christian armies trying to take Palestine from the Muslims

crusade² *v.* [I] to take part in a crusade: +**against/for** *The new mayor is actively crusading against drugs and gangs.* —**crusader** *n.* [C]

crush¹ /krʌʃ/ *v.* [T]
1 PRESS HARD to press someone or something so hard that it breaks or is damaged: *Joe crushed his cigarette into an ashtray.* | *A zookeeper was* ***crushed to death*** *by a hippopotamus.* ►see THESAURUS box at press¹
2 BREAK INTO PIECES to press something in order to break it into very small pieces, or into a powder: *Crush two cloves of garlic.* | *crushed ice* ►see THESAURUS box at cooking¹ → see picture on page A32
3 DEFEAT to completely defeat someone or something that is fighting against you or opposes you: *Seles crushed her opponent in yesterday's match.* | **crush resistance/opposition/a revolt etc.** *The military is determined to crush the student-led uprising.*
4 crush sb's hopes/enthusiasm/confidence etc. to make someone lose all hope, confidence etc.: *Not getting their bonus checks has crushed the staff's morale.*
5 SHOCK/UPSET to make someone feel extremely upset or shocked: *He was crushed by his sister's death.*
6 crush sb to/against you LITERARY to hold someone in your arms very tightly
[**Origin:** 1300–1400 Old French *cruisir*]

crush² *n.* **1** [C] a feeling of romantic love for someone, especially someone you do not know very well, used especially about feelings that young people have: *Actually, I* ***had a*** *big* ***crush on*** *Mel Gibson.* | *a silly* ***schoolgirl crush*** **2** [singular] a crowd of people pressed so close together that it is difficult to move: *the crush of holiday shoppers* **3** [singular] a great amount or number of something: *the crush of media attention*

crush·ing /ˈkrʌʃɪŋ/ *adj.* **1** very hard to deal with, and making you lose hope and confidence: *a crushing blow* **2** a crushing win or loss is very easy and complete: *a crushing defeat* **3** a crushing remark, reply etc. expresses very strong criticism —**crushingly** *adv.*

crust /krʌst/ S3 *n.* [C,U] **1** the hard brown outer surface of bread: *If the oven is too hot the crust will burn.* **2** the baked outer part of foods such as PIES and PIZZAS: *a pizza with a thin crust* **3** a thin hard dry layer on the surface of something: *There was a thin crust of ice on the pond.* **4** SCIENCE the hard outer layer of a PLANET, moon etc., made up mostly of rocks: *the Earth's crust* → see picture at GLOBE

crustacean

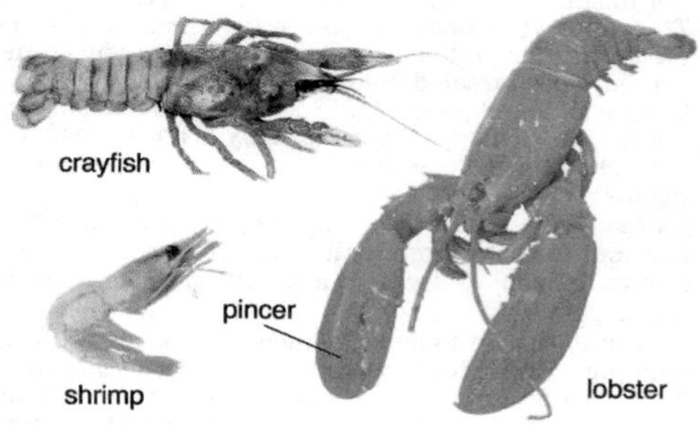

crus·ta·cean /krʌˈsteɪʃən/ *n.* [C] BIOLOGY an animal such as a LOBSTER or a CRAB that has a hard outer shell and several pairs of legs, and usually lives in water —**crustacean** *adj.*

ˌcrustal deforˈmation *n.* [C,U] TECHNICAL SCIENCE large and noticeable changes in the shape of the hard outer surface of the Earth

crust·ed /ˈkrʌstɪd/ *adj.* having a thin hard dry layer on the surface: +**with** *Her boots were crusted with mud.*

crust·y /ˈkrʌsti/ *adj.* **1** having a thin dry hard layer of something on the surface: *a crusty ring around the rim of the ketchup bottle* **2** bread that is crusty is pleasant to eat because it has a hard crust: *a crusty baguette* **3** INFORMAL easily annoyed and impatient: *a crusty old Kansas farmer* —**crustiness** *n.* [U]

crutch /krʌtʃ/ *n.* **1** [C usually plural] a special stick that you put under your arm to support you and help you walk when you have hurt your leg: *I was* ***on crutches*** *for three months after the accident.* **2** something that gives you support or help: *Alcoholics use drinking as a crutch.*

crux /krʌks/ *n.* **the crux** the most important part of a problem, question, argument etc.: ***The crux of the matter*** *is how do we prevent a flood occurring again?*

cry¹ /kraɪ/ S1 W2 *v.* **cries, cried, crying**
1 PRODUCE TEARS [I] to produce tears from your eyes, usually because you are unhappy or hurt: *Don't cry – it's OK.* | *Is the baby crying again?* | +**over/about** *What are you crying about?* | **cry with frustration/rage/relief etc.** *I nearly cried with relief.* | *They* ***cried tears of joy*** *as they sang.* | *Every night at camp, Toby would* ***cry himself to sleep.*** | **cry your eyes/heart out** (=to cry a lot and be very sad)

THESAURUS
weep a literary word for "cry"
sob to cry very hard in a noisy way
be in tears to be crying
be close to tears to be almost crying
hold/fight back (the) tears to make a strong effort not to cry
burst/dissolve into tears to suddenly start crying
break down to start crying after having tried not to cry

2 SAY LOUDLY [T] to shout something loudly SYN cry out: *"Stop!" he cried.* | **cry sth in horror/despair/surprise etc.** *"Yes!" she cried in exasperation.* | **cry for help/mercy** *It sounded like someone crying for help.*
3 for crying out loud SPOKEN used when you feel annoyed or impatient with someone: *It's right in front of you, for crying out loud.*
4 ANIMALS/BIRDS [I] if animals and birds cry, they make a loud sound: *The seagulls on the cliffs were crying loudly.*
5 cry foul to protest because you think something is wrong or not fair: *Conservationists cried foul when public land was put up for sale by the federal government.*
6 it's no use crying over spilled milk used to say that

you should not waste time feeling sorry about an earlier mistake or problem that cannot be changed
7 cry into your beer INFORMAL, DISAPPROVING to feel too much pity for yourself, especially because you think you have been treated unfairly
8 cry wolf to tell people that something bad is happening or going to happen when it really is not, or to make a problem seem worse than it is: *Is he just crying wolf again?*
[**Origin:** 1200–1300 Old French *crier*, from Latin *quiritare* **to shout for help (from a citizen), scream**, from *Quiris* **Roman citizen**] → see also **a shoulder to cry on** at SHOULDER[1] (5)

C

cry out *phr. v.* **1** to make a loud sound of fear, shock, pain etc.: **+in/with** *Even the smallest movement made him cry out in pain.* **2 cry sth ↔ out** to shout something loudly: *He cried out her name.* | **+for** *Chun cried out for his dead daughter.* **3 be crying out for sth** INFORMAL to need something urgently: *The city's in trouble and is crying out for help.*

cry² *n. plural* **cries**
1 SOUND EXPRESSING FEELING [C] a loud sound showing fear, pain, shock etc.: *the baby's cries* | **let out a cry/give a cry** *She let out a cry when she saw him.* | **a cry of delight/surprise/alarm/despair etc.** *Frankie gave a cry of rage.*
2 SHOUT [C] a loud shout: **+of** *We heard a distant cry of warning.* | **a cry for help/mercy/attention** *Who would hear his cries for help?*
3 ANIMAL/BIRD [C] a sound made by a particular animal or bird: **+of** *the cries of monkeys*
4 PUBLIC OPINION [C] something that is being said or a demand that is being made by a lot of people: **+for** *There were cries for Wiggins' resignation.*
5 a cry for help/attention something someone says or does that shows that they are very unhappy and need help: *Janie's suicide attempt was obviously a cry for help.*
6 PHRASE [C] a phrase that is used to unite people in support of a particular action or idea SYN **slogan**: *"Land and liberty" was the rallying cry of revolutionary Mexico.* → see also **be a far cry from sth** at FAR² (4), **in full cry** at FULL¹ (19), HUE AND CRY

cry·ba·by /ˈkraɪˌbeɪbi/ *n. plural* **crybabies** [C] INFORMAL, DISAPPROVING someone, especially a child, who cries or complains too often

cry·ing /ˈkraɪ-ɪŋ/ *adj.* **1 it's a crying shame** used to say you are angry and upset about something: *It's a crying shame how they've let the old neighborhood go.* **2 a crying need for sth** a serious need for something: *The city has a crying need for this kind of housing.*

cry·o·gen·ics /ˌkraɪəˈdʒɛnɪks/ *n.* [U] the scientific study of very low temperatures —**cryogenic** *adj.*

crypt /krɪpt/ *n.* [C] a room under a church, used in past times for burying people

cryp·tic /ˈkrɪptɪk/ *adj.* deliberately mysterious, or having a secret meaning: *a cryptic message* —**cryptically** /-kli/ *adv.*

crypto- /krɪptoʊ, -tə/ *prefix* FORMAL secret or hidden: *a crypto-Communist* [**Origin:** Modern Latin, Greek *kryptos* **hidden**, from *kryptein* **to hide**]

cryp·to·gram /ˈkrɪptəˌgræm/ *n.* [C] a message written in CODE

cryp·tog·ra·phy /krɪpˈtɑgrəfi/ *n.* [U] the study of secret writing and CODES —**cryptographer** *n.* [C]

crys·tal /ˈkrɪstəl/ *n.* **1** [U] clear glass that is of very high quality: *The table was set with the best china and crystal.* | *crystal goblets* **2** [C] PHYSICS a solid substance that has atoms arranged in an ordered repeating pattern: *ice crystals* | *copper sulfate crystals* **3** [C,U] rock that is clear like ice, or a piece of this **4** [C] the clear cover on a clock or watch **5** [U] INFORMAL the illegal drug METHAMPHETAMINE SYN **crystal meth** [**Origin:** 1000–1100 Old French *cristal*, from Latin *crystallum*, from Greek *krystallos* **ice, crystal**]

ˌcrystal ˈball *n.* [C] a glass ball that you can look into to magically see what is going to happen in the future

ˌcrystal ˈclear *adj.* **1** very clearly stated and easy to understand: *crystal clear instructions* **2** completely clean and clear: *The lake's water is crystal clear.*

crys·tal·line /ˈkrɪstələn/ *adj.* **1** LITERARY very clear or transparent, like crystal: *a crystalline blue pool* **2** CHEMISTRY made of crystals: *a hormone in pure crystalline form*

crys·tal·lize /ˈkrɪstəˌlaɪz/ *v.* **1** [I,T] CHEMISTRY to form CRYSTALS, or to make a substance do this: *Sea salt crystallizes from tidal pools when the water evaporates.* **2** [I,T] if an idea, plan etc. crystallizes or if you crystallize it, it becomes very clear in your mind: *The recent events really crystallized my opposition to war.* —**crystallization** /ˌkrɪstələˈzeɪʃən/ *n.* [U]

crys·tal·lized /ˈkrɪstəˌlaɪzd/ *adj.* crystallized fruit is made by a special process which covers it with sugar: *crystallized ginger*

crystal meth /ˌkrɪstəl ˈmɛθ/ *n.* [U] INFORMAL the illegal drug METHAMPHETAMINE

ˈcrystal set *n.* [C] a very simple old-fashioned radio

C.S.A., the /ˌsi ɛs ˈeɪ/ *n.* [singular] HISTORY the abbreviation of CONFEDERATE STATES OF AMERICA

C-section /ˈsi ˌsɛkʃən/ *n.* [C] INFORMAL a CESAREAN

CST the abbreviation of CENTRAL STANDARD TIME

CT **1** a written abbreviation of CONNECTICUT **2** the written abbreviation of CENTRAL TIME

ct. **1** the written abbreviation of CARAT: *a 24ct. gold necklace* **2** a written abbreviation of "cent"

CT scan /si ˈti skæn, ˈkæt skæn/ *n.* [C] a CAT SCAN

CU, cu a short way of writing "see you," used in EMAIL, TEXT MESSAGES, or CHAT ROOMS on the Internet

cu. the written abbreviation of CUBIC: *40 cu. feet*

cub /kʌb/ *n.* [C] the baby of a wild animal such as a lion or a bear: *a seal cub*

Cu·ba /ˈkyubə/ a country which is the largest island in the Caribbean Sea —**Cuban** *n., adj.*

cub·by hole /ˈkʌbi ˌhoʊl/ *n.* [C] a very small space or a small room, used for storing or hiding things: *The letters had been stuffed in a cubbyhole in the desk.*

cube¹ /kyub/ *n.* [C] **1** a solid object with six equal square sides, with each side making a right angle with all of the sides that are next to it: *a sugar cube* | *ice cubes* | *cubes of cheese* ►see THESAURUS box at **shape¹** → see picture at SHAPE¹ **2** SPOKEN, INFORMAL a CUBICLE ►see THESAURUS box at **office** **3 the cube of sth** MATH the number you get when you multiply a number by itself twice. For example, 4 x 4 x 4 = 64, so the cube of 4 is 64. [**Origin:** 1500–1600 Latin *cubus*, from Greek *kybos* **cube, vertebra**]

cube² *v.* [T] **1** MATH to multiply a number by itself twice: *3 cubed is 27* **2** to cut food into cubes SYN **dice**: *The dish is made with cubed pieces of steak.*

ˈcube root *n.* [C] MATH the cube root of a particular number is the number that when multiplied by itself twice will give that number: *The cube root of 125 is 5.*

cu·bic /ˈkyubɪk/ *adj.* **cubic feet/yards/inches etc.** MATH a measurement of space which is calculated by multiplying the length of something by its width and height: *What's the cubic capacity of this engine?*

cu·bi·cle /ˈkyubɪkəl/ *n.* [C] a small partly enclosed part of a room, separated from the rest of the room by thin walls, especially in an office [**Origin:** 1400–1500 Latin *cubiculum*, from *cubare* **to lie**]

cubic zir·co·ni·a /ˌkyubɪk zəˈkoʊniə/ *n. plural* **cubic zirconia** [C,U] an artificial DIAMOND

cub·ism /ˈkyuˌbɪzəm/ *n.* [U] a 20th-century style of art, in which objects and people are represented by GEOMETRIC shapes —**cubist** *adj.*: *cubist paintings* —**cubist** *n.* [C]

cu·bit /ˈkyubɪt/ *n.* [C] OLD USE an ancient measure of length equal to the length of your arm between your wrist and your elbow

ˌcub reˈporter *n.* [C] someone who has just started to work as a REPORTER

ˈCub ˌScout, cub scout *n.* **1 Cub Scouts** [plural] the part of the BOY SCOUTS organization that is for younger boys **2** [C] a young boy who is a member of the Cub Scouts

cuck·old /ˈkʌkəld, -koʊld/ *n.* [C] OLD USE a man whose wife has deceived him by having sex with another man —**cuckold** *v.* [T]

cuck·oo¹ /ˈkuku/ *n.* [C] BIOLOGY a gray European bird that puts its eggs in other birds' nests and that has a call that sounds like its name [**Origin:** 1200–1300 Old French *cucu*, from the sound it makes]

cuckoo² *adj.* [not before noun] INFORMAL crazy or silly: *You're completely cuckoo!*

ˈcuckoo clock *n.* [C] a clock with a wooden bird inside that comes out every hour and makes the sound of a cuckoo to show what time it is

cu·cum·ber /ˈkyuˌkʌmbɚ/ *n.* [C,U] a long thin round vegetable with a dark green skin and a light green inside, usually eaten raw [**Origin:** 1300–1400 Old French *cocombre*, from Latin *cucumis*] → see picture on page A35

cud /kʌd/ *n.* [U] food that a cow has eaten, swallowed, and brought back into its mouth to CHEW a second time

cud·dle¹ /ˈkʌdl/ *v.* [I,T] to hold someone or something very close to you with your arms around them, especially to show that you love them: *Jenny sat on the couch, cuddling a stuffed toy dog.* ►see THESAURUS box at **hug¹**

cuddle up *phr. v.* to lie or sit very close to someone or something: *We cuddled up in bed to watch the movie.*

cuddle² *n.* [C] an act of cuddling someone

cud·dly /ˈkʌdli/ *adj. comparative* **cuddlier**, *superlative* **cuddliest** someone or something that is cuddly looks soft and makes you want to cuddle them: *a cute and cuddly rabbit*

cudg·el¹ /ˈkʌdʒəl/ *n.* **1** [C] a short thick stick used as a weapon SYN **club** **2 take up the cudgels** to start to fight for an idea that you believe in: *One senator has taken up the cudgels on behalf of small farmers.*

cudgel² *v.* [T] to hit someone with a cudgel

cue¹ /kyu/ *n.* [C] **1** an action or event that is a signal for something else to happen: *Use the leash to give the dog cues about what you want him to do.* | **a cue (for sb) to do sth** *My father's remark was the cue for us to change the subject.* | **sb's cue to do sth** *Well, I guess that's my cue to explain why I'm here.* **2** a word or action that is a signal for someone to speak or act in a play, movie etc.: *She stood nervously in the wings waiting for her cue.* | *The audience needs to laugh* **on cue** (=when they are given the signal). | *The star of the show never* **misses a cue.** **3 right on cue** also **as if/though on cue** happening or done at exactly the right moment: *I had been thinking of her, and as though on cue, Maria walked toward me.* **4** a long straight wooden stick used for hitting the ball in games such as POOL and BILLIARDS **5 take your cue from sb** to use someone else's actions or behavior to show you what you should do or how you should behave: *With interest rates, smaller banks take their cue from the Federal Reserve.* **6** ENG. LANG. ARTS a movement of the hand, body, or face that communicates meaning without words: *She was very polite, but she gave nonverbal cues that she wanted us to leave.*

cue² *v.* [T] to give someone a sign that it is the right moment for them to speak or do something, especially during a performance: *The studio manager will cue you when it's your turn to come on.*

ˈcue ball *n.* [C] the white ball which a player hits with the cue in a game such as POOL

cuff¹ /kʌf/ *n.* [C] **1** the end part of a SLEEVE (=the arm of a shirt, dress etc.) that often has a button on it to hold it closed around your wrist **2** a narrow band of cloth turned up at the bottom of your pants **3** an action in which you hit someone lightly on the head with your hand open **4 cuffs** [plural] INFORMAL HANDCUFFS → see also OFF-THE-CUFF

cuff² *v.* [T] **1** to put HANDCUFFS on someone: *His right hand was cuffed to the metal handgrip of the bus seat.* **2** to hit someone lightly, especially in a friendly way: *She cuffed him playfully on the side of the head.*

ˈcuff link *n.* [C] a small piece of jewelry that a man uses instead of a button to hold the cuff on his shirt together

cuff links

cui·rass /kwɪˈræs/ *n.* [C] a piece of metal or leather that covers a soldier's chest and back, worn for protection in battle in past times

Cui·sin·art /ˈkwizɪnˌɑrt/ *n.* [C] TRADEMARK a FOOD PROCESSOR

cui·sine /kwɪˈzin/ *n.* [U] **1** a particular style of cooking: *California cuisine* | **+of** *the cuisine of Mediterranean countries* **2** the food cooked in a particular restaurant or hotel, especially when it is very good: *Enjoy the delicious cuisine created by our award-winning chef.*

CUL, cul, CUL8R a short way of writing "see you later," used in EMAIL, TEXT MESSAGES, or CHAT ROOMS on the Internet

cul-de-sac /ˈkʌl də ˌsæk, ˈkʊl-/ *n. plural* **cul-de-sacs** or **culs-de-sac** [C] **1** a street that is closed at one end so that there is only one way in and out **2** a situation in which you cannot make any more progress: *a career cul-de-sac* [**Origin:** 1800–1900 a French word meaning **bottom of the bag**]

cul·i·nar·y /ˈkʌləˌnɛri, ˈkyu-/ *adj.* [only before noun] FORMAL relating to cooking: *Deep-dish pizza is one of Chicago's culinary traditions.* | *Guests were full of praise for the* **culinary delights** (=excellent food).

cull¹ /kʌl/ *v.* **1** [T] FORMAL to find or choose information from many different places: *Names of potential jurors are culled from voter registration lists.* **2** [I,T] to kill the weakest animals in a group so that the size of the group does not increase too much: *Goats that are larger than average are culled from the herd.*

cull² *n.* [C] the act of killing the weakest animals in a group so that the size of the group does not increase too much

Cul·len /ˈkʌlən/**, Coun·tée** /kaʊnˈteɪ/ (1903–1946) a U.S. poet

cul·mi·nate /ˈkʌlməˌneɪt/ *v.* [T] FORMAL to be the final event or the highest point of development in a long series of events: *Sunday's vote culminated a peaceful democratic revolution.*

culminate in/with sth *phr. v.* **1** to end after a long period of development SYN **end**: *Valerie's months of planning culminated in a beautiful wedding day.* **2** to reach the highest point of development SYN **climax**: *Cold War tensions culminated with the Cuban missile crisis.*

cul·mi·na·tion /ˌkʌlməˈneɪʃən/ *n.* [U] the final or highest point that is reached after a long period of effort or development: *Carnival time in Rio is the culmination of months of preparation.*

cu·lottes /kuˈlɑts, ˈkulɑts/ *n.* [plural] women's pants which stop at the knee and are shaped to look like a skirt

cul·pa·ble /ˈkʌlpəbəl/ *adj.* FORMAL responsible for something bad that has happened and deserving blame SYN **guilty**: *Both men are culpable to some extent.* | **culpable homicide/negligence** *He pleaded guilty to culpable negligence.* —**culpably** *adv.* —**culpability** /ˌkʌlpəˈbɪləṭi/ *n.* [U]

cul·prit /ˈkʌlprɪt/ *n.* [C] **1** someone who is guilty of a crime or of doing something wrong: *The FBI was called in to help track down the culprits.* **2** INFORMAL the reason for or cause of a particular problem or difficulty: *Plaque is the culprit that causes tooth decay.* [**Origin:** 1600–1700 Anglo-French *cul* (from *culpable* **guilty**) + *prit* **ready (to prove it)**]

C

C

cult¹ /kʌlt/ *n.* **1** [C] an extreme religious group that is not part of an established religion: *a religious cult* | *cult members* **2** [C] a fashionable belief, idea, or attitude that influences people's lives: *Diet, therapy, and exercise are all part of the cult of self-improvement.* **3** [C] FORMAL a system of religious beliefs and practices: *The cult of the Virgin Mary remains strong in Mexico.* **4** [singular] a group of people who are very interested in a particular person or thing: *O'Brien has a cult of devoted readers.* → see also PERSONALITY CULT [**Origin:** 1600–1700 French *culte*, from Latin *cultus* **care, worship**]

cult² *adj.* [only before noun] admired or liked very much by some people, but not known or liked by most people: **a cult movie/figure/TV show etc.** *He's become a cult hero among late-night TV viewers.* | *The electric car has acquired a* ***cult following.*** | *a singer from the '60s with* ***cult status***

cul·ti·va·ble /ˈkʌltəvəbəl/ *adj.* cultivable land can be used to grow crops

cul·ti·var /ˈkʌltəˌvɑr/ *n.* [C] a type of plant that has been produced by breeding it over many years

cul·ti·vate /ˈkʌltəˌveɪt/ *v.* [T] **1** to prepare and use land for growing crops and plants SYN **farm**: *The tribe cultivated the land and grew the food.* **2** to grow and take care of a particular crop SYN **grow**: *Dozens of eucalyptus species are cultivated in the arboretum.* **3** to make an effort to help something develop: *Baseball teams spend a lot on cultivating new talent.* **4** to develop a particular skill or quality in yourself: *He's spent years cultivating a knowledge of art.* **5** to make an effort to develop a friendly relationship with someone, especially someone who can help you: *We are cultivating relationships with our economic partners in Asia.*

cul·ti·vat·ed /ˈkʌltəˌveɪt̬ɪd/ *adj.* **1** intelligent and knowing a lot about music, art, literature etc., or containing people like this SYN **cultured** SYN **sophisticated**: *Los Angeles is seen as less cultivated than San Francisco.* **2** cultivated crops or plants are grown in order to be sold: *cultivated mushrooms* **3** cultivated land is used for growing crops or plants: *cultivated fields*

cul·ti·va·tion /ˌkʌltəˈveɪʃən/ *n.* [U] **1** the preparation and use of land for growing crops: *Almost every inch of the land is already* ***under cultivation.*** **2** the process of planting and growing plants and crops: *These fields are used for rice cultivation.* | +**of** *the cultivation of strawberries* **3** the deliberate development of a particular quality or skill: +**of** *the cultivation of good manners in children* **4 the cultivation of sth** the process of developing a friendly relationship with someone, especially someone who can help you: *the cultivation of useful connections*

cul·ti·va·tor /ˈkʌltəˌveɪt̬ɚ/ *n.* [C] **1** FORMAL someone who grows crops or plants, especially a farmer **2** a tool or machine that is used to prepare land for growing crops

cul·tur·al /ˈkʌltʃərəl/ Ac S3 W2 *adj.* **1** relating to a particular society and its way of life: *Our cultural traditions were different.* | **cultural heritage/background** *Japan's unique cultural heritage* | *Puerto Rico has a distinct* ***cultural identity.*** | ***Cultural diversity*** *is a good thing.* **2** ENG. LANG. ARTS relating to art, literature, music etc.: *Houston's cultural offerings are just what we were looking for.* | **cultural events/activities** *dancing, music, and other cultural activities* | *Vienna is a real* ***cultural center*** *for music lovers.*

ˌcultural conˈvergence *n.* [U] TECHNICAL a situation or process in which different CULTURES become more and more similar

ˌcultural difˈfusion *n.* [U] TECHNICAL the spread of ideas, custom etc. between people from different CULTURES

ˌcultural diˈvergence *n.* [U] TECHNICAL a situation in which different CULTURES that have been closely related gradually become separate

ˌcultural diˈversity *n.* [U] the fact that there are many clearly different CULTURES represented in a place, for example within a city or country

ˌcultural instiˈtution *n.* [C] **1** an important custom or practice that has existed in a society or within a social group for a long time: *There was no framework of cultural institutions to draw the different tribes together.* **2** a respected and important CULTURAL, scientific, or historical organization, such as a MUSEUM or university, that has existed for a long time: *The government has pledged to give more funding to cultural institutions.*

ˌcultural ˈlandscape *n.* [C] the activities and objects etc. that are closely connected in people's minds with a particular society and its CULTURE, and the general situation in which CULTURAL activities take place

cul·tur·al·ly /ˈkʌltʃərəli/ Ac *adv.* **1** in a way that is related to the ideas, beliefs, or customs of a society: *a culturally diverse country* | *Lies that protect someone's feelings are often* ***culturally acceptable.*** **2** in a way that is related to art, literature, music etc.: *Culturally, the city has a lot to offer.* | ***culturally deprived*** *children from poor backgrounds*

ˌcultural ˈproduct *n.* [C] something that is produced by the people living in a particular CULTURE, for example a painting, a religious building, or a traditional dance

ˌCultural Reˈvolution *n.* **the Cultural Revolution** HISTORY a period in China, from 1966 to 1969, when its leader Mao Zedong strongly criticized the beliefs and actions of educated Chinese people. Many teachers and artists were physically attacked by the Red Guard, a group of mainly young people who supported Mao's ideas, and many were sent to prison or forced to work on farms.

ˌcultural ˈtrait *n.* [C] a custom, skill, type of behavior etc. that forms part of a CULTURE, or is connected in people's minds with a particular culture: *Japan has always had its own unique cultural traits.*

cul·ture /ˈkʌltʃɚ/ Ac S2 W1 *n.*
1 IN A SOCIETY [C,U] the ideas, beliefs, and customs that are shared and accepted by people in a society: *people from different cultures* | *In my culture, we respect old people.* | **American/Greek/Mexican etc. culture** *She's very interested in Latin American culture.*
2 IN A GROUP [C,U] the attitudes and beliefs about something that are shared by a particular group of people or in a particular organization: *youth culture* | *The culture of the classroom should encourage children to be curious.* | *The two companies have very different* ***corporate cultures.*** | **a culture of violence/dependency etc.** *It is not easy to transform a culture of violence into a culture of peace.* → see also COUNTERCULTURE, SUBCULTURE
3 ART/MUSIC ETC. [U] ENG. LANG. ARTS art, music, literature etc. and the activities related to them: *Old San Juan is rich in history and culture.* | *Superman and Batman have become a part of* ***popular culture.*** → see Word Choice box at CIVILIZATION
4 SOCIETY [C] a society that existed at a particular time in history: *primitive cultures* | *the Ancient Greek and Roman cultures*
5 SCIENCE [C,U] BIOLOGY the process of growing BACTERIA for scientific use, or the BACTERIA produced by this: *The doctor ordered a throat culture.*
6 CROPS [U] TECHNICAL the practice of growing crops: *rice culture*
[**Origin:** 1200–1300 Old French, Latin *cultura*, from *cultus* **care, worship**]

cul·tured /ˈkʌltʃɚd/ Ac *adj.* intelligent, polite, and interested in art, literature, music etc. SYN **cultivated**: *a combination of cultured sophistication and working-class humor*

ˌcultured ˈpearl *n.* [C] a PEARL that has been grown artificially

ˈculture ˌshock *n.* [U] the feelings of surprise or anxiety that someone has when they visit a foreign country or a place for the first time: *I get culture shock every time I come back to this country.*

cul·vert /ˈkʌlvɚt/ *n.* [C] a pipe that takes a stream under a road, railroad etc.

cum /kʊm, kʌm/ *prep.* FORMAL used between two nouns to show that someone or something has two purposes or does two things: *a bookstore-cum-coffeehouse*

Cum·ber·land Pla·teau, the /ˌkʌmbɚlənd plæˈtoʊ/ a part of the southwestern Appalachians, that runs from the state of West Virginia in the U.S. to the state of Alabama

cum·ber·some /ˈkʌmbɚsəm/ *adj.* **1** a cumbersome process or system is slow and difficult: *The system is too cumbersome and expensive.* **2** heavy and difficult to move: *a large, cumbersome machine* **3** cumbersome words or phrases are long or complicated [**Origin:** 1300–1400 *cumber* **to prevent from moving freely, load** (14–20 centuries) (from *encumber*) + *-some*]

cum·in /ˈkyumən/ *n.* [U] the seeds of a plant that have a sweet smell and are used especially in Mexican and Indian cooking, or the plant that they grow on

cum lau·de /kʊm ˈlaʊdə, kʌm-, -di/ *adv.* an expression meaning "with honors," used to show that you have finished high school or college at the third of the three highest levels of achievement that students can reach → see also MAGNA CUM LAUDE, SUMMA CUM LAUDE

cum·mer·bund /ˈkʌmɚˌbʌnd/ *n.* [C] a wide piece of cloth that a man wears around his waist as part of a TUXEDO (=special pants and coat worn on very formal occasions)

cum·mings /ˈkʌmɪŋz/, **e.e.** /i i/ (1894–1962) a U.S. poet known for unusual ways of arranging the words in his poems, and for always using small letters

cu·mu·la·tive /ˈkyumyələt̬ɪv, -ˌleɪt̬ɪv/ *adj.* increasing gradually as more of something is added or happens: *Learning is a cumulative process.* | *The illness is caused by the* ***cumulative effect*** *of stress and overwork.* | **a cumulative grade-point/GPA** (=the average of all grades for all the courses that a student has taken up to a certain point)

ˌcumulative probaˈbility *n.* [U] MATH how likely it is that the value of a RANDOM VARIABLE will be within a particular range of measurements, usually when showing how likely it is that it is less than or equal to a specific number or value

cu·mu·lo·nim·bus /ˌkyumyəloʊˈnɪmbəs/ *n. plural* **cumulonimbuses** or **cumulonimbi** /-baɪ/ [C] EARTH SCIENCE a type of thick large cloud that often produces rain storms or THUNDERSTORMS

cu·mu·lus /ˈkyumyələs/ *n. plural* **cumuli** /-laɪ/ [C,U] EARTH SCIENCE a thick white cloud with a flat bottom edge

cu·ne·i·form /ˈkyuniəˌfɔrm, kyuˈniəˌfɔrm/ *n.* [C] a type of writing used by the people of ancient Mesopotamia whose letters were made using small WEDGES (=triangleshaped objects) —**cuneiform** *adj.*

cun·ning¹ /ˈkʌnɪŋ/ *adj.* **1** DISAPPROVING using clever, but unfair or dishonest ways of getting what you want, especially ways that involve deceiving people: *She was a cold and cunning woman whose victims were lonely men.* ▸see THESAURUS box at **intelligent** **2** using clever methods to achieve something: *a cunning plan* **3** a cunning object or piece of equipment is useful, unusual, and has been designed in a clever way SYN **ingenious**: *a cunning model of the world* **4** OLD-FASHIONED attractive: *a cunning red hat* [**Origin:** 1200–1300 present participle of *cun* **to know**, an early form of *can*] —**cunningly** *adv.*

cunning² *n.* [U] **1** the use of clever methods to achieve something: *They escaped by quick cunning, courage, and luck.* **2** DISAPPROVING the use of unfair or dishonest ways of getting what you want, especially ways that involve deceiving people: *He was fooled by the cunning of the man in the suit.*

Cun·ning·ham /ˈkʌnɪŋhæm/, **Merce** /mɚs/ (1919–) a U.S. dancer and CHOREOGRAPHER of modern dance

cup¹ /kʌp/ S1 W1 *n.* [C]
1 FOR DRINKING a) a small round container with a handle, that you use to drink coffee, tea etc. → see also MUG: *a cup and saucer* | **a coffee cup/teacup** *china coffee cups* **b)** a small round container without a handle, used for drinking: **a plastic/paper cup** *Are there any more paper cups?*
2 DRINK the liquid contained inside a cup: *Would you like another cup?* | **+of** *Let me get you a cup of coffee.*
3 AMOUNT OF LIQUID also **cupful** the amount of liquid or soft food a cup can hold: *He only had a cup of water to shave with.*
4 MEASUREMENT an exact measure of quantity used in cooking, equal to 237 MILLILITERS: *Mix the butter with 1 cup powdered sugar.*
5 ROUND THING something round and hollow that is shaped like a cup: *acorn cups* | **+of** *the cup of a flower* | *She held it in the cup of her hand.*
6 PRIZE a specially shaped container that is given as a prize in a competition, especially a sports competition: *The winner stood on the platform, holding the cup above her head.*
7 COMPETITION a sports competition: *When did Argentina win the World Cup?*
8 GOLF a hole in the ground that you have to try to get the ball into in the game of GOLF SYN **hole**
9 WOMEN'S CLOTHING the part of a BRA that covers a woman's breast
10 MEN'S CLOTHING a hard cover worn by men to protect their sex organs when playing sports
11 not be your cup of tea SPOKEN to not be the type of thing that you like: *Game shows just aren't my cup of tea.*
12 a cup of joe a cup of coffee
13 my cup runneth over used to say that you are very happy and have more than you need → see also LOVING CUP
[**Origin:** Old English *cuppe*, from Late Latin *cuppa*, from Latin *cupa* **barrel**]

cup² *v.* **cupped, cupping** [T] **1** to hold something in your hands, so that your hands form part of a circle around it: *She cupped his face in her hands and kissed him.* **2 cup your hand(s)** to make a shape like a cup with your hand or hands: **+to/under/around/over** *He cupped his hands under the water.* | **cup your hand(s) to your mouth/ear** *"Excuse me?" I said, cupping my hand to my ear.*

cup·board /ˈkʌbɚd/ *n.* [C] a piece of furniture for storing clothes, plates, food etc. that is usually attached to a wall and has shelves and a door SYN **cabinet**: *kitchen cupboards* [**Origin:** 1500–1600 *cupboard* **shelf or table for cups** (14–18 centuries)]

cup·cake /ˈkʌpkeɪk/ *n.* [C] a small round cake

cup·ful /ˈkʌpfʊl/ *n.* [C] the amount that a cup can hold

Cu·pid /ˈkyupɪd/ *n.* **1** [singular] the Roman god of sexual love, usually represented as a beautiful boy with wings who carries a BOW and ARROW **2** [C] also **cupid** an image of this god, used to represent love: *The tablecloth had a pattern of hearts and cupids.* **3 play Cupid** to try to arrange for two people to fall in love with each other: *His attempt at playing Cupid for Selma and Mr. Skinner backfired.*

cu·pid·i·ty /kyuˈpɪdət̬i/ *n.* [U] FORMAL very strong desire for something, especially money or property SYN **greed**

cu·po·la /ˈkyupələ/ *n.* [C] a small round part on the roof of a building, that is shaped like an upside down bowl

cur /kɚ/ *n.* [C] OLD-FASHIONED **1** a dog that is a mix of several breeds and not considered of good quality, especially an unfriendly one SYN **mongrel** **2** a mean man

cur·a·ble /ˈkyʊrəbəl/ *adj.* a curable illness can be cured OPP **incurable**: *The disease is usually curable if it is detected early enough.*

cu·ra·çao /ˈkyʊrəˌsoʊ, ˈkʊr-, ˌkyʊrəˈsaʊ/ *n.* [U] a strong thick alcoholic drink that tastes like oranges

cu·ra·cy /ˈkyʊrəsi/ *n. plural* **curacies** [C] the job or position of curate, or the period of time that someone has this position

cu·ra·re /kyʊˈrɑri/ *n.* [U] a poison made from a tropical plant, used as medicine and on ARROWS as a weapon

cu·rate¹ /ˈkyʊrət/ *n.* [C] a priest of the lowest rank, whose job is to help the priest who is in charge of an area

cu·rate² /ˈkyʊreɪt, kyʊˈreɪt/ *v.* [T] to decide what things will be shown in a MUSEUM, ZOO etc.: *The event was curated by Bill Berkson.*

cu·ra·tive /ˈkyʊrəṭɪv/ *adj.* able to or intended to cure illness: *the plant's curative properties* —**curative** *n.* [C]

C

cu·ra·tor /ˈkyʊˌreɪṭɚ, ˈkyʊrəṭɚ, kyʊˈreɪṭɚ/ *n.* [C] someone who is in charge of and decides what things are shown in a MUSEUM, ZOO etc.: *a curator at a downtown gallery*

curb¹ /kɚb/ *n.* [C] **1** the edge of a street, between where people can walk and cars can drive: *A car was parked at the curb.* ▶see THESAURUS box at **edge¹** **2** something that helps to control or limit something: **+on** *calls for a tighter curb on immigration*

curb² *v.* [T] to control or limit something in order to prevent it from having a harmful effect: *The city is trying new measures to curb pollution.* [**Origin:** 1400–1500 French *courbe* **curve, curved piece of wood or metal**, from Latin *curvus*]

curd /kɚd/ *n.* [C usually plural] the thick substance that forms in milk when it becomes sour, used to make cheese → see also BEAN CURD

cur·dle /ˈkɚdl/ *v.* [I,T] to become thicker or form curds, or to make a liquid do this: *Do not let the sauce boil or it will curdle.* → see also BLOODCURDLING

cure¹ /kyʊɚ/ *v.* [T] **1** to make an illness or an injury better, usually by medical treatment: *Penicillin or other antibiotics will cure most infections.* | *Prostate cancer can be cured if it is caught early.* **2** to solve a problem, or improve a bad situation: *A few small changes won't cure the unemployment problem.* | **cure sb of sth** *What finally cured you of biting your nails?* **3** to make someone who is sick well again: *Can they cure her?* **4** to preserve food, tobacco etc. by drying it, hanging it in smoke, or covering it with salt: *The pork is rubbed with salt to cure it.* [**Origin:** 1200–1300 Old French, Latin *cura* **care**]

WORD CHOICE **cure, heal**

- **Cure** is used about treating someone who has a disease or an illness: *Although doctors can treat AIDS, they cannot yet cure it.*
- **Heal** is usually used when talking about treating someone who has a cut or other injury: *The doctor said the cut should heal soon, and there won't even be a scar.*

cure² *n.* [C] **1** a medicine or medical treatment that can cure an illness: *Prevention is far better than any cure.* | **+for** *Scientists still haven't found a cure for the common cold.* | *Many hope the new drug will prove to be a* ***miracle cure***. **2** something that solves a problem, or improves a bad situation: **+for** *There is no easy cure for loneliness.* **3** the act of making someone well again after an illness: *Miraculous cures have been reported in Lourdes.* **4 take a/the cure** OLD-FASHIONED to go to a special hospital in order to improve your health or to make you stop drinking alcohol

ˈcure-all *n.* [C] something that people think will cure any problem or illness: *Investment is not a cure-all for every economic problem.*

cur·few /ˈkɚfyu/ *n.* **1** [C,U] a law forcing everyone to stay indoors from a particular time in the evening until a particular time in the morning: *During the war, the government* ***imposed a curfew*** *in the capital.* | *All major towns are* ***under curfew***. | *The government has promised to* ***lift the curfew*** *soon.* **2** [U] the time after which everyone must stay indoors, according to this law: *Soldiers found them in the street* ***after curfew***. **3** [C,U] the time by which a child must be indoors or asleep, as decided by their parents: *My curfew is 9:00.* [**Origin:** 1200–1300 Old French *covrefeu* **signal to put out fires, curfew**, from *covrir* **to cover** + *feu* **fire**]

Cu·rie /kyʊˈri/, **Ma·rie** /məˈri/ (1867–1934) a Polish scientist, who with her husband Pierre Curie studied RADIOACTIVITY and discovered two new RADIOACTIVE substances

Curie, Pierre /pyɛr/ (1859–1906) a French scientist who studied RADIOACTIVITY with his wife Marie Curie

cu·ri·o /ˈkyʊriˌoʊ/ *n. plural* **curios** [C] a small object that is interesting or valuable because it is unusual, beautiful, or rare: *souvenirs and curios*

cu·ri·os·i·ty /ˌkyʊriˈɑsəṭi/ *n. plural* **curiosities** **1** [singular, U] the desire to learn about something or to know something: *The children were full of curiosity.* | **+about** *Most people have great curiosity about how nature works.* | *Renee went to the auction just* ***out of curiosity***. | *I had to open the envelope to* ***satisfy my curiosity***. | **pique/spark/arouse sb's curiosity** (=make someone curious about something) **2** [C] something that is interesting because it is unusual or strange: *a house full of old maps and other curiosities* **3 curiosity killed the cat** used to tell someone not to ask questions about something that does not concern them

cu·ri·ous /ˈkyʊriəs/ S2 W3 *adj.* **1** wanting to know or learn about something: *A few curious neighbors came out to see what was going on.* | **+about** *We were all curious about her life overseas.* | **curious to hear/learn/know etc.** *She was curious to know what happened.* | **a curious glance/look** *I got a few curious glances.* | *"Why do you ask?" "No reason.* ***I'm just curious.****"* ▶see THESAURUS box at **interested** **2 the curious** people who are curious: *For the curious, here is a brief history of the building.* **3** FORMAL strange or unusual SYN **odd**: *a curious mixture of joy and fear* | **it's curious that** *It's curious that she left without saying goodbye.* [**Origin:** 1300–1400 Old French *curios*, from Latin *curiosus* **careful, wanting to know**] —**curiously** *adv.*

curl¹ /kɚl/ *n.* **1** [C] a small mass of hair that hangs in a curving shape: *a little girl with long blonde curls* **2** [C] something that forms a curved shape: *chocolate curls on the pie* | **+of** *A curl of smoke rose from her cigarette.* **3** [U] a tendency of your hair to form curls: *The shampoo is supposed to increase curl.* **4** [C] an exercise in which you continuously bend your arms, legs or stomach in order to make the muscles strong: *bicep and tricep curls* **5 a curl of your lip/mouth** a movement of your mouth in which you turn your lips sideways and up to show that you disapprove of someone or something

curl² *v.* **1** [I,T] to form a curl or curls, or to make something do this: *You can curl the ribbon with the edge of the scissors.* | *My hair curls naturally when it rains.* | **curl (sth) around sth** **2** [I always + adv./prep.,T always + adv./prep.] to move, forming a twisted or curved shape, or to make something do this: *Penelope's fingers curled and uncurled nervously in her lap.* | **curl (sth) across/along/around etc. sth** *Morning mists curled across the surface of the river.* | *She had curled the phone cord around her hand.* **3** [I,T] if you curl your lip, or if your lip curls, you move it up and sideways, to show that you disapprove of someone or something: *Her lip curled in contempt.* **4** [I] to slide a special stone toward a marked point on ice in the sport of CURLING → see also **make your hair curl** at HAIR (12), **make sb's toes curl** at TOE¹ (4)

curl up *phr. v.* **1** to lie or sit with your arms and legs bent close to your body: *I love to just curl up with a good book.* | **be curled up** *The cat was curled up in the middle of our bed.* **2** if something flat curls up, its edges start to become curved and point up: *The leaves had turned yellow and curled up at the edges.*

curl·er /ˈkɚlɚ/ *n.* [C usually plural] **1** a small plastic or metal tube used for making hair curl: *She still had a pink curler in her hair.* **2** someone who plays the sport of curling

cur·lew /ˈkɚlyu/ *n.* [C] BIOLOGY a brown and gray bird with long legs and a curved beak, that lives near water or wet areas of land

curl·i·cue, curlycue /ˈkɚliˌkyu/ *n.* [C] a decorative twisted pattern

curl·ing /ˈkɚlɪŋ/ *n.* [U] a sport played on ice by sliding flat heavy stones toward a marked point

ˈcurling iron *n.* [C] a piece of electrical equipment that you heat and use to curl your hair

curl·y /ˈkɚli/ *adj. comparative* **curlier**, *superlative* **curliest** having a lot of curls: *curly red hair* —**curliness** *n.* [U]

ˌcurly ˈendive *n.* [U] an ENDIVE

cur·mudg·eon /kɚˈmʌdʒən/ *n.* [C] OLD-FASHIONED an old person who is often angry or annoyed —**curmudgeonly** *adj.*

cur·rant /ˈkɚənt, ˈkʌr-/ *n.* [C] a small round red or black BERRY used in cooking [**Origin:** 1500–1600 *raison of Coraunte* **raisin of Corinth** (14–17 centuries), from *Corinth* city and area in Greece]

cur·ren·cy /ˈkɚənsi/ Ac W2 *n. plural* **currencies** **1** [C,U] ECONOMICS the system or type of money that a particular country uses: *The Euro has replaced several European currencies.* | *The* ***local currency*** *is the cruzeiro.* | *a currency exchange* → see also HARD CURRENCY ►see THESAURUS box at **money** **2** [U] the state of being generally accepted or used: *"Middle age" is a term which only* ***gained currency*** *after World War I.* | *The idea of time travel enjoys* ***wide currency*** (=is accepted by many people) *in science fiction.* [**Origin:** 1600–1700 Medieval Latin *currentia* **flowing**, from Latin *currere*]

cur·rent¹ /ˈkɚənt/ S2 W1 *adj.* **1** [only before noun] happening or existing now: *What is your current occupation?* | *In its current state, the house is worth around $200,000.* ►see THESAURUS box at **present¹** **2** believed or accepted by a lot of people: *What is the current thinking on this issue?* **3** if a document is current, it gives you the legal right to do something now SYN **valid**: *a current driver's license* [**Origin:** 1200–1300 Old French *curant*, present participle of *courre* **to run**, from Latin *currere*]

current² *n.* [C] **1** EARTH SCIENCE a continuous movement of water or air in a particular direction: *The current in the river was very strong.* | *a current of warm air* **2** PHYSICS a flow of electricity through a wire: *Turn off the current before changing the fuse.* **3** an idea or feeling that a particular group of people has: *a current of discontent*

ˌcurrent eˈvents also **ˌcurrent afˈfairs** *n.* [U] important political events or other events in society that are happening now: *I read the paper to keep up with current events.*

cur·rent·ly /ˈkɚəntli/ W3 *adv.* at the present time: *Ken is currently working as a high school baseball coach.* → see Word Choice box at ACTUALLY

cur·ric·u·lum /kəˈrɪkyələm/ S3 *n. plural* **curricula** /-lə/ or **curriculums** [C] the subjects that are taught at a school, college etc.: *The curriculum includes art and music classes.* [**Origin:** 1800–1900 Modern Latin, Latin, **running, course**, from *currere*] → see also SYLLABUS

curriculum vi·tae /kəˌrɪkyələm ˈviṭə, -ˈviṭi, -ˈvaɪṭi/ ABBREVIATION **C.V.** *n.* [C] a word for a RÉSUMÉ, used especially by people who are APPLYing for a teaching job at a college or university

Cur·ri·er and Ives /ˌkɚiɚ ən ˈaɪvz, ˌkʌr-/ an American business firm, started by Nathaniel Currier (1813–1885) and James Merritt Ives (1824–1895), that produced very popular pictures showing scenes from daily life in 19th-century America

cur·ry¹ /ˈkɚi, ˈkʌri/ *n. plural* **curries** **1** [C,U] a type of food from India consisting of meat or vegetables covered in a thick SPICY liquid: *chicken curry and rice* **2** [U] curry powder

curry² *v.* **curries, curried, currying** [T] **1 curry favor with sb** to try to make someone like you or notice you in order to get something that you want: *Interest groups try to curry favor with lawmakers by donating to their campaigns.* **2** to comb a horse with a special metal comb

ˈcurry ˌpowder also **curry** *n.* [U] a mixture of SPICES that is used for giving food a SPICY taste

curse¹ /kɚs/ *v.* **1** [I] to swear: *A drunk started cursing and spitting.* | **+at** *She cursed at us and threatened us.* **2** [T] to say or think bad things about someone or something because they have made you angry: *I sat in my car, cursing the heavy traffic.* | **curse sb/sth for doing sth** *Elsa cursed herself for being such a fool when it came to men.* **3** [T] to make bad things happen to someone by using magical powers or by asking God to make them happen: *Locals believe witch doctors have the power to bless or curse their lives.*

curse sb ↔ **out** *phr. v.* INFORMAL to swear at someone who has made you angry: *When I disagreed, he cursed me out.*

curse² *n.* [C] **1** a swear word, or words, that you say because you are very angry SYN **swear word**: *He shouted curses at the umpire.* **2** a word or sentence used to ask God or a magical power to do something bad to someone or something, or the result of this: *The witch* ***put a curse on*** *the baby princess.* | *I'm sure there's a curse on this house.* ►see THESAURUS box at **magic¹** **3** something that causes trouble, harm etc.: *Being a war hero has turned out to be both* ***a blessing and a curse.*** **4 the (monthly) curse** OLD-FASHIONED MENSTRUATION

cursed /kɚst/ *adj.* **1 be cursed by/with sth** to suffer because of a problem that you have and cannot get rid of: *The area is cursed with transportation problems.* **2** LITERARY affected by bad things that are caused by God or magical powers: *The cursed jewel was stolen from an idol's eye.* **3** [only before noun] OLD-FASHIONED bad, stupid, or annoying: *Where would we find a hotel in this cursed town?* —**cursedly** *adv.*

cur·sive /ˈkɚsɪv/ *adj.* written in a flowing rounded style of writing with the letters joined together: *cursive script* —**cursive** *n.* [U] *Write your name in cursive.* —**cursively** *adv.*

cur·sor /ˈkɚsɚ/ *n.* [C] COMPUTERS a mark or a small light which can be moved around a computer screen to show where you are working [**Origin:** 1900–2000 *cursor* **messenger, sliding pointer on a scientific instrument** (16–20 centuries), from Latin, **runner**, from *currere*]

cur·so·ry /ˈkɚsəri/ *adj.* quick and done without much attention to detail: **a cursory check/examination/inspection** *Even a cursory inspection would have shown how dangerous the bridge was.* —**cursorily** *adv.*

curt /kɚt/ *adj.* using very few words when you speak to someone, in a way that seems rude: *a curt, three-sentence letter* —**curtly** *adv.* —**curtness** *n.* [U]

cur·tail /kɚˈteɪl/ *v.* [T] FORMAL to reduce or limit something: *Budget cuts forced schools to curtail after-school programs.* [**Origin:** 1400–1500 *curtal* **to cut short an animal's tail** (15–17 centuries), from Old French *courtault* **animal with a shortened tail**; influenced by *tail*] —**curtailment** *n.* [C,U]

cur·tain /ˈkɚtˀn/ S3 *n.* [C] **1** a piece of hanging cloth that can be pulled across to cover a window, divide a room etc.: *a shower curtain* | **close/draw/pull the curtains** *We always close the curtains in the evening.* **2** ENG. LANG. ARTS a sheet of heavy material that can be made to come down across the front of the stage in a theater: *I was shaking as the* ***curtain went up.*** **3** a thick layer of something that stops anything behind it from being seen: *a curtain of fog* **4 draw/bring down/lower etc. the curtains on sth** to do something that stops or ends something else: *The decision brought down the curtain on a 30-year career.* **5 the curtain falls (on sth)** if the curtain falls on an event or period of history, it ends **6 the final curtain a)** the time when the curtain goes down at the end of a performance in a theater **b)** the end of something: *the final curtain of his career* **7 be curtains for sb/sth** INFORMAL used to say that someone will die or be in a lot of trouble, or that something will end: *After 75 years, it's curtains for the town's movie theater.* [**Origin:** 1200–1300 Old French *curtine*, from Late Latin *cortina*, from Latin *cohors* **enclosure, court**]

ˈcurtain call *n.* [C] the time at the end of a performance when the actors, dancers, musicians etc. come out to receive APPLAUSE

'curtain hook *n.* [C] a small hook that you put on the top of a curtain so that you can hang it up

'curtain ˌraiser *n.* [C] **1** a short play, movie, piece of music etc. that is performed or shown before the main one **2** a small event that happens or is done just before a more important event

C

'curtain rod *n.* [C] a long bar of plastic or metal that you hang a curtain on

curt·sy, curtsey /ˈkɚtsi/ *v.* **curtsies, curtsied, curtsying** [I] if a woman curtsies to someone, she bends her knees while putting one foot behind the other as a sign of respect: *Sarah curtsied to the Queen.* [**Origin:** 1500–1600 *courtesy*] —**curtsy** *n.* [C] → see also BOW

cur·va·ceous /kɚˈveɪʃəs/ *adj.* having an attractively curved body shape: *a curvaceous woman* —**curvaceousness** *n.* [U]

cur·va·ture /ˈkɚvətʃɚ/ *n.* [C,U] TECHNICAL **1** the state of being curved, or the degree to which something is curved: +**of** *the curvature of the Earth's surface* **2** a medical condition in which part of someone's body curves in a way that is not natural: +**of** *a curvature of the spine*

curve¹ /kɚv/ *n.* [C] **1** a line or part of an object which gradually bends like part of a circle: *Customers seem to like the car's curves and angles.* | +**of** *the curve of the sword blade* **2** part of a road, river etc. that bends like part of a circle: *a curve in the road* | *I **rounded** the **curve** looking for a place to pull over.* **3** if sales, profits etc. are on a curve, they are increasing or decreasing compared to what they were doing before the gradual increase or decrease of an amount, or the curved line on a GRAPH that shows this increase or decrease: *the normal curve of population growth* **4 throw sb a curve** to surprise someone with a question or problem that is difficult to deal with: *The governor threw them a curve when he announced that funding would be cut.* **5** a method of giving grades based on how a student's work compares with other students' work: *I'll be **grading** the test **on a curve**.* → see also LEARNING CURVE **6** also **curve ball** a throw in baseball toward the BATTER in which the ball spins so that it curves suddenly and is difficult to hit

curve² *v.* [I,T] to bend or move in the shape of a curve, or to make something do this: *His mouth curved upward in a smile.*

curved /kɚvd/ *adj.* having a shape that is rounded and not straight: *a knife with a curved blade*

curv·y /ˈkɚvi/ *adj.* **1** also **curv·ing** /ˈkɚvɪŋ/ having a shape with several curves: *a curvy mountain road* **2** having an attractively curved body shape SYN **curvaceous**

cush·ion¹ /ˈkʊʃən/ *n.* [C] **1** a cloth bag filled with soft material that you put on a chair, the floor etc. to make it more comfortable to sit or lie on → see also PILLOW: *He leaned back against the cushions.* → see also WHOOPEE CUSHION **2** something that stops one thing from hitting another thing: *Good shoes should provide a cushion when running.* | +**of** *a cushion of air* **3** something, especially money, that prevents you from being immediately affected by a bad situation: *The team had a three-point cushion in the second period.* | +**against** *Savings can act as a cushion against unemployment.* **4** the soft rubber edge of the table that is used for playing POOL or BILLIARDS [**Origin:** 1300–1400 Old French *coissin*, from Latin *coxa* **hip**]

cushion² *v.* [T] **1** to make a fall or knock less painful, for example by having something soft in the way: *Mattresses on the ground **cushioned** his **fall**.* **2** to reduce the effects of something bad: **cushion the blow/impact (of sth)** *He made no attempt to cushion the blow of the bad news.*

cush·y /ˈkʊʃi/ *adj.* *comparative* **cushier**, *superlative* **cushiest** INFORMAL **1** a cushy job is easy to do and pays well **2** very comfortable: *a cushy sofa* [**Origin:** 1900–2000 Urdu *khush* **pleasant**, from Persian]

cusp /kʌsp/ *n.* [C] **1** TECHNICAL the point formed by two curves meeting **2 on the cusp of sth** in a situation when something important is about to happen or begin: *He felt this time he was on the cusp of greatness.* **3 on the cusp (of sth)** someone who was born on the cusp was born near the time when one STAR SIGN ends and another one begins

cus·pi·dor /ˈkʌspəˌdɔr/ *n.* [C] FORMAL a SPITTOON

cuss¹ /kʌs/ *v.* SPOKEN **1** [I] to swear because you are annoyed by something SYN **curse**: *He just started yelling and cussing at me.* **2** [T] to say or think bad things about someone or something because they have made you angry SYN **curse**

cuss sb ↔ **out** *phr. v.* to swear and shout at someone because you are angry SYN **curse out**

cuss² *n.* [C] OLD-FASHIONED **a stubborn/stupid/ornery etc. cuss** someone who is annoying because they are STUBBORN, stupid etc.

'cuss word *n.* [C] SPOKEN a SWEAR WORD

cus·tard /ˈkʌstɚd/ *n.* [C,U] a soft mixture of milk, sugar, and eggs, that is usually baked [**Origin:** 1600–1700 *custard*, *crustade* type of pie (14–17 centuries)]

ˌcustard 'pie *n.* [C] a PIE filled with custard, which people throw at each other as a joke in movies, television shows etc.

Cus·ter /ˈkʌstɚ/, **George** (1839–1876) a general in the U.S. Civil War, who was killed by Native Americans from the Sioux tribe in the Battle of the Little Bighorn

cus·to·di·al /kʌˈstoʊdiəl/ *adj.* FORMAL **1** LAW having the legal right to take care of a child: *the custodial parent* **2** relating to the work done by a CUSTODIAN: *the school's custodial staff*

cus·to·di·an /kəˈstoʊdiən/ *n.* [C] **1** someone who takes care of a public building: *a custodian at the stadium* **2** someone who is responsible for taking care of someone or something: *The state was named custodian of the children.*

cus·to·dy /ˈkʌstədi/ *n.* [U] **1** the right to take care of a child, especially when the child's parents are legally separated from each other: *Mrs. Richburn **has custody** of their three children.* | *Doug **got custody** after the divorce.* | *Harper and Moore have **joint custody*** (=they both have the right to take care of their child) *of their six-year-old son.* | **grant/award sb custody** (=if a court grants someone custody, it gives that person the right to take care of a child) | *The twins were placed **in the custody of** their grandparents.* | *a custody dispute* **2** the situation of someone who is being kept in prison by the police until they go to court, because the police think they are guilty of a crime: *The man is now **in custody**.* | *The youth was **put in custody** at juvenile hall.* | **be held/kept in custody** *The defendant will be kept in custody until the appeal.* | *As soon as the plane landed, they were **taken into custody** by waiting FBI men.* **3 in the custody of sb** FORMAL if something is in someone's custody, it is being kept and taken care of by them: *The collection is now in the custody of the university.* [**Origin:** 1400–1500 Latin *custodia* **guarding**, from *custos* **person who guards**]

cus·tom¹ /ˈkʌstəm/ *n.* **1** [C,U] something that is done by people in a particular society because it is traditional: *a society with many ancient customs* | *the book of Jewish law and custom* | **a local/American/Mexican etc. custom** *The guide offers information on local customs.* | ***It is** Asia's **custom to** greet the New Year with firecrackers.* | **the custom of doing sth** *The old custom of sacrificing animals has disappeared.* ▸see THESAURUS box at **habit** **2 customs** [plural] **a)** the place where your bag is checked for illegal goods when you go into a country: *We waited over two hours to **clear customs*** (=be allowed through customs after being checked). **b)** also **customs duty** money that you have to pay as tax when you bring certain types of goods into a country **c)** the government department that checks goods coming into a country and collects taxes on them: *He works for customs.* | *customs officials*

3 sb's custom ESPECIALLY LITERARY something that someone usually does every day, or in a particular situation: *It was his custom to attend Mass every Sunday.* [**Origin:** 1100–1200 Old French *custume*, from Latin *consuetudo*, from *consuescere* **to make someone used to something**]

custom² *adj.* [only before noun] custom products and services are specially designed and made for a particular person or group: *a custom tour of the glacier*

cus·tom·ar·y /ˈkʌstəˌmɛri/ *adj.* **1** something that is customary is normal because it is the way something is usually done: **it is customary to do sth** *It is customary to take off your shoes when entering a house.* **2** someone's customary behavior is the way they usually do things: *Martha's customary brilliance* —**customarily** /ˌkʌstəˈmɛrəli/ *adv.*

ˌcustom-ˈbuilt *adj.* something large that is custom-built is specially designed and made for a particular person: *a custom-built mountain bike* → see also CUSTOM-MADE —**custom-build** *v.* [T]

cus·tom·er /ˈkʌstəmɚ/ S1 W1 *n.* [C] **1** someone who buys goods or services from a store, company etc.: *We don't get many customers on Mondays.* | *a letter of thanks from a **satisfied customer*** | **sb's biggest/best/largest customer** *Business travelers are our best customers.* | *Hemingway was a **regular customer*** (=someone who goes to a store, restaurant etc. often) *of the café.* | *Please call **customer service*** (=help that a company provides for its customers) *with any problems.*

THESAURUS

client someone who pays for a service: *a lawyer meeting with her client*
shopper someone who goes to a store looking for things to buy: *streets full of Christmas shoppers*
consumer anyone who buys goods or uses services: *Consumers are concerned about prices.*
buyer someone who buys something very expensive, such as a car or a house: *first-time home buyers*
guest someone who pays to stay in a hotel: *Guests must register before being given a key.*
→ STORE¹

2 a cool customer INFORMAL someone who is always calm and very confident, but sometimes in a way that is not nice

cus·tom·ize /ˈkʌstəˌmaɪz/ *v.* [T] to change something to make it more appropriate for you, or to make it look special or unusual: *The software is easy to customize.* —**customized** *adj.*

ˌcustom-ˈmade *adj.* custom-made furniture, clothes etc. are specially made for a particular person: *a custom-made guitar* → see also CUSTOM-BUILT

ˈcustoms ˌduty *n.* [C,U] ECONOMICS tax paid to a government on goods that are brought into a country

cut¹ /kʌt/ S1 W1 *v. past tense and past participle* **cut**, **cutting**
1 DIVIDE INTO PIECES [I,T] to use a knife, scissors etc. to divide something into two or more pieces, or to remove a piece from the main part of something: *Let me cut the cake.* | *Using scissors, cut carefully along the dotted lines.* | **cut sth with sth** *He cut the rope with his knife.* | **cut through sth** *We had to cut through the bolt to open the door.* | **cut sth into pieces/slices/chunks etc.** *Cut the apples into four pieces.* | **cut sth in half/two** *They accidentally cut the cable in half.* | **cut sb sth** *Can you cut me a piece of bread too, please?*

THESAURUS

To cut food
chop (up) to cut meat, vegetables, or wood into pieces
slice to cut bread, meat, or vegetables into thin pieces
dice to cut vegetables or meat into small square pieces
peel to cut the outside part off an apple, potato etc.
carve to cut pieces from a large piece of meat
shred to cut vegetables or meat into small thin pieces
grate to cut cheese, vegetables etc. into small pieces using a grater

To cut other things
saw to cut wood, using a saw (=a tool with a row of sharp points)
chop down to make a tree fall down by cutting it
mow to cut grass using a special machine
trim to cut off a small amount of something to make it look neater, for example hair or a bush
clip to cut something out of a newspaper, magazine etc., or to cut small amounts off something
snip to cut something quickly, using scissors

2 REDUCE [T] to reduce the amount of something: *The government has promised to **cut taxes**.* | *This technology could **cut** our operating **costs** significantly.* | *Over 300 **jobs** have been **cut** in the past year.* | **cut sth by $1 million/2%/half etc.** *Local residents may have to cut their water use by half.* | **cut sth off sth** *The new highway cuts an hour off the trip.* | **cut sth from/to sth** *His vacation has been cut from six weeks to just three.* ▸see THESAURUS box at **reduce**
3 WOUND [T] to injure yourself or someone else using a sharp object such as a knife, so that you start bleeding: *His hand was bleeding where the knife had cut him.* | **cut your finger/hand/leg etc. (on sth)** *He cut his hand on some broken glass.* | **cut yourself** *I cut myself shaving this morning.* | *A man who tried to climb the fence **cut open** his leg.*
4 MAKE SHORTER [T] to make something shorter with a knife, scissors etc., especially in order to improve its appearance: *I need to cut my fingernails.* | **have/get your hair cut** *You should get your hair cut today.* | **cut the lawn/grass** *I get two bucks a week for cutting the Gibson's lawn.*
5 MAKE A HOLE [I,T] to make a hole in the surface of something, or to open it by using a sharp tool such as a knife: **+into** *Cut into the meat to see if it is done.* | *Somebody **cut a hole in** the tent and stole our things.* | *Students will **cut open** a frog and dissect it.*
6 TOOLS [I] if a tool cuts well or badly, it is easy or difficult to cut things with it: *These scissors cut really well.* | **cut through sth** *The knife can cut through a tin can.*
7 MAKE WITH TOOLS [T] to make or form something by cutting it from stone, metal, rock, wood etc.: **cut sth from/out of/into sth** *Steps had been cut into the cliff face.*
8 FREE SB [T] to cut something such as a rope or metal in order to let someone escape: **cut sb from sth** *She had to be cut from the wreckage of her car.* | **cut sb free/loose** *The soldiers swiftly cut the prisoners free.*
9 MOVIE/SPEECH/BOOK ETC. [T] **a)** to reduce the length of a movie, speech etc. SYN **shorten**: *The original version was cut by more than 30 minutes.* **b)** to remove part of a movie, speech, or piece of writing, because it is not right or it might offend people SYN **cut out** SYN **edit out**: *The director cut the scenes of cannibalism.* ▸see THESAURUS box at **remove**
10 cut corners to do something in a way that is not perfect, in order to save time, effort, or money: *One airline was accused of cutting corners on safety.*
11 cut your losses to stop trying to do something that is already failing in order to prevent the situation becoming even worse: *We decided to cut our losses and close the business.*
12 IN A LINE [I] to unfairly go in front of other people who are waiting to buy or do something: *People get really angry if you try to **cut in line**.* | **cut in front of sb** *She just cut in front of me.*
13 COMPUTER [I,T] COMPUTERS to remove something from a document on a computer: ***Cut and paste** the picture into a new file* (=remove it from one place and put it somewhere else).

C

14 cut a deal to make an agreement with someone, usually a business deal: *The two sides have been unable to cut a deal.*
15 cut a check to write a check or have one printed: *We'll cut a check for you at the end of the week.*
16 cut class/school to deliberately not go to a class that you ought to go to, or to not go to school when you ought to: *She started cutting classes and fighting with her parents.*
17 cut sth short to stop doing something earlier than was planned: *The mission was cut short when some of the equipment failed.*
18 cut sb short to stop someone from finishing what they wanted to say: *I tried to explain but she cut me short.*
19 sth cuts both ways INFORMAL used to say that something has advantages but also disadvantages: *More money means more work – it cuts both ways.*
20 STOP SUPPLY [T] to stop the supply of something, or to stop something from working: *The power supply has been cut again.*
21 DIVIDE AN AREA [T] to divide an area into two or more parts: *The river **cuts** the valley **in two**.* | **cut through sth** *The new road will cut through a conservation area.*
22 MUSIC/RECORD [T] if a musician cuts a record, they record their music on a record, TAPE etc. SYN **record**: *We cut this track in my studio at home.*
23 cut sth to the bone to reduce costs, services etc. as much as possible: *Our budget has already been cut to the bone.*
24 cut to the chase INFORMAL to immediately start dealing with the most important part of something: *Look, can we cut to the chase now?*

SPOKEN PHRASES

25 cut the crap a) an impolite way of telling someone to stop saying things that are not true: *Come on, cut the crap – I know you were there.* **b)** an impolite way of telling someone to talk only about what is important, instead of wasting time on other things: *Can we just cut the crap and talk about the real issues?*
26 Cut! used by the director of a movie to tell everyone to stop acting, filming etc.
27 not cut it also **not cut the mustard** to not be good enough to do something or deal with something: *Those old excuses won't cut it this time.*
28 cut it close to leave yourself just barely enough time or money to do something: *I don't know – leaving at 6:00 is cutting it kind of close.*
29 cut no ice also **not cut much ice** if something cuts no ice with someone, it will not persuade them to change their mind: *I don't think anything I say will cut much ice with him.*
30 cut the cheese also **cut one** HUMOROUS to make air come out of your BOWELS SYN **fart**

31 TOOTH if a baby cuts a tooth, the tooth starts to grow through the GUMS
32 MAKE A MOVIE [T] to put the parts of a movie together so that they make a continuous story, getting rid of the parts you do not want SYN **edit**
33 CROPS [T] to cut a crop such as wheat, so that the top part can be used SYN **harvest**
34 PLAYING CARDS [I,T] to divide a DECK of cards into two before starting to play
35 cut and run INFORMAL to leave a situation suddenly when it becomes too difficult, especially when you should stay: *We sensed that Borden could cut and run at any moment.*
36 LINE [T] if a line cuts another line, they cross each other at a particular point
37 cut your teeth (on sth) to get your first experience of doing something by practicing on something simple: *He cut his teeth as a tennis player by playing in junior championships.*
38 cut sb to the quick/core LITERARY to upset someone very much by saying something cruel
39 cut a fine/odd etc. figure LITERARY to have an impressive, strange etc. appearance: *With his flowing hair, Zhang cuts a striking figure on stage.*
40 cut the cord to stop depending on someone, especially your parents: *At 18, I figured it was time to cut the cord and move away from home.*
41 ILLEGAL DRUG [T usually passive] to mix an illegal drug such as HEROIN with some other substance
42 not cut the mustard INFORMAL to not be good enough: *Athletes who can't cut the mustard don't make the team.*
[**Origin:** 1200–1300 from an unrecorded Old English *cytan*] → see also **cut it fine** at FINE² (3), **cut/give sb some slack** at SLACK² (3), **cut a swath/swathe through sth** at SWATH, **cut/slit your own throat** at THROAT (5), see also, **have your work cut out (for you)** at WORK² (15)

cut across *phr. v.* **1** if a problem or feeling cuts across different groups of people, they are all affected by it: *Smith's popularity **cuts across** racial **lines**.* **2** to go across an area of land rather than around it SYN **cut through**: *Try not to cut across other people's campsites.*

cut away *phr. v.* **1 cut sth ↔ away** to remove the unwanted or unnecessary parts from something: *Cut away dead or diseased branches.* **2** if a television program or movie cuts away from something, it moves away from or stops showing a particular thing: *Cut away from her face and focus on the puppies.*

cut back *phr. v.* **1 cut sth ↔ back** to reduce the amount, size, cost etc. of something SYN **decrease**: *She cut her class load back to spend more time with her family.* | **+on** *We have had to cut back on spending.* → see also CUTBACK **2** to reduce the amount of something that you eat, drink, or smoke, especially in order to improve your health SYN **cut down**: *You smoke too much. You should cut back.* | **+on** *I'm trying to cut back on fatty foods.* **3 cut sth ↔ back** to remove the top part of a plant in order to help it to grow: *Cut the main branches back in the spring.*

cut down *phr. v.* **1 cut sth ↔ down** to reduce the amount, number, or size of something SYN **decrease**: *We need to do something to cut traffic congestion down.* | **+on** *Reducing the speed limits will help cut down on accidents.* **2** to eat, drink, or smoke less of something that is bad for you, especially in order to improve your health SYN **cut back**: *He still smokes, but he's cut down a lot.* | **+on** *I'm trying to cut down on the amount of coffee I drink.* **3 cut sth ↔ down** to cut through the TRUNK of a tree so that it falls on the ground **4 cut sth ↔ down** to reduce the length of something such as a piece of writing: *Let's try to cut your speech down to six minutes.* **5 cut sb ↔ down** LITERARY to kill or injure someone with a gun, sword, knife etc.: *Dozens of soldiers were cut down as they tried to escape across the river.* **6 cut sb down to size** to make someone realize that they are not as important, successful etc. as they think they are

cut in *phr. v.* **1** to interrupt someone who is speaking or a conversation by saying something: *She was about to ask another question when George cut in.* **2** to suddenly drive into the space between two moving cars in a dangerous way: *A blue Mercedes cut in right in front of me.* **3** if a part of a machine cuts in, it starts to operate when it is needed: *The safety device cuts in automatically when needed.* **4 cut sb in** INFORMAL to allow someone to take part in a plan to make money, especially a secret or illegal plan: **cut sb in on** *They offered to cut me in on the deal.* **5** to ask permission to dance with someone who is already dancing with someone else: *"Do you mind if I cut in?" Mark asked.*

cut into sth *phr. v.* **1** to reduce the amount of time, money etc. that you have available for something, by using up a lot of it: *Simon's job was starting to cut into his social life.* **2** if something such as a rope cuts into your skin, it is so tight that it cuts the skin and hurts it

cut off *phr. v.*
1 PIECE OF STH cut sth ↔ off to separate something by cutting it from the main part: *We had to cut off some of the lower branches.*
2 STOP THE SUPPLY cut sth ↔ off to stop the supply of

something such as electricity, gas, water, money etc.: *The U.S. has cut off economic aid to the country.* | *They're going to cut the electricity off if you don't pay the bill.*

3 PLACE/PEOPLE **be cut off a)** if a place is cut off, it is difficult to get to, for example because it is a long way from any other place or because the weather is bad: *The resort town was cut off by a heavy snowfall.* **b)** to be unable to communicate with other people or countries, for example because they are a long way away or because you are not allowed to: **+from** *The islanders are cut off from the modern world.*

4 STOP SB FROM TALKING **cut sb off** to prevent someone from finishing what they are saying: *Don cut him off before he had a chance to argue.*

5 PREVENT SB FROM ESCAPING **cut sb off** to prevent someone from escaping by getting in their way: *A policeman was waiting to cut him off.*

6 DRIVING **cut sb ↔ off** to suddenly drive in front of a moving car in a dangerous way: *A woman in a green station wagon cut me off at the on-ramp.*

7 TELEPHONE **cut sb ↔ off** to suddenly lose the telephone connection to someone that you were speaking to: *I don't know what happened – we just **got cut off**.*

8 STOP BEING FRIENDLY **cut sb ↔ off** to stop having a friendly relationship with someone: *Don't let your son's divorce cut you off from your grandchildren.*

9 MONEY/PROPERTY **cut sb off** to take away someone's right to receive your money or property, especially when you die: *My parents threatened to **cut me off without a penny** if I married him.*

10 cut off your nose to spite your face to do something because you are angry, even though it will harm you

cut sb **off from** sth *phr. v.* to prevent someone from having or receiving something: *His asthma cuts him off from a lot of activities.*

cut out *phr. v.*

1 REMOVE **cut sth ↔ out** to remove something by cutting: *The tumor had to be cut out.* | *Children love looking at magazines and cutting out pictures.* | **cut sth out of sth** *Rescue workers cut the four men out of the car.*

2 MAKE A SHAPE **cut sth ↔ out** to make a shape by cutting paper, cloth etc.: *First cut out a large circle.*

3 STOP DOING STH **cut sth ↔ out** to stop doing or eating something, especially because it is harmful to you: *I've cut out all expenses that aren't absolutely necessary.* | **+cut sth out of sth** *Sheila's trying to cut sugar out of her diet.*

4 STOP STH FROM HAPPENING **cut sth ↔ out** to stop something from happening or existing SYN **eliminate**: *The goal of these reforms is to cut out fraud.*

5 PIECE OF WRITING/NEWS REPORT ETC. **cut sth ↔ out** to take out part of a piece of writing, a news report etc., especially because it might offend people SYN **edit out**: *They cut out a lot of offensive language.*

6 STOP SB FROM BEING INVOLVED **cut sb out** to prevent someone from being involved in something SYN **exclude**: **cut sb out of sth** *They had cut me out of their plans.* | **cut sb out of your will** (=to remove someone's name from the list of people who will receive your money or property when you die)

7 Cut it/that out! used to angrily tell someone to stop doing something because it is annoying you: *Rusty, cut it out, I'm trying to study in here.*

8 MOTOR if a motor cuts out, it suddenly stops working: *The boat's engine cut out halfway across the lake.*

9 LIGHT/VIEW to prevent light from reaching somewhere, or prevent a particular view from being seen: *Tinted windows help cut out the sun's glare.*

10 not be cut out for sth also **not be cut out to be sth** to not have the qualities that you need for a particular job or activity: *He realized he wasn't cut out to be a police officer.*

11 LEAVE INFORMAL to leave suddenly: *Bob cut out right after the movie.*

cut through sth *phr. v.* **1** to go through a place rather than around it SYN **cut across**: *I usually cut through the parking lot.* **2** to make a path through a place with a lot of plants, by cutting them: *We had to cut through the bushes to get to the house.* **3** to move through something quickly and very easily: *The boat cut effortlessly through the water.* **4** to deal successfully with something that is confusing or difficult so that it is not a problem: *How can we cut through the bureaucracy and get a decision?* **5** LITERARY if a sound cuts through silence or noise, it is heard because it is loud

cut up *phr. v.* **1 cut sth ↔ up** to cut something into smaller pieces SYN **chop up**: *Just cut up the potatoes and throw them in with the meat.* | **cut sth up into pieces/squares/cubes etc.** *She cut the letter up into tiny pieces.* **2** if someone cuts up, they behave loudly, amusingly, and sometimes rudely: *Some of the kids were cutting up in the classroom.*

cut² S2 W2 *n.* [C]

1 REDUCTION [usually plural] a reduction in the size, number, or amount of something that someone has planned to make SYN **reduction** OPP **increase**: *There will be cuts across all levels of the company.* | **+in** *cuts in the number of troops in the area* | **budget/job/tax/pay etc. cuts** *Democrats attacked the proposed spending cuts.* | *The school will have to **make cuts** next year.* | **big/drastic cuts** *drastic cuts in spending on health care* | **+of** *a cut of 1% in interest rates*

2 WOUND a wound that you get if a sharp object cuts your skin: *His arms were covered with **cuts and bruises**.* | **+on** *a bad cut on the forehead* ▸see THESAURUS box at **injury**

3 HAIR [usually singular] **a)** the act of cutting someone's hair SYN **haircut**: *How much do they charge for a cut and blow-dry?* **b)** the style in which your hair has been cut SYN **haircut** SYN **hairstyle**: *a short, stylish cut* → see also CREW CUT

4 HOLE/MARK a hole in something, or a mark in the surface of something, made by something sharp: *Make the first cut fairly shallow.*

5 MONEY [usually singular] INFORMAL someone's share of something, especially money: *How much is my cut going to be?* | **+of** *Schools receive a 34% cut of the money the state lottery earns.*

6 MEAT a piece of meat that is from a particular part of an animal, or the way a piece of meat has been cut: *a particularly tender cut of beef*

7 CLOTHES [usually singular] the style in which your clothes have been made: *The cut of a suit is very important.*

8 make the cut to be good enough to be included in something: *Only six competitors made the final cut.*

9 ACT OF CUTTING an act of cutting something: *With one cut the boat was free.*

10 REMOVING PART OF WRITING/MOVIE ETC. the action of removing part of a speech, piece of writing, movie etc.: *The censors insisted on several cuts.*

11 MOVIE the process of putting together the different parts of a movie and removing the parts that will not be shown: *Spielberg himself oversaw **the final cut**.* | *The DVD includes **the director's cut** of the film.*

12 CHANGE OF SCENE a quick move from one scene in a movie or TV show to another: *a cut to a scene from the man's childhood*

13 REMARK a remark that insults or criticizes someone: *an unkind cut*

14 be a cut above sth to be much better than someone or something else: *Bella Pasta is a cut above the other Italian restaurants in town.*

15 ROAD a road that has been made through a hill

cut³ *adj.* **1** [only before noun] used to describe plants and flowers whose stems have been cut: *cut flowers* | *the smell of cut grass* **2** used to describe a body part that has a cut on it: *a cut finger* **3** INFORMAL having muscles whose edge and shape are clear and easy to see **4** used to describe the way clothes are designed and made: *I don't like the way this jacket is cut.* | **low-cut/high-cut** *a low-cut evening gown* **5** used to describe something that has been cut with a tool: *the cut end of the board*

C

C

ˌcut-and-ˈdried also **ˌcut and ˈdry** *adj.* **1** the result of a situation that is cut-and-dried is known, arranged, or decided before the situation has ended, and is not likely to change SYN **settled**: *The outcome of the case seems cut-and-dried.* **2** not different or not more complicated than usual SYN **straightforward**: *You'll learn the procedure quickly. It's pretty cut-and-dried.*

cut·a·way /ˈkʌt̬əˌweɪ/ *adj.* a cutaway model, drawing etc. is open on one side so that you can see the details inside it

cut·back /ˈkʌt˺bæk/ *n.* [C usually plural] a reduction in something, such as the number of workers in an organization, the amount of money spent by the government etc.: *budget cutbacks* | +**in** *a cutback in employees' workloads* → see also **cut back** at CUT[1]

cute /kyut/ S1 *adj.* INFORMAL **1** a cute child, animal, or object is very pretty or attractive: *a cute, chubby baby* | *Oh, aren't those shoes cute?* ►see THESAURUS box at **attractive**, **beautiful** **2** pretty in a way that you think is sexually attractive: *Who was that cute guy I saw you with?* | *I think she's really cute.* ►see THESAURUS box at **attractive**, **beautiful** **3** cute behavior or words show intelligence but not respect or honesty: *Their lawyer tried a cute trick.* | ***Don't get cute with me*** (=don't speak to me in this way), *young man!* —**cutely** *adv.* —**cuteness** *n.* [U]

cute·sy /ˈkyutsi/ *adj.* something that is cutesy is too pretty in a way you think is annoying: *The cottages all had cutesy names like "Sea Shanty."*

ˌcut ˈglass *n.* [U] glass that has patterns cut into its surface —**cut-glass** *adj.*: *a cut-glass chandelier*

cu·ti·cle /ˈkyut̬ɪkəl/ *n.* [C] BIOLOGY **1** the hard edge of skin around the bottom and sides of your FINGERNAILS and TOENAILS **2** the outer layer of skin on animals with a BACKBONE **3** the protective outer layer of a plant that prevents it from losing too much water

cut·ie, **cutey** /ˈkyut̬i/ *n.* [C] SPOKEN someone who is attractive and nice: *Mike is such a cutie.*

cut·lass /ˈkʌtləs/ *n.* [C] a short sword with a curved blade, used by SAILORS or PIRATES in past times

cut·ler /ˈkʌtlɚ/ *n.* [C] OLD USE someone who makes or sells cutlery

cut·ler·y /ˈkʌtləri/ *n.* [U] knives, forks, spoons, and other tools used for eating with SYN **silverware**

cut·let /ˈkʌtlɪt/ *n.* [C] a small flat piece of meat: *turkey cutlets*

cut·off /ˈkʌt̬ɔf/ *n.* [C] **1** a limit or level at which you must stop doing something: *We can't keep giving them money. There has to be a cutoff.* | *By the* ***cutoff date****, we had received over 9,000 entries.* **2** the act of stopping doing something, especially because it has reached a particular level or limit: +**of** *a cutoff of foreign aid* **3** a SHORTCUT: *Take the San Pablo Ridge cutoff to the right.* **4** a part of a pipe that you open and shut to control the flow of gas or liquid **5 cutoffs** [plural] a pair of SHORTS that you make by cutting off the legs of an old pair of pants

cut·out /ˈkʌt̬aʊt/ *n.* [C] **1** the shape of a person, object etc. that has been cut out of wood or paper: *Colorful cutouts decorated the room.* **2** a piece of equipment that stops a machine when something is not working correctly

ˌcut-ˈprice *adj.* CUT-RATE

cut·purse /ˈkʌtpɚs/ *n.* [C] OLD USE a PICKPOCKET

ˌcut-ˈrate *adj.* **1** sold at less than the usual price: *cut-rate air fares* **2** a cut-rate shop, supermarket etc. sells goods at reduced prices: *a cut-rate men's clothing store* **3** not of good quality: *The book is essentially a cut-rate Stephen King style novel.*

cut·ter /ˈkʌt̬ɚ/ *n.* [C] **1** a small ship **2** [often plural] a tool that is used for cutting: *wire cutters*

cut·throat[1] /ˈkʌt˺θroʊt/ *adj.* willing to do anything to succeed, even if it is unfair: *a cutthroat divorce lawyer* | *The government protects some industries from* ***cutthroat competition****.*

cutthroat[2] *n.* [C] OLD USE a murderer

cut·ting[1] /ˈkʌt̬ɪŋ/ *n.* [C] a stem or leaf that is cut from a plant and put in soil or water to grow into a new plant

cutting[2] *adj.* **1** very unkind and intended to upset someone: *a cutting remark* **2** a cutting wind is very cold and you can feel it through your clothes

ˈcutting board *n.* [C] a large piece of wood or plastic used for cutting meat or vegetables on → see picture at BOARD[1]

ˌcutting ˈedge *n.* **1 at/on the cutting edge (of sth)** working at the most advanced stage or development of something: *The company is at the cutting edge of many new technologies.* **2 the cutting edge** technology or equipment that is the most modern and advanced of its type: +**in** *This system is the cutting edge in digital reproduction.* —**ˈcutting-edge** *adj.*: *cutting-edge technology*

ˈcutting room *n.* [C] a room where the final form of a movie is prepared by cutting the film and putting the different parts into the correct order

ˈcut-up *n.* [C] someone who makes other people laugh by doing amusing things, especially in a situation when they should not do this

Cu·vi·er /ˈkuvieɪ, ˈkyu-/, **Georges** /ʒɔrʒ/ (1769–1832) a French scientist who developed a system for the CLASSIFICATION of animals

cuz /kəz/ *conjunction* SPOKEN, NONSTANDARD a short form of "because"

cwt. the written abbreviation of HUNDREDWEIGHT

-cy /si/ *suffix* [in nouns] **1** the state or quality of being something: *privacy* (=state of being private) | *accuracy* | *bankruptcy* **2** a particular rank or position: *a presidency* (=the rank of a president)

cy·an /ˈsaɪ-æn, -ən/ *adj.* deep greenish blue —**cyan** *n.* [U]

cy·a·nide /ˈsaɪəˌnaɪd/ *n.* [U] a very strong poison

cyber- /saɪbɚ/ *prefix* relating to computers, especially to the messages and information on the Internet

cy·ber·ca·fé, **cyber café** /ˈsaɪbɚkæˌfeɪ/ *n.* [C] a CAFÉ that has computers connected to the Internet for customers to use

cy·ber·crime, **cyber crime** /ˈsaɪbɚˌkraɪm/ *n.* [C,U] COMPUTERS criminal activity that involves the use of computers or the Internet

cy·be·ri·a /saɪˈbɪriə/ *n.* [U] CYBERSPACE

cy·ber·net·ics /ˌsaɪbɚˈnɛt̬ɪks/ *n.* [U] COMPUTERS the scientific study of the way in which information is moved and controlled in machines, the brain, and the NERVOUS SYSTEM —**cybernetic** *adj.*

cy·ber·punk[1] /ˈsaɪbɚˌpʌŋk/ *adj.* [only before noun] relating to computers and people who use computers and TECHNOLOGY but who dislike authority and society, especially in the future: *cyberpunk fiction*

cyberpunk[2] *n.* **1** [U] stories about imaginary events relating to computer science, usually set in the future **2** [C] someone who is able to use computers very well but who dislikes authority and society

ˈcyber rage *n.* [U] HUMOROUS violence and angry behavior by people who are using the Internet

cyber·sex, **cyber sex** /ˈsaɪbɚˌsɛks/ *n.* [U] sexual activity, pictures etc. discussed or shown on the Internet

cy·ber·space /ˈsaɪbɚˌspeɪs/ *n.* [U] COMPUTERS all the connections between computers in different places, considered as a real place where information, messages, pictures etc. exist: *one of the most visited sites in cyberspace*

cy·borg /ˈsaɪbɔrg/ *n.* [C] a creature that is partly human and partly machine

cy·cla·men /ˈsaɪkləmən, ˈsɪ-/ *n.* [C] a plant with pink, red, or white flowers

cy·cle[1] /ˈsaɪkəl/ Ac W3 *n.* [C] **1** a number of related events that happen again and again in the same order: *Scientists studied the animal's* ***sleep cycle*** (=the regular pattern of events that happen when someone is asleep). | +**of** *the cycle of the seasons* | *The program is intended to help people* ***break the cycle of*** (=make a bad or damaging cycle stop repeating itself) *poverty.* → see also **vicious cycle** at LIFE CYCLE → VICIOUS CIRCLE, MENSTRUAL CYCLE **2** PHYSICS one complete process in which something such as a sound wave goes up to its highest point, then down to its lowest point and back to the middle point **3** the period of time needed for a machine to finish a process: *This washing machine has a 28-minute cycle.* **4** ENG. LANG. ARTS a series of poems or songs on the same subject **5** a bicycle or MOTORCYCLE [**Origin:** 1300–1400 French, Late Latin *cyclus*, from Greek *kyklos* **circle, wheel, cycle**]

cycle² Ac *v.* [I] **1** to travel by bicycle SYN **ride**: *I run or cycle at least three times a week.* **2** to go through a series of actions, changes, or events that happen again and again in the same order: *The computer is continually cycling through the data.*

cy·clic /ˈsaɪklɪk, ˈsɪ-/ also **cyc·li·cal** /ˈsaɪklɪkəl, ˈsɪ-/ Ac *adj.* happening in cycles: *a cyclical downturn in the economy* —**cyclically** /-kli/ *adv.*

cy·clist /ˈsaɪklɪst/ *n.* [C] someone who rides a bicycle: *The old creek trail is used by hikers and cyclists.*

cy·clone /ˈsaɪkloʊn/ *n.* [C] EARTH SCIENCE a very strong wind that moves very fast in a circle → see also HURRICANE

ˈCyclone fence *n.* [C] TRADEMARK a type of CHAIN-LINK FENCE

Cy·clops /ˈsaɪklɑps/ *n.* [singular] a very big man in ancient Greek stories who only had one eye in the middle of his FOREHEAD

cyg·net /ˈsɪgnɪt/ *n.* [C] a young SWAN

cyl·in·der /ˈsɪləndɚ/ *n.* [C] **1** MATH a shape which has two circular ends and straight sides ▸see THESAURUS box at shape¹ → see picture at SHAPE¹ **2** an object or container such as a can which is in the shape of a cylinder: *a cylinder of oxygen* **3** the tube within which a PISTON moves forward and backward in an engine: *a four-cylinder engine* **4 run/hit/fire on all cylinders** to be operating or performing very well: *When we're hitting on all cylinders, we're hard to beat.* [**Origin:** 1500–1600 Latin *cylindrus*, from Greek, from *kylindein* **to roll**]

cy·lin·dri·cal /səˈlɪndrɪkəl/ *adj.* in the shape of a cylinder: *a cylindrical oil tank*

cym·bal /ˈsɪmbəl/ *n.* [C] a musical instrument made of a thin round metal plate, played by hitting it with a stick or by hitting two of them together: *the clash of cymbals*

cyn·ic /ˈsɪnɪk/ *n.* [C] someone who is not willing to believe that people have good, honest, or sincere reasons for doing something: *Modern politics has turned voters into cynics.* | **hardened/die-hard cynics** (=someone who is very unwilling to believe that people can be morally good) [**Origin:** 1500–1600 Latin *cynicus*, from Greek *kynikos* **like a dog**] —**cynicism** /ˈsɪnəˌsɪzəm/ *n.* [U]

cyn·i·cal /ˈsɪnɪkəl/ *adj.* **1** unwilling to believe that people have good, honest, or sincere reasons for doing something: *a cynical journalist* | **+about** *Since her divorce, she's become very cynical about men.* **2** unwilling to believe that something can work or be useful: **+about** *Many were cynical about whether the program would work.* **3** cynical behavior shows that you are willing to do things that are unfair or morally wrong in order to get something: *They're using sex in a cynical attempt to sell more books.* —**cynically** /-kli/ *adv.*

cy·no·sure /ˈsaɪnəʃʊr, ˈsɪ-/ *n.* [C usually singular] FORMAL someone or something that everyone is interested in or attracted to

cy·pher /ˈsaɪfɚ/ *n.* [C] another spelling of CIPHER

cy·press /ˈsaɪprəs/ *n.* [C] a tree with dark green leaves and hard wood, that does not lose its leaves in winter

Cy·prus /ˈsaɪprəs/ a large island in the eastern Mediterranean Sea —**Cypriot** /ˈsɪpriət/ *n., adj.*

Cy·ril·lic /səˈrɪlɪk/ *adj.* ENG. LANG. ARTS Cyrillic writing is written in the alphabet used for Russian, Bulgarian, and other Slavonic languages [**Origin:** 1800–1900 Saint *Cyril* (827–69), Greek missionary who is said to have invented the alphabet]

cyst /sɪst/ *n.* [C] MEDICINE a LUMP containing liquid that grows in your body or under your skin: *an ovarian cyst*

cys·tic fi·bro·sis /ˌsɪstɪk faɪˈbroʊsɪs/ *n.* [U] MEDICINE a serious medical condition, especially in children, in which breathing and DIGESTing food is very difficult

cys·ti·tis /sɪˈstaɪt̬ɪs/ *n.* [U] MEDICINE an infection of the BLADDER

cy·to·ki·ne·sis /ˌsaɪt̬oʊkɪˈnisɪs, -kaɪ-/ *n.* [U] BIOLOGY when the cytoplasm in a cell separates and divides as part of the process in which a cell divides into two new cells

cy·tol·o·gy /saɪˈtɑlədʒi/ *n.* [U] BIOLOGY the scientific study of cells from living things —**cytologist** *n.* [C]

cy·to·plasm /ˈsaɪt̬əˌplæzəm/ *n.* [U] BIOLOGY all the material in the cell of a living thing except the NUCLEUS (=central part of a cell)

cy·to·skel·e·ton /ˌsaɪt̬oʊˈskɛlətˀn/ *n.* [C] BIOLOGY a system of very thin connected tubes in the cytoplasm of a cell, that gives the cell its shape and structure

czar /zɑr/ *n.* [C] **1** a male ruler of Russia before 1917 **2 a banking/drug/health etc. czar** someone who is chosen by the government to deal with a particular problem or activity, such as banks, illegal drugs etc. and given a lot of power [**Origin:** 1500–1600 Russian *tsar'*, from Gothic *kaisar* **emperor**, from Greek, from Latin *Caesar*, from Julius *Caesar*]

cza·ri·na /zɑˈrinə/ *n.* [C] a female ruler of Russia before 1917, or the wife of a czar

czarism /ˈzɑrɪzəm/ *n.* [U] a system of government controlled by a czar, especially the system in Russia before 1917 —**czarist** *n.* [C] —**czarist** *adj.*

Czech·o·slo·va·ki·a /ˌtʃɛkəsləˈvɑkiə, -sloʊ-/ a former country in central Europe, which divided in 1993 into two separate countries, the Czech Republic and the Slovak Republic —**Czechoslovakian** *n., adj.*

Czech Re·pub·lic, the /ˌtʃɛk rɪˈpʌblɪk/ a country in central Europe, between Germany, Poland, the Slovak Republic, and Austria —**Czech** *n., adj.*

C

D,d

D[1] /di/ *n. plural* **D's** **1** [C] also **d** *plural* **d's** **a)** the fourth letter of the English alphabet **b)** the sound represented by this letter **2** ENG. LANG. ARTS **a)** [C,U] the second note in the musical SCALE of C MAJOR **b)** [U] the musical KEY based on this note **3** [C] a grade that a teacher gives to a student's work, showing that it is not very good and just above the point of failing

D[2] **1** the number 500 in the system of ROMAN NUMERALS **2** used to show that a television program contains conversations about sex → see also D AND C, D-DAY

'd /d/ *v.* **1** the short form of "would": *I asked if she'd be willing to help.* **2** the short form of "had": *Nobody knew where he'd gone.*

d' /d/ *v.* used in writing to show the way "do" sounds in spoken questions: *D'you know how many people are going to be there?*

d. the written abbreviation of "died": *John Keats d. 1821*

D.A. /ˌdi ˈeɪ/ *n.* [C] LAW the abbreviation of DISTRICT ATTORNEY

dab[1] /dæb/ *n.* [C] **1** a small amount of something that you put onto a surface with your hand, a cloth etc.: **+of** *Add a dab of butter and some parsley.* **2** a light touch with a cloth, SPONGE etc. held in your hand: *He paints with dabs of the brush.*

dab[2] *v.* **dabbed, dabbing** **1** [I,T] to touch something lightly several times with something such as a cloth: *He dabbed his mouth with a napkin.* | **dab at sth** *Mrs. Copeland dabbed at her eyes with a tissue.* **2** [T] to put a small amount of a substance onto something with quick light movements of your hand: **dab sth on/onto/behind etc.** *Diane dabbed perfume behind each ear.*

dab·ble /ˈdæbəl/ *v.* [I] to do something or be involved in something in a way that is not very serious: **+in/with** *He was a stockbroker who dabbled in poetry.*

da·cha /ˈdɑtʃə/ *n.* [C] a large country house in Russia

dachs·hund /ˈdɑkshʊnt, -hʊnd/ *n.* [C] a type of small dog with short legs and a long body [**Origin:** 1800–1900 German **badger-dog** (because it was used to hunt badgers)]

Da·cron /ˈdeɪkrɑn/ *n.* [U] TRADEMARK a type of artificial material used especially for clothing

dac·tyl /ˈdæktl/ *n.* [C] ENG. LANG. ARTS a repeated sound pattern in poetry, consisting of one long sound followed by two short sounds, for example as in the word "carefully" —**dactylic** /dækˈtɪlɪk/ *adj.*

dad, Dad /dæd/ S1 W2 *n.* [C] father: *She lives with her mom and dad.* | *Dad, can I help?* [**Origin:** 1500–1600 from a word used by very young children]

Da·da·ism /ˈdɑdɑˌɪzəm/ *n.* [U] a movement in European art and literature in the early 20th century in which artists and writers aimed to shock people by producing strange new ideas and images

dad·dy, Daddy /ˈdædi/ S1 *n.* [C] a word meaning "father," used especially by or to young children: *My daddy is a pilot.* | *Look, Daddy's home!* → see also SUGAR DADDY

daddy long·legs /ˌdædi ˈlɔŋlɛgz/ *n.* [C] an insect with long legs that is similar to a SPIDER

da·do /ˈdeɪdoʊ/ *n. plural* **dadoes** [C] the lower part of a wall that has a different surface or is decorated differently from the upper part of the wall [**Origin:** 1600–1700 Italian **block, cube**]

dae·mon /ˈdimən/ *n.* [C] a spirit in ancient Greek stories that is less important than the gods → see also DEMON

daf·fo·dil /ˈdæfəˌdɪl/ *n.* [C] a tall yellow spring flower with a tube-shaped part in the middle

daf·fy /ˈdæfi/ *adj. comparative* **daffier**, *superlative* **daffiest** INFORMAL silly or crazy in an amusing way SYN **nutty**

daft /dæft/ *adj.* INFORMAL silly, stupid, or crazy [**Origin:** Old English *gedæfte* **gentle**]

dag·ger /ˈdægɚ/ *n.* [C] a short pointed knife used as a weapon → see also CLOAK-AND-DAGGER

Da·guerre /dəˈgɛr/, **Lou·is** /ˈlui/ (1789–1851) a French artist and early PHOTOGRAPHER who invented the daguerrotype

da·guerr·o·type /dəˈgɛroʊˌtaɪp, -rə-/ *n.* [C,U] an old type of photograph, or the process used to make it

dahl·ia /ˈdælyə/ *n.* [C] a large garden flower with a bright color [**Origin:** 1800–1900 Anders *Dahl* (1751-1789), Swedish plant scientist]

dai·kon /ˈdaɪkɑn/ *n.* [C] a large white Asian RADISH (=type of root vegetable)

dai·ly[1] /ˈdeɪli/ S3 W2 *adj.* [only before noun] **1** happening, done, or produced every day: *a daily newspaper* | *Daily exercise will help keep you healthy.* | *Our website is updated **on a daily basis*** (=every day). ►see THESAURUS box at **regular**[1] **2 daily life** the ordinary things that you usually do or experience: *DVD players have become a part of daily life in North America.* **3** relating to a single day: *The daily rate for parking downtown is $15.*

daily[2] *adv.* done or happening every day: *The zoo is **open daily**, from 9 a.m. to 5 p.m.* | **once/twice daily** *Eat meat only once daily.*

daily[3] *n.* **1** [C usually plural] a newspaper that is printed and sold every day, or every day except Sunday **2 dailies** [plural] ENG. LANG. ARTS the prints of a movie as it is being made, which are looked at every day after filming ends and before changes are made to it; RUSHES

Daim·ler /ˈdaɪmlɚ/, **Gott·lieb** /ˈgɑtlib/ (1834–1900) a German engineer who built one of the first cars

Dai·my·o /ˈdaɪmioʊ/ *n.* [C] HISTORY in Japan during the Middle Ages, a ruler directly below the rank of SHOGUN

dain·ti·ly /ˈdeɪntl-i/ *adv.* done in an extremely careful way, using small movements: *Mrs. Grant daintily sipped her tea.*

dain·ty[1] /ˈdeɪnti/ *adj. comparative* **daintier**, *superlative* **daintiest** **1** small, pretty, and delicate: *a dainty white handkerchief* **2** extremely careful, and using small movements: *a dainty eater* —**daintiness** *n.* [U]

dainty[2] *n. plural* **dainties** [C] OLD-FASHIONED something small that is good to eat, especially something sweet such as a small cake [**Origin:** 1200–1300 Old French *deintié*, from Latin *dignitas* **worth**]

dai·qui·ri /ˈdækəri/ *n.* [C] a sweet alcoholic drink made with RUM and fruit juice

dair·y /ˈdɛri/ *n. plural* **dairies** [C] **1** a company that sells milk and sometimes makes other things from milk, such as cheese **2** a place on a farm where milk is kept and butter and cheese are made [**Origin:** 1200–1300 *dey* **female servant (in a dairy)** (10–19 centuries), from Old English *dæge* **maker of bread**]

ˈdairy ˌcattle *n.* [plural] cows that are kept to produce milk rather than for their meat

ˈdairy cow *n.* [C] a cow that is kept to produce milk rather than for its meat

ˈdairy ˌfarm *n.* [C] a farm that has cows that produce milk

dair·y·maid /ˈdɛriˌmeɪd/ *n.* [C] a woman who worked in a dairy in past times

dair·y·man /ˈdɛrimən, -ˌmæn/ *n.* [C] a man who works in a DAIRY

ˈdairy ˌproduct *n.* [C] milk or a food made from milk, such as butter, cheese, or YOGURT

da•is /'deɪəs/ *n.* [C] a low stage or PLATFORM indoors that you stand or sit on so that people can see and hear you, for example when you are making a speech

dai•sy /'deɪzi/ *n. plural* **daisies** [C] a white flower with a yellow center [**Origin:** Old English *dægeseage* **day's eye**] → see also **be pushing up (the) daisies** at PUSH[1] (19)

'daisy chain *n.* [C] daisies that are attached together to form a string that you can wear around your neck or wrist

Da•kar /'dækɑr, də'kɑr/ the capital and largest city of Senegal

Dal•ai La•ma /ˌdɑli 'lɑmə, ˌdɑleɪ-/ *n.* **the Dalai Lama** the leader of the Tibetan Buddhist religion

dale /deɪl/ *n.* [C] OLD-FASHIONED a valley → see also **over hill and dale** at HILL (6)

Da•li /'dɑli/, **Sal•va•dor** /'sælvədɔr/ (1904–1989) a Spanish painter famous for his work in the style of SURREALISM

Dal•las /'dæləs/ a city in the U.S. state of Texas

dal•li•ance /'dæliəns/ *n.* [C] a sexual relationship between two people that is not considered serious

dal•ly /'dæli/ *v.* **dallies**, **dallied**, **dallying** [I] OLD-FASHIONED to waste time, or do something very slowly: **+over** *Lawmakers have dallied over these major new proposals.* → see also DILLY-DALLY

dally with sth *phr. v.* to be interested or involved in something, but not in a serious way SYN **toy with**: *They dallied with the idea of touring the world.*

dally with sb *phr. v.* OLD-FASHIONED to have a sexual relationship that is not serious with someone SYN **toy with**

Dal•ma•tian, dalmatian /dæl'meɪʃən/ *n.* [C] a large dog with short white hair and black or brown spots

Dal•ton /'dɔltˀn/, **John** (1766–1844) a British scientist who made important discoveries about gases and developed the idea of the existence of atoms

dam[1] /dæm/ *n.* [C] **1** a special wall built across a river, stream etc. to stop the water from flowing, especially to make a lake or produce electricity: *the Hoover Dam in Nevada* **2** [usually singular] TECHNICAL the mother of a four-legged animal, especially a horse → see also SIRE

dam[2] *v.* **dammed**, **damming** [T] to stop the water in a river, stream etc. from flowing by building a special wall across it: *The East Branch River was dammed in 1952.*

dam sth ↔ **up** *phr. v.* to make the water in a river, stream etc. stop flowing by blocking it: *The landslide dammed up the river.*

dam•age[1] /'dæmɪdʒ/ S3 W2 *n.* [U]
1 PHYSICAL HARM physical harm that is done to something or to a part of someone's body, so that is broken or injured: **+to** *There was a lot of damage to both cars.* | **cause/do damage** *The floods caused serious damage to crops.* | **serious/severe/major damage** *The earthquake caused major damage to the freeway system.* | **minor/minimal/superficial damage** (=damage that is not very serious) | **irreparable/irreversible/permanent damage** (=damage that cannot be repaired) | **flood/storm/water etc. damage** (=damage caused by a flood, storm, water etc.) | **brain/liver/lung etc. damage** *The treatment can cause permanent kidney damage.*
2 EMOTIONAL HARM harm that is done to someone's emotions or mind: **psychological/emotional damage** *The death of a parent can cause long-lasting psychological damage in younger children.*
3 BAD EFFECT a bad effect on something: **+to** *The incident resulted in great damage to the city's reputation*
4 damages LAW money that a court orders someone to pay to someone else as a punishment for harming them or their property: *The court* ***awarded*** *the families $33 million* ***in damages****.*
5 the damage is done SPOKEN used to say that something bad has happened that makes it impossible to go back to the way things were before it happened: *Ed apologized later, but the damage was already done.*
6 damage control an attempt to limit the bad effects of something: *Since the scandal broke, the Senator's staff have been busy doing damage control.*
7 What's the damage? SPOKEN, HUMOROUS used to ask how much you have to pay for something

> WORD CHOICE **damage, harm**
> • Things or parts of your body (but NOT people) can be **damaged**: *The engine was too badly damaged to be repaired.* | *Clearly, smoking has damaged your lungs.*
> • Both things and people can be **harmed**: *chemicals that harm the environment* | *I would never do anything to harm you!*
> ►see THESAURUS box at **hurt**

damage[2] W3 *v.* [T] **1** to do physical harm to something or to part of someone's body, so that it is broken or injured: *The storm damaged hundreds of houses.* | *He slipped on some ice and damaged ligaments in his knee.* **2** if the good opinion that people have of a person or organization is damaged, something has happened to make them seem weaker or less important: *The crisis has badly damaged the President's authority.*

'damage conˌtrol *n.* [U] an attempt to limit the bad effects of something, especially by trying to make it seem as if the situation is not as bad as it really is: *Aides were busy with damage control after the President's badly-timed remark.*

dam•aged /'dæmɪdʒd/ *adj.* **1** physically harmed: *his damaged wrist* | **severely/badly/heavily damaged** *heavily damaged railroad lines* **2** having suffered the bad effects of something: *the company's damaged reputation* | *They needed time to repair their damaged relationship.* **3** emotionally or psychologically harmed: *a center for emotionally damaged children* | *She talks about her ex-boyfriend as "damaged goods"* (=someone who has too many emotional problems).

dam•ag•ing /'dæmɪdʒɪŋ/ *adj.* affecting someone or something in a bad way: **+to** *Wigand's statements could be very damaging to the tobacco companies.* | **damaging effects/results/consequences etc.** *the damaging effects of sunlight on the skin*

Da•mas•cus /də'mæskəs/ the capital city of Syria

dam•ask /'dæməsk/ *n.* [U] a type of cloth with a pattern woven in it, often used to cover furniture [**Origin:** 1300–1400 *Damascus*, where it was first made]

Dame /deɪm/ *n.* [C] a title of honor given by the British king or queen to a woman as a reward for the good things she has done: *Dame Judi Dench*

dame /deɪm/ *n.* [C] OLD-FASHIONED a woman [**Origin:** 1200–1300 Old French, Latin *domina* **lady of high rank**] → see also GRANDE DAME

'dame school *n.* [C] CULTURE in the past, a small school with one female teacher where young children were given a basic education in reading, writing, and mathematics, often in the teacher's home

damn /dæm/ *v.*
1 SAY STH IS BAD [T usually passive] to state that something is very bad: *The play was damned by critics after opening night.*
2 be damned to be given the punishment of going to HELL after you die: *The church says that all sinners will be damned.*
3 damn sb with faint praise to show that you think someone or something is not very good, by only praising them a little: *The report damns the proposal with faint praise.*

dam•na•ble /'dæmnəbəl/ *adj.* OLD-FASHIONED very bad or annoying: *That's a damnable lie!* —**damnably** *adv.*

dam•na•tion[1] /dæm'neɪʃən/ *n.* [U] the act of deciding to punish someone by sending them to HELL forever after they die, or the state of being in HELL forever

damnation[2] *interjection* OLD-FASHIONED used to show that you are very angry or annoyed

damned /dæmd/ *n.* **the damned** [plural] the people whom God will send to HELL when they die because they have been so bad

D

damn•ing /ˈdæmɪŋ/ *adj.* proving or showing that something is very bad or wrong: *a damning report on college athletics* | ***Damning evidence** was found in the recordings.*

Dam•o•cles /ˈdæməˌkliz/ → see **a/the sword of Damocles** at SWORD (3)

damp¹ /dæmp/ *adj.* slightly wet, sometimes in a way that is not nice: *Wipe the surface with a damp paper towel.* | *My hair's still a little damp.* ►see THESAURUS box at wet¹ —**dampness** *n.* [U] —**damply** *adv.*

THESAURUS
humid used to say that the weather, especially hot weather, is slightly wet and makes you uncomfortable: *It can be very humid in Florida during the summer.*
moist used to say that something, especially food, is slightly wet, especially in a way that seems nice: *The turkey was moist and tender.* | *a moist chocolate cake*

damp² *v.* [T] **1** to make something less strong or lower in amount SYN dampen: *The economy's slowdown has damped demand for steel.* **2** TECHNICAL to make a sound less loud SYN dampen

damp sth ↔ **down** *phr. v.* to make a fire burn more slowly, often by covering it with ash

damp•en /ˈdæmpən/ *v.* [T] **1** to make something slightly wet: *a cloth dampened with alcohol* **2** to make a feeling such as interest or hope less strong: *My mistakes didn't dampen my enthusiasm for gardening.* **3** to make something weaker or lower in amount: *Demand for gasoline has been dampened by the recession.*

damp•er /ˈdæmpɚ/ *n.* [C] **1 put a damper on sth** to stop something from being enjoyable or from having as good a result as expected: *The burglary put a damper on the family's Christmas.* **2** a small metal door in a FIREPLACE that is opened or closed to control how strongly a fire burns **3** a piece of equipment that stops a piano string from making a sound

dam•sel /ˈdæmzəl/ *n.* [C] **1** OLD-FASHIONED a young woman who is not married **2 damsel in distress** HUMOROUS a young woman who needs help

Dan /dæn/ in the Bible, the head of one of the 12 tribes of Israel

dance¹ /dæns/ S1 W2 *v.* **1** [I] to move your feet and body in a way that matches the style and speed of music: *Do you want to dance?* | +**to** *The audience clapped and danced to the music.* | +**with** *The bride danced with her father.* **2** [T] ENG. LANG. ARTS to do a type of dance: **dance the waltz/tango/samba etc.** *They banged cymbals and danced jigs.* **3** [I,T] ENG. LANG. ARTS to dance in performances, especially in BALLET: *He danced several solos in the "Nutcracker Suite."* | **dance with sth** *She danced with the San Francisco Ballet for six years.* **4** [I] to move up, down, and around quickly in a way that looks like dancing: *Red, white, and blue balloons danced in the wind.* **5** [I] if someone's eyes dance, they show happiness or humor SYN twinkle: *"Shh! Don't tell anyone," he said, his eyes dancing.* **6 dance to sb's tune** to obey someone completely, because they have control over you: *They control all the funding, so we have to dance to their tune.* —**dancing** *n.* [U] *I'd love to **go dancing**.*

dance around sth *phr. v.* DISAPPROVING to avoid discussing something or dealing with it directly: *The governor spent the day dancing around reporters' questions.*

dance² S2 W2 *n.* **1** [C] a special set of movements that matches the style and speed of a particular type of music: *The waltz is an easy dance to learn.* | *I taught her a few **dance steps*** (=the movements of a particular dance). | *Can you teach me how to **do** that **dance**?* **2** [C] a social event where the main activity is dancing: *Alan took Amy to the dance last weekend.* | *school dances*

THESAURUS
ball a large formal occasion where people dance
prom a formal dance party for high school students, usually held at the end of a school year
disco a place where people dance to recorded popular music
club/nightclub a place where people go to dance

3 [C] ENG. LANG. ARTS an act of dancing: *May I have the next dance* (=will you dance with me?)*?* | *Clare did a little dance* (=moved her body as if she were dancing) *of excitement.* **4** [C] ENG. LANG. ARTS a piece of music that you can dance to: *The band was playing a slow dance.* **5** [U] ENG. LANG. ARTS the activity or art of dancing, especially as a performance: *I had always thought I'd pursue dance as my career.* | *a dance troupe* ►see THESAURUS box at theater → see also **a song and dance** at SONG (5)

ˈdance band *n.* [C] a group of musicians who play music that you dance to

ˈdance card *n.* [C] **1 sb's dance card is full** used to say that someone is very busy or has a lot of romantic partners **2** a card with a list of the men that a woman has promised to dance with at a formal party

ˈdance floor *n.* [C] a special floor in a restaurant, club, hotel etc. for people to dance on

ˈdance hall *n.* [C] a large public room where people paid to go and dance in past times

danc•er /ˈdænsɚ/ *n.* [C] **1** someone who dances as a profession: *Her childhood dream was to be a ballet dancer.* **2 be a good/bad dancer** to dance well or badly

D and C /ˌdi ən ˈsi/ *n.* [C] **dilation and curettage** a medical operation to clean out the inside of a woman's UTERUS

dan•de•li•on /ˈdændəˌlaɪən/ *n.* [C] a wild plant with a small bright yellow flower, which later becomes a white ball of seeds that are blown away in the wind [**Origin:** 1400–1500 French *dent de lion* **lion's tooth** (because of the shape of the leaves)]

dan•der /ˈdændɚ/ *n.* [U] **1 get sb's dander up** OLD-FASHIONED or HUMOROUS to make someone angry: *Some recent columns have gotten readers' dander up.* **2** small pieces of dead skin that fall off an animal's body

dan•di•fied /ˈdændɪˌfaɪd/ *adj.* OLD-FASHIONED a man who is dandified wears very fashionable clothes in a way that shows he cares too much about his appearance

dan•dle /ˈdændl/ *v.* [T] OLD-FASHIONED to play with a baby or small child by moving them up and down in your arms or on your knee

dan•druff /ˈdændrəf/ *n.* [U] pieces of dead skin from someone's head that can be seen in their hair or on their shoulders

dan•dy¹ /ˈdændi/ *adj.* SPOKEN very good: *Everything is **fine and dandy**.*

dandy² *n.* [C] OLD-FASHIONED a man who spends a lot of time and money on his clothes and appearance

Dane /deɪn/ *n.* [C] someone from Denmark

dang /dæŋ/ also **ˈdang it!** *interjection* SPOKEN used to show frustration or anger: *Dang, another flat tire!* —**dang** *adj., adv.*: *This software is too dang expensive.*

dan•ger /ˈdeɪndʒɚ/ W2 *n.* **1** [U] a situation in which it is likely that someone or something will be harmed, killed, or destroyed: *Danger! No Swimming.* | *We felt that our lives were **in danger**.* | +**from** *None of the houses were in danger from the volcano's lava flow.* | +**of** *The danger of a fire in the home increases during the holidays.* | **put sb/sth in danger** *If you continue gaining weight, you're putting your health in danger.* | *The five injured soldiers are **out of danger*** (=no longer likely to die). | **great/grave/serious danger** *As the storm continued, we realized the ship was in great danger.*

THESAURUS
risk the chance that something bad may happen: *Smoking greatly increases the risk of lung cancer.*
threat the possibility that something bad will happen: *At that time, there seemed a constant threat of nuclear war.*
hazard something that may be dangerous or cause

accidents, problems etc.: *Oily rags must be disposed off as they are a fire hazard.*

2 [C,U] the possibility that something bad will happen: +**(that)** *I don't think there is any danger that there will be a misunderstanding on this point.* | **the danger of (doing) sth** *There is always the danger of being completely misunderstood.* | **in danger of (doing) sth** *Carlos is in danger of losing his job.* | ***There's no danger of*** *Rob taking the job* (=Rob will definitely not take the job). **3** [C usually plural] something or someone that may harm or kill you: ***the dangers of*** *drug use* | **be/pose a danger to sb** *Police said that Turner is a danger to herself and others.* [**Origin:** 1200–1300 Old French *dangier*, from Vulgar Latin *dominiarium* **power to do harm**]

dan·ger·ous /ˈdeɪndʒərəs/ S2 W2 *adj.* **1** able or likely to harm or kill you → see also HARMFUL OPP safe: *a dangerous road* | *dangerous substances* | *Walking on icy ponds is dangerous.* | +**to** *chemicals that are dangerous to the environment* | +**for** *Salt is dangerous for people with high blood pressure.* | **it is dangerous (for sb) to do sth** *It's dangerous for people to walk alone here at night.* | **very/highly/extremely dangerous** *a highly dangerous situation* **2** involving a lot of risk, or likely to cause problems SYN risky: *The decision was politically dangerous.* | **it is dangerous to do sth** *It is dangerous to assume that the house prices will continue to rise.* **3 dangerous ground/territory** a situation or subject that could make someone very angry or upset: *You're* ***on dangerous ground*** *when you talk politics with Ed.*

dan·ger·ous·ly /ˈdeɪndʒərəsli/ *adv.* **1** [only before an adj] to such a degree that it might cause harm or problems: *We were dangerously close to losing all our money.* | **dangerously high/low** *They found dangerously high levels of mercury in his blood.* **2** in a way that is dangerous: *The plane dipped dangerously several times.* **3 live dangerously** to do things that are risky, often used humorously to say that something is not very risky at all: *"Have another cookie – come on, live dangerously!"*

ˈdanger pay *n.* [U] another word for HAZARD PAY

dan·gle /ˈdæŋgəl/ *v.* **1** [I,T] to hang or swing loosely, or make something do this: +**from** *A cigarette dangled from her mouth.* | **dangle sth over/in sth** *I sat and dangled my legs over the side of the dock.* | **dangle sth by sth** *The phone had been left dangling by its cord.* **2 dangle sth in front of sb** to show or promise something that someone wants in order to make them do what you want → see also TANTALIZE: *Management had dangled a huge pay raise in front of them.* **3 leave sb dangling** DISAPPROVING to give someone no information about what will happen next or in the end: *The author leaves us dangling at the end of every chapter.* **4 leave sth dangling** DISAPPROVING to fail to make a decision about something, so that it still needs to be dealt with: *Too many important issues have been left dangling.*

Dan·iel /ˈdænyəl/ a book in the Old Testament of the Christian Bible

Dan·ish¹ /ˈdeɪnɪʃ/ *n.* **1** [U] the language of Denmark **2** [C] also **Danish pastry** a small sweet type of cake, often with fruit inside

Danish² *adj.* relating to the people or language of Denmark

dank /dæŋk/ *adj.* wet and cold, in a way that does not feel nice: *a dank prison cell* —**dankness** *n.* [U]

Dan·te /ˈdɑnteɪ/ also **Dante A·li·ghie·ri** /-ˌɑliˈgyɛri/ (1265–1321) an Italian poet

Dan·ton /dɑnˈtoʊn/, **Georges Jacques** /ʒɔrʒ ʒɑk/ (1759–1794) a French politician who became one of the leaders of the French Revolution

Dan·ube, the /ˈdænyub/ a long and important river in Eastern Europe, that starts in the Black Forest in Germany and runs through Austria, Hungary, and Romania into the Black Sea

dap·per /ˈdæpɚ/ *adj.* a man who is dapper is nicely dressed, has a neat appearance, and is usually small or thin

dap·ple /ˈdæpəl/ *v.* [T] LITERARY to mark something with spots of color, light, or shade: *Sunlight dappled the dark water.* —**dappled** *adj.*

ˌdapple-ˈgray *n.* [C] a horse that is gray with spots of darker gray

DAR /ˌdi eɪ ˈɑr/ → see DAUGHTERS OF THE AMERICAN REVOLUTION

Dar·da·nelles, the /ˌdɑrdnˈɛlz/ a long narrow area of ocean which connects the European and Asian parts of Turkey and was called the Hellespont in ancient times

dare¹ /dɛr/ W3 *v.* **1** [T] to try to persuade someone to do something dangerous or embarrassing as a way of proving that they are brave: **dare sb to do sth** *The other kids dared me to hit her with a snowball.* | *Yeah, you tell him.* ***I dare you!*** **2** [I not in progressive] a word meaning to be brave enough to do something risky, used especially in questions and negative statements: +**dare (to) do sth** *Who would dare to challenge the King's statement?* | *I* ***didn't dare*** *go home any later.*

SPOKEN PHRASES

3 don't you dare! said to warn someone not to do something because it makes you angry: *Don't you dare hang up on me again!* **4 how dare you** said to show that you are very angry and shocked about what someone has done or said: *How dare you make fun of me like that!* **5 dare I say (it)** FORMAL used when saying something that you think people may not accept or believe: *I found Shaw's play, dare I say it, boring.* **6 I dare say** also **I daresay** OLD-FASHIONED used to say that you think or hope that something may be true: *I dare say things will improve.* **7 dare, double dare** said when you are trying to persuade someone to do something dangerous

dare² *n.* [C] something dangerous or difficult that someone persuades you to do to prove you are brave: *Allen began his career as a comedian* ***on a dare*** (=as a result of a dare) *from a friend in 1979.*

dare·dev·il /ˈdɛrˌdɛvəl/ *n.* [C] someone who likes doing dangerous things —**daredevil** *adj.*: *a daredevil sport*

dare·n't /ˈdɛrənt/ *v.* OLD USE the short form of "I dare not"

Dar·es·Sa·laam /ˌdɑr ɛs səˈlɑm/ the former capital and largest city of Tanzania

dar·ing¹ /ˈdɛrɪŋ/ *adj.* **1** involving danger, or willing to do something that is dangerous or that involves a lot of risk: *a daring rescue attempt* | *a daring pilot* ▸see THESAURUS box at brave¹ **2** new or unusual in a way that is sometimes shocking: *his daring new film* —**daringly** *adv.*

daring² *n.* [U] courage that makes you willing to take risks or do unusual things: *We admired the pilot's skill and daring.* | *the daring shown in the band's music*

dark¹ /dɑrk/ S1 W1 *adj.*

1 PLACE having little or no light OPP light: *The church was dark and quiet.* | *dark winter days* | *Suddenly, the room* ***went dark*** (=became dark) *and somebody screamed.* | *The room was* ***growing darker*** (=becoming less light) *as the sun set.* | *Inside the closet it was* ***pitch dark*** (=completely dark). → see also PITCH-BLACK

2 it gets dark/it is dark used to say that it is becoming night, or that it is night: *Come on, let's go in. It's getting dark.* | *It's only 4:30 and it's already dark outside.* | *We built a fire as* ***it grew dark*** (=it became dark).

3 COLOR closer to black than to white in color OPP light OPP pale: *dark clouds* | **dark blue/green/brown etc.** *a dark blue shirt* ▸see THESAURUS box at color¹

4 HAIR/EYES/SKIN dark hair, eyes, or skin are brown or black in color: *her beautiful dark eyes* ▸see THESAURUS box at hair

5 PERSON if a white person is dark, they have brown or black hair, and often skin that is not very light OPP fair: *a tall dark man*

6 MYSTERIOUS mysterious or secret: *a dark secret* | *a dark hint*
7 EVIL evil and threatening: *the darker side of his personality* | *the dark world of drug trafficking*
8 UNHAPPY TIME a dark time is unhappy or without hope for the future: *the **dark days** of the war* | **sb's darkest hours/moments** *In his darkest moments he felt that no one cared.*
9 WITHOUT HOPE dark feelings and thoughts are sad and show that you do not see any hope for the future: *an extremely dark view of life*
10 HUMOR dark humor deals with sad or upsetting subjects in a funny way SYN black
11 FAR AWAY very far away, or seeming far away, and not usually seen or well understood: **the darkest corners/recesses of sth** *These thoughts had been pushed to the darkest corners of her mind.* | **darkest Africa/South America etc.** OLD-FASHIONED or HUMOROUS (=the parts of Africa etc. that are far away and most people know very little about)
[**Origin:** Old English *deorc*]

dark[2] *n.* **1 the dark** a situation in which there is no light, usually because the sun has gone down: *Children are sometimes afraid of the dark.* | *She walked home alone **in the dark**.* | *We stood outside in **the pitch dark*** (=when there is no light at all). **2 after/before/until dark** after, before, or until the sun goes down at night: *You shouldn't go into the park after dark.* | *We have to be home before dark.* | *I waited until dark to begin.* **3 in the dark** INFORMAL knowing nothing about something important because you have not been told about it: *Board members were **kept in the dark** about the company's financial problems.* → see also **a shot in the dark** at SHOT[1] (13)

'Dark ,Ages *n.* [plural] **the Dark Ages** the period in European history from 476 A.D. to about A.D. 1000

dark·en /ˈdɑrkən/ *v.* [I,T] **1** to become dark, or make something dark OPP lighten: *Age had darkened the wood.* | *The skies darkened, and the wind grew stronger.* **2** to make a situation or someone's attitude less hopeful, or to become less hopeful: *The news darkened their view of the situation.* **3 never darken my door again** OLD-FASHIONED or HUMOROUS used to tell someone that you do not want them in your house again

,dark 'glasses *n.* [plural] SUNGLASSES

,dark 'horse *n.* [C] someone who is not well known and who surprises everyone by winning a competition or election

dark·ly /ˈdɑrkli/ *adv.* **1 darkly funny/humorous/comic etc.** dealing with something that is bad or upsetting in a funny way: *the book's darkly humorous tone* **2** in a sad, angry, or threatening way: *He muttered darkly to himself.* **3** having dark hair, eyes, or skin: *a darkly handsome young man*

'dark ,meat *n.* [U] the darker-colored meat from the legs, THIGHS etc. of a chicken, TURKEY, or other bird → see also WHITE MEAT

dark·ness /ˈdɑrknɪs/ W3 *n.* [U] **1** a place or time when there is no light: *We walked out into the darkness.* | **total/complete/pitch darkness** *She woke in pitch darkness.* | *He was one of the last players on the field as **darkness fell*** (=it became night). | *The clouds moved across the moon, leaving us **in** complete **darkness**.* | *The lights went out and we were **plunged into darkness*** (=suddenly completely without light). | *They escaped **under cover of darkness*** (=hidden by darkness). **2** the dark quality of a color: *the darkness of her skin* **3** sadness and lack of hope: *the darkness of his days in jail* **4 forces/powers of darkness** evil, or the DEVIL

dark·room /ˈdɑrkrum/ *n.* [C] a special room with a red light or no light, where film from a camera is made into photographs

dar·ling[1] /ˈdɑrlɪŋ/ *n.* [C] **1** SPOKEN used when speaking to someone you love: *Hello darling. Did you have a good day?* **2** SPOKEN someone who seems very nice, generous, or friendly: *He's such a darling.* **3 the darling of sth** the most popular person or thing in a particular group: *Charlie was the darling of the New York club scene.*

darling[2] *adj.* SPOKEN **1** used to say that you love someone: *This is my darling little sister.* **2** said when you think someone or something is attractive: *Those pants are darling.*

darn[1] /dɑrn/ *v.* [T]

SPOKEN PHRASES

1 darn (it) said when you are annoyed about something: *Darn, I forgot my purse.* **2 I'll be darned** said when you are surprised about something: *Did they say that? Well, I'll be darned!* **3 (I'll be/I am) darned if...** used for making a strong statement: *I'll be darned if I let my kids talk that way* (=I definitely would not let my kids talk that way). | *"Who's he?" "Darned if I know."* (=used to emphasize that you don't know) **4 darn you/them etc.** used to show that you are extremely angry or annoyed with someone or something

5 to repair a hole in a piece of clothing by stitching it with thread

darn[2] also **darned** /dɑrnd/ *adj.* SPOKEN **1** used to emphasize that you are angry or annoyed: *Darn mosquitoes!* **2** used for emphasis: *That's the biggest darned cat I've ever seen.* | *It's a darn shame he couldn't come.*

darn[3], darned *adv.* used to emphasize how bad or good someone or something is: **pretty darn nice/stupid/exciting etc.** *It's small, but it looks pretty darn good to me!*

darn[4] *n.* [C] a place where a hole in a piece of clothing has been repaired neatly with thread

darn·ing /ˈdɑrnɪŋ/ *n.* [U] OLD-FASHIONED the work of repairing holes in clothing by stitching them with thread, especially done to wool socks

Dar·row /ˈdæroʊ/, **Clar·ence** /ˈklærəns/ (1857–1938) a U.S. lawyer famous for the Scopes Trial, when he defended a teacher who was taken to court for teaching his students about EVOLUTION and the ideas of Charles Darwin

dart[1] /dɑrt/ *v.* **1** [I always + adv./prep.] to move suddenly and quickly in a particular direction: **+across/into/out etc.** *The mouse was darting in and out of its hole.* | *A child darted across the street.* **2** LITERARY to look at someone or something very quickly and suddenly: *His little black eyes darted around my office.*

dart[2] *n.* **1** [C] a small pointed object that is thrown or shot as a weapon or thrown in the game of darts: *Some South American Indians use poison darts for hunting.* **2 darts** [U] a game in which darts are thrown at a circular board with numbers on it **3** [singular] a sudden quick movement in a particular direction: *The cat **made a dart for** (=ran towards) the door.* **4** [C] a small fold sewn into a piece of clothing to make it fit better

dart·board /ˈdɑrt˺bɔrd/ *n.* [C] a circular board used in the game of darts

Charles Darwin

Dar·win /ˈdɑrwɪn/, **Charles** (1809–1882) a British scientist who developed the THEORY of EVOLUTION, the idea that plants and animals develop gradually from simpler to more complicated forms by NATURAL SELECTION

dash[1] /dæʃ/ *v.* **1** [I] to go or run somewhere very quickly: **+into/across/behind etc.** *Duncan dashed across the lawn and climbed the fence.* ►see THESAURUS box at **run[1]**, **rush[1]** **2 dash (sb's) hopes/dreams** to disappoint someone by showing or telling them that what they want

will not happen: *The court's decision dashed our hopes for a new trial.* → see also **raise sb's hopes** at RAISE[1] (6)
3 dash (sth) against/to/into etc. LITERARY to hit violently against something, usually so that it breaks, or to make something do this: *Huge waves dashed the boats against the rocks.* | *Driven by wind, the rain dashed against the thick stone walls.*

dash off *phr. v.* **1 dash sth ↔ off** to write or draw something very quickly: *I dashed off a letter of complaint.* **2** to leave somewhere very quickly: *I called her before dashing off to the airport.*

dash² *n.*
1 SMALL AMOUNT a) [C] a very small amount of a liquid or other substance, especially added to a drink or to food: **a dash of sth** *Add a dash of salt to the beans.* **b)** a small amount of something such as a quality: **a dash of sth** *It's fiction with a dash of history.*
2 RACE [singular] a race to find out who can run the fastest over a short distance: *the 40-yard dash*
3 make a dash for sth to run very quickly in order to get away from something or in order to reach something: *As the fire spread up the walls, Stan made a dash for safety.* | *We heard the whistle and* ***made a mad dash*** (=ran extremely quickly) *for the departing ship.*
4 MARK IN A SENTENCE [C] ENG. LANG. ARTS a mark (–) used in informal writing or when representing spoken language to separate sentences or phrases, for example in the sentence "Don't talk to me now – I'm busy." → see also HYPHEN ►see THESAURUS box at **punctuation mark**
5 CAR [C] INFORMAL a short form of DASHBOARD
6 SOUND [C] a long sound or flash of light used for sending messages in MORSE CODE → see also DOT
7 STYLE [U] OLD-FASHIONED style, energy, and courage in someone such as a soldier

dash·board /ˈdæʃbɔrd/ also **dash** *n.* [C] the board that is in front of the driver of a car and has the controls on it [**Origin:** 1800–1900 *dash* **to strike with small drops of liquid** (17–19 centuries) + *board* (because it was originally a board to stop mud getting into a vehicle)] → see picture on page A36

da·shi·ki /dəˈʃiki, dɑ-/ *n.* [C] a long loose brightly colored piece of clothing, worn especially in Africa

dash·ing /ˈdæʃɪŋ/ *adj.* OLD-FASHIONED a man or a thing that is dashing is very attractive and fashionable: *a dashing young doctor* —**dashingly** *adv.*

das·tard·ly /ˈdæstɚdli/ *adj.* OLD-FASHIONED very cruel or evil

DAT /ˌdi eɪ ˈti, dæt/ *n.* **digital audio tape** a system used to record music, sound, or information in DIGITAL form

da·ta /ˈdeɪt̬ə, ˈdæt̬ə/ Ac S2 W1 *n.* [plural] *singular form* **datum** **1** information or facts that have been gathered in order to be studied: *The data showed that most patients were over 40.* | *data analysis* | **collect/gather data** *You must make these decisions before you start to gather data.* | **+on** *data on the use of pesticides* | **historical/statistical/scientific etc. data** *vast amounts of statistical data* | *The software turns* ***raw data*** (=data that has been collected but not studied, put into groups etc.) *into useable information.* **2** COMPUTERS information in a form that can be stored and used on a computer: *electronic data* | *The program allows your computer and PDA to share data.* | *It's possible to* ***store*** *a lot of* ***data*** *on a DVD.* [**Origin:** 1600–1700 plural of *datum* **fact, piece of information** (17–21 centuries), from Latin, past participle of *dare* **to give**]

ˈdata ˌbank *n.* [C] **1** COMPUTERS a place where information on a particular subject is stored, usually in a computer: *The national genetics data bank will be a storehouse of hundreds of blood samples.* **2** another word for DATABASE

da·ta·base /ˈdeɪt̬əˌbeɪs/ *n.* [C] COMPUTERS a large amount of data stored in a computer system and organized so that you can find and use it easily: *The library has a database of over 21 million book titles.*

ˈdata ˌcapture *n.* [U] COMPUTERS the process of putting information into a computer in a DIGITAL form that the computer can use

ˈdata ˌmining *n.* [U] COMPUTERS the process of using a computer to find new patterns and relationships in large amounts of computer data

ˌdata ˈprocessing *n.* [U] COMPUTERS the use of computers to store and organize data, especially in business

ˌdata reˈtrieval *n.* [U] COMPUTERS the process of searching for and selecting data from where it is stored in a computer

ˈdata ˌtransfer *n.* [U] COMPUTERS the process of moving data from one system or one part of a system to another: *simple and fast data transfer between programs*

date¹ /deɪt/ S1 W2 *n.* [C]
1 DAY a particular day of the month or year, shown by a number: *"What's the date today?" "September 30."* | *The date on the newspaper is October 12, 1966.* | **the date of sth** *The date of the next meeting is April 23.* | **date of birth/birth date** *There is no date of birth listed on the form.* | *Have you* ***set a date*** (=chosen a particular date) *for the wedding?* | **a delivery/departure/launch etc. date** *Can I arrange a delivery date for the furniture?* | *You must apply for a passport at least two months before your* ***date of departure*** (=date you are leaving a country).
2 ROMANTIC an occasion when you arrange to meet someone that you like in a romantic way: *Was that your first date?* | *I* ***have a date*** *tomorrow.* | *We're* ***going on a date*** *Friday night.* → see also BLIND DATE, DOUBLE DATE
3 at...date used to talk about a time in the past or future that is not specified exactly: *The movie will premiere this summer, at a date that has not been specified.* | **at a later date/at some future date** *We'll deal with this problem at a later date.*
4 at this early date at an early time in a long process: *It's hard to tell what will happen at this early date.*
5 to date up to now: *This may be the winery's best Cabernet to date.*
6 SOCIAL an arrangement to meet, especially socially, at a particular time or place: *We* ***made a date*** *to get together with Evan and Debbie for New Year's Eve.* | **a lunch/dinner date** (=an arrangement to meet someone for lunch or dinner) | *We have* ***a play date*** (=an arrangment for young children to play together) *today with one of Katie's friends from school.*
7 FRUIT BIOLOGY a sweet sticky brown fruit with a long hard seed inside
8 PERIOD the period of time when something was built or made: *The church was built in 1392, but the altar is of a much later date.*
9 PERSON someone that you have a date with: *Can I bring my date to the party?*
[**Origin:** (1, 3–5) 1300–1400 French, Late Latin *data* from the past participle of Latin *dare* **to give**] → see also CLOSING DATE, EXPIRATION DATE, OUT-OF-DATE, UP-TO-DATE

date² S2 W3 *v.* **1** [T] to write or print the date on something: *I forgot to date the check.* | *a memo dated November 13* **2** [T] to find out when something very old was made or formed, or when an ancient event happened: *Scientists have not yet dated the bones they found.* **3** [T] to have a romantic relationship with someone: *Is he still dating Sarah?* **4** [T] if something that you say, do, or wear dates you, it shows that you are fairly old: *Yes, I remember the moon landings – that dates me, doesn't it?* **5** [I] if clothing, art etc. dates, it looks old or old-fashioned: *His furniture designs have hardly dated at all.*

date from/date back to *phr. v.* to have existed since a particular time in the past: *This church dates from the 13th century.*

date·book /ˈdeɪt˺bʊk/ *n.* [C] a small book in which you write things you must do, addresses, telephone numbers etc. → see picture at PERSONAL ORGANIZER

dat·ed /ˈdeɪt̬ɪd/ *adj.* looking or seeming old or old-fashioned: *That dress looks dated now.* → see also OUT-OF-DATE

date·line /ˈdeɪt˺laɪn/ *n.* **1** [singular] the INTERNATIONAL DATE LINE **2** [C] the line at the top of a newspaper article that says the date and the city or place where the news is from —**dateline** *v.* [T usually passive]

'date rape *n.* [C,U] a RAPE that is done by someone the woman has met in a social situation —**date rape** *v.* [T] → see also ACQUAINTANCE RAPE

'date stamp *n.* [C] **1** a piece of equipment used for printing the date on letters, documents etc. **2** the mark that is made by this piece of equipment

'dating ˌservice *n.* [C] a business that helps people to meet someone in order to have a romantic relationship with them

da·tive /'deɪṭɪv/ *n.* [C] ENG. LANG. ARTS a particular form of a noun in some languages such as Latin and German, which shows that the noun is the INDIRECT OBJECT of a verb —**dative** *adj.*

D

daub¹ /dɔb/ *v.* [T] to put paint or a soft substance onto a surface, without being very careful [**Origin:** 1300–1400 Old French *dauber*, from Latin *dealbare* **to make white, whitewash**]

daub² *n.* **1** [C] a small amount of a soft or sticky substance: +**of** *a daub of glue* **2** [U] TECHNICAL mud or clay used for making walls

daugh·ter /'dɔṭə/ S1 W1 *n.* [C] **1** someone's female child: *My daughter is three.* | *I have two daughters and a son.* ▸see THESAURUS box at **relative¹** **2** TECHNICAL something new that forms or develops when something else divides or ends: *English is a daughter language of German and Latin.* [**Origin:** Old English *dohtor*]

'daughter-in-law *n. plural* **daughters-in-law** [C] the wife of your son: *I'd like you to meet my daughter-in-law.* → see also SON-IN-LAW

daugh·ter·ly /'dɔṭəli/ *adj.* OLD-FASHIONED behaving in the way that a daughter is supposed to behave

ˌDaughters of the AˌAmerican Revo'lution ABBREVIATION **DAR** an organization for women whose families have been in the U.S. since the American Revolutionary War

daunt /dɔnt, dɑnt/ *v.* [T usually passive] to make someone feel afraid or less confident: *The lightning did little to daunt local golfers.* [**Origin:** 1200–1300 Old French *danter*, from Latin *domitare* **to train (something) so that it obeys**]

daunt·ing /'dɔntɪŋ/ *adj.* frightening in a way that makes you feel less confident: *The interview process can be daunting.* | *Teaching teenagers about art is a* ***daunting task.***

daunt·less /'dɔnt˺lɪs/ *adj.* LITERARY confident and not easily frightened: *dauntless courage* —**dauntlessly** *adv.*

dau·phin /'dɔfən, 'doʊ-/ *n.* [C] the oldest son of a King of France

dau·phine /dɔ'fin, doʊ-/ *n.* [C] the wife of the oldest son of a King of France

da·ven·port /'dævənˌpɔrt/ *n.* [C] a large SOFA, especially one that can be made into a bed

Da·vid /dɑ'vid/**, Jacques-Lou·is** /ʒɑk lu'i/ (1748–1825) a French PAINTER famous for his paintings in the CLASSICAL style that supported the ideas of the French Revolution

Da·vid /'deɪvɪd/**, King** (died around 962 B.C.) in the Bible, one of the Kings of Israel, who is also believed to have written some of the Psalms. When David was a boy, he killed the GIANT (=a very tall strong man) Goliath.

Da·vis /'deɪvɪs/**, Jef·fer·son** /'dʒɛfəsən/ (1808–1889) a U.S. politician who was the President of the Confederacy (=the Southern U.S. states) during the U.S. Civil War

Davis, Miles /maɪlz/ (1926–1991) a U.S. musician who played the TRUMPET and had an important influence on the development of JAZZ

da·vit /'deɪvɪt, 'dæ-/ *n.* [C] one of a pair of long curved poles that SAILORS swing out over the side of a ship in order to lower a boat into the water

daw·dle /'dɔdl/ *v.* [I] to waste time by taking too long to do something or go somewhere: *Hurry up! Quit dawdling!* | +**over** *I dawdled over a second cup of coffee.* —**dawdler** *n.* [C]

dawn¹ /dɔn/ *n.* [C, U] **1** the time at the beginning of the day when light first appears → see also DUSK SYN **daybreak**: *We talked almost until dawn.* | *An ice storm* ***at dawn*** *paralyzed St. Louis traffic.* | *When* ***dawn broke*** (=the first light of the day appeared) *we could see the mountains in the distance.* | *Mom got up* ***at the crack of dawn*** (=very early in the morning) *to put the turkey into the oven.* | *We worked hard* ***from dawn til dusk*** (=all day while it is light). **2 the dawn of sth** the beginning of a period of time, especially one that people feel very positive and hopeful about SYN **birth**: *the dawn of the 21st century* | **the dawn of time/civilization/history** (=the time when people first existed) [**Origin:** 1200–1300 *daw* **to dawn** (10–19 centuries), from Old English *dagian*; related to *day*] → see also FALSE DAWN

dawn² *v.* [I] **1** if day or morning dawns, it begins: *As day dawned, we looked out to see the snow.* | **dawn bright/clear/fresh etc.** *Thursday dawned bright and sunny.* **2** LITERARY if a period of time or situation dawns, it begins: *A new technological era was dawning.* **3** LITERARY if a fact dawns, you realize it or think of it for the first time

dawn on sb *phr. v.* if a fact or idea dawns on you, you realize it or think of it for the first time: *The horrible truth was slowly dawning on me.* | *Gradually* ***it dawned on me that*** *he wasn't going to change.*

day /deɪ/ S1 W1 *n. plural* **days**

1 24 HOURS [C] a period of 24 hours: *"What day is today?" "Friday."* | *We spent four days in Cuba.* | *Tanya left two days ago* (=two days before today). | **on a/the day** *It was raining on the day we got there.* | *He didn't leave the house* ***for days*** (=for several days). | *My mother calls me* ***every day.*** | *Take two pills* ***a day*** (=each day). | *One of my friends was in a car accident* ***the day before yesterday.*** | *I have a meeting with him* ***the day after tomorrow.*** | **Independence/election/Christmas etc. day** *There was rioting on election day.*

2 WHEN IT IS LIGHT [C,U] the period of time between when it becomes light in the morning and the time it becomes dark OPP **night**: *It was sunny all day.* | ***On a hot day*** *it's nice to have ice cream.* | *Morning is my favorite* ***time of day.*** | *Owls usually sleep* ***by day*** (=during the day) *and hunt by night.* | *My neighbor's dog barks* ***day and night*** (=all the time).

3 WHEN YOU'RE AWAKE [C usually singular] the time during the day when you are awake: *His day begins at six.* | *It's been* ***a*** *very* ***long day*** (=a day when you were very busy and awake for a long time). | *Frank eats* ***all day long*** (=continuously during the day). | *We took the kids for* ***a day out*** (=a day when you go somewhere for fun) *at the zoo.*

4 WHEN YOU'RE WORKING [C] the time spent working during a 24-hour period: *I work an eight-hour day.* | **a bad/good day** *I had a terrible day at work today.* | *He never* ***took a day off*** (=had a day of vacation) *in ten years.* → see also WORKDAY

5 PAST [C] used to talk about a time in the past: *That was the day I realized I needed help.* | ***One day*** (=on a day in the past), *he just decided to quit his job.* | *I went to the new library* ***the other day*** (=on a day not too long ago). | *There wasn't much traffic* ***in those days*** (=during a period quite a long time ago). | *Travel was not so easy, before* ***the days of*** *airplanes* (=the time when airplanes began to exist). | ***In the early days of*** (=at the beginning) *our marriage, we lived in New York.* | *McClellan was the best trainer of troops* ***in his day*** (=during the time when he was young and successful). | *The article reflected the thinking* ***of the day*** (=that was happening at a time in the past). | **the (good) old days** (=a time in the past that you think was better that the present time) | **those were the days!** (=used to say that a time in the past was better than the present time)

6 NOW [C] used to talk about the situation that exists now: *I don't have the time to do much exercise* ***these days*** (=now, as opposed to in the past). | *The house*

remains exactly the same **to this day** (=up to now, even though a long time has passed). | **until/up to/to the present day** (=until and including now)
7 FUTURE [C] used to talk about a time in the future: *I can't wait for* **the day when** *I can quit my job.* | **one/some day** *One day, we'll own a big house in country.* | ***One of these days*** (=soon, used to warn that something bad will happen) *I'm going to get mad and hit him.* | *The baby is due* ***any day now*** (=very soon). | **the day will/may come** *The day will finally come when a woman is elected president.*
8 TIME OF SUCCESS [C] a time in someone's life when they are successful, young, or both: ***In my day*** (=when I was young) *school was very different.* | **sb's army/student/working etc. days** *She remembered her childhood days very clearly.* | *Michael knew Annette during* ***her days as*** (=the time when she was) *a Broadway actress.* | **sb's day will come** (=used to say that someone will be successful in the future)
9 make sb's day to make someone very happy: *Your smile makes my day.*
10 day by day slowly and gradually: *Day by day Jeff began to feel better.* | *We'll just* ***take it day by day.***
11 from day one INFORMAL from the beginning of a process, activity etc.: *We've said from day one that we finish on time.*
12 from day to day used when you are comparing the differences that happen to something on different days → see also DAY-TO-DAY: *Property values can vary from day to day.*
13 day after day happening continuously for a long time so that you become annoyed or bored: *The same exercises can get boring if you do them day after day.*
14 day in, day out every day for a long time: *I'm tired of school. It's the same thing day in, day out.*
15 in this day and age used to say what a situation is like, especially when you think it should be different in a modern society: *It seems incredible, in this day and age, that a ship can just disappear.*
16 have an off day to be less successful or happy than usual, for no particular reason: *He was obviously having an off day when he wrote this.*

SPOKEN PHRASES

17 not have all day to not have much time to do something: *Hurry up, we don't have all day!*
18 it's not my/your/his day used when several bad things have happened to someone in one day: *This is just not my day. I was late to work, my computer crashed, and my boss yelled at me.*
19 it's (just) one of those days used to say that everything seems to be going wrong
20 that'll be the day used to say that you think something is very unlikely to happen: *"Bill says he'll wash the dishes tonight." "That'll be the day!"*
21 it's your/his/my lucky day! used when something very good happens to someone: *It must be my lucky day. I just found a $10 bill.*
22 be on days also **be working days** to be working during the day doing a job that you sometimes have to do at night, for example if you work in a hospital: *I'm on days this week.*
23 it's not every day (that) used to say that something does not happen often and is therefore very special: *It's not every day that you see a movie star.*
24 (live to) see the day to experience something that you thought would never happen: *I never thought I'd see the day when we'd have to cut so many jobs.*
25 40/50/60 etc. if sb's a day used to emphasize that someone is at least as old as you are saying, especially because they look old: *She's ninety if she's a day.*
26 make a day of it to decide to spend all day doing something, usually for pleasure: *We were going into New York anyway, so we decided to make a day of it.*

27 have had your/its day to not be successful, powerful, or famous anymore: *It seems as if Communism has had its day.*
28 by day's end by the time it becomes night on a particular day: *By day's end, 1,000 firefighters had been called in.*
29 five/three/nine etc. years to the day exactly five years, three years etc. ago: *It was 25 years to the day after they got married.*
30 sb's days someone's time or someone's whole life: *Mary spends her days writing love letters.* | *She ended her days in poverty.*
31 sb's/sth's days (as sth) are numbered used to say that someone or something will not continue to exist or be effective: *Her days as CEO are numbered.*
32 from one day to the next if something changes from one day to the next, it does not stay the same for very long: *I never know where he'll be from one day to the next.*
33 soup/dish/fish of the day the special soup etc. that a restaurant serves on a particular day
34 the day of reckoning the time when you are punished or made to suffer for the things you have done wrong → see also **call it a day** at CALL[1] (12), DAY JOB, **every dog has its/his day** at DOG[1] (6), **have a field day** at FIELD DAY (1), HALF-DAY, **it's (a little) late in the day** at LATE[1] (11), **save the day** at SAVE[1] (13)

WORD CHOICE from day to day, day by day, day after day
• Something that changes or goes on **day by day** or **from day to day** is a continuous action: *Day by day the weather is getting warmer.* | *Their love grew stronger day by day.* | *The polls can change from day to day.*
• Separate events that are repeated happen **day after day**: *I get tired of listening to their complaints day after day* (=the same thing happens every day).

GRAMMAR
• Remember that **on** is used with the names of days and the word **day** itself: *on Thursday/on that day/on the same day/on the second day* (NOT **in** or **at**). However, **on** is never used with the phrase **the other day**, when you do not say the exact day when something happened: *I went to the beach the other day* (=a few days ago). Compare: *We spent two days in the mountains – on the first day we went hiking and on the second we went fishing.*
• Note that you say **in those days** but **these days** (NOT *in these days*): *In those days, people rode trains, but these days everybody flies.*
• You do not use **the** with **all day**. *Some people watch TV all day* (NOT *all the day*).

Day /deɪ/, **Dor·o·thy** /ˈdɔrəθi/ (1897–1980) a U.S. writer and social REFORMER who started the Catholic Worker magazine and group of CHARITY workers

Da·yan /daɪˈɑn/, **Mosh·e** /ˈmɔʃeɪ/ (1915–1981) an Israeli military leader and politician, who was responsible for Israel's victory in the Arab-Israeli War of 1967, and later became Israel's Foreign Minister

day·bed /ˈdeɪbɛd/ *n.* [C] a bed that can be used as a SOFA

ˈday book *n.* [C] a book with all of a company's financial records in it, including the dates when things were bought, sold, delivered etc.

day·break /ˈdeɪbreɪk/ *n.* [U] the time of day when light first appears: *At daybreak, the police began searching.*

ˈday camp *n.* [C] a place where children go during the day to do activities, sports, art etc. on their summer vacation from school → see also CAMP

day·care, day care /ˈdeɪkɛr/ *n.* [U] **1** the care of babies and young children by people other than their parents, while their parents are at work: *I don't want to* ***put the babies in daycare.*** **2** the care of adults who are too sick or too old to take care of themselves, by someone who is paid to come to their house during the day

ˈday care ˌcenter *n.* [C] a place where babies and young children can be left and taken care of while their parents are at work

daydream

day·dream¹ /ˈdeɪdrim/ *v.* [I] to think about something nice, for example something you would like to happen, especially when this makes you forget what you should be doing: [+ about/of] *Many women daydream about having time to themselves.* ▸see THESAURUS box at **imagine** —**daydreamer** *n.* [C] —**daydreaming** *n.* [U]

daydream² *n.* [C] pleasant thoughts you have while you are awake, that make you forget what you are doing

Day-Glo /ˈdeɪglou/ *adj.* TRADEMARK having a very bright orange, green, yellow, or pink color: *a Day-Glo orange vest*

ˈday job *n.* [C] **1** someone's main job that they do during the day from which they earn most of their money **2 don't quit your day job** SPOKEN, HUMOROUS used to tell someone that you do not think what they are doing is good or that their idea for making money will not be successful

ˈday ˌlabor *n.* [U] physical work that someone is paid to do, one day at a time —**day laborer** *n.* [C]

day·light /ˈdeɪlaɪt/ *n.* [U] **1** the time during the day when it is light: *The robberies usually occur during daylight hours.* | *The air search will continue* ***at daylight*** (=the time when it is first light in the morning) *on Friday.* **2** the light produced by the sun during the day: ***In daylight****, the color looks completely different.* **3 scare/frighten the (living) daylights out of sb** INFORMAL to frighten someone a lot **4 beat/knock/pound the (living) daylights out of sb** INFORMAL **a)** to hit someone a lot and seriously hurt them **b)** to defeat someone in a game, race, election etc. by a large amount: *We got the daylights beaten out of us by Louisiana Tech.* → see also **in broad daylight** at BROAD¹ (6)

ˌdaylight ˈsaving time also **ˌdaylight ˈsavings** *n.* [U] the time from early April to late October when clocks are set one hour ahead of STANDARD TIME

ˌday ˈof ˈjudgment *n.* [singular] JUDGMENT DAY

ˈday room *n.* [C] a room in a hospital where PATIENTS can go to read, watch television etc.

ˈday school *n.* [C,U] a school, especially a PRIVATE SCHOOL, where the students go home in the evening, rather than one where they live → see also BOARDING SCHOOL

day·time /ˈdeɪtaɪm/ *n.* [U] the time during the day between the time when it gets light and the time when it gets dark SYN **day** OPP **nighttime**: *I woke up, thinking it was daytime.* | **in/during the daytime** *Parking in the city is difficult in the daytime.* | *Please include a daytime phone number* (=where you can be called during the day).

ˌday-to-ˈday *adj.* [only before noun] happening every day as a normal part of your life, your job etc.: *The manager is responsible for the day-to-day operations of the hotel.*

Day·ton Ac·cords, the /ˌdeɪtˀn əˈkɔrdz/ HISTORY an agreement between Bosnia, Croatia, and Serbia, signed in 1995 to end the fighting in Bosnia

ˈday ˌtrading *n.* [U] ECONOMICS the activity of buying STOCK and selling it again very quickly in order to try to make a lot of money, which is considered very risky —**day trader** *n.* [C]

daze /deɪz/ *n.* **in a daze** unable to think clearly, especially because you have been shocked, surprised, or hurt: *Survivors wandered through the wreckage in a daze.*

dazed /deɪzd/ *adj.* unable to think clearly, especially because you have been shocked, surprised, or hurt: *Anxious family members sat dazed in the waiting room.* [**Origin:** 1300–1400 Old Norse *dasathr* **very tired**]

daz·zle /ˈdæzəl/ *v.* [T usually passive] **1** to make someone admire someone or something: *We were dazzled by the mountain scenery.* | **dazzle sb with sth** *He dazzles audiences with his talent and wit.* **2** if a very bright light dazzles you, it stops you from seeing well for a short time —**dazzle** *n.* [U]

daz·zling /ˈdæzlɪŋ/ *adj.* **1** very impressive, attractive, or interesting: *dazzling computer graphics* | *a dazzling display of football talent* ▸see THESAURUS box at **impressive** **2** a light that is dazzling makes you unable to see well for a short time: *the dazzling noonday sun* ▸see THESAURUS box at **bright**

dbl. *n., adj.* the written abbreviation of DOUBLE

DC /ˌdi ˈsi/ the abbreviation of DIRECT CURRENT → see also AC

D.C. /ˌdi ˈsi/ **District of Columbia** the area containing the city of Washington, the CAPITAL of the U.S.

D-Day /ˈdi deɪ/ *n.* [C,U] **1** HISTORY June 6, 1944; the day the American army, the British army, and other armies landed in France during World War II **2** INFORMAL a day on which an important action is planned to happen or begin: *Ok everyone, this is D-Day. We have to get this done!*

DDT /ˌdi di ˈti/ *n.* [U] a chemical used to kill insects that harm crops, which is now illegal

DE the written abbreviation of DELAWARE

de- /di, dɪ/ *prefix* **1** in some verbs, nouns, and adjectives, it shows an opposite: *a depopulated area* (=which all or most of the population has left) | *deindustrialization* (=becoming less industrial) **2** in some verbs, it means to remove something or remove things from something: *to debone the fish* (=remove its bones) | *The king was dethroned* (=removed from power). **3** in some verbs, it means to make something less SYN **reduce**: *to devalue the currency*

DEA /ˌdi i ˈeɪ/ *n.* [singular] **Drug Enforcement Agency** an organization in the U.S. government that makes sure people obey the drug laws

dea·con /ˈdikən/ *n.* [C] a religious official in some Christian churches

de·ac·ti·vate /diˈæktəˌveɪt/ *v.* [T] **1** to do something to a system or a piece of equipment so that it cannot be used anymore: *In 1976, the old lighthouse was deactivated.* **2** to remove a person or group from a larger group, such as the army or a sports team, so that they are not a member of the group anymore: *The Giants deactivated their wide receiver in October.*

dead¹ /dɛd/ S1 W1 *adj.*

1 NOT ALIVE not alive anymore → see also LIVE OPP **alive**: *Her mother has been dead for ten years.* | *a dead tree* | ***A dead body*** (=a dead person) *was found in the park.* | *He was* ***found dead*** *in his jail cell.* | *The earthquake* ***left*** *thousands of people* ***dead*** (=caused their deaths). | *She had been attacked and* ***left for dead*** (=left alone to die). | *The men are still missing and* ***presumed dead*** (=used in news reports to say that someone is believed to be dead). | *I'll be* ***dead and gone*** (=dead for a long time) *by the time you're 50.*

THESAURUS

lifeless LITERARY dead or seeming to be dead: *their lifeless bodies*

late/deceased FORMAL dead: *Mrs. Lombard's late husband* | *their recently deceased grandmother*

2 NOT WORKING not working because there is no electrical power: *Is the battery dead?* | *The phones* ***went dead*** *during the storm.*
3 NOT INTERESTING/SUCCESSFUL not interesting, important, or successful any more: *Is feminism dead?* | *a dead debate*
4 PLACE/TIME a place, period of time, or situation that is dead does not have anything interesting happening in it: *The bar is usually dead on weekdays.*
5 a dead language a dead language is not used by ordinary people anymore SYN **living**
6 TIRED SPOKEN very tired SYN **beat**: *I can't go out tonight. I'm dead.* | *The next morning I was* ***half dead*** (=so tired you do not feel well). | *Most of the soldiers were* ***dead on their feet.***
7 BODY PART a part of your body that is dead has no feeling in it for a short time: *Her fingers had* ***gone dead*** *in the cold.*
8 be dead set on/against sth to be determined that something will or will not happen: *Key White House aides are dead set against the proposal.*
9 COMPLETE complete or total: *The car came to a dead stop.* | *There was dead silence in the room.* | **in a dead faint** (=completely unconscious)
10 you're dead (meat)! SPOKEN used to threaten someone with punishment or violence: *If anything happens to the car, you're dead!*
11 beat/flog a dead horse SPOKEN to waste time or effort by trying to do something that is impossible or talking about something that has already been decided
12 LAND/WATER/PLANETS containing no life: *a dead moon of Jupiter* | *the Dead Sea*
13 IN SPORTS when the ball is dead in some games, players must stop playing until the officials start the game again
14 NO EMOTION dead eyes or a dead voice show no emotion SYN **lifeless**
15 dead center the exact center: *Hit the nail dead center so that it doesn't bend.*
16 dead on arrival a) someone who is dead on arrival is DECLARED to be dead as soon as they are brought to a hospital **b)** a law, plan etc. that is dead on arrival is not worth considering even when it is first shown to the public: *The budget was dead on arrival in Congress.*
17 sb wouldn't be caught/seen dead said in order to emphasize that someone would never do something because it would be too embarrassing: **sb wouldn't be caught/seen dead doing sth** *Melanie wouldn't be seen dead wearing a dress like that!* | +**with/at/in** *I wouldn't be caught dead at one of Val's parties.*
18 over my dead body SPOKEN used to say that you are determined not to allow something to happen: *You'll marry him over my dead body!*
19 dead and buried an argument, problem, plan etc. that is dead and buried is not in use anymore, or is not worth considering anymore: *I thought the idea of us moving to New York was dead and buried.*
20 a dead duck INFORMAL **a)** someone who is in trouble or will be punished: *If he's not here on time, he's a dead duck.* **b)** something that is very likely to fail or become less successful: *The news program was once considered a dead duck.*
21 dead to the world very deeply asleep or unconscious
22 dead in the water a plan or idea that is dead in the water has failed and canot possibly succeed in the future
23 a dead ringer someone who looks exactly like someone else: *Dave's a dead ringer for Nicolas Cage.*
24 dead as a doornail SPOKEN **a)** used to say that someone or something is clearly dead: *The rat was dead as a doornail.* **b)** used to say that there is no activity in a place
25 the dead hand of sth a powerful bad influence that makes progress slower: *the dead hand of bureaucracy* —**deadness** *n.* [U] → see also **drop dead** at DROP[1] (12)

WORD CHOICE dead, died
Use **dead** as an adjective to talk about things or people that are no longer alive: *I think this plant is dead.* **Died** is the past tense and past participle of "die": *He died on the way to the hospital.*

dead² *adv.* INFORMAL **1** extremely or completely: *Paula* ***stopped dead*** *when she saw us.* | *The baby was up all night and I'm* ***dead tired.*** | *The Kimballs are* ***dead set against*** (=completely opposed to) *drinking.* **2** [+ adj./adv.] directly or exactly: *You can't miss it – it's* ***dead ahead.*** **3 dead to rights** in the act of doing something wrong: *The FBI got him dead to rights selling illegal weapons.*

dead³ *n.* **1 the dead** [plural] people who have died, especially people who have been killed: *There wasn't even time to bury the dead.* **2 in the dead of night/winter** in the middle of the night or winter when everything is very quiet or cold: *We finally arrived at Aunt Claire's house in the dead of night.* **3 rise from the dead** also **come back from the dead** to become alive again after dying

dead·beat /ˈdɛdbit/ *n.* [C] INFORMAL **1** someone who is lazy and who has no plans in life **2** someone who does not pay their debts: **deadbeat dad/mom** (=a DIVORCED parent who avoids paying money to support his or her family)

dead·bolt /ˈdɛdboʊlt/ also **ˈdeadbolt ˌlock** *n.* [C] a type of lock that is built into a door and is very strong

dead·en /ˈdɛdn/ *v.* [T] to make a feeling or sound less strong: *Carpet will help deaden the noise.*

ˌdead ˈend¹ *n.* [C] **1** also **dead end street/road** a street with no way out at one end **2** a situation from which no more progress is possible: *The negotiations have* ***reached a dead end.*** **3 a dead-end job** a job with low pay and no chance of progress

dead end² *v.* [I] if a road dead ends, there is no way out at one end of it

Dead·head /ˈdɛdhɛd/ *n.* [C] INFORMAL someone who likes the band The Grateful Dead

ˌdead ˈheat *n.* [C usually singular] a race or competition in which two or more competitors are at exactly the same level, speed etc.

ˌdead ˈletter *n.* [C] **1** a law, idea etc. that still exists but that people do not obey or are not interested in anymore **2** a letter that cannot be delivered or returned

dead·line /ˈdɛdlaɪn/ *n.* [C] a date or time by which you have to do or complete something: +**for** *The deadline for applications is March 12.* | +**of** *The committee agreed to a deadline of Dec. 31.* | *Can you* ***meet the 5:00 deadline?*** (=Can you finish by 5:00?) | *She* ***missed the deadline*** (=she was too late) *for entering the race.* | *The department is working under a very* ***tight deadline*** (=a deadline that is difficult to meet). | *Make sure to* ***set a deadline*** (=decide on a deadline) *for making your decision.*

dead·lock¹ /ˈdɛdlɑk/ *n.* [singular, U] a situation in which a disagreement cannot be settled SYN **stalemate**: *The talks have* ***reached a*** *complete* ***deadlock.*** | *a final attempt to* ***break the deadlock*** (=end it) | *Negotiations ended* ***in deadlock.***

deadlock² *v.* [I,T] if a group of people or something such as NEGOTIATIONS deadlock, or if something deadlocks them, they are unable to settle a disagreement: +**on** *The commission deadlocked on the issue.* | +**over** *Congress and the White House deadlocked over balancing the budget.*

dead·locked /ˈdɛdlɑkt/ *adj.* in a situation where it is not possible to settle a disagreement: *the deadlocked U.N. peace plan*

dead·ly¹ /ˈdɛdli/ *adj.* *comparative* **deadlier**, *superlative* **deadliest**
1 VERY DANGEROUS likely to cause death SYN **lethal**: *a deadly poison* | *deadly weapons*
2 BORING SPOKEN not interesting or exciting at all: *His lectures are deadly.*

D

3 a deadly enemy someone who will always be your enemy and who will try to harm you as much as possible
4 VERY EFFECTIVE causing harm in a very effective way: *Hank can shoot with deadly precision.*
5 LIKE DEATH [only before noun] like death in appearance: *Her face had a deadly paleness.*
6 COMPLETE complete or total, often in a bad or frightening way: *We sat in deadly silence.* —**deadliness** *n.* [U]

deadly² *adv.* **deadly serious/quiet/dull etc.** very or extremely serious, quiet, dull etc.: *I'm deadly serious – this isn't a game!*

D

ˌdeadly ˈnightshade *n.* [C,U] a poisonous European plant SYN **belladonna**

ˌdead-man's ˈfloat *n.* [singular] a way of floating in water with your body and face turned down in the water

dead·pan /ˈdɛdpæn/ *adj.* sounding and looking completely serious when you are really joking: *a deadpan expression* —**deadpan** *v.* [I] —**deadpan** *adv.*

ˌdead ˈreckoning *n.* [U] the practice of calculating the position of a ship or airplane without using the sun, moon, or stars

ˌDead ˈSea a large lake between Israel and Jordan that is over 25% salt

ˌdead ˈweight *n.* **1** [C,U] someone or something that prevents you from making progress or being successful: *The smaller stores are dead weight to the supermarket chain.* **2** [C] something that is very heavy and difficult to carry: *the dead weight of the man's body*

dead·wood /ˈdɛdwʊd/ *n.* [U] **1** the people or things within an organization that are useless or not needed anymore: *The reforms should get rid of some of the deadwood.* **2** dead branches or trees

deaf /dɛf/ *adj.* **1** physically unable to hear anything or unable to hear well: *I worry that I'm* ***going deaf*** (=becoming deaf). | *Dad's* ***partially deaf*** *and needs a hearing aid.* | **profoundly/totally deaf** *He was born profoundly deaf.* | *The dog is 14 and* ***deaf as a post*** (=completely deaf). → see also STONE DEAF, TONE-DEAF ►see THESAURUS box at **hear** **2 the deaf** [plural] people who are deaf: *a school for the deaf* **3 deaf to sth** LITERARY unwilling to hear or listen to something: *She was deaf to his warnings.* **4 turn a deaf ear** to be unwilling to listen to what someone is saying or asking: *The factory owners turned a deaf ear to the demands of the workers.* **5 fall on deaf ears** if something you say falls on deaf ears, everyone ignores it: *Their requests fell on deaf ears.* **[Origin:** Old English] —**deafness** *n.* [U]

ˌdeaf and ˈdumb *adj.* OLD-FASHIONED a word meaning "unable to hear or speak," now usually considered offensive

deaf·en /ˈdɛfən/ *v.* [T usually passive] **1** to make it difficult for you to hear anything: *We were deafened by the explosion.* **2** to make someone become deaf: *The injury deafened him for life.*

deaf·en·ing /ˈdɛfənɪŋ/ *adj.* noise or music that is deafening is very loud: *deafening bomb blasts*

ˌdeaf-ˈmute *n.* [C] OLD-FASHIONED a word for someone who is unable to hear or speak, now usually considered offensive

deal¹ /dil/ S1 W1 *n.*
1 AGREEMENT [C] an agreement or arrangement, especially in business or politics, that helps both sides involved: *The deal would create the nation's largest television company.* | *a business deal* | **make/strike/cut a deal** *Lawyers struck a deal before the trial started.* | *I got* ***a really good deal*** *on my car* (=I bought it at a very good price). | **+with** *I'll make a deal with you.* | **+between** *a deal between moderate Democrats and Republicans* | *The singer recently* ***signed a deal*** (=signed a contract) *with Virgin Records.* | *After two months* ***the deal fell through*** (=it was not successfully completed). | *new bands looking for* ***a record deal*** (=an agreement with a record company who will produce and sell their music)
2 a great/good deal a large quantity or amount of something: *He's traveled a great deal in his life.* | **+of** *I've spent a good deal of time thinking about the project.* | *He knows* ***a great deal more*** (=a lot more) *about computers than I do.*
3 TREATMENT [C usually singular] the way someone is treated in a particular situation, often in situations where jobs or pay are involved: *Nurses deserve* ***a better deal.*** | *Teachers are just looking for* ***a fair deal.*** | **get a raw/bum/rough deal** (=be treated unfairly)
4 GAME [singular] the process of giving out cards to players in a card game: *It's your deal, Alison.* → see also DEALER
5 it's a deal used to say that you agree to do something: *"I'll give you $100 for it." "It's a deal."*
6 what's the deal? used when you want to know about a problem or something strange that is happening: *So what's the deal? Why is he so mad?*
7 good deal said when you are pleased by something someone else has just said: *"I've made all the arrangements for the trip." "Good deal."* → see also BIG DEAL

GRAMMAR **A great/good deal of...**

A great/good deal of is used only with uncountable nouns: *a great deal of time/money/difficulty/pressure etc.* Compare *There's been a great deal of change* with *There have been a large number of changes.* You cannot say, "There have been a great deal of changes."

deal² S1 W1 *v. past tense and past participle* **dealt** /dɛlt/ **1** [I,T] to give playing cards to each of the players in a game: *Whose turn is it to deal?* | *Deal three cards to each player.* **2** [I,T] INFORMAL to buy and sell illegal drugs: *He was arrested for dealing cocaine.* **3 deal sb/sth a blow** LITERARY **a)** to make someone or something less successful: **deal a severe/serious/fatal etc. blow** *The recession dealt the steel industry a crippling blow.* **b)** to hit someone or something

deal in sth *phr. v.* **1** to buy and sell a particular type of product: *The store deals in high-quality jewelry.* → see also DEALER **2** to let your work or behavior be guided by specific principles: *As a scientist, I do not deal in speculation.*

deal sb **in** *phr. v.* INFORMAL **1** to include someone in a plan or a deal: *If you decide you want to buy a beach property, you can deal me in.* **2** to deal cards to someone so that they can join your game

deal sth ↔ **out** *phr. v.* **1** to give playing cards to each of the players in a game: *Deal the whole deck out.* **2** to give someone a punishment: *Chinese courts deal out harsh punishments to smugglers.*

deal with *phr. v.* **1 deal with sb/sth** to take the necessary action, especially in order to solve a problem SYN **handle**: *Who's dealing with the Sony account?* | *Teachers will always have difficult students to deal with.*

THESAURUS

handle to deal with someone or something: *He's finding it hard to handle the pressure at work.*
tackle to try to deal with a difficult problem: *There are severe problems which cities need federal help to tackle.*
attend to sth to give attention to someone or something: *I have some business to attend to.*
take care of sth do the work or make the arrangements that are necessary for something to happen: *His secretary took care of the arrangements for the meeting.*

2 deal with sb/sth to succeed in controlling your feelings about an emotional problem so that it does not affect your life: ***I can't deal with*** *any more crying children today.* **3 deal with sb/sth** to do business with someone or have a business connection with someone: *We've been dealing with their company for ten years.* **4 deal with sth** if a book, speech, work of art etc. deals with a particular subject, it is about that subject: *The book deals with art during the French Revolution.*

deal·break·er, deal breaker /ˈdilˌbreɪkɚ/ *n.* [C] INFORMAL something that makes you decide that you do not want a product, relationship, job etc., because you cannot accept that part of it: *The benefits package became a dealbreaker in the negotiations.* | *In every new relationship, there are deal breakers. Mine is a refusal to move to another state.*

deal·er /ˈdilɚ/ W3 *n.* [C] **1** someone who buys and sells a particular product, especially an expensive one: *a car dealer* | *an art dealer* **2** someone who sells illegal drugs **3** someone who gives out playing cards in a game → see also DOUBLE-DEALER

deal·er·ship /ˈdilɚˌʃɪp/ *n.* [C] a business that sells a particular company's product, especially cars: *Ford dealerships*

deal·ing /ˈdilɪŋ/ *n.* **1 dealings** [plural] the business activities or relationships that someone has been involved in: *financial dealings* | *We've **had dealings with** (=had a business relationship with) IBM for the past few years.* | *She is ruthless in **her dealings with** her competitors.* **2** [U] the activity of buying and selling of things, or doing business with people: *the company's reputation for **fair dealing*** | *The mayor wants to end all **drug dealing** in the city.*

dealt /dɛlt/ *v.* the past tense and past participle of DEAL

dean /din/ *n.* [C] **1** someone in a college or university who is in charge of an area of study, or in charge of students and their behavior **2** a priest of high rank, especially in the Episcopal and Catholic Churches, who is in charge of several priests or churches **3** someone in a group of people who do similar things who has more experience than anyone else: *the dean of TV talk show hosts* [**Origin:** 1300–1400 Old French *deien*, from Late Latin *decanus* **person in charge of ten others**]

Dean /din/**, James** (1931–1955) a U.S. movie actor who became very famous, and became even more popular after dying in a car crash at the age of 24

ˈdean's list *n.* [C usually singular] a list of students with high grades at a college or university

dear¹ /dɪr/ *interjection* **Oh dear** said when you are surprised, annoyed, or upset: *Oh dear, I can't find it.*

dear² *n.* [C] SPOKEN **1** used when speaking to someone you love: *How did the interview go, dear?* **2** a friendly way for an old person to speak to a young person: *What's your name, dear?* **3** OLD-FASHIONED someone who is very kind and helpful

dear³ *adj.* **1 Dear** used before someone's name or title when you begin a letter: *Dear Sally,...* | *Dear Dr. Ward:...* **2** FORMAL much loved and very important to you: *a dear friend* | *His sister was very **dear to** him.* **3 for dear life** if you run, hold on, fight etc. for dear life, you do so as fast or as well as you can because you are afraid: *Sherman held onto the bar for dear life.* → see also **hold sth dear** at HOLD¹ (33)

dear·est /ˈdɪrɪst/ *n.* [C] SPOKEN, OLD-FASHIONED used when speaking to someone you love

dear·ie /ˈdɪri/ *n.* [C] OLD-FASHIONED used as a way of speaking to someone you love or someone you want to be friendly to

ˌdear ˈJohn ˌletter *n.* [C] a letter to a man from his wife or GIRLFRIEND, saying that she does not love him anymore

dear·ly /ˈdɪrli/ *adv.* **1** very much: *She **loves** her children **dearly**.* | **sb would dearly like/love to do sth** *It was a day I would dearly love to forget.* **2** in a way that involves a lot of suffering, damage, trouble etc.: *Vandalism **costs** schools **dearly*** (=costs them a lot of money and trouble). | *If we don't take action now, we'll **pay dearly*** (=suffer a lot or pay a lot of money) *later.* **3 dearly beloved** SPOKEN used by a priest or minister when speaking to the people at a Christian religious service, especially a marriage or funeral

dearth /dɚθ/ *n.* [singular] FORMAL a lack of something: +**of** *a dearth of qualified workers*

death /dɛθ/ S2 W1 *n.*
1 THE END OF SB'S LIFE [U] the end of the life of a person or animal OPP **birth**: *Maretti lived in Miami until his death.* | *The death of a child is extremely difficult.* | *Cancer is the leading **cause of death*** (=used in offical reports) *in women.* | **bleed/burn/choke etc. to death** *Several people in the apartment burned to death.* | **shoot/beat etc. sb to death** *Ruby shot Oswald to death with a revolver.* | *He was **close to death** when he wrote his will.* | *The boys' **untimely deaths*** (=deaths at a surprisingly young age) *shocked the town.* | **die a violent/painful/natural etc. death** *Most of the prisoners died slow and painful deaths.* | *Only two of the passengers managed to **escape death*** (=just avoid being killed). | *Charlotte **met her death*** (=died) *in a train wreck.* | *He was found guilty and **sentenced to death*** (=it was decided that he should be killed as a punishment for his crime). | *The horse was so badly injured it had to be **put to death*** (=killed). | *The family is still **mourning her death**.*
2 EXAMPLE OF SB DYING [C] a particular case of someone dying OPP **birth**: *a reduction in the number of traffic deaths* | +**from** *deaths from breast cancer* | *She's not at work because of **a death in the family**.*
3 WAY OF DYING [C] the way in which someone or something dies: **a horrible/terrible/agonizing etc. death** *The pilot and his crew must have died a horrible death.*
4 to death INFORMAL **a)** used to emphasize that a feeling or emotion is very strong: *I'm **sick to death of*** (=extremely annoyed by) *his excuses!* | **scared/frightened/bored to death** *Ron's scared to death of dogs.* | **scare/frighten/bore sb to death** *That class bored me to death.* **b)** ESPECIALLY HUMOROUS used to say that an action is continued with a lot of effort and for as long as possible: *I think the company's trying to **work us to death**!*
5 the death of sth the permanent end of an idea, custom etc. OPP **birth**: *the death of American slavery* | *the death of all our hopes*
6 death blow an action or event that makes something fail or end: *The new law would be a death blow to casinos.*
7 Death a creature that looks like a SKELETON, used in paintings, stories etc. as a sign of death and destruction
8 death's door the point in time when someone is very sick and likely to die: *He looked like a man **at death's door**.*
9 you'll/he'll etc. be the death of me! SPOKEN said about someone who makes you very worried and anxious, especially said in a humorous way: *That boy is going to be the death of me!*
10 you'll catch your death (of cold) SPOKEN, OLD-FASHIONED said as a warning to someone when you think they are likely to become sick because it is wet or cold outside
11 like death warmed over INFORMAL if someone looks or feels like death warmed over, they look or feel very sick or tired → see also BLACK DEATH, **fight to the death** at FIGHT¹ (15), **the kiss of death** at KISS² (2), **sth is a matter of life and death** at MATTER¹ (17)

death·bed /ˈdɛθbɛd/ *n.* [C] the point in time when someone is lying in bed and will die very soon: *My mother was **on her deathbed*** (=close to death) *at the time.*

ˈdeath camp *n.* [C] a place where large numbers of prisoners are killed or die, usually in a war

ˈdeath cerˌtificate *n.* [C] a legal document, signed by a doctor, that states the time and cause of someone's death

death knell /ˈdɛθ nɛl/ *n.* [singular] a sign that something will soon stop existing or stop being used: *Plans for a new bridge **sounded the death knell** for ferry services.*

death·less /ˈdɛθlɪs/ *adj.* LITERARY something that is deathless does not die or go away

death·ly /ˈdɛθli/ *adv.* **1** if you are deathly afraid, or frightened, you are extremely afraid: *Mom's deathly afraid of flying.* **2** in a way that reminds you of death or of a dead body: *Rachel felt deathly cold.* —**deathly** *adj.* [only before noun]

D

'death mask *n.* [C] a model of a dead person's face, made by pressing a soft substance over their face and letting it become hard

'death ˌpenalty *n.* **the death penalty** the legal punishment of being killed, used in some countries for serious crimes: **get/be given/receive the death penalty** *Jurors decided he should get the death penalty.*

'death rate *n.* [C] the number of deaths for every 100 or every 1,000 people in a particular year and in a particular place → see also BIRTHRATE

'death ˌrattle *n.* [C] a strange noise sometimes heard from the throat or chest of someone who is dying

D

death row *n.* [usually singular] the part of a prison where prisoners are kept while waiting to be punished by being killed: *Jones is* ***on death row*** *for murder.*

'death ˌsentence *n.* [C] **1** LAW the punishment of death given by a judge: *Gilmore received a death sentence.* **2** something that causes the end of something or the death of someone: *Cancer is not automatically a death sentence.* | *A golf course will be a death sentence to the local ecosystem.*

'death's head *n.* [C] a human SKULL used as a sign of death

'death squad *n.* [C] a group of people who are ordered by a government to kill people, especially their political opponents

'death throes *n.* [plural] **1** the final stages before something fails or ends: *The regime seems to be in its death throes.* **2** sudden violent movements sometimes made by a person or an animal that is dying

'death toll *n.* [C] the total number of people who die in a particular accident, war etc.: *The death toll from the earthquake continues to rise.*

'death trap *n.* [C] INFORMAL a vehicle or building that is in such bad condition that it is dangerous and might kill someone

ˌDeath 'Valley an area of desert in the U.S. states of Nevada and California

'death ˌwarrant *n.* [C] **1** LAW an official document stating that someone is to be killed as a punishment for their crimes **2 sign your own death warrant** to do something that seems likely to cause you very serious trouble or even to cause your death

'death wish *n.* [singular] a desire to die

deb /dɛb/ *n.* [C] INFORMAL a DEBUTANTE

de·ba·cle /deɪ'bɑkəl, -'bæ-/ *n.* [C] an event or situation that is a complete failure SYN **fiasco**: *The Secretary of State has taken the blame for the debacle.* | **the debacle of sth** *the debacle of the midterm election* [**Origin:** 1800–1900 French *débâcle*, from *débâcler* **to remove a bar**]

de·bar /di'bɑr/ *v.* **debarred, debarring** [T] to officially prevent someone from taking part in something SYN **ban**: **debar sb from sth** *He was debarred from entering the competition.* —**debarment** *n.* [C,U] → see also DISBAR

de·bark /di'bɑrk, di-/ *v.* [I] to DISEMBARK —**debarkation** /ˌdibɑr'keɪʃən/ *n.* [U]

de·base /dɪ'beɪs/ *v.* [T] **1** INFORMAL to reduce the quality or value of something: *Our society has been debased by war and corruption.* | *a debased currency* **2** if something debases you or if you debase yourself, people have less respect for you: *women who debase themselves by selling their bodies* **3** to reduce the value of a particular country's money —**debasement** *n.* [C,U] —**debasing** *adj.*

de·bat·a·ble /dɪ'beɪt̬əbəl/ Ac *adj.* issues or questions that are debatable do not have definite answers, and people have different opinions about what the best answer is: *"I think he made a mistake." "Well, that's debatable."* | ***It is debatable whether*** *nuclear weapons actually prevent war.*

de·bate¹ /dɪ'beɪt/ Ac W2 *n.* **1** [C,U] discussion or argument on a subject that people express different opinions about: *the gun control debate* | **+on/over/about** *public debate on healthcare* | **+between** *the debate between the chemical industry and environmentalists* | **intense/heated/fierce/lively debate** (=discussion involving very strong opinions) | *The question of a third airport is still* ***under debate*** (=being discussed). | *Resolutions* ***up for debate*** (=able or planned to be discussed) *include raising the minimum wage.* | *a book that* ***sparked a debate*** (=started one) *about nuclear power* ►see THESAURUS box at **discussion** **2** [C] **a)** a discussion in which people have a chance to give their opinions, often one that has a set of rules controlling who can speak, when they can speak, and for how long: *The rules were approved after an intense debate in the Senate.* | **+on/about** *a debate in Congress on the issue of Social Security* **b)** a competition in which two people or teams have a debate in front of an audience, in order to decide whose ideas are best: *a presidential debate* | *the school's debate team* | **have/hold a debate** *The Press Club will hold a debate for the two candidates next month.* **3 be open/subject to debate** also **be a matter for debate** if an idea is open to debate, no one has proved yet whether it is true or false: *The question of what a "reasonable price" is, is still open to debate.*

debate² Ac *v.* [I,T] **1** to discuss a subject formally with someone. when you are trying to make a decision or find a solution: *The matter will be debated by the General Assembly.* | **debate whether/what/how etc. (to do sth)** *The council will debate whether to open the park to nonresidents.* | *Her conclusions are* ***hotly debated*** (=argued about strongly) *among academics.* **2** to consider something carefully before making a decision: **debate who/what/how etc. (to do sth)** *I'm still debating what to do.* | **debate doing sth** *For a moment she debated telling Rick the truth.* **3** to take part in a debate in front of an audience: *The candidates will debate on national television.* [**Origin:** 1200–1300 Old French *debatre*, from *batre* **to hit**] —**debater** *n.* [C] —**debating** *n.* [U]

de·bauch /dɪ'bɔtʃ, -'bɑtʃ/ *v.* [T] FORMAL to make someone behave in an immoral way, especially with alcohol, drugs, or sex

de·bauched /dɪ'bɔʃt/ *adj.* someone who is debauched drinks too much alcohol, takes too many drugs, or has an immoral attitude about sex

de·bauch·er·y /dɪ'bɔtʃəri/ *n.* **1** [U] immoral behavior involving drugs, alcohol, sex etc. **2** [C] an occasion when someone behaves in this way

de·ben·ture /dɪ'bɛntʃɚ/ *n.* [C] ECONOMICS an official document given by a company, showing that it has borrowed money and that it will pay a particular rate of INTEREST, whether or not it makes a profit

de·bil·i·tat·ed /dɪ'bɪləˌteɪt̬ɪd/ *adj.* **1** if someone is debilitated, their body or mind is weak from illness, heat etc.: *She was severely debilitated by a brain virus.* **2** if an organization or structure is debilitated, its authority or effectiveness has become weak: *Civil war has left the country debilitated.* —**debilitate** *v.* [T]

de·bil·i·tat·ing /dɪ'bɪləˌteɪt̬ɪŋ/ *adj.* **1** affecting your body or mind in a way that prevents you from doing very much: *a debilitating illness* | *her debilitating shyness* **2** making an organization or system less effective or less powerful: *the debilitating trade war*

de·bil·i·ty /dɪ'bɪləṭi/ *n. plural* **debilities** [C,U] FORMAL weakness, especially as the result of illness: *physical and mental debilities* → see also DISABILITY

deb·it¹ /'dɛbɪt/ *n.* [C] **1** a decrease in the amount of money in a bank account, for example because you have taken money out of it: *a debit of $50* **2** ECONOMICS a record in financial accounts that shows money which has been spent or money that is owed → see also CREDIT, DIRECT DEBIT

debit² *v.* [T] TECHNICAL **1** to take money out of a bank account: *The bank hasn't debited my account yet.* | **debit sth from sth** *The sum of $50 has been debited from your account.* **2** ECONOMICS to record the amount of money taken from a bank account: **debit sth against sth** *Purchases are then debited against the customer's bank account.* → see also CREDIT

'debit card *n.* [C] a special plastic card that you can use to pay for things directly from your bank account → see also CHECK CARD

deb·o·nair /ˌdɛbəˈnɛr/ *adj.* APPROVING a man who is debonair is fashionable and well dressed and behaves in an attractively confident way [**Origin:** 1200–1300 Old French *de bonne aire* **of good family or nature**]

de·brief /diˈbrif/ *v.* [T] to ask someone such as a soldier for information about a job that they have just done or an important experience they have just had: *The returning bomber crews were debriefed.* → see also BRIEF —**debriefing** *n.* [C,U]

de·bris /dɪˈbri/ *n.* [U] **1** all the pieces that are left after something has been destroyed in an accident, explosion etc.: *The explosion sent debris flying in all directions.* **2** pieces of waste material, paper etc. that make a place look untidy and dirty: *The beach was littered with debris.* [**Origin:** 1700–1800 French *débris*, from Old French *débriser* **to break in pieces**]

Debs /dɛbz/, **Eu·gene** /yuˈdʒin, ˈyudʒin/ (1855–1926) a U.S. LABOR leader who led an important railroad STRIKE and was the Socialist Party CANDIDATE for U.S. president in four elections

debt /dɛt/ W2 *n.* **1** [C] money that you owe: +**of** *The company has debts of around $1,000,000.* | *Brian* **ran up** *huge* **debts** (=borrowed a lot of money) *on his credit cards.* | **repay/clear etc. a debt** *Denise finally paid off her debts.* **2** [U] the state of owing money: **be ($10/$100/$1,000) in debt** *They are $40,000 in debt.* | **be heavily/deeply etc. in debt** *He was out of work and deeply in debt.* | **go/get/fall etc. into debt** (=borrow more and more money) | **get out of debt** (=pay back all the money you owe) **3 owe a debt of gratitude/thanks to sb** to be grateful to someone for what they have done for you: *Our club owes a great debt of gratitude to Martha Graham.* **4 be in sb's debt** to be grateful to someone and feel that you must do something for them, because they have done something important for you: *I will be forever in your debt.* **5 a debt to sb/sth** the fact that you have learned from or been influenced by someone else: *the singer's stylistic debt to Tina Turner* [**Origin:** 1200–1300 Old French *dette*, from Latin *debitum*, from *debere* **to owe**] → see also BAD DEBT, NATIONAL DEBT, **sb has paid their debt to society** at PAY[1] (12)

'debt colˌlector *n.* [C] someone whose job is to get back the money that people owe

'debt ˌcrisis *n.* [C,U] ECONOMICS a situation in which a poor country is not able to pay back large amounts of money that it has borrowed from banks or other countries: *He urged the International Community to find a solution to the Third World's debt crisis.*

debt·or /ˈdɛt̬ɚ/ *n.* [C] a person, group, or organization that owes money → see also CREDITOR

'debtor ˌnation *n.* [C] ECONOMICS a country that has borrowed a lot of money or in which other countries have INVESTED more money than that country has invested in other countries → see also CREDITOR NATION

'debt reˌscheduling also **'debt reˌstructuring** *n.* [U] ECONOMICS a situation in which a company or government arranges to pay its debts at a later time or in a different way, usually because it is having problems paying the debt back

'debt reˌtirement *n.* [C,U] the act of paying back all of a sum of money you have borrowed, especially from a bank

de·bug /diˈbʌg/ *v.* **debugged, debugging** [T] **1** COMPUTERS to take the mistakes out of a computer program **2** to find and remove secret listening equipment in a room or building

de·bunk /diˈbʌŋk/ *v.* [T] to show that an idea or belief is false: *The study* **debunks the myth** *that men are better drivers than women.* —**debunker** *n.* [C]

De·bus·sy /ˌdɛbyʊˈsi, ˌdeɪ-/, **Claude** /kloʊd/ (1862–1918) a French musician who wrote CLASSICAL music and developed musical IMPRESSIONISM

de·but[1] /deɪˈbyu, ˈdeɪbyu/ *n.* [C] the first public appearance of someone such as an entertainer or sports player or of something new and important: *Their debut album was recorded in 1991.* | *Ryan* **made her debut** *as a singer in 1990.* | **sb's movie/acting/directorial etc. debut** *The movie was Foster's directorial debut.* [**Origin:** 1700–1800 French *début*, from *débuter* **to begin**, from *but* **starting point**]

debut[2] *v.* **1** [I] to appear in public for the first time or to become available to the public for the first time: *The show debuts Monday night at 8 p.m.* **2** [T] to introduce a product to the public for the first time SYN **launch**: *Ralph Lauren debuted his new collection in Paris last week.* → see also RELEASE

deb·u·tante /ˈdɛbyʊˌtɑnt/ *n.* [C] a young woman who goes to special parties as a way of being formally introduced to rich people's society

Dec. the written abbreviation of DECEMBER

deca- /dɛkə/ *prefix* ten: *decaliter* (=ten liters) | *the decathlon* (=a sports competition with ten different events) [**Origin:** Greek *deka* **ten**]

dec·ade /ˈdɛkeɪd/ Ac W1 *n.* [C] a period of ten years: *By the end of the decade, inflation will have risen by 1.2%.* | **in/over/during the...decade** *Cases of skin cancer have soared in the last decade.* | *changes in education during the next decade* | +**of** *three decades of civil war* [**Origin:** 1400–1500 French *décade*, from Greek *dekas*, from *deka* **ten**]

dec·a·dence /ˈdɛkədəns/ *n.* [U] the state of having low moral standards and being more concerned with pleasure than with serious matters [**Origin:** 1700–1800 French *décadence*, from Latin *decadere* **to fall, sink**]

dec·a·dent /ˈdɛkədənt/ *adj.* having low moral standards and being more concerned with pleasure than with serious matters: *Pop music was condemned as decadent and crude.* —**decadently** *adv.*

de·caf /ˈdikæf/ *n.* [U] SPOKEN decaffeinated coffee

de·caf·fein·at·ed /diˈkæfəˌneɪt̬ɪd/ *adj.* coffee, tea, or COLA that is decaffeinated has had all or most of the CAFFEINE removed

dec·a·gon /ˈdɛkəˌgɑn/ *n.* [C] MATH a flat shape with ten straight sides and ten angles

de·cal /ˈdikæl/ *n.* [C] a piece of paper with a pattern or picture on it that you stick onto another surface

de·camp /dɪˈkæmp/ *v.* [I] **1** if a group of people decamp, they leave a place and go somewhere else to live or work: *The team decamped to Los Angeles in 1981.* **2** to leave a place suddenly, often because you have done something wrong SYN **abscond**

de·cant /dɪˈkænt/ *v.* [T] to pour liquid, especially wine, from one container into another [**Origin:** 1600–1700 Medieval Latin *decantare*, from Latin *cantus* **lip of a pouring container**]

de·cant·er /dɪˈkænt̬ɚ/ *n.* [C] a glass container for alcoholic drinks

de·cap·i·tate /dɪˈkæpəˌteɪt, di-/ *v.* [T] to cut off someone's head —**decapitation** /dɪˌkæpəˈteɪʃən/ *n.* [C,U]

dec·ath·lon /dɪˈkæθlɑn, -lən/ *n.* [C] a competition involving ten running, jumping, and throwing sports → see also HEPTATHLON, PENTATHLON

de·cay[1] /dɪˈkeɪ/ *v.* **decays, decayed, decaying** **1** [I,T] to be slowly destroyed by a natural chemical process, or to make something do this SYN **rot**: *As the plants decay, they give off gases.* | *Avoid sugary foods that decay your teeth.* → see also DECOMPOSE

THESAURUS

rot to decay by a gradual natural process, or to make something do this: *The fruit was left to rot on the ground.*
decompose FORMAL to decay or to make something decay: *leaves decomposing on the forest floor*

2 [I often in progressive] if things such as buildings or areas decay, their condition becomes worse, especially because they are not taken care of: *This decaying city* *was once the busiest port in the world.* **3** [I often in progressive] if a society, a system, standards etc. decay, they gradually become worse in quality or less powerful SYN **decline**: *the decaying moral values of American society* [**Origin:** 1400–1500 Old North French *decaïr*, from Late Latin *decadere* **to fall, sink**]

decay² *n.* [U] **1** the natural chemical change that causes the slow destruction of something: *Organisms in the soil help the process of decay.* | *Fluoride is helpful in fighting* ***tooth decay****.* **2** the gradual destruction of buildings and structures caused by a lack of care: *poverty and urban decay* | *The Civil War-era house was* ***falling into decay*** (=beginning to decay). **3** the process of gradually becoming worse in quality or less powerful SYN **decline**: *moral decay* | +**in** *a decay in educational standards* | *By that time the empire was* ***in decay*** (=becoming less powerful). **4** the part of something that has been destroyed by a gradual chemical change: *There is decay in some of the floorboards.*

de'cay rate *n.* [C] PHYSICS the speed at which a RADIOACTIVE substance breaks apart and sends out ATOMIC PARTICLES or RADIATION

de·ceased /dɪ'sist/ *adj.* FORMAL **1** dead: *Mike's parents are both deceased.* ▸see THESAURUS box at **dead¹** **2 the deceased** someone who has died, especially recently: *The deceased left no will.* [**Origin:** 1300–1400 *decease* **to die** (15–19 centuries), from French *décès* **death**, from Latin *decedere* **to leave, die**]

de·ceit /dɪ'sit/ *n.* [U] behavior that is intended to make someone believe something that is not true: *His political opponents accuse him of corruption and deceit.*

de·ceit·ful /dɪ'sitfəl/ *adj.* intending to make someone believe something that is not true: *a deceitful man* —**deceitfully** *adv.* —**deceitfulness** *n.* [U]

de·ceive /dɪ'siv/ *v.* [I,T] **1** to make someone believe something that is not true in order to get what you want SYN **trick**: *Kahn said voters had been deceived by supporters of the new bill.* | **deceive sb into doing sth** *He deceived young girls into signing movie contracts.* | **deceive sb about sth** *The mayor claims he didn't deceive anyone about the payments he made.* ▸see THESAURUS box at **lie²** **2 looks/appearances can be deceiving** used to say that the way someone or something looks may make you believe something about them that is not true: *With his baby face and cute grin, you might guess he was in his 30s, but looks can be deceiving* (=he is actually older). **3 deceive yourself** to refuse to believe that something is true because the truth is unpleasant: *Many parents deceive themselves about their children's behavior.* **4** if something you see, hear, learn etc. deceives you, it gives you a wrong belief or opinion about something SYN **mislead**: *Don't be deceived by the new packaging. It's still junk food.* [**Origin:** 1200–1300 Old French *deceivre*, from Latin *decipere*] —**deceiver** *n.* [C] → see also DECEPTION

de·cel·er·ate /di'sɛlə,reɪt/ *v.* [I] **1** to go slower, especially in a vehicle OPP **accelerate** **2** if the ECONOMY, sales, business etc. decelerates, it is not growing or improving anymore OPP **accelerate** —**deceleration** /di,sɛlə'reɪʃən/ *n.* [U]

De·cem·ber /dɪ'sɛmbɚ/ WRITTEN ABBREVIATION **Dec.** *n.* [C,U] the twelfth and last month of the year, after November: *The semester ends* ***in December****.* | *Christmas is* ***on December 25****.* | *Emily's baby is due* ***December 10****.* | ***Last December*** *I went to visit my parents.* | *I won't be spending the holidays at home* ***next December****.* [**Origin:** 1200–1300 Old French, Latin, name of the tenth Roman month, from *decem* **ten**] → see Grammar box at JANUARY

De·cem·brist Re·volt, the /dɪ'sɛmbrɪst rɪ,voult/ also **the De'cembrist ,Uprising** HISTORY an occasion in December 1825 when a group of Russian NOBLES, army officers, and soldiers tried and failed to get rid of the government of the CZAR (=Russian ruler)

de·cen·cy /'disənsi/ *n.* [U] polite, honest, and moral behavior and attitudes that show respect for other people: *We treat our employees with respect and decency.* | *Too many broadcasters lack* ***a sense of decency****.* | *The media should* ***have the decency to*** (=behave with decency) *protect a rape victim's identity.* | **public/common/human decency** (=standards of behavior that everyone should have)

de·cent /'disənt/ S3 *adj.* **1** acceptable or good enough: *I need a decent night's sleep.* | *a decent salary* | *a house with a decent-sized yard* | *That new magazine's actually* ***halfway decent*** (=quite good or better than expected). **2** treating people in a fair and kind way: *The coach was a pretty decent guy.* **3** following the standards of moral behavior accepted by most people SYN **respectable**: *Decent working people are frustrated at the level of crime in the cities.* **4** wearing enough clothes to not show too much of your body OPP **indecent**: *Don't come in – I'm not decent!* [**Origin:** 1500–1600 French *décent*, from Latin *decens*, the present participle of *decere* **to be suitable**] —**decently** *adv.*

de·cen·tral·ize /di'sɛntrə,laɪz/ *v.* [T] to move parts of a government, organization etc. from one central place to several different smaller ones —**decentralized** *adj.* —**decentralization** /di,sɛntrələ'zeɪʃən/ *n.* [U]

de·cep·tion /dɪ'sɛpʃən/ *n.* [C,U] the act of tricking someone by making them believe something that is not true: *She was accused of forgery and deception.* | *an elaborate deception*

de·cep·tive /dɪ'sɛptɪv/ *adj.* **1** deliberately intended to make someone believe something that is not true: *deceptive advertising* | *The spokesperson's statements were deceptive.* **2** something that is deceptive is not what it seems to be: *Their music has a deceptive simplicity* (=it seems simple but it is not). —**deceptively** *adj.*: *her deceptively quiet manner* —**deceptiveness** *n.* [U]

deci- /dɛsɪ/ *prefix* 1/10 of a unit: *a deciliter* (=a tenth of a liter) [**Origin:** French *déci-*, from Latin *decimus* **tenth**, from *decem* **ten**]

dec·i·bel /'dɛsə,bɛl, -bəl/ *n.* [C] TECHNICAL a unit of measurement for the loudness of sound: *noise levels above 85 decibels* [**Origin:** 1900–2000 *deci-* + *bel* **unit of sound power** (20–21 centuries), from Alexander Graham *Bell* (1847–1922), U.S. inventor]

de·cide /dɪ'saɪd/ S1 W1 *v.* **1** [I,T] to make a choice or judgment about something, especially after considering all the possibilities or arguments: *"Which one do you want?" "I can't decide."* | *Has the committee decided anything yet?* | **decide to do sth** *Bryant decided to move away from the city.* | **decide (that)** *It was decided that women could compete in the biathlon.* | **decide who/what/whether etc.** *Have you decided what to wear to the wedding?* | *Voters will decide if a new stadium should be built.* | **decide between (doing) sth** *I had to decide between paying the rent and paying for health insurance.* | **decide against (doing) sth** *He eventually decided against telling his mother.* | **decide in favor of (doing) sth** *Management decided in favor of the pay increase.* | **decide for yourself** *Restaurants should be able to decide for themselves* (=make their own choice) *whether to ban smoking.* → see also DECIDING, DECISION

THESAURUS

make up your mind to decide something, especially after thinking about it for a long time: *Have you made up your mind about which college to go to?*
choose to decide which of a number of things, possibilities etc. that you want: *I let the kids choose their own clothes.*
resolve to make a definite decision to do something: *He resolved to quit smoking.*
determine to officially decide what something shall be: *Each department determines its own pay rates.*
come down in favor of sth to decide to support a particular plan, argument etc: *The senator came down in favor of continuing the trade with China.*

2 [T] if an event, action etc. decides something, it influences events so that one particular result will happen: *A three-point basket in the final seconds decided the game.* **3 decide in favor of sth/decide against**

sth if a judge or JURY in a court case decides in favor of someone or against someone, they say that someone is guilty or not guilty [**Origin:** 1300–1400 French *décider*, from Latin *decidere* **to cut off, decide**]

decide on sth *phr. v.* to choose one thing from many possible choices: *Have you decided on a date for your wedding?*

de·cid·ed /dɪˈsaɪdɪd/ *adj.* [only before noun] definite and easily noticed: *The new color is a decided improvement.*

de·cid·ed·ly /dɪˈsaɪdɪdli/ *adv.* **1** [+ adj./adv.] definitely or in a way that is easily noticed SYN **distinctly**: *John was looking decidedly uncomfortable.* **2** in a way that shows that you are very sure and determined about what you want to do: *"No!" said Margaret decidedly.*

de·cid·ing /dɪˈsaɪdɪŋ/ *adj.* [only before noun] a deciding game, vote, goal etc. makes the difference between winning and losing, failing and succeeding, making one decision or another etc.: *the **deciding game** of the tournament* (=the final game that determines the winner of a series of games) | *Myers cast **the deciding vote*** (=the one vote that makes one side win when the votes have been equal). | *Money was **the deciding factor*** (=the thing that most influenced the final decision) *when we had to choose which car to buy.*

de·cid·u·ous /dɪˈsɪdʒuəs/ *adj.* BIOLOGY deciduous trees lose their leaves in winter [**Origin:** 1600–1700 Latin *deciduus*, from *decidere* **to fall off**] → see also EVERGREEN

dec·i·mal¹ /ˈdɛsəməl/ *adj.* MATH a decimal system is based on the number 10

decimal² *n.* [C] MATH a FRACTION (=a number less than one) that is shown as a PERIOD followed by the number of TENTHS, then the number of HUNDREDTHS etc., for example in the numbers 0.5, 0.175, and 0.661

ˌdecimal ˈplace *n.* [C] one of the positions after a decimal point in a decimal number

ˌdecimal ˈpoint *n.* [C] MATH the PERIOD in a decimal, used to separate whole numbers from TENTHS, HUNDREDTHS etc.

ˈdecimal ˌsystem *n.* [C] a system of counting that is based on the number 10 → see also DEWEY DECIMAL SYSTEM

dec·i·mate /ˈdɛsəˌmeɪt/ *v.* [T usually passive] to destroy a large part of something: *The flies have decimated the winter crop.* —**decimation** /ˌdɛsəˈmeɪʃən/ *n.* [U]

de·ci·pher /dɪˈsaɪfɚ/ *v.* [T] **1** to find the meaning of something that is difficult to read or understand: *I couldn't decipher the signature.* **2** to change a message written in a secret code into ordinary language so you can understand it SYN **decode** → see also INDECIPHERABLE

de·ci·sion /dɪˈsɪʒən/ S1 W1 *n.* **1** [C] a choice or judgment that you make after a period of discussion or thought: *The judges' decision is final.* | **decision to do sth** *Navarro said it was his decision to resign.* | **+about** *decisions about medical treatment* | *The committee should **make a decision** this week.* | *The department will make a **final decision** this month.* | **tough/hard/difficult decision** *Leaving my job was a tough decision.* | **come to a decision/reach a decision** *We talked about it for weeks before reaching a decision.* | *Moving to New York was a **big decision*** (=an important decision). **2** [C] an official statement by the court after a court case about whether a person, group etc. is guilty of a crime or not SYN **verdict**: *The Supreme Court **overturned the** lower court's **decision*** (=said that it was incorrect). **3** [U] the ability someone has to make choices or judgments quickly and confidently OPP **indecision**: *the ability to act with speed and decision* **4** [U] the act of deciding something: *The power of decision rests with the Supreme Court.*

de·ci·sion·mak·ing /dɪˈsɪʒənˌmeɪkɪŋ/ *n.* [U] the process of thinking about a problem, idea etc., and then making a choice or judgment

de·ci·sive /dɪˈsaɪsɪv/ *adj.* **1** an action, event etc. that is decisive has a big effect on the way a situation develops: *the decisive battle of the war* | **a decisive factor/effect/role etc.** *His age was a decisive factor in his decision to quit.* | *The U.N. played a decisive role in peace-making.* **2** good at making decisions quickly and with confidence OPP **indecisive**: *a decisive leader* | **decisive action/step etc.** *The U.S. must take decisive action to end the situation.* **3** definite, having a clear result, and not able to be doubted: *His answer to the question was a decisive "no."* | **a decisive victory/result/defeat etc.** *a decisive election victory* —**decisively** *adv.* —**decisiveness** *n.* [U]

deck

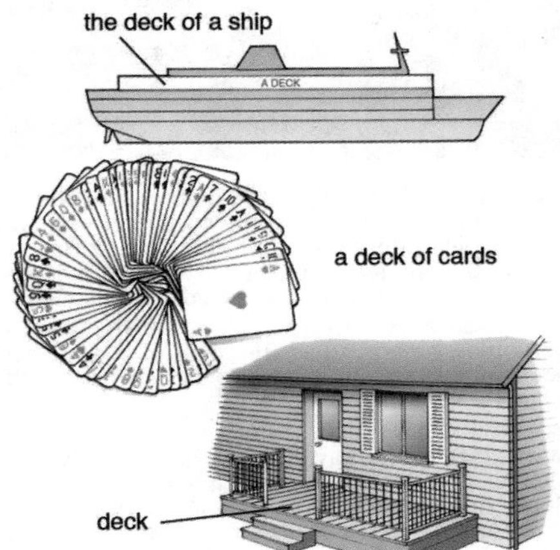

deck¹ /dɛk/ S3 *n.* [C] **1 a)** the outside top level of a ship, that you can walk on: *I left my cabin and went out **on** the main **deck**.* | *The crewmen slept **below deck**.* **b)** one of the levels on a ship, airplane, bus, or in a sports STADIUM: *a seat on the upper deck* **2** a raised wooden floor built out from the back of a house, where you can sit outside and relax **3** a set of playing cards: *Let's open a new **deck of cards**.* **4 cassette/tape/game etc. deck** a machine into which you can put music TAPES, games etc. **5 on deck** if a baseball player is on deck, they have the next chance to hit the ball [**Origin:** 1400–1500 Middle Dutch *dec* **roof, covering**] → see also **clear the decks** at CLEAR² (17), FLIGHT DECK, **hit the ground/deck/dirt** at HIT¹ (25), ON-DECK CIRCLE

deck² *v.* [T] **1** also **deck sth ↔ out** [usually passive] to decorate something with flowers, flags etc., especially for a special occasion: **+in** *The altar was decked in yellow flowers.* | **+with** *The bridge is decked out with lights during Christmas.* **2** SLANG to hit someone so hard that they fall over

deck sb **out** *phr. v.* to dress in fashionable clothes or to dress in a certain style of clothes for a special occasion: **+in** *Adam was decked out in his best suit.*

ˈdeck chair *n.* [C] a folding chair with a long seat made of cloth, used especially on the beach

deck·hand /ˈdɛkhænd/ *n.* [C] someone who does unskilled work on a ship

ˈdeck shoe *n.* [C] a flat shoe made of CANVAS (=heavy cloth), with a rubber bottom

de·claim /dɪˈkleɪm/ *v.* [I,T] FORMAL to speak loudly, sometimes with actions, so that people will notice you —**declamation** /ˌdɛkləˈmeɪʃən/ *n.* [C,U]

de·clam·a·to·ry /dɪˈklæməˌtɔri/ *adj.* FORMAL ENG. LANG. ARTS a declamatory speech or piece of writing expresses your feelings and opinions very strongly

dec·la·ra·tion /ˌdɛkləˈreɪʃən/ *n.* [C,U] **1** an important official statement: *a ceasefire declaration* | **+of** *Congress issued a declaration of war.* **2** an official document giving information, especially about legal or financial matters: *a customs declaration* **3** a statement strongly expressing an idea or belief: +**of** *his declaration of love*

the Declaration of Independence

Decla,ration of Inde'pendence *n.* **the Declaration of Independence** HISTORY the document written in 1776 in which the 13 British colonies (COLONY) in America officially stated that they were an independent nation and would no longer be governed by Britain

de·clar·a·tive /dɪˈklærət̬ɪv, -ˈklɛr-/ *adj.* ENG. LANG. ARTS a declarative sentence has the form of a statement, rather than a question → see also EXCLAMATORY, INTERROGATIVE

de·clare /dɪˈklɛr/ W2 *v.*
1 SAY OFFICIALLY [T] to say officially and publicly that a particular situation exists or that something is true: **declare that** *Doctors declared that Maxwell died of natural causes.* | **declare sb/sth (to be) sth** *Officials declared Jackson the winner.* | **declare sth illegal/unsafe/open etc.** *Police declared the protest illegal.* | **declare sb dead/unfit/insane etc.** *The man was declared dead at the hospital.* | *The college will be forced to* ***declare bankruptcy*** (=state officially that you are unable to pay your debts).
2 declare war (on sb) **a)** to decide and state officially that you will begin fighting another country **b)** to say that you will do everything you can to stop something that is bad or wrong: *The time has come to declare war on cancer.*
3 SAY WHAT YOU THINK/FEEL [T] to say very clearly and publicly what you think or feel: *Most Republicans declared their support for the bill.* | **declare that** *He left, declaring that he would not be forced to retire early.*
4 MONEY/PROPERTY ETC. [T] ECONOMICS to make an official statement saying how much money you have earned, what property you own etc.: *All investment income must be declared.*
5 (Well) I declare! SPOKEN, OLD-FASHIONED used as an expression of surprise
[**Origin:** 1300–1400 Latin *declarare*, from *clarare* **to make clear**] —**declarable** *adj.*

declare for sth *phr. v.* to state publicly that you are going to take part in an election, competition etc.: *He declared for president in a speech in April.*

de·clared /dɪˈklɛrd/ *adj.* **1** a declared rule, intention, wish etc. is one that has been announced publicly: *the state's declared intention to reduce crime* | *the declared winner of the race* **2** a declared candidate has said officially that he or she will run in an election

de·clas·si·fied /diˈklæsəˌfaɪd/ *adj.* official information that is declassified was secret but is not secret anymore: *declassified government documents* —**declassify** *v.* [T]

de·clen·sion /dɪˈklɛnʃən/ *n.* [C] ENG. LANG. ARTS **1** the set of various forms that a noun, PRONOUN, or adjective can have according to whether it is the SUBJECT, OBJECT etc. of a sentence in a language such as Latin or German **2** a particular set of nouns etc. that all have the same type of these forms

de·cline[1] /dɪˈklaɪn/ Ac W2 *v.*
1 BECOME LESS [I,T] to decrease in quantity or importance: *Computer sales declined 2.1 percent this year.* | *The singer's popularity began to decline.* | **decline rapidly/sharply/dramatically/steadily** *The number of members is declining steadily.* ►see THESAURUS box at **decrease**[1]
2 SAY NO [I,T] FORMAL to say "no" politely when someone invites you somewhere, offers you something, or wants you to do something: *They asked me to run the new division, but I declined.* | *The pilot declined medical treatment after the accident.* | **decline an offer/invitation etc.** *I declined his offer of another drink.* | **decline to do sth** *FBI Agent Moran declined to comment.* ►see THESAURUS box at **reject**[1]
3 BECOME WORSE [I] to become gradually worse in quality SYN **deteriorate**: *The general standard of work is declining.* | *Lambeth has been* ***in declining health*** *for several months.*
4 sb's declining years FORMAL the last years of someone's life
5 GRAMMAR ENG. LANG. ARTS **a)** [I] if a noun, PRONOUN, or adjective declines, its form changes according to whether it is the SUBJECT, OBJECT etc. of a sentence **b)** [T] if you decline a noun etc., you show these various forms that it can take

decline[2] Ac W2 *n.* [C usually singular, U] a gradual decrease in the quality, quantity, or importance of something: *Stock markets in Europe showed similar declines.* | +**of** *the decline of the steel industry* | +**in** *a decline in exports* | **a rapid/sharp/steep/dramatic etc. decline** *a dramatic decline in revenues* | **a steady/gradual/long-term etc. decline** *a long-term decline in the teenage marriage rate* | *During the last ten years, the construction industry has been* ***in decline.*** | **go/fall into decline** *The port fell into decline in the 1950s.* | *The number of students entering higher education is* ***on the decline*** (=is decreasing). [**Origin:** 1300–1400 French *décliner*, from Latin *declinare* **to turn aside, inflect**]

de·code /diˈkoʊd/ *v.* [T] **1** to translate a secret or complicated message, some DATA, or a signal into a form that can be easily understood OPP **encode** **2** ENG. LANG. ARTS to understand the meaning of a word rather than use a word to express meaning OPP **encode**

de·cod·er /diˈkoʊdɚ/ *n.* [C] **1** a special machine that translates messages, DATA, or signals into a form that can be understood by people or used by another machine **2** a person who decodes secret messages

dé·col·le·tage /deɪˌkɑləˈtɑʒ/ *n.* [U] the top edge of a woman's dress that is cut very low to show part of her shoulders and breasts —**décolleté** /deɪˌkɑləˈteɪ/ *adj.*

de·col·o·nize /diˈkɑləˌnaɪz/ *v.* [T] POLITICS to make a former COLONY politically independent —**decolonization** /diˌkɑlənəˈzeɪʃən/ *n.* [U]

de·com·mis·sion /ˌdikəˈmɪʃən/ *v.* [T] to officially stop using something such as a ship, airplane, or weapon and take it apart

de·com·pose /ˌdikəmˈpoʊz/ *v.* [I,T] **1** to decay, or to make something decay SYN **rot**: *a partly decomposed body* | *plastics that do not decompose* ►see THESAURUS box at **decay**[1] **2** TECHNICAL to divide into smaller parts, or to make something do this —**decomposition** /ˌdikɑmpəˈzɪʃən/ *n.* [U]

de·com·pos·er /ˌdikəmˈpoʊzɚ/ *n.* [C] BIOLOGY a living thing, such as FUNGUS OR BACTERIA, that feeds on the dead bodies of animals, plants etc., making them gradually decay → see also DETRITIVORE

ˌdecompoˈsition reˌaction *n.* [C] CHEMISTRY a chemical change during which a chemical compound is reduced to two or more simpler chemical substances

de·com·press /ˌdikəmˈprɛs/ *v.* **1** [I,T] to reduce the pressure of air on something: *The fire caused the plane's cabin to decompress.* **2** [T] COMPUTERS to do an operation on a computer that changes stored DATA into a normal form so that a computer can use it —**decompression** /ˌdikəmˈprɛʃən/ *n.* [U]

ˌdecomˈpression ˌchamber *n.* [C] a special room

where people go after they have been deep under water, in order to return slowly to normal air pressure

ˌdecomˈpression ˌsickness *n.* [U] a dangerous medical condition that people get when they come up from deep under water too quickly; the BENDS

de·con·gest·ant /ˌdikənˈdʒɛstənt/ *n.* [C,U] medicine that you can take if you are sick that will help you breathe more easily

de·con·struc·tion /ˌdikənˈstrʌkʃən/ *n.* [U] ENG. LANG. ARTS a method used in PHILOSOPHY and the criticism of literature that says there can be no single explanation of the meaning of a piece of writing —**deconstructionism** *n.* [U] —**deconstructionist** *n.* [C] —**deconstructionist** *adj.* —**deconstruct** /ˌdikənˈstrʌkt/ *v.* [T]

de·con·tam·i·nate /ˌdikənˈtæməˌneɪt/ *v.* [T] to remove a dangerous substance from somewhere: *a company hired to decontaminate nuclear facilities* —**decontamination** /ˌdikənˌtæməˈneɪʃən/ *n.* [U]

de·cor, décor /ˈdeɪkɔr, deɪˈkɔr/ *n.* [C,U] the way that the inside of a building is decorated: *The restaurant's decor is clean and modern.*

dec·o·rate /ˈdɛkəˌreɪt/ *v.* [T] **1** to make something look more attractive by putting something pretty on it: *I'll help you decorate the cake.* | **decorate sth with sth** *Christmas trees were decorated with ornaments and lights.* **2** if something decorates a building, room, wall, tree, food, or other thing, it has been put on it to make it look more attractive: *Fresh fruit decorated the dessert.* **3** to give someone a MEDAL as an official sign of honor: **decorate sb for sth** *Chappell was decorated for heroism.* [**Origin:** 1500–1600 Latin *decoratus*, past participle of *decorare* **to decorate**, from *decus* **honour, decoration**]

decorate

decorating the Christmas tree

dec·o·ra·tion /ˌdɛkəˈreɪʃən/ *n.* **1** [C usually plural, U] something that you put, paint, draw etc. on something else in order to make it more attractive: *Christmas decorations* | *walls with very little architectural decoration* | *The ribbons are just* ***for decoration*** (=for making something pretty, rather than to be used). **2** [U] the activity of making something more attractive by putting, painting, drawing etc. things on it: **+of** *the decoration of palace gardens* **3** [C] something such as a MEDAL that is given to someone as an official sign of honor: *military decorations*

dec·o·ra·tive /ˈdɛkərət̬ɪv/ *adj.* pretty or attractive, but not always necessary or useful: *the house's decorative features* —**decoratively** *adv.*

ˌdecorative ˈarts *n.* [plural] art connected with the design and production of furniture and household objects, such as FABRIC and POTTERY

dec·o·ra·tor /ˈdɛkəˌreɪt̬ɚ/ *n.* [C] someone whose profession is to chose furniture, WALLPAPER, CARPET etc. for houses, offices etc.

dec·o·rous /ˈdɛkərəs, dɪˈkɔrəs/ *adj.* FORMAL having the correct appearance or behavior for a particular occasion —**decorously** *adv.*

de·cor·um /dɪˈkɔrəm/ *n.* [U] FORMAL behavior that shows respect and is correct for a particular occasion: *a strong sense of decorum*

de·coy /ˈdikɔɪ/ *n. plural* **decoys** [C] **1** someone or something used to trick someone into going to a place, so that you can catch them, attack them etc.: *A policewoman acted as a decoy to catch the rapist.* **2** a model of a bird used to attract wild birds so that you can watch them or shoot them [**Origin:** 1500–1600 Dutch *de cooi* **the cage** (= structure of bars for keeping animals in)] —**decoy** /diˈkɔɪ/ *v.* [T]

de·crease¹ /dɪˈkris, ˈdikris/ *v.* [I,T] to become less in number, size, or amount, or to make something do this SYN **go down** SYN **reduce** OPP **increase**: *Sales in Japan steadily decreased last year.* | *Birth control pills* ***decrease the chances of*** *getting pregnant.* | **decrease in number/frequency/size etc.** *The moose are decreasing in number.* | **decrease to sth** *The population has decreased to 5.2 million.* ►see THESAURUS box at **reduce** [**Origin:** 1300–1400 Anglo-French *decreistre*, from Latin *decrescere*, from *crescere* **to grow**] —**decreasing** *adj.*

THESAURUS

go down to become lower or less in level, amount, size, quality etc.: *The number of students enrolled in the class has gone down this semester.*
drop to decrease to a lower level or amount, or to make something decrease: *Sales have dropped 15% this year.*
fall to decrease to a lower level or amount: *Temperatures fell below zero last night.*
plummet to suddenly and quickly decrease in value: *The price of stock plummeted.*
diminish to become smaller or less important: *Union membership diminished from 30,000 at its height to just 20 today.*
decline to decrease in quality, quantity, or importance: *The number of these animals in the wild has declined sharply.*
►see THESAURUS box at **reduce**

de·crease² /ˈdikris/ *n.* [C] the process of reducing something, or the amount by which it reduces SYN **reduction** OPP **increase**: **+in** *a slight decrease in appetite* | *a 19% decrease in prices* | **+of** *a decrease of 5%* | **a drastic/significant/marked/sharp decrease** (=a large decrease)

de·cree¹ /dɪˈkri/ *n.* [C] **1** an official command or decision, especially one made by the ruler of a country: *The president* ***issued a decree*** *imposing a curfew.* | *The tax was imposed* ***by decree*** (=using a decree). **2** LAW a judgment in a court of law: *a court decree* [**Origin:** 1300–1400 Old French *decré*, from Latin *decernere* **to decide**]

decree² *v.* [T] to make an official judgment or give an official command: **decree that** *The king decreed that the army be reduced by 200,000.*

de·crep·it /dɪˈkrɛpɪt/ *adj.* old and in bad condition: *a decrepit subway train* | *I felt old and decrepit.* [**Origin:** 1400–1500 Latin *decrepitus*, from *crepare* **to make a high cracking sound**] —**decrepitude** *n.* [U]

de·crim·i·nal·ize /diˈkrɪmənəˌlaɪz/ *v.* [T] LAW to reduce or remove the punishment for doing a particular illegal thing —**decriminalization** /diˌkrɪmənələˈzeɪʃən/ *n.* [U] → see also LEGALIZE

de·cry /dɪˈkraɪ/ *v.* **decries, decried, decrying** [T] FORMAL to state publicly that you do not approve of something: *Several groups decried the election results.*

ded·i·cate /ˈdɛdəˌkeɪt/ *v.* [T] **1 a)** to say that something such as a book, song, movie etc. has been written, made, or sung to express love, respect etc. for someone: **dedicate sth to sb** *Greene dedicated the book to his mother.* **b)** to state in an official ceremony that something will be given someone's name in order to show respect for them: **dedicate sth to sb** *Murphy Hall is dedicated to one of the university's presidents.* **2 dedicate yourself/your life to sth** to spend most of your time and effort doing one particular thing: *The actress now dedicates herself to charity work.* **3** to use a place, time, money etc. only for a particular purpose SYN **devote**: **dedicate sth to sth** *a magazine dedicated to photography* [**Origin:** 1400–1500 Latin *dedicare*, from *dicare* **to say publicly**]

ded·i·cat·ed /ˈdɛdəˌkeɪt̬ɪd/ *adj.* **1** someone who is dedicated works very hard because they care a lot about their work: *a team of dedicated volunteers* | **+to** *a group dedicated to preserving nature* **2** [only before noun] made or used for only one particular purpose: *a dedicated telephone line*

ded·i·ca·tion /ˌdɛdɪˈkeɪʃən/ *n.* **1** [U] the hard work

D

or effort that someone puts into a particular activity because they care about it a lot: *hard work and dedication* | +**to** *his dedication to community activities* **2** [C] an act or ceremony of dedicating something to someone: *the dedication of the new school* **3** [C] the words used in dedicating something to someone: +**to** *a dedication to his wife*

de·duce /dɪ'dus/ Ac *v.* [T not in progressive] FORMAL to make a judgment about something, based on the information that you have SYN infer: **deduce sth from sth** *We can deduce several facts about the soil from the presence of these plants.* [**Origin:** 1400–1500 Latin *deducere* **to lead out**, from *ducere* **to lead**] —**deducible** *adj.* → see also DEDUCTION

de·duct /dɪ'dʌkt/ *v.* [T] to take away an amount or part from a total SYN subtract: *Can I deduct any of my health insurance costs?* | **deduct sth from sth** *You can deduct the cost of repairs from your rent.*

de·duct·i·ble[1] /dɪ'dʌktəbəl/ *adj.* an amount of money that is deductible can be subtracted from the amount of money you must pay taxes on: *Any contribution is **tax-deductible**.*

deductible[2] *n.* [C] ECONOMICS the amount of money that you must pay a hospital, car repair shop etc. before your insurance company will pay the rest of the bill: *a $200 deductible*

de·duc·tion /dɪ'dʌkʃən/ Ac *n.* [C,U] **1** the process of making a judgment about something, based on the information that you have, or the opinion that comes from this: *The game teaches children logic and deduction.* | *a brilliant deduction* **2** ECONOMICS an amount that you can SUBTRACT (=take away) from your income, on which you do not have to pay taxes: *The standard **tax deduction** for unmarried people is $5,000.* **3** FORMAL the process of taking away an amount from a total, or the amount that is taken away

de·duc·tive /dɪ'dʌktɪv/ *adj.* using the knowledge that you have in order to understand or make a judgment about something: *deductive thinking*

de,ductive 'reasoning *n.* [U] **1** the process by which you form a scientific judgment about something based on existing facts **2** ALGEBRA the process of proving a mathematical statement or solving a mathematical problem using an existing mathematical principle or a series of facts that develop from one to the next in a reasonable or correct way → see also INDUCTIVE REASONING

deed /did/ *n.* **1** [C,U] LITERARY something that you do, especially something that is very good or very bad: *evil deeds* | **sb's good deed for the day** HUMOROUS (=a kind or helpful thing that someone does) | *He was honorable **in word and in deed*** (=in what he said and did). ▸see THESAURUS box at action **2** [C] LAW an official paper that is a record of an agreement, especially an agreement concerning who owns property: *the deed for the land*

deem /dim/ *v.* [T not in progressive] FORMAL to think of or consider something in a particular way SYN consider: **deem sth appropriate/necessary/acceptable etc.** *Judges can give any punishment they deem appropriate.* | **deem that** *Officials deemed that the risks of the mission were too great.*

deep[1] /dip/ S2 W2 *adj.*

1 GOING FAR DOWN going far down from the top or from the surface OPP shallow: *deep snow* | *a deep cut on his arm* | **5 inches/7 feet etc. deep** *The river is 40 feet deep in the middle.* | ***How deep** was the water?*

2 GOING FAR IN going far in from the front edge of something OPP shallow: **5 inches/3 feet etc. deep** *a shelf three feet long and eight inches deep* | ***How deep** do the counter tops need to be?*

3 FEELING/BELIEF [only before noun] a deep feeling or belief is very strong and usually sincere SYN profound: *I felt deep disappointment.* | *his deep faith in God* | *He has a **deep sense of** honor.* | **make/leave a deep impression on sb** (=have an effect on someone that lasts a long time)

4 SEVERE problems that are deep are serious or severe:

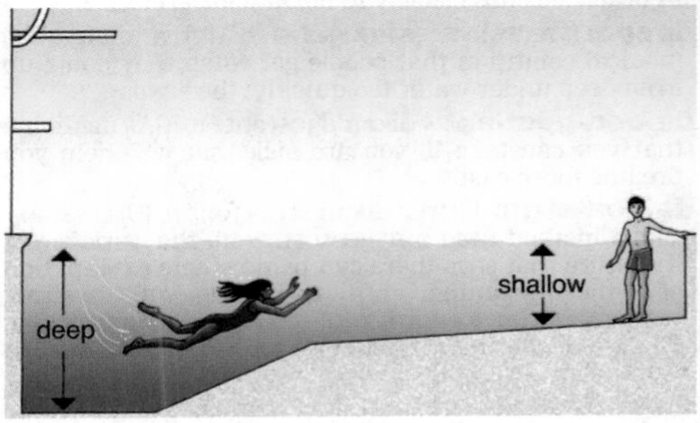

deep divisions in the community | *He fell into a deep depression.*

5 SOUND a deep sound is very low SYN high: *Jones has a strong deep voice.*

6 COLOR a deep color is dark and strong OPP pale OPP light: *a beautiful deep purple* ▸see THESAURUS box at color[1]

7 BREATH breathing a lot of air in or out of your lungs OPP shallow: *a deep sigh* | *It's okay, just relax, **take a deep breath**.*

8 SERIOUS a) someone who is deep is serious and thinks very hard about things, often in a way that other people find difficult to understand OPP shallow: *a deep sensitive person* **b)** involving serious or complicated thoughts, ideas, or feelings: *a deep conversation about religion*

9 deep sleep sleep that is difficult to wake up from: *Finally, her mother **fell into a deep sleep*** (=began to sleep in this way).

10 in deep trouble/water in a bad or difficult situation, especially because you have done something wrong or stupid: *Everyone agrees this city is in deep financial trouble.*

11 deep in thought/conversation etc. thinking so hard, talking so much, or paying so much attention to something that you do not notice anything else that is happening around you: *Moore was deep in prayer.*

12 go off the deep end INFORMAL to suddenly become crazy, angry, or violent: *Sara really went off the deep end, taking drugs and living on the streets.*

13 BALL a deep ball is hit, thrown, or kicked to a far part of the sports field

[**Origin:** Old English *deop*] → see also DEPTH

deep[2] W3 *adv.* **1** [always + adv./prep.] a long way into or below the surface of something: +**down/below/inside etc.** *She pushed her stick deep down into the mud.* | *Crews are working **deep underground**, building a tunnel.* **2 deep down a)** if you know or feel something deep down, that is what you really feel or know even though you do not admit it: *She knew, deep down, that he did not love her.* **b)** if someone is good, evil etc. deep down, that is what they are really like even though they usually hide it: *Deep down, Bill is a very caring person.* **3 deep in debt** owing a lot of money: *The medical bills put us deep in debt.* **4 run/go deep** a feeling that runs deep, is felt very strongly, especially because of things that have happened in the past: *Bitterness runs deep among Kathy's family members.* → see also **still waters run deep** at STILL[2] (4) **5 be in (too) deep** INFORMAL to be very involved in a situation, so that it is difficult to get out of: *I'm in too deep to leave the business now.* **6 two/three/four etc. deep** having two, three, four etc. rows or layers of things or people: *People stood ten deep along the parade route.* **7 deep into the night** until very late: *They talked deep into the night.*

deep[3] *n.* **the deep** POETICAL the ocean

-deep /dip/ [in adjectives] **knee-deep/ankle-deep/waist-deep etc.** deep enough to come up to your knees, ankles, waist etc.: *The water was waist-deep.*

deep·en /'dipən/ *v.* [I,T]

1 BAD SITUATION if a serious situation deepens or something deepens it, it gets worse: *The recession may*

deepen still further. | *The changes will deepen divisions between rich and poor schools.*
2 FEELING/RELATIONSHIP if a feeling or relationship deepens or someone deepens it, it gradually becomes stronger: *We are interested in deepening our economic ties with Japan.*
3 KNOWLEDGE if you deepen your knowledge or understanding of something, you learn more about it and understand it better: *Traveling allows young people to deepen their understanding of other cultures.*
4 COLOR if a color deepens or you deepen it, it becomes or is made darker
5 SOUND if a sound deepens or you deepen it, it becomes lower
6 WATER if a body of water such as a river or lake deepens or someone deepens it, it becomes or is made deeper at a particular place: *The river deepens five feet from the shore.*
7 BREATHING if your breathing deepens or you deepen it, you take more air into your lungs

ˌdeep ˈfreeze *n.* [C] **1** a large metal box in which food can be stored at very low temperatures for a long time SYN freezer **2** very cold weather: *a week-long deep freeze* **3 in a/the deep freeze a)** if something you are working on is in the deep freeze, it is delayed or stopped for a period of time: *The movie was in the deep freeze for almost a year.* **b)** used to describe a difficult relationship between countries, especially when there is very little communication: *U.S. relations with the country have been in the deep freeze for years.*

ˌdeep-ˈfry *v.* [T] to cook food in a lot of hot oil —**deep-fried** *adj.*

deep·ly /ˈdipli/ W3 *adv.* **1** used to emphasize that a belief, feeling, opinion etc. is very strong, serious, important, or sincere: *I am deeply honored.* | *a deeply religious man* | *Congress is deeply concerned about unemployment.* **2** a long way into something, or a long way below the surface: *The seeds were planted too deeply.* **3 breathe/sigh deeply** to completely fill your lungs with air when you breathe, or empty them completely **4 sleep deeply** to sleep very well, so that it is difficult to be woken

ˌdeep-ˈpocketed *adj.* having a lot of money to spend: *the deep-pocketed tobacco industry*

ˌdeep-ˈrooted also **ˌdeeply ˈrooted** *adj.* a deep-rooted habit, idea, belief etc. is so strong in a person or society that it is very difficult to change: *deep-rooted prejudice*

ˌdeep-ˈseated *adj.* a deep-seated attitude, feeling, or idea is strong and is very difficult to change: *a deep-seated distrust of the police*

ˌdeep-ˈset *adj.* deep-set eyes seem to be farther back into the face than most people's

ˌdeep ˈsix *v.* [T] INFORMAL to decide not to use something and to get rid of it: *Why did the company deep-six such a great little camera?*

ˌDeep ˈSouth *n.* **the Deep South** the southeastern part of the U.S., including Alabama, Georgia, Mississippi, Louisiana, and South Carolina

deer

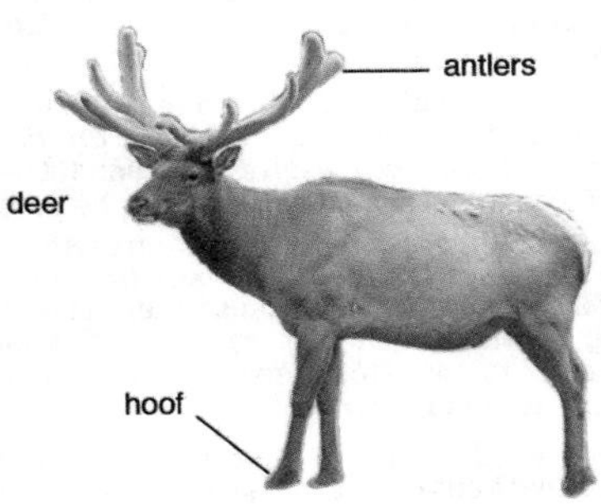

deer /dɪr/ *n. plural* **deer** [C] a large wild animal that lives in forests and has a short tail. The adult male has ANTLERS. [**Origin:** Old English *deor* **animal**] → see also DOE

Deere /dɪr/, **John** (1804–1886) the U.S. inventor of a new kind of PLOW

deer·stalk·er /ˈdɪrˌstɔkɚ/ *n.* [C] a type of soft hat with pieces of cloth that cover your ears

def /dɛf/ *adj.* SLANG very good, fashionable, attractive etc. SYN cool

de·face /dɪˈfeɪs/ *v.* [T] to damage the surface or appearance of something, especially by writing or making marks on it: *Several office buildings were defaced by graffiti.* —**defacement** *n.* [U]

de fac·to /dɪ ˈfæktoʊ, di-/ *adj.* actually existing or happening without being approved of legally or officially: *Hyland is the department's de facto director.* —**de facto** *adv.* → see also DE JURE

def·a·ma·tion /ˌdɛfəˈmeɪʃən/ *n.* [U] FORMAL writing or saying something that makes people have a bad opinion about someone or something: *King sued the show's producers for* ***defamation of character***.

de·fame /dɪˈfeɪm/ *v.* [T] FORMAL to write or say something that makes people have a bad opinion of someone or something: *a novel defaming the Catholic church* —**defamatory** /dɪˈfæməˌtɔri/ *adj.*

de·fault¹ /dɪˈfɔlt/ *n.* **1 by default a)** if something happens by default, it happens because someone did not make a decision or take action: *I became a salesman by default* (=because I did not know what else to do). **b)** if you win a game, competition etc. by default, you win because your opponent did not play or there were no other competitors **2** [C,U] FORMAL failure to do something that you are legally supposed to do or have a duty to do, especially not paying back money: *The loan* ***is in default***. **3** [C] COMPUTERS the way in which things will be arranged on a computer screen unless you decide to change them: *the* ***default settings*** *for my printer* **4 in default of sth** FORMAL because of the lack or absence of something [**Origin:** 1200–1300 Old French *defaute*, from Vulgar Latin *defallere* **to be lacking, fail**]

default² *v.* [I] to not do something that you are legally supposed to, especially not to pay money: +**on** *students who default on their loans* —**defaulter** *n.* [C]

de·feat¹ /dɪˈfit/ *n.* **1** [C,U] failure to win or succeed OPP victory: *an election defeat* | *The team has not* ***suffered a defeat*** *all season.* | *The goalkeeper was blamed for their* ***narrow defeat*** (=defeat by a small amount). | **a humiliating/crushing/heavy etc. defeat** (=one that is very bad and embarrassing) | *Even* ***in defeat****, the General remained optimistic.* | **concede/admit/accept defeat** (=to admit or accept defeat) **2 defeat of sb/sth** victory over someone or something: *the defeat of the military coup*

defeat² W3 *v.* [T] **1** to win a victory over someone in a war, competition, game etc. SYN beat: *his campaign to defeat the President* | *Napoleon was defeated at the battle of Waterloo.* | *Our team was* ***narrowly defeated*** (=by a small number of points) *in the final.* | *He* ***easily defeated*** *his first three opponents.* | **defeat sb by ten points/three runs etc.** *Georgia defeated North Carolina by 13 points.* ▶see THESAURUS box at beat¹ → see also WIN **2** if something defeats you, you cannot understand it, remember it, or deal with it: *The last exam question defeated me.* **3** to prevent something from happening or succeeding: *It was a lack of money that defeated their plan.* | *The legislature defeated the bill.* **4 defeat the purpose (of sth)** if one action defeats the purpose of another action, it make the other action useless or not worth doing: *Eating a fatty cheeseburger with your diet soda defeats the purpose.* [**Origin:** 1300–1400 Anglo-French *defeter* **to destroy**, from Medieval Latin *disfacere*, from Latin *facere* **to do**]

de·feat·ist /dɪˈfitɪst/ *adj.* believing that you will not succeed: *a defeatist attitude* —**defeatist** *n.* [C] —**defeatism** *n.* [U]

def·e·cate /ˈdɛfəˌkeɪt/ *v.* [I] FORMAL to get rid of waste matter from your body out of your ANUS —**defecation** /ˌdɛfəˈkeɪʃən/ *n.* [U]

de·fect¹ /ˈdifɛkt/ *n.* [C] a fault or a lack of something that means that something is not perfect: *All the new cars are tested for defects.* [**Origin:** 1400–1500 Old French, Latin *defectus* **lack**] → see also BIRTH DEFECT ▸see THESAURUS box at **fault¹**

> **THESAURUS**
> **problem** a difficult situation that needs to be dealt with: *There's a problem with the brakes.*
> **flaw** a mark or weakness that makes something not perfect: *a flaw in the glass*
> **bug** a defect in a computer program: *The software developers are trying to get rid of the bugs in the program.*
> **fault** something that is wrong with a machine, design etc., which prevents it from working correctly: *a fault in the power unit*

D

de·fect² /dɪˈfɛkt/ *v.* [I] POLITICS to leave your own country or a group in order to go to or join an opposing one: +**from/to** *Baryshnikov defected from the USSR in 1974.* —**defector** *n.* [C] —**defection** /dɪˈfɛkʃən/ *n.* [C,U]

de·fec·tive /dɪˈfɛktɪv/ *adj.* not made correctly, or not working correctly: *defective merchandise* —**defectively** *adv.* —**defectiveness** *n.* [U]

de·fence /dɪˈfɛns/ *n.* the British and Canadian spelling of DEFENSE

de·fend /dɪˈfɛnd/ [W2] *v.* **1** [I,T] to do something in order to protect someone or something from being attacked [OPP] **attack**: **defend (sb/sth) against sb/sth** *the need to defend the U.S. against a missile attack* | **defend sb/sth from sb/sth** *Rubber bullets were used to defend the police from violent crowds.* | **defend yourself** *Villagers have few weapons to defend themselves.* **2** [T] to say things to support someone or something that is being criticized: *She was quick to defend her husband* | **defend sb/sth against sth** *Hendricks defended himself against the charges.* | **strongly/vigorously defend sth** *The company strongly defends its policy.* **3** to do something to prevent something from failing, stopping, or being taken away: *We are defending the right to demostrate.* **4** [I,T] to protect your GOAL in a sport, to prevent your opponents from getting points [OPP] **attack** **5** [T] LAW to be a lawyer for someone who has been charged with a crime → PROSECUTE : *He had top lawyers to defend him.* **6 defend a title/championship** to try to win a competition that you won last time in order to keep your position as winner: *The boxer will defend his title in New York.* [**Origin:** 1200–1300 Old French *defendre*, from Latin *defendere*, from *fendere* **to hit**]

de·fend·ant /dɪˈfɛndənt/ *n.* [C] LAW the person in a court of law who has been ACCUSED of doing something illegal: *The defendant pleaded guilty.* → see also PLAINTIFF

de·fend·er /dɪˈfɛndɚ/ *n.* [C] **1** someone who defends a particular idea, belief, person etc. → see also PUBLIC DEFENDER **2** one of the players in a sports game who have to defend their team's GOAL from the opposing team

de·fense¹ /dɪˈfɛns/ [W1] *n.*
1 PROTECTING a) [U] the act of protecting something or someone from attack or destruction: +**of** *the defense of the nation* | *The officers claim they fired at Clark* ***in defense of*** *their own lives.* | *Several people saw the attack, but no one* ***came to her defense.*** | *Diet is the first* ***line of defense*** (=thing you do to protect yourself) *against heart disease.* → see also SELF-DEFENSE **b)** [C] something that can be used to protect someone or something against attack or destruction: +**against** *Fire extinguishers are a good defense against small fires.*
2 MILITARY a) [U] the systems, people, weapons etc. that a country uses to protect itself from attack: *the Department of Defense* | *There are plans to increase defense spending* (=money spent on weapons and armies) *by 6%.* **b) defenses** [plural] all the military forces and weapons that are available to defend a place: *The border defenses were weak.*
3 AGAINST CRITICISM [singular, U] something you say or write that supports someone or something that has been criticized, or the act of making this statement: +**of** *his spirited defense of police methods* | *Senator Stevens spoke* ***in defense of*** *the bill.* | **come/go/leap to sb's defense** (=defend someone who has been criticized) | ***In his defense*** (=used before making a statement to support someone), *he is very new to the job.*
4 IN A COURT a) [C,U] the things that are said in a court of law to prove that someone is not guilty of a crime: *Martin decided to speak* ***in his own defense*** (=in support of his own case). | +**for** *He had no defense for the murder charge.* **b) the defense** all the people who are concerned with showing in a court of law that someone is not guilty of a crime: *defense attorneys* | *The defense only has one witness.* → PROSECUTION
5 AGAINST ILLNESS [C] something that your body produces naturally as a way of preventing illness: +**against** *the body's main defense against infection*
6 BEHAVIOR [C] an activity or behavior that that prevents you from being upset or seeming weak: *For me, making people laugh is a kind of defense.* | +**against** *Arrogance is sometimes a defense against fear.*
7 ATTEMPT TO WIN AGAIN sb's defense of sth an attempt by someone to win a competition that they won last time so they keep their position as winner: *Brazil's defense of their World Cup title*

de·fense² /ˈdifɛns/ *n.* **1** [C] the players on a sports team whose main job is to try to prevent the other team from getting points: *the NFL's top-ranked defense* **2** [U] the activity or job of trying to prevent the opposing team in a sport from getting points: *Taylor* ***plays defense*** *for the New York Giants.* | *OK, you guys are* ***on defense.*** → see also OFFENSE

de·fense·less /dɪˈfɛnslɪs/ *adj.* weak and unable to protect yourself from being hurt or criticized: *Troops fired on defenseless civilians.*

deˈfense ˌmechanism *n.* [C] **1** a process in your brain that makes you forget things that are painful for you to think about **2** a reaction in your body that protects you from an illness or danger

de·fen·si·ble /dɪˈfɛnsəbəl/ *adj.* **1** a defensible opinion, idea, or action is one that seems reasonable, and you can easily support it [OPP] **indefensible**: *a legally defensible plan* **2** a defensible building or area is easy to protect against attack or damage —**defensibly** *adv.*

de·fen·sive¹ /dɪˈfɛnsɪv/ [W3] *adj.* **1** used or intended to protect people against attack [OPP] **offensive**: *defensive weapons* **2** behaving in a way that shows you think someone is criticizing you, even if they are not: *It has nothing to do with your work, so don't* ***get defensive.*** **3** relating to stopping the other team from getting points in a game [OPP] **offensive**: *a defensive player* —**defensively** *adv.* —**defensiveness** *n.* [U]

defensive² *n.* **on the defensive** trying to defend yourself because someone is criticizing you: *Her comments* ***put*** *me* ***on the defensive*** (=made me feel I had to defend myself). | **be/go on the defensive** *The mayor has been on the defensive because of the recent scandal.*

de·fer /dɪˈfɚ/ *v.* **deferred, deferring** [T] to delay something until a later date: *The loans are deferred until students finish their degrees.* [**Origin:** 1300–1400 French *différer*, from Latin *differre* **to delay, be different**]

defer to sb/sth *phr. v.* FORMAL to agree to accept someone's opinion or decision because you have respect for that person or because they have power over you: *I will defer to the experts in this matter.* [**Origin:** defer to 1400–1500 French *déférer*, from Late Latin *deferre* **to bring down**]

def·er·ence /ˈdɛfərəns/ *n.* [U] FORMAL polite behavior that shows that you respect someone and are willing to accept what they say or believe: *Visiting officials were treated with great deference.* | **in deference to sth/out of deference to sth** *In deference to local custom, we* *wore longer skirts.* —**deferential** /ˌdɛfəˈrɛnʃəl◂/ *adj.* —**deferentially** *adv.*

de·fer·ment /dɪˈfɚmənt/ *n.* [C,U] FORMAL an occasion when you delay doing something that you have been officially ordered to do, such as join the army or pay back a debt, or the act of officially allowing someone to delay doing something: *In 1946 defense workers were granted draft deferments.*

de·fi·ance /dɪˈfaɪəns/ *n.* [U] behavior that shows you refuse to do what someone tells you to do, especially because you do not respect them: *a look of hatred and defiance* | *Many Americans have visited Cuba* ***in defiance of*** *the law.* → see also DEFY

de·fi·ant /dɪˈfaɪənt/ *adj.* refusing to do what someone tells you to do, especially because you do not respect them: *Her reply was clear and defiant.* | *a defiant gesture* —**defiantly** *adv.*

de·fi·cien·cy /dɪˈfɪʃənsi/ *n. plural* **deficiencies** [C,U] **1** a lack of something that is necessary: *a vitamin deficiency* **2** a weakness or fault in something: *structural deficiencies in the houses*

de·fi·cient /dɪˈfɪʃənt/ *adj.* **1** not containing or having enough of something: **+in** *a diet deficient in calcium* **2** not good enough SYN **inadequate**: *Too many students leave school with deficient basic skills.*

def·i·cit /ˈdɛfəsɪt/ W2 *n.* [C] **1** ECONOMICS the difference between the amount of money that a government spends and the amount that it takes in from taxes and other activities: *The deficit has become so large that our children's children will still be paying it off.* | *a budget deficit of $20 million* → see also TRADE DEFICIT **2** the difference between the amount of something that you have and the higher amount that you need: *The team overcame an 18-point deficit to win 38–30.* [**Origin:** 1700–1800 French *déficit*, from Latin *deficit* **it lacks**, from *deficere*]

ˌdeficit ˈfinancing *n.* [U] ECONOMICS money that a government borrows to pay for the things that it does not pay for with taxes, or a process in which a government does this

ˌdeficit ˈspending *n.* [U] ECONOMICS when a government spends more than it receives in taxes

de·file /dɪˈfaɪl/ *v.* [T] FORMAL to make something less pure, good, or holy, especially by showing no respect: *Gravestones in the cemetery had been defiled.*

de·fine /dɪˈfaɪn/ Ac S2 W2 *v.* [T] **1** to describe something correctly and thoroughly, and to say what standards, limits, qualities etc. it has that make it different from other things: **define sth as sth** *70% of workers can be defined as low-paid.* | **well/clearly defined** *The powers of the President are clearly defined in the Constitution.* | *The contract lists several* ***narrowly defined*** *responsibilities* (=defined in a specific and strictly limiting way). | *my* ***vaguely defined*** (=not very clear or specific) *fears* **2** to explain the exact meaning of a particular word or idea: *Define precisely what you mean by "crime."* | **define sth as sth** *A lie is defined as saying something in order to deceive someone.* | **loosely/broadly defined** (=defined in a way that is not very specific) **3** to show the edge or shape of something clearly: **well/clearly/sharply defined** *The bird has sharply defined black and red markings.* [**Origin:** 1300–1400 Old French *definer*, from Latin *definire*, from *finire* **to limit, end**] —**definable** *adj.*

def·i·nite /ˈdɛfənɪt/ Ac S3 *adj.* **1** clearly known, seen, or stated, and very certain SYN **clear**: *a definite improvement* | *She rarely gives a definite answer.* | *Scientists were not able to reach a definite conclusion in the study.* **2** a definite arrangement, promise etc. will happen in the way that someone has said: *The city has finally given a definite date for the repairs.* | *I don't have any definite plans for the future.* **3** [not before noun] if you are definite about something, you have clearly and firmly decided it or said it, so that there is no question about it: **+about** *We're still not definite about our plans.* | **+that** *The teacher was most definite that Max needed to see a doctor.*

ˌdefinite ˈarticle *n.* [C] ENG. LANG. ARTS **1** the word "the" in English **2** a word in another language that is like "the" → see also ARTICLE (4), INDEFINITE ARTICLE

def·i·nite·ly /ˈdɛfənɪtli/ Ac S1 W3 *adv.* [sentence adverb] **1** certainly and without any doubt: *My watch is definitely broken.* | *Can we say definitely that global temperatures are rising?* | *I'm* ***definitely not*** *coming.* ►see THESAURUS box at **certainly** **2** SPOKEN used to emphasize that you are saying "yes": *"Are you sure you don't want to come?" "Definitely."* **3 definitely not** SPOKEN used to emphasize that you are saying "no": *"Are you going to marry him?" "Definitely not!"* → see **of course** at COURSE[1] (1), SURELY

def·i·ni·tion /ˌdɛfəˈnɪʃən/ Ac S2 W3 *n.* **1** [C] a phrase or sentence that says exactly what a word, phrase, or idea means: **+of** *What's the correct definition of the word "moot"?* | *It depends on your definition of success.* | **a broad/wide definition** (=a meaning of a word that is not too specific) | **a narrow definition** (=a meaning of a word that is exact or limited) **2 by definition** if something has a particular quality by definition, it must have that quality because all things of that type have it: *Writing is, by definition, a lonely job.* **3** [U] the clear edges, shapes, or sound that something has: *This photograph* ***lacks definition*** (=is not clear).

D

de·fin·i·tive /dɪˈfɪnət̬ɪv/ Ac *adj.* **1** [usually before noun] a definitive book, description etc. is considered to be the best and cannot be improved: *the definitive book on modern poetry* **2** a definitive statement, VERDICT etc. is one that will not be changed and cannot be doubted: *a definitive answer* —**definitively** *adv.*

de·flate /dɪˈfleɪt, di-/ *v.* **1** [I,T] if a tire, BALLOON, ball etc. deflates or if you deflate it, it gets smaller because the air or gas inside it comes out OPP **inflate** **2** [T] to make someone feel less important or confident: *Losing your job can really* ***deflate your ego.*** **3** [T] to show that a statement, argument etc. is wrong: *We needed a way to deflate the prosecution's arguments.* **4** [T] ECONOMICS to change the economic rules or conditions in a country so that prices become lower or stop rising OPP **inflate** —**deflation** /dɪˈfleɪʃən/ *n.* [U]

de·flat·ed /dɪˈfleɪt̬ɪd/ *adj.* **1** feeling less cheerful or confident than before: *Zack seemed deflated and shaken by his defeat.* **2** a deflated tire, BALLOON, ball etc. has gotten smaller because the air or gas inside it has come out

de·fla·tion /dɪˈfleɪʃən/ *n.* [U] ECONOMICS a reduction in the amount of money in a country's economy, so that prices fall or stop rising OPP **inflation**

de·fla·tion·ar·y /dɪˈfleɪʃəˌnɛri/ *adj.* ECONOMICS causing a situation in which prices fall or stop rising

de·flect /dɪˈflɛkt/ *v.* **1** [I,T] to turn in a different direction, especially after hitting something else, or to make something do this: *The bomber is designed to deflect radar waves.* | *Volek's shot* ***deflected off*** *the goal.* **2 deflect attention/criticism/anger etc.** to stop people from thinking about something, criticizing something, getting angry about something etc.: *Harris deflected questions about his affair.* **3** [T] to take someone's attention away from something: **deflect sb from sth** *Nothing deflects the lion from the chase.*

de·flec·tion /dɪˈflɛkʃən/ *n.* [C,U] **1** the action of changing direction after hitting something **2** TECHNICAL the degree to which the moving part on a measuring instrument moves away from zero

de·flow·er /diˈflaʊɚ/ *v.* [T] LITERARY to have sex with a woman who has never had sex before

De·foe /dɪˈfoʊ/, **Daniel** (1660–1731) a British writer of NOVELS

de·fog /diˈfɑg/ *v.* **defogged, defogging** [T] to remove the CONDENSATION from the windows inside a car, by using heat or warm air

de·fog·ger /diˈfɑgɚ/ *n.* [C] a piece of electrical equipment in a car, that defogs the windows

de·fo·li·ant /diˈfoʊliənt/ *n.* [C,U] a chemical substance used on plants to make their leaves drop off —**defoliate** *v.* [T]

de·for·es·ta·tion /di,fɔrə'steɪʃən/ *n.* [U] EARTH SCIENCE the cutting or burning down of all the trees in an area OPP afforestation —**deforest** /di'fɔrɪst/ *v.* [T usually passive] —**deforested** *adj.*: *deforested regions around the Amazon*

de·form /dɪ'fɔrm/ *v.* [I,T] to change the usual shape of something so that the thing's usefulness or appearance is spoiled, or to be changed in this way: *Tight shoes can deform a child's feet.* —**deformation** *n.* [C,U]

de·formed /dɪ'fɔrmd/ *adj.* someone or something that is deformed has the wrong shape, especially because they have grown or developed in the wrong way: *a deformed hand*

D

de·form·i·ty /dɪ'fɔrməṭi/ *n. plural* **deformities** [C,U] part of someone's body that is not the normal shape, or the condition of having such a body part

de·fraud /dɪ'frɔd/ *v.* [T] to trick a person or organization in order to get money from them: *a conspiracy to defraud the government* | **defraud sb/sth (out) of sth** *He used his TV show to defraud his followers of $4.8 million.*

de·fray /dɪ'freɪ/ *v.* **defrays, defrayed, defraying** [T] **defray costs/expenses etc.** FORMAL to pay someone's costs, expenses etc.: *The donations **defray the cost of** school trips.*

de·frock /,di'frɑk/ *v.* [T] to officially remove a priest, minister etc. from their job because they did something wrong —**defrocked** *adj.*

de·frost /dɪ'frɔst/ *v.* **1** [I,T] if frozen food defrosts, or if you defrost it, it gets warmer until it is not frozen anymore **2** [I,T] if a FREEZER or REFRIGERATOR defrosts, or if you defrost it, it is turned off so that the ice inside it melts **3** [T] to remove ice from the windows of a car by blowing warm air onto them → see also DEFOG

deft /dɛft/ *adj.* **1** skillful at doing something, or showing skill: *his deft songwriting* **2** a deft movement is skillful, and often quick —**deftly** *adv.* —**deftness** *n.* [U]

de·funct /dɪ'fʌŋkt/ *adj.* not existing or operating anymore: *the **now-defunct** Women's Basketball League* [**Origin:** 1500–1600 Latin *defunctus*, past participle of *defungi* **to finish, die**]

de·fuse /di'fyuz/ *v.* [T] **1** to improve a difficult or dangerous situation, for example by making people less angry: *A joke can often **defuse tension**.* | **defuse a situation/crisis** *Diplomats are trying to defuse the situation.* **2** to prevent a bomb from exploding

de·fy /dɪ'faɪ/ *v.* **defies, defied, defying** [T] **1** to refuse to obey someone or something, or to refuse to do what is expected: *teenagers who **openly defy*** (=not caring if anyone notices) *the law* | *The couple **defied tradition*** (=refused to do what was traditional) *and never married.* ▶see THESAURUS box at **disobey** **2 defy reason/logic/the odds etc.** to not happen according to the principles you would expect: *A 16-week premature baby has defied the odds and survived.* **3 defy description/understanding/categorization etc.** to be almost impossible to describe, understand, categorize etc.: *The beauty of the scene defies description.* **4 I defy sb (to do sth)** SPOKEN, FORMAL used when asking someone to do something that you think they cannot or will not do: *I defy anybody to prove otherwise.* [**Origin:** 1300–1400 Old French *defier*, from Latin *fidere* **to trust**]

deg. the written abbreviation of DEGREE

De·gas /dɪ'gɑ/, **Ed·gar** /'ɛdgɚ/ (1834–1917) a French Impressionist painter, known especially for his pictures of horse racing, theaters, CAFÉS, and women dancing

de Gaulle /dɪ'gɔl, -'goʊl/, **General Charles** (1890–1970) the President of France between 1959 and 1969

de·gen·er·ate[1] /dɪ'dʒɛnə,reɪt/ *v.* [I] to become worse:

deforestation

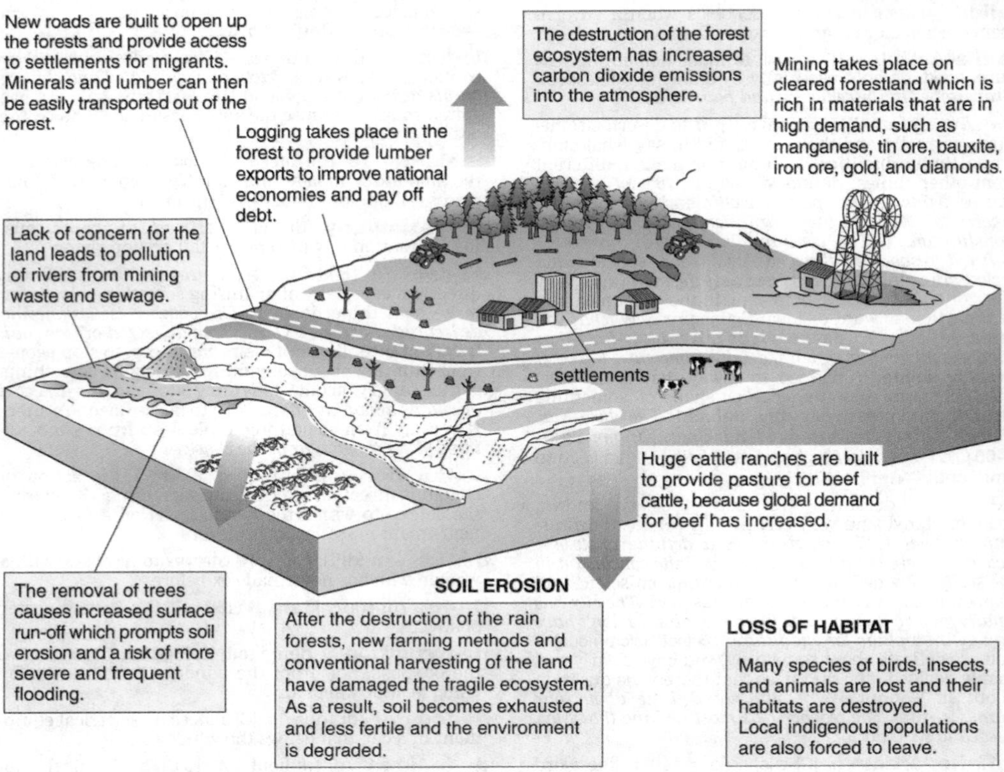

New roads are built to open up the forests and provide access to settlements for migrants. Minerals and lumber can then be easily transported out of the forest.
The destruction of the forest ecosystem has increased carbon dioxide emissions into the atmosphere.
Mining takes place on cleared forestland which is rich in materials that are in high demand, such as manganese, tin ore, bauxite, iron ore, gold, and diamonds.
Logging takes place in the forest to provide lumber exports to improve national economies and pay off debt.
Lack of concern for the land leads to pollution of rivers from mining waste and sewage.
settlements
Huge cattle ranches are built to provide pasture for beef cattle, because global demand for beef has increased.
The removal of trees causes increased surface run-off which prompts soil erosion and a risk of more severe and frequent flooding.
SOIL EROSION
After the destruction of the rain forests, new farming methods and conventional harvesting of the land have damaged the fragile ecosystem. As a result, soil becomes exhausted and less fertile and the environment is degraded.
LOSS OF HABITAT
Many species of birds, insects, and animals are lost and their habitats are destroyed. Local indigenous populations are also forced to leave.

+**into** *These historic buildings are degenerating into slums.* —**degeneration** /dɪˌdʒɛnəˈreɪʃən/ *n.* [U]

de·gen·er·ate² /dɪˈdʒɛnərɪt/ *adj.* **1** having very low standards or moral behavior: *a morally degenerate society* **2** FORMAL worse than before in quality: *a degenerate form of art* —**degeneracy** *n.* [U]

degenerate³ *n.* [C] someone whose behavior is considered to be morally unacceptable

de·gen·er·a·tive /dɪˈdʒɛnərət̮ɪv/ *adj.* MEDICINE a degenerative illness gradually gets worse and cannot be stopped

deg·ra·da·tion /ˌdɛgrəˈdeɪʃən/ *n.* **1** [C,U] an experience, situation, or condition that makes you feel ashamed and angry: *a life of poverty and degradation* **2** [U] the process by which something changes to a worse condition **3** [U] SCIENCE the process by which a substance, chemical etc. changes to a simpler form

de·grade /dɪˈgreɪd, di-/ *v.* **1** [T] to treat someone without respect and make them lose respect for themselves: *The director is accused of degrading women in his movies.* **2** [T] to make a situation or the condition of something worse: *Erosion is degrading the land.* **3** [I,T] SCIENCE if a substance, chemical etc. degrades, or if something degrades it, it changes to a simpler form: *Black plastic starts to degrade upon exposure to sunlight.* → see also BIODEGRADABLE —**degradable** *adj.* —**degradability** /dɪˌgreɪdəˈbɪlət̮i/ *n.* [U]

de·grad·ing /dɪˈgreɪdɪŋ/ *adj.* showing no respect for someone or making them feel very ashamed: *degrading racial comments* | +**to** *Pornography is degrading to women.*

de·gree /dɪˈgri/ [S1] [W1] *n.*
1 TEMPERATURE [C] a unit for measuring temperature or the size of an angle, often represented by the sign (°): *27 degrees Fahrenheit*
2 LEVEL/AMOUNT [C,U] the level or amount of something: +**of** *a small degree of risk* | ***the degree to which*** *exercise influences health* | *He succeeded* ***to a large degree*** (=he was mostly successful). | **to some degree/to a (certain) degree** (=partly or a little) | ***To what degree*** *is this statement true?* (=how much of the statement is true?)
3 ANGLES [C] MATH a unit for measuring the size of an angle, often represented by the sign (°): *an angle of 45 degrees*
4 EDUCATION [C] an official statement that someone has successfully completed a course of study at a college or university: *a law degree* | +**in** *a degree in history* | *Lori* ***has a*** *bachelor's* ***degree*** *from Harvard.* ►see THESAURUS box at **qualification**
5 by degrees very slowly [SYN] **gradually**: *Improvement will come by degrees.*
6 MATH a) the sum of the EXPONENTS of the VARIABLES in a MONOMIAL. For example, the degree of the monomial $3x^2y^2$ is 4. **b)** the sum of the EXPONENTS of the VARIABLES of the TERM with the highest exponents in a POLYNOMIAL expression. For example, the degree of the polynomial $3x^3y^2 + 2x^2 + 6$ is 5.
[**Origin:** 1200–1300 Old French *degré*, from Latin *gradus* **step, grade**] → see FIRST-DEGREE, **to the nth degree** at NTH (1), SECOND-DEGREE, THIRD-DEGREE BURN

ˌdegree of a ˈterm *n.* [singular] MATH the amount you get when you add together the EXPONENTS in one of the TERMS (=parts) of a mathematical or scientific EQUATION

de·hu·man·ize /diˈhyuməˌnaɪz/ *v.* [T often passive] to treat people in a way that makes them not seem to have human qualities: *Is society dehumanized by technology?* —**dehumanizing** *adj.* —**dehumanization** /diˌhyumənəˈzeɪʃən/ *n.* [U]

de·hu·mid·i·fi·er /ˌdihyuˈmɪdəˌfaɪɚ/ *n.* [C] a machine that removes water from the air in a building —**dehumidify** *v.* [T]

de·hy·drate /diˈhaɪdreɪt/ *v.* **1** [I,T] to lose too much water from your body: *The heat will make you dehydrate very quickly.* **2** [T] to remove all the water from something such as food or chemicals —**dehydrated** *adj.* —**dehydration** /ˌdihaɪˈdreɪʃən/ *n.* [U]

de·hy·dro·gen·a·tion /diˌhaɪdrədʒəˈneɪʃən/ *n.* [U] CHEMISTRY the process of removing HYDROGEN from a chemical compound

de-ice /ˌdiˈaɪs/ *v.* [T] to remove the ice from something, especially an airplane

de·i·fy /ˈdeɪəˌfaɪ, ˈdiə-/ *v.* **deifies, deified, deifying** [T] FORMAL to treat someone or something with a lot of admiration, as if they were a god —**deification** /ˌdeɪəfəˈkeɪʃən/ *n.* [U]

deign /deɪn/ *v.* [T] **deign to do sth** HUMOROUS to agree to do something that you think you are too important to do: *Shelly finally deigned to join us for lunch.* [**Origin:** 1200–1300 Old French *deignier*, from Latin *dignus* **deserving admiration**]

D

de·ism /ˈdiɪzəm, ˈdeɪ-/ *n.* [U] the belief in a God who made the world but has no influence on human lives → see also THEISM

de·i·ty /ˈdiət̮i, ˈdeɪ-/ *n. plural* **deities** [C] **1** a god or GODDESS ►see THESAURUS box at **god** **2 the Deity** FORMAL God

dé·jà vu /ˌdeɪʒɑ ˈvu/ *n.* [U] the feeling that what is happening now has happened before in exactly the same way: *I watched them argue with a sense of déjà vu.*

de·ject·ed /dɪˈdʒɛktɪd/ *adj.* unhappy, disappointed, or sad: *He came home looking completely dejected.* [**Origin:** 1400–1500 Latin *dejectus*, from *jacere* **to throw**] —**dejectedly** *adv.* —**dejection** /dɪˈdʒɛkʃən/ *n.* [U]

de ju·re /ˌdi ˈdʒʊreɪ/ *adj.* FORMAL LAW true or right because of a law → see also DE FACTO

de Klerk /də ˈklɚk, -ˈklɛrk/, **F.W.** (1936–) the President of South Africa from 1989 to 1994 who ended the system of APARTHEID

de Koo·ning /də ˈkunɪŋ, -ˈkoʊn-/, **Wil·lem** /ˈwɪləm/ (1904–1997) a Dutch-American PAINTER famous for his ABSTRACT paintings

Del·a·ware /ˈdɛləˌwɛr/ **1** a small state in the northeastern U.S. **2** a Native American tribe from the northeastern area of the U.S.

ˌDelaware ˈRiver a river in the northeastern U.S. that flows southward from the state of New York to the state of Delaware

de·lay¹ /dɪˈleɪ/ [W3] *v.* **delays, delayed, delaying** **1** [I,T] to wait until a later time to do something: *We cannot delay any longer.* | *The manager wanted to* ***delay*** *the bad news* ***until*** *after Christmas.* | **delay doing sth** *He delayed signing the contract for months.*

> **THESAURUS**
> **postpone** to change an event to a later time or date: *The meeting was postponed.*
> **put off** to delay something, or delay doing something, especially something that you do not want to do: *He put off washing the dishes until the morning.*
> **procrastinate** to delay doing something that you ought to do: *A lot of people procrastinate when it comes to doing paperwork.*

2 [T often passive] to make someone or something late: *Our flight was slightly delayed by bad weather.* —**delayed** *adj.*

delay² *n. plural* **delays** **1** [C] a situation in which someone or something is made to wait, or the length of the waiting time: *We asked the court for a delay to continue preparing our defense.* | +**of** *Flight delays of two hours or more are common.* | **a delay in doing sth** *There was some delay in asking for help.* | *There are* ***severe delays*** *on Highway 101 this morning.* | **long/short delay** *The storm has caused long delays at some airports.* | *The reports will* ***be subject to delay*** (=be likely to be delayed). **2** [U] failure to do something quickly: *We had to get him to the hospital* ***without delay*** (=immediately). **3** [C] the time between an event and its result or between one event and the next: +**between** *the delay between braking and coming to a stop* [**Origin:** 1200–1300 Old French *delaier*, from *laier* **to leave**]

de,layed-'action *adj.* [only before noun] designed to work or start only after a particular period of time has passed: *a delayed-action bomb*

de,layed 'broadcast *n.* [C,U] a concert, sports event etc. that is broadcast on television or radio at a time after it originally happens → see also LIVE BROADCAST

de'laying ,tactic *n.* [C usually plural] something that you do deliberately to delay something, in order to gain an advantage for yourself

de·lec·ta·ble /dɪˈlɛktəbəl/ *adj.* FORMAL extremely good to taste or smell: *a delectable chocolate soufflé* —**delectably** *adv.*

D

de·lec·ta·tion /ˌdilɛkˈteɪʃən/ *n.* [U] FORMAL enjoyment, pleasure, or amusement

del·e·gate¹ /ˈdɛləgɪt/ W3 *n.* [C] **1** someone who has been elected or chosen to speak, vote, or make decisions for a group: **+from** *Delegates from 50 colleges attended the conference.* | **+to** *the U.S. delegate to the committee* **2** a member of a House of Delegates in the governments of the U.S. states of Maryland, Virginia, or West Virginia **3** someone who represents a U.S. TERRITORY in the House of Representatives, who is allowed to speak but not to vote [**Origin:** 1400–1500 Medieval Latin *delegatus*, from Latin *legare* **to send as a representative**]

del·e·gate² /ˈdɛləˌgeɪt/ *v.* **1** [I,T] to give part of your work or the things you are responsible for to someone in a lower position than you: *A good manager knows when to delegate.* | **delegate sth to sb** *McConnell delegated authority to the Vice Presidents.* **2** [T] to choose someone to do a particular job, or to be a representative of a group, organization etc.: **delegate sb to do sth** *We were delegated to represent our club at the conference.*

,delegated 'powers *n.* [plural] POLITICS powers given to the U.S. government under the CONSTITUTION. These include the EXPRESSED POWERS, the IMPLIED POWERS, and the INHERENT POWERS.

del·e·ga·tion /ˌdɛləˈgeɪʃən/ *n.* **1** [C] a group of people who represent a company, organization etc.: *a trade delegation from South America* | **+to** *the French delegation to the United Nations* **2** [U] the process of giving power or work to someone else, so that they are responsible for part of what you normally do: **+of** *the delegation of authority*

de·lete /dɪˈlit/ *v.* [T] to remove a letter, word etc. from a piece of writing, or information from a computer's records: *You could delete the second sentence.* | **delete sth from sth** *Matt's name was deleted from the list.* | *He had not deleted the files from his hard drive.* [**Origin:** 1400–1500 Latin *deletus*, past participle of *delere* **to destroy**]

del·e·te·ri·ous /ˌdɛləˈtɪriəs/ *adj.* FORMAL damaging or harmful: *the **deleterious effects** of smoking*

de·le·tion /dɪˈliʃən/ *n.* **1** [U] COMPUTERS the act or process of removing something from a piece of writing or a computer's memory: **+of** *the deletion of unwanted files* **2** [C] a letter, word, sentence etc. that has been removed from a piece of writing

del·i /ˈdɛli/ *n.* [C] a small store, or part of a store that sells cheese, cooked meat, SALADS, breads etc.

de·lib·er·ate¹ /dɪˈlɪbrɪt, -bərɪt/ *adj.* **1** intended or planned SYN **intentional** OPP **accidental**: **a deliberate attempt/effort** *a deliberate attempt to mislead the court* | *a **deliberate act of** cruelty* **2** deliberate speech, thought, or movement is slow and careful: *his deliberate style of speaking* [**Origin:** 1400–1500 Latin *deliberatus*, past participle of *deliberare* **to weigh in the mind**, from *libra* **balance**] —**deliberateness** *n.* [U]

de·lib·e·rate² /dɪˈlɪbəˌreɪt/ *v.* [I,T] to think about or disucss something carefully for a long time, in order to reach a decision: *The jury has been deliberating for three days.* | **+about/on/over** *Six committees deliberate on the budget each year.* | **+what/whether** *I was deliberating whether I should tell her.*

de·lib·er·ate·ly /dɪˈlɪbrɪtli/ *adv.* **1** done in a way that is intended or planned SYN **intentionally** OPP **accidentally**: *Someone had deliberately set fire to the house.*

THESAURUS

on purpose ESPECIALLY SPOKEN deliberately, especially in order to annoy someone or get an advantage for yourself: *I didn't do it on purpose; it was an accident.*

intentionally deliberately, especially in order to have a particular result or effect: *Very few teenagers become pregnant intentionally.*

2 done or said in a slow careful way: *Tom paused deliberately before continuing.*

de·lib·er·a·tion /dɪˌlɪbəˈreɪʃən/ *n.* **1** [U] careful consideration of something: ***After much deliberation,** Diana decided to resign.* **2 deliberations** [plural] discussions of a subject in order to make a decision: *The council concluded its deliberations on Monday.* **3** [U] if you speak or move with deliberation, you speak or move slowly and carefully

de·lib·er·a·tive /dɪˈlɪbəˌreɪt̬ɪv, -brət̬ɪv/ *adj.* existing for the purpose of discussing or planning something: *a deliberative process*

del·i·ca·cy /ˈdɛlɪkəsi/ *n.* **1** [U] a careful and sensitive way of speaking or behaving so that you do not upset anyone SYN **tact**: *The issue is being handled with extreme delicacy.* **2** [U] the quality of being easy to harm, damage, or break SYN **fragility**: *the extreme delicacy of the Roman glass* **3** [U] the quality of being skillfully made with attention to even the smallest details: *the grace and delicacy of his paintings* **4** [U] the quality that a taste, color, or smell has of being pleasant and not too strong: *the delicacy of the aroma* **5** [C] *plural* **delicacies** something good to eat that is expensive or rare: *This fish is considered a delicacy in Italy.* **6** [U] OLD-FASHIONED the quality someone has of being physically weak and likely to be ill SYN **fragility**

del·i·cate /ˈdɛlɪkɪt/ *adj.* **1** easily damaged or broken SYN **fragile**: *The delicate blossoms look like lace.* | *a child's delicate skin* ►see THESAURUS box at **weak¹** **2** needing to be dealt with carefully or sensitively in order to avoid problems or failure: *The delicate operation took more than six hours.* | *delicate peace talks* | *a delicate ecosystem* ►see THESAURUS box at **difficult** **3** gentle and using a lot of care and skill: *He plays the piano with a delicate touch.* **4** a part of the body that is delicate is small, attractive, and graceful: *her delicate hand* **5** made skillfully and with attention to the smallest details: *The china has a delicate pattern of leaves.* **6** a taste, smell, or color that is delicate is pleasant and not too strong OPP **strong**: *delicate pinks and blues* **7** OLD-FASHIONED someone who is delicate is hurt easily or becomes sick easily: *a delicate child* [**Origin:** 1300–1400 Latin *delicatus*] —**delicately** *adv.* → see also INDELICATE

del·i·cates /ˈdɛlɪkɪts/ *n.* [plural] clothes that have to be washed very carefully in cool water because they are made from delicate material

del·i·ca·tes·sen /ˌdɛlɪkəˈtɛsən/ *n.* [C] a DELI [**Origin:** 1800–1900 German, French *délicatesse* **delicacy**, from Latin *delicatus*]

de·li·cious /dɪˈlɪʃəs/ S2 *adj.* **1** having a very enjoyable taste or smell: *The chocolate pie was delicious!* | **smell/look/taste delicious** *The fresh bread smelled delicious.* ►see THESAURUS box at **taste¹** **2** LITERARY extremely pleasant or enjoyable: *He waited in delicious anticipation.* [**Origin:** 1200–1300 Old French, Latin *delicere* **to attract**] —**deliciously** *adv.*

de·light¹ /dɪˈlaɪt/ *n.* **1** [U] a feeling of great pleasure and satisfaction: **with/in delight** *The kids rushed down to the beach, shrieking **with delight**.* | ***To my delight,** my first assignment was in Hawaii.* | *There was a look of **sheer delight** (=very great delight) on her face.* **2** [C] something that makes you feel very happy or satisfied: *culinary delights* | **the delights of sth** *the simple delights of hot sun and good wine* | **it is a delight to do sth** *It was a delight to be back among our old friends.*

3 take delight in (doing) sth to enjoy something very much, often something that annoys someone else: *He took great delight in teasing his younger brother.*

delight² *v.* [T] to give someone a feeling of satisfaction and enjoyment: *This movie classic will delight the whole family.* | **delight sb with sth** *He delighted the crowd with his spectacular talent.* [**Origin:** 1200–1300 Old French *delit*, from Latin *delectare* **to please greatly**]

delight in sth *phr. v.* to enjoy something very much, especially something that makes other people upset or embarrassed: **delight in doing sth** *The twins delighted in confusing other people.*

de·light·ed /dɪˈlaɪt̬ɪd/ *adj.* **1** very pleased or happy: *McCartney sang in front of 50,000 delighted fans.* | **be delighted to do sth** *I'm delighted to have finally met you.* | +**(that)** *We're delighted that you'll be there.* | +**with** *She seemed delighted with her present.* | +**by/at** *They were delighted by the news.* | +**for** *We're all delighted for you!* ▶see THESAURUS box at **happy** **2 I/we would be delighted (to do sth)** used to politely accept an invitation: *Thank you! We'd be delighted to come.* —**delightedly** *adv.*

de·light·ful /dɪˈlaɪtˀfəl/ *adj.* very nice and pleasant: *a delightful young man* | *a delightful wine* —**delightfully** *adv.*

ˈdeli meat *n.* [C,U] cooked meat that is cut in the store and sold in SLICES

de·lim·it /dɪˈlɪmɪt/ *v.* [T] FORMAL to decide or say exactly what the limits of something are —**delimitation** /dɪˌlɪməˈteɪʃən/ *n.* [U]

de·lin·e·ate /dɪˈlɪniˌeɪt/ *v.* [T] FORMAL **1** to describe something carefully so that it is easy to understand: *The document delineates customers' rights.* **2** to show where the edges of an object or an area of land are —**delineation** /dɪˌlɪniˈeɪʃən/ *n.* [U]

de·lin·quen·cy /dɪˈlɪŋkwənsi/ *n. plural* **delinquencies** **1** [U] illegal or socially unacceptable behavior, especially by young people: *problems with vandalism and* ***juvenile delinquency*** (=criminal behavior in young people) **2** [C] FORMAL a debt that has not been paid on time

de·lin·quent¹ /dɪˈlɪŋkwənt/ *adj.* **1** a delinquent debt, account, LOAN etc. has not been paid when it should have been paid: *the collection of delinquent taxes* **2** behaving in a way that is illegal or that society does not approve of: *delinquent teenagers* [**Origin:** 1400–1500 Latin *delinquere* **to fail, offend**, from *linquere* **to leave**]

delinquent² *n.* [C] LAW someone, especially a young person, who has broken the law → see also JUVENILE DELINQUENT

del·i·ques·cent /ˌdɛlɪˈkwɛsənt/ *adj.* CHEMISTRY a substance that is deliquescent is able to take in water from the surrounding air and become a liquid solution —**deliquescence** *n.* [U]

de·lir·i·ous /dɪˈlɪriəs/ *adj.* **1** MEDICINE confused, anxious, excited, and seeing things that are not there, especially because you have a high fever: *One malaria patient became delirious.* **2** extremely excited or happy: +**with** *The freed prisoner was delirious with joy.* —**deliriously** *adv.*

de·lir·i·um /dɪˈlɪriəm/ *n.* [singular, U] **1** MEDICINE a state in which someone is delirious **2** extreme excitement

delirium trem·ens /dɪˌlɪriəm ˈtrɛmənz/ also **D'T's** *n.* [U] MEDICINE a medical condition, caused when someone who usually drinks too much alcohol stops drinking, in which their body shakes and they see things that are not there

de·liv·er /dɪˈlɪvɚ/ S2 W2 *v.*

1 TAKE STH SOMEWHERE [I,T] to take a letter, package, message, goods etc. to a particular place or person: *Ask if the pizza place delivers.* | *That's the woman who delivers our mail.* | **deliver sth to sb/sth** *We will deliver straight to your front door.* | *I* ***had*** *the package* ***delivered to*** (=arranged for someone to deliver it to) *her apartment.*

2 GIVE A SPEECH/PERFORMANCE [T] to give a speech or performance to a lot of people: **deliver a speech/lecture/address/sermon** *Rev. Whitman delivered a powerful sermon.* | *Kidman* ***delivers*** *another outstanding* ***performance*** *in the film.*

3 DO STH YOU ARE SUPPOSED TO DO [I,T] to do or provide the things that you are expected to or that you have promised to: *The state is no longer delivering the services citizens expect.* | *The coach promised a win, but the team couldn't* ***deliver the goods.*** | *Voters are angry that politicians haven't* ***delivered on their promises.***

4 GIVE BIRTH [T] to give birth to a baby: *She delivered a healthy baby girl in April.*

5 HELP SB GIVE BIRTH [T] to help someone give birth to a baby: *Midwives used to deliver all the babies in the area.*

6 JUDGMENT/RULING ETC. [T] to officially state a formal decision, judgment etc., especially in a court of law: **deliver a verdict/judgment/ruling etc.** *The courtroom was silent as the jury delivered their verdict.*

7 VOTES [T] POLITICS to get the votes or support of a particular group of people in an election: *Ford hopes to deliver the black vote in his hometown of Memphis.*

8 BLOW/SHOCK ETC. [T] to give something unpleasant such as a hit, shock, or warning to someone or something: *The fence delivers a mild shock if the animal tries to escape.* | *It's unclear who* ***delivered*** *the first* ***blow*** (=hit sb with a fist).

9 PERSON [T] LITERARY to take someone to a person or place where they will be guarded or taken care of: **deliver sb to sb/sth** *She was safely delivered to her home.*

10 MAKE SB FREE OF **deliver sb from sth** LITERARY or BIBLICAL to help someone escape from a bad situation: *Deliver us from evil.*

[**Origin:** 1200–1300 Old French *delivrer*, from Latin *liberare* **to set free**] —**deliverer** *n.* [C]

deliver sth ↔ **up** *phr. v.* FORMAL to give something to someone: *A bankrupt company must deliver up all its books, papers, and records.*

de·liv·er·ance /dɪˈlɪvərəns/ *n.* [U + from] FORMAL the state of being saved from harm or danger

de·liv·er·y /dɪˈlɪvəri/ S3 W3 *n. plural* **deliveries** **1** [C,U] the act or process of bringing goods, letters etc. to a particular place or person: *Pizza Mondo offers free delivery.* | *mail deliveries* | *a delivery truck* | *We* ***make deliveries*** *in your area in the afternoons.* | *The school* ***took delivery of*** (=received) *two new buses this week.* **2** [C] something that is delivered: *Ask your neighbor to* ***take*** *any* ***deliveries*** *while you are on vacation.* **3** [C] BIOLOGY the process of a baby being born: *She had a quick, easy delivery.* | *We went into the* ***delivery room*** (=hospital room where a baby is born) *at 7:42.* → LABOUR **4** [singular] the way in which someone speaks or performs in public: +**of** *the actor's smooth delivery of his lines* **5** [U] the process of delivering a service: +**of** *the delivery of telecommunications services*

de·liv·er·y·man /dɪˈlɪvərimən, -ˌmæn/ *n.* [C] a man who delivers goods to people

deˈlivery ˌperson *n.* [C] someone who delivers goods to people

dell /dɛl/ *n.* [C] LITERARY a small valley with grass and trees

de·louse /diˈlaʊs/ *v.* [T] to remove lice (LOUSE) from someone's hair, clothes etc.

del·phin·i·um /dɛlˈfɪniəm/ *n.* [C] a tall garden plant with many blue flowers along its stem

del·ta /ˈdɛltə/ *n.* [C] **1** EARTH SCIENCE an area of low land where a river spreads into many smaller rivers near the ocean: *the Mississippi delta* **2** the fourth letter of the Greek alphabet

de·lude /dɪˈlud/ *v.* [T] **1 delude yourself** to choose to believe something that is not true: **delude yourself into doing sth** *We deluded ourselves into thinking we could win.* **2** LITERARY to make someone believe something that is not true SYN **deceive**: *You attempted to delude me!* [**Origin:** 1400–1500 Latin *deludere*, from *ludere* **to play**] —**deluded** *adj.* —**delusive** /dɪˈlusɪv/ *adj.*

del·uge¹ /ˈdɛlyudʒ/ *n.* [C usually singular] **1** a large number of things such as letters or questions that someone has to deal with at the same time: +**of** *the deluge of bills that arrive every month* **2** a heavy rain storm SYN **downpour** **3** LITERARY a flood [**Origin:** 1400–1500 Old French, Latin *diluvium* **flood**]

deluge[2] *v.* [T] **1** to send a lot of letters, questions etc. to someone at the same time SYN **flood**: **deluge sb with sth** *The radio station has been deluged with complaints.* **2** FORMAL to cover something with a lot of water SYN **flood**

de·lu·sion /dɪˈluʒən/ *n.* **1** [C,U] a false belief about something: *He was still* ***under the delusion that*** *we were being cheated.* | ***I have no delusions about*** *my abilities as a writer* (=I realize that I am not a very good writer). **2** something untrue that a person believes is true because they are suffering from a mental illness: *He suffers from delusions.* **3 delusions of grandeur** the belief that you are much more powerful than you really are —**delusional** *adj.*

D

de·luxe /dɪˈlʌks/ *adj.* [usually before noun] of better quality and more expensive than other similar things: *a deluxe hotel room*

delve /dɛlv/ *v.* [I always +adv./prep.] **1** to try to find more information about someone or something: +**into** *Her book delves into the history of traditional Chinese food.* | *I was determined to* ***delve deeper*** *into the matter.* **2** to search for something by putting your hand deeply into a bag, container etc.: +**into** *Laurie delved into her briefcase and pulled out a letter.*

Dem. the written abbreviation of DEMOCRAT or DEMOCRATIC

de·mag·net·ize /diˈmægnəˌtaɪz/ *v.* [T] PHYSICS to take away the MAGNETIC qualities of something —**demagnetization** /diˌmægnətəˈzeɪʃən/ *n.* [U]

dem·a·gogue /ˈdɛməˌgɑg/ *n.* [C] DISAPPROVING POLITICS a political leader who tries to make people feel strong emotions in order to influence their opinions [**Origin:** 1600–1700 Greek *demagogos*, from *demos* **people** + *agogos* **leading**] —**demagogy, demagoguery** *n.* [U] —**demagogic** /ˌdɛməˈgɑdʒɪk/ *adj.*

de·mand[1] /dɪˈmænd/ W1 *n.*

1 NEED FOR STH [U] ECONOMICS the need or desire that people have for particular goods or services, and their willingness to pay for it: +**for** *a growing demand for more economical cars* | *300,000 new houses were needed to* ***meet demand*** (=provide the amount that people want). | *Factories increase production as* ***demand rises*** (=as the amount that people want increases), | *The candle-making class has been* ***in great demand*** (=wanted by a lot of people). → see also SUPPLY AND DEMAND

2 FIRM REQUEST [C] a strong request for something that shows you believe you have the right to get what you ask for: *We do not give in to terrorists' demands.* | +**for** *a demand for the director's resignation* | **demand that** *We received a demand from the bank that we repay the loan.* | *Managers thought that the union was* ***making*** *unreasonable* ***demands***. → see Word Choice box at CLAIM[1]

3 demands [C usually plural] difficult, annoying, or tiring things that need to be done or dealt with SYN **requirements**: +**of** *parents dealing with the conflicting demands of home and job* | +**on** *There are many demands on a doctor's time.* | **put/place/make demands on sb/sth** *The aging population is putting* ***heavy demands*** *on the healthcare system.*

4 by popular demand because a lot of people have asked for something to be done, performed etc.: *The show was brought back by popular demand.*

5 on demand done or given whenever someone asks: *Medical care should be available on demand.*

demand[2] W2 *v.* [T] **1** to ask strongly for something, especially because you feel you have a right to do this: *The President demanded the release of the hostages.* | **demand (that)** *Rainey demanded that his lawyer be called.* | *I* ***demand to know*** *what's going on here!* ►see THESAURUS box at **ask, tell** **2** to ask a question or order something to be done very firmly: *"Did you do this?" Kathryn demanded angrily.* **3 demand sth of sb** to expect someone who you have authority over to do something, especially something difficult SYN **expect**: *Some parents demand too much of their children* (=they ask them to do things they cannot yet do). **4** if something demands your time, skill, attention etc. it makes you use a lot of your time, skill etc. SYN **require**: *The job demands most of Cindy's time.* [**Origin:** 1300–1400 Old French *demander*, from Latin *mandare* **to order**]

deˈmand curve also **ˌmarket deˈmand curve** *n.* [C] ECONOMICS a GRAPH (=drawing with lines showing how sets of measurements are related to each other) showing the different quantities of a product that people buy depending on the price they are charged → see also DEMAND SCHEDULE, SUPPLY CURVE

deˈmand deˌposit *n.* [C] ECONOMICS the money you have in your CHECKING ACCOUNT, which you can take out at any time

de·mand·ing /dɪˈmændɪŋ/ *adj.* **1** making you use a lot of your time, skill, attention etc.: *a very demanding job* | **physically/emotionally/intellectually etc. demanding** *Her novels are intellectually demanding.* **2** a demanding person expects a lot of attention or to have things exactly the way they want them, especially in a way that is not fair: *a demanding boss*

deˌmand-ˈpull ˌtheory *n.* [U] ECONOMICS an idea that says that INFLATION increases when the supply of goods is limited, which then makes the price of the goods rise

deˈmand ˌschedule also **ˌmarket deˈmand ˌschedule** *n.* [C] ECONOMICS a list showing the quantities of a product bought, with different amounts depending on the price charged for the product → see also DEMAND CURVE, SUPPLY SCHEDULE

deˌmand-side ecoˈnomics *n.* [U] ECONOMICS a way for a government to manage a country's ECONOMY that involves changing taxes and interest rates to influence the demand for goods and reduce the number of people who do not have a job → see also SUPPLY-SIDE ECONOMICS

de·mar·cate /diˈmɑrkeɪt, ˈdimɑrˌkeɪt/ *v.* [T] FORMAL to decide or mark the limits of an area, system etc.

de·mar·ca·tion /ˌdimɑrˈkeɪʃən/ *n.* [U] **1** the process of deciding on or marking the border between two areas of land **2** the point at which one area of work, responsibility, activity etc. ends and another begins: +**between** *There should be a clear demarcation between work and play.* [**Origin:** 1700–1800 Spanish *demarcación*, from *marcar* **to mark**]

de·mean /dɪˈmin/ *v.* [T] to behave in a way that shows disrespect for someone or something: *Students demean the graduation ceremony with this inappropriate behavior.* | *I felt I was* ***demeaning myself*** *by asking for money.*

de·mean·ing /dɪˈminɪŋ/ *adj.* showing less respect for someone than they deserve or making them feel embarrassed or ashamed: +**to** *Are beauty pageants demeaning to women?*

de·mean·or /dɪˈminɚ/ *n.* [singular, U] FORMAL the way someone behaves, dresses, speaks etc. that shows what their character is like: *a kind and gentle demeanor* [**Origin:** 1400–1500 *demean* **to behave** (14–21 centuries), from Old French *demener* **to guide**]

de·ment·ed /dɪˈmɛntɪd/ *adj.* **1** crazy or very strange SYN **crazy**: *his demented mind* | *a demented sense of humor* **2** OLD-FASHIONED suffering from dementia [**Origin:** 1600–1700 *dement* **to drive mad** (16–19 centuries), from Latin *mens* **mind**]

de·men·tia /dɪˈmɛnʃə/ *n.* [U] MEDICINE an illness that affects the brain and memory, and makes you gradually lose the ability to think and behave normally

de·mer·it /dɪˈmɛrɪt/ *n.* [C] **1** [usually plural] a bad quality or feature of something: ***the merits and demerits of*** (=the good and bad qualities of) *nuclear power* **2** a warning in the form of a mark that is given to a student to tell them not to do something wrong again

de·mesne /dɪˈmeɪn/ *n.* [C] OLD USE a very big piece of land that one person owns, especially in past times

De·me·ter /dɪˈmit̬ɚ/ in Greek MYTHOLOGY, the goddess of crops

demi- /dɛmi/ *prefix* half: *a demigod* (=half god and half human) | *a demitasse* (=a small cup for serving coffee)

dem·i·god /ˈdɛmiˌgɑd/ *n.* [C] **1** someone who is so important that they are treated like a god **2** a man in ancient stories, who is partly god and partly human

dem·i·god·dess /ˈdɛmiˌgɑdɪs/ *n.* [C] **1** a woman who is so important that she is treated like a goddess **2** a female demigod

de·mil·i·ta·rize /diˈmɪlətəˌraɪz/ *v.* [T] POLITICS to remove the weapons, soldiers etc. from a country or area so that there can be no fighting there: *the* ***demilitarized zone*** *between the two countries* —**demilitarization** /diˌmɪlət̬ərəˈzeɪʃən/ *n.* [U]

deˌmilitarized ˈzone ABBREVIATION **D.M.Z.** *n.* [C] POLITICS an area between two countries where soldiers, weapons, etc. are not allowed as a condition of an official peace agreement between the countries: *the demilitarized zone between North and South Korea*

de Mille /dəˈmɪl/, **Ag·nes** /ˈægnɪs/ (1909–1993) a U.S. dancer and CHOREOGRAPHER of BALLET

DeMille, Ce·cil B. /ˈsisəl bi/ (1881–1959) a U.S. movie producer and director who is famous for making EPICS (=movies about people in the Bible and in history), using hundreds of actors

de·mise /dɪˈmaɪz/ *n.* [U] **1** FORMAL the end of something that used to exist: +**of** *the demise of the Cold War* **2** FORMAL or LAW death: *the demise of the president* [**Origin:** 1400–1500 Anglo-French, Old French *demis* **sent away**]

dem·i·tasse /ˈdɛmiˌtɑs, -ˌtæs/ *n.* [C] a small cup for coffee

dem·o /ˈdɛmoʊ/ *n. plural* **demos** [C] INFORMAL **1** a recording containing an example of someone's music: *a demo tape* **2** a CD-ROM that has a demonstration program on it **3** a DEMONSTRATION: *I'll give you a quick demo.* **4** also **demo model** an example of a product that is used to show how the product works and is later often sold at a lower price

demo- /dɛmə/ *prefix* relating to people or the population: *demographics* (=information about the population of a place)

de·mo·bil·ize /diˈmoʊbəˌlaɪz/ *v.* [I,T usually passive] to send home the members of an army, navy etc., especially at the end of a war: *disarming and demobilizing the rebel troops* —**demobilization** /diˌmoʊbələˈzeɪʃən/ *n.* [U]

de·moc·ra·cy /dɪˈmɑkrəsi/ W2 *n. plural* **democracies** **1** [U] POLITICS a system of government in which every citizen in the country can vote to elect its government officials: *an important step toward democracy* ▸see THESAURUS box at **government** **2** [C] POLITICS a country that allows its people to elect its government officials: *Western democracies* **3** [U] a situation or system in which everyone is equal and has the right to vote, make decisions etc.: *There must be more democracy in the industry.* [**Origin:** 1500–1600 Old French *democratie*, from Greek *demokratia*, from *demos* **people** + *-kratia* **rule**]

dem·o·crat /ˈdɛməˌkræt/ *n.* [C] POLITICS **1 Democrat** a member or supporter of the Democratic Party of the U.S. → see also REPUBLICAN **2** someone who believes in or works to achieve democracy

dem·o·crat·ic /ˌdɛməˈkræt̬ɪk◂/ W3 *adj.* **1** POLITICS based on the system that a government should be elected by the people: *a democratic government* | *the nation's first democratic elections* **2 Democratic** POLITICS belonging to or supporting the Democratic Party of the U.S.: *the Democratic nominee* **3** based on the principle that everyone should have the right to be involved in decision making: *a democratic style of parenting* —**democratically** /-kli/ *adv.*

ˌDemocratic ˈParty *n.* **the Democratic Party** one of the two main political parties of the U.S. → see also REPUBLICAN PARTY

de·moc·ra·tize /dɪˈmɑkrəˌtaɪz/ *v.* [T] POLITICS to change the way in which a government, company etc. is organized, so that it is more democratic —**democratization** /dɪˌmɑkrət̬əˈzeɪʃən/ *n.* [U]

De·moc·ri·tus /dɪˈmɑkrət̬əs/ (460?–?370 B.C.) a Greek PHILOSOPHER

dem·o·graph·ic /ˌdɛməˈgræfɪk◂/ *n.* **1 demographics** [plural] information about the people who live in a particular area, such as how many people there are or what types of people there are: *the changing demographics of Southern California* **2** [singular] a part of the population that is considered as a group, especially for the purpose of advertising or trying to sell goods: *Cable television is focused on the 18 to 49 demographic* (=people who are 18 to 49 years old). —**demographic** *adj.* —**demographically** /-kli/ *adv.*

demoˌgraphic tranˈsition *n.* [C,U] a process in which the population of an area gradually changes from one with high birth and death rates to one with low birth and death rates as it changes from a pre-industrial to to an INDUSTRIALIZED country

de·mog·ra·phy /dɪˈmɑgrəfi/ *n.* **1** [singular] the number and type of people who live in a particular area: *dramatic changes in the region's demography* **2** [U] the study of how human populations change, for example the study of how many births, deaths, marriages etc. happen in a particular place at a particular time —**demographer** *n.* [C]

de·mol·ish /dɪˈmɑlɪʃ/ *v.* [T] **1** to deliberately destroy a building or other structure: *Several houses were demolished to make way for the new road.* ▸see THESAURUS box at **destroy** **2** to destroy a building, structure, vehicle etc. by accident: *Her car was demolished in the accident.* **3** INFORMAL to end or ruin something completely: *The lawyers will demolish his defense.* | *All our hopes were demolished in an instant.* **4** INFORMAL to eat all of something very quickly **5** INFORMAL if you demolish your opponent, you beat them completely [**Origin:** 1500–1600 Old French *demolir*, from Latin *moliri* **to build**]

dem·o·li·tion /ˌdɛməˈlɪʃən/ *n.* [C,U] the act or process of deliberately demolishing a building: *Several housing projects are scheduled for demolition.*

ˌdemolition ˈderby *n.* [C] a competition in which people crash old cars into each other until only one is left driving

de·mon /ˈdimən/ *n.* [C] **1** an evil spirit **2** thoughts and feelings that make you unhappy: *We all have our* ***inner demons.*** **3** HUMOROUS someone who is very good at something: *She's a demon on the hockey field.* [**Origin:** 1200–1300 Late Latin *daemon* **evil spirit**, from Greek *daimon*] → see also SPEED DEMON

de·mo·ni·a·cal /ˌdiməˈnaɪəkəl/ also **de·mo·ni·ac** /dɪˈmoʊniæk/ *adj.* FORMAL wild and evil —**demoniacally** /-kli/ *adv.*

de·mon·ic /dɪˈmɑnɪk/ *adj.* **1** wild and cruel: *demonic laughter* **2** relating to a demon —**demonically** /-kli/ *adv.*

de·mon·ize /ˈdiməˌnaɪz/ *v.* [T] to describe or represent someone as evil: *the government's attempt to demonize immigrants* —**demonization** /ˌdimənəˈzeɪʃən/ *n.* [U]

de·mon·ol·o·gy /ˌdiməˈnɑlədʒi/ *n.* **1** [U] the study of or the belief in DEMONS **2** [C usually singular] a list of people someone disapproves of

de·mon·stra·ble /dɪˈmɑnstrəbəl/ Ac *adj.* FORMAL able to be shown or proved: *There is a demonstrable link between smoking and lung cancer.* —**demonstrably** *adv.* —**demonstrability** /dɪˌmɑnstrəˈbɪlət̬i/ *n.* [U]

dem·on·strate /ˈdɛmənˌstreɪt/ Ac S3 W2 *v.* **1** [T] to show or prove something clearly SYN **show**: *The study demonstrates the link between poverty and malnutrition.* | **demonstrate that** *The President is trying to demonstrate that he is tough on crime.* | **demonstrate how/what/why etc.** *The earthquake demonstrates how little control we have over nature.* |

demonstrate sth to sb *We must do a better job of demonstrating these dangers to the public.*

THESAURUS

show to make it clear that something is true or exists by providing facts or information: *The statistics show that the number of jobs available has fallen.*
mean to be a clear sign that something has happened, or is true: *The lights are on – that means he's still up.*
indicate FORMAL if scientific facts, tests, official figures etc. indicate something, they show that something exists or is likely to be true: *Research indicates that the drug may be linked to birth defects.*
suggest to show that something is probably true, even though there is no proof: *There was nothing in the letter to suggest that he was thinking of suicide.*
prove to show that something is definitely true: *The prosecution is trying to prove that he is guilty.*

2 [T] to show or describe how to do something or how it works SYN **show**: *The ski instructor was demonstrating the correct way to turn.* | **demonstrate how/what etc.** *A trainer came in to demonstrate how to use the new computers.* ▸see THESAURUS box at **explain** **3** [I] to protest or support something in public with a lot of other people: *Supporters demonstrated outside the courtroom during the trial.* | **+against** *Thousands came out to demonstrate against the war.* ▸see THESAURUS box at **protest**[2] **4** [T] if someone demonstrates an ability, quality, or feeling, they show that they have it: *Sloane has demonstrated his ability to work under pressure.* [**Origin:** 1500–1600 Latin *demonstratus*, past participle of *demonstrare*, from *monstrare* **to show**]

dem·on·stra·tion /ˌdɛmənˈstreɪʃən/ Ac W3 *n.* [C] **1** an event at which a lot of people meet to protest or support something in public: *The judge's decision sparked **mass demonstrations*** (=large ones). | **+against** *a demonstration against the war* | *Thousands of young people **took part in the demonstration**.* | **hold/stage a demonstration** (=organize and have one) | *Police **broke up a demonstration*** (=stopped it) *in front of the embassy.* **2** an act of showing people how to do something or how something works: *Laura **gave a demonstration** on how to use the electronic dictionary.* **3 a demonstration of sth a)** something that shows that something else is clearly true: *Today's chaos is a demonstration of the need for better public transportation.* **b)** an action that shows that someone has a feeling, ability, or quality: *I did it as a demonstration of my love for her.*

de·mon·stra·tive /dɪˈmɑnstrət̬ɪv/ Ac *adj.* **1** willing to show how much you care about someone: *Dave's not very demonstrative.* **2** FORMAL showing or explaining something: *graphs used for demonstrative purposes* —**demonstratively** *adv.*

deˌmonstrative ˈpronoun *n.* [C] ENG. LANG. ARTS a PRONOUN such as "that" or "this" that shows which person or thing is meant and separates it from others

dem·on·strat·or /ˈdɛmənˌstreɪt̬ɚ/ Ac *n.* [C] **1** someone who takes part in a DEMONSTRATION: *antiwar demonstrators* **2** someone who shows people how something works or is done: *a computer demonstrator* **3** an example of a product, that shows how it works

de·mor·al·ize /dɪˈmɔrəˌlaɪz, di-, -ˈmɑr-/ *v.* [T] to reduce or destroy someone's courage or confidence: *Boston's early lead demoralized their opponents.* —**demoralized** *adj.*: *exhausted and demoralized refugees* —**demoralizing** *adj.*: *a demoralizing defeat* —**demoralization** /dɪˌmɔrələˈzeɪʃən/ *n.* [U]

De·mos·the·nes /dɪˈmɑsθəˌniz/ (384–322 B.C.) a Greek ORATOR and writer of speeches

de·mote /dɪˈmoʊt, di-/ *v.* [T often passive] to make someone have a lower rank or a less important position than before OPP **promote**: **demote sb to sth** *He was demoted to deputy chairman.* —**demotion** /dɪˈmoʊʃən, di-/ *n.* [C,U]

de·mot·ic /dɪˈmɑt̬ɪk/ *adj.* **1** FORMAL used by or popular with most ordinary people **2 Demotic** HISTORY relating to an ancient form of Egyptian writing called Demotic that was simple and could be used by ordinary people

Demp·sey /ˈdɛmpsi/, **Jack** /dʒæk/ (1895–1983) a U.S. BOXER who was world CHAMPION in 1919–1926

de·mur /dɪˈmɚ/ *v.* **demurred, demurring** [I] FORMAL to say you will not do something or do not agree with something: *When we asked for his help, he demurred.* | **demur at sth** *She liked the house, but demurred at the price.*

de·mure /dɪˈmyʊr/ *adj.* **1** a demure woman or girl is shy and quiet and always behaves well **2** demure clothing is softly colored and does not show much of your body [**Origin:** 1300–1400 Old French *demoré*, past participle of *demorer*, from Latin *morari* **to stay, delay**] —**demurely** *adv.* —**demureness** *n.* [U]

de·mys·ti·fy /diˈmɪstəˌfaɪ/ *v.* **demystifies, demystified, demystifying** [T] to make a subject that seems difficult or complicated easier to understand, especially by explaining it in simpler language: *an attempt to demystify the new technology* —**demystification** /diˌmɪstəfəˈkeɪʃən/ *n.* [U]

den /dɛn/ *n.* [C] **1** a room in a house where people relax, read, watch television etc. **2** the home of some types of animal, for example lions or FOXES **3** a place where secret or illegal activities take place: *a gambling den* **4** a group of CUB SCOUTS **5 den of iniquity** OFTEN HUMOROUS a place where immoral activities happen [**Origin:** Old English *denn*]

De·na·li /dəˈnɑli/ a mountain in central Alaska, which is the highest point in North America. It is also called Mount McKinley.

de·na·tion·al·ize /diˈnæʃənəˌlaɪz/ *v.* [T] POLITICS to sell a business or industry owned by the government, so that it is then owned privately SYN **privatize** —**denationalization** /diˌnæʃənələˈzeɪʃən/ *n.* [U]

de·nat·u·ral·i·za·tion /diˌnætʃərələˈzeɪʃən/ *n.* [U] POLITICS a legal process that takes away someone's rights of CITIZENSHIP —**denaturalize** *v.* [T usually passive]

den·drite /ˈdɛndraɪt/ *n.* [C] BIOLOGY a small part on the body of a nerve cell for bringing electrical signals toward the cell from other cells → see also AXON

Deng Xiao·ping /ˌdʌŋ ʃaʊˈpɪŋ/ (1904–1997) a Chinese politician who was the most powerful person in the Chinese Communist Party from 1977 until his death, and started important changes that helped China to develop its economy and industry

de·ni·al /dɪˈnaɪəl/ Ac *n.* **1** [C,U] a statement saying that something is not true, or the act of making this statement: *Despite his **strong denials**, he has decided to resign.* | *There was no possibility of denial. She did it.* | **+of** *Diaz **issued a** firm **denial** of the rumor* (=officially stated that it was not true). | **+that** *the administration's denials that border security is lax* **2 the denial of sth** the act of refusing to allow someone to have or do something: *the denial of basic human rights* **3** [U] a situation in which something is so bad that you cannot accept, believe, or admit that it exists: *He is still **in denial** about his wife's rape.*

deˌnial of ˈservice atˌtack *n.* [C] COMPUTERS an attempt to make a company's WEBSITE stop working. This is done by sending so much information to the website that the company's computers become unable to work correctly. The result is that customers of the company cannot use the ONLINE services that the company provides.

den·i·grate /ˈdɛnɪˌgreɪt/ *v.* [T] to do or say things to make someone or something seem less important or good: *remarks that denigrate other races* [**Origin:** 1400–1500 Latin *denigrare*, from *niger* **black**] —**denigration** /ˌdɛnɪˈgreɪʃən/ *n.* [U]

den·im /ˈdɛnəm/ *n.* **1** [U] a type of strong cotton cloth, used especially to make JEANS **2 denims** [plural] OLD-FASHIONED a pair of pants made from denim

SYN jeans [**Origin:** 1600–1700 French *(serge) de Nîmes* **(type of cloth) from Nîmes**, French city where it was first made]

de·ni·tri·fi·ca·tion /diˌnaɪtrəfəˈkeɪʃən/ *n.* [U] BIOLOGY a natural process in which the OXYGEN in soil or water containing oxygen and NITROGEN is gradually changed by BACTERIA into nitrogen gas which then goes into the air → see picture at NITROGEN

den·i·zen /ˈdɛnəzən/ *n.* [C + of] LITERARY an animal, plant, or person that lives or is found in a particular place

Den·mark /ˈdɛnmɑrk/ a country in northern Europe, north of Germany and surrounded on three sides by seas → see also DANISH[1]

ˈden ˌmother *n.* [C] a woman who leads a group of CUB SCOUTS

de·nom·i·nate /dɪˈnɑməˌneɪt/ *v.* [T] TECHNICAL to officially set the value of something according to one system or type of money: *loans denominated in dollars*

de·nom·i·na·tion /dɪˌnɑməˈneɪʃən/ *n.* [C] **1** a religious group that has slightly different beliefs from other groups who belong to the same religion, especially Christianity ▸see THESAURUS box at **church**, **religion** **2** the value of a coin, paper money, or a stamp: *U.S. bills **in small denominations*** (=of low value)

de·nom·i·na·tion·al /dɪˌnɑməˈneɪʃənəl/ *adj.* relating or belonging to a particular religious denomination → see also NONDENOMINATIONAL

de·nom·i·na·tor /dɪˈnɑməˌneɪtɚ/ *n.* [C] MATH the number below the line in a FRACTION → see also LOWEST COMMON DENOMINATOR, NUMERATOR

de·no·ta·tion /ˌdinoʊˈteɪʃən/ Ac *n.* [C] ENG. LANG. ARTS the thing that is actually described by a word, rather than the feelings or ideas it suggests → see also CONNOTATION

de·note /dɪˈnoʊt/ Ac *v.* [T] FORMAL **1** to represent or mean something SYN **represent**: *Each X on the map denotes 500 people.* **2** to be a sign or signal of something SYN **indicate**: *Rapid tail movements can denote aggression in cats.* —**denotative** *adj.* → see also CONNOTE

de·noue·ment /ˌdeɪnuˈmɑnt˺, deɪˈnumɑnt˺/ *n.* [C] FORMAL the last part of a story or play that explains what happens after the CLIMAX

de·nounce /dɪˈnaʊns/ *v.* [T] **1** to publicly express disapproval of someone or something: *Residents denounced the plan because of traffic problems.* | **denounce sb/sth as sth** *Catholic bishops denounced the movie as immoral.* **2** to give information to the police or another authority about someone's illegal political activities: **denounce sb to sb** *Anja eventually denounced him to the secret police.* → see also DENUNCIATION

dense /dɛns/ *adj.* **1** made of or containing a lot of things or people that are very close together OPP **sparse**: *the city's **dense population*** | **dense forest/jungle/undergrowth etc.** *miles and miles of dense jungle* | *The lake **is dense with** marine life.* **2** difficult to see through or breathe in: **dense cloud/smoke/fog etc.** *The smoke was becoming denser.* **3** INFORMAL not able to understand things easily SYN **stupid** **4** a dense piece of writing is difficult to understand because it contains a lot of information or uses complicated language **5** PHYSICS a substance that is dense has a lot of MASS in relation to its size: *Water is eight hundred times denser than air.* —**densely** *adv.*: *densely populated areas* | *densely forested hills* —**denseness** *n.* [U]

den·si·ty /ˈdɛnsəti/ *n. plural* **densities** [C,U] **1** the degree to which an area is filled with things or people: *population density* | *The area has **a high density of** houses* (=there are a lot in the area). **2** PHYSICS the relationship between something's MASS and its VOLUME: *bone density*

dent[1] /dɛnt/ *n.* [C] **1** a mark made when you hit or press something so that its surface is bent: **+in** *a dent in the door of the car* **2 make/put a dent in sth** to reduce the amount of something: *The vacation put a big dent in our savings.*

dent[2] *v.* **1** [I,T] if you dent something, or if it dents, you hit or press it so that its surface is bent and marked: *Some idiot dented my car last night.* **2** [T] to harm or reduce something: *Baseball's image was dented by the scandal.*

den·tal /ˈdɛntl/ *adj.* [only before noun] relating to your teeth: *dental treatment* [**Origin:** 1500–1600 Latin *dentalis*, from *dens* **tooth**]

ˈdental asˌsistant *n.* [C] someone whose job is to help a DENTIST

ˌdental ˈfloss *n.* [U] thin string that you use to clean between your teeth

ˌdental ˈhygienist *n.* [C] someone who works with a dentist and cleans people's teeth or gives advice about how to care for teeth

ˈdental ˌsurgeon *n.* [C] a dentist who performs operations in the mouth SYN **oral surgeon**

den·ti·frice /ˈdɛntəˌfrɪs/ *n.* [U] FORMAL a PASTE or powder used to clean teeth

den·tine /ˈdɛntin/ also **den·tin** /ˈdɛntɪn/ *n.* [U] BIOLOGY the type of bone that your teeth are made of → see picture at TOOTH

den·tist /ˈdɛntɪst/ S3 *n.* [C] **1** someone whose job is to treat people's teeth

> **THESAURUS**
> **oral surgeon** a dentist who has special training to operate on people's teeth
> **orthodontist** a dentist who makes teeth straight when they have not been growing correctly
> **dental hygienist/hygienist** someone who is specially trained to help a dentist by cleaning teeth and giving advice about how to keep teeth healthy

2 the dentist/dentist's the place where a dentist works: *I'm **going to the dentist** this afternoon.* | *I saw a poster about gum disease **at the dentist's**.*

den·tis·try /ˈdɛntəstri/ *n.* [U] the medical study of the teeth and the mouth, or the work of a dentist

den·tures /ˈdɛntʃɚz/ *n.* [plural] a set of artificial teeth worn by someone who does not have their own teeth anymore SYN **false teeth**

de·nude /dɪˈnud/ *v.* FORMAL to remove the plants and trees that cover an area of land, or remove the leaves from a plant or tree: *the acid rain that is denuding our forests*

de·nun·ci·a·tion /dɪˌnʌnsiˈeɪʃən/ *n.* [C] a public statement in which you criticize someone or something

Den·ver /ˈdɛnvɚ/ the capital city of the U.S. state of Colorado

ˌDenver ˈboot *n.* [C] a metal object that the police attach to the wheel of an illegally parked car so that it cannot be moved

de·ny /dɪˈnaɪ/ Ac S3 W2 *v.* **denies, denied, denying** [T]

1 NOT TRUE/NOT BELIEVED to say that something someone says is not true, especially something bad that you are accused of: *I saw you do it, so don't try to deny it!* | *She continues to **deny the rumors**.* | **deny (that)** *She denied that she had ever been to Denver.* | **deny doing sth** *Benson denied trying to steal the jewelry.* | **flatly/categorically deny sth** (=deny very strongly) | **deny a charge/allegation/claim** *He has repeatedly denied the allegations against him.* | *The spokeswoman did not **deny the existence of** the report.*

2 NOT ALLOW [often passive] to refuse to allow someone to have or do something: *Parry's appeal to the courts was denied.* | **deny sb sth** *Seven of the actors were denied visas.* | **deny sth to sb** *Women are still denied access to the club.*

3 there's no denying (that) also **sb can't deny (that)** SPOKEN used to say that it is very clear that something is true: *There's no denying that some U.S. workers suffer*

D

because of free trade. | *I can't deny that what she said hurt me.*
4 FEELINGS to refuse to admit to yourself or other people that you are feeling something: *I realized I'd been denying a lot of angry feelings toward my mother.*
5 deny yourself sth to decide not to have something that you would like, especially for moral or religious reasons or because you think it will be good for you in some way: *Jen saved money by denying herself any luxuries.*
6 SAY YOU DO NOT KNOW SB LITERARY to say that you do not know someone when in fact you do, so that they get into trouble
[**Origin:** 1200–1300 Old French *denier*, from Latin *negare* **to deny**]

D

de·o·dor·ant /di'oudərənt/ *n.* [C,U] a substance that you put on the skin under your arms to stop you from smelling bad

de·o·dor·ize /di'oudə,raɪz/ *v.* [T] to remove a bad smell or to make it less noticeable —**deodorizer** *n.* [C]

de·ox·y·ri·bo·nu·cle·ic ac·id /di,ɑksi,raɪbou-nu,kliɪk 'æsɪd/ *n.* [U] → DNA

de·part /dɪ'pɑrt/ *v.* **1** [I,T] to leave, especially when you are starting a trip SYN **leave**: *The flight departs JFK airport every day at 7:05 a.m.* | **depart for sth** *Passengers departing for Tuscon should go to Gate 7.* | **depart from sth** *The train will depart from track 5.* **2 depart this life/earth** FORMAL to die [**Origin:** 1200–1300 Old French *departir*, from *partir* **to divide**] → see also DEPARTURE

depart from sth *phr. v.* to not use the usual way of doing something, and do something different instead: *He* ***departed from tradition*** *by asking for a vote.*

de·part·ed /dɪ'pɑrt̬ɪd/ *adj.* [only before noun] **1** a word meaning "dead," used to avoid saying this directly: *our* ***dearly departed*** *father* **2** LITERARY a time that is departed is gone forever

de·part·ment /dɪ'pɑrt˺mənt/ S1 W1 *n.* [C] **1** one of the parts of a large organization, such as a college, government, or business, that deals with a particular kind of work: *the company's public relations department* | *the Department of Motor Vehicles* ▸see THESAURUS box at **part**[1] **2** an area in a large store where a particular type of product is sold: *the toy department* **3** a particular part of someone's character, a situation, an activity, or subject etc., especially one that you have just mentioned: *The movie tries to be both a comedy and a drama, without success in either department.* | *Don't ask me – cooking* ***is John's department*** (=is the part of house work that John deals with). **4** one of the areas that France is divided into —**departmental** /dɪ,pɑrt˺'mɛntl/ *adj.*: *a departmental meeting* → see also FIRE DEPARTMENT, POLICE DEPARTMENT

de·part·men·tal·ize /dɪ,pɑrt˺'mɛntl,aɪz, ,dipɑrt-/ *v.* [T] to divide something into different departments —**departmentalization** /dɪpɑrt˺,mɛntl-ə'zeɪʃən/ *n.* [U]

De,partment of 'Agriculture, the also **the 'Agriculture De,partment** the U.S. government department that is responsible for farming, food production, and the safety of food products

De,partment of 'Commerce, the also **the 'Commerce De,partment** the U.S. government department that is concerned with trade and economic development

De,partment of De'fense, the also **the De'fense De,partment** the U.S. government department that is responsible for the military forces in the U.S., that is, the Army, Navy, Air Force, Marine Corps, and Coast Guard

De,partment of Edu'cation, the also **the Edu'cation De,partment** the U.S. government department that is responsible for the education system, including education programs, laws for schools and colleges, standards for schools and teachers etc.

De,partment of 'Energy, the also **the 'Energy De,partment** the U.S. government department that is concerned with supplies of FUEL, including coal, oil, gas, and NUCLEAR energy

De,partment of ,Health and ,Human 'Services, the the U.S. government department that is responsible for health programs and providing money and support for people who are poor, have no jobs, or are too old to work

De,partment of ,Housing and ,Urban De'velopment, the → see HUD

De,partment of 'Justice, the also **the 'Justice De,partment** the U.S. government department that deals with the law. Its work includes writing laws, representing the government in courts of law, and searching for information to solve crimes.

De,partment of 'Labor, the also **the 'Labor De,partment** the U.S. government department concerned with how workers are treated by employers. It examines subjects such as fair wages, safety, and the number of hours worked each week.

De,partment of 'State, the also **the 'State De,partment** the part of the U.S. government that deals with the U.S.'s relations with other countries

De,partment of the In'terior, the also **the In'terior De,partment** the part of the U.S. government responsible for protecting the U.S.'s natural RESOURCES such as minerals, water, natural energy etc.

De,partment of the 'Treasury, the also **the 'Treasury De,partment** the U.S. government organization that is responsible for the money system of the country and the money that the government collects and spends

De,partment of Transpor'tation, the also **the Transpor'tation De,partment** the U.S. government department that deals with TRANSPORTATION in the U.S., for example by making laws about road vehicles and airplanes, and by building and repairing roads

De,partment of 'Veterans' Af,fairs, the also **the 'Veterans' De,partment** the U.S. government organization that gives help to soldiers, SAILORS etc. who have fought in a war and to their families

de'partment ,store *n.* [C] a large store that sells many different products such as clothes, kitchen equipment etc.

de·par·ture /dɪ'pɑrtʃɚ/ *n.* **1** [C,U] the act of a plane, bus, train, or boat leaving a place OPP **arrival**: *Please check in two hours before your flight's departure.* | +**from** *a list of departures from Houston* | +**for** *There are several departures for New York every day.* **2** [U] the act of a person leaving a place, usually for a long trip or to live somewhere else OPP **arrival**: +**from** *Mozart's departure from Paris* | +**for** *Our departure for the U.S. was delayed by visa problems.* **3** [C,U] the act of leaving an organization or position: +**from** *He claims his departure from the company was voluntary.* **4 departures** [singular] the part of an airport where people wait to get on planes → see also ARRIVALS **5** [C] a change from what is usual or expected: *The plan is a* ***radical departure from*** (=a big change from) *the original.*

de'parture ,lounge *n.* [C] the place at an airport where people wait until their airplane is ready to leave

de·pend /dɪ'pɛnd/ S1 W2 *v.* **(it/that) depends** SPOKEN used to say that you cannot give a definite answer to something because your answer will be affected by something else: *"Are you going to Karla's party?" "It depends. I might have to work."* | **it depends who/what/how/whether etc.** *"What's the best restaurant in town?" "It depends what kind of food you like."* [**Origin:** 1400–1500 French *dépendre*, from Latin *pendere* **to hang**]

depend on/upon sb/sth *phr. v.* **1** if something depends on something else, it is directly affected or decided by that thing: *The amount you earn depends on your experience.* | **sth depends on who/what/how/whether etc.** *The type of procedure we use depends on where the tumor is.* | **depending on** *Prices vary depending on when you travel.* **2** to need the help or support of someone or something else in order to exist, be successful, be healthy etc. SYN **rely on**: *The* *city depends heavily on tourism.* | +**depend on sb/sth for sth** *I depended on my mother for support.* | **depend on sb/sth to do sth** *Many people depend on Medicaid for their healthcare.*

THESAURUS

rely on/upon to trust or depend on someone or something: *I knew I could rely on David.*
trust to believe that someone is honest and will not do anything bad or wrong: *How can you still trust him when he lied to you?*
count on to depend on someone or something: *Their government was counting on American support.*

3 to trust or have confidence in someone or something SYN rely on: *I know I can depend on you.* | **depend on sb/sth to do sth** *I can depend on my employees to take care of things.*

de·pend·a·ble /dɪˈpɛndəbəl/ *adj.* able to be trusted to do what you need or expect SYN reliable: *a dependable car* —**dependably** *adv.* —**dependability** /dɪˌpɛndəˈbɪləṭi/ *n.* [U]

de·pend·ence /dɪˈpɛndəns/ *n.* [U] **1** the state of depending on the help and support of someone or something else in order to exist or be successful OPP independence: +**on/upon** *We need to reduce our dependence on foreign oil.* **2** the state of being ADDICTED to drugs or alcohol SYN addiction: +**on** *the patient's dependence on tranquilizers* **3** when one thing is strongly affected by another thing: *the mutual dependence of profit and growth*

de·pend·en·cy /dɪˈpɛndənsi/ *n. plural* **dependencies** **1** [U] a state of dependence **2** [C] POLITICS a country that is controlled by another country

de·pend·ent[1] /dɪˈpɛndənt/ *adj.* **1** needing someone or something else in order to exist, be successful, be healthy etc. OPP independent: +**on/upon** *Her elderly mother is dependent on her for everything.* | *The regime is* ***heavily dependent*** (=very dependent) *on foreign aid.* | *an* ***emotionally dependent person*** (=one who depends emotionally on others too much) → see also CO-DEPENDENT **2 be dependent on/upon sth** to be directly affected or decided by something else: *Your success is dependent on how hard you work.* **3** ADDICTED to drugs, alcohol etc.

dependent[2] *n.* [C] someone, especially a child, who depends on you for food, clothes, money etc.

deˌpendent ˈclause *n.* [C] ENG. LANG. ARTS a CLAUSE in a sentence that gives information related to the main clause, but cannot exist alone. For example, in the sentence, "I have hated cleaning since I was a child," the clause "since I was a child" is a dependent clause.

deˌpendent eˈvents *n.* [plural] TECHNICAL two related things that happen, in which the result of the second event is directly affected by the result of the first → see also DISJOINT EVENTS, MUTUALLY EXCLUSIVE EVENTS

deˌpendent ˈsystem *n.* [C] MATH a set of related EQUATIONS that has several possible solutions rather than only one solution → see also INDEPENDENT SYSTEM

deˌpendent ˈvariable *n.* [C] **1** SCIENCE in a scientific EXPERIMENT (=test), a result that is likely to change depending on the different conditions used in the experiment SYN responding variable → see also CONTROLLED VARIABLE, INDEPENDENT VARIABLE **2** MATH in math, a VARIABLE (=mathematical quantity that is not fixed and can be any of several amounts) that depends on the value chosen for another variable for its own value. For example, in the EQUATION $y = 3x + 2$, y is a dependent variable because its value depends on the value chosen for x. → see also INDEPENDENT VARIABLE

de·per·son·al·ize /diˈpɚsənlˌaɪz, -snəˌlaɪz/ *v.* [T] to ignore the human, personal, and individual qualities of a person or group: *Large hospitals can often depersonalize patients.* —**depersonalization** /diˌpɚsnələˈzeɪʃən/ *n.* [U]

de·pict /dɪˈpɪkt/ *v.* [T] to describe or show someone or something using language or pictures: *The state flag depicts a grizzly bear.* | *a book depicting 18th-century Russian life* | **depict sb/sth as sth** *New York used to be depicted as a cold and heartless city.* [**Origin:** 1400–1500 Latin *depictus*, past participle of *depingere*, from *pingere* **to paint**] —**depiction** /dɪˈpɪkʃən/ *n.* [C,U] *a harsh depiction of small-town life*

de·pil·a·to·ry /dɪˈpɪləˌtɔri/ *n. plural* **depilatories** [C] a substance that gets rid of unwanted hair from your body —**depilatory** *adj.* [only before noun]

de·plane /diˈpleɪn/ *v.* [I] to get out of an airplane

de·plete /dɪˈplit/ *v.* [T usually passive] to reduce the amount of something good or necessary, so that there is not enough: *gases that deplete the ozone layer* | *Salmon populations have been* ***severely depleted*** *recently.* [**Origin:** 1800–1900 Latin *depletus*, past participle of *deplere*, from *plere* **to fill**] —**depletion** /dɪˈpliʃən/ *n.* [U] *the depletion of natural resources*

de·plor·a·ble /dɪˈplɔrəbəl/ *adj.* FORMAL very bad, shocking, and deserving strong disapproval: *a deplorable mistake* | *The level of care at the clinic is deplorable.* —**deplorably** *adv.*

de·plore /dɪˈplɔr/ *v.* [T] FORMAL to strongly criticize something that you disapprove of: *The critics deplored the film's violence.* [**Origin:** 1500–1600 French *déplorer*, from Latin *plorare* **to cry out**]

de·ploy /dɪˈplɔɪ/ *v.* **deploys, deployed, deploying** **1** [I,T] to put soldiers, military vehicles, weapons etc. in a particular area or position so that they can fight or do other work, or to get into position in this way: *U.N. troops were deployed in order to keep the peace.* | **deploy to sth** *The Marine battalion was preparing to deploy to the region.* **2** [I,T] if a piece of equipment deploys, or you deploy it, it operates or is used: *The air bags deploy when the car is struck from the side.* **3** [T] FORMAL to use skills, ideas, arguments etc. for a particular purpose: *an argument deployed by the prosecutor* [**Origin:** 1400–1500 French *déployer*, from Latin *displicare* **to scatter**] —**deployment** *n.* [C,U]

de·po·lit·i·cize /ˌdipəˈlɪṭəˌsaɪz/ *v.* [T] to remove political influence or control from a situation

de·pop·u·late /diˈpɑpyəˌleɪt/ *v.* [T usually passive] to greatly reduce the number of people living in a particular area —**depopulation** /diˌpɑpyəˈleɪʃən/ *n.* [U]

de·port /dɪˈpɔrt/ *v.* [T] **1** to make a person from a foreign country return to the country they came from: *Officials deported 300 illegal immigrants last week.* **2 deport yourself** FORMAL to behave in a particular way, especially in the correct way

de·por·ta·tion /ˌdipɔrˈteɪʃən/ *n.* [C,U] the act of deporting someone: *Pascal faces deportation next month.*

de·por·tee /diˌpɔrˈti/ *n.* [C] someone who has been deported or is going to be deported

de·port·ment /dɪˈpɔrtˀmənt/ *n.* [U] FORMAL the way that a person behaves in public

de·pose /dɪˈpoʊz/ *v.* **1** [T] to remove a ruler or political leader from their position of power: *Clemens was deposed in a military coup.* **2** [I,T] LAW to officially give information about something, after you have promised to tell the truth → see also DEPOSITION

de·pos·it[1] /dɪˈpɑzɪt/ S3 *n.* [C] **1** the first part of the money that you pay for something, especially something large or expensive, so that it will not be sold to someone else: +**of** *A deposit of 10% is required.* | *We* ***put a $100 deposit down on*** (=paid a deposit for) *a sofa.* **2** money that you pay when you rent something such as an apartment or car, which will be given back if you do not damage it: *We paid one month's rent, plus a deposit of $500.* | *My landlord only returned half of my* ***security deposit*** (=a deposit on a rented house). **3** an amount of money that is put into a bank account OPP withdrawal: *I* ***made a deposit into*** *my savings account.* **4** EARTH SCIENCE a layer of a mineral, metal etc. that is left in soil or rocks through a natural process: *oil and mineral deposits* **5** an amount or layer of a substance that gradually develops in a particular place: *fatty deposits in the arteries*

deposit² S3 *v.* [T] **1** [always + adv./prep.] to put something down or leave something in a particular place: +**on/in/by etc.** *Litter should be deposited in the green trash cans.* **2** to gradually leave layers of a substance in or on something: **deposit sth on/in/over sth** *The river deposits large amounts of sediment in Lake Powell.* **3** to put money or something valuable in a bank or other place where it will be safe: **deposit sth in/into sth** *I'd like to deposit this in my checking account.*

de'posit ac,count *n.* [C] ECONOMICS a bank account that earns INTEREST → see also CHECKING ACCOUNT, SAVINGS ACCOUNT

D

dep·o·si·tion /ˌdɛpəˈzɪʃən/ *n.* **1** [C] LAW a statement written or recorded for a court of law, by someone who has promised to tell the truth **2** [U] EARTH SCIENCE the natural process of depositing a substance in rocks or soil **3** [C,U] the act of removing a king, queen etc. from a position of power

de·pos·i·tor /dɪˈpɑzɪtə/ *n.* [C] FORMAL ECONOMICS someone who puts money in a bank or other financial organization

de·pos·i·to·ry /dɪˈpɑzəˌtɔri/ *n. plural* **depositories** [C] a place where something can be safely kept —**depository** *adj.*

de'posit slip *n.* [C] a form that you use when you put money into your bank account

de·pot /ˈdipoʊ/ *n.* [C] **1** a place where large amounts of food or other supplies are stored SYN **warehouse**: *a weapons depot* **2** a railroad station or bus station, especially a small one

de·praved /dɪˈpreɪvd/ *adj.* completely evil or morally unacceptable: *a depraved and wicked man* [**Origin:** 1500–1600 *deprave* **to make evil** (14–21 centuries), from French *dépraver*, from Latin *pravus* **bent, bad**]

de·prav·i·ty /dɪˈprævəṭi/ *n.* [U] the state of being evil or morally unacceptable: *sexual depravity* —**depravation** /ˌdɛprəˈveɪʃən/ *n.* [U]

dep·re·cate /ˈdɛprəˌkeɪt/ *v.* [T] FORMAL to disapprove of or criticize something strongly: *Congressional leaders deprecated the military's lack of action.* [**Origin:** 1600–1700 Latin *deprecari* **to keep off by prayer**, from *precari* **to pray**] —**deprecation** /ˌdɛprəˈkeɪʃən/ *n.* [U]

dep·re·cat·ing /ˈdɛprəˌkeɪṭɪŋ/ also **dep·re·ca·to·ry** /ˈdɛprəkəˌtɔri/ *adj.* **1** expressing criticism or disapproval: *a deprecating reference to the administration's economic policies* **2** making something or someone, especially yourself, seem not very important or not very interesting: *a deprecating smile* —**deprecatingly** *adv.* → see also SELF-DEPRECATING

de·pre·ci·ate /dɪˈpriʃiˌeɪt/ *v.* **1** [I] to decrease in value or price OPP **appreciate**: *New cars depreciate quickly in the first two years.* **2** [T] TECHNICAL to reduce the value of something over time, especially for tax purposes: *The bank depreciates its PCs over five years.* **3** [T] LITERARY to make someone or something seem unimportant

de·pre·ci·a·tion /dɪˌpriʃiˈeɪʃən/ *n.* [U] a decrease in the value or price of something: *the depreciation of the dollar* —**depreciatory** /dɪˈpriʃəˌtɔri/ *adj.*

dep·re·da·tion /ˌdɛprəˈdeɪʃən/ *n.* [C usually plural] FORMAL an act of cruelty, violence, or destruction: *the depredations of war*

de·press /dɪˈprɛs/ Ac *v.* [T] **1** to make someone feel very unhappy: *That movie depressed me.* | **it depresses me/him etc.** *It always depresses me to think of the mistakes I made.* **2** to prevent the economy from working correctly or being as active as it usually is: *Higher taxes will depress the state's economy.* **3** to reduce the value of prices or pay: *Falling demand for wheat has depressed its market price.* **4** FORMAL to press something down, especially a part of a machine: *Depress the brake slowly.* [**Origin:** 1300–1400 Old French *depresser*, from Latin *premere* **to press**]

de·pres·sant /dɪˈprɛsənt/ *n.* [C] MEDICINE a substance or drug that acts on your brain and makes your body's processes slower, and makes you feel very relaxed or sleepy —**depressant** *adj.* → see also ANTIDEPRESSANT

de·pressed /dɪˈprɛst/ Ac *adj.* **1 a)** feeling very unhappy: *Some people eat too much when they're depressed.* | +**about/over** *Morgan was depressed about the divorce.* **b)** suffering from a medical condition in which you are so unhappy that you cannot live a normal life: *She was diagnosed as being* ***clinically depressed*** (=shown by a doctor to be suffering in this way). ▸see THESAURUS box at **sad** **2** an area, industry etc. that is depressed does not have enough economic or business activity: *depressed urban areas* **3** a depressed level or amount is lower than normal: *a depressed appetite*

de·press·ing /dɪˈprɛsɪŋ/ Ac *adj.* making you feel very sad: *a depressing gray day* | **it's depressing to do sth** *It's really depressing to watch the political situation go downhill.* —**depressingly** *adv.*: *The idea was depressingly familiar.*

de·pres·sion /dɪˈprɛʃən/ Ac W3 *n.* **1** [C,U] **a)** a feeling of sadness in which you feel there is no hope for the future: *her battle with depression* | *He went into a* ***deep depression*** *when his wife died.* **b)** MEDICINE a medical condition that makes you feel extremely unhappy, so that you cannot live a normal life: *patients suffering from* ***clinical depression*** (=depression that a doctor says is a medical condition) **2** [C,U] ECONOMICS a long period when the economy is not working well and many people do not have jobs: *an economic depression* ▸see THESAURUS box at **recession** → see also RECESSION **3 the Depression** also **the Great Depression** HISTORY the period in the 1930s when the economy was not working well at all and many people had no jobs **4** [C] a part of a surface that is deeper or lower than the other parts: *The turtles leave depressions in the sand.* **5** [C] EARTH SCIENCE a mass of air that has a low pressure and usually causes rain

de·pres·sive¹ /dɪˈprɛsɪv/ *adj.* often feeling depressed, or having signs of depression

depressive² *n.* [C] someone who suffers from DEPRESSION → see also MANIC DEPRESSIVE

de·pres·sur·ize /diˈprɛʃəˌraɪz/ *v.* [I,T] to reduce the pressure of air or gas inside a container or especially in an airplane —**depressurization** /diˌprɛʃərəˈzeɪʃən/ *n.* [U]

dep·ri·va·tion /ˌdɛprəˈveɪʃən/ *n.* [C,U] the lack of something that you need in order to be healthy, comfortable, or happy: *sleep deprivation* | *the deprivations of slavery* (=the lack of freedom, happiness etc. that comes with slavery)

de·prive /dɪˈpraɪv/ *v.*

deprive sb **of** sth *phr. v.* to take something important that someone needs or wants from them: *priosoners who are deprived of their civil rights* | *What happens when the brain is deprived of oxygen?*

de·prived /dɪˈpraɪvd/ *adj.* not having the things that are considered to be necessary for a comfortable or happy life: *deprived children* | *one of the city's most deprived neighborhoods*

de·pro·gram /diˈproʊgræm/ *v.* **deprogrammed, deprogramming** [T] to help someone who has been involved in a religious CULT to stop obeying its orders and to start thinking for themselves again

dept. the written abbreviation of DEPARTMENT

depth /dɛpθ/ W3 *n.*

1 DISTANCE [C,U] **a)** the distance from the top surface of something, such as a river or hole, to the bottom of it: +**of** *the depth of the water* | *Buckeye Lake* ***reaches depths of*** (=gets as deep as) *eight to ten feet.* | **3 feet/2 inches etc. in depth** *The pond is no more than four feet in depth.* | *Dig out the area* ***to a depth of*** *four inches.* | *The fish are found* ***at a depth of*** *50 cm.* **b)** the distance from the front of an object to the back of it: +**of** *The drawers have a depth of 16 inches.*

2 KNOWLEDGE [U] APPROVING the quality of knowing or

giving a lot of important details about a subject: *Network news coverage often lacks depth.* | +**of** *the depth of her knowledge* | *We don't have time to discuss this* ***in great depth*** (=considering lots of detail). → see also IN-DEPTH
3 the depth of sth the great strength or seriousness of an emotion or situation, especially a bad one: *the depth of public concern about the economy* | *We hadn't realized the depth of the problem.*
4 the depths of sth a) the place that is farthest away or most hidden: *the depths of the Amazon rain forest* | **the depths of sb's mind/soul etc.** (=the most hidden, secret parts of a person) **b)** the worst or most extreme part of a situation or feeling: *a family in the depths of despair* | *Europe was in the depths of war.* | **the depths of winter** (=the middle of winter, when it is very cold)
5 be out of your depth to be involved in a situation or activity that is too difficult for you to understand: *I was way out of my depth in chemistry classes.*
6 TEAM [U] a quality of a team or group that contains a large number of very skilled and experienced people: *Their team will have a little more depth this year.*
7 the depths LITERARY the deepest parts of the ocean

'depth charge *n.* [C] a bomb that explodes at a particular depth under water

dep·u·ta·tion /ˌdɛpyəˈteɪʃən/ *n.* [C] FORMAL a group of people who are sent to talk to someone in authority, as representatives of a larger group

de·pute /dɪˈpyut/ *v.* [T] **depute sb to do sth** FORMAL to give someone the authority to do something instead of you

dep·u·tize /ˈdɛpyəˌtaɪz/ *v.* [T] to give someone below you in rank the authority to do your work for a short time, because you need help: *Carter was deputized by Dodge to take command of the tanker.*

dep·u·ty /ˈdɛpyət̬i/ W3 *n. plural* **deputies** [C] **1** someone who is directly below someone else in rank, and who is officially in charge when that person is not there: *She appointed a deputy* | **deputy director/mayor/chief etc.** *the deputy district attorney* **2** LAW someone whose job is to help a SHERIFF [**Origin:** 1400–1500 French *député*, from Latin *deputare* **to give a particular job to someone**]

de·rail /dɪˈreɪl, di-/ *v.* **1** [I,T usually passive] if a train derails, or something derails it, it goes off the tracks: *Forty people were injured when a passenger train derailed.* **2** [T] to spoil or interrupt a plan, agreement etc.: *Radicals are trying to derail the peace process.* —**derailment** *n.* [C,U]

de·rail·leur /dɪˈreɪlɚ/ *n.* [C] the piece of equipment on a bicycle that moves the chain from one GEAR to another

de·ranged /dɪˈreɪndʒd/ *adj.* behaving in a crazy or dangerous way: *a deranged gunman* —**derangement** *n.* [U]

der·by /ˈdɚbi/ *n. plural* **derbies** [C] **1** a type of horse race: *the Kentucky Derby* **2** a special race or competition: *a roller derby* (=a race on ROLLER SKATES) **3** a man's stiff round hat, worn in the past

de·reg·u·late /diˈrɛgyəˌleɪt/ *v.* [T] ECONOMICS to remove government rules and controls from some types of business activity: *The U.S. airline industry has been deregulated since 1978.* —**deregulation** /diˌrɛgyəˈleɪʃən/ *n.* [U]

der·e·lict¹ /ˈdɛrəˌlɪkt/ *adj.* **1** [usually before noun] a building or piece of land that is derelict is in very bad condition because it has not been used for a long time or not been well taken care of: *derelict homes and businesses* **2 be derelict in your duty** to not be doing the things you should be doing or have the responsibility to do [**Origin:** 1600–1700 Latin *derelictus*, past participle of *derelinquere* **to leave something you are responsible for**]

derelict² *n.* [C] DISAPPROVING someone who has no money or home and who has to live on the streets

der·e·lic·tion /ˌdɛrəˈlɪkʃən/ *n.* **1 dereliction of duty** FORMAL failure to do what you should do as part of your job **2** [U] the state of being derelict

de·ride /dɪˈraɪd/ *v.* [T] FORMAL to make statements or jokes that show you have no respect for someone or something: *Gavin has derided the efforts at gun control.* | **deride sb/sth as sth** *Jackson derided the plan as irresponsible.*

de ri·gueur /də riˈgɚ/ *adj.* [not before noun] considered to be necessary and expected by other people: *Tuxedos are de rigueur at the event.*

de·ri·sion /dɪˈrɪʒən/ *n.* [U] statements or actions that show that you have no respect for someone or something: *shouts of derision from the crowd*

de·ri·sive /dɪˈraɪsɪv, -ˈrɪ-/ *adj.* showing that you have no respect for someone or something SYN **contemptuous**: *derisive laughter* —**derisively** *adv.*

de·ri·so·ry /dɪˈraɪsəri, -zə-/ *adj.* **1** an amount of money that is derisory is so small that it is not worth considering seriously: *a derisory pay raise* **2** derisive: *derisory comments* —**derisorily** *adv.*

de·riv·a·tion /ˌdɛrəˈveɪʃən/ Ac *n.* **1** [C,U] the origin of a word SYN **etymology**: *What is the derivation of the word "redshirt"?* **2** [C] a word that comes from another language: *a French derivation* **3** [U] the act of deciding that something is true, based on what you know: *the derivation of conclusions from the available facts*

de·riv·a·tive¹ /dɪˈrɪvət̬ɪv/ Ac *n.* [C] **1** something that has developed or been produced from something else: +**of** *The drug is a derivative of Vitamin A.* **2** ECONOMICS a type of financial INVESTMENT whose value depends on the value of another ASSET: *the derivative market*

derivative² Ac *adj.* DISAPPROVING not new or invented, but copied or taken from something else: *This season's new shows are all pretty derivative.*

de·rive /dɪˈraɪv/ Ac *v.* [T] to come to a solution in a math or science problem using logical or scientific thought processes: *Derive the value of Q in the following equation.* [**Origin:** 1300–1400 French *dériver*, from Latin *derivare* **to draw out water**]

derive from *phr. v.* **1** to get something, especially a good feeling or an advantage, from something: **derive sth from sth** *Children derive comfort from familiar surroundings.* **2** to have something as an origin: **be derived from sth** *Hughes' music is derived from blues and jazz.* | **derive from sth** *The word derives from Latin.* **3** CHEMISTRY to get a chemical substance from another substance: **derive sth from sth** *The enzyme is derived from human blood.*

deˌrived 'character *n.* [C] BIOLOGY a physical feature present in the members of a SPECIES of animal, plant, etc. that are alive now and in those that lived in the recent past, but was not present in members of the same species who lived a long time ago

der·ma·ti·tis /ˌdɚməˈtaɪt̬ɪs/ *n.* [U] MEDICINE a disease of the skin that causes redness, swelling, and pain

der·ma·tol·o·gy /ˌdɚməˈtɑlədʒi/ *n.* [U] the part of medical science that deals with the skin, its diseases, and their treatment —**dermatologist** *n.* [C]

der·mis /ˈdɚmɪs/ *n.* [U] BIOLOGY the layer of skin under the EPIDERMIS → see picture at SKIN¹

der·og·ate /ˈdɛrəˌgeɪt/ *v.* [T] FORMAL to make something seem less important or less good

derogate from sth *phr. v.* FORMAL to change from an expected or planned idea, action, or type of behavior

de·rog·a·to·ry /dɪˈrɑgəˌtɔri/ *adj.* a derogatory word, remark etc. is insulting and disapproving: *She's always making derogatory comments about my weight.* —**derogatorily** *adv.*

der·rick /ˈdɛrɪk/ *n.* [C] **1** a tall tower built over an oil well that is used to raise and lower the DRILL **2** a tall machine used for lifting heavy weights, used especially on ships [**Origin:** 1700–1800 *derrick* **structure for hanging criminals**]

Der·ri·da /ˌdɛriˈdɑ/, **Jacques** /ʒɑk/ (1930–2004) a French PHILOSOPHER

D

der·ri·ère /ˌdɛri'ɛr/ *n.* [C] HUMOROUS the part of the body that you sit on; BUTTOCKS

der·ring-do /ˌdɛrɪŋ 'du/ *n.* [U] HUMOROUS very brave actions like the ones that happen in adventure stories

der·rin·ger /'dɛrɪndʒɚ/ *n.* [C] a small gun with a short BARREL

der·vish /'dɚvɪʃ/ *n.* [C] a member of a Muslim religious group, some of whom dance fast and spin around as part of a religious ceremony

de·sal·i·nate /diˌsælәˌneɪt/ *v.* [T] TECHNICAL to remove the salt from ocean water so that it can be drunk or used by people —**desalination** /diˌsælә'neɪʃәn/ *n.* [U]

D

de·sal·i·nize /di'sælәˌnaɪz/ *v.* [T] TECHNICAL to remove the salt from ocean water so that it can be drunk or used by people —**desalinization** /diˌsælәnә'zeɪʃәn/ *n.v.* [U]

des·cant /'dɛskænt/ *n.* [C] a tune that is played or sung above the main tune in a piece of music

Des·cartes /deɪ'kɑrt/, **Re·né** /rә'neɪ/ (1596–1650) a French mathematician and PHILOSOPHER

de·scend /dɪ'sɛnd/ *v.* **1** [I,T] FORMAL to move from a higher level to a lower one OPP **ascend**: *The plane started to descend.* | *Several climbers were descending the mountain.* | +**from/to/onto** *The elevator descended to the seventh floor, and Anna got out.* **2** [I] if a road, path etc. descends, it slopes downward OPP **ascend**: *After a mile, the road started to descend.* | **descend into/under/from etc. sth** *The tunnel descends 200 feet into the earth.* **3 in descending order** numbers, choices etc. that are in descending order are arranged from the highest or most important to the lowest or least important: *Food manufacturers must list ingredients in descending order by weight.* **4** [I] LITERARY if darkness, night etc. descends, it begins to get dark [**Origin:** 1300–1400 Old French *descendre*, from Latin *scandere* **to climb**]

descend from sb/sth *phr. v.* **1 be descended from sb** to be related to someone who lived a long time ago: *His mother is descended from Cherokee Indians.* **2** to have developed from something that existed in the past: **descend from sth** *ideas that descend from ancient Greek philosophy*

descend into sth *phr. v.* if a situation or place descends into a bad situation, the bad situation happens: *The country finally descended into civil war.*

descend on/upon sb/sth *phr. v.* **1** if a large group of people descends on a place, they go there to visit or stay, often when they are not welcome: *Thousands of students will descend on Florida for spring break.* **2** LITERARY if a feeling descends on someone, they begin to feel it

descend to sth *phr. v.* to behave or speak in an impolite way that is not what people expect from you: *The debate descended to name-calling.* | *Other people will gossip, but don't* ***descend to their level*** (=behave as badly as they do).

de·scend·ant /dɪ'sɛndәnt/ *n.* [C] **1** someone who is related to a person who lived a long time ago: *descendants of the first settlers in America* | *Cristobal Colon is* ***a direct descendant of*** (=from one father or mother to the next) *Columbus.* → see also ANCESTOR **2** something that has been developed from something else: +**of** *The restaurant is* ***a direct descendant of*** *a 1950s diner* (=very closely related to).

de·scent /dɪ'sɛnt/ *n.* **1** [C,U] FORMAL the process of going down OPP **ascent**: +**to/toward/into etc.** *the plane's descent into Miami airport* **2** [U] your family origins, especially in relation to the country where your family came from: **of Russian/Chinese/Spanish etc. descent** *My family is of Scottish descent.* **3 descent into sth** a change to a bad condition or state OPP **ascent**: *a young girl's descent into drug abuse* **4** [C] a path or road that goes steeply down OPP **ascent**: +**to/from** *the descent to the river*

de·scram·bler /di'skræmblɚ/ *n.* [C] a machine that can change a radio, television, or telephone message that has been mixed up into a form that can be understood

de·scribe /dɪ'skraɪb/ S2 W1 *v.* [T] **1** to say what something or someone is like by giving details about them: *The folk tale describes the creation of the Earth.* | **describe sb/sth as sth** *Nick's co-workers described him as fun and outgoing.* | **describe sb/sth to sb** *The woman described her attacker to the police.* | **describe how/what/where etc.** *Children were asked to describe what they saw in the painting.* | **describe doing sth** *She described being lifted into the air by the explosion.* ►see THESAURUS box at **call**[1] **2** FORMAL if something describes a shape, it follows the outside line of that shape: *Her hand described a circle in the air.* [**Origin:** 1400–1500 Latin *describere*, from *scribere* **to write**]

de·scrip·tion /dɪ'skrɪpʃәn/ S2 W3 *n.* **1** [C,U] a piece of writing or speech that gives details about what someone or something is like: +**of** *The writer began with a brief description of the area.* | *The article* ***gives a*** *detailed* ***description*** *of the spider's web.* | *"Outdated" would be an* ***accurate description*** *of the building.* | **match/fit a description** *Whitfield fit the general description of the robbery suspect.* **2** [U] ENG. LANG. ARTS a type of writing or speech that is used to describe someone or something → see also EXPOSITION, NARRATION, PERSUASION **3 be beyond description** also **defy description** to be too good, bad, big etc. to be described easily: *The death and destruction was beyond description.* **4 of every description** also **of all descriptions** of all kinds: *The police found drugs of every description.* **5 of any description** of any kind: *I don't like vegetables of any description.* **6 of some description** used when you are not being exact about the type of thing you mean: *You'll need a computer of some description.*

de·scrip·tive /dɪ'skrɪptɪv/ *adj.* **1** giving a description of something in words or pictures: *a descriptive passage in the novel* **2** ENG. LANG. ARTS describing how the words of a language are actually used, rather than saying how they ought to be used → see also PRESCRIPTIVE —**descriptively** *adv.* —**descriptiveness** *n.* [U]

deˌscriptive sta'tistics *n.* [plural] MATH a method of describing data is a simple way, such as finding the average of a group of numbers or putting the information on a GRAPH

de·scry /dɪ'skraɪ/ *v.* [T] LITERARY to notice or see something, especially when it is a long way away

des·e·crate /'dɛsәˌkreɪt/ *v.* [T] to spoil or damage something holy or respected: *The men admitted desecrating over 100 graves.* [**Origin:** 1600–1700 *de-* + *consecrate*] —**desecration** /ˌdɛsә'kreɪʃәn/ *n.* [U]

de·seg·re·gate /di'sɛgrәˌgeɪt/ *v.* [T] POLITICS to end a system in which people of different races are kept separate OPP **segregate**: *the first attempt to desegregate schools* —**desegregation** /diˌsɛgrә'geɪʃәn/ *n.* [U]

de·sen·si·tize /di'sɛnsәˌtaɪz/ *v.* [T] **1** to make someone react less strongly to something by making them become used to it: +**to** *Do war toys desensitize children to the reality of war?* **2** TECHNICAL to make PHOTOGRAPHIC material less sensitive to light —**desensitization** /diˌsɛnsәṭә'zeɪʃәn/ *n.* [U]

des·ert[1] /'dɛzɚt/ S2 W3 *n.* **1** [C,U] EARTH SCIENCE a large area of land where it is always very hot and dry, there are few plants, and there is often a lot of sand: *the Sahara Desert* → see also DESERT ISLAND **2** [C] a place where there is no activity or where nothing interesting happens: *My hometown is a* ***cultural desert*** (=place where there is not much art, film, music etc.). **3 get your just deserts** to be punished in a way that you deserve [**Origin:** 1100–1200 Old French, Late Latin *desertum*, from Latin *desertus*, past participle of *deserere* **to desert**]

desert[2] /dɪ'zɚt/ *v.* **1** [T] to leave someone alone and refuse to help or support them anymore SYN **abandon**: *Paul feels that his father deserted him after the divorce.* **2** [I] to leave the military without permission: *U.S. officials say 1,000 enemy soldiers have deserted.* **3** [T] to leave a place so that it is completely empty SYN **abandon**: *The house had been deserted by* *its owners.* **4** [T] if a feeling or quality deserts you, you do not have it anymore, especially at a time when you need it: *Mike's confidence seemed to have deserted him.*

de·sert·ed /dɪˈzɚtɪd/ *adj.* empty because people have left SYN **abandoned**: *Now the steel mill stands completely deserted.* | *a deserted street corner*

de·sert·er /dɪˈzɚtɚ/ *n.* [C] a soldier who leaves the military without permission

de·sert·i·fi·ca·tion /dɪˌzɚtəfəˈkeɪʃən/ *n.* [U] a process in which land that is able to produce crops gradually becomes a desert

de·ser·tion /dɪˈzɚʃən/ *n.* **1** [C,U] the act of leaving the military without permission: *a Marine charged with desertion* **2** [U] LAW the act of leaving your wife or husband because you do not want to live with them anymore

ˌdesert ˈisland *n.* [C] a small tropical island that is far away from other places and has no people living on it

ˌdesert ˈscrub *n.* [U] EARTH SCIENCE low bushes and trees that grow in a desert and need very little water in order to stay alive

de·serve /dɪˈzɚv/ S3 W3 *v.* [T] **1** to have earned something by good or bad actions or behavior: *What has he done to deserve this punishment?* | **deserve to do sth** *We didn't really deserve to win.* | *I worked hard for this award, and I* ***deserve it.*** | *He should definitely be in prison. He's just* ***getting what he deserves.*** | *Homeless kids certainly* ***deserve better*** (=deserve nicer treatment). | **deserve a rest/break/drink etc.** *Come on, we've been working hard. We deserve a break.* | **sb richly/thorougly/fully deserves sth** (=someone completely deserves what they are getting) | *Paula* ***deserves a special mention*** *for all her help* (=deserves to be specially thanked). **2** if a suggestion, idea, or plan deserves consideration, attention etc., it is good enough to be considered, paid attention to etc.: *The recommendations in the report certainly deserve further consideration.* **3** used when someone has not been given a reason, answer, or apology for something, to say that they should be given one: *You deserve an apology for the way you were treated.* | *I think I* ***deserve to know*** *exactly what happened to my husband.* **4 sb deserves a medal** HUMOROUS used to say that you admire the way someone has dealt with a difficult situation: *His wife deserves a medal for her patience.* [**Origin:** 1200–1300 Old French, Latin *deservire* **to serve very keenly**, from *servire* **to serve**] → see also **one good turn deserves another** at TURN[2] (16)

de·served /dɪˈzɚvd/ *adj.* earned because of good or bad behavior, skill, work etc.: *his* ***well-deserved*** *reputation as an outstanding athlete*

de·serv·ed·ly /dɪˈzɚvɪdli/ *adv.* **1 deservedly famous/successful/celebrated etc.** famous, successful, celebrated etc. in a way that is right or deserved: *a deservedly popular restaurant* **2 ...(and) deservedly so** used to say that you agree that something is right and deserved: *The play won the Pulitzer Prize for drama, and deservedly so.*

de·serv·ing /dɪˈzɚvɪŋ/ *adj.* **1** [usually before noun] needing help and support, especially financial support: *The state is denying benefits to deserving children.* **2 be deserving of sth** FORMAL to deserve something: *He is certainly deserving of the Heisman Trophy.*

de·sex·u·al·ize /diˈsɛkʃuəˌlaɪz/ *v.* [T] to remove the sexual quality from something —**desexualization** /diˌsɛkʃuələˈzeɪʃən/ *n.* [C,U]

dés·ha·bil·lé /ˌdeɪzæbiˈeɪ/ also **dishabille** *n.* [U] LITERARY or HUMOROUS the state of being only partly dressed, used especially of a woman

des·ic·cant /ˈdɛsɪkənt/ *n.* [C,U] CHEMISTRY a substance that takes water from the air so that other things stay dry

des·ic·cate /ˈdɛsɪˌkeɪt/ *v.* [T] FORMAL to remove all the water from something —**desiccated** *adj.* —**desiccation** /ˌdɛsɪˈkeɪʃən/ *n.* [U]

de·sid·er·a·tum /dɪˌsɪdəˈrɑtəm, -ˈreɪ-/ *n. plural* **desiderata** /-tə/ [C] LITERARY something that is wanted or needed

de·sign[1] /dɪˈzaɪn/ Ac S2 W2 *n.*
1 PATTERN [C] a style or pattern used for decorating something: *Native American designs* | *The ceiling had a hand-painted floral design.* ►see THESAURUS box at **pattern**[1]
2 ARRANGEMENT OF PARTS [C,U] the way that something is made, so that it works a particular way or has a particular appearance: *The car's design has been greatly improved.* | **+of** *There were changes in the designs of several of the machines.* | *dangerous* ***design faults*** *in the aircraft* | *An important* ***design feature*** *is the shape of the handle.*
3 DRAWINGS [C] drawings that show what something will look like when it is made: **+for** *the designs for the new stadium*
4 PROCESS/STUDY [U] the study or process of drawing something to show what it will look like when it is made: *the design of new products* | *She is studying architecture and design.*
5 INTENTION [C,U] a plan that someone has in their mind: *The law firm is all-female, though not* ***by design*** (=intentionally).
6 have designs on sth to want something for yourself and be planning how to get it, especially if it will bring you money: *Several developers have designs on the property.*
7 have designs on sb to want a sexual relationship with someone

design[2] Ac S2 W1 *v.* **1** [I,T] to make a drawing or plan of something to show how it will be made and how it will look and work: *The office complex was designed by Mitchell Benjamin.* | **well-/badly-/specially-designed etc.** *a cheap well-designed subway system* **2** [T usually passive] to plan or develop something for a specific purpose: **design sth to do sth** *These exercises are designed to develop and strengthen muscles.* | **be designed for sth** *The kitchen is designed for two cooks.* | **be designed as sth** *The building was originally designed as a school.* [**Origin:** 1300–1400 French *désigner*, from Latin *designare*, from *signare* **to mark**] → see also DESIGNER[1]

des·ig·nate[1] /ˈdɛzɪɡˌneɪt/ *v.* [T usually passive] **1** to choose someone or something for a particular job or purpose: **designate sth for sth** *Funds were designated for projects in low-income areas.* | **designate sb to do sth** *She has been designated to take over the position of treasurer.* | **designate sth (as) sth** *The area has been designated a national park.* **2** to show or mean something, especially by using a special name or sign: *Buildings are designated by red squares on the map.*

des·ig·nate[2] /ˈdɛzɪɡnət, -ˌneɪt/ *adj.* [only after noun] FORMAL a word used after the name of an official job showing that someone has been chosen for that job but has not yet officially started work: *the ambassador designate*

ˌdesignated ˈdriver *n.* [C] someone who agrees to not drink alcohol when they go out to a party, bar etc., so that they can drive their friends home

ˌdesignated ˈhitter *n.* [C] **1** a baseball player who replaces the PITCHER when it is the PITCHER's turn to hit the ball **2** INFORMAL someone who does a job for someone else, especially in politics or business

des·ig·na·tion /ˌdɛzɪɡˈneɪʃən/ *n.* **1** [U] the act of choosing someone or something for a particular purpose, or of giving them a particular description: *the designation of King's birthday as a national holiday* **2** [C] FORMAL a description or title that someone or something is given

de·sign·er[1] /dɪˈzaɪnɚ/ Ac *n.* [C] someone whose job is to make plans or patterns for clothes, furniture, equipment etc.: *I recommend hiring a professional designer.* | *a software designer*

designer[2] Ac *adj.* [only before noun] made by a well-known and fashionable designer: *designer jeans* ►see THESAURUS box at **fashionable**

ˈdesigner ˌdrug *n.* [C] an drug that has been created

for a specific illegal purpose, for example to help users avoid being caught

de·sign·ing /dɪˈzaɪnɪŋ/ Ac *adj.* [only before noun] someone who is designing tries to deceive people in order to get what they want

de·sir·a·ble /dɪˈzaɪrəbəl/ *adj.* FORMAL **1** something that is desirable has qualities that make you want it OPP **undesirable**: *the city's most desirable neighborhoods* | *Ellman's goal is* ***highly desirable*** (=very desirable), *but not realistic.* | **it is desirable that** *It is desirable that the candidate have relevant experience.* **2** someone who is desirable is sexually attractive —**desirably** *adv.* —**desirability** /dɪˌzaɪrəˈbɪləṭi/ *n.* [U]

D

de·sire¹ /dɪˈzaɪɚ/ S3 W2 *n.* **1** [C,U] a strong hope or wish: **+for** *a teenagers' desire for independence* | **desire to do sth** *a child's strong desire to learn to read* | **desire that** *It was Mr. Hertzog's desire that there be no funeral service.* | *I* ***have no desire to*** (=used to emphasize that you do not want to do something) *work in a restaurant.* | *All my life I've had* ***a burning desire*** (=a very strong desire) *to travel.* | *If either country* ***expresses a desire*** *for peace, this represents progress.* **2** [U + for] FORMAL a strong wish to have sex with someone

desire² W3 *v.* [T not in progressive] **1** FORMAL to want or hope for something very much: *The hotel provides everything you could desire.* | *Add lemon juice* ***if desired*** (=if you want to). **2** FORMAL to want to have sex with someone [**Origin:** 1200–1300 Old French *desirer*, from Latin *desiderare*] —**desired** *adj.* → see also **leave something/a lot/much to be desired** at LEAVE¹ (22)

de·sir·ous /dɪˈzaɪrəs/ *adj.* [+ of] FORMAL wanting something very much

de·sist /dɪˈzɪst, dɪˈsɪst/ *v.* [I] FORMAL to stop doing something: **+from** *The government urged the rebels to desist from their terrorist actions.* → see also **cease and desist** at CEASE¹ (2)

desk /dɛsk/ S1 W2 *n.* [C] **1** a piece of furniture like a table, usually with drawers in it, that you sit at to write and work ►see THESAURUS box at **office** **2** a place where you can get information or use a particular service in a hotel, airport, hospital etc.: *A nurse was seated at the reception desk.* | *the* ***check-in desk*** *at the airport* | *Ask the woman at* ***the front desk.*** **3** an office that deals with a particular subject, especially in newspapers or television: *Lloyd is running the sports desk.* [**Origin:** 1300–1400 Medieval Latin *desca*, from Latin *discus* **dish, disk**]

ˈdesk clerk *n.* [C] someone who works at the main desk in a hotel

de·skill /ˌdiˈskɪl/ *v.* [T] to remove or reduce the need for skill in a job, usually by changing to machinery

ˈdesk job *n.* [C] a job that involves working mostly at a desk in an office

ˈdesk ˌjockey *n.* [C] INFORMAL, HUMOROUS someone who works at a desk instead of doing something that involves physical activity

desk·top /ˈdɛsktɑp/ *n.* [C] **1** COMPUTERS the main area on a computer screen where you can find the ICONS that represent PROGRAMS, and where you can do things to manage the information on the computer: **on the/sb's desktop** *Right click on your desktop.* **2** the top surface of a desk

ˌdesktop comˈputer *n.* [C] a computer that is small enough to be used on a desk → see also LAPTOP

ˌdesktop ˈpublishing *n.* [C] the work of producing magazines, books, signs etc. with a desktop computer

Des Moines /dəˈmɔɪn/ the capital city of the U.S. state of Iowa

des·o·late¹ /ˈdɛsəlɪt/ *adj.* **1** a place that is desolate is empty and looks sad because there are no people there and not much activity: *a desolate stretch of highway* **2** someone who is desolate feels very sad and lonely [**Origin:** 1300–1400 Latin *desolatus*, from *solus* **alone**] —**desolately** *adv.* —**desolation** /ˌdɛsəˈleɪʃən/ *n.* [U]

des·o·late² /ˈdɛsəˌleɪt/ *v.* [T usually passive] LITERARY **1** to make someone feel very sad and lonely **2** to cause so much damage to a place that it is almost completely destroyed: *an economically desolated town*

de So·to, Her·nan·do /dɪˈsoʊtoʊ, hɚˈnɑndoʊ/ (?1500–1542) a Spanish EXPLORER who discovered the Mississippi River

de·spair¹ /dɪˈspɛr/ *n.* [U] **1** a feeling that you have no hope at all: *the* ***deep despair*** *of the dead boy's family* | *Snyder hanged himself* ***in despair*** *over problems in his marriage.* | ***To the despair of*** *15,000 workers, it was announced that eight factories will close.* **2 be the despair of sb** OLD-FASHIONED to make someone feel very worried, upset, or unhappy, especially by your bad behavior

despair² *v.* [I] FORMAL to feel that there is no hope at all because of something bad that is happening: *Despite his illness, Ron never despaired.* | **despair of (doing) sth** *By the end of the day, I despaired of ever learning to ski.* | **despair at sb/sth** *I despair at my students attempts to write.* [**Origin:** 1200–1300 Old French *desperer*, from Latin *desperare*, from *sperare* **to hope**]

de·spair·ing /dɪˈspɛrɪŋ/ *adj.* showing a feeling of despair: *a despairing look* —**despairingly** *adv.*

des·per·a·do /ˌdɛspəˈrɑdoʊ/ *n. plural* **desperadoes** or **desperados** [C] OLD-FASHIONED a violent criminal who is not afraid of danger

des·per·ate /ˈdɛsprɪt, -pərɪt/ *adj.* **1** willing to do anything to change a very bad situation, and not caring about danger: *I had no money left and was desperate.* | *the missing teenager's desperate parents* | **be desperate to do sth** *Many people were desperate to leave the country.* **2** needing or wanting something very much: **+for** *Desperate for ideas, Hollywood often recycles movie plots.* | *The Red Cross said it was* ***in desperate need*** *of blood.* **3** a desperate situation is very bad or serious: *a desperate shortage of doctors* | *The schools are* ***in desperate need of*** *good teachers.* **4** a desperate action is something that you only do because you are in a very bad situation: **desperate attempt/bid/effort** *The prisoners made a desperate atttempt to escape.* | *The country is* ***taking desperate measures*** (=taking desperate actions) *to improve the economy.*

des·per·ate·ly /ˈdɛsprɪtli/ *adv.* **1** in a way that shows you realize the situation is serious: *We're desperately trying to avoid laying off people.* **2** in an extremely strong way: *Lori wanted desperately to have a child.* | *Steady winter rains are* ***desperately needed*** *to bring the city water supply back to normal.*

des·per·a·tion /ˌdɛspəˈreɪʃən/ *n.* [U] a strong feeling that you will do anything to change a very bad situation: *a look of desperation* | *Larson resorted to high-risk investments* ***out of desperation*** (=because of desperation). | ***In desperation*** (=feeling desperation), *the boy grabbed at his rescuer's hands.*

de·spic·a·ble /dɪˈspɪkəbəl/ *adj.* extremely bad, immoral, or cruel: *Abusing a child is a despicable act.* [**Origin:** 1500–1600 Late Latin *despicabilis*, from Latin *despicari* **to look down on**] —**despicably** *adv.*

de·spise /dɪˈspaɪz/ *v.* [T not in progressive] to dislike someone or something very much: *I despised him and everything he did.* [**Origin:** 1200–1300 Old French *despire*, from Latin *despicere* **to look down on**]

de·spite /dɪˈspaɪt/ Ac W1 *prep.* **1** used to say that something happens or is true even though something else might have prevented it SYN **in spite of**: *Despite international pressure, progress has slowed in the peace talks.* | *She was hired* ***despite the fact that*** *she had no background in science.* **2 despite yourself** if you do something despite yourself, you do it although you did not intend to: *Jessie realized that, despite herself, she cared about Edward.*

WORD CHOICE **despite, in spite of, although**

• **Despite** and **in spite of** (prepositions) can only be followed by a noun or gerund: *Marla's a good worker, despite her problems at home.* | *Despite being one of*

the largest cities in the world, Mexico City is relatively safe.
• Unlike **although** (a conjunction), **despite** and **in spite of** cannot introduce a clause that has a finite verb such as "was." Compare: *Despite owning two cars, he can't drive.* | *In spite of owning two cars, he can't drive.* | *Although he owns two cars, he can't drive.*

de·spoil /dɪˈspɔɪl/ *v.* [T] LITERARY **1** to make a place much less attractive by removing or damaging things: *The sandy beaches were despoiled by an oil spill.* **2** to steal from a place or people using force, especially in a war

de·spond·ent /dɪˈspɑndənt/ *adj.* unhappy and without hope SYN **depressed**: **+about/over** *Her husband had been despondent about his cancer.* [**Origin:** 1600–1700 Latin *despondere* **to give up, lose hope**, from *spondere* **to promise**] —**despondency** *n.* [U] —**despondently** *adv.*

des·pot /ˈdɛspət, -pɑt/ *n.* [C] someone such as a ruler who uses power in a cruel and unfair way SYN **tyrant** [**Origin:** 1500–1600 Old French *despote*, from Greek *despotes* **lord**] —**despotic** /dɛˈspɑtɪk, dɪ-/ *adj.* —**despotically** /-kli/ *adv.*

des·pot·ism /ˈdɛspəˌtɪzəm/ *n.* [U] POLITICS rule by a despot

des·sert /dɪˈzɚt/ S2 *n.* [C,U] sweet food served after the main part of a meal: *What's* ***for dessert****, Mom?* [**Origin:** 1500–1600 French *desservir* **to clear the table**, from *servir* **to serve**]

des'sert wine *n.* [C,U] a sweet wine served with dessert

de·sta·bi·lize /diˈsteɪbəˌlaɪz/ *v.* [T] **1** to make something such as a government or ECONOMY weaker and more likely to fail: *an attempt to destabilize the government* **2** to make something physically unsteady or weak: *The train wreck destabilized a gas pipeline that later exploded.* **3** CHEMISTRY to make a chemical separate into simpler ELEMENTS —**destabilization** /diˌsteɪbələˈzeɪʃən/ *n.* [U]

des·ti·na·tion /ˌdɛstəˈneɪʃən/ *n.* [C] the place that someone or something is going to: **sb's destination** *Allow plenty of time to get to your destination.* | *Maui is a popular* ***tourist destination****.* | *The ship stops in Vancouver before going to its* ***final destination****.*

des·tined /ˈdɛstənd/ *adj.* **1** [not before noun] seeming certain to happen at some time in the future: **+for** *She seemed destined for stardom.* | **be destined to do sth** *It was a book he felt destined to write.* **2 (be) destined for sth** to be traveling or taken to a particular place: *exports destined for Europe*

des·ti·ny /ˈdɛstəni/ *n. plural* **destinies** **1** [C usually singular] the things that will happen to someone in the future, especially those that cannot be changed or controlled SYN **fate**: **sb's destiny** *Was it her destiny to marry Peter?* | **have control of/over your own destiny** also **control your (own) destiny** *I wanted to have my own business, control my own destiny.* **2** [U] the power that some people believe decides what will happen to them in the future SYN **fate** [**Origin:** 1300–1400 Old French *destinee*, from Latin *destinare* **to fasten, fix**]

des·ti·tute /ˈdɛstəˌtut/ *adj.* **1** having no money, no food, no place to live etc. SYN **poverty-stricken**: *The floods left many people destitute.* ►see THESAURUS box at **poor** **2 be destitute of sth** LITERARY to be completely without something SYN **devoid of**: *a man destitute of compassion* [**Origin:** 1300–1400 Latin *destitutus*, past participle of *destituere* **to set down, leave**] —**destitution** /ˌdɛstəˈtuʃən/ *n.* [U]

de·stroy /dɪˈstrɔɪ/ S2 W2 *v.* **destroys**, **destroyed**, **destroying** [T] **1** to damage something so badly that it does not exist anymore or cannot be used or repaired SYN **demolish**: *Pollution may destroy the 17th-century shrine.* | *An accident destroyed her ballet career.* | **completely/totally/utterly destroy** *Such an explosion would utterly destroy the entire city.*

THESAURUS

devastate to damage a place very badly or destroy many things in it: *an area devastated by years of war*
flatten to destroy a building or town by knocking it down, bombing it etc.: *The tornado flattened parts of the city.*
demolish to completely destroy a building, deliberately or by accident: *The land was put back to its natural state, which meant demolishing around 150 buildings.*
reduce something to ruins/rubble/ashes to destroy something, especially a building or town, completely: *Dresden was reduced to rubble in the bombings.*
wreck to damage something very badly, often so badly that it cannot be repaired or the harm cannot be put right: *Not oiling the machine will eventually wreck it.*
ruin to spoil something completely: *Fungus may ruin the crop.*

2 destroy sb to ruin someone's life completely, so that they have no hope for the future: *The drugs and alcohol eventually destroyed him.* **3** INFORMAL to defeat an opponent easily or by a large number of points SYN **clobber**: *The Bears destroyed the Detroit Lions, 35–3.* **4** to kill an animal, especially because it is sick or dangerous [**Origin:** 1100–1200 Old French *destruire*, from Latin *destruere*, from *struere* **to build**] → see also DESTRUCTION, **search-and-destroy mission/operation** at SEARCH[2] (7)

de·stroy·er /dɪˈstrɔɪɚ/ *n.* [C] **1** a small fast military ship with guns ►see THESAURUS box at **ship**[1] **2** someone or something that destroys things or people

de·struc·tion /dɪˈstrʌkʃən/ *n.* [U] **1** the act or process of destroying something or of being destroyed: *measures to protect the ozone layer from destruction* | **+of** *Belarus agreed to the destruction of its nuclear weapons.* **2** the damage caused by something SYN **devastation**: *the destruction caused by the earthquake* | *The storms brought* ***death and destruction*** *to the shanty towns.* → see also DESTROY, **weapons of mass destruction** at WEAPON (1)

de·struc·tive /dɪˈstrʌktɪv/ *adj.* causing damage to people or things: *Jealousy is a very destructive emotion.* | *the hurricane's destructive force* —**destructively** *adv.* —**destructiveness** *n.* [U]

deˌstructive interˈference *n.* [U] PHYSICS the combination of two WAVES of energy that are out of PHASE, which results in a wave that is weaker than either of the original ones → see also CONSTRUCTIVE INTERFERENCE

des·ul·to·ry /ˈdɛsəlˌtɔri/ *adj.* FORMAL done without any particular plan or purpose: *a desultory conversation*

Det. the written abbreviation of DETECTIVE

de·tach /dɪˈtætʃ/ *v.* [I,T] **1** if you detach something or if it detaches, it becomes separated from the thing that it was attached to OPP **attach**: *Please detach and fill out the application form.* | **+from** *The skis should detach from the boots if you fall.* | **detach sth from sth** *You can detach the hood from the jacket.* **2 detach yourself (from sb/sth) a)** to try to be less involved with or less concerned about someone or something: *Doctors have to be able to detach themselves from their feelings.* **b)** if you detach yourself from a person or place, you walk away from them: *Her sister detached herself from the group, and came over to her.* [**Origin:** 1600–1700 French *détacher*, from Old French *destachier*, from *atachier* **to attach**]

de·tach·a·ble /dɪˈtætʃəbəl/ *adj.* able to be removed and put back: *The coat has a detachable lining.*

de·tached /dɪˈtætʃt/ *adj.* **1** not reacting to or becoming involved in something in an emotional way: *He sang in a detached passionless way.* | **+from** *He felt strangely detached from the scene.* ►see THESAURUS box at **matter-of-fact** **2** a detached house or garage is not connected to another building on any side **3** no longer attached: *a detached retina*

de·tach·ment /dɪˈtætʃmənt/ *n.* **1** [U] the state of not reacting to or being involved in something in an emotional way: *Doctors need to have some degree of **emotional detachment**.* | **+from** *After taking the drug, he felt a **sense of detachment** from what was happening around him.* **2** [C] a group of soldiers who are sent away from the main group to do a special job **3** [U] the state of being separated from something: **+of** *detachment of the retina*

detail

de·tail¹ /ˈditeɪl, dɪˈteɪl/ S2 W2 *n.* **1** [C,U] a single feature, fact, or piece of information about something: **+of** *Barr would not discuss details of the research.* | *Demand that the house plans show everything, **down to the last detail*** (=completely). | **a small/minor detail** *I need to clear up some minor details in the contract.* **2** [U] all the separate features and pieces of information about something: *Dr. Blount described the process **in detail*** (=using a lot of details). | *She discussed the plan **in great detail**.* | *McDougal was reluctant to **go into detail*** (=give a lot of details) *about the company's earnings.* | *Her hard work and **attention to detail** helped make the store a success.* **3 details** [plural] information that helps to complete what you know about something SYN **particulars**: **+about** *The doctor asked for details about my eating habits.* | **+of** *Applicants should **provide details** of previous jobs.* | *It wasn't until 1945 that the **full details** were revealed.* | *For **further details**, please consult your tax adviser.* **4** [singular, U] TECHNICAL a specific duty that is given to a soldier, or the person or group who have that duty: *a small security detail* [**Origin:** 1600–1700 French *détail*, from Old French *detail* **piece cut off**]

detail² W3 *v.* [T] **1** to list things or give all the facts or information about something: *The story detailed Tyson's charitable donations.* **2** to clean a car very thoroughly, inside and out **3 detail sb to (do) sth** to officially order someone, especially soldiers, to do a particular job: *Vance, you're detailed to the night watch.*

de·tailed /dɪˈteɪld, ˈditeɪld/ *adj.* **1** containing or using a lot of information or details: *detailed lesson plans* | **detailed description/account/instructions etc.** *a detailed analysis of the study's results* **2** having decorations or a lot of small features that are difficult to produce: *beautifully detailed chairs*

de·tail·ing /ˈditeɪlɪŋ/ *n.* [U] **1** decorations that are added to something such as a car or piece of clothing **2** the process of cleaning a car very thoroughly, inside and out

de·tain /dɪˈteɪn/ *v.* [T] **1** to officially prevent someone from leaving a place: *Police detained two suspects for questioning.* **2** to stop someone from leaving a place as soon as they expected SYN **delay**: *She was detained in Washington on urgent business.* —**detainment** *n.* [U]

de·tain·ee /diˌteɪˈni/ *n.* [C] FORMAL someone who is officially kept in a prison, usually because of their political views

de·tan·gle /ˌdiˈtæŋgəl/ *v.* [T] to remove the knots in hair

de·tect /dɪˈtɛkt/ Ac *v.* [T] to notice or discover something, especially something that is not easy to see, hear etc. SYN **discover**: *Many forms of cancer can be cured if detected early.* | *Most people couldn't detect any difference in flavor.* | **difficult/hard/easy etc. to detect** *It was difficult to detect any pattern in the evidence.* [**Origin:** 1400–1500 Latin *detectus*, past participle of *detegere* **to uncover**] —**detectable** *adj.*

de·tec·tion /dɪˈtɛkʃən/ Ac *n.* [U] the process of detecting, or the fact of being detected: **+of** ***Early detection** of the cancer is vital.* | **avoid/escape/evade detection** *By flying low, the plane avoided detection by enemy radar.*

de·tec·tive /dɪˈtɛktɪv/ Ac *n.* [C] **1** a police officer whose job is to discover information about crimes and catch criminals → see also STORE DETECTIVE ▶ see THESAURUS box at **police¹** **2** someone who is paid to discover information about someone or something: *a private detective* **3 detective work** efforts to discover information, find out how something works, answer a difficult question etc.: *It took some detective work to discover the cause of the problem.* **4 detective story/novel etc.** a story, novel etc. about a crime, often a murder, and a detective who tries to find out who did it

de·tect·or /dɪˈtɛktɚ/ Ac *n.* [C] a machine or piece of equipment that finds or measures something: *the **metal detector** at the airport* → see also LIE DETECTOR, SMOKE DETECTOR

dé·tente, detente /deɪˈtɑnt/ *n.* [U] a time or situation in which two countries that are not friendly toward each other agree to behave in a more friendly way: *During a period of détente between the U.S. and the U.S.S.R. two of their spacecraft met in space.*

de·ten·tion /dɪˈtɛnʃən/ *n.* [C,U] **1** the state of being kept in prison, or the time someone is kept in prison: *He was released without charge after five days' detention.* | *500 men remain **in detention**.* **2** a punishment in which children who have behaved badly are forced to stay at school for a short time after the others have gone home: *I **got detention** for talking in class.* | *Those two guys are always **in detention**.*

deˈtention camp *n.* [C] a place where a lot of military prisoners, political prisoners, REFUGEES etc. are kept by a government

deˈtention ˌcenter *n.* [C] a prison, often for a particular type of person

de·ter /dɪˈtɚ/ *v.* **deterred, deterring** [T] to stop something happening, or to stop someone from doing something, by making it seem difficult or threatening people with punishment: *It is not clear whether the death penalty deters crime.* | **deter sb from doing sth** *The study may have deterred women from getting regular checkups.* [**Origin:** 1500–1600 Latin *deterrere*, from *terrere* **to frighten**] → see also DETERRENT

de·ter·gent /dɪˈtɚdʒənt/ *n.* [C,U] a liquid or powder similar to soap, used for washing clothes, dishes etc. [**Origin:** 1600–1700 French *détergent*, from Latin *tergere* **to clean by rubbing**]

de·te·ri·o·rate /dɪˈtɪriəˌreɪt/ *v.* [I] **1** to become worse SYN **worsen**: *Ellen's health has deteriorated rapidly.* | *our deteriorating economy* **2 deteriorate into sth** to develop into a bad situation: *The argument deteriorated into a fistfight.* [**Origin:** 1500–1600 Late Latin *deteriorare*, from Latin *deterior* **worse**] —**deterioration** /dɪˌtɪriəˈreɪʃən/ *n.* [U]

de·ter·mi·nant /dɪˈtɚmɪnənt/ *n.* **1** [C +of] FORMAL something that strongly influences what you do or how you behave **2** [C] MATH a value calculated from a set of numbers in a SQUARE MATRIX. For a 2 x 2 matrix, where a and b are directly above c and d, the determinant is calculated by finding the difference between the PRODUCTS of the DIAGONAL values (ad and bc). Determinants are used to solve sets of EQUATIONS at the same time.

de·ter·mi·nate /dɪˈtɚmənɪt/ *adj.* FORMAL strictly controlled or limited

de·ter·mi·na·tion /dɪˌtɚməˈneɪʃən/ *n.* **1** [U] the quality of trying to do something even when it is difficult: *Success comes from hard work and* *determination.* | **determination to do sth** *She shows great* ***determination*** *to learn English.* | *Hansen has vision and* ***dogged*** (=strong) ***determination.*** **2** [C,U] FORMAL the act of deciding something officially: +**of** *the determination of government policy* | *He had not yet* ***made a determination on*** *whether to keep the U.S. embassy open.* **3** [C] TECHNICAL the act of finding the exact level, amount, or causes of something: +**of** *accurate determination of the temperature* | *The inquiry is trying to* ***make a*** *final* ***determination of*** *what caused the accident.* → see also SELF-DETERMINATION

de·ter·mine /dɪ'tɚmɪn/ S2 W1 *v.* [T] **1** to find out the facts about something SYN **establish**: *Investigators are trying to determine the cause of the fire.* | **determine how/what/who etc.** *Using sonar, they determined exactly where the ship had sunk.* | **determine that** *Experts have determined that the signature was forged.* **2** to officially decide something: *The date of the court case is yet to be determined.* | **determine how/what/who etc.** *The tests will help the doctors determine what treatment to use.* **3** if something determines something else, it directly influences or decides it: *Your votes will determine the outcome of the election.* | **determine how/whether/what etc.** *How hard the swimmers work now will determine how they perform in the Olympics.* ►see THESAURUS box at **decide** **4 determine to do sth** FORMAL to decide to do something, even if it is difficult or not nice: *He determined to work harder.* [**Origin:** 1300–1400 Old French *determiner*, from Latin *terminus* **edge, limit**]

de·ter·mined /dɪ'tɚmɪnd/ W3 *adj.* having or showing a strong desire to do something even if it is difficult SYN **resolute**: *Gwen is a very determined woman.* | **determined to do sth** *She was determined to win.* | **determined (that)** *I was determined that it would never happen again.* | *He* ***made a determined effort*** *to give up smoking.*

de·ter·min·er /dɪ'tɚmənɚ/ *n.* [C] ENG. LANG. ARTS in grammar, a word that is used before a noun in order to show which thing you mean. In the phrases "the car" and "some cars," "the" and "some" are determiners.

de·ter·min·ism /dɪ'tɚmə,nɪzəm/ *n.* [U] the belief that what you do and what happens to you are caused by things that you cannot control —**deterministic** /dɪ,tɚmə'nɪstɪk/ *adj.*

de·ter·rence /dɪ'tɚəns/ *n.* [U] **1** a situation in which a country continues to have a strong army or powerful weapons in order to prevent a military attack from another country, or to make a military attack less likely: *nuclear deterrence* **2** FORMAL the act of stopping people from doing something bad by making them realize it will be difficult or they will be punished: *The death penalty for murder is a combination of punishment and deterrence.*

de·ter·rent /dɪ'tɚənt/ *n.* [C] **1** something that makes someone less likely to do something, by making them realize it will be difficult or have bad results: **serve/act as a deterrent** *The small fines do not act as much of a deterrent.* | +**to** *Car alarms can be an effective deterrent to burglars.* | *the* ***deterrent effect*** *of prison sentences* **2 nuclear deterrent** NUCLEAR weapons that a country has, in order to prevent other countries from attacking it

de·test /dɪ'tɛst/ *v.* [T not in progressive] FORMAL to hate someone or something very much SYN **loathe**: *The other girls detested her.* | *He detested the smell of cigarettes.* [**Origin:** 1400–1500 Latin *detestari*, from *testis* **one who gives information against someone**] —**detestation** /,ditɛs'teɪʃən/ *n.* [U]

de·test·a·ble /dɪ'tɛstəbəl/ *adj.* FORMAL very bad, and deserving to be criticized or hated —**detestably** *adv.*

de·throne /di'θroʊn/ *v.* [T] **1** to remove or defeat someone or something from a position of authority or importance: *an attempt to dethrone the Republican senator* | *Oil dethroned coffee as the country's leading export.* **2** to remove a king or queen from power SYN **depose** —**dethronement** *n.* [U]

det·o·nate /'dɛt̚n,eɪt, -t̬ə,neɪt/ *v.* [I,T] to explode, or to make something explode [**Origin:** 1700–1800 Latin *detonare*, from *tonare* **to thunder**]

det·o·na·tion /,dɛt̚n'eɪʃən, -t̬ə'neɪ-/ *n.* [C,U] an explosion, or the action of making a bomb explode

det·o·na·tor /'dɛt̚n,eɪt̬ɚ, -t̬ə,neɪt̬ɚ/ *n.* [C] a small object that is used to make a bomb explode

de·tour¹ /'ditʊr/ *n.* [C] **1** a way of going from one place to another that is longer than the usual way: *a scenic detour* | **make/take a detour** *We took a detour to avoid the street repairs.* **2** a development or way of doing something that is different from what you planned or expected: *It was a complete detour from anything he had done before.*

detour² *v.* [I] to make a detour

de·tox¹ /'ditɑks/ *n.* [U] INFORMAL a special treatment to help people stop drinking alcohol or taking drugs SYN **rehab**: *She spent a month* ***in detox.***

de·tox² /di'tɑks/ *v.* [I,T] INFORMAL **1** if someone detoxes, they are given special treatment to help them stop drinking alcohol or taking drugs **2** to not eat particular foods or only drink special liquids for a period of time, because you think it will remove harmful substances from your body

de·tox·i·fi·ca·tion /di,tɑksəfə'keɪʃən/ *n.* [U] **1** the process of removing harmful chemicals or poison from something **2** detox: *a detoxification program* —**detoxify** /di'tɑksə,faɪ/ *v.* [T]

de·tract /dɪ'trækt/ *v.* [I] to make something seem less good than it really is: +**from** *The billboards detract from the city's beauty.* —**detraction** /dɪ'trækʃən/ *n.* [C,U]

de·trac·tor /dɪ'træktɚ/ *n.* [C] someone who publicly criticizes someone or something: *Even the President's detractors admit the decision was right.*

det·ri·ment /'dɛtrəmənt/ *n.* [U] FORMAL harm or damage that is done to something: *Americans spend too much time at work,* ***to the detriment of*** *their families.* [**Origin:** 1400–1500 Latin *detrimentum*, from *deterere* **to rub away**]

det·ri·men·tal /,dɛtrə'mɛntl◂ / *adj.* FORMAL causing harm or damage SYN **harmful**: +**to** *Smoking is detrimental to your health.* —**detrimentally** *adv.*

de·tri·ti·vore /dɪ'traɪt̬ə,vɔr/ *n.* [C] BIOLOGY a living thing that feeds on the bodies of dead animals or plants. Detritivores, such as a BACTERIA or EARTHWORMS, help to improve the quality of soil. → see also DECOMPOSER

de·tri·tus /dɪ'traɪt̬əs/ *n.* [U] **1** FORMAL small pieces of waste that remain after something has been broken up or used → see also DEBRIS **2** BIOLOGY very small pieces of the decaying bodies of dead animals, plants etc.

De·troit /dɪ'trɔɪt/ a city in the U.S. state of Michigan

deuce /dus/ *n.* **1** [C] a playing card with the number two on it **2** [U] the situation in tennis when both players have 40 points, after which one of the players must win two more points to win the game **3 a deuce of a time/job etc.** OLD-FASHIONED a very difficult or bad time, job etc. [**Origin:** 1400–1500 Old French *deus* **two**, from Latin *duos*]

deu·te·ri·um /du'tɪriəm/ *n.* [U] CHEMISTRY a type of HYDROGEN that is twice as heavy as normal hydrogen

Deu·ter·on·o·my /,dut̬ə'rɑnəmi/ a book in the Old Testament of the Christian Bible

Deut·sch·mark /'dɔɪtʃmɑrk/ *n.* [C] the standard unit of money used in Germany before the EURO SYN **mark**

de·val·ue /di'vælyu/ *v.* **1** [I,T] ECONOMICS to reduce the value of a country's money, especially in relation to the value of another country's money: *The ruble has been devalued.* **2** [T] to make someone or something seem less important or valuable: *History has tended to devalue the contributions of women.* —**devaluation** /di,vælyu'eɪʃən/ *n.* [C,U]

dev·as·tate /'dɛvə,steɪt/ *v.* [T] **1** to make someone

D

feel extremely shocked and sad: *Her mother's early death from cancer devastated Lianne.* **2** to damage something very badly, or to destroy something completely: *Bombing raids devastated the city of Dresden.* ►see THESAURUS box at **destroy** [**Origin:** 1600–1700 Latin *devastare*, from *vastare* **to lay waste, destroy**] —**devastated** *adj.*

dev·as·tat·ing /ˈdɛvəˌsteɪt̬ɪŋ/ *adj.* **1** badly damaging or destroying something: **devastating effect/impact** *The drought has had a devastating effect on crops.* | **devastating consequences/results** *If a large meteor hit the Earth, it could have devastating consequences.* | *The loss of her job was a* ***devastating blow.*** **2** making someone feel extremely sad or shocked: *The news of her sister's death was devastating.* **3** very impressive or effective: *The movie is a devastating view of the star's life.* **4** extremely attractive: *a devastating smile* —**devastatingly** *adv.*

dev·as·ta·tion /ˌdɛvəˈsteɪʃən/ *n.* [U] **1** very bad damage or complete destruction: *wartime devastation* **2** very bad emotional damage: +**of** *the devastation of divorce*

de·vel·op /dɪˈvɛləp/ S1 W1 *v.*
1 GROW [I,T] to grow or change into something bigger, stronger, more advanced, or more severe, or to make someone or something do this: *Knowledge in the field of genetics has been developing very quickly.* | +**from** *New growth will develop from the bud on the branch.* | +**into** *Scouting helps teenagers develop into responsible adults.* | **develop sth** *These exercises will develop muscle strength.*
2 PLAN/PRODUCT [T] to work on a new idea or product over a period of time: *She had developed new programs to help the students.* | *His company develops software for computers using the Unix operating system.* ►see THESAURUS box at **make**[1]
3 SKILL/ABILITY [I,T] if you develop a skill or ability, or if it develops, it becomes stronger or more advanced: *a class in which students develop their writing skills*
4 FEELING/QUALITY [T] to start to have a feeling, quality, or habit that then becomes stronger: *They promptly developed a strong dislike of each other.* | *The older students develop a sense of responsibility by helping the younger ones.* | *If a bear* ***develops a taste for*** (=begins to like) *human food, it will do almost anything to get it.*
5 DISEASE [I,T] if you develop a disease or illness, or if it develops, you start to have it: *One in nine women will develop breast cancer.*
6 LAND [T] to use land for the things that people need, for example by taking minerals out of it or by building on it: *The land will be developed for low-cost housing.*
7 IDEA/ARGUMENT [T] to make an argument or idea clearer, by studying it more or by speaking or writing about it in more detail: *Bradley develops these ideas further in his book.*
8 PROBLEM/DIFFICULTY [I] if a problem or difficult situation develops, it begins to happen or exist, or it gets worse: *Trouble was developing in the cities.* | +**into** *The incident developed into a full-blown scandal.*
9 PROBLEM/FAULT [T] to gradually begin to have physical problem: *The oil tank had developed a small crack.*
10 START TO HAPPEN [I] to gradually begin to happen, exist, or be noticed: *Clouds are developing over the mountains.*
11 PHOTOGRAPHY [T] to make pictures out of film from a camera
[**Origin:** 1600–1700 French *développer*, from Old French *voloper* **to wrap**]

de·vel·oped /dɪˈvɛləpt/ *adj.* **1** ECONOMICS a developed country is one of the rich countries of the world and has many industries, comfortable living for most people, and usually an elected government: *energy consumption in* ***the developed world*** | **developed country/nation** *Most developed countries have a sizable middle class.* → see also DEVELOPING **2** better, stronger, more advanced, or more severe than others: *plants with* ***well developed*** *root systems* | *A child's social skills aren't* ***fully developed.*** | *her* ***highly developed*** *research skills*

deˌveloped ˈnation *n.* [C] ECONOMICS a rich country with a lot of industry and business activity

de·vel·op·er /dɪˈvɛləpɚ/ *n.* **1** [C] someone who makes money by buying land and then building houses, factories etc. on it: **a real-estate/property/land developer** *a property developer in Florida* **2** [C] a person or an organization that works on a new idea, product etc. to make it successful: *software developers* **3** [C,U] TECHNICAL a chemical substance used for developing photographs → see also **late developer** at LATE[1] (8)

de·vel·op·ing /dɪˈvɛləpɪŋ/ *adj.* **1** a developing country is a poor country that is trying to increase its industry and trade and improve life for its people: *poverty in* ***the developing world*** | **developing country/nation** *aid to developing countries* **2** growing or changing: *the developing crisis in the Middle East* | *a developing fetus* (=unborn baby) → see also DEVELOPED

deˌveloping ˈnation *n.* [C] ECONOMICS a country that is changing its ECONOMY from one based mainly on farming to one based mainly on industry

de·vel·op·ment /dɪˈvɛləpmənt/ S2 W1 *n.*
1 CHANGING [U] the process of becoming bigger, stronger, more advanced, or more severe: *the stages of child development* | *an opportunity for career development* | +**of** *the development of modern religious practices*
2 EVENT [C] a new event that changes a situation: +**in** *recent developments in the former Soviet Union*
3 PLANNING [U] the process of working on a new product, plan, idea etc. to make it successful: *a group responsible for* ***product development*** | **under/in development** *The director has several projects under development.*
4 IMPROVEMENT [C] a change that makes a product, plan, idea etc. better: +**in** *developments in engine design*
5 BUILDING PROCESS [U] the process of planning and building new houses, streets etc. on land: *Several hundred acres have been sold* ***for development.***
6 HOUSES/OFFICES ETC. [C] a group of new buildings that have all been planned and built together on the same piece of land: *a new* ***housing development***
7 ECONOMIC ACTIVITY [U] ECONOMICS the process of increasing business, trade, and industrial activity or of improving the social or political situation of the people in a country: ***economic development*** *in the inner city* —**developmental** /dɪˌvɛləpˈmɛntl/ *adj.* —**developmentally** *adv.*

de·vi·ant /ˈdiviənt/ *adj.* FORMAL different, in a bad way, from what is normal or acceptable SYN **aberrant** —**deviant** *n.* [C] —**deviance, deviancy** *n.* [U]

de·vi·ate[1] /ˈdiviˌeɪt/ Ac *v.* [I] FORMAL to start doing something in a way that does not follow an expected plan, idea, or type of behavior SYN **depart**: +**from** *The screenplay does not deviate very much from the book.* [**Origin:** 1600–1700 Late Latin *deviatus*, from Latin *via* **way**]

de·vi·ate[2] /ˈdiviət/ Ac *adj.* FORMAL deviant —**deviate** *n.* [C]

de·vi·a·tion /ˌdiviˈeɪʃən/ Ac *n.* FORMAL **1** [C,U] a noticeable difference from what is expected or normal: +**from** *Teachers were not allowed any deviation from the curriculum.* **2** [C] MATH a difference between a number or measurement in a set and the average of all the numbers or measurements in that set → see also STANDARD DEVIATION

de·vice /dɪˈvaɪs/ Ac S3 W2 *n.* [C] **1** a machine or small object that does a special job SYN **gadget**: *a safety device* | **device to do sth** *The company makes devices to detect carbon monoxide.* | +**device for doing sth** *a device for separating metal from garbage* | +**that** *a device that allows you to hear a whisper from across the room* ►see THESAURUS box at **machine**[1] **2** a method of achieving something or making people do something: *Direct mail is a common marketing device.* | **device for doing sth** *Testing yourself with information on cards is a useful device for studying.* **3** a bomb or other weapon that explodes: *an explosive device* **4** a trick that gets someone to do what you want: **device to do sth** *The phone call was just a device to keep him from leaving.* **5** ENG. LANG. ARTS the special use of words in literature, or of words, lights etc. in a play, to achieve an effect:

Metaphor is a common literary device. [**Origin:** 1200–1300 Old French *devis, devise* **division, plan**, from *deviser* **to divide, tell**] → see also **leave sb to their own devices** at LEAVE[1] (31)

dev·il /ˈdɛvəl/ *n.*
1 the devil also **the Devil** the most powerful evil spirit in some religions, especially in Christianity SYN **Satan**
2 [C] an evil spirit SYN **demon**: *The villagers believed a devil had taken control of the old woman.*
3 little/old devil INFORMAL, HUMOROUS used to talk about a child or an older man who behaves badly, but who you like

SPOKEN PHRASES

4 lucky/poor etc. devil someone who is lucky, unlucky etc.: *Some lucky devil in Cedar Falls won the lottery.*
5 what/who/why etc. the devil? used to emphasize that you are surprised or annoyed when you are asking a question: *How the devil should I know?*
6 do sth like the devil to do something very fast or using a lot of force: *They rang the doorbell and ran like the devil.*
7 a devil of a time OLD-FASHIONED a very difficult or bad time, job etc.: *We **had a devil of a time** getting the carpet clean again.*
8 the devil made me do it HUMOROUS used to make an excuse for something bad you have done
9 better the devil you know (than the devil you don't) used to say that it is better to deal with someone or something you know, even if you do not like them, than to deal with someone or something new that might be worse

10 play/be (the) devil's advocate to pretend that you disagree with something so that there will be a discussion about it: *Letting people play devil's advocate too much can really slow a meeting down.*
11 BAD PERSON OLD-FASHIONED someone who is very bad or evil
12 have the devil to pay OLD-FASHIONED to have a lot of trouble because of something you have done: *If we don't get this in on time, we'll have the devil to pay.*
13 give the devil his due to praise someone that you do not like for something good they have done: *Give the devil his due – he did a lot for foreign policy.*
[**Origin:** Old English *deofol*, from Greek *diabolos*] → see also **speak of the devil** at SPEAK OF (3)

dev·iled /ˈdɛvəld/ *adj.* deviled food is cooked in or mixed with very hot pepper: *deviled eggs*

dev·il·ish /ˈdɛvəlɪʃ/ *adj.* **1** very bad, difficult, or evil SYN **diabolic**: *devilish torture techniques* **2** seeming likely to cause trouble, but often in a way that is amusing or attractive: *a devilish grin* —**devilishly** *adv.*

ˌdevil-may-ˈcare *adj.* [only before noun] cheerful, careless, and willing to take risks SYN **reckless**: *a reckless **devil-may-care attitude***

dev·il·ment /ˈdɛvəlmənt/ *n.* [U] LITERARY **1** behavior that is intended to cause trouble but no serious harm SYN **mischief**: *He was full of devilment.* **2** extremely cruel and wicked behavior

ˈdevil's food ˌcake *n.* [C,U] a type of chocolate cake

dev·il·try /ˈdɛvəltri/ also **dev·il·ry** /ˈdɛvəlri/ *n.* LITERARY [U] devilment

de·vi·ous /ˈdiviəs/ *adj.* **1** using tricks or lies to get what you want SYN **deceitful**: *a devious and unscrupulous man* **2** FORMAL not going in the most direct way to get to a place SYN **indirect**: *a devious route* [**Origin:** 1500–1600 Latin *devius*, from *via* **way**] —**deviously** *adv.* —**deviousness** *n.* [U]

de·vise /dɪˈvaɪz/ *v.* [T] to plan or invent a way of doing something SYN **concoct**: *A teacher devised the game as a way of making math fun.* | **devise a way/method/plan/system etc.** *He helped devise the campaign strategy.* [**Origin:** 1200–1300 Old French *deviser*, from Latin *divisus*, past participle of *dividere* **to divide**]

de·void /dɪˈvɔɪd/ *adj.* **be devoid of sth** to not have a particular quality at all: *The food was completely devoid of taste.*

dev·o·lu·tion /ˌdɛvəˈluʃən/ *n.* [U] **1** POLITICS the act of giving power from a national government to a group or organization at a lower or more local level: *the devolution of power to the states* **2** the process of becoming worse SYN **degeneration**: *the devolution of TV news into little more than soundbites* —**devolutionist** *adj.*

de·volve /dɪˈvɑlv/ *v.* FORMAL **1** [I,T] if you devolve work, responsibility, power etc. to a person or group at a lower level, or if it devolves to them, it is given to them: **devolve sth to sb/sth** *The federal government has devolved responsibility for welfare to the states.* | **+on/upon** *Half of the cost of the study will devolve upon the firm.* **2** [I] if land, goods etc. devolve to someone, it becomes their property when someone else dies

D

de·vote /dɪˈvoʊt/ Ac *v.* [T] **1** to use all or most of your time, money, attention etc. to do something or help someone: **devote your time/energy/attention etc. to sth** *He wanted to devote more time to his family.* | **devote yourself to sth** *Roper retired and devoted himself to charity work.* **2** to use a particular area, period of time, or amount of space for a specific purpose: **+devote sth to sth** *He devotes a chapter to Iranian history.* [**Origin:** 1500–1600 Latin *devotus*, past participle of *devovere*, from *vovere* **to promise**]

de·vot·ed /dɪˈvoʊt̬ɪd/ Ac *adj.* **1** liking or loving someone or something very much, and giving them a lot of attention: *Mark is a devoted father.* | *a devoted fan* | **+to** *They were obviously devoted to him.* ►see THESAURUS box at **faithful**[1] **2** dealing with, containing, or used for only one thing: **+to** *a museum devoted to photography* —**devotedly** *adv.*

dev·o·tee /ˌdɛvəˈti, -ˈteɪ, -voʊ-/ *n.* [C] **1** someone who enjoys or admires someone or something very much SYN **enthusiast**: *opera devotees* **2** a very religious person: **+of** *a devotee of Buddhism*

de·vo·tion /dɪˈvoʊʃən/ Ac *n.* **1** [U] a strong feeling of love that you show by paying a lot of attention to someone or something: **+to** *his devotion to his wife* **2** [U] the loyalty that you show toward someone or something by spending a lot of time and energy on them SYN **dedication**: **+to** *his devotion to improving education* | *her strong **devotion to duty*** | **+of** *the devotion of the team's fans* **3 devotions** [plural] prayers and other religious acts **4** [U] strong religious feeling

de·vo·tion·al[1] /dɪˈvoʊʃənəl/ *adj.* relating to or used in religious services: *devotional music*

devotional[2] *n.* [C] **1** a short religious reading, or a book containing some of these **2** a short religious meeting

de·vour /dɪˈvaʊə/ *v.* [T] **1** to eat something quickly because you are very hungry: *I sat down and devoured the eggs.* ►see THESAURUS box at **eat** **2** to read something quickly and eagerly: *He devoured science fiction books as a teenager.* **3** to use up a lot of something such as energy or money: *The new fighter plane is devouring public funds.* **4** to destroy someone or something: *The building was devoured by flames.* **5 be devoured by sth** to be filled with a strong feeling that seems to control you: *Howard was devoured by jealousy.* **6 devour sb/sth with your eyes** LITERARY to look eagerly and not very nicely at someone or something and notice everything about them [**Origin:** 1300–1400 Old French *devorer*, from Latin *vorare* **to swallow**]

de·vout /dɪˈvaʊt/ *adj.* **1** having very strong and sincere religious beliefs SYN **pious**: *a devout Muslim* ►see THESAURUS box at **religious** **2** LITERARY a devout hope, wish etc. is one that you feel very strongly and sincerely: *It is my devout hope that we can work together for peace.* —**devoutly** *adv.* —**devoutness** *n.* [U]

de Vries /də ˈvriz/, **Hu·go** /ˈhyugoʊ/ (1848–1935) a Dutch BOTANIST who studied plant GENETICS and developed ideas about EVOLUTION

dew /du/ *n.* [U] the small drops of water that form on outdoor surfaces during the night

dew·drop /ˈdudrɑp/ *n.* [C] a small drop of dew

Dew·ey /ˈdui/, **John** (1859–1952) a U.S. PHILOSOPHER and EDUCATIONIST

ˌDewey ˈDecimal ˌSystem *n.* **the Dewey Decimal System** a system for organizing books in a library in which different subjects are given different numbers

dew·fall /ˈdufɔl/ *n.* [U] LITERARY the forming of DEW or the time when DEW begins to appear

dew·lap /ˈdulæp/ *n.* [C] a fold of loose skin hanging under the throat of an animal such as a cow or dog

ˈdew point *n.* **the dew point** TECHNICAL the temperature at which the air cannot hold any more water, so that DEW forms on surfaces outdoors

dew·y /ˈdui/ *adj.* wet with drops of DEW: *dewy grass*

ˌdewy-ˈeyed *adj.* having eyes that are slightly wet with tears

dex·ter·i·ty /dɛkˈstɛrət̬i/ *n.* [U] **1** skill and speed in doing something, especially with your hands, or in speaking: **manual/physical dexterity** *Computer games can improve children's manual dexterity.* **2** skill in using words or your mind: *his charm and* ***verbal dexterity***

dex·terous /ˈdɛkstrəs/ *adj.* **1** skillful and quick in using your hands or body SYN **deft** **2** skillful in using words or your mind —**dexterously** *adv.*

dex·trose /ˈdɛkstroʊs/ *n.* [U] CHEMISTRY a type of sugar that is found naturally in many sweet fruits

dex·trous /ˈdɛkstrəs/ *adj.* another spelling of DEXTEROUS

Dha·ka /ˈdækə, ˈdɑ-/ the capital and largest city of Bangladesh

dhar·ma /ˈdɑrmə/ *n.* [U] **1** according to the Hindu and Buddhist religions, the force that controls the universe and is present in everyone and everything **2** according to the Hindu religion, a person's duty to follow religious and social laws, and to behave in a moral way **3** according to the Buddhist religion, the teachings of the Buddha

dho·ti /ˈdoʊti/ *n.* [C] a piece of clothing worn by some Hindu men, consisting of a piece of cloth that is wrapped around the waist and between the legs

dhow /daʊ/ *n.* [C] an Arab ship with one large sail

di- /daɪ, dɪ/ *prefix* two SYN **double** SYN **twice**: *a diphthong* (=a vowel made by two sounds) → see also BI-, TRI-

di·a·be·tes /ˌdaɪəˈbit̬iz, -ˈbit̬ɪs/ *n.* [U] MEDICINE a disease in which there is too much sugar in the blood [**Origin:** 1500–1600 Latin, Greek, from *diabainein* **to pass through**]

diabetes mel·li·tus /ˌdaɪəˌbit̬iz məˈlaɪt̬əs/ *n.* [U] MEDICINE **1** also **type 1 diabetes** a severe form of diabetes in which the body does not produce enough INSULIN, found especially in children and young adults **2** also **type 2 diabetes** a form of diabetes that is not severe in which the body produces too much INSULIN, found especially in adults who are OBESE (=very fat in a way that is not healthy)

di·a·bet·ic[1] /ˌdaɪəˈbɛt̬ɪk◂/ *adj.* **1** MEDICINE having diabetes: *Anne is diabetic.* **2** MEDICINE caused by diabetes: *a diabetic coma* **3** produced for people who have diabetes: *diabetic chocolate*

diabetic[2] *n.* [C] MEDICINE someone who has diabetes

di·a·bol·i·cal /ˌdaɪəˈbɑlɪkəl/ also **di·a·bol·ic** /ˌdaɪəˈbɑlɪk/ *adj.* very bad, evil, or cruel: *a diabolical serial killer* [**Origin:** 1300–1400 French *diabolique*, from Greek *diabolos* **devil**] —**diabolically** /-kli/ *adv.*

di·a·chron·ic /ˌdaɪəˈkrɑnɪk/ *adj.* TECHNICAL dealing with something, especially a language, as it changes over time —**diachronically** /-kli/ *adv.*

di·a·crit·ic /ˌdaɪəˈkrɪtɪk/ also **diaˈcritical ˌmark** *n.* [C] TECHNICAL ENG. LANG. ARTS a mark placed over, under, or through a letter in some languages, to show that the letter should be pronounced differently from a letter that does not have the mark [**Origin:** 1600–1700 Greek *diakritikos*, from *krinein* **to separate**] —**diacritical** *adj.*

di·a·dem /ˈdaɪəˌdɛm/ *n.* [C] LITERARY a circle of jewels that you wear on your head, usually to show that you are a queen, PRINCESS etc. SYN **crown**

di·ag·nose /ˌdaɪəgˈnoʊs, ˈdaɪəgˌnoʊs/ *v.* [T usually passive] to find out what illness a person has or what is wrong with something, by examining them closely: *A technician diagnosed a bad pump in the engine.* | **diagnose sb with sth** *Her mother was diagnosed with cancer.* | **diagnose sb as (having) sth** *children who are diagnosed as "learning disabled"* | **diagnose sth as sth** *The headache had been diagnosed as a common migraine.*

di·ag·no·sis /ˌdaɪəgˈnoʊsɪs/ *n. plural* **diagnoses** /-siz/ [C,U] the process or result of discovering what is wrong with someone or something, by examining them closely: +**of** *a diagnosis of heart disease* | *Dr. Pool was unable to* ***make a diagnosis*** (=decide what was wrong). [**Origin:** 1600–1700 Modern Latin, Greek, from *diagignoskein* **to know apart**] → see also PROGNOSIS

di·ag·nos·tic /ˌdaɪəgˈnɑstɪk◂/ *adj.* relating to or used for diagnosis: **diagnostic test/tool/equipment etc.** *a reliable diagnostic test* —**diagnostics** *n.* [U]

di·ag·o·nal /daɪˈægənəl/ *adj.* **1** following a sloping angle: *diagonal parking spaces* **2** a diagonal line is straight and joins two opposite corners of a flat shape that has three or more sides, or a solid shape with three or more sides: *Draw a diagonal line across the square.* [**Origin:** 1500–1600 Latin *diagonalis*, from Greek *diagonios* **from angle to angle**] —**diagonal** *n.* [C] —**diagonally** *adv.* → see also HORIZONTAL → see picture at VERTICAL[1]

di·a·gram[1] /ˈdaɪəˌgræm/ *n.* [C] a drawing that shows how something works, where something is, what something looks like etc.: +**of** *a diagram of the heating system* [**Origin:** 1600–1700 Greek *diagramma*, from *diagraphein* **to mark out with lines**] —**diagrammatic** /ˌdaɪəgrəˈmæt̬ɪk◂/ *adj.*

diagram[2] *v.* [T] **1** to show or represent something in a diagram: *He carefully diagrammed the harbor in his notebook.* **2** ENG. LANG. ARTS **diagram a sentence** to examine and describe the GRAMMATICAL purpose of all the words in a sentence, especially as an exercise in school

dial

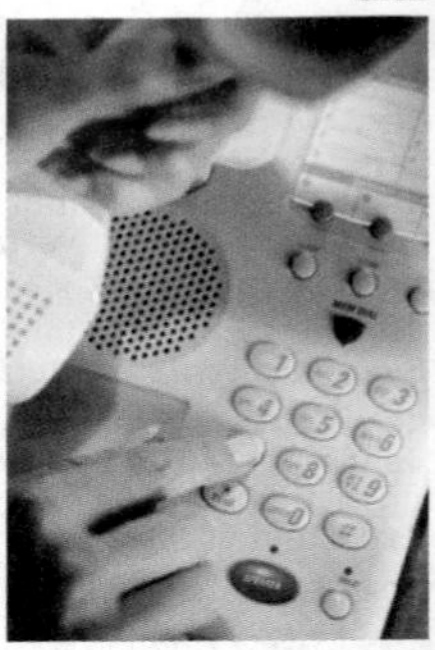

di·al[1] /ˈdaɪəl/ S3 *v.* [I,T] to press the buttons or turn the wheel on a telephone in order to make a telephone call: *She dialed his number again.* [**Origin:** 1300–1400 Old French, Latin *dies* **day**] → SPEED DIAL

dial[2] S3 *n.* [C] **1** the round part of a clock, watch, machine etc. that has numbers that show you the time or a measurement **2** the part of a piece of equipment, such as a radio or THERMOSTAT, that you turn in order to do something, such as find a different station or set the temperature: ***Turn the dial*** *to increase the volume.* **3** the wheel with holes for fingers on some telephones, that you turn to make a call

di·a·lect /ˈdaɪəˌlɛkt/ S2 *n.* [C,U] ENG. LANG. ARTS a form of a language that is spoken in one area, with words or grammar that are slightly different from other areas: +**of** *a dialect of Arabic* | **Chinese/American/Hebrew etc. dialect** | **local/regional dialect** *children speaking the local dialect* [**Origin:** 1500–1600 French *dialecte*, from Greek *dialektos* **conversation, dialect**] → see also ACCENT

di·a·lec·tic /ˌdaɪəˈlɛktɪk/ *n.* [C,U] also **dialectics** [plural] a method of examining and discussing ideas in order to find the truth, in which two opposing ideas are compared in order to find a solution that includes them both —**dialectical** *adj.*

di·a·logue, dialog /ˈdaɪəˌlɔg, -ˌlɑg/ S3 *n.* [C,U] **1** ENG. LANG. ARTS a conversation in a book, play, or movie: *The movie has almost no dialogue.* → see also MONOLOGUE **2** a formal discussion between countries or groups in order to solve problems: +**with/between** *The U.S. wants a deeper dialogue with China.* [**Origin:** 1100–1200 Old French, Greek *dialogos*, from *dialegesthai* **to talk to someone**]

ˈdialogue ˌbox, dialog box *n.* [C] COMPUTERS a box that appears on your computer screen when the program you are using needs to ask you a question before it can continue to do something. You CLICK on one of two or more choices to give your answer.

ˈdial tone *n.* [C] the sound you hear when you pick up a telephone, that lets you know that you can make a call

ˈdial-up *adj.* [only before noun] COMPUTERS relating to a telephone line that is used to send information from one computer to another: *a dial-up connection to the Internet* —**dial-up** *n.* [C]

di·al·y·sis /daɪˈæləsɪs/ *n.* [U] MEDICINE the process of taking harmful substances out of someone's blood using a special machine, because their KIDNEYS do not work correctly: *a dialysis machine* | *He's been* ***on dialysis*** (=receiving dialysis treatments) *for three years.* [**Origin:** 1800–1900 Modern Latin, Greek, **separation**, from *lyein* **to loosen**]

di·am·e·ter /daɪˈæmət̬ɚ/ *n.* [C,U] **1** the width or thickness of something in the shape of a ball or a CYLINDER: *Shape the dough into balls about one inch* ***in diameter*** (=in width). **2** MATH a line or measurement from one side of a circle to the other that passes through the center point [**Origin:** 1300–1400 Old French *diametre*, from Greek *diametros* **measure across**]

diˌameter of a ˈcircle *n.* [singular] MATH a straight line from one side of a circle to the other side, and passing through the center, or the length of this line

di·a·met·ri·cal·ly /ˌdaɪəˈmɛtrɪkli/ *adv.* **diametrically opposed/opposite** completely different or opposite: *The women hold diametrically opposed views on abortion.*

dia·mond /ˈdaɪmənd, ˈdaɪə-/ S3 *n.* **1** [C,U] a clear, very hard valuable stone, used in jewelry and in industry: *a diamond necklace* **2** [C] a shape with four straight sides of equal length that stands on one of its points: *Cut the cookie dough into diamonds.* **3** [C] **a)** the area in a baseball field that is within the diamond shape formed by the four BASES **b)** the whole playing field used in baseball ►see THESAURUS box at sport[1] **4 a) diamonds** one of the four types of cards in a set of playing cards, which had the shape of a red diamond on it: *the two of diamonds* **b)** [C] a card with this shape on it: *Play a diamond.* **5 a diamond in the rough** someone or something that has the possibility of being good, valuable, or attractive, but needs improvement [**Origin:** 1200–1300 Old French *diamant* **hard metal, diamond**, from Greek *adamas*]

ˌdiamond anniˈversary *n.* [C] the date that is exactly 60 or 75 years after the beginning of something, especially a marriage → see also GOLDEN ANNIVERSARY

ˈdiamond ˌlane *n.* [C] a special LANE on a road or street that is marked with a diamond shape and can be used only by buses, taxis etc. and sometimes private cars with more than one passenger

Di·an·a /daɪˈænə/ the Roman name for the goddess Artemis

dia·per /ˈdaɪpɚ, ˈdaɪə-/ S3 *n.* [C] a piece of cloth or soft paper that is put between a baby's legs and fastened around its waist to hold its body wastes: *a* ***dirty diaper*** | *I laid her on the floor to* ***change*** *her* ***diaper*** (=put on a new one). [**Origin:** 1300–1400 Old French *diapre* **fine cloth**, from Medieval Greek *diapras* **pure white**] —**diaper** *v.* [T]

ˈdiaper ˌrash *n.* [U] sore red skin between a baby's legs and on its BUTTOCKS, caused by a wet diaper

di·aph·a·nous /daɪˈæfənəs/ *adj.* LITERARY diaphanous cloth is so fine and thin that you can almost see through it SYN **sheer**

di·a·phragm /ˈdaɪəˌfræm/ *n.* [C] **1** BIOLOGY the muscle between your lungs and your stomach that you use when you breathe → see picture at LUNG **2** a round rubber object that a woman can put inside her VAGINA to stop her from getting PREGNANT **3** TECHNICAL a thin round object, especially in a telephone or LOUDSPEAKER, that is moved by sound or that moves when it produces sound **4** TECHNICAL a round flat part inside a camera that controls the amount of light that enters the camera [**Origin:** 1300–1400 Late Latin *diaphragma*, from Greek *diaphrassein* **to make a fence across, block**]

D

di·ar·rhe·a /ˌdaɪəˈriə/ *n.* [U] an illness in which waste from the BOWELS is watery and comes out often [**Origin:** 1500–1600 Late Latin *diarrhoea*, from Greek *diarrhein* **to flow through**]

di·a·ry /ˈdaɪəri/ *n. plural* **diaries** [C] a book in which you write down important or interesting things that happen to you each day SYN **journal**: ***I kept a diary*** (=wrote in it regularly) *during high school.* [**Origin:** 1500–1600 Latin *diarium*, from *dies* **day**] —**diarist** *n.* [C]

Di·as /ˈdiɑʃ, ˈdiəs/, **Bar·tol·o·me·u** /bɑrˈtɑləmyu/ also **Di·az** (?1450–1500) a Portuguese EXPLORER whose ship was the first to sail around the Cape of Good Hope at the southern end of Africa

di·as·po·ra /daɪˈæspərə/ *n.* **1 the Diaspora a)** HISTORY the movement of the Jewish people away from ancient Palestine, to settle in other countries **b)** all the Jewish people who have moved away from ancient Palestine and live in other countries around the world **2** [U] FORMAL the spreading of people from a national group to other areas: *the African diaspora*

di·a·tom·ic mol·e·cule /ˌdaɪətɑmɪk ˈmɑləkyul/ *n.* [C] CHEMISTRY a MOLECULE made of two atoms

di·a·ton·ic /ˌdaɪəˈtɑnɪk◂/ *adj.* ENG. LANG. ARTS relating to music that uses a set of eight notes with a particular pattern of spaces between them: *the diatonic scale* → see also CHROMATIC

di·a·tribe /ˈdaɪəˌtraɪb/ *n.* [C] FORMAL an angry speech or piece of writing that criticizes someone or something very severely SYN **tirade**: +**against/on** *a diatribe against church policy on women's rights*

dibs /dɪbz/ *n.* [plural] INFORMAL the right to have, use, or do something: *Freshmen* ***have first dibs on*** *dormitory rooms.*

dice[1] /daɪs/ *n.* **1** [plural] *singular* **die** /daɪ/ two or more small blocks of wood, plastic etc. that have six sides with a different number of spots on each side, used in games: *It's your turn to* ***roll the dice.*** **2 no dice** OLD-FASHIONED, SPOKEN said when you refuse to do something: *I asked if I could borrow the car, but she said no dice.* **3** [U] a game of chance that is played with dice **4** [plural] small square pieces of food: *Cut the potatoes into ½" dice.*

GRAMMAR **die, dice**

Die is singular and **dice** is plural. However, many people use the word **dice** when they are speaking about a single **die**.

dice[2] also **dice up** *v.* [T] to cut food into small square pieces ►see THESAURUS box at cut[1] → see picture on page A32

dic·ey /ˈdaɪsi/ *adj.* INFORMAL risky and possibly dangerous: *a dicey situation*

di·chot·o·my /daɪˈkɑt̬əmi/ *n. plural* **dichotomies** [C] FORMAL the difference between two things or ideas that are completely opposite: +**between** *the dichotomy between public and private*

dick /dɪk/ *n.* [C] OLD-FASHIONED **a private dick** a PRIVATE DETECTIVE

D

dick·ens /ˈdɪkənz/ *n.* SPOKEN, OLD-FASHIONED **1 what/who/where the dickens?** used when asking a question to show that you are very surprised or angry: *What the dickens is the matter with her?* **2 as pretty/smart etc. as the dickens** INFORMAL used to emphasize that someone is very pretty, smart etc. **3 have a dickens of a time (doing sth)** SPOKEN to have a difficult time doing something: *I had a dickens of a time trying to get the software to work.*

Dick·ens /ˈdɪkənz/**, Charles** (1812–1870) a British writer famous for his NOVELS which made him the most popular British writer of the 19th century, and which are still very popular today

Dic·ken·si·an /dɪˈkɛnziən/ *adj.* Dickensian buildings, living conditions etc. are poor, dirty, and not nice

dick·er /ˈdɪkɚ/ *v.* [I] INFORMAL to argue about or discuss the conditions of a sale, agreement etc. SYN **haggle**: +**over** *politicians dickering over the budget*

dick·ey /ˈdɪki/ *n.* another spelling of DICKY

Dick·in·son /ˈdɪkənsən/**, Em·i·ly** /ˈɛməli/ (1830–1886) a U.S. poet whose clever and original work is still very popular

Emily Dickinson

dick·y /ˈdɪki/ *n.* [C] **1** a false shirt front or collar sometimes worn under a suit or dress **2** OLD-FASHIONED a small bird

di·cot·y·le·don /ˌdaɪkɑtəˈlidn/ also **di·cot** /ˈdaɪkɑt/ *n.* [C] BIOLOGY a plant that produces seeds that form two seed leaves → see also COTYLEDON

dict. *n.* the abbreviation of DICTIONARY

Dic·ta·phone /ˈdɪktəˌfoʊn/ *n.* [C] TRADEMARK an office machine on which you can record speech so that someone can listen to it and TYPE it later

dic·tate¹ /ˈdɪkteɪt, dɪkˈteɪt/ *v.* **1** [I,T] to say words for someone else to write down: **dictate a letter/memo etc. to sb** *He was dictating a letter to his secretary.* **2** [I,T] to tell someone exactly what they must do or how they must behave SYN **prescribe**: *Fashion designers no longer dictate skirt lengths.* | **dictate sth to sb** *The board does not want to dictate teaching methods to schools.* | **dictate to sb (sth)** *We're not trying to dictate to the governor.* | **dictate who/what/how etc.** *I will not let them dictate how I should run my personal life.* | **dictate that** *Their religious custom dictates that the head be covered.* | *Federal funds have to be used* ***as dictated by*** *Washington.* **3** [T] if something dictates another thing, it controls or influences it SYN **determine**: *The amount of funds we receive dictates what we can do.* | **dictate that** *The laws of physics dictate that what goes up must come down.* [**Origin:** 1500–1600 Latin *dictare* **to say often, say firmly**, from *dicere* **to say**]

dic·tate² /ˈdɪkteɪt/ *n.* [C] FORMAL an order, rule, or principle that you have to obey: +**of** *I had to* ***follow the dictates*** *of my conscience.*

dic·ta·tion /dɪkˈteɪʃən/ *n.* **1** [U] the act of saying words for someone to write down, usually so that they can write a letter, message etc. for you: *As a secretary, I often have to* ***take dictation*** (=to write down the words someone says). **2** [C] a piece of writing that a teacher reads out to test your ability to hear and write the words correctly: *French dictations*

dic·ta·tor /ˈdɪkteɪtɚ/ *n.* [C] **1** a ruler who has complete power over a country, especially when their power has been gained by force: *a military dictator* → see also DESPOT **2** someone who tells other people what they should do, in a way that seems unreasonable: *dictators of fashion*

dic·ta·to·ri·al /ˌdɪktəˈtɔriəl/ *adj.* **1** POLITICS a dictatorial government or ruler has complete power over a country: *a corrupt dictatorial regime* **2** a dictatorial person tells other people what to do in an unreasonable way: *dictatorial parents* | *A Senate chairman cannot be dictatorial.* —**dictatorially** *adv.*

dic·ta·tor·ship /dɪkˈteɪtɚˌʃɪp, ˈdɪkteɪtɚ-/ *n.* POLITICS **1** [C,U] government by a ruler who has complete power: *The country has been moving toward dictatorship.* | *Stalin's dictatorship* ►see THESAURUS box at **government** **2** [C] a country that is ruled by one person who has complete power

dic·tion /ˈdɪkʃən/ *n.* [U] ENG. LANG. ARTS **1** the way in which someone pronounces words: *her perfect diction* **2** the choice and use of words and phrases to express meaning, especially in literature or poetry: *students making an effort to use academic diction*

dic·tion·ar·y /ˈdɪkʃəˌnɛri/ *n. plural* **dictionaries** [C] **1** a book that gives a list of words in alphabetical order and explains their meanings in the same language, or in another language: *a Korean-English dictionary* **2** a book like this that deals with the words and phrases used in a particular subject: *a business dictionary* [**Origin:** 1500–1600 Medieval Latin *dictionarium*, from Late Latin *dictio* **word**]

dic·tum /ˈdɪktəm/ *n. plural* **dicta** /-tə/ or **dictums** [C] **1** a formal statement of opinion by someone who is respected or has authority: *the Catholic Church's dictum against birth control* **2** a short phrase that expresses a general rule or truth: *Gertrude Stein's famous dictum: "a rose is a rose is a rose."*

did /dəd; *strong* dɪd/ *v.* the past tense of DO

di·dac·tic /daɪˈdæktɪk/ *adj.* **1** something such as a speech or movie that is didactic is intended to teach people a moral lesson: *the didactic speeches of the characters* **2** someone who is didactic is too eager to teach people things or give instructions: *a didactic priest* —**didactically** /-kli/ *adv.*

did·dle /ˈdɪdl/ *v.* [I always + adv./prep.] INFORMAL to do something in a way that is not very serious: *He was diddling around on the piano.*

did·dly /ˈdɪdl-i, ˈdɪdli/ also **did·dly·squat** /ˈdɪdliˌskwɑt/ *n.* **not know/mean diddly** INFORMAL to know or mean nothing at all: *Brad doesn't know diddly about baseball.* → see also SQUAT

Di·de·rot /ˌdidəˈroʊ, ˈdidəˌroʊ/**, De·nis** /dɪˈni/ (1713–1784) a French PHILOSOPHER and writer

did·ge·ri·doo /ˌdɪdʒəriˈdu/ *n.* [C] a long wooden musical instrument, played especially in Australia

did·n't /ˈdɪdnt/ *v.* the short form of "did not": *I didn't want to go.*

Did·rik·son (Za·har·i·as) /ˈdidrɪksən zəˈhæriəs/**, Mil·dred** /ˈmɪldrɪd/ also **Babe Didrikson** (1914–1956) a U.S. ATHLETE who is considered one of the best female athletes of this century

didst /dɪdst/ *v.* **thou didst** OLD USE you did

die¹ /daɪ/ S1 W1 *v.* **died, dying** [I]
1 BECOME DEAD to stop living and become dead: *He was very sick and we knew he might die.* | *Her husband had died two years earlier.* | +**of/from** *My mother died of cancer.* | *The youths died from burns and smoke inhalation.* | +**for** *Would you die for your faith?* | **die young/happy/poor etc.** *Franklin died young, at only 32.* | *All four* ***died instantly*** *in the crash.* | **die a hero/martyr/pauper etc.** *Windrich died a hero in World War II.* | **die a natural/horrible/quick etc. death** *Did she die a natural death* (=did she die naturally, or did someone kill her)*?* | *I'll regret it* ***to my dying day*** (=until I die). | **sb's dying breath/wish** (=someone's last breath or wish) *Her husband's dying wish was to be buried at sea.*
2 DISAPPEAR to disappear or stop existing: *Our love will never die.* | *Being the only son, the family name will* ***die with him*** (=disappear or be finished when he dies). | *Real ranchers are a* ***dying breed*** (=a type of person that is no longer common).
3 MACHINES INFORMAL to stop working SYN **break down**: *The engine coughed and died.* | *There I was in*

the middle of the intersection and my car just ***died on me*** (=stopped working while I was using it).

SPOKEN PHRASES

4 be dying for sth to want something very much: *I'm dying for a cup of coffee.*
5 be dying to do sth to want to do something very much, so that it is difficult to wait: *They made a movie out of the book, and I'm dying to see it.*
6 be dying of hunger/thirst to be very hungry or thirsty: *I'm dying of thirst. Do you have anything to drink?*
7 I nearly died also **I could have died** said when you felt very surprised, shocked, or embarrassed: *I checked prices on new models and nearly died!*
8 I'd rather die used to say very strongly that you do not want to do something: *I'd rather die than work for my uncle.*
9 be dying used to say that you are becoming very tired while you doing something: *"I was dying on the last three laps of the race," Feingold said.*
10 be to die for if something is to die for, it is very good: *Their French dip sandwich is to die for.*
11 die laughing to laugh a lot: *Rebecca told me this joke on the phone today, and I almost died laughing.*
12 never say die used to encourage someone to continue doing something that is difficult

13 old habits/prejudices/customs etc. die hard used to say that it takes a long time to change to a new way of doing something
14 die by sb's hand also **die by your own hand** LITERARY to be killed by someone, or to kill yourself
15 die on the vine LITERARY if an idea, process, or business dies on the vine, it fails, especially at an early stage, because of a lack of support
16 die without issue OLD USE or LAW to die before you have any children

die away *phr. v.* if a sound, feeling, wind, or light dies away, it becomes gradually weaker and finally stops: *Her footsteps died away.*

die back *phr. v.* if a plant dies back, it dies above the ground but remains alive at its roots

die down *phr. v.* if something dies down, it becomes less strong, active, or violent: *I hope the wind has died down.* | *when the excitement had died down* | *Rumors still haven't died down.*

die off *phr. v.* if a group of people, animals etc. die off, they die one by one until there are no more of them

die out *phr. v.* to disappear or stop existing completely: *If the ocean becomes too salty, certain types of marine life die out.* | *He predicted that newspapers would die out.* → see Word Choice box at DEAD[1]

WORD CHOICE **die, be dead**
• When you are talking about an event, use **die** **(dying, died, died)**.
• When you are talking about a condition or state, use **be dead**.
Compare: *He died in the ambulance on the way to the hospital.* | *By the time the ambulance reached the hospital, he was dead.*

die² *n.* [C] **1** a metal block used to press or cut something into a particular shape **2** the singular of DICE **3 the die is cast** used to say that a decision has been made and cannot now be changed

'die ˌcasting *n.* [U] the process of making metal objects by putting liquid metal into a hollow container that has a particular shape, and then allowing it to become hard

die•hard, **die-hard** /ˈdaɪhɑrd/ *adj.* **1** opposing change and refusing to accept new ideas: *a diehard opponent of new taxes* **2 die-hard fan/communist/supporter etc.** someone who is very loyal to a team, political party, person etc. —**diehard** *n.* [C] → see also **old habits etc. die hard** at DIE[1] (13)

di•er•esis /daɪˈɛrəsɪs/ *n. plural* **diereses** /-siz/ [C] ENG. LANG. ARTS a sign that is put over the second of two VOWELS to show that it is pronounced separately from the first, for example in the word "naïve"

die•sel /ˈdizəl, -səl/ *n.* **1** [U] a type of heavy oil used instead of gas in a special type of engine: *a tank of diesel for the tractors* | *a diesel truck* **2** [C] INFORMAL a vehicle that uses DIESEL, especially a large truck [**Origin:** 1800–1900 Rudolph *Diesel* (1858–1913), German engineer who invented the engine]

'diesel ˌengine *n.* [C] an engine that burns DIESEL, used especially for buses, trains, and goods vehicles

'diesel ˌfuel also **'diesel ˌoil** *n.* [U] DIESEL

di•et¹ /ˈdaɪət/ S3 W2 *n.* **1** [C,U] the types of food that a person or animal eats each day: *The Italians* ***have*** *a good healthy* ***diet*** *and lifestyle.* | *a vegetarian diet* | **+of** *a dolphin's diet of fish* | **balanced/healthy/good diet** (=one that includes all the foods you need to stay healthy) *the importance of exercise and a balanced diet* | *diseases caused by* ***poor diet*** (=one that is not healthy) | *the amount of fat and sugar* ***in your diet*** **2** [C] a limited type or amount of food that you eat when you want to get thinner or because you have a health problem: **go/be on a diet** *He went on a diet in January.* | *a salt-free diet* **3 a diet of sth** something such as an activity, entertainment, treatment etc. that someone gets, which does not change: *We lived on a* ***steady diet of*** *Dad's criticism.* | *a diet of mysteries and adventure stories* **4** [C] OLD USE an official meeting to discuss political or church matters [**Origin:** 1200–1300 Old French *diete*, from Greek *diaita* **way of living, food to be eaten**]

diet² *v.* [I] to limit the amount and type of food that you eat in order to become thinner: *She dieted, but still wasn't happy with her figure.*

di•e•tar•y /ˈdaɪəˌtɛri/ *adj.* relating to the food someone eats: *dietary guidelines*

di•e•tet•ics /ˌdaɪəˈtɛt̬ɪks/ *n.* [U] MEDICINE the science that is concerned with what people eat and drink and how this affects their health

di•e•ti•cian, **dietitian** /ˌdaɪəˈtɪʃən/ *n.* [C] MEDICINE someone who is specially trained in dietetics

dif•fer /ˈdɪfɚ/ W3 *v.* **1** [I] to be different from something in some way: **+from** *His views differ from those of his partner.* | *Interest rates* ***differ from*** *bank* ***to*** *bank.* | **+in** *packages that differ in size* | **differ greatly/widely** *The amount of preparation students do differs widely.* **2** [I] to have different opinions: **+on/over/about** *Experts differ on how profitable it will be.* [**Origin:** 1300–1400 French *différer* **to delay, be different**, from Latin *differre*] → see also **I beg to differ** at BEG (6)

dif•ference /ˈdɪfrəns/ S1 W1 *n.* **1** [C,U] a way in which two or more things or people are not like each other: *social and class differences* | **+between** *the difference between right and wrong* | *The twins look so alike; how can you* ***tell the difference*** (=see or notice the difference)*?* | **+in** *There was a marked difference in his behavior toward me.* **2** [singular, U] an amount by which one thing is not the same as another: *a five-hour time difference* | **big/small difference** *a big age difference* | **+between** *The trade deficit is the difference between imports and exports.* | **+in** *a small difference in price* | *There's a big* ***difference in*** *maturity level* ***between*** *a 13- and 15-year-old.* | **+of** *There is a temperature difference of up to 15 degrees between the valley and the coast.* → see also **a world of difference** at WORLD[1] (15) **3 make a (big) difference** also **make all the difference** to have an important effect on a thing or a situation: *Working together, we can make a difference.* | **make a difference in sth** *New drugs have made an enormous difference in the way the disease is treated.* | **make a difference to sb/sth** *A salesperson's attitude can make all the difference to a customer.* **4 their/our/your etc. differences** the disagreements that people have: *Charlie and I* ***have*** *our* ***differences.*** | *Penny and Tom have managed to* ***overcome*** *their* ***differences.*** | *They have to find a way to* ***settle*** *their* ***differences.*** **5 difference of opinion** a slight disagreement: *My husband and I* ***have a difference of opinion*** *regarding the kids' bedtimes.* **6 make no difference (to sb/sth) a)** to have no effect at all on a situation:

Unfortunately, the drugs made no difference to the spread of the cancer. **b)** to be unimportant to someone: *Wear what you want; it makes no difference to me.* **7 with a difference** used to express approval about something that is different and better: *a children's book with a difference* → see also **split the difference** at SPLIT[1] (5)

WORD CHOICE difference of, difference in
• **Difference of** is only used to compare numbers. *There is a difference of $500 between the sale price and the regular price.*
• **Difference in** is used to compare particular features, practices, or qualities: *In the U.S., I noticed a big difference in social behavior.*

D

dif·fer·ent /ˈdɪfrənt/ S1 W1 *adj.* **1** not like something or someone else, or not the same as before OPP **similar**: *He looked so different that his own daughter didn't recognize him.* | **+from** *The heat in Arizona is different from the heat here. It's very dry.* | **+than** *College campuses look a lot different than they did years ago.* | **very/entirely/radically/markedly etc. different** *His attitude is markedly different from Benson's.* **2** [only before noun] different things are separate things of the same kind: *He took the photo from three different angles.* | *Alice moved to a different school.* | ***different ways** to approach the problem* | **different kinds/types** *hundreds of different kinds of candy* | **a different sth from sth** *These whales sing a different song from humpback whales in the North Atlantic.* **3** SPOKEN unusual, often in a way that you do not like: *"Do you like my new shoes?" "Well, they sure are different."* **4 different strokes (for different folks)** INFORMAL used to say that different people like different types of thing —**differently** *adv.*: *The twins wear their hair differently.* | *It could have turned out very differently.*

GRAMMAR
We use both **different from** and **different than** to talk about two things that are not the same: *My new school is different from/than my old one.* However, most teachers prefer **different from.** Note that we never say **different of.**

USAGE
The noun is **difference**: *the difference between your country and mine*

dif·fer·en·tial[1] /ˌdɪfəˈrɛnʃəl◂/ *n.* [C] **1** an amount or degree of difference between two quantities, especially relating to money: **wage/price/pay etc. differential** *The wage differential between managers and workers is huge.* **2** a differential gear

differential[2] *adj.* [only before noun] **1** based on or depending on a difference: *Differential pay will be given to teachers who oversee student club meetings.* **2** MATH relating to differential calculus

ˌdifferential ˈcalculus *n.* [U] MATH a type of mathematics that deals with how a mathematical quantity changes according to how other quantities change

ˌdifferential ˈgear *n.* [C] an arrangement of GEARS that allows one back wheel of a car to turn faster than the other when the car goes around a corner

dif·fer·en·ti·ate /ˌdɪfəˈrɛnʃiˌeɪt/ Ac *v.* **1** [I,T] to recognize or express the difference between things or people SYN **distinguish**: **+between** *Most people couldn't differentiate between the two types of soft drink.* | **differentiate sb/sth from sb/sth** *It's easy to differentiate the male birds from the female ones.* **2** [T] to be the quality, feature etc. that makes someone or something clearly different from another SYN **distinguish**: **differentiate sb/sth from sb/sth** *Quality is what differentiates our product from our competitors'.* **3** [I] to behave differently toward someone or something, sometimes in an unfair way SYN **discriminate**: **+between** *Their religion does not differentiate between the rich and poor.* **4** [I] BIOLOGY when cells differentiate, they develop and reach their final adult form

dif·fer·en·ti·a·tion /ˌdɪfəˌrɛnʃiˈeɪʃən/ *n.* [U] **1** the process of recognizing and expressing that there are differences between certain things or people **2** BIOLOGY the process by which cells develop and reach their final adult form

dif·fi·cult /ˈdɪfəˌkʌlt/ S2 W1 *adj.* **1** not easy to do, understand, or deal with SYN **hard** OPP **easy**: *a difficult question* | *A lot of students **find** calculus **difficult**.* | **be difficult (for sb) to do sth** *Tickets for the Super Bowl are always difficult to get.* | *Being too warm can **make it difficult** to sleep.* | ***It was difficult** to believe.*

THESAURUS
hard not at all easy: *hard questions on the test*
tough difficult to do or deal with, especially emotionally: *Doctors have to make tough decisions about who to treat first.*
tricky difficult to deal with or do because it is complicated and full of problems: *The contract negotiations have been tricky.*
awkward fairly difficult to do, use, or deal with: *Reporters are asking awkward questions.*
challenging difficult in an interesting or enjoyable way: *a challenging job*
daunting so difficult that you feel not at all confident about being able to do it: *The task may seem a little daunting.*
delicate needing to be dealt with carefully or sensitively in order to avoid problems or failure: *You must understand that this is a delicate situation and I cannot discuss it publicly.*

2 involving a lot of problems and causing a lot of trouble or worry: *My wife and I have gone through some difficult times.* | **make life/things difficult (for sb)** *The bus strike is making life difficult for commuters.* **3** someone who is difficult is never satisfied, friendly, or helpful: *Stop being difficult!*

dif·fi·cul·ty /ˈdɪfəˌkʌlti/ W2 *n. plural* **difficulties** **1** [U] the quality of being hard to do or understand, or how hard something is: *The books vary in difficulty.* | **+of** *the difficulty of solving these problems* | **have difficulty (in) doing sth** *Stephen's having difficulty finding an apartment.* | *She walks **with difficulty*** (=it is not easy for her to walk). | *He had **great difficulty** catching up.* | *We managed the climb **without difficulty**.* **2** [U] a situation in which you have problems: *Their business is **in** financial **difficulty**.* | *He wasn't prepared, and quickly **ran into difficulty*** (=had problems). **3** [C usually plural] a problem or something that causes trouble: *Many of the children **had difficulties** learning.* | **mechanical/technical difficulties** *Mechanical difficulties caused the flight to be delayed.* | *We **ran into difficulties*** (=had problems) *when we tried to exchange the tickets.* [**Origin:** 1300–1400 Latin *difficultas*, from *difficilis* **difficult**, from *facilis* **easy**]

dif·fi·dent /ˈdɪfədənt/ *adj.* FORMAL shy and not wanting to make people notice you or talk about you, because you lack confidence in your abilities: *his shy and diffident manner* [**Origin:** 1400–1500 Latin, present participle of *diffidere* **to distrust**, from *fidere* **to trust**] —**diffidence** *n.* [U] —**diffidently** *adv.*

dif·frac·tion /dɪˈfrækʃən/ *n.* [U] PHYSICS the process or result of dividing sound or light waves into smaller waves, by sending them around something or through a small hole —**diffract** /dɪˈfrækt/ *v.* [I,T]

difˈfraction ˌgrating *n.* [C] PHYSICS a flat piece of glass or metal with a series of narrow parallel lines cut into its surface, used to separate a beam of light into different bands of color

dif·fuse[1] /dɪˈfyuz/ *v.* **1** [T] TECHNICAL if something diffuses light, it spreads it over a larger area and makes it softer and less bright **2** [I,T] PHYSICS if you diffuse a liquid or a gas, or if it diffuses, it spreads over a larger area and mixes evenly with the surrounding gases or liquids, becoming less strong: *The wind quickly diffused any toxic vapors that may have leaked out.* **3** [T] to spread something over a larger area or to more people, often so that it becomes less strong: *Critics believe that such action will diffuse the power of Congress.* **4** [I,T]

FORMAL to spread ideas or information among a lot of people, or to spread like this: *These stories became diffused throughout the English-speaking world.* **5** [T] FORMAL to make a bad feeling less strong or the effects of a situation, especially a bad one, less severe: *Many presidential candidates have used humor to diffuse criticism.* —**diffused** *adj.*: *diffused lighting* —**diffusion** /dɪˈfyuʒən/ *n.* [U]

dif•fuse² /dɪˈfyus/ *adj.* **1** spread over a large area or in many places: *The organization is large and diffuse.* **2** using a lot of words and not explaining things clearly or directly —**diffusely** *adv.* —**diffuseness** *n.* [U]

dif,fuse re'flection *n.* [U] TECHNICAL PHYSICS the action of light, heat, or sound being sent back from an uneven or rough surface at many different angles

dig¹ /dɪg/ S2 *v. past tense and past participle* **dug** /dʌg/, **digging**

1 MAKE A HOLE [I,T] to break and move earth, stone, snow etc. with a tool, your hands, or a machine, making a hole in it: *Jessica dug in the sand with a small shovel.* | **+down** *We dug down about six feet.* | **+for** *They're digging for dinosaur bones.* | **dig a hole/grave/trench etc.** *The dog had dug a big hole behind the roses.*
2 LOOK FOR STH [I] to put your hand into something in order to search for something: **+for** *She started digging for her keys.* | **+through** *I dug through my drawers until I found the note.* | **+in/into** *Julie dug into her purse for some spare change.* | **+around** *He dug around in the junk drawer for it.*
3 FIND INFORMATION [I] find more information about someone or something: **+into** *I wasn't sure if I really wanted to* ***dig deeper*** *into my family's past.* | **+for** *Journalists are already digging for details.* | **+around** *Reporters had started digging around, trying to find out the truth.*
4 dig a hole for yourself also **dig yourself into a hole** to get yourself into a difficult situation by doing or saying the wrong thing: *The team dug themselves a hole they couldn't climb out of.*
5 REMOVE STH FROM THE GROUND [T] to remove something, especially vegetables, from the ground: *We went with grandpa to dig potatoes.*
6 dig deep to use a lot of effort, money etc. to do something: *I had to dig deep just to get myself out of bed.*
7 dig your own grave to do something that will make you have serious problems later

SPOKEN PHRASES

8 UNDERSTAND STH [I,T] OLD-FASHIONED, SLANG to understand something: *"She says she doesn't like it." "Yeah, I can dig that."*
9 LIKE SB/STH [T] OLD-FASHIONED, SLANG to like someone or something: *I really dig that dress.*
10 Dig that...! [T] OLD-FASHIONED, SLANG used to tell someone to notice or look at someone or something: *Dig that funky hat she has on!*

dig in *phr. v.* **1** SPOKEN, INFORMAL to start eating food that is in front of you: *Come on everyone – dig in!* **2 dig in your heels** also **dig your heels in** to refuse to do or accept something in spite of other people's efforts to persuade you: *a toddler digging in his heels* **3 dig yourself in** if soldiers dig in or dig themselves in, they make a protected place for themselves by digging

dig into *phr. v.* **1 dig (sth) into sth** to push a hard or pointed object into something, especially someone's body, or to press into something: *She* ***dug*** *her* ***nails*** *into my arm.* | *A piece of wood was digging into my side.* **2 dig into sth** to start using a supply of something, especially money: *I'm going to have to dig into my savings again.*

dig out *phr. v.* **1 dig sth ↔ out** to get someone or something out of earth, snow etc. using a tool, your hands, or a machine: *Rescue workers dug survivors out from under the rubble.* **2 dig sth ↔ out** to find something you have not seen for a long time, or that is not easy to find: *Mom dug her wedding dress out of the closet.*

dig sth ↔ up *phr. v.* **1** to remove something from under the ground with a tool, your hands, or a machine: *Beth is out back digging up weeds.* **2** INFORMAL to find hidden or forgotten information by careful searching: *See what you can dig up on the guy.*

dig² *n.* **1** [C] an unkind thing you say to annoy someone: *Sally keeps* ***making digs*** *about my work.* | **+at** *a dig at his opponent* **2 give sb a dig** to push someone quickly and lightly with your finger or an elbow: *He gave me a dig in the ribs.* **3** [C] the process of digging in a place to find ancient objects to study: *an* ***archeological dig*** **4** [C] an act of hitting the ball back up into the air when it is near the ground or floor in VOLLEYBALL **5 digs** [plural] a room or apartment that you pay rent to live in

di•gest¹ /daɪˈdʒɛst, dɪ-/ *v.* **1** [I,T] BIOLOGY if food digests or if you digest it, it changes in the stomach into a form your body can use: *Some babies can't digest cow's milk.* → see also INGEST **2** [T] to understand new information after thinking about it carefully: *It took a while to digest the theory.* [**Origin:** 1300–1400 Latin *digestus*, past participle of *digerere* **to carry apart, arrange, digest**] —**digestible** *adj.*

di•gest² /ˈdaɪdʒɛst/ *n.* [C] a short piece of writing that gives the most important facts from a book, report etc.

di•ges•tion /daɪˈdʒɛstʃən/ *n.* [U] the process of digesting food, or your ability to digest it: *Fiber is good for your digestion.*

di•ges•tive /daɪˈdʒɛstɪv/ *adj.* [only before noun] BIOLOGY relating to the process of digestion

di'gestive ,system *n.* [C] the system of organs in your body that DIGESTS food

dig•ger /ˈdɪgə/ *n.* [C] **1** a person who digs: *a clam digger* **2** a machine or tool that is used to dig → see also GOLD DIGGER

dig•gings /ˈdɪgɪŋz/ *n.* [plural] a place where people are digging for metal, especially gold

dig•it /ˈdɪdʒɪt/ *n.* [C] **1** MATH one of the written signs that represent the numbers from 0 to 9: *a seven-digit phone number* **2** BIOLOGY a finger or toe [**Origin:** 1300–1400 Latin *digitus* **finger, toe**]

dig•i•tal /ˈdɪdʒɪtl/ S3 W3 *adj.* **1** using a system in which information is represented in the form of numbers, usually numbers in the BINARY system: *a digital camera* **2** giving information in the form of numbers OPP **analog**: *a digital clock* **3** BIOLOGY relating to the fingers and toes

,digital 'audiotape *n.* [C] a DAT

dig•i•tal•is /,dɪdʒəˈtælɪs/ *n.* [U] a medicine made from FOXGLOVES that makes your heart beat faster

dig•i•tal•ly /ˈdɪdʒɪtl-i/ *adv.* COMPUTERS in a way that uses a system of BINARY numbers: *Data was captured digitally and stored on two separate hard drives.*

dig•i•tize /ˈdɪdʒə,taɪz/ *v.* [T] to put information into a digital form: *Engineers digitize the film and then create the special effects.*

dig•ni•fied /ˈdɪgnə,faɪd/ *adj.* behaving in a calm controlled way, even in a difficult situation, which makes people respect you: *a dignified old lady*

dig•ni•fy /ˈdɪgnə,faɪ/ *v.* **dignifies, dignified, dignifying** [T] to make something or someone seem better, more impressive, or more important than they really are, especially by reacting to them in a particular way or calling them a good name: *A huge portrait dignified the living room wall.* | **dignify sb/sth with sth** *I'm not even going to dignify that last comment with a response.*

dig•ni•tar•y /ˈdɪgnə,tɛri/ *n. plural* **dignitaries** [C] someone who has an important official position: *foreign dignitaries from 20 countries*

dig•ni•ty /ˈdɪgnəti/ *n.* [U] **1** the ability to behave in a calm controlled way even in a difficult situation: *a woman of compassion and dignity* | *She bore the difficulties* ***with dignity***. **2** respect that other people have for you or that you have for yourself: *Prisoners must be treated with regard to their* ***human dignity***. | **maintain/retain your dignity** *Old people need to retain* *their dignity and independence.* **3** the quality of being serious, formal, and respectable: *Lawyers must respect the dignity of the court.* **4 be beneath sb's dignity** if something is beneath your dignity, you think you are too good or important to do it: *It seemed that doing his own laundry was beneath his dignity.* [**Origin:** 1100–1200 Old French *dignité*, from Latin *dignitas* **worth**]

di·graph /ˈdaɪgræf/ *n.* [C] ENG. LANG. ARTS a pair of letters that represent one sound, such as "ea" in "head" and "ph" in "phrase"

di·gress /daɪˈgrɛs, dɪ-/ *v.* [I] FORMAL to talk or write about something that is not your main subject: *Miller often digressed to give the history behind each theory.* [**Origin:** 1500–1600 Latin *digressus*, past participle of *digredi* **to step aside**] —**digression** /daɪˈgrɛʃən/ *n.* [C,U] —**digressive** /daɪˈgrɛsɪv/ *adj.*

D

dike, **dyke** /daɪk/ *n.* [C] a wall or bank built to keep back water and prevent flooding

dik·tat /dɪkˈtɑt/ *n.* [C,U] an order that is forced on people by a ruler or government: *a diktat from the Soviet leader*

di·lap·i·dat·ed /dəˈlæpəˌdeɪt̬ɪd/ *adj.* a dilapidated building, vehicle etc. is old, broken, and in very bad condition [**Origin:** 1500–1600 Latin *dilapidare* **to scatter like stones, misuse, destroy**, from *lapidare* **to throw stones**] —**dilapidation** /dəˌlæpəˈdeɪʃən/ *n.* [U]

di·late /daɪˈleɪt, ˈdaɪleɪt/ *v.* [I,T] to become wider or more open, or to cause something to do this: *The drops dilate the patient's pupils.* [**Origin:** 1300–1400 French *dilater*, from Latin *latus* **wide**]

dilate on/upon sth *phr. v.* FORMAL to speak or write a lot about something: *He dilated upon their piety.*

di·la·tion /dɪˈleɪʃən, daɪ-/ *n.* TECHNICAL **1** [U] the process of becoming wider or more open: *the dilation of blood vessels in the brain* **2** [C,U] MATH a change in the size of a shape, so that the size of the original shape and the size of the new shape are directly related to each other

dil·a·to·ry /ˈdɪləˌtɔri/ *adj.* FORMAL slow and tending to delay decisions or actions

di·lem·ma /dəˈlɛmə/ *n.* [C] a situation in which you have to make a difficult choice between actions which are equally good or equally bad: *Many parents are* ***faced with the dilemma*** *of choosing between work and family commitments.* | *We're* ***in a dilemma*** *about whether to move or not.* | **pose/create a dilemma** *The situation posed a dilemma for the White House.* [**Origin:** 1500–1600 Greek **double statement**, from *lemma* **statement**] → see also **be on the horns of a dilemma** at HORN[1] (7)

dil·et·tante /ˈdɪləˌtɑnt/ *n.* [C] FORMAL, DISAPPROVING someone who is interested in a subject or activity but who does not study it thoroughly and is not serious about what they are doing —**dilettante** *adj.* —**dilettantism** *n.* [U]

dil·i·gent /ˈdɪlədʒənt/ *adj.* **1** someone who is diligent works hard and carefully: *a diligent student* **2** carefully and thoroughly done: *The book required ten years of diligent research.* [**Origin:** 1300–1400 French, Latin, present participle of *diligere* **to put high value on, love**] —**diligence** *n.* [U] —**diligently** *adv.*

dill /dɪl/ *n.* [U] a plant whose seeds and leaves are used in cooking

Dil·lin·ger /ˈdɪlɪndʒɚ/, **John** (1903–1934) a famous U.S. bank ROBBER and murderer

ˌdill ˈpickle *n.* [C] a CUCUMBER that has been preserved in VINEGAR (=a sour-tasting liquid)

dil·ly /ˈdɪli/ *n.* [C] OLD-FASHIONED someone or something that is exciting or special: *Hey, listen to this joke – it's a dilly.*

ˌdilly-ˈdally *v.* **dilly-dallied, dilly-dallying** [I] INFORMAL to waste time or do something very slowly, especially

digestive system

1) Digestion begins in the mouth as the saliva containing the enzyme amylase helps moisten the food, and starts the breakdown of starches.

2) Chewed lumps of food from the mouth then pass along the esophagus to the stomach.

3) The food stays in the stomach for several hours while the initial digestion of protein takes place. The stomach wall secretes hydrochloric acid which makes the stomach contents very acidic. This part of the process plays an important role as it kills bacteria that are taken into the gut along with the food, helping to protect us from food poisoning.

4) Semi-digested food is held back in the stomach by the sphincter muscle, and when this relaxes, the food is released into the duodenum. Several digestive enzymes are added to the food in the duodenum. These are made by the pancreas, and digest starch, proteins, and lipids.

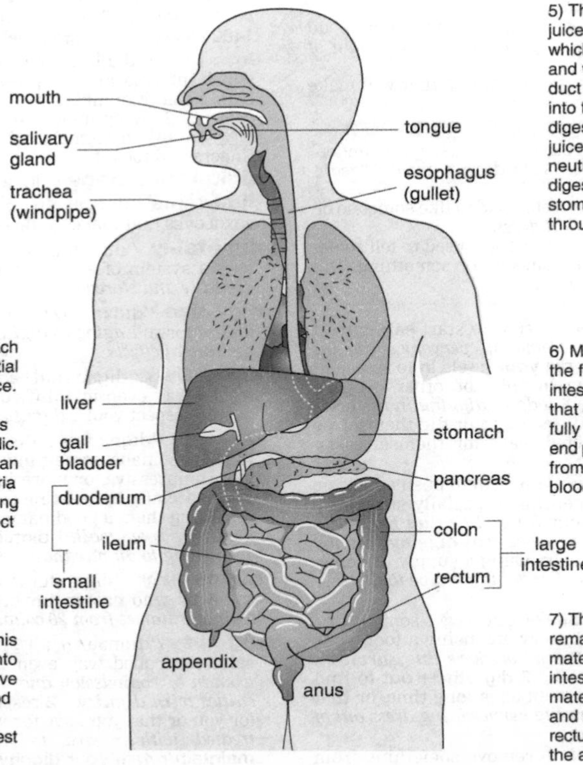

5) The liver makes a digestive juice called bile - a green liquid which is stored in the gall bladder and which passes down the bile duct onto the food. Bile turns fat into tiny droplets for easier digestion. Bile and pancreatic juices are also alkaline, which neutæli e the acidic semi-digested food leaving the stomach before it continues through the gut.

6) More enzymes are added as the food continues along the intestine until the parts of the food that can be digested have been fully broken down into soluble end products which are absorbed from the ileum and then into the blood stream.

7) The colon absorbs most of the remaining water from the waste materials entering the large intestine. A semi-solid waste material called feces remains, and this is then stored in the rectum, until it is expelled through the anus.

because you cannot decide about something: *Stop dilly-dallying and get dressed!*

di·lute¹ /dɪˈlut, daɪ-/ *v.* [T] **1** to make a liquid weaker by adding water or another liquid: *Add some red wine to dilute the tomato sauce.* | **dilute sth with sth** *Dilute the paint with a little oil.* **2** to make a quality, belief etc. weaker or less effective, especially by adding something: *Opening NATO to new members may dilute its strength.* [**Origin:** 1500–1600 Latin *dilutus*, past participle of *diluere* **to wash away**] —**diluted** *adj.*: *diluted fruit juice* —**dilution** /dɪˈluʃən/ *n.* [U]

dilute² *adj.* [only before noun] a dilute liquid has been made weaker by the addition of water or another substance: *dilute hydrochloric acid*

diˌlute soˈlution *n.* [C] CHEMISTRY a liquid that contains a SOLUTE (=substance that has mixed with and become part a liquid)

dim¹ /dɪm/ *adj. comparative* **dimmer**, *superlative* **dimmest**

1 DARK fairly dark or not giving much light, so that you cannot see well OPP **bright**: *a dim hallway* | *The lights were dim.*

2 SHAPE a dim shape is not easy to see well because it is far away or there is not enough light SYN **faint**: *the dim outline of a ship in the distance*

3 a dim recollection/awareness etc. something that is difficult for someone to remember, understand etc. SYN **vague**: *Laura had only a dim memory of the conversation.*

4 take a dim view of sth to disapprove of something: *Management took a dim view of union organizing efforts.*

5 FUTURE CHANCES if your chances of success in the future are dim, they are not good: *Prospects for an early settlement of the dispute are dim.*

6 UNINTELLIGENT INFORMAL not intelligent SYN **stupid**: *You can be really dim sometimes!* → see also DIMWIT

7 LONG AGO long ago and not related to the present time: *For many students the 1970s are dim history.*

8 EYES LITERARY dim eyes are weak and cannot see well —**dimly** *adv.*: *a dimly lit room* | *She was only dimly aware of the risk.* —**dimness** *n.* [U]

dim² *v.* **dimmed, dimming** **1** [I,T] if a light dims, or if you dim it, it becomes less bright: *The lights dimmed, and the curtain rose.* **2** [I,T] if a feeling or quality dims, or if something dims it, it grows weaker: *Nothing could dim their enthusiasm.* | *Hopes for a peaceful settlement have dimmed.* **3 dim your headlights/lights** to lower the angle of the front lights of your car, especially when someone is driving toward you

Di Mag·gio /dɪˈmædʒioʊ/, **Joe** /dʒoʊ/ (1914–1999) a U.S. baseball player who is considered one of the greatest players ever

dime /daɪm/ S3 *n.* [C] **1** a coin worth ten cents (=1/10 of a dollar), used in the U.S. and Canada ►see THESAURUS box at **money** **2 be a dime a dozen** to be very common and not valuable: *Jobs like his are a dime a dozen.* **3 not a dime** no money at all: *It didn't cost me a dime.* **4 on a dime** within a very small space, or within a very short period of time: *Her new car can stop on a dime.* [**Origin:** 1300–1400 Old French **tenth part**, from Latin *decima*]

ˈdime ˌnovel *n.* [C] a cheap book with a story that contains a lot of exciting events

di·men·sion /dɪˈmɛnʃən, daɪ-/ Ac *n.* **1** [C] a part of a situation that affects the way you think about it SYN **aspect**: **+to** *There's a social dimension to education.* | **a new/an extra/another etc. dimension** *His coaching has* ***added*** *another* ***dimension to*** *my game.* | *The baby has* ***brought*** *another* ***dimension to*** *their lives.* | *Stacy is also Tom's twin, which adds* ***another dimension*** *to the story.* | **the political/human/spiritual etc. dimension** *the historical dimensions of these issues* **2** [C usually plural] MATH the length, height, width, depth, or DIAMETER of something: *a rectangle with the dimensions 5 cm x 2 cm* | **+of** *the exact dimensions of the room* **3** a direction in space that is at an agle of 90 degrees to two other directions: *A diagram represents things in only two dimensions.* → see also FOURTH DIMENSION **4** [C,U] how great or serious a problem is: *a catastrophe of enormous dimensions* [**Origin:** 1300–1400 Old French, Latin *dimetiri* **to measure out**]

ˈdime store *n.* [C] a store that sells many different types of inexpensive goods, especially for the house SYN **five-and-dime**

di·min·ish /dɪˈmɪnɪʃ/ Ac *v.* **1** [I,T] to become smaller or less important, or to make something do this SYN **reduce** SYN **lessen**: *His anxiety slowly diminished.* | *The fences may diminish property values in the neighborhood.* **2** [T] to deliberately make someone or something appear less important or valuable than they really are: *This is not to diminish the importance of what social workers achieve.* ►see THESAURUS box at **decrease¹** **3 diminishing returns** the point when the profits or advantages you are getting from something stop increasing in relation to the effort you are making [**Origin:** 1400–1500 *diminue* (14–16 centuries), from Old French *diminuer*, from Latin *minuere* **to make less**]

diˌminished caˈpacity also **diˌminished responsiˈbility** *n.* [U] LAW a condition in which someone is not considered to be responsible for their actions because they are mentally ill or because they are below a normal level of intelligence

diˌminishing ˌmarginal reˈturns also **diˌminishing reˈturns** *n.* [plural] ECONOMICS a rule about systems for making products in which everything but one INPUT is fixed. The more you add additional units of the unfixed input, the less product you will produce.

di·min·u·en·do /dɪˌmɪnyuˈɛndoʊ/ *n.* [C] TECHNICAL a part in a piece of music where it becomes gradually quieter OPP **crescendo**

dim·i·nu·tion /ˌdɪməˈnuʃən/ Ac *n.* [C,U] FORMAL a reduction in the size, number, or amount of something: **+of/in** *a diminution of citizens' freedom*

di·min·u·tive¹ /dɪˈmɪnyəṭɪv/ *adj.* FORMAL very small or short: *a diminutive man*

diminutive² *n.* [C] ENG. LANG. ARTS a word formed by adding a DIMINUTIVE SUFFIX

diˌminutive ˈsuffix *n.* [C] ENG. LANG. ARTS an ending that is added to a word to express smallness, for example "-ling" added to "duck" to make "duckling"

dim·mer /ˈdɪmɚ/ also **ˈdimmer ˌswitch** *n.* [C] an electric SWITCH that can change the brightness of a light

dim·ple /ˈdɪmpəl/ *n.* [C] **1** a small hollow place on your cheek or chin, especially one that forms when you smile **2** a small hollow place on a surface —**dimpled** *adj.*: *dimpled cheeks*

dim sum /ˌdɪm ˈsʌm/ *n.* [U] a Chinese meal in which small amounts of many different types of food are served, usually a few at a time

dim·wit /ˈdɪmwɪt/ *n.* [C] SPOKEN a stupid person —**dimwitted** *adj.*

din¹ /dɪn/ *n.* [singular, U] FORMAL a loud continuous noise that sounds bad SYN **uproar**: *We couldn't hear ourselves talk* ***above the din.***

din² *v.* **dinned, dinning**

din sth **into** sb *phr. v.* FORMAL to make someone learn and remember something by repeating it to them again and again: *Respect for our elders was dinned into us in school.*

di·nar /ˈdinɑr, dɪˈnɑr/ *n.* [C] the standard unit of money used in the former Yugoslavia and in some Middle Eastern countries

dine /daɪn/ *v.* [I] FORMAL to eat dinner, especially at a formal occasion: *We dined at the Ritz.* → see also **wine and dine sb** at WINE²

dine on sth *phr. v.* FORMAL to eat a particular kind of food for dinner, especially expensive food: *We dined on lobster.*

dine out *phr. v.* FORMAL to eat dinner in a restaurant SYN **eat out**: *They would dine out together once a month.*

D

din·er /ˈdaɪnɚ/ *n.* [C] **1** a small restaurant that serves inexpensive meals: *an all-night diner* ▶see THESAURUS box at **restaurant** **2** someone who is eating in a restaurant

di·nette /daɪˈnɛt/ *n.* [C] a small area, usually in or near the kitchen in a house, where people eat meals

diˈnette set *n.* [C] a table and matching chairs

ding¹ /dɪŋ/ *n.* [C] **1** a small hollow area in the surface of something, usually caused by something hitting it: *a few dings in the car door* **2** a sharp ringing sound, usually from a bell or piece of metal

ding² *v.* INFORMAL **1** [T] to damage something slightly by hitting it: *Pete just dinged the rear bumper.* **2** [I,T] to make a sound like a bell, or to make a bell do this **3** [T usually passive] to refuse to accept someone for a job, school etc. SYN **reject**: *I* ***got dinged*** *by all the colleges I applied to.*

ding-a-ling /ˈdɪŋ ə ˌlɪŋ/ *n.* [C] SPOKEN a stupid person

ding·bat /ˈdɪŋbæt/ *n.* [C] SPOKEN a stupid person

ding-dong /ˈdɪŋ dɔŋ, -dɑŋ/ *n.* **1** [U] the sound made by a bell **2** [C] SPOKEN a stupid person

dinghy

din·ghy /ˈdɪŋi/ *n. plural* **dinghies** [C] a small open boat used for pleasure, or for taking people between a ship and the shore [**Origin:** 1800–1900 Hindi *dingi* **small boat**, from *dinga* **boat**]

din·go /ˈdɪŋgoʊ/ *n. plural* **dingoes** [C] an Australian wild dog

din·gy /ˈdɪndʒi/ *adj. comparative* **dingier**, *superlative* **dingiest** a dingy room, street, or place is dirty and in bad condition: *a dark dingy basement* —**dinginess** *n.* [U]

ˈdining car *n.* [C] a special car on a train where meals are served

ˈdining room S3 *n.* [C] a room where you eat meals in a house, hotel etc.

ˈdining ˌtable also **ˈdining room ˌtable** *n.* [C] a table at which you eat meals → see also DINNER TABLE

dink¹ /dɪŋk/ *v.*

dink around *phr. v.* SPOKEN to waste time doing something unimportant: *Stop dinking around and get to work.*

dink² *n.* [C] SPOKEN a stupid person → see also RINKY-DINK

din·ky /ˈdɪŋki/ *adj. comparative* **dinkier**, *superlative* **dinkiest** SPOKEN too small, and often of poor quality: *I can't believe they charge $8.95 for this dinky salad!*

din·ner /ˈdɪnɚ/ S1 W2 *n.* **1** [C,U] the main meal of the day, usually eaten in the evening, but sometimes in the middle of the day: *We're having fish* ***for dinner*** *tonight.* | **have/eat dinner** *What time do you usually eat dinner?* | *Let's* ***go out for dinner*** *tonight.* | *She* ***took*** *me* ***out to dinner*** *on my birthday.* ▶see THESAURUS box at **meal** **2 Sunday/Christmas/Thanksgiving etc. dinner** a special meal eaten on Sunday, at Christmas, at Thanksgiving etc.: *We had some friends over for Sunday dinner.* **3** [C] a formal occasion when an evening meal is eaten, often to celebrate something: *the club's annual dinner* [**Origin:** 1200–1300 Old French *diner*, from *diner* **to eat**] → see also TV DINNER

ˈdinner ˌdance *n.* [C] a social event in the evening, that includes a formal meal and music for dancing

ˈdinner ˌjacket *n.* [C] a black or white JACKET worn by men on very formal occasions, usually with a BOW TIE as part of a TUXEDO

ˈdinner ˌparty *n.* [C] a social event when people are invited to someone's house for an evening meal

ˈdinner ˌservice also **ˈdinner set** *n.* [C] a complete set of plates, dishes etc., used for serving meals

ˈdinner ˌtable *n.* **the dinner table 1** an occasion when people are eating dinner together: *Many of the photographs are not suitable for the dinner table.* **2** the table at which people eat dinner SYN **dining table**

ˈdinner ˌtheater *n.* [C,U] a restaurant in which you see a play after your meal, or this type of entertainment

din·ner·time /ˈdɪnɚˌtaɪm/ *n.* [U] the time when you usually have dinner, usually between 5 p.m. and 7 p.m. or between noon and 1 p.m.: *He always seems to call me at dinnertime.*

dinosaur

di·no·saur /ˈdaɪnəˌsɔr/ S3 *n.* [C] **1** BIOLOGY one of many types of REPTILE that lived millions of years ago **2** something very large and old-fashioned that does not work well or effectively anymore: *The Maine dam is a dinosaur which should be removed.* **3** INFORMAL an insulting way of describing someone who is old and does not have modern ideas: *Some of the dinosaurs of heavy metal music will be on tour this summer.* [**Origin:** 1800–1900 Greek *deinos* **terrible** + *sauros* **lizard**]

dint /dɪnt/ *n.* **by dint of sth** by using a particular method: *By dint of hard work, she got the manager's job.*

di·o·cese /ˈdaɪəsɪs, -ˌsiz/ *n.* [C] the area under the control of a BISHOP in some Christian churches —**diocesan** /daɪˈɑsəsən/ *adj.*

di·ode /ˈdaɪoʊd/ *n.* [C] PHYSICS a piece of electrical equipment that makes an electrical current flow in one direction

Di·og·e·nes /daɪˈɑdʒəniz/ (?412–?323 B.C.) an ancient Greek PHILOSOPHER

Di·o·ny·sus /ˌdaɪəˈnaɪsəs/ in Greek MYTHOLOGY, the god of wine and FERTILITY, usually connected with uncontrolled behavior involving drinking, parties, and sex

di·o·ram·a /ˌdaɪəˈræmə, -ˈrɑmə/ *n.* [C] a box or glass case that contains a model of a scene from history or from a story, often made by children in school

di·ox·ide /daɪˈɑksaɪd/ *n.* [C,U] CHEMISTRY a chemical compound containing two atoms of oxygen to every atom of another ELEMENT → see also CARBON DIOXIDE

di·ox·in /daɪˈɑksɪn/ *n.* [C,U] a very poisonous chemical used for killing plants

dip¹ /dɪp/ S3 *v.* **dipped**, **dipping** **1** [T] to put something into a liquid and quickly lift it out again: **dip sth in/into sth** *Dip vegetables into the batter before frying.* → see picture on page A32 **2** [I] if the amount or level of something dips, it goes down to a lower level, usually for a short time: *Housing prices dipped again last month.* | *Temperatures may dip to –2 degrees overnight.* **3** [I always + adv./prep.,T] to move to a lower position, or to make something do this: *She dipped her head to avoid a low branch.* | **+in/into/down etc.** *The sun dipped below the horizon.* **4** [T] to put pets or other animals in a bath containing a chemical that kills insects on their skin [**Origin:** Old English *dyppan*] → see also SKINNY-DIPPING

dip into sth *phr. v.* **1** to use some of an amount of money that you have: *City officials were forced to dip into other funds to pay for snow removal.* | *Teachers are having to* ***dip into their pockets*** (=pay for something with their own money) *for new school supplies.* **2** to take something from inside something such as a box or container: *He kept dipping into the bag of candy.* **3** to read short parts of a book, magazine etc., but not the whole thing: *It's the kind of book you can dip into now and again.*

dip² *n.*
1 FOOD [C,U] a thick mixture that you can dip food into before you eat it: *an avocado dip for chips*
2 SWIM [C] INFORMAL a quick swim: *Let's* ***take a quick dip*** *in the pool.* | *She* ***went for a dip in the lake.***
3 DECREASE [C] a slight decrease in the amount of something: **+in** *a dip in the exchange rate*
4 IN A SURFACE [C] a place where the surface of something goes down suddenly, and then goes up again: **+in** *a dip in the road*
5 PERSON [C] SPOKEN a stupid person
6 FOR ANIMALS [C,U] a liquid that contains a chemical which kills insects on pets and other animals

diph·the·ri·a /dɪfˈθɪriə, dɪp-/ *n.* [U] MEDICINE a serious infectious throat disease that makes breathing difficult [**Origin:** 1800–1900 Modern Latin, Greek *diphthera* **leather**; because of the hardened skin in the throat]

diph·thong /ˈdɪfθɔŋ, ˈdɪp-/ *n.* [C] ENG. LANG. ARTS **1** a vowel sound made by pronouncing two vowels quickly one after the other; for example, the vowel sound in "my" is a diphthong **2** a DIGRAPH [**Origin:** 1400–1500 French, Late Latin *diphthongus* **two sounds**, from Greek *phthongos* **voice, sound**]

dip·loid /ˈdɪplɔɪd/ *n.* [C] BIOLOGY a cell or ORGANISM that contains two complete sets of CHROMOSOMES, one from each parent —**diploid** *adj.*

di·plo·ma /dɪˈploʊmə/ *n.* [C] an official paper showing that a student has successfully completed their HIGH SCHOOL or college education: *a high school diploma* [**Origin:** 1600–1700 Latin **passport, diploma**, from Greek, **folded paper**]

di·plo·ma·cy /dɪˈploʊməsi/ *n.* [U] **1** POLITICS the management of relationships between countries: *We hope to end the conflict through diplomacy rather than force.* **2** skill in dealing with people and persuading them to agree to something without upsetting them: *The job requires tact and diplomacy.* → see also GUNBOAT DIPLOMACY

dip·lo·mat /ˈdɪpləˌmæt/ *n.* [C] **1** someone who officially represents their government in a foreign country **2** someone who is good at dealing with people without upsetting them: *Karen is a natural diplomat.*

dip·lo·mat·ic /ˌdɪpləˈmætɪk◂/ *adj.* **1** relating to the work of diplomats: *Robert's next diplomatic assignment was at the Paris embassy.* **2** good at dealing with people politely and skillfully without upsetting them: *Jen tried to be diplomatic as she explained the problem.* | *a diplomatic answer* —**diplomatically** /-kli/ *adv.*

diploˈmatic ˌcorps *n.* [U] all the diplomats working in a particular country

ˌdiplomatic imˈmunity *n.* [U] LAW, POLITICS a diplomat's special rights in the country where they are working, which protect them from local taxes and PROSECUTION

ˌdiplomatic reˈlations also **ˌdiplomatic ˈties** the arrangement between two countries that each should keep representatives at an EMBASSY in the other's country: *The two countries* ***established diplomatic relations*** *last year.* | *The U.S.* ***broke off diplomatic ties*** *with Cuba in the early 1960s.*

di·plo·ma·tist /dɪˈploʊmətɪst/ *n.* [C] FORMAL a DIPLOMAT

di·pole /ˈdaɪpoʊl/ *n.* [C] CHEMISTRY two equal and opposite electrical CHARGES separated by a short distance, for example the positive and negative forces on a MAGNET or a MOLECULE

dip·per /ˈdɪpɚ/ *n.* [C] **1** a large spoon with a long handle, used for taking liquid out of a container **2** BIOLOGY a small bird that feeds in quick-moving streams → see also BIG DIPPER, LITTLE DIPPER

dip·py /ˈdɪpi/ *adj.* *comparative* **dippier**, *superlative* **dippiest** INFORMAL silly or crazy

dip·so·ma·ni·ac /ˌdɪpsəˈmeɪniæk/ *n.* [C] TECHNICAL someone who has a very strong desire for alcoholic drinks, which they cannot control —**dipsomania** *n.* [U] → see also ALCOHOLIC

dip·stick /ˈdɪpstɪk/ *n.* [C] **1** a stick used for measuring the amount of liquid in a container, especially the amount of oil in a car's engine **2** SPOKEN a stupid person

dip·tych /ˈdɪptɪk/ *n.* [C] a picture made in two parts which can be closed like a book → see also TRIPTYCH

dire /daɪɚ/ *adj.* **1** extremely serious or terrible: *The situation doesn't seem as dire as you described it.* | *At the time, rebels were* ***in dire need of*** *arms.* | *Increasing housing prices will have* ***dire consequences*** *for the poor.* | *Peggy was* ***in dire*** *financial* ***straits*** (=in an extremely difficult or serious situation) *when her husband died.* **2 a dire warning/prediction/outlook** something that warns people about something terrible that will happen in the future: *Analysts' dire predictions about the economy have failed to come true.*

di·rect¹ /dəˈrɛkt, daɪ-/ S3 W2 *adj.*
1 WITHOUT INVOLVING OTHERS [usually before noun] done without involving other people, actions, processes etc. OPP **indirect**: *I'm not in direct contact with them.* | *Sue has direct control over the business.* | **a direct effect/impact** *Cutbacks in defense spending will have a direct impact on 80,000 jobs.* | **a direct link/connection** *There is a direct link between poverty and ill-health.* | **a direct result/consequence (of sth)** *At least 32 people died as a direct result of the explosion.*
2 FROM ONE PLACE TO ANOTHER going straight from one place to another, without stopping or changing direction OPP **indirect**: *a direct route to the freeway* | *We can get a* ***direct flight*** *to New York.*
3 BEHAVIOR/ATTITUDE saying exactly what you mean in an honest clear way OPP **indirect**: *It's best to be direct when talking with the management.* | **a direct question/answer** *He wouldn't give me a direct answer.* ▶see THESAURUS box at **honest**
4 EXACT [only before noun] exact, complete, or total: *The results of this study are* ***in direct contrast to*** *earlier findings.* | *Weight increases* ***in direct proportion to*** *mass.* | *The article contains* ***direct quotes*** (=their exact words) *from witnesses.*
5 a direct hit an occasion when something such as a bomb or a very bad storm exactly hits a place, causing a lot of damage: *A direct hit destroyed the bridge.*
6 a direct descendant someone who is the child, GRANDCHILD, GREAT-GRANDCHILD etc. of someone else, and not a NIECE, NEPHEW etc.: *a direct descendant of Benjamin Franklin*
7 direct sunlight/heat strong sunlight or heat without anything between it and someone or something else OPP **indirect**: *Keep the plant away from direct sunlight.*
[**Origin:** 1300–1400 Latin *directus*, past participle of *dirigere* **to set straight, guide**]

direct² S3 W2 *v.*
1 [T always + adv./prep.] to aim something in a particular direction or at a particular person, group etc.: **+at/toward/away from etc.** *Her angry comments were not directed at us.* | *How could scientists direct deadly meteorites away from the earth?* | *I'd like to* ***direct*** *your* ***attention to*** *paragraph four.*
2 [T] to be in charge of something or control it: *Mr. Turner is directing the investigation.* ▶see THESAURUS box at **control¹**
3 [I,T] ENG. LANG. ARTS to give the actors in a play, movie, or television program instructions about what they should do: *The play was directed by Frank Hauser.*
4 [T] FORMAL to tell someone the way to a place: **direct sb to sth** *A nurse directed us to the waiting room.* | *A police officer was* ***directing traffic*** *after a truck accident.* ▶see THESAURUS box at **lead¹**
5 TELL SB TO DO STH [T] FORMAL to tell someone what they should do SYN **order**: **direct sb to do sth** *The border guard directed me to hand over my passport.* | **direct that** *Burns' will directed that the money be used for college scholarships.*

D

direct³ *adv.* **1** without stopping or changing direction SYN **directly**: *I'm flying direct to Dallas from Los Angeles.* **2** without dealing with anyone else first SYN **directly**: *It's usually cheaper to buy the goods direct from the wholesaler.*

di͵rect 'action *n.* [U] an action such as a STRIKE or a protest which is intended to make a company or government make changes such as increasing workers' pay or stopping something from being built

di͵rect 'current ABBREVIATION **DC** *n.* [U] PHYSICS a flow of electricity that moves in one direction → see also ALTERNATING CURRENT

di͵rect 'debit *n.* [C,U] an method of having a bank regularly pay your bills for you directly from your bank account —**direct debit** *v.* [T]

di͵rect de'mocracy *n.* [U] POLITICS a system of government in which groups of citizens discuss and vote on every plan or action to be carried out by the government, rather than have the decisions made by elected government officials

di͵rect de'posit *n.* [U] a method of paying someone's salary directly into their bank account —**direct deposit** *v.* [T]

di͵rect 'discourse *n.* [U] DIRECT SPEECH

di·rec·tion /dəˈrɛkʃən, daɪ-/ S2 W1 *n.*
1 TOWARD [C] the way something or someone moves, faces, or is aimed: *Did you see which direction they went?* | *I was hoping they wouldn't look* ***in** our **direction**.* | *The trucks headed* ***in the direction of*** (=toward) *town.* | *A car coming* ***in the opposite direction*** *struck Sandi's car.* | *Hurricanes can* ***change direction*** *in a matter of hours.* | *I saw smoke coming* ***from the direction of*** *the parking lot.* | *People started running* ***in all directions.*** | **in a northerly/easterly etc. direction** *Continue in a southerly direction until you reach the road.*
2 WAY STH DEVELOPS [C] the general way in which someone or something changes or develops: *Our lives started to go in different directions.* | **take a different/new/exciting etc. direction** *We decided that the campaign should take a different direction.* | **move/head/go in the right direction** *We didn't feel that the country was going in the right direction.*
3 directions [plural] **a)** instructions about how to get from one place to another: *Could you* ***give*** *me* ***directions to*** *Times Square?* | *Why do men always hate to* ***ask for directions?*** **b)** instructions on how to do something SYN **instructions**: *You'd better read the directions first.* | *Just* ***follow the directions*** *on the package.*
4 CONTROL [U] control, management, or advice: *The company has been successful* ***under*** *Meyer's* ***direction.***
5 PURPOSE [U] a general purpose or aim: *Rachel's father felt her life lacked direction.*
6 MOVIE [U] ENG. LANG. ARTS the instructions and advice given to actors and other people in a movie, play etc. → see also **sense of direction** at SENSE¹ (11)

di·rec·tion·al /dəˈrɛkʃənəl, daɪ-/ *adj.* [only before noun] TECHNICAL **1** pointing in a particular direction: *a directional beam of light* **2** a directional piece of equipment receives or gives out radio signals from some directions more strongly than others: *a directional antenna*

di͵rectional se'lection *n.* [U] BIOLOGY a form of NATURAL SELECTION in which a single group within a SPECIES with a particular physical feature continues to exist and produce children, while members of the species without this feature gradually stop existing → see also DISRUPTIVE SELECTION

di·rec·tive¹ /dəˈrɛktɪv/ *n.* [C] an official order or instruction to do something: *a government directive on food labeling*

directive² *adj.* giving instructions: *a directive approach to management*

di·rect·ly /dəˈrɛktli, daɪ-/ S2 W2 *adv.* **1** with no other person, action, process etc. involved OPP **indirectly**: *New evidence directly linked Nathanson to the killing.* | *The new law won't affect us directly.* **2** exactly SYN **right**: *Have you noticed how he never looks directly at you?* | *Mike and his wife sat directly behind us.* **3 speak/ask/answer etc. directly** to say exactly what you mean without trying to hide anything: *Strauss refused to comment directly on the board meeting.*

di͵rect 'mail *n.* [U] advertisements that are sent by mail to many people

di͵rect 'method *n.* [singular] a method of teaching a foreign language without using the student's own language

͵direct 'object *n.* [C] ENG. LANG. ARTS in grammar, the person or thing that receives the direct action of a TRANSITIVE verb. In the sentence "He eats bread," "bread" is the direct object. → see also INDIRECT OBJECT

di·rec·tor /dəˈrɛktɚ, daɪ-/ S2 W1 *n.* [C] **1** ENG. LANG. ARTS the person who gives instructions to the actors, CAMERAMAN etc. in a movie, play etc. → see also PRODUCER ►see THESAURUS box at **movie** **2** someone who controls or manages a company, organization, or activity: *a sales director* | *the board of directors*

di·rec·tor·ate /dəˈrɛktərɪt/ *n.* [C] the BOARD (=committee) of directors of a company, or the people who are in charge of a large government AGENCY: *the CIA's Operations Directorate*

di·rec·tor·ship /dəˈrɛktɚ͵ʃɪp/ *n.* [C,U] the position of being in charge of a company, organization, or activity: *Sales increased by 25% under Danoff's directorship.*

di·rec·to·ry /dəˈrɛktəri, daɪ-/ *n. plural* **directories** [C] **1** a book or list of names, facts etc., usually arranged in alphabetical order: *the telephone directory* | *a directory of all baseball clubs worldwide* **2** a sign in a building or department store that tells you where to find something or someone **3** COMPUTERS a WEBSITE where you can find contact information for people or businesses **4** COMPUTERS a list of computer FILES kept on a DISK or in the part of the computer where information is stored

di͵rectory as'sistance *n.* [U] a service on the telephone network that you can use to find out someone's telephone number SYN **information**

di͵rect 'primary *n.* [C] POLITICS an election in the U.S. in which all citizens in an area can vote to choose a political party's CANDIDATES for political positions → see also BLANKET PRIMARY

di·rec·trix /dɪˈrɛktrɪks, daɪ-/ *n. plural* **directrixes** or **directrices** /-trɪsiz/ [C] MATH a straight line drawn below a PARABOLA (=deep curve with steep sides), which is used to describe the shape of the curve. Each point on the curve is equal to its distance from the directrix divided by its distance from another fixed point inside the curve.

di͵rect 'rule *n.* [U] POLITICS a system of government in which an area or country is under the political control of the government of a more powerful country or under the control of a central government

di͵rect 'speech *n.* [U] ENG. LANG. ARTS the style used to report what someone says by giving their actual words, for example, "Julie said, 'I don't want to go.'" → see also INDIRECT SPEECH

di͵rect 'tax *n.* [C,U] ECONOMICS a tax, such as income tax, which is collected from the person who pays it, rather than a tax on goods or services which companies pay OPP **indirect tax** —**direct taxation** *n.* [U]

di͵rect vari'ation *n.* [U] MATH the relationship between two VARIABLES (=mathematical quantities which can represent any of several different amounts) that can be written as $y = kx$, where k is a quantity that stays the same. As one of the variables increases, so does the other by the same amount or to the same degree. → see also INVERSE VARIATION

dirge /dɚdʒ/ *n.* [C] **1** a slow sad song that is sung or played at a funeral **2** a song or piece of music that is too slow and boring

dir·i·gi·ble /ˈdɪrədʒəbəl, dəˈrɪ-/ *n.* [C] an AIRSHIP → see also BLIMP (1)

dirt /dɚt/ S2 W3 *n.* [U] **1** earth or soil: *Put the seeds in* *the pot and cover them with dirt.* | *A dog was rolling around* ***in the dirt***. | *They live at the end of a dirt road* (=with a surface made of dirt). ▸see THESAURUS box at **ground**[1] **2** any substance that makes things dirty, such as mud or dust: *The floor was covered with dirt.* **3** INFORMAL information about someone's private life or activities which could give people a bad opinion of them if it became known: *Reporters contacted Cox's former girlfriend, trying to* ***dig up dirt on*** (=find embarrassing things about) *him.* **4** talk, writing, movies etc. that are considered bad or immoral because they are about sex [SYN] **filth** [**Origin:** 1200–1300 Old Norse *drit*] → see also **dish the dirt** at DISH (2), **hit the ground/deck/dirt** at HIT[1] (25), **hit paydirt** at PAY DIRT (1)

'dirt bag, dirtbag *n.* [C] a person who is disgusting and immoral, who does bad things to other people, and who you do not respect

'dirt bike *n.* [C] a small MOTORCYCLE for young people, usually ridden on rough paths or fields

dirt-'cheap *adj., adv.* INFORMAL extremely inexpensive: *Air fares to Chicago are dirt-cheap right now.*

'dirt ˌfarmer *n.* [C] a poor farmer who works to feed himself and his family, without paying anyone else to help

'dirt-poor *adj.* INFORMAL extremely poor

dirt·y[1] /ˈdəṭi/ [S2] [W3] *adj. comparative* **dirtier**, *superlative* **dirtiest**

1 NOT CLEAN not clean [OPP] **clean**: *How did the floor get so dirty?* | *a stack of* ***dirty dishes*** | *Put your* ***dirty clothes*** *in the washing machine.*

THESAURUS

filthy very dirty: *The carpet was filthy.*
dusty covered with dust: *piles of dusty books*
muddy covered in mud: *muddy hiking boots*
grimy dirty: *The glass in the windows was grimy.*
grubby INFORMAL fairly dirty: *a grubby pair of jeans*
greasy covered with a lot of oil or grease (=a thick oily substance): *greasy fingermarks on the table*
soiled FORMAL made dirty, especially by waste from your body: *The sheets were soiled.*
contaminated made dirty by a dangerous substance or bacteria: *contaminated food*
polluted used about land, water, or air that has been made dirty: *a polluted lake*

2 SEX relating to sex, in a way that is considered bad or immoral: *dirty magazines* | *a* ***dirty joke*** | *That's not what I meant! You* ***have such a dirty mind***.
3 BAD/IMMORAL used to emphasize that you think something is bad, dishonest, or immoral: *Having to lay employees off is a dirty job.* | *He* ***played a dirty trick on*** *me.* | *Journalists have discovered the mayor's* ***dirty little secret***: *his criminal record for drug possession.*
4 give sb a dirty look to look at someone in a very disapproving way: *My cell phone rang during the meeting and Jack gave me a really dirty look.*
5 sth is a dirty word, sth has become a dirty word used to say that people believe something is a bad thing even if they do not know or think much about it: *"Liberal" has somehow become a dirty word in America.*
6 dirty tricks dishonest or illegal activities, especially done by a government, political group, or company, such as spreading false information about their competitors or opponents
7 do sb's dirty work to do a bad or dishonest job for someone so that they do not have to do it themselves: *Tell Fran I'm not going to do her dirty work for her.*
8 it's a dirty job, but someone has to do it used to say that something is unpleasant to do, but that it is necessary
9 wash your dirty laundry/linen in public also **air your dirty laundry/linen in public** to discuss something embarrassing or bad about yourself where everyone can know, see, or hear
10 dirty pool unfair or dishonest behavior: *They shouldn't charge you for that. It's just dirty pool.*
11 DRUGS SLANG containing or possessing illegal drugs

dirty[2] *adv.* **1 dirty rotten** SPOKEN extremely dishonest or unkind: *What a dirty rotten trick!* **2 play dirty** INFORMAL **a)** to behave in a very unfair and dishonest way: *Warren was willing to play dirty in order to get the job.* **b)** to cheat in a game: *I hate playing basketball with Bill – he always plays dirty.* **3 talk dirty** INFORMAL to talk about sex using words that are offensive or OBSCENE

dirty[3] *v.* **dirties, dirtied, dirtying** [T] **1** to make something dirty: *You can borrow my gloves, but please try not to dirty them.* **2** to make someone feel or seem bad, dishonest, or immoral [SYN] **sully**: *The army's actions dirtied its reputation.* **3 dirty your hands (with sth)** to do hard work, especially physical work in which your your hands get dirty: *Why dirty your hands when you can hire someone to do the work?*

ˌdirty 'blond *adj.* dirty blond hair is a dull light brown color —**dirty blond** *n.* [C]

ˌdirty old 'man *n.* [C] INFORMAL, DISAPPROVING an older man who is too sexually interested in younger women

ˌDirty 'War *n.* **the Dirty War** HISTORY in Argentina, the period between 1976 and 1983 when the country was ruled by a military government, during which the army and police force carried out many violent attacks against Argentine citizens, and thousands of people the government considered to be a threat to the state disappeared or were put in prison without a TRIAL

dis /dɪs/ *v.* **dissed, dissing** [T] SLANG to make unfair and unkind remarks about someone

dis- /dɪs/ *prefix* **1** [in nouns, verbs, and adjectives] shows an opposite or negative: *I disapprove* (=do not approve). | *dishonesty* (=lack of honesty) | *a discontented look* **2** [in verbs] shows the stopping or removing of a condition: *Disconnect the machine from the electrical supply* (=so that it is no longer connected). | *Disinfect the wound first.*

dis·a·bil·i·ty /ˌdɪsəˈbɪləṭi/ [S3] *n. plural* **disabilities**
1 [C] a physical or mental condition that makes it difficult for someone to do the things most people are able to do [SYN] **handicap**: *a severe disability* | **people/children with disabilities** *help for children with disabilities* | **a learning/physical/mental etc. disability** *She manages to lead a normal life in spite of her physical disabilities.* **2** [U] money that is given by the government to people who are disabled: *He has been living* ***on disability*** *for ten years.* **3** [U] the state of having a disability, especially not being able to use parts of your body: *The group is for people who are learning to live with disability.*

dis·a·ble /dɪsˈeɪbəl/ *v.* [T] **1** [often passive] to make someone unable to use a part of their body in a way that most people can: *Don was permanently disabled in a car accident.* ▸see THESAURUS box at **hurt**[1] **2** to deliberately stop a machine or piece of equipment from working: *Somehow, the robbers were able to disable the gallery's alarm system.* —**disablement** *n.* [C,U]

dis·a·bled /dɪsˈeɪbəld/ *adj.* **1** someone who is disabled cannot use a part of their body in a way that most people can: *One of their daughters is* ***severely disabled***.

THESAURUS

handicapped if someone is handicapped, a part of their body or their mind has been permanently injured or damaged. This word is old-fashioned and is considered offensive by some people.
wheelchair user someone who is in a wheelchair because they cannot walk
paraplegic someone who is unable to move the lower part of their body, including their legs
quadriplegic someone who is permanently unable to move any part of their body below their neck
special needs people with special needs need special help or equipment or different teaching methods because of their mental or physical condition

learning difficulties people with learning difficulties have a mental problem that affects their ability to learn

2 the disabled [plural] people who are disabled: *Doors should be wide enough to provide access for the disabled.* **3** [only before noun] intended to be used by physically disabled people: *a disabled parking permit* → see Usage note at HANDICAPPED

dis'abled list *n.* **the disabled list** the players on a professional sports team who are unable to play because of injuries

D

dis·a·buse /ˌdɪsəˈbyuz/ *v.* [T] FORMAL to persuade someone that what they believe is untrue: **disabuse sb of sth** *I hope to disabuse you of the notion that all employees are lazy.*

di·sac·cha·ride /daɪˈsækəˌraɪd/ *n.* [C] CHEMISTRY a sugar that contains two MONOSACCHARIDES (=simple sugars that do not separate and form other sugars)

dis·ad·van·tage /ˌdɪsədˈvæntɪdʒ/ *n.* [C,U] **1** something that may make someone less successful than other people OPP advantage: *Your main disadvantage is your lack of job experience.* | *Anyone who can't use a computer is **at a disadvantage**.* | *Jen's small size **puts** her **at a disadvantage** in the game.* | *The present system **works to the disadvantage of** the consumer.* **2** something that is not favorable, or that causes problems OPP advantage: **+of** *The biggest disadvantage of her job is the long hours.* | *Both methods have their **advantages and disadvantages**.* | **+to** *One disadvantage to this plan is that you can't choose your own doctor.*

dis·ad·van·taged /ˌdɪsədˈvæntɪdʒd/ *adj.* **1** having social problems, such as a lack of money or education, which make it more difficult for you to succeed than other people: *racial minorities and other disadvantaged groups* ►see THESAURUS box at poor **2 the disadvantaged** [plural] people who are disadvantaged: *health programs for the disadvantaged*

dis·ad·van·ta·geous /ˌdɪsædvænˈteɪdʒəs, -vən-/ *adj.* [+ to/for] unfavorable and likely to cause problems for you OPP advantageous —**disadvantageously** *adv.*

dis·af·fect·ed /ˌdɪsəˈfɛktɪd◂/ *adj.* FORMAL not loyal anymore because you are not satisfied with your leader, ruler etc.: *disaffected voters* —**disaffection** /ˌdɪsəˈfɛkʃən/ *n.* [U]

dis·af·fil·i·ate /ˌdɪsəˈfɪliˌeɪt/ *v.* [I,T + from] if an organization disaffiliates from another organization or is disaffiliated from it, it breaks the official connection between them —**disaffiliation** /ˌdɪsəfɪliˈeɪʃən/ *n.* [U]

dis·a·gree /ˌdɪsəˈgri/ S3 *v.* [I] **1** to have or express a different opinion from someone else OPP agree: *I totally disagree, Mike. It's not a problem at all.* | **+with** *Charlie didn't like it when I disagreed with him.* | **+on/about** *We often disagree on politics.* | *Jane and Rob disagreed about how to use the money they won.* **2** if two or more sets of statements, reports, or numbers which are about the same thing disagree, they are different from each other OPP agree: **+with** *The results of the new study disagree with the findings of an earlier study.*

disagree with sb *phr. v.* if something such as food or weather disagrees with you, it has a bad effect on you or makes you sick OPP agree with: *Spicy food really disagrees with me.*

dis·a·gree·a·ble /ˌdɪsəˈgriəbəl/ *adj.* FORMAL **1** unfriendly and in a bad mood: *He's the most disagreeable man I've ever met.* **2** not enjoyable or pleasant: *a very disagreeable task* —**disagreeably** *adv.*

dis·a·gree·ment /ˌdɪsəˈgrimənt/ *n.* **1** [C,U] a situation in which people express different opinions about something and sometimes argue OPP agreement: **+about/over** *disagreements about money* | **+with** *She left her job after a disagreement with her boss.* | **+among/between** *There is a lot of disagreement among doctors about the best way to treat the disease.* | *We've **had** a few **disagreements**, but we're still good friends.* **2** [U] differences between two statements, reports, numbers etc. that ought to be similar OPP agreement: **+between** *considerable disagreement between the two estimates*

dis·al·low /ˌdɪsəˈlaʊ/ *v.* [T] to officially refuse to allow something such as a tax BENEFIT, an action in a court of law, or a GOAL in sports because of a rule OPP allow: *The judge disallowed evidence containing confidential information.*

dis·ap·pear /ˌdɪsəˈpɪr/ S3 W2 *v.* [I] **1** to become impossible to see anymore: *The scars will disappear in a year or two.* | **+into/behind/from etc.** *The railway tracks disappear into a hole in the side of the mountain.* | **disappear from sight/view** *She watched the car slowly disappear from view.* | *The magician **made** the rabbits **disappear**.* **2** to become impossible to find or to be lost: *The two girls disappeared while walking home from school.* | *The video quickly disappeared from the stores* (=it sold so quickly that it was impossible to find it in the stores). | *His wallet had **disappeared without a trace**.* → see Word Choice box at LOSE **3** to stop existing: *Small companies will disappear by being merged into big ones.*

dis·ap·pear·ance /ˌdɪsəˈpɪrəns/ *n.* [C,U] **1** the act or state of becoming impossible to see or find: *He notified the police of the girl's disappearance.* **2** the state of not existing anymore: *the disappearance of ancient forests*

dis·ap·point /ˌdɪsəˈpɔɪnt/ *v.* [I,T] **1** to make someone feel unhappy because something they hoped for does not happen or is not as good as they expected: *He didn't want to disappoint his parents.* | *New York is a city that never disappoints.* **2 disappoint sb's hopes/plans/expectations** FORMAL to fail to make something happen, or to prevent something from happening, that someone hoped for or expected: *A return to the old system would disappoint all our hopes.* [**Origin:** 1400–1500 Old French *desapointier*, from *apointier* **to arrange**]

dis·ap·point·ed /ˌdɪsəˈpɔɪntɪd/ S3 *adj.* **1** unhappy because something you hoped for did not happen, or because someone or something was not as good as you expected: *She was disappointed when she failed her test.* | *Hundreds of disappointed fans were unable to get tickets.* | **disappointed (that)** *Steve is very disappointed that he couldn't go.* | **+with/at/about/by** *She was disappointed with her performance.* | *We are saddened and disappointed about this decision.* | **+in** *I'm very disappointed in you.* | **disappointed to hear/see/learn etc.** *We are very disappointed to see her go.* | **deeply/terribly/bitterly disappointed** *Arnold said he was deeply disappointed by the verdict.* **2 a disappointed hope/plan/expectation** something you hope for, plan, or expect that does not happen or is not as good as you expected

dis·ap·point·ing /ˌdɪsəˈpɔɪntɪŋ/ *adj.* not as good as you expected or hoped something would be: *The team had a disappointing season.* | *The show was pretty disappointing in the end.* —**disappointingly** *adv.*

dis·ap·point·ment /ˌdɪsəˈpɔɪntˀmənt/ *n.* **1** [U] a feeling of sadness because something is not as good as you expected or has not happened in the way you hoped: *Julie tried to hide her disappointment.* | **+at/over/with/about** *Several people expressed disappointment at the delay.* | **disappointment (that)** *It was a **great disappointment** that my marriage didn't work.* | **+in** *disappointment in the current administration* | *McGee **expressed disappointment** at not being chosen for the job.* | ***To** her great **disappointment*** (=she was very disappointed), *she was turned down for the transfer.* | **deep/bitter disappointment** *The mood among the staff was one of deep disappointment.* **2** [C] someone or something that is not as good as you hoped or expected: *The movie was a real disappointment.* | **+to** *Kate feels like she's a disappointment to her family.* | **+for** *Low sales of the album have been a disappointment for the band.* | **a big/major/huge disappointment** *The news came as a big disappointment.*

dis·ap·pro·ba·tion /ˌdɪsæprəˈbeɪʃən/ *n.* [U] FORMAL disapproval of someone or something because you think they are morally wrong

dis·ap·prov·al /ˌdɪsəˈpruvəl/ *n.* [U] a feeling or opinion that someone is behaving badly or that something is bad OPP approval: +**of** *Public disapproval of smoking has increased.* | *Marion shook her head **in disapproval**.* | ***strong disapproval** of the country's human rights record*

dis·ap·prove /ˌdɪsəˈpruv/ *v.* **1** [I] to think that someone or something is bad, wrong etc. OPP approve: +**of** *Careful – Janet really disapproves of gossip.* | *All her friends disapproved of her new boyfriend.* | *My grandmother **strongly disapproves** of couples living together before marriage.* **2** [T] FORMAL to not agree to something that has been suggested OPP approve: *The board of directors disapproved the sale.*

dis·ap·prov·ing /ˌdɪsəˈpruvɪŋ◂/ *adj.* showing that you think someone or something is bad, wrong etc. OPP approving: *a disapproving look* —**disapprovingly** *adv.*

dis·arm /dɪsˈɑrm/ *v.* **1** [I] to reduce the size of your army, navy etc. and the number of your weapons: *Both sides must disarm before the peace talks.* **2** [T] to take away someone's weapons OPP arm: *U.N. peacekeepers will disarm both forces.* **3** [T] to make someone less angry and more friendly OPP arm: *She uses humor to disarm people.* → see also DISARMING **4** [T] to take the explosives out of a bomb, MISSILE etc.

dis·ar·ma·ment /dɪsˈɑrməmənt/ *n.* [U] the reduction in numbers or size of a country's weapons, army, navy etc.: *a commitment to worldwide **nuclear disarmament*** (=a reduction in the number of atomic weapons) → see also ARMAMENT

dis·arm·ing /dɪsˈɑrmɪŋ/ *adj.* making you feel less angry and more friendly or trusting: *a disarming smile* —**disarmingly** *adv.*

dis·ar·range /ˌdɪsəˈreɪndʒ/ *v.* [T] FORMAL to spoil the organization of something, or to make something messy —**disarrangement** *n.* [U]

dis·ar·ray /ˌdɪsəˈreɪ/ *n.* [U] FORMAL the state of being messy or not organized: *The company's files were **in disarray**.* | *The delay **threw** the entire timetable **into disarray**.* | *After she left him, his whole life **fell into disarray**.*

dis·as·sem·ble /ˌdɪsəˈsɛmbəl/ *v.* [T] to take apart something that is made of many connected pieces OPP assemble: *You'll have to disassemble the bed frame in order to move it.* —**disassembly** *n.* [U]

dis·as·so·ci·ate /ˌdɪsəˈsoʊʃiˌeɪt, -siˌeɪt/ *v.* [T] another form of DISSOCIATE

dis·as·ter /dɪˈzæstɚ/ W3 *n.* **1** [C,U] a sudden event such as a flood, storm, or accident that causes great harm or damage: *a nuclear disaster* | *120 people died in China's worst **air disaster*** (=airplane crash). | *The country has been hit by a series of **natural disasters**.* | +**for** *The oil spill was a disaster for marine life.* | *If **disaster strikes** during a school day, Newark elementary students know what to do.* ►see THESAURUS box at accident **2** [C,U] a complete failure: *The party was a disaster.* | **a complete/total/unmitigated disaster** *Because of the weather, the parade was a total disaster.* | *The marriage **ended in disaster**.* | *Five small boys on skis is **a recipe for disaster**.* **3 be a disaster waiting to happen** to be very likely to produce a very bad result: *These environmental policies are a disaster waiting to happen.* **4** [C] INFORMAL something that is very messy or dirty, or that looks very bad: *I'd invite you in, but my place is a disaster.* [**Origin:** 1500–1600 French *désastre*, from Italian *disastro*, from *astro* **star** (from the idea of luck coming from the stars)]

diˈsaster ˌarea *n.* [C] **1** a place where a flood, storm, fire etc. has happened and caused a lot of damage, used especially when the government agrees to give disaster relief: *The town was **declared a disaster area** after the floods.* **2** INFORMAL a place that is very messy or dirty: *Her bedroom is a disaster area.*

diˈsaster reˌlief *n.* [U] money and supplies that are given to people after their property has been damaged by a very bad flood, storm, fire etc.: *disaster relief to the hurricane victims*

dis·as·trous /dɪˈzæstrəs/ *adj.* very bad, or ending in failure: *disastrous floods* | *a disastrous early marriage* | **disastrous effects/consequences** *The attack failed, with disastrous consequences.* —**disastrously** *adv.*

dis·a·vow /ˌdɪsəˈvaʊ/ *v.* [T] FORMAL to say that you are not responsible for something, that you do not know about it, or that you are not involved with it: *The group has disavowed any involvement in the violence.* —**disavowal** *n.* [C,U]

dis·band /dɪsˈbænd/ *v.* [I,T] to stop existing as an organization, or to make something do this: *The group officially disbanded in 1995.*

dis·bar /dɪsˈbɑr/ *v.* **disbarred, disbarring** [T] LAW to make a lawyer leave the legal profession because he or she has done something wrong: *Estrada was fired from his job and disbarred.* → see also DEBAR —**disbarment** *n.* [U]

dis·be·lief /ˌdɪsbəˈlif/ *n.* [U] a feeling that something is not true or does not exist: *Her first reaction to winning the award was disbelief.* | *Bill stared at him **in disbelief**.* OPP belief → see also UNBELIEF

dis·be·lieve /ˌdɪsbəˈliv/ *v.* [I,T] FORMAL to not believe something or someone: *The jury had no reason to disbelieve the witnesses.* —**disbelieving** *adj.* —**disbelievingly** *adv.*

dis·burse /dɪsˈbɚs/ *v.* [T] FORMAL to pay out money, especially from a large sum that is available for a special purpose: *The bank disbursed a record $2.5 billion in loans last year.* —**disbursement** *n.* [C,U] —**disbursal** *n.* [C,U]

disc /dɪsk/ S3 *n.* [C] another spelling of DISK → see also COMPACT DISC, LASER DISC

dis·card[1] /dɪˈskɑrd/ *v.* **1** [T] to get rid of something SYN throw away: *Cut the olives into small slices and discard the pits.* **2** [I,T] to put down unwanted cards in a card game: *Wait! You forgot to discard.* —**discarded** *adj.*

dis·card[2] /ˈdɪskɑrd/ *n.* [C] **1** something that you get rid of because you do not want it anymore **2** an unwanted card that is put down in a card game

ˈdisc brakes *n.* [plural] BRAKES that work by means of a pair of hard surfaces pressing against a DISK in the center of a car wheel

dis·cern /dɪˈsɚn, dɪˈzɚn/ *v.* [T not in progressive] FORMAL **1** to notice or understand something, especially after thinking about it carefully: *Two distinct trends may be discerned.* | **discern what/whether/how etc.** *Officials were anxious to discern how much public support there was.* **2** to see or hear something, especially something that is not easy to see or hear SYN perceive: *The telescope can discern objects incredibly distant in space.* [**Origin:** 1300–1400 Latin *discernere* **to separate**, from *cernere* **to sift**] —**discernible** *adj.* —**discernibly** *adv.*

dis·cern·ing /dɪˈsɚnɪŋ/ *adj.* APPROVING able to make good judgments about people, styles, and things: *The book will charm discerning readers.* | **the discerning ear/eye/nose etc.** (=someone who is able to make good judgments about what they hear, see, smell etc.)

dis·cern·ment /dɪˈsɚnmənt/ *n.* [U] FORMAL the ability to make good judgments about people, styles, and things

dis·charge[1] /dɪsˈtʃɑrdʒ/ *v.*
1 SEND SB AWAY [T] to officially allow someone to go or to send them away from a place, especially after they have been in a hospital or working in the Army, Navy etc.: **discharge sb from sth** *When do you expect Mom to be discharged from the hospital?* | **be honorably/dishonorably discharged** *Harris was honorably discharged from the Army in 1998.*
2 LET STH OUT [I always + adv./prep., T usually passive] to send, pour, or let out something from something else, especially a liquid or a gas: +**into** *The pond discharges into Matadero Creek.* | **discharge sth into sth** *Raw sewage was discharged into the ocean.*
3 SHOOT [I,T] FORMAL if you discharge a gun, or if it discharges, it shoots a bullet: *Jefferson's gun accidentally discharged, killing him.*

4 DUTY/RESPONSIBILITY [T] FORMAL to perform a duty or keep a promise etc.: *The soldiers discharged their duty with honor.*
5 ELECTRICITY [I,T] PHYSICS if a piece of electrical equipment discharges or is discharged, it sends out electricity
6 A WOUND [T] MEDICINE if a wound or body part discharges a substance such as PUS (=infected liquid), the substance slowly comes out of it
7 DEBT [T] FORMAL to pay a debt
8 GOODS/PASSENGERS [T] FORMAL to unload goods or passengers from a ship, airplane etc.: *The captain gave the order to discharge the cargo.*
[**Origin:** 1300–1400 Old French *descharger*, from Late Latin *carricare* **to load**]

D

dis·charge² /ˈdɪstʃɑrdʒ/ *n.* **1** [U] the action of officially sending someone or something away, especially from the hospital or the Army, Navy etc.: *Some soldiers were given a medical discharge.* | **+from** *After his discharge from the army, Jim got married.* → see also DISHONORABLE DISCHARGE, HONORABLE DISCHARGE **2** [C,U] the act of sending a substance out of something else, or the substance that comes out: **+of** *The discharge of harmful chemicals into drinking water is banned.* **3** [U] MEDICINE a substance that comes out of a wound or out of a part of your body such as your nose: *Nasal discharge may mean the patient has a sinus infection.* **4** [U] the act of shooting a gun: *the discharge of a firearm* **5** [C,U] PHYSICS electricity that is sent out by a piece of equipment, a storm etc. **6** [U] FORMAL the act of doing a duty **7** [U] FORMAL the act of paying a debt

dis·ci·ple /dɪˈsaɪpəl/ *n.* [C] **1** a follower of a great teacher or leader, especially a religious one: *a disciple of Freud* **2** one of the 12 original followers of Jesus Christ [**Origin:** 800–900 Latin *discipulus* **pupil**]

dis·ci·ple·ship /dɪˈsaɪpəlˌʃɪp/ *n.* [U] the period of time when someone is a disciple, or the state of being a disciple

dis·ci·pli·nar·i·an /ˌdɪsəpləˈnɛriən/ *n.* [C] someone who believes that people should obey orders and rules, and who makes them do this: *My father was a strict disciplinarian.*

dis·ci·pli·nar·y /ˈdɪsəpləˌnɛri/ *adj.* relating to trying to make someone obey rules, or to the punishment of someone who has not obeyed rules: **disciplinary action/measures** *The department is considering disciplinary action against the officers.*

dis·ci·pline¹ /ˈdɪsəplɪn/ W3 *n.* **1** [U] a way of training someone so that they learn to control their behavior and obey rules, which involves punishing them if they do not obey rules: *Children need discipline.* **2** [U] controlled behavior in which people obey rules and orders, especially in institutions such as schools, the Army etc.: *There was a lack of discipline in some army units.* | *He **imposed** tough **discipline** and demanded better results.* | *Teachers are expected to **maintain discipline**.* **3** [U] the ability to control your own behavior and way of working: *Working from home requires a good deal of discipline.* | *Martial arts teach respect, discipline, and cooperation.* → see also SELF-DISCIPLINE **4** [C] a way of training your mind or learning to control your behavior: *Disciplines such as yoga improve mental and physical fitness.* | **+for** *Learning poetry is a good discipline for the memory.* **5** [U] punishment for not obeying rules SYN **punishment**: *Employees who joined the strike face discipline.* **6** [C] an area of knowledge or teaching, especially one such as history, chemistry, mathematics etc. that is studied at a college or university: *the basic scientific disciplines of physics and chemistry* [**Origin:** 1200–1300 Old French *descepline*, from Latin *disciplina* **teaching, learning**]

discipline² *v.* [T] **1** to punish someone for not obeying rules: *Six workers were disciplined last year for not doing their jobs.* **2** to train someone to obey rules and control their own behavior: *It is the parents' duty to discipline their children.* **3 discipline yourself (to do sth)** to control the way you work or how regularly you do something, because you know it is good for you

dis·ci·plined /ˈdɪsəplɪnd/ *adj.* obeying rules and controlling your behavior OPP **undisciplined**: *a loyal and disciplined army* | *We're very disciplined when it comes to money.*

ˈdisc jockey *n.* [C] someone whose job is to play the music on a radio show or in a club where you can dance

dis·claim /dɪsˈkleɪm/ *v.* [T] FORMAL to state, especially officially, that you are not responsible for something, that you do not know about it, or that you are not involved with it: *The group has disclaimed all responsibility for the attack.*

dis·claim·er /dɪsˈkleɪmɚ/ *n.* [C] a statement that you are not responsible for something, that you do not know about it etc., often used in advertising: *The disclaimer states that past performance is no guarantee of future results.*

dis·close /dɪsˈkloʊz/ *v.* [T] **1** to make something known publicly, especially after it has been kept secret SYN **reveal**: *The company did not disclose details of the agreement.* | **disclose that** *Officials disclosed that the delays had been caused by computer errors.* **2** FORMAL to show something by removing the thing that covers it [**Origin:** 1400–1500 Old French *desclore*, from Medieval Latin *disclaudere* **to open**]

dis·clo·sure /dɪsˈkloʊʒɚ/ *n.* [C,U] a secret that someone tells people, or the act of telling this secret: *The recent disclosures have been very embarrassing for the president.* | *the disclosure of classified information*

dis·co /ˈdɪskoʊ/ *n. plural* **discos** [C] **1** a type of dance music with a strong repeating beat that was first popular in the 1970s **2** a place where people can dance to recorded popular music ►see THESAURUS box at **dance²**

dis·cog·ra·phy /dɪˈskɑgrəfi/ *n.* [C] a list of the music and songs recorded by a musician or musical group

dis·col·or /dɪsˈkʌlɚ/ *v.* [I,T] to change color, or to make something change color, so that it looks unattractive: *Smoking had discolored his teeth.* —**discolored** *adj.*

dis·col·or·a·tion /dɪsˌkʌləˈreɪʃən/ *n.* **1** [C] a place on the surface of something where it has become discolored: *There was a slight discoloration on the back of his jacket.* **2** [U] the process of becoming discolored

dis·com·bob·u·lat·ed /ˌdɪskəmˈbɑbyəˌleɪtɪd/ *adj.* HUMOROUS completely confused or upset —**discombobulate** *v.* [T]

dis·com·fit /dɪsˈkʌmfɪt/ *v.* [T] FORMAL to make someone feel uncomfortable, annoyed, or embarrassed SYN **unsettle**: *The announcement discomfited some Democrats.* —**discomfited** *adj.* —**discomfiting** *adj.* —**discomfiture** /dɪsˈkʌmfətʃɚ/ *n.* [U]

dis·com·fort /dɪsˈkʌmfɚt/ *n.* **1** [U] slight pain or a bad feeling OPP **comfort**: *You may experience some slight discomfort.* **2** [U] a feeling of embarrassment, shame, or worry: *The personal questions increased my discomfort.* | **+at** *I noticed her discomfort at hearing these cruel remarks.* **3** [C] something that makes you uncomfortable: **+of** *the discomforts of air travel* —**discomfort** *v.* [T] —**discomforting** *adj.*

dis·com·mode /ˌdɪskəˈmoʊd/ *v.* [T] FORMAL to cause trouble or difficulties for someone

dis·com·po·sure /ˌdɪskəmˈpoʊʒɚ/ *n.* [U] FORMAL the state of feeling worried and not calm anymore —**discompose** *v.* [T]

dis·con·cert /ˌdɪskənˈsɚt/ *v.* [T] to make someone feel slightly confused, worried, or embarrassed [**Origin:** 1600–1700 Old French *desconcerter*, from *concerter* **to bring into agreement**]

dis·con·cert·ed /ˌdɪskənˈsɚṭɪd◂/ *adj.* feeling slightly confused, worried, or embarrassed: *There was a disconcerted expression on her face.*

dis·con·cert·ing /ˌdɪskənˈsɚṭɪŋ/ *adj.* making you feel slightly confused, worried, or embarrassed: *She has a disconcerting habit of staring at people.* —**disconcertingly** *adv.*

dis·con·nect¹ /ˌdɪskəˈnɛkt/ *v.* **1** [T] to remove the supply of power from a machine or piece of equipment OPP **connect**: *The family agreed to disconnect the life* *support system.* | **disconnect sth from sth** *First disconnect the machine from the electricity supply.* **2** [I,T] to separate something from the thing it is connected to, or to become separated OPP **connect**: +**disconnect (sth) from sth** *Two freight cars disconnected from the train engine.* **3** [T] to stop supplying a service, such as water, telephone, electricity, or gas, to a house or other building SYN **cut off** OPP **connect**: *I tried to call the company, but the phone had been disconnected.* **4** [T] to break the telephone connection between two people or computers SYN **cut off** OPP **connect**: *I'll have to call him back – we **got disconnected**.* **5** [I] if you disconnect from your feelings, family, society etc., you no longer feel as though you belong or have a relationship with them —**disconnection** /ˌdɪskəˈnɛkʃən/ *n.* [C,U]

disconnect² *n.* [singular] **1** a surprising difference between two people, ideas, actions etc.: +**between** *There's a big disconnect between what she says and what she does.* **2** a feeling of not having a relationship with other people: *an emotional disconnect*

dis·con·nect·ed /ˌdɪskəˈnɛktɪd◂ / *adj.* **1** not related to anything else, and often difficult to understand SYN **unrelated**: *disconnected thoughts* **2** feeling that you no longer have a relationship with other people: *emotionally disconnected families*

dis·con·so·late /dɪsˈkɑnsəlɪt/ *adj.* extremely sad and hopeless: *A few disconsolate men sat with their hats in their hands.* —**disconsolately** *adv.*

dis·con·tent /ˌdɪskənˈtɛnt/ also **dis·con·tent·ment** /ˌdɪskənˈtɛnt˺mənt/ *n.* [U] a feeling of not being happy or satisfied OPP **contentment**: +**with** *Discontent with the administration is strong.* | +**over/at** *There is widespread discontent over math instruction.* —**discontent** *v.* [T]

dis·con·tent·ed /ˌdɪskənˈtɛntɪd/ *adj.* unhappy or not satisfied: *Discontented workers joined the protests.*

dis·con·tin·ue /ˌdɪskənˈtɪnyu/ *v.* [T] to stop doing, producing, or providing something: *The airline plans to discontinue daily flights from L.A. to Osaka.* —**discontinued** *adj.*: *a discontinued china pattern* —**discontinuance** *n.* [U] —**discontinuation** /ˌdɪskəntɪnyuˈeɪʃən/ *n.* [U]

dis·con·ti·nu·i·ty /ˌdɪskɑnt˺nˈuəṭi -təˈnuəṭi/ *n.* FORMAL **1** [U] the fact of a process not being continuous **2** [C] a sudden change or pause in a process

dis·con·tin·u·ous /ˌdɪskənˈtɪnyuəs◂ / *adj.* FORMAL not continuous

dis·cord /ˈdɪskɔrd/ *n.* **1** [U] FORMAL disagreement between people OPP **harmony**: *The verdict has increased racial discord in the country.* **2** [C,U] an annoying sound produced by a group of musical notes that do not go together well → see also HARMONY

dis·cor·dant /dɪsˈkɔrdnt/ *adj.* **1** LITERARY something that is discordant seems strange, wrong, or inappropriate in relation to everything around it: *discordant colors* | *The modern decor **strikes a discordant note** in this 17th-century building.* **2** FORMAL not in agreement: *The two experiments gave us discordant results.* **3** a discordant sound is annoying because it is made up of musical notes that do not go together well: *strange discordant music*

dis·co·theque /ˈdɪskəˌtɛk, ˌdɪskəˈtɛk/ *n.* [C] a DISCO

dis·count¹ /ˈdɪskaʊnt/ S3 W3 *n.* [C] a reduction in the usual price of something: *Tickets are $9, with a $2 discount for kids.* | +**on** *a discount on rail travel* | *Employees can buy books **at a discount**.* | *Rochelle gets a 15% **employee discount*** (=a discount for workers at a particular place). | **a discount fare/price** *discount airfares to Europe* | *Wal-Mart quickly became one of the largest **discount stores*** (=stores where you can buy goods cheaply) *in the nation.*

dis·count² /ˈdɪskaʊnt, dɪsˈkaʊnt/ *v.* [T] to reduce the price of something: *Some videos were discounted to sell for as little as $5.*

dis·count³ /dɪsˈkaʊnt/ *v.* [T] to regard something as unlikely to be true or important: *Scientists discounted his method of predicting earthquakes.* | *We cannot **discount the possibility** that he was lying.*

dis·coun·te·nance /dɪsˈkaʊnt˺n-əns/ *v.* [T] FORMAL to show your disapproval of something or of someone's behavior: *The Russians were anxious to discountenance the war.*

dis·count·er /ˈdɪskaʊntɚ/ *n.* [C] a store or a person that sells goods cheaply

ˈdiscount ˌrate *n.* **the discount rate** the interest rate that the Federal Reserve Bank charges other banks

dis·cour·age /dɪˈskɚɪdʒ, -ˈskʌr-/ *v.* [T] **1** to persuade someone not to do something, especially by making it seem difficult or bad OPP **encourage**: *The cameras should discourage shoplifters.* | **discourage sb from doing sth** *My father tried to discourage me from becoming a lawyer.* **2** to make someone less confident or less willing to do something OPP **encourage**: *You shouldn't let one failure discourage you.* **3** to make something become less likely to happen OPP **encourage**: *Put the plant in a cold room to discourage growth.*

dis·cour·aged /dɪˈskɚɪdʒd/ *adj.* no longer having the confidence you need to continue doing something: *Students may **get discouraged** if they are criticized too often.*

disˌcouraged ˈworker *n.* [C] ECONOMICS someone without a job who has stopped trying to get one because he or she believes that there are no jobs available or that he or she does not have the necessary skills or ability to do the jobs that are available

dis·cour·age·ment /dɪˈskɚɪdʒmənt/ *n.* **1** [U] a feeling of being discouraged: *a feeling of discouragement and disappointment* **2** [U] the act of trying to discourage someone from doing something OPP **encouragement**: *the country's discouragement of religion* **3** [C] something that discourages you: *Despite early discouragements, she eventually became a successful songwriter.*

dis·cour·a·ging /dɪˈskɚɪdʒɪŋ/ *adj.* making you lose the confidence you need to continue doing something: *a discouraging report on the economy*

dis·course¹ /ˈdɪskɔrs/ *n.* **1** [U] serious discussions between people, especially about a particular subject: +**on** *Rational discourse on public policy is vital to a democracy.* | *Racist language is not acceptable in **public discourse*** (=discussions of subjects by politicians, business leaders etc.). **2** [C] a serious speech or piece of writing on a particular subject: +**on/upon** *a discourse on 18th-century poetry* **3** [U] the language used in particular kinds of speech or writing: *spoken and written discourse* [**Origin:** 1400–1500 Late Latin *discursus* **conversation**]

dis·course² /dɪsˈkɔrs, ˈdɪskɔrs/ *v.*

discourse on/upon sth *phr. v.* to make a long formal speech about something, or to discuss something seriously

dis·cour·te·ous /dɪsˈkɚṭiəs/ *adj.* FORMAL not polite, and not showing respect for other people SYN **rude** OPP **courteous**: *The sales staff were discourteous and slow.* —**discourteousness** *n.* [U] —**discourteously** *adv.*

dis·cour·te·sy /dɪsˈkɚṭəsi/ *n.* [C,U] FORMAL an action or behavior that is not polite or does not show respect OPP **courtesy**

dis·cov·er /dɪˈskʌvɚ/ S2 W1 *v.* [T] **1** to find that something exists, when no one else has found it before: *The island was first discovered by Captain Cook.* | *Scientists believe that they may have discovered a cure for the disease.* ►see THESAURUS box at **find¹** → see also INVENT **2** to find someone or something that was lost or hidden: *Police discovered 500 pounds of dynamite in the house.* **3** to find out information that you did not know about before: **discover that** *He soon discovered that the job wasn't as easy as he'd expected.* | **discover who/what/how etc.** *Did you ever discover who sent you the flowers?* **4** to notice or try something for the first time and start to enjoy it: *At 14, Veronica discovered boys.* **5** to notice someone who is very good at something and help them to become successful and well-known: *She* *used to go to Hollywood parties, hoping to be discovered.* [**Origin:** 1300–1400 Old French *descovrir*, from Late Latin *discooperire* **to uncover**] —**discoverer** *n.* [C]

dis·cov·er·y /dɪˈskʌvri, -vəri/ W3 *n.* *plural* **discoveries** **1** [C] a fact or thing that someone finds out about, when it was not known about before: *recent archeological discoveries* | +**about** *new scientific discoveries about genes* | **discovery that** *We were all shocked by the discovery that he had been having an affair.* **2** [C,U] the act of discovering something that was hidden or not known before: +**of** *the discovery of oil in Alaska* | *Einstein* ***made an*** *important* ***discovery*** *about the nature of energy.* **3** [C] someone who you think has a lot of TALENT (=special abilities), who you have found out about, especially before they become really famous: *He just signed a recording contract with his latest discovery.* **4** [U] LAW the process by which EVIDENCE is made available for the opposing side in a court case to look at, before the case begins

dis·cred·it¹ /dɪsˈkrɛdɪt/ *v.* [T] **1** to make someone or something less respected or trusted: *Defense lawyers tried to discredit her testimony.* **2** [usually passive] to cause an idea not to be believed anymore: *Some of Freud's theories have now been discredited.*

discredit² *n.* the loss of other people's respect or trust: *Wilson's actions* ***brought discredit on*** *the entire Senate.*

dis·cred·it·a·ble /dɪsˈkrɛdɪt̬əbəl/ *adj.* bad or wrong, and making people lose respect for you or trust in you

dis·creet /dɪˈskrit/ *adj.* **1** careful about what you say or do so that you do not upset or embarrass people, especially by keeping a secret OPP **indiscreet**: *Andrew's very discreet – he won't tell anyone.* | +**about** *He was always discreet about his love affairs.* **2** done, said, or shown in a careful or polite way so that you do not upset or embarrass people: *a discreet nod* | *I made discreet inquiries among his friends.* **3** APPROVING small and showing good taste or judgment: *a discreet gold necklace* —**discreetly** *adv.* → see also DISCRETE, DISCRETION

dis·crep·an·cy /dɪˈskrɛpənsi/ *n.* *plural* **discrepancies** [C,U] a difference between two amounts, details etc. that should be the same: +**in** *There were discrepancies in the expense accounts.* | +**between** *An employee noticed a discrepancy between the two signatures.* [**Origin:** 1400–1500 Latin *discrepare* **to make unpleasant sounds that do not go together**]

dis·crete /dɪˈskrit/ Ac *adj.* FORMAL clearly separate SYN **distinct**: *The developing insect passes through several discrete stages.* → see also DISCREET

dis,crete 'data *n.* [U] MATH data representing facts that can be counted, for example the number of people who live in a city or the number of vehicles using a particular road → see also CATEGORICAL DATA

dis·cre·tion /dɪˈskrɛʃən/ Ac *n.* [U] **1** the ability to deal with situations in a way that does not offend or embarrass people, especially by keeping other people's secrets: *The hotel has built a reputation on its discretion.* | *I'm sure I can rely on your discretion.* → see also **be the soul of discretion** at SOUL (7) **2** the ability and right to decide what should be done in a particular situation: *Hiring is* ***at the discretion of*** *fire department administrators.* | *Decisions about attendance policies are* ***left to the discretion of*** *individual schools* (=each school can decide). | *I'm not giving you instructions – I want you to* ***use your discretion.*** | **the discretion to do sth** *The committee has discretion to make changes in the rules.* **3 parental/viewer discretion is advised** SPOKEN said on television before programs that might offend some people because they contain violence, swearing, sex etc. **4 discretion is the better part of valor** used to say that it is better to be careful than to take unnecessary risks

dis·cre·tion·a·ry /dɪˈskrɛʃəˌnɛri/ Ac *adj.* **1** not controlled by strict rules, but left for someone to make a decision about in each particular situation: *the discretionary sentencing powers of judges* **2 discretionary income/money** money that you can spend in any way you want, as opposed to money that must be used to pay bills, rent etc.

dis,cretionary 'spending *n.* [U] ECONOMICS **1** the money a company or government spends, on which it can make choices about how much to spend and what to spend it on **2** the amount of money that people spend on things they want, such as entertainment or a vacation, rather than on things that they need, such as food

dis·crim·i·nant /dɪˈskrɪmənənt/ *n.* [C] MATH a relationship between the COEFFICIENTS (=the number that does not change in an expression that has a variable, for example 8 in 8x) in an EQUATION, that allows you to calculate the roots of a QUADRATIC EQUATION or a POLYNOMIAL

dis·crim·i·nate /dɪˈskrɪməˌneɪt/ Ac *v.* **1** [I] to treat a person or a group differently from another in an unfair way: +**against** *The policies discriminate against disabled people.* | +**in** *discrimination in hiring* | **discriminate on the grounds/basis of sth** *It was found that the company discriminated on the grounds of race.* | *Employers may not* ***discriminate in favor of*** (=give better treatment to) *younger applicants.* **2** [I,T] to recognize a difference between things SYN **differentiate**: +**between** *Young babies can discriminate between pleasant and unpleasant odors.* | **discriminate sth from sth** *You need to learn to discriminate fact from opinion.* [**Origin:** 1600–1700 Latin *discriminare* **to divide**, from *discernere* **to separate**]

dis·crim·i·nat·ing /dɪˈskrɪməˌneɪt̬ɪŋ/ Ac *adj.* APPROVING able to judge what is of good quality and what is not SYN **discerning**: *The store will attract discriminating customers.*

dis·crim·i·na·tion /dɪˌskrɪməˈneɪʃən/ Ac W3 *n.* [U] **1** the practice of treating a person or a group differently from another in an unfair way: *laws against discrimination* | +**against** *discrimination against people with disabilities* | **racial/sex/religious etc. discrimination** *Many women still face sex discrimination in the military.* | *The university does not allow* ***discrimination in favor of*** (=better treatment of) *or against anyone on the basis of race.* → see also REVERSE DISCRIMINATION ►see THESAURUS box at **prejudice¹** **2** the ability to judge what is of good quality and what is not: *He showed almost no discrimination in his choice of partners.*

dis·crim·i·na·tor·y /dɪˈskrɪmənəˌtɔri/ *adj.* tending to treat a person or a group of people differently from other people in an unfair way: *a discriminatory hiring policy*

di·scur·sive /dɪˈskɚsɪv/ *adj.* discussing many different ideas, facts etc. rather than keeping to a single subject: *a rambling discursive style* —**discursively** *adv.* —**discursiveness** *n.* [U]

dis·cus /ˈdɪskəs/ *n.* [C] **1** a heavy plate-shaped object which is thrown as far as possible for sport **2** the sport in which this object is thrown

dis·cuss /dɪˈskʌs/ S2 W1 *v.* [T] **1** to talk about something with someone or a group in order to exchange ideas or decide something: *Can we discuss this later?* | *The two leaders discussed a range of issues.* | **discuss sth with sb** *Doctors should discuss possible treatments with the patient.* | **discuss what/who/where etc.** *We need to discuss what to do next.* ►see THESAURUS box at **talk¹** **2** to talk or write about something in detail and consider different ideas or opinions about it: *This topic will be discussed further in Chapter 4.* [**Origin:** 1300–1400 Latin *discussus*, past participle of *discutere* **to shake to pieces**]

dis·cus·sant /dɪˈskʌsənt/ *n.* [C] FORMAL someone who is part of a formal discussion

dis·cus·sion /dɪˈskʌʃən/ S2 W2 *n.* [C,U] **1** the act of discussing something, or a conversation in which people discuss something: *She* ***had a*** *long* ***discussion with*** *her husband.* | +**about/on** *heated discussions about money* | +**of** *the discussion of important issues* | +**between** *discussions between the two governments* |

Changes in the airline's mileage program ***are now under discussion*** (=being discussed).

THESAURUS

negotiations official discussions between two groups who are trying to agree on something: *Contract negotiations are continuing between the union and Amtrak.*
debate a formal discussion of a subject, during which people express different opinions: *the debate between the presidential candidates*
talks formal discussions between governments, organizations etc.: *a new start to the peace talks*
conference a large formal meeting at which members of an organization, profession etc. discuss things related to their work: *a conference for teachers of English*

2 a piece of writing about a subject that considers different ideas or opinions about it: *The report includes a discussion of global warming.*

dis·dain[1] /dɪsˈdeɪn/ *n.* [U] FORMAL a complete lack of respect that you show for someone or something because you think they are not important or good enough SYN **contempt**: +**for** *They expressed disdain for Western pop culture.* | *She spoke of her ex-husband* ***with disdain.***

disdain[2] *v.* **1** [T] to not like or to have no respect for someone or something, because you think they are not important or good enough: *He disdains New York and the art that is produced there.* **2 disdain to do sth** to refuse to do something because you are too proud to do it: *Tom Butler disdained to reply to such a trivial question.*

dis·dain·ful /dɪsˈdeɪnfəl/ *adj.* showing that you do not respect someone or something because you think they are not important or good enough SYN **scornful**: *a long disdainful look* | +**of** *They were disdainful of popular entertainment.* —**disdainfully** *adv.*

dis·ease /dɪˈziz/ S3 W1 *n.* **1** [C,U] MEDICINE an illness or unhealthy condition of the body or mind, which can be named: *Thousands of people are dying of hunger and disease.* | **heart/lung/liver etc. disease** *Heart disease is a leading cause of death in the U.S.* | *Tina* ***suffers from a*** *rare brain* ***disease.*** | *Scientists are working to block the viruses that* ***cause disease.*** | *She* ***contracted the*** *fatal* ***disease*** (=she became infected with the disease) *through a blood transfusion.* | *Unclean drinking water can* ***spread disease*** (=cause other people to become infected). | **infectious/contagious/communicable disease** (=disease that is passed from one person to another) ►see THESAURUS box at **illness** **2** [C] a bad or harmful condition or behavior of a group, such as society: *Loneliness is a disease of our urban communities.* [**Origin:** 1300–1400 Old French *desaise*, from *aise* **relaxed feeling, comfort**] —**diseased** *adj.* → see also HEART DISEASE, ILLNESS, SOCIAL DISEASE, VENEREAL DISEASE

dis·em·bark /ˌdɪsɪmˈbɑrk/ *v.* [I,T] FORMAL to get off a vehicle, such as a ship or airplane, or to let people off or take goods off: +**from** *The passengers began to disembark from the plane.* —**disembarkation** /ˌdɪsɪmbɑrˈkeɪʃən/ *n.* [U]

dis·em·bod·ied /ˌdɪsɪmˈbɑdid◂/ *adj.* **1** a disembodied sound or voice comes from someone who cannot be seen **2** without a body or separated from a body: *disembodied spirits*

dis·em·bow·el /ˌdɪsɪmˈbaʊəl/ *v.* [T] to remove someone's BOWELS —**disembowelment** *n.* [U]

dis·en·chant·ed /ˌdɪsɪnˈtʃæntɪd/ *adj.* disappointed with someone or something, and not believing in their value anymore: +**with** *Voters seem disenchanted with government in general.* —**disenchantment** *n.* [U]

dis·en·fran·chised /ˌdɪsɪnˈfræntʃaɪzd/ *adj.* **1** not having any rights, especially the right to vote, and not feeling part of society: *Disenfranchised voters are believed to number at least 100,000.* **2 the disenfranchised** people who are disenfranchised —**disenfranchise** *v.* [T] —**disenfranchisement** *n.* [U]

dis·en·gage /ˌdɪsɪnˈgeɪdʒ/ *v.* **1** [I,T] if you disengage a machine or DEVICE, or if it disengages, it stops operating because two parts are separated from each other OPP **engage**: *Disengage the gears before you start the car.* | *The cruise control does not disengage when it should.* **2** [I] to deliberately stop being involved with a group or activity: +**from** *The council pressured Pike to disengage from the project.* **3** [I,T] if an army disengages, or if someone disengages it, it stops fighting and removes its soldiers from the area OPP **engage**: *Troops moved in Thursday to disengage the two warring factions.* **4** [T] to separate someone or something from someone or something else that was holding them or connected to them: *He removed the screws and disengaged the back panel.* | **disengage sb/sth from sth** *Yoko disengaged herself from John's embrace.* —**disengagement** *n.* [U]

dis·en·gaged /ˌdɪsɪnˈgeɪdʒd/ *adj.* not involved with someone or something, and feeling separate from them: +**from** *The singer seemed completely disengaged from the audience.*

dis·en·tan·gle /ˌdɪsɪnˈtæŋgəl/ *v.* [T] **1** to separate different things, especially ideas or pieces of information, that have become confused together: *Investigators had to disentangle Maxwell's complicated financial affairs.* **2 disentangle yourself (from sb/sth)** to remove yourself from a complicated situation that you are involved in SYN **extricate**: *The President was eager to disentangle himself from the scandal.* **3** to separate ropes, strings etc. that have become twisted or tied together —**disentanglement** *n.* [U]

dis·e·qui·lib·ri·um /ˌdɪsikwəˈlɪbriəm/ *n.* [U] **1** FORMAL a lack of balance in something, or a lack of equality between two opposing things OPP **equilibrium** **2** ECONOMICS a situation in which the supply and DEMAND (=desire or need) for a good or service are not equal OPP **equilibrium**

dis·es·tab·lish /ˌdɪsəˈstæblɪʃ/ Ac *v.* [T] FORMAL to officially decide that a particular system, organization, or church is not the official system, organization, or church of your state or country anymore —**disestablishment** *n.* [U]

dis·fa·vor /dɪsˈfeɪvɚ/ *n.* [U] FORMAL a feeling of dislike and disapproval: *Coal* ***fell into disfavor*** (=became unpopular) *because burning it caused pollution.* | *He was regarded* ***with disfavor*** *by the commanding officer.*

dis·fig·ure /dɪsˈfɪgyɚ/ *v.* [T] to ruin the appearance of someone or something —**disfiguring** *adj.*: *a disfiguring disease* —**disfigurement** *n.* [C,U]

dis·fig·ured /dɪsˈfɪgyɚd/ *adj.* ruined in appearance: *horribly disfigured bodies*

dis·fran·chise /dɪsˈfræntʃaɪz/ *v.* [T] another form of DISENFRANCHISE —**disfranchisement** *n.* [U]

dis·gorge /dɪsˈgɔrdʒ/ *v.* **1** [T] LITERARY if a vehicle or building disgorges people, they come out of it in a large group: *Black limousines disgorged movie stars.* **2** [T] if something disgorges what was inside it, it lets it pour out: *Chimneys in the valley were disgorging smoke into the air.* **3** [T] to give back something that you have taken illegally: *The trustee was forced to disgorge the funds.* **4** [T] to bring food back up from your stomach through your mouth **5** [I,T] if a river disgorges, it flows into the ocean —**disgorgement** *n.* [U]

dis·grace[1] /dɪsˈgreɪs/ *n.* **1** [singular] something or someone that is so bad, wrong, or unacceptable that the people should feel ashamed or upset about them: **it is a disgrace that** *It is a disgrace that we've been cutting down these ancient trees.* | *The public schools here are* ***an absolute disgrace.*** **2** [U] the loss of other people's respect because you have done something they strongly disapprove of: *Smith faced total public disgrace after the incident.* | *Athletes caught using drugs were sent home* ***in disgrace.*** | *Her actions* ***brought disgrace on*** *the family.* **3 be a disgrace (to sb/sth)** to have a very bad effect on the opinion that people have of your family or the group that you belong to: *Players who only think of their paychecks are a disgrace to the game of baseball.*

D

4 no disgrace used to say that you should not feel ashamed about a particular situation or action: *It's no disgrace to be out of work.*

disgrace² *v.* [T] **1** to do something so bad that people lose respect for your family or for the group you belong to: *How could you disgrace us all like that?* | **disgrace yourself** *She disgraced herself by getting completely drunk.* **2 be disgraced** to lose the respect of people because they disapprove of something you have done: *He was publicly disgraced and driven from power.*

dis·grace·ful /dɪsˈgreɪsfəl/ *adj.* so bad, wrong, or unacceptable that people should feel ashamed or upset: *Their behavior was absolutely disgraceful.* —**disgracefully** *adv.*

D

dis·grun·tled /dɪsˈgrʌntld/ *adj.* annoyed and not satisfied because things have not happened in the way that you wanted: *Disgruntled employees are leaving to work for other firms.* [**Origin:** 1600–1700 *gruntle* **to complain** (15–19 centuries), from *grunt*]

dis·guise¹ /dɪsˈgaɪz/ *v.* [T] **1** to change your appearance so that people cannot recognize you: **disguise yourself as sb/sth** *To get into the building, I disguised myself as a reporter.* | **be disguised as sb/sth** *The two women were disguised as nuns.* ▸see THESAURUS box at **hide¹** **2** to change the usual appearance, sound, taste etc. of something so that people do not recognize it: *The park's waterfalls disguise the traffic noise from the freeway.* | **disguise sth as sth** *Well, it may be hard to disguise junk as health food.* | *The game is a* ***thinly disguised*** *form of gambling.* **3** to hide a fact or feeling so that people will not notice it: *Dan tried to disguise his feelings for Katie.* | *His* ***thinly disguised*** (=not well hidden at all) *hatred of rock-n-roll was well known.* | *Spices helped* ***disguise the fact that*** *food was not fresh.* [**Origin:** 1300–1400 Old French *desguiser*, from *guise* **appearance**]

disguise² *n.* [C,U] **1** something that you wear to change your appearance and hide who you are, or the act of wearing this: *The dark glasses were part of her disguise.* | *The woman was really a police officer* ***in disguise.*** | **a master of disguise** (=someone who is very good at changing their appearance in different ways) **2** something that hides what something else is really like: *His charming manner was a clever disguise for his evil intentions.* | *"Tax reform" is just a tax increase* ***in disguise.*** → see also **a blessing in disguise** at BLESSING (5)

dis·gust¹ /dɪsˈgʌst/ *n.* [U] **1** the feeling you have when you are annoyed or upset because a situation or someone's behavior is completely unacceptable: *Martha gave him a look of disgust.* | **+with** *voters' disgust with politics as usual* | **+at/with** *The fans showed their disgust at the umpire's decision.* | *Barber walked out of the meeting* ***in disgust.*** | ***To my disgust,*** *I found that there were no nonsmoking tables available.* **2** a very strong feeling of dislike that almost makes you sick because something is so bad: *She looked at the horrifying pictures* ***with disgust.***

disgust² *v.* [T] **1** to make someone feel very annoyed or upset about something that they think is completely unacceptable: *All the violence on TV disgusts me.* **2** to be so bad to see, feel, think about etc. that it makes someone feel almost sick: *The smell of beer disgusted her.* [**Origin:** 1500–1600 Old French *desgouster*, from *goust* **taste**]

dis·gust·ed /dɪsˈgʌstɪd/ *adj.* annoyed or upset because of something that you think is completely unacceptable: *Disgusted parents gathered to protest.* | *a disgusted look* | **+at/with** *We were disgusted at the way we'd been treated.*

dis·gust·ing /dɪsˈgʌstɪŋ/ S2 *adj.* **1** extremely unpleasant, and making you feel sick: *Chewing tobacco is a disgusting habit.* | *The food smelled disgusting.* ▸see THESAURUS box at **horrible, taste¹** **2** shocking, or completely unacceptable: *They shouldn't treat people like that – it's absolutely disgusting.* —**disgustingly** *adv.*: *They're disgustingly rich.* → see also NAUSEATING

dish¹ /dɪʃ/ S2 W3 *n.* [C] **1** a round container with low sides, used for holding food: *Pass me your dish.* | *a serving dish* → see also BOWL, PLATE¹ (1) **2 the dishes** all the plates, cups, bowls etc. that have been used during a meal: *Could you put away the dishes for me?* | **do/wash the dishes** *We never wash the dishes until morning.* **3** food cooked or prepared in a particular way as a meal: *a classic Creole dish* | *This salad is substantial enough to be served as a* ***main dish.*** → see also SIDE DISH **4** OLD-FASHIONED a sexually attractive person, especially a woman [**Origin:** Old English *disc*, from Latin *discus* **disk, plate**] → see also SATELLITE DISH

dish² *v.* [I] INFORMAL also **dish the dirt** to spend time talking about other people's private lives and saying unkind or shocking things about them: *He goes on to dish the dirt on all his fellow Hollywood stars.*

dish sth ↔ **out** *phr. v.* **1** INFORMAL to give advice, criticism, or punishments to people: *My uncle's always dishing out unwanted advice.* **2** to serve food to people: *Can you dish out the ice cream?* **3** INFORMAL to give something to a number of people in a careless way: *Banks are dishing out loans to practically anyone these days.* **4** to pass the ball or PUCK to another player in basketball or HOCKEY so that they can SCORE points easily: *Fields scored 17 points, made nine steals, and dished out six assists.* **5 sb can dish it out, but they can't take it** used to say that someone often treats other people in a particular way, for example by criticizing them, but does not like to be treated that way by others

dish sth ↔ **up** *phr. v.* to put food for a meal onto dishes, or to serve food to people: *Hand me your plate and I'll dish up some rice for you.*

dis·ha·bille /ˌdɪsəˈbil/ *n.* [U] another form of the word DÉSHABILLÉ

dis·har·mo·ny /dɪsˈharməni/ *n.* [U] FORMAL disagreement about important things, which makes people be unfriendly to each other OPP **harmony**: *marital disharmony* —**disharmonious** /ˌdɪsharˈmoʊniəs/ *adj.*

dish·cloth /ˈdɪʃklɔθ/ *n.* [C] a cloth used for washing dishes

ˈdish drain *n.* [C] a DRAINER

dis·heart·ened /dɪsˈhartˀnd/ *adj.* FORMAL disappointed, so that you lose hope and do not feel determined to continue doing something anymore: *Try not to feel disheartened.* —**dishearten** *v.* [T]

dis·heart·en·ing /dɪsˈhartˀn-ɪŋ/ *adj.* making you lose hope and determination: *disheartening news* | **disheartening to hear/see/know etc.** *It's disheartening to see what little progress has been made.*

di·shev·eled /dɪˈʃɛvəld/ *adj.* if someone or what they are wearing is disheveled, they look very messy: *Clarke appeared tired and disheveled.* [**Origin:** 1300–1400 Old French *deschevelé*, from *chevel* **hair**]

dis·hon·est /dɪsˈɑnɪst/ *adj.* not honest OPP **honest**: *Do you think he was being deliberately dishonest?* | *a dishonest lawyer* —**dishonestly** *adv.*

dis·hon·est·y /dɪsˈɑnɪsti/ *n.* [U] behavior in which someone lies or tries to hide the truth from others: *Are you accusing me of dishonesty?*

dis·hon·or¹ /dɪsˈɑnɚ/ *n.* [U] FORMAL loss of respect from other people because you have behaved in an unacceptable way or have done something immoral OPP **honor**: *He knew that suicide would* ***bring dishonor on*** *his family.*

dishonor² *v.* [T] **1** FORMAL to make your family, country, profession etc. lose the respect of other people OPP **honor**: *Failure to build a memorial would dishonor the soldiers who gave their lives.* **2** TECHNICAL if a bank dishonors a check, it refuses to pay out money for it OPP **honor** **3** to refuse to keep an agreement or promise OPP **honor**

dis·hon·or·a·ble /dɪsˈɑnərəbəl/ *adj.* not morally correct or acceptable: *dishonorable conduct*

disˌhonorable ˈdischarge *n.* [C,U] an order to someone to leave the military because they have behaved in a morally unacceptable way: *The sergeant was given a dishonorable discharge.*

dish·pan /ˈdɪʃpæn/ *n.* [C] **1** a large bowl that you wash dishes in **2 dishpan hands** INFORMAL hands that look dry and old because you wash dishes a lot

ˈdish rack *n.* [C] an object that holds dishes while they dry, that is usually kept next to the kitchen SINK

dish·rag /ˈdɪʃræg/ *n.* [C] an old cloth that is used for washing dishes

ˈdish ˌtowel *n.* [C] a cloth used for drying dishes

dish·ware /ˈdɪʃwɛr/ *n.* [U] a set of dishes, cups, bowls etc.

dish·wash·er /ˈdɪʃˌwɑʃɚ/ S3 *n.* [C] **1** a machine that washes dishes **2** someone whose job is to wash dirty dishes in a restaurant

ˌdishwashing deˈtergent *n.* [U] soap used to wash dishes, especially in a dishwasher

ˌdishwashing ˈliquid *n.* [U] liquid soap used to wash dishes

dish·wa·ter /ˈdɪʃˌwɔtɚ/ *n.* [U] dirty water that dishes have been washed in → see also **(as) dull as dishwater** at DULL[1] (1)

ˌdishwater ˈblond *adj.* OLD-FASHIONED dishwater blond hair is a dull pale brown color → see also DIRTY BLOND

dish·y /ˈdɪʃi/ *adj.* OLD-FASHIONED sexually attractive

dis·il·lu·sion /ˌdɪsəˈluʒən/ *v.* [T] to make someone realize that something that they thought was true or good is not really true or good: *I hate to disillusion you, but you'll probably never get your money back.* —**disillusionment** *n.* [U]

dis·il·lu·sioned /ˌdɪsəˈluʒənd/ *adj.* disappointed because you have lost your belief that someone or something is good or right: **+by/with** *Laura was growing increasingly disillusioned with politics.*

dis·in·cen·tive /ˌdɪsɪnˈsɛntɪv/ *n.* [C] something that makes people not want to continue doing something anymore OPP **incentive**: **+to** *Higher taxes may act as a disincentive to savings and investment.*

dis·in·clined /ˌdɪsɪnˈklaɪnd/ *adj.* **be/feel disinclined to do sth** FORMAL to be unwilling to do something OPP **inclined**: *The President said that he was disinclined to send in American troops.* —**disinclination** /ˌdɪsɪŋkləˈneɪʃən/ *n.* [C,U]

dis·in·fect /ˌdɪsɪnˈfɛkt/ *v.* [T] to clean something with a chemical that destroys BACTERIA: *First, use some iodine to disinfect the wound.*

dis·in·fect·ant /ˌdɪsɪnˈfɛktənt/ *n.* [C,U] a chemical or a cleaning product that destroys BACTERIA

dis·in·for·ma·tion /ˌdɪsɪnfɚˈmeɪʃən/ *n.* [U] false information which is given deliberately in order to hide the truth or confuse people, especially in political situations: *Wallace says his job was to spread government disinformation to extremist groups.* → see also MISINFORMATION

dis·in·gen·u·ous /ˌdɪsɪnˈdʒɛnyuəs/ *adj.* FORMAL not sincere and slightly dishonest, perhaps trying to trick people: *It's disingenuous of politicians to blame reporters for leaks that appear in the press.* —**disingenuously** *adv.*

dis·in·her·it /ˌdɪsɪnˈhɛrɪt/ *v.* [T] to prevent someone, especially your children, from receiving any of your money or property after your death —**disinheritance** *n.* [U]

dis·in·te·grate /dɪsˈɪntəˌgreɪt/ *v.* **1** [I,T] to break into very small pieces and be destroyed, or to make something do this: *The plane caught fire and disintegrated in the air.* **2** [I] to become weaker or less united and be gradually destroyed: *Support for the party had begun to disintegrate.* —**disintegration** /dɪsˌɪntəˈgreɪʃən/ *n.*: *the disintegration of the Soviet empire into separate republics*

dis·in·ter /ˌdɪsɪnˈtɚ/ *v.* **disinterred, disinterring** [T] FORMAL to remove a dead body from a grave OPP **inter** —**disinterment** *n.* [U]

dis·in·terest /dɪsˈɪntrɪst/ *n.* [U] **1** a lack of interest: **+in** *Americans' disinterest in foreign news* **2** the quality of being able to judge a situation fairly because you are not involved in it SYN **impartiality** SYN **objectivity**

dis·in·terest·ed /dɪsˈɪntrɪstɪd, -ˈɪntəˌrɛstɪd/ *adj.* **1** not interested SYN **uninterested** OPP **interested**: **+in** *Police appeared disinterested in halting the fighting.* **2** not personally involved in a situation, and therefore able to judge the situation fairly SYN **impartial** SYN **unbiased** SYN **objective** OPP **interested**: *a disinterested observer*

dis·in·vest·ment /ˌdɪsɪnˈvɛstmənt/ *n.* [U] ECONOMICS DIVESTMENT

dis·joint·ed /dɪsˈdʒɔɪntɪd/ *adj.* disjointed speaking or writing is not easy to understand because it has parts that do not seem well connected or are not arranged well: *His evidence was disjointed and sometimes contradictory.* —**disjointedly** *adv.* —**disjointedness** *n.* [U]

dis·joint e·vents /dɪsˌdʒɔɪnt ɪˈvɛnts/ *n.* [plural] TECHNICAL two events that cannot happen at the same time – for example the event of becoming 18 years old and the event of becoming 30 years old → see also DEPENDENT EVENTS

disk /dɪsk/ S2 *n.* [C] **1 a)** COMPUTERS a computer's HARD DISK: *Are you sure you have enough disk space?* **b)** a FLOPPY DISK: *Insert a blank disk into your disk drive.* | *All the information is stored **on disk**.* **2** a small flat round piece of plastic or metal, such as a CD, used for storing DIGITAL information: *You can play an entire 135-minute motion picture from a single disk.* **3** a round flat shape or object: *small colored disks for a children's game* **4** BIOLOGY a flat piece of CARTILAGE between the bones in your back → see also **slip a disk** at SLIP[1] (14), SLIPPED DISK [**Origin:** 1600–1700 Latin *discus* **disk, plate**]

ˈdisk brakes *n.* [plural] another spelling of DISC BRAKES

ˈdisk drive *n.* [C] COMPUTERS a piece of equipment in a computer that is used to get information from a disk or to store information on it

disk·ette /dɪˈskɛt/ *n.* [C] COMPUTERS a FLOPPY DISK

dis·like[1] /dɪsˈlaɪk/ *v.* [T, not in progressive] to not like someone or something: *Why do you dislike her so much?* | **dislike doing sth** *Many men dislike shopping.* | *I **disliked** the movie **intensely**.*

dislike[2] *n.* **1** [C,U] a feeling of not liking someone or something: **+of** *She shared her mother's dislike of housework.* | **+for** *Their dislike for each other was obvious.* | *He seemed to **take an instant dislike to** to me.* **2** [C usually plural] something that you do not like: *Describe your **likes and dislikes** and the type of person you'd like to meet.*

dis·lo·cate /dɪsˈloʊkeɪt, ˈdɪsloʊˌkeɪt/ *v.* [T] **1** MEDICINE to injure a joint so that the bone at the joint is moved out of its normal position: *I dislocated my shoulder playing football.* ▸see THESAURUS box at **hurt**[1] **2** to cause so many changes to a system or to someone's life that things cannot continue normally: *Thousands of workers have been dislocated by recent military base closures.* —**dislocation** /ˌdɪsloʊˈkeɪʃən/ *n.* [C,U]

dis·lodge /dɪsˈlɑdʒ/ *v.* [T] **1** to force or knock something out of a place where it was held or stuck: *Heavy rains had dislodged a boulder at the mouth of Thompson Canyon.* **2** to make someone leave a place or lose a position of power: *Police used tear gas to dislodge protesters who had taken over the building.* → see also LODGE —**dislodgement** *n.* [U]

dis·loy·al /dɪsˈlɔɪəl/ *adj.* doing or saying things that do not support your friends, your country, or the group you belong to OPP **loyal**: **+to** *He felt he had been disloyal to his friends.* —**disloyalty** *n.* [C,U]

dis·mal /ˈdɪzməl/ *adj.* if a situation or place is dismal, it is so bad that it makes you feel very unhappy and hopeless: *They lived in a dismal apartment in the poorest part of town.* | *a dismal gray afternoon* | *dismal economic news* | *Mitchell called the policy a **dismal failure**.* [**Origin:** 1300–1400 Anglo-French, Medieval Latin *dies mali* **evil days**] —**dismally** *adv.*

dis·man·tle /dɪsˈmæntl/ *v.* [T] **1** to take a machine or piece of equipment apart so that it is in separate pieces SYN **take apart** OPP **assemble**: *Chris had dismantled* *the entire bike in five minutes.* **2** to get rid of a system or organization, especially in a gradual way: *No one is suggesting that we dismantle the Social Security system.* **3** to defeat an opponent in a game by a large number of points: *The Detroit Tigers dismantled the Chicago White Sox 16–0.* [**Origin:** 1500–1600 Old French *desmanteler*, from *mantel* **cloak**]

dis·may¹ /dɪsˈmeɪ/ *n.* [U] the worry, disappointment, or unhappiness you feel when something bad happens: *Many women discover* ***with dismay*** *that their salaries will not pay for child care.* | *Neighbors stared* ***in dismay*** *at the damage the tornado had caused.* | ***To the dismay of*** *his parents, he's moving back in with them.* | *Members of Congress* ***expressed dismay*** *at the cost of the new bombers.*

D

dismay² *v.* [T] to make someone feel worried, disappointed, and upset: *The horrible pictures on TV dismayed the American public.*

dis·mayed /dɪsˈmeɪd/ *adj.* worried, disappointed, and upset: **+at** *School officials were dismayed at the test results.* | **dismayed that** *We are dismayed that the demonstration was allowed to take place.* | **dismayed to see/hear/read etc.** *Ruth was dismayed to see how thin he had gotten.*

dis·mem·ber /dɪsˈmɛmbɚ/ *v.* [T] FORMAL **1** to cut or tear a body into pieces: *He is charged with dismembering and disposing of the body.* **2** to divide a country, area, or organization into smaller parts: *The company will probably have to be dismembered.* —**dismemberment** *n.* [U]

dis·miss /dɪsˈmɪs/ W3 *v.* [T] **1** to refuse to consider someone or something seriously because you think they are silly or not important: *Richards dismissed suggestions that he planned to resign.* | **dismiss sth as sth** *She dismissed the idea as ridiculous.* | *They routinely* ***dismiss*** *any advice* ***out of hand*** (=dismiss it without even thinking about it). **2** [usually passive] LAW if a court CASE is dismissed, a judge decides that it should not continue, often because there is not enough information available to make a decision about the case: *The murder charge against Beckwith has been dismissed.* **3** to remove someone from their job or position SYN **fire**: **+dismiss sb from sth** *She was dismissed from her teaching job.* | **+dismiss sb for sth** *Employees may be dismissed for using illegal drugs.* **4** if someone in authority dismisses a person or a group, they send them away or allow them to leave: *You all know your homework assignment? All right,* ***class dismissed.*** [**Origin:** 1400–1500 Latin *dimissus*, past participle of *dimittere* **to send away**]

dis·miss·al /dɪsˈmɪsəl/ *n.* **1** [C,U] the act of removing someone from their job or position: **+from** *Randall now faces dismissal from her job.* | *Staff were warned that theft would be* ***grounds for dismissal.*** **2** [C,U] the act of stopping a court CASE from continuing: *the dismissal of a lawsuit* **3** [U] the act of refusing to consider someone or something seriously: *one critic's dismissal of the book as "386 pages of garbage"* **4** [C,U] the act of allowing someone to leave, or of sending them away

dis·mis·sive /dɪsˈmɪsɪv/ *adj.* DISAPPROVING refusing to consider someone or something seriously: *Collins has been criticized for her dismissive attitude toward the investigations.* —**dismissively** *adv.*

dis·mount¹ /dɪsˈmaʊnt/ *v.* **1** [I] to get off a horse, bicycle, or MOTORCYCLE OPP **mount**: *Seidman's horse reared up when he tried to dismount.* **2** [T] to take something, especially a gun, out of its base or support

dis·mount² /ˈdɪsmaʊnt/ *n.* [C] the final movements that a GYMNAST performs in a particular event, especially to get off a piece of equipment

Dis·ney /ˈdɪzni/, **Walt** /wɔlt/ (1901–1966) a U.S. PRODUCER who is famous for making CARTOON movies for children, and for inventing cartoon characters including Mickey Mouse and Donald Duck

dis·o·be·di·ent /ˌdɪsəˈbidiənt/ *adj.* deliberately not doing what you are told to do by your parents, teacher, employer etc. OPP **obedient**: *a disobedient child* —**disobedience** *n.* [U] → see also CIVIL DISOBEDIENCE

dis·o·bey /ˌdɪsəˈbeɪ/ *v.* **disobeys, disobeyed, disobeying** [I,T] to refuse to do what someone in authority tells you to do, or refuse to obey a rule or law OPP **obey**: *Pilots who disobey orders to land can face up to five years in prison.*

THESAURUS

break a rule/law to disobey a rule or law: *What happens if you break the rules?*
rebel to oppose or fight against someone who is in authority: *Part of growing up is rebelling against your parents, your teachers, and other authority figures.*
defy to refuse to obey someone or something: *He would never dare to defy his father.*
violate to disobey or do something against a law, rule, agreement etc.: *Using the money in this way clearly violates the tax laws.*

dis·or·der /dɪsˈɔrdɚ/ W2 *n.* **1** [C] MEDICINE a mental or physical problem that can affect your health for a long time SYN **condition**: *a serious heart disorder* | *Her daughter* ***suffered from*** *an eating* ***disorder.*** **2** [U] a situation in which many people disobey the law, especially in a violent way, and are difficult to control: *There is a risk of serious* ***civil disorder.*** **3** [U] a situation in which things are not organized at all SYN **chaos**: *Papers were scattered all over the office* ***in disorder.***

dis·or·dered /dɪsˈɔrdɚd/ *adj.* **1** not arranged, planned, or done neatly or in a clear order: *a disordered kitchen* **2** if someone is mentally disordered, their mind is not working in a normal and healthy way

dis·or·der·ly /dɪsˈɔrdɚli/ *adj.* **1** behaving in a noisy way and causing trouble in a public place: *Cole was arrested for* ***disorderly conduct.*** **2** messy or lacking order OPP **orderly**: *Papers were stacked in disorderly piles.* —**disorderliness** *n.* [U]

dis·or·ga·nized /dɪsˈɔrgəˌnaɪzd/ *adj.* **1** not arranged or planned in a clear order: *The meeting was completely disorganized.* **2** not planning or organizing things in a clear way: *I'm sorry I'm so disorganized – I just haven't had time to get everything ready.* → see also UNORGANIZED

dis·o·ri·ent /dɪsˈɔriˌɛnt/ *v.* [T] **1** to make someone uncertain about what is happening around them and unable to think clearly: *Grandpa's doctor told me the medicine might disorient him.* **2** to make someone not know which direction they have come from or are going in: *The smoke disoriented rescuers.* —**disorienting** *adj.* —**disorientation** /dɪsˌɔriənˈteɪʃən/ *n.* [U]

dis·o·ri·ent·ed /dɪsˈɔriˌɛntɪd/ *adj.* **1** confused and not understanding what is happening around you: *Don't be surprised if she seems a little disoriented after the surgery.* **2** confused about which direction you are facing or which direction you should go: *The pilot became disoriented in bad weather.*

dis·own /dɪsˈoʊn/ *v.* [T not in progressive] to say that you do not want to have any connection with someone or something anymore, especially a member or members of your family: *Jen's parents threatened to disown her if she married Bill.*

dis·par·age /dɪˈspærɪdʒ/ *v.* [T] FORMAL to criticize someone or something in a way that shows you do not think they are very good or important: *He never missed the opportunity to disparage his coworkers.* [**Origin:** 1200–1300 Old French *desparagier* **to marry below one's social class**, from *parage* **rank**] —**disparagement** *n.* [C,U]

dis·par·a·ging /dɪˈspærədʒɪŋ/ *adj.* criticizing someone or something, and showing that you do not think they are very good or important: *Tyler also made* ***disparaging remarks*** *about her ex-husband on a national talk show.* —**disparagingly** *adv.*

dis·par·ate /ˈdɪspərɪt/ *adj.* FORMAL very different and not related to each other: *Many disparate forms of* *information can be linked together in the database.* —**disparately** *adv.*

dis·par·i·ty /dɪˈspærət̬i/ *n. plural* **disparities** [C,U] FORMAL a difference between things, especially an unfair difference: +**in/between** *a disparity between men's and women's salaries* → see also PARITY

dis·pas·sion·ate /dɪsˈpæʃənɪt/ *adj.* not easily influenced by personal feelings: *a dispassionate analysis of the conflict* —**dispassionately** *adv.*

dis·patch[1] /dɪˈspætʃ/ *v.* [T] **1** to officially send someone or something somewhere for a particular purpose: *Goods are normally dispatched within 24 hours.* | **dispatch sb/sth to sth** *Specialist officers were immediately dispatched to the scene.* **2** to deal with someone or something or get rid of them quickly and effectively: *Sampras quickly dispatched his opponent in straight sets.* **3** LITERARY to deliberately kill a person or animal **4** OLD-FASHIONED to finish all of something [**Origin:** 1500–1600 Italian *dispacciare*, from Old French *despeechier* **to set free**]

dispatch[2] *n.* **1** [C] a message sent between military or government officials: *Our unit received a dispatch from headquarters.* **2** [C] a report sent to a newspaper from one of its writers who is in another town or country: *a news dispatch from Tokyo* **3** the act of sending people or things to a particular place: +**of** *the dispatch of warships to the region* **4 with dispatch** FORMAL if you do something with dispatch, you do it well and quickly: *Most cases are investigated with dispatch.*

dis·patch·er /dɪˈspætʃɚ/ *n.* [C] someone whose job is to send out vehicles such as police cars, taxis, or AMBULANCES to places where they are needed

dis·pel /dɪˈspɛl/ *v.* **dispelled, dispelling** [T] FORMAL to stop someone from believing or feeling something, especially because it is harmful or not correct: **dispel an idea/a myth/a rumor etc.** *Technology is helping to dispel the myth that people with disabilities cannot work.* | **dispel (sb's) fears/concerns/doubts etc.** *The doctor was able to dispel my concerns about my son's development.*

di·spen·sa·ble /dɪˈspɛnsəbəl/ *adj.* not really needed, and therefore easy to get rid of OPP **indispensable**: *Part-time workers are considered dispensable in times of recession.*

dis·pen·sa·ry /dɪˈspɛnsəri/ *n. plural* **dispensaries** [C] a place where medicines are prepared and given out, especially in a hospital → see also PHARMACY

dis·pen·sa·tion /ˌdɪspənˈseɪʃən, -pɛn-/ *n.* **1** [C,U] special permission from someone in authority or from a religious leader to do something that is not usually allowed: *You may be able to get* ***special dispensation*** *from a rabbi to eat non-kosher food.* **2** [U] FORMAL the act of providing people with something as part of an official process: *the dispensation of justice* **3** [C] POLITICS a religious or political system that has control over people's lives at a particular time in history

dis·pense /dɪˈspɛns/ *v.* [T] **1** FORMAL to give out or supply people with something, especially in particular amounts: *Ann dispensed orange juice in plastic cups.* | **dispense sth to sb** *Volunteers helped dispense food and blankets to people.* **2** FORMAL to officially provide something for people, especially a service: *The lawyers' group dispensed free legal advice.* **3** if a machine dispenses a product or substance, it gives you a particular amount of the product when you press a button or put money in the machine: *ATMs dispense cash 24 hours a day.* **4** to officially provide medicine to people: *The clinic dispenses medication and makes referrals.* [**Origin:** 1300–1400 Latin *dispensare* **to share out**, from *pendere* **to weigh**]

dispense with sth *phr. v.* FORMAL **1** to not use or do something that you usually use or do, because it is not necessary anymore: *Let's dispense with the formalities. Can I call you John?* **2** to do or finish something, especially as quickly as possible, so that you can continue with something else: *Once the speeches had been dispensed with, it was time to start drinking.*

dis·pens·er /dɪˈspɛnsɚ/ *n.* [C] a machine that provides a particular amount of a product or substance when you press a button or put money into it: *a soap dispenser* | *a candy dispenser*

di·sper·sal /dɪˈspɚsəl/ *n.* [U] the act of spreading something over a wide area or to a large number of people: *the role of birds in the dispersal of seeds*

dis·perse /dɪˈspɚs/ *v.* [I,T] **1** if a group of people disperses or is dispersed, they separate and go away in different directions: *The student protesters dispersed peacefully.* **2** if something disperses or is dispersed, it spreads thinly and evenly over a wide area: *The oil had been dispersed by chemicals sprayed on the water.*

dis·per·sion /dɪsˈpɚʒən/ *n.* [U] **1** the state of being spread over a wide area or between a wide group of people SYN **dispersal**: *The success of the system depends upon the dispersion of economic power.* **2** MATH the way in which data is arranged around a central number, usually the middle number in a set or the average of the set **3** PHYSICS the separation of white light into different bands of colored light, that happens when light passes through a PRISM or water

dis'persion ˌforces *n.* [C] CHEMISTRY a force that exists between MOLECULES, which makes them move toward or away from each other, caused by ELECTRONS moving around the NUCLEUS within each atom

dis·pir·it·ed /dɪˈspɪrɪt̬ɪd/ *adj.* FORMAL without hope or confidence: *He felt tired and dispirited.*

dis·place /dɪsˈpleɪs/ Ac *v.* [T] **1** to make a group of people or animals have to leave the place where they normally live: *An estimated 500,000 refugees have been displaced by the civil war.* | *Flooding caused by the dam may displace up to a million people.* **2** to take the place or position of someone or something else: *Compact discs displaced records in the late 1980s.* | *Millions of workers have been displaced by immigrants.* **3** to force something from its usual place or position: *The earthquake displaced the water that caused the tsunami.*

disˌplaced 'person *n. plural* **displaced persons** [C] FORMAL someone who has been forced to leave their country because of war or cruel treatment SYN **refugee**

dis·place·ment /dɪsˈpleɪsmənt/ Ac *n.* **1** [U] the act of forcing a group of people or animals to leave the place where they usually live: *the displacement of native peoples* **2** [U] the process of someone or something taking the place or position of someone or something else: *the displacement of oil by natural gas* **3** [singular, U] PHYSICS the amount of liquid that something such as a ship takes the place of when it floats on that liquid, used especially as a way of describing how large or heavy that object is **4** [singular, U] TECHNICAL the state of changing the connection of a feeling from the person or thing that originally caused it to someone or something else

dis'placement reˌaction *n.* [C] TECHNICAL CHEMISTRY a SINGLE-REPLACEMENT REACTION

dis·play[1] /dɪˈspleɪ/ Ac W2 *n. plural* **displays**
1 ARRANGEMENT [C] an arrangement of things for people to look at: *The fruit and vegetables made a beautiful display.* | +**of** *a dazzling display of flowers* | *a brightly lit* ***window display*** *of expensive fashions*
2 PERFORMANCE [C] a public performance of something that is intended to entertain people: *a fireworks display* | +**of** *a display of traditional dance*
3 on display a) something that is on display is in a place where people can look at it: *Children's artwork is on display in all the classrooms.* | *Owen said the fossil would be* ***put on display*** *in about a month.* | *Winning entries will* ***go on display*** *in the public library.* **b)** a quality, feeling etc. that is on display is shown very clearly and is easy to notice: *There's a tremendous amount of creativity on display in this school.*
4 a display of anger/affection/loyalty etc. an occasion when someone clearly shows a particular feeling, attitude, or quality: *He hated public displays of emotion.*
5 ON EQUIPMENT [C] COMPUTERS a part of a piece of equipment that shows changing information, for example the screen of a computer

6 **BIRD/ANIMAL** [C] a set pattern of behavior by a male bird or animal as a signal to other birds or animals

display² Ac W3 *v.* **displays, displayed, displaying** [T] **1** to show an object or a specially arranged group of objects to people, or to put them where people can easily see them: *The museum will display 135 of Van Gogh's paintings.* **2** to clearly show a feeling, attitude, or quality by what you do or say: *The accused man displayed little emotion in court.* | *Early in life, Frederick displayed an interest in poetry.* **3** if a computer or notice displays information, it shows information in a way that can be clearly seen: *Local train and bus times are displayed on the screen.* **4** if a person or animal displays signs of an illness, there is evidence that they have the illness [**Origin:** 1500–1600 Anglo-French *despleier*, from Latin *displicare* **to unfold**]

D

dis·pleased /dɪs'plizd/ *adj.* FORMAL very unhappy and fairly angry about something OPP **pleased**: +**with** *City officials are displeased with the lack of progress.* —**displease** *v.* [T]

dis·pleas·ure /dɪs'plɛʒɚ/ *n.* [U] FORMAL the feeling of being unhappy and fairly angry with someone or something: +**with/over** *The letter expressed his displeasure with the management.*

dis·port /dɪ'spɔrt/ *v.* **disport yourself** OLD-FASHIONED to amuse yourself by doing active enjoyable things

dis·pos·a·ble /dɪ'spoʊzəbəl/ Ac *adj.* **1** intended to be used once or for a short time and then thrown away: *disposable diapers* **2 disposable income** the amount of money you have left to spend after you have paid your taxes, bills etc. **3** DISAPPROVING not interesting, of poor quality, and not likely to be remembered for very long: *disposable pop songs*

dis·pos·al /dɪ'spoʊzəl/ Ac *n.* **1** [U] the act of getting rid of something: +**of** *the disposal of hazardous waste* **2 at sb's disposal** available for someone to use: *He'll use every means at his disposal to win.* **3** [C] a GARBAGE DISPOSAL **4** [U] FORMAL the way that an amount of money is used: *the disposal of funds* **5** [U] FORMAL the act of putting people or things in a particular place or in a particular order

dis·pose /dɪ'spoʊz/ Ac *v.*

dispose of *phr. v.* **1 dispose of sth** to get rid of something, especially something that is difficult to get rid of SYN **get rid of**: *How did he dispose of the body?* **2 dispose of sth** to defeat an opponent: *Hingis disposed of Williams in three straight sets.* **3 dispose of sb** INFORMAL to kill someone **4 dispose of sth** to deal with something such as a problem or question successfully

dis·posed /dɪ'spoʊzd/ Ac *adj.* **1 be/feel disposed to do sth** FORMAL to feel willing to do something or behave in a particular way SYN **inclined**: *Johnson disagreed but did not feel disposed to argue.* **2 be favorably/well/pleasantly etc. disposed toward sth** to like or approve of something such as an idea or plan: *Management is favorably disposed to the idea of job-sharing.* **3 be disposed to sth** FORMAL to tend to do, have, or use something SYN **prone**: **be naturally/genetically disposed to sth** *The new drug could help men who are genetically disposed to baldness.*

dis·po·si·tion /ˌdɪspə'zɪʃən/ *n.* FORMAL **1** [C] the way someone tends to behave: SYN **temperament**: **have a nervous/cheerful/sunny etc. disposition** *Thena has such a sweet disposition.* **2** [singular] someone's willingness to do something: **have/show a disposition to do sth** *Neither side shows a disposition to compromise.* **3** [U] the act of selling or giving away property: +**of** *the disposition of an individual's assets after death* **4** [U] the way that a situation is dealt with or that things are arranged: +**of** *his skillful disposition of the matter*

dis·pos·sess /ˌdɪspə'zɛs/ *v.* [T usually passive] FORMAL to take land or other property away from someone: **be dispossessed of sth** *Many black South Africans had been dispossessed of their homes.* —**dispossession** /ˌdɪspə'zɛʃən/ *n.* [U]

dis·pos·sessed /ˌdɪspə'zɛst◂/ *n.* **the dispossessed** [plural] FORMAL people who have had their land or other property taken away from them

dis·pro·por·tion /ˌdɪsprə'pɔrʃən/ Ac *n.* [C,U] FORMAL a situation in which two or more things do not have an equal or appropriate relationship

dis·pro·por·tion·ate /ˌdɪsprə'pɔrʃənɪt/ Ac *adj.* too much or too little in relation to something else: **a disproportinate number/amount** *A disproportionate number of women do unskilled low-paid work.* —**disproportionately** *adv.*: *Local farmers have been disproportionately affected by the new regulations.*

dis·prove /dɪs'pruv/ *v.* [T] to prove that something is false or wrong OPP **prove**: *These figures disproved Smith's argument.*

di·sput·a·ble /dɪ'spyuṭəbəl/ *adj.* something that is disputable is not definitely true or correct, and therefore is something that you can argue about SYN **debatable** OPP **indisputable** —**disputably** *adv.*

dis·pu·ta·tion /ˌdɪspyə'teɪʃən/ *n.* [C,U] FORMAL a formal discussion about a subject which people cannot agree on

dis·pu·ta·tious /ˌdɪspyə'teɪʃəs/ *adj.* FORMAL tending to argue a lot, or involving a lot of argument SYN **argumentative**

dis·pute¹ /dɪ'spyut/ W3 *n.* **1** [C,U] a serious argument or disagreement: +**between** *Several disputes have broken out between businesses competing for the best locations.* | +**over** *Kahane killed the man in a dispute over money.* | *The key issue* ***in dispute*** (=being argued about) *is the church's plan to expand its bookstore.* | *Several unions are* ***in dispute with*** *the company over retirement benefits.* | *Employees are involved in a* ***labor dispute*** (=argument between a union and a company) *with GenCo and may go on strike.* **2 be beyond dispute** FORMAL if something is beyond dispute, everyone agrees that it is true or that it really happened: *Ellen's honesty is beyond dispute.*

dispute² *v.* **1** [T] to say that you think something such as a statement or idea is not correct or true: *The main facts have never been disputed* | **dispute that** *No one disputes that jazz started in the U.S.* | **dispute sth with sb** *I disputed the charges with my credit card company.* **2** [I,T] to argue or disagree with someone: *Historians still dispute what really happened.* | *What happened next is* ***hotly disputed*** (=argued about with strong feelings). **3** [T] to argue with another country, group, or person about who owns or controls something: *The two countries continue to dispute ownership of the islands.* [**Origin:** 1500–1600 Old French *desputer*, from Latin *disputare* **to discuss**] —**disputed** *adj.*: *a disputed territory*

dis·qual·i·fy /dɪs'kwɑləˌfaɪ/ *v.* **disqualifies, disqualified, disqualifying** [T usually passive] to stop someone from taking part in an activity or competition, or from doing a job, usually because they have broken a rule or do not meet a particular standard: **disqualify sb for sth** *He was disqualified for kicking his opponent.* | **disqualify sb from sth** *Certain crimes could disqualify you from entering the United States.* —**disqualification** /dɪsˌkwɑləfə'keɪʃən/ *n.* [C,U]

dis·qui·et /dɪs'kwaɪət/ *n.* [U] FORMAL feelings of being anxious or not satisfied about something: *a growing sense of disquiet over crime in the neighborhood*

dis·qui·si·tion /ˌdɪskwə'zɪʃən/ *n.* [C] FORMAL a long speech or written report

Dis·rae·li /dɪz'reɪli/, **Benjamin** (1804–1881) a British politician who was Prime Minister in 1868 and from 1874 to 1880

dis·re·gard¹ /ˌdɪsrɪ'gɑrd/ *v.* [T] to ignore something or treat it as unimportant: *Please disregard any notes written in the margins.*

disregard² *n.* [singular, U] the act of ignoring something, in a way that annoys other people because they think it is important: +**for/of** *He showed total disregard for her feelings.* | **blatant/reckless/flagrant disregard** *a blatant disregard of party rules*

dis·re·pair /ˌdɪsrɪ'pɛr/ *n.* [U] buildings, roads etc. that are in disrepair are in bad condition because they have not been repaired or cared for: *The old hotel has **fallen into disrepair**.*

dis·rep·u·ta·ble /dɪs'rɛpyəṭəbəl/ *adj.* FORMAL not respected, and often thought to be involved in dishonest or illegal activities OPP **reputable**: *They haven't done anything disreputable.* —**disreputably** *adv.*

dis·re·pute /ˌdɪsrə'pyut/ *n.* [U] a situation in which people do not trust or respect a person or an idea: *Today, such ideas have **fallen into disrepute**.* | *The charges have **brought** the whole office **into disrepute**.*

dis·re·spect[1] /ˌdɪsrɪ'spɛkt/ *n.* [U] **1** lack of respect for someone or for something such as the law OPP **respect**: +**for** *disrepect for authority* | *Putting your feet on the table **shows disrespect**.* **2 no disrespect (to sb)** SPOKEN used when you are disagreeing with or criticizing someone or something to show that you do not want to seem impolite: *No disrespect to your son, but I think it's better for an adult to do this.* —**disrespectful** *adj.* —**disrespectfully** *adv.*

disrespect[2] *v.* [T] INFORMAL to show a lack of respect to someone, especially by saying impolite things to them: *Don't disrespect your mother like that.*

dis·robe /dɪs'roʊb/ *v.* [I] FORMAL to take off your clothes

dis·rupt /dɪs'rʌpt/ *v.* [T] to prevent a situation, event, system etc. from continuing in its usual way by causing problems: *We hope the move won't disrupt the kids' schooling too much.* [**Origin:** 1400–1500 Latin *disruptus*, from *rumpere* **to break**]

dis·rup·tion /dɪs'rʌpʃən/ *n.* [C,U] a situation in which something is prevented from continuing in its usual way because of problems and difficulties: +**to** *The strike caused widespread disruption to flight schedules.*

dis·rup·tive /dɪs'rʌptɪv/ *adj.* causing a lot of problems, and preventing something from being able to continue in its usual way: *disruptive behavior* | +**to** *Having a new baby can be so disruptive to family life.* —**disruptively** *adv.*

disˌruptive se'lection *n.* [U] BIOLOGY a form of NATURAL SELECTION in which two separate groups within a SPECIES, each with very different and opposite physical features, both continue to exist and produce children, while members of the species in the middle of the range gradually stop existing → see also DIRECTIONAL SELECTION

diss /dɪs/ another spelling of DIS

dis·sat·is·fac·tion /dɪˌsæṭɪs'fækʃən, dɪsˌsæ-/ *n.* [U] a feeling of not being satisfied, especially because something is not as good as you had expected OPP **satisfaction**: +**with** *Many of the guests expressed dissatisfaction with the service.*

dis·sat·is·fied /dɪ'sæṭɪsˌfaɪd/ *adj.* not satisfied, especially because something is not as good as you had expected OPP **satisfied**: +**with** *If you are dissatisfied with our service, please let us know.* —**dissatisfying** *adj.*

dis·sect /dɪ'sɛkt, daɪ-/ *v.* [T] **1** SCIENCE to cut up the body of a dead animal or person to study it **2** to examine something in great detail so that you discover its faults or understand it better: *The book dissects Napoleon's military strategy.*

dis·sec·tion /dɪ'sɛkʃən/ *n.* [C,U] **1** the act of cutting up the body of a dead animal or person to study it **2** the process of examining something in great detail so that you discover its faults or understand it better

dis·sem·ble /dɪ'sɛmbəl/ *v.* [I,T] FORMAL to hide your true feelings, ideas, desires etc. especially in order to deceive someone

dis·sem·i·nate /dɪ'sɛməˌneɪt/ *v.* [T] FORMAL to spread information, ideas etc. to as many people as possible, especially in order to influence them: *False information was being disseminated among investors.* —**dissemination** /dɪˌsɛmə'neɪʃən/ *n.* [U]

dis·sen·sion /dɪ'sɛnʃən/ *n.* [C,U] FORMAL disagreement and argument among a group of people: *Recent defeats has caused dissension in the army ranks.*

dis·sent[1] /dɪ'sɛnt/ *n.* **1** [C,U] disagreement with an official rule or law, or with an opinion that most people accept: *the government's efforts to suppress **political dissent*** **2** [C] LAW a judge's written statement, giving reasons for disagreeing with the other judges in a law CASE **3** [U] OLD USE a disagreement with accepted religious beliefs, especially one that makes someone leave an established church → see also CONSENT

dissent[2] *v.* [I] to say that you strongly disagree with an official opinion or decision, or one that is accepted by most people: +**from** *Four of the panel's members dissented from the majority's opinion.* —**dissenter** *n.* [C]

Dis·sent·er /dɪ'sɛntɚ/ *n.* [C] HISTORY a PROTESTANT in England during the 17th and 18th century who disagreed with the religious teachings and practices of the Church of England. Many Dissenters left the established church to start their own religious groups.

disˌsenting o'pinion *n.* [C] LAW a written document that states the opinion of one or more judges who disagree with a decision reached by a larger group of judges

dis·ser·ta·tion /ˌdɪsɚ'teɪʃən/ *n.* [C] a long piece of writing about a particular subject, especially one that you write as part of your work for a Ph.D. degree from a university [**Origin:** 1600–1700 Latin *dissertatio*, from *dissertare* **to discuss**]

dis·serv·ice /dɪ'sɚvɪs, dɪs'sɚ-/ *n.* **do sb/sth a disservice** to do something that harms someone or something, especially by giving other people a bad opinion about them: *You're doing your patients a great disservice if you don't help them lose weight.*

dis·si·dent /'dɪsədənt/ *n.* [C] POLITICS someone who publicly criticizes a government or political party in a country where this is not allowed: *political dissidents* [**Origin:** 1500–1600 Latin *dissidere* **to sit apart, disagree**, from *sedere* **to sit**] —**dissident** *adj.*: *a group of dissident writers* —**dissidence** *n.* [U]

dis·sim·i·lar /dɪ'sɪmələ̠, dɪs'sɪ-/ Ac *adj.* FORMAL very different OPP **similar**: *Their social backgrounds are very dissimilar.* | *Several countries have legal systems which are **not dissimilar to** (=similar to) our own.* —**dissimilarity** /dɪˌsɪmə'lærəṭi/ *n.* [C,U]

dis·sim·u·late /dɪ'sɪmyəˌleɪt/ *v.* [I,T] FORMAL to hide your true feelings or intentions, especially by lying to people

dis·si·pate /'dɪsəˌpeɪt/ *v.* FORMAL **1** [I,T] to scatter or disappear, or to make something do this: *The gas cloud had dissipated by late morning.* **2** [I,T] if feelings dissipate or something dissipates them, they gradually become weaker until you do not feel them anymore: *Exercise can help dissipate stress.* **3** [T] DISAPPROVING to gradually waste something such as money or energy by trying to do a lot of different or unnecessary things: *She had dissipated her fortune by the time she was 25.*

dis·si·pat·ed /'dɪsəˌpeɪṭɪd/ *adj.*, LITERARY DISAPPROVING spending too much time on physical pleasures such as drinking, smoking etc., in a way that is harmful to your health SYN **debauched**

dis·si·pa·tion /ˌdɪsə'peɪʃən/ *n.* [U] FORMAL **1** the process of making something disappear or scatter: *the dissipation of heat* **2** DISAPPROVING the enjoyment of physical pleasures that are harmful to your health SYN **debauchery**: *a life of luxury and dissipation* **3** DISAPPROVING the act of wasting money, time, energy etc.

dis·so·ci·ate /dɪ'soʊʃiˌeɪt, -siˌeɪt/ also **disassociate** *v.* [T] FORMAL **1 dissociate yourself from sb/sth** to do or say something to show that you do not agree with a person, organization, or action, especially so that you avoid being criticized or blamed SYN **distance** OPP **associate**: *The President quickly dissociated himself from the Secretary of State's remarks.* **2 dissociate sb/sth from sb/sth** to consider two things or people as separate and not related to each other: *His work could never be dissociated from his political beliefs.* **3** TECHNICAL to completely separate different mental processes or parts of your PERSONALITY as part of a mental illness

—**dissociation** /dɪˌsoʊʃiˈeɪʃən/ *n.* [U] —**dissociative** /dɪˈsoʊʃiət̬ɪv/ *adj.*

dis·so·lute /ˈdɪsəˌlut/ *adj.*, FORMAL DISAPPROVING having an immoral way of life, for example by drinking too much alcohol, having sex with many people etc. —**dissolutely** *adv.*

dis·so·lu·tion /ˌdɪsəˈluʃən/ *n.* [U] **1** LAW the act of formally ending a marriage or legal agreement: *the dissolution of a 13-year marriage* **2** POLITICS the act of ending a LEGISLATURE or PARLIAMENT, especially by a PRIME MINISTER before an election **3** the act of breaking up an organization, institution etc. so that it no longer exists: *the dissolution of a labor union* **4** the process by which something gradually becomes weaker and disappears: *the dissolution of the American dream*

D

dis·solve /dɪˈzɑlv/ *v.*
1 STH SOLID [I] CHEMISTRY if something solid dissolves or is dissolved in a liquid, it mixes with a liquid and becomes part of it: *Stir the mixture until the sugar has dissolved completely.* | **dissolve (sth) in sth** *Dissolve the yeast in lukewarm water.*
2 MARRIAGE/AGREEMENT [T usually passive] LAW to formally end a marriage, business arrangement etc.: *The lawsuit began after the marriage had been dissolved.*
3 ORGANIZATION a) [I,T] if an organization dissolves or is dissolved, it closes down and stops existing: *The committee was dissolved, and a new organization was set up to manage the event.* **b)** [T] to formally end a LEGISLATURE or PARLIAMENT, especially before an election
4 BECOME WEAKER [I,T] to become weaker and disappear, or to make something do this: *Maria's objections to the plan began to dissolve.*
5 dissolve into laughter/tears LITERARY to start to laugh or cry: *When Harriet learned about Edward's affair, she dissolved into tears.*

dis·so·nance /ˈdɪsənəns/ *n.* **1** [C usually singular, U] FORMAL a lack of agreement between ideas, opinions, or facts: +**between** *the dissonance between her orderly school life and chaotic home* **2** [C,U] ENG. LANG. ARTS an annoying sound made by a group of musical notes that do not go together well SYN **discord** OPP **consonance** OPP **harmony**: *a choral piece full of dissonance and odd rhythms* —**dissonant** *adj.*

dis·suade /dɪˈsweɪd/ *v.* [T] to make someone decide not to do something: *He wanted to come with me, and nothing I said could dissuade him.* | **dissuade sb from doing sth** *We hope the ads will dissuade teenagers from smoking.* → see also PERSUADE —**dissuasion** /dɪˈsweɪʒən/ *n.* [U]

dis·tance[1] /ˈdɪstəns/ S2 W2 *n.*
1 HOW FAR [C,U] the amount of space between two places or things: +**from/to** *Measure the distance from the top of the closet to the floor.* | +**between** *The distance between St. Petersburg and Moscow is 593 miles.* | **a short/long distance** *Police found the body a short distance from the scene of the crime.* | *The town is still **some distance*** (=a fairly long distance) *away.* | *Bird feeders should be placed **at a distance of** at least six feet from a bush or tree.*
2 A PLACE THAT IS FAR [singular] a point or place that is far away, but close enough to be seen or heard: *The ruins look impressive **from a distance**.* | *We heard church bells **in the distance**.* | *Even **at a distance** he could see she was in a bad mood.*
3 within walking/driving/striking etc. distance near enough to walk to, drive to, hit etc.: +**of** *The subway is within walking distance of my house.*
4 keep your distance a) to stay far enough away from someone or something to be safe: *Shots were fired into the air to force the police to keep their distance.* **b)** also **keep sb at a distance** to avoid becoming too friendly with someone or too closely involved in something: *Men tend to keep their children at more of a distance than women.*
5 DIFFERENCE [C usually singular] a difference or separation between two things: +**between** *the economic distance between rich and poor* | *Simmons was quick to **put some distance between** himself and his colleagues' remark* (=he emphasized what the differences were).
6 TIME [U] the amount of time between two events: *Now that there's some distance between us and the accident, it's easier to talk about.*
7 UNFRIENDLY FEELING [C usually singular] a situation in which two people do not tell each other what they really think or feel, in a way that seems unfriendly: +**between** *There was still a certain distance between me and my father.*
8 go the distance INFORMAL if you go the distance in a sport or competition, you continue playing or competing until the end → see also LONG-DISTANCE, MIDDLE DISTANCE

distance[2] *v.* **1 distance yourself (from sth)** to say that you are not involved with someone or something, or to try to become less involved with someone or something: *Rosen tried to distance himself from the controversy over fund-raising.* **2 distance yourself (from sb)** to avoid becoming involved with someone, or behave in a way that shows you do not want to be involved with them: *As a doctor, you have to learn to distance yourself.* **3** [T] to make someone have a less friendly relationship with someone else or a less positive attitude toward something: **distance sb from sb** *My work has distanced me from my family.*

ˈdistance ˌlearning *n.* [U] a method of studying that involves watching television programs, using the Internet etc. and sending work to teachers instead of going to school

dis·tant /ˈdɪstənt/ W3 *adj.*
1 FAR AWAY far away from where you are now: *the distant roar of the ocean* | *travelers from distant lands* | +**from** *The galaxy is very distant from ours.*
2 IN TIME at a time that was very long ago, or that will be very far in the future: *The book tells about societies **in the distant past*** (=from a long time ago). | *Their love affair was now a **distant memory**.* | *Wilder believes there will be an African American president **in the not-too-distant future*** (=sometime fairly soon).
3 NOT FRIENDLY seeming unfriendly, but still polite, and showing no emotion: *Jeff's been kind of distant lately.*
4 NOT PAYING ATTENTION showing that you are thinking about something else: *She had a distant look in her eyes.*
5 RELATIVE [only before noun] not very closely related to you OPP **close**: *a distant relative*
6 a distant second/third etc. someone who finishes seond, third etc. in a competition but is much worse, slower etc. than the one in front of them: *Rolley finished the tournament a distant second.*
[**Origin:** 1300–1400 Latin *distans*, present participle of *distare* **to stand apart**] —**distantly** *adv.*

dis·taste /dɪsˈteɪst/ *n.* [U] a feeling of dislike for someone or something that you think is annoying or offensive: +**for** *a distaste for violence in any form*

dis·taste·ful /dɪsˈteɪstfəl/ *adj.* unpleasant in a way that is rather shocking or rude: *Some viewers **found** the program **distasteful**.* —**distastefully** *adv.* —**distastefulness** *n.* [U]

dis·tem·per /dɪsˈtɛmpɚ/ *n.* [U] MEDICINE an infectious disease that affects dogs and cats

dis·tended /dɪˈstɛnd/ *adj.* stretched larger than the normal size because of pressure from inside: *the distended bellies of famine victims* —**distend** *v.* [I,T] —**distention**, **distension** /dɪˈstɛnʃən/ *n.* [U]

dis·till /dɪˈstɪl/ *v.* [T] **1** to make a strong alcoholic drink by heating alcohol until it becomes a gas and then letting it cool: **distill sth from sth** *You can distill brandy from wine.* **2** SCIENCE to make a liquid purer by heating it so that it becomes a gas, and then letting it cool: *It's not difficult to distill water.* **3** to get specific ideas, information etc. from a large amount of knowledge or experience: **distill sth from sth** *Our organization attempts to distill information from a variety of sources.* **4** SCIENCE to get a substance from a plant by heating and cooling it [**Origin:** 1300–1400 Old French *distiller*, from Latin *stillare* **to fall in drops**] —**distilled** *adj.*: *distilled water* —**distillation** /ˌdɪstəˈleɪʃən/ *n.* [C,U]

dis·til·late /ˈdɪstəlɪt, -ˌleɪt, dɪˈstɪlɪt/ *n.* [C] TECHNICAL a liquid that has been distilled from another liquid, for example GASOLINE that has been made from oil

dis·till·er /dɪˈstɪlɚ/ *n.* [C] a person or company that makes strong alcoholic drinks such as WHISKEY

dis·till·er·y /dɪˈstɪləri/ *n. plural* **distilleries** [C] a factory where strong alcoholic drinks are produced by distilling

dis·tinct /dɪˈstɪŋkt/ Ac *adj.* **1** clearly different or separate: *African and Asian elephants are distinct species.* | *two very distinct musical styles* | **+from** *The hill people are ethnically distinct from lowland Laotians.* | *"Animal desires" relate to the physical* ***as distinct from*** *the spiritual nature of people.* **2** clearly seen, heard, understood etc.: *I have a distinct memory of our conversation.* | *a distinct smell of burning leaves* **3** [only before noun] a distinct possibility, feeling, quality etc. is definite, obvious, and impossible to ignore: *I get the distinct impression that you don't like her very much.* | *a distinct advantage*

dis·tinc·tion /dɪˈstɪŋkʃən/ Ac S3 W3 *n.* **1** [C] a clear difference between things: **+between** *the distinction between fiction and nonfiction* | **make/draw a distinction** (=to be careful to say what the difference between two or more people or things is) **2** [C] something that makes a person or thing special: *Neil Armstrong* ***had the distinction of*** *being the first man on the moon.* | *The school holds the* ***dubious distinction of*** (=something that is bad or embarrassing) *the worst test scores in the county.*

dis·tinc·tive /dɪˈstɪŋktɪv/ Ac *adj.* having a special quality, character, or appearance that is easy to recognize and is different from others of the same type: *the spider's distinctive markings* —**distinctively** *adv.* —**distinctiveness** *n.* [U]

dis·tinct·ly /dɪˈstɪŋktli/ Ac *adv.* **1** clearly, and without any doubt: *I distinctly told you to be home before 11:00.* | **distinctly remember/recall** *Several witnesses distinctly remember Sanders starting the fight.* | **distinctly see/hear/feel etc.** *I distinctly heard someone say my name.* **2** WRITTEN used with adjectives to emphasize that something is clear, easy to recognize, or important SYN **decidedly**: *She looked distinctly uncomfortable.* **3** carefully and clearly: *She read each name slowly and distinctly.*

dis·tin·guish /dɪˈstɪŋgwɪʃ/ W3 *v.* **1** [I,T] to recognize or understand the difference between two similar things, people etc.: **+between** *the ability to distinguish between different speech sounds* | **distinguish sb/sth from sb/sth** *The twins are so alike it's difficult to distinguish one from the other.* **2** [T not in progressive] to be the thing that makes someone or something different from other people or things: **distinguish sb/sth from sb/sth** *Language distinguishes humans from other animals.* **3 distinguish yourself** to do something so well that people notice you, praise you, or remember you: *He distinguished himself as an actor before becoming a director.* **4** [T not in progressive] to be able to see, hear, or taste something, even if this is difficult: *I couldn't distinguish the words, but his tone was clear.* [**Origin:** 1500–1600 French *distinguer*, from Latin *distinguere* **to separate using a sharp pointed object**] —**distinguishing** *adj.* [only before noun] *a distinguishing feature*

dis·tin·guish·a·ble /dɪˈstɪŋgwɪʃəbəl/ *adj.* **1** easy to notice or to recognize as being different from other things or people: *Her work is instantly distinguishable from that of her fellow artists.* **2** easy to see, smell, taste, notice etc.: *The comet should be distinguishable in the night sky.*

dis·tin·guished /dɪˈstɪŋgwɪʃt/ *adj.* **1** very successful and therefore respected and admired: *a long and distinguished career* | *one of the country's most distinguished authors* ►see THESAURUS box at **famous** **2** looking important and serious in a way that makes people respect you: *He looked very distinguished in his black suit.*

dis·tort /dɪˈstɔrt/ Ac *v.* **1** [T] DISAPPROVING to explain or report information in a way that is incorrect or untrue, or that makes something seem different from what it really is: *The movie has clearly distorted historical fact.* ►see THESAURUS box at **change**[1] **2** [I,T] if a sound, shape, or character distorts, or someone distorts it, it changes so that it is strange, unclear, or difficult to recognize: *The intense heat had distorted the building's steel supports.* [**Origin:** 1400–1500 Latin *distortus*, past participle of *distorquere* **to twist out of shape**] —**distorted** *adj.*: *a badly distorted TV picture* —**distortion** /dɪˈstɔrʃən/ *n.* [U]

dis·tract /dɪˈstrækt/ S3 *v.* [T] to do something that takes someone's attention away from what they should be paying attention to: *Don't distract me while I'm driving!* | **distract sb from sth** *Jack's music was distracting me from my book.* | *Events overseas have* ***distracted attention from*** *the economy.* [**Origin:** 1300–1400 Latin *distractus*, past participle of *distrahere* **to pull apart**] —**distracting** *adj.*

dis·tract·ed /dɪˈstræktɪd/ *adj.* unable to pay attention to what you are doing, because you are worried or thinking about something else: *She was inattentive and easily distracted in class.* —**distractedly** *adv.*

dis·trac·tion /dɪˈstrækʃən/ *n.* **1** [C,U] something that takes your attention away from what you are doing: *I can't work at home – there are too many distractions.* | **+from** *a distraction from the work at hand* **2** [C] a pleasant and not very serious activity that you do for amusement: *Tennis has become a welcome distraction for Rudy.* **3 drive sb to distraction** to annoy someone so much that they become angry, upset, and not able to think clearly anymore: *He drove all his teachers to distraction.*

dis·traught /dɪˈstrɔt/ *adj.* so anxious or upset that you cannot think clearly: **+over/about** *He was distraught over the breakup of his marriage.*

dis·tress[1] /dɪˈstrɛs/ *n.* [U] **1** a feeling of being extremely worried and upset: *Children suffer emotional distress when their parents divorce.* | **+over/about** *distress over the loss of a loved one* | *The girl was crying and clearly* ***in distress.*** **2** a situation in which someone or something needs help, for example because they are in a dangerous situation or they do not have food or money: *The Shelter meets the needs of families* ***in distress.*** | **a distress signal/call** (=a signal made by a ship or plane, asking for other ships or planes to come and help) **3** FORMAL severe physical pain, or injury to the muscles: *abdominal distress* [**Origin:** 1200–1300 Old French *destresse*, from Latin *districtus*, past participle of *distringere* **to pull apart, prevent from acting or leaving**]

distress[2] *v.* [T] to make someone feel extremely upset and worried: *The thought of a painful death distresses most people.* | **it distresses sb to hear/see/learn etc.** *It distressed him to see her cry.* | **it distresses sb that** *It distressed her that women could not be members.*

dis·tressed /dɪˈstrɛst/ *adj.* **1** extremely worried or upset: **+about/at/over/by** *Homeowners are already distressed about their high property taxes.* | *When he came to see me, he was* ***deeply distressed.*** | **distressed to hear/see/learn etc.** *We were all distressed to hear of her death.* | **distressed that** *I am distressed that so little progress has been made.* ►see THESAURUS box at **sad** **2** FORMAL needing help, money etc.: *distressed urban neighborhoods* **3** distressed furniture or cloth has been deliberately treated in a way that makes it look old and used **4** experiencing a lot of pain: *The animal was clearly distressed.* **5** distressed property is offered for sale at a lower than usual price because the owner cannot afford to keep it: *distressed real estate*

dis·tress·ing /dɪˈstrɛsɪŋ/ also **dis·tress·ful** /dɪˈstrɛsfəl/ *adj.* making you feel extremely worried or upset: *a distressing experience* —**distressingly** *adv.*

dis·trib·ute /dɪˈstrɪbyət/ Ac W1 *v.* **1 GIVE OUT** [T] to give something such as food, medicine, or information to each person in a group: *Copies of the report were distributed shortly after the meeting.* | **distribute sth to/among sb** *The Red Cross is distributing* *food and clothing to the refugees.* ►see THESAURUS box at give[1]

2 SUPPLY GOODS [T] to supply goods to stores, companies etc. so that they can be sold: *The firm distributes paper and other office supplies.*

3 DIVIDE [T] to divide something such as power or an amount of money fairly among different people or organizations so that they can share it: *The Foundation is responsible for distributing the grant money.* | **distribute sth between/among sb** *The prize money was distributed equally between the winners.*

4 SPREAD [T] to spread something over an area or through a substance: *Each panel distributes sound evenly in all directions.*

D

5 SELL DRUGS [I,T] LAW to sell illegal drugs to other people: *He pleaded guilty to possession with intent to distribute.*

[**Origin:** 1400–1500 Latin *distribuere* **to give out**, from *tribuere* **to give to a particular person**]

dis·trib·ut·ed /dɪˈstrɪbyət̬ɪd/ *adj.* **1** existing in particular numbers or amounts within a particular area or group: *Their factories are **widely distributed** throughout the region.* | **equally/evenly distributed** *Unemployment was evenly distributed between males and females.* **2** COMPUTERS [only before noun] a distributed computer system or network uses several computers in different places, rather than one central computer

dis·tri·bu·tion /ˌdɪstrəˈbyuʃən/ Ac W3 *n.* **1** [U] the process of giving something such as food, medicine, or information to each person in a group: **+of** *the distribution of medical supplies to the refugees* **2** [U] the process of supplying goods to stores, companies etc. area so that they can be sold: *The cost of packaging and distribution ranges from $3 to $4 per videotape.* | *a distribution center* **3** [C,U] the way in which people or things are spread out over an area or through a substance, or the process of spreading them: *the population distribution of Canada* | *the distribution of pollen by the wind* **4** [U] the way in which money, property etc. is shared among different groups: *calls for a more equitable distribution of wealth* **5** [C,U] MATH a set of numbers and how often they appear in a set of data, especially as shown in a GRAPH or TABLE —**distributional** *adj.* —**distributive** /ˌdɪstrəˈbyut̬ɪv/ *adj.*

dis·trib·u·tor /dɪˈstrɪbyət̬ɚ/ Ac *n.* [C] **1** a company or person that supplies goods to stores or other companies **2** the part of a car's engine that sends electricity to the SPARK PLUGS

dis·trib·u·tor·ship /dɪˈstrɪbyət̬ɚˌʃɪp/ *n.* [C] a company that supplies goods to stores or other companies

dis·trict /ˈdɪstrɪkt/ S2 W1 *n.* [C] a particular area of a city, country etc., especially an area that is officially divided from others: *Blaine works in the financial district.* [**Origin:** 1600–1700 French, Medieval Latin *districtus* **area under control of a lord or judge**, from *districtus* **taken hold of, forced**] ►see THESAURUS box at area

ˌdistrict atˈtorney *n.* [C] LAW a lawyer who works for the government in a particular district and brings people who may be criminals to court

ˌdistrict ˈcourt *n.* [C] LAW a U.S. court of law where people are judged in situations that involve national rather than state law

ˌDistrict of Coˈlumbia, the ABBREVIATION **D.C.** the special area of the eastern U.S. next to Maryland and Virginia, which includes Washington, the capital of the U.S.

dis·trust¹ /dɪsˈtrʌst/ *n.* [U] a feeling that you cannot trust someone: *Many people regard politicians with distrust.* | **+of** *a deep distrust of authority* → see also MISTRUST —**distrustful** *adj.*

distrust² *v.* [T] to not trust someone or something: *He distrusts banks.*

dis·turb /dɪˈstɚb/ S3 W3 *v.* [T] **1** to annoy someone or interrupt what they are doing by making noise, asking a question etc.: *If she's sleeping, don't disturb her.* | *a **Do Not Disturb** sign* (=that you put on your hotel door to tell people not to wake you up) | ***I'm sorry to disturb you,** but we need your advice.* **2** to make someone feel worried or upset: *What disturbs you most about this decision?* **3** to do something that changes the position or condition of things, usually in a bad way: *I was careful not to disturb anything in his office.* | *Cutting down rainforests disturbs the Earth's balance.* **4 disturb the peace** LAW to behave in a noisy and annoying way in public [**Origin:** 1100–1200 Old French *destourber*, from Latin *turbare* **to put into disorder**]

dis·turb·ance /dɪˈstɚbəns/ *n.* **1** [C,U] something that annoys you or interrupts you so that you cannot continue what you are doing, or the act of annoying or interrupting someone: *It was enough of a disturbance to wake me.* | *Residents complained of disturbance from the aircraft.* **2** [C] a situation in which people fight or behave violently in public: *Police violence sparked civil disturbances.* | **create/cause a disturbance** *Several people tried to create a disturbance in the courtroom.* **3** [C,U] a change in the normal condition or position of something: *There is a fast-moving weather disturbance passing through Utah.* **4** [C,U] a mental or emotional problem that makes you unable to behave normally: *a history of mental disturbances*

dis·turbed /dɪˈstɚbd/ *adj.* **1** worried or upset: **+about/by/at** *He was deeply disturbed by what he saw.* | **disturbed to hear/read/learn etc.** *We were disturbed to learn she's using drugs.* | **disturbed that** *His parents are disturbed that he's dating a much older woman.* **2** not behaving in a normal way because of mental or emotional problems: *The defendant is mentally and emotionally disturbed.* ►see THESAURUS box at crazy[1]

dis·turb·ing /dɪˈstɚbɪŋ/ *adj.* making you feel worried or upset: *It's very disturbing, the way they're getting rid of older employees.*

dis·u·nit·ed /ˌdɪsyuˈnaɪt̬ɪd/ *adj.* FORMAL not working together the way the members of a group should OPP **united**: *a disunited political party* —**disunite** *v.* [I,T]

dis·u·ni·ty /dɪsˈyunət̬i/ *n.* [U] FORMAL a state in which a group of people cannot agree with each other or work together OPP **unity**: *Disunity damaged the party in the election.*

dis·use /dɪsˈyus/ *n.* [U] a situation in which something is not used anymore: *A lot of farmland **fell into disuse** (=stopped being used) during the war.* —**disused** /ˌdɪsˈyuzd◂/ *adj.*

di·syl·lab·ic /ˌdaɪsəˈlæbɪk◂/ *adj.* ENG. LANG. ARTS having two SYLLABLES

ditch¹ /dɪtʃ/ *n.* [C] a long narrow open hole that is dug in the ground for water to flow through, usually at the side of a road or in a field: *I accidentally drove my car into a ditch.* | **a drainage ditch/an irrigation ditch** *a drainage ditch blocked with leaves and mud* → see also LAST-DITCH

ditch² *v.* **1** [T] INFORMAL to get rid of something or stop using or considering it because it is not useful to you anymore: *He ditched the car and escaped on foot.* **2** [T] SPOKEN, INFORMAL to not go to school, class etc. when you should SYN **skip**: *Let's ditch school and go to the park.* **3** [T] SPOKEN, INFORMAL to leave someone somewhere without telling them that you are leaving: *I'm mad at Charlene – she ditched me at the party last night.* **4** [T] SPOKEN, INFORMAL to end a romantic relationship with someone SYN **dump**: *If I were you, I'd ditch her.* **5** [I,T] to land an airplane on water in a controlled crash: *The pilot had no choice but to ditch the plane.*

dith·er¹ /ˈdɪðɚ/ *v.* [I] to keep changing your opinion or decision about something, especially to avoid making a final decision: **+on/over** *They're still dithering over the date of the wedding.* [**Origin:** 1600–1700 *didder* **to shake** (14–19 centuries)] —**ditherer** *n.* [C]

dither² *n.* **be/get (all) in a dither** to be nervous and confused because you cannot decide what to do: *I was all in a dither about my mother-in-law's visit.*

dit·sy /ˈdɪtsi/ *adj.* another spelling of DITZY

dit·to¹ /ˈdɪt̬oʊ/ *interjection* used to say that you have exactly the same opinion as someone else about something, or that something is also true for you: *"I find his classes really boring." "Ditto."*

ditto² *adv.* used to say that what is true about one thing or situation is also true about another: *The pets all need to be fed – **ditto for** the kids.* [**Origin:** 1600–1700 Italian, past participle of *dire* **to say**]

ditto³ *n. plural* **dittos** [C] **1** also **'ditto mark** ENG. LANG. ARTS a mark (") that you write beneath a word in a list so that you do not have to write the same word again **2** a copy of a letter, form etc. made on an old-fashioned machine that was used before PHOTOCOPIERS

dit·ty /'dɪṭi/ *n. plural* **ditties** [C] HUMOROUS a short simple poem or song

ditz /dɪts/ *n.* [C] SPOKEN someone who is silly, forgetful, or stupid: *My art teacher is a total ditz.*

dit·zy /'dɪtsi/ *adj.* INFORMAL silly, forgetful, or stupid: *I like her, but she's kind of ditzy.*

di·u·ret·ic /ˌdaɪyə'rɛṭɪk/ *n.* [C] a substance that increases the flow of URINE —**diuretic** *adj.*

di·ur·nal /daɪ'ɚnl/ *adj.* TECHNICAL **1** being active in the daytime OPP **nocturnal**: *diurnal animals* **2** happening or existing during the day OPP **nocturnal**: *diurnal temperatures* **3** happening every day or during one day

Div. *n.* the written abbreviation of DIVISION

di·va /'divə/ *n.* [C] a woman who is a very good singer, especially of OPERA music [**Origin:** 1800–1900 Italian **female god**] → see also PRIMA DONNA

di·van /dɪ'væn, 'daɪvæn/ *n.* [C] OLD-FASHIONED a long low soft seat that has no back or arms, which is often used as a bed

dive¹ /daɪv/ *v. past tense* **dived** or **dove** /doʊv/, *past participle* **dived** [I]

1 JUMP INTO WATER to jump into the water with your head and arms going in first: **+in/into/off etc.** *She ran to the edge of the pool and dived in.* | *Diving off the cliffs is very dangerous.*

THESAURUS

plunge to move, fall, or be thrown or pushed suddenly forward or downward: *The car swerved and plunged off the cliff.*
submerge to put something completely under the surface of the water: *Global warming may cause coastal cities to be submerged by rising sea levels.*
sink to go down below the surface of water, mud etc., or to make something do this: *The ship was hit by a torpedo and sank very quickly.*

►see THESAURUS box at **jump¹**

2 JUMP/MOVE QUICKLY [always + adv./prep.] to jump or move quickly in a particular direction or into a particular place: **+after/under/aside etc.** *Ripken dived to his left and caught the ball.* | *We all **dove for cover** under a table.*

3 SWIM UNDER WATER to swim under water using special equipment to help you breathe: **+for** *The men use scuba gear to dive for abalone.*

4 GO DEEPER to go deeper under water: *Slowly, the submarine began to dive.*

5 AIRCRAFT/BIRD if an airplane or a bird dives, it suddenly flies toward the ground very steeply: *The bird suddenly spotted its prey and dived.*

6 NUMBERS if numbers, prices etc. dive, they fall very quickly and suddenly SYN **plummet**: *Stock prices have dived to their lowest level this year.*

7 SOCCER INFORMAL in SOCCER, to fall to the ground in a dishonest attempt to persuade the referee that an opponent has done something wrong

[**Origin:** Old English *dufan* **to sink** and *dyfan* **to put into liquid**] → see also DIVING, NOSEDIVE², SCUBA DIVING, SKYDIVING

dive in *phr. v.* **1** to immediately start doing something eagerly and with a lot of energy: *Harry dived in and started asking questions.* **2** SPOKEN, INFORMAL start eating a meal eagerly with a lot of energy

dive into sth *phr. v.* to quickly become completely involved in an activity, a subject etc.: *Plummer was eager to dive into the kind of opportunity the college offers.*

dive² *n.* [C]

1 SUDDEN MOVEMENT a jump or sudden movement in a particular direction or into a particular place: *Vincenze **made a dive for** the ball.*

2 AMOUNT/VALUE a sudden drop in the amount or value of something: *Their sales have **taken a dive**.*

3 JUMP a jump into deep water with your head and arms going in first: *a graceful dive*

4 BAR/HOTEL/RESTAURANT INFORMAL a place such as a bar or a hotel that is cheap and dirty: *We're not staying in this dive.*

5 AIRPLANE/BIRD an occasion when an airplane or a bird suddenly flies toward the ground very steeply: *The plane **went into a dive** shortly after takeoff.*

6 take a dive to deliberately do something in order to lose a game, competition etc.: *He was supposed to take a dive in the fourth round.*

7 SWIM an occasion when someone swims under water using special equipment to breathe

8 SUBMARINE an occasion when a SUBMARINE goes deeper under the water

9 SOCCER in SOCCER, an occasion when a player deliberately falls to the ground in a dishonest attempt to persuade the referee that an opponent has done something wrong → see also NOSEDIVE¹

'dive-bomb *v.* [I,T] **1** to attack someone or something by flying down toward them and dropping a bomb: *The plane grew louder as it dive-bombed a bunker.* **2** INFORMAL if a bird dive-bombs someone or something, it quickly flies down and attacks them

'dive ˌbomber *n.* [C] a type of military airplane that flies low over a place and drops bombs on it

div·er /'daɪvɚ/ *n.* [C] **1** someone who swims or works underwater using special equipment to breathe: *a deep sea diver* **2** someone who jumps into deep water with their head and arms first

di·verge /də'vɚdʒ, daɪ-/ *v.* [I] **1** if similar things diverge, they develop in different ways and so are not similar anymore OPP **converge**: *The two species diverged millions of years ago.* **2** if people's opinions, interests etc. diverge, they are different from each other: *Their political views **diverge sharply**.* **3 diverge from sth** to change from your current attitude or your current way of doing something: *Russia does not intend to diverge from its position.* **4** if two lines or paths that are next to each other diverge, they begin to go in different directions OPP **converge** [**Origin:** 1600–1700 Medieval Latin *divergere*, from Latin *vergere* **to lean**]

di·ver·gence /də'vɚdʒəns/ *n.* [C,U] a difference between two or more things such as opinions or interests: **+between** *political divergence between the U.S. and Europe*

di·ver·gent /də'vɚdʒənt/ *adj.* divergent opinions, ideas, interests etc. are very different from each other: *divergent views on drugs*

diˌverging 'lens *n.* [C] PHYSICS a piece of glass or plastic which causes a narrow beam of light passing through it to spread out in different directions → see also CONVERGING LENS

di·vers /'daɪvɚz/ *adj.* [only before noun] OLD-FASHIONED of many different kinds SYN **various**

di·verse /də'vɚs, daɪ-/ Ac *adj.* **1** very different from each other: *topics as diverse as pop music and architecture* **2** a place or group that is diverse has many different types of people or things in it: *New York is one of the most **culturally diverse** cities in the world.*

di·ver·si·fy /də'vɚsəˌfaɪ/ Ac *v.* **diversifies, diversified, diversifying** **1** [I,T] ECONOMICS if a company or a country's ECONOMY diversifies, or if someone diversifies it, it begins to make a larger range of products or to become involved in new types of business: *Singapore has diversified its economy to embrace a wider range of industries.* | **+into** *The company survived by diversifying into other areas.* **2** [I,T] ECONOMICS to put your money into several different types of INVESTMENT instead of only one or two: *Reduce risk by diversifying your investment portfolio.* **3** [I,T] to increase the variety of things that you do: *She began to diversify, performing songs in many languages.* **4** [I] to develop in different ways so that new forms or types are created —**diversification** /dəˌvɚsəfəˈkeɪʃən/ *n.* [U]

di·ver·sion /dəˈvɚʒən, daɪ-/ *n.* **1** [C,U] a change in the usual or intended way that something such as money is used, or the act of changing this: +**of** *an illegal diversion of public funds* **2** [C,U] a change in the direction of the flow of something: *water diversions such as dams and canals* **3** [C] something that takes your attention away from something that you should be giving your attention to: *Four prisoners* ***created a diversion*** *to allow the others time to escape.* **4** [C,U] an enjoyable activity that you do so that you are not bored: +**from** *The course was a welcome diversion from work.*

D

di·ver·sion·a·ry /dəˈvɚʒəˌnɛri/ *adj.* intended to take someone's attention away from something: *Most children are skilled in* ***diversionary tactics****.*

di·ver·si·ty /dəˈvɚsəṭi, daɪ-/ Ac *n.* **1** [U] the quality of being made up of a range of different people, ideas, or things: *Pop music's main problem is its lack of diversity.* | +**of** *The laws should reflect the diversity of the country.* | **cultural/ethnic/linguistic etc. diversity** *The school prides itself on its ethnic diversity.* **2** [C usually singular] a range of different people, ideas, or things SYN **variety**: +**of** *It's natural that there is a diversity of opinions within the organization.*

di·vert /dəˈvɚt, daɪ-/ *v.* [T] **1** to change what something such as money or time is used for: **divert sth to/into sth** *Voters do not want to divert public tax dollars into private education.* | **divert sth from sth** *Police resources are being diverted from investigating real crimes.* **2** to make a vehicle change direction and travel a different way: *Traffic has been diverted because of an accident.* | **divert sth to/away from/along etc. sth** *Planes are being diverted to Philadelphia airport.* **3** to change the direction in which something flows: *Farmers were illegally diverting water to save their crops.* **4** to stop someone from paying attention to something, by giving them something else to notice SYN **distract**: **divert attention/suspicion from sb/sth** *The story was an attempt to divert attention from the scandal.* **5** FORMAL to amuse or entertain someone: *Take games on the plane to divert the children.* [**Origin:** 1400–1500 Old French *divertir*, from Latin *divertere*, from *vertere* **to turn**]

di·vert·ing /dəˈvɚṭɪŋ/ *adj.* FORMAL entertaining and amusing

di·vest /dəˈvɛst, daɪ-/ *v.* [I,T] ECONOMICS if a person, company etc. divests, or divests their ASSETS or INVESTMENTS, they sell them: *We will divest all non-core units.*

divest sb **of** sth *phr. v.* **1** ECONOMICS to sell a company or an INVESTMENT: **divest yourself of sth** *The company is divesting itself of $120 million in unprofitable business.* **2** FORMAL to take away someone's rights, power, or authority **3** FORMAL to take away something that someone is wearing or carrying —**divestment** *n.*

di·ves·ti·ture /dəˈvɛstɪtʃɚ/ *n.* [C,U] ECONOMICS the act of selling a company or an INVESTMENT

di·vide¹ /dəˈvaɪd/ S2 W2 *v.*

1 SEPARATE [I,T] to separate something into two or more parts, groups etc., or to become separated in this way: *Cancer cells divide rapidly.* | **divide (sth) into sth** *Divide the dough into four parts and make each into a ball.* | *The class divided into groups of four and five.* ▸see THESAURUS box at **separate²**

2 KEEP SEPARATE [T] to keep two areas separate from each other: *A river divides the two states.* | **divide sth from sth** *Only a curtain divides the kitchen from the bedroom.*

3 SHARE [T] also **divide up** to separate something into two or more parts and share it among two or more people, groups, places etc.: *How will the money be divided?* | **divide sth between sth and sth** *She divides her time between New York and Paris.* | **divide sth among sb/sth** *The money will be divided up equally among his children.*

4 MATHEMATICS a) [I,T] to calculate how many times one number contains a smaller number: **divide (sth) by sth** *Divide 21 by 3.* | *12 divided by 4 is 3.* | *Add 15, then divide by 10.* **b)** [I] to be contained in another number one or more times: +**into** *8 divides into 64 eight times.* ▸see THESAURUS box at **calculate** → see also MULTIPLY

5 DISAGREE [T] to make people disagree with each other and form groups with different opinions: *The incident has divided the community.* | **be divided over/about sth** *Congress is divided over what to do.*

6 FORM SEPARATE GROUPS [I] if people divide, they disagree with each other and form groups with different opinions: **divide along racial/ethnic/party etc. lines** *On this issue people tend to divide along racial lines.*

7 divide and conquer/rule to defeat or control people by making them argue or fight with each other instead of opposing you: *The authorities continued to practice divide and rule policies.*

[**Origin:** 1300–1400 Latin *dividere*, from *videre* **to separate**] —**divided** *adj.*

divide² *n.* [C usually singular] **1** a strong difference between two groups of people, especially in their beliefs or way of life, that separates them and can result in fighting: *The racial divide between the city and its suburbs is deepening.* **2** EARTH SCIENCE a line of very high ground from which water flows to two different river systems SYN **watershed**

diˌvided ˈhighway *n.* [C] a main road on which the traffic traveling in opposite directions is kept apart by a piece of land or a low wall

div·i·dend /ˈdɪvəˌdɛnd, -dənd/ W3 *n.* [C] **1** ECONOMICS a part of a company's profit that is paid to people who have SHARES in the company **2** MATH a number that is to be divided by another number → see also DIVISOR, **pay dividends** at PAY¹ (6)

di·vid·er /dəˈvaɪdɚ/ *n.* [C] **1** something such as a wall or SCREEN that separates one room or part of a room from another: *a room divider* **2** a wall, fence, piece of land etc. that separates the traffic moving in opposite directions on a main road **3** a piece of stiff paper used to keep pages separate: *a set of notebook dividers* **4 dividers** [plural] GEOMETRY an instrument used for measuring or marking lines or angles, that consists of two pointed pieces of metal joined together at the top

diˈviding ˌline *n.* [C] **1** the difference between two types or groups of similar things: +**between** *It's hard to* ***draw a dividing line between*** *scientific issues and moral and religious ones.* **2** a line or border that separates two areas or things: *The car swerved across the dividing line of a two-lane highway.*

div·i·na·tion /ˌdɪvəˈneɪʃən/ *n.* [U] FORMAL the act of finding out what will happen in the future by using special powers, or the practice of doing this

di·vine¹ /dəˈvaɪn/ *adj.* **1** coming from God or a god: *Only* ***divine intervention*** *would help me now.* | *He thought his illness was* ***divine retribution*** *for his misdeeds.* **2** relating to God or a god, or like a god: *man's belief in divine beings* **3** OLD-FASHIONED unusually good SYN **wonderful**: *The food was simply divine.* [**Origin:** 1300–1400 Old French *divin*, from Latin *divus* **god**]

divine² *v.* **1** [T] LITERARY to discover or guess something: *They divined the truth immediately.* **2** [I] to search for water or minerals that are under the ground using a special Y-shaped stick —**diviner** *n.* [C]

divine³ *n.* **1 the Divine** God, or someone who has qualities like a god's: *St. John the Divine* **2** [C] FORMAL a priest or minister

diˌvine ˈright *n.* [singular] **1** INFORMAL the right to do what you want without having to ask permission: *Some bicyclists apparently think they have a divine right to ride wherever they want.* **2** the right given to a king or queen by God to rule a country, that in past times could not be questioned or opposed

diˌvine ˌright of ˈkings *n.* [singular] HISTORY the idea that a king's right to rule comes directly from God, not from the people of a country

div·ing /ˈdaɪvɪŋ/ *n.* [U] **1** the sport of swimming under water using special equipment to breathe: *They **went diving** in the Florida Keys on their vacation.* **2** the activity of jumping into water with your head and arms first: *a diving competition*

ˈdiving bell *n.* [C] a metal container shaped like a bell, in which people can work under water

ˈdiving board *n.* [C] a board above a SWIMMING POOL from which you can jump into the water

ˈdiving suit *n.* [C] a special protective suit that is worn when someone is swimming deep under water

diˈvining rod *n.* [C] a special stick shaped like the letter Y that some people use to find water and minerals that are under the ground

di·vin·i·ty /dəˈvɪnəṭi/ *n. plural* **divinities** **1** [U] the study of God and religious beliefs [SYN] **theology**: *a Master of Divinity degree* **2** [U] the state of being a god, or the quality of being like a god: *the divinity of Christ* **3** [C] God or a god: *Celtic divinities* ►see THESAURUS box at **god** **4** also **divinity candy** [U] a soft white candy, often containing nuts

diˈvinity school *n.* [C] a college where students study to become priests or ministers

di·vis·i·ble /dəˈvɪzəbəl/ *adj.* able to be divided, especially by another number: **+by** *Fifteen is divisible by 3.* **—divisibility** /dəˌvɪzəˈbɪləṭi/ *n.* [U]

di·vi·sion /dəˈvɪʒən/ [S3] [W2] *n.*
1 SEPARATION [C,U] the act of separating something into two or more parts or groups, or the way that these parts are separated or shared: *the process of cell division* | **+of** *the division of Korea in 1948* | **division of sth between/among sb** *the division of the estate among the man's children* | **division of sth into sth** *the division of words into syllables*
2 PART OF AN ORGANIZATION [C] a group that does a particular job within a large company, organization etc.: *the TV network's news division*
3 DISAGREEMENT [C,U] a disagreement among the members of a group: *The controversy has revealed a **deep division within** the church.* | **+between/among** *There are divisions among the band's members.* | **+over/about** *growing divisions about the best policy*
4 DIFFERENCE [C] a difference in the way that people within the same country or community live: *class divisions* | **+between** *the division between rich and poor*
5 MATHEMATICS [U] the process of finding out how many times one number contains a smaller number → see also LONG DIVISION, MULTIPLICATION
6 SPORTS [C] a group of teams that a sports LEAGUE or competition is divided into: *The team is currently first in the Pacific division.*
7 MILITARY [C] a large military group: *The entire division of 18,000 troops will be home.*

di·vi·sion·al /dəˈvɪʒənl/ *adj.* relating to a sports, military, or organizational division: *the divisional playoffs*

diˌvision of ˈlabor *n.* [C,U] a way of organizing work in which each member of a group has a particular job to do

di·vi·sive /dəˈvaɪsɪv, -ˈvɪs-/ *adj.* causing a lot of disagreement among people: *Abortion is one of the most divisive issues in America.*

di·vi·sor /dəˈvaɪzɚ/ *n.* [C] MATH the number by which another number is to be divided → see also DIVIDEND

di·vorce¹ /dəˈvɔrs/ [S3] [W3] *n.* **1** [C,U] the legal ending of a marriage: *Half the marriages in this country end in divorce.* | *Tony and Karen are **getting a divorce**.* | *His wife **filed for divorce*** (=began the divorce process). | **a messy/bitter divorce** *a prolonged and bitter divorce* | *He had to pay her $10 million as part of the **divorce settlement*** (=the legal decision about how much money, property etc. each person gets after a divorce). → see also SEPARATION **2** [C] a separation of ideas, subjects, values etc.: **+between** *a divorce between theory and practice* [**Origin:** 1300–1400 French, Latin *divertere* **to divert, leave one's husband**]

divorce² [S2] *v.* **1** [I,T] to legally end a marriage: *We divorced after six years of marriage.* | *She threatened to divorce me.* | **+be divorced from sb** *Trent was divorced from his wife in 1974.*

THESAURUS
separate to start to live apart from your husband or wife: *They separated six months ago.*
split up/break up to end a marriage or a long romantic relationship: *When Andy was nine, his parents split up.* | *He broke up with his girlfriend.*
leave sb to stop living with your husband, wife, or partner: *Her husband left her after 27 years of marriage.*

2 [T] to separate two ideas, values, organizations etc.: **divorce sth from sth** *You can't completely divorce society from religion.* **3 divorce yourself from sth** to stop being involved with an activity, an organization etc.

di·vorced /dəˈvɔrst/ *adj.* **1** not married to your former wife or husband anymore: *a divorced woman* | **+from** *He's been divorced from Delores for years.* | *My parents **got divorced*** (=legally ended their marriage) *when I was ten.* ►see THESAURUS box at **married** **2 divorced from sth** not connected or related to something: *Some of his ideas **are completely divorced from reality*** (=not based on real experience or sensible thinking).

di·vor·cee, **divorcée** /dəˌvɔrˈsi, -ˈseɪ/ *n.* [C] a woman who has legally ended her marriage

div·ot /ˈdɪvət/ *n.* [C] a small piece of earth and grass that you dig out accidentally while playing GOLF

di·vulge /dəˈvʌldʒ, daɪ-/ *v.* [T] to give someone information, especially about something that was secret: *The FBI has not divulged information on any suspects.* | **divulge sth to sb** *She would not divulge her plans to anyone.* | **divulge what/where/whether etc.** *The Navy refuses to divulge whether any of the ships are carrying nuclear weapons.* [**Origin:** 1400–1500 Latin *divulgare* **to make widely known to everyone**, from *vulgus* **the common people**]

div·vy /ˈdɪvi/ *v.* **divvies**, **divvied**, **divvying**
divvy sth ↔ **up** *phr. v.* INFORMAL to divide something among two or more people: *Divvy up the cookies between you.*

Dix /dɪks/, **Do·ro·the·a** /ˌdɔrəˈthiə, ˌdɑr-/ (1802–1887) a U.S. social REFORMER who worked to improve conditions for people who were in prison or mentally ill

Dix·ie /ˈdɪksi/ *n.* [U] INFORMAL the southeastern states of the U.S. that fought against the North in the U.S. Civil War

dix·ie·land /ˈdɪksiˌlænd/ also **ˈdixieland ˌjazz** *n.* [U] a type of JAZZ with a strong RHYTHM

diz·zy /ˈdɪzi/ *adj. comparative* **dizzier**, *superlative* **dizziest** **1** having a feeling of not being able to balance, especially after spinning around or because you feel sick: *I'd better sit down – I feel dizzy.* | *She suffers from high blood pressure and **dizzy spells*** (=short periods when you feel dizzy). **2** confused or excited: **+from/with** *We were all dizzy with excitement.* **3** INFORMAL silly or stupid [SYN] **ditzy**: *a dizzy blonde* **4** DIZZYING [**Origin:** Old English *dysig* **stupid**] **—dizzily** *adv.* **—dizziness** *n.* [U]

diz·zy·ing /ˈdɪziɪŋ/ *adj.* **1** making someone feel confused or excited: *a dizzying number of choices* **2** making someone feel unable to balance: *The view from the top of the building is dizzying.* **—dizzy** *v.* [T]

DJ /ˈdi dʒeɪ/ *n.* [C] a DISC JOCKEY

Dji·bou·ti /dʒɪˈbuṭi/ a small country on the coast of northeast Africa **—Djiboutian** *n., adj.*

djinn /dʒɪn/ *n.* [C] a magical spirit in Islamic stories that can appear as a human or an animal and influence people in good or bad ways → see also GENIE

DMV /ˌdi ɛm ˈvi/ *n.* **the Department of Motor Vehicles the DMV** the organization in many U.S. states where you can get a DRIVER'S LICENSE, REGISTER your car etc.

DMZ /ˌdi ɛm ˈzi/ *n.* [C] **Demilitarized Zone** POLITICS a phrase meaning an area from which all weapons, soldiers etc. have been removed so that there can be no fighting there, used especially about the area between North and South Korea

DNA /ˌdi ɛn ˈeɪ/ *n.* [U] **deoxyribonucleic acid** BIOLOGY an acid found in the cells of living things, that holds GENETIC information: *a strand of DNA* | *DNA samples*

DNA pol·y·mer·ase /ˌdi ɛn eɪ ˈpɑləməˌreɪs/ *n.* [U] BIOLOGY a chemical substance in the bodies of animals and plants which repairs and produces new DNA → see also ENZYME

D

ˌDNA ˈprofiling also **ˌDNA ˈfingerprinting** *n.* [U] the act of examining DNA, especially to find out who did a particular crime or whether two people are related

do¹ /də; *strong* du/ S1 W1 *auxiliary verb* **does** /dəz; *strong* dʌz/, *past tense* **did** /dɪd/, *past participle* **done** /dʌn/ **1** used with another verb to form questions or negatives: *Do you know Nancy?* | *We don't eat much red meat.* | *How does this machine work?* | *Don't make a lot of noise.* | *Doesn't Rosie look fat?* | *I didn't say anything.* **2** SPOKEN used at the end of a sentence to make a question or to show that you expect someone to agree with it: *You didn't go alone, did you?* | *It looks just like new, doesn't it?* **3** used to emphasize the main verb in a sentence: *I don't have any brothers, but I do have a sister.* | *"Why didn't you tell me?" "I did tell you – you just forgot."* **4** used to avoid repeating another verb: *She speaks much better English than I do.* | *"You broke my glasses!" "No, I didn't."* | *"Which train goes to Tokyo?" "That one does."* | *"I love this place." "I **do** too."* | *"I speak French and **so does** my wife."* | *"You didn't eat much." "**Neither did** you."* **5** used to change the order of the subject and the verb for literary effect, especially when a negative adverb or adverbial phrase starts a sentence: *Not only did she tell lies, but she also stole things.* **6** used before a verb instead of "should" in questions asking for instructions or suggestions: *What do I say if someone asks me where you are?* [**Origin:** Old English *don*]

do² /du/ S1 W1 *v.*

1 ACTION/ACTIVITY a) [T] to perform an action or an activity: *Do your homework before you watch TV.* | *You should do more exercise.* | *"What are you doing?" "Making cookies."* | *All he does is watch TV.* | **do the dishes/laundry/ironing etc.** *It's Jim's turn to do the dishes.* | *It's a pleasure **doing business** with you.* → see Word Choice box at MAKE¹ **b) do something/anything (about sth)** to take necessary action to stop or improve a bad situation: *He's hurt! Do something!* | *Can't you do anything about it?*

2 SUCCEED/FAIL [I only in progressive] used to ask or say whether someone is being successful SYN **get along**: *How are you doing? Are you nearly finished?* | **+with** *How is Erica doing with the new baby?* | **do well/badly/okay etc.** *Neil is doing very well at school this year.*

3 HAVE AN EFFECT [T] to have a particular effect on someone or something: *This could do serious damage to your career.* | *The new car factory has **done a lot for*** (=had a good effect on) *the local economy.* | *The changes have **done nothing** to improve the situation.* | *If she doesn't like Kevin, you can't **do anything about** that* (=you cannot change that). | *Come on, let's go to the beach. It'll **do you good*** (=make you feel better or happier). | *I don't think one more cookie will **do any harm*** (=cause problems). | **not do anything/a thing for sb** *Red doesn't do a thing for her* (=it doesn't make her look good). | *Moving to the city has **done wonders for*** (=has really improved) *my social life.*

4 JOB [T] to have a particular type of job or work: *What do you want to do when you finish school?* | *She hopes to do something in education.* | ***What** does Ann **do for a living*** (=what is her job)?

5 do sb's hair/nails/makeup etc. to spend time arranging someone's hair, painting their nails etc.: *It takes her a half an hour to do her hair in the morning.*

6 TRAVEL FAST/FAR [T] to travel at a particular speed, or to travel a particular distance: *I'm only doing 50 miles an hour.* | *We did 300 miles on the first day.*

7 BE ACCEPTABLE/ENOUGH [I,T not in progressive] to be acceptable or be enough: *The recipe calls for butter, but margarine will do.* | *I wanted to get a new dress for the wedding, but my blue one **will have to do**.* | *"Do you want a glass this size?" "Yeah, **that'll do**."* | **sth will do sb** *Just a sandwich will do me for lunch.* ▶see THESAURUS box at **adequate**

8 SPEND TIME [T] INFORMAL to spend a period of time doing something difficult or something that you have to do: *He did three years in the army.* → see also **do time** at TIME¹ (41)

9 MAKE FOOD [T] INFORMAL to make a particular type of food SYN **make**: *I was thinking of doing a casserole tonight.*

10 PROVIDE A SERVICE [T] to provide a particular service: *They do music for weddings mostly.* | *We do both interior and exterior design.*

11 VISIT [T] INFORMAL to visit a particular place, especially when you are going to see a lot of other places: *Let's do the Empire State Building tomorrow.*

12 TAKE A DRUG [T] to use an illegal drug, especially regularly: *I would never do drugs.*

13 COPY [T] INFORMAL to copy someone's behavior, in order to entertain people SYN **imitate**: *He does Bush very well.*

14 BEHAVE [I] to behave in a particular way: *They think they can do as they please.* | *Do as you're told.*

15 PERFORM A PLAY [T] to perform a particular play: *They did "Hamlet" last year.*

SPOKEN PHRASES

16 what is sb/sth doing...? used to ask why someone or something is doing something or why they are in a particular place, especially when you do not approve: *What's this cake doing on the floor?* | *What are you doing eating that cookie when I'm about to fix dinner?*

17 do lunch/a meeting/a movie etc. INFORMAL to have lunch, have a meeting, see a movie etc. with someone else: *Let's do lunch next week.*

18 do it a phrase meaning "have sex," used humorously or when you do not want to say this directly

19 that'll do used to tell a child that you want them to stop being noisy, angry, excited etc.: *That'll do, you two. Stop arguing.*

20 what will you do for sth? used to ask someone what arrangements they have made to deal with something: *If you quit your job, what will you do for money?*

21 what can I do you for? HUMOROUS used to ask someone what you can do to help them

22 HAPPEN [I only in progressive] SLANG to happen: *What's doing at your place tonight?*

23 sb would do well to do sth used to advise someone that they should do something: *She would do well to keep her political views to herself.*

24 DECORATE [T] to paint or decorate something, such as a room or a house: *We're going to do my office in blue.*

25 CHANGE [T] INFORMAL to change in a particular way: *We'll have to wait and see what the weather does.*

26 do sth to death to talk about or do something so often that it becomes boring: *That joke has been done to death.*

27 sth (just) won't do used to say that something is not good enough or is not acceptable: *I'm afraid that apology just won't do.*

28 do well/right by sb to treat someone well: *He's left home, but he still does well by his kids.* → see also **be done for** at DONE² (5), DO-OR-DIE, **how do you do** at HOW (22)

do away with *phr. v.* **1 do away with sth** to get rid of something: *Maybe it's time we did away with the old system.* **2 do away with sb** INFORMAL to kill someone: *She hired two men to do away with her husband.*

do sb **in** *phr. v.* **1** to make someone feel extremely tired: *That bike ride really did me in.* **2** INFORMAL to kill someone or kill yourself: *Do you really think Stan would do himself in?*

do sb **out of** sth *phr. v.* INFORMAL to cheat someone by not giving them something that they deserve, or something that they are owed: *The waiter tried to do us out of $10.*

do sth **over** *phr. v.* **1** to do something again, especially because you did it wrong the first time: *I had to* *do the test over.* | ***If I had it to do over**, I'd have given myself more time to relax.* **2** to decorate a room, wall etc. in a different way than before: *We're doing over the whole apartment.*

do up *phr. v.* **1 do sth ↔ up** to tie or arrange your hair in a particular way: *She had done her hair up with a ribbon.* **2 do sb ↔ up** to make yourself or another person look neat and attractive, or to dress them in a particular way: *Sue took forever doing herself up for her date.* | *The girls were **all done up in** white robes and tinsel for the Christmas procession.* **3 do sth ↔ up** to decorate something so that it looks attractive: *The bar was done up like a plush salon from 100 years ago.* **4 do sth ↔ up** to fasten a piece of clothing in a particular way, or to be fastened or tied in that way: *I don't like blouses that do up in the back.*

do with sth *phr. v.* **1 have to do with sth** to be about something, related to something, or involved in something: *What does this have to do with our situation?* | *The overdose **had nothing to do with** the patient's death* (=it was not related to the death). | *The problem **has something to do with** the computer system* (=it is related to the computer system, but they are not sure exactly how). | *Do our moods **have anything to do with** our temperature?* **2 have nothing to do with sb** to not concern or involve someone: *My private life has nothing to do with you.*

SPOKEN PHRASES

3 what have you/has he etc. done with sth? used to ask where someone has put something: *What have you done with the scissors?* **4 what sb does with himself/herself** what someone spends their time doing: *What will you do with yourself over the summer?* **5 what is sb doing with sth?** used to ask why someone has something: *What are you doing with my wallet?* **6 what should/do I do with sth?** used to ask what you should use something for, or where you should put it: *Mom, what should I do with this frying pan?* **7 sb could do with sth** used to say that someone needs or wants something: *I could do with a cold drink.*

do without *phr. v.* **1 do without sth** to manage to continue living or doing something without having a particular thing: *City residents need to think about what services they can do without.* **2 I can/could do without sth** SPOKEN used to say that something is annoying you or making things difficult for you: *I could do without that constant racket in the next room.*

USAGE

Do is used in many phrases and expressions in English. If you do not find the expression you are looking for here, look at the next important word in the phrase. For example, you can find **do sb a favor** at **favor**.

USAGE **Phrases with "do"**

- If someone asks you what you have **done to** something, you have probably changed it in some way: *"What did you do to your hair?"* However, if someone asks you what you have **done with** something, they want to know where it is: *"What did you do with my book?"*
- If someone asks you what you **do**, they want to know what type of work you do: *"What do you do, Sally?" "I'm a doctor."*
However, if they ask you what you **are doing**, they want to know what activity you are doing at that particular moment: *"What are you doing, Sally?" "I'm making lunch."*
- In some phrases, **do** is the only word that can be used: *They want to do more research on that.* (Don't say, *They want to make more research.*) In other phrases, you can use **do** instead of another verb: *I have to do my bills this afternoon.* (= *I have to pay my bills this afternoon.*)

do³ *n.* [C] INFORMAL **1 dos and don'ts** things that you should or should not do in a particular situation: *the dos and don'ts of office dating* **2** a party or other social event: *a family do* **3** a HAIRDO

do⁴, doh /doʊ/ *n.* [singular, U] ENG. LANG. ARTS the first note in a musical SCALE according to the SOL-FA system

DOA /ˌdi oʊ 'eɪ/ *adj.* **dead on arrival** → see **dead on arrival** at DEAD¹ (16)

do·a·ble /'duəbəl/ *adj.* INFORMAL able to be completed or done: *The first task seems doable.*

d.o.b. *n.* the written abbreviation of "date of birth"

Do·ber·man pin·scher /ˌdoʊbɚmən 'pɪntʃɚ/ also **doberman** *n.* [C] a large black and brown dog with very short hair, often used for guarding houses or buildings

doc /dɑk/ *n.* [C] SPOKEN a short form of DOCTOR

do·cent /'doʊsənt/ *n.* [C] someone who guides visitors through a MUSEUM, church, garden etc.

doc·ile /'dɑsəl/ *adj.* quiet, calm, and easy to control: *Kangaroos are not as docile as they look.* [**Origin:** 1400–1500 Latin *docilis*, from *docere* **to teach**] —**docilely** /'dɑsəl-li/ *adv.* —**docility** /dɑ'sɪləṭi/ *n.* [U]

dock¹ /dɑk/ *n.* **1** [C,U] an area of water in a port where ships stay while goods are being loaded and unloaded, while passengers get on or off, or where repairs are done: *The ship never even left the dock.* | *The ship is now **in dock** for repairs.* → see also DRY DOCK **2** [C] a structure around a port or built out into an area of water from which boats or ships are loaded or unloaded or from which passengers get on and off SYN **pier** SYN **wharf**: *A crowd was waiting on the dock to greet them.* **3 the docks** [plural] all the offices and other buildings used for loading, unloading, and repairing ships, and the land and water around them: *an old apartment building near the docks* **4** [C] a LOADING DOCK **5 the dock** LAW an enclosed area in some law courts where the DEFENDANT (=person charged with a crime) sits or stands [**Origin:** 1300–1400 Middle Dutch *docke*]

dock² *v.* **1** [I,T] if a ship docks or you dock it, it sails into a dock: *The ship docked in Honolulu on November 1.* **2** to reduce the amount of money you pay someone, especially because they have done something wrong: *Roman was docked two hours' pay for the incident.* | **dock sb's wages/pay** *If you don't repay the money, they'll dock your wages.* **3** [I] if two spaceships dock, they join together in space: *The repair ship docked with the space station last night.* **4** [T] COMPUTERS to connect a computer to another computer or a computer network **5** [T] to cut an animal's tail short

dock·et /'dɑkɪt/ *n.* [C] **1** LAW a list of legal cases that will take place in a particular court: *There were 415 cases on the docket that day.* **2** a list of things to be done or discussed SYN **agenda**: *So what's **on the docket** for today's meeting?* **3** TECHNICAL a short document that shows what is in a package or describes goods that are being delivered

dock·side /'dɑksaɪd/ *n.* [singular] the area around the place in a port where ships are loaded and UNLOADed

dock·work·er /'dɑkˌwɚkɚ/ *n.* [C] someone who works on a DOCK, especially loading and UNLOADing ships

dock·yard /'dɑkyɑrd/ *n.* [C] a place where ships are repaired or built

doc·tor¹, Doctor /'dɑktɚ/ S1 W1 WRITTEN ABBREVIATION **Dr.** *n.* [C] **1** someone whose job is to treat people who are sick, or the title of such a person: *He trained as a doctor.* | *Good afternoon, Doctor Singh.* | **go to the doctor/see a doctor** *See a doctor if the fever lasts more than three days.*

THESAURUS

physician FORMAL a doctor: *our family physician*
surgeon a doctor who does operations in a hospital

specialist a doctor who knows a lot about a particular area of medicine
psychiatrist a doctor who treats mental illness
psychologist someone who is specially trained to treat mental illnesses
pediatrician a doctor who treats children who are sick
gynecologist a doctor who treats medical conditions and illnesses that affect only women
obstetrician a doctor who deals with the birth of children
medical student a student who is studying to be a doctor
intern a student who has almost finished studying to be a doctor, and who is working in a hospital
→ DENTIST, OPTOMETRIST

D

2 someone who has a DOCTORATE, or the title of such a person: *a Doctor of Law* [**Origin:** 1300–1400 Old French *doctour*, from Latin *doctor* **teacher**]

doctor² *v.* [T] **1** to change something, especially in a way that is not honest: *Photographs can easily be doctored.* **2** to add a substance, especially a drug or poison, to food or drink SYN **spike**: *Paul suspected that his drink had been doctored.* **3** to give medical treatment to someone or something: *Gina gently doctored Clint's injured hand.*

doc·tor·al /ˈdɑktərəl/ *adj.* [only before noun] relating to or done as part of work for the university degree of DOCTOR: *a doctoral dissertation*

doc·tor·ate /ˈdɑktərɪt/ *n.* [C] a university degree of the highest level

ˌDoctor of Phiˈlosophy *n.* [C] a PH.D.

ˈdoctor's deˌgree *n.* [C] INFORMAL a doctorate

doc·tri·naire /ˌdɑktrəˈnɛr◂/ *adj.* FORMAL certain that your beliefs or opinions are completely correct, and not willing to change them: *the most doctrinaire of the court's conservative judges*

doc·trine /ˈdɑktrɪn/ *n.* [C] **1** a strong belief or set of beliefs that form an important part of a religion or system of ideas: *the Hindu doctrine of the immortality of the soul* **2** POLITICS a formal statement of the government's way of dealing with something, especially other countries: *the Monroe Doctrine* [**Origin:** 1300–1400 French, Latin *doctrina*, from *doctor* **teacher**] —**doctrinal** /ˈdɑktrɪnl, dɑkˈtraɪnl/ *adj.*

doc·u·dra·ma /ˈdɑkyəˌdrɑmə/ *n.* [C] a movie, usually for television, that is based on a true story

doc·u·ment¹ /ˈdɑkyəmənt/ Ac S3 W2 *n.* [C] **1** a piece of paper that has official information written on it, or a set of these papers: *legal documents* | *a 55-page document detailing the criminal charges* **2** COMPUTERS a piece of work that you write on a computer, which is saved in a single file: *If you try to close the document, the program will prompt you to save it.* [**Origin:** 1400–1500 French, Late Latin *documentum*, from Latin *docere* **to teach**]

doc·u·ment² /ˈdɑkyəˌmɛnt/ Ac *v.* [T] **1** to write about something, film it, photograph it etc. in order to record information about it: *The journal documents his cross-country trip.* | **document sth with sth** *He documented his research with a video camera.* | **document sth in sth** *The findings were documented in her report.* **2** to support something with facts: *The effects of smoking have been* ***well documented***. **3** to provide someone with official documents, especially so they can work legally —**documented** *adj.*

doc·u·men·ta·ry¹ /ˌdɑkyəˈmɛntri, -ˈmɛntəri/ *n.* *plural* **documentaries** [C] a movie or television program that gives facts and information about something: **+on/about** *a documentary on whales* ►see THESAURUS box at **television**

documentary² *adj.* **1 documentary film/program** ENG. LANG. ARTS a movie or television program that gives facts and information about something **2** [only before noun] documentary proof or EVIDENCE is proof in the form of documents

doc·u·men·ta·tion /ˌdɑkyəmənˈteɪʃən/ Ac *n.* [U] **1** official documents, reports etc. that are used to prove that something is true or correct: *There was no formal documentation of their business partnership.* | *You must provide the necessary documentation when opening a bank account.* **2** the process of writing about something, filming it, photographing it etc. in order to record information about it, or the papers, photographs etc. that are produced: *The library wants documentation of the fire for its history exhibit.* **3** COMPUTERS written instructions about how to use a computer or computer program

DOD /ˌdi oʊ ˈdi/ the abbreviation of the DEPARTMENT OF DEFENSE

dod·der /ˈdɑdɚ/ *v.* [I] to walk in an unsteady way while shaking slightly, especially because you are very old

dod·der·ing /ˈdɑdərɪŋ/ *adj.* shaking slightly, walking with difficulty, and often confused because you are old or sick: *a doddering old man*

do·dec·a·gon /doʊˈdɛkəˌgɑn/ *n.* [C] MATH a flat shape with 12 straight sides

dodge¹ /dɑdʒ/ *v.* **1** [I,T] to move quickly, especially to avoid being hit by something or being seen by someone: *They ran quickly, dodging the bullets.* | **+into/out/behind etc.** *George dodged around the truck.* **2** [T] to avoid talking about something or doing something that you do not want to do: *The senator skillfully dodged the reporter's question.* | *When asked about his enormous salary, he* ***dodged the issue****, saying, "I don't like discussing cash."* **3** [T] to avoid paying taxes that you should pay by using dishonest methods **4 dodge a bullet** to avoid something that could hurt you or make you fail: *Marshall dodged a bullet by avoiding criminal charges.*

dodge² *n.* [C] **1** INFORMAL something dishonest that you do to avoid a responsibility or a law: *He used his medical condition as a dodge to avoid testifying.* | *IRS attorneys have called the "charity" a* ***tax dodge*** (=a way to avoid paying taxes). **2** a sudden forward or sideways movement to avoid someone or something

ˈdodge ball *n.* [U] a game played by children in which you try to avoid being hit by a large rubber ball thrown by the other players

Dodge Cit·y /ˌdɑdʒ ˈsɪt̬i/ a city in the U.S. state of Kansas

dodg·er /ˈdɑdʒɚ/ *n.* [C] **a tax/draft dodger** someone who uses dishonest methods to avoid paying taxes or serving in the army

do·do /ˈdoʊdoʊ/ *n.* [C] **1** BIOLOGY a large bird that was unable to fly and does not exist anymore **2** INFORMAL a stupid person [**Origin:** 1600–1700 Portuguese *doudo* **stupid person**]

doe /doʊ/ *n.* [C] a female DEER, rabbit, and some other animals → see also BUCK

do·er /ˈduɚ/ *n.* [C] someone who does things instead of just thinking or talking about them: *The people of our grandparents' generation were doers, not talkers.* → see also EVILDOER, WRONGDOER

does /dəz; *strong* dʌz/ *v.* the third person singular of the present tense of DO

does·n't /ˈdʌzənt/ *v.* the short form of "does not": *She doesn't want to go.*

doff /dɑf, dɔf/ *v.* [T] OLD-FASHIONED to take off a piece of clothing, especially your hat OPP **don**: *He doffed his cap and bowed.*

dog¹ /dɔg/ S1 W1 *n.* [C]
1 ANIMAL BIOLOGY a very common animal with four legs that is often kept as a pet or used for guarding buildings: *I could hear a dog barking.* | *I saw her in the park* ***walking the dog***. | ***Stray dogs*** *roamed the streets.* | *What breed of dog is it?*
2 UNPLEASANT MAN also **dirty dog** INFORMAL a man who behaves badly and treats others badly: *He's such a dog. I can't believe he would cheat on you like that.*
3 be going to the dogs INFORMAL if an organization, company etc. is going to the dogs, it is getting much worse and will be difficult to improve: *This country's really going to the dogs.*

4 dog eat dog used when describing a situation in which people compete against each other and will do anything to get what they want: *It's a dog-eat-dog world out there.*
5 every dog has its/his day an expression used to mean that even the most unimportant person has a time in their life when they are successful and noticed
6 FOOD INFORMAL a HOT DOG
7 it's a dog's life SPOKEN used to say that life is difficult and full of hard work and worry, with very little pleasure
8 POOR QUALITY INFORMAL something that is not of good quality: *It was a dog of a movie.*
9 put on the dog OLD-FASHIONED to behave or dress in a way that makes people notice how wealthy, intelligent etc. you are, especially when this annoys people
10 a dog in the manger someone who will not let other people use or have something, even though they do not need it themselves
11 FEET dogs [plural] INFORMAL feet
12 a dog and pony show INFORMAL a very impressive event, usually organized to help sell a product
13 MALE ANIMAL BIOLOGY a male dog, FOX, and some other animals → see also BITCH
[**Origin:** Old English *docga*] → see also **be in the doghouse** at DOGHOUSE (2), **a/the hair of the dog (that bit you)** at HAIR (13), **(you) lucky dog!** at LUCKY (8), SHAGGY-DOG STORY, **let sleeping dogs lie** at SLEEP[1] (7), **it's (a case of) the tail wagging the dog** at TAIL[1] (12), **top dog** at TOP[2] (5)

dog² *v.* **dogged, dogging** [T] **1** if a problem, bad luck etc. dogs you, it does not go away and causes trouble for a long time: *She was dogged by injuries all season.* **2** to follow closely behind someone: *The press dogged him relentlessly.* **3** [T] SLANG **a)** to make jokes about someone and laugh at them in order to embarrass them **b)** to defeat someone badly, especially in a sport or a game **4 dog it** INFORMAL to not try as hard as you should or need to in order to do something

'dog ˌbiscuit *n.* [C] a small dry hard cookie for dogs

dog·catch·er /ˈdɔgˌkætʃə/ *n.* [C] someone whose job is to catch dogs that are loose or that do not have owners

'dog ˌcollar *n.* [C] **1** a collar worn by dogs, onto which a LEASH (=a piece of rope used to control a dog) can be attached **2** INFORMAL a stiff round white collar worn by priests

'dog days *n.* [plural] LITERARY **1** the hot uncomfortable days in July and August: *the dog days of summer* **2** a period of time when not very much is done or when someone is not successful

'dog door *n.* [C] a small door cut in a door of the house that a dog or cat can go in and out of

doge /doʊdʒ/ *n.* [C] the highest government official in Venice and in Genoa in the past

'dog-eared *adj.* dog-eared books or papers have been used so much that the corners are turned down or torn: *a dog-eared Bible* —**dog-ear** *v.* [T]

dog·fight /ˈdɔgfaɪt/ *n.* [C] **1** an organized fight between dogs **2** a fight between armed airplanes

dog·fish /ˈdɔgˌfɪʃ/ *n. plural* **dogfish** [C] a type of small SHARK

dog·ged /ˈdɔgɪd/ *adj.* dogged actions or behavior show that you are very determined to continue doing something: *a dogged determination to succeed* —**doggedly** *adv.* —**doggedness** *n.* [U]

dog·ge·rel /ˈdɔgərəl, ˈdɑ-/ *n.* [U] poetry that is silly or funny and not intended to be serious: *a few verses of doggerel*

dog·gie /ˈdɔgi/ *n.* [C] another spelling of DOGGY

dog·gone /ˌdɔˈgɔn◂/ *v.* [T] SPOKEN **doggone it** used when you are annoyed: *Doggone it! I can't find my purse.* —**doggone, doggoned** SPOKEN *adj., adv.*

dog·gy, doggie /ˈdɔgi/ *n.* [C] a word meaning "dog", used especially by or when speaking to young children

'doggy bag *n.* [C] a small bag for taking home food that is left over from a meal, especially from a restaurant

'doggy ˌpaddle *n.* [C] DOG PADDLE

'dog ˌhandler *n.* [C] a police officer who works with a trained dog

dog·house /ˈdɔghaʊs/ *n.* **1** [C] a small house made for a dog to sleep in **2 be in the doghouse** INFORMAL to be in a situation in which someone is annoyed with you because you have done something wrong: *I'm in the doghouse for forgetting Valentine's Day.*

do·gie /ˈdoʊgi/ *n.* [C] a CALF (=baby cow) without a mother

dog·leg /ˈdɔglɛg/ *n.* [C] a place in a road, path etc. where it changes direction suddenly —**dogleg** *v.* [I]

dog·ma /ˈdɔgmə, ˈdɑgmə/ *n.* [C,U] POLITICS a particular belief or set of beliefs that people are expected to accept without questioning them: *traditional Christian dogma*

dog·mat·ic /dɔgˈmætɪk/ *adj.* having ideas or beliefs that you will not change and that you expect other people to accept: *Her employees find her bossy and dogmatic.* —**dogmatically** /-kli/ *adv.*

dog·ma·tis·m /ˈdɔgməˌtɪzəm/ [U] attitudes or behavior that are dogmatic —**dogmatist** *n.* [C]

dog·ma·tize /ˈdɔgməˌtaɪz/ *v.* [I] to speak, write, or act in a dogmatic way

do-good·er /ˈdu ˌgʊdə/ *n.* [C] someone who does things to help people who are poor or need help, but who sometimes is annoying because they get involved when they are not wanted

'dog ˌpaddle also **'doggy ˌpaddle** INFORMAL *n.* [singular] a simple way of swimming by moving your legs and arms like a swimming dog

'dog show *n.* [C] a competition in which dogs are judged according to their appearance and sometimes according to the things they can do

dog·sled /ˈdɔgslɛd/ *n.* [C] a SLED (=low flat vehicle on metal blades) pulled by dogs over snow

'dog tag *n.* [C] a small piece of metal that soldiers wear on a chain around their necks that has their name, blood type, and number written on it

ˌdog-'tired *adj.* INFORMAL extremely tired

dog·wood /ˈdɔgwʊd/ *n.* [C,U] an eastern North American tree or bush with flat white or pink flowers

d'oh /doʊ/ *interjection* HUMOROUS said when you have just realized that you did something stupid

Do·ha /ˈdoʊhɑ/ the capital city of Qatar

doi·ly /ˈdɔɪli/ *n. plural* **doilies** [C] a circle of paper or cloth with a pattern cut into it, used for decoration, especially on a plate before you put cakes etc. on it [**Origin:** 1700–1800 the name of a 17th-century London cloth-seller]

Doi moi /ˌdɔɪ ˈmɔɪ/ *n.* [U] HISTORY a Vietnamese word used to describe the social, political, and economic changes that happened in Vietnam from 1986, which led to improvements in people's living standards and personal freedom

do·ing /ˈduɪŋ/ *n.* **1 be sb's (own) doing** if something bad is someone's doing, they did it or did things that caused it: *Your problems are all your own doing.* **2 take some doing** to be hard work: *Getting this old car to run is going to take some doing.* **3 doings** [plural] INFORMAL events or activities that someone is involved in: *the daily doings of Hollywood stars*

ˌdo-it-your'self *adj.* **1** a do-it-yourself job, repair etc. is one that you do yourself instead of paying someone else to do it: *a do-it-yourself remodeling job* **2** a do-it-yourself book, store etc. tells you how to make or repair things yourself, sells you things you need to do this etc.: *a do-it-yourself manual*

Dol·by /ˈdoʊlbi/ *n.* [U] TRADEMARK a system for reducing unwanted noise when you record music or sounds

dol·drums /ˈdoʊldrəmz, ˈdɑl-/ *n.* [plural] INFORMAL **1** a state in which something is not improving or developing: *The stock market has recovered completely from its recent doldrums.* | *The manufacturing sector is still* ***in***

the doldrums, analysts say. **2** a state in which you feel sad and bored: *Beat the summer doldrums by spending a day at the zoo.* | *Tom has been* ***in the doldrums.*** **3 the doldrums** an area in the ocean just north of the EQUATOR where the weather can be so calm that sailing ships cannot move

dole[1] /doʊl/ *v.*

dole sth ↔ **out** *phr. v.* INFORMAL to give something such as money, food, advice etc. in small amounts to a lot of people: **dole sth out to sb** *The proposal would involve doling out $850 million to school districts around the country.*

dole[2] *n.* BRITISH **the dole** money given by the government to people who need financial help

dole·ful /ˈdoʊlfəl/ *adj.* very sad: *a doleful look* —**dolefully** *adv.* —**dolefulness** *n.* [U]

doll[1] /dɑl/ S3 *n.* [C] **1** a child's toy that looks like a small person or baby **2** a very nice person: *Thanks. You're a doll.* **3** also **dollface** OLD-FASHIONED a word used to talk to an attractive young woman, now considered offensive [**Origin:** 1500–1600 the female name *Doll*, from *Dorothy*]

doll[2] *v.*

doll yourself **up** *phr. v.* INFORMAL if a woman dolls herself up, she puts on attractive clothes and MAKEUP: *I got all* ***dolled up*** *for the party.*

dol·lar /ˈdɑlɚ/ S1 W1 *n.* [C] **1** SYMBOL **$** the standard unit of money in the U.S., Canada, Australia, New Zealand, and other countries: *These pants cost 30 dollars.* **2** a piece of paper money or a coin of this value: *He gave me a dollar.* **3 the dollar** ECONOMICS the value of U.S. money in relation to the money of other countries: *The yen rose against the dollar.* → see also **you can bet your bottom dollar** at BET[1] (5), **feel/look like a million bucks/dollars** at MILLION (6)

USAGE

We say "a two billion dollar debt" or "a fifty dollar loan," but we write "a $2 billion debt" or "a $50 loan."

ˌdollar diˈplomacy *n.* [U] a way of getting support from other countries for American ideas and aims, by giving them money or by INVESTING in them

dol·lar·i·za·tion /ˌdɑlərəˈzeɪʃən/ *n.* [U] the process by which a country's ECONOMY becomes dependent on the U.S. dollar instead of its own money: *the dollarization of the country's economy*

ˌdollars-and-ˈcents *adj.* considered in a financial way: *From a dollars-and-cents point of view, it's a good idea.*

ˈdollar sign *n.* [C] **1** a symbol ($) that means "dollar" or "dollars": *$1* (=one dollar) | *$3* (=three dollars) **2 see dollar signs** to think that a situation is likely to give you an opportunity to make a lot of money: *Some are unsure about the product, but others see dollar signs.*

doll·house /ˈdɑlhaʊs/ *n.* [C] a small toy house for DOLLS

dol·lop /ˈdɑləp/ *n.* [C] a small amount of soft food, usually dropped from a spoon in a rounded shape: +**of** *a large dollop of whipped cream* [**Origin:** 1500–1600 from a Scandinavian language; related to Norwegian *dolp* **piece**] —**dollop** *v.* [T]

dol·ly /ˈdɑli/ *n. plural* **dollies** [C] **1** another word for a DOLL, used by children and when talking to children **2** TECHNICAL a flat frame on wheels used for moving heavy objects

dol·men /ˈdoʊlmən, ˈdɑl-/ *n.* [C] two or more large upright stones supporting a large flat piece of stone, built in ancient times

dol·phin /ˈdɑlfɪn, ˈdɔl-/ *n.* [C] BIOLOGY an intelligent ocean animal like a large gray fish with a long pointed nose [**Origin:** 1300–1400 Old French *dalfin*, from Greek *delphis*]

ˈdolphin-safe *adj.* dolphin-safe fish are caught in a way that does not harm DOLPHINS

dolt /doʊlt/ *n.* [C] OLD-FASHIONED a silly or stupid person —**doltish** *adj.* —**doltishly** *adv.*

-dom /dəm/ *suffix* **1** [in U nouns] the state of being in a particular condition or having a particular quality: *freedom* (=state of being free) | *boredom* (=state of being bored) | *wisdom* (=state of being wise) **2** [in C nouns] **a)** an area ruled in a particular way: *a kingdom* (=place ruled by a king) **b)** a particular rank: *He was rewarded with a dukedom* (=was made a DUKE). **3** [in U nouns] INFORMAL all the people who share the same set of interests, have the same job etc.: *officialdom* (=all government officials)

do·main /doʊˈmeɪn, də-/ AC *n.* [C] FORMAL **1** a particular activity that is controlled by one person, group, organization etc.: *Housework was thought to be a woman's domain.* | *The matter* ***falls outside the domain of*** (=is not part of the domain of) *local government.* **2** a particular area of activity or life: *The issue has moved into the political domain.* → see also EMINENT DOMAIN, PUBLIC DOMAIN **3** an area of land owned or controlled by one person, group, or government, especially in the past: *the royal domain* **4** MATH all the possible values that can be used as INDEPENDENT VARIABLES in a mathematical FUNCTION → see also RANGE **5** BIOLOGY one of the groups into which scientists divide animals or plants, in which the animals or plants are closely related but cannot produce babies or more plants together. A domain is larger than a KINGDOM. → see also FAMILY, GENUS, SPECIES

dome /doʊm/ *n.* [C] **1** a round roof on a building or room **2** a shape like a ball cut in half: *the dome of his bald head* [**Origin:** 1600–1700 French *dôme* **dome, cathedral**, from Latin *domus* **house**]

dome

domed /doʊmd/ *adj.* covered with a dome, or shaped like a dome: *a domed stadium*

do·mes·tic[1] /dəˈmɛstɪk/ W2 *adj.* **1** happening or produced within one country and not involving any other countries: *Most Americans listed domestic issues as their top priority.* | *The airline serves mainly domestic routes.* | *domestic wine* **2** [only before noun] relating to family relationships and life at home: *domestic responsibilities* | *Manley was arrested for assault and* ***domestic violence*** (=violence between husband and wife). **3** someone who is domestic enjoys spending time at home and is good at cooking, cleaning etc. **4** [only before noun] a domestic animal lives on a farm or in someone's home OPP **wild** **5** used in people's homes: *a manufacturer of* ***domestic appliances*** (=machines such as washing machines, stoves etc.) [**Origin:** 1400–1500 French *domestique*, from Latin *domesticus*, from *domus* **house**] —**domestically** /-kli/ *adv.*

domestic[2] AC *n.* [C] OLD-FASHIONED a servant who works in a house

do·mes·ti·cate /dəˈmɛstɪˌkeɪt/ AC *v.* [T] to make an animal able to live with people as a pet or to work for them, for example on a farm → see also TAME —**domestication** /dəˌmɛstɪˈkeɪʃən/ *n.* [U]

do·mes·ti·cat·ed /dəˈmɛstɪˌkeɪt̬ɪd/ AC *adj.* animals or plants that are domesticated are raised by people and are able to be used for work or food OPP **wild:** *domesticated birds*

do·mes·tic·i·ty /ˌdoʊmɛˈstɪsət̬i/ *n.* [U] life at home with your family, or the state of enjoying this life: *a scene of happy domesticity*

doˌmestic ˈpartner *n.* [C] a phrase meaning someone that you live with and have a romantic relationship with, but whom you are not married to —**domestic partnership** *n.* [C,U]

doˌmestic ˈpolicy *n.* [U] POLITICS a government's decisions, actions etc. relating to the country it governs, and not involving any other countries: *America's domestic policy* → see also FOREIGN POLICY

dom·i·cile /ˈdɑmə,saɪl, ˈdoʊ-/ *n.* [C] LAW a place where someone lives

dom·i·ciled /ˈdɑmə,saɪld/ *adj.* LAW **be domiciled in** to live in a particular place

dom·i·cil·i·a·ry /,dɑməˈsɪli,ɛri/ *adj.* FORMAL **domiciliary services/care/visits etc.** care or services at someone's home

dom·i·nance /ˈdɑmənəns/ Ac *n.* [U] the fact of being more powerful, more important, or more noticeable than other people or things: *military dominance* | +**in** *the company's dominance in the software market* | +**over** *the Rockets' dominance over Boston in last night's game* | +**of** *the dominance of Hollywood's film industry*

dom·i·nant¹ /ˈdɑmənənt/ Ac *adj.* **1** stronger, more important, more common, or more noticeable than other people or things: *TV is the dominant source of information in our society.* **2** controlling other people or things, or showing this quality: *dominant and aggressive behavior* ▶see THESAURUS box at **powerful** **3** BIOLOGY a dominant GENE is expressed as a physical feature even if it has been passed on from only one parent OPP **recessive**: *The gene for brown eyes is dominant.*

dominant² Ac *n.* [singular] ENG. LANG. ARTS the fifth note of a musical SCALE of eight notes

dom·i·nate /ˈdɑmə,neɪt/ Ac W2 *v.* **1** [I,T] to have more power than other people, so that you control a situation, especially when you have more control than is considered good: *Movie directing is a profession dominated by men.* | *She tends to dominate other children her age.* **2** [I,T] to be the most important feature of something: *The murder trial has dominated the news this week.* **3** [T] to be larger or more noticeable than anything else in a place or situation: *A pair of gold boots dominated the display.* **4** [I,T] to play much better than your opponent in a sports game: *New Orleans dominated throughout the game.* [**Origin:** 1600–1700 Latin *dominatus*, past participle of *dominari* **to rule**] —**dominating** /ˈdɑmə,neɪṭɪŋ/ *adj.* —**domination** /,dɑməˈneɪʃən/ *n.* [U]

dom·i·neer·ing /,dɑməˈnɪrɪŋ/ *adj.* trying to control other people without considering how they feel or what they want: *a domineering mother* —**domineer** *v.* [I]

Dom·i·nic /ˈdɑmɪnɪk/, **Saint** (?1170–1221) a Spanish religious leader who started the Dominican group of Christian FRIARS

Dom·i·ni·ca /,dɑməˈnikə, dəˈmɪnɪkə/ a country which is an island in the Caribbean Sea —**Dominican** *n., adj.*

Do·min·i·can /dəˈmɪnɪkən/ *n.* [C] **1** someone from the Dominican Republic **2** a member of a Christian religious group who leads a holy life —**Dominican** *adj.*

Do·min·i·can Re·pub·lic, the /də,mɪnɪkən rɪˈpʌblɪk/ a country in the Caribbean Sea on the island of Hispaniola, which it shares with Haiti

Do·min·i·cans, the /dəˈmɪnɪkənz/ a Christian religious ORDER of MONKS —**Dominican** *adj.*

do·min·ion /dəˈmɪnyən/ *n.* **1** [U] LITERARY the power or right to rule people or control something: **have/hold dominion over** *Alexander the Great held dominion over a vast area.* **2** also **Dominion** [C] HISTORY one of the countries that was a member of the British Commonwealth in past times: *Canada became a self-governing dominion of Great Britain in 1867.* **3** [C] HISTORY a large area of land owned or controlled by one person or a government SYN **realm** → see also COLONY (1), PROTECTORATE

dom·i·no /ˈdɑmə,noʊ/ *n. plural* **dominoes** **1** [C] a small rectangular piece of wood, plastic etc. with a number of spots on each half of its top side, used in playing a game **2 a/the domino effect** a situation in which one event or action causes several other things to happen, one after the other: *The workers' strike **had a domino effect on** several other deadlines.* **3 the domino theory** the idea that one event or action causes several other things to happen

dom·i·noes /ˈdɑmə,noʊz/ *n.* [U] the game played using dominoes

dominoes

ˈdomino ,theory *n.* [U] POLITICS the idea that if one country becomes Communist, then other countries in the same area will also become Communist

don¹ /dɑn/ *v.* **donned**, **donning** [T] FORMAL to put on a hat or piece of clothing OPP **doff**

don² *n.* [C] the leader of a Mafia organization

do·na·ta·ri·o /,doʊnəˈtɛrioʊ/ *n.* [C] HISTORY a Portuguese man who owned very large amounts of land in Brazil in the past

do·nate /ˈdoʊneɪt, doʊˈneɪt/ S3 *v.* [I,T] **1** to give something useful to a person or an organization that needs help: **donate sth to sb/sth** *One school donated $500 to the Red Cross.* | **donate to sb/sth** *I never donate to charities who call me on the phone.* ▶see THESAURUS box at **give¹** **2 donate blood/organs etc.** to give some of your blood or part of your body to be used for medical purposes: *We are looking for people to donate blood.*

do·na·tion /doʊˈneɪʃən/ S3 *n.* **1** [C] something, especially money, that you give to a person or an organization that needs help: +**of** *donations of toys and clothing* | *Please **make a donation to** UNICEF.* **2** [U] the act of giving something to help a person or an organization: *We receive 50% of our funds through donation.* | *The booklet provides information about **organ donation** and transplants.* [**Origin:** 1400–1500 Latin *donare* **to give**]

done¹ /dʌn/ *v.* the past participle of DO

done² *adj.* [not before noun, no comparative] **1** finished or completed: *The job's almost done.* | *I'll be glad when my exams are **over and done with*** (=used to emphasize that something is done).

THESAURUS

finished done, and dealt with in the way you wanted: *She showed him the finished drawing.*
complete finished, and having all the necessary parts: *Six months later the job was complete.*
over if an event, activity, or period of time is over, it is finished: *Practice is over at 4:30. Can you pick me up then?*
through if you are through with something, you have finished using it or doing it: *Are you through with those scissors?*

2 someone who is done has finished doing or using something: *Well, I'm done. I'm going home.* | **be done with sth** *Do you want to read this magazine? I'm done with it.* **3** cooked enough to be eaten: *I think the hamburgers are done.* → see also OVERDONE **4 it's a done deal** INFORMAL used to mean that an agreement has been made and it cannot be changed **5 be done for** INFORMAL to be in serious trouble and likely to fail or die: *If we get caught we're done for.* **6 be done in** INFORMAL to be extremely tired: *I've got to sit down – I'm done in.* **7 just not be done** to be considered unacceptable behavior in social situations: *Showing affection in public just isn't done in Japan.* **8 be done with it** used to tell someone to stop talking about something: *Oh, buy it and be done with it!* → see also DO²

done³ *interjection* said in order to accept a deal that someone offers you: *"How about I give you $25 for it?" "Done!"*

dong /dɑŋ, dɔŋ/ *n.* [C] the unit of money in Vietnam

don·gle /ˈdɑŋgəl, ˈdɔŋ-/ *n.* [C] a small piece of equipment that you attach to a computer in order to use particular SOFTWARE

Don Juan /,dɑn ˈwɑn/ *n.* [C] a man who is good at persuading women to have sex with him

don·key /ˈdɑŋki, ˈdʌŋ-, ˈdɔŋ-/ *n. plural* **donkeys** [C] a gray or brown animal similar to a horse, but smaller and with long ears

Donne /dʌn/, **John** (?1572–1631) an English poet known for his love poetry and religious poems

do·nor /ˈdoʊnɚ/ *n.* [C] **1** a person, group etc. that gives something, especially money, to help an organization: *The museum received $10,000 from an anonymous donor.* **2** MEDICINE someone who gives some of their blood or part of their body to be used for medical purposes: *Finding a liver donor may be difficult.*

ˈdonor ˌcard *n.* [C] a card that you carry to show that when you die, a doctor can take parts of your body to use for medical purposes

D

ˈdo-ˌnothing *adj.* [only before noun] INFORMAL lazy or unwilling to make any changes, especially in politics: *People are tired of this do-nothing Congress.* —**do-nothing** *n.* [C]

Don Qui·xo·te /ˌdɑn kiˈoʊṭi, -ˈhoʊṭi/ *n.* [singular] someone who is determined to change what is wrong, but who does it in a way that is silly or not practical → see also QUIXOTIC

don't /doʊnt/ *v.* **1** the short form of "do not": *Don't worry!* | *You know him, don't you?* → see also **dos and don'ts** at DO[3] **2** SPOKEN, NONSTANDARD an incorrect short form of "does not": *She don't like it.*

do·nut /ˈdoʊnʌt/ *n.* [C] another spelling of DOUGHNUT

doo·bie /ˈdubi/ *n.* [C] OLD-FASHIONED, SLANG a MARIJUANA cigarette

doo·dad /ˈdudæd/ *n.* [C] INFORMAL a small and unnecessary object, especially one whose name you have forgotten or do not know: *a gift shop selling postcards and tourist doodads*

doo·dle /ˈdudl/ *v.* [I,T] to draw shapes, lines, or patterns without really thinking about what you are doing: *Margo was doodling on a legal pad.* ►see THESAURUS box at **draw**[1] —**doodle** *n.* [C]

doo-doo /ˈdudu/ *n.* [U] INFORMAL a word for solid waste from your body, used especially by or when speaking to children —**doo-doo** *v.* [I]

doo·fus /ˈdufəs/ *n.* [C] INFORMAL a silly or stupid person

doo·hick·ey /ˈduˌhɪki/ *n.* [C] a small object whose name you have forgotten or do not know, especially a part of a machine

doom[1] /dum/ *v.* [T usually passive] to make someone or something certain to fail, be destroyed, or die: *The threat of a costly legal battle doomed the proposal.* | **doom sb/sth to do sth** *Are we doomed to lose our memory as we get older?* | **doom sb/sth to sth** *Over 50,000 species a year are being doomed to extinction.* | *The marriage seems* ***doomed to failure***. —**doomed** *adj.*

doom[2] *n.* [U] **1** destruction, death, or failure that you are unable to avoid: *I sat there with a sense of* ***imminent doom*** (=doom that will come very soon). | *The poor performances do not necessarily* ***spell doom for*** *the movie* (=mean that it will fail). | *Thousands of soldiers* ***met their doom*** (=died) *on this field.* **2 doom and gloom** HUMOROUS a state or attitude in which there is no hope for the future: *The article is full of doom and gloom about the environment.*

doom·say·er /ˈdumˌseɪɚ/ *n.* [C] someone who always says that bad things are going to happen: *Doomsayers tell us that one day California will tumble into the sea.*

Dooms·day /ˈdumzdeɪ/ *n.* [C,U] **1 till/until Doomsday** INFORMAL used to emphasize that you mean a very long time: *You could wait till Doomsday and he'd never show up.* **2** the last day of the Earth's existence

door /dɔr/ S1 W1 *n.* [C] **1** the large flat piece of wood, glass, metal etc. that you push or pull in order to go into a building, room, car etc.: *Is the car door locked?* | **+of** *the door of his office* | **+to** *This is the door to the fitness center.* | *Could you* ***open the door*** *for me, please?* | **close/shut the door** *She closed the garage door and headed to the house.* | **front/back/side door** *A Christmas wreath hung on the front door.* | **kitchen/bathroom/office etc. door** *Leave the bathroom door open when you're done in the shower.* | *I think there's somebody* ***at the door*** (=waiting for the door to be opened). | **knock on/at the door** *I knocked on the door, but there was no answer.* | **answer/get the door** (=open it because someone has knocked on it or rung the bell) | *He* ***slammed the door*** (=shut it very hard) *and stormed off.* | *Here, let me* ***get the door for*** (=open the door for) *you.* → see also GATE **2** the space made by an open door SYN **doorway**: **out/through a door** *Go out the doors and turn left.* | *I knew when he came* ***in the door*** (=through the door) *there was something wrong.* **3** an opportunity or the possibility to start doing something SYN **opportunity**: *This ruling could* ***open the door to*** *other lawsuits* (=make other lawsuits possible). | *Changes in the labor market* ***opened doors for*** (=gave opportunities to) *women.* | *The accident* ***shut the door on*** *her ballet career* (=made it impossible). **4 two/three etc. doors down** a place that is a particular number of rooms, houses etc. away from where you are: *Her office is two doors down.* **5 (from) door to door a)** between one place and another: *If you drive, it should take you 20 minutes door to door.* **b)** going to each house in a street or area to sell something, collect money etc.: *We went door to door asking people to sponsor us in the race.* → see also DOOR-TO-DOOR **6 show/see sb to the door** to walk with someone to the main door of a building: *My secretary will show you to the door.* **7 out of doors** outside SYN **outdoors**
[**Origin:** Old English *duru* **door** and *dor* **gate**] → see also **answer the phone/the door/a call** at ANSWER[1] (3), BACK DOOR, **behind closed doors** at CLOSED (7), **at death's door** at DEATH (8), FRONT DOOR, **lay sth at sb's door** at LAY[1] (18), NEXT DOOR, OPEN DOOR POLICY, **show sb the door** at SHOW[1] (15), **work the door** at WORK[1] (26)

door·bell /ˈdɔrbɛl/ *n.* [C] a button outside a house or apartment that you push so that people inside know you are there, or the bell that this button rings: *I* ***rang the doorbell*** *and waited.*

ˌdo-or-ˈdie, **do or die** *adj.* something do-or-die has to be done or you will fail completely: *a do-or-die effort to save the company* | *Ok, this is do or die. Let's try it.*

door·jamb /ˈdɔrdʒæm/ *n.* [C] one of two upright posts on either side of a doorway SYN **doorpost**

door·keep·er /ˈdɔrˌkipɚ/ *n.* [C] someone who guards the main door of a large building and lets people in and out

door·knob /ˈdɔrnɑb/ *n.* [C] a round handle that you turn to open a door

door·knock·er /ˈdɔrˌnɑkɚ/ *n.* [C] a heavy metal ring or bar on a door, that visitors use to knock with

door·man /ˈdɔrmæn, -mən/ *n. plural* **doormen** /-mɛn, -mən/ [C] a man who works in a hotel or apartment building watching the door, helping people find taxis etc. → see also PORTER

door·mat /ˈdɔrmæt/ *n.* [C] **1** a thick piece of material just outside or inside a door for you to clean your shoes on **2** INFORMAL someone who lets other people treat them badly and who never complains about it

door·nail /ˈdɔrneɪl/ *n.* [singular] → see **dead as a doornail** at DEAD[1] (24)

door·plate /ˈdɔrpleɪt/ *n.* [C] a flat piece of metal attached to the door of a house or building, showing the name of the person or company that lives or works inside

door·post /ˈdɔrpoʊst/ *n.* [C] a DOORJAMB

ˈdoor prize *n.* [C] a prize given to someone who has the winning number on their ticket for a show, dance etc.

door·sill /ˈdɔrˌsɪl/ *n.* [C] the part of a door frame that you step across when you go through a DOORWAY

door·step /ˈdɔrstɛp/ *n.* [C] **1** a step just outside a door to a house or building: *A cat sat patiently on the doorstep.* **2 on/at sb's doorstep a)** at your home, or very near to it: *Janet turned up on her sister's doorstep, needing a place to stay.* **b)** affecting a particular person or group, rather than happening somewhere far away: *Today, there's a new racial conflict on our doorstep.*

door·stop /ˈdɔrstɑp/ *n.* [C] **1** something you put under or against a door to keep it open: *They'd been using the encyclopedia as a doorstop.* **2** a rubber object attached to a wall to stop a door from hitting it when it is opened

ˌdoor-to-ˈdoor, **door to door** *adj., adv.* visiting each house in a street or area, usually to sell something, collect money, or ask for votes: *a door-to-door salesman* | *In 1964, I campaigned door to door for Lyndon Johnson.*

door·way /ˈdɔrweɪ/ *n.* [C] **1** the space where a door opens into a room or building: *a wide doorway into the kitchen* **2** a way for you to get what you want in order to succeed: *Large corporations are seeking a doorway to the markets of the Far East.*

door·yard /ˈdɔryɑrd/ *n.* [C] OLD-FASHIONED the area in front of the door of a house

doo·zy, **doozie** /ˈduzi/ *n.* [C] INFORMAL something that is extremely good, bad, strange, big etc.: *The storm is going to be a real doozy* (=a very big one).

do·pa·mine /ˈdoʊpəˌmin/ *n.* [U] a chemical in the brain that is necessary for the normal control of muscle movements

dope[1] /doʊp/ *n.* INFORMAL **1** [C] SPOKEN someone who is stupid or has done something stupid: *I felt like such a dope!* **2** [U] a drug that is not legal **3** [U] new information about someone or something, especially information that not many people know: +**on** *Reporters were looking for the latest dope on the steroid scandal.* **4** [U] medicine, especially medicine that makes you sleep easily

dope[2] also **dope sb up** *v.* [T] INFORMAL to take a drug or to give a person or animal a drug, in order to sleep, feel better, or work better: *They dope the elephants in order to tag them.* → see also DOPING

dope[3] *adj.* SLANG good or satisfactory: *If we got to be friends, that'd be dope.*

dope·head /ˈdoʊphɛd/ *n.* [C] SLANG someone who takes a lot of illegal drugs

dop·ey /ˈdoʊpi/ *adj.* INFORMAL **1** slow to react mentally or physically, as if you have taken a drug: *I feel really dopey, and I've had a headache all day.* **2** slightly stupid: *What a dopey thing to do.*

dop·ing /ˈdoʊpɪŋ/ *n.* [U] the practice of taking drugs to improve your performance in a sport: *Several athletes failed a doping test.*

dop·pel·gang·er /ˈdɑpəlˌgæŋɚ, -ˌgɛŋɚ/ *n.* [C] **1** an imaginary spirit that looks exactly like a living person **2** someone who looks exactly like someone else

Dop·pler ef·fect /ˈdɑplɚ ɪˌfɛkt/ *n.* [singular] a change in how someone hears a sound or sees a light that is moving toward or away from them, so that a sound seems higher as it is moving closer to them, and a light seems more blue

Do·ri·an /ˈdɔriən/ *n.* [C] one of the people that lived in the southern part of ancient Greece from the 11th century B.C.

Dor·ic /ˈdɔrɪk, ˈdɑr-/ *adj.* in the oldest and simplest of the Greek building styles: *a Doric column* → see also CORINTHIAN

dork /dɔrk/ *n.* [C] INFORMAL someone who you think is stupid, because they behave strangely or wear strange clothes —**dorky** *adj.*

dorm /dɔrm/ *n.* [C] INFORMAL a DORMITORY: *Yeah, I know him. He lived in my dorm.* | *a dorm room*

dor·man·cy /ˈdɔrmənsi/ *n.* [U] **1** the state of being not active for some time **2** BIOLOGY the period of time during which a seed is alive but not growing

dor·mant /ˈdɔrmənt/ *adj.* **1** not active or not growing right now, but able to be active later: *a dormant volcano* | *The virus can* ***lie dormant*** *in the blood for up to 12 years.* **2** not used or not active for a period of time: *Accounts that* ***remain dormant*** *for three years must be reported to the state.* **3** BIOLOGY seeds that are dormant are alive but not growing at the moment

dor·mer /ˈdɔrmɚ/ also **ˈdormer ˌwindow** *n.* [C] a window built upright in the slope of a roof, so that it sticks out from the roof

dor·mi·to·ry /ˈdɔrməˌtɔri/ *n. plural* **dormitories** [C] **1** a large building at a college or university where students live **2** a large room for several people to sleep in, for example in a prison or a HOSTEL

dor·mouse /ˈdɔrmaʊs/ *n. plural* **dormice** /-maɪs/ [C] a small European forest animal similar to a mouse, with a long furry tail

dor·sal /ˈdɔrsəl/ *adj.* [only before noun] BIOLOGY relating to the back of an animal or fish: *a shark's dorsal fin* → see also VENTRAL

do·ry /ˈdɔri/ *n. plural* **dories** [C] a boat that has a flat bottom and is used for fishing → see also HUNKY-DORY

DOS /dɑs, dɔs/ *n.* [U] COMPUTERS **Disk Operating System** SOFTWARE that is loaded onto a computer system to make all the different parts work together

dos·age /ˈdoʊsɪdʒ/ *n.* [C usually singular] the amount of medicine that you should take at one time: *Lowering the dosage can stop some side effects.*

dose[1] /doʊs/ *n.* [C] **1** MEDICINE a measured amount of a medicine: +**of** *a dose of heart medicine* | *Doctors say that a* ***low dose*** *is just as effective as a* ***high dose****, and causes fewer side effects.* **2** an amount of something such as a chemical or poison that affects you: +**of** *a dangerous dose of radiation* | *Niacin can be harmful if used* ***in large doses*** (=if you take a lot each time). **3** an amount of something that you do or experience at one time: *The banks need a healthy dose of competition.* | *It's a very amusing book if read* ***in small doses*** (=a little at a time). [**Origin:** 1400–1500 French, Greek *dosis*, from *didonai* **to give**]

dose[2] *v.* [T] also **dose sb up** to give medicine or another type of drug to an animal or person: +**with** *The patients were all dosed with sleeping pills.*

do-si-do /ˌdoʊ si ˈdoʊ/ *n.* [singular] an action in SQUARE DANCING in which partners walk around each other with their backs toward each other —**do-si-do** *v.* [I]

Dos Pas·sos /dɑs ˈpæsəs/, **John** (1896–1970) a U.S. writer of NOVELS

dos·si·er /ˈdɑsiˌeɪ, ˈdɔ-/ *n.* [C] a set of papers containing detailed information about a person or subject SYN file: *The U.S. government* ***kept a*** *secret* ***dossier on*** *him for 27 years.*

dost /dʌst/ *v.* **thou dost** OLD USE or BIBLICAL you do

Dos·to·yev·sky, **Dostoevsky** /ˌdɑstəˈyɛfski, ˌdɑstɔɪ-/, **Fy·o·dor** /ˈfiədɔr/ (1821–1881) a Russian writer, famous for his NOVELS

dot[1] /dɑt/ S3 *n.* **1** [C] a round mark or spot: *blue material decorated with colored dots* | +**of** *tiny dots of ink* → see also **connect the dots** at CONNECT (8), POLKA DOT, SPOT **2** [C] SPOKEN what you say when you read the sign (.) in an Internet address or a computer CODE: *You can visit our website at www.longman.com* (=said as, "w-w-w dot Longman dot com"). **3 on the dot** INFORMAL exactly at a particular time: *I'm leaving work at 12:30 on the dot.* **4** [C] something that looks like a small spot because it is so far away: *The plane was just a dot in the sky.* **5** [C] a short sound or flash of light used when sending messages by MORSE CODE → see also DASH [**Origin:** Old English *dott* **top of a spot on the skin**]

dot[2] *v.* **dotted**, **dotting** [T] **1** to mark something by putting a dot on it or above it: *She never dots her i's.* **2** [usually passive] to be spread far apart from each other over a wide area: *Chalet-style homes dot the landscape.* | **be dotted around sth** *Little piles of toys were dotted around the room.* **3 be dotted with sth** if an area is dotted with things, a number of those things are found throughout the area, each one far apart from the others: *The hills are dotted with California live oaks.* **4** to put a very small amount of something on a surface, or in several places on a surface: *Dot the apples with butter.* **5 dot the i's and cross the t's** INFORMAL to deal with all the details when you are finishing something: *We haven't dotted all the i's and crossed the t's, but the* *contract's almost ready.* —**dotted** *adj.* → see also DOTTED LINE

dot·age /ˈdoʊt̬ɪdʒ/ *n.* **in your dotage** when you are old: *Thurmond is as mean in his dotage as he was in his younger days.*

dot-com, dot com /ˌdɑt ˈkɑm/ *n.* a company whose business involves the Internet —**dot-com** *adj.* [only before noun]

dote /doʊt/ *v.*

dote on/upon sb *phr. v.* to love someone very much and to show this: *He dotes on his six-year-old niece.* —**doting** *adj. a doting parent* —**dotingly** *adv.*

doth /dʌθ/ *v.* OLD USE or BIBLICAL an old form of "does"

ˈdot-matrix ˌprinter *n.* [C] COMPUTERS a machine connected to a computer, that prints letters, numbers etc. using many small DOTS

ˈdot ˌproduct *n.* [C] MATH a SCALAR PRODUCT

ˌdotted ˈline *n.* [C] a series of printed or drawn DOTS that form a line: *Cut along the dotted lines.*

dot·ty /ˈdɑt̬i/ *adj.* OLD-FASHIONED slightly crazy or likely to behave strangely: *a dotty old lady*

dou·ble[1] /ˈdʌbəl/ S3 W2 *adj.*

1 OF TWO PARTS consisting of two parts that are similar or exactly the same: *Double doors lead into the backyard.* | *the double yellow line in the middle of the road*

2 TWICE AS BIG twice as big, twice as much, or twice as many as usual: *Leave the dough to rise until it is double in size.* | *I'm working a double shift today.* | *a double cheeseburger* (=one with two layers of meat)

3 FOR TWO PEOPLE made to be used by two people → see also SINGLE: *a double room*

4 COMBINING TWO THINGS combining or involving two separate things or events of the same type SYN **dual**: *a double murder case* | *I have a double major in history and political science.* | *The sofa* ***does double duty*** (=is used for two purposes) *as a place to sit and a bed.*

5 SAME THING WITH DIFFERENT QUALITIES involving two things of the same type, which have different or opposite qualities from each other SYN **dual**: *The title has* ***a double meaning*** (=it can mean two different things). | *It was a shock to find out that Dad was* ***leading a double life*** (=had two very different ways of living, that were secret from each other).

6 FLOWER a double flower has more than the usual number of PETALS

[**Origin:** 1100–1200 Old French, Latin *duplus*, from *duo* **two** + *-plus* **multiplied by**] → see also DOUBLY

double[2] S3 *n.*

1 TWICE THE SIZE [C,U] something that is twice the size, quantity, value, or strength of something else: *Scotch and water, please – make it a double.* | *She offered to pay me double* (=twice the amount of money).

2 SIMILAR PERSON [C] someone who looks very much like someone else: *Caroline is virtually her mother's double.*

3 IN MOVIES [C] ENG. LANG. ARTS an actor who takes the place of another actor in a movie, especially because the acting involves doing something dangerous: *He was John Wayne's stunt double in the movie.*

4 BASEBALL [C] a hit in baseball that allows the BATTER to reach second BASE: *Harper led the inning with a double.*

5 TENNIS doubles [U] a game played between two pairs of players: *the men's doubles* → see also MIXED DOUBLES, SINGLES

6 ROOM a room in a hotel for two people: *Rooms cost $95 for a double.*

7 on the double very quickly and without any delay: *I headed for the Commander's office on the double.*

8 roll a double to throw a pair of DICE so that they each show the same number

9 double or nothing a decision in GAMBLING which will either win you twice as much money or make you lose it all

double[3] S3 *v.* **1** [I,T] to become twice as large or twice as much, or to make something twice as large or twice as much: *Building costs have doubled since then.* | *The company doubled its profits in three years.* | **double in size/value/volume etc.** *Our house has doubled in value since we bought it.* | **double the number/amount/size (of sth)** *The mayor doubled the number of police on the streets.* ▸see THESAURUS box at **increase**[1] **2** also **double sth over/up** [T] to fold something in half, so that it has two layers: *Take a sheet of paper and double it.* **3** [I] if a BATTER in a game of baseball doubles, he hits the ball far enough to run safely to second BASE **4 double your fists** to curl your fingers tightly to make FISTS, usually in order to be ready to fight

double as sb/sth *phr. v.* to have a second use, job, or purpose as something else: *Schools doubled as hospitals during the war.*

double back *phr. v.* also **double back on yourself** to turn around and go back the way you have come: *I doubled back and headed south.*

double up *phr. v.* **1** also **double over, double sb up** to suddenly and uncontrollably bend forward at the waist because of pain, laughter etc.: *We doubled over, laughing so hard it hurt.* | **be doubled up/over with** *He was doubled up with cramps.* **2** to share something, especially a house or a BEDROOM: +**with** *You'll have to double up with Kyle while your aunt is here.* **3** to fold something in half: **double sth ↔ up** *He doubled up the blankets and put them away.*

double[4] *adv.* **1 see double** to have something wrong with your eyes so that you see two things instead of one: *Selma complained of seeing double.* **2 be bent double** to be bent over a long way: *The old man was bent double under his load.* **3 fold sth double** to fold something in half to make it twice as thick

double[5] S3 *quantifier* twice as much or twice as many: *The painting is worth double what we paid for it.* | **double the size/number/amount etc.** *an increase that is almost double the rate of inflation* | *No, he earns* ***double that!*** (=double an amount already mentioned)

ˈdouble-act *n.* [C] two actors, especially COMEDIANS, who perform together

ˌdouble ˈagent *n.* [C] someone who finds out an enemy country's secrets for their own country, but who also gives secrets to the enemy → see also SPY

ˌdouble-ˈbarreled **1** a double-barreled gun has two places where the BULLETS come out **2** with two purposes: *a double-barreled question* **3** very strong or using a lot of force: *a double-barreled threat*

double bass /ˌdʌbəl ˈbeɪs/ also **bass** *n.* [C] a very large musical instrument shaped like a VIOLIN that the musician plays standing up

double bass

ˌdouble ˈbed *n.* [C] a bed made for two people to sleep in

ˌdouble ˈbill *n.* [C] an occasion when two plays, performances, movies etc. are shown or performed one after the other: *a double bill of horror movies* → see also DOUBLE FEATURE

ˌdouble ˈbind *n.* [C usually singular] a situation in which any choice you make will have bad results

ˌdouble-ˈblind *adj.* SCIENCE a double-blind EXPERIMENT or study compares two or more groups in which neither the scientists nor the people being studied know which group is being tested and which group is not

ˌdouble ˈbluff *n.* [C] an attempt to deceive someone by telling them the truth, hoping that they will think you are lying

ˌdouble ˈboiler *n.* [C] a pot for cooking food, consisting of one pan resting on top of another pan with hot water in it

ˌdouble-ˈbook *v.* [I,T] to promise the same seat in a

theater, on an airplane etc. to more than one person —**double-booking** *n.* [U]

ˌdouble-ˈbreasted *adj.* a double-breasted JACKET, coat etc. has two sets of buttons → see also SINGLE-BREASTED

ˌdouble-ˈcheck *v.* [I,T] to check something again so that you are completely sure that it is safe, ready, correct etc.: *Double-check that all the information was copied correctly.* | **double-check (that)** *I double-checked that I had my passport.*

ˌdouble ˈchin *n.* [C] a fold of loose skin under someone's chin that looks like a second chin

ˌdouble-ˈclick *v.* [I,T] to press a button on a computer mouse twice in order to send an instruction to the computer: **+on** *If you double-click on the word, it becomes highlighted.*

ˌdouble coˌvalent ˈbond *n.* [C] CHEMISTRY a chemical BOND between two pairs of atoms, that forms when the atoms share two pairs of ELECTRONS

ˌdouble ˈcropping *n.* [U] the practice of growing more than one crop on the same piece of land in the same year

ˌdouble-ˈcross *v.* [T] to cheat someone, especially after you have already agreed to do something dishonest with them: *He was killed for double-crossing his Mob bosses.* —**double cross** *n.* [C] —**double-crosser** *n.* [C]

ˌdouble ˈdate *n.* [C] an occasion when two COUPLES meet to go to a movie, restaurant etc. together —**double-date** *v.* [I,T]

Dou·ble·day /ˈdʌbəlˌdeɪ/, **Ab·ner** /ˈæbnɚ/ (1819–1893) a U.S. army officer who is known as the inventor of baseball

ˌdouble-ˈdealer *n.* [C] INFORMAL someone who deceives other people —**double-dealing** *n.* [U]

ˌdouble-ˈdecker *n.* [C] **1** a bus with two levels **2** a SANDWICH made with meat, cheese etc. between three pieces of bread

ˌdouble-ˈdigit *adj.* relating to the numbers 10 to 99, especially as a PERCENTAGE: *double-digit inflation* → see also DOUBLE FIGURES

ˌdouble-ˈdip[1] *n.* [C] an ICE CREAM CONE with two balls of ice cream

double-dip[2] *v.* [I] to get money from two places at once, usually in a way that is not legal or not approved of: *Some farmers double-dip into federal funds.*

ˌdouble-dip reˈcession *n.* [C usually singular] INFORMAL a situation in which a country's ECONOMY is weak, starts to get strong again, then becomes weak again

ˌdouble-ˈdutch *n.* [U] a game in which one child jumps over two long ropes that are being swung around in a circle by other children

ˌdouble-ˈedged *adj.* **1 a double-edged sword** something good that also has a bad effect: *Being famous is often a double-edged sword.* **2** having two very different meanings: *a double-edged remark* **3** having two different parts [SYN] two-pronged: *a double-edged attack on global warming* **4** having two cutting edges: *a double-edged knife*

dou·ble en·ten·dre /ˌdubəl ɑnˈtɑndrə, ˌdʌbəl-/ *n.* [C] a word or phrase that may be understood in two different ways, one of which is often sexual

ˌdouble ˈfault *n.* [C] two mistakes, one after another, when you are serving (SERVE) in tennis, that make you lose a point

ˌdouble ˈfeature *n.* [C] ENG. LANG. ARTS **1** an occasion when two movies are shown one after the other at a theater **2** a VIDEO or a DVD with two movies on it: *a double feature of two early John Wayne westerns*

ˌdouble ˈfigures *n.* [plural] a number such as 10, 25, 43 etc., that is made up of two figures: *Inflation reached double figures.* | *Five players scored* ***in double figures.*** → see also DOUBLE-DIGIT

ˌdouble-ˈheader *n.* [C] two baseball games played one after the other

ˌdouble ˈhelix *n.* [C] BIOLOGY a shape consisting of two parallel SPIRALS that twist around the same center, found especially in the structure of DNA

ˌdouble inˈdemnity *n.* [U] LAW a feature of a life insurance POLICY that allows twice the value of the contract to be paid in the case of death by accident

ˌdouble ˈjeopardy *n.* [U] LAW the act of taking someone to court a second time for the same offense. This is not allowed by the U.S. Constitution if the person has already been found not guilty.

ˌdouble-ˈjointed *adj.* able to move the joints in your fingers, arms etc. backward as well as forward

ˌdouble ˈnegative *n.* [C] ENG. LANG. ARTS a sentence in which two NEGATIVE words are used when only one is needed in correct English grammar, for example in the sentence "I don't want nobody to help me!"

ˌdouble-ˈpark *v.* [I,T] to illegally leave a vehicle beside a vehicle that is legally parked at the side of a road, so that your car is in the path of people driving

ˌdouble ˈplay *n.* [C] the action of making two runners in a game of baseball have to leave the field by throwing the ball quickly from one BASE to another before the runners reach either one

ˌdouble-ˈspaced *adj.* double-spaced lines of words on a printed page have one empty line between them, rather than being close together —**double-space** *v.* [T] —**double spacing** *n.* [U] → see also SINGLE-SPACED

ˌdouble ˈstandard *n.* [C] a rule, principle etc. that is unfair because it treats one group or type of people more severely than another in the same situation: *Society's double standard says that teen sex is natural for boys but forbidden for girls.*

dou·blet /ˈdʌblɪt/ *n.* [C] a man's shirt, worn in Europe from about 1400 to the middle 1600s

ˌdouble ˈtake *n.* [C] **do a double take** to look at someone or something again because you are surprised by what you originally saw or heard

ˈdouble-talk *n.* [U] INFORMAL speech that seems to be serious and sincere, but has another meaning or is a mixture of sense and nonsense: *legal double-talk* —**double-talk** *v.* [I,T] —**double-talker** *n.* [C]

dou·ble·think /ˈdʌbəlˌθɪŋk/ *n.* [U] a belief in or acceptance of two opposing ideas at the same time, sometimes deliberately in order to trick people

ˌdouble ˈtime *n.* [U] **1** twice the amount of regular pay given when someone works on a day or at a time when people do not normally work → see also TIME AND A HALF **2** a fast military march

ˈdouble-time, double time *adj., adv.* twice as fast as usual, or as quickly as possible: *We were working double-time to finish on time.*

ˌdouble ˈvision *n.* [U] a medical condition in which you see two of everything

double wham·my /ˌdʌbəl ˈwæmi/ *n.* [C] INFORMAL two bad things that happen together, or one after the other: *Farmers have faced the double whammy of a freeze and a drought this year.*

double ˈwhole note *n.* [C] a musical note that continues for twice the length of a WHOLE NOTE

ˈdouble-wide also **ˌdouble-wide ˈtrailer** *n.* [C] a type of MOBILE HOME consisting of two pieces that have been fastened together along their longest sides

dou·bloon /dʌˈblun/ *n.* [C] a gold coin used in the past in Spain and Spanish America

dou·bly /ˈdʌbli/ *adv.* **1** by twice the amount, or to twice the degree: *Be doubly careful when driving in fog.* **2** in two ways or for two reasons: *You are doubly mistaken.*

doubt[1] /daʊt/ [S3] [W2] *n.* **1** [C,U] the feeling of being unable to trust or believe in someone or something: **+about/as to** *We have strong doubts about his effectiveness as a leader.* | **doubt whether/who/what etc.** *There was doubt whether he would be well enough to play.* | **doubt (that)** *Our team has little doubt that this deal will be made.* | *Several scientists* ***expressed*** *serious* ***doubts***

about the study. | *I* **have doubts** *about his qualifications for the job.* | *The recent bombing errors have* **raised doubts about** *the military's competence.* | *The case has been proved* **beyond a shadow of a doubt** (=there is no doubt at all). | *There is an* **element of doubt** (=a slight doubt) *as to whether the deaths were accidental.* | *Neighbors quickly* **cast doubt on** *Hill's version of the story* (=said that it might not be true). | *Bradley says he'll be ready to play, but the coach* **has his doubts** (=has reasons for not being sure about this). **2 no doubt** used when emphasizing that you think something is probably true: *No doubt you'll have your own ideas.* | *The budget cuts will hurt,* **no doubt about it** (=it is certainly true). **3 if/when (you're) in doubt...** used when advising someone what to do: *If you're in doubt about what to wear to the interview, dress conservatively.* **4 be in doubt a)** to not be certain what will happen or what to do: *The outcome of the case never seemed in doubt.* **b)** to not be sure that something will be able to succeed or continue: *Prospects for progress in the peace talks are very much in doubt.* **5 be beyond doubt** if something is beyond doubt, it is completely certain: *The test showed beyond doubt that Granger was the girl's father.* **6 reasonable doubt** LAW something that makes you think that a law case has not been completely proved: *The jurors felt there was reasonable doubt.* | *They proved* **beyond a reasonable doubt** (=they showed that it was certain) *that alcohol played a part in the accident.* **7 without doubt** FORMAL used to emphasize an opinion: *She is, without doubt, one of the best runners I've ever seen.* → see also **the benefit of the doubt** at BENEFIT[1] (4), **be open to question/doubt** at OPEN[1] (20), SELF-DOUBT

GRAMMAR

When you use the verb **doubt** in a statement, it can be followed by the words "that," "if," or "whether": *I doubt that they would be willing to pay $20 each.* | *Sara doubted if/whether Al would show up.* However, if **doubt** is used with a negative, it can only be followed by "that" or a clause: *I never doubted (that) Jake would be able to help us* (=I always believed that he would be able to help). When you use the noun **doubt** after "no" or "not," it is always followed by "that" or a clause: *There is no doubt that Jenkins is guilty.*

doubt[2] S2 W3 *v.* [T not in progressive] **1** to think that something may not be true or that it is unlikely: *I never doubted his story.* | **doubt (that)** *Doctors doubted that surgery would be necessary.* | **doubt if/whether** *Researchers doubted if any of the eggs would hatch.* | *He might show up later, but* **I doubt it** (=I don't think he will). | *I have no reason to* **doubt his word** (=think that he is lying). **2** to not trust or have confidence in someone: *Do you have any reason to doubt her?* | *I never* **doubted myself**. *I knew I could win.* [**Origin:** 1200–1300 French *douter*, from Latin *dubitare*] **—doubter** *n.* [C]

doubt·ful /ˈdaʊt˺fəl/ *adj.* **1** something that is doubtful is not certain or not likely to happen: *Prospects for peace remain doubtful.* | **it is doubtful if/whether** *It is doubtful whether the budget will be passed before the elections in July.* | **it is doubtful that** *It is doubtful that voters will approve the bill.* **2** not sure or not certain about something: *Holmes still looked doubtful.* | **doubtful if/whether** *I was doubtful whether you'd even notice the difference.* **3** not good SYN **dubious**: *The tap water here is of doubtful quality.* | *an old lady in doubtful health* **4** unable to be trusted or believed: *documents of doubtful authenticity* | *his doubtful loyalties* **5** [not before noun] if a sports player is doubtful for a game, it is not likely that they will play, especially because they are injured **—doubtfully** *adv.*

ˌdoubting ˈThomas *n.* [C] someone who tends to doubt things if they have not seen proof of them [**Origin:** 1800–1900 *Thomas* the follower of Christ who did not believe he had come back to life]

doubt·less /ˈdaʊt˺lɪs/ *adv.* FORMAL very likely: *The majority will doubtless agree with him.*

douche /duʃ/ *n.* [C usually singular] a mixture of water and something such as VINEGAR, that a woman can use to wash her VAGINA, or the instrument that is used to do this **—douche** *v.* [I,T]

dough /doʊ/ *n.* **1** [singular, U] a mixture of flour and water ready to be baked into bread, PASTRY etc.: *Leave the dough to rise.* **2** [U] INFORMAL money

dough·nut, donut /ˈdoʊnʌt/ *n.* [C] **1** a small round cake, often in the form of a ring **2 do doughnuts** INFORMAL to make a car spin around in circles

dough·ty /ˈdaʊt̬i/ *adj.* [only before noun] LITERARY brave and determined

dough·y /ˈdoʊi/ *adj.* **1** looking and feeling like DOUGH **2** doughy skin is pale and soft and looks unhealthy

Doug·lass /ˈdʌgləs/, **Fred·erick** /ˈfrɛdrɪk/ (1817–1895) an African-American who was born a SLAVE, famous for working to get rid of SLAVERY (=the practice of having slaves), and writing a book about his life

dour /ˈdaʊɚ, dʊɚ/ *adj.* **1** severe and never smiling SYN **grim**: *her dour expression* **2** making you feel anxious or afraid SYN **grim**: *a dour reminder* [**Origin:** 1300–1400 Gaelic *dur*] **—dourly** *adv.*

douse, dowse /daʊs/ *v.* [T] **1** to put out a fire by pouring water on it **2** to cover something in water or other liquid

dove[1] /dʌv/ *n.* [C] **1** BIOLOGY a small white bird, often used as a sign of peace **2** POLITICS someone in politics who prefers peace and discussion to war OPP **hawk** [**Origin:** Old English *dufe*]

dove[2] /doʊv/ *v.* a past tense of DIVE

dove·cote /ˈdʌvkoʊt, -kɑt/ *n.* [C] a small house built for doves to live in

Do·ver /ˈdoʊvɚ/ the capital city of the U.S. state of Delaware

dove·tail[1] /ˈdʌvteɪl/ *v.* **1** [I,T] if two plans, ideas etc. dovetail or you dovetail them, they fit together perfectly: *The two objectives dovetail nicely.* | **+with** *My vacation plans dovetailed perfectly with Joyce's.* **2** [T + together] to join two pieces of wood by means of dovetail joints

dovetail[2] also **ˈdovetail ˌjoint** *n.* [C] a type of JOINT fastening two pieces of wood together

dov·ish /ˈdʌvɪʃ/ *adj.* preferring peace and discussion to war

Dow /daʊ/ *n.* **The Dow** ECONOMICS the DOW JONES INDUSTRIAL AVERAGE

dow·a·ger /ˈdaʊədʒɚ/ *n.* [C] **1** a woman from a high social class who has land or a title from her dead husband **2** INFORMAL a respected and impressive old lady

dow·dy /ˈdaʊdi/ *adj.* **1** unattractive or unfashionable SYN **frumpy**: *a dowdy uniform* **2** a dowdy woman wears clothes that are old-fashioned or that are not attractive **—dowdily** *adv.* **—dowdiness** *n.* [U]

dow·el /ˈdaʊəl/ *n.* [C] a wooden pin for holding two pieces of wood, metal, or stone together

ˌDow Jones Inˌdustrial ˈAverage, the also **the ˌDow Jones ˈAverage** *n.* ECONOMICS an economic measurement tool that gives the average STOCK prices of 30 important businesses in the U.S. each day, used for showing the strength of economic performance of U.S. industry in general: *The Dow Jones Industrial Average fell 12 points early in the day but closed higher.*

down[1] /daʊn/ S1 W1 *adv.*

1 FROM HIGHER TO LOWER from a higher place or position toward a lower place or position OPP **up**: *David looked down at his feet.* | *The sun was beating down on our backs.* | *Do you want me to* **take** *that poster* **down** (=take it off the wall) *for you?* | *Ken fell asleep* **face down** (=with his face toward the ground) *on the couch.*

2 FROM STANDING TO LYING/SITTING from a position in which someone or something is standing into a position in which they are lying flat or sitting: *Angie, why don't you sit down and relax?* | *I think I'll go and lie down for a while.* | *Trees were blown down onto houses when the tornado hit.*

3 TO THE SOUTH toward or in the south: *They have a*

house down near the Mexican border. | **+to** *We drove down to Albuquerque.*
4 FROM MORE TO LESS at or toward a lower level or amount: *Keep your speed down* (=don't drive fast). | *Can I* ***turn*** *the TV* ***down*** (=make it quieter) *a little?* | *Sales were down last month.* | **+to** *Prices have gone down to their lowest level in ten years.* | **+by** *Profits are down by 3%.*
5 DESTROYED to a state in which something is completely destroyed: *They tore the old school down.* | *The factory burned down in 1900.*
6 FROM BIGGER TO SMALLER to a smaller size: *Sand can wear down the moving parts in your bike.* | **+to** *Sharif cut his report down to only three pages.*
7 IN A LOWER PLACE in a lower place or position: *There's a parking lot down at the bottom of the hill.* | *I'll be down* (=on a lower floor of a building) *in a minute.*
8 RECORDED in the form of writing, especially on a list, or some other recorded form: *I have it all down on tape.* | *Ok,* ***write*** *"return library books"* ***down*** *on your list.* | **down to do sth** ***Put*** *me* ***down to*** (=write on a list that I will) *bring the dessert.* | *Let me* ***take down*** *your number and I'll call you back.*
9 FIRMLY firmly and tightly into a place or position: *We could tape the mat down with duct tape.*
10 FARTHER ALONG in or to a place that is farther along something such as a road or river: *There's a hotel a little farther down.* | **two/three etc. doors down (from sb)** *our neighbor who lives two doors down*

SPOKEN PHRASES

11 LOCAL PLACE in or to a place that is fairly near: *I saw him down at the bus station.*
12 Down! used to tell a dog not to jump on you or someone else
13 Down with...! used to say that you strongly oppose a government, leader etc. and do not want them to have any power anymore: *Hundreds of students were shouting, "Down with dictatorship!"*

14 be down to sth to have only a small amount left from a larger amount: *Now we're down to our last eight dollars.*
15 TO LATER TIMES to people living in a later time in history: **pass/hand sth down** *Chu's recipes have been handed down through generations.*
16 TO LOWER RANK to someone with a lower position or rank: *a command passed down through the chain of command*
17 (from sb) down to sb including something or someone at a low level or rank: *Everyone uses the cafeteria, from the CEO down to the mailroom staff.*
18 INTO STOMACH in or into your stomach as a result of swallowing: *He gulped down his coffee.* | **get/keep sth down** *I was so sick, I couldn't keep anything down.*
19 go/come/be down to the wire to have very little time left to finish or achieve something: *We were in a couple of games that went right down to the wire.*
20 IN PAYMENT paid to someone immediately in CASH as part of the payment for something: *Lease a new SUV today for no money down.* → see also **come down to sth**[1], **come down with sth**[1], DOWN PAYMENT

USAGE

The word **down** is often used to make phrasal verbs. Some of these verbs show that you have moved from a higher level to a lower one. For example, **quiet down** means "to become quieter after being noisy," **calm down** means "to become more calm after being excited," and **dumb down** is an informal phrasal verb that means "to make something much easier to understand than it was." Another common use of **down** as a phrasal verb is to show that something is done very thoroughly. For example, **wash down** means to wash something completely using a lot of water.

down[2] S2 *adj.*
1 SAD [not before noun] INFORMAL sad and without confidence SYN **depressed**: *I've been feeling really down lately.* | **down in the mouth/dumps** (=very sad) ▸see THESAURUS box at **sad**
2 IN A GAME [not before noun] behind an opponent by a particular number of points: *We were down by 17 points at half-time.*
3 COMPUTER [not before noun] if a computer is down, it is not working because there is something wrong with the NETWORK it is connected to OPP **up**: *Our computers are down right now. Could you call back?*
4 LESS/LOWER [not before noun] less in amount than before, or at a lower level or place than before: *At lunchtime, the stock market was down 77 points.* | *The lake level is down but fishing is still good.*

SPOKEN PHRASES

5 be down on sb/sth to have a bad opinion of someone or something: *Don't be so down on yourself!*
6 COMPLETED [not before noun] used to say that a particular number of things have been finished, when there are more things left to do: *"One down, five to go," I thought, as I started on the next one.*
7 be down with sth SLANG to agree with or accept something: *Yeah, I'm down with that.*

8 be down on your luck to have very little money because you have had a lot of bad luck recently: *He helped me out when I was down on my luck.*
9 a down escalator an ESCALATOR (=set of moving stairs) that takes you down to a lower floor
[Origin: (1–2) 1300–1400 Old Norse *dúnn*]

down[3] S1 *prep.* **1** toward the ground or a lower place, or in a lower position: *Tears were running down his cheeks.* | *Do you want to go down the slide?* | *The hospital is just down the hill.* **2** along something, or toward the far end of something: *Look who's coming down the hall.* | *There's a great Vietnamese restaurant down the street.* | *We were driving really fast down the freeway.* **3** along the side of a place towards the south: *They sailed down the east coast of Africa.* | *a chain of mountains down the west side of South America* **4 down the road/line/pike** INFORMAL at some time in the future: *The situation is likely to be worse, six months down the road.* **5** in the direction of a river's current: *An empty boat was floating down the river.* | *We traveled down the Mississippi.*

down[4] *v.* [T] **1** to drink or eat something very quickly: *Jack downed three beers with his steak and fries.* **2** to defeat an opponent in sports: *Utah downed Orlando in Salt Lake City.* **3** to make something that is usually upright or in the air fall to the ground: *More than 60 electric lines were downed by the wet heavy snow.* **4** to force an airplane to crash by shooting it or exploding it: *He claimed the rebels downed 35 government aircraft.*

down[5] *n.* **1** [U] the soft fine feathers of a bird, often used between layers of material to make warm clothes and bed covers: *a down jacket* | *a pillow filled with down* → see also EIDERDOWN, GOOSEDOWN **2** [C] one of the four chances that a football team has to move forward at least ten YARDS in order to keep the ball: *It's second down with six yards to go.* **3** [U] soft hair like a baby's **4 downs** [plural] low round hills covered with grass → see also **ups and downs** at UP[4] (1)

down- /daʊn/ *prefix* **1** toward a lower position, or toward the bottom of something: *downstairs* | *downriver* (=nearer to where it flows into an ocean or lake) **2** used to show that something is being made smaller or less important: *to downsize a company* (=reduce the number of jobs in it) | *to downgrade a job* (=make it less important) **3** used to show that something is bad or negative: *the downside of a situation* (=the negative part of it) → see also UP-

ˌdown-and-ˈout *adj.* INFORMAL having no luck or money: *a down-and-out actor* —**down-and-outer** *n.* [C]

down·beat[1] /ˈdaʊnbit/ *adj.* not hopeful that the future will be good OPP **upbeat**: *a downbeat assessment of the situation*

downbeat[2] *n.* [C] **1** the first note in a MEASURE of music **2** ENG. LANG. ARTS the movement a CONDUCTOR makes to show when this note is to be played or sung

down·cast /ˈdaʊnkæst/ *adj.* **1** sad or upset because something bad has happened: *The team seemed down-*

D

cast after their fourth loss in a row. **2** downcast eyes are looking down: *He said nothing and kept his eyes downcast.*

down•draft /ˈdaʊndræft/ *n.* [C] **1** a DOWNWARD movement of air: *The plane experienced a sudden downdraft.* **2** a situation in which prices, STOCKS etc. go down, or when business becomes worse → see also UPDRAFT

Down ˈEast *adv.* INFORMAL in or to New England, especially the state of Maine —**Down Easter** *n.* [C]

down•er /ˈdaʊnɚ/ *n.* [C] INFORMAL **1** [usually singular] a person or situation that stops you from feeling cheerful or happy: *The book is a real downer.* **2** a drug that makes you feel very relaxed or sleepy → see also UPPER

D

down•fall /ˈdaʊnfɔl/ *n.* [singular] **1** the complete loss of your money, moral standards, social position etc., or the sudden failure of an organization: *the scandal that led to his downfall* **2** something that causes a complete failure or loss of someone's money, moral standards, social position etc.: *Greed would later prove to be Barnett's downfall.*

down•grade¹ /ˈdaʊngreɪd/ *v.* [T] **1** to make a job less important, or to move someone to a less important job SYN **demote** OPP **upgrade**: *After the merger, many reporters were reassigned or downgraded.* | **downgrade sb/sth to sth** *Harris was downgraded to assistant manager.* **2** to treat something as less important, valuable, or serious than before, or than it really is OPP **upgrade**: *The police were accused of downgrading the seriousness of violence against women.* | **downgrade sth to sth** *Hurricane Bob was downgraded to a tropical storm late Monday.*

downgrade² *n.* [C] TECHNICAL the angle at which something such as a hill or a road goes down

down•heart•ed /ˌdaʊnˈhɑrt̬ɪd◂/ *adj.* sad or hopeless: *When no job offers came, I began to feel downhearted.*

down•hill¹ /ˌdaʊnˈhɪl/ *adv.* **1** toward the bottom of a hill or lower land OPP **uphill**: *The truck rolled downhill into a parked car.* **2 go downhill** to become worse: *After he lost his job, things went downhill.*

downhill² *adj.* **1** on a slope that goes down to a lower point OPP **uphill**: *a downhill slope* | *It's a long walk, but it's all downhill.* **2 be (all) downhill a)** to become easier to do, especially after you have been doing something difficult: *You've done the hardest part. **It's all downhill from here**.* **b)** to become worse: *The best growth rates were in 2002, and it's been downhill ever since.*

ˈdownhill ˌskiing *n.* [U] the sport of moving fast down a mountain on SKIS → see also CROSS-COUNTRY SKIING

ˈdown-home *adj.* [only before noun] relating to the simple values and customs of people who live in the COUNTRYSIDE, especially in the southern U.S.: *authentic down-home cooking*

down•load /ˈdaʊnloʊd/ *v.* [I,T] COMPUTERS if information, a program etc. downloads, or if you download it, you move it from a large computer system to a computer which is connected to the system: *Download your favorite games here.* | **+from/off** *It's easy to download music from the Internet.* ►see THESAURUS box at **camera** —**download** *n.* [C] → see also UPLOAD

down•mar•ket /ˈdaʊnˌmɑrkɪt/ *adj.* DOWNSCALE OPP **upmarket**

ˌdown ˈpayment *n.* [C] the first payment that you make on something expensive, which you will continue to pay for over a longer period of time: *We almost have enough to **make a down payment on** a house.*

down•play /ˈdaʊnpleɪ/ *v.* **downplays, downplayed, downplaying** [T] to make something seem less important than it really is SYN **play down**: *Mom downplays the seriousness of her health problems.*

down•pour /ˈdaʊnpɔr/ *n.* [C usually singular] a lot of rain that falls in a short time

down•range /ˌdaʊnˈreɪndʒ/ *adv.* in the direction away from where something such as a MISSILE or gun is fired: *The rockets dropped into the Atlantic about 130 miles downrange.*

down•right /ˈdaʊnraɪt/ *adv.* [+ adj./adv.] INFORMAL used to emphasize that someone or something is completely good, bad etc.: *Tom can be downright nasty sometimes.* —**downright** *adj.* [only before noun] *a downright lie*

down•riv•er /ˌdaʊnˈrɪvɚ/ *adv.* in the direction that the water in a river is flowing OPP **upriver**: *The bridge was a mile downriver.* → see also DOWNSTREAM

down•scale¹ /ˈdaʊnskeɪl/ *adj.* not expensive, and usually not of good quality OPP **upscale**: *a downscale motel*

downscale² *v.* [T] to reduce something in size, or to make something less expensive: *The military forces have been downscaled since the end of the Cold War.*

down•shift /ˈdaʊnʃɪft/ *v.* [I,T] to move the GEAR SHIFT in a car or truck to a lower GEAR

down•side /ˈdaʊnsaɪd/ *n.* [singular] the negative part or disadvantage of something OPP **upside**: *It's a really good deal, but the downside is there's a waiting list.* | **+of/to** *The downside of the album is its excessive length.*

down•size /ˈdaʊnsaɪz/ *v.* [I,T] if a company or organization downsizes, or downsizes its operations, it reduces the number of people it employs in order to reduce costs —**downsizing** *n.* [U] → see also RIGHTSIZE

down•spout /ˈdaʊnspaʊt/ *n.* [C] a pipe that carries water away from the roof of a building SYN **drainpipe**

Down's syn•drome /ˈdaʊnz ˌsɪndroʊm/ *n.* [U] MEDICINE a condition that someone is born with, that stops them from developing in a normal way, both mentally and physically

down•stage /ˌdaʊnˈsteɪdʒ/ *adv.* toward or near the front of the stage in a theater —**downstage** /ˈdaʊnsteɪdʒ/ *adj.* → see also UPSTAGE

down•stairs /ˌdaʊnˈstɛrz/ S2 *adv.* to or on a lower floor of a building, especially a house: *Rosie ran downstairs to answer the door.* | *The washing machine is downstairs.* —**downstairs** /ˈdaʊnstɛrz/ *adj.* [only before noun] *a downstairs bedroom* → see also UPSTAIRS

down•state /ˌdaʊnˈsteɪt/ *adv.* in or to the southern part of a state —**downstate** /ˈdaʊnsteɪt/ *adj.* [only before noun] *downstate Illinois* → see also UPSTATE

down•stream /ˌdaʊnˈstrim/ *adv.* in the direction the water in a river or stream is flowing OPP **upstream**: *The body had drifted three miles downstream.*

down•swing /ˈdaʊnswɪŋ/ *n.* [C usually singular] a time during which business activity is reduced and conditions become worse OPP **upswing**: *a downswing in lumber prices*

down•time /ˈdaʊntaɪm/ *n.* [U] **1** the time when a machine, a factory, or equipment is not working **2** INFORMAL time spent relaxing: *You need some more downtime.*

ˌdown-to-ˈearth *adj.* practical and direct in a sensible honest way: *Fran's a very friendly down-to-earth person.*

down•town /ˌdaʊnˈtaʊn/ S2 W3 *adv.* to or in the main business area of a town or city: *Stacy works downtown.* | *I have to **go downtown** later.* —**downtown** /ˈdaʊntaʊn/ *adj.* [only before noun] *downtown restaurants* → see also UPTOWN

down•trend /ˈdaʊntrɛnd/ *n.* [C] a time in which business activities, prices etc. decrease OPP **uptrend**: **+in** *an eight-month downtrend in the car market*

down•trod•den /ˈdaʊnˌtrɑdn/ *adj.* LITERARY downtrodden people, workers etc. are treated badly and without respect by people who have power over them

down•turn /ˈdaʊntɚn/ *n.* [C usually singular] ECONOMICS a time during which business activity, production etc. is reduced and conditions become worse OPP **upturn**: **+in** *an economic downturn in the textile industry*

Down ˈUnder *adv.* in or to Australia or New Zealand

down•ward¹ /ˈdaʊnwɚd/ also **downwards** *adv.* **1** toward the ground or toward a lower place SYN **down** OPP **upward** OPP **up**: *Push the handle downward.* | *Tim pointed downward to his shoes.* | *He was lying **face downward** in the grass* (=with the front of his body touching the ground). **2** to a lower level, value, amount etc. SYN **down** OPP **upward** OPP **up**:

The temperature continued to drift downward. | *The dollar moved downward against the Euro.* **3 from sb downward** including a senior person down to and including people of lower rank or status: *The changes affect everyone from the CEO downward.*

downward² *adj.* [only before noun] **1** moving toward the ground or toward a lower place OPP **upward**: *a gentle downward slope* **2** falling to a lower level, value, amount etc. OPP **upward**: *Stock prices continued their downward trend.* | *the economy's long* ***downward spiral*** (=fall to very low levels)

down·wind /ˌdaʊnˈwɪnd/ *adv.* in the direction that the wind is moving: *Residents who lived downwind from the explosion were evacuated.*

down·y /ˈdaʊni/ *adj.* covered in, filled with, or made of soft fine hair or feathers: *a baby's downy hair*

dow·ry /ˈdaʊri/ *n. plural* **dowries** [C,U] property and money that a woman gives to her husband when they marry in some societies

dowse¹ /daʊz/ *v.* [I + for] to look for water or minerals under the ground using a special stick that points to where they are SYN **divine** —**dowser** *n.* [C]

dowse² /daʊs/ *v.* [T] another spelling of DOUSE

ˈdowsing rod *n.* [C] a special stick in the shape of a Y, used for dowsing for water or minerals

dox·ol·o·gy /dɑkˈsɑlədʒi/ *n.* [C] a special Christian HYMN or prayer used to praise God

doy·en /ˈdɔɪən, ˈdwɑyɛn/ *n.* [C] the oldest, most respected, or most experienced member of a group: *the doyen of sports commentators*

doy·enne /dɔɪˈɛn, dwɑˈyɛn/ *n.* [C] the oldest, most respected, or most experienced woman in a group: *the doyenne of Wallstreet*

Doyle /dɔɪl/**, Sir Ar·thur Con·an** /ˈɑrθɚ ˈkɑnən/ (1859–1930) a British doctor and writer of stories about the DETECTIVE Sherlock Holmes

doz. the written abbreviation of DOZEN

doze /doʊz/ *v.* [I] to sleep lightly for a short time: *Kevin was dozing in his chair after lunch.* [**Origin:** 1600–1700 from a Scandinavian language; related to Old Norse *dúsa* **to sleep lightly**]

doze off *phr. v.* to go to sleep, especially when you did not intend to: *I was just dozing off when the phone rang.*

doz·en /ˈdʌzən/ S3 W1 WRITTEN ABBREVIATION **doz.** *n.* **1 a/two/three dozen etc. (sth)** one, two, three etc. groups of 12: *two dozen eggs* | *He made* ***half a dozen*** (=six, or approximately six) *phone calls.* **2 dozens (of sth)** INFORMAL a lot, but not hundreds: *Dozens were injured in the fire.* | **+of** *She's had dozens of boyfriends.* → see also BAKER'S DOZEN, **a dime a dozen** at DIME (2), **it's six of one and half a dozen of the other** at SIX (3)

> USAGE **plural forms: dozen, dozens (of)**
> **Dozen**, without an "s," is used after numbers. **Dozens (of)** is used in an informal way when the exact number of what you are talking about is not important.
> Compare: *I bought two dozen apples* (=24 apples) and *I bought dozens of apples* (=a lot of apples).

do·zy /ˈdoʊzi/ *adj.* INFORMAL not feeling very awake

DP the abbreviation of DATA PROCESSING

D.Phil. /di ˈfɪl/ an abbreviation of DOCTOR OF PHILOSOPHY

DPT /ˌdi pi ˈti/ also **DTP** *n.* [U] MEDICINE a VACCINE against the diseases DIPHTHERIA, TETANUS, and PERTUSSIS

Dr. **1** the written abbreviation of DOCTOR **2** the written abbreviation of DRIVE: *88 Park Dr.*

drab /dræb/ *adj.* **1** not bright in color: *a drab green* **2** boring: *Paul grew tired of his drab depressing life.* [**Origin:** 1500–1600 *drab* **(dull-colored) cloth** , from Old French *drap* **cloth**] → see also DRIBS AND DRABS

drach·ma /ˈdrækmə, ˈdrɑk-/ *n. plural* **drachmas** or **drachmae** /-mi/ [C] **1** the unit of money in modern Greece before the Euro was introduced **2** an ancient Greek silver coin and weight

dra·co·ni·an /dræˈkoʊniən/ *adj.* FORMAL very strict and cruel: **draconian laws/measures/methods etc.** *The hospital has been forced to make draconian budget cuts.* [**Origin:** 1800–1900 Greek *Drakon* **Draco**, ancient Greek judge who had criminals killed for very small crimes]

draft¹ /dræft/ Ac *n.*
1 UNFINISHED FORM [C] a piece of writing, a drawing, or a plan that is not yet in its finished form: *a draft of the first chapter* | **a first/rough draft** (=the first plan for something)
2 a/the final draft the finished form of a piece of writing, a drawing, or a plan
3 MILITARY the draft a system in which people must join the military, especially when there is a war
4 AIR [C] a current of air, especially cold air, that comes into a room and feels unpleasant: *Could you close the window? There's a draft in here.*
5 SPORTS [C usually singular] a system in some sports in which professional teams choose players from colleges to join their teams
6 MONEY [C] a written order for money to be paid by a bank, especially from one bank to another
7 BEER [C] a beer in a bar that is served from a barrel rather than a bottle or can
8 on draft beer that is on draft is served from a large container, rather than from a bottle or can SYN **on tap**

draft² Ac *v.* [T] **1** to write a plan, letter, report etc. that will need to be changed before it is in its finished form: **draft a speech/letter/bill etc.** *We drafted a proposal to be presented to the school board.* **2** [usually passive] to order someone to serve in their country's military, especially during a war: **be/get drafted into sth** *My dad was 18 when he got drafted into the army.* **3** to choose an ATHLETE to play for a professional sports team: *He was the first player drafted by the Chicago Blackhawks.*

draft sb into sth *phr. v.* to choose someone to do something, especially something they did not want or expect to do: **draft sb into doing sth** *Somehow my boss drafted me into filing these reports.*

draft³ Ac *adj.* **1 a draft proposal/copy/version etc.** a piece of writing that is not yet in its finished form: *The draft report was given to managers for their comments.* **2** a draft horse or animal is used for pulling heavy loads

ˌdraft ˈbeer *n.* [U] beer that is served from a large container, rather than a bottle or can

ˈdraft board *n.* [C] the committee that decides who will be ordered to join the military

ˈdraft card *n.* [C] a card that is sent to someone, telling them they have been ordered to join the military

ˈdraft ˌdodger *n.* [C] someone who illegally avoids joining the military, even though they have been ordered to join → see also CONSCIENTIOUS OBJECTOR

draft·ee /dræfˈti/ *n.* [C] someone who has been ordered to join the military

ˈdraft pick *n.* [C] a person who has been chosen to play for a professional sports team during a DRAFT

drafts·man /ˈdræftsmən/ *n. plural* **draftsmen** /-mən/ [C] **1** someone whose job is to make detailed drawings of a building, machine etc. that is being planned **2** LAW someone who puts a suggested law or a new law into the correct words

draft·y /ˈdræfti/ *adj. comparative* **draftier**, *superlative* **draftiest** a drafty room or building has unpleasantly cold air blowing through it: *a drafty old house*

drag¹ /dræg/ S2 W3 *v.* **dragged, dragging**
1 PULL ALONG THE GROUND [T] to pull someone or something along the ground, often because they are too heavy to carry: *We couldn't lift it, so we dragged it.* | **drag sb/sth away/along/off etc.** *Wild animals had dragged the carcass away.* | **drag sb/sth into/to/across etc.** *I managed to drag the table into the kitchen.* ▸see THESAURUS box at pull¹
2 NOT GENTLY [T always + adv./prep.] to pull someone or something somewhere in a way that hurts or damages

D

them: *Several protesters were dragged away by police.* | *Secret Service agents* ***dragged*** *the man* ***to the ground*** (=pulled the man down to the ground).
3 drag yourself up/down/into etc. to move somewhere with difficulty: *Jacob was so tired he could hardly drag himself up the stairs.*
4 PERSUADE SB TO GO [T always + adv./prep.] INFORMAL to persuade or force someone to come somewhere when they do not want to: *Mom dragged us to a classical concert last night.* | *Can you* ***drag yourself away from*** *that video game for a few minutes?*
5 COMPUTER [T always + adv./prep.] COMPUTERS to move something on a computer screen by pulling it along with the MOUSE: ***Drag and drop*** *the icon into the new folder.*
6 TOUCH THE GROUND [I] if something is dragging along the ground, part of it is touching the ground as you move: **drag along/in/on sth** *Your coat's dragging in the mud.*
7 BORING [I] if time or an event drags, it seems to go very slowly because nothing interesting is happening: *The last two hours of the play really dragged.*
8 BODY PART [T] if you drag your leg, foot etc., you cannot lift it off the ground as you walk because it is injured: *The bird was dragging its broken wing.*
9 drag your feet INFORMAL to take too much time to do something because you do not want to do it: *The police have been accused of dragging their feet on the investigation.*
10 drag a lake/river/pond etc. to look for something in a lake, river, pond etc. by pulling a heavy net along the bottom: *They dragged the lake for the missing girl's body.*
11 drag sb's name through the mud to tell about the bad things that someone has done, so that others will have a bad opinion of them
12 drag sb kicking and screaming into sth HUMOROUS to force someone to do something or become involved in something that they do not want to: *The company has been dragged kicking and screaming into the 21st century.*
13 BOAT [T] if a boat drags its ANCHOR, it pulls the anchor away from its place on the bottom of a lake, river etc.
[**Origin:** 1300–1400 Old Norse *draga* or Old English *dragan*]

drag sb/sth ↔ **down** *phr. v.* **1** to make the price, level, or quality of something go down: *The widespread decline in stocks dragged down computer share prices.* **2** to make someone feel unhappy: *Fuhr said that losing his job dragged him and his whole family down.* **3** if someone or something bad drags you down, they make your behavior worse: *Don't let them* ***drag you down to their level*** (=make you behave as badly as they do).

drag sb/sth **in** *phr. v.* to start to talk about someone or something that is not connected with what you are talking or arguing about: *They're trying to drag in all kinds of other issues to distract us.* → see also **look like something the cat dragged in** at CAT (4), **look what the cat dragged in!** at LOOK[1] (18)

drag sb/sth **into** sth *phr. v.* to make someone or an organization get involved in a particular situation, discussion etc., even though they do not want to: *I'm sorry I dragged you into this mess.*

drag on *phr. v.* if an event drags on, it seems to continue for longer than is necessary, often because you are bored: **+for/into** *The board's discussions dragged on for several hours.* | *The meeting dragged on into the evening.*

drag sth ↔ **out** *phr. v.* to make a meeting, an argument etc. last longer than is necessary: *How long are you going to drag this discussion out?*

drag sth **out of** sb *phr. v.* to make someone tell you something when they had not intended to or were not supposed to do so: *It took me all day to drag it out of her.*

drag sth **up** *phr. v.* to mention an unpleasant or embarrassing story from the past, even though it upsets someone: *Why does he have to drag that up again?*

drag[2] S3 *n.*
1 a drag INFORMAL **a)** something or someone that is boring: *Don't be such a drag! Come to the party.* **b)** something that is annoying and continues for a long time: *It's a drag having to share a bathroom with four people.*
2 be a drag on sb/sth a person or thing that is a drag on someone makes it hard for them to make progress toward what they want: *Maggie thinks marriage would be a drag on her career.*
3 CIGARETTE [C] the act of breathing in smoke from a cigarette: *Frank* ***took a*** *deep* ***drag on*** *his cigarette.*
4 the main drag INFORMAL the biggest or longest street that goes through a town, especially the middle of a town: *Our hotel is right on the main drag.*
5 in drag INFORMAL wearing clothes that are intended for people of the opposite sex, especially for fun or entertainment
6 FORCE [singular, U] the force of air that pushes against an airplane or a vehicle that is moving forward: *The car's low profile and rounded edges reduce its drag.*

drag·gled /ˈdrægəld/ *adj.* LITERARY → see BEDRAGGLED

drag·gy /ˈdrægi/ *adj.* INFORMAL if something is draggy, it is boring or seems to happen too slowly: *a long draggy afternoon*

drag·net /ˈdrægnɛt/ *n.* [C] **1** a net that is pulled along the bottom of a river or lake, to bring up things that may be there **2** a system in which the police look for criminals, using very thorough methods: *a police dragnet*

drag·on /ˈdrægən/ *n.* [C] a large imaginary animal that is like a LIZARD with wings and a long tail and can breathe out fire [**Origin:** 1200–1300 Old French, Greek *drakon* **large snake**]

drag·on·fly /ˈdrægənˌflaɪ/ *n. plural* **dragonflies** [C] a brightly colored insect with a long thin body and transparent wings

ˈdragon ˌlady *n.* [C] HUMOROUS a woman with power who is cruel toward other people

dra·goon[1] /drəˈgun, dræ-/ *n.* [C] HISTORY a European soldier in past times who rode a horse and carried a gun and sword [**Origin:** 1600–1700 French *dragon* **dragon, gun, soldier with a gun**]

dragoon[2] *v.*
dragoon sb **into** sth *phr. v.* to force someone to do something they do not want to do: *Monica was dragooned into helping her sister move.*

ˈdrag race *n.* [C] a car race over a very short distance —**drag racing** *n.* [U]

drag·ster /ˈdrægstɚ/ *n.* [C] a long narrow low car used in drag races

drain[1] /dreɪn/ S3 *v.*
1 LIQUID a) [I,T] if liquid drains, or you drain it, it flows out of a container: **drain sth from sth** *Brad drained all the oil from the engine.* | **+away/off** *After the floodwaters drained away, Shahar returned to her village.* **b)** [I,T] if a container, area, object etc. drains or you drain it, all the liquid flows out of or off it: *Open ditches drain very efficiently.* | *They drained the pond in order to search the bottom.* | **well/poorly etc. drained** *Carrots grow best in well-drained soil.* → see picture on page A32
2 MAKE TIRED [T] to make someone feel very tired: *Listening to customers' complaints all day really drains me.*
3 USE TOO MUCH [T usually passive] to use too much of something so that there is not enough left: *Over $15 million a year is being drained from federal resources.* | **be drained of sth** *Parents can become so drained of energy that they just give up.*
4 the color/blood drains from sb's face used to say that someone becomes very pale usually because they are frightened or shocked: *All the blood drained from Collins' face as the verdict was read.*
5 FEELING if a feeling drains away from you, it is

reduced until you don't feel it anymore: *Suddenly all her anger **drained away**.*
6 **drain a glass/cup etc.** to drink all the liquid in a glass, cup etc.: *Lori quickly drained her cup.*
[**Origin:** Old English *dreahnian*]

drain sth **off** *phr. v.* to make all the water or a liquid flow off something: *Drain off the fat from the meat after frying.*

drain² *n.* [C] **1** a pipe or hole that dirty water or waste liquids flow into: *The drain in the bathtub is clogged.* **2 a drain on sth** something that continuously uses time, money, strength etc.: *Owning this boat is a big drain on my finances.* **3 down the drain** INFORMAL **a)** wasted or having no result: *Well, there's another 50 dollars down the drain.* **b) go down the drain** if an organization, country etc. goes down the drain, it becomes worse or fails → see also BRAIN DRAIN

drain·age /ˈdreɪnɪdʒ/ *n.* [U] **1** a system of pipes or passages in the ground for carrying away water or waste liquids: *drainage ditches* **2** the process by which water or waste liquid flows away: *a way to improve drainage*

ˈdrainage ˌbasin *n.* [C] EARTH SCIENCE an area of land where the water that falls as rain flows into a river

ˈdrain board also **ˈdraining board** *n.* [C] a slightly sloping flat area next to a SINK where you put dishes to dry

drained /dreɪnd/ *adj.* **1** very tired, and without any energy: *Steve felt so drained he could hardly make it to the car.* **2 be drained of color/emotion/energy etc.** to have lost all your color, emotion, energy etc.: *Her voice was drained of emotion.*

drain·er /ˈdreɪnɚ/ *n.* [C] a flat object made of RUBBER that you put under a DISH RACK to catch the water from wet dishes

drain·pipe /ˈdreɪnpaɪp/ *n.* [C] **1** a pipe that carries waste water away from buildings **2** a pipe that carries rain water away from the roof of a building

drake /dreɪk/ *n.* [C] BIOLOGY a male duck

Drake /dreɪk/, **Sir Fran·cis** /ˈfrænsɪs/ (?1540–1596) an English sailor and EXPLORER, who was the first English man to sail around the world, and was one of the leaders of the English navy when it defeated the Spanish Armada in 1588

dram /dræm/ *n.* [C] a small unit of weight or of liquid

dra·ma /ˈdrɑmə, ˈdræmə/ Ac W3 *n.* **1** [C] ENG. LANG. ARTS a movie, television program, play etc. that is serious rather than humorous: *an award-winning TV drama* → see also COMEDY **2** [U] ENG. LANG. ARTS the study of acting and plays: *students studying drama* | *drama school* **3** [C,U] an exciting and unusual situation or set of events: *The drama of this year's World Series helped ticket sales.* [**Origin:** 1500–1600 Late Latin, Greek, **action, theater plays**, from *dran* **to do**]

ˈdrama queen *n.* [C] DISAPPROVING **a)** a woman, especially an actress, who demands too much attention by trying to make situations seem worse than they are **b)** a HOMOSEXUAL man who behaves this way

dra·mat·ic /drəˈmæṭɪk/ Ac W2 *adj.* **1** sudden, surprising, and often impressive: *The results were dramatic.* | **dramatic change/improvement/shift** *a dramatic improvement in her appearance* | **a dramatic increase/rise/fall/drop etc.** *a dramatic rise in the cost of living* **2** exciting and impressive: *a dramatic rescue* | *the dramatic scenery of the Grand Canyon* ▸see THESAURUS box at **exciting** **3** ENG. LANG. ARTS connected with drama or the theater: *a collection of Shakespeare's dramatic works* **4** showing a lot of emotion in a way that makes other people notice: *Stop being so dramatic. It's embarrassing.* —**dramatically** /-kli/ *adv.*: *Output has increased dramatically.*

draˌmatic ˈirony *n.* [U] ENG. LANG. ARTS a way of giving information in a play in which the people watching know something that the characters in the play do not, and can understand the real importance or meaning of what is happening

dra·mat·ics /drəˈmæṭɪks/ *n.* **1** [plural] behavior that shows too much feeling, and that is often insincere SYN **histrionics**: *I've had enough of your dramatics.* **2** [U] the study or practice of skills used in drama, such as acting

dram·a·tis per·so·nae /ˌdræməṭɪs pɚˈsoʊni, -naɪ/ *n.* [plural] FORMAL ENG. LANG. ARTS the characters in a play

dram·a·tist /ˈdræməṭɪst, ˈdrɑ-/ Ac *n.* [C] someone who writes plays, especially serious ones SYN **playwright**

dram·a·tize /ˈdræməˌtaɪz/ Ac *v.* [T] **1** ENG. LANG. ARTS to make a book or event into a play, movie, television program etc.: *a novel dramatized for TV* **2** DISAPPROVING to make a situation seem more exciting, terrible etc. than it really is: *Some newspapers tend to dramatize reports of robberies.* **3** to make something more noticeable SYN **highlight**: *This incident dramatizes the difficulties of the project.* —**dramatization** /ˌdræməṭəˈzeɪʃən/ *n.* [C,U]

dra·me·dy /ˈdrɑmədi, ˈdræ-/ *n.* [C] INFORMAL a television program that is both serious and humorous

drank /dræŋk/ *v.* the past tense of DRINK

drape /dreɪp/ *v.* [T usually passive] **1** to put something somewhere so that it hangs or lies loosely: **drape sth over/around/across etc. sth** *His clothes were draped over the back of the chair.* **2** to cover or decorate something with a cloth: **drape sb/sth with/in etc. sth** *The soldiers' coffins were draped with American flags.* **3** to rest yourself or part of your body somewhere so that you or it hangs or lies loosely in a relaxed way: **drape sth over/around/across sth** *He draped his arm around my shoulders.* | **drape yourself over/across etc. sth** *Molly draped herself across the sofa.*

drap·er·y /ˈdreɪpəri/ *n.* **1 draperies** [plural] long heavy curtains **2** [U] cloth that is arranged in folds

drapes /dreɪps/ *n.* [plural] long heavy curtains

dras·tic /ˈdræstɪk/ *adj.* strong, sudden, and often severe: **drastic action/measures** *NATO threatened to take drastic action.* [**Origin:** 1600–1700 Greek *drastikos*, from *dran* **to do**] —**drastically** /-kli/ *adv.*: *The size of the army was drastically cut.*

drat /dræt/ *interjection* OLD-FASHIONED used to show you are annoyed

draught /dræft/ *n.* [C] the British spelling of DRAFT

draw¹ /drɔ/ S1 W1 *v.* past tense **drew** /dru/, *past participle* **drawn** /drɔn/
1 PICTURE [I,T] to make a picture of something with a pencil or pen: *Amy loves to draw.* | **draw sb sth** *Could you draw me a diagram?* | **draw sth for sb** *I'll draw a map for you.*

> **THESAURUS**
> **sketch** to draw something quickly and without a lot of detail: *Students were sketching a model in the center of the room.*
> **doodle** to draw shapes or patterns without really thinking about what you are doing: *A lot of people doodle during meetings.*
> **scribble** to draw or write something quickly in a messy way: *She scribbled her name and phone number on the back of the card.*
> **trace** to copy a picture by putting a piece of thin paper over it and drawing the lines that you can see through the paper: *The kids were tracing designs on the paper.*

2 NOTICE [T] if something draws your attention, your gaze, your eyes etc., it makes you notice it: **draw (sb's) attention** *The case drew international attention.* | **draw (sb's) attention to sth** *I'd like to draw your attention to the wonderful paintings on the ceiling.* | **draw attention to yourself** *I didn't want to draw attention to myself.* | **draw sb's eye/gaze** (=make someone pay attention to something)
3 DECIDE STH IS TRUE to decide that a particular fact or principle is true after thinking carefully about it: **draw a conclusion/inference (from sth)** *There's only one conclusion that can be drawn from the evidence.*
4 **draw a distinction/comparison/analogy etc.** to

D

show why two things are different from or similar to each other: +**between** *The law draws a distinction between murder and manslaughter.* | *People often try to* ***draw parallels between*** *computers and our brains* (=show that they are the similar).

5 GET A REACTION to get a particular kind of reaction from someone because of something you have said or done: **draw praise/criticism** *Phillips drew criticism recently for canceling a national concert tour.* | *The development plans have* ***drawn fire from*** (=been criticized by) *local residents.* | *His remarks* ***drew*** *an angry* ***response*** *from Democrats.*

6 draw the line (at sth) to set a limit on what you are willing to do, or refuse to do something, especially because you disapprove of something: *He wanted to succeed, but he drew the line at cheating.* | *Is 50 too old to have a baby? Where do you draw the line?*

D

7 ATTRACT [T] to attract someone and make them want to do something, go somewhere, or be with someone: *Tourists are drawn by the beautiful beaches.* | **draw sb to sb/sth** *I was drawn to engineering from a young age.* | *People were always drawn to him, even as a child.* | *The new Children's Museum is* ***drawing*** *huge* ***crowds.***

8 draw a line in the sand to warn someone that if they do something you have told them not to do, they will have to fight you or be punished by you: *It's time to draw a line in the sand and stop any more cuts to education.*

9 draw blood a) to take blood from someone, especially at a hospital: +**from** *The nurse drew some blood from Toni's arm.* **b)** to make someone BLEED: *The tiny insects swarm and bite, sometimes drawing blood.* **c)** to have a very negative effect on something, especially in business or politics: *The next social program cuts will draw blood.*

10 TAKE OUT [T always + adv./prep.] to remove something from its place or from a container: **draw sth out/from sth** *She reached into her purse and drew out a silver cigarette case.* | **draw a gun/knife/sword etc.** *Suddenly he drew a knife and pointed it at me.*

11 MOVE IN ONE DIRECTION [I always + adv./prep.] to move steadily in a particular direction, especially toward someone or something: *The crowd drew back to allow the police to enter.* | **draw near/close** *Maria grew nervous as the men drew closer.* | **draw alongside/beside/toward etc.** *The crowd shouted as the boat drew away from the dock.*

12 PULL CURTAINS/SHEETS ETC. [T] to move something such as curtains or sheets by pulling it: **draw sth back** *He drew back the sheet to look at his son.* | **draw sth around sb/sth** *She drew the shawl around her shoulders.* | **draw the curtains/blinds** (=close them by pulling them)

13 PULL A VEHICLE if an animal draws a vehicle, it pulls it along: *The carriage was drawn by six white horses.*

14 draw a blank SPOKEN to not be able to think of or find an answer to a question: *I just drew a blank on the last test question.*

15 GET STH IMPORTANT [T] to get something, especially a feeling, that you need or that is important from someone or something: **draw comfort/satisfaction/pleasure etc. from sth** *I drew a lot of comfort from her kind words.* | **draw ideas/inspiration from sth** *Many artists have drawn inspiration from this landscape.*

16 BE PAID [T] to receive an amount of money regularly from your employer or from the government: *I've been* ***drawing unemployment*** *for six months.*

17 draw a check (on sth) to write a check for taking money out of a bank: *He drew a check on a Swiss bank account.*

18 LIQUID [T] to take water, beer etc. from a well or container

19 BREATHE IN [T] LITERARY to take air or smoke into your lungs [SYN] **take**: *She drew a deep breath.*

20 draw (sb) a picture to describe something in detail, in speech or in writing: *It was impossible to draw a complete picture of the damage.*

21 PLAYING CARD/TICKET [I,T] to choose a card, ticket etc. by chance: *The winning lottery numbers will be drawn on Saturday evening.*

22 draw to a stop/end/close FORMAL to gradually stop or finish

23 draw near/close to become closer in time: *Summer vacation is drawing near.*

24 draw straws to decide who will do something by having each person pick one STRAW, stick, pencil etc. from a group of different-sized ones, with the loser being the person who picks the shortest one: *The players drew straws to decide who went first.*

25 draw the short straw used to say that someone has been unlucky because they were chosen by chance to do a job that no one wants to do: *I'm only here because I drew the short straw.*

26 draw lots to decide who will do something by taking pieces of paper etc. out of a container: *We drew lots to see who would go first.*

27 draw a bath LITERARY to fill a BATHTUB with water

28 draw a bow to bend a BOW by pulling back the string in order to shoot an ARROW

[**Origin:** Old English *dragan*]

draw sb aside *phr. v.* to stop someone so that you can talk to them: *Jackie drew me aside to ask what was wrong.*

draw back from sth *phr. v.* to decide not to do something: *The company drew back from its initial agreement of a 3% pay raise.*

draw sb in also **draw sb into sth** *phr. v.* to attract someone or involve them in something, often when they do not really want to take part: *Keith refused to be drawn into the argument.* | *We hope our lower prices will draw in more first-time Internet users.*

draw sth off *phr. v.* to remove some liquid from a larger supply: *Some of the river water will be drawn off into a network of canals.*

draw on sth *phr. v.* **1** also **draw upon sth** to use supplies, experiences etc. for a particular purpose: *She has 20 years of teaching experience to draw on.* **2** to take money out of a particular account: *The courts prohibit us from drawing on that line of credit.* **3 draw on a cigarette/cigar etc.** FORMAL to breathe in smoke from a cigarette etc.

draw sb/sth ↔ out *phr. v.* **1** to make an event last longer than usual: *The final questions drew the meeting out for another hour.* **2** to make someone feel less nervous and more willing to talk: *Mr. Monroe has helped draw Billy out of his shyness.* **3** to remove money from a bank account [SYN] **withdraw**: *She went to the bank and drew out all the money they had saved.*

draw up *phr. v.*

1 LIST/CONTRACT ETC. draw sth ↔ up to prepare a written document: *The committee has drawn up a list of finalists.*

2 VEHICLE to arrive somewhere and stop: *A huge black limousine drew up outside the gates.*

3 draw up a chair also **draw a chair up** to move a chair so that you are sitting close to someone or something

4 draw yourself up (to your full height) to stand up very straight because you are angry or determined about something

5 SOLDIERS draw sb up to arrange people in a special order: *The troops were drawn up in ranks for inspection.*

draw² [S3] *n.* [C] **1** a person, thing, or place that a lot of people are interested in seeing or going to: *The Statue of Liberty is always a big draw for tourists.* **2** a TIE in a game or competition: *The third game in the chess tournament* ***ended in a draw.*** **3** the act of choosing someone or something by chance, especially in a game or LOTTERY: *The jackpot for Saturday's draw is over $5 million.* → see also **the luck of the draw** at LUCK¹ (15), **be quick on the draw** at QUICK¹ (12), **a quick draw** at QUICK¹ (13)

draw·back /ˈdrɔbæk/ *n.* [C] a disadvantage of a situation, product etc.: +**to/of** *The major drawback of being famous is the lack of privacy.*

draw·bridge /ˈdrɔbrɪdʒ/ *n.* [C] a bridge that can be pulled up to let ships go under it, or to stop people from entering or attacking a castle

draw·down /ˈdrɔdaʊn/ *n.* [C] the act, process, or result of reducing the level or amount of something: *a large drawdown in world grain supplies*

drawer /drɔr/ S2 *n.* **1** [C] part of a piece of furniture, such as a desk, that is like a box that slides in and out and that you can keep things in: *She opened the drawer and took out a pair of scissors.* | *an underwear drawer* | **the bottom/top drawer** *There are some pens in the top drawer.* → see also TOP-DRAWER **2 drawers** [plural] OLD-FASHIONED underwear worn between the waist and the top of the legs

draw·ing /ˈdrɔ-ɪŋ/ *n.* **1** [C] ENG. LANG. ARTS a picture that you make with a pencil, pen etc.: *da Vinci's drawings* | **+of** *a drawing of the building*

THESAURUS

picture a drawing, painting, or photograph: *On the refrigerator were pictures the kids had drawn.*
sketch a drawing that you do quickly and without a lot of details: *When she was traveling, she drew quick sketches of the places she'd been.*
comic strip a series of pictures that are drawn inside boxes and tell a story: *The Doonesbury comic strip comments on political and social events.*
cartoon a funny drawing in a newspaper, usually about someone or something that is in the news: *An editorial cartoon showed him as a baby throwing a tantrum.*

2 [U] ENG. LANG. ARTS the art or skill of making pictures with a pen, pencil etc.: *I've never been very good at drawing.* ►see THESAURUS box at **art¹** **3** [C] a contest in which a winning number, ticket etc. is chosen by chance: *The church social will include a* ***prize drawing***.

ˈdrawing board *n.* **1 (go) back to the drawing board** to start working on a plan or idea again after an idea that you have tried has failed, or to make someone do this: *Voters rejected the plans, so it's back to the drawing board for city engineers.* **2 on the drawing board** in the process of being planned or prepared: *A remake of the movie is on the drawing board.* **3** [C] a large flat board that artists and DESIGNERS work on

ˈdrawing card *n.* [C] a feature that attracts people to an area, a concert, a competition etc.: *The hotel spa is a real drawing card.*

ˈdrawing room *n.* [C] OLD-FASHIONED a room, especially in a large house, where you can entertain guests or relax

drawl /drɔl/ *n.* [singular] a way of speaking in which vowels are longer than normal: *a Texas drawl* —**drawl** *v.* [I,T]

drawn¹ /drɔn/ *v.* the past participle of DRAW

drawn² *adj.* someone who looks drawn has a thin pale face, usually because they are sick or worried

ˌdrawn-ˈout *adj.* taking more time than usual or more time than you would like: *Getting parents involved in schools is* ***a long drawn-out process***.

draw·string /ˈdrɔstrɪŋ/ *n.* [C] a string through the top of a bag, piece of clothing etc. that you can pull tight or make loose

dray /dreɪ/ *n.* [C] a flat CART with four wheels that was used in the past for carrying heavy loads, especially BARRELS of beer

dread¹ /drɛd/ *v.* [T] to feel anxious about or afraid of something, especially something in the future: *I was coming to dread my parents' visits.* | **dread doing sth** *I'm dreading going back to work.* | **dread the thought/prospect of (doing) sth** *He dreaded the prospect of being all alone in that house.* | ***I dread to think*** (=I do not want to think about it because I think it will be bad) *what might happen if he finds out.*

dread² *n.* **1** [U] strong fear of something, especially something in the future: *I felt a sense of dread as I walked into the interview.* | *The prospect of flying* ***filled me with dread***. **2 dreads** [plural] INFORMAL DREADLOCKS

dread·ed /ˈdrɛdɪd/ also **dread** LITERARY or HUMOROUS *adj.* [only before noun] making you feel anxious or afraid: *cancer and other dreaded diseases*

dread·ful /ˈdrɛdfəl/ *adj.* FORMAL very bad or very unpleasant: *a dreadful mistake* | *Michelle felt absolutely dreadful.*

dread·ful·ly /ˈdrɛdfəli/ *adv.* FORMAL **1** [+ adj./adv.] extremely: *I am dreadfully sorry for any damage I may have caused.* **2** very badly: *The team played dreadfully.*

dread·locks /ˈdrɛdlɑks/ *n.* [plural] hair that hangs in a lot of thick pieces that look like rope → see picture at HAIRSTYLE

dream¹ /drim/ S1 W2 *n.*

1 IMAGES WHILE SLEEPING [C] a series of thoughts, pictures, and feelings that you have when you are asleep: **+about** *a dream about work* | *I* ***had a*** *really weird* ***dream*** *last night.* | *Horror movies give me* ***bad dreams*** (=frightening dreams). | ***In*** *my* ***dream*** *I was flying.*

2 WISH [C] something you hope for and want to happen very much: *His dream was to be a professional ball player.* | **+of** *dreams of world travel* | *The store has succeeded* ***beyond*** *our* ***wildest dreams*** (=better than anything we hoped or imagined). | **fulfill/realize a dream** *She realized her lifelong dream of opening a little boutique.* | *In law school Stuart met the woman* ***of*** *his* ***dreams***.

3 a/sb's dream (come true) something that is perfect for someone, or something that they have wanted to happen for a long time: *The food festival is a pasta lover's dream come true.* | *Our evening together was so perfect – it was like a dream.*

4 OTHER THOUGHTS [C usually singular] a set of thoughts that make you forget about the things happening around you SYN **daydream**: *Ben seemed lost in a dream.*

5 a dream car/job/vacation etc. the best car, job etc. that you can imagine → see also AMERICAN DREAM, **pipe dream** at PIPE DREAM

SPOKEN PHRASES

6 be/live in a dream world to have ideas or hopes that are not practical or likely to happen: *If you think he'll change, you're living in a dream world.*

7 never in my wildest dreams used to say that you could not possibly have imagined or expected something: *Never in my wildest dreams did I expect him to apologize.*

8 in your dreams used to say in a rude way that something is not likely to happen: *"I can beat you, no problem." "Yeah, in your dreams."*

9 like a dream extremely well or effectively: *The new car drives like a dream.*

10 a dream OLD-FASHIONED, INFORMAL a very attractive person or thing: *Her latest boyfriend is an absolute dream.*

[**Origin:** Old English *dream* **noise, great happiness**]

dream² S3 W2 *v. past tense and past participle* **dreamed** or **dreamt** /drɛmt/ **1** [I,T] to have a dream while you are asleep: **+about** *I dreamt about her last night.* | **dream (that)** *I often dream that I'm falling.* **2** [I,T] to think about something that you would like to happen: **+of/about** *It was the kind of vacation I'd always dreamed about.* | **dream (that)** *I used to dream that someday I would be famous.* | *I* ***never dreamed*** *I'd end up living in L.A.* **3** [I,T] to imagine that you do, see, or hear something that you really do not: *I was sure I mailed the letter yesterday, but I must have dreamed it.* **4** to think about something else and not give your attention to what is happening around you SYN **daydream**: *I was dreaming and not listening to what she was saying.* **5 sb wouldn't dream of (doing) sth** SPOKEN used to say that you would never do something, because you do not approve of it or think it is bad: *I wouldn't dream of going without you!*

dream sth ↔ **away** *phr. v.* to waste time by thinking about what may happen: *Don't dream your life away!*

dream on *phr. v.* SPOKEN used to tell someone that

they are hoping for something that will not happen: *You think I'm going to help you move? Dream on!*

dream sth ↔ **up** *phr. v.* to think of a plan or idea, especially an unusual one: *Who dreams up these silly TV commercials?*

dream·boat /ˈdrimboʊt/ *n.* [C] INFORMAL, OLD-FASHIONED someone who is very good-looking and attractive

dream·er /ˈdrimɚ/ *n.* [C] **1** someone who has ideas or plans that are not practical: *She's a dreamer, not a realist.* **2** someone who dreams

dream·i·ly /ˈdriməli/ *adv.* thinking about pleasant things and not about what is actually happening: *She looked dreamily at the sky.*

D

dream·land /ˈdrimlænd/ *n.* [U] **1** a happy place or situation that exists only in your imagination **2** INFORMAL sleep: *Most of the kids were on their way to dreamland.*

dream·less /ˈdrimlɪs/ *adj.* dreamless sleep is very deep and peaceful

dream·like /ˈdrimlaɪk/ *adj.* as if happening or appearing in a dream: *The film had a dreamlike quality.*

dreamt /drɛmt/ *v.* a past tense and past participle of DREAM

dream·y /ˈdrimi/ *adj. comparative* **dreamier**, *superlative* **dreamiest** **1** pleasant, peaceful, and relaxing: *dreamy melodies* **2** having a quality like a dream: *The photos have a dreamy look.* **3** someone who is dreamy likes to imagine things: *a dreamy 14-year-old girl* **4** OLD-FASHIONED, INFORMAL very attractive and desirable: *a dreamy new sports car* —**dreaminess** *n.* [U]

drear·y /ˈdrɪri/ also **drear** /drɪr/ *adj. comparative* **drearier**, *superlative* **dreariest** LITERARY dull, uninteresting, and not cheerful: *dreary weather* [**Origin:** Old English *dreorig* **bloody, sad**]

dreck /drɛk/ *n.* [U] INFORMAL something that is of very bad quality: *There's just so much dreck on TV these days.* [**Origin:** 1900–2000 Yiddish *drek* **dirt, crap**]

dredge /drɛdʒ/ *v.* **1** [I,T] to remove mud or sand from the bottom of a river, HARBOR etc., or to search for something by doing this: *Fearing more floods, the state had the river dredged.* **2** [T] to cover food lightly with flour, sugar etc.

dredge sth ↔ **up** *phr. v.* **1** INFORMAL to start talking or thinking again about something that happened a long time ago, or to make people do this: *Why do the papers have to dredge up that old story?* **2** to pull something up from the bottom of a river: *Weapons crews dredged up the unexploded bombs.*

dredg·er /ˈdrɛdʒɚ/ also **dredge** *n.* [C] a machine or ship used for digging or removing mud and sand from the bottom of a river, HARBOR etc.

Dred Scott v. Sand·ford /ˌdrɛd ˌskɑt vɚsəs ˈsændfɚd/ also **the ˌDred ˈScott Case** HISTORY a U.S. Supreme Court decision made in 1857 that stated that SLAVES (=people owned by other people and forced to work for them) were not citizens and that living in a free state or area did not mean a slave was free. This decision is often given as an important cause of the Civil War.

dregs /drɛgz/ *n.* **1** [plural] small solid pieces in a liquid such as wine or coffee that sink to the bottom of the cup, bottle etc. **2 the dregs of society/humanity etc.** people that are considered by the person speaking to be the least important or useful in society

drei·del /ˈdreɪdl/ *n.* [C] a TOP (=toy that you spin) with a Hebrew letter on each of its four sides and a point at the bottom, used in a game played during Hanukkah

Drei·ser /ˈdraɪsɚ, -zɚ/, **The·o·dore** /ˈθiəˌdɔr/ (1871–1945) a U.S. writer of NOVELS

drench /drɛntʃ/ *v.* [T] to make something or someone completely wet: *He turned the hose on us and drenched us all.* [**Origin:** Old English *drencan*; related to *drink*] —**drenching** *adj.*

drenched /drɛntʃt/ *adj.* **1** completely wet: +**with/in** *I was drenched in sweat from mowing the lawn.* ▸see THESAURUS box at **wet**[1] **2** completely covered in something: +**in/with** *She was drenched in cheap perfume.* | **sun-drenched/syrup-drenched etc.** *Phoenix is a sun-drenched city of one million inhabitants.*

dress

He got dressed.

He put on a jacket.

He wore a dark suit.

dress[1] /drɛs/ S1 W2 *v.*

1 PUT ON CLOTHES [I,T] to put clothes on yourself SYN **get dressed**: *I dressed quickly.* | **dress yourself** *Patty's just learning to dress herself.* | +**for** *We went upstairs to dress for dinner.*

THESAURUS

get dressed to put on all your clothes: *Get dressed! It's almost time to leave for school!*
put on to put on a particular piece of clothing, jewelry etc.: *Wait – I just have to put my shoes on.*
dress up to put on more formal clothes than you usually wear, or to put on special clothes for fun: *We always used to dress up to go to church.* | *He dressed up as a pirate for the party.*
dress yourself to put on your clothes – used when this is difficult, because you are a child, sick, injured etc.: *He hurt his arm so badly that he can't dress himself.*
have sth on to be wearing a particular piece of clothing, jewelry etc.: *He had on a red tie and a gray jacket.*
wear to have clothes on your body, especially a particular piece of clothing or a particular style of clothing: *All visitors to the site must wear a protective helmet.* | *She always wears black.*

2 PUT CLOTHES ON SB [T] to put clothes on someone else: *Can you dress the kids while I make breakfast?* | **dress sb in sth** *She dressed him in a T-shirt and shorts.*

3 WEAR CLOTHES [I] to wear a particular kind of clothes SYN **be dressed**: *How do most of the people dress at your office?* | *Dress warmly – it's cold out.* | +**in** *She always dresses in black.* | +**as** *She decided to dress as an astronaut for the party.* | *He once taught a course in how to* ***dress for success*** (=dress in a way that will help you be successful in business).

4 WOUND/CUT ETC. [T] to put medicine and BANDAGES on a wound: *Clean the area thoroughly before dressing the wound.*

5 MAKE CLOTHES FOR SB [T] to make or choose clothes for someone: *The designer dressed some of the most famous people in Hollywood.*

6 MEAT/CHICKEN/FISH [T] to clean and prepare a dead

animal so that it is ready to cook or eat: *Ask Mom if she needs help dressing the turkey.*
7 VEGETABLES [T] to put a DRESSING, salt etc. onto a SALAD: *Dress the salad with lemon, olive oil, and a little black pepper.*
8 WINDOW [T] to put an attractive arrangement in a store window
9 HORSE [T] to brush a horse in order to make it clean
10 SOLDIERS [I,T] TECHNICAL to stand in a line, or to make soldiers do this
11 HAIR [T] FORMAL to arrange someone's hair into a special style

dress down *phr. v.* **1** to wear clothes that are more informal than you would usually wear: *Many offices dress down on Fridays.* **2 dress sb ↔ down** to speak angrily or severely to someone about something they have done wrong SYN **tell off**: *Carter had no problem dressing down his staff.* → see also DRESSING DOWN

dress up *phr. v.* **1 dress sb ↔ up** to wear special clothes, shoes etc. for fun, or to put such clothes on someone: **dress (sb) up as sb/sth** *We dressed the kids up as tigers for Halloween.* | **dress (sb) up in sth** *I keep a box of old clothes for the kids to dress up in.* **2** to wear clothes that are more formal than you would usually wear: *Do we have to dress up?* **3 dress sth up** to make something more interesting or attractive, often in a way that is slightly dishonest: **dress sth up with sth** *Buy simple cards and dress them up at home with glue and glitter.* | *To dress this up as an environmentally friendly tax is nonsense.*

dress² S2 W2 *n.* **1** [C] a piece of clothing worn by a woman or girl, that covers the top of her body and some or all of her legs: *Do you like my new dress?* | *a woman* ***in a*** *white* ***dress*** → see also SKIRT **2** [U] clothes for men or women of a particular type or for a particular occasion: **casual/informal/formal dress etc.** *Informal dress is not appropriate for this occasion.* | **evening/national etc. dress** *All of the dancers wore traditional Austrian dress.* [**Origin:** 1300–1400 Old French *dresser* **to arrange**, from Latin *directus* **straight**] ►see THESAURUS box at **clothes**

dress³ *adj.* [only before noun] **a dress shirt/dress shoes/dress pants etc.** clothes that are appropriate for formal occasions

dres·sage /drəˈsɑʒ, drɛ-/ *n.* [U] a competition in which a horse performs a complicated series of actions in answer to signals from its rider

ˈdress code *n.* [C] a set of rules for what you should wear for a particular situation: *More schools are starting strict dress codes.*

dressed /drɛst/ *adj.* **1 get dressed** to put your clothes on: *Rob got dressed in a hurry.* **2** having your clothes on, or wearing a particular type of clothes: *Aren't you dressed yet?* | **+in** *The marchers were all dressed in white.* | **+as** *He was dressed as a police officer.* | *Mrs. Russell is always* ***neatly dressed.*** | **half/fully dressed** (=with half or all of your clothes on) **3 dressed up** wearing more attractive or formal clothes than you would usually wear: *What are you doing all dressed up?* **4 dressed up** wearing a costume so that you look like a particular type of person, as a disguise or for fun: *He was dressed up as a cowboy.* **5 dressed to kill** INFORMAL wearing very attractive clothes so that everyone notices you: *In her black velvet cocktail dress, Elaine was dressed to kill.* **6 dressed to the nines** INFORMAL wearing your best or most formal clothes → see also WELL-DRESSED

dress·er /ˈdrɛsɚ/ *n.* [C] **1** a piece of furniture with drawers for storing clothes, sometimes with a mirror on top SYN **chest of drawers** **2 a fashionable/stylish/sloppy etc. dresser** someone who dresses in a fashionable, stylish etc. way: *Kendall is known as a sharp dresser.* **3** someone who takes care of someone's clothes and helps them dress, especially someone who helps an actor in the theater → see also HAIRDRESSER

dress·ing /ˈdrɛsɪŋ/ *n.* **1** [U] a mixture of liquids, often made from oil and VINEGAR, that you put on raw vegetables or SALAD → see also FRENCH DRESSING, SALAD DRESSING **2** [C,U] STUFFING **3** [C,U] MEDICINE a special piece of material used to cover and protect a wound: *Change the dressing twice a day.* → see also WINDOW DRESSING

dressing ˈdown *n.* [singular] an act of talking angrily to someone and criticizing them because they have done something wrong: *Dad* ***gave me a dressing down*** *for not calling sooner.*

ˈdressing gown *n.* [C] FORMAL a ROBE

ˈdressing room *n.* [C] **1** an area in a store where you can put on clothes to see how they look SYN **fitting room** **2** ENG. LANG. ARTS a room where an actor, performer, sports team etc. can get ready, before going on stage, appearing on television, playing a game etc. **3** a small room in some houses where you get dressed, put on MAKEUP etc.

D

ˈdressing ˌtable *n.* [C] a piece of furniture that you use when you are brushing your hair, putting on MAKEUP etc., that is like a table with a mirror on top and sometimes has drawers

dress·mak·er /ˈdrɛsˌmeɪkɚ/ *n.* [C] someone who makes clothes for other people as a job → see also SEAMSTRESS —**dressmaking** *n.* [U]

ˈdress reˌhearsal *n.* [C] the last time actors practice a play, OPERA etc., using all the clothes, objects etc. that will be used in the real performance

ˈdress ˌuniform *n.* [C,U] a uniform that officers in the army, navy etc. wear for formal occasions or ceremonies

ˈdress-up *n.* [U] a children's game in which they put on special clothes and pretend that they are someone else ►see THESAURUS box at **dress¹**

dress·y /ˈdrɛsi/ *adj. comparative* **dressier**, *superlative* **dressiest** **1** formal and fashionable: *a dressy silk suit* **2** someone who is dressy likes to wear very attractive or formal clothes: *Older customers are dressier than most teenagers.*

drew /dru/ *v.* the past tense of DRAW

drib·ble¹ /ˈdrɪbəl/ *v.* **1** [I,T] to have liquid or soft food come out of your mouth onto your face in a small stream: *Watch out – the baby's dribbling on your shirt!* **2** [I always + adv./prep.] if a liquid dribbles, it flows in a thin irregular stream: **+down/from/out etc.** *Sweat was dribbling down my face.* **3** [I,T] to move a ball or PUCK forward by bouncing (BOUNCE), kicking, or hitting it: *Mullin dribbled the ball down the floor.* **4** [I always +adv./prep.] if something such as money or news dribbles somewhere, it comes or goes in small irregular amounts: *Money is finally dribbling back into the country now.* **5** [T] to pour something out slowly in an irregular way: *She dribbled cream in her coffee.* [**Origin:** 1500–1600 *drib* **to fall in small drops**]

dribble² *n.* **1** [U] a small amount of liquid or soft food that has come out of your mouth **2** [C] a small amount of liquid: *The oil spill sent dribbles of tar onto beaches in New Jersey.* **3** [C] an act of bouncing (BOUNCE) or kicking a ball, or of hitting a PUCK to move it forward

dribs and drabs /ˌdrɪbz ən ˈdræbz/ *n.* [plural] **in dribs and drabs** in small irregular amounts or numbers over a period of time: *News of the accident is coming in in dribs and drabs.*

dried /draɪd/ *adj.* dried substances, such as food or flowers, have had the water removed

ˌdried ˈmilk *n.* [U] milk that is made into a powder and can be used by adding water

dri·er /ˈdraɪɚ/ *n.* [C] another spelling of DRYER

drift¹ /drɪft/ *v.* **1** [I] to be moved slowly and quietly through the air or on the surface of water: **+out/toward/along etc.** *The boat had drifted out to sea.* | *Black clouds of smoke drifted over the city.* **2** [I always + adv./prep.] to happen, change, or do something without any plan or purpose: **+around/along/by etc.** *Many of these kids will drift though life without any goals.* | *Another hour drifted by.* | **drift from sth to sth** *For five years he drifted from one job to another.* | **+into** *He had somehow drifted into an affair with a coworker.* **3** [I always + adv./prep.] to move or go somewhere without any plan or purpose: **+around/along/toward etc.** *Jenni spent the year drifting around Europe.* | **drift off/away** *The crowd of people slowly drifted away.* **4** [I] to gradually change from being in one condition, situation etc. into another: *All night Julie drifted in and out of consciousness.* | *His politics gradually drifted to the right.* **5** [I] if values, prices, STOCKS etc. drift, they gradually change: *The dollar drifted lower against the yen today.* **6** [I] if a sound or smell drifts somewhere, you notice it but it is not very loud or strong: *The scent of roses drifted through the windows.* **7** [I,T] if snow, sand etc. drifts, or if the wind drifts it, the wind blows it into large piles

D

drift apart *phr. v.* if people drift apart, their relationship gradually ends: *After college, we both got busy and just drifted apart.*

drift off *phr. v.* to gradually fall asleep, or to stop giving attention to something: *I kissed her goodnight as she* ***drifted off to sleep.***

drift² *n.* **1** [C] a large pile of snow, sand etc. that has been blown by the wind: *All the roads were blocked by snow drifts.* **2 catch/get the drift (of sth)** INFORMAL to understand the general meaning of what someone is saying: *I heard enough of the speech to get the drift of it.* | *She was very friendly to me –* ***if you catch my drift*** (=I hope you understand what I am trying to say). **3** [singular] a gradual change or development in a situation, people's opinion etc.: *The party has experienced a drift toward the right in the last two years.* **4** [U] very slow movement, especially movement caused by wind or water → see also CONTINENTAL DRIFT

drift·er /ˈdrɪftɚ/ *n.* [C] **1** someone who is always moving from one job or place to another **2** a fishing boat that uses a floating net

ˈdrift ice *n.* [U] pieces of broken ice floating in an ocean, river etc.

drift·wood /ˈdrɪftwʊd/ *n.* [U] wood floating in the ocean or left on the shore

drill¹ /drɪl/ *n.* **1** [C] a tool or machine used for making holes in something: *an electric drill* | *a dentist's drill* **2** [C] a method of teaching students, soldiers, sports players etc. something by making them repeat the same lesson, exercise etc. many times: *multiplication drills* | *a marching drill* **3 fire/emergency etc. drill** an occasion when you practice what you should do during a dangerous situation such as a fire **4 the drill** the usual expected way that something is done: ***You know the drill*** *– Christmas at my parents' and New Year's at Aunt Jill's.* **5** [U] a type of strong cotton cloth **6** [C] a machine for planting seeds in rows **7** [C] a row of seeds planted by machine, or the long narrow hole that they are planted in

drill² *v.* **1** [I,T] to make a hole in something using a drill: *The dentist started drilling, but I couldn't feel anything.* | *We'll have to* ***drill*** *some more* ***holes.*** | **+into/through** *We finally managed to drill through the wall.* | *Oil companies still* ***drill for oil*** (=make a hole in the earth to find oil) *off the coast here.* ▸see THESAURUS box at **hole¹**, **pierce** **2** [T] to teach students, soldiers, sports players etc. something by making them repeat the same exercise, lesson etc. many times: **drill sb in sth** *The game is designed to drill children in the letters of the alphabet.* | *Our flight crew is* ***well-drilled*** *in handling emergencies.* ▸see THESAURUS box at **practice²** **3** [T] to plant seeds in rows using a machine

drill sth **into** sb *phr. v.* to keep telling someone something until they know it very well: *Mom drilled it into my head that I should never talk to strangers.*

ˈdrilling ˌplatform *n.* [C] a large structure in the ocean used for drilling for oil, gas etc.

ˈdrill team *n.* [C] a team in a school, the army, navy etc. whose members perform together a series of complicated movements with their bodies or with pieces of equipment

dri·ly /ˈdraɪli/ *adv.* another spelling of DRYLY

drink¹ /drɪŋk/ [S1] [W1] *v. past tense* **drank** /dræŋk/, *past participle* **drunk** /drʌŋk/ **1** [I,T] to pour a liquid into your mouth and swallow it: *What do you want to drink?* | *Charlie drinks way too much coffee.* | **drink (sth) from sth** *He was drinking vodka straight from the bottle.* | *Do you want* ***something to drink?***

> **THESAURUS**
>
> **sip/take a sip** to drink something very slowly
> **slurp** INFORMAL to drink something in a noisy way
> **gulp sth down** also **down sth** INFORMAL to drink all of something very quickly: *I downed my beer and left.*
> **knock sth back** INFORMAL to drink all of an alcoholic drink very quickly
> **swig** INFORMAL also **take/have a swig** INFORMAL to drink something quickly by taking large amounts into your mouth, especially from a bottle: *He took a swig of his Coke.*
> → EAT

2 [I] to drink alcohol, especially too much or too often: *My parents don't drink.* | *You really shouldn't* ***drink and drive*** (=drive after you have drunk too much alcohol). | *He's been* ***drinking heavily*** *since his wife died.* | *Luke* ***drinks like a fish*** (=regularly drinks a lot of alcohol). | *Robin can* ***drink*** *any man* ***under the table*** (=drink more alcohol than them without becoming as drunk as them). | *The pressure of work* ***drove*** *him* ***to drink.*** **3 drink yourself unconscious/silly etc.** to drink so much alcohol that you become unconscious, silly etc.: *I'm going out tonight and drink myself silly.* [**Origin:** Old English *drincan*]

drink sth ↔ **in** *phr. v.* LITERARY to listen, look at, feel, or smell something in order to enjoy it: *From the balcony, I drank in the beauty of the valley below.*

drink to sth *phr. v.* **1** to have an alcoholic drink after wishing someone success, good luck, good health etc.: *Let's drink to the bride and groom.* **2 I'll drink to that!** SPOKEN used to agree with what someone has said

drink sth ↔ **up** *phr. v.* to finish drinking something, or to drink all of something: *Drink up – they're closing.* | *Drink up your milk, Kelsey.*

drink² [S2] [W2] *n.* **1** [C,U] liquid that you can drink, or an amount of liquid that you drink: *a drink of water* | *There will be plenty of food and drink available at the fair.* | **a hot/cold drink** *Would you like a cold drink?* | *Can I* ***have a drink, please?*** | *He* ***took a drink of*** *his coffee.* **2** [C,U] alcohol, or an alcoholic drink: *There's a nice bar nearby where we can* ***have a drink.*** | *We* ***went for a drink*** *after work.* | *Why don't we* ***meet for drinks*** *tomorrow?* **3 the drink** INFORMAL the ocean, a lake, or another large area of water: *The car rolled down the hill and ended up in the drink.* → see also SOFT DRINK, **a stiff drink/whiskey etc.** at STIFF¹ (6)

drink·a·ble /ˈdrɪŋkəbəl/ *adj.* **1** water that is drinkable is safe to drink [SYN] **potable** **2** wine, beer etc. that is drinkable is of good quality and tastes good

drink·er /ˈdrɪŋkɚ/ *n.* [C] **1** someone who regularly drinks alcohol, especially too much of it: *Greg's always been a* ***heavy drinker*** (=has always drunk a lot of alcohol). **2 a coffee/wine/beer etc. drinker** someone who regularly drinks coffee, wine, beer etc.

ˈdrinking ˌfountain *n.* [C] a piece of equipment in a public place that produces a stream of water for you to drink from [SYN] **water fountain**

ˈdrinking ˌwater *n.* [U] water that is pure enough for you to drink

drip¹ /drɪp/ *v.* **dripped, dripping** **1** [I] to fall in the shape of a small drop: **+down/from etc.** *Sweat was dripping off his forehead.* ▸see THESAURUS box at **flow¹** **2** [I,T] to let liquid fall in the shape of small drops: *The faucet's dripping again – you'd better call the plumber.* | *A cut on her hand was dripping blood.* | **be dripping with blood/water/sweat etc.** *Our clothes were dripping with sweat.* ▸see THESAURUS box at **pour** **3 be dripping with sth a)** to be filled with a strong emotion, or to show this emotion clearly: *Mulroy's voice was dripping with sarcasm.* **b)** to have, wear etc. a lot or too much of something: *As usual Ms. Vanderwegh arrived dripping with jewels.*

drip² *n.* **1** [C] one of the small drops of liquid that falls from something: *Before painting, lay a cloth on the floor to catch any drips.* **2** [singular, U] the sound or action of a liquid falling in very small drops: *the drip of rain from the roof* **3** [C] MEDICINE an IV **4** [C] INFORMAL someone who is boring and annoying

drip-'dry *adj.* drip-dry clothing can be hung up wet and dried without needing to be IRONed —**drip-dry** *v.* [I,T]

'drip irri,gation *n.* [U] a method used for supplying crops in hot dry areas with an exact amount of water by having drops of water fall directly onto plants from pipes

drip·ping /'drɪpɪŋ/ also **,dripping 'wet** *adj.* extremely wet: *Take off that jacket, you're* ***dripping wet.***

drip·pings /'drɪpɪŋz/ *n.* [plural] the oil and liquid that comes out of meat when you cook it

drip·py /'drɪpi/ *adj. comparative* **drippier**, *superlative* **drippiest** very emotional in a silly way: *The movie is nothing but a drippy melodrama.*

drive[1] /draɪv/ S1 W1 *v. past tense* **drove** /droʊv/, *past participle* **driven** /'drɪvən/

1 OPERATE A VEHICLE [I,T] to make a car, truck, bus etc. move and control where it goes: *I've never driven a truck before.* | *I* ***learned how to drive*** *when I was fifteen.* | **drive sth into/out of/through etc. sth** *She drove the car into the garage.*

THESAURUS

When you get into a car, you **buckle/fasten your seatbelt**, then put the key in the **ignition** and turn it to **start the engine**.
You **release** the **parking/emergency brake**, and put the car in **drive**. You **check your mirrors** (=look into them) before driving onto the street. You press the **gas pedal** with your foot to make the car **accelerate** (=go faster).
When you turn right or left, you must **indicate/put on your turn signals**. When you want to slow down, you press the **brake (pedal)** with your foot. When you **park** your car, you put the car **in park** and **set/put on the parking brake**.

2 TRAVEL SOMEWHERE [I] to travel somewhere in a car, truck etc.: *On our trip to Florida, I drove 300 miles in one day.* | **+to/from/into/back etc.** *Do you drive to work or go by bus?* | **+up/down/over to** *We're driving down to Chicago this weekend.* ►see THESAURUS box at **travel**[1]

3 TAKE SB SOMEWHERE [T] to take someone somewhere in a car, truck etc.: *Can you drive me to the airport next Friday?* | *I drove myself to the hospital.* | *Let me* ***drive*** *you* ***home.***

4 VEHICLE MOVES SOMEWHERE [I always + adv./prep.] if a car, truck, bus etc. drives somewhere, it goes there with someone driving it: **+into/out of/past etc.** *A strange car drove into the driveway.*

5 OWN A VEHICLE [T] to own a particular type of car, truck etc. and drive it regularly: *Jeff drives a green Volvo.*

6 FORCE SB/STH TO LEAVE [T] to force people, organizations, activities etc. to leave and go somewhere else: **drive sb/sth away/from/back etc.** *The floods drove many people from their homes.* | *Crime has driven many businesses out of the neighborhood.*

7 FORCE SB INTO A BAD STATE [T] to make someone get into a bad or extreme state or situation, usually an emotional one: **drive sb to (do) sth** *His financial losses drove him to suicide.* | *The noise* ***is driving*** *me* ***to distraction*** (=it's really annoying me). | *The thought of losing her business* ***drove*** *her* ***to despair*** (=made her lose all hope).

8 **drive sb crazy/nuts/insane etc.** to make someone feel very annoyed and angry: *I can't remember his name and it's driving me crazy.*

9 **drive sb crazy/wild** to make someone feel very sexually excited: *Her tight dresses drive all the guys wild.*

10 **sb/sth drives sb up the wall** also **sb/sth drives sb out of their mind** to make someone feel very annoyed and angry: *All that barking is driving me up the wall!*

11 MAKE SB DETERMINED [T] to make someone feel determined and want to work hard to succeed: *My love of competition is what drives me.* | *He was driven by a desire to improve himself.*

12 MAKE SB/STH WORK [T] to make someone or something work hard: **drive yourself** *Don't drive yourself too hard.*

13 HIT STH INTO STH [T] to hit something, such as a nail, into something else: **drive sth into sth** *Drive the nail downward into the wall.*

14 SPORTS [I,T] **a)** to move a ball or PUCK in a game of baseball, GOLF, HOCKEY etc. by hitting or kicking it hard and fast: *Bonds drove the ball into right field.* **b)** to run with the ball toward the GOAL in sports such as basketball or football

15 PROVIDE POWER [T] to provide the power for something: *The ship is driven by nuclear energy.*

16 MAKE ANIMALS MOVE [T] to make animals move somewhere by chasing them or hitting them: *The dog drives stray sheep back to the shepherd.*

17 RAIN/WIND ETC. [I always + adv./prep.] if rain, snow, wind etc. drives somewhere, it moves very quickly in that direction: *Snow drove against the windows.*

18 **drive a hard bargain** to demand a lot or refuse to give too much when making an agreement: *Well, you drive a hard bargain, but you've got yourself a deal.*

19 **drive sth home** to make something completely clear: *He showed us some pictures of the accident to drive his point home.*

20 **drive a wedge between sb/sth** to do something that makes people or groups disagree or start to dislike each other: *My husband says I'm trying to drive a wedge between him and his mother.*

[**Origin:** Old English *drifan*]

drive at sth *phr. v.* **what sb is driving at** the thing someone is really trying to say SYN **get at**: *She didn't mention the money, but I knew what she was driving at.*

drive sb/sth **away** *phr. v.* to make someone or something leave or stay away from someone or something: *His heavy drinking eventually drove Beth away.* | **+from** *Such strict laws drive drug addicts away from getting treatment.*

drive sth ↔ **down** *phr. v.* to make prices, costs etc. decrease OPP **drive up**: *The policy will likely drive down interest rates.*

drive sb/sth ↔ **in** *phr. v.* to hit the ball so that another player can SCORE a RUN in baseball

drive off *phr. v.* **1** if a driver or a car drives off, they leave: *After the accident, the other car just drove off.* **2** **drive sb/sth** ↔ **off** to force someone or something to go away from you: *The army used tear gas to drive off the rioting crowds.*

drive sb/sth ↔ **out** *phr. v.* to force someone or something to leave a place: *Cattle tend to drive out wild animals that eat the same grass.*

drive sth ↔ **up** *phr. v.* to make prices, costs etc. increase OPP **drive down**: *The war has driven up the price of oil.*

drive[2] S2 W2 *n.*

1 IN A CAR [C] a trip in a car: *It's only a 20-minute drive to the beach.* | *Let's* ***go for a drive*** *this afternoon.* | *He* ***took us for a drive*** *in his new car.*

2 EFFORT [C singular] an effort to achieve something, especially an effort by an organization for a particular purpose SYN **campaign**: *Union High School is holding a* ***blood drive*** (=an effort to collect blood) *on December 19.* | **+for** *The drive for civil rights is an on-going process.* | **a drive to do sth** *a drive to get more women into top jobs*

3 COMPUTERS [C] COMPUTERS a piece of equipment in a computer that is used to get information from a FLOPPY DISK, a CD-ROM etc. or to store information on it: *Put your disk in the "A" drive and click on "save."* → see also DISK DRIVE

4 NATURAL NEED [C] a strong natural need, such as the need for food, that people or animals must satisfy: *The male sex drive is not necessarily stronger than the female.*

5 DETERMINATION [U] determination and energy to suc-

ceed: *She certainly **has** a lot of **drive**.* | **drive to do sth** *Greg has the drive to become a good lawyer.*
6 ROAD [C] **a)** a road for cars and other vehicles, especially a beautiful one or one between another road and someone's house: *a long tree-lined drive* | *You can park in the drive.* **b) Drive** ABBREVIATION, **Dr.** used in the name of some streets: *We live on Crescent Drive.*
7 POWER [U] the power from an engine that makes the wheels of a car, bus etc. turn: *The pickup has four-wheel drive.*
8 BASEBALL/TENNIS ETC. [C] an act of hitting a ball hard, especially in baseball, tennis, soccer, or GOLF: *Griffey hit a long high drive to right field.*
9 MILITARY ATTACK [C] a series of military attacks: *They made a drive deep into enemy territory.*
10 ANIMALS [C] an act of bringing animals such as cows or sheep together and making them move in a particular direction: *a cattle drive*

D

ˌdrive-by ˈshooting also **ˈdrive-by** *n.* [C] a situation in which someone shoots someone else from a moving car

ˈdrive-in *n.* [C] **1** a place where you can watch movies outdoors while sitting in your car **2** a restaurant where you are served and eat in your car —**drive-in** *adj.* [only before noun]

driv•el /ˈdrɪvəl/ *n.* [U] something that is said or written that is stupid, silly, or does not mean anything: *Most of these essays are just full of drivel.* —**drivel** *v.* [I]

driv•en¹ /ˈdrɪvən/ *v.* the past participle of DRIVE

driven² *adj.* **1** trying extremely hard to achieve what you want: *John is a very driven young man.* **2** driven snow is snow that has been blown by the wind and is in piles → see also **as pure as the driven snow** at PURE (11)

driv•er /ˈdraɪvɚ/ S2 W2 *n.* [C] **1** someone who drives a car, bus etc.: *She's a very good driver.* | **a bus/taxi/truck/train etc. driver** *His dad is a taxi driver.*

THESAURUS
motorist WRITTEN someone who drives a car, usually their own car
chauffeur someone whose job is to drive someone else to places in a car

2 COMPUTERS a piece of computer SOFTWARE that makes a computer work with another piece of equipment such as a PRINTER or a MOUSE **3 in the driver's seat** in control of a situation: *The law would put big business back in the driver's seat.* **4** a GOLF CLUB with a wooden head → see also **back seat driver** at BACK SEAT (2), SLAVE DRIVER

ˌdriver's eduˈcation also **ˌdriver's ˈed** *n.* [U] a course that teaches you how to drive, which you usually take in high school

ˈdriver's ˌlicense *n.* [C] an official document or card that says you are legally allowed to drive, which has your name and address on it, and usually a picture of you

ˈdrive shaft *n.* [C] TECHNICAL a part of a car, truck etc. that takes power from the GEARBOX to the wheels

ˈdrive-through also **drive-thru** NONSTANDARD *adj.* [only before noun] a drive-through restaurant, bank etc. can be used without getting out of your car: *We'll just get a couple of burgers at the drive-through window.* —**drive-through** *n.* [C]

drive•way /ˈdraɪvweɪ/ S3 *n. plural* **driveways** [C] the area or road for cars between a house and the street

driv•ing /ˈdraɪvɪŋ/ *adj.* **1 driving rain/snow** rain or snow that falls very hard and fast **2 the driving force** someone or something that strongly influences people or situations and makes them do something or change: *Hawksworth was **the driving force behind** the project.* **3 driving ambition** a strong determination to succeed in something

ˈdriving range *n.* [C] an open outdoor area where people practice hitting GOLF balls

ˈdriving school *n.* [C] a business that teaches you to how to drive a car

ˈdriving test *n.* [C] the official test that you must pass in order to be legally allowed to drive

driz•zle¹ /ˈdrɪzəl/ *v.* **1 it drizzles** if it drizzles, light rain and mist come out of the sky: *It's been drizzling all day.* **2** [T] to let a liquid fall on something else in a small stream or small drops, or to cover something with a liquid in this way: *Drizzle chocolate sauce over the sliced bananas.*

drizzle² *n.* [singular, U] weather that is a combination of mist and light rain: *A light drizzle had started by the time we left.* ▸see THESAURUS box at **rain¹** —**drizzly** *adj.*

droll /droʊl/ *adj.* amusing in an unusual way —**drolly** *adv.* —**drollness** *n.* [U]

drom•e•dar•y /ˈdrɑməˌdɛri/ *n. plural* **dromedaries** [C] a CAMEL with one raised HUMP on its back

drone¹ /droʊn/ *v.* [I] **1** to make a continuous low noise: *A plane droned overhead.* **2** also **drone on** to speak in a boring way, usually for a long time: **+about** *Tom was droning on and on about work.*

drone² *n.* **1** [U] a continuous low noise: **+of** *the drone of the traffic* **2** [C] BIOLOGY a male BEE that does no work **3** [C] someone who does a lot of dull work without many rewards: *Shelby was one of the drones on the factory floor.* **4** [C] an airplane or piece of equipment that does not have a person inside it, but is operated by radio: *The police use high-tech radar drones to catch speeders.* **5** [C] someone who has a good life but does not work to earn it: *She was labeled a welfare drone.*

drool¹ /drul/ *v.* [I] **1** to have SALIVA (=the liquid in your mouth) come out of your mouth: *This stupid dog drools all over the place.* → see also DRIBBLE, SLOBBER **2** to show in a silly way that you like someone or something a lot: **+over** *Sarah was drooling over the lead singer through the whole concert.*

drool² *n.* [U] a flow of SALIVA (=the liquid in your mouth) that comes out of your mouth

droop /drup/ *v.* **1** [I,T] to hang or bend down, or to make something do this: *Can you water the plants? They're starting to droop.* | *His **eyelids** were beginning to **droop*** (=because he was sleepy). **2** [I] to become sad or weak: *Our spirits drooped as we faced the long trip home.* —**droop** *n.* [singular] —**droopy** *adj.*

drop¹ /drɑp/ S1 W1 *v.* **dropped, dropping**
1 LET STH FALL [T] **a)** to deliberately stop holding or carrying something, so that it falls: *Police ordered him to drop the gun.* | **drop sth into/onto/off etc. sth** *U.S. planes began dropping bombs on the city.* | *Liz dropped an ice cube into her drink.* **b)** to accidentally stop holding or carrying something, so that it falls: *Excuse me – I think you dropped your glove.*
2 FALL [I] to fall, especially from a high place: *The bottle rolled off the table and dropped to the floor.*
3 LOWER YOUR BODY [I always + adv./prep.,T] to lower yourself suddenly: **+to/into/down etc.** *The blow was so hard that he dropped to his knees.*
4 LOWER PART OF YOUR BODY [I,T] if part of your body drops or you drop it, it moves downward SYN **lower**: *He let his hand drop to his side.* | *Drop your head and roll it from side to side.* | **drop your eyes/gaze** *They dropped their eyes and pretended not to notice him.*
5 TAKE SB SOMEWHERE [T always + adv./prep.] to take someone to a place in a car when you are going on to another place SYN **drop off**: *I'll drop you at the corner, okay?*
6 DECREASE [I,T] to decrease to a lower level, amount, temperature etc., or to make something do this: *Stock prices **dropped sharply** Wednesday.* | *The major phone companies have all dropped their prices.* | **+to/from/by** *The temperature dropped to 50 below zero.* | **+below** *Wages have dropped below the national average.* ▸see THESAURUS box at **decrease¹**
7 STOP DOING STH [T] to stop doing something or stop planning to do something: *The proposal was later dropped.* | *You can't expect me to **drop everything*** (=stopped everything I'm doing) *whenever you're in town.* | *Police have **dropped charges** against Walters.*
8 MOVE TO A LOWER POSITION [I] to move to a lower

position in relation to someone or something else, especially in a competition: **+to/from** *Georgia dropped from 18th to 21st after losing to Virginia.*
9 LEAVE STH SOMEWHERE [T always + adv./prep.] to take something to a place and leave it there, especially when you are going on to another place SYN **drop off**: *You can drop your stuff at my place.*
10 STOP INCLUDING/USING [T] to decide not to include or use someone or something: **+drop sb/sth from sth** *Morris has been dropped from the team.*
11 STOP DISCUSSING [I,T] to stop talking about something, especially because it is upsetting someone: *Can we just* ***drop the subject****? | She didn't understand, so I* ***let it drop****. |* ***Drop it****, man. It's late and I'm tired.*
12 drop dead a) to die suddenly: *One day he just dropped dead in the street.* **b)** SPOKEN said when you are angry with someone to tell them rudely to stop annoying you, go away etc.
13 STOP STUDYING STH [T] to stop taking a course at a high school or college, or to stop studying a particular subject: *I think I'm going to drop one of my classes.*
14 LOSE WEIGHT [I,T] to lose a particular amount of weight: *I have to drop 25 pounds to fit in the costume.*
15 END A RELATIONSHIP [T] to stop having a relationship with someone, especially suddenly: *Marian has dropped all her old friends since she started college. | After a few dates, he* ***dropped*** *her* ***like a hot potato*** (=ended his relationship with her very suddenly).
16 work/run/shop etc. till you drop INFORMAL to do something until you are extremely tired
17 drop sb a line/note to write and send a short letter to someone: *Drop us a line sometime.*
18 drop a hint to say something in a way that is not direct: *I've dropped a few hints about what I want for my birthday.*
19 drop the ball to not do a job that you are expected to do, especially because you make mistakes: *Investigators dropped the ball in the murder investigation.*
20 AIRPLANE [T] to drop someone from an airplane with a PARACHUTE: *Soldiers were dropped behind enemy lines.*
21 drop your pants/trousers to pull down your pants, usually as a joke or to be rude
22 be dropping like flies INFORMAL used to say that a lot of people are dying or getting sick at the same time: *Players from both teams are dropping like flies.*
23 SLOPE [I always + adv./prep.] if a path, land etc. drops, it goes down suddenly, forming a steep slope: *The road crosses the highway and then drops down to the lake.*
24 NOT PRONOUNCE A LETTER [T] to not pronounce a particular sound: *Not all Southerners drop their r's.*
25 drop a bombshell INFORMAL to suddenly tell someone a shocking piece of news: *Last week Reynolds dropped the bombshell that she would resign.*
26 LOWER YOUR VOICE [I,T] if your voice drops, or if you drop it, you speak more quietly or lower: *She dropped her voice so Nick wouldn't hear.*
27 LOSE/SPEND MONEY [T] INFORMAL to lose money in business, a game etc., or to spend a lot of money on something: *Pearl dropped $600 at the casino.*
28 LOSE GAMES [T] to lose a point, game etc. in a sports competition
29 drop anchor to lower a boat's ANCHOR to the bottom of the ocean, lake etc. so that the boat stays in the same place
30 KNOCK SB DOWN [T] to hit someone so hard that they fall down SYN **knock down**: *Getz dropped McCallum with a right blow to the jaw.*
31 drop names to use the names of famous or important people in conversations to make yourself seem important
32 drop a stitch to let the YARN fall off the needle when you are KNITting
[**Origin:** Old English *droppian*]

drop back *phr. v.* to move backward, especially in football before throwing the ball: *Jeff dropped back to pass.*

drop by *phr. v.* to visit someone when you have not arranged to come at a particular time SYN **drop in** SYN **stop by**: *Doris and Ed dropped by on Saturday.*

drop behind *phr. v.* to move or make progress more slowly than other people or things, so that they move ahead of you SYN **fall behind**: *An hour into the hike, two of the boys had already dropped behind.*

drop in *phr. v.* to visit someone when you have not arranged to come at a particular time SYN **drop by** SYN **stop in**: **drop in on sb** *Every now and then I drop in on my brother Art.*

drop off *phr. v.* **1** to begin to sleep: *The baby* ***dropped off to sleep*** *in the car.* **2 drop sb/sth ↔ off** to take someone or something to a place in a car when you are going on to another place OPP **pick up**: *I'll drop you off on my way home.* **3** to become lower in level or amount: *Interest in the new movie soon dropped off.*

drop out *phr. v.* **1** to stop going to school or stop an activity before you have finished it: *The group gets smaller as members move away or drop out. |* **+of** *Kelly dropped out of college after one semester.* **2** to move away from or refuse to take part in society, because you do not agree with its principles **3** if a word or expression drops out of a language, it is not used anymore → see also DROPOUT

drop² S2 W3 *n.*
1 LIQUID [C] a very small amount of liquid that falls in a round shape: **+of** *Big drops of rain splashed on the sidewalk.* → see also TEARDROP
2 A SMALL AMOUNT [C] INFORMAL a small amount of liquid, especially an alcoholic drink: **+of** *a drop of whiskey*
3 drops [plural] medicine that you put in your eye, ear, nose etc. in drops: **eye/ear/nose etc. drops** *a bottle of eye drops*
4 DECREASE IN AMOUNT [singular] a decrease in the amount, level, or number of something SYN **fall**: **+in** *a sharp drop in temperature*
5 DISTANCE [singular] a distance from the top of something that is high to the bottom of it: *It's a 25-foot drop from this cliff.*
6 A FALL [C] a fall from a higher position to a lower position: *a sudden drop in the plane's altitude*
7 a drop in the bucket/ocean an amount of something that is too small to have any effect: *$5,000 is a drop in the bucket compared to the $14 million we need.*
8 at the drop of a hat at any time without preparation or warning: *He's ready to throw a party at the drop of a hat.*
9 DELIVER [C] an act of dropping or leaving something, such as food or medical supplies, especially from an airplane: *Air drops of food aid were made to the region yesterday.* → see also MAIL DROP
10 a lemon/chocolate/fruit etc. drop a small piece of candy that tastes like or is made of LEMON, chocolate, fruit etc. → see also COUGH DROP
11 drops [plural] special liquid medicine that you put in your eyes, ears, or nose in small drops → see also EAR DROPS, EYE DROPS
12 not touch a drop to not drink any alcohol at all: *I haven't touched a drop in years.*
[**Origin:** Old English *dropa*]

ˈdrop cloth *n.* [C] a large cloth for covering furniture, floors etc. in order to protect them from dust or paint

ˈdrop-dead *adv.* SPOKEN extremely: *drop-dead gorgeous*

ˈdrop-in *adj.* [only before noun] a drop-in place or time is a place where you can go or a time that you can go there without having to make arrangements first: *a drop-in counseling center*

ˈdrop kick *n.* [C] a kick made by dropping a ball and kicking it immediately —**drop-kick** *v.* [T]

drop·let /ˈdrɑplɪt/ *n.* [C] a very small drop of liquid

ˈdrop-off¹ *n.* [C] **1** a decrease in something SYN **drop**: *the recent drop-off in customers* **2** a place where the level of the land goes down sharply SYN **drop**: *a 50-foot drop-off* **3** the act of leaving or delivering someone or something somewhere: *airport parking for drop-off and pick-up* **4** a place where you leave something for someone else

drop-off² *adj.* [only before noun] a drop-off place or

container is a place where something can be left for someone else: *Local malls will set up drop-off bins for toys for needy kids.*

drop·out /ˈdrɑp-aʊt/ *n.* **1** [C] someone who leaves school or college before they have finished: *high-school dropouts* **2** [C] someone who refuses to be involved in ordinary society, because they do not agree with its social practices, moral standards etc. **3** [C,U] TECHNICAL a short loss of signal when an electronic machine is working

drop·per /ˈdrɑpɚ/ *n.* [C] a short glass tube with a hollow rubber part at one end, used for measuring liquid in drops

drop·pings /ˈdrɑpɪŋz/ *n.* [plural] solid waste from birds or other animals

ˈdrop shot *n.* [C] an action of hitting the ball very lightly in sports such as tennis so that it barely goes over the net

drop·sy /ˈdrɑpsi/ *n.* [U] OLD-FASHIONED, NOT TECHNICAL a medical condition in which liquid forms in parts of your body SYN **edema**

dross /drɑs, drɔs/ *n.* [U] **1** something of very bad quality **2** waste or useless substances, especially the waste separated from gold when gold is REFINED

drought /draʊt/ *n.* [C,U] a long period of dry weather when there is not enough water

drove¹ /droʊv/ *v.* the past tense of DRIVE

drove² *n.* **1** [C] a group of animals that are being moved together **2 droves** [plural] a large crowd of people or animals: *The sunny weather has brought out boaters* ***in droves.***

drov·er /ˈdroʊvɚ/ *n.* [C] someone who moves cattle or sheep from one place to another in groups

drown /draʊn/ *v.* **1** [I,T] to die from being under water for too long, or to kill someone in this way: *He nearly drowned before friends rescued him.* | *The floods drowned scores of livestock.* **2** [T] to cover something completely with liquid: **drown sth in/with sth** *The beef was drowned in gravy.* **3 drown your sorrows** to drink a lot of alcohol in order to forget your problems —**drowning** *n.* [C,U]

drown in sth *phr. v.* to have so much of something bad that it is almost impossible to deal with, or to put someone in this situation: *The country is drowning in debt.*

drown sb/sth ↔ **out** *phr. v.* to prevent a sound from being heard by making a loud noise or sound: *His voice was drowned out by the traffic.*

drowse /draʊz/ *v.* [I] to be in a light sleep: *We were content to drowse in the warm sunlight on the beach.*

drows·y /ˈdraʊzi/ *adj. comparative* **drowsier**, *superlative* **drowsiest** **1** tired and almost asleep, sometimes because you have eaten, taken drugs, or because you are in a warm place: *Cold medicines can make you feel drowsy.* **2** so peaceful that you feel relaxed and sleepy: *a drowsy rice-farming village* —**drowsily** *adv.* —**drowsiness** *n.* [U]

drub·bing /ˈdrʌbɪŋ/ *n.* [C] INFORMAL **1** an occasion when something or someone is criticized a lot: *Taylor's latest movie has* ***taken a drubbing*** *from the critics.* **2** an occasion when one team easily beats another team in a game —**drub** *v.* [T]

drudge /drʌdʒ/ *n.* [C] someone who does hard boring work —**drudge** *v.* [I]

drudg·er·y /ˈdrʌdʒəri/ *n.* [U] hard boring work: *the endless drudgery of housework*

drug¹ /drʌg/ S1 W1 *n.* [C] **1 a)** an illegal chemical substance that people take, smoke, INJECT etc. for pleasure: *Four teenagers were arrested for selling drugs.* | **take/use/do drugs** *My cousin's been using drugs for years.* | *Look for signs that your child may be* ***on drugs*** (=using drugs). | ***illegal drugs*** *such as heroin and cocaine* | *drug smuggling* **b)** a chemical substance that people take in order to illegally improve their ability to do sports: *performance-enhancing drugs* | *a drug test* **c)** any chemical substance that you can take to affect your mind, mood, or body: *Alcohol and nicotine are drugs.* **2** MEDICINE a medicine or a substance for making medicines: +**for** *a drug for treating allergies* | *Did the doctor* ***prescribe*** *any* ***drugs****?* [**Origin:** 1300–1400 Old French *drogue*] ►see THESAURUS box at **medicine** → see also DESIGNER DRUG, DRUG ABUSE

drug² *v.* **drugged**, **drugging** [T] **1** to give a person or animal a drug, especially in order to make feel them tired or go to sleep: *He usually drugged his victims first.* **2** to add drugs to someone's food or drink to make them feel tired or go to sleep: *The wine had been drugged.* —**drugged** *adj.*

drug³ *v.* NONSTANDARD a past tense and past participle of DRAG

ˈdrug aˌbuse *n.* [U] the use of illegal drugs, or the use of other drugs in way that is not good for you

ˈdrug ˌaddict *n.* [C] someone who cannot stop taking drugs, especially illegal drugs —**drug addiction** *n.* [U]

ˈdrug czar *n.* [C] a government official of very high rank whose job is to try to stop the illegal drug trade

ˈdrug ˌdealer *n.* [C] someone who sells illegal drugs

ˌDrug Enˈforcement Adminiˌstration, the a U.S. government organization which makes sure that people and companies obey the laws about dangerous drugs

ˌdrugged-ˈout *adj.* INFORMAL using drugs a lot or being influenced by drugs: *a drugged-out hippie*

drug·get /ˈdrʌgɪt/ *n.* [C,U] rough heavy cloth used especially as a floor covering, or a piece of this material

drug·gie /ˈdrʌgi/ *n.* [C] INFORMAL someone who often takes illegal drugs

drug·gist /ˈdrʌgɪst/ *n.* [C] OLD-FASHIONED a PHARMACIST

ˈdrug lord *n.* [C] someone who leads an organization that sells large quantities of illegal drugs

ˈdrug rehabiliˌtation also **ˈdrug ˌrehab** *n.* [U] the process of helping someone to live without drugs after they have been ADDICTED to them

ˈdrug ˌrunner *n.* [C] someone who brings illegal drugs from one country to another

drug·store /ˈdrʌgstɔr/ *n.* [C] a store where you can buy medicine, beauty products etc. SYN **pharmacy**

dru·id, Druid /ˈdruɪd/ *n.* [C] a member of an ancient Celtic group of priests, in Great Britain, Ireland, and France, before the Christian religion, or a member of the modern religious group with similar beliefs [**Origin:** 1500–1600 Latin *druides*, from Gaulish; related to *tree*] —**Druidism** *n.* [U]

drum

drum¹ /drʌm/ S3 *n.* [C] **1** ENG. LANG. ARTS a musical instrument with a skin stretched over a circular frame, that you play by hitting it with your hand or a stick: *a snare drum* | *Who's* ***on drums*** (=playing the drums) *tonight?* | **play (the) drums** *Jones quit school to play drums with a band.* | *Protestors* ***beat drums*** *and carried signs.* **2** a large round container for storing liquids such as oil, chemicals etc.: *an oil drum* | *a 50-gallon drum of paint thinner* → see picture at CONTAINER **3** something that looks like a drum, especially part of a machine: *brake drums* **4** the low continuous sound of something hitting something else again and a again: *the drum of horses' hooves* → see also **beat sb like a drum** at BEAT¹ (22), **beat the drum for sb/sth** at BEAT¹ (21), DRUM ROLL

drum² *v.* **drummed**, **drumming** **1** [I] ENG. LANG. ARTS to play a drum **2** [I,T] to hit something again and again in a way that sounds like a drum: *Rain drummed on the windows.* | *He* ***drummed his fingers*** (=hit lightly with his fingers) *on the wood box a few times.*

drum sth **into** sb *phr. v.* to keep telling someone

something until they cannot forget it SYN **drill into**: *Patriotism was drummed into us at school.*

drum sb **out of** sth *phr. v.* to force someone to leave an organization: *He was drummed out of football for writing a very revealing book.*

drum sth **up** *phr. v.* to make an effort to obtain something such as support or business: *We've been working hard to drum up business on the East Coast.*

drum·beat /ˈdrʌmbit/ *n.* [C] the sound made by hitting a drum

ˈdrum brake *n.* [C usually plural] a system used for stopping a vehicle which uses two BRAKE SHOES that press against a metal CYLINDER that looks like a drum

ˌdrum ˈmajor *n.* [C] the leader of a MARCHING BAND

ˌdrum majorˈette *n.* [C] a MAJORETTE

drum·mer /ˈdrʌmɚ/ *n.* [C] someone who plays drums

drum·ming /ˈdrʌmɪŋ/ *n.* [U] the act of playing a drum or the sound a drum makes

ˈdrum roll *n.* [C] a quick continuous beating of a drum, usually used to introduce an important event

drum·stick /ˈdrʌmˌstɪk/ *n.* [C] **1** the leg of a chicken or other bird, cooked as food **2** ENG. LANG. ARTS a stick that you use to hit a drum

drunk[1] /drʌŋk/ *v.* the past participle of DRINK

drunk[2] *adj.* **1** [not before noun] unable to control your behavior, speech etc. because you have drunk too much alcohol: *He gets in fights when he's drunk.* | *One of the salesman* ***got drunk*** *while entertaining clients.* | *Michael's* ***drunk as a skunk*** (=very drunk). **2 drunk and disorderly** LAW the crime of behaving in a violent noisy way in a public place when you are drunk **3 drunk on/with sth** so excited by a feeling that you behave in a strange way: *We were drunk with freedom.* → see also DRUNKEN, PUNCH-DRUNK, **roaring drunk** at ROARING (3), SOBER[1] (1)

drunk[3] also **drunk·ard** /ˈdrʌŋkɚd/ *n.* [C] someone who is drunk or often gets drunk → see also ALCOHOLIC

ˈdrunk ˌdriver also **ˌdrunken ˈdriver** *n.* [C] someone who illegally drives while drunk on alcohol

drunk·driv·ing /ˌdrʌŋkˈdraɪvɪŋ/ also **ˌdrunken ˈdriving** *n.* [U] the crime of driving a car after having drunk too much alcohol —**drunk-driving** *adj.*: *a drunk-driving accident*

drunk·en /ˈdrʌŋkən/ *adj.* [only before noun] **1** drunk, or showing that you are drunk: *A drunken teenager was arrested for vandalism.* | *a drunken rage* **2 a drunken party/brawl/orgy etc.** a party, brawl, orgy etc. at or in which people are drunk: *Two men were killed in a drunken brawl inside a cafe.* —**drunkenly** *adv.* —**drunkenness** *n.* [U]

ˈdrunk tank *n.* [C] INFORMAL a room in a prison for people who have drunk too much alcohol

druth·ers /ˈdrʌðɚz/ *n.* **if I had my druthers...** also **given my druthers...** SPOKEN used to say what you would wish if you could have whatever you wanted: *If I had my druthers, I wouldn't even take the trip.*

Druze, Druse /druz/ *n. plural* **Druze** [C] a member of a group of people in Syria, Lebanon, and Israel whose religion includes features from Islam, Christianity, and Judaism —**Druze** *adj.*

dry[1] /draɪ/ S2 W2 *adj. comparative* **drier**, *superlative* **driest**

1 NOT WET having no water or liquid inside or on the surface OPP **wet**: *Are the clothes dry yet?* | *Store disks in a dry place.* | *Wait until the paint is completely dry.* | **wipe/shake/rub etc. sth dry** *Pat the lettuce dry with a paper towel.* | *The ground was* ***as dry as a bone*** (=very dry).

2 WEATHER having very little rain or MOISTURE: *The weather tomorrow will be sunny and dry.* | *a dry winter* | *The recent* ***dry spell*** *has led to water shortages.*

3 MOUTH, SKIN, LIPS ETC. not having enough of the normal liquid or MOISTURE that is usually in your mouth, skin etc.: *His mouth was dry, and he swallowed nervously.* | *a shampoo for dry hair*

4 FOOD dry food does not have much liquid such as fat or juice in it OPP **moist**: *The chicken was dry and tough.*

5 dry wit/humor also **a dry sense of humor** someone with a dry sense of humor pretends to be serious when they are really joking: *We all enjoy Mike's dry wit.* → see also DRYLY

6 BORING someone or something such as a movie or book that is dry is boring and too serious: *a dry and uninteresting subject*

7 dry wine/sherry etc. wine, sherry etc. that is not sweet: *I prefer a dry white wine with fish dishes.*

8 a dry cough a cough that does not produce any PHLEGM

9 run/go dry if a lake, river etc. runs dry, all the water gradually disappears, especially because there has been no rain: *The reservoir ran dry during the drought.*

10 dry toast TOASTed bread that does not have butter or JAM on it

11 not a dry eye in the house used to say that everyone was crying because something was very sad: *There wasn't a dry eye in the house after Marvin finished his speech.*

12 dry land land rather than water: *After three weeks at sea we were glad to be back on dry land again.*

13 the dry heaves the action of continuing to VOMIT even though nothing comes out through your mouth anymore

14 TOWN/COUNTY not allowing any alcohol to be sold there: *Conway is in a dry county.*

[**Origin:** Old English *dryge*] —**dryness** *n.* [U] → see also DRIP-DRY

dry[2] S2 W3 *v.* **dries, dried, drying** [I,T] **1** to become dry, or to make something dry: *Let the glue dry for at least an hour.* | *It'll only take a few minutes to dry my hair.* **2** to rub plates, dishes etc. with a cloth until they are dry after you have washed them: *You wash and I'll dry.* ▸see THESAURUS box at **clean**[2] → see also CUT AND DRIED, DRIED

dry off *phr. v.* **dry sb/sth ↔ off** to become dry, or to make something dry, especially on the surface: *The best time to moisturize the skin is after you shower and dry off.* | *He dried his bicycle seat off with a towel.*

dry out *phr. v.* **1 dry sth ↔ out** to become completely dry or make something completely dry after it has been very wet: *Farmers now have to wait for fields to dry out.* | *Hang your towel over the chair to dry it out.* **2 dry sb out** to stop drinking alcohol after you have become an ALCOHOLIC, or to help someone do this: *Miller spent a month drying out at the Betty Ford Center.*

dry up *phr. v.* **1 dry sth ↔ up** if something dries up or is dried up, it stops having liquid in it or on it: *The river dried up completely that summer.* **2** if supplies or money dry up, they come to an end and there is no more available: *After a few months the work dried up.*

dry·ad /ˈdraɪæd, -əd/ *n.* [C] a female spirit who lives in a tree, in ancient Greek stories

ˈdry ˌbattery also **ˈdry cell** *n.* [C] PHYSICS an electric BATTERY in which the substance through which the electricity passes is a slightly wet solid

ˌdry-ˈclean, dry clean *v.* [T] to clean clothes, BLANKETS etc. with chemicals instead of water

ˈdry ˌcleaners *n.* [C] a store where you can take clothes to be dry-cleaned

Dry·den /ˈdraɪdn/, **John** (1631–1700) an English writer of poetry and plays

ˈdry dock *n.* [C] a place where a ship can be taken out of the water for repairs

dry·er /ˈdraɪɚ/ S3 *n.* [C] a machine that dries things, especially clothes

ˌdry-ˈeyed *adj.* not crying

ˌdry ˈfarming *n.* [U] a farming method in dry areas in which crops that do not need much water are planted and MULCH is used to keep water in the soil, so that farmers do not need to water the plants

ˈdry goods *n.* [plural] things that are made from cloth, such as clothes, sheets, and curtains: *a dry goods store*

ˌ**dry ˈice** *n.* [U] CARBON DIOXIDE in a solid form, often used to keep food and other things cold or used to make mist in a theater or NIGHTCLUB

dry·ly, drily /ˈdraɪli/ *adv.* speaking seriously, although you are really joking: *"I hear you're a hero," Philip said dryly.*

ˌ**dry ˈmeasure** *n.* [U] a system of measuring the VOLUME, instead of the weight, of things such as grain, fruit, and vegetables → see also BUSHEL, PECK² (3)

ˌ**dry ˈrot** *n.* [U] a disease in wood that turns it into powder

ˌ**dry ˈrun** *n.* [C] an event that you use as a way of practicing for a more important event: *a dry run for the debate*

D

ˌ**dry-ˈshod** *adv.* LITERARY without getting your feet wet

dry·wall /ˈdraɪwɔl/ *n.* [U] a type of board made of two large sheets of CARDBOARD with PLASTER between them, used to cover walls and ceilings —**dry-wall** *v.* [I,T]

DST /ˌdi ɛs ˈti/ *n.* [U] the abbreviation of DAYLIGHT SAVING TIME

DTP /ˌdi ti ˈpi/ *n.* [U] **1** MEDICINE DPT **2** the abbreviation of DESKTOP PUBLISHING

DT's /ˌdi ˈtiz/ *n.* **the DT's** HUMOROUS DELIRIUM TREMENS

du·al /ˈduəl/ *adj.* [only before noun] having parts, qualities etc. at the same time: **a dual role/purpose/function** *The bridge has a dual role, carrying both cars and trains.* | **dual nationality/citizenship** (=the state of being a citizen of two countries at the same time) —**duality** /duˈæləti/ *n.* [U]

dub /dʌb/ *v.* **dubbed, dubbing** [T] **1** [usually passive] to give something or someone a humorous name that describes their character: *The body found in the Alps was dubbed "the Iceman."* **2** ENG. LANG. ARTS to replace the original sound recording of a movie, television show etc. with another sound recording, especially in another language: **dub sth into sth** *Most martial arts movies are poorly dubbed into English.* **3** to copy a recording from a tape or CD to another tape or CD **4** LITERARY if a king or queen dubs someone, they give the title of KNIGHT to that person in a special ceremony

du·bi·e·ty /duˈbaɪəti/ *n.* [U] FORMAL a feeling of doubt

du·bi·ous /ˈdubiəs/ *adj.* **1** probably not honest, true, or right: *dubious accounting practices* **2** probably not good or not of good quality: *The room was decorated in dubious taste.* **3** [not before noun] not sure whether something is good or true SYN **doubtful**: **+about** *Many people are dubious about whether the airport will ever be built.* **4 the dubious honor/distinction/pleasure etc. (of doing sth)** something that is actually bad or the opposite of an honor etc.: *He had the dubious distinction of having the worst voting record in the Senate.* [**Origin:** 1500–1600 Latin *dubius*, from *dubare* to be unable to decide] —**dubiously** *adv.* —**dubiousness** *n.* [U]

Dub·lin /ˈdʌblɪn/ the capital and largest city of the Republic of Ireland

Du Bois /duˈbɔɪs/, **W.E.B.** (1868–1963) an African-American writer and educator who helped to start the NAACP

du·cal /ˈdukəl/ *adj.* relating or belonging to a DUKE

duc·at /ˈdʌkət/ *n.* [C] a gold coin that was used in several European countries in the past

Du·champ /duˈʃɑmp/, **Mar·cel** /mɑrˈsɛl/ (1887–1968) a French PAINTER famous for his work in the style of Cubism and Dadaism

duch·ess /ˈdʌtʃɪs/ *n.* [C] a woman with the highest social rank below a PRINCESS, or the wife of a DUKE

duch·y /ˈdʌtʃi/ *n. plural* **duchies** [C] the land and property of a DUKE or DUCHESS SYN **dukedom**

duck¹ /dʌk/ S3 W3 *n.* **1** [C] BIOLOGY a common water bird with short legs and a wide beak: *We went to the pond to feed the ducks.* **2** [C] BIOLOGY a female duck → see also DRAKE **3** [U] the meat of this bird used as food: *roast duck* [**Origin:** Old English *duce*] → see also **a dead duck** at DEAD¹ (20), LAME DUCK, **take to sth like a duck to water** at TAKE TO (4), **like water off a duck's back** at WATER¹ (8)

duck² *v.* **1** [I,T] to lower your head or body very quickly, especially to avoid being seen or hit: *If she hadn't ducked, the ball would have hit her.* | **+under** *The children quickly ducked under their desks.* | *Lewis* ***ducked his head*** *to avoid the ball.* **2** [I] to go quickly into or behind something, especially to avoid being seen or to get away from someone: **+into** *The three men ducked into a subway entrance and disappeared.* **3** [I] to visit a place, especially for only a short time: **+into** *She ducked into a drugstore to buy a pair of sunglasses.* **4** [T] to try to avoid something, especially a difficult duty or something that you do not want to do: *Benson* ***ducked a question*** *about his involvement in the bank scandal.* **5** [T] OLD-FASHIONED to push someone or something under the water SYN **dunk**

duck out *phr. v.* INFORMAL **1** to avoid doing something that you have to do or have promised to do: **+of/on** *You can't duck out on your promise now.* **2** to leave quickly, especially without anyone noticing: **+of** *He ducked out of the meeting early.*

duck-billed plat·y·pus /ˌdʌkbɪld ˈplætəpʊs, -pəs/ *n.* [C] a PLATYPUS

duck·boards /ˈdʌkbɔrdz/ *n.* [plural] long narrow boards that you use to make a path over muddy ground

ˈ**ducking stool** *n.* [C] HISTORY a seat on the end of a long pole, used to DUCK a person in water as a punishment in the past

duck·ling /ˈdʌklɪŋ/ *n.* [C] a small young duck

duck·weed /ˈdʌkwid/ *n.* [U] a plant that grows on the surface of fresh water

duck·y¹ /ˈdʌki/ *n. plural* **duckies** [C] INFORMAL a word meaning a duck, used especially when speaking to children: *a rubber ducky for the bathtub*

ducky² *adj.* OLD-FASHIONED perfect or satisfactory

duct /dʌkt/ *n.* [C] **1** SCIENCE a pipe or tube for carrying liquids, air, CABLES etc.: *a heating duct* **2** BIOLOGY a thin narrow tube that carries air, liquid etc. inside your body, in a plant etc.: *tear ducts*

duc·tile /ˈdʌktl, -taɪl/ *adj.* ductile substances can be pressed or pulled into shape without breaking —**ductility** /dʌkˈtɪləti/ *n.* [U]

duct·less gland /ˌdʌktlɪs ˈglænd/ *n.* [C] an ENDOCRINE GLAND

ˈ**duct tape** *n.* [U] a silver-gray cloth TAPE that is used for repairs in a house such as PLUMBING

dud /dʌd/ *n.* [C] INFORMAL **1** something that is useless, especially because it does not work correctly: *Several of the bombs were duds.* **2** a person, movie, book etc. that is not interesting, entertaining, or successful —**dud** *adj.* → see also DUDS

dude /dud/ S1 *n.* [C] **1** SLANG used as a way of speaking to someone, especially a man: *Dude, look at that car!* **2** SLANG a man: *Who's that dude over there?* **3** OLD-FASHIONED a man from a city, who is living in or visiting the COUNTRYSIDE, especially a RANCH

ˈ**dude ranch** *n.* [C] a vacation place where you can ride horses and live like a COWBOY

dudg·eon /ˈdʌdʒən/ *n.* **in high dudgeon** FORMAL angry because someone has treated you badly: *Simons left the interview in high dudgeon.*

duds /dʌdz/ *n.* [plural] OLD-FASHIONED clothes

due¹ /du/ S2 W2 *adj.* [no comparative]

1 be due a) to be expected to happen or arrive at a certain time or date: *When is your baby due* (=expected to be born)? | *The bus is due any minute now.* | **+at/on etc.** *The flight from Chicago is due at 6:30 p.m.* | **+for** *The video is due for release in July.* | **be due to do sth** *The theme park is due to open next year.* | **be due back/out/in etc.** *Mike is due back today.* **b)** to need to be paid or given on a particular date: **+at/on/by etc.** *The next payment is due on Friday.* | *My library books aren't due until next week.*

2 due to sth because of: *Her success is due to her hard work.* | *Our flight was delayed due to fog.* | *The fall in* *population is **due largely to** a drop in the birthrate.* | *Our failure was **due in part to** bad management.*

3 be due for sth if someone or something is due for something, they should have it now because a lot of time has passed since the last one they had: *You're about due for a raise, aren't you?*

4 OWED [not before noun] owed to someone either as a debt or because they have a right to it: *Please send the amount due immediately.* | *He gives praise when it's due.* | +**to** *After he was fired, the company failed to pay him the commissions due to him.*

5 with (all) due respect (to sb) SPOKEN used when you disagree with someone or criticize them in a polite way: *With all due respect, that's not really relevant.*

6 in due time/course at some time in the future when it is the right time, especially after a process has been completed: *The results of the survey will be published in due time.*

7 APPROPRIATE [only before noun] FORMAL appropriate or correct: *The community association must use **due care** to make responsible decisions.* | *They acted without **due regard** for the needs of patients.*

[**Origin:** 1200–1300 Old French *deu* **owed**, past participle of *devoir* **to owe**, from Latin *debere*] → see also DULY

due² *adv.* **due north/south/east/west** directly or exactly north, south, east, or west: *The storm was 150 miles due east of New York City.*

due³ *n.* **1 sb's due** things such as respect, money, justice etc. that someone deserves: *Women composers rarely **get their due**.* **2 dues** [plural] regular payments you make to an organization of which you are a member: *They **pay** union **dues** of about $8 a week.* → see also **pay your dues** at PAY¹ (16) **3 give sb his/her due** to admit that someone has good qualities even though you often criticize them: *Let's give the man his due – he's very good at turning a profit.* → see also **give the devil his due** at DEVIL (13)

ˌdue ˈdate *n.* [usually singular] **1** the date on which a baby is expected to be born, which is calculated by a doctor **2** a DEADLINE

ˌdue ˈdiligence *n.* [U] LAW a legal standard that is used to judge whether someone tried hard enough to avoid harming another person or their property, for example in a business deal: *Before a company can sell its stock on the stock market, it must **do due diligence** to make sure that all its financial matters are in order.*

du·el¹ /ˈduəl/ *n.* [C] **1** a fight with weapons between two people, used in past times to settle an argument: *The officer challenged him to a duel.* **2** a situation in which two ATHLETES or teams compete very hard against each other: *The World Cup final has been called "the duel of the champions."* **3** a situation in which two people or groups are involved in an angry disagreement: *a verbal duel between representatives of the two companies*

duel² *v.* **dueled, dueling** also **duelled, duelling** [I + with] to fight a duel

ˌdue ˈprocess also **due ˌprocess of ˈlaw** *n.* [U] LAW the correct process that should be followed in law and that is designed to protect someone's legal rights

du·et /duˈɛt/ *n.* [C] a piece of music for two performers → see also QUARTET, SOLO¹ (1), TRIO (3)

duff /dʌf/ *n.* [C usually singular] INFORMAL **1 get off your duff** used to say that someone should stop being lazy and start doing something: *Tell him to get off his duff and get a job!* **2** your BUTTOCKS

duf·fel bag, duffle bag /ˈdʌfəl ˌbæg/ *n.* [C] a cloth bag with a round bottom and a string at the top to tie it closed

duffel coat, duffle coat /ˈdʌfəl ˌkoʊt/ *n.* [C] a coat made of rough heavy cloth, usually with a HOOD and TOGGLES (=a type of long button)

duff·er /ˈdʌfɚ/ *n.* [C] **1** INFORMAL someone who plays GOLF fairly badly **2 old duffer** INFORMAL an old man who cannot think clearly anymore **3** OLD-FASHIONED someone who is stupid or not very good at something

dug /dʌg/ *v.* the past tense and past participle of DIG

dug·out /ˈdʌgaʊt/ *n.* [C] **1** a low shelter at the side of a sports field, especially a baseball field, where players and COACHes sit **2** also **dugout canoe** a small boat made by cutting out a hollow space in a tree TRUNK

duh /dʌ/ also **no duh** *interjection* INFORMAL used to say that what someone else has just said or asked is stupid or unnecessary because it is very easy to understand: *"You mean I can't park there?" "Duh, that's what the big sign says."*

DUI /ˌdi yu ˈaɪ/ *n.* [C,U] **driving under the influence** the crime of driving when you have drunk too much alcohol

du jour /du ˈʒʊr, də ˈʒɚ/ *adj.* [only after noun] used in restaurants to show that a dish is not part of the usual MENU but has been specially made for that day: *soup du jour*

duke¹ /duk/ *n.* [C] **1** a man with the highest social rank below a PRINCE: *the Duke of Norfolk* → see also DUCHESS **2 put up your dukes** INFORMAL to hold up your FISTS to get ready to fight [**Origin:** 1100–1200 Old French *duc*, from Latin *dux* **leader**]

duke² *v.* INFORMAL **duke it out (with sb)** to fight or compete: *The teams are duking it out for first place.*

duke·dom /ˈdukdəm/ *n.* [C] **1** the rank of a DUKE **2** the land and property belonging to a DUKE

Duke of Wel·ling·ton, the /ˌduk əv ˈwɛlɪŋtən/ (1769–1852) a British soldier and politician, famous for defeating Napoleon at the Battle of Waterloo in 1815

dul·cet /ˈdʌlsɪt/ *adj.* **1 sb's dulcet tones** HUMOROUS someone's voice **2** LITERARY dulcet sounds are soft and pleasant to hear

dul·ci·mer /ˈdʌlsəmɚ/ *n.* [C] ENG. LANG. ARTS **1** a musical instrument with up to 100 strings, played with light hammers **2** a small instrument with strings that is popular in American FOLK MUSIC, and is played with it sitting across your knees

dull¹ /dʌl/ *adj.*

1 BORING not interesting or exciting SYN **boring** OPP **interesting**: *This place gets really dull at times.* | *an extremely dull book* | *The play is **as dull as dishwater*** (=very boring). ►see THESAURUS box at **boring**

2 never a dull moment USUALLY HUMOROUS used to say that a lot of interesting things are happening or that you are very busy: *There's never a dull moment in our house.*

3 COLOR/LIGHT not bright or shiny OPP **bright**: *The leaves were a dull gray-green.* | *dull lifeless hair*

4 SOUND not clear or loud: *His head hit the floor with a dull thud.*

5 PAIN a dull pain is not severe but does not stop: *a dull headache*

6 KNIFE/BLADE not sharp OPP **sharp**: *Here, use this knife – that one's dull.* → see picture at SHARP¹

7 NOT INTELLIGENT OLD-FASHIONED not able to think quickly or understand things easily: *a dull student*

8 TRADE if business on the Stock Exchange is dull, few people are buying and selling OPP **active**: *dull trading*

[**Origin:** Old English *dol*] —**dullness** *n.* [U] —**dully** *adv.*

dull² *v.* [T] **1** to make something such as pain or a feeling become less sharp, less clear etc.: *Medication helped dull her back pain.* **2** to make someone less able to think or notice things clearly: *The drugs had dulled his wits.* **3** to make something less shiny or bright **4** to make the edge of something such as a knife less sharp OPP **sharpen**

dull·ard /ˈdʌlɚd/ *n.* [C] OLD-FASHIONED someone who is stupid and has no imagination

du·ly /ˈduli/ *adv.* in the appropriate or expected way: *Williams' absence was **duly noted** by teammates.*

Du·ma /ˈdumə/ *n.* [singular] POLITICS the elected national institution in modern Russia with the power to make and change laws

Du·mas /duˈmɑ/, **Al·ex·an·dre** /ˌælɪgˈzɑndrə/ (1802–1870) a French writer of NOVELS and plays

dumb¹ /dʌm/ S2 *adj.* **1** INFORMAL stupid: *That's a dumb idea.* | *I can't get my dumb car to start.* | *She's just a **dumb blonde*** (=an offensive expression for a woman with BLONDE hair who is pretty, but seems stupid). **2** unable to speak, because you are angry, surprised, shocked etc.: *The crowd was* ***struck dumb*** *by the sight of the hanging.* **3** OLD-FASHIONED a word used to describe someone who is permanently unable to speak, now considered offensive by most people SYN **mute** → see also DEAF AND DUMB **4 dumb luck** the way in which something good happens in a completely unexpected way, especially if it is not deserved: *It was just dumb luck that we found the place at all.* **5 dumb animals/creatures** an expression used to emphasize that animals cannot speak and that people often treat them badly —**dumbly** *adv.* —**dumbness** *n.* [U]

D

dumb² *v.*

dumb sth ↔ **down** *phr. v.* INFORMAL, DISAPPROVING to make something very simple, so that anyone can understand it: *They've dumbed down the TV news so much it's not really worth watching anymore.*

dumb·bell /ˈdʌmbɛl/ *n.* [C] two weights connected by a short bar, that you can lift in each hand to strengthen your arms and shoulders

ˈdumbbell ˌtenement *n.* [C] a type of TENEMENT building (=a large building divided into apartments) built in the past, that was narrower in the middle than at the sides, with open passages in the middle that were intended to allow air and light into the apartments

dumb·found /dʌmˈfaʊnd, ˈdʌmfaʊnd/ *v.* [T] to shock or surprise someone so much that they are very confused

dumb·found·ed /ˈdʌmˌfaʊndɪd/ *adj.* so surprised that you are confused and cannot speak: *He was dumbfounded when Martin didn't apologize.*

dumb·struck /ˈdʌmstrʌk/ *adj.* so shocked or surprised that you cannot speak: *Millions of Americans were dumbstruck by the news of the bombing.*

ˈdumb ˌterminal *n.* [C] a type of computer that is not able to store information or do things without being connected to another computer → see also INTELLIGENT TERMINAL

dumb·wait·er /dʌmˈweɪt̬ɚ/ *n.* [C] a small ELEVATOR used to move food, plates etc. from one floor of a restaurant, hotel etc. to another

dum-dum /ˈdʌm dʌm/ also **ˈdum-dum ˌbullet** *n.* [C] a soft bullet that causes serious wounds because it breaks into pieces when it hits you

dum·my¹ /ˈdʌmi/ *n. plural* **dummies** [C] **1** a large model in the shape of a person, used especially when you are making clothes, show clothes in a store, or testing the safety of cars: *a crash test dummy* **2** also **ventriloquist's dummy** a large DOLL in the shape of a person, which has a mouth that can be moved so that it looks as though it is talking **3** a stupid person: *She's no dummy.* **4** an object that is made to look like a tool, weapon, vehicle etc. but which you cannot use **5** also **dummy hand** cards that are placed on the table by one player for all the other players to see in a game of BRIDGE

dummy² *adj.* [only before noun] a dummy tool, weapon, vehicle etc. is made to look like a real one, but you cannot use it: *a dummy rifle*

dummy³ *v.* **dummies, dummied, dummying**

dummy up *phr. v.* SLANG to stay silent and not speak

dump¹ /dʌmp/ S2 *v.*

1 PUT STH SOMEWHERE [T always + adv./prep.] to pour something out or put something somewhere in a careless, messy, or quick way: **dump sth in/on/under etc. sth** *Just dump your bags over there in the corner.* | *He found a can of soup and dumped it in a saucepan to heat.* ►see THESAURUS box at **put, shove¹**

2 END RELATIONSHIP [T] to end a romantic relationship, especially in a sudden way that shows you do not care about that person: *He just dumped her without any warning.*

3 THROW AWAY [T] to get rid of something you do not want, especially by pouring it out: *Should I dump this coffee? It's cold.* | *Hill had to drive six miles just to dump her garden waste.*

4 COPY INFORMATION [T] COMPUTERS to copy information stored in a computer's memory onto a DISK or MAGNETIC TAPE

5 SELL GOODS [T] to sell goods at a very low price, when they should cost much more, in order to beat the competition: *They were accused of dumping computer chips on the U.S. market.*

dump on *phr. v.* INFORMAL **1 dump on sb** to criticize someone very strongly and often unfairly: *Students will always dump on the teachers.* **2 dump on sb** to tell someone all your problems: *Sorry to dump on you like that – I just needed someone to listen.* **3 dump sb/sth on sb** to give someone an unwanted job or responsibility: *Don't dump your kids on me. I've got work to do.*

dump² *n.* [C] **1** a place where unwanted waste is taken and left: *a garbage dump* **2** INFORMAL a place that is not nice to live in because it is dirty, ugly, messy etc.: *How can you live here? This place is a dump.* **3** a place where military supplies are stored, or the supplies themselves: *an ammunition dump* **4** COMPUTERS the act of printing or copying the information from a computer onto something else, such as a DISK: *a screen dump* → see also **be down in the dumps** at DOWN² (1)

ˈdumping ˌground *n.* [C] a place where you send people or things that you want to get rid of: *The school has become a dumping ground for difficult students.*

dump·ling /ˈdʌmplɪŋ/ *n.* [C] **1** a small round mass of flour and fat mixed with water, cooked in boiling liquid and served with meat: *chicken and dumplings* **2** a small ball of meat, vegetables etc. wrapped in a thin sheet of a flour and water mixture, often served steamed: *Chinese dumplings* **3** a sweet dish made of PASTRY filled with fruit: *apple dumplings*

Dump·ster /ˈdʌmpstɚ/ *n.* [C] TRADEMARK a large metal container used for waste

ˈDumpster ˌdiving *n.* [U] INFORMAL the activity of looking through Dumpsters for used clothes, food, furniture etc. that other people have thrown away

ˈdump truck *n.* [C] a vehicle with a large open container at the back that can move up at one end to pour sand, soil etc. onto the ground

dump·y /ˈdʌmpi/ *adj.* INFORMAL someone who is dumpy is fat, short, and unattractive: *a dumpy little man*

dun /dʌn/ *n.* [C,U] a dull brownish-gray color —**dun** *adj.*

Dun·bar /ˈdʌnbɑr/, **Paul** (1872–1906) a U.S. poet famous as one of the first African-American writers to become well known

Dun·can /ˈdʌŋkən/, **Is·a·do·ra** /ˌɪzəˈdɔrə/ (1878–1927) a U.S. dancer who had a great influence on modern dance

dunce /dʌns/ *n.* [C] OLD-FASHIONED someone who is slow at learning things: *the dunce of the class*

ˈdunce cap *n.* [C] a tall pointed hat that a stupid student had to wear in school in the past

dun·der·head /ˈdʌndɚˌhɛd/ *n.* [C] OLD-FASHIONED someone who is stupid

dune /dun/ *n.* [C] EARTH SCIENCE a hill made of sand near the ocean or in the desert SYN **sand dune**

ˈdune ˌbuggy *n. plural* **dune buggies** [C] a car with big wheels and no roof, that you can drive across sand

dung /dʌŋ/ *n.* [U] solid waste from animals, especially cows

dun·ga·rees /ˌdʌŋgəˈriz, ˈdʌŋgəˌriz/ *n.* [plural] OLD-FASHIONED heavy cotton pants used for working in SYN **jeans**

dun·geon /ˈdʌndʒən/ *n.* [C] a dark prison that is below the surface of the earth, especially under a castle, used in the past [**Origin:** 1300–1400 Old French *donjon* **central part of a castle**, from Latin *dominus* **lord**]

dunk /dʌŋk/ *v.* **1** [T] to quickly put something into a liquid and take it out again, especially something you are eating: **dunk sth in/into sth** *The old man dunked a donut into his coffee.* **2** [I,T] to jump up toward the basket and throw the ball down into it in the game of basketball: *I've tried, but I can't dunk the ball.* **3** [T] to push someone under water for a short time, especially as a joke [**Origin:** 1900–2000 Pennsylvania German *dunke*, from Middle High German *dunken*] —**dunk** *n.* [C] → see also SLAM DUNK

dun·no /də'noʊ/ WRITTEN, NONSTANDARD a way of writing "don't know" that looks like it sounds in "I don't know": *"What are you doing tonight?" "I dunno."*

du·o /'duoʊ/ *n. plural* **duos** [C] two people who do something together, especially sing or play music

du·o·dec·i·mal /ˌduə'dɛsəməl◂ / *adj.* MATH a duodecimal system of numbers is based on the number 12, instead of the usual system based on ten

du·o·de·num /ˌduə'dinəm, du'ɑdn-əm/ *n.* [C] BIOLOGY the beginning part of your SMALL INTESTINE, below your stomach [**Origin:** 1300–1400 Medieval Latin, Latin *duodeni* **12 each** (because it is 12 finger-widths long)] —**duodenal** /ˌduə'dinl, du'ɑdnəl/ *adj.* → see picture at DIGESTIVE SYSTEM

du·op·o·ly /du'ɑpəli/ *n. plural* **duopolies** [C usually singular] TECHNICAL the control of all or most of a business activity by only two companies, so that other organizations cannot easily compete with them → see also MONOPOLY

dupe¹ /dup/ *n.* [C] **1** someone who is tricked, especially into becoming involved in something illegal **2** the act of duping someone [**Origin:** 1600–1700 French]

dupe² *v.* [T usually passive] to trick or deceive someone: **dupe sb into doing sth** *Many elderly people have been duped into buying worthless insurance.*

du·plex /'duplɛks/ *n.* [C] a type of house that is divided so that it has two separate homes in it

du·pli·cate¹ /'dupləkɪt/ *n.* [C] **1** an exact copy of something that you can use in the same way: *a duplicate of the key* **2 in duplicate** if something is written in duplicate, there are two copies of it —**duplicate** *adj.*: *a duplicate copy*

du·pli·cate² /'dupləˌkeɪt/ *v.* [T] **1** to copy something exactly SYN **copy**: *The video had been duplicated illegally.* | *The bright lights duplicate outdoor conditions.* **2** FORMAL to succeed in repeating something in exactly the same way SYN **replicate**: *Scientists raced to duplicate the experiment.* —**duplication** /ˌduplə'keɪʃən/ *n.* [U]

du·plic·i·ty /du'plɪsət̬i/ *n.* [U] FORMAL dishonest behavior that is intended to deceive someone —**duplicitous** *adj.*

Du Pont /du'pɑnt/, **Pierre Sam·u·el** /pyɛr 'sæmyuəl/ (1870–1954) a U.S. businessman who greatly developed the Du Pont company, especially by adding the making of chemicals to its activities

Du Pont de Ne·mours /duˌpɑnt də nə'mʊr/, **El·eu·thère** /ˌɛlu'θɛr/ (1771–1834) a U.S. businessman, born in France, who made explosives and started the Du Pont company

dur·a·ble /'dʊrəbəl/ *adj.* **1** staying in good condition for a long time, even if used a lot: *Plastic window frames are more durable than wood.* ►see THESAURUS box at **strong** **2** continuing for a long time: *We hope this will be a durable peace.* —**durably** *adv.* —**durability** /ˌdʊrə'bɪlət̬i/ *n.* [U]

'durable ˌgoods *n.* [plural] ECONOMICS large expensive products such as televisions or cars that people do not buy regularly or often SYN **durables** → see also NON-DURABLE GOODS

dur·a·bles /'dʊrəbəlz/ *n.* [plural] ECONOMICS DURABLE GOODS

Du·rant /dʊ'rænt/, **William** (1861–1947) a U.S. businessman who organized the car companies Buick, Chevrolet, and General Motors

du·ra·tion /dʊ'reɪʃən/ Ac *n.* [U] FORMAL the length of time that something continues: *To avoid injuries, increase the duration of your exercise gradually.* | *The site manager will be in Japan* ***for the duration of*** *the project* (=until the end of the project).

Dü·rer /'dʊrɚ/, **Al·brecht** /'ælbrɛkt/ (1471–1528) a German artist famous for his drawings and ENGRAVINGS

du·ress /dʊ'rɛs/ *n.* [U] FORMAL illegal or unfair threats: *The confession was made* ***under duress*** (=as a result of illegal or unfair threats). [**Origin:** 1300–1400 Old French *duresce*, from Latin *durus* **hard**]

dur·ing /'dʊrɪŋ/ S1 W1 *prep.* **1** all through a period of time: *During the summer, she worked as a lifeguard.* | *Some animals sleep during the day.* **2** at some point in a period of time: *I met him during his recent visit.* | *During the second week in December, the jobless rate fell by two percent.*

WORD CHOICE during, for

- **During** can be used to answer the question "when?": *"When did you learn Italian?" "I learned it during my year abroad in Venice."*
- **For** can be used to answer the question "how long?": *"How long have you been in the U.S.?" "I've been here for three months."*
- When you want to talk about the time within which something happens, you use **during**: *Call me sometime during your trip.* | *Thieves broke in during the night.* When you are talking about how long something lasts, you use **for**: *I was only out of the room for a few minutes.* | *They were married for 29 years.*
- **During** is common with words for something that continues for a length of time: *during the program/the semester/the war.* You also use it to talk about specific periods of time: *during office hours/the day/that year/the '90s.* **For** is more usual with phrases used to measure the length of time: *for two hours/a week/many years.*

GRAMMAR

During is never used in a clause instead of **while**: *While I was at home, I saw Jerri.* You can say: *During my time at home,..* but NOT *During I was at home,...* Also, you can say: *I did the dishes while you were asleep* (NOT *during you were asleep*).

Durk·heim /'dʊrkhaɪm/, **É·mile** /eɪ'mil/ (1858–1917) a French university teacher who helped to establish the principles of SOCIOLOGY

durst /dɚst/ *v.* OLD USE a past tense of DARE

Du·shan·be /du'ʃɑmbə, -'ʃæm-/ the capital city of Tajikistan

dusk /dʌsk/ *n.* [U] the time just before it gets dark, when the sky is becoming darker SYN **twilight**: *The street lights go on* ***at dusk***. [**Origin:** Old English *dox*] → see also DAWN

dusk·y /'dʌski/ *adj.* dark or not very bright in color: *a dusky museum* | **dusky pink/orange/blue etc.** *a dusky pink room*

dust¹ /dʌst/ S3 W3 *n.* **1** [U] extremely small pieces of dirt that are in buildings on furniture, floors etc. if they are not kept clean: *A thick* ***layer of dust*** *covered the furniture.* | *There was not* ***a speck of dust*** *anywhere.* | **gather/collect dust** *The books just sit on the shelf collecting dust.* **2** [U] extremely small pieces of dirt, sand etc. that are like a dry powder on the ground or in the air: *He lay on his face in the dust.* | *A car sped past in a* ***cloud of dust***. **3 gold/coal/pollen etc. dust** [U] powder consisting of extremely small pieces of gold, COAL, POLLEN etc. **4 the dust settles** used to say that the details of a situation become clearer and less confused: ***When the dust*** *finally* ***settled*** *after the layoffs, only two managers were left in the department.* | *We'll just have to* ***wait for the dust to settle***. [**Origin:** Old English] → see also **bite the dust** at BITE¹ (7), DUSTY, **leave sb in the dust** at LEAVE¹ (32)

dust² *v.* **1** [I,T] to clean the dust from a surface by moving something such as a soft cloth across it: *Help me dust the furniture.* ►see THESAURUS box at **clean²** **2** [T] to cover something with a fine powder: **dust sth with sth** *Dust the top of the cake with cinnamon.*

dust off *phr. v.* **1 dust sb/sth ↔ off** to clean something by brushing it or rubbing it with a cloth or with your hands: *She dusted the snow off Billy's coat.* | **dust yourself off** *Smitty stood up and dusted himself off.* **2 dust sth ↔ off** to get something ready in order to use it again after not using it for a long time: *Investors are dusting off their check books as the economy recovers.* **3 dust sth off sth** also **dust sth from sth** to remove something such as dust or dirt from your clothes or another surface by brushing them with your hands: *She dusted crumbs from her skirt.*

'dust bowl *n.* [C] EARTH SCIENCE an area of land that has DUST STORMS and very long periods without rain, especially the area in the southern-central U.S. that suffered from severe lack of rain in the 1930s

D

'dust ˌbunny *n. plural* **dust bunnies** [C] INFORMAL a small ball of dust that forms in a place that is not cleaned regularly, such as under a piece of furniture SYN **dust mouse**

'dust ˌcover *n.* [C] a DUST JACKET

dust·er /'dʌstɚ/ *n.* [C] **1** a cloth or piece of equipment used for removing dust from furniture: *a feather duster* **2** a light coat that you wear to protect your clothes from dust **3** INFORMAL a DUST STORM

'dust ˌjacket *n.* [C] **1** a folded paper cover that fits over the cover of a book, used to protect it SYN **dust cover** **2** a CARDBOARD cover that a record is sold in

'dust mouse *n. plural* **dust mice** [C] a DUST BUNNY

dust·pan /'dʌstpæn/ *n.* [C] a flat container with a handle, that you use with a brush to remove dust and waste from the floor

'dust storm *n.* [C] EARTH SCIENCE a storm with strong winds that carries large amounts of dust

'dust-up *n.* [C] OLD-FASHIONED, INFORMAL a fight or argument

dust·y /'dʌsti/ *adj. comparative* **dustier**, *superlative* **dustiest** **1** covered with dust: *The shelves are really dusty.* | *a dusty road* ▸see THESAURUS box at **dirty**[1] **2 dusty blue/pink etc.** blue, pink etc. that is not bright but is slightly gray

Dutch[1] /dʌtʃ/ *n.* **1** [U] the language of the Netherlands **2 the Dutch** [plural] people from the Netherlands → see also DOUBLE-DUTCH

Dutch[2] *adj.* **1** from or relating to the Netherlands **2 go Dutch (with sb)** INFORMAL to share the cost of a meal in a restaurant: *My boyfriend and I always go Dutch.* **3 Dutch treat** an occasion when you share the cost of something such as a meal in a restaurant

ˌDutch 'elm disˌease *n.* [U] a disease that kills ELM trees

Dutch·man /'dʌtʃmən/ *n.* [C] someone from the Netherlands

ˌDutch 'oven *n.* [C] a large heavy pot with a lid, used for cooking

du·ti·a·ble /'dut̬iəbəl/ *adj.* dutiable goods are those that you must pay DUTY on

du·ti·ful /'dut̬ɪfəl/ *adj.* always obeying other people, doing what you are supposed to do, and behaving in a loyal way: *an obedient dutiful daughter*

du·ti·ful·ly /'dut̬ɪfəli/ *adv.* if you do something dutifully, you do it because you think it is the correct way to behave: *I dutifully wrote down every word.*

du·ty /'dut̬i/ S2 W2 *n. plural* **duties**
1 STH YOU MUST DO [C,U] something that you have to do because it is the right thing for you to do in your position: **+to/toward** *Dennis feels a sense of duty toward his parents.* | *Parents* ***have a duty to*** *make sure their kids behave in school.* | **it is sb's duty to do sth** *We feel it is our duty to help her.* | *You must* ***do your duty*** *and report him to the police.* | *Lawyers have a* ***legal*** *and* ***moral duty*** *to represent their clients as best they can.* → see also JURY DUTY
2 PART OF YOUR JOB [C usually plural, U] something you have to do as part of your job: *My duties include answering the telephone.* | **carry out/perform duties** *He had to perform his duties correctly.* | ***Report for duty*** *at General Peckham's office* (=go to the office to work or to be told what to do). | *Eldrige devoted too much of his time to* ***official duties*** *and not enough to his family.* → see also **do double duty** at DOUBLE[1] (4), **in the line of duty** at LINE[1] (24), TOUR OF DUTY
3 be on/off duty to be working or not working at a particular time, especially in a job which people take turns to do so that someone is always doing it: *The night shift goes off duty at 6 a.m.* | *Two officers were on duty at the police station.* → see also **active duty/service** at ACTIVE[1] (7)
4 TAX [C,U] ECONOMICS a tax you pay on something you buy, especially goods you bought in another country: **+on** *the duty on cigarettes* | *You'll have to* ***pay duty*** *on that watch.* | *Last month the* ***customs duty*** *was raised on luxury cars.*
5 kitchen/laundry/garbage etc. duty a job, especially in the house, that you must do: *My wife has me on kitchen duty tonight* (=I have to cook dinner, wash the dishes etc.).
6 do duty as/for sth to be used as something: *The breakfast nook can also do duty as a home office.*
[**Origin:** 1200–1300 Anglo-French *dueté*, from Old French *deu*]

'duty-bound *adj.* having to do something because of a feeling of duty: *Agency employees are duty-bound to enforce the rules.*

ˌduty-'free *adj.* **1** ECONOMICS duty-free goods can be brought into a country without paying tax on them: *duty-free cigarettes* **2** [only before noun] used to describe a place where duty-free goods are sold: *the duty-free shop* —**duty-free** *adv.*

du·vet /du'veɪ/ *n.* [C] a COMFORTER [**Origin:** 1700–1800 French **soft feathers**]

DVD /ˌdi vi 'di/ *n.* [C] **Digital Versatile (or Video) Disc** a special type of CD that can store large amounts of DATA such as movies, music, or computer information

DVD-ROM /ˌdi vi di 'rɑm/ *n.* [C] **Digital Versatile (or Video) Disc Read-Only Memory** a DVD that stores a lot of information that can be read but not changed

Dvoř·ák /'dvɔrʒɑk/, **An·to·nín** /'æntənin/ (1841–1904) a Czech musician who wrote CLASSICAL music

dwarf[1] /dwɔrf/ *n. plural* **dwarves** /dwɔrvz/ or **dwarfs** [C] **1** an imaginary creature that looks like a small man: *Snow White and the Seven Dwarfs* **2** a word meaning someone who does not grow to a normal height because of a medical condition, considered offensive by some people

dwarf[2] *adj.* [only before noun] BIOLOGY a dwarf plant or animal is much smaller than the usual size: *a dwarf cherry tree*

dwarf[3] *v.* [T usually passive] to be so big that other things are made to seem very small: *The cathedral is dwarfed by the surrounding skyscrapers.*

dweeb /dwib/ *n.* [C] SLANG a weak slightly strange person who is not popular or fashionable

dwell /dwɛl/ *v. past tense and past participle* **dwelled** or **dwelt** /dwɛlt/ [I] LITERARY to live in a particular place: *A woodsman dwelled in the middle of the forest.*
dwell on/upon sth *phr. v.* to think or talk for too long about something, especially something unpleasant: *Quit dwelling on the past.*

dwell·er /'dwɛlɚ/ *n.* [C] **a city/town/cave/forest etc. dweller** a person or animal that lives in a city, town etc.: *City dwellers suffer from higher pollution levels.*

dwell·ing /'dwɛlɪŋ/ *n.* [C] FORMAL a house, apartment etc. where people live

dwelt /dwɛlt/ *v.* a past tense and past participle of DWELL

DWI /ˌdi dʌbəlyu 'aɪ/ *n.* [C,U] **driving while intoxicated** → see also DUI

dwin·dle /'dwɪndl/ *v.* [I] also **dwindle away** to gradually become less and less or smaller and smaller: *The money available to build new parks has dwindled.* | **dwindle (away) to nothing/one/two etc.** *Attendance at meetings had dwindled to only four or five people.* —**dwindling** *adj.*: *a dwindling population*

Dyck /daɪk/, **An·tho·ny Van** /ˈænθəni væn/ → see VAN DYCK, SIR ANTHONY

dye¹ /daɪ/ *n.* [C,U] **1** a substance you use to change the color of your clothes, hair etc.: *hair dye* **2 a dye job** INFORMAL someone who has had a dye job has used a substance to change the color of their hair

dye² *v.* **dyes, dyed, dyeing** [T] to give something a different color using a dye: *Do you think she dyes her hair?* | **dye sth black/blue/blond etc.** *Priscilla's hair was dyed jet black.* —**dyed** *adj.*

ˌdyed-in-the-ˈwool *adj.* having strong beliefs, likes, or opinions that will never change: *a dyed-in-the-wool environmentalist*

dy·ing /ˈdaɪ-ɪŋ/ the present participle of DIE

dyke /daɪk/ *n.* [C] another spelling of DIKE

Dy·lan /ˈdɪlən/, **Bob** /bɑb/ (1941–) a U.S. singer and SONGWRITER famous for his songs from the 1960s on the subjects of war and the CIVIL RIGHTS movement

Bob Dylan

dy·nam·ic¹ /daɪˈnæmɪk/ *adj.* **1** APPROVING full of energy and new ideas, and determined to succeed: *a dynamic young businesswoman* ►see THESAURUS box at **energetic** **2** continuously changing, growing, or developing [OPP] **static**: *Markets are dynamic and a company must learn to adapt.* **3** PHYSICS relating to a force or power that causes movement: *the dynamic force of a volcanic eruption* **4** COMPUTERS needing electrical charges at regular INTERVALS to avoid losing computer information: *dynamic memory* [**Origin:** 1800–1900 French *dynamique*, from Greek *dynamikos* **powerful**] —**dynamically** /-kli/ *adv.*

dynamic² [Ac] *n.* **1 dynamics a)** [plural] the way in which things or people behave, react, and affect each other: *With Kathy's death, the family dynamics changed forever.* | **+of** *the dynamics of capitalist economies* → see also GROUP DYNAMICS **b)** [U] the science concerned with the movement of objects and with the forces related to movement **c)** [plural] changes in how loudly music is played or sung **2** [singular] FORMAL something that causes action or change: *Feminism is seen as a dynamic of social change.*

dyˌnamic ˈcharacter *n.* [C] ENG. LANG. ARTS a person in a book, play etc. whose character, opinion, or behavior etc. changes during the course of a story

dy·na·mism /ˈdaɪnəˌmɪzəm/ *n.* [U] the quality of being dynamic

dy·na·mite¹ /ˈdaɪnəˌmaɪt/ *n.* [U] **1** a powerful explosive used especially for breaking rock: *a stick of dynamite* **2** someone or something that is likely to cause a lot of trouble: *The new hiring policy is political dynamite.* **3** OLD-FASHIONED something or someone that is very exciting or impressive: *The band is dynamite.*

dynamite² *v.* [T] to damage or destroy something with dynamite

dy·na·mo /ˈdaɪnəˌmoʊ/ *n. plural* **dynamos** [C] **1** INFORMAL someone who has a lot of energy and is excited about what they do **2** something that has a very strong effect on something else, and that makes things happen: *Oil production is the dynamo that drives the nation's economy.* **3** PHYSICS a machine that changes some other form of power directly into electricity: *Bicycle lights are usually powered by a dynamo.*

D

dy·nas·ty /ˈdaɪnəsti/ *n. plural* **dynasties** [C] **1** POLITICS a family of kings or other rulers whose parents, grandparents etc. have ruled the country for many years: *the Habsburg dynasty of Austria* **2** a period of time when a particular family ruled a country or area: *the vase is from the Ming dynasty* **3** INFORMAL a group or family that controls a particular business or organization for a long period of time: *a banking dynasty* [**Origin:** 1300–1400 Late Latin *dynastia*, from Greek *dynastes* **lord**] —**dynastic** /daɪˈnæstɪk/ *adj.*

dys·en·ter·y /ˈdɪsənˌtɛri/ *n.* [U] MEDICINE a serious disease of your BOWELS that makes them bleed and pass much more waste than usual [**Origin:** 1300–1400 Latin *dysenteria*, from Greek, from *dys-* **bad** + *enteron* **bowels**]

dys·func·tion·al /dɪsˈfʌŋkʃənl/ *adj.* **1** showing an inability to behave in a normal way, accomplish things, get along with other people, or have a satisfactory life: *a dysfunctional family* **2** a dysfunctional organization or system is one that does not work correctly and accomplish what it is meant to [SYN] **functional**: *a dysfunctional welfare program* **3** TECHNICAL not working correctly or normally

dys·lex·i·a /dɪsˈlɛksiə/ *n.* [U] a condition that makes it difficult for someone to read —**dyslexic** *adj.*: *a dyslexic child*

dys·pep·si·a /dɪsˈpɛpsiə, -ˈpɛpʃə/ *n.* [U] MEDICINE a problem that your body has in dealing with the food you eat [SYN] **indigestion**

dys·pep·tic /dɪsˈpɛptɪk/ *adj.* **1** MEDICINE suffering from or caused by dyspepsia: *a dyspeptic ulcer* **2** OLD-FASHIONED in a bad mood

dy·sto·pi·a /dɪsˈtoʊpiə/ *n.* [C] an imaginary place where life is extremely difficult and a lot of unfair or immoral things happen —**dystopian**, **dystopic** *adj.* → see also UTOPIA

dys·tro·phy /ˈdɪstrəfi/ → see MUSCULAR DYSTROPHY

E,e

E /i/ *plural* **E's** *n.* **1** also **e** *plural* **e's** [C] **a)** the fifth letter of the English alphabet **b)** a sound represented by this letter **2** ENG. LANG. ARTS **a)** [C,U] the third note in the musical SCALE of C MAJOR **b)** [U] the musical KEY based on this note **3** [C,U] SLANG the illegal drug ECSTASY, or a pill of this drug

E., **E** /i/ the written abbreviation of EAST or EASTERN

e-, **E-** /i/ *prefix* **electronic** relating to the Internet or computers: *e-commerce* (=business on the Internet) → see also CYBER-, EMAIL

each[1] /itʃ/ S1 W1 *quantifier, pron.* **1** every one of two or more things or people, considered separately: *She had a bag in each hand.* | *There are four bedrooms, each with its own shower.* | *John and I have each been to Greece twice.* | *We each have a job to do.* | *They paid us each $100.* | *There are three blocks of stone, and* ***each one*** *weighs a ton.* | +**of** *Each of the children got a piece of candy.* | **one/two/half etc. of each** *"There are chocolate chip cookies and brownies." "Can I have one of each?"* | **each day/week/month etc.** *25 million viewers watch the show each week.* | *The trip takes an hour* ***each way*** (=going and returning). | *I'm proud of* ***each and every*** *member of the team.* | *a series of adventures,* ***each more*** *exciting* ***than the last*** **2 to each his own** used to mean that we all have different ideas about how to do things, what we like etc.: *I would have chosen a more modern style, but to each his own.* [**Origin:** Old English *ælc*]

> **WORD CHOICE** **each, every, both, all**
> • Use **each** and **every** with a singular countable noun to mean "every person or thing in a group": *Each/Every child got a balloon to take home.*
> • Use **both** with a plural countable noun to mean "the two things or people in a pair, considered together": *I have blisters on both feet.*
> • Use **all** with a plural countable noun to mean "every member of a group of three or more things or people": *All the leaves have fallen off the trees.* Compare: *Both our children are in college* (=we have two children). | *All our children are married* (=we have more than two children).

> **GRAMMAR** **each, every**
> • You can use **each** or **every** before a singular countable noun, and the verb that follows is always singular: *Each/every part of the country has* (NOT *have*) *had unusual weather this year.*
> • You can use **each of** or **every one of** before plural nouns or pronouns. Most teachers think that the verb that follows should be singular: *Each of the girls was wearing a red and white uniform.* | *Every one of them has promised to help.* In informal English, however, people sometimes use a plural verb in these sentences, especially when there are a lot of words between **each of** and the verb: *Each of the kids arriving for the first time are shown around the school.*
> • If **each** comes after a plural noun or pronoun, the verb is also always plural: *They each have their own phone line.* | *The kids each drink about two glasses of milk a day.*

each[2] S2 W1 *adv.* to, for, or by every one in a group: *The tickets cost $10 each.* | *You get two cookies each.*

each 'other S1 W1 *pron.* [not used as the subject of a sentence] used to show that each of two or more people does something to the other or others or has the same relationship with them: *José and his uncle hate each other.* | *The two kids played happily with each other.* | *It's normal for people to ignore each other in an elevator.* | *We sit next to each other in class.* → see also **be at each other's throats** at THROAT (4)

> **WORD CHOICE** **each other, one another**
> Some teachers prefer to use **each other** when talking about two people or things, and **one another** when talking about more than two: *The two leaders shook hands with each other.* | *All the leaders shook hands with one another.* **One another** is more formal than **each other**.

ea·ger /ˈigɚ/ W3 *adj.* **1** having a strong desire to do, have, or experience something: *a group of eager volunteers* | +**for** *Everyone was eager for news.* | **eager to do sth** *The students here are eager to learn.* **2 eager to please** willing to do anything to be helpful to people: *Mika is a very hard worker and very eager to please.* **3 an eager beaver** INFORMAL someone who works harder and is more excited about the work than others who are doing the same thing [**Origin:** 1200–1300 Old French *aigre*, from Latin *acer* **sharp**] —**eagerly** *adv.*: *Her new novel has been eagerly awaited for over a year.* —**eagerness** *n.* [U]

ea·gle /ˈigəl/ *n.* [C] BIOLOGY a very large strong bird with a beak like a hook that eats small animals [**Origin:** 1300–1400 Old French *aigle*, from Latin *aquila*]

ˌeagle-ˈeyed *adj.* very good at seeing or noticing things: *The error was caught by an eagle-eyed employee.*

ea·glet /ˈiglɪt/ *n.* [C] a young EAGLE

Ea·kins /ˈeɪkɪnz/, **Thomas** (1844–1916) a U.S. PAINTER famous for his REALISTIC style

-ean /iən/ *suffix* [in adjectives and nouns] another form of the SUFFIX -AN: *Mozartean* (=of or like Mozart)

ear

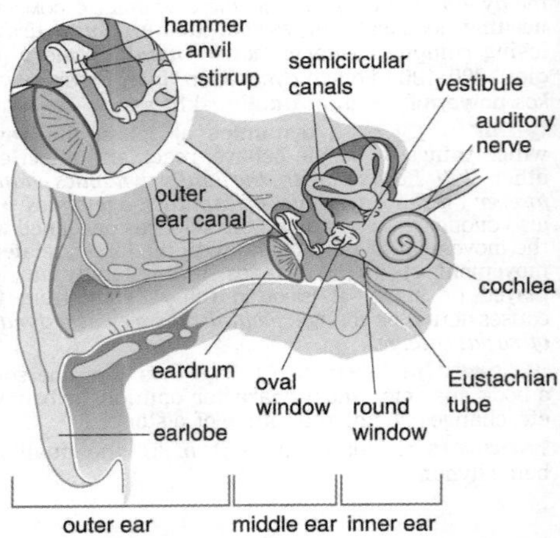

1) The eardrum vibrates as it detects sound waves.

2) These are passed on to the cochlea by the three bones in the ear (hammer, anvil, and stirrup).

3) When the hair cells located in the cochlea receive vibrations, a nerve impulse is generated in the auditory nerve.

4) These impulses are then sent to the brain.

ear /ɪr/ S1 W2 *n.*
1 PART OF YOUR BODY [C] BIOLOGY one of the two organs on either side of your head that you hear with, or just the part of these organs that you can see from the outside: *a boy with big ears* | *Stop shouting* ***in my ear!*** | *an infection in the* ***inner ear***
2 HEARING [C,U] the ability to hear sounds: *The new recording technique fools* ***the ear*** *into thinking sounds are coming from different parts of the room.* | *Wow, you really* ***have good ears****. I didn't hear anything at all.* | ***To*** *my untrained* ***ears****, the music sounded wonderful.*
3 CORN [C] BIOLOGY the part of a CEREAL plant, especially a corn plant, where the grain grows: *an ear of corn*

4 **have an ear for music/languages etc.** also **have a good ear for music/languages etc.** to be very good at hearing, recognizing, and copying sounds from music, languages etc.: *The author has an ear for the way present-day New Yorkers talk.*
5 **grin/smile etc. from ear to ear** to smile a lot because you are very happy: *Brandon came in grinning from ear to ear.*
6 **go in one ear and out the other** INFORMAL to be heard and then forgotten immediately: *Whatever I say to him goes in one ear and out the other.*
7 **by ear** by listening, and without looking at something written down: *He learned to **play** the piano **by ear**.* → see also **play it by ear** at PLAY¹ (11)
8 **be up to your ears in sth** to be very busy with something, or to have too much of something: *I'm up to my ears in work right now. Can I call you back?*
9 **be all ears** INFORMAL to be very interested in listening to someone: *Go ahead – I'm all ears.*
10 **have sth coming out your ears** INFORMAL to have so much of something that you cannot deal with it all: *We've got tomatoes coming out our ears this summer.*
11 **be out on your ear** INFORMAL to be forced to leave a place, especially because of something you have done wrong: *If we can't pay the rent we'll be out on our ear.*
12 **have sb's ear** to be able to get someone important to listen to what you have to say, especially because they trust you: *He claims to have the president's ear.*
13 **keep your/an ear to the ground** also **keep an ear open** to make sure that you always know what is happening or is going to happen in a situation: *I haven't heard anything, but I'll keep my ear to the ground.*
14 **shut/close your ears to sth** to refuse to listen to something, especially to bad news: *The administration has closed its ears to economists who criticize its policies.*
15 **sb's ears are burning** HUMOROUS used to say that you are talking about someone who is not with you and who cannot hear you: *I bet your ears were burning – Tom and I were just talking about you.*
[**Origin:** (1, 2) Old English *eare*] → see also **bend sb's ear** at BEND¹ (6), **turn a deaf ear** at DEAF (4), **lend an ear** at LEND (6), **be music to sb's ears** at MUSIC (4), **wet behind the ears** at WET¹ (4)

ear·ache /ˈɪreɪk/ *n.* [C usually singular] a pain inside your ear

ˈear drops *n.* [plural] liquid medicine to put in your ear

ear·drum /ˈɪrdrʌm/ *n.* [C] BIOLOGY a tight thin MEMBRANE (=layer like skin) over the inside of your ear that allows you to hear sound

-eared /ɪrd/ *suffix* **long-eared/short-eared etc.** having long, short etc. ears: *a long-eared rabbit*

ear·ful /ˈɪrfʊl/ *n.* INFORMAL **1 get an earful (from sb)** to be told by someone about something they are upset or angry about: *The chancellor got an earful when he asked the students for feedback.* **2 give sb an earful** to tell someone about something you are upset or angry about

Amelia Earhart

Ear·hart /ˈɛrhɑrt/, **A·me·li·a** /əˈmiliə/ (1898–1937) a U.S. pilot known for being the first woman to fly across the Atlantic Ocean alone, and for mysteriously disappearing while flying across the Pacific Ocean

earl /ɚl/ *n.* [C] a man with a high social rank in Europe, especially in the United Kingdom: *the Earl of Warwick*

ear·li·est /ˈɚliɪst/ *n.* **the earliest** the soonest time that is possible: *The earliest I can meet you is 4:00.* | *He'll arrive on Monday **at the earliest**.*

ear·lobe /ˈɪrloʊb/ *n.* [C] the soft piece of flesh at the bottom of your ear

ear·ly¹ /ˈɚli/ S1 W1 *adj.* *comparative* **earlier**, *superlative* **earliest**
1 BEFORE THE USUAL TIME arriving, happening, ready etc. before the usual or expected time: *The train was ten minutes early.* | *Hey, you're early! It's only five o'clock.* | **an hour/10 minutes etc. early** *The train was five minutes early.* | **+for** *Am I early for my appointment?*
2 NEAR THE BEGINNING [only before noun] near the beginning of a period of time, event, story, or process: *Early detection of cancer improves the chances of survival.* | **early spring/summer/fall/winter** *We were enjoying the early summer sunshine.* | **the early morning/afternoon/evening** *We had a drink in the early evening.* | **in sb's early twenties/thirties etc.** *a man in his early twenties* | **the early 1960s/1820s etc.** (=the years from 1960–1964, 1820–1824 etc.)
3 IN THE MORNING near the beginning of the day, especially before most people have gotten up: *"I usually get up at 6." "That's so early!"* | *The meetings are usually **early in the morning**.* | **an early train/bus/plane etc.** *She took the early train.* | *My dad has always been an **early riser*** (=someone who gets up early). | *Order was restored in the prison **in the early hours*** (=between midnight and morning) *of June 25th.*
4 WHEN SB IS YOUNG [only before noun] during the period of time when someone is young: *the early years of a child's life* | **at/from an early age** *He knew from an early age that he wanted to be an actor.* | *My **earliest memories** are of the house where I was born.*
5 BEFORE OTHERS [only before noun] existing or happening before other people, machines, events etc. of the same kind: *early automobiles* | *Many of the earliest settlers here were from Sweden.*
6 **the early days** the time when something has just started to be done or exist: *In the early days of the company, our office was in my garage.*
7 **an early night** a night when you go to bed earlier than usual: *I think I'm going to **make it an early night** tonight.*
8 **an early warning system/aircraft/radar etc.** a system, airplane etc. that gives a warning when something bad, especially an enemy attack, is going to happen
9 **get (off to) an early start** also **make an early start** to start an activity, trip etc. very early in the day: *If we want to get to Las Vegas by noon, we'll have to make an early start.*
10 **an early bird** someone who gets up early or arrives early, or something that is made for or given to someone like this: *There will be some wonderful bargains for the early birds.*
11 **the early bird gets/catches the worm** SPOKEN used to say that someone is successful because they were the first to be somewhere or to do something
12 **an early grave** a death that comes before it should: *Heroin was responsible for sending Morrison to an early grave.*
[**Origin:** Old English *ærlice*, from *ær* **early, soon**]

early² S1 W2 *adv.* *comparative* **earlier**, *superlative* **earliest** **1** before the usual, arranged, or expected time: *You should get there early if you want a good seat.* | **five minutes/two hours etc. early** *The bus arrived five minutes early.* | **+for** *I got there a few minutes early for my interview.* **2** near the beginning of the day: *I usually get up very early.* | *We need to leave **as early as possible** tomorrow.* | *The plane left **early in the morning**.* **3** near the beginning of a period of time, event, story, process etc.: *He'll be back early next month.* | *I realized **early on** that the relationship wasn't going to work.* | **+in** *The flowers were planted earlier in the spring.* | *They took the lead early in the game.* | *She became a star very **early in life**.* **4 as early as a)** used

E

when giving a date, to say how long ago something started: *Wine was being made as early as 2500 B.C.* **b)** used when giving a date, to say how soon something will finish or be ready

ear·mark¹ /ˈɪrmɑrk/ *v.* [T usually passive] to decide that something, especially money, will be used for a particular purpose in the future: **earmark sth for sth** *$40,000 will be earmarked for education.*

earmark² *n.* [C] a feature that makes something easy to recognize: *The case has all the earmarks of a political cover-up.*

ear·muffs /ˈɪrmʌfs/ *n.* [plural] two pieces of material attached to the ends of a band that you wear over your head to keep your ears warm

earn /ɚn/ S2 W1 *v.*

1 GET MONEY [T] to get money by working: *Alan earns $50,000 a year.* | *It's hard to* ***earn a living*** (=make money to pay for the things you need) *as a writer.*

THESAURUS

make to earn or get money: *Debbie makes a little money by babysitting.*
get to receive money for doing work or selling something: *How much do you get an hour?*
be/get paid to be given money for doing a job: *I get paid monthly.*
clear INFORMAL to earn a particular amount of money after taxes have been paid on it: *The business clears $450,000 a year.*

2 MAKE A PROFIT [T] ECONOMICS to make a profit from business or from putting money in a bank, lending it etc.: *The company earned $187 million last year.* | **earn sth from sth** *I earn a lot of money from my investments.*
3 GET STH YOU DESERVE [T] to get something that you deserve, because of your qualities or actions: *Enjoy your vacation – you've earned it!* | **earn yourself sth** *Gail earned herself a place on the team by practicing hard.* | *Chavez* ***earned a reputation*** *for being unfair.* ►see THESAURUS box at **get**
4 earn your keep to do jobs as a way of paying the owner of the place where you live: *I don't mind you staying with us, but you'll have to earn your keep.*
5 earn your stripes INFORMAL to do something to deserve a particular rank or position
6 earn sb/sth the name to cause someone to be called a particular name: *His large glasses earned him the name "four eyes."*
[**Origin:** Old English *earnian*]

ˌearned ˈincome *n.* [U] money that you receive for work you have done, used on official documents such as tax forms → see also UNEARNED

earn·er /ˈɚnɚ/ *n.* [C] **1 the main/top/worst etc. earner** something that earns you the most, least etc. money: *The portable radio is the company's second highest earner.* **2** someone who earns money for the job that they do: **high-income/low-income/high-wage etc. earners** *Taxes rose for low-income earners last year.* → see also WAGE EARNER

ear·nest¹ /ˈɚnɪst/ *adj.* **1** very serious and sincere: *an earnest, hard-working young man* **2** felt or done sincerely and with a lot of energy: *It was his earnest desire to make a difference in the world.* —**earnestly** *adv.* —**earnestness** *n.* [U]

earnest² *n.* **1 in earnest** happening more seriously or with greater effort than before: *On Monday your training begins in earnest!* **2 be in earnest** FORMAL to be serious about what you are saying

Earn·hardt /ˈɚnhɑrt/, **Dale** /deɪl/ (1952–2001) a U.S. race car driver who has been STOCK CAR racing champion seven times

earn·ings /ˈɚnɪŋz/ W2 *n.* [plural] **1** the money that you get by working: *The average worker's earnings have not kept up with inflation.* ►see THESAURUS box at **pay²** **2** the profit that a company makes: *Company earnings are up 18% over last year's.*

Earp /ɚp/, **Wy·att** /ˈwaɪət/ (1848–1929) a famous U.S. MARSHAL (=law official) and GAMBLER who lived in the western U.S.

ear·phone /ˈɪrfoʊn/ *n.* [C usually plural] a piece of electrical equipment that you put over or in your ear to listen to a radio, MP3 PLAYER etc.

ear·piece /ˈɪrpis/ *n.* [C] **1** a piece of electrical equipment that you put into your ear to hear a recording, message etc. **2** the part of a telephone that you listen through **3** one of the two pieces at the side of a pair of glasses that go over your ears

ear·plug /ˈɪrplʌg/ *n.* [C usually plural] a small piece of rubber, FOAM etc. put inside your ear to keep out noise or water

ear·ring /ˈɪrɪŋ/ S3 *n.* [C] a piece of jewelry that you fasten to your ear: *She was wearing a pair of diamond earrings.*

ear·shot /ˈɪrʃɑt/ *n.* **1 within earshot (of sb)** near enough to hear what someone is saying: *I looked around to make sure she wasn't within earshot.* **2 out of earshot (of sb)** not near enough to hear what someone is saying: *She waited till they were out earshot to start complaining*

ˈear-ˌsplitting *adj.* very loud: *ear-splitting music*

earth /ɚθ/ S2 W1 *n.*

1 WORLD [singular] also **(the) Earth** PHYSICS the world that we live in, especially considered as a PLANET, or its surface → see also WORLD: *the planet Earth* | *the earth's surface* | *The comet will pass close to Earth next year.* | *clues to the origins of life* ***on earth*** | *The space shuttle will return* ***to earth*** *next week.* → see picture at SOLAR SYSTEM

THESAURUS

earth the planet we live on, as compared to the moon, the sun, other planets, etc.: *The earth moves around the sun.*
world the planet we live on, considered as a place where there are people and countries, mountains and oceans, etc.: *It's one of the largest countries in the world.*
You can use **earth** to mean "the world": *It's the highest mountain on earth.* | *It's the highest mountain in the world.*
When you compare the earth's surface to the ocean, use **land**: *After weeks at sea, the sailors saw land.*
When you compare the earth's surface to the sky, use **earth**: *The space shuttle returned to earth safely.*

2 the biggest/tallest/most expensive etc. on earth the biggest, tallest etc. example of something that exists: *She's the most beautiful woman on earth.*
3 what/why/how etc. on earth...? SPOKEN said when you are asking a question about something that you are very surprised or annoyed about: *What on earth did you do to your hair?*
4 nothing/nowhere etc. on earth used to emphasize that you mean nothing, nowhere etc. at all: *There is no place on earth I would rather be.*
5 SOIL [U] BIOLOGY the substance that plants, trees etc. grow in: *She picked up a handful of earth.* ►see THESAURUS box at **ground¹**
6 (back) down to earth back to a more sensible or practical way of thinking, behaving, or living: *The surprise defeat quickly* ***brought the team back down to earth.***
7 earth to sb! SPOKEN used to tell someone that you think they are being unreasonable or are not paying attention to what is happening: *Earth to Cathy! You're not the only one with problems.*
[**Origin:** Old English *eorthe*] → see also DOWN-TO-EARTH, **move heaven and earth** at HEAVEN (11), **the salt of the earth** at SALT¹ (2)

earth·bound /ˈɚθbaʊnd/ *adj.* **1** unable to move away from the surface of the Earth: *earthbound astronomers* **2** having very little imagination and thinking too much about practical things

earth·en /ˈɚθən, -ðən/ *adj.* [only before noun] made of dirt or baked clay: *an earthen floor* | *an earthen pot*

earth·en·ware /ˈɚθənwɛr, -ðən-/ *adj.* an earthenware cup, plate etc. is made of very hard baked clay —**earthenware** *n.* [U]

earth·ling /ˈɚθlɪŋ/ *n.* [C] a word used by creatures from other worlds in SCIENCE FICTION stories, to talk about a human

earth·ly /ˈɚθli/ *adj.* **1 no earthly reason/use/solution etc.** no reason, use etc. at all: *I have no earthly idea she is.* **2** [only before noun] LITERARY relating to life on earth rather than in heaven: *Buddha taught that earthly existence is full of suffering.*

ˈearth ˌmother *n.* [C] a woman who has a natural appearance and does not wear much MAKEUP, who cares about other people, especially children, and who is interested in SPIRITUAL things and nature → see also MOTHER EARTH

earth·quake /ˈɚθkweɪk/ *n.* [C] EARTH SCIENCE a sudden shaking of the earth's surface that often causes a lot of damage: *More than 1,000 people were killed when the earthquake struck.*

earth·shaking /ˈɚθˌʃeɪkɪŋ/ *adj.* **1** surprising or shocking and very important: *Results of the research were interesting, but nothing earthshaking.* **2** making the earth shake: *an earthshaking explosion*

ˈearth-ˌshattering *adj.* surprising, upsetting, or shocking and very important: *Being diagnosed with cancer was an earth-shattering experience.*

ˈearth tone *n.* [C usually plural] one of the colors within the range of brownish colors

earth·ward /ˈɚθwɚd/ also **earthwards** *adv.* in a direction toward the earth's surface: *The missile fell earthward.* —**earthward** *adj.*

earth·work /ˈɚθwɚk/ *n.* [C usually plural] a large long pile of dirt used to stop attacks

earth·worm /ˈɚθwɚm/ *n.* [C] a common type of long thin light brown WORM that lives in soil

earth·y /ˈɚθi/ *adj.* *comparative* **earthier**, *superlative* **earthiest** **1** tasting, smelling, or looking like earth or soil **2** natural, relaxed, and enjoying life: *a practical, earthy woman* **3** talking in a direct and impolite way, usually about sex and the human body: *an earthy sense of humor* —**earthiness** *n.* [U]

ˈear ˌtrumpet *n.* [C] a type of tube that is wide at one end, used by old people in the past to help them hear

ear·wig /ˈɪrˌwɪg/ *n.* [C] a long brown insect with two curved pointed parts at the back of its body [**Origin:** Old English *earwicga* **ear-insect**; because it used to be believed that these insects get into people's ears]

ease¹ /iz/ W3 *n.* [U] **1 at ease a)** feeling relaxed in a situation in which most people might feel a little nervous: *Mr. Pratt uses games to make the new students* ***feel at ease.*** | *Dave always looks* ***ill at ease*** (=not relaxed) *in a suit.* | *News of their safe return* ***put*** *everyone* ***at ease.*** | *His explanation* ***put*** *my* ***mind at ease*** (=made me feel less worried and nervous). **b)** SPOKEN used by officers in the military to tell soldiers to stand in a relaxed way with their feet apart **2** the quality of doing something easily or of being done easily: *Randy learns new languages* ***with ease.*** | *I was impressed by the ease with which he made friends.* **3 a life of ease** a comfortable life, without problems or worries: *Rachel has always lived a life of ease.* **4** the ability to feel or behave in a natural or relaxed way: *There was a growing* ***sense of ease*** *as we got to know each other.* **5 ease of use/application etc.** how easy it is to use, APPLY etc. something: *Ease of use and price are two main factors in buying a computer.*

ease² *v.*

1 BECOME LESS SEVERE [I,T] if something bad eases, or if you ease it, it gradually becomes less severe: *Tensions in the region have eased slightly.* | *Increased police patrols have helped ease the fears of residents.* | *He was given drugs to* ***ease the pain.*** ►see THESAURUS box at reduce

2 MAKE LESS STRICT [T] to make rules, control, a punishment etc. less strict and severe: *The U.N. has agreed to ease sanctions.*

3 MAKE EASIER [T] to make something, especially a process, happen more easily: *She will stay for a month to ease the transition.* | *The central bank* ***eased credit*** (=made it easier to borrow money) *twice last year.*

4 MOVE STH [I,T always + adv./prep.] to move slowly and carefully into another place, or to move something this way: **ease (sth) into/onto etc.** *The train slowly eased forward.* | *She eased herself onto the couch.*

5 ease your grip (on sth) a) to allow your control of something to become weaker: *The military has no plans to ease its grip on the region.* **b)** to hold something less tightly

6 ease sb's mind to make someone feel calmer and less nervous or worried about something: *Knowing that he's getting good medical care does ease my mind.*

ease into *phr. v.* **ease (sb) into sth** to start doing a new job, activity etc. gradually, or to help someone do this: **ease yourself into sth** *After the baby, she eased herself back into work.*

ease sb ↔ **out** *phr. v.* to deliberately try to make someone leave a job, a position of authority etc. without officially saying anything: *They're trying to ease out some of the older staff to save money.*

ease up *phr. v.* **1** also **ease off** if something, especially something bad or annoying, eases up or eases off, it becomes less or gets better: *The rain is starting to ease up.* → see also LET UP **2** to stop demanding so much from someone: **+on** *Ease up on Sean – he's trying really hard.* **3** to do something more slowly or with less effort than before, especially because you have been going too fast, working too hard etc.: *Doctors have told him to ease up in practice to avoid further injury.* **4** to stop pressing so hard on something: **+on** *If your tires start to skid, ease up on the brakes.* **5** to start doing or using something less: **+on** *You should ease off on the whiskey.*

ea·sel /ˈizəl/ *n.* [C] a frame that you put a painting on while you paint it [**Origin:** 1500–1600 Dutch *ezel* **donkey**; because an easel carries a painting as a donkey carries a person]

ease·ment /ˈizmənt/ *n.* [C] LAW **1** an agreement that allows a person, organization, or government to use land that belongs to someone else **2** the area of land that is being used

eas·i·ly /ˈizəli/ S2 W2 *adv.* **1** without problems or difficulties: *We won easily.* | *The bike can easily be assembled in thirty minutes.* **2 easily the best/most/highest etc.** without doubt the best, most etc. SYN **definitely**: *He is easily the highest paid player in baseball.* **3** used to say that something is possible or is very likely to happen: *Gambling* ***can easily*** *become an addiction.* | *You* ***could easily*** *get lost in the city's narrow streets.* | *Wounds become infected* ***all too easily*** *in a hot climate.* **4** in a relaxed way: *She smiled easily when I asked about her hometown.* **5** reacting in a bad or extreme way with very little cause: *She cries easily.* → see also **breathe again/easy/easily** at BREATHE (7)

east¹, East /ist/ S2 W3 *n.* **1** [U] WRITTEN ABBREVIATION **E.** the direction from which the sun rises, that is on the right of a person facing north: *Which way is east?* | *The wind was blowing* ***from the east.*** | *The lake is five miles* ***to the east of*** *the cabin.* **2 the east** the eastern part of a country: **+of** *The rebel strongholds are located in the east of the republic.* **3 the East a)** the part of the U.S. east of the Allegheny Mountains, especially the states north of Washington, D.C.: *She was born in the East but now lives in California.* **b)** the countries in Asia, especially China, Japan, and Korea: *The martial arts originated in the East.* **c)** the countries in the eastern part of Europe, especially when they used to have Communist governments **4 East-West relations/trade etc.** political relations, trade etc. between countries in eastern Europe or Asia and those in Europe or North America [**Origin:** Old English] → see also FAR EAST,

E

MIDDLE EAST, NEAR EAST → see Word Choice box at NORTH[1]

east² *adj.* **1** WRITTEN ABBREVIATION **E.** [only before noun] in, to, or facing the east: *the east coast of Africa* **2** an east wind comes from the east

east³ S3 W3 *adv.* **1** toward the east: *Go east on I-80 to Omaha.* | *The apartment faces east.* **2 east of sth** in a place to the east of a place: *The town is 12 miles east of Portland.* **3 back East** in or to the northeast part of the U.S. especially after being further west: *Glen went to college back East.* → see also OUT WEST

ˌEast ˌAsian ˈTigers, the ECONOMICS a name for Hong Kong, Singapore, South Korea, and Taiwan, countries that developed a lot of industry quickly between the 1960s and 1990s

ˌEast ˈbloc, East Bloc *n.* [singular] the former name for the group of countries including the former Soviet Union and other eastern European countries with Communist governments, that had a close military and trade relationship

east·bound /ˈistbaʊnd/ *adj., adv.* traveling or leading toward the east: *eastbound traffic* | *The truck was traveling eastbound on Blossom Hill Road.*

ˌEast ˈCoast *n.* **the East Coast** the part of the U.S. that is next to the Atlantic Ocean, especially the states north of Washington, D.C.

Eas·ter /ˈistɚ/ *n.* [C,U] **1** a Christian holiday on a Sunday in March or April to celebrate Jesus Christ's return to life after his death **2** the period of time just before and after this day: *We went skiing in Vermont at Easter.* [**Origin:** from Old English *eastre*]

ˈEaster ˌBunny *n.* **the Easter Bunny** an imaginary rabbit that children believe brings colored eggs and chocolate at Easter

ˈEaster egg *n.* [C] **1** an egg that has been colored and decorated, to celebrate Easter **2** chocolate in the shape of an egg, eaten around the time of Easter

ˈEaster ˌIsland a small island in the Pacific Ocean, which belongs to Chile

east·er·ly /ˈistɚli/ *adj.* **1** in or toward the east **2** an easterly wind comes from the east

Eastern /ˈistɚn/ *n.* SPOKEN a short form of Eastern Time (=the time used in the eastern part of the U.S.)

east·ern /ˈistɚn/ W2 *adj.* [only before noun] **1** in or from the east of a country or area: *eastern Minnesota* **2** in or from the countries in Asia, especially China, Japan, or Korea: *Eastern philosophies* **3** in or from the countries in the east part of Europe, especially the countries that used to have Communist governments

ˌEastern ˈDaylight Time ABBREVIATION **EDT** *n.* [U] the time that is used in the eastern part of the U.S. for over half the year, including the summer, when clocks are one hour ahead of Eastern Standard Time

East·ern·er /ˈistɚnɚ/ *n.* [C] someone who lives in or comes from the eastern U.S., north of Washington, D.C.

ˌEastern ˈEurope *n.* the eastern part of Europe, especially the countries that used to have Communist governments, such as Poland and Bulgaria → see also CENTRAL EUROPE

east·ern·most /ˈistɚnˌmoʊst/ *adj.* farthest east: *the easternmost point of the island*

ˌEastern ˌOrthodox ˈChurch, the the group of Christian churches that include the Greek Orthodox Church and the Russian Orthodox Church

ˌEastern ˈStandard ˌTime ABBREVIATION **EST** *n.* [U] the time that is used in the Eastern U.S. for almost half the year, including the winter → see also EASTERN DAYLIGHT TIME

ˌEastern ˈStar, Order of the an organization of Masons and women related to them, that does CHARITY work

ˈEastern ˌTime ABBREVIATION **ET** *n.* [U] the time that is used in the eastern part of the U.S.

East In·dies, the /ist ˈɪndiz/ **1** Indonesia **2** a name that was formerly given to the countries of Southeast Asia and, before that, to the Indian SUBCONTINENT

East·man /ˈistmən/, **George** (1854–1932) a U.S. inventor and businessman who started the Kodak company, and made the first camera that was cheap and easy to use → see picture on page A25

ˈEast ˌRiver, the a river in the northeastern U.S. that flows into New York Harbor, separating Manhattan from Long Island

east·ward /ˈistwɚd/ also **eastwards** *adj.* toward the east: *The storm moved eastward.* —**eastward** *adj.*

eas·y¹ /ˈizi/ S1 W2 *adj. comparative* **easier**, *superlative* **easiest**

1 NOT DIFFICULT not difficult, and not needing much physical or mental effort SYN **simple** OPP **hard** OPP **difficult**: *The test was really easy.* | *There's no easy way to solve this problem.* | **sth is easy (for sb) to do** *Choose a code that will be easy for you to remember.* | **it is easy (for sb) to do sth** *It's easy to cook good meals if you just take a little time.* | *A personal assistant will definitely* ***make things*** *a lot* ***easier*** *at work.* | *The shopping center is* ***within easy walking distance*** (=near enough to walk to) *of the stadium.* ▶see THESAURUS box at **simple**

2 WITH NO PROBLEMS an easy time is a time when you do not have any problems or difficulties and do not have to work too hard OPP **hard** OPP **difficult**: *I've had a really easy time at work recently.* | *Very few people have an* ***easy life.*** | *A booming economy has* ***made life easy*** *for the president.* | *She hasn't* ***had an easy time of it*** *since Jack left.*

3 NOT STRICT not strict, or not making many demands OPP **hard**: *Mr. Taylor is an easy teacher.* | **+on** *The judge has been criticized for being too easy on drug users.*

4 RELAXED relaxed, comfortable, and not nervous or worried OPP **uneasy**: *an easy smile* | **+about** *I feel a lot easier about it now.*

5 NATURAL OR COMMON natural or common to do, but not necessarily right: *It's an* ***easy mistake*** *to make.* | **it is easy (for sb) to do sth** *It's easy to forget that we were all young once.* | *It's* ***all too easy to*** *blame other people for our own shortcomings.*

6 I'm easy SPOKEN used to say that you do not mind what choice is made: *"What movie do you want to see?" "I'm easy."*

7 take the easy way out to end a difficult situation in a way that seems easy, but is not the best or smartest way: *She took the easy way out and resigned.*

8 that's easy for you to say SPOKEN said when someone has given you some advice that would be difficult for you to follow: *"Just ignore them if they make fun of you." "That's easy for you to say."*

9 an easy target someone or something that can be easily attacked or criticized: *Politicians are always an easy target in the press.*

10 easy money/pickings money that you do not have to work hard to get: *The thought of easy money draws some people to drug dealing.*

11 easy prey also **an easy mark** someone who can be easily attacked, tricked, treated badly etc.: *The elderly are often easy prey for conmen.*

12 easy on the eye/ear pleasant to look at or listen to: *I like jazz because it's usually easy on the ear.*

13 an easy ride a period of time during which people treat you kindly and do not criticize you: *They* ***gave*** *him* ***an easy ride*** *during the question period.*

14 easy as pie SPOKEN very easy

15 it's as easy as falling off a log SPOKEN used to say that something is very easy to do

16 SEX OLD-FASHIONED, DISAPPROVING having a lot of sexual partners

17 be (living) on easy street OLD-FASHIONED to be in a situation in which you have plenty of money

[**Origin:** 1100–1200 Old French *aisié*, from *aise* **comfort**]
—**easiness** *n.* [U] → see also EASE[1], EASILY, OVER-EASY

easy[2] S1 *adv. comparative* **easier**, *superlative* **easiest** INFORMAL **1 take it easy a)** also **take things easy** to relax and not do very much: *I'm going to take it easy this weekend.* **b)** SPOKEN used to tell someone to slow down or become less upset or angry: *Take it easy – everything's going to be just fine.* **c)** SPOKEN used to say goodbye to someone: *"See you next week." "Yeah, take it easy."* **2 go easy on/with sth** to not use or do too much of something: *Go easy on the cheese – it has a lot of fat.* **3 go easy on sb** to be more gentle and less strict or angry with someone: *Go easy on Peter – he's having a hard time at school.* **4 get off easy** to escape severe punishment for something that you have done wrong: *You got off pretty easy if you only had to pay a $33 fine.* **5 easier said than done** used to say that it would be difficult to actually do what someone has suggested: *I should just move the shelves myself, but that's easier said than done.* **6 easy does it** SPOKEN used to tell someone to be careful, especially when they are moving something **7 easy come, easy go** said when something, especially money, was easily obtained and is quickly used, spent, or taken away **8 rest/sleep/breathe easy** to stop worrying: *I won't rest easy until I know she's safe.*

'easy chair *n.* [C] a large comfortable chair with arms, which is covered with soft material

eas·y·go·ing /ˌiziˈgoʊɪŋ◂/ *adj.* not easily upset, annoyed, or worried: *an easygoing guy*

ˌeasy 'listening *n.* [U] music that is relaxing to listen to

ˌeasy 'money ˌpolicy *n.* [C] ECONOMICS a plan by which a government tries to increase the supply of money and make it available at low INTEREST RATES

eat /it/ S1 W1 *v. past tense* **ate** /eɪt/, *past participle* **eaten** /ˈitˀn/

1 FOOD [I,T] to put food in your mouth and swallow it: *Eat your sandwich.* | *Would you like* ***something to eat*** (=some food)? | *I try to exercise and* ***eat right*** (=eat food that keeps you healthy). | *We stopped for* ***a bite to eat*** (=a small amount of food).

THESAURUS

devour WRITTEN, **gobble something up** INFORMAL, **wolf something down** INFORMAL to eat something very quickly
munch to eat something with quite big movements of your mouth
nibble (on) something to take small bites and eat only a little bit of something
pick at something to eat only a little bit of your food because you are not hungry
be dieting/be on a diet to be eating less than normal in order to become thinner
fast to not eat for a period of time, often for religious reasons
→ DRINK

2 MEAL [I,T] to have a meal: *What time do we eat?* | **eat breakfast/lunch/dinner** *Let's eat dinner in the dining room tonight.* | **+at** *We don't eat at restaurants very often.*

3 eat your words to admit that what you said was wrong: *He'll have to eat his words if she wins.*

4 eat your heart out! HUMOROUS used to say that someone should be upset or ENVIOUS because you are better than them or have something that they want: *You should see my latest painting. Pablo Picasso, eat your heart out!*

5 eat sb alive also **eat sb for breakfast** to show that you are very angry with someone, or to defeat them completely: *I can't tell him that. He'll eat me alive!*

6 USE [I always + adv./prep., T] to use a lot of something SYN **eat up**: *That big old car of mine just eats money.*

7 eat sb out of house and home to eat a lot of someone's supply of food, especially when you are living with them: *Our sixteen-year-old is eating us out of house and home.*

8 eat crow also **eat humble pie** to admit that you were wrong, especially in an embarrassing situation: *Critics who said the plan wouldn't work are now eating crow.*

9 eating out of sb's hand very willing to believe someone or to do what they want: *Young and beautiful, Lamour* ***had*** *the world* ***eating out of her hand.***

SPOKEN PHRASES

10 what's eating you? used to ask why someone seems annoyed or upset
11 I could eat a horse used to say you are very hungry
12 sb eats like a horse if someone eats like a horse, they eat a lot
13 sb eats like a pig if someone eats like a pig, they eat a lot quickly in a messy way
14 sb eats like a bird if someone eats like a bird, they eat very little
15 if ..., I'll eat my hat OLD-FASHIONED used to say that you think something is not true or will not happen
16 I couldn't eat another bite/thing used to say that you are full

[**Origin:** Old English *etan*] → see also EATS

eat sth ↔ **away** *phr. v.* to gradually destroy something until it is gone: *The acid can eat away clothes and burn your skin.*

eat away at *phr. v.* **1 eat away at sth** to gradually remove or reduce the amount of something: *Rising production costs are eating away at profits.* **2 eat away at sb** to make someone feel very worried or upset over a long period of time: *Her doubts kept eating away at her.* **3 eat away at sth** to gradually destroy something

eat in *phr. v.* to eat at home instead of going to a restaurant: *We usually eat in.*

eat into sth *phr. v.* **1** to gradually reduce the amount of time, money etc. that is available: *The cost of car repairs are eating into my savings.* **2** to damage or destroy something: *The acid eats into the surface of the metal.*

eat out *phr. v.* to eat a meal in a restaurant: *I don't feel like cooking. Let's eat out tonight.*

eat up *phr. v.* **1 eat sth ↔ up** SPOKEN to eat all of something: *Come on, Katie, eat up!* | *Who ate up all the cookies I baked for the party?* **2 eat sth ↔ up** INFORMAL to use a lot of something or all of something until it is gone: *The program eats up a lot of memory.* **3 eat it up** to enjoy something very much: *Everyone complimented her, and she just ate it up.* **4 eat sb up** to make someone feel very upset and full of sadness: *It eats me up to see those starving kids on TV.* **5 be eaten up with anger/jealousy/curiosity etc.** to be very angry, JEALOUS etc., so that you cannot think about anything else

eat·a·ble /ˈit̬əbəl/ *adj.* in a good enough condition to be eaten → see also EDIBLE

eat·en /ˈitˀn/ the past participle of EAT

eat·er /ˈit̬ɚ/ *n.* [C] **a big/light/fussy etc. eater** someone who eats a lot, not much, only particular things etc.: *Stacy's not much of a meat eater.*

eat·e·ry /ˈit̬əri/ *n. plural* **eateries** [C] INFORMAL a restaurant or other place to eat

'eating ˌapple *n.* [C] an apple that you eat raw rather than cooked → see also COOKING APPLE

'eating disˌorder *n.* [C] MEDICINE a medical condition in which you do not eat normal amounts of food or do not eat regularly → see also ANOREXIA, BULIMIA

eats /its/ *n.* [plural] INFORMAL food, especially for a party

eau de co·logne /ˌoʊ də kəˈloʊn/ *n.* [U] COLOGNE

eaves /ivz/ *n.* [plural] the edges of a roof that stick out beyond the walls: *Birds had nested under the eaves.*

eaves·drop /ˈivzdrɑp/ *v.* **eavesdropped**, **eavesdropping** [I] to listen secretly to other people's conversations: **+on** *I'm sure Sheri was eavesdropping on us.* [**Origin:** 1600–1700 *eavesdropper* **someone who stands close to a wall, where rainwater drops from the eaves, in order to listen secretly**] → see also OVERHEAR —**eavesdropper** *n.* [C]

eavesdrop

eaves·trough /ˈivzˌtrɔf/ *n.* [C] ESPECIALLY CANADIAN a GUTTER on the edge of a roof

ebb¹ /ɛb/ *n.* **1 ebb and flow** a situation or state in which something increases and decreases in a type of pattern: *the ebb and flow of consumer demand* **2 be at a low ebb** to be in a bad state or condition: *I was at my lowest ebb after the kidney surgery.* **3** a decrease in the amount of something: *the ebb in the governor's influence* **4** [singular] also **ebb tide** EARTH SCIENCE the flow of the ocean away from the shore, when the TIDE goes out OPP **flood tide**

ebb² *v.* [I] **1** also **ebb away** to gradually decrease: *I could feel my courage ebbing away.* **2** EARTH SCIENCE if the TIDE ebbs, it flows away from the shore

E·bon·ics, ebonics /iˈbɑnɪks/ *n.* [U] BLACK ENGLISH

eb·o·ny¹ /ˈɛbəni/ *n.* [U] a type of hard black wood

ebony² *adj.* LITERARY black: *She had long ebony hair.*

Eb·ro, the /ˈibroʊ/ a river that flows through Spain from mountains near its northern coast to the Mediterranean Sea

e·bul·lient /ɪˈbʌlyənt, ɪˈbʊl-/ *adj.* very happy and excited: *an ebullient personality* [**Origin:** 1500–1600 Latin *ebullire* **to bubble out**] —**ebullience** *n.* [U]

EC /ˌi ˈsi◂ / *n.* **the EC the European Community** the former name of the EUROPEAN UNION

ec·cen·tric¹ /ɪkˈsɛntrɪk/ *adj.* **1** behaving or appearing in a way that is unusual and different from most people: *an eccentric millionaire* ►see THESAURUS box at **strange¹** **2** MATH eccentric circles do not have the same center point → see also CONCENTRIC [**Origin:** 1500–1600 Late Latin *eccentricus*, from Greek *ekkentros* **out of the center**] —**eccentrically** /-kli/ *adv.*

eccentric² *n.* [C] someone who behaves in a way that is different from what is usual or socially accepted

ec·cen·tric·i·ty /ˌɛksɛnˈtrɪsəṭi/ *n. plural* **eccentricities** **1** [U] strange or unusual behavior: *Kate's mother had a reputation for eccentricity.* **2** [C] a feature, action, or opinion that is strange or unusual: *the eccentricities of the English language*

Ec·cle·si·as·tes /ɪˌkliziˈæstiz/ a book in the Old Testament of the Christian Bible

ec·cle·si·as·tic /ɪˌkliziˈæstɪk/ *n.* [C] FORMAL a priest or minister, usually in a Christian church

ec·cle·si·as·ti·cal /ɪˌkliziˈæstɪkəl/ also **ecclesiastic** *adj.* relating to the Christian church or its priests or ministers: *ecclesiastical history*

Ec·cle·si·as·ti·cus /ɪˌkliziˈæstɪkəs/ a book in the Apocrypha of the Protestant Bible and in the Old Testament of the Catholic Bible

ECG /ˌi si ˈdʒi/ *n.* [C] an EKG

ech·e·lon /ˈɛʃəˌlɑn/ *n.* [C] **1** also **echelons** [plural] a rank or level of responsibility in an organization, business etc., or the people at that level: **upper/higher/top/lower etc. echelons (of sth)** *the highest echelons of society* **2** TECHNICAL a line of ships, soldiers, airplanes etc. arranged in a pattern that looks like a series of steps

ech·o¹ /ˈɛkoʊ/ *v.* **echoes**, **echoed** **1** [I] if a sound echoes, it is heard again, sometimes repeatedly, because it was made near something such as a wall or hill: **+off/through/across etc.** *Their voices echoed through the cave.* **2** [T] to repeat or copy an idea, a style, or what someone has said or done: *Results of the study echo the findings of recent newspaper polls.* **3 echo with sth** LITERARY if a place echoes with a sound, it is filled with it: *The theater echoed with laughter and applause.* **4** [I] if a place echoes, or it echoes in a place, sounds that are made there are heard again, sometimes repeatedly: *Hey, listen –* ***it echoes in here.***

echo² *n. plural* **echoes** [C] **1** a sound that you hear again, sometimes repeatedly, because it was made near something such as a wall or a hill: *the echo of her footsteps on the wooden floor* **2** something that is very similar to something that has happened or been said before: **+of** *The uprising was an echo of the student protests in the '60s.*

é·clair /eɪˈklɛr, ɪ-/ *n.* [C] a small cake with a long narrow shape, covered with chocolate and filled with whipped cream

é·clat /eɪˈklɑ/ *n.* [U] LITERARY great skill, ability, or success: *Pinckney has served in Congress with ability and éclat.*

e·clec·tic¹ /ɪˈklɛktɪk/ *adj.* including a mixture of many different things or people, especially so that you can use the best of all of them: *an eclectic range of musical styles* [**Origin:** 1600–1700 Greek *eklektikos*, from *eklegein* **to choose**] —**eclectically** /-kli/ *adv.* —**eclecticism** /ɪˈklɛktəˌsɪzəm/ *n.* [U]

eclectic² *n.* [C] FORMAL someone who chooses the best or most useful parts from many different ideas, methods etc.

e·clipse¹ /ɪˈklɪps/ *n.* **1 a)** [C] an occasion when the Sun or the Moon cannot be seen because one of them is passing between the other one and the Earth: ***a total eclipse of the sun*** (=an occasion when the Sun is completely blocked by the Moon so that the sun cannot be seen) → see also LUNAR ECLIPSE, SOLAR ECLIPSE **b)** an occasion when the view of a star, PLANET, moon etc. is blocked by another planet, moon etc. **2** [U] FORMAL a situation in which someone or something loses their power or fame, because someone or something else has become more powerful or famous: *the eclipse of Europe's prestige after World War I* **3 be in eclipse/go into eclipse** FORMAL to be or become less famous or powerful than before [**Origin:** 1200–1300 Old French, Greek *ekleipsis*, from *ekleipein* **to leave out, fail**]

eclipse² *v.* [T] **1** to become more important, powerful, famous etc. than someone or something else, so that they are not noticed anymore: *Gray's Anatomy eclipsed all other reference books of its type.* **2 a)** if the Moon eclipses the Sun or the Earth eclipses the Moon, the Sun or the Moon cannot be seen for a short time because the Moon or Earth passes in front of it **b)** SCIENCE if a PLANET, moon etc. eclipses a star, planet etc. it blocks someone's view of it

e·clip·tic /ɪˈklɪptɪk/ *n.* [singular] SCIENCE the path along which the sun seems to move

eco- /ikoʊ/ *prefix* concerned with the environment, or not harmful to the environment: *eco-education* | *eco-toys*

e·co·friend·ly /ˌikoʊ ˈfrɛndli◂ / *adj.* not harmful to the environment: *ecofriendly detergents*

E. co·li /ˌi ˈkoʊlaɪ/ *n.* [U] a type of BACTERIA that can make you very sick if you eat food that contains it

e·co·log·i·cal /ˌikəˈlɑdʒɪkəl, ˌɛ-/ *adj.* [only before noun] **1** BIOLOGY relating to how plants, animals, and people are related to each other and to their environment: *an ecological disaster* **2** interested in protecting the environment: *ecological groups* —**ecologically** /-kli/ *adv.*

ˌecological ˈpyramid *n.* [C] BIOLOGY a drawing in the shape of a PYRAMID that shows how the relative number of animals, plants, or other living things decreases at each stage of the cycle in which plants are eaten by insects or animals, which are then eaten by other animals and so on → see also FOOD CHAIN

ˌecological sucˈcession *n.* [U] BIOLOGY the process

in which the particular group of animals, plants, etc. living in a particular area is replaced again and again over a long period of time by others until a state is reached in which no more changes happen

e·col·o·gist /ɪˈkɑlədʒɪst/ *n.* [C] EARTH SCIENCE a scientist who studies ecology

e·col·o·gy /ɪˈkɑlədʒi/ *n.* [singular, U] BIOLOGY EARTH SCIENCE the way in which plants, animals, and people are related to each other and to their environment, or the scientific study of this: *the ecology of the Red Sea* [**Origin:** 1800–1900 Greek *oikos* **house, living place**]

e-com·merce /ˈi ˌkɑmɚs/ *n.* [U] COMPUTERS the activity of doing business using the Internet

e·con /ˈikɑn/ *n.* [U] SPOKEN, ECONOMICS, especially as a subject of study at a college or university

ec·o·nom·ic /ˌɛkəˈnɑmɪk◂, ˌi-/ Ac W1 *adj.* **1** [only before noun] relating to trade, industry, and the management of money: **economic growth/development/recovery etc.** *The country's remarkable economic growth has produced millions of new jobs.* | *The country faces an* ***economic crisis.*** | *a difficult* ***economic climate*** **2** relating to money or to making a profit SYN **financial**: *The school lost three teachers for economic reasons.*

WORD CHOICE **economy, economic, economical**
The adjective of the word **economy** [C], referring to the economy of a country or region, is **economic** (NOT **economical**): *We are faced with a deepening economic crisis.* | The adverb of both **economic** and **economical** is **economically**: *The country is not economically stable.* | *You can live here very economically.*

ec·o·nom·i·cal /ˌɛkəˈnɑmɪkəl/ Ac *adj.* **1** not costing a lot of money: *an economical car* | *Hiring and training your own staff would be more economical.* **2** using money carefully without wasting any: *an economical shopper* **3** using only as much energy, effort, words etc. as necessary: *economical movements* → see Word Choice box at ECONOMIC

ec·o·nom·i·cally /ˌɛkəˈnɑmɪkli/ Ac *adv.* **1** in a way that is related to systems of money, trade, or business: *economically depressed areas* | [sentence adverb] *Economically, our city has never been stronger.* **2** in a way that relates to money: *an economically wise decision* **3** in a way that does not cost a lot of money: *We produce food as economically as possible.* **4** in a way that uses only as much energy, effort, words etc. as necessary

ˌeconomic imˈperialism *n.* [U] DISAPPROVING ECONOMICS control of one country by another using economic programs instead of military action → see also IMPERIALISM: *Several smaller countries do not want any more American-made products on their shelves and are charging the U.S. with economic imperialism.*

ec·o·nom·ics /ˌɛkəˈnɑmɪks/ Ac W3 *n.* **1** [U] the study of the way in which money and goods are produced and used **2** [plural] the way in which money influences whether a plan, business etc. will work effectively: *The economics of building new subway lines are being studied.* → see also HOME ECONOMICS

WORD CHOICE **economics, economy**
The study of economies and their money systems is called **economics** (uncountable): *Tammy majored in history and economics* (NOT **economic** or **economy**). | *Economics is my favorite subject* (NOT *are my favorite subject*).

ˌeconomic ˈsanctions *n.* [plural] ECONOMICS another word for SANCTIONS

eˌconomies of ˈscale *n.* [plural] ECONOMICS in economics, the decrease in cost of each product that happens as the total number of products produced increases: *Small stores are threatened by the economies of scale that large supermarket chains can achieve.*

e·con·o·mist /ɪˈkɑnəmɪst/ Ac W2 *n.* [C] ECONOMICS someone who studies the way in which money and goods are produced and used, and the systems of business and trade

e·con·o·mize /ɪˈkɑnəˌmaɪz/ *v.* [I] to reduce the amount of money, time, goods etc. that you use: +**on** *Higher taxes encourage people to economize on fuel.*

e·con·o·my[1] /ɪˈkɑnəmi/ Ac W1 *n. plural* **economies** **1** [C] ECONOMICS the system by which a country's money and goods are produced and used, or a country considered in this way: *a capitalist economy* | *Low interest rates will help* ***boost the economy.*** | **the global/world/international economy** *a slowdown in the world economy* **2** [U] ECONOMY CLASS **3** [U] the careful use of money, time, goods etc. so that nothing is wasted: *For reasons of economy, only a few copies were made.* **4** [U] the use of only as much energy, effort, words etc. as necessary: *ecomony of movement* **5 a false economy** something that seems cheaper than something else at first, but which will cause you to spend more money later: *Not insuring your belongings is a false economy.* **6 economies of scale** ECONOMICS the financial advantages of producing something in very large quantities, because the cost per piece is lower [**Origin:** 1400–1500 French, Greek *oikonomia*, from *oikonomos* **manager of a house**] → see also MARKET ECONOMY, MIXED ECONOMY → see Word Choice box at ECONOMIC, ECONOMICS

economy[2] Ac *adj.* [only before noun] **an economy size/pack/package etc.** a large product that costs less per pound, piece etc. compared to smaller-sized packages

eˈconomy class *n.* [U] the cheapest type of seats in an airplane SYN **economy** → see also BUSINESS CLASS —**economy class** *adj.*: *economy class seats*

e·co·pol·i·tics /ˌikoʊˈpɑlətɪks/ *n.* [U] a type of political activity that is concerned with preserving the world's environment

e·co·sys·tem /ˈikoʊˌsɪstəm/ *n.* [C] BIOLOGY EARTH SCIENCE a particular place and all the living things in it, along with the way they react to each other and to the place itself

eco·tour·ism /ˌikoʊˈtʊrɪzəm, ˈikoʊˌtʊrɪzəm/ *n.* [U] the business and activity of traveling to places on vacation, being careful not to damage the natural environment

ec·ru /ˈɛkru, ˈeɪkru/ *n.* [U] a very light brown color [**Origin:** 1800–1900 French *écru* **not made white**] —**ecru** *adj.*

ec·sta·sy /ˈɛkstəsi/ *n. plural* **ecstasies** **1** [C,U] a feeling of extreme happiness: *The fans shouted out* ***in ecstasy.*** **2** also **Ecstasy** [U] an illegal drug, usually in the form of a PILL, which is taken to give a feeling of happiness, love, and energy **3** [C,U] a state in which you have very strong religious feelings and do not know what is happening around you **4 go into ecstasies over sth** to say that you like something a lot in a very excited way [**Origin:** 1300–1400 Old French, Greek *ekstasis*, from *existanai* **to make mad**]

ec·stat·ic /ɪkˈstæṭɪk, ɛk-/ *adj.* feeling extremely happy and excited: *Jacqueline was ecstatic to see her old friends again.* —**ecstatically** /-kli/ *adv.*

ECT /ˌi si ˈti/ *n.* [U] **electroconvulsive therapy** another word for ELECTROSHOCK

ec·to·derm /ˈɛktəˌdɚm/ *n.* [singular, U] BIOLOGY the outer layer of cells around an EMBRYO, which develops to form the outside layer of a person's or animal's skin and organs → see also ENDODERM

-ectomy /ɛktəmi/ *suffix* [in nouns] the removing of a particular part of someone's body by an operation: *an appendectomy* (=removing the appendix)

ec·to·therm /ˈɛktoʊˌθɚm/ *n.* [C] BIOLOGY an animal that depends on the sun or the heat from its environment to raise and control the temperature of its body. All animals except birds and MAMMALS are ectotherms. → see also ENDOTHERM

Ec·ua·dor /ˈɛkwəˌdɔr/ a country in northern South America, between Peru and Colombia, and next to the Pacific Ocean —**Ecuadorian** /ˌɛkwəˈdɔriən/ *n., adj.*

ec·u·men·i·cal /ˌɛkyəˈmɛnɪkəl/ *adj.* supporting the idea of uniting the different branches of the Christian religion [**Origin:** 1500–1600 Late Latin *oecumenicus*, from Greek *oikoumene* **the whole world in which people live**] **—ecumenically** /-kli/ *adv.*

ec·ze·ma /ˈɛksəmə, ˈɛɡzəmə, ɪɡˈzimə/ *n.* [U] MEDICINE a condition in which your skin becomes dry, red, swollen, and ITCHY [**Origin:** 1700–1800 Modern Latin, Greek *ekzema*, from *ekzein* **to boil out, erupt**]

-ed /d, ɪd, t/ *suffix* [in adjectives] having a particular thing: *a bearded man* (=a man with a beard) | *a red-haired girl*

ed /ɛd/ *n.* [U] INFORMAL, SPOKEN education as a subject of study: *We learned how to check the oil in* ***drivers' ed*** *class.*

ed. **1** the written abbreviation of EDUCATION **2** the written abbreviation of EDITION **3** the written abbreviation of EDITOR

E·dam /ˈidəm, -dæm/ *n.* [U] a type of yellow cheese from the Netherlands, usually covered in red WAX [**Origin:** 1800–1900 *Edam*, Dutch town where the cheese was first made]

ed·dy¹ /ˈɛdi/ *n. plural* **eddies** [C] a circular movement of water, wind, dust etc.

eddy² *v.* **eddies, eddied, eddying** [I + **around**] if water, wind, dust etc. eddies, it moves around with a circular movement

Ed·dy /ˈɛdi/, **Ma·ry Ba·ker** /ˈmɛri ˈbeɪkɚ/ (1821–1910) a U.S. religious leader, who started a new form of Christianity called Christian Science in 1866

e·de·ma /ɪˈdimə/ *n.* [U] a medical condition in which a part of the body, such as the legs, lungs, or brain, becomes swollen and filled with liquid

E·den /ˈidn/ *n.* [U] **1** also **the Garden of Eden** in the Bible story, the garden where Adam and Eve, the first humans, lived **2** [singular] a place of happiness, INNOCENCE, or beauty: *In those days, California seemed like an agricultural Eden.*

edge¹ /ɛdʒ/ S2 W2 *n.* [C]

1 SIDE the part of an object or an area that is farthest from its center: *Don't put your glass so close to the edge of the table.* | *My uncle's house is on the edge of town near the freeway.*

THESAURUS

border the official line that separates two countries, states, or areas: *the border between Mexico and the United States*
rim the outside edge of something, especially something circular such as a glass: *a chip on the rim of the glass*

edge

on the edge of a cliff

at the water's edge

margin the empty space at the side of a printed page: *I wrote some notes in the margins.*
hem the edge of a piece of cloth that is turned under and stitched down, especially the lower edge of a skirt, pair of pants, etc.: *The hem of her dress was coming down.*
curb the edge of the sidewalk, next to the street: *If the curb is painted red, you may not park next to it.*

2 KNIFE the thin sharp part of a blade or tool that is used for cutting: *You'll need a knife with a very sharp edge.*

3 ADVANTAGE a quality that you have, that gives you an advantage over other people: *Some athletes lose their edge by their mid-20s.* | *American companies* ***have an edge over*** *their competition in this technology.*

4 be on edge to be nervous, especially because you are expecting something bad to happen: *What's wrong, Sue? You've been on edge all morning.*

5 an edge (of sth) a small amount of a particular quality, such as an emotion: *Jenny's voice took on an edge of impatience.*

6 be on the edge to be behaving in a way that makes it seem as if you are going crazy

7 be on the edge of your seat to be very excited and interested in something that is happening: *Star Trek fans will be waiting on the edge of their seats for the next movie.*

ecosystem

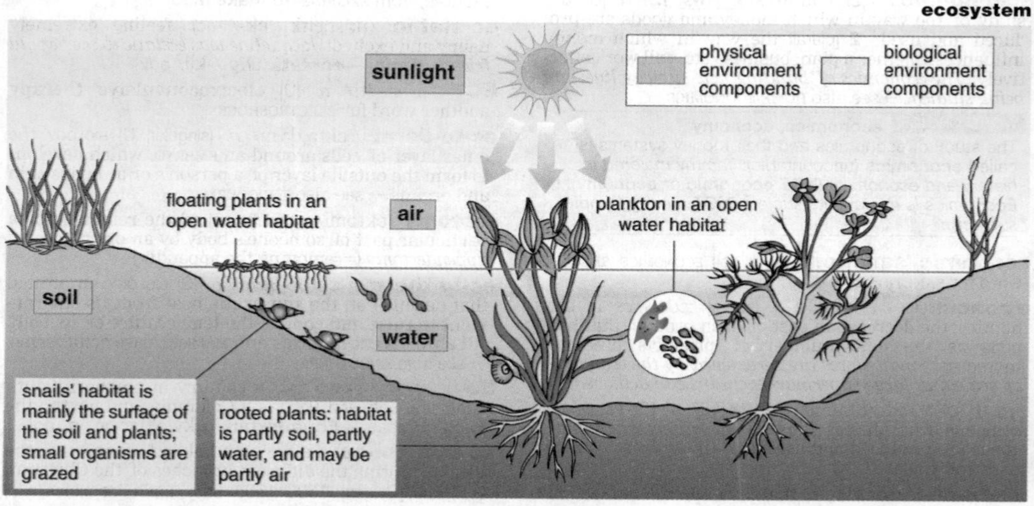

8 the edge of sth the limit of something, or the point at which it may start to happen: *She and her family live on the edge of poverty.*
9 take the edge off (sth) to make something less bad, strong etc.: *Try this. It should take the edge off the pain.*
10 go over the edge to go crazy or have a NERVOUS BREAKDOWN: *Nick needs to get some help before he goes completely over the edge.*
[**Origin:** Old English *ecg*] → see also CUTTING EDGE, **have rough edges** at ROUGH[1] (8)

edge² *v.* **1** [I,T always + adv./prep.] to move slowly and gradually, or to make something do this: *As he edged closer, Jan became more nervous.* | **edge sth in/across/toward etc.** *Dan edged his chair closer to the fireplace.* **2** [I,T always + adv./prep.] to develop gradually, or to make something do this: **edge (sth) up/down/toward etc.** *The dollar edged lower against the Japanese yen.* **3** [T usually passive] to have or put something on the edge or border of something: **edge sth with/in sth** *The sleeves were edged with lace.* **4** [T] to defeat someone by a small number of points or by a short distance: *Fontes edged Gibbs in the voting for NFL Coach of the Year.* **5** [T] to cut the edges of an area of grass so that they are neat and straight

edge sb/sth ↔ **out** *phr. v.* to win by a small number of points or by a short distance: *Carr edged out Durelle in a battle for second place.*

edge·wise /ˈɛdʒwaɪz/ *adv.* with the edge or thinnest part forward SYN **sideways** → see also **not get a word in edgewise/edgeways** at WORD[1] (22)

edg·ing /ˈɛdʒɪŋ/ *n.* [C,U] something that forms an edge or border: *a white handkerchief with blue edging*

edg·y /ˈɛdʒi/ *adj. comparative* **edgier**, *superlative* **edgiest** nervous and worried: *Residents are still edgy over a series of student killings last summer.*

ed·i·ble /ˈɛdəbəl/ *adj.* something that is edible can be eaten OPP **inedible**: *The meal was barely edible.* | *edible plants* [**Origin:** 1600–1700 Late Latin *edibilis*, from Latin *edere* **to eat**]

e·dict /ˈidɪkt/ *n.* [C] FORMAL an official public order made by someone in a position of power, sometimes unfairly: *Perpich learned how much state employees resented edicts sent down from the senior management.*

ed·i·fice /ˈɛdəfɪs/ *n.* [C] FORMAL **1** a building or structure, especially a large one: *The Times is housed in an imposing edifice on 1st Street.* **2** a complicated system of beliefs or ideas: *The whole edifice of the family's thinking rested on the notion of hard work.* [**Origin:** 1300–1400 French, Latin *aedificium*, from *aedificare* **to build a house**]

ed·i·fy /ˈɛdəˌfaɪ/ *v.* **edifies, edified, edifying** [T] FORMAL to be good for your mind or moral character by teaching you something: *The movie neither edifies nor entertains its viewers.* —**edifying** *adj.* —**edification** /ˌɛdəfəˈkeɪʃən/ *n.* [U] FORMAL OR HUMOROUS: *For your edification, I'm enclosing an article on our local fishing festival.*

Ed·in·burgh /ˈɛdnbərə/ the capital city of Scotland

Ed·i·son /ˈɛdɪsən/, **Thom·as Al·va** /ˈtɑməs ˈælvə/ (1847–1931) a U.S. inventor who made over 1300 electrical inventions and is most famous for inventing the LIGHT BULB → see picture on page A25

ed·it /ˈɛdɪt/ Ac S2 *v.* [T] ENG. LANG. ARTS **1** to remove mistakes or inappropriate parts from a book, article, television program etc.: *Viewing and editing documents on screen can be much quicker than working on paper.* **2** to prepare a book, article etc. for printing by deciding what to include and how to arrange and put together the parts **3** to be in charge of a newspaper, magazine etc. and make decisions about what types of information to include: *Gupta founded and edited a newspaper in colonial East Africa.* **4** to arrange and put together the parts of a movie, television program, or sound recording —**edit** *n.* [C]

edit sth ↔ **out** *phr. v.* ENG. LANG. ARTS to remove something when you are preparing a book, piece of film etc. for printing or broadcasting: *If you make a mistake, don't worry – we can edit it out before the interview is shown.*

e·di·tion /ɪˈdɪʃən/ Ac *n.* [C] **1** the form in which a book, newspaper, product etc. is printed or made at a particular time: *Vogel's textbook is now in its fourth edition.* | *Publishers expect to bring out a paperback edition later in the year.* **2** the number of copies of a particular book, newspaper, product etc. that are printed or made at one time: *This beautiful hand-painted plate is available in an edition of 5,000.* **3** one copy of a book, newspaper etc.: *Wilson owns a rare 1853 edition of the poetry collection.* **4** one television or radio program that is part of a series: *I saw a report on cancer treatments on Thursday's edition of the local news.* [**Origin:** 1400–1500 Latin *editus*, past participle of *edere* **to give out, produce**] → see also LIMITED EDITION

ed·i·tor /ˈɛdət̬ɚ/ Ac W2 *n.* [C] **1** the person who is in charge of a newspaper, magazine etc. and decides what should be included in it ►see THESAURUS box at newspaper **2** ENG. LANG. ARTS someone who prepares a book, article etc. for printing by deciding what to include and by checking for any mistakes **3** ENG. LANG. ARTS someone who arranges and puts together the parts of a movie, television program, or sound recording **4** ENG. LANG. ARTS someone who decides what should be included in a television or radio program, especially a news program **5** COMPUTERS a computer program that is used to make changes in FILES

ed·i·to·ri·al¹ /ˌɛdəˈtɔriəl/ Ac *adj.* **1** relating to the work of an editor: *Sharon is an editorial assistant in the sports department.* **2** [only before noun] expressing an opinion, rather than just giving facts: *the editorial pages in the newspaper* | *editorial comments*

editorial² Ac *n.* [C] a piece of writing in a newspaper that gives the editor's opinion about something, rather than just reporting facts

ed·i·to·ri·al·ize /ˌɛdəˈtɔriəˌlaɪz/ *v.* [I] to give your opinion and not just the facts about something, especially publicly: **+on/about/against etc.** *The Clarion-Ledger has editorialized in favor of increased funding for AIDS drugs.*

ed·i·tor·ship /ˈɛdət̬ɚˌʃɪp/ *n.* [U] the position of being the editor of a newspaper or magazine, or the time during which someone is an editor

Ed·mon·ton /ˈɛdməntən/ the capital city of the Canadian PROVINCE of Alberta

EDT the abbreviation of EASTERN DAYLIGHT TIME

edu /ˌi di ˈyu/ the abbreviation for educational institution, used in U.S. Internet addresses

ed·u·ca·ble /ˈɛdʒəkəbəl/ *adj.* able to learn or be educated: *educable mentally handicapped students*

ed·u·cate /ˈɛdʒəˌkeɪt/ S3 *v.* [T] **1** to teach or train someone, especially at a school or college: *Many of the women had been educated at the best universities abroad.* **2** to give someone information about a particular subject, or to show them a better way to do something: **educate sb about sth** *Young people need to be educated about the dangers of alcohol abuse.* [**Origin:** 1400–1500 Latin, past participle of *educare* **to bring up, educate**]

ed·u·cat·ed /ˈɛdʒəˌkeɪt̬ɪd/ *adj.* **1** having knowledge as a result of studying or being taught: *The First Lady was also a* ***highly educated*** *woman.* | **college-educated/Harvard-educated/high-school-educated etc.** *Young is the Berkeley-educated son of an immigrant.* **2 an educated guess** a guess that is likely to be correct because you have enough information: *Dearborn was* ***making an educated guess*** *when he said that 170 positions would be cut over six months.*

ed·u·ca·tion /ˌɛdʒəˈkeɪʃən/ S2 W1 *n.* **1** [singular, U] the process by which your mind develops through learning at a school or college: *It can cost a lot to give your kids a college education.* | *Jody's grandmother only had five years of* ***formal education*** (=education in a school). **2** [U] the general area of work or study connected with teaching: *He earned his bachelor's degree in elementary education.* → see also HIGHER EDUCATION, SPECIAL EDUCATION

ed·u·ca·tion·al /ˌɛdʒəˈkeɪʃənəl/ W3 *adj.* **1** relating to education: *After retiring, he remained active in educational programs at the laboratory.* **2** teaching you something you did not know before: *educational TV programs*

ed·u·ca·tionist /ˌɛdʒəˈkeɪʃənɪst/ also **ed·u·ca·tion·al·ist** /ˌɛdʒəˈkeɪʃənlˌɪst/ *n.* [C] FORMAL an EDUCATOR

ed·u·ca·tor /ˈɛdʒəˌkeɪtɚ/ *n.* [C] FORMAL **1** a teacher **2** someone who knows a lot about methods of education

ed·u·tain·ment /ˌɛdʒuˈteɪnmənt/ *n.* [U] movies, television programs, or computer SOFTWARE that educate and entertain at the same time

Ed·ward·i·an /ɛdˈwɑrdiən, -ˈwɔr-/ *adj.* relating to the time of King Edward VII of Great Britain (1901–1910): *Edwardian furniture*

Ed·wards /ˈɛdwɚdz/, **Jon·a·than** /ˈdʒɑnəθən/ (1703–1758) a U.S. THEOLOGIAN and religious leader, who succeeded in persuading large numbers of people to become Christians

-ee /i/ *suffix* [in nouns] **1** someone who is being treated in a particular way: *a payee* (=someone who is paid) | *a trainee* | *an employee* **2** someone who is in a particular state or who is doing something: *an absentee* (=someone who is absent) | *an escapee*

EEC /ˌi i ˈsi/ *n.* **the EEC** the European Economic Community; the former name for the EC and a former name of the EU

EEG /ˌi i ˈdʒi/ *n.* [C] **1 electroencephalograph** a piece of equipment that records the electrical activity of your brain **2 electroencephalogram** a drawing made by an ELECTROENCEPHALOGRAPH

eek /ik/ *interjection* an expression of sudden fear and surprise: *Eek! A mouse!*

eel /il/ *n.* [C] BIOLOGY a long thin fish that looks like a snake and can be eaten

e'en /in/ *adv.* POETIC the short form of EVEN

ee·ny /ˈini/ **eeny meeny miny mo** SPOKEN the first line of a short poem that children say to help them choose between different possibilities

EEO /ˌi i ˈoʊ/ *n.* [U] equal employment opportunity; the principle that some businesses follow, stating that a person's race, sex, religion etc. cannot be a reason for not getting the job

EEOC /ˌi i oʊ ˈsi/ → see EQUAL EMPLOYMENT OPPORTUNITIES COMMISSION, THE

-eer /ɪr/ *suffix* [in nouns] someone who does or makes a particular thing, often something bad: *an auctioneer* (=someone who runs auction sales) | *a profiteer* (=someone who makes unfair profits)

e'er /ɛr/ *adv.* POETIC the short form of "ever"

ee·rie /ˈɪri/ *adj.* strange and frightening: *The wind made an eerie sound outside.* [**Origin:** 1200–1300 Old English *earg* **not brave, full of fear**]

ef·face /ɪˈfeɪs/ *v.* [T] **1** FORMAL to destroy or remove something so that it cannot be seen or noticed: *Carbon dioxide and moisture threaten to efface the Lascaux cave drawings.* | *Communist historians tried to efface whole segments of their nation's past.* **2 efface yourself** LITERARY to behave in a way that makes other people not notice you → see also SELF-EFFACING

ef·fect¹ /ɪˈfɛkt/ S2 W1 *n.*

1 CHANGE/RESULT [C,U] the way in which an event, action, or person changes someone or something: +**of** *Most people are aware of the harmful effects of smoking.* | *Seeing my father in such pain really* ***had an effect on*** *my mom.* | *In order to* ***produce the desired effect*** (=achieve the result you want) *of losing weight permanently, you must alter your eating habits.* | **to good/great/little etc. effect** *Arai mixes and sculpts the metallic fibers to breathtaking effect.* → see also SIDE EFFECT ►see THESAURUS box at **result¹**

2 put/bring sth into effect to make a plan or idea happen: *The council will need more money to put the regulations into effect.*

3 go/come into effect if a new law, rule, or system goes into effect, it officially starts: *The treaty went into effect in May 1997.*

4 take effect a) to start to produce results: *It will be a few minutes before the drugs start to take effect.* **b)** if a law, rule, or system takes effect, it officially begins: *The controversial bike-helmet law will take effect January 1.*

5 be in effect if a law, rule, or system is in effect, it must be obeyed now or it is being used now: *The benefits listed are those in effect as of December 16.*

6 in effect used when you are describing what the real situation is, especially when it is different from the way that it seems to be: *In effect we're earning less than last year because of inflation.*

7 to this/that/the effect used when you are giving the general meaning of what someone says, rather than the exact words: *Barkley's response was, "Go away," or* ***words to that effect.*** | *The letter said* ***something to the effect that*** *her job was no longer safe.*

8 IDEA/FEELING [C usually singular] an idea or feeling that an artist, speaker, book etc. tries to make you think of or feel: *Storni's use of rhythm creates an effect of tension in her poems.*

9 for effect if someone does something for effect, they do it in order to make people notice: *Dangerfield rolled his eyes for effect as he told the joke.*

10 MOVIE [C usually plural] an unusual or impressive sound or image that is artificially produced for a movie, play, or television or radio program

11 effects [plural] the things that someone owns SYN **belongings**: *Don's few* ***personal effects*** *were in a suitcase under the bed.*

12 with immediate effect FORMAL beginning immediately: *Both armies were ordered to cease all attacks with immediate effect.*

[**Origin:** 1300–1400 Old French, Latin *effectus*, past participle of *efficere* **to cause to happen**] → see also SOUND EFFECTS, SPECIAL EFFECT → see Word Choice box at AFFECT²

effect² *v.* [T] FORMAL to make something happen: *Conley saw religion as a way to* ***effect*** *real* ***change*** *in her family life.*

ef·fec·tive /ɪˈfɛktɪv/ S3 W2 *adj.* **1** producing the result that was wanted or intended OPP **ineffective**: *The less expensive drugs were just as effective in treating arthritis.* **2** [no comparative] if a law, agreement, or system becomes effective, it officially starts: *His resignation is effective April 8.* **3** done with skill, or having a skillful way of doing things: *The effective use of color can make a small room look much bigger.* **4** [no comparative; only before noun] real, rather than what is officially intended or generally believed: *Rapid advancements in technology have reduced the effective lifespans of computers.* —**effectiveness** *n.* [U]

ef·fec·tive·ly /ɪˈfɛktɪvli/ W3 *adv.* **1** in a way that produces the result that was intended: *Unlike many academics, Rice can communicate her knowledge effectively.* **2** used to describe what the real situation is as a result of something that has happened: *Most of the urban poor are effectively excluded from politics.*

ef·fec·tu·al /ɪˈfɛktʃuəl/ *adj.* FORMAL producing the result that was wanted or intended OPP **ineffectual** SYN **effective** —**effectually** *adv.*

ef·fec·tu·ate /ɪˈfɛktʃuˌeɪt/ *v.* [T] FORMAL to make something happen

ef·fem·i·nate /ɪˈfɛmənɪt/ *adj.* a man who is effeminate looks or behaves like a woman —**effeminacy** *n.* [U] —**effeminately** *adv.*

ef·fer·vesce /ˌɛfɚˈvɛs/ *v.* [I] TECHNICAL a liquid that effervesces produces small BUBBLES of gas [**Origin:** 1700–1800 Latin *effervescere*, from *fervescere* **to begin to boil**]

ef·fer·ves·cent /ˌɛfɚˈvɛsənt/ *adj.* **1** CHEMISTRY a liquid that is effervescent produces small BUBBLES of gas **2** someone who is effervescent is very cheerful and active: *an effervescent personality* —**effervescence** *n.* [U]

ef·fete /ɛˈfit, ɪ-/ *adj.* FORMAL **1** an effete man looks or behaves like a woman **2** weak and powerless in a way that you dislike: *the effete intellectuals in New York society* —**effetely** *adv.*

ef·fi·ca·cious /ˌɛfəˈkeɪʃəs◂/ *adj.* FORMAL producing the result that was intended, especially when dealing with an illness or a problem: *More efficacious treatments may soon be available.* —**efficaciously** *adv.* —**efficacy** /ˈɛfɪkəsi/ *n.* [U]

ef·fi·cien·cy /ɪˈfɪʃənsi/ *n.* **1** [U] the quality of doing or using something well and effectively, without wasting time, money, or energy: *The company will focus on improving the efficiency of its operations.* | *I admired her for her efficiency and cheerfulness.* **2 efficiencies** [plural] the amounts of money, supplies etc. that are saved by finding a better or cheaper way of doing something: *Using new technology has helped us achieve dramatic efficiencies in production.* **3** [C] an efficiency apartment **4** PHYSICS the measurement of the amount of work a machine or system does compared to the amount of energy that it uses: *A new furnace would give greater efficiency and more heat output.* | **fuel/energy efficiency** | *This system could increase the fuel efficiency of today's cars by 50%.*

efˈficiency aˌpartment *n.* [C] a small apartment, usually with only one room, that is meant to be easy to take care of

ef·fi·cient /ɪˈfɪʃənt/ S3 *adj.* a person, machine, or organization that is efficient works well and effectively without wasting time, money, or energy: *Service at the restaurant is efficient and friendly.* | **fuel-/energy-efficient** *an energy-efficient heating system* [**Origin:** 1300–1400 Latin, present participle of *efficere* **to cause to happen**] —**efficiently** *adv.*

ef·fi·gy /ˈɛfədʒi/ *n. plural* **effigies** [C] **1** a figure made of wood, paper, stone etc., that looks like a person, especially one that makes the person look ugly or funny: +**of** *Protesters unveiled an effigy of the mayor.* **2 burn/hang sb in effigy** to burn or hang a figure of someone at a political DEMONSTRATION because you hate them

ef·flo·resce /ˌɛfləˈrɛs/ *v.* [I] CHEMISTRY if a chemical substance in the form of CRYSTALS containing water effloresces, it loses all its water and becomes a powder: *The crystal will effloresce when exposed in air, so it is wrapped in layer of gel.*

ef·flo·res·cence /ˌɛfləˈrɛsəns/ *n.* [U] FORMAL OR TECHNICAL the action of flowers, art etc. forming and developing, or the period of time when this happens

ef·flu·ent /ˈɛfluənt/ *n.* [plural, U] liquid waste, especially chemicals or SEWAGE

ef·fort /ˈɛfɚt/ S2 W1 *n.*
1 PHYSICAL/MENTAL ENERGY [U] the physical or mental energy that is needed to do something: *Starting an exercise program* ***takes a lot of effort.*** | *City management needs to* ***put*** *more* ***effort into*** *promoting our airport.* | *Driving an automatic* ***takes all the effort out of*** *driving* (=makes it much easier).
2 ATTEMPT [C,U] an attempt to do something, especially when this involves a lot of hard work or determination: +**at** *Further efforts at negotiation have broken down.* | **effort(s) to do sth** *Tom's efforts to lose weight haven't been very successful.* | *Team officials continue to negotiate* ***in an effort to*** *reach an agreement with Parcells.* | *We should* ***make an effort*** (=try very hard) *to include everyone in the process.* | *Board members* ***made no effort*** (=did not try at all) *to hide their disgust.*
3 be an effort to be difficult or painful to do: *I was so weak that even standing up was an effort.*
4 a good/bad/poor etc. effort something that has been done well, badly etc.: *That's a good effort for a beginner!*
5 an effort of will/imagination/concentration etc. FORMAL the determination needed to do something: *Birdwatching requires a real effort of patience sometimes.*
[**Origin:** 1400–1500 Old French *esfort*, from *esforcier* **to force**]

ef·fort·less /ˈɛfɚtlɪs/ *adj.* done in a skillful way that makes it seem easy: *Garner's effortless performance makes the show a pleasure to watch.* —**effortlessly** *adv.*: *It was amazing how she could run effortlessly mile after mile.*

ef·front·er·y /ɪˈfrʌntəri/ *n.* [U] OLD-FASHIONED behavior that you think someone should be ashamed of, although they do not seem to be: *I can't believe that they* ***have the effrontery to*** *ask us to help.*

ef·ful·gent /ɪˈfʊldʒənt/ *adj.* LITERARY beautiful and bright

ef·fu·sion /ɪˈfyuʒən/ *n.* [C,U] **1** LITERARY an uncontrolled expression of strong feelings: *His letters were filled with effusions of love.* **2** PHYSICS the process that happens when a gas escapes through a small hole in its container

ef·fu·sive /ɪˈfyusɪv/ *adj.* showing strong excited feelings: *Simpson began his speech with effusive praise for his wife.* —**effusively** *adv.* —**effusiveness** *n.* [U]

E

EFL /ˌi ɛf ˈɛl/ *n.* [U] English as a foreign language; the methods used for teaching English to people whose first language is not English, and who do not live in an English-speaking country → see also ESL

EFT /ˌi ɛf ˈti/ *n.* [C,U] an ELECTRONIC FUNDS TRANSFER

e.g. /ˌi ˈdʒi/ a written abbreviation of "for example": *midwestern states, e.g., Iowa and Illinois*

e·gal·i·tar·i·an /ɪˌgæləˈtɛriən/ *adj.* believing that everyone is equal and should have equal rights: *an egalitarian society* —**egalitarianism** *n.* [U]

egg[1] /ɛg/ S1 W2 *n.* [C]
1 BIRD BIOLOGY a round object with a hard SHELL, that contains a baby bird, snake, insect etc. and which comes out of a female bird, snake, or insect: *Blackbirds usually* ***lay*** *their* ***eggs*** *in March.* | *an ostrich egg*
2 FOOD an egg, especially one from a chicken, that is used for food: *We had fried eggs for breakfast.*
3 ANIMALS/PEOPLE also **egg cell** BIOLOGY a cell produced by a woman or female animal that combines with SPERM (=male cell) to make a baby
4 put/have all your eggs in one basket to depend completely on one thing or one course of action in order to get success: *When planning your investments, it's unwise to put all your eggs in one basket.*
5 have egg on your face if someone, especially someone in authority, has egg on their face, they look silly because something embarrassing has happened: *Economists who had predicted a recession emerged with egg on their faces after news of the stock market boom.*
6 a good egg OLD-FASHIONED someone who you can depend on to be honest, nice etc.
[**Origin:** 1300–1400 Old Norse] → see also **lay an egg** at LAY[1] (20)

egg[2] *v.*
egg sb ↔ **on** *phr. v.* to encourage someone to do something, especially something that they should not do or do not want to do: *Susan didn't want to ask Bob on a date, but her friends kept egging her on.*

ˈegg cream *n.* [C] a drink made with chocolate SYRUP, milk, and CARBONATED water (=water that has a lot of BUBBLES in it)

egg·cup /ˈɛgkʌp/ *n.* [C] a small container that holds a boiled egg while you eat it

egg·head /ˈɛghɛd/ *n.* [C] HUMOROUS someone who is very intelligent, and only interested in ideas and books

egg·nog /ˈɛgnɑg/ *n.* [U] a drink made with milk, eggs, SPICES, and often alcohol such as BRANDY, drunk mainly in the winter

egg·plant /ˈɛgplænt/ *n.* **1** [C,U] a large vegetable with smooth purple skin → see picture on page A35 **2** [U] a dark purple color

ˌegg ˈroll *n.* [C] a type of Chinese food consisting of vegetables and sometimes meat rolled inside a piece of thin DOUGH that is then cooked in oil

eggs Ben·e·dict /ˌɛgz ˈbɛnəˌdɪkt/ *n.* [U] a dish made with a POACHED egg on an ENGLISH MUFFIN with a piece of HAM, with a white SAUCE poured over it

egg·shell /ˈɛgʃɛl/ *n.* **1** [C,U] the hard outside part of a bird's egg **2** [U] a very pale yellowish-white color **3 eggshell paint** a type of paint that is slightly shiny when it is dry → see also **be walking on eggshells/eggs** at WALK[1] (8)

ˈegg ˌtimer *n.* [C] a small glass container with sand in it that runs from one part to the other in about 3 to 5 minutes, used for measuring the time it takes to boil an egg

ˈegg white *n.* [C,U] the transparent part inside an egg that turns white when it is cooked → see also YOLK → see picture at EGG

e·go /ˈigoʊ/ *n. plural* **egos** [C] **1** the opinion that you have about yourself: *Skinner* ***has a big ego*** (=thinks he is very smart and important). | *Losing 50 pounds was the* ***ego boost*** (=something that makes you feel good about yourself) *he needed.* | *Jan's co-workers became increasingly annoyed with her* ***inflated ego*** (=the thought that you are smarter or more important than you are). → see also ALTER EGO **2 an ego trip** INFORMAL something that you do because it makes you feel important: *Phillips has been* ***on an ego trip*** *ever since he got promoted to vice president.* **3** [usually singular] TECHNICAL the part of your mind with which you think and take action, according to Freudian PSYCHOLOGY → see also ID

e·go·cen·tric /ˌigoʊˈsɛntrɪk◂/ *adj.* thinking only about yourself and not thinking about what other people might need or want —**egocentric** *n.* [C] —**egocentricity** /ˌigoʊsɛnˈtrɪsət̬i/ *n.* [U]

e·go·ism /ˈigoʊˌɪzəm/ *n.* [U] EGOTISM —**egoist** *n.* [C] —**egoistic** /ˌigoʊˈɪstɪk◂/ *adj.*

e·go·ma·ni·ac /ˌigoʊˈmeɪniˌæk/ *n.* [C] someone who thinks that they are very important, and tries to get advantages for themselves without caring about how this affects other people

e·go·tism /ˈigəˌtɪzəm/ *n.* [U] the belief that you are much better or more important than other people, or behavior that shows this

e·go·tis·ti·cal /ˌigəˈtɪstɪkəl/ *adj.* believing that you are much better or more important than other people: *Rigby often seems egotistical and arrogant.*

e·gre·gious /ɪˈgridʒəs/ *adj.* FORMAL an egregious mistake, failure, problem etc. is extremely bad and noticeable: *The situation at Zefco was one of the most egregious examples of discrimination we have seen.* —**egregiously** *adv.*

e·gress /ˈigrɛs/ *n.* [U] FORMAL OR LAW the act of leaving a building or place, or the right to do this

e·gret /ˈigrət, -ɛt/ *n.* [C] BIOLOGY a bird that lives near water and has long legs and long white tail feathers → see picture on page A31

E·gypt /ˈidʒɪpt/ a country in northeast Africa, next to the Mediterranean Sea and the Red Sea

E·gyp·tian[1] /ɪˈdʒɪpʃən/ *n.* [C] someone from Egypt

Egyptian[2] *adj.* from or relating to Egypt

E·gyp·tol·o·gy /ˌidʒɪpˈtɑlədʒi/ *n.* [U] the study of the history, society, buildings, and language of ancient Egypt —**Egyptologist** *n.* [C]

eh /eɪ, ɛ/ *interjection* SPOKEN used when you want someone to reply to you or agree with something you have said: *Pretty cold out, eh?*

ei·der·down /ˈaɪdɚˌdaʊn/ *n.* **1** [U] the soft fine feathers of a particular type of DUCK **2** [C] OLD-FASHIONED a thick warm cover for a bed, filled with feathers

Eif·fel /ˈaɪfəl/, **Gus·tave** /ˈgustɑv/ (1832–1923) a French engineer who built many bridges and the Eiffel Tower

ˌEiffel ˈTower, the a 300 meter-high metal tower in Paris, completed in 1889

eight /eɪt/ *number* **1** 8 **2** 8 o'clock: *Let's have breakfast* ***at eight***. **3 be behind the eight ball** SPOKEN to be in a difficult or risky situation: *We can't afford to lose any more money – we're behind the eight ball already.* [**Origin:** Old English *eahta*]

eight·een /ˌeɪˈtin◂/ *number* 18

eight·eenth[1] /ˌeɪˈtinθ◂/ *adj.* 18th; next after the seventeenth: *the eighteenth century*

eighteenth[2] *pron.* **the eighteenth** the 18th thing in a series: *Let's have dinner on the eighteenth* (=the 18th day of the month).

ˌEighteenth Aˈmendment, the HISTORY an addition to the U.S. Constitution in 1917 that made it illegal to make or sell alcoholic drinks. This rule was changed by the Twenty-first Amendment in 1933.

ˌeighteen-ˈwheeler *n.* [C] a large truck consisting of two connected parts, used for carrying goods over long distances

eighth[1] /eɪtθ/ *adj.* 8th; next after the seventh: *This is the eighth day in a row that he has been late.*

eighth[2] *pron.* **the eighth** the 8th thing in a series: *Classes start on the eighth* (=the 8th day of the month).

eighth[3] *n.* [C] 1/8; one of eight equal parts: *Divide the pie into eighths.* | ***An eighth of*** *the students said they had no opinion on the subject.* | **one-eighth/three-eighths/seven-eighths etc.** *Shares fell five-eighths of a point yesterday.*

ˈeighth note *n.* [C] a musical note that continues for an eighth of the length of a WHOLE NOTE

eight·i·eth[1] /ˈeɪt̬iɪθ/ *adj.* 80th; next after the seventy-ninth: *It's my grandmother's eightieth birthday tomorrow.*

eightieth[2] *pron.* **the eightieth** the 80th thing in a series

eight·y /ˈeɪt̬i/ *number* **1** 80 **2 the eighties** also **the '80s** the years from 1980 through 1989 **3 sb's eighties** the time when someone is 80 to 89 years old: **in your early/mid/late eighties** *My grandfather's in his early eighties.* **4 in the eighties** if the temperature is in the eighties, it is between 80° and 89° FAHRENHEIT: **in the high/low eighties** *The temperature was in the low eighties and sunny.*

ˌeighty-ˈsix *v.* [T] INFORMAL to refuse to serve a customer, or to make them leave a bar or restaurant: *Rob got eighty-sixed from the club for not wearing a jacket.*

Ein·stein /ˈaɪnstaɪn/ *n.* [C usually singular] INFORMAL a name you call someone who is very smart, or that you use humorously when someone has just done or said something stupid: *You don't have to be an Einstein to know it's not going to work.*

Einstein, Al·bert /ˈælbɚt/ (1879–1955) a U.S. PHYSICIST and MATHEMATICIAN born in Germany, who developed the THEORY of RELATIVITY, which completely changed the way that scientists understand space and time

Ei·sen·how·er /ˈaɪzənˌhaʊɚ/, **Dwight Da·vid** /dwaɪt ˈdeɪvɪd/ (1890–1969) the 34th President of the U.S., who had been a general in the U.S. Army during World War II

Ei·sen·stein /ˈaɪzənˌstaɪn/, **Ser·gei Mi·khai·lo·vich** /ˈsɛrgeɪ mɪˈkeɪləvɪtʃ/ (1898–1948) a Russian movie DIRECTOR who is considered one of the greatest directors ever

ei·ther[1] /ˈiðɚ, ˈaɪ-/ S1 W2 *conjunction* used to begin a list of two or more possibilities, separated by "or" → see also OR: *You can choose either french fries, baked potato, or mashed potatoes.* | *Either eat some more, or take some of those meatballs home with you.* → see Word Choice box at ALSO

GRAMMAR **either...or and neither...nor**

When you use these phrases in formal speech or writing, use a singular verb if the second noun is singular: *If either my parents or Will calls, tell them I'm not here.* | *Neither Brad nor Mike was at the party.* If the second noun is plural, use a plural verb: *If either my sister or my parents come, can you let them in?* In informal speech, the verb is usually plural.

either² S2 W3 *determiner* **1** one or the other of two things or people: *Do you have insurance on either one of these cars?* → see also ANY, NEITHER¹ **2** one and the other of two things or people SYN **each**: *Sandy's brothers were standing on either side of her.* | *There are gas stations at either end of the block.* **3 either way** SPOKEN used to say that something will be the same, whichever of two possible choices you make: *Either way, it's going to be expensive.* **4 within two feet/ten years/one hour etc. either way** two feet, ten years etc. more or less than the correct amount or measurement: *Chris says he can guess anyone's age within two years either way.* **5 sth could go either way** if a situation could go either way, both results are equally possible: *The race for governor could still go either way.* **6 an either-or situation** a situation in which you cannot avoid having to make a decision or choice

GRAMMAR **either, neither, none, any**
In formal speech and writing, use these pronouns with a singular verb: *None/Neither of us has seen the show.* In informal speech and writing, you can use a plural verb: *Have either of you ever been to New York?*

either³ S2 *pron.* one or the other of two things or people: *I brought chocolate and vanilla ice cream — you can have either.* | *Do either of you have 50 cents I could borrow?*

either⁴ S1 W2 *adv.* **1** [only in negatives] also: *"I didn't know you could go skiing in Hawaii." "I didn't either."* | *"Didn't she tell you her name?" "No, and I didn't introduce myself, either."* **2 me either** SPOKEN, NONSTANDARD used to say that something is also true about you: *"I've never had a broken bone." "Me either."* → see also NEITHER

e·jac·u·late /ɪˈdʒækyəˌleɪt/ *v.* [I,T] **1** BIOLOGY when a man ejaculates, SEMEN comes out of his PENIS **2** OLD-FASHIONED to suddenly shout or say something, especially because you are surprised —**ejaculation** /ɪˌdʒækyəˈleɪʃən/ *n.* [C,U]

e·ject /ɪˈdʒɛkt/ *v.* **1** [T] to push or throw out with force: *The driver was ejected when the car hit an embankment and rolled over.* **2** [I] to jump out of an airplane when it is going to crash **3** [T] to make something come out of a machine by pressing a button: *Press the stop button again to eject the tape.* **4** [T] to make someone leave a place or building by using force: **+from** *Protesters were ejected from the courtroom for shouting obscenities.* [**Origin:** 1400–1500 Latin *ejectus*, past participle of *eicere* **to throw out**] —**ejection** /ɪˈdʒɛkʃən/ *n.* [C,U]

eˈjection seat *n.* [C] a special seat that throws the pilot out of an airplane when it is going to crash

eke /ik/ *v.* [**Origin:** Old English *iecan, ecan* **to increase**]

eke sth ↔ **out** *phr. v.* LITERARY **1 eke out a living/existence** to succeed in getting the things you need to live, even though you have very little money or food: *Cliff's family worked in the cotton fields to eke out a meager living.* **2 eke out a profit/victory etc.** to just barely succeed in making a profit, winning a competition etc.: *If they're lucky, they might eke out a tiny profit for the year.* **3** to make a small supply of something such as food or money last longer by carefully using small amounts of it: *The library has worked hard to eke out extra space for books.*

EKG /ˌi keɪ ˈdʒi/ *n.* [C] **1** a piece of equipment that records electrical changes in your heart SYN **electrocardiograph** **2** a drawing produced by an ELECTROCARDIOGRAPH SYN **electrocardiogram**

e·lab·o·rate¹ /ɪˈlæbrɪt/ *adj.* **1** having a lot of small details or parts that are connected to each other in a complicated way: *an elaborate tattoo of an eagle* **2** carefully planned and produced with many details: *Cho and Lee celebrated their new partnership at an elaborate banquet.* [**Origin:** 1400–1500 Latin *elaboratus*, past participle of *elaborare* **to work out**] —**elaborately** *adv.*: *an elaborately carved statue* —**elaborateness** *n.* [U]

e·lab·o·rate² /ɪˈlæbəˌreɪt/ *v.* [I] to give more details or new information about something: **+on** *Lally refused to elaborate on her earlier statement.* —**elaboration** /ɪˌlæbəˈreɪʃən/ *n.* [U]

é·lan /eɪˈlɑn/ *n.* [U] LITERARY a style that is full of energy and determination: *Collins' story was filmed with real intelligence and élan.*

e·lapse /ɪˈlæps/ *v.* [I not in progressive] FORMAL if a particular period of time elapses, it passes: *More than five years have elapsed since the kidnapping.* [**Origin:** 1500–1600 Latin *elapsus*, past participle of *elabi* **to slip away**]

e·las·tic¹ /ɪˈlæstɪk/ *n.* **1** [U] a type of rubber material that can stretch and then return to its usual length or size: *The gloves have elastic at the wrist for a snug fit.* **2** ESPECIALLY CANADIAN [C] a RUBBER BAND

elastic² *adj.* **1** made of elastic: *an elastic waistband* **2** a material that is elastic can stretch or bend and then go back to its usual length, size, or shape: *Children's bones are far more elastic than adults'.* **3** ECONOMICS an elastic supply of or demand for changes according to price: *The demand for air travel is less elastic in the Caribbean.* **4** a system or plan that is elastic can change or be changed easily

e·las·tic·i·ty /iˌlæˈstɪsət̬i, ˌilæ-/ *n.* [U] the ability of an object or material to return to its normal shape or size after it has been stretched or pressed: *the elasticity of skin*

elasˌticity of deˈmand *n.* [U] ECONOMICS the degree to which people's desire for a good or service changes in reaction to a change in price

elasˌticity of supˈply *n.* [U] ECONOMICS the degree to which the supply of a good or service changes in reaction to a change in price

eˌlastic ˈlimit *n.* [C] PHYSICS the furthest point to which you can stretch or press a material without permanently changing its shape or breaking it

e·lat·ed /ɪˈleɪt̬ɪd/ *adj.* extremely happy and excited, especially because you have been successful: *We were elated to find out Sue was pregnant again.* [**Origin:** 1500–1600 Latin *elatus*, past participle of *efferre* **to carry up**]

e·la·tion /ɪˈleɪʃən/ *n.* [U] a feeling of extreme happiness and excitement

el·bow¹ /ˈɛlboʊ/ S3 *n.* [C] **1** BIOLOGY the joint where your arm bends **2** the part of a shirt, coat etc. that covers your elbow **3 give sb the elbow** INFORMAL to tell someone that you do not like them or want them to work for you anymore, and that they should leave **4 elbow grease** INFORMAL hard work and effort, especially when cleaning or polishing something: *You'll need to use some elbow grease to get that floor clean.* **5 elbow room** enough space in which to move easily: *Let's sit in a booth. There's more elbow room there.* **6** a curved part of a pipe [**Origin:** Old English *elboga*]

elbow² *v.* [T] to push someone with your elbows, especially in order to move past them: *Greene had to leave the game after being elbowed in the face.* ►see THESAURUS box at **push¹**

El·brus, Mount also **Elbruz, Mount** /ˈɛlbrus/ the highest mountain in the Caucasus Mountains

El Cid /ɛl ˈsɪd/ (?1043–1099) a Spanish soldier who appears in many stories and poems as a perfect example of CHIVALRY, Christian values, and love of his country

el·der¹ /ˈɛldɚ/ *adj.* **1** OLD-FASHIONED OR FORMAL **an elder brother/daughter/sister etc.** an older brother, daughter etc.: *John's elder brother died in the war.* **2 the elder a)** OLD-FASHIONED OR FORMAL the older one of two people: *The elder of his two daughters sat next to him.* **b) the Elder** used after the name of a famous person who lived in the past, to show that they are the

E

older of two people with the same name, usually a father and son: *Pliny the Elder* → see also YOUNGER → see Word Choice box at OLD

elder² *n.* [C] **1** a member of a tribe or other social group who is important and respected because they are old: *the tribal elders* **2 your elders** people who are older than you are: *Young people should have respect for their elders.* **3** someone who has an official position of responsibility in some Christian churches **4 elder abuse** the crime of harming an old person **5** BIOLOGY a small wild tree with white flowers and black berries

USAGE **elder, eldest**
Elder and **eldest** are fairly formal words and were used more in the past. **Older** and **oldest** are used more often now. Note that you CANNOT say "elder than": *My sister is two years older* (NOT "elder") *than I am.*

E

el·der·ber·ry /ˈɛldɚˌbɛri/ *n.* [C] BIOLOGY the fruit of the elder tree

el·der·care /ˈɛldɚˌkɛr/ *n.* [U] medical care for old people

el·der·ly /ˈɛldɚli/ W3 *adj.* **1** old, especially used in order to be polite: *Some elderly residents cited concerns over crime levels.* **2 the elderly** [plural] people who are old: *What services are available for the elderly in this neighborhood?* ▸see THESAURUS box at **old**

ˌelder ˈstatesman *n.* [C] someone old and respected, especially a politician, who people ask for advice because of his knowledge and experience

el·dest /ˈɛldɪst/ *adj.* OLD-FASHIONED OR FORMAL **1 the eldest son/sister/child etc.** the oldest son, sister etc. among a group of people, especially brothers and sisters: *Her eldest child is at college now.* **2 the eldest** the oldest one in a group of people, especially brothers and sisters: *I have two brothers, but I'm the eldest.*

e·lect¹ /ɪˈlɛkt/ W2 *v.* **1** [T usually passive] POLITICS to choose someone for an official position by voting: **elect sb to sth** *Brock was elected to the state legislature.* | **elect sb president/governor etc.** *Brown was elected mayor two years ago.* **2 elect to do sth** FORMAL to choose to do something: *The committee elected not to fire Johnson.* [**Origin:** 1400–1500 Latin *electus*, past participle of *eligere* **to choose**]

elect² *adj.* **president-elect/governor-elect/mayor-elect etc.** the person who has been elected as president etc., but who has not yet officially started their job

e·lec·tion /ɪˈlɛkʃən/ W1 *n.* **1** [C] POLITICS an occasion when people vote to choose someone for an official position: *This year's presidential election will take place on November 4.* **2** [U] POLITICS the fact of being elected to an official position: *This is Sanders' fourth trip to Washington since his election as governor.* → see also GENERAL ELECTION

e·lec·tion·eer·ing /ɪˌlɛkʃəˈnɪrɪŋ/ *n.* [U] POLITICS speeches and other activities intended to persuade people to vote for a particular person or political party —**electioneer** *n.* [C]

e·lec·tive¹ /ɪˈlɛktɪv/ *n.* [C] a course students can choose to take, but they do not have to take in order to GRADUATE

elective² *adj.* FORMAL **1** POLITICS an elective position or organization is one for which there is an election **2** elective medical treatment is treatment that you choose to have, although you do not have to

e·lec·tor /ɪˈlɛktɚ, -tɔr/ *n.* [C] **1** POLITICS someone who has the right to vote in an election **2** POLITICS a member of the Electoral College

e·lec·tor·al /ɪˈlɛktərəl/ *adj.* [only before noun] **1** POLITICS relating to elections and voting: *the electoral system* **2** POLITICS relating to the people who are allowed to vote in an election: *an electoral list*

eˌlectoral ˈcollege *n.* POLITICS **1 the Electoral College** an official group of people who come together to elect the U.S. President and Vice President, based on the votes of people in each state **2** [C] a similar group in other countries

e·lec·tor·ate /ɪˈlɛktərɪt/ *n.* [singular] POLITICS all the people who are allowed to vote in an election

E·lec·tra com·plex /ɪˈlɛktrə ˌkɑmplɛks/ *n.* [C usually singular] TECHNICAL the unconscious sexual feelings that a girl has toward her father, according to the ideas of Sigmund Freud → see also OEDIPUS COMPLEX

e·lec·tric /ɪˈlɛktrɪk/ S3 W3 *adj.* **1** PHYSICS using, carrying, or producedy by electricity: *There were no electric lights.* | *Is the stove electric or gas?* | *an electric shock* | *an electric cable* **2** making people feel very excited: *The atmosphere in the stadium was electric.* ▸see THESAURUS box at **exciting** [**Origin:** 1600–1700 Modern Latin *electricus*, from Latin *electrum* **amber**; because electricity was first made by rubbing amber]

WORD CHOICE **electric, electronic, electrical**
• Use **electric** as an adjective with the names of things that need electricity to work or that carry electricity: *an electric guitar* | *electric lights*.
• Use **electronic** for equipment that uses electricity, but in a special way by passing the electricity through smaller more complicated pieces of equipment: *an electronic game* | *an electronic calculator*.
• Use **electrical** as a more general word to talk about people and their work, or about general types of things that use or produce electricity: *an electrical engineer* | *My dad's company imports electrical goods.*

e·lec·tri·cal /ɪˈlɛktrɪkəl/ S3 *adj.* **1** using, carrying, or produced by electricity: *electrical equipment* | *electrical wiring* | *The changing magnetic fields create an electrical current.* | **electrical power/energy** *The train runs on electrical power.* | **an electrical charge/surge/current etc.** *Protect computer equipment from electrical surges.* → see Word Choice box at ELECTRIC **2** relating to electricity or electrical equipment: *an electrical technician* | *The fire was caused by an electrical fault.* —**electrically** /-kli/ *adv.*

eˌlectrical ˈforce an ELECTROMAGNETIC FORCE

eˌlectrically ˈpolarized *adj.* PHYSICS used for describing an ATOM or MOLECULE with an electric CHARGE that is slightly more positive or negative on one side than on the opposite side

eˌlectrical poˈtential *n.* [U] CHEMISTRY **1** the ability of a PRIMARY CELL to produce electricity **2** the energy that is likely to be produced by something that produces electricity SYN **voltage**

eˌlectrical reˈsistance also **eˌlectric reˈsistance** *n.* [U] PHYSICS how hard it is for an electric current to flow through a particular material or object. Electrical resistance is usually measured in OHMS: *the electrical resistance of conductors and insulators*

eˌlectrical ˈstorm *n.* [C] a violent storm with a lot of LIGHTNING

eˌlectric ˈblanket *n.* [C] a special BLANKET (=large cloth on a bed) with electric wires in it, used for making a bed warm

eˈlectric ˌblue *adj.* very bright blue —**electric blue** *n.* [C,U]

eˌlectric ˈchair *n.* **the electric chair** a chair in which criminals are killed using electricity, in order to punish them for crimes such as murder

eˌlectric ˈeel *n.* [C] BIOLOGY a large South American fish that looks like a snake, and can give an electric shock

eˌlectric ˈeye *n.* [C] NOT TECHNICAL a PHOTOELECTRIC CELL

eˌlectric ˈfield *n.* [C] PHYSICS an area of force that surrounds something with an electric charge or is connected with a changing MAGNETIC FIELD, which affects other electric charges

eˌlectric ˈforce *n.* [C] PHYSICS a force that exists between two objects with an electric charge

e·lec·tri·cian /ɪˌlɛkˈtrɪʃən, i-/ *n.* [C] someone whose job is to connect or repair electrical wires or equipment

e·lec·tric·i·ty /ɪˌlɛkˈtrɪsət̬i/ S3 *n.* [U] **1** PHYSICS power in the form of electric current that is carried by wires, CABLES etc. and is used to provide light or heat, to make machines work etc.: *the electricity supply* | *an electricity bill* | ***The electricity went out*** (=it stopped working) *during the storm.* | **generate/produce electricity** *Wind can be used to produce electricity.* **2** a form of energy that is caused by moving PARTICLES (=very small things) with electric charge → see also STATIC ELECTRICITY **3** a feeling of excitement: *You could feel the electricity in the air.*

e,lectric 'power *n.* [U] **1** electricity produced from something such as coal, gas, water, etc.: *the generation of electric power from sunlight* **2** PHYSICS the rate at which electricity produces another form of energy such as light or heat. Electric power is measured in WATTS.

e,lectric re'sistance *n.* [U] TECHNICAL ELECTRICAL RESISTANCE

e·lec·tri·fy /ɪˈlɛktrəˌfaɪ/ *v.* **electrified, electrifying** [T] **1** to make people feel very excited or interested: *His speech electrified the entire convention.* **2** to start supplying a building, area etc. with electricity: *The rural areas have not been electrified yet.* **3** to change a railroad or other system so that it uses electrical power: *Mackenzie had electrified the Toronto streetcar system.* —**electrifying** *adj.*: *an electrifying performance* —**electrification** /ɪˌlɛktrəfəˈkeɪʃən/ *n.* [U]

electro- /ɪlɛktroʊ, -trə/ *prefix* TECHNICAL **1** relating to electricity, or made to work by electricity: *an electromagnet* | *to electrocute someone* (=kill them with electricity) **2** electric and something else: *electromechanical*

e·lec·tro·car·di·o·gram /ɪˌlɛktroʊˈkɑrdiəˌgræm/ *n.* [C] TECHNICAL an EKG

e·lec·tro·car·di·o·graph /ɪˌlɛktroʊˈkɑrdiəˌgræf/ *n.* [C] TECHNICAL an EKG

e·lec·tro·chem·i·cal cell /ɪˌlɛktroʊˌkɛmɪkəl ˈsɛl/ *n.* [C] CHEMISTRY a piece of equipment containing chemicals, such as a BATTERY, that produces electrical energy from the reaction between the chemicals or changes electrical energy into chemical energy

e,lectrochemical 'process *n.* [C,U] CHEMISTRY the process by which the chemicals stored inside an electrochemical cell are changed into electrical power or electrical power is changed into chemical energy

e·lec·tro·con·vul·sive therapy /ɪˌlɛktroʊkənˌvʌlsɪv ˈθɛrəpi/ *n.* [U] TECHNICAL ELECTROSHOCK

e·lec·tro·cute /ɪˈlɛktrəˌkyut/ *v.* [T usually passive] to kill someone by passing electricity through their body —**electrocution** /ɪˌlɛktrəˈkyuʃən/ *n.* [U]

e·lec·trode /ɪˈlɛktroʊd/ *n.* [C] PHYSICS one of the two parts, often marked (+) or (-), through which electricity flows to or from a part of an electrical CIRCUIT that is not metal, as in a BATTERY → see also ANODE: *Doctors attached electrodes to his chest to measure his heart rate.*

e·lec·tro·en·ceph·a·lo·gram /ɪˌlɛktroʊɪnˈsɛfələˌgræm/ *n.* [C] TECHNICAL an EEG

e·lec·tro·en·ceph·a·lo·graph /ɪˌlɛktroʊɪnˈsɛfələˌgræf/ *n.* [C] TECHNICAL an EEG

e·lec·trol·y·sis /ɪˌlɛkˈtrɑlɪsɪs/ *n.* [U] **1** the process of using electricity to destroy hair roots and remove hair from your face, legs etc. **2** PHYSICS the process of separating or changing the chemical parts of a substance by passing an electric current through it

e·lec·tro·lyte /ɪˈlɛktrəˌlaɪt/ *n.* [C] CHEMISTRY a liquid or solid substance that allows electricity to pass through it by the movement of IONS

e·lec·tro·lyt·ic cell /ɪˌlɛktroʊˌlɪṭɪk ˈsɛl/ *n.* [C] CHEMISTRY a piece of equipment containing an electrolyte, that separates or changes the chemical parts of the liquid when an electric current passes through it

e·lec·tro·mag·net /ɪˌlɛktroʊˈmægnɪt, ɪˈlɛktroʊˌmægnɪt/ *n.* [C] PHYSICS a type of MAGNET that usually consists of a piece of wire wound around some metal. It becomes MAGNETIC when an electric current is passed through the wire. —**electromagnetic** /ɪˌlɛɛktroʊmægˈnɛṭɪk/ *adj.*

e,lectromag,netic 'force also **e,lectrical 'force** *n.* [U] PHYSICS the force that affects PARTICLES that have an electric CHARGE. When the charges are the same, they REPEL each other (=push each other away). When the charges are opposite, they attract each other.

e,lectromangnetic in'duction *n.* [U] PHYSICS the production of an electric current in a CONDUCTOR caused by changes or movements in a MAGNETIC FIELD near the conductor

e,lectromagnetic radi'ation *n.* [U] PHYSICS energy in the form of electromagnetic waves, such as heat, light, or X-RAYS that contains both electric and MAGNETIC fields

e,lectromagnetic 'spectrum *n.* [C] PHYSICS all the different forms of electromagnetic waves

e,lectromagnetic 'wave *n.* [C] PHYSICS a wave of electric and MAGNETIC energy that moves through space, for example a radio wave or a light wave

e·lec·tro·mag·net·ism /ɪˌlɛktroʊˈmægnəˌtɪzəm/ *n.* [U] PHYSICS a force relating to electric and MAGNETIC FIELDS, or the study of this force

e·lec·tron /ɪˈlɛktrɑn/ *n.* [C] PHYSICS a PARTICLE (=very small piece of matter) with a negative electrical CHARGE that moves around the NUCLEUS (=central part) of an atom → see also NEUTRON, PROTON → see picture at ATOM

electricity

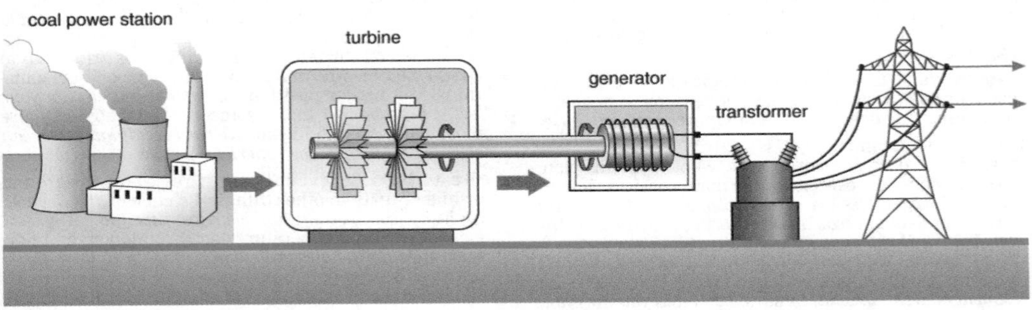

1 In many power stations, fossil fuels are burned to release energy. This is used to heat water to produce steam.

2 The steam is forced through large fans called turbines, making them turn.

3 The turbines turn generators. These are large magnets inside massive coils of wire. A moving magnet inside a coil of wire creates an electric current.

4 The electricity flows along cables.

e·lec·tro·neg·a·tiv·i·ty /ɪˌlɛktroʊˌnɛgəˈtɪvət̬i/ *n.* [U] CHEMISTRY a measurement of whether an atom in a MOLECULE is likely or able to attract ELECTRONS

e·lec·tron·ic /ɪˌlɛkˈtrɑnɪk/ W2 *adj.* **1** PHYSICS electronic equipment, such as computers or televisions, uses electricity that has passed through CHIPS, TRANSISTORS etc.: *an electronic keyboard* → see Word Choice box at ELECTRIC **2** using or produced by electronic equipment: *electronic banking* | *electronic music* —**electronically** /-kli/ *adv.*

elecˌtronic ˈfunds ˌtransfer ABBREVIATION **EFT** *n.* [C,U] the process by which money is moved from one bank account, business etc. to another using the telephone or a computer

elecˌtronic ˈmail *n.* [U] EMAIL

elecˌtronic ˈmusic *n.* [U] a style of modern popular music that is made using electronic instruments and equipment and has a very strong fast beat

elecˌtronic ˈorganizer *n.* [C] a small piece of electronic equipment that you can use to record addresses, telephone numbers, meetings etc.

elecˌtronic ˈpublishing *n.* [U] the business or activity of producing books, magazines, or newspapers that are designed to be read using a computer

e·lec·tron·ics /ɪˌlɛkˈtrɑnɪks/ *n.* **1** [U] the study or industry of making equipment, such as computers or televisions, that uses electricity that has passed through CHIPS, TRANSISTORS etc. **2** [plural] electronic equipment: *consumer electronics* | *American homes are filled with VCRs and other electronics.*

eˌlectron ˈmicroscope *n.* [C] PHYSICS a very powerful MICROSCOPE (=scientific instrument used for looking at small objects) that uses beams of ELECTRONS instead of light to make things look larger

e·lec·tro·plate /ɪˈlɛktrəˌpleɪt/ *v.* [T usually passive] to put a very thin layer of metal onto the surface of an object, using ELECTROLYSIS

e·lec·tro·shock /ɪˈlɛktroʊˌʃɑk/ also **eˌlectroshock ˈtherapy** *n.* [U] a method of treatment for mental illness that involves sending electricity through someone's brain

e·lec·tro·stat·ics /ɪˌlɛktroʊˈstæt̬ɪks/ *n.* [plural] PHYSICS the area of physics that studies STATIC ELECTRICITY

el·e·gant /ˈɛləgənt/ *adj.* **1** very beautiful, stylish, and graceful: *She was tall and elegant.* | *an elegant black dress* **2** an elegant idea or a plan is very intelligent yet simple: *an elegant solution* [**Origin:** 1400–1500 French, Latin *elegans* **specially chosen as being of good quality**] —**elegantly** *adv.* —**elegance** *n.* [U]

el·e·gi·ac /ˌɛləˈdʒaɪək◂ / *adj.* LITERARY **1** showing that you feel sad about something that happened in the past, someone who has died, or something that no longer exists: *the film's elegiac mood* **2** relating to elegies: *elegiac verse*

el·e·gy /ˈɛlədʒi/ *n.* [C] *plural* **elegies** ENG. LANG. ARTS a poem or song written to show sadness for someone or something that does not exist anymore: *a funeral elegy*

el·e·ment /ˈɛləmənt/ Ac S3 W2 *n.* [C]

1 PART one part or feature of a whole system, plan, piece of work etc., especially one that is basic or important: +**of** *Vegetables are a vital element of the human diet.* | +**in** *Religion was an element in the dispute.* | *The movie has* ***all the elements of*** *a great love story.*

2 an element of danger/truth/risk etc. a definite amount, usually small, of danger, truth etc.: *There's an element of truth in what he says.* | *If I told you the plan, that would spoil* ***the element of surprise.***

3 CHEMISTRY CHEMISTRY a substance that consists of only one type of atom and which cannot be changed into a simpler substance. CARBON gold, and oxygen are elements. → see also COMPOUND: *chemical elements*

4 PEOPLE USUALLY DISAPPROVING a group of people who can be recognized by particular behavior or beliefs: *The clubs also tend to attract a* ***criminal element*** (=people who do illegal things).

5 the elements weather, especially bad weather: *The tent was their only protection from the elements.*

6 the elements of sth the most basic and important features of something, or the things that you have to learn first about a subject: *His imaginative stories use the elements of poetry – rhythm, rhyme, alliteration.*

7 be in your element to be in a situation that you enjoy because you are good at it: *Dad was in his element, building a fire and grilling the steaks.*

8 be out of your element to be in a situation that makes you uncomfortable because you are not good at it: *Miller is completely out of her element in this sci-fi role.*

9 HEAT the part of a STOVE or other piece of electrical equipment that produces heat

10 EARTH/AIR/FIRE/WATER one of the four substances from which people used to believe that everything was made

11 MATH a number that is a single part of a mathematical set or MATRIX

12 CHURCH **the Elements** [plural] the bread and wine used in Communion in some Christian church services

[**Origin:** 1300–1400 Old French, Latin *elementum*]

el·e·men·tal /ˌɛləˈmɛntəl/ *adj.* **1** elemental fears, forces or emotions are the most basic and natural ones simple, basic, and important: *Love and fear are two of the most elemental human emotions.* **2** TECHNICAL existing as a simple chemical element that has not been combined with anything else: *elemental carbon*

el·e·men·tary /ˌɛləˈmɛntri, -ˈmɛntəri/ *adj.* **1** [only before noun] relating to elementary school: *elementary education* **2** [only before noun] relating to the first and easiest part of a subject: *Billy is taking elementary algebra this year.* **3** simple or basic: *elementary principles of justice* | *an elementary mistake*

ˌelementary ˈparticle *n.* [C] PHYSICS one of the types of pieces of matter, including ELECTRONS, NEUTRONS, and PROTONS that make up atoms and are not made up of anything smaller

ˌelementary reˈaction *n.* [C,U] CHEMISTRY a change that happens in a single step when different chemical substances are mixed together

eleˈmentary ˌschool *n.* [C] a school in the U.S. that is typically for the first six years of a child's education SYN **grade school**

el·e·phant /ˈɛləfənt/ *n.* [C] a very large gray animal with four legs, big ears, and a TRUNK (=very long nose) that it can use to pick things up [**Origin:** 1200–1300 Old French *oliphant*, from Greek *elephas* **elephant, ivory**] → see also WHITE ELEPHANT

el·e·phan·tine /ˌɛləˈfæntin, -taɪn/ *adj.* FORMAL very large, or slow and awkward: *elephantine bureaucracy*

el·e·vate /ˈɛləˌveɪt/ *v.* [T] **1** FORMAL to move someone or something to a higher or more important level or rank, or make them better than before: *Store owners hope to elevate the mall's image to help improve business.* | **elevate sb/sth to sth** *Sloane was elevated to the rank of captain.* **2** to increase the amount, temperature, pressure etc. of something: *This drug tends to elevate body temperature.* **3** to lift someone or something to a higher position: *Lie down and elevate your feet.* **4** FORMAL to make someone feel happier, more moral, or more intelligent: *We need candidates who can elevate and inspire the American people.*

el·e·vat·ed /ˈɛləˌveɪt̬ɪd/ *adj.* **1** raised off the ground or higher up than other things: *A section of the elevated highway collapsed.* | *an elevated pipeline* **2** FORMAL elevated levels, temperatures etc. are higher than normal: *Elevated cholesterol levels may lead to a heart attack.* **3** elevated thoughts, words etc. seem to be intelligent or of a high moral standard: *Jack had more elevated interests than his colleagues' drinking parties.* **4** [only before noun] an elevated position or rank is very important and respected: *He reached an elevated position within the hierarchy.*

el·e·va·tion /ˌɛləˈveɪʃən/ *n.* **1** [C] a height above the level of the ocean: +**of** *We camped at an elevation of 10,000 feet.* **2** [U] FORMAL an act of moving someone to a more important rank or position: +**to** *the judge's elevation to the Supreme Court* **3** [C,U] FORMAL an increase in the amount or level of something: *Elevation of blood pressure can cause headaches.* | **+in** *a marked elevation in the blood calcium level* **4** [C] TECHNICAL an upright side of a building, as shown in a drawing done by an ARCHITECT (=person who plans buildings): *the front elevation of a house* **5** [C] TECHNICAL the angle made with the HORIZON by pointing a gun: *The cannon was fired at an elevation of 60 degrees.*

el·e·va·tor /ˈɛləˌveɪtɚ/ *n.* [C] **1** a machine in a building that takes people and goods from one level to another: *We'll have to* ***take the elevator***. **2** a tall building used for storing and lifting grain

ˈelevator ˌmusic *n.* [U] INFORMAL the type of soft music that is often played in stores and public places, and is usually thought to be boring

e·lev·en /ɪˈlɛvən/ *number* **1** 11 **2** 11 o'clock: *I have an appointment* ***at eleven***. [**Origin:** Old English *endleofan*]

e·lev·enth¹ /ɪˈlɛvənθ/ *adj.* **1** 11th; next after the tenth: *Tomorrow is her eleventh birthday.* **2 at the eleventh hour** at the latest possible time: *The arrival of additional troops at the eleventh hour turned a potential catastrophe into a victory.*

eleventh² *pron.* **the eleventh** the 11th thing in a series: *The meeting is on the eleventh* (=the 11th day of the month).

ELF /ˌi ɛl ˈɛf/ *n.* [U] TECHNICAL extremely low frequency; a type of RADIATION (=energy wave) that comes from electrical equipment such as computer screens and televisions

elf /ɛlf/ *n. plural* **elves** /ɛlvz/ [C] a small imaginary person with pointed ears and magical powers

el·fin /ˈɛlfɪn/ *adj.* **1** someone who looks elfin is small and delicate: *a small, elfin face with pale skin and big eyes* **2** liking to have fun, especially by playing tricks on other people: *an elfin charm*

El·gar /ˈɛlgɑr/**, Ed·ward** /ˈɛdwɚd/ (1857–1934) a British musician who wrote CLASSICAL music

El Gre·co /ɛl ˈgrɛkoʊ/ (1541–1614) a Spanish PAINTER famous for his paintings of religious subjects

e·lic·it /ɪˈlɪsɪt/ *v.* [T] FORMAL to get information, a reaction etc. from someone, especially when this is difficult: *Short questions are more likely to elicit a response.* | **elicit sth from sb** *The circus act elicited "oohs" and "ahs" from the crowd.* [**Origin:** 1600–1700 Latin *elicitus*, past participle of *elicere* **to draw out**] —**elicitation** /ɪˌlɪsɪˈteɪʃən/ *n.* [U]

e·lide /ɪˈlaɪd/ *v.* [T] ENG. LANG. ARTS to leave out the sound of a letter or of a part of a word: *Most English speakers elide the first "d" in Wednesday.* —**elision** /ɪˈlɪʒən/ *n.* [C,U]

el·i·gi·ble /ˈɛlədʒəbəl/ *adj.* **1** able or allowed to do something: **+for** *Part-time students are not eligible for a loan.* | **eligible to do sth** *You're eligible to vote when you turn 18.* **2** [only before noun] an eligible man or woman would be good to marry because they are rich, attractive etc. and not married: *an eligible bachelor* —**eligibility** /ˌɛlədʒəˈbɪləti/ *n.* [U]

e·lim·i·nate /ɪˈlɪməˌneɪt/ Ac W2 *v.* [T] **1** to completely get rid of something that is unnecessary or unwanted: *The company it will eliminate 74,000 jobs over the next four years.* | **eliminate sth from sth** *Try to eliminate high-calorie foods from your diet.* **2** to decide that a choice or possibility is not correct or not appropriate, and therefore does not need to be considered any more: *First eliminate any answers that are clearly wrong.* | *Have you* ***eliminated the possibility*** *that he might have a hearing defect?* **3** [usually passive] to defeat a team or person in a competition, so that they do not take part in it anymore: *The Colts were eliminated in the first round of the playoffs.* **4** to kill someone in order to prevent them from causing trouble: *The dictator eliminated anyone who might be a threat to him.* [**Origin:** 1500–1600 Latin *eliminatus*, past participle of *eliminare* **to put out of doors**]

e·lim·i·na·tion /ɪˌlɪməˈneɪʃən/ Ac *n.*
1 REMOVAL OF STH [U] the removal or destruction of something that is unnecessary or unwanted: **+of** *the elimination of lead in gasoline*
2 DEFEAT [C,U] the defeat of a team or player in a competition, so that they may not take part anymore: *His elimination in the first round was a surprise.*
3 KILLING [U] the act of killing someone, especially to prevent them from causing trouble: **+of** *The elimination of Gustavo has weakened the drug cartel.*
4 BODY PROCESS [U] TECHNICAL the process of getting rid of substances that your body does not need anymore → see also **process of elimination** at PROCESS¹ (4)

eˌlimiˈnation ˌmethod *n.* [C] MATH a method for solving a system of LINEAR EQUATIONS that involves adding or SUBTRACTING the equations in order to remove the VARIABLES (=quantities that can represent any of several different amounts)

El·i·ot /ˈɛliət/**, George** (1819–1880) a British woman writer, famous for her NOVELS, whose real name was Mary Ann (or Marian) Evans

Eliot, T.S. (1888–1965) a U.S. poet who lived in England, and is considered one of the most important writers of the 20th century

e·li·sion /ɪˈlɪʒən/ ENG. LANG. ARTS the leaving out of the sound of a letter when pronouncing a word

e·lite¹, élite /eɪˈlit, ɪ-/ *adj.* [only before noun] limited to a small number of the best, most skilled, most experienced etc. people: *an elite group of athletes*

elite², élite *n.* [C also + plural verb] a small group of people who are powerful or important because they have money, knowledge, special skills etc.: *The ruling elite has resisted all attempts at reform.*

e·lit·ist /eɪˈlitɪst/ *adj.* DISAPPROVING an elitist system, government etc. is one in which a small group of people have much more power or advantages than other people —**elitism** *n.* [U] —**elitist** *n.* [C]

e·lix·ir /ɪˈlɪksɚ/ *n.* **1** [C] something that is supposed to solve problems as if by magic: *Nutritionists warn that artificial fat is no magic elixir for weight loss.* **2** [C,U] LITERARY OR HUMOROUS a magical liquid that is supposed to cure people of illness, make them younger etc. **3** [C,U] TECHNICAL a type of sweet liquid medicine

E·liz·a·be·than /ɪˌlɪzəˈbiθən/ *adj.* relating to the period 1558–1603 when Elizabeth I was the Queen of England: *Elizabethan drama* —**Elizabethan** *n.* [C]

E·liz·a·beth I, Queen /ɪˌlɪzəbəθ ðə ˈfɚst/ (1533–1603) the Queen of England from 1558 until her death

Elizabeth II, Queen /ɪˌlɪzəbəθ ðə ˈsɛkənd/ (1926–) the British Queen since 1952, and also head of the British Commonwealth. She is married to Prince Philip, and they have four children.

elk /ɛlk/ *n.* [C] **1** *plural* **elk** or **elks** BIOLOGY a large DEER with a lot of hair around its neck → see also MOOSE **2 Elk** a member of the Elks

Elks /ɛlks/ **the Elks** an organization for men which does charity work, with groups in many small towns and cities in the U.S.

El·ling·ton /ˈɛlɪŋtən/**, Duke** /duk/ (1899–1974) a U.S. JAZZ musician who played the piano, wrote music, and was a band leader

el·lipse /ɪˈlɪps/ *n.* [C] MATH a curved shape that looks like a circle, but with two sides that are longer and flatter, formed by a PLANE (=flat surface) crossing completely through a CONE at an angle, so that the sum of the distances from any point on the curve to two fixed points inside the ellipse is always the same → see also CONIC SECTION, HYPERBOLA, OVAL, PARABOLA

el·lip·sis /ɪˈlɪpsɪs/ *n. plural* **ellipses** /-siz/ **1** [C] ENG. LANG. ARTS the sign (...) in writing, used to show that some words have deliberately been left out of a sentence ▶see THESAURUS box at **punctuation mark** **2** [C,U] ENG. LANG. ARTS an occasion when words are deliberately left out of a sentence, though the meaning can still be understood

el·lip·ti·cal /ɪˈlɪptɪkəl/ also **el·lip·tic** /ɪˈlɪptɪk/ *adj.* **1** MATH having the shape of an ellipse: *the elliptical orbits of the planets* **2** ENG. LANG. ARTS elliptical speech or writing is difficult to understand because more is meant than is actually said: *His writing is often elliptical and ambiguous.*

El·li·son /ˈɛlɪsən/, **Ralph** /rælf/ (1914–1994) a U.S. writer famous for his NOVEL "The Invisible Man"

Ells·worth /ˈɛlzwɚθ/, **Ol·i·ver** /ˈɑlɪvɚ/ (1745–1807) a CHIEF JUSTICE on the U.S. Supreme Court

elm /ɛlm/ *n.* [C,U] a type of large tree with broad leaves, or the wood from this tree

El Niño /ɛl ˈninyoʊ/ *n.* EARTH SCIENCE a rise in the temperature in the CURRENT in the Pacific Ocean off the west coast of South America that happens every three to eight years, leading to severe changes in the weather in many parts of the world, especially to countries in or near the Pacific Ocean

el·o·cu·tion /ˌɛləˈkyuʃən/ *n.* [U] good clear speaking in public, involving voice control, pronunciation etc.: *elocution lessons* —**elocutionary** *adj.* —**elocutionist** *n.* [C]

E

e·lon·gate /ɪˈlɔŋgeɪt, i-/ *v.* [I,T] to become longer, or make something longer than normal: *Wearing high-heeled shoes elongates the leg.* —**elongation** /ɪˌlɔŋˈgeɪʃən/ *n.* [C,U]

e·lon·gat·ed /ɪˈlɔŋˌgeɪṭɪd/ *adj.* longer and thinner than normal: *The picture shows two elongated figures.*

e·lope /ɪˈloʊp/ *v.* [I] to go away secretly with someone in order to get married: *My parents didn't approve, so we eloped.* —**elopement** *n.* [C,U]

el·o·quent /ˈɛləkwənt/ *adj.* **1** able to express your ideas or opinions well, especially in a way that influences people: *an eloquent speech* **2** showing a feeling or meaning clearly without using words: *The photographs are an eloquent reminder of the horrors of war.* [**Origin:** 1300–1400 French, Latin, present participle of *eloqui* **to speak out**] —**eloquently** *adv.* —**eloquence** *n.* [U]

El Sal·va·dor /ɛl ˈsælvəˌdɔr/ a country in Central America, on the coast of the Pacific Ocean —**Salvadorean** /ˌsælvəˈdɔriən/ *n., adj.*

else /ɛls/ S1 W1 *adv.* **1** a word meaning "in addition" or "besides," used especially after words beginning with "any-," "every-," "no-," or "some-," and after question words: *Clayton needs someone else to help him.* | *There's nothing else to do.* | *What else can I get you?* | *Everyone else gets to go – why can't I?* | ***If all else fails** get professional help.* → see also **above all (else)** at ABOVE[1] (3) **2** a word meaning "different" or "instead," used after words beginning with "any-" or "some-," and after question words: *I don't like pizza. Is there anything else to eat?* | *I'm sorry, I thought you were somebody else.* | *She's wearing someone else's coat* (=not her coat). | *He must be at work – where else could he be?* **3 or else...** **a)** used when saying what the result of not doing something will be: *They said she'd have to pay, or else she'd go to jail.* **b)** used when saying what another possibility might be: *She'll be here any minute, or else she's gotten lost again.* **c)** used for saying that a situation would be different if something were not true: *I'm sure the baby's sleeping, or else we'd hear him.* [**Origin:** Old English *elles*]

SPOKEN PHRASES

4 anything else? used to ask someone if they want to buy another thing, say another thing etc.: *"I'll have a cheeseburger, please." "Anything else?" "No, thanks."* **5 if nothing else** used to say that a situation gives you one opportunity, or has one good result, even though there are no others: *It's boring, but if nothing else, I can get my homework done.* **6 what else?/who else?/where else? etc.** used to say that it is easy to notice that the thing, person, place etc. that has been mentioned is the only one possible: *"Was he with Andrea?" "Of course, who else?"* **7 what else can sb do/say?** used to say that it is impossible to do or say anything apart from what you have mentioned: *I told her it looked good. What else could I say?* **8 ...or else!** used to threaten someone: *You'd better not tell Mom, or else!*

else·where /ˈɛlswɛr/ W3 *adv.* FORMAL in, at, or to another place: *She is becoming famous in France and elsewhere.* | *We had to **look elsewhere** for answers.*

e·lu·ci·date /ɪˈlusəˌdeɪt/ *v.* [I,T] FORMAL to explain very clearly something that is difficult to understand: *Further research is required to elucidate the reasons for these differences.* —**elucidation** /ɪˌlusəˈdeɪʃən/ *n.* [C,U]

e·lude /ɪˈlud/ *v.* [T] **1** to avoid being found or caught by someone, especially by tricking them SYN **avoid**: *Jones eluded the police for six weeks.* | **elude arrest/capture/discovery etc.** *She hid in the bushes to elude detection.* **2** if something that you want eludes you, you fail to find, catch, or achieve it: *Till now a college degree has eluded her.* **3** if a fact, idea etc. eludes you, you cannot completely understand or remember it SYN **escape**: *The distinction between the two philosophies largely eludes me.* [**Origin:** 1500–1600 Latin *eludere*, from *ludere* **to play**]

e·lu·sive /ɪˈlusɪv/ *adj.* **1** difficult to find, or not often seen: *The fox is a sly elusive animal.* **2** an elusive idea or quality is difficult to describe, understand, or remember: *the elusive key to corporate success* **3** an elusive result is difficult to achieve: *The team came within one game of the elusive state championship.* —**elusively** *adv.* —**elusiveness** *n.* [U]

elves /ɛlvz/ the plural of ELF

'em /əm/ *pron.* SPOKEN, INFORMAL a short form of "them": *Tell the kids I'll pick 'em up after school.*

em- /ɪm, ɛm/ *prefix* used instead of EN- before the letters "b," "m," and "p": *an embittered man* (=made to feel extremely disappointed) | *empowerment* (=when someone is given control of something)

e·ma·ci·at·ed /ɪˈmeɪʃiˌeɪṭɪd/ *adj.* extremely thin from lack of food or illness: *The prisoners were sick and emaciated.* —**emaciate** *v.* [I,T] —**emaciation** /ɪˌmeɪʃiˈeɪʃən/ *n.* [U]

e·mail, e-mail, E-mail /ˈimeɪl/ S2 W2 *n.* **1** [U] COMPUTERS **electronic mail** a system that allows you to send and receive messages by computer: *You can contact us **by email**.* | *an email account* ▸see THESAURUS box at **Internet** **2** [C,U] a message that is sent from one person to another using this system, or all messages you receive this way: *Send me an email about the meeting.* | *I just want to check my email.* —**email** *v.* [I,T]: *Ryan emailed me as soon as he arrived in Japan.*

em·a·nate /ˈɛməˌneɪt/ *v.* **1** [I] to come from or out of something: +**from** *Wonderful smells were emanating from the kitchen.* **2** [T] to produce a smell, light, heat etc., or to show a particular quality: *She emanates calmness and confidence.* —**emanation** /ˌɛməˈneɪʃən/ *n.* [C,U]

e·man·ci·pate /ɪˈmænsəˌpeɪt/ *v.* [T] FORMAL to make someone free from social, political, or legal restrictions that limit what they can do [**Origin:** 1600–1700 Latin *emancipatus*, past participle of *emancipare*, from *mancipium* **ownership**] —**emancipation** /ɪˌmænsəˈpeɪʃən/ *n.* [U] *the emancipation of slaves*

e·man·ci·pat·ed /ɪˈmænsəˌpeɪṭɪd/ *adj.* **1** socially, politically, or legally free **2** an emancipated woman is not influenced by old-fashioned ideas about how women should behave

Eˌmanciˈpation Proclaˌmation, the *n.* [singular] HISTORY the DECREE (=official order from the President of the U.S.) given by President Abraham Lincoln in 1863 that freed the SLAVES in the southern states

e·mas·cu·late /ɪˈmæskyəˌleɪt/ *v.* [T often passive] **1** to make someone or something weaker or less effective: *The bill has been emasculated by Congress.* **2** to make a man feel weaker and less male: *Some men feel emasculated if they work for a woman.* **3** TECHNICAL to remove all or part of a male's sex organs SYN **castrate** —**emasculation** /ɪˌmæskyəˈleɪʃən/ *n.* [U]

em·balm /ɪmˈbɑm/ *v.* [T] to treat a dead body with chemicals, oils etc. to prevent it from decaying —**embalmer** *n.* [C]

em·bank·ment /ɪmˈbæŋkmənt/ *n.* [C] a wide wall of earth or stones built to stop water from flooding an area, or to support a road or railroad

em·bar·go¹ /ɪm'bɑrgoʊ/ *n. plural* **embargoes** [C] an official order to stop trade with another country: +**on** *an embargo on wheat* | +**against** *a trade embargo against the dictatorship* | *The UN* ***imposed an*** *arms* ***embargo*** *against the country.* | *Many allies are pushing to* ***lift the*** *oil* ***embargo*** (=end it). [**Origin:** 1500–1600 Spanish *embargar* **to stop, prevent, seize**]

embargo² *v.* [T] POLITICS to officially stop particular goods from being traded with another country: *Several countries embargoed arms shipments to the region.*

em·bark /ɪm'bɑrk/ *v.* **1** [I,T] to go onto a ship or an airplane, or to put or take something onto a ship or an airplane OPP **disembark**: *He stood on the pier to watch me embark.* **2** to begin a trip: +**for** *The ship embarks for Honolulu at 10:00.* [**Origin:** 1500–1600 French *embarquer*, from *barque* **ship**] —**embarkation** /ˌɛmbɑr'keɪʃən/ *n.* [C,U]

embark on/upon sth *phr. v.* to start something, especially something new, difficult, or exciting: *Hal is embarking on a new career.*

em·bar·rass /ɪm'bærəs/ *v.* [T] **1** to make someone feel ashamed, nervous, or uncomfortable, especially in front of other people: *I hope my little dance didn't embarrass you.* **2** to do something that causes problems for a government, political organization, or politician, and makes it look bad: *The revelations have embarrassed the administration.* [**Origin:** 1600–1700 French *embarrasser*, from Spanish *embarazar*]

em·bar·rassed /ɪm'bærəst/ S3 *adj.* ashamed, nervous, or uncomfortable, especially in front of others: *He looked really embarrassed when he realized I'd heard* | *an embarrassed grin* | *Lori's a good singer, but she* ***gets embarrassed*** *if we ask her to sing.* | **be embarrassed to do sth** *He was embarrassed to ask for help.* | +**about** *I felt embarrassed about how dirty my house was.*

THESAURUS

uncomfortable/awkward unable to relax because you are embarrassed: *There was an awkward silence between us.*
sheepish slightly uncomfortable or embarrassed because you know that you have done something silly or wrong: *She looked sheepish, and started to apologize.*
red-faced a word meaning "embarrassed" that is used mainly in newspapers: *The doctors looked red-faced and distinctly uncomfortable.*
mortified extremely embarrassed: *I had to walk in late, and I was mortified when everyone looked at me.*

em·bar·ras·sing /ɪm'bærəsɪŋ/ *adj.* **1** making you feel ashamed, nervous, or uncomfortable: *She asked embarrassing questions.* | +**for/to** *The videotape is very embarrassing for me.* | **it is embarrassing to do sth** *It's embarrassing to ask for money.* | **an embarrassing moment/incident** *It was one of those truly embarrassing moments.* **2** making a government, political organization, or politician, look bad and so causing problems for them: *embarrassing political revelations* —**embarrassingly** *adv.*: *Student numbers are embarrassingly low in our department.*

em·bar·rass·ment /ɪm'bærəsmənt/ *n.* **1** [U] the feeling you have when you are embarrassed: *His face was red with embarrassment.* | +**at** *Ron's embarrassment at his children's rudeness* **2** [C] an event or action that causes a government, political organization etc. problems, and makes it look bad: *The allegations have been an acute embarrassment to the administration.* **3** [C] someone who behaves in a way that makes you feel ashamed, nervous, or uncomfortable, or their behavior: +**to** *Tim's drinking has made him an embarrassment to the whole family.* **4 an embarrassment of riches** so many good things that it is difficult to decide which one you want

em·bas·sy /'ɛmbəsi/ *n.* [C] *plural* **embassies** a group of officials who represent their government in a foreign country, or the building they work in: *the American Embassy in Paris*

em·bat·tled /ɪm'bætḷd/ *adj.* FORMAL **1** [only before noun] an embattled person, organization, etc. has many problems or difficulties: *The embattled mayor explained his position to the press.* **2** surrounded by enemies, especially in war or fighting: *refugees from the embattled villages*

em·bed /ɪm'bɛd/ *v.* **embedded**, **embedding** **1** [I,T usually passive] to put something firmly and deeply into something else, or to be put into something else in this way: +**in** *Part of the club broke off and embedded in his skull.* | **be embedded in sth** *A piece of glass was embedded in her hand.* **2** [T usually passive] to make something an important or basic part of something else, or to make it difficult to remove: *Her feelings of guilt are deeply embedded in her personality.* **3** [T] COMPUTERS to make images, sound, or computer software a part of other software

emˌbedded 'journalist also **emˌbedded re'porter** *n.* [C] a JOURNALIST (=someone who reports the news) who stays with a part of the army, navy, etc. during a war in order to report directly about the fighting

em·bel·lish /ɪm'bɛlɪʃ/ *v.* [T] **1** to make a story or statement more interesting by adding details that are not true: *Lynn couldn't help embellishing the story.* **2** to make something more beautiful by adding decorations to it: +**embellish sth with sth** *The dress is embellished with gold threads.* [**Origin:** 1300–1400 Old French *embelir*, from *bel* **beautiful**] —**embellishment** *n.* [C,U]

em·ber /'ɛmbɚ/ *n.* [C usually plural] a piece of wood or coal that stays red and very hot after a fire has stopped burning

em·bez·zle /ɪm'bɛzəl/ *v.* [I,T] to steal money from a place where you work: *The director was charged with embezzling public funds.* [**Origin:** 1400–1500 Anglo-French *embeseiller*, from Old French *besillier* **to destroy**] —**embezzlement** *n.* [U] —**embezzler** *n.* [C]

em·bit·tered /ɪm'bɪtɚd/ *adj.* angry, sad, or full of hate because of bad or unfair things that have happened to you: *an angry, embittered man* —**embitter** *v.* [T]

em·bla·zon /ɪm'bleɪzən/ *v.* [T usually passive] to put a name, design etc. on something so that it can easily be seen: **be emblazoned with sth** *The T-shirts were emblazoned with political slogans.*

em·blem /'ɛmbləm/ *n.* [C] **1** a picture, shape, or object that is used to represent a country, organization etc.: +**of** *The fish was a familiar emblem of the early Christians.* **2** something that represents an idea, principle, or situation: +**of** *Expensive cars are seen as an emblem of success.* [**Origin:** 1400–1500 Latin *emblema* **design set into a surface**, from Greek *emballein* **to put in**] → see also SYMBOL

em·blem·at·ic /ˌɛmblə'mætɪk/ *adj.* FORMAL seeming to represent or be a sign of something: +**of** *The cowboy is emblematic of not only an era, but a nation.*

em·bod·i·ment /ɪm'bɑdɪmənt/ *n.* **the embodiment of sth** someone or something that represents or is very typical of an idea or quality: *Many people think Wall Street is the embodiment of greed.*

em·bod·y /ɪm'bɑdi/ *v.* **embodied**, **embodying** [T] **1** to be a very good example of an idea or quality: *Mrs. Miller embodies everything I admire in a teacher.* **2** FORMAL to include something: *The latest model embodies many new improvements.*

em·bold·en /ɪm'boʊldən/ *v.* [T] FORMAL to give someone more courage: *My earlier comments had emboldened him.*

em·bo·lism /'ɛmbəˌlɪzəm/ *n.* [C] MEDICINE something such as a hard mass of blood or a small amount of air that blocks a VESSEL carrying blood through the body: *a coronary embolism*

em·boss /ɪm'bɔs, ɪm'bɑs/ *v.* [T usually passive] to decorate the surface of metal, paper, leather etc. with a raised pattern: **be embossed with sth** *The Bible had*

E

been embossed with her name. —**embossed** *adj.*: *embossed stationery*

em·brace¹ /ɪmˈbreɪs/ *v.* **1** [I,T] to put your arms around someone and hold them in a caring way: *Jack warmly embraced his son.* | *They ran to each other and embraced.* ►see THESAURUS box at **hug¹** **2** [T] FORMAL to eagerly accept new ideas, opinions, religions etc.: *We hope these regions will embrace democratic reforms.* **3** [T] FORMAL to include something as part of a subject, discussion etc.: *This course embraces several different aspects of psychology.* [**Origin:** 1300–1400 Old French *embracier*, from *brace* **two arms**] → see also ALL-EMBRACING

embrace² *n.* [C] an act of holding someone close to you, especially as a sign of love: *They held each other in a tender embrace.*

em·broi·der /ɪmˈbrɔɪdɚ/ *v.* **1** [I,T] to decorate cloth by sewing a picture, a pattern, or words on it with colored threads **2** [T] to make a story or report of events more interesting or exciting by adding details that are not true SYN **embellish**: *He embroidered his stories and kept us entertained for hours.* —**embroidered** *adj.*: *a richly embroidered jacket*

embroider

an embroidered hat

em·broi·der·y /ɪmˈbrɔɪdəri/ *n.* [U] **1** a decoration, pattern, or words sewn onto cloth, or the act of making this **2** imaginary details that are added to make a story seem more interesting or exciting

emˈbroidery floss *n.* [U] silk or cotton thread used in embroidery

emˈbroidery hoop *n.* [C] a circular wooden frame used to hold cloth firmly in place while patterns are being sewn into it

em·broil /ɪmˈbrɔɪl/ *v.* [T usually passive] to involve someone or something in a difficult situation: **be/become embroiled in sth** *Morgan is embroiled in a child custody battle with her ex-husband.*

em·bry·o /ˈɛmbriˌoʊ/ *n. plural* **embryos** [C] BIOLOGY an animal or human that has not yet been born, and has just begun to develop. In humans, an embryo becomes a FETUS after eight weeks of development. → see also FETUS [**Origin:** 1300–1400 Medieval Latin, Greek *embryon*, from *bryein* **to swell**]

em·bry·ol·o·gy /ˌɛmbriˈɑlədʒi/ *n.* [U] BIOLOGY the scientific study of embryos —**embryologist** *n.* [C]

em·bry·o·nic /ˌɛmbriˈɑnɪk◂/ *adj.* **1** in a very early stage of development: *Her plan is still in the embryonic stage.* **2** [only before noun] BIOLOGY relating to EMBRYOS

em·cee /ˌɛmˈsi/ *n.* [C] **master of ceremonies** someone who introduces the performers on a television or radio program or at a social event: *an emcee for a beauty pageant* —**emcee** *v.* [I,T]

e·mend /iˈmɛnd/ *v.* [T] FORMAL to take the mistakes out of something that has been written → see also AMEND —**emendation** /iˌmɛnˈdeɪʃən, ˌimɛn-/ *n.* [C,U]

em·er·ald /ˈɛmərəld/ *n.* **1** [C] a valuable bright green stone that is often used in jewelry **2** [U] a bright green color —**emerald** *adj.*

e·merge /ɪˈmɚdʒ/ Ac W2 *v.* [I] **1** to appear or come out from somewhere: *Insects emerge in the spring.* | +**from** *The sun emerged from behind the clouds.* **2** if facts emerge, they become known after being hidden or secret: *More details of the plan emerged at yesterday's meeting.* | **it emerges that** *After the crash, it emerged that bomb warnings had been issued to airlines.* **3** to come out of a difficult experience, often with a new quality or position: +**from** *She emerged from the divorce a stronger person.* **4** to begin to be known or noticed: *Marlena is emerging as a top fundraiser for the charity.* [**Origin:** 1500–1600 Latin *emergere*, from *mergere* **to dive**] → see also EMERGENT, EMERGING

e·mer·gen·cy /ɪˈmɚdʒənsi/ S3 W3 *n. plural* **emergencies** [C] an unexpected and dangerous situation that you must deal with immediately: *Don't call me unless it's an emergency.* | *We need to know what to do* ***in an emergency.*** | ***In case of emergency,*** *press the alarm button.* | *Who should we call in a* ***medical emergency.*** | **emergency exit/supplies/surgery etc.** (=done or used in an emergency) [**Origin:** 1600–1700 From the idea of something suddenly **emerging** or happening] → see also STATE OF EMERGENCY

eˈmergency ˌbrake *n.* [C] a piece of equipment in a car that stops the car from moving or rolling down a slope if the regular BRAKES fail → see picture on page A36

eˌmergency ˌmedical techˈnician *n.* [C] an EMT

eˈmergency ˌroom ABBREVIATION **ER** *n.* [C] the part of a hospital that immediately treats people who have been hurt in accidents or who are extremely sick

eˈmergency ˌservices *n.* [plural] the official organizations, such as the police or the fire department, that deal with crime, fires, and injuries

e·mer·gent /ɪˈmɚdʒənt/ Ac *adj.* [only before noun] beginning to develop and be noticeable: *the country's emergent democratic institutions*

e·merg·ing /ɪˈmɚdʒɪŋ/ Ac *adj.* [only before noun] in an early state of development: *the emerging economies of Southeast Asia*

e·mer·i·ta /ɪˈmɛrət̬ə/ *adj.* **a professor/director etc. emerita** a woman who is RETIRED, but has kept her previous job title as an honor

e·mer·i·tus /ɪˈmɛrət̬əs/ *adj.* **a professor/director etc. emeritus** a man who is RETIRED, but has kept his previous job title as an honor

Em·er·son /ˈɛmɚsən/, **Ralph Wal·do** /rælf ˈwɔldoʊ/ (1803–1882) a U.S. poet and writer who had great influence on the religious and PHILOSOPHICAL thought of his time

em·er·y /ˈɛməri/ *n.* [U] a very hard mineral that is used for polishing things and making them smooth

ˈemery board *n.* [C] a NAIL FILE made from a piece of stiff paper with emery powder on it

e·met·ic /ɪˈmɛt̬ɪk/ *n.* [C] MEDICINE something that you eat or drink in order to make yourself VOMIT (=bring up food from your stomach) —**emetic** *adj.*

em·i·grant /ˈɛməgrənt/ *n.* [C] someone who leaves their own country to live in another country → see also IMMIGRANT

em·i·grate /ˈɛməˌgreɪt/ *v.* [I] to leave your own country in order to live in another country: +**from/to** *Maria emigrated from Mexico three years ago.* → see also IMMIGRATE → see Thesaurus Box at IMMIGRATE

em·i·gra·tion /ˌɛməˈgreɪʃən/ *n.* [C,U] **1** the movement of people out of one country to go and live in other countries **2** BIOLOGY the permanent movement of animals out of a particular area

é·mi·gré /ˈɛmɪˌgreɪ/ *n.* [C] someone who leaves their own country to live in another, usually for political reasons: *Many Cuban émigrés have made Miami their home.*

em·i·nence /ˈɛmɪnəns/ *n.* **1** [U] the quality of being famous and important: *He has risen to a level of eminence in the medical field.* **2 your/his Eminence** a title used when talking to or about a CARDINAL (=priest of high rank in the Catholic church) **3** [C] a hill or area of high ground

em·i·nence grise /ˌɛmɪnɑns ˈgriz/ *n.* [C] someone who has a lot of power in an organization, but who often works secretly or in an unofficial way

em·i·nent /ˈɛmənənt/ *adj.* famous and admired by many people: *an eminent anthropologist* [**Origin:** 1400–1500 Latin, present participle of *eminere* **to stand out**] → see also IMMANENT

ˌeminent doˈmain *n.* [U] LAW the right of the government to take private property for public use, usually by paying for it

em·i·nent·ly /ˈɛmənəntli/ *adv.* FORMAL, APPROVING completely and without a doubt: *Woods is eminently qualified for the job.*

e·mir /ɛ'mɪə˞, i-/ *n.* [C] a Muslim ruler in some countries: *the emir of Bahrain*

em·ir·ate /'ɛmərɪt, ɪ'mɪrət/ *n.* [C] the country ruled by an emir, or his position

em·is·sar·y /'ɛmə,sɛri/ *n. plural* **emissaries** [C] someone who is sent with an official message, or who must do other official work: *Japan is sending two emissaries to Washington to discuss trade issues.*

e·mis·sion /ɪ'mɪʃən/ *n.* **1** [C usually plural] a gas or other substance that is sent out into the air: +**of** *U.S. emissions of carbon dioxide are still increasing.* | *Your car has to pass an **emissions test*** (=a test to make sure the gases your car sends out are at the right level). **2** [U] the act of sending out light, heat, gas, sound etc.

e·mit /ɪ'mɪt/ *v.* **emitted**, **emitting** [T] to send out gas, heat, light, sound etc.: *The kettle emitted a shrill whistle.* | *He emitted a snort of laughter.* [**Origin:** 1600–1700 Latin *emittere*, from *mittere* **to send**]

Em·my /'ɛmi/ *n. plural* **Emmys** [C] a prize given every year to the best programs, actors etc. on U.S. television

e·mol·lient /ɪ'mɑlyənt/ *adj.* FORMAL **1** making something, especially your skin, softer and smoother **2** making you feel calmer when you have been angry: *emollient words* —**emollient** *n.* [C]

e·mol·u·ment /ɪ'mɑlyəmənt/ *n.* [C] FORMAL money or another form of payment for work you have done

e·mote /ɪ'moʊt/ *v.* [I] to clearly show emotion, especially when you are acting: *The children emote to the music as they dance.*

e·mo·ti·con /ɪ'moʊṭɪ,kɑn/ *n.* [C] a set of special signs that are used to show emotions in EMAIL and on the Internet, often by making a picture that you look at sideways. For example, the emoticon :-) looks like a smiling face and means that you have made a joke. SYN **smiley**

e·mo·tion /ɪ'moʊʃən/ W2 *n.* [C,U] a strong human feeling such as love, hate, or anger: *David usually tries to hide his emotions.* | *Her voice was full of emotion as she spoke.* | **express/show (an) emotion** *He showed no emotion as the verdict was read.* | **conflicting/mixed emotions** (=opposite feelings about the same thing at the same time) | ***Emotions were running high*** *in the city after the attacks.* [**Origin:** 1500–1600 French *émouvoir* **to cause to have strong feelings**, from Latin *movere* **to move**]

e·mo·tion·al /ɪ'moʊʃənəl/ S3 W2 *adj.* **1** making people have strong feelings: *It was an emotional reunion for all of us.*

THESAURUS

moving making you feel strong emotions, especially sadness or sympathy: *The movie was very moving.*
touching making you feel sympathy or sadness: *There was a touching note from my daughter inside the card.*
poignant making you feel sad or full of pity: *poignant memories*
sentimental and **schmalzy** INFORMAL showing emotions such as love, pity, and sadness too strongly: *a sentimental love song*

2 having strong feelings and showing them to other people, especially by crying: *He's an emotional guy.* | *Please don't **get emotional*** (=start crying). **3** [only before noun] relating to your feelings or how they are controlled: *Ann suffered from a number of emotional disturbances.* **4** influenced by what you feel, rather than what you know: *an emotional response to the busing proposal* **5 an emotional cripple** DISAPPROVING someone who is not able to deal with their own or other people's feelings **6 emotional blackmail** DISAPPROVING a method of trying to persuade a person to do something by making them feel guilty —**emotionally** *adv.*

e·mo·tion·al·ism /ɪ'moʊʃənə,lɪzəm/ *n.* [U] a tendency to show or feel too much emotion

e·mo·tion·less /ɪ'moʊʃənlɪs/ *adj.* not feeling or showing your emotions: *a precise, emotionless speech*

e·mo·tive /ɪ'moʊṭɪv/ *adj.* making people have strong feelings: *an emotive drama*

em·pa·na·da /,ɛmpə'nɑdə/ *n.* [C] a food made with DOUGH which is filled with meat or something sweet, folded, and fried (FRY)

em·pan·el /ɪm'pænl/ *v.* [T] another spelling of IMPANEL

em·pa·thize /'ɛmpə,θaɪz/ *v.* [I] to be able to understand someone else's feelings, problems etc., especially because you have had similar experiences: **empathize with sb** *My mother died last year, so I can empathize with you.* → see also SYMPATHIZE

em·pa·thy /'ɛmpəθi/ *n.* [U] the ability to understand other people's feelings and problems: +**for/with** *We have a lot of empathy for people in financial trouble.* [**Origin:** 1900–2000 Greek *empatheia*, from *pathos* **suffering, feeling**] —**empathetic** /,ɛmpə'θɛṭɪk/ also **empathic** /ɛm'pæθɪk/ *adj.* → see also SYMPATHY

em·per·or /'ɛmpərə˞/ *n.* [C] a man who is the ruler of an EMPIRE [**Origin:** 1100–1200 Old French *empereor*, from Latin *imperare* **to command**] → see also EMPRESS

em·pha·sis /'ɛmfəsɪs/ Ac W3 *n. plural* **emphases** /-siz/ [C,U] **1** special attention or importance: +**on** *It is a varied menu, with an emphasis on fresh fish.* | *The class **places emphasis on** practical work.* **2** ENG. LANG. ARTS special importance that is given to a word or phrase by saying it louder or higher, or by printing it in a special way SYN **stress**: *The emphasis should be on the first syllable.* [**Origin:** 1500–1600 Latin, Greek, from *emphainein* **to show**]

em·pha·size /'ɛmfə,saɪz/ Ac W2 *v.* [T] **1** to show that an opinion, idea, quality etc. is especially important: *My parents emphasized the importance of college.* | *I want to emphasize how expensive this process is.* | **emphasize that** *Both leaders emphasized that there are no plans to raise taxes.* **2** to say a word or phrase louder or higher than others to give it more importance SYN **stress**: *She said it again slowly, emphasizing each word.* **3** to make something more noticeable SYN **accentuate**: *The dress emphasized the shape of her body.*

THESAURUS

stress to emphasize a statement, fact, or idea: *I cannot stress the need for safety improvements enough.*
highlight to make a problem, subject, etc. easy to notice so people will pay attention to it: *Your résumé should highlight your skills and experience.*
underline to show that something is important: *The test results underline the need to improve academic standards.*
accentuate to make something easier to notice: *The thinness of his face accentuated the wrinkles around his eyes.*
underscore to emphasize that something is important: *The president's speech repeatedly underscored the progress that has been made.*

em·phat·ic /ɪm'fæṭɪk/ Ac *adj.* **1** done or said in a way that clearly shows something is important or should not be doubted: *Dale's answer was an emphatic "No!"* | +**about** *The director is emphatic about the need for change.* | +**that** *My mother was emphatic that we should go without her.* **2** used to describe a situation in which one person or group wins a game, contest etc. by a very large amount or in a very clear way: **an emphatic win/victory defeat etc.** *the Republicans' emphatic victory in the last election* —**emphatically** /-kli/ *adv.*

em·phy·se·ma /,ɛmfə'zimə, -'si-/ *n.* [U] MEDICINE a serious disease that affects the lungs, making it difficult to breathe

em·pire /ˈɛmpaɪɚ/ W3 *n.* [C] **1** POLITICS a group of countries that are all controlled by one ruler or government: *the Roman empire* **2** a group of organizations that are all controlled by one person or company: **a business/media/publishing etc. empire** *Rupert Murdoch's media empire*

ˌEmpire ˈState ˌBuilding, the also **the ˌEmpire ˈState** a famous very tall office building in New York City, which has 102 floors. It was built in 1931, and for many years it was the tallest building in the world.

the Empire State

em·pir·i·cal /ɪmˈpɪrɪkəl, ɛm-/ Ac *adj.* [only before noun] based on scientific testing or practical experience: *empirical evidence* [**Origin:** 1500–1600 *empiric* **person who puts trust only in practical experience** (16–21 centuries), from Latin *empiricus*] —**empirically** /-kli/ *adv.*

emˌpirical ˈformula *n.* [C] CHEMISTRY a series of letters and numbers that represent the relative amounts of each type of atom in a chemical compound, rather than the exact number of each type of atom in the compound → see also MOLECULAR FORMULA

em·pir·i·cism /ɪmˈpɪrəˌsɪzəm, ɛm-/ Ac *n.* [U] the belief in basing your ideas on practical experience —**empiricist** *n.* [C]

em·place·ment /ɪmˈpleɪsmənt/ *n.* [C] a special position prepared for a gun or other large piece of military equipment

em·ploy¹ /ɪmˈplɔɪ/ W2 *v.* **employs, employed, employing** [T] **1** to pay someone to work for you: *The factory employs over 2000 people.* | **employ sb as sth** *Kelly is currently employed as a motorcycle mechanic.* | **employ sb to do sth** *She employed an agent to handle publicity for her.* → see also SELF-EMPLOYED, UNEMPLOYED¹ **2** to use a particular object, method, skill etc. in order to achieve something: *They employ modern marketing strategies.* | **employ sth to do sth** *Helicopters were employed to move troops.* **3** FORMAL to spend your time doing a particular thing: *There must be better ways to employ your time.* [**Origin:** 1400–1500 French *emploier* **to use**, from Latin *implicare*]

employ² *n.* [U] **in sb's employ** FORMAL working for someone

em·ploy·a·ble /ɪmˈplɔɪəbəl/ *adj.* having skills or qualities that are necessary to get a job: *highly employable graduates*

em·ploy·ee /ɪmˈplɔɪ-i, ˌɪmplɔɪˈi, ˌɛm-/ S2 W1 *n.* [C] someone who is paid to work for someone else: *The restrooms are for employees only.* | *a government employee* | **+of** *an employee of the airline*

em·ploy·er /ɪmˈplɔɪɚ/ S3 W2 *n.* [C] a person, company, or organization that employs people: *The shoe factory is the largest employer in this area.*

em·ploy·ment /ɪmˈplɔɪmənt/ S3 W2 *n.* [U] **1** the state of having work for which you earn money: *She was offered employment in the sales office.* | *employment opportunities* | **full-time/part-time employment** *Steve's still looking for full-time employment.* | *income from **paid employment*** **2** the number of people who have jobs OPP **unemployment**: *rising levels of employment in the country* **3** the act of paying someone to work for you: *an expert in employment law* | **+of** *the employment of illegal immigrants* **4** FORMAL the use of a particular object, method, skill etc. to achieve something SYN **use**: **+of** *the employment of economic sanctions*

emˈployment ˌagency *n.* [C] a business that makes money by finding jobs for people

em·po·ri·um /ɪmˈpɔriəm/ *n. plural* **emporiums** or **emporia** /-riə/ [C] a large store

em·pow·er /ɪmˈpaʊɚ/ *v.* [T] **1** to give someone more control over their own life or situation: *laws that empower minority groups* **2 empower sb to do sth** to give a person or organization the official power or legal right to do something: **be empowered to do sth** *The President is empowered to appoint judges to the Supreme Court.* —**empowerment** *n.* [U]

em·press /ˈɛmprɪs/ *n.* [C] a female ruler of an EMPIRE, or the wife of an EMPEROR

emp·ties /ˈɛmptiz/ *n.* [plural] bottles or cans that are empty and can be thrown away

emp·ti·ness /ˈɛmptinɪs/ *n.* [U] **1** a feeling of great sadness and loneliness: *the emptiness of his life in prison* **2** the state of being empty or containing nothing in a place: **+of** *the barren emptiness of the huge desert*

emp·ty¹ /ˈɛmpti/ S2 W2 *adj.* *comparative* **emptier**, *superlative* **emptiest**

1 CONTAINER having nothing inside: *an empty beer can* | *an empty space* | *The gas tank's almost empty.*

2 PLACE an empty place does not have any people in it: *I hate coming home to an empty house.* | *The streets were empty.* | *The plane was **half empty*** (=used to emphasize that something was not full). | *The beach was **empty of** people.*

THESAURUS

bare used about a room or area that has very little in it: *The cupboards were completely bare.*
deserted used about a place or building that is empty and quiet because no people are there: *The town, so busy during the Gold Rush, is now deserted.* | *a deserted beach*
uninhabited used about a place that has no people living in it: *an uninhabited island*
free used about a seat, space, or room that no one is using: *Is this seat free?*
hollow used about something that has an empty space inside: *a hollow tree*
blank used about a computer screen, a page, a piece of paper, or a wall that has no writing or pictures on it: *a room with blank walls*

3 NOT USED not being used by anyone SYN **vacant**: *Is this seat empty?* | *The building still **stands empty** after 20 years.*

4 PERSON/LIFE unhappy because nothing seems interesting or important, or because you feel your life has no purpose: *After the divorce, he felt empty.* | *an empty life*

5 empty words/promises/gestures etc. words, promises etc. that are not sincere, or have no effect: *an empty threat* | *His repeated promises were just empty words.*

6 do sth on an empty stomach to do something without having eaten any food first: *I overslept and had to take the test on an empty stomach.*

7 empty nest also **empty nest syndrome** a situation in which parents become sad because their children have grown up and moved out of their house

8 be empty of sth to not have a particular quality: *His tired face was empty of expression.*

[**Origin:** Old English *æmettig*] —**emptily** *adv.* → see also EMPTIES

empty² *v.* **empties, emptied, emptying 1** [T] also **empty out** to remove or pour out everything that is inside of something: *Did you empty the dishwasher?* | *I emptied my pockets, looking for the card.* | **empty sth into/onto etc.** *Empty the muffin mix into a medium bowl.* **2** [I,T] to leave a place, or to make everyone leave a place: *The streets began to empty.*

empty into sth *phr. v.* if a river empties into a larger area of water, it flows into it: *The Mississippi River empties into the Gulf of Mexico.*

ˌempty-ˈhanded *adj.* without getting what you hoped or expected to get: *The bank robbers were forced to leave the bank empty-handed.*

ˌempty-ˈheaded *adj.* INFORMAL stupid, silly, and unable to think or behave seriously

EMS /ˌi ɛm ˈɛs/ *n.* [U] **emergency medical services** an organization that gives medical treatment to people at the place where they were injured or became sick, before taking them to a hospital

EMT /ˌi ɛm ˈti/ *n.* [C] **emergency medical technician** a person who is trained to give medical treatment to people at the place where they were injured or became sick, before they are taken to a hospital

e·mu /ˈimyu/ *n.* [C] BIOLOGY a large Australian bird that can run very fast, but cannot fly

em·u·late /ˈɛmyəˌleɪt/ *v.* [T] **1** to try to do something or behave in the same way as someone else, especially because you admire them: *He wanted to emulate the style of trumpet player Bobby Hackett.* → see also IMITATE **2** TECHNICAL if one computer or piece of electronic equipment emulates another, it works in a similar way [**Origin:** 1500–1600 Latin *aemulatus*, past participle of *aemulari* **to (try to) be as good as another**] —**emulation** /ˌɛmyəˈleɪʃən/ *n.* [U]

e·mul·si·fi·er /ɪˈmʌlsəˌfaɪɚ/ *n.* [C] a substance that is added, especially to food, to prevent liquids and solids from separating

e·mul·si·fy /ɪˈmʌlsəˌfaɪ/ *v.* **emulsifies, emulsified, emulsifying** [I,T] to combine to become a smooth mixture, or to make two liquids do this: *Stir in the oil until the mixture emulsifies.*

e·mul·sion /ɪˈmʌlʃən/ *n.* [C,U] **1** CHEMISTRY a mixture of liquids, such as oil and water, that contains very small drops of one liquid floating in the other rather than completely combined with it → see also SUSPENSION **2** the substance on the surface of photographic film or paper that makes it react to light

-en /ən/ *suffix* **1** [in adjectives] made of a particular material or substance: *a golden crown* | *wooden seats* **2** [in verbs] to make something have a particular quality: *to darken* (=make or become dark) | *ripening fruit* | *This strengthened his resolve* (=made it stronger).

en- /ɪn, ɛn/ *prefix* [in verbs] **1** to make someone or something be in a particular state, or have a particular quality: *to enlarge* (=make something bigger) | *to endanger* (=put someone in danger) | *to enrich* (=make better) **2** to go completely around something, or include all of it: *to encircle* (=surround everything)

en·a·ble /ɪˈneɪbəl/ Ac W3 *v.* [T] to make it possible for someone to do something, or for something to happen: **enable sb/sth to do sth** *The loan enabled us to buy the house.* | *A longer runway will enable huge airliners to land.*

en·a·bler /ɪˈneɪblɚ/ *n.* [C] **1** DISAPPROVING someone who makes it possible for someone else to continue behaving badly, for example by dealing with their problems for them **2** someone or something that makes it possible for someone to do something or for something to happen: *the idea of a teacher as an enabler*

en·a·bling /ɪˈneɪblɪŋ/ Ac *adj.* [only before noun] LAW an enabling law is one that makes something possible or gives someone special legal powers

en·act /ɪˈnækt/ *v.* [T] **1** LAW to make a new rule or law: *Congress has never enacted a law of this kind.* **2** ENG. LANG. ARTS to perform a play or story by acting → see also RE-ENACT —**enactment** *n.* [C,U]

en·am·el¹ /ɪˈnæməl/ *n.* [U] **1** a glass-like substance that is put on metal, clay etc. for decoration or protection **2** BIOLOGY the hard, smooth outer surface of your teeth → see picture at TOOTH **3** a type of paint that produces a shiny surface when it is dry —**enamel** *adj.*

enamel² *v.* [T usually passive] to cover or decorate something with enamel

en·am·ored /ɪˈnæmɚd/ *adj.* [not before noun] **1** liking something very much: **+of/with** *Charley was never really enamored of Paris.* **2** in love with someone, or caring about them very much: **+of/with** *He tends to become enamored of pretty young women.*

en bloc /ɑn ˈblɑk/ *adv.* all together as a single unit, rather than separately: *You cannot dismiss these stories en bloc.*

en·camp /ɪnˈkæmp/ *v.* **be encamped** to be staying in a camp, especially a military one, somewhere: *Troops are encamped two miles from the border.*

en·camp·ment /ɪnˈkæmp¬mənt/ *n.* [C] a large temporary camp, especially of soldiers: *a military encampment*

en·cap·su·late /ɪnˈkæpsəˌleɪt/ *v.* [T] **1** to put the main facts or ideas of something in a short form or a small space: *The song neatly encapsulates the songwriter's philosophy.* | **encapsulate sth in sth** *The teachings of Zen were encapsulated in short statements.* **2** to completely cover something with something else, especially in order to protect it: **encapsulate sth in sth** *The leaking fuel rods must be encapsulated in lead.* —**encapsulation** /ɪnˌkæpsəˈleɪʃən/ *n.* [C,U]

en·case /ɪnˈkeɪs/ *v.* [T often passive] to cover or surround something completely: **encase sth in sth** *Andre's right arm was encased in a cast.*

-ence /əns/ *suffix* [in nouns] **1** used to make nouns from verbs, to show a state, a quality, or a fact: *existence* (=the fact of existing) | *an occurrence* (=something that has happened) | *dependence* (=the state of depending on someone or something) **2** used to make nouns from adjectives ending in -ENT: *permanence* (=from PERMANENT) → see also -ANCE

en·ceph·a·li·tis /ɪnˌsɛfəˈlaɪt̬ɪs/ *n.* [U] MEDICINE a serious medical condition carried by insects which involves swelling of the brain

en·chant /ɪnˈtʃænt/ *v.* [T usually passive] **1** to attract and hold someone's attention and make them feel very interested, happy, or excited: *a story that has enchanted children for centuries* **2** LITERARY to use magic on something or someone [**Origin:** 1300–1400 Old French *enchanter*, from Latin *cantare* **to sing**]

en·chant·ed /ɪnˈtʃæntɪd/ *adj.* **1** attracted to someone in a way that makes you feel happy and excited: **+by/with** *From the moment we met, I was enchanted with her.* → see also DISENCHANTED **2** an enchanted object or place has been changed by magic, so that it has special powers SYN **bewitched**: *an enchanted castle*

en·chant·er /ɪnˈtʃæntɚ/ *n.* [C] LITERARY someone who uses magic on people and things

en·chant·ing /ɪnˈtʃæntɪŋ/ *adj.* very pleasant or attractive in a way that makes you feel very interested, happy, or excited: *an enchanting tale* | *his enchanting eyes* —**enchantingly** *adv.*

en·chant·ment /ɪnˈtʃænt¬mənt/ *n.* **1** [U] a feeling of pleasure or excitement that strongly interests or attracts you: **+with** *her enchantment with island life* **2** [C,U] a quality or feature of something that is very attractive: *a ballet performance full of enchantment* **3** [C,U] LITERARY a piece of magic, or a change caused by magic SYN **spell**

en·chant·ress /ɪnˈtʃæntrɪs/ *n.* [C] **1** OLD-FASHIONED a woman whom men find very attractive and interesting **2** LITERARY a woman who uses magic on people and things

en·chi·la·da /ˌɛntʃəˈlɑdə/ *n.* [C] **1** a Mexican food consisting of a rolled up TORTILLA (=flat piece of bread), filled with meat or cheese and covered with a sauce **2 the big enchilada** INFORMAL something that is the most important or biggest of its type: *Our products are aimed at the big enchilada – the home computer market.* **3 the whole enchilada** INFORMAL all of something: *I'd advise you to sell the whole enchilada.* [**Origin:** 1800–1900 American Spanish, past participle of *enchilar* **to put chili into**]

en·cir·cle /ɪnˈsɚkəl/ *v.* [T] to surround someone or something completely: *The city is encircled by rebel troops.* —**encirclement** *n.* [U]

encl. the written abbreviation of ENCLOSURE, used in formal letters to show that something else has been included in the envelope

en·clave /ˈɛnkleɪv, ˈɑŋ-/ *n.* [C] a place or a group of people that is surrounded by people or areas that are different from it: *an Armenian enclave in the region* |

E

the city's gay enclave [**Origin:** 1800–1900 French, Old French *enclaver* **to enclose**]

en·close /ɪn'kloʊz/ *v.* [T] **1** to put something inside an envelope with a letter: *I am enclosing my résumé.* → see also ATTACH **2** [usually passive] to surround something, especially with a fence or wall, in order to make it separate: *The pool area is enclosed by a six-foot wall.* —**enclosed** *adj.*: *an enclosed area of land*

en·clo·sure /ɪn'kloʊʒɚ/ *n.* **1** [C] an area surrounded by a wall or fence, and used for a particular purpose: *The animals were placed in a large enclosure.* **2** [U] the act of making an area separate by putting a wall or fence around it: +**of** *the enclosure of land for pastures* **3** [C] something that is put inside an envelope with a letter: *You should say at the bottom of the letter how many enclosures there are in the envelope.* **4** HISTORY in England from the 12th century to the 19th century, the process of dividing up land that was previously public so that the land can be used for private use

E

en·code /ɪn'koʊd/ *v.* **1** [T] to put a message or other information into a different form, often called a CODE SYN **encrypt** OPP **decode** **2** [T] COMPUTERS to change computer data or software into a form that a computer can use **3** [I,T] ENG. LANG. ARTS to express what you want to say in a particular language or form

en·co·mi·en·da /ɛnˌkoʊmi'ɛndə/ *n.* **1** [U] a system that started in 1503 by which Spain gave land in North and South America to Spanish people along with control of the Native Americans who lived there and the right to collect taxes from them **2** [C] land given through this system

en·com·pass /ɪn'kʌmpəs/ *v.* [T] **1** to include a wide range of ideas, subjects, etc.: *His career encompassed television, radio, and newspapers.* **2** to completely cover or surround something: *The Presidio encompasses 1,400 acres.*

en·core[1] /'ɑŋkɔr/ *n.* [C] an short musical performance given after the main performance because the audiences wants to hear more: *The band came back for two encores.*

encore[2] *interjection* said when you have enjoyed a musical performance very much and want the performer to sing or play more

en·coun·ter[1] /ɪn'kaʊntɚ/ Ac W3 *v.* [T] **1** to experience problems, difficulties, or opposition when you are trying to do something: **encounter problems/difficulties/obstacles etc.** *This was easily the best website we encountered during our search of the real estate agents.* | **encounter opposition/resistance** *The reforms have encountered fierce opposition.* **2** FORMAL to meet someone or experience something without planning to: *the best website we've encountered so far* [**Origin:** 1200–1300 Old French *encontrer*, from Late Latin *incontra* **toward**]

encounter[2] Ac *n.* [C] **1** an occasion when you meet someone, especially when you did not plan or expect to: +**with** *an encounter with an old friend* | *The conductor and the young student met in* ***a chance encounter*** (=a meeting that happened by luck or chance). **2** an occasion when two opposing groups of people meet and fight or argue with each other: +**with** *the first encounter with the enemy* | +**between** *News footage showed a hostile encounter between police and protestors.* **3** an occasion when you experience something, especially for the first time: +**with** *a child's first encounter with books* | ***We had a close encounter*** (=an occasion when you experience something dangerous) *with a rattlesnake.* **4** also **sexual/casual encounter** an unplanned occasion when people who do not know each other have sex

en'counter group *n.* [C] a group of people, usually led by someone with special training, that meets to discuss emotional and personal problems

en·cour·age /ɪn'kɚɪdʒ, -'kʌr-/ S2 W2 *v.* [T] **1** to say or do something that helps someone have the courage or confidence to do something OPP **discourage**: *The company tries to encourage creativity.* | **encourage sb to do sth** *Barber's parents encouraged her to stay in school.* | **encourage sb in sth** *She encouraged me in my ambitions.* **2** to provide or create the conditions that make something more likely to happen OPP **discourage**: *Damp conditions encourage the growth of mold.* | *an economic climate that does not encourage investment* —**encouragement** *n.* [C,U]: *Harry squeezed her hand for encouragement*

en·cour·ag·ing /ɪn'kɚɪdʒɪŋ/ *adj.* giving you hope and confidence: *I have some encouraging news.* | *His condition after the surgery looks very encouraging.* —**encouragingly** *adv.*

en·croach /ɪn'kroʊtʃ/ *v.* [I always + prep.] DISAPPROVING **1** to gradually cover or use more of an area, so that something is affected or threatened: **encroach on/upon sth** *Urban development is encroaching on rural land.* | *gang members who encroach on other gangs' territory* **2** to gradually take more and more control of someone's time, possessions, rights etc.: +**on/upon** *She doesn't allow her political activities to encroach on her writing.* —**encroaching** *adj.*: *The road curved through the encroaching jungle.* —**encroachment** *n.* [C,U]

en·crust·ed /ɪn'krʌstɪd/ *adj.* covered with a hard layer of something, or covered all over with small hard things: +**with/in** *The ship's hull was encrusted with ice.* | **jewel-encrusted/ice-encrusted/mud-encrusted etc.** *a diamond-encrusted bracelet* —**encrustation** /ɪnˌkrʌs'teɪʃən/ *n.* [C,U]

en·crypt /ɪn'krɪpt/ *v.* [I,T] COMPUTERS to change the form of computer information so that it cannot be read by people who are not supposed to see it —**encryption** *n.* [U]

en·cum·ber /ɪn'kʌmbɚ/ *v.* [T usually passive] **1** to make it more difficult for someone or something to develop or make progress SYN **hinder**: **be encumbered by/with** *The whole process is encumbered with bureaucracy.* **2** FORMAL to make it difficult for someone to move easily SYN **hinder**: *She ran slowly, encumbered by her wet skirt.* —**encumbrance** *n.* [C]

-ency /ənsi/ *suffix* [in nouns] the state or action of doing something, or the quality of being a particular way: *the Presidency* (=the state of being President) | *fluency in French* (=the ability to speak it very well) → see also -ANCY

en·cy·clo·pe·di·a /ɪnˌsaɪklə'pidiə/ *n.* [C] a book or CD, or a set of these containing facts about many different subjects, or containing detailed facts about one subject: +**of** *an encyclopedia of Music* [**Origin:** 1500–1600 Medieval Latin *encyclopaedia* **course of general education**, from Greek *enkyklios paideia* **general education**]

en·cy·clo·pe·dic /ɪnˌsaɪklə'pidɪk/ *adj.* used to emphasize that someone's knowledge, memory etc. is very impressive because they know or remember lots of facts: *his encyclopedic knowledge of baseball*

end[1] /ɛnd/ S1 W1 *n.*

1 LAST PART [singular] the last part of something such as a period of time, activity, book, or movie: *I liked the play, especially the end.* | ***At the end****, the hero dies.* | **the end of sth** *Rob's moving to Maine at the end of September.* | *We have to hire a new teacher by the end of the semester.* | *We didn't leave until* ***the very end*** (=the final part of something). | *I played the tape* ***from beginning to end.***

2 FARTHEST POINT [C] the farthest point of a place or thing: *a long hall with a door at the end* | +**of** *We went to the end of the line.* | *a town at* ***the far end*** *of the lake* (=the furthest part from where you are) | *They were sitting* ***at opposite ends*** *of the couch.* | *Put the two tables* ***end to end*** (=in a line with the ends touching). | *The boat measured 40 feet from end to end.*

THESAURUS

point the sharp end of something: *The point of the pencil broke.*
tip the end of something, especially something pointed: *the tip of your nose*

3 FINISH [singular] a situation in which something is finished or does not exist anymore: **the end of sth** *An injury could mean the end of her career.* | **an end to sth** *There is no sign of an end to the war.* | *This could mean the party's 75 years of power* ***are at an end****.* | *The long legal battle has finally* ***come to an end****.* | **put/bring an end to sth** also **bring sth to an end** *The fall of the Berlin Wall brought an end to the Cold War.* | *a country locked in civil war with* ***no end in sight*** (=there seems to be no end)
4 GOAL [C] an aim or purpose, or the result that you hope to achieve: *He wants to cut costs, and* ***to that end*** (=to achieve that) *is trying to improve efficiency.* | *Ryan didn't realize Thompson would use the information* ***for his own ends****.* | **for political/military/commercial etc. ends** *Most of the research is done for military ends.* | *Learning to play the piano was* ***an end in itself*** (=something you do because you want to, not for any other advantage). | *We've had decades of school reform,* ***to what end*** (=what are the goals or results)*?* | *terrorists who believe that* ***the end justifies the means*** (=it is acceptable to do even bad things to achieve your goal)
5 RANGE [C] one of the two points that begin or end a range or scale: **the top/higher etc. end (of sth)** *the top end of the income scale* | **the bottom/lower/cheaper etc. end (of sth)** *the cheaper end of the car market* | **at one end of the scale/spectrum...at the other end** *At the other end of the scale, seats in the front can cost $1,000.* | *The two men are* ***at opposite ends of*** *the political spectrum.*
6 CONNECTION [C] one of two places that are connected by a telephone line, a trip etc.: *Someone will be there to meet you at the other end.* | **the end of the phone/line** *There was silence on the other end of the phone.* | *How are things* ***at your end*** (=where you are)?
7 in the end after a period of time [SYN] **finally**: *In the end, we decided to go to Florida.*
8 make ends meet to have just enough money to buy what you need: *a young mother struggling to make ends meet*
9 for days/hours/weeks etc. on end for many days, hours etc. without stopping: *Sometimes he doesn't call for weeks on end.*
10 to no end SPOKEN very much: *That kind of thing annoys me to no end.*
11 no end of sth a lot of something, especially something bad: *This will cause no end of trouble.*
12 the end of the road/line the end of a process or activity: *Our marriage had reached the end of the line.*
13 put/stand sth on end to put something in a position so that its longest edge is upright → see also **make sb's hair stand on end** at HAIR (11)
14 PART OF AN ACTIVITY INFORMAL the particular part of a job, activity, place etc. that you are involved in, or that affects you [SYN] **side**: *She works in the sales end of the company.* | **sb's end of the deal/bargain** *Let's hope they keep their end of the bargain.*
15 be at the end of your rope to have no more PATIENCE or strength to deal with something: *I'm at the end of my rope here. What should I do?*
16 it's not the end of the world SPOKEN used to say that a possible problem is not really as bad or serious as someone thinks: *If you don't get the job, it's not the end of the world.*
17 at the end of the day SPOKEN used to give your final opinion after considering all the possibilities: *At the end of the day, it's just too much money to spend.*
18 end of story SPOKEN used to say that you do not want to say anymore about something, especially something embarrassing or secret: *I'm fine. I just tripped and fell. End of story.*
19 the end justifies the means used to say that the result you want makes it acceptable to do bad things in order to get it
20 DEATH [C usually singular] INFORMAL a word meaning "death," used because you want to avoid saying this directly: *James was with his father at the end.*
21 until/till/to the end of time LITERARY forever: *He promised to love her till the end of time.*
22 sb would go to the ends of the earth to do everything you can, even if it is very difficult, in order to achieve something: *Brad would go to the ends of the earth to make his wife happy.*
23 go to such/those ends to do sth to use a lot of effort in order to achieve something: *Most women would not go to those ends to make their house look nice.*
24 sb is the living end SPOKEN used as an expression of strong approval or disapproval about someone who does things that seem a little crazy
[**Origin:** Old English *ende*] → see also **the be-all (and end-all)** at BE[2] (13), **to/until the bitter end** at BITTER (7), DEAD END[1], **go off the deep end** at DEEP[1] (12), **be at loose ends** at LOOSE[1] (14), **loose ends** at LOOSE[1] (11), ODDS AND ENDS, **get the short end of the stick** at SHORT[1] (20), **the tail end of sth** at TAIL[1] (7), **be at your wits' end** at WIT (5)

end[2] [S1] [W1] *v.* **1** [I,T] if a situation or activity ends, or someone ends it, it finishes or stops: *The conference ends on Saturday.* | *The war ended in 1945.* | *A knee injury ended his basketball season.* | **end (sth) with sth** *The festival will end with fireworks.* | **end (sth) by doing sth** *He ended the speech with a call for change.* **2** [I always + adv./prep.] if a situation, activity, story etc. ends in a particular way or state, or something ends it, this is how it is when it reaches its final point: *Does the story end happily?* | *He ended the race 2 seconds behind the leader.* | **end the day/year etc.** *Stock prices ended the week up 2%.* **3 end your life** also **end it all** to kill yourself: *Mabel tried to end her life after her husband died.* **4 end your days** if you end your days in a particular place or doing a particular activity, you spend the last part of your life there or doing that: *Unfortunately he ended his days in prison.* **5 the sth to end all sths** used to describe something that is the best, most important, or most exciting of its kind: *This movie has the car chase to end all car chases.*

end in sth *phr. v.* to have a particular result, or finish in a particular way: *His first three marriages ended in divorce.* | *protests that end in violence*

end up *phr. v.* INFORMAL **1** to come to be in a particular situation or state, especially when you did not plan it: *You could end up dead if you're not careful.* | **+with/in/on etc.** *Cochrane ended up with 12 percent of the vote.* | **end up doing sth** *I always end up paying the bill for your dinner!* | **end up as sth** *He could end up as president.* | **end up like sb/sth** *I don't want to end up like my parents.* **2** to arrive in a place you did not plan to go to: *I was traveling to Florida, but ended up in New Orleans.*

en·dan·ger /ɪnˈdeɪndʒɚ/ *v.* [T] to put someone or something in a dangerous situation: *Smoking during pregnancy endangers your baby's health.*

en·dan·gered /ɪnˈdeɪndʒɚd/ *adj.* in danger of being killed or destroyed, or of not existing anymore: *endangered forests*

en,dangered 'species *n.* [C] a type of animal or plant that may soon not exist anymore

en·dear /ɪnˈdɪr/ *v.*

endear sb **to** sb *phr. v.* to make someone popular and liked: **endear sb to sb** *The emperor was trying to endear himself to his people.* | **sth won't endear sb to sb** *Comments like that won't endear him to my father.*

en·dear·ing /ɪnˈdɪrɪŋ/ *adj.* making someone love or like you: *Will's sense of humor is one of his most endearing qualities.* —**endearingly** *adv.*

en·dear·ment /ɪnˈdɪrmənt/ *n.* [C,U] an action or word that expresses your love for someone: *She never used* ***terms of endearment*** (=special names for someone you love) *for anyone in the family.*

en·deav·or[1] /ɪnˈdɛvɚ/ *n.* **1** [C] FORMAL an attempt or effort to do something new or different: *His latest endeavor* (=attempt to start a business) *is a Chinese restaurant.* **2** [U] efforts or activities that have a special purpose: **scientific/creative/artistic etc. endeavor** *the highest forms of artistic endeavor* | *Almost every area of* ***human endeavor*** (=all the activities that people do) *is now influenced by computers.*

E

endeavor² *v.* [I] FORMAL to try very hard: **endeavor to do sth** *We always endeavor to please our customers.* ►see THESAURUS box at try¹

en·dem·ic /ɛnˈdɛmɪk, ɪn-/ *adj.* an endemic disease or problem is always present in a particular place, or among a particular group of people: **+in/to** *Violent crime is now endemic in the area.* → see also EPIDEMIC

end·game /ˈɛndgeɪm/ *n.* [C usually singular] the last part of a long process or series of events

end·ing /ˈɛndɪŋ/ *n.* **1** [C] the way in which a story, movie etc. finishes: **a happy/sad/surprise ending** *The story has a surprise ending.* **2** [singular, U] the act of permanently ending a process, situation, or activity: **+of** *the ending of sanctions* **3** [C] a part that can be added to the end of a word: *Gerunds have the ending "-ing."* → see also NERVE ENDINGS

E

en·dive /ˈɛndaɪv/ *n.* [C,U] **1** also **Belgian endive** BIOLOGY a vegetable with long, pointed, mostly white, bitter-tasting leaves that is eaten raw or cooked **2** also **curly endive** BIOLOGY a vegetable with curly bitter-tasting leaves that is eaten raw in SALADS SYN frisee

end·less /ˈɛndlɪs/ *adj.* **1** never stopping or coming to an end, or seeming to be this way: *We had to sit through endless meetings.* ►see THESAURUS box at long¹ **2** used to emphasize that something is very large or too large in amount, size, or number: *The possibilities for the use of plastics seem endless.* | **an endless stream/succession/supply etc. of sth** *an endless stream of visitors* | *He's been arrested so many times – for drugs, guns, blackmail –* ***the list is endless.*** (=used to say that there are many things you could add) **—endlessly** *adv.*: *Mrs. Allen talked endlessly about her grandchildren.*

en·do·crine /ˈɛndəkrɪn/ *adj.* [only before noun] BIOLOGY relating to HORMONES in your blood: *an endocrine gland*

ˈendocrine ˌgland *n.* [C] BIOLOGY a GLAND in the body which produces HORMONES that are sent directly into the blood flowing in the body → see also EXOCRINE GLAND

en·do·cri·nol·o·gy /ˌɛndəkrəˈnɑlədʒi/ *n.* [U] the scientific and medical study of the GLANDS (=a type of organ) in the body and the HORMONES that they produce **—endocrinologist** *n.* [C]

en·do·derm /ˈɛndəˌdɚm/ *n.* [U] BIOLOGY the inner layer of cells around an EMBRYO → see also ECTODERM

en·do·der·mis /ˌɛndəˈdɚmɪs/ *n.* [U] BIOLOGY a layer of cells between the CORTEX and the hard central part of a plant's root or stem

en·dor·phin /ɛnˈdɔrfɪn/ *n.* [U, plural] a chemical produced by the brain, that reduces the feeling of pain and can affect emotions

en·dorse /ɪnˈdɔrs/ W3 *v.* [T] **1** to officially say that you support or approve of someone or something: *The Pentagon endorsed a new strategy that creates smaller military forces.* | **endorse a view/comment/idea etc.** (=say publicly that you endorse a particular opinion, remark etc.) **2** to say publicly that you support someone, especially a candidate in an election: *Officially, the mayor has not endorsed any candidate.* **3** if a famous person endorses a product or service, they say in an advertisement that they like it and that it is good: *retired athletes who are paid to endorse products* **4** to prove that something is true or right, especially when you suspected that it was: *These numbers endorse the company's marketing strategy.* **5 endorse a check** to sign your name on the back of a check [**Origin:** 1400–1500 Old French *endosser* **to put on the back**, from *dos* **back**] **—endorsement** *n.* [C,U]

en·do·skel·e·ton /ˈɛndoʊˌskɛlətˀn/ *n.* [C] BIOLOGY the structure on the inside of the bodies of living creatures that have a BACKBONE, consisting of all the bones in their body → see also EXOSKELETON

en·do·sperm /ˈɛndəˌspɚm/ *n.* [U] BIOLOGY the part of a seed that contains the necessary supply of food for the growing seed

en·do·therm /ˈɛndəˌθɚm/ *n.* [C] BIOLOGY an animal that produces heat inside its body and is able to control the temperature of its body when the temperature of its environment changes. Birds and MAMMALS are endotherms. → see also ECTOTHERM

en·do·ther·mic /ˌɛndəˈθɚmɪk◂/ *adj.* CHEMISTRY relating to or describing a chemical reaction in which heat is taken in from the surrounding area: *an endothermic reaction* → see also EXOTHERMIC

en·dow /ɪnˈdaʊ/ *v.* [T] to donate a large amount of money to a college, hospital, school etc.: *Her parents endowed a scholarship fund in her name.*

endow sb **with** sth *phr. v.* **1 be endowed with sth** to naturally have a good feature or quality: *She was endowed with both good looks and brains.* **2** FORMAL to make someone or something have a good quality or ability: *This law does not endow judges with special powers.* [**Origin:** 1300–1400 Anglo-French *endouer*, from Latin *dotare* **to give**] → see also WELL-ENDOWED

en·dow·ment /ɪnˈdaʊmənt/ *n.* **1** [C,U] a large sum of money or other valuable gift that someone gives to a college, hospital, school etc. or the act of giving this money **2** [C] a quality or ability that someone or something has naturally: *the island's natural endowments*

end·point /ˈɛndpɔɪnt/ *n.* [C] the place or stage at which something ends: *Has the trend toward smaller cell phones reached its endpoint?*

ˌend ˈproduct *n.* [C] the final result of a series of a process or activity, especially a manufacturing process: *The jets were the end product of a 35-year research program.* → see also BYPRODUCT

ˌend reˈsult *n.* [C usually singular] the final result of a process or activity: *We worked hard, but the end result was still disappointing.*

ˈend ˌtable *n.* [C] a small low table, usually used in a LIVING ROOM next to a SOFA or chair

en·due /ɪnˈdu/ *v.*

endue sb **with** sth *phr. v.* LITERARY to give someone a good quality SYN endow

en·dur·ance /ɪnˈdʊrəns/ *n.* [U] the ability to continue doing something that is physically painful or mentally difficult for a long time: *ways to increase your strength and endurance* | **physical/mental endurance** *A marathon is a test of both physical and mental endurance.*

en·dure /ɪnˈdʊr/ *v.* **1** [T] to suffer pain or deal with a very bad situation for a long time, especially with strength and patience: *Cancer patients often have to endure great pain.* **2** [I] to continue to exist for a long time: *Scott's popularity endured well beyond his death in 1832.* [**Origin:** 1300–1400 French *endurer*, from Latin *durare* **to harden**] **—endurable** *adj.*

en·dur·ing /ɪnˈdʊrɪŋ/ *adj.* continuing to exist for a long time, especially in spite of difficulties: *the enduring appeal of Shakespeare's plays* | *Is an enduring peace in the region possible?*

ˈend ˌuser *n.* [C] the person who actually uses a particular product: *We try to get as much feedback from the end users as possible.*

end·ways /ˈɛndweɪz/ *adv.* SPOKEN with the end forward: *Will it fit in the car endways?*

ˈend zone *n.* [C] the place at each end of a football field where players take the ball in order to gain points

en·e·ma /ˈɛnəmə/ *n.* [C] the process of putting a liquid into someone's RECTUM in order to make them empty their BOWELS, or the liquid that is used in this process

en·e·my /ˈɛnəmi/ W2 *n. plural* **enemies** [C] **1** someone who hates you and wants to harm you: *He didn't have any enemies.* | *Collins* ***made quite a few enemies.*** | *For years, the two men were* ***bitter enemies*** (=enemies who hate each other very much). | *Taylor has been Johnson's* ***sworn enemy*** (=an enemy that is determined never to end their disagreement) *since that dispute.* **2** someone who opposes or competes against you SYN rival: *The teams are* ***old enemies*** (=they have been competing hard against each other for many years). | *He said that his* ***political enemies*** *are behind the rumor.* **3** [often singular] the person or group of people you are fighting against in a war: ***The enemy** is likely to attack after dark.* | **enemy soldiers/missiles etc.** *Enemy aircraft were spotted 20 miles east of the border.* | *There are reports that **enemy forces*** (=the enemy's army, navy etc.) *have entered the capital.* **4 the enemy of sth** LITERARY something that changes something else or makes it weaker: *Jealousy is the enemy of love.* [**Origin:** 1200–1300 Old French *enemi*, from Latin *inimicus*, from *amicus* **friend**] → see also **With friends like that, who needs enemies?** at FRIEND (7), NATURAL ENEMY, **sb is his/her own worst enemy** at WORST[1] (2)

en·er·get·ic /ˌɛnɚˈdʒɛt̬ɪk/ Ac *adj.* **1** very active because you have a lot of energy: *an intelligent and energetic young officer* | *energetic dancing* | *I **feel** so much more **energetic** since I lost the weight.*

THESAURUS

full of energy having a lot of energy: *Kids were running around the playground, full of energy.*
vigorous using a lot of energy and strength or determination: *a vigorous opponent of capital punishment*
dynamic interesting, exciting, and full of energy and determination to succeed: *the city's dynamic new mayor*
hyperactive too active, and not able to keep still or quiet for very long: *a hyperactive child*
tireless working very hard in a determined way: *her tireless effort to help homeless children*

2 very determined and working hard to acheive something: *an energetic supporter of reform* | **energetic in (doing) sth** *We need to be more energetic in promoting our products.* —**energetically** /-kli/ *adv.*: *They are working energetically on local problems that affect our daily lives.*

en·er·gize /ˈɛnɚˌdʒaɪz/ *v.* [T] **1** to make someone feel more determined and energetic: *She energized the audience with a rousing speech.* **2** [usually passive] SCIENCE to make a machine work: *The cars' electric motors are energized by solar cells.* —**energizing** *adj.*

en·er·gy /ˈɛnɚdʒi/ Ac S2 W1 *n.* **1** [U] the physical and mental strength that makes you able to do things: *Kids have so much energy.* | *She came back **full of energy** after her vacation.* | *I didn't **have the energy to** argue with him.* | *It **takes** a lot of **energy** to keep yourself fully informed.* | *We **put** a lot of time and **energy into** this project.* | *I'm not going to **expend** any more **energy** worrying about this.* | *Joking around is often a sign of **nervous energy*** (=energy that comes from feeling nervous). **2** [U] power that is used to produce heat and make machines work: *the world's energy resources* | **+from** *energy from the sun* | **solar/wind/nuclear etc. energy** (=energy from the sun, wind etc.) | *a source of **renewable energy*** (=power produced from sources that will not run out) **3** [C,U] PHYSICS in PHYSICS, the ability of something to do work, move, or produce heat: *kinetic energy* **4 energies** [plural] the effort that you use to do things: *I quit my job to devote **all of my energies** to our children.* **5** [U] a special unseen force that can influence thoughts, emotions etc., that some people believe exists in people, places, and things: **negative/positive energy** *There's a lot of negative energy in this building.* [**Origin:** 1500–1600 Late Latin *energia*, from Greek *energeia* **activity**]

en·er·vat·ed /ˈɛnɚˌveɪt̬ɪd/ *adj.* FORMAL feeling weak, tired, and without energy

en·er·vat·ing /ˈɛnɚˌveɪt̬ɪŋ/ *adj.* FORMAL making you feel weak, tired, and without energy

en·fant ter·ri·ble /ˌɑnfɑn tɛˈriblə/ *n.* [C] LITERARY a young person, especially a performer, artist etc., who is very skilled or intelligent but behaves in a way that shocks and amuses other people: *the enfant terrible of the architectural world*

en·fee·ble /ɪnˈfibəl/ *v.* [T] LITERARY to make someone weak —**enfeebled** *adj.*

en·fold /ɪnˈfoʊld/ *v.* [T] LITERARY to enclose or surround someone or something: **enfold sb/sth in sth** *He enfolded her in his arms.*

en·force /ɪnˈfɔrs/ Ac W3 *v.* [T] **1** to make people obey a rule or law, especially by punishing those who do not obey it: *The police are strict about enforcing the speed limit.* **2** to cause a particular type of behavior or a situation to exist by using threats or force: *the difficulties of enforcing discipline* | **enforce sth on sb** *She enforced strict order on her children.* —**enforceable** *adj.* —**enforcement** *n.* [U] → see also LAW ENFORCEMENT

En'forcement ˌActs, the *n.* [singular] HISTORY three laws passed by the U.S. Congress in 1870 and 1871 to protect the voting rights of African Americans by making it illegal to use violence against black voters

en·forc·er /ɪnˈfɔrsɚ/ *n.* [C] **1** someone such as a police officer who makes sure that people obey rules and laws: *the police and other law enforcers* **2** a player in sports such as basketball and hockey who plays roughly in order to make his opponents afraid to get close to the GOAL

en·fran·chise /ɪnˈfrænˌtʃaɪz/ *v.* [T] **1** POLITICS to give a group of people rights, especially the right to vote OPP **disenfranchise** **2** OLD USE to free a slave —**enfranchisement** *n.* [U]

en·gage /ɪnˈgeɪdʒ/ S3 W2 *v.* FORMAL **1** [T] to attract someone and keep their interest: **engage sb's interest/attention/imagination** *a storyteller who can engage children's imagination* **2** [T] FORMAL to arrange to employ someone SYN **hire**: **engage sb to do sth** *The board engaged Thompson to run a series of seminars.* | **engage sb as sth** *The King engaged him as his personal physician.* **3** [I,T] to make one part fit into another part of a machine OPP **disengage**: *Push the pedal to engage the clutch.* | **+with** *The wheel engages with the cog and turns it.* **4** [I,T] to begin to fight with an enemy: *The two armies engaged at dawn.* | **engage sb in battle/combat** *two swordsmen engaged in battle* [**Origin:** 1500–1600 French *engager*, from *gage* **something given as a promise**]

engage in sth FORMAL *phr. v.* **1** to do or take part in an activity: *The two companies then engaged in a price war.* **2** to make someone become involved in a particular activity, especially by trying to make them feel interested in it: **engage sb in sth** *The nurses try hard to engage patients in the activities.* | **engage sb in conversation** (=to start having a conversation with someone)

engage with sb *phr. v.* to get involved with other people so that you know about them and understand them: *I'm always too tired to really engage with my kids.*

en·gaged /ɪnˈgeɪdʒd/ *adj.* **1** two people who are engaged have agreed to get married: *They've been engaged for six months.* | **+to** *Shari's engaged to Joe.* | *Vicki and Tyler **got engaged** last week.* ►see THESAURUS box at **married** **2** [not before noun] interested in and aware of what is happening, for example in politics: *Woman are more politically engaged than ever before.* **3 be otherwise engaged** FORMAL OR HUMOROUS unable to do something because you have arranged to do something else

en·gage·ment /ɪnˈgeɪdʒmənt/ *n.* **1** [C,U] a promise between two people to marry each other: *They've officially announced their engagement.* | **+to** *her engagement to Stewart* | *Carla and I have **broken off our engagement*** (=said we do not want to get married anymore). **2** [C] FORMAL an arrangement to do something or meet someone: *The Senator has a **speaking engagement*** (=an occasion when you give a speech) *in Ohio.* | **a previous/prior engagement** (=an arrangement you have already made that prevents you from doing something else) **3** [U] APPROVING the process of becoming more involved with someone or something so that you understand them better: **+in** *an active engagement in civic life* | **+with** *the benefits of engagement with the local community* **4** [C] TECHNICAL a battle between armies, navies etc. **5** [U] the state of being joined together with other working parts of a machine

E

en'gagement ring *n.* [C] a ring that a man gives to a woman when they decide to get married

en·gag·ing /ɪn'geɪdʒɪŋ/ *adj.* attracting people's attention and interest: *her engaging personality* | *an engaging story* —**engagingly** *adv.*

En·gels /'ɛŋgəlz/, **Frie·drich** /'fridrɪk/ (1820–1895) a German political thinker and REVOLUTIONARY who, together with Karl Marx, wrote "The Communist Manifesto" and developed the political system of Communism

en·gen·der /ɪn'dʒɛndɚ/ *v.* [T] FORMAL to be the cause of something such as a situation, action, or emotion: **engender sth in/among sb** *Good teachers try to engender enthusiasm in their students.*

en·gine /'ɛndʒɪn/ S3 W2 *n.* [C] **1** a piece of machinery with moving parts that changes power from steam, electricity, oil etc. into movement: *a jet engine* | *The engine won't start.* | *Alex* ***turned off the engine.*** | *The car's* ***engine was running*** (=it was operating). → see also MOTOR **2** a vehicle that pulls a train: *a diesel engine* → see also LOCOMOTIVE **3 an engine of change/destruction etc.** FORMAL something that causes change etc.: *Investments will be the engine of growth for the future.* [**Origin:** 1300–1400 Old French *engin* **cleverness, machine**, from Latin *ingenium* **abilities you are born with**] → see also FIRE ENGINE, SEARCH ENGINE

en·gi·neer¹ /ˌɛndʒə'nɪr/ S3 W2 *n.* [C] **1** someone who designs the way roads, bridges, machines etc. are built: *a civil engineer* | *a software engineer* **2** someone who drives a train **3** someone who controls the engines on a ship or airplane: *a flight engineer* **4** a soldier in the army who designs and builds roads, bridges etc. **5 the engineer of sth** someone who plans something and uses skill to make it happen: *the engineer of many Republican victories in Texas* → see also CIVIL ENGINEER, MECHANICAL ENGINEER

engineer² *v.* [T] **1** to arrange something by skillful secret planning: *He engineered the escape of 480 prisoners of war.* **2** [usually passive] to design, plan, and make roads, bridges, machines etc.: *poorly engineered machine parts* **3** [T] to change the genetic structure of a plant, animal etc.: *genetically engineered corn*

en·gi·neer·ing /ˌɛndʒə'nɪrɪŋ/ W3 *n.* [U] the profession and activity of designing the way roads, bridges, machines etc. are built → see also CIVIL ENGINEERING, GENETIC ENGINEERING, SOCIAL ENGINEERING

Eng·land /'ɪŋglənd/ the largest country in the U.K.

En·glish¹ /'ɪŋglɪʃ/ *n.* [U] **1** the language used in countries such as the U.S., the U.K., Canada, and Australia **2** the study of the English language and its literature, or a course in this: *an English teacher* | *Did you major in English?* **3 the English** [plural] people from England

English² *adj.* **1** from or relating to England **2** relating to the English language: *English grammar*

ˌEnglish Bill of 'Rights, the HISTORY the BILL OF RIGHTS

ˌEnglish 'horn a musical instrument similar to an OBOE, but larger

Eng·lish·man /'ɪŋglɪʃmən/ *n. plural* **Englishmen** /-mən/ [C] a man from England

ˌEnglish 'muffin *n.* [C] a round thick flat piece of bread with holes inside it that you cut in half and TOAST before eating

Eng·lish·wom·an /'ɪŋglɪʃˌwʊmən/ *n. plural* **Englishwomen** /-ˌwɪmɪn/ [C] a woman from England

en·gorged /ɪn'gɔrdʒd/ *adj.* having become larger or filled with something: **+with** *a river engorged with water from the storm* —**engorgement** *n.* [U] —**engorge** *v.* [T]

en·grave /ɪn'greɪv/ *v.* **1** [T] ENG. LANG. ARTS to cut words or pictures into the surface of metal, wood, glass etc.: **engrave sth on sth** *The soldiers' names are engraved on two marble walls.* | **engrave sth with sth** *a thin gold bracelet engraved with her initials* **2 be engraved in your memory/mind/heart** FORMAL to be impossible to forget: *Their last conversation is deeply engraved in my memory.* **3** [I,T] ENG. LANG. ARTS to make an image that will be printed by burning the shape into a special metal plate, using acid —**engraver** *n.* [C]

en·grav·ing /ɪn'greɪvɪŋ/ *n.* ENG. LANG. ARTS **1** [C] a picture printed from an engraved metal plate **2** [U] the art or work of cutting words or pictures into the surfaces of things

en·gross /ɪn'groʊs/ *v.* [T] **1 be engrossed in/with sth** to be so interested in something that you do not notice anything else: *She was too engrossed in her phone conversation to notice.* **2** to be or become very interesting to someone, so that they do not notice anything else: *The murder trial had engrossed the small Ohio town for months.* [**Origin:** 1300–1400 Anglo-French *engrosser*, from French *en gros* **in a mass, by wholesale**] —**engrossing** *adj.*: *an engrossing story*

en·gulf /ɪn'gʌlf/ *v.* [T] **1** to suddenly affect someone so strongly that they feel nothing else: *Fear engulfed him as he approached the microphone.* **2** if a war, social change etc. engulfs a place, it affects it so much that the place changes completely: *Civil war has completely engulfed the country.* **3** [usually passive] to completely surround or cover something: *a surfer engulfed by a wave* | *The boat was immediately* ***engulfed in flames.***

en·hance /ɪn'hæns/ Ac W3 *v.* [T] to improve something: *We're using technology to enhance our service.* | *Herbs enhance the flavor of the meat.* [**Origin:** 1200–1300 Anglo-French *enhauncer*, from Vulgar Latin *inaltiare* **to raise**] —**enhancement** *n.* [C,U]

e·nig·ma /ɪ'nɪgmə/ *n.* [C] a person, thing, or event that is strange or mysterious and difficult to understand or explain [**Origin:** 1500–1600 Latin *aenigma*, from Greek, from *ainos* **story**]

en·ig·mat·ic /ˌɛnɪg'mæṭɪk◂/ *adj.* mysterious, and difficult to understand or explain: *an enigmatic smile* —**enigmatically** /-kli/ *adv.*: *"You'll find out soon," she said enigmatically.*

en·join /ɪn'dʒɔɪn/ *v.* [T] **1** LAW to legally forbid an activity **2** FORMAL to order someone to do something

en·joy /ɪn'dʒɔɪ/ S1 W1 *v.* **enjoys, enjoyed, enjoying** [T] **1** to get pleasure from something: *Greg says he enjoys his new job.* | *Enjoy your dessert!* | **enjoy doing sth** *Thena enjoys working with children.* | **enjoy yourself** *Everyone seemed to enjoy themselves at the party.* | **enjoy every minute/moment (of sth)** *The show was great. I enjoyed every minute!*

THESAURUS

like to enjoy something, or think that it is nice or good: *Do you like Mexican food?*
love to like something very much, or enjoy doing something very much: *My father loved to travel.*
have a good/great time to have experiences that you enjoy: *Did you have a good time at the party?*
have fun to enjoy doing something: *The kids had fun at the park.*

2 to have something good such as success or a particular ability or advantage: *The team has enjoyed some success this season.* | *workers who enjoy a high level of job security* **3 enjoy!** SPOKEN used when you give someone something and you want them to get pleasure from it: *Here's your dinner. Enjoy!* [**Origin:** 1300–1400 Old French *enjoir*, from Latin *gaudere* **to show great happiness**]

GRAMMAR

Enjoy is almost always followed by a noun phrase, a pronoun, or by a verb with *-ing*: *"Did you enjoy your vacation?" "Yes, I enjoyed it a lot."* (NOT *I enjoyed with/of it.*) | *I really enjoyed myself last night at the party* (NOT *I enjoyed at the party*). | *He enjoys playing golf very much* (NOT *He enjoys to play golf*).

en·joy·a·ble /ɪn'dʒɔɪəbəl/ *adj.* giving you pleasure:

an enjoyable afternoon | *How do we make learning more enjoyable?* —**enjoyably** *adv.*

en·joy·ment /ɪnˈdʒɔɪmənt/ *n.* **1** [U] the pleasure that you get from something: *I now play the piano mostly* ***for enjoyment.*** | +**of** *his enjoyment of good wine* | **get enjoyment out of/from sth** *I get a lot of enjoyment from working with teenagers.* **2** [U] FORMAL the fact of having something: *the enjoyment of civil rights* **3** [C usually plural] FORMAL something that you enjoy doing: *social enjoyments*

en·large /ɪnˈlɑrdʒ/ *v.* [I,T] to become bigger, or to make something bigger: *How do I enlarge the picture?* | *The diet causes the liver to enlarge.* | *Enlarge your vocabulary by reading the newspaper.*

enlarge on/upon sth *phr. v.* FORMAL to provide more facts or details about something you have already mentioned: *She didn't enlarge on her reasons for leaving.*

en·large·ment /ɪnˈlɑrdʒmənt/ *n.* **1** [C] a photograph that has been printed again in a larger size OPP **reduction** ▸see THESAURUS box at **camera** **2** [C,U] an increase in size or amount

en·larg·er /ɪnˈlɑrdʒɚ/ *n.* [C] a piece of equipment used for making photographs larger

en·light·en /ɪnˈlaɪt̚n/ *v.* [T] FORMAL to explain something to someone: *The website tries to both enlighten and entertain kids.* —**enlightening** *adj.*: *an enlightening experience*

en·light·ened /ɪnˈlaɪt̚nd/ *adj.* **1** treating people in a kind and fair way and understanding their needs and problems: *an enlightened, progressive company* **2** showing a good understanding of something, and not believing things about it that are false: *enlightened readers*

en,lightened 'despot also **be,nevolent 'despot** *n.* [C] HISTORY a ruler of a country who uses his or her power to bring social or political change to the country, especially by allowing more political and religious freedom

en·light·en·ment /ɪnˈlaɪt̚nmənt/ *n.* [U] **1 the Enlightenment** a period in the 18th century when many writers and scientists believed that science and knowledge, not religion, could improve people's lives **2** FORMAL the state of understanding something clearly, or the act of making someone understand something clearly **3** the state in the Buddhist and Hindu religions, of not having any more human desires, so that your spirit is united with the universe

en·list /ɪnˈlɪst/ *v.* **1** [I,T] to join the army, navy etc., or be accepted into the army, navy etc.: **enlist in sth** *Her brother just enlisted in the Marines.* ▸see THESAURUS box at **army** **2** [T] to persuade someone to help you: **enlist sb to do sth** *I've been enlisted to collect the money.* | **enlist sb's help/support** *I enlisted the help of some friends when I moved.* | **enlist sb in sth** *The mayor enlisted townspeople in his efforts to rebuild the library.* —**enlistment** *n.* [C,U]

en·list·ed /ɪnˈlɪstɪd/ *adj.* **an enlisted man/woman** someone in the army, navy etc. whose rank is below that of an officer

en·liv·en /ɪnˈlaɪvən/ *v.* [T] to make something more interesting or amusing: *His humor enlivened the dull math classes.*

en masse /ɑn ˈmæs, -ˈmɑs, ɛn-/ *adv.* if a group of people do something en masse, they all do it together: *The senior management resigned en masse.*

en·meshed /ɪnˈmɛʃt/ *adj.* [not before noun] **1** involved in a bad or complicated situation, so that it is difficult to get out: +**in** *Congress is worried about becoming enmeshed in a foreign war.* **2** physically stuck in something, so that it is difficult to get out: +**in** *dolphins which become enmeshed in fishing nets*

en·mi·ty /ˈɛnməṭi/ *n. plural* **enmities** [C,U] FORMAL the feeling of hatred or anger toward someone: *deep enmity between the two ethnic groups*

en·no·ble /ɪˈnoʊbəl, ɛ-/ *v.* [T] FORMAL **1** if something ennobles you, it improves your character **2** [usually passive] to give someone an official title and make them part of the NOBILITY —**ennoblement** *n.* [U] —**ennobling** *adj.*

en·nui /ɑnˈwi/ *n.* [U] LITERARY a feeling of being tired and bored, especially as a result of having nothing to do

e·nor·mi·ty /ɪˈnɔrməṭi/ Ac *n.* [U] the great size, seriousness, or amount of influence of something: *How do we deal with problems of this enormity?* | **the enormity of sth** *the enormity of the agency's task* | *the enormity of his actions*

e·nor·mous /ɪˈnɔrməs/ Ac W2 *adj.* extremely large in size or amount: *an enormous house* | *The country's problems are enormous.* | **an enormous amount/number of sth** *an enormous amount of money* [**Origin:** 1500–1600 Latin *enormis* **out of the ordinary,** from *norma* **rule**] —**enormousness** *n.* [U]

e·nor·mous·ly /ɪˈnɔrməsli/ Ac *adv.* **1** [only before adj.] extremely or very: *I'm enormously proud of my son.* | *He was enormously popular.* **2** to a very great extent: *The town's Hispanic population has grown enormously.* | *Prices vary enormously.*

e·nough[1] /ɪˈnʌf/ S1 W1 *adv.* **1** as much as is necessary: *It's late, and you two have talked enough for one day.* | **tall/nice/fast etc. enough** *I couldn't see well enough to read the sign.* | +**for** *Our car wasn't big enough for six people.* | *The song is easy enough for a child to learn.* | *You'll have to rewrite this paper – it's just* ***not good enough*** (=not satisfactory or acceptable). ▸see THESAURUS box at **adequate**

> **THESAURUS**
> **plenty** a large amount that is enough or more than enough: *Try to eat plenty of fruits and vegetables.*
> **sufficient** as much as you need for a particular purpose: *The bill does not have sufficient support in Congress to pass.*
> **adequate** enough in quantity or good enough in quality for a particular purpose: *The workers had not been given adequate safety training.*

2 not very, but in an acceptable way: *She seemed nice enough.* **3 strangely/oddly/funnily enough** used to say that although something seems unlikely, it is true: *Oddly enough, both authors begin their stories with the same incident.* **4 bad/hard/difficult enough** used to say that a situation is already bad or difficult and you do not want anything to make it worse: *It's bad enough losing your job. I don't need your criticism too.* **5 sb is stupid/silly/foolish etc. enough to do sth** used to say that someone does something stupid: *I was stupid enough to believe everything she said.* **6 sb is lucky/unlucky enough to do sth** used to say that someone is lucky or unlucky: *I was lucky enough to meet someone who is perfect for me.* → see also, **fair enough** at FAIR[1] (11), **sure enough** at SURE[2] (1)

> **GRAMMAR**
> **Enough** comes after adjectives and adverbs: *He's not tall enough* (NOT *He's not enough tall*). | *I can't walk fast enough to keep up with you.* | *They're rich enough to own three houses.* **Enough** usually comes before a plural or uncountable noun: *enough teachers/space.* In sentences with "there" as the subject, **enough** can also be used after uncountable nouns, but it can sound slightly formal or old-fashioned: *There was food enough for everyone.*

enough[2] S1 W1 *determiner, pron.* **1** as much or as many as may be necessary: *I don't have enough time.* | **enough of sb/sth** *Are there enough of us to play football?* | **enough (sth) for sb/sth** *Don't grab. There's enough food for everyone.* | *Is there enough space for a swimming pool?* | **enough sth to do sth** *We didn't win enough games to go to the play-offs.* | *We have* ***nowhere near enough*** *room in our car for everyone's suitcase.* | *Two years of college were* ***more than enough*** (=too much). | *Ten years was* ***time enough*** *for the forest to* *recover from the fire.* | **enough to do/eat etc.** *There are too many children who don't have enough to eat.*

SPOKEN PHRASES

2 have had enough (of sth) to be very annoyed with someone or something: *I'd had enough of the neighbors' noise, so I called the police.* **3 be enough to do sth** used to emphasize how annoying or impressive something is: *The noise is enough to drive you crazy!* **4 enough is enough** also **I've had enough (of sth)** used for saying that you are not going to allow a bad situation to continue: *Finally my mother said, "Enough is enough," and left him after 35 years.* **5 enough about sb/sth** used to say that you want to stop talking about someone or something: *Enough about politics. Let's talk about sports.* **6 that's enough** used to say that you want someone to stop doing something annoying: *That's enough! No more complaining.* **7 enough said** used to say that there is no need to say any more because you understand everything: *"Of course he got the job. His father's a Senator." "Enough said."* **8 enough already** used to show that you are annoyed and want something to stop: *You've complained about the food, the heat, and the beds – **enough already**!*

E

en·quire /ɪnˈkwaɪɚ/ *v.* [I,T] another spelling of INQUIRE

en·quir·y /ɪnˈkwaɪəri, ˈɪŋkwəri/ *n. plural* **enquiries** [C,U] another spelling of INQUIRY

en·rage /ɪnˈreɪdʒ/ *v.* [T] to make someone extremely angry: *The governor's comments enraged civil rights activists.* —**enraged** *adj.*: *an enraged bull*

en·rap·ture /ɪnˈræptʃɚ/ *v.* [T usually passive] FORMAL to make someone feel such pleasure and happiness that they cannot think of anything else —**enraptured** *adj.*

en·rich /ɪnˈrɪtʃ/ *v.* [T] **1** to improve the quality of something: *The goal of the class is to enrich our understanding of other cultures.* | *Fertilizer is added to enrich the soil.* **2 enrich yourself** DISAPPROVING to make yourself richer —**enrichment** *n.* [U]

en·roll /ɪnˈroʊl/ *v.* **1** [I,T] to officially arrange to join a school, college, class, organization etc., or to accept someone as a member of a college, class etc.: **enroll in sth** *He plans to enroll in a vocational school.* | *The college only enrolled 14 new students.* **2 enroll sb in sth** to arrange for someone else to join a school, college, class, organization etc.: *They enrolled their son in a private school.*

en·roll·ment /ɪnˈroʊlmənt/ *n.* **1** [U] the process of arranging to join a school, college, class, organization etc. **2** [C] the number of people who have arranged to join a school, college, class, organization etc.: *College enrollments are up again this fall.*

en route /ɑn ˈrut, ɛn-/ *adv.* **1** in the process of traveling somewhere SYN **on the way**: *We'll stop at the store en route.* | **+to/from** *a bus en route to Denver* **2** as a stage in the process of winning a game, an election etc SYN **on the way**: **+to** *The team scored 31 final-period points en route to a 90–70 win.*

en·sconce /ɪnˈskɑns/ *v.* to get into a comfortable place or good position, in which you plan to stay: **ensconce yourself in sth** *My aunt had ensconced herself in the best bedroom.* | **be ensconced in sth** *Gavigan was firmly ensconced in the top job in sales.*

en·sem·ble /ɑnˈsɑmbəl/ *n.* **1** [C] ENG. LANG. ARTS a small group of musicians who play together regularly: *a jazz ensemble* **2** [C usually singular] a set of clothes, jewelry etc. that are worn together **3** [C usually singular] a set of people, organizations, or things that work together or are used together

en·shrine /ɪnˈʃraɪn/ *v.* [T usually passive] **1** FORMAL if a belief, right, or tradition is enshrined in law, it is preserved as part of the law: **be enshrined in sth** *The right of free speech is enshrined in the U.S. Constitution.* **2** if someone is enshrined in a place, their picture or possessions are placed in a public place so that people will remember them: **be enshrined in sth** *players who are enshrined in the Baseball Hall of Fame*

en·shroud /ɪnˈʃraʊd/ *v.* [T] LITERARY to cover or hide something: *A dense fog enshrouded the mountain peaks.*

en·sign /ˈɛnsən/ *n.* [C] **1** a low rank in the U.S. Navy, or an officer who has this rank **2** a flag on a ship that shows what country the ship belongs to **3** a small piece of metal on your uniform that shows your rank

en·slave /ɪnˈsleɪv/ *v.* [T usually passive] **1** FORMAL to trap someone in a situation that they cannot easily escape from: *Many Americans are enslaved in credit-card debt.* **2** to make someone into a slave —**enslavement** *n.* [U]

en·snare /ɪnˈsnɛr/ *v.* [T] **1** FORMAL to catch someone in a dangerous, illegal, or unpleasant situation SYN **trap**: *businessmen ensnared in an investment scandal* **2** to catch an animal or person in a TRAP, net, or similar thing so that they cannot escape SYN **trap**

en·sue /ɪnˈsu/ *v.* [I] to happen after something, especially as a result of it: *When police told them to leave, an argument ensued.* | **the ensuing year/months/weeks etc.** *In the ensuing weeks, she began to get disturbing phone calls at night.* | **the ensuing battle/argument/panic etc.** *Fred was knocked to the ground in the ensuing fight.* [**Origin:** 1300–1400 Old French *ensuivre*, from *suivre* **to follow**]

en·sure /ɪnˈʃʊr/ Ac W3 *v.* [T] to make certain that something will happen: *All the necessary steps had been taken to ensure their safety.* | **+that** *The new law will ensure that criminals serve their full prison terms.* → see also INSURE → see Word Choice box at INSURE

-ent /ənt/ *suffix* [in adjectives and nouns] someone or something that does something, or that has a particular quality: *local residents* (=people who live here) | *different* → see also -ANT

en·tail /ɪnˈteɪl/ *v.* [T] **1** to make it necessary to do something: *Repairs would entail the closure of the bridge for six months.* | **entail doing sth** *The surgery entailed placing a screw into a bone in her wrist.* **2** OLD USE to arrange for your property to become the property of a particular person, especially your son, after your death [**Origin:** 1300–1400 Anglo-French *taile* **legal limitation**, from Old French *taillier* **to cut, limit**]

en·tan·gle /ɪnˈtæŋgəl/ *v.* [T usually passive, always + adv./prep.] **1** to become involved in an argument, a situation that is difficult to escape from, or a relationship that causes problems etc.: **entangle sb in sth** *They lost all their money after getting entangled in a bad real estate deal.* | **entangle sb with sb** *Sue became romantically entangled with her boss.* **2** to become twisted and caught in a rope, net etc.: **+in/with** *Penguins have been found entangled in lengths of fishing net.* —**entangled** *adj.*

en·tan·gle·ment /ɪnˈtæŋgəlmənt/ *n.* [C,U] a difficult situation or relationship that is hard to escape from: *political entanglements*

en·ten·dre /ɑnˈtɑndrə/ [C] *n.* → see DOUBLE ENTENDRE

en·tente /ɑnˈtɑnt/ *n.* [C,U] a situation in which two countries agree to work together in some areas, even though they may not be friendly with each other

en·ter /ˈɛntɚ/ S2 W1 *v.*

1 GO INTO a) [I,T] to go or come into a place: *When the bride entered the church, everyone stood up.* | *Army tanks entered the main square of the city.* **b)** [T] if an object or disease enters part of something, it goes inside it: *The infection hasn't entered the bloodstream.*

THESAURUS

go in to move into a particular place: *Frank opened the door, and we went in.*
come in to enter a room or house: *Come in and sit down.*
barge in to interrupt someone or go into a place when you were not invited: *Mom just barged into my room without knocking.*
sneak in to go somewhere quietly and secretly: *They snuck in to the auditorium to watch the rehearsals.*

get in to be allowed or able to enter a place: *You can't get in without ID.*
trespass to go onto someone's land without permission: *He was arrested for trespassing on federal land.*

2 START WORKING [T] to start working in a particular profession or organization, or to start studying at a college or university: *Jason plans to enter the Navy.* | *This fall she will enter the University of North Carolina.* | *graduates* ***entering*** *the teaching* ***profession***
3 START AN ACTIVITY [T] to start to take part in an activity or become involved in a situation: *Reese entered the game with five minutes left.* | *new competitors* ***entering the*** *computer games* ***market*** | *Last week, the governor* ***entered the*** *public* ***debate*** *on health-care reform.* | *Rebels have refused to* ***enter negotiations.***
4 COMPUTER [T] **a)** COMPUTERS to put information into a computer by pressing the keys: *Enter your user name and password.* **b)** if you enter a computer system, you are given permission to use it by the system
5 WRITE INFORMATION [T] to write information on a particular part of a form, document etc.: *Enter your address in the spaces provided.*
6 COMPETITION/EXAM [I,T] to arrange to take part in something such as a competition, or to arrange for someone else to take part: *She entered the drawing competition and won.* | *A friend of mine entered me in the 10K race.*
7 PERIOD OF TIME [T] to begin a period of time when something happens: *Our economy is entering a period of growth.* | **sth enters its third week/sixth day/second year etc.** *The hostage crisis has now entered its third day.*
8 a) enter a plea (of guilty/of not guilty) LAW to officially say that you are guilty or not guilty of a particular crime in a court of law: *Sarkin is scheduled to enter a plea Tuesday.* **b)** to officially give something to a court of law, such as EVIDENCE for a TRIAL: *Judge Laney allowed them to enter the knife as evidence.* → see also SUBMIT (1)
9 sth never entered my mind/head SPOKEN used to say that you have not considered a possibility, especially when you are surprised that something has happened: *It never entered my mind that I might win.*
10 CHANGE [T] if a particular quality enters something, it starts to exist in it and change it, especially suddenly: *A note of panic entered her voice.*
11 sb/sth enters sb's life if someone or something enters your life, you start to know them or be affected by them: *Everything's changed since our children entered our lives.*
12 enter an offer/complaint/objection etc. FORMAL to officially make an offer, complaint etc.
[**Origin:** 1200–1300 Old French *entrer*, from Latin *intra* **inside**]

enter into sth *phr. v.* **1 enter into an agreement/contract etc.** to officially make an agreement to do something: *The media giant entered into a partnership agreement with an unknown company.* **2** to start doing something, especially discussing or studying something: *Lawyers often avoid entering into discussions about personal and legal ethics.* **3** to affect a situation and be something that you must consider when you make a choice: *Money didn't enter into my decision to leave the company.* **4 enter into the spirit of it/things** to take part in a game, party etc. in an eager way

enter upon/on sth *phr. v.* FORMAL to start doing something or being involved in it

en·ter·i·tis /ˌɛntəˈraɪt̬ɪs/ *n.* [U] MEDICINE a painful condition that affects your INTESTINES

en·ter·prise /ˈɛntɚˌpraɪz/ W3 *n.* **1** [C] a company, organization, or business, especially a new one: *a multimillion-dollar enterprise* **2** [U] the activity of starting and running businesses: ***Private enterprise*** *is the backbone of this country.* **3** [C] a large and complicated plan or process that is done with other people or groups: *a new scientific enterprise* **4** [U] the ability to think of new activities or ideas and make them work: *She's a woman of great enterprise and creativity.* [**Origin:** 1400–1500 Old French *entreprise*, from *entreprendre* **to undertake**] → see also FREE ENTERPRISE, PRIVATE ENTERPRISE

ˈenterprise ˌzone *n.* [C] ECONOMICS an area where companies do not have to pay particular taxes and are given other advantages in order to encourage them to do business there

en·ter·pris·ing /ˈɛntɚˌpraɪzɪŋ/ *adj.* able and willing to think of new activities or ideas, and make them work: *An enterprising student was selling copies of the answers to the test.* —**enterprisingly** *adv.*

en·ter·tain /ˌɛntɚˈteɪn/ S3 *v.* **1** [I,T] to do something that amuses or interests people: *It is a movie that will inspire and entertain you.* | **entertain sb with sth** *He used to entertain his family with jokes and songs.* **2 entertain yourself** to do something that keeps you busy and interested: *Some children can entertain themselves quietly with books or games.* **3** [I,T] to spend time with people that you have invited to a dinner, party etc. for pleasure or business: *Mike often gets home late when he's entertaining business clients.* **4 entertain an idea/thought/doubt etc.** to allow yourself to consider or think about something: *Since last year, he's been* ***entertaining the idea of*** *retiring.* [**Origin:** 1400–1500 Old French *entretenir* **to hold together, support**, from *tenir* **to hold**]

en·ter·tain·er /ˌɛntɚˈteɪnɚ/ *n.* [C] someone who tells jokes, sings etc. to amuse people: *a nightclub entertainer*

en·ter·tain·ing[1] /ˌɛntɚˈteɪnɪŋ/ *adj.* amusing and interesting: *an entertaining show*

entertaining[2] *n.* [U] the practice of inviting people for dinners or to parties, especially for business reasons

en·ter·tain·ment /ˌɛntɚˈteɪnmənt/ W2 *n.* [U] performances or activities that people enjoy, or the pleasure gained from them: *Movies are one of the most popular forms of entertainment.* | *The game provided hours of entertainment.*

en·thal·py /ˈɛnˌθælpi, ɛnˈθælpi/ SYMBOL **H** *n.* [C] PHYSICS a measurement of the total amount of heat inside a system, which is calculated by adding the amount of energy within the system to the outside pressure multiplied by the VOLUME

en·thrall /ɪnˈθrɔl/ *v.* [T] if something enthralls you, you find it extremely interesting or exciting: *The new video game has enthralled millions of children.* —**enthralling** *adj.*: *an enthralling story*

en·throne /ɪnˈθroʊn/ *v.* [T usually passive] to officially give power to a new king, queen, or religious leader, in a ceremony in which they sit on a THRONE (=special chair) —**enthronement** *n.* [C,U]

en·thuse /ɪnˈθuz/ *v.* **1** [I,T] to talk about something in a way that shows you are very excited: *"It's a great opportunity," enthused Rossi.* | **enthuse about/over sth** *Rick was enthusing about life in Australia.* **2** [T] to make someone interested in something or excited by it: *The owners were definitely enthused by the offer.*

en·thused /ɪnˈθuzd/ *adj.* [not before noun] excited about or interested in something: **+about** *We're enthused about students' response to the new textbooks.*

en·thu·si·asm /ɪnˈθuziˌæzəm/ *n.* **1** [U] a strong feeling of interest and enjoyment about something, and an eagerness to be involved in it: *She sang the national anthem* ***with great enthusiasm.*** | **+for** *Marcus' enthusiasm for Jazz* | *We returned from the meeting* ***full of enthusiasm.*** | **show some/little/no enthusiasm** *Employers showed little enthusiasm for the new regulations.* | *The cold weather* ***dampened our enthusiasm*** (=made us feel less of it) *for the camping trip.* **2** [C] an activity or subject that someone is very interested in: *His latest enthusiasm is climbing.* [**Origin:** 1500–1600 Greek *enthousiasmos*, from *entheos* **filled (by a god) with sudden strong abilities**]

en·thu·si·ast /ɪnˈθuziˌæst/ *n.* [C] someone who is very interested in a particular activity or subject: *a sports enthusiast*

en·thu·si·as·tic /ɪnˌθuziˈæstɪk◂/ *adj.* showing a lot

of interest and excitement about something: *an enthusiastic supporter of the President's plan* | *The crowd gave the band an enthusiastic welcome.* | **+about** *Rachel is enthusiastic about going to kindergarten.* —**enthusiastically** /-kli/ *adv.*

en·tice /ɪn'taɪs/ *v.* [T] to persuade someone to do something by offering them something nice: **entice sb to do sth** *His aunt tried to entice him to eat.* | **entice sb into/away from sth** *low prices that will entice shoppers away from their favorite stores* [**Origin:** 1200–1300 Old French *enticier*, from Latin *titio* **large burning piece of wood**] —**enticement** *n.* [C,U]

en·tic·ing /ɪn'taɪsɪŋ/ *adj.* very pleasant or interesting, so that you feel strongly attracted: *the enticing smell of fresh bread* —**enticingly** *adv.*

en·tire /ɪn'taɪɚ/ S2 W1 *adj.* [only before noun] whole or complete, used to emphasize what you are saying: *Dad spent the entire day in the kitchen.* | *Gary ate the entire chicken.* [**Origin:** 1300–1400 Old French *entier*, from Latin *integer* **whole, complete**]

en·tire·ly /ɪn'taɪɚli/ S3 W2 *adv.* completely and in every possible way: *people from entirely different backgrounds* | *a sculpture made entirely of old tires.* | *Schilling's ankle was **not entirely** healed.*

en·tire·ty /ɪn'taɪɚṭi, -'taɪrəṭi/ *n.* **in its/their entirety** FORMAL as a whole, and including every part: *The speech will be shown tonight in its entirety.*

en·ti·tle /ɪn'taɪṭl/ *v.* [T] **1 entitle sb to (do) sth** to give someone the right to have or do something: *Membership entitles you to the use of the pool and the gym.* **2 be entitled to (do) sth** to have the right to have or do something: *Only full-time employees are entitled to receive health insurance.* **3 be entitled sth** if a book, play etc. is entitled something, that is its name: *The last song is entitled "Into the Woods."*

en·ti·tle·ment /ɪn'taɪṭlmənt/ *n.* **1** [C,U] the official right to have or receive something, or the amount that you receive: **+to** *workers' entitlement to benefits* **2** [C] ECONOMICS an entitlement program

en'titlement ˌprogram *n.* [C] a government program or system that gives money or help to particular groups in society, for example old people or poor people SYN **entitlement**: *Social Security is the largest entitlement program.*

en·ti·ty /'ɛntəṭi/ Ac S3 *n. plural* **entities** [C] something that exists as a single and complete unit: *The two school districts are **separate** legal **entities**.* | *The two books can be considered **a single entity*** (=they can be considered as one thing).

en·tomb /ɪn'tum/ *v.* [T often in passive] LITERARY to bury or trap someone under the ground

en·to·mol·o·gy /ˌɛntə'mɑlədʒi/ *n.* [U] BIOLOGY the scientific study of insects —**entomologist** *n.* [C] —**entomological** /ˌɛntəmə'lɑdʒɪkəl/ *adj.*

en·tou·rage /ˌɑntʊ'rɑʒ/ *n.* [C usually singular] a group of people who travel with an important person: *Mr. Stallone and his entourage*

en·trails /'ɛntreɪlz/ *n.* [plural] the inside parts of an animal or person's body, especially their INTESTINES

en·trance¹ /'ɛntrəns/ *n.* **1** [C] a door, gate etc. that you go through to enter a place OPP **exit**: **+to/of** *the main entrance to the school* | *The entrance gate was closed.* | **a back/side entrance** (=one at the back or side of a building) **2** [U] permission to become a member of or become involved in a profession, university, organization etc.: *college entrance examinations* | *In 1987, Walls **gained entrance to** Yale.* **3** [U] the right or ability to go into a place: *Entrance to the museum is free.* | *an entrance fee* | *No one is sure how the men **gained entrance to*** (=got into) *the factory.* **4** [C] the time when a person, country, organization etc. first becomes involved in a particular area of activity: **+into** *the company's entrance into the software market* **5** [C usually singular] the act of entering a place or room, especially in a way that people notice OPP **exit**: *We were interrupted by the entrance of four visitors.* | **make your/an entrance** *At 4 p.m., the bride made her entrance.* | *He is a leader who likes to make **a grand entrance*** (=an impressive one). **6** [C usually singular] the act of coming onto the stage in a play OPP **exit**: *the moment when the hero **makes his entrance***

en·trance² /ɪn'træns/ *v.* [T usually passive] to seem very interesting and attractive, so that people will be sure to pay attention: *I was entranced by her sheer beauty.* —**entrancing** *adj.*

en·trant /'ɛntrənt/ *n.* [C] someone who enters a competition, race etc.

en·trap /ɪn'træp/ *v.* **entrapped**, **entrapping** [T] **1** to catch a criminal by persuading him or her to do something illegal **2** FORMAL to trick someone so that they are trapped in a situation they cannot escape from

en·trap·ment /ɪn'træp˺mənt/ *n.* [U] the act of catching a criminal by persuading him or her to do something illegal

en·treat /ɪn'trit/ *v.* [T] FORMAL to ask someone, in a very emotional way, to do something for you: **entreat sb to do sth** *Rayburn entreated them to drop their guns.*

en·treat·y /ɪn'triṭi/ *n. plural* **entreaties** [C,U] FORMAL a serious request in which you ask someone to do something for you

en·trée, entree /'ɑntreɪ/ *n.* **1** [C] the main dish of a meal **2** [C,U] FORMAL the right or freedom to enter a place or to join a group of people: **+to/into** *They use their connections to **gain entree to** the White House.*

en·trenched /ɪn'trɛntʃt/ *adj.* **1** entrenched ideas are strongly established and not likely to change: *entrenched attitudes* | **deeply/strongly entrenched** *deeply entrenched racism* **2** unlikely to change your belief or situation: **+in** *a political party entrenched in power*

en·trench·ment /ɪn'trɛntʃmənt/ *n.* [U] the process in which an attitude, belief etc. becomes firmly established

en·tre·pot /'ɑntrəˌpoʊ/ *n.* [C] TECHNICAL a place where large quantities of goods are stored before they are sent somewhere else

en·tre·pre·neur /ˌɑntrəprə'nɚ, -'nʊr/ W3 *n.* [C] someone who starts a company, arranges business deals, and takes risks in order to make a profit —**entrepreneurial** *adj.*: *entrepreneurial skills*

en·tre·pre·neur·ship /ˌɑntrəprə'nɚʃɪp/ *n.* [U] FORMAL the skill and practice of taking risks in order to start a company, arrange business deals, and make a lot of profit

en·tro·py /'ɛntrəpi/ *n.* [U] **1** TECHNICAL a measure of the lack of order in a system **2** PHYSICS a measure of the energy in a system that is not available to do work **3** PHYSICS the tendency of all MATTER and energy in the universe to develop toward a state where everything is inactive and the same **4** FORMAL a process by which a system or society becomes less organized

en·trust /ɪn'trʌst/ *v.* [T] to ask someone who you trust to do something important: **entrust sb with (doing) sth** *Bergen was entrusted with looking after the money.* | **entrust sth to sb** *Carter entrusted the negotiations to Richard Holbrooke.*

en·try /'ɛntri/ W3 *n. plural* **entries**

1 ACT OF ENTERING [C,U] the act of coming or going into something, or the right to do this: **+into** *There is no record of his entry into the country.* | **+to** *Entry to the film is included in the price.* | *The thieves **gained entry*** (=got into a place) *through an open kitchen window.* | *A huge sign said **No Entry**.* | **refuse/deny sb entry** (=not allow someone to enter)

2 BECOMING INVOLVED [C,U] a situation in which someone starts to take part in a system, a particular kind of work etc., or joins a group of people: *the entry of women into the work force during the war* | *Several Eastern European countries hope to soon **gain entry*** (=become involved) *to the European Union.*

3 DICTIONARY [C] a short piece of writing in a dictionary, list etc.: *Find the entry for "Impressionism" in the encyclopedia*

4 a) COMPETITION [C] something such as a perfor-

mance, set of answers, a picture etc. that is intended to win a competition: *The winning entry was a short film from France.* **b)** [C usually singular] a group of people or things who take part in a competition
5 COMPUTER [U] COMPUTERS the act of writing of information onto a computer: *data entry*
6 DOOR [C] a door, gate, or passage that you go through to enter a place → see also ENTRANCE[1]

'entry-ˌlevel *adj.* [only before noun] an entry-level job, activity, course etc. is for people with little or no experience

en·try·way /ˈɛntriˌweɪ/ *n.* [C] a passage or small room that you go through to enter a place

en·twine /ɪnˈtwaɪn/ *v.* [I,T often passive] **1** to twist two things together, or to wind one thing around another: *Flowers were entwined in her hair.* **2 be entwined (with sth)** to be closely connected with something in a complicated way

e·nu·mer·ate /ɪˈnuməˌreɪt/ *v.* [T] FORMAL to name a list of things one by one: *Hunt enumerates several reasons for the changes.*

eˌnumerated 'powers *n.* [plural] POLITICS another name for EXPRESSED POWERS

e·nun·ci·ate /ɪˈnʌnsiˌeɪt/ *v.* **1** [I,T] ENG. LANG. ARTS to pronounce words clearly and carefully → see also ARTICULATE[2] (2) **2** [T] FORMAL to express an idea clearly and exactly: *Here, Paul utilizes the principle he enunciated in Chapter 3.* —**enunciation** /ɪˌnʌnsiˈeɪʃən/ *n.* [U]

en·ured /ɪˈnʊrd/ *v.* [T] another spelling of INURED

en·vel·op /ɪnˈvɛləp/ *v.* [T] to cover something, or wrap it up completely: **envelop sth in/with sth** *The hills were enveloped in thick mist.* —**envelopment** *n.* [U]

en·ve·lope /ˈɛnvəˌloʊp, ˈɑn-/ S2 *n.* [C] **1** a thin paper cover in which you put a letter: *I tore open the envelope.* | *She* ***sealed the envelope*** (=stuck it shut) *and put a stamp on it.* **2** a layer of something that surrounds something else: +**of** *the envelope of gases that surround Earth* **3 push the envelope** to try to do more than what people think is possible, sensible, or right: *The CEO is known for pushing the envelope and getting results.* [**Origin:** 1700–1800 French *enveloppe*, from Old French *voloper* **to wrap**]

en·vi·a·ble /ˈɛnviəbəl/ *adj.* [only before noun] an enviable quality, position, or possession is good and other people would like to have it: *Burns is now* ***in the enviable position of*** *being able to make any film he wants.* —**enviably** *adv.*

en·vi·ous /ˈɛnviəs/ *adj.* wishing you had something that someone else has: +**of** *I was always envious of her long blond hair.* → see also JEALOUS → see Word Choice box at JEALOUS —**enviously** *adv.*

en·vi·ron·ment /ɪnˈvaɪənmənt/ Ac S2 W2 *n.* [C] **1 the environment** the air, water, and land in which people, animals, and plants live: *chemicals that damage the environment*

THESAURUS

Things that are harmful to the environment
pollution damage caused to air, water, soil etc. by harmful chemicals and waste
the greenhouse effect the warming of the air around the Earth as a result of the sun's heat being trapped by pollution
global warming an increase in world temperatures, caused by pollution in the air
acid rain rain that contains acid chemicals from factory smoke and cars etc.
deforestation when all the trees in an area are cut down or destroyed
Describing things that are good for the environment
environmentally friendly/eco-friendly products that are environmentally friendly or eco-friendly are not harmful to the environment
recycle if materials such as glass or paper are recycled, they are put through a special process so that they can be used again
biodegradable a material that is biodegradable can be destroyed by natural processes, in a way that does not harm the environment
organic organic food or organic farming does not use chemicals that are harmful to the environment

2 all the situations, events, people etc. that influence the way in which people live or work: *a pleasant work environment* | *It's not a very safe environment for children.* **3** an area of land or water, considered in terms of its natural features: *a harsh desert environment* **4** [C] BIOLOGY the physical, chemical, natural etc. conditions that affect the way a living thing lives or develops: *The moths were able to adapt to their new environment.* [**Origin:** 1600–1700 *environ* **to surround** (14–21 centuries), from Old French *environer*]

en·vi·ron·men·tal /ɪnˌvaɪənˈmɛntl◂/ Ac W2 *adj.* **1** EARTH SCIENCE concerning or affecting the air, land, or water on Earth: *environmental issues* | *the White House's environmental policies* | **environmental damage/impact** *the environmental impact of the war* | *Several* ***environmental groups*** (=organizations trying to protect the environment) *came out to protest.* **2** concerning the things and people around you in your life: *environmental factors that cause stress* —**environmentally** *adv.* → see also ENVIRONMENTALLY FRIENDLY

enˌvironmental 'impact ˌstatement *n.* [C] a document in which the environmental effects of a future project are explained

en·vi·ron·men·tal·ist /ɪnˌvaɪənˈmɛntl-ɪst/ Ac *n.* [C] EARTH SCIENCE someone who is concerned about protecting the environment —**environmentalism** *n.* [U]

enˌvironmentally 'friendly also **enˌvironment-'friendly** *adj.* EARTH SCIENCE products that are environmentally friendly do not harm the environment

enˌvironmental 'print *n.* [U] ENG. LANG. ARTS writing that is not in books but all around us, for example, words and SYMBOLS on signs, medicine bottles, food LABELS etc.

Enˌvironmental Pro'tection ˌAgency, the the EPA

en·vi·rons /ɪnˈvaɪrənz, ɛn-/ *n.* [plural] FORMAL the area surrounding a place: *Boston and its environs*

en·vis·age /ɪnˈvɪzɪdʒ/ *v.* [T] FORMAL to imagine something that will happen in the future: *The effects have been greater than we envisaged.*

en·vi·sion /ɪnˈvɪʒən/ *v.* [T] to imagine something, especially as a future possibility: *He envisions a day when every home will have access to the Internet.*

en·voy /ˈɛnvɔɪ, ˈɑn-/ *n. plural* **envoys** [C] someone who is sent to another country as an official representative of their government [**Origin:** 1600–1700 French *envoyé*, past participle of *envoyer* **to send**]

en·vy[1] /ˈɛnvi/ *v.* **envied, envying** [T] **1** to wish that you had someone else's possessions, abilities, qualities etc.: *Our classmates envied our freedom from rules.* **2 not envy sb sth** used to say that you are glad you do not have to have or deal with something that someone else does: *We don't envy them their difficult task.*

envy[2] *n.* [U] **1** the feeling of wanting something that someone else has: **with/in envy** *She stared with envy at Cara's new boyfriend.* **2 be the envy of sb/sth** to be something that other people admire and want to have very much: *Our living standards are the envy of the world.* [**Origin:** 1200–1300 Old French *envie*, from Latin *invidere* **to look at with bad feelings**] → see also **be green with envy** at GREEN[1] (5), JEALOUSY

en·zyme /ˈɛnzaɪm/ *n.* [C] CHEMISTRY a protein in a plant or animal that helps some chemical processes, but which does not change itself during the processes [**Origin:** 1800–1900 German *enzym*, from Greek *zyme* **substance that makes a flour-and-water mixture swell**]

e·on /ˈiən, ˈiɑn/ *n.* [C usually plural] **1** an extremely long period of time **2** a very long period of time in the history of the Earth: *The Precambrian eon started* *about 3.8 billion years ago, and finished about 550 million years ago.*

-eous /iəs/ *suffix* [in adjectives] used to make adjectives SYN -ous: *gaseous* (=in the form of a gas) | *beauteous* (=having great beauty) → see also -IOUS

EPA, the /ˌi pi ˈeɪ/ **Environmental Protection Agency** the U.S. government organization that works to reduce POLLUTION and protect the environment

ep·au·let, epaulette /ˌɛpəˈlɛt, ˈɛpəˌlɛt/ *n.* [C] a shoulder decoration on a shirt or military uniform

é·pée, epee /ˈɛpeɪ, eɪˈpeɪ/ *n.* [C] a narrow sword with a sharp point, used in the sport of FENCING

e·phem·er·a /ɪˈfɛmərə/ *n.* [plural] things such as newspapers, letters etc. that are only popular or important for a short time

e·phem·er·al /ɪˈfɛmərəl/ *adj.* FORMAL existing for only a short time [**Origin:** 1500–1600 Greek *ephemeros* **lasting a day**, from *hemera* **day**] —**ephemerally** *adv.*

E·phe·sians /ɪˈfiʒənz/ a book in the New Testament of the Christian Bible

ep·ic¹ /ˈɛpɪk/ *n.* [C] ENG. LANG. ARTS **1** a book, movie etc. that tells a long story that is full of action and events **2** a long poem that tells the story of what gods or important people did in ancient times

epic² *adj.* [only before noun] **1** ENG. LANG. ARTS epic stories, poems, movies etc. are long and full of action and events **2 of epic proportions** very big or impressive: *a famine of epic proportions* [**Origin:** 1500–1600 Latin *epicus*, from Greek *epikos*, from *epos* **word, speech, poem**]

ep·i·cen·ter /ˈɛpəˌsɛntə/ *n.* [C usually singular] EARTH SCIENCE a place on the Earth's surface that is above the point where an EARTHQUAKE begins

ep·i·cure /ˈɛpɪˌkyʊr/ *n.* [C] LITERARY someone who enjoys good food and drinks SYN **gourmet**

ep·i·cu·re·an /ˌɛpɪkyʊˈriən, -ˈkyʊriən/ *adj.* LITERARY gaining or giving pleasure through the senses, especially through good food and drinks —**epicurean** *n.* [C]

ep·i·dem·ic /ˌɛpəˈdɛmɪk/ *n.* [C] **1** MEDICINE a large number of cases of a particular infectious disease happening at the same time: *a cholera epidemic* **2** a sudden increase in the amount of times that something bad happens: +**of** *There has been a recent epidemic of car thefts.* [**Origin:** 1600–1700 French *épidémique*, from Greek *epidemos* **visiting**] —**epidemic** *adj.*: *Violence is reaching **epidemic proportions** in the inner cities.*

ep·i·de·mi·ol·o·gy /ˌɛpəˌdimiˈɑlədʒi/ *n.* [U] the study of the causes and control of diseases among people —**epidemiologist** *n.* [C] —**epidemiological** /ˌɛpəˌdimiəˈlɑdʒɪkəl/ *adj.*

ˌepidermal ˈcell *n.* [C] BIOLOGY any cell that is part of the EPIDERMIS of an animal or plant

ep·i·der·mis /ˌɛpəˈdəmɪs/ *n.* [C,U] BIOLOGY **1** the outer layer of skin on a person or animal, formed by a layer of cells → see picture at SKIN¹ **2** the outside surface of a plant, formed by a layer of cells —**epidermal** *adj.*

ep·i·dur·al /ˌɛpɪˈdʊrəl◂/ *n.* [C usually singular] a medical process in which a drug is put into your lower back to prevent you from feeling pain, especially when you are having a baby

ep·i·glot·tis /ˌɛpəˈglɑtɪs/ *n.* [C] BIOLOGY a thin piece of flesh at the back of your throat, that covers part of your throat when you swallow

ep·i·gram /ˈɛpəˌgræm/ *n.* [C] ENG. LANG. ARTS a short poem or phrase that expresses an idea in an amusing way —**epigrammatic** /ˌɛpəgrəˈmætɪk/ *adj.* —**epigrammatically** /-kli/ *adv.*

ep·i·lep·sy /ˈɛpəˌlɛpsi/ *n.* [U] MEDICINE a medical condition in the brain that can suddenly make you become unconscious, and often make you move your body in an uncontrolled way

ep·i·lep·tic¹ /ˌɛpəˈlɛptɪk◂/ *adj.* MEDICINE caused by epilepsy: *an epileptic seizure*

epileptic² *n.* [C] MEDICINE someone who has epilepsy

ep·i·logue, epilog /ˈɛpəˌlɑg, -ˌlɔg/ *n.* [C] ENG. LANG. ARTS a speech or piece of writing added to the end of a book, movie, or play to give more information about what happened later → see also PROLOGUE

e·piph·a·ny /ɪˈpɪfəni/ *n.* **1** *plural* **epiphanies** [C] a moment of sudden very strong emotions, when someone suddenly understands something **2 Epiphany** a Christian holy day on January 6 that celebrates the Three Wise Men's visit to the baby Jesus Christ [**Origin:** 1600–1700 French *épiphanie*, from Greek *epiphaneia* **appearance**]

ep·i·phyte /ˈɛpɪˌfaɪt/ *n.* [U] BIOLOGY a plant that grows on or is supported by a bigger plant but does not depend on it for food

e·pis·co·pa·cy /ɪˈpɪskəpəsi/ also **e·pis·co·pate** /ɪˈpɪskəpət/ *n.* [U] TECHNICAL **1** the rank of a BISHOP, or the time during which someone is bishop **2** all the bishops, or the system of the church government by bishops

e·pis·co·pal /ɪˈpɪskəpəl/ *adj.* **1 Episcopal** relating to the Episcopal Church **2** TECHNICAL relating to a BISHOP

Eˌpiscopal ˈChurch *n.* **the Episcopal Church** a PROTESTANT church in America that developed from the official Church of England

E·pis·co·pa·li·an /ɪˌpɪskəˈpeɪliən/ *n.* [C] a member of an Episcopal church —**Episcopalian** *adj.*

ep·i·sode /ˈɛpəˌsoʊd/ W3 *n.* [C] **1** a television or radio program that is one of a series of programs telling one story: *The final episode will be broadcast next week.* ▸see THESAURUS box at **television** **2** an event or a short period of time during which something specific happened: *Susan has had several episodes of depression lately.* [**Origin:** 1600–1700 Greek *epeisodion*, from *epeisodios* **coming in besides**]

ep·i·sod·ic /ˌɛpəˈsɑdɪk/ *adj.* FORMAL **1** happening at times that are not regular: *episodic neck pain* **2** consisting of separate parts which together form a series: *an episodic TV program* —**episodically** /-kli/ *adv.*

e·pis·tle /ɪˈpɪsəl/ *n.* [C] **1** FORMAL a long or important letter **2 Epistle** one of the letters written by the first Christians which are in the New Testament of the Bible

e·pis·to·lar·y /ɪˈpɪstəˌlɛri/ *adj.* ENG. LANG. ARTS an epistolary book is written in the form of a series of letters

ep·i·taph /ˈɛpəˌtæf/ *n.* [C] a short piece of writing on the stone over someone's grave

ep·i·the·li·al tis·sue /ˌɛpəθiliəl ˈtɪʃu/ *n.* [U] BIOLOGY material consisting of cells, that forms a thin protective layer on the inner surfaces of the body and around organs

ep·i·thet /ˈɛpəˌθɛt/ *n.* [C] a word or short phrase used to describe someone, especially when saying something bad about them: *Perez was the target of a **racial epithet*** (=something negative said about someone's race).

e·pit·o·me /ɪˈpɪtəmi/ *n.* **the epitome of sth** the best possible example of something: *Haneberg is the epitome of the successful executive.*

e·pit·o·mize /ɪˈpɪtəˌmaɪz/ *v.* [T not in progressive] to be a very typical example of something: *Cass Avenue epitomizes the city's economic and social depression.*

e plu·ri·bus u·num /i ˌplʊrəbəs ˈyunəm/ a Latin phrase meaning "out of the many, one," printed on U.S. money. It expresses the idea that many different people can work together under a single government.

ep·och /ˈɛpək/ *n.* [C] a period of history, especially one in which important events take place: *The Russian Revolution marked the beginning of a new epoch in history.* → see also ERA

e·poch·mak·ing /ˈɛpəkˌmeɪkɪŋ/ *adj.* [only before noun] very important in changing or developing people's lives: *an epoch-making event*

e·pon·y·mous /ɪˈpɑnəməs/ *adj.* [only before noun] an eponymous television show, CD, book etc. takes its name from a person, group, character etc. involved in it: *The Indigo Girls' eponymous album* (=it was called "The Indigo Girls") —**eponymously** *adv.*

ep·ox·y /ɪˈpɑksi/ *n.* [U] a type of very strong glue

Ep·som salts /ˈɛpsəm ˌsɔlts/ *n.* [plural] a white powder that can be mixed with water and used as a medicine, especially for stomach problems

eq·ua·ble /ˈɛkwəbəl/ *adj.* **1** FORMAL calm and not easily annoyed: *her equable temperament* **2** TECHNICAL having weather or conditions that are neither too hot nor too cold: *an equable climate* —**equably** *adv.* —**equability** /ˌɛkwəˈbɪləṭi/ *n.* [U]

e·qual[1] /ˈikwəl/ S3 W2 *adj.*
1 SIZE/VALUE/NUMBER the same in size, value, amount, number etc. as someone or something else: *Divide the dough into three equal parts.* | **sth is equal to sth** *The rent was equal to half his monthly income.* | **of equal height/weight/strength etc.** *They want three people of equal height for the show.* | **an equal number/amount of sth** *The two candidates received an equal number of votes.* | **equal value/importance** *We place equal value on both partners' careers.*
2 HAVING SAME RIGHTS having the same rights, opportunities etc. as everyone else, whatever their race, religion, sex etc.: *We are equal partners in the business.* | *The Declaration of Independence states that all people are equal.*
3 GIVING PEOPLE SAME RIGHTS giving people the same rights, opportunities etc. as everyone else, whatever their race, religion, sex etc.: *The fight for* ***equal rights*** *for women has been pushed to one side.* | *Our schools must provide* ***equal opportunities*** *for children of all races and religions.*
4 on an equal footing also **on equal terms** with neither side having any advantage over the other: *Small businesses cannot compete on equal terms with huge corporations.*
5 be equal to sth a) to be able to deal with a problem, piece of work etc. successfully: *I'm not sure he's equal to the job.* **b)** to have as high a standard or quality as something else: *The museum's collection is equal to any in Europe.*
6 all (other) things being equal SPOKEN used to say what a situation will be like if everything is normal and there are no special facts to consider: *All other things being equal, a small car will cost less than a large one.*
[**Origin:** 1300–1400 Latin *aequalis*, from *aequus* **level, equal**]

equal[2] S3 *v.* **equaled, equaling 1** [linking verb] to be the same in size, number, or amount as something else: *Three plus three equals six.* | *Prices will be more stable when supply equals demand.* **2** [T] to be as good as someone or something else: *Thompson equaled the world record.* **3** [T] to directly produce a particular result or effect: *A highly trained work force equals high productivity.*

equal[3] *n.* [C] **1** someone who is as important, intelligent etc. as you are, or who has the same rights and opportunities as you do: *My boss treats her employees as equals.* | **+in** *He's not her equal in intelligence.* **2 be without equal** also **have no equal** FORMAL to be better than everyone or everything else of the same type: *His paintings are without equal in the Western world.* **3 be the equal of sb/sth** to be as good as someone or something else: *The company proved to be the equal of its U.S. competitors.*

ˌequal-ˈarea ˌmap *n.* [C] a map on which areas that are the same size as each other in the world are also shown the same size, although their shapes are changed

ˌEqual Emˌployment Opporˈtunities Comˌmission, the a U.S. government organization whose aim is to make sure that people are not prevented from getting jobs because of their race, religion, age, sex etc., and to make sure that all workers are treated fairly and equally

e·qual·i·ty /ɪˈkwɑləṭi/ *n.* [U] the state of having the same rights, opportunities etc. as everyone else OPP **inequality**: **+between** *equality between men and women* | **+in** *the fight for equality in the workplace* | **racial/sexual/economic etc. equality** *He believed that socialism was the best way to social and economic equality.*

e·qual·ize /ˈikwəˌlaɪz/ *v.* [T] to make two or more things the same in size, value, amount etc.: *We try to equalize the workload between our teachers.* —**equalization** /ˌikwələˈzeɪʃən/ *n.* [U]

e·qual·iz·er /ˈikwəˌlaɪzɚ/ *n.* [C] **1** something that affects all people or groups the same way, even if their position in society is very different: *Computers are* ***great equalizers*** *for many people with disabilities.* (=computers allow them to do what everyone else does) **2** the part of a piece of electronic equipment such as a radio, that you use to change the quality of high and low sounds

e·qual·ly /ˈikwəli/ W3 *adv.* **1** [+ adj./adv.] to the same degree or amount: *The candidates are equally qualified for the job.* **2** in parts or amounts that are the same size: *We'll divide the money equally.* **3** in the same way: *He treats all the customers equally.* **4** [sentence adverb] also **equally important** used when introducing a second idea or statement that is as important as your first one: *We want the economy to grow, but equally we want low inflation.*

E

ˌequal proˈtection *n.* [U] LAW the principle that the government must treat all people and groups of people in a fair and equal way, as promised in the Equal Protection CLAUSE of the Fourteenth Amendment of the U.S Constitution

ˈequal sign *n.* [C] a sign (=) used in mathematics to show that two things are the same size, number, or amount

e·qua·nim·i·ty /ˌikwəˈnɪməṭi, ˌɛk-/ *n.* [U] FORMAL calmness in a difficult situation: *He received the news with surprising equanimity.* [**Origin:** 1600–1700 Latin *aequanimitas*, from *aequo animo* **with level mind**]

e·quate /ɪˈkweɪt/ Ac *v.* [T] to consider that one thing is the same as something else: **equate sth with sth** *Most people equate wealth with success.*
equate to sth *phr. v.* to be equal to sth: *a rate of pay that equates to $6 per hour*

e·qua·tion /ɪˈkweɪʒən/ Ac *n.* **1** [C] MATH a statement in mathematics, science etc., showing that two quantities are equal, for example $2x + 4 = 10$: *a mathematical equation* | ***Solve the following equation.*** **2** [U] a problem or situation with many different parts that all affect each other: *If you're trying to lose weight, exercise must* ***be part of the equation.*** | *The job applicant's sex does not* ***enter into the equation*** (=affect the situation) *when we decide who to hire.* **3** [U] the act of equating two things

e·qua·tor, Equator /ɪˈkweɪṭɚ/ *n.* **the equator** an imaginary line around the Earth, that divides it equally into its northern and southern halves → see picture at GLOBE

e·qua·to·ri·al /ˌɛkwəˈtɔriəl◂/ *adj.* EARTH SCIENCE relating to the equator, or near the equator: *an equatorial rainforest*

E·qua·to·ri·al Guin·ea /ˌɛkwətɔriəl ˈgɪni/ a small country in west central Africa north of Gabon —**Equatorial Guinean** *n., adj.*

eq·uer·ry /ˈɛkwəri, ɪˈkwɛri/ *n.* [C] a personal servant to a powerful person, especially a member of the British royal family

e·ques·tri·an /ɪˈkwɛstriən/ *adj.* relating to horse riding: *equestrian events* —**equestrian** *n.* [C]

equi- /ikwə, ɛkwə/ *prefix* equal or equally

e·qui·an·gu·lar /ˌikwiˈæŋgyəlɚ, ˌɛk-/ *adj.* MATH equiangular TRIANGLES or other shapes have angles of the same size → see also CONGRUENT

e·qui·dis·tant /ˌikwəˈdɪstənt◂, ˌɛkwə-/ *adj.* FORMAL at an equal distance from or between two places: **+from/between** *a point that is equidistant from Jupiter and the Sun*

e·qui·lat·er·al /ˌikwəˈlæṭərəl/ *adj.* MATH having all

sides the same length: *an equilateral triangle* —**equilateral** *n.* [C] → see picture at TRIANGLE

e·qui·lib·ri·um /ˌikwəˈlɪbriəm/ *n.* [singular, U] **1** a balance between opposing forces, influences etc. that makes a situation stable OPP **disequilibrium**: **upset/disturb etc. the equilibrium** *Too much rain entering the soil disturbs the equilibrium.* **2** ECONOMICS the point at which the supply of a good or service is equal to people's DEMAND (=need or desire) for it OPP **disequilibrium**: *The supply and the demand for money must be kept* ***in equilibrium*** *to avoid inflation.* **3** a state in which you are calm and not angry or upset: *She struggled to regain her equilibrium.* **4** BIOLOGY a state of balance between the substances in a chemical solution after a chemical reaction OPP **disequilibrium**

E

equiˈlibrium ˌprice *n.* [C] ECONOMICS a MARKET CLEARING PRICE

equiˈlibrium ˌwage *n.* [C] ECONOMICS the rate of pay for a particular job that produces a situation in which there are no jobs without workers and no workers without jobs

e·quine /ˈikwaɪn, ˈɛ-/ *adj.* FORMAL relating to horses, or looking like a horse

e·qui·nox /ˈikwəˌnɑks, ˈɛ-/ *n.* [C] one of the two times in a year when day and night are equal in length everywhere —**equinoctial** /ˌikwəˈnɑkʃəl/ *adj.* → see also SOLSTICE

e·quip /ɪˈkwɪp/ Ac *v.* **equipped**, **equipping** [T usually passive] **1** to provide a person or place with the things that are needed for a particular activity or type of work: **be equipped with sth** *Every room is equipped with a video camera.* | **be equipped to do sth** *The hospital is not equipped to provide the care the veterans need.* | **be equipped for sth** *Guides are equipped for any emergency.* | **fully/well/poorly equipped** *a fully equipped kitchen.* | *The report says city police are poorly equipped and underpaid.* **2** to provide someone with the skills, training, or education that they need for a particular purpose: **equip sb for sth** *training that will equip you for the job* | **equip sb with sth** *equipping young people with vocational skills* | **be equipped to do sth** *He is not emotionally equipped to deal with the real world.* | **well/ill equipped** *Carolyn is well equipped to manage independently.* [**Origin:** 1500–1600 French *équiper*] → see also ILL-EQUIPPED

e·quip·ment /ɪˈkwɪpˀmənt/ Ac S2 W2 *n.* [U] **1** the special tools, machines etc. that you need for a particular activity or type of work: *sports equipment* | *medical equipment* | *We bought several new* ***pieces of equipment*** *for the chemistry lab.* **2** the process of equipping someone or something

eq·ui·ta·ble /ˈɛkwət̬əbəl/ *adj.* FORMAL treating everyone equally and fairly —**equitably** *adv.*

Eq·ui·ty /ˈɛkwət̬i/ a UNION for actors and other theater workers in the U.S.

eq·ui·ty /ˈɛkwət̬i/ W3 *n.* **1** [U] ECONOMICS the amount of money you would have left if you sold something you own, such as a house, and paid back the money you still owe on it: *We have a lot of equity in our house.* **2** [U] the quality of treating everyone fairly, and dealing with situations in a fair way: *the ideals of equity, justice, and community* **3 equities** [plural] ECONOMICS STOCK in a company (=shares that show you own part of it) [**Origin:** 1300–1400 French *équité*, from Latin *aequitas*, from *aequus* **level, equal**]

e·quiv·a·len·cy /ɪˈkwɪvələnsi/ *n. plural* **equivalencies** [C,U] **1 equivalency degree/diploma/certificate etc.** a test that you take to show that you have the same knowledge or skills as other people who have GRADUATED from a particular school or college → see also GED **2** the state of being equal in value, meaning, or effect to something else

e·quiv·a·lent¹ /ɪˈkwɪvələnt/ Ac *n.* [C] something that has the same value, size, purpose etc. as something else: *Some Thai words have no English equivalents.* | **the equivalent of sth** *They earn the equivalent of $2 per day.* [**Origin:** 1400–1500 French, Late Latin, from *aequivalere* **to have equal power**]

equivalent² Ac *adj.* equal in value, purpose, rank etc. to someone or something else: *I offered him an equivalent amount in euros.* | **+to** *Each barrel of oil is equivalent to about 40 gallons of gasoline.* | **equivalent in size/value/meaning etc.** *Dolphins' brains are roughly equivalent in size to a human brain.* —**equivalence** *n.* [U] —**equivalently** *adv.*

eˌquivalent eˈquations *n.* [plural] MATH two or more EQUATIONS that have the same set of solutions

eˌquivalent ineˈqualities *n.* [plural] MATH two or more INEQUALITIES (=mathematical statement about quantities that are not equal) that have the same set of solutions

eˌquivalent ˈsystems *n.* [plural] MATH two or more systems of EQUATIONS that all have the same set of solutions

e·quiv·o·cal /ɪˈkwɪvəkəl/ *adj.* **1** deliberately not clear or definite in meaning OPP **unequivocal**: *an equivocal answer* **2** information that is equivocal is difficult to understand or explain OPP **unequivocal**: *The results of the test were equivocal.* —**equivocally** /-kli/ *adv.* → see also AMBIGUOUS

e·quiv·o·cate /ɪˈkwɪvəˌkeɪt/ *v.* [I] FORMAL to say something that has more than one possible meaning, in order to avoid giving a clear or direct answer —**equivocation** /ɪˌkwɪvəˈkeɪʃən/ *n.* [C,U]

-er /ɚ/ *suffix* **1** [in adjectives] used to form the COMPARATIVE of many short adjectives and adverbs: *hot, hotter* | *My car is fast, but hers is faster.* → see also -IER **2** [in nouns] someone who does something or who is doing something: *a dancer* (=someone who dances or is dancing) | *the diners* (=people having dinner) **3** [in nouns] something that does something: *a dishwasher* (=machine that washes dishes) **4** [in nouns] someone who makes a particular type of thing: *a potter* (=someone who makes things from clay) **5** [in nouns] someone who lives in or comes from a particular place: *a New Yorker* (=someone from New York) | *the villagers* (=people who live in the village) **6** [in nouns] someone skilled in a particular subject: *a geographer* (=someone who studies GEOGRAPHY) **7** [in nouns] something that has something: *a three-wheeler* (=a vehicle with three wheels) → see also -AR, -IER, -OR

ER /i ˈɑr/ *n.* [C] TECHNICAL the abbreviation of EMERGENCY ROOM

er /ɚ/ *interjection* a sound you make when you pause to correct something you have just said, or when you do not know exactly what to say: *We'll never forgive – er, forget – her accomplishments.*

e·ra /ˈɪrə, ˈɛrə/ W2 *n.* [C] **1** a period of time that is associated with particular events or qualities, or that begins with a particular date or event: *the post Cold War era* | **+of** *We live in an era of instant communication.* **2** EARTH SCIENCE one of the three long periods of time that the history of the earth is divided into, starting 550 million years ago: *the dinosaurs of the Mesozoic Era* [**Origin:** 1600–1700 Late Latin *aera* **number for calculating from**, from Latin, **counters**, plural of *aes* **copper, money**] → see also EPOCH

e·rad·i·cate /ɪˈrædəˌkeɪt/ *v.* [T] to completely get rid of or destroy something: *He spoke about what is necessary to eradicate AIDS.* | **eradicate sth from sth** *an attempt to eradicate bullying from the school* [**Origin:** 1400–1500 Latin, past participle of *eradicare* **to pull out by the root**, from *radix* **root**] —**eradication** /ɪˌrædəˈkeɪʃən/ *n.* [U]

e·rase /ɪˈreɪs/ S3 *v.* [T] **1** to completely remove information from a computer memory or recorded sounds from a TAPE: *The computer's hard drive had been erased.* ►see THESAURUS box at **remove** **2** to remove marks or writing so that they cannot be seen anymore: *Erase all incorrect answers.* **3** FORMAL to get rid of something so that it is completely gone and no signs of it exist: *Today's fall in prices erases yesterday's gains.* **4 erase sth from your mind/memory** to make yourself forget something bad that has happened: *He couldn't erase the* *horrible image from his mind.* [**Origin:** 1500–1600 Latin, past participle of *eradere*, from *radere* **to rub roughly, scrape**]

e·ras·er /ɪˈreɪsɚ/ *n.* [C] **1** a piece of rubber used to remove pencil or pen marks from paper **2** an object used for cleaning marks from a BLACKBOARD or WHITEBOARD

E·ras·mus /ɪˈræzməs/, **Des·i·der·i·us** /ˌdɛzɪˈdɛriəs/ (1466?–1536) a Dutch writer and teacher who criticized the Catholic Church but opposed the Protestant Reformation

e·ra·sure /ɪˈreɪʃɚ/ *n.* FORMAL **1** [C] a mark that is left when words or letters are removed with an eraser **2** [U] the act of completely removing or destroying something: *the erasure of the debt*

ere /ɛr/ *prep., conjunction* OLD USE OR POETIC before

Er·e·bus, Mount /ˈɛrəbəs/ a mountain on Ross Island in Antarctica that is an active VOLCANO

e·rect¹ /ɪˈrɛkt/ *v.* [T] FORMAL **1** to build a building, wall, STATUE etc.: *A monument will be erected in the firefighters' honor.* ►see THESAURUS box at **build¹** **2** to attach all the pieces of something together, and put it in an upright position SYN **put up**: *The tents for the fair were erected overnight.* **3** to establish something such as a system or institution: **erect barriers/obstacles etc.** *His policy would erect trade barriers to protect American jobs.*

erect² *adj.* **1** in a straight upright position: **stand/sit erect** *The 8-year-olds sat erect at their desks.* **2** BIOLOGY an erect PENIS or NIPPLE is stiff and bigger than it usually is, usually because of sexual excitement [**Origin:** 1300–1400 Latin *erectus*, past participle of *erigere* **to erect**] **—erectly** *adv.* **—erectness** *n.* [U]

e·rec·tile /ɪˈrɛktl, -taɪl/ *adj.* TECHNICAL relating to a man's erection

e·rec·tion /ɪˈrɛkʃən/ *n.* **1 have an erection** BIOLOGY if a man has an erection his PENIS becomes stiff because he is sexually excited **2** [U] the act of building something or putting it in an upright position

erg /ɚg/ *n.* [C] TECHNICAL a unit used to measure work or energy

er·go /ˈɛrgoʊ, ˈɚgoʊ/ *adv.* FORMAL [sentence adverb] therefore

er·go·nom·ics /ˌɚgəˈnɑmɪks/ *n.* [U] the study of how the design of equipment affects how well, quickly, and comfortably people can use it **—ergonomic** *adj.* **—ergonomically** /-kli/ *adv.*

Er·ics·son, **Eriksson** /ˈɛrɪksən/, **Leif** /lif/ (10th century A.D.) an EXPLORER from Norway, who was probably the first European to discover America. He landed in Newfoundland in the late 10th century.

Er·ic the Red /ˌɛrɪk ðə ˈrɛd/ (10th century) a Norwegian EXPLORER who sailed along the coast of Greenland and brought people to settle there

E·rie, Lake /ˈiri/ one of the Great Lakes of North America, between the U.S. and Canada

ˌErie Caˈnal, the a CANAL in the U.S. state of New York that connects Lake Erie and the Hudson River

Er·i·tre·a /ˌɛrɪˈtriə/ a country in northeast Africa, south of Sudan and north of Ethiopia **—Eritrean** *n., adj.*

er·mine /ˈɚmən/ *n.* **1** [U] an expensive white fur, used especially for the clothes of judges, kings, and queens **2** [C] BIOLOGY a small thin animal of the WEASEL family whose fur is white in winter

Ernst /ɛrnst/, **Max** /mæks/ (1891–1976) a German PAINTER famous for his work in Dadaism and Surrealism

e·rode /ɪˈroʊd/ Ac *v.* **1** [I,T] if the weather or water erodes rock or soil, or it erodes, it is gradually destroyed or washed away: *Hard rains have eroded topsoil in the Midwest.* | *The south beach has eroded significantly.* **2** [I,T] if someone's power, authority, confidence etc. erodes, or something erodes it, it is gradually reduced or becomes weaker: *Failure had eroded her confidence.* [**Origin:** 1600–1700 Latin *erodere* **to eat away**, from *rodere*] → see also EROSION

e·rog·e·nous zone /ɪˌrɑdʒənəs ˈzoʊn/ *adj.* a part of your body that gives you sexual pleasure when it is touched

Er·os /ˈɛrɑs, ˈɛroʊs, ˈɪr-/ **1** in Greek MYTHOLOGY, the god of sexual and romantic love **2** [U] sexual love

e·ro·sion /ɪˈroʊʒən/ Ac *n.* [U] **1** the process by which rock or soil is gradually washed away by wind, rain, or water: *soil erosion* | +**of** *the gradual erosion of the cliffs* **2** the process of gradually making something weaker: *the erosion of civil liberties* **—erosive** /ɪˈroʊsɪv/ *adj.*

e·rot·ic /ɪˈrɑṭɪk/ *adj.* relating to sex, or making you feel sexually excited: *erotic pictures* [**Origin:** 1600–1700 Greek *erotikos*, from *eros* **sexual love**] **—erotically** /-kli/ *adv.*

e·rot·i·ca /ɪˈrɑṭɪkə/ *n.* [U] erotic writing, drawings etc. → see also PORNOGRAPHY

e·rot·i·cism /ɪˈrɑṭəˌsɪzəm/ *n.* [U] a style or quality that expresses strong feelings of sexual love and desire, especially in works of art: *the eroticism of her poetry*

err /ɛr, ɚ/ *v.* [I] **1 err on the side of caution/mercy etc.** to be more careful, safe etc. than is necessary rather than risk making a mistake **2** FORMAL to make a mistake: *The editors now admit that they erred in their decision.* **3 to err is human, (to forgive divine)** used to say that it is very easy to make mistakes, so we should all try to forgive them

er·rand /ˈɛrənd/ *n.* [C] a short trip that you take to deliver a message, buy something etc.: **run/do an errand** *Could you run an errand for Grandma?* | *His mother **sent him on an errand**.*

er·rant /ˈɛrənt/ *adj.* [only before noun] FORMAL OR HUMOROUS **1** behaving in a bad or irresponsible way: *an errant husband* **2** moving in the wrong direction: *Rainer caught the errant pass.*

er·rat·ic /ɪˈræṭɪk/ *adj.* changing often and without warning, or done without planning in a way that does not follow a pattern: *erratic winds* | *It was hard to deal with his erratic behavior.* **—erratically** /-kli/ *adv.*: *Police observed him driving erratically.*

er·ra·tum /ɛˈrɑṭəm/ *n. plural* **errata** /-ṭə/ [C] TECHNICAL a mistake in a book, shown in a list that is added after the book is printed

er·ro·ne·ous /ɪˈroʊniəs/ Ac *adj.* FORMAL incorrect or wrong: *The report contained erroneous information.* **—erroneously** *adv.*

er·ror /ˈɛrɚ/ Ac S3 W3 *n.* **1** [C,U] a mistake, especially one that causes problems: *a spelling error* | +**in** *an error in the calculations* | *She **made** several **errors** on the typing test.* | *We know now that the plane crash was the result of **human error*** (=by a person rather than a machine). | *Kovitz apologized yesterday for his **error in judgment*** (=a decision that was a mistake). | **computer/technical/administrative etc. error** *The company says a **computer error** was responsible for the enormous bill.* | **grave/serious/grievous/fatal error** (=a very bad one) **2 see the error of your ways** LITERARY OR HUMOROUS to realize that you have been behaving badly and decide to stop **3** a throw or catch in baseball that you do not make successfully when you should have: **make/commit an error** *They committed two errors in the first inning.* **4 be in error** FORMAL to be wrong or have made a mistake: *The company has admitted that it was in error.* **5 do sth in error** FORMAL to do something that is wrong without intending to do it: *The bank had withdrawn the funds in error.* [**Origin:** 1200–1300 Old French *errour*, from Latin *error*, from *errare*] → see also **by/through trial and error** at TRIAL (4)

WORD CHOICE **error, mistake**

• **Mistake** is a word for something that you do by accident or that is the result of not knowing or understanding something: *I'm sorry – I took your pen by mistake.* | *Maybe we made a mistake in buying the car.*

• **Error** is a more formal word than **mistake**. It is used more frequently in writing than in speech, especially in phrases like the ones shown in the entry above.

er·satz /ˈɛrsɑts, ˈɛrzɑts/ *adj.* [usually before noun] artificial, and not as good as the real thing: *ersatz coffee* [**Origin:** 1800–1900 German **something used instead of something else**]

erst·while /ˈɚstwaɪl/ *adj.* [only before noun] FORMAL former or in the past: *his erstwhile critics* [**Origin:** 1500–1600 *erst* **formerly** (11–19 centuries) from Old English *ærest* **earliest** + *while*]

er·u·dite /ˈɛryəˌdaɪt, ˈɛrə-/ *adj.* showing a lot of knowledge: *a complex and erudite work* [**Origin:** 1400–1500 Latin, past participle of *erudire* **to give instruction to**, from *rudis* **rude, uneducated**] —**erudition** /ˌɛryəˈdɪʃən/ *n.* [U]

E

e·rupt /ɪˈrʌpt/ *v.* [I] **1** if an argument, fighting etc. erupts, it starts suddenly: *A political crisis has erupted in Italy.* | *Violence erupted when police confronted protestors.* **2** EARTH SCIENCE if a VOLCANO erupts, it explodes and sends smoke, fire, and rock into the sky **3** if a place, situation, or group erupts, there is a sudden increase in activity or strong emotion: **erupt into sth** *The memorial service for the slain leader erupted into chaos.* | *The audience erupted into laughter.* **4** if something erupts, it suddenly explodes SYN **explode**: *Gunfire erupted all around us.* | *There was a crash and the train* ***erupted into flames.*** **5** if spots erupt on your body, they suddenly appear on your skin [**Origin:** 1600–1700 Latin, past participle of *erumpere* **to burst out**] —**eruption** /ɪˈrʌpʃən/ *n.* [C,U]

-ery /əri/ *suffix* [in nouns] **1** a quality or condition: *bravery* (=quality of being brave) | *slavery* (=condition of being a slave) **2** things of a particular kind: *modern machinery* (=different types of machines) | *her finery* (=beautiful clothes) **3** a place where a particular activity happens: *a bakery* (=where bread is baked) | *an oil refinery* | *a fish hatchery* → see also -ARY

es·ca·late /ˈɛskəˌleɪt/ *v.* [I,T] **1** if fighting, violence, or a bad situation escalates, or if someone escalates it, it becomes much worse: **escalate into sth** *A dispute on the dance floor quickly escalated into violence.* **2** to become higher or increase, or to make something do this: *Land costs are escalating rapidly.* —**escalation** /ˌɛskəˈleɪʃən/ *n.* [C, U]

es·ca·la·tor /ˈɛskəˌleɪtɚ/ *n.* [C] a set of stairs that move and carry people from one level within a building to another

escalator

es·ca·pade /ˈɛskəˌpeɪd/ *n.* [C] **1** an adventure, trick, or series of events that is exciting or risky: *In her wildest escapade, she faked her own death.* **2** a sexual relationship that is exciting or risky, but that is not considered serious

es·cape¹ /ɪˈskeɪp/ W2 *v.* **1** GET AWAY [I,T] **a)** to get away from a place or situation where you are in danger, or when someone is trying to stop you: *The man was shot as he attempted to escape with the money.* | *She managed to escape her kidnappers.* | **+from/through/over etc.** *She managed to escape from the car unharmed.* | *The family escaped to Switzerland.* **b)** to get away from a boring or unpleasant situation: *They went to the mountains to escape the summer heat.* | **escape from sth** *Education helps people escape from poverty.*

erosion

1 First, waves break on the cliffs in a process called hydraulic action. The erosion process begins as the force and impact of the waves loosens the rocks and air (a) which are trapped in the cliff's joints and faults.

2 Next, the new rock is worn away by the pebbles and sand that are flung against the cliffs. As a result of this process, known as corrosion, wave-cut notches (b) are created under the cliffs. Eventually wave-cut platforms consisting of material from the eroded cliff are also produced.

3 The erosion process continues with a process called attrition in which cliff-fall material (c) (=material from the eroded cliff that has fallen down) is ground down into smaller particles until they are small enough for the ocean to move them away (d).

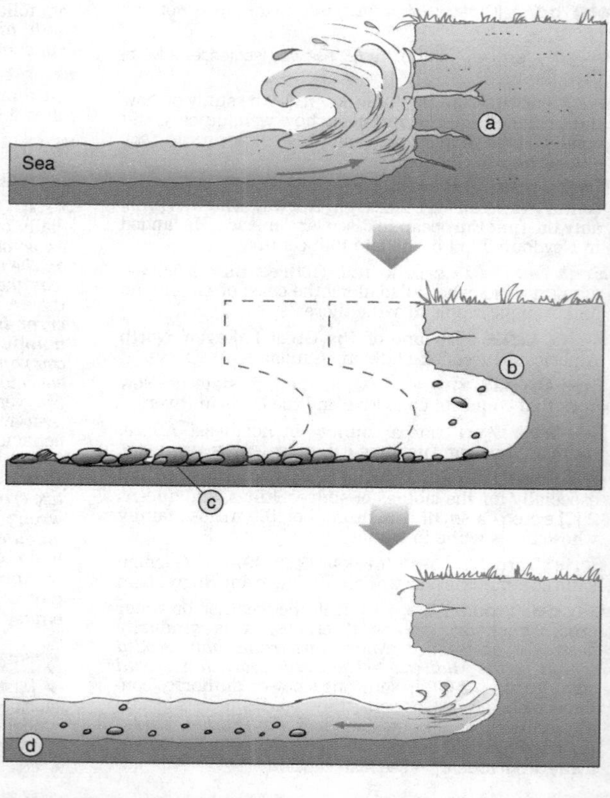

THESAURUS

get away to escape from someone who is chasing you: *He grabbed the man's legs and stopped him getting away.*
flee to leave somewhere very quickly in order to escape from danger: *refugees who were forced to flee their country*
get out to escape from a place: *He was locked in the room and couldn't get out.*
break out to escape from prison: *Several inmates have broken out of the state penitentiary.*
break free/break away to escape from someone who is trying to hold you: *She broke free and started running.*
abscond FORMAL to escape from a place where you are being kept: *Patients at the mental hospital found it all too easy to abscond.*
fly OLD-FASHIONED to leave somewhere in order to escape: *They were forced to fly the country in 1939.*

2 AVOID [I,T] to avoid something bad happening to you: *Until now he has managed to escape criticism.* | *The doctors said I was lucky to escape with only minor injuries.* | *The couple* ***narrowly escaped*** *death in the crash* (=they came very close to dying). | **escape unharmed/unhurt** *The woman in the car escaped unhurt.*
3 FORGET [I,T] to do something else in order to forget a bad situation for a short time: *People are willing to pay $10 for a movie ticket to escape their problems.*
4 the name/date/title escapes me used to say that you cannot remember a name, date etc.: *I've met him before, but his name escapes me.*
5 GAS/LIQUID ETC. [I] if gas, liquid, light, heat etc. escapes from somewhere, it comes out, especially when you do not want it to: *A cloud of poisonous gas escaped from the chemical plant.*
6 escape (sb's) attention/notice to not be noticed by someone: *Nothing escapes Bill's attention.*
7 SOUND [I,T] if a sound escapes from someone's mouth, they accidentally make that sound: *A tired sigh* ***escaped from his lips.***
8 there's no escaping the fact that used to say that something is definitely true, even if you would like to avoid thinking about it: *There's no escaping the fact that our bodies deteriorate as we get older.*
[**Origin:** 1200–1300 Old North French *escaper*, from Late Latin *cappa* **head-covering**; from the idea of throwing off something that limits your movement] —**escaped** *adj.* [only before noun]: *escaped prisoners*

escape² *n.* **1** [C,U] **a)** the act of getting away from a place or situation where you are in danger, or when someone is trying to stop you: *The boy had no chance of escape.* | +**from** *her miraculous escape from the burning plane* | *The three men* ***made a*** *daring* ***escape*** *from jail.* **b)** the act of getting away from a boring or unpleasant situation: +**from** *There is no escape from the difficulties of growing up.* **2** [singular, U] a way to forget about a bad situation for a short time: *Books are a good form of escape.* **3** [C] the act of avoiding a bad or unpleasant situation that could have affected you: +**from** *the company's* ***narrow escape*** (=a situation in which it almost did not escape) *from bankruptcy* **4** [singular, U] an amount of gas, liquid etc. that comes out of a place where it is being kept, or an occasion when this happens: *the escape of heat from the atmosphere* → see also FIRE ESCAPE

es'cape clause *n.* [C] a part of a contract that explains the conditions under which the person who signs it would not have to obey the contract

es·cap·ee /ɪˌskeɪˈpi, ˌɛskeɪˈpi/ *n.* [C] someone who has escaped from somewhere

es'cape route *n.* [C] a way to get out of a dangerous place: *The fire was between us and our escape route.*

es·cap·ism /ɪˈskeɪpˌɪzəm/ *n.* [U] activities or entertainment that help you forget about bad or boring things for a short time: *The world looks to Hollywood for escapism.* —**escapist** *adj.*

es·cap·ol·o·gy /ɪˌskeɪˈpɑlədʒi, ˌɛskə-/ *n.* [U] the skill of escaping from ropes, chains etc. as part of a performance —**escapologist** *n.* [C]

es·car·got /ˌɛskɑrˈgoʊ/ *n.* [C] a SNAIL that has been prepared for you to eat

es·ca·role /ˈɛskəˌroʊl/ *n.* [U] a vegetable like LETTUCE with curly leaves

es·carp·ment /ɪˈskɑrpmənt/ *n.* [C] a high steep slope or cliff that joins two levels on a hill or mountain

es·cheat /ɪsˈtʃit/ *n.* [C] LAW a legal process in which someone's money and property is given to the state after they die if they do not have a WILL, or if there is not someone else with the legal rights to their property

es·chew /ɛsˈtʃu/ *v.* [T] FORMAL to deliberately avoid doing, using, or having something: *a man who eschews violence*

es·cort¹ /ɪˈskɔrt, ˈɛskɔrt/ *v.* [T] **1** to go somewhere with someone to protect or guard them: **escort sb in/into/through etc. sth** *Armed guards escorted the prisoners into the courthouse.* **2** to go somewhere with someone to show them the way, show them a place etc.: *I escorted the visitors on a tour of the house.* ►see THESAURUS box at **lead¹** **3** OLD-FASHIONED to go with someone to a social event

es·cort² /ˈɛskɔrt/ *n.* [C] **1** a person or a group of people or vehicles that go with someone in order to protect or guard them: *The governor travels with* ***a police escort.*** | *The three were sent back to Baghdad* ***under escort*** (=with an escort). **2** someone who goes with someone to a formal social event: *Lou agreed to be my escort for the evening.* **3** someone who is paid to go out with someone socially **4** someone who is paid to go out with someone to social events, often someone who is also a PROSTITUTE [**Origin:** 1500–1600 French *escorte*, from Italian *scorgere* **to guide**, from Latin *corrigere*]

'escort ˌservice also **'escort ˌagency** *n.* [C] a business that arranges occasions for people to meet escorts or PROSTITUTES

es·cri·toire /ˈɛskrəˌtwɑr/ *n.* [C] a small writing desk

es·crow /ˈɛskroʊ/ *n.* [U] LAW something such as a written contract, money etc. that is held by someone who is not directly involved in an agreement until a particular goal is achieved

es·cudo /ɪˈskudoʊ/ *n.* [C] the unit of money used in Portugal [**Origin:** 1800–1900 Spanish and Portuguese, **shield**]

es·cutch·eon /ɪˈskʌtʃən/ *n.* [C] FORMAL a SHIELD on which someone's COAT OF ARMS (=family sign) is painted

-ese /iz, is/ *suffix* **1** [in nouns] a person from a particular country or place, or their language: *the Taiwanese* (=people from Taiwan) | *learning Japanese* (=language of Japan) **2** [in adjectives] belonging to a particular country or place: *Chinese music* **3** [in nouns] language or words used by a particular group, especially when it is difficult to understand: *journalese* (=language used in newspapers) | *officialese* (=language used in official or legal writing)

Es·ki·mo /ˈɛskəˌmoʊ/ *n. plural* **Eskimo** or **Eskimos** [C] a word for a member of one of the Native American tribes in Alaska, northern Canada etc., that may be considered offensive [**Origin:** 1500–1600 Danish *Eskimo* and French *Esquimaux*, from Algonquian] → see also INUK

ESL /ˌi ɛs ˈɛl/ *n.* [U] **English as a second language** the teaching of English to people whose first language is not English, who are living in an English-speaking country → see also EFL

ESOL /ˌi ɛs oʊ ˈɛl, ˈisɔl/ *n.* [U] **English for speakers of other languages** → see also TESOL

e·soph·a·gus /ɪˈsɑfəgəs/ *n.* [C] the tube that connects the mouth to the stomach in people and animals → see picture at DIGESTIVE SYSTEM

es·o·ter·ic /ˌɛsəˈtɛrɪk◂/ *adj.* known and understood by only a few people who have special knowledge about something: *esoteric religious teachings* [**Origin:** 1600–

1700 Greek *esoterikos*, from *esotero* **further inside**] —**esoterically** /-kli/ *adv.*

ESP /ˌi ɛs ˈpi/ *n.* [U] **1 extrasensory perception** the ability to know what another person is thinking, or to know what will happen in the future, not by seeing or hearing things, but in a way that cannot be explained **2** English for special purposes; the teaching of technical English to business people, scientists etc.

esp. the written abbreviation of ESPECIALLY

es·pa·drille /ˈɛspəˌdrɪl/ *n.* [C] a light shoe that is made of cloth and rope [**Origin:** 1800–1900 French, Latin *spartum* name of a type of grass from which it was first made]

es·pe·cial /ɪˈspɛʃəl/ *adj.* FORMAL → see SPECIAL

es·pe·cial·ly /ɪˈspɛʃəli/ S1 W1 *adv.* **1** [sentence adverb] used to emphasize that something is more important than usual, or that something happens to a higher degree with one particular person, group, or thing than with others: *Drive carefully, especially with all this fog.* | *Everyone's excited about the trip, especially Wendy.* | **especially if/when** *You have to be polite, especially when customers are yelling.* **2** to a particularly high degree, or much more than usual SYN **particularly**: *I especially like this picture.* | *I wasn't especially happy at that school.* | *"Do you want to help me paint?" "**Not especially**."* **3** for a particular person, purpose etc.: +**for** *I bought a new dress especially for the occasion.* → see also SPECIALLY

Es·pe·ran·to /ˌɛspəˈræntoʊ, -ˈrɑntoʊ/ *n.* [U] a language invented in 1887 to help people from different countries in the world speak to each other [**Origin:** 1800–1900 Dr *Esperanto* (from Latin *sperare* **to hope**), name taken by Ludwik Zamenhof, who invented the language]

es·pi·o·nage /ˈɛspiəˌnɑʒ/ *n.* [U] the activity of finding out secret information and giving it to a country's enemies or a company's competitors

es·pla·nade /ˈɛspləˌneɪd, ˌɛspləˈneɪd/ *n.* [C] a flat open space or wide street, especially next to the ocean in a town

ESPN /ˌi ɛs pi ˈɛn/ *n.* [singular, not with "the"] a CABLE TELEVISION station that broadcasts sports programs

es·pouse /ɛˈspaʊz, ɪ-/ *v.* [T] **1** FORMAL to believe in and support a political, religious etc. idea or PHILOSOPHY: **espouse a cause/principle etc.** *Christian organizations that espouse human rights issues* **2** OLD USE to marry —**espousal** *n.* [singular, U]

es·pres·so /ɛˈsprɛsoʊ/ *n. plural* **espressos** [C,U] very strong coffee that you drink in small cups [**Origin:** 1900–2000 Italian *caffè espresso* **pressed-out coffee**]

es·prit de corps /ɛˌspri də ˈkɔr/ *n.* [U] feelings of loyalty toward people who are all involved in the same activity as you

es·py /ɪˈspaɪ/ *v.* [T] LITERARY to see someone or something that is far away or difficult to see

Esq. /ˈɛskwaɪɚ/ **Esquire** a title of respect that is put after the names of lawyers

-esque /ɛsk/ *suffix* [in adjectives] **1** in the manner or style of a particular person, group, or place: *Kafkaesque* (=in the style of the writer Franz Kafka) **2** having a particular quality: *picturesque* (=pleasant to look at)

Es·quire /ˈɛskwaɪr, ɪˈskwaɪr/ *n.* ESQ.

-ess /ɛs, ɪs/ *suffix* [in nouns] a woman who does something, or a female: *an actress* (=female actor) | *a waitress* | *two lionesses*

es·say[1] /ˈɛseɪ/ S3 *n. plural* **essays** [C] **1** a short piece of writing about a particular subject done for a class at school or college: +**on/about** *an essay on democracy and education* | *Her teacher asked her to **write an essay** about Winter.* ►see THESAURUS box at **school**[1] **2** a short piece of writing giving someone's ideas about politics, society etc.: +**on** *Rousseau's Essay on the Origin of Languages* **3** FORMAL an attempt to do something: +**into** *his first essay into politics* [**Origin:** 1400–1500 Old French *essai*, from Late Latin *exagium* **act of weighing**]

es·say[2] *v.* [T] FORMAL to attempt to do something: *She essayed a little dance step.*

es·say·ist /ˈɛseɪ-ɪst/ *n.* [C] someone who writes essays, especially as a form of literature

es·sence /ˈɛsəns/ *n.* **1** [U] the most basic and important quality of something: **the essence of sth** *The essence of his teachings is "know yourself."* **2 in essence** FORMAL used to emphasize the most basic and important part of a statement, idea, or situation: *The organization was, in essence, a revolutionary one.* **3** [C,U] a liquid obtained from a plant, flower etc. that has a strong smell or taste and is used especially in cooking: *essence of garlic* **4 sth is of the essence** used to say that something is the most important thing: *Speed is of the essence, so that people can see progress.* [**Origin:** 1300–1400 French, Latin *essentia*, from *esse* **to be**]

es·sen·tial[1] /ɪˈsɛnʃəl/ W3 *adj.* **1** important and necessary OPP **nonessential**: *A compass is essential in the mountains.* | +**for/to** *Respect and trust are absolutely essential for a good relationship.* | **it is essential (that)** *In a crisis situation, it is essential that the pilot remain calm.* | **it is essential to do sth** *It is essential to set realistic goals.* ►see THESAURUS box at **important**, **necessary** **2** an essential part, quality, or feature of something is the most basic one SYN **fundamental**: *What is the essential difference between the two designs?* | *one of the essential features of his comedy* ►see THESAURUS box at **basic** → see also ESSENTIAL OIL

essential[2] *n.* **1** [C usually plural] something that is important and necessary: *food, transportation, and other essentials* | *We provide the homeless with **the bare essentials*** (=the most basic and necessary things) *such as food and clothing.* **2 the essentials** [plural] the basic and most important information or facts about a particular subject: *the essentials of English grammar*

es·sen·tial·ly /ɪˈsɛnʃəli/ S2 W3 *adv.* in the most important or basic form or state: *Polk believes that the world is essentially a good place.* | [sentence adverb] *Essentially, they have 90 days to leave the country.*

esˌsential ˈoil *n.* [C] an oil from a plant that has a strong smell and is used for making PERFUME or in AROMATHERAPY etc.

-est /ɪst/ *suffix* used to form the SUPERLATIVE of many short adjectives and adverbs: *cold, colder, coldest* | *the survival of the fittest* → see also -ER, -IEST

EST /ˌi ɛs ˈti/ the abbreviation of EASTERN STANDARD TIME

est. **1** the written abbreviation of ESTABLISHED used after the names of a business to show when it was started: *H. Perkins and Company, est. 1869* **2** the written abbreviation of ESTIMATED

es·tab·lish /ɪˈstæblɪʃ/ AC S3 W1 *v.* [T] **1** to start a company, organization, system etc. that is intended to exist or continue for a long time SYN **set up** SYN **found**: *The university was established in 1922.* | *the difficulties of establishing a new democracy* **2** to begin a relationship with someone or a situation that will continue: *I have **established** strong **relationships** with most of my clients.* | *The two countries **established diplomatic relations** in 2005.* **3** to find out facts that will prove that something is true SYN **find out**: *Investigators have not established a reason for the attack.* | **establish (that)** *The autopsy established that he had been murdered.* | **establish a cause/relationship etc.** *Science has established a link between smoking and cancer.* | **establish whether/if** *The police never established whether her story was true.* **4** to make people accept that you can do something, or that you have a particular quality: **establish yourself (as sth)** *Stevens has established himself as an expert in the field.* | **establish a reputation (as sth)** *She's already begun to establish a reputation as a tough journalist.* [**Origin:** 1300–1400 Old French *establir*, from Latin *stabilire* **to make firm**]

es·tab·lished /ɪˈstæblɪʃt/ Ac *adj.* [only before noun] **1** already in use or existing for a long period of time: *an old, established company* | *a* ***well-established*** *teaching method* **2** known to do a particular job well, because you have done it for a long time: *an established scientist*

es,tablished 'church *n.* [C] POLITICS a church that is given official STATUS and support by the government: *The U.S. does not have an established church.*

es·tab·lish·ment /ɪˈstæblɪʃmənt/ Ac W3 *n.* **1** [C] FORMAL a business, store, institution etc.: *small retail establishments* **2 the establishment** the organizations and people in a society who have a lot of power and influence, and are often opposed to change and new ideas: **the medical/legal/military etc. establishment** (=the people who control the medical, legal etc. system) **3** [U] the act of establishing an organization, relationship, system etc.: **+of** *the establishment of NATO in 1949*

es·tate /ɪˈsteɪt/ Ac *n.* **1** [C usually singular] all of someone's property and money, especially everything that is left after they die **2** [C] a large area of land in the country, usually with one large house on it and one owner → see also FOURTH ESTATE, REAL ESTATE

es'tate sale *n.* [C] a sale of used furniture, clothes etc. from someone's house, usually after the owner has died

es'tate tax *n.* [C,U] tax that is paid on someone's money, property etc, after they die → .see also INHERITANCE TAX

es·teem¹ /ɪˈstim/ *n.* [U] a feeling of respect and admiration for someone: *The drama critics* ***held him in high esteem*** (=had a very good opinion of him). | *Please accept this gift* ***as a token of our esteem*** (=as a sign of our respect for you). → see also SELF-ESTEEM

esteem² *v.* [T usually passive] to respect and admire someone: *No writer is more* ***highly esteemed*** *by the Japanese than Soseki.* | *He was esteemed as a literary wit.*

es·ter /ˈɛstɚ/ *n.* [C] CHEMISTRY a chemical compound formed when an acid and an alcohol react, and water is removed: *Esters are responsible for the smell of many fruits and vegetables.*

Es·ther /ˈɛstɚ/ a book in the Old Testament of the Christian Bible

es·thete /ˈɛsθit/ *n.* [C] another spelling of AESTHETE

es·thet·ic /ɛsˈθɛt̬ɪk/ *adj.* another spelling of AESTHETIC —**esthetically** /-kli/ *adv.*

es·thet·ics /ɛsˈθɛt̬ɪks/ *n.* [U] another spelling of AESTHETICS

es·ti·ma·ble /ˈɛstəməbəl/ *adj.* [only before noun] FORMAL deserving respect and admiration

es·ti·mate¹ /ˈɛstə,meɪt/ Ac W2 *v.* [T] to try to judge the value, size, speed, cost etc. of something, partly by calculating and partly by guessing: *The committee did not estimate how much such a program would cost.* | **estimate (that)** *We estimate that over 75% of our customers are women.* | **be estimated to be/do sth** *The tree is estimated to be at least 700 years old.* | **estimate sth at sth** *Organizers estimated the crowd at 50,000.* —**estimated** *adj.*: *the estimated cost of the project* | ***An estimated*** *one billion people watch the World Cup on TV.* —**estimator** *n.* [C]

es·ti·mate² /ˈɛstəmɪt/ Ac W3 *n.* [C] **1** a calculation or judgment of the value, size, amount etc. of something: *Some estimates put the number of deaths at several thousand.* | *Give us* ***a rough estimate*** (=not an exact calculation) *of how long the job will take.* | *It will cost at least $300,000, and that's a* ***conservative estimate*** (=a deliberately low one). → see also GUESSTIMATE **2** a statement of how much it will probably cost to build or repair something: *We got two or three estimates on the car.* [**Origin:** 1500–1600 Latin, past participle of *aestimare* **to think important**]

es·ti·ma·tion /,ɛstəˈmeɪʃən/ Ac *n.* **1** [U] your opinion or judgment of the value, nature etc. of someone or something SYN **opinion**: ***In my estimation****, he has been a great mayor.* | **sb's estimation of sth** *Her estimation of the company has never been very positive.* **2** [C,U] a calculation or judgment about a number, amount, price etc. that is not exact: *an estimation of moving costs* **3** [U] FORMAL respect or admiration for someone SYN **esteem**

Es·to·ni·a /ɛˈstoʊniə/ a small country in northeastern Europe on the Baltic Sea, west of Russia and north of Latvia —**Estonian** *n., adj.*

es·trange /ɪˈstreɪndʒ/ *v.* [T] to behave in a way that makes other people unfriendly toward you SYN **alienate**

es·tranged /ɪˈstreɪndʒd/ *adj.* **1** not having any connection anymore with a relative or friend, especially because of an argument: **+from** *Nagle became estranged from her family after her marriage.* | **sb's estranged husband/wife/father etc.** *His estranged wife declined to comment.* ►see THESAURUS box at **married** **2** not feeling any connection anymore with something that used to be important in your life SYN **alienated**: **+from** *young adults who feel estranged from the Church* —**estrangement** *n.* [C,U]

es·tro·gen /ˈɛstrədʒən/ *n.* [U] a sex HORMONE (=chemical substance) that is produced in a woman's body

es·tu·ar·y /ˈɛstʃu,ɛri/ *n. plural* **estuaries** [C] EARTH SCIENCE the wide part of a river where it goes into the ocean [**Origin:** 1500–1600 Latin *aestuarium*, from *aestus* **boiling, tide**]

ET the written abbreviation of EASTERN TIME

ETA /,i ti ˈeɪ/ *n.* FORMAL OR HUMOROUS **estimated time of arrival** the time when a person or an airplane, ship etc. is expected to arrive

et al. /,ɛt̬ ˈæl, ,ɛt̬ ˈɑl/ *adv.* FORMAL written after a list of names to mean that other people are also involved in something: *The authors are listed as P. Raynes, Charles Hayworth et al.*

etc. /ɛt ˈsɛtrə, -t̬ərə/ *adv.* the written abbreviation of ET CETERA, used after a list to show that there are many other similar things or people that could be added: *fruit juices such as orange, pineapple etc.* | *Simpson has traveled all over the country: Boston, Memphis, Dallas* ***etc.*** (=used to emphasize that a list is very long or too long)

et cet·er·a /ɛt ˈsɛtrə, -t̬ərə/ *adv.* FORMAL the full form of ETC.

etch /ɛtʃ/ *v.* **1** [I,T] ENG. LANG. ARTS to cut lines on the surface of a metal plate, piece of glass, stone etc. in order to write something or make a picture or design: **etch sth onto/into sth** *The design is etched onto the glasses using a laser.* **2 be etched in your memory/mind** LITERARY if an experience, name etc. is etched in your memory or mind, you cannot forget it and you think of it often **3 be etched with sth** LITERARY if someone's face is etched with pain, sadness etc. you can see these feelings from their expression [**Origin:** 1600–1700 Dutch *etsen*, from German *ätzen* **to feed**; because originally the lines were **eaten** into the metal with acid] —**etched** *adj.*: *etched glass* —**etcher** *n.* [C,U] → see also **not be carved/etched in stone** at STONE¹ (7)

etch·ing /ˈɛtʃɪŋ/ *n.* [C] a picture made by printing from an etched metal plate

e·ter·nal /ɪˈtɚnl/ *adj.* **1** continuing forever or staying the same forever: *people searching for eternal youth* | *My sister is* ***an eternal optimist*** (=she always believes that good things will happen). **2** seeming to continue forever, especially because of being boring or annoying SYN **never-ending**: *I was tired of the eternal arguments between my wife and son.* **3 eternal truths** FORMAL principles that are always true → see also **hope springs eternal** at HOPE² (7)

e·ter·nal·ly /ɪˈtɚnl-i/ *adv.* **1** without end SYN **forever**: *Her memory will remain with us eternally.* **2** very often or all the time: *He's eternally arguing with the referee.* **3 be eternally grateful** to be very grateful for something someone has done for you

e·ter·ni·ty /ɪˈtɚnət̬i/ *n.* [U] **1 an eternity** a very long time, or a period of time that seems very long because you are annoyed, anxious etc.: *We only waited five minutes, but it seemed like an eternity.* **2** the whole of

E

time, without any end: *The cause of the crash will continue to be a mystery* **for all eternity**. **3** the state of existence after death that some people believe continues forever

-eth /ɪθ/ *suffix* also **-th** OLD USE OR BIBLICAL used to form the third person singular of verbs: *he goeth* (=he goes)

eth·a·nol /ˈɛθəˌnɔl, -ˌnoʊl/ *n.* [U] TECHNICAL → see ETHYL ALCOHOL

e·ther /ˈiθɚ/ *n.* **1** [U] CHEMISTRY a chemical compound that was used in past times as an ANESTHETIC (=substance to make people sleep during surgery) **2 the ether** LITERARY the air or the sky

e·the·re·al /ɪˈθɪriəl/ *adj.* LITERARY very delicate and light, in a way that does not seem real: *ethereal beauty* —**ethereally** *adv.*

e·ther·net /ˈiθɚˌnɛt/ *n.* [U] TRADEMARK a special system of wires used for connecting computers into a network in an office, building etc.

eth·ic /ˈɛθɪk/ Ac W2 *n.* **1** [singular] a general idea or set of moral beliefs that influences people's behavior and attitudes: *the Judeo-Christian ethic* → see also WORK ETHIC **2 ethics** [plural] moral rules or principles of behavior for deciding what is right and wrong: *Mallett is highly respected for his **professional ethics*** (=the moral rules relating to a particular profession). **3 ethics** [U] the study of the moral rules and principles of behavior in society, and how they influence the choices people make

eth·i·cal /ˈɛθɪkəl/ Ac *adj.* **1** relating to principles of what is right and wrong: *the hospital's high ethical standards* → see also MORAL **2** morally good or correct OPP **unethical**: *This type of advertisement may be legal, but is it ethical?* —**ethically** /-kli/ *adv.*

E·thi·o·pi·a /ˌiθiˈoʊpiə/ a country in northeast Africa on the Red Sea —**Ethiopian** *n., adj.*

eth·nic /ˈɛθnɪk/ Ac W3 *adj.* **1** relating to a group of people who have the same customs and traditions based on their race, nationality, religion or culture: *students of different ethnic backgrounds* | **ethnic group/minority** *Asian-Americans are the largest ethnic group at the university.* **2 ethnic cooking/food/clothes etc.** cooking, food etc. from different countries or races that are considered very different and unusual **3 an ethnic joke/remark/slur etc.** a joke, remark etc. that insults people of a particular race or nationality [**Origin:** 1300–1400 Late Latin *ethnicus*, from Greek *ethnos* **nation, people**] —**ethnically** /-kli/ *adv.*

ˌethnic ˈcleansing *n.* [U] the act of forcing people to leave their homes or killing them because they belong to a particular RACIAL, religious, or national group

eth·nic·i·ty /ɛθˈnɪsət̬i/ Ac *n. plural* **ethnicities** [C,U] the race or national group that someone belongs to

eth·no·cen·tric /ˌɛθnoʊˈsɛntrɪk◂ / *adj.* DISAPPROVING thinking about things in a way that is based only on your own culture and race, and not considering or including the culture, traditions etc. of other groups —**ethnocentrism** *n.* [U] —**ethnocentricity** /ˌɛθnoʊsɛnˈtrɪsət̬i/ *n.* [U]

eth·noc·ra·cy /ɛθˈnɑkrəsi/ *n. plural* **ethnocracies** [C,U] POLITICS a form of government in which one ETHNIC group rules over others and holds all the important government jobs

eth·nog·ra·pher /ɛθˈnɑgrəfɚ/ *n.* [C] someone who studies ethnography

eth·nog·ra·phy /ɛθˈnɑgrəfi/ *n.* [U] the scientific study of different races of people —**ethnographic** /ˌɛθnəˈgræfɪk◂ / *adj.* —**ethnographically** /-kli/ *adv.*

eth·nol·o·gy /ɛθˈnɑlədʒi/ *n.* [U] the scientific study and comparison of the origins and organization of different races of people → see also ANTHROPOLOGY, SOCIOLOGY —**ethnologist** *n.* [C] —**ethnological** /ˌɛθnəˈlɑdʒɪkəl/ *adj.* —**ethnologically** /-kli/ *adv.*

e·thos /ˈiθɑs/ *n.* [singular] the set of ideas and moral attitudes belonging to a person or group: *the community's ethos of sharing and caring* [**Origin:** 1800–1900 Greek **custom, character**]

eth·yl al·co·hol /ˌɛθəl ˈælkəhɔl/ *n.* [U] TECHNICAL the type of alcohol in alcoholic drinks

eth·y·lene /ˈɛθəlin/ *n.* [U] BIOLOGY a gas found in natural gas, fruit that is becoming RIPE, and PETROLEUM. It is used to help fruit to become ripe.

E-tick·et /ˈi ˌtɪkɪt/ *n.* [C] **electronic ticket** COMPUTERS a ticket, especially for an airplane, that is stored in a computer and is not given to the customer in the form of paper

e·ti·o·lat·ed /ˈit̬iəˌleɪt̬ɪd/ *adj.* **1** LITERARY pale and weak **2** BIOLOGY a plant that is etiolated is white because it has not received enough light —**etiolation** /ˌit̬iəˈleɪʃən/ *n.* [U]

e·ti·ol·o·gy /ˌit̬iˈɑlədʒi/ *n. plural* **etiologies** [C,U] MEDICINE the cause of a disease, or the scientific study of the causes of diseases —**etiological** /ˌit̬iəˈlɑdʒɪkəl/ *adj.* —**etiologically** /-kli/ *adv.*

et·i·quette /ˈɛt̬ɪkɪt/ *n.* [U] the formal rules for polite behavior in society or in a particular group [**Origin:** 1700–1800 French *étiquette* **ticket**]

Et·na /ˈɛtnə/ also **Mount Etna** a mountain in Sicily, southern Italy, which is an active VOLCANO

é·touf·fée, etouffee /ˌeɪtuˈfeɪ/ *n.* [U] a SPICY dish popular in traditional Cajun cooking made with SEAFOOD and vegetables cooked in liquid

E·trus·can /ɪˈtrʌskən/ one of the people that lived in northern Italy from the eighth century to the fourth century B.C.

-ette /ɛt/ *suffix* [in nouns] **1** a small thing of a particular type: *a kitchenette* (=small kitchen) | *a statuette* (=small statue) **2** OLD-FASHIONED a woman who does a particular job: *an usherette* (=a female USHER)

e·tude /ˈeɪtud/ *n.* [C] a piece of music that is intended to improve your skill at playing an instrument

et·y·mol·o·gy /ˌɛt̬əˈmɑlədʒi/ *n.* ENG. LANG. ARTS **1** [U] the study of the origins, history, and changing meanings of words **2** [C] *plural* **etymologies** a description of the history of a particular word [**Origin:** 1300–1400 Latin *etymologia*, from Greek, from *etymon* **original meaning**] —**etymologist** *n.* [C] —**etymological** /ˌɛt̬əməˈlɑdʒɪkəl/ *adj.* —**etymologically** /-kli/ *adv.*

EU /ˌi ˈyu/ the abbreviation of the EUROPEAN UNION

eu·ca·lyp·tus /ˌyukəˈlɪptəs/ *n.* [C,U] a tall tree, originally from Australia, that produces an oil with a strong smell which is used in medicines [**Origin:** 1800–1900 Modern Latin *eu-* **well, good** + Greek *kalyptos* **covered**; from the covering on the tree's buds]

Eu·cha·rist /ˈyukərɪst/ *n.* **the Eucharist** the holy bread and wine, representing Jesus Christ's body and blood, used during a Christian ceremony, or the ceremony itself —**Eucharistic** /ˌyukəˈrɪstɪk/ *adj.*

Eu·clid /ˈyuklɪd/ (about 300 B.C.) a Greek MATHEMATICIAN who developed a system of GEOMETRY (=the study of angles, shapes, lines etc.) called Euclidean geometry

Eu·clid·e·an /yuˈklɪdiən/ *adj.* relating to the GEOMETRY described by Euclid, who made statements about what was possible by connecting facts and reasons in a clear and sensible way

eu·gen·ics /yuˈdʒɛnɪks/ *n.* [U] the scientific idea that it is possible to improve the mental and physical abilities of human beings by selecting who will be allowed to be a parent

eu·kar·y·a /yuˈkæriə/ *n.* [U] BIOLOGY one of the classes into which scientists group animals, plants, and other living creatures whose cells have a NUCLEUS

eu·kar·y·ote, eucaryote /yuˈkæriˌoʊt/ *n.* [C] BIOLOGY a living creature with a cell or cells that have the GENETIC material in a NUCLEUS

eu·lo·gize /ˈyuləˌdʒaɪz/ *v.* [I,T] to praise someone or something very much, especially at a funeral —**eulogist** *n.* [C] —**eulogistic** /ˌyuləˈdʒɪstɪk/ *adj.* —**eulogistically** /-kli/ *adv.*

eu·lo·gy /ˈyulədʒi/ *n. plural* **eulogies** [C,U] a speech or piece of writing in which you praise someone or something very much, especially at a funeral

eu•nuch /ˈyunək/ *n.* [C] a man whose TESTICLES have been removed, especially someone who guarded a king's wives in some Eastern countries in past times

eu•phe•mism /ˈyufəˌmɪzəm/ *n.* [C] ENG. LANG. ARTS a polite word or expression that you use instead of a more direct one, to avoid shocking or upsetting someone: *"Pass away" is a euphemism for "die."* [**Origin:** 1500–1600 Greek *euphemismos*, from *euphemos* **sounding good**, from *pheme* **speech**]

eu•phe•mis•tic /ˌyufəˈmɪstɪk◂/ *adj.* ENG. LANG. ARTS using polite words and expressions to avoid shocking or upsetting people: *euphemistic descriptions* —**euphemistically** /-kli/ *adv.*

eu•pho•ni•ous /yuˈfoʊniəs/ *adj.* LITERARY words or sounds that are euphonious are pleasant to listen to

eu•pho•ri•a /yuˈfɔriə/ *n.* [U] a feeling of extreme happiness and excitement [**Origin:** 1600–1700 Greek *euphoros* **healthy**]

eu•phor•ic /yuˈfɔrɪk/ *adj.* feeling very happy and excited —**euphorically** /-kli/ *adv.*

Eu•phra•tes, the /yuˈfreɪt̬iz/ a long river that flows from Turkey through Syria and Iraq into the Persian Gulf

Eur•a•sia /yʊˈreɪʒə/ the large area of land that consists of the CONTINENTS of Europe and Asia

Eur•a•sian[1] /yʊˈreɪʒən/ *adj.* relating to both Europe and Asia

Eurasian[2] *n.* [C] OLD-FASHIONED someone who has one white parent and one Asian parent

eu•re•ka /yʊˈrikə/ *interjection* OFTEN HUMOROUS used to show how happy you are that you have discovered the answer to a problem, found something etc. [**Origin:** 1600–1700 Greek *heureka* **I have found**, said by the Greek scientist Archimedes when he discovered a method of testing the purity of gold]

Eu•rip•i•des /yʊˈrɪpəˌdiz/ (?480–406 B.C.) an ancient Greek writer of plays

Euro- /yʊroʊ/ *prefix* **a)** relating to Europe, especially western Europe: *Europop* (=European popular music) | *Euromoney* **b)** European and something else: *Euro-American relations*

eu•ro /ˈyʊroʊ/ *n. plural* **euros** [C] the unit of money used in the European Union

Eu•rope /ˈyʊrəp/ *n.* one of the seven CONTINENTS, that includes land north of the Mediterranean Sea and west of the Ural Mountains

Eu•ro•pe•an[1] /ˌyʊrəˈpiən◂/ *adj.* from or connected with Europe: *European law* | *European governments*

European[2] *n.* [C] someone from Europe: *Many Europeans oppose the changes.*

ˌEuropean ˈUnion ABBREVIATION **EU** *n.* **the European Union** a European political and economic organization that encourages trade between the countries that are members, and makes laws for all these countries

Euro•trash /ˈyʊroʊˌtræʃ/ *n.* [U] SLANG an insulting word for rich, fashionable Europeans who are considered lazy and too interested in their social lives

Eu•sta•chian tube /yuˈsteɪʃən ˌtub, -ʃiən-/ *n.* [C] BIOLOGY one of the pair of tubes inside your head and neck that connect your ears to your throat

eu•tha•na•sia /ˌyuθəˈneɪʒə/ *n.* [U] the painless killing of people who are very sick or very old in order to stop them from suffering SYN **mercy killing** [**Origin:** 1600–1700 Greek **easy death**, from *thanatos* **death**]

eu•than•ize /ˈyuθəˌnaɪz/ *v.* [T] to kill animals or people in a painless way, especially because they are very sick or old

e•vac•u•ate /ɪˈvækyuˌeɪt/ *v.* **1** [I,T] to leave a building or area because it is dangerous, or to make someone do this: *Police evacuated the stock exchange after receiving a bomb threat.* | **evacuate sb from/to** *2,500 campers were evacuated from Yosemite due to a wildfire.* **2** [T] to make people leave the place they live in because it has become too dangerous, for example because of a war: **evacuate sb to sth** *Refugees were evacuated to camps in neighboring countries.* **3** [T] TECHNICAL to empty your BOWELS [**Origin:** 1300–1400 Latin, past participle of *evacuare*, from *vacuus* **empty**] —**evacuation** /ɪˌvækyuˈeɪʃən/ *n.* [C,U]

e•vac•u•ee /ɪˌvækyuˈi/ *n.* [C] someone who is moved away from a place that is dangerous, for example because there is a war

e•vade /ɪˈveɪd/ *v.* [T] **1 evade the subject/question/issue etc.** to avoid talking about something, especially because you are trying to hide some information SYN **avoid**: *The mayor kept evading the question.* **2** to avoid paying money that you ought to pay, especially tax: *Fisher pleaded guilty to evading taxes on $51,000 of income.* **3** to avoid being caught or hurt by someone or something: *For six years, Harris has* ***evaded capture*** (=avoided being caught). **4** to not do or deal with something that you should do: *Jones is now doing everything he can to* ***evade responsibility*** *for his mistake.* **5** FORMAL if something evades you, you cannot do it, achieve it, or understand it [**Origin:** 1500–1600 French *évader*, from Latin *evadere*, from *vadere* **to go, walk**]

e•val•u•ate /ɪˈvælyuˌeɪt/ Ac *v.* [T] **1** to judge how good, useful, or successful something is SYN **assess**: *Your work will be evaluated by the management team.* | *We are evaluating the success of the campaign* ►see THESAURUS box at **judge**[2] **2** MATH to calculate the value of a mathematical expression

e•val•u•a•tion /ɪˌvælyuˈeɪʃən/ Ac S3 *n.* [C,U] a judgment about how good, useful, or successful something is: *They took some samples for evaluation.* | **+of** *a thorough evaluation of the project's progress* [**Origin:** 1700–1800 French *évaluation*, from *évaluer* **to evaluate**, from *value* **value**]

eˌvaluative ˈquestion *n.* [C] ENG. LANG. ARTS a question that asks someone to give their opinion or make a judgment about something, especially something they have read → see also INFERENTIAL QUESTION, LITERAL QUESTION

ev•a•nes•cent /ˌɛvəˈnɛsənt/ *adj.* LITERARY something that is evanescent disappears quickly

e•van•gel•i•cal[1] /ˌivænˈdʒɛlɪkəl, ˌɛvən-/ *adj.* **1** evangelical Christians and beliefs emphasize a personal relationship with God, the importance of the Bible, and the importance of telling others about these ideas **2** very eager to talk about your ideas and beliefs in order to persuade people to accept them: *Kemp is evangelical about eating healthy food.*

evangelical[2] *n.* [C] a person who is a member of an evangelical Christian church

e•van•ge•list /ɪˈvændʒəlɪst/ *n.* [C] **1** someone who travels from place to place, trying to persuade people that they should become Christians **2 Evangelist** Matthew, Mark, Luke, or John, one of the four writers of the books in the Bible called the Gospels [**Origin:** 1100–1200 Old French *evangeliste*, from Greek *euangelion* **good news, gospel**] —**evangelism** *n.* [U] —**evangelistic** /ɪˌvændʒəˈlɪstɪk/ *adj.*

e•van•gel•ize /ɪˈvændʒəˌlaɪz/ *v.* [I,T] to try to persuade people that they should become Christians

E•vans /ˈɛvənz/, **Mar•y Ann** /ˈmɛri æn/ the real name of the writer George Eliot

e•vap•o•rate /ɪˈvæpəˌreɪt/ *v.* **1** [I,T] if a liquid evaporates, or if heat evaporates it, it changes into a VAPOR (=mass of very small drops of a liquid which float in the air) gas: *Add wine and cook until the liquid evaporates.* **2** [I] if a feeling evaporates, it slowly disappears: *Support for the idea had evaporated by that time.*

eˌvaporated ˈmilk *n.* [U] milk which has been made thicker and sweeter by removing some of the water from it → see also CONDENSED MILK

e•vap•o•ra•tion /ɪˌvæpəˈreɪʃən/ *n.* [U] CHEMISTRY VAPOR (=very small drops of a liquid in air) that forms when a liquid is heated below the temperature at which it will boil, or the process by which this happens

e·va·sion /ɪˈveɪʒən/ *n.* **1** [U] the act of avoiding doing something that you should do: *Henning went to prison on charges of **tax evasion*** (=not paying taxes). **2** [C,U] an act of deliberately avoiding talking about something or dealing with something: *I'm tired of his lies and evasions.*

e·va·sive /ɪˈveɪsɪv/ *adj.* **1** not willing to answer questions directly: *an evasive answer* **2 evasive action** action to avoid being injured or harmed: *The pilots **took evasive action** to avoid hitting the other plane.* —**evasively** *adv.* —**evasiveness** *n.* [U]

Eve /iv/ in the Bible, the first woman, who lived in the Garden of Eden with Adam, the first man

E

eve /iv/ *n.* **1** [C usually singular] the night or day before an important religious day or holiday: *Christmas Eve* (=December 24) | *New Year's Eve* (=December 31) **2 the eve of sth** the time just before an important event: *the eve of the election* **3** [C usually singular] POETIC evening: *one summer's eve*

e·ven¹ /ˈivən/ S1 W1 *adv.* **1** used to emphasize something that is unexpected or surprising: *The house is always warm, even in Winter.* | *Even the youngest children enjoyed the concert.* | **not/never even** *They never even said goodbye.* **2 even bigger/better/worse etc.** used to emphasize a comparison: *Jeff knows even less than I do about cars.* **3 even though** used for introducing a fact that makes the main statement in your sentence seem very surprising: *I haven't lost any weight, even though I've been exercising a lot.* **4 even if** used to say that something will not have any effect on a situation: *I'll never speak to her again, even if she apologizes* **5 even so** used for introducing something that is true although it might seem surprising after what you have just said: *"This is the cheapest hotel." "Even so, it costs $200 a night."* **6 even with sth** despite something: *Even with all this rain, the grass is still yellow.* **7 even as** used to emphasize that something happens at the same time as something else: *He realized, even as he said it, that no-one would believe him.* **8 even as we speak** used for emphasizing that something is happening now: *The news is being published even as we speak.* **9 even now/then** in spite of what has happened, what you have done, or what is true: *Even now I find it hard to believe Brenda's story.* | *She will have an operation, but even then she may not recover.* **10** used just before or just after an adjective that makes what you are saying stronger: *He could be very unkind, cruel even.* [**Origin:** Old English *efne*, from *efen*]

even² *adj.*
1 SURFACE completely flat, level, or smooth SYN **flat**: *Make sure the floor is even before you lay the carpet.* | *an even stretch of road* ▸see THESAURUS box at **flat¹**
2 be even (with sth) to be at the same height or level as something SYN **level**: *Line up the boards so their ends are even.* | *The top of the picture should be even with the window frame.*
3 NOT CHANGING an even rate, temperature etc. is steady and does not change much SYN **steady**: *The chemicals must be stored at an even temperature.* | *Run at a nice, even pace.*
4 DIVIDED EQUALLY divided equally, so that there is the same amount of something in each place, for each person etc. SYN **equal**: *Shape the dough into eight even pieces.* | *an even distribution of wealth*
5 EQUAL equal or identical in amount, size, length etc. SYN **equal**: *Make sure the hem is an even length all the way around.* | **+in** *The boys were even in height.*
6 EXACT an even amount, measurement, price etc. can be expressed as an exact number of units: *Our grocery bill came to an even $30.00.*
7 even number MATH a number that can be divided exactly by two, such as 2, 4, 6, 8 etc. OPP **odd**
8 CALM calm and controlled, and not extreme: *her even temper* | *"Calm down," he said in an even voice.*
9 COMPETITION having teams or competitors that are equally good so that everyone has a chance of winning OPP **uneven**: **an even game/contest/match** *It should be a fairly even contest.*
10 LINE OF THINGS regularly spaced and neat-looking: *an even row of telephone poles*
11 get even (with sb) to harm someone just as much as they have harmed you: *I'll get even with you — just wait!*
12 be even INFORMAL to not owe someone something anymore, especially money: *If you pay for my ticket, we'll be even.* —**evenness** *n.* [U] → see also **break even** at BREAK¹ (13), EVEN-TEMPERED, **stay/remain on an even keel** at KEEL¹ (2), UNEVEN

even³ *v.* **even the score** to do something to punish or embarrass someone, because they have done something bad to you: *I was humiliated, and I wanted to even the score with my sister.*

even out *phr. v.* to become equal or level, or to make something do this: *The differences in their income should even out over time.* | **even sth ↔ out** *Use a brush to even out the variations in color.*

even sth ↔ up *phr. v.* to make a situation or competition equal: *O'Malley hit a home run to even up the score.*

ˌeven-ˈhanded *adj.* giving fair and equal treatment to everyone SYN **impartial**: *an even-handed documentary* —**even-handedly** *adv.*

eve·ning /ˈivnɪŋ/ S1 W2 *n.* **1** [C,U] the late part of the day between about 6:00 and the time when most people go to bed: *the evening news* | *I'll see you **this evening*** (=today in the evening). | **(on) Monday/Tuesday/Friday etc. evening** *I have a class Thursday evening.* | **yesterday/tomorrow evening** *Peter left yesterday evening.* | *We like to go for walks **in the evening**.* | *I'm going out **for the evening**.* | **early/late evening** *Their flight didn't arrive until late evening.* → see also AFTERNOON **2 Good evening** SPOKEN, FORMAL also **Evening** said as a greeting in the evening: *Good evening, ladies and gentlemen!* **3** [C] a social event, performance etc. that takes place in the evening: **+of** *an evening of music and dance* [**Origin:** Old English *æfnung*, from *æfen* **evening**]

ˈevening dress *n.* **1** [C] an evening gown **2** [U] EVENING WEAR

ˈevening gown *n.* [C] a long dress worn by women to formal meals, parties etc. in the evening

eve·nings /ˈivnɪŋz/ *adv.* during the evening: *This month I'll be working evenings.*

ˌevening ˈstar *n.* **the evening star** the PLANET Venus, seen as a bright star in the western sky in the evening before the other stars can be seen → see also MORNING STAR

ˈevening wear *n.* [U] special clothes that you wear for formal occasions in the evening

e·ven·ly /ˈivənli/ *adv.* **1** covering or affecting all parts of something equally SYN **equally**: *Spread the coating evenly over the entire surface.* | *Turn the chicken so that it cooks evenly.* **2** divided equally among a group of people SYN **equally**: *The money was divided evenly among all four brothers.* **3** in a steady or regular way SYN **regularly**: *The patient was breathing evenly.* | ***evenly spaced** rows of desks* **4 evenly matched** if two competitors are evenly matched, they have an equal chance of winning **5** if you say something evenly, you say it in a calm way, trying not to show any emotion

even-ste·ven /ˌivən ˈstivən/ *adj.* SPOKEN if you are even-steven with someone, you do not owe them anything

e·vent /ɪˈvɛnt/ S1 W1 *n.* [C]
1 INTERESTING/EXCITING something that happens, especially something important, interesting, or unusual: *one of the most important events of the century* | ***the sequence of events*** (=the order in which events happened) *that led to the plane crash* | **a chain of events** (=a series of events, each of which causes the next one to happen) | *We couldn't have done anything to change **the course of events*** (=the way that things happen). → see also CURRENT EVENTS

THESAURUS

occurrence FORMAL something that happens: *These children have witnessed violence as a routine occurrence.*
incident something unusual, serious, or violent that happens: *an upsetting incident*
happening something that happens, especially a strange event: *There have been reports of strange happenings in the town.*
phenomenon something that happens or exists in society, science, or nature that is unusual or difficult to understand: *Homelessness is not a new phenomenon.*

2 COMPETITION/PERFORMANCE/PARTY an important performance, sports competition, party etc. which has been arranged for a particular date and time: *The award ceremony is* ***an annual event*** (=one that takes place every year). | *The presidential victory party was the* ***social event*** *of the year.* | *The Tour de France is the world's biggest single* ***sporting event***.
3 IN A SPORTS COMPETITION any of the races, competitions etc. arranged as part of a day's sports: *The next event will be the men's 100-meter dash.*
4 **in any event** used just before or after a statement to emphasize that it is true or will happen, even if something else is not clear SYN **in any case**: *The show could have been a fake. In any event, it was good television.*
5 **in either event** if either of two things happens or is true SYN **in either case**: *Who knows if we'll win or lose. In either event, I'm happy we're here.*
6 **in the event of** also **in the event that** used to tell people what they should do or what will happen if something else happens, often something unpleasant: *In the event of fire, the boat is equipped with fire extinguishers.*
7 MATH the possible results of a test done to find out how likely it is that particular things will happen. For example, in an experiment on rolling a dice, the possible events are rolling a 1, 2, 3, 4, 5, or 6. → see also OUTCOME
[**Origin:** 1500–1600 Latin *eventus*, from the past participle of *evenire* **to happen**]

ˌeven-ˈtempered *adj.* not becoming angry easily SYN **calm**

e·vent·ful /ɪˈvɛntˀfəl/ *adj.* full of interesting or important events: *She's led a very eventful life.* | *an eventful meeting* —**eventfully** *adv.*

e·ven·tide /ˈivənˌtaɪd/ *n.* [U] POETIC evening

e·ven·tu·al /ɪˈvɛntʃuəl/ Ac *adj.* [only before noun] happening or achieving something at the end of a process: *the eventual winner of the tournament* | *No one was sure what the eventual outcome of the war would be.*
[**Origin:** 1600–1700 French *éventuel*, from Latin *eventus* **what happens in the end**]

e·ven·tu·al·i·ty /ɪˌvɛntʃuˈæləṭi/ Ac *n. plural* **eventualities** [C] FORMAL a possible event or result, especially a bad one: *We have to be prepared for every eventuality.*

e·ven·tual·ly /ɪˈvɛntʃəli, -tʃuəli/ Ac S2 W2 *adv.* after a long time, especially after a long delay or a lot of problems: *He eventually escaped and made his way back to Mexico.* | *Eventually, I got a job at a bank.*

e·ven·tu·ate /ɪˈvɛntʃuˌeɪt/ *v.*
eventuate in sth *phr. v.* FORMAL to have something as a final result: *The experiments did not eventuate in any published work.*

ev·er /ˈɛvɚ/ S1 W1 *adv.*
1 ANYTIME a word meaning "at any time," used mostly in questions, negatives, comparisons, or sentences with "if": *I don't remember ever seeing him before.* | *If you're ever in Wilmington, give us a call.* | *Nothing ever makes Ted mad.* | *Don't ever do that again!* | ***Have you ever*** *eaten snails?* | *It's hotter* ***than ever*** (=than it has ever been) *outside.* | *Mrs. Russell is* ***as*** *talkative* ***as ever*** (=as she has always been). | *Brent* ***hardly ever*** (=almost never) *calls me anymore.* | *He* ***rarely, if ever*** (=almost never) *gets here on time.* | *This is my* ***first*** *time* ***ever*** (=used for emphasis) *on a plane.*
2 IN COMPARISONS used for emphasis in comparisons: **the best/biggest/worst etc. ever** *her best performance ever* | *That's the biggest fish I've ever seen.* | **more/bigger/better etc. than ever** *You look more beautiful than ever.* | **as good/big/bad etc. as ever** *The food was as bad as ever.*
3 **ever since** continuously since a time or event in the past: *Ever since the accident, Martha's been too afraid to drive.* | *We moved here in 1985 and have lived here ever since.*
4 ALWAYS always: *Ever optimistic, Jen gave him another chance.* | *Stan, ever the leader, made all the decisions.* | **ever-growing/-increasing/-worsening etc.** *We need to keep up with ever-changing trends in the market.*
5 **ever so slightly** very little; by a very small amount: *Meg looked at us and smiled ever so slightly.*
6 **if ever there was (one)** used to say that someone or something is a typical example of something: *He's a genius if ever there was one.* | *If ever there was an avoidable war, that was it.*
7 **was sb ever...!** SPOKEN used to add force to a statement: *Boy, was he ever mad* (=he was extremely angry)*!*
8 **did you ever** OLD-FASHIONED used to show your surprise, disbelief etc.: *Did you ever hear of such a thing?*
[**Origin:** Old English *æfre*]

E

Ev·er·est /ˈɛvərɪst/ also **Mount Everest** a mountain in the Himalayas, on the border between Tibet and Nepal, that is the highest mountain in the world

ev·er·glade /ˈɛvɚˌgleɪd/ *n.* [C] an area of low flat land that is covered with water and tall grass

Ev·er·glades, the /ˈɛvɚˌgleɪdz/ an area of low, wet, warm land in the southeastern U.S., in the state of Florida, covering about 5,000 square miles and famous for its special plants and animals

ev·er·green[1] /ˈɛvɚˌgrin/ *n.* [C] a tree or bush that does not lose its leaves in the winter ▸see THESAURUS box at **tree**

evergreen[2] *adj.* **1** BIOLOGY an evergreen tree or bush does not lose its leaves in winter → see also DECIDUOUS **2** always popular and never becoming unfashionable: *The group's name matches the evergreen quality of Farrar's songs.*

ev·er·last·ing /ˌɛvɚˈlæstɪŋ◂/ *adj.* a word used especially in religious writing, meaning continuing to exist forever SYN **eternal**: *everlasting love*

Ev·ers /ˈɛvɚz/, **Med·gar** /ˈmɛdgɚ/ (1925–1963) a U.S. CIVIL RIGHTS worker in Mississippi who was shot dead by a member of the Ku Klux Klan

Ev·ert /ˈɛvɚt/, **Chris** /krɪs/ (1954–) a U.S. tennis player famous for winning many women's tennis CHAMPIONSHIPS

ev·ery /ˈɛvri/ S1 W1 *quantifier* **1** used for referring to all the people or things in a particular group or to all the parts of something: *Every athlete will take a drug test.* | *Every one of the bags has a hole in it.* | *These two dresses are identical* ***in every way***, *except for the price tag.* | ***Every single*** (=used for emphasis) *person in the office has a cold.* | *He drank* ***every last*** (=used for emphasis) *drop of the medicine.* | ***Not every*** (=used to say that something is not true in all cases) *teenager likes pop music.* **2** used for saying how often something that occurs more than once happens: **every day/week/month etc.** *They see each other every day.* | *The roof leaks* ***every time*** *it rains* (=whenever it rains). | **every few seconds/five minutes/ten days etc.** *Take the medicine every four hours.* | **every now and then/every so often** (=sometimes, but not often or regularly) | **every other day/week/month etc.** (=regularly, with one day, week, month etc. between each event) **3** **one in every hundred/two out of every thousand/five for every thousand etc.** used to say how common something is: *One in every three marriages ends in divorce.* | *There was one priest for every 220 inhabitants.* **4** **every few feet/ten yards etc.** used for saying how much distance there is between each thing in a series: *There were traffic lights every 200 yards.* **5** **every which way** INFORMAL in every direction: *People were running every which way when the fire* *started.* **6 every bit as good/important/much etc.** used to emphasize that something is just as good, important as something else: *The cake was every bit as good as I remembered.* **7 every chance/reason/opportunity etc.** as much chance, reason etc. as possible: *We **have every reason to believe** that Melinda is still alive.* **8 every Tom, Dick, and Harry** SPOKEN everyone or anyone [**Origin:** Old English *æfre ælc* **ever each**] → see Word Choice box at EACH[1] → see Grammar box at EACH[1]

ev·ery·bod·y /ˈɛvriˌbɑdi, -ˌbʌdi/ S1 W2 *pron.* everyone → see Usage note at EVERYONE → see Grammar box at EVERYONE

ev·ery·day /ˈɛvriˌdeɪ/ *adj.* [only before noun] ordinary, usual, or happening every day: *simple, everyday language* | *Stress is just part of **everyday life**.*

> USAGE **SPELLING**
> **Every day** is spelled as two words as an adverb, but only one word as an adjective: *She swims every day.* | *the everyday life of a business executive.* Note that you never say **every days**.

Eve·ry·man /ˈɛvriˌmæn/ *n.* [singular] LITERARY a typical ordinary person

ev·ery·one /ˈɛvriˌwʌn/ S1 W1 *pron.* **1** every person involved in a particular activity or in a particular place SYN **everybody**: *Is everyone ready to go?* | *Everyone who ran in the race got a T-shirt.* | *I was still awake, but **everyone else*** (=all the other people) *had gone to bed.* | ***Not everyone** agreed with me* (=some people there disagreed with me). | ***Everyone but*** (=all the people except) *Lisa got there on time.* → see also ANYONE **2** all people in general: *Everyone needs love.* | ***Not everyone** likes fancy food.*

> USAGE **SPELLING**
> **Everyone**, written as one word, means "all the people in one group": *Everyone is waiting for you.* **Every one**, written as two words, means "each single thing or person in a group.": *Every one of the books has a torn page.* | *There are torn pages in every one (of them).* **Everybody** is written as one word. **Every body** written as two words means "every dead body."

> GRAMMAR
> Note that words like **everyone**, **everybody**, and **everything** must be used with a singular verb: *Everybody was* (NOT *were*) *glad to be home.*

ev·ery·place /ˈɛvriˌpleɪs/ *adv.* SPOKEN everywhere

ev·ery·thing /ˈɛvriˌθɪŋ/ S1 W1 *pron.* **1** each thing, or all things: *Everything was covered in dust.* | *I decided to tell her everything.* | *Her photo album was saved, but she lost **everything else*** (=all her other things) *in the fire.* **2** used to talk about a whole situation or to life in general: *"How's everything at work?" "Very busy."* | *Everything seems to be going wrong.* **3 be/mean everything (to sb)** to be the thing that is most important to you and that you care about the most: *Greg's family means everything to him.* **4 ...and everything** SPOKEN and a lot of related things: *Ben's all worried about getting married and everything.* **5 have everything going for you** to have all the qualities that are likely to make you succeed: *Dan seemed to have everything going for him in college.* → see also **everything but the kitchen sink** at KITCHEN (2)

ev·ery·where /ˈɛvriˌwɛr/ S2 W2 *adv.* **1** in, at, or to every place: *They looked everywhere for Jen's keys.* | *Everywhere I go, I hear people worrying about the future.* | *People here are the same as **everywhere else*** (=in every other place).

> THESAURUS
> **all over** everywhere on a surface or in a place: *Jack's clothes were all over the floor.*
> **worldwide** everywhere in the world: *The Olympic Games are watched by people worldwide.*
> **nationwide** everywhere in a particular nation: *a nationwide study of adolescents*
> **everyplace** SPOKEN everywhere: *There you are. I've been looking for you everyplace.*

2 be everywhere to be very common: *Online advertising is everywhere.* → see also NOWHERE

e·vict /ɪˈvɪkt/ *v.* [T] to legally force someone to leave the house they are living in: **evict sb from sth** *Frank was evicted from his apartment four months ago.* [**Origin:** 1500–1600 Latin, past participle of *evincere*, from *vincere* **to defeat**] —**eviction** /ɪˈvɪkʃən/ *n.* [C,U]

ev·i·dence[1] /ˈɛvədəns/ Ac S3 W1 *n.* **1** [U] facts, objects, or signs that make you believe that something exists or is true: +**of** *At present we have no evidence of life on other planets.* | +**for** *There is some evidence for* (=in support of) *this theory.* | +**(that)** *There is no evidence that the treatment works.* | *You will need to **provide evidence of** your citizenship.* | *The study produced one interesting **piece of evidence**.* | **medical/scientific evidence** (=evidence that is good because it has been done scientifically) ►see THESAURUS box at **sign**[1] **2** [U] LAW information, statements, and objects that are given in a court of law in order to prove that someone is guilty or not guilty: *The new evidence helped to convict Hayes of murder.* | +**against** *There was no evidence against her.* | *He refused to **give evidence** at the trial.* **3 be in evidence** FORMAL to be present and easily seen or noticed: *The police were very much in evidence at the protest.* → see also STATE'S EVIDENCE

evidence[2] Ac *v.* [T usually passive] FORMAL to show that something exists or is true: *The volcano is still active, **as evidenced by** the recent eruption.*

ev·i·dent /ˈɛvədənt/ Ac *adj.* easily noticed or understood SYN **obvious**: *Carlos' frustration was evident in his comments.* | **it is evident (that)** *It was evident that she was unhappy.* [**Origin:** 1300–1400 French, Latin *evidens*, from *e-* **out** + the present participle of *videre* **to see**] → see also SELF-EVIDENT

ev·i·dent·ly /ˈɛvədəntli, ˌɛvəˈdɛntli/ Ac *adv.* **1** used to say that you believe something because you have learned that it is true: *The man next to him was evidently his father.* | *Evidently, the two of them have gotten back together.* **2** used to say that you know something because you could see it: *Amelio evidently liked what he saw during Carey's concert.*

e·vil[1] /ˈivəl/ S2 W3 *adj.* **1** someone who is evil deliberately does very cruel things to harm other people: *an evil dictator* **2** morally bad and having a very harmful influence on people: *The police called it a brutal and evil attack.* ►see THESAURUS box at **bad**[1] **3** connected with the Devil or having special powers to harm people: *evil spirits* **4** very bad or disgusting: *There's an evil smell coming from the fridge.* **5 the evil eye** the power which some people believe makes particular people able to harm others by looking at them [**Origin:** Old English *yfel*] —**evilly** *adv.*

evil[2] *n.* **1** [U] actions and behavior that are morally wrong and cruel, or the power that makes people do bad things OPP **good**: *It's a classic tale about the struggle between **good and evil**.* **2** [C] something that has a very bad or harmful influence or effect: *Dad gave us a lecture on **the evils of** smoking.* → see also **the lesser of two evils** at LESSER (2), **necessary evil** at NECESSARY (2)

e·vil·do·er /ˌivəlˈduɚ/ *n.* [C] OLD-FASHIONED someone who does evil things

ˌevil-ˈminded *adj.* an evil-minded person is always thinking of evil things to do

e·vince /ɪˈvɪns/ *v.* [T] FORMAL to show a feeling or quality very clearly in what you do or say: *He has evinced little interest in the job so far.*

e·vis·cer·ate /ɪˈvɪsəˌreɪt/ *v.* [T] FORMAL OR TECHNICAL to cut the organs out of a body

e·voc·a·tive /ɪˈvɑkət̬ɪv/ *adj.* producing a strong feeling in someone, either by reminding them of something or making them imagine something: *an evocative description* | +**of** *the car's styling is evocative of the 1930s*

e·voke /ɪˈvoʊk/ *v.* [T] to produce a strong feeling or memory in someone: *The word "cancer" evokes fear in most people.* [**Origin:** 1600–1700 French *évoquer*, from Latin *evocare* **to call out**] —**evocation** /ˌivəˈkeɪʃən, ˌɛvə-/ *n.* [C,U]

ev·o·lu·tion /ˌɛvəˈluʃən/ Ac *n.* [U] **1** BIOLOGY the natural process of change in which plants and animals develop and change their form gradually over a long period of time **2** the gradual change and development of an idea, situation, object, system etc.: *the evolution of the English alphabet*

ev·o·lu·tion·ar·y /ˌɛvəˈluʃəˌnɛri/ Ac *adj.* **1** BIOLOGY connected with scientific evolution: *the evolutionary development of birds* **2** connected with gradual change and development: *Social change is an evolutionary process.*

evoˌlutionary classifiˈcation *n.* [U] BIOLOGY a scientific system of putting living things into particular groups or classes, according to the way they EVOLVED (=develop and change over very long periods)

e·volve /ɪˈvɑlv/ Ac W3 *v.* [I,T] **1** to develop by gradually changing, or to make something do this: *The school has evolved its own teaching methods.* | +**from/into** *a small family store that evolved into a national supermarket chain* **2** to change gradually, developing new features, over a long period of time through the process of scientific evolution: *Bears have evolved huge claws for catching their prey.* | **evolve from sth** *Fish evolved from prehistoric sea creatures.* | **evolve into sth** *dinosaurs that evolved into birds*

ewe /yu/ *n.* [C] BIOLOGY a female sheep

ex /ɛks/ *n.* [C usually singular] **sb's ex** INFORMAL someone's former wife, husband, GIRLFRIEND, or BOYFRIEND: *I didn't know my ex was going to be at the party.*

ex- /ɛks/ *prefix* **1** no longer in a particular relationship or position, but still alive: *my ex-wife* | *an ex-President* → see also FORMER **2** out of something, or away from something: *to exhale* (=let the air out of your lungs) | *to be excommunicated* (=not be allowed to remain a member of a church)

ex·ac·er·bate /ɪgˈzæsɚˌbeɪt/ *v.* [T] FORMAL to make a bad situation worse: *Tiredness can exacerbate the symptoms.* | *His comments have exacerbated racial tensions in the city.* [**Origin:** 1600–1700 Latin, past participle of *exacerbare*, from *acerbus* **bitter**] —**exacerbation** /ɪgˌzæsɚˈbeɪʃən/ *n.* [U]

ex·act[1] /ɪgˈzækt/ S2 *adj.*

1 CORRECT completely correct in every detail SYN **precise**: *Doctors do not know the exact cause of the disease.* | *What were his exact words?* | **the exact location/position/spot etc.** *The exact location of the hostages is not known.* | **the exact date/time/number/amount etc.** *Her birthday is in July, but I can't remember the exact date.*

2 the exact color/moment/type etc. used to emphasize that something is the same as something else: *That's the exact color I've been looking for.* | *He came in at the exact moment I mentioned his name.* | *Carla was saying the **exact same thing** (=spoken) yesterday.*

3 to be exact FORMAL used to emphasize that what you are saying is correct in every detail: *It was more than 20 years ago, to be exact.*

4 the exact opposite someone or something that is as different as possible from another person or thing: +**of** *Gina's the exact opposite of her little sister.*

5 sth is not an exact science used to say that an activity involves opinions, guessing etc. rather than just calculating and measuring things: *Predicting the weather is not an exact science.*

6 CAREFUL PERSON someone who is exact is very careful and thorough in what they do SYN **precise**

[**Origin:** 1500–1600 Latin *exactus*, past participle of *exigere*]

exact[2] *v.* [T] **1** FORMAL to demand and get something from someone by using threats, force etc.: **exact sth from sb** *He exacted a promise from us that we wouldn't tell anyone.* **2 exact revenge on sb** to do something to get revenge for something bad that someone has done to you **3 exact a high price/a heavy toll** to have a very bad or harmful effect: *The years of war have exacted a heavy price.*

ex·act·ing /ɪgˈzæktɪŋ/ *adj.* demanding a lot of effort, careful work, or skill SYN **demanding**: *She was an exacting woman to work for.* | **exacting standards/demands/requirements etc.** *He could never live up to his father's exacting standards.* —**exactingly** *adv.*

ex·ac·ti·tude /ɪgˈzæktəˌtud/ *n.* [U] FORMAL the state of being exact

ex·act·ly /ɪgˈzæktli/ S1 W2 *adv.* **1** in every detail or way SYN **precisely**: *That's exactly right.* | **exactly where/what/when etc.** *I can't remember exactly what she said.* | *Her shoes are **exactly the same as** mine.* | *She looks **exactly like** her mother.* | *At school he's very quiet, but at home he's **exactly the opposite**.* **2** no more or no less than a particular amount or number SYN **precisely**: *I've been here exactly a year.* | *The baby weighed seven pounds exactly.* → see also APPROXIMATELY

E

SPOKEN PHRASES

3 exactly used to say that you agree with what someone has said: *"So you're saying there's no money left?" "Exactly."* **4 not exactly a)** used to say that the opposite of something is true: *He's not exactly the most intelligent person* (=he is stupid). | *Well, they didn't exactly rush over to help us* (=they came very slowly, or not at all). **b)** used to say that what someone has said is not completely correct or true: *"Is anything wrong?" "Not exactly, I'm just a little worried."* **5 why/what/where etc. exactly...?** used with question words to ask someone to give you more precise information: *What exactly do you do at your company?*

ex·ag·ger·ate /ɪgˈzædʒəˌreɪt/ *v.* [I,T] to make something seem better, larger, worse etc. than it really is: *Rob said he caught a 20-pound fish, but I think he was exaggerating.* | *The problem has been exaggerated by the media.* [**Origin:** 1500–1600 Latin, past participle of *exaggerare* **to make into a pile**]

ex·ag·ger·at·ed /ɪgˈzædʒəˌreɪt̬ɪd/ *adj.* **1** described as better, more important etc. than is really true: *greatly exaggerated reports* **2** an exaggerated sound or movement is emphasized to make people notice it: *exaggerated hand gestures* —**exaggeratedly** *adv.*

ex·ag·ger·a·tion /ɪgˌzædʒəˈreɪʃən/ *n.* [C,U] a statement or way of saying something that makes something seem better, more important etc. than it really is: *Jim's not exactly fat – that's a slight exaggeration.* | **it is an exaggeration to say sth** *It would be an exaggeration to say that we were close friends.*

ex·alt /ɪgˈzɔlt/ *v.* [T] FORMAL to praise or admire someone or something very much: *a poem exalting the Roman empire*

ex·al·ta·tion /ˌɛgzɔlˈteɪʃən, ˌɛksɔl-/ *n.* [C,U] FORMAL **1** very high praise, or something that expresses this **2** a very strong feeling of happiness, power etc.

ex·alt·ed /ɪgˈzɔltɪd/ *adj.* FORMAL **1** having a very high rank and highly respected **2** filled with a feeling of great happiness

ex·am /ɪgˈzæm/ S2 *n.* [C] **1** a spoken or written test of knowledge, especially an important one at the end of a school year or course of study : *a difficult exam question* | *Only fifteen students **passed the exam**.* | *One of the kids cheated **on an exam**.* | **fail/flunk an exam** *I failed my Chemistry exam.* | *Do you have to **take an exam** today?* | *When are your **final exams**?* | **a history/biology/English etc. exam** *My English exam is Tuesday.* → see also TEST **2** the paper on which the questions for an exam are written, or on which you write your answers **3** a set of medical tests: *an eye exam*

ex·am·i·na·tion /ɪgˌzæməˈneɪʃən/ *n.* **1** [C,U] the process of looking at and thinking about something carefully in order to see what it is like or to see how good it is: +**of** *an examination of the wreckage* | *an* *examination of U.S. foreign policy* | ***a detailed examination** of the organization's financial records* | *The proposals are still **under examination*** (=being examined). | ***Upon closer examination*** (=after looking more carefully), *technicians found several more defective parts.* **2** [C] FORMAL a spoken or written test of knowledge SYN **exam**: *The examination scores will be announced next week.* **3** [C] FORMAL an occasion when a doctor or nurse looks at your body and does a set of medical tests SYN **exam**: *All patients are **given a** complete physical **examination**.* **4** [C,U] LAW the process of asking questions in a court of law: *the prosecution's examination of the witness*

examine

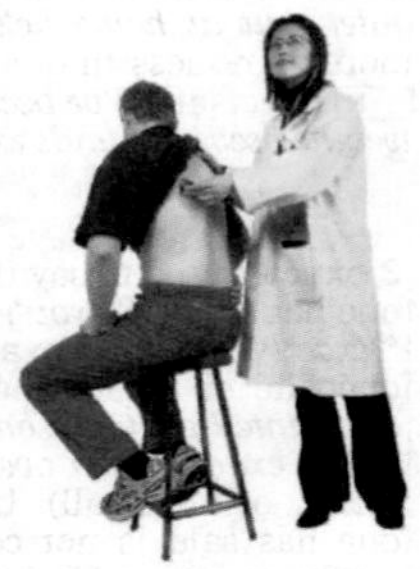

examining a patient

ex·am·ine /ɪgˈzæmɪn/ W2 *v.* [T] **1** to look at, consider, or study something in order to find out about it: *The study examines the emotional effects of unemployment.* | **examine sth closely/carefully** *Pat examined the picture closely.* | **examine sth for sth** *Investigators examined the gun for fingerprints.* | **examine how/whether/what etc.** *We need to examine how we can improve the service.* ►see THESAURUS box at **check**¹ **2** if a doctor examines you, he or she looks at your body to check that you are healthy **3** LAW to officially ask someone questions in a court of law **4** FORMAL to ask someone questions to test their knowledge of a subject: *Students will be examined on these four topics.* [**Origin:** 1300–1400 French *examiner*, from Latin *examinare*, from *examen* **weighing out**] → see also CROSS-EXAMINE

ex·am·in·er /ɪgˈzæmɪnɚ/ *n.* [C] **1** someone whose job is to check something carefully, especially accounts: *a bank examiner* **2** someone who tests someone's knowledge in an examination → see also MEDICAL EXAMINER

ex·am·ple /ɪgˈzæmpəl/ S1 W1 *n.* [C] **1** a specific fact, idea, person, or thing that is used to explain or support a general idea, or to show what is typical of a larger group: **+of** *Can anyone **give me an example of** a transitive verb?* | *She **cited** a number of recent **examples** to support her theory.* | **a good/typical/classic etc. example of sth** *This church is a good example of Roman architecture.* **2 for example** used before mentioning something that shows what you mean or shows that your idea is true: *Many countries, for example Mexico and Japan, have a lot of earthquakes.* **3** a person or way of behaving that you think other people should copy: **be an example to sb** *His determination is an example to us all.* | *Parents should **set a good example for** their children* (=behave well so that the children copy them). | *I suggest you **follow** Rosie's **example*** (=copy her behavior) *and get more exercise.* | *She is a **a shining example of*** (=an excellent example) *how to be a good manager.* **4 make an example of sb** to punish someone so that other people will be afraid to do the same thing [**Origin:** 1300–1400 Old French, Latin *exemplum*, from *eximere* **to take out**]

ex·as·per·ate /ɪgˈzæspəˌreɪt/ *v.* [T] to make someone very annoyed by continuing to do something that upsets them: *His refusal to cooperate has exasperated his lawyers.* [**Origin:** 1500–1600 Latin, past participle of *exasperare*, from *asper* **rough**] —**exasperation** /ɪgˌzæspəˈreɪʃən/ *n.* [U]

ex·as·pe·rat·ed /ɪgˈzæspəˌreɪtɪd/ *adj.* very annoyed and upset: *an exasperated look* | **+with** *Cindy was completely exasperated with her son.* —**exasperatedly** *adv.*

ex·as·per·at·ing /ɪgˈzæspəˌreɪtɪŋ/ *adj.* extremely annoying: *her exasperating habit of talking like a child* —**exasperatingly** *adv.*

Ex·cal·i·bur /ɛksˈkælɪbɚ/ the name of the sword belonging to King Arthur

ex·ca·vate /ˈɛkskəˌveɪt/ *v.* [I,T] **1** if a scientist or ARCHAEOLOGIST excavates an area of land, they dig carefully to find ancient objects, bones etc.: *Work is under way to excavate the ancient city.* **2** to dig a large hole, TUNNEL etc. in the ground [**Origin:** 1500–1600 Latin, past participle of *excavare*, from *cavus* **hollow**] —**excavation** /ˌɛkskəˈveɪʃən/ *n.* [C,U]

ex·ca·va·tor /ˈɛkskəˌveɪtɚ/ *n.* [C] **1** a large machine that digs and moves earth and soil **2** someone who digs to find things that have been buried under the ground for a long time

ex·ceed /ɪkˈsid/ AC W3 *v.* [T] **1** to be more than a particular number, amount etc.: *Construction costs could exceed $230 million.* **2** to go beyond what rules or laws say you are allowed to do: *The city's air pollution exceeds federal standards.* **3 exceed sb's expectations** to do or achieve more than someone expects: *a talented young player who has exceeded everyone's expectations* **4 exceed your authority** to do something that your authority or power does not allow you to do [**Origin:** 1300–1400 Old French *exceder*, from Latin *excedere*, from *cedere* **to go**]

ex·ceed·ing·ly /ɪkˈsidɪŋli/ *adv.* extremely: *an exceedingly rare occurrence* | *His parents are exceedingly worried.*

ex·cel /ɪkˈsɛl/ *v.* **excelled, excelling** [I not in progressive] to do something very well, or much better than most people: **+at/in** *Rick has always excelled at foreign languages.* [**Origin:** 1400–1500 Latin *excellere*, from *-cellere* **to rise, stick up**]

ex·cel·lence /ˈɛksələns/ *n.* [U] the quality of being excellent: *Our company is committed to excellence.*

Ex·cel·len·cy /ˈɛksələnsi/ *n.* **your/his/her Excellency** FORMAL a way of talking to or about someone who has a high position in the government or the church: *his Excellency the Spanish Ambassador*

ex·cel·lent /ˈɛksələnt/ S2 W3 *adj.* **1** extremely good or of very high quality: *Nancy's in excellent health.* | *an excellent idea* | *Dinner was excellent!* ►see THESAURUS box at **good**¹ **2** SPOKEN said when you are pleased about something: *"I'll bring the CDs over tonight." "Excellent."* —**excellently** *adv.*

ex·cept¹ /ɪkˈsɛpt/ S1 W3 *prep.* also **except for** used before the people or things that are not included in a statement: *We're open every day except Monday.* | *Everyone except Scott went to the show.* | **+in/by/up etc.** *They have a TV in every room, except in the bathroom.*

except² S3 W3 *conjunction* **1** used for giving a reason why something is not true or not completely true: **except (that)** *I have earrings just like those, except they're blue.* | *They told us nothing except that the plane was late.* | **except (to) do sth** *He didn't mention work, except to say that he was very busy.* | *We couldn't do anything except wait and hope.* | **except when/what/where etc.** *I don't smoke except when I'm drinking.* | *I like the summer, except when it's hot at night.* **2** used to give the reason why something was not done or did not happen: *Liz would have run, except that she didn't want to appear to be in a hurry.*

except³ *v.* [T usually passive] FORMAL to not include something: **be excepted from sth** *High-technology equipment would be excepted from the trade agreement.*

ex·cept·ed /ɪkˈsɛptɪd/ *adj.* **sb/sth excepted** used to mean that someone or something is not included in a statement: *Fred's not interested in anything, politics excepted.* → see also **present company excepted** at PRESENT¹ (5)

ex·cept·ing /ɪkˈsɛptɪŋ/ *prep.* FORMAL except: *It is a desert with no animals of any kind, excepting a few lizards.*

ex·cep·tion /ɪkˈsɛpʃən/ S3 W3 *n.* [C,U] **1** someone or something that is not included in a rule, does not follow the expected pattern etc.: *It's been very cold, but today's an exception.* | *We don't usually accept checks, but for you we'll **make an exception*** (=not include you in this rule). | *Most cities have high crime rates and New York **is no exception**.* | *We all laughed **with the exception of** Ann.* | *While most of the city's high schools* *are overcrowded, East High School* ***is the exception to the rule****.* | *Most of the top teams played in the competition, with a few* ***notable exceptions****.* | *Successful two-career couples with children are still* ***the exception rather than the rule*** (=used to emphasize that something is unusual). **2 take exception to sth** to be offended and angry about what someone says and complain about it: *Jones took exception to a comment I made about his weight.* **3 without exception** used to say that something is true of all the people or things in a group: *Without exception, the company's directors are all under 40.* **4 sb/sth is the exception that proves the rule** SPOKEN used to say that a statement is usually true even though you are mentioning something that seems to disagree with it: *Books seldom make great movies, but this one is the exception that proves the rule.*

ex·cep·tion·a·ble /ɪkˈsɛpʃənəbəl/ *adj.* FORMAL an exceptionable remark, criticism etc. is a statement that other people will probably disagree with

ex·cep·tion·al /ɪkˈsɛpʃənəl/ *adj.* **1** unusually good or impressive: *an exceptional athlete* ►see THESAURUS box at good[1] **2** unusual or not likely to happen often: *exceptional weather conditions* | *Promotion in the first year is only given* ***in exceptional circumstances****.* **3** having mental or physical problems that make it necessary to go to a special school: *a class for exceptional children*

ex·cep·tion·al·ly /ɪkˈsɛpʃənəli/ *adv.* [+ adj./adv.] unusually or extremely: *Gloria is an exceptionally gifted singer.*

ex·cerpt /ˈɛksɚpt/ *n.* [C] a short part taken from a book, poem, piece of music etc.: **+of/from** *An excerpt of the speech appeared in the Sunday paper.* [**Origin:** 1500–1600 Latin, past participle of *excerpere*, from *carpere* **to gather, pick**] —**excerpt** /ɪkˈsɚpt/ *v.* [T]

ex·cess¹ /ˈɛksɛs, ɪkˈsɛs/ *adj.* [only before noun] additional and more than is needed or allowed: *a $75 charge for excess baggage* | *Cut any excess fat from the meat before cooking.*

excess² *n.* **1 in excess of sth** more than a particular amount: *The director earns an annual salary in excess of $100,000.* **2** [singular, U] a larger amount of something than usual, needed, or allowed: **+of** *There is an excess of writer-actors in Los Angeles.* **3 do sth to excess** to do something too much or too often, so that it may harm you: *He would frequently drink to excess.* **4 excesses** [plural] actions that are socially or morally unacceptable because they are too harmful or too extreme: *The people have not forgotten the excesses of the military regime.* **5** [U] behavior that is not acceptable because it is too harmful or extreme: *a lifetime of excess*

ˌexcess deˈmand *n.* [C,U] ECONOMICS a situation in which people want to buy more of a good or service than is available

ex·ces·sive /ɪkˈsɛsɪv/ *adj.* much more than is reasonable or necessary: *Don's wife left him because of his excessive gambling.*

ˌexcess reˈserves *n.* [plural] ECONOMICS an amount of money that a bank has that is more than the law says it needs to have

ˌexcess supˈply *n.* [C,U] ECONOMICS a situation in which there is more of a good or service than people want to buy

ex·change¹ /ɪksˈtʃeɪndʒ/ [S3] [W2] *n.*
1 GIVING/RECEIVING [C,U] the act of giving someone one thing and receiving something else from them at the same time [SYN] trade [SYN] swap: *a fair exchange* | **+of** *Negotiators are considering the exchange of land for peace.* | *I gave Larry my bike* ***in exchange for*** *some video games.*
2 STH YOU BUY [C,U] the act of giving something you have bought back to the store where you bought it, for example because it does not work, fit etc., and taking something else instead: *The store does not allow returns or exchanges.*
3 ARGUMENT/DISCUSSION [C] a short conversation, usually between two people who are angry with each other: **+between** *an angry exchange between the two men* | *There were several* ***heated exchanges*** (=angry arguments) *but no injuries during the demonstration.* | **an exchange of words/views** *Collins had a brief exchange of words with some reporters.*
4 an exchange of ideas/information etc. an act of discussing or sharing ideas, information etc., or the situation in which this happens: *The organization is dedicated to the free exchange of information.*
5 FINANCIAL CENTER [C] a place where things are bought, sold, or traded: *a commodities exchange* → see also STOCK EXCHANGE
6 STUDENTS/TEACHERS [C,U] an arrangement in which a student, teacher etc. visits another school or country to work or study: *I first went to Germany* ***on an exchange****.* → see also EXCHANGE PROGRAM, EXCHANGE STUDENT
7 JOBS/HOMES ETC. [C] an arrangement in which you stay in someone's home, do someone's job etc. for a short time while that person stays in your home, does your job etc. [SYN] swap: *an apartment exchange* | *Kate's in New York* ***on an*** *employee* ***exchange****.*
8 GUNS [C] an occasion during which two people, armies etc. use weapons against each other: *an exchange of gunfire*
9 MONEY a) [U] ECONOMICS the process in which you change money from one CURRENCY to another: *international currency exchange* | *exchange facilities* | *The* ***rate of exchange*** *is currently very favorable.* **b)** [C] the EXCHANGE RATE
10 TELEPHONE a TELEPHONE EXCHANGE

exchange² *v.* [T]
1 GIVE/RECEIVE to give someone something and receive the same kind of thing from them: *My family still exchanges gifts at Christmas.* | *We exchanged phone numbers before he left.*
2 TAKE BACK TO A STORE to take something back to the place where you bought it and change it for something else: *This shirt is too big. Can I exchange it?* | **exchange sth for sth** *I took the ring back and exchanged it for a silver chain.*
3 CHANGE FOR STH DIFFERENT to give someone something and receive something different instead [SYN] trade [SYN] swap: **exchange sth for sth** *He managed to exchange his horse for some food and clothing.*

> **THESAURUS**
>
> **trade** to exchange something that you have for something that someone else has: *He traded records with friends and acquaintances until he had an unsurpassed collection.*
> **swap** to give something to someone, who gives you something similar: *The two schools use the Internet to swap pictures, stories, and jokes.*
> **in exchange/return (for sth)** if you give something in exchange or in return for something else, you give it in order to get something else back: *Williams will plead guilty in exchange for a reduced sentence.*

4 DO THE SAME THING if two or more people exchange something, they do the same thing to each other: *City council members* ***exchanged greetings with*** *the group of business leaders.* | *The two men* ***exchanged a few words*** (=talked to each other) *and then left the park in opposite directions.* | **exchange glances/looks/smiles etc.** *The two women exchanged glances and laughed.* | **exchange blows/insults etc.** *While the men exchanged blows, the girl struck Diane from behind.*
5 CHANGE MONEY to change money from one type of CURRENCY to another: *Did you exchange any money before your trip?* | **exchange sth for sth** *I need to exchange these dollars for pesos.*
6 exchange information/ideas etc. to discuss something or share information, ideas etc.: *It's a place where people can chat and exchange ideas.*
7 exchange words (with sb) to argue with someone: *The pitcher exchanged words with the umpire and was thrown out of the game.* —**exchangeable** *adj.*

exˈchange ˌprogram *n.* [C] a program in which people, especially students, travel to another country to work or study for a particular length of time → see also FOREIGN EXCHANGE

ex'change rate *n.* [C] the value of the money of one country compared to the money of another country

ex'change ˌstudent *n.* [C] a student who goes to a foreign country to study, usually as part of a program

ex·cheq·uer, Exchequer /ˈɛksˌtʃɛkɚ, ɪkˈstʃɛkɚ/ *n.* [C usually singular] ECONOMICS a government department in Great Britain and Northern Ireland that controls the money that the country collects and spends → see also TREASURY

ex·cise¹ /ˈɛksaɪz, -saɪs/ also **ˈexcise ˌtax** *n.* [C,U] ECONOMICS a government tax that is put on particular goods produced and used inside a country

ex·cise² /ˈɛksaɪz, ɪkˈsaɪz/ *v.* [T] FORMAL to remove or get rid of something, especially by cutting it out: *Offensive scenes were excised from the film.* —**excision** /ɪkˈsɪʒən/ *n.* [C,U]

E

ex·cit·a·ble /ɪkˈsaɪt̬əbəl/ *adj.* easily excited: *an excitable, quick-tempered person* —**excitability** /ɪkˌsaɪt̬əˈbɪlət̬i/ *n.* [U]

ex·cite /ɪkˈsaɪt/ *v.* [T] **1** [not in progressive] to make someone feel very happy, interested, or eager because of something good: *The movie was okay, but it didn't excite me that much.* **2** to cause a particular feeling or reaction SYN **arouse**: **excite interest/curiosity/sympathy etc.** *The murder trial has excited a lot of public interest.* **3** [not in progressive] to make someone feel nervous or upset: *Don't excite him – he needs his rest.* **4** TECHNICAL to make an organ, nerve etc. in your body react or increase its activity: *The signal excites the neurons in the brain.* **5** to make someone feel sexual desire SYN **arouse** [**Origin:** 1300–1400 French *exciter*, from Latin *excitare*, from *citare* **to set in movement**]

ex·cit·ed /ɪkˈsaɪt̬ɪd/ S2 *adj.* **1** feeling very happy, interested, or eager because of something good: *Police tried to hold back the excited crowd.* | *Before the first day of school, I* ***get*** *so* ***excited*** *that I can't sleep.* | +**about** *The kids are really excited about our trip to Mexico.* | *His latest novel is* ***nothing to get excited about*** (=not very good or interesting). | +**by** *Everyone was excited by Alton's discovery.* | **excited to do sth** *We're excited to be here tonight.* | **excited (that)** *I'm very excited that our song was chosen.* **2** worried, angry, or upset about something: +**about** *People don't* ***get*** *as* ***excited*** *about pollution as they probably should.* | +**by** *He never lets himself become excited by rumors.* **3** feeling sexual desire —**excitedly** *adv.*: *They ran excitedly to the lake and jumped in.* → see also EXCITING

ex·cite·ment /ɪkˈsaɪt˺mənt/ *n.* **1** [U] the feeling of being excited: *She longed for some excitement in her life.* | +**of** *the excitement of living in a big city* | +**at** *Anna felt great excitement at the thought of meeting him.* | *Her cheeks were flushed* ***with excitement***. | ***In*** *his* ***excitement****, he knocked over a lamp.* **2** [C usually plural] an exciting event or situation: *The excitements of the day had tired him.* **3** [U] the feeling that you want to have sex SYN **arousal**

ex·cit·ing /ɪkˈsaɪt̬ɪŋ/ S2 W3 *adj.* making you feel very happy, interested, or eager: *exciting news* | **exciting to do sth** *It must have been so exciting to watch the first men land on the moon.* | **an exciting opportunity/possibility/prospect etc.** *an exciting job opportunity* —**excitingly** *adv.* → see also EXCITED

THESAURUS

thrilling exciting and interesting: *the most thrilling day of his sports career*
gripping a gripping movie, story etc. is very exciting and interesting: *a gripping story of love, death, and deception*
dramatic used about something that is exciting to watch or hear about as it happens: *the dramatic events of the past week*
exhilarating making you feel happy, excited, and full of energy: *an exhilarating sense of freedom*
electric making you feel very excited: *There was an almost electric atmosphere in the stadium.*
nail-biting very exciting, especially because you do not know what is going to happen next: *a nail-biting finish*

ex·claim /ɪkˈskleɪm/ *v.* [I,T] to say something suddenly because you are surprised, excited, or angry: *"What a beautiful house!" she exclaimed.*

ex·cla·ma·tion /ˌɛkskləˈmeɪʃən/ *n.* [C] a sound, word, or short sentence that you say suddenly because you are surprised, excited, or angry: +**of** *an exclamation of surprise*

excla'mation ˌpoint also **excla'mation ˌmark** *n.* [C] the mark (!) used in writing after a sentence or word that expresses surprise, excitement, or anger

ex·clam·a·to·ry /ɪkˈsklæməˌtɔri/ *adj.* ENG. LANG. ARTS an exclamatory sentence expresses a strong opinion or emotion and ends with an EXCLAMATION POINT (=!) → see also DECLARATIVE, INTERROGATIVE

ex·clude /ɪkˈsklud/ Ac *v.* [T] **1** to not allow someone to enter a place or to do something OPP **include**: *The club used to exclude women.* | **exclude sb from (doing) sth** *Reporters were excluded from the event.* **2** to deliberately not include something OPP **include**: *The diet excludes all dairy products.* | **exclude sth from sth** *Several of the incidents were excluded from the report.* **3** to decide that something is not a possibility: *France has refused to* ***exclude the possibility of*** *a military attack.* [**Origin:** 1300–1400 Latin *excludere*, from *claudere* **to close**]

ex·clud·ing /ɪkˈskludɪŋ/ Ac *prep.* not including something OPP **including**: *The trip costs $1,300, excluding airfare.*

ex·clu·sion /ɪkˈskluʒən/ Ac *n.* **1** [C,U] the act of not allowing someone to do something or of not including something, or a situation in which this happens OPP **inclusion**: *She was annoyed at her exclusion from the meeting.* | +**of** *the exclusion of professional athletes from the competition* **2** [C] something that is deliberately not included in a contract or an agreement: *exclusions in an insurance policy* **3 do sth to the exclusion of sth** to do something so much that you do not do, include, consider, or have time for something else: *The school concentrates on academic subjects to the exclusion of sports and music.* —**exclusionary** *adj.*: *exclusionary business practices*

ex'clusion ˌlaws *n.* [plural] LAW laws that stop people from particular countries or areas from coming to live and work somewhere: *Exclusion laws barred the Chinese from coming to the U.S for half a century.*

ex'clusion ˌzone *n.* [C] an area that the government does not allow people to enter, because it is dangerous or because secret things happen there: *a military exclusion zone*

ex·clu·sive¹ /ɪkˈsklusɪv, -zɪv/ Ac *adj.* **1** available to only one person or group, and not shared: *an exclusive offer* | **exclusive interview/report/coverage etc.** *an exclusive interview with the convicted murderer* | *We have* ***the exclusive right*** *to publish her work.* | *Hotel residents have* ***exclusive use*** *of the hotel's private beach.* **2** an exclusive group, organization etc. is difficult to be part of: *These students are part of an exclusive group of high achievers.* **3** exclusive restaurants, hotels etc. are for people who have a lot of money, or who belong to a high social class: *an exclusive Manhattan hotel* **4** deliberately not allowing someone to do something or be part of a group OPP **inclusive**: *a racially exclusive hiring policy* **5** [only before noun] concerned with only one thing: *the company's exclusive focus on profits* **6 exclusive of sth** not including: *All prices are exclusive of tax.* —**exclusiveness** *n.* [U] —**exclusivity** /ˌɛkskluˈsɪvət̬i, ˌɪks-/ *n.* [U] → see also **mutually exclusive/contradictory** at MUTUALLY (2)

exclusive² Ac *n.* [C] an important news story that is in only one newspaper, magazine, television news program etc.

ex·clu·sive·ly /ɪkˈsklusɪvli/ Ac *adv.* made of, including, or involving only one thing or group SYN **only**: *The office staff is almost exclusively female.*

exˌclusive 'powers *n.* [plural] POLITICS the legal right to do particular things that only one part of the government has: *One of the exclusive powers of the federal government is the printing of money.*

ex·com·mu·ni·cate /ˌɛkskəˈmyunəˌkeɪt/ *v.* [T] to punish someone by not allowing them to be a member of the Catholic Church anymore —**excommunication** /ˌɛkskəˌmyunəˈkeɪʃən/ *n.* [C,U]

ex-con /ˌɛks ˈkɑn/ *n.* [C] INFORMAL a criminal who has been in prison but who is now free → see also CONVICT

ex·co·ri·ate /ɪkˈskɔriˌeɪt/ *v.* [T] FORMAL to express a very bad opinion of a book, play, person etc.: *The book was excoriated in the press.* —**excoriation** /ɪkˌskɔriˈeɪʃən/ *n.* [C,U]

ex·cre·ment /ˈɛkskrəmənt/ *n.* [U] FORMAL the solid waste material from a person's or animal's BOWELS

ex·cres·cence /ɪkˈskrɛsəns/ *n.* [C] FORMAL **1** an addition that is not wanted or not needed **2** BIOLOGY an ugly growth on an animal or plant

ex·cre·ta /ɪkˈskritə/ *n.* [plural] BIOLOGY the solid or liquid waste material that people and animals produce and get rid of from their bodies

ex·crete /ɪkˈskrit/ *v.* [I,T] BIOLOGY to get rid of waste material from your body through your BOWELS, your skin etc. [**Origin:** 1600–1700 Latin *excretus*, past participle of *excernere* **to separate out**] —**excretory** /ˈɛkskrɪˌtɔri/ *adj.* → see also SECRETE

ex·cre·tion /ɪkˈskriʃən/ *n.* **1** [U] BIOLOGY the process of getting rid of waste material from your body **2** [C,U] BIOLOGY the waste material that people or animals get rid of from their bodies

ex·cru·ci·at·ing /ɪkˈskruʃiˌeɪt̬ɪŋ/ *adj.* **1** extremely painful: *The pain in my knee was excruciating.* **2** extreme in a negative, unpleasant, or upsetting way: *Witnesses described the brutal attack in excruciating detail.* [**Origin:** 1500–1600 *excruciate* **to cause great pain to** (16–21 centuries), from Latin *excruciare*, from *cruciare* **to crucify**] —**excruciatingly** *adv.*

ex·cul·pate /ˈɛkskəlˌpeɪt/ *v.* [T] FORMAL to prove or decide that someone is not guilty of something —**exculpatory** /ɪkˈskʌlpəˌtɔri/ *adj.*: *exculpatory evidence* —**exculpation** /ˌɛkskəlˈpeɪʃən/ *n.* [U]

ex·cur·sion /ɪkˈskɚʒən/ *n.* [C] **1** a short trip, usually made by a group of people: **+to** *a three-day excursion to Disneyland.* ►see THESAURUS box at **trip**[1] **2 an excursion into sth** FORMAL an attempt to experience, learn, or talk about something, especially something that is new to you: *He returned to the stage after a brief excursion into TV.* [**Origin:** 1500–1600 Latin *excursio*, from *excurrere* **to run out**]

ex·cus·a·ble /ɪkˈskyuzəbəl/ *adj.* excusable behavior or reasons are easy to forgive [OPP] **inexcusable**

ex·cuse[1] /ɪkˈskyuz/ [S1] *v.* [T]

1 excuse me SPOKEN **a)** said when you want to politely get someone's attention or interrupt them, especially to ask a question: *Excuse me. Is this the right bus to the airport?* **b)** used to say that you are sorry when you have done something embarrassing or impolite: *Oh, excuse me. I didn't know you were standing in line.* **c)** used to politely tell someone that you are leaving a place: *Excuse me for a minute. I'll be right back.* **d)** used to ask someone to repeat something that they have just said: *"What time is it?" "Excuse me?" "I asked what time it is."* **e)** used to politely ask someone to move so that you can walk past: *Excuse me. Could I just squeeze past?* **f)** used to show that you disagree with someone or are very surprised or upset by what they have just said: *"You're older than Sue, right?" "Excuse me? She's five years older than I am."* **g)** used to disagree with someone in a polite way: *Excuse me, but I don't think that's what he meant.*

2 FORGIVE to forgive someone, usually for something that is not very serious: *Please excuse my bad handwriting.* | **excuse sb for (doing) sth** *You'll have to excuse me for being late – my car broke down.* | *After the way the team played last Friday, he **can be excused for being** upset.*

3 EXPLAIN to make someone's bad or unusual behavior seem more acceptable by giving reasons for it [SYN] **justify**: *I'm sorry, but that explanation doesn't excuse what he did.* | **excuse yourself** *There was nothing she could say to excuse herself.*

4 FROM A PLACE to give someone permission to leave a place: **excuse sb from sth** *May I please be excused from the table?*

5 excuse yourself to say politely that you need to leave a place: *Richard excused himself and went to his room.*

6 FROM A DUTY to allow someone not to do a duty or not to do something they are supposed to do: **excuse sb from (doing) sth** *Please excuse Sherry from gym class today. She has had the flu.*

7 excuse me (for living)! SPOKEN said in an angry way when someone has offended you or told you that you have done something wrong

[**Origin:** 1400–1500 Old French *excuser*, from Latin *excusare*, from *causa* **cause, explanation**]

WORD CHOICE (I'm) sorry, excuse me, pardon (me), (I) beg your pardon

- Say **(I'm) sorry** or **excuse me** to someone if you accidentally get in their way, touch them, or push against them, or if you make a small mistake: *Sorry. I didn't mean to bump you.* | *"You're blocking the doorway." "Oh, excuse me."*
- Use **I'm sorry** when you have done something more seriously wrong or have upset someone: *I'm sorry I didn't call you – I forgot.* If you are late, it is polite to say **I'm sorry** and give a reason: *I'm sorry I'm late. The traffic was bad.*
- Say **excuse me** to get someone's attention or before speaking to someone you don't know: *Excuse me. Can you tell me where the post office is?*
- Say **sorry, excuse me, pardon (me)** or **(I) beg your pardon** (old-fashioned) as a question if you want someone to repeat something, especially because you did not understand it or hear it correctly: *"Hi, my name's Maria Dallaglio." "Sorry?" "Maria Dallaglio."*

excuse[2] /ɪkˈskyus/ [S3] *n.* [C] **1** a reason that you give to explain why you did something wrong: *What's your excuse this time?* | **+for** *His excuse for being late wasn't very good.* | ***There's no excuse for** yelling in a restaurant like that.* | *I'm sure Mike **has a** good **excuse** for not coming to practice.* | *You're always **making excuses for** him.* ►see THESAURUS box at **reason**[1] **2** a false reason that you give to explain why you are or are not doing something: **an excuse to do sth** *I need an excuse to call her.* | **+for** *I think this vacation is just an excuse for her to buy new clothes.* | *The conference **gives** me **an excuse** to visit Atlanta.* | *She continually **uses** her sick mother **as an excuse**.* **3 a poor/bad etc. excuse for sth** used when you think someone is very bad at something they are doing or at their job: *Her paintings are a pretty poor excuse for artwork.* **4** a note written by one of your parents or a doctor explaining why you were not at school on a particular day **5 make your excuses** to say politely that you cannot come somewhere you have been invited or that you have to leave: *I made my excuses and left the party.*

ex·ec /ɪgˈzɛk/ *n.* [C] INFORMAL an EXECUTIVE

ex·e·cra·ble /ˈɛksɪkrəbəl/ *adj.* FORMAL extremely bad: *execrable wine*

ex·e·crate /ˈɛksəˌkreɪt/ *v.* [T] LITERARY to express strong disapproval or hatred for someone or something

ex·e·cute /ˈɛksɪˌkyut/ *v.* [T] **1** to kill someone, especially legally as a punishment for a serious crime: **execute sb for sth** *The general was executed for war crimes.* → see Thesaurus box at KILL[1] **2** FORMAL to do something that has been planned or agreed to [SYN] **carry out**: *Franklin is in charge of executing the company's reorganization plan.* **3** FORMAL to perform something, especially a difficult action or movement: *The show's dance routines were executed extremely well.* **4** COMPUTERS if a computer executes a program or a COMMAND (=instruction), it makes the program or command work or happen: *This program automatically executes the commands once a day.* **5** LAW to make sure that the instructions in a legal document are followed:

Brock's attorney has yet to execute the will. **6** ENG. LANG. ARTS to produce a painting, movie, book etc.: *Some of his most important works were executed during the war.*

ex·e·cu·tion /ˌɛksɪˈkyuʃən/ *n.* **1** [C,U] the act of killing someone, especially as a legal punishment for a serious crime: *The execution has been delayed one month.* | *He was found guilty and now faces execution.* **2** [U] FORMAL a process in which you do something that has been planned or agreed to: +**of** *We do not want to delay the execution of the building work.* **3** [U] FORMAL the performance of something, especially a difficult action or movement: *Davis' execution on his last jump was perfect.* **4** [U] LAW the process of making sure that the instructions in a legal document are followed: *the execution of a search warrant* **5** [U] ENG. LANG. ARTS the act of producing a painting, movie, book etc., or the way it is produced: *Many of Dali's paintings are witty in design and execution.* **6** [C,U] COMPUTERS the act or result of making a computer program work, or a COMMAND (=instruction) happen

E

ex·e·cu·tion·er /ˌɛksɪˈkyuʃənɚ/ *n.* [C] someone whose job is to legally kill someone else as a punishment for a serious crime

ex·ec·u·tive¹ /ɪgˈzɛkyət̬ɪv/ W2 *n.* **1** [C] someone who manages others in an organization, especially a business or company, or helps decide what the organization will do: *a senior marketing executive* **2 the executive** POLITICS the executive branch of government → see also CHIEF EXECUTIVE

executive² W2 *adj.* [only before noun] **1** relating to making decisions and organizing, especially in a company or a business: *the executive producer of a popular TV show* | *The committee does not have* ***executive powers.*** → see also CHIEF EXECUTIVE OFFICER **2** for the use of people who are important managers in a company or organization: *the executive washroom* **3 the executive branch** the part of a government that approves decisions and laws and is responsible for making them work → see also JUDICIAL BRANCH, **legislative branch** at LEGISLATIVE (2)

exˌecutive aˈgreement *n.* [C] POLITICS an agreement between the U.S. government and the government of another country that does not need approval by the SENATE

exˌecutive ˈprivilege *n.* [C] POLITICS the right of a president or other government leaders to keep official records and papers secret

ex·ec·u·tor /ɪgˈzɛkyət̬ɚ/ *n.* [C] LAW someone who deals with the instructions in someone's WILL

ex·e·ge·sis /ˌɛksəˈdʒisəs/ *n.* [C,U] ENG. LANG. ARTS a detailed explanation of a piece of writing, especially one about the Bible

ex·em·plar /ɪgˈzɛmplɑr, -plɚ/ *n.* [C] FORMAL a good or typical example

ex·em·pla·ry /ɪgˈzɛmpləri/ *adj.* **1** excellent and used as an example to follow: *exemplary leadership skills* **2** [only before noun] severe and used as a warning: *an exemplary punishment*

ex·em·pli·fy /ɪgˈzɛmpləˌfaɪ/ *v.* **exemplifies, exemplified, exemplifying** [T] **1** to be a very typical example of something, or to give an example like this: *Moore's case exemplifies the difficulty in diagnosing unusual illnesses.* **2** to give an example of something: *These problems are exemplified clearly in the report.* —**exemplification** /ɪgˌzɛmpləfəˈkeɪʃən/ *n.* [C,U]

ex·empt¹ /ɪgˈzɛmpt/ *adj.* having special permission not to do a duty, pay for something etc.: +**from** *Their income is exempt from state taxes.*

exempt² *v.* [T] to give someone special permission not to do a duty, pay for something etc.: **exempt sb from sth** *Disabled students are exempted from paying the fee.*

ex·emp·tion /ɪgˈzɛmpʃən/ *n.* [C] **1** ECONOMICS an amount of money that you do not have to pay tax on in a particular year: *a tax exemption for a dependent child* **2** [C,U] special permission not to do a duty, pay for something etc.

ex·er·cise¹ /ˈɛksɚˌsaɪz/ S2 W2 *n.*
1 FOR HEALTH [U] physical activity that you do in order to stay healthy and become stronger: *Let's walk. It'll be good exercise.* | *aerobic exercise* | *I don't* ***get*** *a lot of* ***exercise*** *during the week.* | **strenuous/vigorous exercise** *Try to do twenty minutes of vigorous exercise each day.*
2 FOR A BODY PART [C] a movement or set of movements that you do regularly in order to keep your body strong and healthy: *a stretching exercise for my back* | *Have you* ***done*** *your stomach* ***exercises*** *today?*
3 FOR SCHOOL [C] a set of written questions that test your skill or knowledge: *For homework,* ***do exercises*** *1 and 2.*
4 FOR A SKILL [C] an activity or process that helps you practice a particular skill, such as playing a musical instrument or singing: *fingering exercises for the piano* | *He was* ***doing*** *some breathing* ***exercises*** *to help him relax.*
5 WITH A QUALITY/RESULT [C usually singular] an activity or situation that has a particular quality or result: *a cost-cutting exercise* | +**in** *Fighting the rising waters was an exercise in futility.*
6 ARMY/NAVY ETC. [C] a set of military actions that are not part of a war, but that allow soldiers to practice their skills: *naval exercises*
7 USE [C,U] FORMAL the use of power, a right etc.: +**of** *the exercise of our freedom of speech*
[**Origin:** 1300–1400 French *exercice*, from Latin *exercere* **to drive on, keep busy**]

exercise² S3 W3 *v.* **1** [I] to do physical activities so that you stay strong and healthy: *Karl exercises by playing racquetball twice a week.*

THESAURUS

stay/keep/get in shape to stay or to become physically healthy and strong
work out to do exercise in order to be healthy and strong, especially to exercise regularly
warm up to do gentle exercises to prepare your body for more active exercise
stretch to reach your arms, legs, or body out to full length, in order to make your muscles as long as possible, so that you do not injure them when you exercise
gym/health club a place you go to exercise

2 [T] to make a particular part of your body move in order to make it stronger: *Swimming exercises all the major muscle groups.* **3** FORMAL to use power, a right etc.: *Our manager exercised her influence to get Rigby the position.* **4** FORMAL to use a skill or quality that you have when you are doing something or making a decision: *I think we should exercise caution.* **5** [T] to make an animal walk or run in order to keep it healthy and strong **6** [T] FORMAL to make someone worry or think about something a lot

ˈexercise ˌbike also **ˈexercise ˌbicycle** *n.* [C] a bicycle that does not move and is used indoors for exercise

ex·ert /ɪgˈzɚt/ *v.* [T] **1 exert authority/influence etc.** to use your authority, influence etc. to make something happen: *The U.N. is exerting pressure on the countries' leaders to stop the war.* **2 exert yourself** to make a strong physical or mental effort: *She's still quite weak, so she shouldn't exert herself.* **3** to have an effect on something: *The book has exerted a lasting impact.* [**Origin:** 1600–1700 Latin *exsertus*, past participle of *exserere* **to push out**]

ex·er·tion /ɪgˈzɚʃən/ *n.* [C,U] **1** strong physical or mental effort: *If you are not used to physical exertion, start slowly.* **2** the use of authority, influence etc. to make something happen: +**of** *the exertion of legislative power*

ex·e·unt /ˈɛksiˌʌnt/ *v.* [I] a word written in the instructions of a play to tell two or more actors to leave the stage

ex·hale /ɛksˈheɪl, ɛkˈseɪl/ *v.* [I,T] to breathe air, smoke etc. out of your mouth or nose OPP **inhale**: *Take a* *deep breath; then exhale slowly.* —**exhalation** /ˌɛksəˈleɪʃən, ˌɛkshə-/ *n.* [U]

ex•haust[1] /ɪgˈzɔst/ *v.* [T] **1** to make someone very tired: *The trip totally exhausted us.* | **it exhausts sb to do sth** *It exhausts me to think of all the things I have to do before the move.* **2** to use all of something: **exhaust a supply/stock/reserve** *We are in danger of exhausting the world's oil supply.* **3** to try all the possible options in a situation so that there is nothing left to try: *We haven't yet **exhausted the possibilities** of the technology.* **4 exhaust a subject/topic** to talk about something so much that you have nothing more to say about it: *Well, it looks like we've exhausted that topic. Let's move on to the next question.* [**Origin:** 1500–1600 Latin *exhaustus*, past participle of *exhaurire*, from *haurire* **to draw off liquid, drain**]

exhaust[2] *n.* **1** [U] SCIENCE the gas or steam that is produced when a machine is working **2 the exhaust** also **the exhaust system** the parts of a car or machine that exhaust passes through as it leaves the engine

ex•haust•ed /ɪgˈzɔstɪd/ *adj.* **1** extremely tired and having no energy: **+from/by** *Ron was exhausted from studying all night.* ▶see THESAURUS box at **tired** **2** having or containing no more of a particular thing or substance: *an exhausted coal mine*

ex•haust•ing /ɪgˈzɔstɪŋ/ *adj.* making you feel extremely tired: *an exhausting trip*

ex•haus•tion /ɪgˈzɔstʃən/ *n.* [U] **1** a state of being extremely tired: **mental/physical exhaustion** *Neil is suffering from mental exhaustion.* **2** a situation in which all of something has been used, so that there is none left: **+of** *Poor farming techniques have led to the exhaustion of the soil.*

ex•haus•tive /ɪgˈzɔstɪv/ *adj.* extremely thorough: *an exhaustive investigation* —**exhaustively** *adv.*

exˈhaust pipe *n.* [C] a pipe on a car or a machine that gas or steam comes out of → see picture on page A36

ex•hib•it[1] /ɪgˈzɪbɪt/ Ac *v.* **1** [I,T] to put something in a public place so that people can see it, learn about it etc.: *The gallery will exhibit some of Monet's paintings.* | *She was invited to exhibit at a local gallery.* **2** [T] FORMAL to show a particular quality, sign, emotion etc. so that it is easy to notice: *Some of the patients exhibit violent behavior.* [**Origin:** 1400–1500 Latin *exhibitus*, past participle of *exhibere* **to hold out, show**]

exhibit[2] Ac S3 *n.* [C] **1** an exhibition: *a new sculpture exhibit at the museum* **2** a thing or a collection of things that is put in a public place so that people can see it, learn about it etc.: *The children's museum has several hands-on exhibits.* **3** LAW an object, piece of clothing etc. that is used in a court of law to prove that someone is guilty or not guilty: *Exhibit A is the bloody glove.* **4 on exhibit** ENG. LANG. ARTS if something such as a painting or other object is on exhibit, it is put in a public place for people to see: *The painting is currently on exhibit at the local museum.*

ex•hi•bi•tion /ˌɛksəˈbɪʃən/ Ac *n.* **1** [C] a public show where you put something so that people can go to see it SYN **exhibit**: **+of** *an exhibition of Impressionist painters* **2** [U] the act of showing something such as a painting in a public place: **+of** *the exhibition of her sculptures* | *A collection of rare books is **on exhibition** at the city library.* **3 an exhibition of rudeness/jealousy/temper etc.** behavior that shows rudeness, jealousy etc.: *Stilwell's actions were a startling exhibition of his disregard for others.* **4** a situation in which someone shows a particular skill or quality: *The show provides an exhibition of her skill as a dancer.* **5 make an exhibition of yourself** behave in a silly or embarrassing way: *Sam got drunk and made an exhibition of himself.*

ex•hi•bi•tion•ism /ˌɛksəˈbɪʃəˌnɪzəm/ *n.* [U] **1** behavior that makes people notice you, but that most people think is not acceptable: *Getting up and singing like that is pure exhibitionism.* **2** a mental problem which makes someone like to show their sexual organs to other people in public places —**exhibitionist** *n.* [C] —**exhibitionistic** /ˌɛksəˌbɪʃəˈnɪstɪk/ *adj.*

ex•hib•i•tor /ɪgˈzɪbɪtɚ/ *n.* [C] someone who is showing something in a public place so that people can see it, learn about it etc.: *an exhibitor at a trade show*

ex•hil•a•rat•ed /ɪgˈzɪləˌreɪt̬ɪd/ *adj.* feeling extremely happy and excited: *We were tired but exhilarated when we reached the top.* —**exhilarate** *v.* [T] —**exhilaration** /ɪgˌzɪləˈreɪʃən/ *n.* [U]

ex•hil•a•ra•ting /ɪgˈzɪləˌreɪt̬ɪŋ/ *adj.* making you feel extremely happy and excited: *Sky-diving is an exhilarating experience.* —**exhilaratingly** *adv.*

ex•hort /ɪgˈzɔrt/ *v.* [T] FORMAL to try very hard to persuade someone to do something, especially through a speech: **exhort sb to do sth** *He exhorted the workers to end the strike.* —**exhortation** /ˌɛksɔrˈteɪʃən, ˌɛgzɚ-/ *n.* [C,U]

ex•hume /ɪgˈzum, ɛksˈhyum/ *v.* [T usually passive] FORMAL to remove a dead body from the ground after it has been buried —**exhumation** /ˌɛkshyuˈmeɪʃən, ˌɛgzu-/ *n.* [C,U]

E

ex•i•gen•cy /ˈɛksədʒənsi, ɪgˈzɪdʒənsi/ also **ex•igence** /-dʒəns/ *n.* FORMAL **1** [C usually plural] what you need to do to deal with a particular situation: *the exigencies of war* **2** [U] the quality of being urgent and needing to be dealt with

ex•i•gent /ˈɛksədʒənt/ *adj.* FORMAL an exigent situation is urgent, so that you must deal with it very quickly

ex•ig•u•ous /ɪgˈzɪguəs/ *adj.* FORMAL very small in amount: *exiguous earnings*

ex•ile[1] /ˈɛgzaɪl, ˈɛksaɪl/ *n.* **1** [singular, U] a situation in which someone is forced to leave their country to live in another country, especially for political reasons: *She wrote the novel while living **in exile**.* | *The King **went into exile** after the revolution.* | *The house was raided and the family was **forced into exile**.* **2** [C] someone who has been forced to live in exile [**Origin:** 1300–1400 French *exil*, from Latin *exul* **person sent away**]

exile[2] *v.* [T usually passive] to force someone to leave their country, especially for political reasons: **exile sb to sth** *Several of the student leaders have been exiled to France.* —**exiled** *adj.* [only before noun]

ex•ist /ɪgˈzɪst/ S2 W2 *v.* [I not in progressive] **1** to happen or be present in a particular situation or place: *Stop pretending that the problem doesn't exist.* | *By 1950 the organization had **ceased to exist**.* **2** to be real, or to be alive: *Do ghosts really exist?* **3** to stay alive, especially in difficult conditions: *Poor families in our city are barely able to exist during the winter.* | **+on** *Brian exists on pizza and soft drinks.* [**Origin:** 1600–1700 Latin *exsistere* **to come into being, exist**, from *sistere* **to stand**]

ex•ist•ence /ɪgˈzɪstəns/ W2 *n.* **1** [U] the state of existing: **+of** *Do you believe in the existence of God?* | *Similar laws are already **in existence**.* | *The museum's **very existence** depends on contributions like yours.* | *Scientists have many theories about how the universe first **came into existence*** (=started to exist). **2** [C usually singular] the type of life that someone has, especially when it is bad or unhappy: *Pablo **led a** lonely **existence** when he first moved to San Juan.* → see also **eke out a living/existence** at EKE OUT

ex•is•tent /ɪgˈzɪstənt/ *adj.* FORMAL existing now → see also NONEXISTENT

ex•is•ten•tial /ˌɛgzɪˈstɛnʃəl◂/ *adj.* [only before noun] **1** also **existentialist** relating to existentialism: *an existential novel* **2** relating to the existence of humans and human experience

ex•is•ten•tial•ism /ˌɛgzɪˈstɛnʃəˌlɪzəm/ *n.* [U] the belief that people are responsible for their own actions and experiences, and that the world has no particular meaning —**existentialist** *n.* [C]

ex•ist•ing /ɪgˈzɪstɪŋ/ W3 *adj.* [only before noun] present or being used now: *The service is available to existing customers.*

ex•it[1] /ˈɛgzɪt, ˈɛksɪt/ S3 *n.* [C] **1** a door or space through which you can leave a room, building etc.

OPP entrance: *There are two exits at the back of the plane.* | *an emergency exit* **2** [usually singular] the act of leaving a place such as a room or theater stage OPP entrance: **+from** *A car was blocking her exit from the parking lot.* | *Kennedy* ***made a*** *quick* ***exit*** *after his speech.* **3** a small road that you drive on to leave a larger road: *Take the 14th Street exit and then turn right.* **4** [usually singular] an occasion when someone stops being involved in a competition, profession, organization etc., especially because they have not been successful: *Pratt* ***made an*** *early* ***exit*** *from the tournament.* [**Origin:** 1500–1600 Latin *exitus*, from the past participle of *exire* **to go out**]

exit² *v.* **1** [I] to leave a place: **+from/through** *The band exited through a door behind the stage.* **2** [I,T] COMPUTERS to stop using a computer program: *Click on the "X" to exit.* **3** [I,T] to leave a road and join another one: **exit (sth) at sth** *He exited the freeway at Imperial Beach.* **4** [I] ENG. LANG. ARTS a word used in the instructions of a play to tell an actor to leave the stage

'exit poll *n.* [C] POLITICS a process of asking people how they have voted as they leave a voting place in order to discover the likely result of the election

ex·o·crine gland /'ɛksəkrɪn ˌglænd/ *n.* [C] BIOLOGY a GLAND in the body that produces a SECRETION (=liquid in the body with a particular function) that travels through special tubes to the outside of the body, for example a gland that produces SWEAT → see also ENDOCRINE GLAND

Ex·o·dus /'ɛksədəs/ the second book in the Old Testament of the Christian Bible

ex·o·dus /'ɛksədəs/ *n.* [singular] a situation in which a lot of people leave a particular place at the same time: **+of** *the exodus of refugees* | **+from/to** *the exodus from the countryside to the towns in the 19th century* | *I joined the* ***mass exodus*** *for drinks at intermission.* [**Origin:** 1600–1700 *Exodus*, which describes how the Israelites left Egypt]

Ex·o·dus·ter /'ɛksədəstɚ/ *n.* [C] HISTORY the Exodusters were African Americans who left the South after the American Civil War and moved west, especially to Kansas

ex of·fi·ci·o /ˌɛks ə'fɪʃiˌoʊ/ *adj.* FORMAL an ex-officio member of an organization is only a member because of their rank or position —**ex officio** *adv.*

ex·on·er·ate /ɪg'zɑnəˌreɪt/ *v.* [T] FORMAL to officially say that someone who has been blamed for something is not guilty: **exonerate sb of sth** *Ross was exonerated of all charges.* [**Origin:** 1400–1500 Latin, past participle of *exonerare*, from *onus* **load**] —**exoneration** /ɪgˌzɑnə'reɪʃən/ *n.* [U]

ex·or·bi·tant /ɪg'zɔrbət̬ənt/ *adj.* an exorbitant price, demand etc. is much higher or greater than is reasonable or usual: *exorbitant interest rates on loans* [**Origin:** 1400–1500 French, Late Latin, present participle of *exorbitare* **to leave the track**] —**exorbitance** *n.* [U] —**exorbitantly** *adv.*

ex·or·cise /'ɛksɔrˌsaɪz, -sɚ-/ *v.* [T] **1** to forget or be able to deal with bad memories or bad experiences, or to make someone do this: **exorcise demons/ghosts etc.** *Starting my own family has helped exorcise the demons of my past.* **2** to try to force evil spirits to leave a place or someone's body by using special words and ceremonies

ex·or·cism /'ɛksɔrˌsɪzəm/ *n.* [C,U] **1** a process by which someone tries to force evil spirits to leave a place or someone's body by using special words and ceremonies **2** the process of making yourself forget a bad memory or experience

ex·or·cist /'ɛksɔrsɪst/ *n.* [C] someone who tries to force evil spirits to leave a place or someone's body

ex·o·skel·e·ton /'ɛksoʊˌskɛlət̚n/ *n.* [C] BIOLOGY hard structure on the outside of the body of some living creatures such as TURTLES, that protects and supports the creature's body instead of a BACKBONE → see also ENDOSKELETON

ex·o·ther·mic /ˌɛksoʊ'θɚmɪk/ *adj.* CHEMISTRY relating to or describing a chemical reaction that produces or sends out heat: *an exothermic process* → see also ENDOTHERMIC

ex·ot·ic /ɪg'zɑt̬ɪk/ *adj.* APPROVING unusual and exciting because of a connection with a foreign country: *exotic birds from New Guinea* | *exotic places* [**Origin:** 1500–1600 Latin *exoticus*, from Greek *exotikos*, from *exo* **outside**] —**exotically** /-kli/ *adv.*

ex·ot·i·ca /ɪg'zɑt̬ɪkə/ *n.* [plural] unusual and exciting things, especially ones that come from foreign countries

exˌotic 'dancer *n.* [C] a dancer who takes off his or her clothes while dancing SYN stripper

ex·pand /ɪk'spænd/ Ac S3 W2 *v.* **1** [I,T] to become larger in size, number, or amount, or to make something become larger OPP contract: *The population was expanding rapidly.* | *This exercise is a good way to expand the chest.* | **expand the number/range of sth** *The college is expanding its range of evening courses.* **2** [I,T] if a company, business etc. expands or if someone expands it, they open new stores, factories etc.: *The company has aggressive plans to expand overseas.* | **expand (sth) into sth** *We plan to expand our operations into Europe.* [**Origin:** 1400–1500 Latin *expandere*, from *pandere* **to spread**] —**expandable** *adj.*: *an expandable garment bag*

expand on/upon sth *phr. v.* to add more details or information to something that has already been said: *Wilson refused to expand upon what action would be taken.*

ex·panse /ɪk'spæns/ *n.* [C] a very large area of water, sky, land etc.: **+of** *the vast expanse of the Pacific Ocean*

ex·pan·sion /ɪk'spænʃən/ Ac W3 *n.* **1** [C,U] the act or process of increasing in size, number, amount, or range: **+of** *the continuing expansion of the Internet* | *the expansion of the British Empire* **2** [C,U] ECONOMICS a period of increased business activity and economic growth: *Most regions are enjoying rapid economic expansion.* **3** [U] the act or process of making a company or business larger by opening new shops, factories etc.: **+into** *The airline has plans for expansion into Asia.* **4** [C] a detailed idea, story etc. that is based on one that is simpler or more general: *The novel is an expansion of an earlier short story.*

ex·pan·sion·ar·y /ɪ'spænʃəˌnɛri/ *adj.* FORMAL ECONOMICS encouraging a business or economy to become bigger and more successful: *the government's expansionary monetary policies*

ex'pansion ˌcard also **ex'pansion ˌboard** *n.* [C] COMPUTERS a piece of electronic equipment that allows a computer to do more things, such as make sounds, receive FAXES, and play CD-ROMS

ex·pan·sion·ism /ɪk'spænʃəˌnɪzəm/ Ac *n.* [U] the practice of increasing the amount of land or power that a country has, used especially when you disapprove of this —**expansionist** *adj.* —**expansionist** *n.* [C]

ex'pansion ˌteam *n.* [C] a new professional sports team in the U.S. whose members usually come from other teams

ex·pan·sive /ɪk'spænsɪv/ Ac *adj.* **1** very large in area, or including a large variety of things: *an expansive view of the beach* | *an expansive selection of food* **2** very friendly and willing to talk a lot: *Our visitors became more expansive after a few beers.* **3** relating to the ability of a business to grow: *expansive economic policies* —**expansively** *adv.* —**expansiveness** *n.* [U]

ex·pat /'ɛksˌpæt/ *n.* [C] INFORMAL an EXPATRIATE

ex·pa·ti·ate /ɛk'speɪʃiˌeɪt/ *v.*

expatiate on/upon sth *phr. v.* FORMAL to speak or write in detail about a particular subject: *Bill likes to expatiate on the benefits of a free market economy.*

ex·pa·tri·ate /ɛks'peɪtriɪt/ *n.* [C] someone who lives in a foreign country —**expatriate** *adj.* [only before noun] *Hong Kong's expatriate community*

ex·pa·tri·a·tion /ɛksˌpeɪtri'eɪʃən/ *n.* [U] a situation in which someone leaves or is forced to leave their country and go to live in another country, especially because they have broken the law —**expatriate** /ɛks'peɪtri,eɪt/ *v.* [T] → see also EXILE

ex·pect /ɪk'spɛkt/ S1 W1 *v.* [T]
1 THINK STH WILL HAPPEN to think that something will happen or will be true, because it seems likely or has been planned: *The police were expecting trouble.* | **expect sb/sth to do sth** *I didn't expect him to stay.* | **expect to do sth** *She expects to graduate next spring.* | **expect (that)** *Analysts expect that stock prices will improve this year.* | *She **fully expected** to be criticized for her decision.* | ***As expected,** Williams won the game* (=everyone knew this would happen). | *This type of weather damage **is to be expected*** (=is not surprising) *with older houses.* | *Change comes **when you least expect it**.*
2 DEMAND to demand that someone do something, especially because it is their duty: *At these prices, I expect better service.* | **expect sb to do sth** *You are expected to return all books by Monday.* | **expect sth of sb/sth** *Good behavior is expected of all our students.* | *Wanda's parents **expect too much of** her* (=think she should do more than she really can). | *I suppose **it was too much to expect** that he'd pay on time.*
3 be expecting (a baby) to be going to have a baby soon: *They're expecting their first child September 5.*
4 THINK to think that you will find that someone or something has a particular quality or does a particular thing: *She's shorter than I expected.*
5 BE WAITING FOR SB/STH to believe that someone or something is going to arrive: *How many people are you expecting?* | *I'm expecting a call from him soon.*
6 what do/can you expect? SPOKEN used to say that something should not surprise you: *"The hotel was awful." "Well, what do you expect for that price?"*
7 how do/can you expect...? used to say that it is unreasonable to think that something will happen or be true: *How can you expect me to study with all that noise?*
8 half expect to think that something might happen, although you know it really will not: *I **half expected** the kids to burn down the house while we were gone.*
9 I expect SPOKEN used to say that you think something is probably true: *I expect you're right.* | *"Do you think he'll go?" "I **expect so**."*
[**Origin:** 1500–1600 Latin *exspectare* **to look forward to**, from *spectare* **to look at**] ▸see THESAURUS box at wait[1]

ex·pect·an·cy /ɪk'spɛktənsi/ *n.* [U] the feeling that something pleasant or exciting is going to happen: *a look of expectancy in the children's eyes* → see also LIFE EXPECTANCY

ex·pect·ant /ɪk'spɛktənt/ *adj.* **1 expectant mother/father/couple** a mother, father etc. whose baby will be born soon **2** hopeful that something good or exciting will happen, or showing this: *an expectant crowd* —**expectantly** *adv.*

ex·pec·ta·tion /,ɛkspɛk'teɪʃən/ S3 W2 *n.* **1** [C usually plural, U] what you think or hope will happen: **expectation that** *We always had the expectation that we would succeed.* | **+of** *expectations of a rise in interest rates* | *The size of the audience was far **below expectations*** (=worse than expected). | *Gina has succeeded **beyond** our **expectations**.* | *Meetings between the two leaders have **raised expectations*** (=made people more hopeful) *that an agreement is likely.* | *Viking fans **have high expectations** for this season* (=they expect the team to be successful). | *Sales results have **exceeded expectations*** (=been much better than expected). | *Sandbags were placed **in expectation of** the river rising another foot.* **2** [C usually plural] a feeling or belief about the way something should be or how someone should behave: *The two partners went into the business with completely different expectations.* | **+of** *He had unrealistic expectations of marriage.* | **meet sb's expectations/live up to sb's expectations** (=be as good as someone thinks it should be)

ex·pect·ed /ɪk'spɛktɪd/ S3 W3 *adj.* [only before noun] **1** an expected event or result is one you think will happen: *an expected daytime temperature of 50 degrees* **2** an expected person or group is one you think will arrive: *an expected crowd of 80,000*

ex·pec·to·rant /ɪk'spɛktərənt/ *n.* [U] MEDICINE a type of medicine that you take to help you cough up PHLEGM (=a sticky substance) from your lungs

ex·pec·to·rate /ɪk'spɛktə,reɪt/ *v.* [I] FORMAL to force liquid out of your mouth SYN spit

ex·pe·di·en·cy /ɪk'spidiənsi/ also **ex·pe·di·ence** /-diəns/ *n. plural* **expediencies** [C,U] what is quickest or most effective to do in a particular situation, rather than what is morally right: *The decision was made on the basis of political expediency.*

ex·pe·di·ent[1] /ɪk'spidiənt/ *adj.* **1** quick and effective, but sometimes not morally right OPP inexpedient: *a politically expedient compromise* **2** useful or appropriate for a particular situation OPP inexpedient: **expedient to do sth** *It proved expedient to fly via Paris rather than London.* —**expediently** *adv.*

expedient[2] *n.* [C] a quick and effective way of dealing with a problem

ex·pe·dite /'ɛkspə,daɪt/ *v.* [T] to make a process, action etc. happen more quickly: *More money would expedite the construction.*

ex·pe·di·tion /,ɛkspə'dɪʃən/ *n.* **1** [C] a long and carefully organized trip, especially to a dangerous or unfamiliar place, or the people that make this trip: *an expedition to the North Pole* ▸see THESAURUS box at trip[1] **2** [C] a short trip, usually made for a particular purpose: *a shopping expedition* **3** [U] the act of doing something more quickly than you would usually

ex·pe·di·tion·ar·y /,ɛkspə'dɪʃə,nɛri/ *adj.* **1 expeditionary army/force etc.** an army, group of soldiers etc. that is sent to a battle in another country **2** relating to an expedition

ex·pe·di·tious·ly /,ɛkspə'dɪʃəsli/ *adv.* FORMAL in a quick and effective way: *The board must resolve this issue expeditiously.* —**expeditious** *adj.*

ex·pel /ɪk'spɛl/ *v.* **expelled**, **expelling** [T] **1** to officially make someone leave a school, organization, country etc., especially because they have broken rules: *The government is trying to expel all foreign journalists.* | **expel sb from sth** *Jakes had been expelled from the Communist Party.* | **expel sb for doing sth** *Leon was expelled for bringing a knife to school.* → see also SUSPEND **2** to force air, water, gas etc. out of something → see also EXPULSION

ex·pend /ɪk'spɛnd/ *v.* [T] FORMAL to use money, time, energy etc. to do something: *Manufacturers have expended a lot of time and effort trying to improve computer security.* | **expend sth on sth** *Billions of dollars have been expended on research.*

ex·pend·a·ble /ɪk'spɛndəbəl/ *adj.* **1** not needed enough to be kept or saved SYN dispensable: *No one's job is safe – everyone is expendable.* **2** able to be spent: *expendable income*

ex·pend·i·ture /ɪk'spɛndətʃɚ/ *n.* [C,U] FORMAL **1** ECONOMICS the total amount of money that a government, organization, or person spends : **+on** *the state's expenditure on welfare* → see also INCOME, PUBLIC FUNDING **2** the action of spending or using time, money, energy etc.: *unnecessary expenditure of time and money*

ex·pense /ɪk'spɛns/ W2 *n.* **1** [C,U] the amount of money that you spend on something: *Most of my paycheck just goes to **living expenses*** (=what it costs to pay for food, a house etc.). | **medical/legal etc. expenses** *He offered to pay my medical expenses.* | *Melissa's parents **spared no expense** on her wedding* (=they spent all the money necessary to buy the best things). | *The airfare is a bona fide **business expense**.* | **go to considerable/great expense** (=spend a lot of money) ▸see THESAURUS box at cost[1] **2 expenses** [plural] money that you spend on travel, hotels, meals etc. as part of your job, and that your employer gives back to you later: *travel expenses* **3 at the expense of sb/sth** if something is done at the expense of someone or something else, it is only achieved by doing something that could harm the other person or thing: *He devoted more and more time to his business at the expense of his*

E

family **4 at sb's expense a)** if you do something at someone's expense, they pay for you to do it: *Several state senators traveled to Asia at taxpayers' expense.* **b)** if you make jokes at someone's expense, you laugh about them and make them seem stupid or silly: *Louis kept making jokes at his wife's expense.* **5 all expenses paid** having all of your costs for hotels, travel, meals etc. paid for by someone else: *The prize was a weekend in Hawaii, all expenses paid.*

ex'pense ac,count *n.* [C] money that is available to someone who works for a company so that they can pay for meals, hotels etc. when traveling or entertaining people for work

ex·pen·sive /ɪk'spɛnsɪv/ S1 W2 *adj.* costing a lot of money: *Gas has gotten really expensive.* | *an expensive restaurant* | **expensive to maintain/keep/run etc.** *Children's hospitals are expensive to run.* —**expensively** *adv.*

E

THESAURUS

high used about prices or amounts that are greater than normal or usual: *Gas prices are very high right now.*
pricey INFORMAL expensive: *a pricey restaurant*
overpriced something that is overpriced is more expensive than it should be: *overpriced souvenirs*
be a ripoff INFORMAL if something is a ripoff, it is more expensive than it should be: *$125 for a shirt. What a ripoff!*
extortionate/astronomical/exorbitant used about things that are much too expensive: *Housing prices in New York are exorbitant.*
fancy used about fashionable restaurants, cars, clothes etc. that look expensive: *a fancy sports car*
posh INFORMAL used about expensive hotels, restaurants, schools etc. that are used by rich people: *a posh five-star hotel*
cost a lot to be expensive: *It costs a lot of money to go to medical school.*
cost a fortune INFORMAL to be very expensive: *It cost a fortune to get the car fixed.*
→ CHEAP

ex·pe·ri·ence¹ /ɪk'spɪriəns/ S1 W1 *n.*
1 KNOWLEDGE/SKILL [U] knowledge or skill that you gain from doing a job or activity, or the process of gaining this: *The job requires two years of teaching experience.* | **+in/with** *Do you have any previous experience in sales?* | *He didn't get the job because of his* ***lack of experience*** *with computers.* | **gain/get experience** *Chuck gained valuable work experience while he was still in college.*
2 KNOWLEDGE OF LIFE [U] knowledge that you gain about life and the world by being in different situations and meeting different people, or the process of gaining this: ***In my experience****, it's best not to discuss politics with Kate.* | **know/learn/speak from experience** *I know from experience that being a parent is not easy.* | **personal/past/first-hand experience** *Robbins wrote a story about climbing based on personal experience.* | **experience shows/suggests that** *Experience shows that older adults can quit smoking as successfully as young ones.*
3 STH THAT HAPPENS [C] something that happens to you or something that you do, especially when this has an effect on what you feel or think: *childhood experiences* | *I* ***had*** *a similar* ***experience*** *last year.* | **+of/with** *Nothing had fully prepared me for the experience of childbirth.* | **+for** *Losing the tournament was a difficult experience for her.* | **a memorable/unforgettable experience** *A trip down the Colorado River is an unforgettable experience.*
4 the American/immigrant/black etc. experience events or knowledge shared by the members of a particular society or group of people
[**Origin:** 1300–1400 French, Latin *experientia* **act of trying**, from *experiri* **to try out**]

experience² S2 W2 *v.* [T] **1** if you experience a problem, event, situation etc., you are involved with it and it influences or affects you: *Many regions are experiencing a shortage of food.* | *As it grew, the city experienced an increase in crime.* | *You have to* ***experience*** *skydiving* ***first hand*** *to know what it's like.* **2** to feel a particular emotion, pain etc.: *You may experience some dizziness after taking the medicine.*

ex·pe·ri·enced /ɪk'spɪriənst/ *adj.* having particular skills or knowledge because you have done something often or for a long time: *an experienced skier* | **+in** *Blake's very experienced in treating sports injuries.*

ex·pe·ri·en·tial /ɪk,spɪri'ɛnʃəl/ *adj.* based on experience, or relating to experience: *experiential approaches to learning*

ex·per·i·ment¹ /ɪk'spɛrəmənt/ S3 W3 *n.* [C,U] **1** a scientific test that can be repeated at another time, done to find out how something will react in a particular situation, or to find out if a particular idea is true: *medical experiments* | **+on/with** *laboratory experiments on animals* | **an experiment to see/test/learn etc.** *an experiment to test the ability of dogs to see color* | **carry out/perform/conduct/do an experiment** *They are doing experiments to learn more about the effects of alcohol.* **2** a process in which you try a new idea, method etc. to find out if it is useful or effective: *I decided to try a little experiment to see if it was quicker to walk to work.* | **+in** *an experiment in communal living* [**Origin:** 1300–1400 Old French, Latin *experimentum*, from *experiri* **to try out**]

ex·per·i·ment² /ɪk'spɛrə,mɛnt/ *v.* [I] **1** to try using various ideas, methods, materials etc. to find out how good or effective they are: **+with** *Artists like to experiment with different media.* **2** to do a scientific test to find out if a particular idea is true or to obtain more information: **+on** *The lab experiments on rats and guinea pigs.* **3** to try something such as an illegal drug or sex to find out what it feels like: **+with** *Several politicians admitted experimenting with marijuana.* —**experimenter** *n.* [C]

ex·per·i·men·tal /ɪk,spɛrə'mɛntəl/ *adj.* **1** used for, relating to, or resulting from experiments: *an experimental drug* | *experimental research* **2** using new ideas or methods: *an experimental theater group* —**experimentally** *adv.*

ex,perimental proba'bility *n.* [U] MATH the number of times an event actually happens in a test, considered in relation to the number of tests carried out to find out if the event will happen

ex·per·i·men·ta·tion /ɪk,spɛrəmɛn'teɪʃən/ *n.* [U] **1** the process of testing various ideas, methods, materials etc. to find out how good or effective they are: **+with/in** *experimentation with computer-assisted language learning* **2** the process of performing scientific tests to find out if a particular idea is true or to obtain more information: **+on** *medical experimentation on cats* **3** the activity of trying something such as an illegal drug or sex to find out what it feels like

ex·pert¹ /'ɛkspət/ Ac W2 *n.* [C] someone who has a special skill or special knowledge of a subject, gained as a result of training or experience: **+on/in** *an expert on ancient Egyptian art* | **+at** *Mrs. Taus became an expert at making desserts.* | **a medical/technical/legal etc. expert** *Legal experts say the ruling will likely be overturned.* [**Origin:** Old French, Latin *expertus*, past participle of *experiri* **to try out**]

THESAURUS

specialist someone who knows a lot about something because she or he has studied it for a long time: *the school's reading specialist*
authority someone who is very respected because she or he knows more about a subject than other people: *the senator who is the leading authority on welfare policies*
connoisseur someone who knows a lot about something such as art, food, or music: *a connoisseur of fine wines*
buff used after a noun to mean someone who knows a lot about something such as movies or music: *a film buff*

expert² Ac *adj.* **1** having a special skill or special knowledge of a subject: *an expert watchmaker* **2** relating to or coming from an expert: *expert advice* | *They worked under the* ***expert eye*** *of their professor.* —**expertly** *adv.* —**expertness** *n.* [U]

ex·per·tise /ˌɛkspɚˈtiz/ Ac *n.* [U] special skills or knowledge in a particular subject, that you learn by experience or training: *medical expertise* | **+in** *expertise in hotel management* | **the expertise to do sth** *Many individuals do not have the expertise to make wise investments.*

ˌexpert ˈsystem *n.* [C] COMPUTERS a computer system containing a lot of information about one particular subject, so that it can help someone find an answer to a problem

ˌexpert ˈwitness *n.* [C] someone with special knowledge about a subject who is asked to give their opinion about something relating to that subject in a court of law

ex·pi·ate /ˈɛkspiˌeɪt/ *v.* [T] FORMAL to do something to show that you are sorry and to improve the situation after you have done something wrong: *Maybe he was looking for a way to expiate his guilt.* —**expiation** /ˌɛkspiˈeɪʃən/ *n.* [U]

ex·pi·ra·tion /ˌɛkspəˈreɪʃən/ *n.* [U] the end of a period of time during which an official document or agreement is allowed to be used: *the expiration of the treaty*

expiˈration date *n.* [C] the date after which something is not safe to eat or cannot be used or sold anymore: *Write in the credit card number and the expiration date.*

ex·pire /ɪkˈspaɪɚ/ *v.* [I] **1** if a document, agreement, contract etc. expires, it cannot be legally used anymore: **+on/at/in** *My driver's license expires on October 12.* **2** if a period of time when someone has a particular authority expires, it ends: *The mayor's term of office expires at the end of March.* **3** LITERARY to die **4** FORMAL to breathe out air SYN **exhale**

ex·plain /ɪkˈspleɪn/ S1 W1 *v.* **1** [T] to describe something in a way that makes it clear or easier to understand: *Our lawyer carefully explained the process.* | *It's not that complicated – let me explain.* | **explain sth to sb** *Could you explain the rules to me again?* | **explain (to sb) why/how/what etc.** *The guide explains how to identify edible mushrooms.* | **explain that** *The doctor explained that my ear problem was related to my sinuses.*

> **THESAURUS**
>
> **tell** to give someone facts or information in speech or writing: *Dan told me about the meeting.*
> **show** to tell someone how to do something or where something is: *Ellen showed me how to work the coffee maker.*
> **demonstrate** to show or describe how to use or do something: *Demonstrate the experiment first, then get the students to try.*
> **go through sth** to explain something carefully, especially one step at a time: *Mrs. Riddell went through the homework assignment.*

2 [I,T] to give a reason for something, or to be a reason for it: *Wait! I can explain.* | *How can you explain this sort of behavior?* | **explain why/how/what etc.** *Let me explain why I don't believe your story.* | **explain that** *Marta explained that she had been sick.* **3** [T] to be the piece of information that helps someone understand the reason for something: *Oh, I see. That explains it.* | **explain why/how/what etc.** *He was obviously drunk, which explains why he was acting strange.* **4 explain yourself a)** to tell someone who is angry or upset with you the reasons why you did something: *I think you'd better explain yourself.* **b)** to say clearly what you mean: *I'm sorry. I guess I didn't explain myself very well.* [**Origin:** 1500–1600 Latin *explanare* **to make level, unfold**, from *planus* **level, flat**]

explain sth ↔ **away** *phr. v.* to make something seem less important, or not your fault, by giving reasons for it: *Children will often try to explain away bruises caused by abuse.*

ex·pla·na·tion /ˌɛkspləˈneɪʃən/ W3 *n.* **1** [C,U] the reasons you give for why something happened or why you did something: *Were you satisfied with his explanation?* | **+for/of** *There was no apparent explanation for the attack.* | **give/provide an explanation** *There was a long delay for which no explanation has been given.* | *I think you* ***owe*** *him an* ***explanation.*** ►see THESAURUS box at **reason**[1] **2** [C] what you say or write to make something easier to understand: *a detailed scientific explanation* | **+of** *She gave the kids an explanation of how butter was made.*

ex·plan·a·to·ry /ɪkˈsplænəˌtɔri/ *adj.* giving information about something or describing how something works, in order to make it easier to understand: *explanatory pamphlets* → see also SELF-EXPLANATORY

ex·ple·tive /ˈɛkspləṭɪv/ *n.* [C] FORMAL a strong impolite word that you use when you are angry or in pain, for example "DAMN" [**Origin:** 1600–1700 Late Latin *expletivus*, from Latin *explere* **to fill out**; because the words fill a space in a sentence without adding to the meaning]

ex·pli·ca·ble /ɪkˈsplɪkəbəl, ˈɛksplɪ-/ *adj.* [often in negatives] able to be easily understood or explained OPP **inexplicable**

ex·pli·cate /ˈɛkspləˌkeɪt/ *v.* [T] FORMAL to explain a work of literature, an idea etc. in detail: *It's not easy to explicate a poem.* —**explication** /ˌɛkspləˈkeɪʃən/ *n.* [C,U]

ex·plic·it /ɪkˈsplɪsɪt/ Ac *adj.* **1** language or pictures that are explicit describe or show sex or violence very clearly: *movies with explicit love scenes* **2** expressed in a way that is very clear: *explicit instructions* → see also IMPLICIT **3** very clear and direct in what you say: *Be explicit when you talk about money with your family.* | **+about** *Angela was very explicit about her reasons for wanting a divorce.* —**explicitly** *adv.* —**explicitness** *n.* [U]

exˌplicit ˈformula also **exˌplicit ˌformula of a ˈsequence** *n.* [C] MATH a FORMULA for calculating the value of any TERM in a mathematical SEQUENCE

exˌplicit ˈteaching *n.* [U] a method of teaching in which a teacher clearly leads students through each step of what is being taught

ex·plode /ɪkˈsploʊd/ W3 *v.*

1 BURST [I,T] to burst into small pieces, usually making a loud noise and causing damage, or to make something do this → see also IMPLODE SYN **blow up**: *A car exploded in a crowded street this morning, killing five people.* | *Police were called in to explode the bomb.*

2 INCREASE SUDDENLY [I] to suddenly increase greatly in number, amount, or degree: *Florida's population exploded after World War II.*

3 GET ANGRY [I] to suddenly become angry: *When the sales manager gave the job to Jane, Frank exploded.* | **+with/into** *Without warning, she exploded into rage.*

4 BECOME DANGEROUS [I] if a situation explodes, it is suddenly not controlled anymore, and is often violent: *Riots could explode at any time.* | **+in/with/into** *The continued tension could explode into more violence.*

5 explode the myth to prove that something which is believed by many people is actually wrong or not true: *The report explodes the myth that pollution is only a problem for rich countries.*

6 MAKE A LOUD NOISE [I] to make a very loud noise: *A clap of thunder exploded overhead.* | **+into** *The entire room exploded into applause.*

7 DO STH SUDDENLY [I] to suddenly begin moving or doing something very quickly: **+into** *Startled, the birds exploded into flight.*

[**Origin:** 1500–1600 Latin *explodere* **to drive off the stage by clapping**, from *plaudere* **to clap**]

exˌploded ˈview *n.* [C] TECHNICAL a drawing, model etc. that shows the parts of something separately, but in a way that shows how they are related or put together

ex·ploit[1] /ɪkˈsplɔɪt/ Ac *v.* [T] **1** DISAPPROVING to treat someone unfairly in order to earn money or gain an advantage: *Many employers exploit illegal workers.* **2** DISAPPROVING to use a situation for your own advan-

E

tage, even when this is morally wrong: *Extremists try to exploit people's fears.* **3** to use something effectively: *The new hotel failed to exploit its prime location.* **4** to develop and use minerals, forests, oil etc. for business or industry: *We need to do a better job of exploiting our natural resources.* [**Origin:** 1500–1600 Old French *esploit* **result, success**, from Latin *explicitus*] —**exploitable** *adj.* —**exploiter** *n.* [C]

ex·ploit² /ˈɛksplɔɪt/ Ac *n.* [C usually plural] a brave, exciting, and interesting action: *stories about the sailor's exploits*

ex·ploi·ta·tion /ˌɛksplɔɪˈteɪʃən/ Ac *n.* [U] **1** DISAPPROVING a situation in which someone treats someone else unfairly in order to earn money or gain an advantage: +**of** *the exploitation of child workers* **2** the development and use of minerals, forests, oil etc. for business or industry: +**of** *the controlled exploitation of the rainforests* **3** DISAPPROVING an attempt to use a situation for your own advantage, even when this is morally wrong: +**of** *the exploitation of religion for political ends* **4** the effective use of something: +**of** *the exploitation of new business opportunities*

ex·ploit·a·tive /ɪkˈsplɔɪt̬ət̬ɪv/ *adj.* treating people unfairly to earn money or gain an advantage: *a sexually exploitative movie*

ex·plo·ra·tion /ˌɛkspləˈreɪʃən/ *n.* **1 a)** [U] the process of traveling through a place in order to find out about it or find something such as oil or gold in it: *oil exploration* | +**of** *the exploration of space* **b)** [C] a trip that is made in order to do this: *explorations of the Japan Sea* **2** [C,U] the act of trying to find out more about something by discussing it, thinking about it etc.: +**of/into** *an exploration of spiritual issues*

ex·plo·ra·to·ry /ɪkˈsplɔrəˌtɔri/ *adj.* done in order to find out more about something: *exploratory surgery*

ex·plore /ɪkˈsplɔr/ W3 *v.* **1** [I,T] to travel around an unfamiliar area to find out what it is like: *We explored the city on foot.* | **explore (sth) for oil/gold/minerals etc.** *The company has been exploring for oil in Algeria for years.* **2** [T] to discuss, examine, or think about something carefully: *Maybe we should explore this idea further.* | *I want to* ***explore the possiblity*** *of part-time work.* [**Origin:** 1500–1600 Latin *explorare*, from *plorare* **to cry out**]

ex·plor·er /ɪkˈsplɔrə/ *n.* [C] someone who travels through an area about which little is known or which has not been visited before

ex·plo·sion /ɪkˈsploʊʒən/ W3 *n.* **1** [C,U] the action of something exploding, or the act of making something explode: *a nuclear explosion* | +**of** *No one has claimed responsibility for the explosion of the bomb.* **2** [C] a sudden or quick increase in the number or amount of something: *a population explostion* | +**of** *an explosion of interest in Latin music and dance* | +**in** *an explosion in housing prices* **3** [C] a sudden increase in anger, violence, disagreement etc.: *an explosion of rage* **4** [C] a sudden very loud noise: *an explosion of laughter*

ex·plo·sive¹ /ɪkˈsploʊsɪv/ *adj.* **1** able or likely to explode: *Dynamite is* ***highly explosive.*** | *an explosive device* (=that can explode or make a bomb explode) **2** likely to suddenly become violent: *an explosive situation* | *a man with an explosive temper* **3** able to make people argue and become angry: *the explosive issue of abortion* **4** increasing suddenly or quickly in amount, number, or degree: *the explosive growth of the computer industry* **5** relating to or like an explosion: *an explosive force of 15,000 tons of TNT* —**explosively** *adv.* —**explosiveness** *n.* [U]

explosive² *n.* [C] a substance that can cause an explosion → see also HIGH EXPLOSIVE, PLASTIC EXPLOSIVE

ex·po /ˈɛkspoʊ/ *n.* [C] INFORMAL an EXPOSITION

ex·po·nent /ɪkˈspoʊnənt, ˈɛkspoʊ-/ *n.* [C] **1** someone who supports or explains an idea, belief etc.: +**of** *an early exponent of the theory* → see also PROPONENT **2** MATH a sign written above and to the right of a number or letter to show how many times that quantity is to be multiplied by itself, for example 2^2 **3** someone whose work or methods provide a good example of a particular skill, idea, or activity: +**of** *The poet is a supreme exponent of the Romantic style.*

ex·po·nen·tial /ˌɛkspəˈnɛnʃəl/ *adj.* **1 exponential growth/increase** a rate of growth that becomes faster as the amount of the thing that is growing increases: *Analysts agree the tax-deferred funds are a major force behind the exponential growth in stock prices.* | *the exponential growth of the world's population* **2** MATH using a sign that shows how many times a number is to be multiplied by itself, such as y^3 —**exponentially** *adv.*

expoˌnential eˈquation *n.* [C] MATH an EQUATION in which an EXPONENT (=sign that shows how many times a number is to be multiplied by itself) includes a VARIABLE (=mathematical quantity that can represent several different amounts). Exponential equations are solved by finding the LOGARITHM of each side of the equation.

expoˌnential ˈfunction *n.* [C] MATH a mathematical FUNCTION in which the original quantity is multiplied by the same number a particular number of times → see also LOGARITHMIC FUNCTION

ex·port¹ /ˈɛkspɔrt/ Ac W3 *n.* **1** [U] the business of selling and sending goods to other countries OPP **import**: +**of** *the export of manufactured goods* | *The crops are grown mainly* ***for export.*** | *Mexico is California's third largest* ***export market.*** **2** [C] a product that is sold and sent to another country OPP **import**: *Wheat is one of our country's chief exports.*

ex·port² /ɛkˈspɔrt, ˈɛkspɔrt/ Ac *v.* **1** [I,T] to sell and send goods to another country OPP **import**: **export sth to sb** *The U.S. hopes to export more cars to Asia next year.* ▸see THESAURUS box at **sell¹** **2** [T] to introduce an activity, idea etc. to another place or country OPP **import**: *The Italian style of cooking has been exported all over the world.* **3** [T] COMPUTERS to move computer information from a computer or computer program you are working on to another one OPP **import** [**Origin:** 1400–1500 Latin *exportare*, from *portare* **to carry**] —**exportation** /ˌɛkspɔrˈteɪʃən/ *n.* [U]

ex·port·er /ɪkˈspɔrt̬ə, ˈɛkspɔrt̬ə/ Ac *n.* [C] a person, company, or country that sells and sends goods to another country OPP **importer**

ex·pose /ɪkˈspoʊz/ Ac W3 *v.* [T]

1 PUT IN DANGER to put someone or something in a situation or position where something could affect them, usually something harmful or unpleasant: **expose sb/sth to sth** *Workers charge that the company exposed them to toxic chemicals.* | *The colors will fade if they are exposed to sunlight.*

2 SHOW to uncover or show something that is usually covered or not able to be seen: *The boy lifted his T-shirt to expose a scar across his belly.*

3 LET SB EXPERIENCE STH to make it possible for someone to experience ideas, events, methods etc. that are new to them: **expose sb to sth** *Many children are never exposed to classical music.*

4 TELL THE TRUTH to tell people the truth about an event or situation that is not acceptable, especially because it involves something dishonest or illegal: *Two reporters exposed corruption in Philadelphia's court system.* | **expose sb as sth** *He was exposed as a spy.*

5 expose yourself to deliberately show your sexual organs to someone in a public place, usually because of mental illness

6 MAKE A PHOTOGRAPH to allow light onto a piece of film in a camera in order to take a photograph

7 SHOW FEELINGS to show other people feelings that you usually hide, especially when this is not planned: *I'm afraid to expose my innermost thoughts and emotions to anyone.*

[**Origin:** 1400–1500 French *exposer*, from Latin *exponere* **to put out, explain**] → see also EXPOSURE

ex·po·sé /ˌɛkspoʊˈzeɪ/ *n.* [C] a television program, newspaper story, or movie that tells people the truth about an event or situation in which someone did something dishonest or illegal: +**of** *an exposé of human rights abuses*

ex·posed /ɪkˈspoʊzd/ Ac *adj.* not covered or protected from harm or danger: *All exposed skin should be covered with protective cream.*

ex·po·si·tion /ˌɛkspəˈzɪʃən/ *n.* **1** [C] a large public event at which you show or sell products, art etc.: *the Chicago International Art Exposition* **2** [C,U] the act of giving a clear and detailed explanation, or the explanation itself: *a professor of Bible exposition* **3** [U] ENG. LANG. ARTS a type of writing or speech that explains something → see also DESCRIPTION, NARRATION, PERSUASION

ex·pos·i·to·ry /ɪkˈspɑzəˌtɔri/ *adj.* ENG. LANG. ARTS relating to exposition in writing or speech: *expository writing*

ex post fac·to law /ˌɛks poʊst ˌfæktoʊ ˈlɔ/ *n.* [C] LAW LAW a law that makes a particular action into a crime, and then punishes people who took that action before it had legally become a crime

ex·pos·tu·late /ɪkˈspɑstʃəˌleɪt/ *v.* [I] FORMAL to say something angrily because you do not agree with something, disapprove of it, or are not satisfied with it

ex·po·sure /ɪkˈspoʊʒə/ Ac *n.*
1 DANGER [C,U] the state of being put into a harmful or bad situation or position without having any protection against what may happen: *radiation exposure* | **+to** *Skin cancer is often caused by too much exposure to the sun.*
2 EXPERIENCE [C,U] the opportunity to experience ideas, events, methods etc. that are new to you: **+to** *Exposure to a second language should take place in elementary school.*
3 TRUTH [C,U] the action of telling people about a dishonest person, event, or situation: *By talking about the affair he risked exposure.* | **+of** *the newspaper's exposure of the school scandal*
4 PUBLIC ATTENTION [U] things that are said and written on television and in newspapers that make a person or event known to a lot of people: *media exposure* | *The issue of bullying at school has* ***gotten*** *a lot of* ***exposure*** *recently.*
5 EFFECT OF COLD WEATHER [U] the harmful effects on your body that happen when you stay outside for a long time when the weather is extremely cold: *Three climbers died of exposure in the Himalayas this weekend.*
6 PHOTOGRAPHY a) [C] a length of film in a camera that is used for producing one photograph: *a roll of 36-exposure film* (=that has enough space for 36 photographs to be taken) **b)** [C] the amount of time a piece of film is EXPOSED to the light when making a photograph: *a timed exposure*
7 DIRECTION [C usually singular] the direction in which a building, hill etc. faces: *a room with a southern exposure*
8 BUSINESS RISK [C,U] the amount of financial risk that a company has
9 SHOW [C] the act of exposing or showing something that is usually covered or unable to be seen → see also INDECENT EXPOSURE

ex·pound /ɪkˈspaʊnd/ *v.* [I,T] FORMAL to explain or talk about something in detail: **+on/upon** *texts that expound on Jewish beliefs*

ex·press[1] /ɪkˈsprɛs/ S3 W2 *v.* [T]
1 FEELINGS to tell or show what you are thinking or feeling by using words, actions, looks etc.: *She doesn't express her emotions as much as he does.* | **express sth in/by/through sth** *Your father may be expressing his wish to die by refusing to eat.* | **express yourself** *It's hard sometimes for children to express themselves* (=say what they think or feel). | **express your views/opinions** *Even people who knew little about the subject were ready to express their opinions.* | *She* ***expressed an interest in*** *seeing the old map.* | **express gratitude/thanks for sth** *Hector expressed his thanks for the help the community had given his family.* | ***Words cannot express*** (=it is impossible to describe) *how much we miss her.* ►see THESAURUS box at say[1]
2 sth expresses itself if a feeling expresses itself, it becomes noticeable: *Sometimes public outrage expresses itself in extreme ways.*
3 WORDS/ART/MUSIC to show or describe a particular feeling: *Many of Munch's paintings express a deep feeling of despair.*
4 MATHEMATICS to show a mathematical idea in a particular form: *Express three-quarters as a decimal.*
5 SEND to send something using a service that will deliver it very quickly: *I'll express the documents to her.*
6 MILK if a woman expresses milk, she presses milk out of her breast in order to feed it to her baby later
[**Origin:** 1300–1400 Early French *expresser*, from Latin *expressus*, past participle of *exprimere* **to press out**]

express[2] *adj.* [only before noun] **1** designed to help you move through a place more quickly: *express lanes on the freeway* **2** sent more quickly than usual: *an express package* **3 express train/bus** a train or bus that does not stop in many places and therefore can travel more quickly → see also LOCAL TRAIN/BUS **4** an express command, desire, aim etc. is very clear and very specific, so that everyone understands exactly what it means: *It was her express wish that you inherit her house.* → see also EXPRESSLY

E

express[3] *n.* **1** [C usually singular] a train or bus that does not stop in many places, and can therefore travel more quickly → see also LOCAL **2** [U] a service that delivers letters and packages very quickly: *We'll send it by express.* → see also EXPRESS MAIL

express[4] *adv.* **send/deliver sth express** to send or deliver a letter, package etc. quickly using a special mail service

exˌpressed ˈpowers *n.* [plural] POLITICS the powers given to the U.S government that are clearly stated in the CONSTITUTION SYN **enumerated powers** → see also DELEGATED POWERS, IMPLIED POWERS, INHERENT POWERS

ex·pres·sion /ɪkˈsprɛʃən/ S3 W2 *n.*
1 A LOOK [C] a look on someone's face that shows what they are thinking or feeling: *facial expressions* | *His expression became serious as he listened to her story.* | **+of** *an expression of mild amusement*
2 WORDS/ACTIONS ETC. [C,U] something you say, write, do, or make that shows what you think or feel: **+of** *Crying is an acceptable and healthy expression of grief.* | *Student leaders also have demanded greater* ***freedom of expression*** (=the right to say what you think without being punished). | **political/artistic/religious expression** *Painting is her main means of artistic expression.* | *The film* ***gave expression to*** *the way many people in her community felt.*
3 A WORD/PHRASE [C] ENG. LANG. ARTS a word or phrase that is used to express a particular idea or feeling: *You use the expression "break a leg" to wish an actor good luck.* ►see THESAURUS box at phrase[1]
4 MUSIC [U] ENG. LANG. ARTS the quality of singing or playing a musical instrument with feeling: *Try to put a little more expression into the slow passage.*
5 MATHEMATICS [C] a sign or group of signs that show a mathematical idea in a particular form: *$x^3 + 4$ is an algebraic expression.*
6 (if you'll) pardon/forgive/excuse the expression SPOKEN said when you have used a word that you think may offend someone: *He's a pain in the butt, if you'll pardon the expression.*

ex·pres·sion·ism /ɪkˈsprɛʃəˌnɪzəm/ *n.* [U] ENG. LANG. ARTS a style of art and literature that uses unusual images, colors, and forms to emphasize feelings, rather than showing images or telling stories in a traditional way —**expressionist** *n.* [C] —**expressionist** *adj.*

ex·pres·sion·less /ɪkˈsprɛʃənlɪs/ *adj.* an expressionless face, feature, or voice does not show what someone thinks or feels: *dark expressionless eyes* —**expressionlessly** *adv.*

ex·pres·sive /ɪkˈsprɛsɪv/ *adj.* **1** showing what someone thinks or feels: *She has large, expressive eyes.* **2 be expressive of sth** showing a particular feeling or influence: *Art deco designs are expressive of the modern technology of the 1920s.* —**expressiveness** *n.* [U] —**expressively** *adv.*

ex·press·ly /ɪkˈsprɛsli/ *adv.* FORMAL **1** in a detailed or exact way: *Congress had* ***expressly forbidden*** *sending arms to the region.* **2** for a specific purpose: *The building is expressly designed to conserve energy.*

ex'press ˌmail *n.* [U] a mail service that delivers letters and packages very quickly

ex·press·way /ɪk'spresˌweɪ/ *n.* [C] a wide road in a city on which cars can travel very quickly without stopping → see also FREEWAY

ex·pro·pri·ate /ɛks'proʊpriˌeɪt/ *v.* [T] FORMAL LAW to take away someone's private property, especially for public use: *The city wanted to expropriate a three-mile strip along the river.* —**expropriation** /ɛksˌproʊpri'eɪʃən/ *n.* [C, U]

ex·pul·sion /ɪk'spʌlʃən/ *n.* [C,U] FORMAL **1** the official act of making someone leave a country, school, organization etc.: **+from** *All the students responsible for the prank face expulsion from school.* **2** the process of sending a person or group of people away from a place, often by using force: **+from** *the expulsion of rebel forces from the area* **3** the act of forcing air, water, or gas out of something: **+from** *the expulsion of air from the lungs* → see also EXPEL

E

ex·punge /ɪk'spʌndʒ/ *v.* [T] FORMAL **1** to remove something such as a name or piece of information from a list, book etc.: *Their criminal records were expunged in return for their testimony.* **2** to forget something bad: **expunge sth from sth** *Howard tried to expunge the whole episode from his memory.*

ex·pur·gat·ed /'ɛkspɚˌgeɪt̬ɪd/ *adv.* FORMAL an expurgated book, play etc. has had some parts removed because they are considered harmful or offensive OPP **unexpurgated**: *an expurgated version of "A Streetcar Named Desire"* → see also ABRIDGED —**expurgate** *v.* [T]

ex·quis·ite /ɪk'skwɪzɪt, 'ɛkskwɪ-/ *adj.* **1** extremely beautiful or delicate, and seeming to be perfect: *an exquisite piece of jewelry* **2** very sensitive and nearly perfect in the way you do things, or showing this: *Sophie has exquisite taste.* **3** LITERARY exquisite pain or pleasure is felt extremely strongly [**Origin:** 1500–1600 Latin *exquisitus*, past participle of *exquirere* **to search out**] —**exquisitely** *adv.* —**exquisiteness** *n.* [U]

ext. *n.* the written abbreviation of EXTENSION

ex·tant /'ɛkstənt, ɛk'stænt/ *adj.* FORMAL still existing in spite of being very old SYN **surviving**: *one of the few extant manuscripts*

ex·tem·po·ra·ne·ous /ɪkˌstɛmpə'reɪniəs, ɛk-/ *adj.* spoken or done without any preparation or practice: *an extemporaneous speech* —**extemporaneously** *adv.*

ex·tem·po·re /ɪk'stɛmpəri/ *adj.* FORMAL spoken or done without any preparation or practice: *extempore remarks* —**extempore** *adv.*

ex·tem·po·rize /ɪk'stɛmpəˌraɪz/ *v.* [I] FORMAL to speak without preparation, especially during a performance SYN **ad-lib** —**extemporization** /ɪkˌstɛmpərə'zeɪʃən/ *n.* [C,U]

ex·tend /ɪk'stɛnd/ S3 W2 *v.*

1 AFFECT MORE THAN BEFORE [T] to make something affect more people, situations, areas etc. than before: *Derkin vows to fight any effort to extend sales taxes on food.* | **extend sth to sb/sth** *The government is looking for ways to extend health care to all Americans.*

2 CONTINUE LONGER [I always + adv./prep., T] to continue to happen or exist for a longer period of time than planned or expected, or to make something do this: *The committee has agreed to extend the deadline.* | **extend sth for/by/until etc.** *The current contract will be extended to next year.* | **+for/into/over etc.** *The hot weather extended into late September.* ►see THESAURUS box at **prolong**

3 REACH/SPREAD [I always + adv./prep.] to reach a particular distance, or spread over a particular area: **+across/over/through etc.** *The forest extends across 7,500 acres.* | **extend 5 inches/six feet/40 miles etc. from sth** *The shelf extends six inches from the wall.*

4 AFFECT/INCLUDE [I always + adv./prep.] to affect or include people, things, or places: **+to/beyond/over etc.** *His influence extends far beyond the company where he works.*

5 OFFER/GIVE [T] FORMAL to offer or give help, sympathy, thanks etc. to someone: *We'd like to* ***extend a warm welcome to*** *our Mongolian visitors.* | *A German bank has* ***extended credit to*** *the city for most of the cost of the project* (=has allowed it to borrow money).

6 ARMS/LEGS ETC. [T] to stretch out a part of your body: *"Hello, Tom," he said, extending his hand.*

7 MAKE STH BIGGER [T] to make a room, building, road etc. bigger or longer: *The developer plans to extend Thomas Road to meet 10th Street.* | **extend sth by sth** *We plan to extend the kitchen by six feet.*

8 extend your lead (to/by sth) to increase the number of points, games etc. by which one person or team is ahead of other competitors: *With the shot, the team extended its lead to 77–66.*

9 FURNITURE [I,T] if a table, LADDER etc. extends, or you can extend it, it can be made longer

[**Origin:** 1300–1400 Latin *extendere*, from *tendere* **to stretch**] → see also OVEREXTEND

ex·tend·ed /ɪk'stɛndɪd/ *adj.* [only before noun] **1** an extended period of time is fairly long or longer than expected: *an extended business trip* **2** long and detailed: *an extended analysis of the movie*

exˌtended 'family *n.* [C] a family group that includes not only parents and children but also grandparents, AUNTS, UNCLES etc. → see also NUCLEAR FAMILY

ex·ten·sion /ɪk'stɛnʃən/ S3 *n.*

1 MORE TIME [C] an additional period of time that is given to do something: *a contract extension* | **+on** *My professor gave me a one-week extension on my paper.*

2 TELEPHONE a) [C] one of many telephone lines connected to a central system in a large building such as an office, which all have different numbers: *Hello, I'd like extension 2807, please.* **b)** [C] one of the telephones in a house that all have the same number

3 MAKING STH BIGGER/LONGER [C,U] the process of making something bigger or longer, or the part that is added in this process: *The city is building an extension to the subway line.*

4 by extension used to say that something that is true about one thing is also true about another thing that is related to it: *Women lawyers, and by extension all professional women, looked for ways to balance family and work.*

5 AFFECTING MORE [singular, U] the development of something in order to make it affect more people, situations, areas etc. than before: **+of** *an extension of copyright laws to cover on-line materials*

6 DEVELOPMENT FROM STH [C] something that develops from a particular custom, activity, idea etc.: **+of** *Business entertainment seems a natural extension of Japan's gift-giving culture.*

7 UNIVERSITY/COLLEGE [U] part of a university or college that offers courses to people who are not regular students: *an extension course*

8 COMPUTER [C] a set of three letters that follow the name of a computer FILE to show what type of file it is. For example, the extension ".doc" shows that a file is a written document.

9 OFFERING/GIVING [U] FORMAL the act of offering or giving something to someone: *the extension of credit to newer customers*

10 HAIR extensions long pieces of artificial hair that can be fastened to your own hair to make it look longer

11 STRETCHING AN ARM/LEG ETC. [U] the position of a part of the body when it is stretched, or the process of stretching it

ex'tension cord *n.* [C] an additional electric CORD that you attach to another cord to make it longer

ex·ten·sive /ɪk'stɛnsɪv/ W3 *adj.* **1** containing a lot of information, details, work etc.: *extensive research into the effects of stress* **2** very large in size, amount, or degree: *Logging has caused extensive damage to the forests.* —**extensively** *adv.*: *He read extensively on the subject.* —**extensiveness** *n.* [U]

ex·tent /ɪk'stɛnt/ S3 W3 *n.* **1** [singular] how large, important, or serious something is, especially something such as a problem or injury: **+of** *the extent of American influence in Europe* | *We were shocked by the* ***full extent*** *of the damage.* **2** [singular] used to talk about how true something is or how great an effect or change is: *The schools have deteriorated* ***to such an***

extent that they are unsafe. | *Violence increased* ***to the extent that*** (=so much that) *people were afraid to leave their homes.* | **to a great/large extent** *To a large extent, he owed his sporting career to his father.* | **to a certain extent/to some extent/to an extent** (=partly) *I agree with him to a certain extent.* | *They examined* ***the extent to which*** (=how much) *age affected language-learning ability.* | ***To what extent*** (=how much) *did she influence his decision?* | **to a greater/lesser extent** *All the schools were, to a greater or lesser extent, run by the church.* **3** [U] the length or size of something: *the extent of the palace grounds* | *a small wildlife refuge, four acres* ***in extent***

ex·ten·u·at·ing /ɪkˈstɛnyuˌeɪt̬ɪŋ/ *adj.* **extenuating circumstances** FORMAL facts about a situation which make a wrong or illegal action easier to understand or excuse —**extenuate** *v.* [T]

ex·te·ri·or¹ /ɪkˈstɪriɚ/ *n.* [C] **1** [usually singular] the outside surface of something, especially a building OPP **interior**: *the exterior of a house* **2** behavior that others see, but which often hides a different feeling or attitude: *Belle finds a sweet soul behind his gruff exterior.* **3** an outdoor scene in a picture, part of a movie etc. OPP **interior**

exterior² *adj.* **1** on the outside of something SYN **outer** OPP **interior**: *the car's sleek exterior design* **2** appropriate for use outside OPP **interior**: *exterior paint* **3** exterior scenes in a movie are filmed outdoors OPP **interior**

exˌterior ˈangle *n.* [C] MATH an angle outside a POLYGON (=flat shape with straight sides) that is formed from one of the sides of the polygon and a line continuing out from a side that is next to the first side → see also INTERIOR ANGLE

ex·ter·mi·nate /ɪkˈstɚməˌneɪt/ *v.* [T] to kill large numbers of a particular group of people, animals, or insects of a particular type SYN **eliminate**: *ranchers trying to exterminate prairie dogs* —**extermination** /ɪkˌstɚməˈneɪʃən/ *n.* [C,U]

ex·ter·mi·na·tor /ɪkˈstɚməˌneɪt̬ɚ/ *n.* [C] someone whose job is to kill insects or small animals that have been causing problems in buildings

ex·tern /ˈɛkstɚn/ *n.* [C] a university student who works in a particular type of job for a short time in order to gain experience of that type of work → INTERN

ex·ter·nal /ɪkˈstɚnl/ Ac *adj.* **1** coming from outside something such as an organization, group, or business OPP **internal**: *He faced external pressure to resign.* | *information from external sources* **2** relating to the outside of something OPP **internal**: *This medicine is* ***for external use only*** (=to be used on the outside of the body and not swallowed). **3** relating to a person or thing's environment or situation, rather than to its own qualities, ideas etc.: *The surface of Mercury has largely been shaped by external forces.* | *Men and women face external pressure to conform to society.* **4** relating to foreign countries OPP **internal**: *external affairs* [**Origin:** 1500–1600 Latin *externus*, from *exter* **on the outside**] —**externally** *adv.*

exˌternal fertiliˈzation *n.* [U] BIOLOGY a process in which an egg cell (=cell that can become a baby) combines with SPERM (=male cells) on the outside of a female's body, for example in some fish → see also INTERNAL FERTILIZATION

ex·ter·nal·ize /ɪkˈstɚnlˌaɪz/ Ac *v.* [T] FORMAL to express your feelings in words or actions OPP **internalize** —**externalization** /ɪkˌstɚnl-əˈzeɪʃən/ *n.* [C,U]

ex·ter·nals /ɪkˈstɚnlz/ *n.* [plural] the way that a situation or thing appears to be, although this may not be true: *Don't judge by externals.*

ex·tinct /ɪkˈstɪŋkt/ *adj.* **1** BIOLOGY an extinct animal or plant does not exist anymore: *Dinosaurs have been extinct for millions of years.* | *Pandas may* ***become extinct*** *in the wild.* **2** if a type of person, custom, skill etc. is extinct, it does not exist in society any more: *an extinct language* **3** EARTH SCIENCE an extinct VOLCANO does not ERUPT anymore OPP **active**

ex·tinc·tion /ɪkˈstɪŋkʃən/ *n.* [U] **1** BIOLOGY the disappearance of a whole SPECIES, so that no more animals of that sort exist any more: *Greenpeace believes that whales are* ***in danger of extinction.*** | **the brink/edge/verge of extinction** *Alligators had been hunted to the brink of extinction.* | *The bison was* ***threatened with extinction.*** | *The zoo has worked to* ***save*** *the birds* ***from extinction.*** **2** the state of no longer existing in society any more: *Their traditional way of life seems doomed to extinction.*

ex·tin·guish /ɪkˈstɪŋgwɪʃ/ *v.* [T] FORMAL **1** to make a fire or light stop burning or shining SYN **put out**: *Please extinguish all cigarettes.* ▸see THESAURUS box at **burn¹** **2** LITERARY to make an idea or feeling stop existing: *The news extinguished all hope of his return.* [**Origin:** 1500–1600 Latin *exstinguere*, from *stinguere* **to extinguish**]

ex·tin·guish·er /ɪkˈstɪŋgwɪʃɚ/ *n.* [C] INFORMAL a FIRE EXTINGUISHER

ex·tir·pate /ˈɛkstɚˌpeɪt/ *v.* [T] FORMAL to completely destroy something that is bad or not wanted

ex·tol /ɪkˈstoʊl/ *v. past tense and past participle* **extolled, extolling** [T] FORMAL to praise something very much: *Scott was* ***extolling the virtues of*** *being a vegetarian.* [**Origin:** 1500–1600 Latin *extollere*, from *tollere* **to lift up**]

ex·tort /ɪkˈstɔrt/ *v.* [T] to illegally force someone to give you money by threatening them: **extort sth from sth** *The police officers were actually extorting money from drug dealers.* [**Origin:** 1400–1500 Latin, past participle of *extorquere*, from *torquere* **to twist**] —**extortion** /ɪkˈstɔrʃən/ *n.* [U] —**extortionist** *n.* [C]

ex·tor·tion·ate /ɪkˈstɔrʃənɪt/ also **ex·tor·tion·a·ry** /ɪkˈstɔrʃəˌnɛri/ *adj.* an extortionate price, demand etc. is extremely high or unfair SYN **exorbitant**: *an extortionate price for car insurance* —**extortionately** *adv.*

ex·tra¹ /ˈɛkstrə/ S1 W2 *adj.* **1** [only before noun] more of something, in addition to the usual or standard amount or number SYN **additional**: *a large pizza with extra cheese* | *I need some extra time to finish.* | *an extra napkin* | *The service costs an extra $5 a week.* ▸see THESAURUS box at **addition, more²** **2** [not before noun] if something is extra, it is not included in the price of something and you have to pay more for it: *Hotels are included in the cost, but meals are extra.*

extra² *adv.* **1** extremely: *If you're extra good, I'll buy you an ice cream cone.* | *He worked extra hard that semester.* **2** in addition to the usual things or the usual amount: *This team just seems to have* ***something extra,*** *something special.* | **one/a few etc. extra** *I bought a few extra in case anyone else decides to come.* | *Whipped cream is 50 cents extra.* **3 extra large/small** used in sizes to show that something is extremely large or small

extra³ S3 *n.* [C] **1** something that is added to a basic product or service and that usually costs more: *a car with extras such as a sun roof and CD player* **2** ENG. LANG. ARTS an actor in a TV program or movie who does not say anything but is part of a crowd **3** a special EDITION of a newspaper containing important news: *Extra! Extra! Read all about it!*

extra⁴ *pron.* an amount of something, especially money, in addition to the usual, basic, or necessary amount: **cost/pay/charge etc. extra** *Workers are paid extra for any overtime.* | *Here, have a hamburger; I made extra.*

extra- /ɛkstrə/ *prefix* **1** outside of or beyond: *extracurricular activities* (=activities a student does in addition to their usual classes) **2** very, or more than usual: *extra-special*

ex·tra·cel·lu·lar /ˌɛkstrəˈsɛlyəlɚ/ *n.* [U] BIOLOGY happening or existing outside a cell rather than inside it: *extracellular fluid*

ex·tract¹ /ɪkˈstrækt/ Ac *v.* [T] FORMAL **1** to remove an object from somewhere, especially by pulling it SYN **draw (out)**: *I'm having my wisdom teeth extracted.* | **extract sth from sth** *He extracted an enve-*

E

lope from his inside pocket. **2** to remove a substance from something which contains it, using a machine, chemical process etc.: **extract sth from sth** *The laboratories are able to extract DNA from bones and teeth.* **3** to make someone give you information, money etc. that they do not want to give: **extract sth from sb** *The police extracted a confession from him.* **4 extract yourself (from sth)** to leave a place or situation that is difficult to leave: *The singer finally extracted himself from the crowd of admirers.* **5** to get an advantage or good thing from a situation: **extract sth from sth** *They aim to extract the maximum political benefit from the Games.* **6** to take information or a short piece of writing from a report, book, poem etc., especially in order to use it as an example SYN **excerpt** [**Origin:** 1400–1500 Latin, past participle of *extrahere*, from *trahere* **to pull**] —**extractor** *n.* [C]

E

ex·tract² /ˈɛkstrækt/ Ac *n.* **1** [C,U] a substance that is removed from a root, flower etc. by a special process: *vanilla extract* **2** [C] ENG. LANG. ARTS a short piece of writing taken from a story, poem, song etc. SYN **excerpt**: +**from** *an extract from "A Midsummer Night's Dream"*

ex·trac·tion /ɪkˈstrækʃən/ Ac *n.* **1** [C,U] the process of removing an object or substance from something else: +**of** *the extraction of coal and other natural resources* **2 be of German/Chinese/Indian etc. extraction** to be part of a family that comes from a particular country, even though you were not born in that country SYN **ancestry** SYN **descent**

ex·tra·cur·ric·u·lar /ˌɛkstrəkəˈrɪkyələ˞/ *adj.* extracurricular activities are sports or other activities that are not part of students' usual classes

ex·tra·dit·a·ble /ˈɛkstrəˌdaɪṭəbəl/ *adj.* FORMAL an extraditable crime is one for which someone can be extradited

ex·tra·dite /ˈɛkstrəˌdaɪt/ *v.* [T] LAW to use a legal process to send someone who may be guilty of a crime back to the country or state where the crime happened, so that they can be judged in a court of law: **extradite sb to/from** *Drexel was arrested and extradited to Germany.* —**extradition** /ˌɛkstrəˈdɪʃən/ *n.* [C,U]

ex·tra·ju·di·cial /ˌɛkstrədʒuˈdɪʃəl/ *adj.* FORMAL LAW beyond or outside the ordinary powers of the law

ex·tra·mar·i·tal /ˌɛkstrəˈmærəṭl◂/ *adj.* an extramarital sexual relationship is one that a married person has with someone who is not their husband or wife

ex·tra·mu·ral /ˌɛkstrəˈmyʊrəl◂/ *adj.* **1** involving students from different schools: *extramural sports* → see also INTRAMURAL **2** relating to a place or organization, but happening or done outside it: *the director of extramural research* (=research for a company that is done outside the company)

ex·tra·ne·ous /ɪkˈstreɪniəs/ *adj.* FORMAL **1** not important, or not directly related to a particular subject or problem SYN **irrelevant**: *extraneous details* **2** coming from outside: *extraneous military forces*

exˌtraneous soˈlution *n.* [C] MATH the correct answer to a simplified (SIMPLIFY) form of an EQUATION that is not a solution to the original form of the equation

ex·tra·net /ˈɛkstrəˌnɛt/ *n.* [C] COMPUTERS a computer system in a company that allows better communication between the company and its customers by combining Internet and INTRANET systems, so that some customers can view some of the company's private information that is not normally available on the Internet

ex·traor·di·naire /ɪkˌstrɔrdnˈɛr/ *adj.* [only after noun] able to do something very well: *a violin player extraordinaire*

ex·traor·di·nar·i·ly /ɪkˌstrɔrdnˈɛrəli/ *adv.* [+ adj./adv.] extremely and in an unusual way: *She looks extraordinarily beautiful tonight.* | *an extraordinarily intelligent man*

ex·traor·di·nar·y /ɪkˈstrɔrdnˌɛri/ W3 *adj.* **1** very much greater or more impressive than usual: *He's the most extraordinary man I've ever met.* | *The show's ratings were extraordinary.* **2** very unusual or surprising SYN **amazing**: *He had an extraordinary tale to tell.* | *Something quite extraordinary had happened.* ►see THESAURUS box at **surprising** **3 extraordinary meeting/session etc.** FORMAL a meeting that takes place in addition to the usual ones **4 envoy/ambassador/minister extraordinary** an official who is employed for a special purpose, in addition to the usual officials [**Origin:** 1400–1500 Latin *extraordinarius*, from *extra ordinem* **out of the usual course**, from *ordo* **order**]

ex·trap·o·late /ɪkˈstræpəˌleɪt/ *v.* [I,T] **1** to use facts that you already know about a situation or group in order to make a guess about the future or about other situations or groups: **extrapolate from sth to sth** *We may foresee some developments by extrapolating from current trends.* **2** TECHNICAL to guess a value that you do not know by continuing a curve which is based on values that you already know —**extrapolation** /ɪkˌstræpəˈleɪʃən/ *n.* [C, U]

ex·tra·sen·so·ry per·cep·tion /ˌɛkstrəsɛnsəri pəˈsɛpʃən/ *n.* [U] ESP

ex·tra·ter·res·tri·al¹ /ˌɛkstrətəˈrɛstriəl/ *n.* [C] a living creature that people think may live on another PLANET

extraterrestrial² *adj.* relating to things that do not come from Earth, or do not exist or happen on Earth: *extraterrestrial exploration*

ex·tra·ter·ri·to·ri·al /ˌɛkstrəˌtɛrəˈtɔriəl/ *adj.* LAW existing or coming from an area outside a particular country: *extraterritorial legislation* —**extraterritoriality** /ˌɛkstrəˌtɛrəˌtɔriˈæləṭi/ *n.* [U]

ex·trav·a·gant /ɪkˈstrævəgənt/ *adj.* **1** spending a lot of money, especially on things that are not necessary or that you cannot afford: *His personal life was notably extravagant.* **2** very impressive because of being very expensive, beautiful etc.: *The gifts, though not extravagant, were nice.* | *extravagant celebrations* **3** extreme, and not reasonable, true, or real: *extravagant marketing claims* **4** doing or using something too much or more than is necessary: *an extravagant display of loyalty* | +**with** *Don't be too extravagant with the wine.* [**Origin:** 1300–1400 Medieval Latin, Latin *vagans*, present participle of *vagari* **to wander about**] —**extravagantly** *adv.* —**extravagance** *n.* [C,U]

ex·trav·a·gan·za /ɪkˌstrævəˈgænzə/ *n.* [C] an event or performance that is very large and impressive SYN **spectacular**: *a fireworks extravaganza*

ex·tra·vert /ˈɛkstrəˌvə˞t/ *n.* [C] another spelling of EXTROVERT

ˌextra ˌvirgin ˈolive oil *n.* [U] oil that is taken from OLIVES the first time they are pressed, without using any heat

ex·tre·ma /ɪkˈstrimə/ *n.* MATH a plural of EXTREMUM

ex·treme¹ /ɪkˈstrim/ *adj.* **1** [only before noun] very great in degree: *The refugees face a winter of extreme hardship.* | *extreme temperatures* | *Proceed with extreme caution.* **2** very unusual and severe or serious: *scenes of extreme violence* | *extreme weather conditions* | **an extreme example/case** *an extreme example of child abuse* **3** extreme opinions, beliefs, or organizations, especially political ones, are considered by most people to be very unusual and unreasonable: *His views are extreme.* | *extreme nationalists* **4** relating to a sport such as ROCK CLIMBING or SNOWBOARDING that is exciting but dangerous **5 extreme athlete/surfer/skier etc.** someone who takes part in an extreme sport **6 extreme south/end/limits etc.** the extreme south etc. is the place furthest toward the south, closest to the end etc. SYN **farthest** [**Origin:** 1400–1500 French *extrême*, from Latin *extremus* **most outward**]

extreme² *n.* [C] **1** a situation, quality, idea etc. which has a feature to as great or small a degree as possible, especially when this makes very different from something you are comparing it to: +**of** *the extremes of temperature found in desert climates* | *The truth lies between the two extremes.* | **the other/opposite extreme** *The school teaches the children of migrant farm workers and, at the other extreme, the children of* *millionaires.* | *Her feelings swung* ***from one extreme to the other*** (=change from being very happy to very sad). **2 in the extreme** to a very great degree: *Conditions were horrible in the extreme.* **3 go to extremes, take/carry/push sth to extremes** if someone does something to extremes, they do it to a point beyond what is normal or acceptable: *Mrs. Norris takes saving money to extremes.*

ex·treme·ly /ɪk'strimli/ S2 W2 *adv.* to a very great degree: *an extremely difficult decision*

ex,tremely low 'frequency *n.* [U] TECHNICAL → see ELF

extreme unc·tion /ɪk,strim 'ʌŋkʃən/ *n.* [U] LAST RITES

ex·tre·mis /ɪk'strimɪs/ *n.* → see IN EXTREMIS

ex·trem·ism /ɪk'stri,mɪzəm/ *n.* [U] opinions, ideas, and actions, especially political or religious ones, that most people think are unreasonable and unacceptable

ex·trem·ist /ɪk'strimɪst/ *n.* [C] someone who has extreme political opinions and aims, and who is willing to do unusual or illegal things in order to achieve them: *right-wing political extremists* —**extremist** *adj.*

ex·trem·i·ty /ɪk'strɛməṭi/ *n. plural* **extremities** **1** [C usually plural] one of the parts of your body that is furthest away from the center, for example your hands and feet **2** [U] the degree to which a belief, opinion, situation, or action goes beyond what is usually thought to be acceptable or usual: *the extremity of the proposal* **3** [C] the part that is furthest away from the center of something: *Alviso is a mostly Hispanic area in the city's northern extremity.*

ex·tre·mum /ɪk'striməm/ *plural* **extrema** /-mə/ or **extremums** *n.* [C] MATH the largest or smallest possible value of a mathematical FUNCTION

ex·tri·cate /'ɛkstrə,keɪt/ *v.* [T] **1** to remove someone or something from a place in which they are trapped: *Firemen extricated the driver from the wrecked car.* **2** to escape from a difficult, embarrassing, bad etc. situation: +**from** *She spent more than $57,000 extricating her husband from jail.* | **extricate yourself from sth** *Fewer women manage to extricate themselves from low-paying jobs.* —**extrication** /,ɛkstrə'keɪʃən/ *n.* [U]

ex·trin·sic /ɛk'strɪnzɪk/ *adj.* coming from the outside, or not directly related to something OPP **intrinsic**: *Some students need extrinsic rewards to motivate them to learn* (=they need rewards such as money or gifts, instead of the reward of learning something).

ex·tro·vert /'ɛkstrə,vɚt/ *n.* [C] someone who is active and confident, and who enjoys being with other people OPP **introvert**: *Willie is a total extrovert.* —**extrovert** *adj.* —**extroversion** /,ɛkstrə'vɚʒən/ *n.* [U]

ex·tro·vert·ed /'ɛkstrə,vɚṭɪd/ *adj.* confident and enjoying being with other people SYN **outgoing** OPP **introverted**: *an extroverted teenager*

ex·trude /ɪk'strud/ *v.* [T] FORMAL **1** to push or force something out through a hole **2** TECHNICAL to force plastic or metal through a hole so that it has a particular shape —**extrusion** /ɪk'struʒən/ *n.* [C,U]

ex·u·ber·ant /ɪg'zubərənt/ *adj.* **1** happy and cheerful, and full of energy and excitement SYN **ebullient**: *He is energetic and exuberant.* | *an exuberant celebration* **2** seeming full of energy and excitement: *exuberant paintings, full of color and life* [**Origin:** 1400–1500 French, Latin, present participle of *exuberare* **to exist in large quantities**, from *uber* **producing a lot**] —**exuberance** *n.* [U] —**exuberantly** *adv.*

ex·ude /ɪg'zud/ *v.* FORMAL **1** if you exude a particular quality or feeling, it is easy to see that you have a lot of it or feel it strongly SYN **ooze**: **exude confidence/warmth/optimism etc.** *He exudes enough confidence for us both.* **2** [I,T] to flow out slowly and steadily, or to push a liquid out in this way SYN **ooze**: *The plant exudes a sticky liquid.* [**Origin:** 1500–1600 Latin *exsudare*, from *sudare* **to have liquid coming out through the skin**]

ex·ult /ɪg'zʌlt/ *v.* [I] FORMAL to show that you are very happy and proud, especially because you have succeeded in doing something SYN **rejoice**: *"It was a great day," Martin exulted.* | +**in/over/at** *Republicans exulted in the election results.* —**exultation** /,ɛksəl'teɪʃən, ,ɛgzəl-/ *n.* [U]

ex·ul·tant /ɪg'zʌltənt/ *adj.* FORMAL very happy or proud, especially because you have succeeded in doing something: *Crowds of exultant people waved flags and sang.* —**exultantly** *adv.*

-ey /i/ *suffix* [in adjectives] used to show that something has a particular quality: *gooey candy*

Eyck /aɪk/, **Jan van** /yɑn væn/ (1390?–1441) a Flemish PAINTER famous as the first important northern European painter of the early Renaissance, who painted pictures of people with bright colors and a lot of detail

eye

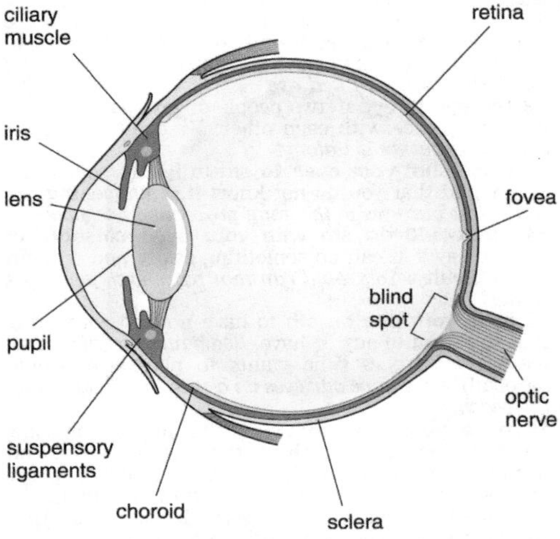

eye¹ /aɪ/ S1 W1 *n.*

1 BODY PART [C] BIOLOGY one of the two parts of the body that you see with: *Erica has green eyes.* | *Her eyes were bright with happiness.* | ***Close your eyes*** *and go to sleep.* | *Tom* ***opened*** *his* ***eyes.*** | *There were* ***tears in her eyes.*** | **your eyes widen/narrow** (=you open your eyes wider, or close them slightly, in order to express an emotion) *Louise's eyes widened in surprise.*

2 WAY OF SEEING/UNDERSTANDING [C usually singular] a particular way of seeing, judging, or understanding something: **critical/trained eye** *Always read your work again with a critical eye.* | *The story is told* ***through the eyes of*** (=from the point of view of) *a child.* | *More interesting,* ***to my eyes,*** *are his landscape paintings.* | *He became a hero* ***in the eyes of*** (=in the opinion of) *millions of Americans.*

3 keep an eye on sb/sth INFORMAL **a)** to carefully watch someone or something, especially because you expect something bad to happen: *Firefighters kept a wary eye on the dry hills.* **b)** to take care of someone or something and make sure that they are safe: *Could you keep an eye on my luggage?* | *I'll keep an eye on the kids for you.* **c)** to carefully watch something, especially in order to do something with it: *Keep your eye on the ball and swing the bat evenly.*

4 lay/set eyes on sb/sth to see something or meet someone, especially for the first time: *We loved the house from the moment we set eyes on it.*

5 eye contact if you have eye contact with someone, you look directly at them and they look directly at you: *People who are lying often don't* ***make eye contact.***

6 all eyes are on sb/sth, all eyes focus on sb/sth used to say that everyone is looking at or paying attention to something or someone: *The score was 3–3,*

and all eyes were on the batter. | All eyes were on the White House during the recent crisis.
7 keep an/your eye out/open/peeled (for sth) to watch carefully so that you will notice someone or something when it appears: *Art dealers are being asked to keep an eye out for the stolen paintings.* | *Keep your eyes peeled for bargains at the farmers' market.* | *I kept my eyes open for an opportunity.*
8 with your eyes open knowing fully what the problems, difficulties, results etc. of a situation might be: *They went into the deal with their eyes open.*
9 have a (good) eye for sth to be good at noticing and recognizing a particular type of thing, especially something attractive, valuable etc.: *Greene has an eye for detail.*
10 cannot take your eyes off sb/sth to be unable to stop looking at someone or something, especially because they are very attractive or interesting: *She was so beautiful I simply couldn't take my eyes off her.*
11 the naked eye if you can see something with the naked eye, you can see it without using any artificial help such as a TELESCOPE or MICROSCOPE: *The comet will be* ***visible to the naked eye.***
12 see eye to eye if two people or groups see eye to eye, they agree with each other: *We don't always see eye to eye, but we get along.*
13 close/shut your eyes to sth to ignore something or pretend that you do not know it is happening: *We can't close our eyes to the gang problems in schools.*
14 can/could do sth with your eyes closed/shut used to say you can do something easily and without any difficulty: *You could run that place with your eyes shut.*
15 have your eye on sth to have noticed something that you want to buy or have: *Rodrigues has his eye on the major leagues* (=he wants to play professional baseball). | *We have our eyes on a nice little house near the beach.*
16 have your eye on sb a) to notice someone, especially because you think they are attractive and want to have a relationship with them: *I've had my eye on my sister's roommate for a while.* **b)** to notice someone and consider them suitable for a job: *Ailey had his eye on a couple of Jamaican dancers.*
17 with an eye to/toward (doing) sth if you do something with an eye to something else, you do it in order that a second thing will happen: *Most novels are published with an eye to commercial success.*
18 eye to eye where you can see someone, especially because they are in the same room: *A lot of business people prefer doing business eye to eye.*

SPOKEN PHRASES

19 in front of/before your (very) eyes happening where you can clearly see something, used especially when what you see is surprising or shocking: *The Soviet Union fell apart before our eyes.*
20 sb has eyes bigger than their stomach, sb's eyes are bigger than their stomach said when you take more food than you are able to eat
21 not be able to believe your eyes said when you see something very surprising: *Then Mark walked in. She couldn't believe her eyes!*
22 have eyes in the back of your head to know what is happening all around you, even when this might seem impossible: *You need to have eyes in the back of your head to be a teacher.*
23 have eyes like a hawk to notice every small detail or everything that is happening, and therefore to be difficult to deceive: *My mother had eyes like a hawk.*
24 my eye!, in a pig's eye! OLD-FASHIONED said when you do not believe what someone has just said: *A diamond necklace my eye! That was glass!*

25 drop/lower your eyes to look down, especially because you are shy, embarrassed, or ashamed: *Suzanne dropped her eyes and blushed.*
26 eyes pop (out of your head) INFORMAL used when you are very surprised, excited, or shocked by something you see: *Grillo spotted a 16-year-old hockey player who* ***made his eyes pop out.***
27 make eyes at sb to look at someone in a way that shows you find them sexually attractive: *She's making eyes at you.*
28 an eye for an eye the idea that people should be punished by hurting them in the same way as they hurt someone else: *eye-for-an-eye justice*
29 keep/have one eye on sth (and the other on sth) to be paying attention to one thing while you are also doing something else: *Responsible companies should keep one eye on profits and the other on the environment.*
30 NEEDLE [C] the hole in a needle that you put thread through
31 be all eyes to watch carefully what is happening or what someone is doing: *Five-year-old Ryan was all eyes during his first trip to the ballpark.*
32 sb's eyes glued to sth if your eyes are glued to something, you watch it so carefully that you do not notice anything else: *Their eyes were glued to the news report on TV.*
33 under the (watchful/stern etc.) eye of sb while being watched by someone who is making sure you behave or do something correctly: *The eldest daughter cooked dinner under the watchful eye of her mother.*
34 take your eye off sth to stop watching something carefully: *Don't take your eye off the ball.*
35 POTATO [C] a dark spot on a potato from which a new plant can grow
36 CAMERA [singular] the eye of the camera is the part that you look through
37 only have eyes for sb if someone only has eyes for someone else, they only love and are interested in that one person
38 run/cast your eye over sth to look at something quickly: *Archer ran his eye over the headlines.*
39 (for your) eyes only said or written when something is secret and must only be seen by one particular person
40 STORM [singular] the calm center of a storm, especially a HURRICANE or CYCLONE
41 CLOTHING [C] a small circle or U-shaped piece of metal used together with a hook for fastening clothes
[**Origin:** Old English *eage*] → see also **be the apple of sb's eye** at APPLE (2), **not bat an eye/eyelid** at BAT² (3), BIRD'S-EYE VIEW, BLACK EYE, **turn a blind eye (to sth)** at BLIND¹ (3), **catch sb's eye** at CATCH¹ (19), **see sth out of the corner of your eye** at CORNER¹ (8), **the evil eye** at EVIL¹ (5), -EYED, **look sb in the eye/face** at LOOK¹ (12), **there's more to sb/sth than meets the eye** at MEET¹ (15), **in your mind's eye** at MIND¹ (47), **here's mud in your eye** at MUD (3), **open sb's eyes (to sth)** at OPEN² (3), PRIVATE EYE, RED-EYE, **a sight for sore eyes** at SIGHT¹ (13), SNAKE EYES, **in the twinkling of an eye** at TWINKLING (1), **keep a weather eye on sth** at WEATHER¹ (5), **pull the wool over sb's eyes** at WOOL (4)

eye² *v.* **eyeing** or **eying** [T] to look at someone or something with interest, especially because you do not trust them, you think they are attractive, or because you want something: *Sandy eyed him suspiciously.*

THESAURUS

watch to look at and pay attention to something that is moving or happening
stare to look at someone or something for a long time
keep an eye out for sb/sth to watch carefully for something or someone so that you will notice it when it appears
keep an eye on sb/sth to carefully watch someone or something, especially because you expect something bad to happen
observe to watch someone or something carefully, especially in order to find out something
scrutinize to examine something thoroughly and carefully

eye·ball¹ /ˈaɪbɔl/ *n.* [C] **1** the round ball that forms the whole of your eye, including the part inside your head **2 eyeball-to-eyeball** if two people are eyeball-to-eyeball, they are directly facing each other, especially in an angry or threatening way **3 be up to the/your eyeballs in sth** INFORMAL to have more of something than you can deal with: *We're up to our eyeballs in work.*

eyeball² *v.* [T] **1** INFORMAL to look directly and closely at something or someone: *They eyeballed each other suspiciously.* **2** to guess the size, length etc. of something by just looking at it, without using any measuring tools

eye·brow /ˈaɪbraʊ/ *n.* [C] **1** the line of short hairs above your eye **2 raise your eyebrows** to move your eyebrows up in order to show surprise or disapproval **3 be up to your eyebrows in sth** SPOKEN to have a lot of things to do or to deal with: *Stein is up to his eyebrows in debt.*

ˈeyebrow ˌpencil *n.* [C,U] a special pencil you can use to make your eyebrows darker

ˈeye ˌcandy *n.* [U] INFORMAL someone or something that is attractive to look at, but is not serious or important

ˈeye-ˌcatching *adj.* something eye-catching is unusual or attractive in a way that makes you notice it: *an eye-catching dress* —**eye-catchingly** *adv.*

-eyed /aɪd/ [in adjectives] **blue-eyed/one-eyed/bright-eyed etc.** having blue eyes, one eye, bright eyes etc.

ˈeye drops *n.* [plural] a special liquid that you put in your eyes when they feel dry or sore

eye·ful /ˈaɪfʊl/ *n.* [C] **1 get an eyeful** SPOKEN to see something shocking or surprising **2** an amount of liquid, dust, or sand that has gone into someone's eye **3 an eyeful** OLD-FASHIONED something or someone, especially a woman, who is very attractive to look at

eye·glass /ˈaɪglæs/ *n.* [C] **1** a MONOCLE **2** an EYEPIECE

eye·glass·es /ˈaɪˌglæsɪz/ *n.* [plural] a pair of GLASSES

eye·lash /ˈaɪlæʃ/ *n.* [C usually plural] **1** one of the small hairs that grow along the edge of your EYELIDS **2 flutter/bat your eyelashes** if a woman flutters her eyelashes, she moves them up and down very quickly, especially in order to look sexually attractive

eye·less /ˈaɪlɪs/ *adj.* having no eyes

eye·let /ˈaɪlɪt/ *n.* **1** [C] a hole surrounded by a metal ring, which is put in leather or cloth so that a string can be passed through it, especially in a shoe **2** [U] a type of cloth with small holes in it

ˈeye ˌlevel *n.* [singular] a height equal to the level of your eyes: *Pictures should be hung **at eye level**.*

eye·lid /ˈaɪˌlɪd/ *n.* [C] a piece of skin that covers your eye when it is closed: *Her **eyelids grew heavy*** (=she felt sleepy). | *I looked at him, his **eyelids fluttering*** (=moving up and down quickly) *in his sleep.* → see also **not bat an eye/eyelid** at BAT² (3)

eye·lin·er /ˈaɪˌlaɪnɚ/ *n.* [C,U] a colored substance that you put along the edges of your eyelids to make your eyes look bigger or more noticeable

ˈeyeliner ˌpencil *n.* [C,U] a type of pencil used for putting on eyeliner

ˈeye-ˌopener *n.* [C] an experience from which you learn something surprising or new: *A visit to a farm is an eye-opener to a city child.* → see also **open sb's eyes (to sth)** at OPEN² (3)

ˈeye patch *n.* [C] a piece of material worn over one eye, usually because that eye has been damaged

eye·piece /ˈaɪpis/ *n.* [C] the glass piece that you look through in a MICROSCOPE or TELESCOPE

ˈeye ˌshadow *n.* [C,U] a colored substance that you put on your EYELIDS to make your eyes look more attractive → see picture at MAKEUP

eye·sight /ˈaɪsaɪt/ *n.* [U] your ability to see SYN **vision**: **poor/failing/good eyesight** *a child with poor eyesight*

eye·sore /ˈaɪsɔr/ *n.* [C] something that is very ugly, especially a building surrounded by other things that are not ugly: *The old house is an eyesore.*

ˈeye strain *n.* [U] a pain you feel in your eyes, for example because you are tired or have been reading a lot

ˈeye tooth *n.* [C] **1** BIOLOGY one of the long pointed teeth at the corner of your mouth SYN **canine tooth** **2 give your eye teeth for sth** SPOKEN used when you want something very much: *I'd give my eye teeth to be able to play the piano like her.*

eye·wit·ness /ˌaɪˈwɪtˀnɪs, ˈaɪˌwɪtˀnɪs/ *n.* [C] someone who has seen something such as a crime happen, and is able to describe it later SYN **witness**: **+to** *There were no eyewitnesses to the shootings.* | **eyewitness account/report/testimony** *an eyewitness account of the battle*

ey·ing /ˈaɪ-ɪŋ/ *v.* the present participle of EYE

E·ze·ki·el /ɪˈzikiəl/ a book in the Old Testament of the Christian Bible

Ez·ra /ˈɛzrə/ a book in the Old Testament of the Christian Bible

E

F,f

F¹ /ɛf/ *n. plural* **F's** **1** also **f** *plural* **f's** [C] **a)** the sixth letter of the English alphabet **b)** the sound represented by this letter **2** ENG. LANG. ARTS **a)** [C,U] the fourth note in the musical SCALE of C MAJOR **b)** [U] the musical KEY based on this note **3** [C] a grade given to a student's work, showing that the student has failed: *Tony got an F in chemistry.*

F² **1** the written abbreviation of FAHRENHEIT: *Water boils at 212°F.* **2** the written abbreviation of FEMALE **3** the written abbreviation of FALSE

f the written abbreviation of FORTE

fa /fɑ/ *n.* [singular] the fourth note in a musical SCALE, according to the SOL-FA system

F

FAA /ˌɛf eɪ ˈeɪ/ → see FEDERAL AVIATION ADMINISTRATION

fab /fæb/ *adj.* [no comparative] OLD-FASHIONED extremely good

Fa·ber·gé /ˌfæbɚˈʒeɪ/, **Peter** (1846–1920) a Russian GOLDSMITH and JEWELER famous for making beautiful Easter eggs decorated with jewels for the Russian royal family

fa·ble /ˈfeɪbəl/ *n.* ENG. LANG. ARTS **1** [C] a traditional short story, often about animals, that teaches a moral lesson: *the fable of the race between the tortoise and the hare* ►see THESAURUS box at **story** **2** [U] such stories considered as a group: *monsters of fable and legend* [**Origin:** 1200–1300 Old French, Latin *fabula* **conversation, story**]

fa·bled /ˈfeɪbəld/ *adj.* [only before noun] famous and often mentioned in traditional stories SYN **legendary**: *statues of fabled warriors*

fab·ric /ˈfæbrɪk/ *n.* **1** [C,U] cloth used for making clothes, curtains etc. SYN **material**: *a thin silk fabric* | *special fabric for Christmas decorations* → see Word Choice box at CLOTH **2** [singular] the fabric of a society or particular group of people is its basic structure, its way of life, and its relationships and traditions: **+ of** *Has easy divorce weakened the fabric of the family?* | *Computers have become woven into the fabric of our daily life.* | **social/moral/spiritual etc. fabric** *the economic and social fabric of the nation* [**Origin:** 1400–1500 Old French *fabrique*, from Latin *fabrica* **thing made, place where things are made**]

fab·ri·cate /ˈfæbrəˌkeɪt/ *v.* [T] **1** to invent a story, piece of information etc. in order to deceive someone SYN **make up**: *Branson later admitted that he had fabricated the whole story.* **2** TECHNICAL to make or produce goods or equipment SYN **manufacture**: *The discs are expensive to fabricate.*

fab·ri·ca·tion /ˌfæbrɪˈkeɪʃən/ *n.* **1** [C,U] a piece of information or a story that someone has invented in order to deceive people SYN **lie**: **pure/complete/sheer etc. fabrication** *The accusation turned out to be pure fabrication.* **2** [U] TECHNICAL the process of making or producing something SYN **manufacture**

ˈfabric ˌsoftener *n.* [C,U] a liquid that you put in water when washing clothes in order to make them feel softer

fab·u·lous /ˈfæbyələs/ S3 *adj.* **1** extremely good or impressive SYN **marvelous**: *You look fabulous!* | *a fabulous meal* **2** [only before noun] FORMAL unusually large SYN **huge**: *The painting was sold for a fabulous sum.* **3** LITERARY [only before noun] fabulous creatures, places etc. are mentioned in traditional stories, but do not really exist

fab·u·lous·ly /ˈfæbyələsli/ *adv.* **fabulously expensive/rich/successful etc.** extremely expensive, rich, successful etc. SYN **incredibly**

fa·cade, façade /fəˈsɑd/ *n.* **1** [C usually singular] a way of behaving that hides your real feelings or character: ***Behind** her cheerful **facade**, she's really a lonely person.* **2** [C] the front of a building, especially a large and important one: *the building's marble facade* | **+of** *the facade of the Fairmont Hotel*

face¹ /feɪs/ S1 W1 *n.* [C,U]

1 FRONT OF YOUR HEAD the front part of your head, where your eyes, nose, and mouth are: *Jodi has such a pretty face.* | *One of the victims had scratches all over his face.* | *A smile spread across her face.* | *You have some jam on your face.* | **look/expression on sb's face** *Uncle Gene **had a** surprised **look on his face**.*

2 EXPRESSION an expression on someone's face: *the children's happy faces* | *Matt, stop **making faces at** your sister* (=making expressions with his face to annoy her or make her laugh). | ***You should have seen his face*** (=used to say how angry, surprised etc. someone looked) *when I told him I was leaving the company.* | **with a smile/frown/grin etc. on sb's face** *Sally watched him with a smile on her face.* | *I could see by their **blank faces*** (=an expression that shows you do not know or understand something) *that they didn't understand.* | *Joan's **face brightened*** (=she started to smile and look happy) *when I told her how much I liked her painting.* | *The kids' **faces lit up*** (=they started to smile and look happy) *when they saw Santa Claus.* | *Darren's **face fell*** (=he started to look disappointed or upset) *when I told him about the test results.* | *She was afraid, you could **see it in her face**.* | *Hey, Eddie, why the **long face*** (=unhappy or worried expression)*?*

3 in the face of sth ESPECIALLY WRITTEN in a situation where there are many problems, difficulties, or dangers: *He has persisted in the face of strong opposition.*

4 face to face a) if two people are face to face, they are very close and in front of each other: *Actually, I've never **met** her **face to face**.* | *"Call me." "No, I want to **talk to you face to face**."* | *He suddenly **came face to face with*** (=met him, in a surprising or upsetting way) *Stafford, whom he had been avoiding.* **b)** in a situation where you have to accept or deal with something bad: *It was the first time he'd ever **come face to face with** death.* | *This **brought** him **face to face with** the limits of his authority.* → see also FACE-TO-FACE

5 PERSON a person: **a new/different face** (=someone you have not seen before) *There were a few new faces in class.* | *She looked around at the **sea of faces** in the cafeteria.* | *Eddie nodded to a few **familiar faces*** (=people he knows or has seen before). | **a famous/well-known face** *a restaurant full of famous faces*

6 lose face if you lose face, you do something which makes you seem weak or stupid, so that other people respect you less: *They want to negotiate a ceasefire without either side losing face.*

7 save face if you do something to save face, you do it so that people will not lose their respect for you: *Franklin compromised in order to save face.*

8 MOUNTAIN/CLIFF a steep, high side of a mountain, cliff etc.: *the north face of Mount Rainier* | *climbers on the **rock face*** | *an image of Buddha carved into the **cliff face***

9 CLOCK the front of a clock, where the numbers are

10 face down/downward with the face or front toward the ground: *The body was lying face down on the carpet.*

11 face up/upward with the face or front toward the sky: *She laid the cards out face upward.*

12 on the face of it used to say that something seems true but that you think there may be other facts about it which are not yet clear: *It looks, on the face of it, like a pretty minor change in the regulations.*

13 say sth to sb's face, **tell sb sth to their face** to say something to someone directly: *I'd never say it to her face, but her hair looks terrible.*

14 the face of sth a) the nature or character of an organization, industry, system etc., or the way it appears to people: *Roosevelt's bold policies **changed the face of** the nation.* | *the **new face of** an old company* | **the acceptable/unacceptable face of sth** (=the qualities of an organization etc. that people think are good or not good) *Sweatshops are part of the unacceptable*

face of capitalism. **b)** the general appearance of a particular place: *the **changing face of** the suburbs*
15 OUTSIDE SURFACE a) one of the outside surfaces of an object or building: *the western face of the palace* **b)** one of the outside surfaces of a THREE-DIMENSIONAL GEOMETRIC shape: *A cube has six faces.*
16 the face of the Earth a) EARTH SCIENCE the outside part of the Earth: *It's one of the last unexplored places on the face of the Earth.* **b)** used to emphasize that something affects everyone on Earth: *The polio vaccine lifted a terrible curse from the face of this Earth.* **c)** used when you are emphasizing a statement: *It's the greatest adventure **on the face of the Earth**.*
17 disappear/vanish from the face of the Earth INFORMAL used to say that you do not know where someone is because you have not seen them in a long time, or that someone or something no longer exists: *It was like the woman vanished from the face of the Earth for 19 years.* | *animal species that have now disappeared from the face of the Earth*
18 in your face SPOKEN INFORMAL behavior, remarks etc. that are in your face are very direct and often make people feel shocked or surprised: *Bingham has a real "in your face" writing style.*
19 get in sb's face SPOKEN INFORMAL to annoy someone and try to tell them what to do
20 SPORTS the part of a RACKET, GOLF CLUB etc. that you use to hit the ball
21 get out of my face SPOKEN INFORMAL used to tell someone in an impolite way to go away because they are annoying you
22 put your face on INFORMAL to put MAKEUP on: *Jill's still busy putting on her face.*
23 MINE the part of a mine from which coal, stone etc. is cut
[**Origin:** 1200–1300 Old French, Latin *facies* **form, face,** from *facere* **to make**] → see also **blow up in sb's face** at BLOW UP (6), **do sth till you're blue in the face** at BLUE[1] (3), **put on a brave face** at BRAVE[1] (2), **have egg on your face** at EGG[1] (5), -FACED, **fly in the face of sth** at FLY[1] (19), **laugh in sb's face** at LAUGH[1] (2), **not just another/a pretty face** at PRETTY[2] (5), **show your face** at SHOW[1] (19), **shut your mouth/trap/face!** at SHUT[1] (3), **a slap in the face** at SLAP[2] (2), **be staring sb in the face** at STARE[1] (2), **a straight face** at STRAIGHT[2] (5), **what's-her-face** at WHAT'S-HER-NAME, **what's-his-face** at WHAT'S-HIS-NAME, **wipe the smile/grin off sb's face** at WIPE[1] (4), **have sth written all over your face** at WRITE (8)

face² S2 W1 *v.* [T]
1 DIFFICULT SITUATION if you face a difficult situation, or if a difficult situation faces you, it is going to affect you and you must deal with it: **face a problem/challenge/task etc.** *Weber is facing the biggest challenge of his career.* | *If found guilty, Jones could face up to 20 years in jail.* | *The company is facing stiff competition.* | *He has faced growing criticism of his role in the affair.* | *He may **face** criminal **charges**.* | **face a dilemma/decision/choice** *Government officials face a dilemma.* | **be faced with sth** *The city council is faced with the task of making budget cuts.*
2 ADMIT A PROBLEM EXISTS to accept that a difficult situation or problem exists, even though you would prefer to ignore it SYN **acknowledge**: *We have to **face the fact that** we'll be playing teams that are better than we are.* | ***Let's face it**, people change.* | *Arts groups don't like the funding cuts, but they have to **face facts**.* | *He had to **face the** awful **truth** that there was no cure for the disease.*
3 can't face sth if you cannot face something, you feel unable to do it because it seems too bad or difficult: *I don't want to go back to school again – I just can't face it.* | *She couldn't **face the thought** of seeing him again.* | **can't face doing sth** *Mr. MacArthur can't face selling the store.*
4 POINT IN A PARTICULAR DIRECTION to be turned or pointed in a particular direction or toward someone or something: *Dean turned to face me.* | *My house faces the bay.* | **face east/north/up/down etc.** *The bedroom window faces west.* → see Word Choice box at FRONT
5 OPPONENT/TEAM to play against an opponent or team in a game or competition: *The Jets face the Dolphins in two weeks.*
6 TALK/DEAL WITH SB to deal with someone who is difficult to deal with, or talk to someone who you do not want to talk to: *You're going to have to face her sooner or later.* | *Are you ready to **face the world** (=deal with the ordinary problems of life)?*
7 face the music INFORMAL to accept criticism or punishment for something you have done
8 be faced with stone/concrete etc. a building that is faced with stone, CONCRETE etc. has a layer of that material on its outside surface

face sb ↔ **down** *phr. v.* to deal in a strong and confident way with someone who opposes you: *Harrison successfully faced down the mob of angry workers.*

face off *phr. v.* to fight, argue, or compete with someone, or to get into a position in which you are ready to do this: *The two candidates will face off in a televised debate on Friday.* → see also FACE-OFF

face up to sth *phr. v.* to accept and deal with a difficult fact or problem: *Kids need to face up to the consequences of their actions.* | *Company leaders must **face up to the fact** that they have responsibilities to the environment.*

ˈface card *n.* [C] the king, queen, or JACK in a set of playing cards

-faced /feɪst/ [in adjectives] **1 pale-faced/round-faced/hawk-faced etc.** having a face that has a particular shape or color: *a round-faced boy* → see also RED-FACED **2 grim-faced/sad-faced/solemn-faced etc.** showing a particular expression on your face: *happy-faced children* → see also BAREFACED, POKER-FACED, STONE-FACED, TWO-FACED

face•less /ˈfeɪslɪs/ *adj.* a faceless person, organization, or building is boring, not easily noticed, or not known: *These victims should not remain faceless.* | *a faceless new suburb*

face•lift, face-lift /ˈfeɪslɪft/ *n.* [C] **1** work or repairs that make a building or place look newer or better: *The theatre will be **given a** $10 million **facelift**.* **2** a medical operation in which doctors make loose skin tighter on someone's face in order to make them look younger: *She denied that she has **had a face-lift**.*

ˈface-off *n.* [C] **1** INFORMAL a fight or argument: *a face-off between police and rioters* → see also **face off** at FACE[2] **2** the start of play in a game of HOCKEY

ˈface-ˌsaving *adj.* a face-saving action or arrangement prevents you from losing other people's respect: *a face-saving deal* —**face saver** *n.* [C usually singular] → see also **save face** at FACE[1] (7)

fac•et /ˈfæsɪt/ *n.* [C] **1** one of several parts of someone's character, a situation etc. SYN **aspect**: **+of** *the many facets of New York life* **2** one of the flat sides of a cut jewel

-faceted /fæsət̬ɪd/ [in adjectives] **multi-faceted/many-faceted** consisting of many different parts: *The problem is complex and multi-faceted.*

ˈface time *n.* [U] **1** time that you spend at your job because you want other people, especially your manager, to see you there, whether or not you are actually doing good work **2** time that you spend with someone in order to talk to them: **+with** *In return for a donation, he wanted face time with the President.*

fa•ce•tious /fəˈsiʃəs/ *adj.* saying things that are intended to be funny but which are really silly and annoying and not appropriate in a serious situation SYN **tongue-in-cheek**: *The comment was clearly meant to be facetious.* —**facetiously** *adv.* —**facetiousness** *n.* [U]

ˌface-to-ˈface *adj.* [only before noun] a face-to-face meeting, conversation etc. is one where you are actually with another person and talking to them: *the first face-to-face meeting the two leaders had*

ˌface ˈvalue *n.* **1** [C,U] the value that is written on something such as a coin, STOCK etc., but that may not actually be what the coin etc. is worth: *Super Bowl*

F

tickets with a face value of $300 are being sold for $2,000. **2 take sth at face value** to accept a situation or accept what someone says, without thinking there may be a hidden meaning: *Would you take at face value everything a politician says?*

fa·cial¹ /ˈfeɪʃəl/ *adj.* on the face, or relating to the face: *facial hair* | *gestures and **facial expressions***

facial² *n.* [C] a beauty treatment in which creams are rubbed into your face in order to clean and improve your skin: *I **had a facial**.*

fac·ile /ˈfæsəl/ *adj.* FORMAL **1** a facile remark, argument etc. is too simple and shows a lack of careful thought or understanding: *a facile judgment* **2** [only before noun] a facile achievement or success has been obtained very easily, so that it is not respected or satisfying SYN **easy**: *a facile victory* —**facilely** *adv.* —**facileness** *n.* [U]

fa·cil·i·tate /fəˈsɪləˌteɪt/ Ac *v.* [T] to make it easier for a process or activity to happen: *Dividing students into small groups helps facilitate discussion.* —**facilitation** /fəˌsɪləˈteɪʃən/ *n.* [U]

F

fa·cil·i·ta·tor /fəˈsɪləˌteɪtə/ Ac *n.* [C] **1** someone who helps a group of people discuss things with each other or do something effectively **2** TECHNICAL something that helps a process to take place

fa·cil·i·ty /fəˈsɪləti/ Ac W2 *n. plural* **facilities** **1** [C] a place or building used for a particular activity or industry, or for providing a particular type of service: *a new sports facility* | *The college has excellent research facilities.* **2 facilities** [plural] rooms, equipment, or services that are provided for a particular purpose: *parks and recreational facilities* | *Most campgrounds have laundry facilities.* **3** [singular] a natural ability to do or learn something easily and well SYN **talent**: **+for** *a facility for languages* | *He writes with great facility.* **4** [C usually singular] FORMAL a feature of a system or piece of equipment that makes it possible to do something: *a phone with a call-back facility* **5 the facilities** SPOKEN a word meaning the "toilet," used to be polite

fac·ing /ˈfeɪsɪŋ/ *n.* [C,U] **1** an outer surface of a wall or building that is made of a different material from the rest, in order to make it look attractive **2** material fastened to the inside of a piece of clothing to strengthen it

fac·sim·i·le /fækˈsɪməli/ *n.* [C] **1** an exact copy of a picture, piece of writing etc. SYN **copy** **2** FORMAL a FAX —**facsimile** *adj.*

fact /fækt/ S1 W1 *n.*

1 TRUE INFORMATION [C] a piece of information that is known to be true: *Newspapers have a duty to provide readers with the facts.* | **+of/in** *What are the facts of this case?* | **+about** *The book is full of interesting facts about plants.* | **get your facts right/straight** (=make sure you are right about something) | **stick/keep to the facts** (=only say what you know is true) *Witnesses must stick to the facts.* | ***It's a** well-known **fact that** smoking causes cancer.* | **simple/basic/plain fact** *The simple fact is we didn't have the money.* | ***I know for a fact that*** (=used to say that you definitely know that something is true) *he didn't go when he said he did.* | *I've never seen anything like it before, and **that's a fact*** (=used to emphasize that something is true). → see also **the bare facts/truth** at BARE¹ (4), **hard facts/information/evidence etc.** at HARD¹ (8)

2 the fact (that) used when talking about a situation and saying that it is true: *I don't deny the fact that things occasionally go wrong.* | *He refused to help me, **despite the fact that** I've done a lot for him.* | **due to the fact (that)/owing to the fact (that)** (=because) *The company's problems are largely due to the fact that the price of raw materials has increased dramatically.* | **given the fact (that)/in view of the fact (that)** (=used when saying that a particular fact influences your judgment) *Given the fact that this was their first game, they did pretty well.*

3 REAL EVENTS/NOT A STORY [U] situations, events etc. that really happened and have not been invented: *Much of the novel is based on fact.* | *Kids need to learn to separate **fact from fiction**.*

4 in fact also **in actual fact a)** used when you are adding something, especially something surprising, to emphasize what you have just said: *Yes, I know the mayor – in fact, I had dinner with her last week.* **b)** used to say what the real truth of a situation is, especially when this is different from what people think or say it is: *In fact, it's cheaper to fly than it is to drive.* | *Her teachers said she was a slow learner, but in actual fact she was partially deaf.*

5 the fact is also **the fact of the matter is** SPOKEN used when you are telling someone what is actually true in a particular situation, especially when this may be difficult to accept or different from what people believe: *The fact of the matter is that without government help this industry couldn't survive.*

6 facts and figures the basic details, numbers etc. relating to a particular situation or subject: *some facts and figures about the Saturn Corporation*

7 sth is a fact of life used to say that a situation exists and must be accepted: *Violent crime just seems to have become a fact of life.*

8 the facts of life the details about sex and how babies are born: *Most parents have difficulty talking to their children about the facts of life.*

9 is that a fact? SPOKEN used to reply to a statement that you think is surprising or interesting

10 the facts speak for themselves used to say that the things that have happened or the things someone has done show clearly that something is true: *She obviously knows what she's doing – the facts speak for themselves.*

11 the fact remains used to emphasize that a situation is true and people must realize this: *The fact remains that without raising taxes we won't be able to pay for any of these programs.*

12 after the fact after something has happened or been done, especially after a mistake has been made: *Few people even heard about the concert until after the fact.*

[**Origin:** 1400–1500 Latin *factum* **thing done**, from *facere* **to do, make**] → see also **as a matter of fact** at MATTER¹ (7), **in point of fact** at POINT¹ (16)

ˈfact-ˌfinding *adj.* **a fact-finding trip/tour/mission etc.** a trip during which you try to find out facts and information about something for your organization, government etc.

fac·tion /ˈfækʃən/ *n.* **1** [C] POLITICS a small group of people within a larger group, who have ideas that are different or that directly disagree with the larger group: *The leaders of the **warring factions*** (=disagreeing factions) *within the Socialist party met with each other today.* **2** [U] FORMAL disagreement or fighting within a group or a political party [**Origin:** 1400–1500 French, Latin *factio* **act of making**] —**factional** *adj.*

fac·ti·tious /fækˈtɪʃəs/ *adj.* FORMAL made to happen artificially by people, rather than happening naturally SYN **contrived**: *a factitious public outcry*

fac·toid /ˈfæktɔɪd/ *n.* [C] INFORMAL a small interesting piece of information, that is often not important

fac·tor¹ /ˈfæktə/ Ac S3 W2 *n.* [C] **1** one of several things that influence or cause a situation: *a rise in crime due to social and economic factors* | **+in** *The weather could be a factor in tomorrow's game.* | **a key/crucial/important etc. factor** *a major factor in children's poverty* | **the deciding/decisive/determining factor** *We liked both cars, but the price was the deciding factor.* **2** a particular level on a scale that measures how strong or effective something is: *factor 30 sun lotion* | *With **the wind chill factor*** (=the degree to which the air feels colder because of the wind), *it feels like 20 below zero.* **3 by a factor of five/ten etc.** if something increases or decreases by a factor of five, ten etc., it increases or decreases by five times, ten times etc.: *This increases the force level by a factor of five.* **4** MATH a number that divides into another number exactly: *3 is a factor of 15.* **5** TECHNICAL a financial company that pays a business for all the money it is owed by other companies, in return for a small PERCENTAGE, and that then collects the money owed for itself

factor² Ac *v.* [T] MATH to calculate the factors of a number

factor sth ↔ **in** also **factor sth into sth** *phr. v.* to include a particular thing in your calculations about how long something will take, how much it will cost etc.: *Interest payments will have to be factored in.*

factor sth ↔ **out** *phr. v.* to not include something in your calculations about how long something will take, how much it will cost etc.: *Real wages, after factoring out inflation, rose eleven percent.*

fac·to·ri·al /fæk'tɔriəl/ *n.* [C] MATH the result when you multiply a whole number by all the numbers below or equal to it. The factorial for any number "n," called n factorial, is shown as n!: *factorial 3 = 3 × 2 × 1*

fac·tor·ing /'fæktərɪŋ/ Ac *n.* [C] the business of being a FACTOR

'factor ˌmarket *n.* [C] ECONOMICS a place where FACTORS OF PRODUCTION, such as LABOR and CAPITAL, are bought and sold

ˌfactor of pro'duction *n.* [C] ECONOMICS any of the things that can result in the production of goods or services. These things are generally considered to be land, CAPITAL (=money and goods used to produce other goods, such as machines), LABOR (=human effort), and sometimes ENTREPRENEURS (=people who organize business)

'factor ˌtheorem *n.* [C] MATH a mathematical rule for calculating the FACTORS (=numbers or algebraic expressions that divide into another number) of a POLYNOMIAL

fac·to·ry /'fæktəri/ S3 W3 *n. plural* **factories** [C] a building or group of buildings in which goods are produced in large quantities, using machines: *a shoe factory* | *factory workers*

'factory farm *n.* [C] a farm where animals such as chickens or pigs are kept inside, in small spaces or small CAGES, and made to produce eggs or grow very quickly —**factory farming** *n.* [U]

ˌfactory 'floor *n.* **the factory floor a)** the ordinary workers in a company, rather than the managers: *There's talk* ***on the factory floor*** *of more layoffs.* **b)** the area in a factory where goods are made

'factory ˌsystem *n.* [C] **the factory system** HISTORY the system that began in England during the Industrial Revolution in which large numbers of workers and machines were brought together to produce goods

fac·to·tum /fæk'toʊt̬əm/ *n.* [C] FORMAL a servant or worker who has to do many different kinds of jobs for someone

'fact sheet *n.* [C] a piece of paper giving all the most important information about something

fac·tu·al /'fæktʃuəl/ *adj.* [no comparative] based on facts or relating to facts: *Keep your account of events factual and specific.* | ***factual information*** *presented in a graph* | *The report contained a number of* ***factual errors*** (=pieces of information that are wrong). —**factually** *adv.*

fac·ul·ta·tive an·ae·robe /ˌfækəlteɪt̬ɪv 'ænəˌroʊb/ *n.* [C] BIOLOGY a very small living thing that can exist with or without oxygen → see also ANAEROBE

fac·ul·ty /'fækəlti/ S3 *n. plural* **faculties** **1** [C,U] all the teachers in a particular school or college, or in a particular department of a school or college: *Both students and faculty have protested.* | *faculty members* | **+of** *the Faculty of Social Sciences* **2** [C] FORMAL a particular skill that someone has SYN **talent**: **+for** *She has a great faculty for absorbing information.* **3** [C] FORMAL a natural ability, such as the ability to see, hear, or think clearly: *the patient's mental faculties* | **+of** *the faculty of hearing* | *Mrs. Darwin is no longer* ***in full possession of all*** *her* ***faculties*** (=able to see, hear, think etc. well).

fad /fæd/ *n.* [C] something that someone likes or does for a short time, or that is fashionable for a short time SYN **craze**: *The popularity of organic food is not just a* ***passing fad*** (=a fad that will soon end). —**faddish** *adj.* —**faddishness** *n.* [U]

fade /feɪd/ S3 W3 *v.* **1** [I] also **fade away** to gradually disappear: *Hopes of peace settlement are beginning to fade.* | *Over the years her beauty had faded a little.* **2** [I,T] to lose color or brightness, or to make something do this: *faded jeans* | *The sun had faded the curtains.* **3** [I] if someone fades, they stop doing something as well as they did before: *The Broncos faded in the second half.* **4** also **fade away** [I] to become weaker physically, especially so that you become very sick or die

fade in *phr. v.* **fade sth** ↔ **in** to appear slowly or become louder, or to make a picture or sound do this [**Origin:** 1300–1400 French *fader*, from Latin *fatuus* **stupid, tasteless**] —**'fade-in** *n.*

fade out *phr. v.* **fade sth** ↔ **out** to disappear slowly or become quieter, or to make a picture or sound do this: *The radio signal faded out.* —**'fade-out** *n.*

faer·ie, faery /'fɛri/ *n.* [C] OLD USE a FAIRY

Fahr·en·heit /'færənˌhaɪt/ *n.* [U] a scale of temperature in which water freezes at 32° and boils at 212° [**Origin:** 1700–1800 Gabriel *Fahrenheit* (1686–1736), German scientist]

fail¹ /feɪl/ S3 W1 *v.*

1 NOT SUCCEED [I] to not succeed in achieving something OPP **succeed**: *Peace talks between the two countries have failed.* | **fail to do sth** *Doctors failed to save the girl's life.* | **+in** *He* ***failed in*** *his first* ***attempt*** *to win a seat in the State Assembly.* | *He has tried to quit smoking and* ***failed miserably*** (=been completely unsuccessful). | ***If all else fails****, you can declare bankruptcy.*

2 NOT DO STH [I] to not do what is expected, needed, or wanted: **fail to do sth** *Larry failed to submit his proposal on time.* | **fail in sb's duty/responsibility** *Schools are failing in their duty to educate children.*

3 EXAM/TEST a) [I,T] to not pass a test or examination OPP **pass**: *I failed my math test.* **b)** [T] to decide that someone has not passed a test or examination OPP **pass**: *I had no choice but to fail her.*

4 I fail to see/understand used to show that you are annoyed by something that you do not accept or understand: *I fail to see the humor in this situation.*

5 BANK/COMPANY [I] ECONOMICS if a bank, company etc. fails, it has to stop operating because of a lack of money SYN **go out of business**: *Many small businesses fail within their first year.*

6 MACHINE/BODY PART [I] if a part of a machine or an organ in your body fails, it stops working: *The engine failed just after the plane took off.* | *His heart was failing.*

7 HEALTH [I] if your sight, memory, health etc. is failing, it is becoming worse

8 never fail (to do sth) to do something or happen so regularly that people expect it: *His use of the term never failed to annoy her.* | ***Never fails****, the light always turns red just as you get there.*

9 fail sb to not do what someone has trusted you to do SYN **let sb down**: *I felt that I had failed my children by not spending more time with them.* → see also **words fail me** at WORD¹ (36)

10 CROPS [I] if crops fail, they do not grow or produce food: *The corn crop failed due to the drought.*

11 your courage/nerve fails (you) if your courage, nerve etc. fails or fails you, you suddenly do not have it when you need it: *At the last minute his courage failed him.*

12 RAINS [I] if the RAINS (=a lot of rain that happens at a particular time each year) fail, they do not come when expected or it does not rain enough

[**Origin:** 1200–1300 Old French *faillir*, from Latin *fallere* **to deceive, disappoint**]

fail² *n.* **without fail a)** if you do something without fail, you always do it: *Danny comes over every Sunday without fail.* **b)** used when telling someone that they must do something: *I want that work finished by tomorrow, without fail!*

failed /feɪld/ *adj.* [only before noun] **a failed actor/writer etc.** someone who wanted to be an actor, writer etc. but was not successful

fail·ing¹ /'feɪlɪŋ/ *n.* [C] a fault or weakness SYN **shortcoming**: *He loved her in spite of her failings.*

F

failing² *prep.* used to say that if one thing is not possible or available, there is another one you could try: *She wanted to make the team hate losing, or **failing that**, hate the consequences of losing.*

ˈfail-safe *adj.* **1** a fail-safe machine, piece of equipment etc. contains a system that makes the machine stop working if one part of it fails **2** a fail-safe plan is certain to succeed

fail·ure /ˈfeɪlyɚ/ W2 *n.*
1 LACK OF SUCCESS [C,U] a lack of success in achieving or doing something OPP success: *Winston is not someone who accepts failure easily.* | **end/result in failure** *His last attempt ended in failure.* | **+of** *the failure of the peace talks* | **failure to do sth** *the failure to find a vaccine against the disease*
2 UNSUCCESSFUL PERSON/THING [C] someone or something that is not successful OPP success: *I feel like such a failure.* | **a total/complete failure** *The advertising campaign was a total failure.*
3 MACHINE/BODY PART [C,U] an occasion when a machine or part of your body stops working in the correct way: *The plane may have suffered engine failure before the crash.* | **heart/liver/kidney etc. failure** *The cause of death was listed as heart failure.* | **+in** *a failure in the computer system*
4 failure to do sth an act of not doing something that should be done or that people expect you to do: *Failure to show proof of car insurance to an officer will result in a fine.*
5 BANK/COMPANY [C,U] ECONOMICS a situation in which a bank, company etc. has to stop operating because of a lack of money: *the most expensive bank failure in U.S. history*
6 CROPS [C,U] a situation in which crops do not grow and no food is produced, for example because of bad weather: *a series of **crop failures***

F

fain /feɪn/ *adv.* OLD USE **sb would fain do sth** if someone would fain do something, they would like to do it

faint¹ /feɪnt/ *adj.* **1** difficult to see, hear, smell etc.: *a faint noise* | *the faint outline of the cliffs* | *She gave a faint smile.* **2 a faint possibility/chance etc.** a very small or slight possibility etc.: *There's still a faint hope that they might be alive.* **3 not have the faintest idea** to not know anything at all about something: *I don't have the faintest idea what you're talking about.* **4 sth is not for the faint of heart** HUMOROUS used to say that a particular activity or job is not good for people who are nervous or easily frightened: *Being an inner-city cop is not for the faint of heart.* → see also FAINT-HEARTED **5** feeling weak and as if you are about to become unconscious because you are very sick, tired, or hungry: *The shock made her **feel faint**.* | **+with** *He was faint with hunger.* [**Origin:** 1200–1300 Old French *faindre, feindre* **to pretend**] —**faintly** *adv.*: *a wine with a faintly sweet taste* —**faintness** *n.* [U] → see also **damn sb with faint praise** at DAMN⁴ (3)

faint² *v.* [I] **1** to suddenly become unconscious for a short time SYN pass out: *It was hot and crowded, and several people fainted.* **2 I almost fainted** SPOKEN used to say that you were very surprised by something: *I almost fainted when they told me the price.*

faint³ *n.* [C usually singular] an act of becoming unconscious: *She fell down **in a faint**.*

ˌfaint-ˈhearted, fainthearted *adj.* **1** not trying very hard, because you do not want to do something, or because you are not confident that you can succeed SYN half-hearted: *She made a rather faint-hearted attempt to stop him from leaving.* **2 sth is not for the faint-hearted** HUMOROUS used to say that a particular activity or job is not good for people who are nervous or easily frightened → see also **sth is not for the faint of heart** at FAINT¹ (4)

fair¹ /fɛr/ S2 W2 *adj.*
1 REASONABLE AND ACCEPTABLE a fair situation, system, or way of treating people seems reasonable, acceptable, and right OPP unfair: *What do you think is the fairest solution?* | *All we're asking for is a fair wage.* | *the right to a fair trial* | **be fair to do sth** *It seems fair to give them a second chance.* | ***It's only fair that** she get something in return.* | **seem/sound fair** *That sounds fair to me.*
2 TREATING EVERYONE EQUALLY treating everyone in a way that is right or equal OPP unfair: *Life isn't fair.* | *Mrs. Anderson is strict but she's fair.* | *Why does Eric get to go and I don't? **It's not fair!*** | *The law was not always **fair to** women.* | ***It's only fair that** everyone has access to the same information.*

THESAURUS
just morally right and fair: *a just ruler*
reasonable fair and sensible: *a reasonable request*
equitable FORMAL fair and equal to everyone involved: *an equitable solution*
balanced fair and sensible: *balanced reporting of the news*
even-handed giving fair and equal treatment to everyone: *an even-handed documentary about capital punishment*

3 ACCORDING TO THE RULES a fair fight, game, or election is one that is played or done according to the rules OPP unfair: *free and fair elections*
4 LEVEL OF ABILITY neither particularly good nor particularly bad SYN average: *Jenny excels in science, but her grades in English are just fair.*
5 have had more than your fair share of sth to have had more of something, especially something bad, than seems reasonable or fair: *Tim's had more than his fair share of bad luck this year.*
6 SKIN/HAIR someone who is fair, or has fair skin or hair, has skin or hair that is light in color OPP dark: *Julia has blue eyes and fair hair.* | *Both her children are very fair.* ►see THESAURUS box at **hair**
7 WEATHER weather that is fair is pleasant and not windy, rainy etc. SYN fine: *It should be generally fair and warm for at least the next three days.* ►see THESAURUS box at **sunshine**
8 it's fair to say (that) used when you think what you are saying is correct or reasonable: *It's fair to say that most of our customers are well-educated.*
9 give/get a fair shake INFORMAL to treat someone, or to be treated, fairly, so that everyone has the same chances as everyone else: *It's true that women don't always get a fair shake in business.*
10 a fair size/number/amount/distance etc. INFORMAL a fairly large size, number, amount, distance etc.: *There's a fair amount of unemployment around here.*

SPOKEN PHRASES
11 fair enough used to say that you agree with someone's suggestion or that something seems reasonable: *"You'd better do it yourself." "Okay, fair enough."*
12 to be fair used after you have just criticized someone, in order to add something that explains their behavior or performance SYN in fairness: *He's not playing well but, to be fair, he did have a serious injury.*
13 be fair! used to tell someone not to be unreasonable or criticize someone too much: *Come on, be fair, the poor girl's trying her hardest!*
14 fair's fair said when you think it is fair that someone should do something, especially because of something that has happened earlier: *Come on, fair's fair – I paid last time, so it's your turn.*

15 BEAUTY LITERARY beautiful: *a fair maiden*
16 have a fair idea of sth to know a lot about something: *I think I have a pretty fair idea of what she's like.*
17 all's fair in love and war used to say that in some situations any method of getting what you want is acceptable
18 by fair means or foul using any method to get what you want, including dishonest or illegal methods
[**Origin:** Old English *fæger* **beautiful**]

fair² S2 *n.* [C] **1** an outdoor event, at which there may be large machines to ride on, games to play, music, and sometimes farm animals being judged and sold: **a state/county fair** (=a fair for the whole state or county) | *a **street fair** with dozens of booths featuring food and crafts* **2** a small outdoor event with games and things to eat and drink, usually organized to get money for a school, club etc.: *a booth at the school fair* **3** an event at which people or businesses show and sell their products: *a craft fair in the park* | *the Frankfurt Book Fair* | *the annual* ***trade fair*** *in March* **4** an event where people can get information about something: *a health fair where you can get a cholesterol test* | *a job fair at the college* [**Origin:** 1200–1300 Old French *feire*, from Latin *feriae* **holidays**] → SCIENCE FAIR

fair³ *adv.* **1 fair and square** in a fair and honest way: *They* ***won fair and square****.* **2 play fair** to do something in a fair and honest way: *In international trade, very few countries play fair.*

Fair·banks /ˈfɛrbæŋks/, **Doug·las** /ˈdʌgləs/ (1883–1939) a U.S. actor famous for performing in movies

ˌfairer ˈsex *n.* [U] OLD-FASHIONED **the fairer sex** also **the fair sex** women

ˌfair ˈgame *n.* [U] if someone or something is fair game, it is acceptable, reasonable, or right to criticize or attack them: *Politicians are fair game for the press.*

fair·ground /ˈfɛrgraʊnd/ *n.* [C] an open space on which a fair takes place

ˌfair-haired ˈboy *n.* [C] INFORMAL someone who is likely to succeed because someone in authority likes them

fair·ly /ˈfɛrli/ S2 W3 *adv.* **1** more than a little, but much less than very: *The house has a fairly large yard.* | *She speaks English fairly well.* ►see THESAURUS box at **rather** **2** in a way that is fair, honest, and reasonable SYN **justly**: *I felt I hadn't been treated fairly.*

ˌfair-ˈminded *adj.* able to understand and judge situations fairly and always considering other people's opinions: *a fair-minded man*

fair·ness /ˈfɛrnɪs/ *n.* [U] **1** the quality of being fair: *principles of decency and fairness* **2 in fairness (to sb)** used after you have just criticized someone, in order to add something that explains their behavior or performance SYN **to be fair**: *In fairness, I don't think she meant for it to happen.*

ˌfair ˈplay *n.* [U] **1** playing according to the rules of a game, without cheating **2** fair treatment of people, without cheating or being dishonest: *Claiming credit for other people's work violates our society's* ***sense of fair play****.* → see also **turnabout is fair play** at TURNABOUT (1)

ˌfair ˈsex *n.* **the fair sex** OLD-FASHIONED another phrase for FAIRER SEX

ˌfair-to-ˈmiddling *adj.* INFORMAL neither particularly good nor particularly bad SYN **so-so**: *a fair-to-middling saxophone player*

fair·way /ˈfɛrweɪ/ *n.* [C] the part of a GOLF COURSE that you hit the ball along toward the hole

ˌfair-weather ˈfriend *n.* [C] someone who only wants to be your friend when you are successful

fair·y /ˈfɛri/ *n. plural* **fairies** [C] a very small imaginary creature with magic powers, that looks like a small person with wings [**Origin:** 1300–1400 Old French *faerie* **fairyland**, from *fae* **fairy**, from Latin *fatum* **fate**]

ˌfairy ˈgodmother *n.* [C] a woman with magic powers who saves people from trouble, especially in children's stories

fair·y·land /ˈfɛriˌlænd/ *n.* **1** [U] an imaginary place where fairies live **2** [singular] a place that looks very beautiful and special: *At Christmas, the downtown area is a fairyland.*

ˈfairy tale *n.* [C] **1** ENG. LANG. ARTS a story for children in which magical things happen: *traditional fairy tales* **2** a story that someone has invented and that is difficult to believe

fai·ry·tale /ˈfɛriˌteɪl/ *adj.* [only before noun] **1** extremely happy, lucky etc. in a way that usually only happens in children's stories: *a fairytale romance* **2** beautiful, and like something from a fairy tale: *a fairytale cottage*

fait ac·com·pli /ˌfeɪt̬ əkɑmˈpli, ˌfɛt̬ ækɔmˈpli/ *n.* [singular] FORMAL something that has already happened or been done and cannot be changed

faith /feɪθ/ S3 W2 *n.*

1 TRUST/BELIEF IN SB/STH [U] a strong feeling of trust or confidence in someone or something: *I* ***have*** *a lot of* ***faith in*** *her.* | **destroy/restore faith in** *It has helped restore my faith in human nature.* | *The public has* ***lost faith in*** *the political process.* | *Allowing Ken to run the project was* ***an act of faith*** (=something that shows you trust someone). | *Starting her own business required a* ***leap of faith*** (=a chance you take because you are confident about something).

2 BELIEF IN GOD/RELIGION **a)** [U] belief and trust in God: *He's a man of deep religious faith.* | +**in** *Her faith in God is unshakable.* **b)** [C] one of the main religions in the world: *people from all faiths* | **the Jewish/Hindu/Muslim etc. faith** *members of the Jewish faith*

THESAURUS

religion belief in one or more gods, or a particular system of beliefs in one or more gods: *a book about world religions*
belief an idea or set of ideas that you think are true: *She has strong religious beliefs.*
creed a set of beliefs or principles: *Nonviolence was part of Gandhi's creed of personal ethics.*

►see THESAURUS box at **religion**

3 good/bad faith honest and sincere intentions, or intentions that are not sincere and honest: *There must be communication and good faith on both sides.* | **in good/bad faith** *Can it be shown that the reporter* ***acted in bad faith****?*

4 break faith with sb/sth to stop supporting or believing in a person, organization, or idea: *Has the U.S. broken faith with the island's government?*

5 keep faith with sb/sth to continue to support or believe in a person, organization, or idea: *Investors have so far kept faith with the company.*

6 keep the faith used to encourage someone to continue to believe in a principle, religion etc.

ˈfaith comˌmunity *n.* [C] a group of people who share a particular set of religious beliefs

faith·ful¹ /ˈfeɪθfəl/ *adj.* **1** remaining loyal to a person, belief, political party etc. and continuing to support them: *a faithful Catholic* | *Mary's always been a* ***faithful friend****.* | +**to** *Reynolds has* ***remained faithful*** *to his principles.*

THESAURUS

loyal always supporting a particular person, set of beliefs, or country: *a loyal friend*
devoted giving someone or something a lot of love, concern, and attention: *her devoted fans*
staunch/steadfast very loyal: staunch supporters of the president

2 representing an event or an image in a way that is exactly true or that looks exactly the same: *a faithful account of what happened* | *It's a faithful reproduction of the original picture.* **3** if you are faithful to your wife, husband, BOYFRIEND etc., you are not having a sexual relationship with anyone else: +**to** *She hasn't always been faithful to me.* | *Married partners are supposed to* ***remain faithful****.* **4** [only before noun] able to be trusted or depended upon SYN **reliable**: *a faithful servant* | *my faithful old car* —**faithfulness** *n.* [U]

faithful² *n.* **1 the faithful** **a)** the people who are very loyal to a leader, political party etc. and continue to support them: *the support of* ***the party faithful*** **b)** the people who believe in a religion: *bells calling the faithful to prayer* **2** [C] a loyal follower, supporter, or member: *A handful of* ***old faithfuls*** *came to the meeting.*

faith·ful·ly /ˈfeɪθfəli/ *adv.* **1** in a loyal and honest way: *Anne promised faithfully never to tell.* | *He performed his duties faithfully.* **2** in a regular way: *She wrote faithfully in her diary.* **3** if a copy, account, or TRANSLATION of something is done faithfully, it is done

F

very carefully and exactly: *The artist reproduced the picture faithfully.*

ˈfaith ˌhealing *n.* [U] a method of treating illnesses by praying —**faith healer** *n.* [C]

faith·less /ˈfeɪθlɪs/ *adj.* FORMAL someone who is faithless cannot be trusted —**faithlessly** *adv.* —**faithlessness** *n.* [U]

fa·ji·ta /fəˈhiṭə, fɑ-/ *n.* [C usually plural] a TEX-MEX food made with GRILLED onions, peppers, and chicken or meat that are put in a TORTILLA

fake¹ /feɪk/ *n.* [C] **1** a copy of a valuable object, painting etc. that is intended to deceive people: *Beware of fakes when buying antiques.* **2** someone who is not what they claim to be or does not have the skills they say they have SYN **imposter**: *It turned out her doctor was a fake.* **3** an action in which you pretend to move in one direction when you are really moving in another, or that makes you think one thing is happening when something else is really happening

F

fake² *adj.* [usually before noun] **1** made to look like a real material or object, usually in order to deceive people SYN **counterfeit**: *a fake ID card* | *a fake fur coat* ►see THESAURUS box at **artificial** **2** seeming to be real, but not being real, in order to deceive people: *a fake tan* | *He gave a fake name.*

THESAURUS

false made to look like something real, sometimes in order to deceive people: *false teeth* | *a false passport*
imitation made to look and seem like something else: *imitation leather*
counterfeit counterfeit money or a counterfeit product is made to look real in order to deceive people: *counterfeit credit cards* | *counterfeit lottery tickets* | *a million dollars in counterfeit bills*
phony not real and intended to deceive people: *He got the job using a phony job history and references.*
forged used about writing or documents that have been illegally copied in order to deceive people: *a forged signature on the letter*
ersatz artificial, and not as good as the real thing: *ersatz coffee*
→ ARTIFICIAL

fake³ *v.* **1** [I,T] to pretend to be sick, or to be interested, pleased etc., when you are not: *I thought he was hurt, but he was just **faking it**.* | *He faked some enthusiasm for the idea.* **2** [T] to make something seem real in order to deceive people: *He faked his grandfather's signature on the check.* | *The hospital records had been faked.* **3** [I,T] to pretend to move in one direction, but then move in another, especially when playing a sport: *Elway faked a pass and ran with the ball.*

fake sb **out** *phr. v.* to deceive someone by making them think you are planning to do one thing when you are really planning to do something else

fa·kir /fəˈkɪr, ˈfeɪkɚ/ *n.* [C] a traveling Hindu or Muslim holy man

fal·con /ˈfælkən, ˈfɔl-/ *n.* [C] BIOLOGY a large bird that kills and eats other animals and can be trained to hunt

fal·con·er /ˈfælkənɚ, ˈfɔl-/ *n.* [C] someone who trains falcons to hunt

fal·con·ry /ˈfælkənri, ˈfɔl-/ *n.* [U] the skill or sport of using falcons to hunt

Falk·land Is·lands, the /ˌfɔklənd ˈaɪləndz/ also **the Falklands** a group of islands, under British control, in the Atlantic Ocean off the coast of Argentina. The Argentineans believe that the islands belong to Argentina, and call them the Malvinas.

fall¹ /fɔl/ S1 W1 *v.* past tense **fell** /fɛl/, past participle **fallen** /ˈfɔlən/

1 MOVE DOWNWARD [I] to move or drop down from a higher position to a lower position: *Outside, the rain was falling steadily.* | +**out of/from/on** *We picked up the apples that had fallen from the trees.* | *The little boat **rose and fell** with the movement of the waves.*

2 PERSON FALLING [I] to suddenly go down onto the ground, especially without intending to, after you have been standing, walking, or running SYN **fall down**: *Katie fell and scraped her knee.* | *Don't worry – I'll catch you if you fall.* | +**on/into/down etc.** *Dennis lost his balance and fell into the water.* | **slip/stumble/trip etc. and fall** *She slipped and fell on the ice.* | *She **fell flat on her face*** (=fell so that her face was against the ground) *in the mud.*

THESAURUS

trip to hit your foot against something, so that you fall or nearly fall: *He tripped over a crack in the sidewalk.*
slip to slide on something that is wet or icy, so that you fall or nearly fall: *There was water on the floor, and she slipped and fell.*
stumble to put your foot down in an awkward way, so that you nearly fall: *She stumbled backwards and hit her head on the bed.*
lose your balance to fall when you are standing on something small or unsteady, or leaning over: *Someone bumped into him and made him lose his balance.*

3 LOWER AMOUNT/LEVEL ETC. [I] to become lower in price, amount, level etc. SYN **drop** OPP **rise**: *Temperatures should fall below zero tonight.* | **fall to/from/by etc.** *The number of traffic fatalities fell by 15%* (=was 15% lower) *last year.* | **fall sharply/steeply** (=quickly become lower) ►see THESAURUS box at **decrease¹**

4 BECOME [linking verb] to start to be in a new or different state: *I **fell asleep** at 9:00.* | **fall in love (with sb/sth)** *They met on vacation and fell in love immediately.* | *I fell in love with New York the first time I visited.* | *Everyone **fell silent** as Beth walked in.* | *The duchess had **fallen out of favor** with the King* (=he did not like or approve of her anymore).

5 GROUP/PATTERN [I] to be part of a particular group, pattern, or range of things or people: **fall into sth** *These substances fall into two categories.* | **fall under sth** *Her novels fall under the heading of historical fiction.* | **fall within/outside sth** *topics that fall outside the scope of our study*

6 HAPPEN [I] to happen on a particular day or date: **fall on sth** *Christmas falls on a Thursday this year.*

7 night/darkness/dusk falls LITERARY used to say that the night begins and that it starts to become dark: *The lights came on as darkness fell on the city.*

8 LIGHT/SHADOW [I always + adv./prep.] to shine or appear on a surface: *The last rays of sunlight were falling on the fields.* | *A shadow fell across his face.*

9 HANG DOWN [I always + adv./prep.] to hang down loosely: *Maria's hair fell over her shoulders.*

10 fall short (of sth) to fail to achieve the result, amount, or standard that is needed or that you want: *Her newest book fell short of many critics' expectations.*

11 fall flat if a joke, remark, or performance falls flat, it fails to interest or amuse people: *My attempts to entertain her all fell flat.*

12 fall to pieces a) to become damaged or not be able to work well SYN **fall apart**: *Without reforms, the economy will simply fall to pieces.* **b)** to become so sad and upset that you cannot do anything SYN **fall apart**: *Stacy would fall to pieces if she knew Gary was cheating on her.*

13 falling to pieces in very bad condition, especially because of being very old SYN **falling apart**: *The old building was falling to pieces.*

14 BE KILLED [I] LITERARY to be killed in a war SYN **die**: *a memorial to those who fell in battle*

15 LOSE POWER [I] POLITICS if a leader or a government falls, they lose their position of power: *The previous regime fell after only 6 months in power.*

16 TAKE CONTROL OF A PLACE [I] if a place falls in a war or an election, a group of soldiers or a political party takes control of it: **fall to sb** *The city finally fell to the advancing rebel army.*

17 fall victim/prey to sth to get a very serious illness: *While in Africa, she fell victim to a rare blood disorder.*

18 fall victim/prey to sb to be attacked or deceived by

someone: *The elderly are most likely to fall prey to con men.*
19 fall back into your old ways to start behaving in the way that you used to, especially when other people disapprove of this
20 fall by the wayside if something falls by the wayside, it stops being done or considered, or stops being successful: *Congress has let many important issues fall by the wayside this session.*
21 fall from grace/favor to stop being liked by people in authority: *I don't think she'll get the promotion – she's kind of fallen from grace recently.*
22 fall foul of sb/sth to do something that makes someone angry or that breaks a rule, with the result that you are punished: *Edwards fell foul of the authorities and was ordered to leave the country.*
23 VOICE/SOUND [I] if someone's voice or a sound falls, it becomes quieter or lower
24 silence/sadness/calm etc. falls LITERARY used to say that a group of people or a place becomes quiet, sad, calm etc.: **+on/upon** *As she entered the ballroom, a great silence fell on the crowd.*
25 the stress/accent/beat falls on sth used to say that a particular part of a word, phrase, or piece of music is emphasized or is played more loudly than the rest: *In the word "spoken," the stress falls on the first syllable.*
26 HIT [I always + adv./prep.] to hit a particular place or a particular part of someone's body: *The first punch fell right on his nose.*
27 I almost fell off my chair SPOKEN used to say that you were very surprised when something happened
28 fall to your knees move into a position in which you are on your knees, usually intentionally: *The priest fell to his knees to pray.*
29 fall at sb's feet to kneel in front of someone, especially to ask them to do something or to show your respect
30 fall from sb's lips LITERARY if words fall from someone's lips, they say them
[**Origin:** Old English *feallan*] → see also **it's as easy as falling off a log** at EASY[1] (15), **stand or fall by/on** at STAND[1] (40)

fall apart *phr. v.* **1** to separate into small pieces: *The old book fell apart in my hands.* **2** if an organization, system etc. falls apart, it stops working effectively and has a lot of problems: *Our department is **falling apart at the seams**.* **3 be falling apart** to be in very bad condition: *That car of yours is falling apart.* **4** if your life, your world etc. falls apart, you suddenly have a lot of personal problems: *When she left me, my world just fell apart.*

fall away *phr. v.* **1** if something such as a feeling, a quality, or a noise falls away, it gradually becomes weaker or quieter and disappears: *I closed the door, and the music outside fell away.* **2** to become separated from something after being attached to it: *There were places where the plaster had fallen away from the walls.* **3** to become fewer in number and stop being able to be seen as you move through an area: *As we drove, the rows of houses started to fall away and we could see open farmland.* **4** LITERARY to slope down: *Here, the road falls away to the valley.*

fall back *phr. v.* **1** if soldiers fall back, they move back because they are being attacked: *He ordered the men to fall back.* **2** LITERARY to move backward because you are very surprised, frightened etc.: *They fell back in horror.*

fall back on sth *phr. v.* **1** to use something that you would prefer not to use when dealing with a difficult situation, especially because other methods have failed: *In the end we had to fall back on our original plan.* | *Well, at least she **has** her father's money **to fall back on**.* **2** to use a particular method, argument etc. because it seems simple and easy, not because it is the best one to use: *They tend to fall back on the same old excuses.*

fall behind *phr. v.* **1** to fail to finish a piece of work or fail to pay someone money that you owe them at the right time OPP **keep up**: *The manufacturers have **fallen behind schedule**.* | **fall behind with/on sth** *We fell behind with the payments on the car.* **2** to become less successful than someone else OPP **keep up**: *If you don't come to class regularly, you'll fall behind.* | **fall behind sb/sth** *If we don't release the new software soon, we wil fall behind our competitors.* **3** to go more slowly than other people, so that they gradually move further ahead of you OPP **keep up**: *The older walkers soon fell behind.*

fall down *phr. v.* **1 be falling down** if a building is falling down, it is in very bad condition **2** if someone's pants, underpants etc. fall down, they fall downward from someone's waist, especially accidentally **3** if an argument, plan, system etc. falls down, it fails to work because of a particular fault: *That's where the whole argument falls down.* **4 fall down on the job** INFORMAL to fail to do what you should be doing in your job: *The city is falling down on the job of keeping the streets clean.*

fall for *phr. v.* INFORMAL **1 fall for sth** to be tricked into believing something that is not true: *We told him we were French, and he fell for it!* | *He said I'd double my money in six months and I **fell for it hook, line, and sinker*** (=was completely deceived). **2 fall for sb** to suddenly feel romantic love for someone: *Jackie's fallen for a man half her age.*

fall in *phr. v.* **1** if the roof, ceiling etc. falls in, it falls onto the ground SYN **collapse** SYN **cave in** **2** to start walking behind or to form a line behind other people OPP **fall out**: **fall in behind sb** *The students fell in behind the leaders.*

fall into sth *phr. v.* **1 fall into place a)** if parts of a situation that you have been trying to understand fall into place, you start to understand how they are related to each other: *Suddenly all the clues started falling into place.* **b)** if the parts of something that you want to happen fall into place, they start to happen in the way that you want: *Things are finally falling into place for the team.* **2 fall into the habit of sth** to start doing something, especially something that you should not do: *He fell into the habit of stopping at the bar every night before going home.* **3** to move somewhere quickly by relaxing your body and letting it fall on or against something: *We came home and fell into bed.* | *She fell into his arms.* **4** INFORMAL to start doing something, especially by chance and not by trying to: *I kind of fell into this job.* **5 fall into sb's lap** if an opportunity or something good falls into your lap, you get it by chance and good luck, without trying to get it: *It was the perfect movie role, and it just fell into his lap.* **6** to start to have a particular mood, especially suddenly: *She's unstable and liable to fall into sudden fits of rage.* **7 fall into a conversation/discussion/argument etc.** FORMAL to start talking or arguing with someone: *Half an hour after we met, Kirk and I fell into a heated discussion about the space program.* **8 fall into ruin/disrepair/decay/disrepute etc.** to start being in a state that is worse than before: *Over the years the house had fallen into disrepair.* **9 fall into step with sb/sth a)** to start doing something in the same way as the other members of a group: *The other countries on the Security Council are expected to fall into step with France.* **b)** to start to walk next to someone else, at the same speed as them **10 fall into a trap** also **fall into the trap of sth** to make a mistake that many people make: *Don't fall into the trap of thinking you're smarter than everyone else.* **11 fall into line** to obey someone or do what other people want you to do, especially when you do not want to do it at first: *If you can persuade her, the others will soon fall into line.* **12 fall into the hands/clutches of sb** if something or someone falls into the hands of an enemy or dangerous person, the enemy, dangerous person etc. gets control or possession of them: *Somehow, the plans fell into the hands of an enemy spy.*

fall in with sb *phr. v.* to begin to spend time with someone, especially someone who is bad or does illegal things: *I don't like the crowd he's fallen in with.*

fall off *phr. v.* **1** if part of something falls off, it becomes separated from the main part SYN **drop off**:

F

This button keeps falling off. | *A branch had fallen off the tree.* **2** if the amount, rate, or quality of something falls off, it becomes less: *Demand for records has fallen off dramatically.*

fall on/upon *phr. v.* **1 fall on/upon sb** FORMAL if a duty or responsibility falls on you, you are given that duty or responsibility SYN **fall to**: *Responsibility for childcare usually falls on the mother.* | **it falls on sb to do sth** *It fell on him to make the announcement.* **2 sb's eyes/gaze/glance falls on/upon sth** used to say that someone sees something when they are looking at or for something else: *As I looked around, my eyes fell on a young woman in a corner.* **3 fall on/upon deaf ears** if someone's words fall on deaf ears, no one pays any attention to them: *His pleas for mercy fell on deaf ears.* **4 fall on/upon hard times** to have problems because you do not have enough money: *The factory eventually fell on hard times, and he was forced to declare bankruptcy.* **5 fall on/upon sb** LITERARY to suddenly attack or get hold of someone: *Rebel forces fell upon the small outpost during the night.* **6 fall on/upon sth** LITERARY to eagerly start eating or using something: *The kids fell upon the pizza as if they hadn't eaten in weeks.*

F

fall out *phr. v.* **1** if something such as a tooth or your hair falls out, it comes out: *My dad's hair fell out when he was only 30.* **2** to have an argument with someone, so that you do not agree with them anymore or are not friendly with them anymore: **fall out with sb** *Walker has recently fallen out with his publisher.* **3** if a group of soldiers who are standing together fall out, they leave and go to different places

fall over *phr. v.* **1** if someone falls over or if they fall over something, they fall onto the ground: *I got dizzy and fell over.* | *Tommy fell over one of the electric cables.* **2** if something falls over, it falls from an upright position onto its side: *The fence fell over in the wind.* **3 be falling over yourself to do sth** to be very eager to do something, especially something you do not usually do: *Sylvia was falling over herself to be nice to me.*

fall through *phr. v.* if an agreement, plan etc. falls through, it is not completed successfully: *The deal fell through at the last minute.*

fall to *phr. v.* **1 fall to sb** FORMAL if a duty, especially a difficult one, falls to someone, it is their responsibility to do it SYN **fall on**: *The job fell to me to give her the bad news about her father.* **2 fall to sth** FORMAL to start doing something with a lot of effort: *We immediately fell to work on the project.* **3 fall to doing something** LITERARY to start doing something: *When things started going wrong, they fell to arguing among themselves.*

fall[2] S2 W1 *n.*
1 SEASON [singular, U] the season between summer and winter, when the weather becomes cooler SYN **autumn**: *Fall is my favorite season.* | *fall fashions* | *Brad's going to Georgia Tech* ***in the fall***. | **the fall of 2007/1978/2015 etc.** *They were married in the fall of 1957.* | *I met her* ***last fall*** (=the last time it was fall). | *The new building opens* ***next fall*** (=the next time it will be fall).
2 DECREASE [C] a decrease in the amount, level, price etc. of something SYN **drop** OPP **rise**: +**in** *a sudden fall in temperature overnight* | +**of** *a fall of almost 20%* | **a sharp/steep/dramatic etc. fall** *a sharp fall in the birth rate*
3 MOVEMENT DOWNWARD [C] movement down toward the ground or toward a lower position: *the fall of the rain on the roof* | *A few years ago Don* ***had a*** *bad* ***fall*** (=he fell onto the ground and hurt himself) *from a ladder.* | *Luckily the bushes next to the house* ***broke*** *my* ***fall*** (=prevented me from falling too hard).
4 WATER falls [plural] a place where a river suddenly goes straight down over a cliff: *Niagara Falls*
5 LOSE POWER/BECOME UNSUCCESSFUL [singular] a situation in which someone or something loses their position of power or becomes unsuccessful: +**of** *the fall of the Soviet Union* | *the party's* ***fall from power*** | *It's a book about* ***the rise and fall*** (=the period of success and then failure) *of communism in eastern Europe.*
6 DEFEAT [singular] a situation in which a country, city etc. is defeated by an enemy: **the fall of sth (to sb)** *a movie about the fall of France in 1940*
7 fall from grace/favor a situation in which someone stops being respected by other people or loses their position of authority, especially because they have done something wrong
8 AMOUNT OF SNOW ETC. [C] an amount of snow, rocks etc. that has fallen onto the ground: +**of** *a heavy fall of snow*
9 take the fall (for sth) to be blamed and punished for a mistake or a crime, although you did not do it: *Don't expect me to take the fall for this.*
10 SPORTS [C] an act of forcing your opponent onto the ground in WRESTLING or JUDO
11 the fall the occasion in the Bible when Adam and Eve did not obey God, and as punishment they had to leave the Garden of Eden

fal·la·cious /fə'leɪʃəs/ *adj.* FORMAL containing or based on false ideas: *a fallacious argument* —**fallaciously** *adv.*

fal·la·cy /'fæləsi/ *n. plural* **fallacies** **1** [C] a false idea or belief, especially one that a lot of people believe is true: +**that** *It's a fallacy that money brings happiness.* **2** [C,U] FORMAL a weakness in someone's argument or idea that is caused by a mistake in the way they have thought about that argument or idea: +**of** *the basic fallacy of his argument*

fall·back /'fɔlbæk/ *n.* [C] something that can be used if the usual supply, method etc. fails: *Do you have an alternative plan to use as a fallback?* | *a fallback strategy*

fall·en[1] /'fɔlən/ *v.* the past participle of FALL

fallen[2] *adj.* **1** on the ground after falling down: *The road was blocked by a fallen tree.* **2 the fallen** FORMAL soldiers who have been killed in a war **3 fallen angel** someone who has behaved in a bad or immoral way, but who was an honest, good person before **4 a fallen woman** OLD-FASHIONED a woman who has had a sexual relationship with someone she is not married to

'fall guy *n.* [C] INFORMAL **1** someone who is punished for someone else's crime or mistake SYN **scapegoat**: *The company was looking for a fall guy to take the blame.* **2** someone who is easily tricked or made to seem stupid

fal·li·ble /'fæləbəl/ *adj.* [no comparative] able to make mistakes or be wrong OPP **infallible**: *The trial showed Americans that the justice system is fallible.* —**fallibility** /ˌfælə'bɪləṭi/ *n.* [U]

ˌfalling-'out *n.* INFORMAL a bad argument with someone: +**over** *The brothers* ***had a falling-out over*** *their inheritance.*

ˌfalling 'star *n.* [C] a SHOOTING STAR

'fall line *n.* [C] **1** the natural course for going down a slope between any two points on a hill **2** EARTH SCIENCE an imaginary line along which rivers naturally form WATERFALLS and RAPIDS as they move from high land to low land: *the fall line between the Appalachian Mountains and the Atlantic Coast*

fall·off, **fall-off** /'fɔlɔf/ *n.* [C] a quick decrease in the level, amount, or number of something: *the recent falloff in technology stock prices*

fal·lo·pi·an tube /fəˌloʊpiən 'tub/ *n.* [C] BIOLOGY one of the two tubes in a female's body through which her eggs move to her UTERUS [**Origin:** 1700–1800 Gabriel *Fallopius* (1523-1562), Italian scientist who studied the structure of bodies]

fall·out /'fɔlaʊt/ *n.* [U] **1** the bad results or effects of a particular event, especially when they are unexpected: *The fallout from the scandal cost him his job.* **2** PHYSICS the dangerous RADIOACTIVE dust that is left in the air after a NUCLEAR explosion and that slowly falls to earth

'fallout ˌshelter *n.* [C] a building under the ground where people can go to protect themselves from a NUCLEAR attack

fal·low /'fæloʊ/ *adj.* **1** fallow land is dug or PLOWED but is not used for growing crops: *The land* ***lies fallow***

(=is left unused) *for two years.* **2** not doing anything or not working SYN **inactive**: *a two-year fallow period*

false /fɔls/ W3 *adj.*
1 NOT TRUE a statement, story etc. that is false is not true at all OPP **true**: *false information* | *Rosenberg had supplied a false name and address* (=in order to trick someone). | *Please decide whether the following statements are* ***true or false.*** ►see THESAURUS box at **wrong**[1]
2 WRONG based on incorrect information or ideas: *Many false assumptions were made about the planet Jupiter.* | *The article gives* ***a totally false impression*** *of life in Japan.* | *The wine had given her* ***a false sense of security*** (=a feeling of being safe when you are really not). | *The marketing of the drug raised* ***false hopes*** *that a cure was available.*
3 ARTIFICIAL made to look like something real, often in order to deceive people SYN **fake**: *false eyelashes* | *a false passport* ►see THESAURUS box at **artificial**, **fake**[2]
4 NOT SINCERE not sincere or honest, and pretending to have feelings that you do not really have OPP **genuine**: *Her smile and welcome seemed false.* | *It would be* ***false modesty*** *to say that we win games on luck alone.*
5 a false move/step a movement or action that has bad results: *One false move, and I'll shoot!* | *He was just waiting for me to* ***make a false step,*** *so he could report me.*
6 under/by false pretenses by deceiving people: *The reporter got the information under false pretenses.*
7 false imprisonment/arrest the illegal act of putting someone in prison or ARRESTing them for a crime they have not done
8 a false positive/negative a scientific test that has a positive or negative result that is not correct: *A number of drugs can cause false positives on the screening tests.*
9 under false colors pretending to be something that you are not
[**Origin:** 900–1000 Latin *falsus*, from *fallere* **to deceive**]

ˌfalse aˈlarm *n.* [C] a situation in which people think that something bad is going to happen, when this is a mistake: *She thought she was pregnant, but it was a false alarm.*

ˌfalse ˈbottom *n.* [C] a part of a container that looks like the bottom of it, but is used to cover a small space for hiding things: *a suitcase with a false bottom*

ˌfalse ˈdawn *n.* [C] a situation in which something good seems likely to happen, but it does not: *The first quarter's sales figures were sort of a false dawn.*

ˌfalse eˈconomy *n.* [C] something that you think will save money but that will really cost you more: *To cut the city's budget for waste disposal is a false economy.*

ˌfalse ˈfriend *n.* [C] a word in a foreign language that is similar to one in your own, so that you wrongly think they both mean the same thing

false·hood /ˈfɔlshʊd/ *n.* FORMAL **1** [C] a statement that is not true SYN **lie** **2** [U] the practice of telling lies

ˌfalse ˈstart *n.* [C] **1** an unsuccessful attempt to begin a process or event: *After several false starts, the concert finally began.* **2** a situation at the beginning of a race when one competitor starts too soon and the race has to start again

ˌfalse ˈteeth *n.* [plural] a set of artificial teeth worn by someone who has lost their natural teeth SYN **dentures**

fal·set·to /fɔlˈsɛt̬oʊ/ *n. plural* **falsettos** [C] a very high male singing or speaking voice, that is much higher than the man's normal voice —**falsetto** *adj., adv.*

fals·ies /ˈfɔlsiz/ *n.* [plural] INFORMAL pieces of material inside a BRA, used to make a woman's breasts look larger

fal·si·fy /ˈfɔlsəˌfaɪ/ *v.* **falsified, falsifying** [T] to change figures, records etc. so that they contain false information: *Mitchell joined the Navy at 16 by falsifying his birth certificate.* —**falsification** /ˌfɔlsəfəˈkeɪʃən/ *n.* [C,U]

fal·si·ty /ˈfɔlsət̬i/ *n.* [U] FORMAL the quality of being not true OPP **truth**

fal·ter /ˈfɔltɚ/ *v.* [I] **1** to become weaker and unable to continue in an effective way: *The peace talks seem to be faltering.* **2** if someone or their voice falters, it sounds weak and uncertain, and keeps stopping: *Laurie's voice faltered as she thanked him.* **3** to become less certain and less determined that you want to do something: *Just for a moment, her confidence faltered.* **4** FORMAL to walk in an unsteady way because you suddenly feel weak or afraid: *Langetta faltered as he made his way up the steps.*

fal·ter·ing /ˈfɔltərɪŋ/ *adj.* nervous and uncertain or unsteady: *With faltering steps, the old lady left the office.* —**falteringly** *adv.*

fame /feɪm/ *n.* [U] the state of being known about by a lot of people because of your achievements: *The novel's main character has a choice between fame and love.* | **win fame/rise to fame/gain fame** *Elizabeth Taylor first rose to fame in the movie "National Velvet."* | *In 1967, the Beatles were* ***at the height of*** *their* ***fame.*** | *Lee set off for California to find* ***fame and fortune.*** | *the Cleaver family* ***of*** *1950s television* ***fame*** (=used to show what someone is famous for) → see also **sb's/sth's claim to fame** at CLAIM[2] (4)

famed /feɪmd/ *adj.* known about by a lot of people SYN **famous**: **+for** *The Blue Ridge Mountains are famed for their beauty.* | **+as** *a town famed as a center of European learning*

fa·mil·ial /fəˈmɪliəl/ *adj.* [only before noun] FORMAL relating to a family or typical of a family: *familial relationships*

fa·mil·iar[1] /fəˈmɪlyɚ/ S2 W2 *adj.*
1 EASY TO RECOGNIZE well-known to you and easy to recognize: *It was a relief to be back in familiar surroundings.* | **look/sound/seem familiar** *His face looks familiar to me.* | *There was something* ***vaguely familiar*** (=a little familiar) *about her.* | *She is a* ***familiar figure*** (=well-known person) *in New York's clubs.* | *Stories of environmental damage are becoming* ***all-too-familiar*** (=very familiar, in a way that is sad or upsetting).
2 be familiar with sth to know something well because you have seen it, read it, or used it many times before: *Are you familiar with his books?*
3 INFORMAL STYLE informal and friendly in speech, writing etc.: *Sanders has an easy, familiar style of writing.*
4 FRIENDLY/INFORMAL talking to someone in a friendly and informal way that you use with people you know well: **+with** *Hotel staff should not be too familiar with guests.* | *He's* ***on familiar terms with*** (=knows them well enough to be friendly and informal) *all the teachers.* → see also FAMILIARLY

familiar[2] *n.* **1** [C] a cat or other animal that is controlled by an evil spirit, and is used by a WITCH to do magic **2 familiars** OLD USE close friends

fa·mil·iar·i·ty /fəˌmɪlˈyærət̬i, -ˌmɪliˈær-/ *n.* [U] **1** a good knowledge of a particular subject or place: **+with** *Familiarity with these software packages is required for the job.* **2** the quality of being well-known to you, especially in a way that makes you feel comfortable: **+of** *Sometimes I really miss the familiarity of home.* **3** a relaxed way of speaking to someone or behaving with someone that you would use with a friend: *He treated us all with easy familiarity.* **4 familiarity breeds contempt** an expression meaning that if you know someone or something too well, you find out their faults and respect them less

fa·mil·iar·ize /fəˈmɪlyəˌraɪz/ *v.* **familiarize sb/yourself etc. with sth** to learn about something so that you understand it, or to teach someone else about something so that they understand it: *The introduction helps to familiarize students with the technology.* | *I spent the first week* ***familiarizing myself*** *with the neighborhood.* —**familiarization** /fəˌmɪlyərəˈzeɪʃən/ *n.* [U]

fa·mil·iar·ly /fəˈmɪlyɚli/ *adv.* in an informal or friendly way

fam·ily[1] /ˈfæmli, -məli/ S1 W1 *n. plural* **families**
1 PEOPLE WHO ARE CLOSELY RELATED [U] a group of people who are related to each other and usually live

F

together, especially a mother, father, and their children: *Do you know the family next door?* | *the Webb family* | **a family of four/five/seven etc.** *The house is big enough for a family of five.* | *We've never been a very **close family*** (=one who likes each other and talks to each other often). | *It is often easier to talk to someone outside your **immediate family*** (=your most closely related family, such as your parents, sisters, and brothers). | **one-parent family/single-parent family** (=a family in which there is only one parent) → see also EXTENDED FAMILY, NUCLEAR FAMILY
2 ALL YOUR RELATIVES [C,U] all the people you are related to, including those who are now dead: *She's visiting family in Vancouver.* | **sth has been in sb's family** *The house has been in my family for over 200 years.* | *Heart disease **runs in our family*** (=is common in our family). | **a member of the family/family members** *We didn't invite any family members to our wedding.* | **a friend of the family/a family friend** *The Wilsons are old family friends.* | *Terry wants to work in the **family business*** (=a small business owned by one family). | *I don't want to ask him to pay because **he's family*** (=used to emphasize someone's relationship to you). | *The report deals with the suspect's **family background*** (=information about the kind of family someone comes from). | *Uncle Jack's not really related to us, but he's **like one of the family*** (=treated like one).

THESAURUS
relative a member of your family: *Most of my relatives are in California.*
relation a member of your family: *Hugh is a distant relation of mine.*
folks your parents or family: *My folks are coming to visit.*
→ RELATIVE⁴

3 CHILDREN [C] someone's children: *a young couple and their family* | *Steve and Linda want to **start a family*** (=have children) *next year.* | *When you first have children, you don't know anything about the problems of **raising a family*** (=educating and caring for children). | **family movies/shows/restaurants etc.** (=movies, shows, restaurants etc. that are appropriate for children as well as adults)
4 GROUP OF ANIMALS/PLANTS [C] BIOLOGY one of the groups into which scientists divide animals and plants. A family is larger than a GENUS, but smaller than an ORDER.: *tigers and other members of the cat family*
5 GROUP OF LANGUAGES [C] ENG. LANG. ARTS a group of languages that have a lot of similarities because they share the same origins: *Spanish and Italian are part of the Romance language family.*
6 be in the family way OLD-FASHIONED to be PREGNANT
[**Origin:** 1400–1500 *familia* **people living in a house**, from Latin *famulus* **servant**]

family² *adj.* [only before noun] used about products or containers that contain enough of the product for a large family to use: **a family pack/size etc.** *I buy the family packs of chicken breasts.*

ˌfamily ˈcircle *n.* [C usually singular] a group of people who are related to each other, especially a mother, father, and their children

ˌfamily ˈdoctor *n.* [C] a doctor trained to treat the general health problems of families and people of all ages

ˈfamily ˌman *n.* [C] **1** a man who enjoys being with his wife and children **2** a man with a wife and children

ˈfamily ˌname *n.* [C] the name someone shares with all the members of their family SYN **last name**

ˌfamily ˈplanning *n.* [U] the practice of controlling the number of children that are born by using CONTRACEPTIVES

ˌfamily ˈpractice *n.* [U] a part of medical practice in the U.S. in which doctors learn to treat general health problems of families and people of all ages

ˌfamily pracˈtitioner *n.* [C] a FAMILY DOCTOR

ˈfamily ˌroom *n.* [C] a room in a house where the family can play games, watch television etc.

ˌfamily ˈtree *n.* [C] a drawing that gives the names of all the members of a family over a long period of time, and shows how they are related to each other

ˌfamily ˈvalues *n.* [plural] traditional ideas about what a family should be like and how people should behave, which emphasize the importance of marriage, used especially in politics

fam·ine /ˈfæmɪn/ *n.* [C,U] a situation in which a large number of people have little or no food for a long time and many people die

fam·ished /ˈfæmɪʃt/ *adj.* [not before noun] INFORMAL extremely hungry: *What's for dinner? I'm famished.*

fam·ous /ˈfeɪməs/ S2 W2 *adj.* **1** known about or recognized by a lot of people: *a famous actor* | **+for** *Yosemite is famous for its giant sequoia trees.* | **+as** *Lake Winnebago is famous as a fishing destination.* → see also WORLD-FAMOUS

THESAURUS
well-known fairly famous or known about by a lot of people: *a well-known local businessman* | *It's a well-known fact that smoking causes cancer.*
legendary very famous and admired by many people for a long time: *the legendary blues guitarist, BB King*
infamous/notorious famous for doing something bad: *an infamous criminal*
celebrated famous and often impressive or important: *the celebrated black leader Nelson Mandela*
renowned/noted famous, especially for a particular quality, skill etc: *a renowned civil rights attorney* | *The lake is noted for its bird population.*
distinguished/eminent well-known, especially for serious work in science, the arts etc.: *a distinguished author* | *an eminent professor*
star a famous actor, musician, or sports player: *basketball stars*
celebrity someone who the public knows about, especially someone who appears on television: *newspaper stories about celebrities*

2 the famous people who are famous: *an old hotel where **the rich and famous** used to stay* **3 famous last words** SPOKEN said when someone says too confidently that they can do something or that something will happen, because you do not believe them: *Then he said those famous last words, "Don't worry, everything will be fine."* **4** OLD-FASHIONED very good SYN **excellent**
[**Origin:** 1300–1400 Old French *fameus*, from Latin *fama* **report, fame**]

fa·mous·ly /ˈfeɪməsli/ *adv.* **1 get along famously** OLD-FASHIONED to have a friendly relationship with someone **2** FORMAL in a way that is famous: *He was famously bad-tempered.*

fan

electric fan

fan

fan¹ /fæn/ S2 W2 *n.* [C] **1** someone who likes a particular sport, kind of music etc. very much, or who admires a famous person: *Thousands of fans called in to buy tickets.* | *He's **a big fan of** Elvis Presley.* | **a sports/music/movie etc. fan** *The event will be a real treat for country music fans.* | *I'm not a baseball fan.* **2** a machine with blades that turn and make the air move, in order to make a room feel cooler: *an electric fan* **3** an object that you wave with your hand in order to make yourself feel cooler: *a beautiful, delicate Japanese fan* **4** something that is arranged in a shape which looks like a part of a circle: *He arranged his cards in a fan.* [**Origin:** (1) 1800–1900 *fanatic*] → see also FAN CLUB, FAN MAIL

fan² *v.* **fanned, fanning** [T] **1** to make air move around by waving a fan, piece of paper etc. so that you feel cooler: *Gina **fanned herself** with a newspaper.* **2** also **fan out** to spread something out, especially a group of things, so that they make the shape of a half-circle: *The bird fans its tail to impress females.* **3** to encourage someone to feel something more strongly, or to do something more: *His statement fanned the rumors that say he is about to resign.* | *Comments like that will only **fan the flames of** distrust and fear* (=make these bad feelings worse). **4 fan a fire/blaze** to make a fire burn more strongly, for example by blowing on it: *Fanned by a steady wind, the fire spread quickly.*

fan out *phr. v.* **1** if a group of people fan out, they walk forward while spreading over a wide area **2 fan sth ↔ out** to spread out a group of things that you are holding so that they make a half-circle: *Fan the cards out, then pick one.* **3** if something such as hair or clothing fans out, it spreads out in many directions

fa·nat·ic /fəˈnætɪk/ *n.* [C] **1** someone who has extreme political or religious ideas and is often dangerous SYN **extremist**: *Gandhi was killed by a religious fanatic.* **2** someone who likes a particular thing or activity very much and uses or does it a lot SYN **enthusiast**: *an exercise fanatic* —**fanatical** *adj.* —**fanatically** /-kli/ *adv.*

fa·nat·i·cism /fəˈnætəˌsɪzəm/ *n.* [U] extreme political or religious beliefs that are often dangerous SYN **extremism**

ˈfan belt *n.* [C] the belt that operates a FAN which keeps a car engine cool

fan·ci·er /ˈfænsiɚ/ *n.* **cat/wine/opera etc. fancier** someone who is very interested in cats, wine, OPERA etc.

fan·ci·ful /ˈfænsɪfəl/ *adj.* **1** imagined rather than based on facts: *I dismissed the rumors as fanciful.* | *a fanciful idea* **2** full of unusual and very detailed shapes or complicated designs: *fanciful costumes* —**fancifully** *adv.*

ˈfan club *n.* an organization for FANS of a particular team, famous person etc.

fan·cy¹ /ˈfænsi/ S2 *adj. comparative* **fancier**, *superlative* **fanciest** **1** fancy hotels, restaurants, cars etc. are expensive and fashionable: *We stayed in this really fancy hotel in the mountains.* ►see THESAURUS box at **expensive** **2** made in a special or complicated way: *fancy soaps in seashell shapes* | *The restaurant's food is **nothing fancy*** (=it's not special), *but it's good and cheap.* **3** complicated and needing a lot of skill: *fancy skiing* **4** [only before noun] fancy food is very high quality: *fancy butter*

fancy² *n.* OLD-FASHIONED **1** [singular] a feeling that you would like something or someone: *Cora **took a fancy to** John, and eventually married him.* | *The idea about going to Mexico was just a **passing fancy*** (=an idea that does not last long). **2** [C,U] imagination or something that you imagine: *the poet's brilliant fancies* → see also **flight of fancy** at FLIGHT (6) **3 tickle sb's fancy** to seem attractive or amusing to someone **4 sth takes/strikes/catches your fancy** used to say that you like something or want to have it

fancy³ *v.* **fancies, fancied, fancying** [T] OLD-FASHIONED **1** to believe that something is true, even if it is not really SYN **imagine**: *Archer fancied that she knew of his coming.* | *She **fancies herself** an intellectual.* **2** to like or want something, or want to do something SYN **feel like**: *Do you fancy a walk in the park, Estelle?*

ˌfancy-ˈfree *adj.* [not before noun] able to do anything you like because you do not have a family or other responsibilities: *No, I'm not married – still **footloose and fancy-free**.*

fan·cy·work /ˈfænsiwɚk/ *n.* [U] pretty sewing SYN **embroidery**

fan·dan·go /fænˈdæŋgoʊ/ *n.* [C] a fast Spanish or South American dance, or the music for this dance

fan·fare /ˈfænfɛr/ *n.* [C] **1** a lot of public activity, attention, or discussion relating to an event: **with/without fanfare** *Goldin resigned last week with little fanfare.* **2** ENG. LANG. ARTS a short, loud piece of music played on a TRUMPET to introduce an important person or event [**Origin:** 1700–1800 French]

fang /fæŋ/ *n.* [C] a long sharp tooth of an animal such as a snake or dog

fan·light /ˈfænlaɪt/ *n.* [C] **1** a small window above a door or a larger window SYN **transom** **2** a window shaped like a half circle

ˈfan mail *n.* [U] letters sent to famous people by their FANS

fan·ny /ˈfæni/ *n. plural* **fannies** [C] INFORMAL the part of your body that you sit on SYN **bottom** SYN **butt**

ˈfanny pack *n.* [C] a small bag that someone wears around their waist to carry money, keys etc.

fan·ta·sia /fænˈteɪʒə/ *n.* [C] ENG. LANG. ARTS **1** a piece of music that does not have a regular form or style **2** ENG. LANG. ARTS a piece of music consisting of a collection of well-known tunes

F

fan·ta·size /ˈfæntəˌsaɪz/ *v.* [I,T] to imagine something that is very pleasant or exciting, but that is very unlikely to happen: **fantasize about sth** *Kids idolize athletes, and fantasize about playing in the pros.* | **fantasize (that)** *I used to fantasize that my sons would grow up to be doctors.*

fan·tas·tic /fænˈtæstɪk/ S3 *adj.* **1** extremely good, attractive, enjoyable etc. SYN **wonderful**: *My mom's sixty, but she still looks fantastic.* | *He's done a fantastic job.* | *a hotel with fantastic views* ►see THESAURUS box at **good¹**, **nice** **2** SPOKEN used when someone has just told you something good SYN **excellent** SYN **wonderful**: *"He got a scholarship." "Fantastic!"* **3** [only before noun] a fantastic amount is extremely large SYN **huge**: *Teenagers spend fantastic amounts of money on clothes.* **4** [only before noun] a fantastic story, creature, or place is very strange, magical, or unreal: *fantastic stories of invisible men* **5** a plan, suggestion etc. that is fantastic is not likely to be possible: *fantastic schemes for making money* —**fantastically** /-kli/ *adv.*

fan·tas·ti·cal /fænˈtæstɪkəl/ *adj.* strange, magical, and unreal: *a fantastical world populated by mermaids*

fan·ta·sy /ˈfæntəsi, -zi/ W3 *n. plural* **fantasies** **1** [C,U] an exciting and unusual experience or situation that you imagine happening, but that will probably never happen: *Sometimes I **have this fantasy about** opening a campground there.* | *Young children sometimes can't distinguish between fantasy and reality.* | *a young woman's romantic fantasies* | *Carlos retreats into a **fantasy world** in which everyone adores him.* **2** [singular, U] an idea or belief that is not based on real facts: *Psychologists say that memories can sometimes be pure fantasy.* **3** [C,U] ENG. LANG. ARTS a story, film etc that is based on imagination and not facts, or these types of stories, films etc.: *works of fantasy and science fiction* [**Origin:** 1300–1400 Old French *fantasie*, from Latin *phantasia*, from Greek, **appearance, imagination**]

fan·zine /ˈfænzin/ *n.* [C] a magazine written by and for people who admire and support a popular musician, a sports team etc.

FAQ /ˌɛf eɪ ˈkyu, fæk/ *n.* [C usually plural] a frequently asked question

far¹ /fɑr/ S1 W1 *adv. comparative* **farther** or **further**, *superlative* **farthest** or **furthest**

1 LONG DISTANCE over a long distance: *I don't want to drive very far.* | *As a parent, I think two miles is **too far** for a small child to walk to school.* | *Let's see who can swim **the farthest**.* | ***How far away** does Sue live?* | *I've started parking **farther away from** the office in order to get a cheaper rate.* | **far above/below/across etc.** *We heard laughter far above us, on the canyon's rim.* | *There was nothing but snow covered peaks **as far as the eye could see*** (=up to the longest distance that you can see).

2 as far as sth up to a particular point or distance: *Goods were traded up the Missouri River as far as Yellowstone.*
3 MUCH to a great degree or extent SYN **much**: **far too much/long/busy etc.** *I'm afraid this gift is far too expensive.* | **far stronger/faster/sooner/more etc.** *Jake has a far bigger appetite than I do.* | *The new system is far better than the old one.* | **far more/less** *I enjoyed the movie far more than I expected to.* | **far above/below/beyond etc.** *The students scored far below average on the test.* | *The operation was successful far beyond all expectations.* | *Life on the farm is* ***far removed from*** (=very different from) *the hustle and bustle of life in the city.*
4 by far also **far and away** used before a superlative to emphasize that something is much better, worse etc. than anything else: *She's by far the best player on the team.*
5 PROGRESS used for talking about the progress that someone or something makes: *We won't* ***get far*** *if we don't work together.* | ***How far have you gotten with*** *painting the kitchen?* | *We've only* ***gotten as far as*** *buying the paint.* | ***Things have gone too far*** (=a situation has progressed to a point that is too advanced) *for us to change our minds now.*
6 LONG TIME a long time in the past or the future, or a long time into a particular period: *I can't remember* ***that far back*** (=a time so long ago). | ***As far back as*** (=used for emphasizing how long ago something happened) *400 B.C. doctors were using herbs to treat disease.* | **far away/off** *Spring is not far off* (=it is coming soon). | *We haven't been able to plan very* ***far in advance*** (=far into the future). → see also FAR-OFF
7 so far up to a particular time, point, degree etc.: *I think he's done a great job so far.*
8 sb will/should go far used to say that you think someone will be successful in the future: *The Panther's newest player should go far in the league.*
9 as far as sth (goes) used to show which particular subject or thing you are talking about: *As far as science is concerned, the schools are not doing a good enough job.*
10 go so/as far as to do sth to behave in a way that seems surprising or extreme: *The government went as far as to arrest its opponents.*
11 go too far also **take/carry sth too far** to do something too much or in an extreme way, especially so that people get angry: *He's always joking, but one day he'll go too far.*
12 not go far a) if money does not go far you cannot buy very much with it: *A dollar doesn't go very far these days.* **b)** if a supply of something does not go far, it is not enough: *This pizza won't go far if everyone wants some.* **c) not go far enough** if a policy, law etc. does not go far enough, it has a smaller effect than people wanted or expected: *The reforms do not go far enough toward protecting human rights.*
13 as far as possible as much as possible: *We try, as far as possible, to use local produce.*

SPOKEN PHRASES

14 as far as I know also **as far as I can tell/remember** said when you think that something is true, although you do not know or cannot remember all the facts: *He's planning to be there for Christmas, as far as I know.* | *As far as I could tell, she wasn't mad.*
15 so far so good used to say that things have been happening successfully until now: *"How's your new job?" "So far so good."*
16 go so/as far as to say sth used when you give a particular idea or opinion, in order to show that the opinion is extreme or unlikely to be true: *Some people go so far as to say this discovery is more significant than the telephone.* | ***I wouldn't go so far as to say*** *he's a coward.*
17 far from it used to say that the opposite of what someone says is true; certainly not: *"Did you enjoy yourself?" "Far from it!"*
18 far be it from me to do sth used when you are pretending that you do not wish to criticize, advise etc., when this is exactly what you are doing: *Far be it from me to tell you what to wear.*

19 far from used to say that the opposite of something is true, or the opposite of what you expect happens: **far from doing/being sth** *Far from helping the situation, she made it worse.* | *The company's troubles are* ***far from over.*** | **far from pleased/happy etc.** *Critics are far from satisfied.*
20 as far as it goes used to say that an idea, suggestion, plan etc. is satisfactory, but only to a limited degree: *What Kroll said was accurate, as far as it goes.*
21 far and wide over or from a large area: **travel/wander etc. far and wide** *I have traveled far and wide, and have never eaten at a worse diner.* | **hunt/search far and wide** *We've been searching far and wide for new talent.*
22 not be far off/wrong INFORMAL to be almost correct: *His estimates weren't too far off.*
[**Origin:** Old English *feorr*] → see also **as far as sb is concerned** at CONCERNED (4), **as far as sth is concerned** at CONCERNED (5), INSOFAR AS

far² S2 *adj. comparative* **farther** or **further**, *superlative* **farthest** or **furthest** **1** used for talking about distance: *We can walk if it's not far.* | *Denver's* ***farther away*** *than I thought.* | *Aim at the target that's* ***farthest from*** *you.* | *Excuse me,* ***how far*** *is it to Times Square?* | **the far end/side etc.** *There's a TV at the far end of the bar.* | *The car is in the far corner of the parking lot.* **2 the far north/south etc.** the part of a country or area that is farthest in the direction of north, south etc.: *The plains are in the far west of the country.* **3 the far left/right** people who have extreme LEFT-WING or RIGHT-WING political opinions **4 be a far cry from sth** to be very different from something else: *The reward was a far cry from what we'd expected.*

far·a·way /ˈfɑrəˌweɪ/ *adj.* **1** [only before noun] LITERARY distant: *She was alone in a faraway place.* | *faraway noises* **2 a faraway look/expression** an expression on your face which shows that you are not thinking about what is around you but thinking about something very different

farce /fɑrs/ *n.* **1** [singular] an event or a situation that is badly organized and does not happen in the way that it should, so that it seems silly: *The interview was a complete farce. I should've stayed home.* **2** [C,U] ENG. LANG. ARTS a humorous play in which people are involved in silly situations, or the style of writing used in this type of play [**Origin:** 1500–1600 French, Latin *farcire* **to stuff** (=fill with a mixture of cut-up food); because early religious plays often had humorous parts put into them]

far·ci·cal /ˈfɑrsɪkəl/ *adj.* **1** extremely silly and badly organized: *a farcical trial* **2** having the qualities of a farce: *farcical characters* —**farcically** /-kli/ *adv.*

fare¹ /fɛr/ *n.* **1** [C] the price you pay to travel by bus, train, airplane etc.: *The fare is cheaper on Saturdays and Sundays.* | **air/bus/train/cab fare** *The company is paying my air fare.* ▸see THESAURUS box at **cost¹** **2** [U] food, especially food that you can buy in a restaurant or that you eat on a special occasion: *Goose, duck, and turkey are typical holiday fare in the Netherlands.* **3** [U] entertainment that someone else provides for you: *The movie is suitable family fare.* **4** [C] a passenger in a taxi **5 a fare beater** INFORMAL someone who avoids paying for a ticket on a train, SUBWAY, or bus [**Origin:** Old English *faru* **journey**]

fare² *v.* **fare well/badly/better etc.** FORMAL to be successful, unsuccessful etc.: *The show is faring well in the ratings.*

ˌFar ˈEast *n.* **the Far East** the countries in the eastern part of Asia, such as China, Japan, Korea etc. —**Far Eastern** *adj.* → see also MIDDLE EAST, NEAR EAST

fare·well¹ /ˌfɛrˈwɛl/ *n.* [C,U] the action of saying goodbye: *a farewell speech* | *Grantson met with employees to* ***bid them farewell*** (=say goodbye to them). | **a farewell party/drink** (=a party you have because someone is leaving a job, city etc.)

farewell² *interjection* OLD-FASHIONED goodbye

ˌfarewell adˈdress *n.* [C] POLITICS a formal speech given by a politician, especially a president, when he or she leaves his or her government job

ˌfar-ˈfetched *adj.* extremely unlikely to be true or to happen: *At the time, his ideas were considered far-fetched.*

ˌfar-ˈflung *adj.* **1** very distant: *He's off hiking in some far-flung corner of Alaska.* **2** spread out over a very large area: *The company operates a number of far-flung offices.*

Far·go /ˈfɑrgoʊ/ the largest city in the U.S. state of North Dakota

ˌfar ˈgone *adj.* [not before noun] INFORMAL very sick, drunk, crazy etc.: *She's too far gone to understand what's happening.*

farm¹ /fɑrm/ S2 W2 *n.* [C] an area of land, used for growing crops or keeping animals: *a farm in southern Alberta* | *farm animals* | **live/work etc. on a farm** *He grew up on a farm in Iowa.* | **a chicken/pig/wheat etc. farm** *a rice farm in Thailand* [**Origin:** 1300–1400 Old French *ferme* **rent, lease,** from Latin *firmus* **firm, fixed**] → see also **bet the ranch/farm** at BET¹ (6), FACTORY FARM, FARM TEAM, FISH FARM, FUNNY FARM

farm² *v.* [I,T] **1** to use land for growing crops, keeping animals etc.: *My family has farmed here since 1901.* **2 farmed fish/salmon/trout etc.** fish that have been raised in a special place in order to be sold as food, rather than fish that live in the wild

farm out *phr. v.* **1 farm sth ↔ out** to send work to other people instead of doing it yourself: **farm sth out to sb** *Most of the editing is farmed out to freelancers.* **2 farm sb ↔ out** to send someone, especially a child, to a different place or person where they will be taken care of: **farm sb out to sb** *They used to farm me out to relatives in the summer.*

ˈfarm ˌbelt *n.* [C] an area of a country where there are many farms

farm·er /ˈfɑrmɚ/ S3 W2 *n.* [C] someone who owns or manages a farm: *a local farmer* | **a sheep/cattle/pig etc. farmer** *Many pig farmers have been affected by the decision.*

ˈfarmers' ˌmarket *n.* [C] a place where farmers bring their fruit and vegetables to sell directly to people

ˌfarmer's ˈtan *n.* [C] areas of darker skin that appear on the parts of your neck and arms that are not protected from the sun by a T-SHIRT

farm·hand /ˈfɑrmhænd/ *n.* [C] someone who is employed to work on a farm

farm·house /ˈfɑrmhaʊs/ *n.* [C] the main house on a farm, where the farmer lives

farm·ing /ˈfɑrmɪŋ/ *n.* [U] the practice or business of growing crops or keeping animals on a farm

farm·land /ˈfɑrmlænd/ *n.* [U] land used for farming

farm·stead /ˈfɑrmstɛd/ *n.* [C] a farmhouse and the buildings around it

ˈfarm team *n.* [C] a MINOR LEAGUE baseball team that trains players for a particular MAJOR LEAGUE team

farm·yard /ˈfɑrmyɑrd/ *n.* [C] the area next to or around farm buildings

ˈfar-off *adj.* LITERARY **1** a long way from where you are: *travelers from a far-off land* **2** a long time ago: *those far-off days when we were young*

ˌfar-ˈout *adj.* **1** very strange or unusual: *Dave has some pretty far-out beliefs about UFOs.* **2** OLD-FASHIONED SLANG extremely good

Far·ra·khan /ˈfærəˌkɑn/, **Lou·is** /ˈluɪs/ (1933–) the leader of the Nation of Islam

ˌfar-ˈreaching *adj.* having a big influence or effect: *a far-reaching human rights law*

far·ri·er /ˈfæriɚ/ *n.* [C] someone who makes special metal shoes for horses' feet

Far·si /ˈfɑrsi/ *n.* [U] the language of Iran SYN Persian

far·sight·ed /ˈfɑrˌsaɪṭɪd/ *adj.* **1** able to see or read things clearly only when they are far away from you OPP nearsighted **2** APPROVING considering what will happen in the future: *Even farsighted advisers were surprised by the speed of political change.* —**farsightedly** *adv.* —**farsightedness** *n.* [U]

fart¹ /fɑrt/ *v.* [I] IMPOLITE to make air come out of your BOWELS

fart² *n.* IMPOLITE an act of making air come out of your BOWELS

far·ther /ˈfɑrðɚ/ *adj., adv* the COMPARATIVE of FAR

> **WORD CHOICE** **farther and further**
> • Use **farther** to talk about distance: *I can't run any farther.* | *There's a gas station a few miles farther down the road.*
> • Use **further** to talk about time, quantities, or amounts: *Prices will probably increase further next year.* | *Patty refused to discuss the matter any further.* People often use **further** to talk about distance, but many teachers consider this use incorrect.

far·thest /ˈfɑrðɪst/ *adj., adv* the SUPERLATIVE of FAR

far·thing /ˈfɑrðɪŋ/ *n.* [C] a British coin, used in past times, that was worth one quarter of a PENNY

fas·ci·a /ˈfeɪʃə/ *n. plural* **fascias** or **fasciae** /-ʃi-i/ [C] **1** the flat outside surface of a building, which is meant to be pretty rather than being part of the structure of the building **2** a band of material in your body that separates, attaches, or surrounds muscles, organs etc.

fas·ci·nate /ˈfæsəˌneɪt/ *v.* [I,T not in progressive] to attract or interest someone very much: *Insects have always fascinated me.* | *The Mona Lisa has the power to fascinate and impress.* [**Origin:** 1500–1600 Latin *fascinatus*, from *fascinum* **use of (evil) magic**]

fas·ci·nat·ed /ˈfæsəˌneɪṭɪd/ *adj.* [not before noun] extremely interested by something or someone: *As a schoolboy, Martin was fascinated by aviation.* | **be fascinated to discover/hear/learn etc.** *We were fascinated to learn she had grown up in Kenya.*

fas·ci·nat·ing /ˈfæsəˌneɪṭɪŋ/ *adj.* extremely interesting: *a fascinating woman* | ***I found** Rutherfurd's book on Russia **fascinating**.* | **it is fascinating to see/hear/watch etc. sth** *It was fascinating to watch how the garments were made.* —**fascinatingly** *adv.*

fas·ci·na·tion /ˌfæsəˈneɪʃən/ *n.* **1** [singular, U] the state of being very interested in something, so that you want to look at it, learn about it etc.: **have a fascination with/for sth** *Kucher **has had a fascination with** bugs since childhood.* | **in/with fascination** *The children watched him **with fascination**.* **2** [C,U] the quality that an object, event, or person has of being very interesting to people, or something that is very interesting to people: **have/hold fascination for sb** *The idea of space travel will always hold great fascination for me.*

fas·cism /ˈfæʃɪzəm/ *n.* [U] POLITICS an extreme political system in which people's lives are controlled by the state and no political opposition is allowed

fas·cist /ˈfæʃɪst/ *n.* [C] **1** POLITICS someone who supports fascism **2** INFORMAL someone who is cruel and unfair and does not like people to argue with them: *My children have occasionally accused me of being a fascist.* [**Origin:** 1900–2000 Italian *Fascista*, from *fascio* **group of things tied together**] —**fascist** *adj.*

fash·ion¹ /ˈfæʃən/ S3 W3 *n.* **1** [C,U] the fact that something is popular or thought to be good at a particular time: *The color black is always **in fashion**.* | *Harper carries classic styles that never **go out of fashion*** (=stop being popular). | *His ideas are **coming back into fashion**.* | *Bottled mineral water **was the fashion** in the late 1980s.* **2** [C,U] a style of clothes, hair etc. that is popular at a particular time: *this year's men's fashions* | *These bags are this year's biggest fashion accessory.* | *She always buys **the latest fashions**.* | *Nightclubbers and teenagers prompted **the fashion of** body piercing.* | *The store is a temple of **high fashion*** (=the most modern and expensive fashions). | *Our typical customer is very **fashion conscious*** (=always wanting to wear the newest fashions). **3** [U] the business or study of making and selling clothes, shoes etc. in new and changing styles: *the assistant fashion editor at "Vogue"* | *one of the biggest names in fashion* | *a fashion magazine* | *She is studying fashion and hopes to* *work in* ***the fashion industry***. | *The judges are some of the world's best known* ***fashion designers***. **4 in a... fashion** FORMAL in a particular way: *The books were arranged* ***in an orderly fashion*** (=neatly). **5 like it's going out of fashion** INFORMAL if you eat, drink, or use something like it's going out of fashion, you eat, drink, or use a lot of it: *She's been spending money like it's going out of fashion.* **6 after/in the fashion of sb** in a style that is typical of a particular person: *His first novels are very much after the fashion of Faulkner and O'Connor.* **7 after a fashion** FORMAL if you do something after a fashion, you can do it, but not very well: *The group learns to ride and lasso after a fashion.* [**Origin:** 1300–1400 Old French *façon*, from Latin *factio* **act of making**] → see also FASHION PLATE, FASHION SENSE, FASHION SHOW, FASHION VICTIM

fashion² *v.* [T] **1** FORMAL to shape or make something, using your hands or only a few tools: **fashion sth from sth** *Several prisoners were armed with weapons fashioned from razor blades.* | **fashion sth into sth** *As a boy, he had fashioned pieces of wood into homemade baseball bats.* **2** [usually passive] to influence and form someone's ideas and opinions or a particular situation: *Our attitudes to politics are fashioned by the media.*

-fashion /fæʃən/ *suffix* [in adverbs] like something, or in the way that a particular group of people does something: *They ate Indian-fashion, using their fingers.*

fash·ion·a·ble /ˈfæʃənəbəl/ *adj.* **1** popular, especially for a short period of time OPP **unfashionable**: *fashionable clothes* | *shoes for children in fashionable colors*

THESAURUS

trendy modern and fashionable: *trendy restaurants*
stylish attractive in a fashionable way: *a store selling stylish furniture*
designer designer clothes, watches etc. are made by someone who is famous for designing fashionable things: *a pair of designer jeans*
be in style/fashion to be fashionable during a particular period of time: *What colors are in style for this fall?* | *Western movies were then in fashion.*
be in INFORMAL to be fashionable at the present time: *Long skirts are in this summer.*

►see THESAURUS box at **clothes** **2** popular with, or used by, rich people: *a very fashionable restaurant* **3** someone who is fashionable wears good clothes, goes to expensive restaurants etc. OPP **unfashionable**: *a young, fashionable crowd* —**fashionably** *adv.*

fash·ion·ably /ˈfæʃənəbli/ *adv.* **1 fashionably late** a little late, especially because you want people who are waiting for you to pay special attention to your arrival: *Lucy and Rose arrived fashionably late.* **2** according to the current style: *You don't have to dress fashionably, just warmly.*

ˈfashion house *n.* [C] a company that produces new and expensive styles of clothes

ˈfashion plate *n.* [C] INFORMAL someone who likes to wear very fashionable clothes

ˈfashion sense *n.* [U] the ability to choose clothes that make you look attractive

ˈfashion show *n.* [C] an event at which new styles of clothes are shown to the public

ˈfashion ˌstatement *n.* [C] an unusual way of wearing clothes that makes people notice you and shows them what your feelings, attitudes, or opinions are: *She wears old army uniforms as a fashion statement.*

ˈfashion ˌvictim *n.* [C] INFORMAL someone who always tries to wear what is fashionable, even though it makes them look bad

fast¹ /fæst/ S2 *adj.*
1 MOVING QUICKLY a) moving or traveling quickly OPP **slow**: *He's one of the fastest sprinters in the world.* | *The first pitch was fast and hard.* **b)** able to travel or move very quickly OPP **slow**: *The new convertible is fast and fun to drive.*
2 IN A SHORT TIME a) doing something or happening in a short time OPP **slow**: *The subway is the fastest way to get downtown.* | *We hope Arlene will make a fast recovery.* **b)** able to do something in a short time OPP **slow**: *I'm a pretty fast reader.* **c)** happening without delay OPP **slow**: *One man's fast response saved the victim's life.*
3 CLOCK [not before noun] a clock that is fast shows a later time than the real time OPP **slow**: *Is it really 6:45, or is my watch fast?* | *I keep the clock five minutes fast, so I won't be late.*
4 fast film/lens a film or LENS on a camera that can be used when there is not much light, or when something is moving very quickly
5 COLOR a color that is fast will not change when clothes are washed → see also COLORFAST
6 SPORTS a fast surface is one on which a ball moves very quickly, or one on which a person, horse, or dog can run very quickly
7 fast talker someone who talks very quickly and easily but may not be sincere or honest: *He's a fast talker who asks and answers his own questions.*
8 fast friends LITERARY two people who are very friendly for a long time
9 a fast worker INFORMAL someone who gets what they want very quickly, especially someone who starts a sexual relationship very quickly
10 WOMAN OLD-FASHIONED becoming involved quickly in sexual relationships with men
11 make sth fast to tie something such as a boat or tent firmly to something else → see also **make a fast buck** at BUCK¹ (1), FAST FOOD, FAST FORWARD, FAST TRACK, **pull a fast one** at PULL¹ (12)

fast² S1 W3 *adv.*
1 QUICKLY moving quickly OPP **slowly**: *The car was going pretty fast when it went off the road.* | *Burglars work fast.* | *Just keep skiing* ***as fast as you can***. | *Johnny ran off* ***as fast as his legs could carry him*** (=running as quickly as he could).

THESAURUS

quickly/swiftly used especially about movement: *I ran quickly down the stairs.* | *The police reacted swiftly to the threat.*
rapidly/speedily used especially about the speed at which something happens: *Unemployment rose rapidly.* | *We need to resolve this issue speedily.*
at high/great speed used about movement: *The car went around the corner at high speed.*
at a rapid rate used especially about a change: *The world is changing at a rapid rate.*

2 IN A SHORT TIME a) in a short time OPP **slowly**: *Prices aren't rising as fast as they were a year ago.* | *Kids grow up so fast these days.* | *a fast-growing community* | **be fast becoming/developing/disappearing** | *Many Asian countries are fast becoming real economic powers.* **b)** soon and without delay OPP **slowly**: *Two of these will get rid of your headache fast.* | *How fast can you get it ready?*
3 fast asleep sleeping very deeply: *Most of the household was still fast asleep.*
4 TIGHTLY firmly or tightly, and unable to move: *The front of the boat was* ***stuck fast*** *in the mud.* | *The gun was* ***held fast*** *in his hand.*
5 hold fast (to sth) to continue to believe in or support an idea, principle etc.: *Bush urged the party to hold fast to its traditions.*
6 not so fast SPOKEN used to tell someone not to be too eager to do or believe something: *"Not so fast!" he said as she tried to leave.*
7 fast and furious happening or changing very quickly with a lot of energy: *With elections a year away, proposals for tax cuts are coming fast and furious.*
[**Origin:** Old English *fæst* **firm**] → see also **play fast and loose with sb/sth** at PLAY¹ (32), **stand fast/firm** at STAND¹ (20), **thick and fast** at THICK² (3)

fast³ *v.* [I] to eat little or no food for a period of time, especially for religious reasons: *Muslims fast during Ramadan.* ►see THESAURUS box at **eat**

fast⁴ *n.* [C] a period during which someone eats little or no food, especially for religious reasons: *a one-day fast for charity* | *The group will **break its fast** (=end the fast by eating or drinking something) tomorrow.*

fast·ball /ˈfæstbɔl/ *n.* [C] a ball that is thrown very hard and quickly toward the BATTER in a game of baseball

ˈfast ˌday *n.* [C] a day when you do not eat any food, especially for religious reasons

fas·ten /ˈfæsən/ *v.*
1 CLOTHES/BAG ETC. also **fasten up a)** [T] to join together the two sides of a coat, shirt, bag etc. so that it is closed OPP **unfasten**: *Please fasten your seat belts.* | *With the strap fastened, you should not be able to get the bike helmet off.* **b)** [I] to become joined together with buttons, hooks etc.: *Does the dress fasten in the back?* | *Many children's shoes now fasten with Velcro.*
2 ATTACH STH TO STH [T] to attach something firmly to another object or surface: **fasten sth to/onto sth** *A pulley is fastened to the ceiling of the warehouse.* | **fasten sth together** *He fastened the two ends of the rope together*

THESAURUS
attach to fasten something firmly to another object or surface
join to connect or fasten things together
glue to join things together using glue
tape to fasten something using tape
staple to fasten something using staples (=small pieces of bent wire that go through paper)
clip to fasten things together using a clip (=a small object that goes over paper to hold it together)
tie to fasten a tie or shoes etc. by making a knot
button (up) to fasten the buttons on a shirt, coat etc.
zip (up) to fasten clothes, bags etc. with a zipper
unfasten, **untie**, **undo**, **unbutton**, **unzip** to open something that is fastened

3 fasten your eyes on sb/sth to look at someone or something for a long time: *Her dark eyes fastened on Arthur's face.*
4 fasten your attention on sth to think a lot about one particular thing
5 WINDOW/GATE ETC. [I,T] to firmly close a window, gate etc. so that it will not open, or to become firmly closed OPP **unfasten**: *Make sure all the windows are securely fastened before you leave.*
6 fasten blame on sb/sth to blame someone or something, often in a way that is not fair
7 HANDS/ARMS ETC. [I,T] if your hand, arms etc. fasten around someone or something, or you fasten them, they close tightly around the person or thing: *I felt his hands fastening around my throat.*
ˈfasten on/upon sth *phr. v.* to concentrate attention on one particular thing because you think it is the most important: *Brennan's campaign has fastened on budget problems as a way to get voters' attention.*

fasteners

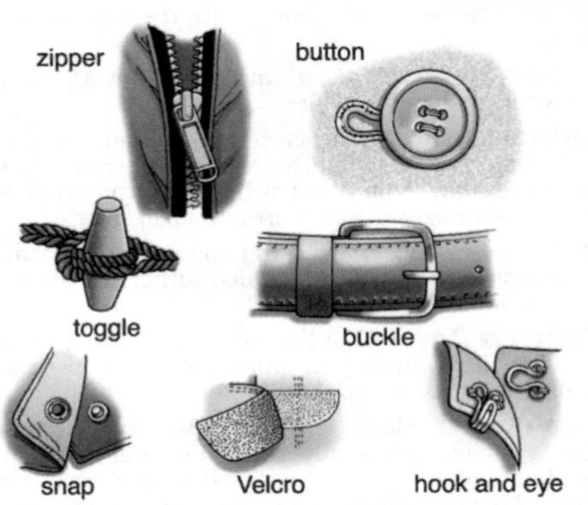

fas·ten·er /ˈfæsənɚ/ also **fas·ten·ing** /ˈfæsənɪŋ/ *n.* [C] something that you use to join something together, for example a button on a piece of clothing: *a Velcro fastener*

ˈfast food *n.* [U] inexpensive food, for example HAMBURGERS, that is prepared and served quickly in a restaurant: *a fast-food restaurant*

ˌfast ˈforward, fast-forward *v.* **1** [I,T] to wind a TAPE forward quickly in a machine by pressing a button: *Listeners can fast forward and rewind the taped audio.* **2** [I] to move quickly to a later point in a story or stage of development: *Now fast forward to 1976 when Bolin met his future wife.* —**fast forward** *n.* [U] *He watched the whole movie on fast forward.*

fas·tid·i·ous /fæˈstɪdiəs, fə-/ *adj.* very careful about small details in your appearance, work etc.: *A cat is a fastidious animal that washes itself frequently.* [**Origin:** 1400–1500 Latin *fastidiosus*, from *fastidium* **strong dislike**] —**fastidiously** *adv.* —**fastidiousness** *n.* [U] → see also FUSSY

ˈfast lane *n.* [singular] **the fast lane a)** the part of a big road where people drive fastest **b)** an exciting way of living that involves dangerous or expensive activities: *He lived **life in the fast lane**, and died young.*

fast·ness /ˈfæstnɪs/ *n.* [C] LITERARY a safe place that is difficult to reach SYN **stronghold**: *mountain fastnesses*

ˈfast track *n.* [singular] a way of achieving something more quickly than it is normally done: *The company developed a fast track for Internet customers.* | **on the fast track (to sth)** *employees on the fast track to management positions*

fat¹ /fæt/ S1 W2 *adj. comparative* **fatter**, *superlative* **fattest**
1 FLESH weighing too much because you have too much flesh on your body: *He's short and fat.* | *I always look so fat in pictures.* | *a **big fat** kid* | *The cat's starting to **get fat**.*

THESAURUS
You can call yourself **fat**, but it is not polite to directly tell someone else that they are fat: *I'm getting really fat.*
overweight used as a more polite way of describing someone who is fat: *He's a little overweight.*
big, **heavy**, **large** used as polite ways to describe someone who is big, strong, or fat: *a heavy woman in her fifties* | *He's a pretty big guy.*
obese used about someone who is extremely fat in a way that is dangerous to their health: *the health risks of being obese*
chubby used about someone, especially a baby or a child, who is slightly fat: *a chubby blond boy*
plump used to say that someone, especially a woman or a child, is slightly fat in a pleasant way: *Her grandmother was a plump, kindly woman.*
stout used to say that an adult is slightly fat: *a stout woman in her sixties*
tubby used about someone who is short and fat, especially around the stomach: *a somewhat tubby little man*
→ THIN

2 THICK OR WIDE thick or wide: *There was a fat envelope waiting for him on his desk.* | *fat red plastic earrings*
3 MONEY [only before noun] INFORMAL containing or worth a large amount of money: *He left the waitress a nice fat tip.* | *a fat profit*
4 a fat lip a lip that is swollen because it has been injured
5 fat cat INFORMAL, DISAPPROVING someone who earns a lot of money because they have a very senior job in a company, organization etc., used when you think they earn too much money
6 grow fat on sth WRITTEN to become rich because of something: *These stock brokers grow fat on other people's money.*

SPOKEN PHRASES

7 fat chance used to say that something is very unlikely to happen: *You want tickets for the big game? Fat chance.*
8 be in fat city OLD-FASHIONED to have plenty of money
9 a fat lot of good/use if something is a fat lot of good, it is not useful and does not help you at all: *I practiced a lot, but a fat lot of good it did me* (=the practice did not help).
10 a fat lot sb cares (about sb/sth) used to say that someone does not care at all

[**Origin:** Old English *fætt*] —**fatness** *n.* [U] → see also PHAT

fat² *n.*
1 PERSON OR ANIMAL [U] BIOLOGY a white or yellow TISSUE in the body of people and animals that protects the ORGANS, stores energy, and helps to keep them warm: *a layer of fat under the skin*
2 BIOLOGY the layer of tissue under the skin that develops too much and hides the natural shape of the body when a person or animal eats too much: ***A roll of fat*** (=a fold of fat in someone's skin who is very fat) *bulged over his belt.*
3 ON MEAT [U] the soft white substance that is attached to meat: *Cut off the fat before cooking the chicken breasts.*
4 IN FOOD [C,U] an oily substance in some foods: *A can of tuna packed in water contains 1.2 grams of fat.* | **high/low in fat** *Try to avoid foods that are high in fat.* | **high-/low-fat** *low-fat cottage cheese*
5 FOR COOKING [C,U] an oily substance taken from animals or plants and used in cooking: *Fry the potatoes in oil or bacon fat.*
6 MONEY [U] money used to buy things that you do not really need: *Most people are trying to **trim the fat** out of their budgets this Christmas.*
7 the fat is in the fire used to say that there will be trouble because of something that has happened
8 live off the fat of the land to get enough money to live comfortably without doing much work
9 run/go to fat to start to become fat, especially because you are getting older or do not do much exercise: *He was in his mid fifties and running to fat.* → see also BABY FAT, **chew the fat** at CHEW¹ (4), **not have an ounce of fat on you** at OUNCE (4)

fa·tal /ˈfeɪtl/ *adj.* **1** resulting in someone's death: *The gas can be fatal if inhaled in large amounts.* | **a fatal accident/illness/injury etc.** *a fatal climbing accident* | *German measles can **prove fatal*** (=make someone die) *to an unborn baby.* **2** having a very bad effect, especially making someone fail or stop what they are doing: **be/prove fatal to sth** *The loss could **prove fatal to** their championship hopes.* | *Her **fatal mistake** was to marry too young.* | *The developments dealt **a fatal blow** to the government's peace plan.* | *There are **fatal flaws*** (=serious weaknesses) *in this computer program.* **3** a fatal error is one that stops a computer program from working correctly

fa·tal·ism /ˈfeɪtlˌɪzəm/ *n.* [U] the belief that there is nothing you can do to prevent events from happening —**fatalist** *n.* [C]

fa·tal·is·tic /ˌfeɪtlˈɪstɪk/ *adj.* believing that there is nothing you can do to prevent things from happening: *Emma was fatalistic about her future.* —**fatalistically** /-kli/ *adv.*

fa·tal·i·ty /feɪˈtæləti, fə-/ *n. plural* **fatalities** **1** [C,U] a death in an accident or violent attack: *This year there have been 15% fewer traffic fatalities.* | *Airplane **fatality rates** are low.* **2** [U] FORMAL the fact that a disease is certain to cause death: *New drugs have reduced the fatality of the disease.* **3** [U] FORMAL the feeling that you cannot control what happens to you

fa·tal·ly /ˈfeɪtl-i/ *adv.* **1** in a way that causes death: **fatally wounded/injured/burned etc.** *Eight children were fatally injured in the explosion.* **2** in a way that will make something fail or be unable to continue: *The strategy is **fatally flawed**.*

fate /feɪt/ W3 *n.* **1** [C] the things that will happen to someone or something, especially bad events: **+of** *These rulings will affect the fate of more than 6,000 refugees.* | **decide/settle/seal sb's fate** *A three-man, three-woman jury will decide Chambers' fate.* | *So far, the video game has not **suffered the same fate** as other toy fads* (=it has not become unpopular). | **leave/abandon sb to their fate** (=leave someone when something bad is likely to happen to them) **2** [U] also **Fate** a power that is believed to control what happens in people's lives → see also PROVIDENCE: *He felt that fate had been very unfair to him.* | *By a lucky **twist of fate*** (=completely unexpected event), *we were on the same plane.* **3 a fate worse than death** HUMOROUS an experience that seems like the worst thing that could happen to you: *I knew that Grandma's visit would be a fate worse than death.* **4 the Fates** the three GODDESSES who, according to the ancient Greeks, controlled what happened to people [**Origin:** 1300–1400 French, Latin *fatum* **what has been spoken (by the gods)**, from *fari* **to speak**] → see also **tempt fate** at TEMPT (3)

fat·ed /ˈfeɪtɪd/ *adj.* LITERARY **be fated to do sth** certain to happen or to do something because of fate: *Achilles was fated to die after Hector.* → see also ILL-FATED

fate·ful /ˈfeɪtfəl/ *adj.* having an important, usually bad, effect on future events: *that **fateful day** when President Kennedy was killed* —**fatefully** *adv.*

ˈfat farm *n.* [C] INFORMAL a place where people who are fat can go to lose weight and improve their health

ˌfat-ˈfree *adj.* food that is fat-free does not have any fat in it: *fat-free yogurt*

fat·head /ˈfæthɛd/ *n.* [C] SLANG a stupid person —**fat-headed** *adj.*

fa·ther¹ /ˈfɑðɚ/ S1 W1 *n.* **1** [C] a male parent: *I'd like you to meet my father.* | **a father of two/three etc.** *Hernandez, the father of five, has not been able to work since July.* ►see THESAURUS box at **relative¹**
2 Father a) a priest, especially in the Catholic church: *Have you met Father Simmons?* **b)** a way of speaking to or about God, used in the Christian religion: *Heavenly Father, please forgive us our sins.* **3 the father of sth** the man who was responsible for starting something: *George Washington is the father of our country.*
4 father figure an older man who you trust and respect
5 like father, like son used to say that a boy behaves like his father, especially when this behavior is bad
6 fathers [plural] LITERARY people related to you who lived a long time ago; ANCESTORS: *Our fathers came to a new country with new hope.* [**Origin:** Old English *fæder*] → see also CITY FATHER, FOREFATHER

father² *v.* [T] **1** to make a woman have a baby: *Taylor denies fathering her 4-month-old son.* **2** to start an important new idea or system: *Roosevelt fathered the concept of Social Security.*

ˈfather ˌfigure *n.* [C] an older man who you trust and respect to give you help or advice in life: *Ken was a father figure to all of us.*

fa·ther·hood /ˈfɑðɚˌhʊd/ *n.* [U] the state of being a father

ˈfather-in-ˌlaw *n. plural* **fathers-in-law** [C] the father of your husband or wife

fa·ther·land /ˈfɑðɚˌlænd/ *n.* [singular] the country where you or your family were born, especially when you live away from it but still feel a strong connection to it → see also MOTHER COUNTRY, MOTHERLAND

fa·ther·ly /ˈfɑðɚli/ *adj.* kind and gentle in a way that is considered typical of a good father: *He spoke in a warm, fatherly tone.*

ˈFather's Day *n.* [C] a holiday in the U.S. and Canada on the third Sunday of June, on which people give cards and presents to their father

fath·om¹ /ˈfæðəm/ *v.* [T] to understand what something means, especially something very difficult to understand, after thinking about it carefully: *The jury had difficulty fathoming the technical details.* | **fathom how/why/where etc.** *Mark couldn't fathom why she hated him so much.*

fathom[2] *n.* [C] a unit for measuring how deep water is, equal to 6 feet or 1.83 meters

fath•om•less /ˈfæðəmlɪs/ *adj.* LITERARY **1** too deep to be measured **2** too complicated to be understood

fa•tigue /fəˈtig/ *n.* [U] **1** extreme tiredness: *Stoklos was showing signs of fatigue after a difficult game.* **2** TECHNICAL weakness in a substance such as metal, caused when it is bent or stretched many times, which is likely to make it break **3 fatigues** [plural] loose-fitting army clothes —**fatigue** *v.* [T] FORMAL → see also COMBAT FATIGUE

fa•tigued /fəˈtigd/ *adj.* [T] FORMAL extremely tired

fat•so /ˈfætsoʊ/ *n.* [C] SPOKEN an insulting word for someone who is fat

fat•ten /ˈfætˀn/ *v.* **1** [I,T] to make an animal become fatter so that it is ready to eat, or to become fat and ready to eat **2** [T] to make an amount larger: *Increased profits will fatten the bonuses of the partners.*

fatten sb/sth ↔ **up** *phr. v.* to make a thin person or animal fatter: *Cattle are sent to the feedlot to be fattened up.*

fat•ten•ing /ˈfætˀn-ɪŋ/ *adj.* likely to make you fat: *a fattening dessert*

fat•ty[1] /ˈfæti/ *adj.* *comparative* **fattier**, *superlative* **fattiest** containing a lot of fat: *fatty foods*

fatty[2] *n.* [C] SPOKEN an insulting word for someone who is fat

ˌfatty ˈacid *n.* [C] BIOLOGY an acid that is obtained from natural substances, such as oil, fat, and plant material, which the cells of your body need to use food effectively

fat•u•ous /ˈfætʃuəs/ *adj.* FORMAL stupid or FOOLISH: *fatuous speeches* —**fatuously** *adv.* —**fatuousness** *n.* [U]

fat•wa /ˈfɑtwɑ/ *n.* [C] an official order made by an important Islamic religious leader

fau•cet /ˈfɔsɪt/ *n.* [C] the piece of equipment that you turn on and off to control the flow of water from a pipe SYN **tap** [**Origin:** 1300–1400 Old French *fausset* **something that closes a hole in a container**, from Late Latin *falsare* **to make false**]

Faulk•ner /ˈfɔknɚ/, **William** (1897–1962) a U.S. writer of NOVELS about the Deep South of the U.S.

fault[1] /fɔlt/ S2 W3 *n.*

1 responsibility that you have for something bad that has happened because you caused it or failed to stop it: **be sb's fault** *The accident was my fault.* | **be sb's fault (that)** *It's your fault we're late.* | **be sb's fault for doing sth** *It was Greg's fault for leaving the window open.* | ***It's partly their own fault** if they don't get promoted.* | *He lost his job **through no fault of** his **own**.* | *I think **the fault lies with** parents who are too permissive.*

2 at fault a person, organization, or system that is at fault is responsible for something bad that has happened: *Both drivers were at fault because they were driving too fast.*

3 STH WRONG WITH STH [C] **a)** something that is wrong with something, which could be improved: *The main fault of her writing is that it lacks detail.* | *The treaty was a great achievement, **for all its faults*** (=in spite of its faults). **b)** something that is wrong with a machine, system, design etc., which prevents it from working correctly: +**in** *a fault in the airplane's fuel system* | **an electrical/a mechanical/a technical fault** *The fire was caused by an electrical fault.* ►see THESAURUS box at defect[1]

THESAURUS

defect a fault in something that is there because of the way it was made or designed: *a structural defect in the building*
flaw a mistake, mark, or bad feature that makes something not perfect: *the flaw in the argument*
weakness a fault in a system, organization, design etc.: *Comment on the strengths and weaknesses of each method.*
bug a fault in a computer program: *The new software has a few bugs in it.*
mistake something that is wrong in someone's spelling, grammar, calculations etc.: *I think you've made a mistake here – it should be 133, not 121.*

4 SB'S CHARACTER [C] a bad or weak part of someone's character: *He's a nice boy, although he has his faults.* | ***For all her faults*** (=in spite of her faults), *I still love her.*

5 CRACK [C] EARTH SCIENCE a large crack in the rocks that form the Earth's surface: *the San Andreas fault*

6 generous/kind/honest etc. to a fault extremely generous, kind etc., especially to a degree that is unnecessary: *Our cat is friendly to a fault.*

7 TENNIS [C] a mistake made when a player is serving the ball in a game of tennis

[**Origin:** 1200–1300 Old French *faute*, from Latin *fallere* **to deceive, disappoint**] → see also **find fault with sb/sth** at FIND[1] (14)

fault[2] *v.* [T] to criticize someone or something for doing something wrong: *You can't fault him for a lack of effort.* | *The meal was a little bland, but you **couldn't fault** the service* (=the service was good).

fault•less /ˈfɔltlɪs/ *adj.* having no mistakes SYN **perfect**: *a faultless memory* —**faultlessly** *adv.* —**faultlessness** *n.* [U]

fault•y /ˈfɔlti/ *adj.* **1** something such as a machine that is faulty has something wrong with it that stops it from working correctly, or it was not made correctly: *faulty electrical wiring* **2** a faulty way of thinking about something contains a mistake that results in a wrong decision: *The article was full of faulty reasoning.* —**faultily** *adv.*

faun /fɔn, fɑn/ *n.* [C] an ancient Roman god with the body of a man and the legs and horns of a goat

fau•na /ˈfɔnə, ˈfɑ-/ *n.* [C,U] BIOLOGY all the animals living in a particular place or at a particular time in history [**Origin:** 1700–1800 Late Latin *Fauna* **wife or sister of Faunus** (Roman god of nature and farms)] → see also FLORA

Faust /faʊst/, **Jo•hann** /ˈyoʊhɑn/ also **Dr. Faustus** /ˌdɑktɚ ˈfaʊstəs/ a German doctor and SCHOLAR of the early 16th century, who appears in many stories, plays etc. as a man who sold his soul to the Devil in exchange for knowledge and power

fauv•ism /ˈfoʊˌvɪzəm/ *n.* [U] a style of painting that uses pure bright colors, which was developed in the early 20th century —**fauvist** *n.* [C]

faux /foʊ/ *adj.* [only before noun] artificial, but made to look real: *faux pearls*

faux pas /ˌfoʊ ˈpɑ/ *n.* [C] an embarrassing mistake in a social situation: *Talking business at dinner is a faux pas in France.*

fa•va bean /ˈfɑvə ˌbin/ *n.* [C] a large flat pale green bean

fave /feɪv/ *n.* [C] INFORMAL a favorite person or thing: *The band is a local fave.* —**fave** *adj.*

fa•ve•la /fəˈvelə/ *n.* [C] a Brazilian SLUM (=place in a city where many poor people live) → see also BARRIO

fa•vor[1] /ˈfeɪvɚ/ S3 W2 *n.*

1 HELP [C] something that you do for someone in order to help them or be kind to them: *Could you **do me a favor** and watch the baby for half an hour?* | *I need to **ask** you both **for a** huge **favor**.* | *I **have a favor to ask** – could you call Eric for me?* | *I'll repair the bike **as a favor to** you.* | *I **owed** him **a favor** so I couldn't refuse.* | *Thanks for all your help – I'll **return the favor*** (=help you because you have helped me) *sometime!* | *I would consider it a **personal favor** if you came.*

2 SUPPORT/APPROVAL [U] support or approval for someone or something such as a plan, idea, or system: *A number of politicians have said they **are in favor of** term limits.* | *I'm **all in favor of*** (=completely approve of) *the changes.* | *Several teachers have **spoken in favor of** closing the school.* | *Will **all in favor say aye*** (=used when taking a vote)? | *Plans to increase spending have **lost favor*** (=stopped being supported) *among the president's inner circle.* | *We're hoping the board will **look***

F

with favor on (=use its power to help something succeed) *our plan.* | **find/gain/win favor** *It's hoped that the proposal will gain favor with local residents.* | **find/rule in favor of sb/sth** (=make a legal decision that supports someone or something)
3 reject/abandon/avoid sth in favor of sth to stop using one person, plan, idea, or system and choose another because you think it is better: *The tunnel was abandoned in favor of a bridge.*
4 in sb's favor if something is in someone's favor, it gives them an advantage over someone else: *The vote was 60–54 in Warren's favor.* | *In an interview, a good first impression* ***works in your favor*** (=gives you an advantage). | *Everyone knows that you can't win in gambling because* ***the odds are stacked in*** *the dealer's* ***favor*** (=he has a big advantage).
5 POPULAR [U] if someone or something is in favor or out of favor, people like and approve of them at the present time, or do not like and approve of them anymore: *He isn't* ***in favor with*** *the team's management.* | *More traditional teaching methods are* ***back in favor*** (=popular again). | *Although he's* ***out of favor****, some people still read his books.* | **fall/go out of favor** *The theory fell out of favor in the 1980s.*
6 be thankful/grateful for small favors to be pleased that a bad situation is not as bad as it could be
7 do me/us a favor SPOKEN used to tell someone angrily that you want them to do something: *Do us a favor and leave us alone!*
8 do yourself a favor SPOKEN used when giving someone advice about what they should do: *Do yourself a favor and stop seeing him.*
9 GIFT [C] a small gift given to guests at a party: *inexpensive party favors in plastic bags*
10 don't do me any favors INFORMAL used to say that someone's offer is not very helpful or generous: *"If you want, you can rent my car from me while you're here." "Don't do me any favors."*
11 SEX favors [plural] OLD-FASHIONED a sexual relationship that a woman agrees to have with a man: *Several women had been pressured for* ***sexual favors****.*
12 UNFAIR SUPPORT [U] support that is given to one person or group and not to others in a way that does not seem fair SYN **favoritism** → see also **curry favor with sb** at CURRY[2] (1), **without fear or favor** at FEAR[1] (5)

favor² *v.* [T]
1 PREFER/SUPPORT to prefer or support one person or thing, especially when there are several to choose from: *The president is believed to favor further tax cuts.* | **favor sb/sth over sb/sth** *Voters favored Rankin over Hall by a small margin.*
2 GIVE AN ADVANTAGE to treat someone much better than someone else, in an unfair way: *Many teachers favor boys without even realizing it.*
3 HELP to provide the right conditions for something to happen: *The current economy does not favor the creation of small businesses.*
4 LOOK LIKE OLD-FASHIONED to look like one of your parents or grandparents: *I think he favors his Uncle Dean.*
favor sb **with** sth *phr. v.* FORMAL to give someone something that gives them an advantage or that pleases them: *Maybe Cindy will favor us with a song.*

fa·vor·a·ble /ˈfeɪvərəbəl/ *adj.* **1** a favorable report, opinion, or reaction shows that you think that someone or something is good or that you agree with them: *a favorable court ruling* | *The reviews have all been quite favorable.* **2** appropriate and likely to make something happen or succeed OPP **unfavorable**: **+for/to** *Are conditions favorable for flying?* **3** reasonable and not too expensive or difficult: *favorable interest rates* **4** making people like or approve of someone or something: *Dress appropriately in order to* ***make a favorable impression****.* **5** treating someone or something much better than someone or something else, in an unfair way: *Finch claims he received no* ***favorable treatment*** *from the government.* —**favorably** *adv.*

fa·vored /ˈfeɪvərd/ *adj.* [only before noun] **1** receiving special attention, help, or treatment, especially in an unfair way: *Congress approved "most favored nation" trade status for the country.* **2** chosen or preferred by many people: *"Time out," rather than spanking, is now the favored form of discipline for many parents.* **3** a favored team, player etc. is one that is expected to win: *Kansas City is favored by 4 points.* → see also ILL-FAVORED

fa·vor·ite¹ /ˈfeɪvrɪt, -vərɪt/ S3 W3 *adj.* **1** [only before noun] someone or something that you like more than any other one of its kind: *What's your favorite color?* | *Science was my* ***least favorite*** *subject in school.* | *"The Wizard of Oz" is my* ***all-time favorite*** *movie.* **2 a favorite son** a politician, sports player etc. who is popular with people in the area that they come from

favorite² S2 W2 *n.* [C] **1** something that you like more than other things of the same kind: *Apple fritters are my favorite.* | *This song is* ***an old favorite*** *of mine.* **2** someone who receives more attention and approval than is fair: *Parents shouldn't have favorites.* | *A good teacher never* ***plays favorites****.* → see also FAVORITISM **3** the team, person etc. that is expected to win a race or competition: *Which horse is the favorite?* | **a favorite to do sth** *Italy was the favorite to win the World Cup.*

fa·vor·it·ism /ˈfeɪvrəˌtɪzəm/ *n.* [U] a way of treating one person or group better than others in an unfair way: *School district employees believed that promotions were based on favoritism.*

fa·vour /ˈfeɪvər/ *n., v.* the British and Canadian spelling of FAVOR, also used in the words "favourable," "favoured," "favourite," and "favouritism"

fawn¹ /fɔn, fɑn/ *v.* [I] to praise someone and be friendly to them in an insincere way, because you want them to like you or give you something: **+on/over** *People were fawning over him, hoping for tickets.*

fawn² *n.* **1** [C] BIOLOGY a young DEER **2** [U] a pale yellow-brown color

fawn³ *adj.* having a pale yellow-brown color

fax¹ /fæks/ S3 *n.* **1** [C] a document that is sent in electronic form through a telephone line and then printed using a special machine: *Did you get my fax?* **2** [C] also **ˈfax maˌchine** a machine used for sending and receiving faxes: *Do you have a fax?* | *a fax number* **3** [U] the system of sending documents using a fax machine: *Send the letter* ***by fax****.*

fax² S3 *v.* [T] to send someone a document using a fax machine: **fax sb sth** *She said they'll fax us the contract by 4:30.* | **fax sth to sb** *Can you fax the order to Reynolds as soon as possible?*

fay /feɪ/ *n.* [C] POETIC a FAIRY

faze /feɪz/ *v.* [T] INFORMAL if a new or difficult situation fazes you, it makes you feel confused or shocked: *Nothing seems to faze him.* [**Origin:** 1800–1900 *feeze* **to drive away, frighten**, from Old English *fesian*]

FBI, the /ˌɛf bi ˈaɪ/ *n.* **the Federal Bureau of Investigation** the police department of the U.S. government that collects information about crime and is concerned with FEDERAL law rather than state law → see also CIA

FCC, the /ˌɛf si ˈsi/ → see FEDERAL COMMUNICATIONS COMMISSION

FDA, the /ˌɛf di ˈeɪ/ *n.* **Food and Drug Administration** a U.S. government organization which makes sure that foods and drugs are safe enough to be sold

fe·al·ty /ˈfiəlti/ *n.* [U] OLD-FASHIONED loyalty to a king, queen, president, political party etc.

fear¹ /fɪr/ S3 W1 *n.* **1** [C,U] the feeling you get when you are afraid or worried that something bad is going to happen: *The boy's eyes were full of fear.* | *Fear is no excuse for violence.* | **+of** *a fear of snakes* | *Fear of flying is quite common.* | **+about** *fears about disease* | *He* ***lives in fear of*** (=is always afraid of) *being caught.* | *A small boy was crouched* ***in fear*** (=feeling afraid) *behind a tree.* | *He managed to* ***overcome his fear*** *of heights.* | **in fear of/for your life** (=afraid that someone will try to kill you) | *I was* ***filled with fear*** *when I saw their guns.* | **shake/tremble with fear** *I was trembling with fear.*

THESAURUS

terror a feeling of extreme fear
fright a sudden feeling of fear
panic a sudden strong feeling of fear or nervousness that makes you unable to think clearly or behave sensibly
alarm a feeling of fear or worry because something bad or dangerous might happen
phobia a permanent strong unreasonable fear of a type of thing or experience
→ FRIGHTENED

2 [C,U] something bad that might happen, which makes you feel afraid or worried: **fear that** *There was always the fear that the crisis could get worse.* | **sb's biggest/greatest fear** *My greatest fear is that I might lose my job.* | *What are your* ***hopes and fears*** *for the future?* **3 for fear of sth** also **for fear (that)** because you are worried that you will make something happen: *She would not give her name, for fear that her abusive husband would find her.* **4 put the fear of God into sb** INFORMAL to make someone feel that they must do something, by making sure they know the bad things that will happen if they do not do it **5 without fear or favor** FORMAL in a fair way [**Origin:** Old English *fær* **sudden danger**]

fear² W2 *v.* **1** [I,T] to feel afraid or worried that something bad may happen: *Fearing a blizzard, many people stayed home.* | **fear (that)** *Police fear that there may be further terrorist attacks.* | *Hundreds of people are* ***feared dead*** *in the ferry disaster.* | **+for** *I'm not afraid for myself, but I fear for my daughter.* | *Sometimes I* ***fear for the future*** *of this country.* | **fear for sb's safety/life** *Residents fear for their children's safety on the busy road.* | **fear to do sth** *People feared to go out at night.* **2 fear the worst** to think that the worst possible thing has happened or might happen: *Rescuers feared the worst for the men trapped in the mine.* **3** [T] to be afraid of someone or something and what they might do: *The dictator was feared by the entire country.* **4 I fear** FORMAL used when telling someone that you think that something bad has happened or is true: ***I fear that*** *we must accept the limitations of medicine.* **5 fear not** also **never fear** OLD-FASHIONED used to tell someone not to worry: *Never fear, we'll fix it somehow.* → see also GOD-FEARING

fear·ful /ˈfɪrfəl/ *adj.* **1** FORMAL frightened that something might happen: **+of** *Even doctors are fearful of getting the disease.* | **fearful (that)** *Officials are fearful that the demonstrations will cause new violence.* **2** OLD-FASHIONED [only before noun] frightening: *a fearful noise* —**fearfulness** *n.* [U]

fear·ful·ly /ˈfɪrfəli/ *adv.* **1** in a way that shows you are afraid: *She glanced fearfully over her shoulder.* **2** [+ adj./adv.] OLD-FASHIONED extremely

fear·less /ˈfɪrlɪs/ *adj.* not afraid of anything: *a fearless explorer* —**fearlessly** *adv.* —**fearlessness** *n.* [U]

fear·some /ˈfɪrsəm/ *adj.* very frightening: *fearsome soldiers*

fea·si·ble /ˈfizəbəl/ *adj.* a plan, idea, or method that is feasible is possible and is likely to work: *Solar heating is technically and economically feasible.* [**Origin:** 1400–1500 French *faisible*, from *faire* **to do, make**] —**feasibly** *adv.* —**feasibility** /ˌfizəˈbɪləṭi/ *n.* [U]

feast¹ /fist/ *n.* [C] **1** a large meal for a lot of people, to celebrate a special occasion: *The king promised a great feast for all citizens.* **2** a very good, large meal: *What a feast!* **3** an occasion when there are a lot of enjoyable things to see or do: **+for** *The wonderful illustrations are a feast for the eyes.* **4** also **feast day** a day or period when there is a special religious celebration [**Origin:** 1100–1200 Old French *feste* **occasion of celebration**, from Latin *festum*]

feast² *v.* **1** [I] to eat and drink a lot to celebrate something: *On the first Thanksgiving, the Pilgrims feasted for three days.* **2 feast your eyes on sb/sth** to look at someone or something with great pleasure: *Just feast your eyes on the car's leather seats.* **3** [T usually passive] FORMAL to treat someone with a lot of respect by giving them a special meal

feast on/upon sth *phr. v.* to eat a lot of a particular food with great enjoyment: *We feasted on chicken and mashed potatoes.*

feat /fit/ *n.* [C] something that someone does that is impressive because it needs a lot of skill, strength etc.: *acrobatic circus feats* | **a feat of memory/strength/engineering etc.** *The tunnel is a remarkable feat of engineering.* | **perform/accomplish/achieve a feat** *How did he accomplish such an astounding feat?* | **no mean/small/easy feat** (=something that is very difficult to do) [**Origin:** 1300–1400 Old French *fait* **thing done**, from Latin *factum*]

feath·er¹ /ˈfɛðɚ/ *n.* [C] **1** BIOLOGY one of the light soft things that cover a bird's body: *an eagle feather* | **a feather bed/pillow/comforter etc.** (=a bed etc. that is filled with feathers) **2 a feather in your cap** something you have done that you should be proud of [**Origin:** Old English *fether*] → see also **birds of a feather** at BIRD (5), **light as air/as light as a feather** at LIGHT² (2)

feather² *v.* [T] **1** to cut hair in thin layers **2 feather your nest/bed** to get money by dishonest methods **3** OLD-FASHIONED to put feathers on an ARROW → see also **tar and feather sb** at TAR² (4)

ˈfeather ˌbedding *n.* [U] DISAPPROVING INFORMAL the practice of letting workers keep their jobs even if they are not needed or do not work well

ˌfeather ˈboa *n.* [C] a long SCARF made of feathers and worn around someone's neck

ˈfeather-brained *adj.* extremely silly: *a feather-brained scheme*

ˌfeather ˈduster *n.* [C] a stick with feathers on the end, used for removing dust

feath·ered /ˈfɛðɚd/ *adj.* **1** having feathers, or made from feathers **2** feathered hair has been cut in thin layers **3 a feathered friend** a bird

feath·er·weight /ˈfɛðɚˌweɪt/ *n.* [C] a BOXER who is heavier than a BANTAMWEIGHT but lighter than a LIGHTWEIGHT

feath·er·y /ˈfɛðəri/ *adj.* looking or feeling light and soft, like a feather: *The plant has feathery leaves.*

fea·ture¹ /ˈfitʃɚ/ Ac S3 W2 *n.* [C] **1** an important, interesting, or typical part of something: *Air bags are a standard feature in most new cars.* | **+of** *one of the best features of the design* | *The crescent moon is a* ***common feature*** *of the flags of Islamic countries.* | *The red leaves are a* ***distinguishing feature*** *of this tree.* ►see THESAURUS box at **characteristic¹** **2** [usually plural] a part of someone's face such as their eyes, nose etc.: *Her eyes are her best feature.* | *He had a small face with delicate features.* **3** a piece of writing about a subject in a newspaper or a magazine, or a special treatment of a subject on television or the radio: **+on** *a special feature on vacations abroad* | *a feature article* **4** ENG. LANG. ARTS a movie being shown at a theater: *The Plaza Theater is showing a science fiction* ***double feature*** (=two movies the same evening). **5** a part of the land, especially part that you can see: *The maps show mountains, rivers, and other* ***geographical features***. [**Origin:** 1300–1400 Old French *feture* **shape, form**, from Latin *facere* **to do, make**]

feature² Ac W2 *v.* **1** [T] to show a particular person or thing in a movie, magazine, show etc.: *The exhibit features paintings by contemporary artists.* | **feature sb as sth** *The movie features Frank Sinatra as Nathan Detroit.* | **be featured in sth** *Their house was featured in "Ebony" magazine last month.* **2** [I] to be included in something and be an important part of it: **+in** *Violence features too strongly in many TV shows.* **3** [T] a word meaning "to include something new or unusual," used especially in advertisements: *The device features a phone, keyboard, and camera.* **4** to show a movie, play etc.: *The opera company is featuring two operas by Puccini.* **5** [T] to show or advertise a particular kind of

F

product: *The vacuum cleaner has been featured in a series of commercials.*

ˈfeature ˌfilm *n.* [C] a movie that has a story and is acted by professional actors, which people would usually go to see in a theater

fea·ture·less /ˈfitʃəlɪs/ *adj.* a featureless place has no interesting parts: *a large featureless expanse of desert*

feb·rile /ˈfibraɪl, ˈfɛ-/ *adj.* **1** LITERARY full of nervous excitement or activity: *a febrile atmosphere* **2** TECHNICAL relating to or caused by a fever

Feb·ru·ar·y /ˈfɛbyuˌɛri, ˈfɛbruˌɛri/ WRITTEN ABBREVIATION **Feb.** *n.* [C,U] the second month of the year, between January and March: *Eric's new job starts on February 4.* | *Our game is February 25th.* | *We often get snow **in February**.* | *I came back **last February**.* | *I'm going to France **next February**.* → see Grammar box at JANUARY [**Origin:** 1300–1400 Latin *Februarius*, from *Februa*, Roman religious ceremony in February to make things pure]

F

fe·ces /ˈfisiz/ *n.* [plural] FORMAL solid waste material from the BOWELS [**Origin:** 1300–1400 Latin, plural of *faex* **waste material**] —**fecal** /ˈfikəl/ *adj.*

feck·less /ˈfɛklɪs/ *adj.* FORMAL lacking determination, and not achieving anything in your life: *a feckless young man* [**Origin:** 1500–1600 Scottish English *feck* **effect, larger part**, from *effect*] —**fecklessly** *adv.* —**fecklessness** *n.* [U]

fe·cund /ˈfikənd, ˈfɛkənd/ *adj.* FORMAL able to produce many children, young animals, or crops SYN **fertile**: *fecund agricultural land* —**fecundity** *n.* [U]

Fed /fɛd/ *n.* **the Fed** INFORMAL **a)** the FEDERAL RESERVE SYSTEM **b)** the FEDERAL RESERVE BOARD

fed[1] /fɛd/ *v.* the past tense and past participle of FEED → see also FED UP

fed[2] *n.* [C] INFORMAL a police officer in the FBI

fed·er·al /ˈfɛdərəl/ Ac S3 W1 *adj.* **1** POLITICS relating to the central government of a country such as the U.S., rather than to the government of one of its states: *federal law* | *federal income tax* **2** POLITICS a federal country or system of government consists of a group of states that control their own affairs but are controlled by a central government: *a federal republic* [**Origin:** 1600–1700 Latin *foedus* **formal agreement or joining together**]

ˌFederal Aviˈation Adminiˌstration, the *n.* a U.S. government organization which is responsible for making sure that aircraft and airports are safe for people to use

ˌfederal ˈbudget *n.* [C] ECONOMICS the FEDERAL government's plan for how it will spend money in the next year

ˌFederal ˌBureau of Investiˈgation, the *n.* the FBI

ˌFederal Communiˈcations Comˌmission, the *n.* a U.S. government organization which makes rules that control broadcasting on radio, television, CABLE and SATELLITE television in the U.S.

ˌfederal ˈdebt *n.* [U] ECONOMICS the total amount of money owed by the government of a country SYN **national debt** SYN **public debt**: *increases in the federal debt*

ˌFederal Deˌposit Inˈsurance Comˌmission, the *n.* a U.S. government department that provides insurance against the failure of banks and controls their activities

ˌfederal ˈfunds rate *n.* [C] ECONOMICS the rate of INTEREST that banks charge other banks and which affects other interest rates in the country

ˌfederal ˈgovernment *n.* [C,U] **1 the federal government** POLITICS the national government of the U.S.: *States should not expect the federal government to solve all their problems.* **2** POLITICS a system of government in which power is divided between a central government and local governments

fed·er·al·ism /ˈfɛdərəˌlɪzəm/ *n.* [U] **1** POLITICS a system of governing a country that divides the power between the national government and the states: *the U.S. concept of federalism* **2** POLITICS belief in or support for a federal system of government —**federalist** *n.* [C]

fed·e·ral·ist /ˈfɛdərəlɪst/ *n.* [C] **1** someone who believes in or supports a federal system of government (=one which consists of a group of states that control their own affairs but are controlled by a central government) **2 Federalist** HISTORY one of a group of people who between 1787 and 1788 supported signing the Constitution of the United States because they wanted America to have a strong central government → see also ANTI-FEDERALIST

ˈFederalist ˌParty *n.* [C] HISTORY an early U.S. political party that supported a strong national government

ˌFederal ˌOpen ˈMarket Comˌmittee, the ABBREVIATION **FOMC** ECONOMICS the group that sets INTEREST RATES and makes rules about borrowing money for the Federal Reserve System

ˌfederal reˈpublic *n.* [C] POLITICS a government in which the power is divided between a national government and state governments: *The U.S. is a federal republic.*

ˌFederal Reˈserve Bank *n.* [C] one of the 12 banks that are part of the Federal Reserve System

ˌFederal ˈReserve Board *n.* **the Federal Reserve Board** the official organization that controls the Federal Reserve System

ˌFederal Reˈserve ˌdistrict *n.* [C] ECONOMICS one of the 12 areas that are part of the Federal Reserve System

ˌFederal Reˈserve ˌnote *n.* [C] ECONOMICS a piece of paper money that is given out by the Federal Reserve

ˌFederal Reˈserve ˌSystem *n.* **the Federal Reserve System** the main system of banks in the U.S., in which a group of seven officials and 12 banks control the way the country's banks work

ˌFederal ˈTrade Comˌmission, the *n.* [C] the FTC

fed·er·ate /ˈfɛdəˌreɪt/ *v.* [I + with] POLITICS if a group of states federate, they join together to form a federation

fed·er·a·tion /ˌfɛdəˈreɪʃən/ Ac *n.* **1** [C] a group of organizations, clubs, or people that have joined together: *the U.S. Gymnastics Federation in Indianapolis* **2** [C] POLITICS a group of states that have joined together to form a single government which decides important political matters, such as defense or foreign affairs. Each state also has its own independent government for deciding local matters.: *the Russian Federation* **3** [U] the act of joining together to form a group

ˌfed ˈup *adj.* [not before noun] INFORMAL annoyed or bored, and wanting something to change: +**with** *City golfers are fed up with conditions on the course.* | *In the end, she just **got fed up** and left.*

fee /fi/ Ac S2 W2 *n.* [C] **1** an amount of money that you pay to do something: *a membership fee* | *a shipping fee* | +**for** *The fee for the course is $250.* | *The bank **charges a fee** of $10 for the service.* | *Cable TV subscribers **pay monthly fees**.* | *The 10K run has an **entry fee*** (=a fee to take part) *of $15.* | *State parks charge a small **entrance fee*** (=a fee to enter a place). | *You'll be charged a **flat fee** for each transaction.* ►see THESAURUS box at **cost**[1] **2** an amount of money that you pay to a professional person for their work: *Insurance covered most of the doctor's fees.* | **legal/medical etc. fees** *Losers of the suit will have to pay the winner's legal fees.* [**Origin:** 1300–1400 Old French *fé*, *fief*, from Medieval Latin *feudum* **land given in return for service**]

fee·ble /ˈfibəl/ *adj.* **1** extremely weak: *a feeble old woman* ►see THESAURUS box at **weak**[1] **2** a feeble light or sound is not bright or loud: *a feeble voice* **3** not very good or effective: *a feeble excuse* [**Origin:** 1100–1200 Old French *feble*, from Latin *flebilis* **causing tears, weak**]

ˈfeeble-ˌminded *adj.* **1** unable to think clearly and decide what to do **2** OLD-FASHIONED having much less than average intelligence —**feeble-mindedly** *adv.* —**feeble-mindedness** *n.* [U]

feed¹ /fid/ S1 W2 *v. past tense and past participle* **fed** /fɛd/

feed

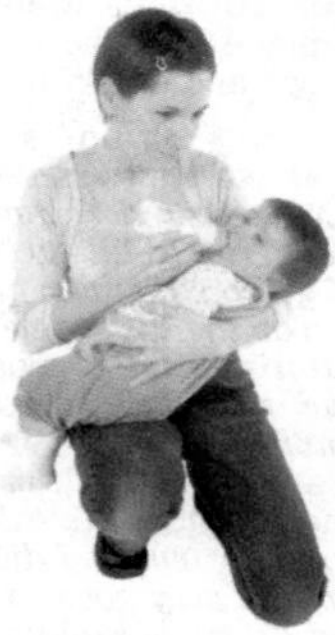

1 GIVE FOOD [T] **a)** to give food to a person or animal: *Did you feed the dog?* | **feed sth to sb** *We fed the scraps to the pig.* | **feed yourself** *She was too weak to feed herself.* **b)** to provide enough food for a group of people: *His wages are hardly enough to feed his family.* | *This recipe feeds six.*
2 SUPPLY STH [T] to supply something, especially a liquid or gas, in a continuous flow: *Small streams feed the main river.* | **feed sth to/into sth** *The sound is fed directly to the headphones.* | **feed sth with sth** *She fed the fire with logs.*
3 ANIMAL/BABY [I] if a baby or an animal feeds, they eat: *Frogs generally feed at night.*
4 PLANT [T] to give a special substance to a plant, which makes it grow: **feed sth with sth** *Feed the plant with liquid fertilizer.*
5 INCREASE STH [T] to do something that increases an activity or makes something bigger or stronger: *There has been a boom in tourism, fed by publicity about the movie filmed there.* | **feed sth with sth** *Blanca fed the fire with sticks she had brought in.*
6 PUT STH INTO STH [T] to put something such as a tube or a wire slowly into something else: **feed sth in** *With this printer you have to feed the paper in by hand.* | **feed sth through sth** *Feed the fabric through the sewing machine.* | **feed sth into sth** *The tube was fed into the patient's stomach.*
7 COMPUTER [T] COMPUTERS to put information into a computer over a period of time: **feed sth into sth** *The locations of the icebergs are fed into computer models.*
8 NEED/DEMAND ETC. [T] to try to satisfy a need, demand, ADDICTION etc.: *He started stealing to feed his drug addiction.*
9 INFORMATION [T] to give someone information or ideas over a period of time, especially false information: **feed sth to sb** *She fed celebrity gossip to the magazine.*
10 feed your face INFORMAL to eat a lot of food
11 feed sb's guilt/vanity/paranoia etc. to make someone's feelings, especially negative feelings, stronger: *Having nothing to do fed my anxiety.*
12 feed sb's ego to do something to make someone feel important: *Compliments like those just feed his ego.*
13 feed lines/jokes to sb to say things to another performer so that they can make jokes
14 feed sb a line INFORMAL to tell someone something which is not true so that they will do what you want: *She fed him a line about being busy on Saturday.*
15 SPORTS [T] to throw or hit a ball or a PUCK to someone else on your team, especially so that they can make a point: *Johnson fed the ball to Kyman, who scored.*
16 feed a meter to keep putting money into a machine so that you can park your car
17 TV/RADIO [T] to send a television or radio program somewhere so that it can be broadcast
[**Origin:** Old English *fedan*; related to *food*] → see also BREAST-FEED, FEEDING, FORCE-FEED, **mouth to feed** at MOUTH¹ (8), SPOON-FEED, UNDERFED, WELL-FED

feed back ↔ sth *phr. v.* to give advice, criticism, comments etc. to someone about something they have done so that they can improve: *Thanks to all those who fed back their comments.* | **feed sth back to sb** *The results of the survey will be fed back to employers.*

feed into sth *phr. v.* **1** to flow or move into something that is larger, or to provide it with something: *Six elementary schools feed into Jefferson High.* **2** to have an effect on something or help to make it happen: *The influence of designer fashion feeds into sports fashion.*

feed off sth *phr. v.* **1** if an animal feeds off something, it gets food from it: *The bears are feeding off the town's garbage.* **2** to use something to increase, become stronger, or succeed: *When the two are together, they feed off each other's energy.* **3** DISAPPROVING to use something bad or negative to help you succeed, or use something in a bad or negative way to help you succeed: *People think he's feeding off his father's reputation as a writer.*

feed on sth *phr. v.* **1** if an animal feeds on a particular food, it usually eats that food: *The young fish feed on brine shrimp.* **2** to use something to increase, become stronger, or succeed: *Prejudice feeds on ignorance.*

feed² *n.* **1** [U] food for animals: *cattle feed* **2** [C] an action of sending a television or radio program somewhere so that it can be broadcast, or the connection that is used to do this: *a live satellite feed* **3** [C] a tube which supplies a machine with FUEL **4** [C] OLD-FASHIONED a big meal → see also CHICKEN FEED

feed·back /ˈfidbæk/ S3 *n.* [U] **1** advice, criticism etc. about how successful or useful something is: **+on** *Employees should be given frequent feedback on their work.* | **+from** *We rely on feedback from the public.* **2** a high noise that is not nice to listen to, heard when a MICROPHONE is too close to an AMPLIFIER

feed·bag /ˈfidbæg/ *n.* [C] a bag put around a horse's head, containing food

feed·er /ˈfidɚ/ *n.* [C] **1** a container with food for animals or birds **2** a small road or railroad line that takes traffic onto a main road or railroad line

ˈfeeder ˌschool *n.* [C] a school from which many students go to a high school in the same area

feed·ing /ˈfidɪŋ/ *n.* [C] one of the times when you give milk to a small baby: *a midnight feeding*

ˈfeeding ˌfrenzy *n.* [C] **1** INFORMAL a situation in which many people try very hard to get the same thing, and behave in an uncontrolled, excited, or unpleasant way: *the media feeding frenzy surrounding the trial* **2** a situation in which a group of animals, especially SHARKS, attack and eat something

ˈfeeding ground *n.* [C] a place where a group of animals or birds find food to eat

feel¹ /fil/ S1 W1 *v. past tense and past participle* **felt** /fɛlt/
1 FEELING/EMOTION [linking verb, T] to experience a particular feeling or emotion: *Stop running if you feel any pain.* | **feel guilty/sorry/happy etc.** *I feel sorry for her.* | **feel hungry/tired/sick etc.** *I don't really feel hungry yet.* | **+like** *The Lees made me feel like their own son.* | **+as if/though** *He felt as if he had been hit.* | **feel guilt/anger/relief etc.** *He felt great sadness that his marriage had failed.*
2 PHYSICAL [linking verb] to make someone have a particular physical feeling, especially when touched or held: **feel smooth/rough/cold etc.** *The clothes still feel slightly damp.* | *The room felt cool and comfortable.* | **+like** *Her hands felt like ice.* | **+as if/though** *The sheets feel as if they were made of silk.*
3 EXPERIENCE/EVENT [linking verb] if a situation, event etc. feels good, strange etc., that is the emotion or feeling that it gives you: *Getting a little exercise always feels good.* | *How does it feel to be home?* | *It felt kind of weird being back in school.* | **+like** *It felt like I'd known them all my life.*
4 HAVE AN OPINION [linking verb, T not usually in progressive] to have a particular opinion, especially one that is based on your feelings, not on facts: **+about** *The survey asked what students felt about school.* | **feel (that)** *I felt I should've helped more.* | **+like** *I feel like I'm being treated unfairly.* | *He* ***feels strongly*** *about the issue.* | *"I think it's a good idea." "I hope you still* ***feel that way*** *tomorrow."* | **feel sure/certain (that)** *I felt certain that the other jurors agreed with me.* ▸see THESAURUS box at **think**
5 TOUCH [T] to touch something with your fingers to find out about it: *Dr. Wright felt the baby's stomach.* | *Feel this material – it's so soft.* | **feel how hard/soft/**

F

rough etc. sth is *Can you feel how smooth it is now that it's been sanded?* ▸see THESAURUS box at **touch**[1]
6 NOTICE STH TOUCHING [T not in progressive] to notice something because it is touching you or having an effect on you: *He felt a hand on his shoulder.* | *The earthquake was felt 300 miles away.* | **feel sb/sth do sth** *Ann felt him brush against her and turned to face him.*
7 NOTICE BODY CHANGES [T not in progressive] to notice that something is suddenly happening to your body that you cannot control: **feel sb/sth do sth** *She felt her mouth go dry.* | **feel yourself do/doing sth** *I felt myself blushing.*
8 NOTICE STH YOU CAN'T SEE [T not in progressive] to notice something although you cannot see, hear etc. it SYN **sense**: *You could feel the tension in the crowd.* | **feel sb doing sth** *He could feel her watching him.*

SPOKEN PHRASES

9 feel like (doing) sth to want to have something or do something: *I don't feel like going to work.* | *Joe says he feels like Mexican food.*
10 feel free used to tell someone that they can do something if they want to: *"Could I use your phone for a minute?" "Feel free."* | **feel free to do sth** *Feel free to add your own ingredients.*
11 I know how you feel said to express sympathy with a remark someone has just made: *"I'm so embarrassed." "I know how you feel."*
12 not feel yourself to not feel as healthy or happy as usual: *I just haven't been feeling myself lately.*

13 feel the force/effects/benefits etc. of sth to experience the good or bad results of something: *Patients will feel the effects of the operation for weeks.*
14 feel your way a) to move carefully with your hands out in front of you because you cannot see well: *He felt his way across the room, and found the door handle.* **b)** to do something slowly and carefully because you are not certain of the best way to do it: *They were feeling their way toward an agreement.*
15 feel around/on/in etc. sth (for sth) to search for something with your fingers: *Ben felt in his pocket for a handkerchief.*
16 feel the need to do sth to have the feeling that you need to do something: *Some magazines feel the need to be controversial.*
17 feel your age to realize that you are not as young or active as you used to be: *Spending time with the kids really makes me feel my age.*
18 feel your oats INFORMAL to feel full of energy
19 feel the cold to suffer because of cold weather: *Old people tend to feel the cold more.*
20 feel a death/loss etc. to react very strongly to a bad event, especially someone's death
[**Origin:** Old English *felan*]
feel for sb *phr. v.* to feel sympathy for someone: *She looked tired and he really felt for her.*
feel sb/sth ↔ **out** *phr. v.* INFORMAL to find out what someone's opinions or feelings are without asking them directly: *I thought I'd feel out some of my colleagues before the meeting.*
feel sb ↔ **up** *phr. v.* SPOKEN to touch someone sexually
feel up to sth *phr. v.* INFORMAL to have the strength, energy etc. to do something: *I don't really feel up to going out tonight.*

feel[2] *n.* [singular] **1** a quality that something has that makes you feel or think a particular way about it: *The movie has the feel of a big summer hit.* | *The house had a nice **feel about it**.* **2** the way that something feels when you touch it: *I love **the feel of** leather.* **3 have/get a feel for sth** INFORMAL to have or develop an understanding of something, or skill in doing something: *I read the local newspapers, trying to get a feel for the place.* **4 get the feel of sth** to become comfortable with something: *You'll soon get the feel of the car.* **5 a feel for sth** an understanding of something, or a skill in doing something: *He has a good feel for the game.*

feel·er /ˈfilɚ/ *n.* **1 put/send out feelers** to start to try to discover what people think about something that you want to do: *Possible presidential candidates are already putting out feelers.* **2** [C usually plural] BIOLOGY one of the two long things on an insect's head that it uses to feel or touch things

ˈfeel-good *adj.* **feel-good movie/program/music etc.** a movie etc. whose main purpose is to make you feel happy and cheerful

feel·ing[1] /ˈfilɪŋ/ S1 W2 *n.*
1 ANGER/SADNESS/HAPPINESS ETC. [C] something that you feel such as anger, sadness, or happiness: *It's a wonderful feeling to be home.* | **+of** *I had terrible feelings of guilt.* | *Exercise gives a feeling of accomplishment.* | *It was the last game of the season, and **feelings were running high*** (=people were very angry or excited). | *I had **mixed feelings*** (=some good, some bad) *about leaving the job.*
2 sb's feelings [plural] someone's thoughts, emotions, and attitudes: *You don't care about anybody's feelings but your own.* | *I didn't mean to **hurt your feelings**.* | *I'm not very good at **putting** my **feelings into words**, but I'll try to explain.*
3 OPINION [C] a belief or opinion about something, especially one that is influenced by your emotions: *My personal feeling is that most voters just don't care.* | **+on** *She has strong feelings on the subject.* | **+about** *What's your feeling about the president's economic plan?* | *Employees have expressed **mixed feelings*** (=are not sure what they feel or think) *about the project.* | *My **gut feeling*** (=an opinion without any evidence) *is that something is wrong.*
4 have the/a feeling (that) also **get the/a feeling (that)** to think that something is probably true, or will probably happen: *Mike got the feeling that she didn't believe him.*
5 have a bad feeling about sb/sth to think that someone or something is not good or that something bad will happen: *I had a bad feeling about him from the beginning.*
6 GENERAL ATTITUDE [singular, U] a general attitude among a group of people about a subject: *The feeling is that he should resign.* | **+against** *Leaders underestimated the strength of public feeling against the war.*
7 SENSATION IN BODY [C] something that you feel in your body such as heat, cold, pain etc. SYN **sensation**: *He had a tight feeling in his chest.* | **+of** *feelings of dizziness*
8 ABILITY TO FEEL [U] the ability to feel heat, cold, pain etc. in part of your body: *She has no feeling in her legs.* | *He had **lost the feeling in** his toes.*
9 the feeling is mutual SPOKEN said when you have the same feeling about someone as they have toward you: *Well, if Dave doesn't want to see me, then the feeling is mutual.*
10 with feeling in a way that shows you feel very angry, happy etc.: *Baktiar spoke of Iran with deep feeling.*
11 bad/ill feelings also **bad/ill feeling** anger, lack of trust etc. between people, especially after an argument or unfair decision: *The argument created bad feeling among department members.* | **harbor/bear ill feelings (toward sb)** (=to be angry or unhappy with someone)
12 I know the feeling SPOKEN said when you understand how someone feels because you have had the same feeling: *"She makes me so mad I could scream!" "I know the feeling."*
13 EFFECT OF A PLACE/BOOK ETC. [singular] the effect that a place, book, movie etc. has on people and the way it makes them feel: *There was a friendly feeling about the place.*
14 a feeling (for sth) a) an ability to do something or understand a subject, which you get from experience: *The experiments give kids a better feeling for what magnetism is.* **b)** a natural ability to do something: *She has a natural feeling for languages.*
15 EMOTIONS NOT THOUGHT [U] a way of reacting to things using your emotions, instead of thinking about them carefully: *The Romantic writers valued feeling above all else.* → see also **hard feelings** at HARD[1] (13), **have/get a sinking feeling (that)** at SINK[1] (13)

feeling[2] *adj.* showing strong feelings: *A feeling look came across her face.* —**feelingly** *adv.*

feet /fit/ *n.* the plural of FOOT → see also **get/have cold**

feet at COLD[1] (7), **have feet of clay** at FOOT[1] (24), **have itchy feet** at ITCHY (4)

feign /feɪn/ *v.* [T] FORMAL to pretend to have a particular feeling or to be sick, asleep etc.: *Christina feigned interest.* [**Origin:** 1200–1300 Old French *feindre*, from Latin *fingere* **to shape, pretend**]

feint[1] /feɪnt/ *n.* [C] a movement or an attack that is intended to deceive an opponent, especially in BOXING

feint[2] *v.* [I,T] to pretend to hit someone in BOXING

feist·y /ˈfaɪsti/ *adj. comparative* **feistier**, *superlative* **feistiest** APPROVING having a strong, determined character and being willing to argue with people: *She's a pretty feisty kid, isn't she?* [**Origin:** 1800–1900 *feist* **small dog**]

feld·spar /ˈfɛldspɑr/ *n.* [U] EARTH SCIENCE a type of gray or white mineral

fe·lic·i·ta·tions /fɪˌlɪsəˈteɪʃənz/ *interjection* FORMAL said to wish someone happiness

fe·lic·i·tous /fɪˈlɪsət̬əs/ *adj.* FORMAL well-chosen, appropriate, and pleasing: *Lincoln's felicitous words about government* —**felicitously** *adv.*

fe·lic·i·ty /fɪˈlɪsət̬i/ *n.* FORMAL **1** [U] happiness: *domestic felicity* **2** [singular, U] the quality of being well-chosen, appropriate, and pleasing: *a felicity of language*

fe·line[1] /ˈfilaɪn/ *adj.* **1** BIOLOGY relating to cats or other members of the cat family, such as lions or tigers **2** looking like or moving like a cat: *A feline grin spread over his face.*

feline[2] *n.* [C] BIOLOGY a cat or a member of the cat family, such as a lion or a tiger

fell[1] /fɛl/ *v.* the past tense of FALL

fell[2] *v.* [T] **1** to cut down a tree **2** to knock someone down with a lot of force

fell[3] *adj.* **in one fell swoop** doing a lot of things at the same time, using only one action: *The deal could solve all our financial problems in one fell swoop.*

fel·la /ˈfɛlə/ *n.* [C] SPOKEN, OLD-FASHIONED **1** a man **2** a boy or man with whom you have a romantic relationship SYN **boyfriend**

fel·lah /ˈfɛlə, -lɑ/ *n. plural* **fellaheen** /-hin/ [C] someone who owns a small farm or works on a farm in Egypt or another Arab country

fel·ler /ˈfɛlɚ/ *n.* [C] SPOKEN, OLD-FASHIONED a man

Fel·li·ni /fəˈlini/, **Fed·e·ri·co** /ˌfɛdəˈrikoʊ/ (1920–1993) an Italian movie DIRECTOR who had an important influence on the cinema

fel·low[1] /ˈfɛloʊ/ S2 W2 *n.* [C] **1** OLD-FASHIONED a man: *He said a fellow named LeRoy was the best pilot.* **2** a GRADUATE student who has a fellowship in a university **3** a member of an ACADEMIC society [**Origin:** Old English *feolaga* **partner**]

fellow[2] *adj.* **1 fellow workers/students/countrymen etc.** people who work, study etc. with you: *Try to maintain good relationships with your fellow workers.* **2 our fellow man** other people in general: *We must all help our fellow man.* **3 fellow feeling** LITERARY a feeling of sympathy and friendship toward someone because they are like you

fel·low·ship /ˈfɛloʊˌʃɪp, -lə-/ *n.* **1** [C] **a)** money given to a student to allow him or her to continue studying at an advanced level: *She has been awarded a fellowship at Harvard.* **b)** a group of officials who decide which students will receive this money **2** [C] a group of people who share an interest or belief, especially Christians who have religious ceremonies together **3** [U] a feeling of friendship resulting from shared interests or experiences: *a sense of fellowship*

ˈfellow ˌtraveler *n.* [C] **1** DISAPPROVING someone who supports Communism, or another organization that you disagree with **2** someone who is traveling with you

fel·on /ˈfɛlən/ *n.* [C] LAW someone who is guilty of a serious crime: *Our prisons are so overcrowded that convicted felons walk free.*

fel·o·ny /ˈfɛləni/ *n. plural* **felonies** [C,U] LAW a serious crime such as murder → see also MISDEMEANOR

felt[1] /fɛlt/ *v.* the past tense and past participle of FEEL

felt[2] *n.* [U] a thick soft material made of wool, hair, or fur that has been pressed flat

ˈfelt tip pen *n.* [C] a pen that has a hard piece of felt at the end that the ink comes through

fem. *adj.* the written abbreviation of FEMALE or FEMININE

fe·male[1] /ˈfimeɪl/ S3 W3 *n.* [C] **1** BIOLOGY an animal that belongs to the sex that can have babies or produce eggs OPP **male**: *Male birds display their feathers to attract females.* **2** BIOLOGY a woman or a girl OPP **male**: *As a group, females performed better on the test than males.* ►see THESAURUS box at **woman** **3** BIOLOGY a plant that produces flowers or fruit OPP **male**

female[2] S3 W2 *adj.* **1** BIOLOGY belonging to the sex that can have babies or produce eggs OPP **male**: *a female spider* **2** BIOLOGY relating to women or girls → see also FEMININE OPP **male**: *female voters* ►see THESAURUS box at **woman** **3** BIOLOGY a female plant or flower produces fruit OPP **male** **4** TECHNICAL a female part of a piece of equipment has a hole into which another part fits SYN **male** [**Origin:** 1300–1400 Old French *femelle* (influenced by *male*), from Latin *femella* **girl**] —**femaleness** *n.* [U] → see Word Choice box at MASCULINE

ˌfemale ˈcondom *n.* [C] a loose rubber tube with one end closed, that fits inside a woman's VAGINA when she is having sex, so that she will not have a baby

fem·i·nine /ˈfɛmənɪn/ *adj.* **1** having qualities that are considered to be typical of women, especially by being gentle, delicate and pretty: *I'd like my hair cut in a softer, more feminine style.* | *The way she dresses isn't very feminine.* **2** relating to being female: *a feminine point of view* **3** ENG. LANG. ARTS a feminine noun or PRONOUN has a special form that means it REFERS to a female, such as "actress" or "her" → see also FEMALE → see Word Choice box at MASCULINE

ˌfeminine ˈhygiene *n.* [U] methods that women use when they are having their monthly PERIOD, or that they use to clean their sexual organs: *feminine hygiene products*

fem·i·nin·i·ty /ˌfɛməˈnɪnət̬i/ *n.* [U] qualities that are considered to be typical of women, especially qualities that are gentle, delicate, and pretty: *The color pink is associated with femininity.* → see also MASCULINITY

fem·i·nism /ˈfɛməˌnɪzəm/ *n.* [U] the belief that women should have the same rights and opportunities as men —**feminist** *adj.*: *feminist principles*

fem·i·nist /ˈfɛmənɪst/ *n.* [C] someone who supports the idea that women should have the same rights and opportunities as men: *She's been an outspoken feminist for over 20 years.*

ˈfeminist ˌmovement, the *n.* [singular] POLITICS the organized attempts, which began in the middle of the 19th century, to obtain the same rights for women that men had, including the right to vote, the right to do the same work for the same pay as men, and many other rights

femme fa·tale /ˌfɛm fəˈtɑl, -ˈtæl/ *n.* [C] a beautiful woman who men find very attractive, even though she may make them unhappy

fe·mur /ˈfimɚ/ *n.* [C] BIOLOGY the bone in your THIGH —**femoral** /ˈfɛmərəl/ *adj.* → see picture at SKELETON[1]

fence[1] /fɛns/ S2 *n.* **1** [C] a structure made of wood, metal etc. that surrounds a piece of land: *a chain-link fence* **2** [C] INFORMAL someone who buys and sells stolen goods **3** [C] a wall or other structure that horses jump over in a race or competition → see also **mend (your) fences** at MEND[1] (4), **sit on the fence** at SIT (10)

fence[2] *v.* **1** [T] to put a fence around something **2** [I] to fight with a long thin sword as a sport **3** [I + with] to answer someone's questions in a skilled way in order to get an advantage in an argument **4** [I,T] INFORMAL to buy stolen goods from the people who have stolen them, and then sell them to other people for a profit

fence in *phr. v.* **1 fence sth ↔ in** to surround a place with a fence: *They fenced the field in with barbed wire.* **2 fence sb ↔ in** to make someone feel that they cannot leave a place or do what they want: *As kids we were fenced in by rules and regulations.* —**fenced-in** *adj.*

fence sb/sth ↔ off *phr. v.* to separate one area from another area with a fence: *We've fenced off the back of the property.*

fenc·er /ˈfɛnsɚ/ *n.* [C] someone who fights with a long thin sword as a sport

ˈfence-ˌsitter *n.* [C] someone who avoids saying which side of an argument they support or what their opinion is about a particular subject: *He faces a challenge winning over the fence-sitters.* —**fence-sitting** *n.* [U] → see also **sit on the fence** at SIT (10)

fenc·ing /ˈfɛnsɪŋ/ *n.* [U] **1** the sport of fighting with a long thin sword **2** fences, or the pieces of wood, metal etc. used to make them

F

fend /fɛnd/ *v.* **fend for yourself** to take care of yourself without help from other people: *Young birds are left to fend for themselves soon after they hatch.*

fend sb/sth ↔ off *phr. v.* **1** to defend yourself against someone who is attacking you: *Mrs. Spencer tried to fend off the mugger with her umbrella.* **2** to defend yourself from something such as competition, difficult questions, or a situation you do not want to deal with: *The company managed to fend off the hostile takeover bid.*

fend·er /ˈfɛndɚ/ *n.* [C] **1** the part of a car's body that covers the wheels → see picture on page A36 **2** a curved piece of metal over the wheel of a bicycle → see picture at BICYCLE[1] **3** a low metal wall around a FIREPLACE that prevents burning wood or coal from falling out **4** an object such as an old tire used to protect the side of a boat

ˈfender-ˌbender *n.* [C] INFORMAL a car accident in which little damage is done

feng shui /ˌfɛŋ ˈʃweɪ/ *n.* [U] a Chinese system of organizing the furniture and other things in a house or building in a way that people believe will bring good luck and happiness [**Origin:** 1700–1800 a Chinese phrase meaning **wind water**]

fen·nel /ˈfɛnl/ *n.* [U] a pale green plant whose seeds are used to give a special taste to food and which can also be eaten as a vegetable

fe·ral /ˈfɛrəl, ˈfɪrəl/ *adj.* feral animals used to live with humans but have become wild: *a pack of feral dogs*

Fer·di·nand and Is·a·bel·la /ˌfɚdn-ænd ənd ɪzəˈbɛlə/ King Ferdinand of Spain (1452–1516) and his wife, Queen Isabella of Spain (1451–1504), who are famous for giving Christopher Columbus the money and ships to make the trip on which he discovered America

fer·ment¹ /fɚˈmɛnt/ *v.* [I,T] if fruit, beer, wine etc. ferments or if it is fermented, the sugar in it changes to alcohol —**fermented** *adj.*

fer·ment² /ˈfɚmɛnt/ *n.* [U] a situation of great excitement or trouble in a country, especially caused by political change: *In the 1960s, American society was* ***in ferment.*** | **political/intellectual/social etc. ferment** *a period of intense political ferment*

fer·men·ta·tion /ˌfɚmənˈteɪʃən/ *n.* [U] CHEMISTRY a process in which the sugar contained in fruit, beer, wine etc. is gradually changed into alcohol by the action of YEAST or BACTERIA

Fer·mi /ˈfɛrmi/, **En·ri·co** /ɛnˈrikoʊ/ (1901–1954) a U.S. scientist, born in Italy, who did important work on RADIOACTIVITY and produced the first controlled NUCLEAR REACTION

fern /fɚn/ *n.* [C] a type of plant with green leaves shaped like large feathers, but no flowers —**ferny** *adj.*

fe·ro·cious /fəˈroʊʃəs/ *adj.* **1** violent, dangerous, and frightening: *ferocious acts of violence* | *a ferocious shark* **2** very strong, severe, and unpleasant: *a ferocious critic* **3** a ferocious emotion is felt very strongly: *He has a ferocious determination to succeed.* [**Origin:** 1600–1700 Latin *ferox* **wild-looking**, from *ferus* **wild**] —**ferociously** *adv.* —**ferociousness** *n.* [U]

fe·roc·i·ty /fəˈrɑsət̬i/ *n.* [U] the state of being extremely violent, cruel, and severe: *the ferocity of the storm*

fer·ret¹ /ˈfɛrɪt/ *v.* [**Origin:** 1300–1400 Old French *furet*, from Latin *fur* **thief**]

ferret out *phr. v.* **1 ferret sth ↔ out** to succeed in finding a piece of information that is difficult to find: *Reporters have somehow managed to ferret out the facts in the case.* **2 ferret sb/sth ↔ out** to find and usually get rid of someone or something that is causing a problem: *The new program is meant to ferret out problem cops.*

ferret² *n.* [C] a small animal with a pointed nose and soft fur, used for hunting rats and rabbits

fer·ris wheel /ˈfɛrɪs ˌwil/ *n.* [C] a very large upright wheel with seats on it for people to ride on in an AMUSEMENT PARK

fer·rous /ˈfɛrəs/ *adj.* CHEMISTRY containing iron, or relating to iron: *ferrous metals*

fer·rule /ˈfɛrəl/ *n.* [C] a piece of metal or rubber put around a stick or pipe to make it stronger

fer·ry¹ /ˈfɛri/ *n. plural* **ferries** [C] a boat that carries people or goods across a river or a narrow area of water ►see THESAURUS box at ship¹

ferry² *v.* **ferries, ferried, ferrying** [T always + adv./prep.] to carry people or goods a short distance from one place to another in a boat or other vehicle: **ferry sth (from sth) to sb/sth** *Four helicopters ferried food, medicine, and blankets to the survivors.*

fer·ry·boat /ˈfɛriˌboʊt/ *n.* [C] a FERRY

fer·ry·man /ˈfɛrimən/ *n.* [C] someone who guides a ferry across a river

fer·ti·ga·tion /ˌfɚtəˈgeɪʃən/ *n.* [C] the process of supplying water and FERTILIZER directly to the roots of plants to help them grow

fer·tile /ˈfɚt̬l/ *adj.* **1** fertile land or soil is able to produce good crops: *fertile farmland* **2** BIOLOGY able to produce babies, young animals, or new plants OPP **infertile** **3 a fertile imagination/mind** an imagination that is able to produce a lot of interesting and unusual ideas **4 fertile ground/field/territory etc.** a situation where new ideas, political groups etc. can easily develop and succeed: *The South remains fertile ground for conservative politicians.* [**Origin:** 1400–1500 French, Latin *ferre* **to carry, bear**]

ˌFertile ˈCrescent, the *n.* [singular] HISTORY an area in what is now the Middle East, from the Nile Valley to the Tigris and Euphrates Rivers where the first organized, highly developed societies began

fer·til·i·ty /fɚˈtɪləti/ *n.* [U] **1** the ability of the land or soil to produce good crops **2** BIOLOGY the ability of a person, animal, or plant to produce babies, young animals, or seeds OPP **infertility**

ferˈtility ˌdrug *n.* [C] a drug given to a woman to help her have a baby

fer·til·ize /ˈfɚt̬lˌaɪz/ *v.* [T] **1** to put fertilizer on the soil to help plants grow **2** BIOLOGY to make new animal or plant life develop: *After the egg has been fertilized, it will hatch in about six weeks.* —**fertilization** /ˌfɚt̬l-əˈzeɪʃən/ *n.* [U]

fer·til·iz·er /ˈfɚt̬lˌaɪzɚ/ *n.* [C,U] a substance that is put on the soil to help plants grow

fer·vent /ˈfɚvənt/ *adj.* believing or feeling something very strongly and sincerely: *It is my fervent hope that this matter is now ended.* | **a fervent believer/admirer/supporter etc.** *a fervent supporter of human rights* —**fervency** *n.* [U] —**fervently** *adv.*

fer·vid /ˈfɚvɪd/ *adj.* FORMAL believing or feeling something extremely strongly —**fervidly** *adv.*

fer·vor /ˈfɚvɚ/ *n.* [U] very strong belief or feeling:

patriotic fervor [**Origin:** 1300–1400 Old French *ferveur*, from Latin *fervor*, from *fervere* **to boil**]

'fess /fɛs/ *v.*

'fess up *phr. v.* SPOKEN to admit that you have done something wrong, although it is not very serious: *Come on, 'fess up! Who ate that last cookie?*

fest /fɛst/ *n.* **a beer/song/food etc. fest** an informal occasion when a lot of people do a fun activity together, such as drinking beer, singing songs, or eating food → see also LOVEFEST, SLUGFEST

fes·ter /ˈfɛstɚ/ *v.* [I] **1** if a bad feeling or problem festers, it gets worse because it has not been dealt with: *Resentments have festered between the two ethnic groups for centuries.* **2** MEDICINE if a wound festers, it becomes infected **3** if waste material or dirty objects fester, they decay and smell bad: *Rotting meat was left to fester in the hot sun.*

fes·ti·val /ˈfɛstəvəl/ S3 W3 *n.* [C] **1** ENG. LANG. ARTS an occasion when there are performances of many movies, plays, pieces of music etc., which happens in the same place every year: **a film/music/dance etc. festival** *the Cannes Film Festival* **2** a special occasion when people celebrate something such as a religious event: *Hannukah is an eight-day Jewish festival.* [**Origin:** 1300–1400 Old French, Latin *festivus*, from *festum* **ceremony of celebration**]

fes·tive /ˈfɛstɪv/ *adj.* **1** looking or feeling bright and cheerful in a way that seems appropriate for celebrating something: *a festive atmosphere* **2 a festive occasion** a day when you celebrate something special, such as a holiday **3 the festive season** the period around Christmas

fes·tiv·i·ty /fɛˈstɪvət̬i/ *n.* [U] **1** a happy and cheerful feeling that exists when people celebrate something: *There was an air of festivity in the village.* **2 festivities** [plural] things such as drinking, dancing, or eating that are done to celebrate a special occasion: *Fourth of July festivities at Huntington Beach*

fes·toon[1] /fɛˈstun/ *v.* [T usually passive] to cover something with flowers, long pieces of material etc., especially as a decoration: **be festooned with sth** *The steps of the courthouse were festooned with banners and flags.*

festoon[2] *n.* [C] FORMAL a long thin piece of material, used especially as a decoration

fet·a /ˈfɛt̬ə/ *n.* [U] a white cheese from Greece made from sheep's milk or goat's milk [**Origin:** 1900–2000 Modern Greek, Italian *fetta* **piece cut off**]

fe·tal /ˈfit̬l/ *adj.* BIOLOGY relating to a FETUS

'fetal po,sition *n.* [C] a body position in which your body is curled up, and your arms and legs are pulled up against your chest

fetch[1] /fɛtʃ/ *v.* [T] **1** to be sold for a particular amount of money, especially at a public sale: *Some properties have fetched prices in the $4 million range.* ►see THESAURUS box at cost[2] **2** OLD-FASHIONED to go and get something, and bring it back: *Rushworth went to fetch the key to the gate.* | **fetch sth from sth** *She fetched water from the well.* **3 fetch and carry** OLD-FASHIONED to do simple and boring jobs for someone as if you were their servant [**Origin:** Old English *fetian*, *feccan*]

fetch[2] *n.* **play fetch** if you play fetch with a dog, you throw something for the dog to bring back to you

fetch·ing /ˈfɛtʃɪŋ/ *adj.* OLD-FASHIONED attractive: *a fetching young woman* —**fetchingly** *adv.*

fete[1] /feɪt/ *v.* [T usually passive] to honor someone by having a public celebration for them: *Baker will be feted at a government banquet.*

fete[2] *n.* [C] a special occasion to celebrate something: *a farewell fete in honor of the mayor*

fet·id /ˈfɛt̬ɪd/ *adj.* FORMAL having a strong, bad smell: *the fetid streets of the slum*

fet·ish /ˈfɛt̬ɪʃ/ *n.* [C] **1** a desire for sex that comes from seeing a particular type of object or doing a particular activity, especially when the object or activity are considered unusual: *a foot fetish* **2** something you are always thinking about, or spending too much time doing: *The suspect has* **had a** *gun* **fetish** *for a long time.* **3** an object that is treated like a god and is thought to have magical powers [**Origin:** 1600–1700 French *fétiche*, from Portuguese *feitiço* **artificial, false**]

fet·ish·ist /ˈfɛt̬ɪʃɪst/ *n.* [C] someone who gets sexual pleasure from unusual objects or activities —**fetishism** *n.* [U] —**fetishistic** /ˌfɛt̬ɪˈʃɪstɪk/ *adj.*

fet·lock /ˈfɛtlɑk/ *n.* [C] the back part of a horse's leg, just above the HOOF

fet·ter /ˈfɛt̬ɚ/ *v.* [T usually passive] FORMAL **1** to restrict someone's freedom and prevent them from doing what they want to do: *The industry is fettered by debt.* **2** to put chains on a prisoner's hands or feet

fet·ters /ˈfɛt̬ɚz/ *n.* [plural] **1** LITERARY the things that prevent someone from doing what they want to do: *He wanted to free their minds from the fetters of old ideas.* **2** chains that were put around a prisoner's feet in past times

fet·tle /ˈfɛt̬l/ *n.* **in fine fettle** OLD-FASHIONED healthy or working correctly

fet·tuc·ci·ne /ˌfɛt̬əˈtʃini/ *n.* [U] thin, long, flat pieces of PASTA

fe·tus /ˈfit̬əs/ *n.* [C] BIOLOGY a young human or animal before birth. In humans, an EMBRYO becomes a fetus after eight weeks of development [**Origin:** 1300–1400 Latin **giving birth, things born**] → see also EMBRYO

feud[1] /fyud/ *n.* [C] an angry and often violent argument between two people or groups that continues for a long time: **+with/between** *a long-running feud between the two brothers* | **+over** *a bitter feud over money* [**Origin:** 1200–1300 Old French *feide*]

feud[2] *v.* [I] to continue arguing for a long time, often in a violent way: **feud (with sb) over sth** *The two countries have long been feuding over the island.*

feud·al /ˈfyudl/ *adj.* [only before noun] relating to feudalism: *the feudal system*

feu·dal·is·m /ˈfyudlˌɪzəm/ *n.* [U] HISTORY a system that existed in the Middle Ages, in which people received land and protection from someone of a higher rank when they worked and fought for him

feu·dal·is·tic /ˌfyudlˈɪstɪk◂/ *adj.* POLITICS based on a system in which only a few people have all the power

fe·ver /ˈfivɚ/ *n.* **1** [C,U] MEDICINE an illness or a medical condition in which you have a very high temperature: *I think you* **have a fever**. | *She's* **running a fever** (=has a fever). | **a high/low/slight fever** *The illness begins with a high fever, followed by a rash.* → see also HAY FEVER, SCARLET FEVER, YELLOW FEVER **2** [U] a state in which a lot of people are excited about something in a crazy way: *Academy Award fever is taking over Hollywood.* | *The incident raised racial tensions to a* **fever pitch** (=an extreme level of excitement) *in the city.* [**Origin:** 900–1000 Latin *febris*] → see also CABIN FEVER

'fever ,blister *n.* [C] a COLD SORE

fe·vered /ˈfivɚd/ *adj.* [only before noun] LITERARY **1** extremely excited or worried: *the band's fevered fans* **2** MEDICINE suffering from a fever SYN **feverish**: *She smoothed the child's* **fevered brow** (=a hot forehead caused by a fever). **3 a fevered imagination/mind** someone who has a fevered imagination imagines strange things and cannot control their thoughts

fe·ver·ish /ˈfivərɪʃ/ *adj.* **1** MEDICINE suffering from a fever: *He suddenly felt feverish.* **2** very excited or worried about something: *two days of feverish activity* —**feverishly** *adv.*

few /fyu/ S1 W1 *quantifier, pron., adj.* **1 a few** [no comparative] a small number of something OPP **a lot**: *The bus is usually a few minutes late.* | *I just need to buy a few things at the store.* | *Most of the pictures were good, and a few were excellent.* | **just/only a few** *The ceremony will begin in just a few minutes.* | *There are* **a few more** *things I'd like to talk about before we go.* | **+of** *I've seen a few of those new cars around.* | *A few of us are organizing a party.* **2 quite a few** a fairly large number of people or things: *Quite a few people came to* the meeting. | *"How many countries has he visited?" "Quite a few."* **3** not many or not enough people or things OPP **many**: *There may be few options open to you.* | *Many people expressed concern, but few were willing to help.* | *Give me the dessert with* ***the fewest*** *calories.* | ***Very few*** *people agreed with me.* | +**of** *Few of the teachers actually live here.* | *Why are there* ***so few*** *women in these jobs?* | *It is surprising* ***how few*** *students fail.* | *We have* ***too few*** *people to do the work.* | ***Fewer and fewer*** (=a decreasing number) *students are choosing to study chemistry.* | *We have had* ***far fewer*** *complaints recently.* | *There were* ***precious few*** (=very few) *opportunities for older actresses.* **4 the/these/those/sb's few** used for referring to a particular small group, set, or series of things or people: *She enjoyed her few days in Paris.* | *Most people agreed, and those few who disagreed left the meeting.* | *Grant's* ***one of the few*** *people I know who can tell stories well.* | **the first/last/next few** *They've lost their last few games.* | *Read the next few pages carefully.* **5 be few and far between** to be rare, or to be not happening or available often: *Good jobs are few and far between these days.* **6 every few days/weeks/years etc.** happening again after a period of a few days, weeks etc.: *The plants need to be watered every few days.* **7 every few feet/miles etc.** appearing or existing in a series after a distance of a few feet, miles etc.: *There was a gas station every few miles.* **8 as few as** used to emphasize how small a number is: *As few as 20 out of 500 candidates passed the test.* **9 no fewer than** used to emphasize how large a number is; at least: *I tried to contact him no fewer than ten times.* → see Grammar box at LESS[1] **10 have had a few (too many)** INFORMAL to have too much alcohol to drink: *It looks like you've had a few too many.* [**Origin:** Old English *feawa*] → see also **the chosen few** at CHOSEN[2] (2), **to name (but) a few** at NAME[2] (5)

WORD CHOICE **few, a few, little, a little**

- Use **few** with plural countable nouns to mean "not many": *Few people actually bother to get involved.* **Few** used alone is fairly formal, and you would most often use it with **very**: *Very few people come here now.*
- Use **a few** with plural countable nouns to mean "some": *A few people arrived late, but most of them got there on time.* With words for time, use **a few**: *After a few minutes I decided to leave.* | *I didn't see her again until a few years later.*
- Use **little** with uncountable nouns to mean "not much": *Unfortunately he now has little money left.* **Little** used alone is fairly formal, and you would most often use it with **very**: *There's usually very little traffic this early in the morning.*
- Use **a little** with uncountable nouns to mean "some, but not a lot": *There's only a little ice cream left.*

fey /feɪ/ *adj.* someone who is fey is attractive or interesting but in a slightly strange or childish way

Feyn·man /ˈfaɪnmən/, **Richard** (1918–1988) a U.S. scientist who did important work on RADIOACTIVITY and won a Nobel Prize

fez /fɛz/ *n.* [C] a round red hat with a flat top and no BRIM

ff the written abbreviation of "and following," used in a book to mean the pages after the one you have mentioned: *Please see pages 54ff.*

fi·an·cé /ˌfiɑnˈseɪ, fiˈɑnseɪ/ *n.* [C] the man whom a woman is going to marry

fi·an·cée /ˌfiɑnˈseɪ, fiˈɑnseɪ/ *n.* [C] the woman whom a man is going to marry

fi·as·co /fiˈæskoʊ/ *n. plural* **fiascoes** or **fiascos** [C,U] something that is completely unsuccessful, in a way that is very embarrassing or disappointing: *The new mall has been an economic fiasco.* [**Origin:** 1800–1900 Italian *(far) fiasco* **(to make) a bottle, to fail in a performance**]

fi·at /ˈfiæt, -ɑt, -ət/ *n.* [C] FORMAL an official command given by someone in a position of authority, without considering what other people want: *Public policy issues cannot be settled* ***by fiat.***

ˈfiat ˌmoney *n.* [U] ECONOMICS money that a government says has value, but which is not based on gold or silver and cannot be exchanged for gold or silver

fib[1] /fɪb/ *n.* [C] INFORMAL a small unimportant lie: *His mother says that he sometimes* ***tells fibs.*** ►see THESAURUS box at **lie[3]**

fib[2] *v.* **fibbed, fibbing** [I] INFORMAL to tell a small unimportant lie: *He fibbed about his age.* —**fibber** *n.* [C]

fi·ber /ˈfaɪbɚ/ *n.* **1** [U] parts of plants that you eat but cannot DIGEST, which help food to move quickly through your body: *Eat foods that are high in fiber.* **2** [C,U] the part of some plants that is used for making materials such as rope or cloth: *plant fibers* **3** [C] a type of thread or cloth: **a synthetic/man-made/artificial fiber** *Nylon is a man-made fiber.* | *I prefer* ***natural fibers*** *against my skin.* **4 nerve/muscle fibers** [plural] the thin pieces of flesh that form the nerves or muscles in your body **5 with every fiber of your being** LITERARY if you feel something with every fiber of your being, you feel it very strongly: *I regret my decision with every fiber of my being.*

fi·ber·board /ˈfaɪbɚˌbɔrd/ *n.* [U] a special type of board made from wood fibers pressed together

fi·ber·fill /ˈfaɪbɚˌfɪl/ *n.* [U] an artificial substance used to fill PILLOWS, SLEEPING BAGS etc.

fi·ber·glass /ˈfaɪbɚˌglæs/ *n.* [U] a light material made from small glass threads pressed together, used for making racing cars, small boats etc.

ˈfiber ˌoptics *n.* [U] the use of long thin threads of glass or plastic to carry information in the form of light, especially on telephone lines —**fiber-optic** *adj.*: *fiber-optic cables*

fi·brous /ˈfaɪbrəs/ *adj.* consisting of many fibers or looking like fibers: *the fibrous outer shell of a coconut*

ˌfibrous ˈroot *n.* [C] BIOLOGY a system of roots that is made up of many small thin branches of about the same length, for example the roots of many grasses

fib·u·la /ˈfɪbyələ/ *n.* [C] BIOLOGY the outer bone of the two bones in your leg below your knee [**Origin:** 1500–1600 Latin **piece of jewelry for fastening clothes** (because of the shape of the two bones)] → see picture at SKELETON[1]

FICA /ˈfikə/ *n.* [U] **Federal Insurance Contributions Act** ECONOMICS a tax that workers pay on the money they earn that supports the Social Security system

fiche /fiʃ/ *n.* [C,U] a MICROFICHE

fick·le /ˈfɪkəl/ *adj.* **1** someone who is fickle is always changing their opinions or feelings about what they like or want, so that you cannot depend on them: *Teenagers are fickle and switch brands frequently.* **2** something that is fickle, such as weather, often changes suddenly: *fickle winds* —**fickleness** *n.* [U]

fic·tion /ˈfɪkʃən/ *n.* **1** [U] ENG. LANG. ARTS books and stories about imaginary people and events OPP **nonfiction**: *I rarely read fiction* | *science-fiction novels* | **romantic/crime/historical etc. fiction** *Anthony's first books were historical fiction.* | *This book is his first* ***work of fiction.*** ►see THESAURUS box at **book[1]** **2** [C] something that someone wants you to believe is true, but which is not true: *Free elections are a fiction in this region.* [**Origin:** 1300–1400 Old French, Latin *fictus*, past participle of *fingere* **to shape, make**]

fic·tion·al /ˈfɪkʃənəl/ *adj.* fictional people, events etc. are imaginary and from a book or story: *a fictional character*

fic·tion·al·ize /ˈfɪkʃənəˌlaɪz/ *v.* [T] to make a movie or story about a real event, changing some details and adding some imaginary characters: *The play fictionalizes the life of Hoffmann.* —**fictionalization** /ˌfɪkʃənələˈzeɪʃən/ *n.* [C,U]

fic·ti·tious /fɪkˈtɪʃəs/ *adj.* not true, or not real: *He gave a fictitious address.*

fic·tive /ˈfɪktɪv/ *adj.* fictive events, people etc. are imaginary and not real

fid·dle[1] /ˈfɪdl/ *v.* [I] **1** to keep moving and touching things, especially because you are bored or nervous: *I sat and fiddled at the computer for a while.* **2** INFORMAL to play a VIOLIN

fiddle around *phr. v.* to waste time by doing things that are not important: *If you keep fiddling around we're going to be late!*

fiddle around with sth *phr. v.* **1** to move the parts of a machine in order to try to make it work or repair it: *I've been fiddling around with this old car for months but I still can't get it to work.* **2** to keep making changes to something, especially in a way that is stupid, annoying, or dangerous

fiddle with sth *phr. v.* **1** to keep moving something or touching something with your fingers because you are bored, nervous, or want to change something: *He kept fiddling with his tie.* **2** to move part of a machine in order to make it work, without knowing exactly what you should do: *Rosie fiddled with the lock, trying different combinations.* **3** to keep making changes to something, especially in a way that is stupid, annoying, or dangerous: *The bus company is always fiddling with the schedules.* **4** to move or touch something that you should not move or touch in an annoying way: *Who's been fiddling with my stuff?*

fiddle² *n.* [C] INFORMAL a VIOLIN → see also **fit as a fiddle** at FIT³ (3), **play second fiddle (to sb)** at PLAY¹ (22)

fid·dle-fad·dle /ˈfɪdl ˌfædl/ *n.* [U] OLD-FASHIONED nonsense

fid·dler /ˈfɪdlɚ/ *n.* [C] someone who plays the VIOLIN, especially someone who plays FOLK MUSIC

fid·dle·sticks /ˈfɪdlˌstɪks/ *interjection* OLD-FASHIONED said when you are slightly angry or annoyed about something

fid·dling¹ /ˈfɪdlɪŋ/ *n.* [U] the activity of playing the fiddle

fiddling² *adj.* [only before noun] unimportant and annoying: *a fiddling little job*

fi·del·i·ty /fəˈdɛləṭi, faɪ-/ *n.* [U] **1** FORMAL the quality of not changing something when you are producing it again in a different form, by recording, translating, making a movie etc.: +**of** *the incredible sound fidelity of CDs* | +**to** *the movie's fidelity to the original novel* **2** loyalty to your husband, wife etc., shown by having sex only with them [OPP] **infidelity**: *Kip was beginning to doubt Jessica's fidelity.* **3** the quality of being faithful and loyal, or of not doing anything that is against your beliefs [SYN] **loyalty** [SYN] **faithfulness**: *fidelity to religious beliefs* [**Origin:** 1400–1500 French *fidélité*, from Latin *fidelitas*, from *fides* **faith, trust**] → HIGH FIDELITY

fidg·et¹ /ˈfɪdʒɪt/ *v.* [I] to keep moving your hands or feet, especially because you are bored or nervous: *A few students fidgeted nervously in their chairs.* | **fidget with sth** *He was fidgeting with a pen.*

fidget² *n.* [C] INFORMAL someone who keeps moving and is not able to sit or stand still

fidg·et·y /ˈfɪdʒəṭi/ *adj.* INFORMAL tending to fidget a lot: *fidgety boys*

fi·du·ci·a·ry¹ /fɪˈduʃiˌɛri/ *n.* [C] TECHNICAL someone who has legal control of the money or property belonging to other people, a company, or an organization

fiduciary² *adj.* TECHNICAL relating to the legal control of someone else's money or property

fie /faɪ/ *interjection* OLD USE **fie on sb** used to express anger or disapproval toward someone

fief /fif/ *n.* [C] HISTORY in past times, an area of land that a LORD gave to someone who promised to work and fight for him

field¹ /fild/ [S1] [W1] *n.*

1 FARM [C] an area of land where crops are grown or animals feed on grass: +**of** *fields of cotton* | **a corn/wheat/rice etc. field** (=an area of land where corn, wheat, rice etc. is grown)

2 SPORTS a) [C] an area of ground where outdoor games such as baseball or football are played: *The fans cheered as he walked off the field.* | *The Trojans will **take the field*** (=go onto the field in order to begin a game) *against Arizona State this afternoon.* | **a baseball/football/soccer field** *Students gathered at the side of the football field before the game.* | **on/off the field** *Team members have had a bad year both on and off the field.* **b) the field** the team that is throwing and catching the ball in a game such as baseball, rather than the team that is hitting ►see THESAURUS box at **sport¹**

3 SUBJECT [C] a subject that people study or are involved in as part of their work [SYN] **area**: *We both work in the same field.* | +**of** *new developments in the field of computer science* | *He's an expert **in his field**.* | *Her **field of study** is neurobiology.*

4 PRACTICAL WORK [singular] work or study that is done in the field is done in the real world or in the area where something is happening, rather than in a CLASSROOM or LABORATORY: *Firefighters **in the field** called for more help.* | **field testing/trial/research etc.** *Seven months of field testing have shown the device to be reliable.* → see also FIELD TEST

5 COMPETITORS [singular] **a)** all the people, companies, or products who are competing against each other: *a strong field of candidates for the job* | *The company **leads the field*** (=is the most successful company) *in wireless communication devices.* **b)** all the horses or runners in a race: *Dusty Nell is **leading the field** as they come around the final bend.*

6 COMPUTERS [C] an amount of space made available for a particular type of information: *The field for the user's name is 25 characters long.*

7 coal/oil/gas field a large area where coal, oil, or gas is found

8 an area that a person or a piece of equipment can see at one time: *the camera's depth of field* | **field of view/vision** *The goggles limit your field of vision.*

9 a magnetic/gravitational/force field an area where a natural force is felt or has an effect

10 the field (of battle) the time or place where there is fighting in a war [SYN] **battlefield**: *Civilians walked miles to villages away from the field of battle.* | *The new tank has yet to be used **in the field**.*

11 a snow/an ice field a large area covered with snow or ice

12 a field of fire the area that you can hit by shooting from a particular position

[**Origin:** Old English *feld*] → see also **play the field** at PLAY¹ (30)

field² *v.* **1** [T] to deal with questions, telephone calls etc, especially when there are a lot of them or they are difficult to deal with: *The senator **fielded questions** on Social Security reform.* | *The college spokeswoman has **fielded** numerous **calls** from the media.* **2** [T] if you field a team, or an army, they represent you or fight for you in a competition or war: *We've fielded a team of highly talented basketball players.* **3** [T] if you field the ball in a game of baseball, you stop it after it has been hit: *Carlton fielded all five grounders hit his way.* **4 be fielding** the team that is fielding in a game of baseball is the one that is throwing and catching the ball, rather than the one hitting it

ˈfield corn *n.* [U] corn that is grown to use as grain or to feed to animals, rather than to be eaten by people

ˈfield day *n.* [C] **1 have a field day** INFORMAL to have a chance to do a lot of something you enjoy, especially a chance to criticize someone or something: *The newspapers have had a field day covering the trial.* **2** a day when students at a school have sports competitions outside

field·er /ˈfildɚ/ *n.* [C] one of the players who tries to catch the ball in a game of baseball

ˈfield eˌvent *n.* [C] a sports activity such as jumping over bars or throwing heavy things, that is part of an outdoor competition → see also TRACK EVENT

ˈfield ˌglasses *n.* [plural] BINOCULARS

ˈfield goal *n.* [C] **1** the act of kicking the ball over the bar of the GOAL for three points in football **2** the act of putting the ball through the BASKET to get points in basketball

ˈfield hand *n.* [C] someone who works in the field on a farm

F

ˈfield ˌhockey *n.* [U] an outdoor game in which two teams of 11 players using special sticks try to hit a ball into their opponents' GOAL

ˈfield house *n.* [C] a large building used for indoor sports events such as basketball

ˈfield test *n.* [C] SCIENCE a test of a new product or system that is done outside the LABORATORY in real conditions —**field-test** *v.* [T]

ˈfield trip *n.* [C] an occasion when students go somewhere to learn about a particular subject: *The class **went on a field trip to** a recycling factory.*

field·work /ˈfildwɚk/ *n.* [U] **1** the study of scientific or social subjects that is done outside the CLASSROOM or LABORATORY **2** work that is done in farmers' fields to help crops grow —**fieldworker** *n.* [C]

fiend /find/ *n.* [C] **1 a dope/drug/cocaine etc. fiend** someone who takes drugs regularly **2 a sex fiend** DISAPPROVING someone who wants to have sex a lot **3** someone who likes something much more than other people do: *a sports fiend* **4** a very cruel or evil person **5** LITERARY an evil spirit

F

fiend·ish /ˈfindɪʃ/ *adj.* **1** LITERARY very bad in a way that seems evil: *a fiendish murder* **2** FORMAL extremely difficult or bad: *a plot of fiendish complexity* —**fiendishly** *adv.*

fierce /fɪrs/ *adj.* **1** done with a lot of energy and often violent: *fierce resistance* | *The **fiercest fighting** took place in the north.* | **a fierce attack/battle/clash etc.** *They launched a fierce attack on the rebels.* **2** a fierce person or animal is angry or ready to attack, and looks very frightening: *a fierce guard dog* **3** involving strong feelings and a lot of energy or activity: *Rogers has a fierce love for the game of baseball.* | *The company faces **fierce competition** from abroad.* | **a fierce argument/debate etc.** *They had a fierce argument over money.* | **fierce opposition/criticism/attack etc.** *There has been fierce opposition to the plan.* **4** fierce cold, heat, or weather is much colder, hotter etc. than usual: *the fierce heat of the desert* **5 something fierce** SPOKEN more loudly, strongly etc. than usual: *It rained something fierce.* [**Origin:** 1200–1300 Old French *fiers*, from Latin *ferus* **wild**] —**fiercely** *adv.* —**fierceness** *n.* [U]

fi·er·y /ˈfaɪəri/ *adj.* **1** containing or looking like fire: *a fiery sunset* **2** making people feel strong emotions such as anger or excitement, or showing these types of emotion: *a fiery labor leader* | *music with a fiery rhythm* **3** becoming angry very quickly: *Nansen is fiery and emotional.* **4** fiery foods taste very strong and hot **5** bright red: *He has fiery red hair.*

fi·es·ta /fiˈɛstə/ *n.* [C] **1** a religious holiday with dancing, music etc., especially in Spain and Latin America **2** a party

fife /faɪf/ *n.* [C] a small musical instrument like a FLUTE, often played in military bands

fif·teen /ˌfɪfˈtin◂ / *number* 15

fif·teenth¹ /ˌfɪfˈtinθ◂ / *adj.* 15th; next after the fourteenth: *the fifteenth century*

fifteenth² *pron.* **the fifteenth** the 15th thing in a series: *Let's have dinner on the fifteenth* (=the 15th day of the month).

ˌFifteenth Aˈmendment, the *n.* [singular] HISTORY an AMENDMENT (=official addition) to the U.S. Constitution, made in 1870, that gave all male citizens the right to vote, giving African-Americans the same voting rights as white people

fifth¹ /fɪfθ/ *adj.* 5th; next after the fourth: *fifth place in the race* | *her fifth birthday*

fifth² *pron.* **1 the fifth** the 5th thing in a series: *Her party is on the fifth* (=the 5th day of the month). **2 take/plead the fifth (amendment)** to refuse to answer a question about a crime in a court of law, because you think that by answering you might give the court information that would show you are guilty

fifth³ *n.* [C] **1** 1/5; one of five equal parts of something: *Only **a fifth of** the students are boys.* | **one-fifth/two-fifths/three-fifths etc.** *two-fifths of the pie* **2** an amount of alcohol equal to 1/5 of a gallon, sold in bottles: *a fifth of bourbon*

ˌfifth ˈcolumn *n.* [C] a group of people who work secretly to help the enemies of the country they live in, especially during a war —**fifth columnist** *n.* [C]

ˌfifth ˈwheel *n.* [C] **1 feel like a fifth wheel** INFORMAL to feel that the people you are with do not want you to be there **2** a piece of equipment, shaped like a wheel on its side, used to attach a TRAILER to a large vehicle such as a truck

fif·ti·eth¹ /ˈfɪftiɪθ/ *adj.* 50th; next after the forty-ninth: *my parents' fiftieth anniversary*

fiftieth² *pron.* **the fiftieth** the 50th thing in a series

fif·ty /ˈfɪfti/ *number, n.* **1** 50 **2 the fifties** also **the '50s** the years from 1950 through 1959: *Were you born in the fifties?* | **the early/late/mid fifties** *popular music in the late fifties* **3 sb's fifties** the time when someone is 50 to 59 years old: **early/mid/late fifties** *He's **in** his early **fifties**.* **4 in the fifties** if the temperature is in the fifties, it is between 50° and 59° FAHRENHEIT: **in the high/low fifties** *It will be cloudy, with temperatures in the low fifties.* **5** [C] a piece of paper money worth $50: *a fifty and two tens*

ˌfifty-ˈfifty *adj., adv.* SPOKEN **1** divided or shared equally between two people: *We **split** the money **fifty-fifty**.* **2** having an equal chance of happening or not happening in a particular way: *I think we have a **fifty-fifty chance** of winning.*

fig /fɪg/ *n.* [C] **1** BIOLOGY a soft sweet fruit with a lot of small seeds, often eaten dried, or the tree on which this fruit grows → see picture at FRUIT¹ **2 not care/give a fig (about sb/sth)** SPOKEN, OLD-FASHIONED to not care at all about someone or something

fig. **1** the written abbreviation of FIGURE **2** the written abbreviation of FIGURATIVE

fight¹ /faɪt/ S1 W1 *past tense and past participle* **fought** /fɔt/ *v.*

1 WAR [I,T] to take part in a war or battle: *Pancho Villa fought a battle near here.* | **+in** *My grandfather fought in the Pacific during World War II.* | **+against/with** *He fought against the Nazis.* | **+about/over/for** *They fought for control of the islands.* | **fight sb** *Vietnam fought France and then the U.S. over 30 years.* | *North and South Korea **fought a** three-year **war** in the early 1950s.*

2 HIT PEOPLE [I,T] if someone fights another person, or if two people fight, they hit and kick each other in order to hurt each other: *The children fought and pushed in line.* | **+with** *The two boys are always fighting with each other.* | **+about/over/for** *They were fighting over a woman.* | *She and her brother used to **fight like cats and dogs*** (=fight violently).

3 ARGUE [I] to argue about something SYN **quarrel**: *My mother and my grandmother fight all the time.* | **+with** *The kids seem to fight with each other constantly.* | **+about/over** *Most married couples fight occasionally about money.* ►see THESAURUS box at **argue**

4 TRY TO DO STH [I,T] to try hard to get, change, or prevent something: *Civil rights groups have vowed to fight the changes.* | **+for/against** *The union fought for a better health care package.* | **fight to do sth** *I had to really fight to stay awake.* | **fight sb (on sth)** *Citizens' groups intend to fight the mayor on the freeway plan.* | *The closing of the school was **fought tooth and nail*** (=fought against in a very determined way) *by neighborhood groups.* | *He **fought** his **way** back to the starting lineup.*

5 COMPETE [I,T] to compete strongly for something, especially a job or political position or in a sport: **+for** *Party members are fighting for power.* | **fight sb for sth** *He had to fight several other applicants for the job.*

6 SPORT [I,T] to hit someone as a sport SYN **box**

7 fight a fire/blaze etc. to try to stop a fire from burning

8 EMOTION [T] also **fight back** to try very hard not to show your feelings or not to do something you want to do: *I had to fight the impulse to slap her.*

9 fight your way (into/through/past etc. sb/sth) to move somewhere with difficulty, for example because

there are so many people around you: *John fought his way through the crowd.*
10 be fighting for your life to be very sick or injured and likely to die: *Collins is fighting for his life against stomach cancer.*
11 have a fighting chance to have a chance to do something or achieve something if you work very hard at it: *All children must have a fighting chance at a good education.*
12 fight fire with fire to use the same methods as your opponents in an argument, competition etc.
13 fighting spirit the desire to fight or compete
14 fighting words something you say that makes someone want to fight or argue with you: *To Chapman, **those are fighting words**.*
15 fight to the death a) to fight until one person is killed **b)** to fight very hard to achieve something even if it means that you suffer
16 fight your own battles to try hard to get what you want or need, without needing help from other people: *a strong woman who can fight her own battles*
[**Origin:** Old English *feohtan*] → see also **fight/wage/be a losing battle** at BATTLE[1] (3)

fight back *phr. v.* **1** to use violence or arguments against someone who has attacked you or argued with you: *If you're mugged, don't fight back. Give them your wallet.* **2** to work hard to achieve or oppose something, especially in a situation where you are losing: *Victims of discrimination often don't have the power to fight back.* **3 fight sth ↔ back** to try hard not to have or show a feeling: *"I'm devastated," Weston said, **fighting back tears**.*

fight sth ↔ **down** *phr. v.* to try hard not to have or show a feeling: *She fought down her panic.*

fight sb/sth ↔ **off** *phr. v.* **1** to push someone away when they are attacking you: *She fought off his clumsy advances.* **2** to succeed in preventing someone from doing something, or to prevent something from happening: *The company managed to fight off a hostile takeover attempt.* **3** to try hard to get rid of something, especially an illness or a feeling: *White blood cells help to fight off infections.* | *He fought off the boredom by doodling.*

fight sth **out** *phr. v.* to argue or use violence until a disagreement is settled: *The two groups will **fight it out** in the courts.*

fight[2] S2 W2 *n.*

1 HIT [C] a situation in which two people or groups hit, push etc. each other: **+between** *A fight between them left Paula with a black eye.* | **+over/about** *What was the fight about?* | **+with** *He'd **had a fight** with a boy from school.* | *You **got in a fight**? Are you all right?* | **pick/start a fight** *A drunk tried to pick a fight with him.*

THESAURUS

brawl a noisy fight among a lot of people
free-for-all a fight or argument involving a lot of people, but having no particular purpose
scuffle a short fight that is not very violent
scrap INFORMAL a short fight

2 BATTLE [C] a battle between two armies, especially the fighting that happens at one particular place and time: **+for** *the fight for Bunker Hill*

THESAURUS

battle an attempt to stop something happening or to achieve something difficult: *the battle for equal rights*
campaign a series of actions that are intended to achieve a particular result: *a campaign in schools against teenage pregnancy*
struggle a long, hard fight for freedom, political rights etc.: *the country's struggle for independence*

3 ARGUMENT [C] an argument SYN **quarrel**: *A good fight once in a while can clear the air.* | **+about/over** *The kids used to **have fights** about who got to sit in the front seat.* | **+with** *I had a fight with my boyfriend.*
4 ACHIEVE/PREVENT STH [singular] the process of trying to achieve something, change something, or prevent something SYN **struggle**: **+against** *her long fight against cancer* | **+for** *the fight for equality and justice* | **fight to do sth** *the fight to prevent drunk driving* | *He'll **have a fight on his hands** (=it will be difficult) to get Malone acquitted.*
5 SPORTS [C] an act of fighting as a sport, in BOXING: *Are you going to watch the **big fight** (=important fight)?*
6 ENERGY [U] the energy and desire to keep working hard for something you want to achieve: *They're not going to give up – they **have a lot of fight left** in them.*
7 sb's fight for life a struggle to stay alive when someone is badly injured or very sick
8 put up a good fight to work very hard to fight or compete in a difficult situation
9 a fight to the finish/death a fight that continues until one side is completely defeated

fight·er /ˈfaɪtə/ W3 *n.* [C]

1 someone who keeps trying to achieve something in difficult situations: *Dad was a fighter, but he couldn't beat cancer.* | *a crime fighter* **2** someone who fights as a sport SYN **boxer** **3** also **a fighter plane/jet** a small, fast military airplane that can destroy other planes → see also FIREFIGHTER, FREEDOM FIGHTER

F

ˈfig leaf *n.* [C]

1 the large leaf of the FIG tree, sometimes shown in paintings as covering people's sex organs **2** INFORMAL something that is intended to hide embarrassing facts

fig·ment /ˈfɪgmənt/ *n.* [C]

a figment of sb's imagination something that you imagine to be real, but does not exist

fig·u·ra·tive /ˈfɪgyərətɪv/ *adj.* ENG. LANG. ARTS

1 a figurative word or expression is used in a different way from its usual meaning, to give you a particular idea or picture in your mind SYN **metaphorical**: *He is my son, in a **figurative sense**.* → see also LITERAL **2** figurative art shows objects, people, or nature in the way they really look → see also ABSTRACT —**figuratively** *adv.*

ˌfigurative ˈlanguage *n.* [U] ENG. LANG. ARTS

writing or speech that uses figurative words or expressions to give people a particular picture or idea in their minds

fig·ure[1] /ˈfɪgyə/ S1 W1 *n.* [C]

1 NUMBER a) a number representing an amount, especially an official number: *sales figures* | *Ohio's employment figures for December* **b)** a number from 0 to 9, written as a sign rather than spelled with letters SYN **numeral**: *Five players scored in **double figures*** (=numbers between 10 and 99).
2 AMOUNT OF MONEY a particular amount of money: *a figure of $140 million* | **a five-/six-figure salary/income/paycheck etc.** (=an amount of money in the ten thousands, hundred thousands etc.) *Carl was earning a six-figure salary.* | **five/six figures** (=an amount of money in the ten thousands, hundred thousands etc.) *They paid six figures for the movie rights.*
3 IMPORTANT PERSON someone who is important or famous in a particular way: **political/public/sports etc. figure** *Ali was one of the great sports figures of the last century.* | **central/leading/key etc. figure** *The central figure of the movie is a 13-year-old girl.*
4 WOMAN'S BODY the shape of a woman's body, used when describing how attractive it is SYN **body**: *Caroline really **has** a terrific **figure**.* | **keep/lose your figure** (=keep your body in an attractive shape as you get older, or to not do this) ▸see THESAURUS box at **body**
5 father/mother/authority figure someone who is considered to be like a father or mother, or to represent authority, because of their character or behavior: *He had been both a coach and a father figure to Reid.*
6 give an exact figure also **put an exact figure on it** to say exactly how much something is worth, or how much or how many of something you are talking about: *It's worth a lot but I couldn't give you an exact figure.*
7 PERSON'S SHAPE the shape of a person, especially one that is far away or is difficult to see SYN **form**: *a figure in a red robe* | *Freddy's bent figure*
8 DRAWING a numbered drawing or a DIAGRAM in a book

9 MATHEMATICAL SHAPE a GEOMETRIC shape: *A hexagon is a six-sided figure.*
10 a fine figure of a man/woman OLD-FASHIONED someone who is tall and has a good body
11 PAINTING/MODEL a person in a painting, a model of a person, or a small STATUE → see also FIGURINE: *a rare 16th century Japanese figure* | *Star Wars* ***action figures*** (=a toy shaped like a person)
12 ON ICE a pattern formed in FIGURE SKATING
13 a figure of fun someone who people laugh at
[**Origin:** 1200–1300 French, Latin *figura*, from *fingere* **to shape, make**]

figure² S1 W2 *v.* **1** [I] to be an important part of a process, event, or situation, or to be included in something: +**in** *Lott* ***figured prominently*** *in the Chiefs' win last night.* | *Trade issues* ***figure heavily*** *on the agenda.* **2** [T] to calculate an amount: *I'm just figuring my expenses.*

SPOKEN PHRASES

3 [T] INFORMAL to form a particular opinion after thinking about a situation: **figure (that)** *I figure it's easier to do it myself.* | *She figured that it was just going to take more time.* ▸see THESAURUS box at **think** **4 that figures** also **(it) figures a)** said when something happens or someone behaves in a way that you expect, but do not like: *"They're out of hot chocolate." "Figures."* **b)** used to say that something is reasonable or makes sense: *Well, it sort of figures that she'd be mad at you after what you did.* **5 go figure** said to show that you think something is strange or difficult to explain: *"He didn't even leave a message." "Go figure."*

figure on sth *phr. v.* SPOKEN to expect something, especially a number or a time, and include it in your plans: *Figure on 40 minutes from Gilroy to Tamian Station.* | **figure on doing sth** *You should figure on spending $150 a day.*

figure sb/sth ↔ **out** *phr. v.* **1** to think about a problem or situation until you find the answer or understand what has happened: *If I have a map, I can figure it out.* | *Don't worry, we'll figure something out* (=find a way to solve the problem). | **figure out how/what/why** *Let's figure out what we're doing first.* **2** to understand why someone behaves in the way they do: *Women. I just can't figure them out.*

fig·ured /ˈfɪgyɚd/ *adj.* [only before noun] FORMAL decorated with a small pattern

ˌfigure ˈeight *n.* [C] the pattern or shape of a number eight, as seen in a knot, dance, SKATING etc.

fig·ure·head /ˈfɪgyɚˌhɛd/ *n.* [C] **1** someone who seems to be the leader of a country or organization, but who has no real power: *Norway's King Harald V is a figurehead.* **2** a wooden model of a woman that used to be placed on the front of ships

ˌfigure of ˈspeech *n.* [C] a word or expression that is used in a different way from the usual meanings of the words, in order to give you an idea or picture in your mind

ˈfigure ˌskating *n.* [C] a sport in which you SKATE in patterns on ice —**figure skater** *n.* [C]

fig·u·rine /ˌfɪgyəˈrin/ *n.* [C] a small model of a person or animal made of CHINA (=baked clay), used as a decoration SYN **statuette** → see also FIGURE

Fi·ji /ˈfidʒi/ a country in the southwestern Pacific Ocean made up of two main islands and hundreds of smaller islands —**Fijian** *n., adj.*

fil·a·ment /ˈfɪləmənt/ *n.* [C] **1** a very thin thread, especially the thin wire in a LIGHT BULB **2** BIOLOGY the stem of a flower's STAMEN (=the male part of a flower), that supports the ANTHER (=the part that carries the pollen) → see picture at FLOWER¹ **3** BIOLOGY a long thin structure consisting of many cells joined together, found in ALGAE and certain types of BACTERIA

fil·bert /ˈfɪlbɚt/ *n.* [C] a HAZELNUT

filch /fɪltʃ/ *v.* [T] INFORMAL to steal something, especially something small or not very expensive SYN **snitch** [**Origin:** 1200–1300 Perhaps from Old English *fylcan* **to arrange soldiers, attack, take**]

file¹ /faɪl/ Ac S1 W2 *n.* [C] **1** a set of papers, records etc. that contain information about a particular person or subject SYN **dossier**: *I put Callahan's file back in the drawer.* | +**on** *Mendoza read over the file on the murders.* | *The CIA does not* ***keep files on*** (=collect and keep information on) *American citizens.* ▸see THESAURUS box at **record¹** **2** COMPUTERS a collection of information on a computer that is stored under a particular name: **a text/data file** *downloading a text file* | **copy/delete/open/save etc. a file** *It's a good idea to save a file often.* **3 on file a)** kept in a file so that it can be used later: *Some of the information on file is confidential.* **b)** officially recorded: *More than four million patents are on file in the U.S.* **4** a box or folded piece of heavy paper that is used to keep papers organized or separate from other papers: *a stack of blue and yellow files* **5** a metal tool with a rough surface, used to make other surfaces smooth or to cut through wood, metal etc. → see also NAIL FILE, RANK AND FILE, SINGLE FILE [**Origin:** (1–4) 1500–1600 French *fil* **thread** (because documents were stored on pieces of string)]

file² Ac S2 W2 *v.* **1** [I always + adv./prep., T] to officially record something such as a complaint, law case, official document etc.: *Married couples can file separate tax returns.* | +**for** *She decided to file for divorce.* | *The district attorney* ***filed charges*** *against him.* | **file a claim/suit** *O'Brien will file a $1 million civil damage suit.* | **file sth against sb** *a lawsuit filed against the L.A. Unified school system* **2** [T] also **file away** to keep papers with information on them in a particular place, so that you can find them easily: *Slawa filed a copy of the contract he'd signed.* ▸see THESAURUS box at **keep¹** **3** [T] to give or send an official report or news story to your employer: *The officer left the scene without* ***filing a report.*** **4** [I always + adv./prep.] to walk in a line of people, one behind the other: +**past/into/through etc.** *The kids filed out.* **5** [I always + adv./prep., T] to rub something with a metal tool or a NAIL FILE to make it smooth or cut it: *Alice was filing her nails.* | +**through/away/down etc.** *File down the sharp edges.*

ˈfile ˌcabinet *n.* [C] a FILING CABINET

ˈfile exˌtension *n.* [C] TECHNICAL an EXTENSION

file·name /ˈfaɪlneɪm/ *n.* [C] the name of a particular computer FILE

fi·let /fɪˈleɪ/ *n.* [C] a piece of meat or fish without bones: *salmon filets*

ˈfile ˌtransfer *n.* [C] TECHNICAL the process by which computer information is sent from one computer to another, especially over the Internet

fil·i·al /ˈfɪliəl/ *adj.* FORMAL relating to the way in which a son or daughter should behave toward their parents: *filial duty*

fil·i·bus·ter /ˈfɪləˌbʌstɚ/ *v.* [I] POLITICS to try to delay action in the Senate by making very long speeches [**Origin:** 1800–1900 Spanish *filibustero* **pirate**] —**filibuster** *n.* [C]

fil·i·gree /ˈfɪləˌgri/ *n.* [U] delicate decoration made of gold or silver wire

fil·ing /ˈfaɪlɪŋ/ Ac *n.* [U] **1** the activity of putting papers or documents into the correct FILES **2** [C] a document, report etc. that is officially recorded: *a bankruptcy filing* **3 filings** [plural] very small sharp pieces that come off a piece of metal when it is FILED

ˈfiling ˌcabinet *n.* [C] a piece of office furniture with drawers for keeping letters, reports etc.

Fil·i·pi·no /ˌfɪlɪˈpinoʊ/ *n.* [C] someone from the Philippines —**Filipino** *adj.*

fill¹ /fɪl/ S1 W1 *v.*
1 BECOME/MAKE FULL [I,T] also **fill up** if a container or place fills, or if you fill it, enough of something goes into it to make it full: *He filled a glass for her.* | *After heavy rains, the reservoirs began to fill up.* | **fill sth with sth** *George filled a couple of sacks with newspapers.* | +**with** *The washing machine began to fill with water.* | *a soup bowl* ***filled to the brim*** | *Miller's band was filling*

dancehalls (=attracting a lot of people to dance) *all over the country.*
2 NOT LEAVE ANY SPACE [T] also **fill up** if a lot of people or things fill a place, there are so many of them that there is no space left: *Computers used to fill entire rooms.* | **be filled with sth** *Crowded stores were filled with shoppers.* | *The room was* ***filled to capacity*** (=all the seats were full) *that night.* | *Pictures* ***filled*** *every available* ***space.***
3 HOLE/CRACK [T] also **fill in** to put a substance in a hole or crack in order to make a surface smooth again: *He had three cavities filled* (=in his teeth). | *Fill the hole with a mixture of compost and sand.*
4 SOUND/SMELL/LIGHT [T] if a sound, smell, or light fills a place or space, you notice it because it is very loud or strong: *The smell of smoke filled the house.* | **be filled with sth** *days filled with sunshine*
5 PROVIDE STH [T] to provide something that is missing, and that is needed or wanted: **fill a need/demand (for sth)** *The project will fill a need for affordable housing.* | **fill a gap/hole/vacuum etc.** *A number of projects try to fill the gaps left by social service programs.* | *People with low self-esteem often try to fill the void by criticizing other people.*
6 PERFORM A JOB [T] to perform a particular job, activity, or purpose in an organization, or to find someone or something to do this: **fill a position/job/vacancy etc.** | *Women do not fill combat positions in the military.* | *Roberts is expected to* ***fill a*** *significant* ***role*** *in Michigan's offense.*
7 EMOTIONS [T] if you are filled with an emotion, or if it fills you, you feel it very strongly: *A feeling of joy filled his heart.* | **be filled with sth** *He gave me a smile that was filled with pride.* | **fill sb with sth** *The sound filled her with terror.*
8 sb's eyes fill with tears if someone's eyes fill with tears, they start to cry
9 TIME [T] if you fill a period of time with a particular activity, you spend that time doing it: **fill sth with sth** *I filled every minute with activity, trying to forget.* | **fill sth doing sth** *I fill most of my spare time reading and listening to music.*
10 fill sb's shoes to be able to do a job as well as the person who did it before you: *New mayor Susan Hammer had to prove she could fill McEnery's shoes.*
11 fill yourself also **fill yourself up** INFORMAL to eat so much food that you cannot eat any more: **fill yourself with sth** *Don't fill yourself up with candy, it's almost dinner time.*
12 fill an order to supply the goods a customer has asked for
13 SAIL [I,T] if a sail fills or the wind fills a sail, the sail has a rounded shape rather than hanging down loosely [**Origin:** Old English *fyllan*] → see also **fill the bill/fit the bill** at BILL[1] (5)

fill in *phr. v.* **1 fill sth ↔ in** to make something more complete, especially by giving more information: *His imagination filled in the details.* | **fill in the gaps/blanks/holes etc.** *Scientists may not be able to fill in all the gaps in the fossil record.* **2 fill sb ↔ in** to tell someone about things that have happened recently, especially because they have been away from a place: **fill sb in on sth** *Helen filled me in on what I'd missed.* **3 fill sth ↔ in** to write all the necessary information in special places on a document: ***Fill in the blanks*** *on page two.* **4 fill sth ↔ in** to paint or draw over the space inside a shape **5** to do someone's job or work because they are not there to do it: **fill in for sb** *Beth will fill in for Tina while she's on vacation.* **6 fill sth ↔ in** to put a substance into a hole, crack etc. so that it is full and level

fill out *phr. v.* **1 fill sth ↔ out** to write all the necessary information on a document: **fill out a form/application/questionnaire etc.** *Joe filled out an application form.* **2 fill sth ↔ in** to add more details to a description, story, idea etc. **3** if a young person fills out, their body becomes more like an adult's body, for example by developing bigger muscles, developing breasts etc.: *At puberty, a girl's body begins to fill out.*

fill up *phr. v.* **1 fill sb up** INFORMAL food that fills you up makes you feel you have eaten a lot when you have only eaten a small amount: *Hot oatmeal will fill you up in the morning.* **2 fill sth ↔ up** if a container or place fills up, or if you fill it up, it becomes full: *I filled up my plate with food.* | **+with** *After school, the pool starts filling up with kids.* **3 fill yourself up** to eat so much food that you cannot eat any more: **+on** *Toddlers may fill up on juice, and not eat a balanced diet.*

fill[2] *n.* **1 have your fill of sth** to have done or experienced something, especially something you do not like, so that you do not want any more: *I've had my fill of noisy, smoky parties.* **2 eat/drink your fill** to eat or drink as much as you want or need

ˌfilled ˈgold *n.* [U] filled gold jewelry is made of an inexpensive metal such as COPPER covered with a thin layer of gold

fill·er /ˈfɪlɚ/ *n.* [U] **1** stories, information, drawings, songs etc. that are not important but are used to fill space in a newspaper or magazine, on a CD etc.: *His latest album consists of two great singles and ten tracks of filler.* **2** something that is added to food in order to increase its weight or size, so that the food can be sold cheaply: *The crab cakes were 80% crab, with very little filler.* **3** a substance used to fill cracks in wood, walls etc., especially before you paint them SYN **spackle** **4** also **fill** a soft substance such as cotton or feathers used to fill PILLOWS, COMFORTERS etc.

fil·let[1] /fɪˈleɪ/ *n.* [C] a piece of meat or fish without bones: *salmon fillets*

fillet[2] *v.* [T] to remove the bones from a piece of meat or fish: *Salmon is a relatively easy fish to fillet.*

ˈfill-in *n.* [C] someone who does someone else's job while they are away, sick etc.

fill·ing[1] /ˈfɪlɪŋ/ *n.* **1** [C] a small amount of metal that is put into your tooth to replace a decayed part that has been removed **2** [C,U] the food that is put inside something such as a PIE, cake etc.: *Roll the tortilla around the filling.*

filling[2] *adj.* food that is filling makes your stomach feel full: *A casserole makes a basic but filling meal.*

ˈfilling ˌstation *n.* [C] a GAS STATION

fil·lip /ˈfɪlɪp/ *n.* [singular] something that adds excitement or interest to something: *a designer who knows how to* ***give a fillip to*** *classic styles*

Fill·more /ˈfɪlmɔr/, **Mil·lard** /ˈmɪlɚd/ (1800–1874) the 13th President of the U.S.

fil·ly /ˈfɪli/ *n. plural* **fillies** [C] **1** BIOLOGY a young female horse → see also COLT **2** OLD-FASHIONED a young girl who has a lot of energy

film[1] /fɪlm/ S1 W1 *n.* **1** [U] the thin plastic used in a camera for taking photographs or recording movies: *five* ***rolls of film*** | *I need to get this* ***film developed*** (=made into photographs). | **capture/record/preserve etc. sth on film** *An onlooker captured the Kennedy assassination on film.* **2** [C] ENG. LANG. ARTS a MOVIE: *classic French films* ▸see THESAURUS box at **movie**, **television** **3** [U] ENG. LANG. ARTS the work of making movies, considered as an art or a business: *He was well-known in film and television.* | *the Hollywood film industry* **4** [U] moving pictures of real events that are shown on television, in a movie theater etc.: *Film at eleven!* (=we will show the film of the event during the news) **5** [singular, U] a very thin layer of liquid, powder etc. on the surface of something else: **+of** *A film of perspiration appeared on his forehead.* [**Origin:** Old English *filmen* **thin skin**]

film[2] S3 *v.* [I,T] to use a camera to record a story or real events so that it can be shown in movie theaters or on television: *The movie was filmed in Ireland.*

ˈfilm ˌfestival *n.* [C] an event at which a lot of movies are shown, and sometimes prizes are given for the best ones: *the Cannes film festival*

film·mak·er /ˈfɪlmˌmeɪkɚ/ *n.* [C] someone who makes movies, especially a DIRECTOR or PRODUCER —**filmmaking** *n.* [U]

film noir /ˌfɪlm ˈnwɑr/ *n. plural* **films noir** /ˌfɪlm ˈnwɑr/ [C,U] a type of movie that is usually filmed with

F

a lot of shadows or at night in a large city, and in which the characters are often dishonest or immoral

ˈfilm star *n.* [C] OLD-FASHIONED a MOVIE STAR

film·strip /ˈfɪlmˌstrɪp/ *n.* [C] a photographic film that shows photographs, drawings etc. one at a time, not as moving pictures, especially used in a class

fi·lo dough /ˈfiloʊ ˌdoʊ/ *n.* [U] another spelling of PHYLLO DOUGH

fil·ter¹ /ˈfɪltɚ/ S3 *n.* [C] **1** something that you put gas or liquid through, in order to remove unwanted substances: *a water filter* | *a coffee filter* **2** COMPUTERS a computer program that only allows certain types of information to pass through it: *an Internet filter used to prevent children looking at sex sites* **3** a piece of glass or plastic that changes the amount or color of light allowed into a camera or TELESCOPE **4** a piece of equipment that only allows certain sounds to pass through it [**Origin:** 1300–1400 Old French *filtre* **piece of felt (=thick material) used as a filter**, from Medieval Latin *filtrum*]

F

filter² *v.* **1** [T] to remove unwanted substances from a liquid or gas by passing it through a special substance or piece of equipment: *Filter the water before drinking it.* **2** [I always + adv./prep.] if news or information filters somewhere, people gradually hear about it: +**back/through etc.** *Unofficial reports of the violence began to filter out of the capital within days.* **3** [I always + adv./prep.] if people filter somewhere, they move gradually to that place through a door, passage etc.: +**in/out etc.** *People began filtering into the auditorium.* **4** [I always + adv./prep.] if light or sound filters into a place, it can be seen or heard only slightly: +**through/into** *Sunshine filtered through a stained glass window.*

filter sth ↔ **out** *phr. v.* **1** to remove something by using a filter: *The system filters out chemicals that are harmful to fish.* **2** to remove people, things, information etc. that you do not need or want: *The software can filter out unwanted advertisements.* | *Tests are used to filter out unqualified applicants.*

ˈfilter tip *n.* [C] the special end of a cigarette that removes some of the harmful substances from the smoke, or a cigarette that has this special end —**filter-tipped** *adj.*

filth /fɪlθ/ *n.* [U] **1** an extremely dirty substance: *filth in the streets* **2** very offensive language, stories, or pictures about sex: *some of the filth they show on television*

filth·y¹ /ˈfɪlθi/ *adj.* *comparative* **filthier**, *superlative* **filthiest** **1** extremely dirty SYN **foul**: *filthy clothes* | *The bathroom was absolutely filthy.* ►see THESAURUS box at **dirty¹** **2** showing or describing sexual acts in a very offensive way SYN **obscene**: *filthy language* —**filthily** *adv.* —**filthiness** *n.* [U]

filthy² *adv.* **1 filthy rich** INFORMAL an expression meaning "extremely rich," used when you think someone has too much money **2 filthy dirty** SPOKEN extremely dirty

fil·trate /ˈfɪltreɪt/ *n.* [C] TECHNICAL a substance that has been removed from something else, by using a FILTER

fil·tra·tion /fɪlˈtreɪʃən/ *n.* [U] BIOLOGY the process of cleaning a liquid or gas by passing it through a FILTER: *a water filtration system*

fin /fɪn/ *n.* **1** [C] BIOLOGY one of the thin body parts that a fish uses to swim → see picture at FISH¹ **2** [C] part of an airplane that sticks up at the back and helps it to fly smoothly **3** [C] also **tailfin** a thin piece of metal that sticks out from something such as a car, as a decoration **4** [C usually plural] a FLIPPER

fi·na·gle /fəˈneɪgəl/ *v.* [T] INFORMAL to obtain something that is difficult to get by using unusual or unfair methods: *How he finagled four front row seats to the game, I'll never know.* —**finagling** *n.* [U]

fi·nal¹ /ˈfaɪnl/ Ac S3 W1 *adj.* **1** [only before noun] last in a series of actions, events, parts of a story etc.: *Mulligan will coach his final game on Saturday.* | *final exams* | *He scored twice in the final minutes of the game.* | *the final stage of the trial* **2** if a decision, offer, agreement etc. is final, it cannot be changed: *The **final decision** rests with the client.* | *When it comes to discipline, parents **have the final say**.* | *You can't go, **and that's final!*** **3** [only before noun] being the result at the end of a process: *the final outcome of the negotiations* | *What was the final score?* **4 final buzzer/whistle** the sound that tells you that a game is over [**Origin:** 1300–1400 French, Latin *finalis*, from *finis* **end**] → see also **in the final/last analysis** at ANALYSIS (4), **last/final straw** at STRAW¹ (3), **finishing/final touches** at TOUCH² (12)

final² Ac S3 *n.* [C] **1** an important test that you take at the end of a particular class in high school or college: *my biology final* | *finals week for the fall quarter* **2** [usually plural] the last and most important game, race, or set of games in a competition: *hockey's Stanley Cup final* | ***the NBA finals*** | *Johnson failed to **make the finals** in the 100-meter backstroke.* | *The team **reached the finals** for three years straight.*

fi·nal·e /fɪˈnæli, -ˈnɑ-/ *n.* [C] the last part of a piece of music, a performance etc.: *the finale of the show* | *The concert's **grand finale** was accompanied by fireworks.*

fi·nal·ist /ˈfaɪnl-ɪst/ *n.* [C] one of the people or teams that reaches the final part in a competition or set of sports games

fi·nal·i·ty /faɪˈnæləṭi, fə-/ Ac *n.* [U] FORMAL the quality that something has when you know it is finished or done and cannot be changed: *Small children do not understand the finality of death.*

fi·nal·ize /ˈfaɪnlˌaɪz/ Ac *v.* [T] to finish the last part of a plan, business deal etc.: *The deal is expected to be finalized this week.* —**finalization** /ˌfaɪnl-əˈzeɪʃən/ *n.* [U]

fi·nal·ly /ˈfaɪnl-i/ Ac S1 W1 *adv.* **1** after a long time SYN **eventually**: *The plane finally took off three hours later.* | *We finally found an apartment close to campus.* | *Finally, she came back.* ►see THESAURUS box at **lastly** **2** [sentence adverb] used to introduce the last of a series of things OPP **firstly**: *Finally, I'd like to thank you all for your hard work.* | ***And finally**, here's Jane with the weather.* ►see THESAURUS box at **lastly** **3** used when talking about the last in a series of actions: *She ran down the court, caught the pass, faked, and finally put the ball in the basket.* **4** FORMAL in a way that does not allow further change: *The case has not been finally settled.*

fi·nance¹ /fəˈnæns, ˈfaɪnæns/ Ac W2 *n.* **1** [U] ECONOMICS the management of money, especially money controlled by a government, company, or large organization: *corporate finance and budgeting* | *articles on **personal finance*** (=managing your own bank accounts etc.) **2 finances** [plural] ECONOMICS the money that a person, company, organization etc. has available, or the way they manage this money: *the school's finances* | *Mason is going to help me straighten out my finances.* **3** [U] ECONOMICS money provided by a bank, organization etc. to help buy or do something SYN **funding**: *campaign finance laws* [**Origin:** 1300–1400 French *finer* **to end, settle (a debt)**]

finance² Ac W2 *v.* [T] **1** ECONOMICS to provide money, especially a large amount of money, to pay for something SYN **fund**: *research financed by the Foundation* **2** [T] ECONOMICS to make an arrangement to pay for something over a long period of time: *We financed the new house through the credit union.*

fiˈnance ˌcharge *n.* [C] the money that a bank or finance company charges someone who has borrowed money from them to start a business, buy something etc. → see also INTEREST

fiˈnance ˌcompany *n.* [C] ECONOMICS a company that lends money, especially to businesses

fi·nan·cial /fəˈnænʃəl, faɪ-/ Ac S3 W1 *adj.* relating to money, or the management of money: *my financial advisor* | *the U.S. financial system* | *a company with major financial problems* | *estate planning and other financial services* | *Boston's **financial district*** (=the part of a city where many banks, financial institutions etc. are located) —**financially** *adv.*: *a financially suc-*

cessful lawyer | *She had saved enough to be* ***financially secure.***

fi,nancial 'aid *n.* [U] money that is given or lent to college or university students to pay for their education

fi,nancial insti'tution *n.* [C] a business or organization that lends and borrows money, for example a bank

fi,nancial inter'mediary *n.* [C] ECONOMICS an institution or person that helps money move from people who are saving or INVESTING it to people who want to borrow it

fi,nancial 'market *n.* [C usually plural] ECONOMICS a bank or other financial institution that makes business contracts with other similar organizations

fi,nancial 'year *n.* [C] ECONOMICS a FISCAL YEAR

fin·an·cier /ˌfaɪnæn'sɪr, fəˌnæn-, ˌfɪnən-/ Ac *n.* [C] someone who controls or lends large sums of money

fi·nanc·ing /'faɪnænsɪŋ/ Ac *n.* [U] money that you borrow from a bank or FINANCE COMPANY to start a business, buy something etc., and which you pay back over an agreed period of time: +**for** *the financing for the project*

finch /fɪntʃ/ *n.* [C] BIOLOGY a small wild bird with a short beak

find[1] /faɪnd/ S1 W1 *past tense and past participle* **found** /faʊnd/ *v.* [T]

1 DISCOVER STH to discover, see, or get something, either by searching for it or by chance: *I found a wallet in the parking lot.* | *Have you found your plane ticket yet?* | *He found a small apartment in Santa Monica.* | *I have a better chance of winning the lottery than of finding a man to marry.* | **find sb sth** *I found Trudy a nice blouse for her birthday.* | *Kathy was* ***nowhere to be found*** (=could not be found).

THESAURUS

discover to find something that was hidden or that people did not know about before: *A Mayan pyramid was discovered deep in the jungle.*
trace to find someone or something that has disappeared: *She had given up all hope of tracing her missing daughter.*
locate to find the exact position of something: *No one was able to locate the file or any of the documents in it.*
track sb/sth down to find someone or something after searching in different places: *The F.B.I. tracked him down in Europe.*
turn sth up to find something by searching for it thoroughly: *The investigation hasn't turned up any new evidence.*
unearth to find out information or the truth about something: *It was years before the full story was unearthed.*

2 BY STUDY to discover or learn something by study, tests, or thinking about a problem: *Scientists still haven't found a cure for AIDS.* | **be found to do/be sth** *Yellow fever was found to be carried by mosquitoes.* | +**that** *Researchers have found that 67% of all American mothers now work outside the home.*

3 BY EXPERIENCE to learn or know something by experience: +**(that)** *She's found that people aren't always eager for change.* | *One thing I found was that people were more friendly than I expected.* | **find sb/sth to be sth** *Ross found her to be very intelligent.*

4 DISCOVER STATE OF SB/STH to discover that someone or something is in a particular condition or doing a particular thing when you arrive or first see them: *When he finished, he was surprised to find it was two a.m.* | *She tried the door and found it unlocked.* | **find sb doing sth** *He found her crying in her room.* | **find (that)** *We looked in, and found that she was hard at work.*

5 THINK/FEEL to have a particular feeling, opinion, or idea about something: **find sth easy/difficult etc.** *Some children find it difficult to concentrate.* | *He found the class very challenging.* | *I found Stan's comments offensive.* | **find sb appealing/annoying etc.** *Lots of women I know find him attractive.*

6 MONEY/TIME/ENERGY to succeed in getting enough money, time, energy etc. to be able to do something: *I'd love to learn a foreign language, but I can't find the time right now.* | *Where will she find the money to send her son to college?*

7 DO STH WITHOUT MEANING TO to notice or realize something, or to be in a particular state or do a particular thing, when you did not expect or intend to do it: **find yourself in/at/back etc.** *After wandering around, we found ourselves back at the hotel.* | *Despite your efforts, you may find yourself in a very difficult situation.* | +**(that)** *He found that he was shivering.* | *I found I was really looking forward to going back to work.* | **find yourself/your mind etc. doing sth** *When he left, Karen found herself heaving a sigh of relief.* | *He found himself attracted to her.*

8 EXIST IN A PLACE **be found** [always + adv./prep.] if something is found somewhere, it lives or exists there: *This species of butterfly is only found in West Africa.*

9 **find your way** to reach a place by discovering the right way to get there: *I wasn't sure I'd be able to find my way back.*

10 **find its way** [always + adv./prep.] if something finds its way somewhere, it arrives or gets there after some time or in a way that is not clear: *Some water had found its way between the boards and warped the wood.* | *Virtually every major U.S. newspaper has found its way onto the Internet.*

11 **find yourself** OFTEN HUMOROUS to discover what you are really like and what you want to do: *She went to India to find herself.*

12 COURT OF LAW to officially decide that someone is guilty or not guilty of something: **find sb guilty/not guilty/innocent** *Galbraith was found not guilty and set free.* | +**of** *Morgan was found guilty of kidnapping.* | *The jury* ***found in favor of*** *the defendant.*

13 HAVE A FEELING to experience a good feeling because of something: **find comfort/pleasure/satisfaction etc. in sth** *He found a certain satisfaction in making his own bread.*

14 **find fault with sb/sth** to criticize someone or something, often unfairly and frequently: *The sergeant seemed to find fault with everything Maddox did.*

15 **find favor with sb** be liked or approved of by someone: *The film received mixed reviews from critics, but has found favor with audiences.*

16 **be found wanting** FORMAL to not be considered good enough: *The policy has been severely tested over the last 16 months and has been found wanting.*

17 **find its mark/target** if an ARROW, bullet etc. finds its target, it hits what it is supposed to hit

18 **find your voice** **a)** also **find your tongue** to become able to speak again after being too nervous, surprised etc. to say anything **b)** if a writer, speaker, politician etc. finds their voice, they decide what they want to say and how to say it effectively

19 **find your feet** to get used to a new situation, especially one that is difficult at first: *Robson is still finding his feet as a coach.*

20 **find it in your heart to do sth** LITERARY to feel able or willing to do sth: *Helen couldn't find it in her heart to tell him.*

[Origin: Old English *findan*]

find against sb *phr. v.* LAW to judge that someone is wrong or guilty: *The defendants realized that the jury might find against them.*

find for sb *phr. v.* LAW to judge that someone is right or not guilty: *The jury found for the plaintiffs on both counts.*

find out *phr. v.* **1 find sth ↔ out** to learn information, either by chance or after trying to discover it: *To find out more, visit our website.* | +**who/what/how etc.** *Have you found out how much it will cost?* | +**(that)** *When I got to the airport, I found out that the flight had been canceled.* | *She's just found out she has cancer.* | +**about** *You find out a lot about people on these trips.* | +**if/whether** *I had some tests done to find out if I have any food allergies.* | +**from** *I found out from Lisa that Robert had lied about where he'd been.* **2 find sb out** to discover that someone has been doing something dishonest or illegal SYN **catch**: *After years* *of stealing from the company, Andrews was finally found out.*

find² *n.* [C usually singular] **1** something very good or valuable that you discover by chance: *That little Greek restaurant was a real find.* **2** something that someone finds, especially by digging or searching under water: *important archeological finds*

find·er /ˈfaɪndɚ/ *n.* [C] **1** someone who finds something, especially something that was lost or stolen **2 finders keepers (losers weepers)** SPOKEN used to say that if someone finds something, they have the right to keep it, even if the person who lost it is unhappy about this **3 finder's fee** money that is paid to someone who finds something for someone else, or who introduces people to each other so that they can make a business deal

fin de siè·cle, fin-de-siècle /ˌfæn də siˈɛklə◂/ *adj.* [only before noun] typical of the end of the 19th century, especially typical of the art, literature, and attitudes of the time

F

find·ing /ˈfaɪndɪŋ/ W3 *n.* [C] **1** [usually plural] the information that someone has learned as a result of their studies, work etc.: *The findings show a high level of alcohol abuse among teenagers.* **2** LAW a decision made by a judge or JURY

fine¹ /faɪn/ S1 W2 *adj.*

SPOKEN PHRASES

1 ACCEPTABLE satisfactory, acceptable, or good enough SYN **all right**: *"The meeting's at eight." "Okay, fine."* | **be fine with/by sb** *Just a sandwich is fine with me.* | **sound/look/seem fine** *"Why don't we get takeout tonight?" "That sounds fine."* | *If she wants to do it herself,* ***that's fine.*** | *"How's your meal?"* ***"It's fine,*** *thanks."* | *"Did you want some more coffee?" "No,* ***I'm fine*** (=what I have is satisfactory; I do not want any more), *thank you."*
2 HEALTHY healthy and well: *"How are you?" "Fine, thanks."* | *So far, mother and baby are both* ***just fine.*** | *I felt fine during the game.* ▸see THESAURUS box at **healthy**
3 ANGRY used when you are angry because you really think that something is not good or satisfactory at all: *Fine, then, I'll do it myself.* | *That's a fine mess you've gotten yourself into.* | *Well, that's* ***just fine.*** *What are you going to do about it?*
4 ATTRACTIVE SLANG used when you think someone is attractive: *I met this fine Italian girl at school.*

5 VERY GOOD of a very high quality or standard, or very expensive: *Many people regard Beethoven's fifth symphony as his finest work.* | *Trinity Church is a* ***fine example*** *of Gothic architecture.* | *fine wines* | *It handles like a fine sports car.*
6 THIN/SMALL very thin or narrow, or in small pieces or drops: *Cut the onion into fine slices.* | *A fine coating of dust covered most of the furniture.* | *Her hair is very fine.* → see also FINE PRINT ▸see THESAURUS box at **hair**
7 SMALL DETAILS fine differences, changes, or details are very small and therefore difficult to understand or notice: *the fine tuning on the radio* | *the fine distinctions between levels of sleep depth* | *They were discussing some of the* ***finer points*** *of the law.*
8 WEATHER bright and not raining: *The weather was fine.* | **fine day/morning/afternoon etc.** *a fine day in mid-October* ▸see THESAURUS box at **sunshine**
9 DELICATE attractive, neat, and delicate: *a dress made of fine silk* | *the* ***fine features*** *of her face*
10 SMALL HOLES having very small holes or spaces: *a fine-tooth comb* | *a fine mesh screen*
11 a fine line if you say that there is a fine line between two different things, you mean that there is a point at which one can easily become the other: *There's a fine line between bravery and recklessness.*
12 walk a fine line to try to get or keep a balance between two things that are closely connected: *His novels have always* ***walked a fine line between*** *fiction and fact.*
13 WORDS [only before noun] fine words sound important or impressive, but are probably not true or honest
14 a fine man/woman/person a good person that you have a lot of respect for: *Your father is a fine man, a real gentleman.*
15 not to put too fine a point on it FORMAL used to show that you are going to criticize something in a plain and direct way: *The dishes we tried tasted, not to put too fine a point on it, awful.*
16 sb's/sth's finest hour an occasion when someone or something does something very well or successfully: *The festival's finest hour was the production of "Henry V."*
[**Origin:** 1200–1300 French *fin*, from Latin *finis* **end**]
→ see also **a fine figure of a man/woman** at FIGURE¹ (10)

fine² S1 *adv.* **1** SPOKEN in a way that is satisfactory SYN **all right**: *"How's it going?" "Fine, thanks."* | *Of course the TV worked fine when the repairman tried it.* | *The dress fit me fine.* **2 do fine** SPOKEN to be good enough, or to do something well enough: *Don't worry, you're doing just fine.* **3 cut it fine** INFORMAL to leave yourself just barely enough time to do something

fine³ S2 *v.* [T] to make someone pay money as a punishment: **fine sb for (doing) sth** *Hill was fined $115 for speeding.*

fine⁴ S3 W3 *n.* [C] money that you have to pay as a punishment: *a $75 fine* | *The newspaper was forced to* ***pay a fine*** *of $1,000.* | *If convicted, they will face prison and $25,000* ***in fines.*** | **heavy/hefty/huge fine** (=a large fine) *The penalty is a jail sentence and a hefty fine.* ▸see THESAURUS box at **punishment**

ˌfine ˈart *n.* **1** [U] paintings, drawings, music, SCULPTURE etc. that are of very good quality and have serious artistic value: *a dealer in fine art* **2 fine arts** [plural] activities such as painting, music, and SCULPTURE that are concerned with producing beautiful rather than useful things **3** [singular] something you are very good at, because you have practiced it a lot: **the fine art of doing sth** *the fine art of riding the waves* | **develop/hone/raise sth to a fine art** *Tropical resorts have honed honeymoon planning to a fine art.*

fine·ly /ˈfaɪnli/ *adv.* **1** into very thin or very small pieces: *Finely chop the peppers and onions.* **2** in a very careful, delicate or exact way: *a finely polished mirror* | **finely tuned/honed** (=prepared or developed in a very careful way) *a finely tuned athlete* **3** beautifully and delicately: *finely detailed furniture*

ˌfine ˈprint *n.* [U] part of a contract or other document that has important information and details, which you may not notice because it is written in very small letters: *Before you buy insurance, make sure you* ***read the fine print.***

fi·ne·ry /ˈfaɪnəri/ *n.* [U] FORMAL clothes and jewelry that are beautiful or very expensive, and are worn for a special occasion

fi·nesse¹ /fɪˈnɛs/ *n.* [U] if you do something with finesse, you do it with a lot of skill and style

finesse² *v.* [T] **1** to handle a situation well, but in a way that is slightly deceitful **2** to do something with a lot of style and skill

ˌfine-toothed ˈcomb also **ˌfine-tooth ˈcomb** *n.* [C] **go through/over sth with a fine-toothed comb** to examine something very carefully and thoroughly

ˌfine-ˈtune *v.* [T] to make very small changes to something such as a machine, system, or plan, so that it works as well as possible: *The program will be fine-tuned to suit each school.* —**fine tuning** *n.* [U]

fin·ger¹ /ˈfɪŋgɚ/ S2 W2 *n.* [C]
1 PART OF YOUR HAND one of the four long thin parts on your hand, not including your thumb: *a ring on her finger* | *We ate with our fingers.* | *The* ***tips of your fingers*** *are very sensitive.* | *She* ***ran*** *her* ***fingers*** *through her hair.* | *"Who hit you?" "He did," said Mike,* ***pointing his finger*** *at Ben.* → see also INDEX FINGER, LITTLE FINGER, MIDDLE FINGER, RING FINGER
2 cross your fingers a) to hope that something will happen the way you want: ***Keep your fingers crossed*** *that I get this job.* **b)** if someone, especially a child,

crosses their fingers, they secretly put one finger over another finger, because they are telling a lie: *"We won't," said Ann, crossing her fingers behind her back.*
3 not lift a finger to not make any effort to help someone with their work: *I do all the work around the house – Frank never lifts a finger.*
4 put your finger on sth to know or be able to explain exactly what is wrong, different, or unusual about a situation: *I can't put my finger on it, but there's something different about you.*
5 LONG THIN SHAPE anything that is long and thin, like the shape of a finger, especially a piece of land, an area of water, or a piece of food: *Fingers of flame spread in all directions.*
6 GLOVE the part of a GLOVE that covers your finger
7 DRINK an amount of an alcoholic drink that is as high in the glass as the width of someone's finger: *In the glass was a finger of pale gold wine.*
8 have/keep your finger on the pulse (of sth) to always know about the most recent changes or developments in a situation or organization: *Brokers have to keep their fingers on the pulse of the international markets.*
9 twist/wrap sb around your little finger to be able to persuade someone to do anything that you want: *Before long, Jennifer had Carlos wrapped around her little finger.*
10 have a finger in every pie to be involved in many activities and have influence over them, used especially when you think someone has too much influence
[**Origin:** Old English] → see also **burn your fingers** at BURN¹ (17), -FINGERED, **have a green thumb** at GREEN¹ (7), **lay a finger/hand on sb** at LAY¹ (5), **point the finger at sb** at POINT² (7), **slip through your fingers** at SLIP¹ (10), **snap your fingers** at SNAP¹ (6), **have sticky fingers** at STICKY (4), **work your fingers to the bone** at WORK¹ (25)

finger² *v.* [T] **1** to touch or handle something with your fingers: *She fingered the beautiful cloth with envy.* **2** SLANG if someone, especially a criminal, fingers another criminal, they tell the police what the other person has done SYN **inform**

'finger bowl *n.* [C] a small bowl in which you wash your fingers at the table during a formal meal

-fingered /fɪŋgəd/ [in adjectives] **1 long-fingered/delicate-fingered etc.** having long fingers, delicate fingers etc. → see also LIGHT-FINGERED **2 two-fingered/three-fingered etc.** using two, three etc. fingers to do something: *two-fingered typing*

fin·ger·ing /ˈfɪŋgərɪŋ/ *n.* [U] the positions in which a musician puts his or her fingers to play a piece of music, or the order in which he or she uses the fingers

fin·ger·nail /ˈfɪŋgəˌneɪl/ *n.* [C] the hard flat part that covers the top end of your finger: *Stop biting your fingernails.*

'finger paint *n.* [U] special paint that children paint pictures with, using their fingers —**finger-paint** *v.* [I] —**finger painting** *n.* [U]

fin·ger·print¹ /ˈfɪŋgəˌprɪnt/ *n.* **1** [C usually plural] the mark made by the pattern of lines at the end of a person's finger: *His fingerprints were all over the gun.* | *Detective Blake* ***took the suspects' fingerprints*** (=made a record of them). **2** [C] a mark or special feature that can be used to correctly name something or someone: *DNA testing provides a genetic fingerprint.* | *This policy has McBride's fingerprints all over it* (=it is obvious that he was involved in it).

fingerprint² *v.* [T] to press someone's finger on ink and then press it onto paper in order to make a picture of the pattern of the lines at the end of the finger —**fingerprinting** *n.* [U]

fin·ger·tip /ˈfɪŋgəˌtɪp/ *n.* [C] **1** the end of a finger: *She touched his cheek gently with her fingertips.* **2 at your/their fingertips** if you have something at your fingertips, it is ready and available to use very easily: *Keep your travel information at your fingertips.*

fin·ick·y /ˈfɪnɪki/ *adj.* **1** very concerned with small details, only liking particular things, and difficult to please SYN **fussy** SYN **picky**: *a finicky eater* **2** needing to be dealt with very carefully, while paying attention to small details: *a finicky classification system*

fin·ish¹ /ˈfɪnɪʃ/ S1 W1 *v.*
1 STOP DOING STH [I,T] to come to the end of doing or making something, so that it is complete: *Marv moved to New York when he finished college.* | *Have you finished your homework?* | *Just leave it on the table when you finish.* | **finish doing sth** *You can play after you finish eating.*
2 COMPLETE [I,T] also **finish off** to complete an event, performance, piece of work etc. by doing one final thing: **finish (sth) by doing sth** *In 1953, the engineers finished the job by building a flood control channel.* | **finish (sth) with sth** *We finished dinner with fresh fruit.* | *The concert finished with "You're a Grand Old Flag."*
3 EAT/DRINK [T] also **finish up/off** to eat or drink all of something, so there is none left: *Let me just finish my beer.*
4 RACE [I,T] to be in a particular position at the end of a race, competition etc. SYN **come in**: **finish first/second etc.** *He finished fourth in the race.*
5 SURFACE [T] to give the surface of something a particular appearance by painting, polishing, or covering it: *The furniture had been attractively finished in a walnut veneer.*
6 the finishing/final touch the final detail that makes something complete: *The hat* ***added the finishing touch to*** *her outfit.*
[**Origin:** 1300–1400 French *finir*, from Latin *finire*, from *finis* **end**]

finish off *phr. v.* **1 finish sth ↔ off** to use or eat all of something, so there is none left: *Who finished off the cake?* **2 finish sb/sth ↔ off** to kill or defeat a person or animal when they are weak or wounded **3 finish sth ↔ off** to end a performance, event etc. by doing one final thing: **+with** *We finished off the trip with a visit to the spectacular harbor.* **4 finish sb off** to take away all of someone's strength, energy etc.: *The last hill just about finished me off.*

finish sth ↔ **up** *phr. v.* **1** to eat or drink all the rest of something: *Why don't you finish up the pie?* **2** to end an event, situation etc. by doing one final thing: *He finished up his summer with a week on the Cape.*

finish with sth *phr. v.* **1** to not need something that you have been using anymore: *Can you hand me the scissors when you finish with them?* **2 be finished with sb** to have finished talking to someone or having a relationship with them, especially when you are angry with them: *Sit down. I'm not finished with you yet.* | *I'm finished with him – he's a jerk.*

finish² *n.* **1** [C] the end or last part of something: *the finish of the show* | **a first/second/third place finish** *a second place finish in the race* | *It was a* ***close finish*** (=an end of a race where two competitors are very close to each other), *but Jarrett won.* | *Their new album is good* ***from start to finish.*** | *Gray's* ***strong finish*** *in the Iowa elections* **2** [C,U] the appearance of the surface of something after it has been painted, polished etc.: *The paint dries to a glossy finish.* **3 a fight to the finish** a fight, game, competition etc. in which teams or competitors struggle until one is completely defeated **4** the FINISH LINE

fin·ished /ˈfɪnɪʃt/ *adj.* **1** [not before noun] not doing, dealing with, or using something any more SYN **done**: *I'm almost finished.* | **+with** *Are you finished with my tools yet?* ►see THESAURUS box at **done²** **2** [only before noun] fully made or completed OPP **unfinished**: *It took a long time to do, but the* ***finished product*** *was worth it.* **3** [not before noun] not able to do something successfully anymore: *If the bank refuses to give us the loan, we're finished!*

'finishing ˌschool *n.* [C] a private school where girls from rich families go to learn social skills

'finish line *n.* **the finish line** the line at which a race ends → see also STARTING LINE

fi·nite /ˈfaɪnaɪt/ AC *adj.* **1** having an end or a limit OPP **infinite**: *Oil is a finite resource.* **2** ENG. LANG. ARTS a

F

finite verb form shows a particular tense or time. "Am," "was," and "are" are examples of finite verb forms, but "being" and "been" are non-finite.

fink¹ /fɪŋk/ *n.* [C] OLD-FASHIONED, INFORMAL **1** someone who tells the police, a teacher, or a parent when someone else breaks a rule or a law **2** a person who you do not like or respect

fink² *v.* [I] OLD-FASHIONED, INFORMAL to tell the police, a teacher, or a parent that someone has broken a rule or a law: **+on** *I would never fink on a friend.*

Fin·land /ˈfɪnlənd/ a country in northeast Europe that is west of Russia and east of Sweden —**Finnish** *n., adj.*

fi·ord /fyɔrd/ *n.* [C] another spelling of FJORD

fir /fɚ/ *n.* [C] a tree with leaves shaped like needles that do not fall off in the winter

fire

Joe lit the fire.
Al set fire to the leaves.
The curtain caught fire.

fire¹ /faɪɚ/ S1 W1 *n.*
1 BURNING [C,U] the flames, light, and heat produced when something burns, especially in an uncontrolled way: *the incredible heat of the fire* | *a building destroyed by fire* | *Winds quickly spread the fire across the valley.* | *The house is* **on fire** (=burning)*!* | *One of the plane's engines had* **caught fire** (=started to burn). | *A spark from the fireplace* **set** *the curtains* **on fire** (=made them start to burn). | *Rioters* **set fire to** (=made it start to burn) *a whole row of stores.* | *Police believe the* **fire** *in the store was* **started** *deliberately.* | *A* **fire broke out** *in the apartment around 2 a.m.* | *It took firemen several hours to* **put out the fire** (=stop it burning). | *Lightning increases the possibility of* **forest fires**. | **brush fires** (=fires in grassy areas) *in the hills above Los Angeles*

THESAURUS
flames the bright parts of a fire that you see burning in the air
blaze the flames from a fire, or a large and dangerous fire: *Firemen fought to keep the blaze under control.*
inferno LITERARY a very large and very dangerous fire: *The fire on the train spread to 14 cars, creating an inferno that reached 2,700 degrees.*
bonfire a large outdoor fire: *a bonfire at the beach*
campfire a fire that you build outdoors when you are camping

2 FOR HEATING/COOKING ETC. [C] a pile of burning material, such as wood, coal etc., used to heat a room, cook food etc.: *He put another log on the fire.* | **build/light a fire** (=make a fire, or start burning one) *Matt built a fire to dry his wet clothes.* | *a* **roaring fire** *in the fireplace* | *We roasted marshmallows over the* **open fire**. | *She curled up in an armchair* **by the fire**.
3 SHOOTING [U] shots coming from a gun, especially from many guns at the same time: *Soldiers* **opened fire** (=started shooting) *as soon as the enemy came within range.* | *The truck she was in* **came under fire** (=was shot at). | *casualties due to accidents and* **friendly fire** (=shots fired by your own side) | **Hold** *your* **fire** (=stop shooting)*!*
4 **be/come under fire** to be criticized very strongly: *Campbell came under fire for his handling of the negotiations.*
5 EMOTION [U] a very strong emotion that makes you want to think about nothing else: **+of** *the fire of his enthusiasm*
6 **a fire in your belly** INFORMAL a strong desire to achieve something
7 INJURY a part of your body that is on fire feels very painful: *My feet were* **on fire** *after the trek up the mountain.*
8 **set the world on fire** to have a big effect or be very successful: *His last movie didn't exactly set the world on fire.*
9 **light a fire under sb** SPOKEN to do something that makes someone who is being lazy start doing their work
10 **fire and brimstone** a phrase describing Hell, used by some religious people
[**Origin:** Old English *fyr*] → see also CEASE-FIRE, **fight fire with fire** at FIGHT¹ (12), **do sth like a house on fire** at HOUSE¹ (13), **be in the line of fire** at LINE¹ (34), **play with fire** at PLAY¹ (23), **where there's smoke there's fire** at SMOKE¹ (6)

fire² S2 W2 *v.*
1 JOB [T] to force someone to leave their job SYN **dismiss**: *Are you going to fire him?* | **fire sb for sth** *The airline fired him for being drunk on duty.* | **fire sb from sth** *She was fired from her job when she got pregnant.* | *Brad* **got fired** *last week.*
2 SHOOT [I,T] to shoot bullets from a gun, or to shoot small bombs: *He aimed and fired.* | **+at/on/into** *Several missiles were fired at the army base.* | **fire a gun/rifle/weapon etc.** *the sound of a gun being fired* | **fire sth at sb** *The police officer* **fired** *two* **shots** *at the suspects before they surrendered.*
3 QUESTIONS [T] to ask someone a lot of questions quickly, often in order to criticize them: **fire sth at sb** *Dozens of reporters* **fired** *non-stop* **questions** *at him.*
4 EXCITE [T] also **fire up** to make someone feel very excited or interested in something SYN **inspire**: **be fired with sth** *kids* **fired with an enthusiasm** *for learning* | *stories that* **fire** *children's* **imaginations**
5 ENGINE [I] if a vehicle's engine fires, the gas is lit to make the engine work
6 CLAY [T] to bake clay pots etc. in very high heat in a KILN: *fired earthenware*
7 **not firing on all cylinders** HUMOROUS acting strangely, or not thinking sensibly
8 **be firing on all cylinders** INFORMAL to be thinking or doing something well

fire away *phr. v.* SPOKEN used to tell someone that you are ready to answer questions: *"I have a few questions." "Fire away."*

fire back sth *phr. v.* to quickly and angrily answer a question or remark: *"This is dirty politics," he fired back.*

fire sth ↔ **off** *phr. v.* **1** to shoot a weapon, often so that there are no bullets etc. left: *People were firing off pistols in New Year's Eve celebrations.* **2** to quickly send an angry letter to someone: *She fired off a heated memo to her boss.*

fire sth/sb ↔ **up** *phr. v.* INFORMAL **1** to start a machine or piece of equipment, especially one that burns gas: *Dad fired up the grill.* **2** to make someone very excited and eager: *a speech meant to fire up the players* | *Kelly came home* **all fired up**.

ˈfire aˌlarm *n.* [C] a piece of equipment that makes a loud noise to warn people of a fire in a building: *He heard the hotel **fire alarm go off**.*

ˈfire ant *n.* [C] a type of insect that lives in groups. They live in large piles of earth that they build, and can give a very painful bite.

fire·arm /ˈfaɪɚɑrm/ *n.* [C usually plural] FORMAL a gun: *the illegal possession of a firearm*

fire·ball /ˈfaɪɚbɔl/ *n.* [C] a large, hot fire, such as the very hot cloud of burning gases formed by an atomic explosion

fire·bomb¹ /ˈfaɪɚbɑm/ *n.* [C] a bomb that makes a fire start burning when it explodes

firebomb² *v.* [T] to attack a place with a firebomb —**firebombing** *n.* [C]

fire·brand /ˈfaɪɚbrænd/ *n.* [C] FORMAL **1** someone who tries to make people angry about a law, government etc. so that they will try to change it **2** LITERARY a large burning piece of wood

fire·break /ˈfaɪɚbreɪk/ *n.* [C] a narrow piece of land where all the plants and trees have been removed, made to prevent fires from spreading

fire·brick /ˈfaɪɚˌbrɪk/ *n.* [C] a brick that is not damaged by heat, used in CHIMNEYS

ˈfire briˌgade *n.* [C] a group of people who work together to stop fires, but are not paid to do this

fire·bug /ˈfaɪɚbʌɡ/ *n.* [C] INFORMAL someone who deliberately starts fires to destroy property SYN arsonist

ˈfire ˌchief *n.* [C] someone who is in charge of all the fire departments in a city or area

fire·crack·er /ˈfaɪɚˌkrækɚ/ *n.* [C] **1** a small FIREWORK that explodes loudly **2** INFORMAL someone who has a lot of energy and likes to make things happen: *Erica was the firecracker of the bunch.*

ˈfire deˌpartment *n.* [C] an organization that works to prevent fires and stop them from burning

ˈfire ˌdoor *n.* [C] a heavy door in a building that is kept closed to help to prevent a fire from spreading

ˈfire drill *n.* [C] an occasion when people practice how to leave a burning building safely

ˈfire ˌeater *n.* [C] an entertainer who puts burning sticks into his or her mouth —**fire eating** *n.* [U]

ˈfire ˌengine *n.* [C] a special large truck that carries people and the equipment they use to stop fires burning

ˈfire esˌcape *n.* [C] metal stairs on the outside of a building, that people can use to escape from the building if there is a fire

ˈfire ˌexit *n.* [C] a door that is used to let people out of a building such as a movie theater, hotel, restaurant, etc. when there is a fire

ˈfire exˌtinguisher *n.* [C] a metal container with water or chemicals in it, used for stopping small fires

fire·fight /ˈfaɪɚfaɪt/ *n.* [C] a short gun battle, usually involving soldiers or the police

fire·fight·er /ˈfaɪɚˌfaɪt̬ɚ/ *n.* [C] someone whose job is to stop fires from burning SYN fireman —**firefighting** *n.* [U]

fire·fly /ˈfaɪɚflaɪ/ *n. plural* **fireflies** [C] an insect with a tail that shines in the dark SYN lightning bug

fire·house /ˈfaɪɚhaʊs/ *n.* [C] a small FIRE STATION, especially in a small town

ˈfire ˌhydrant *n.* [C] a piece of equipment near a street and connected to a large water pipe under the ground, used to get water for stopping fires from burning

ˈfire ˌiron *n.* [C] a metal tool used for arranging a fire in a FIREPLACE

fire·light /ˈfaɪɚlaɪt/ *n.* [U] the light produced by a small fire

fire·man /ˈfaɪɚmən/ *n.* [C] **1** a man whose job is to stop fires from burning SYN firefighter **2** someone who takes care of the fire in a steam train engine or a FURNACE

fire·place /ˈfaɪɚpleɪs/ *n.* [C] a special place in the wall of a room, connected to a CHIMNEY, where you can make a fire

fire·plug /ˈfaɪɚplʌɡ/ *n.* [C] INFORMAL a FIRE HYDRANT

fire·pow·er /ˈfaɪɚˌpaʊɚ/ *n.* [U] TECHNICAL **1** the number of weapons that an army, military vehicle etc. has available: *The battle was won by classic military tactics and superior firepower.* **2** an amount of something important or necessary that someone can use to achieve something: *the firepower of their political opponents*

fire·proof /ˈfaɪɚpruf/ *adj.* a building, piece of cloth etc. that is fireproof cannot be badly damaged by fire —**fireproof** *v.* [T]

ˈfire sale *n.* [C] a sale of things that have been slightly damaged by a fire, or of goods that cannot be stored because of a fire

ˈfire screen *n.* [C] a large frame with woven wire in the middle that is put in front of a FIREPLACE to protect people

fire·side /ˈfaɪɚsaɪd/ *n.* [C usually singular] the area close to or around a small fire, especially in a home: *a cat dozing by the fireside*

ˌfireside ˈchat *n.* [C] an informal talk given by a U.S. president to the country on television or radio

ˈfire ˌstation *n.* [C] a building where the equipment used to stop fires from burning is kept, and where FIREFIGHTERS stay until they are needed

fire·storm /ˈfaɪɚstɔrm/ *n.* [C] **1** a very large fire that is kept burning by the high winds that it causes **2** a lot of protests, complaints, or arguments that happen suddenly because of something such as a plan or decision SYN storm: +**of** *The court's ruling provoked a firestorm of criticism.*

fire·trap /ˈfaɪɚtræp/ *n.* [C] a building that would be difficult to escape from if a fire started there

ˈfire truck *n.* [C] a FIRE ENGINE

fire·wall /ˈfaɪɚwɔl/ *n.* [C] **1** a wall that will not burn, used to keep a fire from spreading **2** COMPUTERS a system that protects a computer network from being used or looked at by people who do not have permission to do so, especially over the Internet **3** a system that is used by large financial or law companies to stop secret information from being passed from one department to another

fire·wa·ter /ˈfaɪɚˌwɔt̬ɚ/ *n.* [U] INFORMAL strong alcohol, such as WHISKEY

fire·wood /ˈfaɪɚwʊd/ *n.* [U] wood that has been cut or collected in order to be burned

fire·work /ˈfaɪɚwɚk/ *n.* [C usually plural] **1** a small container filled with powder that burns or explodes to produce colored lights and noise in the sky: *a Fourth of July **fireworks display*** **2** SPOKEN used to say that someone will be angry: ***There'll be fireworks** if your dad finds out.*

ˈfiring line *n.* **be on the firing line** to be in a position or situation in which you can be attacked or criticized: *As spokesman, Hall is constantly on the firing line.*

ˈfiring squad *n.* [C] a group of soldiers whose duty is to punish prisoners by shooting and killing them

firm¹ /fɚm/ W1 *n.* [C] ECONOMICS a business or company, especially a small one that does not make goods SYN company: **a law/engineering/design etc. firm** *an architectural firm in Chicago* ▸see THESAURUS box at company [**Origin:** 1700–1800 Italian *firma* **signature**, from Latin *firmare* **to show to be true**]

firm² *adj.*

1 HARD not completely hard, but not soft and not easy to bend: *What you need is a firmer mattress.* | *Cook macaroni until tender but still firm.* | *a firm red tomato* ▸see THESAURUS box at hard¹

2 IN CONTROL showing that you are in control of a situation and not likely to change your mind about something: *Cal replied with a polite but firm "no."* | *firm leadership* | **be firm with sb** *You must be firm but fair with your children.*

3 NO CHANGE not likely to change: *a firm commitment to*

peace | *A firm decision will not be made until later today.* | *a* ***firm believer*** *in equal rights* | *Both sides* ***held firm*** (=did not change) *about their demands.* | *Peters* ***took a firm stand*** (=would not change his opinion) *against the changes.* | *a* ***firm offer*** *for the ranch*
4 NOT LIKELY TO MOVE strongly fastened or placed in position, and not likely to move or break SYN **secure**: *Make sure the ladder is firm before you climb up.* | *The dam* ***held firm*** *during the earthquake.*
5 a firm grip/hold/grasp etc. a) if you have something in a firm grip etc., you are holding it tightly and strongly: *He* ***took a firm grip of*** *my arm and marched me toward the door.* | *a* ***firm handshake*** **b)** if you have a firm grasp etc. of something, you understand it well: +**on/of** *a firm grasp on the problems that are likely to arise*
6 INFORMATION [only before noun] true and based on facts: *There is firm evidence that the economy is improving.* | *The experiments showed that his ideas had a* ***firm basis*** *in fact.*
7 MONEY ECONOMICS not falling in value: *The dollar began Friday on a firm note.* —**firmly** *adv.*: *"No," Brenda said firmly.* | *His reputation was firmly established.* —**firmness** *n.* [U]

F

firm³ *v.* [T] to make something harder or more solid, especially by pressing down on it
firm sth ↔ **up** *phr. v.* **1** to make arrangements, ideas etc. more definite and exact: *Jane will call later to firm up the details.* **2** to make a part of your body have more muscle and less fat by exercising **3** if a company or organization firms up the price or value of something, it does something to keep it at a particular level: *a need to firm up interest rates*

fir·ma·ment /ˈfɚməmənt/ *n.* LITERARY **the firmament** the sky or heaven

firm·ware /ˈfɚmwɛr/ *n.* [U] COMPUTERS instructions to computers that are stored on CHIPS so that they can be done much faster, and cannot be changed or lost → see also HARDWARE

first¹ /fɚst/ S1 W1 *adj.*
1 happening or coming before all the other things or people in a series SYN **initial**: *her first appearance on stage* | *Was that* ***the first time*** *that you met Ted?* | *I only read the first chapter.* | **first two/three/few etc.** *a child's development during the first two years of life* | *his first wife* | **first Monday/Saturday etc.** *Admission is free on the first Monday of every month.*
2 most important SYN **main**: *Our first priority is to maintain the quality of the product.*
3 for the first time used to say that something has never happened or been done before: *For the first time in my life, I felt happy.* | *Jody wondered,* ***not for the first time***, *whether he'd been lying.*
4 first and last used to emphasize that something happened only once: *It was the first and last time I ever saw him.*
5 at first sight/glance a) the first time you see someone: *Do you believe in* ***love at first sight***? **b)** when you first start considering something, without noticing much detail: *At first sight, it may seem strange to treat these as a group.*

SPOKEN PHRASES

6 first thing as soon as you get up in the morning, or as soon as you start work: *Sharon wants that report first thing tomorrow.* | *I'll call her first thing in the morning.*
7 in the first place a) used to give the first in a list of reasons or points: *Well, in the first place, Quinn would never say that.* **b)** used to talk about the beginning of a situation, or the situation before something happened: *Why did you agree to go in the first place?*
8 not know the first thing about sth to not know anything about a subject, or not know how to do something: *My dad doesn't know the first thing about sports.*
9 first things first used to say that something should be done or dealt with first because it is the most important: *Okay, first things first: does everybody have a safety helmet?*

10 first choice the thing or person you like best: *Which college is your first choice?*
11 (at) first hand if you hear or experience something first hand, you hear or experience it yourself, rather than other people telling you about it: *Students in the program are exposed first hand to the workplace.* → see also FIRST-HAND
12 first prize/place the prize that is given to the best person or thing in a competition
13 make the first move to be the person who starts to do something when everyone else is too nervous or embarrassed to do it
14 first light the time when the sun is just beginning to appear, very early in the morning SYN **dawn** SYN **daybreak**: *They left camp* ***at first light.***
15 there's a first time for everything used to say that something has never happened before and that it is surprising or unlikely: *"Maybe Jane will help." "There's a first time for everything."*
16 JOB TITLE used in the title of someone's job or position to show that they have a high rank: *the first officer*
17 in the first instance FORMAL at the start of a situation or series of actions: *The Supreme Court will decide the case in the first instance.*
18 first among equals someone who is officially on the same level as other people, but who really has more power
[**Origin:** Old English *fyrst*]

first² S1 W1 *adv.* **1** before anything or anyone else: *It's mine – I saw it first.* | *Who's going first?* | *Johnson finished first in the 100-meter dash.* **2** at the beginning of a situation or activity SYN **initially**: *When we were first married, we lived in Toronto.* | *We first became friends when we were teenagers.* **3** done for the first time: *Simmons' book was first published last year.* **4** before doing anything else, or before anything else happens: *I'm coming, but I need to make a phone call first.* | ***First of all***, *we'd better make sure we have everything we need.* **5** [sentence adverb] used before saying the first of several things you want to say SYN **firstly**: *First, I'd like to thank everyone for coming.* **6** used to show what is most important to someone: *Work always* ***came first***, *and family came second.* | *a school district that* ***puts*** *quality education* ***first*** | *The festival is about music,* ***first and foremost*** (=used to emphasize the most important thing). **7 come in first** to win a race, competition etc.: *Johnson came in first in the 100 meters.* **8 first off** INFORMAL **a)** used before saying the first of several things you want to say, especially when you are annoyed: *First off, you have to get the repairman back and get it done right.* **b)** before doing anything else: *First off, I'd like to thank you all for coming.* **9 first come, first served** used to say that the first people who arrive somewhere, ask for something etc. will be dealt with before others: *Seating is available* ***on a first come, first served basis.***

WORD CHOICE **first, first of all, at first**
• **First** and **first of all** are used at the beginning of a sentence to talk about the first or most important thing in a series of things: *First, we have to notify the police.* | *First of all, you have to figure out how much money you have available.*
• Use **at first** to talk about what happened at the beginning of an event or situation: *At first I didn't recognize the voice on the phone, but then I realized it was my old buddy Tyler from college.*

first³ *n.* **1 at first** used to talk about the beginning of a situation, especially when it is different now SYN **in the beginning**: *At first, he said very little.* | *He watched from a distance at first.* → compare AT LAST **2** [C usually singular] something that has never been done or happened before: *This project is* ***a first*** *for the city.* | *"Dad washed the dishes." "****That's a first.****"* **3 from the (very) first** FORMAL from the beginning: *The relationship was doomed to failure from the first.*

first⁴ *pron.* **1 the first** the first person to do something, or the first thing to happen: *Others have now climbed Everest, but he was the first.* | *Can we meet on the first* (=the 1st day of the month)? | **be the first to do sth**

She's the first in her family to go to college. **2 the First** ABBREVIATION **I** used after the name of a king, queen, POPE etc. when other later ones have the same name: *Queen Elizabeth the First* (=written as "Queen Elizabeth I") **3 the first I (have) heard of sth** SPOKEN used when you have just found out about something that other people already know, and are slightly annoyed about it: *The first I heard of it was on the night of August 23.*

ˌfirst ˈaid *n.* [U] basic medical treatment that is given as soon as possible to someone who is injured or who suddenly becomes sick: *The victims were all **given first aid** at the scene of the accident.*

ˌfirst-ˈaid ˌkit *n.* [C] a special box containing BANDAGES and medicines to treat people who are injured or suddenly become sick

ˌFirst Aˈmendment, the HISTORY the first addition to the U.S. Constitution, which promises people the right to say, write, and read what they want, to follow the religion they choose, to gather together, and to complain to the government —**First Amendment** *adj.* [only before noun] *First Amendment rights*

ˌfirst ˈbase *n.* [C] **1 a)** the first of the four places in a game of baseball that a player must touch before gaining a point **b)** the position of a defending player near this place: *He **plays first base**.* **2 get to first base a)** to reach the first stage of success in an attempt to achieve something: *If you get an interview, you've gotten to first base.* **b)** OLD-FASHIONED, INFORMAL an expression meaning "to kiss or hold someone in a sexual way," used especially by young men

ˌFirst ˌBattle of Bull ˈRun, the *n.* [singular] HISTORY the first land battle of the American Civil War, fought on July 21, 1861, at Manassas, Virginia

first·born /ˈfɚstbɔrn/ *n.* [singular] your first child —**firstborn** *adj.*

first ˈclass *n.* **1** [U] the best and most expensive seats or rooms on an airplane, boat etc. → see also BUSINESS CLASS **2** [U] the class of mail used in the U.S. for ordinary business and personal letters → see also SECOND CLASS

ˈfirst-class *adj.* **1** of very good quality, and much better than other things of the same type: *a first-class wine* | *Her performance was first-class.* ►see THESAURUS box at **good**[1] **2** using the first class of mail: *a first-class package* **3** relating to the first class of seats and rooms in an airplane, boat etc.: *a first-class passenger* —**first class** *adv.*

ˌFirst ˌContinental ˈCongress, the *n.* [singular] HISTORY a meeting in Philadelphia in September 1774 of 55 representatives from 12 of the colonies (COLONY) in North America in which they agreed to stop buying British goods or selling goods to Britain to protest King George III's governing of the colonies. This meeting was an important step toward the Revolutionary War.

ˌfirst ˈcousin *n.* [C] a child of your AUNT or UNCLE SYN **cousin**

ˌfirst-deˈgree *adj.* [always before noun] **1 first-degree murder** murder of the most serious type, in which someone deliberately kills someone else → see also MANSLAUGHTER **2 first-degree burn** a burn that is not very serious

ˌfirst eˈdition *n.* [C] one of the first copies of a book, which is often valuable —**first-edition** *adj.*

ˌfirst-ˈever *adj.* [only before noun] happening for the first time: *It was the first-ever visit to China by an American president.*

ˌfirst ˈfamily, First Family *n.* [C usually singular] the family of the President of the U.S.

ˌfirst geneˈration *n.* [singular] **1** people who have moved to live in a new country, or the children of these people **2** the first type of a machine to be developed: **+of** *the first generation of digital TV sets* **3** the first people to do something: **+of** *the first generation of feminists* —**first-generation** *adj.*: *first-generation Americans*

ˈfirst-hand *adj.* [only before noun] **first-hand experience/knowledge/account etc.** experience, knowledge, an account etc. that has been learned or gained by doing something yourself: *his first-hand experience of war* → see also **(at) first hand** at FIRST[1] (11), SECONDHAND

ˌfirst ˈlady, First Lady W3 *n.* [C usually singular] the wife of the President of the U.S., or of the GOVERNOR of a U.S. state

ˌfirst ˌlaw of ˌthermodyˈnamics *n.* [singular] PHYSICS the scientific principle that states that the total amount of energy in a system does not change, although the form of the energy may change

ˌfirst lieuˈtenant *n.* [C] a middle rank in the U.S. Army, Marines, or Air Force, or someone who has this rank

first·ly /ˈfɚstli/ *adv.* [sentence adverb] used to say that the fact or reason that you are going to mention is the first one and will be followed by others SYN **first** OPP **finally**: *Firstly, I would like to thank everyone.*

ˌfirst ˈmate *n.* [C] the officer who has the rank just below CAPTAIN on a ship that is not a military ship

ˈfirst name S2 *n.* [C] **1** the name that comes before your family name: *What's your mom's first name?* **2 be on a first-name basis** to know someone well enough to call them by their first name → see also LAST NAME

ˌfirst ofˈfender *n.* [C] someone who is guilty of breaking the law for the first time

ˌfirst ˈofficer *n.* [C] a FIRST MATE

ˌfirst ˈperson *n.* TECHNICAL **1 the first person** ENG. LANG. ARTS a form of a verb or a pronoun that is used to show that you are the speaker. For example, "I," "me," "we," and "us" are pronouns in the first person, and "I am" is the first person singular of the verb "to be." **2 in the first person** ENG. LANG. ARTS a story in the first person is told as if the writer or speaker were involved in the story —**ˈfirst-person** *adj.* [only before noun] *a first-person narrative* → see also SECOND PERSON

ˌfirst ˌpostulate of ˌspecial relaˈtivity *n.* [singular] PHYSICS the scientific statement that all the laws of PHYSICS are the same in any system, and this does not depend on the system's position or speed

ˌfirst-ˈrate *adj.* of the very best quality SYN **excellent**: *a first-rate surgeon*

ˌfirst reˈsponder *n.* [C] someone who works for the police, fire department, or AMBULANCE service who is specially trained to be the first person to go to a very serious accident or to an extremely dangerous and unexpected situation that must be dealt with quickly

ˌfirst-ˈstring *adj.* [only before noun] a first-string player on a team plays when the game begins because they are one of the best players → see also SECOND-STRING

ˌfirst-time ˈbuyer *n.* [C] someone who is buying something such as a house or a car for the first time

ˌFirst ˈWorld *n.* **the First World** the rich industrial countries of the world —**first-world** *adj.* [always before noun] → see also THIRD WORLD

ˌFirst World ˈWar *n.* **the First World War** HISTORY WORLD WAR I

fis·cal /ˈfɪskəl/ W3 *adj.* FORMAL ECONOMICS relating to money, taxes, debts etc., especially those relating to the government: *a sound fiscal policy* [**Origin:** 1500–1600 Latin *fiscus* **basket, money bag**] —**fiscally** *adv.*

ˌfiscal ˈpolicy *n.* [C] ECONOMICS a government's plan for dealing with taxes, spending, and borrowing

ˌfiscal ˈyear *n.* [C] ECONOMICS a 12-month-long period of time over which a company calculates its profits and losses, or a government calculates its income and spending

F

fish

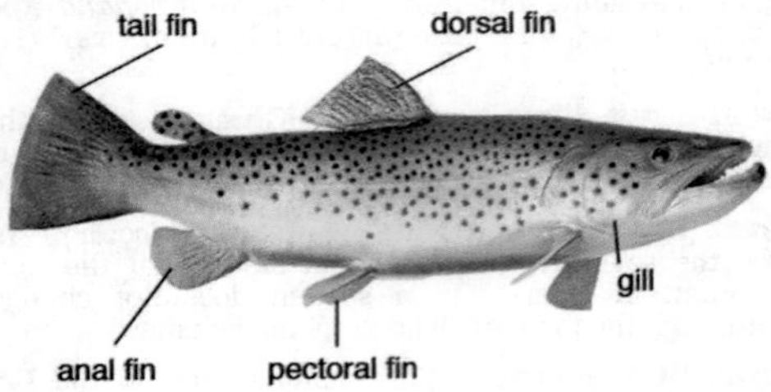

fish¹ /fɪʃ/ S1 W2 *n. plural* **fish** or **fishes** [C] **1** BIOLOGY an animal that lives in water, takes in oxygen through the GILLS on the side of its body, and uses its FINS and tail to swim: *Ronny **caught** three huge **fish** this afternoon.* | **a freshwater/saltwater/tropical fish** *a colorful tropical fish* | *A **school of fish** swam by.* **2** [U] the flesh of a fish used as food: *fried fish* | *I don't eat fish.* **3 feel/be like a fish out of water** to feel uncomfortable because you are in an unfamiliar place or situation: *I'd feel like a fish out of water if I had to live in the big city.* **4 there are more/other fish in the sea** also **there are plenty (more) fish in the sea** used to tell someone whose relationship has ended that there are other people they can have a relationship with **5 have other/bigger fish to fry** INFORMAL to have other things to do, especially more important things: *I can't deal with this now – I've got other fish to fry.* **6 a cold fish** an unfriendly person who seems to have no strong feelings **7 a big fish in a small pond** someone who is important or who has influence over a very small area **8 neither fish nor fowl** neither one thing nor another: *We were caught between two generations, neither fish nor fowl.* [**Origin:** Old English *fisc*; related to *Pisces*]

fish² S3 *v.* **1** [I] to try to catch fish: +**for** *We're fishing for trout.* **2** [I always + adv./prep.] to search through a bag, pocket, container etc. trying to find something: +**in** *She fished in her bag and produced a plastic card.* | +**for** *She fished around in her purse and pulled out a picture.* **3 be fishing for compliments** to try to make someone say something nice about you, usually by asking a question: *I'm not fishing for compliments. I just want an honest opinion.* **4 fish or cut bait** SPOKEN used to tell someone to do something they say they will, when they have been talking about doing it for too long **5** [T] FORMAL to try to catch fish in a particular area of water: *Other nations are forbidden to fish the waters within 200 miles of the coast.* **6 be fishing for information/news/gossip etc.** to try to find out secret information: *He was fishing for information about her previous boyfriends.*

fish out *phr. v.* **1 fish sb/sth ↔ out** to pull someone or something out of water: **fish sb/sth out of sth** *Police divers fished the body out of the East River a week later.* **2 fish sth ↔ out** to take something out of a bag, pocket, container etc. after searching inside for it: *Eric reached in the bag and fished out a piece of candy.*

ˌfish and ˈchips *n.* [U] a meal consisting of fish covered with a mixture of flour and milk and cooked in oil, served with thick FRENCH FRIES

fish·bowl /ˈfɪʃboʊl/ *n.* [C] **1** a glass bowl that you can keep fish in **2** a place or situation in which you cannot do anything in private: *In a small town like this, you're **in a fishbowl**.*

fish·cake /ˈfɪʃkeɪk/ *n.* [C] a small round flat food consisting of cooked fish mixed with cooked potato

fish·er·man /ˈfɪʃəmən/ *n. plural* **fishermen** /-mən/ [C] someone who catches fish as a sport or as a job

fish·er·y /ˈfɪʃəri/ *n. plural* **fisheries** [C] a part of the ocean where fish are caught as a business

fish·eye lens /ˌfɪʃaɪ ˈlɛnz/ *n.* [C] a type of curved LENS (=piece of glass on the front of a camera) that allows you to take photographs of a wide area

ˈfish ˌfarm *n.* [C] a place where fish are bred as a business

ˈfish fry *n.* [C] an event, usually held outdoors to raise money for an organization, at which fish is fried and eaten with other foods

fish·hook /ˈfɪʃhʊk/ *n.* [C] a small hook with a sharp point at one end, that is fastened to the end of a long string in order to catch fish

fish·ing /ˈfɪʃɪŋ/ *n.* [U] **1** the sport or business of catching fish: *Fishing is one of Mike's hobbies.* | *Terry's **going fishing** next weekend.* **2 be on a fishing expedition** INFORMAL to try to find out secret information

ˈfishing line *n.* [U] very long string made of strong material and used for catching fish

ˈfishing rod also **ˈfishing pole** *n.* [C] a long thin pole with a long string and a hook attached to it, used for catching fish

ˈfishing ˌtackle *n.* [U] equipment used for fishing, such as hooks and BAIT

ˈfish meal *n.* [U] dried fish that have been crushed into a powder, in order to be put on the land to help plants grow or used as food for farm animals

fish·mon·ger /ˈfɪʃˌmɑŋgə, -ˌmʌŋ-/ *n.* [C] OLD-FASHIONED someone who sells fish

fish·net /ˈfɪʃnɛt/ *n.* [U] a type of material with a pattern of small holes that look like a net: *fishnet stockings*

ˈfish stick *n.* [C] a long piece of fish that has been covered with small pieces of dried bread, usually sold frozen to be cooked at home

fish·tail /ˈfɪʃteɪl/ *v.* [I] if a vehicle or airplane fishtails, it slides from side to side, usually because the tires are sliding on water or ice

fish·y /ˈfɪʃi/ *adj.* **1** INFORMAL seeming bad or dishonest: *There's something very fishy about his business deals.* **2** tasting or smelling like fish

fis·sile /ˈfɪsəl/ *adj.* TECHNICAL **1** PHYSICS able to be split by atomic fission **2** tending to split along natural lines of weakness

fis·sion /ˈfɪʃən/ *n.* [U] TECHNICAL **1** PHYSICS the process of splitting the NUCLEUS of an atom to produce large amounts of energy SYN **nuclear fission** **2** BIOLOGY the process that happens when a living ORGANISM divides into two halves, and each half then develops into a new organism → see also FUSION

fis·sure /ˈfɪʃə/ *n.* [C] a deep crack, especially in rock or earth

fist /fɪst/ *n.* [C] a hand with the fingers curled in toward the PALM, especially in order to express anger or to hit someone: *She held the money tightly in her fist.* | *Mark **clenched** his **fists*** (=held his fists very tightly closed) *in rage.* | *He was **shaking** his **fist** at the taxi driver.* [**Origin:** Old English *fyst*] → see also HAM-FISTED, **make/spend/lose money hand over fist** at HAND¹ (26), TIGHT-FISTED

fist·fight /ˈfɪstfaɪt/ *n.* [C] a fight in which you use your BARE hands to hit someone

fist·ful /ˈfɪstfʊl/ *n.* [C] an amount that is as much as you can hold in your hand: +**of** *a fistful of cash*

fist·i·cuffs /ˈfɪstɪˌkʌfs/ *n.* [plural] OLD-FASHIONED a fist-fight

fit¹ /fɪt/ S1 W2 *v. past tense and past participle* **fit** or **fitted, fitting**

1 CLOTHES [I,T not in progressive] to be the right size and shape for someone or something: *The pants fit fine, but the jacket's too small.* | *My jeans don't fit me anymore.* | *I tried it on and it **fits like a glove*** (=fits perfectly).

2 BE RIGHT SIZE/SHAPE [I always + adv./prep., not in progressive,T] to be the right size and shape for a particular space, and not be too big or too small: *I couldn't find a key that fit the lock.* | *I wanted to put the desk next to the window, but it won't fit.* | +**in/into/under/through etc.** *A queen-sized bed will never fit in this room.*

3 FIND SPACE FOR [T always + adv./prep.] to find enough space for something in a room, vehicle, container etc.: **fit sth in/into/through etc.** *We couldn't fit the armchair through the door.* | *I don't think we'll be able to fit any more people into the car.*
4 MATCH/BE APPROPRIATE [I,T not in progressive] to have the qualities, experience etc. that are appropriate for a particular situation, job etc. If something fits another thing, it is similar to it or appropriate for it: *The punishment should fit the crime.* | **+with** *How does the job description fit with what you actually do?* | *Police said the car* ***fits the description of*** *the stolen vehicle.* | *We wanted an experienced writer, and Watts* ***fit the bill*** (=had the right qualities or experience). → see also FITTING
5 PUT IN PLACE [T always + adv./prep.] to put or join something in a particular place where it is meant to go: **fit sth in/over/on etc.** *You have to fit the plastic cover over the frame.* | *I tried to fit them together like the directions said, but I couldn't.*
6 EQUIPMENT/PART [T] to put a small piece of equipment into a place, or a new part onto a machine, so that it is ready to be used: **fit sth on/to etc. sth** *I need to fit a lock on the bathroom door.* | **be fitted with sth** *All the new cars are fitted with airbags.*
7 TRY CLOTHES/EQUIPMENT ON SB [T usually passive] to make a piece of clothing or equipment exactly the right size and specification for someone: **fit sb for sth** *I'm being fitted for a new suit tomorrow.* | **be fitted with sth** *She may need to be fitted with a hearing aid.* → see also FITTED, FITTING², **if the shoe fits (, wear it)** at SHOE¹ (4)

GRAMMAR
Although both **fit** and **fitted** can be used in the past tense, most people use **fit**: *Two years ago, these pants fit me perfectly.*

fit in *phr. v.* **1** to be accepted by other people in a group because you have the same attitudes and interests: *I never really fit in at school.* | **+with** *Lonnie doesn't seem to fit in with the other children.* **2 fit sb/sth ↔ in** to manage to do something or see someone, even though you have a lot of other things to do: *Dr. Lincoln can fit you in on Monday at 4:00.* **3** if something fits in with other things, it is similar to them or goes well with them: *I don't know quite how this new course will fit in.* | **+with** *A new building must fit in with its surroundings.*

fit into sth *phr. v.* **1** to be able to be a part of a group or system: *These items don't fit into any of our existing categories.* **2** to be accepted by the people in a group or organization: *I don't think she'll really fit into our family.*

fit sb/sth ↔ **out** *phr. v.* to provide a person or place with the equipment, furniture, or clothes that they need: *The office had been fitted out in style.* | **fit sb/sth out with sth** *New recruits are fitted out with uniforms and weapons.*

fit together *phr. v.* **1 fit sth together** if something fits together or you fit it together, different pieces can be joined to make something: *Look, the tubes fit together like this.* **2** if a story, set of facts, set of ideas etc. fit together, they make sense when considered together: *The pieces of evidence don't seem to fit together.*

fit² S3 *n.*
1 have/throw a fit SPOKEN to become very angry or shocked and shout a lot: *When I refused he threw a fit.*
2 EMOTION [C] a very strong emotion that you cannot control: **a fit of rage/anger/jealousy etc.** *She killed him in a fit of anger.*
3 SIZE [singular] the way in which something fits on your body or fits into a space: *the fit of the jacket* | **a good/tight/close etc. fit** *I thought they'd be too big, but these shelves are a perfect fit.*
4 LAUGH/COUGH [C] a period during which you laugh or cough a lot: **a coughing/sneezing fit** *He had a violent coughing fit.* | **+of** *a fit of the giggles* | *Her stories had us all* ***in fits*** (=laughing a lot).
5 STOP BEING CONSCIOUS [C] MEDICINE a short period of time when someone stops being conscious and cannot control their body because their brain is not working correctly: *He sometimes* ***has*** *epileptic* ***fits***.
6 in/by fits and starts repeatedly starting and stopping: *Electoral reform is moving ahead in fits and starts.*
7 APPROPRIATE [singular] FORMAL a relationship between two things, systems, organizations etc. in which they match each other or are appropriate for each other: **+between** *There must be a fit between the children's needs and the education they receive.*

fit³ *adj. comparative* **fitter**, *superlative* **fittest**
1 APPROPRIATE having the qualities that are appropriate for a particular job, occasion, purpose etc. OPP **unfit**: **+for** *The meat was not fit for human consumption.* | **fit to do sth** *That woman's not fit to be a mother!* | **be fit to eat/drink** *The local water is not fit to drink.* | *That dinner was* ***fit for a king*** (=of the highest quality).
2 see/think fit (to do sth) an expression meaning to decide that it is right or appropriate to do a particular thing, used especially when you do not agree with this decision: *They did not see fit to inform us of the change.*
3 STRONG healthy and strong, especially because you exercise regularly: *I stay fit by swimming every morning.* | *Rowers have to be extremely* ***physically fit***. | *She's 86, but* ***fit as a fiddle*** (=completely healthy).
4 fit to be tied SPOKEN very angry, anxious, or upset: *I was absolutely fit to be tied when I found out who got the promotion.*
5 be in a fit state/condition (to do sth) to be healthy enough, after being sick or drunk, to be able to do something: *You clearly aren't in a fit state to drive.*
6 fit to wake the dead OLD-FASHIONED a noise that is fit to wake the dead is extremely loud
[**Origin:** Old English *fitt* **disagreement, opposition, fighting**] → see also **survival of the fittest** at SURVIVAL (3)

fit·ful /ˈfɪtfəl/ *adj.* happening for short and irregular periods of time: *He finally fell into a fitful sleep.* —**fitfully** *adv.*

fit·ness /ˈfɪt˺nɪs/ *n.* [U] **1** the condition of being healthy and strong enough to do hard work or sports: *Join a health club to improve your fitness.* | *Running marathons requires a high level of* ***physical fitness***. **2** the quality of being appropriate or good enough for a particular situation or purpose: **+for** *They were still unsure of his fitness for the priesthood.* | **fitness to do sth** *Wyatt questioned Lindsey's fitness to serve as judge.* **3** BIOLOGY the ability of an ORGANISM to carry on living and to create new organisms

fit·ted /ˈfɪt̬ɪd/ *adj.* **1** fitted clothes are designed so that they fit closely to someone's body: *a fitted black jacket* **2 be fitted (out) with sth** to have or include something as a permanent part: *All new buildings are fitted with water meters.*

ˌfitted ˈsheet *n.* [C] a sheet that has ELASTIC at the corners to hold it on a MATTRESS on a bed

fit·ting¹ /ˈfɪt̬ɪŋ/ *adj.* FORMAL right or appropriate for a particular situation or occasion: *a fitting punishment* | *The victory was a* ***fitting end*** *to a near-perfect season.* | ***It's only fitting that*** *the convention center be named after the mayor.*

fitting² *n.* [C] **1** an occasion when you put on a piece of clothing that is being made for you to find out if it fits **2** [usually plural] a part of a piece of equipment that makes it possible for you to use it: *a new sink with chrome fittings*

ˈfitting room *n.* [C] a DRESSING ROOM

Fitz·ger·ald, El·la /fɪtsˈdʒɛrəld, ˈɛlə/ (1918–1996) a U.S. JAZZ singer famous for her beautiful voice and her skill in SCAT singing

F

Fitzgerald, F. Scott /ɛf skɑt/ (1896–1940) a U.S. writer of NOVELS

F. Scott Fitzgerald

five¹ /faɪv/ *number* **1** 5 **2** 5 o'clock: *Meet me **at five**.* [**Origin:** Old English *fif*] → see also HIGH-FIVE, NINE-TO-FIVE

five² *n.* [C] **1** a piece of paper money worth $5: *Do you have two fives for a ten?* **2 give sb five** INFORMAL to hit the inside of someone's hand with the inside of your hand to show that you are very pleased about something **3 take five** SPOKEN used to tell people to stop working and rest for a few minutes

ˌfive-and-ˈdime also **ˌfive-and-ˈten (cent store)** *n.* [C] OLD-FASHIONED a DIME STORE

five oˈclock ˈshadow *n.* [singular] the dark color on a man's face where the hair has grown during the day

ˈfive-spot *n.* [C] OLD-FASHIONED a piece of paper money worth $5

ˈfive-star *adj.* [only before noun] a five-star hotel or restaurant is very good

ˌfive star ˈgeneral *n.* [C] the highest rank in the Army

fix¹ /fɪks/ S1 W2 *v.* [T]

1 REPAIR to repair something that is broken or not working correctly: *He's outside fixing his bike.* | **get/have sth fixed** *We just had the roof fixed.* ►see THESAURUS box at **repair¹**

2 PREPARE to prepare a meal or drinks SYN **make**: *I have to fix dinner now.* | **fix sb sth** *Sit down. I'll fix you a drink.* ►see THESAURUS box at **cook¹**

3 fix a time/day/place etc. to decide on a particular time etc. when something will happen: *Have you fixed a date for the wedding yet?*

4 LIMIT to decide on a limit for something, especially prices, costs etc., so that they do not change SYN **set**: **fix sth at sth** *The interest rate has been fixed at 6.5%.*

5 HAIR/FACE to make your hair or MAKEUP look neat and attractive: *Let me fix my hair first and then we can go.* | *Terry was in the bathroom, **fixing her face*** (=putting makeup on it to make it look attractive).

6 ARRANGE to make arrangements for something SYN **arrange**: *If you want a chance to meet the Senator, I can fix it.* | **fix it for sb to do sth** *I've fixed for you to see him this afternoon at four.*

7 ATTACH to attach something firmly to something else, so that it stays there permanently: **fix sth to/on sth** *We fixed the shelves to the wall with steel bolts.*

8 INJURY INFORMAL to treat an injury on your body so that it is completely better: *The doctors don't know if they can fix my kneecap.*

9 CAT/DOG INFORMAL to do a medical operation on a cat or dog so that it cannot have babies

10 RESULT to make dishonest arrangements so that an election, game etc. has the result that you want: *The government clearly fixed the elections.*

11 PUNISH SPOKEN to harm or punish someone for something they have done: *I'll fix her! Just you wait!*

12 fix sth in your mind to do something to make sure you will remember something: *Mick looked again to fix the scene in his mind.*

13 fix sb with a stare/glare/look etc. to look directly into someone's eyes for a long time: *Rachel fixed him with an icy stare.*

14 PAINTINGS/PHOTOGRAPHS to use a chemical process on paintings, photographs etc. that makes the colors or images permanent

15 be fixing to do sth NONSTANDARD SPOKEN to prepare to do something

[**Origin:** 1400–1500 Latin *fixus*, past participle of *figere* **to fasten**]

fix on sth/sb *phr. v.* **1** to choose an appropriate thing or person, especially after thinking about it carefully: *We've finally fixed on a date for the family reunion.* **2 fix your attention/eyes/mind etc. on sb/sth** to think about or look at someone or something carefully: *All eyes were fixed on the new girl.*

fix up *phr. v.* **1 fix sth ↔ up** to make a place look attractive by doing small repairs, decorating it again etc.: *We fixed up the guest bedroom before my parents came to stay.* **2 fix sb ↔ up** INFORMAL to find a romantic partner for someone: *Your friend's kind of cute – could you fix us up?* | **fix sb up with sb** *Dean fixed him up with a girl from his class.* **3 fix sb ↔ up** to provide someone with something they want: **fix sb with sth** *Can you fix me up with a bed for the night?*

fix² *n.* **1** [C usually singular] an amount of something, such as an illegal drug, that you often use and badly want: *my morning coffee fix* | *drug addicts looking for a fix* **2** [C] something that solves a problem: *a technical fix* | *No one expects a **quick fix** to the problem of terrorism.* **3** a problem or situation that is difficult to solve: *We're going to **be in a** real **fix** if we miss the last bus.* **4 get a fix on sb/sth a)** to find out exactly where someone or something is: *Have you managed to get a fix on the plane's position?* **b)** to understand what someone or something is really like: *I sat there, trying to get a fix on the situation.* **5** [singular] something that has been dishonestly arranged: *People think the election was a fix.*

fix·ate /ˈfɪkseɪt/ *v.*

fixate on sb/sth *phr. v.* to always think or talk about one particular person or thing

fix·at·ed /ˈfɪkˌseɪt̬ɪd/ *adj.* **1** always thinking or talking about one particular thing: **+on** *She becomes fixated on losing weight.* **2** TECHNICAL having stopped developing emotionally or mentally

fix·a·tion /fɪkˈseɪʃən/ *n.* [C] **1** an extreme, unhealthy interest in or love for someone or something: **+on/about/with** *a fixation on money* **2** TECHNICAL a type of mental illness in which someone's mind or emotions stop developing, so that they are like a child

fix·a·tive /ˈfɪksət̬ɪv/ *n.* [C,U] **1** a substance used to glue things together or to hold things such as hair or false teeth in place **2** ENG. LANG. ARTS a chemical used on a painting or photograph so that the colors do not change

fixed /fɪkst/ *adj.* **1** not changing or not able to be changed: *The symbols must be used in a fixed order.* | **a fixed amount/rate** *Workers are paid a fixed rate per hour.* | **a fixed position/location** *The satellite maintains a fixed position above the Earth.* **2** firmly fastened to something and in a particular position: **be fixed to/in/on sth** *The ship's tables are fixed to the floor.* **3 fixed ideas/opinions etc.** ideas or opinions which you will not change and that are often unreasonable: *Lloyd **has very fixed ideas about** religion.* **4 a fixed expression/smile/frown etc.** a fixed expression, smile, frown etc. does not change and does not seem to express real emotions **5 of no fixed address/abode** without a permanent place to live **6 how are you fixed for sth?** SPOKEN used to ask someone how much of something they have: *Hey Mark, how are you fixed for cash?*

ˌfixed ˈassets *n.* [plural] ECONOMICS land, buildings, or equipment that a business owns and uses

ˌfixed ˈcapital *n.* [U] TECHNICAL buildings or machines that a business owns and that can be used for a long time to produce goods

ˌfixed ˈcharge *n.* [C] TECHNICAL a business cost that does not change and must be paid regularly

ˌfixed ˈcost *n.* [C usually plural] also **fixed expenses** [plural] TECHNICAL money, such as rent, that a business has to pay even when it is not producing anything

fix·ed·ly /ˈfɪksɪdli/ *adv.* without looking at or thinking about anything else: *She stared fixedly at the highway.*

fix·er /ˈfɪksɚ/ *n.* [C] someone who is good at arranging events, situations etc. for other people so that they have the results they want, especially by using dishonest or illegal methods

fix·ings /ˈfɪksɪŋz/ *n.* **the fixings** the vegetables, bread etc. that are eaten with meat at a large meal: *turkey with all the fixings*

fix·i·ty /ˈfɪksət̬i/ *n.* [U] FORMAL the state of not changing or not becoming weaker

fix·ture /ˈfɪkstʃɚ/ *n.* **1** [C usually plural] a piece of equipment that is attached inside a house or building, such as an electric light or a toilet, and is sold as part of the house **2 be a (permanent) fixture** to be always present and not likely to move or go away: *He is a permanent fixture of the Washington political and social scene.*

fizz¹ /fɪz/ *n.* [singular, U] the BUBBLES of gas in some kinds of drink, or the sound that they make —**fizzy** *adj.*

fizz² *v.* [I] if a liquid fizzes, it produces a lot of BUBBLES and makes a continuous sound: *The champagne fizzed in the glasses.*

fiz·zle /ˈfɪzəl/ also **fizzle out** *v.* [I] INFORMAL to gradually end, fail, or disappear in a weak or disappointing way, especially after a good start: *After a few months, the romance fizzled out.*

fjord /fyɔrd/ *n.* [C] EARTH SCIENCE a narrow area of ocean between high cliffs

FL a written abbreviation of FLORIDA

flab /flæb/ *n.* [U] INFORMAL soft, loose fat on a person's body

flab·ber·gast·ed /ˈflæbɚˌgæstɪd/ *adj.* INFORMAL extremely surprised or shocked: *I was absolutely flabbergasted by her attitude.*

flab·by /ˈflæbi/ *adj. comparative* **flabbier**, *superlative* **flabbiest** INFORMAL **1** having too much soft loose fat instead of strong muscles: *She's gotten flabby since she stopped swimming.* **2** a flabby argument, excuse etc. is weak and not effective —**flabbiness** *n.* [U]

flac·cid /ˈflæsɪd/ *adj.* TECHNICAL soft and weak instead of firm: *flaccid muscles* —**flaccidity** /flæˈsɪdət̬i/ *n.* [U]

flack /flæk/ *n.* [U] another spelling of FLAK

flag¹ /flæg/ [S2] [W3] *n.* [C] **1** a piece of cloth with a colored pattern or picture on it, that represents a particular country or organization: *the Spanish flag* | *Children **waved flags** as the president's car drove by.* | ***Flags were flying*** (=they were shown on poles) *at half-mast after the bombing of the embassy.* **2** a colored piece of cloth used as a signal: *The flag went down, and the race began.* **3 the flag** an expression meaning a country or organization and its beliefs, values, and people: *loyalty to the flag* **4 under the flag of sth a)** as a representative of a country or organization: *The troops operate under the flag of the United Nations.* **b)** as a citizen or part of a country: *Florida came under the U.S. flag in 1819.* **5 keep the flag flying** to achieve success for your country in a competition **6 show/wave the flag** to show that you are proud of your country or organization **7** a FLAGSTONE → see also RED FLAG, WHITE FLAG

flag² *v.* **flagged, flagging** **1** [I] to become tired, weak, or less interested in something: *By the end of the day her enthusiasm had begun to flag.* **2** [T] make a mark next to something in a piece of writing to show that it is important: *I've flagged the sections I have questions about.* **3** [T] to draw attention to something: *We must flag any problems that arise.*

flag sb/sth ↔ **down** *phr. v.* to make the driver of a vehicle stop by waving at them: *She tried to flag down a passing car.*

flag·el·lant /ˈflædʒələnt, fləˈdʒɛlənt/ *n.* [C] FORMAL someone who whips themselves as a religious punishment

flag·el·late /ˈflædʒəˌleɪt/ *v.* [T] FORMAL to whip yourself or someone else, especially as a religious punishment

fla·gel·lum /fləˈdʒɛləm/ *n. plural* **flagella** /-lə/ [C] BIOLOGY a thin hair-like structure that grows from the surface of some cells and from some small living things, such as BACTERIA. It is used in order to help the cell or living thing move around. → see picture at BACTERIUM

ˈflag ˌfootball *n.* [U] a game like football in which players tear off flags from around other players' waists instead of knocking them down → see also TOUCH FOOTBALL

flag·ging /ˈflægɪŋ/ *adj.* becoming tired, weaker, or less interested: *the nation's flagging economy*

flag·on /ˈflægən/ *n.* [C] a large container for liquids, used in the past

flag·pole /ˈflægpoʊl/ *n.* [C] a tall pole used for hanging flags

fla·grant /ˈfleɪgrənt/ *adj.* a flagrant action is shocking because it is done in a way that is easily noticed and shows no respect for laws, truth, someone's feelings etc.: *The arrests are a **flagrant violation** of human rights.* [**Origin:** 1400–1500 Latin *flagrare* **to burn**] —**flagrantly** *adv.*

flag·ship /ˈflægˌʃɪp/ *n.* [C] **1** the most important ship in a group of Navy ships, on which the ADMIRAL sails **2** the best and most important product, building etc. that a company owns or produces: *the flagship of the new line of cars*

flag·staff /ˈflægstæf/ *n.* [C] FORMAL a flagpole

flag·stone /ˈflægstoʊn/ *n.* [C] a smooth flat piece of stone used for floors, paths etc.

ˈflag-ˌwaving *n.* [U] the expression of strong feelings of support for your country, especially when these feelings seem too extreme

flail¹ /fleɪl/ *v.* **1** [I,T] if you flail your arms or legs, or if they flail, you wave them in a fast and uncontrolled way: *The little boy flailed his arms, knocking over the vase.* **2** [I] to do something in an uncontrolled way, especially because you do not know exactly how to do it or do not have a plan: **+around** *Lasch flailed around, trying to answer the question.* **3** [T] to beat someone or something violently, usually with a stick **4** [I,T] to beat grain with a flail

flail² *n.* [C] a tool consisting of a stick that swings from a long handle, used in the past to separate grain from wheat by beating it

flair /flɛr/ *n.* **1** [singular] a natural ability to do something very well: *Joe **has a flair for** math.* ►see THESAURUS box at **ability** **2** [U] a way of doing things that is interesting and shows imagination: *Bates is bringing her comedic flair to the show.* [**Origin:** 1800–1900 French **sense of smell**]

flak /flæk/ *n.* [U] **1** INFORMAL strong criticism: **get/take/catch flak** *He's taken a lot of flak for his decisions.* **2** bullets or SHELLS that are shot from guns on the ground at enemy airplanes [**Origin:** 1900–2000 German *FLiegerAbwehrKanone* **flyer defence guns**] → see also FLAK JACKET

flake¹ /fleɪk/ *v.* **1** [I] also **flake off** to break off or come off in small thin pieces: *Paint was flaking off the doors and window frames.* **2** [I,T] to break fish or another food into small thin pieces, or to break in this way: *Poach the fish until it flakes easily.* **3** [I] also **flake out** SPOKEN to do something strange or forgetful, or to not do what you said you would do: **flake (out) on sb** *Kathy said she'd help but she flaked out on us.* [**Origin:** 1300–1400 From a Scandinavian language; related to Norwegian *flak* **disk**]

flake² *n.* [C] **1** a very small flat thin piece that breaks off easily from something else: *flakes of chocolate on a cake* **2** SPOKEN someone who easily forgets things, does strange things, or does not do what they say they will do: *He's such a flake, but he's fun to work with.* → see also SNOWFLAKE

ˈflak ˌjacket *n.* [C] a special coat made of heavy material with metal inside it to protect soldiers and police officers from bullets

flak·y /ˈfleɪki/ *adj. comparative* **flakier**, *superlative* **flakiest** **1** tending to break into small thin pieces: *flaky pastries* **2** SPOKEN tending to easily forget things or do strange things: *Carrie's pretty flaky but everyone likes her.* —**flakiness** *n.* [U]

F

flam·bé /flɑm'beɪ/ also **flam·béed** /flɑm'beɪd/ *adj.* food that is flambéed has an alcoholic drink such as BRANDY poured over it and then is lit to produce flames

flam·boy·ant /flæm'bɔɪənt/ *adj.* **1** behaving or dressing in a confident or surprising way that makes people notice you: *a flamboyant Hollywood lawyer* **2** brightly colored, expensive, big etc., and therefore easily noticed: *a flamboyant red sequined dress* [**Origin:** 1800–1900 French, present participle of *flamboyer* **to flame**] —**flamboyantly** *adv.* —**flamboyance** *n.* [U]

flame[1] /fleɪm/ *n.* [C,U] **1** hot bright burning gas that you see when something is on fire: *a candle flame* | *Flames poured out of the windows.* | *The plane crashed and* ***burst into flames*** (=began burning suddenly and strongly). | *A large part of the building was* ***in flames*** (=burning strongly). | *The whole house* ***went up in*** *flames.* → see picture at CANDLE **2 a flame of passion/desire/vengeance etc.** LITERARY a strong feeling **3** [C] an angry or insulting email → see also **naked flame** at NAKED (4), **old flame** at OLD (7)

flame[2] *v.* **1** [I] LITERARY to become or be bright red or orange: *Erica's cheeks flamed with anger.* **2** [I] also **flame up** to suddenly burn more strongly or brightly: *A fire flamed in the fireplace.* **3** [T] to send someone an angry or insulting message by EMAIL or on the Internet, especially using only CAPITAL letters

fla·men·co /flə'mɛŋkoʊ/ *n.* [C,U] a fast and exciting Spanish dance, or the music that is played for this dance [**Origin:** 1800–1900 Spanish **person from Flanders**; in former times the people of Flanders wore bright clothes and were often thought to look like gypsy dancers]

flame·proof /'fleɪmpruf/ *adj.* **1** flameproof cooking dishes can be used in a hot oven or on a stove **2** flame resistant

'flame re,sistant *adj.* something that is flame resistant is specially made or treated with chemicals so that it does not burn easily

flame·throw·er /'fleɪm,θroʊɚ/ *n.* [C] a machine like a gun that shoots flames or burning liquid, used as a weapon or for burning away plants

flam·ing /'fleɪmɪŋ/ *adj.* [only before noun] **1** very bright red or orange: *flaming red hair* **2** burning strongly and brightly: *the flaming wreckage of the helicopter*

fla·min·go /flə'mɪŋgoʊ/ *n. plural* **flamingos** or **flamingoes** [C] BIOLOGY a tall tropical bird with very long thin legs, pink feathers, and a long neck [**Origin:** 1500–1600 Portuguese *flamengo*, from Provençal *flamenc* **flamingo, fire-bird**]

flam·ma·ble /'flæməbəl/ *adj.* something that is flammable burns very easily SYN **inflammable** OPP **nonflammable**: *Caution! Highly flammable chemicals.*

> **WORD CHOICE flammable, inflammable**
> Both of these words mean the same thing, but we usually use **flammable** to avoid confusion. The opposite of both of these words is **nonflammable**.

flan /flæn, flɑn/ *n.* [C] a sweet soft baked food made with eggs, milk, and sugar [**Origin:** 1800–1900 French, Latin *flado* **flat cake**]

Flan·ders /'flændɚz/ a flat area consisting of part of Belgium, the Netherlands, and northern France. It is known for the many battles that were fought there in World War I.

flange /flændʒ/ *n.* [C] the flat edge that stands out from the main surface of an object such as the wheel on a railroad car, to keep it in the right position

flank[1] /flæŋk/ *n.* [C] **1** BIOLOGY the side of an animal's or person's body, between the RIBS and the HIP **2** the side of an army in a battle or war: *We were attacked on our left flank.* **3** FORMAL the side of a hill, mountain, or very large building

flank[2] *v.* [T usually passive] to be on both sides of someone or something: **be flanked by sb/sth** *Lewis was flanked by police bodyguards.*

flan·nel /'flænl/ *n.* [U] soft light cotton or wool cloth that is used for making warm clothes: *a flannel shirt*

flan·nel·ette /,flænl'ɛt/ *n.* [U] soft cotton cloth used especially for baby clothes and sheets

flap[1] /flæp/ *v.* **flapped, flapping** **1** [I,T] if a bird flaps its wings or if the wings flap, it moves its wings up and down in order to fly: *The bird flapped its wings and took flight.* **2** [I] if a piece of cloth, paper etc. flaps, it moves around quickly and makes noise: *The ship's sails flapped in the wind.* **3** [I,T] if you flap your arms, hands, or legs, or if they flap, they move quickly up and down or backward and forward: *He flapped his arms against his coat.* **4 flap your lips/gums** SPOKEN to talk a lot without saying anything important

flap[2] *n.* **1** [C] a thin flat piece of cloth, paper, skin etc. that is attached by one edge to a surface, which you can lift up easily: *Make sure you zip up the tent flap.* **2** [C] INFORMAL a situation in which people are excited, confused, and upset: *Kelly resigned over a flap about vacation time.* **3** [singular] the noisy movement of something such as cloth in the air: *All we could hear was the flap of the sails.* **4** [C] a part of the wing of an airplane that can be raised or lowered to help the airplane go up or down

flap·jack /'flæpdʒæk/ *n.* [C] a PANCAKE

flap·per /'flæpɚ/ *n.* [C] a fashionable young woman in the late 1920s who wore short dresses, had short hair, and had ideas that were considered very modern

flare[1] /flɛr/ *v.* **1** [I] also **flare up** to suddenly begin to burn, or to burn more brightly for a short time: *A match flared in the darkness.* **2** [I] also **flare up** if strong feelings flare, people suddenly become angry, violent etc.: *Violence has flared up again in the Middle East.* **3** [I] also **flare up** if a disease or illness flares, it suddenly becomes worse: *My allergies tend to flare up in humid weather.* **4** [I,T] if a person or animal flares their NOSTRILS, or their NOSTRILS flare, they become wider, especially because they are feeling strong emotion: *The bull flared its nostrils and charged.* **5** [I always + adv./prep.] also **flare out** to become wider toward one end: *The dress flares out at the hip.*

flare[2] *n.* **1** [C] a piece of equipment that produces a bright flame, or the flame itself, used outdoors as a signal: *Flares marked the landing site.* **2** [C usually singular] a sudden bright flame **3 flares** [plural] pants that become wide near the bottom of the leg

'flare path *n.* [C] a path for an airplane to land on that is lit with special lights

'flare-up *n.* [C] **1** a situation in which a person or group suddenly becomes angry or violent, especially when they have not been violent for a period of time: *a flare-up between the two tribes* **2** a situation in which a disease or illness suddenly becomes bad again, after not causing any problems for a long time: *a flare-up of arthritis*

flash[1] /flæʃ/ *v.*
1 SHINE [I,T] to shine suddenly and brightly for a very short time, or to make something shine in this way: *The police car's lights were flashing.* | **flash sth into/at/toward sb** *Why did that guy flash his headlights at me?* | *A big red warning light* ***flashed on and off*** (=shone for a short time and then stopped shining).
► see THESAURUS box at **shine**[1]
2 PICTURES [I always + adv./prep.] to be shown quickly on television or in a movie etc.: **+across/onto/past etc.** *Images of the war flashed across the screen.*
3 MEMORIES/IMAGES [I always + adv./prep.] if thoughts, images, memories etc. flash through your mind, you suddenly think of them or remember them: **+across/through/into** *Warnings that her mother had given her flashed through her mind.*
4 flash a smile/glance/look/sign etc. at sb to smile or look at someone quickly, or to make a quick movement with a particular meaning: *Collins flashed a broad grin and waved to reporters.* | *Reed flashed a "V" for victory sign.*

5 SHOW STH QUICKLY [T] to show something to someone for only a short time: *The detective flashed his badge as he walked through the door.*
6 NEWS/INFORMATION [T always + adv./prep.] to send news or information somewhere quickly by radio, computer, or SATELLITE: **flash sth across/over etc. sth** *Brady's comments flashed across the newswires.*
7 MOVE QUICKLY [I always + adv./prep.] to move very quickly: **+by/past** *An ambulance flashed past.*
8 EYES [I] if your eyes flash, they seem to be very bright for a moment, especially because of a sudden emotion: **flash with anger/excitement/hatred etc.** *Anne's eyes flashed with excitement.*
9 SEX ORGANS [I,T] INFORMAL if a man flashes or flashes someone, he shows his sexual organs in public
10 **sb's life flashes before their eyes** if someone's life flashes before their eyes, they suddenly remember many events from their life, especially because they are in great danger and might die
11 TIME [I always + adv./prep.] if a period of time flashes by, past etc., it seems to end very quickly: **+by/past** *Our vacation seemed to just flash by.*
[**Origin:** 1200–1300 Originally (of liquid) **to strike a surface**; from the sound]

flash sth **around** *phr. v.* DISAPPROVING to use something in a way that will make people notice you and think you have a lot of money: *He's always flashing his money around.*

flash back *phr. v.* to think about or show something that happened in the past, especially in a movie, book etc.: **+to** *The movie flashes back to Billy's first meeting with Schultz.*

flash forward *phr. v.* if a movie, book etc. flashes forward, it shows what is happening in the future: **+to** *The next chapter flashes forward to their daughter's fifth birthday.*

flash² *n.*
1 LIGHT [C] a bright light that shines for a short time and then stops shining: *a flash of lightning*
2 CAMERA [C,U] a special bright light used with a camera when taking photographs indoors or when there is not enough light: *Did the flash go off?* ▶see THESAURUS box at camera
3 **in/like a flash** also **quick as a flash** very quickly: *He was gone in a flash.*
4 **a flash of brilliance/inspiration/anger etc.** if someone has a flash of brilliance, anger etc., they suddenly have a very good idea or suddenly have a particular feeling: *His work shows occasional flashes of brilliance.*
5 **a flash in the pan** a sudden success that ends quickly and is unlikely to happen again: *Beene's new novel proves that he isn't just a flash in the pan.*
6 BRIGHT COLOR/STH SHINY [C] if there is a flash of something brightly colored or shiny, it appears suddenly for a short time: **+of** *The bird vanished in a flash of blue.*
7 SIGNAL [C] the act of shining a light as a signal: *Two flashes mean danger.* → see also HOT FLASH

flash³ *adj.* [only before noun] happening very quickly or suddenly, and continuing for only a short time: *Flash fires swept through the area last night.* → see also FLASH FLOOD

flash·back /ˈflæʃbæk/ *n.* **1** [C,U] ENG. LANG. ARTS a scene in a movie, play, book etc. that shows something that happened before that point in the story: *The hero's childhood is shown as a series of flashbacks.* **2** [C] a sudden very clear memory of something that happened to you in the past: *Amado **has flashbacks** to his experiences in the war.* **3** [C] an occasion when someone has the same bad feeling that they had when they took an illegal drug in the past: *Many users of the drug experience flashbacks.* **4** [C] CHEMISTRY a burning gas or liquid that moves back into a tube or container

ˈflash bulb *n.* [C] a small BULB (=a bright light) used when you take photographs indoors or when there is not enough light

ˈflash burn *n.* [C] a burn that you get from being near a sudden, very hot flame, for example an explosion

flash·card /ˈflæʃkɑrd/ *n.* [C] a card with a word or picture on it, used in teaching

flash·er /ˈflæʃɚ/ *n.* [C] **1** INFORMAL a man who shows his sex organs to women in public **2** a light that flashes on and off on a vehicle as a warning signal

ˌflash ˈflood *n.* [C] a sudden flood that is caused by a lot of rain falling in a short period of time

ˌflash ˈfreeze *v.* [T] to freeze food quickly so that its quality is not damaged

flash·gun /ˈflæʃɡʌn/ *n.* [C] a piece of equipment that lights a special bright light when you press the button on a camera to take a photograph

flash·light /ˈflæʃlaɪt/ *n.* [C] a small electric light that you can carry in your hand

flash·point /ˈflæʃpɔɪnt/ *n.* [C] **1** a place where trouble or violence might easily develop suddenly and be hard to control: *The city was one of the flashpoints during the war.* **2** [usually singular] TECHNICAL the lowest temperature at which a liquid such as oil will produce enough gas to burn if a flame is put near it

flash·y /ˈflæʃi/ *adj.* *comparative* **flashier**, *superlative* **flashiest** INFORMAL too big, bright, or expensive in a way that other people disapprove of: *a flashy new sports car*

flask /flæsk/ *n.* [C] **1** a small flat bottle used to carry alcohol in your pocket **2** SCIENCE a glass bottle with a narrow top, used in a LABORATORY

flat¹ /flæt/ S2 W2 *adj.* *comparative* **flatter**, *superlative* **flattest**
1 SURFACE smooth and level, without raised or hollow areas, and not sloping or curving: *Stack the crepes on a flat plate.* | *You need to work on a clean flat surface.* | *That part of the state is **as flat as a pancake*** (=very flat).

THESAURUS

level a surface or area that is level does not slope in any direction, so that every part of it is at the same height: *Construction workers poured the concrete floor and made sure it was level.*
smooth having an even surface, without any holes or raised areas: *Sand the wood until it is smooth.*
even flat, level, and smooth: *The paint is best applied to an even surface.*
horizontal a horizontal line, position, or surface is straight, flat, and not sloping: *horizontal layers of rock*

2 TIRE/BALL a tire or ball that is flat has no air or not enough air inside it: *Can you change a **flat tire**?*
3 NOT DEEP not very deep, thick, or high, especially in comparison to its width or length: *a flat panel computer monitor* | *The cake came out of the oven flat, not fluffy.*
4 DRINK a drink that is flat does not taste fresh because it has no more BUBBLES of gas in it: *This soda is completely flat.*
5 BUSINESS/TRADE ECONOMICS if prices, economic conditions, trade etc. are flat, they have not increased or gotten better over a period of time: *Home prices have stayed flat for the past year.*
6 MUSICAL SOUND ENG. LANG. ARTS a musical note that is flat is played or sung slightly lower than it should be: *The horn was a little flat.*
7 **E flat/B flat/A flat etc.** ENG. LANG. ARTS a musical note that is one half STEP lower than the note E, B, A etc.
8 **a flat rate/price/fee etc.** a flat rate, price, amount of money etc. that you pay that does not change or have anything added to it: *We charge a flat fee of $2 a day for each DVD.*
9 NOT INTERESTING [not before noun] a performance, book etc. that is flat seems fairly boring: *The first episode of the show was flat and boring.*
10 VOICE not showing much emotion, or not changing much in sound as you speak: *"He's dead," she said in a flat voice.*
11 **a flat refusal/denial etc.** something you say that is definite and that you will definitely not change: *Our requests were met with a flat refusal.*

12 be flat on your back a) to be lying down so that all of your back is touching the floor or the ground: *Arthur was flat on his back under the car.* **b)** to be very sick so that you have to stay in bed for a period of time: *I've been flat on my back with the flu all week.*
13 SHOES flat shoes have very low heels
14 LIGHT having little variety of light and dark: *Flat lighting is typical of Avedon's portraits.*
[**Origin:** 1200–1300 Old Norse *flatr*] —**flatness** *n.* [U]

flat² S3 *adv.*
1 FLAT POSITION in a straight position or stretched against a flat surface: *Put your hands flat on the floor.* | *I have to* ***lie flat on my back*** *when I sleep.* | *My first time out on the ice I* ***fell flat on my face*** (=fell so I was lying on my chest).
2 in 10 seconds/two minutes etc. flat INFORMAL in exactly ten seconds, two minutes etc.: *I was out of the house in ten minutes flat.*
3 fall flat INFORMAL **a)** if a joke or story falls flat, people are not amused by it: *His little joke fell flat.* **b)** if something you have planned falls flat, it is unsuccessful or does not have the result you wanted: *A lot of people expected the team to* ***fall flat on its face*** (=be unsuccessful in an embarrassing way).
4 MUSIC ENG. LANG. ARTS if you sing or play music flat, you sing or play slightly lower than the correct note so that it sounds bad → see also SHARP
5 be flat broke INFORMAL to have no money at all
6 flat out INFORMAL **a)** as fast as possible: *They were working flat out to get the job done on time.* **b)** completely, or in a direct way: *He said flat out that he thought I was lying.*

flat³ *n.* [C] **1** a tire that does not have enough air inside it **2 a)** ENG. LANG. ARTS a musical note that is one HALF STEP lower than a particular note → see also NATURAL **b)** the sign (♭) in written music that shows that a note is one HALF STEP lower than a particular note → SHARP³ (1) **3 flats** [plural] **a)** a pair of women's shoes with very low heels **b)** an area of land that is at a low level, especially near water: *the mud flats near the beach* **4 the flat of sth** the flat part or flat side of something: *She hit me with the flat of her hand.* **5** BRITISH an APARTMENT

flat·boat /ˈflæt,boʊt/ *n.* [C] a boat with a flat bottom used for carrying heavy things on rivers and lakes

flat·car /ˈflæt˺kɑr/ *n.* [C] a railroad car without a roof or sides, used for carrying goods

ˌflat ˈcharacter *n.* [C] ENG. LANG. ARTS a character in a piece of literature with only one or two important features or CHARACTERISTICS, who does not change the way the story develops → see also ROUND CHARACTER

ˌflat-ˈchested *adj.* a woman who is flat-chested has small breasts

ˌflat ˈfeet *n.* [plural] a medical condition in which someone's feet rest flat on the ground because the middle of each foot is not as curved as it should be

flat·fish /ˈflæt,fɪʃ/ *n.* [C] BIOLOGY a type of ocean fish with a thin flat body, such as COD or SOLE

ˌflat-ˈfooted *adj.* **1 catch sb flat-footed** to surprise someone so that they cannot do something in the way they ought to: *The president's announcement seemed to catch Democrats flat-footed.* **2** having flat feet **3** INFORMAL dealing with situations in a way that is not sensitive to other people's thoughts or feelings

Flat·head /ˈflæthɛd/ a Native American tribe from the northwestern area of the U.S.

flat·i·ron /ˈflæt,aɪɚn/ *n.* [C] a type of IRON (=object that you use to make your clothes smooth) used in the past that was not heated by electricity

flat·ly /ˈflætli/ *adv.* **1 flatly refuse/deny/oppose etc.** to say something in a direct and definite way that is not likely to change: *He flatly rejected calls for his resignation.* **2** without showing any emotion: *He said flatly that there was no chance of a reconciliation.*

ˈflat screen *n.* [C] a very thin flat television or computer screen with a very sharp clear picture → see also PLASMA SCREEN

flat·ten /ˈflæt˺n/ *v.* **1** [I,T] also **flatten out** to make something flat or flatter, or to become flat or flatter: *Flatten the cardboard boxes and stack them in the corner.* | *The hills flatten out near the coast.* **2** [T] to destroy a building or town by knocking it down, bombing it etc.: *More than 10,000 houses were flattened by the quake.* ▸see THESAURUS box at **destroy** **3** [T] INFORMAL to defeat someone completely and easily in a game, argument etc.: *The Packers flattened the Saints 42–6.* **4 flatten yourself against sth** to press your body against something: *I flattened myself against the wall.* **5** [T] INFORMAL to hit someone very hard and knock them down: *Shut up or I'll flatten you!*

flat·tened /ˈflæt˺nd/ *adj.* [not before noun] unhappy and embarrassed because of what someone has said about you

flat·ter /ˈflæt̬ɚ/ *v.* **1** [T] to praise someone in order to please them or get something from them, even though you do not really mean it: *Don't try to flatter me!* ▸see THESAURUS box at **praise¹** **2** [T] to make someone look as attractive as they can: *That dress really flatters your figure.* **3 flatter yourself** to think that you have a good quality or ability, although you may not have it: *"I think you like me more than you'll admit." "Don't flatter yourself."* **4 you flatter me** SPOKEN FORMAL used to say that something nice someone has just said about you is not true: *"You know how popular you are with the ladies." "You flatter me."* **5** [T] to make something look or seem more important or better than it really is: *The novel doesn't flatter Midwestern attitudes and morals.* [**Origin:** 1100–1200 Old French *flater* **to move the tongue against, flatter**]

flat·tered /ˈflæt̬ɚd/ *adj.* [not before noun] pleased because someone has shown you that they like or admire you: *If a woman called me for a date I'd be flattered.*

flat·ter·er /ˈflæt̬ərɚ/ *n.* [C] someone who FLATTERS people

flat·ter·ing /ˈflæt̬ərɪŋ/ *adj.* clothes, pictures etc. that are flattering make someone look as attractive as they can or make something as good as possible, even if it is not really very good: *It's not a very flattering photograph, is it?*

flat·ter·y /ˈflæt̬əri/ *n.* [U] praise that you do not really mean

flat·top /ˈflæt˺tɑp/ *n.* [C] a type of hair style that is very short and looks flat on top

flat·u·lence /ˈflætʃələns/ *n.* [U] FORMAL the condition of having too much gas in your stomach —**flatulent** *adj.*

flat·ware /ˈflæt˺wɛr/ *n.* [U] a word meaning knives, forks, and spoons SYN **cutlery**

Flau·bert /floʊˈbɛr/, **Gus·tave** /ˈgʊstɑv/ (1821–1880) a French writer of NOVELS

flaunt /flɔnt, flɑnt/ *v.* [T] **1** to show your money, success, beauty etc. so that other people notice it: *She's always flaunting her jewelry.* **2 if you've got it, flaunt it** SPOKEN, HUMOROUS used to tell someone not to hide their beauty, wealth, or abilities

flau·tist /ˈflaʊt̬ɪst/ *n.* [C] a FLUTIST

fla·vor¹ /ˈfleɪvɚ/ S2 W3 *n.* **1** [C] the particular taste of a food or drink: *Chocolate is my favorite flavor.* | *The dessert has a tangy citrus flavor.* | **a strong/mild/full/distinctive etc. flavor** *Cranberry juice has a strong flavor.* **2** [U] the quality of tasting good: *The meat was tender and full of flavor.* | **add/give flavor (to sth)** *A pinch of herbs will add flavor to any dish.* **3** [C,U] a substance used to give something a particular taste, especially an artificial substance SYN **flavoring**: *Too many foods contain artificial flavors.* **4** [singular] a quality or feature that makes something have a particular style or character: *The music had a strong Spanish flavor.* **5** [U] an idea of what the typical qualities of something are: *The free trial lesson will give you the* *flavor of the course.* **6 flavor of the month** the idea, person, style etc. that is the most popular one for a short time: *Environmentalism seems to have become Hollywood's flavor of the month.*

flavor² *v.* [T] to give something a particular taste or more taste: **flavor sth with sth** *Before roasting, flavor the beef with garlic.*

fla·vored /ˈfleɪvɚd/ *adj.* having had a flavor added: *flavored coffees*

-flavored /fleɪvɚd/ [in adjectives] **chocolate-flavored/strawberry-flavored etc.** tasting like chocolate, strawberries etc.: *cheese-flavored crackers*

fla·vor·ful /ˈfleɪvɚfəl/ *adj.* having a strong pleasant taste: *a flavorful Mexican dish*

fla·vor·ing /ˈfleɪvərɪŋ/ *n.* [C,U] a substance used to give something a particular flavor SYN **flavor**: *This yogurt contains no artificial flavorings.*

fla·vour /ˈfleɪvɚ/ the British and Canadian spelling of FLAVOR, also used in the words "flavoured," "flavourful," and "flavouring"

flaw /flɔ/ *n.* [C] **1** a mistake, mark, or weakness that makes something not perfect SYN **defect**: *It was half price because of a slight flaw.* | +**in** *There was a flaw in the glass.* ▸see THESAURUS box at **defect¹**, **fault¹** **2** a mistake in an argument, plan, or set of ideas: +**in** *a flaw in Baker's argument* | *There are **fatal flaws*** (=very important mistakes that make something certain to fail) *in this program that make it unworkable.* | *The report illustrates a **fundamental flaw** in our product development process.* **3** a fault in someone's character: *a character flaw*

flawed /flɔd/ *adj.* spoiled by having mistakes, weaknesses, or damage: *a flawed but entertaining movie*

flaw·less /ˈflɔlɪs/ *adj.* perfect, with no mistakes, marks, or weaknesses SYN **perfect**: *He spoke flawless Spanish.* | *flawless skin* —**flawlessly** *adv.*

flax /flæks/ *n.* [U] **1** BIOLOGY a plant with blue flowers, used for making cloth and oil **2** the thread made from this plant, used for making LINEN

flax·en /ˈflæksən/ *adj.* LITERARY flaxen hair is very light in color

flay /fleɪ/ *v.* **flays, flayed, flaying** [T] **1** FORMAL to criticize someone very severely: *Congressmen have flayed the president for neglecting domestic issues.* **2** LITERARY to whip or beat someone very severely **3** FORMAL to remove the skin from an animal or person, especially one that is dead

flea /fli/ *n.* [C] a very small insect without wings that jumps and bites animals and people to eat their blood

flea·bag /ˈflibæg/ *n.* [C] INFORMAL a cheap dirty hotel

flea·bite /ˈflibaɪt/ *n.* [C] the bite of a flea

ˈflea ˌcollar *n.* [C] a special collar, worn by a dog or cat, that contains chemicals to keep fleas away from them

ˈflea ˌmarket *n.* [C] a market, usually in the street, where old or used goods are sold

flea·pit /ˈfliˌpɪt/ *n.* [C] OLD-FASHIONED, HUMOROUS a cheap dirty place, especially a movie theater

fleck /flɛk/ *n.* [C] a small mark or spot: +**of** *Kathy's eyes have flecks of gray in them.*

flecked /flɛkt/ *adj.* having small marks or spots: *Her hands were flecked with white paint.*

fledged /flɛdʒd/ → see FULL-FLEDGED

fledg·ling¹ /ˈflɛdʒlɪŋ/ *adj.* [only before noun] a fledgling state, organization etc. has only recently been formed and is still developing: *a fledgling democracy*

fledgling² *n.* [C] a young bird that is learning to fly

fledglings

flee /fli/ W3 *v. past tense and past participle* **fled** /flɛd/ [I,T] to leave somewhere very quickly, in order to escape from danger: *When they saw the police car, his attackers turned and fled.* | +**from/to/into** *Thousands of people have fled from the area.* | *The president was forced to **flee the country** after the revolution.* [**Origin:** Old English *flean*]

fleece¹ /flis/ *n.* [C] **1** the woolly coat of a sheep, especially the wool and skin of a sheep when it has been made into a piece of clothing: *fleece-lined slippers* **2** an artificial soft material used to make warm clothes

fleece² *v.* [T] INFORMAL to charge someone too much money for something, usually by tricking them: *If you paid $40 for that ring, you were fleeced.*

fleec·y /ˈflisi/ *adj.* soft and woolly, or looking soft and woolly: *a fleecy bathrobe*

fleet¹ /flit/ *n.* [C] **1** a group of ships, or all the ships in a navy: *the U.S. Seventh Fleet* **2** a group of vehicles that are controlled or owned by one company: *We have the largest fleet of trucks in the state.*

fleet² *adj.* LITERARY very fast or quick: *He was not young, but was still **fleet of foot**.*

ˈfleet ˌadmiral, **Fleet Admiral** *n.* [C] the highest rank in the Navy, or someone who has this rank

fleet·ing /ˈflitɪŋ/ *adj.* [usually before noun] continuing for only a short time: *I caught a fleeting glimpse of them as they drove past.* —**fleetingly** *adv.*

Flem·ing /ˈflɛmɪŋ/**, Alexander** (1881–1955) a British scientist who discovered PENICILLIN, a substance that is used as a medicine to destroy BACTERIA

Fleming, Peg·gy /ˈpɛgi/ (1948–) a U.S. woman who was world FIGURE SKATING CHAMPION in 1966–1968

Flem·ish /ˈflɛmɪʃ/ *n.* [U] a language like Dutch that is spoken in northern Belgium —**Flemish** *adj.*

flesh¹ /flɛʃ/ *n.* [U] **1** BIOLOGY the soft part of the body of a person or animal that is between the skin and the bones: *The lion tore the animal's flesh with its teeth.* **2** BIOLOGY the outer skin of the human body: *His flesh was red and covered in sores.* **3** BIOLOGY the soft part of a fruit or vegetable that can be eaten: *Cut the melon in half and scoop out the flesh.* **4 see/meet sb in the flesh** if you see or meet someone in the flesh, you see or meet someone who you previously had only seen in pictures, in movies etc.: *I never thought I'd actually meet him in the flesh.* **5 your own flesh and blood** someone who is part of your family: *He raised those kids like they were his own flesh and blood.* **6 make sb's flesh crawl/creep** to make someone feel very frightened, nervous, or uncomfortable: *His touch makes my flesh crawl.* **7 the flesh** LITERARY the physical human body, as opposed to the mind or spirit: **the temptations/pleasures of the flesh** (=things such as drinking, eating a lot, or having sex) **8 be (only) flesh and blood** to be human: *What more can I do? I'm only flesh and blood.* **9 put flesh on sth** to give more details about something to make it clear, more interesting etc.: *Medical experts put flesh on the statistical data for the audience.* **10 more than flesh and blood can stand/bear** used to describe something that you find too bad, difficult etc. to think about **11 go the way of all flesh** LITERARY to die → see also **get/take etc. a pound of flesh** at POUND¹ (5), **press the flesh** at PRESS¹ (13), **the spirit is willing but the flesh is weak** at SPIRIT¹ (14)

flesh² *v.*
flesh sth ↔ **out** *phr. v.* to add more details to some-

thing in order to improve it: *It's a good idea, but you need to flesh it out a bit more.*

ˈflesh-colored *adj.* having a slightly pink color like that of white people's skin: *flesh-colored pantyhose*

flesh·ly /ˈflɛʃli/ *adj.* [only before noun] LITERARY physical, especially sexual

flesh·pots /ˈflɛʃpɑts/ *n.* [plural] INFORMAL areas in a city or town where there are many places that people go to for pleasure, especially sexual pleasure: *the fleshpots of the south side of the city*

ˈflesh wound *n.* [C] a wound that cuts the skin but does not injure the organs and bones inside the body

flesh·y /ˈflɛʃi/ *adj.* **1** having a lot of flesh: *a round, fleshy face* **2** having a soft, thick inner part: *The plant has dark green fleshy leaves.*

flew /flu/ *v.* the past tense of FLY

flex /flɛks/ *v.* [T] **1** to bend or move part of your body so that your muscles become tight **2 flex your muscles** to show your ability to do something, especially your skill or power: *This new position should give you the chance to really flex your muscles.*

flex·i·bil·i·ty /ˌflɛksəˈbɪləṭi/ Ac *n.* [U] **1** the ability to change or be changed easily to suit a different situation: *There is some flexibility in the schedule.* **2** the ability to bend or be bent easily: *Stretching exercises will help your flexibility.*

flex·i·ble /ˈflɛksəbəl/ Ac *adj.* **1** a person, plan etc. that is flexible can change or be changed easily to suit any new situation OPP **inflexible**: *My work schedule is fairly flexible.* **2** something that is flexible can bend or be bent easily: *shoes with flexible rubber soles* —**flexibly** *adv.*

flexible

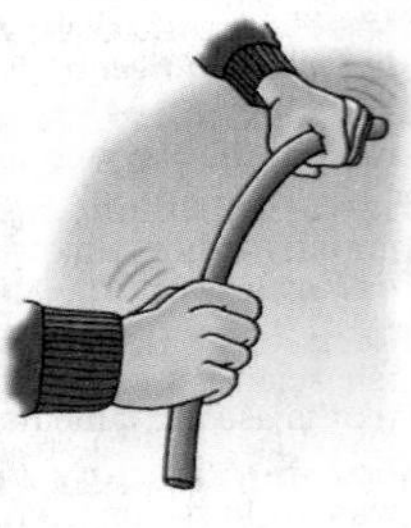

flex·time /ˈflɛks-taɪm/ *n.* [U] a system in which people work a particular number of hours each week or month, but can change the times at which they start and finish working each day

flick[1] /flɪk/ *v.* **1** [T] to make something move by hitting or pushing it suddenly or quickly, especially with your thumb and finger: **flick sth from/off/into etc. sth** *He flicked the cigarette out the window.* **2** [I always + adv./prep., T always + adv./prep.] to move with a sudden, quick movement, or to make something move in this way: **+from/up/down** *The cow's tail flicked from side to side.* | **flick sth up/into/down etc.** *Jackie flicked her long hair back.* **3** [T] to make a light, machine etc. stop or start working by moving a SWITCH or pressing a button: **flick sth on/off** *She flicked the light off.* **4** [T] if you flick something such as a whip or rope, you move it so that the end moves quickly away from you: *Ricky, stop flicking that towel at me!*
[**Origin:** 1400–1500 From the sound of a light blow]

flick

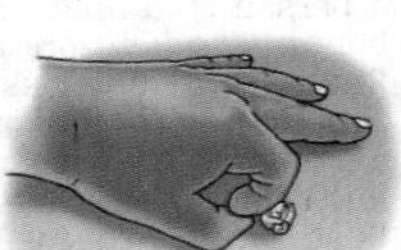

flick through sth *phr. v.* to look at a book, magazine, set of photographs etc. quickly

flick[2] *n.* **1** [C] INFORMAL a movie: *an action flick* ►see THESAURUS box at **movie** **2** [C] a short, light, sudden movement or hit with your hand, a whip etc.: **+of** *a flick of the wrist* **3 a flick of a switch** used to emphasize how easy it is to start a machine and use it: *Brokers can move huge amounts of stock* ***with the flick of a switch.***

flick·er[1] /ˈflɪkɚ/ *v.* [I] **1** to burn or shine with an unsteady light that goes on and off quickly: *The overhead lights suddenly flickered and went out.* ►see THESAURUS box at **shine**[1] **2** [always + adv./prep.] if an emotion or expression flickers on someone's face or through their mind, it exists or is shown for only a short time: **+across/through/on etc.** *A look of pleasure flickered across her face.* **3** to quickly make a sudden small movement or series of movements: *Penny's eyelids flickered for a moment, and then she slept.*

flicker[2] *n.* [C] **1** an unsteady light that goes on and off quickly: **+of** *the flicker of firelight* **2 a flicker of interest/remorse/guilt etc.** a feeling or expression that continues for a very short time: *As the verdict was read, Farley showed not even a flicker of emotion.* **3** a quick sudden movement or series of movements

fli·er /ˈflaɪɚ/ *n.* [C] **1** a piece of paper advertising something, which is given to people in the street, sent in the mail etc. ►see THESAURUS box at **advertisement** **2** INFORMAL a pilot or someone who travels on an airplane → see also FREQUENT FLIER

flies /flaɪz/ *n.* the plural of FLY

flight /flaɪt/ S3 W2 *n.*
1 TRAVEL [C] a trip in an airplane or space vehicle: *It's only an hour's flight to Detroit from here.* | *flight delays* | **an international/a domestic flight** *You should get to the airport two hours before international flights.* | **a nonstop/direct flight** (=a flight that does not stop or require you to change planes) ►see THESAURUS box at **trip**[1]
2 PLANE [C] an airplane making a particular trip: *Flight 202 from Denver is now arriving.* | *We need to hurry or we'll* ***miss*** *our* ***flight.*** | *Bernstein* ***caught*** *the first* ***flight*** *out of Washington.* | *We only had twenty minutes to make our* ***connecting flight.*** → see also CHARTER FLIGHT
3 FLYING [U] the act of flying through the air: *a photograph of eagles* ***in flight*** | *Thousands of birds* ***took flight*** (=began flying) *at our approach.*
4 STAIRS [C] a set of stairs between one floor and the next: *The bathroom is one flight up.* | *She fell down a* ***flight of stairs.***
5 ESCAPE [U] the act of avoiding a dangerous or difficult situation by leaving or escaping: **+from/across/through etc.** *the flight of refugees across the border* | *Residents* ***took flight*** (=ran away in order to escape) *to escape the fighting.*
6 flight of imagination/fancy/fantasy thoughts, ideas etc. that are full of imagination but that are not practical or sensible
7 BIRDS [C] LITERARY a group of birds all flying together
8 ABILITY TO FLY [U] the ability to fly through the air: *mankind's desire for flight*
9 put sb to flight OLD-FASHIONED to make someone run away in order to try and escape
[**Origin:** Old English *flyht*] → see also IN-FLIGHT, TOP-FLIGHT

ˈflight atˌtendant *n.* [C] someone who is responsible for the comfort and safety of the passengers on an airplane

ˈflight deck *n.* [C] **1** the room in an airplane where the pilot sits to control the airplane **2** the flat surface of a ship from which military airplanes can fly into the air

flight·less /ˈflaɪtlɪs/ *adj.* a flightless bird is unable to fly

ˈflight path *n.* [C] the course that an airplane or space vehicle travels along

ˈflight reˌcorder *n.* [C] a piece of equipment on an airplane that records what happens and how the airplane operates during a flight SYN **black box**

ˈflight ˌsimulator *n.* [C] a machine that copies the movements of an airplane, used to train pilots

flight·y /ˈflaɪṭi/ *adj.* someone who is flighty changes their ideas or activities a lot without finishing them or being serious about them —**flightiness** *n.* [U]

flim·flam /ˈflɪmflæm/ *n.* OLD-FASHIONED, INFORMAL **1** [U] stories, information etc. that do not seem serious or true **2** [C usually singular] a trick intended to cheat someone —**flimflam** *v.* [T]

flim·sy /ˈflɪmzi/ *adj. comparative* **flimsier**, *superlative* **flimsiest** DISAPPROVING **1** flimsy cloth or clothing is light and thin, and can tear easily: *a flimsy summer* dress **2** flimsy equipment, buildings etc. are not made very well and are easily broken: *a shantytown of flimsy wood and tin structures* ▸see THESAURUS box at **weak**[1] **3** a flimsy argument, excuse etc. is hard to believe: *The evidence against him is very flimsy.* —**flimsily** *adv.* —**flimsiness** *n.* [U]

flinch /flɪntʃ/ *v.* [I] **1** to make a sudden small backward movement when you are hurt or afraid of something: *Everyone flinched as shells exploded all around us.* **2** to avoid doing something because you dislike it or are afraid of it: **flinch from doing sth** *He never flinched from doing his duty.* **3** to feel upset, shocked, or frightened when you experience something, or to show with your facial expression that this is how you feel: *McCracken* ***didn't even flinch*** *when he heard the price.* [**Origin:** 1500–1600 Old French *flenchir* **to turn aside**]

fling[1] /flɪŋ/ *v. past tense and past participle* **flung** /flʌŋ/ [T]
1 THROW [always + adv./prep.] to throw something quickly with a lot of force SYN **throw**: **fling sth at/into/on etc. sb/sth** *She flung the letter into the river.* ▸see THESAURUS box at **throw**[1]
2 BODY [always + adv./prep.] to move yourself or part of your body suddenly and with a lot of force SYN **throw**: **fling sth around/toward/back etc. sb/sth** *When I came in, Katie flung her arms around me and kissed me.* | **fling yourself on/into/at etc. sb/sth** *Polly flung herself down on the bed beside him.*
3 PUSH [always + adv./prep.] to push someone roughly, especially so that they fall to the ground: *He grabbed her arm and flung her to the ground.*
4 **fling yourself into sth** to begin to do something using a lot of effort: *After the divorce he flung himself into his work.*
5 **fling a door/window etc. open** also **fling open a door/window etc.** to quickly and suddenly open a door, window etc.: *She flung open her cabin door and waved.*
6 **fling sb in prison/jail** to put someone in prison, often without having a good reason
fling sth ↔ **off** *phr. v.* to take off a piece of clothing in a hurried way: *He flung off his clothes and lay down.*
fling sth ↔ **on** *phr. v.* to put on a piece of clothing in a hurried way

fling[2] *n.* [C usually singular] **1** a short and not very serious sexual relationship: *We* ***had*** *a* ***brief fling*** *twenty years ago.* **2** a short period of time during which you enjoy yourself or are interested in something: *Do you regret your fling with alcohol and drugs?*

flint /flɪnt/ *n.* **1** [C,U] EARTH SCIENCE a type of smooth hard black or gray stone, or a piece of this stone **2** [C] a piece of this stone or a small piece of metal that makes a small flame when you strike it with steel

flint·lock /ˈflɪntlɑk/ *n.* [C] a gun used in past times

flint·y /ˈflɪnti/ *adj.* a flinty expression or person does not show emotions

flip[1] /flɪp/ S2 *v.* **flipped, flipping** **1** [I,T] to turn something over or put into a different position with a quick, sudden movement, or to turn over in this way: **+over** *The helicopter flipped over and landed in a field upside down.* | **flip sth back/across/over etc.** *She flipped her hair across one shoulder.* | *Flip the tortilla over and cook for 1 to 2 minutes.* **2** [T] to throw something flat such as a coin up so that it turns over in the air SYN **toss**: *In the end we* ***flipped a coin*** (=tossed a coin in the air to help decide something, according to which side lands upward). **3 flip burgers** INFORMAL to work in a FAST FOOD restaurant, cooking food such as HAMBURGERS: *He used to flip burgers at one of the local fast food restaurants.* **4** [I] also **flip your lid** INFORMAL to suddenly become very angry or upset, or start behaving in a crazy way SYN **flip out**: *When Dad finds out, he'll flip.* **5** [T] to quickly start or stop electrical equipment by moving a SWITCH or pressing a button: **flip sth on/off** *I flipped the answering machine off.*
flip for *phr. v.* INFORMAL **1 flip for sb** to suddenly begin to like someone very much: *Ben has really flipped for Laura, hasn't he?* **2 flip sb for sth, flip for sth** to flip a coin in the air to decide who will get something: *We couldn't decide who would get the tickets, so we flipped for them.*
flip out *phr. v.* INFORMAL to suddenly become very angry or upset, or start behaving in a crazy way: *The guy just flipped out and started shooting.*
flip over sth *phr. v.* INFORMAL to feel very excited and like something very much
flip through sth *phr. v.* to look at a book, magazine etc. quickly

flip[2] *n.* [C] **1** a movement in which you jump up and turn over in the air, so that your feet go over your head: *a backward flip* **2** a quick, light hit with your thumb or finger, especially one that makes a flat object turn over in the air: *It'll be decided by a flip of a coin.*

flip[3] *adj.* INFORMAL FLIPPANT

ˈflip chart *n.* [C] large pieces of paper that are connected at the top so that the pages can be turned over to present information to groups of people

ˈflip-flop[1] *n.* **1** [C] INFORMAL an occasion when someone changes their opinion or decision about something: **+on** *an embarrassing flip-flop on the government's domestic policy* **2** [C usually plural] a summer shoe, usually made of rubber, with only a V-shaped band across the front to hold your feet SYN **thong** **3** a movement in GYMNASTICS in which you flip over backward with your hands touching the floor

flip-flop[2] *v.* [I] INFORMAL to change your opinion or decision about something

flip·pant /ˈflɪpənt/ *adj.* not serious about something that other people think you should be serious about, so that they think you do not care SYN **flip**: *a flippant remark* —**flippantly** *adv.* —**flippancy** *n.* [U]

flip·per /ˈflɪpɚ/ *n.* [C] **1** BIOLOGY a flat part on the body of some large sea animals, used for pushing themselves through water **2** a large flat rubber shoe that you use to help you swim faster

ˈflip side *n.* [singular] **1** used when you describe the good or bad parts or effects of something, after you have just described the opposiste parts or effects: ***On the flip side****, the medicine may cause nausea.* **2** the side of a record that has a song on it that is less popular than the song on the other side

flirt[1] /flɚt/ *v.* [I] to behave toward and talk to someone as though you are sexually attracted to them, but not in a very serious way: *We flirted a little but that's all.* | **+with** *The waitress was flirting with a customer.*
flirt with sth *phr. v.* **1** to consider doing something, but not be very serious about it: *He had flirted with the idea of quitting his job.* **2** to be involved in something but not in a serious way or not for a long time: *Some of the athletes had flirted with drugs.* **3 flirt with danger/disaster etc.** to take an unnecessary risk and not be worried about it

flirt[2] *n.* [C] someone who often behaves toward and talks to people as though she or he is sexually attracted to them, but not in a very serious way

flir·ta·tion /flɚˈteɪʃən/ *n.* **1** [U] behavior that shows a sexual attraction to someone, though not in a serious way **2** [C] a short period of time during which you are interested in something or in which you try something: **+with** *the magazine's flirtation with taboo topics* **3** [C] a short sexual relationship which is not serious

flir·ta·tious /flɚˈteɪʃəs/ *adj.* behaving in a way that deliberately tries to attract sexual attention, but not in a serious way: *a flirtatious smile* —**flirtatiously** *adv.* —**flirtatiousness** *n.* [U]

flit /flɪt/ *v.* **flitted, flitting** [I always + adv./prep.] to move lightly or quickly from one place to another: *Birds were flitting from branch to branch.* [**Origin:** 1100–1200 Old Norse *flytja* **to carry around**]

float

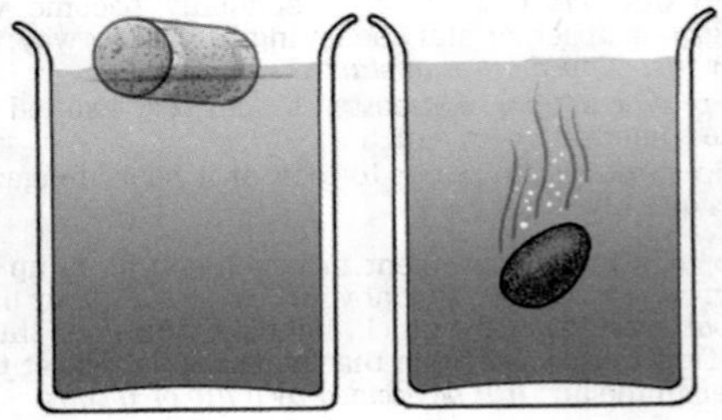

float sink

float¹ /floʊt/ S3 W3 *v.*
1 ON WATER [I] **a)** to stay or move on the surface of a liquid without sinking: *I wasn't sure if the raft would float.* | **+on/in** *Tim was floating on his back in the pool.* | **+along/down/past etc.** *A dead branch floated past the dock.* **b)** [T] to put something on the surface of a liquid so that it does not sink: *Children were floating small boats made of banana leaves.*
2 IN THE AIR [I always + adv./prep.] if something floats, especially something very light or filled with air, it moves slowly in the air or stays up in the air: **+up/down/through etc.** *He watched sadly as his balloon floated away.* | **float in the sky/air** *I looked up at the clouds floating in the sky.*
3 SOUNDS/SMELLS [I always + adv./prep.] if sounds, smells etc. float somewhere, people in another place can hear or smell them: **+up/down/toward/into etc.** *His voice floated up to her.*
4 MOVE GRACEFULLY [I always + adv./prep.] to move gracefully and lightly: *Laura floated down the stairs toward him.*
5 SUGGEST [T] to suggest an idea or plan, especially in order to find out what people think about it: *We first floated the idea back in 1998.*
6 COMPANY [T] ECONOMICS to sell STOCK in a company or business to the public for the first time
7 MONEY [I,T] ECONOMICS if a country floats its money or its money floats, the value of the money is allowed to change freely in relation to money from other countries: *The government decided to allow the peso to float freely.*
8 NO DEFINITE PURPOSE [I always + adv./prep.] to keep changing what you are doing without having any particular ideas or plans: *Speck was a drifter who had floated in and out of trouble for most of his life.*
9 float sb a loan INFORMAL to allow someone to borrow money from you
10 float a check to write a check that you do not have enough money in the bank to pay
[**Origin:** Old English *flotian*] —**floater** *n.* [C] → see also **whatever floats your boat** at WHATEVER¹ (8)
float around *phr. v.* **float around sth** to be present in a place: *There are a lot of rumors floating around.*

float² *n.* [C] **1** a large vehicle that is decorated to be part of a PARADE: *The children were decorating a float for the parade.* **2** a SOFT DRINK that has ICE CREAM floating in it: *a root-beer float* **3** a small amount of money that a bank, store etc. keeps so that they have enough money to pay for things, give change to people etc. **4** a small light object that floats on the surface of the water, used by people trying to catch fish to show where their line is **5** a light object that floats on the water or other liquid in a container

float·ing /ˈfloʊtɪŋ/ *adj.* **1** changing according to what the situation is at a particular time: *Employees get three floating holidays a year.* **2** TECHNICAL an organ or part of your body that is floating is not connected correctly or is not in the usual place

flock¹ /flɑk/ *n.* **1** [C] a group of sheep, goats, or birds: *a flock of geese* → see also HERD ▸see THESAURUS box at **group¹** **2** [C usually singular] a priest or minister's flock is the group of people who regularly attend his church **3** [C usually singular] a large group of the same kind of people: **+of** *a noisy flock of children* ▸see THESAURUS box at **group¹** **4** [U] FORMAL small pieces of wool, cotton etc. used for filling the CUSHIONS of chairs and other furniture **5** [U] also **flocking** a soft woolly substance used to make patterns on the surface of WALLPAPER, curtains etc. [**Origin:** (1–3) Old English *flocc* **crowd**]

flock² *v.* [I always + adv./prep.] to go to a place in large numbers because something interesting or exciting is happening there: **+to/into/around etc.** *People have been flocking to the exhibit.*

flocked /flɑkt/ *adj.* decorated with patterns made of a soft woolly material: *flocked wallpaper*

floe /floʊ/ *n.* [C] an ICE FLOE

flog /flɑg, flɔg/ *v.* **flogged, flogging** [T] **1** to beat a person or animal with a whip or stick as a punishment: *People caught breaking the liquor laws may be flogged.* **2** INFORMAL to sell something: *He's been on a lot of TV shows, flogging his new book.* → see also **beat/flog a dead horse** at DEAD¹ (11)

flog·ging /ˈflɑgɪŋ/ *n.* [C] a punishment in which someone is severely beaten with a whip or stick

flood¹ /flʌd/ *v.*
1 COVER WITH WATER [I,T] to make a place become covered with water, or to become covered with water: *Farmers flood the fields in order to grow rice.* | *The whole town flooded last summer.*
2 RIVER [I] if a river floods, water rises up over its edges and covers the land around it: *The river usually floods once or twice a year.*
3 ARRIVE/GO IN LARGE NUMBERS [I always + adv./prep.] to arrive or go somewhere in large numbers or amounts: **+in/into/out/across etc.** *Refugees flooded across the border.* | *Offers of help soon started flooding in.*
4 SEND IN LARGE AMOUNTS [T] to send or give a large number of something to a person, organization, country etc., especially so many that it is difficult for them to deal with them all: **flood sb/sth with sth** *Voters flooded Congress with letters of protest.* | *The office has been flooded with applications for the job.*
5 flood the market to sell something or be sold in very large numbers or amounts, especially so that the price goes down: *Special sports drinks are now flooding the market.* | **+with** *Producers have recently flooded the market with crude oil.*
6 LIGHT [I,T] LITERARY if light floods a place or floods into it, it makes it very light and bright: *The small room was flooded with light.*
7 be flooded out to be forced to leave your home because of a flood
8 ENGINE [I,T] if an engine floods or you flood it, it has too much gas in it, so that it will not start
9 sb's eyes flood with tears also **tears flood sb's eyes** LITERARY used to say that someone begins to cry a lot
10 FEELING [I,T] LITERARY if a feeling or memory floods someone, they feel or remember it very strongly: **+over/back/through** *He saw her and relief flooded over him.* | *Her childhood memories **came flooding back**.*
11 COLOR [I,T] LITERARY if color floods your face or cheeks or your face or cheeks flood with color, your face suddenly turns red because of a strong emotion

flood² *n.* **1** [C,U] a very large amount of water that covers an area that is usually dry: *The town was completely destroyed by floods.* | *aid for flood victims* **2 a flood of sb/sth** a very large number or amount of people or things that arrive at the same time: *The station has received a flood of complaints about last night's show.* | *The door opened, letting in **a flood of light**.* **3 the Flood** the great flood described in the Bible story, that covered the world → see also FLASH FLOOD

flood·gate /ˈflʌdgeɪt/ *n.* **1 open the floodgates** to suddenly make it possible for a lot of people to do something, by removing laws and rules which had previously prevented or controlled it: *Any change in the law could open the floodgates to increased immigration.* **2** [C usually plural] a gate used to control the flow of water from a large lake, river etc.

flood·ing /ˈflʌdɪŋ/ *n.* [U] a situation in which an area of land becomes covered with water, for example because of heavy rain → see picture on page A30

flood·light /ˈflʌdlaɪt/ *n.* [C usually plural] a very bright light, used at night to light the outside of buildings, sports fields etc.

flood·lit /ˈflʌdˌlɪt/ *adj.* lit at night by floodlights: *a floodlit football field*

ˈflood plain *n.* [C] EARTH SCIENCE the large area of flat land on either side of a river that is sometimes covered with water

ˈflood tide *n.* [C] **1** EARTH SCIENCE the flow of the TIDE in toward the land → see also EBB TIDE **2 the flood tide of sth** a very large number or amount of something that arrives at the same time: *There is a flood tide of public interest in this issue.*

flood·wa·ter /ˈflʌdˌwɔt̬ɚ/ *n.* [U, plural] water that covers an area during a flood: *2500 residents were forced out of their homes by floodwaters.*

floor[1] /flɔr/ S1 W1 *n.*
1 FLAT SURFACE [C] the flat surface on which you stand indoors: *a dirt floor* | **the kitchen/bathroom/bedroom etc. floor** *I just mopped the kitchen floor.* ►see THESAURUS box at **ground**[1]
2 LEVEL IN BUILDING [C] one of the levels in a building SYN **story**: *My office is **on the third floor**.* | *a fourth-floor apartment*
3 GROUND the ground at the bottom of the ocean, a forest, a cave etc.: *The floor of the cave was wet.* | **the ocean/forest/valley floor** *These sea creatures live on the ocean floor.*
4 the floor a) the place where discussions or debates take place in a government institution or public meeting place: *The delegates crowded the floor of the House.* **b)** the people attending a public meeting: *Are there any questions from the floor?* **c)** the right to speak at an important public meeting, or the action of speaking: *Mr. Springer **took the floor** to explain his plan.* | *The senator from Wyoming **has the floor**.*
5 FOR DANCING [C] an area in a restaurant, hotel etc. where people can dance SYN **dance floor**: *There were two or three couples **on the floor**.* | *The bride and groom **took the floor** for the first dance.*
6 AREA FOR PARTICULAR PURPOSE [C] a large area on one level in a building, used for a particular purpose, especially work: *The stock market floor was wildly busy.* | *The manager's office is above the **shop floor*** (=the area in a factory where people work using machines).
7 go through the floor if a price, amount etc. goes through the floor, it becomes very low OPP **go through the roof**: *In the past year, stock prices have gone through the floor.*
8 LIMIT [singular] an officially agreed limit so that something cannot go below a certain value OPP **ceiling**: *The Federal Bank was accused of **putting a floor under** share prices.*
[**Origin:** Old English *flor*] → see also **be/get in on the ground floor** at GROUND FLOOR (2), **wipe the floor with sb** at WIPE[1] (7)

floor[2] *v.* [T] **1** to surprise or shock someone so much that they do not know what to say or do: *His response totally floored me.* **2** to hit someone so hard that they fall down: *The champion floored Watson with a single punch.* **3** INFORMAL to make a car go as fast as possible by pressing the ACCELERATOR all the way down: *She floored the Audi and took off.* | *I jumped in the car and **floored it**.* **4** to put down some type of material to make or cover the floor of a room

floor·board /ˈflɔrbɔrd/ *n.* [C] **1** [usually plural] a board in a wooden floor **2** the floor in a car

floor·ing /ˈflɔrɪŋ/ *n.* [U] material used to make or cover floors: *vinyl flooring*

ˈfloor lamp *n.* [C] a tall lamp that stands on the floor

ˌfloor ˈleader *n.* [C] POLITICS an important officer in the House of Representatives or the Senate who is chosen by his or her political party to organize the party's activities there, so that the bills that the party supports are passed and become law

ˈfloor-length *adj.* [only before noun] long enough to reach the floor: *a floor-length evening gown*

ˈfloor ˌmodel *n.* [C] a piece of furniture or equipment for the home, such as a washing machine, that has been in a store for people to look at and is often sold at a cheaper price because it may have been slightly damaged

ˈfloor plan *n.* [C] a drawing that shows the shape of a room or rooms in a building and the positions of things in it, as seen from above

ˈfloor price *n.* [C] ECONOMICS PRICE FLOOR

ˈfloor show *n.* [C] a performance by singers, dancers etc. at a NIGHTCLUB

floo·zy, floozie /ˈfluzi/ *n. plural* **floozies** [C] INFORMAL, DISAPPROVING a woman who has sexual relationships with a lot of different men

flop[1] /flɑp/ *v.* **flopped, flopping 1** [I always + adv./prep.] also **flop down** to sit or lie down in a relaxed way, by letting all your weight fall heavily onto a chair etc.: +**in/onto/across etc.** *Karl came in and flopped onto the sofa.* **2** [I always + adv./prep.] to hang or fall in an awkward or uncontrolled way: +**around/along/onto etc.** *His head flopped back pathetically.* | *Her blonde hair flopped over her eyes.* **3** INFORMAL if something such as a product, play, or plan flops, it is completely unsuccessful: *The musical flopped after its first week on Broadway.*

flop[2] *n.* **1** [C] INFORMAL a movie, play, product etc. that is completely unsuccessful OPP **hit**: *His first play was a flop.* | *The movie was a **box-office flop*** (=very few people went to see it). **2** [singular] a heavy falling movement or the noise that something makes when it falls heavily: *He landed with a flop in the water.* → see also BELLY FLOP, FLIP-FLOP[1]

flop·house /ˈflɑphaʊs/ *n.* [C] a cheap dirty hotel, that often has many beds in one room

flop·py /ˈflɑpi/ *adj. comparative* **floppier**, *superlative* **floppiest** soft and hanging down loosely: *a dog with long, floppy ears* | *a floppy hat* —**floppiness** *n.* [U]

ˌfloppy ˈdisk also **floppy** *n.* [C] COMPUTERS a small square plastic object with a DISK in it, that can be put into a computer and used for storing or moving information → see also HARD DISK

flo·ra /ˈflɔrə/ *n.* [U] BIOLOGY all the plants of a particular place, or of a particular period of time: *the flora of the Alps* [**Origin:** 1500–1600 Modern Latin, Latin *Flora* Roman female god of flowers, from *flos* **flower**] → see also FAUNA

flo·ral /ˈflɔrəl/ *adj.* decorated with or made of flowers: *floral designs on the curtains* | *a floral display*

Flor·en·tine /ˈflɔrəntin, -taɪn/ *adj.* **1** relating to or coming from Florence, Italy **2** [only after noun] made with SPINACH: *eggs Florentine*

flor·et /ˈflɔrət/ *n.* [C usually plural] one of the small flower-like parts of a plant or a vegetable such as BROCCOLI or CAULIFLOWER

flor·id /ˈflɔrɪd, ˈflɑrɪd/ *adj.* LITERARY **1** having too much decoration or detail: *a florid romance novel* **2** skin that is florid is red: *florid cheeks* —**floridly** *adv.*

Flor·i·da /ˈflɔrɪdə, ˈflɑr-/ ABBREVIATION **FL** a state in the southeastern U.S.

flo·rist /ˈflɔrɪst, ˈflɑr-/ *n.* [C] **1** someone who owns or works in a store that sells flowers **2** a store that sells flowers: *Dean stopped at the florist on the way home.*

floss[1] /flɔs, flɑs/ *n.* [U] **1** DENTAL FLOSS **2** EMBROIDERY FLOSS

floss[2] *v.* [I,T] to clean between your teeth with DENTAL FLOSS

flo·ta·tion /floʊˈteɪʃən/ *n.* [C,U] **1 flotation ring/compartment/device etc.** something that helps something or someone float in water: *Every boat carries one flotation device per passenger.* **2** ECONOMICS a time when STOCK in a company is made available for people to buy for the first time: *the company's flotation on the stock market*

flo·til·la /floʊˈtɪlə/ *n.* [C] a group of small ships [**Origin:** 1700–1800 Spanish *flota* **group of ships**]

F

flot·sam /ˈflɑtsəm/ *n.* [U] **1** broken pieces of wood, plastic etc. that are floating in the ocean or scattered on the shore → see also JETSAM **2** also **flotsam and jetsam** things that are not useful or needed anymore: *the plastic foam flotsam of fast-food restaurants*

flounce¹ /flaʊns/ *v.* [I always + adv./prep.] to walk quickly while making a big movement with your head or shoulders, especially to show that you are angry: +**out/off/past etc.** *Sandra frowned and flounced out of the room.*

flounce² *n.* [C] a band of cloth that is stitched into folds as a decoration on a piece of clothing, furniture etc.

flounced /flaʊnst/ *adj.* decorated with flounces

floun·der¹ /ˈflaʊndɚ/ *v.* [I] **1** to have a lot of problems and be likely to fail completely: *Brando's career was floundering when he was offered the role.* **2** [always + adv./prep.] to move awkwardly or with difficulty, especially in water, mud etc.: *The lifeguard saw some of the kids floundering in the waves.* **3** to not know what to say or do because you feel confused or upset: *I found myself floundering as I tried to answer her questions.*

F

flounder² *n. plural* **flounder** or **flounders** [C,U] BIOLOGY a flat ocean fish, or the meat of this fish

flour¹ /flaʊɚ/ *n.* [U] a powder made from grain, usually wheat, and used for making bread, cake etc.: *Mix the flour and sugar.* | **whole wheat/corn/rice etc. flour** *bread made with whole wheat flour* [**Origin:** 1200–1300 *flower* **best part**; because it is the best of the grain]

flour² *v.* [T] to cover a surface with flour: *a lightly floured board*

flour·ish¹ /ˈflɚɪʃ, ˈflʌrɪʃ/ *v.* **1** [I] to develop well and be successful SYN **thrive**: *a flourishing black market* | *Foley's career has flourished.* **2** [I] to grow well and be very healthy SYN **thrive**: *The plants flourished in the warm sun.* **3** [T] to wave something in your hand in order to make people notice it: *Ellie ran in, flourishing her acceptance letter.* [**Origin:** 1200–1300 Old French *florir* **to produce flowers**, from Latin *flos* **flower**]

flourish² *n.* **1** [C] something such as a decoration or detail that is not necessary: *Lucas' speech was full of rhetorical flourishes.* **2 with a flourish** with a large confident movement that makes people notice you: *The old gentleman took off his hat* ***with a flourish.*** **3** [C] a curved line in writing, done for decoration **4** [C] a loud part of a piece of music, played especially when an important person enters: *a flourish of trumpets*

flour·y /ˈflaʊri/ *adj.* covered with flour, or tasting or feeling like flour

flout /flaʊt/ *v.* [T] FORMAL to deliberately disobey a law, rule etc.: *Too many people regularly flout traffic laws.*

flow¹ /floʊ/ W3 *v.* [I]

1 LIQUID/GAS/ELECTRICITY if a liquid, gas, or electricity flows, it moves in a steady continuous stream: *The river flows more slowly here.* | +**over/down/through etc.** *Water was flowing over the top of the dam.* | *Lava flowed from the volcano.* | *a surge of power flowing through the cable* | *If the windows are shut, air cannot* ***flow freely.***

THESAURUS

run to flow: *Tears ran down her cheeks.*
pour to flow in large quantities: *Oil is pouring out of the broken pipeline.*
gush to flow out quickly in very large quantities: *Water gushed from the hydrant.*
spurt to flow out suddenly with a lot of force: *Blood spurted from the wound.*
trickle to flow slowly in drops or in a thin stream: *Tears were trickling down his cheeks.*
leak to flow in or out through a small hole or crack, usually when this is not meant to happen: *The faucet was leaking.*
ooze to flow from something very slowly: *Sticky sap was oozing from the cut end of the stick.*
drip to fall in drops: *Sweat was dripping from my forehead into my eyes.*

►see THESAURUS box at **pour**

2 GOODS/INFORMATION/CARS ETC. to move or be supplied easily, smoothly, and continuously and in large numbers or amounts from one place to another: *The widened freeway should help keep traffic flowing.* | +**in/out/through/from etc.** *Money has been flowing into the country from aid agencies.* | *Refugees were flowing out of the war zone.*

3 ALCOHOL if alcohol flows at a party, people drink a lot and there is a lot available: *That night the wine* ***flowed freely.***

4 WORDS/IDEAS a) if conversation or ideas flow, people talk or have ideas without being interrupted: *The conversation flowed from one topic to another.* **b)** if the ideas or words of a speech or piece of writing flow, they seem to follow each other in a way that is pleasing and makes sense: *If I change this paragraph, do you think it will flow better?*

5 CLOTHES/HAIR if clothing, hair etc. flows, it hangs loosely and gracefully

6 FEELINGS if an emotion flows, someone feels it strongly: +**through/into/from etc.** *He let all his anger flow out of him.*

7 OCEAN if the TIDE flows, it moves toward the land → see also EBB

flow from sth *phr. v.* FORMAL to happen as a result of something: *the political consequences that flowed from this decision*

flow² W3 *n.*

1 MOVEMENT OF LIQUID [C usually singular] a smooth steady movement of liquid, gas, or electricity: +**of** *the flow of blood to the brain* | **blood/water/air etc. flow** *The air flow is then stopped.*

2 SUPPLY/MOVEMENT [C usually singular] a continuous supply or movement of something from one place to another: *The road repairs should not affect traffic flow.* | +**of** *the flow of food and medicine into areas affected by the flood* | ***the free flow of*** (=ability of something to move without being restricted) *goods between our countries*

3 WORDS/IDEAS [U] actions, words, or ideas that are produced continuously: +**of** *the flow of your speech*

4 OCEAN [singular] the regular movement of the ocean toward the land: *the ebb and flow* (=movement away and toward land) *of the tide*

5 go with the flow INFORMAL **a)** to do what is easiest in your situation, and not try to do something difficult or different: *If you want to stay sane, just go with the flow.* **b)** to do what other people are doing

6 go against the flow INFORMAL to do something very different from what other people are doing

[**Origin:** Old English *flowan*] → see also CASH FLOW, **ebb and flow** at EBB¹ (1)

ˈflow chart also **ˈflow ˌdiagram** *n.* [C] a drawing that uses shapes and ARROWS to show how a series of actions or parts of a system are related to each other

flower

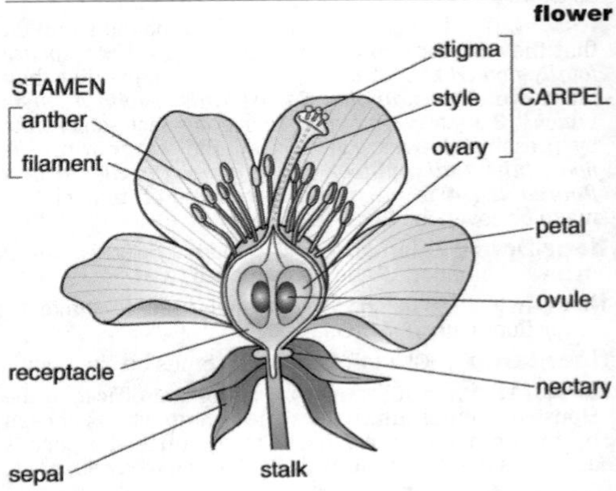

flow·er¹ /ˈflaʊɚ/ S2 W2 *n.* **1** [C] BIOLOGY the colored part of a plant or tree that produces seeds: *a tree with* *delicate pink flowers* **2** [C] a flower with its stem that has been removed from a plant: *I'll just put the flowers in some water.* | **a bunch/bouquet of flowers** *The boy gave me a bouquet of flowers.* | *She bent down and* ***picked a flower*** (=pulled it off the plant). | *They always* ***send me flowers*** *on my birthday.* **3** [C] a plant that is grown for the beauty of the flowers: *We planted a few flowers in the front yard.* **4 in flower** a plant or tree that is in flower has flowers on it: *It was May and the apple trees were all in flower.* **5 come into flower** to begin to have flowers: *Roses come into flower in June.* **6 the flower of sth** LITERARY the best or most perfect part of something: *the flower of the nation's youth* [**Origin:** 1100–1200 Old French *flor, flour*, from Latin *flos*]

flower² *v.* [I] **1** BIOLOGY to produce flowers: *The azaleas are already flowering.* **2** FORMAL to develop and reach a high level of achievement: *Communal living flowered briefly in the 1960s.*

'flower ar,ranging *n.* [U] the art of arranging flowers in an attractive way

flow·er·bed, flower bed /'flaʊɚˌbɛd/ *n.* [C] an area of ground in which flowers are grown

'flower child *n. plural* **flower children** [C] a young person in the 1960s and 1970s who wanted peace and love in society

flow·ered /'flaʊɚd/ *adj.* decorated with pictures of flowers: *a flowered dress*

flow·er·et /'flaʊərət, ˌflaʊə'rɛt/ *n.* [C] a FLORET

'flower girl *n.* [C] a young girl who carries flowers in a wedding ceremony → see also BRIDESMAID

flow·er·ing /'flaʊərɪŋ/ *n.* **the flowering of sth** a successful period in the development of something: *the flowering of 17th century science*

flow·er·pot /'flaʊɚˌpɑt/ *n.* [C] a pot in which you grow plants

'flower ,power *n.* [U] the ideas of young people in the 1960s and 1970s who believed that peace and love were the most important things in life

flow·er·y /'flaʊəri/ *adj.* **1** decorated with pictures of flowers: *flowery fabrics* **2** ENG. LANG. ARTS flowery speech or writing uses complicated and rare words instead of simple clear language: *a flowery description*

flow·ing /'floʊɪŋ/ *adj.* [usually before noun] moving, curving, or hanging gracefully: *long, flowing white hair* | *the flowing lines of the car's design*

flown /floʊn/ *v.* the past participle of FLY

'flow ,resource *n.* [C] TECHNICAL a RESOURCE (=something from nature that people use), such as wind, light from the sun, or flowing water, that must be used at the time or place that it exists → see also NONRENEWABLE RESOURCE, RENEWABLE RESOURCE

fl. oz. *n.* the written abbreviation of FLUID OUNCE

flu /flu/ *n.* [U] MEDICINE a common infectious disease that makes your throat sore, makes it difficult for you to breathe, gives you a fever, and makes you feel very tired SYN **influenza**: *Arlene* ***has the flu.*** | *Glen is home sick* ***with the flu.*** | *Flu shots are recommended for people 55 and older.*

flub /flʌb/ *v.* **flubbed, flubbing** [T] INFORMAL to make a mistake or do something badly: *Several cast members flubbed their lines.*

flub up *phr. v.* INFORMAL to make a mistake or do something badly

fluc·tu·ate /'flʌktʃuˌeɪt/ Ac *v.* [I] to change very often, especially from a high level to a low one and back again: **+between** *Temperatures in the valley fluctuate between 90 and 110 degrees.* | **fluctuate from sth to sth** *His weight fluctuates from 265 to 285 pounds.* | **sth fluctuates with sth** *The state's income from sales taxes fluctuates with the economy.* | **fluctuate wildly/greatly** *Stock prices fluctuated wildly in the following weeks.* [**Origin:** 1600–1700 Latin *fluctuare*, from *fluere* **to flow**]

fluc·tu·a·tion /ˌflʌktʃu'eɪʃən/ Ac *n.* [C,U] a sudden change in the amount, level, or price of something: *price fluctuations* | **+in** *The plants are affected by fluctuations in temperature.*

flue /flu/ *n.* [C] a pipe through which smoke or heat from a fire can pass out of a building: *a chimney flue*

flu·ent /'fluənt/ *adj.* **1** able to speak a language very well: **+in** *Sutherland is fluent in French.* **2 fluent French/Japanese etc.** someone who speaks fluent French, Japanese etc. speaks it like a person from that country: *They were surprised when I gave my speech in fluent Chinese.* **3** speaking, reading, writing, or playing a musical instrument confidently and without long pauses: *Johansson is a fluent and expressive fiddler.* [**Origin:** 1500–1600 Latin, present participle of *fluere* **to flow**] —**fluently** *adv.* —**fluency** *n.* [U]

fluff¹ /flʌf/ *n.* [U] **1** something that is pretty or interesting, but not really serious or important: *The magazine is a mix of fashion, fluff, and some serious journalism.* **2** small soft light pieces of thread or dust that have come from clothing or other materials: *fluff under the bed* **3** soft light hair or feathers, especially from a young bird or animal → see also DOWN

fluff² *v.* [T] also **fluff up, fluff out** **1** to make something soft appear larger by shaking or brushing it: *Fluff the couscous with a fork.* | *We made the bed and fluffed up the pillows.* **2** if a bird fluffs its feathers, it raises them to keep warm or to make itself look bigger

F

fluff·y /'flʌfi/ *adj. comparative* **fluffier**, *superlative* **fluffiest** **1** made of or covered with something soft and light, such as wool, hair, or feathers: *a fluffy little kitten* | *He had fluffy white hair.* **2** food that is fluffy is made soft and light by shaking, or beating so that air is mixed into it: *Mix the butter and sugar until fluffy.* | *a light, fluffy cheesecake* —**fluffiness** *n.* [U]

flu·id¹ /'fluɪd/ *n.* [C,U] a liquid: *Be sure and drink plenty of fluids.* | *brake fluid* | **body/bodily fluids** (=liquids that come from your body, such as blood or URINE)

fluid² *adj.* **1** fluid movements are relaxed and graceful: *Clark throws with a fluid motion.* **2** having a moving, flowing quality: *the sculpture's round shapes and fluid lines* | *a fluid guitar solo* **3** [not before noun] likely to change often, or able to change: *Our plans for the project are still somewhat fluid.* —**fluidity** /flu'ɪdəṭi/ *n.* [U]

,fluid 'ounce *n.* [C] WRITTEN ABBREVIATION **fl. oz.** a unit for measuring liquids, equal to 1/16 of a PINT or 0.0296 liters

fluke /fluk/ *n.* [C] **1** INFORMAL something that only happens because of chance or luck: *We wanted to show that the win was not just a fluke.* **2** TECHNICAL one of the two flat parts of a WHALE'S tail —**fluky** *adj.*

flume /flum/ *n.* [C] a long narrow structure built for water to slide down, used to move water or LOGS from one place to another or for people to slide down for fun

flum·mox /'flʌməks/ *v.* [T usually passive] to completely confuse someone: *I was totally flummoxed by his last question.*

flung /flʌŋ/ *v.* the past tense and past participle of FLING

flunk /flʌŋk/ *v.* INFORMAL **1** [I,T] to fail a test or class: *Tony flunked chemistry last semester.* | *Yesterday I took my driver's test and flunked.* **2** [T] if a teacher flunks someone, he or she gives them a failing grade for a test or class: *She didn't do any of the work, so I flunked her.*

flunk out *phr. v.* INFORMAL to be forced to leave a school or college because your work is not good enough: **+of** *Leo flunked out of Yale in his junior year.*

flun·ky /'flʌŋki/ *n. plural* **flunkies** [C] INFORMAL **1** someone who does the boring or physical work that someone else tells them to do: *the office flunky* **2** DISAPPROVING someone who is always with an important person and treats them with too much respect

flu·o·res·cent /flʊ'rɛsənt, flɔ-/ *adj.* **1** fluorescent colors are very bright: *a fluorescent pink T-shirt* **2 fluorescent light/lamp** PHYSICS a light that contains a gas-filled tube that produces a very bright light when electricity is passed through it **3** PHYSICS a fluorescent substance produces light when hit by ELECTRONS or

RADIATION [**Origin:** 1800–1900 *fluorspar*, type of fluorescent mineral (18–21 centuries), from Modern Latin *fluor* **mineral used for melting**] —**fluorescence** *n.* [U]

fluor·i·date /ˈflɔrəˌdeɪt, ˈflʊ-/ *v.* [T usually passive] to add fluoride to water in order to protect people's teeth —**fluoridation** /ˌflɔrəˈdeɪʃən/ *n.* [U]

fluor·ide /ˈflɔraɪd/ *n.* [U] CHEMISTRY a chemical that helps to protect teeth against decay

fluor·ine /ˈflɔrin, ˈflʊ-/ *n.* [U] SYMBOL **F** CHEMISTRY a chemical substance that is an ELEMENT and is usually in the form of a poisonous gas

fluor·o·car·bon /ˌflʊroʊˈkɑrbən, ˈflɔroʊˌkɑrbən/ *n.* [C] CHEMISTRY any chemical that contains the substances fluorine and CARBON → see also CFC

flur·ry /ˈflɚi, ˈflʌri/ *n. plural* **flurries** **1 a flurry of sth** a sudden short period of activity, movement, emotion, excitement, or interest: *a flurry of activity* | *After his statement, Orr's office received a flurry of phone calls.* **2** [usually plural] also **snow flurries** a small amount of snow that falls: *A few flurries are expected tonight.*

F

flush¹ /flʌʃ/ *v.* **1** [I,T] if you flush a toilet or if it flushes, you make water go through it to clean it: *Don't forget to flush the toilet.* | *I can't get the toilet to flush.* | *Joe **flushed** the dead goldfish **down the toilet**.* **2** [I] to become red in the face: *Flushing slightly, Lesley looked away.* **3** [T] also **flush out** to clean something by forcing water or another liquid through it: *Drink water after exercise to flush out the wastes released from the muscles.*

flush sb ↔ **out** *phr. v.* to make someone leave the place where they are hiding: *Police used tear gas to flush out the gunmen.*

flush² *n.* **1 the (first) flush of youth/success etc.** LITERARY the period when something is still new and exciting: *The family bought a new house and car in the first flush of affluence.* **2 a flush of pride/embarrassment etc.** a sudden feeling of pride, excitement etc. SYN **surge** **3** [C] the act of flushing a toilet: *Most toilets use 5 gallons of water per flush.* **4** [singular] a red color that appears on your face or body, especially because you are embarrassed, sick, or excited **5** [C] card games, a flush is a set of cards that are all of the same SUIT

flush³ *adj.* **1** if two surfaces are flush, they are at exactly the same level, so that the place where they meet is flat: **+with** *Make sure that the shelf is flush with the wall.* **2** INFORMAL if someone or an organization is flush, they have plenty of money: *Jamie has $600 saved; Adam isn't quite so flush.* **3 flush with success/pride/optimism etc.** feeling a sudden strong feeling of happiness, pride etc., especially after achieving something: *The explorers arrived home flush with their success.*

flush⁴ *adv.* **1** fitting together so that the place where two surfaces meet is flat: *The door should fit flush into its frame.* **2** directly onto something: *Williams was hit flush on the chin.*

flushed /flʌʃt/ *adj.* red in the face: *Nona was feverish and flushed.* | **+with** *Her face was flushed with pride.*

flus·tered /ˈflʌstɚd/ *adj.* feeling confused and nervous: *Jay **got all flustered** and forgot what he was going to say.* —**fluster** *v.* [T]

flute /flut/ *n.* [C] **1** ENG. LANG. ARTS a musical instrument shaped like a pipe, that you play by holding it across your lips, blowing into it, and pressing KEYS to change the notes **2** also **champagne flute** a tall narrow glass used for some alcoholic drinks, especially CHAMPAGNE [**Origin:** 1300–1400 Old French *flahute*, from Old Provençal *flaut*]

flut·ed /ˈflut̬ɪd/ *adj.* decorated with long narrow upright curves or folds: *a fluted cake pan*

flut·ist /ˈflut̬ɪst/ *n.* [C] someone who plays the flute

flut·ter¹ /ˈflʌt̬ɚ/ *v.* **1** [I,T] if a bird or insect flutters its wings or if its wings flutter, its wings move quickly and lightly up and down: *Butterflies fluttered from flower to flower.* **2** [I] to wave or move gently in the air: *Flags from a hundred nations fluttered in the breeze.* **3** [I,T] if your stomach or your heart flutters, you feel very excited or nervous **4** if your heart flutters, it beats in a rapid or irregular way **5 flutter your eyelashes (at sb)** if a woman flutters her eyelashes at a man, she uses her sexual attractiveness to influence him

flutter² *n.* **1** [C usually singular] a fluttering movement: *a flutter of wings* **2** [singular] the state of being nervous, confused, or excited: *Laurie was **in a flutter of** excitement at the idea of a party.* **3** [C] TECHNICAL an irregular heart beat **4** [U] TECHNICAL a shaking movement that stops a machine from working correctly

flu·vi·al /ˈfluviəl/ *adj.* EARTH SCIENCE relating to or produced by rivers

flux /flʌks/ *n.* [U] **be in (a state of) flux** to be always changing so that you cannot be sure what will happen: *Fashion is always in flux.* | *The country's economy is in a state of flux.*

fly¹ /flaɪ/ S1 W1 *v. past tense* **flew** /flu/, *past participle* **flown** /floʊn/

1 THROUGH AIR [I] **a)** if a vehicle such as a plane flies, it moves through the air: *Fighter jets fly at incredibly high speeds.* | **fly over sth** *The plane was flying over the desert.* **b)** if a bird or insect flies, it moves through the air using its wings: *Flocks of seagulls flew overhead.* | **fly away/off** *The butterfly flew away.*

2 TRAVEL [I] to travel by airplane: *Are you going to fly or drive?* | **fly to sth** *We're flying nonstop to Orlando.* | **fly from sth/fly out of sth** *He flew out of JFK yesterday.* ►see THESAURUS box at **escape¹**, **travel¹**

3 PILOT [I,T] to be the pilot of an airplane: *Brenda's learning to fly.* | *Stan flew helicopters in Vietnam.*

4 AIRLINE [I,T] to use a particular AIRLINE or use a particular type of ticket when flying: *I flew Aeroflot out of Moscow.* | *We usually fly coach.*

5 SEND GOODS/PEOPLE [T] to carry or send goods or people by airplane: **fly sth into/out of** *Food and medicine are being flown into the area.*

6 OVER/ACROSS AN AREA [T] to fly an airplane over a large area: *Lindbergh was the first man to fly the Atlantic.*

7 MOVE [I always + adv./prep.] to suddenly move somewhere quickly: **+down/across/out of etc.** *Timmy flew down the stairs and out the door.* | **+open/shut/back etc.** *The door suddenly flew open.*

8 MOVE THROUGH AIR [I] to move quickly and suddenly through the air: *Debris was flying everywhere.* | *The vase shattered and **sent** glass **flying** across the room.* | *He tripped on a crack in the sidewalk and **went flying**.*

9 TIME if time flies, it passes very quickly: *Is it 5:30 already? Boy, **time** sure **flies**!* | **fly past/by** *Last week just seemed to fly past.*

10 FLAG [I,T] if a flag flies, or if you fly it, it is fastened to a pole or a building, ship etc.: *The ship is flying the Dutch flag.*

11 TOY [T] to make something such as a toy plane or KITE move through the air: *Kids were flying kites in the park.*

12 HAIR/COAT [I] if your hair, coat etc. is flying, it moves freely and loosely in the air: *Her long hair was flying in the wind.*

13 be flying high to be very successful, and often to feel very happy about it: *The team is flying high after winning the Super Bowl again.*

14 fly off the handle INFORMAL to suddenly become angry, especially about something that does not seem very important: *Linda called me back and apologized for flying off the handle.*

15 fly into a temper/rage to suddenly become extremely angry: *He flew into a rage and demanded his money back.*

16 rumors/accusations etc. fly used to say that people are talking about something a lot, saying things that may be untrue, criticizing it etc.: *Rumors are flying about a possible military takeover.*

17 PLAN [I] INFORMAL a plan that will fly is good or useful: *Is their idea really going to fly?*

18 let fly INFORMAL **a)** to suddenly say something angrily to someone: **+with** *Hayes let fly with some unprintable swear words.* **b)** to suddenly attack someone: **+with** *The boys let fly with a torrent of rocks.*

19 fly in the face of sth to be the opposite of what most people think is reasonable, sensible, or normal: *His claim flies in the face of all the evidence.*
20 go fly a kite SPOKEN said when you want someone to go away because they are being annoying
21 fly a kite to make a suggestion to see what people will think of it
22 fly the coop INFORMAL to leave or escape from a place where you were not free: *All my children have flown the coop now.*
23 ESCAPE [T] OLD-FASHIONED to leave somewhere in order to escape: *They were forced to fly the country in 1939.*
→ see also **as the crow flies** at CROW[1] (3), **sparks fly** at SPARK[1] (7)
fly at sb also **fly into** sb *phr. v.* to suddenly rush toward someone because you are very angry with them: *The old man flew at her in rage.*

fly² *n. plural* **flies** [C]
1 INSECT BIOLOGY a small flying insect with two wings, often found around garbage: *The flies were swarming around the garbage cans.*
2 PANTS the part at the front of a pair of pants that you can open: *Your fly is unzipped.*
3 BASEBALL a fly ball
4 FISHING a hook that is made to look like an insect, used for catching fish
5 on the fly while you are doing something else: *Sometimes you have to make decisions on the fly.*
6 sb wouldn't hurt a fly SPOKEN used to say that someone is very gentle and is not likely to hurt anyone: *Duane wouldn't hurt a fly. I can't imagine him fighting in a war.*
7 drop/die like flies INFORMAL used to say that a lot of people are becoming sick, or that a lot of people are dying
8 a fly in the ointment INFORMAL the only thing that spoils something and prevents it from being successful
9 be a fly on the wall to be able to watch what happens without other people knowing that you are there: *I wish I'd been a fly on the wall during that conversation.*

fly³ *v.* **flied, flying** [I] to hit a baseball high into the air, especially so that the ball is caught by the other team: *Harper flied to left field.*

fly⁴ *adj.* SLANG very fashionable, attractive, relaxed etc. SYN **cool**: *That Sharlene is one fly girl.*

'fly ball *n.* [C] a ball that has been hit high into the air in a baseball game

fly·boy /'flaɪbɔɪ/ *n. plural* **flyboys** [C] OLD-FASHIONED a pilot

fly·by /'flaɪbaɪ/ *n. plural* **flybys** [C] **1** an occasion when a space vehicle or SATELLITE passes a PLANET: *During the flyby, the spacecraft will measure gases in the atmosphere.* **2** an occasion when a plane flies over a particular position

'fly-by-,night *adj.* [only before noun] INFORMAL a fly-by-night organization cannot be trusted and is not likely to exist very long

fly·er /'flaɪɚ/ *n.* [C] a FLIER

'fly ,fishing *n.* [U] the sport of fishing in a river or lake, using special hooks that are made to look like insects

fly·ing¹ /'flaɪ-ɪŋ/ *adj.* [only before noun] **1** able to fly: *a flying insect* **2 with flying colors** if you do something with flying colors, you are very successful at it: *The president passed his health exam with flying colors.* **3 get off to a flying start** to begin something such as a job or race very well **4 a flying jump/leap** a long high jump made while you are running

flying² *n.* [U] the activity of traveling by plane or of being a pilot: *She's afraid of flying.*

,flying 'buttress *n.* [C] part of an ARCH that sticks out from and supports the top of an outside wall of a large building such as a church

,flying 'fish *n.* [C] BIOLOGY a tropical fish that can jump out of the water

,flying 'fox *n.* [C] BIOLOGY a FRUIT BAT

,flying 'saucer *n.* [C] a space vehicle shaped like a plate, that some people believe carries creatures from another world SYN **UFO**

'fly leaf *n.* [C] a page at the beginning or end of a book, on which there is usually no printing

fly·o·ver /'flaɪ,oʊvɚ/ *n.* [C] a group of planes that fly close together for people to watch on a special occasion

fly·pa·per /'flaɪ,peɪpɚ/ *n.* [U] paper that is covered with a sticky substance and is used to catch and kill flies

fly·speck /'flaɪspɛk/ *n.* [C] **1** something that is very small: *The islands are just flyspecks in the ocean.* **2** a small spot of waste matter from a fly

fly·swat·ter /'flaɪ,swɑt̬ɚ/ *n.* [C] a plastic square fastened to a long handle, used for killing flies

fly·weight /'flaɪweɪt/ *n.* [C] a BOXER who belongs to the lightest class of BOXERS and weighs under 112 pounds

fly·wheel /'flaɪwil/ *n.* [C] a heavy wheel that keeps a machine working at a steady speed because of its weight

FM /,ɛf 'ɛm/ *n.* [U] a system of broadcasting radio programs which produces a clear sound → see also AM

F

foal¹ /foʊl/ *n.* [C] a very young horse

foal² *v.* [I] to give birth to a foal

foam¹ /foʊm/ *n.* [U] **1** a lot of very small BUBBLES on the surface of something SYN **froth**: *the white foam on top of the waves* **2** a light solid substance filled with many very small BUBBLES of air: *foam packing material* | *an old foam mattress* **3** a soft liquid substance made of very small BUBBLES: *The fire extinguisher uses a chemical foam.* —**foamy** *adj.* → see also STYROFOAM

foam² *v.* [I] **1** to produce foam: *Beat the cream until it foams.* **2 foam at the mouth a)** to have a lot of very small BUBBLES come out of your mouth because you are sick **b)** to be very angry: *Some senators are foaming at the mouth over what they say is obscene art.*

,foam 'rubber *n.* [U] soft rubber full of air BUBBLES that is used in PILLOWS, chair seats, beds etc.

fob¹ /fɑb/ *v.* **fobbed, fobbing** [**Origin:** 1500–1600 *fob* **to deceive** (16–19 centuries)]
fob sth **off** *phr. v.* to get rid of something that is broken or of poor quality by tricking someone: **fob sth off on sb** *Don't let them fob off a cheap brand on you.*

fob² *n.* [C] a short chain or piece of cloth to which a fob watch is fastened

'fob watch *n.* [C] a watch that fits into a pocket, or is pinned to a woman's dress

fo·cac·cia /foʊ'kɑtʃə/ *n.* [U] a type of Italian bread

fo·cal length /'foʊkəl ,lɛŋθ/ *n.* [C] TECHNICAL the distance between the center of a LENS and the focal point

fo·cal point /'foʊkəl ,pɔɪnt/ *n.* **1** the thing, activity, or person in a situation that is the most interesting or most important: *The kitchen is usually the focal point of the home.* **2** PHYSICS the point where light, sound, or heat RAYS meet SYN **focus**

fo·cus¹ /'foʊkəs/ Ac S2 W1 *v.* [I,T] **1** to pay special attention to a particular person or thing instead of others: *He stopped writing, trying to focus.* | **focus on sth** *The gallery's show focuses on works painted after 1945.* | *The recent civil war has* ***focused attention on*** (=caused people to pay attention to) *the southern region.* | **focus your mind/thoughts/efforts etc. on sth** *Try to focus your efforts on achievable goals.* **2** to change the position of the LENS on a camera, TELESCOPE etc., so that you can see something clearly: **focus sth on sth** *He focused his binoculars on the building opposite.* | **focus on sth** *She turned the camera and focused on Martin's face.* ►see THESAURUS box at **camera**
3 if your eyes focus, or if you focus your eyes, you become able to see something clearly **4** PHYSICS if beams of light focus, or you focus them, they pass through a lens and meet at a point [**Origin:** 1600–1700 Latin **hearth** (=place for a fire in a house)]

focus

focus² Ac S3 W2 *n.* **1** [singular, U] a subject or situation that is the most important part of something or that people pay special attention to: *The organization has a simple focus – keeping kids in school.* | **+of** *The war became the focus of worldwide attention.* | **sb's focus is on sth** *The company's focus is on growth.* | *This small village became the* ***focus of worldwide attention.*** | *The House's actions today will* ***shift the focus*** (=change it) *back to the budget.* **2** [U] serious concentration on a particular goal without wasting time or energy on other things: *He's a talented tennis player, but he lacks focus.* **3** [singular] the part of an instrument such as a camera or telescope that you turn until the image that you are looking at is clear: *She* ***adjusted the focus*** *on the camera.* **4** how clear or unclear an image is when it is seen through a camera, TELESCOPE etc.: *I adjusted the lens until the image was* ***in focus*** (=clear). | *Almost every picture she took was* ***out of focus*** (=unclear). | *We turned the telescope until the stars* ***came into focus*** (=became clear). **5 bring sth into focus** to make people become aware of an issue or subject and start to think and talk about it: *The case has brought the problem of child abuse sharply into focus.* **6** [C] EARTH SCIENCE the center of an EARTHQUAKE **7** [C] *plural* **foci** /ˈfoʊsaɪ/ PHYSICS the point at which RAYS of light, sound, or heat meet each other SYN **focal point**: *the focus of a lens* **8 a)** PHYSICS one of two fixed points inside an ELLIPSE for which the sum of the distances from these points to any point on the ellipse is always the same **b)** PHYSICS one of the two fixed points inside the curves of a HYPERBOLA for which the difference between the distances from these points to any point on the hyperbola is the same **c)** PHYSICS a fixed point inside a PARABOLA for which the distance between that point and any point on the parabola is the same as the distance from that point on the parabola and the DIRECTRIX (=a particular line outside the parabola)

fo·cused /ˈfoʊkəst/ Ac *adj.* paying careful attention to what you are doing, in a way that shows you are determined to succeed: *I have to stay focused if I want to win.*

ˈfocus group *n.* [C] a group of people who are asked, for example by a company or political party, their opinions about a particular product or subject

fod·der /ˈfɑdɚ/ *n.* [U] **1** DISAPPROVING something for people to talk or write about: **+for** *Her love life has always been fodder for the gossip columnists.* **2** food for farm animals → see also CANNON FODDER

foe /foʊ/ *n.* [C] LITERARY an enemy

fog¹ /fɑg, fɔg/ *n.* **1** [C,U] thick cloudy air near the ground that is difficult to see through → see also MIST: **thick/heavy/dense fog** *Thick fog is making driving dangerous.* | **fog lifts/clears** *The fog lifted later in the day.* → see picture on page A30 **2** INFORMAL confused and unable to think clearly: *a fog of depression* | *Stillman seems to be* ***in a fog.***

fog² *v.* **fogged, fogging 1** also **fog up** [I,T] if glass fogs or becomes fogged, it becomes covered in very small drops of water so you cannot see through it: *My glasses fogged up as soon as I stepped outside.* **2 be fogged in** to be completely surrounded by fog: *Kennedy Airport was fogged in, so we landed in Newark.* **3 fog the issue** to deliberately make something confusing or difficult to understand

fog·bound /ˈfɑgbaʊnd/ *adj.* prevented from traveling or working normally because of fog: *Interstate 5 was fogbound this morning.*

fo·gey, fogy /ˈfoʊgi/ *n.* → see OLD FOGEY

fog·gy /ˈfɑgi/ *adj. comparative* **foggier**, *superlative* **foggiest 1** not clear because of fog: *a damp and foggy morning* **2 not have the foggiest (idea)** SPOKEN said to emphasize that you do not know something: *I don't have the foggiest idea what his address is.* —**foggily** *adv.* —**fogginess** *n.* [U]

Fog·gy Bot·tom /ˈfɑgi ˌbɑṭəm/ the part of Washington, D.C. where the offices of the U.S. State Department are

fog·horn /ˈfɑghɔrn/ *n.* [C] **1** a loud horn used by ships in fog to warn other ships of their position **2 like a foghorn** HUMOROUS very loud: *He has a voice like a foghorn.*

ˈfog light also **ˈfog lamp** *n.* [C usually plural] a strong light on a car that helps drivers to see and be seen in fog → see picture on page A36

foi·ble /ˈfɔɪbəl/ *n.* [C usually plural] FORMAL a small weakness or strange habit that someone has, which does not harm anyone else: *We all have our little foibles.*

foie gras /ˌfwɑ ˈgrɑ/ *n.* [U] the LIVER of a duck or GOOSE, usually eaten as a PÂTÉ

foil¹ /fɔɪl/ *n.* **1** [U] metal sheets that are thin like paper, used for wrapping food: *Cover the turkey with foil.* **2 be a foil for/to sb/sth** to make the good qualities of someone or something more noticeable, especially by being very different from them: *Roasted red peppers are a sweet foil to the slightly bitter spinach.* **3** [C] a light narrow sword used in FENCING

foil² *v.* [T often passive] to prevent someone from doing something they had planned to do, especially to prevent someone from doing something illegal: *The escape attempt was foiled by police guards.*

foist /fɔɪst/ *v.*

foist sth **on/upon** sb *phr. v.* to make someone accept something they do not want: *He tried to foist some of his work on me at the last minute.*

-fold /foʊld/ *suffix* **1** [in adjectives] relating to a particular number of kinds: *The purpose of our mission is three-fold* (=it has three related purposes). **2** [in adverbs] a particular number of times: *Profits have increased fourfold* (=they are four times as much as before).

fold¹ /foʊld/ S3 W3 *v.*

1 BEND [T] to bend a piece of paper, cloth etc. so that one part covers another part: *Fold the paper along the dotted line.* | *Roll the dough out and* ***fold it in half.*** | **fold sth under/over/down etc.** (=take one side and fold it in a particular direction so it is covered by the other side)

2 MAKE STH SMALLER/NEATER [T] also **fold up** to fold something several times so that it makes a small neat shape: *Fold up your clothes, and put them away.* | *The blankets were folded at the bottom of the bed.*

3 FURNITURE ETC. [I,T] if something such as a piece of furniture folds or you fold it, you make it smaller or move it to a different position by bending it or closing it: *The chairs fold flat for easy storage.* | **fold sth forward/up/down etc.** *Fold the seat forward so Becky can get in.* | **+away/up/down etc.** *The computer screen folds down over the keyboard.* | *The sofa folds out into a bed.*

4 fold your arms to bend your arms so they are resting across your chest: *George stood silently with his arms folded.*

5 BUSINESS [I] if a business folds, it fails and is not able to continue: *One of the biggest newspapers in the region has folded.*

6 COVER [T] to cover something, especially by wrapping it in material: **fold sth in sth** *Some old pennies were folded in the handkerchief.*

7 LEGS [I] if your legs fold, they suddenly become too

weak to support you so that you fall to the ground: *The fawn's legs **folded under her**, and she fell.*
8 **fold sb in your arms** LITERARY to hold someone closely by putting your arms around them
9 **ROCKS** [I,T] EARTH SCIENCE if a layer of rock folds or something folds it, it bends or becomes curved
[**Origin:** Old English *fealdan*]

fold sth **in/into** *phr. v.* to gently mix another substance into a mixture when you are preparing food: *Whip the cream and fold it into the cooled custard.*

fold up *phr. v.* **1 fold sth ↔ up** to fold something several times so that it makes a small neat shape: *She folded up the letter and put it in her pocket.* **2** if something such as a piece of furniture folds up, you can make it smaller or move it to a different position by bending it or closing it: *My umbrella folds up and fits in my purse.* **3 fold sth ↔ up** to make something such as a piece of furniture smaller or move it to a different position by bending it or closing it: *Fold up the ironing board please.*

fold² *n.* [C]
1 LOOSE SKIN/MATERIAL [usually plural] the folds in material, skin etc. are the loose parts that hang over other parts of it: +**of** *He hid the knife in the folds of his robe.*
2 LINE a line made in paper, cloth etc. when you fold one part of it over another: *Cut the cardboard along the fold.*
3 the fold a group of people who have shared aims or beliefs, or who work together: *Democrats have to find some way to make voters **return to the fold*** (=vote for them again). | *The Church is happy to have him back **in the fold**.*
4 SHEEP LITERARY a small area of a field where sheep are kept for safety
5 ROCK EARTH SCIENCE a bend in layers of rock, caused by movements under the earth

fold·a·way /ˈfoʊldəˌweɪ/ *adj.* [only before noun] a foldaway bed, table etc. can be folded so that it uses less space

fold·er /ˈfoʊldɚ/ S2 *n.* [C] **1** a large folded piece of strong paper or plastic, in which you keep loose paper **2** COMPUTERS a picture on a computer screen that shows you where a FILE is kept: *Put the new documents in a separate folder.*

fold·ing /ˈfoʊldɪŋ/ *adj.* [only before noun] **1** a folding bicycle, bed, chair etc. can be folded so that it is smaller and easier to carry or store **2 folding money** HUMOROUS paper money, as opposed to coins of small value

fo·li·age /ˈfoʊliɪdʒ/ *n.* [U] the leaves of a plant: *the plant's dark green foliage* | **dense/thick foliage** (=many leaves that are close together)

fo·li·o /ˈfoʊlioʊ/ *n. plural* **folios** [C] TECHNICAL **1** a book made with very large sheets of paper **2** a single numbered sheet of paper from a book

folk¹ /foʊk/ S1 *n.* **1** also **folks** [plural] INFORMAL people: *Most folks around here are pretty friendly.* | **young/old folks** *a meeting place for old folks* | *Congressmen are trying hard to please **the folks back home**.* | **country/city/farming etc. folk(s)** *We don't see many city folk around here.* **2 folks** SPOKEN said when you are talking to a group of people in a friendly way: *Hi folks, it's good to see you all here tonight!* **3 sb's folks** somone's parents: *I need to call my folks sometime this weekend.* **4** [U] ENG. LANG. ARTS FOLK MUSIC [**Origin:** Old English *folc*]

folk² *adj.* [only before noun] **1** ENG. LANG. ARTS folk art, dance, knowledge etc. is traditional and typical of the ordinary people who live in a particular area: *folk tales* | *Spanish folk songs* **2 folk medicine/remedy** a traditional type of medical treatment that uses plants etc. rather than modern scientific methods

ˈfolk dance *n.* [C] a traditional dance from a particular area, or a piece of music for this dance —**folk dancer** *n.* [C] —**folk dancing** *n.* [U]

ˈfolk ˌhero *n.* [C] someone who people in a particular place admire very much because of something they have done

folk·ie /ˈfoʊki/ *n.* [C] INFORMAL someone who sings or who likes folk music

folk·lore /ˈfoʊk-lɔr/ *n.* [U] the traditional stories, customs etc. of the ordinary people of a particular area: *Hawaiian folklore* —**folkloric** *adj.*

ˈfolk ˌmusic *n.* [U] ENG. LANG. ARTS **1** traditional music that has been played by the ordinary people in a particular area for a long time: *Russian folk music* **2** a type of modern popular music developed from traditional folk music, with songs about personal or social subjects, usually played without electronic equipment or instruments

folk·sy /ˈfoʊksi/ *adj.* INFORMAL **1** friendly and informal: *the town's folksy charm* **2** in a style that is typical of traditional country speech or customs: *a funny folksy radio show*

folk·way /ˈfoʊkweɪ/ *n.* [C usually plural] the way a group of people who live in a particular area behave: *Southern folkways*

fol·li·cle /ˈfɑlɪkəl/ *n.* [C] **1** BIOLOGY a group of cells in the skin that a hair grows from → see picture at SKIN¹ **2** BIOLOGY a space around an egg and the cells that surround it, that is developing inside a female animal or human: *The follicles prepare each ovum for release into the reproductive system where it can be fertilized.*

fol·low /ˈfɑloʊ/ S1 W1 *v.*
1 COME BEHIND [I,T] to walk, drive, run etc. behind or after someone else: *They followed us in their car.* | *The president was followed by a crowd of photographers.* | **follow sb up/into/out etc.** *Jack had followed her into the kitchen.* **2 HAPPEN AFTER** [I,T] to happen immediately after something else: *the years following World War I* | *the huge fire that followed the 1906 San Francisco earthquake* | *Thunderstorms today will **be followed by** more rain.* | *The wedding is at 2:30, with a reception **to follow**.* | ***In the days/weeks that followed**, the police received hundreds of calls.* → see also FOLLOWING¹
3 IN ORDER TO WATCH SB [T] to go closely behind someone in order to watch them and find out where they go: *The man followed her home.*

THESAURUS
chase to quickly follow someone or something in order to catch him, her, or it: *The neighbor's dog was chasing a boy on a bike.*
pursue FORMAL to chase or follow someone or something in order to catch him, her, or it: *We ran faster, but he continued to pursue us.*
run after to chase someone or something: *She started to leave, and Smith ran after her.*
tail INFORMAL to secretly watch and follow someone such as a criminal: *He had been tailed by the secret police for months.*
stalk to follow a person or animal quietly in order to catch, attack, or kill him, her, or it: *a tiger stalking its prey*
give chase ESPECIALLY WRITTEN to chase someone or something: *The guards spotted him and gave chase.*

4 COME AFTER [I,T] to come immediately after something else, for example in a book or a series of things: *A full report follows this chapter.* | *In English the letter "Q" **is always followed by** a "U."*
5 WISHES/RULES/INSTRUCTIONS to do what someone wants you to do, or do what the rules or instructions say you should do: *Investors who **followed** Murphy's **advice** made a large profit.* | **follow the rules/instructions/guidelines etc.** *Did you follow the instructions on the box?* | *I should have **followed my instincts*** (=done what I first wanted to do) *and not listened to you.* | *Her father encouraged her to **follow her heart*** (=do what she most wanted to do) *and become a singer.* | *If you **follow** the recipe **to the letter*** (=exactly), *you'll get perfect cookies.*
6 follow signs/directions to go in the direction that the signs say you should go or that someone has told you to go: *Turn right and follow the signs down the hallway.* | *Your directions were very easy to follow.*
7 GO IN A PARTICULAR DIRECTION [T] **a)** to continue along a particular road, river etc.: *Follow the trail until*

you reach the shore. **b)** to go in the same direction as something else, especially something that is very close: *The road follows the river for the next six miles.*
8 DO THE SAME THING [I,T] to do the same thing or the same type of thing as someone else: **follow sb into sth** *Cox's son Robert followed him into the family business.* | *He encouraged others to* ***follow her example*** (=do the same things as her) *of non-violence.* | *When Allied Stores reduced their prices, other companies were forced to* ***follow suit*** (=do the same thing). | *Will the U.S.* ***follow*** *Europe's economic* ***lead*** (=do the same thing econmically)? | **follow the herd/crowd** (=do the same thing as other people, without thinking about what is best for you)
9 follow (in) sb's footsteps to do the same job or live in the same way as someone else, especially a member of your family: *She followed in her mother's footsteps and started her own business.*
10 UNDERSTAND [I,T] to understand something such as an explanation or story: *Sorry,* ***I don't follow you.*** | *The plot was pretty* ***hard to follow.*** ▶see THESAURUS box at **understand**

F

11 BE INTERESTED [T] to be interested in something, especially a sport, and pay attention to it: *Do you follow baseball at all?*
12 BELIEVE/OBEY [T] to believe in and obey a particular set of religious or political ideas, or a leader who teaches these ideas: *They still follow the teachings of Gandhi.*
13 RESULT [I,T] FORMAL if something follows, it must be true as a result of something else that is true: *Interest rates are going down, so* ***it follows that*** *house sales will improve.* | **follow from sth** *the consequences that follow from his view of the problem*
14 follow a trend/pattern/course etc. to continue to happen or develop in a particular way: *In Australia, the weather follows a fairly predictable pattern.*
15 BE ABOUT [T] to show or describe someone's life or a series of events, for example in a movie or book: *The novel follows a group of students during the sixties.*
16 THINK ABOUT/STUDY [T] to study or think about a particular idea or subject and try to find out more about it: *Several biotech companies are following the same line of research.*
17 WATCH CAREFULLY [T] to carefully watch someone move: *The dogs in the pens followed her with their eyes as she passed.*
18 as follows FORMAL used to introduce a list of names, things, instructions etc.: *The forms should be completed as follows.*
19 follow your nose INFORMAL **a)** to do something in the way that you feel is right: *I don't really have a career plan – I just follow my nose.* **b)** to go straight forward: *Turn left on 6th Avenue, then just follow your nose.*
[**Origin:** Old English *folgian*] → see also **a hard/tough act to follow** at ACT[1] (7), FOLLOW-THROUGH

follow along *phr. v.* to read a book or written document while someone says or sings the words in it out loud: +**with** *Jurors were given a typed transcript to follow along with the tape.*

follow sb **around** *phr. v.* to keep following someone everywhere they go, in an annoying way: *Jamie follows Andrew around everywhere.*

follow through *phr. v.* **1** to do what needs to be done to complete something or make it successful: **follow sth ↔ through** *The college will make every effort to follow the proposal through.* | +**on** *The airline apparently didn't follow through on its promise.* | +**with** *The president intends to follow through with his plans to travel to Russia.* **2** to continue moving your arm after you hit the ball in tennis, GOLF etc.

follow up *phr. v.* to find out more about something, or to do more about something: +**on** *Did Jay ever follow up on that job possibility in Tucson?* | **follow sth up** *I saw the email, but I never followed it up.* | **follow sth up with sth** *Follow up the letters with a phone call.* → see also FOLLOW-UP[1]

fol·low·er /ˈfɑloʊɚ/ *n.* [C] someone who believes or supports a particular leader, team, or set of ideas: *The governor's followers are eager for him to run again.* | +**of** *The early followers of Jesus were mostly Jews.*

fol·low·ing[1] /ˈfɑloʊɪŋ/ *adj.* **1 the following day/year/chapter etc.** the next day, year, chapter etc. SYN **next** OPP **preceding**: *The following day, he felt much better.* ▶see THESAURUS box at **later[2]** **2 the following sth** used for introducing something, often a list of things, that you are going to say or mention next OPP **preceding**: *Give the following information: name, address, and birth date.* **3 a following wind** TECHNICAL a wind that is blowing in the same direction as a ship, and helps it to move faster

following[2] *prep.* immediately after an event or as a result of it SYN **after**: *There will be time for questions following the lecture.* | *Thousands of refugees left the country following the outbreak of civil war.* ▶see THESAURUS box at **next[1]**

following[3] *n.* **1** [C usually singular] a group of people who support or admire someone such as a performer: *The band has a big following in Europe.* **2 the following** [plural] the people or things that you are going to mention next: *You will need the following: paper, pencil, scissors, glue.*

ˈfollow-on *adj.* [only before noun] done or existing in addition to something or in order to continue something that was done before: *a follow-on program*

ˌfollow-the-ˈleader *n.* [U] **1** a children's game in which one of the players does actions which all the other players must copy **2** if companies or groups play follow-the-leader, they all do something that one of them has done, especially because they are competing

ˈfollow-through *n.* [singular] **1** the continued movement of your arm after you have thrown a ball or hit the ball in tennis, GOLF and other sports **2** the things that someone does in order to complete a plan: *The budget covers not only the main project but the follow-through.*

ˈfollow-up *n.* **1** [C,U] something that is done to make sure that earlier actions have been successful or effective: *We're fairly sure the data is accurate, but we will be doing a follow-up.* | *a follow-up study* **2** [C] a book, movie, article etc. that comes after another one that has the same subject or characters: *Spielberg says he's planning to do a follow-up next year.*

fol·ly /ˈfɑli/ *n. plural* **follies** **1** [C,U] FORMAL a very stupid thing to do: +**of** *the follies of youth* | *In 1914, President Wilson said* ***it would be folly to*** *enter the war.* **2** [C] LITERARY an unusual building that was built in past times as a decoration, not to be used or lived in **3 Follies** used in the name of a theater show that has dancing, singing, and other types of entertainment: *the Greenwich Village Follies*

fo·ment /ˈfoʊmɛnt, foʊˈmɛnt/ *v.* FORMAL **foment war/revolution/unrest etc.** to do something that encourages people to cause a lot of trouble in a society: *The students were accused of fomenting rebellion.* —**fomentation** /ˌfoʊmənˈteɪʃən/ *n.* [U]

fond /fɑnd/ *adj.* **1 be fond of sb** to like someone very much, especially when you have known them for a long time and almost feel love for them: *I'm very fond of Ed.* | *Over the years we've* ***grown*** *very* ***fond of*** *each other.* **2 be fond of sth** to like something, especially something you have liked for a long time: *I'd* ***grown fond of*** *Burlington and it was difficult to leave.* | **be fond of doing sth** *She was fond of reading biographies.* **3 fond memories** a memory that makes you happy when you think of it: *I have fond memories of my first trip to Europe.* **4 sb is fond of doing sth** used to say that someone does something all the time: *My father is fond of giving advice to anyone who will listen.* **5** [only before noun] a fond look, smile, action etc. shows you like someone very much SYN **affectionate**: *We wish* *you a fond farewell.* **6 a fond belief/hope** FORMAL a belief or hope that something will happen, which seems silly because it is very unlikely to happen [**Origin:** 1300–1400 *fonne* **stupid person** (12–16 centuries)] —**fondness** *n.* [U] → see also FONDLY

fon·dle /ˈfɑndl/ *v.* [T] **1** DISAPPROVING to touch someone's body in a sexual way **2** FORMAL to touch someone or something in a gentle way that shows love ►see THESAURUS box at **touch**[1]

fond·ly /ˈfɑndli/ *adv.* **1** in a way that shows you like someone or something very much: *Greta smiled fondly at him.* | *Both sisters spoke fondly of their daredevil brother.* **2 fondly remember/recall** to feel happy when you remember what you like about a person or place: *The brothers fondly recalled the games they played as children.* **3 fondly imagine/believe/hope etc.** FORMAL to believe something that is untrue, hope for something that will probably not happen etc.: *Some people fondly believe that these herbs will cure them.*

fon·due /fɑnˈdu/ *n.* [U] a hot food made of melted cheese or chocolate, into which you DIP small pieces of meat, fruit etc. on the end of a stick or fork

Fon·ga·fa·le /ˈfɔŋgəˌfɑleɪ/ the capital city of Tuvalu

font /fɑnt/ *n.* [C] **1** a set of letters of a particular size and style, used for printing books, newspapers etc. or on a computer screen **2** a stone container for the water used in the ceremony of BAPTISM in a Christian church

food /fud/ S1 W1 *n.* **1** [U] things that people and animals eat, such as vegetables, fruit, meat, rice etc.: *The hotel's food is great, and it's not that expensive.* | *The refugee camps need more food and water.* **2** [C,U] a particular type of food: *I'd never tried Indian food before.* | *fatty foods* | **frozen/canned/packaged etc. food** *Our freezer is full of frozen food.* | *It's a* ***fast food*** (=food in a restaurant that is ready immediately) *restaurant.* | *Tim eats way too much* ***junk food*** (=food that is not healthy for you). | *There's a* ***health food*** (=food that is healthy for you) *store on Lassen Street.* | **cat/dog/fish etc. food** (=food for cats, dogs, fish etc.) **3 food for thought** something that makes you think carefully: *The study on poverty certainly provides food for thought.* [**Origin:** Old English *foda*]

ˌFood and ˈDrug Adminiˌstration, the → see FDA

ˈfood bank *n.* [C] a place that gives food to poor people

food chain

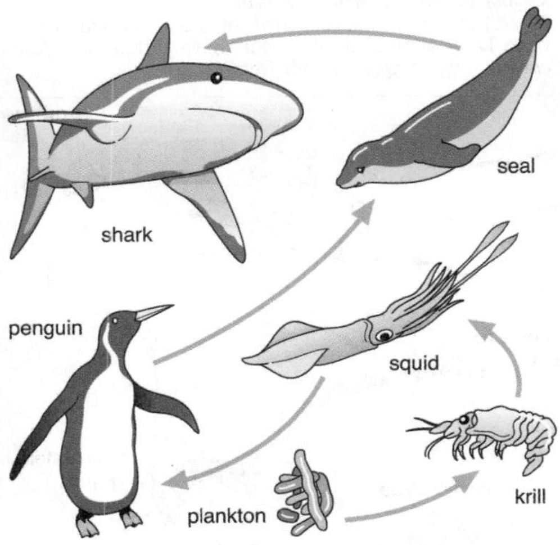

ˈfood chain *n.* **the food chain a)** BIOLOGY animals, insects, and plants considered as a group in which a plant is eaten by an insect or animal, which is then eaten by another animal and so on: *Pollution is having a negative effect on the food chain in the bay.* **b)** HUMOROUS the system in society or an organization in which people at each rank have authority and control over the people in the rank below them: *I was near the bottom of the company food chain.*

ˈfood ˌcoloring *n.* [U] a special colored liquid used to give cookies, FROSTING, and other foods a color

ˈfood court *n.* [C] the area in a shopping MALL where there are many small restaurants

ˈfood drive *n.* [C] an event at a business, school, church etc. at which people can give food in cans to help poor people

ˈfood group *n.* [C] one of the groups that types of food are divided into, such as meat, vegetables, or milk products: *A balanced diet includes foods from all the food groups.*

food·ie /ˈfudi/ *n.* [C] INFORMAL someone who is very interested in cooking and eating good-quality food

ˈfood ˌpoisoning *n.* [U] MEDICINE an illness caused by eating food that contains harmful BACTERIA, in which you usually VOMIT often

ˈfood ˌprocessor *n.* [C] a piece of electrical equipment for preparing food, that cuts or mixes food very quickly

ˈfood ˌservice *n.* [U] the department of a school, hospital etc. whose job is to provide food: *Food service officials say that pizza is kids' favorite food.*

ˈfood stamp *n.* [C] an official piece of paper that the US government gives to poor people so they can buy food

food·stuff /ˈfudstʌf/ *n.* [C usually plural, U] a word meaning "food," used especially when talking about supplying, producing, or selling food: *Prices of most foodstuffs and consumer goods have gone down.*

ˈfood web *n.* [C] SCIENCE all the connected and dependent FOOD CHAINS (=all the animals, plants, insects etc. that are eaten by other animals etc., considered as a group) in a particular place → see picture on page 626

fool[1] /ful/ S3 *n.* [C]
1 STUPID PERSON a stupid person: *What does that fool think he's doing?* | ***Like a fool,*** *I believed every word she said.* | ***I felt like such a fool*** *when I locked my keys in the car.*
2 make a fool of yourself to do something that makes you seem stupid or silly in front of other people: *I met Sylvester Stallone one time and made a complete fool of myself.*
3 make a fool of sb to deliberately try to make someone seem stupid: *Why did you try to make a fool of me in public?*
4 be no fool/be nobody's fool to be difficult to trick or deceive, because you have a lot of experience and knowledge about something: *Claire is no fool – she knows how to take care of herself.*
5 any fool can do sth/any fool knows sth SPOKEN used to say that it is very easy to do something or that it is easy to see that something is true: *Any fool can make a baby, but it takes a real man to raise his children.*
6 ENTERTAINER a man whose job was to entertain a king or other powerful person in past times, by doing tricks, singing funny songs etc.
7 fools rush in (where angels fear to tread) used to say that people are stupid to do something quickly without thinking about it first
8 play/act the fool to behave in a silly or stupid way
9 be living in a fool's paradise FORMAL to feel happy and satisfied, and believe there are no problems, when in fact this is not true
10 send sb on a fool's errand FORMAL to make someone go somewhere or do something for no good reason
11 a fool and his money are soon parted OLD-FASHIONED used to say that stupid people spend money quickly without thinking about it
[**Origin:** 1200–1300 Old French *fol*, from Latin *follis* **bag for blowing air**] → see also APRIL FOOL

fool[2] S3 *v.* **1** [T] to trick or deceive someone: *Even the art experts were fooled.* | **fool sb into doing sth** *Don't be*

F

fooled into buying more insurance than you need. | *For a moment or two she* ***had me fooled*** (=she tricked me into believing her).

SPOKEN PHRASES

2 be fooling yourself to make yourself believe something you know is not really true: *Maybe I was just fooling myself, but I really thought he liked me.* **3 you could have fooled me** said when you do not believe what someone has told you: *"We're doing our best to fix it." "Well, you could have fooled me."* **4 no fooling** used to say that what you have just said is really true, even though it seems unlikely: *She really did ask me to marry her. No fooling!* **5 sb is just fooling** used to say that someone is not serious and is only pretending that something is true: *Don't pay any attention to Henry. He's just fooling.*

fool around *phr. v.* **1** to spend time doing something that you enjoy: *We spent the day fooling around at the beach.* **2** to waste time by doing things that are not important: *Stop fooling around and start studying!* | *It was an intensive training session – the teachers* ***didn't fool around***. **3** to behave in a silly or careless way: **+with** *Stop fooling around with those scissors before you hurt yourself!* **4** to have a sexual relationship with someone who is not your wife, husband, girlfriend, or boyfriend: **+with** *Matt thinks his wife is fooling around with someone.*

fool with sth *phr. v.* INFORMAL to touch or play with something in a careless or irresponsible way that could cause trouble: *Who's been fooling with the radio settings?*

fool[3] *adj.* [only before noun] SPOKEN silly or stupid: *What did you say a fool thing like that for?*

fool·er·y /ˈfuləri/ *n.* [U] OLD-FASHIONED silly or stupid behavior

fool·har·dy /ˈfulˌhɑrdi/ *adj.* taking stupid and unnecessary risks SYN **foolish**: *It was foolhardy to take the plane up alone, with so little flying experience.* —**foolhardiness** *n.* [U]

fool·ish /ˈfulɪʃ/ *adj.* **1** not sensible or wise SYN **stupid**: *a foolish decision* | **it is foolish to do sth** *It's foolish to ride a motorcycle without a helmet.* | **sb is foolish to do sth** *Jack was foolish to give up his job.* | *The place is guarded by dogs who will attack anyone* ***foolish enough*** *to try to get in.* **2** silly, so that people are likely to laugh at you SYN **stupid**: *a foolish grin* | *She* ***felt foolish*** *for running away.* | *The other kids were trying to make me* ***look foolish***. —**foolishly** *adv.*: *She foolishly agreed to go with them.* —**foolishness** *n.* [U]

fool·proof /ˈfulpruf/ *adj.* a foolproof method, plan, system etc. is certain to be successful SYN **infallible**: *There is no foolproof method of winning a bet.*

fools·cap /ˈfulskæp/ *n.* [U] a large size of paper, especially paper used for writing

ˌfool's ˈgold *n.* [U] **1** a kind of yellow metal that exists in some rocks and looks like gold, but is not valuable; iron PYRITE **2** something that you think will be very exciting, very attractive etc. but in fact is not

Foos·ball /ˈfusbɔl/ *n.* [U] TRADEMARK a game played on a special table, in which two players move rods with small figures of SOCCER players on them, in order to hit a ball toward a hole at the end of the table

foot[1] /fʊt/ S1 W1 *n.* [C]

1 BODY PART *plural* **feet** /fit/ BIOLOGY the part of your body that you stand on and walk on: *My foot hurts.* | *Stop tickling my feet!* | *He crept downstairs in his* ***bare feet*** (=without shoes or socks on). | *A dog sat* ***at her feet*** (=on the ground by her feet). | **foot pedal/brake/pump etc.** (=a machine or part of a machine that you operate using your feet) → see also **shuffle your feet** at SHUFFLE[1] (5), **stamp your foot** at STAMP[2] (2)

2 MEASUREMENT WRITTEN ABBREVIATION **ft.** *plural* **feet** or **foot** a unit for measuring length, equal to 12 inches or 0.3048 meters: *He's six feet tall, with blonde hair and a mustache.* | *She's about five foot three* (=five feet and three inches tall). | *a two-foot-long board* | *They were standing a few feet away.* | **square foot/cubic foot** *15,000 square feet of office space*

3 on foot if you go somewhere on foot, you walk there: *The best way to see Yosemite is on foot.*

4 BOTTOM PART the foot of sth the lowest part of something such as a mountain, tree, or set of stairs, or the end of a bed OPP **top**: *Our dog sleeps at the foot of the bed.* | *a stunningly beautiful lake at the foot of the mountain*

5 on your feet a) standing or walking for a long time without having time to sit down: *Waitresses are on their feet all day.* **b)** having enough money again, or successful again after having problems: *Dan got a job, so we should be* ***back on our feet*** *soon.* **c)** feeling better again after being sick and in bed: *It's good to see you on your feet again!* **d)** standing up: *Ellis was hurt but managed to* ***stay on his feet*** (=remain standing).

6 off your feet sitting or lying down, rather than standing or walking: *It was a relief to get off my feet for a while.* | *The doctor told me to* ***stay off my feet*** *for a few days.*

7 set foot in sth to go into a place: *The last time Molly set foot in that house was 26 years ago.*

8 get/jump/rise etc. to your feet to stand up after you have been sitting or after you have fallen: *The fans cheered and jumped to their feet.*

food web

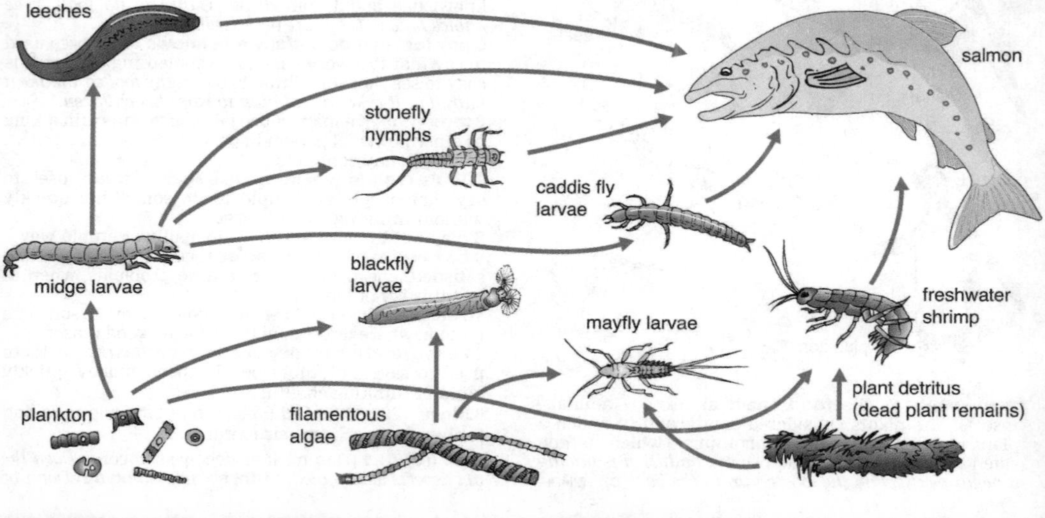

9 put your feet up INFORMAL to relax and rest, especially by sitting with your feet supported on something
10 put your foot down to say very firmly what someone must do or must not do: *I wanted to take a year off before college, but my mother put her foot down.*
11 get your foot in the door to get your first opportunity to work in a particular organization or industry: *I auditioned for a commercial and got it, and that's how I got my foot in the door.*
12 get your feet wet to do something for the first time, especially when you are learning to do something: *You have to be willing to stand up in front of the class and get your feet wet.*
13 put your foot in your mouth to say something that is embarrassing or that upsets someone, because you have not thought carefully about what you are saying
14 feet first a) with your feet coming before the rest of your body as you move somewhere: *Competitors slide down the hill feet first.* **b)** if you do something feet first, you do it quickly and without thinking about the consequences carefully: *She jumped into the argument feet first, without checking her facts first.* **c) leave sth feet first** INFORMAL if someone leaves a place feet first, they are carried out dead
15 have one foot in the grave HUMOROUS to be old: *She sounded like she had one foot in the grave.*
16 be/get under your feet to annoy you by always being in the same place as you and preventing you from doing what you want: *The kids have been under my feet all day long.*
17 get/start off on the wrong foot to start a relationship or activity badly: *The interview got off on the wrong foot and never got any better.*
18 get/start off on the right foot to start a relationship or activity well: *I was pleased to help get things off on the right foot.*
19 put your best foot forward to try to be polite, helpful etc. so that other people will have a good opinion of you from the beginning
20 have/keep both feet on the ground to be sensible and practical in the way you do things: *She's really creative, but she also has her feet firmly on the ground.*
21 not/never put a foot wrong to make no mistakes: *From the beginning to the end of the book, the author never puts a foot wrong.*
22 have a foot in both camps to be friendly with or have sympathy for both sides in an argument or dispute
23 have two left feet INFORMAL to be very CLUMSY and unable to dance well
24 have feet of clay if you realize that someone you admire has feet of clay, you realize they have faults that you did not know about before
25 foot soldier/patrol a soldier or a group of soldiers that walks and does not use horses or vehicles
26 SOCK the part of a sock that covers your foot: *There's a run in the foot of my nylons.*
27 POETRY TECHNICAL a part of a line of poetry in which there is one strong BEAT and one or two weaker ones
28 ON SEA/LAND ANIMAL BIOLOGY a muscle on the lower part of a sea or land animal that has a soft body covered by a hard shell, which it uses to move forward
[**Origin:** Old English *fot*] → see also **get/have cold feet** at COLD[1] (7), **drag your feet** at DRAG[1] (9), **find your feet** at FIND[1] (19), -FOOTED, **(from) head to foot/toe** at HEAD[1] (7), **land on your feet** at LAND[2] (8), **quick on your feet** at QUICK[1] (9), **stand on your own two feet** at STAND[1] (35), **sweep sb off their feet** at SWEEP[1] (10), UNDERFOOT

foot[2] *v.* **foot the bill (for sth)** INFORMAL to pay for something, especially something expensive: *Our insurance company should foot the bill for the damage.*

foot·age /ˈfʊt̬ɪdʒ/ *n.* [U] film that shows a particular event: **+of** *black-and-white footage of the 1936 Olympics*

ˌfoot-and-ˈmouth disˌease *n.* [U] a serious disease that kills cows and sheep

foot·ball /ˈfʊt˺bɔl/ S2 W2 *n.* **1** [U] a game in which two teams of 11 players carry, kick or throw an OVAL ball into an area at the end of a field to win points → see also SOCCER: *college football games* **2** [C] the OVAL ball used in this game **3** [U] BRITISH SOCCER → see also FLAG FOOTBALL, **political football** at POLITICAL (4)

foot·bridge /ˈfʊtˌbrɪdʒ/ *n.* [C] a narrow bridge that people can walk over

foot-drag·ging /ˈfʊtˌdrægɪŋ/ *n.* [U] the act of deliberately being slow to do something: *The police were accused of foot-dragging on the investigation.*

-footed /fʊt̬ɪd/ [in adjectives] SUFFIX **flat-footed/four-footed etc.** having a particular type or number of feet: *a four-footed animal* | *a flat-footed man*

foot·er /ˈfʊt̬ɚ/ *n.* **1 six-footer/eighteen-footer etc.** someone or something that measures six feet tall, eighteen feet long etc.: *The fish must have been an eight-footer, at least!* **2** [C] information at the bottom of a page, especially things such as page numbers that appear on each page in a document

foot·fall /ˈfʊtfɔl/ *n.* [C,U] LITERARY the sound of each step when someone is walking SYN **footstep**

ˈfoot fault *n.* [C] a mistake in tennis when the person who is serving (SERVE) is not standing behind the line

foot·hill /ˈfʊtˌhɪl/ *n.* [C usually plural] one of the low hills at the bottom of a group of high mountains: *the foothills of the Rockies*

foot·hold /ˈfʊthoʊld/ *n.* [C] **1** [usually singular] a position from which you can start to make progress and achieve your aims: *The sport is* ***gaining a foothold*** *in Northern California.* **2** a place where you can safely put your foot when climbing a rock or mountain

foot·ing /ˈfʊt̬ɪŋ/ *n.* **1** [singular] the conditions or arrangements under which something exists or operates: **on a...footing** *The city hopes to start the new year on a stronger financial footing.* | *The law puts women* ***on an equal*** *legal* ***footing*** *with men.* | **a solid/firm footing** *the company's solid footing in the software market* **2** [singular] a firm hold with your feet on a SLIPPERY or dangerous surface: *The boy* ***lost his footing*** *and fell 200 feet down a steep bank.* | *We were struggling to* ***keep our footing*** *on the icy trail.* **3** [C] a base that supports a bridge or structure and fastens it firmly to the ground: *concrete footings*

foot·lights /ˈfʊtlaɪts/ *n.* [plural] a row of lights along the front of the stage in a theater

ˈfoot ˌlocker *n.* [C] a large strong plain box that you can keep your things in, used especially by soldiers

foot·loose /ˈfʊtlus/ *adj.* OLD-FASHIONED able to do what you want and enjoy yourself because you have no responsibilities: *Europe is filled with footloose students every summer.* | *No, I'm not married – still* ***footloose and fancy free!***

foot·man /ˈfʊt˺mən/ *n. plural* **footmen** /-mən/ [C] a male servant in past times who opened the front door, announced the names of visitors etc.

foot·note /ˈfʊt˺noʊt/ *n.* [C] **1** a note at the bottom of the page in a book, that gives more information about something on that page **2** something that is not very important but that is mentioned because it is interesting or helps you understand something: *The event is no more than an interesting historical footnote.*

foot·path /ˈfʊtpæθ/ *n.* [C] a TRAIL

foot·print /ˈfʊtˌprɪnt/ *n.* [C] **1** a mark made by a foot or shoe: *a deer's footprints in the snow* **2** the amount of space that a structure or object such as a building or computer takes up on the ground or on a surface: *a computer with a footprint the size of a yogurt container*

footprint

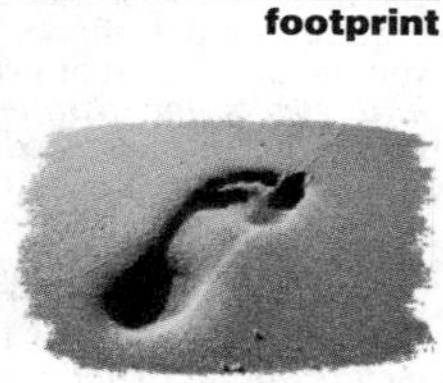

foot·rest /ˈfʊt˺rɛst/ *n.* [C] a part of a chair that you can raise or lower in order to support your feet when you are sitting down

foot·sie /ˈfʊtsi/ *n.* **play footsie** INFORMAL **a)** to secretly touch someone's feet with your feet under a table, especially someone who you are sexually attracted to **b)** to work together and help each other in a dishonest way: +**with** *Blanford continued to play footsie with prominent Republicans.*

foot·step /ˈfʊtstɛp/ *n.* [C] the sound of each step when someone is walking: *He heard someone's footsteps in the hall.* → see also **follow (in) sb's footsteps** at FOLLOW (9)

foot·stool /ˈfʊtstul/ *n.* [C] a low piece of furniture used to support your feet when you are sitting down

foot·wear /ˈfʊt˺wɛr/ *n.* [U] things that people wear on their feet, such as shoes or boots: *athletic footwear*

foot·work /ˈfʊt˺wɚk/ *n.* [U] **1** skillful use of your feet when dancing or playing a sport **2** skillful methods that you use to achieve something: *Government attorneys' **fancy** legal **footwork** has raised doubts about their motives.*

fop /fɑp/ *n.* [C] OLD-FASHIONED, DISAPPROVING a man who is too interested in his clothes and appearance —**foppish** *adj.* —**foppishness** *n.* [U]

F

for[1] /fɚ; *strong* fɔr/ S1 W1 *prep.* **1** intended to be given to or used by a particular person or group: *I have a present for you.* | *Save a piece of cake for Noah.* **2** intended to be used in a particular situation: *Leave the chairs out – they're for the concert.* | *We made cookies for the party.* **3** used to show the purpose of an object, action etc.: *a knife for cutting bread* | *The dining room is just large enough for the table and four chairs.* | ***What** did you **do** that **for*** (=why did you do it?)? | ***What's** this gadget **for*** (=what is its purpose?)? **4** in order to have, do, or get something: *Alison is looking for a job.* | *Several people were standing there, waiting for the bus.* | *Are the Gardiners coming for dinner tonight?* | *You should see a lawyer for some advice.* | *For more information, write to the address below.* | *Let's **go for** a walk.* | *We just play poker **for fun**, not for money.* **5 for sale/rent** used to show that something is available to be sold or rented: *They've just put their house up for sale.* **6** in order to help someone: *I'm babysitting for Jo on Friday night.* | *Let me lift that box for you.* | *The doctor said that there was nothing he could do for her* (=he could not make her well). | ***What can I do for you*** (=used by someone in a store, in order to ask if they can help you)? **7** used to show the time when something is planned to happen: *I made an appointment for October 18th.* | ***It's time for** supper* (=we are going to have supper now). **8** used to express a length of time: *Bake the cake for 40 minutes.* | *I've known Kim for a long time.* | *Can I borrow your drill **for a while**?* | *We've lived here **for years*** (=for quite a long time). → see Word Choice box at DURING, SINCE[1] **9** because of or as a result of something: *The award for the highest sales goes to Pete McGregor.* | *It won't print pictures for some reason.* | **for doing sth** *Mia got a ticket for driving through a red light.* **10** used to state where a person, vehicle etc. is going: *I usually leave for work at 7:30.* | *The plane for Las Vegas took off an hour late.* **11** used to express a distance: *We walked for miles.* | *The mountains went on for as far as the eye could see.* **12** used to show a price or amount: *a check for a hundred dollars* | *He placed an order for 200 copies.* | **for free/nothing** *I got this stereo for nothing from my cousin.* **13 for breakfast/lunch/dinner etc.** used in order to say what you ate or will eat at breakfast, LUNCH, DINNER etc.: *We **had** steaks **for dinner** last night.* | ***"What's for lunch?"** "Chicken noodle soup."* **14 for Christmas/sb's birthday etc.** in order to celebrate Christmas, someone's birthday etc.: *What did you get for your birthday?* | *We went to my grandmother's for Thanksgiving last year.* **15 for now** used to say that a situation is temporary and can be changed later: *Just put the pictures in a box for now.* **16** if you work for a company, play for a team etc., the one mentioned is the one in which you work, play etc.: *Amelia worked for Exxon until last year.* | *He writes for the "Washington Post."* **17 for sb/sth to do sth a)** used when discussing what is happening, what may happen, or what can happen: *The plan is for us to leave on Friday to pick up Joe.* | *It's unusual for it to be so cold in June.* | *There's nothing worse than for a parent to hit a child.* | *The cat is too high in the tree for me to reach her.* **b)** used when you are saying what someone or something is able to do: *It's easy for a computer to keep a record of this information.* | *The dolphin was close enough for me to reach out and touch it.* | *It's too difficult for me to explain.* **c)** used when you are explaining a reason for something: *He must have had some bad news for him to be so quiet.* | *I left my coat for it to be cleaned.* **18** supporting or agreeing with someone or something: *How many people voted for Mulhoney?* | *Please discuss the case for and against nuclear energy.* | *Three cheers for Mr. Sheridan!* | ***I'm all for*** (=I strongly approve of) *getting started right now.* **19** when you consider a particular fact: *It's cold for this time of year.* | *Libby is very tall for her age.* | *For someone who is supposed to have very good taste, Jo wears some strange clothes.* **20** relating to or concerning someone or something: *I'm sure she's the ideal person for the job.* | *Fortunately for Tim, he can swim.* | *Congratulations! I'm really happy for you.* | *Nate has a lot of respect for his teachers.* | *The success rates for each task are given in Table 4.* | **too difficult/long/hot etc. for sb/sth** *You're too quick **for me*** (=used to say that someone does something much more quickly than you do)! | **good/big/warm etc. enough for sb/sth** *Jill isn't old enough for school yet.* | *City life is **not for me**.* **21** meaning or representing something: *What's the Spanish word for "oil"?* | *Red is for stop, green is for go.* **22 for all I know/care** SPOKEN used to say that you really do not know or care: *For all I know, the story just could be true.* | *Their religion doesn't matter; they can howl at the moon for all I care.* **23 for all a)** considering how little: *For all the good I did, I shouldn't have even tried to help.* **b)** considering how much or how many: *For all the plays Ruby's seen, she still hasn't seen "Hamlet."* | *For all his expensive education, Leo doesn't know very much.* **24 for each/every sth** used to say something happens or is true each or every time another thing happens or is true: *For each mistake, you'll lose half a point.* | *For every three people who agree, you'll find five who don't.* **25 I wouldn't do sth for anything** SPOKEN used to emphasize that you definitely would not do something: *I would not go through that again for anything.* **26 I, for one...** SPOKEN used to say what your opinion is or what you will do: *I, for one, believe that many sports stars are not good role models.* | *As a resident, I, for one, will refuse to participate.* **27 for one thing... (and for another)** used when you are giving reasons for a statement you have made: *I'm not going to buy it. For one thing I don't like the color, and for another it's way too expensive.* **28 now for sb/sth** SPOKEN used to introduce a new subject: *Okay, now for the news.* | *Now for the first graders, each one needs a bag lunch.* **29 if it weren't for/if it hadn't been for sb/sth** if something had not happened, or if a situation were different: *If it hadn't been for you, I would not be alive now.* | *If it weren't for Michelle's help, we'd never get this job done.* **30 that's/there's...for you!** SPOKEN **a)** used to say that something is typical of a particular type of thing, especially when you expect that thing to be of low quality: *She won't listen, but I guess that's just teenagers for you.* **b)** used to say that something is the complete opposite of what you were saying: *She didn't even thank me; there's gratitude for you!* **31 be in for it** to be likely to be blamed or punished, or to have something bad happen to you: *The hills are very dry; if we get any more hot winds we could be in for it* (=there could be fires). [**Origin:** Old English] → see also **once and for all** at ONCE[1] (10), **for sure** at SURE[1] (7)

USAGE

Use verbs such as "buy" or "make" without **for** only when you are talking about buying or making something for a person or animal: *He bought a new dish for his dog* or *He bought his dog a new dish.* | *She made a new dress for her daughter* or *She made her daughter a new dress.* If you are talking about buying or making something for an object, you must use **for**: *I bought a new tablecloth for the kitchen table.* Don't say "I bought the table a new tablecloth."

for[2] S1 W2 *conjunction* LITERARY used to introduce the reason for something SYN because: *He found it increasingly difficult to read, for his eyes were failing.*

for·age¹ /ˈfɔrɪdʒ, ˈfɑr-/ v. [I] **1** to go around searching for food or other supplies: +**for** *squirrels foraging for nuts and seeds* **2** to search for something, especially with your hands: +**for** *People foraged in the dump for materials to build with.* —**forager** n. [C]

forage² n. [U] food supplies for horses and cattle

for·ay /ˈfɔreɪ, ˈfɑreɪ/ n. plural **forays** [C] **1** a short attempt at doing a particular job or activity, especially one that is very different from what you usually do: +**into** *an unsuccessful foray into politics* | *She **made** her first **foray** into theater in the 1990s.* **2** a short sudden attack by a group of soldiers, especially in order to get food or supplies SYN raid: +**into** *The soldiers **made** nightly **forays** into enemy territory.* **3** a short trip somewhere in order to get something or do something: +**into** *her **first foray** into the mountains.* —**foray** v. [I]

for·bade /fɚˈbæd/ v. a past tense of FORBID

for·bear¹ /fɔrˈbɛr, fɚ-/ v. *past tense* **forbore** /-ˈbɔr/, *past participle* **forborne** /-ˈbɔrn/ [I] LITERARY to not do something that you could do because you think it is wiser not to SYN refrain from: **forbear to do sth** *She forbore to participate.* | +**from** *He forbore from commenting on my appearance.*

for·bear² /ˈfɔrbɛr/ n. [C] another spelling of FOREBEAR

for·bear·ance /fɔrˈbɛrəns, fɚ-/ n. [U] LITERARY the quality of being patient, having control over your emotions, and being willing to forgive someone

for·bear·ing /fɔrˈbɛrɪŋ/ adj. FORMAL patient and willing to forgive

for·bid /fɚˈbɪd/ v. *past tense* **forbade** /-ˈbæd/ or **forbid**, *past participle* **forbidden** /-ˈbɪdn/, **forbidding** [T] **1** to officially state that something is not allowed, for example because of a law, rule, custom etc. SYN prohibit OPP permit: *At that time, the state law forbade the teaching of evolution.* | **forbid sb from doing sth** *Women are forbidden from going out without a veil.* | **forbid sb to do sth** *Post Office rules forbid employees to accept tips.* | **strictly/expressly/explicitly forbid** *The law strictly forbids racial or sexual discrimination in hiring.*

THESAURUS

not allow/permit/let to say that someone must not do something, and stop him or her doing it: *People are not allowed to sell food or drinks along the parade route.*
ban to officially say that people must not do something or that something is not allowed: *Campfires are banned during the dry season.*
prohibit to say officially that an action is illegal or not allowed: *In the sea near the reef, the use of anchors is prohibited.*
bar to officially prevent someone from doing something: *Firms are barred from doing business with Cuba.*
→ ALLOW

2 God/Heaven forbid SPOKEN said in order to emphasize that you hope that something will not happen: *God forbid you should have an accident.* **3** FORMAL to make it impossible for someone to do something SYN prevent: *Lack of space forbids the listing of all those who contributed.* [**Origin:** Old English *forbeodan*]

for·bid·den /fɚˈbɪdn/ adj. **1** not allowed, especially because of an official rule SYN prohibited: *Alcohol is forbidden in the dormitories.* | *Smoking inside the hospital is **strictly forbidden**.* | **be forbidden to do sth** *a book she was forbidden to read* | **be forbidden from sth** *The union is forbidden from striking.* | ***It is forbidden to** marry someone outside the faith.* **2** a forbidden place is one that you are not allowed to go to: +**to** *The Great Mosque is forbidden to Christians.* **3** a forbidden activity, object etc. is one that people think you should not do, talk about etc., often in a way that makes you more interested: *Sex was a forbidden topic.* | ***forbidden fruit*** (=something you should not have, but that you want)

for·bid·ding /fɚˈbɪdɪŋ/ adj. having a frightening or unfriendly appearance: **forbidding mountain/desert/place etc.** *the dark and forbidding mountains* | *His face was stern and forbidding.* —**forbiddingly** adv.

for·bore /fɔrˈbɔr, fɚ-/ v. the past tense of FORBEAR

for·borne /fɔrˈbɔrn, fɚ-/ v. the past participle of FORBEAR

force¹ /fɔrs/ S2 W1 n.

1 MILITARY [C] a group of people who have been trained to do military or police work: *the Air Force* | *the St. Paul Police Force.* | **armed/miltary/peacekeeping etc. force** *the U.N. peacekeeping force in Bosnia* | ***Rebel forces** are seeking to overthrow the government.*

2 MILITARY ACTION [U] military action used as a way of achieving your aims: *The UN tries to limit **the use of force** in conflicts.* | *Change must come by negotiation, not **by force**.*

3 VIOLENCE [U] violent physical action used to get what you want: *The police **used force** to break up the demonstration.* | *A ten-year-old girl was taken away **by force** outside a local supermarket.* | *They had to use **brute force** to get the door open.*

4 PHYSICAL POWER [U] the amount of physical power with which something moves or hits another thing: +**of** *The force of the explosion shook buildings several blocks away.* | *Waves were hitting the rocks **with** tremendous **force**.*

THESAURUS

force the natural power that something has: *The force of the wind knocked the fence down.*
power the physical strength of something such as an explosion, or the energy produced by a natural force: *the power of the storm* | *Their home is heated by solar power.*
strength the physical quality that makes you strong: *I still can't walk far; I don't have the strength.*

5 NATURAL POWER [C,U] PHYSICS an action or influence on an object that changes its movement or shape: *Centrifugal force can be greater than the force of gravity.*

6 SB/STH THAT INFLUENCES [C] something or someone that has a strong influence or a lot of power: *Mandela was the **driving force** behind the changes* (=the one who made them happen). | **a force for change/good/peace etc.** | *He has emerged as a strong force for political reform.* | *Kessler has made the agency **a force to be reckoned with*** (=an organization with a lot of power and influence). | *Americans have been frightened by job losses and other **forces beyond their control**.*

7 STRONG EFFECT [U] the powerful effect of what someone says or does: *Even after 30 years, the play has lost none of its force.* | *The force of public opinion stopped the highway project.*

8 ORGANIZED GROUP [C] a group of people who have been trained and organized to do a particular job: *the company's sales force* | *the college's teaching force*

9 join/combine forces to join together so that you can deal with a problem, defend yourselves etc.: **join forces to do sth** *Local churches have joined forces to help the homeless.* | +**with** *Workers are joining forces with the students to protest the new bill.*

10 in force a) if a law or a rule is in force, it exists and must be obeyed: *Similar rules are in force at other amusement parks.* | *A curfew **went into force*** (=started to operate) *on May 31.* **b)** in a large group: *The mosquitoes were **out in force** tonight.*

11 the forces of evil/darkness also **dark forces** LITERARY someone or something, especially the Devil, that has a strong bad influence on a person or situation: *a battle against the forces of evil*

12 by/from force of habit because you have always done a particular thing: *Ken puts salt on everything from force of habit.*

13 the forces of nature, **natural forces** things such as wind, rain, or EARTHQUAKES that are caused by nature

14 gale/hurricane force wind an extremely strong wind that does a lot of damage

F

[**Origin:** 1200–1300 Old French, Latin *fortis* **strong**] → see also LABOR FORCE, TASK FORCE, TOUR DE FORCE

force² S2 W1 *v.* [T]
1 MAKE SB DO STH if a person or situation forces you to do something, it makes you do something you do not want to do: *The economy has forced a lot of companies out of business.* | **force sb to do sth** *Nobody's forcing you to get married.* | *The storms forced people to flee their homes.* | **force sb/sth into doing sth** *Illness forced her into canceling the concert.* | **force yourself (to do sth)** *I had to force myself to get up this morning.*

THESAURUS
make to force someone to do something: *I wish there were something I could do to make her quit smoking.*
coerce FORMAL to force someone to do something by threatening him or her: *Her parents tried to coerce her into an arranged marriage.*
compel to force someone to do something: *She felt compelled to resign because of the scandal.*
pressure to try to make someone do something by using influence, arguments, threats etc.: *He was pressured by his parents into joining the family business.*

2 MAKE SB/STH MOVE to make someone or something move in a particular direction or into a different position or place, especially using physical force: *Some idiot forced Laura off the road yesterday.* | **force sb into/out of sth** *Prisoners were forced into concentration camps.* | *He was forced out of his car and taken hostage.* | *Thieves **forced open** a kitchen window.*
3 MAKE STH HAPPEN to make something happen or change, especially more quickly than was planned or expected: *Democrats are trying to force a vote on the issue.* | *The Bears forced three fumbles during the game.* | *Market pressures are sure to force prices down.* | *The governor is trying to **force** the legislature's **hand*** (=make them do something unwillingly or earlier than planned) *on this issue.* | *Time was running out, and I had to **force the issue*** (=make someone make a decision or take action) *with him.*
4 force your way in/out/through etc. to push and use physical force in order to get somewhere: *Four men, wearing masks, forced their way into the house.*
5 OPEN STH to use physical force to open something: **force a door/lock/window** *Firefighters had to force the lock.*
6 force a smile/laugh etc. to make yourself smile, laugh etc. even though you feel upset or annoyed

force sth ↔ **back** *phr. v.* to stop yourself from showing that you are upset or frightened, especially with difficulty: *Janet forced back her tears.*

force sth ↔ **down** *phr. v.* **1** to make yourself eat or drink something, although you do not want it: *I managed to force down a piece of toast.* **2** to make a plane have to land by threatening to attack it

force sth **on/upon** sb *phr. v.* to make someone accept something even though they do not want it: *Many children have piano lessons forced upon them.* | *No man has the right to **force himself upon** a woman* (=make her have sex with him).

force sth ↔ **out of** sb *phr. v.* to make someone tell you something by asking them many times, threatening them etc.: *I wasn't going to tell Matt, but he forced it out of me.*

forced /fɔrst/ *adj.* **1** done because you must do something, not because of any sincere feeling: *The applause seemed forced.* | *a forced smile* **2** done suddenly and quickly, because a situation makes it necessary: *The plane had to make a forced landing in a field.*

ˈforce-feed *v.* **force-fed** [T] to force someone to eat by putting food or liquid down their throat —**force-feeding** *n.* [U]

ˈforce field *n.* [C] PHYSICS an area in space in which a force such as electricity, GRAVITY etc. has an effect: *the Earth's gravitational force field*

force·ful /ˈfɔrsfəl/ *adj.* **1** a forceful person expresses their opinions very strongly and clearly and people are easily persuaded by them SYN **strong**: *Gage is outspoken and forceful.* | *a forceful leader* **2** forceful arguments, reasons etc. are strongly and clearly expressed SYN **powerful**: *He made a forceful denial.* **3** doing things in a determined way so that you are likely to change a situation: *a forceful attempt to change the laws* **4** using physical force —**forcefully** *adv.* —**forcefulness** *n.* [U]

force ma·jeure /ˌfɔrs mɑˈʒɚ/ *n.* [U] LAW unexpected events that prevent you from doing what you intended or promised

for·ceps /ˈfɔrsəps, -sɛps/ *n.* [plural] a medical tool used for picking up, pulling, or holding things

forc·i·bly /ˈfɔrsəbli/ *adv.* **1** using physical force: *The police threatened to forcibly remove the protesters.* **2** in a way that has a strong clear effect SYN **powerfully**: *a forcibly expressed opinion* —**forcible** *adj.*

ford¹ /fɔrd/ *n.* [C] a place in a river that is not deep, so that you can walk or drive across it

ford² *v.* [T] to walk or drive across a river at a place where the water is not deep

Ford /fɔrd,/, **Ger·ald** /ˈdʒɛrəld/ (1913–2006) the 38th President of the U.S.

Ford, Henry (1863–1947) a U.S. businessman and engineer, who established the Ford Motor Company, and developed the idea of the ASSEMBLY LINE for producing cars in large numbers → see picture on page A25

Ford, John (1895–1973) a U.S. movie DIRECTOR known especially for his WESTERNS (=films about the American west in the 19th century)

ˈFord Founˌdation *n.* an organization that gives money and supports programs to improve social conditions and opportunities for education and employment, in the U.S. and other countries

fore¹ /fɔr/ *n.* **to the fore** in a position of importance or influence: *Environmental issues **came to the fore*** (=became important) *in the 1980s.* | *This case has **brought to the fore** a lot of racial tensions.*

fore² *adj.* [only before noun] TECHNICAL the fore parts of a ship, plane, or animal are the parts at the front OPP **aft**

fore³ *interjection* used in the game of GOLF to warn people that you have hit the ball toward them

fore- /fɔr/ *prefix* **1** before: *to forewarn someone* | *forethought* (=careful thinking before you do something) **2** at the front, or in the most important position: *a horse's forelegs* **3** in the most important position: *the factory foreman* (=the person in charge of a group of people) **4** the front part of something: *his strong forearms* (=the lower part of his arms) | *in the foreground* (=in the nearest part of a picture)

fore·arm /ˈfɔrɑrm/ *n.* [C] the lower part of the arm, between the hand and the elbow → see also **forewarned is forearmed** at FOREWARN (2)

fore·bear /ˈfɔrbɛr/ *n.* [C usually plural] FORMAL someone who was a member of your family a long time in the past SYN **ancestor**

fore·bod·ing /fɔrˈboʊdɪŋ/ *n.* [U] a feeling that something bad is going to happen soon: *We waited for news with a **sense of foreboding**.*

fore·cast¹ /ˈfɔrkæst/ *n.* [C] a description of what is likely to happen in the future, based on information you have now SYN **prediction**: *the **weather forecast*** | **sales/profit/earnings etc. forecast** *the company's annual sales forecast*

forecast² *v. past tense and past participle* **forecast** or **forecasted** [T] to make a statement saying what is likely to happen in the future, based on information that you have now SYN **predict**: *Rain has been forecast for this weekend.* | **forecast (that)** *The Federal Reserve Bank forecast that the economy will grow by 2% this year.* ►see THESAURUS box at **predict** [**Origin:** 1400–1500 *fore-* + *cast* **to arrange cleverly** (14–19 centuries)]

fore·cast·er /ˈfɔrkæstɚ/ *n.* [C] someone whose job is

to say what is likely to happen in the future, especially what kind of weather is expected

fore·cas·tle /ˈfoʊksəl, ˈfɔrˌkæsəl/ *n.* [C] TECHNICAL the front part of a ship, where the SAILORS live

fore·close /fɔrˈkloʊz/ *v.* [I] ECONOMICS if a bank forecloses, it takes away someone's property because they have not paid back the money that they borrowed to buy it: +**on** *The mortgage company has threatened to foreclose on their home.* —**foreclosure** /fɔrˈkloʊʒɚ/ *n.* [C,U]

fore·fa·ther /ˈfɔrˌfɑðɚ/ *n.* [C usually plural] **1** the people, especially men, who were part of your family a long time in the past SYN **ancestor**: *None of David's forefathers died in World War I.* **2** someone in the past who did something important that influences your life today: *Two hundred years ago our forefathers established a new nation.*

fore·fin·ger /ˈfɔrˌfɪŋgɚ/ *n.* [C] the finger next to your thumb SYN **index finger**

fore·front /ˈfɔrfrʌnt/ *n.* **1 in/at/to the forefront (of sth)** in a leading position in an important activity whose purpose is to achieve something or develop new ideas: *The department is at the forefront of research into the disease.* **2 in/at the forefront of sb's mind/thoughts etc.** being thought about most or a great deal: *Isaac was always at the forefront of her thoughts.*

fore·go /fɔrˈgoʊ/ *v.* [T] another spelling of FORGO

fore·go·ing /ˈfɔrˌgoʊɪŋ/ *adj., n.* **the foregoing (sth)** FORMAL something that has just been mentioned, read, dealt with etc. SYN **preceding** OPP **following**: *the foregoing examples*

fore·gone con·clu·sion /ˌfɔrgɔn kənˈkluʒən/ *n.* **be a foregone conclusion** if something is a foregone conclusion, it is certain to have a particular result, even though it has not yet happened: *The election result was a foregone conclusion.*

fore·ground /ˈfɔrgraʊnd/ *n.* **1 the foreground** the closest part of a scene in a picture or a photograph OPP **background**: *the figures in the foreground* **2 in/to the foreground** regarded as important and receiving a lot of attention: *Trade issues are currently in the foreground of the talks.*

fore·hand /ˈfɔrhænd/ *n.* [singular] a way of hitting the ball in tennis, with the flat part of your hand facing the direction of the ball OPP **backhand** —**forehand** *adj.*

fore·head /ˈfɔrhɛd, ˈfɔrɪd, ˈfɑrɪd/ *n.* [C] the part of your face above your eyes and below your hair

for·eign /ˈfɑrɪn, ˈfɔrɪn/ S3 W1 *adj.* **1** from or relating to a country that is not your own: *The bus tour goes through seven foreign countries in two weeks.* | *the best foreign-language film* | *Toyota is the leading foreign car company.* **2** [only before noun] involving or dealing with other countries: *The budget calls for cuts in foreign aid.* | *the Chinese Foreign Ministry* **3 be foreign to sb** FORMAL **a)** to seem strange and not familiar to someone SYN **unfamiliar**: *I knew the tune, but the words were foreign to me.* **b)** to not be typical of someone's usual character: *Aggression is completely* ***foreign to*** *his* ***nature.*** **4 foreign body/matter/object** FORMAL something that is inside something else, especially inside someone's body, but should not be there: *Make sure you remove all foreign matter from the wound.* [**Origin:** 1200–1300 Old French *forein*, from Latin *foris* **outside**] —**foreignness** *n.* [U]

ˌforeign afˈfairs *n.* [plural] POLITICS politics, business matters etc. that affect or concern the relationship between your country and other countries

ˌforeign ˈaid *n.* [U] POLITICS money, goods, or military help that one country gives to another country → see also AID: *Millions of dollars were donated in foreign aid.*

ˌforeign ˈdebt *n.* [C] ECONOMICS money that a country owes to another country or a foreign bank

for·eign·er /ˈfɑrənɚ/ *n.* [C] someone who comes from a different country: *About 40 million foreigners visited the U.S. last year.*

> **USAGE**
> It is not polite to call someone from another country a **foreigner**. You should say that someone is "from Canada/Japan/Russia" or use a noun referring to their nationality instead: *Many Norwegians emigrated to the United States around that time.*

ˌforeign exˈchange *n.* **1** [U] ECONOMICS the system of buying and selling foreign money: *the foreign exchange markets* **2** [U] ECONOMICS foreign money, especially money obtained by selling goods to a foreign country: *Coffee is a valuable source of foreign exchange for Uganda.* **3** [C] also **exchange** a program in which people, especially students, travel to another country to work or study for a particular length of time: *a* ***foreign exchange student***

ˌforeign ˈminister *n.* [C] POLITICS a government official who is in charge of a country's FOREIGN AFFAIRS

ˌforeign ˈpolicy *n.* [U] POLITICS a government's decisions, actions, etc. relating to other countries → see also DOMESTIC POLICY: *changes in the U.S. foreign policy in the Middle East*

fore·knowl·edge /ˈfɔrˌnɑlɪdʒ/ *n.* [U] FORMAL knowledge that something is going to happen before it actually does

fore·leg /ˈfɔrlɛg/ *n.* [C] TECHNICAL one of the two front legs of an animal with four legs

fore·lock /ˈfɔrlɑk/ *n.* [C] LITERARY a piece of hair that falls over someone's FOREHEAD

fore·man /ˈfɔrmən/ *n. plural* **foremen** /-mən/ [C] **1** a worker who is in charge of a group of other workers, for example in a factory: *Her father is a retired mining foreman.* **2** LAW the leader of a JURY, who announces the jury's decision in court

Fore·man /ˈfɔrmən/**, George** (1949–) a U.S. BOXER who was world CHAMPION in 1973–1974 and again in 1994–1995

fore·most /ˈfɔrmoʊst/ *adj.* **1** the best or most important in a particular activity SYN **leading** SYN **top**: **foremost authority/expert** *Campbell was the foremost authority on mythology.* | *the world's foremost cellist* **2** the most important idea or thing: *Economic concerns are foremost on many voters' minds.* → see also **first and foremost** at FIRST[2] (6)

fo·ren·sic /fəˈrɛnsɪk, -zɪk/ *adj.* [only before noun] **1** relating to the scientific methods for finding out about a crime: *DNA tests have revolutionized forensic science.* | *the* ***forensic evidence*** **2** relating to arguments and DEBATE: *a politician's forensic skill* [**Origin:** 1600–1700 Latin *forensis* **of a court or forum**] —**forensics** *n.* [U]

fore·or·dain /ˌfɔrɔrˈdeɪn/ *v.* [T usually passive] FORMAL to decide or arrange how something will happen before it actually happens SYN **destine** —**foreordained** *adj.*

fore·per·son /ˈfɔrˌpɚsən/ *n.* [C] the leader of a JURY, who announces the jury's decision in court

fore·play /ˈfɔrpleɪ/ *n.* [U] sexual activity such as kissing and touching the sexual organs, before having sex

fore·run·ner /ˈfɔrˌrʌnɚ/ *n.* [C] **1** someone or something that existed before something similar that developed or came later SYN **predecessor**: +**of** *The league was a forerunner of the NBA.* **2** a sign or warning that something is going to happen: +**of** *Cirrus clouds are usually forerunners of a cold front.*

fore·see /fɔrˈsi/ *v. past tense* **foresaw** /-ˈsɔ/, *past participle* **foreseen** /-ˈsin/ [T] FORMAL to know that something will happen before it happens: *I don't foresee any problems.* | **foresee that** *Few analysts foresaw that oil prices would rise so steeply.* | +**what** *No one could have foreseen what would happen.*

fore·see·a·ble /fɔrˈsiəbəl/ *adj.* **1 for the foreseeable future** for as long as anyone can know what is likely to happen: *There are no plans to change, at least for the foreseeable future.* **2 in the foreseeable future** fairly soon: *There may be water shortages in the forsee-*

able future. **3** foreseeable difficulties, events etc. are ones that you know will happen in the future: *foreseeable dangers*

fore·shad·ow /fɔr'ʃædoʊ/ *v.* [T] to be a sign of something that will happen in the future: *The events in Spain in the 1930s foreshadowed the rise of Nazi Germany.*

fore·shad·ow·ing /fɔr'ʃædoʊɪŋ/ *n.* [U] the method of giving signs that suggest what will happen later in a story, or the signs themselves: *There was a lot of foreshadowing in the movie, so I wasn't surprised when the main character shot his wife.*

fore·short·ened /fɔr'ʃɔrt¬nd/ *adj.* objects, places etc. that are foreshortened appear to be smaller, shorter, or closer together than they really are —**foreshorten** *v.* [T]

fore·sight /'fɔrsaɪt/ *n.* [U] the ability to imagine what will probably happen, and to consider this in your plans for the future: *a man of intelligence and foresight* | **foresight to do sth** *At least she'd **had the foresight** to take extra food.* | *the **lack of foresight** shown by city planners* → see also FORETHOUGHT

F

fore·skin /'fɔr,skɪn/ *n.* [C] a loose fold of skin covering the end of a man's PENIS

for·est /'fɔrɪst, 'fɑr-/ S3 W2 *n.* [C,U] **1** a very large area of land that is covered with trees SYN **woodland**: *Much of Scandinavia is covered in dense pine forest.* | *a forest fire* | *spring flowers on the **forest floor*** (=the ground) ▸see THESAURUS box at **tree** → see picture on page A31

THESAURUS

the woods a large area with many trees
woodland an area of land that is covered with trees
forest a very large area with a lot of trees growing closely together
rain forest a tropical forest with tall trees, in an area where it rains a lot
jungle a tropical forest with trees and large plants

2 not see the forest for the trees to not notice what is important about something because you give too much of your attention to small details [**Origin:** 1200–1300 Old French, Latin *foris* **outside** (because it was outside the main fenced area of woods)]

fore·stall /fɔr'stɔl/ *v.* [T] FORMAL to prevent an action or situation by doing something first SYN **prevent**: *The National Guard was sent in to forestall any trouble.*

for·est·er /'fɔrəstɚ/ *n.* [C] someone who works in a forest taking care of, planting, and cutting down the trees

,forest 'ranger *n.* [C] someone whose job is to protect or manage a forest owned by the government

for·est·ry /'fɔrəstri/ *n.* [U] the science and skill of taking care of and managing the use of forests

'Forest ,Service, the an organization that is responsible for taking care of forests in the U.S.

fore·taste /'fɔrteɪst/ *n.* **be a foretaste of sth** FORMAL to be a sign of something that is likely to happen in the future, especially something that is more important or impressive: *The violence on the streets was only **a foretaste of what** was to come.*

fore·tell /fɔr'tɛl/ *v.* **foretold** /-'toʊld/ [T] to say what will happen in the future, especially by using special magic powers SYN **predict**

fore·thought /'fɔrθɔt/ *n.* [U] careful thought or planning before you do something: *A long backpacking trip requires a lot of forethought.* → see also FORESIGHT

fore·told /fɔr'toʊld/ *v.* the past tense and past participle of FORETELL

for·ev·er /fə'rɛvɚ, fɔ-/ S1 W2 *adv.* **1** for all future time SYN **always**: *I'll remember you forever.* | *You can't avoid him forever, you know.* | *Many valuable works of art were lost forever.* ▸see THESAURUS box at **always** **2** SPOKEN for a very long time: *That ice cream has been in the freezer forever.* | *She **takes forever*** (=takes a very long time) *to get ready to go anywhere.* | *The meeting seemed to last **forever and a day*** (=a very long time). **3 go on forever** to be extremely long or large: *The train just seemed to go on forever.* **4 be forever doing sth** LITERARY to do something often or without stopping, sometimes in an annoying way: *Mama was forever telling stories of her childhood.* **5 forever and ever** a phrase meaning "forever," used especially in stories

for·ev·er·more /fə,rɛvɚ'mɔr/ *adv.* LITERARY forever

fore·warn /fɔr'wɔrn/ *v.* [T often passive] **1** to warn someone about something dangerous or bad before it happens SYN **warn**: **forewarn sb of/about/against sth** *We'd been forewarned about the dangers of traveling at night.* | ***Be forewarned** – it's not an easy hike.* **2 forewarned is forearmed** SPOKEN used to say that if you know about something before it happens, you can prepare for it —**forewarning** *n.* [C,U]

fore·went, forwent /fɔr'wɛnt/ *v.* past tense of FORGO

fore·wom·an /fɔr,wʊmən/ *n.* [C] **1** a woman who is in charge of a group of other workers, for example in a factory **2** LAW a woman who is the leader of a JURY and who announces the jury's decision in court

fore·word /'fɔrwɚd/ *n.* [C] ENG. LANG. ARTS a short piece of writing at the beginning of a book that introduces the book or the person who wrote it SYN **preface** → see also AFTERWORD

for·feit¹ /'fɔrfɪt/ *v.* [T] to give something up or have it taken away from you, because of a law or rule: *Convicted criminals **forfeit the right** to vote.* —**forfeiture** /'fɔrfɪtʃɚ/ *n.* [U]

forfeit² *n.* [C,U] something that is taken away from you or that you give up, because you have broken a law or rule: *The Dorsey High football team was declared the winner by forfeit* (=the other team broke a rule and had to give up the game). [**Origin:** 1200–1300 Old French *forfet*, past participle of *forfaire* **to do a crime**]

forfeit³ *adj.* **be forfeit** LAW to be legally or officially taken away from you as a punishment

for·gave /fɚ'geɪv/ *v.* the past tense of FORGIVE

forge¹ /fɔrdʒ/ *v.* **1** [T] to illegally copy something, for example a document, a painting, or money, to make people think that it is real: *Someone stole my credit card and forged my signature.* | *a forged passport* ▸see THESAURUS box at **copy²** **2** [T] to develop a strong relationship with other people, groups, or countries: **forge a relationship/alliance/links etc.** *He has forged a strong relationship with his own daughter.* | *The program will forge closer ties between schools and the workplace.* **3** [T] to produce or make something, especially after a long time or a lot of discussion: *Women engineers have to forge their careers in a field dominated by men.* **4** [I always + adv./prep.] to move somewhere or continue doing something in a steady determined way: **+through** *He forged through the biting, blinding snow.* | **+on** *Baker forged on, asking yet another question.* **5** [T] to make something from a piece of metal by heating the metal and shaping it

forge ahead *phr. v.* **1** to make progress, especially quickly: *The company has forged ahead with its plans.* **2** to move forward in a strong and powerful way

forge² *n.* [C] **1** a place where metal is heated and shaped into objects **2** a large piece of equipment that produces high temperatures, used for heating and shaping metal objects

forg·er /'fɔrdʒɚ/ *n.* [C] someone who illegally copies documents, money, paintings etc., to try to make people think they are real

for·ger·y /'fɔrdʒəri/ *n.* *plural* **forgeries** **1** [C] a document, painting, or piece of paper money that has been copied illegally SYN **fake**: *An art dealer insisted that the portrait is a forgery.* **2** [U] the crime or act of copying official documents, money etc. ▸see THESAURUS box at **crime**

for·get /fɚ'gɛt/ S1 W1 *v.* *past tense* **forgot** /-'gɑt/, *past participle* **forgotten** /-'gɑt¬n/, **forgetting**
1 FACTS/INFORMATION [I,T] to not remember facts, information, or people or things from the past: *I've forgotten*

her name. | These events will never be forgotten. | As soon as I stood up to speak, I forgot everything I'd meant to say. | +**(that)** *Don't forget that Linda's birthday is on Tuesday.* | +**about** *I'd completely forgotten about our bet until Bill reminded me.* | +**how/what/when/why etc.** *Most adults seem to forget what it's like to be a teenager.*
2 STH YOU SHOULD DO [I,T] to not remember to do something that you should do: *I'd better put that on the calendar so I don't forget.* | **forget to do sth** *Someone's forgotten to turn off their headlights.* | +**about** *He said he'd call me, but he forgot about it.* | **forget (that)** *Dan forgot that he was supposed to pick up the kids after school.* | *Let me get your phone number, **before I forget*** (=forget to get it). | *I was supposed to meet them there, but I **forgot all about** it.*
3 LEAVE STH BEHIND [T] to not remember to bring something with you that you intended to bring: *"Why did Carol come back?" "She forgot her purse."* | ***Don't let me forget** my sunglasses* (=remind me to bring my sunglasses).
4 STOP THINKING ABOUT STH [I,T] to stop thinking, worrying, or caring about someone or something: *Forget him, he's not worth it.* | **+ (that)** *After a while, you forget you're wearing contact lenses.* | +**about** *Forget about fashion, just keep yourself warm.* | *Once they have money, some people forget about all their old friends.*
5 STOP A PLAN [I,T] to stop planning to do or get something, because it is not possible or sensible: **forget doing sth** *If you don't finish your homework, you can forget going out this weekend.* | +**about** *You can forget about getting tickets – they're sold out.* | *If you're in a bad mood, **forget it**; don't try and train your dog then.*
6 forget yourself LITERARY to do something stupid or embarrassing, especially by losing control of your emotions: *Veronica was worried that she might forget herself and confess her true feelings.*
[**Origin:** Old English *forgietan*]

SPOKEN PHRASES

7 don't forget a) used to remind someone to do something: *Don't forget, we have to be there by five o'clock.* | **don't forget to do sth** *Don't forget to call Steve today, okay?* **b)** used to remind someone about an important fact or detail that they should consider: *Don't forget that you'll have to pay interest on the loan.* **c)** used to remind someone to take something with them: *Don't forget your lunch – it's on the counter.*
8 forget it a) used to tell someone that something is not important and they do not need to worry about it: *"Here, let me pay you back." "No, forget it."* **b)** used to tell someone to stop asking or talking about something, because it is annoying you: *I'm not buying you that bike, so just forget it.* **c)** used when someone asks you what you just said and you do not want to repeat it: *"What'd you say?" "Nothing, just forget it."* **d)** also **forget that** used to tell someone that you refuse to do something or that it will be impossible to do something: *"Can I borrow $25?" "Forget it!"* | *Drive to the airport in this snow? Forget that!* **9 I forget** NONSTANDARD used when you cannot remember a particular detail about something: *How old is Kristen again? I forget.* | *You know that guy we met last week – I forget his name.* | **I forget what/how/where etc.** *I forget what he said, but she got really embarrassed.* **10 I'll never forget** used to say that you will always remember something from the past, because it was sad, funny, enjoyable etc.: *I'll never forget the look on Ben's face!* | *I'll never forget that summer.* **11 ...and don't you forget it** used to remind someone angrily about something important that should make them behave differently: *I'm your father, and don't you forget it!*
12 Aren't you forgetting (to do) sth? used to tell someone that they have not remembered something important: *Aren't you forgetting something? You were supposed to help me clean the house today.* **13 forget that** used to tell someone to ignore what you have just said because it is not correct, important etc.: *Then mix a cup of milk, no, forget that, a half a cup of milk.*

for·get·ful /fɚˈgɛtfəl/ *adj.* often forgetting things: *My grandfather is getting more forgetful.* —**forgetfully** *adv.* —**forgetfulness** *n.* [U]

forˈget-me-ˌnot *n.* [C] a small plant with pale blue flowers

for·get·ta·ble /fɚˈgɛt̬əbəl/ *adj.* not very interesting or good: *a completely forgettable movie*

for·giv·a·ble /fɚˈgɪvəbəl/ *adj.* if something bad is forgivable, you can understand how it happened and you can easily forgive it

for·give /fɚˈgɪv/ *v. past tense* **forgave** /-ˈgeɪv/, *past participle* **forgiven** /-ˈgɪvən/ [I,T] **1** to stop blaming someone or being angry with them, although they have done something wrong: *Years later, Deanna was finally able to forgive her father.* | **forgive sb for (doing) sth** *I can't forgive him for what he said.* | *He can't forgive her for leaving him.* | **forgive sb sth** *Lord, please forgive us our sins.* | *If anything happened to the kids **I'd never forgive myself**.* | *"I'm sorry." "That's okay, **you're forgiven*** (=used to say you are not angry with someone)." | *Maybe you can **forgive and forget*** (=forgive someone and behave as if they had never done anything wrong), *but I can't.* **2 forgive a loan/debt** if a country or organization forgives a LOAN, it says that the money does not have to be paid back SYN **write off**: *The U.S. has forgiven the country's $42 million debt.* **3 forgive me** SPOKEN used when you are going to say or ask something that might seem impolite or offensive, and you want it to seem more polite: ***Forgive me, but** that's not exactly a new idea.* | ***Forgive me for saying so**, but yellow doesn't look good on you.* **4 sb can be forgiven for thinking/wondering/feeling sth** used to say that it is easy to understand why someone would think, believe, or do something: *You could be forgiven for thinking it was a joke.* [**Origin:** Old English *forgifan*]

for·give·ness /fɚˈgɪvnɪs/ *n.* [U] the act of forgiving someone: **beg/pray/ask for (sb's) forgiveness** *He confessed and begged her forgiveness.*

for·giv·ing /fɚˈgɪvɪŋ/ *adj.* **1** willing to forgive: *My father was a kind and forgiving man.* **2** if something is forgiving, it does not matter if you make small mistakes with it: *This recipe is very forgiving.*

for·go, **forego** /fɔrˈgoʊ/ *v. past tense* **forwent** /-ˈwɛnt/, *past participle* **forgone** /-ˈgɔn/ [T] FORMAL to not do or have something, especially something enjoyable: *Council members were asked to forgo their pay raises.*

for·got /fɚˈgɑt/ *v.* the past tense of FORGET

for·got·ten¹ /fɚˈgɑtˀn/ *v.* the past participle of FORGET

forgotten² *adj.* [usually before noun] relating to something that people have forgotten about or do not pay much attention to anymore: *a song that is a forgotten gem*

fork¹ /fɔrk/ S2 *n.* [C] **1** a tool used for picking up and eating food, with a handle and three or four points: *knives, forks, and spoons* **2** a place where a road or river divides into two or more parts, or one of the parts it divides into: *Turn left at the fork in the road.* | *the middle fork of the Klamath River* **3** a PITCHFORK **4** the parallel metal bars between which the front wheel of a bicycle or MOTORCYCLE is attached [**Origin:** Old English *forca*, from Latin *furca*] → see also TUNING FORK

fork² *v.* **1** [I] if a road, path, or river forks, it divides into two parts SYN **divide** **2 fork left/right** to travel toward the left or right part of a road when it divides into two parts **3** [T] to pick up, carry, or turn something over using a fork: *Anna forked some more potatoes onto her plate.*

fork sth ↔ **over/out** *phr. v.* INFORMAL to spend a lot of money on something because you have to: *A customer forked over his $25 membership fee.* | +**for/on** *He forked out $150 on tickets for the game.*

forked /fɔrkt/ *adj.* **1** having one end divided into two or more parts: *Snakes have forked tongues.* **2 speak with forked tongue** also **have a forked tongue** an expression meaning to tell lies, which may be considered offensive

ˌforked ˈlightning *n.* [U] lightning that looks like a line of light that divides into several smaller lines near the bottom → see also HEAT LIGHTNING

fork·lift /ˈfɔrklɪft/ also **ˈforklift ˌtruck** *n.* [C] a small vehicle with special equipment on the front for lifting and moving heavy things, for example in a factory

for·lorn /fɚˈlɔrn, fɔr-/ *adj.* LITERARY **1** sad and lonely: *A forlorn line of refugees stood near the truck.* **2** a place or thing that is forlorn seems empty and sad, and is often in bad condition: *The banners and ribbons looked forlorn in the rain.* **3** [only before noun] a forlorn hope, attempt, struggle etc. is not going to be successful: *We continued negotiating in the* ***forlorn hope*** *of finding a peace formula.* [**Origin:** Old English, past participle of *forleosan* **to lose**]

form¹ /fɔrm/ S1 W1 *n.*

1 TYPE [C] a particular type of something that exists in many different types SYN **kind**: **+of** *a rare form of cancer* | *Swimming is a great form of exercise.* | *Please bring two forms of identification, such as a passport or driver's license.*

2 WAY STH IS/APPEARS [C] the way in which something exists or appears: *We oppose racism in all its forms.* | *Vitamin C comes* ***in*** *tablet or liquid* ***form.*** | *Children help the family* ***in the form of*** *chores.* | *The project* ***took the form of*** *a math book written by the kids for younger students.*

3 DOCUMENT [C] an official document with spaces where you write information, especially about yourself: *The nurse asked her to sign the consent form.* | *a college application form* | ***Fill out the*** *order* ***form*** (=write your address etc. on the form) *and send it back with your check.*

4 SHAPE [C] a shape SYN **figure**: *the ideal female form* | *Dark forms seemed to hide behind the trees.* | *The main staircase was* ***in the form of*** *a large "S."*

5 ART/LITERATURE [U] ENG. LANG. ARTS the structure of a work of art or piece of writing, rather than the ideas it expresses or events it describes: *Writers such as Henry James are concerned with form as well as content.* | *The story is told* ***in the form of*** *a ship's log.*

6 PERFORMANCE [U] how well a sports person, team, musician etc. is performing: *Johnson is far from his past form* (=he is not playing, running etc. as well as he did in the past). | **in good/fine form** *The band was in good form that night.*

7 bad form FORMAL OR HUMOROUS behavior that is not socially acceptable: *It's bad form to talk about money.*

8 GRAMMAR [C] ENG. LANG. ARTS a way of writing or saying a word that shows its number, tense etc. For example, "was" is a past form of the verb "to be."

9 take form a) to begin to exist or develop SYN **take shape**: *An idea started to take form.* **b)** to start to become a particular shape SYN **take shape**: *Slowly the building began to take form.*

10 OBJECT GIVING A SHAPE [C] an object that makes something have a particular shape: *Pour the cement into the wooden form.*

[**Origin:** 1200–1300 Old French *forme*, from Latin *forma*] → see also **not in any way, shape, or form** at WAY¹ (61)

form² S2 W1 *v.*

1 START TO EXIST [I,T often passive] to start to exist, or make something start to exist, especially as the result of a natural process: *The rocks were formed more than 4 billion years ago.* | *Aspirin stops heart attacks by preventing blood clots from forming.* | *Ice was already forming on the roads.*

2 SHAPE/LINE [I,T, linking verb] to come together in a particular shape or a line, or to make something have a particular shape: *Long lines formed outside the ticket offices.* | *Our house and the barn form a big "L."* | **form sth into sth** *Form the dough into a ball, then roll it out.*

3 ESTABLISH [T] to start a new organization, government, country etc. SYN **establish**: *The United Nations was formed in 1945.* | *IBM formed an alliance with Lotus, a software maker.*

4 BE PART OF [linking verb] to be the thing, or one of the things, that makes up something else: *Newton's theories* ***form the basis of*** *modern mathematics.* | *Rice* ***forms*** *the most important* ***part of*** *their diet.* | *The Rio Grande forms the boundary between Texas and Mexico.*

5 form an opinion/impression/idea to use the information that you have in order to develop or reach an opinion or idea: *During the trial, jurors form an opinion as to the defendant's guilt or innocence.*

6 RELATIONSHIP [T] to establish and develop a relationship with someone: **form a relationship/attachment/bond etc.** *Autistic children have difficulty forming close relationships.* | *The two girls have formed a close friendship.*

7 MAKE/PRODUCE [T] to make something by combining two or more parts: *In English the past tense is usually formed by adding "ed."* | *The two chemicals combine to form acid rain.*

8 INFLUENCE [T] to have a strong influence on how someone's character develops and the type of person they become: *Events in early childhood help to form our personalities in later life.*

for·mal¹ /ˈfɔrməl/ S3 W3 *adj.*

1 OFFICIAL [usually before noun] made or done officially or publicly OPP **informal**: *On July 19th a formal declaration of war was made.* | *They filed a formal complaint.* | *a formal announcement*

2 formal education/training/qualification education in a subject or skill that you get in school rather than by practical experience: *My grandfather had little formal education.*

3 BEHAVIOR formal behavior is very polite, and is used in official or important situations, or with people you do not know well OPP **informal**: *His parents are very formal.* | *Classrooms have become less formal.*

4 LANGUAGE ENG. LANG. ARTS formal language or writing is used for official or serious situations OPP **informal**: *a formal letter* | *What should I call your mom? "Mrs. Dunlap" seems too formal.*

5 EVENT/OCCASION a formal event is important, and people who go to it wear special clothes and behave very politely: *He was dressed for a* ***formal occasion.*** | *a formal dance*

6 CLOTHES formal clothes, such as a TUXEDO or long dress, are worn to formal events OPP **informal** OPP **casual**: *men's formal wear*

7 ORGANIZED done in a very organized way OPP **informal**: *The class includes formal lectures as well as field trips.*

8 GARDEN/PARK a formal garden, park, or room is arranged in a very orderly way: *Paris has a number of beautiful formal parks.* → see also FORMALLY

formal² *n.* [C] **1** a dance at which you have to wear formal clothes SYN **ball**: *the school's winter formal* **2** an expensive and usually long dress that women wear on formal occasions

ˌformal aˈmendment *n.* [U] LAW POLITICS the process of officially changing a part of the Constitution, rather than just choosing to understand it in a new way → see also INFORMAL AMENDMENT

for·mal·de·hyde /fɚˈmældəˌhaɪd, fɔr-/ *n.* [U] CHEMISTRY a strong-smelling gas that can be mixed with water and used for preserving things, especially dead animals or body parts that are examined in science

ˌformal ˈdress *n.* [U] clothes worn for formal social occasions, especially TUXEDOS for men and long dresses for women

for·ma·lin /ˈfɔrməlɪn/ *n.* [U] a liquid made by mixing formaldehyde and water, used for preserving things such as dead animals or body parts that are examined in science

form·al·ism /ˈfɔrməˌlɪzəm/ *n.* [U] ENG. LANG. ARTS a style or method in art, religion, or science that pays a lot of attention to rules and correct forms of something, rather than to meaning —**formalist** *n., adj.*

for·mal·i·ty /fɔrˈmæləṭi/ *n. plural* **formalities** **1** [C] something formal or official that you must do as part of an activity or process: *The couple will complete the adoption formalities this weekend.* | **just/merely/purely a formality** *We've already decided to hire you; the inter-*

view is just a formality. **2** [U] careful attention to polite behavior and language in formal situations: *The after-class meetings didn't have the formality of a classroom.*

for·mal·ize /ˈfɔrməˌlaɪz/ *v.* [T] to make a plan, decision, or idea official, especially by deciding and clearly describing all the details: *The contracts must be formalized within a month.* —**formalization** /ˌfɔrmələˈzeɪʃən/ *n.* [U]

for·mal·ly /ˈfɔrməli/ *adv.* **1** officially OPP **informally**: *Taiwan formally calls itself the Republic of China.* **2** in a polite way: *Mr. Takaki bowed formally to each guest in turn.*

for·mat¹ /ˈfɔrmæt/ Ac S3 *n.* [C] **1** the way in which something such as a computer document, television show, or meeting is organized or arranged: *The interview was written in a question and answer format.* **2** the size, shape, design etc. in which something such as a book or magazine is produced: *a large-format book of photographs* **3** the type of equipment that a VIDEO, music recording, or piece of computer SOFTWARE is designed to use: *a video camera using an 8mm format*

format² Ac *v.* **formatted**, **formatting** [T] **1** COMPUTERS to organize the space on a computer DISK so that information can be stored on it **2** to arrange a book, page etc. according to a particular design or plan: *a better way to format your spreadsheets* —**formatted** *adj.* —**formatting** *n.* [U]

for·ma·tion /fɔrˈmeɪʃən/ *n.* **1** [U] the process of starting a new organization or group: *the formation of a community environmental group* **2** [U] the process by which something develops into a particular thing or shape: *Astronomers were able to observe a galaxy still in the process of formation.* | +**of** *Burning plastics were responsible for the formation of toxic smoke.* **3** [C] the way in which a group of things are arranged to form a pattern or shape: *The players lined up in a T formation.* **4 in formation** if a group of planes, ships, soldiers etc. are moving in formation, they are marching, flying etc. in a particular order or pattern: *The planes were flying in formation.* **5** [C] something that is formed in a particular shape, or the shape in which it is formed: *the natural rock formations of Bryce Canyon* **6** [C,U] society, politics etc. seen as a system of practices and beliefs: **social/political/cultural etc. formation** *the history of American social formations*

form·a·tive /ˈfɔrmət̬ɪv/ *adj.* [only before noun] having an important influence on the way something or someone develops: *The plan is still in a* ***formative stage.*** | *The Marines were a formative experience for Bernie.* | *Weiss spent her* ***formative years*** (=the time when she was growing up) *in Italy.*

for·mer¹ /ˈfɔrmɚ/ *adj.* [only before noun] **1** having a particular position in the past SYN **ex-**: *her former husband* | *an adviser to former President Clinton* **2** happening or existing before, but not now: *Canada is a former British colony.* | *Their farm has been reduced to half its former size.* ►see THESAURUS box at **last¹** **3 sb's/sth's former self** what someone or something was like before they were changed by age, illness, trouble etc.: *She seems more like her former self.* | *So many people had moved away that the town was just* ***a shadow of its former self*** (=much less lively, exciting etc. than it used to be). **4 former times/years** the past: ***In former times,*** *Latin was spoken by all educated men.*

former² *n.* **the former** FORMAL the first of two people or things that are mentioned OPP **latter**: *Of the two possibilities, the former seems more likely.*

for·mer·ly /ˈfɔrmɚli/ *adv.* in earlier times SYN **previously**: *Peru was formerly ruled by the Spanish.* | *Churkin, 43, was formerly a deputy foreign minister.* | *"Voyagers" is a 70-year-old program* ***formerly known as*** *"Indian Guides."*

ˈform-fitting *adj.* form-fitting clothes fit closely around the body

For·mi·ca /fɔrˈmaɪkə/ *n.* [U] TRADEMARK strong plastic made in thin sheets and fastened to the top of tables, COUNTERS etc.

for·mic ac·id /ˌfɔrmɪk ˈæsɪd/ *n.* [U] an acid used especially for coloring cloth and making leather

for·mi·da·ble /ˈfɔrmədəbəl, fɔrˈmɪdə-/ *adj.* **1** very powerful or impressive: *a formidable opponent* | *Russia still has a formidable nuclear arsenal.* **2** difficult to deal with and needing a lot of effort or skill: *They face the formidable task of working out a peace plan.* [**Origin:** 1300–1400 Latin *formidabilis*, from *formido* **fear**] —**formidably** *adv.*

form·less /ˈfɔrmlɪs/ *adj.* without a definite shape or idea: *a child's formless fears* —**formlessly** *adv.* —**formlessness** *n.* [U]

ˈform ˌletter *n.* [C] a standard letter that is sent to a number of people

for·mu·la /ˈfɔrmyələ/ Ac *n. plural* **formulas** or **formulae** /-li/ **1** [C, usually singular] a method or set of principles that you use to solve a problem or to make sure that something is successful: *the proven formula of investing money to make money* | +**for** *A sensible diet and plenty of exercise is the formula for weight loss.* | *O'Brien has no* ***magic formula*** (=a method that is certain to work) *for success, other than hard work.* | *a comedy with a* ***winning formula*** (=a successful formula) **2** [C] MATH a series of numbers or letters that represent a mathematical or scientific rule: +**for** *the formula for calculating distance* **3** [C] a list of the substances used to make a medicine, FUEL, drink etc., showing the amounts of each substance that should be used: *Coca-Cola's patented formula* **4** [U] a liquid food for babies that is similar to a woman's breast milk **5** [C] a set of words that is familiar to everyone and that seems meaningless or insincere: *a speech full of formulas and clichés*

F

for·mu·la·ic /ˌfɔrmyəˈleɪ-ɪk/ *adj.* FORMAL, DISAPPROVING containing or made from ideas or expressions that have been used many times before and are therefore not very new or interesting: *a formulaic mystery novel*

ˌFormula ˈOne *n.* [U] a type of car racing in very fast cars with powerful engines

for·mu·late /ˈfɔrmyəˌleɪt/ Ac *v.* [T] **1** to develop something such as a plan or set of rules, and decide all the details of how it will be done: **formulate a policy/plan/strategy etc.** *Carville helped formulate the campaign strategy.* | **formulate a theory/hypothesis/idea etc.** *He had formulated a theory on the relation of your body type to your personality.* **2** to think carefully about what you want to say, and say it clearly: *Jackie paused to formulate her reply.* **3** to make something using particular amounts of different substances: *The gasoline is formulated to burn more cleanly, producing less pollution.* —**formulation** /ˌfɔrmyəˈleɪʃən/ *n.* [C,U]

for·ni·cate /ˈfɔrnəˌkeɪt/ *v.* [I] LITERARY, DISAPPROVING to have sex with someone you are not married to —**fornication** /ˌfɔrnəˈkeɪʃən/ *n.* [U]

for·sake /fɚˈseɪk, fɔr-/ *v. past tense* **forsook** /-ˈsʊk/ *past participle* **forsaken** /-ˈseɪkən/ [T] **1** FORMAL to stop doing or having something that you enjoy or which is good SYN **give up**: *These men and women have forsaken retirement to help at local schools.* **2** LITERARY to leave someone, especially when you should stay because they need you SYN **abandon** SYN **desert**: *He felt that all his friends had forsaken him.* **3** to leave a place, especially when you do not want to: *John forsook the farm for the unknown life of the city.* → see also GODFORSAKEN

for·sooth /fɚˈsuθ/ *adv.* OLD USE certainly

For·ster /ˈfɔrstɚ/, **E.M.** (1879–1970) a British writer of NOVELS

for·swear /fɔrˈswɛr/ *v. past tense* **forswore** /-ˈswɔr/, *past participle* **forsworn** /-ˈswɔrn/ [T] LITERARY to stop doing something, or to promise that you will stop doing something SYN **renounce**: *Both sides agreed to forswear all acts of terrorism.*

for·syth·i·a /fɚˈsɪθiə/ *n.* [C,U] a bush that is covered with bright yellow flowers in early spring

fort /fɔrt/ *n.* [C] **1** a strong building or group of buildings used by soldiers or an army for defending an important place: *a fort in the Dakota territory* **2** a permanent place where an army lives or trains: *soldiers from Fort Bragg* [**Origin:** 1400–1500 French, Latin *fortis* **strong**] → see also **hold the fort** at HOLD[1] (31)

forte[1] /fɔrt, ˈfɔrteɪ/ *n.* [C] **1 be sb's forte** to be something that someone is good at doing SYN **specialty**: *Cooking has never been Kelly's forte.* **2** ENG. LANG. ARTS a note or line of music played or sung loudly OPP **piano**

for·te[2] /ˈfɔrteɪ/ *adj., adv.* music that is forte is played or sung loudly OPP **piano**

for·te·pi·an·o /ˌfɔrteɪpiˈænoʊ/ *n. plural* **fortepianos** [C] an old-fashioned musical instrument like a piano that was popular in the 18th century

forth /fɔrθ/ S1 W2 *adv.* LITERARY **1 from this/that day/time/moment forth** LITERARY beginning on that day or at that time: *From this day forth you shall speak to no one.* **2** [only after verb] LITERARY going out or away from where you are, or from a particular point SYN **forward**: *They marched forth into battle.* → see also **back and forth** at BACK[1] (11), **hold forth** at HOLD[1], **and so on/forth** at SO[1] (5)

F

forth·com·ing /ˌfɔrθˈkʌmɪŋ◂/ Ac *adj.* **1** [only before noun] happening or coming soon: *Irving's forthcoming novel* | *the forthcoming meeting in October* **2** [not before noun] given or offered when needed: *When no response was forthcoming, she wrote again.* **3** [not before noun] willing to give information about something OPP **unforthcoming**: +**about** *The charity has not been forthcoming about its finances.*

forth·right /ˈfɔrθraɪt/ *adj.* APPROVING saying honestly what you think, in a way that may seem impolite SYN **frank**: +**in** *He has been forthright in his criticism.*

forth·with /fɔrθˈwɪθ/ *adv.* FORMAL immediately SYN **at once**: *Sanctions will take effect forthwith.*

for·ti·eth[1] /ˈfɔrt̬iɪθ/ *adj.* 40th; next after the thirty-ninth: *It's our fortieth anniversary next week.*

fortieth[2] *pron.* **the fortieth** the 40th thing in a series

fortieth[3] *n.* [C] one of forty equal parts of something

for·ti·fi·ca·tion /ˌfɔrt̬əfəˈkeɪʃən/ *n.* **1** [U] the process of making something stronger or more effective **2 fortifications** [plural] towers, walls etc. built around a place in order to protect it or defend it: *battlefield fortifications*

for·ti·fied /ˈfɔrt̬əˌfaɪd/ *adj.* **1** made stronger and easier to defend: *The border is the most* ***heavily fortified*** *in the world.* **2** if food or drinks are fortified, they have VITAMINS added to them to make them more healthy: *vitamin-fortified cereals*

ˌfortified ˈwine *n.* [C,U] wine such as SHERRY that has strong alcohol added

for·ti·fy /ˈfɔrt̬əˌfaɪ/ *v.* **fortifies, fortified, fortifying** [T] **1** to build towers, walls etc. around an area or city in order to defend it: *Concrete blocks were piled high to fortify the government center.* **2** to encourage an attitude or feeling and make it stronger SYN **strengthen**: **fortify sb with sth** *His mother was a heroic woman who fortified her children with faith in the future.* **3** [usually passive] to make food or drinks more healthy by adding VITAMINS to them: **fortify sth with sth** *orange juice fortified with calcium* **4** to make someone feel physically or mentally stronger: **fortify yourself** *Several performers fortified themselves at the bar* (=drank alcohol to make themselves feel stronger) *before going on stage.*

for·tis·si·mo /fɔrˈtɪsəˌmoʊ/ *adj., adv.* music that is fortissimo is played or sung very loudly OPP **pianissimo** → see also FORTE

for·ti·tude /ˈfɔrt̬əˌtud/ *n.* [U] courage shown when you are in pain or having a lot of trouble SYN **strength**: *Janet met each challenge with fortitude and a wry good humor.* → see also **intestinal fortitude** at INTESTINAL (2)

fort·night /ˈfɔrtˀnaɪt/ *n.* [C usually singular] LITERARY two weeks [**Origin:** Old English *feowertyne niht* **fourteen nights**]

for·tress /ˈfɔrtrɪs/ *n.* [C] a large, strong building used for defending an important place

Fort Sum·ter /ˌfɔrt ˈsʌmtɚ/ a FORT in Charleston, South Carolina, where the first battle of the American Civil War was fought in 1861

for·tu·i·tous /fɔrˈtuət̬əs/ *adj.* FORMAL lucky and happening by chance: *a fortuitous meeting* [**Origin:** 1600–1700 Latin *fortuitus*, from *fors* **chance, luck**] —**fortuitously** *adv.*

for·tu·nate /ˈfɔrtʃənɪt/ *adj.* **1** [not before noun] someone who is fortunate has something good happen to them, or is in a good situation SYN **lucky** OPP **unfortunate**: *People have been very helpful – I'm very fortunate.* | **fortunate to do sth** *I've been fortunate to have done a lot of traveling.* | **fortunate that** *We were fortunate that there were no serious injuries.* | *We were* ***fortunate enough*** *to get tickets for Saturday's playoff game.* | **less/more fortunate** *Kelly was more fortunate than many pregnant teens – she has supportive parents.* **2 the less fortunate** people who are poor: *The organization is collecting canned food to help the less fortunate.* **3** [only before noun] a fortunate event is one in which something good happens by chance, especially when this saves you from trouble or danger SYN **lucky** OPP **unfortunate**: *It was a fortunate coincidence that the police were passing by just then.*

for·tu·nate·ly /ˈfɔrtʃənɪtli/ *adv.* [sentence adverb] happening because of good luck SYN **luckily** OPP **unfortunately**: *Fortunately, she hadn't gone far before she was found.*

for·tune /ˈfɔrtʃən/ W3 *n.*

1 MONEY [C] a very large amount of money: *To a four-year-old, $10 seems like a fortune.* | *Julia must have* ***spent a fortune*** *on her wedding dress.* | *A car like that* ***costs a fortune.*** | *His family* ***made a fortune*** (=earned a lot of money) *in railroads.* | *His Senate campaign was financed by his* ***personal fortune.*** | *The painting is now* ***worth a fortune.*** | *Mrs. Foy made* ***a small fortune*** (=a lot of money, but not a very large amount) *buying and selling real estate.*

2 CHANCE [U] chance or luck, and the good or bad effect that it has on your life: *It was useless to struggle against fortune.* | *Elizabeth told me of their* ***good fortune.*** | *I consider myself privileged to* ***have had the fortune to*** *know him.* | *She felt that not stopping to pray was to risk* ***bad fortune.***

3 WHAT HAPPENS TO YOU [C usually plural] the good or bad things that happen in life: *This defeat marked a* ***change in*** *the team's* ***fortunes.*** | **sinking/declining/slumping fortunes** *the company's declining fortunes* | *The young soldier, once full of life, is now destroyed by the* ***fortunes of war*** (=the things that can happen during a war).

4 sb's fortune [C,U] what is supposed to happen to someone in the future SYN **destiny**: *A woman at the fair was* ***telling*** *people's* ***fortunes*** (=using special cards or looking at people's hands to tell them what will happen to them).

5 fortune smiles on sth/sb LITERARY used to say that someone or something is lucky

[**Origin:** 1200–1300 French, Latin *fortuna*] → see also **fame and fortune** at FAME, **seek your fortune** at SEEK (4), SOLDIER OF FORTUNE

ˈfortune ˌcookie *n.* [C] a cookie with a piece of paper inside it that tells you what is supposed to happen in your future, often served after a meal in Chinese restaurants in the U.S.

ˈfortune ˌhunter *n.* [C] someone who wants to make a lot of money quickly and easily: *Fortune hunters went to the hills in search of gold.*

ˈfortune ˌteller *n.* [C] someone who uses cards or looks at people's hands in order to tell them what will happen to them in the future —**fortune telling** *n.* [U]

Fort Worth /ˌfɔrt ˈwɚθ/ a city in the U.S. state of Texas

for·ty /ˈfɔrt̮i/ *number* **1** the number 40 **2 the forties** also **the '40s** the years from 1940 through 1949 **3 sb's forties** the time when someone is 40 to 49 years old: **in your early/mid/late forties** *a man in his mid forties* **4 in the forties** if the temperature is in the forties, it is between 40° and 49° Fahrenheit: **in the high/low forties** *The temperature was in the low forties.* **5 forty winks** a very short sleep

ˌforty-ˈfive *n.* [C] INFORMAL **1** also **45** a small record with one song on each side **2** also **.45, Colt 45** TRADEMARK a small gun

forty-nin·er /ˌfɔrt̮i ˈnaɪnɚ/ *n.* [C] HISTORY a MINER who went to California in 1849 to look for gold during the California Gold Rush

fo·rum /ˈfɔrəm/ W3 *n.* [C] **1** an organization, meeting, report etc. in which people have a chance to publicly discuss an important subject: **+for** *The United Nations should be a forum for solving international problems.* | **+on** *A large number of mayors attended the forum on crime.* **2** COMPUTERS a group of computer users who are interested in a subject and discuss it using EMAIL or the Internet → see also NEWSGROUP ▸see THESAURUS box at **Internet** **3** HISTORY a large outdoor public place in ancient Rome used for business and discussion [**Origin:** 1400–1500 Latin]

for·ward¹ /ˈfɔrwɚd/ S2 W2 *adv.* **1** also **forwards** toward a place or position that is in front of you OPP **backward**: *Greg leaned forward to hear what they were saying.* | *The truck was moving forwards into the road.* **2** toward more progress, improvement, or development: *Negotiators are trying to find a* ***way forward*** *in the peace talks.* | *NASA's project cannot* ***go forward*** *without more money.* | *Diplomats recommended* ***moving forward*** *with an aid program.* **3** toward the future in a way that is hopeful OPP **backward**: *Companies must* ***look forward*** (=make plans for the future) *and invest in new technologies.* **4 from this/that day/time/moment etc. forward** beginning on that day or at that time OPP **backward**: *They never met again from that day forward.* **5** in or toward the front part of a ship → see also **backward and forward** at BACKWARD¹ (6), FAST FORWARD, **look forward to** at LOOK¹

forward² *adj.* **1** [only before noun] closer to a person, place, or position that is in front of you OPP **backward**: *Army roadblocks prevented any further forward movement.* | *Troops were moved to a forward position on the battlefield.* **2 forward planning/thinking/progress etc.** plans, ideas etc. that are helpful in a way that prepares you for the future: *The company is suffering from a lack of forward planning.* **3 no further forward** not having made much progress, especially compared to what was expected: *The talks are no further forward than they were two weeks ago.* **4** [only before noun] at the front part of a ship, vehicle, plane etc.: *We got a forward cabin.* **5** too confident and friendly in dealing with people you do not know very well: *Kirstie did not wish to sound too forward.* [**Origin:** Old English *foreweard*, from *fore-* + *-ward*] → see also BACKWARD

forward³ *v.* **1** [T] to send a letter, message etc. that you have received to another person: *The e-mail service forwards your messages but removes the address.* | **forward sth to sb** *The Post Office will be forwarding my mail to my new address.* | *Bernie's complaint was forwarded to the city manager.* **2** [T] FORMAL to help something to develop so that it becomes successful: *This new responsibility is a good chance to forward my career.*

forward⁴ *n.* [C] **1** in basketball, one of two players whose main job is to SHOOT the ball at the other team's BASKET **2** an attacking player on a team in sports such as SOCCER

ˈforwarding adˌdress *n.* [C] an address that you give to someone when you move so that they can send your mail to you: *Did she* ***leave a forwarding address****?*

ˈforward-ˌlooking *adj.* planning for and thinking about the future in a positive way, especially by being willing to try new ideas: *Help with childcare costs is offered by some forward-looking companies.*

for·ward·ness /ˈfɔrwɚdnɪs/ *n.* [U] behavior that is too confident or friendly

Dian Fossey

for·wards /ˈfɔrwɚdz/ *adv.* FORWARD

ˈforward slash *n.* [C] a line (/) used in writing to separate words, numbers, or letters → BACKSLASH

ˈforward-ˌthinking *adj.* FORWARD-LOOKING

for·went /fɔrˈwɛnt/ *v.* another spelling of FOREWENT

Fos·sey /ˈfɔsi/, **Di·an** /daɪˈæn/ (1932–1985) a U.S. ZOOLOGIST who lived near GORILLAS in Africa and studied them for many years

fossil

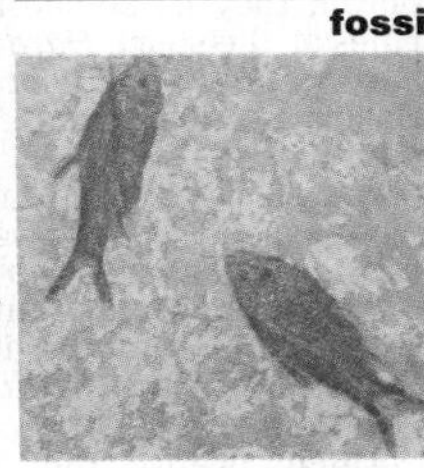

fos·sil /ˈfɑsəl/ *n.* [C] **1** part of an animal or plant that lived millions of years ago and that has been preserved, or the shape of one of these plants or animals that is preserved in rock: *Several dinosaur fossils were found in Montana.* | *the appearance of species in the* ***fossil record*** (=all the fossils that have been discovered and recorded by scientists) **2** INFORMAL an insulting word for an old person [**Origin:** 1500–1600 Latin *fossilis* **dug up**, from *fodere* **to dig**]

ˈfossil ˌfuel *n.* [C,U] EARTH SCIENCE a FUEL such as coal, oil, or natural gas that is formed from decayed animals and plants that lived millions of years ago

fos·sil·ize /ˈfɑsəˌlaɪz/ *v.* [I,T usually passive] **1** EARTH SCIENCE to become or form a FOSSIL by being preserved in rock: *fossilized dinosaur bones* **2** if people, ideas, systems etc. fossilize or are fossilized, they never change or develop, even though there are good reasons why they should change: *He feels that unions in America have become fossilized.* —**fossilization** /ˌfɑsələˈzeɪʃən/ *n.* [U]

ˈfossil ˌrecord *n.* [C] BIOLOGY information about the animals and other creatures that lived many thousands of years ago, what they looked like, what they ate, and the kind of environment they lived in etc., which is obtained from their fossils

fos·ter¹ /ˈfɔstɚ, ˈfɑ-/ *v.* **1** [T] FORMAL to help to develop a skill, feeling, idea etc. over a period of time: *The workshops can foster better communication between husbands and wives.* **2** [I,T] to take care of someone else's child for a period of time and have them live with you, without becoming their legal parent → see also ADOPT: *The Hammonds fostered a little boy for a few months.*

foster² *adj.* **1 foster mother/father/parents/family** the person or people who foster a child **2 foster brother/sister** someone who has different parents than you, but who is fostered in the same family **3 foster child** a child who is fostered **4 foster home** a person's or family's home where a child is fostered [**Origin:** Old English *fostor-*, from *fostor* **food, feeding**]

Fou·cault /fuˈkoʊ/, **Jean Ber·nard Lé·on** /ʒɑn bɛrˈnɑr leɪˈɑn/ (1819–1868) a French scientist who studied the speed of light

fought /fɔt/ *v.* the past tense and past participle of FIGHT

foul¹ /faʊl/ *adj.*
1 SMELL/TASTE a foul smell or taste is very bad SYN **disgusting** SYN **horrible**: *Residents have complained of foul odors from the factory.* | *a pile of foul-smelling garbage* ▸see THESAURUS box at **horrible**
2 foul language impolite and offensive words

F

SYN swear words: *Never use foul language to a customer.*
3 have a foul mouth INFORMAL to use a lot of SWEAR WORDS and offensive language
4 SPORTS not within the rules of a sport or not within the limits of the playing field or COURT: *Sanchez hit three* ***foul balls*** *before connecting with a line drive to right field.*
5 AIR/WATER very dirty: *the foul haze of pollution over the city*
6 in a foul mood in a very bad mood and likely to get angry: *She was in a foul mood the next morning.*
7 WEATHER foul weather is stormy and windy, with a lot of rain or snow: *All that night the foul weather continued.*
8 EVIL LITERARY evil or cruel: *foul deeds*
[**Origin:** Old English *ful*] —**foully** *adv.* —**foulness** *n.* [U]
→ see also **cry foul** at CRY[1] (5), **by fair means or foul** at FAIR[1] (18), **fall foul of sb/sth** at FALL[1] (22)

foul² *v.* **1** [I,T] **a)** if a sports player fouls another player, they do something that is not allowed by the rules of the sport: *Hardaway was fouled while trying to make a three-point shot* (=another player tried to stop Hardaway by doing something that was not allowed). **b)** to hit a ball outside the limit of the playing area in BASEBALL **2** [T] to make something very dirty, especially with waste SYN **pollute**: *The oil spill has fouled at least four beaches.* **3** [I,T] also **foul up** TECHNICAL if a rope, chain, or part of a machine fouls or if something fouls it, it twists or cannot move as it should: *Check that nothing can foul the moving parts.*

foul out *phr. v.* **a)** in baseball, to hit a ball outside the playing area that is caught by a player on the other team, so that your turn to try to hit the ball is over **b)** in basketball, to make more than five fouls in a game, so that you are not allowed to play in that game anymore

foul up *phr. v.* INFORMAL **foul sth ↔ up** to do something wrong or to spoil something by making a mistake: *Someone had fouled up the accounts.* | *You've totally fouled up this time.*

foul³ *n.* [C] **1** an action in a sport that is against the rules: *He'd committed three fouls by half-time.* **2** in baseball, a ball that has been hit outside the playing area → see also STRIKE

'foul line *n.* [C] a line marked on a sports field, outside of which a ball cannot be legally played

,foul-'mouthed *adj.* swearing too much: *a foul-mouthed man*

,foul 'play *n.* [U] **1** if the police think someone's death was caused by foul play, they think that person was murdered: *The autopsy report showed no evidence of foul play.* **2** an action that is dishonest, unfair, or illegal: *There have been rumors of foul play in the last election.*

'foul-up *n.* [C] INFORMAL a problem caused by a stupid or careless mistake: *The papers were lost in a bureaucratic foul-up.*

found¹ /faʊnd/ Ac S3 *v.* the past tense and past participle of FIND

found² Ac W2 *v.* [T] **1** to start something such as an organization, institution, company or city SYN **establish**: *Founded in 1935, Alcoholics Anonymous is now a world-wide organization.* | *The Baptists founded many churches in the southern U.S.* **2 be founded on/upon sth a)** to be the main idea, belief etc. that something else develops from SYN **be based on sth**: *Racism is not founded on rational thought, but on fear.* | *The Soviet Union was originally founded on Socialism.* **b)** to be the solid layer of CEMENT, stones etc. that a building is built on: *The castle is founded on solid rock.* **3** TECHNICAL to melt metal and pour it into a MOLD (=a hollow shape), to make things such as tools, parts for machines etc. [**Origin:** 1300–1400 Old French *fonder*, from Latin *fundus* **bottom**] —**founding** *n.* [U] *the founding of the University of Chicago* → see also FOUNDATION, WELL-FOUNDED

foun·da·tion /faʊnˈdeɪʃən/ Ac W2 *n.*
1 BUILDING [C] the solid layer of CEMENT, bricks, stones etc. that is under a building to support it: *There were cracks in the foundation of the house.* | *It should take them about three weeks to* ***lay the foundation*** (=build it).
2 BASIC IDEA [C] a basic idea, principle, situation etc. that something develops from SYN **base**: *Reading, writing, and arithmetic provide* ***a solid foundation*** *for a child's education.* | *The Chinese diet is* ***built on a foundation of*** *rice, with only small amounts of meat.*
3 ORGANIZATION [C] an organization that gives or collects money to be used for special purposes, especially for CHARITY or research: *The Heritage Foundation is a conservative political research organization.* | *the National Foundation for the Arts*
4 be without foundation also **have no foundation** FORMAL if a statement, idea etc. is without foundation, there is no proof that it is true SYN **be groundless**: *His fears were not completely without foundation.*
5 ESTABLISHMENT [C,U] the establishment of an organization, business, school etc. SYN **founding**: *This school has served the community since its foundation in 1835.*
6 lay/provide the foundation(s) for sth to provide the conditions that will make it possible for something to be successful: *Tests on healthy people may lay the foundation for a vaccine to prevent the disease.*
7 SKIN [U] a cream in the same color as your skin that you put on before the rest of your MAKEUP
8 shake/rock sth to its foundations to completely change the way something is done or the way people think by having a completely new idea: *Darwin's theory rocked the scientific establishment to its foundations.*

foun'dation ,garment *n.* [C] OLD-FASHIONED a piece of clothing worn by women under their clothes to give shape to their bodies

foun'dation ,stone *n.* [C] **1** a large stone placed at the bottom of an important building, usually as part of a ceremony **2** the facts, ideas, principles etc. that form the base from which something else develops or begins: *Greek and Latin were once considered the foundation stones of a good education.*

found·er¹ /ˈfaʊndɚ/ Ac *n.* [C] someone who establishes a business, organization, school etc.: *The shop is still run by the founder and his two sons.*

founder² Ac *v.* [I] FORMAL **1** if a ship or boat founders, it fills with water and sinks **2** to fail after a period of time because something has gone wrong → see also FLOUNDER: **+on** *The program foundered on legal problems.*

,founding 'father *n.* [C] **1** someone who begins something such as a new way of thinking or a new organization: **+of** *one of the founding fathers of modern science* **2 the Founding Fathers** [plural] the group of men who wrote the American Constitution and Bill of Rights and started the U.S. as a country

found·ling /ˈfaʊndlɪŋ/ *n.* [C] OLD-FASHIONED a baby who has been left by its parents, and is found and taken care of by other people

found·ry /ˈfaʊndri/ *n. plural* **foundries** [C] a place where metals are melted and made into new parts for machines, tools etc.

fount /faʊnt/ *n.* [C usually singular] a place, person, idea etc. that provides a large supply of something SYN **source**: **a fount of information/knowledge** *The book is a fount of information for new parents.*

foun·tain /ˈfaʊntˀn/ *n.* [C] **1** a structure from which water is pushed up into the air, used as a decoration **2** also **water fountain** a piece of equipment in a public place that produces a stream of water for you to drink from SYN **drinking fountain** **3** a flow of liquid, or of something bright and colorful, that goes straight up into the air: **+of** *A fountain of lava burst from the volcano.* **4 fountain of sth** WRITTEN a SOURCE or supply of something: *People have accused the Internet of being a fountain of misinformation.* [**Origin:** 1300–1400 French *fontaine*, from Latin *fons* **place where water comes out of the ground**] → see also SODA FOUNTAIN

foun·tain·head /ˈfaʊntˀnˌhɛd/ *n.* [singular + of] the origin of something SYN **source**

ˌfountain of ˈyouth *n.* [C usually singular] something that many people believe will keep you young

ˈfountain pen *n.* [C] a pen that you fill with liquid ink

four /fɔr/ *number* **1** the number 4 **2** 4 o'clock: *I get off work **at four**.* **3 on all fours** supporting your body with your hands and knees: *Billy was down on all fours playing with the puppy.* **4 the four corners of the Earth/world** LITERARY places or countries that are very far away from each other: *For centuries, the Spanish traveled to the four corners of the Earth in search of new lands.* **5 four on the floor** INFORMAL if a car has four on the floor, it has four GEARS that you change using a GEAR SHIFT [**Origin:** Old English *feower*] → see also **be scattered to the four winds** at SCATTER (3), TWO-BY-FOUR

ˌfour-by-ˈfour usually written as **4 X 4** *n.* [C] a vehicle that has four wheels and FOUR-WHEEL DRIVE

ˈfour eyes *n.* [singular] an insulting word for someone who wears glasses, used especially by children —**four-eyed** *adj.*

ˌfour-leaf ˈclover *n.* [C] a CLOVER plant that has four leaves instead of the usual three, and that people consider to be lucky

ˌfour-letter ˈword *n.* [C] **1** a word that is considered very offensive, especially one relating to sex or body wastes SYN **swear word** **2** [usually singular] HUMOROUS a word that expresses an idea that people do not like or agree with: *"Diet" has become a four-letter word to many women.*

ˌFour Moderniˈzations, the HISTORY the program of Deng Xiaoping beginning in 1978 to develop China's farming, industry, science and TECHNOLOGY, and military and make them more modern

ˌfour-one-ˈone *n.* **the 411** SLANG information: *What's the 411 on that show Friday night?*

ˌfour-poster ˈbed also **ˌfour-ˈposter** *n.* [C] a bed with four tall posts at the corners, usually with a cover attached at the top of the posts and curtains around the sides

four·some /ˈfɔrsəm/ *n.* [C] a group of four people who are together to play a game such as BRIDGE or GOLF

four·square[1] /fɔrˈskwɛr/ *adj.* a building that is foursquare is solidly and plainly built, and square in shape

foursquare[2] , **four-square** *adv.* firmly and completely: *Seymour said he would stand **foursquare behind** (=strongly supporting) the President's policies.*

foursquare[3] *n.* [U] a game played by four people on a square area divided into four smaller squares, in which the players each stand in a square and BOUNCE a ball into the other squares

four·star gen·e·ral /ˌfɔrstɑr ˈdʒɛnərəl/ *n.* [C] an officer with a very high rank in the army

ˌfour-stroke ˈengine *n.* [C] an engine that works with two up and two down movements of a PISTON

four·teen /ˌfɔrˈtin◂ / *number* the number 14

four·teenth[1] /ˌfɔrˈtinθ◂ / *adj.* 14th; next after the thirteenth: *the fourteenth century*

fourteenth[2] *pron.* **the fourteenth** the 14th thing in a series: *Let's have dinner on the fourteenth* (=the 14th day of the month).

ˌFourteenth Aˈmendment, the HISTORY a written change to the U.S. CONSTITUTION, which gives all citizens the same right to be protected by law. The Fourteenth Amendment was made in 1868.

fourth[1] /fɔrθ/ *adj.* 4th; after the third: *Her apartment was on the fourth floor.* | *fourth grade*

fourth[2] *pron.* **the fourth** the 4th thing in a series: *Does your flight leave on the fourth* (=the 4th day of the month)*?*

fourth[3] *n.* [C] 1/4; one of four equal parts: **one-fourth/three-fourths** *Three-fourths of the class read very well.* → see also QUARTER[3]

ˌfourth diˈmension *n.* **a) the fourth dimension** an expression meaning "time," used especially by scientists and writers of SCIENCE FICTION **b)** [singular] a type of experience that is outside normal human experience

ˌfourth esˈtate *n.* **the fourth estate** newspapers, news magazines, television and radio news, the people who work for them, and the political influence that they have SYN **press**

ˌFourth of Juˈly *n.* **the Fourth of July** Independence Day: *a Fourth of July picnic*

ˌfour-wheel ˈdrive WRITTEN ABBREVIATION **4WD** *n.* [C,U] a system in a vehicle that gives the power of the engine to all four wheels to make it easier to drive, or a vehicle that has this type of system —**four-wheel drive** *adj.*

ˌfour-ˈwheeler *n.* [C] **1** a small vehicle, like a MOTORCYCLE but with four fat wheels, that people ride for fun **2** INFORMAL a vehicle with four-wheel drive —**four-wheeling** *n.* [U]

fo·ve·a /ˈfoʊviə/ *n* [C] BIOLOGY a part of the eye that consists of a small hollow in the RETINA. It is the area where we are able to see things most clearly. → see picture at EYE[1]

fowl /faʊl/ *n. plural* **fowls** or **fowl** [C,U] a bird, especially a chicken, that is kept for its meat and eggs SYN **poultry** → see also **neither fish nor fowl** at FISH[1] (8)

Fox /fɑks/ a Native American tribe from the northeastern area of the U.S.

fox /fɑks/ *n.* **1** [C] BIOLOGY a wild animal like a dog, with reddish-brown fur, a pointed face, and a thick tail **2** [C] INFORMAL someone who is sexually attractive: *She's such a fox!* **3** [C] someone who is intelligent and good at deceiving people: *He was **a sly old fox**.* **4 crazy like a fox** if someone is crazy like a fox, they behave in a way that makes people think they are strange or crazy, in order to get something **5** [U] the skin and fur of a fox, used to make clothes

fox·glove /ˈfɑksglʌv/ *n.* [C] a tall plant with many bell-shaped flowers, whose leaves are used to make a medicine for heart problems

fox·hole /ˈfɑkshoʊl/ *n.* [C] **1** a hole in the ground that soldiers dig for protection **2** a hole in the ground where a fox lives

fox·hound /ˈfɑkshaʊnd/ *n.* [C] a dog with a very good sense of smell, trained to hunt and kill FOXES

fox·hunt·ing /ˈfɑksˌhʌntɪŋ/ *n.* [U] the sport of hunting FOXES with dogs while riding on a horse —**foxhunt** *n.* [C]

ˌfox ˈterrier *n.* [C] BIOLOGY a small dog with short hair

fox·trot /ˈfɑkstrɑt/ *n.* [C] a type of formal dance which combines short, quick steps with long slow steps, or a piece of music for this dance —**foxtrot** *v.* [I]

fox·y /ˈfɑksi/ *adj. comparative* **foxier**, *superlative* **foxiest** **1** INFORMAL sexually attractive: *Regina is a truly foxy lady.* **2** skillful at deceiving people SYN **cunning**: *a foxy old man* **3** like a FOX in appearance

foy·er /ˈfɔɪɚ/ *n.* [C] **1** a large room or hall at the entrance to a public building SYN **lobby**: *the main foyer of the hotel* **2** a room or hall at the entrance to a house or apartment

FPO /ˌɛf pi ˈoʊ/ *n.* [C] an abbreviation of **fleet post office** or **field post office**, used as part of the address of someone in the navy or army

Fr. **1** a written abbreviation of "Father", used in front of the name of a priest: *Fr. Edmond Lavalle* **2 fr.** a written abbreviation of "from" **3** a written abbreviation of "French" or "France"

frac·as /ˈfrækəs, ˈfreɪ-/ *n.* [singular] a short, noisy fight involving several people: *Eight people were injured in the fracas.* [**Origin:** 1700–1800 French, Italian *fracassare* **to break in pieces**]

frac·tal /ˈfræktl/ *n.* [C] TECHNICAL a pattern, usually produced by a computer, that is made by repeating the same shape many times at smaller and smaller sizes —**fractal** *adj.*: *fractal geometry*

frac·tion /ˈfrækʃən/ *n.* [C] **1** a very small amount of

F

something: +**of** *I got these shoes at a fraction of the original price.* **2** MATH a part of a whole number in mathematics, such as ½ or ¾ [**Origin:** 1300–1400 Late Latin *fractio*, from Latin *fractus*, past participle of *frangere* **to break**] → see also COMMON FRACTION, IMPROPER FRACTION, PROPER FRACTION

frac·tion·al /ˈfrækʃənl/ *adj.* **1** very small in amount: *a fractional sales increase in December* **2** MATH relating to fractions, in mathematics **3** TECHNICAL happening or done in a series of steps: *fractional distillation* —**fractionally** *adv.*

frac·tious /ˈfrækʃəs/ *adj.* someone who is fractious gets angry very easily and tends to start fights: *Maggie grew up in a large, fractious family.* [**Origin:** 1600–1700 *fraction* **lack of agreement** (16–18 centuries)] —**fractiousness** *n.* [U]

frac·ture¹ /ˈfræktʃɚ/ *v.* **1** [I,T] if a bone or other hard substance fractures or is fractured, it breaks or cracks SYN **break**: *Ron fractured his finger in the first half of the game.* **2** [I,T] if a group, organization etc. fractures or is fractured, the people in it disagree and do not work well together anymore: *The country has already been fractured by bitter ethnic and political clashes.* **3** [T usually passive] to use something such as language in a way that is not correct, or to do something without following the correct rules: *a politician who fractured the language* | **fractured syntax/English etc.** *the girl's fractured English*

fracture² *n.* [C] a crack or broken part in a bone or other hard substance: *X-rays showed no fractures in his leg.* | *a **hairline fracture*** (=very thin crack) | *a **stress fracture** in his left foot* (=a crack caused by using it too much) ►see THESAURUS box at **injury**

frag /fræg/ *v.* **fragged, fragging** [T] SLANG a word meaning "to completely destroy an enemy," used especially by people in the army, or when talking about computer games

frag·ile /ˈfrædʒəl/ *adj.* **1** easily broken, damaged, or ruined SYN **delicate** OPP **strong**: *Be careful with that vase – it's very fragile.* ►see THESAURUS box at **weak¹** **2** easily harmed → see also FRAIL: *Ed's already fragile health deteriorated after he left the hospital.* | *Mike's fragile ego* | *an environmentally fragile area* **3** a fragile situation is one that is weak or uncertain, and likely to become worse easily: *the country's fragile economy* | *the **fragile peace** in the region* [**Origin:** 1400–1500 Latin *fragilis*, from *frangere* **to break**] —**fragility** /frəˈdʒɪləṭi/ *n.* [U]

frag·ment¹ /ˈfrægmənt/ *n.* [C] a small piece of something that has broken off or that comes from something larger: *glass fragments from a smashed window* | +**of** *Doctors found fragments of metal embedded in his legs.* ►see THESAURUS box at **piece¹**

frag·ment² /ˈfrægˌmɛnt/ *v.* [I,T] to break something, or be broken into a lot of small, separate parts: *His day was fragmented by interruptions and phone calls.* —**fragmentation** /ˌfrægmənˈteɪʃən/ *n.* [U]

frag·men·tar·y /ˈfrægmənˌtɛri/ *adj.* consisting of many different small parts: *the fragmentary picture we have of human evolution*

ˌfragmenˈtation ˌbomb *n.* [C] a bomb that sends many small metal pieces out over a large area when it explodes to cause as much damage and injury as possible

frag·ment·ed /ˈfrægˌmɛntɪd/ *adj.* separated into many parts, groups, or events, and not seeming to have a clear purpose: *a fragmented market*

fra·grance /ˈfreɪgrəns/ *n.* **1** [C,U] a nice smell → see also AROMA SYN **scent**: *the rich fragrance of a garden flower* ►see THESAURUS box at **smell¹** **2** [C] a liquid that you put on your body to make it smell nice SYN **perfume**

fra·grant /ˈfreɪgrənt/ *adj.* having a nice smell: *a fragrant rose garden* —**fragrantly** *adv.*

fraid·y cat /ˈfreɪdi ˌkæt/ *n.* [C] INFORMAL a word meaning someone who is too afraid to do something, used especially by children SYN **scaredy-cat**

frail /freɪl/ *adj.* **1** someone who is frail is thin and weak, because they are old or sick: *He looked old and frail.* | *my mother's **frail health*** ►see THESAURUS box at **weak¹** **2** not strongly made or built, and therefore easily damaged: *A fierce storm engulfed the frail ship.* [**Origin:** 1300–1400 Old French *fraile*, from Latin *fragilis*, from *frangere* **to break**] → see also FRAGILE

frail·ty /ˈfreɪlti/ *n. plural* **frailties** **1** [C,U] something bad or weak in your character SYN **weakness** SYN **fault**: *a novel that is compassionate in its treatment of our **human frailties*** **2** [U] the lack of strength or health SYN **weakness**: +**of** *the frailty of his body* | *the frailty of the peace agreement*

frame¹ /freɪm/ S2 W3 *n.*

1 PICTURE/MIRROR [C] a firm structure that holds something such as a picture or mirror, and provides a border for it: *a picture in a silver frame* | *Do you have any small **picture frames**?*

2 WINDOW/DOOR [C] the firm structure around a window or door: **a window/door frame** *He leaned against the door frame.*

3 STRUCTURE [C] the structure or main supporting parts of a piece of furniture, vehicle, or other object: *a bicycle frame* | *the wooden frame of the bed*

4 BODY [C] the general shape formed by the bones of someone's body: *The clothes were too small for his large frame.*

5 GLASSES [C usually plural] the metal or plastic part of a pair of GLASSES that holds the LENSES: *The frames of his glasses were held together with tape.*

6 frame of mind the attitude you have at a particular time: **be in a good/bad etc. frame of mind** *You just need to be in the right frame of mind to win.*

7 MAIN FACTS/IDEAS [C usually singular] the main ideas, facts etc. that something is based on: *A clear explanation provides a frame on which a deeper understanding can be built.* | *Some comments may be understood as harassment, depending on your **frame of reference*** (=knowledge and beliefs that influence the way you think).

8 FILM [C] an area of film that contains one photograph, or one of the series of separate photographs that make up a movie: *Movies are shot at 24 frames per second.*

9 SPORTS [C] a complete part in the game of BOWLING

10 COMPUTER [C] one of the areas on a computer screen that some programs are divided into, which can be moved separately from the other areas → see also TIME FRAME

frame² S3 *v.* [T] **1** to put a picture in a structure that will hold it firmly: *I might get the print framed and put it on the wall.* **2** to surround something with a border so that it looks nice, or so that you can see it clearly: *Her pretty face was framed by dark curls.* **3** to deliberately make someone seem guilty of a crime when they are not guilty, by providing things that seem like proof: *Needham's lawyers claimed that he had been framed by the police.* → see also FRAME-UP **4** FORMAL to carefully plan the way you are going to say a question, statement etc.: *She wondered how she was going to frame the question.* **5** FORMAL to organize and develop a plan, system etc.: *Newman played a central role in framing the new law.* **6** to decide what to include when you are taking a photograph: *He frames his shots beautifully.* [**Origin:** Old English *framian* **to be helpful to, make progress**]

-framed /freɪmd/ [in adjectives] **1** having a particular type of frame: **gold-framed/wood-framed etc.** *a gold-framed mirror* **2** having a particular body shape: **small-framed/large-framed etc.** *small-framed adults*

ˈframe house *n.* [C] a house whose main structure is made of wood

ˌframe of ˈreference *n. plural* **frames of reference** [C] **1** a set of ideas, beliefs, experiences etc. that you use to judge or understand something **2** MATH a set of AXES (=two or more lines that cross each other), from which measurements about the size, position, or movement of something can be made

fram·er /ˈfreɪmɚ/ *n.* [C] **1** someone whose job is to frame pictures: *a picture framer* **2** [usually plural] also **Framer** HISTORY one of the people who wrote the U.S. Constitution

ˈframe-up *n.* [C] a plan to make someone seem guilty of a crime when they are not guilty

frame·work /ˈfreɪmwɚk/ Ac *n.* [C] **1** [usually singular] a set of facts, ideas etc. from which more complicated ideas are developed, or on which decisions are based: +**of** *We must act within the framework of the Constitution.* | +**for** *The report could serve as the possible framework for a compromise.* **2 political/legal/social etc. framework** the structure of a society, a legal or political system etc.: *We as residents have the right, within the legal framework, to decide what the city will look like.* **3** the main supporting parts of a building, vehicle, or object: *A rigid metal framework supported the sculpture.*

franc /fræŋk/ *n.* [C] the standard unit of money in Switzerland and some African countries. Francs also used to be used in France and Belgium

France /fræns/ a country in western Europe

France /fræns, frɑns/**, An·a·tole** /ˈænəˌtoʊl/ (1844–1924) a French writer of short stories and NOVELS

fran·chise¹ /ˈfræntʃaɪz/ *n.* **1** also **business franchise** [C] a business that sells a particular company's products or services under a special agreement: *fast-food franchises* **2** [C] a professional sports team: *a Major League baseball franchise* **3** [C] permission that a company gives to a person or group so that they can sell the company's products or services: *The government has said it will not renew the company's franchise.* **4** [U] POLITICS the legal right to vote in your country's elections [**Origin:** 1300–1400 Old French *franchir* **to set free**]

franchise² *v.* [T] to give or sell a franchise to someone: *The corporation plans to franchise the treatment nationally.*

fran·chis·ee /ˌfræntʃaɪˈzi/ *n.* [C] someone who is given or sold a franchise to sell a company's products or services

fran·chis·er, franchisor /ˈfræntʃaɪzɚ/ *n.* [C] a company that gives people or businesses permission to sell its products or services to the public

Fran·cis·cans /frænˈsɪskənz/ *n.* [plural] a Christian religious group begun by St. Francis of Assisi in 1209, whose members live a holy life according to strict rules —**Franciscan** *adj.*

Fran·cis Fer·di·nand /ˌfrænsɪs ˈfɚdnˌænd/ (1863–1914) an Austrian ARCHDUKE who was killed by a Serbian ASSASSIN and whose death started World War I

Francis of As·si·si, St. /ˌfrænsɪs əv əˈsisi/ (1182–1226) an Italian Christian leader who started the Franciscan religious ORDER

Francis Xa·vi·er, St. /ˌfrænsɪs ˈzeɪviɚ/ → see XAVIER, ST. FRANCIS

fran·ci·um /ˈfrænsiəm/ *n.* [U] SYMBOL **Fr** CHEMISTRY a heavy RADIOACTIVE metal that is an ELEMENT. Francium is found naturally in URANIUM or can be produced as part of a NUCLEAR REACTION.

Franck /frɑŋk/**, Cé·sar** /ˈseɪzɑr/ (1822–1890) a French musician, born in Belgium, who wrote CLASSICAL music

Franco- /fræŋkoʊ, fræŋkə/ *prefix* [in nouns and adjectives] **1** relating to France SYN **French**: *a francophone* (=French-speaking) *population* **2** French and something else: *a Franco-German proposal*

Fran·co /ˈfræŋkoʊ/**, Fran·cis·co** /frænˈsɪskoʊ/ (1892–1975) a Spanish military leader and RIGHT-WING politician, who led the Nationalist side in the Spanish Civil War, and ruled Spain as a DICTATOR until his death

fran·co·phone /ˈfræŋkəˌfoʊn, -koʊ-/ *n.* [C] someone who speaks French as their first language —**francophone** *adj.*

Fran·glais /ˌfrɑŋˈgleɪ/ *n.* [U] INFORMAL a mixture of the French and English languages

Frank /fræŋk/ *n.* one of the people that lived in Germany in the third century A.D. and ruled much of western Europe from the fifth century to the ninth century A.D.

frank¹ /fræŋk/ *adj.* **1** honest and truthful: *a frank and open discussion* | +**with** *I'll be frank with you, David – you could have done better.* ►see THESAURUS box at **honest** **2 to be frank** SPOKEN used when you are saying something true that other people may not like: *To be frank, business isn't going very well.* [**Origin:** 1300–1400 French **free, generous**, from Late Latin *Francus* **Frank** (because the Franks, an ancient German people, were given political freedom in France)] —**frankness** *n.* [U]

frank² *n.* [C] a long cooked SAUSAGE, usually eaten in a long piece of bread SYN **wiener**

frank³ *v.* [T] to print a sign on an envelope showing that the cost of sending it has been paid: *The date was franked on the envelope.*

Frank, Anne /æn/ (1929–1945) a Jewish girl who wrote a famous DIARY, in which she describes her life while she and her family were hiding from the Nazis in Amsterdam

Frank·fort /ˈfræŋkfɚt/ the capital city of the U.S. state of Kentucky

frank·fur·ter /ˈfræŋkˌfɚt̬ɚ/ *n.* [C] FORMAL a FRANK

frank·in·cense /ˈfræŋkənˌsɛns/ *n.* [U] a substance that is burnt to give a sweet smell, especially at religious ceremonies

ˈfranking maˌchine *n.* [C] a POSTAGE METER

Frank·lin /ˈfræŋklɪn/**, Benjamin** (1760–1790) a U.S. politician, writer, and scientist, who was involved in writing the Declaration of Independence and the U.S. Constitution → see picture on page A25

frank·ly /ˈfræŋkli/ *adv.* **1** [sentence adverb] used to show that you are saying what you really think about something: ***Quite frankly**, I'm worried about him.* **2** honestly and directly: *She spoke frankly of the difficulties she'd experienced.*

fran·tic /ˈfræntɪk/ *adj.* **1** extremely worried and frightened about a situation, so that you cannot control your feelings: *People were frantic, trying to call relatives after the earthquake.* **2** extremely hurried and using a lot of energy, but not very organized: *I spent three frantic days getting everything ready for Christmas.* → see also FRENETIC —**frantically** /-kli/ *adv.*

frap·pé /fræˈpeɪ/ *n.* [C] **1** a drink served over very thin pieces of ice **2 frappe** /fræp/ a MILKSHAKE

frat /fræt/ *n.* [C] INFORMAL a FRATERNITY: *a frat boy* (=a member of a fraternity)

fra·ter·nal /frəˈtɚnl/ *adj.* FORMAL **1** showing a special friendliness to other people because you share interests or ideas with them: *a fraternal spirit among the workers* **2** [only before noun] relating to an organization formed of people who share interests: *a fraternal organization* **3** relating to brothers: *fraternal loyalty* [**Origin:** 1400–1500 Medieval Latin *fraternalis*, from Latin *frater* **brother**] —**fraternally** *adv.*

fraˌternal ˈtwin *n.* [C usually plural] one of a pair of babies born at the same time to the same mother, but who develop from different EGGS → see also IDENTICAL TWIN

fra·ter·ni·ty /frəˈtɚnət̬i/ *n. plural* **fraternities** **1** [C] a club at a college or university that has only male members → see also SORORITY: *He was president of his college fraternity.* **2** [U] a feeling of friendship between members of a group: *fraternity between nations* **3 the educational/scientific etc. fraternity** all the people who work in a particular profession: *the views of the medical fraternity*

frat·er·nize /ˈfræt̬ɚˌnaɪz/ *v.* [I] to be friendly with someone who is not allowed to be your friend: +**with** *The troops were forbidden to fraternize with the enemy.* —**fraternization** /ˌfræt̬ɚnəˈzeɪʃən/ *n.* [U]

frat·ri·cide /ˈfrætrəˌsaɪd/ *n.* [C,U] TECHNICAL the crime of murdering your brother or sister

fraud /frɔd/ W3 *n.* **1** [C,U] the illegal action of deceiving people in order to gain money, power etc.: **bank/**

F

tax/mail etc. fraud *a rise in credit card fraud* | **election/electoral/voter fraud** *Widespread electoral fraud has been reported.* ►see THESAURUS box at **crime**
2 [C] someone who pretends to be someone else in order to gain money, friendship etc.: *He was finally exposed as a fraud.* | *Pretending to support him makes me* ***feel like a fraud.*** **3** [C] something that is not what it is claimed to be SYN **fake**: *He insisted that the photo was a fraud.* [**Origin:** 1300–1400 Old French *fraude*, from Latin *fraus* **deceiving**]

fraud·u·lent /ˈfrɔdʒələnt/ *adj.* intended to deceive people in an illegal way, in order to gain money, power etc.: *a fraudulent insurance claim* —**fraudulently** *adv.* —**fraudulence** *n.* [U]

fraught /frɔt/ *adj.* full of something, especially problems or negative feelings: **fraught with peril/danger/risk/problems etc.** *Either course of action seemed fraught with danger.* [**Origin:** 1300–1400 Past participle of *fraught* **to load, fill** (14–19 centuries), from Middle Dutch *vracht* **load**]

F

fray¹ /freɪ/ *n.* **1** [C] an argument, fight, or uncontrolled situation: *Three civilians were injured during the fray.* | **enter/join the fray** *Several national organizations have joined the fray, backing Harrison's position.* | **jump/step/leap into the fray** *Then Merton jumped into the fray and tried to persuade company bosses to lower prices.* **2 be/stay above the fray** to not be involved in a fight or argument: *Watkins always tried to stay above the political fray and concentrate on her work.*

fray² *v.* **frays, frayed, fraying** [I,T] **1** if cloth or other material frays or if you fray it, the threads become loose because the material is old: *The jacket's collar had started to fray.* **2** if someone's temper or nerves fray or something frays them, they become annoyed: *It was only 3:00 and tempers were already beginning to fray.* —**frayed** *adj.*

Fra·zier /ˈfreɪʒɚ/, **Joe** /dʒoʊ/ (1944–) a U.S. BOXER who was world CHAMPION in 1970–1973

fraz·zle /ˈfræzəl/ *n.* **be worn to a frazzle** to be extremely tired after doing something: *I'm worn to a frazzle trying to deal with all this publicity.*

fraz·zled /ˈfræzəld/ *adj.* INFORMAL extremely tired and unable to deal with problems or difficulties, especially because you have been very busy: *Some parents say they feel frazzled most nights.*

FRB /ˌɛf ɑr ˈbi/ → see FEDERAL RESERVE BANK

freak¹ /frik/ *n.* [C] **1 computer/fitness/jazz etc. freak** INFORMAL someone who is very interested in a particular thing or activity, or likes something a lot SYN **fanatic** SYN **nut**: *I've been a huge health freak since my daughter was born.* **2** someone who looks very strange or behaves in a very unusual way SYN **weirdo**: *That haircut makes him look like a freak.* **3** something in nature, such as a strangely shaped plant or animal, that is very unusual: *The two headed snake is a* ***freak of nature.*** **4** an unexpected and very unusual event: *By some* ***freak of fate*** *he walked away from the crash completely unhurt.* → see also CONTROL FREAK

freak² *adj.* [only before noun] **a freak accident/storm etc.** an accident, storm etc. that is unexpected and very unusual: *The first day of spring brought rain and freak weather across much of the state.*

freak³ S2 *v.* [I] SPOKEN, INFORMAL to become suddenly angry or afraid, especially so that you cannot control your behavior: *When I told Ben about the accident, he just freaked.*

freak out *phr. v.* INFORMAL **freak sb ↔ out** to become very anxious, upset, or afraid, or to make someone very anxious, upset or afraid: *These actors would all completely freak out and panic in a real medical emergency.* | *Those people really* ***freak me out.***

freak·ish /ˈfrikɪʃ/ *adj.* very unusual and strange, and sometimes frightening: *a freakish eight-foot-tall woman with four arms* —**freakishly** *adv.* —**freakishness** *n.* [U]

ˈfreak show *n.* [C] **1** a place or occasion when people can look at people or animals that look strange or behave in an unusual way: *a circus freak show* **2** a very unusual and strange performance or event which people watch with interest

freak·y /ˈfriki/ *adj. comparative* **freakier**, *superlative* **freakiest** SPOKEN strange and slightly frightening: *It was kind of freaky to meet all of his old girlfriends.*

freck·le /ˈfrɛkəl/ *n.* [C usually plural] a small brown spot on someone's skin, especially the face, usually caused by the sun: *a little girl with red hair and freckles*

freck·led /ˈfrɛkəld/ *adj.* having freckles: *a lightly freckled face*

Fred·ericks·burg /ˈfrɛdrɪksˌbɚg/ a city in the U.S. state of Virginia where the Confederate general Robert E. Lee defeated a Union army in the American Civil War

free¹ /fri/ S1 W1 *adj.*
1 WITHOUT COST not costing any money: *free bus service* | *Admission is free for children.*
2 NOT BUSY if you are free, or have some free time, you have no work, and nothing else that you must do: *I'm free next weekend.* | **+for** *Are you free for lunch on Tuesday?* | *My husband and I never seem to have any* ***free time*** *together.* | **a free morning/afternoon etc.** *I'll give you a call if I have a free evening next week.*
3 WITHOUT RESTRICTIONS without restrictions or controls: *a free exchange of information* | *The country is holding the first* ***free elections*** *in over sixty years.* | **+from/of** *The newspapers are free from government control.* | *the right of* ***free speech*** (=the right to say whatever you want) | *He was given* ***free access to*** *the documents.*
4 ABLE TO DO WHAT YOU WANT allowed to do or say whatever you want without being controlled or restricted: *They dreamed of a day when the country would be free.* | **free to do sth** *The kids are free to come and go as they please.* | **a free country/society** *The government of a free country must conduct its business openly.*
5 NOT BEING USED something that you want to use is free if no one else is using it: *Excuse me, is this seat free?* | **sb's free arm/hand** *He grabbed a knife with his free hand.* ►see THESAURUS box at **empty¹**
6 NOT A PRISONER not a prisoner: *He walked out of the courtroom a free man.* | *She was* ***set free*** *after four years.* | *The boy managed to* ***break free*** *and ran off.* | *The charges were dropped and he* ***walked free*** (=was not put in prison).
7 ANIMALS not kept in a CAGE or controlled by humans: *They* ***set*** *the birds* ***free.*** | *The animals are allowed to* ***run free*** *in the park.*
8 free from/of sth without something that you do not want to have: *Lydia is now completely free from cancer.* | *He longed to be free of obligations.*
9 free of sth/sb away from something or someone, and happy about it: *I was glad to be free of that dismal office at last.*
10 break free to stop being influenced, affected, or controlled by something: **+of/from** *Women are struggling to break free from tradition.*
11 NOT ATTACHED loose and not fastened to anything or held by anything or anyone: *The free end of the flag has been torn by the wind.* | **work/pull/tear etc. free** *Some of the shutters on the windows had broken free of their hinges.*
12 NOT BLOCKED free movement is not blocked or controlled by anything: *We opened both doors to allow a free flow of air through the building.*
13 feel free (to do sth) SPOKEN used to tell someone that they can do something: *If you have any questions, feel free to call me.*
14 get/be given/enjoy a free ride to get something without having to pay for it, because someone else is paying for it: *Big corporations are getting a free ride at taxpayers' expense.*
15 there's no free lunch also **there's no such thing as a free lunch** HUMOROUS used to say that you should not expect to get something good or valuable without having to pay for it or make any effort
16 give sb a free hand also **give sb (a) free rein** to let

someone do whatever they want or need to do in a particular situation: *Managers are given free rein in their departments.*
17 free and easy relaxed, friendly, and without many rules: *a free and easy lifestyle*
18 be free with sth to be generous with something, and possibly more generous than people think you should be: *She is always free with her advice.*
19 it's a free country SPOKEN, HUMOROUS used to say that you are or should be allowed to do something, after someone has said that you should not do it: *I can say whatever I want – it's a free country.*
20 TRANSLATION a free translation gives a general idea of a piece of writing rather than translating every word exactly
21 free of tax/duty etc. not taxed: *The import items are free of customs duty.*
22 NOT SHOWING RESPECT OLD-FASHIONED too friendly, in a way that does not show enough respect: *Your son's manner is rather free.*
23 CHEMISTRY TECHNICAL not combined with any other chemical substance SYN pure: *free oxygen* → see also FREE RADICAL

free² W3 *v.* [T]
1 RELEASE to allow a person or animal to leave prison or a place where they have been kept by force: *The kidnappers freed two of the hostages.*
2 NOT CONTROL to allow someone to say and do what they want by removing restrictions: **free sb/sth from sth** *We were determined to free our country from foreign rule.* | **free sb/sth of sth** *I just wish I were free of some of these duties.*
3 ALLOW SB/STH TO MOVE to release something or someone from a place where they are firmly fastened or trapped: *We're going to need some rope to help free the girl.* | **free yourself** *He struggled to free himself, but the ropes were too tight.* | **free sb/sth from sth** *All the passengers have now been freed from the wreckage.*
4 MAKE AVAILABLE also **free up** to make something available so that it can be used: *Working from home will free up more time to spend with your family.*
5 GET RID OF STH to help someone by removing something bad or harmful, or something that restricts them in some way: **free sb from sth** *Treatment has freed Jenna from her drug addiction.*
6 GIVE SB TIME also **free up** to give someone time to do something, by taking away other jobs that they have to do: **free sb (up) to do sth** *We have freed some staff up to deal with the extra work.*

free³ S3 *adv.* **1** also **for free** without payment: *Children under four can travel free.* | *Gary told me he would do the work for free.* | *We deliver **free of charge**.* **2** not fixed or held in a particular place or position: *The ropes were hanging free.* → see also FREELY, SCOT-FREE

-free /fri/ *suffix* [in adjectives and adverbs] without something that you do not want: *a salt-free diet* | *a trouble-free trip* | *a smoke-free restaurant* (=where you are not allowed to smoke)

ˌfree ˈagent *n.* [C] **1** someone who has no responsibilities to anyone else and can do what they want: *When you are self-employed, you are a free agent.* **2** a professional sports player who does not have a contract with any team

ˌfree associˈation *n.* [U] a method of finding out about someone's mind by asking them to say the first word they think of when you say a particular word —**ˌfree-asˈsociate** *v.* [I]

free·base /ˈfribeɪs/ *v.* [I,T] to smoke the illegal drug COCAINE after heating it over a flame

free·bie /ˈfribi/ *n.* [C] INFORMAL something that you are given free, usually something small and not expensive: *They were ofering baseball caps and other freebies.*

ˌfree-ˈbody ˌdiagram *n.* [C] PHYSICS a DIAGRAM that shows all the forces that have an effect on an object

free·boot·er /ˈfriˌbuṭə/ *n.* [C] OLD USE someone who joins in a war in order to steal other people's goods and money —**freeboot** *v.* [I]

free·born /ˌfriˈbɔrn◂ / *adj.* OLD USE not born as a slave

freed·man /ˈfridmən, -mæn/ *n. plural* **freedmen** /-mən, -mɛn/ [C] OLD USE someone who was born a slave, but has been set free

free·dom /ˈfridəm/ S2 W2 *n.* **1** [C,U] the right to do what you want without being controlled or restricted by anyone: *In those days people had very little freedom.* | *the rights and freedoms of citizens* | **freedom to do sth** *We take our freedom to choose our own husband or wife for granted.* | **political/religious/academic freedom** *The policy will limit academic freedom.* | **freedom of speech/religion/expression etc.** *All students have the right to exercise freedom of speech.* | *Democracy requires **freedom of the press**.* **2** [U] the state of being free and allowed to do what you want: *Cars give people a great sense of freedom.* | **freedom to do sth** *Thanks to the Internet, more and more people have the freedom to work from home.* | **+of** *I like the freedom of being my own boss.* **3** [U] the state of being free because you are not in prison: *Davis celebrated his freedom with a beer.* **4 freedom from sth** the state of not being affected by something that makes you worried, unhappy, afraid etc.: *freedom from hunger* **5 freedom of choice** the right or ability to choose whatever you want to do or have: *The regulations limit freedom of choice for patients.* **6 freedom of information** the availability to everyone of information that a government has about people and organizations → see also LIBERTY

ˈfreedom ˌfighter *n.* [C] someone who fights in a war against an unfair or dishonest government, army etc. → see also GUERRILLA

ˌfreedom of the ˈpress *n.* [U] the right to publish newspapers, magazines etc. and not be controlled or limited by the government, as promised in the First Amendment of the U.S. Constitution

ˈFreedom ˌRiders, the *n.* [C] HISTORY a group of young African-American and white people who took buses all over the southern U.S. in 1961 to test whether new laws were being followed that made it illegal to SEGREGATE (=make separate areas for blacks and whites) public places and services

free ˈenterprise *n.* [U] ECONOMICS the principle and practice of allowing private business to operate without much government control → see also PRIVATE ENTERPRISE

ˌFree ˈExercise ˌClause, the *n.* POLITICS the part of the First Amendment to the U.S. Constitution that promises the people freedom of religion

ˈfree fall, freefall *n.* [C,U] **1** the movement of someone or something through the air without engine power, for example when someone jumps out of an airplane before the PARACHUTE opens **2** a very fast and uncontrolled fall in the value of something: *The economy is **in freefall** and there are no signs that it will stop.* —**free-fall** *v.* [I] —**free-falling** *adj.*

ˈfree-ˌfloating *adj.* not connected to or influenced by anything: *a free-floating presidential adviser*

ˌfree-for-ˈall *n.* [singular] **1** a noisy fight or argument that a lot of people join: *The meeting turned into a free-for-all.* ▸see THESAURUS box at fight² **2** DISAPPROVING a situation in which there is total freedom and anything can happen: *the free-for-all of sexual activity in the 1970s* —**free-for-all** *adj.* [only before noun]

ˈfree-form *adj.* [only before noun] having a shape or structure that is not regular or fixed: *free-form designs*

free·hand /ˈfrihænd/ *adj.* drawn without any special tools, by using just your hands and a pen or pencil: *a freehand sketch* —**freehand** *adv.*

free ˈkick *n.* [C] a chance for a player on a SOCCER team to kick the ball without opposition because the other team did something wrong

free·lance /ˈfrilæns/ *adj., adv.* working independently for different companies rather than having a job with just one: *a freelance journalist* | *Steve plans to start working freelance this year.* [**Origin:** 1800–1900 *free lance* **soldier in former times who sold his fighting skills to anyone**] —**freelance** *v.* [I] *Fran freelances for* *several translation agencies.* —**freelance** also **freelancer** *n.* [C]

free·load·er /ˈfriloʊdɚ/ *n.* [C] DISAPPROVING INFORMAL someone who regularly takes food or other things from other people, without giving anything in return, in a way that is annoying —**freeload** *v.* [I] DISAPPROVING INFORMAL: *Nicole is still freeloading off her boyfriend.*

ˌfree ˈlove *n.* [U] an expression meaning the practice or principle of having sex with many different people without being married, used especially in the 1960s and 1970s

free·ly /ˈfrili/ *adv.* **1** without anyone stopping or limiting something: *the country's first freely elected president* | **talk/speak freely** *Thomas could not find anyone with whom he could speak freely.* **2** if something moves freely, it moves smoothly and nothing prevents it from doing this: *If your muscles are tense and tight, blood cannot circulate freely.* **3 freely available** very easy to obtain: *Information is freely available on the Internet.* **4 freely admit/acknowledge** to agree that something is true, especially when this is difficult SYN **openly**: *I freely admit I made many mistakes.* **5** if a piece of writing is translated freely, the translation does not attempt to translate the original words exactly, but gives the general meaning **6** generously, or in large quantities: *Sugar is given away freely in restaurants.*

F

free·man /ˈfrimən/ *n.* [C] OLD USE someone who is not a slave

ˌfree ˈmarket *n.* [C] an economic system in which prices are not controlled or limited by the government or any other powerful group: *a free-market economy*

ˌfree marketˈeer *n.* [C] ECONOMICS someone who thinks that prices should be allowed to rise and fall naturally and should not be controlled by the government or any other powerful group

Free·ma·son /ˈfriˌmeɪsən/ *n.* [C] FORMAL a Mason

Free·ma·son·ry /ˌfriˈmeɪsənri/ *n.* [U] the system and practices of Masons

ˈfree port *n.* [C] a port where goods from all countries can be brought in and taken out without being taxed

ˌfree ˈradical *n.* [C] TECHNICAL an atom or group of atoms with at least one free ELECTRON, which combines with other atoms very easily

ˌfree-ˈrange *adj.* [only before noun] **1** free-range farm animals are not kept in small CAGES but are allowed to move around in a large area: *free-range hens* **2** free-range meat or eggs come from these farm animals: *a free-range turkey*

free·sia /ˈfriʒə/ *n.* [C] a plant with nice-smelling flowers [**Origin:** 1800–1900 F. H. T. *Freese*, 19th-century German doctor]

ˌfree ˈspirit *n.* [C] someone who lives the way they want to rather than in the way that society considers normal: *Max is a free spirit and doesn't care what people think of him.*

free·stand·ing /ˌfriˈstændɪŋ◂/ *adj.* standing alone without being fastened to a frame, wall, or other support: *a freestanding storage unit*

free·style /ˈfristaɪl/ *n.* **1** [singular] a swimming competition in which swimmers can use whatever style they want, but swimmers always choose the CRAWL (=fast style of swimming): *the 100-meter freestyle* **2** [singular] a sports competition, for example in SKIing, WRESTLING etc. in which all types of movement are allowed **3** [C] a RAP song in which the artist sings words directly from their imagination, without planning or writing them first

free·think·er /ˌfriˈθɪŋkɚ/ *n.* [C] someone who does not accept official opinions or ideas, especially about religion —**freethinking** *adj.*

ˌfree ˈthrow *n.* [C] a chance for one player on a basketball team to throw the ball without any opposition, because a player on the other team did something wrong

Free·town /ˈfritaʊn/ the capital and largest city of Sierra Leone

ˌfree ˈtrade *n.* [U] ECONOMICS a situation in which the goods coming into or going out of a country are not controlled or taxed

ˌfree ˈverse *n.* [U] ENG. LANG. ARTS poetry that does not follow a definite structure and does not RHYME at the end of lines → see also BLANK VERSE

free·ware /ˈfriwɛr/ *n.* [U] COMPUTERS free computer SOFTWARE, often available on the Internet → see also SHAREWARE

free·way /ˈfriweɪ/ S3 *n. plural* **freeways** [C] a very wide road in the U.S., built for fast travel: *a six-lane freeway* | *My car broke down on the freeway.* → see also EXPRESSWAY

free·wheel /ˌfriˈwil/ *v.* [I] to ride a bicycle or drive a vehicle toward the bottom of a hill, without using power from your legs or the engine SYN **coast**

free·wheel·ing /ˌfriˈwilɪŋ◂/ *adj.* [only before noun] without a lot of rules, or not worried about rules: *a freewheeling discussion*

ˌfree ˈwill *n.* [U] **1 do sth of your own free will** to do something because you want to, not because someone else has forced you to: *Bronson gave us his confession of his own free will.* **2** human effort, which some people believe affects what happens in life more than God or FATE

ˌfree ˈworld *n.* **the free world** a name for the DEMOCRATIC countries of the world, especially as opposed to COMMUNIST countries: *The U.S. is often seen as the leader of the free world.*

freeze¹ /friz/ S1 *v. past tense* **froze** /froʊz/ *past participle* **frozen** /ˈfroʊzən/

1 BECOME ICE [I,T] if a liquid or something that contains liquid freezes, it becomes hard and solid because it is very cold → see also MELT: *Water freezes at 32 degrees Fahrenheit.* | *The ground had* ***frozen solid.***

2 FOOD [I,T] to make food extremely cold so that you can preserve it for a long time, or to be able to be preserved in this way: *You can freeze any leftover chili for another meal.* | *Tomatoes don't freeze well.*

3 MACHINE/PIPE/LOCK [I,T] if a machine, pipe, or lock freezes or something freezes it, the liquid and parts inside it become solid with cold, so that it does not work properly SYN **freeze up**: *Run a thin stream of water to help keep the pipes from freezing.* | *The cold weather froze firefighters' hoses.*

4 FEEL COLD [I] SPOKEN if someone freezes, they feel very cold: *You'll freeze if you don't put a coat on.* | *We almost* ***froze to death*** (=felt extremely cold) *at the football game.*

5 WAGES/PRICES [T] to officially stop something from happening in order to prevent money from being spent, or prevent prices, pay etc. from being increased: *He has introduced a plan to freeze state spending and cut taxes.*

6 MONEY/PROPERTY [T] to legally prevent money in a bank from being spent, property from being sold etc.: *The court issued an order* ***freezing*** *the company's* ***assets*** *temporarily.*

7 STOP MOVING [I] to stop moving suddenly and stay completely still and quiet: *His hand froze in mid-air.* | *Freeze! Drop your weapons!*

8 BE UNABLE TO SPEAK [I] if you freeze, you feel so nervous especially when you are speaking in public, that you cannot think of what it was that you meant to say SYN **freeze up**: *When she got up to speak, she just froze.*

9 COMPUTER [I] if a computer or a computer screen freezes, the image on the screen will not change because of a problem with the computer: *The computer froze briefly then started working again.*

10 MOVIE [T] to stop a DVD or video in order to be able to look at a particular image: *When you use the pause button, it freezes a scene.* → see also FREEZE-FRAME

11 PRESERVE [T] if something such as part of an animal, plant or human body is frozen, it is stored at very low temperatures to preserve it: *The embryos are frozen for later use.*

12 freeze to death to become so cold that you die

[**Origin:** Old English *freosan*]

freeze sb ↔ **out** *phr. v.* to deliberately prevent someone from being involved in something by making it difficult for them, not being nice to them etc.: **freeze sb out of sth** *He claims he was frozen out of the decision making process.*

freeze over *phr. v.* if an area or pool of water freezes over, its surface turns into ice: *We'll go skating tomorrow if the lake freezes over.*

freeze up *phr. v.* **1** if something such as a machine, engine, or pipe freezes up, the liquid inside becomes solid with cold so that it does not work properly **2** to suddenly be unable to speak or act normally: *I freeze up every time I try to talk to him.*

freeze² *n.* **1** [C] an occasion when prices or pay are not allowed to be increased: **a price/wage freeze** *The unions have agreed to a wage freeze.* **2** [C usually singular] a short period of time, especially at night, when the temperature is extremely low: *My pansies didn't survive the first **hard freeze** of the season.* **3** [C] a situation in which a company, government etc. decides to stop an activity or process for a period of time: *a hiring freeze* | **+on** *a temporary freeze on immigration* → see also DEEP FREEZE

'freeze-dry *v.* **freeze-dries, freeze-dried, freeze-drying** [T usually passive] to preserve food by freezing and drying it very quickly —**freeze-dried** *adj.*: *freeze-dried instant coffee*

'freeze-frame *n.* [C,U] the process of stopping the action on a DVD or VIDEO at one particular place, or the place where you stop the action —**freeze-frame** *v.* [T]

freez•er /'frizɚ/ S3 *n.* [C] a large piece of electrical equipment that is usually part of a REFRIGERATOR, in which food can be stored at very low temperatures for a long time: *I think there's some fish in the freezer.* → see also DEEP FREEZE

freez•ing¹ /'frizɪŋ/ *n.* [U] **above/below freezing** above or below 32° F or 0° C, the temperature at which water freezes: *Temperatures remained below freezing during the afternoon.*

freezing² *adj.* extremely cold, or feeling extremely cold: *Close the window – it's freezing in here.* | *We were **freezing cold** in the tent last night.*

'freezing ˌpoint *n.* [C usually singular] **1** the temperature at which water turns into ice, 32° F or 0° C **2** the temperature at which a particular liquid freezes: *Alcohol has a lower freezing point than water.* → see also BOILING POINT

freight¹ /freɪt/ *n.* **1** [U] goods that are carried by train, airplane, or ship: *a carrier of passengers, freight, and mail* **2** [U] the money charged for sending goods by train, airplane, or ship: *The basic model is listed at $16,298 plus $500 freight.* **3** [U] the system of sending goods by train, airplane, or ship **4** [C] a FREIGHT TRAIN [**Origin:** 1400–1500 Middle Dutch *vracht, vrecht*]

freight² *v.* [T] to send goods by train, airplane, or ship

freight•er /'freɪṭɚ/ *n.* [C] a large ship that carries goods

'freight train *n.* [C] a train that carries goods, not passengers

Fré•mont /'frimɑnt/, **John C.** (1813–1890) a U.S. soldier, politician, and EXPLORER, who traveled across the western part of North America and made maps of this area. He encouraged U.S. citizens to move to these places, which are now the states of Idaho, Nevada, Washington, Oregon, and California.

French¹ /frɛntʃ/ *n.* **1** the language of France, and some other countries: *Do you speak French?* | *How do you say "mushrooms" **in French**?* **2 the French** the people of France: *The territory was originally colonized by the French.* **3 pardon/excuse my French** SPOKEN INFORMAL used to say that you are sorry that you just used an offensive word

French² *adj.* **1** relating to France or its people: *French wine* | *My boyfriend is French.* **2** relating to the French language: *a French accent*

ˌFrench and ˌIndian 'War, the *n.* [singular] HISTORY the last of four wars fought to gain power in North America that took place from 1754–1763 between Britain and its colonies (COLONY) and France and its colonies, each side having help from Native Americans. Britain won.

ˌFrench 'bread *n.* [U] white bread that is baked in a long narrow shape

ˌFrench Ca'nadian *n.* [C] a person from Canada whose first language is French —**French-Canadian** *adj.*

ˌFrench 'doors *n.* [plural] a pair of doors with many pieces of glass in a frame

ˌFrench 'dressing *n.* [U] a special SAUCE for SALADS that is reddish-orange

ˌFrench-'fried *adj.* cooked in hot oil: *French-fried onions*

ˌFrench 'fry *n. plural* **French fries** [C usually plural] a thin piece of potato that has been cooked in hot oil

French Gui•a•na /ˌfrɛntʃ gi'ɑnə, -'ænə/ a country in northeast South America that is ruled by France

ˌFrench 'horn *n.* [C] a musical instrument that is shaped like a circle, with a wide bell-like opening

ˌFrench 'kiss *n.* [C] a romantic kiss between two people with their mouths open and with their tongues touching —**French-kiss** *v.* [I,T]

French•man /'frɛntʃmən/ *n. plural* **Frenchmen** /-mən/ [C] a man from France

ˌFrench Revo'lution, the *n.* HISTORY the event beginning in 1789 during which the French people got rid of their king and made France a REPUBLIC for the first time

ˌFrench 'toast *n.* [U] pieces of bread put into a mixture of eggs and milk and then cooked in hot oil

ˌFrench 'windows *n.* [plural] FRENCH DOORS

French•wom•an /'frɛntʃˌwʊmən/ *n. plural* **Frenchwomen** /-ˌwɪmɪn/ [C] a woman from France

fre•ne•tic /frə'nɛṭɪk/ *adj.* frenetic activity is fast, exciting, and not very organized: **frenetic pace/activity/motion** *the frenetic pace of life in the city* [**Origin:** 1300–1400 French *frénétique*, from Latin *phreneticus*, from Greek *phren* **mind**]

fren•zied /'frɛnzid/ *adj.* frenzied activity is done with a lot of anxiety or excitement and not much control: *frenzied applause* —**frenziedly** *adv.*

fren•zy /'frɛnzi/ *n. plural* **frenzies** **1** [C,U] the state of being very anxious, excited, and unable to control your behavior: *Gaetz's last minute goal sent the crowd **into a frenzy**.* | **+of** *a frenzy of looting and killing* **2** [C usually singular] a period in which people do a lot of things very quickly: **+of** *Rumors of their divorce stirred up a frenzy of media attention.* | **a buying/selling/shopping etc. frenzy** *The price drop set off a selling frenzy of the company's shares.* → see also FEEDING FRENZY

Fre•on /'friɑn/ *n.* [U] TRADEMARK a chemical that was used for cooling in equipment such as REFRIGERATORS and AIR CONDITIONERS until it was found to be harmful to the environment

freq. the written abbreviation of FREQUENCY or FREQUENTLY

fre•quen•cy /'frikwənsi/ S3 *n. plural* **frequencies** **1** [C,U] the number of times that something happens within a particular period or within a particular group of people: **+of** *the frequency of serious road accidents* | *Her memory lapses are happening **with increasing frequency**.* | **high/low frequency** *Developed countries have a much lower frequency of infant mortality.* **2** [U] the fact that something happens a lot: **+of** *We are concerned about the frequency of crime in the area.* | **with alarming/surprising/depressing etc. frequency** *Businesses come and go with alarming frequency.* **3** [C] the number of radio waves broadcast per second by a particular station, used to express where to find a station on the radio **4** [C,U] PHYSICS the number of sound, light, or radio WAVES that pass any point per second, which is determined by the WAVELENGTH (=the distance between two points on the wave): ***high frequency sounds***

F

ˈfrequency disˌtribution *n.* [C] MATH a GRAPH or table that shows how frequently a particular value appears or exists in a set of data

ˈfrequency ˌtable *n.* [C] MATH a TABLE (=organized list) that shows how often a number, a range of numbers, or any other sort of information appears in a set of data

fre·quent[1] /ˈfrikwənt/ W3 *adj.* happening or doing something often OPP **infrequent**: *His absences became more frequent.* | **a frequent flier/traveler/visitor etc.** *Shaw's Market is offering a discount to frequent shoppers.* [**Origin:** 1400–1500 French, Latin *frequens* **crowded, full**]

frequent[2] *v.* [T usually passive] FORMAL to go to a particular place often: *The hotel is* ***frequented by*** *American tourists.*

ˌfrequent ˈflier *n.* [C] someone who is often a passenger on a particular AIRLINE, so that they receive free flight tickets, a more comfortable place to sit etc.: **frequent flier program/mileage/award etc.** *Employers allow business travelers to keep frequent flier miles for their own use.*

F

fre·quent·ly /ˈfrikwəntli/ S3 W2 *adv.* very often or many times SYN **often**: *Stir the sauce frequently to avoid burning.* | *You see her pretty frequently, don't you?*

fres·co /ˈfrɛskoʊ/ *n. plural* **frescoes** or **frescos** [C] a painting made on a wall, on a surface of wet PLASTER → see also MURAL

fresh /frɛʃ/ S2 W2 *adj.*
1 FOOD/FLOWERS a) fresh food is very recently produced, picked, or prepared and tastes good: *fresh vegetables* | *a fresh pot of coffee* | *You can use fresh or frozen strawberries.* | **+from** *The beans are fresh from the garden.* | *The cookies were* ***fresh out of the oven.*** | **stay/keep/remain fresh** *The bread will stay fresh for several days.* **b)** fresh flowers have recently been picked: *a vase of fresh flowers* ▸see THESAURUS box at **new**
2 NEW new and clean or unused, and replacing something that was there before: *I'll bring you a fresh glass.* | *Will you put* ***fresh sheets*** (=clean sheets) *on the beds in the guest room?* | *Brighten up your home with a* ***fresh coat of paint.***
3 RECENT made, done, experienced, or having happened recently: *fresh lion tracks* | *fresh snow* | *It's a good idea to reread the notes you take in class while they are still* ***fresh in your mind.***
4 fresh air air from outside, especially away from a city where the air is cleaner: *I leave the window open at night to get some fresh air.*
5 INTERESTING something fresh is good or interesting because it has not been done, seen, read etc. before: *Their music is fresh and exciting.* | *Ryan will bring a* ***fresh approach*** *to the job.* | *We need some* ***fresh ideas.*** | *Let's* ***take a fresh look at*** *the problem.*
6 NOT TIRED full of energy because you are not tired: *Go to bed early so that you'll be fresh in the morning.* | *Despite her busy day, she arrived looking* ***fresh as a daisy*** (=not tired and ready to do things).
7 fresh from sth a) also **fresh out of sth** having just finished something such as your education or training, and often not having a lot of experience: *She got the job fresh out of law school.* **b)** having just come from a particular place or experience: *The team is fresh from their victory over Colorado.*
8 WATER fresh water contains no salt and comes from rivers and lakes
9 COOL/CLEAN looking, feeling, smelling, or tasting pleasantly clean or cool: *a fresh minty taste*
10 be fresh out of sth SPOKEN to have just used your last supplies of something: *Sorry, we're fresh out of swordfish.*
11 a fresh start an act of starting something again in a completely new and different way after being unsuccessful: *She moved to California to* ***make a fresh start.***
12 APPEARANCE clean, pleasant, and bright: *bright, fresh colors* | *a fresh complexion*
13 WEATHER wind or weather that is fresh feels fairly cold: *a fresh breeze*
14 get/be fresh with sb a) to behave or speak in a way that does not show respect for someone: *Don't you get fresh with me, son!* **b)** to show someone in a confident but impolite way that you think they are sexually attractive: *He started getting fresh with me.*
15 PERSON SLANG a person or thing that is fresh is very good or attractive SYN **cool**: *The party was fresh.*
[**Origin:** 1200–1300 Old French *freis*] → see also **new/fresh blood** at BLOOD (3) —**freshness** *n.* [U]

fresh- /frɛʃ/ *prefix* [+ past participle] **fresh-made/fresh-cut/fresh-grated etc.** having just been made, cut, grated etc.: *fresh-squeezed orange juice* → see also FRESHLY

fresh·en /ˈfrɛʃən/ *v.* **1** [T] to make something look clean, new, and attractive, or smell nice SYN **freshen up**: *We were looking for a way to freshen the company's image.* **2** [T] to add more of a drink to someone's glass or cup: *Can I freshen your drink?* **3** [I] if wind or the weather freshens, it gets colder

freshen up *phr. v.* **1 freshen yourself up** to wash your hands and face in order to feel clean and comfortable: *Sara hurried into the bathroom to freshen up before the meeting.* **2 freshen sth ↔ up** to make something look clean, new, and attractive, or smell nice: *I'm going to buy some white paint to freshen up the bathroom walls.*

ˈfresh-faced *adj.* having a young, healthy-looking face, and often seeming to have little experience or knowledge of the world: *a fresh-faced teenager*

fresh·ly /ˈfrɛʃli/ *adv.* [+ past participle] very recently: *freshly ground black pepper* | *freshly painted walls*

fresh·man /ˈfrɛʃmən/ S2 *n. plural* **freshmen** /-mən/ [C] a student in the first year of HIGH SCHOOL or college → see also JUNIOR

fresh·wa·ter /ˈfrɛʃˌwɔt̬ɚ/ *adj.* [only before noun] BIOLOGY relating to or coming from rivers or lakes, rather than the ocean: *freshwater lakes* | *freshwater crabs* → see also SALTWATER

fret[1] /frɛt/ *v.* **fretted, fretting** [I] to feel worried about small or unimportant things: *Don't fret – everything will be all right.* | **+about/over** *She's always fretting about the children.* [**Origin:** Old English *fretan* **to eat**]

fret[2] *n.* [C] one of the raised lines on the NECK (=long straight part) of a GUITAR, BANJO etc.

fret·ful /ˈfrɛtfəl/ *adj.* anxious and complaining, especially about small or unimportant things: *The baby was tired and fretful.* —**fretfully** *adv.* —**fretfulness** *n.* [U]

fret·ted /ˈfrɛt̬ɪd/ *adj.* TECHNICAL cut or shaped into complicated patterns as decoration

fret·work /ˈfrɛtˀwɚk/ *n.* [U] patterns cut into thin wood, or the activity of making these patterns

Freud /frɔɪd/, **Sig·mund** /ˈsɪgmənd/ (1856–1939) an Austrian doctor who developed a new system for understanding the way that people's minds work, and a new way of treating mental illness called PSYCHOANALYSIS. His ideas have had a very great influence on the way that people think in the 20th century.

Freud·i·an /ˈfrɔɪdiən/ *adj.* **1** relating to Sigmund Freud's ideas about the way the mind works, and the way it can be studied **2** a Freudian remark or action is connected with the ideas about sex that people have in their minds but do not usually talk about

ˌFreudian ˈslip *n.* [C] something you say that is different from what you intended to say, but shows your true thoughts

Fri. a written abbreviation of FRIDAY

fri·a·ble /ˈfraɪəbəl/ *adj.* EARTH SCIENCE friable rocks or soil are easily broken into very small pieces or into powder

fri·ar /ˈfraɪɚ/ *n.* [C] a man who belongs to a Catholic group, whose members in past times traveled around teaching about religion and who were very poor → see also MONK

fric·as·see /ˈfrɪkəˌsi/ *n.* [C,U] a dish made of small pieces of meat in a thick SAUCE —**fricassee** *v.* [T]

fric·a·tive /ˈfrɪkət̬ɪv/ *n.* [C] ENG. LANG. ARTS a sound, such as /f/ or /z/, made by forcing your breath through a narrow opening between your lips, or between your tongue and your lips, teeth, or the top of your mouth

fric·tion /ˈfrɪkʃən/ *n.* **1** [C usually plural, U] disagreement or angry feelings between people: **+with/between** *We want to avoid unnecessary friction with our neighbors.* **2** [U] the action of one surface rubbing against another: *Friction against the rock can wear through your rope.* **3** [U] PHYSICS the natural force that prevents one surface from sliding easily over another surface: *Putting oil on both surfaces reduces friction.* [**Origin:** 1500–1600 French, Latin *frictio*, from *fricare* **to rub**]

Fri·day /ˈfraɪdi, -deɪ/ WRITTEN ABBREVIATION **Fri.** *n.* [C,U] the sixth day of the week, between Thursday and Saturday: *Our Spanish class has a test Friday.* | *Richard's birthday is* ***on Friday****.* | *Mom said she mailed the letter* ***last Friday****.* | *We're having a huge party* ***next Friday****!* | *It is supposed to rain* ***this Friday*** (=the next Friday that is coming). | *Jody only works* ***on Fridays*** (=each Friday). | **Friday morning/afternoon/night etc.** *I've set aside a time for you on Friday morning.* [**Origin:** Old English *frigedæg* **day of Frigg, female god of love**] → see Grammar box at SUNDAY

fridge /frɪdʒ/ S3 *n.* [C] INFORMAL a REFRIGERATOR

fried /fraɪd/ the PAST TENSE and PAST PARTICIPLE of FRY

Frie·dan /ˈfridn/, **Bet·ty** /ˈbɛti/ (1921–2006) a U.S. writer whose ideas were important in starting the modern WOMEN'S MOVEMENT

Fried·man /ˈfridmən/, **Milton** (1912–2006) a U.S. ECONOMIST who helped to develop the idea of MONETARISM

friend /frɛnd/ S1 W1 *n.* [C]
1 PERSON YOU LIKE someone who you like very much and like to spend time with: *Jerry, I'd like to introduce you to my friend Lucinda.* | **be friends with sb** *Billy's parents are friends with my dad.* | *I'm going to visit* ***a friend of mine*** *in New York.* | *They've been* ***best friends*** *since kindergarten.* | *I ran into* ***an old friend*** (=someone who has been your friend for a long time) *last night.* | **good/close friends** *We've always been good friends.* | *I met my husband through* ***a friend of a friend****.* | *A* ***friend of the family*** *is taking care of Greg.* | *I wish I had a larger* ***circle of friends****.*
2 **make friends** to meet someone and become friendly with them: *Did you make any new friends at school today?* | **+with** *A little boy came over and tried to make friends with Tommy.*
3 **be just (good) friends** SPOKEN used to say that you are friendly with someone but are not having a romantic relationship with them: *I'm not going out with Nathan, you know – we're just friends.*
4 SUPPORTER someone who supports a theater, arts organization, CHARITY etc. by giving money or help: **+of** *Carol is chairman of the Friends of the Library committee.*
5 NOT AN ENEMY someone who is not an enemy and will not harm you or cause trouble for you: *our friends and allies around the world* | *Don't worry, you're among friends here.*
6 **have friends in high places** to know important people who can help you: *I just happened to have friends in high places who could arrange a meeting with the mayor.*
7 **With friends like that, who needs enemies?** SPOKEN, HUMOROUS used to say that someone who you thought was your friend has done something to you that was not nice
8 **be no friend of sth** to oppose someone or something: *I've never been a friend of conservative politics.*
9 **our/your/my friend** SPOKEN used to talk about someone you do not know, who is doing something annoying: *Our friend with the loud voice is back.*
10 AT PUBLIC OCCASION SPOKEN used to speak to a group of people in a meeting or other formal public occasion: *Friends, we are gathered here today to witness the marriage of John and Beth.*
11 **Friend** a member of the Society of Friends SYN **Quaker**
12 **a friend in need (is a friend indeed)** FORMAL used to say that someone who helps you when you need it is truly a friend
[**Origin:** Old English *freond*]

friend·less /ˈfrɛndlɪs/ *adj.* having no friends and no one to help you

friend·ly /ˈfrɛndli/ S2 W3 *adj.* *comparative* **friendlier**, *superlative* **friendliest** **1** behaving toward someone in a way that shows you like them and are ready to talk to them or help them: *The receptionist was very friendly.* | *a friendly smile* | **+to/toward** *She was always kind and friendly to me.*

THESAURUS

warm friendly: *Sonya's a very warm person.*
nice friendly and kind: *Everyone seemed really nice.*
amiable friendly and easy to like: *a big, amiable kid*
cordial friendly and polite but formal: *The two nations have always maintained cordial relations.*
welcoming making you feel happy and relaxed: *a welcoming atmosphere*
hospitable friendly, welcoming, and generous to visitors: *They were very kind and hospitable to us.*

2 people who are friendly are friends: *I didn't know that you and Ken were so friendly.* | **+with** *Betty's very friendly with the Jacksons.* | *My ex-wife and I are still* ***on friendly terms****.* **3** not at war with your own country, or not opposing you: *friendly nations* **4** used to describe a situation in which people who are friends compete with each other without getting angry: *a friendly game of poker* | *a friendly rivalry* → see also ENVIRONMENTALLY FRIENDLY —**friendliness** *n.* [U]

GRAMMAR

Although **friendly** ends in "ly," it is an adjective and not an adverb: *Amy is a very friendly girl.* | *We aim to treat all our clients in a friendly, courteous manner.*

-friendly /frɛndli/ *suffix* [in adjectives] **1** appropriate, helpful, or easy to use for a particular group of people: *user-friendly software* | *family-friendly hotels* | *business-friendly laws* **2** not harming something: *eco-friendly paper products* (=not harming the environment)

ˌfriendly ˈfire *n.* [U] bombs, bullets etc. that accidentally kill people who are fighting on the same side

friend·ship /ˈfrɛndʃɪp/ *n.* **1** [C] a relationship between friends: *Our friendship developed quickly over the weeks that followed.* | **+with/between** *The friendship between the two women began in college.* | *I envied their* ***close friendship****.* | *The two boys* ***formed a*** *deep and lasting* ***friendship****.* **2** [U] the feelings and behavior that exist between friends: *I could always rely on her for friendship and support.* | **sb's friendship** *I have always treasured Patsy's friendship.* **3** [C,U] a good relationship between two countries in which they support and help each other and do not fight with each other: *the long friendship between the two countries* | *a treaty of friendship and cooperation*

fri·er /ˈfraɪɚ/ *n.* [C] another spelling of FRYER

fries /fraɪz/ **1** the plural of FRY **2** the third person singular form of the verb FRY

frieze /friz/ *n.* [C] a thin border along the top of the wall of a building or in a room, usually decorated with pictures, patterns etc.

frig·ate /ˈfrɪgɪt/ *n.* [C] a small, fast ship used in wars, especially for protecting other ships

fright /fraɪt/ *n.* **1** [singular, U] a sudden feeling of fear: *Darren was pale with fright.* | **give sb a fright** *The heart attack gave Dick quite a fright, but he's doing well.* ▶see THESAURUS box at **fear**[1] **2** **look a fright** OLD-FASHIONED to look unattractive, or much worse than usual → see also STAGE FRIGHT

fright·en /ˈfraɪtˀn/ *v.* [T] to make someone feel afraid: *Travis, you just frighten the dog when you play that music.* | *The driver was frightened by the shots.*
frighten sb ↔ **away** *phr. v.* to make a person or

animal feel so afraid or nervous that they go or stay away or do not do something that they were going to do: *Our yelling and screaming frightened the bear away.*

frighten sb **into** (doing) sth *phr. v.* to persuade someone to do something by making them afraid: *Mrs. Fenn tried to frighten the boy into telling her who had broken her window.*

frighten sb/sth ↔ **off** *phr. v.* to make a person or animal feel so afraid or nervous that they go or stay away or do not do something that they were going to do: *They believe that banging on pots will frighten off evil spirits.*

frighten sb **out of** (doing) sth *phr. v.* to persuade someone not to do something by making them afraid: *The crash frightened small investors out of the market.*

fright·ened /ˈfraɪtˀnd/ *adj.* feeling afraid SYN **scared**: *a frightened animal* | **+of** *He was very frightened of being left alone.* | **frightened that** *I was frightened I'd lose my job.* | **frightened to do sth** *I am frightened to go back home.* | *She was* ***too frightened to*** *testify against the man that attacked her.* | *I was* ***frightened to death*** (=very scared) *when I saw a burglar in the house.* → see Word Choice box at ADJECTIVE

THESAURUS

afraid/scared frightened because you think that you may get hurt or that something bad may happen: *It sounded awful, and I was afraid to look.* | *She was scared of her father.*
terrified very frightened: *I'm terrified of heights.*
petrified very frightened, often so that you cannot move: *He stood petrified as the dogs approached.*

fright·en·ing /ˈfraɪtˀnɪŋ/ *adj.* making you feel afraid or nervous: *The crime rate in this city is frightening.* | *Going into the hospital can be very frightening.* | **it is frightening to do sth** *It's frightening to think that such evil people exist.* → see Word Choice box at ADJECTIVE —**frighteningly** *adv.*: *The ice seemed frighteningly thin.*

fright·ful /ˈfraɪtfəl/ *adj.* OLD-FASHIONED very bad, or not nice: *a frightful accident* —**frightfulness** *n.* [U]

fright·ful·ly /ˈfraɪtfəli/ *adv.* [+ adj.] OLD-FASHIONED very: *Lawrence was frightfully strict with the children.*

frig·id /ˈfrɪdʒɪd/ *adj.* **1** very cold: *frigid winds* **2** a woman who is frigid does not like having sex **3** LITERARY not friendly or nice: *a frigid look* —**frigidly** *adv.* —**frigidity** /frɪˈdʒɪdəti/ *n.* [U]

frill /frɪl/ *n.* [C] **1** additional features that are nice but not necessary: *Some cheaper airlines offer few frills.* | *If you need to save money, choose a well-made,* ***no-frills*** *model.* **2** an edge on a piece of cloth that has many small folds in it and that is used as decoration: *Cindy's dress was covered with frills and bows.*

frill·y /ˈfrɪli/ *adj. comparative* **frillier**, *superlative* **frilliest** having many frills: *a frilly nightgown*

fringe[1] /frɪndʒ/ *n.* [C] **1** a row of threads or thin pieces of material that are attached at one end to the edge of a curtain, piece of clothing etc. for decoration **2** people, activities, or parts of a society that are different from what most people think is normal or acceptable: *Hockey moved from the fringe to become a mainstream sport.* | *a small group* ***on the fringes of*** *the art world* | **the nationalist/radical etc. fringe** *activists on the political fringe of the union* → see also **the lunatic fringe** at LUNATIC (3) **3** the part of a thing or place that is farthest from the center: **+of** *It was easier to move around on the fringe of the crowd.*

fringe[2] *adj.* [only before noun] different from the most usual or accepted way of thinking or doing things: **fringe activists/groups/movements etc.** *The government coalition included several smaller fringe parties.* → see also FRINGE BENEFIT

fringe[3] *v.* [T] to be around the edge of something SYN **border**: *A line of trees fringed the pool.*

ˈfringe ˌbenefit *n.* [C usually plural] a service or advantage that you are given with a job, in addition to your pay, such as health insurance, a company car etc.

frip·per·y /ˈfrɪpəri/ *n. plural* **fripperies** [C usually plural] an unnecessary and useless object or decoration [**Origin:** 1500–1600 French *friperie* **old clothes or pieces of cloth**, from Medieval Latin *faluppa* **piece of dried grass**]

Fris·bee, **frisbee** /ˈfrɪzbi/ *n.* [C,U] TRADEMARK a piece of plastic shaped like a plate that you throw to someone else to catch as a game

frisk /frɪsk/ *v.* **1** [T] to search someone for hidden weapons, drugs etc. by passing your hands over their body: *Visitors to the ceremony were frisked.* **2** [I] OLD-FASHIONED to run and jump in a playful way: *A puppy frisked at his heels.*

frisk·y /ˈfrɪski/ *adj. comparative* **friskier**, *superlative* **friskiest** **1** full of energy, fun, and cheerfulness: *a frisky colt* **2** INFORMAL feeling sexually excited —**friskily** *adv.* —**friskiness** *n.* [U]

fris·son /friˈsoʊn/ *n.* [C usually singular] a sudden feeling of excitement or fear: **+of** *A frisson of alarm went down my back.*

frit·ter[1] /ˈfrɪtɚ/ *n.* [C] a thin piece of fruit, vegetable, or meat covered with a mixture of eggs and flour and cooked in hot oil: *apple fritters*

fritter[2]

fritter sth ↔ **away** *phr. v.* to waste time, money, or effort on something small or unimportant, so that you gradually have none left: **fritter sth ↔ away on sth** *He's just frittering away his money on booze and poker.*

fritz /frɪts/ *n.* **be/go on the fritz** INFORMAL if something is or goes on the fritz, it is not working correctly: *My TV is on the fritz again.*

fri·vol·i·ty /frɪˈvɑləti/ *n. plural* **frivolities** [C,U] behavior or activities that are not serious or sensible: *Frivolity is out of place on such a solemn occasion.*

friv·o·lous /ˈfrɪvələs/ *adj.* **1** not serious or sensible, especially in a way that is not appropriate for a particular occasion: *Work time is too valuable to waste on frivolous games.* | *New York is trying to limit the number of* ***frivolous lawsuits.*** **2** a frivolous person likes having fun rather than doing serious or sensible things: *Having all that money had turned Maria into a frivolous person.* —**frivolously** *adv.*

frizz /frɪz/ *v.* [I,T] INFORMAL if your hair frizzes or you frizz it, it curls very tightly and looks messy —**frizz** *n.* [U]

friz·zle /ˈfrɪzəl/ *v.* [I,T] INFORMAL also **frizzle up** to dry or burn something, or to be dried or burned, especially into a curly shape

frizz·y /ˈfrɪzi/ *adj. comparative* **frizzier**, *superlative* **frizziest** frizzy hair is tightly curled and looks a little messy

fro /froʊ/ *adv.* → see TO AND FRO[1]

frock /frɑk/ *n.* [C] **1** OLD-FASHIONED a woman's or girl's dress: *a party frock* **2** a long loose piece of clothing worn by some Christian MONKS

ˌfrock ˈcoat *n.* [C] a knee-length coat for men, worn in the 19th century

frog /frɔg, frɑg/ *n.* [C] **1** a small green animal that lives near water and has long legs for jumping → see also TOAD **2 have a frog in your throat** INFORMAL to have difficulty speaking because of a sore throat **3 Frog** an insulting word for a French person [**Origin:** Old English *frogga*]

frog·man /ˈfrɔgmən/ *n. plural* **frogmen** /-mən/ [C] someone who swims under water using special equipment to help them breathe, especially as a job

frol·ic[1] /ˈfrɑlɪk/ *v. past tense and past participle* **frolicked**, **frolicking** [I] to play in an active, happy way: *The penguins were frolicking in the icy waters.* [**Origin:** 1500–1600 Dutch *vroolijk* **happy**]

frolic[2] *n.* [C often plural] a cheerful, enjoyable game or activity: *two weeks of fun and frolics*

frol·ic·some /ˈfrɑlɪksəm/ *adj.* LITERARY active and liking to play: *frolicsome kittens*

from /frəm; *strong* frʌm/ S1 W1 *prep.*
1 WHERE SB/STH STARTS starting at a particular place or position: *a flight from Atlanta* | *the main road from the south* | *Where did he fall from?* | **from sth to sth** *How do I get from the airport to the university?* | **away from sth** *He walked slowly away from the car.* | **from behind/under etc. sth** *Come out from behind that tree.* | *He was grinning* ***from ear to ear***. | *Reilly was encased* ***from head to toe*** (=all over his body) *in plaster and gauze.*
2 DISTANCE used to express a distance: *We live about five miles from Boston.* | **away from sb/sth** *He was only a few feet away from me.*
3 WHEN STH STARTS starting at a particular time: *He'll be here tomorrow from about seven o'clock onward.* | **from sth to sth** *I was only there from 11:30 to 1 o'clock.* | ***From now on*** (=starting now and continuing into the future), *I'm only going to work in the mornings.* | *The TV was on constantly,* ***from morning till night***.
4 HOW LONG AFTER used to say how long after a particular time something will happen: *My birthday is two weeks from tomorrow.* | *I'll call you back about an hour from now.*
5 WHERE YOU DO STH if you see, watch, or do something from a place, this is where you are when you see, watch, or do it: *From the top of the hill, you can see for miles.* | *He called me yesterday from Paris.* | **from behind sth** *Sandi looked at me disapprovingly from behind her desk.*
6 ORIGIN used to say what the origin of something is: *She got the idea from her sister.* | *I caught the flu from another student in my class.* | *music from the movie "Star Wars"*
7 SENT/GIVEN BY SB sent or given by someone: *We got a message from Fred yesterday.* | *You need to get permission from your parents.* | *A bill from the hospital arrived today.* | *Have you heard anything from Gary yet?*
8 RANGE starting at a particular limit or price: **from sth to sth** *The sizes range from small to extra-large.* | *This process can take anything from a few weeks to a few months.*
9 ORIGINAL STATE starting in a particular condition or state before changing: *The story has been translated from French.* | **from sth to/into sth** *The price had risen from $25 to $40.* | *Things have gone* ***from bad to worse*** *since Tara moved in.*
10 PLACE someone who comes from a particular place was born there or lives, works, or belongs there: *I'm from Texas.* | *The guy from the toy store called.* | *Where are you from?*
11 REMOVING if something is moved or taken from a place or person, it is removed, taken away or taken out: *He took a notebook from his pocket.* | **away from sb/sth** *I tried to take the knife away from him.* | **from behind/under etc. sth** *She pulled another bag out from under the table.*
12 REASON FOR STH used for saying what made you form a particular opinion or judgment: *I speak from experience.* | *From what I understand, you all did pretty well on the test.*
13 CAUSE OF STH used to state the cause of something: *Death rates from accidents have declined.* | **from doing sth** *I've gained a lot of weight this winter from not doing any exercise.*
14 PROGRESS used to talk about progress or development with relation to where you started or where you will finish: *How far are you from finishing?*
15 STOP STH used after words such as "protect," "prevent," or "keep," to introduce the situation or action that is stopped, avoided, or prevented: *Get a hat that offers good protection from the sun.* | **from doing sth** *Winston's bad eyesight prevented him from driving.*
16 from place to place/house to house etc. going to a number of different places, houses etc.: *He walked from place to place selling his goods.*
17 from day to day/minute to minute etc. used for saying that something keeps changing: *My health is improving from day to day.*
18 vary/differ from sth to sth to be different in each individual situation: *The treatment will vary from patient to patient.*
19 DIFFERENCE used for talking about differences between people or things: *She's quite different from her sister.* | *Our two cats are so much alike, I can never tell one from the other.*
20 SEPARATION used for expressing the idea of separation: *The children had been separated from their mothers.*
21 MADE OF STH used to state the substance that is used to make something: *Our Christmas tree* ***is made from*** *recycled plastic.*
22 SELECTION used for stating the group that is the source of a selection: *There are many different colors to choose from.*
23 SUBTRACTION used for stating a number or amount that is reduced by a smaller number or amount: *Subtract three from fifteen.*
[**Origin:** Old English]

WORD CHOICE from and since
Use **from** when you are referring to the length of time during which something happened in the past: *She lived in France from 1988 to 1995.* Use **since** when you want to say that something has been happening from a particular time in the past until now: *She's been back in the U.S. since 1995.*

F

Fromm /frɑm/, **Er·ich** /ˈɛrɪk/ (1900–1980) a U.S. PSYCHOLOGIST, born in Germany, who wrote about the way that social conditions and arrangements affect human behavior

frond /frɑnd/ *n.* [C] BIOLOGY the type of leaf which is divided into smaller parts that a FERN or PALM has

front

Joe ran in front of the bus. Joe got a seat at the front of the bus.

front¹ /frʌnt/ S1 W1 *n.*
1 PART THAT IS FARTHEST FORWARD the front the part of something that is farthest forward in the direction that it faces or moves OPP **back**: **+of** *He stepped forward to the front of the stage.* | *I pushed my way toward the front of the crowd.* | *She always sits* ***at the front of*** *the class.* | *Can I sit* ***in front*** (=in the front part of a car), *Mom?* | *When we finally got to* ***the front of the line***, *the tickets were sold out.*
2 FORWARD SIDE/SURFACE the front the side or surface of something that is in the direction that it faces or moves OPP **back**: **+of** *Ben had just finished painting the front of the house.* | *The front of the coin has a picture of an eagle on it.* | *Where did the scratch* ***on the front of*** *the car come from?* | *His sweater had a stain* ***down the front***.
3 FIRST PAGES the front the first pages of a book, newspaper etc., especially inside the front cover OPP **back**: *Her name is* ***in the front of*** *the book.*
4 in front of sth a) near the side of something that is in the direction that it faces or moves OPP **behind**: *They've set up some food booths in front of the museum.* | *I parked in front of Paul's car.* **b)** near the entrance to a building: *He dropped me off* ***right in front of*** *the building.* **c)** facing something, so that you can see it if you look forward: *She sat down in front of the mirror.* | **in front of the TV/computer etc.** *The average child spends three to four hours a day in front of the TV.* **d)** in a position where a car, train etc. is likely to run you down and seriously injure or kill you: *She ran out in front of the car.*
5 in front of sb a) ahead of someone, in the direction

that they are facing or moving OPP **behind**: *This really tall guy came and sat in front of me.* **b)** when someone is where they can see or hear you: *I didn't want to say anything in front of the kids.* **c)** when a group of people are watching or listening to you: *The band played in front of a crowd of 8,000.* **d)** if you have problems or difficulties in front of you, you will need to deal with them soon
6 the front the most important side or surface of something, that you look at first → see also REAR OPP **back**: *The postcard had a picture of our hotel on the front.* | **+of** *His picture is on the front of the book.*
7 in front a) ahead of something or someone SYN **ahead** OPP **behind**: *He drove straight into the car in front.* **b)** winning something such as a competition or an election SYN **ahead** OPP **behind**: *Opinion polls show the Democrats way out in front.* **c)** in the area at the front of a building OPP **in back**: *a house with a tree in front*
8 out front a) outside in front of a house or other building, usually near the main entrance OPP **out back**: *Two cars were parked out front.* **b)** in the part of a theater, restaurant etc. where the public is
9 WEATHER [C] EARTH SCIENCE the place where two areas of air of different temperatures meet, often shown as a line on weather maps: **a warm/cold front** (=the edge of an area of warm or cold air)
10 up front INFORMAL **a)** money that is paid up front is paid before work is done, or before goods are supplied: *We need $200 up front.* **b)** directly and clearly from the start: *I told her up front that I wasn't interested.* → see also UPFRONT **c)** in the part of a car where the driver sits
11 TYPE OF ACTIVITY [C] a particular area or activity: **on the political/economic etc. front** *Things did not look good on the economic front.* | *Excellent teamwork has brought improvement* ***on all fronts***.
12 ILLEGAL BUSINESS [C] something that hides a secret or an illegal activity: **+for** *The cafe was being used as a front for prostitution.*
13 HIDE FEELINGS [C usually singular] a way of behaving that shows what you want people to see, rather than what you feel: *His arrogance is just a front. Deep down he's really insecure.* | *I know you're scared, but you've got to* ***put up a*** *brave* ***front***. | *When disciplining children, it is important that parents present* ***a united front***.
14 ORGANIZATION [singular] used in the name of a political party or unofficial military organization: *the People's Liberation Front*
15 WAR [C] the area where fighting happens in a war SYN **front line**: *Trucks are heading toward the front with fresh supplies.* → see also HOME FRONT
16 BODY sb's front someone's chest, or the part of their body that faces forward: *You've spilled juice all down your front!*
[**Origin:** 1200–1300 French, Latin *frons* **forehead (=top of the face), front**]

> **WORD CHOICE** **in front of, behind, in back of, at/in the front of, at/in the back of, face, across from**
> • **In front of** (opposite **behind** or **in back of**) is used when one thing is separate from the other: *A boy ran out in front of the bus* (=in the street outside the bus).
> • **At/in the front of** (opposite **at/in the back of**) is used when one thing is inside or part of the other: *The boy took a seat at/in the front of the bus* (=in the front part of the bus).
> • If you can see something from the front part of a building, the building **faces** that thing: *Our hotel faced the central square.*
> • A person or place that faces another one exactly, with a space between, is **across from** it. If the bus stop is *across from the school*, it is not *in front of the school* but on the other side of the street. *I live across from Greg.*

front² S1 W2 *adj.* [only before noun] **1** at, on, or in the front of something OPP **back**: *There was a "For Sale" sign in the* ***front yard***. | *You only need one key for both the* ***front door*** *and the back door.* | *Let's sit in the* ***front row***. | *The title is on the* ***front cover*** *of the book.* **2** a front man or organization acts legally in business as a way of hiding a secret or illegal activity: *a front organization for importing heroin* **3** TECHNICAL a front vowel sound is made by raising your tongue at the front of your mouth, such as the vowel sound in "see" OPP **back**

front³ *v.* **1** [I,T] if a building fronts something or fronts onto it, the front of the building faces it: **+on/onto** *The hotel fronts onto a busy road.* **2** [T] to be the leader or main representative of a particular group: *Genesis was originally fronted by Peter Gabriel.* **3** [T] to be in front of something: *The mansion is fronted by a huge lawn.*
front for sb/sth *phr. v.* INFORMAL to be the person or organization that hides the real nature of a secret or illegal activity: *He denied that he is fronting for the tobacco companies.*

front·age /ˈfrʌntɪdʒ/ *n.* [U] the part of a building or piece of land that is along a road, river etc.

ˈfrontage ˌroad *n.* [C] a small road next to a large road such as a FREEWAY or EXPRESSWAY, that lets you drive to the buildings that are near the larger road but cannot be reached directly from it

fron·tal /ˈfrʌntəl/ *adj.* [only before noun] FORMAL **1** toward the front of something: *a frontal attack on the enemy* **2** relating to the front part of something: *the right frontal lobe of the brain* **3 full frontal nudity** the fact of showing the front of people's bodies with no clothes on, in movies, pictures etc. —**frontally** *adv.*

ˈfrontal ˌsystem *n.* [C] EARTH SCIENCE a weather FRONT

ˌfront and ˈcenter *adj., adv.* in a very important position, where something will receive attention: *Their aim is to move environmental concerns front and center.*

front ˈdoor *n.* [C usually singular] the main entrance door to a house, at the front → see also BACK DOOR

-fronted /frʌntɪd/ [in adjectives] **glass-fronted/marble-fronted etc.** having a particular substance on the front surface of something: *glass-fronted cabinets*

ˌfront-end ˈloader *n.* [C] a large vehicle that is used for lifting and moving piles of dirt, rocks etc.

fron·tier /frʌnˈtɪr/ *n.* **1 the frontier** the area beyond the places that people know well or live in, especially in the western U.S. in the 19th century: *pioneers of the American frontier* | *Alaska is known as the last frontier.* **2** [C] the limit of what is known about something: *Researchers are pushing back* ***the frontiers of science***. **3** [C] POLITICS the border of a country, or the area near the border: *a picturesque village near the Italian frontier* | **+between/with** *The frontier between France and Spain runs along the river here.*

fron·tiers·man /frʌnˈtɪrzmən/ *n. plural* **frontiersmen** /-mən/ [C] a man who lived on the American frontier, especially in the 19th century

fron·tiers·wom·an /frʌnˈtɪrzˌwʊmən/ *n. plural* **frontierswomen** / -ˌwɪmɪn/ [C] a woman who lived on the American frontier, especially in the 19th century

fron·tis·piece /ˈfrʌntɪsˌpis/ *n.* [C] a picture or photograph at the beginning of a book, facing the page that has the title on it

ˈfront line *n.* [C] **1** the place where fighting happens in a war SYN **front**: *68% of people approve of women fighting on the front lines.* **2** a position in which you are doing something important or difficult that has not been done before: *Researchers concluded that the front line of HIV prevention had shifted to smaller cities.* —**front-line** *adj.* [only before noun] *front-line conditions*

ˈfront man *n.* [C usually singular] **1** a person who speaks for an organization, often an illegal one, but is not the leader of it: *a Mafia front man* **2** the leader, and usually the singer, of a musical group

ˈfront ˌmoney *n.* [U] money that is paid for something before you get it

ˈfront ˌoffice *n.* [singular] the group of people who manage a company

ˈfront page *n.* [C usually singular] the first page of a newspaper: *The story made the front page of the New York Times.*

ˈfront-page *adj.* [only before noun] **front-page story/news/article etc.** something that is printed on the first page of a newspaper because it is very important or exciting

ˌfront ˈroom *n.* [C usually singular] a LIVING ROOM: *Maureen was lying on the sofa in the front room.*

front·run·ner, front-runner /ˈfrʌntˌrʌnɚ/ *n.* [C] the person or thing that is most likely to win a competition: *the frontrunner in November's election*

ˈfront-wheel ˌdrive *n.* [C,U] a system in a vehicle which sends the power of the engine to the front wheels only —**front-wheel drive** *adj.*

frosh /frɑʃ/ *n. plural* **frosh** [C] OLD-FASHIONED a student who is in their first year at a high school, college, or university SYN **freshman**

frost¹ /frɔst/ *n.* **1** [U] ice that looks white and powdery and covers things outside when the temperature is very low: *The ground was white with frost.* ►see THESAURUS box at **snow¹** **2** [U] the ice that forms on the inside of a REFRIGERATOR or FREEZER **3** [C] an occasion when the weather is so cold that water freezes: *There might be* ***a light frost*** *tonight.* | *The only thing that could hurt the crop now is* ***an early frost.*** | *frost damage* → see also FROSTED, FROSTY

frost² *v.* **1** [T] to cover a cake with FROSTING **2** [I,T] to cover something with frost, or to become covered with frost: **+over/up** *All the windows had frosted over during the night.* **3** [T] to make some parts of your hair lighter than the rest by using chemicals

Frost /frɔst/, **Rob·ert** /ˈrɑbɚt/ (1874–1963) a U.S. poet

ˈFrost Belt *n.* **the Frost Belt** the northern or northeastern parts of the U.S., where the weather is very cold in the winter → see also SUN BELT

frost·bite /ˈfrɔstˌbaɪt/ *n.* [U] a condition caused by extreme cold, that makes your fingers, toes etc. swell, become darker and sometimes fall off —**frostbitten** *adj.*

frost·ed /ˈfrɔstɪd/ *adj.* **1** covered with FROST, or with something that looks like frost: *Alice poured her beer into a tall, frosted mug.* **2** covered with FROSTING: *frosted cookies* **3** frosted hair has parts that have been made much lighter than others by using chemicals

ˌfrosted ˈglass *n.* [U] glass whose surface has been made rough, so that it is not transparent

ˈfrost-free *adj.* a frost-free REFRIGERATOR or FREEZER gets slightly warm at times to make the ice inside it disappear, so that you do not have to remove the ice yourself

ˈfrost heave *n.* [U] a situation in which the surface of a road breaks apart because water has entered it and then frozen

frost·ing /ˈfrɔstɪŋ/ *n.* [U] a sweet substance that is put on cakes, made from sugar and butter → see also ICING

ˈfrost line *n.* [C usually singular] the lowest level under the earth's surface that FROST reaches

frost·y /ˈfrɔsti/ *adj. comparative* **frostier**, *superlative* **frostiest** **1** very cold, or covered with FROST: *a frosty windowpane* | *frosty air* ►see THESAURUS box at **cold¹** **2** unfriendly: **a frosty stare/look/welcome** *Pat gave him a frosty, calculating stare.* —**frostily** *adv.* —**frostiness** *n.* [U]

froth¹ /frɔθ/ *n.* [U] **1** a mass of small BUBBLES that form on top of a liquid: *Skim the froth off the top of the melted butter.* **2** small, white BUBBLES of SALIVA around a person's or animal's mouth **3** [U] words or ideas that are attractive, but have no real value or meaning: *The play is an enjoyable bit of holiday froth.*

froth² *v.* [I] **1 be frothing at the mouth** INFORMAL to be extremely angry or excited about something: *She was frothing at the mouth when we finally got back.* **2** if a liquid froths, it produces or contains a lot of small BUBBLES on top: *The beer frothed as he opened the can.* **3** if someone's mouth froths, SALIVA comes out as a lot of small white BUBBLES: *Hal and his friends played Frisbee with the dog until she was* ***frothing at the mouth.***

froth·y /ˈfrɔθi, -ði/ *adj. comparative* **frothier**, *superlative* **frothiest** **1** a liquid that is frothy has a lot of small BUBBLES on top: *a frothy cappuccino* **2** a frothy book, movie etc. is enjoyable but not serious or important —**frothily** *adv.*

frown¹ /fraʊn/ *v.* [I] to make an angry, unhappy, or confused expression by turning down the ends of your mouth or moving your EYEBROWS together: *She frowned, trying to remember.* | **+at** *Mattie stood frowning at the mess.* **[Origin:** 1300–1400 Old French *froignier*]

frown on/upon sb/sth *phr. v.* to disapprove of something, especially someone's behavior: *Second marriages were legal but frowned upon.*

frown² *n.* [C usually singular] the expression on your face when you frown: *"What do you mean?" she asked* ***with a frown.***

fro·yo /ˈfroʊyoʊ/ *n.* [U] INFORMAL frozen YOGURT

froze /froʊz/ the past tense of FREEZE

fro·zen¹ /ˈfroʊzən/ the past participle of FREEZE

frozen² *adj.* **1** frozen food has been stored at a very low temperature in order to preserve it: *Could you buy a couple of frozen pizzas?* | *frozen peas* **2** made very hard or turned to ice because of cold temperatures: *The ground was frozen beneath our feet.* | *frozen pipes* | **frozen stiff/solid** *Rosen's body was found frozen stiff by the railroad tracks.* **3 be frozen** SPOKEN to feel very cold: *He went out without a jacket – he must be frozen.* **4 be frozen with fear/terror/fright** to be so afraid, shocked etc. that you cannot move

fruc·ti·fy /ˈfrʌktəˌfaɪ, ˈfrʊk-/ *v.* **fructifies, fructified, fructifying** [I,T] BIOLOGY to produce fruit or to make a plant produce fruit —**fructification** /ˌfrʌktəfəˈkeɪʃən/ *n.* [U]

fruc·tose /ˈfrʊktoʊs, ˈfrʌk-/ *n.* [U] CHEMISTRY a type of natural sugar in fruit juices and HONEY

fru·gal /ˈfrugəl/ *adj.* **1** careful to only buy what is necessary OPP **extravagant**: *She's too frugal to buy new clothes.* **2** a frugal meal is a small meal of plain food [**Origin:** 1500–1600 French, Latin *frux* **fruit, value**] —**frugally** *adv.* —**frugality** /fruˈgæləṭi/ *n.* [U]

fruit¹ /frut/ S2 W3 *n. plural* **fruit** or **fruits** **1** [C,U] BIOLOGY the part of a plant or tree that contains seeds and is often eaten as food: *We usually eat fresh fruit after dinner.* | *Jack grows a variety of fruits and vegetables in the garden.* | *You should eat a few* ***pieces of fruit*** *every day.* **2 the fruit/fruits of sth** the good results that you have from something, after you have worked very hard: *They had little time to enjoy* ***the fruits of their labors.*** **3 in fruit** BIOLOGY trees and plants that are in fruit are producing their fruit **4 the fruits of the earth/nature** BIOLOGY all the natural things that the earth produces, such as fruit, vegetables, or minerals **5 the fruit of sb's loins** BIBLICAL OR HUMOROUS someone's children [**Origin:** 1100–1200 Old French, Latin *fructus*, from *frui* **to enjoy, have the use of**] → see also **bear fruit** at BEAR¹ (8)

fruit² *v.* [I] TECHNICAL if a tree or a plant fruits, it produces fruit

ˈfruit bat *n.* [C] BIOLOGY a large BAT (=small animal like a flying mouse) that lives in hot countries and eats fruit

fruit·cake /ˈfrut˺keɪk/ *n.* **1** [C,U] a type of heavy cake that has pieces of dried fruit in it **2** [C] INFORMAL someone who seems to be mentally ill or who behaves in a strange way: *You're starting to sound like a fruitcake.*

ˈfruit ˌcocktail *n.* [U] a mixture of small pieces of fruit, sold in cans

ˈfruit fly *n. plural* **fruit flies** [C] BIOLOGY a small fly that eats fruit or decaying plants

fruit·ful /ˈfrutfəl/ *adj.* **1** producing good results OPP **fruitless**: *a very fruitful discussion* **2** LITERARY land that is fruitful produces a lot of grain, vegetables, fruit etc. **3** BIBLICAL producing a lot of babies —**fruitfully** *adv.* —**fruitfulness** *n.* [U]

fru·i·tion /fruˈɪʃən/ *n.* [U] FORMAL the successful result of a plan, idea etc.: *She died without seeing her plan* ***come to fruition.***

F

fruit·less /ˈfrutlɪs/ *adj.* FORMAL failing to achieve what was wanted, especially after much effort [OPP] **fruitful**: *a fruitless attempt to find gold* —**fruitlessly** *adv.* —**fruitlessness** *n.* [U]

ˌfruit ˈsalad *n.* [C,U] a mixture of many different types of fruit that have been cut into small pieces

fruit·y /ˈfruṭi/ *adj. comparative* **fruitier**, *superlative* **fruitiest** **1** tasting or smelling strongly like fruit: *a fruity red wine* **2** INFORMAL silly or stupid: *This must be one of Mike's fruity ideas.*

frump /frʌmp/ *n.* [C] a woman who is frumpy

frump·y /ˈfrʌmpi/ *adj. comparative* **frumpier**, *superlative* **frumpiest** a frumpy woman looks unattractive because she dresses in old-fashioned clothes that do not fit her well: *a frumpy housewife*

frus·trate /ˈfrʌstreɪt/ *v.* [T] **1** [usually passive] if something frustrates you, it makes you feel annoyed or angry because you are unable to do what you want: *What frustrates voters is the slow pace of change.* **2** to prevent someone's plans, efforts or attempts from succeeding: *Thick fog frustrated their attempt to land on the tiny island.* [**Origin:** 1400–1500 Latin *frustrare*, from *frustra* **without effect**]

frus·trat·ed /ˈfrʌstreɪṭɪd/ *adj.* **1** feeling annoyed, upset, and impatient, because you cannot control or change a situation, or achieve something: *Frustrated customers are seeking refunds.* | **+with/at** *We got frustrated with the lack of progress.* | **frustrated that** *Many parents are frustrated that their children don't read more.* **2 sexually frustrated** not satisfied because you do not have any opportunity to have sex **3 a frustrated poet/actor/dancer etc.** someone who wants to develop a particular skill but has not been able to do this

frus·trat·ing /ˈfrʌstreɪṭɪŋ/ *adj.* making you feel annoyed, upset, or impatient because you cannot do what you want to do: *It's so frustrating not to have a car to get around.* | *a frustrating experience*

frus·tra·tion /frʌˈstreɪʃən/ *n.* **1** [C,U] the feeling of being annoyed, upset, or impatient, because you cannot control or change a situation, or achieve something: *tears of anger and frustration* | *She threw her pen across the room* ***in frustration.*** **2** [U] the fact of being prevented from achieving what you are trying to achieve: **+of** *the frustration of all his ambitions*

fry¹ /fraɪ/ [S2] *v.* **fries, fried, frying** **1** [I,T] to cook something in hot oil or fat, or to be cooked in hot oil or fat: *Fry the pork for five minutes.* | *I could smell the onions frying.* ▸see THESAURUS box at **cook¹** **2** [I,T] SLANG to kill someone, or to be killed, as a punishment in the ELECTRIC CHAIR [**Origin:** 1200–1300 Old French *frire*, from Latin *frigere*] —**fried** *adj.* → see also DEEP-FRY, FRENCH FRY, STIR-FRY

fry² [S2] *n. plural* **fries** **1** [C usually plural] a long thin piece of potato that has been cooked in hot oil [SYN] **French fry** **2** [C] an amount of fries that are served together, especially in a FAST FOOD restaurant: *I'll have a cheeseburger and a large fry.* **3 fry** [plural] BIOLOGY very young fish → see also SMALL FRY

fry·er /ˈfraɪɚ/ *n.* [C] **1** a special pan or piece of electrical equipment for frying food **2** a chicken that has been specially bred to be fried

ˈfrying ˌpan *n.* [C] **1** a round flat pan with a long handle, used for frying food [SYN] **skillet** → see picture at PAN **2 out of the frying pan (and) into the fire** SPOKEN from a bad situation to one that is even worse

FSLIC /ˌɛf ɛs ˌɛl aɪ ˈsi/ *n.* [singular] **Federal Savings and Loan Insurance Corporation** an official government organization that insures the money you keep in a SAVINGS AND LOAN association

f-stop /ˈɛf stɑp/ *n.* [C] a position of the opening in a camera LENS that controls how much light can enter the camera

ft. **1** the written abbreviation of FOOT or feet **2 Ft.** the written abbreviation of FORT, used in the names of places: *Ft. Lauderdale*

FTC /ˌɛf ti ˈsi/ *n.* [singular] **Federal Trade Commission** **the FTC** an official government organization that makes sure that businesses do not do anything illegal or unfair

FTP /ˌɛf ti ˈpi/ *n.* [U] COMPUTERS **file transfer protocol** a standard for sending information from one computer to another over the Internet

fuch·sia¹ /ˈfyuʃə/ *n.* **1** [U] a bright pink color **2** [C,U] BIOLOGY a type of bush with hanging bell-shaped flowers in red, pink, or white [**Origin:** 1700–1800 Leonhard *Fuchs* (1501–66), German plant scientist]

fuchsia² *adj.* bright pink

fud·dy-dud·dy /ˈfʌdi ˌdʌdi/ *n. plural* **fuddy-duddies** [C] INFORMAL someone who has old-fashioned ideas and attitudes: *That dress makes you look like such a fuddy-duddy.*

fudge¹ /fʌdʒ/ *n.* [U] a type of soft candy, made with milk, butter, sugar, and usually chocolate

fudge² *v.* [I,T] **1** to change important figures or facts in order to deceive people: *Smithson has been fudging his data for years now.* **2** to avoid giving exact details or a clear answer about something: **+on** *A lot of people fudged on their answers about exercise.*

fudge³ *interjection* used when you are angry, annoyed, or disappointed, instead of saying a more offensive word: *Oh, fudge! I forgot to mail Janet's birthday card.*

fudg·y /ˈfʌdʒi/ *adj.* slightly sticky with a strong sweet chocolate taste: *fudgy brownies*

fueh·rer /ˈfyʊrɚ/ *n.* another spelling of FUHRER

fuel¹ /fyul, ˈfyuəl/ [W3] *n.* **1** [C,U] a substance such as coal, gas, or oil that can be burned to produce heat or energy: *The plane was running low on fuel.* | *Coal has always been a cheap fuel.* | *a fuel tank* **2** [U] a fact, statement etc. that someone can use to support an argument: *You're giving the other side fuel for their argument.* [**Origin:** 1100–1200 Old French *fouaille*, from *feu* **fire**, from Latin *focus* **hearth**] → see also **add fuel to sth** at ADD (5), FOSSIL FUEL

fuel² *v.* **1** [T] to make something happen, grow, increase etc., or to encourage someone to do something: *Easy credit terms helped fuel the economic expansion.* | **fuel fears/worry/speculation etc.** *The slow pace of work fueled concern that the stadium would not be finished on time.* **2** [I,T] also **fuel up** to take fuel into a vehicle, or to provide a vehicle with fuel: *Workers began fueling the spaceship for liftoff.*

ˈfuel cell *n.* [C] CHEMISTRY a piece of equipment that combines a FUEL such as HYDROGEN with oxygen to produce electricity

ˈfuel-efˌficient *adj.* a fuel-efficient engine or vehicle burns fuel in a more effective way than usual, so that it uses less fuel

ˈfuel inˌjection *n.* [U] a method of using pressure to put fuel such as gasoline directly into an engine, which allows a vehicle to burn the fuel in a more effective way —**fuel-injected** *adj.*

ˈfuel oil *n.* [U] a type of oil that is burned to produce heat or power

Fu·en·tes /fʊˈɛnteɪs/**, Car·los** /ˈkɑrloʊs/ (1928–) a Mexican writer of NOVELS

fu·gi·tive¹ /ˈfyudʒəṭɪv/ *n.* [C] someone who is trying to avoid being caught, especially by the police: **+from** *a fugitive from U.S. justice*

fugitive² *adj.* [only before noun] **1** trying to avoid being caught, especially by the police: *The fugitive leader was captured last night.* **2** LITERARY continuing for a very short time: *They shared a fugitive embrace.* [**Origin:** 1300–1400 French *fugitif*, from Latin *fugere* **to run away**]

ˌFugitive ˈSlave ˌAct, the *n.* [singular] HISTORY a law passed by the U.S. Congress in 1850 telling all citizens to help to catch and return people who had escaped from SLAVERY to their owners in the South, which was very unpopular in the North

fugue /fyug/ *n.* [C] a piece of serious music in which a tune is repeated regularly by different instruments, voices etc. with small changes each time

fuh·rer /ˈfyʊrɚ/ *n.* **the Fuhrer, the Führer** Adolf Hitler, the leader of the Nazi party in Germany in the 1930s and early 1940s during World War II

Fu·ji, Mount /ˈfudʒi/ also **Fu·ji·ya·ma** /ˌfudʒiˈɑmə/ a VOLCANO on the largest island in Japan, southwest of Tokyo, that is the highest mountain in Japan

-ful¹ /fəl/ *suffix* [in adjectives] **1** having a particular quality: *a beautiful girl* | *Is it painful?* | *a skillful driver* **2** full of something: *a gleeful smile* | *an eventful day* —**-fully** /fəli, fli/ *suffix* [in adverbs] *a delightfully fruity wine*

-ful² /fʊl/ *suffix* [in nouns] **1** the amount of a substance needed to fill a particular container: *a cupful of milk* **2** as much as can be carried by, or contained in, a particular part of the body: *an armful of flowers* | *a mouthful of water*

Ful·a·ni /ˈfulɑni/ *plural* **Fulani** or **Fulanis** also **Fu·la** /ˈfulə/ *plural* **Fula** or **Fulas** *n.* **1** [C] a member of a group of mainly Muslim people who live in northern Nigeria, Mali, and other parts of West Africa **2** [U] the language of the Fulani

Ful·bright /ˈfʊlbraɪt/, **J. William** (1905–1995) a U.S. politician who established the FULBRIGHT SCHOLARSHIPS

ˌFulbright ˈScholarship *n.* [C] money provided for U.S. university students and teachers so that they can study in other countries, and for students and teachers from other countries so that they can study in the U.S. —**Fulbright Scholar** *n.* [C]

ful·crum /ˈfʊlkrəm, ˈfʌl-/ *n.* [C] the point on which a LEVER turns, balances, or is supported when it is turning or lifting something

ful·fill /fʊlˈfɪl/ *v.* [T] **1** to achieve a goal, wish, or aim: *The couple fulfilled their dream of getting married in Tahiti.* | *None of the trainees have* ***fulfilled*** *our* ***expectations.*** | *The program helps to* ***fulfill*** *parents'* ***hopes*** *for their children's education.* **2** to do something that is useful or necessary: **fulfill a function/role/need etc.** *The church fulfills an important role in daily life.* **3** to do something because it is required by a rule or law, or because it is your duty: *I took the class to fulfill the science requirement.* | **fulfill a role/function/duty etc.** *In trying to fulfill his role as leader, he has alienated his own supporters.* **4** FORMAL to do what you said you would do: **fulfill a promise/pledge/commitment** *Will the government fulfill its pledge to hold free elections?* **5** if your work fulfills you, it makes you feel satisfied because you are using all your skills, qualities etc. **6 fulfill yourself** to feel satisfied because you are using all your skills, qualities etc.: *She succeeded in fulfilling herself both as an actress and as a mother.* **7 fulfill your potential/promise** to be as successful as you possibly can be: *He never fulfilled his potential as a basketball player.* **8 fulfill a prophecy** if a PROPHECY is fulfilled, something happens that someone said would happen → see also SELF-FULFILLING PROPHECY

ful·filled /fʊlˈfɪld/ *adj.* satisfied with your life, job etc. because you feel that it is interesting, useful, or important, and you are using all your skills: *I don't need to have a boyfriend to be fulfilled.*

ful·fill·ing /fʊlˈfɪlɪŋ/ *adj.* a job, relationship etc. that is fulfilling makes you feel satisfied because it allows you to use all your skills and personal qualities: *I had a long and fulfilling career as an architect.*

ful·fill·ment /fʊlˈfɪlmənt/ *n.* [U] **1** the feeling of being satisfied, especially in your job, because you are using all your skills and personal qualities: *I get a real* ***sense of fulfillment*** *when I go out and perform.* **2** the act or state of meeting a need, demand, or condition: +**of** *the fulfillment of a promise*

full¹ /fʊl/ S1 W1 *adj.*

1 CONTAINER/ROOM/PLACE ETC. holding or containing as much of something as possible, or as many things or people as possible OPP **empty**: *a full box of cereal* | *The restaurant was already full when we got there.* | *Fill the muffin cups about* ***half full.*** | **chock/crammed full of sth** (=so full that there is no extra room) | *The glass was* ***full to the brim*** (=to the very top).

THESAURUS

filled with sth full of something: *a shopping cart filled with groceries*
packed (with sth) extremely full of people or things: *The trial took place in front of a packed courtroom.* | *a small book that's packed with information*
crammed (with sth) full of people or things: *The garage was crammed with junk.*
stuffed (full of sth) full of things: *The bookcase was stuffed full of paperbacks.*
bursting (with sth) very full of something: *a muffin bursting with blueberries*
overflowing a container that is overflowing is so full that the liquid or things inside it come out over the top: *a sink overflowing with dirty dishes*
overloaded if a vehicle or ship is overloaded, too many people or things have been put in it: *The ferry in the disaster had been overloaded.*
teeming (with sth) full of people, animals etc. that are all moving around: *The river was teeming with fish.*

2 INCLUDING EVERYTHING [only before noun] including all parts or details SYN **complete** OPP **partial**: *Please give your full name and address.* | *Salcido gave a full confession to the police.* | *We sell* ***the full range of*** *kitchen appliances* (=everything available). | *We are not being told* ***the full story*** (=everything someone knows about something) *by our political leaders.*

3 HIGHEST LEVEL [only before noun] being the highest level or greatest amount that is possible SYN **total**: *I never pay full price for anything.* | *She turned the radio up to full volume.* | *He was driving* ***at full speed*** (=as fast as possible) *when he hit the tree.* | *The heat was on* ***full blast*** (=as strongly as possible) *in the car.* | *The roses are now* ***in full bloom*** (=the flowers are all open).

4 be full of sth a) to contain a large number of things, or a large amount of something: *Dan's garage is full of half-finished projects.* | *brochures full of information* | *My jeans are all full of holes.* **b)** to feel or express a strong emotion, or have a lot of a particular quality: *Boston's streets are full of history.* | *We were full of admiration for Kim's talent.*

5 FOOD [not before noun] SPOKEN having eaten so much food that you cannot eat any more: *"Do you want more noodles?" "No, thanks.* ***I'm full.****"* | *Don't go swimming* ***on a full stomach*** (=while your stomach is full of food).

6 be full of yourself to think or talk about yourself all the time, in a way that other people find annoying

7 TIME a) [only before noun] used to emphasize that something continues for a long time: *He sat on the witness stand for four full days.* **b)** busy and filled with many activities: *I've had a full week at work.* | *My grandfather* ***lived a full life.***

8 be in full swing if an event or process is in full swing it has reached its highest level of activity: *The college football season is now in full swing.*

9 RANK [only before noun] having all the rights, duties etc. relating to a particular rank or position, because you have reached the necessary standard: **a full professor/member/colonel etc.** *Watson has been a full member for six years.*

10 (at) full speed/tilt as fast or as strongly as possible: *We will be working at full tilt during the final days of the campaign.*

11 full speed/steam ahead with as much energy and eagerness as possible: *The three cruise lines are moving full speed ahead with major expansion plans.*

12 SOUND/TASTE ETC. a quality such as a sound, taste etc. that is full is pleasantly strong: *Cheddar cheese ages well to produce a full, rich aroma.*

13 CLOTHING a full skirt, pair of pants etc. is made with a lot of material and fits loosely: *full sleeves* | *a dress with a full skirt*

14 BODY a full face, body etc. is rounded, large, or fat

15 come/go full circle to end in the same situation in which you began, even though there have been

F

changes in the time in between: *Ideas on how to teach reading have come full circle since the 1960s.*
16 in full view of sb/sth so that everyone watching can see everything: *The fight occurred in full view of the fans who arrived early.*
17 to the fullest in the best or most complete way: *His disabilities don't stop him from enjoying life to the fullest.*
18 draw yourself up to your full height also **rise to your full height** to stand up very straight
19 in full cry if a group of people are in full cry, they are criticizing someone very strongly: *By that time, the press was in full cry, insisting that there had been illegal activities.*
[**Origin:** Old English] → see also FULLY, **have your hands full** at HAND[1] (22)

full[2] *n.* **in full** if you pay an amount of money in full, you pay the whole amount: *The balance must be paid in full each month.*

full[3] *adv.* directly: **+on/in** *The door struck me full in the face.* → see also **know full well** at KNOW[1] (4)

F

full·back /ˈfʊlbæk/ *n.* [C] **1** a player on a football team who lines up behind the quarterback, and who blocks players on the other team **2** a player on a soccer or hockey team who helps defend the goal

ˌfull-ˈblooded *adj.* [only before noun, no comparative] having parents, grandparents etc. from only one race of people, especially a race that is not the main one in a particular society: *a full-blooded Cherokee Indian*

ˈfull-blown *adj.* [only before noun, no comparative] a full-blown illness, problem, bad situation etc. is in its most fully developed or advanced stage: *The oil spill has become a full-blown environmental disaster.* | *full-blown AIDS*

ˌfull-ˈbodied *adj.* tasting strong, in a pleasant way: *a full-bodied beer*

ˌfull ˈbore *adv.* if someone is doing something full bore, they are doing it as hard and with as much energy as possible: *They plan to proceed full bore with building the airport extension.* —**full-bore** *adj.* [only before noun]

ˈfull-color *adj.* [only before noun] printed using colored inks, so that pictures and photographs look REALISTIC: *a 76-page, full-color brochure*

ˌfull-court ˈpress *n.* [singular] **1** a method of defending in a fierce way across the whole COURT in basketball **2** the use of pressure or influence by several groups on someone: *the government's full-court press on drug barons*

ˌfull ˈdress *n.* [U] special clothes that are worn for official occasions and ceremonies —**full-dress** *adj.*: *a full-dress military ceremony*

Ful·ler /ˈfʊlɚ/, **Mel·ville** /ˈmɛlvɪl/ (1833–1910) a CHIEF JUSTICE on the U.S. Supreme Court

Fuller, R. Buck·min·ster /ɑr ˈbʌkmɪnstɚ/ (1895–1983) a U.S. ARCHITECT and engineer, famous for inventing the GEODESIC DOME

ˈfull-face *adj.* a full-face photograph or picture of someone shows their whole face → see also PROFILE

ˌfull-ˈfigured *adj.* used to politely describe a woman who is slightly fat and has large breasts

ˌfull-ˈfledged *adj.* completely developed, trained, or established: *the youngest full-fledged member of the board of directors*

ˌfull-ˈgrown *adj.* a full-grown animal, plant, or person has developed to their full size and will not grow any bigger: *full-grown female whales*

ˌfull ˈhouse *n.* [C usually singular] **1** an occasion at a movie theater, concert hall, sports field etc. when every seat has someone sitting in it: *Organizers expect a full house for tonight's game.* **2** a combination of three cards of one value and a pair of another value in a game of POKER

ˌfull ˈlength *adv.* [only after verb] someone who is lying full length is lying flat with their legs straight out: *Alison was stretched out full length on the couch.*

ˈfull-length *adj.* **1 full-length mirror/photograph/portrait etc.** a mirror, photograph etc. that shows all of a person, from their head to their feet **2 full-length skirt/dress/coat etc.** a skirt, dress, coat etc. that reaches the ground, or is the longest possible for that particular type of clothing: *a full-length evening dress* **3 full-length play/book/movie etc.** a play, book, movie etc. of the normal length

ˌfull ˈmoon *n.* [singular] the moon when it looks completely round → see also HALF MOON

full·ness /ˈfʊlnɪs/ *n.* [U] **1** the condition of being full: *the body's natural feelings of hunger and fullness* **2** the quality of being large and round in an attractive way: *the fullness of her lips* **3** LITERARY the quality of being complete: *the fullness of the information provided* **4** the quality of having a pleasantly deep sound: *the instrument's fullness of tone* **5** the quality of having a pleasantly strong taste: *the wine's freshness and fullness* **6 in the fullness of time** when the best or right time comes SYN **eventually**: *I'm sure he'll tell us everything in the fullness of time.*

ˌfull-ˈpage *adj.* [only before noun] covering all of one page, especially in a newspaper or magazine: *a full-page anti-smoking ad*

ˌfull proˈfessor *n.* [C] a teacher of the highest rank at a U.S. college or university

ˈfull-scale *adj.* [only before noun] **1** as complete as possible, or to the greatest degree possible: *The country is on the brink of full-scale civil war.* **2** a full-scale drawing, model, copy etc. of something is the same size as the thing it represents

ˌfull-ˈsize also **ˌfull-ˈsized** *adj.* **1** of the normal, usual, or largest possible size: *The new laptop features a full-size keyboard.* **2 a)** a full-size bed is 54 inches (=137 cm) wide and 75 inches (=191 cm) long → see also KING-SIZE **b)** full-size sheets, BLANKETS etc. are made to be used on a full-size bed

ˌfull ˈstop *n.* [C] BRITISH a PERIOD

ˌfull-ˈterm *adj.* relating to a PREGNANCY of a normal length: **a full-term infant/pregnancy/birth etc.** *a full-term baby* → see also PREMATURE

ˌfull-ˈtime *adj., adv.* **1** working or studying for the number of hours that work is usually done: *Janine attends high school full-time and works part-time.* | *Only **full-time employees** get health coverage.* **2 a full-time job a)** a job that you do for all the normal working hours in a week **b)** INFORMAL hard work that you are not being paid for that takes a lot of your time: *I raise my children, and that's a full-time job.* → see also PART-TIME

ful·ly /ˈfʊli/ S3 W2 *adv.* **1** completely: *The President is fully aware of the problem.* | *a fully equipped kitchen* | *The concept is discussed more fully in Chapter 9.* **2** FORMAL used to emphasize how big a number is, and to say that it could possibly be even bigger: *Fully half of engineering students left the program after their first year.*

ˌfully-ˈgrown *adj.* FULL-GROWN

ful·mi·nate /ˈfʊlməˌneɪt, ˈfʌl-/ *v.* [I] FORMAL to speak angrily against something: **+against/about** *Politicians still fulminate against the war crimes.* —**fulmination** /ˌfʊlməˈneɪʃən, ˌfʌl-/ *n.* [C,U]

ful·some /ˈfʊlsəm/ *adj.* FORMAL a fulsome piece of writing, speech etc. gives a lot of praise, especially in a way that does not seem sincere: *The book contains a fulsome dedication to his wife.* —**fulsomely** *adv.* —**fulsomeness** *n.* [U]

Ful·ton /ˈfʊltˀn/, **Rob·ert** /ˈrɑbɚt/ (1765–1815) a U.S. engineer and inventor who designed and built several STEAMSHIPS

fum·ble[1] /ˈfʌmbəl/ *v.* **1** [I] to hold or try to move something with your hands carelessly or awkwardly: **fumble (in sth) for sth** *I fumbled in my pockets for a box of matches.* | **fumble with sth** *Her cold fingers fumbled with the buttons.* **2** [I,T] to drop the ball after catching it in a game of football **3** [I] if you fumble your words when you are speaking, you have difficulty saying something: **fumble for sth** *The group fumbled for a response to the accusations.*

fumble² *n.* [C] an act of dropping a football after catching it, or an occasion when this happens: *Scott's fumble gave Atlanta a last minute chance.*

fume /fyum/ *v.* [I] **1** to be angry, usually without saying anything: *"They have no right to be in my house," she fumed.* | **fume over/about/at sth** *He left, fuming over the department's inefficiency.* **2** to give off smoke or gases [**Origin:** 1300–1400 French *fumer*, from Latin *fumus* **smoke**]

fumes /fyumz/ *n.* [plural] strong-smelling gas or smoke that is bad to breathe in: *paint fumes*

fu·mi·gate /ˈfyuməˌgeɪt/ *v.* [I,T] to clear disease, BACTERIA, insects etc. from somewhere using smoke or chemical gases —**fumigation** /ˌfyuməˈgeɪʃən/ *n.* [U]

fun¹ /fʌn/ S1 W2 *n.* **1** [U] an experience or activity that is very enjoyable and exciting: *The class was very hard, but fun too.* | *Did you* ***have fun*** *at Denny's the other night?* | ***It's no fun*** *to be sick when you're on vacation.* | *That* ***sounds like fun****. What kind of movie is it?* | *I decided to come out and* ***join in the fun****, instead of just watching.* | **it's fun (doing sth/to do sth)** *It was fun seeing all my old friends again.* **2 make fun of sb/sth** to make jokes about someone that are insulting or make them feel bad: *Stop it – I don't make fun of the way you talk, do I?* **3** happiness and enjoyment: **do sth for fun/for the fun of it** *Encourage your child to read all kinds of books just for fun.* | *It was just a joke! Where's your* ***sense of fun****?* | *He called me a gorilla, but I knew it was just* ***in fun*** (=as a joke). **4 fun and games** playful activities: *It started out as fun and games but became a successful business.* | *Of course, college* ***is not all fun and games*** *– you have to work hard too.* **5 sb's idea of fun** used to talk about an activity, situation etc. that is exciting or interesting to someone else, but not to you: *Larsen's idea of fun is to paddle a canoe around all day.* | *Running in the August heat* ***is not my idea of fun****.* **6 like fun** OLD-FASHIONED used to disagree with someone, when you think something will not happen, or when something is not true [**Origin:** 1600–1700 *fun* **to play a trick on**] → see also **figure of fun** at FIGURE¹ (13), FUNNY, **poke fun at sb/sth** at POKE¹ (4) → see Word Choice box at FUNNY

fun² S2 *adj.* **1** a fun activity, experience, or place is enjoyable: *The weight training class is really fun.* | *Have a fun Labor Day!* | *Boulder is a fun place to live.* **2** someone who is fun is enjoyable to be with because they are cheerful and amusing: *Randy's a really fun guy to be around.*

func·tion¹ /ˈfʌŋkʃən/ Ac S3 W2 *n.*
1 PURPOSE [C] the purpose that something has, or the job that someone or something does: *The filter's function is to remove pollution from the air.* | **+of** *Consistent exercise changes the function of the heart.* | *The main function of the press is to provide information.* | **perform/fulfill a function** *The organization fulfills a valuable social function.* | *Bauhaus architects thought that function was more important than form.*
2 EVENT [C] a large party or ceremonial event, especially for an important or official occasion: *weddings and other social functions*
3 be a function of sth if one thing is a function of another, it is produced by or changes according to the other thing: *The fog is a function of the cooler air moving in.*
4 MATH [C] **a)** SYMBOL **f** a relation between two sets of values, for which each value of the DOMAIN (=first set) has a single related value in the RANGE (=second set). For example, $f(x) = \sqrt{x}$ is a function because each value "x" has only one SQUARE ROOT. **b)** a mathematical quantity that changes according to how another mathematical quantity changes. For example, in $x = 5y$, x is a function of y, and the possible solutions for x directly relate to the possible solutions for y.
5 COMPUTERS [C] one of the basic operations performed by a computer
[**Origin:** 1500–1600 Latin *functio*, from *fungi* **to perform**]

function² Ac W3 *v.* [I] **1** if something functions, it works correctly or in a particular way: *The alarm system was not functioning when the paintings were stolen.* | *Ancient Egyptians used herbs to help the stomach function naturally.* **2 not function** if someone cannot function, they cannot do the activities that people normally do: *You can't really function in society if you can't read.*

function as sth *phr. v.* to be or work as something: *The ranch functions as a ski resort in winter.*

func·tion·al /ˈfʌŋkʃənəl/ Ac *adj.* **1** designed to be useful: *These tin cookie cutters are both functional and decorative.* **2** working in the way that something is supposed to: *The tiny machine is a* ***fully functional*** *computer.* **3** having a useful purpose: *The company was divided into four main functional areas.* —**functionally** *adv.*

ˈfunctional ˌdocument *n.* [C] ENG. LANG. ARTS a piece of writing that helps you do something, for example, a list, a book about how to make something, a SCHEDULE etc. → see also CONSUMER DOCUMENT → INFORMATIONAL DOCUMENT, PUBLIC DOCUMENT, WORKPLACE DOCUMENT

ˈfunctional ˌgroup *n.* [C] CHEMISTRY a group of atoms that are responsible for the chemical structure and qualities of a chemical compound, such as the ways it reacts with other chemicals

ˌfunctional ilˈliterate *n.* [C] someone who may be able to read a little, but cannot read well enough to do many things in society, such as getting a good job

func·tion·al·ism /ˈfʌŋkʃənəˌlɪzəm/ *n.* [U] the idea that the most important thing about a building, piece of furniture etc. is that it is useful —**functionalist** *n.* [C] —**functionalist** *adj.*

func·tion·ar·y /ˈfʌŋkʃəˌneri/ *n. plural* **functionaries** [C] someone who has a job doing unimportant or boring official duties

ˈfunction key *n.* [C] COMPUTERS a button on the KEYBOARD of a computer that tells the machine to perform a particular function

ˈfunction noˌtation *n.* [C,U] MATH the sign f(x) which is used to represent a mathematical FUNCTION

ˈfunction ˌrule *n.* [C] MATH an EQUATION that describes a FUNCTION (=mathematical relation in which one quantity changes according to how another quantity changes)

ˈfunction word *n.* [C] ENG. LANG. ARTS a word such as a PRONOUN or PREPOSITION that is used in place of another word, or that shows the relationship between two words. For example, in the sentences "The cat is hungry. It hasn't been fed yet," "it" is a function word.

fund¹ /fʌnd/ Ac S2 W1 *n.* **1** [C] an amount of money that is collected and kept for a particular purpose: *The government created a fund to help develop rural areas.* | *Carol wants to* ***set up*** *an investment* ***fund****.* → see also FUNDING, SLUSH FUND, TRUST FUND **2 funds** [plural] the money needed to do something: *Where are we going to get the funds to do all this?* | *Many state programs are running short of funds.* **3** [C] an organization that is responsible for collecting and spending money for a particular purpose → see also CHARITY: *the Cancer Research Fund* **4 a fund of sth** a large supply of something: *a man with a fund of funny stories* [**Origin:** 1600–1700 Latin *fundus* **bottom, piece of land**]

fund² Ac S2 W1 *v.* [T] **1** to provide money for an activity, organization, event etc.: *The women's shelter is funded entirely by the church.* | **publicly/privately/federally etc. funded** *privately funded research* **2** TECHNICAL to change the arrangements for paying a debt, so that you have more time to pay

fun·da·men·tal¹ /ˌfʌndəˈmɛntl/ Ac W3 *adj.* **1** relating to the most basic and important parts of something: *fundamental principles of human rights* | *a fundamental difference of opinion* | *fundamental changes in the company's structure* | *The Red Sox made a fundamental mistake in the sixth inning.* | **a fundamental flaw/weakness** (=a problem with the most basic parts or ideas of something) ▶see THESAURUS box at basic **2 be fundamental to sth** to be necessary if something is to happen, exist, or succeed: *Water is*

F

fundamental to survival. | *Competition is fundamental to keeping prices down.*

fundamental² Ac *n.* [C usually plural] the most important ideas, rules etc. that something is based on: +**of** *The cookbook gives readers the fundamentals of cooking.*

fun·da·men·tal·ism /ˌfʌndəˈmɛntl̩ˌɪzəm/ *n.* [U] **1** the practice of following religious laws very strictly: *Islamic fundamentalism* **2** a belief of some Christians that everything in the Bible is completely true

fun·da·men·tal·ist /ˌfʌndəˈmɛntl-ɪst/ *n.* [C] **1** someone who follows religious laws very strictly **2** a Christian who believes that everything in the Bible is completely true —**fundamentalist** *adj.*: *fundamentalist beliefs*

fun·da·men·tal·ly /ˌfʌndəˈmɛntl-i/ Ac *adv.* **1** in every way that is important or basic: *The two sides remain fundamentally divided on key issues.* | *Military dicatorships behave in a fundamentally different way from elected governments.* | *the* ***fundamentally flawed*** *logic in his argument* **2** [sentence adverb] when you consider the most important or basic parts: *Fundamentally, we have a good safety program.*

F

fund·ing /ˈfʌndɪŋ/ Ac *n.* [U] an amount of money for a specific purpose: *Were you able to get funding to finish your dissertation?* | **federal/state/government/private etc. funding** *$30 million in taxpayer funding*

fund·rais·er /ˈfʌndˌreɪzɚ/ *n.* [C] **1** an event that is held to collect money for a specific purpose such as a CHARITY or political party **2** a person who collects money for a specific purpose such as a CHARITY or a political party, for example by arranging social events that people pay to attend

fund·rais·ing /ˈfʌndˌreɪzɪŋ/ *n.* [U] the activity of collecting money for a specific purpose such as a CHARITY or a political party: *a fundraising dinner* | +**for** *She's very involved in fundraising for the school.*

fu·ner·al /ˈfyunərəl/ S3 W3 *n.* [C] a ceremony for burying or burning a dead person: *Over 200 people came to the funeral.* | *The* ***funeral was held*** (=took place) *in his hometown.* | *Private* ***funeral services*** *are scheduled for Saturday.* | *She refused to* ***attend*** *his* ***funeral*** (=go to it). [**Origin:** 1300–1400 Late Latin *funeralis*, from Latin *funus* **funeral**]

THESAURUS

burial the act or ceremony of putting a dead body in the ground
cremation the act or ceremony of burning a dead body
coffin/casket a long box in which a dead body is buried or burned
hearse a large car used to carry a dead body in a coffin at a funeral
grave the place in the ground where a dead body is buried
graveyard an area of ground where people are buried
cemetery an area of ground where people are buried, usually not belonging to a church
crematorium a building in which the bodies of dead people are burned at a funeral ceremony
funeral director someone whose job is to arrange funerals
undertaker/mortician someone whose job is to prepare bodies for burial or burning
mourners the people who attend a funeral, especially relatives of the dead person

ˈfuneral diˌrector *n.* [C] someone whose job is to organize funerals

ˈfuneral home also **ˈfuneral ˌparlor** *n.* [C] the place where a body is kept before a funeral and where the funeral is sometimes held

fu·ner·ar·y /ˈfyunəˌrɛri/ *adj.* [only before noun] FORMAL relating to a funeral or a grave: *the funerary procession*

fu·ne·re·al /fyʊˈnɪriəl/ *adj.* FORMAL **1** [only before noun] sad, slow, and appropriate for a funeral: *funereal music* **2** making it difficult to feel hopeful or happy: *The local weather was funereal.* —**funereally** *adv.*

fun·gal /ˈfʌŋgəl/ *adj.* TECHNICAL relating to or caused by a fungus: *a fungal infection*

fun·gi·cide /ˈfʌŋgəˌsaɪd, ˈfʌndʒə-/ *n.* [C,U] a chemical used for destroying fungus

fun·goid /ˈfʌŋgɔɪd/ *adj.* TECHNICAL like a fungus: *fungoid growths*

fun·gus /ˈfʌŋgəs/ *n.* *plural* **fungi** /-gaɪ, -dʒaɪ/ or **funguses** **1** [C,U] BIOLOGY a simple fast-growing ORGANISM, such as a MUSHROOM or MOLD **2** [U] this type of living thing, especially considered as a disease

ˈfun house *n.* [C] a building at a FAIR in which there are things that amuse or shock people

fu·nic·u·lar /fyʊˈnɪkyəlɚ, fə-/ also **fuˌnicular ˈrailway** *n.* [C] a small vehicle that goes up a hill or a mountain, pulled by a thick metal rope

funk /fʌŋk/ *n.* [U] **1** ENG. LANG. ARTS a style of music with a strong RHYTHM that is based on JAZZ and African music **2 in a (blue) funk** INFORMAL very unhappy, worried, or afraid about something: *Sam drove off in a funk.* **3** INFORMAL a strong smell, especially one that comes from someone's body

funk·y /ˈfʌŋki/ S3 *adj.* *comparative* **funkier**, *superlative* **funkiest** INFORMAL **1** fashionable and interesting in a way that is different from the usual: *All these people were wearing funky leather outfits.* **2** ENG. LANG. ARTS funky music is simple with a strong BASS beat that is easy to dance to **3** having a bad, dirty smell or appearance: *This water looks a little funky.*

fun·nel¹ /ˈfʌnl/ *n.* [C] a tube that is wide at one end and narrow at the other end, used for pouring liquids or powders into a container with a narrow opening

funnel² *v.* **1** [I,T] to pass or be passed through a narrow opening: +**to/through/into** *Solar cells collect and funnel energy to the batteries.* | *The four-lane highway funnels into a two-lane road.* **2** [T] to send a large number of things or money from different places to a particular place: *Economic aid from 24 countries will be funneled into the region.*

fun·nies /ˈfʌniz/ *n.* INFORMAL **the funnies** the part of a newspaper with many different CARTOONS

fun·ni·ly /ˈfʌnl-i/ *adv.* in an odd or unusual way: *He was behaving funnily that day.* → see also **strangely/oddly/funnily enough** at ENOUGH¹ (3)

fun·ny /ˈfʌni/ S1 W2 *adj.* *comparative* **funnier**, *superlative* **funniest**

1 AMUSING making you laugh: *You'll like Alan – he's really funny.* | *Bob tells the funniest jokes.* | *I don't* ***find*** *his type of humor* ***funny*** (=it doesn't make me laugh). | *Once I calmed down, I could* ***see the funny side of*** *the situation.*

THESAURUS

hilarious/hysterical extremely funny: *The movie is a hilarious look at the fashion industry.*
witty using words in a funny and intelligent way: *witty remarks*
corny corny jokes, songs etc. have been done many times or are so silly that they are not funny: *a corny birthday card*
amusing/humorous slightly more formal ways to say that something is funny: *Luckily, Joe thought my son's behavior was amusing rather than annoying.*
comedy a movie, play, or television program that is intended to make people laugh

2 STRANGE strange and unusual, and difficult to explain: *I always thought that was a funny place to have a house.* | *a funny smell* | ***It's funny that*** *he and Gloria have never gotten married.* | ***It's funny how*** *two sisters can be so different.* | ***That's funny.*** *I'm sure I put my wallet down there, and now it's gone.* ►see THESAURUS box at **strange¹**

3 DISHONEST seeming to be illegal or dishonest, although you are not exactly sure why: *There's some-*

thing funny going on here. | *I don't want any **funny business** going on while I'm gone.*
4 feel funny to feel slightly sick: *Nicole says her stomach feels funny.*

SPOKEN PHRASES

5 the funny thing is used to say what the strangest or most amusing part of a story or situation is: *My uncle Dan taught us how to do a lot of illegal stuff. And the funny thing is, his son's a police officer.*
6 it's not funny used to tell someone not to laugh at or make jokes about something you think is very serious: *It's not funny to be making jokes about fat people all the time.*
7 very funny! used when someone is laughing at you or making a joke and you do not think it is funny: *Oh, that's very funny. I know you're in there.* | *Very funny! Who hid my car keys?*
8 what's so funny? used when someone is laughing and you want to know why: *"What's so funny?" "Marcia just spilled purple paint all over herself!"*
9 funny little... used to describe something or someone that is small and unusual: *I like the funny little way Maury has of smiling.*
10 funny old... used to describe something or someone that is strange but that you like or think is interesting: *Like they say, it's a funny old game.*
11 funny weird/strange or funny ha ha? used when someone has described something as funny, and you want to know if they mean that it is strange or amusing: *"Tim's a funny guy." "Funny weird or funny ha ha?"*

WORD CHOICE **fun and funny**
• Use **fun** to talk about things or events that you enjoy: *We had a fun time at the dance.* | *That sounds like fun.*
• Use **funny** to talk about people or things that make you laugh: *Jim Carrey is a funny guy.* | *The skits were so funny last night.*

ˈfunny bone *n.* [singular] **1** BIOLOGY the soft part of your elbow that hurts a lot when you hit it hard **2** your sense of humor: *Bennett's latest show is guaranteed to **tickle your funny bone*** (=make you laugh).

ˈfunny farm *n.* [C] INFORMAL an expression meaning a hospital for people who are mentally ill, that is usually considered offensive

ˈfunny-ˌlooking *adj.* INFORMAL having a strange or amusing appearance: *Jon was a really funny-looking little kid.*

fun·ny·man /ˈfʌniˌmæn/ *n. plural* **funnymen** /-ˌmɛn/ [C] a man who acts in funny movies or television shows, or works as a COMEDIAN

ˈfunny ˌmoney *n.* [U] INFORMAL money that has been printed illegally → see also COUNTERFEIT

ˈfunny ˌpapers *n.* [plural] INFORMAL another expression meaning FUNNIES

fun·ny·wom·an /ˈfʌniˌwʊmən/ *n. plural* **funnywomen** /-ˌwɪmɪn/ [C] a woman who acts in funny movies or television shows, or works as a COMEDIAN

ˈfun ˌrun *n.* [C] an event in which people run a long distance in order to collect money, usually for CHARITY

fur /fɚ/ *n.* **1** [U] BIOLOGY the thick soft hair that covers the bodies of some types of animal, for example cats or dogs → see also HAIR: *There was cat fur all over the chair.* **2** [C,U] the fur-covered skin of an animal, especially used for making clothes: *Furs were exchanged for cotton and other goods.* | *the fur industry* | *a fur coat* | *a **fake fur** jacket* (=one made of artificial material that looks like fur) **3** [C] a coat or piece of clothing made of fur: *Mrs. Welland was putting on her fur.* **4 the fur flies** used to say that an angry argument or fight starts: *She found out where Keith was all night, and that's when the fur really started to fly.* [**Origin:** 1300–1400 *fur* **to cover the inside of sth with fur** (14–19 centuries), from Old French *forre* **inside covering**] → see also FURRY

Fu·ries /ˈfyʊriz/ *n.* **the Furies** [plural] the three GODDESSES in ancient Greek stories, who punish people for their crimes

fu·ri·ous /ˈfyʊriəs/ *adj.* **1** extremely angry → see also ANGRY: *Tony was furious when Bobbie admitted the truth.* | *Williams got a call that day from a furious Larry Parnes.* | +**with** *My parents were furious with me.* | +**at/about** *They were furious at finding no doctors on duty at the hospital.* | +**that** *She was furious that they had seen her cry.* ▶see THESAURUS box at **angry** **2** [only before noun] done with a lot of energy, effort, or anger: *a furious fight* | *They headed through the woods **at a furious pace*** (=very fast and with a lot of energy). | *The following round of questions for the President was **fast and furious**.* [**Origin:** 1300–1400 Old French *furieus*, from Latin *furia* **fury**] **—furiously** *adv.*

furl /fɚl/ *v.* [T] LITERARY to roll or fold something such as a flag, UMBRELLA, or sail OPP **unfurl** **—furled** *adj.*

fur·long /ˈfɚlɔŋ/ *n.* [C] a unit for measuring length used in horse racing, equal to 220 yards or 201 meters

fur·lough /ˈfɚloʊ/ *n.* [C,U] **1** a period of time when a soldier or someone working in another country can return to their own country: *He was home **on furlough** in July.* **2** a temporary period of time when a worker is told not to work, especially because there is not enough work or not enough money to pay them → see also LAYOFF: *a four-day furlough for 26,000 city employees* **3** a short period of time when a prisoner is allowed to leave prison before returning

fur·nace /ˈfɚnɪs/ *n.* [C] **1** a piece of equipment that is used to heat a house or building **2** a large container in which a very hot fire is made, to produce power or heat, or to melt metals → see also BLAST FURNACE **3 be (like) a furnace** to be extremely hot

fur·nish /ˈfɚnɪʃ/ *v.* [T] **1** [usually passive] to put furniture and other things into a house or room: *a beautifully furnished house* | **furnish sth with sth** *The Inn is furnished with antiques.* **2** FORMAL to supply or provide something SYN **provide**: *Buyers of any gun must furnish two pieces of identification.* | **furnish sb with sth** *The embassy can furnish you with a list of local hospitals.* **—furnished** *adj.*: *a furnished apartment*

fur·nish·ing /ˈfɚnɪʃɪŋ/ *n.* [U, plural] the furniture and other things in a room, such as curtains, decorations etc.: *home furnishings*

fur·ni·ture /ˈfɚnɪtʃɚ/ S2 W3 *n.* [U] large objects that you have in your house or office, such as chairs, tables, beds, and cupboards: *antique furniture* | *office furniture* | *The former owners had left behind several **pieces of furniture**.* [**Origin:** 1500–1600 French *fourniture*, from Old French *furnir* **to complete, provide equipment**] → see also **part of the furniture** at PART[1] (23)

fu·ror /ˈfyʊrɔr/ *n.* [singular] a sudden expression of anger or excitement among a large group of people about something: *The security leaks have caused a national furor.* | +**about/over** *the furor over her new book*

fur·ri·er /ˈfɚiɚ, ˈfʌriɚ/ *n.* [C] someone who makes or sells fur clothing

fur·row[1] /ˈfɚoʊ, ˈfʌroʊ/ *n.* [C] **1** a deep line or fold in the skin of someone's face, especially on the top front part of their head **2** a long narrow cut made in the surface of a field with a PLOW **3** a long, narrow cut or hollow area in the surface of something: *The river cuts a long furrow between the hills.*

furrow[2] *v.* **1** [I,T] to make the skin on your face form deep lines or folds, especially because you are worried, angry, or thinking hard: *Ralph **furrowed his brow**, trying to work everything out.* **2** [T] to make a deep cut or hollow area in something **—furrowed** *adj.*: *a furrowed brow*

fur·ry /ˈfɚi/ *adj. comparative* **furrier**, *superlative* **furriest** covered with fur, or looking or feeling as if covered with fur: *a furry puppy* | *a furry cap*

fur·ther[1] /ˈfɚðɚ/ S2 W2 *adv.*
1 MORE more, or to a greater degree: *Safety will be further improved.* | *I won't trouble you any further.* |

+**into/away etc.** *The company is sliding* ***further and further*** *into debt.* | **even/still further** *His explanation confused me even further.*
2 DISTANCE a longer distance, or a longer distance away SYN **farther**: *Let's walk a little further.* | +**up/away/along/from etc.** *a few miles further down the road* | *Our house is further from the river.* | **further north/south etc.** *They've never been further south than San Diego.* | *The balloon floated* ***further and further*** *away.*
3 take sth further to take action at a more serious or higher level, especially in order to get the result that you want: *We try to take it further than just saying "Don't do drugs."* | *If we do not receive payment by May 5, we will* ***take the matter further****.*
4 go (one step) further to do or say more than before: *A few days later the department went one step further and filed a lawsuit.*
5 TIME further back/on/ahead etc. a longer way in the past or future: *Five years further on, a cure has still not been found.* | *The records don't go further back than to 1970.* | *He'll come up with a different idea* ***further down the road*** (=in the future).
6 PROGRESS continuing or progressing beyond a particular stage SYN **farther**: *Have discussions progressed any further?* | *I didn't* ***get*** *any* ***farther*** (=make any more progress) *than asking her name.*
7 IN ADDITION [sentence adverb] FORMAL used to introduce something additional that you want to talk about SYN **furthermore**: *These men are dangerous. Further, they have already committed serious crimes abroad.*
8 go further a) to say or do something that is more extreme: *The laws need to go further and ban guns altogether.* | *I'd go even further and use the word "evil."* **b)** to continue talking about something: *She interrupted me before I could go any further.*
9 nothing could be further from the truth used when you want to say that something is completely untrue: *People think he's stupid, but nothing could be further from the truth.*
[**Origin:** Old English *furthor*; related to *forth*] → see Word Choice box at FARTHER

further² W2 *adj.* [only before noun] **1** more or additional: *For further information, travelers may contact the consulate.* | *Are there any further questions?* | **a further 5 minutes/ten miles etc.** *Add the sesame seeds, and bake for a further 20 minutes.* ▸see THESAURUS box at **more²** **2 until further notice** until you are told that something has changed: *All three schools are closed until further notice.*

further³ *v.* [T] to help something succeed or be achieved: *Rodney had no opportunities to further his education.*

fur·ther·ance /ˈfɚðərəns/ *n.* [U] FORMAL **1 the furtherance of sth** the development or progress of something: *the furtherance of human rights* **2 in furtherance of sth** in order to help something progress or become complete

fur·ther·more /ˈfɚðɚˌmɔr/ Ac *adv.* [sentence adverb] FORMAL in addition to what has already been said: *The drug has powerful side effects. Furthermore, it can be addictive.*

fur·thest /ˈfɚðɪst/ *adj., adv.* **1** at the greatest distance from a place or point in time: *the furthest corners of the universe* | +**away/from etc.** *Whose house is furthest away?* | *the planet that is furthest from the sun* | *This is* ***the furthest*** *I've ever ridden in a day.* **2** most, or to the greatest degree: *The space program has been developed furthest in the US.* **3** to the most distant time in the past or the future: ***The furthest*** *back that I can remember is when I was three.* **4 the furthest thing from my mind** used to emphasize that you were not thinking about or intending something: *Politics was the furthest thing from my mind when they asked me to run.*

fur·tive /ˈfɚṭɪv/ *adj.* behaving as if you want to keep something secret: *She was having a furtive affair with a cameraman.* | *Tim and Joanie exchanged* ***furtive glances*** *across the room.* [**Origin:** 1600–1700 French *furtif*, from Latin *fur* **thief**] —**furtively** *adv.* —**furtiveness** *n.* [U]

fu·ry /ˈfyʊri/ *n.* **1** [singular, U] a state or feeling of extreme, often uncontrolled anger SYN **rage**: *Shaking* ***with fury****, I stood up to confront him.* | +**at/over** *She did not hide her fury at their incompetence.* **2 a fury of sth** a state of very busy activity or strong feeling: *She drove down the road in a fury of emotion.* **3 the fury of the wind/sea/waves etc.** LITERARY used to describe bad weather conditions: *the devastating fury of the storm*

fuse¹ /fyuz/ *n.* [C] **1** PHYSICS a short thin piece of wire that is inside electrical equipment and prevents damage by melting and stopping the electricity when there is too much power: *Suddenly,* ***a fuse blew*** *and the whole house went dark.* | *The electronic scoreboard* ***blew a fuse*** *and the display disappeared.* **2** also **fuze** a part of a bomb, FIREWORKS etc. that delays the explosion until you are a safe distance away, or makes it explode at a particular time **3 have a short fuse** to get angry very easily: *Dad has a very short fuse.* → see also **blow a fuse** at BLOW¹ (9)

fuse² *v.* [I,T] **1** to join together, or to make things join together, to become a single thing: *Getz was one of the first musicians to fuse jazz and Latin rhythms.* | *King sought to fuse the civil rights movement with anti-war activists.* **2** CHEMISTRY if metals, rocks etc. fuse or if you fuse them, they become joined together by being heated: *The radio's wires had been fused by the heat.* **3** CHEMISTRY if a rock or metal fuses or if you fuse it, it becomes liquid by being heated

ˈfuse box *n.* [C] a box that contains the fuses of the electrical system of a house or other building

fu·se·lage /ˈfyusəˌlɑʒ, -lɪdʒ, -zə-/ *n.* [C] the main part of an airplane, in which people sit or goods are carried

fu·sil·lade /ˈfyuzəˌleɪd/ *n.* [C usually singular] **1** a rapid series of loud noises, especially shots from a gun: +**of** *a fusillade of bullets* **2** a rapid series of questions or remarks: +**of** *a fusillade of hostile questions for the mayor*

fu·sion /ˈfyuʒən/ *n.* **1** [singular, U] the combination or joining together of separate things, ideas, or groups: *The restaurant serves a fusion of Japanese and Californian cooking.* **2** [U] CHEMISTRY the process of joining together the nuclei (NUCLEUS) of atoms, producing heavier atoms and a lot of energy → see also FISSION: +**of** *the fusion of hydrogen atoms* **3** also **fusion jazz** [U] a style of music that combines JAZZ and ROCK → see also NUCLEAR FUSION

ˈfusion bomb *n.* [C] another word for a HYDROGEN BOMB

fuss¹ /fʌs/ *n.* **1** [singular, U] attention or excitement that makes something seem more serious or important than it is: +**about** *There's been a lot of fuss in the media about the latest crime figures.* **2 make a fuss/kick up a fuss** also **raise a fuss** to complain or become angry about something, especially in a way that is stronger than necessary: *Davis kicked up a fuss when the waiter forgot her order.* **3 make a fuss over sb/sth** to pay too much attention to someone or something that you like: *People always make such a fuss over babies.* **4 not see/understand etc. what all the fuss was about** used to say that you do not understand why people are so excited about or interested in something: *Until I heard her sing live, I didn't see what all the fuss was about.*

fuss² *v.* [I] **1** if a baby fusses, it cries or seems unhappy: *The baby was fussing and whining.* **2** to worry a lot about things that may not be very important: **fuss about/over sth** *Mom's still fussing over the seating arrangements.*

fuss over sb/sth *phr. v.* to pay a lot of, or too much, attention to someone or something that you like: *Mrs. Wilson fussed over the little dog in her lap.*

fuss with sth *phr. v.* to touch or handle something continuously in a nervous way: *Stop fussing with your hair!*

fuss·budg·et /ˈfʌsˌbʌdʒɪt/ *n.* [C] OLD-FASHIONED someone who is always too concerned or worried about small, unimportant details

F

fuss·y /ˈfʌsi/ *adj.* *comparative* **fussier**, *superlative* **fussiest** **1** too concerned or worried about small, usually unimportant details → see also FASTIDIOUS: *I've become much more fussy about how I draw the characters.* **2** unhappy or difficult to please: *a fussy baby* | *Children nowadays are very* ***fussy eaters.*** **3 not be fussy** SPOKEN used to say that you do not mind what decision is made, where you go etc.: *"What would you like to eat?" "Oh, whatever – I'm not fussy."* **4** fussy clothes, objects, buildings etc. are too detailed and decorated: *fussy wallpaper* —**fussily** *adv.* —**fussiness** *n.* [U]

fus·tian /ˈfʌstʃən/ *n.* [U] **1** a type of rough heavy cotton cloth, worn especially in past times **2** LITERARY words that sound important but have very little meaning —**fustian** *adj.*

fus·ty /ˈfʌsti/ *adj.* **1** OLD-FASHIONED if rooms, clothes, buildings etc. are fusty, they have a bad smell, because they have not been used for a long time **2** ideas or people that are fusty are old-fashioned: *A number of young economists, impatient with such fusty arguments, began searching for new models.* [**Origin:** 1400–1500 *fust* **wooden wine container** (15–16 centuries), from Old French, from Latin *fustis*] —**fustiness** *n.* [U]

fu·tile /ˈfyutl̩/ *adj.* actions that are futile are useless because they have no chance of being successful: *Rescue workers made a* ***futile attempt*** *to save the people trapped in the collapsed building.* [**Origin:** 1500–1600 Latin *futilis* **that pours out easily, useless**] —**futility** /fyuˈtɪləṭi/ *n.* [U]

fu·ton /ˈfutɑn/ *n.* [C] a type of bed that you can roll up when you are not using it, originally from Japan [**Origin:** 1800–1900 Japanese]

fu·ture¹ /ˈfyutʃɚ/ S2 W1 *n.* **1 the future** the time after the present OPP **past**: *What are your plans for the future?* | *What do you think life* ***in the future*** *will be like?* | **in the near/immediate/not-too-distant future** *It is unlikely that we will achieve any profits in the near future.* | *We will not be hiring anyone else* ***in the foreseeable future*** (=for as long as you can imagine or plan for). | *None of us knows* ***what the future holds for*** (=what will happen in the future to) *us.* | *They believed that dreams could* ***predict the future*** (=tell what will happen in the future). **2** [C usually singular] what someone or something will do or what will happen to them in the future OPP **past**: *Gabby assured me that she is confident about her future.* | +**of** *Ferguson is optimistic about the future of the business.* | **determine/shape/decide the future of sth** *a leader who will determine the future of the organization* **3** [singular, U] a chance or possibility of success at a later time: **have a/no future** *I think she has a future in the newspaper business.* | **there is a/no future in sth** *He felt there was no future in farming.* | **have a great/promising/bright future** *This team has a very bright future.* **4 futures** [plural] TECHNICAL legal agreements to buy or sell goods, money, land etc in the future at a time and price that have been agreed **5 the future** also **the future tense** TECHNICAL in grammar, the form of a verb that shows that something will happen or exist at a later time. In the sentence "I will leave tomorrow," "will leave" is in the future. [**Origin:** 1300–1400 Old French *futur*, from Latin *futurus* **going to be**]

future² W3 *adj.* [only before noun] **1** happening, existing, or expected to happen or exist at a time after the present: *He is being talked about as a future president.* | *future plans for the show* | **sb's future wife/husband/son-in-law etc.** (=someone who will be your wife, husband, son-in-law etc.) | **at a/some future date** *We'll make a final decision at some future date.* | *We want to preserve this land* ***for future generations*** (=for the members of our family who will come after us). ►see THESAURUS box at **later²** **2 for future reference a)** something kept for future reference is kept in order to be used or looked at in the future: *He took notes for future reference.* **b)** used for telling someone something that you want them to do or remember in the future, especially when you are annoyed with them for forgetting now: *For future reference, everyone who is a member must attend the meetings.*

ˌfuture ˈperfect *n.* ENG. LANG. ARTS **the future perfect** in grammar, the form of a verb that shows that an action will be complete before a particular time in the future, formed in English by "will have." In the sentence, "I will have finished my finals by next Friday," "will have finished" is in the future perfect. —**future perfect** *adj.*

fu·tur·ism /ˈfyutʃəˌrɪzəm/ *n.* [U] **1** ENG. LANG. ARTS a style of painting, music, and literature from the early 20th century that expresses the violent, active qualities of modern life, machines, science etc. **2** the act of imagining what may happen in the future, especially through scientific developments or politics: *an interest in futurism and technology* —**futurist** *n.* [C]

fu·tur·is·tic /ˌfyutʃəˈrɪstɪk/ *adj.* **1** a building, movie, design etc. that is futuristic is so unusual and modern in appearance that it looks as if it belongs in the future instead of the present time: *the car's futuristic styling* **2** futuristic ideas, books etc. imagine what may happen in the future, especially through scientific developments: *a futuristic thriller starring Bruce Willis*

fu·tu·ri·ty /fyʊˈtʊrəṭi, -ˈtʃʊr-/ *n.* *plural* **futurities** **1** [U] FORMAL the time after the present; the FUTURE **2** [C] a type of horse race in which the horses are entered in the competition at the time they are born

futz /fʌts/ *v.*

futz around *phr. v.* INFORMAL **1** to waste time, especially by doing small, unimportant jobs slowly: *Yolanda futzed around upstairs while the rest of us waited.* **2** to make changes or move things around, especially without knowing the right way to do it SYN **fiddle with sth**: +**with** *Brad spent a couple of hours futzing around with the speaker connections.*

fuze /fyuz/ *n.* [C] another spelling of FUSE

fuzz¹ /fʌz/ *n.* [U] **1** thin soft hair or a substance like hair that covers something: *The baby's hair was a soft fuzz.* **2** a small amount of soft material that has come from clothing etc.: *the dust and fuzz that gathers behind the computer*

fuzz² *v.* [T usually passive] to make something fuzzy

Fuzz·Bust·er /ˈfʌzˌbʌstɚ/ *n.* [C] TRADEMARK a machine in your car that warns you when there are any police cars nearby, so that you know that you should not drive too fast

fuzz·y /ˈfʌzi/ *adj.* *comparative* **fuzzier**, *superlative* **fuzziest** **1** unclear or confused and lacking details: *Clarence had only a few fuzzy memories of his grandparents.* **2** having a lot of very small thin hairs, fur etc. that look very soft: *a fuzzy hat* **3** if a picture or sound is fuzzy, it is unclear → see also BLURRED: *a fuzzy videotape of the bank robbery* → see also **warm (and) fuzzy** at WARM¹ (7) —**fuzzily** *adv.* —**fuzziness** *n.* [U]

ˌfuzzy ˈlogic *n.* [U] COMPUTERS a machine, computer, or piece of equipment that uses fuzzy logic is able to change for particular situations in order to do a job better, rather than always doing things in exactly the same way

FWIW, fwiw a written abbreviation of **for what it's worth**, used in EMAIL, or by people communicating in CHAT ROOMS on the Internet

fwy. the written abbreviation of FREEWAY

FX **1** an abbreviation of SPECIAL EFFECTS **2** an abbreviation of FOREIGN EXCHANGE

FY the abbreviation of FISCAL YEAR

-fy /faɪ/ *suffix* [in verbs] to affect or change someone or something in a particular way: *stupefy* (=make you feel very surprised or bored) → see also -IFY

FYI the abbreviation of **for your information**, used especially in short business notes and EMAILS

G,g

G¹ /dʒi/ *n. plural* **G's** **1** also **g** *plural* **g's** [C] **a)** the seventh letter of the English alphabet **b)** a sound represented by this letter **2** ENG. LANG. ARTS **a)** [C,U] the fifth note in the musical SCALE of C MAJOR **b)** [U] the musical KEY based on this note **3** [C,U] **general** used to show that a movie is appropriate for people of any age → see also PG **4** [C,U] SPOKEN A GRAND (=$1,000)

G² PHYSICS the symbol that represents the fixed relationship between force, mass, and distance, according to Newton's law of GRAVITATION

g¹ **1** the written abbreviation of GRAM **2** PHYSICS a unit that measures the rate at which an object ACCELERATES (=increases its speed) as a result of the effect of GRAVITY: *Near the Earth's surface, all objects accelerate downwards at a rate of g= 9.81 meters per second.*

g² *n.* [C] PHYSICS the amount of force caused by GRAVITY on an object that is on the surface of the Earth: *The MiG-29 fighter jet can take nine g's* (=nine times the force of gravity).

G

G8 /dʒi ˈeɪt/ *n.* **the G8** eight of the wealthiest industrial nations in the world (Canada, France, Germany, Britain, Italy, Japan, Russia, and the U.S.) who meet to discuss world political and economic problems

GA the written abbreviation of GEORGIA

gab /gæb/ *v.* **gabbed, gabbing** [I] INFORMAL to talk continuously, usually about things that are not important: *They spend too much time gabbing instead of working.* → see also **the gift of gab** at GIFT¹ (4) —**gab** *n.* [U] —**gabby** *adj.*

gab·ar·dine /ˈgæbɚˌdin/ *n.* [U] a type of cloth that is made of tightly woven wool, cotton, or POLYESTER, especially used for making clothes

gab·ble¹ /ˈgæbəl/ *v.* **gabbled, gabbling** [I,T] **1** to say something so quickly that people cannot hear you or understand you well **2** to make the sound that a group of geese or similar bird makes

gabble² *n.* [singular, U] a lot of talking that is difficult to understand, especially when several people are talking at the same time SYN **babble**: *the gabble of the audience before the show*

gab·er·dine /ˈgæbɚˌdin/ *n.* [U] another spelling of GABARDINE

ga·ble /ˈgeɪbəl/ *n.* [C] the top part of a wall of a house where it joins with a sloping roof and makes a shape like a TRIANGLE

ga·bled /ˈgeɪbəld/ *adj.* having one or more gables: *a gabled roof*

Ga·bon /gæˈbɑn, -ˈboʊn/ a country in west central Africa on the Atlantic Ocean —**Gabonese** /ˌgæbəˈniz◂ , -ˈnis◂ / *n., adj.*

Ga·bo·ro·ne /ˌgɑbəˈroʊni/ the capital city of Botswana

Ga·bri·el /ˈgeɪbriəl/ in the Bible, an ARCHANGEL who brings messages from God to people on Earth. In the Muslim religion, Gabriel gave Muhammad the messages from Allah which form the KORAN.

Gad /gæd/ *interjection* a word used instead of "God" to emphasize what you are saying: *Gad, what was I doing so far from home?*

gad /gæd/ *v.* **gadded, gadding**

gad around OLD-FASHIONED to go out and enjoy yourself, going to many different places, especially when you should be doing something else

gad·a·bout /ˈgædəˌbaʊt/ *n.* [C] OLD-FASHIONED someone who goes out a lot or travels a lot in order to enjoy themselves, instead of behaving responsibly

Gad·da·fi /gəˈdɑfi/, **Colonel Mu·am·mar al-** /ˈmoʊəmɑr æl/ → see QADDAFI, COLONEL MUAMMAR AL-

gad·fly /ˈgædflaɪ/ *n. plural* **gadflies** [C] **1** someone who annoys other people by criticizing them: *a political gadfly* **2** BIOLOGY a fly that bites cattle and HORSES

gadg·et /ˈgædʒɪt/ *n.* [C] a word meaning a small machine or tool designed for a specific purpose: *kitchen gadgets such as avocado peelers*

gadg·et·ry /ˈgædʒɪtri/ *n.* [U] a word meaning small modern tools and machines in general that is often used when you think the machines are complicated or not necessary: *high-tech medical gadgetry*

Gads·den Pur·chase, the /ˌgædzdən ˈpɚtʃɪs/ HISTORY an area that is now part of Arizona and New Mexico, which was bought from Mexico by the U.S. in 1853

gad·zooks /gædˈzuks/ *interjection* OLD-FASHIONED used to show that you are surprised about something

Gae·a, Gaia /ˈgaɪə, ˈdʒiə/ in Greek MYTHOLOGY, the goddess of the Earth

Gael·ic¹ /ˈgeɪlɪk, ˈgælɪk/ *n.* [U] one of the Celtic languages, especially spoken in parts of Scotland and in Ireland

Gaelic² *adj.* speaking Gaelic, or relating to Gaelic

gaff¹ /gæf/ *n.* [C] a stick with a hook at the end, used to pull big fish out of the water

gaff² *v.* [T] to pull big fish out of the water with a gaff

gaffe /gæf/ *n.* [C] an embarrassing mistake, especially something you say, that is made in public SYN **faux pas**: *The consul's comments were a major diplomatic gaffe.*

gaf·fer /ˈgæfɚ/ *n.* [C] **1** the person who is in charge of the lighting in making a movie **2** HUMOROUS an old man

gag¹ /gæg/ *v.* **gagged, gagging** **1** [I] to feel sick in a way that makes you feel as though you might VOMIT (=bring food from your stomach back through your mouth): *The smell made her gag.* | **gag on sth** *A customer gagged on a piece of meat.* **2** [T] to put a piece of cloth over someone's mouth to stop them making a noise: *Five of the occupants were* ***bound and gagged*** (=tied and gagged) *by the robbers.* **3** [T] to stop people saying what they want to say and expressing their opinions: *The mayor was accused of trying to gag the media.* **4** [I] INFORMAL to feel surprised and annoyed about something you think is not fair: *The price of these tickets is enough to make anyone gag.*

gag² *n.* [C] **1** INFORMAL a joke, funny story, or trick that is done to make someone look silly: *He wrote gags for the Jack Benny show.* | *The movie has some good* ***sight gags*** (=things that are funny to watch rather than jokes). ▸see THESAURUS box at **joke¹** **2** a piece of cloth put over someone's mouth to stop them making a noise

ga·ga /ˈgɑgɑ/ *adj.* [not before noun] INFORMAL **1** having a strong but often temporary feeling of love for someone, or having a strong liking for something: *Customers have* ***gone gaga over*** *our cheese steak sandwiches.* **2** used to describe someone who is acting confused or slightly crazy: *I'm going gaga, studying for all these exams.*

Ga·ga·rin /gəˈgɑrɪn/, **Yu·ri** /ˈyʊri/ (1934–1968) a Soviet ASTRONAUT who became the first man in space when he traveled round the Earth in 1961

gage /geɪdʒ/ *n.* another spelling of GAUGE

gag·gle /ˈgægəl/ *n.* **1 a gaggle of tourists/children etc.** HUMOROUS a noisy group of people **2 a gaggle of geese** a group of geese (GOOSE)

ˈgag ˌorder *n.* [C] LAW an order made by a court of law, that stops people from reporting on what is happening in a TRIAL that is still being considered by the court

ˈgag rule *n.* [C] **1** a rule or law that stops people from talking about a subject during a particular time or in a particular place **2** HISTORY a rule passed by the House of Representatives in 1836 that prevented any speeches or other documents that were against SLAVERY to be read or dealt with in the House

gai·e·ty /ˈgeɪəṭi/ *n.* OLD-FASHIONED **1** [U] a feeling of cheerfulness and fun: *the warmth and gaiety of a family reunion* **2 gaieties** [plural] enjoyable events or activities: *Elaine missed the gaieties of life in Paris.* → see also GAY[1]

gai·ly /ˈgeɪli/ *adv.* OLD-FASHIONED **1 gaily colored/painted/decorated etc.** having bright cheerful colors: *a gaily wrapped package* **2** in a happy cheerful way: *Marge waved gaily at us.*

gain[1] /geɪn/ S3 W1 *v.*
1 GET STH [T] to get, win, or achieve something important or valuable, often after trying hard: *The country gained independence in 1957.* | *Detroit gained a spot in the finals with a 4–0 victory over Toronto.* | **gain power/control** *The army gained control of the foothills.* ►see THESAURUS box at **get**
2 GET GRADUALLY [I,T] to gradually get more and more of a useful or valuable quality, skill etc. OPP **lose**: *an opportunity to* ***gain experience*** *in a real-life work environment* | *a bid by Democrats to* ***gain public support*** *for their budget plan* | *Taylor has* ***gained a reputation*** (=become known) *for making profitable business decisions.* | **gain in popularity/confidence/efficiency etc.** *The sport has gained in popularity over the last three years.* | **gain an understanding/impression of sth** *We are hoping to gain a better understanding of the process.* | **gain (an) insight into sth** (=get a better understanding of something)
3 GET AN ADVANTAGE [I,T] to get an advantage from a situation, opportunity, or event OPP **lose**: *We* ***gained an advantage*** *through better use of technology.* | **gain (sth) from (doing) sth** *People with higher incomes clearly gained the most from the tax cuts.* | *The family* ***stands to gain*** (=would gain, if the situation works for them) *a couple of million dollars.* | ***There's nothing to be gained from*** (=it will not help you) *losing your temper.*
4 gain weight/speed/height to increase in weight, speed, or height OPP **lose**: *I've gained a lot of weight recently.*
5 gain access (to sth) a) to be able to enter a building or place: *Prison officials wouldn't say how the inmates gained access to the roof.* **b)** to be allowed to see someone or use something that is usually private or secret: *Lawyers are trying to gain access to the confidential files.*
6 gain entrance/entry a) to enter a building that is locked: *Police had to break the door down to gain entry into the building.* **b)** to join or become part of a system or organization: *The company is trying hard to gain entry to the Japanese market.* **c)** to be allowed to come into a country: *The two men used fake passports to gain entry into Germany.*
7 gain ground make steady progress and become more popular, more successful etc.: *In the currency markets, the dollar gained ground in Japan and Europe.*
8 gain time to deliberately do something to give yourself more time to think or to do something: *I was just trying to gain time before answering the question.*
9 gain currency FORMAL to become more popular or more accepted: *an idea that has gained currency in recent years*
10 CLOCK [I,T] if a clock or watch gains or gains time, it goes too fast OPP **lose**
11 ARRIVE [T] FORMAL OR LITERARY to reach a place after a lot of effort or difficulty: *The swimmer finally gained the river bank.*
[**Origin:** 1400–1500 French *gagner*, from Old French *gaaignier* **to prepare the ground for growing crops, earn, gain**] → see also **nothing ventured, nothing gained** at VENTURE[2] (3)

gain on/upon sb/sth *phr. v.* **1** to gradually get closer to a person, car etc. that you are chasing: *Gant was gaining on Allison in the final few laps.* **2** to gradually become almost as successful as someone or something else: *Right now we're the best Internet service provider, but the competition is gaining on us.*

gain[2] W2 *n.* **1** [C,U] an increase in the amount or level of something OPP **loss**: *weight gain* | *Women have* ***made*** *economic, legal, and social* ***gains.*** | **+in** *the show's gain in popularity* | *The Party won 150 seats,* ***a net gain of*** (=the total gain, after all gains and losses have been calculated) *two seats.* **2** [C,U] financial profit OPP **loss**: *short-term gains* | **+of** *a pre-tax gain of $20 million* | **do sth for personal/financial/economic gain** (=do something only in order to make money) **3** [C] an advantage or improvement, especially one achieved by planning or effort: *significant gains in medical technology* | **+from** *the possible gains from improved marketing* **4 ill-gotten gains** HUMOROUS money or advantages that someone obtains dishonestly → see also CAPITAL GAINS

gain·ful /ˈgeɪnfəl/ *adj.* **gainful employment/work/activity** FORMAL work or activity for which you are paid —**gainfully** *adv.*

gain·say /ˌgeɪnˈseɪ/ *v.* **gainsaid** /-ˈsɛd/ [T usually in negatives] FORMAL to say that something is not true, or to disagree with someone: *It may be very difficult to gainsay the claim.*

Gains·bor·ough /ˈgeɪnzbərə/, **Thomas** (1727–1788) a British artist best known for his PORTRAITS (=pictures of people) and LANDSCAPES (=pictures of the countryside)

gait /geɪt/ *n.* [singular] the way someone walks: *the old man's slow, shuffling gait* [**Origin:** 1400–1500 *gate* **way** (13–21 centuries), from Old Norse *gata* **road**]

gai·ter /ˈgeɪṭə/ *n.* [C usually plural] a cloth or leather covering that covers your lower leg or ANKLE and stops mud and water from going into your boots

gal /gæl/ S3 *n.* [C] INFORMAL a girl or woman: *She's a great gal.*

gal. the written abbreviation of "gallon"

ga·la /ˈgælə, ˈgeɪlə/ *n.* [C] an event at which a lot of people are entertained and celebrate a special occasion [**Origin:** 1600–1700 Italian, Old French *gale* **fun and enjoyment**]

ga·lac·tic /gəˈlæktɪk/ *adj.* relating to a galaxy

Ga·lap·a·gos Is·lands, the /gəˈlæpəgoʊs ˌaɪləndz, -ˈlɑ-/ a group of islands in the east Pacific Ocean that belong to Ecuador

Ga·la·tians /gəˈleɪʃənz/ a book in the New Testament of the Christian Bible

gal·ax·y /ˈgæləksi/ *n. plural* **galaxies** [C] **1** PHYSICS any of the large groups of stars that make up the universe ►see THESAURUS box at **space**[1] **2 the Galaxy** PHYSICS the large group of stars that the Earth's sun and stars are a part of **3** [singular] a large number of things that are similar: *Lane was awarded a galaxy of medals for her bravery.* [**Origin:** 1300–1400 Late Latin *galaxias*, from Greek, from *gala* **milk**; because the Galaxy looks milky white from the Earth]

Gal·braith /ˈgælbreɪθ/, **John Ken·neth** /dʒɑn ˈkɛnɪθ/ (1908–2006) an American ECONOMIST, born in Canada, who wrote several books about the way society is developing and changing

gale /geɪl/ *n.* [C] **1** a very strong wind: *The ship sank in the gale.* ►see THESAURUS box at **wind**[1] **2 gales of laughter** a lot of loud laughter: *The audience applauded in gales of laughter.*

ˈgale-force *adj.* a gale-force wind is strong enough to be dangerous or cause damage —**gale-force** *adv.*

Ga·len /ˈgeɪlən/ (?130–?201) a Greek doctor and writer whose ideas had a great influence on doctors in Europe until the Renaissance

Ga·li·le·o /ˌgæləˈlioʊ, -ˈleɪ-/, **Galileo Gal·i·lei** /-ˈleɪi/ (1564–1642) an Italian ASTRONOMER, mathematician, and PHYSICIST whose many discoveries had a great influence on modern science. He was punished by the Catholic Church because he believed that the Sun, not the Earth, was the center of the universe.

gall[1] /gɔl/ *n.* **1 have the gall to do sth** DISAPPROVING to do something impolite and unreasonable that most people would be too embarrassed to do: *Congress actually had the gall to vote for a pay raise for themselves.* **2** [U] OLD-FASHIONED anger and hate that will not go away **3** [U] OLD USE → see BILE **4** [C] a swelling on a tree or plant caused by damage from insects or infection **5** [C]

G

a painful place on an animal's skin, caused by something rubbing against it

gall² *v.* [T] to make someone feel upset and angry because of something that is unfair: **it galls sb (that)** *It galls me that she's never apologized for what she said.*

gal·lant¹ /ˈgælənt/ *adj.* **1** brave: *gallant deeds* **2** OLD-FASHIONED a man who is gallant is kind and polite toward women [**Origin:** 1300–1400 Old French *galer* **to have a good time**, from *gale* **fun and enjoyment**] —**gallantly** *adv.*

gal·lant² /gəˈlænt, ˈgælənt/ *n.* [C] OLD USE a well-dressed young man who is kind and polite toward women

gal·lant·ry /ˈgæləntri/ *n.* [U] FORMAL **1** courage, especially in a battle: *a medal for gallantry* **2** polite attention given to women by men

ˈgall ˌbladder *n.* [C] BIOLOGY the organ in your body in which BILE is stored → see picture at DIGESTIVE SYSTEM

gal·le·on /ˈgæliən/ *n.* [C] HISTORY a sailing ship used mainly by the Spanish from the 15th to the 17th century

gal·ler·y /ˈgæləri/ *n. plural* **galleries** [C] **1 a)** ENG. LANG. ARTS a room, hall, or building where people can see famous pieces of art: *the National Portrait Gallery in Washington* | *the museum's newest gallery* **b)** [C] a small store or STUDIO where you can see and buy pieces of art: *a craft gallery downtown* **2** [C] an upper floor like a BALCONY in an AUDITORIUM, theater, or church, from which people can watch a performance, DEBATE etc.: *the public gallery in Congress* **3 the gallery** the people sitting in a gallery **4 play to the gallery** to do or say something just because you think it will please people and make you popular **5** [C] a level passage under the ground in a mine or CAVE [**Origin:** 1400–1500 Medieval Latin *galeria*] → see also PRESS GALLERY, SHOOTING GALLERY

gal·ley /ˈgæli/ *n. plural* **galleys** [C] **1** a kitchen on a ship **2** HISTORY a long low Greek or Roman ship with sails that was rowed by SLAVES in past times **3 a)** a TRAY used by printers that holds TYPE **b)** also **galley proof** a sheet of paper on which a PRINTER prints a book so that mistakes can be corrected before it is printed to be sold

Gal·lic /ˈgælɪk/ *adj.* relating to France or French people

gall·ing /ˈgɔlɪŋ/ *adj.* making you feel upset and angry because of something that is unfair: *It's galling when people blame the victim for being careless.*

gal·li·vant /ˈgæləˌvænt/ *v.* [I] INFORMAL OR HUMOROUS to spend time enjoying yourself and going from place to place for pleasure: +**around** *She spent six months gallivanting around Europe.*

gal·lon /ˈgælən/ S3 *n.* [C] a unit for measuring liquids, equal to 4 QUARTS or 3.785 liters: *a gallon of water* | *a 20 gallon fish tank* | *The car gets about 47* ***miles to the gallon*** (=you can drive 47 miles with each gallon of gas). [**Origin:** 1200–1300 Old North French, Medieval Latin *galeta* **liquid container, liquid measure**]

gal·lop¹ /ˈgæləp/ *v.* **1** [I,T] if a horse gallops, it runs as fast as it can, with all its feet leaving the ground together: *A thoroughbred can gallop a mile in about 90 seconds.* | +**along/across/toward etc.** *Wild horses galloped through the canyon.* **2** [I,T] if you gallop or gallop a horse, you ride very fast on a horse or you make it run very fast: +**along/across/toward etc.** *Mounted police galloped down Main Street with drawn pistols.* **3** [I always + adv./prep.] to move or do something very quickly: +**through/past etc.** *This is a bill that will gallop through Congress.*

gallop² *n.* **1 a)** [singular] the movement of a horse running as fast as it can, with all four feet leaving the ground together: *The horse took off* ***at full gallop*** (=as fast as possible). **b)** [C] a ride on a horse when it is galloping **2** [singular] a very fast speed: *The project began at a gallop.*

gal·lop·ing /ˈgæləpɪŋ/ *adj.* [only before noun] increasing or developing very quickly: *the galloping cost of health care*

gal·lows /ˈgæloʊz/ *n. plural* **gallows** [C] a structure used for killing criminals by hanging them from a rope

ˈgallows ˌhumor *n.* [U] humor that makes very bad or serious things seem funny: *In hospitals where staff deal with death every day, gallows humor is common.*

gall·stone /ˈgɔlstoʊn/ *n.* [C] BIOLOGY a hard stone that can form in your GALL BLADDER

Gal·lup /ˈgæləp/, **George** (1901–1984) a U.S. public opinion ANALYST who developed the Gallup poll

ga·loot /gəˈlut/ *n.* [C] OLD-FASHIONED someone who is not graceful at all, and does not dress neatly

ga·lore /gəˈlɔr/ *adj.* [only after noun] in large amounts or numbers: *At the flea market, there were quilts, furniture, and books galore.* [**Origin:** 1600–1700 Irish Gaelic *go leor* **enough**]

ga·losh·es /gəˈlɑʃɪz/ *n.* [plural] OLD-FASHIONED rubber shoes worn over ordinary shoes when it rains or snows

ga·lumph /gəˈlʌmf/ *v.* [I always + adv./prep.] INFORMAL to move in a noisy, heavy, and awkward way: *Children were galumphing around the stage.*

gal·van·ic /gælˈvænɪk/ *adj.* **1** FORMAL making people react suddenly with strong feelings or actions: *a galvanic experience* **2** PHYSICS relating to the production of electricity by the action of acid on metal

gal·va·nism /ˈgælvəˌnɪzəm/ *n.* [U] PHYSICS the production of electricity by the use of chemicals, especially as in a BATTERY

gal·va·nize /ˈgælvəˌnaɪz/ *v.* [T] to shock or surprise someone so that they do something to solve a problem, improve a situation etc.: *King's great speeches galvanized the African American community.* | **galvanize sb into (doing) sth** *The possibility of defeat finally galvanized us into action.* —**galvanizing** *adj.*: *a galvanizing experience*

gal·va·nized /ˈgælvəˌnaɪzd/ *adj.* **galvanized iron/metal etc.** galvanized iron etc. has a covering of ZINC so that it does not RUST

gal·va·nom·e·ter /ˌgælvəˈnɑmət̬ɚ/ *n.* [C] an instrument that measures small electrical currents

Gam·bi·a, the /ˈgæmbiə/ a country on the coast of West Africa next to Senegal —**Gambian** *n., adj.*

gam·bit /ˈgæmbɪt/ *n.* [C] **1** something that you do or say that you hope will give you an advantage in an argument, conversation, or meeting: *a political gambit* | *This may be* ***the opening gambit*** (=the first thing that is said or done in a difficult situation) *in the trade negotiations.* **2** a planned series of moves at the beginning of a game of CHESS [**Origin:** 1600–1700 Italian *gambetto* **act of making someone fall over**, from *gamba* **leg**]

gam·ble¹ /ˈgæmbəl/ *v.* **1** [I] to risk money or possessions because you might win more if a card game, race etc. has the result you want → see also BET: *I don't drink or gamble.* | **gamble (sth) on sth** *He illegally gambled on a college basketball game.* **2** [I,T] to do something risky in order to get something you want: *The president is hoping he has gambled correctly.* | **gamble (sth) on sth** *We're gambling on the weather being nice for our outdoor wedding.* | **gamble with sth** *Doctors can't gamble with patients' lives just to test new drugs.* | **gamble (that)** *She was gambling that they wouldn't see her leave.*

gamble sth ↔ **away** *phr. v.* to lose money by gambling: *Nielsen gambled all his money away.*

gamble² *n.* [singular] an action or plan that is risky but that you hope will succeed: *It was a big gamble to leave the band and go for a solo career.* | **take a gamble (on sb)** *Getz had little experience, but they took a gamble on him.* | *Luckily,* ***the gamble paid off*** (=the risk achieved the result), *and she got the job.*

gam·bler /ˈgæmblɚ/ *n.* [C] someone who gambles

gam·bling /ˈgæmblɪŋ/ *n.* [U] **1** the practice of risking money or possessions because you might win a lot more if a card game, race etc. has the result you want: *Gambling is still illegal in Arkansas.* | *gambling debts*

2 gambling den a place where people go to gamble illegally

gam·bol /ˈgæmbəl/ *v.* [I always + adv./prep.] to jump or run around in an excited active way: *lambs gamboling in the fields* —**gambol** *n.* [C]

games

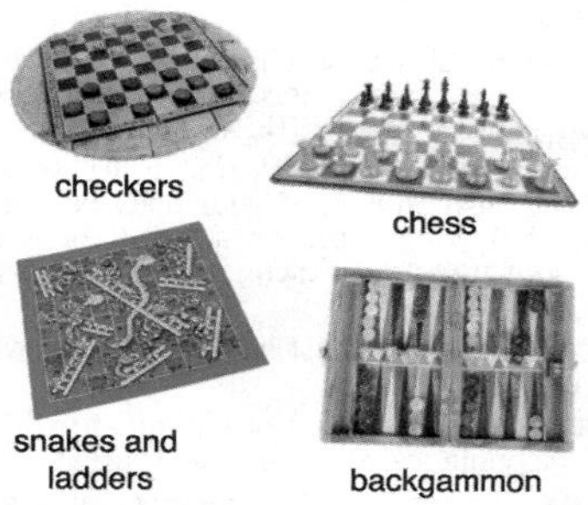

game[1] /geɪm/ S1 W1 *n.*

1 ACTIVITY OR SPORT [C] an activity or sport in which people compete with each other according to agreed rules: *a video game* | *What are the rules of the game?* | **+of** *the game of football* | *We spent the evening* ***playing*** *card* ***games***. | *Do you like* ***board games***? | **a game of chance** (=a game in which you risk money on the result)

THESAURUS

game a particular competition in a sport, or a competition that involves mental skill, knowledge, or luck: *Who won the football game?* | *a game of cards*
sport a physical activity in which people or teams play against each other and try to win: *Girls who are involved in sports tend to be more confident.*
recreation all the activities that people do in order to relax: *the city's parks and recreation department*
hobby an activity that you do in your free time: *Her hobbies are reading and music.*

2 PARTICULAR OCCASION [C] an occasion when a game is played: *He scored two touchdowns in last night's game.* | **+of** *Let's* ***play a game of*** *chess.* | **+against** *the Red Sox's game against the Baltimore Orioles* | **win/lose a game** *We lost the game 5–3.* | **home/away game** (=a game that is played on the team's own field or away at the opposing team's field)
3 PART OF A COMPETITION [C] one of the parts into which a single competition is divided, for example in tennis → see also MATCH: *Sampras leads, two games to one.*
4 CHILDREN'S PLAY [C] a children's activity in which they play with toys, pretend to be someone else etc.: **+of** *a game of hide-and-seek* | *The boys were* ***playing a game*** *in the backyard.*
5 SPORTS EVENT the games [plural] a large organized sports event that includes many different sports: *the Olympic Games*
6 TYPE OF WORK/ACTIVITY [singular] INFORMAL an area of work or activity: *I'm still new to the game. I have a lot to learn.* | *I've been in this game for over ten years.* | **the advertising/public relations etc. game** (=the profession of advertising etc.)
7 be (just) a game (to sb) if something is just a game, you do not consider it to be serious or important: *I really loved him, but to him it was just a game.*
8 play games (with sb) a) to behave in a dishonest or unfair way in order to get what you want: *Many taxpayers try to play games on their tax returns.* **b)** to not be serious about doing something: *We want an agreement. We're not interested in playing games.*
9 give the game away to spoil a surprise or secret by doing or saying something that lets someone guess what the secret is: *Don't say any more or you'll give the game away.*
10 ANIMALS/BIRDS [U] wild animals, birds, and fish that are hunted for food, especially as a sport → see also BIG GAME ►see THESAURUS box at **meat**
11 be the only game in town used to say that something is the only possible choice in a situation: *Cotton was still an important crop, but it was no longer the only game in town.*
12 sb's game how skillfully someone plays a particular sport: *Lisa's taking lessons to improve her tennis game.* | *The champion was clearly* ***off his game*** (=not playing with the usual skill) *yesterday.*
13 beat sb at their own game to beat someone or fight back against them by using the same methods that they use
14 the game's up SPOKEN INFORMAL used to tell someone that something wrong or dishonest that they have done has been discovered: *The game's up. Come on out.*
15 sb got game SPOKEN NONSTANDARD used to say that someone is very skillful at doing something, especially playing a sport → see also **ahead of the game/curve** at AHEAD (11), FAIR GAME, **fun and games** at FUN[1] (4), **the name of the game** at NAME[1] (8), **two can play at that game** at TWO (9)
[**Origin:** Old English *gamen*]

game[2] *adj.* willing to try something new, difficult, or dangerous: **+for** *Helen was game for any new challenge.* | **game to do sth** *Are you game to go rock climbing with us?* —**gamely** *adv.*

game[3] *v.* **game the system** to use rules or laws to your advantage in an unfair but legal way so that you get what you want: *companies accused of gaming the system to increase profits*

ˈgame cock *n.* [C] a ROOSTER (=male chicken) that is trained to fight other roosters

game·keep·er /ˈgeɪmˌkipɚ/ *n.* [C] someone whose job is to take care of the wild animals and birds that are kept to be hunted on private land

gam·e·lan /ˈgæməlæn/ *n.* [C] a traditional ORCHESTRA (=group of musicians and instruments) of southeast Asia, especially Indonesia, which includes a lot of PERCUSSION instruments (=instruments that you hit)

ˈgame park *n.* [C] a GAME RESERVE

ˈgame plan *n.* [C] a plan for achieving success, especially in business or sports: *If we stick to the game plan, there's no way we'll lose.*

ˈgame ˌpoint *n.* [C,U] the situation in a game such as tennis in which one player will win the game if they win the next point → see also MATCH POINT

ˈgame preˌserve *n.* [C] a game reserve

gam·er /ˈgeɪmɚ/ *n.* [C] **1** SLANG someone who likes to play VIDEO GAMES **2** INFORMAL a person who plays a sport very well, and can help a team win games

ˈgame reˌserve *n.* [C] a large area of land where wild animals can live safely

ˈgame show *n.* [C] a television program in which people play games or answer questions to win money and prizes

games·man·ship /ˈgeɪmzmənˌʃɪp/ *n.* [U] **1** the ability to influence events or people so that you gain an advantage: *political gamesmanship* **2** the ability to succeed by using the rules of a game to your own advantage

gam·ete /ˈgæmit/ *n.* [C] BIOLOGY a type of cell that joins with another cell, starting the development of a baby or other young creature

ˈgame ˌwarden *n.* [C] someone whose job is to take care of wild animals in a GAME RESERVE

gam·ey /ˈgeɪmi/ *adj.* another spelling of GAMY

gam·in /ˈgæmɪn/ *n.* [C] OLD USE a young boy who lives on the streets

ga·mine /gæˈmin, ˈgæmin/ *n.* [C] **1** a small thin girl or woman who looks like a boy **2** OLD USE a young girl who lives on the streets —**gamine** *adj.*: *a gamine hairstyle*

gam·ing /ˈgeɪmɪŋ/ *n.* [U] playing cards or other games of chance for money SYN **gambling**: *gaming tables*

G

gam·ma /ˈgæmə/ *n.* [C] the third letter of the Greek alphabet

ˌgamma ˈglobulin *n.* [U] BIOLOGY a natural substance in your body that is a type of ANTIBODY and gives protection against some diseases

ˈgamma ray *n.* [C usually plural] PHYSICS a type of RADIATION that is the result of NUCLEAR FISSION, and involves high-energy PHOTONS

gam·ut /ˈgæmət/ *n.* **the gamut** the complete range of possibilities: +**of** *The movie uses the gamut of computerized special effects.* | *Riesling wines* ***run the gamut from** dry **to** sweet* (=include the complete range of possibilities). [**Origin:** 1400–1500 Medieval Latin *gamma ut*, names given to the highest and lowest notes on the musical scale]

gam·y, gamey /ˈgeɪmi/ *adj. comparative* **gamier**, *superlative* **gamiest** having the strong taste or smell of wild animals

-gamy /gəmi/ *suffix* [in U nouns] marriage to a particular number or type of people: *monogamy* (=marriage to one person) | *bigamy* (=marriage to two people) —**-gamous** *suffix* [in adjectives]

gan·der /ˈgændə˞/ *n.* [C] **1** BIOLOGY a male GOOSE **2 have/take a gander at sth** SPOKEN to look at something: *Take a gander at this letter I just got from Janet.* → see also **what's good/sauce for the goose is good/sauce for the gander** at GOOSE[1] (3)

Gan·dhi, In·di·ra /ˈgɑndi/, /ˈɪndɪrə/ (1917–1984) a PRIME MINISTER of India

Gandhi, Mo·han·das (Ma·hat·ma) /ˌmoʊhənˈdɑs məˈhɑtmə/ (1869–1948) an Indian leader who helped India gain its independence from Great Britain

Gandhi

gang[1] /gæŋ/ S3 W3 *n.* **1** a group of young people who spend time together, and often cause trouble and fight against other groups: *a motorcycle gang* | *gang warfare* | *Several* ***gang members*** (=people who belong to a gang) *were arrested.* | +**of** *a gang of teenage boys* | *He belongs to one of Chicago's* ***street gangs*** (=gang that claims control over a particular area of a city). ►see THESAURUS box at **group**[1] **2** [C] a group of criminals who work together: *Several gangs were operating in the area.* | +**of** *a gang of thieves* **3** INFORMAL a group of friends, especially young people: *She went out with Sarah and the gang.* **4** a group of workers or prisoners doing physical work together [**Origin:** Old English **way, journey**; the modern meaning comes from the idea of a group of people "going" together] → see also CHAIN GANG

gang[2] *v.*

gang up on sb *phr. v.* to join together into a group to attack or criticize someone, especially in a way that seems unfair: *You two stop ganging up on your sister!*

ˈgang-ˌbanging *n.* [U] the activity of gangs fighting with other gangs —**gang-banger** *n.* [C]

gang·bust·ers /ˈgæŋˌbʌstə˞z/ *n.* **like gangbusters** INFORMAL doing something very eagerly and with a lot of energy, or happening very quickly: *Fraser's historical novels are selling like gangbusters.*

Gan·ges, the /ˈgændʒiz/ a long river that flows through northern India and Bangladesh. To the Hindus, the Ganges is a holy river.

gang·land /ˈgæŋlænd/ *adj.* **a gangland killing/murder/shooting etc.** a killing etc. that is related to the activities of violent gangs or ORGANIZED CRIME

gan·gling /ˈgæŋglɪŋ/ *adj.* gangly

gan·gli·on /ˈgæŋgliən/ *n.* [C] TECHNICAL **1** a painful raised area of skin that is full of liquid, often on the back of your wrist **2** BIOLOGY a mass of nerve cells

gan·gly /ˈgæŋgli/ *adj. comparative* **ganglier**, *superlative* **gangliest** unusually tall and thin, and not able to move gracefully: *a gangly sixteen-year-old boy*

gang·plank /ˈgæŋplæŋk/ *n.* [C] a board for walking on between a boat and the shore, or between one boat and another

ˈgang ˌrape *n.* [C] a criminal act when several men attack a woman or man to force her or him to have sex with them —**gang-rape** *v.* [T]

gan·grene /ˈgæŋgrin, gæŋˈgrin/ *n.* [U] MEDICINE the decay of the flesh on part of your body because blood has stopped flowing there as a result of illness or injury —**gangrenous** /ˈgæŋgrənəs/ *adj.*: *a gangrenous foot*

gang·sta /ˈgæŋstə/ *n.* [C] SLANG someone who is a member of a gang

ˈgangsta ˌrap *n.* [U] a type of RAP music with words about drugs, violence, and life in poor areas of cities

gang·ster /ˈgæŋstə˞/ *n.* [C] a member of a group of violent criminals

gang·way /ˈgæŋweɪ/ *n.* [C] **1** a large GANGPLANK **2 gangway!** SPOKEN used to tell people in a crowd to let someone go through **3** a narrow path between two things such as rooms or rows of seats

gan·net /ˈgænɪt/ *n.* [C] BIOLOGY a large sea bird that lives in large groups on cliffs

gan·try /ˈgæntri/ *n. plural* **gantries** [C] a large metal frame that is used to support heavy machinery or railroad signals

gap /gæp/ W3 *n.* [C]

1 A SPACE an empty space between two objects or two parts of something, especially because something is missing: +**in** *a gap in the fence* | *The sun shone through a gap in the clouds* | +**between** *There's a big gap between the tub and the wall.* ►see THESAURUS box at **hole**[1]

2 DIFFERENCE a big difference between two situations, amounts, groups of people etc.: +**between** *The gap between the rich and the poor is widening.* | *This program exists to* ***bridge the gap*** (=reduce the amount of difference) *between environmentalists and businesses.* → see also GENERATION GAP

3 STH MISSING something that is missing that stops something else from being good or complete: +**in** *a serious gap in medical technology* | *There are huge gaps in my knowledge of European history.* | *Venezuela has increased oil production to help* ***fill the gap*** *in world supplies.*

4 IN TIME a period of time when nothing is happening, that exists between two other periods of time: +**in** *an uncomfortable gap in the conversation* | +**between** *The gaps between his visits got longer and longer.*

5 IN A MOUNTAIN a low place between two higher parts of a mountain, often used in the names of these places: *the Cumberland Gap*

6 a gap in the market a product or service that does not exist, so that there is an opportunity to develop that product or service and sell it

[**Origin:** 1300–1400 Old Norse **hole, deep narrow valley**]

gape /geɪp/ *v.* [I] **1** to look at something for a long time, especially with your mouth open, because you are very surprised or shocked → see also GAZE: **gape at sth** *A group of small boys gaped at the scene in awe.* ►see THESAURUS box at **look**[1] **2** also **gape open** to come apart or to open widely: *The wound on his neck gaped open.* —**gape** *n.* [C]

gap·ing /ˈgeɪpɪŋ/ *adj.* [only before noun] a gaping hole, wound, or mouth is very wide and open

ˌgap-ˈtoothed *adj.* having wide spaces between your teeth

ga·rage /gəˈrɑʒ, gəˈrɑdʒ/ S2 *n.* [C] **1** a building for keeping a car in, usually next to or attached to a house → see also CARPORT: *a two-car garage* **2** a place where cars are repaired: *My car's at the garage.* [**Origin:** 1900–2000 French *garer* **to shelter**]

ga'rage ˌband *n.* [C] a group of musicians who play loud ROCK music and practice in a garage

ga'rage ˌsale *n.* [C] a sale of used furniture, clothes etc. from people's houses, usually done in someone's garage → see also YARD SALE

garb¹ /gɑrb/ *n.* [U] FORMAL OR LITERARY a particular style of clothing, especially clothes that show your type of work or that look unusual: *green surgical garb*

garb² *v.* **be garbed in sth** LITERARY to be dressed in a particular type of clothes: *The men were garbed in Army uniforms.*

gar·bage /'gɑrbɪdʒ/ S2 *n.* **1** [singular, U] waste material that is thrown away, such as paper, empty containers, and old food SYN **trash**: *Can you* ***take out the garbage*** *when you go out?*

THESAURUS

trash things that you throw away, such as old food, dirty paper etc.: *garbage cans overflowing with trash*
refuse FORMAL things that you throw away, such as old food, dirty paper etc.: *the money spent on refuse collection*
litter garbage, especially pieces of paper, food containers etc., that people leave on the ground in public places: *There was litter all over the beach.*
waste unwanted things or substances that are left after you have used something: *the safe disposal of nuclear waste*

2 [singular] the container this is put in: *The garbage is under the sink.* **3** [U] stupid words, ideas etc.: *You're talking garbage.* **4 garbage in, garbage out** used to say that if you put bad information into a computer, you will get bad results [**Origin:** 1400–1500 Anglo-French]

'garbage ˌbag *n.* [C] a large plastic bag for holding waste material

'garbage ˌcan *n.* [C] a plastic or metal container with a lid that is used for holding waste until it can be taken away

THESAURUS

wastebasket a small container inside a building where you put paper and things you do not want
dumpster a large metal container outside a building, for example an office or store, used for things people throw away

'garbage colˌlection *n.* [U] the act of taking waste from houses and businesses

'garbage colˌlector *n.* [C] someone whose job is to remove waste from garbage cans and take it away to a garbage dump

'garbage disˌposal *n.* [C] a small machine in the kitchen SINK that cuts food waste into small pieces so that it can be washed down the DRAIN of the sink

'garbage dump *n.* [C] a place in a city or town where waste is taken and stored

'garbage man *n.* [C] a garbage collector

'garbage ˌtruck *n.* [C] a large vehicle that goes from house to house to collect the garbage from garbage cans

gar·ban·zo /gɑr'bɑnzoʊ/ also **gar'banzo ˌbean** *n. plural* **garbanzos** [C] another word for CHICKPEA, used especially in the western U.S.

gar·bled /'gɑrbəld/ *adj.* **1** very unclear and confusing, and often not giving correct information SYN **confused**: *The newspapers had some garbled version of the story.* **2** difficult to hear or understand: *The voice on the tape was too garbled to understand.* [**Origin:** 1400–1500 *garble* **to remove impure parts by putting through a container with small holes** (15–19 centuries), from Old Italian *garbellare*]

Gar·cí·a Lor·ca /gɑrˌsiə 'lɔrkə/, **Fed·e·ri·co** /ˌfɛdə'rɪkoʊ/ (1898–1936) a Spanish poet and writer of plays

García Már·quez /gɑrˌsiə 'mɑrkɛs/, **Gabriel** (1928–) a Colombian writer of NOVELS

gar·çon /gɑr'soʊn/ *n.* [C] a WAITER, especially in a French restaurant

gar·den¹ /'gɑrdn/ S2 W2 *n.* **1** [C] the part of the land around or next to a house that has flowers and plants in it: *a vegetable garden* | *a flower garden* **2 gardens** [plural] a public park where a lot of unusual plants and flowers are grown: *the Brooklyn Botanical Gardens* [**Origin:** 1300–1400 Old North French]

garden² *v.* [I] to work in a garden, keeping it clean, making plants grow etc.: *Stephen's mom loves to garden in her spare time.* —**gardening** *n.* [U]

gar·den·er /'gɑrdnɚ/ *n.* [C] **1** someone whose job is to work in gardens **2** someone who enjoys growing flowers and plants

gar·de·nia /gɑr'dinyə/ *n.* [C] a large white nice-smelling flower that grows on a bush [**Origin:** 1700–1800 Alexander *Garden* (1730–1791), Scottish plant scientist]

'garden-vaˌriety *adj.* [only before noun] very ordinary and not very interesting: *This is not your garden-variety case of fraud.*

Gar·field /'gɑrfild/, **James** (1831–1881) the 20th President of the U.S.

G

gar·gan·tu·an /gɑr'gæntʃuən/ *adj.* extremely large: *a gargantuan task* [**Origin:** 1500–1600 *Gargantua*, name of a giant in the book "Gargantua" (1534) by François Rabelais]

gar·gle¹ /'gɑrgəl/ *v.* [I,T] to clean the inside of your mouth and throat by blowing air through water or medicine in the back of your throat: +**with** *Gargle with salt water to help your sore throat.*

gargle² *n.* **1** [C,U] liquid that you gargle with **2** [singular] the act of gargling

gar·goyle /'gɑrgɔɪl/ *n.* [C] a stone figure with the face of a strange and ugly creature, that carries rain water from the roof of an old building, especially a church [**Origin:** 1400–1500 Old French *gargouille* **throat**; because the water appears to come out of the creature's throat]

Gar·i·bal·di /ˌgærə'bɔldi/, **Giu·sep·pe** /dʒʊ'sɛpi/ (1807–1882) an Italian military leader who helped Italy to become a united independent country by taking control of Sicily and Naples in 1860

gar·ish /'gærɪʃ, 'gɛr-/ *adj.* very brightly colored in a way that is annoying to look at: *a garish necktie* —**garishly** *adv.* —**garishness** *n.* [U]

gar·land¹ /'gɑrlənd/ *n.* [C] a ring of flowers or leaves, worn on your head or around your neck for decoration or for a special ceremony

garland² *v.* [T] LITERARY to decorate someone or something, especially with flowers

gar·lic /'gɑrlɪk/ S2 *n.* [U] a plant like a small onion with a very strong taste, used in cooking: ***a clove of garlic*** (=a single section of it) [**Origin:** Old English *garleac*, from *gar* **spear** + *leac*] —**garlicky** *adj.*

'garlic ˌpress *n.* [C] a kitchen tool used to crush garlic

gar·ment /'gɑrmənt/ *n.* [C] FORMAL a piece of clothing [**Origin:** 1300–1400 French *garnement* **equipment**, from *garnir* **to warn, provide with equipment, garnish**]

'garment ˌbag *n.* [C] a special SUITCASE (=bag) used to carry clothes such as suits and dresses

gar·ner /'gɑrnɚ/ *v.* [T] FORMAL to take or get something, especially information or support: *The party garnered 70 percent of the vote.*

gar·net /'gɑrnɪt/ *n.* **1** [C] a dark red stone used as a jewel **2** [U] a dark red color

gar·nish¹ /'gɑrnɪʃ/ *v.* [T] **1** to add something to food in order to decorate it: **garnish sth with sth** *roasted turkey garnished with fresh orange and lemon slices* **2** also **garnishee** TECHNICAL to take money from someone's salary because they have not paid their debts: *The* *state* ***garnished my wages*** *to pay for the parking tickets.*

garnish² *n.* [C] something that you add to food to decorate it [**Origin:** 1300–1400 French *garnir* **to warn, provide with equipment, garnish**]

gar·ret /'gærɪt/ *n.* [C] a small room at the top of a house → see also ATTIC

gar·ri·son¹ /'gærəsən/ *n.* [C] a group of soldiers living in a town or FORT in order to defend it

garrison² *v.* [T] to send a group of soldiers to defend or guard a place

Gar·ri·son /'gærɪsən/, **William** (1805–1879) a U.S. newspaper writer and PUBLISHER famous for working to end SLAVERY in the U.S.

gar·rotte /gə'rɑt/ *v.* [T] to kill someone using a metal collar or wire that is pulled tightly around their neck —**garrotte** *n.* [C]

gar·ru·lous /'gærələs/ *adj.* always talking a lot: *a garrulous young man*

gar·ter /'gɑrtə/ *n.* [C] **1** one of four pieces of ELASTIC attached to a woman's underwear and to her STOCKINGS to hold them up, used especially in past times **2** a band of ELASTIC (=material that stretches) worn around your leg to keep a sock or STOCKING up

G

'garter ˌbelt *n.* [C] a piece of women's underwear with garters hanging down from it that fasten onto STOCKINGS and holds them up, used especially in past times

'garter ˌsnake *n.* [C] BIOLOGY a harmless snake with colored lines along its back, which lives in North and Central America

Gar·vey /'gɑrvi/, **Mar·cus** /'mɑrkəs/ (1887–1940) an African-American who started the "Back to Africa" movement to encourage other African-Americans to establish a society of their own in Africa

gas¹ /gæs/ S1 W2 *n.* **1** [U] also **gasoline** a liquid made from PETROLEUM, used mainly for producing power in the engines of cars, trucks etc.: *I probably spend over $200 a month on gas.* | *The mechanic found a hole in the* ***gas tank.*** **2** *plural* **gases** or **gasses** [C,U] PHYSICS a substance such as air that is not solid or liquid, does not have a definite shape or VOLUME (=measurement of the amount of space it fills), and cannot usually be seen: *hydrogen gas* | *greenhouse gases* **3** [U] a clear substance like air that is burned for heating or cooking: *a gas stove* **4** [U] INFORMAL the condition of having a lot of air in your stomach **5 the gas** the gas PEDAL of a car SYN **accelerator**: *The driver* ***stepped on the gas*** (=pushed down the gas pedal and made the car go faster) *and tried to escape.* **6** [singular] OLD-FASHIONED something that is fun and makes you laugh a lot [**Origin:** (2–3) 1600–1700 Modern Latin, Greek *khaos* **empty space**]

gas² *v.* **gassed, gassing** **1** [T] to poison or kill someone with gas: *5,000 civilians were gassed to death by the army.* **2** [I] OLD-FASHIONED to talk for a long time about unimportant or boring things

gas sth ↔ **up** *phr. v.* to put gas in a car: *I need to gas up the car before we go.*

gas·bag /'gæsbæg/ *n.* [C] INFORMAL someone who talks too much

'gas ˌchamber *n.* [C] a large room in which people or animals are killed with poisonous gas

gas·e·ous /'gæsiəs, 'gæʃəs/ *adj.* like gas or in the form of gas

'gas-fired *adj.* OLD-FASHIONED using gas as a FUEL: *a gas-fired heater*

'gas-ˌguzzler *n.* [C] INFORMAL a car that uses a lot of gas —**gas-guzzling** *adj.*

gash /gæʃ/ *n.* [C] **1** a large deep wound from a cut: *a gash above his eye* **2** a long deep hole in something: *a gash in the sidewall of a tire* —**gash** *v.* [T]

gas·i·fy /'gæsəˌfaɪ/ *v.* **gasifies, gasified, gasifying** [I,T] to change into a gas, or to make something do this —**gasification** /ˌgæsəfə'keɪʃən/ *n.* [U]

gas·ket /'gæskɪt/ *n.* [C] **1** a flat piece of rubber placed between two surfaces of a machine, especially an engine, that prevents steam, oil, gas etc. from escaping **2 blow a gasket a)** if a vehicle blows a gasket, the gasket breaks and steam or gas escapes **b)** INFORMAL to become very angry

gas·light /'gæs-laɪt/ *n.* **1** [U] the light produced from burning GAS **2** also **'gas lamp** [C] a lamp in a house or on the street that gives light from burning GAS

'gas main *n.* [C] a pipe that supplies GAS to buildings and houses, and is buried under the ground

'gas mask *n.* [C] a piece of equipment worn over your face to protect you from poisonous gases, especially during a war

'gas ˌmeter *n.* [C] a piece of equipment that measures how much GAS is used in a building or house

gas·o·hol /'gæsəhɔl/ *n.* [U] gas with a small amount of alcohol in it, which can be used in special cars and is cheaper than regular gas

gas·o·line /ˌgæsə'lin, 'gæsəˌlin/ *n.* [U] GAS

gasp¹ /gæsp/ *v.* [I] **1** to breathe in suddenly in a way that can be heard, especially because you are surprised or shocked: **gasp in/with sth** *The crowd gasped in astonishment.* | **gasp at sth** *Everyone gasped at the sight of a two-headed dog.* **2** to breathe quickly because you are having difficulty breathing: **gasp for air/breath** *I kept climbing gasping for breath.* [**Origin:** 1300–1400 Old Norse *geispa* **to yawn**]

gasp² *n.* [C] **1** an act of taking in your breath suddenly in a way that can be heard, especially because you are surprised or shocked: **+of** *a gasp of pain* **2** an act of taking in air quickly because you are having difficulty breathing: *short gasps of breath* **3 sb's/sth's last gasp** something that is done when someone is about to die, or about to stop happening or existing: *This cold spell appears to be winter's last gasp for the year.*

'gas ˌpedal *n.* [C] the thing that you press with your foot to make a car go faster SYN **accelerator** → see picture on page A36

ˌgas ˌpermeable 'lens *n.* [C] a type of CONTACT LENS that allows oxygen to reach your eyes

'gas pump *n.* [C] a machine at a GAS STATION that is used to put gasoline into cars

'gas ˌstation *n.* [C] a place where you can buy gas and oil for cars, trucks etc.

gas·sy /'gæsi/ *adj. comparative* **gassier**, *superlative* **gassiest** INFORMAL having a lot of air in your stomach

gas·tric /'gæstrɪk/ *adj.* [only before noun] BIOLOGY **1** relating to your stomach: *gastric ulcers* **2 gastric juices** the acids in your stomach that break food into smaller parts

gas·tri·tis /gæ'straɪtɪs/ *n.* [U] MEDICINE an illness that makes the inside of your stomach become swollen, so that you feel a burning pain

gas·tro·en·ter·i·tis /ˌgæstroʊˌɛntə'raɪtɪs/ *n.* [U] MEDICINE an illness that makes your stomach and INTESTINES become swollen

gas·tro·in·tes·ti·nal /ˌgæstroʊɪn'tɛstɪnl/ *adj.* BIOLOGY of or relating to the stomach and INTESTINES

gas·tro·nom·ic /ˌgæstrə'nɑmɪk/ *adj.* [only before noun] relating to the art of cooking good food or the pleasure of eating it: *a gastronomic tour of European restaurants*

gas·tron·o·my /gæ'strɑnəmi/ *n.* [U] the art and science of cooking and eating good food

ˌgas 'turbine *n.* [C] an engine in which a wheel of special blades is pushed around at high speed by hot gases

gas·works /'gæswəks/ *n. plural* **gasworks** [C] a place where gas is made from coal

gat /gæt/ *n.* [C] SLANG a gun

gate /geɪt/ S2 W3 *n.* [C] **1** the part of a fence or outside wall that you can open and close like a door → see also DOOR: *a garden gate* **2** the place where you leave an airport building to get on an airplane: *Air France flight 76 leaves from gate 6A.* **3 -gate** INFORMAL used with the name of a place or a person to give a name to an event involving dishonest behavior by a politician or other public official: *the Watergate scandal* **4 a)** the amount of money that is made from a sports event, concert, movie etc.: *The new Disney movie took a gate of $4.6 million.* **b)** the number of people who go in to see a sports event or concert [**Origin:** Old English *geat*]

gate·crash·er /ˈgeɪtˀˌkræʃɚ/ *n.* [C] someone who goes to a party or event that they have not been invited to or do not have a ticket to —**gatecrash** *v.* [I,T]

ˌgated comˈmunity *n. plural* **gated communities** [C] an area of expensive houses, stores, tennis courts etc. with a fence or wall around it and an entrance that is guarded

gate·house /ˈgeɪthaʊs/ *n.* [C] **1** a small building next to the gate of a park, castle, large house etc. **2** the building where the controls for a DAM or CANAL are

gate·keep·er /ˈgeɪtˀˌkipɚ/ *n.* [C] **1** someone whose job is to open and close a gate and control who comes in or out **2** a person or organization with the power to make decisions about which people get certain jobs or opportunities in a company or profession: *Law schools are the gatekeepers of the profession.*

ˌgate-leg ˈtable *n.* [C] a table that can be made larger by moving a leg out to support a folding part

gate·post /ˈgeɪtˀpoʊst/ *n.* [C] one of two strong upright poles set in the ground to support a gate

Gates /geɪts/, **Bill** /bɪl/ (1955–) a U.S. computer programmer and businessman, who started the Microsoft computer company and is famous for being the richest man in the world

gate·way /ˈgeɪtˀweɪ/ *n. plural* **gateways** [C] **1** the opening in a fence, wall etc. that can be closed by a gate **2 the gateway to sth a)** a place, especially a city, that you can go through in order to reach another place: *St. Louis was once the gateway to the West.* **b)** a way of achieving something: *Hard work is the gateway to success.* **3** COMPUTERS a way of connecting two different computer NETWORKS that helps them to work together

gath·er¹ /ˈgæðɚ/ S3 W2 *v.*
1 COME TOGETHER [I,T] to come together and form a group, or to make a group do this: **gather (sb) to do sth** *The group gathers daily at the senior center to sing songs.* | **gather (sb) together** *The bridesmaids gathered together for a picture.* | *We gathered the employees together to make the announcement.* | **gather around (sth)** *A crowd gathered around the spot to watch the fight.* | **be gathered** *Around fifty protesters were gathered in the park.* ►see THESAURUS box at **meet¹**
2 KNOW/THINK [T not in progressive] to believe that something is true, because of what you have seen or heard: *Jack was not happy about the news, I gather.* | **I/we gather (that)** *I gather that you really don't want to be here.* | **from what I can gather/as far as I can gather** (=from the information you have heard) | *"It's not the first time it's happened." "So I gather."* (=I have heard that this is true)
3 gather speed/force/momentum etc. to move faster, become stronger, get more support etc. SYN **gain**: *The plane gathered speed down the runway.* | *The international relief effort appears to be gathering momentum.*
4 COLLECT [I,T] to get things from different places and put them together in one place SYN **collect**: *Researchers have gathered information on a variety of diseases.* | **gather (sth) together/up** *Debbie gathered up the clothes and got in line to pay for them.*
5 gather yourself (together) also **gather your thoughts/strength etc.** to prepare yourself for something you are going to do, especially something difficult: *I took a few moments to gather my thoughts before going into the meeting.*
6 gather dust a) if something useful gathers dust, it is not being used: *We sold our piano because it was just gathering dust.* **b)** if something gathers dust, dust sticks to it easily
7 CLOTH [T] **a)** to pull cloth into small folds at the edge: *Gather the material and baste it.* **b)** to pull cloth or a piece of clothing closer to you: *I gathered my coat around me and went outside.*
8 CLOUDS [I] if clouds gather, they start to appear and cover the sky
9 the gathering darkness/dusk/shadows etc. LITERARY the time in the evening when it is getting dark
10 gather sb to you/gather sb up OLD-FASHIONED to take someone into your arms and hold them in order to protect them or show them love
[**Origin:** Old English *gaderian*]

gather² *n.* [C] a small fold produced by pulling cloth together at the edge

gath·ered /ˈgæðɚd/ *adj.* having small folds produced by pulling the edge of a piece of cloth together: *The skirt is gathered at the waist.*

gath·er·ing /ˈgæðərɪŋ/ *n.* [C] **1** a meeting of a group of people: *a large gathering of war veterans* **2** a fold or group of folds in cloth

ga·tor /ˈgeɪt̬ɚ/ *n.* [C] INFORMAL an ALLIGATOR

GATT /gæt/ **General Agreement on Tariffs and Trade** an organization of about 80 countries whose aim was to make agreements that would encourage international trade and remove rules or restrictions that make trade more difficult. GATT was replaced in 1995 by a new organization with similar aims, called WTO (=the World Trade Organization).

gauche /goʊʃ/ *adj.* INFORMAL doing or saying wrong or impolite things, especially because you do not know the right way to behave: *a gauche adolescent boy* [**Origin:** 1700–1800 French **left, left-handed**]

gau·cho /ˈgaʊtʃoʊ/ *n. plural* **gauchos** [C] a South American COWBOY [**Origin:** 1800–1900 American Spanish]

gaud·y /ˈgɔdi/ *adj. comparative* **gaudier**, *superlative* **gaudiest** clothes, decorations, colors etc. that are gaudy are too bright and look cheap: *a gaudy neon sign* [**Origin:** 1400–1500 *gaud* **bright decorative object**] —**gaudily** *adv.* —**gaudiness** *n.* [U]

gauge¹, gage /geɪdʒ/ *n.* [C]
1 INSTRUMENT an instrument for measuring the amount or size of something: *the car's gas gauge* | *an oil pressure gauge*
2 WIDTH/THICKNESS a) the width of thin metal objects such as wire or screws: *a narrow-gauge screw* **b)** the thickness of thin material such as metal or plastic sheets: *heavy gauge black polythene*
3 STANDARD a standard by which something is measured: **+of** *Exports are an important gauge of economic activity.*
4 GUN the width of the BARREL of a gun: *a 12-gauge shotgun*
5 RAILROAD the distance between the lines of a railroad or between the wheels of a train: *a narrow-gauge track*

gauge² *v.* [T] **1** to judge how people feel about something or what they are likely to do SYN **judge**: **gauge what/how etc.** *It's difficult to gauge how the public will respond to this product.* ►see THESAURUS box at **judge²** **2** to measure or calculate something by using a particular method or instrument SYN **measure**: *a new method for gauging the effectiveness of drug rehab programs*

Gau·guin /goʊˈgæn/, **Paul** (1848–1903) a French PAINTER famous for his brightly colored paintings of the people of Tahiti

gaunt /gɔnt, gɑnt/ *adj.* **1** very thin and pale, especially because of sickness or worry: *his gaunt face* **2** a building, mountain etc. that is gaunt looks very plain and ugly

gaunt·let /ˈgɔntˀlɪt, ˈgɑntˀ-/ *n.* **1 throw down the gauntlet** to invite someone to fight or compete over a disagreement: *The girls threw down the gauntlet and challenged the boys to a basketball game* **2 take up the gauntlet** to accept the invitation to fight or compete over a disagreement **3 run the gauntlet (of sb/sth)** to go through a long and difficult experience, especially one in which a group of difficult or dangerous people are trying to approach you: *He had to run the gauntlet of fans to get to his car.* **4** [C] a long GLOVE that covers

G

someone's wrist and protects their hand, worn for example by workers in a factory **5** [C] a GLOVE covered in metal, used for protection by soldiers in past times

Gau·ta·ma Bud·dha /ˌgaʊtəmə ˈbudə, ˌgoʊ-/ the Buddha

gauze /gɔz/ *n.* [U] **1** also **gauze bandage** thin cotton with very small holes in it that is used for wrapping around a wound **2** very thin transparent cloth with very small holes in it, often used for curtains [**Origin:** 1500–1600 French *gaze*] —**gauzy** *adj.*: *a gauzy blouse*

gave /geɪv/ *v.* the past tense of GIVE

gav·el /ˈgævəl/ *n.* [C] a small hammer that the person in charge of a meeting, court of law, AUCTION etc. hits on a table in order to get people's attention

ga·votte /gəˈvɑt/ *n.* [C] a fast, cheerful French dance, or the music for this dance

gawd /gɔd/ *interjection* NONSTANDARD another spelling and pronunciation of the word "God," which is said when you are surprised, upset etc.

gawk /gɔk/ *v.* [I] to look at something for a long time, in a way that seems stupid: **gawk at sth** *Drivers slowed to gawk at the accident.*

G

gawk·y /ˈgɔki/ *adj. comparative* **gawkier**, *superlative* **gawkiest** moving in a nervous and awkward way, as if you cannot control your arms and legs: *a gawky, long-legged teenager* —**gawkiness** *n.* [U]

gay¹ /geɪ/ S2 W2 *adj.* **1** sexually attracted to people of the same sex as yourself, or relating to this SYN **homosexual**: *the gay community* | ***gay and lesbian** couples* **2** OLD-FASHIONED bright or attractive **3** OLD-FASHIONED cheerful and excited **4 with gay abandon** in a careless and thoughtless way [**Origin:** 1200–1300 Old French *gai* **happy**] → see also GAIETY, GAILY —**gayness** *n.* [U]

gay² *n. plural* **gays** [C] someone who is HOMOSEXUAL, especially a man → see also LESBIAN

gay·dar /ˈgeɪdɑr/ *n.* [U] SPOKEN, HUMOROUS an ability that some people think they have to recognize someone who is HOMOSEXUAL

Gay-Lus·sac's law /ˌgeɪ luˈsɑks lɔ/ PHYSICS a scientific principle that says the pressure of a gas is in direct relation to its temperature and VOLUME

Ga·za Strip, the /ˈgɑzə strɪp/ an area of land on the eastern coast of the Mediterranean Sea between Israel and Egypt where many Palestinians live. Israel controls its coast and its AIRSPACE, but Palestinians are responsible for the government within the area.

gaze¹ /geɪz/ *v.* [I always + adv./prep.] to look at someone or something for a long time, especially without realizing you are doing it: **gaze into/at etc.** *He sat for hours gazing out the kitchen window.* | *We gazed up at the stars.* ►see THESAURUS box at **look¹**

gaze² *n.* [singular] a long steady look: *She felt uncomfortable under his **steady gaze**.* | *My mother was mad, and I didn't dare **meet her gaze*** (=look directly into her eyes). | **lower/drop your gaze** (=look down because you are embarrassed or shy)

ga·ze·bo /gəˈziboʊ/ *n. plural* **gazebos** [C] a small building in a garden or park, where you can sit

ga·zelle /gəˈzɛl/ *n.* [C] an animal like a small DEER, which moves and jumps very quickly and gracefully

ga·zette /gəˈzɛt/ *n.* [C] a newspaper or magazine [**Origin:** 1600–1700 French, Italian *gazzetta*, from Italian dialect *gazeta* **small coin** (the price of the newspaper)]

gaz·et·teer /ˌgæzəˈtɪr/ *n.* [C] a list of names of places, printed for example in a dictionary or as a list at the end of a book of maps

GB the written abbreviation of Great Britain

Gb the written abbreviation of GIGABYTE

GDP /ˌdʒi di ˈpi/ GROSS DOMESTIC PRODUCT → see also GNP

gear¹ /gɪr/ S3 *n.*

1 IN CARS ETC. [C,U] the machinery in a vehicle that turns power from the engine into movement: *Put the car **in gear*** (=move the stick that connects the engine to the gear that turns the wheels). | *Don't leave the car **out of gear*** (=stop the connection between the engine and the gear that turns the wheels) *on a hill.* | **low/high gear** (=the gear used for going slowly or going fast) | **shift/change gear** (=move from one gear to another)

2 EQUIPMENT/CLOTHES ETC. equipment, clothes, tools etc. that you need for a particular activity: *He's crazy about photography – he's got all the gear.* | *camping gear* | *You'll probably need to bring your **rain gear*** (=clothes that keep you dry when it rains).

3 in high gear a) using the gear for high speeds **b)** doing something with the greatest possible effort and energy: *The first session of Congress swings into high gear this week.*

4 shift/switch/change gears to start doing something in a different way, especially using more or less energy or effort: *We shifted gears in the second half and started to play better.*

5 MACHINERY a piece of machinery that performs a particular job: *the landing gear of a plane*

[**Origin:** Old English *gearwe*]

gear² *v.* [T] **be geared to sb/sth** also **be geared toward sb/sth** to be organized in a way that is appropriate for a particular purpose or situation: *The new air fares are geared toward business travelers.* | **be geared to do sth** *Oil refineries generally are geared to take only a certain type of oil.*

gear up *phr. v.* to prepare for something, or prepare to do something, especially something unusual or difficult: **gear up to do sth** *Taxi companies geared up to give free rides home on New Year's Eve.* | **gear up for sth** *The organization is gearing up for its four-day convention in Boston.* | **be geared up to do sth/for sth** *I was all geared up to go to Africa.*

gear·box /ˈgɪrbɑks/ *n.* [C] a metal box containing the gears of a vehicle

ˈgear shift *n.* [C] a metal ROD that you move in order to control the gears of a vehicle → see picture on page A36

geck·o /ˈgɛkoʊ/ *n. plural* **geckos** or **geckoes** [C] a type of small LIZARD

GED /ˌdʒi i ˈdi/ *n.* [C] **General Equivalency Diploma** a DIPLOMA (=piece of paper that shows you have finished a particular level of education) that people who did not finish high school can obtain by taking a test

gee /dʒi/ S1 *interjection* used to show that you are surprised or annoyed: *Gee, I didn't realize we were so late.* [**Origin:** 1800–1900 *Jesus*]

geek /gik/ *n.* [C] SLANG someone who is not popular, wears unfashionable clothes, behaves awkwardly in social situations, and is interested in things that most people think are strange —**geeky** *adj.*

geese /gis/ *n.* the plural of GOOSE

gee whiz /ˌdʒi ˈwɪz/ *interjection* OLD-FASHIONED used to show that you are surprised or annoyed

geez /dʒiz/ *interjection* another spelling of JEEZ

gee·zer /ˈgizɚ/ *n.* [C] INFORMAL an old man

Geh·rig /ˈgɛrɪg/, **Lou** /lu/ (1903–1941) a baseball player famous for playing in more CONSECUTIVE games than any other player before him, and who died of a serious muscle disease which is now called "Lou Gehrig's Disease"

Gei·ger count·er /ˈgaɪgɚ ˌkaʊntɚ/ *n.* [C] PHYSICS an instrument for finding and measuring RADIOACTIVITY

gei·sha /ˈgeɪʃə, ˈgiʃə/ also **ˈgeisha girl** *n.* [C] a Japanese woman who is trained in the art of dancing, singing, and providing entertainment, especially for men [**Origin:** 1800–1900 Japanese *gei* **art** + *-sha* **person**]

gel¹ /dʒɛl/ *n.* [C,U] a thick, wet substance that is used in beauty or cleaning products: *hair gel* | *a gel toothpaste*

gel² *v.* **gelled, gelling 1** [I] another spelling of JELL **2** [T] to put hair gel into your hair

gel·a·tin, gelatine /ˈdʒɛlətɪn, -lətˀn/ *n.* **1** [U] a clear substance obtained from boiled animal bones, used for making liquid food more solid and in sweet foods such as JELL-O **2** [C] a piece of colored plastic that is put over a light to change its color

ge·lat·i·nous /dʒəˈlætˀn-əs/ *adj.* in a state between solid and liquid, like a gel

geld /gɛld/ *v.* [T] to remove the TESTICLES of a horse

geld·ing /ˈgɛldɪŋ/ *n.* [C] a horse that has been gelded

gel·id /ˈdʒɛlɪd/ *adj.* very cold

gel·ig·nite /ˈdʒɛlɪgˌnaɪt/ *n.* [U] a very powerful explosive

gem /dʒɛm/ *n.* [C] **1** also **ˈgem stone** a beautiful stone that has been cut into a special shape SYN **jewel** **2** something that is very special or beautiful: *The city is one of the gems of eastern Europe.* **3** a very helpful or special person: *Ben, you're a real gem!*

Gem·i·ni /ˈdʒɛməˌnaɪ/ *n.* **1** [singular] the third sign of the ZODIAC, represented by TWINS and believed to affect the character and life of people born between May 21 and June 21 **2** [C] someone who was born between May 21 and June 21: *Bob's a Gemini.*

gem·ol·o·gy /dʒɛˈmɑlədʒi/ *n.* [U] the study of gems —**gemologist** *n.* [C]

Gen. a written abbreviation of General

-genarian /dʒənɛriən/ *suffix* [in nouns and adjectives] someone who is a particular number of DECADES (=periods of ten years) old: *an octogenarian* (=between 80 and 89 years old) | *a septuagenarian* (=between 70 and 79 years old)

gen·darme /ˈʒɑndɑrm/ *n.* [C] a French police officer

gen·der /ˈdʒɛndɚ/ Ac W3 *n.* **1** [C,U] FORMAL the fact of being male or female: *people of the same gender* | *traditional gender roles* **2 a)** [U] ENG. LANG. ARTS a category such as MASCULINE, FEMININE, or NEUTER into which words are divided in some languages **b)** [C] males or females, considered as a group: *the differences between the genders* [**Origin:** 1300–1400 Old French *gendre*, from Latin *genus* **birth, race, type**]

ˈgender ˌbending *n.* [U] the act of dressing or behaving in a way that is typical of the opposite sex

ˈgender discrimiˌnation *n.* [U] SEX DISCRIMINATION

ˈgender ˌgap *n.* [C] a large difference between the ideas of men and women and the way they vote

ˈgender-ˌneutral *adj.* [usually before noun] gender-neutral language or words do not specifically mention men or women, and so can be understood to include everyone: *Use the gender-neutral "humankind" rather than "mankind."* → see also GENDER-SPECIFIC

ˌgender-speˈcific *adj.* relating to or for males only, or relating to or for females only → see also GENDER-NEUTRAL: *gender-specific roles*

gene /dʒin/ W3 *n.* [C] BIOLOGY a unit of DNA on a CHROMOSOME that contains information which is used to control the development of the qualities that are passed on to a living thing from its parents: +**for** *the gene for asthma* | *Some women* ***carry a gene*** (=have a gene) *that increases the risk of breast cancer.* [**Origin:** 1900–2000 German *gen*, from Greek *genos* **birth, kind**]

ge·ne·al·o·gy /ˌdʒiniˈɑlədʒi/ *n. plural* **genealogies** **1** [U] the study of the history of families **2** [C] an account of the history of a family, especially one that shows how each person is related to the others —**genealogist** *n.* [C] —**genealogical** /ˌdʒiniəˈlɑdʒɪkəl/ *adj.*

ˈgene map *n.* [C] BIOLOGY a drawing showing the position of all the known GENES along a CHROMOSOME (=the part of every living cell that is shaped like a thread and contains genes)

ˈgene pool *n.* [C] BIOLOGY all of the genes in a particular POPULATION at a particular time

gen·er·a /ˈdʒɛnərə/ *n.* the plural of GENUS

gen·er·al[1] /ˈdʒɛnərəl, ˈdʒɛnrəl/ S1 *adj.*

1 MOST IMPORTANT FEATURES describing only the main features or parts of something, not the details: *This class is a general introduction to finance.* | *I have* ***a general idea*** *of how I want the room to look.* | *He described the theory only* ***in general terms*** (=without details).

2 AS A WHOLE involving the whole of a situation, group, or thing, rather than specific parts of it: *a general decline in educational standards* | *ways to improve your general health*

3 as a general rule used to say what usually happens in most cases: *As a general rule, it takes a month to learn the whole system.*

4 MOST PEOPLE shared by or affecting most people, or most of the people in a group: *The drug is now available for general use.* | *topics of* ***general interest*** (=that most people are interested in) | ***The general opinion*** *is that a bridge is necessary.* | ***There was general agreement that*** *the tests were too difficult.* → see Word Choice box at COMMON[2]

5 ORDINARY ordinary or usual: *The oil is fine for general cooking and baking.*

6 JOB used in the name of a job to show that the person who does this job has complete responsibility: *the general manager* | *the Attorney General*

7 the general public/population ordinary people, who do not have important positions or belong to specific groups: *The cave is closed to the general public.*

8 NOT LIMITED not limited to one subject, service, product etc. OPP **specialized**: *a good general education* | *a general fertilizer*

9 APPROXIMATE used to talk about an approximate area or direction: *I've lived* ***in the general area*** *for ten years.* | *They started walking* ***in the general direction*** *of the restaurant.*

[**Origin:** 1100–1200 French, Latin *generalis* **of the whole type**, from *genus* **birth, race, type**] → see also GENERALLY, **as a (general) rule** at RULE[1] (4)

general[2] W3 *n.* [C] **1 in general a)** usually or in most situations: *In general, this type of camera costs under $300.* **b)** used when talking about the whole of a situation, group, or thing, rather than specific parts of it: *She's dissatisfied with her job and* ***life in general.*** | *The conference is focusing on the environment* ***in general and*** *air pollution* ***in particular.*** **2** an officer of very high rank in the Army, Marines, or Air Force: *General Eisenhower* | *He was* ***made a general*** (=given the rank of general) *in 1878.*

ˌGeneral Acˈcounting ˌOffice, the a U.S. government department that checks and examines all records of U.S. government spending

ˌgeneral anesˈthetic *n.* [C] a medicine that makes you unconscious and keeps you from feeling pain, used during a medical operation

ˌGeneral Asˈsembly *n.* [C] **1 the General Assembly** the group of countries that make up the United Nations **2** the group of people who make laws in a state LEGISLATURE

ˌgeneral ˈcounsel *n.* [C] **1** LAW the chief legal officer of a company **2** LAW a firm of lawyers that gives general legal advice

ˌgeneral deˈlivery *n.* [U] a post office department that keeps someone's letters until that person comes to get them

ˌgeneral eˈlection *n.* [C] POLITICS an election in which all the people in a country who can vote elect a political party, president, GOVERNOR, SENATOR etc.

ˌgeneral ˈheadquarters *n.* [plural] the place from which the actions of an organization, especially a military one, are controlled

gen·er·al·ist /ˈdʒɛnərəlɪst/ *n.* [C] a person who knows about many different things and can do many things well

gen·er·al·i·ty /ˌdʒɛnəˈrælət̬i/ *n. plural* **generalities** **1** [C often plural] a very general statement that avoids mentioning details or specific cases: *Strock would only talk about the plan* ***in generalities.*** **2** [U] FORMAL the quality of being true or useful in most situations

gen·er·al·i·za·tion /ˌdʒɛnərələˈzeɪʃən/ *n.* **1** [C] a statement that may be true in some or many situations but is not true all of the time: +**about** *You can't make*

G

***generalizations** about what men or women are like.* | **broad/sweeping/gross generalization** (=a statement that says something is always true, when it is not true in every case) **2** [U] the act of making generalizations: *The students' different backgrounds make generalization difficult.*

gen·er·al·ize /ˈdʒɛnərəˌlaɪz/ *v.* **1** [I,T] to form a general principle or opinion after considering only a small number of facts or examples: *Be careful not to generalize too much.* | +**about** *It is difficult to generalize about China because it's such a huge country.* | +**from** *We can generalize from the samples and make some conclusions.* **2** [I] to make a statement about a number of different things or people without mentioning any details: +**about** *It's impossible to generalize about such a complicated subject.* **3** [T] FORMAL to put a principle, statement, or rule into a more general form so that it covers a larger number of examples: *Can we generalize the data on aspirin's effect on men to women?*

ˌgeneral ˈknowledge *n.* [U] knowledge of facts about many different subjects that most people know about

gen·er·al·ly /ˈdʒɛnərəli/ S2 W2 *adv.* **1** considering something as a whole, without details or specific cases: *It was generally a positive conversation.* | [sentence adverb] *Generally, the team has been more successful at home.* **2** by or to most people SYN **widely**: *The problem is larger than is generally realized.* | **generally regarded/accepted/known etc.** *He is generally regarded as New York's best defensive player.* **3** usually or most of the time SYN **usually**: *The quality of the food here is generally good.* **4 generally speaking** used to introduce a statement that is true in most cases but not always: *Generally speaking, the more expensive models are the best.*

ˌgeneral ˈpartner *n.* [C] ECONOMICS a partner who is a full member of a either a LIMITED PARTNERSHIP or a GENERAL PARTNERSHIP, and is responsible for the partnership's debts, without any limit → see also LIMITED PARTNER

ˌgeneral ˈpartnership *n.* [C] ECONOMICS a PARTNERSHIP (=business owned by two or more partners who share the profits and losses) in which all the partners are responsible for the partnership's debts, without any limit → see also LIMITED PARTNERSHIP

ˌgeneral ˈpractice *n.* [U] OLD-FASHIONED the work of a doctor who deals with all the ordinary types of illnesses, rather than one specific type

ˌgeneral pracˈtitioner *n.* [C] a doctor who is trained in general medicine

ˌgeneral-ˈpurpose *adj.* [only before noun] a general-purpose product, vehicle etc. is appropriate for most situations or jobs that such things are normally used for: *a general-purpose fertilizer*

gen·er·al·ship /ˈdʒɛnərəlˌʃɪp/ *n.* [U] the skill of leading an army and developing plans for battle

ˌgeneral ˈstaff *n.* **the general staff** the group of military officers who work for a commanding officer

ˈgeneral ˌstore *n.* [C] a shop that sells a wide variety of goods, especially one in a small town

ˌgeneral ˈstrike *n.* [C] a situation when most of the workers in a country refuse to work in order to protest something

ˌgeneral ˌtheory of relaˈtivity *n.* [singular] PHYSICS the second of Einstein's scientific descriptions of the relationship between time, space, and movement, which includes the effect of GRAVITY on the shape of space and the flow of time → see also SPECIAL THEORY OF RELATIVITY

gen·er·ate /ˈdʒɛnəˌreɪt/ Ac S3 W2 *v.* [T] **1** to produce or make something: *a way of generating new ideas* | *The computer industry generated many new jobs in the area.* | **generate revenue/profits/income etc.** *Tourism generates income for local people.* | **generate excitement/interest/support etc.** *Their success in the Olympics generated a lot of interest in women's team sports.* **2** to produce heat, electricity, or another form of energy: *The engine generates 138 horsepower.* [**Origin:** 1500–1600 Latin, past participle of *generare* **to produce children**, from *genus* **birth, race, type**]

gen·er·a·tion /ˌdʒɛnəˈreɪʃən/ Ac S2 W2 *n.* **1** [C] a group consisting of all the people in a society who are about the same age: *people of my generation* | *We want to preserve the planet for **future generations**.* | **the older/younger generation** *The younger generation don't know what hard work is.* | +**of** *a new generation of writers* **2** [C] all the members of a family of about the same age: +**of** *a photograph showing four generations of the family* **3** [C] the average period of time between the birth of a person and the birth of that person's children: *A generation ago, this was still farmland.* | *The house has been in my family **for generations**.* **4** [C] all the members of a group of things which have been developed from a previous group: +**of** *the next generation of cell phones* **5** [U] the process of producing something or making something happen: *the generation of electricity* → see also -GENERATION

-generation /dʒɛnəreɪʃən/ [in adjectives] **first-generation/second-generation a)** someone who is a first-generation American, Canadian etc. was born in the U.S., Canada etc. but their parents were not. A second-generation American, Canadian etc. has parents who were born in the U.S., Canada, etc. but their grandparents were not. **b)** a first-generation, second-generation etc. computer, cell phone etc. belongs to the first, second etc. type of computers, cell phones etc. that were developed

gen·er·a·tion·al /ˌdʒɛnəˈreɪʃənl/ *adj.* connected with a particular generation or the relationship between different generations: *generational differences*

generˈation gap *n.* [singular] the lack of understanding or the differences between older people and younger people, caused by their different attitudes and experiences: *Is the generation gap widening?*

Generation X /ˌdʒɛnəreɪʃən ˈɛks/ *n.* [U] the group of people who were born during the late 1960s and 1970s in the U.S.

Generation Y /ˌdʒɛnəreɪʃən ˈwaɪ/ *n.* [U] the group of people born in or after 1980 in the U.S.

gen·er·a·tive /ˈdʒɛnərət̬ɪv/ *adj.* FORMAL able to produce something: *Knowledge from research is often generative.*

ˌgenerative ˈgrammar *n.* [C,U] the description of a language by rules that produce all the possible correct sentences of the language

gen·er·a·tor /ˈdʒɛnəˌreɪt̬ɚ/ *n.* [C] a machine that produces electricity → see picture at ELECTRICITY

ge·ner·ic /dʒəˈnɛrɪk/ *adj.* **1** a generic product does not have a special name to show that it is made by a particular company: *generic drugs* **2** relating to a whole group of things rather than to one thing in particular: *Fine Arts is a **generic term** for subjects such as painting, music, and sculpture.* —**generically** /-kli/ *adv.*

gen·er·os·i·ty /ˌdʒɛnəˈrɑsət̬i/ *n.* [C,U] willingness to give money, time etc. in order to help or please someone, or something you do that shows this quality: +**of** *The generosity of Mr. and Mrs. Kaplan made the museum project possible.* | +**to/toward** *his generosity toward the poor*

gen·er·ous /ˈdʒɛnərəs/ *adj.* **1** willing to give more money, time etc. than is expected to help someone or give them pleasure OPP **stingy**: *She's a very generous woman.* | +**to/toward** *Josh is very generous to the kids.* | +**with** *My grandfather has always been very generous with his money.* | **it is generous of sb to do sth** *It's very generous of you to help.* | **a generous offer/donation/gift etc.** *Thank you for your generous donation to our campaign.* **2** [usually before noun] larger or more than the usual or expected amount: *a generous slice of cake* | *a generous pension plan* **3** sympathetic in the way you deal with people, and tending to see the good qualities in them not the bad: *a generous comment* [**Origin:** 1500–1600 French *généreux*, from Latin *generosus* **born into a high rank**] → see also **generous/kind etc. to a fault** at FAULT[1] (6) —**generously** *adv.*

G

Gen·e·sis /ˈdʒɛnəsɪs/ the first book of the Bible

gen·e·sis /ˈdʒɛnəsɪs/ *n.* FORMAL **the genesis** the beginning or origin of something: +**of** *the genesis of the company's problems*

ˈgene ˌtherapy *n.* [U] a way of treating certain diseases by using GENETIC ENGINEERING

ge·net·ic /dʒəˈnɛṭɪk/ *adj.* BIOLOGY relating to GENES or GENETICS: *genetic defects* | *a genetic test for the disease* —**genetically** /-kli/ *adv.*: *genetically transmitted characteristics*

geˌnetic ˈcode *n.* [C] BIOLOGY the arrangement of chemicals on a CHROMOSOME that controls the way in which features are passed on from parents to their young

geˌnetic diˈversity *n.* [U] BIOLOGY the fact that there are many slightly different genetic types within a group of ORGANISMS (=living creatures) that are very similar in most ways, which helps the organism to be able to stay alive in a particular area, because, for example, if a disease kills some of the types it will not kill all of them: *The Irish potato famine was probably caused by the lack of genetic diversity in the potato crop.*

geˌnetic ˈdrift *n.* [U] BIOLOGY changes that happen by chance in the GENE POOL of a group of people, animals, plants etc. that are separated from others of their kind, which lead to certain genes being lost or preserved over a long period of time

geˌnetic enginˈeer *n.* [C] BIOLOGY a scientist who works in the field of genetic modification —**genetically engineered** *adj.*

geˌnetic equiˈlibrium *n.* [U] BIOLOGY a state in which a population of humans, animals, plants etc. does not EVOLVE (=change gradually over a long period), which is very rare

geˌnetic ˈfingerprint *n.* [C] the pattern of GENES that is different for each person or animal

geˌnetic ˈfingerprinting *n.* [U] SCIENCE the process of examining the pattern of someone's GENES, especially in order to find out if they are guilty of a crime

geˌnetic ˈmarker *n.* [C] BIOLOGY a GENE or a group of genes that is known for typically producing particular physical qualities, behavior, diseases etc.

geˌnetic modifiˈcation also **geˌnetic enginˈeering** *n.* [U] the process of changing the genetic structure of an ORGANISM by adding genetic material from another organism

ge·net·ics /dʒəˈnɛṭɪks/ *n.* [plural] BIOLOGY the study of how the qualities of living things are controlled and passed on by GENES —**geneticist** /dʒəˈnɛṭəsɪst/ *n.* [C]

Ge·ne·va /dʒəˈnivə/ a city in Switzerland which is the main base for several important international organizations

Geneva, Lake a lake in southwest Switzerland that is the largest lake in central Europe

Geˌneva Acˈcords, the HISTORY an agreement in 1954 by which Vietnam was divided into two countries

Geˌneva Conˈvention *n.* [C] LAW one of a series of international agreements containing rules for the treatment of prisoners of war, sick and wounded soldiers, and CIVILIANS in wartime, made in 1864, 1929, and 1949

Gen·ghis Khan /ˌgɛŋgɪs ˈkɑn, ˌdʒɛŋ-/ (?1160–1227) the ruler of the Mongol tribe in China, who took control of northern India and sent his armies as far west as the Black Sea

ge·nial /ˈdʒinyəl, -niəl/ *adj.* cheerful, kind, and friendly: *a genial old man* —**geniality** /ˌdʒiniˈæləṭi/ *n.* [U]

ge·nie /ˈdʒini/ *n.* [C] a magical spirit, especially in Arabian stories, that will do what you want when you call it

gen·i·tal /ˈdʒɛnəṭl/ *adj.* [only before noun] BIOLOGY relating to or affecting the outer sex organs: *genital herpes* —**genitally** *adv.*

gen·i·tals /ˈdʒɛnəṭlz/ also **gen·i·ta·li·a** /ˌdʒɛnəˈteɪlyə/ *n.* [plural] BIOLOGY the outer sex organs

gen·i·tive /ˈdʒɛnəṭɪv/ *n.* [C] ENG. LANG. ARTS a form of the noun in some languages, which shows a relationship of possession or origin between one thing and another —**genitive** *adj.*

ge·nius /ˈdʒinyəs/ *n.* **1** [C] someone who has an unusually high level of intelligence, mental skill, or artistic ability: +**at** *Sandra's a genius at crossword puzzles.* | **a musical/comic/mathematical etc. genius** *a literary genius* **2** [U] a very high level of intelligence, mental skill, or artistic ability, which only a few people have: *Her teachers recognized her genius early on.* | **a work/writer/man etc. of genius** *The film is a work of genius.* **3 a genius for (doing) sth** a special ability or talent for doing something: *Kimble has a genius for motivating his employees.* [**Origin:** 1300–1400 Latin **spirit who guards a person or place**, from *gignere*] → see also **a stroke of genius/inspiration etc.** at STROKE[1] (6)

gen·o·cide /ˈdʒɛnəˌsaɪd/ *n.* [U] the deliberate murder of a whole group or race of people —**genocidal** /ˌdʒɛnəˈsaɪdl◂/ *adj.*

ge·nome /ˈdʒinoʊm/ *n.* [C] BIOLOGY the total of all the GENES that are found in one type of living thing: *the human genome*

ge·no·type /ˈdʒinəˌtaɪp/ *n.* [C] BIOLOGY the GENETIC nature of a particular living thing or type of living thing, as opposed to its physical appearance → see also PHENOTYPE

gen·re /ˈʒɑnrə/ *n.* [C] ENG. LANG. ARTS a particular type of art, writing, music etc., which has certain features that all examples of this type share: *Science fiction is a relatively new genre.* | +**of** *R & B is my favorite genre of music.*

gent /dʒɛnt/ *n.* [C] OLD-FASHIONED, INFORMAL a GENTLEMAN

gen·teel /dʒɛnˈtil/ *adj.* **1** polite, gentle, or graceful: *The town has a genteel southern charm.* **2** OLD-FASHIONED from or relating to a good social class: *a genteel family*

gen·tian /ˈdʒɛnʃən/ *n.* [C] a small plant with blue or purple flowers that grows in mountain areas

gen·tile /ˈdʒɛntaɪl/ *n.* [C] a word meaning someone who is not Jewish, used by Jewish people —**gentile** *adj.*

gen·til·i·ty /dʒɛnˈtɪləṭi/ *n.* [U] FORMAL the quality of being polite, gentle, or graceful: *Beaufort, an old Southern town, is a picture of gentility.*

gen·tle /ˈdʒɛntl/ *adj.* **1** kind and careful in the way you behave, so that you do not hurt or damage anyone or anything: *a gentle person* | *a gentle smile* | +**with** *Be gentle with the baby.* **2** not too strong or forceful, or not using too much effort: *gentle exercise* | *the gentle pressure of her hand* | *the gentle warmth of the fire* **3** a gentle wind or rain is soft and light SYN **light**: *a gentle breeze* **4** a gentle hill or slope is not very steep or sharp OPP **steep** [**Origin:** 1200–1300 French *gentil*, from Latin *gentilis* **of a family, of the same family**] → see also GENTLY —**gentleness** *n.* [U]

gen·tle·folk /ˈdʒɛntlˌfoʊk/ *n.* [plural] OLD USE people belonging to the higher social classes

gen·tle·man /ˈdʒɛntlmən/ S3 *n. plural* **gentlemen** /-mən/ [C] **1** a polite word meaning a "man," used especially when talking to or about a man you do not know: *Please show this gentleman to his seat.* | ***Ladies and gentlemen*** (=used to talk to a large group of people), *welcome to the show!* ►see THESAURUS box at man[1] **2** a man who is polite and behaves well toward other people: *Roland was a **perfect gentleman** last night.* **3** OLD-FASHIONED a man from a high social class, especially one whose family owns a lot of property **4 sb's gentleman friend** OLD-FASHIONED a woman's male friend SYN **boyfriend** —**gentlemanly** *adj.*

ˌgentleman ˈfarmer *n.* [C] a man with a lot of money who owns and runs a farm for pleasure rather than as his job

ˌgentleman's aˈgreement *n.* [C] an agreement that is not written down, made between people who trust each other

gen·tle·wom·an /ˈdʒɛntl,wʊmən/ *n. plural* **gentlewomen** /-ˌwɪmɪn/ [C] OLD USE a woman who belongs to a high social class

gen·tly /ˈdʒɛntˀli/ *adv.* in a gentle way: *Don gently kissed her on the cheek.*

gen·tri·fi·ca·tion /ˌdʒɛntrəfəˈkeɪʃən/ *n.* [U] the gradual process of changing an area from an area in bad condition where poor people live, to one in better condition where people with more money want to live —**gentrify** /ˈdʒɛntrəˌfaɪ/ *v.* [T usually passive]

gen·try /ˈdʒɛntri/ *n.* [plural] people who belong to a high social class, own land, and are wealthy enough to employ other people: *the **landed gentry*** (=those who own land)

gen·u·flect /ˈdʒɛnyəˌflɛkt/ *v.* [I] to bend one knee when in a church or a holy place, as a sign of respect —**genuflection** /ˌdʒɛnyəˈflɛkʃən/ *n.* [C,U]

gen·u·ine /ˈdʒɛnyuɪn/ *adj.* **1** a genuine feeling, desire etc. is one that you really have, not one that you pretend to have SYN **real** SYN **sincere**: *genuine fear* | *Mrs. Liu showed a **genuine concern for** the children.* **2** [no comparative] something genuine really is what it seems to be SYN **real**: *a genuine diamond* **3** someone who is genuine is honest, has good intentions, and can be trusted SYN **sincere** **4 the genuine article** INFORMAL a person, or sometimes a thing, that is a true example of their type: *If you want to meet a cowgirl, Katy is the genuine article.* —**genuinely** *adv.*: *He genuinely believes in what he sells.* —**genuineness** *n.* [U]

ge·nus /ˈdʒinəs/ *n. plural* **genera** /ˈdʒɛnərə/ [C] BIOLOGY one of the groups into which scientists divide animals and plants. A genus is larger than a SPECIES, but smaller than a FAMILY. [**Origin:** 1500–1600 Latin **birth, race, type**]

Gen X /ˌdʒɛn ˈɛks/ *n.* [U] INFORMAL → see GENERATION X

geo- /dʒioʊ, dʒiə/ *prefix* TECHNICAL relating to the Earth or its surface: *geophysics* | *geopolitical*

ge·o·cen·tric /ˌdʒioʊˈsɛntrɪk◂/ *adj.* having the Earth as the central point, or measured from the center of the Earth: *a geocentric model of the universe*

geode /ˈdʒioʊd/ *n.* [C] a round stone that is hollow, and that often has CRYSTALS inside

ge·o·de·sic /ˌdʒiəˈdizɪk/ *adj.* TECHNICAL a geodesic shape or structure consists of small flat pieces, usually triangles or pentagons, that together form curves

ge·o·gra·phi·cal /ˌdʒiəˈgræfɪkəl/ also **ge·o·graph·ic** /-ˈgræfɪk/ *adj.* relating to geography: *The rebels have control over a large geographical area.* —**geographically** /-kli/ *adv.*

geoˌgraphic isoˈlation *n.* [U] BIOLOGY a situation in which a natural physical object, such as a river or a mountain, keeps two populations of people, animals etc. apart, so that they develop different GENES and become a separate SPECIES

ge·og·ra·phy /dʒiˈɑgrəfi/ *n.* [U] **1** the study of the countries, oceans, rivers, mountains, cities etc., as well as populations, industry, agriculture, and the economies of different areas of the world: *a geography lesson* | *I studied geography in college.* → see also PHYSICAL GEOGRAPHY, POLITICAL GEOGRAPHY **2** the way the parts of a place are arranged, such as where the streets, mountains, rivers etc. are: *What effects has geography had on the population?* | ***the geography of** the planet* **3** the way that the buildings, streets etc. within an area are arranged: *Explain the town's geography to me.* [**Origin:** 1400–1500 Latin *geographia*, from Greek, **describing the Earth**] —**geographer** *n.* [C]

ge·ol·o·gy /dʒiˈɑlədʒi/ *n.* [U] EARTH SCIENCE the study of materials such as rocks, soil, and minerals, and the way they have changed since the Earth was formed —**geologist** *n.* [C] —**geological** /ˌdʒiəˈlɑdʒɪkəl/ also **geologic** *adj.*: *geological periods* —**geologically** /-kli/ *adv.*

ge·o·met·ric /ˌdʒiəˈmɛtrɪk◂/ also **ge·o·met·ri·cal** /-ˈmɛtrɪkəl/ *adj.* **1** having or using lines or shapes from GEOMETRY, such as circles or squares, especially when these are used in regular patterns: *a geometric design* **2** relating to GEOMETRY —**geometrically** /-kli/ *adv.*

ˌgeometric ˈfigure *n.* [C] MATH any point or set of points on a PLANE (=flat surface) or in space, such as a line, an angle, a circle, a POLYGON (=flat shape with many straight sides), a SOLID (=shape with length, width, and height) etc.

ˌgeometric ˈmean *n.* [singular] MATH an average value of a set of numbers that you calculate by multiplying together all the numbers in the set that are greater than 0 and then finding the ROOT of that PRODUCT whose INDEX is equal to the number of numbers in the set. For example, for a set of three numbers, you find the CUBE ROOT (=$\sqrt[3]{}$) of the product of the three numbers.

ˌgeometric ˈpattern *n.* [C] **1** MATH a COMMON RATIO **2** a pattern of geometric shapes

geoˌmetric probaˈbility *n.* [U] MATH the study of the PROBABILITY involved in GEOMETRY problems, for example, how likely particular lengths, areas etc. are to appear for particular shapes in particular conditions

geoˌmetric proˈgression *n.* [U] MATH a set of numbers in order, in which each is multiplied by a specific number to produce the next number in the series, for example as in 1, 2, 4, 8, 16,..., in which each number is multiplied by two → see also ARITHMETIC PROGRESSION

ˌgeometric ˈsequence *n.* [C] MATH a list of related numbers formed by multiplying or dividing each previous number in the list by one particular number. For example, in the geometric sequence 2, 4, 8, 16, each number is multiplied by 2 to get the next number in the sequence. In the sequence 36, 12, 4, each number is divided by 3 to get the next number in the sequence.

ˌgeometric ˈseries *n.* [C] MATH the sum of the numbers in a geometric sequence

ge·om·e·try /dʒiˈɑmətri/ *n.* [U] MATH the study in MATHEMATICS of the form and relationships of angles, lines, curves, shapes, and solid objects

ge·o·phys·ics /ˌdʒioʊˈfɪzɪks/ *n.* [U] EARTH SCIENCE the study of the movements of parts of the Earth, and the forces involved with this, including the weather, oceans etc. —**geophysical** *adj.* —**geophysicist** *n.* [C]

ge·o·pol·i·tics /ˌdʒioʊˈpɑlətɪks/ *n.* [U] the study of the effects of a country's position, population etc. on its political character and development —**geopolitical** /ˌdʒioʊpəˈlɪṭɪkəl/ *adj.*

George /dʒɔrdʒ/ *n.* **by George!** OLD-FASHIONED, SPOKEN used when you are pleasantly surprised

George III, King /ˌdʒɔrdʒ ðə ˈθɚd/ (1738–1820) a king of Great Britain and Ireland, who is remembered as the British king at the time of the Revolutionary War

George·town /ˈdʒɔrdʒtaʊn/ **1** a fashionable area of the city of Washington, D.C. **2** the capital and largest city of Guyana **3** the capital and largest city of the Cayman Islands

geor·gette /dʒɔrˈdʒɛt/ *n.* [U] a light strong material, used for making clothes

Geor·gia /ˈdʒɔrdʒə/ **1** WRITTEN ABBREVIATION **GA** a state in the southeastern U.S. **2** a country in western Asia, east of the Black Sea —**Georgian** *n., adj.*

ge·o·sta·tion·ar·y /ˌdʒioʊˈsteɪʃəˌnɛri/ also **ge·o·syn·chro·nous** /ˌdʒioʊˈsɪŋkrənəs/ *adj.* a geostationary SPACECRAFT or SATELLITE goes around the Earth at the same speed as the Earth moves, so that it is always above the same place on the Earth

ge·o·ther·mal /ˌdʒioʊˈθɚməl/ *adj.* relating to or coming from the heat inside the earth: *a geothermal energy plant*

ge·ra·ni·um /dʒəˈreɪniəm/ *n.* [C] a common house plant with colorful flowers and large round leaves [**Origin:** 1500–1600 Latin, Greek *geranion*, from *geranos* **crane**; because the plant's seed-case looks like a crane's long beak]

ger·bil /ˈdʒɚbəl/ *n.* [C] a small animal with soft fur and a long tail that is kept as a pet

ger·i·at·ric /ˌdʒɛriˈætrɪk/ *adj.* **1** [only before noun] MEDICINE relating to the medical care and treatment of old people: *geriatric medicine* **2** HUMOROUS used about a machine that is too old to work well

ger·i·at·rics /ˌdʒeriˈætrɪks/ *n.* [U] the medical treatment and care of old people → see also GERONTOLOGY —**geriatrician** /ˌdʒeriəˈtrɪʃən/ *n.* [C]

germ /dʒɚm/ *n.* [C] **1** BIOLOGY a very small living thing that can make you sick SYN **bacteria**: *You spread germs every time you cough.* **2 the germ of an idea/hope etc.** the beginning of an idea that may develop into something else: *The germ of the scandal first appeared last month.* [**Origin:** 1400–1500 French *germe*, from Latin *germen* **seed, bud, germ**] → see also GERM WARFARE, WHEATGERM

Ger·man¹ /ˈdʒɚmən/ *adj.* **1** relating to or coming from Germany **2** relating to the German language

German² *n.* **1** [U] the language used in Germany, Austria, parts of Switzerland etc. **2** [C] someone from Germany

ger·mane /dʒɚˈmeɪn/ *adj.* FORMAL an idea, remark etc. that is germane to something is related to it in an important and appropriate way SYN **relevant**: +**to** *information germane to the case*

Ger·man·ic /dʒɚˈmænɪk/ *adj.* **1** ENG. LANG. ARTS relating to the language family that includes German, Dutch, Swedish, and English **2** typical of Germany or the Germans

ˌGerman ˈmeasles *n.* [U] MEDICINE an infectious disease that causes red spots on your body SYN **rubella**

ˌGerman ˈshepherd *n.* [C] a large dog that looks like a WOLF, often used by the police, for guarding property etc.

Ger·ma·ny /ˈdʒɚməni/ a country in central Europe

ger·mi·cide /ˈdʒɚməˌsaɪd/ *n.* [C,U] a substance that kills BACTERIA

ger·mi·nate /ˈdʒɚməˌneɪt/ *v.* **1** [I,T] BIOLOGY if a seed, SPORE, or grain of POLLEN germinates or is germinated, it begins to grow **2** [I] if an idea, feeling etc. germinates, it begins to develop: *The idea of the business began to germinate in his mind.*

ger·mi·na·tion /ˌdʒɚməˈneɪʃən/ *n.* [U] BIOLOGY the beginning of the growth of a seed, SPORE, or grain of POLLEN

ˌgerm ˈwarfare *n.* [U] the use of harmful BACTERIA in war to cause illness and death among the enemy

Ge·ron·i·mo /dʒəˈrɑnəˌmoʊ/ (1829–1909) an Apache chief famous for fighting to keep his people on their own land in New Mexico and Arizona, until the U.S. army forced them to move to Oklahoma

ge·ron·i·mo /dʒəˈrɑnəˌmoʊ/ *interjection* a shout used by U.S. PARATROOPERS when they jump out of airplanes and by children when jumping from a high place

ger·on·toc·ra·cy /ˌdʒerənˈtɑkrəsi/ *n.* [C,U] government by old people, or a government that consists of old people

ger·on·tol·o·gy /ˌdʒerənˈtɑlədʒi/ *n.* [U] MEDICINE the scientific study of old age and the changes it causes in the body → see also GERIATRICS —**gerontologist** *n.* [C] —**gerontological** /ˌdʒerəntəˈlɑdʒɪkəl/ *adj.*

ger·ry·man·der·ing /ˈdʒeriˌmændərɪŋ/ *n.* [U] POLITICS the action of changing the borders of an area before an election so that one person, group, or party has an unfair advantage [**Origin:** 1800–1900 Elbridge *Gerry* (1744–1818), US politician + *salamander*; because a voting area he made to help his own party win an election was said to be shaped like a salamander] —**gerrymander** *v.* [I,T]

Gersh·win /ˈgɚʃwɪn/, **George** (1898–1937) a U.S. musician who wrote both CLASSICAL music and popular songs and tunes. His brother Ira Gershwin (1896–1983) wrote the words for many of his popular songs.

ger·und /ˈdʒerənd/ *n.* [C] ENG. LANG. ARTS in grammar, a noun in the form of the PRESENT PARTICIPLE of a verb, such as "reading" in the sentence "He enjoys reading." [**Origin:** 1500–1600 Late Latin *gerundium*, from Latin *gerere* **to bear, carry on**]

ge·stalt /gəˈʃtɑlt, -ˈʃtɑlt/ *n.* [C] TECHNICAL a whole thing that cannot easily be divided into its separate parts, and that has qualities that are not present in any of its parts by themselves: *gestalt psychology*

Ge·sta·po /gəˈstɑpoʊ/ *n.* [U] the secret police force used by the state in Germany during the NAZI period

ges·ta·tion /dʒeˈsteɪʃən/ *n.* [U] **1** BIOLOGY the process of a child or young animal developing inside its mother's body, or the period of time when this happens: *Humans have a nine-month **gestation period**.* **2** the process of developing a new idea, piece of work etc., or the period of time when this happens: *The gestation of the biotechnology industry was short.*

ges·tic·u·late /dʒeˈstɪkyəˌleɪt/ *v.* [I] to make movements with your arms and hands, usually while speaking, because you are excited, angry, or cannot think of the right words to use: *Jane shouted and gesticulated wildly.* —**gesticulation** /dʒeˌstɪkyəˈleɪʃən/ *n.* [C,U]

ges·ture¹ /ˈdʒestʃɚ, ˈdʒeʃtʃɚ/ *n.* **1** [C,U] a movement of your arms, hands, or head that shows what you mean or how you feel: *He **made a** rude **gesture at** us as he drove by.* **2** [C] something that you do or say to show how you feel about someone or something: *The flowers were really a nice gesture.* | +**of** *A flag was burned as a gesture of protest.* —**gestural** *adj.*

gesture² *v.* [I always + adv./prep.] to move your arms, hands, or head to tell someone something: **gesture to/toward/at sth** *Brad gestured toward the door. "Get out."* | **gesture for sb to do sth** *Robin gestured for me to move out of the way.*

ge·sund·heit /gəˈzʊnthaɪt/ *interjection* used to wish someone good health when they have just SNEEZED

get

getting away from it all

get /get/ S1 W1 *v. past tense* **got** /gɑt/, *past participle* **gotten** /ˈgɑtˈn/, **getting**

1 OBTAIN [T not in passive] to obtain something by finding it, asking for it, being given it etc. SYN **obtain**: *I need to get a new job.* | **get sb sth** *His dad got him work in the factory.* | **get sth for sb/sth** *The librarian should be able to get the article for you.* | **get sth from/out of/off of sth** *I got the information from the Internet.* | *I need to get some money out of the bank.* | **get help/advice/permission** *You should get some professional advice.* | *If you buy one, you **get** one **free**.* ▶see THESAURUS box at **earn**

THESAURUS

obtain/acquire formal words for "get": *These statistics were obtained from the police department.* | *The program helps adults acquire skills that lead to jobs.*
gain to get something useful or necessary: *I've gained a lot of useful experience.*
earn to get something because you deserve it: *He had earned a reputation as a peacemaker.*

2 BUY [T not in passive] to buy something SYN **buy**: | **get sb sth** *Her boyfriend got her a big bunch of flowers.* | **get sth for sb** *My parents got this T-shirt for me in Switzerland.* | **get sth from sb/sth** *I get all our groceries from this store.* | **get sth for sth** *You can get a DVD*

G

for about $12. | **get sth cheap** *I got my coat cheap in a sale.* ▸see THESAURUS box at **buy**[1]
3 RECEIVE [T not in passive] to receive something that someone gives or sends you SYN **receive**: *I got your message.* | *We haven't gotten any mail for three days.* | **get sth from sb** *How much money did you get from Grandma?*
4 BECOME [linking verb] to change from one state, feeling etc. to another SYN **become**: *Vicky got really mad at him.* | *If I wear wool, my skin gets all red.* | *Don't worry, I won't get lost.* | *The weather had suddenly gotten cold.* | *Mom told you you'd get hurt if you did that!* ▸see THESAURUS box at **become**
5 MOVE [I always + adv./prep.] to move to a different place or position, often when this is difficult: **+off/onto/into etc.** *How did the guy get into their house?* | *The gunman told everybody to get down on the floor.* | *It felt good to get out of the city.* | *Colleen* ***got to her feet*** (=stood up) *slowly and went to the window.*
6 MAKE STH MOVE/FIT [T always + adv./prep. not in passive] to make something move or fit somewhere, especially when this is difficult: *Can you get the ladder into the car?* | *I don't think we'll be able to get that through the door.* | *I can't get the disk out of the computer.*
7 REACH A PLACE [I always + adv./prep.] to reach a particular place, position, or stage: *What time will we get there?* | *She got downstairs and found him lying on the floor.* | **+to** *You might be disappointed when you get to the end of the book.*
8 BRING [T not in passive] to bring someone or something back from somewhere: *Run upstairs and get my glasses.* | **get sb/sth from sth** *I'm going to go get the kids from the babysitter's.* | **get sb sth/get sth for sb** *Get me a towel, please.* | *Could you* ***go and get*** *a doctor, please?* ▸see THESAURUS box at **bring**
9 MAKE SB/STH DO STH [not in passive] to persuade someone or make something do what you want them to do or what they are supposed to do: **get sb/sth to do sth** *Bonnie couldn't get the light to work.* | *I tried to get Teresa to come out tonight, but she can't.* | **get sb/sth doing sth** *We'll get the TV working again.*
10 EARN [T not in passive] to earn a particular amount of money, especially as an hourly rate or for a particular job SYN **earn**: *Jennifer gets $19 an hour at her new job.* | *I got $5 for washing my dad's car.*
11 RECEIVE MONEY FOR STH SOLD [T not in passive] to receive a particular amount of money for something you sell: *You should get a good price.* | **get sth for sth** *How much can you get for a house this size?*
12 HAVE THE OPPORTUNITY TO DO STH [T] to have the opportunity to do something that you want to do: **get to do sth** *Tom gets to go to Disneyland this summer.* | *I didn't get to sit down all day.* | **get the chance/opportunity (to do sth)** *I never got the chance to say "thank you."* | *I don't really* ***get the time to*** *read.*
13 get sb upset/excited/mad etc. to make someone feel a particular way, or to make something happen to them: *Mom got really mad.* | *Don't let the illness* ***get you down*** (=make you unhappy).
14 CAUSE SB/STH TO BE IN A STATE OR CONDITION [T not in passive] to make someone or something be in a particular state or condition: *Don't get your clothes dirty!* | *She has to get two papers written by tomorrow afternoon.* | *She got her finger caught in the door.*
15 ARRANGE TO HAVE SB DO STH get sth cut/fixed/done etc. to arrange for someone to fix, cut, do etc. something for you: *I'm getting my hair cut on Tuesday.* | *We have to get the car fixed before we go.*
16 ILLNESS [T not in passive] to catch an illness, especially one that is not very serious: *I got the flu when we were on vacation.* | **get a headache/backache/stomachache etc.** *I got a headache halfway through class.*
17 FEELING/IDEA to start to feel, think etc. something: *She gets a lot of* ***pleasure*** *from playing the piano.* | *Where'd you* ***get that idea*** (=what made you think that)*?* | **get the feeling/impression (that)** *I get the feeling you don't like her very much.* | **get a shock/surprise** *I got a big surprise when I opened the bill.*
18 HAPPEN/EXIST sb/sth gets sth INFORMAL used in order to say that something happens or exists where you are: *We get a lot of rain around here in the summer.* | *Denver gets a lot of visitors for conferences.*
19 UNDERSTAND [T not in passive or progressive] INFORMAL to understand something: *Tracy didn't get the joke.* | **get what/how/who etc.** *He still doesn't get what we were trying to tell him.* | *I kept trying to explain, but he didn't* ***get the point*** (=understand the most important part of something). | **get the message/hint** *Okay, I get the message – you want me to leave now.* | *Oh, now I* ***get it*** *– you have to divide 489 by 3.*
20 BEGIN DOING STH [T] to begin doing something, or make someone or something begin doing something: *We* ***got talking*** *about our school days.* | **get going/moving** *We'd better get going, or we'll be late.* | *The lawyers immediately* ***got to work on*** *the contracts.* | **get sb/sth doing sth** *He got the engine running.* | *You know, our conversation last night got me thinking.*
21 get to know/like etc. sb/sth to gradually begin to know, like etc. someone or something: *As you get to know the city, I'm sure you'll like it better.*
22 RADIO/TELEVISION [T not in passive or progressive] to be able to receive a particular radio signal or television station SYN **receive**: *We don't get Channel 24.*
23 get a bus/train etc. to leave on a bus or train, or to travel on it: *We need to get the next bus if we're going to be there by six.*
24 CALL [T not in passive] to call someone on the telephone and be able to talk to them: *Hi, I'm trying to get the customer services department.* | **get sb sb** *Sarah, would you get me Ms. Jones, please?*
25 MEAL [T not in passive] to prepare a meal: *She gets breakfast for all four children before sending them to school.*

SPOKEN PHRASES

26 have got a) used to say that you have something: *Mike's got a wife and three kids.* **b)** used to say that you need to do something or you must do something: *I've got to go to the bathroom.*
27 get the phone/door to answer the telephone, or open the door to see who is there: *Val, can you get the phone, please – I'm making dinner.*
28 get it to be punished for something bad you have done: *You're really going to get it when Dad gets home.*
29 get sth on/off to put a piece of clothing on or take it off SYN **put on**: *Get your shoes on – it's time to go.*
30 FOOL/SURPRISE [T not in passive or progressive] to trick or surprise someone: *I really* ***got you good*** *that time, didn't I?*
31 ATTACK/PUNISH SB [T not in passive or progressive] to do something bad to someone, such as attack, punish, or cause trouble for them, especially because they have done something bad to you: *That stupid dog tried to get me.* | *She thinks they are all* ***out to get her*** (=trying to cause trouble for her). | **get sb for sth** *I'll get you for that, you little brat!*
32 you('ve) got me used to say you do not know the answer to something: *"Why did he attack him?" "You got me."*
33 HEAR to hear something, or to hear something clearly: *I'm sorry, I didn't get your name.*
34 it (really) gets me used to say that something really annoys you: *It really gets me the way he acts like he knows everything.*
35 get this said when telling someone something that is surprising: *And the whole thing only cost – get this – $12.95.*
36 PAY FOR STH [T not in passive] to pay for something: *I'll get dinner if you get the movie.* | *That's okay, I'll get it.*
37 get you/him/her used to say that you think someone is trying to seem more important, intelligent etc. than they really are: *Get you, in that fancy suit.*

[**Origin:** 1200–1300 Old Norse *geta*]

get sth ↔ **across** *phr. v.* if an idea or piece of information gets across, or you get it across, it is explained to someone and they understand it: **get (sth) across to sb** *It was difficult to get my idea across to the committee.* | *The message just isn't getting across to young people.*

get ahead *phr. v.* to be successful, especially in your job: **+in** *It's not easy to get ahead in the movie business.*

get along *phr. v.* **1** to have a friendly relationship with someone or a group of people: *Dave and Vince get along really well.* | **+with** *Rachel doesn't get along with Cyrus at all.* **2** to deal with a situation, for example a new job, school etc., especially when you do it successfully and make progress: *Is Sam getting along ok at college?* | **+without** *We get along without much help from the main office.* **3** SPOKEN to leave a place: *Well, I guess I'd better be getting along before it gets too late.*

get around *phr. v.* **1 get around sth** to find a way of dealing with a problem or a person, often by avoiding them: *We'll find some way of getting around the problem.* **2 get around sth** if you get around a law or rule, you find a legal way of doing something that the law or rule was intended to prevent: *They've hired an accountant to help them get around the new tax laws.* **3** to move or travel to different places: *His new wheelchair lets him get around more easily.* **4** to travel around a city or area: **get around sth** *It's easy to get around New York.* **5** if news or information gets around, a lot of people hear about it: *If this news gets around, we'll have reporters calling us all day.* | *We're expecting more business as* ***word gets around*** (=people hear about us). **6 get around sth** to avoid admitting that something is true: *You can't get around the fact there are very few stores left downtown.*

get around to (doing) sth *phr. v.* to do something that you have been intending to do for some time: *I meant to go to the bookstore, but I never got around to it.*

get at sth *phr. v.* **1** to try to explain something, especially something difficult: *Did you understand what he was getting at?* **2 get at the meaning/facts etc.** to discover the meaning of something, the facts about someone or something etc.: *The judge asked a few questions to try to get at the truth.* **3 get at sb/sth** to be able to reach something: *I could see the ring stuck under there, but I couldn't get at it.*

get away *phr. v.* **1** to leave a place, especially when this is difficult: *Barry had to work late and couldn't get away till 9:00.* **2** to escape from someone who is chasing you or trying to catch you: *The two men got away in a blue pickup truck.* | **+from** *He managed to get away from the attacker.* **3** INFORMAL to go on vacation: *Are you going to be able to get away this summer?*

get away from sth *phr. v.* **1** to begin to talk about other things rather than the subject you are supposed to be discussing: *I think we're getting away from the main issue.* **2 get away from it all** to leave behind your normal life or problems, especially on vacation: *Get away from it all in sunny Barbados.*

get away with (doing) sth *phr. v.* **1** to not be noticed, caught, or punished when you have done something wrong: *Students will cheat if they think they can get away with it.* | *His parents let him* ***get away with murder*** (=do very bad things and not get caught or punished). **2** to do something without experiencing any problems or difficulties, even though it is not the best thing to do: *Do you think we can get away with just one coat of paint?* **3** SPOKEN to be able to do something that other people cannot, because you have enough confidence or because you have the right kind of PERSONALITY, social position etc.: *Only Susan could get away with wearing a bikini like that.*

get sb **back** *phr. v.* **1** INFORMAL also **get back at sb** to do something to hurt or embarrass someone who has hurt or embarrassed you: **get sb back for sth** *Jerry's just trying to get back at her for leaving him.* **2** to persuade a lover, wife etc. who has left you to start having a relationship with you again: *Do you think she's trying to get him back?*

get back to *phr. v.* **1 get back to sth** to start doing something again after a short period when you did not do it: *I have to get back to work.* **2 get back to sb** to talk or write to someone at a later time because you are busy, or do not know how to answer their question: *I'll try to get back to you later today.* **3 get back to sth** change to a previous state or condition again: *I couldn't get back to sleep after that.* | *I just want things to* ***get back to normal*** (=I want the situation to return to the way it was).

get back together *phr. v.* if two people who had a romantic relationship, marriage etc. get back together, they start having a relationship again

get behind *phr. v.* **1** if you get behind with a job, with payments etc, you do not do or pay what you should have by a particular time: **get behind with/on sth** *We got behind with the rent, and they kicked us out.* **2 get behind sb** to support someone: *The fans were great. They really got behind the team.*

get by *phr. v.* **1** to have enough money to buy the things you need, but no more: *He only earns enough to get by.* | **get by on sth** *Somehow they manage to get by on $800 a month.* **2** to manage to do something, although you do not have a lot of knowledge, talent, or other things you need: *"Do you speak Spanish?" "Just enough to get by."* | **get by on sth** *He gets by on five hours of sleep a night.*

get down *phr. v.* **1 get sth ↔ down** to write something down on paper, especially quickly: *Let me get your number down before I forget it.* **2 get sth ↔ down** to succeed in reducing the amount or number of sth: *an attempt to get costs down* | **+to** *They've gotten the rate of inflation down to 4%.* **3 get sb down** to make someone feel unhappy SYN depress: *His work is really getting him down.* | *Don't* ***let her get you down.*** *She's just being mean.* **4 get sth down** to succeed in swallowing food or drink **5** SLANG to dance in a skillful stylish way

get down to sth *phr. v.* to finally start doing something that will take a lot of time or effort: *By the time we finally got down to work, it was already 10:00.*

get in *phr. v.* **1 get (sb) in** to be allowed or able to enter a place, or to make it possible for someone to do this: *The door was locked, and he couldn't get in.* | *You have to be 21 to get in.* | **get (sb) in to do sth** *I'll see if I can get you in to see the band.* **2** if a plane, train, bus etc. gets in or a person gets in on a plane, train etc., they arrive at a particular place: *What time does your plane get in?* | *Steve just got in a few minutes ago.* | **get in to sth** *We get in to Dallas around noon.* **3 get sth in** to send or give something to a particular person, company etc.: *Make sure you get your homework in by Thursday.* **4** to be elected to a position of political power: *It's unlikely Coogan will get in again.* **5 get sth ↔ in** to gather together something such as crops and bring them to a sheltered place: *They're trying to get the rest of the corn in before it rains.* **6 get sth ↔ in** to manage to do something even though you do not have much time: *I want to get a couple of hours' work in before we go out.* **7 get sth ↔ in** if a store gets a product in, the store gets a supply of the product, so that it can be sold to people: *We should be getting some more in tomorrow.*

get (sb) **in on** sth *phr. v.* INFORMAL to become involved in something that other people are doing or planning: *I wanted to make sure we get your department in on the planning.* | *Democrats want tax cuts – now Republicans want to* ***get in on the act*** (=get involved in doing something).

get into **1 get into sth** to be allowed to go to a school, college, or university: *Lori got into the graduate program at Cornell.* **2 what's gotten into sb?** also **something's gotten into sb** SPOKEN used to express surprise that someone is behaving very differently from the way they usually behave: *You're so grouchy! What's gotten into you?* **3 get into sth** to begin to have a discussion about something: *Let's not get into it right now. I'm tired.* | **get into a discussion/debate (about/on sth)** *We got into a debate about the war.* **4 get (sb) into trouble/difficulties etc.** to do something that causes trouble for yourself or for someone else: *I was always getting into trouble at school.* **5 get into sth** to start doing something regularly: **get into the habit/routine etc. of** *I tried to get into the habit of walking to the office in the mornings.* **6 get (sb) into sth** to become interested in an activity, or make someone do this: *Many young black Americans are getting into older black music.* **7 get into sth** to put clothes on: *I can't get into these pants anymore.* **8 get into pairs/groups etc.** if people get into pairs, groups etc. they form small groups

get off *phr. v.* **1 get off sth** to leave a bus, train, plane, boat etc. OPP **get on**: *I got off at the next stop* (=bus stop). | *We all got off the plane.* **2 get off sth** to finish working at your work place: *What time do you get off work?* | *Shelly gets off at 5:30.* **3 get (sb) off** to get little or no punishment for a crime, or to help someone escape punishment: *I can't believe his lawyers managed to get him off.* | **get off with sth** *He got off with just a small fine.* **4 get (sb) off sth** to stop depending on something that you used to have regularly: *He got himself off drugs, and he's doing well.* **5 get off sth** to stop talking about what you had been talking about: *Can we **get off the subject** of death, please?* **6 where does sb get off (doing sth)?** SPOKEN said when you think someone has done something to you that they do not have a right to do: *Where does he get off telling me how to live my life?* **7 get off on the wrong foot** to start a job, relationship etc. badly by doing something that annoys people: *We just got off on the wrong foot the other day.* **8 get off to a good/bad start** to start well or badly: *The day had gotten off to a very bad start*

G

get on *phr. v.* **1 get on sth** to go onto a bus, plane, train etc. OPP **get off**: *She got on the plane to San Francisco.* | *I got on at the first stop.* **2 be getting on (in years)** INFORMAL to be old: *Dad's getting on in years, but he's still healthy.* **3 get on the subject (of sth)** to start talking about something: *How did we get on the subject of eating habits?* **4 get on the phone to sb** to call someone on the phone, especially to discuss something: *He got on the phone to his lawyer immediately.*

get on with sth *phr. v.* **1** to continue doing something after you have stopped doing it for a while: *Let's get on with the meeting, so we can go home on time.* **2 get on with it!** used to tell someone to hurry: *Get on with it will you? I don't have all day!*

get onto sb/sth *phr. v.* **1** to start talking about a particular subject after you have been talking about something else: *Then we **got onto the subject** of women in the military.* **2 get onto sth** to get elected onto a committee, a political organization etc.: *When did she get onto the committee?* **3** SPOKEN to criticize someone about something they have done: **get onto sb for sth** *Mrs. Prichett got onto me for turning my homework in late.*

get out *phr. v.* **1** to leave a place, room, or building: *Get out! And don't come back.* | *It feels good to get out in the fresh air.* | **+of** *We'd better get out of here fast!* **2 get sth ↔ out** to take something from the place where it is kept SYN **take out**: *Get out your books.* | **get sth out of sth** *She took her violin out of the case.* **3 get sb out** to be allowed to leave a place, or to make it possible for someone to do this: *He got out after serving a 12-year sentence for manslaughter.* | **get (sb) out of sth** *I got Sam out of school early on Thursday.* **4 get sb out** to escape from a place, or help someone do this: *The dog got out again.* **5 get sb out** to leave and escape from an unpleasant situation, that is dangerous, boring, or makes you unhappy, or to help someone do this: **get (sb) out of sth** *You've got to help me get out of this mess.* **6** if information gets out, a lot of people learn about it, even though it is meant to be secret: *If this gets out, we might lose our jobs.* | **get out that** ***Word got out*** *that the band was staying at the Hilton, and a huge crowd of fans showed up.* **7 get sth ↔ out** to succeed in saying something, especially when this is very difficult: *I wanted to apologize, but couldn't get the words out.* **8** to go to different places in order to meet people and enjoy yourself: *You should get out more.* **9 get sth ↔ out** to produce or PUBLISH something: *We plan to get the book out next month.*

get out of *phr. v.* **1 get (sb) out of sth** to avoid doing something you have promised to do or are supposed to do, or help someone do this: *Dana couldn't get out of the meeting, so she canceled dinner.* | **get (sb) out of doing sth** *Joe tried to get out of cleaning the bathroom.* | *I'll see if I can get you out of having to testify.* **2 get sth out of sth** to feel a particular way, learn something etc. because of something you do: *Are you getting anything out of your classes?* | **get sth out of doing sth** *She gets a lot of pleasure out of painting.* **3 get out of sth** to stop doing or being involved in something: *Dave wants to get out of teaching.* **4 get sth out of sb** to force or persuade someone to tell you something or give you something: *I'll get the truth out of him.* | *His ex-wife is always trying to get money out of him.* **5 get out of sth** to take off a set of clothes so that you can put on more comfortable ones: *Get out of those wet clothes!* **6 Get out of here!** SPOKEN used to say that you don't believe someone

get over **1 get over sth** to start to feel better after an emotional experience that has caused a lot of sadness or disappointment: *The family still hadn't gotten over the shock of Jennifer's death.* **2 get over sth** to become well again after you have been ill: *It took him a week to get over the flu.* **3 get over sb** to stop feeling upset about a romantic relationship with someone that has just ended: *You'll get over her.* **4 get over sth** to no longer have feelings of nervousness, shyness, lack of self-confidence etc. SYN **overcome**: *She seems to have gotten over her confidence problems.* **5 sb can't/couldn't get over sth** SPOKEN used to say that someone is very surprised, shocked, or amused by something: *I can't get over how thin you are!* **6 get over it!** SPOKEN used to tell someone to stop being upset or complaining about something, because they are annoying you

get sth **over with** *phr. v.* to finish doing something you do not like doing as quickly as possible: *"The shot should only hurt a little." "OK. Just get it over with."*

get through *phr. v.* **1 get (sb) through sth** to manage to deal with a difficult or bad experience until it ends, or help someone do this: *I was so embarrassed, I don't know how I got through the rest of dinner.* | *Her love got me through my illness.* **2** to succeed in reaching someone by telephone: *I couldn't get through the first time I called.* | **get through to sb/sth** *Did you get through to the manager?* **3 get sth through** if a law gets through Congress or another official organization, or if someone gets it through, it is officially accepted **4 get sth through your head** to understand or believe something: *Get it through your head – I am not interested in her!* **5 get through sth** to finish doing something: *I want to get through this chapter before I go to bed.* **6** if someone or something gets through or gets something through to a place that is hard to reach, they succeed in sending supplies, food, money etc. to people in that place: *Trucks carrying medical supplies were unable to get through.* | **get sth through (to sb)** *Aid workers got the food through to the refugees.*

get through to *phr. v.* **1 get through to sb** to be able to make someone understand something, especially when this is difficult: *Sometimes it's like I just can't get through to her.* **2 get through to sth** to succeed in reaching the next stage of a game or competition: *The team got through to the final round.*

get to *phr. v.* INFORMAL **1 get to sb** to upset or annoy someone: *Don't let him get to you, honey.* **2 get to doing sth** SPOKEN INFORMAL to start doing something: *We got to talking about old friends from school.*

get together *phr. v.* **1** to meet with someone or with a group of people: *We should really get together for lunch sometime.* | **get together with sb** *Every time he gets together with Murphy, they argue.* **2** to start a romantic relationship with someone: *Those two should get together – they have a lot in common.* **3 get yourself together** also **get your life together** SPOKEN to begin to be in control of your life, your emotions etc.: *After my husband left, it took a year for me to get myself together.* **4 get it together** also **get your act**

together to become organized and successful in a situation, your life etc., so that you can be successful: *He can't seem to get it together and get himself a job.*

get up *phr. v.* **1 get sb up** to wake up and get out of your bed, especially in the morning, or to make someone do this SYN **wake up**: *What time do you want to get up?* | *Could you get me up at 8:00?* | **get up early/late** *I have to get up early tomorrow.* **2** to stand up: *Tom got up to make some more coffee.*

get·a·way /ˈgɛt̬əˌweɪ/ *n.* [C] **1** an escape from a place or a bad situation, especially after you have done something illegal: *The bank robber **made** his **getaway** in a red truck.* | *a **getaway car*** (=a car used by criminals to escape after a crime) **2** a short trip that you take as a vacation, or the place where you go: *Bear Lake is a popular weekend getaway.*

ˈget-go *n.* **from the get-go** INFORMAL from the beginning: *Harry's been involved in the project from the get-go.*

ˌget-rich-ˈquick *adj.* [only before noun] relating to the desire to earn a lot of money quickly, or relating to a method of doing this: *a get-rich-quick scheme*

get·ter /ˈgɛt̬ɚ/ *n.* [C usually singular] something or someone that gets or receives something: *Gilroy was the top vote-getter.* | *It's fun to drive – it's an attention-getter.* → see also GO-GETTER

ˈget-toˌgether *n.* [C] a friendly informal meeting or party: *a family get-together*

Get·ty /ˈgɛt̬i/, **J. Paul** /dʒeɪ pɔl/ (1892–1976) a U.S. businessman who owned an oil company and became one of the richest men in the world. He built the Getty Museum in Malibu, California.

Get·tys·burg /ˈgɛt̬izˌbɚg/ a town in the U.S. state of Pennsylvania where the Confederate general Robert E. Lee was defeated by a Union army in the American Civil War

ˌGettysburg Adˈdress, the HISTORY a famous speech made by Abraham Lincoln at Gettysburg in 1863, about the Union soldiers who had died in the Civil War

get·up /ˈgɛt̬ʌp/ *n.* [C] INFORMAL strange or unusual clothes that someone is wearing: *a 1920s gangster getup*

ˌget-up-and-ˈgo *n.* [U] INFORMAL energy and determination to do things

gew·gaw /ˈgyugɔ, ˈgu-/ *n.* [C] a cheap brightly colored piece of jewelry or decoration

gey·ser /ˈgaɪzɚ/ *n.* [C] EARTH SCIENCE a natural spring that sends hot water and steam into the air from a hole in the ground

Gha·na /ˈgɑnə/ a country in west Africa east of Ivory Coast —**Ghanaian** /gɑˈneɪən/ *n., adj.*

ghast·ly /ˈgæstli/ *adj. comparative* **ghastlier**, *superlative* **ghastliest** **1** extremely bad, shocking, or upsetting: *ghastly pictures of the accident* | *a ghastly mistake* **2** FORMAL looking or feeling very sick, upset, or unhappy: *She felt ghastly afterwards.*

Ghats, the /gɑts, gɔts/ two RANGES of mountains in central India

GHB /ˌdʒi eɪtʃ ˈbi/ *n.* [U] a chemical substance that is taken as a drug by some people, especially at parties and dance clubs

gher·kin /ˈgɚkɪn/ *n.* [C] a small type of CUCUMBER that is often made into a PICKLE [**Origin:** 1600–1700 Dutch *gurken* **cucumbers**, from Polish *ogurek*, from Medieval Greek *agouros* **watermelon**]

ghet·to /ˈgɛt̬oʊ/ *n. plural* **ghettos** or **ghettos** [C] **1** a part of a city where people from a particular race or group, especially people who are poor, live separately from the rest of the people in the city. This word is sometimes considered offensive: *Rap music began in the ghettos.* ▶see THESAURUS box at **area** **2** a part of a city where people who belonged to a particular race were forced to live by a government, especially in the past: *the Jewish ghetto in Warsaw* **3** an area or environment that is limited to a particular group of people: *His office marked the edge of the executive ghetto.* [**Origin:** 1600–1700 Italian]

ˈghetto ˌblaster *n.* [C] OLD-FASHIONED a word for a BOOM BOX, now considered offensive

ghet·to·ize /ˈgɛt̬oʊˌaɪz/ *v.* [T] **1** to make part of a town become a ghetto **2** to force someone to live in a ghetto

ghost¹ /goʊst/ *n.* [C]
1 SPIRIT the spirit of a dead person, that some people believe they can see or feel in a place SYN **spirit** SYN **spook**: *They say the captain's **ghost** still **haunts** the waterfront.* | +**of** *the ghosts of Civil War soldiers* | *He looked like he'd **seen a ghost*** (=he looked frightened). → see also HOLY GHOST

THESAURUS
spirit a creature without a physical body, such as an angel or ghost
phantom/specter/apparition LITERARY a ghost

2 MEMORY/EFFECT the memory or effect of someone or something bad that lived, existed, or happened in the past: +**of** *The ghost of Stalinism still affects life in Russia today.*
3 not a ghost of a chance not even a slight chance of doing something, or of something happening: *There's not a ghost of a chance that we'll get there on time now.*
4 give up the ghost HUMOROUS **a)** if a machine gives up the ghost, it does not work anymore and cannot be repaired: *My old car's finally given up the ghost.* **b)** to die
5 TELEVISION/COMPUTER a second image that is not clear on a television or computer screen
6 the ghost of a smile/sound etc. a smile, sound etc. that is so slight you are not sure it happened: *He had the ghost of a smile on his lips.*
7 a GHOST WRITER

ghost² *v.* [I,T] INFORMAL to write something as a GHOST WRITER

ghost·ly /ˈgoʊstli/ *adj.* slightly frightening and seeming to be related to ghosts or spirits: *a ghostly voice*

ˈghost ˌstory *n.* [C] a story about ghosts that is intended to frighten people

ˈghost town *n.* [C] a town that used to have many people living and working in it, but now has very few or none: *The place where Jake was born became a ghost town, because when the mine closed down, there were no jobs and everybdy left.*

ˈghost ˌwriter, ghostwriter *n.* [C] someone who is paid to write a book or story for another person, who then says it is their own work —**ghostwrite** *v.* [I,T]

ghoul /gul/ *n.* [C] **1** an evil spirit in stories, that takes bodies from graves and eats them **2** someone who gets pleasure from unpleasant things such as accidents, which shock other people —**ghoulish** *adj.*

GHQ /ˌdʒi eɪtʃ ˈkyu/ *n.* [U] **General Headquarters** the place that a large military operation is controlled from

GI, G.I. /ˌdʒi ˈaɪ/ *n.* [C] **Government Issue** a soldier in the U.S. army

Gia·co·met·ti /ˌdʒɑkəˈmɛt̬i/, **Al·ber·to** /ælˈbɛrtoʊ/ (1901–1966) a Swiss SCULPTOR and PAINTER, famous for his work in the style of SURREALISM

gi·ant¹ /ˈdʒaɪənt/ S3 W3 *adj.* extremely big, and much bigger than other things of the same type SYN **huge**: *a giant TV screen*

giant² *n.* [C] **1** a very tall strong man who is often bad and cruel, in children's stories **2** a very successful or important person or company: +**of** *He is one of the giants of the music industry.* | *companies such as the software giant, Microsoft* **3** a very big man, animal, plant etc. [**Origin:** 1200–1300 Old French *geant*, from Greek *gigas*]

gi·ant·ess /ˈdʒaɪəntɪs/ *n.* [C] an extremely tall woman, especially a tall, strong woman who is often bad and cruel in childrens' stories

ˌgiant ˈpanda *n.* [C] a PANDA

gib·ber /ˈdʒɪbɚ/ *v.* [I] to speak quickly in a way that is difficult to understand, especially because you are frightened, shocked, or excited: +**with** *He was gibbering with rage.*

gib·ber·ish /ˈdʒɪbərɪʃ/ *n.* [U] something you write or say that has no meaning, or is very difficult to understand SYN **nonsense**: *Most of what she said was gibberish.*

gib·bet /ˈdʒɪbɪt/ *n.* [C] a wooden frame on which criminals were HANGed in past times using a rope around their neck SYN **gallows**

gib·bon /ˈgɪbən/ *n.* [C] a small animal like a monkey, with long arms and no tail, that lives in trees in Asia

gibe /dʒaɪb/ *n.* [C] another spelling of JIBE

ˌGI ˌBill of ˈRights, the HISTORY a U.S. law passed in 1944 to help people returning from World War II to buy homes and pay for higher education

gib·lets /ˈdʒɪblɪts/ *n.* [plural] organs such as the heart and LIVER, that you remove from a bird before cooking it

Gi·bral·tar /dʒɪˈbrɔltɚ/ a town on the Rock of Gibraltar on the southern coast of Spain

Gibraltar, the Strait of a narrow piece of sea that connects the Mediterranean Sea at its western end with the Atlantic Ocean

G

Gib·ran /dʒɪˈbrɑn/, **Kah·lil** /kɑˈlil/ (1883–1931) a Lebanese poet

gid·dy[1] /ˈgɪdi/ *adj. comparative* **giddier**, *superlative* **giddiest** **1** feeling silly, happy, and excited, or showing this feeling: *giddy laughter* | +**with** *The children are giddy with excitement.* **2** feeling slightly sick and unable to balance, because everything seems to be moving SYN **dizzy**: *Just watching those kids spinning makes me **feel giddy**.* **3** OLD-FASHIONED silly and not interested in serious things: *a giddy girl* [**Origin:** Old English *gydig* **mentally ill**] —**giddily** *adv.* —**giddiness** *n.* [U]

giddy[2] *v.*
giddy up *phr. v.* used to command a horse to go faster

Gide /ʒid/, **André** /ˈɑndreɪ/ (1869–1951) a French writer famous especially for his NOVELS

Gid·e·on Bi·ble /ˌgɪdiən ˈbaɪbəl/ a Bible that is put in a hotel room by a Christian organization called Gideons International, so that people staying there can read it

GIF /gɪf/ *n.* [C] **Graphics Interchange Format** COMPUTERS a type of computer FILE used on the Internet that contains pictures, photographs, or other images

gift[1] /gɪft/ S1 W2 *n.* [C] **1** something that you give someone, for example to thank them or because you like them, especially on a special occasion SYN **present**: *The earrings were a gift from my boyfriend for my birthday.* | **birthday/wedding/Christmas gift** *We **gave** her the photo as a Christmas **gift**.* | *The Machon family **made a** substantial **gift of** land **to** the college.* | *You receive **a free gift*** (=something that you do not have to pay for) *with any purchase of $20 or more.* **2 a)** a natural ability SYN **talent**: +**for** *Elena sure has a gift for telling stories.* | +**of** *She has the gift of being able to laugh at herself.* → see also GIFTED **b)** an ability that is given to you by God: +**of** *the gift of prophecy* | *spiritual gifts* ►see THESAURUS box at **ability** **3 a gift (from God)** something good you receive or something good that happens to you, even though you might not deserve it **4 the gift of gab** INFORMAL an ability to speak easily and confidently with other people: *You cannot be a salesperson without the gift of gab.* **5 don't look a gift horse in the mouth** SPOKEN used to tell someone to be thankful for something that has been given to them, instead of asking questions about it or finding something wrong with it [**Origin:** 1200–1300 Old Norse] → see also **God's gift to sb/sth etc.** at GOD (5)

gift[2] *v.* [T] INFORMAL NONSTANDARD to give someone something as a gift: **gift sb with sth** *He gifted us each with $100.*

ˈgift cerˌtificate *n.* [C] a special piece of paper worth a particular amount of money when exchanged for goods in a particular store, that you can give someone as a gift: *On his birthday he received a $25 gift certificate for the bookstore.*

gift·ed /ˈgɪftɪd/ *adj.* **1** having a natural ability to do one or more things extremely well SYN **talented**: *a gifted poet* | **athletically/musically etc. gifted** *a school for artistically gifted children* | **be gifted with sth** *Elaine is gifted with a superb singing voice.* **2** very intelligent: *a special class for gifted children* ►see THESAURUS box at **intelligent**

ˈgift shop *n.* [C] a store that sells small things that are appropriate for giving as presents

ˈgift wrap[1] also **ˈgift ˌwrapping** *n.* [U] attractive colored paper for wrapping presents in SYN **wrapping paper**

gift wrap[2], **gift-wrap** *v.* **gift wrapped**, **gift wrapping** [T] to wrap a present with colored paper, especially at a store

gig[1] /gɪg/ *n.* [C] **1** a performance by musicians, especially musicians who play popular music or JAZZ, or a performance by a COMEDIAN: *The band has a gig at the Blues Bar next week.* **2** INFORMAL a job, especially one that does not last for a long time: *Working for a TV show is a pretty good gig.* **3** INFORMAL a gigabyte **4** a small carriage with two wheels that is pulled by one horse

gig[2] *v.* **gigged**, **gigging** [I] to give a performance of modern popular music, JAZZ etc., for which you are paid

gig·a·byte /ˈgɪgəˌbaɪt/ WRITTEN ABBREVIATION **Gb** *n.* [C] COMPUTERS a unit for measuring the amount of information a computer can store or use, equal to 1024 MEGABYTES and used less exactly to mean a BILLION BYTES

gi·gan·tic /dʒaɪˈgæntɪk/ *adj.* [no comparative] extremely large SYN **huge** SYN **enormous**: *a gigantic statue of Buddha*

gig·gle[1] /ˈgɪgəl/ *v.* **giggled**, **giggling** [I] to laugh quickly and quietly in a high voice because you think something is very funny or because you are nervous: *What are you two girls giggling about?* ►see THESAURUS box at **laugh**[1] [**Origin:** 1500–1600 From the sound] —**giggly** *adj.*

giggle[2] *n.* [C] a quick quiet high-sounding laugh: *a nervous giggle* | *One of the boys **got the giggles*** (=was unable to stop giggling) *during dinner.* —**giggly** *adj.*

gig·o·lo /ˈdʒɪgəˌloʊ/ *n. plural* **gigolos** [C] a man who is paid by a rich woman, especially an older woman, to have sex with her [**Origin:** 1900–2000 French *gigolette* **girl who goes to dances, prostitute**, from *gigue* **dance**]

Gi·ku·yu /gɪˈkuyu/ another form of KIKUYU

Gi·la monster, **gila monster** /ˈhilə ˌmɑnstɚ/ *n.* [C] a large orange and black LIZARD that is poisonous and lives in the deserts of the southwestern U.S. and western Mexico

gild /gɪld/ *v.* [T] **1** to cover something with a thin layer of gold or gold paint: *a gilded picture frame* **2** LITERARY to make something look as if it is covered in gold: *The autumn sun gilded the lake.* **3 gild the lily** to spoil something by trying to improve it when it is already good enough

gill[1] /gɪl/ *n.* [C] **1** BIOLOGY one of the organs on the sides of a fish through which it breathes → see picture at FISH[1] **2** BIOLOGY one of the thin structures like a blade on the under side of some fungi (FUNGUS) such as MUSHROOMS that carry the SPORES **3 packed/stuffed/full etc. to the gills** completely full: *The plane was packed to the gills with relief supplies.*

gill[2] /dʒɪl/ *n.* [C] a measure of liquid equal to ¼ of a PINT

Gil·man /ˈgɪlmən/, **Char·lotte Per·kins** /ˈʃɑrlət ˈpɚkənz/ (1860–1935) a U.S. writer who supported women's rights, famous for her book on women and ECONOMICS

gilt[1] /gɪlt/ *adj.* [only before noun] covered with a thin layer of gold or gold-colored paint: *gilt lettering*

gilt² *n.* **1** [U] a thin layer of gold or gold-colored paint, used to cover objects for decoration **2** [C] BIOLOGY a young female pig **3** [C] ECONOMICS a STOCK or SHARE that is gilt-edged

ˌgilt-ˈedged *adj.* **1** having gilt on the edges **2** ECONOMICS gilt-edged STOCKS or SHARES do not give you much INTEREST (=additional money) but are considered very safe because they are sold mainly by governments **3** extremely good or respected: *a gilt-edged credit history*

gim·let /ˈgɪmlɪt/ *n.* [C] **1** an alcoholic drink made with GIN or VODKA and LIME juice **2 gimlet-eyed** also **gimlet eyes** if someone is gimlet-eyed or has gimlet eyes, they look at things very closely and notice every detail **3** a tool that is used to make small holes in wood so that you can put screws in easily

gim·me¹ /ˈgɪmi/ NONSTANDARD a way of writing the spoken short form of "give me": *Gimme that ball back!*

gimme² *n.* [C] INFORMAL something that is so easy to do or succeed at that you do not even have to try: *The victory was a gimme for the New York Yankees.*

gim·mick /ˈgɪmɪk/ *n.* [C] DISAPPROVING a trick or something unusual that you do to make people notice someone or something: *advertising gimmicks* —**gimmicky** *adj.* DISAPPROVING —**gimmickry** *n.* [U] DISAPPROVING

gimp·y /ˈgɪmpi/ also **gimp** /gɪmp/ *adj.* INFORMAL **1** a gimpy leg or knee does not work normally, especially because it is hurt **2** a gimpy person cannot walk normally, either because one or both of their legs are hurt, or because they are physically unable to use them —**gimp** *n.* [C]

gin /dʒɪn/ *n.* **1** [C,U] a strong alcoholic drink made mainly from grain, or a glass of this drink → see also GIN AND TONIC **2** [U] the situation in the game of GIN RUMMY when all the cards in your hand are matched in sets and you win **3** [U] GIN RUMMY [**Origin:** 1700–1800 *geneva* **gin** (18–20 centuries), from Dutch *genever*, from Latin *juniperus* **juniper**, plant used to give gin its taste] → see also COTTON GIN

ˌgin and ˈtonic *n.* [C,U] an alcoholic drink made with gin and TONIC (=a special type of water), served with ice and a thin piece of LEMON or LIME

gin·ger /ˈdʒɪndʒɚ/ *n.* [U] **1** a light brown root with a strong hot taste, or the powder made from this root, that is used in cooking **2** BIOLOGY the plant that this root comes from

ˈginger ale *n.* [C,U] a SOFT DRINK with a ginger taste

gin·ger·bread /ˈdʒɪndʒɚˌbrɛd/ *n.* [U] **1** a type of cookie with ginger and sweet SPICES in it, that is usually cut into shapes before baking it: *a **gingerbread house/man*** (=a piece of gingerbread in the shape of a house or a person) **2** complicated decorations on the outside of a house: *a Victorian mansion decorated with gingerbread* **3** a heavy cake that has GINGER and MOLASSES in it

gin·ger·ly /ˈdʒɪndʒɚli/ *adv.* if you do something gingerly, you do it very slowly, carefully, and gently, because you are afraid it will be dangerous or painful SYN **cautiously**: *They gingerly loaded the patient into the ambulance.* —**gingerly** *adj.*

ˈginger snap *n.* [C] a hard cookie with GINGER in it

ging·ham /ˈgɪŋəm/ *n.* [U] cotton cloth that has a pattern of small white and colored squares on it: *a red and white gingham tablecloth*

gin·gi·vi·tis /ˌdʒɪndʒəˈvaɪṭɪs/ *n.* [U] MEDICINE a medical condition in which your GUMS are red, swollen, and painful

gink·go, gingko /ˈgɪŋkoʊ/ *n.* [C] a type of tree from China with leaves that are shaped like small FANS

ˌgin ˈrummy *n.* [U] a type of RUMMY (=card game)

Gins·berg /ˈgɪnzbɚg/, **Al·len** /ˈælən/ (1926–1997) a U.S. poet and leader of the Beat Generation

gin·seng /ˈdʒɪnsɛŋ, -sɪŋ/ *n.* [U] medicine made from the root of a Chinese plant, that some people think keeps you young and healthy [**Origin:** 1600–1700 Chinese *renshen*]

Giot·to /ˈdʒɔtoʊ/ (?1266–1337) an Italian painter and ARCHITECT who was one of the most important painters of his time

gip·sy /ˈdʒɪpsi/ *n.* [C] another spelling of GYPSY

gi·raffe /dʒəˈræf/ *n.* [C] a tall African animal with a very long neck and legs and dark spots on its yellow-brown fur

gird /gɚd/ *v.* *past tense and past participle* **girded** or **girt** /gɚt/ **1** [I,T] if you gird for something, or gird yourself for something, especially something difficult, you prepare for it: +**for** *District officials are girding for a tough campaign.* **2 gird (up) your loins** HUMOROUS OR BIBLICAL to get ready to do something, especially to fight **3** FORMAL to put or fasten something around something else, especially to give it support or protection: *Roman walls still gird the Old City.*

gird·er /ˈgɚdɚ/ *n.* [C] a strong beam, made of iron or steel, that supports a floor, roof, or bridge

gir·dle /ˈgɚdl/ *n.* [C] a piece of women's underwear which fits tightly around her stomach, bottom, and HIPS to make her look thinner

girl /gɚl/ S1 W1 *n.* [C]
1 CHILD a female child: *She's tall for a girl her age.* | *a seven-year-old girl* | *I lived in Colorado when I was **a little girl**.* | *A **small girl** hugged her mother's legs.* | *a group of **boys and girls*** ▸see THESAURUS box at **woman**
2 DAUGHTER a daughter: *They have two girls and a boy.* | *How old is your **little girl**?*
3 WOMAN a word meaning a woman, which is considered offensive by some people: *A nice girl like you needs a husband.*
4 the girls INFORMAL a woman's female friends: *I'm going out with the girls tonight.*
5 ANIMAL used to speak to a female animal, such as a horse, cat, or dog: *Bring me the stick. Good girl!*
6 girl SPOKEN used by a woman to address another woman that she knows well: *Hey, girl. What's up?*
7 (you) go, girl! SLANG used to encourage a girl or woman, or to say that you agree with what she is saying
8 RELATIONSHIP OLD-FASHIONED a woman who you are having a romantic relationship with SYN **girlfriend**: *She's my girl.*
9 EMPLOYEE OLD-FASHIONED a word for a female worker, especially in an office, now considered offensive by most people: *I'll have my girl send it over.*
10 SERVANT OLD-FASHIONED a woman servant
[**Origin:** 1500–1600 *gurle*, *girle* **child, young person** (13–15 centuries), of unknown origin]

ˌgirl ˈFriday *n.* [C] a girl or woman worker who does several different jobs in an office

girl·friend /ˈgɚlfrɛnd/ S2 *n.* [C] **1** a girl or woman with whom you have a romantic relationship: *Sam's new girlfriend* | *Does Jim **have a girlfriend**?* | *an ex-girlfriend* (=a former girlfriend) **2** a woman's female friend: *She's out with one of her girlfriends.* → see also BOYFRIEND

girl·hood /ˈgɚlhʊd/ *n.* [U] the period of a woman's life when she is a girl → see also BOYHOOD

girl·ie¹, **girly** /ˈgɚli/ *adj.* **1** INFORMAL **a girlie magazine/calendar etc.** a magazine etc. with pictures of women with no clothes on **2** SPOKEN relating to or more appropriate for girls than men or boys: *girlie names such as Natasha*

girlie² *n.* [C] OLD-FASHIONED an offensive word used especially by men to talk to a woman who they think is less sensible or intelligent than they are

girl·ish /ˈgɚlɪʃ/ *adj.* behaving like a girl, or looking like a girl, or appropriate for a girl: *girlish laughter* → see also BOYISH —**girlishly** *adv.*

ˈGirl Scout *n.* **1** [C] a member of the Girl Scouts **2 the Girl Scouts** an organization for girls that teaches them practical skills and helps to develop their character → see also BOY SCOUT

girl·y /ˈgɚli/ *adj.* another spelling of GIRLIE

girt /gɚt/ *v.* a past participle of GIRD

G

girth /gɚθ/ *n.* **1** [C,U] the distance around the middle of someone or something: *the enormous girth of a redwood tree's trunk* | *She is a woman of substantial girth* (=she is fat). **2** [C] a band of leather that is passed tightly around the middle of a horse to keep a SADDLE or load firmly in position

GIS /ˌdʒi aɪ ˈɛs/ *n.* [singular] EARTH SCIENCE **geographic information system** a computer system for storing and examining information about the natural features of the Earth's surface: *GIS software*

gist /dʒɪst/ *n.* **the gist** the main idea or meaning of what someone has said or written: *I don't speak much French, but I* ***got the gist of*** (=understood the main ideas of) *what she said.* [**Origin:** 1700–1800 Anglo-French **it lies, it can be presented in a court of law,** from Old French *gesir* **to lie**]

Giu·li·a·ni /ˌdʒuliˈɑni/, **Ru·dolph** /ˈrudɔlf/ (1944–) the MAYOR of New York City from 1994 to 2001, including the time of the TERRORIST attacks on the World Trade Center

G

give[1] /gɪv/ S1 W1 *v. past tense* **gave** /geɪv/, *past participle* **given** /ˈgɪvən/

1 PUT IN SB'S HAND [T] to put something near someone or in their hand so that they can use it, hold it etc.: **give sb sth** *Here, give me your coat.* | **give sth to sb** *Give the keys to Daddy, Amanda.* | *I gave the money to her on Wednesday.*

THESAURUS

pass to take something and put it in someone's hand: *Could you pass me the salt?*
hand to pass something to someone: *Hand me those scissors, will you?*
hand out/pass out to give something to each of the people in a group: *Mr. Goodmanson handed out the test.* | *Tony filled the glasses and passed them out.*
share to divide something into equal parts and give a part to each person: *She made a cake and shared it with the children.*
distribute to give things to a large number of people, especially on the street: *Anti-war protesters were distributing leaflets.*

2 PROVIDE [T] to provide or supply someone with a thing, a service etc.: **give sb sth** *Dan gave me a ride to work.* | *The doctor gave him something for the pain.* | **give sth to sb** *They gave the job to some guy from Texas.*

3 LET SB HAVE/DO STH to allow or make it possible for someone to do or have something: **give sb sth** *They never* ***gave*** *me a* ***chance*** *to explain.* | *The teacher finally* ***gave*** *us* ***permission*** *to leave.* | *Women were given the right to vote in the early 1900s.* | **give sth to sb** *The plan gives control of the firm to an Indonesian company.*

4 PRESENT [T] to provide someone with something as a present: *What are you giving Mom for Christmas?* | **give sb sth** *Aunt Jo gave Alex a telescope.* | **give sth to sb** *He gave a dozen roses to his wife on their anniversary.*

5 TELL SB STH [T] to tell someone information or details about something, or tell someone to do something: *The police asked him to give a description of the man.* | *You may have to give evidence in court.* | **give sb sth** *Would you give Kim a message for me?* | *Let me* ***give*** *you some* ***advice***. | **give orders/instruction** *Who gave the order to shoot?*

6 DO AN ACTION to do something by making a movement with your hand, face, body etc.: *Come on, give Grandpa a hug.* | **give a smile/laugh/frown/yawn etc.** *The boy gave Lynn a big smile.* | **give a wave/signal/sign etc.** *As he left the building, he gave the crowd a thumbs-up sign.* | **give sth a shake/rattle/tug etc.** *She gave the package an experimental shake.*

7 MAKE SB HAVE PROBLEMS [T] to do something that causes problems or makes a situation difficult for someone: **give sb problems/trouble/difficulties** *The machines in the lab are giving us trouble.* | *Stop* ***giving*** *me* ***a hard time*** (=stop criticizing me).

8 FEELING [T] to make someone have a particular physical or emotional feeling: *The applause gave her the confidence to continue.* | **give sb sth** *The noise is giving me a headache.* | **give sth to sb** *Their music has given pleasure to a lot of people.*

9 ILLNESS [T] to infect someone with the same illness you have: **give sb sth** *The kids are always giving me colds.* | **give sth to sb** *It is very unlikely that a doctor could give HIV to a patient.*

10 SPEECH/TALK/PERFORMANCE [T] to talk, play an instrument etc. in front of a group of people: **give a talk/speech/lecture etc.** *Each student has to give a short talk.* | **give a performance/display/concert** *Yo Yo Ma gave a wonderful performance last night.*

11 MONEY [I,T] to give money, food etc. in order to help others: *He gives generously to the church.* | **give sth to sb/sth** *They gave $25 to the memorial fund.*

THESAURUS

donate to give money or other things to an organization that uses it to help people: *Profits from the book sale are being donated to a local homeless shelter.*
leave also **bequeath** FORMAL to give something to people after you die: *This house was left to me by my aunt.*
award to officially give money or a prize to someone: *Heaney was awarded the Nobel Prize for Literature.*
present to formally or officially give something to someone, in person: *They presented her with a bouquet of flowers.*

12 QUALITY/SHAPE ETC. [T not in progressive] to make someone have a particular quality, shape, look etc.: **give sb/sth sth** *The color of the room gives it a warm cozy feeling.*

13 MAKE SB THINK STH to make someone think about something in a particular way, or have a particular idea about something: **give sb the impression/feeling/sense etc.** *He gave me the impression that he wasn't happy with work.* | **give sb an idea/a picture/a view etc.** *The report gives an accurate picture of life in the inner cities.*

14 give sb loyalty/obedience/respect etc. to behave in a loyal, respectful etc. way toward someone: *If you give children respect, they will respect you.*

15 PAY [T] to pay a particular amount of money for something: **give sb sth for sth** *I'll give you $75 for the oak desk.*

16 BEND/STRETCH [I] if a material gives, it bends or stretches when you put pressure on it: *The leather will give slightly when you start wearing the boots.*

17 give or take a few minutes/a mile/a penny etc. used in order to show that a number or amount is not exact: *The show lasts about an hour, give or take five minutes.*

18 PARTY/DANCE/SOCIAL EVENT to organize a social event such as a party, especially at your own home: *Julie is giving a birthday party for Lori next Saturday.*

19 give (sb/sth) credit/respect/priority etc. to treat something or someone in a way that shows you think they have done something well, that they are important etc.: *You have to give him credit for trying.* | *Top priority should be given to finishing on schedule.*

20 PRODUCE AN EFFECT [T] to produce a particular effect, solution, result etc.: *The field goal gave the team a two-point lead over Fullerton.*

21 MAKE SB DO STH [T] to ask or tell someone to do a job or piece of work: **give sb work/homework/chores etc.** *Our English teacher always gives us a lot of homework.* | *If you're bored, I'll give you something to do.*

22 give sb/sth time to allow time for someone to do something or something to happen: *Give her some time. She'll make the right decision.* | **give sb/sth**

time to do sth *Can you give me a few more days to finish my report?*

SPOKEN PHRASES

23 don't give me that! INFORMAL said when you do not believe someone's excuse or explanation: *"I'm too tired." "Oh, don't give me that! You just don't want to come."*
24 sb would give anything/a lot/their right arm etc. said to emphasize that someone wants something very much: *I'd give anything to get tickets.*
25 give me sth (any day/time) used to say that you like something much more than something else: *I don't like those fancy desserts. Give me a bowl of ice cream any day.*
26 give sth six weeks/a month etc. used to say that you think that something is not going to continue successfully for very long: *They're moving in together? I give it about two months.*
27 give it to sb to angrily criticize or punish someone: *He's going to give it to you when he finds out.*
28 give it to sb straight to tell someone something in a clear direct way
29 What gives? used to ask someone what is happening when there is a problem or when something is confusing: *"Scott quit yesterday." "What gives?"*
30 give as good as you get to fight or argue with someone, using the same amount of skill or force that they are using: *The youngest of three sons, Dave can give as good as he gets.*
31 I'll give you that used to say that you accept that something is true, even though you do not like it or disagree with other parts of it: *It's nice – I'll give you that – but I still wouldn't want to live there.*
32 give sb what for OLD-FASHIONED, INFORMAL to tell someone angrily that you are annoyed with them

33 give (sth) thought/attention/consideration etc. to spend some time thinking about something carefully: *He is giving serious consideration to running again for president.* | ***Don't give it a second thought** – I'll take care of everything.*
34 give (sb) a hand INFORMAL to help someone do something: *Can you give me a hand, here?* | +**with** *Do you want a hand with your luggage?*
35 give sb a call/buzz INFORMAL to call someone on the telephone: *I'll give you a call before I leave, okay?*
36 PUNISHMENT [T] to officially say that someone must have a particular punishment: **give sb 6 months/3 years etc.** *Jones was given thirty years for the murder.* | **give sb a fine/sentence** *You could be given a fine of up to $1,000.*
37 GRADE/SCORE [T] to decide that someone should have a particular grade or score for something they have done: **give sb sth** *Mr. Morris gave me a B on my report.* | *One judge gave her a 9.8 on her balance beam routine.*
38 CHANGE [I] to be willing to change what you think or do in a situation according to what else happens: *Both sides need to give a little.* | *I'm willing to compromise somewhat, but he won't **give an inch*** (=change what he thinks).
39 give sth a try/shot/whirl to try to do something, especially something you have not done before: *I don't know; it might work. I'll give it a try.*
40 give and take INFORMAL to help other people and do things for them as well as expecting them to do things for you: *You have to learn to give and take in any relationship.*
41 give way a) also **give** to break because of too much weight or pressure: *More than 50 homes were flooded when the dam gave way.* | *The branch suddenly gave beneath him.* **b) give way to sth** to change to something newer, better, or different: *Many movie houses closed down, giving way to smaller theaters.* | *October gave way to November.* **c)** to agree to do what someone else wants to do, instead of what you wanted to do: *It is unlikely that either side will give way in the dispute over the islands.* **d)** to YIELD
42 BE CARING [I] to be caring and generous, especially in a relationship: *She's looking for a man who knows how to give.*
43 something has to give used to say that a situation cannot remain as it is and that something must change: *With 800 refugees arriving every day, something has to give.*
44 give sb a/the name to name someone: *We gave him the nickname "Spanky."*
45 TELEPHONE [T] to make a telephone connection for someone: *Operator, could you give me extension 103, please?*
46 HAVE A BABY [T] OLD-FASHIONED to have a baby for a man: *She gave him three sons.*
47 give sb to understand/believe that FORMAL to make someone believe that something will happen or is true: *I was given to understand that I would be offered a permanent job.*
[**Origin:** Old English *giefan*] → see also **give up the ghost** at GHOST[1] (4)

give away *phr. v.* **1 give sth ↔ away** to give something to someone because you do not want or need it for yourself: *I'm going to give some of these old clothes away.* **2 give sth ↔ away** to give something to someone without asking for any money, rather than selling it to them: **give sth away to sb/sth** *The store is giving away a toaster to the first 50 customers.* **3 give sb/sth ↔ away** to do or say something that shows thoughts, feelings, or actions that you want to keep secret SYN **reveal**: *He said he hadn't told her, but his face gave him away* (=showed that he had told her). | *I was afraid the kids would give the surprise party away.* **4 give sth ↔ away** to lose a game or competition by doing something badly or making mistakes: *I swear the Democrats are just giving away this election.* **5 give sb ↔ away** when a man, especially the BRIDE 's father, gives the bride away, he walks with her to the front of the church and formally gives permission for her to marry

give back *phr. v.* **1 give sth ↔ back** to return something to the person who it belongs to or to the person who gave it to you: **give sth back to sb** *I'll give the keys back to you tomorrow morning.* | **give sb sth ↔ back** *He gave me back my books.* | *Give Jane her doll back, Katie.* **2** to give something to someone or do something for them because they have helped you in the past: *Anytime you do volunteer work, you give back to the community.* | **give sth ↔ back** *I hope to give back to Scouting what it has given me.* **3 give sth ↔ back** to make it possible for someone to have or do something again, after a time when they have not been able to SYN **restore**: **give sb sth ↔ back** *The operation gave him back his sight.* | *The company finally agreed to give the women their old jobs back.*

give in *phr. v.* **1** to agree to something you were unwilling to agree to before, especially because someone has forced or persuaded you to: *Randy asked her out for months before she finally gave in.* | +**to** *We will never give in to terrorist demands.* **2** to accept that you are or will be defeated and stop playing, fighting etc.: *Despite a bad first half, Iowa didn't give in and went on to win 85–65.*

give in to sth *phr. v.* to stop being able to control a strong need, emotion, or desire: *They refuse to give in to despair.* | *Don't have cookies in the cupboard – you're bound to give in to temptation.*

give of sth *phr. v.* if you give of yourself, your time, or your money, you do things for other people without expecting them to do anything for you: *These professionals give of their free time to help poor children.*

give off sth *phr. v.* to produce a smell, light, heat, a sound etc. SYN **emit**: *The factory gives off a terrible smell.*

give on/onto sth *phr. v.* FORMAL if a window, door, building etc. gives on or onto a particular place, it leads to that place or you can see that place from it: *The door gave on a cement stairway leading down.*

give out *phr. v.* **1 give sth ↔ out** to give something to a number of different people SYN **hand out**: *She* *gave out copies of the report before the meeting.* | *You shouldn't have given my phone number out.* **2** to stop working correctly: *My voice gave out halfway through the song.* | *The fuel pump gave out on the freeway.* **3** if a supply of something gives out, there is none left: *After two hours, my patience gave out.*

give sb/sth **over to** sth *phr. v.* **1 be given over to sth** to be used for a particular purpose: *The upstairs bedroom is given over to her collection of antique dolls.* **2 give yourself over to sth** also **give your life over to sth** to spend all your time doing something: *You have to give yourself over to football if you want to be good at it.* **3** to give the responsibility for something or someone to a particular person, organization etc.: *His mother gave him over to his uncle's care when he was very small.*

give up *phr. v.*

1 STOP TRYING to stop trying to do something, especially something difficult, without completing it: *I looked everywhere for the keys – finally I just gave up.* | **give up doing sth** *Vladimir has given up trying to teach her Russian.* | **give up ↔ sth** *She refused to give up the search.*

2 STOP DOING to stop doing or having something, especially something that you do or have regularly SYN **quit**: **give sth ↔ up** *She gave up her job, and started writing full time.* | *Ed has given up his dream of becoming a professional athlete.* | **give up doing sth** *I gave up smoking when I got pregnant.*

3 I give up SPOKEN used when you do not know the answer to a question or joke: *"Why did the chicken cross the road?" "I give up. Why?"*

4 TO POLICE give sb up to allow yourself or someone else to be caught by the police or enemy soldiers: **give yourself up** *One of the men gave himself up to police on Thursday.*

5 LET SB HAVE give sb/sth ↔ up to let someone else have something that is yours: *She gave up her first child for adoption.* | **give sth up to sb** *Peggy gave up her seat to an old woman on the bus.*

6 GIVE TIME give up sth to agree to use your free time to do something else: *Carol has generously given up two evenings a week to help us on this project.*

7 give sb up for dead/lost etc. to believe that someone is dead and stop looking for them: *The ship sank and the crew was given up for dead.*

8 give it up (for sb) SPOKEN, INFORMAL to APPLAUD (=hit your open hands together) for someone: *Come on everybody, let's give it up for Elton John!*

give up on sb/sth *phr. v.* to stop hoping that someone or something will change or improve: *I'd been in trouble so many times that my teachers had given up on me.*

give yourself **up to** sth *phr. v.* LITERARY to allow yourself to feel an emotion completely without trying to control it: *She gave herself up to passion.*

give² *n.* [U] the ability of a material to bend or stretch when it is under pressure: *A climbing rope must **have** some **give** to it.*

ˌgive-and-ˈtake, give and take *n.* [U] a situation in which two people or groups are each willing to let the other have or do some of the things they want: *In every successful marriage there is a certain amount of give and take.*

give·a·way¹ /ˈgɪvəˌweɪ/ *n. plural* **giveaways** **1** [singular] something that makes it easy for you to guess something: *Vince was lying. His red face was a **dead giveaway**.* **2** [C] something that is given away for free, especially something that a store or bank gives its customers **3** [C] an act of giving something away: *Critics said the tax plan was a giveaway to the rich.*

giveaway² *adj.* [only before noun] **1** giveaway prices are extremely low **2** given away for free by a store, bank etc. as a way of advertising: *a giveaway calendar*

give·back /ˈgɪvbæk/ *n.* [C] a reduction of pay or other advantages that a union accepts for its members because the economic situation is bad or because they are given other advantages

giv·en¹ /ˈgɪvən/ *v.* the past participle of GIVE

given² *adj.* [only before noun] **1 any/a given...** any particular time, idea, thing etc. that is being used as an example: ***On any given** day, half the hospital beds are empty.* | **at any given time/moment etc.** *At any given moment, millions of people are connected to the Internet.* **2** previously arranged or agreed on: *Students prepare a speech on a given topic.* **3 be given to (doing) sth** to tend to do something, especially something that you should not do SYN **prone to**: *Some adults are still given to temper tantrums.*

given³ *prep.* used to say that something is not surprising when you consider the situation it happened in SYN **considering**: *Given the number of people we invited, I'm surprised so few came.* | **+that** *I think I did all right, given that I didn't study much.*

given⁴ *n.* **a given** a basic fact that you accept as being true: *Sandra will be at least 15 minutes late – that's a given.*

ˈgiven name *n.* [C] your FIRST NAME

giving /ˈgɪvɪŋ/ *adj.* kind, caring, and generous: *She's a very giving person.*

Giza

Gi·za /ˈgizə/ HISTORY a city in ancient Egypt on the west bank of the Nile, where the Great Pyramid and the Sphinx were built

giz·mo, gismo /ˈgɪzmoʊ/ *n. plural* **gizmos** [C] INFORMAL a GADGET

giz·zard /ˈgɪzɚd/ *n.* [C] BIOLOGY an organ near a bird's stomach that helps it break down food

gla·cial /ˈgleɪʃəl/ *adj.* **1** EARTH SCIENCE relating to ice or glaciers, or formed by glaciers: *a glacial valley* **2** a glacial look or expression is extremely unfriendly SYN **icy** **3** extremely slow: *Progress was being made, but at a **glacial pace**.* **4** extremely cold SYN **icy**: *a glacial wind* —**glacially** *adv.*

gla·ci·a·tion /ˌgleɪʃiˈeɪʃən, -si-/ *n.* [U] EARTH SCIENCE the process in which land is covered by glaciers, or the effect this process has

gla·cier /ˈgleɪʃɚ/ *n.* [C] EARTH SCIENCE a large mass of ice that moves slowly over an area of land

glad¹ /glæd/ *adj.* [no comparative] **1** [not before noun] happy or satisfied about something SYN **pleased**: **glad (that)** *We're really glad that you could come tonight.* | **glad to do sth** *I'm glad to be home.* | **glad to see/hear etc.** *I'm glad to hear that you're feeling better.* | **glad when** *We'll be glad when this is all over.* | **+for/about** *He's glad for the opportunity to practice his English.* ►see THESAURUS box at **happy** **2 be glad to do sth** to be willing to do something: *We'd be glad to send you any information you need.* | *"Can you give me a hand?" "Sure, **I'd be glad to.**"* **3 be glad of sth** OLD-FASHIONED to be grateful for something: *It was cold, and she was glad of her coat.* **4** making people feel happy: *It was a glad day for everyone.* **5 glad tidings** OLD-FASHIONED OR BIBLICAL good news **[Origin:** Old English *glæd* **bright, shining, happy]** → see also GLAD-HAND, GLADLY —**gladness** *n.* [U]

glad² *n.* [C] INFORMAL a GLADIOLUS

glad·den /ˈglædn/ *v.* [T] OLD-FASHIONED to make someone feel pleased and happy: *It **gladdens** my **heart** to see young people doing volunteer work.*

glade /gleɪd/ *n.* [C] LITERARY a small open space inside a forest → see also MEADOW

'glad-hand *v.* [I,T] to talk to or welcome people in a very friendly way, especially when this is not sincere: *Candidates were busy glad-handing voters.*

glad·i·a·tor /ˈglædiˌeɪtɚ/ *n.* [C] HISTORY a strong man who fought other men or animals as a public entertainment in ancient Rome —**gladiatorial** /ˌglædiəˈtɔriəl/ *adj.*

glad·i·o·lus /ˌglædiˈoʊləs/ also **glad·i·o·la** /ˌglædiˈoʊlə/ *n. plural* **gladioli** /-laɪ/ or **gladiolas** [C] a garden plant with long leaves and many brightly colored flowers that grow on a long stem

glad·ly /ˈglædli/ *adv.* **1** willingly or eagerly: *My parents would gladly loan us the money.* **2** happily: *"Here's Michelle!" he said gladly.*

'glad rags *n.* [plural] OLD-FASHIONED your best clothes that you wear for special occasions

Glad·stone, **Wil·liam Ew·art** /ˈglædstoʊn/, /ˈwɪlyəm ˈyuɚt/ (1809–1898) a British politician, who was Prime Minister four times (1868–1874, 1880–85, 1886, 1892–1894)

glam·or /ˈglæmɚ/ *n.* [U] another spelling of GLAMOUR

glam·or·ize /ˈglæməˌraɪz/ *v.* [T] to make something seem more attractive or exciting than it really is: *Hollywood has always glamorized drinking.* —**glamorization** /ˌglæmərəˈzeɪʃən/ *n.* [U]

glam·or·ous /ˈglæmərəs/ *adj.* attractive, exciting, and relating to wealth and success: *On television she looks so beautiful and glamorous.* | *glamorous clothes*

glam·our, **glamor** /ˈglæmɚ/ *n.* **1** [U] the attractive and exciting quality that is related to being rich and successful: *the movie industry's dazzle and glamour* | +**of** *the thrill and glamour of traveling the world* **2 a glamour girl/boy** someone who is young, attractive, and wears fashionable clothes [**Origin:** 1700–1800 Scottish English **magic**, from English *grammar*; because of an old association of knowledge with magic]

glance¹ /glæns/ *v.* [I always + adv./prep.] **1** to quickly look at someone or something: +**at/toward/up etc.** *He glanced at his watch.* | *Gary glanced over his shoulder.* ▸see THESAURUS box at **look¹** **2** to read something very quickly: +**at/over etc.** *Susan glanced at the menu.*

glance off *phr. v.* **1** to hit a surface at an angle and then move away from it in another direction: *The bullet glanced off the side of the car.* **2** if light glances off something, it flashes or shines back from it: *The beam of his flashlight glanced off something in the water.*

glance² *n.* **1** [C] an occasion when you look quickly at someone or something: *He **gave her a glance** as she walked by.* | *The sisters **exchanged glances** (=looked at each other quickly) and started to laugh.* | **take/shoot/throw a glance at sb** *She shot a glance at the man behind her.* **2 at a glance a)** in a short form that is easy to see or read quickly: *the football scores at a glance* **b)** as soon as you see or look at something: *I saw at a glance that something was wrong.* **3 at first glance** when you see or think about something for the first time: *At first glance, the paintings all look the same.*

glanc·ing /ˈglænsɪŋ/ *adj.* **1 a glancing blow** a hit that partly misses, so that it does not have its full force **2 glancing mention/treatment etc.** a short or indirect reference to someone or something —**glancingly** *adv.*

gland /glænd/ *n.* [C] BIOLOGY an organ of the body that produces a substance that the body needs, for example HORMONES, SWEAT, or SALIVA [**Origin:** 1600–1700 French *glande*, from Latin *glans* **acorn**] —**glandular** /ˈglændʒəlɚ/ *adj.*

glare¹ /glɛr/ *v.* [I] **1** to angrily look at someone or something for a long time: +**at** *Lilly just glared at me when I asked her what was wrong.* **2** [always + adv./prep.] to shine with such a strong light that it hurts your eyes: +**through/in/off** *Sunlight glared off the hood of the car.* [**Origin:** 1200–1300 Middle Low German *glaren* **to shine dully**]

glare² *n.* **1** [singular, U] a light that is too bright and hurts your eyes: *Polarized sunglasses reduce glare.* | +**of** *the glare of the sun* **2** [C] a long angry look: *She gave him an icy glare.* **3 the glare of publicity/the spotlight/media attention etc.** the full attention of newspapers, television etc., especially when you do not want it

'glare screen *n.* [C] a piece of glass that is put in front of a computer screen to protect your eyes from the strong light that comes from it

glar·ing /ˈglɛrɪŋ/ *adj.* **1** very bad and very easy to notice: SYN **obvious**: **a glaring mistake/error/omission etc.** *The report contained a number of glaring errors.* | *a **glaring example** of corruption* **2** too bright to look at: *the glaring sun*

glar·ing·ly /ˈglɛrɪŋli/ *adv.* in a way that is very clear and easy to notice: *Some of the clues were **glaringly obvious**.*

Glas·gow /ˈglæsgoʊ, ˈglæz-/ the largest city in Scotland

glas·nost /ˈglæznoʊst, ˈglɑz-/ *n.* [U] POLITICS the POLICY begun by Mikhail Gorbachev in the former U.S.S.R. during the 1980s that allowed discussion of the country's political, economic, and social problems [**Origin:** 1900–2000 a Russian word meaning **openness**, from *glas* **voice**]

G

glass /glæs/ S1 W1 *n.*

1 TRANSPARENT MATERIAL [U] a hard transparent material that is used for making windows, bottles etc.: *a glass bowl* | *a piece of broken glass* | *a new **pane of glass*** (=a flat piece of glass with straight edges) *for the window*

2 FOR DRINKING [C] a container without a handle used for drinking liquids, usually made out of glass: *wine glasses* | *She set down her empty glass.*

3 AMOUNT OF LIQUID [C] the amount of a drink contained in a glass: +**of** *a glass of milk*

4 FOR EYES glasses [plural] two pieces of specially cut glass or plastic in a FRAME, that you wear in front of your eyes to see more clearly SYN **eyeglasses** SYN **spectacles**: *I need **a new pair of glasses**.* | *He had dark hair and **wore glasses**.* | *As you get older, you may need **reading glasses**.* → see also DARK GLASSES, FIELD GLASSES, OPERA GLASSES, SUNGLASSES

5 GLASS OBJECTS [U] objects made of glass: *a collection of Venetian glass*

6 people (who live) in glass houses shouldn't throw stones used to say that you should not criticize someone for having a fault if you have the same fault yourself

7 MIRROR [C] OLD USE a mirror

[**Origin:** Old English *glæs*] → see also CUT GLASS, GROUND GLASS, LOOKING GLASS, MAGNIFYING GLASS, PLATE GLASS, **raise your glass (to sth)** at RAISE¹ (21), SPYGLASS, STAINED GLASS

Glass, **Phil·ip** /glæs/, /ˈfɪlɪp/ (1937–) a U.S. musician who writes modern CLASSICAL music and is known for his MINIMALIST style

glass·blow·er /ˈglæsˌbloʊɚ/ *n.* [C] someone who shapes hot glass by blowing air through a tube

ˌglass 'ceiling *n.* [singular] the attitudes and practices that prevent women or people from MINORITY groups from getting high level jobs, even though there are no actual laws or rules to stop them

glassed-in /ˌglæst ˈɪn◂/ *adj.* surrounded by a glass structure: *a glassed-in back porch*

glass·ful /ˈglæsfʊl/ *n.* [C] the amount of liquid a glass will hold

glass·ware /ˈglæswɛr/ *n.* [U] glass objects, especially ones that you drink from

glass·y /ˈglæsi/ *adj.* *comparative* **glassier**, *superlative* **glassiest** **1** smooth and shiny, like glass: *the glassy surface of the lake* **2** glassy eyes do not show any feeling or understanding, and are shiny SYN **expressionless**

ˌglassy-'eyed *adj.* having eyes that do not show any

expression, because you are tired, sick, or taking drugs: *Many of the students were glassy-eyed from studying all night.*

glau·co·ma /glaʊˈkoʊmə, glɔ-/ *n.* [U] MEDICINE an eye disease in which increased pressure inside your eye gradually makes you lose your ability to see

glaze¹ /gleɪz/ *v.* **1** [I] also **glaze over** if your eyes glaze over, they show no expression, usually because you are very bored or tired: *By the second chapter, your eyes begin to glaze.* **2** [T] to cover food with a liquid that gives it an attractive shiny surface: *The rolls are glazed with egg before they are baked.* **3** [T] to cover clay pots, bowls etc. with a thin liquid that is then dried in a very hot OVEN, in order to give them a shiny surface **4** [T] to cover something such as a road with a thin layer of ice: *Temperatures fell suddenly, glazing the highways.* **5** [T] to put glass into window frames in a house, door etc.

glaze² *n.* **1** [C,U] a liquid that is put on clay pots, bowls etc. and then dried in a hot OVEN, in order to give them a shiny surface **2** [C,U] a liquid that is put on food to give it an attractive shiny surface **3** [C] a thin layer of ice, for example on a road **4** [C,U] a transparent covering of oil paint spread over a painting

glazed /gleɪzd/ *adj.* **glazed look/eyes/expression etc.** if you have a glazed look, eyes etc., your eyes show no expression, usually because you are very bored or tired

gla·zier /ˈgleɪʒɚ, -ziɚ/ *n.* [C] someone whose job is to put glass into window frames

glaz·ing /ˈgleɪzɪŋ/ *n.* [U] glass that has been put into windows, or the activity of putting glass in windows

gleam¹ /glim/ *v.* [I] **1** to shine softly, especially because of being clean or polished: *The dining table gleamed in the candlelight.* | **+with** *The engine gleamed with oil.* ►see THESAURUS box at **shine¹** **2** if your eyes or face gleam, they show that something pleases you: **+with** *Her eyes gleamed with amusement.* —**gleaming** *adj.*

gleam² *n.* **1** [C usually singular] an emotion or expression that appears for a moment on someone's face: **+of** *a gleam of happiness on his face* | *There was a mischievous **gleam in her eye**.* **2** [C usually singular] the shiny quality that something has when light shines on it SYN **glint**: **+of** *a gleam of gold from his watch* **3** [C usually singular] a small pale light, especially one that shines for a short time SYN **glimmer**: **+of** *the gleam of a flashlight* **4 sth is (just) a gleam in sb's eye** SPOKEN used to say that at a particular time something is being planned or thought about, but does not yet exist: *Back then, CD-ROMs were just a gleam in the eye of some young engineer.* **5 sb was (just) a gleam in sb's father's/daddy's eye** SPOKEN used to say that at a particular time in the past someone was not yet born

glean /glin/ *v.* **1** [T] to find out information, even though this is difficult and takes time: **glean sth from sb/sth** *Several lessons can be gleaned from our experience so far.* **2** [I,T] to collect grain that has been left behind in a field after the crops have been cut SYN **gather**

glean·ings /ˈglinɪŋz/ *n.* [plural] **1** small pieces of information that you have found out, even though it was difficult **2** grain that is left behind in a field after the crops have been cut, which is then collected

glee /gli/ *n.* [U] a feeling of happy excitement and satisfaction, sometimes because something bad has happened to someone you do not like SYN **delight**: *The kids shouted **with glee** when they saw Santa.*

ˈglee club *n.* [C] a group of people who sing together for enjoyment

glee·ful /ˈglifəl/ *adj.* happily excited and satisfied, sometimes because something bad has happened to someone you do not like: *A gleeful grin crossed his face.* —**gleefully** *adv.*

glen /glɛn/ *n.* [C] LITERARY a deep narrow valley

Glenn /glɛn/**, John** (1921–) a U.S. ASTRONAUT who became the first American to make a journey in space in 1962

glib /glɪb/ *adj.* **1** said without thinking about all the problems in something, or about how your remarks will affect someone: *the lawyer's glib advice* **2** spoken easily and smoothly, but usually not sincerely, and without considering things carefully SYN **smooth-talking**: *a glib talk show host* —**glibly** *adv.*

glide¹ /glaɪd/ *v.* **1** [I always + adv./prep.] to move smoothly and quietly, as if no effort is being made: **+across/over etc.** *Sailboats glided across the lake.* ►see THESAURUS box at **slide¹** **2** [I] if a bird glides, it flies without moving its wings **3** [I always + adv./prep.,T] to fly without engine power, or to make something fly in this way: *The plane glided through heavy clouds.* **4** [I always + adv./prep.] to smoothly move from one subject, activity, song etc. to another without stopping: *The pianist glided easily into another song.* **5** [I always + adv./prep.] to do or achieve things easily: **+through** *He glided through his time in college.*

glide² *n.* [C] **1** a smooth, quiet movement that seems to take no effort **2** ENG. LANG. ARTS the act of moving from one musical note to another without a break in sound **3** ENG. LANG. ARTS a vowel sound which is made by moving your tongue from one position to another one, for example "i" /aɪ/ → see also DIPHTHONG

glid·er /ˈglaɪdɚ/ *n.* [C] a light airplane that flies without an engine

glid·ing /ˈglaɪdɪŋ/ *n.* [U] the sport of flying in a glider → see also HANG GLIDING

glim·mer¹ /ˈglɪmɚ/ *n.* [U] **1 a glimmer of hope/doubt/recognition** a small sign of hope, doubt etc.: *Rochester offers her a glimmer of hope for a better life.* **2** a light that does not shine very brightly SYN **gleam**: **+of** *the glimmer of a candle*

glimmer² *v.* [I] to shine weakly with a pale light

glim·mer·ing /ˈglɪmərɪŋ/ *n.* [C often plural] a small sign of something such as a thought or feeling: *the first glimmerings of democracy in the region*

glimpse¹ /glɪmps/ *n.* [C] **1** a quick look at someone or something that does not allow you to see them clearly: **get/catch a glimpse of** *Fans waited to catch a glimpse of their favorite stars.* | **brief/fleeting/quick glimpse** *We got a quick glimpse of the mountains before the clouds covered them again.* **2** a short experience of something that helps you begin to understand it: *a glimpse of what life was like for the early settlers*

glimpse² *v.* [T] **1** to see someone or something for a moment, without getting a complete view of them SYN **catch sight of sth**: *We glimpsed the coastline through the clouds.* ►see THESAURUS box at **see¹** **2** to begin to understand something for a moment: *He glimpsed the despair that she must have felt.*

glint¹ /glɪnt/ *v.* [I] **1** if something that is shiny or smooth glints, it flashes or throws back a small amount of light SYN **glitter**: *His badge glinted in the sun.* ►see THESAURUS box at **shine¹** **2** if your eyes glint, they shine and show an unfriendly feeling: *Derek's eyes glinted when he saw the money.* **3** if light glints off a surface, it shines back off it: **+off/on** *Sunlight glinted off the windows.*

glint² *n.* [C] **1** a small flash of light from a shiny surface: *the glint of his gold watch* **2** a look in someone's eyes that shows a particular emotion SYN **gleam**: *I saw the glint of hope in her eyes.*

glis·san·do /glɪˈsɑndoʊ/ *n.* [C] TECHNICAL a smooth series of musical notes that is played, for example, by sliding a finger rapidly over the keys of a piano —**glissando** *adj., adv.*

glis·ten /ˈglɪsən/ *v.* [I] to shine and look wet or oily: *the glistening wet streets* | **+with** *His chest glistened with sweat.*

glitch /glɪtʃ/ *n.* [C] **1** a small problem that prevents something from working or happening correctly: *Company records were lost due to a computer glitch.* **2** a sudden change or increase in the supply of electric power

glit·ter[1] /ˈglɪt̬ɚ/ *v.* [I] **1** to shine with a lot of small flashes of light [SYN] **sparkle**: *Fresh snow glittered in the morning light.* ►see THESAURUS box at **shine**[1] **2** if someone's eyes glitter, they shine brightly and show a particular strong emotion: +**with** *His eyes glittered with anger.*

glitter[2] *n.* [U] **1** a lot of small flashes of light [SYN] **sparkle**: *the glitter of her diamond necklace* **2** very small pieces of shiny plastic or metal that you glue onto paper, cards etc. for decoration **3** the exciting attractive quality of a place, way of life etc. that is related to rich, famous, or fashionable people: *the glitter of Hollywood* —**glittery** *adj.*

glit·te·ra·ti /ˌglɪt̬əˈrɑt̬i/ *n.* [plural] rich, famous, and fashionable people whose activities are often reported in newspapers and magazines

glit·ter·ing /ˈglɪt̬ərɪŋ/ *adj.* **1** giving off many small flashes of light [SYN] **sparkling**: *glittering jewels* **2** very successful: *a glittering career* **3** relating to rich, famous, or important people: *a glittering Hollywood premiere* —**glitteringly** *adv.*

glitz /glɪts/ *n.* [U] DISAPPROVING an exciting and attractive quality that something or someone rich, famous, or fashionable has: *show business glitz* —**glitzy** *adj.*

gloam·ing /ˈgloʊmɪŋ/ *n.* [U] **the gloaming** POETIC the time in the early evening when it is becoming dark [SYN] **dusk**

gloat /gloʊt/ *v.* [I] to show in an annoying way that you are proud of your success, or happy about someone else's failure: +**over** *Jason's still gloating over beating me at chess.*

glob /glɑb/ *n.* [C] INFORMAL a small amount of a soft substance or thick liquid, that has a round shape: *a glob of ketchup*

glob·al /ˈgloʊbəl/ [Ac] [W2] *adj.* **1** affecting the whole world, or relating to the whole world [SYN] **worldwide**: *a slowdown in the global economy* | *Climate change is a global problem which needs a global response.* **2** considering all parts of a problem or a situation together: *a global view of social problems such as poverty* **3** COMPUTERS affecting or relating to a whole computer system, program, or FILE: *a global search* —**globally** *adv.*

glob·al·i·za·tion /ˌgloʊbələˈzeɪʃən/ [Ac] *n.* [U] **1** the idea that the world is developing as a single economy and culture, as very large businesses become more powerful: *There have been mass protests about globalization.* **2** the process of making something such as a business operate in a lot of different countries all around the world, or the result of this: *the globalization of world markets* —**globalize** /ˈgloʊbəˌlaɪz/ *v.* [I,T]

ˌglobal ˈvillage *n.* [singular] an expression meaning the world, used to emphasize the way in which every part of the world is connected and each part depends on the other: *In today's global village, events in Japan or Kuwait affect everyone.*

ˌglobal ˈwarming *n.* [U] EARTH SCIENCE a general increase in world temperatures caused by increased amounts of CARBON DIOXIDE around the Earth → see also GREENHOUSE EFFECT, GREENHOUSE GAS

globe /gloʊb/ [Ac] [W3] *n.* [C] **1 the globe** the world: *Our company has offices all around the globe.* **2** a round object with a map of the Earth on it **3** an object shaped like a ball [SYN] **sphere** [**Origin:** 1500–1600 French, Latin *globus*]

globe·trot·ter /ˈgloʊbˌtrɑt̬ɚ/ *n.* [C] INFORMAL someone who spends a lot of their time traveling to many different countries —**globe-trotting** *adj.*

glob·u·lar /ˈglɑbyəlɚ/ *adj.* in the shape of a globule or a globe

glob·ule /ˈglɑbyul/ *n.* [C] a small round drop of a liquid or a melted substance [SYN] **glob**

glob·u·lin /ˈglɑbyəlɪn/ *n.* [U] TECHNICAL one of a type of PROTEINS that are found in blood, muscle, milk, and plants → see also GAMMA GLOBULIN

glock·en·spiel /ˈglɑkənˌspil, -ˌʃpil/ *n.* [C] a musical instrument consisting of many flat metal bars of different lengths, that you play with special hammers

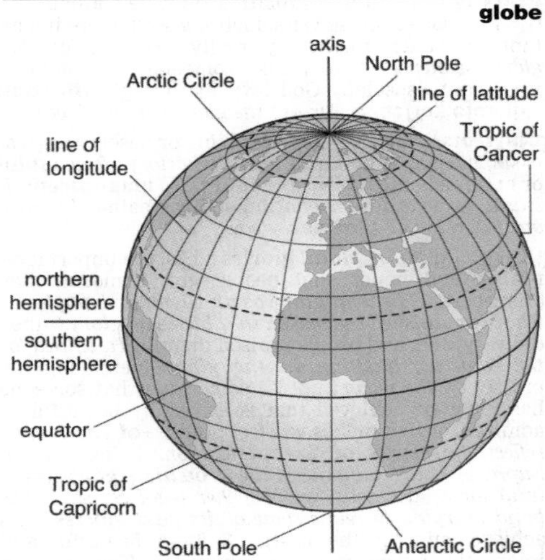

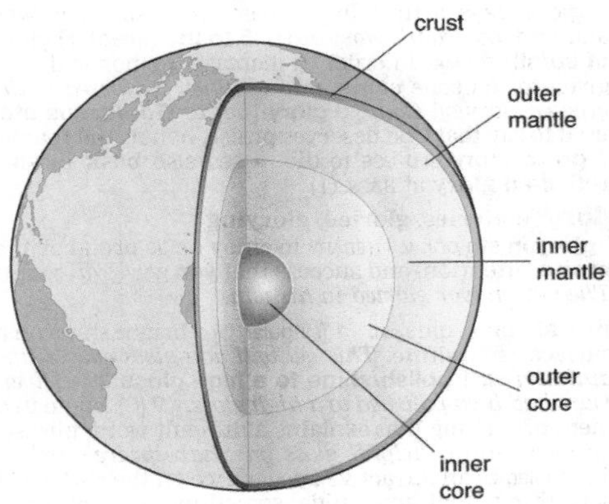

glom /glɑm/ *v.* **glommed, glomming** INFORMAL
glom onto sb/sth *phr. v.* **1** to become attached to someone or something so strongly that it is difficult to break the attachment: *The antibodies glom onto the virus and destroy it.* **2** to be very attracted to an idea, opinion, style etc.: *College students have glommed onto the new styles.*

gloom /glum/ *n.* [singular, U] **1** LITERARY darkness that you can hardly see through [SYN] **dimness**: *the dim gloom of the warehouse* **2** a feeling of great sadness and lack of hope: *a time of high unemployment and economic gloom*

gloom·y /ˈglumi/ *adj. comparative* **gloomier**, *superlative* **gloomiest** **1** making you feel sad because things will not improve [SYN] **depressing**: *a gloomy outlook for the future* | *a* ***gloomy picture*** *of the economy* **2** dark, especially in a way that makes you feel sad: *The woods were dark and gloomy.* **3** sad because you do not think a situation will improve [SYN] **depressed**: *the gloomy faces of the men* ►see THESAURUS box at **sad** —**gloomily** *adv.* —**gloominess** *n.* [U]

glop /glɑp/ *n.* [U] INFORMAL a thick soft wet mass of something, especially of something disgusting: *"What is this glop?" "Tuna casserole."* —**gloppy** *adj.*

glo·ri·fied /ˈglɔrəˌfaɪd/ *adj.* [only before noun] DISAPPROVING used when saying what something is really like, when other people try to make it seem more important: *Teachers are often treated like glorified baby-sitters.*

glo·ri·fy /ˈglɔrəˌfaɪ/ *v.* **glorifies, glorified, glorifying** [T] **1** to make someone or something seem more important or better than they really are: *movies that glorify violence* **2** to praise someone or something important, especially God SYN **exalt** —**glorification** /ˌglɔrəfəˈkeɪʃən/ *n.* [U]: +**of** *the glorification of war*

glo·ri·ous /ˈglɔriəs/ *adj.* **1** having or deserving great FAME, praise, or honor: *a glorious victory* **2** beautiful or extremely nice SYN **splendid** SYN **magnificent**: *It was a glorious day* (=beautiful sunny weather)*!* | *glorious fall colors* —**gloriously** *adv.*

glo·ry[1] /ˈglɔri/ *n. plural* **glories** **1** [U] the importance, praise, and honor that people give someone they admire: *At 19 he* ***won glory*** *as an Olympic champion.* | *The team finished the season* ***in a blaze of glory*** (=they did very well, and people praised them). | *He smiled for the cameras,* ***basking in the glory*** (=enjoying the praise) *of the victory.* **2** [C] something that someone has made or achieved that is especially beautiful or admired, or that makes you feel proud: +**of** *The designs reflect the glories of French fashion.* | *Becoming a Supreme Court judge was the* ***crowning glory*** (=the final most successful part) *of her legal career.* | *The band is trying to relive some of its* ***past glories*** (=its achievements in the past). **3** [U] a beautiful and impressive appearance SYN **splendor**: *They restored the Grand Theater to its* ***former glory***. | *The sun emerged from behind the clouds* ***in all its glory***. **4 glory days** a time in the past when someone was admired: *the team's glory days* **5 to the (greater) glory of sb/sth** FORMAL in order to increase the honor that is given to someone or something: *Bach composed to the greater glory of God.* **6 glory (be) to God/Jesus etc.** used to say that God deserves praise, honor, and thanks **7 go to glory** OLD USE to die → see also **bask in sb's reflected glory** at BASK (1)

glory[2] *v.* **glories, gloried, glorying**

glory in sth *phr. v.* LITERARY to enjoy or be proud of the praise, attention, and success that you get SYN **exult**: *The new mayor gloried in his win.*

gloss[1] /glɔs, glɑs/ *n.* **1** [singular, U] a bright shine on a surface SYN **shine**: *This gel will add gloss even to the dullest hair.* | **polish/shine to a high gloss** *The silverware had been polished to a high gloss.* **2** [C] a note in a piece of writing that explains a difficult word, phrase, or idea: +**on** *a helpful gloss on Shakespeare's sonnet* **3** [singular, U] an attractive appearance on the surface of something, that may hide something less pleasant SYN **façade**: *The regime held elections in October, giving itself a gloss of democracy.* **4 gloss finish/print/paint etc.** a surface, photograph, paint etc. that is shiny [**Origin:** (3–4) 1500–1600 Old French *glose*, from Latin *glossa* **unusual word that needs explaining**] → see also MATTE, LIP GLOSS

gloss[2] *v.* [T] to provide a note in a piece of writing, explaining a difficult word, phrase, or idea

gloss over sth *phr. v.* to deliberately avoid talking about something unpleasant, or say as little as possible about it: *The report glossed over the company's financial problems.*

glos·sa·ry /ˈglɔsəri, ˈglɑ-/ *n. plural* **glossaries** [C] a list of special words and explanations of what they mean, usually at the end of a book

gloss·y[1] /ˈglɔsi/ *adj. comparative* **glossier**, *superlative* **glossiest** **1** shiny and smooth SYN **shiny**: *her glossy black hair* **2 a glossy magazine/brochure etc.** a magazine etc. that is printed on good quality, shiny paper, usually with lots of color pictures **3** something is glossy if it is designed to look attractive or perfect, even though it is not really this way: *Film critics are calling the movie a glossy melodrama.* —**glossiness** *n.* [U]

glossy[2] *n. plural* **glossies** [C] a photograph printed on shiny paper: *an 8" by 10" glossy of the actor*

glot·tal stop /ˌglɑtl ˈstɑp/ *n.* [C] ENG. LANG. ARTS a speech sound made by completely closing and then opening your glottis, which in some forms of spoken English may take the place of a /t/ between vowel sounds or may be used before a vowel sound

glot·tis /ˈglɑṭɪs/ *n.* [C] BIOLOGY the space between your VOCAL CORDS. The opening and closing of this space helps produce the sound of your voice. —**glottal** *adj.*

gloves

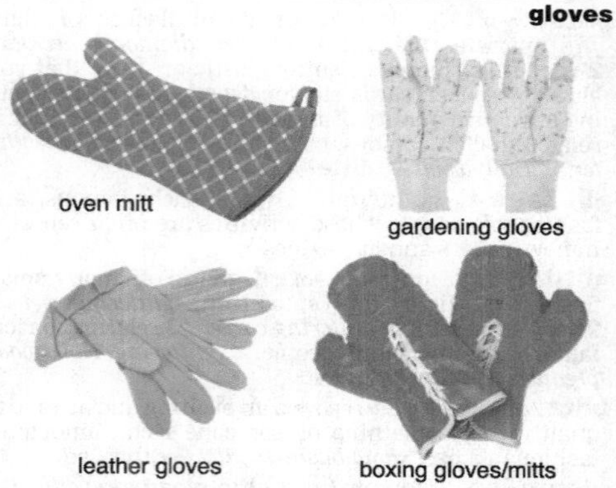

glove /glʌv/ S3 *n.* [C] **1** a piece of clothing worn on your hand, with separate parts to cover your thumb and each finger → see also MITTEN: *a* ***pair of*** *warm* ***gloves*** | **rubber/leather/latex etc. gloves** *Wear rubber gloves to protect your hands.* **2** a large leather glove used in BOXING, which does not have separate parts for your fingers **3** a large leather glove used to catch the ball in BASEBALL [**Origin:** Old English *glof*] → see also **fit like a glove** at FIT[1] (1)

ˈglove comˌpartment also **ˈglove box** *n.* [C] a small cupboard in a car in front of the passenger seat, where small things such as maps can be kept → see picture on page A36

gloved /glʌvd/ *adj.* wearing a glove or gloves

glow[1] /gloʊ/ *n.* [singular] **1** a soft steady light: *the golden glow of candlelight* | *the glow from the fire* **2** the bright color your face or body has because you are healthy, proud, or very happy: *Her skin had a* ***healthy glow***. **3** a strong feeling of pleasure, satisfaction etc.: **a glow of pride/satisfaction/pleasure etc.** *She felt a glow of pride in her daughter's achievement.* | *He* ***basked in the glow*** (=enjoyed the feeling of pleasure) *of his success.*

glow[2] *v.* [I] **1** to shine with, REFLECT, or produce a soft steady light SYN **shine**: *The church walls glowed in the candlelight.* ►see THESAURUS box at **shine**[1] **2** to look very happy because you feel proud, good etc.: *Evie laughed, and her eyes glowed.* | **glow with pride/joy/pleasure etc.** *Her parents were glowing with pride.* **3** if your face or body glows, it is pink or hot because you are healthy, have been doing exercise, or are feeling a strong emotion: *children* ***glowing with health*** **4 glow in the dark** if something glows in the dark, it produces a soft light in the dark → see also GLOW-IN-THE-DARK

glow·er /ˈglaʊɚ/ *v.* [I] to look at someone in an angry way SYN **glare**: +**at** *Mrs. Smith glowered at them disapprovingly.* —**gloweringly** *adv.*

glow·ing /ˈgloʊɪŋ/ *adj.* **1 glowing report/recommendation/description etc.** a report etc. that is full of praise: *The play has received glowing reviews.* **2 in glowing terms** using a lot of praise: *The two men speak of their friendship in glowing terms.* —**glowingly** *adv.*

ˌglow-in-the-ˈdark *adj.* **a glow-in-the-dark ring/ball/toy etc.** a glow-in-the-dark ring, ball etc. can be seen in the dark because it produces a soft light

glow·stick /ˈgloʊstɪk/ *n.* [C] a LIGHTSTICK

glow·worm /ˈgloʊwɚm/ *n.* [C] an insect that produces a small amount of light from its body

glu·cose /ˈglukoʊs/ *n.* [U] CHEMISTRY a natural form of sugar that exists in fruit [**Origin:** 1800–1900 French, Greek *gleukos* **sweet wine**]

glue¹ /glu/ *n.* [C,U] a sticky substance used for joining things together

glue² *v.* **gluing** or **glueing** [T] **1** to join two things together using glue: **glue sth (back) together** *The boards are glued together.* | *He glued the pieces back together.* | **glue sth to sth** *The shells are glued to the frame of the mirror.* ►see THESAURUS box at **fasten** **2** to join things together so that they are not easily separated or so that they work well together: **glue sth together** *Parts of different songs are glued together in a new arrangement.* **3 be glued to sth** INFORMAL **a)** to look at something with all your attention: *Americans were glued to their TVs during the televised trial.* **b)** to not move because you are very interested, surprised, frightened etc.: *We were glued to our chairs, listening.*

ˈglue ˌsniffing *n.* [U] the act or habit of breathing in dangerous gases from glues in order to produce a state of excitement or happiness —**glue sniffer** *n.* [C]

glu·ey /ˈglui/ *adj.* **1** sticky like glue **2** covered with glue

glum /glʌm/ *adj.* sad and quiet, especially because you are upset about something SYN **gloomy**: *Anna **looked glum**.* | *The place was full of glum men with no jobs.*

glut¹ /glʌt/ *n.* [C usually singular] a supply of something, especially a product or crop, that is more than is needed SYN **excess** OPP **shortage**: **+of** *a glut of new cars on the market*

glut² *v.* **glutted**, **glutting** [T] to make something have too much of something: **be glutted with sth** *They are flooding a **market** already **glutted with** beef.*

glu·ten /ˈglutˀn/ *n.* [U] a sticky PROTEIN substance that is found in wheat flour

glu·ti·nous /ˈglutˀn-əs/ *adj.* very sticky

glut·ton /ˈglʌtˀn/ *n.* [C] **1** someone who eats too much **2 a glutton for punishment** someone who seems to enjoy working hard or doing something that is not pleasant —**gluttonous** *adj.*

glut·ton·y /ˈglʌtˀn-i/ *n.* [U] FORMAL the bad habit of eating and drinking too much

glyc·er·in, **glycerine** /ˈglɪsərɪn/ *n.* [U] a thick colorless liquid used in soaps, medicines, explosives, and foods

glyc·er·ol /ˈglɪsəˌrɔl/ *n.* [U] TECHNICAL a chemical substance that is used to make foods sweeter and is used in products such as soap and explosives

gly·col·y·sis /glaɪˈkɑləsɪs/ *n.* [U] BIOLOGY the first stage of a chemical process in all living cells through which living creatures obtain energy from GLUCOSE (=natural form of sugar)

glyph /glɪf/ *n.* [C] a SYMBOL, especially one cut into stone

GMAT /ˈdʒi mæt/ *n.* [U] TRADEMARK **Graduate Management Admissions Test** a test that you take when you APPLY to study in a business program at a university after you have finished your first degree

GMO /ˌdʒi ɛm ˈoʊ/ *n.* [C] **genetically modified organism** a plant or other living thing whose GENES have been changed by scientists, especially in order to make it stronger, less likely to get diseases etc. —**GMO** *adj.* [only before noun] *GMO crops*

GMT /ˌdʒi ɛm ˈti/ *n.* [U] **Greenwich Mean Time** the time as measured at Greenwich in London, England, that is used as an international standard for measuring time

gnarled /nɑrld/ *adj.* **1** a gnarled tree or branch is rough and twisted **2** gnarled hands or fingers are twisted, rough, and difficult to move, usually because they are old

gnarl·y /ˈnɑrli/ *adj.* **1** a gnarly tree or branch is rough and twisted SYN **gnarled** **2** gnarly hands or fingers are twisted, rough, and difficult to move, usually because they are old SYN **gnarled** **3** SLANG a word meaning "very good" or "excellent," used by young people: *"Look at the size of that wave." "Gnarly!"* **4** SLANG a word meaning "very bad," used by young people: *a gnarly car wreck*

gnash /næʃ/ *v.* [T] LITERARY **gnash your teeth** to move your teeth against each other so that they make a noise, especially because you are unhappy or angry

gnat /næt/ *n.* [C] a small flying insect that bites

gnaw /nɔ/ *v.* [I always + adv./prep., T] to keep biting something hard SYN **chew**: *A rat had gnawed a hole in the box.* | **+away/at/on** *a puppy gnawing on a bone*

gnaw at sb *phr. v.* to make someone feel worried or frightened: *The thought of being fired gnawed at him all day.*

gnaw·ing /ˈnɔ-ɪŋ/ *adj.* [only before noun] worrying or painful, especially for a long time: *gnawing doubts*

gnome /noʊm/ *n.* [C] **1** a creature in children's stories who looks like a little old man and lives under the ground **2** a stone or plastic figure representing one of these creatures: *a garden gnome* **3** someone who helps decide financial plans in a country: *the gnomes who work in the U.S. Treasury*

gno·mic /ˈnoʊmɪk/ *adj.* gnomic remarks are short, intelligent, and difficult to understand

GNP /ˌdʒi ɛn ˈpi/ *n.* [singular] ECONOMICS the abbreviation of GROSS NATIONAL PRODUCT

gnu /nu/ *n.* [C] a WILDEBEEST

go¹ /goʊ/ S1 W1 *v.* **goes** /goʊz/, *past tense* **went** /wɛnt/ *past participle* **gone** /gɔn, gɑn/

1 MOVE/TRAVEL [I always + adv./prep.] to travel or move in a particular way, to a particular place, or for a particular distance: *Where are you going?* | **+to** *We're going to my parents' for Christmas.* | **+into/over/around etc.** *He went into his office.* | *The ball went over the wall.* | **+by/past** *Several cars went by very quickly.* | *I want to **go home**.* | **go by car/bus/plane etc.** (=use a car etc. to travel somewhere) | **go 10 miles/200 meters/a long way etc.** *He went a few yards then stopped.*

2 LEAVE SOMEWHERE [I] to leave the place where the speaker is in order to move to somewhere else SYN **leave**: *I wanted to go, but Anna wanted to stay.* | *Come on, Joe, it's time to go.* | **be/get going** *It's late – I should be going.*

3 a) VISIT past participle also **been** [I] to visit a place and then leave it: *Barcelona is beautiful – you should go there.* | *Nancy has gone to Paris* (=she is in Paris now). | *Luke has been to Moscow* (=he has visited Moscow in the past) *a few times.* | **+to** *Are you going to the museum this weekend?* | **go (to) see/visit** *I'll go visit Barbara when I'm in Los Angeles.* **b) go to the doctor/dentist/hospital etc.** to visit a doctor, dentist etc. for medical treatment: *You should go to the doctor if you still feel sick.*

4 be going to do sth a) to intend to do something: *I'm going to tell him what you said.* **b)** to be certain or expected to happen in the future: *It looks like it's going to rain.* → see also GONNA → see Word Choice box at WILL¹

5 ATTEND [I] to attend something such as a party, a concert, or a school: *There's a party tonight – do you want to go?* | **+to** *I used to go to concerts a lot.* | **go to school/college/church etc.** *She's not old enough to go to school.*

6 go shopping/swimming/fishing etc. to go somewhere in order to shop, swim etc.: *Let's go jogging tomorrow.*

7 go for a walk/swim etc. to spend time walking, swimming etc.: *Do you want to go for a walk along the river?*

8 go to jail/prison to be sent to jail or prison as punishment: *He went to prison for murder.*

9 DIRECTION [I always + adv./prep., not in progressive] if a road or path goes somewhere, it passes in that direction or leads to that place: **+to/up/along etc.** *Does this road go to the station?* | *A path goes through the middle of the forest.*

10 REACH [I always + adv./prep., not in progressive] to reach as far as a particular place: *The pond doesn't go very deep.* | **+to/from/down etc.** *This belt won't go around my waist.* | *The trees go right up to the beach.* ►see THESAURUS box at **reach**

11 BELONG/FIT [I always + adv./prep., not in progressive] to belong or fit in a particular place or position: *Where do*

G

these plates go? | +**in/under/on etc.** *The sofa can go against the wall.* | *I don't think all of this will go in the trunk.*

12 BE SENT [I] to be sent or passed on: +**to** *The email went to everyone in the company.* | +**by/through etc.** *The package was late because it had to go through customs.*

13 BECOME [linking verb] to become something different, especially something not as good, either naturally or by changing deliberately: **go bald/deaf/blind etc.** (=lose your hair, hearing, sight etc.) | **go red/white/brown etc.** *He went red with embarrassment.* | **go wild/crazy** *The crowd went wild.* | **go sour/bad** *The milk had gone sour.* | *The company **went bankrupt** last year.* ►see THESAURUS box at **become**

14 BE IN A STATE [linking verb] to be or remain in a particular state, especially a bad one: *The mother bird will often **go hungry*** (=have nothing to eat) *to keep her babies alive.* | **go unheard/unanswered/unnoticed etc.** *Unfortunately, his cries for help went unheard.* | **go barefoot/naked** *He usually goes barefoot around the house.*

15 HAPPEN [I always + adv./prep.] to happen or develop in a particular way: *How are your driving lessons going?* | **go well/fine/smoothly etc.** *The party went well.* | *Everything seems to **go wrong** for her.* | *Most of us are satisfied with **the way things are going** with the project.*

16 SONG/STORY [I always + adv./prep., T, not in progressive] to be said or sung in a particular way: *I don't exactly remember how the song goes.* | **the story/argument etc. goes that** *The story goes that he was poisoned by his wife.*

17 go running/laughing/crashing etc. to move in a particular way, or to do something as you are moving: *John went rushing down the hall.* | *The ball went flying over my head.*

18 BE SPENT [I] if money or time or another supply goes, it is spent or used up: *I don't know where all my money goes!* | *The food went really quickly.* | *Katherine is three already – the time goes so fast.* | +**on/for** *Half her salary goes on rent.* | +**toward** *The money will go toward a new clinic.*

19 MAKE A SOUND [T] to make a particular sound: *Cats go "meow."*

20 to go a) still remaining before something happens: *We have only two weeks to go before our trip to Hawaii!* **b)** still to be dealt with before you have finished what you are doing: *I have ten more pages to go until I'm finished with the book.* **c)** still to travel before you reach the place you are going to: *We still have five more miles to go.* **d)** if you buy food from a restaurant to go, you buy it to take away and eat at home or somewhere else: *I'll have a burger and fries to go, please.* → see also TAKEOUT

21 GET RID OF [I] if someone or something goes, you get rid of them: *Two hundred jobs will go at the factory.* | *This ugly old couch **has to go**.* | *"Do you want to keep these papers?" "No, they **can go**."*

22 WORK CORRECTLY [I] INFORMAL if a machine goes, it works in the way that it should: *I can't get the lawnmower to go.*

23 go out of your way to do sth to do something that you do not have to do and that involves making an effort: *They went out of their way to make me feel welcome.*

24 STOP WORKING [I] to become weaker or damaged and stop working correctly: *That lamp in the bathroom is about to go.* | *I think my hearing is **starting to go**.*

25 BE SOLD [I] to be sold: +**to** *The jewels will go to the highest bidder.* | +**for** *The painting should go for about $200.* | *I bought some mugs that **were going cheap*** (=were being sold at a low price).

26 START [I] to start doing something, especially after a wait or delay: *The builders are **ready to go**, but their boss hasn't arrived yet.* | *The party doesn't usually **get going** till after midnight.*

27 MAKE A MOVEMENT [I always + adv./prep.] to make a particular movement: *She went like this with her pen.* | +**up/down etc.** *All of the children's hands went up.*

28 BE GIVEN TO SB [I always + adv./prep.] to be given to someone as a prize or INHERITANCE: +**to** *Who will the Oscar go to?*

29 MATCH [I] to look or taste good together: *Do you think this goes?* | +**with** *Does red wine go with chicken?* | +**together** *Those colors don't go together well.*

30 DIE [I] to die: *When I go, this will all be yours.*

31 PAY MONEY [I] to be willing to pay an amount of money for something: *I can't go any higher than $500.*

SPOKEN PHRASES

32 how are things going?/how's it going?/how goes it? used to ask how someone's situation is or how things are developing, especially used as a greeting: *"Hey, Al, how's it going?" "Fine."*

33 go and do sth a) to go somewhere in order to do something: *I'll go and get the car for you.* **b)** to do something unexpected, and usually bad: *He went and sold the car without telling me.* | *Tom's really **gone and done it*** (=made a really big mistake) *this time.*

34 SAY [T] to say something: *Then she goes, "Sorry for interrupting your dinner."*

35 go (to the bathroom) to make waste come out of your body, especially to URINATE: *I drank three beers and now I really **have to go**.*

36 don't go doing sth used to tell someone not to do something, especially something that is wrong or bad: *It's a secret, so don't go telling everyone.*

37 sth (just) goes to show/prove used to say that something helps to prove that something is true: *It just goes to show, anything can happen in America.*

38 what sb says goes used to say that someone is in authority and other people must do as they say: *I'm in charge here and what I say goes.*

39 here/there sb goes (again) used when someone has annoyed you by continuing to do something they know you do not like: *There he goes again – telling those stupid jokes of his.*

40 not go there used to say that you do not want to talk or think about something: *"What if the two of them actually..." "**Don't even go there.**"* | *As for his personal hygiene problems – **let's not go there**.*

41 you go, girl! INFORMAL said to encourage a girl or a woman to continue doing or saying something you approve of

42 go do sth used to tell someone to go away when you are angry: *Go fly a kite!*

43 go (sb) one better to do something better than someone else had done it, or get something better than they have: *He bought a bike, so she went one better and got a car.*

44 go too far to go beyond the limits of what is reasonable or acceptable: *This time you've gone too far!*

45 go all out (to do sth) to try as hard as you can to do or get something: *The company will be going all out to improve sales.*

46 go all the way (with sb) INFORMAL to have sex with someone

47 go far to succeed in whatever you choose to do: *He's a very bright kid and he'll go far.*

48 not go far if an amount of money does not go far, you cannot buy much with it: *$20 dollars doesn't go as far as it used to.*

49 going, going, gone used to say something has been sold at an AUCTION

50 as sb/sth goes INFORMAL compared with the average person or thing of that type: *He's not bad, as politicians go.*

51 go it alone to do something, especially start a business, alone: *Sayles hasn't regretted his decision to go it alone as a filmmaker.*

[**Origin:** Old English *gan*] → see also **anything goes** at ANYTHING (7), GOING[1], GOING[2], GONE[2], **here goes (nothing)/here we go** at HERE[1] (17), **there goes sth** at THERE[2] (13), **there (you go)** at THERE[2] (9), **go to waste** at WASTE[1] (3) , **the way things are (going)** at WAY[1] (54)

go about sth *phr. v.* **1** to do something or begin working at something SYN **tackle**: *What's the best way to go about it?* | **go about (doing) sth** *The booklet explains how to go about making a will.* **2** to do something in the way that you usually do: *People were calmly **going about** their **business** as if nothing had happened.*

go after *phr. v.* **1 go after sb/sth** to follow or chase someone or something because you want to catch them: *Joe went after her to make sure she was OK.* **2 go after sth** to try to get something: *Several people were going after the same apartment.*

go against *phr. v.* **1 go against sth** if something goes against your beliefs, principles etc., it is opposite to them: *This goes against everything I believe in.* **2 go against sb/sth** to do the opposite of what someone wants or advises you to do: *Nobody ever dared go against her.* **3 go against sb** if a decision, judgment, vote etc. goes against you, you do not get the result you want: *The ruling went against us.*

go ahead *phr. v.* **1** SPOKEN said in order to politely give someone permission to do something, or to let someone speak first: *"Do you mind if I smoke?" "No, **go right ahead.**" | Go ahead, I'm listening.* **2** to do something that you have been planning or preparing to do: +**with** *They decided to go ahead with the wedding.* | **go ahead and do sth** *The newspaper decided to go ahead and publish the story.* **3** if something that has been planned goes ahead, it takes place: *Work on the new building will go ahead in May.* **4** to go somewhere before the other people in your group SYN **go on**: *You can go ahead and we'll catch up with you later.* | +**of** *He stood back to let Sue go ahead of him.*

go along *phr. v.* **1** to go with someone to a place or event: *They're going to a movie later, and I thought I might go along.* **2** if something is going along in a particular way, it is happening or progressing in that way: *Things were going along nicely.* **3 as sb goes along** if you do something as you go along, you do it without preparing or planning it: *I just made up the story as I went along.* **4** to continue with a plan, activity etc.: **go along doing sth** *I went along making the same mistake for weeks.*

go along with sb/sth *phr. v.* to agree with or support someone or something: *You'll never get Mom to go along with your idea.*

go around *phr. v.* **1 go around doing sth** if you go around doing something, especially something people do not approve of, you often do it: *You can't go around calling people liars.* **2 go around sth** to usually dress or behave in a particular way: *It's so embarrassing the way he goes around with his pants unzipped. | I can't believe how she goes around town in that funny hat.* **3 go around sth** if an illness, some news etc. is going around, it is being passed from one person to another: *There's a rumor going around the office that Randy's having an affair. | Last week, I had that stomach virus that's being going around.* **4 enough/plenty to go around** to be enough for everyone to have some: *There should be enough ice-cream bars to go around.* **5** to move in a circular way: *The wheels went around faster and faster.* → see also **go/run around in circles** at CIRCLE[1] (5) **6 what goes around comes around** an expression meaning that if you do something bad, something bad will happen to you some day

go at sth/sb *phr. v.* INFORMAL to attack someone or start to fight: *The two dogs went at each other as soon as I opened the gate. | The boxers **went at it** until officials pulled them apart.*

go away *phr. v.* **1** to leave a place or person: *Go away! Leave me alone!* **2** to leave to spend some time somewhere else, especially on vacation: *We're going away for seven days. | Dad used to **go away on business** a lot.* **3** if a problem, bad feeling etc. goes away, it disappears or does not happen any longer: *Has your headache gone away yet?*

go back *phr. v.* **1** to return to a place that you have just come from SYN **return**: *I think we ought to go back now.* | +**for** *I had to go back for my passport.* | +**to/into/out etc.** *It's cold out here – let's go back to the kitchen.* **2 go back a long way** also **go way back** INFORMAL if two people go back a long way, they have known each other for a long time: *Bill and I go back a long way.* **3** to have been made, built, or started at some time in the past SYN **date back**: *Their family history goes back to the 16th century.* **4 there's no going back** used to say it is impossible to return to the way things were before: *Once you've made the decision, I'm afraid there's no going back.*

go back on sth *phr. v.* to not do what you said you would do: *They went back on the agreement.* | **go back on your promise/word** *I have a hard time trusting Jack – he's gone back on his word too many times.*

go back over sth *phr. v.* **1** to examine or consider something again, especially in a thorough way so that you do not miss anything: *The jury went back over all the evidence.* **2** to repeat something again so that someone understands it

go back to *phr. v.* **1 go back to sth** to start to do something again that you were doing before, or that you used to do in the past SYN **return to**: *He went back to sleep.* | **go back to doing sth** *After they finished speaking, he went back to watching TV.* **2 go back to sth** to return to a situation or state that used to exist before something happened SYN **return to**: *Things soon went back to normal.* **3 go back to sth** to start talking about a subject again SYN **return to**: *Can we go back to your original point?* **4 go back to sb** if you go back to someone that you used to have a sexual relationship with, you start to have a relationship with them again: *He went back to his wife.*

go before *phr. v.* **1 go before sb/sth** if something goes before a judge, group of people in authority etc., they consider it before making a decision: *The case will go before the court next week* **2** to happen or exist before something else: *The new system is an improvement on what went before.*

go beyond sth *phr. v.* to be much better, worse, more serious etc. than something else: *Their relationship has gone beyond friendship.*

go by *phr. v.* **1** if time goes by, it passes: *The morning went by so slowly. | Things will get easier **as time goes by**.* **2 go by sth** to use the information or advice you get from a person, a book, a set of rules etc.: *Don't go by that old map – it's out of date. | Taylor is a tough, good cop who always **goes by the book*** (=obeys the rules very strictly). **3 go by sth** to use a particular name: *She goes by the name of Lara now.* **4 go by sth** to form an opinion or judgment of someone or something from something else: *You can't always go by appearances.*

go down *phr. v.*
1 BECOME LOWER to not be as expensive, high etc. as before: *The price of computers keeps going down. | The water level in the pool has gone down quite a bit.* | **go down in price/value** *Oil has gone down in price.*
2 MOVE ALONG **go down sth** to move along a street, path etc. in order to get somewhere: *Go down the street and turn right at the corner.*
3 GO SOMEWHERE NEARBY to go to a place near where you live: *I'm going down to the library.*
4 GO TO A LOWER PLACE to go to a lower place or a lower floor of a building: *Are you going down for lunch anytime soon?*
5 GO SOUTH to go to a place that is further south: +**to** *She went down to Mexico for the weekend.*
6 BECOME WORSE if something goes down, its quality or standard gets worse: *This neighborhood has really gone down in the last few years.* | **go down in sb's estimation/opinion** (=someone is respected less)
7 go down well/badly etc. to get a particular sort of reaction from someone: *Marsha's joke about Canadians didn't go down well at the party.*
8 SUN if the sun goes down, you cannot see it above the ground anymore, and it becomes night
9 SINK if a ship goes down, it sinks: *Ten men died when the ship went down.*
10 AIRPLANE if an airplane goes down, it suddenly falls to the ground
11 BECOME FLATTER to become less swollen or lose air: *Put some ice on your knee to make the swelling go down.*
12 BE REMEMBERED to be recorded or remembered in a particular way: +**as/in** *The talks went down as a landmark in the peace process. | This day will surely **go down in history*** (=be remembered for a long time).
13 COMPUTER to stop working for a short time: *My computer went down an hour ago.*
14 FOOD/DRINK to pass down your throat: *My throat was so sore that I couldn't get the pill to go down.*

G

15 **LIGHTS** if lights go down, they become less bright: *The lights went down and the curtain rose on an empty stage.*
16 **HAPPEN** INFORMAL to happen: *Nobody really knows what went down that day.*
17 **SPORTS** **a)** to lose a game or competition: *Chang went down to Sampras in the third set.* **b)** to move down to a lower position in an official list of teams or players: **+to** *Dallas has gone down to second place in the NFL.*

go for *phr. v.* **1 go for sth** to try to get or win something: *He is going for his second gold medal.* → see also **go for broke** at BROKE[2] (3) **2 go for it!** SPOKEN said when you want to encourage someone to do something **3 I could go for sth** SPOKEN used to say that you want to have something: *I could really go for a taco right now.* **4 that goes for sb/sth, too** also **the same goes for sb/sth** SPOKEN used to say that something is true about someone or something else: *Peter, you need to be quiet and listen, and that goes for you, too, Steve* (=Steve needs to be quiet and listen also). **5 go for sb/sth**SPOKEN to usually like a particular type of person or thing, or to usually choose a particular type of person or thing: *I tend to go for bright colored ties.* **6 have a lot going for you** also **have everything going for you** to have a lot of good features or qualities: *This town has a lot going for it.* **7 have nothing going for you** also **not have anything/much going for you, have very little going for you** to have no good features or qualities, or very few: *He's not rich or handsome – he has nothing going for him.*

go in for sth *phr. v.* **1** to like something or become interested in something: *Our family don't really go in for big formal meals.* **2** to get medical treatment at a hospital or CLINIC: *She's gone in for some tests.*

go in with sb *phr. v.* to join someone in a business relationship: *Ellie's going in with a friend who's just started a café.*

go into sth *phr. v.*
1 **JOB** to enter a particular profession or business: *Vivian wants to go into politics.* | *I might* ***go into business*** (=begin a business) *with Brian.*
2 **GO TO WORK** to go to work: *Are you going into work today?*
3 **ENTER A STATE OR CONDITION** to start being in a particular state or condition: *Severe pain can make you faint or go into shock.* | *The family* ***went*** *deeper and deeper* ***into debt.***
4 **TIME/MONEY/EFFORT** to be used in order make something work or happen: *It's obvious that a lot of money has gone into this house.*
5 **DISCUSS** to explain, describe, or talk about something in detail: *I don't want to go into the matter now.* | *Clare wouldn't* ***go into details*** *about her divorce.*
6 **HIT** if a vehicle goes into a tree, wall, or another vehicle, it hits it: *The driver lost control and went into the median.*
7 **BEGIN A MOVEMENT** if someone or something goes into a particular movement, they start to do it: *The plane went into a steep descent.*
8 **BE INCLUDED** to be used in something you are making or preparing: *Most of the ingredients that go into this recipe are easy to obtain.*
9 **DIVIDE** INFORMAL if a number goes into another number, the second number can be divided by the first: *12 goes into 60 five times.*
10 **COMPUTER** to open a particular computer program or file

go off *phr. v.*
1 **LEAVE** to leave a place, especially in order to do sth: *You shouldn't go off on your own like that.*
2 **EXPLODE** to explode: *Fireworks went off all over the city last night.*
3 **GUN** if a gun goes off, it fires: *The gun went off accidentally.*
4 **ALARM** to make a loud noise: *I overslept because my alarm clock didn't go off.*
5 **STOP WORKING** if a machine goes off, it stops working: *Suddenly, all the lights went off.*
6 **go off well/badly etc.** to happen in a particular way: *We hope the party goes off well.*
7 **LINE/ROAD** if a line, road, path etc. goes off another one, it separates from it and goes in a different direction

go off on sb/sth *phr. v.* INFORMAL to show your anger at someone or about something by saying what you really think: *Lisa called him a bad name, so Brett just went off on her.*

go off with sb/sth *phr. v.* INFORMAL **1** to leave your husband, wife, partner etc. in order to have a relationship with someone else: *She's gone off with her husband's best friend.* **2** to take something away from a place without having permission: *Apparently someone's gone off with my notebook.*

go on *phr. v.*
1 **CONTINUE AN ACTION** to continue happening or doing something without stopping or changing: **+with** *I just want to go on with my life and forget the whole experience.* | **go on doing sth** *We can't go on fighting like this.* | *Sometimes I feel that* ***I can't go on.***
2 **CONTINUE TALKING** to continue talking, especially after stopping or changing to a different subject: *Go on, I'm listening.* | **+with** *After a pause Maria went on with her story.* | **go on to do sth** *He went on to explain why he had left his job.*
3 **CONTINUE TRAVELING** to continue traveling or moving toward a place or in a particular direction: *They went on until they reached Morocco.* | **+to** *We're stopping in Chicago and then going on to New York.*
4 **DO STH NEXT** to do something after you have finished doing something else: **+to** *When you've finished, go on to question 5.* | **go on to do sth** *She went on to write several children's books.*
5 **HAPPEN** to take place or happen: *I thought that there was something suspicious going on.* | ***What's going on*** *in there?* | *She didn't really understand* ***what was going on.*** | **+with** *What's going on with Seth?* → see also GOINGS-ON
6 **BEGIN TO WORK** if a machine goes on, it begins to operate: *Our coffeemaker is set to go on at 7 a.m.*
7 **USE AS PROOF** **go on sth** to base an opinion or judgment on something: *Police* ***don't have much to go on*** *in their hunt for the killer.*
8 **TIME** to pass: *As time went on, I began to like him more.*
9 **BE ALMOST** **be going on sth** to be nearly a time, age, number etc.: *It's going on 10 o'clock.* | *Jenny's 16 going on 70* (=she behaves older than she is).
10 **MEDICINE** **go on sth** to begin to take a type of medicine: *Dani's too young to* ***go on the pill.***
11 **GO IN FRONT OF** to go somewhere before the other people you are with SYN go ahead: *You go on – don't wait for me.* | **+ahead** *Dad told me to go on ahead and he would meet me at the restaurant.*
12 **TALK TOO MUCH** INFORMAL to talk or complain too much: **+about** *I wish you'd stop going on about my haircut.* | *Grandpa* ***went on and on*** *about how good he was at golf.*
13 **go on** SPOKEN used to encourage someone to do something: *Go on, have another cookie.*

go out *phr. v.*
1 **LEAVE A BUILDING/ROOM ETC.** to leave a building room etc. in order to go somewhere else: *She got up and went out.*
2 **FOR ENTERTAINMENT** to leave your house, especially in order to enjoy yourself: *Are you going out tonight?* | **go out doing sth** *She goes out partying every weekend.* | **go out and do sth** *Can I go out and play now?* | **go out for dinner/lunch etc.** *We went out for dinner a couple of times.*
3 **WITH BOY/GIRL** to have a romantic relationship with someone: *They've been going out for six months.* | **+with** *Leah's still going out with Colin.*
4 **FIRE/LIGHT** to stop burning or shining: *Our campfire went out while we were sleeping.*
5 **go out like a light** INFORMAL to go to sleep very quickly: *As soon as his head hit the pillow, he went out like a light.*
6 **TIDE** if the tide goes out, the water at the edge of the

ocean goes back to its lower level OPP come in: *The tide's going out.*
7 STOP BEING FASHIONABLE to stop being fashionable or popular: *Haircuts like that went out in the 1990s.* | **go out of style/fashion** *Leisure suits went of out style over 30 years ago.*
8 our heart/thoughts/sympathies go out to sb used to say that you have a lot of sympathy for someone else: *Our hearts go out to the victim's family.*
9 TRAVEL to travel to a place that is far away, in order to live there: *I'm going out to Malysia to set up a new branch.*
10 MAKE PUBLIC to be sent or told to people: *An appeal went out for food and medicines.*
11 go out and do sth to do something, even though it is difficult and needs a lot of effort: *We're going to go out and win the championship.*
12 TIME LITERARY to end: *Spring went out with a bang.*
go out of sb/sth *phr. v.* if a fun or lively quality goes out of someone or something, they lose that quality: *All the fun had gone out of the game.*
go over *phr. v.*
1 GO NEAR SB/STH to go nearer to someone or something: *Brad went over and got a drink.* | **+to** *We went over to the man to ask for directions.* | **go over to do sth** *I think I'll go over to thank them for the gift.*
2 EXAMINE **go over sth** to look at something or think about something carefully: *The jury spent hours going over all the evidence.*
3 SEARCH **go over sth** to search something or a place very carefully: *Investigators have gone over every square inch of the area looking for clues.*
4 REPEAT STH **go over sth** to read, say, or think about something again in order to learn it, understand it, or explain it: *I keep going over what happened in my mind.* | *Could you go over the instructions one more time?*
5 go over well/badly etc. if a speech, performance, type of behavior etc. goes over well, badly etc., people like it, do not like it etc.: *Her presentation went over well.*
6 CLEAN to clean something: *You need to go over the floor with a damp mop.*
go over to *phr. v.* **1 go over to sth** to change to a new belief, religion, habit, job etc.: *One of the Democratic senators has gone over to the Republicans.* **2 go over to sb/sth** to change from being broadcast from one person or place to being broadcast from another person or place: *Now we'll go over to Bryant in Atlanta.*
go through *phr. v.*
1 SUFFER **go through sth** to suffer or experience something bad: *She's been through a lot this year.*
2 EXPERIENCE **go through sth** to experience a period or process: *Japan went through a period of rapid economic growth.*
3 LOOK AT/FOR STH **go through sth** to look at or for something carefully: *I went through all of our closets and I still can't find my tennis racket.*
4 READ CAREFULLY **go through sth** to carefully read something and check it: *Go through your work and check your spelling.*
5 EXPLAIN **go through sth** to talk about all the details of something to someone, in order to make sure that they understand it: *Do you want me to go through the main points again?*
6 USE ALL OF STH **go through sth** to use something and have none left: *We went through a quart of milk today.*
7 sth goes through sb's mind/head used to say that someone thinks about something: *The thought went through my mind that she might be lying.*
8 LAW **go through sth** if a law goes through or goes through a LEGISLATIVE institution, it is officially accepted: *Everyone expects this bill to go through Congress quickly.*
9 BE APPROVED OFFICIALLY if a deal or agreement goes through, it is officially accepted: *Did the loan go through?*
10 PRACTICE STH **go through sth** to practice something, for example for a performance: *Let's go through the song one more time.*
go through with sth *phr. v.* to do something you had promised or planned to do, even though it causes problems or you are not sure you want to do it anymore: *Rich said he didn't want to go through with the wedding.*
go to sth *phr. v.* **1 go to great lengths/pains** also **go to a lot of trouble/effort** to use a lot of effort to get something or to do something: *Your dad went to a lot of trouble to get you these baseball cards.* **2 go to sleep/war etc.** to begin sleeping, fighting a war etc.: *Shh! The baby's trying to go to sleep.* **3 go to great expense** to spend a lot of money for something or to do something: *Some people go to great expense to decorate their homes.*
go together *phr. v.* **1** if two things go together, they exist together or are connected in some way: *Drug abuse and mental illness often go together.* **2** if two people are going together, they are having a romantic relationship
go under *phr. v.* **1** if a business goes under, it has serious problems and fails: *Paul's roofing business went under last year.* **2** if a ship or something that is floating goes under, it sinks beneath the surface: *The Titanic finally went under.* **3** to become unconscious because you have been given a drug
go up *phr. v.*
1 INCREASE to increase in number or amount: *The price of gas continues to go up.* | **+by** *Unemployment went up by 1.5%.*
2 MOVE NEAR SB/STH to move near to someone or something: *I went up and said "Hi."*
3 GO TO A HIGHER PLACE to go to a higher position or a higher floor in a building: *I'll just go up and check on the kids.*
4 BE BUILT to be built: *The new civic center went up last month.*
5 EXPLODE/BURN to explode or be destroyed in a fire: *The factory **went up in flames** before the firemen arrived.* → see also **go up in smoke** at SMOKE[1] (4)
6 TRAVEL NORTH to travel to a place that is further north: **+to** *He goes up to Canada each summer.*
7 LIGHTS if lights go up, they become brighter: *The lights went up at the end of the performance.*
8 SHOUT if a shout or a CHEER goes up, people start to shout or CHEER
go with *phr. v.* **1 go with sth** to be included as part of something: *The company car goes with the job.* **2 go with sth** to choose something or choose to do something: *I think I'll go with the green tie instead.* **3 go with sb** to have someone as your BOYFRIEND or GIRLFRIEND
go without *phr. v.* **1 go without sth** to be able to live without something or without doing something: *He had gone without sleep for two days.* **2 it goes without saying** used to say that something is understood by everyone and that it does not need to be said: *It goes without saying that he has no talent.*

go² S3 *n.* **1 make a go of sth** INFORMAL to try to make a business, marriage etc. succeed: *They both want to make a go of their relationship.* | *His family believes he can **make a go of it** in the computer business.* **2 on the go** INFORMAL very busy or working all the time: *My kids keep me always on the go.* **3** [singular] INFORMAL an attempt to do something: *He's going to **have a go at** the role of Romeo.* | *I've never skied before, but I'd like to **give it a go**.* **4** [C] someone's turn in a game: *It's your go.* **5** [U] a Japanese game that is played by two players, one with black pieces and the other with white pieces **6 sth is a go** SPOKEN used to say that things are working correctly, or that you have permission to do something: *I just got word from our boss, and the trip to London is a go.* **7 sth is (a) no go** SPOKEN used to say that something has not happened or that it will not happen: *I asked for a raise but it was a no go.* **8 all systems are go** SPOKEN used to say that everything is working the way that it should **9 in/at one go** at the same time: *It would be good to finish all the work at one go.* → see also GET-UP-AND-GO

goad¹ /goʊd/ *v.* [T] **1** to make someone do something by annoying them or encouraging them until they do it: **goad sb into (doing) sth** *Several boys surrounded* *him and goaded him into a fight.* | **goad sb on** *They goaded him on with insults.* **2** to push animals ahead of you with a sharp stick

goad² *n.* [C] **1** a sharp stick for making animals, especially cattle, move forward **2** something that forces someone to do something

'go-ahead¹ *n.* **the go-ahead** permission to do something: *The council is expected to **give the go-ahead** next week.* | *We are confident that the project will **get the go-ahead**.*

go-ahead² *adj.* **a go-ahead goal/touchdown/basket etc.** a go-ahead goal, touchdown etc. in sports is one that puts a team ahead in points in a game: *He scored the go-ahead run on an error by the first baseman.*

goal /goʊl/ Ac S2 W1 *n.* [C] **1** something that you hope to achieve in the future SYN **aim**: *We are all working toward a common goal.* | **+of** *We have set ourselves a goal of raising $100,000.* | **sb's/sth's goal is to do sth** *Our goal is to stop the spread of AIDS.* | **achieve/reach a goal** *Our division reached its sales goal for the month.* | *I try to **set goals** for myself every day.* | *My **long-term goal** is to make a million dollars by my 40th birthday.* ▶see THESAURUS box at **purpose¹** **2** the action of making the ball go into a particular area to win a point in games such as football or SOCCER, or the point won by doing this: *the game's winning goal* | *Ronaldo **scored** three **goals** for Brazil.* **3** the area between two posts where the ball must go for a point to be won [**Origin:** 1500–1600 *gol* **limit, boundary** (1300–1400)]

G

goal·ie /'goʊli/ *n.* [C] INFORMAL a GOALKEEPER

goal·keep·er /'goʊl,kipɚ/ *n.* [C] the player on a sports team who tries to stop the ball from going into his team's goal

'goal line *n.* [C] a line that marks the end of a playing area, where the goal is placed

goal·mouth /'goʊlmaʊθ/ *n.* [C] the area directly in front of the GOAL

goal·post /'goʊlpoʊst/ *n.* [C usually plural] one of the two posts, with a bar along the top or across the middle, that form the GOAL in games such as football or SOCCER

goal·ten·der /'goʊl,tɛndɚ/ *n.* [C] a GOALKEEPER

goat /goʊt/ *n.* [C] **1** BIOLOGY an animal that has horns on top of its head and long hair under its chin, and that can climb steep hills and rocks **2 get sb's goat** SPOKEN to make someone very angry or annoyed: *Relax – don't let him get your goat.* **3 old goat** INFORMAL an old man who is not nice, especially one who annoys women in a sexual way [**Origin:** Old English *gat*] → see also BILLY GOAT

goat·ee /goʊ'ti/ *n.* [C] a small pointed BEARD on the end of a man's chin

goat·herd /'goʊthɚd/ *n.* [C] someone who takes care of a group of goats

goat·skin /'goʊt,skɪn/ *n.* **1** [C,U] leather made from the skin of a goat, or a wine container made from this **2** [C] the skin of a goat

gob /gɑb/ *n.* [C] INFORMAL **1** a mass of something wet and sticky: **+of** *a gob of gum under the chair* **2 gobs** [plural] INFORMAL a large amount of something: **+of** *The Johnsons must have gobs of money.* [**Origin:** 1300–1400 Old French *gobe* **large piece of food**]

gob·bet /'gɑbɪt/ *n.* [C] OLD USE a small piece of something, especially food

gob·ble /'gɑbəl/ *v.* INFORMAL **1** [I,T] also **gobble up** to eat something very quickly or in a way that people do not consider polite: *We gobbled up all of the cake in one evening.* **2** [T] also **gobble up** to use a supply of something quickly: *Housing costs gobble up almost half of our budget.* **3** [I] to make a sound like a TURKEY —**gobble** *n.* [C]

gob·ble·dy·gook, gobbledegook /'gɑbəldi,guk/ *n.* [U] INFORMAL complicated language that seems to have no meaning, especially language used in an official document

gob·bler /'gɑblɚ/ *n.* [C] INFORMAL a male TURKEY

'go-be,tween *n.* [C] someone who takes messages from one person or group to another, because the two sides cannot meet or do not wish to meet: **act/serve as a go-between** *It has been agreed that a United Nations representative will act as a go-between for leaders of the two countries.*

Go·bi Des·ert, the /,goʊbi 'dɛzɚt/ also **the Gobi** one of the largest deserts in the world. It is partly in northern China and partly in Mongolia.

gob·let /'gɑblɪt/ *n.* [C] a cup made of glass or metal, with a base and a long stem but no handle

'gob·let ,cell *n.* [C] BIOLOGY a type of cell in the stomach, INTESTINES, and lungs that produces MUCUS

gob·lin /'gɑblɪn/ *n.* [C] a small ugly creature in children's stories that likes to trick people

'go-cart *n.* [C] a small car made of an open frame on four wheels, that people race for fun

god /gɑd/ S1 W1 *n.* **1 God** [singular, not with the] the spirit or BEING whom Christians, Jews, and Muslims believe created the universe, and to whom they pray: *Do you **believe in God**?* | *I put my faith in God.* | *We believe the bible is the Word of God.* | *If it is the Will of God, you cannot stop it.* **2** [C] a male spirit or BEING who is believed to control the world or part of it, or who represents a particular quality: **+of** *the Hindu god of destruction* | **a Greek/Roman/Norse god** *Mars was the Roman god of war.* → see also GODDESS

THESAURUS

deity/divinity a god or goddess
idol an image or object that people pray to as a god

3 [C] someone who is admired very much: *To his fans he is a god.* **4 play God** to behave as though you have the power to do whatever you like: *more and more people are beginning to think that geneticists are playing God.* **5 God's gift to sb/sth** someone who thinks they are perfect or extremely attractive: *John thinks he's God's gift to women.*

SPOKEN PHRASES

6 I swear/hope/pray etc. to God used to emphasize that you promise, hope etc. that something is true or that something happens: *I hope to God that she'll make it home safely.* **7 honest to God** used to emphasize that you are not lying or joking: *Honest to God, I didn't tell her!* **8 God forbid (that)** used when you very much hope that something will not happen: *God forbid anything should happen to her.* **9 God help sb** used when you think that something bad is going to happen or that someone is in a bad situation: *God help you if you spill anything on the carpet.* **10 God bless (you)** used to say that you hope someone will be safe and happy, used especially when you are saying goodbye: *Good night and God bless.* **11 God willing** used to say that you hope there will be no problems: *God willing, the war will end soon.* **12 God rest his/her soul** OLD-FASHIONED used to show respect when speaking about someone who is dead

13 the gods [plural] the force that some people believe controls their lives, bringing them good or bad luck: *The gods are against me!* **14** [C] something to which you give too much importance or respect: *Money was his god.* [**Origin:** Old English] → see also **act of God** at ACT¹ (9), **by the grace of God** at GRACE¹ (5), **so help me (God)** at HELP¹ (10), **thank God/goodness/heavens** at THANK (3)

GRAMMAR

God is not used with *the*: *I pray to God* (NOT *the God*) *every night.*

Go·dard /goʊ'dɑr/, **Jean-Luc** /ʒɑn luk/ (1930–) a French movie writer and DIRECTOR who is known for using new and unusual methods of making films

ˌgod-'awful, God-awful, godawful *adj.* [only before noun] INFORMAL very bad or annoying: *What is that god-awful smell?*

god·child /ˈɡɑdtʃaɪld/ *n. plural* **godchildren** /-ˌtʃɪldrən/ [C] a child that a GODPARENT promises to help and to teach Christian values to

God·dard /ˈɡɑdəd/**, Rob·ert** /ˈrɑbət/ (1882–1945) a U.S. scientist who developed the first ROCKET that used liquid fuel

god·daugh·ter /ˈɡɑdˌdɔtə/ *n.* [C] a girl that a GODPARENT promises to help and to teach Christian values to

god·dess /ˈɡɑdɪs/ *n.* [C] **1** a female spirit or BEING who is believed to control the world or part of it, or represents a particular quality: **+of** *Aphrodite, the Greek goddess of love* **2** a woman who is admired very much → see also GOD, SEX GODDESS

god·fa·ther /ˈɡɑdˌfɑðə/ *n.* [C] **1** a man who promises to help a child and to teach him or her Christian values **2** INFORMAL the head of a criminal organization or MAFIA group

'God-ˌfearing *adj.* OLD-FASHIONED leading a good life and following the rules of the Christian religion: *God-fearing Christians*

god·for·sak·en, Godforsaken /ˈɡɑdfəˌseɪkən/ *adj.* a godforsaken place is far away from where people live and contains nothing interesting, attractive, or cheerful in it: *How can you live in this godforsaken place?*

'God-ˌgiven *adj.* received from God: *She has a God-given talent for singing.* | *The cowboys think it's their* ***God-given right*** *to carry a gun.*

God·head /ˈɡɑdhɛd/ *n.* **the Godhead** FORMAL a word that Christians use to mean the Father, the Son, and the Holy Spirit, whom they consider to be one God in three parts

god·hood, Godhood /ˈɡɑdhʊd/ *n.* [U] the quality or state of being God or a god

god·less /ˈɡɑdlɪs/ *adj.* OLD-FASHIONED not showing respect for God or not having a belief in a god: *godless Communists* —**godlessly** *adv.*

god·like /ˈɡɑdlaɪk/ *adj.* having a quality like God or a god: *godlike heroes*

god·ly /ˈɡɑdli/ *adj.* OLD-FASHIONED obeying God and leading a good life —**godliness** *n.* [U]

god·moth·er /ˈɡɑdˌmʌðə/ *n.* [C] a woman who promises to help a child, and to teach him or her Christian values

god·par·ent /ˈɡɑdˌpɛrənt/ *n.* [C] someone who promises to help a child, and to teach him or her Christian values

god·send /ˈɡɑdsɛnd/ *n.* [singular] something good that happens to you when you really need it: *The good weather has been a real godsend for construction companies.*

god·son /ˈɡɑdsʌn/ *n.* [C] a boy that a godparent promises to help and to teach Christian values to

god·speed, Godspeed /ˌɡɑdˈspid/ *n.* [U] OLD USE used to wish someone good luck, especially before a trip

-goer /ɡoʊə/ *suffix* [in nouns] **movie-goer/concert-goer/theater-goer etc.** someone who goes to movies, concerts etc.

Goe·the /ˈɡəṭə/**, Jo·hann Wolf·gang von** /ˈyoʊhɑn ˈwʊlfɡɑŋ vɑn/ (1749–1832) a German poet, scientist, and writer of plays and NOVELS

go·fer /ˈɡoʊfə/ *n.* [C] INFORMAL someone who carries messages or gets or takes things for their employer

ˌgo-'getter *n.* [C] someone who is likely to be successful because they are very determined and have a lot of energy: *She's a real go-getter.*

gog·gle /ˈɡɑɡəl/ *v.* **goggled, goggling** [I] to look at something with your eyes wide open in surprise or shock: **+at** *Everyone in the class was goggling at us as if we were freaks.*

ˌgoggle-'eyed *adj.* with your eyes wide open because you are surprised or shocked

goggles

ski goggles

swimming goggles

gog·gles /ˈɡɑɡəlz/ *n.* [plural] something that protects your eyes, made of glass or plastic with a rubber or plastic edge that fits against your skin: *safety goggles*

'go-go *adj.* INFORMAL **1** a go-go period of time is one in which prices and salaries increase very quickly: *the go-go 1980s* **2** go-go STOCKS increase in value very quickly in a short period of time, but are risky

'go-go ˌdancer *n.* [C] someone who dances with sexy movements in a bar or NIGHTCLUB —**go-go dancing** *n.* [U]

Go·gol /ˈɡoʊɡəl, -ɡɔl/**, Nik·o·lai** /ˈnɪkəˌlaɪ/ (1809-1852) a Russian writer of plays and NOVELS

go·ing¹ /ˈɡoʊɪŋ/ *n.* [U] **1 rough/hard/heavy etc. going** the difficulty or speed with which something is done: *The first two years of their marriage were tough going.* | *I'm getting the work done, but it's slow going.* | *We climbed the mountain in three hours, which was pretty good going.* **2** the act of leaving a place SYN **departure**: *His going will be no great loss to the company.* **3 when the going gets tough, the tough get going** used for saying that in difficult situations the best people will make more effort to succeed and will not stop trying **4 while the going's good** before someone stops you from doing what you want or before something becomes difficult: *Let's get out while the going's good.* → see also **sb's comings and goings** at COMING¹ (2)

going² *adj.* **1 the going rate/price/salary etc.** the usual cost of a service or job: **+for** *Thirty dollars an hour is the going rate for a math tutor.* **2 the best/fastest/cheapest etc. sth going** INFORMAL the best, fastest etc. thing of a particular kind that is available or able to be found: *We think we make the best computers going.* **3 a going concern** a business that is making a profit and is expected to continue to do so

-going /ɡoʊɪŋ/ *suffix* [in adjectives] **theater-going/church-going/movie-going etc.** regularly attending the theater, church etc.: *the theater-going public*

ˌgoing-'over *n.* [singular] INFORMAL a thorough examination of something to make sure it is all right: *Our lawyers will* ***give*** *the contract* ***a good going-over****.*

ˌgoings-'on *n.* [plural] activities or events that are strange or interesting, especially ones that involve something illegal: *He was shocked at some of the strange goings-on in the house.*

goi·ter /ˈɡɔɪṭə/ *n.* [C,U] a disease of the THYROID GLAND that makes your neck very swollen

gold¹ /ɡoʊld/ S3 W2 *n.* **1** [U] SYMBOL **Au** CHEMISTRY a valuable soft yellow metal that is an ELEMENT and is used for making coins, jewelry etc.: *an ounce of gold* | **pure/solid gold** *a statue made of solid gold* | **9/18/22/24 etc. carat gold** *beautiful earrings in 18 carat gold* → see also **strike gold/oil etc.** at STRIKE¹ (14) **2** [U] coins, jewelry etc. made of this metal **3** [C,U] the color of this metal: *The flag's colors are red, gold, and blue.* **4** [C,U] INFORMAL a GOLD MEDAL: *He* ***won the gold*** *in the 100-meter dash.* | *She'll be* ***going for gold*** *in the 50-meter breast stroke.* [**Origin:** Old English] → see also **have a heart of gold** at HEART (32)

gold² S3 W2 *adj.* **1** made of gold: *a gold necklace*

2 having the color of gold: *gold nail polish* → see also GOLDEN

Gold·berg /ˈgoʊldbɚg/, **Rube** /rub/ (1883–1970) a U.S. artist famous for his CARTOONS of strange and extremely complicated machines that are designed to do very simple jobs

gold·brick /ˈgoʊldˌbrɪk/ also **gold·brick·er** /ˈgoʊldˌbrɪkɚ/ *n.* [C] INFORMAL, DISAPPROVING someone who stays away from their work, and especially using the false excuse that they are sick —**goldbrick** *v.* [I]

ˈgold card *n.* [C] a special CREDIT CARD that gives you additional advantages or services, such as a high spending limit

ˈgold ˌdigger *n.* [C] **1** SLANG a woman who tries to attract rich men in order to get their money **2** OLD-FASHIONED someone who dug for gold in past times

ˈgold dust *n.* [U] gold in the form of a fine powder

gold·en /ˈgoʊldən/ W2 *adj.* **1** having a bright rich yellow color, like gold: *golden sunlight* | *golden hair* **2** made of gold: *a golden statue* **3 a golden opportunity** a good chance to get something valuable or to be very successful: *The trip presented a golden opportunity to improve my Spanish.* **4 sb is golden** SPOKEN, INFORMAL used to say that someone is in a very good situation: *If the right editor looks at your article, you're golden.* **5 sb's/the golden years** old age: *I want to enjoy my golden years.* **6 sb's/the golden boy/girl** someone who is popular and successful: *She's Hollywood's current golden girl.*

G

ˈgolden age *n.* [usually singular] the time when something was at its best: *the golden age of radio*

ˌgolden anniˈversary *n.* [C] the date that is exactly 50 years after the beginning of something, especially a marriage → see also DIAMOND ANNIVERSARY

ˌgolden ˈbrown *adj.* a light brown color: *Bake the cookies until they're golden brown.*

ˌgolden ˈeagle *n.* [C] BIOLOGY a large light brown bird that lives in northern parts of the world

ˌGolden ˈGate, the an area of water on the western coast of the U.S. that connects San Francisco Bay in California with the Pacific Ocean. It is crossed by the Golden Gate Bridge.

ˌgolden ˈhandcuffs *n.* [plural] INFORMAL something that companies give to important EMPLOYEES to make them less likely to leave their job for a different one, because they will not make as much money or receive as many advantages: *Stock options are used as golden handcuffs to keep executives with the company.*

ˌgolden ˈhandshake *n.* [C] a large amount of money given to someone when they leave their job

ˌgolden ˈoldie *n.* [C] a song, movie etc. which is old but is still liked by many people: *The radio station plays golden oldies.*

ˌgolden ˈparachute *n.* [C] part of a business person's contract that states that they will be paid a large amount of money when their contract ends or when they leave the company

ˌgolden ˈraisin *n.* [C] a RAISIN made from white GRAPES

ˌgolden ˈratio also **ˌgolden ˈmean** *n.* [C] MATH the RATIO (=relationship) of the length of a golden rectangle to its width, equal to about 1.62

ˌgolden ˈrectangle *n.* [C] MATH a RECTANGLE that can be divided into a square and a rectangle that is SIMILAR (=with the same relationship between the side lengths) to the original rectangle

ˌgolden reˈtriever *n.* [C] a large dog with light brown fur, especially used for hunting

gold·en·rod /ˈgoʊldənˌrɑd/ *n.* **1** [C] a plant with small yellow flowers **2** [U] a yellow-orange color

ˌgolden ˈrule *n.* [usually singular] **1 the Golden Rule** a principle which states that you should treat others as you want them to treat you **2** a very important principle, way of behaving etc. that should be remembered: *My golden rule of cooking is to use only fresh ingredients.*

gold·field /ˈgoʊldfild/ *n.* [C usually plural] an area of land where gold can be found

gold·finch /ˈgoʊldˌfɪntʃ/ *n.* [C] BIOLOGY a small singing bird with yellow feathers on its wings

gold·fish /ˈgoʊldˌfɪʃ/ *n.* [C] BIOLOGY a small shiny orange fish often kept as a pet

ˈgoldfish ˌbowl *n.* [C] **1** a round glass bowl in which fish are kept as pets **2 live in a goldfish bowl** to be in a situation in which people can know everything about your life: *Living in small towns can be like living in a goldfish bowl.*

Gold·ing /ˈgoʊldɪŋ/, **William** (1911–1993) a British writer of NOVELS

ˌgold ˈleaf *n.* [U] gold in extremely thin sheets that is used to cover things such as picture frames for decoration

Gold·man /ˈgoʊldmən/, **Em·ma** /ˈɛmə/ (1869–1940) a U.S. political writer, speaker and organizer, born in Lithuania, who was an ANARCHIST, supported BIRTH CONTROL, and opposed military CONSCRIPTION

ˌgold ˈmedal *n.* [C] a prize made of gold that is given to someone for a special achievement, especially for winning a race or competition: *He won a gold medal in volleyball.* → see also BRONZE MEDAL, SILVER MEDAL

ˌgold ˈmedalist *n.* [C] someone who has won a gold medal

gold·mine /ˈgoʊldmaɪn/ *n.* [C] **1** INFORMAL a business or activity that produces large profits: *His printing business has turned out to be a real goldmine.* **2** a deep hole or system of holes under the ground from which rock containing gold is taken **3 be sitting on a goldmine** to own something very valuable, especially without realizing this

ˌgold ˈplate *n.* [U] **1** a layer of gold on top of another metal **2** dishes, spoons etc. made of or covered with gold —**gold-plated** *adj.*: *Is it solid gold or gold-plated?*

ˌgold-ˈrimmed *adj.* having a gold edge or border: *gold-rimmed glasses*

ˈgold rush *n.* [C] a situation when a lot of people hurry to a place where gold has just been discovered: *the California gold rush*

gold·smith /ˈgoʊldˌsmɪθ/ *n.* [C] someone who makes things out of gold

ˈgold ˌstandard *n.* **1 the gold standard** the use of the value of gold as a standard on which the value of money is based **2 the gold standard of sth** something that is very good and used as a standard against which everything else or everyone else of the same type is compared: *The university considers itself to be the gold standard of education in this country.*

Gold·wyn /ˈgoʊldwɪn/, **Samuel** (1882–1974) a U.S. movie PRODUCER, born in Poland, who started the company that became MGM and had an important part in the development of the Hollywood movie industry

go·lem /ˈgoʊləm/ *n.* [C] a creature in Jewish stories that is made of dirt and brought to life by using magic

golf /gɑlf, gɔlf/ S3 W3 *n.* [U] a game in which the players hit a small white ball into holes in the ground with a set of golf clubs: *He **plays golf** on Sundays.* | ***a round of golf*** (=a complete game of golf) —**golfer** *n.* [C]

ˈgolf ball *n.* [C] a small hard white ball used in the game of golf

ˈgolf cart *n.* [C] a small vehicle that people use to drive around a golf course when they are playing golf

ˈgolf club *n.* [C] **1** a long wooden or metal stick used for hitting the ball in the game of golf **2** an organization of people who play golf, or the land and buildings where a golf course is

ˈgolf course *n.* [C] an area of land that golf is played on

golf·ing /ˈgɑlfɪŋ/ *n.* [U] the activity of playing golf: *Holt loves to **go golfing**.*

ˈgolf links *n.* [plural] a golf course SYN links

Go·li·ath /gəˈlaɪəθ/ *n.* **1** in the Bible, a GIANT (=a very big strong man) who was killed by a boy who later became King David **2 goliath** [C] a person or organization that is very large and powerful: *How can a small* *computer company compete with the goliaths of the industry?*

gol·ly /ˈgɑli/ *interjection* OLD-FASHIONED said when you are surprised

-gon /gɑn, gən/ *suffix* [in nouns] a shape with a particular number of sides and angles: *a hexagon* (=with six sides) | *a polygon* (=with many sides)

go·nad /ˈgoʊnæd/ *n.* [C] BIOLOGY the male or female sex organ in which the SPERM or eggs are produced

gon·do·la /ˈgɑndələ, gɑnˈdoʊlə/ *n.* [C] **1** a long narrow boat with a flat bottom and high points at each end, used on the CANALS in Venice in Italy **2** the enclosed part of a CABLE CAR where the passengers sit **3** the place where passengers sit that hangs beneath an AIRSHIP or HOT-AIR BALLOON [**Origin:** 1500–1600 Italian]

gon·do·lier /ˌgɑndəˈlɪr/ *n.* [C] a man who rows a gondola in Venice

gone¹ /gɔn, gɑn/ *v.* the past participle of GO¹

gone² *adj.* [not before noun] **1** no longer in a particular place: *I turned around for my bag and it was gone.* | *She was* ***long gone*** *by the time I got home.* **2** absent for a period of time: *How long will you be gone?* **3** no longer in existence: *Many of the old houses are gone now.* | *Kids used to be able to play safely in the streets, but* ***those days are gone.*** **4 all gone** completely used up, eaten, or drunk: *Are there any cookies left?" "No, they're all gone."* **5** dead: *Now that his wife is gone, he doesn't get out very much.* **6** INFORMAL unconscious or unable to think normally, because of the effect of alcohol or drugs, or because you are very tired: *Look at Michelle – she's totally gone!*

gon·er /ˈgɔnɚ/ *n.* [C] INFORMAL someone who will soon die, or who is in a bad situation and will definitely fail: *When one of the plane's engines went out, I thought I was a goner.*

gong /gɔŋ, gɑŋ/ *n.* [C] a round piece of metal that hangs in a frame and is hit with a stick to make a loud sound, especially as a signal

gon·na /ˈgɔnə, gənə/ NONSTANDARD a written form of the spoken short form of "going to": *What are you gonna do this weekend?*

gon·or·rhe·a /ˌgɑnəˈriə/ *n.* [U] MEDICINE a disease of the sex organs that is passed on during sex

gon·zo jour·nal·ism /ˈgɑnzoʊ ˌdʒɚnl-ɪzəm/ *n.* [U] INFORMAL reporting in newspapers that is concerned with shocking or exciting the reader and not with giving true information —**gonzo journalist** *n.* [C]

goo /gu/ *n.* [U] INFORMAL **1** a disgusting sticky substance: *My shoes were covered in oily goo.* **2** words or feelings that are too emotional or romantic → see also GOOEY

goo·ber /ˈgubɚ/ *n.* [C] INFORMAL **1** also **ˈgoober pea** a PEANUT **2** a stupid person

good¹ /gʊd/ S1 W1 *adj. comparative* **better**, *superlative* **best**

1 OF A HIGH STANDARD of a high standard or quality OPP **bad**: *a good hotel* | *a really good book* | *Terry's always been a good father to Denise.* | *My French is better than my Spanish.* | *I bought the best big-screen TV I could find.* | *a* ***good quality*** *car* | *Your work's simply* ***not good enough.***

THESAURUS

great ESPECIALLY SPOKEN very good: *That's a great idea!*
excellent very good: *The play was excellent.*
wonderful very good: *a wonderful place for a picnic*
fantastic extremely good: *The movie's special effects were fantastic.*
superb extremely good: *a superb performance*
outstanding very good, and better than other people or things: *an award for outstanding teaching*
exceptional unusually good: *Ruth's an exceptional student.*
first-class good and of very high quality: *He's a first-class player.*
ace INFORMAL very good: *an ace guitarist*
→ BAD

2 SKILLFUL able to do something well OPP **bad**: *Andrea is a good cook.* | **+at** *Alex is very good at languages.* | *She's good at making friends.* | **+with** *Mona is good with children.*

3 NICE enjoyable and pleasant: *good weather* | *Have a good weekend!* | *We really* ***had a good time*** *in Mexico.* | **be good to do sth** *It's good to see you again.* → see also **good/big etc. old** at OLD (9)

4 LOOK/TASTE/SMELL ETC. looking, tasting, smelling, or feeling attractive or pleasant: *Her new haircut looks really good.* | *Mm, that tastes good.* | *It* ***feels good to*** *lie down.*

5 APPROPRIATE a) useful or appropriate for a particular purpose OPP **bad**: *Today's a good day for going to the beach.* | **be good for (doing) sth** *Aluminum or steel pans are best for baking.* **b)** convenient for someone OPP **bad**: **be good for sb** *Ten o'clock is good for me.* | **a good time/place etc. to do sth** *Is this a good time to talk?*

6 HAVING A POSITIVE EFFECT needed and having a positive effect on someone or something OPP **bad**: **+for** *The publicity has been good for business.* | *That's* ***good news!***

7 MAKING YOU HEALTHY likely to improve your physical or mental health: **be good for sb** *Eating junk food all the time isn't good for you.*

8 HEALTHY healthy OPP **bad**: *You don't look so good. You should go home.* | *He'll* ***feel better*** *in the morning.*

9 HAPPY happy, pleased, or satisfied OPP **bad**: ***I feel*** *really good about what we've accomplished.* | *She's in a* ***good mood*** *this morning.*

10 EFFECTIVE likely to give the result that you want OPP **bad**: *The best thing you can do is wait here.* | *What's the best way to do this?* | *What a* ***good idea!*** | *He gave me some* ***good advice.***

11 WELL-BEHAVED well-behaved, used especially about a child: *Be a good boy and eat your vegetables.* | *She's the author of five books on good manners.* | *Both children* ***were on*** *their* ***best behavior*** (=they were deliberately behaving well).

12 CORRECT correct or true SYN **accurate**: *a good guess* | *I* ***have*** *a pretty* ***good idea*** *of what it will be like.*

13 IN SATISFACTORY CONDITION in a satisfactory condition for use; not broken, damaged etc. OPP **bad**: *Are these batteries still good?* | **in good shape/condition** *The car's still in pretty good shape.* | *There, now the table is* ***as good as new*** (=fixed so that it looks new again). | **sb's good arm/leg/eye** (=the arm, leg, or eye that has not been injured or damaged)

14 SENSIBLE sensible or useful: *John has very good judgment.* | *The best reason to visit in wintertime is the lack of tourists.*

15 ABLE TO BE USED able to be used for a particular period of time: **+for** *The warranty for my stereo is good for one year.*

16 KIND kind and concerned about what other people need or want: **+about** *Ann's been really good about the whole thing.* | **+to** *Mrs. Russell has always been good to me.* | **good of sb (to do sth)** *It was good of her to offer us a ride home.*

17 a good friend someone who you know very well and like very much: *The two girls are* ***best friends.***

18 MORALLY RIGHT morally right in what someone believes or does OPP **bad**: *a good woman* | *Mr. Amos lived a good life.* | *That's my* ***good deed*** (=something you do to help someone) *for the day.* | *He was trying to portray himself as* ***the good guy.***

19 LARGE/LONG large in amount, area, or range: *I'd walked a good distance that day.* | *a good selection of desserts* | *The bedrooms are all good size.* | *They've been gone* ***a good while*** (=a long time). | **a good number/amount of sth** *There were a good number of empty seats.*

20 COMPLETE complete and thorough: *The dog definitely needs a good bath.* | ***Take a good look at*** *this picture.*

21 RESPECTABLE [only before noun] respected or having a high position in a society, or used by people like this: *She comes from a very good family.* | *They thought she wasn't good enough for their son.*

22 as good as almost: *He's as good as admitted it.* | **as good as done/finished etc.** *The work is as good as*

G

finished. | **as good as dead/ruined/useless etc.** *The carpet's as good as ruined.*

23 LIKELY TO HAPPEN likely to happen SYN **strong** OPP **poor**: *There's a good chance of rain tomorrow.*

24 BELIEVABLE likely to be believed or persuade people: *You'd better have a good explanation for being late.*

25 SPORTS a ball that is good in a game such as tennis falls within the allowed playing area

SPOKEN PHRASES

26 good a) said to show that you are pleased that something has happened or is done: *Good. I'm glad that's finished.* | *"I got an A in Biology." "**Oh, good.**"* **b)** said to tell someone that you think their work or what they are doing is of a high quality or standard: *"Is the answer five?" "Good! That's right."*

27 good idea/point/question etc. said when someone says or suggests something interesting or important that you had not thought of before: *Uh, good question. I'll have to find out for you.*

28 good luck said to tell someone that you hope that they will be successful, or that something good will happen to them: *Good luck on your job interview tomorrow.*

29 that's good said to show that you approve of something: *"We're going to buy a house." "Oh, that's good!"*

30 good for sb said to show that you approve of or are pleased with what someone has done or decided: *"I made the team!" "Good for you!"*

31 it's a good thing (that) said when you are glad something has happened, because there would have been problems if it had not happened: *It's a good thing you remembered to bring napkins.*

32 all good things must come to an end used to say that something pleasant, enjoyable, or lucky ended or will have to end

33 good grief/Lord/heavens/gracious! said to express surprise, anger, or other strong feelings: *Good grief! I forgot my keys again.*

34 have a good one! used to say goodbye and wish someone a nice day

35 good enough said when you are satisfied with something: *"Is that okay?" "Yeah, good enough."*

36 as good a time/place etc. as any said to show that although a time etc. is not perfect, there will not be a better one: *Well, I suppose this is as good a spot as any to set up camp.*

37 that's a good one said to tell someone that you do not believe something they have said and think it is a joke or a trick: *You won $50,000? Boy, that's a good one!*

38 (what a) good girl/boy/dog etc. said to tell a child or animal that it has behaved well or done something well: *You picked up all of your toys. What a good boy!*

39 good and ready completely prepared and willing to do something: *Don't rush me! I'll call her when I'm good and ready.*

40 be good for a laugh to be enjoyable or amusing: *Let's go watch Brent play volleyball. That'll be good for a laugh.*

41 all in good time said when someone wants you to hurry but you are not going to: *"When are you going to pay me?" "All in good time."*

42 if you know what's good for you used to threaten someone and to say that something bad will happen to them if they do not do something: *If you know what's good for you, you'll do what I tell you.*

43 it's all good SLANG used to say that a situation is good or acceptable, or not a problem: *Don't worry about it, man – it's all good.*

44 be good to go to be ready to do something: *I've got my shoes on and I'm good to go.*

45 would you be good enough to do sth also **would you be so good as to do sth** OLD-FASHIONED used to ask someone very politely to do something: *Would you be good enough to get my glasses for me?*

46 a good three miles/ten years etc. at least three miles, ten years etc., and probably more: *He's a good ten years younger than her.*

47 be good for another three years/hundred miles etc. something that is good for a particular length of time will probably be able to be used for that length of time: *This old truck is good for another 100,000 miles.*

48 the good old days the good times in the past: *We talked for hours about the good old days.*

49 a good many INFORMAL a fairly large number of people or things: *A good many people are upset about the new gas tax.*

50 too much of a good thing no longer pleasant or enjoyable because you have too much of something or it continues for too long: *Spending an entire month at the beach was too much of a good thing.*

51 be too good for sb if someone is too good for someone, they have a better character than the other person: *Why is Kate going out with him? She's too good for him.*

52 good old John/Karen etc. used to praise someone, especially because they have behaved in the way that you would expect them to: *Good old Jake! I knew he'd come.*

53 be too good to be true also **be too good to last** INFORMAL to seem to be so good that you think something must be wrong, or expect something bad to happen: *"She found out he was married." "I knew he was too good to be true!"*

54 in sb's own good time INFORMAL someone who does something in their own good time does it when they are ready, not when other people want them to do it

55 good for nothing INFORMAL someone or something that is good for nothing is completely useless and worthless → see also GOOD-FOR-NOTHING

56 be in sb's good graces/books INFORMAL if you are in someone's good graces or books, they like you or approve of you more than they usually do: *He's trying to get back in his wife's good graces.*

57 give as good as you get INFORMAL to react to someone who attacks or harms you by attacking or harming them in a way that is equally strong

58 have a good thing going to be doing something that is successful: *They've got a good thing going with that little business of theirs.*

59 be as good as your word to keep your promise

60 be good for a meal/a few drinks etc. INFORMAL to be likely to give someone something: *My uncle should be good for a few bucks.*

61 a good word for sb/sth a favorable remark about someone or something: *Stacey **put in a good word for me** at her company, so I might get a job there.*

62 the good life a simple, natural way of living

[**Origin:** Old English *god*] → see also **a great/good deal** at DEAL[1] (2), **so far so good** at FAR[1] (15), **while the going's good** at GOING[1] (4), **for good measure** at MEASURE[1] (7), **pay good money for sth** at MONEY (12), **be onto a good thing** at ONTO (5), **that's/it's (all) well and good** at WELL[3] (3)

WORD CHOICE **good, well**

Use **good** as an adjective to talk about the quality of someone or something: *She's a good singer.* Use **well** as an adverb to talk about the way that something is done: *She sings very well.* In spoken English, **good** is sometimes used as an adverb instead of **well**: *You did good.* However, many people think this is incorrect English.

good[2] S3 W2 *n.*

1 ADVANTAGE something that improves a situation or gives you an advantage: *It'll **do you good** (=make you feel better) to have a vacation.* | ***For his own good**, I told him he was completely wrong.* | **do/cause more harm than good** *Having the tumor removed may do more harm than good.* | *He's **too ambitious for his own good** (=his ambition may cause him problems rather than being an advantage).* | *Drunk-driving laws were made for **the common good** (=the advantage of everyone in society).* → see also **do sb a world of good** at WORLD[1] (14)

2 no good/not any good/not much good a) not very skillful or of a very high quality SYN **bad**: *The food was no good.* | **+at** *I'm not much good at public speaking.* **b)** not useful, appropriate, or convenient: *That* pan's no good – it's too small.* | +**for** *This paper's no good for taking notes.* | +**to** *A car's not much good to me since I can't drive anymore.* | *"How about Thursday?" "**That's no good** – I leave Wednesday."* **c)** not likely to be successful, to improve a situation, or to produce a result: *You can talk to him all you want, but I don't think it'll **do any good**.* | **it's no good doing sth** *It's no good trying to adjust the radio, one of the speakers is broken.* **d)** damaging someone or something SYN **bad**: +**for** *All these late nights are no good for me.* | *All those chemicals can't **do your body any good**.*

3 any good a) used to ask or express uncertainty about the quality or skill of someone or something: *Was the movie any good?* | *I don't know if this pie is any good.* **b)** used to ask whether something is useful, appropriate or convenient: *Is next Tuesday any good?*

4 PRODUCTS goods [plural] things that are produced in order to be sold → see also SERVICE: *The cost of goods and services has soared.* | *fresh **baked goods*** (=bread, cake etc.) | *Organizers are collecting **canned goods*** (=food that is packaged in cans) *for the local homeless shelter.* | *Imports of **consumer goods*** (=televisions, washing machines etc.) *have risen.* | *a growing demand for **goods and services***

5 GOOD BEHAVIOR [U] actions or behavior that are morally right or that follow religious principles → see also DO-GOODER: *She sees the good in everyone.* | *the battle between **good and evil***

6 PLEASANT PART the good [singular] the pleasant or enjoyable parts of something: *No job is perfect – you've got to **take the good with the bad**.*

7 for good permanently: *I'd like to stay in Colorado for good.*

8 GOOD PEOPLE the good [plural] good people in general, or people who do what is right

9 What good is sth? also **What's the good of sth?** INFORMAL used to say that having or doing something brings you no advantage: *What good is money when you don't have any friends?*

10 What good is sb? used to say rudely that someone is not useful or helpful

11 make good on a promise/threat/pledge etc. to do what you say you are going to do: *No one had any doubt that he would make good his threat.*

12 make good on a debt/loss etc. to pay back money that you owe, or replace money that has been lost

13 be up to no good INFORMAL to be doing or planning something wrong or dishonest: *Those guys look like they're up to no good.*

14 make good to become successful after being poor: *He made good as a reporter in New York.*

15 come up with the goods also **deliver the goods** to do what other people need or expect: *He promised so much but couldn't deliver the goods.*

16 be (all) to the good to have a positive result or a positive effect on something: *If further improvements can be made, that would be all to the good.*

17 have/get the goods on sb to have or find proof that someone is guilty of a crime: *Face it – they've got the goods on you.*

18 make good your escape LITERARY to succeed in escaping → see also DRY GOODS, **sb's worldly goods/possessions** at WORLDLY (1)

good³ *adv.* SPOKEN NONSTANDARD well: *Listen to me good!*

good ˌafterˈnoon S2 *interjection, n.* [C] FORMAL used to say hello when you are greeting someone in the afternoon, especially someone you do not know

ˌGood ˈBook *n.* OLD-FASHIONED **the Good Book** the Christian Bible

good·bye /gʊdˈbaɪ, gədˈbaɪ/ *interjection, n.* [C] **1** used when you are leaving someone, or when they are leaving SYN **bye** OPP **hello**: *"Goodbye, Mrs. Anderson."* | *I just have to **say goodbye** to Erika.* | **kiss/wave goodbye** *I kissed her goodbye at the door.* | *We **said our goodbyes** and left.* **2 say/wave/kiss sth goodbye** INFORMAL to not get, achieve, or keep something: *If he's late again, he can kiss this job goodbye.* **3 goodbye to sth** used when you have to stop doing or being something: *The injury meant he had to **say goodbye to** football.* [**Origin:** 1500–1600 *God be with you*]

good ˈday *interjection* OLD-FASHIONED used to say hello or goodbye, especially in the morning or afternoon

good ˈevening *interjection, n.* [C] FORMAL used to say hello when you are greeting someone in the evening, especially someone you do not know → see also GOOD NIGHT

ˌgood ˈfaith *n.* [U] the state of doing something honestly and sincerely, with no intention to deceive anyone: *Union leaders have **acted in good faith** during the negotiations.* —**good-faith** *adj.*: *a good-faith effort*

ˌgood-for-ˈnothing *adj.* a good-for-nothing person is lazy or has no skills SYN **worthless** —**good-for-nothing** *n.* [C]

ˌGood ˈFriday *n.* [C,U] the Friday before the Christian holiday of EASTER, that Christians remember as the day Jesus Christ was CRUCIFIED

ˌgood-ˈhearted *adj.* kind and generous SYN **kind-hearted**

ˌgood-ˈhumored *adj.* naturally cheerful and friendly SYN **good-natured**: *a good-humored, intelligent woman*

good·ie /ˈgʊdi/ *n.* [C] another spelling of GOODY

ˌgood-ˈlooking *adj.* someone who is good-looking is attractive SYN **beautiful** SYN **handsome**: *a tall, good-looking man* —**good-looker** *n.* [C]

ˌgood ˈlooks *n.* [plural] the attractive appearance of someone's face SYN **beauty**: *He had the blond good looks of a surfer.*

good·ly /ˈgʊdli/ *adj.* [only before noun] **1 a goodly number/sum/amount etc.** OLD-FASHIONED a large amount SYN **considerable** **2** OLD USE pleasant in appearance or good in quality

good ˈmorning S2 also **morning** *interjection, n.* [C] used to say hello when you are greeting someone in the morning

ˌgood-ˈnatured *adj.* naturally kind and helpful and not easily made angry SYN **good-humored** —**good-naturedly** *adv.*

good·ness /ˈgʊdnɪs/ S1 *n.* [U]

SPOKEN PHRASES

1 my goodness/goodness (gracious) said when you are surprised or annoyed: *My goodness, this house is big.* **2 for goodness' sake** said when you are annoyed or surprised, especially when you are telling someone to do something: *For goodness' sake, be quiet!* **3 goodness (only) knows** used to emphasize that you are not sure about something, or to make a statement stronger: *Goodness knows we don't need any more trouble.*

4 the quality of being good: *Anne believes in the basic goodness of all people.* **5** the part of food that tastes good or is good for your health: *the crunchy goodness of an apple* **6 out of the goodness of sb's heart** used when someone has done something in order to be kind or helpful to other people → see also HONEST-TO-GOODNESS, **thank God/goodness/heavens** at THANK (3)

good ˈnight S3 *interjection, n.* [C] used to say goodbye when you are leaving someone or they are leaving at night, or before going to bed: *Good night. Sleep well.* → see also GOOD EVENING, **night, night** at NIGHT (6)

ˌgood old ˈboy also **good ol' boy** /ˌgʊd oʊl ˈbɔɪ/ *n.* [C] INFORMAL a white man from the southern U.S. who is loud, friendly, and has rough manners, and who is often considered to be uneducated or RACIST by people who are not like this

Good Sa·mar·i·tan, **good Samaritan** /ˌgʊd səˈmærət¬n/ *n.* [C] a person who helps people, especially strangers, who need help

ˌgood-ˈtempered *adj.* cheerful, kind, and not easily made angry OPP **bad-tempered**

G

good·will /gʊd'wɪl/ *n.* [U] **1** kind feelings toward or between people and a willingness to be helpful: *The principal has the goodwill and respect of the teachers.* | *The president's words were seen as a* ***goodwill gesture***. **2** the success of a company, and its good relationship with its customers, considered as part of its value: *The changes put the company's goodwill at risk.*

good·y¹ /'gʊdi/ *n. plural* **goodies** [C usually plural] INFORMAL **1** something that is nice to eat: *We brought lots of goodies for the picnic.* **2** something that is desirable to have: *You could win all sorts of goodies.*

goody² *interjection* INFORMAL said especially by children to express pleasure or excitement: *Oh, goody — ice cream!*

Good·year /'gʊdyɪr/**, Charles** (1800–1860) a U.S. inventor who discovered how to VULCANIZE rubber and make it strong enough for car tires

'goody-goody also **,goody-'two-shoes** *n. plural* **goody-goodies** [C] DISAPPROVING an expression meaning someone who tries hard to be very good and helpful in order to please their parents, teachers etc., used especially by children

goo·ey /'gui/ *adj.* INFORMAL **1** sticky and soft: *gooey chocolate cakes* **2** expressing love or emotions in a way that other people think is silly SYN **sentimental**: *a gooey love song*

G

goof¹ /guf/ also **goof up** *v.* [I] INFORMAL to make a silly mistake: *Somebody goofed and entered the wrong amount.* | **goof sth ↔ up** *The printer goofed up my business cards.*

goof around *phr. v.* INFORMAL to spend time doing silly things or not doing very much SYN **mess around**: *We were just goofing around the mall.*

goof off *phr. v.* INFORMAL to waste time or avoid doing any work: *He was goofing off in school.* —**goof-off** *n.*

goof² *n.* [C] INFORMAL **1** a silly mistake: *The goof could cost the city $5 million.* **2** someone who is silly

goof·ball /'gufbɔl/ *n.* [C] INFORMAL someone who is silly or stupid

goof·y /'gufi/ *adj.* INFORMAL stupid or silly: *He gave a goofy grin.* —**goofily** *adv.* —**goofiness** *n.* [U]

goo·gol /'gugɔl/ *n.* [C] TECHNICAL the number that is written as the number 1 followed by 100 zeros

goo·gol·plex /'gugɔl,plɛks/ *n.* [C] TECHNICAL the number that is written as the number 1 followed by a googol of zeros

'goo goo *n.* [C] a word used for a sound that babies make

'goo-goo ,eyes *n.* [plural] HUMOROUS a silly look that shows that you love someone —**goo-goo-eyed** *adj.*

goon /gun/ *n.* [C] INFORMAL **1** a violent criminal who is paid to frighten or attack people **2** a silly or stupid person

goop /gup/ *n.* [U] INFORMAL a thick soft slightly sticky substance

goose¹ /gus/ *n.* **1 a)** *plural* **geese** /gis/ [C] BIOLOGY a bird that is similar to a duck but is larger and makes loud noises → see also GANDER **b)** a female goose **2** [U] the cooked meat of this bird **3 what's good/sauce for the goose is good/sauce for the gander** used to say that what is fair for one person is fair for other people too **4** OLD-FASHIONED a silly person [**Origin:** Old English *gos*] → see also **kill the goose that lays the golden egg** at KILL¹ (13), WILD GOOSE CHASE

goose² *v.* [T] INFORMAL to hit or press someone on their BUTTOCKS as an impolite joke

goose·ber·ry /'gus,bɛri/ *n. plural* **gooseberries** [C] BIOLOGY a small round green fruit with a sour taste that grows on a bush

goose·bumps /'gusbʌmps/ *n.* [plural] small raised spots on your skin that you get when you are cold, afraid, or excited: *I get* ***goosebumps*** *every time I think about it.*

goose·down /'gusdaʊn/ *n.* [U] the soft fine feathers of a GOOSE, often used between layers of material to make warm clothes and bed covers

'goose egg *n.* [singular] INFORMAL zero

goose·flesh /'gusflɛʃ/ *n.* [U] goosebumps

goose·step /'gus-stɛp/ *n.* **the goosestep** a way of marching, used by soldiers in some countries, in which they lift their legs quite high and do not bend their knees —**goosestep** *v.* [I]

GOP /,dʒi oʊ 'pi/ *n.* **the GOP the Grand Old Party** another name for the Republican Party in U.S. politics

go·pher /'goʊfɚ/ *n.* [C] **1** BIOLOGY a North and Central American animal that looks similar to a large SQUIRREL and lives in holes in the ground, and that often damages crops **2** another spelling of GOFER **3** also **Gopher** COMPUTERS a program that helps computer users find and use information quickly on the Internet

Gor·ba·chev /'gɔrbə,tʃɔf/**, Mi·khail** /mɪ'kaɪl/ (1931–) the President of the Soviet Union from 1985 to 1991, who started the process of economic and political change which improved his country's relationship with the West and resulted in the end of Communism in the Soviet Union and Eastern Europe

Gor·di·an knot /,gɔrdiən 'nɑt/ *n.* **cut the Gordian knot** to quickly solve a difficult problem by determined action

Gor·di·mer /'gɔrdɪmɚ/**, Na·dine** /næ'din/ (1923–) a South African writer of NOVELS

gore¹ /gɔr/ *v.* [T] if an animal gores someone, it wounds them with its horns or TUSKS

gore² *n.* **1** [U] LITERARY thick dark blood that has flowed from a wound: *a video game full of* ***blood and gore*** → see also GORY **2** [C] a piece of material that gets wider toward the bottom, used in making a skirt

Gore /gɔr/**, Al·bert** /'ælbɚt/ **(Al)** /æl/ (1948–) a U.S. POLITICIAN who was Vice President under Bill Clinton and a CANDIDATE for U.S. President in 2000

gorge¹ /gɔrdʒ/ *n.* [C] EARTH SCIENCE a deep narrow valley with steep sides SYN **canyon**

gorge² *v.* **1 gorge yourself (on/with sth)** to eat until you are too full to eat any more SYN **stuff yourself**: *We gorged ourselves on hot dogs at the game.* **2 be gorged with sth a)** to be too full of something: *The Chari River is gorged with water during the rainy season.* **b)** to have eaten so much of something that you are completely full: *The insect sucks until it is gorged with blood.*

gor·geous /'gɔrdʒəs/ S2 *adj.* INFORMAL **1** extremely beautiful or attractive: *Liz is* ***absolutely gorgeous***. | *the gorgeous fall colors of the trees* ►see THESAURUS box at **attractive**, **beautiful** **2** extremely pleasant or enjoyable SYN **glorious** SYN **wonderful**: *What a gorgeous day* (=a day with warm and sunny weather)! [**Origin:** 1400–1500 Old French *gorgias* **stylish**] —**gorgeously** *adv.*

Gor·gon /'gɔrgən/ *n.* [C] one of the three sisters in ancient Greek stories, who had snakes on their heads that made anyone who looked at them change into stone

go·ril·la /gə'rɪlə/ *n.* [C] **1** BIOLOGY a very large African monkey that is the largest of the APES **2** SLANG an ugly strong man who looks as if he might become violent [**Origin:** 1800–1900 Greek *Gorillai*, name of an African tribe of hairy women in old stories]

Gor·ky /'gɔrki/**, Max·im** /'mæksɪm/ (1868–1936) a Russian writer of NOVELS, famous especially for his book about his own life

gorse /gɔrs/ *n.* [U] a bush with bright yellow flowers and sharp pointed parts on its stems, which grows in Europe

gor·y /'gɔri/ *adj. comparative* **gorier**, *superlative* **goriest** **1** INFORMAL clearly describing or showing violence, blood, and killing: *a gory movie* **2 the gory details** HUMOROUS all the interesting details about an event, especially a bad one: *Come on, I want to hear all the gory details.* **3** LITERARY covered in blood → see also GORE²

gosh /gɑʃ/ *interjection* INFORMAL used to express surprise: *Gosh, it's cold.* | ***My gosh**, it's so big!*

gos·ling /ˈgɑzlɪŋ/ *n.* [C] a young GOOSE

gos·pel /ˈgɑspəl/ *n.* **1 Gospel** [C] one of the four books in the Bible about Christ's life: **+of** *the Gospel of John* **2** [singular] also **Gospel** the life of Christ and the ideas that he taught: **preach/spread the gospel** (=tell people about Jesus) *Missionaries were sent to spread the Gospel.* **3** [C usually singular] a particular set of ideas that someone believes in very strongly and tries to persuade other people to accept: **preach/spread the gospel (of sth)** *Young is tireless in preaching his gospel of economic growth.* **4** [U] also **gospel truth** something that is completely true: *Don't **take** what Ellen says **as gospel**.* **5** [U] also **gospel music** ENG. LANG. ARTS a style of Christian music usually performed by black singers, in which religious songs are sung strongly and loudly: *a gospel singer* [**Origin:** Old English *godspel*, from *god* **good** + *spell* **story, news**]

gos·sa·mer /ˈgɑsəmɚ/ *n.* [U] **1** LITERARY a very light thin material: *a gossamer silk dress* **2** something that is light and delicate **3** BIOLOGY light silky thread which SPIDERS leave on grass and bushes

gos·sip¹ /ˈgɑsəp/ *n.* **1** [C,U] information that is told by one person to another about other people's behavior and private lives, and that often includes remarks that are not true or not nice: *an interesting **piece of gossip** about Miss Smith* | *She always knows all the **juicy gossip*** (=interesting and often shocking information). | ***idle gossip*** (=gossip not based on facts) | **office/neighborhood/local etc. gossip** *People stood around the coffee machine, **exchanging** office **gossip**.* **2 the gossip mill** the people who start gossip **3** [C] also **gossiper** DISAPPROVING someone who likes talking about other people's private lives [**Origin:** Old English *godsibb* **godparent, close friend**, from *god* **god** + *sibb* **relative**]

gossip² *v.* [I] to talk or write gossip about someone or something: **+about** *They're all gossiping about you.* ► see THESAURUS box at **talk¹**

ˈgossip ˌcolumn *n.* [C] a regular article in a newspaper or magazine about the behavior and private lives of famous people —**gossip columnist** *n.* [C]

gos·sip·y /ˈgɑsəpi/ *adj.* INFORMAL **1** talk or writing that is gossipy is informal and full of gossip: *a gossipy magazine* **2** a gossipy person likes to gossip

got /gɑt/ *v.* **1** the past tense of GET **2** a past participle of GET

WORD CHOICE got, gotten, have got, have
- Use **gotten** as the past participle of **get**: *I have gotten up early every day this week.*
- You can use **got** instead of "became": *Kim just got engaged.*
- You can use **have got** to mean "possess" or "own": *They've got three cars.* But it is more usual to use **have** in this meaning: *They have three cars.*

got·cha /ˈgɑtʃə/ *interjection* INFORMAL **1** a short form of "I've got you," said when you catch someone or when you have gained an advantage over them: *"Did he really say that?" "Gotcha (=I fooled you)!"* | *Gotcha, Katie! Now I'm gonna tickle you!* **2** a word meaning "I understand" or "all right": *"You have to be there by five." "Gotcha."*

Goth /gɑθ/ one of the people from central Europe, in what is now Germany, who attacked and moved into the Roman Empire several times between the 3rd and 5th centuries A.D.

goth /gɑθ/ *n.* **1** [U] a type of loud, slow, and sad popular music that is played on electric GUITARS and KEYBOARDS **2** [C] someone who likes goth music and dresses in a style that includes having very pale skin and wearing dark eye MAKEUP and black clothes

Goth·ic /ˈgɑθɪk/ *adj.* ENG. LANG. ARTS **1** the Gothic style of building was common in Western Europe between the 12th and 16th centuries. Its main features were pointed ARCHES, tall PILLARS, and tall thin pointed windows. **2** a Gothic story, movie etc. is about frightening things that happen in mysterious old buildings and lonely places, especially stories that were popular in the early 19th century **3** Gothic writing, printing etc. has thick decorated letters

ˈgo-to *adj.* [only before noun] INFORMAL **go-to guy/go-to man/go-to woman** someone who you can always ask to do something specific for you, because he or she is good at doing it: *If you have problems with your computer, Chris is the go-to guy.*

got·ta /ˈgɑt̬ə/ SPOKEN, NONSTANDARD a short form of "got to," "have got to," "has got to," "have got a," or "has got": *I gotta go now.* | *Bob, you gotta minute to talk to Randy?*

got·ten /ˈgɑtˀn/ *v.* the past participle of GET: *You've gotten us into a lot of trouble.*

gou·ache /gʊˈɑʃ, gwɑʃ/ *n.* ENG. LANG. ARTS **1** [U] a method of painting using colors that are mixed with water and made thicker with a type of GUM **2** [C] a picture produced by this method

Gou·da /ˈgudə/ *n.* [U] a yellow Dutch cheese that does not have a very strong taste

gouge¹ /gaʊdʒ/ *v.* [T] **1** to make a deep hole or cut in the surface of something: *Bombs had gouged huge craters in the city.* **2** INFORMAL to make people spend too much money for something you are selling: *Hotels are ready to gouge Olympic visitors by raising room prices.*

gouge sth ↔ **out** *phr. v.* **1** to make a hole in something such as rock etc. by removing material that is on the surface: *The waterfall has gouged out a deep bowl at its foot.* **2 gouge sb's eyes out** to remove someone's eyes with a pointed weapon

gouge² *n.* [C] a hole or cut made in something, usually by a sharp tool or weapon

gou·lash /ˈgulɑʃ, -læʃ/ *n.* [C,U] a dish made of meat cooked in liquid with PAPRIKA (=hot tasting pepper), originally from Hungary

Gou·nod /guˈnoʊ/, **Charles** (1818–1893) a French musician who wrote CLASSICAL music

gourd /gɔrd, gʊrd/ *n.* [C] **1** BIOLOGY a round fruit with a hard outer shell that is sometimes used as a container **2** a container made from this fruit

gour·mand /ˈgʊrmɑnd/ *n.* [C] DISAPPROVING someone who enjoys good food and drink very much, but who sometimes eats too much → see also GOURMET

gour·met¹ /gʊrˈmeɪ, ˈgʊrmeɪ/ *adj.* [only before noun] producing or relating to very good food and drink: *a gourmet restaurant*

gourmet² *n.* [C] someone who knows a lot about food and wine and who enjoys good food and wine

gout /gaʊt/ *n.* [U] MEDICINE a disease that makes your toes, fingers, and knees swollen and painful [**Origin:** 1200–1300 Old French *goute*, from Latin *gutta* **drop**; because it used to be believed that it was caused by drops of disease in the blood] —**gouty** *adj.*

gov·ern /ˈgʌvɚn/ **W3** *v.* **1** [I,T] to officially and legally control a country and make all the decisions about taxes, laws, public services etc. SYN **rule**: *the military leaders who govern the country* **2** [T] if rules, principles etc. govern the way a system or situation works, they control how it happens or what happens: **rules/laws/principles etc. that govern sth** *new regulations governing the disposal of toxic waste* **3** [T] OLD-FASHIONED to control a strong or dangerous emotion SYN **restrain** [**Origin:** 1200–1300 Old French *governer*, from Latin *gubernare*, from Greek *kybernan* **to control the direction of something**]

gov·ern·ess /ˈgʌvɚnɪs/ *n.* [C] a female teacher in past times, who lived with a rich family and taught their children at home

gov·ern·ing /ˈgʌvɚnɪŋ/ *adj.* **1** [only before noun] having the power to control an organization, country etc. SYN **ruling**: *FIFA is the **governing body** (=the group of people controlling an organization) of world soccer.* | *the leader of the **governing party** (=the political party that is governing a country)* **2 governing principle** a principle that has the most important influence on something: *Freedom of speech is one of the governing principles in a democracy.* → see also SELF-GOVERNING

gov·ern·ment /ˈgʌvɚmənt, ˈgʌvɚnmənt/ S2 W1 *n.* **1** [C] also **Government** the group of people who govern a country or state: *the French government* | *The government said that Iceland has no plans to resume whaling.* | **government policies/funding/statistics etc.** *Government figures show that bankruptcies have increased.* | **local/state/federal government** (=the government of a city or town, the state, or of the U.S.) *The federal government will supply part of the funding.* | *It has been difficult for the* ***central government*** (=the government of a whole country) *to conduct elections in remote regions.* **2** [C,U] a form, system, or process by which a country or state is governed: *the establishment of a* ***democratic government*** | *Term limits mean we are electing more people who have no experience of government* (=no experience in the process by which a country is governed). | *The voters just want good government.* | *In Britain, Labor has* ***been in government*** (=been governing) *for many years.* | *Conservatives have protested against* ***big government*** (=when the government controls many activities) *and federal spending.*

G

THESAURUS

democracy a political system in which everyone can vote to choose the government, or a country that has this system
republic a country that has an elected government, and does not have a king or queen
monarchy a country that has a king or queen as the head of state, and which may or may not also have an elected government
regime a government, especially one that was not elected fairly or that you disapprove of
dictatorship a political system in which a dictator (=a leader who has complete power and who has not been elected) controls a country, or a country that has this system
totalitarian country/state etc. a country in which the government has complete control over everything
police state a country where the government strictly controls people's freedom, for example to travel or to talk about politics
→ POLITICIAN

gov·er·nor, Governor /ˈgʌvənɚ, -vɚ-/ W2 *n.* [C] **1 a)** the person in charge of governing a state in the U.S.: *the governor of South Dakota* | *Governor Brown* **b)** the person in charge of governing a country that is under the political control of another country: *the former governor of Hong Kong* **2** a part of a machine that controls how the machine works, especially by limiting it in some way → see also GUBERNATORIAL

ˌGovernor-ˈGeneral *n.* [C] someone who represents the King or Queen of Great Britain in other Commonwealth countries which are not REPUBLICS: *the Governor-General of Australia*

gov·er·nor·ship /ˈgʌvənɚˌʃɪp/ *n.* [U] the position of being governor, or the period during which someone is governor

govt. a written abbreviation of GOVERNMENT

gown /gaʊn/ *n.* [C] **1** a long dress that a woman wears on formal occasions SYN **evening dress**: **a wedding/evening/ball gown** *a silk evening gown* **2** a long loose piece of clothing worn by someone staying in a hospital **3** a long loose piece of clothing worn for special ceremonies by people such as judges or teachers at universities SYN **robe**

goy /gɔɪ/ *n. plural* **goyim** /ˈgɔɪ-ɪm/ or **goys** [C] DISAPPROVING a word used by Jewish people to talk about someone who is not Jewish

Go·ya /ˈgɔɪə/, **Fran·cis·co de** /frɑnˈsɪskoʊ dɪ/ (1746–1828) a Spanish artist famous for his pictures of members of the royal families of Spain

G.P. /ˌdʒi ˈpi/ *n.* [C] the abbreviation of GENERAL PRACTITIONER

GPA /ˌdʒi pi ˈeɪ/ *n.* [C] **grade point average** a number representing the average of all a student's grades, in which an A is 4 points, a B is 3, a C is 2, a D is 1, and an F is 0: *Applicants need at least a 3.1 GPA.*

grab¹ /græb/ S1 W3 *v.* **grabbed, grabbing** [T] **1** to take hold of someone or something with a sudden or violent movement SYN **snatch** SYN **seize**: *Two men grabbed her and pushed her to the ground.* | **grab sth from sb/sth** *Stuart grabbed a flashlight from his car.* | *He* ***grabbed hold of*** *my arm.* **2** INFORMAL to get some food or sleep quickly because you are busy SYN **snatch**: *Let me grab a cup of coffee first.* | *Do we have time to* ***grab a bite to eat*** *before the movie?* **3** to get someone's attention: *The photo* ***grabbed*** *her* ***attention***. | *The case* ***grabbed*** *national* ***headlines*** (=was an important story in the news). **4** to take something for yourself when you have a chance to do this, sometimes in an unfair way: *The firm is trying to grab a share of the market.* | *Could you grab some good seats for us?* | **grab a chance/opportunity** *Sylvia* ***grabbed the chance*** *to work in Italy for the summer.* | *Tompkins* ***grabbed the lead*** (=he took first place in a race) *from Barve.* **5 how does sth grab you?** SPOKEN used to ask someone if they would be interested in doing a particular thing: *How does going to Hawaii for Christmas grab you?* [**Origin:** 1500–1600 Middle Dutch, Middle Low German *grabben*]

grab at/for sth *phr. v.* to quickly and suddenly put out your hand in order to take hold of something SYN **snatch at**: *The child grabbed at her mother's skirt.* | *Susan grabbed for the money.*

grab on *phr. v.* **1** to take hold of someone or something with your hand, with a quick or violent movement: **grab on to sth** *He grabbed on to the rope to stop himself falling.* **2** to use something as support for an idea or an understanding of something: **grab on to sth** *People grabbed on to the report as proof that global warming was happening.*

grab² *n.* **1 make a grab for/at sth** to suddenly try to take hold of something: *He made a grab for the knife.* **2 be up for grabs** INFORMAL if a job, prize, opportunity etc. is up for grabs, it is available for anyone who wants to try to have it **3** [C] the act of getting something quickly, especially dishonestly: *a power grab within the company*

ˈgrab ˌbag *n.* **1** [C] a container filled with small presents, into which you put your hand to pick one out **2** [singular] a mixture of different things or styles: **+of** *The treaty covers a grab bag of issues.* **3** [singular] INFORMAL a situation in which things are decided by chance

grab·by /ˈgræbi/ *adj.* INFORMAL someone who is grabby is SELFISH and impolite because they take things that are not their own, or they take more than they deserve

gra·ben /ˈgrɑbən/ *n.* [C] EARTH SCIENCE a long area of lower land between two FAULTS (=very large cracks) in the rocks that form the Earth's surface, caused by movement of the faults in the past → see also RIFT VALLEY

grace¹ /greɪs/ S3 *n.*
1 WAY OF MOVING [U] a smooth way of moving that seems natural, relaxed, and attractive SYN **gracefulness**: *She moved with the grace of a dancer.*
2 BEHAVIOR a) [U] polite and pleasant behavior: *The princess always handled herself with grace and dignity.* | **have the grace to do sth** *At least he had the grace to admit he was wrong.* **b) graces** [plural] the skills needed to behave in a way that is considered polite and socially acceptable: *Kids need to be taught social graces.*
3 MORE TIME [U] also **grace period** more time that is allowed so that someone can finish a piece of work, pay a debt etc.: *There is a six-month grace period before payments are required on the loan.* | **a day's/week's etc. grace** *My professor gave me a few days' grace to finish my essay.*
4 with good/bad grace willingly and cheerfully, or in

an unwilling and angry way: *Kevin accepted defeat with good grace.*
5 GOD'S KINDNESS [U] God's kindness, shown to people because he loves them: *You are saved by grace alone, not by good works.* | ***By the grace of God*** (=because of God's kindness), *Alan wasn't hurt.*
6 PRAYER [C,U] a prayer thanking God, said before a meal: *Frank, would you **say grace** for us?*
7 SOUL [U] the state of someone's soul when it has been freed from evil, according to Christian belief: *a **state of grace*** (=when God has forgiven you for the wrong things you have done)
8 Your/His etc. Grace used as a title for talking to or about a DUKE, DUCHESS, or ARCHBISHOP
9 the Graces three beautiful Greek GODDESSES who often appear in art
[**Origin:** 1100–1200 Old French, Latin *gratia* **pleasing quality, kindness**, from *gratus*] → see also **fall from grace/favor** at FALL[1] (21), **be in sb's good graces/book** at GOOD[1] (56), **saving grace** at SAVE[1] (12)

grace² *v.* [T] **1 grace sb/sth with your presence** HUMOROUS an expression meaning to bring honor to an occasion or group of people by being present, said when someone arrives late, or when someone arrives who does not often come to events **2** to make a place or an object look more attractive: *His portrait now graces the wall of the drawing room.*

grace·ful /'greɪsfəl/ *adj.* **1** moving in a smooth and attractive way, or having a smooth attractive shape: *a graceful dancer* | *The branches formed a graceful curve.* **2** behaving in a polite and pleasant way: *a graceful acceptance of defeat* —**gracefully** *adv.* —**gracefulness** *n.* [U]

grace·less /'greɪslɪs/ *adj.* **1** moving or doing something in a way that seems awkward SYN **awkward** OPP **graceful**: *his graceless movements* **2** something that is graceless is unattractive to look at OPP **graceful**: *a graceless three-story building* —**gracelessness** *n.* [U]

gra·cious¹ /'greɪʃəs/ *adj.* **1** behaving in a polite, kind, and generous way: *a gracious hostess* **2** having the type of expensive style, comfort, and beauty that only rich people can afford: *a gracious country home* | *gracious living* (=an easy way of life enjoyed by rich people) **3** a word meaning "kind and forgiving," used to describe God's actions SYN **merciful** —**graciously** *adv.* —**graciousness** *n.* [U]

gracious² also **goodness gracious** *interjection* OLD-FASHIONED used to express surprise or to emphasize "yes" or "no"

grack·le /'grækəl/ *n.* [C] BIOLOGY a type of bird with shiny black feathers

grad¹ /græd/ *n.* [C] INFORMAL **1** a GRADUATE **2** CANADIAN INFORMAL a dance to celebrate students' GRADUATION from high school

grad² *adj.* [only before noun] INFORMAL relating to or involved in studies done at a university after completing a first degree: *a grad student*

grad·a·ble /'greɪdəbəl/ *adj.* ENG. LANG. ARTS a gradable adjective or adverb can be used in the COMPARATIVE or SUPERLATIVE forms, or with words such as "very," "fairly," and "almost" —**gradability** /ˌgreɪdə'bɪləṭi/ *n.* [U]

gra·da·tion /greɪ'deɪʃən, grə-/ *n.* [C] FORMAL a small change or difference between points on a scale: *gradations of color*

grade¹ /greɪd/ Ac S1 W2 *n.*
1 SCHOOL YEAR [C] one of the 12 years you are in school in the U.S., or the students in a particular year: *What grade are you in?* | *a fifth-grade teacher* | **be in first/sixth etc. grade** *My brother is in tenth grade.*
2 NUMBER/LETTER IN SCHOOL [C] a number or letter that shows how well you have done in school, college etc. SYN **mark**: *Ellen always **gets good grades**.*
3 STANDARD [C,U] a particular standard, measurement, or level of quality that a product, material etc. has: *Grade A beef* | *weapons-grade nuclear material* | *a low-grade fever* (=a fever with a slightly high temperature)
4 make the grade to succeed or reach the necessary standard: *Only a few athletes make the grade in professional sports.*
5 SLOPE [C] a slope or a degree of slope, especially in a road or railroad tracks SYN **gradient**: *a steep grade*
6 COMPANY [C,U] the level of importance you have or the level of pay you receive in a company or organization: *The pay scale is based on grade and length of service.*
[**Origin:** 1500–1600 French, Latin *gradus* **step, degree**]

grade² Ac S3 *v.* [T] **1** to give a grade to a test or to a piece of school work SYN **mark**: *I spent the weekend grading tests.* **2** to say what level of quality something has, or what standard it is: *Beef is graded on the basis of its fat content.* **3** to make something such as a road or hill less steep: *The hillsides must be graded to prevent erosion.*

'grade ˌcrossing *n.* [C] a place where a road and railroad tracks cross each other at the same level, often with gates that close the road while the train passes

grad·ed /'greɪdɪd/ Ac *adj.* **1** designed to suit different levels of learning: *graded textbooks* **2** made level or less steep: *graded highways*

ˌgrade point 'average *n.* [C] GPA

-grader /greɪdə/ *n.* [C] a student in a particular grade of school: *a cute little first-grader*

'grade ˌschool *n.* [C] an ELEMENTARY SCHOOL

gra·di·ent /'greɪdiənt/ *n.* [C] **1** a GRADE **2** TECHNICAL the rate of change of pressure, temperature etc. in relation to something else, especially distance, or a curved line representing this

grad·ing /'greɪdɪŋ/ Ac *n.* [U] the activity of checking students' written work and giving it a grade

'grad school *n.* [C] INFORMAL a GRADUATE SCHOOL

grad·u·al /'grædʒuəl/ *adj.* **1** happening, developing, or changing slowly over a long time OPP **sudden**: *the gradual process of evolution* | *There have been gradual changes in her behavior.* **2** a gradual slope is not steep

grad·u·al·ly /'grædʒuəli, -dʒəli/ W3 *adv.* slowly, over a long period of time OPP **suddenly**: *Gradually mix in the milk.* | *My ankle gradually got better.*

grad·u·ate¹ /'grædʒuɪt/ S2 *n.* [C] someone who has successfully completed their studies at a school, college, or university SYN **alumnus** → see also UNDERGRADUATE: *a high school graduate* | +**of** *a graduate of Ohio State University*

grad·u·ate² /'grædʒuˌeɪt/ S2 W3 *v.* **1** [I] to obtain a DIPLOMA or a degree by completing your studies at a school, college, or university: +**from** *Ruth graduated from Princeton.* **2 graduate (from sth) to sth** to start doing something that is better, more advanced, or more important: *Bob played college baseball but never graduated to the majors.* **3** [T] to give a DIPLOMA or a degree to someone who has completed a course of study: *We expect to graduate nearly 300 students this year.*

grad·u·ate³ /'grædʒuɪt/ *adj.* [only before noun] relating to or involved in studies done at a university after completing a first degree: *a graduate student*

grad·u·at·ed /'grædʒuˌeɪṭɪd/ *adj.* **1** divided into different levels or GRADES: *graduated rates of income tax* **2** a graduated tool or container has small marks on it showing measurements

ˌgraduated 'income tax *n.* [C,U] ECONOMICS a method of taxing money that people earn by which higher rates are charged on larger amounts of income

'graduate ˌschool *n.* [C] a college or university where you can study for a MASTER'S DEGREE or a DOCTORATE after receiving your first degree, or the period of time when you study for these degrees

grad·u·a·tion /ˌgrædʒu'eɪʃən/ S3 *n.* **1** [U] the time when you complete a college or university degree or high school education: **after/upon/following graduation** *After graduation, Jayne went to nursing school.* | *the classes required for graduation* **2** [U] a ceremony at which you receive a DIPLOMA or degree SYN **commencement**: *Graduation is on Saturday.*

3 [C] a mark showing measurement on an instrument or container for measuring

graf·fi·ti /grəˈfit̬i/ *n.* [U] writing and pictures illegally drawn on the walls of buildings, trains etc.: *There was racist graffiti on the walls.* [**Origin:** 1800–1900 Italian *graffiare* **to make marks in a surface**]

graft¹ /græft/ *n.* **1** [C] a piece of healthy skin or bone taken from someone's body and put in or on another part of their body that has been damaged: *One burn victim has already had several* ***skin grafts***. **2** [C] a piece cut from one plant and attached to another plant, so that it grows there **3** [U] the practice of dishonestly using your position or influence to get money or advantages: *Six politicians were accused of* ***graft and corruption***. [**Origin:** 1400–1500 *graff* **graft** (14–19 centuries), from Old French *grafe* **pencil, graft**; because a plant graft looks like a pencil]

graft² *v.* [T] **1** to remove a piece of skin or bone from one part of someone's body and put it onto or into another part that has been damaged: **graft sth onto sth** *Doctors grafted skin from Mike's arm onto his face.* **2** to join a part of a flower, plant, or tree onto another flower, plant, or tree **3** to add something very different to something else, so that the two things become combined: **graft sth onto sth** *The new system is not one you can graft onto your existing system; you have to change it.*

graft off sb *phr. v.* to get money or advantages from someone by dishonestly using your position or influence, especially political influence: *The bosses grafted off the men.*

Gra·ham /ˈgreɪəm/, **Bil·ly** /ˈbɪli/ (1918–) a U.S. religious leader and EVANGELIST, who travels around the world and tries to persuade people to follow the Christian religion

Graham, Mar·tha /ˈmɑrθə/ (1894–1991) a U.S. dancer and CHOREOGRAPHER known especially for her work in developing modern dance

graham cracker /ˈgræm ˌkrækɚ/ *n.* [C] a type of sweet brown CRACKER that is made from WHOLE WHEAT flour

Grail /greɪl/ *n.* **the Grail** → see HOLY GRAIL

grain /greɪn/ *n.*
1 FOOD a) [U] the seeds of crops such as corn, wheat, or rice that are gathered for use as food, or the crops themselves: *fields of grain* | *the grain harvest* **b)** [C] a single seed of wheat, rice etc.
2 SMALL PIECE [C] a single, very small piece of a substance such as sand, salt etc.
3 the grain the lines or patterns you can see in things such as wood, rock, or flesh, which are part of its structure: *Split the wood along the grain.*
4 against the grain if something goes against the grain, it is not what normally happens or what you would expect: **go/run/cut against the grain** *She's an honest person, and it went against the grain to lie.*
5 a grain of sth a very small amount of something: **grain of truth/doubt etc.** *There's more than a grain of truth in what Spencer said.* | *Anyone with a* ***grain of sense*** *would have known it wasn't true!*
6 take sth with a grain of salt to not completely believe what someone tells you because you know that they often lie or are wrong: *Sometimes you have to take what Kevin says with a grain of salt.*
7 MEASURE [C] TECHNICAL the smallest measure of weight, used in weighing medicines, equal to 0.002285 OUNCES or 0.0648 grams
[**Origin:** 1200–1300 Old French, Latin *granum* **seed**]

grain·y /ˈgreɪni/ *adj. comparative* **grainier**, *superlative* **grainiest** **1** a photograph that is grainy has a rough appearance, as if the images are made up of spots **2** a grainy substance feels rough when you touch it or eat it because it contains many small pieces, seeds, or grains: *grainy mustard*

gram /græm/ WRITTEN ABBREVIATION **g** or **gm** *n.* [C] a unit for measuring weight in the METRIC system, equal to 1/1,000 of a kilogram or 0.035 OUNCES

-gram /græm/ *suffix* [in nouns] something that is written or drawn: *a diagram* | *a telegram*

gram·mar /ˈgræmɚ/ S3 *n.* ENG. LANG. ARTS **1** [U] the rules by which the words of a language change their forms and are combined into sentences, or the study or use of these rules: *English grammar is very different from Japanese grammar.* | *Check your grammar and spelling.* **2** [C] a particular description of grammar, or a book that describes grammar rules: *a good French grammar* [**Origin:** 1300–1400 Old French *gramaire*, from Latin *grammatica*, from Greek *grammatikos* **of letters**]

gram·mar·ian /grəˈmɛriən/ *n.* [C] someone who studies and knows about grammar

ˈgrammar ˌschool *n.* [C] OLD-FASHIONED an ELEMENTARY SCHOOL

gram·mat·i·cal /grəˈmæt̬ɪkəl/ *adj.* ENG. LANG. ARTS **1** [only before noun] relating to the use of grammar: *grammatical errors* **2** correct according to the rules of grammar OPP **ungrammatical**: *a grammatical sentence* —**grammatically** /-kli/ *adv.*

Gram·my /ˈgræmi/ *n. plural* **Grammys** or **Grammies** [C] a prize given in the U.S. every year to the best song, the best singer etc. in the music industry

gram·o·phone /ˈgræməˌfoʊn/ *n.* [C] OLD-FASHIONED a RECORD PLAYER

Gramps /græmps/ *n.* SPOKEN INFORMAL grandfather

gran·a·ry /ˈgreɪnəri, ˈgræ-/ *n. plural* **granaries** [C] **1** a place where grain is stored **2** an area that produces a lot of grain: *The U.S. is one of the world's leading granaries.*

grand¹ /grænd/ S3 W2 *adj.* **1** big and very impressive: *the grand prize* | *the grand houses along the beach* | *The CIA began operating* ***on a grand scale*** *during the 1950s.* | *The president* ***made a grand entrance*** *into the Senate chamber.* **2 grand total** the final total you get when you add up several numbers or amounts **3** aiming or intending to achieve something very impressive: **grand plan/scheme/design etc.** *a grand plan to improve the urban landscape* | *his grand vision for the future* **4** well-known, impressive, and respected: *He has taken the grand tradition of adventure novels several steps further.* | *the* ***grand old*** *art of oil painting* | *the* ***grand old man*** *of country music* **5** important, or having an important position: *the grand marshal of the Rose Parade* | *The opera deals with the grand theme of good versus evil.* **6 Grand a)** used in the titles of buildings or places that are big and impressive: *Grand Central Station* | *the Grand Canyon* **b)** used in the titles of some people who belong to the highest social class in Europe: *the Grand Duke of Tuscany* **7** OLD-FASHIONED very good, pleasant, or enjoyable [**Origin:** 1500–1600 Old French **large, great**, from Latin *grandis*] —**grandly** *adv.* —**grandness** *n.* [U]

grand² *n.* [C] **1** *plural* **grand** INFORMAL a thousand dollars: *She made 60 grand last year.* **2** a GRAND PIANO

the Grand Canyon

ˌGrand ˈCanyon, the a very large, deep GORGE in the southwestern U.S., in the state of Arizona

grand·child /ˈgræntʃaɪld/ S3 *n. plural* **grandchildren** /-ˌtʃɪldrən/ [C] the child of your son or daughter

Grand Cou·lee Dam, the /ˌgrænd ˌkuli ˈdæm/ a DAM built across the Columbia River in the U.S. state of Washington

grand·dad /ˈgrændæd/ *n.* [C] INFORMAL grandfather

grand·dad·dy /ˈgrænˌdædi/ *n. plural* **granddaddies** [C] INFORMAL **1** grandfather **2 the granddaddy of sth** the first or greatest example of something: *Aspirin is the granddaddy of pain relievers.*

grand·daugh·ter /ˈgrænˌdɔṭɚ/ *n.* [C] the daughter of your son or daughter

grande dame /ˌgrɑn ˈdɑm/ *n. plural* **grandes dames** or **grande dames** /ˌgrɑn ˈdɑm/ [C] a respected older woman who has a lot of experience in a particular subject: *a grande dame of American theater*

gran·dee /grænˈdi/ *n.* [C] **1** a Spanish or Portuguese NOBLEMAN of the highest rank **2** someone who has a lot of influence or power, especially in politics

gran·deur /ˈgrændʒɚ, -dʒʊr/ *n.* [U] impressive beauty, power, or size: *the grandeur of the Rocky Mountains* → see also **delusions of grandeur** at DELUSION (3)

grand·fa·ther[1] /ˈgrændˌfɑðɚ/ S2 W3 *n.* [C] the father of your father or mother ▸see THESAURUS box at relative[1]

grandfather[2] also **grandfather** sb/sth ↔ **in** *v.* [T] to give someone or something special permission not to obey a new law or rule, and continue what they have been doing: *Even though the new owners banned pets, they grandfathered my cat so I could stay.*

ˈgrandfather ˌclause *n.* [C] a part of a new law or rule that gives a particular group of people special permission not to obey it, and to continue what they have been doing

ˈgrandfather ˌclock *n.* [C] a tall clock in a wooden case that stands on the floor

grandfather clock

ˌgrand fiˈnale *n.* [C] the last and most impressive or exciting part of a show or performance

gran·dil·o·quent /grænˈdɪləkwənt/ *adj.* FORMAL using words that are too long and formal, in order to sound important SYN **pompous**: *a grandiloquent prose style* —**grandiloquence** *n.* [U]

gran·di·ose /ˈgrændiˌoʊs, ˌgrændiˈoʊs/ *adj.* grandiose plans, buildings, thoughts etc. seem very important or impressive but are not practical: *grandiose claims for the drug's effectiveness*

ˌgrand ˈjury *n.* [C] LAW a group of people who decide whether someone who may be guilty of a crime should be judged in a court of law —**grand juror** *n.* [C]

ˌgrand ˈlarceny *n.* [U] LAW the crime of stealing very valuable goods

grand·ma /ˈgrændmɑ, ˈgræmɑ/ S2 *n.* [C] INFORMAL **1** grandmother ▸see THESAURUS box at relative[1] **2** an insulting word for an old woman: *Hey, grandma, learn how to drive!*

grand mal /ˈgrɑn mɑl, -mæl/ *n.* [U] MEDICINE a serious form of EPILEPSY → see also PETIT MAL

ˌgrand ˈmaster *n.* [C] a CHESS player who plays at a very high standard

grand·moth·er /ˈgrændˌmʌðɚ/ S2 W2 *n.* [C] the mother of your mother or father

ˌgrand ˈopera *n.* [C,U] an OPERA with a serious subject, and in which all the words are sung

grand·pa /ˈgrændpɑ, ˈgræmpɑ/ S2 *n.* [C] INFORMAL **1** grandfather ▸see THESAURUS box at relative[1] **2** an insulting word for an old man: *Watch what you're doing, grandpa.*

grand·par·ent /ˈgrændˌpɛrənt/ *n.* [C usually plural] one of the parents of your mother or father: *My grandparents live in Oregon.*

ˌgrand piˈano also **grand** *n.* [C] the type of large piano often used in concerts, with strings in a horizontal position → see also UPRIGHT PIANO

grand prix /ˌgrɑn ˈpri/ *n.* [C] one of a set of international races, especially a car race

ˌgrand ˈslam *n.* [C] **1** a hit in baseball that gets four points because it is a HOME RUN and there are players on all the BASES **2** the act of winning all of a set of important sports competitions in the same year **3** the winning of all of the TRICKS possible in one game of cards, especially in BRIDGE

grand·son /ˈgrændsʌn/ *n.* [C] the son of your son or daughter

grand·stand /ˈgrændstænd/ *n.* [C] a large structure that has many rows of seats and a roof, where people sit and watch sports competitions, games, or races → see also BLEACHERS

grand·stand·ing /ˈgrændˌstændɪŋ/ *n.* [U] actions that are intended to make people notice you or think you are important: *a lot of grandstanding by the lawyers* —**grandstand** *v.* [I] —**grandstand** *adj.* [only before noun]

ˌgrand ˈtour *n.* [C] **1** an occasion when someone takes you through all the rooms in a building to show it to you: *They took us on a grand tour of their new house.* **2 the grand tour** a trip around Europe made in past times by young English or American people from rich families, as part of their education

grange /greɪndʒ/ *n.* [C] OLD-FASHIONED a farm, including the main house and the buildings near it

gran·ite /ˈgrænɪt/ *n.* [U] EARTH SCIENCE a very hard gray rock, often used in buildings

gran·ny[1], **grannie** /ˈgræni/ *n. plural* **grannies** [C] INFORMAL **1** grandmother **2** an insulting word for an old woman

granny[2], **grannie** *adj.* [only before noun] having a style typically used by old women: *granny shoes*

ˈgranny ˌglasses *n.* [plural] INFORMAL GLASSes that have two very small round pieces of glass for the eyes and a thin metal FRAME

ˈgranny ˌknot *n.* [C] a SQUARE KNOT in which the two pieces of string are crossed in the wrong way so that the knot does not hold well

gra·no·la[1] /grəˈnoʊlə/ *n.* [U] breakfast food made from mixed nuts, grains, and seeds

granola[2] *adj.* [only before noun] INFORMAL HUMOROUS a granola person eats healthy food, is concerned about the environment, and wears very loose comfortable clothing

grant[1] /grænt/ Ac S2 W3 *n.* [C] an amount of money given to a person or organization, especially by the government, for a particular purpose: *The medical school has received a grant for cancer research.* | *The high school has* ***applied for a grant*** *to run the program.* | **+from** *a grant from the Rockefeller Foundation* | *The magazine is run on grant money.* [**Origin:** 1200–1300 Old French *creanter, graanter*, from Latin *credere* **to believe**]

grant[2] Ac S3 W2 *v.* **1 take sb/sth for granted** to expect that someone or something will always be there when you need them, so that you do not pay attention to them or think how important or useful they are: *Most people take their health for granted.* | *Children tend to take their parents for granted.* | *We* ***take it for granted*** *that we can talk to anyone, anywhere, at any time.* **2 take it for granted (that)** to believe that something is true without making sure SYN **assume**: *We just took it for granted that the $1,000 was part of the normal fee for buying a house.* **3** [T] FORMAL to give someone something that they have asked for, especially official permission to do something: **grant sb sth** *Ching Hua was granted American citizenship last year.* | **grant sth to sb** *The Constitution grants authority to the President in times of emergency.* | *She refused to* ***grant*** *our* ***request*** *for interview.* **4** [I,T] to admit that something is true although it does not make much

G

difference to your opinion SYN **concede**: *He has talent, **I grant you**, but he doesn't work hard enough.* —**grantor, granter** *n.* [C]

Grant /grænt/, **U·lys·ses** /yuˈlɪsiz/ (1822–1885) the 18th President of the U.S., who had commanded the army of the Union during the American Civil War

gran·ted /ˈgræntɪd/ *adv.* [sentence adverb] used when you admit that something is true: *Granted, I don't make as much money, but I'm a lot happier.*

grant·ee /grænˈti/ *n.* [C] a person or organization that receives a grant

gran·u·lar /ˈgrænyələ/ *adj.* consisting of or covered with granules: *granular fertilizer*

gran·u·lat·ed /ˈgrænyəˌleɪtɪd/ *adj.* granulated sugar is in the form of small white grains

gran·ule /ˈgrænyul/ *n.* [C] a small hard piece of something SYN **grain**: *instant coffee granules*

grape /greɪp/ S3 *n.* [C] BIOLOGY a small round green or purple fruit that grows in groups on a VINE and is often used for making wine: *a **bunch of grapes*** [**Origin:** 1200–1300 Old French *crape*, *grape* **hook, bunch of grapes**]

G

grape·fruit /ˈgreɪpfrut/ *n.* [C] a round yellow or pink CITRUS fruit with a thick skin, which tastes slightly bitter and looks like a large orange

grape·vine /ˈgreɪpvaɪn/ *n.* [C] **1 hear sth through the grapevine** to hear news because it has been passed from one person to another in conversation: *I heard through the grapevine that you'd gotten the job.* **2** BIOLOGY a climbing plant on which grapes grow SYN **vine**

graph /græf/ *n.* [C] MATH a drawing that uses a line or lines to show how two or more sets of measurements are related to each other: *The graph shows population growth over the past 50 years.* —**graph** *v.* [T] → see picture at CHART[1]

graph·ic[1] /ˈgræfɪk/ *adj.* **1** a graphic account or description of an event is very clear and gives a lot of details, especially bad ones: **graphic account/description/example etc.** *a graphic description of physical abuse* | *The movie portrays the battlefield **in graphic detail**.* **2** graphic language uses a lot of swearing and sexual words **3** [only before noun] ENG. LANG. ARTS relating to drawing or printing: *a graphic artist* → see also GRAPHICAL

graphic[2] *n.* **1** [C] a drawing, graph etc., especially one that is used to help you understand something **2 graphics** [plural] drawings or images that are designed to represent objects or facts, especially in a computer program, or the activity of drawing them: *The computer program allows you to combine text with graphics.*

graph·i·cal /ˈgræfɪkəl/ *adj.* relating to or using GRAPHICS, especially on a computer: *a graphical user interface* (=the pictures on a computer screen that you use to open programs) → see also GRAPHIC

graph·i·cally /ˈgræfɪkli/ *adv.* **1** clearly describing something, especially something bad, and using a lot of detail SYN **vividly**: *an ad that graphically warns against driving drunk* **2** FORMAL using a graph or GRAPHICS

ˌgraphic ˈarts *n.* [plural] the activity of drawing, painting, making prints etc.

ˌgraphic deˈsign *n.* [U] the art of combining pictures, words, and decoration in the production of books, magazines etc. —**graphic designer** *n.* [C]

ˌgraphic ˈorganizer *n.* [C] ENG. LANG. ARTS a picture, GRAPH, DIAGRAM etc. that helps you organize information in a way that is easy to see: *The graphic organizer can help you arrange the ideas for your essay.*

graph·ite /ˈgræfaɪt/ *n.* [U] a soft black substance that is a type of CARBON and is used in pencils, paints, and electrical equipment

gra·phol·o·gy /græˈfɑlədʒi/ *n.* [U] the study of HANDWRITING in order to understand people's characters —**graphologist** *n.* [C]

ˈgraph ˌpaper *n.* [U] paper with many squares printed on it, used for drawing GRAPHS

-graphy /grəfi/ *suffix* [in nouns] used in nouns to mean a way of making a copy, picture, or record of something: *photography* | *a bibliography*

grap·nel /ˈgræpnəl/ *n.* [C] **1** an ANCHOR with three or more hooks **2** a GRAPPLING HOOK

grap·ple /ˈgræpəl/ *v.* [I] to fight or struggle with someone, holding them tightly SYN **wrestle**: +**with** *A man was grappling with the guard.*

grapple with sth *phr. v.* to try hard to deal with or understand something difficult: *Schools have had to grapple with violence on campus.*

ˈgrappling hook also **ˈgrappling ˌiron** *n.* [C] an iron tool with several hooks on it, that you tie to a rope and use to hold a boat still, look for objects on the bottom of a river etc.

grasp[1] /græsp/ *v.* [T] **1** to take something and hold it firmly SYN **grip**: *Alan grasped her arm firmly.* ▸see THESAURUS box at **hold**[1] **2** [not in progressive] to completely understand something, especially a complicated fact or idea SYN **understand** SYN **comprehend**: *Some scientific concepts can be difficult to grasp.* | *She **grasped the significance** of the change immediately.* | **grasp what/how etc.** *People were so shocked that it took them some time to grasp what had happened.* | **grasp that** *I don't think he'd really grasped that we were going.* ▸see THESAURUS box at **understand** → see also **be grasping/clutching at straws** at STRAW[1] (4)

grasp at sth *phr. v.* **1** to eagerly try to use an opportunity: *Desperate patients may grasp at any experimental treatment.* **2** to try to reach something: *The crowd grasped at the money.*

grasp[2] *n.* [singular] **1** the ability to understand a complicated idea or situation SYN **understanding** SYN **comprehension**: **have a good/poor etc. grasp of sth** *MacMillan has a good grasp of the issues facing the city.* | *Some of the ideas presented are **beyond the grasp*** (=too difficult to understand) *of young children.* | +**on** *He didn't have a **firm grasp** on the subject.* **2** your ability to achieve or gain something: *Control of the whole program was now **within her grasp*** (=achievable). | *It looks like the election is **beyond his grasp*** (=he cannot be elected). **3** a hold on something, or your ability to hold it: +**on/of** *Take a firm grasp on the rope.* **4** control of a situation: *Recent moves have weakened his grasp on power.*

grasp·ing /ˈgræspɪŋ/ *adj.* too eager to get money and unwilling to give any of it away or spend it: *Hanson was a hard, grasping man.*

grass /græs/ S2 W2 *n.* **1** [U] BIOLOGY a very common plant with thin green leaves that covers the ground in yards, parks, fields etc., and which is often eaten by animals: *the feeling of the grass beneath her feet* | *a **blade of grass*** (=single leaf) **2 the grass** an area of grass, especially one where the grass is kept cut short: *Please keep off the grass.* | *Will you mow the grass?* **3** [C] a particular type of grass: *wild grasses* **4** [U] INFORMAL MARIJUANA **5 the grass is (always) greener (on the other side)** used to say that other people's situations always seem better than yours, although they may not really be better **6 not let the grass grow under your feet** to not waste time or delay starting something [**Origin:** Old English *græs*] → see also GRASSROOTS, **snake in the grass** at SNAKE[1] (2)

Grass /grɑs/, **Gün·ter** /ˈgʊntə/ (1927–) a German writer of NOVELS

grass·hop·per /ˈgræsˌhɑpə/ *n.* [C] an insect that has long back legs for jumping and that makes short loud noises → see also **knee-high to a grasshopper** at KNEE-HIGH[1] (2)

grass·land /ˈgræslænd/ *n.* [U] also **grasslands** [plural] EARTH SCIENCE large areas of land covered with wild grass SYN **prairie** → see also WETLAND, WOODLAND

ˌgrass ˈroots *n.* **the grass roots** the ordinary people in an organization, rather than the leaders —**grass-roots** *adj.*: *a grass-roots campaign*

ˈgrass snake *n.* [C] BIOLOGY a common snake that is not poisonous

gras·sy /ˈgræsi/ *adj.* covered with grass: *a grassy hill*

grate¹ /greɪt/ *v.* **1** [T] to rub cheese, fruit etc. against a rough or sharp surface in order to break it into small pieces: *The Parmesan cheese was freshly grated.* ▶see THESAURUS box at **cooking¹**, **cut¹** → see picture on page A32 **2** [I,T] to make an unpleasant sound by rubbing against another hard surface, or to make something do this: **+on/against** *chalk grating against a blackboard* **3** [I] to annoy someone SYN **irritate**: **+on** *Her high voice began to* ***grate on my nerves***. → see also GRATING²

grate² *n.* [C] **1** the frame and metal bars that hold the wood, coal etc. in a FIREPLACE **2** a metal frame with bars across it that covers a hole, window etc.: *The homeless slept on subway grates to keep warm.*

grate·ful /ˈgreɪtfəl/ *adj.* **1** feeling that you want to thank someone because of something kind that they have done, or showing this feeling SYN **thankful** OPP **ungrateful**: *a grateful patient of Dr. Watson* | *He gave her a grateful look.* | **+for** *They'd be grateful for your help.* | **grateful to sb (for sth)** *Mona was grateful to him for his support.* | **grateful that** *I'm grateful that I have a steady job that I enjoy.* | **be deeply/eternally/extremely grateful** *I am deeply grateful for everything you have done.* **2 I/we would be grateful if sb would/could...** used in formal situations or letters to make a request: *I would be grateful if you would allow me to visit your school.* [**Origin:** 1500–1600 *grate* **pleasing, thankful** (16–17 centuries), from Latin *gratus*] —**gratefully** *adv.*: *We gratefully accepted their offer.*

grat·er /ˈgreɪtɚ/ *n.* [C] a tool used for grating food

grat·i·fy /ˈgræt̬əˌfaɪ/ *v.* **gratifies, gratified, gratifying** [T] FORMAL **1** to satisfy a desire, need etc. SYN **satisfy**: *I do not intend to gratify the public's curiosity.* **2** [usually passive] to make someone feel pleased and satisfied: **+by** *She is gratified by all the public support.* | **be gratified (that)** *We are gratified that the court has agreed to hear our case.* | **be gratified to see/hear/learn etc.** *I was gratified to hear that they like my work.* —**gratification** /ˌgræt̬əfəˈkeɪʃən/ *n.* [C,U]

grat·i·fy·ing /ˈgræt̬əˌfaɪ-ɪŋ/ *adj.* pleasing and satisfying: **it's gratifying to do sth** *It's gratifying to note that progress has been made.*

grat·ing¹ /ˈgreɪt̬ɪŋ/ *n.* [C] a GRATE

grating² *adj.* **1** a grating sound is annoying and not nice to listen to SYN **irritating**: *a grating voice* **2** tending to annoy people SYN **irritating**: *a grating personality* —**gratingly** *adv.*

gra·tis /ˈgrætɪs, ˈgrɑ-/ *adj., adv.* done or given without payment SYN **free**: *Medical advice was provided gratis.*

grat·i·tude /ˈgræt̬əˌtud/ *n.* [U] the feeling of being grateful OPP **ingratitude**: **+for** *She expressed her gratitude for their continuing friendship.* | **with/in gratitude** *My father looked at him with gratitude.* | **gratitude to/toward sb** *I would like to* ***express*** *my* ***gratitude*** *to everyone who has helped today.* → see also **owe a debt (of gratitude) to sb** at DEBT (3)

gra·tu·i·tous /grəˈtuət̬əs/ *adj.* said or done without a good reason, in a way that offends someone SYN **unnecessry**: *movies full of* ***gratuitous violence*** —**gratuitously** *adv.*

gra·tu·i·ty /grəˈtuət̬i/ *n. plural* **gratuities** [C] FORMAL a TIP

grave¹ /greɪv/ *n.* [C] **1** the place in the ground where a dead body is buried → see also TOMB ▶see THESAURUS box at **funeral** **2 sb would turn/roll over in their grave** used to say that someone who is dead would strongly disapprove of something happening now: *Mozart would roll over in his grave if he heard this music.* **3 the grave** ESPECIALLY LITERARY death: *He took that secret to the grave.* [**Origin:** Old English *græf*] → see also **from (the) cradle to (the) grave** at CRADLE¹ (3), **dig your own grave** at DIG¹ (7), **have one foot in the grave** at FOOT¹ (15), **a watery grave** at WATERY (4)

grave² *adj.* FORMAL **1** very serious and worrying: *The situation is grave.* | *They are making a* ***grave mistake***. | *a* ***grave danger*** *to national security* | **grave doubts/concerns etc.** *He had grave doubts about the marriage.* **2** looking or sounding very serious, especially because something important or worrying has happened SYN **somber**: *Dr. Fromm looked grave. "I have some bad news," he said.* —**gravely** *adv.* → see also GRAVITY

grave³ *adj.* ENG. LANG. ARTS a grave ACCENT is a mark put above a letter in some languages, such as French, to show the pronunciation, for example è → see also ACUTE

grave·dig·ger /ˈgreɪvˌdɪgɚ/ *n.* [C] someone whose job is to dig graves

grav·el /ˈgrævəl/ *n.* [U] small stones used to make a surface for paths, roads etc.: *a gravel driveway* | *a* ***gravel pit*** (=a place where gravel is dug out of the ground) —**gravel** *v.* [T]

grav·el·ly /ˈgrævəli/ *adj.* **1** a gravelly voice has a low, rough sound **2** covered with or mixed with gravel: *gravelly soil*

grav·en /ˈgreɪvən/ *adj.* **a graven image** LITERARY an image or figure that has been made out of stone, wood, or metal

ˈgrave ˌrobber *n.* [C] someone who digs up graves to steal valuable things or the dead bodies inside

grave·side /ˈgreɪvsaɪd/ *n.* **at the graveside** beside a grave, especially when someone is being buried there —**graveside** *adj.* [only before noun] *graveside services*

grave·stone /ˈgreɪvstoʊn/ *n.* [C] a TOMBSTONE

grave·yard /ˈgreɪvyɑrd/ *n.* [C] **1** an area of ground where people are buried, often near a church → see also CEMETERY, CHURCHYARD ▶see THESAURUS box at **funeral** **2** a place where things that are no longer wanted are left: *a graveyard for old cars* **3** a place or situation where people or things fail: *Florida was the graveyard of his presidential ambition* (=he lost the election in Florida).

ˈgraveyard ˌshift *n.* [C] a period of time at night when people regularly work, especially in a factory, hospital etc.

grav·i·tate /ˈgrævəˌteɪt/ *v.* [I always + adv./prep.] FORMAL to be attracted to someone or something and therefore move toward it or become involved with it: **+to/toward** *Other people just naturally gravitated toward him.*

grav·i·ta·tion /ˌgrævəˈteɪʃən/ *n.* [U] PHYSICS the force that makes two objects move toward each other because of their MASS. The greater the mass, the greater the force of gravity.

grav·i·ta·tion·al /ˌgrævəˈteɪʃənl/ *adj.* [usually before noun] PHYSICS relating to or resulting from the force of gravity: *the Earth's* ***gravitational pull***

graviˌtational ˈfield *n.* [C] PHYSICS an area in space around every large mass such as a PLANET or star, that attracts other objects toward it

gra·vi·tro·pism /græˈvɪtrəˌpɪzəm/ *n.* [U] BIOLOGY the way a plant moves or grows as a reaction to gravity → see also PHOTOTROPISM, THIGMOTROPISM, TROPISM

grav·i·ty /ˈgrævət̬i/ *n.* [U] **1** PHYSICS the force that pulls one object toward another, especially the force that pulls objects toward the surface of the Earth or other PLANETS: *Mars' gravity is only about 38% of Earth's.* | **the law/force of gravity** **2** FORMAL the seriousness or importance of a situation etc.: **+of** *Do you understand the gravity of the situation?* **3** an extremely serious way of behaving, speaking etc. SYN **solemnity**: *They spoke with gravity.* → see also CENTER OF GRAVITY

gra·vy /ˈgreɪvi/ S3 *n. plural* **gravies** [C,U] **1** SAUCE made from the juice that comes from meat as it cooks, mixed with flour and water **2** INFORMAL something good that is more than you expected to get: *When you have a small baby, any sleep you get* ***is gravy***.

ˈgravy boat *n.* [C] a long bowl that you pour gravy from

ˈgravy ˌtrain *n.* **the gravy train** INFORMAL an organization, activity, or business from which many people can make money or profit without much effort

gray¹ /greɪ/ S2 W3 *adj.* **1** having a color of black

G

mixed with white, like rain clouds: *the icy gray waters of the Atlantic* ►see THESAURUS box at **hair** **2** having gray hair: **turn/go gray** *Ryan went gray when he was only 40.* **3** if the weather is gray, the sky is full of clouds and the sun is not bright SYN **dreary** ►see THESAURUS box at **sunshine** **4 a gray area** used to talk about a situation or subject in which something is not clearly a particular thing, so that people are not sure how to deal with it: *Many laws contain gray areas when applied to the Internet.* **5** looking pale because you are tired, frightened, or sick SYN **ashen**: *His face went gray with shock.* **6** boring and unattractive OPP **colorful**: *gray faceless bureaucrats*

gray² *n.* **1** [C,U] the color of smoke and rain clouds, between black and white **2** an animal, especially a horse or a WHALE, that is gray

gray³ *v.* [I] if someone grays or their hair grays, their hair becomes gray

gray·ing /ˈgreɪ-ɪŋ/ *n.* **the graying of sth** the situation in which the average age of a group of people increases, so that there are more old people than there were in the past: *the graying of America*

gray·ish /ˈgreɪ-ɪʃ/ *adj.* slightly gray

G

ˈgray ˌmarket *n.* [C] **1** the system by which people buy and sell goods that are hard to find, in a way that is legal, but that is not morally good or correct **2** TECHNICAL a situation in which people are buying and selling SHARES just before they are officially made available to be sold for the first time → see also BLACK MARKET

ˈgray ˌmatter *n.* [U] INFORMAL your intelligence, or your brain

ˌGray ˈPanthers an organization of older and RETIRED people

graze¹ /greɪz/ *v.* **1** [I,T] if an animal grazes or if you graze it, it eats grass that is growing: *sheep grazing in the field* | *Ranchers pay to graze their cattle on public land.* **2** [T] to touch something lightly while passing it, sometimes damaging it: *A bullet grazed his arm.* **3** [T] to break the surface of your skin by rubbing it against something rough SYN **scrape**: *Billy grazed his knee on the sidewalk.* **4** [I] INFORMAL to eat small amounts of food, usually all through the day, instead of having a full regular meal

graze² *n.* [C] a wound caused by rubbing, which slightly breaks the surface of your skin SYN **scrape**

GRE /ˌdʒi ɑr ˈi/ *n.* [C] TRADEMARK **Graduate Record Examination** a test taken by students who have completed a first degree and want to go to GRADUATE SCHOOL

grease¹ /gris/ *n.* [U] **1** a thick oily substance that is put on the moving parts of a car, machine etc. to make it run or move smoothly **2** soft fat from animals or vegetables, especially after it has melted: *bacon grease* **3** an oily substance that is produced by your skin [**Origin:** 1200–1300 Old French *craisse*, *graisse*, from Latin *crassus* **thick, fat**]

grease² *v.* [T] **1** to put grease on something: *Grease the pan before you pour the batter in.* **2 grease sb's palm** to give someone money in a secret or dishonest way in order to persuade them to do something **3 like greased lightning** INFORMAL extremely fast

ˈgrease gun *n.* [C] a tool for forcing grease into machinery

ˈgrease ˌmonkey *n.* [C] INFORMAL someone who repairs car engines or other machinery SYN **mechanic**

grease·paint /ˈgris-peɪnt/ *n.* [U] a thick soft kind of paint that actors use on their face or body

greas·er /ˈgrisɚ, -zɚ/ *n.* [C] OLD-FASHIONED a young man who is very interested in MOTORCYCLES and cars, and who behaves in a rough way

greas·y /ˈgrisi, -zi/ *adj.* *comparative* **greasier**, *superlative* **greasiest** covered in grease or oil, or full of grease SYN **oily**: *greasy French fries* | *long greasy hair* —**greasiness** *n.* [U]

ˌgreasy ˈspoon *n.* [C] INFORMAL a small cheap restaurant that mainly serves FRIED food

great¹ /greɪt/ S1 W1 *adj.*

1 EXTREME [usually before noun] very large in amount or degree: *The show was a great success.* | *The cost was considered to be too great.* | *He was in great pain.* | *It gives me great pleasure to introduce my next guest.* | ***A great many** people died.* | *The explosion caused **a great deal** (=a lot) of damage.* ►see THESAURUS box at **big**

2 VERY GOOD very good SYN **excellent**: *That was a great dinner.* | *It's great to be home.* | *It'd be great if you could come.* | **look/feel/sound great** *Your trip sounds great.* ►see THESAURUS box at **good¹**, **nice**

3 SKILLFUL able to do something well or deal with someone or something well: *Mrs. Townsend's a great teacher.* | +**at** *Candy's great at swimming.* | +**with** *He's great with babies.*

4 USEFUL INFORMAL very useful or appropriate for something, or giving you an advantage: +**for** *This stuff's great for getting stains out of clothes.* | ***The great thing about** eating out is that you don't have to wash dishes.*

5 LARGE USUALLY WRITTEN very large in size: *the Great Lakes* | *a great fireplace filled one wall* | *the great white shark* (=a type of shark that is larger than other sharks)

6 IMPORTANT [only before noun] important and having a lot of influence: *a great scientific achievement* | *the Great Powers of Europe* (=the countries with the most power and influence)

7 FAMOUS [only before noun] famous and admired by a lot of people, because of doing something very well: *one of the great writers of the 20th century*

8 IN GOOD HEALTH feeling or looking well and happy: **feel/look/sound great** *I feel great this morning!* | *You look great!*

SPOKEN PHRASES

9 EXPRESSION OF PLEASURE used when you are pleased about something that someone has just said: *Hey, that's great! Congratulations.* | *"I'll see you tomorrow." "Great!"*

10 EXPRESSION OF ANNOYANCE said when you are disappointed or annoyed about something: *"Your car won't be ready until next week." "Oh, great!"*

11 great minds think alike used humorously when you and another person have the same idea at the same time

12 it'd be great if... used to ask someone politely to do something to help you: *It'd be great if you could get here by 8:30 tomorrow.*

13 be no great shakes to not be very good or interesting, or not very skillful: *The food was no great shakes.*

14 Great Scott! OLD-FASHIONED used to express surprise

15 STRONGLY INTERESTED used to emphasize that someone is strongly interested in someone or something or does something a lot: *I'm a great fan of his.* | *My uncle's a great joker.* | *My grandfather was a **great believer** in education.* | *She was a **great admirer** of Eleanor Roosevelt.*

16 IMPORTANT EVENTS used in the title of an event of period of history that was very important: *the Great Depression of the 1930s*

17 the great outdoors the country, mountains, beaches etc., considered as enjoyable and healthy places to be

18 the Great used in the name or title of someone or something to show their importance: *Alexander the Great* | *the Great Houdini*

19 go great guns INFORMAL to do something very fast and successfully: *The business is going great guns.*

20 ADMIRABLE good or generous in a way that should be admired: *a great humanitarian gesture* | *a great lady*

21 Greater used before the name of a city to mean the city and its outer areas: *Greater Los Angeles*

[**Origin:** Old English] —**greatness** *n.* [U] → see also **be heavy/great/big with child** at CHILD (6)

great² S3 *adv.* INFORMAL **1** very well: *I can see great with these glasses.* **2 great big** very big: *a great big box of toys*

great³ *n.* [C usually plural] a very famous and successful person in a particular sport, profession etc.: *Jack Nicklaus is one of the* ***all-time greats*** *of golf.*

great- /greɪt/ *prefix* **1 great-granddaughter/great-nephew etc.** the GRANDDAUGHTER, NEPHEW etc. of your child **2 great-grandmother/great-uncle etc.** the grandmother, uncle etc. of one of your parents

ˌGreat ˌBarrier ˈReef, the the largest CORAL REEF in the world, off the northeast coast of Australia

ˌgreat ˈcircle *n.* [C] MATH a circle around the surface of a SPHERE (=round object) that is the INTERSECTION of the sphere and a PLANE (=flat surface) that passes through the center of the sphere

great·coat /ˈgreɪt˺koʊt/ *n.* [C] a long heavy coat

ˌGreat ˈCompromise, the HISTORY a proposal at the U.S. Constitutional Convention in 1787 that there should be a two-part LEGISLATURE, with one part having representatives according to the population of each state and the other having an equal number of representatives for each state

ˌGreat ˈCrash, the HISTORY the occasion in 1929 when the STOCKS in the U.S. STOCK MARKET suddenly lost a lot of their value, which led to great economic problems

ˌGreat Diˈviding ˈRange, the a system of mountain RANGES in Australia that follows the line of the east coast through the states of Victoria, New South Wales, and Queensland

ˌgreatest ˌcommon ˈfactor ABBREVIATION **GCF** *n.* [singular] MATH the largest positive INTEGER (=1, 2, 3, 4 etc.) that divides exactly into each of a set of numbers → see also LEAST COMMON MULTIPLE

ˌGreat ˈLakes, the a group of five lakes along the border between the U.S. and Canada, which consists of Lake Superior, Lake Michigan, Lake Huron, Lake Erie, and Lake Ontario

ˌGreat Leap ˈForward, the HISTORY the failed economic and social plan from 1958 to 1960 that tried to quickly change China into a modern INDUSTRIALIZED country

great·ly /ˈgreɪtli/ *adv.* FORMAL [usually before verb or participle] extremely or very much: *The money you sent us was greatly appreciated.* | *His work is greatly improved.* | *The colors vary greatly.*

ˌGreat ˈPlains *n.* **the Great Plains** the MIDWESTERN parts of the U.S. and Canada, where there is a lot of flat land that is used for farming

ˌGreat Salt ˈLake, the a lake in the U.S. state of Utah which is about 70 miles long and has very salty water

ˌGreat ˌSmoky ˈMountains, the also **the ˌGreat ˈSmokies, the Smokies** a range of mountains in the southeastern U.S. along the border between the states of North Carolina and Tennessee

ˌGreat ˈWar, the HISTORY another name for WORLD WAR I

grebe /grib/ *n.* [C] BIOLOGY a bird similar to a duck

Gre·cian /ˈgriʃən/ *adj.* LITERARY from ancient Greece, or having a style or appearance that is considered typical of ancient Greece: *a Grecian urn*

Greco- /grɛkoʊ/ *prefix* **1** relating to ancient Greece SYN **Greek** **2** ancient Greek and something else: *Greco-Roman art*

Gre·co, El /ˈgrɛkoʊ, ɛl/ → see EL GRECO

Greece /gris/ a country in southeast Europe on the Mediterranean Sea

greed /grid/ *n.* [U] a strong desire for more money, power, possessions etc. than you need SYN **avarice**

greed·y /ˈgridi/ *adj. comparative* **greedier**, *superlative* **greediest** DISAPPROVING **1** always wanting more money, power, possessions etc. SYN **avaricious**: *greedy lawyers* | *You're being greedy and selfish.* **2** wanting more food or drink than you need **—greedily** *adv.* **—greediness** *n.* [U]

Greek¹ /grik/ *adj.* **1** relating to or coming from Greece **2** relating to the Greek language **3 Greek god** INFORMAL a very attractive man

Greek² *n.* **1** [U] the language of modern or ancient Greece **2** [C] someone from Greece **3** [C] a member of a SORORITY or FRATERNITY at an American college or university **4 it's all Greek to me** INFORMAL used to say that you cannot understand something

ˌGreek ˈOrthodox ˈChurch, the a branch of the Christian Church in east Europe and southwest Asia, which split away from the western (now Catholic) church in the year 1054

green¹ /grin/ S1 W1 *adj.*

1 COLOR having the color of grass or leaves: *Go! The light's green.* | *green eyes* | **dark/light/bright etc. green** *a dark green shirt*

2 GRASSY covered with grass, trees, bushes etc.: *green fields*

3 FRUIT/PLANT not ready to be eaten, or very young: *green bananas*

4 ENVIRONMENT a) also **Green** relating to the environment or its protection: *green politics* **b)** harming the environment as little as possible: *better, greener cleaning products*

5 be green with envy to want very much something that someone else has

6 WITHOUT EXPERIENCE INFORMAL young and lacking experience SYN **naive**: *When I first went to New York I was still pretty green.*

7 have a green thumb to be good at making plants grow

8 ILL INFORMAL looking pale and unhealthy because you are sick: *George turned greener with each rock of the boat.*

9 the green-eyed monster HUMOROUS OR LITERARY JEALOUSY

10 the green stuff INFORMAL money

[**Origin:** Old English *grene*]

green² S3 W3 *n.* **1** [C,U] the color of grass and leaves: *different shades of green* **2** [C] a smooth flat area of grass around each hole on a GOLF COURSE **3 greens** [plural] **a)** vegetables with large green leaves: *Eat your greens, they're good for you.* **b)** leaves and branches used for decoration, especially at Christmas → see also GREENERY **4 Green** [C] POLITICS someone who belongs to or supports a political party which thinks that the protection of the environment is very important **5** [C] a level area of grass, especially in the middle of a small town → see also BOWLING GREEN

green³ *v.* [T] INFORMAL **1** also **green up** to fill an area with growing plants in order to make it more attractive **2** also **green up** if plants green or green up, they become green, especially in spring → see also GREENING

green·back /ˈgrinbæk/ *n.* [C] INFORMAL a dollar BILL

ˈgreen bean *n.* [C] a long thin green vegetable which is picked before the beans inside it grow → see picture on page A35

ˈgreen belt *n.* [C,U] an area of trees, fields etc. around a city, where no building is allowed

ˌGreen Beˈret *n.* [C] a member of the U.S. Special Army Forces

ˌgreen ˈcard *n.* [C] an official document that shows that someone who is not a citizen can legally live and work in the U.S.

Greene /grin/, **Gra·ham** /ˈgreɪəm/ (1904–1991) a British writer of NOVELS and plays

green·er·y /ˈgrinəri/ *n.* [U] green leaves and plants, often used as decoration

green·fly /ˈgrinflaɪ/ *n. plural* **greenflies** [C] a very small green insect that feeds on and damages young plants

green·gro·cer /ˈgrinˌgroʊsɚ, -ˌgroʊʃɚ/ *n.* [C] someone who sells fresh fruit and vegetables

green·horn /ˈgrinhɔrn/ *n.* [C] INFORMAL someone who lacks experience and can be easily deceived

green·house /ˈgrinhaʊs/ *n.* [C] a glass building used for growing plants that need warmth, light, and protection

ˈgreenhouse efˌfect *n.* [singular] EARTH SCIENCE the gradual warming of the air surrounding the Earth as a result of heat being trapped by an increase in gases such as CARBON DIOXIDE → see also GLOBAL WARMING

ˈgreenhouse ˌgas *n.* [C] EARTH SCIENCE a gas, especially CARBON DIOXIDE or METHANE, that is thought to trap heat above the Earth and cause the greenhouse effect

green·ing /ˈgrinɪŋ/ *n.* INFORMAL **the greening of sb/sth** the process of making a person or organization realize the importance of environmental problems

green·ish /ˈgrinɪʃ/ *adj.* slightly green

Green·land /ˈgrinlənd, -lænd/ a large island in the North Atlantic Ocean, near northeast Canada, which belongs to Denmark but has its own government

Green·land·ic /grinˈlændɪk/ *n.* [U] a language spoken by the Inuit people in Greenland —**Greenlandic** *adj.*

ˌgreen ˈlight *n.* [C] **1** a TRAFFIC LIGHT that shows cars they can go forward **2 give sb/sth the green light** to allow a piece of work, plan etc. to begin: *The board just gave us the green light to begin research.*

green·mail /ˈgrinmeɪl/ *n.* [U] the practice of buying STOCK in your own company, usually at a high price, from someone who is trying to take control of your company, or the money paid to do this

ˈGreen ˌMountains, the a part of the northern Appalachians that runs from southeastern Canada to the U.S. state of Massachusetts

ˌgreen ˈonion *n.* [C] an onion with a small white round part and a long green stem, usually eaten raw

Green·peace /ˈgrinpis/ an international organization whose members work to protect the environment from damage caused by industrial processes or military activities

ˌgreen ˈpepper *n.* [C] a vegetable with green flesh and white seeds, that you can cook or eat raw

ˌgreen revoˈlution *n.* [singular] **1** BIOLOGY a large increase in the amount of crops, such as wheat or rice, that are produced because of improved scientific methods of farming **2** the interest in protecting the environment that has developed in many parts of the world

ˈgreen room *n.* **the green room** the room in a theater, television STUDIO etc. in which performers wait when they are not on stage performing

ˌgreen ˈsalad *n.* [C] a SALAD made with LETTUCE and other raw green vegetables

ˌgreen ˈtea *n.* [U] light-colored tea made from leaves that have been heated with steam, especially popular in eastern Asia

Green·wich Mean Time /ˌgrɛnɪtʃ min ˈtaɪm, ˌgrɛnɪtʃ ˈmin ˌtaɪm/ ABBREVIATION **GMT** *n.* [U] the time as measured at Greenwich in London, England, which is used as a standard to set times all over the world

Greenwich Vil·lage /ˌgrɛnɪtʃ ˈvɪlɪdʒ/ an area of New York City known for being the home of many artists

greet /grit/ W3 *v.* [T] **1** to say hello to someone or welcome them SYN **welcome**: *Diana greeted them warmly.* | **greet sb with sth** *Roz's mother greeted her with hugs and kisses.* **2** [always + adv./prep.] to react to something in a particular way: **greet sth with/by sth** *The proposal was greeted with loud laughter.* **3** to be the first thing you see or hear when you arrive somewhere: *As we entered, complete chaos greeted us.* [**Origin:** Old English *gretan*]

greet·ing /ˈgriṭɪŋ/ *n.* [C] **1** something you say or do when you meet someone: *a warm greeting* | *He offered me his hand **in greeting**.* | *The two men **exchanged greetings*** (=said hello to each other). **2 birthday/Christmas etc. greetings** a message saying that you hope someone will be happy and healthy on their BIRTHDAY, at Christmas etc. **3 greetings** FORMAL or HUMOROUS used to say hello to someone

ˈgreeting card *n.* [C] a card that you send to someone on their BIRTHDAY, at Christmas etc.

gre·gar·i·ous /grɪˈgɛriəs/ *adj.* **1** someone who is gregarious is friendly and enjoys being with other people: *a gregarious child* ►see THESAURUS box at **sociable** **2** TECHNICAL gregarious animals tend to live in a group [**Origin:** 1600–1700 *gregarius*, from *grex* **group of animals**]

Gre·go·ri·an cal·en·dar /grɪˌgɔriən ˈkæləndɚ/ *n.* **the Gregorian calendar** the system of arranging the 365 days of the year in months and giving numbers to the years from the birth of Jesus Christ, used in the West since 1582

Greˌgorian ˈchant *n.* [C,U] a type of church music for voices alone

Greg·o·ry XIII, Pope /ˌgrɛgəri ðə θɚˈtinθ/ (1502–1585) the POPE who introduced the Gregorian calendar

grem·lin /ˈgrɛmlən/ *n.* [C] an imaginary evil spirit that is blamed for problems in machinery

Gre·na·da /grəˈneɪdə/ a country in the Caribbean Sea consisting of the island of Grenada and some of a group of small islands called the Grenadines —**Grenadian** *n., adj.*

gre·nade /grəˈneɪd/ *n.* [C] a small bomb that can be thrown by hand or fired from a gun: *a hand grenade*

gren·a·dier /ˌgrɛnəˈdɪr/ *n.* [C] a soldier in a special CORPS or REGIMENT

gren·a·dine /ˈgrɛnəˌdin, ˌgrɛnəˈdin/ *n.* [U] a sweet liquid made from POMEGRANATES that is used in drinks

greenhouse effect

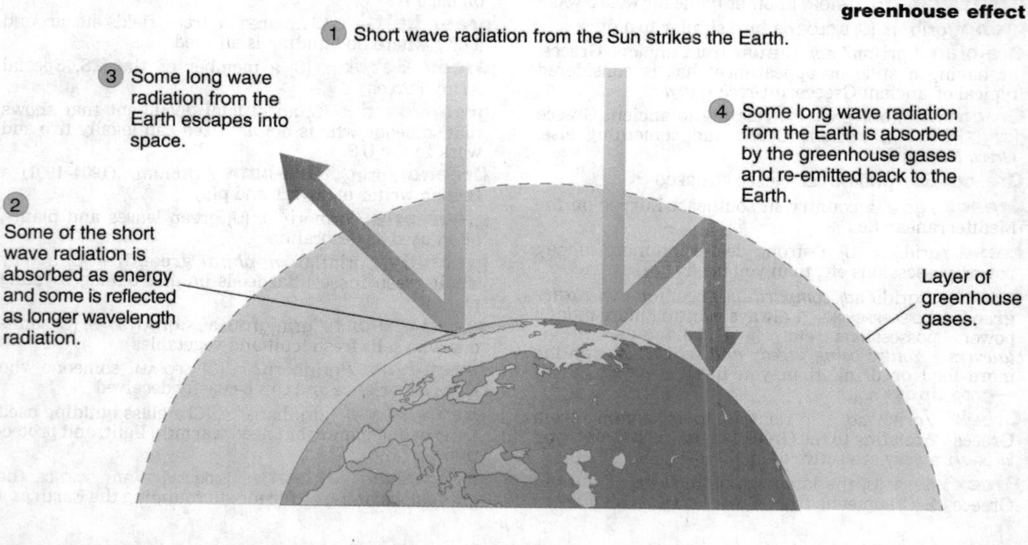

1 Short wave radiation from the Sun strikes the Earth.
2 Some of the short wave radiation is absorbed as energy and some is reflected as longer wavelength radiation.
3 Some long wave radiation from the Earth escapes into space.
4 Some long wave radiation from the Earth is absorbed by the greenhouse gases and re-emitted back to the Earth.
Layer of greenhouse gases.

Gretz·ky /ˈgrɛtski/, **Wayne** /weɪn/ (1961–) a Canadian HOCKEY player

grew /gru/ *v.* the past tense of GROW

grey /greɪ/ *adj.* another spelling of GRAY

grey·hound /ˈgreɪhaʊnd/ *n.* [C] a type of thin dog that can run very fast and is used in races

grid /grɪd/ *n.* **1** [C] a pattern of straight lines that cross each other and form squares: *The city's streets are organized in a grid.* **2** [C] a system of numbered squares printed on a map so that the exact position of any place can be found **3** the network of electricity supply wires that connects POWER STATIONS and provides electricity to buildings in an area: *a power grid* **4** [C] a set of starting positions for all the cars in a motor race

grid·dle /ˈgrɪdl/ *n.* [C] a flat metal plate that is used for cooking on top of a STOVE or over a fire

grid·dle·cake /ˈgrɪdlˌkeɪk/ *n.* [C] a PANCAKE

grid·i·ron /ˈgrɪdaɪərn/ *n.* [C] **1** a football field **2** an open frame of metal bars for cooking meat or fish over a very hot fire

grid·lock /ˈgrɪdlɑk/ *n.* [singular, U] **1** a situation in which streets in a city are so full of cars that they cannot move: *We spent two hours stuck* ***in gridlock.*** **2** a situation in which nothing can happen, usually because people disagree strongly —**gridlocked** *adj.*

grief /grif/ *n.* **1** [U] extreme sadness, especially because someone you love has died: *She was overcome with grief.* | **+at/over** *the man's grief over the death of his wife* **2 give sb grief (about sth)** INFORMAL to criticize someone in an annoying way: *Frank always gives me grief about my sloppy handwriting.* **3 good grief!** SPOKEN used when you are slightly surprised or annoyed: *Good grief! Look the mess in here!* **4** [U] INFORMAL trouble or problems: *Don't argue with him. It's not worth the grief.* [**Origin:** 1200–1300 Old French *gref*, from Latin *gravis*]

grief·strick·en /ˈgrɪfˌstrɪkən/ also **grief·struck** /-ˌstrʌk/ *adj.* feeling very sad because of something that has happened

Grieg /grig/, **Ed·vard** /ˈɛdvɑrd/ (1843–1907) a Norwegian musician who wrote CLASSICAL music

griev·ance /ˈgrivəns/ *n.* [C,U] a complaint about an unfair situation or event that affects and upsets you, or the belief that you have been treated unfairly: **+against** *Smith has a legitimate grievance against the company.* | *One woman* ***filed a grievance*** (=officially complained) *after she was refused a promotion.* | *a deep* ***sense of grievance***

grieve /griv/ *v.* **1** [I,T] to feel extremely sad, especially because someone you love has died: *We are still grieving the death of our mother.* | **+over/for** *I felt like I would never stop grieving over my dead brother.* **2** [T] if something grieves you, it makes you feel very unhappy: **it grieves sb to think/say/see etc.** *It grieves me to see him wasting his talent like that.*

grieved /grivd/ *adj.* LITERARY very sad and upset: *The whole community is deeply grieved by her tragic death.*

griev·ous /ˈgrivəs/ *adj.* **1** FORMAL very serious and likely to be very harmful: *a grievous error* **2** ESPECIALLY LITERARY a grievous wound or pain is severe and hurts a lot —**grievously** *adv.*

grif·fin, gryphon /ˈgrɪfən/ *n.* [C] an imaginary animal in stories that has a lion's body and an EAGLE's wings and head

Grif·fith /ˈgrɪfɪθ/, **D.W.** (1875–1948) a U.S. movie DIRECTOR, famous especially for inventing new ways of making movies and of using the camera

grift·er /ˈgrɪftər/ *n.* [C] INFORMAL someone who dishonestly obtains something, especially money —**grift** *v.* [T]

grill¹ /grɪl/ *v.* **1** [I,T] if you grill something, you cook it by putting it on a flat metal frame with bars across it, over very strong direct heat → see also BROIL: *The chicken is grilled over an open flame.* ▸see THESAURUS box at **cook¹** **2** [T] to ask someone a lot of difficult questions in order to make them explain their actions, opinions etc.: *Officers grilled the men for two hours.* | **+on/about** *My mom always grills me about where I've been.*

grill² *n.* [C] **1** a flat metal frame with bars across it that can be put over strong direct heat, so that food can be cooked on it **2** a place where you can buy and eat grilled food: *Baker's Bar and Grill* **3** also **grille** a frame with metal bars or wire across it that is put in front of a window or door for protection **4** also **grille** the metal bars at the front of a car that protect the RADIATOR

grilled /grɪld/ *adj.* something that is grilled has been cooked on a grill: *grilled chicken*

grill·ing /ˈgrɪlɪŋ/ *n.* [C] the process of asking someone a lot of difficult questions in order to make them explain their actions or opinions

grim /grɪm/ *adj.* *comparative* **grimmer**, *superlative* **grimmest** **1** making you feel worried and unhappy: *a grim economic situation* | *The future of public schools in America* ***looks pretty grim.*** | ***the grim reality of*** *war* **2** looking or sounding very serious because the situation is very bad: *a grim-faced policeman* | *It was their* ***grim determination*** (=serious determination in spite of difficulties or dangers) *that got them to the top of Mount Everest.* | *Rosen came out of the meeting* ***looking grim*** (=looking serious and worried). **3** ugly and unattractive: *a grim industrial town* —**grimly** *adv.*: *a grimly realistic movie*

grim·ace¹ /ˈgrɪməs/ *v.* [I] to twist your face in an ugly way because you do not like something, because you are feeling pain, or because you are trying to be funny: **+at** *She grimaced at her reflection in the mirror.* | *Duran bent over and* ***grimaced in pain.***

grimace² *n.* [C] an expression you make by twisting your face because you do not like something or because you are feeling pain: *Bernie gave a grimace of disgust and left the room.*

grime /graɪm/ *n.* [U] oily dirt that forms a black layer on surfaces: *His hands were black with grime from working on the car.*

Grimm /grɪm/ the family name of two German brothers, Jakob Grimm (1785–1863) and Wilhelm Grimm (1786–1859), famous for writing "Grimm's Fairy Tales", a collection of nearly 200 stories

ˌGrim ˈReaper *n.* **the Grim Reaper** a figure, usually a SKELETON in a black ROBE holding a SCYTHE, who represents death, especially in stories and poems

grim·y /ˈgraɪmi/ *adj.* *comparative* **grimier**, *superlative* **grimiest** covered with black oily dirt: *grimy factories*

grin¹ /grɪn/ *v.* **grinned, grinning** [I] **1** to smile widely: *She grinned with delight.* | **+at** *Every time I walk by him, he just grins at me.* | *Thomas was* ***grinning from ear to ear*** (=grinning very widely) *as he received the trophy.* ▸see THESAURUS box at **smile¹** **2 grin and bear it** to accept a bad or difficult situation without complaining, especially because you realize there is nothing you can do to make it better

grin² *n.* [C] a wide smile: *a friendly grin* → see also **wipe the smile/grin off sb's face** at WIPE¹ (4)

grind¹ /graɪnd/ *v.* *past tense and past participle* **ground** /graʊnd/

1 INTO SMALL PIECES [T] **a)** to break something such as grain or coffee beans into small pieces or powder, either in a machine or between two hard surfaces SYN **grind up**: *Grind some black pepper over the salad.* **b)** to cut food, especially raw meat, into very small pieces by putting it through a machine SYN **mince** ▸see THESAURUS box at **press¹**

2 SMOOTH/SHARP [T] to make something smooth or sharp by rubbing it on a hard surface or by using a machine: *The lenses are ground to a high standard of precision.*

3 PRESS STH DOWN [T always + adv./prep.] to press something down into a surface and rub it with a strong twisting movement: **grind sth into/in sth** *He ground his cigarette butt into the ashtray.*

4 PRESS AGAINST STH [I always + adv./prep.] to press and rub against something: **+against** *I hate the sound of metal grinding against metal.*

G

5 grind your teeth to rub your upper and lower teeth together, making a noise
6 grind to a halt a) if a vehicle or traffic grinds to a halt, it stops gradually: *Traffic ground to a halt as we got closer to the accident.* **b)** if a country, organization, or process grinds to a halt, it gradually stops working: *Production ground to a halt at five of the factories.* → see also **have an ax to grind** at AX[1] (3)

grind sb ↔ **down** *phr. v.* to make someone lose all courage, hope, or energy, especially by treating them badly: *The air attacks are grinding down the enemy's ability to fight.*

grind on *phr. v.* to continue for a long time, which seems longer than necessary: *The trial has been grinding on for six months now.*

grind sth ↔ **out** *phr. v.* **1** to produce information, writing, music etc. in such large amounts that it becomes boring: *Franklin just keeps grinding out detective stories.* **2** to do something with a lot of effort: *We just barely ground out a win.*

grind sth ↔ **up** *phr. v.* to break something such as grain or coffee beans into small pieces or powder, either in a machine or between two hard surfaces: *Could you grind up some coffee beans for me?*

grind² *n.* **1** [singular] something that is hard work and physically or mentally tiring or boring: *All the paperwork I have to do is* ***a real grind.*** | ***the daily grind*** (=things that you have to do every day that are tiring or boring) **2** [C] DISAPPROVING INFORMAL a student who never does anything except study

grind·er /ˈgraɪndɚ/ *n.* [C] **1** a machine used to break up or cut food into small pieces: *a coffee grinder* **2** a HERO SANDWICH → see also ORGAN GRINDER

grind·ing /ˈgraɪndɪŋ/ *adj.* [only before noun] **1 grinding poverty/work etc.** a bad situation that makes your life very difficult and unhappy, and never seems to improve **2** a grinding noise is the continuous annoying noise of machinery parts rubbing together

grind·stone /ˈgraɪndstoʊn/ *n.* [C] a large round stone that is turned like a wheel, used for making tools, knives etc. sharp → see also **keep your nose to the grindstone** at NOSE[1] (7)

gri·ot /ˈgrioʊ/ *n.* [C] ENG. LANG. ARTS someone whose job is to tell history and stories in western Africa

grip¹ /grɪp/ *n.*
1 FIRM HOLD [C usually singular] the way you hold something tightly, or your ability to do this: *He has a firm grip.* | **+on** *It's hard to get a good grip on this box.* | *Ruth* ***tightened*** *her* ***grip on*** *his arm.*
2 POWER [singular] power and control over someone or something: **have/keep a grip on sth** *He struggled to keep a grip on his temper.* | **a tight/firm/strong/iron etc grip** *He ruled the country with an iron grip.* | *The army has* ***tightened*** *its* ***grip on*** *the city.*
3 come to grips with sth to understand and deal with a difficult problem or situation: *Eric still hasn't come to grips with his alcoholism.*
4 get a grip (on sth) SPOKEN to start controlling your emotions when you have been very upset: *Get a grip – you're overreacting.*
5 lose your grip (on sth) INFORMAL to become less confident and less able to deal with a situation: *Unfortunately, lately her mother seems to have lost her grip on reality.*
6 be in the grip/grips of sth to be experiencing a very bad situation that cannot be controlled or stopped: *Our economy is deep in the grips of a recession.*
7 PART OF OBJECT FOR HOLDING [C] a special part of a handle that has a rough surface so that you can hold it firmly without it slipping: *a pen with a rubber grip*
8 TIRES/SHOES [C,U] the ability of something to stay on a surface without slipping: *tires with good grip*
9 CAMERAMAN [C] someone whose job is to move the cameras around while a television show or movie is being made
10 BAG [C] OLD-FASHIONED a bag used for traveling SYN **suitcase**

grip² *v.* **gripped, gripping** [T] **1** to hold something very tightly: **grip sth tightly/firmly** *He gripped my arm so tightly that it hurt.* ►see THESAURUS box at **hold¹** **2** to have a strong effect on someone or something: *I was suddenly gripped by fear.* **3** to hold someone's attention and interest: *The book gripped me from start to finish.* **4** if something grips a surface, it stays on it without slipping: *Radial tires grip the road well.* → see also GRIPPING

gripe¹ /graɪp/ *v.* [I] to complain about something continuously and in an annoying way: **+about** *What are you griping about now?*

gripe² *n.* INFORMAL **1** [C] something unimportant that you complain about: *Students' main gripe is the poor quality of the dorm food.* **2 the gripes** OLD-FASHIONED sudden bad stomach pains

grippe, grip /grɪp/ *n.* [singular] OLD USE the FLU

grip·ping /ˈgrɪpɪŋ/ *adj.* a gripping movie, story etc. is very exciting and interesting and keeps your attention

gris·ly /ˈgrɪzli/ *adj. comparative* **grislier**, *superlative* **grisliest** extremely nasty and bad, especially because death or violence is involved: *a grisly murder*

grist /grɪst/ *n.* **grist for the mill** something that is useful in a particular situation: *The star's love life has long been grist for the tabloid mill.*

gris·tle /ˈgrɪsəl/ *n.* [U] the part of a piece of meat that is not soft enough to eat —**gristly** *adj.*

grit¹ /grɪt/ *n.* **1** [U] very small pieces of stone or sand **2** [U] INFORMAL determination and courage **3 grits** [plural] crushed HOMINY grain that is cooked and often eaten for breakfast **4 Grit** CANADIAN a member of the Liberal Party in Canada —**gritty** *adj.*

grit² *v.* **gritted, gritting** [T] **1 grit your teeth** to use all your determination to continue in spite of difficulties: *I guess I'll have to just grit my teeth and hope for the best.* **2** to scatter grit on a frozen road to make it less slippery

grit·ty /ˈgrɪti/ *adj. comparative* **grittier**, *superlative* **grittiest** **1** having a lot of courage or determination: *a gritty football player* **2** full of dirt, small stones, or sand: *a gritty dust storm* **3** showing a difficult or unpleasant situation as it really is: *gritty realism*

griz·zled /ˈgrɪzəld/ *adj.* LITERARY having gray or grayish hair

griz·zly bear /ˈgrɪzli ˌbɛr/ also **grizzly** *n.* [C] a very large brown bear that lives in the Northwest of North America → see picture on page A34

groan¹ /groʊn/ *v.* **1** [I] to make a long deep sound to express pain, disappointment, or sexual pleasure SYN **moan**: *Everyone groaned as Scott began to tell another one of his stupid jokes.* **2** [I] if something groans, it makes a long low deep sound as it moves or as it holds something heavy: *The bed groaned as he climbed in.* **3** [I,T] to complain about something: *"It's too hot," he groaned.* **4** [I] if a table groans with food, there is a very large amount of food on it

groan² *n.* [C] **1** a long deep sound that you make when to express pain, disappointment, or sexual pleasure SYN **moan**: *The crowd* ***let out a groan*** *when he dropped the ball.* **2** LITERARY a long low sound like someone groaning: *The door opened with a groan.*

groats /groʊts/ *n.* [plural] grain, especially OATS with the outer shell removed

gro·cer /ˈgroʊsɚ, -ʃɚ/ *n.* [C] someone who owns or works in a grocery store [**Origin:** 1200–1300 Old French *grossier* **person who sells in large quantities**, from *gros* **big, thick**]

gro·cer·ies /ˈgroʊsəriz, ˈgroʊʃriz/ *n.* [plural] food and other things used in the home that are sold at a grocery store or SUPERMARKET

ˈgrocery ˌshopping *n.* [U] the activity of buying food and other things at a grocery store

ˈgrocery store also **grocery** S3 *n.* [C] a store that sells food and other things used in the home SYN **supermarket**

gro·dy /ˈgroʊdi/ *adj.* SPOKEN a word meaning "very bad" or "offensive," used especially by children

grog /grɑg/ *n.* [U] **1** a mixture of strong alcoholic drinks, especially RUM, and water **2** INFORMAL any alcoholic drink [**Origin:** 1700–1800 *Old Grog*, a name given (because he wore a coat of *grogram*, a type of rough cloth) to Edward Vernon, the 18th-century British navy officer who started the practice of giving sailors rum and water to drink]

grog·gy /ˈgrɑgi/ *adj. comparative* **groggier**, *superlative* **groggiest** weak and unable to walk steadily or think clearly because you are sick or very tired: *Bill looked groggy after studying all night.*

groin /grɔɪn/ *n.* [C] the place where the tops of your legs meet the front of your body [**Origin:** Old English *grynde* **valley**; influenced by *groin* **animal's nose** (14–19 centuries)]

grom·met /ˈgrɑmɪt/ *n.* [C] **1** a small metal ring used to make a hole in cloth or leather stronger **2** MEDICINE a small piece of plastic put into a child's ear in order to remove liquid from it

groom¹ /grum/ *v.* **1** [T] to prepare someone for an important job or position in society by training them over a long period: **groom sb to do sth** *Graham's son was being groomed to take over the business.* | **groom sb as/for sth** *They're grooming Tim for a managerial position.* **2** [T] to take care of animals, especially horses, by cleaning and brushing them **3** [I,T] to take care of your own appearance by keeping your hair and clothes clean and neat **4** [T] to prepare an area for a particular activity: *The ski runs are groomed daily.* **5** [I,T] if an animal grooms itself or another animal, it cleans its own fur and skin or that of the other animal **6** [T] to take care of plants by cutting off leaves or branches —**grooming** *n.* [U] → see also WELL-GROOMED

groom² *n.* [C] **1** a man at the time he gets married, or just after he is married SYN **bridegroom** ►see THESAURUS box at **wedding** **2** someone whose job is to feed, clean, and take care of horses

grooms·man /ˈgrumzmən/ *n.* [C] a friend of a GROOM who has special duties at a wedding

groove¹ /gruv/ *n.* [C] **1** a thin line cut into a surface, especially to guide the movement of something: *The bolt slid easily into the groove.* **2 be/get in the groove** INFORMAL to begin to do an activity well and without much effort or thought, especially for a period of time: *We got in a groove in the second half and won the game.* **3** INFORMAL the beat of a piece of popular music, especially one that you can dance to: *the music's hypnotic grooves* **4 be in a groove** to be living or working in a comfortable situation that has been the same for a long time and that is unlikely to change, so that it is easy for you

groove² *v.* [T] to make a long narrow track in something —**grooved** *adj.*

groov·y /ˈgruvi/ *adj. comparative* **groovier**, *superlative* **grooviest** OLD-FASHIONED INFORMAL fashionable, modern, and fun

grope¹ /groʊp/ *v.* **1** [I always + adv./prep.] to try to find something that you cannot see by feeling with your hands: +**for/through/around etc.** *He groped for the light switch.* **2 grope your way along/across etc.** to go somewhere by feeling the way with your hands, because you cannot see: *I groped my way down the hallway till I found my room.* **3** [I] to try hard to find the right words to say, or the right solution to a problem, but without any real idea of how to do this: +**for** *He groped for something to say.* **4** [T] INFORMAL to touch or GRAB someone's body in a sexual way, when they do not like it ►see THESAURUS box at **touch¹**

grope² *n.* [C] INFORMAL an act of groping

Gro·pi·us /ˈgroʊpiəs/, **Wal·ter** /ˈwɔltɚ/ (1883–1969) a German-American ARCHITECT famous for starting and directing the Bauhaus school of design

gross¹ /groʊs/ S2 *adj.* **1** SPOKEN very disgusting to look at or think about SYN **disgusting**: *Ooh, gross! The dog just threw up on the carpet!* **2** ECONOMICS a gross amount of money is the total amount before any taxes or costs have been subtracted: *a gross income of $150,000* | **gross receipts/sales/revenues etc.** *The chain had gross sales totaling $10 million.* → see also NET **3 gross negligence/misconduct/injustice etc.** wrong and unacceptable in a way that is very clear or extreme: *gross inequalities in salaries* **4** [only before noun] gross weight is the total weight of something, including its wrapping → see also NET **5** extremely fat and unattractive [**Origin:** 1300–1400 Old French *gros* **big, thick**, from Latin *grossus*] —**grossly** *adv.*: *grossly overweight* —**grossness** *n.* [U]

gross² *adv.* **make/earn $25,000 etc. gross** to earn a particular amount of money before taxes have been subtracted: *Henry makes more than $30,000 gross.*

gross³ *v.* [T] to gain an amount as a total profit, or earn it as a total amount, before taxes have been subtracted: *The movie grossed $7.7 million.*

gross sb ↔ out *phr. v.* SPOKEN to make someone feel sick because of something you say or do: *You guys totally gross me out.*

gross⁴ *determiner, n. plural* **gross** [C] **1** a total profit before taxes have been subtracted: *a gross of $2 million* **2** a quantity of 144 of something: *a gross of pencils*

ˌgross doˌmestic ˈproduct ABBREVIATION **GDP** *n.* **the gross domestic product** ECONOMICS the total value of all the goods and services produced in a country, except for income received from abroad → see also GROSS NATIONAL PRODUCT

ˌgross ˈmargin *n.* [C] TECHNICAL the financial difference between what something costs to produce and what it is sold for

ˌgross ˌnational ˈproduct ABBREVIATION **GNP** *n.* **the gross national product** ECONOMICS the total value of all the goods and services produced in a country, including income from abroad → see also GROSS DOMESTIC PRODUCT

ˌgross ˈprofit *n.* [C] GROSS MARGIN

Gros Ventre /ˈgroʊ vɑnt/ another name for the Atsina and Hidatsa tribes of Native Americans

gro·tesque¹ /groʊˈtɛsk/ *adj.* **1** extremely ugly in a strange or unnatural way: *grotesque lumps on the skin* **2** strange or unusual in a way that is shocking or offensive: *a grotesque act of cruelty* [**Origin:** 1500–1600 French, Old Italian *(pittura) grottesca* **cave painting**, from *grotta*] —**grotesquely** *adv.*

grotesque² *n.* [C] an image in art of someone who is strangely ugly

grot·to /ˈgrɑt̬oʊ/ *n. plural* **grottoes** or **grottos** [C] a small natural CAVE, or one that someone has made

grouch¹ /graʊtʃ/ *n.* [C] INFORMAL someone who is always slightly angry or complaining: *Dad's such a grouch in the morning.*

grouch² *v.* [I + about] INFORMAL to complain in a slightly angry way SYN **grumble**

grouch·y /ˈgraʊtʃi/ *adj. comparative* **grouchier**, *superlative* **grouchiest** in a bad mood, especially because you are tired —**grouchiness** *n.* [U]

ground¹ /graʊnd/ S1 W1 *n.*
1 EARTH [singular, U] **a)** the surface of the Earth → see also FLOOR: ***The ground** was covered with snow.* | *A large branch was lying **on the ground**.* | *The platform is at least four inches **off the ground*** (=above the ground). | **below/under/above ground** *Miners work 10-hour shifts below ground.* **b)** the soil on and under the surface of the earth: ***The ground** is too hard to plant trees now.* | *marshy ground*

THESAURUS

ground the surface under your feet when you are outside: *It was so cold the ground was frozen.*
floor the surface under your feet when you are inside a building: *the kitchen floor*
land is an area of ground that is owned by someone or used for something, or that is not covered by water: *land used for growing corn*
bed the ground at the bottom of a river, lake, ocean, etc.: *During the summer the river bed is dry.*

G

dirt/earth/soil the substance that plants grow in: *fertile soil*
mud very wet soil: *the mud in the fields after the rain*

2 AREA OF LAND a) [C] a large area of land or ocean that is used for a particular activity or sport: **a hunting/feeding/burial etc. ground** *The forest is a feeding ground for moose and deer.* **b) grounds** [plural] the land or gardens around a building: *prison grounds* **c)** [U] an area of land, usually without many trees or buildings on it: *This ground is considered sacred by local tribes.* | *Residents went to* ***higher ground*** (=a hill, for example) *to escape the flood.*
3 SUBJECT [U] a particular subject, topic, set of opinions, area of experience etc.: *Scientists are* ***breaking new ground*** (=discovering new ideas) *in surgical techniques.* | *Vaughn's book* ***covers*** *much of* ***the same ground*** (=the same things) *as Graham's.* | *Keith's* ***on familiar ground*** (=dealing with a subject he knows a lot about) *with computers.* | *His speech* ***covered a lot of ground.*** | *He's* ***on dangerous ground*** (=talking about something that might be offensive or embarrassing) *here in terms of political correctness.* | *At this point, I must admit I'm* ***on shaky ground*** (=talking about something you are not sure about). | **on firm/solid/safe ground** (=discussing a subject that you know a lot about and that is unlikely to offend anyone)
4 lose ground to lose an advantage and become less successful: *The radicals have steadily lost ground to the moderates.*
5 gain ground a) to get an advantage and become more successful: *Stock prices gained ground in late trading today.* **b)** if an idea, belief etc. gains ground, it starts to become accepted or believed by more people: *Respect for human rights continues to gain ground.*
6 REASON grounds [plural, U] a reason, especially one that makes you think that something is true or correct: **+for** *Mental cruelty can be grounds for divorce.* | *My opposition of the war is based* ***on moral grounds.*** | *They have no* ***legal grounds*** *to file a lawsuit.* | *Zoe was awarded compensation* ***on the grounds that*** *the doctor had been negligent.*
7 common/middle ground an area of opinion that two people or groups share: *The two candidates found little common ground.*
8 get (sth) off the ground if a plan, a business idea etc. gets off the ground, or if you get it off the ground, it starts to be successful: *Construction of the theme park never got off the ground.*
9 stand/hold your ground a) to refuse to change your opinion in spite of opposition: *Kessler vowed to stand his ground and fight for justice.* **b)** to stay where you are when someone threatens you, in order to show them that you are not afraid
10 give ground to change your opinion, or to agree that someone else is right about something: *Neither side gave ground in the budget battle.*
11 cover a lot of ground to travel a very long distance: *We covered a lot of ground in two weeks.*
12 to the ground until nothing is left standing: *The whole building burnt to the ground.*
13 SMALL PIECES grounds [plural] the small pieces of something such as coffee which sink to the bottom of a liquid: *coffee grounds*
14 from the ground up starting with the most basic things or the least important people and moving all the way up through the most important: *They say they're going to reorganize the whole company from the ground up.*
15 fertile ground/breeding ground a situation in which it is easy for something to develop: *The housing projects are fertile ground for drug dealers.*
16 on the ground in the actual place where something, especially a war, is happening, rather than in another place where it is being discussed: *While the talks continue, the situation on the ground is worsening.*
17 work/drive/run yourself into the ground to work so hard that you become extremely tired: *Kay's working herself into the ground trying to meet her deadlines.*
18 on your own ground also **on home ground** in the place or situation that is most familiar to you, or where you feel the most comfortable: *I wouldn't dream of meeting my ex-husband again unless I was on home ground.*
19 ELECTRICAL [singular] PHYSICS a wire that connects a piece of electrical equipment to the ground for safety
20 BACKGROUND [C] TECHNICAL the background for a design, painting etc. SYN **background**
[Origin: Old English *grund*] → see also **break fresh/new ground** at BREAK[1] (37), **have/keep both feet on the ground** at FOOT[1] (20), **hit the ground running** at HIT[1] (26), **take/claim/seize etc. the moral high ground** at MORAL[1] (4)

ground² *v.* **1** [T usually passive] to refuse to allow an aircraft or pilot to fly: *All planes are grounded until the fog clears.* **2 be grounded in/on sth** to be based on something: *Our beliefs are firmly grounded in reality.* **3** [T] INFORMAL to punish a child by making them stay home and not allowing them to see their friends for a particular period of time: *You'll be grounded for a week if I catch you smoking again.* **4** [T] PHYSICS to make a piece of electrical equipment safe by connecting it to the ground with a wire: *Ground the black cable to the engine block.* **5** [I,T] if you ground a boat or if it grounds, it hits ground where the water is not very deep, so that it cannot move → see also WELL-GROUNDED
ground sb **in** sth *phr. v.* to teach someone the basic things they should know in order to be able to do something: *Most parents want their children to be grounded in the basics of reading and writing.*
ground out *phr. v.* to hit a ball in baseball so that it goes over the ground to a player who throws the ball to first base before you get there, so that you are OUT

ground³ *adj.* [only before noun] **1 ground beef/turkey/pork etc.** meat that has been cut up into very small pieces, often formed into a shape to be cooked, for example for HAMBURGERS **2** ground coffee or nuts have been broken up into powder or very small pieces, using a special machine

ground⁴ *v.* the past tense and past participle of GRIND

'ground ball *n.* [C] a GROUNDER

ground·break·ing /ˈgraʊndˌbreɪkɪŋ/ *adj.* **1** groundbreaking work involves making new discoveries, using new methods etc.: *groundbreaking research* **2** the act of digging up the ground in order to start building something

'ground cloth *n.* [C] a piece of material that water cannot pass through, which people sleep on or put under a tent when they are camping

'ground conˌtrol *n.* [U] the people on the ground who are responsible for guiding the flight of SPACECRAFT or aircraft

'ground ˌcover *n.* [U] plants that cover the soil

'ground crew *n.* [C] the group of people who work at an airport and take care of the aircraft

ground·er /ˈgraʊndɚ/ *n.* [C] a ball hit along the ground in baseball

'ground floor *n.* [C] **1** the first floor of a building that is at the same level as the ground **2 be/get in on the ground floor** to become involved in a plan, business activity etc. from the beginning

'ground ˌforces *n.* [plural] military groups that fight on the ground rather than at sea or in the air

ˌground 'glass *n.* [U] **1** glass that has been made into a powder **2** glass that has been rubbed on the surface so that you cannot see through it, but light passes through it

ground·hog /ˈgraʊndhɑg/ *n.* [C] a small North American animal that has thick brown fur and lives in holes in the ground SYN **woodchuck**

'Groundhog ˌDay *n.* [C] February 2; according to stories, if the groundhog sees its shadow when it comes out of its hole on this day, there will be six more weeks of winter. If it does not, good weather will come early.

ground·ing¹ /ˈgraʊndɪŋ/ *n.* **1** [singular] training in the basic parts of a subject or skill: +**in** *She had a good grounding in mathematics.* **2** [C] a punishment for a child's bad behavior in which they are not allowed to go out with their friends for a period of time **3** [U] the process of officially stopping an aircraft or spacecraft from flying, especially because it is not safe to fly **4** [U] a situation in which a boat or ship hits ground where the water is not very deep and becomes stuck **5** PHYSICS the system of connecting electrical equipment to the ground, especially for safety

grounding² *adj.* PHYSICS connecting electrical equipment to the ground, especially for safety: *grounding wire*

ground·less /ˈgraʊndlɪs/ *adj.* groundless fears, worries, claims etc. are unnecessary because there are no facts or reasons to base them on: *The charges against him are groundless.*

ˈground ˌlevel *n.* [singular] the same level as the surface of the earth, rather than above it or below it

ground·nut /ˈgraʊndnʌt/ *n.* [C] TECHNICAL a PEANUT or PEANUT plant

ˈground plan *n.* [C] **1** a drawing of how a building is arranged at ground level, showing the size, position, and shape of walls, rooms etc. **2** a basic plan for doing something in the future

ˈground rules *n.* [plural] the basic rules or principles on which future actions or behavior should be based: *Let's establish some ground rules first.*

grounds·keep·er /ˈgraʊndzˌkipɚ/ *n.* [C] someone whose job is to take care of an area of land such as a garden or sports field

ˈground ˌsquirrel *n.* [C] a GOPHER

ˈground staff *n.* [C] GROUND CREW

ˈground state *n.* [C usually singular] PHYSICS the lowest possible energy state of an atom, PARTICLE, or MOLECULE

ˈground ˌstroke *n.* [C] a way of hitting the ball after it has hit the ground in tennis and similar games

ground·swell /ˈgraʊndswɛl/ *n.* **1 groundswell of support/enthusiasm etc.** a sudden increase in how strongly people feel about something: *a groundswell of interest in organic foods* **2** [singular, U] the strong movement of the ocean that continues after a storm or strong winds

ground·wa·ter, ground water /ˈgraʊndˌwɔt̬ɚ/ *n.* [U] water that is under the ground that supplies water to WELLS, lakes, streams etc.

ground·work /ˈgraʊndwɚk/ *n.* [U] important work that has to take place before another activity, plan etc. can be successful: *The groundwork for next year's conference has already begun.*

ˌground ˈzero *n.* [U] **1** the place where a large bomb explodes, where the most severe damage happens **2 Ground Zero** the place in New York City where the World Trade Center buildings were destroyed by TERRORISTS on September 11, 2001

group¹ /grup/ S1 W1 *n.* [C] **1** several people or things that are all together in the same place: +**of** *a group of tall trees* | **groups of three/six/ten etc.** *Get into groups of four.* | *Men stood* ***in groups*** *on the sidewalk.* | *a group photo* | *a group discussion*

THESAURUS

Group of people
crowd a large group of people in one place: *She had gotten separated from her little boy in the crowd.*
team a group of people who work together: *a team of doctors* | *the basketball team*
crew a group of people who all work together, especially on a ship or airplane: *the flight crew*
bunch INFORMAL a group of people: *They're a nice bunch of kids.*
gang a group of young people, especially a group that often causes trouble and fights: *The school has had trouble with gangs.* | *her gang of friends*
mob a large noisy group of people, especially one that is angry and violent: *the mob outside the courtroom*
horde a large group of people moving in a noisy uncontrolled way: *There were hordes of people coming out of the subway.*
flock a large group of people of the same type: *a flock of tourists*
mass a large group of people all close together in one place: *A mass of people gathered outside the White House.*
party a group of people who have been organized to do something together: *a search party*

Group of animals
herd of cows/deer/elephants
flock of sheep/birds
school/shoal of fish/dolphins/herring etc.
pack of dogs
litter of puppies/kittens (=a group of baby animals born from the same mother at the same time)

Group of things
bunch of flowers/grapes/keys etc. (=several flowers, etc. tied or held together)
bundle of papers/clothes/sticks (=several papers, etc. tied or held together)

2 a set of people who join together for a particular purpose or activity: *terrorist groups* | *an Internet discussion group* | +**of** *a group of concerned citizens* | *Marian* ***joined*** *a support* ***group*** *after her father's death.* **3** several people or things that share particular characteristics: *food from the various food groups* | +**of** *a group of irregular verbs* | **ethnic/age/income etc. group** (=people with the same races, ages etc.) **4** ENG. LANG. ARTS a number of musicians or singers who perform together, usually playing popular music: *a rock group* **5** several companies that all have the same owner: *The Pearson Group owns a diverse array of companies.* **6** CHEMISTRY a COLUMN of ELEMENTS in the PERIODIC TABLE, which all have similar ATOMIC structures and chemical properties (PROPERTY): *The alkali metals are the elements located in Group IA of the periodic table.* [**Origin:** 1600–1700 French *groupe*, from Italian *gruppo*] → see also AGE GROUP, INTEREST GROUP, PLAY GROUP

group² S3 W3 *v.* **1** [T always + adv./prep.] to put people or things into groups or types according to a system SYN **classify**: **group sb/sth according to sth** *The plates were grouped according to color and size.* | **group sb/sth together** *The dialects can be grouped together as a single language.* | **group sb/sth into sth** *All minerals have been grouped into eight types.* **2** [I,T] to gather together in a group SYN **gather**: +**on/in/together etc.** *Reporters were grouped on the steps below him.* | **group yourself around/about/into etc.** *The tourists grouped themselves around the statue.* **3** [T] to arrange people or objects in specific positions in a group SYN **arrange**: *The chairs were grouped closely together.*

ˌgroup dyˈnamics *n.* [plural] the way in which the members of a group behave toward and react to each other

group·ie /ˈgrupi/ *n.* [C] someone, especially a young woman, who likes a musician, movie star, or sports star and follows them around hoping to meet them

group·ing /ˈgrupɪŋ/ *n.* **1** [C] a set of people, things, or organizations that have the same interests, qualities, or features: *a loose grouping of states* **2** [U] the act of putting people or things into groups

ˌgroup ˈpractice *n.* [C,U] a group of doctors who work together in the same building

ˌgroup ˈtherapy *n.* [U] a method of treating people with emotional or PSYCHOLOGICAL problems by bringing them together in groups to talk about their problems

group·ware /ˈgrupwɛr/ *n.* [U] COMPUTERS a special type of computer SOFTWARE that allows several computers on a network to work on the same computer DOCUMENT at the same time

grouse¹ /graʊs/ *v.* [I] INFORMAL to complain about some-

G

thing: *He was always grousing about his aches and pains.*

grouse² *n.* [C,U] BIOLOGY a small fat bird that is hunted and shot for food and sport, or the meat of this bird

grove /groʊv/ *n.* **1** [C] a group of trees: *the redwood groves of Northern California* **2** [C] an area of land planted with a particular type of fruit tree, especially LEMON or orange trees → see also ORCHARD: *a lemon grove*

grov·el /ˈgrɑvəl, ˈgrʌ-/ *v.* [I] **1** to behave with too much respect toward someone, because you are asking them to help or forgive you: *There's nothing worse than seeing a man grovel just to keep his job.* **2** to lie or move flat on the ground because you are afraid of someone, or as a way of showing that you will obey them: *The prisoner groveled at the king's feet.*

grow /groʊ/ S1 W1 *v. past tense* **grew** /gru/, *past participle* **grown** /groʊn/

1 PERSON/ANIMAL [I] to become bigger and develop over a period of time: *It's hard to believe how much the kids have grown.* | **grow an inch/a foot etc.** *Jamie's grown three inches this year.* | **a growing boy/girl** *Of course he eats a lot. He's a growing boy!* | **grow to a size/length/height of sth** *The fish grows to a length of 8 inches.* | *Jerry's* ***growing like a weed*** (=growing very quickly).

2 PLANTS/CROPS a) [I] to exist and develop somewhere in a natural way: *Our lawn has all kinds of weeds growing in it.* | *It's too cold for orchids to grow here.* | **+to** *Redwood trees can grow to 300 feet.* **b)** [T] to make plants or crops grow by taking care of them: *We're trying to grow roses in our garden this year.*

3 HAIR/NAILS a) [I] if hair, FINGERNAILS etc. grow, they become longer: *My hair grows very quickly.* **b)** [T] if you grow your hair, FINGERNAILS etc., you do not cut them: *Are you growing a beard?*

4 BUSINESS [I,T] if a business, economy etc. grows, or if you grow it, it becomes larger or more successful: *Mark's business grew rapidly in the first year.*

5 INCREASE [I] to increase in amount, size, or degree: *The world's population is growing at an alarming rate.* | *Her confidence has grown steadily.* | **+from/to** *The number of students has grown from 200 to over 500.* | **grow in size/importance/popularity etc.** *Bicycling has grown in popularity.* | ***A growing number of*** *people are buying handguns for protection.* ►see THESAURUS box at increase¹

6 BECOME [linking verb] LITERARY to gradually develop a feeling, opinion, or more of a particular quality over a period of time: *The sound grew louder.* **grow to like/fear/respect etc.** *After three years here, I've grown to like Dallas.*

7 IMPROVE [I] to improve in ability or character: *Beth has grown quite a bit as an actress.*

8 sth doesn't grow on trees SPOKEN used to say that someone should not waste money or something else that is valuable because it is hard to get

[**Origin:** Old English *growan*]

grow apart *phr. v.* if two people grow apart, their relationship becomes less close: *The couple had been growing apart for years.*

grow away from *phr. v.* **1 grow away from sb** to begin gradually to have a less close relationship with someone that you loved: *My son began to grow away from me the year he left for college.* **2 grow away from sth** to gradually become less closely related to something: *Rural economies have grown away from a reliance on agriculture.*

grow into sth *phr. v.* **1** to develop over a period of time and become a particular kind of person or thing: *She's grown into a beautiful young woman.* **2** if a child grows into clothes, they become big enough to wear them: *He'll grow into the coat by winter.* **3** to gradually learn how to do a job or deal with a situation successfully

grow on sb *phr. v.* if someone or something grows on you, you like them more and more: *I didn't like his music at first, but it grows on you.*

grow out *phr. v.* **1 grow sth ↔ out** if you grow out your hair or it grows out, it grows long: *It took me months to grow my hair out.* **2 grow sth ↔ out** if you grow out a hair style or it grows out, it disappears as your hair becomes longer: *You'll have to wait till the dye grows out.*

grow out of sth *phr. v.* **1** if a child grows out of clothes, they become too big to wear them: *Kids grow out of their shoes so quickly.* **2** if a child grows out of a habit, they stop doing it as they get older: *He sucked his thumb till he was six, but he grew out of it eventually.* **3** to develop from something small or simple into something bigger or more complicated: *The union grew out of worker dissatisfaction.*

grow up *phr. v.* **1** BIOLOGY to develop from being a child to being an adult: *I grew up in Chicago.* | *What do you want to do when you grow up?* **2** to start thinking and behaving more like an adult instead of acting foolish and irresponsible: *Some men just refuse to grow up.* **3** to start to exist and become bigger or more important: *Trading settlements grew up by the river.*

grow·er /ˈgroʊə/ *n.* [C] **1** a person or company that grows fruit, vegetables etc. in order to sell them: *potato growers* **2** a plant that grows and develops in a particular way: *This species is a very fast grower.*

ˈgrowing ˌpains *n.* [plural] **1** pain that children can sometimes feel in their arms and legs when they are growing **2** problems and difficulties that are experienced at the beginning of a new activity: *Any new show goes through a lot of growing pains.*

ˈgrowing ˌseason *n.* [C] the period during the year from the time when crops start to grow until they become fully grown, considered by farmers to be the average number of days between the last FROST (=period of very cold weather when the ground and water freezes) of spring and the first frost of fall

growl /graʊl/ *v.* **1** [I] if an animal growls, it makes a long deep angry sound: *Their dog growls at everyone.* **2** [I,T] to say something in a low angry voice: *"Leave that alone," she growled.* ►see THESAURUS box at say¹ —**growl** *n.* [C]

grown¹ /groʊn/ *v.* the past participle of GROW

grown² *adj.* [only before noun] **1 a grown man/woman** an expression meaning an adult man or woman, used especially when you think someone is not behaving as an adult should: *He had never seen a grown man cry before.* **2 a grown son/daughter/child** a son or daughter who is now an adult → see also FULL-GROWN

ˈgrown-up¹ *adj.* **1** fully developed as an adult SYN **adult**: *They have three grown-up children.* **2** behaving or looking like an adult: *You're looking very grown-up.* **3** typical of an adult or appropriate for an adult SYN **adult**: *The play deals with grown-up subjects like sex and war.*

grown-up² *n.* [C] a word meaning an "adult person," used especially by children or when speaking to children SYN **adult**: *He listened while the grown-ups talked.*

growth /groʊθ/ W1 *n.*

1 INCREASE IN AMOUNT [U] an increase in amount, size, or degree: *population growth* | **+in** *a growth in exports* | *obstacles to* ***economic growth*** | *The economy's annual* ***growth rate*** *was 3.5%.* | **a growth area/industry** (=an area of business that is growing very quickly)

2 PERSON/ANIMAL/PLANT [U] BIOLOGY the development of the physical size, strength etc. of a person, animal, or plant over a period of time: *Vitamins are essential for healthy growth.*

3 INCREASE IN IMPORTANCE [singular, U] the gradual development and increase in the importance or influence of something: **+of** *the growth of modern technology*

4 PERSONAL DEVELOPMENT [U] the development of someone's character, intelligence, emotions etc.: *The job provides opportunities for personal growth.*

5 SWELLING [C] MEDICINE a swelling on your body or under your skin, caused by disease: *a cancerous growth*

6 GROWING THING [C,U] something that is growing: *There are signs of new growth on the tree.*

Groz·ny /ˈgroʊzni/ the capital and largest city of Chechnya

grub¹ /grʌb/ *n.* **1** [U] INFORMAL food **2** [C] BIOLOGY an insect when it is in the form of a small soft white worm

grub² [I always + adv./prep.] **1** INFORMAL to ask for something rather than buying it or working for it yourself: +**for** *All the candidates are busy grubbing for money.* → see also MONEY-GRUBBING **2** INFORMAL to look for something, especially by moving things, looking under them etc.: +**for** *The pigs are behind the barn grubbing for roots.*

grub sth ↔ **up/out** *phr. v.* to dig around something and then pull it out of the ground: *Farmers grubbed the sagebrush up by hand.*

grub·by /ˈgrʌbi/ *adj. comparative* **grubbier**, *superlative* **grubbiest** **1** dirty: *grubby clothes* ►see THESAURUS box at dirty¹ **2** not respectable, or morally unacceptable: *the grubby world of politics* **3 sb's grubby hands/mitts/paws etc.** used to talk about someone else's hands, when you are angry because you do not want them to touch something or someone: *Get your grubby mitts off my stuff.* —**grubbiness** *n.* [U]

grub·stake /ˈgrʌbˌsteɪk/ *n.* [U] ECONOMICS money that someone gives to help develop a new business, in return for a share of the profits

grudge¹ /grʌdʒ/ *n.* [C] **1** a feeling of anger or dislike you have for someone who has harmed you: +**against** *She's got a grudge against me.* | **hold/harbor/nurse a grudge** (=continue to be angry with someone) **2 a grudge fight/match** a fight or competition in sports between two people who dislike each other very much

grudge² *v.* [T] **1** to feel a little angry that you have to do or give something SYN **begrudge**: *I grudged the time I had to spend doing housework.* **2** to be JEALOUS of someone because they have something good or are in a good situation SYN **begrudge**

grudg·ing /ˈgrʌdʒɪŋ/ *adj.* done or given in a very unwilling way: *a grudging apology* —**grudgingly** *adv.*

gru·el /ˈgruəl/ *n.* [U] thin OATMEAL that was eaten in the past by poor or sick people

gru·el·ing /ˈgruəlɪŋ/ *adj.* very tiring because you have to use a lot of effort for a long time: *a grueling three-hour climb* [**Origin:** 1800–1900 *gruel* **to punish** from *gruel* **food**; because people were given gruel as a punishment] —**gruelingly** *adv.*

grue·some /ˈgrusəm/ *adj.* very upsetting or bad to look at or hear about, and usually involving death or injury: *a gruesome accident* [**Origin:** 1500–1600 *grue* **to shake (with fear)** (14–19 centuries), from Middle Dutch *gruwen*]

gruff /grʌf/ *adj.* **1** unfriendly or annoyed, especially in the way you speak: *Dad can be gruff and impatient at times.* **2** a gruff voice sounds low and rough, as if the speaker does not want to talk or is annoyed —**gruffly** *adv.*

grum·ble¹ /ˈgrʌmbəl/ *v.* [I] **1** to complain in a quiet but slightly angry way: +**about/at/over** *She's always grumbling about her work.* ►see THESAURUS box at complain **2** to make a very low sound that continuously gets quieter then louder then quieter: *Thunder grumbled in the distance.* —**grumbler** *n.* [C]

grumble² *n.* [C] **1** a complaint **2** a low continuous sound that gets quieter then louder then quieter

grump·y /ˈgrʌmpi/ *adj. comparative* **grumpier**, *superlative* **grumpiest** easily annoyed and tending to complain: *a grumpy old man* —**grump** *n.* [C] —**grumpily** *adv.* —**grumpiness** *n.* [U]

THESAURUS

cranky/crabby/grouchy INFORMAL easily annoyed and complaining a lot: *The kids were tired and crabby.*
cantankerous easily annoyed and complaining a lot, especially when this is part of your character: *a cantankerous old man*
irritable easily annoyed or made angry: *He seemed irritable and restless.*
touchy easily offended or annoyed: *She's touchy about her weight.*

grunge /grʌndʒ/ *n.* [U] **1** a type of loud music played with electric GUITARS, popular in the early 1990s **2** a style of fashion popular with young people in the early 1990s, in which they wore clothes that looked dirty and messy **3** INFORMAL dirt and GREASE SYN **grime**

grun·gy /ˈgrʌndʒi/ *adj. comparative* **grungier**, *superlative* **grungiest** INFORMAL dirty and sometimes smelling bad: *grungy jeans*

grunt¹ /grʌnt/ *v.* **1** [I,T] to make short sounds or say only a few words in a low rough voice, when you do not want to talk: *He just grunted "Hi" and kept walking.* **2** [I] if someone or an animal, especially a pig, grunts, they make a short low sound in their throat

grunt² *n.* [C] **1** a short low sound made in your throat, or a similar sound that an animal makes, especially a pig: *He stood up with a grunt.* **2** SLANG an INFANTRY soldier

ˈgrunt work *n.* [U] INFORMAL the hard uninteresting part of a job or PROJECT

Gru·yère /gruˈyɛr/ *n.* [U] a type of hard Swiss cheese with holes in it

gryph·on /ˈgrɪfən/ *n.* [C] another spelling of GRIFFIN

G-string /ˈdʒi ˌstrɪŋ/ *n.* [C] very small underwear that does not cover the BUTTOCKS

gua·ca·mo·le /ˌgwɑkəˈmoʊleɪ/ *n.* [U] a Mexican dish made with crushed AVOCADOS [**Origin:** 1900–2000 American Spanish, Nahuatl, from *ahuacatl* **avocado** + *molli* **sauce**]

Gua·dal·ca·nal /ˌgwɑdlkəˈnæl/ the largest of the Solomon Islands in the western Pacific Ocean

Gua·de·loupe /ˌgwɑdəˈlup, ˈgwɑdəˌlup/ a country consisting of a group of islands in the Caribbean Sea, which is ruled by France

Guam /gwɑm/ a U.S. TERRITORY that is the largest of the Mariana Islands in the western Pacific Ocean

gua·no /ˈgwɑnoʊ/ *n.* [U] solid waste from sea birds that is often put on soil to help plants grow

Guan·tan·a·mo Bay /gwɑnˌtɑnəmoʊ ˈbeɪ/ a U.S. naval base in Cuba, which the U.S. uses as a prison holding possible TERRORISTS

guar·an·tee¹ /ˌgærənˈti/ Ac S3 W3 *v.* [T]
1 PROMISE to promise that you will do something, that something will happen, or that someone will have or get something SYN **promise**: **guarantee (that)** *I can't guarantee this will work, but let's try.* | **guarantee sb sth** *Even if you complete your training, I can't guarantee you a job.* | **guarantee to do sth** *The diet guarantees to get rid of those extra pounds.* ►see THESAURUS box at promise¹
2 MAKE STH CERTAIN to make it certain that something will happen SYN **ensure**: **guarantee sb sth** *A good education doesn't guarantee you a good job.* | **guarantee (that)** *No set of rules can absolutely guarantee all children will be protected.* | *The slow economy* ***virtually guarantees*** *that schools will suffer.*
3 PRODUCT to make a formal written promise to repair or replace a product if it has a fault within a specific period of time after you buy it: **guarantee sth against sth** *All parts are guaranteed against failure for a year.*
4 be guaranteed to do sth to be certain to behave, work, or happen in a particular way: *Going out with friends is guaranteed to cheer you up.*
5 LEGAL to make yourself legally responsible for the payment of money: *The loans are guaranteed by the government.*
6 PROTECT to provide complete protection against harm or damage: **guarantee sth against sth** *This protective coating guarantees your car against corrosion.*

guarantee² Ac W3 *n.* [C] **1** a formal promise, especially in writing, that a product will please the customer or perform in a particular way for a specific length of time SYN **warranty**: +**on** *a two-year guaran-*

G

tee on all electrical goods | *Our laptops* **come with** *a 12-month* **guarantee.** | *The microwave comes with* **a money-back guarantee** (=a promise to return your money if it does not work). **2** a formal promise that something will happen or be allowed to happen SYN **promise**: +**of** *the Constitution's guarantee of free speech* | **guarantee that** *an international guarantee that the borders will remain open* | *Can you* **give** *me a* **guarantee** *that the work will be finished on time?* **3** an action, situation etc. that makes it certain that something else will happen: +**of** *Hard work is no guarantee of success.* | ***There's no guarantee that*** *the peace will last* (=it is not sure to happen). **4 a)** an agreement to be responsible for someone else's promise, especially a promise to pay a debt: *a loan guarantee* → see also SECURITY **b)** something valuable that is given to someone to keep until the owner has kept their promise, especially to pay a debt

guar·an·tor /ˌgærən'tɔr, 'gærəntɚ/ *n.* [C] someone who promises that they will pay for something if the person who should pay for it does not

guar·an·ty /'gærənti/ *n.* [C] LAW a GUARANTEE

guard¹ /gɑrd/ S2 W2 *n.*

1 PERSON [C] someone whose job is to protect people, places, or objects, so that they are not attacked or stolen: *Two guards stopped us at the gate.* | *The trucks were accompanied by* ***armed guards.*** → see also BODYGUARD, SECURITY GUARD ▸see THESAURUS box at **protect**

2 IN A PRISON [C] someone whose job is to prevent prisoners from escaping: *He claims the guards beat him.*

3 be on guard to be responsible for guarding a place or person for a specific period of time: *Hogan was on guard the night the prisoners escaped.*

4 stand/keep guard (over sb/sth) to guard or watch a person or place: *Thousands of police stood guard over today's ceremony.*

5 be under (armed) guard to be guarded by a group of people with weapons: *City hall was under tight guard all night.*

6 catch/take/throw sb off guard to surprise someone by doing or saying something that they are not ready to deal with: *The sudden snowstorm caught weather forecasters off guard.*

7 sb's guard the state of paying careful attention to what is happening, in order to avoid being tricked or getting into danger: *Tina's not going to* ***let down*** *her* ***guard*** (=relax because a threat is gone). | *Hanson's dismissal has* ***put*** *others in the department* ***on*** *their* ***gurd.*** | **sb's guard is up/down** (=someone is or is not paying careful attention to what is happening so that they are not or are easy to attack, trick, or deal with)

8 EQUIPMENT [C] something that covers and protects someone or something: *All hockey players must wear face guards.*

9 the old guard people who belong to a group which wants to do things the way they have always been done in the past: *the old guard of the Communist Party*

10 BASKETBALL [C] one of two players on a basketball team who is responsible for moving the ball so that it is easy for their team to gain points

11 FOOTBALL [C] one of two players on a football team who play on either side of the CENTER

12 FIGHTING [C] the position of holding your hands or arms up in fighting to defend yourself, or the position in which you hold a sword to defend yourself: *If you want to be a successful boxer, you have to* ***keep your guard up.***

13 GROUP [singular] a group of people, especially soldiers, who guard someone or something: *In London, we watched the changing of the guard.* | *the National Guard*

[**Origin:** 1400–1500 French *garde*]

guard² W3 *v.* [T]

1 PROTECT to protect a person, place, or valuable object by staying near them and watching them: *A dog guards the house.* | **guard sb/sth against sth** *Troops guarded the area against possible attack.*

2 PREVENT ESCAPE to watch a prisoner and prevent them from escaping: *The hostages were guarded night and day.*

3 TRY TO KEEP to try very hard to keep something that is important to you and that other people might try to take away: **jealously/fiercely guard sth** *The country has guarded its independence fiercely.*

4 KEEP SECRET to not tell information or a secret to anyone: **a closely/carefully guarded secret** *His real identity is a closely guarded secret.*

5 SPORTS to prevent a player from another sports team from gaining points or moving forward, or to defend a part of the playing field: *Richards will guard Davis in tonight's game.*

6 guard your tongue OLD-FASHIONED used to tell someone to be careful about what they say, so that they do not tell a secret

guard against *phr. v.* **1 guard against sth** to try to prevent something from happening by being careful: *It's important to guard against tiredness when you're driving.* **2 guard (yourself) against sth** to provide protection from something bad, or to prevent it from happening: *Exercise can help guard against a number of serious illnesses.*

'guard cell *n.* [C] BIOLOGY one of a pair of cells that surround a small natural hole in the surface of a leaf and make it open and close

'guard dog *n.* [C] a dog that is trained to guard a place

guard·ed /'gɑrdɪd/ *adj.* careful not too say too much or show too much emotion: *Baker spoke with guarded enthusiasm.* —**guardedly** *adv.*

guard·house /'gɑrdhaʊs/ *n.* [C] a building for soldiers who are guarding the entrance to a military camp

guard·i·an /'gɑrdiən/ *n.* [C] **1** someone who is legally responsible for someone else, especially a child **2** FORMAL a person or organization that tries to protect laws, moral principles, traditional ways of doing things etc.: +**of** *Saudi Arabia sees itself as the guardian of Islam.*

ˌguardian 'angel *n.* [C] **1** an ANGEL (=good spirit) who is believed to protect a person or place **2** someone who helps or protects someone else when they are in trouble

ˌGuardian 'Angels, the *n.* an organization whose members try to protect people from being attacked or robbed, especially when they are traveling on SUBWAYS in big cities

guard·i·an·ship /'gɑrdiənˌʃɪp/ *n.* [U] **1** LAW the position of being legally responsible for someone else, especially a child, or the period during which you have this position **2** FORMAL the position or fact of being responsible for someone or something, especially in order to protect them from harm or damage

guard·rail /'gɑrd-reɪl/ *n.* [C] a long metal bar that is intended to prevent cars or people from falling over the edge of a road, boat, or high structure

guards·man /'gɑrdzmən/ *n. plural* **guardsmen** /-mən/ [C] a member of the U.S. National Guard

Gua·te·ma·la /ˌgwɑt̬ə'mɑlə/ a country in Central America, between the Pacific and Atlantic Oceans —**Guatemalan** *n., adj.*

ˌGuatemala 'City the capital and largest city of Guatemala

gua·va /'gwɑvə/ *n.* [C] BIOLOGY a small tropical fruit with pink flesh and many seeds inside [**Origin:** 1500–1600 Spanish *guayaba*, from an Arawakan language]

gu·ber·na·to·ri·al /ˌgubɚnə'tɔriəl/ *adj.* FORMAL relating to the position of being a GOVERNOR

guer·ril·la, guerilla /gə'rɪlə/ *n.* [C] a member of an independent fighting group that fights for political reasons, usually against their government, and attacks the enemy in small groups: *The rebels have used* ***guerrilla warfare*** (=attacks by small groups) *to fight the government.* [**Origin:** 1800–1900 Spanish *guerra* **war**] → see also FREEDOM FIGHTER, TERRORIST

guess¹ /gɛs/ S1 W2 *v.*

1 WITHOUT BEING SURE [I,T] to try to answer a question or make a judgment about something without knowing all the facts, so that you are not sure whether you are correct: *I think she's about 30, but I'm only guessing.* |

guess who/what/why etc. *Guess who I saw at the store today.* | **guess (that)** *I guessed that it was about 4 a.m.* | **+at** *He guessed at the answer, but got it wrong.*
2 GUESS CORRECTLY [I,T] to guess something correctly: *"Don't tell me – you got the job." "How'd you guess?"* | *She managed to guess the answer.* | **guess (that)** *I would never have guessed they were a couple.* | **guess who/what/why etc.** *Her accent makes it easy to guess where she comes from.* | *They told us they were getting married, but we'd already* ***guessed as much*** (=guessed correctly before they told us).
3 keep sb guessing to not tell someone what is going to happen next: *Our supervisor likes to keep everyone guessing.*

SPOKEN PHRASES

4 I guess a) said when you think something is true or likely, but you are not completely sure: *His light's on, so I guess he's still up.* **b)** said to show that you do not feel very strongly about what you are planning or agreeing to do: *I guess I'll stay home tonight.* **c)** said to show that you know about a situation, because someone else has told you about it rather than because you were there yourself: *I guess his dad had to work two jobs when they were little.*
5 I guess so/not used to say yes or no when you are not very sure, or when you are making your decision based on what someone else has told you: *"She wasn't happy?" "I guess not."*
6 guess what! also **you'll never guess who/what/where etc.** used when you are about to tell someone something that will surprise them: *Guess what! I won a free trip to Europe!* | *You'll never guess what she was wearing.*
7 let me guess used when you think you know what someone is going to say, and you want to say it before they tell you: *Let me guess – you got lost.*
8 you guessed it used when someone probably knows something before you say it because it is so obvious: *He showed up with his wife, his kids, and you guessed it ... the dog.*

guess² S3 *n.* [C] **1** an attempt to guess something: *I'll give you three guesses.* | *Just* ***take a guess.*** | *It was* ***a wild guess*** (=made without much thought)*, but I got the right answer.* | *"How did you know I liked pasta?" "It was just* ***a lucky guess.****"* **2** an opinion formed by guessing: ***My guess is that*** *Dan won't come today.* | *What's your* ***best guess?*** **3 be anybody's guess** to be something that no one knows: *It's anybody's guess where he's gone.* **4 your guess is as good as mine** SPOKEN said to tell someone that you do not know any more than they do about something: *"When's the next bus coming?" "Your guess is as good as mine."*

guess·ti·mate /ˈgɛstəmɪt/ *n.* [C] SPOKEN INFORMAL an attempt to judge a quantity by guessing it —**guesstimate** /ˈgɛstəˌmeɪt/ *v.* [I,T]

guess·work /ˈgɛswɚk/ *n.* [U] the way of trying to find the answer to something by guessing: *Many of the estimates are based on guesswork.*

guest¹ /gɛst/ S2 W2 *n.* [C]
1 AT A PARTY/MEAL/SPECIAL OCCASION someone who is invited to a meal, party, or special occasion, especially a very big or important one: *They invited over 100 guests to the wedding.* | *a dinner guest* | *Ambassador Harris was* ***the guest of honor*** *at the ball.*
2 AT YOUR HOUSE someone who you have invited to your home to stay for a short time: *We're having guests this weekend.*
3 AT A HOTEL/RESTAURANT someone who is paying to stay in a hotel or eat in a restaurant: *The hotel can accommodate up to 300 guests.* ►see THESAURUS box at **customer**
4 ON A SHOW someone famous who is invited to take part in a show, concert etc., in addition to those who usually take part: **+on** *a guest on the late-night talk show* | *Tonight's* ***special guest*** *will be Mel Gibson.*
5 WHEN YOU PAY FOR SB someone who is invited to a restaurant, theater, club etc. by someone else who pays for them: *You don't need to pay – you're my guest.*
6 SB WHO IS NOT A MEMBER someone you invite to come with you to a club or organization that you are a member of: *Members can bring two guests with them.*
7 be my guest SPOKEN said when giving someone permission to do what they have asked to do: *"Could I use your phone?" "Be my guest."*
8 IN A FOREIGN COUNTRY someone who visits another country for a short period of time: *We want our guests from Asia to feel welcome.*
[**Origin:** 1200–1300 Old Norse *gestr*] → see also HOST

guest² *adj.* **1 a guest speaker/star/artist etc.** someone who is invited to speak on a subject or take part in a performance, in addition to those who usually take part **2** [only before noun] for guests to use: *the guest room* | *guest towels* **3 a guest appearance** a performance that is given by someone who is invited to take part in a show, concert etc., in addition to those who usually take part

guest³ *v.* [I] to take part in a show, concert etc. as a guest performer

ˈguest book *n.* [C] a book in which everyone who comes to a formal occasion or stays at a hotel writes their name

guest·house /ˈgɛsthaʊs/ *n.* [C] a small building next to a main house that visitors can stay in

ˈguest star, **guest-star** *v.* [I] to perform on a television show along with the people who normally take part in the show —**guest star** *n.* [C]

ˈguest ˌworker *n.* [C] a foreign worker, usually from a poor country, working in another country for a particular period of time

Gue·va·ra /gɛˈvɑrə/, **Er·nes·to (Ché)** /ɚˈnɛstoʊ tʃeɪ/ (1928–1967) a Marxist military leader, born in Argentina, who developed the method of fighting known as GUERRILLA warfare and helped Fidel Castro to gain control of Cuba

guff /gʌf/ *n.* [U] SPOKEN stupid or annoying behavior or talk: *Don't* ***take any guff*** *from those guys.*

guf·faw /gəˈfɔ/ *v.* [I] to laugh loudly ►see THESAURUS box at **laugh¹** —**guffaw** *n.* [C]

Gug·gen·heim /ˈgugənˌhaɪm/, **Sol·o·mon** /ˈsɑləmən/ (1861–1949) a U.S. INDUSTRIALIST who started a FOUNDATION for modern art that later built the Guggenheim Museum in New York City

GUI /ˈgui/ *n.* [U] **graphical user interface** COMPUTERS a way of arranging computer information on a screen using pictures, which makes it easier for users to tell the computer what to do

guid·ance /ˈgaɪdns/ *n.* [U] **1** helpful advice given to someone about their work, education, personal life etc.: **+on/about** *Tutors provide students with guidance about careers.* | **spiritual/moral guidance** *I often turn to the Bible for spiritual guidance.* ►see THESAURUS box at **advice** **2** the activity of leading, influencing, or directing someone or something: *Spitz started training* ***under the guidance of*** *Coach Ballatore.* **3** the process of directing a MISSILE in flight: *The missiles have an electronic guidance system.*

ˈguidance ˌcounselor *n.* [C] someone who works in a school, whose job is to give advice to students about what subjects to study and help them with personal problems

guide¹ /gaɪd/ S3 W3 *n.* [C]
1 CITY/BUILDING someone whose job is to show tourists around a city, MUSEUM etc.: *a tour guide*
2 OUTDOORS someone who takes you somewhere outdoors, especially a place that is difficult or dangerous to reach: *an experienced mountain guide*
3 BOOK a) a book, PAMPHLET etc. that provides information on a particular subject or explains how to do something SYN **handbook**: **+to** *"The Complete Guide to Computer Literacy"* | **+for** *a guide for new parents* **b)** a GUIDEBOOK: *a travel guide*
4 FOR DOING STH CORRECTLY something that gives you information about the right direction to go in or the right way to do something: *You can* ***use*** *these sample essays* ***as a guide for*** *your own writing.*

G

5 FOR MAKING DECISIONS something that gives you an idea about what is likely to happen or helps you to make a decision about what to do: *A friend's experience isn't always the best guide for you.*
6 ADVISER someone who helps you decide what to do by giving you advice, or by giving you a good example to follow: *a spiritual guide*
[**Origin:** 1300–1400 French, Old Provençal *guida*]

guide[2] W3 *v.* [T] **1** to take someone to or through a place that you know very well, showing them the way: **guide sb along/through/to etc. sth** *He guided us through the narrow streets.* ►see THESAURUS box at **lead**[1] **2** to help someone or something to move in a particular direction: **guide sth into/onto/down etc.** *The pilot guided the plane to a safe landing.* | **guide sb into/toward etc. sth** *He jumped up and guided her toward the armchair.* **3** to strongly influence someone's behavior, thoughts etc., or help them make a decision: *Teenagers need adults to guide them.* **4** to show someone the right way to do something, especially something difficult or complicated: **guide sb through sth** *Tax-preparation programs guide you through the tax form.* **5** to make something develop in a particular way: *I tried to guide the discussion back to the main topic.* → see also GUIDING

guide·book /ˈgaɪdbʊk/ *n.* [C] a special book about a city, area etc. that gives details about the place and its history

ˌguided ˈmissile *n.* [C] a MISSILE that can be controlled electronically while it is flying

ˈguide dog *n.* [C] a dog trained to guide a blind person

ˌguided ˈtour *n.* [C] a trip around a city, building etc., led by someone who tells people about the place: *a guided tour of the palace*

guide·line /ˈgaɪdlaɪn/ Ac *n.* [C often plural] a rule, principle, or instruction about the best way to do something: **+for/on** *federal guidelines on TV violence* | *Teachers should **follow** the new **guidelines**.*

guide·post /ˈgaɪdpoʊst/ *n.* [C] **1** something that helps you decide what to do or the best way to do it: *History is an important guidepost for leaders.* **2** a sign beside a road, path etc. that tells people which way to go

guid·ing /ˈgaɪdɪŋ/ *adj.* **a guiding principle/star/light** a principle, idea, or person that you follow in order to help you decide what you should do in a difficult situation

guild /gɪld/ *n.* [C] HISTORY an organization of people who share the same interests, skills, or profession, especially one in Medieval times for people who had a particular skill or trade: *the writer's guild*

guil·der /ˈgɪldɚ/ *n.* [C] the unit of money used in the past in the Netherlands

guild·hall /ˈgɪldhɔl/ *n.* [C] a large building in which members of a guild met in past times

guile /gaɪl/ *n.* [U] FORMAL the use of smart but dishonest methods to deceive someone: *With a little guile, she might get what she wants.* —**guileful** *adj.*

guile·less /ˈgaɪl-lɪs/ *adj.* behaving in an honest way, without trying to hide anything or deceive people

guil·lo·tine[1] /ˈgɪləˌtin, ˈgiə-, ˌgiəˈtin/ *n.* [C] HISTORY a piece of equipment used to cut off the heads of criminals in past times, especially in France [**Origin:** 1700–1800 French, from Joseph *Guillotin* (1738–1814), French doctor who invented it]

guillotine[2] *v.* [T] to cut off someone's head using a guillotine

guilt[1] /gɪlt/ *n.* [U] **1** a feeling of shame and sadness when you know or believe you have done something wrong: **+about/at/over** *She had a sense of guilt about the way she'd behaved.* | **a pang/twinge of guilt** *Sometimes I felt little pangs of guilt.* **2** LAW the fact of having broken an official law or moral rule OPP **innocence**: *He made no attempt to deny his guilt.* **3 a guilt trip** INFORMAL a feeling of guilt about something, when this is unreasonable: *I wish my parents would stop **laying a guilt trip on** me* (=stop trying to make me feel guilty) *about not going to college.* **4** the state of being responsible for something bad that has happened: *Most of the guilt for failure lies with him.* [**Origin:** Old English *gylt*]

> **THESAURUS**
> **shame** the feeling of being guilty or embarrassed that you have after doing something that is wrong: *I was too scared to help him, and I was filled with shame.*
> **remorse** a strong feeling of being sorry for doing something very bad: *a murderer who showed no remorse*
> **conscience** the set of feelings that tell you whether what you are doing is morally right or wrong: *If what I did harmed her, I could not be happy with that on my conscience.*

guilt[2] *v.*
guilt sb **into (doing)** sth *phr. v.* INFORMAL to try to make someone feel guilty, especially so they will do what you want: *Her parents guilted her into moving home.*

guilt·less /ˈgɪltlɪs/ *adj.* not responsible for a crime or for having done something wrong SYN **innocent** —**guiltlessly** *adv.*

ˈguilt-ˌridden *adj.* feeling so guilty about something that you cannot think about anything else: **+over/about** *She was guilt-ridden over the incident.*

guilt·y /ˈgɪlti/ S3 W3 *adj.* *comparative* **guiltier**, *superlative* **guiltiest** **1** ashamed and sad because you know or believe you have done something wrong: *I **feel guilty about** not inviting her.* | *His **guilty conscience** kept him awake at night.*

> **THESAURUS**
> **ashamed** unhappy and disappointed with yourself because you have done something wrong or unpleasant: *You should be ashamed of yourself for lying to your mother.*
> **embarrassed** feeling slightly worried about what people will think of you because you have done something stupid or silly: *I was embarrassed to be caught looking in his drawers.*

2 having done something that is a crime OPP **innocent**: *He's obviously guilty.* | *The court **found** him **guilty of*** (=officially decided that he was guilty of) *fraud.* | *He plans to **plead not guilty*** (=say in a court of law that he was not guilty) *to the murder charges.* | *Both defendants were found **guilty as charged*** (=guilty of the illegal action that someone said they did). **3** responsible for behavior that is morally or socially unacceptable or for something bad that has happened: **guilty of (doing) sth** *These officials are guilty of arrogance and greed.* **4 the guilty party** the person who has done something illegal or wrong **5 a/sb's guilty pleasure** something that someone likes but that they feel slightly embarrassed about liking: *Night-time soap operas are my guilty pleasure.* —**guiltily** *adv.* —**guiltiness** *n.* [U]

Guin·ea /ˈgɪni/ a country in west Africa north and east of Sierra Leone —**Guinean** *n., adj.*

Guinea-Bis·sau /ˌgɪni bɪˈsaʊ/ a small country in west Africa between Guinea and Senegal —**Guinean** *n., adj.*

guinea fowl /ˈgɪni ˌfaʊl/ *n.* [C] BIOLOGY a gray African bird that is often used for food

guin·ea pig /ˈgɪni ˌpɪg/ *n.* [C] **1** BIOLOGY a small animal like a large rat with long fur, short ears, and no tail, which is often kept as a pet **2** INFORMAL someone who is used in a test to see how successful or safe a new product, system etc. is: *Soldiers were used as guinea pigs to test chemical weapons.*

Guin·e·vere /ˈgwɪnəˌvɪr, ˈgwɛ-/ in old stories the wife of King Arthur, who had a sexual relationship with Sir Lancelot

guise /gaɪz/ *n.* [C] FORMAL the way someone or something seems to be, which is meant to hide the truth:

in/under the guise of sth *He raised large amounts of political money in the guise of charitable contributions.*

gui·tar /gɪˈtɑr/ S2 *n.* [C] a musical instrument that has six or twelve strings, a long neck, and a wooden body, which is played by pulling on the strings with your fingers or a PICK: *Jack* ***plays the guitar***. [**Origin:** 1600–1700 French *guitare*, from Spanish *guitarra*, from Arabic *qitar*, from Greek *kithara* type of stringed instrument] —**guitarist** *n.* [C]

gu·lag /ˈgulɑg/ *n.* [C] one of a group of prison camps in the former U.S.S.R., where conditions were very bad

gulch /gʌltʃ/ *n.* [C] EARTH SCIENCE a narrow deep valley formed by flowing water, but that is usually dry

gulf /gʌlf/ *n.* [C] **1** EARTH SCIENCE a large area of ocean partly enclosed by land: *the Gulf of Mexico* **2** a great difference and lack of understanding between two groups of people, especially in their beliefs, opinions, and way of life: +**between** *the gulf between rich and poor* **3** EARTH SCIENCE a deep hollow place in the Earth's surface [**Origin:** 1300–1400 French *golfe*, from Greek *kolpos* **arms folded around, bay**]

ˌGulf of ˈMexico, the an area of the Atlantic Ocean that is south of the U.S., east of Mexico, and west of Cuba

Gulf of Ton·kin Res·o·lu·tion, the /ˌgʌlf əv ˌtɑŋkɪn rɛzəˈluʃən/ a decision by Congress in 1964 allowing President Johnson to take military action in Vietnam

ˈGulf states *n.* **the Gulf States** the southern states of the U.S. that are next to the Gulf of Mexico

ˈGulf Stream *n.* **the Gulf Stream** a current of warm water that flows northeastward in the Atlantic Ocean from the Gulf of Mexico toward Europe

ˌGulf ˈWar, the HISTORY a war which began in 1991, after Iraq attacked Kuwait and took control of it. A United Nations force led by the U.S. attacked Iraq and forced the Iraqi army out of Kuwait.

gull[1] /gʌl/ *n.* [C] **1** a SEAGULL **2** LITERARY someone who is easily deceived

gull[2] *v.* [T] OLD USE to cheat or deceive someone

Gul·lah /ˈgʌlə/ *n.* [U] **1** a language spoken by the Gullah people in the southeastern U.S., which is a mixture of English and West African languages **2** a member of the group of African Americans who live on the Sea Islands and in the coastal areas of the southeastern U.S.

gul·let /ˈgʌlɪt/ *n.* [C] OLD-FASHIONED the tube through which food goes down your throat

gul·ley /ˈgʌli/ *n.* [C] another spelling of gully

gul·li·ble /ˈgʌləbəl/ *adj.* too ready to believe what other people say, and therefore easy to trick: *a group of gullible tourists* —**gullibility** /ˌgʌləˈbɪləṭi/ *n.* [U]

gul·ly /ˈgʌli/ *n. plural* **gullies** [C] **1** EARTH SCIENCE a small narrow valley, usually formed by a lot of rain flowing down the side of a hill **2** a deep DITCH

gulp[1] /gʌlp/ *v.* **1** [T] also **gulp sth ↔ down** to swallow something quickly: *She gulped her coffee and ran for the bus.* **2** [T] also **gulp sth ↔ in** to take in quick large breaths of air: *Steve swam up to the surface and gulped in air.* **3** [I] to swallow suddenly because you are surprised or nervous: *Mandy read the test questions and gulped.* **4 gulp back tears** to try to prevent yourself from crying: *He gulped back tears as he spoke.*

gulp[2] *n.* [C] an act of swallowing something quickly, or the amount swallowed: *Rachel* ***took a gulp*** *of soda.* | *He drank the rest of the beer* ***in one gulp***.

gum[1] /gʌm/ S2 *n.* **1** a sweet sticky type of candy that you chew for a long time but do not swallow: *He's always* ***chewing gum***. **2** [C usually plural] BIOLOGY the firm pink part inside your mouth that holds your teeth: *healthy gums* → see picture at TOOTH **3** [U] BIOLOGY a sticky substance found in the stems of some trees **4** [C] a GUM TREE [**Origin:** (1) Old English goma]

gum[2] *v.* **gummed, gumming**

gum sth ↔ up *phr. v.* INFORMAL to prevent something from working correctly by covering it with a sticky substance: *How did this lock get so gummed up?*

gum·ball /ˈgʌmbɔl/ *n.* [C] gum in the form of a small brightly colored ball

gum·bo /ˈgʌmboʊ/ *n.* [U] **1** a thick soup made with meat, fish, and OKRA **2** another word for OKRA, used in some parts of the U.S.

gum·drop /ˈgʌmdrɑp/ *n.* [C] a small CHEWY candy

gum·my /ˈgʌmi/ *adj. comparative* **gummier**, *superlative* **gummiest** **1** sticky, or covered in GUM: *a baby's gummy fingers* **2** a gummy smile shows the GUMS in your mouth

gump·tion /ˈgʌmpʃən/ *n.* [U] INFORMAL the ability and determination to decide what needs to be done and do it

gum·shoe /ˈgʌmˌʃu/ *n.* [C] OLD-FASHIONED a DETECTIVE

ˈgum tree *n.* [C] a tall tree that produces a strong-smelling oil used in medicine

gun[1] /gʌn/ S2 W2 *n.* [C]

1 WEAPON a weapon that fires bullets or SHELLS (=large metal objects), especially one that can be carried: *Someone* ***fired a gun***. | *The* ***gun went off*** *accidentally.* | *Should ordinary citizens* ***carry guns***?

2 TOOL a tool or object used to send out objects or a liquid by using pressure: *a paint gun* → see also FLASHGUN, SPRAY GUN

3 the big/top gun INFORMAL someone who controls an organization, or who is the most successful person in a group: *All the big guns were at the meeting.*

4 under the gun (to do sth) INFORMAL if you are under the gun, you are in a difficult situation under a lot of pressure, and you do not know if you can succeed: *To remain competitive, companies are under the gun to cut costs.*

5 a hired gun INFORMAL someone who is paid to shoot someone else or to protect someone

6 a 21-gun salute an act of shooting guns as a sign of respect

7 hold/put a gun to sb's head INFORMAL to force someone to do something they do not want to do → see also **go great guns** at GREAT[1] (19), **jump the gun** at JUMP[1] (11), SON OF A GUN, **stick to your guns** at STICK TO (6)

gun[2] *v.* **gunned, gunning** [T] INFORMAL to make a car go very fast by pressing the ACCELERATOR very hard

gun sb ↔ down *phr. v.* to shoot someone and badly injure or kill them, especially someone who cannot defend themselves: *Two people were gunned down in the drive-by shooting.*

gun for *phr. v.* **1 be gunning for sth** to be trying very hard to obtain something: *Someone else is gunning for his job.* **2 be gunning for sb** to be looking for an opportunity to criticize or harm someone

gun·boat /ˈgʌnboʊt/ *n.* [C] a small military ship that is used near a coast

ˌgunboat diˈplomacy *n.* [U] the practice of threatening to use force against a smaller country in order to make it agree to your demands

ˈgun ˌcarriage *n.* [C] a frame with wheels on which a heavy gun is moved around

ˈgun conˌtrol *n.* [U] laws that restrict the possession and use of guns

gun·fight /ˈgʌnfaɪt/ *n.* [C] a fight between people using guns —**gunfighter** *n.* [C]

gun·fire /ˈgʌnfaɪɚ/ *n.* [U] the repeated firing of guns, or the noise made by this: *enemy gunfire*

gung-ho /ˌgʌŋ ˈhoʊ/ *adj.* INFORMAL very eager or too eager to do something: *gung-ho supporters* [**Origin:** 1900–2000 Chinese *gonghe*, from *jongguo gongye hozo she* **Chinese Industrial Cooperatives Society**, used as a battle cry (meaning "work together") by U.S. soldiers in World War II]

gunk[1] /gʌŋk/ *n.* [U] INFORMAL any substance that is thick, dirty, and sticky: *The drain was full of gunk.* [**Origin:** 1900–2000 *Gunk*, a trademark for a type of soap] —**gunky** *adj.*

G

gunk² *v.* **be gunked up (with sth)** INFORMAL to be blocked with a dirty sticky substance

gun·man /ˈgʌnmən/ *n.* [C] a criminal or TERRORIST who uses a gun

gun·met·al /ˈgʌnˌmɛtl/ *n.* [U] **1** a dull gray-colored metal that is a mixture of COPPER, TIN, and ZINC **2** the dull gray color of gunmetal —**gunmetal** *adj.*: *gunmetal skies*

gun·ner /ˈgʌnɚ/ *n.* [C] a soldier, sailor etc. whose job is to aim or fire a large gun

gun·ner·y /ˈgʌnəri/ *n.* [U] the science and practice of shooting with heavy guns: *a gunnery officer*

gun·ny·sack /ˈgʌniˌsæk/ *n.* [C] INFORMAL a large BURLAP bag used for storing and sending grain, coffee etc.

gun·point /ˈgʌnpɔɪnt/ *n.* **at gunpoint** while threatening people with a gun, or while being threatened with a gun: *She was **held at gunpoint** for 37 hours.*

gun·pow·der /ˈgʌnˌpaʊdɚ/ *n.* [U] an explosive substance in the form of powder

ˈgun-ˌrunning *n.* [U] the activity of taking guns into a country secretly and illegally, especially so that they can be used to fight the government —**gun-runner** *n.* [C]

G

gun·ship /ˈgʌnˌʃɪp/ *n.* [C] a military aircraft such as a HELICOPTER, that is used to protect soldiers who are fighting and to destroy enemy guns

gun·shot /ˈgʌnʃɑt/ *n.* **1** [C] the action of shooting a gun, or the sound that this makes **2** [U] the bullets fired from a gun: *a gunshot wound*

ˈgun-ˌshy *adj.* **1** very careful or frightened about doing something, because of a bad experience in the past: *Cecile is still a little gun-shy about traveling alone.* **2** a hunting dog that is gun-shy is easily frightened by the noise of a gun

gun·sling·er /ˈgʌnˌslɪŋɚ/ *n.* [C] someone who is very skillful at using guns, especially a criminal in past times —**gun-slinging** *adj.* [only before noun]

gun·smith /ˈgʌnˌsmɪθ/ *n.* [C] someone who makes and repairs guns

gun·wale /ˈgʌnl/ *n.* [C] TECHNICAL the upper edge of the side of a boat or small ship

Guo·min·dang /ˌgwoʊmɪnˈdɑŋ/ → another form of KUOMINTANG

gup·py /ˈgʌpi/ *n. plural* **guppies** [C] BIOLOGY a very small brightly-colored tropical fish

gur·gle /ˈgɚgəl/ *v.* [I] **1** if something such as a stream gurgles, it makes a pleasant low sound, like water flowing through a pipe **2** if a baby gurgles, it makes this kind of sound in its throat —**gurgle** *n.* [C]

gur·ney /ˈgɚni/ *n. plural* **gurneys** [C] a long narrow table with wheels, used for moving sick people in a hospital [**Origin:** 1800–1900 *Gurney cab* (19–20 centuries), a type of horse-drawn vehicle invented by J. T. *Gurney* of Boston, Massachusetts]

gu·ru /ˈguru, ˈgʊru/ *n.* [C] **1** INFORMAL someone who knows a lot about a particular subject, and to whom people go for advice: *a nutrition guru* **2** a Hindu religious teacher or leader

gush¹ /gʌʃ/ *v.* **1** [I always + adv./prep.,T] if a liquid gushes from something, or if something gushes it, it flows or pours out quickly in large quantities: *His wound was gushing blood.* | +**out/from/down etc.** *Oil gushed from the broken pipeline.* ►see THESAURUS box at **flow¹**, **pour** **2** [I,T] to express your admiration, pleasure etc. in a way that other people think is too strong: *"I just love your outfit," she gushed.*

gush² *n.* **1** a large quantity of liquid that suddenly flows from somewhere: *a gush of water* **2 a gush of relief/pride/ideas etc.** a sudden feeling or expression of emotion, ideas etc.

gush·er /ˈgʌʃɚ/ *n.* [C] INFORMAL an OIL WELL where the natural flow of oil out of the well is very strong, so that a pump is not needed

gush·ing /ˈgʌʃɪŋ/ also **gush·y** /ˈgʌʃi/ *adj.* INFORMAL expressing admiration, pleasure etc. in a way that other people think is too strong: *a gushing speech*

gus·set /ˈgʌsɪt/ *n.* [C] a small piece of material stitched into a piece of clothing to make it stronger, wider, or more comfortable in a particular place

gus·sy /ˈgʌsi/ *v.* **gussies, gussied, gussying**
gussy sb/sth ↔ **up** *phr. v.* INFORMAL to make someone look attractive by dressing them in their best clothes, or to make something look attractive by decorating it etc.: *They **got all gussied up** for the performance.*

gust¹ /gʌst/ *n.* [C] **1** a sudden strong movement of wind, air, snow etc.: *a gust of wind* ►see THESAURUS box at **wind¹** **2** a sudden strong feeling or expression of anger, excitement etc.: *A gust of rage swept over him.* —**gusty** *adj.*

gust² *v.* [I] if the wind gusts, it blows strongly with sudden short movements: *Winds were gusting up to 46 miles per hour.*

gus·ta·to·ry /ˈgʌstəˌtɔri/ *adj.* [only before noun] FORMAL relating to taste or tasting: *gustatory pleasures*

gus·to /ˈgʌstoʊ/ *n.* [U] **with gusto** with a lot of eagerness and energy: *Elizabeth sang with gusto.*

gut¹ /gʌt/ S3 *n.*
1 a gut reaction/feeling/instinct etc. INFORMAL a reaction or feeling that you are sure is right although you cannot give a reason for it: *My gut reaction is that it's a bad idea.*
2 COURAGE guts [plural] INFORMAL the courage you need to do something difficult or something that you do not want to do: *Rich didn't **have the guts to** say what he really thought.*
3 STOMACH [C] INFORMAL your stomach: *He hit me right in the gut.* | *Phil has a huge **beer gut*** (=unattractive fat stomach caused by drinking too much beer).
4 INSIDE YOUR BODY NOT TECHNICAL **a) guts** [plural] the organs inside your body, especially the INTESTINES **b)** [C] the tube through which food passes when it leaves your stomach SYN **intestine**
5 work/run etc. your guts out INFORMAL to work, run etc. very hard
6 MACHINE/EQUIPMENT guts [plural] INFORMAL the parts inside a machine, piece of equipment, factory etc.: *The guts of the airplane were torn out by the explosion.*
7 at gut level if you know or feel something at gut level, you feel sure about it, although you can not give a reason for it: *She knew at gut level that he was lying.*
8 MOST IMPORTANT PARTS guts [plural] INFORMAL the most important or basic parts of something: *the guts of the problem*
9 STRING [U] a type of strong string made from the INTESTINE of an animal
[**Origin:** Old English *guttas* (plural)] → see also BLOOD-AND-GUTS, **bust a gut** at BUST¹ (5), CATGUT, **hate sb's guts** at HATE¹ (2), **spill your guts** at SPILL¹ (5)

gut² *v.* **gutted, gutting** [T] **1** to completely destroy the inside of a building, especially by fire: *The fire gutted St. Mary's church.* **2** to change something by removing some of the most important parts: *Democrats have gutted the anti-crime bill.* **3** to remove the organs from inside a fish or animal in order to prepare it for cooking: *Gut and clean all the fish before cooking.*

Gu·ten·berg /ˈgutˀnˌbɚg/, **Jo·han·nes** /yoʊˈhɑnɪs/ (1397–1468) a German printer who is considered to have invented the method of printing that uses movable letters

Guth·rie /ˈgʌθri/, **Wood·y** /ˈwʊdi/ (1912–1967) a singer and writer of FOLK MUSIC, known especially for his songs about working people

gut·less /ˈgʌtlɪs/ *adj.* INFORMAL **1** lacking courage: *a gutless decision* **2 gutless wonder** someone with no courage at all

gut·sy /ˈgʌtsi/ *adj. comparative* **gutsier**, *superlative* **gutsiest** INFORMAL brave or showing that you are willing to take risks: *a gutsy decision*

gut·ter¹ /ˈgʌtɚ/ *n.* **1** [C] an open pipe at the edge of a roof for collecting and carrying away rain water **2** [C] the low place along the edge of a road, where water collects and flows away **3 the gutter** dirty and difficult conditions that you experience because of lack of care or money: *I was on drugs and living in the gutter.* **4 gutter mouth/talk/language** someone who has a gutter mouth, or uses gutter talk, uses offensive words, especially relating to sex **5** the low area on both sides of a LANE in a BOWLING ALLEY: *a gutter ball* (=a ball that goes in the gutter)

gutter² *v.* [I] LITERARY if a CANDLE gutters, it burns with an unsteady flame

gut·ter·snipe /ˈgʌtɚˌsnaɪp/ *n.* [C] OLD-FASHIONED **1** a dirty, badly-behaved child who lives on the street **2** someone from the poorest social class

gut·tur·al /ˈgʌtərəl/ *adj.* a guttural sound is produced deep in the throat

guy /gaɪ/ S1 W1 *n.* [C] **1** INFORMAL a man, especially a young man: *Dave's a nice guy.* | *There's a guy on the phone who wants to talk to you.* ▸see THESAURUS box at **man¹** **2 (you/those) guys** SPOKEN said when talking to or about two or more people, male or female: *We'll see you guys Sunday, okay?* → see also Y'ALL **3** also **guy rope** a rope that stretches from the top or side of a tent, pole, or structure to the ground to keep it in the right position [**Origin:** (1–2) 1800–1900 *Guy* Fawkes (1570–1606), who tried to blow up the English parliament] → see also **no more Mr. Nice Guy!** at MR (4), **wise guy** at WISE GUY

Guy·an·a /gaɪˈɑnə/ a country in northeastern South America on the Atlantic Ocean, east of Venezuela —**Guyanese** /ˌgaɪəˈnɪz◂ , -ˈnis◂ / *n., adj.*

guz·zle /ˈgʌzəl/ *v.* [I,T] INFORMAL to drink a lot of something, eagerly and quickly: *Chris has been guzzling beer all evening.* → see also GAS-GUZZLER

gym /dʒɪm/ S3 *n.* INFORMAL **1** [C] a special building or room that has equipment for doing physical exercise or playing sports: *the boys' gym at the high school* ▸see THESAURUS box at **sport¹** **2** [U] exercises done indoors for physical development and as a sport, especially as a school subject: *We played basketball in gym.* [**Origin:** 1800–1900 *gymnasium* Latin, Greek *gymnasion*, from *gymnazein* **to exercise with no clothes on**]

gym·na·si·um /dʒɪmˈneɪziəm/ *n.* [C] a GYM

gym·nast /ˈdʒɪmnæst, -nəst/ *n.* [C] someone who does gymnastics as a sport, especially someone who competes against other people

gym·nas·tics /dʒɪmˈnæstɪks/ *n.* [U] **1** a sport involving physical exercises and movements that need skill, strength, and control, and that are often performed in competitions: *gymnastics competitions* **2 mental/intellectual/verbal etc. gymnastics** thinking, speaking etc. that is very quick, complicated, and skillful **3** movements that are quick, complicated, and skillful —**gymnastic** *adj.*

gym·no·sperm /ˈdʒɪmnəˌspɚm/ *n.* [C] BIOLOGY a plant producing seeds that are contained in a CONE. Trees that grow in cold countries and keep their leaves all year, such as PINE TREES and FIR TREES, are gymnosperms. → see also ANGIOSPERM

ˈgym shoe *n.* [C] a shoe that is appropriate to wear for playing sports

gyn- /gaɪn/ *prefix* TECHNICAL relating to women: *gynecology*

gy·ne·col·o·gy /ˌgaɪnəˈkɑlədʒi/ *n.* [U] the study and treatment of medical conditions and illnesses affecting only women —**gynecologist** *n.* [C] —**gynecological** /ˌgaɪnəkəˈlɑdʒɪkəl/ *adj.*

gyp¹ /dʒɪp/ *v.* **gypped, gypping** [T] SPOKEN to cheat or trick someone: ***I got gypped out of $50!***

gyp² *n.* [singular] SPOKEN something that you were tricked into buying, or a situation in which you feel you have been cheated: *What a gyp!*

gyp·sum /ˈdʒɪpsəm/ *n.* [U] a soft white substance, usually in the form of powder, that is used to make PLASTER OF PARIS, which becomes hard after it has been mixed with water and has dried

gyp·sy /ˈdʒɪpsi/ *n. plural* **gypsies** [C] **1** a member of a group of people originally from northern India, who used to live and travel around in CARAVANS, and now live in many countries all over the world → see also ROMANY (1) **2** someone who does not like to stay in the same place for a long time

ˈgypsy moth *n.* [C] a type of MOTH whose CATERPILLARS eat leaves and damage trees

gy·rate /ˈdʒaɪreɪt/ *v.* [I] to turn around fast in circles: *The dancers gyrated wildly to the music.* —**gyration** /dʒaɪˈreɪʃən/ *n.*

gy·ro¹ /ˈdʒaɪroʊ/ *n.* [C] INFORMAL GYROSCOPE

gy·ro² /ˈdʒaɪroʊ, ˈyiroʊ/ *n. plural* **gyros** [C] a Greek SANDWICH usually made of lamb, onion, and TOMATO in PITA BREAD

gy·ro·scope /ˈdʒaɪrəˌskoʊp/ *n.* [C] a wheel that spins inside a frame, and is used for keeping ships and aircraft steady —**gyroscopic** /ˌdʒaɪrəˈskɑpɪk/ *adj.*

G

H,h

H, h /eɪtʃ/ *n. plural* **H's, h's** [C] **a)** the eighth letter of the English alphabet **b)** a sound represented by this letter → see also H-BOMB

h **1** a written abbreviation of HOUR SYN **hr.** **2** PHYSICS the symbol for PLANCK'S CONSTANT

H_2O /ˌeɪtʃ tu ˈoʊ/ *n.* [U] TECHNICAL the chemical sign for water

ha, hah /hɑ/ *interjection* used when you are surprised or have discovered something interesting: *Ha! I told you it wouldn't work.* → see also AHA, HA HA

ha. the written abbreviation of HECTARES

Ha·bak·kuk /ˈhæbəˌkʌk, həˈbækək/ a book in the Old Testament of the Christian Bible

ha·be·as cor·pus /ˌheɪbiəs ˈkɔrpəs/ *n.* [U] LAW the right of someone in prison to come to a court of law so that the court can decide whether they should stay in prison

hab·er·dash·er /ˈhæbɚˌdæʃɚ/ *n.* [C] OLD-FASHIONED someone who works in or owns a store that sells men's clothes

hab·er·dash·er·y /ˈhæbɚˌdæʃəri/ *n.* [C,U] OLD-FASHIONED a store or part of a store that sells men's clothing, especially hats, or the clothes and hats sold there

hab·it /ˈhæbɪt/ S2 W3 *n.*

1 STH YOU DO REGULARLY [C,U] something that you do regularly, often without thinking about it because you have done it so many times before: *healthy eating habits* | **a good/bad/annoying etc. habit** *good work habits* | *I know biting my nails is a bad habit, but I can't stop.* | *I guess I still eat there* ***out of habit****, not because the food is good.* | **have a habit of doing sth** *She has a habit of twisting her hair on her finger.* | **break/kick the habit** (=stop a bad habit) | *You should* ***get into the habit of*** *exercising when you're young.*

THESAURUS

custom something that people in a particular society do because it is traditional, or something that people think is the normal and polite thing to do: *the Japanese custom of taking off your shoes when you enter a house*
tradition a belief, custom, or way of doing something that has existed for a long time: *In many countries it's a tradition for the bride to wear white.* | *a family tradition*
practice something that people often do, especially as part of their work or daily life: *the practice of dividing children into high and low reading groups*
convention a rule of behavior that most people in a society accept: *It is a matter of convention for people attending funerals to wear dark clothes.*

2 DRUGS [C usually singular] a strong physical need to keep taking a drug regularly: *Many addicts get into petty crime to support their habit.* | *He quit his four-pack-a-day* ***cigarette habit****.*

3 CLOTHES [C] a long loose piece of clothing worn by people in some religious groups: *a nun's habit*

SPOKEN PHRASES

4 don't make a habit of (doing) sth used to tell someone who has done something bad or wrong that they should not do it again: *You can turn your paper in late this time, but don't make a habit of it.*
5 I'm not in the habit of doing sth used when you are offended because someone has suggested that you have done something that you have not done: *I'm not in the habit of lying to my friends.*
6 old habits die hard used to say that it is difficult to make people change their attitudes or behavior

[**Origin:** 1100–1200 Old French, Latin *habitus* **condition, character**, from *habere* **to have**] → see also **a creature of habit** at CREATURE (3), **by/from force of habit** at FORCE[1] (12)

hab·it·a·ble /ˈhæbət̬əbəl/ *adj.* good enough for people to live in: *It would cost a fortune to make the house habitable.* —**habitability** /ˌhæbət̬əˈbɪlət̬i/ *n.* [U]

hab·i·tat /ˈhæbəˌtæt/ *n.* [C] BIOLOGY the natural environment of a plant or animal: *the owl's* ***natural habitat*** *is in the forests of the Northwest.*

ˌHabitat for Huˈmanity an organization that helps poor people to build and own their own homes

ˈhabitat fragmenˌtation *n.* [U] BIOLOGY a process of environmental change in which a large area of land, that was the natural habitat for particular animals and plants, becomes divided into many small separate parts, each of which has a different environment. This process can happen naturally or when land is developed for farming or new houses.

hab·i·ta·tion /ˌhæbəˈteɪʃən/ *n.* FORMAL **1** [U] the act of living in a place: *Will we ever have permanent habitation in space?* | *Many of the housing projects are* ***unfit for human habitation*** (=not safe or healthy for people to live in). **2** [C] LITERARY a house or place to live in

ˈhabit-ˌforming *adj.* a drug or activity that is habit-forming makes you want to keep taking it, keep doing it etc.: *Video games can be habit-forming.*

ha·bit·u·al /həˈbɪtʃuəl/ *adj.* **1** done as a habit or doing something from habit: *Many of the patients are habitual liars.* **2** [only before noun] usual or typical of someone: *James took his habitual morning walk around the park.* —**habitually** *adv.*

ha·bit·u·at·ed /həˈbɪtʃuˌeɪt/ *v.* [T usually passive] FORMAL **habituated to sth** used to something or in the habit of doing something because you have experienced or done it many times before: *The bears have become habituated to people feeding them.*

ha·bit·u·ation /həˌbɪtʃuˈeɪʃən/ *n.* [U] BIOLOGY a basic learning process by which the reaction of a person, animal, or other living thing to a STIMULUS (=something that makes them move or react) gradually becomes less strong, so that after a period of time the person, animal etc. does not react at all: *During the process of habituation, the organism learns not to respond to an apparently harmless stimulus.*

ha·bit·u·é /həˈbɪtʃuˌeɪ, həˌbɪtʃuˈeɪ/ *n.* [C] FORMAL someone who regularly goes to a particular place or event

ha·ci·en·da /ˌhɑsiˈɛndə/ *n.* [C] a large farm in Spanish-speaking countries

hack¹ /hæk/ *v.* **1** [I always + adv./prep., T always + adv./prep.] to cut something into pieces roughly or violently: *The bodies of the men had been* ***hacked to pieces****.* | **hack (away) at sth** *She hacked at the huge turkey.* | **hack through/into sth** *Explorers hacked their way through the jungle with machetes.* | **hack sth off** *He hacked off the buffalo's head.* **2 can't hack sth** SPOKEN to feel that you cannot do something that is difficult or boring: *Debbie just couldn't hack Mr. Temple's physics class.* **3** [I] COMPUTERS to use a computer to enter someone else's computer system without their permission: **+into** *A teenage boy managed to hack into military computer networks.* **4** [I] to cough very loudly and painfully: *I couldn't stop hacking last night.* —**hacking** *n.* [U]

hack² *n.* [C] **1** a writer who does a lot of low-quality work, especially writing newspaper articles: *the hacks who write TV movies* **2** someone who does whatever they need to in order to be an artist, musician, politician etc., even if this means doing low-quality or boring work: *a political hack* **3** INFORMAL a taxi, or a taxi driver **4** an old tired horse

hack·er /ˈhækɚ/ *n.* [C] COMPUTERS someone who uses computers a lot, especially in order to secretly use or change the information in another person's computer system

ˌ**hacking 'cough** *n.* [usually singular] a repeated painful cough with a loud sound

hack·les /ˈhækəlz/ *n.* [plural] **1 raise sb's hackles** to say or do something that makes someone very angry: *The proposal to build 135 new homes has raised environmentalists' hackles.* **2** BIOLOGY the long feathers or hairs on the back of the neck of some animals and birds, which stand up straight when they are in danger

hack·neyed /ˈhæknid/ *adj.* a hackneyed phrase, statement etc. is boring and does not have much meaning, because it has been used so often [**Origin:** 1700–1800 *hackney* **to use (a horse) for ordinary riding, to use (something) too much** (16–19 centuries), from *hackney* **horse for ordinary riding**]

hack·saw /ˈhæksɔ/ *n.* [C] a type of SAW (=cutting tool) with small teeth on its blade, used especially for cutting metal

had /əd, həd; *strong* hæd/ *v.* **1** the past tense and past participle of HAVE **2 be had** INFORMAL to be tricked or cheated and made to look stupid: *When they looked closely at the watch, they realized they'd been had.* **3 have had it a)** to be very tired and not want to do something anymore: *I've had it. Let's go home.* **b)** to be very annoyed about something or what someone is doing, and not want it to continue: *I've had it with you!*

had·dock /ˈhædək/ *n. plural* **haddock** [C,U] BIOLOGY a common fish that lives in northern oceans and is often used as food

Ha·des /ˈheɪdiz/ *n.* [U] the place where people went after they died in the stories of ancient Greece SYN **hell**

had·n't /ˈhædnt/ *v.* the short form of "had not": *I went to visit a friend I hadn't seen for years.*

haft /hæft/ *n.* [C] TECHNICAL a long handle on an AX or on other weapons

hag /hæg/ *n.* [C] an ugly or mean woman, especially one who is old or looks like a WITCH

Hag·gai /ˈhægaɪ, -giˌaɪ/ a book in the Old Testament of the Christian Bible

hag·gard /ˈhægəd/ *adj.* having lines on your face and dark marks around your eyes, because you are sick, worried, or very tired: *The jurors looked haggard on their tenth day of deliberations.* [**Origin:** 1500–1600 French *hagard* **wild**]

hag·gle /ˈhægəl/ *v.* [I] **1** to argue about the amount of money you will pay for something: **haggle over sth** *I hate having to haggle over prices.* | **haggle with sb** *Ted was haggling with the street sellers.* **2** to argue with someone about the details of something: **haggle over sth** *Let's let the lawyers haggle over the details.* [**Origin:** 1500–1600 *hag* **to cut** (14–19 centuries)] —**haggling** *n.* [U]

hag·i·og·ra·phy /ˌhægiˈɑgrəfi, ˌhædʒi-/ *n.* [C,U] **1** a book about the lives of SAINTS **2** a book about someone that describes them as better than they really are

Hague, The /heɪg/ a city in the Netherlands. The country's government is in The Hague, but its capital city is Amsterdam.

hah /hɑ/ *interjection* another spelling of HA

ha ha /hɑ ˈhɑ/ *interjection* **1** used in writing to represent a shout of laughter **2** SPOKEN used, sometimes angrily, to show that you do not think something is funny: *Oh, very funny, John, ha ha.* → see also **funny weird/strange or funny ha ha** at FUNNY (11)

Hai·da /ˈhaɪdə/ a Native American tribe from the coast of northwest Canada and Alaska

hai·ku /ˈhaɪku/ *n. plural* **haiku** [C] ENG. LANG. ARTS a type of Japanese poem with three lines consisting of five, seven, and five SYLLABLES [**Origin:** 1800–1900 Japanese *haikai no ku* **not serious poem**]

hail[1] /heɪl/ *v.* **1** [I] if it hails, small balls of ice fall from the clouds ►see THESAURUS box at **snow**[1] **2** [T] to call to someone in order to attract their attention: **hail a taxi/cab** *The hotel doorman will hail a cab for you.*

hail sb/sth **as** sth *phr. v.* to describe someone or something as being very good, especially in newspapers, magazines etc.: *Lang's first film was immediately hailed as a masterpiece.*

hail from sth *phr. v.* OLD-FASHIONED to have been born in a particular place: *What part of the world do you hail from?*

hail[2] *n.* **1** [U] frozen rain that falls as balls of ice: *Hail the size of golf balls fell in Andrews, Texas.* ►see THESAURUS box at **rain**[1] **2 a hail of bullets/stones etc.** a large number of bullets, stones etc. thrown or fired at someone: *A hail of enemy fire forced them back into the trenches.* **3 a hail of criticism/abuse** a lot of criticism about something someone says or does

hail[3] *interjection* LITERARY used to greet someone: *Hail to the King!*

Hail Ma·ry /ˌheɪl ˈmɛri/ *n.* [C] a special Catholic prayer to Mary, the mother of Jesus Christ

hail·stone /ˈheɪlstoʊn/ *n.* [C] a small ball of frozen rain

hail·storm /ˈheɪlstɔrm/ *n.* [C] a storm when a lot of HAIL falls

hair /hɛr/ S1 W1 *n.*

1 ON HEAD [U] BIOLOGY the mass of thin things like threads that grow on your head: *gray hair* | *Don't forget to brush your hair.* | **long/short etc. hair** *Brandi has nice long hair.* | **blonde/dark/black etc. hair** *a young woman with short red hair* | **get/have your hair done** (=have it cut or given a particular style) → see picture at SKIN[1]

THESAURUS

Words used to describe hair
short, **long**, **shoulder-length**
straight, **curly**, **wavy** (=with loose curls), **frizzy** (=tightly curled)
thin used to say that someone does not have much hair
receding used to say that a man's hair is becoming thin
thick used to say that someone has a lot of hair
fine each hair is thin
wiry each hair is thick and strong
lank thin, straight, and unattractive
greasy covered in grease

Color of hair
fair/blonde (=yellow or very light)
towhead someone with very blonde hair
dark/brown
brunette someone with brown hair
black
red/auburn
strawberry blonde a light red-blonde
redhead someone with red hair
gray/white

2 ON BODY [U] BIOLOGY the short thin things like thread that grow on some parts of your body, for example on your legs or under your arms: *facial hair*
3 ON ANIMALS [U] BIOLOGY a word meaning hair that grows on the bodies of some animals, used especially when it has come off the animal's body → see also FUR: *cat hair*
4 ONE HAIR [C] BIOLOGY one human or animal hair: *Yuck! There's a hair in my sandwich.* | *dog hairs*
5 tear/pull your hair out INFORMAL to be very anxious or angry about something: *I was pulling my hair out trying to find someone to help me.*
6 not harm/touch a hair on sb's head used to emphasize that a person or animal would not harm someone in any way: *The dog wouldn't harm a hair on the kid's head.*
7 a hair a small amount: *Larson won the race by a hair.*
8 not have a hair out of place to have a very neat appearance: *Joel never has a hair out of place.*
9 let your hair down INFORMAL to enjoy yourself and start to relax, especially after working very hard: *Come out with us tonight and let your hair down a little.*
10 a bad hair day HUMOROUS **a)** a day on which your

hair will not do what you want it to do **b)** a day when everything seems to go wrong for you

11 make sb's hair stand on end to make someone very frightened: *The thought of a lawsuit was enough to make his hair stand on end.*

12 make your hair curl INFORMAL if a story, experience etc. makes your hair curl, it is very surprising, frightening, or shocking: *The stories they tell about him would make your hair curl.*

13 a/the hair of the dog (that bit you) HUMOROUS an alcoholic drink that is supposed to make you feel better after drinking too much alcohol the night before

[**Origin:** Old English *hær*] → see also -HAIRED, **a head of hair** at HEAD[1] (30), **not see hide nor hair of sb** at HIDE[2] (3), **split hairs** at SPLIT[1] (9)

hair·ball /ˈhɛrbɔl/ *n.* [C] a ball of hair that forms in the stomach of animals such as cats that LICK their fur

hair·breadth /ˈhɛrbrɛtθ, -brɛdθ/ *n.* [singular] another spelling of HAIR'S BREADTH

hair·brush /ˈhɛrbrʌʃ/ *n.* [C] a brush you use on your hair to make it look neat → see picture at BRUSH[1]

ˈhair-care *adj.* relating to the things people do and use to keep their hair clean, healthy, and attractive: *hair-care products* —**hair care, haircare** *n.* [U]

hair·cloth /ˈhɛrklɔθ/ *n.* [U] rough material made from animal hair, especially from horses or CAMELS

hair·cut /ˈhɛrkʌt/ *n.* [C] **1** the act of having your hair cut by someone: *I'm going to **get a haircut** later on today.* **2** the style your hair has when it has been cut recently: *Do you like my new haircut?*

H

hair·do /ˈhɛrdu/ *n. plural* **hairdos** [C] INFORMAL a woman's HAIRSTYLE

hair·dress·er /ˈhɛrˌdrɛsɚ/ *n.* [C] a person who washes, cuts, and arranges people's hair in particular styles: *I'm going to the hairdresser after work.* → see also BARBER —**hairdressing** *n.* [U]

hair·dry·er, hairdrier /ˈhɛrˌdraɪɚ/ *n.* [C] **1** a BLOW DRYER **2** a machine that you sit under that blows out hot air, used for drying hair

-haired /hɛrd/ *suffix* [in adjectives] **red-haired/curly-haired/long-haired etc.** having a particular type or color of hair: *a tall, red-haired woman*

hair·less /ˈhɛrlɪs/ *adj.* with no hair: *his hairless chin*

hair·line¹ /ˈhɛrlaɪn/ *n.* [C] the area around the top of your face where your hair starts growing: *Bruce is embarrassed about his **receding hairline*** (=the fact that he is losing hair).

hairline² *adj.* **a hairline crack/fracture** a very thin crack in something hard: *She had a hairline fracture in her leg.*

hair·net /ˈhɛrnɛt/ *n.* [C] a very thin net that stretches over your hair to keep it in place or to keep hairs from falling onto something

hair·piece /ˈhɛrpis/ *n.* [C] a piece of false hair used to cover a BALD place on your head, or to make your own hair look thicker

hair·pin /ˈhɛrˌpɪn/ *n.* [C] a pin used to hold hair in a particular position, that is made of wire bent into a U-shape

ˈhairpin turn also **ˈhairpin curve** *n.* [C] a very sharp U-shaped curve in a road, especially on a steep hill

ˈhair-ˌraising *adj.* frightening in a way that is exciting: *a hair-raising ride through the mountains*

ˈhair reˌstorer *n.* [C,U] a substance or liquid that is supposed to make hair grow again

ˈhair's breadth *n.* [singular] a very small amount or distance: *I came within a hair's breadth of losing my life.*

ˌhair ˈshirt *n.* [C] a shirt made of rough uncomfortable cloth that contains hair, worn in past times by some religious people as a punishment

ˈhair-ˌsplitting *n.* [U] the act of paying too much attention to small differences and unimportant details: *It is this kind of hair-splitting that gives politics a bad name.* → see also **split hairs** at SPLIT[1] (9)

ˈhair spray, hairspray *n.* [U] a sticky liquid that you SPRAY on your hair to make it stay in place

hairstyle

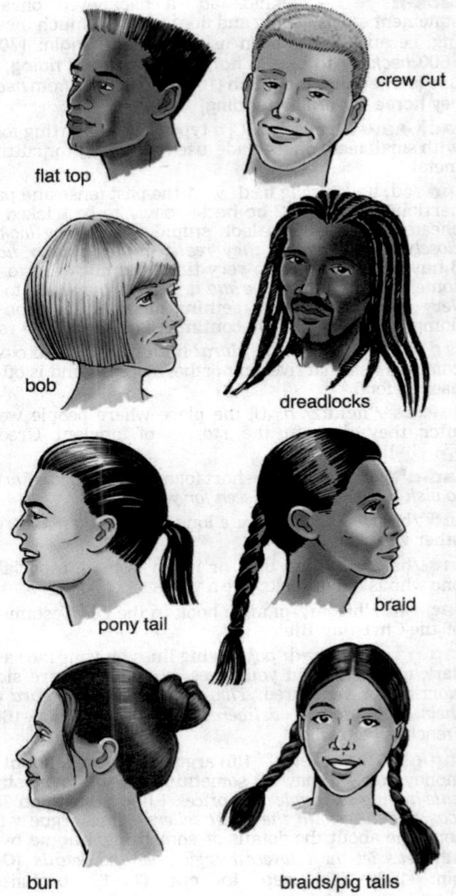

hair·style /ˈhɛrstaɪl/ *n.* [C] the style in which someone's hair has been cut or shaped

ˈhair ˌtonic *n.* [C,U] a liquid that is supposed to make hair grow on an area of your head that is BALD (=hairless)

ˈhair-trigger¹ *n.* [C] a TRIGGER on a gun that needs very little pressure to fire the gun

hair-trigger² *adj.* reacting to very slight things in a strong way: *a hair-trigger temper*

ˈhair weave *n.* [C] a piece of artificial hair that is attached to your own hair to make it look longer or thicker

hair·y /ˈhɛri/ *adj. comparative* **hairier**, *superlative* **hairiest 1** having a lot of body hair: *his hairy arms* | *a big hairy spider* **2** INFORMAL dangerous or frightening, often in a way that is exciting: *It got pretty hairy climbing down the cliff.* —**hairiness** *n.* [U]

Hai·ti /ˈheɪţi/ a country in the Caribbean Sea on the island of Hispaniola, which it shares with the Dominican Republic —**Haitian** /ˈheɪʃən/ *n., adj.*

hajj, haj /hɑdʒ/ *n.* [C] a trip to Mecca for religious reasons, that all Muslims try to make at least once in their life

haj·ji, **hadji** /ˈhɑdʒi/ *n.* [C] used as a title for a Muslim who has made a hajj

hake /heɪk/ *n. plural* **hake** [C,U] BIOLOGY an ocean fish, used as food

ha·lal, **hallal** /həˈlɑl/ *adj.* [U] halal meat is meat from an animal that has been killed in a way that is approved by Muslim law [**Origin:** 1800–1900 Arabic **that which is lawful**]

hal·berd /ˈhɑlbɚd/ *n.* [C] a weapon with a blade on a long handle, used in past times

hal·cy·on /ˈhælsiən/ *adj.* [only before noun] **halcyon days/years/era etc.** LITERARY the happiest and most peaceful time of someone's life: *the halcyon days of her youth* [**Origin:** 1500–1600 *halcyon* **bird believed to bring good weather at sea** (14–19 centuries), from Latin, from Greek *alkyon* **kingfisher**]

hale /heɪl/ *adj.* LITERARY someone, especially an old person, who is hale is very healthy and active: *The professor is still **hale and hearty** at age 88.*

Hale /heɪl/, **Na·than** /ˈneɪθən/ (1755–1776) a U.S. soldier who was caught by the British and hanged for being a SPY during the Revolutionary War

half¹ /hæf/ S1 W1 *quantifier, adj.* [only before noun] **1** 50% of an amount, time, distance, number etc.: *a half a bottle of beer* | *Only half the audience stayed.* | **half the cost/size/amount etc.** *It costs the same but it's half the size.* | **half an hour/a mile/a pound etc.** *The farm is half a mile down the road.* | **a half hour/mile/pound etc.** *I'll wait for another half hour.* **2** if something is half one thing and half something else, it is a combination of those two things: *Lacey's mother is half Chinese and half Portuguese.* **3 half a chance** a small opportunity to do something, especially one which someone would take eagerly: *I'd leave tomorrow if I had half a chance.* **4 half a dozen a)** six: *half a dozen eggs* **b)** several or many: *He had rewritten the story half a dozen times.* **5 half a minute/second** SPOKEN a very short time: *This will only take half a minute.* **6 be half the battle** SPOKEN used to say that when you have done the most difficult part of an activity, everything else is easier: *Getting Jeff to listen to me is half the battle.* **7 half the...** used to emphasize that you mean a very large part of an amount, time, group etc.: *She seems to be asleep half the time.* | *For kids, getting dirty is half the fun.* **8 half the story** an explanation that is not complete, used especially to say that someone is trying to keep something secret: *How could you side with them after hearing only half the story?* **9 have half a mind to do sth** SPOKEN used to say, often in a threatening way, that you would like to do something but you probably will not do it: *I have half a mind to tell her I don't want her at my house.* → see also HALF MEASURES

half² S1 W1 *n., pron. plural* **halves** /hævz/ [C]
1 50% one of two equal parts of something: *Cut it down the middle, and we'll each have a half.* | **half of sth** *the second half of the chapter* | *two halves of an orange* | **a week/month/year etc. and a half** *I talked to Susan about a week and a half ago.* | **top/bottom/northern etc. half** *the southern half of the country* | *She tore the piece of paper **in half*** (=into two pieces). | **cut/reduce sth by half** (=make something 50% smaller)
2 SPORTS EVENT either of the two parts into which a sports event is divided: **the first/second half** *Johnson scored 15 points in the second half.*
3 NUMBER the number ½: *Four halves make 2.* | **one/two/three etc. and a half** *The insect is two and a half inches long.* | *Rachel is four and a half years old.*
4 go halves (on sth) to share something, especially the cost of something, equally between two people: *Do you want to go halves on a pizza?*
5 half past one/two/three etc. *BrE* thirty minutes after the hour mentioned: *It's already half past twelve!*
6 and a half SPOKEN used to emphasize that someone has a quality very strongly: *He's a flirt and a half, isn't he?*
7 not do sth by halves OLD-FASHIONED to do something very eagerly and using a lot of care and effort
8 your better/other half HUMOROUS your husband, wife or partner in a relationship
9 you don't know the half of it SPOKEN used to emphasize that a situation is more difficult, more complicated, or worse than people realize: *"It sounds like it was horrible." "Oh, you don't know the half of it."*
10 how the other half lives how people who are much richer or much poorer than you manage their lives, work, money etc.: *Try taking the bus, and see how the other half lives.*

half³ S2 W3 *adv.* **1** partly, but not completely: *Her first album is now half finished.* | *The door was only half closed.* | *I half hoped they wouldn't come.* | *I said it half jokingly.* (=I wasn't completely serious.) | **half-filled/half-empty etc.** *A half-filled wine glass stood on the table.* | **half awake/asleep** *It was ten o'clock and I was half asleep.* **2** used to emphasize something, especially when a situation is extremely bad: *The kitten looked half starved.* | *I was half out of my mind with worry.* **3 not half as good/interesting etc. (as)** much less good, less interesting etc. than someone or something else: *The movie wasn't half as entertaining as the book.* **4 half as much/big etc.** half the size, amount etc. of something else: *The new computer has all the same functions, but is only half as large.* **5 not half bad** an expression meaning "good," used especially when you are surprised that something is good: *The pizza here isn't half bad.* **6 half and half** partly one thing and partly another: *It looked like the crowd was about half and half, men and women.*

ˌhalf-and-ˈhalf *n.* [U] a mixture that is half milk and half cream, used in coffee

half·back /ˈhæfbæk/ *n.* [C] **1** one of two players in football who, at the start of play, are behind the front line of players and next to the FULLBACK **2** a player who plays in the middle part of the field, in SOCCER, RUGBY etc.

ˌhalf-ˈbaked *adj.* a half-baked idea, suggestion, plan etc. has not been thought about and planned carefully

ˈhalf ˌbrother *n.* [C] a brother who is the son of only one of your parents

ˌhalf-ˈcocked *adj.* **go off half-cocked** to do something without enough thought or preparation, so that it is not successful: *You ought to talk to her before you go off half-cocked.*

ˌhalf-ˈcrazed, **half crazed** *adj.* behaving in a slightly crazy uncontrolled way: +**with** *The prisoners were half crazed with terror and hunger.*

ˌhalf-ˈcup *n.* [C] a small container used to measure a specific amount of food or liquid when cooking, or the amount that this holds: *Add a half-cup of sugar.*

ˈhalf-day *n.* [C] a day when you work or go to school either in the morning or the afternoon, but not all day: *I'm working only half-days now.*

ˌhalf ˈdollar *n.* [C] a coin worth 50 cents

half-ˈgallon *n.* [C] one half of a GALLON, equal to two QUARTS: *a half-gallon of milk*

ˌhalf-ˈhearted *adj.* done without much effort and without much interest in the result: *She made a **half-hearted attempt** to be friendly to the new girl.* —**half-heartedly** *adv.* —**half-heartedness** *n.* [U]

ˌhalf-ˈhour, **half hour** *n.* [C] a period of time that is thirty minutes long: *I got off work a half-hour ago.* —**half-hour** *adj.*: *Buses arrive here at half-hour intervals.*

ˌhalf-ˈinch *n.* [C] one half of an inch: *She's grown a half-inch this month.*

ˌhalf-ˈlength *adj.* a half-length painting or picture shows the top half of someone's body

ˈhalf-life *n.* [C] PHYSICS the length of time needed for half the atoms in a RADIOACTIVE substance to decay into material that is no longer radioactive

ˈhalf-light *n.* [U] the dull gray light you see when it is almost dark, but not completely dark: *the misty half-light of dawn*

ˌhalf-ˈmast *n.* **be/fly at half-mast** a flag that is at half-mast has been raised only to the middle of the pole in order to show respect and sadness for someone important who has died

ˈhalf ˌmeasures *n.* [plural] actions or methods that do not deal with something well or completely enough: *Half-measures will not fix America's healthcare crisis.*

half-ˈmile *n.* [C] **1** one half of a mile: *There's a gas station about a half-mile down the road.* **2** a race in which you run this length

ˈhalf moon *n.* [C] the shape of the moon when only half of it can be seen → see also FULL MOON, NEW MOON

half nel·son /ˌhæf ˈnɛlsən/ *n.* [C] a way of holding your opponent's arm behind their back in the sport of WRESTLING

ˈhalf note *n.* [C] TECHNICAL a musical note that continues for half the length of a WHOLE NOTE

half-ˈpound *n.* [C] one half of a pound in weight: *a half-pound of hamburger*

ˌhalf ˈprice *adv.* SPOKEN at half the usual price: *I got the stereo system half price.* —**half-price** *adj.*: *half-price tickets*

ˈhalf-ˌsister *n.* [C] a sister who is the daughter of only one of your parents

ˈhalf step *n.* [C] TECHNICAL the difference in PITCH between any two notes that are next to each other on a piano

ˌhalf-ˈtimbered *adj.* a half-timbered house is usually old and shows the wooden structure of the building on the outside walls

H

ˌhalf-ˈtime *adj., adv.* working half the usual amount of time each week in a particular job: *Louisville Housing Services employs only one half-time consultant.*

half·time, half-time /ˈhæftaɪm/ *n.* [U] a short period of rest between two parts of a game, such as football or basketball: *The score at halftime was 34–7.*

ˈhalf-truth *n.* [C] a statement that is only partly true, especially one that is intended to keep something secret: *The article is full of lies and half-truths.*

half·way /ˌhæfˈweɪ◂ / *adj., adv.* [no comparative] **1** at the middle point in space or time between two things: *I filled my glass only halfway with orange juice.* | **+across/through/up etc.** *He started crying halfway through his speech.* | *They drove halfway across the country to visit us.* | **halfway between sth and sth** *It's halfway between Baton Rouge and New Orleans.* | **the halfway point/mark** *the halfway point of the race* **2 be halfway there** to be half the way to achieving something: *Construction on the civic center is halfway there.* **3** [only before noun] INFORMAL to a satisfactory degree SYN **fairly**: *This is halfway decent coffee.* | *I'd like a chance to live a halfway normal life.* **4 be/go halfway to doing sth** to achieve something partly but not completely: *The Foundation is halfway toward its goal of raising $10,000.* → see also **meet sb halfway** at MEET[1] (17)

ˌhalfway ˈhouse *n.* [C] a place for people who have had mental illnesses or drug problems or who have been in prison, where they can live until they are ready to live on their own

ˈhalf-wit, halfwit *n.* [C] a stupid person or someone who has done something stupid —**half-witted** *adj.* —**half-wittedly** *adv.*

hal·i·but /ˈhæləbət/ *n. plural* **halibut** [C] BIOLOGY a large flat ocean fish used as food [**Origin:** 1400–1500 *holy* + *butte* **flat fish** (13–19 centuries); because it was eaten on holy days]

Hal·i·fax /ˈhæləˌfæks/ the capital and largest city of the Canadian PROVINCE of Nova Scotia

hal·i·to·sis /ˌhæləˈtoʊsɪs/ *n.* [U] TECHNICAL a condition in which someone's breath smells very bad

hall /hɔl/ S2 W2 *n.* [C] **1** a passage in a building or house that leads to many of the rooms: *This hall leads to the stairs.* | *We heard the principal* **coming down the hall** (=walking toward us in the hall). **2** a building or large room for public events such as meetings or dances → see also CITY HALL, DANCE HALL, TOWN HALL **3** used in the names of dormitories (DORMITORY): *Drummond Hall* **4** a HALLWAY [**Origin:** Old English *heall*]

hal·le·lu·jah /ˌhæləˈluyə/ *interjection* said in order to express thanks, JOY, or praise to God —**hallelujah** *n.* [C]

Hal·ley /ˈheɪli/, **Ed·mond** /ˈɛdmənd/ (1656–1742) a British ASTRONOMER who was the first to calculate the time that a COMET would return and be seen again from Earth

hall·mark[1] /ˈhɔlmɑrk/ *n.* [C] **1** an idea, method, or quality that is typical of a particular person or thing: **+of** *Clog dancing is a hallmark of Appalachian culture.* | **sth has/bears all the hallmarks of sth** *Oates's new novel has all the hallmarks of her earlier work.* **2** a mark put on silver, gold, or PLATINUM that shows the quality of the metal, and where and when it was made [**Origin:** 1700–1800 Goldsmiths' *Hall* in London, England where gold and silver articles were tested and marked]

hallmark[2] *v.* [T] to put a hallmark on silver, gold, or PLATINUM

ˌHall of ˈFame *n.* [C] a list of famous sports players, or the building where their uniforms, sports equipment, and information about them are shown

hal·lowed /ˈhæloʊd/ *adj.* **1** holy or made holy: *For Muslims, Mecca is* **hallowed ground** (=land that is holy). **2** important and respected: *the hallowed Blue Note jazz label*

Hal·low·een, Hallowe'en /ˌhæləˈwin, ˌhɑ-/ *n.* [U] a holiday on the night of October 31, when children wear COSTUMES and walk from house to house asking for candy and sometimes playing tricks [**Origin:** 1700–1800 *All Hallow Even* **All Saints' Eve**] → see also TRICK OR TREAT

hal·lu·ci·nate /həˈlusəˌneɪt/ *v.* [I] to see, feel, or hear things that are not really there, for example because you are sick, mentally ill, or taking drugs

hal·lu·ci·na·tion /həˌlusəˈneɪʃən/ *n.* [C,U] something you see, feel, or hear that is not really there, or the experience of this, usually caused by a drug or mental illness: *Doctors believe the medication was the cause of her hallucinations.*

hal·lu·ci·na·to·ry /həˈlusənəˌtɔri/ *adj.* FORMAL **1** causing hallucinations or resulting from hallucinations: *hallucinatory drugs* **2** using strange images, sounds etc. like those experienced in a hallucination: *the movie's hallucinatory ending*

hal·lu·cin·o·gen /həˈlusənədʒɪn/ *n.* [C] something that causes hallucinations: *LSD is a dangerous hallucinogen.*

hal·lu·ci·no·gen·ic /həˌlusənəˈdʒɛnɪk/ *adj.* causing hallucinations: *hallucinogenic mushrooms*

hall·way /ˈhɔlweɪ/ S3 *n. plural* **hallways** [C] **1** the area just inside the door of a house or other building that leads to other rooms **2** a passage in a building or house that leads to many of the rooms; SYN **corridor** SYN **hall**

ha·lo /ˈheɪloʊ/ *n. plural* **halos** [C] **1** a bright circle that is often shown above or around the heads of holy people in religious art **2** a bright circle of light around a person or thing, or something that looks similar: *a halo of blonde curls around her face*

hal·o·car·bon /ˈhæləˌkɑrbən/ *n.* [C] CHEMISTRY a chemical compound that contains CARBON and a halogen

hal·o·gen[1] /ˈhælədʒɪn/ *n.* [U] CHEMISTRY one of a group of five simple chemical substances that make compounds easily. They are: CHLORINE, FLOURINE, IODINE, BROMINE, and ASTETINE.

halogen[2] *adj.* **a halogen lamp/light/bulb etc.** a type of lamp or LIGHT BULB that uses halogen gas to produce light

halt[1] /hɔlt/ *n.* [singular] a stop or pause: **bring sth to a halt** *The snow and ice brought traffic to a halt.* | *The train* **came to a halt** (=stopped), *and the passengers stepped out.* | **grind/screech/skid etc. to a halt** *The car* screeched to a halt. | The protestors were ***calling for a halt to*** the violence (=saying that it should stop). | Management ***called a halt to*** the negotiations (=stopped them).

halt² *v.* **1** [I,T] WRITTEN to stop continuing or developing, or prevent something from continuing or developing SYN **stop**: *measures to halt the spread of HIV* | *Construction on the road halted in 1999.* **2** [I,T] WRITTEN to stop moving, or cause something to stop moving SYN **stop**: *Heavy rain halted five railroad lines in the Tokyo area.* | *The taxi halted in front of the hotel.* **3 halt!** used as a military command to order someone to stop moving or soldiers to stop marching: *Company halt!*

hal·ter /ˈhɔltɚ/ *n.* [C] **1** also **halter top** a type of clothing for women that covers the chest and ties behind the neck and waist, so that the arms and back are not covered **2** a rope or leather band that fastens around a horse's head, usually used to lead the horse

halt·ing /ˈhɔltɪŋ/ *adj.* if your speech or movements are halting, you stop for a moment between words or movements, especially because you are not confident: ***In halting English,*** *he gave us directions to the museum.* —**haltingly** *adv.*

halve /hæv/ *v.* [T] **1** to cut or divide something into two equal pieces: *Halve the eggplant lengthwise.* **2** to reduce something by a half: *His 13-year prison term was halved because of good behavior.*

halves /hævz/ *n.* the plural of HALF → see also **go halves (on sth)** at HALF² (4), **not do sth by halves** at HALF² (7)

hal·yard /ˈhælyɚd/ *n.* [C] TECHNICAL a rope used to raise or lower a flag or sail

ham¹ /hæm/ S3 *n.* **1** [C,U] the upper part of a pig's leg used as meat and preserved with salt or smoke: *a ham sandwich* | *We bought two small hams for dinner.* ►see THESAURUS box at **meat** **2** [C] an actor who performs with too much false emotion **3** [C] someone who receives and sends radio messages for fun [**Origin:** (2) 1800–1900 *ham-fatter* **bad actor** (19–20 centuries), from the song "The Ham-fat Man."]

ham² *v.* **hammed, hamming ham it up** INFORMAL to perform or behave with too much false emotion, especially in order to be funny: *Dad put on his Santa suit and hammed it up for the kids.*

ham·burg·er /ˈhæmˌbɚgɚ/ S3 *n.* **1** [C] a SANDWICH with cooked BEEF in a flat circular shape, eaten between pieces of round bread **2** [U] BEEF that has been ground (GRIND) into very small pieces: *a pound of hamburger* [**Origin:** 1800–1900 German **of Hamburg, city in Germany**]

ˌham-ˈfisted also **ˌham-ˈhanded** *adj.* INFORMAL **1** not skillful or careful at all in the way that you do something: *Employees protested at the ham-fisted way that Simmons was fired.* **2** not skillful at all with your hands SYN **clumsy** —**ham-fistedly, ham-handedly** *adv.*

Ham·il·ton /ˈhæməltən/ the capital city of Bermuda

Hamilton, Alexander (1755–1804) a U.S. politician who helped to write the U.S. Constitution and became the first U.S. Secretary of the Treasury

ham·let /ˈhæmlɪt/ *n.* [C] a very small town

Ham·mar·skjöld /ˈhæmɚʃəld/**, Dag** /dɑg/ (1905–1961) the Secretary General of the United Nations from 1953 until his death in 1961

ham·mer¹ /ˈhæmɚ/ *n.* [C]
1 TOOL a) a tool with a heavy metal part on a long handle, used for hitting nails into wood **b)** a tool like this with a wooden head, used to make something flat, make a noise etc.: *an auctioneer's hammer*
2 come/go under the hammer to be offered for sale at an AUCTION
3 GUN the part of a gun that hits the explosive CHARGE that fires a bullet
4 SPORT a heavy metal ball on a wire with a handle that is thrown as far as possible, as a sport
5 hammer and tongs INFORMAL with a lot of force, effort, or violence: *Republicans attacked Mr. Daniels hammer and tongs.*
6 PIANO ENG. LANG. ARTS a wooden part of a piano that hits the strings inside to make a musical sound

hammer² *v.*
1 HIT WITH HAMMER [I,T] to hit something with a hammer in order to force it into a particular position or shape: *The carpenters were hammering on the roof.* | **hammer sth into sth** *He hammered the nail into the board with one blow.* | *The copper is* ***hammered into shape*** *with a mallet.*
2 WITH FISTS [I] to bang on something repeatedly with your fists, making a loud noise SYN **bang** SYN **pound**: **hammer at/on sth** *Someone was hammering on the door.* ►see THESAURUS box at **hit¹**
3 RAIN/HEART [I] to hit something or beat repeatedly, especially making a loud noise SYN **pound**: *I stood up, my heart hammering.* | **+against/on** *The rain was hammering against the window.*
4 HURT WITH PROBLEMS [T] to hurt someone or damage something by causing them a lot of problems: *The economy has been hammered by the recession.*
5 SAY STH REPEATEDLY [I,T] to say something repeatedly until you are sure that people understand or accept what you mean: **hammer away at sth** *She kept hammering away at one simple question.* | *The Senator* ***hammered home*** *his point in a rousing speech.*
6 CRITICIZE [T] to strongly criticize or attack someone for something they have said or done: **be hammered for (doing) sth** *The President has been hammered for his lack of leadership.*
7 DEFEAT [T] INFORMAL to defeat someone completely in a war or at a sport: *Chicago hammered San Diego 13–2.* | *We* ***got hammered*** *last night.*
8 HIT/KICK A BALL [T always + adv./prep.] INFORMAL to hit or kick a ball very hard

hammer sth **in/into** sb *phr. v.* to say something repeatedly until people completely understand it: *The coach hammered the concept of teamwork into the squad.*

hammer sth ↔ **out** *phr. v.* to decide on an agreement, contract etc. after a lot of discussion and disagreement: *Officials met Thursday to try to hammer out an agreement.*

ˌhammer and ˈsickle *n.* [singular] HISTORY the sign of a hammer crossing a SICKLE on a red background, used on the flag of the former Soviet Union

ham·mered /ˈhæmɚd/ *adj.* [only before noun] **1** hammered silver, gold etc. has a pattern of small hollow areas on its surface **2** SPOKEN very drunk

ham·mer·ing /ˈhæmərɪŋ/ *n.* **1 take a hammering** to be attacked very severely: *Dresden took a real hammering during the war.* **2** [U] the action or sound of someone hitting something with a hammer or with their FISTS (=closed hands): *I heard hammering outside the building.*

Ham·mer·stein II /ˈhæmɚstaɪn/**, Os·car** /ˈɑskɚ/ (1895–1960) a U.S. writer who worked with the musician Richard Rodgers to produce many famous MUSICALS

ham·mock /ˈhæmək/ *n.* [C] a large piece of material or a net that you can sleep on, that hangs between two trees or poles [**Origin:** 1500–1600 Spanish *hamaca*, from Taino]

ham·per¹ /ˈhæmpɚ/ *v.* [T] to restrict someone's movements, activities, or achievements by causing difficulties for them: *The expedition* ***was hampered by*** *bad weather.*

hamper² *n.* [C] **1** a large basket that you put dirty clothes in until they can be washed **2** a basket with a lid, often used for carrying food → see picture at BASKET

ham·ster /ˈhæmstɚ/ *n.* [C] a small animal like a mouse, often kept as a pet

ham·string¹ /ˈhæmˌstrɪŋ/ *n.* [C] BIOLOGY a TENDON behind your knee

hamstring² *v.* past tense and past participle **hamstrung** /-ˌstrʌŋ/ [T] to cause a person or group to have difficulty doing or achieving something: *Excessive regulations tend to hamstring honest businesses.*

Han·cock /ˈhænkɑk/, **John** (1737–1793) a U.S. politician who was the President of the Continental Congress, and was the first person to write his name on the Declaration of Independence → see also JOHN HANCOCK

hand¹ /hænd/ S1 W1 *n.*
1 BODY PART [C] BIOLOGY the part at the end of a person's arm, including the fingers and thumb, used to pick up or keep hold of things: *Go wash your hands.* | *What's that **in your hand**?* | *The old lady led me **by the hand** to the kitchen.* | *The couple were **holding hands*** (=holding one of each other's hands with one of their hands). | *Jack **took my hand*** (=held my hand with one of his) *and led me down the hall.* | *"Hello," she said **shaking my hand*** (=moving someone's hand up and down with one of yours as a polite greeting). | *I was **on my hands and knees*** (=kneeling with your hands on the floor) *looking for my ring.*
2 a hand help with something you are doing, especially something that involves physical work: **give/lend sb a hand** *Can you give your brother a hand up in the attic?* | *She's always the first to volunteer to help when I **need a hand**.* | *I'm always happy to **lend a hand*** (=help) *with the yard work.* ►see THESAURUS box at **help¹**
3 (on the one hand. . .) on the other hand used when comparing two different or opposite facts or ideas: *Gary, on the other hand, used to be very thin.* | *On the one hand, they work slowly, but on the other hand they do a great job.*
4 on hand INFORMAL close by and ready when needed: *There is always a nurse on hand in case of any injuries.*
5 get out of hand to become impossible to control: *Pull or spray garden weeds before they get out of hand.* | *It was a practical joke that got a little out of hand.*
6 in the hands of sb also **in sb's hands** being dealt with or controlled by someone: *The decision is in your hands.* | *The area is already in the hands of the rebels.*
7 be good with your hands skillful at making things
8 hand in hand holding each other's hand, especially to show love: *They strolled hand in hand through the flower garden.*
9 have a hand in sth to influence or be involved in something: *Thorpe has had a hand in restoring the 21 houses.*
10 in hand being dealt with and controlled: *Officer Rogers said he has the situation in hand.*
11 in good/safe/capable etc. hands being dealt with or taken care of by someone who can be trusted: *Every parent wants to make sure they're leaving their child in safe hands.*
12 by hand a) done or made by a person, not a machine: *The rug was made by hand.* **b)** delivered from one person to another, not sent through the mail: *They delivered their wedding invitations by hand.*
13 off your hands not your responsibility anymore, so that you feel happier: *By the time we're 50, the kids will be off our hands.*
14 out of your hands if something is out of your hands you are not in charge of it anymore, or do not deal with it anymore: *I'm sorry. The decision is out of my hands now.*
15 have sb/sth on your hands to have a difficult job, problem, or responsibility that you must deal with: *I think you have enough trouble on your hands already.*
16 at hand FORMAL **a)** happening soon: *Graduation day **is close at hand**.* **b)** close by and ready when needed: *Make sure you have your notes at hand.* **c)** needing to be dealt with now: *Let's focus on the task at hand.*
17 WORKER [C] someone who does physical work on a farm, in a factory etc.: *a hired hand*
18 hands down easily: *Harry would have **won hands down**, if he hadn't hurt his ankle.*
19 can/could do sth with one hand (tied) behind your back SPOKEN used to say that you can do something easily and well: *I could beat them with one hand tied behind my back.*
20 get/lay your hands on sth to find or obtain something: *It's $150 for the best seats, if you can get your hands on a ticket.*
21 get your hands on sb to catch someone you are angry with in order to punish them: *I'd love to get my hands on the guy who slashed my tires.*
22 have your hands full to be very busy or too busy: *Diane has her hands full with a new baby.*
23 have sth on your hands if you have something on your hands, you have to deal with it: *We have a big problem on our hands.*
24 sb's hands are tied if someone's hands are tied, they cannot do what they want because a rule, law, or situation prevents it: *We'd really like to help you, but our hands are tied.*
25 go hand in hand to be closely related, or happen together: *Diet and exercise should go hand in hand.*
26 make/spend/lose money hand over fist INFORMAL to gain, spend, or lose money very quickly and in large amounts: *For years they were making money hand over fist.*
27 CARD GAME [C] **a)** a set of playing cards held by one person in a game: *a winning hand* **b)** a game of cards: *We played a couple of hands of poker.*
28 ON A CLOCK [C] one of the long thin pieces of metal that point at the numbers on a clock: *the hour hand* | **big/little hand** (=used when talking to children about the hands on a clock)
29 give sb a (big) hand to CLAP loudly in order to show your approval of a performer or speaker
30 at the hands of sb if you suffer at the hands of someone, they treat you badly: *He told of the abuse he had suffered at the hands of prison guards.*
31 refuse/reject/dismiss etc. sth out of hand if you refuse, reject etc. something out of hand, you refuse, reject it immediately and completely: *My request for more vacation time was rejected out of hand.*
32 a firm hand strict control of someone: *Active kids need a firm hand* (=they need to be controlled).
33 sb's hand (in marriage) OLD-FASHIONED permission or agreement for a man to marry a particular woman: *He finally asked for her hand in marriage.*
34 turn your hand to sth to start doing something new or practicing a new skill: *After 25 years in broadcasting, she decided to turn her hand to writing.*
35 HORSE [C] a unit for measuring the height of a horse, equal to four inches
36 tie/bind sb hand and foot a) to tie someone's hands and feet **b)** to severely restrict someone's freedom to make decisions: *We're bound hand and foot by all these safety regulations.*
37 WRITING [singular] the way you write SYN **handwriting**: *The letter was written in a neat hand.*
38 keep your hand in (sth) to keep doing something so you do not lose your skill: *I'd like to keep my hand in as a coach on a professional team.*
39 hand in glove LITERARY closely related to someone or something: *Temperamentally and ideologically, the two men fit hand in glove.* → see also **bite the hand that feeds you** at BITE¹ (6), **(at) first hand** at FIRST¹ (11), **force sb's hand** at FORCE² (3), FREEHAND, HANDS-ON, HANDS UP, LEFT-HAND, LEFT-HANDED, LEFT-HANDER, **have time on your hands** at TIME¹ (17), **be an old hand (at sth)** at OLD (15), **overplay your hand** at OVERPLAY (3), RIGHT-HAND, RIGHT-HANDED, RIGHT-HANDER, **shake hands (with sb)** at SHAKE¹ (4), **wash your hands of sth** at WASH¹ (5), **win hands down** at WIN¹ (1)

hand² S1 W2 *v.* [T] **1** to pass something to someone else SYN **give**: **hand sb sth** *Hand me the newspaper, will you?* | **hand sth to sb** *I handed the package to the security guard.* ►see THESAURUS box at **give¹** **2 you have to hand it to sb** SPOKEN used to say that you admire someone: *You have to hand it to her. She's really made a success of that company.*

hand sth ↔ **back** *phr. v.* **1** to pass something back to someone: **hand sth back to sb** *The guard looked at my papers and handed them back to me.* **2** to give something back to someone it used to belong to: **hand sth back to sb** *Hong Kong was handed back to China in 1997.*

hand sth ↔ **down** *phr. v.* **1 hand down a decision/ruling/sentence etc.** to officially announce a decision, a punishment etc.: *The sentence was handed down on Monday.* **2** to give or leave something to people who are younger than you or live after you: **hand sth down to sb** *The recipe was handed down to me by my grandmother.* → see also HAND-ME-DOWN **3** to pass something to someone who is below you: *Can you hand that box down to me?*

hand sth ↔ **in** *phr. v.* to give something to a person in authority: *He handed in his essay three days late.* | *I* ***handed in my resignation*** (=told my employer I was going to leave my job) *yesterday.*

hand sth ↔ **out** *phr. v.* to give something to each member of a group of people SYN **pass out** SYN **give out** SYN **distribute**: *A guy in a Santa Claus suit was handing out candy.* → see also HANDOUT

hand over *phr. v.* **1 hand sb/sth ↔ over** to give someone or something to someone else to take care of or to control: **hand sth over to sb** *I reluctantly handed the $25 over to my brother.* **2 hand sth ↔ over** to give power or responsibility to someone else: *The captain was unwilling to hand over the command of his ship.* **3 hand over to sb** to let another person speak in a discussion, report etc. after you have finished talking: *Now I'm going to hand over to our chairman, Mary Pressley.*

hand·bag /ˈhændbæg/ *n.* [C] a PURSE

hand·ball /ˈhændbɔl/ *n.* **1** [U] a game in which you hit a ball against a wall with your hand **2** [C] the ball used in this game

hand·bas·ket /ˈhændˌbæskɪt/ *n.* [C] OLD-FASHIONED a small basket with a handle

hand·bill /ˈhændˌbɪl/ *n.* [C] a small printed notice or advertisement that is usually given by one person to other people

hand·book /ˈhændbʊk/ *n.* [C] a short book giving information or instructions: *a handbook for new employees*

hand·brake /ˈhændbreɪk/ *n.* [C] EMERGENCY BRAKE

hand·car /ˈhændkɑr/ *n.* [C] a small railroad vehicle operated by pushing large handles up and down to make it move forward and back

hand·cart /ˈhændkɑrt/ *n.* [C] a small vehicle used for carrying goods, that is pushed or pulled by hand

hand·craft·ed /ˈhændˌkræftɪd/ *adj.* skillfully made by hand, not by machine: *handcrafted jewelry*

hand·cuff /ˈhændkʌf/ *v.* [T] to put handcuffs on someone: *The man was handcuffed and led away.*

hand·cuffs /ˈhændkʌfs/ *n.* [plural] a pair of metal rings joined by a chain or bar, used for holding a prisoner's wrists together

Han·del /ˈhændl/, **George Fred·erick** /dʒɔrdʒ ˈfrɛdrɪk/ (1685–1759) a British musician, originally from Germany, who wrote CLASSICAL music

ˌhand-eye coordiˈnation *n.* [U] the way in which your hands and eyes work together to make you able to do things well, for example to make you able to catch, hit, kick etc. a ball or to write or draw

hand·ful /ˈhændfʊl/ *n.* **1** [C] an amount that you can hold in your hand: +**of** *I scooped up a handful of white sand.* **2** a very small number of people or things: *They played a handful of tunes from their new album.* **3 a handful** INFORMAL someone, especially a child, who is difficult to control: *3-year-old Matilda is a handful.*

ˈhand greˌnade *n.* [C] a small bomb that is thrown by a person rather than shot from a machine

hand·gun /ˈhændgʌn/ *n.* [C] a small gun that you hold in one hand when you shoot

hand·held /ˈhændhɛld/ *n.* [C] a computer, piece of electronic equipment etc. that is small enough to hold in your hand when you use it: *a review of new handhelds on the market* —**handheld** *adj.*: *handheld devices*

hand·hold /ˈhændhoʊld/ *n.* [C] a place where you can safely put your hand when climbing a rock or mountain → see also FOOTHOLD, TOEHOLD

hand·i·cap[1] /ˈhændiˌkæp/ *n.* [C] **1** a condition or situation that makes it difficult for someone to do something: *His lack of experience on Wall Street may prove to be a handicap.* **2** OLD-FASHIONED an inability to use part of your body or mind because it has been damaged SYN **disability** **3** in GOLF, an advantage given to someone who is not very good, in order to make the competition fair **4** a handicap horse race is one in which some of the horses carry more weight in order to make the competition fair [**Origin:** 1700–1800 *handicap* **game in which people put their hand, holding money for a bet, into a hat** (1600–1700), from *hand in cap*]

handicap[2] *v.* **handicapped** [T] to make it difficult for someone to do something: *His business plans were handicapped by lack of money.*

hand·i·capped /ˈhændiˌkæpt/ *adj.* OLD-FASHIONED **1** not able to use part of your body or mind fully because it has been damaged SYN **disabled** ▸see THESAURUS box at **disabled** **2 the handicapped** people who are physically or mentally handicapped SYN **the disabled**

USAGE

Using the word **handicapped** to talk about someone who cannot use part of their body or mind normally may be considered offensive by some people. The word **disabled** is commonly used, but some people consider it more polite to say **challenged** or **impaired**: *physically challenged* | *visually impaired.*

hand·i·cap·per /ˈhændiˌkæpɚ/ *n.* [C] someone who tries to guess what the results of a competition such as a horse race will be, especially as a job

hand·i·craft /ˈhændiˌkræft/ also **craft** *n.* [C usually plural] a skill needing careful use of your hands, such as SEWING, making baskets etc.

hand·i·ly /ˈhændəli/ *adv.* if you handily win something or defeat someone, you do it easily: *She handily defeated Davis in the election.*

hand·i·work /ˈhændiˌwɚk/ *n.* [U] **1** something that someone makes, especially something you make using your hands: *She stepped back to admire her handiwork.* **2** something that someone has done or caused: *Officials believe that the bomb was the handiwork of a local terrorist group.*

hand·ker·chief /ˈhæŋkɚtʃɪf, -ˌtʃif/ *n.* [C] a piece of cloth used for drying your nose or eyes

han·dle[1] /ˈhændl/ S1 W2 *v.*

1 DEAL WITH STH [T] to deal with a situation or problem: *I don't think I can handle the pressure.* | *We were impressed with the way he handled a very difficult situation.*

2 DEAL WITH SB [T] to deal with people or behave toward them in a particular way: *You'll receive training on how to handle angry customers.* | *I can only handle Dan for about fifteen minutes.*

3 handle yourself to be able to behave well or calmly in a difficult situation: *I know you're worried, but he can handle himself.* | *She has handled herself well in the last two games.*

4 HOLD [T] to pick up, touch, or feel something with your hands: *You should wash your hands after handling raw meat.* ▸see THESAURUS box at **touch**[1]

5 CONTROL WITH YOUR HANDS [I,T] to control the movement of a vehicle, tool etc., or to be controlled: *Carver handles the basketball with confidence and skill.* | *The car was comfortable and* ***handled well.***

6 IN CHARGE OF [T] to organize or be in charge of something: *HPC Architects handled the architectural work.* | *Jones has handled a wide variety of criminal cases.*

7 MACHINES/SYSTEMS [T] to have the power, equipment, or systems that are necessary to deal with a particular amount of work, number of people etc.: *At one time, AT&T handled over 70% of the nation's long-distance calls.*

H

8 BUY/SELL [T] to buy, sell, or deal with goods or services in business or trade: *Bennet was charged with handling stolen goods.*

handle² S3 *n.* [C] **1** the part of a door, drawer, window etc. that you pull, push etc. to open it: *Pull on the handle to open the window.* **2** the part of an object that you use for holding it: *a knife with an ivory handle* | *The bag's handle was broken.* | **a broom/saucepan/ax etc. handle** *The broom handle unscrews from the bottom.* **3 get/have a handle on sth** to start to understand a person, situation etc.: *At least they have a handle on what caused the power failure.* **4** INFORMAL a name used by someone, especially by a user of a CB radio [**Origin:** Old English] → see also **fly off the handle** at FLY¹ (14)

'handlebar ˌmustache *n.* [C] a long thick MUSTACHE that curves up at both ends

han·dle·bars /ˈhændlˌbɑrz/ *n.* [plural] also **handlebar** [singular] the bar above the front wheel of a bicycle or MOTORCYCLE that you hold and use to control the direction it goes in → see picture at BICYCLE¹

han·dler /ˈhændlɚ/ *n.* [C] **1** someone whose job is to deal with a particular type of object, especially to move it or lift it: *baggage handlers for the airline* **2** someone whose job is to protect, advise, and represent a famous person or politician: *White House handlers* **3** someone who trains an animal, especially a dog

H

'hand-ˌlettered *adj.* written by hand in large letters or with carefully made letters: *a hand-lettered invitation*

han·dling /ˈhændlɪŋ/ *n.* [U] **1** the way in which a problem or person is treated or dealt with: **sb's handling of sth** *Police have been criticized for their handling of the Stuart murder case.* **2** the act of picking something up, or touching or feeling it with your hands: *Most of these chemicals require special handling.* **3** the process of packing and moving goods that are to be delivered: *You only pay $4 for* ***shipping and handling.***

'handling ˌcharge *n.* [C] the amount charged for dealing with goods or moving them from one place to another

hand·loom /ˈhændlum/ *n.* [C] a small machine for weaving by hand

'hand ˌluggage *n.* [U] the small bags that you carry with you when you travel, especially on an airplane

hand·made /ˌhændˈmeɪd◂/ *adj.* made by hand, not by machine: *The table is handmade.* | *handmade shoes*

hand·maid·en /ˈhændˌmeɪdn/ also **hand·maid** /ˈhændˌmeɪd/ *n.* [C] **1** OLD USE a female servant **2 the handmaiden of sth** FORMAL something that supports an idea, system, or way of life: *Aquinas belived that reason should be the handmaiden of religious faith.*

'hand-me-down *n.* [C usually plural] a piece of clothing that has been used by someone and then given to another person in the family: *I always had to wear my sister's hand-me-downs.*

hand·out /ˈhændaʊt/ *n.* [C] **1** money or goods that are given to someone, for example because they are poor: *My parents refused to take handouts from the government.* **2** a piece of paper with information on it that is given to people who are attending a class, meeting etc.: *a four-page handout*

hand·o·ver /ˈhændˌoʊvɚ/ *n.* [C] **1** the act of giving someone control of a place or person: *Arrangements for the handover of prisoners have been made.* **2** the act of officially giving something to someone: *Lawyers have arranged for the handover of documents to take place tomorrow.* → see also **hand over** at HAND²

hand·picked /ˌhændˈpɪkt◂/ *adj.* someone who is handpicked has been carefully chosen for a special purpose: *Dawson was the Mayor's handpicked successor.* —**handpick** *v.* [T]

hand·rail /ˈhændreɪl/ *n.* [C] a long bar fastened to a wall for people to hold while they walk, for example up the stairs

hand·saw /ˈhændsɔ/ *n.* [C] a small tool for cutting wood etc. that has a flat blade and sharp V-shaped parts on the edge of the blade

hand·set /ˈhændsɛt/ *n.* [C] the part of a telephone that you hold with your hand to your ear and mouth

hands·free /ˌhændzˈfri◂/ *adj.* [only before noun] a handsfree machine is one that you operate without using your hands: *a handsfree cell phone for the car*

hand·shake /ˈhændʃeɪk/ *n.* [C] **1** the act of taking someone's right hand and shaking it, which people do when they meet or leave each other or when they have made an agreement **2** the way that someone does this: *Nancy has a nice firm handshake.* → see also GOLDEN HANDSHAKE

ˌhands 'off¹ *interjection* used to warn someone not to touch something: *Hands off, that's my candy bar!*

'hands off² *adj.* [only before noun] letting other people do what they want and make decisions, without telling them what to do: *Kohler's hands-off style of management*

hand·some /ˈhænsəm/ *adj.* **1 a)** a man who is handsome is attractive SYN **good-looking**: *Roy is still as handsome as ever.* **b)** a woman who is handsome is attractive in a strong healthy way: *a handsome gray-haired woman* ►see THESAURUS box at **attractive**, **beautiful** **2** an object, building etc. that is handsome is attractive and well made: *a handsome colonial house* **3 a handsome profit/salary/sum etc.** a large amount of money: *She inherited a handsome fortune.* **4 a handsome gift/offer etc.** a generous or valuable gift etc. [**Origin:** 1500–1600 *handsome* **easy to handle** (15–17 centuries), from *hand*] —**handsomely** *adv.*

'hands-on *adj.* [only before noun] providing practical experience of something by letting people do it themselves: *Students are getting hands-on experience in a hospital.*

hand·spring /ˈhændˌsprɪŋ/ *n.* [C] a quick movement in which you turn yourself over completely, so that your feet go up in the air as your hands touch the ground, and then you jump into an upright position

hand·stand /ˈhændstænd/ *n.* [C] a movement in which you put your hands on the ground and your legs into the air

ˌhands 'up *interjection* used when threatening someone with a gun

ˌhand-to-'hand, hand to hand *adj., adv.* **hand-to-hand fighting/combat** a way of fighting in a war using hands, knives etc. rather than guns

ˌhand to 'mouth *adv.* **live hand to mouth** to live with just barely enough money and food and nothing for the future —**ˌhand-to-'mouth** *adj.*: *a hand-to-mouth existence*

'hand tool *n.* [C] a tool that you can use with your hands, especially a tool that is not electric

'hand ˌtowel *n.* [C] a small TOWEL for drying your hands

'hand-ˌwringing *n.* [U] the state or activity of worrying and feeling nervous: *There was a lot of hand-wringing among Democrats before the election.*

hand·writ·ing /ˈhændˌraɪt̬ɪŋ/ *n.* [U] **1** the style of someone's writing: *I recognized her handwriting on the envelope.* **2 the handwriting is on the wall** also **see/read the handwriting on the wall** used to say that it seems very likely that something will not exist much longer or that someone will fail: *The leadership should have seen the handwriting on the wall and acted sooner.*

hand·writ·ten /ˌhændˈrɪtˀn◂/ *adj.* written with a pen or pencil, not printed: *a handwritten letter*

hand·y /ˈhændi/ S3 *adj.* *comparative* **handier**, *superlative* **handiest** **1** useful and simple to use: *There's a handy cup holder under the car radio.* **2** INFORMAL near and easy to reach: *Add a rail to keep kitchen equipment handy.* **3 come in handy** to be useful: *I'm keeping the instructions – they might come in handy someday.*

4 good at using something, especially a tool: **+with** *He's handy with a screwdriver.*

ˈhandy-ˌdandy *adj.* [only before noun] SPOKEN HUMOROUS very simple and easy to use

hand·y·man /ˈhændiˌmæn/ *n. plural* **handymen** /-ˌmɛn/ [C] someone who is good at doing repairs and practical jobs in the house

hang

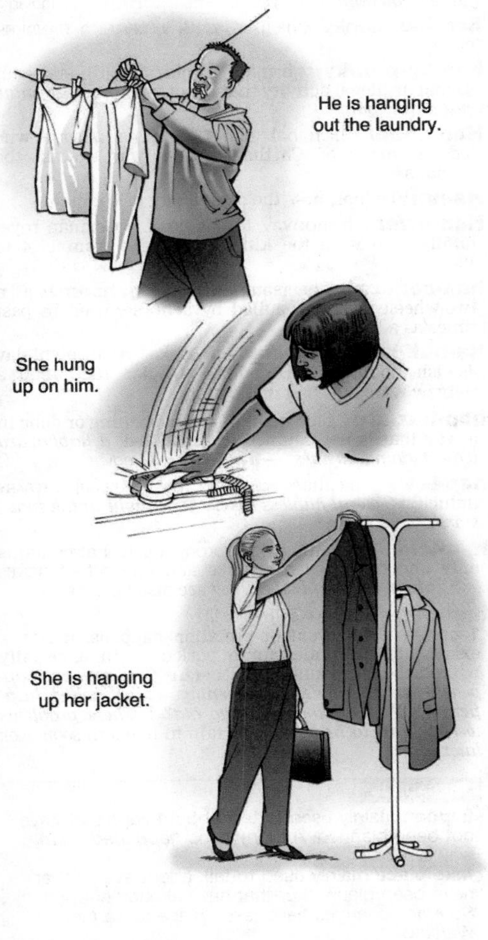
He is hanging out the laundry.
She hung up on him.
She is hanging up her jacket.

hang[1] /hæŋ/ S1 W1 *v. past tense and past participle* **hung** /hʌŋ/

1 HANG FROM ABOVE [I,T] to put something somewhere so that its top part is firmly fastened but its bottom part is free to move, or to be in this position: *We found the kite hanging in a tree.* | **hang (sth) on sth** *Hang your coat on the hook.* | **hang (sth) from sth** *A single bulb hung from the ceiling.* | *His hair* ***hung down*** (=used to show how far down something hangs) *in front of his eyes.*

2 PICTURE/PHOTOGRAPH a) [I always + adv./prep., T] to fasten a picture, photograph etc. to a wall, or to be fastened this way: *We could hang the mirror in the hall.* | **hang (sth) on/over/near etc. sth** *A portrait of his mother hung on the wall over the fireplace.* **b)** [I always + adv./prep., T] to show a picture publicly, or to be shown publicly: *A small study for the painting hangs in the J. Paul Getty Museum.* **c) be hung with sth** if the walls of a room are hung with pictures or decorations, the pictures, decorations etc. are on the walls: *The theater was hung with the flags of the United States and France.*

3 hang in the balance to be in a situation in which the result is not certain, and something bad may happen: *Peace in the region is hanging in the balance.*

SPOKEN PHRASES

4 hang in there also **hang tough** to remain determined to succeed, even in a difficult situation: *I know it's hard, but it's worth hanging in there.*

5 SPEND TIME [I] INFORMAL to spend a lot of time in a particular place or with particular people: *Most of the time we hang at my house.* | **+with** *We saw Pamela hanging with Connie.* → see also **hang out** at HANG[1]

6 hang a right/left used to tell the driver of a car to turn right or left: *Go straight on Vista for two blocks then hang a left.*

7 hang loose used to tell someone to stay calm and relaxed

8 PAPER [T] to put WALLPAPER on a wall

9 MIST/SMOKE/SMELL [T] to stay in the air in the same place for a long time: *A cloud of smoky fog hung over the town.*

10 hang by a thread to be in a very dangerous situation: *For weeks her life hung by a thread.*

11 hang your head to look ashamed and embarrassed: *Kevin hung his head and left the room in silence.*

12 DOOR/WINDOW [T] to put a door or window in position → see also **leave sb/sth hanging** at LEAVE[1] (33)

hang around *phr. v.* INFORMAL **1 hang around sb** to wait or stay somewhere with no real purpose: *A bunch of kids were hanging around outside the store.* | *What are you going to do – just hang around until six thirty?* **2 hang around with sb** to spend a lot of time with someone: *He's been hanging around with Randy a lot lately.*

hang back *phr. v.* **1** to not move forward or closer to someone or something, often because you are shy or afraid: *The villagers hung back at a safe distance.* **2** to be unwilling to do or try something: *Investors tend to hang back in times of recession.*

hang on *phr. v.* **1** to hold something tightly SYN **hold on**: *Hang on tight!* | **+to** *Hang on to the rail or you'll fall.* **2 hang on** SPOKEN used to ask or tell someone to wait SYN **hold on**: **hang on a minute/second** *Hang on a second, let me ask the nurse what's happening.* **3 hang on sb's every word** to pay close attention to everything someone is saying, especially because you admire or respect them: *The students hung on his every word.* **4** to continue doing something in spite of difficulties: *She hung on for five weeks before her kidneys failed.* **5 hang on sth** to depend on something: *His fate hangs on the legal negotiations.*

hang on to sb/sth *phr. v.* to keep something, or continue a relationship with someone: *You can hang on to the book until you're finished.* | *I don't think the Prime Minister can hang on to power much longer.*

hang out *phr. v.* **1** INFORMAL to spend a lot of time in a particular place or with particular people: *I just want to hang out, eat pizza, and watch TV.* | **+with** *Who does she usually hang out with?* → see also HANGOUT **2 hang sth ↔ out** to hang clothes on a piece of string outside in order to dry them: *He's outside hanging out the laundry.* | ***Hang*** *the blanket* ***out to dry*** *in the backyard.* **3 hang sb out to dry** to severely criticize someone for something they have said or done: *The press has really hung Smith out to dry.*

hang over sb/sth *phr. v.* if something bad hangs over you, you are worried because it is likely to happen soon: *The prospect of famine hangs over the whole area.* | *He has a six-month jail sentence* ***hanging over his head.***

hang together *phr. v.* **1** if a plan, story, set of ideas

H

etc. hangs together, it is well-organized and makes sense: *Make sure that your paragraphs hang together well.* **2** to help each other and work together to achieve an aim: *The band hung together for over ten years, before breaking up last month.*

hang up *phr. v.* **1** to finish a telephone conversation by putting the RECEIVER (=the part you speak into) down: *Please hang up and dial again.* | *Why did you **hang up on me** (=put the phone down before I was finished speaking)?* **2 hang sth ↔ up** to put something such as clothes on a hook or HANGER: *Amanda, hang up your clothes before you go to bed.* **3 be hung up on/about sth** SPOKEN to be thinking or worrying about someone or something so much that you cannot deal with other things: *He's still hung up on his ex-wife.* | *The media is hung up on this one tiny incident.* **4 get hung up** INFORMAL to be delayed: *Sorry I'm late, I got hung up in a meeting.* **5 hang up your cleats/badge/gear etc.** to stop doing a job or activity after a long time: *He's finally hanging up his badge* (=policeman's badge) *after a long career.* → see also HANG-UP

hang² *v. past tense and past participle* **hanged** [I,T] to kill someone by dropping them with a rope around their neck, or to die in this way: *During the Civil War, Milligan was hanged for treason.*

hang³ [S3] *n.* **get the hang of something** INFORMAL to learn how to do something or use something: *I still haven't gotten the hang of being a salesman.*

hang·ar /ˈhæŋɚ, ˈhæŋgɚ/ *n.* [C] a very large building where aircraft are kept

hang·dog /ˈhæŋdɔg/ *adj.* a hangdog expression on your face shows you feel sorry or ashamed about something

hang·er /ˈhæŋɚ/ *n.* [C] a curved piece of wood, plastic, or metal with a hook on it, on which you hang clothes

ˌhanger-ˈon *n. plural* **hangers-on** [C] someone who spends a lot of time with a person who is important, famous, or rich, because they hope to get some advantage: *The artist's friends and hangers-on were interviewed for the film.*

ˈhang ˌglider *n.* [C] a large frame covered with cloth, which you hang from in order to fly

ˈhang ˌgliding *n.* [U] the sport of flying using a hang glider

hang·ing /ˈhæŋɪŋ/ *n.* **1** [C,U] the action of killing someone by putting a rope around their neck and dropping them, used as a punishment **2** [C] a large piece of cloth hung on a wall as a decoration: *wall hangings*

hang·man /ˈhæŋmən/ *n.* **1** [U] a game in which one player tries to guess a word the other player has chosen, by guessing letters one by one **2** [C] OLD-FASHIONED someone whose job is to kill criminals by hanging them

hang·nail /ˈhæŋneɪl/ *n.* [C] a piece of skin that has become loose on the bottom or sides of the FINGERNAIL

hang·out /ˈhæŋaʊt/ *n.* [C] INFORMAL a place someone likes to go to often, especially with a particular group of people: *The park is the neighborhood hangout for teenagers.*

hang·o·ver /ˈhæŋˌoʊvɚ/ *n.* [C] **1** the feeling of sickness you get the day after you have drunk too much alcohol: *I **have a** really bad **hangover**.* **2 a hangover from sth** an action, feeling, or idea that has continued from the past into the present time: *The institution is a hangover from the Cold War era.*

han·gul /ˌhɑŋˈgul/ *n.* [U] ENG. LANG. ARTS the alphabet used for writing Korean

ˈhang-up *n.* [C] **1** INFORMAL if you have a hang-up about something, you feel worried or embarrassed about it in an unreasonable way: *All the characters **have** some weird psychological **hang-ups**.* **2** a problem that delays something: *There were a few technical hang-ups in the making of the movie.* → see also **hang up** at HANG¹

hank /hæŋk/ *n.* [C] an amount of YARN, thread, or hair that has been wound into a loose ball

hank·er /ˈhæŋkɚ/ *v.* [I,T] INFORMAL to have a strong desire for something over a period of time: **hanker for/after sth** *Voters seem to be hankering for change.* | **hanker to do sth** *I've been hankering to visit my father's birthplace for years.* —**hankering** *n.* [singular]

han·kie, hanky /ˈhæŋki/ *n.* [C] INFORMAL a HANDKERCHIEF

han·ky-pan·ky /ˌhæŋki ˈpæŋki/ *n.* [U] HUMOROUS sexual or illegal activity that is not very serious: *financial hanky-panky*

Han·ni·bal /ˈhænəbəl/ (247–183 B.C.) a GENERAL who led the army of Carthage in its war against the Romans

Ha·noi /hæˈnɔɪ, hə-/ the capital city of Vietnam

Han·o·ver /ˈhænoʊvɚ/ the name of a German royal family who were the kings of Britain from 1714 to 1901

han·som cab /ˈhænsəm ˌkæb/ also **hansom** *n.* [C] a two-wheeled vehicle pulled by a horse, used in past times as a taxi

Ha·nuk·kah, Chanukah /ˈhɑnəkə/ *n.* an eight-day Jewish holiday in December [**Origin:** 1800–1900 a Hebrew word meaning **dedication**]

hap·haz·ard /ˌhæpˈhæzɚd/ *adj.* happening or done in a way that is not planned or organized: *a haphazard way of doing business* —**haphazardly** *adv.*

hap·less /ˈhæplɪs/ *adj.* [only before noun] LITERARY unlucky: *Several hapless hikers got caught in the snowstorm.*

hap·loid /ˈhæplɔɪd/ *n.* [C] BIOLOGY a cell that contains only one set of CHROMOSOMES and one set of GENES —**haploid** *adj.*: *haploid cells* → see also DIPLOID

hap·pen /ˈhæpən/ [S1] [W1] *v.* [I]

1 OCCUR if an event or situation happens, it starts, exists, and continues for a period of time, usually without being planned [SYN] **occur**: *The accident happened early on Tuesday morning.* | *Hey, **what happened**? Why did the lights go out?* | *These problems were **bound to happen** (=certain to happen) sooner or later.*

THESAURUS

happen mainly used to talk about things that have not been planned: *A funny thing happened on my way to work.*
take place mainly used to talk about events that have been planned or that have already happened: *So many changes have taken place since I left Warsaw.*
occur FORMAL used especially to say that something happens in a particular place or situation: *The accident occurred around 9 p.m.*

2 RESULT to be caused as the result of an event or action: *Look, when I turn the key, nothing happens.* | ***What happens if** your parents find out?* | *I know they're losing, but it's early in the game. Let's just **see what happens** (=wait and find out what the final result is).*
3 sth happens to sb used to say that an event, action, or change affects someone or something: *Kids often don't believe anything bad could happen to them.*
4 whatever/what happened to...? **a)** used to complain that something good does not seem to exist anymore or has been forgotten: *Whatever happened to plain common courtesy?* **b)** used to ask where someone or something is or what someone is doing now: *Whatever happened to Jeanne, anyway?* | *What happened to my keys?*
5 happen to do sth to do or have something by chance: *I happened to see Hannah at the store today.*
6 as it happens used to say what really is true in a

situation: *Sam thought he'd find work right away, but as it happened, he was unemployed for months.*

SPOKEN PHRASES

7 what's happening? SLANG used when you meet someone you know well, to ask them how they are and what they have been doing: *Hey Carl, what's happening, man?*
8 sb/sth happens to be... said when you are angry or annoyed, to emphasize what you are saying: *That happens to be my foot you're standing on!*
9 whatever happens used to say that no matter what else happens, one thing will certainly happen: *We'll be thinking about you, whatever happens.*
10 it (just) so happens that used to tell someone something that is surprising, interesting, or useful: *They needed a painter, and it just so happened that Tom's friend is one.*
11 these things happen used to tell someone not to worry about a mistake they have made, an accident they have caused etc.: *It was a tough loss, but these things happen.*
12 anything can happen used to say that it is impossible to know what will happen: *Anything can happen when children are left alone in the house.*
13 you don't happen to...? also **do you happen to...?** used politely to ask someone if they have or know something: *You don't happen to know his address, do you?*

[**Origin:** 1300–1400 *hap* **chance, luck** (13–20 centuries), from Old Norse *happ*] → see also **accidents happen** at ACCIDENT (7)

happen across sth *phr. v.* to find something by chance: *Turner happened across a photo of his parents in an old magazine.*

happen by *phr. v.* to find a place or thing by chance: *The boat's captain points out any sea animals that happen by.*

happen on/upon sb/sth *phr. v.* to find something or meet someone by chance: *If you happen on a good sale, stock up.*

hap·pen·ing¹ /ˈhæpənɪŋ/ *n.* [C] **1** something that happens: *The paper has a listing of the day's happenings.* ►see THESAURUS box at **event** **2** OLD-FASHIONED an artistic event that takes place without much planning, and that the people watching or listening can PARTICIPATE in

happening² *adj.* SLANG fashionable and exciting: *a happening club*

hap·pen·stance /ˈhæpənˌstæns/ *n.* [U] FORMAL something that happens by chance: *The similarities between the two books could not have occurred **by happenstance**.*

hap·pi·ly /ˈhæpəli/ *adv.* **1** in a happy way: *Sally smiled happily.* | *a happily married couple* **2** [sentence adverb] fortunately: *Happily, Bruce's injuries were not serious.* **3** very willingly: *I'd happily go pick up the kids for you.* **4 live happily ever after** used at the end of children's stories to say that someone was happy for the rest of their life: *The prince and princess got married and lived happily ever after.*

hap·pi·ness /ˈhæpinɪs/ *n.* [U] the state of being happy: *Money is not the key to happiness.* | *He was flushed with happiness.*

hap·py /ˈhæpi/ S1 W1 *adj.* *comparative* **happier**, *superlative* **happiest**
1 FEELING having feelings of pleasure, often because something good has happened to you OPP **sad**: *a happy baby* | *You look a lot happier today.* | *I just wanted to **make** her **happy**.* | **be/feel happy for sb** *Congratulations, I'm really happy for you.* | **happy (that)** *We're happy that things have worked out so well.* | **happy to do sth** *Margo was really happy to see you.* | **happy to be doing sth** *Part of me is sad, but another part is happy to be leaving.*

THESAURUS

glad pleased about a situation or something that has happened: *I'm so glad you were able to come.*
pleased happy and satisfied with something that has happened: *Margaret smiled and looked pleased to see him.*
content/contented happy and satisfied: *We're usually content to stay at home and read or watch TV.* | *a contented baby*
delighted/thrilled/overjoyed extremely happy because something good has happened: *We were delighted when she had a baby girl.*
ecstatic extremely happy and excited: *The girls had won, by thirty points, and they were ecstatic.*
cheerful behaving in a way that shows you are happy: *He looked cheerful and relaxed.*
in a good mood happy at a particular time, and therefore friendly to other people: *I'll ask him sometime when he's in a good mood.*

2 be happy to do sth to be very willing to do something, especially to help someone: *I'd be happy to cook if you want me to.*
3 HAPPY TIME a happy time, place, occasion etc. is one that makes you feel happy: *Those were the happiest years of my life.* | *a lot of happy memories* | *Most fairy tales have a **happy ending**.*
4 SATISFIED [not before noun] satisfied or not worried: **+about** *I'm not happy about Dave buying a motorcycle.* | **+with** *Anne wasn't very happy with their decision.* | *The restaurant is determined to **keep** its customers **happy**.*
5 Happy Birthday/New Year/Anniversary etc. used to wish someone happiness on a special occasion: *Happy Thanksgiving, everyone.*
6 LUCKY fortunate or lucky: *By a **happy coincidence**, James was also there that weekend.* | *I'm in the happy position of not having to work.*
7 a happy medium a way of doing something that is not extreme but is somewhere between two possible choices: *Your house doesn't need to be perfect: find a happy medium between design and comfort.*
8 a happy camper HUMOROUS someone who is pleased about a situation: *I won't be a very happy camper if I have to do yard work all weekend.*
9 the happy event OLD-FASHIONED the time when a baby is born or when two people get married
10 as happy as a lark OLD-FASHIONED very happy
11 APPROPRIATE FORMAL appropriate for a particular situation: *His choice of words was not a very happy one.*
[**Origin:** 1300–1400 *hap* **chance, luck** (13–20 centuries), from Old Norse *happ*]

ˌhappy-go-ˈlucky *adj.* enjoying life and not worrying about things: *Jim's a happy-go-lucky kind of person.*

ˈhappy hour *n.* [U] a special time, usually in the early evening, when a bar sells alcoholic drinks at lower prices

Haps·burg /ˈhæpsbɚg/ the name of an important European royal family, who ruled in Austria from 1278 to 1918 and in Spain from 1516 to 1700. The German spelling of the name is Habsburg. —**Hapsburg** *adj.*

har /hɑr/ *interjection* used to represent the sound of laughter, especially when you do not really think something is funny

har·a·kiri /ˌhærɪˈkɪri/ *n.* [U] a way of killing yourself by cutting open your stomach, used in past times in Japan to avoid losing honor

ha·rangue¹ /həˈræŋ/ *v.* [T] to speak in an angry way, often for a long time, in order to criticize someone or persuade them that you are right SYN **lecture**: **harangue sb about sth** *Teachers must constantly harangue the kids about good behavior.*

harangue² *n.* [C] an angry speech that criticizes or blames people, or tries to persuade them that you are right: *anti-abortion harangues*

Ha·ra·re /həˈrɑreɪ/ the capital and largest city of Zimbabwe

ha·rass /həˈræs, ˈhærəs/ *v.* [T] **1** to annoy or threaten someone again and again SYN **hassle**: *Black teenagers are being constantly harassed by the police.* | *He denied*

H

sexually harassing *her.* **2** to annoy someone by interrupting them again and again over a long period of time SYN **pester**: *parents harassed by their kids* **3** to attack an enemy many times [**Origin:** 1600–1700 French *harasser*, from *harer* **to set a dog on**] —**harasser** *n.* [C]

ha•rass•ment /hə'ræsmənt, 'hærəs-/ *n.* [U] behavior that is threatening or offensive to other people: *There have been inquiries into* ***sexual harassment*** *at the college.* | *complaints of police harassment* | +**of** *the harassment of minorities*

har•bin•ger /'hɑrbɪndʒɚ/ *n.* [C] LITERARY a sign that something is going to happen soon SYN **herald**: +**of** *The increase in home prices may be a harbinger of better economic times.*

har•bor¹ /'hɑrbɚ/ *n.* [C] an area of water next to the land where the water is calm, so that ships are safe when they are inside it, and can be left there

harbor² *v.* [T] **1** to keep bad thoughts, fears, or hopes in your mind for a long time: *Ralph harbors no bitterness toward his ex-wife.* **2** to contain something, especially something hidden and dangerous: *Dirty towels can harbor germs.* **3** to protect someone by hiding them from the police

har•bour /'hɑrbɚ/ the British spelling of HARBOR

hard¹ /hɑrd/ S1 W1 *adj.*

1 FIRM TO TOUCH firm and stiff, and difficult to press down, break, or cut OPP **soft**: *Diamond is the hardest substance known to man.* | *a piece of hard candy* | *a hard wooden chair*

THESAURUS

firm not completely hard, but not soft and not easy to bend: *Brownies are done when the edges are firm but the middle is still soft.*
stiff difficult to bend or move: *Men in those days wore stiff, starched collars.*
solid firm and usually hard, without spaces or holes: *They blasted the tunnel through solid rock.*
rigid stiff and impossible to bend: *The disease made all her joints rigid.*
crisp used especially about food that is pleasantly hard: *a crisp apple*

2 DIFFICULT difficult to do or understand SYN **difficult** OPP **easy**: *Chemistry was one of the hardest classes I've ever taken.* | **be hard for sb** *It was hard for him, as he didn't speak any English.* | **be hard to do sth** *The print was small and hard to read.* | ***The hard part is*** *going to be telling my mother.* | *We lost the game in the last few seconds; that was really* ***hard to take*** (=difficult to accept or believe). | **it is hard to believe/imagine/see etc.** *It's hard to believe that no one saw what happened.* | **hard to tell/say/know** (=difficult to know) *It was hard to tell whether Katie really wanted to go.* | **have a hard time doing sth** *I had a hard time finding his house.* | *I was* ***finding it hard to*** *concentrate.* | *Jobs were* ***hard to come by*** (=difficult to find) *then.* ►see THESAURUS box at **difficult**

3 A LOT OF EFFORT [usually before noun] using or involving a lot of mental or physical effort: *Give the door a hard push.* | *She's earned a spot on the team with* ***hard work.*** | *She had a really* ***hard day*** *at school.* | *He knows how to have fun after a* ***hard day's work.***

4 be hard on sb a) to treat someone in a way that is unfair or too strict, especially by criticizing them: *You're harder on Donald than you are on Monica.* **b)** to cause someone problems: *It's going to be hard on the kids if you move away.*

5 be hard on sth to have a bad effect on something: *Aspirin can be hard on your stomach.*

6 PROBLEMS a situation or time that is hard is one in which you have a lot of problems or bad experiences, especially when you do not have enough money: ***Times were hard,*** *and we were forced to sell our home.* | *She's* ***had a hard life.*** | **fall on/come on hard times** *The family had fallen on hard times.* | *He's* ***had a hard time*** *in school, but he's doing better now.*

7 NOT NICE showing no feelings of kindness or sympathy: *He's a hard man to work for, but he's fair.* | *Her voice was hard and cold.*

8 hard facts/information/evidence etc. facts, information etc. that are definitely true and can be proven: *There is now hard evidence that global warming is happening.*

9 hard news news stories that are about serious and important subjects or events

10 learn/do sth the hard way INFORMAL **a)** to learn about something by a bad experience or by making mistakes: *I* ***learned the hard way*** *that my computer didn't have enough memory.* **b)** to learn or achieve something by working and having a lot of experience: *Kate Forrest had earned her position in the company the hard way.*

11 give sb a hard time INFORMAL **a)** to deliberately make someone feel uncomfortable or embarrassed, especially by joking: +**about** *Bob was giving her a hard time about her new boyfriend.* **b)** to treat someone badly or cause problems for them: *Is your boss giving you a hard time again?* **c)** to criticize someone a lot: *It's not my fault, John. Don't give me a hard time.*

12 hard-earned/hard-won achieved after a lot of effort: *your hard-earned dollars*

13 hard feelings a) anger between people because of something that has happened: *Sarcasm can lead to arguments and hard feelings.* **b) No hard feelings** SPOKEN used to tell someone after an argument that you do not want to be angry with them or for them to be angry with you

14 WATER hard water contains a lot of minerals and does not mix easily with soap OPP **soft**

15 DRUGS/ALCOHOL very strong, difficult to stop using, and sometimes illegal: *I never touch* ***the hard stuff*** (=strong alcohol). | *beer and* ***hard liquor*** | *the risks of* ***hard drugs***

16 hard line a strict way of dealing with someone or something: *They've* ***taken a hard line*** *in contract negotiations.*

17 hard winter a very cold winter OPP **mild**

18 take a (long) hard look at sth to think about something carefully without being influenced by your feelings, with the result that you change your opinions or behavior: *We need to take a long hard look at the whole system of welfare payments.*

19 hard left/right a) a sharp turn to the left or right: ***Make a hard left*** *just after crossing Lindley Avenue.* **b)** people who have extreme LEFT-WING or RIGHT-WING political aims and ideas: *Is the Republican Party moving to the hard right?*

20 hard-luck story if someone tells you a hard-luck story, they tell you about all the bad things that have happened to them in order to make you feel sorry for them

21 hard-luck kids/town etc. someone or something that has had a lot of bad things happen to them

22 PRONUNCIATION ENG. LANG. ARTS a hard "c" is pronounced /k/ rather than /s/; a hard "g" is pronounced /g/ rather than /dz/

23 LIGHT LITERARY hard light is bright and unpleasant SYN **harsh**

[**Origin:** Old English *heard*] —**hardness** *n.* [U] → see also **drive a hard bargain** at DRIVE¹ (18)

hard² S1 W2 *adv.*

1 USING ENERGY/EFFORT using a lot of effort, energy, or attention: *Elaine had been* ***working hard*** *all morning.* | *We* ***try hard*** *to keep our customers happy.* | *You need to think hard about what you want to do next.*

2 WITH FORCE with a lot of force: *It's raining hard.* | *Tyson hit him hard on the chin.* | *She ran all that way and she wasn't even breathing hard.*

3 baked/set hard made firm and stiff by being heated, glued etc.

4 be hard hit also **be hit hard** to be badly affected by something that has happened: *Bridgeport was hard hit by economic troubles.*

5 be hard pressed/put/pushed (to do sth) INFORMAL to have difficulty doing something: *Small companies are hard pressed to provide health insurance for their employees.*

6 laugh/cry etc. hard to laugh, cry etc. a lot and loudly: *We were laughing so hard we could hardly breathe.*

7 take sth hard INFORMAL to feel upset about something, especially bad news: *Dad didn't say much, but I could tell he took it hard.*
8 hard on the heels of sth happening soon after something: *The warm weather has come hard on the heels of the coldest December on record.*
9 be hard on sb's heels to follow close behind or soon after someone → see also HARD UP, **play hard to get** at PLAY¹ (24)

WORD CHOICE hard, hardly
- Use **hard** as an adverb to say that something is done using a lot of effort or force: *We studied hard for the test.* | *You have to push hard or the door won't open.*
- Use **hardly** to mean "almost not": *I could hardly believe it.* | *Laura hardly studied for the test, so it was no big surprise that she failed.*

ˌhard-and-ˈfast *adj.* clear, definite, always able to be used, and not able to be changed SYN **set**: *The school doesn't have any **hard-and-fast rules** about what children should wear.*

hard·back /ˈhɑrdbæk/ *n.* [C] a HARDCOVER ► see THESAURUS box at **book**¹ —**hardback** *adj.*

hard·ball /ˈhɑrdbɔl/ *n.* [U] **play hardball** INFORMAL to be very determined to get what you want, especially in business or politics

ˌhard-ˈbitten *adj.* not easily shocked or upset, because you have had a lot of experience SYN **tough**: *a hard-bitten detective*

hard·board /ˈhɑrdbɔrd/ *n.* [U] a building material made from small pieces of wood pressed together to form a board

ˌhard-ˈboiled *adj.* **1** a hard-boiled egg has been boiled until it becomes solid → see also SOFT-BOILED **2** INFORMAL **a)** not showing your emotions and not influenced by your feelings in what you do SYN **tough**: *a hard-boiled businesswoman* **b) hard-boiled fiction/novels etc.** a book etc. that deals with people who do not show their emotions: *hard-boiled detective stories*

hard·bound /ˈhɑrdbaʊnd/ *adj.* a hardbound book has a strong stiff cover

ˌhard ˈcash *n.* [U] paper money and coins, not checks or CREDIT CARDS

ˈhard ˌcopy *n.* [C,U] information from a computer that is printed onto paper, or the papers themselves

hard·core, hard-core /ˈhɑrdkɔr/ *adj.* **1** [only before noun] having an extremely strong belief, opinion, or behavior that is unlikely to change: *hardcore criminals* | *hard-core Republicans* **2 hardcore pornography** magazines, movies etc. that show the details of sexual behavior, often in a way that people think is too violent or shocking **3** hardcore PUNK or ROCK music is played very fast and loudly

hard·cov·er /ˈhɑrdˌkʌvɚ/ *n.* [C] a book that has a strong stiff cover ►see THESAURUS box at **book**¹ —**hardcover** *adj.* → see also PAPERBACK

ˌhard ˈcurrency *n.* [C,U] ECONOMICS money that is from a country that has a strong ECONOMY, and is therefore unlikely to lose its value

ˌhard ˈdisk *n.* [C] COMPUTERS a stiff DISK inside a computer, used for permanently storing a large amount of information → see also FLOPPY DISK

ˈhard-ˌdrinking *adj.* drinking a lot of alcohol: *a hard-drinking man*

ˈhard drive *n.* [C] COMPUTERS the part of a computer where information and PROGRAMS are stored, consisting of HARD DISKS and the electronic equipment that reads what is stored on them → see picture at COMPUTER

ˌhard-ˈedged *adj.* dealing with difficult subjects or criticizing someone severely in a way that may offend some people: *hard-edged, realistic stories*

hard·en /ˈhɑrdn/ *v.* **1** [I,T] to become firm or stiff, or to make something firm or stiff OPP **soften**: *The clay needs to harden first.* | *Harden the chocolates by putting them in the fridge.* **2** [I,T] to become or sound more strict and determined and less sympathetic, or to make someone become this way OPP **soften**: *Opposition to the peace talks has hardened since the attack.* | *The death of a parent can harden young people.* **3** WRITTEN if your face or voice hardens, or if something hardens it, you look or sound less sympathetic or happy OPP **soften**: *With each missed shot, her face hardens.* **4 harden your heart** to make yourself not feel pity or sympathy for someone

hard·ened /ˈhɑrdnd/ *adj.* **1 hardened criminal/police officer etc.** a criminal, officer etc. who has had a lot of experience with things that are shocking and is therefore less affected by them **2 become hardened toward/to sth** to become used to something shocking because you have seen it many times: *Many inner-city residents have become almost hardened to the violence.*

ˈhard hat *n.* [C] a protective hat, worn especially by workers in places where buildings are being built → see picture at HAT

ˌhard-ˈheaded *adj.* practical and able to make difficult decisions without being influenced by your emotions: *a hard-headed manager* —**hard-headedness** *n.* [U]

ˌhard-ˈhearted *adj.* not caring about other people's feelings SYN **unfeeling** —**hard-heartedness** *n.* [U]

ˌhard-ˈhitting *adj.* criticizing someone or something in a strong and effective way: *a hard-hitting TV documentary*

har·di·ness /ˈhɑrdinɪs/ *n.* [U] the ability to bear difficult or severe conditions: *This type of wheat is noted for its hardiness.*

Hard·ing /ˈhɑrdɪŋ/, **War·ren** /ˈwɔrən/ (1865–1923) the 29th President of the U.S.

hard ˈlabor *n.* [U] punishment in prison that consists of hard physical work

ˌhard-ˈline *adj.* having extreme political beliefs, and refusing to change them: *the candidate's hard-line views* → see also **take a hard line** at HARD¹ (16)

hard·lin·er /ˌhɑrdˈlaɪnɚ◂/ *n.* [C] a politician who wants political problems to be dealt with in a strong and extreme way

hard·ly /ˈhɑrdli/ S2 W2 *adv.* **1** almost not SYN **barely**: *I hardly know her.* | *I was so tired I **could hardly** walk.* | *I **can hardly** wait!* | ***Hardly anyone*** (=almost no one) *likes liver.* | *There's **hardly any*** (=very little) *difference in price.* | *What do you mean? I **hardly even*** (=almost not at all) *know the guy!* | *We **hardly ever*** (=almost never) *go out to eat.* | **can hardly believe your ears/eyes** (=be surprised by what you hear or see) *Sam could hardly believe his eyes. Was it really his brother standing there?* → see Word Choice box at ALMOST **2** used to say that something is not true, appropriate, possible etc. at all, when you think the person you are speaking to will agree with you SYN **scarcely**: **be hardly the time/place/person etc.** *This is hardly the ideal time to buy a house.* | *The results of the survey were **hardly surprising**.* | *It **hardly seems** likely that he'll resign.* | *You **can hardly** blame her for being angry.* | *The program **could hardly be** easier to use.* **3** used to say that something had just happened or someone had just done something when something else happened SYN **just**: *The day had hardly begun, and he felt exhausted already.* | *She had **hardly** sat down **when** the phone rang.*

GRAMMAR

Do not use **hardly** with "not" or "no" or other negative words. Say *The city has hardly any pollution* or *I could hardly believe they were sisters*, NOT *The city has hardly no pollution* and NOT *I couldn't hardly believe they were sisters.* **Hardly** usually comes just before the main verb: *I could hardly hear her* (NOT *I hardly could hear her*).
Hardly is used at the beginning of sentences only in very formal or old-fashioned writing. People usually say *The game had hardly begun when it started to rain* rather than *Hardly had the game begun when it began to rain*, which sounds old-fashioned and literary. **Hardly** is not the adverb of **hard**. Say *She works very hard* (NOT *She works very hardly*).

ˈhard ˌmoney *n.* [U] money that is given to a politician by his or her supporters for an election campaign. The amount that can be given is limited by the government. → see also SOFT MONEY

ˌhard-ˈnosed *adj.* [usually before noun] not affected by emotions, and determined to get what you want SYN **hard-headed**: *a hard-nosed negotiator*

ˌhard of ˈhearing *adj.* [not before noun] **1** unable to hear very well **2 the hard of hearing** people who are not able to hear very well

ˌhard ˈpalate *n.* [C] the hard part of the top of your mouth that is at the front behind your teeth → see also SOFT PALATE

ˌhard-ˈpressed *adj.* having a lot of problems and not enough money or time: *The clinic provides help for hard-pressed families.* → see also **be hard pressed/put/pushed (to do sth)** at HARD² (5)

ˌhard ˈrock *n.* [U] a type of ROCK MUSIC that is played loudly, has a strong beat, and uses electric instruments

hard·scrab·ble /ˈhɑrdˌskræbəl/ *adj.* **1** hardscrabble land is difficult to grow crops on **2** working hard without earning much money, especially because you are working on bad land: *his hardscrabble childhood in Kansas*

ˌhard ˈsell *n.* [singular] **1** a way of selling something in which you try very hard to persuade someone to buy it OPP **soft sell**: *Brittan was **giving the hard sell** to a farmer.* **2** if an idea or product is a hard sell, it is difficult to sell because people do not accept it: *Back then, California wines were a hard sell.* **3 sb is a hard sell** used to say that it is difficult to persuade someone to buy or do something: *I was a hard sell at first, but now I'm glad we moved.*

hard·ship /ˈhɑrdˌʃɪp/ *n.* [C,U] something that makes your life very difficult, especially not having enough money or food: *economic hardships* | **endure/suffer hardship** *Early settlers endured great hardship.* | *The new taxes are **creating** extreme **hardship for** poor families.*

hard·tack /ˈhɑrdtæk/ *n.* [U] a hard CRACKER, eaten especially in past times on ships

hard·top /ˈhɑrdtɑp/ *n.* [C] a car's metal roof, which cannot be removed, or a car with this type of roof → see also CONVERTIBLE

ˌhard ˈup *adj.* not having something that you want or need, especially money: *Scott was pretty hard up, so I lent him $20.* | *"How about going out with Tom?" "No thanks, I'm not that hard up."*

hard·ware /ˈhɑrdwɛr/ *n.* [U] **1** COMPUTERS computer equipment and machinery → see also SOFTWARE **2** equipment and tools, such as a hammer and nails, that you use in your home and yard **3** the machinery and equipment needed to do something: *tanks and other military hardware*

ˌhard-ˈwired *adj.* COMPUTERS computer systems that are hard-wired are controlled by HARDWARE rather than SOFTWARE and therefore cannot be easily changed by the user

hard·wood /ˈhɑrdwʊd/ *n.* **1** [C,U] strong heavy wood from trees such as OAKS, used for making furniture ►see THESAURUS box at **tree** **2** [C] a tree that takes a long time to grow and that produces this kind of wood → see also SOFTWOOD

ˌhard-ˈworking *adj.* working seriously and with a lot of effort: *a hard-working teacher*

har·dy /ˈhɑrdi/ *adj.* *comparative* **hardier**, *superlative* **hardiest** **1** strong and healthy, and able to deal with difficult living conditions: *Red deer are hardy animals.* **2** BIOLOGY a hardy plant is able to live through the winter

hare /hɛr/ *n.* [C] an animal like a rabbit, but larger and with longer ears and longer back legs, that can run very quickly

hare·brained /ˈhɛrbreɪnd/ *adj.* not sensible or practical SYN **foolish**: *a harebrained scheme*

Ha·re Krish·na /ˌhæri ˈkrɪʃnə/ *n.* **1** a branch of the HINDU religion worshipping the god Krishna **2** [C] a member of Hare Krishna

hare·lip /ˈhɛrˌlɪp/ *n.* [singular] MEDICINE the condition of having a top lip that is divided into two parts, because it did not develop correctly before birth —**harelipped** *adj.*

har·em /ˈhɛrəm, ˈhærəm/ *n.* [C] **1** the group of wives or women who lived with a rich or powerful man in some Muslim societies in past times **2** the rooms in a Muslim home where the women live [**Origin:** 1600–1700 Arabic *harim* **something forbidden**]

ˈharem pants *n.* [plural] loose-fitting women's pants made from thin cloth

Har·ing /ˈhærɪŋ/, **Keith** /kiθ/ (1958–1990) a modern U.S. PAINTER who used the style of GRAFFITI art

hark¹ /hɑrk/ *v.*

hark back to sth *phr. v.* to be similar to something in the past, or remind people of something in the past

hark to sth *phr. v.* LITERARY to listen or pay attention to something

hark² *interjection* OLD USE used to tell someone to listen

har·ken /ˈhɑrkən/ *v.* [I]

harken back to sth *phr. v.* to hark back to sth

harken to sth *phr. v.* to hark to sth

Har·lem Hell Fight·ers, the /ˌhɑrləm ˈhɛl ˌfaɪtɚz/ HISTORY the informal name of the 369th Infantry Regiment, a group of African-American soldiers from New York City that fought with the French Army during World War II

Har·lem Ren·ais·sance, the /ˌhɑrləm ˈrɛnəˌzɑns/ ENG. LANG. ARTS a period in the 1920s and 1930s of great achievements in African-American art, music, and literature. The center of the movement was Harlem, a part of New York City, where many African Americans live.

har·le·quin /ˈhɑrləˌkwɪn/ *n.* [C] **1** a harlequin pattern is made up of DIAMOND shapes **2** ENG. LANG. ARTS a character in a type of traditional Italian play who wears brightly colored clothes and plays tricks

har·lot /ˈhɑrlət/ *n.* [C] LITERARY a PROSTITUTE SYN **whore**

harm¹ /hɑrm/ *n.* [U] **1** damage, injury, or trouble caused by someone's actions or by an event: *Several people were injured, but most escaped harm.* | **do/cause harm** *A little wine won't do you any harm.* | *Some types of diets **do more harm than good*** (=cause more problems than they solve). | *We must protect these children from **mental** or **physical harm**.* → see Word Choice box at DAMAGE¹ **2 mean no harm** also **not mean any harm** to have no intention of hurting, offending, or upsetting anyone: *I know he meant no harm, but it was a very personal question.*

SPOKEN PHRASES

3 there's no harm in doing sth also **it does no harm to do sth** used to suggest that someone should do something: *There's no harm in trying.* | *It does no harm to ask.* **4 it wouldn't do sb any harm to do sth** used to suggest that it would be helpful or useful to someone if they did something: *It wouldn't do you any harm to get some experience first.* **5 no harm done** said in order to tell someone that you are not upset by something they have done or said, or that no damage or trouble was caused: *Don't worry, I'll clean it up. No harm done.* **6 what's the harm in (doing) sth?** used to ask what problems would be caused by something, especially after someone has criticized you: *What's the harm in letting a child watch a little TV?*

7 in harm's way in a place where something dangerous can happen: *Employees should never be put in harm's way.* **8 out of harm's way** in a safe place: *Move valuable objects out of harm's way when children are visiting.* **9 come to no harm** also **not come to any harm** to not be hurt or damaged: *With relief, she saw that none of the children had come to any harm.* [**Origin:** Old English *hearm*] → see also HURT

harm² *v.* [T] **1** to damage something: *Will the trade agreement harm the economy?* **2** to hurt someone or an animal: *fishing methods that do not harm dolphins* **3 harm sb's image/reputation** to make people have a worse opinion of a person or group

harm·ful /ˈhɑrmfəl/ *adj.* causing harm, or likely to cause harm: *the harmful effects of smoking* | *harmful bacteria* | **+to** *Some pesticides are harmful to the environment.* —**harmfully** *adv.* —**harmfulness** *n.* [U]

THESAURUS

poisonous/toxic containing a substance that can kill you or make you sick if you eat it breathe it etc.: *a poisonous snake* | *toxic fumes from burning tires*
detrimental FORMAL harmful or damaging to something: *It was felt that the trade deal was detrimental to U.S. interests.*
damaging having a bad effect on someone or something: *the damaging effects of sunlight on your skin*

harm·less /ˈhɑrmlɪs/ *adj.* **1** unable or unlikely to hurt anyone or cause damage: *Don't worry, the dog's harmless.* **2** not likely to upset or offend anyone SYN **innocuous**: *harmless fun* —**harmlessly** *adv.* —**harmlessness** *n.* [U]

har·mon·ic /hɑrˈmɑnɪk/ *adj.* TECHNICAL relating to the way notes are played or sung together to give a pleasing sound: *harmonic scales*

har·mon·i·ca /hɑrˈmɑnɪkə/ *n.* [C] a small musical instrument that you play by blowing or sucking air into it with your mouth and moving it from side to side SYN **mouth organ**

har·mo·ni·ous /hɑrˈmoʊniəs/ *adj.* **1** harmonious relationships, agreements etc. are ones in which people are friendly and helpful to one another **2** looking good or working well together: *The garden is a harmonious blend of art and nature.* | *harmonious flavors* **3** sounds that are harmonious sound good together and are pleasant —**harmoniously** *adv.* —**harmoniousness** *n.* [U]

har·mo·ni·um /hɑrˈmoʊniəm/ *n.* [C] a musical instrument like a small ORGAN worked by pumped air

har·mo·nize /ˈhɑrməˌnaɪz/ *v.* **1** [I] if two or more things harmonize, they work well together or look good together: **+with** *Buildings should harmonize with their natural surroundings.* **2** [T] to make two or more sets of rules, taxes etc. the same: *Countries need to work to harmonize standards on pesticides.* **3** [I] ENG. LANG. ARTS to sing or play music in HARMONY

har·mo·ny /ˈhɑrməni/ *n. plural* **harmonies** **1** [C usually plural, U] ENG. LANG. ARTS notes of music combined together in a pleasant way OPP **dissonance**: *four-part harmony* | *a choir singing **in perfect harmony*** **2** [U] a situation in which people live or work together without fighting or disagreeing with each other: *an effort to restore family harmony* | **live/work in harmony** *The mayor appealed for people to live in racial harmony.* **3 be in harmony (with sth)** FORMAL to agree with another idea, feeling etc.: **+with** *His religious ideas are **in harmony** with Hinduism.* | *The Indians are seen as **living in harmony with** nature.* **4** [U] the pleasant effect made by different things that form an attractive whole: *the harmony of sea and sky* | *The buildings are **in harmony with** their natural surroundings.* → see also DISCORD

har·ness¹ /ˈhɑrnɪs/ *n.* [C,U] **1** a set of leather bands used to control a horse or to attach it to a vehicle the horse is pulling **2** a set of bands used to hold someone in a place or to stop them from falling: *A climbing harness attaches you to the safety rope.* [**Origin:** 1200–1300 Old French *herneis* **bags, equipment**]

harness² *v.* [T] **1** to control and use the natural force or power of something: *The power of the Missouri River is harnessed to produce electricity.* **2** to fasten two animals together, or to fasten an animal to something using a harness **3** to put a harness on a horse

harp¹ /hɑrp/ *n.* [C] a large musical instrument with strings that are stretched on a frame with three corners, and that you play with your fingers —**harpist** *n.* [C]

harp

harp² *v.*

harp on sb/sth *phr. v.* INFORMAL to complain or talk about something a lot: *The press has been harping on the problem all month.*

Har·per's Fer·ry /ˌhɑrpɚz ˈfɛri/ a place in the U.S. state of West Virginia where the ABOLITIONIST John Brown took over a government weapons establishment in 1859

har·poon /hɑrˈpun/ *n.* [C] a weapon used for hunting WHALES or large fish —**harpoon** *v.* [T]

harp·si·chord /ˈhɑrpsɪˌkɔrd/ *n.* [C] a musical instrument like a PIANO, used especially in CLASSICAL MUSIC

har·py /ˈhɑrpi/ *n. plural* **harpies** [C] LITERARY a cruel woman

har·ri·dan /ˈhærɪdən/ *n.* [C] OLD-FASHIONED a woman who is not nice and is always in a bad mood

har·ried /ˈhærid/ *adj.* very busy and worried, especially because other people keep asking you to do things: *Robinson's harried secretary was on the phone.*

Har·ris /ˈhærɪs/, **Joel Chan·dler** /dʒoʊl ˈtʃændlɚ/ (1848–1908) a U.S. writer famous for his books for children in which Uncle Remus tells stories about Brer Rabbit

Har·ris·burg /ˈhærɪsˌbɚg/ the capital city of the U.S. state of Pennsylvania

Har·ris·on /ˈhærɪsən/, **Benjamin** (1833–1901) the 23rd President of the U.S.

Harrison, William (1773–1841) the ninth President of the U.S.

har·row /ˈhæroʊ/ *n.* [C] a farming machine with sharp round metal blades, used to break up the soil before planting crops —**harrow** *v.* [I,T]

har·rowed /ˈhæroʊd/ *adj.* a harrowed look or expression shows that you are very worried or afraid

har·row·ing /ˈhæroʊɪŋ/ *adj.* very frightening or shocking and making you feel very upset: *a harrowing account of childhood abuse*

har·rumph /həˈrʌmf/ *v.* [I,T] to make a sound that shows you are annoyed or that you disapprove of something —**harrumph** *interjection*

har·ry /ˈhæri/ *v.* **harries**, **harried**, **harrying** [T] LITERARY **1** to keep asking someone for something in a way that is upsetting or annoying SYN **pressure** SYN **pester** **2** to attack an enemy again and again

harsh¹ /hɑrʃ/ *adj.* **1** harsh conditions are difficult to live in and very uncomfortable SYN **severe**: *the harsh conditions in the refugee camps* | **harsh winter/weather/climate** *the harsh Canadian winters* | *the **harsh realities** of life in the inner cities* **2** cruel, or strict, or not nice: *They suspended him? That seems pretty harsh.* | *the **harsh treatment** of women in this culture* | *The movie has received **harsh criticism**.* | *He had **harsh words*** (=strong criticism) *for Republican leaders.* **3** unpleasantly loud and rough OPP **soft**: *a harsh voice* **4** unpleasantly bright OPP **soft**: *The stage lighting is harsh.* **5** ugly and not nice to look at: *the harsh outline of the factories against the sky* **6** a cleaning substance that is harsh is too strong and likely to damage the thing you are cleaning —**harshly** *adv.* —**harshness** *n.* [U]

harsh² *v.*

harsh on sb *phr. v.* SLANG to criticize someone or say things to them that are not nice

H

hart /hɑrt/ *n.* [C] OLD USE a male DEER

Hart /hɑrt/, **Lor·enz Mil·ton** /ˈlɔrənts ˈmɪltˀn/ (1895–1943) a U.S. SONGWRITER famous for writing MUSICALS with Richard Rodgers

Hart, Moss /mɔs/ (1904–1961) a U.S. writer and DIRECTOR of plays and MUSICALS

Hart·ford /ˈhɑrtˀfəd/ the capital city of the U.S. state of Connecticut

har·um-scar·um /ˌhɛrəm ˈskɛrəm/ *adj.* OLD-FASHIONED someone who is harum-scarum does things without thinking about what the results might be: *a pair of harum-scarum boys* —**harum-scarum** *adv.*

har·vest[1] /ˈhɑrvɪst/ *n.* **1** [C,U] the time when crops are gathered from the fields, or the act of gathering them: *September is usually harvest time.* | *the wheat harvest* **2** [C] the amount or quality of the crops that have been gathered: **good/bumper/poor/bad harvest** *It should be a good harvest this year.* **3 reap a rich/bitter etc. harvest** to get good or bad results: *Fathers who ignore their children will reap a bitter harvest.*

harvest[2] *v.* [I,T] to gather crops from the fields

har·vest·er /ˈhɑrvɪstə/ *n.* [C] **1** a farm machine that gathers crops **2** someone who gathers crops, fruit etc.

ˌharvest ˈmoon *n.* [usually singular] the FULL MOON in the fall

has /əz, həz; *strong* hæz/ *v.* the third person singular of the present tense of HAVE

H

ˈhas-been *n.* [C] INFORMAL someone who was important or popular, but who has now been forgotten

hash[1] /hæʃ/ *n.* [U] **1** a dish made with cooked meat and potatoes: *corned-beef hash* **2** INFORMAL hashish **3 make hash (out) of sth** to do something very badly: *The scriptwriters have made hash out of the story.* → see also REHASH, **sling hash** at SLING[1] (3)

hash[2] *v.*

hash sth ↔ **out** *phr. v.* INFORMAL to discuss something very thoroughly and carefully, especially until you reach an agreement SYN **discuss**: *They spent hundreds of hours hashing out a compromise.*

hash sth ↔ **over** *phr. v.* INFORMAL to talk a lot about something that has happened SYN **talk over**: *We watched a video of the game as the coach hashed over our mistakes.* → see also REHASH

ˌhash ˈbrowns *n.* [plural] potatoes that are cut into very small pieces, pressed together, and cooked in oil

hash·ish /ˈhæʃiʃ, hæˈʃiʃ/ *n.* [U] the strongest form of the illegal drug MARIJUANA

ˈhash mark *n.* [C] **1** one of the lines on a football field that marks a YARD **2** a mark that shows rank that is put on a soldier's uniform SLEEVE

Ha·sid /ˈhæsɪd/ *n. plural* **Hasidim** /hæˈsɪdɪm/ *n.* a member of a Jewish religious group who wear special clothes and believe in coming close to God through prayer —**Hasidism** *n.*

has·n't /ˈhæzənt/ *v.* the short form of "has not": *She hasn't seen Bruce in five years.*

hasp /hæsp/ *n.* [C] a flat piece of metal used to fasten a door, lid etc.

has·sle[1] /ˈhæsəl/ *n.* **1** [C,U] something that is annoying, because it causes problems or is difficult to do: *Driving downtown is just too much hassle.* ►see THESAURUS box at **problem**[1] **2** [C] INFORMAL an argument between two people or groups: *An experienced real estate agent will be able to avoid legal hassles.*

hassle[2] *v.* INFORMAL [T] **1** to argue with someone or annoy them: *A man was hassling motorists at the traffic lights.* **2** to ask someone again and again to do something, in a way that annoys them: **hassle sb to do sth** *I got tired of my parents hassling me to do my homework.*

has·sock /ˈhæsək/ *n.* [C] **1** a soft round piece of furniture used as a seat or for resting your feet on SYN **footstool** **2** a small CUSHION that you kneel on in a church

hast /həst; *strong* hæst/ *v.* **thou hast** OLD USE a way of saying "you have"

haste /heɪst/ *n.* [U] **1** great speed in doing something, especially because you do not have enough time SYN **hurry**: ***In her haste to** get to the airport, Mindy forgot the tickets.* **2 in haste** FORMAL quickly or in a hurry: *The army retreated in haste.* **3 make haste** OLD-FASHIONED to hurry or do something quickly **4 haste makes waste** used to say that if you do something too quickly, you make mistakes and it does not turn out well

has·ten /ˈheɪsən/ *v.* **1** [T] to make something happen faster or sooner SYN **quicken**: *The agency hoped to hasten the approval process for new drugs.* **2 hasten to do sth** to do or say something quickly or without delay: *Barbara hastened to tell him that she was all right.* **3 hasten to add** if someone hastens to add something to what they have said, they say something more when they think they may have not have been understood correctly: *He hastened to add that their behavior had not been typical.* **4** [I always + adv./prep.] FORMAL to go somewhere quickly SYN **hurry**: *We hastened toward shelter.*

hast·y /ˈheɪsti/ *adj. comparative* **hastier**, *superlative* **hastiest** **1** done in a hurry, especially with bad results SYN **hurried**: *He'd been pressured into making a hasty decision.* ►see THESAURUS box at **impulsive** **2 be hasty** to do something too soon, without thinking carefully enough first: *He cautioned them not to be too hasty.* —**hastily** *adv.* —**hastiness** *n.* [U]

hat

hat /hæt/ S2 W2 *n.* [C] **1** a piece of clothing that you wear on your head: ***Put your hat on** – it's cold.* | *She was **wearing a** big straw **hat**.* | **cowboy/bowler/top etc. hat** *a man in a black cowboy hat* **2 hats off to sb** also **take your hat off to sb** INFORMAL used when you want to praise someone for their achievement: *I take my hat off to him – he's a good lawyer.* **3 throw/toss your hat into the ring** to officially announce that you will compete or take part in something: *He threw his hat into the ring for the job of chief officer.* **4 keep something under your hat** INFORMAL to keep information secret **5 be wearing your manager's/teacher's etc. hat** also **have your manager's/teacher's etc. hat on** INFORMAL to be doing your work as a manager etc., which is not your only work **6 my hat!** OLD-FASHIONED used to express great surprise [**Origin:** Old English *hæt*] → see also **at the drop of a hat** at DROP² (8), HARD HAT, -HATTED, **pull sth/a rabbit out of a hat** at PULL² (9)

hat·box /ˈhætbɑks/ *n.* [C] a special round box in which you keep a hat to protect it

hatch¹ /hætʃ/ *v.* **1** [I,T] BIOLOGY if an egg hatches or is hatched, it breaks and a baby bird, fish, or insect is born: *The eggs should hatch any day now.* **2** [I,T] also **hatch out** BIOLOGY if a young bird, insect etc. hatches, or if it is hatched, it breaks through its egg in order to be born: *Millions of mosquitoes will have hatched out by May.* **3 hatch a plot/plan/idea etc.** to think of a plan, idea etc., often secretly

hatch² *n.* [C] **1** a hole in a ship or aircraft, used for loading goods, or the door that covers it: *a hatch on the submarine* **2** a hatchback **3 escape hatch a)** a door on a ship or aircraft that you can leave from if there is an accident **b)** something that allows you to avoid a bad situation: *Kids are looking for an escape hatch from the pressures of home.* **4** the act of hatching eggs, or the animals that have hatched, considered as a group: *The oil spill will affect next spring's hatch.* **5 down the hatch** SPOKEN used when you drinking something, especially an alcoholic drink **6** a HATCHWAY → see also BOOBY HATCH

hatch·back /ˈhætʃbæk/ *n.* [C] a car with a door at the back that opens up

hat·check /ˈhæt-tʃɛk/ *n.* [C] OLD-FASHIONED the place in a restaurant, theater etc. where you can leave your coat

hatch·er·y /ˈhætʃəri/ *n. plural* **hatcheries** [C] a place for hatching eggs, especially fish eggs

hatch·et /ˈhætʃɪt/ *n.* [C] a small AX with a short handle → see also **bury the hatchet** at BURY (9)

ˈhatchet-ˌfaced *adj.* having a thin ugly face with sharp features

ˈhatchet job *n.* [C] INFORMAL a newspaper article, television program etc. that criticizes someone severely and unfairly

ˈhatchet ˌman *n.* [C] INFORMAL someone who is employed to make unpopular changes in an organization

hatch·ing /ˈhætʃɪŋ/ *n.* [U] fine lines drawn on or cut into a surface

hatch·way /ˈhætʃweɪ/ *n. plural* **hatchways** [C] a small hole in the wall, floor, or ceiling of a room, or the door that covers it: *the hatchway into the attic*

hate¹ /heɪt/ S1 W2 *v.* [T not in progressive] **1** INFORMAL to dislike something very much SYN **detest** OPP **love**: *It's the kind of movie you either love or hate.* | *Pat hates her job.* | **hate doing sth** *Paul hates having his picture taken.* | **hate to do sth** *I hate to just leave stuff here.* | **hate sb doing sth** *Jenny's mother hates her staying out late.* | ***I hate it when*** *she calls me at work.* **2** to dislike someone very much and feel angry toward them SYN **loathe** OPP **love**: *Jill really hates her stepfather.* | **hate yourself** *I hate myself, but I can't stop taking drugs.* | **hate sb for (doing) sth** *She hates him for what he did to her.* | *The two of them* ***hate*** *each other's* ***guts*** (=dislike each other very much).

THESAURUS

can't stand/bear to hate someone or something: *I can't stand being late.*
detest FORMAL to hate someone or something very much: *I was going out with a boy my mother detested.*
loathe to hate something or someone very much: *She had once loved him, but now she began to loathe him.*
despise to hate someone very much and not respect him or her at all: *I despised him for his arrogance.*
abhor FORMAL to hate something because you think it is morally wrong: *He abhors violence of any kind.*
→ LOVE

SPOKEN PHRASES

3 I hate to say sth also **I hate to tell you...** used when saying something that is slightly embarrassing or not polite: *I hate to say it, but I think he's really boring.* **4 I'd hate (for) sb/sth to do sth** used to emphasize that you really do not want something to happen: *I'd hate all that food to spoil.* **5 I hate to disturb/bother/interrupt, but...** used to show that you are sorry that you have to say something, interrupt someone etc.: *I hate to interrupt, but it's urgent.* **6 I hate to think...** used when you feel sure that something would have a bad result, or when an idea is not nice to think about: **I hate to think what/how/where etc.** *I hate to think what would happen if he dropped out of school.* | **+of** *I hate to think of the struggles ahead of me.* **7 I'd/I would hate to think (that)...** used to say that you hope that something is not true or that it will not happen: *I'd hate to think someone set the fire on purpose.*

—**hated** *adj.*: *the hated dictator*

hate² *n.* [U] an angry feeling that someone has when they hate someone SYN **hatred** OPP **love**: *a look of hate* [**Origin:** Old English *hete*]

ˈhate crime *n.* [U] a crime that is COMMITted against someone only because they belong to a particular race, religion etc.

hate·ful /ˈheɪtfəl/ *adj.* very bad or expressing a lot of hate: *a hateful letter* —**hatefully** *adv.*

hate·mon·ger /ˈheɪtˀˌmʌŋgɚ, -ˌmɑŋ-/ *n.* [C] someone who tries to make other people fear or hate people from another race, religion, country etc.

hath /həθ; *strong* hæθ/ *v.* OLD USE has

hat·pin /ˈhætˀˌpɪn/ *n.* [C] a long pin that is used to make a woman's hat stay on her head

ha·tred /ˈheɪtrɪd/ *n.* [U] an angry feeling of extreme dislike for someone or something SYN **hate** OPP **love**: **+of** *the group's hatred of foreigners* | **+for/toward** *her hatred for her father* | **pure/sheer hatred** *She gave him a look of pure hatred.*

ˈhat stand also **ˈhat rack** *n.* [C] a tall pole with hooks at the top that you can hang coats and hats on

-hatted /hæt̬ɪd/ *suffix* [in adjectives] **fur-hatted/top-hatted etc.** wearing a particular type of hat

hat·ter /ˈhæt̬ɚ/ *n.* [C] OLD-FASHIONED **1** someone who makes or sells hats **2 as mad as a hatter** INFORMAL behaving in a way that is crazy or very strange

ˈhat trick *n.* [C] three GOALS made by the same person in a single game of SOCCER or HOCKEY

haugh·ty /ˈhɔt̬i/ *adj.* proud and unfriendly SYN **stuck-up**: *a haughty laugh* —**haughtily** *adv.* —**haughtiness** *n.* [U]

haul¹ /hɔl/ S3 *v.* [I always + adv./prep., T] **1** to carry or pull something heavy: **haul sth along/in/across etc.** *I was hauling boxes into the new house.* ►see THESAURUS box at **carry¹**, **pull¹** **2** to carry a large amount of something in a truck or ship SYN **transport**: *The ship was hauling a load of iron ore.* | **haul sth ↔ away/in/off etc.** *Trucks haul away garbage to the landfill.* **3 haul yourself up/out of etc.** to move yourself somewhere using a lot of effort: *Welles hauled himself up the rock face.* [**Origin:** 1200–1300 French *haler* **to pull**]

haul sth ↔ **in** *phr. v.* INFORMAL to earn a lot of money: *The movie hauled in $2 million in just one weekend.*

haul off *phr. v.* **1 haul sb ↔ off** to take someone somewhere they do not want to go, especially to prison: *Mahoney was hauled off for questioning.* **2 haul off and hit/punch/kick sb** INFORMAL to try to hit someone very hard

haul² *n.* [C] **1** a large amount of illegal or stolen goods: **+ of** *Police have seized a large haul of cocaine.* **2 the long/short haul** the long or short time that it takes to achieve something or for something to happen: *They offer guaranteed savings* ***over the short haul.*** | ***In the long haul****, these changes will improve our children's education.* | *We're in this project* ***for the long haul.*** **3 a long haul** a long distance to travel: *It's a long haul from here to Boise.* **4** the amount of fish caught when fishing with a net SYN **catch** → see also LONG-HAUL, SHORT-HAUL

haul·age /ˈhɔlɪdʒ/ *n.* [U] the business of carrying goods in trucks or trains for other companies

haul·er /ˈhɔlɚ/ *n.* [C] a company that carries goods in trucks or trains for other companies

haunch /hɔntʃ, hɑntʃ/ *n.* [C usually plural] **1** BIOLOGY one of the back legs of a four-legged animal, especially when it is used as meat **2 sb's haunches** BIOLOGY the part of your body at the back that includes your bottom, your HIPS, and the tops of your legs: *The coach squatted on his haunches, giving instructions to the players on the bench.*

haunt¹ /hɔnt, hɑnt/ *v.* [T not in progressive] **1** if the spirit of a dead person haunts a place, it appears there often: *People say the house is haunted by a former slave.* **2** if something haunts you, you keep remembering it and it makes you worry and feel sad: *Memories of the war still haunt her.* **3** to cause problems for someone over a long period of time: *All your mistakes will* ***come back to haunt*** *you.*

H

haunt² *n.* [C] a place that someone likes to go to often: **sb's old/usual/favorite haunt** *a bar that is the favorite haunt of local writers*

haunt·ed /ˈhɔntɪd/ *adj.* **1** a haunted place is one where the spirits of dead people are believed to stay: *a haunted house* **2 haunted expression/look etc.** a worried or frightened expression

haunt·ing /ˈhɔntɪŋ/ *adj.* sad but also beautiful and staying in your thoughts for a long time: *a haunting melody* —**hauntingly** *adv.*

Hau·sa /ˈhaʊsə, -zə/ *n. plural* **Hausa** or **Hausas** **1** [C] a member of a group of mainly Muslim people who live in northern Nigeria and southern Niger **2** [U] the language of the Hausa

haute cou·ture /ˌoʊt kuˈtʊr/ *n.* [U] the business of making and selling very expensive and fashionable clothes for women

haute cui·sine /ˌoʊt kwɪˈzin/ *n.* [U] cooking of a very high standard, especially French cooking

hau·teur /hɔˈtɚ, oʊˈtɚ/ *n.* [U] LITERARY a proud, very unfriendly manner

Ha·van·a¹ /həˈvænə/ the capital and largest city of Cuba

Havana² *n.* a type of CIGAR made in Cuba

Ha·va·su·pai /ˌhɑvəˈsupaɪ/ a Native American tribe from the southwestern area of the U.S.

have¹ /əv, həv; *strong* hæv/ S1 W1 *auxiliary verb* **has** /əz, həz; *strong* hæz/, **had** /əd, həd; *strong* hæd/ **1** used with the PAST PARTICIPLE of another verb to form the perfect tense: *She had lived in Peru for 30 years.* | *Has anyone called?* | *I've read the book already.* | *I don't think you've been telling me the truth.* **2** used with some MODAL VERBS and a PAST PARTICIPLE to make a past MODAL: *I must have left my wallet at home.* | *You should've been nicer to her.* **3 had better** used to give advice, or to say what is the best thing to do SYN **ought to** SYN **should**: *You'd better phone Julie to say you'll be late.* | *I'd better not go out tonight; I'm really tired.* **4 have had it** SPOKEN **a)** said when something is so old or damaged that it cannot be used anymore: *It looks like your stereo's had it.* **b)** used to say that someone is tired: *We'd better find a motel – the kids have just about had it.* **c)** used to say that if someone does something, it will cause problems or cause them trouble: *If you press the wrong button, you've had it.* **d) I've had it with sb/sth** said when you are so annoyed by someone or something that you do not want to deal with them any longer: *I've just about had it with you two – be quiet!* **5 had sb done sth** if someone had done something: *Had we known earlier, we could have gotten a babysitter.* [**Origin:** Old English *habban*]

have² S1 W1 *v.* [T not usually in passive]

1 FEATURES/QUALITIES [not in progressive] used when saying what someone or something looks like, or what qualities or features they possess: *Ruby has dark hair and brown eyes.* | *The stereo doesn't have a CD player.* | *Teachers need to have a lot of patience.*

2 OWN OR USE [not in progressive] to own something or to be able to use something: *They used to have three dogs.* | *The school doesn't have room for any more students.* | *Can I have the car tonight, Mom?* ▶see THESAURUS box at own²

3 have got used instead of "have" to mean "possess": *I've got four tickets to the Twins game on Saturday.*

4 INCLUDE/CONTAIN [not in progressive] to include or contain something or a particular number of things or people: *Japan has a population of over 120 million.* | *Our old apartment had a huge kitchen.* | *How many pages* ***does it have?*** | *Does the tank still* ***have*** *water* ***in it?***

5 EAT/DRINK/SMOKE to eat, drink, or smoke: *Why don't you have a beer with us?* | *We had steak for dinner last night.* | **have lunch/dinner/a meal etc.** *I usually have lunch around noon.*

6 EXPERIENCE/DO to experience something, do something, or be affected by something: *I have a meeting in fifteen minutes.* | *We* ***had a great time*** *in Florida.* | *We've been* ***having*** *a lot of* ***problems*** *with the new computer system.*

7 RECEIVE to receive something: *Jenny! You have a phone call!* | *I had three letters from credit card companies this morning.* | *He had some help from his dad.*

8 IN A POSITION/STATE [not in progressive] to put or keep something in a particular position or state: *I had my eyes half-closed.* | *I like to have the windows open.* | *Why do you always* ***have*** *the TV* ***on*** *so loud?*

9 may I have, can I have, I'll have SPOKEN said when politely asking for something: *I'll have two hot dogs to go, please.* | *May I have your name, please?* | *Could we have our ball back?*

10 SELL/MAKE AVAILABLE [not in progressive] to sell something, or make it available for people to use: *Do you have any single rooms?* | *They didn't have the sweater I liked in my size.*

11 FAMILY/FRIENDS ETC. [not in progressive] to know someone, or to be related to someone: *She has an uncle who lives in Wisconsin.* | *Chris has a friend who knows Randy Travis.*

12 AMOUNT OF TIME [not in progressive] if you have time or a particular amount of time, it is available for you to do something: *Will you vacuum if you have time?* | **have time to do sth** *I wish I had more time to talk to you.* | *You have 30 minutes to finish the test.* | *Do you have a minute? I have a question.*

13 DISEASE/INJURY/PAIN [not in progressive] to suffer from a disease, injury, or pain: *Sarah has a broken leg.* | *Many older men have high cholesterol.*

14 IDEA/THOUGHT/FEELING [not in progressive] to think of something, realize something, or experience a particular feeling: *If you have any good ideas for presents, let me know.* | *Survivors often have a deep feeling of guilt.*

15 have your hair cut/have your car repaired etc. to employ someone to cut your hair, fix your car etc.: *We're having the house painted this week.* | *I just had it fixed.*

16 have sth ready/done/finished etc. to make something ready to be used, or to finish something: *They should have the car ready by Monday.* | *I'll have it done soon.*

17 CARRY WITH YOU [not in progressive] to be carrying something with you: *Do you have your purse?* | *I thought I* ***had*** *my keys* ***with me****, but I must have left them at home.* | *How much cash do you* ***have on you?***

18 OFFER used in the IMPERATIVE to offer someone something: *Here, Tina, have some popcorn.* | *Please* ***have a seat*** (=sit down), *and the doctor will be right with you.*

19 GUESTS to be with someone, or be visited by someone: *I'll call back later – I didn't realize you had guests.* | **have sb with you** *Barry had an Australian guy with* *him.* | *It looks like the Hammills* ***have company*** *tonight.*

20 have an effect/influence/result etc. to influence someone or something, or cause a particular effect: *The fall in stock prices could have a disastrous effect.* | **have an effect etc. on sth** *Folk songs had a great influence on Bartok's music.*

21 have a baby/twins etc. to give birth: *Anna had a healthy baby boy on Tuesday.*

22 MEDICINE **have an operation/treatment etc.** to be given an operation, treatment etc. for a medical problem: *She had to have chemotherapy for about nine months.*

23 have a job/position/role etc. if you have a particular job, position etc., it is yours and you are the one who does it: *She has a job as a manager for a printing company.*

24 have a duty/responsibility etc. to be responsible for doing something: *We have a duty to the public to ensure safe food preparation.*

25 have sth stolen/broken/taken etc. if you have something stolen, broken etc., someone steals it, breaks it etc.: *She had her bike stolen from outside the house.* | *Coffey had his nose broken in the fight.*

26 have a party/concert etc. to hold an event such as a party: *We're having a party on Saturday.*

27 have the chance/opportunity/honor etc. to be able to do something: *Go see the new Coen brothers movie if you have a chance.* | **have the chance etc. to do sth** *I had the opportunity to work with some of the nation's top designers.* | **have the chance etc. of doing sth** *My mother had the honor of meeting the President when she was in college.*

28 EMPLOY/BE IN CHARGE OF [not in progressive] to employ or be in charge of a group of workers: *Ahmad has five employees under him.*

29 HOLD SB **have sb by sth** to hold someone violently by a part of their body: *They had him by the throat.*

30 MAKE SB DO STH [not in progressive] **a)** to make someone start doing something: **have sb doing sth** *Within minutes he had the whole audience laughing and clapping.* **b)** to persuade or order someone to do something: **have sb doing sth** *She had me doing all kinds of jobs for her.* | **have sb do sth** *I'll have the bellboy take up your bags.*

SPOKEN PHRASES

31 have it coming used to say someone deserved the bad thing that happened to them: *Tom got grounded for a week, but I guess he had it coming.*

32 have it in for sb/sth to want to harm someone or something or make life difficult for them: *I swear the garbage collectors have it in for my trash cans.*

33 I've got it used to say you have suddenly thought of the solution to a problem or suddenly understand something

34 NOT ALLOW **sb can't/won't have sth** used to say that someone will not allow something to happen: **can't/won't have sb doing sth** *We can't have you walking home alone; it's too late at night.* | *I won't have any kid leaving my class thinking he's stupid.*

35 you have me there also **you've got me there** used to say that you do not know the answer to a question

36 I'll have you know used to start to tell someone something when you are annoyed with them: *I'll have you know I speak six languages.*

37 have sth/sb (all) to yourself to be the only person or people in a place, using something, talking to someone else etc.: *For once I had the house to myself.*

38 have it (that) to say or be told that something is true: ***Rumor has it*** *he's going out with Michele.* | *I* ***have it on good authority*** *that Congress will soon debate the issue.*

39 have it in you to have a particular quality, skill, or ability: *Look at Steve dance – I didn't know he had it in him!*

40 DO STH a word meaning to do something: *He said it was interesting, so I had a look.* | *I had a shower this morning.*

41 SEX [not in progressive] INFORMAL to have sex with someone

42 have done with sth to finish or settle an argument or a difficult situation

have sth **against** sb/sth *phr. v.* to dislike or be opposed to someone or something for a particular reason: *I don't know what it is, but Roger has something against women.* | *I don't understand what he has against the idea.* | *I* ***have nothing against*** *him, I just don't like what he does for a living.*

have on *phr. v.* **1 have sth ↔ on** to be wearing a piece of clothing or type of clothing: *Chad had a blue shirt on.* | *Jimmy* ***had nothing on*** (=was wearing no clothes) *except his socks.* **2 have sth on sb** to know about something bad that someone has done: *Do the police have anything on Tonya?* **3 have nothing on sb/sth** to not be nearly as good as someone or something else: *Most restaurant versions of fried chicken have nothing on my mother's.*

have sth out *phr. v.* **1 have a tooth/appendix etc. out** to have a tooth etc. removed in a medical operation: *Gwen had her tonsils out when she was nine.* **2 have it out with sb** INFORMAL to settle a disagreement or difficult situation by talking to the person involved, especially when you are angry with them

have sb **over** *phr. v.* if you have someone over, they come to your house for a meal, a drink etc. because you have invited them: **have sb over for sth** *We had them over for dinner last week.*

ha·ven /ˈheɪvən/ *n.* [C] **1** a place where people or animals go to be safe and live peacefully: +**for** *a haven for refugees* **2** a place where people go because it helps them feel happy: +**for** *The town is a haven for artists.*

ˌhave-ˈnots *n.* **the have-nots** the poor people in a country or society OPP **the haves**

have·n't /ˈhævənt/ *v.* the short form of "have not": *I haven't seen her in five years.*

hav·er·sack /ˈhævɚˌsæk/ *n.* [C] OLD-FASHIONED a bag that you carry on your back SYN **knapsack** [**Origin:** 1700–1800 French *havresac*, from German *habersack*, from *haber* **oats** + *sack* **bag**]

Ha·ver·sian ca·nal /həˌvɚʒən kəˈnæl/ *n.* [C] BIOLOGY one of network of small tubes in the bones of a person or animal, that contain BLOOD VESSELS and nerve FIBERS (=thin pieces of flesh that form the nerves)

haves /hævz/ *n.* **the haves** the rich people in a country or society OPP **the have-nots**: *the gap between the haves and the have-nots*

have to /ˈhæftə; *strong* ˈhæftu/ S1 W1 also **have ˈgot to** *modal verb* **1** to be forced to do something because someone makes you do it, or because a situation makes it necessary: *You don't have to answer that question.* | *We had to put her in a nursing home.* | *I hate having to get up early.*

THESAURUS

have to used to say that doing something is necessary, and you do not have a choice about it: *I have to study for my test.*
must used in more formal writing to say that doing something is necessary because a government, law, or person in authority says it is necessary: *All visitors must report to the office.*
have got to used to emphasize how important it is to do something: *I've got to talk to him today.*
gotta SPOKEN INFORMAL used instead of "have got to": *I gotta talk to him today.*
The past tense of **have to, have got to**, and **must** is **had to**: *I had to talk to him.*

2 used when saying that it is important that something happens: *There has to be an end to the violence.* | *You've got to believe me!* | *You'll have to be nice to Aunt Lynn.* **3** used when telling someone how to do something: *First of all, you have to mix the sugar and the butter.* **4** used when saying that you are sure that something will happen or is true: *The price of houses has to go up*

H

sooner or later. | *Mark has to be stuck in traffic – he wouldn't be late otherwise.*

SPOKEN PHRASES

5 used when talking about an annoying event which happens in a way that causes you problems: *Of course it had to happen on a Sunday, when the veterinarian's office is closed.* **6 do you have to do sth?** used to ask someone to stop doing something that annoys you: *Bobby, do you have to keep making that noise?* **7** used to say that only one thing or person is good enough or right for someone: *Wanda always has to have the best.* **8** used to suggest that someone should do something, because it would be enjoyable or useful: *You'll have to come visit us this summer.* **9 I have to say/admit/confess** used when speaking honestly about something awkward or embarrassing: *I have to say I don't know anything about computers.*

→ see also MUST[1]

hav·oc /ˈhævək/ *n.* [U] a situation in which there is a lot of confusion or damage: **cause/creat havoc** *A strike will cause havoc for commuters.* | *The insects have been* ***wreaking havoc on*** (=causing a lot of damage to) *crops.* | *A poor harvest could* ***play havoc with*** (=cause great harm to) *the country's economy.* [**Origin:** 1400–1500 Anglo-French, Old French *havot* **destruction, disorder**]

haw /hɔ/ *interjection* another spelling of HA

H

Ha·wai·i /həˈwaɪ-i/ **1** WRITTEN ABBREVIATION **HI** a U.S. state which consists of eight main islands in the Pacific Ocean **2** the largest of the islands in the Pacific Ocean that form the U.S. state of Hawaii

Ha,waii 'Standard Time ABBREVIATION **HST** *n.* [U] the time that is used in Hawaii

Ha'waii Time ABBREVIATION **HT** *n.* [U] another word for HAWAII STANDARD TIME

hawk[1] /hɔk/ *n.* [C] **1** BIOLOGY a large wild bird that eats small birds and animals **2** POLITICS a politician who believes in using military force OPP **dove**: *the hawks in the President's cabinet* **3 watch sb like a hawk** to watch someone very carefully **4 news hawk** a REPORTER **5 have eyes like a hawk** to be quick to notice things, especially small details

hawk[2] *v.* **1** [T] to try to sell goods, usually by talking about them and often going from place to place SYN **peddle**: *a man hawking souvenirs* **2 hawk a loogie** SLANG to cough up PHLEGM (=thick sticky liquid), and then SPIT it out

hawk·er /ˈhɔkɚ/ *n.* [C] someone who carries goods from place to place and tries to sell them SYN **peddler**

'hawk-eyed *adj.* quick to notice small details: *hawk-eyed customs officers*

hawk·ish /ˈhɔkɪʃ/ *adj.* supporting the use of military force OPP **dovish** —**hawkishness** *n.* [U]

'hawk-nosed *adj.* having a nose that is large and curves down at the end

Hawks /hɔks/, **How·ard** /ˈhaʊɚd/ (1896–1977) a U.S. movie DIRECTOR

haw·ser /ˈhɔzɚ/ *n.* [C] TECHNICAL a thick rope or steel CABLE used on a ship

haw·thorn /ˈhɔθɔrn/ *n.* [C,U] a small tree that has small white flowers and red berries

Haw·thorne /ˈhɔθɔrn/, **Na·than·iel** /nəˈθænyəl/ (1804–1864) a U.S. writer of NOVELS and short stories

hay /heɪ/ *n.* [U] **1** a type of long grass that has been cut and dried, often used as food for cattle and horses: *a* ***bale of hay*** **2 make hay (while the sun shines)** to take the opportunity to do something while you are able to, especially in order to get an advantage from a situation: *Democrats are trying to make hay over the president's mistakes.* **3 hit the hay** INFORMAL to go to bed **4 sth isn't/ain't hay** HUMOROUS used to say that an amount is large: *Earning 2 percent on a $17 billion investment sure ain't hay.* → see also **a roll in the hay** at ROLL[1] (8)

Hay·dn /ˈhaɪdn/, **Joseph** (1732–1809) an Austrian musician who wrote CLASSICAL music

Hayes /heɪz/, **Hel·en** /ˈhɛlən/ (1900–1993) a U.S. actress, famous for appearing in plays and movies

Hayes, Ruth·er·ford /ˈrʌðɚfɚd/ (1822–1893) the 19th President of the U.S.

'hay ,fever, hayfever *n.* [U] a medical condition in which you SNEEZE a lot and your eyes produce water, that is caused by breathing in POLLEN (=dust from plants)

hay·loft /ˈheɪlɔft/ *n.* [C] the top part of a farm building where hay is stored

hay·mak·ing /ˈheɪˌmeɪkɪŋ/ *n.* [U] the process of cutting and drying hay

hay·ride /ˈheɪraɪd/ *n.* [C] a ride in a WAGON filled with hay, usually as part of a social event

hay·seed /ˈheɪsid/ *n.* [C] INFORMAL someone from a country area, who does not know how to behave in the city —**hayseed** *adj.*

hay·stack /ˈheɪstæk/ *n.* [C] a large firmly built pile of hay → see also **sth is like looking for a needle in a haystack** at NEEDLE[1] (8)

hay·wire /ˈheɪwaɪɚ/ *adj.* **go haywire** INFORMAL to start working in completely the wrong way: *My computer has gone haywire again.* [**Origin:** 1900–2000 from the use of hay-tying wire for quick repairs]

haz·ard[1] /ˈhæzɚd/ *n.* [C] **1** something that may be dangerous, or that may cause accidents, problems etc. SYN **danger**: *Ice on the road is a major hazard.* | **+to/for** *The small parts pose a choking hazard for small children.* | *The leaves are a* ***fire hazard*** (=something that may cause a fire). | **health/safety hazard** *The lead in old paints is a real health hazard.* ▶see THESAURUS box at **danger** **2** a risk that cannot be avoided: **+of** *the economic hazards of running a small farm* | *Burnout seems to be an* ***occupational hazard*** (=a danger that exists in a job) *for teachers.* [**Origin:** 1200–1300 Old French *hasard* **game of chance played with dice**, from Arabic *az-zahr* **the chance**]

hazard[2] *v.* [T] **1** to say something that is only a suggestion or guess SYN **venture**: *I don't really know, but I could* ***hazard a guess.*** **2** FORMAL to risk losing your money, property etc. in an attempt to gain something SYN **gamble**

'hazard ,light *n.* [C usually plural] a special light on a vehicle that flashes to warn other drivers of danger

haz·ard·ous /ˈhæzɚdəs/ *adj.* **1** dangerous, especially to people's health or safety SYN **dangerous**: **+to** *Smoking is hazardous to your health.* | *the disposal of* ***hazardous waste*** **2** involving danger: *a hazardous occupation*

'hazard pay *n.* [U] the money someone is paid for doing dangerous work, in addition to their usual pay

haze[1] /heɪz/ *n.* [singular, U] **1** smoke, dust, or MIST in the air that is difficult to see through: *a haze of cigarette smoke* **2** the feeling of being very confused and unable to think clearly: *The family is* ***in a haze*** *of shock and grief.*

haze[2] *v.* [T] to play tricks on a new student or to make them do silly or dangerous things, as part of joining the school or a club at the school —**hazing** *n.* [U]

ha·zel[1] /ˈheɪzəl/ *adj.* hazel eyes are a green-brown color

hazel[2] *n.* **1** [C,U] BIOLOGY a small tree that produces nuts **2** [U] the green-brown color of some people's eyes

ha·zel·nut /ˈheɪzəlˌnʌt/ *n.* [C] the nut of the hazel tree → see picture at NUT

haz·mat, HazMat /ˈhæzmæt/ *n.* [U] **hazardous material** substances that are dangerous to people's health, and that cannot be thrown away in the usual garbage collection: *Paint can be taken to a hazmat center for disposal.*

haz·y /ˈheɪzi/ *adj.* *comparative* **hazier**, *superlative* **haziest** **1** air that is hazy is not clear because there is a lot of smoke, dust, or mist in it: *hazy sunshine* **2** an idea, memory, explanation etc. that is hazy is not clear, exact, or detailed SYN vague: *Greg's memory of the accident is a little hazy.* | +**about** *Officials were hazy about the details.* —**hazily** *adv.* —**haziness** *n.* [U]

HBO *n.* TRADEMARK **Home Box Office** a CABLE television company that shows mainly movies

H-bomb /ˈeɪtʃ bɑm/ *n.* [C] INFORMAL a HYDROGEN BOMB

HCF MATH the abbreviation of HIGHEST COMMON FACTOR

HD *adj.* **High Definition** a type of television and VIDEO equipment that produces a much clearer picture than standard equipment: *HD video systems*

HDTV *n.* [U] **high definition television** a type of DIGITAL television broadcasting in which the picture and sound are much clearer than ordinary television

he[1] /i; *strong* hi/ S1 W1 *pron.* [used as subject of a verb] **1** a male person or animal that has already been mentioned or is already known about: *"Does Josh still live in New York?" "No, he moved to Ohio."* | *How old is he?* | *He's my brother.* **2** used to talk about anyone or about people in general, whether male or female: *Everyone should do what he considers best.* **3 He** used when writing about God [**Origin:** Old English]

USAGE

He can be used to mean either a man or a woman when the sex of the person in the sentence is not known or does not matter, for example in the sentence *Each person should do what he thinks is best.*
Many people, however, do not like using **he** in this way because it seems unfair to women, and they prefer to use **he** or **she** or, in writing only, **s/he**: *Each person should do what he or she thinks is best.* | *Each person should do what s/he thinks is best.*
Many people use **they** instead of **he**, especially in speech and less formal writing: *Each person should do what they think is best.* But other people do not think this is correct, because *each person* is singular and *they* is plural. Often you can avoid the problem by writing the sentence in a different way: *People should all do what they think is best.*

he[2] *n.* [singular] a male: *I couldn't tell if the cat was a he or a she.*

he- /hi/ *prefix* [in nouns] OLD-FASHIONED a male, especially a male animal: *a he-goat*

head[1] /hɛd/ S1 W1 *n.*
1 TOP OF BODY [C] BIOLOGY the top part of your body that has your face at the front and your brain in it: *He turned his head to kiss her.* | *severe head injuries* | *Campbell **nodded his head*** (=moved it up and down to show agreement or say yes). | *Several people **shook their heads*** (=moved them from side to side to say no or show disagreement). | **raise/lift your head** (=look up) *Bob lifted his head to look at her.* | **lower/bend/bow your head** (=look down) *They bowed their heads in prayer.*
2 MIND [C] your mind or mental ability SYN mind: *Troy's head is just full of ideas.* | *I have a picture of what it should be like **in my head**.* | *I can **do** the addition **in my head**.* | *Come on, **use** your **head*** (=think about something)*! You can figure this out!* | **come/pop into sb's head** (=to think of something suddenly) *The name just popped into my head.* | *It **never entered** my **head*** (=I never thought) *that Bruce would steal.* | ***I couldn't get** the tune **out of my head*** (=not be able to stop thinking about it). | *What **put** that idea **into** your **head*** (=made you think or believe it)*?* | **have a head for figures/facts/business etc.** (=to be good at doing calculations, remembering facts etc.)
3 LEADER [C] the leader or person in charge of a group or organization, or the most important person in a group: *Professor Calder is the department head.* | +**of** *Eileen is head of the family now.* | *the European **heads of state*** (=leaders of countries) | **head waiter/chef/gardener etc.**
4 POSITION the head the top or front of something, or the most important position: +**of** *the head of the bed* | *The bride and groom sat at **the head of the table**.*
5 ON A TOOL [C] the widest or top part of something such as a piece of equipment or a tool: *a shower head* | +**of** *the head of a hammer*
6 PLANT [C] BIOLOGY the top of a plant where its leaves and flowers grow: *a head of lettuce*
7 (from) head to foot/toe over your whole body: *The kids were covered head to foot in mud.*
8 keep your head above water to just manage to live or keep your business working when you are having money problems: *I work full time, but we're still just keeping our heads above water.*
9 come to a head also **bring sth to a head** if a problem or difficult situation comes to a head, or if something brings it to a head, it suddenly becomes worse and you have to do something about it immediately: *The situation came to a head when the workers went out on strike.*
10 laugh/shout/scream your head off INFORMAL to laugh, shout etc. very loudly: *Fans were screaming their heads off.*
11 put your heads together INFORMAL to discuss a difficult problem together: *We need to put our heads together and make a decision.*
12 a clear/cool head the ability to think clearly or calmly in a difficult or dangerous situation: *The situation is tense, and cool heads are needed.*
13 get/be in over your head to be doing something that is more difficult or risky than you are able to deal with: *New kayakers can easily get in over their heads.*
14 keep/lose your head to remain calm in a difficult or dangerous situation, or to be unable to remain calm: *I just lost my head and started shouting.*
15 be over your head in debt to owe so much money that there is no possibility of paying it all back
16 go over sb's head a) to be too difficult for someone to understand: *The explanation went right over the kids' heads.* **b)** to do something without discussing it with someone first, when you should discuss it with them
17 can't make head(s) nor tail(s) of sth to be completely unable to understand something: *I couldn't make heads or tails of the book.*
18 go to sb's head INFORMAL **a)** if success goes to someone's head, it makes them feel more important than they really are: *Dave really let his promotion go to his head.* **b)** if alcohol goes to your head, it quickly makes you feel slightly drunk: *The wine **went straight to my head**.*

SPOKEN PHRASES

19 heads up! used to warn people that something is falling from above, or that something is being thrown to them
20 have a good head on your shoulders to be sensible or intelligent
21 get your head together to start behaving in a sensible and responsible way: *I got off drugs and started to get my head together.*
22 have your head screwed on (right/straight) also **keep your head on straight** to be sensible and able to deal with difficult situations: *Even as a kid, Yolanda had her head screwed on right.*
23 get sth into your head to understand and realize something: *I wish he'd get it into his head that school is important.*
24 need your head examined to be crazy: *Anybody who believes in UFOs needs their head examined.*
25 heads will roll used to say that some people will be punished severely for something that has happened
26 on your own head be it used to tell someone that they will be blamed if the thing they are planning to do has bad results

27 not be right in the head to be mentally ill or not as intelligent as a normal person
28 not bother/trouble your head about sth to not worry about something, because you think it is unimportant or too difficult to understand: *Hale doesn't bother his head about the opinions of strangers.*
29 heads the side of a coin that has a picture of a person's head on it OPP tails
30 a head of hair a lot of hair on your head: *Roy's **full head of hair** is mostly gray.*

H

31 a head/per head for each person: *The meal will cost $7 a head.*
32 keep your head down to try not to be noticed or not to get involved in something: *When Ali's parents are fighting, he just tries to keep his head down.*
33 have your head in the clouds to not be thinking in a practical or sensible way
34 be/fall head over heels in love to love or start loving someone very much: *Sam was obviously head over heels in love with his new bride.*
35 go head to head with sb to deal with someone in a very direct and determined way: *Jim finally went head to head with his boss.*
36 have no head for heights to be unable to look down from high places without feeling nervous
37 BEER [C usually singular] the layer of small white BUBBLES on the top of a glass of beer
38 ELECTRONICS [C] a piece of equipment that changes information on something MAGNETIC, such as a recording TAPE or a computer HARD DISK, into electrical messages that electronic equipment can use
39 head of cattle/sheep etc. a particular number of cows, sheep etc.: *a small farm with 20 head of cattle*
40 be out of your head INFORMAL to not know what you are doing because you have taken illegal drugs or drunk too much alcohol
41 be (like) banging your head against a brick wall SPOKEN to seem like you are making no progress at all when you are trying to do something: *Talking to her is like banging my head against a brick wall.*
42 take it into your head to do sth to suddenly decide to do something that does not seem sensible: *Neil suddenly took it into his head to go to Japan.*
43 turn/stand sth on its head to make people think about something in the opposite way from the way it was intended: *"You stand logic on its head when you use arms control as an argument for a larger defense budget," the senator said.*
44 be head and shoulders above the rest/others to be much better at something than everyone else
45 INFECTION [C] the center of a swollen spot on your skin
46 head of water/steam pressure that is made when water or steam is kept in an enclosed space
47 RIVER/STREAM [C] the beginning of a river or stream
[**Origin:** Old English *heafod*] → see also **bite sb's head off** at BITE[1] (5), **bury your head in the sand** at BURY (11), **eyes pop out (of your head)** at EYE[1] (26), **hang your head** at HANG[1] (11), **hold your head up/high** at HOLD[1] (38), **nod your head** at NOD[1] (1), **a roof over your head** at ROOF[1] (2), **shake your head** at SHAKE[1] (3), **do sth standing on your head** at STAND[1] (16), **off the top of your head** at TOP[1] (13), **turn sb's head** at TURN[1] (26)

head² S2 W1 *v.*
1 GO TOWARD [I always + adv./prep.] to go or make something go in a particular direction: **be headed** *Where are you guys headed?* | **+for/toward/across etc.** *A line of trucks was heading out of town.* | *We were just* ***heading home.*** | **head north/south etc.** *They were going up the hill, heading west.*
2 BE IN CHARGE [T] also **head up** to be in charge of a government, organization, or group of people: *Most single-parent families are headed by women.* | *The commission was headed up by Barry Kerr.*
3 BE LIKELY TO HAPPEN **be heading** also **be headed** if you are heading for a situation, especially a bad one, it is likely to happen: **+for** *You're heading for trouble.* | *Where is your life heading?*
4 BE AT THE TOP [T] **a)** to be at the top of a list or group of people or things: *The movie heads the list of Oscar nominations.* | *a good cast headed by John Malkovich* **b) be headed** if a page is headed with a particular word or sentence, it has it on the top: *The page was headed "Expenses."*
5 BE AT THE FRONT [T usually passive] to be at the front of a line of people: *The march was headed by the Reverend Martin Luther King.*
6 SOCCER [T] to hit the ball with your head, especially in SOCCER

head off *phr. v.* **1** to leave to go to another place: *Where are you heading off to?* **2 head sth ↔ off** to prevent something from happening: *The budget agreement headed off some painful spending cuts.* **3 head sb ↔ off** to stop someone going somewhere by moving in front of them: *Soldiers headed them off at the border.* **4 head sb off at the pass** HUMOROUS to take action quickly in order to prevent someone from doing something that you do not want them to do

head³ *adj.* [only before noun, no comparative] most important, or highest in rank: *the head coach* | *the bank's head office*

-head /hɛd/ *suffix* [in nouns] **1** the top of something: *a letterhead* (=name and address printed at the top of a letter) **2** the place where something begins SYN **source**: *a fountainhead* (=source of a river or stream)

head·ache /ˈhɛdeɪk/ S3 *n.* [C] **1** MEDICINE a pain in your head: *I* ***had a*** *really bad* ***headache*** *and couldn't eat anything.* | **a splitting/pounding headache** (=a very bad headache) **2** INFORMAL a problem that is annoying or difficult to deal with: *The paperwork is such a headache.*

head·band /ˈhɛdbænd/ *n.* [C] a band that you wear around your head to keep your hair off your face or as a decoration

head·bang·er /ˈhɛdˌbæŋɚ/ *n.* [C] INFORMAL someone who enjoys HEAVY METAL music and moves their head around violently to the beat of the music —**headbang** *v.* [I] —**headbanging** *n.* [U]

head·board /ˈhɛdbɔrd/ *n.* [C] the upright board at the end of a bed where your head is

head·butt /ˈhɛdbʌt/ *v.* [T] to deliberately hit someone with your head

head·cheese /ˈhɛdtʃiz/ *n.* [U] a food made from pieces of meat from the head of a pig that are boiled and put in GELATIN, then served in thin pieces

ˈhead cold *n.* [C] a COLD that makes it very difficult for you to breathe

ˈhead count, headcount *n.* [C] a count of how many people are present in a particular place at one time

head·dress /ˈhɛd-drɛs/ *n.* [C] something that someone wears on their head for decoration on a special occasion: *a feathered headdress*

-headed /hɛdɪd/ [in adjectives] **1 red-headed/gray-headed etc.** having red hair, gray hair etc. **2 two-headed/three-headed etc.** having two heads, three heads etc.

head·er /ˈhɛdɚ/ *n.* [C] **1** information at the top of a page, especially things such as page numbers that appear on each page in a document **2** COMPUTERS information at the beginning of an EMAIL message that shows when it was written or sent, who wrote or sent it etc. **3** a shot in SOCCER made by hitting the ball with your head → see also DOUBLE-HEADER

head·first, head-first /ˌhɛdˈfɚst/ *adv.* **1** moving forward with the rest of your body following your head SYN **headlong**: *He jumped headfirst through a window.* **2** to start doing something too quickly, without thinking carefully SYN **headlong**: *Coe dove into the problem headfirst.*

ˈhead game *n.* [C usually plural] INFORMAL something you say or do that makes someone confused and annoyed, because it does not seem sensible or honest to them: *He's obviously* ***playing headgames*** *with you.*

head·gear /ˈhɛdgɪr/ *n.* [U] hats and other things that you wear on your head

head·hunt·er /ˈhɛdˌhʌntɚ/ *n.* [C] **1** someone who finds people with the right skills and experience to do particular jobs **2** a member of a tribe of people who cut off and keep the heads of their enemies —**headhunt** *v.* [T]

head·ing /ˈhɛdɪŋ/ *n.* [C] **1** the title written at the top of a piece of writing **2** a particular direction on a COMPASS, toward which someone is traveling

H

head·lamp /ˈhɛdlæmp/ *n.* [C usually plural] a HEADLIGHT

head·land /ˈhɛdlənd, -lænd/ *n.* [C] EARTH SCIENCE an area of land that sticks out from the coast into the ocean → see picture on page A31

head·less /ˈhɛdlɪs/ *adj.* without a head: *a headless corpse*

head·light /ˈhɛdlaɪt/ *n.* [C usually plural] one of the large lights at the front of a vehicle SYN **headlamp** → see picture on page A36

head·line[1] /ˈhɛdlaɪn/ *n.* [C] **1** the title of a newspaper article, printed in large letters above the article: *newspaper headlines* **2 make/grab (the) headlines** also **be in/hit the headlines** to be widely reported in newspapers and on television and radio: *Woods' success has made headlines nationwide.*

headline[2] *v.* **1** [T usually passive] to give a headline to an article or story: *The report was headlined "Big Changes at City Hall."* **2** [I,T] ENG. LANG. ARTS to appear as the main performer in a show: *Eminem is headlining at the festival this year.*

head·lin·er /ˈhɛdlaɪnɚ/ *n.* [C] someone who is the main performer at a show

head·lock /ˈhɛdlɑk/ *n.* [C] a way of holding someone around their neck so that they cannot move: *He had me **in a headlock** and I couldn't move.*

head·long /ˈhɛdlɔŋ, ˌhɛdˈlɔŋ◂/ *adv.* **1 rush/plunge headlong into sth** to start doing something too quickly, without thinking carefully about it first SYN **headfirst**: *Stockbrokers should prevent their clients from plunging headlong into trouble.* **2** falling with your head going first and the rest of your body following SYN **headfirst**: *Miller slid headlong into second base.* —**headlong** *adj.*

head·man /ˌhɛdˈmæn, ˈhɛdmæn/ *n. plural* **headmen** /-mɛn/ [C] a chief of a small town where a tribe lives

head·mas·ter /ˈhɛdˌmæstɚ/ *n.* [C] a PRINCIPAL in a private school

head·mis·tress /ˈhɛdˌmɪstrɪs/ *n.* [C] a female PRINCIPAL in a private school

ˌhead of ˈstate *n. plural* **heads of state** [C] POLITICS the main representative of a country, such as a queen, king, or president

ˈhead-ˌon *adv.* **1 meet/crash etc. head-on** if two vehicles meet or hit head-on, the front part of one vehicle comes toward or hits the front part of the other vehicle: *The cars crashed head-on in one of the northbound lanes.* **2** if someone deals with a problem head-on, they deal with it in a direct and determined way: **face/tackle/meet/confront sth head-on** *Athletics is tackling the drug problem head-on.* —**head-on** *adj.*: *a head-on collision*

head·phones /ˈhɛdfoʊnz/ *n.* [plural] a piece of equipment that you wear over your ears to listen to a radio or recording

headphones

head·piece /ˈhɛdpis/ *n.* [C] something you wear on your head

head·quar·tered /ˈhɛdˌkwɔrt̬ɚd/ *adj.* **be headquartered** to have your headquarters at a particular place: *The combined company will be headquartered in Houston.*

head·quar·ters /ˈhɛdˌkwɔrt̬ɚz/ W3 *n. plural* **headquarters** [C] **1** the main building or offices used by a large organization **2** ABBREVIATION **HQ** the place from which military operations are controlled

head·rest /ˈhɛdrɛst/ *n.* [C] the top part of a chair or of a seat in a car, airplane etc. that supports the back of your head → see picture on page A36

head·room /ˈhɛd-rum/ *n.* [U] the amount of space above your head inside a car or room, in a DOORWAY etc.

head·scarf /ˈhɛdskɑrf/ *n. plural* **headscarves** /-skɑrvz/ [C] a square piece of cloth that women wear on their heads, tied under their chin

head·set /ˈhɛdsɛt/ *n.* [C] a set of HEADPHONES, often with a MICROPHONE attached

head·stand, head stand /ˈhɛdstænd/ *n.* [C] a position in which you turn your body upside down, with your head and hands on the floor and your legs and feet in the air: *Come on, **do a headstand**.*

ˌHead ˈStart *n.* POLITICS a government program for poor children, that helps prepare them to start school as well as giving families advice about health and about social services that are available to them

ˌhead ˈstart *n.* [C usually singular] **1** an advantage that helps you to be successful: *The class **gives** kids **a head start** in learning a foreign language.* **2** a start in a race in which you begin earlier or further ahead than someone else

head·stone /ˈhɛdstoʊn/ *n.* [C] a TOMBSTONE

head·strong /ˈhɛdstrɔŋ/ *adj.* very determined to do what you want, even when other people advise you not to do it: *a headstrong child*

ˈheads-up[1] *adj.* [only before noun] INFORMAL paying close attention to something and able to act on what you see: *McCartney was playing heads-up ball out there.*

heads-up[2] *n.* [singular] INFORMAL a warning that something may happen: *Here's a heads-up for investors in real-estate stocks.*

ˌhead ˈtable *n.* [C] a table at a formal meal where the most important people or the people who are going to give speeches sit

ˌhead-to-ˈhead *adv.* directly competing with another person or group: *Courier companies are **going head-to-head with** the Post Office.* —**head-to-head** *adj.*: *head-to-head competition*

ˈhead trip *n.* [C] SLANG an experience that has a strong effect on your mind, as if you had taken a drug: *The whole movie is like a massive head trip.*

head·wait·er, head waiter /ˌhɛdˈweɪt̬ɚ/ *n.* [C] the WAITER who is in charge of the other WAITERS in a restaurant

head·wa·ters /ˈhɛdˌwɔt̬ɚz/ *n.* [plural] EARTH SCIENCE the place where a stream starts before it flows into a river

head·way /ˈhɛdweɪ/ *n.* **make headway a)** to make progress toward achieving something even when it is difficult: **+toward/in/with etc.** *Foreign firms have made little headway in the U.S. market.* **b)** to move forward: *The ship had trouble making headway because of the storms.*

head·wind /ˈhɛdˌwɪnd/ *n.* [C,U] a wind that blows directly toward you when you are moving

head·word /ˈhɛdˌwɚd/ *n.* [C] TECHNICAL one of the words whose meaning is explained in a dictionary

head·y /ˈhɛdi/ *adj. comparative* **headier**, *superlative* **headiest** [usually before noun] **1** very exciting in a way that makes you feel you can do anything: *the heady years of fame* **2** a heady smell, drink etc. is pleasantly strong and seems to affect your senses: *a heady aroma*

heal /hil/ S3 *v.* **1** [I,T] to make a wound or a broken bone healthy again, or to become healthy again: *A sprain usually takes longer to heal than a broken bone.* **2** [T] to cure someone who is sick: *He claims to be able to heal the sick.* → see Word Choice box at CURE[1] **3** [I,T] to return or help someone return to a healthy mental and emotional state after a bad or shocking experience: *Her mental scars will take time to heal.* | *Time heals all wounds.* **4 heal the wounds/breach/divisions** to make people stop being angry with each other [**Origin:** Old English *hælan*]

heal over *phr. v.* if a wound or an area of broken skin heals over, new skin grows over it and it becomes healthy again

heal up *phr. v.* if an injury or wound heals up, it becomes healthy again

heal·er /ˈhilɚ/ *n.* [C] someone who is believed to have the natural ability to cure people

heal·ing /ˈhilɪŋ/ *n.* [U] the process of becoming well again after an illness or of feeling happy again after a bad experience, or the process of helping someone to do this: *nontraditional forms of healing* | *The healing process may take a long time.* → see also FAITH HEALING

health /hɛlθ/ S2 W1 *n.* [U] **1** the general condition of your body, and how healthy you are: *Betty's worried about her husband's health.* | **in good/poor/ill health** *She's 92 but she's in good health.* | *My parents are* ***not in the best of health*** (=they are not very healthy). | **good/bad for sb's health** *Eating lots of fiber is good for your health.* | *His* ***mental health*** *had suffered considerably.* | **health improves/declines/deteriorates** *Her health has improved rapidly.* | *Tyler has some serious* ***health problems.*** | **health risk/hazard** *Excess body fat is a health hazard.* **2** the work of providing medical services to keep people healthy: *government spending on health* | *health insurance* **3** the state of being without illness or disease: *I wish you health and happiness.* **4** how successful an ECONOMY, business, or organization is: +**of** *the health of the economy* [**Origin:** Old English *hælth*, from *hal* **healthy, unhurt, complete**] → see also **a clean bill of health** at CLEAN¹ (8)

ˈhealth care W2, **healthcare** *n.* [U] the service of taking care of people's health and giving them medical treatment: *the rising cost of health care*

ˈhealth ˌcenter *n.* [C] **1** a place where college students go to get medical treatment or advice **2** a place where several doctors have their offices, and people can go for medical treatment or advice

ˈhealth club *n.* [C] a place where people who have paid to become members can go to exercise

ˈhealth food *n.* [C,U] food that contains only natural substances, and that is healthy to eat

health·ful /ˈhɛlθfəl/ *adj.* likely to make you healthy: *healthful mountain air*

ˈhealth ˌmaintenance organiˌzation *n.* [C] an HMO

ˈhealth ˌspa *n.* [C] a SPA

health·y /ˈhɛlθi/ S2 W2 *adj. comparative* **healthier**, *superlative* **healthiest**

1 PERSON/ANIMAL physically strong and not likely to become sick OPP **unhealthy**: *a healthy baby* | *I've always been* ***perfectly healthy*** *until now.*

THESAURUS

well healthy, used especially when describing how someone feels or looks: *Andrew doesn't look very well – is he feeling all right?*
fine SPOKEN healthy, used when someone has asked you how you feel and you are replying that you feel well: *"Hi, Tom, how are you?" "Fine, thanks."*
better less sick than you were, or no longer sick: *She had a fever yesterday, but she's much better today.*
in (good) shape in a good state of health and physically strong: *We were in good enough shape to keep playing hard.*
physically fit healthy and having a strong body: *Even kids need exercise to be physically fit.*

2 MAKING YOU HEALTHY good for your physical health, and making you healthy SYN **healthful** OPP **unhealthy**: *a healthy diet* | *Regular exercise can be healthy and enjoyable.*

3 COMPANY/RELATIONSHIP ETC. a healthy company, society, relationship etc. is working effectively and successfully OPP **sick**: *a healthy economy* | *a healthy marriage*

4 SHOWING GOOD HEALTH showing that you are healthy OPP **unhealthy**: *Her face had a healthy glow.* | *healthy skin* | *All my kids have* ***healthy appetites.***

5 NATURAL/NORMAL natural and normal in a way that is sensible or to be expected: *Fear is a natural and healthy response to danger.* | **a healthy respect/attitude/curiosity etc.** *Surfers should have a healthy respect for the ocean.*

6 GOOD FOR YOUR MIND/EMOTIONS good for your mental or emotional state OPP **unhealthy**: **it's not healthy (for sb) to do sth** *It's not healthy to spend so much time alone.*

7 AMOUNT fairly large and good: *a healthy profit* | ***a healthy dose of*** *optimism* —**healthily** *adv.* —**healthiness** *n.* [U]

heap¹ /hip/ *n.* [C] **1** a large messy pile of things: *a garbage heap* | +**of** *a heap of newspapers* | *His clothes lay* ***in a heap*** *on the floor.* ►see THESAURUS box at **pile¹** **2 the heap** all similar people or things and their status or ranking with relation to each other: *He rose from* ***the bottom of the heap*** *to become a senior manager.* | *They want to be recognized as being* ***top of the heap.*** **3 a heap of sth** also **heaps of sth** SPOKEN a lot of something: *You're going to be in a heap of trouble.* **4 fall/collapse/lie etc. in a heap** to fall down and lie without moving: *Exhausted, she fell in a heap on the floor.* **5 the ash/dust/scrap etc. heap of history** HUMOROUS all the things that happened in the past that people have forgotten about or do not admire or respect anymore: *The old building is destined for the ash heap of history.* **6** HUMOROUS an old car that is in bad condition

heap² *v.* [T] **1** also **heap up** to put a lot of things on top of each other in a messy way: *Piles of garbage were heaped everywhere.* | **heap sth on/onto sth** *Heap the blueberries on top of the filling.* **2 heap praise/abuse/criticism etc. on sb** to praise, criticize etc. someone a lot: *Officials have heaped praise on the school's anti-drug program.* **3 be heaped with sth a)** if a plate is heaped with food, it has a lot on it **b)** covered with messy piles of things

heap·ing /ˈhipɪŋ/ *adj.* [only before noun] used to describe an amount of food in a spoon, on a plate etc. that is the most it can contain and forms a curved shape on the top of it: **a heaping teaspoon/tablespoon** *two heaping tablespoons of cocoa*

hear /hɪr/ S1 W1 *v. past tense and past participle* **heard** /hɚd/

1 HEAR SOUNDS/WORDS ETC. [I,T not in progressive] to know that a sound is being made, using your ears: *I heard footsteps.* | *Grandma doesn't hear as well as she used to.* | **hear sb/sth doing sth** *We heard some people shouting.* | **hear sb/sth do sth** *No one heard him come in.* | **hear what** *Did you hear what I said?* | **not hear a word/thing** *I can't hear a word you're saying.*

THESAURUS

audible loud enough to be heard
inaudible too quiet to be heard
clear easy to hear: *her clear voice*
be drowned out if something is drowned out by a noise, you cannot hear it because of the noise: *He said something that was drowned out by the traffic.*
within earshot near enough to hear or be heard: *Everyone within earshot was listening to our conversation.*
out of earshot not near enough to hear or be heard: *I waited until he was out of earshot.*

Unable to hear
deaf not able to hear anything at all
hard of hearing/hearing impaired not able to hear very well because of a physical problem with your ears

2 LISTEN TO SB/STH [T not usually in progressive] to listen to what someone is saying, the music they are playing etc.: *Did you hear the speech on the radio?* | *Jen didn't wait to hear an answer.* | **hear sb do sth** *We went to hear Todd's band play at Mr. B's.* | **hear what** *I want to hear what the doctor says.* | **hear sb/sth do sth** *Have you heard Billy sing?*

3 BE TOLD STH [I,T not usually in progressive] to be told or find out a piece of information: *I've heard rumors that she's going to quit.* | **hear (that)** *I heard that the show's been canceled.* | *I hear Tom got a job.* | **+about** *How did you hear about it?* | **hear sth about sb** *It's nice to meet you. I've heard a lot about you.* | **hear what/how/who etc.** *Did you hear what Sam's latest idea is?* | **be glad/sorry/relieved etc. to hear (that)** *I'm glad to hear your mother's feeling better.* | **from what I hear/from what I've heard** *From what I hear according to what people have told me, she's really strict.* | *"Nina quit her job." "Yeah,* ***so I heard*** (=I was told this information before)*."* | *I've* ***heard it said*** (=heard people say) *that animals love you unconditionally.*
4 IN COURT [T] LAW to listen to what is said in a court of law, and make a decision: *The case will be heard on July 16.* | *The committee will* ***hear evidence*** *from both sides.*
5 REPORTING [T] used for reporting what other people say or do by speaking: *You never hear her arguing.* | **be heard to say/remark/complain etc.** *He was heard to say that the plan would fail.*
6 make yourself heard to speak loudly enough so people can hear you: *He had to shout to make himself heard.*
7 sb has heard it all before used to say that someone has often been told something before so that it is no longer believable or interesting: *Don't bother making excuses! I've heard it all before.*

SPOKEN PHRASES

8 (do) you hear (me)? said when you are giving someone an order and want to be certain that they will obey you: *Be home by ten, you hear?*
9 I hear you a) used to say that you understand what someone has told you to do and you will obey them: *"We have to finish on time." "Okay, I hear you."* **b)** also **I heard that!** used to say that you agree strongly with what someone just said: *"Sneakers have sure gotten expensive." "I heard that!"*
10 have not heard the last of sb used to say that someone or something will cause more problems for you: *I'm going to sue him. He hasn't heard the last of me.*
11 sb will never hear the end of it used to say that someone will criticize or make jokes about something you have done: *If you make a mistake you'll never hear the end of it.*
12 be hearing things to imagine you can hear a sound when really there is no sound: *You must be hearing things. There's no one there.*
13 sb can't hear himself/herself think said when the place where someone is is too noisy: *Just be quiet! I can't even hear myself think.*
14 let's hear it used for telling someone to say what it is they want to say: *"I was wondering if I could ask a favor." "Let's hear it."*
15 have you heard the one/joke/story about...? used when asking someone if they know a joke: *Have you heard the one about the traveling salesman?*
16 let's hear it for sb/sth! used to say that you think someone or something deserves praise or admiration: *Let's hear it for strong women!*
17 you could hear a pin drop used to say that a place was extremely quiet: *You could hear a pin drop when Willis started his speech.*
18 now hear this! OLD USE used to introduce an important official announcement
19 Hear! Hear! said after a speech or in a meeting when you agree with the person who is speaking

[**Origin:** Old English *hieran*] → see also **hear sth through the grapevine** at GRAPEVINE, see also UNHEARD OF

hear from sb *phr. v.* **1** to get a letter, phone call, email etc. from someone: *Have you heard from Francis at all?* **2** to listen to someone giving their opinion: *We'll be hearing from Bill after the break.*

hear of *phr. v.* **1 have heard of sb/sth** to know that someone or something exists because you have been told about them: *Have you ever heard of a band called Big Star?* **2 hear of sth** to find out about something that has happened or is happening: *Well, this is* ***the first I've heard of*** *your objections.* **3 hear of sb** to receive news about someone: *She went to Europe and that's* ***the last*** *anyone* ***heard of*** *her.* **4 sb won't/wouldn't hear of it** used to say that someone will not accept or allow something: *I offered to help, but Dennis wouldn't hear of it.*

hear sb **out** *phr. v.* to listen to all of what someone wants to tell you, without interrupting them: *I know you're mad, but hear me out.*

WORD CHOICE hear, listen
- Use **hear** when you mean that a sound comes to your ears: *I heard loud music coming from the room next door.*
- Use **listen** when you mean you want to hear something and pay attention to it: *I was listening to music when the phone rang.*

hear·er /ˈhɪrɚ/ *n.* [C] someone who hears something

hear·ing /ˈhɪrɪŋ/ S3 W2 *n.* **1** [U] BIOLOGY the sense which you use to hear sounds: *Very loud music can damage your hearing.* | *hearing loss* → see also HARD OF HEARING **2** [C] LAW a meeting of a court or special committee to find out the facts about a case: *a public hearing on the policy change* **3** [singular] an opportunity for someone to explain their actions, ideas, or opinions: *The ideas deserve a full hearing.* | **get/receive/be given a (fair) hearing** *We will make sure everyone gets a fair hearing.* **4 in sb's hearing** FORMAL if you say something in someone's hearing, you say it where they can hear you: *I never complained in my father's hearing.*

ˈhearing aid *n.* [C] a small piece of equipment that you put in or behind your ear to make sounds louder if you cannot hear well

ˈhearing-imˌpaired *adj.* unable to hear well **—the hearing-impaired** *n.* [plural]

hear·ken, harken /ˈhɑrkən/ *v.* [I] LITERARY to listen

hear·say /ˈhɪrseɪ/ *n.* [U] something that you have heard about from other people, but do not know to be true: *Hearsay is not allowed as evidence in court.*

hearse /hɚs/ *n.* [C] a large car used to carry a dead body in a CASKET at a funeral [**Origin:** 1200–1300 Old French *herce* **frame for holding candles, farm tool for breaking up soil**, from Latin *hirpex*]

Hearst /hɚst/, **Wil·liam Ran·dolph** /ˈwɪlyəm ˈrændɔlf/ (1863–1951) a U.S. businessman who owned many popular newspapers

heart /hɑrt/ S1 W1 *n.*
1 BODY [C] BIOLOGY the part of your body in your chest that pumps blood through your body: *Regular exercise is good for the heart.* | *His* ***heart*** *was* ***beating*** *faster now.* | *My* ***heart raced*** (=beat quickly) *as we flew over the canyon.* | *He's had* ***heart trouble*** *for years.*
2 EMOTIONS [C] the part of you that is able to feel strong emotions: *I knew* ***in my heart*** *that I wouldn't see him again.* | *Leonard was clearly speaking* ***from the heart.*** | *We must win the* ***hearts and minds*** *of ordinary voters.* | *I was hoping* ***with all*** *my* ***heart*** *that you would win.* | *It would* ***break*** *his* ***heart*** (=make him very sad) *to move out of his own home.* | *I believe* ***with my heart and soul*** *that we will overcome this* (=I believe it completely). | *The movie really* ***touched*** *my* ***heart.*** | **listen to/follow your heart** (=to base your decisions and actions on your emotions rather than what seems sensible)
3 LOVE [singular] the part of you that feels romantic love: *It* ***broke*** *her heart when Doug left her.* | *Tess's* ***heart ached*** *to be with her husband.* | **affairs/matters of the heart** (=things that relate to love)
4 the heart of sth a) the main or most important part of something: *The issue is* ***at the heart of*** *Reddin's campaign.* | *Eckert wants to* ***get to the heart of*** *the problem, so it can be prevented in the future.* **b)** the

heart

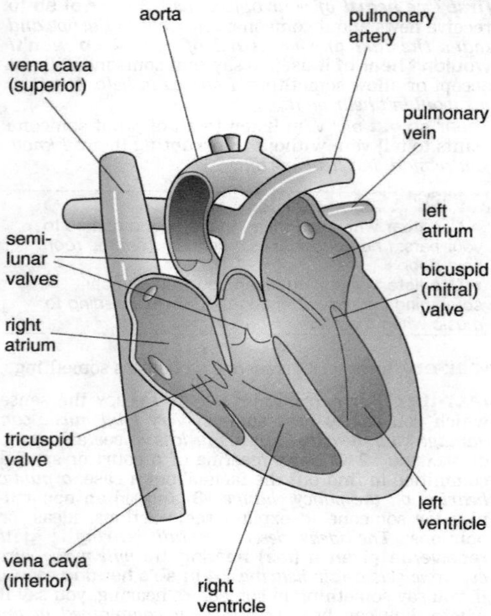

middle or the busiest part of an area: *The hotel is* ***in the heart of*** *the downtown area.*
5 YOUR CHEST [C usually singular] the part of your chest near your heart: *Put your hand on your heart and repeat after me.*
6 SHAPE [C] a shape with two curved parts on top and a point at the bottom, used to represent love
7 WILLINGNESS TO TRY [U] a feeling of being ready and willing to try hard to do something: *The win proves that the team has heart.* | *She got up and sang the song* ***with heart.***
8 HOPEFULNESS [U] confidence and hopefulness about what you can achieve: *Don't* ***lose heart*** *if some of the plants don't grow.* | ***Take heart*** *– we can fix this easily.*
9 **know/learn something by heart** to know or learn something so that you can remember all of it correctly: *He knew her phone number by heart.*
10 **at heart** if you are a particular kind of person at heart, that is the type of person you really are: *I guess I'm just a kid at heart.* → see also **have sb's (best) interests at heart** at INTEREST[1] (5), **young at heart** at YOUNG[1] (7)
11 CARD GAMES **a)** [C] a playing card with one or more red heart shapes on it **b) hearts** [plural] the set of playing cards that have these shapes on them: *the ace of hearts*
12 **have a good/kind/warm etc. heart** to be a good, kind etc. person: *Whatever his faults, he had a good heart.*
13 **put your heart into sth** to give a lot of energy and effort to something: *The kids have really put their hearts into the play.*
14 **sing/dance/play etc. your heart out** INFORMAL to sing, dance etc. with all your energy
15 **win/capture/steal sb's heart** to make someone love you or fall in love with you
16 **tear/rip sb's heart out** to make someone feel extremely upset: *It just tears your heart out to see how they live.*
17 **sb's heart sinks** used to say that someone suddenly loses hope and begins to feel sad: *My heart sank when I saw the mess the house was in.*
18 **take sth to heart** to be listen carefully to what someone says to you, and try to do what they say: *Jack took his father's advice to heart.*
19 **do sth to your heart's content/desire** to do something as much as you want to: *On the farm, the children can run around to their heart's content.*

SPOKEN PHRASES

20 **not have the heart to do something** to be unable to do something because you do not want to make someone unhappy: *I didn't have the heart to tell my daughter we couldn't keep the puppy.*
21 **sb's heart goes out to sb** used to say that someone feels a lot of sympathy for someone else: *My heart just went out to those poor children.*
22 **a man/woman after my own heart** said when someone has the same opinion as you: *She loves eating out in restaurants – a woman after my own heart.*
23 **my heart stopped** also **my heart was in my mouth** used to say that you suddenly felt very afraid: *My heart stopped when I got that phone call.*
24 **sb's heart isn't in it** used to say that someone does not really want to do something or does not care about what they are doing: *She was doing the best she could, but her heart just wasn't in it.*
25 **have a heart!** used to tell someone to be nicer or not to be too strict: *Have a heart! I'll never get all that done.*
26 **it does sb's heart good to see/hear sth** used to say that something makes you feel happy: *It does my heart good to see him running around again.*
27 **my heart bleeds (for sb)** used to say that you feel a lot of sympathy for someone, but often said in a joking way when you do not think someone deserves any sympathy

28 **sb's heart skips/misses a beat** used to say that someone is very excited, surprised, or afraid: *Frank's heart skipped a beat when he heard someone come in.*
29 **the heart and soul of sth** the most important part of something: *Miller is the heart and soul of the team.*
30 **in your heart of hearts** if you know, feel, or believe something in your heart of hearts, you definitely know, feel, or believe it although you may not admit it: *I know in my heart of hearts that what we're doing is right.*
31 **sb's heart is in the right place** INFORMAL used to say that someone is really a kind person, even though they may not appear to be: *Mike's a little grouchy sometimes, but his heart's in the right place.*
32 **have a heart of gold** to have a very nice, generous character, though not seeming nice on the outside: *Watling is a tough guy with a heart of gold.*
33 **set your heart on sth** also **have your heart set on sth** to want something very much: *He's set his heart on a new bike for Christmas.*
34 **have a heart of stone** to be very cruel or unsympathetic
35 **close/dear to sb's heart** very important to someone
36 **sb's heart leaps** LITERARY used to say that someone suddenly feels happy and full of hope
37 **know the way to sb's heart** HUMOROUS to know the way to please someone: *What a great meal! You certainly know the way to a man's heart!*
38 VEGETABLE [C] the firm middle part of some vegetables: *artichoke hearts*
39 **your heart's desire** also **everything your heart could desire** something that someone wants very much
40 **give/lose your heart to sb** OLD-FASHIONED to fall in love with someone
[**Origin:** Old English *heorte*] → see also **from the bottom of sb's heart** at BOTTOM[1] (13), **a broken heart** at BROKEN[2] (9), **have a change of heart** at CHANGE[2] (1), **cross my heart (and hope to die)** at CROSS[1] (10), **eat your heart out** at EAT (4), **with a heavy heart** at HEAVY[1] (30), **sick at heart** at SICK[1] (8), **wear your heart on your sleeve** at WEAR[1] (8)

heart·ache /ˈhɑrt̮eɪk/ *n.* [U] a strong feeling of sadness

ˈheart atˌtack S3 *n.* [C] **1** MEDICINE a serious medical condition in which someone's heart suddenly stops working, either for a short time or permanently: *a massive heart attack* | **have/suffer a heart attack** *Marv recently suffered his second heart attack.* **2** SPOKEN a sudden feeling of shock or a frightening experience: *I almost* ***had a heart attack*** *when they called my name.* | *You just about* ***gave me a heart attack*** *there, Dave.*

heart·beat /ˈhɑrt˺bit/ *n.* [C,U] **1** the action or sound of your heart as it pumps blood through your body: *A baby's heartbeat is nearly twice as fast as an adult's.*

2 be a heartbeat away from sth to be very close to a particular position or condition: *The team is only a heartbeat away from the championship.* **3 in a heartbeat** very quickly, or without thinking about something first: *I'd do it again in a heartbeat.* **4 the heartbeat of sth** the main origin of activity, interest, or excitement in a place or organization: *Broadway has long been the heartbeat of the American musical.*

heart·break /ˈhɑrt˺breɪk/ *n.* [U] a strong feeling of sadness or disappointment: *the heartbreak of the death of a child*

heart·break·ing /ˈhɑrt˺ˌbreɪkɪŋ/ *adj.* making you feel very upset, sad, or disappointed: *a heartbreaking story about a man dying of cancer* —**heartbreakingly** *adv.*

heart·bro·ken /ˈhɑrt˺ˌbroʊkən/ *adj.* very sad because someone or something has disappointed you: *Amy was heartbroken when her puppy was lost.*

heart·burn /ˈhɑrt˺bɚn/ *n.* [U] a slightly painful burning feeling in your stomach or chest caused by INDIGESTION

ˈheart disˌease *n.* [U] MEDICINE a medical condition in which a person's heart has difficulty pumping blood

-hearted /hɑrt̬ɪd/ *suffix* [in adjectives] **kind-/cold-/light-hearted etc.** having a particular type of character: *a kind-hearted woman*

heart·en /ˈhɑrt˺n/ *v.* [T usually passive] to make someone feel happier and more hopeful OPP **dishearten**: *We were heartened by the news of his return.* —**heartening** *adj.*: *It's very heartening to see more jobs coming to our area.* —**hearteningly** *adv.* → see also DISHEARTENING

ˈheart ˌfailure *n.* [U] the failure of the heart to continue working, which causes death

heart·felt /ˈhɑrtfɛlt/ *adj.* very strongly felt and sincere: *a heartfelt apology*

hearth /hɑrθ/ *n.* [C] **1** the area of floor around a FIREPLACE in a house **2 hearth and home** LITERARY your home and family: *the joys of hearth and home*

heart·i·ly /ˈhɑrt̬l-i/ *adv.* **1** loudly and cheerfully: *Ryan laughed heartily.* **2** completely or very much: *I **heartily agree**.* **3 eat/drink heartily** to eat or drink a large amount

heart·land /ˈhɑrtlænd/ *n.* [singular] **1** the central part of a country or area, usually considered to be the place where people live in a way that represents the basic values of that country: +**of** *the heartland of America* **2** the most important part of a country or area for a particular activity, or the part where a political group has most support: *America's industrial heartland*

heart·less /ˈhɑrtlɪs/ *adj.* cruel or not feeling any pity: *Todd's father was cold and heartless.* —**heartlessly** *adv.* —**heartlessness** *n.* [U]

ˌheart-ˈlung maˌchine *n.* [C] a machine that pumps blood and oxygen around someone's body during a medical operation

ˈheart rate *n.* [C] the speed at which your heart beats

heart·rend·ing /ˈhɑrtˌrɛndɪŋ/ *adj.* making you feel great pity: *a heartrending sob*

heart·sick /ˈhɑrtˌsɪk/ *adj.* very unhappy or disappointed

heart·strings /ˈhɑrtˌstrɪŋz/ *n.* [plural] **tug/pull at sb's heartstrings** also **play on sb's heartstrings** to make someone feel a lot of pity or love: *The young girl's story pulled at the nation's heartstrings.*

heart·throb /ˈhɑrtθrɑb/ *n.* [C] a famous person who many young people feel romantic love for: *teenage heartthrobs*

ˌheart-to-ˈheart *n.* [C] a conversation in which two people honestly express their feelings or opinions about something: *It was time for a heart-to-heart with my daughter.* —**heart-to-heart** *adj.* [only before noun] *a heart-to-heart conversation*

heart·warm·ing /ˈhɑrt˺ˌwɔrmɪŋ/ *adj.* making you feel happy, calm, and hopeful: *a heartwarming holiday story* —**heartwarmingly** *adv.*

heart·wood /ˈhɑrt˺wʊd/ *n.* [U] BIOLOGY the older, harder wood at the center of a tree which provides support but does not carry any SAP

heart·worm /ˈhɑrt˺wɚm/ *n.* [C,U] a type of WORM that lives in the heart of dogs and some other animals, or the condition of having these worms

heart·y /ˈhɑrt̬i/ *adj.* *comparative* **heartier**, *superlative* **heartiest** **1** cheerful and friendly, and usually loud: *a hearty laugh* | *We received a hearty welcome.* **2** a hearty meal or food is satisfying and large: *a hearty soup* **3** if someone is a hearty EATER or if they have a hearty APPETITE, they eat a lot **4** hearty feelings are strong and sincere: *Board members expressed their **hearty approval** for Meyer's plan.* **5** OLD-FASHIONED strong and healthy —**heartiness** *n.* [U] → see also **hale and hearty** at HALE, HEARTILY

heat¹ /hit/ S2 W2 *n.*

1 WARMTH [U] warmth or the quality of being hot: *heat from a lamp* | *a heat source* ►see THESAURUS box at **competition**

2 WEATHER [U] very hot weather: *I'm just not used to this kind of heat.* | *The heat in the desert was unbearable.*

3 SYSTEM IN A HOUSE/BUILDING [U] the system in a house, building, or car that keeps it warm, or the heat that comes from it: *We had no heat or water.* | **turn the heat on/off** *How do you turn the heat on?* | **turn the heat up/down** *Can you turn the heat up? I'm freezing.*

4 COOKING [C usually singular, U] the heat that comes from an OVEN or STOVE when you are cooking or heating something: **(a) low/medium/high heat** *Cook the soup at a low heat.* | ***Reduce the heat** and stir the pasta.*

5 PRESSURE [U] strong pressure or attention on someone: **the heat is on/off** *The heat is on as we reach the final stages of the competition.* | *His problems with the landlord have **taken the heat off** the rest of us.* | *Critics continue to **turn up the heat on** the government.*

6 in the heat of the moment/argument/battle etc. during a situation in which there is a lot of excitement, anger, or other strong feelings: *In the heat of the moment, I said some things I didn't mean.*

7 take the heat to deal with difficulties in a situation, especially by saying that you are responsible for them: *The coach took the heat from the press over the loss.*

8 in heat if a female animal is in heat, her body is ready to have sex with a male

9 FOOD [U] a SPICY taste from food, that makes your mouth feel hot: *The chilies gave the sauce some heat.*

10 IN A RACE [C] one of the parts of a race or competition from which the winners are chosen to compete against each other in the next part

11 ENERGY [U] CHEMISTRY energy that moves from one object to another when there is a difference in temperature between the objects: *The bigger the difference in temperature between two objects, the faster heat flows between them.*

12 if you can't stand/take the heat, get out of the kitchen used to say that if you cannot deal with problems, criticism, or other difficult things, then you should not become involved

[**Origin:** Old English *hætu*] → see also DEAD HEAT, **be packing a gun/heat/a piece** at PACK¹ (8), WHITE HEAT

heat² S2 W3 *v.* [I,T] to make something become warm or hot: *Heat the milk until it boils.*

heat up *phr. v.* **1 heat sth ↔ up** to become warm or hot, or to make something become warm or hot: *I heated up some leftover spaghetti sauce.* | *An electric stove takes a while to heat up.* **2** if a situation heats up, it becomes more exciting or dangerous, with a lot more activity: *Gang activity is heating up.*

heat sth **through** *phr. v.* to heat food thoroughly

ˈheat caˌpacity *n.* [C] CHEMISTRY the amount of heat needed in order to raise the temperature of an object or system by one degree CELSIUS → see also CALORIE SYN **thermal capacity**: *The heat capacity of pure water is 1 cal/g iC.*

heat·ed /ˈhit̬ɪd/ *adj.* **1** kept warm by a heater: *a heated swimming pool* **2 a heated argument/debate/**

H

discussion etc. an argument etc. in which people become very angry and excited —**heatedly** *adv.*

heat·er /ˈhitɚ/ S3 *n.* [C] a machine that makes air or water hotter: *Did you turn the heater off? | a water heater*

ˈheat exˌhaustion *n.* [U] weakness and sickness caused by doing too much work, exercise etc. when it is hot

heath /hiθ/ *n.* [C] an area of open land where grass, bushes, and other small plants grow

hea·then¹ /ˈhiðən/ *adj.* OLD-FASHIONED not related or belonging to the Christian religion or any of the large established religions

heathen² *n. plural* **heathen** [C] **1** OLD-FASHIONED someone who is not a member of the Christian religion or any of the large established religions **2** HUMOROUS someone who refuses to believe in something, or does not know about art, literature etc.

heath·er /ˈhɛðɚ/ *n.* [U] a low plant with small purple, pink, or white flowers, that grows on hills

ˈheat ˌindex *n.* **the heat index** a measure of the combination of hot weather and HUMIDITY that makes the weather feel hotter: *The heat index is 100 degrees.*

heat·ing /ˈhit̬ɪŋ/ *n.* [U] a system for making a room or building warm SYN **heat**: *the heating and air conditioning*

ˈheat ˌlightning *n.* [U] LIGHTNING without THUNDER or rain, usually seen in the evenings during hot weather

heat·proof /ˈhit˺pruf/ *adj.* heatproof material cannot be damaged by heat

ˈheat pump *n.* [C] a piece of equipment that can make a building warmer or cooler by taking heat from one place to another

ˈheat rash *n.* [C,U] painful or ITCHY red marks on someone's skin that are caused by heat

ˈheat-reˌsistant *adj.* not easily damaged by heat

ˈheat-ˌseeking *adj.* a heat-seeking weapon is able to find and move toward the hot gases from an aircraft or ROCKET and destroy it: *heat-seeking missiles*

heat·stroke /ˈhitstroʊk/ *n.* [U] fever and weakness caused by being outside in the heat of the sun for too long → see also SUNSTROKE

ˈheat wave *n.* [C usually singular] a period of unusually hot weather, especially one that continues for a long time

heave¹ /hiv/ *v.*

1 THROW [T] to throw something heavy using a lot of effort: **heave sth at sb/sth** *Rioters heaved rocks at the police.* | **heave sth onto/into/toward etc. sth** *He took the box and heaved it into the river.*

2 heave a sigh to breathe out loudly, especially because you have stopped worrying about something: *We **heaved a sigh of relief** when it was over.*

3 CHEST/SHOULDERS [I] if someone's chest or shoulders heave, they are breathing very hard: *My chest was heaving with the effort.*

4 OCEAN/GROUND [I] if the ocean or the ground heaves, it moves up and down with very strong movements: *Suddenly the ground heaved under their feet.*

5 PULL/LIFT [I,T] to pull or lift something very heavy with a lot of effort: *The girls grabbed the man's hand and heaved him upright.* | **heave at/on sth** *Joe was heaving on the rope when it snapped.* ▸see THESAURUS box at **pull¹**

6 VOMIT [I] SLANG to VOMIT

7 heave into sight/view *past tense and past participle* **hove** LITERARY to appear, especially by getting closer from a distance: *A few moments later a barge hove into view.*

heave to *phr. v. past tense and past participle* **hove to** TECHNICAL if a ship heaves to, it stops moving

heave² *n.* **1** [C] a strong pulling, pushing, or lifting movement: *With one giant heave, they loaded the sack onto the trailer.* **2 the heaves** an occasion when you are VOMITing: *Shelly had **the dry heaves*** (=vomiting with nothing coming out of her mouth). **3** [U] LITERARY a strong rising or falling movement

ˌheave-ˈho *n.* [singular] **give someone the (old) heave-ho** INFORMAL to end a relationship with someone, or to make someone leave their job

heav·en /ˈhɛvən/ S3 W3 *n.* **1** also **Heaven** [singular, not with the] according to some religions, the place where God or the gods live and where good people go after they die: *Do you think you'll **go to heaven** when you die?* **2** [U] INFORMAL a very good thing, situation, or place: *Sitting by the pool with a good book is my idea of heaven. | Star Trek fans were **in heaven** today at the Science Fiction Convention. | The fresh crab was so good **I thought I'd died and gone to heaven**.* **3 the heavens** LITERARY **a)** the sky **b)** the home of the gods

SPOKEN PHRASES

4 for heaven's sake also **for heaven sakes a)** said when you are annoyed or angry: *Where was the kid's mother, for heaven's sake?* **b)** used to emphasize a question or request: *For heaven's sake, don't tell him my age!* **5 (Good) Heavens!** also **Heavens above**, **Heavens to Betsy!** OLD-FASHIONED said when you are surprised or slightly annoyed: *Good Heavens, what a mess!* **6 heaven forbid/forfend** used to emphasize that you hope something will not happen: *Heaven forbid you should have an accident!* **7 heaven knows a)** also **heaven only knows** used to say that you do not know something: *Heaven knows what the true unemployment rate is.* **b)** used to emphasize what you are saying: *Heaven knows, plenty of children need more attention.* **8 heaven help sb** used to say that something will cause problems or be dangerous if it happens: *Heaven help us if it snows again.* **9 what/how/why etc. in heaven's name...?** used when asking a surprised and angry question: *Where in heaven's name have you been?*

10 the heavens open LITERARY used to say that it starts to rain very hard **11 move heaven and earth** to try very hard to achieve something [**Origin:** Old English *heofon*] → see also **be in seventh heaven** at SEVENTH¹ (2), **thank God/goodness/heaven(s)** at THANK (3)

heav·en·ly /ˈhɛvənli/ *adj.* **1** OLD-FASHIONED very beautiful or enjoyable: *What a heavenly sound!* **2** [only before noun] WRITTEN existing in or belonging to heaven: *a heavenly choir of angels | Pray to our **heavenly Father*** (=God). | *The **Heavenly Host*** (=all the angels) *were praising God.* **3** LITERARY existing in or relating to the sky or stars

ˌheavenly ˈbody *n.* [C] LITERARY a star, PLANET, or the moon

ˌheaven-ˈsent *adj.* happening luckily at exactly the right time: *a heaven-sent opportunity*

heav·en·ward /ˈhɛvənwɚd/ also **heavenwards** *adv.* LITERARY toward the sky

heav·i·ly /ˈhɛvəli/ W3 *adv.* **1** a lot or in large amounts: *It's been raining heavily all day. | She's been **drinking heavily** recently. | Street gangs are often **heavily armed*** (=they have a lot of guns). **2** very or very much: *Fifty houses were heavily damaged in the hurricane. | The southern region is heavily dependent on tourism.* **3** if you sleep heavily, you cannot be woken easily: *Joe slept heavily for eight hours.* **4 breathe heavily** to breathe slowly and loudly **5 heavily built** having a large broad body that looks strong **6** if you do or say something heavily, you do it slowly and with a lot of effort, especially because you are sad or bored: *He was walking heavily, his head down.*

heav·y¹ /ˈhɛvi/ S2 W2 *adj.* *comparative* **heavier**, *superlative* **heaviest**

1 WEIGHT weighing a lot OPP **light**: *a heavy suitcase | The box is extremely heavy.*

2 HOW HEAVY used to talk about how much someone or something weighs: *How heavy is the package?*

3 FAT PERSON used to politely describe someone who is

fat: *Brian's gotten very heavy lately.* ▶see THESAURUS box at fat[1]

4 A LOT unusually large in amount or quantity: *The traffic was heavier than normal.* | *a heavy workload* | *Roads were closed due to the* ***heavy snow****.* | *The police made* ***heavy use of*** *firearms.* | *Illegal parking carries a* ***heavy fine*** (=you will have to pay a lot of money). | *Most insurance companies suffered* ***heavy losses*** (=they lost a lot of money) *last year.* | *There was* ***heavy fighting*** *in the capital yesterday.* | **heavy reliance/dependence on sb/sth** *a heavy reliance on imported materials*
5 SEVERE very severe: **a heavy defeat/blow** *She suffered the heaviest defeat of her career.* | **a heavy load/burden/responsibility etc.** *Rent increases put a heavy burden on some families' budgets.* | **a heavy price/toll** *The bombing took a heavy toll.* | *She's in bed with a* ***heavy cold****.*
6 MATERIAL/CLOTHES ETC. material, clothes, jewelry, shoes etc. that are heavy are large, thick, and solid OPP light OPP lightweight: *a heavy winter coat*
7 NEEDING PHYSICAL EFFORT needing a lot of physical strength and effort OPP light: *I can't do any heavy lifting.* | *heavy manual work*
8 NEEDING MENTAL EFFORT very complicated or serious and needing a lot of mental effort OPP light: *I want something to read on vacation – nothing too heavy.* | *a heavy discussion* | *I found her last novel rather* ***heavy going***
9 GUNS/EQUIPMENT [only before noun] large and powerful OPP light: *tanks and heavy weaponry* | *heavy machinery*
10 a heavy smoker/drinker someone who smokes a lot or drinks a lot of alcohol
11 heavy accent if someone speaks with a heavy accent, it is difficult to understand what they say because they use the sounds of their own language when they are speaking a different language: *Ricky's mother has a heavy Spanish accent.*
12 BUSY a day etc. in which you have a lot to do in a short time OPP light: *I had a pretty* ***heavy day*** *at the office.*
13 FOOD solid or containing a lot of fat, and making your stomach feel full and uncomfortable OPP light: *a heavy meal* | *heavy cream*
14 a heavy sleeper someone who does not wake easily OPP a light sleeper
15 WITH FORCE hitting something or falling with a lot of force or weight: *the sound of heavy footsteps* | *a heavy blow to the jaw*
16 heavy breathing a) breathing that is slow and loud: *I could hear Carl's heavy breathing coming from the bedroom.* **b)** the act of breathing loudly while on the telephone, in order to frighten someone: *The calls were filled with heavy breathing and dirty language.*
17 BODY/FACE having a large, broad, or thick appearance: *a large, heavy-featured woman* | *Kyle is a tall man with a* ***heavy build*** (=a large broad body).
18 be heavy on sth INFORMAL to use a lot or too much of something: *Many computer games are heavy on fighting.*
19 heavy clouds/skies LITERARY dark and gray clouds that make it look as though it will rain soon
20 GROUND heavy soil is thick and solid
21 AIR too warm and with no wind: *the damp heavy atmosphere of the rainforest*
22 SMELL strong and usually sweet: *a heavy fragrance* | **+with** *The garden was heavy with the scent of summer.*
23 TIRED if your head, arms, legs or eyes are heavy, it is difficult to use them, hold them up, or keep them open, because you are very tired: *My eyes were so heavy, I couldn't keep them open.*
24 INVOLVING SERIOUS EMOTIONS INFORMAL involving serious or strong emotions OPP light: *She didn't want things to get too heavy.*
25 a heavy date a very important DATE that is likely to involve romantic or sexual activity
26 the heavy hand of sth used to say that someone or something has a lot of authority and uses it in an unreasonable way: *the heavy hand of the law*
27 a heavy sigh a deep SIGH (=act of letting your breath out) that shows you are very upset or sad
28 a heavy silence/atmosphere a situation in which people feel sad, anxious, or embarrassed: *A heavy silence fell upon the room.*
29 heavy seas big waves on the surface of the ocean
30 with a heavy heart LITERARY feeling very sad: *It was with a heavy heart that Kate kissed her children goodbye.*
31 be heavy with fruit/blossom etc. LITERARY if trees are heavy with fruit etc. they have a lot of fruit etc. on them
32 heavy irony/sarcasm remarks that very clearly say the opposite of what you really feel
33 have a heavy foot INFORMAL to drive too fast
34 SERIOUS/WORRYING SLANG a situation that is heavy makes you feel that people are very angry or have very strong feelings: *It was a pretty heavy scene.*
35 a heavy cold a very bad cold: *She's in bed with a heavy cold.*
[**Origin:** Old English *hefig*] —**heaviness** *n.* [U]

heavy[2] *adv.* **1 time hangs/lies heavy on your hands** LITERARY if time hangs or lies heavy on your hands, it seems to pass slowly because you are bored or have nothing to do **2 lie/weigh heavy on sb/sth** LITERARY to make you feel continuously worried or uncomfortable **3 be heavy into sth** SPOKEN, NONSTANDARD to be very involved in an activity, especially one that is not good for you: *Eric was real heavy into drugs for a while.*

heavy[3] *n. plural* **heavies** [C] **1** a bad male character in a play or movie SYN villain **2** INFORMAL [usually plural] a large strong man who is paid to protect someone or to threaten other people

ˌheavy-'duty *adj.* [no comparative] **1** designed to be strong enough for hard work or a lot of use: *heavy-duty plastic garbage bags* ▶see THESAURUS box at strong **2** INFORMAL said when you want to emphasize how complicated, serious etc. someone or something is: *heavy-duty maintenance* | *a heavy-duty conversation*

ˌheavy-'handed *adj.* **1** strict, unfair, and not considering other people's feelings: *a heavy-handed style of management* **2** done in an awkward way: *heavy-handed symbolism* —**heavy-handedly** *adv.* —**heavy-handedness** *n.* [U]

ˌheavy-'hearted *adj.* LITERARY very sad

ˌheavy 'hitter *n.* [C] INFORMAL **1** someone or organization that has a lot of power, especially in business or politics: *corporate heavy hitters* **2** a baseball player who hits the ball very hard —**heavy-hitting** *adj.*

ˌheavy 'industry *n.* [C,U] ECONOMICS industry and industrial activity on a large scale, including, for example, producing goods such as cars in large quantities, taking things such as coal from the ground, or making steel

ˌheavy-'laden *adj.* LITERARY **1** carrying or supporting something very heavy **2** having many worries or problems

ˌheavy-'lidded *adj.* [only before noun] having EYELIDS that seem to hang down over the eyes: *heavy-lidded eyes*

ˌheavy 'metal *n.* **1** [U] ENG. LANG. ARTS a type of ROCK music with a strong beat that is played very loudly on electric GUITARS **2** [C] CHEMISTRY a very DENSE metal, especially one that is poisonous, such as MERCURY or LEAD

ˌheavy 'petting *n.* [U] OLD-FASHIONED sexual activities that do not involve actually having sex

ˌheavy-'set *adj.* someone who is heavy-set is large and looks strong or fat

ˌheavy 'water *n.* [U] a special type of water that is used in NUCLEAR REACTORS

heav·y·weight /ˈhɛviˌweɪt/ *n.* [C] **1** someone or organization that is important and that has a lot of power and experience in a particular business or job: *political heavyweights* **2** someone who BOXES or WRESTLES in the heaviest weight group —**heavyweight** *adj.* [only before noun] *a heavyweight boxer*

He·bra·ic /hɪˈbreɪ-ɪk/ *adj.* relating to the Hebrew language or people: *Hebraic literature*

He·brew /ˈhibru/ *n.* **1** [U] the language traditionally used by the Jewish people **2** [C] a member of the Jewish people, especially in ancient times —**Hebrew** *adj.*

He·brews /ˈhibruz/ a book in the New Testament of the Christian Bible

heck¹ /hɛk/ *n.* SPOKEN INFORMAL **1 a heck of a sth** used to emphasize that something is very big, very good, very bad etc.: *It cost a heck of a lot of money.* **2 who/what/where etc. the heck** used to emphasize a question, especially to show you are confused or surprised: *Where the heck are we?* **3 what the heck** said when you do something you probably should not do: *"Want another piece of pie?" "Sure, what the heck."* **4 hard/funny/cold etc. as heck** said to emphasize what you are saying: *It was August, so of course it was as hot as heck outside.* **5 for the heck of it** for no particular reason or purpose, or only for fun: *Let's go in and take a look around just for the heck of it.* **6 run/work/hurt etc. like heck** to run, work etc. very quickly or very much: *We just shut the door and ran like heck.*

heck² *interjection* INFORMAL used to show that you are annoyed: *Aw, heck, I can't do this.*

heck·le /ˈhɛkəl/ *v.* [I,T] to interrupt and try to embarrass someone who is speaking or performing in public —**heckler** *n.* [C] —**heckling** *n.* [U]

heck·uv·a /ˈhɛkəvə/ *adj.* INFORMAL a way of spelling "heck of a" to show how it sounds when it is spoken; used to emphasize how big, good, bad etc. something is: *That was a heckuva storm last night.*

hec·tare /ˈhɛktɛr/ *n.* [C] a unit for measuring an area of land, equal to 10,000 square meters or 2.471 ACRES

H

hec·tic /ˈhɛktɪk/ *adj.* very busy or full of activity, and often slightly exciting: *It's been pretty hectic around here.* | *a hectic social life* [**Origin:** 1300–1400 Old French *etique*, from Greek *hektikos* **done as a habit, suffering from tuberculosis**] —**hectically** /-kli/ *adv.*

hecto- /hɛktoʊ, hɛktə/ *prefix* 100 times a particular unit of measurement: *a hectometer* (=100 meters)

hec·tor /ˈhɛktɚ/ *v.* [I,T] FORMAL to speak to someone in an angry, threatening way: *Brooks had hectored employees who refused to work overtime.* —**hectoring** *adj.*: *a hectoring tone*

he'd /id; *strong* hid/ **1** the short form of "he had" when you are using the past perfect tense: *He'd never been a very good dancer.* **2** the short form of "he would": *I'm sure he'd drive you there.*

hedge¹ /hɛdʒ/ *n.* [C] **1** a row of small bushes or trees growing close together, used as a border around a yard or between two yards **2** something that helps avoid problems, losing a lot of money etc.: **+against** *People are buying houses as a hedge against inflation.* [**Origin:** Old English *hecg*]

hedge² *v.* **1** [I] to avoid giving a direct answer to a question: **+on** *He hedged on the question of whether the trials were fair.* **2 hedge your bets** to reduce your chances of failing or losing money by trying several different possibilities instead of one: *It's a good idea to hedge your bets by applying to more than one college.*

hedge against sth *phr. v.* to try to protect yourself against possible problems, especially financial loss: *Smart managers will hedge against price increases.*

hedge sb/sth **in** *phr. v.* **be hedged in a)** to be surrounded or enclosed by something: *The building was hedged in by trees.* **b)** if you feel hedged in by something, you feel that your freedom is restricted by it

hedge·hog /ˈhɛdʒhɑg, -hɔg/ *n.* [C] a small brown European animal whose body is round and covered with sharp needle-like hairs

hedge·row /ˈhɛdʒroʊ/ *n.* [C] LITERARY a line of bushes or small trees growing along the edge of a field or road

hed·on·ist /ˈhɛdn-ɪst/ *n.* [C] someone who believes that pleasure is the most important thing in life [**Origin:** 1800–1900 Greek *hedone* **pleasure**] —**hedonism** *n.* [U] —**hedonistic** /ˌhɛdnˈɪstɪk/ *adj.*

hee·bie-jee·bies /ˌhibi ˈdʒibiz/ *n.* **give sb the heebie-jeebies** INFORMAL to make someone feel nervous or frightened

heed¹ /hid/ *v.* [T] FORMAL to pay attention to someone's advice or warning: *If she had **heeded my advice**, none of this would have happened.*

heed² *n.* [U] FORMAL **pay heed (to sth)** also **take heed (of sth)** to pay attention to something and seriously consider it: *Tom **paid no heed to** her warnings.*

heed·less /ˈhidlɪs/ *adj.* FORMAL not paying attention to something important: **+of** *Heedless of danger, he ran out into the street.*

hee-haw /ˈhi hɔ/ *n.* [C] the sound made by a DONKEY

heel¹ /hil/ S3 *n.* [C]

1 FOOT BIOLOGY the curved back part of your foot

2 SHOE the raised part of a shoe that is under the back of your foot: *red pumps with three-inch heels* | *black boots with **high heels***

3 heels [plural] a pair of women's shoes with high heels: *I just can't walk in heels.*

4 HAND the raised part of your hand, near your wrist: *Using **the heel of your hand**, press the dough firmly into shape.*

5 SOCK the part of a sock that covers your heel

6 on the heels of sth very soon after something: *Often one storm will **come on the heels of** another.*

7 (hard/hot/close) on sb's heels a) following closely behind someone, especially in order to catch or attack them: *A man raced past, with a police officer hot on his heels.* **b)** to be close behind someone in a competition, election, race etc.

8 at sb's heels following closely behind someone: *The dog trotted happily at Troy's heels.*

9 take to your heels LITERARY to start running as fast as possible: *The boys jumped down and took to their heels.*

10 bring sb to heel FORMAL to force someone to behave in the way that you want them to: *Party leaders are attempting to bring rebel members to heel.*

11 turn/spin on your heel to suddenly turn away from someone, especially in an angry or impolite way: *He turned on his heel and stomped away in anger.*

12 under the heel of sb/sth completely controlled by a government or group: *The country is once more under the heel of a dictator.*

13 BAD MAN OLD-FASHIONED a man who behaves badly toward other people

[**Origin:** Old English *hæla*] → see also ACHILLES' HEEL, **cool your heels** at COOL² (4), **dig in your heels** at DIG IN (2), **be hard on sb's heels** at HARD² (9), **be head over heels in love** at HEAD¹ (34), **be hot on sb's heels** at HOT (19), **kick up your heels** at KICK UP (2), WELL-HEELED

heel² *v.* **1 heel!** SPOKEN used to tell your dog to walk next to you **2** [T] to put a heel on a shoe **3** [I] also **heel over** if a boat heels or heels over, it leans to one side as if it is going to fall SYN **list**: *The ship was heeling over in the wind.*

-heeled /hild/ *suffix* [in adjectives] **high-heeled/low-heeled etc.** high-heeled or low-heeled shoes have high or low heels → see also WELL-HEELED

heft¹ /hɛft/ *n.* [U] **1** how heavy someone or something is: *I like the heft of these glasses.* **2** influence or power: *The movie lacks the emotional heft of his earlier works.*

heft² *v.* [T] **1** to lift something heavy **2** to lift something or hold it in your hand in order to judge how heavy it is

heft·y /ˈhɛfti/ *adj. comparative* **heftier**, *superlative* **heftiest** **1** big, heavy, or strong: *a hefty slice of pie* | *He's a hefty guy.* **2** a hefty amount of something such as money is very large: *a hefty fine* —**heftily** *adv.*

He·gel /ˈheɪgəl/, **Ge·org Wil·helm Frie·drich** /ˈgeɪɔrg ˈvɪlhɛlm ˈfridrɪk/ (1770–1831) a German PHILOSOPHER

he·gem·o·ny /hɪˈdʒɛməni, -ˈgɛ-, ˈhɛdʒəˌmoʊni/ *n.* [U] POLITICS a situation in which one state, country, or group has much more power than any other

He·gi·ra, Hejira /ˈhɛdʒərə, hɪˈdʒaɪrə/ *n.* **the Hegira** the escape of Mohammed from Mecca to Medina in A.D. 622

ˌHegira ˈcalendar *n.* [singular] the Muslim system of dividing a year of 354 days into 12 months and starting to count the years from the Hegira

Hei·deg·ger /ˈhaɪdɪgɚ/, **Mar·tin** /ˈmɑrtˀn/ (1889–1976) a German PHILOSOPHER

heif·er /ˈhɛfɚ/ *n.* [C] a young cow that has not yet given birth to a CALF (=baby cow) → see also OX

heigh-ho /ˌhaɪ ˈhoʊ, ˌheɪ-/ *interjection* OLD-FASHIONED used when you have to accept something that is boring, or to show that you are surprised or excited

height /haɪt/ S3 W3 *n.*
1 HOW TALL [C,U] **a)** how tall someone is: *Sam's about my height.* | *You have to be a certain height to get on some of the rides.* | *When I'm wearing heels I'm* ***the same height as*** *he is.* **b)** the distance between the base and the top of something: *Sunflowers can grow to* ***a height of*** *fifteen feet.* | *Some of the pyramids are over 200 feet* ***in height.***
2 HOW HIGH [C] a particular distance above the ground: *Raise your arms to shoulder height.* | *A small plane can fly at* ***a height of*** *about 10,000 feet.* | **gain/lose height** *The plane was rapidly losing height.*
3 heights [plural] places that are a long way above the ground: *I'm afraid of heights.*
4 heights [plural] a particular high place: *the Golan Heights*
5 MOST EXTREME TIME [singular] the part of a period of time that is the busiest, hottest etc., or when there is the most activity: *We wanted to avoid* ***the height of*** *the tourist season.* | *At that time, the Cold War was* ***at its height.***
6 new/great/dizzy heights a) a higher level of achievement or success than anyone has ever reached before: *Jones has* ***reached new heights*** *in the world of music.* | *The restaurant* ***takes*** *the humble meatloaf* ***to new heights.*** **b)** a greater level or degree than anyone has ever reached before: *Stock market prices* ***jumped to new heights*** *Tuesday.*
7 at the height of sb's success/fame/powers etc. at the time when someone is most successful, famous etc.: *Kennedy was killed at the height of his political career.*
8 be the height of fashion/stupidity/luxury etc. to be extremely fashionable, stupid etc.: *Long skirts were the height of fashion in those days.*
[**Origin:** Old English *hiehthu*]

height·en /ˈhaɪtˀn/ *v.* [I,T] if a feeling, effect etc. heightens or something heightens it, it increases SYN **intensify**: *A high-fat diet may heighten the risk of cancer.* | *Tensions between the two countries heightened.* | *The campaign has* ***heightened*** *people's* ***awareness*** *of mental illness.*

Heim·lich ma·neu·ver /ˈhaɪmlɪk məˌnuvɚ/ *n.* [C usually singular] a method of stopping someone from choking (CHOKE) on food, in which you stand behind them, put both your hands on the upper part of their stomach, and press suddenly toward a higher position in order to force the food out of their throat

hei·nie /ˈhaɪni/ *n.* [C] HUMOROUS the part of your body that you sit on

hei·nous /ˈheɪnəs/ *adj.* **1** FORMAL very shocking and immoral: *a heinous crime* **2** SPOKEN INFORMAL extremely bad: *The food in the cafeteria is pretty heinous.* [**Origin:** 1300–1400 Old French *haineus*, from *haine* **hate**] —**heinously** *adv.* —**heinousness** *n.* [U]

Heinz /haɪnz/, **Henry** (1844–1919) a U.S. food MANUFACTURER who started the H.J. Heinz Company

heir /ɛr/ *n.* [C] **1** someone who will legally receive or has received money, property etc. from someone else after that person's death: *The man's heirs are selling the ranch.* | **+to** *John was the sole heir to a large estate.* **2** the person who will take over a position or job after you, or who does things or thinks in a similar way: *Reagan's political heirs*

ˌheir apˈparent *n. plural* **heirs apparent** [C] **1** an heir whose right to receive the family property, money, or title cannot be taken away **2** someone who seems very likely to take over a job, position etc. after a particular person: *Huston is considered the governor's political heir apparent.*

heir·ess /ˈɛrɪs/ *n.* [C] a woman who will legally receive or has received a lot of money, property, etc. after the death of an older member of her family

heir·loom /ˈɛrlum/ *n.* [C] a valuable object that has been owned by a family for many years and that is passed from the older members to the younger members

Hei·sen·berg /ˈhaɪzənˌbɚg/, **Wer·ner** /ˈvɛrnɚ/ (1901–1976) a German PHYSICIST who studied the behavior of atoms, and is best known for developing the UNCERTAINTY principle

ˌHeisenberg unˈcertainty ˌprinciple, the PHYSICS a scientific principle that says it is not possible to calculate both the position of a PARTICLE and the speed at which it is moving in a particular direction at the same time

heist /haɪst/ *n.* [C] an act of robbing something very valuable from a store, bank etc.: *a jewelry heist* —**heist** *v.* [T]

He·ji·ra /ˈhɛdʒərə, hɪˈdʒaɪrə/ *n.* another spelling of HEGIRA

held /hɛld/ *v.* the past tense and past participle of HOLD

Hel·e·na /ˈhɛlənə/ the capital city of the U.S. state of Montana

Hel·en of Troy /ˌhɛlən əv ˈtrɔɪ/ the wife of the Menelaus, the king of Sparta, in ancient Greek stories, who was famous for her great beauty

hel·i·cop·ter /ˈhɛlɪˌkɑptɚ/ S3 *n.* [C] a type of aircraft with large metal blades on top that spin very fast to make it fly [**Origin:** 1800–1900 French *hélicoptère*, from Greek *heliko-* + *pteron* **wing**] —**helicopter** *v.* [I,T]

ˈhelicopter ˌpad *n.* [C] a helipad

he·li·o·cen·tric /ˌhilioʊˈsɛntrɪk/ *adj.* SCIENCE having the sun at the center: *the idea of a heliocentric universe*

he·li·o·trope /ˈhiliəˌtroʊp/ *n.* **1** [C] BIOLOGY a plant that has nice-smelling pale purple flowers **2** [U] a pale purple color

hel·i·pad /ˈhɛləˌpæd/ *n.* [C] an area where HELICOPTERS can land, either on the ground or on top of a building

hel·i·port /ˈhɛləˌpɔrt/ *n.* [C] a small airport for HELICOPTERS

hel·i-ski·ing /ˈhɛləˌskiɪŋ/ *n.* [U] the sport of flying by HELICOPTER to a place in the mountains where you can SKI on deep snow that no one else has skied on

he·li·um /ˈhiliəm/ SYMBOL **He** *n.* [U] CHEMISTRY a gas that is an ELEMENT and that is lighter than air, often used in order to make BALLOONS float [**Origin:** 1800–1900 Greek *helios* **sun**; because it was discovered in the sun's spectrum]

he·lix /ˈhilɪks/ *n. plural* **helices** /-lɪsiz/ [C] MATH a line that curves and rises around a central line SYN **spiral** → see also DOUBLE HELIX

he'll /ɪl, il, hɪl; *strong* hil/ the short form of "he will": *Mike called to say he'll be late this morning.* | *He'll do it.*

hell /hɛl/ W2 *n.* **1** also **Hell** [singular, not with the] the place where bad people will be punished after death, according to some religions: *Do you believe some people* ***go to hell*** *when they die?* **2** [singular, U] a situation, experience, or place that is very unpleasant or causes a lot of suffering: *My parents* ***went through hell,*** *thinking I was dead.* [**Origin:** Old English] → see also **like a bat out of hell** at BAT[1] (6)

hel·la·cious /hɛˈleɪʃəs/ *adj.* **1** extremely bad **2** SPOKEN INFORMAL used to emphasize that something is very good: *a hellacious party*

Hel·lene /ˈhɛlin/ *n.* [C] LITERARY a Greek, especially an ancient Greek

Hel·len·ic /hɛˈlɛnɪk, hə-/ *adj.* relating to the history, society, art etc. of the ancient Greeks

Hel·le·nis·tic /ˌhɛləˈnɪstɪk◂/ *adj.* HISTORY relating to the ancient Greeks between the years of the death of Alexander the Great in 323 B.C. and the defeat of Antony and Cleopatra by Octavian in 31 B.C.

ˌHellenistic civiliˈzation *n.* [U] HISTORY the ancient

H

CIVILIZATION that combined Greek customs with the customs of the Middle East

hell·hole, hell hole /ˈhɛlhoʊl/ *n.* [C] a very dirty, ugly, and disgusting place

hell·ish /ˈhɛlɪʃ/ *adj.* INFORMAL extremely bad or difficult: *five hellish months in the prison* —**hellishly** *adv.*

Hell·man /ˈhɛlmən/**, Lil·li·an** /ˈlɪliən/ (1907–84) a U.S. writer of plays

hel·lo /həˈloʊ, hɛˈloʊ, ˈhɛloʊ/ S1 *interjection* **1** used when meeting or greeting someone: *Hello! How are you doing?* | ***Say hello** to Sarah for me.* | *Well, **hello there** Mr. Walker.* **2** used when answering the telephone or starting a telephone conversation: *Hello, may I speak to Terry, please?* **3** used when calling to get someone's attention: *Hello! Is anybody home?* **4** INFORMAL used when you think someone is not acting sensibly or has said something stupid: *You really thought she would just give you the money? Hello!* **5 say hello** to have a quick conversation with someone: *She just called to say hello.* [**Origin:** 1800–1900 *hollo* a shout to call attention (16–19 centuries)]

helm /hɛlm/ *n.* **1 at the helm a)** in charge of something: *The company has a new CEO at the helm.* **b)** guiding a ship or boat **2** [C] the wheel or TILLER which guides a ship or boat **3** [C] OLD USE a helmet

H

hel·met /ˈhɛlmɪt/ *n.* [C] a hard hat that covers and protects your head → see also CRASH HELMET, PITH HELMET

hel·met·ed /ˈhɛlmɪt̬ɪd/ *adj.* wearing a helmet

helms·man /ˈhɛlmzmən/ *n. plural* **helmsmen** /-mən/ [C] someone who guides a ship or boat

help¹ /hɛlp/ S1 W1 *v.*

1 PEOPLE [I,T] to make it possible or easier for someone to do something, by doing part of their work or giving them something they need: *If there's anything I can do to help, just call me.* | *I'll help you as soon as I finish this.* | **help sb (to) do sth** *I helped her carry her suitcases upstairs.* | **help (to) do sth** *Would you mind staying to help clean up?* | **help (sb) with sth** *I'm helping with the Mardi Gras Ball this weekend.*

THESAURUS

give sb a hand (with sth) to help someone do something: *Can you give me a hand moving these boxes?*
need a hand to need help doing something: *Give me a call if you need a hand with anything.*
lend a hand (with sth) to help someone, especially when there are not enough people to do something: *I went over to see if I could lend a hand.*
assist/aid FORMAL to help someone, especially when you use special skills: *There is much local governments can do to assist people in starting small businesses.*

2 SITUATIONS [I,T] to make a situation better, easier, or less painful: *Crying won't help.* | *Increased tourism would help the economy.* | **it helps to do sth** *It helped to know that someone understood how I felt.*
3 sb can't help (doing) sth also **sb can't help but do sth** used to say that someone is unable to change their behavior or feelings, or to prevent themselves from doing something: *Ron can't help the way he feels about her.* | *You can't help but like Mike. He's so funny.* | *I **can't help it**. I hear that song and I have to dance.* | **can't help wondering/thinking/feeling etc.** *I can't help wondering what happened to that little girl.* | *I fell in love. I **couldn't help myself**.*
4 HELP SB MOVE [T always + adv./prep.] to help someone move to a particular place, especially because they are old, sick, or hurt: **help sb into/up/across/off etc.** *Can you help me up, please?*
5 help sb on/off with sth to help someone put on or take off a piece of clothing: *Let me help you on with your coat.*

SPOKEN PHRASES

6 Help (me)! used to call people and ask for help when you are in danger
7 help yourself (to sth) a) used to invite someone to take something that they want, especially food: *Go ahead and help yourselves to a drink.* **b)** INFORMAL to steal something: *She helped herself to some money from the register.*
8 it can't be helped used to say that there is nothing you can do to change a bad situation: *It's not an ideal solution, but it can't be helped.*
9 not if I can help it used to say that you will try very hard to avoid doing something or to prevent something: *"Are you going to stay very long?" "Not if I can help it."*
10 so help me (God) used when making a serious promise, especially in a court of law

[**Origin:** Old English *helpan*] → see also **God help sb (if...)** at GOD (9)

GRAMMAR

Help can be followed by a verb in the *to* form or the basic form: *Ollie helps his brothers milk the cows* (or *...to milk the cows*). But after **can't help...** meaning "cannot stop yourself," the verb that follows it is in the *-ing* form: *I couldn't help laughing* (NOT *to laugh*).

help sth ↔ **along** *phr. v.* to make a process or activity happen more quickly or easily: *She asked a few questions to help the conversation along.*

help out *phr. v.* **1** to help someone who is busy by doing some of their work for them: *We're hired a couple of people to help out in the store.* | **help sb ↔ out** *Carol started helping Mom out when I moved away.* **2 help sb ↔ out** to give help and support to someone who has problems: *It's an organization that helps out people in need.*

help² S1 W2 *n.* **1** [U] things you do to make it easier or possible for someone to do something: *Thank you for all your help.* | **+with** *Do you need some help with the stroller?* | **give (sb) help** *Could you give me some help with dinner?* | **with sb's help/with the help of sb** *We managed to move her with the help of a nurse.* | *She screamed at them to go and **get help*** (=because someone is hurt or in danger).

THESAURUS

assistance help with something you are doing, especially help that is the easier or less important part of a job: *The governor has asked for federal assistance to deal with the flood damage.*
aid money, food, medicine etc. that is given to countries or to people that need them because they are poor or have serious problems: *Aid is being sent to areas affected by the earthquake.*

2 [singular, U] the fact of being useful or making something easier to do: *Kelly hasn't been much help either.* | *We got it open **with the help of** a knife.* | **be a big/great/real help (to sb)** *I think those picture dictionaries are a real help.* | **be of (any/little/no) help** *Let me know if I can be of any help.* **3** [U] advice, treatment, information, or money which is given to people who need it: *We're here to give help and advice.* | **professional/medical/financial etc. help** *A lot of these children need professional help.* | **+with** *The company gives help with travel costs.* **4** [U] COMPUTERS a part of a computer program that gives additional information about how to use it: *the help menu* **5** [singular] OLD-FASHIONED also **the help** someone's servant or servants

ˈhelp desk *n.* [C] a department of a company that other workers or customers call for help with computer problems they are having

help·er /ˈhɛlpɚ/ *n.* [C] someone who helps another person or does this as a job

help·ful /ˈhɛlpfəl/ S3 *adj.* **1** providing useful help in making a situation better or easier: **it is helpful to do sth** *Sometimes it's helpful to make a list of everything you have to do.* | *Here's **a helpful hint** for cooking fish.*

2 willing to help: *a helpful child* | *I'm sure he was just trying to be helpful.* —**helpfully** *adv.* —**helpfulness** *n.* [U]

help·ing¹ /ˈhɛlpɪŋ/ *n.* [C] the amount of food that you are given or that you take SYN **serving**: *He took a huge helping of potatoes.*

helping² *adj.* **a helping hand** help that you give to someone, especially someone who really needs it: **lend/give/extend a helping hand** *He's always ready to lend a helping hand to those in need.*

ˈhelping verb *n.* [C] INFORMAL an AUXILIARY VERB

help·less /ˈhɛlplɪs/ *adj.* **1** unable to take care of yourself or to do anything to help yourself: *helpless baby animals* | **helpless to do sth** *Doctors are helpless to stop disease without any supplies.* **2** unable to control a strong feeling that you have: +**with** *The audience was helpless with laughter.* | **helpless laughter/rage/tears etc.** *He kicked the door in helpless rage.* —**helplessly** *adv.* —**helplessness** *n.* [U]

help·line /ˈhɛlplaɪn/ *n.* [C] a telephone number that you can call if you need advice or information

help·mate /ˈhɛlpmeɪt/ also **help·meet** /ˈhɛlpmit/ *n.* [C] LITERARY a helpful partner, usually a wife

Hel·sin·ki /hɛlˈsɪŋki, ˈhɛlsɪŋki/ the capital and largest city of Finland

hel·ter-skel·ter /ˌhɛltɚˈskɛltɚ/ *adv., adj.* done in a disorganized, confusing, and hurried way: *People ran helter-skelter down the street.*

hem¹ /hɛm/ *n.* [C] the edge of a piece of a cloth that is turned under and sewn down, especially the lower edge of a skirt, pants etc. ▸see THESAURUS box at **edge¹**

hem² *v.* **hemmed, hemming** **1** [T] to turn under the edge of a piece of material or clothing and sew it in place **2 hem and haw** to keep pausing before saying something, and avoid saying it directly: *Doug hemmed and hawed when I asked him where he'd been.*

hem sb ↔ **in** *phr. v.* **1** to surround someone closely, in a way that prevents them from moving: *They were hemmed in by steep mountains on all sides.* **2** to make someone feel that they are not free to do what they want to do: *Employees don't want to be hemmed in by regulations.*

ˈhe-man *n. plural* **he-men** [C] HUMOROUS a strong man with powerful muscles

he·ma·tol·o·gy /ˌhiməˈtɑlədʒi/ *n.* [U] the scientific study of blood

Ernest Hemingway

Hem·ing·way /ˈhɛmɪŋˌweɪ/, **Er·nest** /ˈɚnɪst/ (1899–1961) a U.S. writer famous for his NOVELS and short stories that are written in a simple and direct style

hem·i·sphere /ˈhɛməˌsfɪr/ *n.* [C] **1** EARTH SCIENCE one of the halves of the Earth, especially the northern or southern parts above and below the EQUATOR: *the Northern hemisphere* → see also WESTERN HEMISPHERE → see picture at GLOBE **2** BIOLOGY one of the two halves of your brain **3** MATH half of a SPHERE (=an object which is round like a ball) that is made by a PLANE going through the center of the sphere

hem·line /ˈhɛmlaɪn/ *n.* [C] the bottom edge of a dress, skirt, or pants, used especially when talking about their length: *a knee-length hemline*

hem·lock /ˈhɛmlɑk/ *n.* [C,U] a very poisonous plant, or the poison that is made from it

hemo- /himoʊ, himə/ *prefix* relating to blood: *hemorrhage* (=an occasion when you bleed too much)

he·mo·glo·bin /ˈhiməˌgloʊbɪn/ *n.* [U] BIOLOGY a red substance in the blood that contains iron and carries oxygen from the LUNGS to other parts of the body

he·mo·phil·i·a /ˌhiməˈfɪliə, -ˈfilyə/ *n.* [U] a serious disease that prevents the blood from becoming thick, so that the person loses too much blood after being cut or wounded

he·mo·phil·i·ac /ˌhiməˈfɪliæk/ *n.* [C] someone who suffers from hemophilia

hem·or·rhage /ˈhɛmərɪdʒ/ *n.* [C,U] a serious medical condition in which a person bleeds a lot, often inside the body

hem·or·rhoid /ˈhɛməˌrɔɪd/ *n.* [C usually plural] a painfully swollen BLOOD VESSEL at the ANUS

hemp /hɛmp/ *n.* [U] a type of plant that is used to make rope, strong cloth, and the drug CANNABIS

hen /hɛn/ *n.* [C] **1** BIOLOGY an adult female chicken **2** BIOLOGY a fully grown female bird

hence /hɛns/ Ac *adv.* FORMAL **1** [sentence adverb] used to show that what you are about to say is a result of what you have just said: *People are dying, hence the need for urgent action.* **2 ten days/two weeks/six months etc. hence** FORMAL ten days, two weeks etc. from now **3** OLD USE from this place

hence·forth /ˈhɛnsfɔrθ, ˌhɛnsˈfɔrθ/ also **hence·forward** /hɛnsˈfɔrwɚd/ *adv.* FORMAL from this time on: *Henceforth, death row inmates will have an automatic right to appeal.*

hench·man /ˈhɛntʃmən/ *n. plural* **henchmen** /-mən/ [C] DISAPPROVING someone who faithfully obeys a powerful person such as a politician or a criminal

Jimi Hendrix

Hen·drix /ˈhɛndrɪks/, **Jim·i** /ˈdʒɪmi/ (1942–1970) a U.S. musician and singer who played the GUITAR in a completely new way, and was known for his exciting performances

hen·house /ˈhɛnhaʊs/ *n.* [C] a small building where chickens are kept

hen·na /ˈhɛnə/ *n.* [U] a reddish-brown substance used to change the color of hair or to DYE the skin —**henna** *v.* [T]

hen·pecked /ˈhɛnpɛkt/ *adj.* a man who is henpecked is always being told what to do by his wife, and is afraid to disagree with her

Hen·ry /ˈhɛnri/, **John** a character in American stories and FOLK songs who worked on railways and was very strong

Henry, O. (1862–1910) a U.S. writer of short stories, whose real name was William Sydney Porter

Henry, Pat·rick /ˈpætrɪk/ (1736–1799) a U.S. politician who was one of the leaders of the fight for independence during the Revolutionary War

ˈHenry's ˌlaw CHEMISTRY a scientific principle that says the amount of gas that can be ABSORBED by a liquid will increase if the pressure of the gas above the liquid increases and the temperature remains the same

Henry V, King /ˌhɛnri ðə ˈfɪfθ/ (1387–1422) a king of England who is remembered especially for defeating the French at the Battle of Agincourt

Henry VIII, King /ˌhɛnri ði ˈeɪtθ/ (1491–1547) a king of England, who had six wives and made himself the head of the Church in England. This started the Reformation in England, in which the Protestant Church was established.

hep /hɛp/ *adj.* OLD-FASHIONED → see HIP³

he·pat·ic /hɪˈpætɪk/ *adj.* [only before noun] TECHNICAL relating to your LIVER

hep·a·ti·tis /ˌhɛpəˈtaɪtɪs/ *n.* [U] MEDICINE a disease of the LIVER that causes fever and makes the skin yellow. There are several types of hepatitis: hepatitis A, which is less severe, and hepatitis B and C which are much more serious

Hep·burn, Kath·arine /ˈhɛpbən/, /ˈkæθrɪn/ (1907–2003) a U.S. movie and theater actress, known for appearing as strong, brave, and determined characters

Katharine Hepburn

He·phaes·tus /hɪˈfɛstəs/ in Greek MYTHOLOGY, the god of fire and METALWORK, who made weapons for the gods

hep·ta·gon /ˈhɛptəˌgɑn/ *n.* [C] MATH a flat shape with seven sides —**heptagonal** /hɛpˈtægənl/ *adj.*

hep·tath·lon /hɛpˈtæθlən, -lɑn/ *n.* [singular] a women's sports competition involving seven running, jumping, and throwing events → see also DECATHLON, PENTATHLON

her¹ /ɚ; *strong* hɚ/ S1 W1 *possessive adj.* [possessive form of "she"] **1** belonging to or relating to a woman, girl, or female animal that has been mentioned or is known about: *Maria locked her keys in the car.* | *her first appearance on Broadway* | *She makes **her own** clothes.* **2** OLD-FASHIONED relating to a country, ship, or car that has been mentioned: *Her top speed is about 110 miles an hour.*

her² S1 W1 *pron.* [object form of "she"] **1** a woman, girl, or female animal that has been mentioned or is known about: *Where did you meet her?* | *There's a picture of her in here.* | *I owe her $25.* **2** OLD-FASHIONED a country, ship, or car that has been mentioned: *God bless this ship and all who sail in her.* [**Origin:** Old English *hiere*]

H

He·ra /ˈhɛrə, ˈhɪrə/ in Greek MYTHOLOGY, the goddess of women and marriage. She was the wife of Zeus.

Her·a·cli·tus /ˌhɛrəˈklaɪt̬əs/ (6th–5th century B.C.) a Greek PHILOSOPHER

Her·a·kles /ˈhɛrəˌkliz/ the Greek name for the HERO Hercules

her·ald¹ /ˈhɛrəld/ *v.* [T] FORMAL **1** to be a sign of something that is going to come or happen soon: *The first red leaves appeared, heralding autumn.* **2 to be heralded as sth** to be publicly called good or important: *She has been heralded as one of the country's finest musicians.* → see also MUCH-HERALDED

herald² *n.* [C] **1** HISTORY someone who carried messages from a ruler in past times **2** a sign that something is soon going to happen: **+of** *The tiny flowers are a herald of spring.*

her·ald·ry /ˈhɛrəldri/ *n.* [U] COATS OF ARMS and other family SYMBOLS, or the study or skill of making them —**heraldic** *adj.*

herb /ɚb/ *n.* [C] a small plant that is used to improve the taste of food, or to make medicine [**Origin:** 1200–1300 Old French *erbe*, from Latin *herba* **grass, herb**]

her·ba·ceous /hɚˈbeɪʃəs, ɚˈbeɪ-/ *adj.* BIOLOGY herbaceous plants have soft stems rather than wood-like stems

herb·al /ˈɚbəl/ *adj.* made of or relating to herbs: *herbal tea*

herb·al·ist /ˈɚbəlɪst, ˈhɚ-/ *n.* [C] someone who grows, sells, or uses herbs to treat illness

ˌherbal ˈmedicine *n.* MEDICINE **1** [U] the practice of treating illness using plants **2** [C,U] medicine made from plants

ˈherb ˌgarden *n.* [C] a garden in which only HERBS are grown

her·bi·cide /ˈhɚbəˌsaɪd, ˈɚ-/ *n.* [C,U] TECHNICAL a substance used to kill unwanted plants

herb·i·vore /ˈhɚbəˌvɔr, ˈɚbə-/ *n.* [C] BIOLOGY an animal that eats only plants —**herbivorous** /hɚˈbɪvərəs/ *adj.* → see also CARNIVORE, OMNIVORE

Her·cu·le·an, herculean /ˌhɚkyʊˈliən◂, hɚˈkyuliən/ *adj.* needing great strength or determination: *a Herculean effort*

Her·cu·les /ˈhɚkyəˌliz/ in Roman MYTHOLOGY a HERO known for his very great strength and for performing twelve very difficult and dangerous jobs known as the Labors of Hercules

herd¹ /hɚd/ *n.* [C] **1** a group of animals of one kind that lives and feeds together → see also FLOCK: **+of** *a herd of elephants* ▸see THESAURUS box at **group¹** **2 the herd** DISAPPROVING people generally, especially when thought of as being easily influenced by others: *Why **follow the herd**? You decide what you want to do.*

herd² *v.* **1** [T always + adv./prep.] to move people together in a large group, especially roughly: **herd sb into/through etc.** *Police officers herded the protesters away.* **2** [T] to make animals move together in a group: *Cowboys herded the steers north to Reno.*

ˈherd menˌtality *n.* [C usually singular] an attitude or way of thinking in which people decide to do things because other people are doing them

herds·man /ˈhɚdzmən/ *n. plural* **herdsmen** /-mən/ [C] a man who takes care of a herd of animals

here¹ /hɪr/ S1 W1 *adv.* **1** in or to the place where you are or where you are pointing → see also THERE: *Ken was supposed to be here at ten.* | *Sign your name here.* | *Come here for a minute.* | *How far is Denver from here?* | *Push this button here.* | *I'm not from **around here*** (=I don't live in or near this place). | *We're **over here**!* | **out/in here** *It's so cold in here.* **2** at this point in time or in a situation: *It will get easier from here.* | *There isn't time here to give a full explanation.* **3** used to say that a period of time, a situation, or an event has begun or is happening now: *Spring is here!* **4 here and there** scattered around in several different places: *Wild roses were blooming here and there.* **5 the here and now** the present time: *You need to live in the here and now and stop worrying about the future.* **6 here to stay** if something is here to stay, it has become a part of life and will continue to be so **7 sb/sth is here to do sth** used to say what someone or something's duty or purpose is: *We're here to serve you.*

SPOKEN PHRASES

8 here is sth a) also **here it is** said when you are giving something to someone, or showing something to them: *Here's your twenty dollars.* | *Here are some pictures of our trip to Texas.* **b)** also **here she/he/it etc. is** said when you have found someone or something you were looking for: *Have you seen my glasses? Oh, here they are.* | *Here you are! Where were you?* **c)** also **here is sb** used for introducing something that you are going to say, or something that someone is going to do: *Here are the results of the competition.* | *Here is Emily Moore singing "Tomorrow."* **9** used for saying that someone or something is arriving or has just arrived: **sb/sth is here** *Mr. Nichols, your client is here to see you.* | *Is the mail here yet?* | **here is sb/sth** *Here's the mailman now.* | ***Here comes** your mother – be quiet!* **10 here we go a)** also **here we go again** said when something bad or annoying is beginning to happen again: *Here we go again. More tears!* **b)** said when you are starting to do something or move in a particular direction: *Let's do that again. Ready? Here we go.* **11 here I am** said to tell someone where you are when they are looking for you: *"Mindy, where are you?" "Here I am, Mommy!"* **12 here you go/are** said when you are giving something to someone: *Here you go – two lattes.* **13 here he/she etc. is (doing sth)** used to describe the present situation that someone is in: *Here I am, 69 years old with no money in the bank.* **14 here we are a)** said when you have finally arrived somewhere you were traveling to: *Here we are, home again!* **b)** also **here we go** said when you have found something you were looking for: *Here we go! It's at the bottom of page 78.* **15 here's to sb** said when you are going to drink something to wish someone good luck, show respect for them etc.: *Here's to the happy couple.* **16 I'm/we're out of here** INFORMAL used to say that you are going to leave a place because you do not like what is happening: *As soon as the speeches are over, I'm out of here!* **17 here goes (nothing)** also **here we go** said when you are going to try something that is exciting or dangerous and you do not know what will happen: *O.K. Here goes. Move back everyone.* **18 here, there, and everywhere** in or to many different places: *The rabbits were running here, there, and everywhere.*

[**Origin:** Old English *her*] → see also **be neither here nor there** at NEITHER³ (2)

here² S1 *interjection* used when you are giving or offering something to someone: *Here, have some more cake.* | *Here, let me help you with that.*

here·a·bouts /ˈhɪrəˌbaʊts, ˌhɪrəˈbaʊts/ *adv.* INFORMAL somewhere near the place where you are: *I've lived hereabouts since I was born.*

here·af·ter¹ /ˌhɪrˈæftɚ/ *adv.* **1** [sentence adverb] FORMAL from this time or in the future: *Hereafter the comittee shall report to the council.* **2** in a later part of a legal document **3** FORMAL after death: *a life hereafter*

hereafter² *n.* **the hereafter** a life after death

here·by /ˌhɪrˈbaɪ, ˈhɪrbaɪ/ *adv.* LAW as a result of this statement: *I hereby submit my resignation.*

he·red·i·tar·y /həˈrɛdəˌtɛri/ *adj.* **1** BIOLOGY a hereditary mental or physical quality, or disease is passed to a child from the GENES of their parents: *Some forms of deafness are hereditary.* **2** a hereditary position, rank, or title can be passed from an older to a younger person in the same family, usually when the older one dies

he·red·i·ty /həˈrɛdəṭi/ *n.* [U] BIOLOGY MEDICINE the process of passing on features that are controlled by GENES from parents to a child [**Origin:** 1500–1600 French *hérédité*, from Latin *hereditas*]

here·in /ˌhɪrˈɪn/ *adv.* FORMAL in this place, situation, document etc.: *the conditions stated herein* (=referring to conditions in a legal document) → see also THEREIN

here·in·af·ter /ˌhɪrɪnˈæftɚ/ *adv.* LAW later in this official statement, document etc.

here·of /ˌhɪrˈʌv/ *adv.* FORMAL relating to this → see also THEREOF

her·e·sy /ˈhɛrəsi/ *n. plural* **heresies** [C,U] **1** a belief that disagrees with the official principles of a particular religion **2** HUMOROUS a belief, statement etc. that disagrees with what a group of people believe to be right SYN **sacrilege**: *It's heresy to consider changing the rules of baseball.*

her·e·tic /ˈhɛrəˌtɪk/ *n.* [C] someone who is guilty of heresy —**heretical** /həˈrɛṭɪkəl/ *adj.*

here·to /ˌhɪrˈtu/ *adv.* FORMAL to this: *the document attached hereto*

here·to·fore /ˌhɪrtəˈfɔr, ˈhɪrtəˌfɔr/ *adv.* FORMAL before this time: *a feat which heretofore seemed impossible*

here·up·on /ˌhɪrəˈpɑn, ˈhɪrəˌpɑn/ *adv.* FORMAL at or after this moment → see also THEREUPON

here·with /ˌhɪrˈwɪθ, -ˈwɪð/ *adv.* FORMAL with this letter or document: *Enclosed herewith is a copy of the contract.*

her·i·ta·ble /ˈhɛrəṭəbəl/ *adj.* **1** BIOLOGY a physical or mental feature that is heritable can be passed from a parent to his or her children: *They claim that IQ is heritable.* | *the possibility that a heritable cancer gene may exist* **2** [usually before noun] LAW heritable property, land etc. can legally be left to someone when you die → see also INHERIT

her·it·age /ˈhɛrəṭɪdʒ/ *n.* [singular, U] the traditions, values, arts etc. that are passed down over many years within a country, society, or family: +**of** *the musical heritage of the southern states* | **American/Greek/Jewish etc. heritage** *These beatutiful murals make people proud of their Latin heritage.* | **cultural/architectural etc. heritage** *European literary heritage* | *The three groups share* ***a common heritage*** (=the same traditional culture, beliefs etc.).

her·maph·ro·dite /hɚˈmæfrəˌdaɪt/ *n.* [C] BIOLOGY a living thing that has both male and female sexual organs [**Origin:** 1400–1500 Latin *hermaphroditus*, from Greek *Hermaphroditos*, the son of the ancient Greek god Hermes and the goddess Aphrodite, who became joined in body with the female nature spirit Salmacis] —**hermaphrodite** *adj.* —**hermaphroditic** /hɚˌmæfrəˈdɪṭɪk/ *adj.*

Her·mes /ˈhɚmiz/ in Greek MYTHOLOGY, the god who is the MESSENGER of the gods. He is usually shown in pictures with wings on his shoes and on his HELMET

her·met·i·cally /hɚˈmɛṭɪkli/ *adv.* **hermetically sealed** very tightly closed so that air cannot get in or out —**hermetic** *adj.*

her·mit /ˈhɚmɪt/ *n.* [C] someone who prefers to live far away from other people, usually for religious reasons [**Origin:** 1100–1200 Old French *eremite*, from Greek *eremites* **living in the desert**, from *eremos* **lonely**] → see also RECLUSE

her·mit·age /ˈhɚmɪṭɪdʒ/ *n.* [C] a place where a hermit lives or has lived

ˈhermit ˌcrab *n.* [C] a type of CRAB that lives in the empty shells of other sea creatures

ˈhermit ˌkingdom *n.* [C] **1 the Hermit Kingdom** HISTORY a name used for Korea during the period from about 1637 to 1876, when it did not have relations with countries other than China **2** POLITICS any country that has limited relations with other countries

her·ni·a /ˈhɚniə/ *n.* [C,U] MEDICINE a medical condition in which an organ pushes through the skin or muscles that cover it

he·ro /ˈhɪroʊ/ W2 *n. plural* **heroes** [C] **1** someone who is admired for doing something extremely brave: *Conway is a local* ***war hero.*** | *one of America's* ***national heroes*** **2** someone, especially a man or boy, who is the main character in a book, movie, play etc. OPP **villain**: *The hero of the story is a young soldier.* **3** someone who is admired very much for a particular skill or quality etc.: *sports heroes* | **your/my/her etc. hero** *Michael Jordan was my hero when I was little.* **4** a SANDWICH made of a long LOAF of bread filled with meat, cheese etc. [**Origin:** 1500–1600 Latin *heros*, from Greek] → see also HEROINE

He·rod·o·tus /hɪˈrɑdəṭəs/ (485?–425 B.C.) a Greek writer of history

he·ro·ic /hɪˈroʊɪk/ *adj.* **1** extremely brave or determined, and admired by many people SYN **courageous**: *heroic deeds* | *Soldiers made* ***heroic efforts*** *to get all the civilians out of the city.* ►see THESAURUS box at **brave¹** **2** ENG. LANG. ARTS a heroic story, poem etc. has a hero in it, usually from ancient LEGENDS **3 on a heroic scale** or **of heroic proportions** very large or great: *a battle on a heroic scale* —**heroically** /-kli/ *adv.*

heˌroic ˈcouplet *n.* [C] ENG. LANG. ARTS a pair of lines in poetry which end with the same sound and have five main beats in each line

he·ro·ics /hɪˈroʊɪks/ *n.* [plural] brave actions or words, often ones that are meant to seem impressive to other people: *We don't need any heroics. Everyone stay calm.*

her·o·in /ˈhɛroʊɪn/ *n.* [U] a powerful illegal drug that people usually take by putting it into their arms with a special needle: *a heroin addict* [**Origin:** 1800–1900 German, Greek *heros*; because taking it is said to make people feel heroic]

her·o·ine /ˈhɛroʊɪn/ *n.* [C] **1** the woman or girl who is the main character in a book, movie, play etc.: *the novel's heroine* **2** a woman who is extremely brave and is admired by many people: *a heroine of the French Resistance* **3** a woman you admire very much for her intelligence, skill etc.: *I finally got to meet my heroine, Maya Angelou.* → see also HERO

her·o·ism /ˈhɛroʊˌɪzəm/ *n.* [U] very great courage: *He won the Medal of Honor for heroism in Vietnam.*

her·on /ˈhɛrən/ *n.* [C] BIOLOGY a large bird with very long legs and a long beak, that lives near water

ˈhero ˌworship *n.* [U] great admiration for someone you think is very brave, good, skillful etc., sometimes when the person does not deserve this: *the hero worship of sports stars* —**hero-worship** *v.* [T]

her·pes /ˈhɚpiz/ *n.* [U] MEDICINE a very infectious disease that causes spots on the skin, for example on the

H

sexual organs or face [**Origin:** 1300–1400 Latin, Greek, from *herpein* **to move slowly and quietly**]

her·ring /ˈhɛrɪŋ/ *n. plural* **herrings, herring** [C,U] BIOLOGY a long thin silver ocean fish, or the meat from this fish → see also RED HERRING

her·ring·bone /ˈhɛrɪŋˌboʊn/ *n.* [U] a pattern consisting of a continuous line of V shapes, used on cloth, or a type of cloth with this pattern on it

hers /hɚz/ S2 *possessive pron.* [possessive form of "she"] the thing or things belonging to or relating to a female person or animal that has been mentioned or is known about: *This is my coat. Hers* (=her coat) *is over there.* | *My shoes are brown, and hers are red.* | *Paul is a friend **of hers**.*

her·self /ɚˈsɛlf; *strong* hɚˈsɛlf/ S2 W1 **1** the REFLEXIVE form of "she": *She hurt herself.* | *I think she really enjoyed herself.* **2** the strong form of "she," used to emphasize the subject or object of a sentence: *Bridget made her dress herself.* | *Sandy just got back herself.* **3 (all) by herself a)** alone: *She was sitting at a table by herself.* **b)** without help from anyone else: *She raised her daughter by herself.* **4 have sth (all) to herself** if a woman or girl has something to herself, she does not have to share it with anyone: *She had the house to herself all day.* **5 not feel/look/seem like herself** if a woman or girl is not feeling like herself, she does not feel or behave as she usually does, for example because she is upset or sick: *Charlotte just doesn't look like herself today.*

H

hertz /hɚts/ *n. plural* **hertz** [C] WRITTEN ABBREVIATION **Hz** PHYSICS a unit used to measure FREQUENCY. One hertz is one CYCLE each second. [**Origin:** 1800–1900 Heinrich *Hertz* (1857–94), German scientist who worked on energy waves]

Her·zl /ˈhɛrtsəl/, **The·o·dor** /ˈteɪədɔr/ (1860–1904) an Austrian politician who started Zionism

he's /iz; *strong* hiz/ **1** the short form of "he is": *He's in kindergarten already.* | *He's from Spain.* **2** the short form of "he has": *He's had three months of training.*

He·si·od /ˈhisiəd, ˈhɛ-/ (8th century B.C.) a Greek poet

hes·i·tan·cy /ˈhɛzət̬ənsi/ also **hes·i·tance** /ˈhɛzət̬əns/ *n.* [U] the quality of being uncertain or slow in doing or saying something: *He showed no hesitancy in answering some difficult questions.*

hes·i·tant /ˈhɛzət̬ənt/ *adj.* uncertain about what to do or say because you are nervous or unwilling: *his shy, hesitant manner.* | **be hesitant to do sth** *I'm hesitant to draw conclusions until the study is over.* | **be hesitant about doing sth** *They seemed hesitant about coming in.* —**hesitantly** *adv.*

hes·i·tate /ˈhɛzəˌteɪt/ *v.* **1** [I] to pause before saying or doing something because you are nervous or not sure: *Paul hesitated for a minute, searching for the right words.* | **hesitate over/about (doing) sth** *He was still hesitating over whether to stay or go.* **2 not hesitate to do sth** to be willing to do something because you are sure that it is right: *He does not hesitate to criticize the country's politicians.* **3 don't hesitate to do sth** used to tell someone that they can do something, such as ask for help, without worrying about it: *Don't hesitate to call me if you need any help.* [**Origin:** 1600–1700 Latin, past participle of *haesitare* **to stick firmly, hesitate**, from *haerere* **to stick**] —**hesitatingly** *adv.*

hes·i·ta·tion /ˌhɛzəˈteɪʃən/ *n.* [C,U] a pause before someone says or does something because they are nervous or not sure: *After some hesitation, one boy spoke.* | *Ice cream is one food that most kids will eat **without hesitation**.* | *She **had no hesitation** in accepting their job offer.* | *After **a moment's hesitation** the other kids jumped in the car.*

Hes·se /ˈhɛsə/, **Her·man** /ˈhɚmən/ (1877–1962) a German writer and poet famous for his NOVELS

Hes·ti·a /ˈhɛstiə, ˈhɛstʃə/ in Greek MYTHOLOGY, the goddess of the HEARTH who protects people's homes

hetero- /hɛt̬əroʊ, -rə/ *prefix* FORMAL OR TECHNICAL the opposite of something, or different from something: *heterosexual* (=attracted to someone of the opposite sex) | *a heterogeneous mixture* (=a mixture of things that are not alike)

het·er·o·ge·ne·ous /ˌhɛt̬ərəˈdʒiniəs, -nyəs/ also **het·e·rog·e·nous** /ˌhɛt̬əˈrɑdʒənəs/ *adj.* FORMAL consisting of parts or members that are very different from each other: *The U.S. has a very heterogeneous population.* —**heterogeneity** /ˌhɛt̬əroʊdʒɪˈniət̬i/ *n.* [U] —**heterogeneously** /ˌhɛt̬ərəˈdʒiniəsli/ *adv.* → see also HOMOGENEOUS

hetero,geneous 'mixture *n.* [C] CHEMISTRY a substance consisting of two or more different substances that remain physically separate, so that all parts of the mixture look different → see also EMULSION, HOMOGENEOUS MIXTURE, SUSPENSION

het·er·o·sex·u·al /ˌhɛt̬ərəˈsɛkʃuəl/ *adj.* FORMAL sexually attracted to people of the opposite sex: *heterosexual relationships* —**heterosexual** *n.* [C] —**heterosexually** *adv.* —**heterosexuality** /ˌhɛt̬ərəˌsɛkʃuˈælət̬i/ *n.* [U] → see also BISEXUAL

het·e·ro·troph /ˈhɛt̬ərəˌtrɑf, -ˌtroʊf/ *n.* [C] BIOLOGY a living creature that obtains the energy it needs in order to live, grow, and stay healthy from the foods it eats, rather than by PHOTOSYNTHESIS

het·e·ro·zy·gous /ˌhɛt̬ərəˈzaɪgəs/ *adj.* BIOLOGY relating to a cell or ORGANISM which has two or more different forms of a particular GENE → see also HOMOZYGOUS

heu·ris·tic /hyʊˈrɪstɪk/ *adj.* TECHNICAL **1** heuristic education is based on discovering and experiencing things for yourself **2** helping you in the process of learning or discovery —**heuristically** /-kli/ *adv.*

heu·ris·tics /hyʊˈrɪstɪks/ *n.* [U] TECHNICAL the study of how people use their experience to find answers to questions or to improve performance

hew /hyu/ *v.* **hewed, hewed** or **hewn** /hyun/ LITERARY [I,T] to cut something with a cutting tool: *roughly hewn wooden beams*

hew to sth *phr. v.* FORMAL to obey someone, or to do something according to the rules or instructions SYN **adhere to**: *She hews closely to tradition in her art.* → see also ROUGH-HEWN

hewn /hyun/ the past participle of HEW

hex¹ /hɛks/ *n.* [C] an evil CURSE that brings trouble ▸see THESAURUS box at **magic¹**

hex² *v.* [T] to use magic powers to make bad things happen to someone SYN **curse**

hex·a·dec·i·mal /ˌhɛksəˈdɛsəməl◂/ also **hex** *adj.* COMPUTERS hexadecimal numbers are based on the number 16 and are mainly used on computers

hex·a·gon /ˈhɛksəˌgɑn/ *n.* [C] MATH a flat shape with six sides —**hexagonal** /hɛkˈsægənl/ *adj.* → see picture at SHAPE¹

hex·a·gram /ˈhɛksəˌgræm/ *n.* [C] a star shape with six points, made from two TRIANGLES

hex·am·e·ter /hɛkˈsæmət̬ɚ/ *n.* [C] ENG. LANG. ARTS a line of poetry with six main beats

hey /heɪ/ S1 *interjection* **1** a shout used to get someone's attention or to express surprise, interest, or annoyance: *Hey, wait a minute!* | *Hey, those are mine.* **2** INFORMAL hello: *Hey, girl, what's up?*

hey·day /ˈheɪdeɪ/ *n.* [C usually singular] the time when someone or something was most popular, successful, or powerful: *a picture of the actress **in her heyday*** [**Origin:** 1500–1600 *heyda* a shout of happiness (16–17 centuries); influenced by day]

Hey·er·dahl /ˈhaɪɚˌdɑl/, **Thor** /θɔr/ (1914–2002) a Norwegian ANTHROPOLOGIST famous for crossing the Pacific on a RAFT, the Kon-Tiki, to prove that people might have come to Polynesia from Peru

HI the written abbreviation of HAWAII

hi /haɪ/ S1 *interjection* hello: *Hi! How are you?* | ***Hi there**, Charlie.*

hi·a·tus /haɪˈeɪtəs/ *n.* [singular, U] a break in an activity, or a time when something does not happen or exist for a while SYN **break**: *The show is **on hiatus** this season.* [**Origin:** 1500–1600 Latin *hiare* **to yawn**]

Hi·a·wa·tha /ˌhaɪəˈwɑθə/ a Native American chief who, in the 16th century, helped to unite the Iroquois into a single group called the Five Nations

hi·ba·chi /hɪˈbɑtʃi/ *n.* [C] a small piece of equipment for cooking food outdoors, over burning CHARCOAL

hi·ber·nate /ˈhaɪbɚˌneɪt/ *v.* [I] BIOLOGY if an animal hibernates, it sleeps all the time during the winter —**hibernation** /ˌhaɪbɚˈneɪʃən/ *n.* [U]

hi·bis·cus /hɪˈbɪskəs, haɪ-/ *n.* [C,U] a tropical plant with large brightly colored flowers

hic·cough /ˈhɪkʌp/ *n.* [C usually plural] OLD-FASHIONED another spelling of HICCUP

hic·cup¹ /ˈhɪkʌp/ *n.* [C] **1** [usually plural] a sudden repeated stopping of the breath, usually caused by eating or drinking too fast: *Do you **have the hiccups**?* **2** a small problem or delay: *Except for a few hiccups, the project went well.* | +**in** *a hiccup in the negotiations* [**Origin:** 1500–1600 from the sound]

hiccup² *v. past tense and past participle* **hiccupped**, **hiccupping** [I] to have the hiccups

hick /hɪk/ *n.* [C] DISAPPROVING someone who lives in the country and is thought to be uneducated or stupid [**Origin:** 1500–1600 *Hick*, a man's name, from *Richard*]

hick·ey /ˈhɪki/ *n. plural* **hickeys** or **hickies** [C] INFORMAL a dark red or purple mark on someone's skin, especially on their neck, caused by someone else sucking it as a sexual act

Hick·ok /ˈhɪkɑk/, **Wild Bill** /waɪld bɪl/ (1837–1876) a U.S. soldier who was one of the first white Americans to live in the western U.S. where he became a MARSHAL

hick·o·ry /ˈhɪkəri/ *n. plural* **hickories** [C,U] a North American tree that produces nuts, or the wood that comes from this tree [**Origin:** 1600–1700 Algonquian *pawcohiccora* **food made from crushed nuts**]

hid /hɪd/ the past tense of HIDE¹

Hi·dat·sa /hɪˈdɑtsə/ a Native American tribe from the northern central area of the U.S.

hid·den¹ /ˈhɪdn/ the past participle of HIDE¹

hidden² *adj.* **1** not easy to notice or realize: *the hidden costs of owning a car* **2** difficult to see or find SYN **concealed**: *Hidden video cameras were used to improve security.* | *She **kept** the candy **hidden** from the children.*

ˌhidden aˈgenda *n.* [C] an intended result of a plan or activity that you do not tell other people about

hide¹ /haɪd/ S2 W2 *v. past tense* **hid** /hɪd/, *past participle* **hidden** /ˈhɪdn/ **1** [T] to deliberately put or keep something in a place where it cannot easily be seen or found SYN **conceal**: **hide sth in/under/behind etc.** *Marcia hid the pictures in her desk drawer.* | **hide sth from sb** *I tried to hide the letter from my mother.*

THESAURUS

conceal FORMAL to hide something carefully: *He tried to conceal how he felt.*
cover/cover up to put something over the top of something else in order to hide it: *A green blanket covered the old chair.*
disguise to change your appearance or voice so that people cannot recognize you: *In the story, the queen disguises herself as an old woman.*
mask to hide a smell or taste, your feelings, or the truth: *The scented candles masked the cooking smells from the kitchen.*

2 [I] to go or stay in a place where no one will see or find you: *She's coming – we'd better hide!* | +**in/under/behind etc.** *The cat was hiding among the plants.* | **hide from sb** *Weiss spent two years hiding from the Nazis.* **3** [T] to cover something so that it cannot be seen clearly SYN **conceal** OPP **reveal**: *The house was hidden by the trees.* | **hide sth from view/sight** *The swimming pool was hidden from view.* **4** [T] to not show your feelings to people SYN **conceal** OPP **show**: *José couldn't hide his embarrassment.* | **hide sth from sb** *She tried to hide her nervousness from his family.* **5** [T] to help someone stay in a place where other people will not find them SYN **conceal**: *The old woman hid him in her cellar for three days.* | **hide sb from sb** *We had to hide him from the soldiers.* **6** [T] to deliberately not let people find out about something OPP **reveal**: *an attempt to hide the truth* | **hide sth (from sb)** *Don't try to hide anything from me.* **7 have nothing to hide** to not be worried about what people will discover about you, because you have done nothing wrong or immoral: *You can ask me anything. I have nothing to hide.* [**Origin:** Old English *hydan*]

hide away *phr. v.* **1 hide sth ↔ away** to put or keep something in a place so that people cannot find or see it: *The documents had been hidden away in a closet.* **2** to go or stay in a place where no one will see or find you: *Wild animals hide away when they are injured.*

hide behind sb/sth *phr. v.* DISAPPROVING to use someone or something in order to protect yourself from criticism: *The White House is hiding behind its legal advisors.*

hide out *phr. v.* to stay in a place where people who are looking for you will not be able to find you: **hide out in/at/under etc.** *They gangsters were found hiding out on a farm.*

hide² *n.* **1** [C] an animal's skin, especially when it is removed to be used for leather: *a buffalo hide* **2 have/tan sb's hide** SPOKEN, HUMOROUS to punish someone severely **3 not see hide nor hair of sb** SPOKEN to not see someone anywhere for a period of time: *I haven't seen hide nor hair of him in months.*

ˌhide-and-ˈseek also **ˌhide-and-go-ˈseek** *n.* [U] a children's game in which one player shuts their eyes while the others hide, and then goes to look for them

hide·a·way /ˈhaɪdəˌweɪ/ *n. plural* **hideaways** [C] **1** a place where you can go to be alone and relax, for example on vacation: *a romantic hideaway in the mountains* **2** a place where you can go to hide SYN **hideout**

hide·bound /ˈhaɪdbaʊnd/ *adj.* DISAPPROVING having old-fashioned attitudes and ideas

hid·e·ous /ˈhɪdiəs/ *adj.* **1** extremely ugly: *a hideous dress* **2** extremely bad: *a hideous crime* [**Origin:** 1300–1400 Old French *hidous*, from *hide* **terror**] —**hideously** *adv.* —**hideousness** *n.* [U]

hide·out /ˈhaɪdaʊt/ *n.* [C] a place where someone goes because they do not want anyone to find them: *the neighborhood kids' hideout*

hid·ing /ˈhaɪdɪŋ/ *n.* **1** [U] the state of staying somewhere in secret because you have done something illegal or are in danger: *He is believed to **be in hiding** somewhere in Mexico.* | *He **went into hiding** in 1973.* **2 a hiding** OLD-FASHIONED a severe physical punishment

ˈhiding ˌplace *n.* [C] a place where you can hide, or where you can hide something

hie /haɪ/ *v.* [I,T] OLD USE to make yourself hurry, or go quickly

hi·er·ar·chy /ˈhaɪəˌrɑrki/ AC *n. plural* **hierarchies** **1** [C,U] a system of organization in which people or things are divided into levels of importance: *a rigid social hierarchy* | +**of** *the hierarchy of the company* **2** [C usually singular] the most important and powerful members of an organization: *Smith has the support of the Republican hierarchy.* **3** [C] a series of things arranged according to importance: +**of** *a hierarchy of priorities* [**Origin:** 1300–1400 Old French *ierarchie*, from Latin, from Greek *hierarches*, from *hieros* **holy** + *-arches* **ruler**] —**hierarchical** /ˌhaɪəˈrɑrkɪkəl/ *adj.* —**hierarchically** /-kli/ *adv.*

H

hieroglyphics

hier·o·glyph·ics /ˌhaɪrəˈglɪfɪks/ also **hier·o·glyphs** /ˈhaɪrəˌglɪfs/ *n.* [U, plural] a system of writing, especially one from ancient Egypt, that uses pictures to represent words —**hieroglyphic** *adj.*

hi-fi¹ /ˌhaɪ ˈfaɪ◂/ *n. plural* **hi-fis** [C] OLD-FASHIONED a STEREO

hi-fi² *adj.* [only before noun] HIGH FIDELITY

hig·gle·dy-pig·gle·dy /ˌhɪgəldi ˈpɪgəldi/ *adj.* things that are higgledy-piggledy are mixed together in a way that is not very neat —**higgledy-piggledy** *adv.*

high

a high shelf

a tall building

high¹ /haɪ/ S1 W1 *adj.*

1 FROM BOTTOM TO TOP something that is high measures a long distance from its bottom to its top → see also TALL OPP **low**: *a high wall* | *Mount Rainier is Washington's highest point.* | ***How high** is the Eiffel Tower?* | **10 feet/5 yards etc. high** *The fountain shot a stream of water 15 feet high.* ►see THESAURUS box at **tall**

2 ABOVE THE GROUND in a position that is a long way, or a longer way than usual, above the ground, floor etc. OPP **low**: *an apartment with high ceilings* | *a high shelf* | *There was a squirrel **high up** in the tree.*

3 LARGE NUMBER large in amount, number, or level, or larger than usual OPP **low**: *the highest score* | *Temperatures will be in the high eighties.* | *a car traveling **at high speed*** | **a high price/cost** *the high cost of living in the city* | *The cable company's prices are too high.* | **a high percentage/proportion** *A high percentage of children have not learned geography.* | **a high level/degree/rate (of sth)** *There is a higher rate of the disease amongst men.* ►see THESAURUS box at **expensive**

4 CONTAINING A LOT containing a lot of a particular substance, or having a lot of a particular quality: *high pollution levels* | **high in sth** *foods that are high in calories*

5 RANK/POSITION having an important or powerful position in society or in an organization: *people in the highest levels of management* | *I know a guy who's **high up** in the Greenpeace organization.* | *They've been trying to get into **high office** for years now.* → see also **have friends in high places** at FRIEND (6)

6 GOOD excellent in quality or standard: *The fabric is of very high quality.* | *the hotel's high standards of service* | *I **have a** very **high opinion** of him.* | *She **has** extremely **high standards** when it comes to food.* (=she only wants the best quality) | **hold sb/sth in high regard/esteem** (=respect someone very much) | **high ideals/principles** (=someone's strong beliefs that people should behave in an honest and morally good way)

7 be high on the list/agenda also **be a high priority** to be important, or need to be dealt with quickly: *Democracy in the region will be high on the agenda of both meetings.*

8 SOUND near the top of the range of sounds that humans can hear: *I can't sing the high notes.* → see also HIGH-PITCHED

> **THESAURUS**
> **high-pitched** higher than most sounds or voices: *a high-pitched voice*
> **piercing** very high and loud in a way that is not nice to listen to: *a piercing scream*
> **shrill** high and unpleasant: *a shrill, unpleasant laugh*
> **squeaky** making very high noises that are not loud: *squeaky shoes*

9 EXTREME being the greatest or most extreme example or part of something: *high fashion* | *tales of high adventure* | *an afternoon of **high drama*** (=very exciting events and situations)

10 ADVANCED advanced and often complicated: *high finance* | *the benefits of high technology* | **higher animals/mammals/organisms etc.** (=animals etc. that are more intelligent or advanced than others)

11 have high hopes/expectations to hope for or expect very good results or great success: *Teachers should have high expectations for their students.*

12 the high point/spot the best part of an activity or occasion: *the high point of the baseball season*

13 DRUGS [not before noun] behaving in an unusually excited or relaxed way because of taking drugs: *the problem of kids **getting high** at school*

14 high spirits feelings of happiness and energy, especially when you are having fun: *Despite the rain, everyone was **in high spirits**.*

15 it is high time sb did sth used to say that something should have been done already: *It's high time we stopped all these arguments.*

16 TIME [only before noun] the middle or the most important part of a particular period of time: *high summer* → see also HIGH SEASON

17 be/get on your high horse to behave or talk as if you are better than other people: *He gets on his high horse and starts telling people what to do.*

18 high and mighty talking or behaving as if you think you are more important than other people: *Don't act so high and mighty!*

19 leave sb high and dry INFORMAL to leave someone without any help or without the things that they need: *Michael quit, leaving Elliot high and dry to run the new company.*

20 a high wind a strong wind

21 HAPPY/EXCITED OLD-FASHIONED happy and excited

[**Origin:** Old English *heah*] → see also HIGH GEAR, HIGHLY, HIGH SEAS, **in high dudgeon** at DUDGEON

high² S2 W3 *adv.*

1 ABOVE THE GROUND at or to a level high above the ground OPP **low**: *Garbage had been **piled high** on the sidewalk.* | **+into/above etc.** *Paula threw the ball high into the air.* | *He held the trophy high above his head.*

2 VALUE/COST/AMOUNT at or to a high value, cost, amount etc. OPP **low**: *Tom scored higher than anyone else in the class.* | *The dollar climbed higher against the yen today.*

3 SOUND with a high sound OPP **low**: *I can't sing that high.*

4 ACHIEVEMENT to a high rank or level of achievement,

especially in an organization, business etc.: *Sandy continued to rise higher in Zefco's ranks.*
5 look/search high and low to try to find someone or something by looking everywhere: *We looked high and low for the dog but couldn't find her.* **hold your head up/high** at HOLD[1] (38), **live high on the hog** at LIVE[1] (3) → see also, **be riding high** at RIDE[1] (4), **be running high** at RUN[1] (39)

high[3] W3 *n.*
1 NUMBER/AMOUNT [C] the highest number, level, temperature etc. that has ever been recorded OPP **low**: **hit/reach a high (of sth)** *The shares hit a high of $36.75 last year.* | **a new/record/all-time etc. high** *The price of oil reached a new high this week.*
2 WEATHER [C] **a)** the highest temperature in a particular day, week, month etc., used in weather reports → see also LOW OPP **low**: *Highs tomorrow will be in the mid-90s.* | **+of** *Today we had a high of 70 degrees.* **b)** an area of HIGH PRESSURE that affects the weather: *another high moving in from the Atlantic*
3 DRUGS [C] a feeling of pleasure or excitement produced by some drugs: *the high a user gets from cocaine*
4 EXCITEMENT [C usually singular] INFORMAL a feeling of happiness or excitement you get from doing something you enjoy: *The team* ***was on a high*** *after winning the state championship.*
5 MACHINE [U] the position on the controls of a machine that makes it work hardest, go fastest, become the hottest etc. OPP **low**: *Set the fan to high.* | *The toaster was* ***on high****, so the bagels burned.*
6 High a short form of "high school," used in the name of a school: *I went to Reseda High.*
7 from on high HUMOROUS from someone in a position of authority: *an email from on high*
8 on high BIBLICAL in, to, or from heaven or a high place

high·ball /ˈhaɪbɔl/ *n.* [C] an alcoholic drink, especially WHISKEY or BRANDY mixed with water or SODA

high ˈbeam *n.* **1 high beams** [plural] the HEADLIGHTS of a vehicle that shine higher and brighter than the regular lights in order to help you see things far away **2 on high beam** if your car lights are on high beam, they are brighter than the normal lights, so that you can see farther → see also ON LOW BEAM

high ˈblood ˌpressure *n.* [U] a serious medical condition in which your BLOOD PRESSURE is too high

ˌhigh-ˈborn *adj.* FORMAL born into the highest social class

high·boy /ˈhaɪbɔɪ/ *n. plural* **highboys** [C] a piece of wooden furniture with drawers and tall thin legs

high·brow /ˈhaɪbraʊ/ *adj.* **1** a highbrow book, movie etc. is intended for intelligent people who have an interest in serious ideas, art etc. → see also MIDDLEBROW SYN **intellectual** OPP **lowbrow** **2** someone who is highbrow has an interest in highbrow things SYN **intellectual** —**highbrow** *n.* [C]

high·chair /ˈhaɪtʃɛr/ *n.* [C] a special tall chair that a young child sits in to eat → see picture at CHAIR[1]

ˌHigh ˈChurch *n.* **the High Church** used to describe some Christian churches that have very traditional formal ceremonies

ˌhigh-ˈclass *adj.* [usually before noun] of good quality and style, and usually expensive SYN **upscale**: *a high-class hotel* → see also CLASSY

ˌhigh comˈmand *n.* [singular] the most important leaders of a country's army, navy etc.: *the Army High Command*

ˌhigh comˈmission *n.* [C] POLITICS a group of people working for a government or an international organization to deal with a specific problem: *the UN High Commission for Refugees* —**High Commissioner** *n.* [C]

ˌhigh-defiˈnition ABBREVIATION **HD** *adj.* [only before noun] a high-definition television or computer MONITOR shows images very clearly

ˈhigh-end *adj.* [usually before noun] relating to products or services that are more expensive and of better quality than other products of the same type: *high-end computer memory chips* → see also LOW-END

high·er /ˈhaɪɚ/ *adj.* the COMPARATIVE of HIGH

ˌhigher eduˈcation *n.* [U] education at a college or university, after leaving HIGH SCHOOL

ˈhigher-ˌend *adj.* [usually before noun] HIGH-END

ˌhigher-ˈup *n.* [C usually plural] INFORMAL someone who has a high rank in an organization

ˌhighest ˌcommon ˈfactor *n.* [C] MATH the largest number that a set of numbers can all be divided by exactly: *The highest common factor of 12, 24 and 30 is 6.*

ˌhigh exˈplosive *n.* [C,U] a substance that explodes with great power and violence

high·fa·lu·tin, highfalutin' /ˌhaɪfəˈlutˀn◂/ *adj.* INFORMAL, DISAPPROVING **1** highfalutin language, ideas etc. are meant to be impressive but actually sound silly because they are not appropriate in the situation SYN **pretentious** SYN **grandiose**: *He tried to impress us with some highfalutin words.* **2** a highfalutin person behaves in a way that shows they think they are more important than other people SYN **pretentious**

ˌhigh fiˈdelity *adj.* [usually before noun] high fidelity recording equipment produces sound that is very clear → see also HI-FI[2]

ˌhigh-ˈfive *n.* [singular] the action of hitting someone's open hand with your own above your heads, used as an informal greeting, or to show that you are happy about something: *My son gave me a high five, and said, "Great work, Dad!"* —**high-five** *v.* [I,T]

ˌhigh-ˈflier *n.* [C] a person or organization that is extremely successful, especially in business, work, or school: *a high-flier in the software industry* —**high-flying** *adj.*

ˌhigh-ˈflown *adj.* high-flown language, ideas etc. seem very impressive, but are often too complicated and not useful → see also LOFTY: *high-flown ideas about saving the world*

ˌhigh ˈfrequency *n.* [U] a radio FREQUENCY in the range of 3 to 30 MEGAHERTZ → see also LOW FREQUENCY —**high-frequency** *adj.*: *high-frequency broadcasts*

high-ˌfrequency ˈword *n.* [C] ENG. LANG. ARTS a word that is used much more often than most words in speaking or writing: *high-frequency words such as "the" and "and"*

high ˈgear *n.* [U] **1** one of a vehicle's GEARS that you use when you are driving at fast speeds **2 in high gear** if a situation is in high gear, it is happening or changing very quickly or people are working very hard: **kick/move/swing into high gear** *The flu season usually swings into high gear in November.*

ˈhigh-grade *adj.* [only before noun] of the best quality: *high-grade oil*

ˈhigh ground *n.* [U] **1** an area of land that is higher than the land around it: *Farmers moved livestock to high ground as the river flooded.* **2** if someone or a group has the high ground in an argument, they have the advantage: *Workers have regained the high ground in the negotiations.* → see also **take/claim/seize etc. the moral high ground** at MORAL[1] (4)

ˌhigh-ˈhanded *adj.* using your authority in an unreasonable way, without considering other people's feelings or opinions: *the company's high-handed treatment of clients* —**high-handedly** *adv.* —**high-handedness** *n.* [U]

ˌhigh ˈheels *n.* [plural] women's shoes with high heels —**high-heeled** *adj.*

ˌhigh ˈisland *n.* [C] EARTH SCIENCE an island in the ocean that is formed by a VOLCANO → see also LOW ISLAND

high jinks, hijinks /ˈhaɪ dʒɪŋks/ *n.* [U] OLD-FASHIONED noisy, silly, or excited behavior or activities which happen when people are having fun

ˈhigh jump *n.* **the high jump** a sports event in which someone runs and jumps over a pole that is raised higher each time they jump —**high jumper** *n.* [C]

high·land /ˈhaɪlənd/ *adj.* [only before noun] **1** relating to an area with a lot of mountains: *the highland city of Puno* **2** coming from or relating to the Scottish Highlands: *highland dancing*

H

High·land·er /ˈhaɪləndɚ/ *n.* [C] someone from the Scottish Highlands

high·lands /ˈhaɪləndz/ *n.* [plural] an area of a country where there are a lot of mountains: *the Andean highlands* → see also LOWLANDS

ˌhigh ˈlatitudes *n.* [plural] the areas north of the Arctic Circle and south of the Antarctic Circle → see also LOW LATITUDES → MIDDLE LATITUDES

ˌhigh-ˈlevel *adj.* [only before noun] **1** in a powerful position or job, or involving people who are in powerful positions or jobs OPP low-level: *a high-level attorney* | *high-level positions in the company* **2** to a high degree or strength OPP low-level: *high-level pollution* | *The virus has shown high-level resistance to penicillin.* **3** involving advanced ideas or an advanced level of skill: *a high-level philosophical discussion* **4** COMPUTERS a high-level computer language is similar to human language rather than machine language OPP low-level

ˈhigh life *n.* **the high life** a way of life that involves a lot of parties, and expensive food, wine, travel etc.: *We lived the high life for a couple of years.*

high·light[1] /ˈhaɪlaɪt/ Ac S3 *v.* [T] **1** to make something easy to notice so that people pay attention to it: *Your resumé should highlight your skills and achievements.* ▸see THESAURUS box at **emphasize** **2** to mark written words with a special colored pen, or in a different color on a computer, so that you can see them easily: *Highlight the text by pressing Alt-F4.* **3** to make some parts of your hair a lighter color than the rest —**highlighting** *n.* [U]

highlight[2] Ac *n.* [C] **1** the most important, interesting, or enjoyable part of an activity or period of time: *Venice was definitely **the highlight of** our trip.* **2 highlights** [plural] **a)** areas of hair that have been made a lighter color than the rest **b)** the most exciting parts of a sports game broadcast after the event has taken place **3** ENG. LANG. ARTS a light bright area on a painting or photograph

high·light·er /ˈhaɪlaɪt̬ɚ/ *n.* [C] a special light-colored pen used for marking words in a book, article etc.

high·ly /ˈhaɪli/ S3 W2 *adv.* **1** [+ adj./adv.] very: *a highly flammable liquid* | *a highly successful businessman* | **highly unlikely/likely/improbable/probable** *It seems highly unlikely that the project will continue.* **2** [+ adj./adv.] to a high level, standard, or degree: *highly educated workers* | *a highly developed sense of smell* | *a highly respected artist* | *I **highly recommend*** (=recommend strongly) *his new restaurant.* **3 speak/think highly of sb** to tell other people how good someone is at doing something or to think they are very good at doing something: *Mr. Lloyd speaks highly of you.* **4 highly placed** in an important or powerful position: *highly placed public officials*

ˌHigh ˈMass *n.* [C,U] a very formal church ceremony in the Catholic Church

ˌhigh-ˈminded *adj.* having or showing very high moral standards: *high-minded academic ideas* —**high-mindedly** *adv.* —**high-mindedness** *n.* [U]

High·ness /ˈhaɪnɪs/ *n. plural* **Highnesses** [C] **Your/Her/His Highness** used to speak to or about a king, queen, prince etc.

ˌhigh-ˈoctane *adj.* high-octane GASOLINE is of a very high quality —**high-octane** *n.* [U] → see also OCTANE

ˌhigh-perˈformance *adj.* **high-performance cars/computers/tires etc.** cars, computers etc. that are able to go faster, do more work etc. than normal ones

ˌhigh-ˈpitched *adj.* a high-pitched voice or sound is higher than usual: *a high-pitched scream*

ˌhigh-ˈpowered *adj.* [usually before noun] **1** a high-powered machine, vehicle, or piece of equipment is very powerful → see also LOW-POWERED: *a high-powered rifle* **2** very important or successful: *a high-powered law firm*

ˌhigh ˈpressure *n.* [U] EARTH SCIENCE an area of high air pressure in the sky, which usually brings warm weather: *an area of high pressure over the Atlantic*

ˈhigh-ˌpressure *adj.* [only before noun] **1** a high-pressure job or situation is one in which you have to work very hard **2** DISAPPROVING using very direct and forceful methods of persuading people to buy something or do something: *high-pressure sales techniques* **3** containing or using a very high force of water, gas, air etc.: *high-pressure hoses* **4 a high-pressure system** HIGH PRESSURE

ˌhigh-ˈpriced *adj.* costing a lot of money: *high-priced apartments* | *high-priced lawyers*

ˌhigh ˈpriest *n.* [C] **1** INFORMAL a man who is famous for being the best at something such as a type of art or music: *the high priest of hip hop* **2** the most important PRIEST in some religions

ˌhigh ˈpriestess *n.* [C] **1** INFORMAL a woman who is famous for being the best at something such as a type of art or music: *the high priestess of fashion* **2** the most important PRIESTESS in some religions

ˌhigh-ˈprincipled *adj.* a high-principled person has high moral standards → see also MORAL SYN principled

ˌhigh-ˈprofile *adj.* [only before noun] often mentioned in newspapers and in television and radio programs, and known about by most people: *a high-profile trial* —**high profile** *n.* [singular]

ˌhigh-ˈranking *adj.* [only before noun] having a high position in a government or other organization: *high-ranking military officials*

ˌhigh reˈlief *n.* [U] **1** ENG. LANG. ARTS a form of art in which figures cut in stone or wood stand out from the surface → see also BAS-RELIEF **2 throw/bring sth into high relief** to make something very clear and easy to notice

ˈhigh-rise, highrise *n.* [C] a tall building, for example an office building or an apartment building —**high-rise** *adj.* [only before noun] → see also LOW-RISE

ˈhigh-risk *adj.* [only before noun] involving a lot of risk: *a high-risk investment* | *The drug reduces strokes in **high-risk patients*** (=patients who have a high risk of illness or dying). → see also AT-RISK

ˈhigh road *n.* **1 take the (moral) high road** to do what you believe is right according to your beliefs, even when others criticize or oppose you **2** [C] OLD-FASHIONED a main road

ˌhigh ˈroller *n.* [C] INFORMAL someone who spends a lot of money, especially by BETting on games, horse races etc.

ˈhigh school S1 W1 *n.* **1** [C,U] a school in the U.S. and Canada for students between the ages of 14 and 18: *high school graduates* | *Where did you **go to high school**?* **2** [U] the period of time in your life when you go to high school: *They got married right after high school.* | *Both of my kids are **in high school**.*

ˌhigh ˈseas *n.* **the high seas** LITERARY the areas of ocean that are far from land and do not belong to any particular country

ˌhigh ˈseason *n.* [singular, U] the time of year when businesses make a lot of money and prices are high because there are a lot of tourists

ˌhigh-ˈsounding *adj.* [only before noun] high-sounding language, ideas etc. seem very impressive, but are often too complicated and not helpful or useful

ˈhigh-speed *adj.* [only before noun] **1** designed to travel or operate very fast: *a high-speed train* **2 a high-speed chase** a situation when the police drive very fast to try to catch someone who is in a car

ˌhigh-ˈspirited *adj.* **1** someone who is high-spirited has a lot of energy and enjoys fun and adventure **2** a horse that is high-spirited is nervous and difficult to control

ˌhigh-ˈstrung *adj.* nervous and easily upset or excited

high·tail /ˈhaɪteɪl/ *v.* INFORMAL **hightail it** to leave a place quickly: *They ended up hightailing it across the border.*

ˈhigh tech also **ˌhigh techˈnology** *n.* [U] the most

modern and advanced technology: *advances in high tech*

ˌhigh-ˈtech *adj.* [usually before noun] using the most modern information, machines, methods etc. OPP **low-tech**: *high-tech weapons* | *high-tech industries* → see Word Choice box at TECHNIQUE

ˌhigh-ˈtension *adj.* **high-tension wires/lines etc.** wires, lines etc. that have a powerful electric current going through them

ˌhigh ˈtide *n.* **1** [C,U] EARTH SCIENCE the point or time at which the ocean reaches its highest level OPP **low tide**: *The beach disappears **at high tide**.* **2** [singular] the time when something is busiest, most successful, or most impressive: *the high tide of the Cultural Revolution in China*

ˌhigh-ˈtoned *adj.* someone or something that is high-toned shows a lot of intelligence or too much intelligence: *high-toned language*

ˈhigh-tops *n.* [plural] INFORMAL sports shoes that cover your ANKLES —**high-top** *adj.*: *high-top basketball shoes*

ˌhigh ˈtreason *n.* [U] LAW the crime of putting your country's government or leader in great danger, for example by giving military secrets to an enemy

ˈhigh-ˌvoltage *adj.* [only before noun] **1** containing a lot of electrical force: *high-voltage power lines* **2** having or showing a lot of energy: *a high-voltage performer*

ˌhigh ˈwater *n.* [U] the time when the water in a river, lake etc. is at its highest level OPP **low water**

ˌhigh-ˈwater mark *n.* [singular] **1** the mark that shows the highest level that the ocean or a river reaches **2** the time when someone or something is most successful: *the high-water mark of American journalism*

high·way /ˈhaɪweɪ/ S3 W2 *n. plural* **highways** [C] **1** a wide fast road that connects cities or towns together → see also FREEWAY: *a four-lane highway* | *an accident **on the highway*** → EXPRESSWAY ►see THESAURUS box at **road** **2 highway robbery** INFORMAL a situation in which something costs you a lot more than it should: *Sixty dollars for a textbook? That's highway robbery.*

high·way·man /ˈhaɪweɪmən/ *n. plural* **highwaymen** /-mən/ [C] OLD USE HISTORY someone who stopped people and carriages on the roads and robbed them

ˈhighway paˌtrol *n.* **the highway patrol** the police who make sure that people obey the rules on HIGHWAYS in the U.S.

ˈhigh wire *n.* [C] a tightly stretched rope or wire high above the ground that someone walks along, usually as part of a CIRCUS performance

hi·jab /hɪˈdʒɑb/ *n.* **1** [U] the practice of Muslim women of wearing clothing that covers most of their body **2** [C] a piece of cloth worn by a Muslim woman to cover her head

hi·jack /ˈhaɪdʒæk/ *v.* [T] **1** to use violence or threats to take control of an airplane, vehicle, or ship: *The ship was hijacked by four young terrorists.* **2** to take control of something and use it for your own purposes: *Radical students hijacked the street protests.* —**hijacker** *n.* [C]

hi·jack·ing /ˈhaɪˌdʒækɪŋ/ *n.* **1** [C,U] the use of violence or threats to take control of an airplane or vehicle: *One person was killed during the hijacking.* → see also CARJACKING **2** [U] the act of taking control of something so you can use it for your own purposes: *the hijacking of the meeting by a few noisy individuals*

hi·jinks /ˈhaɪdʒɪŋks/ *n.* [plural] another spelling of HIGH JINKS

Hij·ra /ˈhɪdʒrə/ *n.* another form of HEGIRA

hike¹ /haɪk/ S2 *n.* [C] **1** a long walk in the country, mountains etc. for pleasure: *a hike in the hills* **2** a large increase in something: +**in** *another hike in the price of gasoline* | **price/rate/tax etc. hikes** *Several airlines have announced fare hikes.* **3** a long walk that soldiers do for training **4 take a hike** SPOKEN an impolite way of telling someone to go away

hike² S2 *v.* **1** [I,T] to take a long walk in the country, mountains etc.: *We hiked for miles.* | *I've hiked the canyon four times.* → see also HIKING ►see THESAURUS box at **travel¹**, **walk¹** **2** [T] also **hike sth ↔ up** to increase something such as a price or tax by a large amount: *The President wants to hike spending for foreign aid.*

hike sth ↔ **up** *phr. v.* to pull or lift up a piece of your clothing: *She hiked her skirt up to climb the stairs.*

hik·er /ˈhaɪkɚ/ *n.* [C] someone who takes long walks in the country, mountains etc. for pleasure or exercise

hik·ing /ˈhaɪkɪŋ/ *n.* [U] an outdoor activity in which you take long walks in the mountains or country: *We're going to do some hiking this summer.* | *Southeast Utah is a great place to **go hiking** and mountain biking.*

hi·lar·i·ous /hɪˈlɛriəs, -ˈlær-/ S3 *adj.* extremely funny: *His new show is hilarious.* [**Origin:** 1800–1900 Latin *hilarus* **cheerful**, from Greek *hilaros*] —**hilariously** *adv.*

hi·lar·i·ty /hɪˈlærəṭi/ *n.* [U] the behavior of people who are laughing a lot or having fun

hill /hɪl/ S2 W2 *n.* [C] **1** an area of land that is higher than the land around it, like a mountain but smaller → see also VALLEY: *a beautiful view of the hills* | *We climbed up to the top of a steep hill.* | *The hotel is up **on a hill**, overlooking the town.* | *We went for a walk **in the hills*** (=in an area where there are hills). | **the bottom/foot of the hill** *We stopped at the bottom of the hill to rest.* | *the **rolling hills*** (=hills with long slopes that are not very steep) *of southern Spain* → see picture on page A31 **2** a slope on a road or path: *The car started rolling back down the hill.* **3 the Hill** another word for CAPITOL HILL used especially by politicians and journalists: *He was trying to influence key people **on the Hill*** (=in the U.S. Congress). **4 over the hill** INFORMAL too old for something or too old to do something well: *At 38, a professional boxer may be considered over the hill.* **5 it doesn't amount to a hill of beans** SPOKEN it is not important **6 over hill and dale** OLD-FASHIONED for a long distance, up and down hills [**Origin:** Old English *hyll*]

Hil·la·ry /ˈhɪləri/**, Sir Ed·mund** /ˈɛdmənd/ (1919–) a New Zealand mountain climber known for being the first person, with Tenzing Norgay, to reach the top of Mount Everest in 1953

hill·bil·ly /ˈhɪlˌbɪli/ *n. plural* **hillbillies** [U] a type of music that was developed by white people in the mountains of the southern United States

hill·ock /ˈhɪlək/ *n.* [C] a small hill

hill·side /ˈhɪlsaɪd/ *n.* [C] the sloping side of a hill: *Her house was built on a hillside.*

hill·y /ˈhɪli/ *adj. comparative* **hillier**, *superlative* **hilliest** having a lot of hills: *hilly roads*

hilt /hɪlt/ *n.* [C] **1** the handle of a sword or knife that is used as a weapon **2 (up) to the hilt** as much as possible or to a high level: *Everything I have is mortgaged to the hilt.* | *Troy lived each day to the hilt.*

him /ɪm; *strong* hɪm/ S1 W1 *pron.* **1** the object form of "he": *I took him to lunch yesterday.* | *She's in love with him.* | *Why don't you just ask him yourself?* **2** OLD-FASHIONED used to talk about anyone or about people in general, whether male or female: *Everyone should choose what is best for him.* → see Usage note at HIS **3 Him** used to talk about God: *Let us praise Him.* [**Origin:** Old English]

Him·a·la·yas, the /ˌhɪməˈleɪəz/ a long range of mountains in southern Asia, northeast of India, that includes the highest mountain in the world, Mount Everest

him·self /ɪmˈsɛlf; *strong* hɪmˈsɛlf/ S1 W1 *pron.* **1 a)** the REFLEXIVE form of "he": *I don't think he hurt himself when he fell* | *Mikey calls himself Michael these days.* | *Peter considers himself a poet.* **b)** the REFLEXIVE form of "he," used after words like "everyone," "anyone," "no one" etc.: *Everyone here should decide for himself.* **2** the strong form of "he," used to emphasize the subject or object of a sentence: *Steve himself is just* *recovering from surgery.* | *He built the closets himself.* **3 (all) by himself a)** alone: *Don's traveling by himself.* **b)** without help from anyone else: *He's standing up by himself already.* **4 have sth (all) to himself** if a man or boy has something to himself, he does not have to share it with anyone: *Jerry wanted to have the company all to himself.* **5 not feel/look/seem like himself** if a man or boy is not feeling, looking etc. like himself, he does not feel or behave in the way that he usually does because he is nervous, upset, or sick: *Doug hasn't been himself lately.* → see also YOURSELF

hind /haɪnd/ *adj.* the hind legs, feet etc. of an animal or insect are the ones at the back

hin·der /ˈhɪndɚ/ *v.* [T] to make it difficult for someone to do something or for something to develop SYN **hamper**: *Problems at home may hinder a child's learning.* [**Origin:** Old English *hindrian*]

Hin·di /ˈhɪndi/ *n.* [U] one of the official languages of India

hind·most /ˈhaɪndmoʊst/ *adj.* OLD USE farthest behind

hind·quar·ters /ˈhaɪndˌkwɔrṭɚz/ *n.* [plural] the back part of an animal, including the back legs

hin·drance /ˈhɪndrəns/ *n.* **1** [C] something or someone that makes it difficult for you to do something successfully: *He feels marriage would be **a hindrance to** his career.* **2** [U] FORMAL the act of making it difficult for someone to do something: *They should be allowed to do their job **without hindrance**.*

H

hind·sight /ˈhaɪndsaɪt/ *n.* [U] the ability to understand facts about a situation only after it has happened: *It's easy to say **in hindsight*** (=after something has happened) *that I should have done things differently.* | **with the benefit/wisdom of hindsight** *With the wisdom of hindsight, I now realize that he was unhappy.* → see also **20/20 hindsight** at TWENTY-TWENTY (2)

Hin·du /ˈhɪndu/ *n. plural* **Hindus** [C] someone who believes in Hinduism —**Hindu** *adj.*: *a Hindu temple*

Hin·du·ism /ˈhɪnduˌɪzəm/ *n.* [U] the main religion in India, which includes belief in many gods and in REINCARNATION

hinge¹ /hɪndʒ/ *n.* [C] a metal part used to fasten a door to its frame, a lid to a box etc., so that it can swing open and closed

hinge² *v.*

hinge on/upon sth *phr. v.* if a result hinges on something happening, it depends on it completely: *The case hinges on whether the jury believed the defendants.*

hinged /hɪndʒd/ *adj.* joined by a hinge: *a hinged lid*

hint¹ /hɪnt/ *n.* [C] **1** something that you say or do that helps someone guess what you really want or mean: *Come on, just **give me a hint**.* | *He's been **dropping hints*** (=giving hints indirectly) *that he might not return next year.* | *I said I was busy but he didn't **take the hint*** (=understand my hint, and go away). | **a strong/heavy/clear hint** (=hint in which it is very clear what someone means) **2** a very small amount or sign of something: +**of** *a hint of anger in his voice* | *a hint of sweetness in the wine* | *At **the first hint of** trouble, he left.* | *There is **no hint of** humor in the book* (=no humor at all). **3** a useful piece of advice about how to do something: +**on** *hints on how to avoid injuring your back* | **handy/helpful hints** (=useful hints)

hint² *v.* [I,T] to say something in an indirect way, but so that someone can guess what you mean: +**at** *What are you hinting at?* | **hint (that)** *I think she was hinting that I might be offered a contract.*

hint at sth *phr. v.* to be a sign that something exists or will happen: *Nothing in his childhood hinted at the unusual life he would have.*

hin·ter·land /ˈhɪntɚˌlænd/ *n.* [C usually plural] **1** a less developed area that is far from big cities, especially in the middle of a country **2** an area of land next to a city or area along a coast: *The port cities relied on their immediate rural hinterlands for food.*

hip¹ /hɪp/ S3 *n.* [C] **1** BIOLOGY one of the two parts on each side of your body between the top of your leg and your waist: *his narrow hips* **2** BIOLOGY one of the two joints on each side of your body between the top of your leg and your waist: *She fell and broke her hip.* **3** [usually plural] BIOLOGY the red fruit of some kinds of ROSE bushes SYN **rose hip** [**Origin:** (1, 2) Old English *hype*] → see also **shoot from the hip** at SHOOT¹ (19)

hip² *adj. comparative* **hipper**, *superlative* **hippest** INFORMAL **1** fashionable SYN **cool**: *a hip new dance club* **2 be/get hip to sth** INFORMAL to know about something new and understand it

hip³ *interjection* **hip, hip, hooray!** used as a shout of approval

ˈhip flask *n.* [C] a small container for strong alcoholic drinks, made to fit in your pocket

ˈhip-hop *n.* [U] **1** a type of dance music with a strong regular BEAT and spoken words → see also RAP **2** a type of popular CULTURE among young people in big cities which includes RAP music, dancing, and GRAFFITI art, especially popular among African-American young people: *hip hop culture*

hip·hug·gers /ˈhɪpˌhʌgɚz/ *n.* [plural] pants that fit tightly around your HIPS and do not cover your waist

hip·pie, hippy /ˈhɪpi/ *n. plural* **hippies** [C] someone, especially in the 1960s, who opposed war and the traditional values of society, and often wore unusual clothes, had long hair, and took drugs for pleasure —**hippie** *adj.*: *hippie clothes*

hip·po /ˈhɪpoʊ/ *n. plural* **hippos** [C] INFORMAL a hippopotamus

ˌhip ˈpocket *n.* [C] a back pocket in a pair of pants or a skirt

Hip·poc·ra·tes /hɪˈpɑkrəˌtiz/ (?460–?377 B.C.) a doctor in ancient Greece who is considered to have begun the study of modern medicine

Hip·po·crat·ic oath /ˌhɪpəkræṭɪk ˈoʊθ/ *n.* [singular] the promise made by doctors that they will obey the principles of the medical profession

hip·po·pot·a·mus /ˌhɪpəˈpɑṭəməs/ *n. plural* **hippopotamuses** or **hippopotami** /-maɪ/ [C] a large African animal with a large head, a wide mouth, and thick gray skin, that lives in and near water [**Origin:** 1500–1600 Latin, Greek, from *hippos* **horse** + *potamos* **river**]

hip·py /ˈhɪpi/ *n.* [C] another spelling of HIPPIE

hip·ster /ˈhɪpstɚ/ *n.* [C] INFORMAL someone who is very HIP

hire¹ /haɪɚ/ S1 W2 *v.* [T] **1** to employ someone to work in a job SYN **employ** OPP **fire**: *The school plans to hire more teachers.* | *The first hurdle for young people is **getting hired**.* | **hire sb as sth** *The restaurant was one of the first to hire women as chefs.* | **hire sb to do sth** *They hired an accounting firm to process the results.* **2** BRITISH to rent something

hire on *phr. v.* to start to work somewhere or for someone: *The firefighters hire on only for the wildfire season.*

hire sb ↔ out *phr. v.* to arrange for someone to work somewhere for a short period of time: **hire yourself out** *They hired themselves out as farm workers.*

hire² *n.* **for-hire** [combined with nouns] done for money or employment: *a sex-for-hire business* | *a local helicopter pilot-for-hire* → see also **murder-for-hire** at MURDER¹ (5)

ˌhired ˈhand *n.* [C] someone who is employed to help on a farm

hire·ling /ˈhaɪɚlɪŋ/ *n.* [C] DISAPPROVING someone who will work for anyone who is willing to pay

Hi·ro·hi·to /ˌhɪroʊˈhitoʊ/ (1901–1989) the EMPEROR of Japan from 1926 to 1989

hir·sute /ˈhɚsut, ˈhɪr-, hɚˈsut/ *adj.* LITERARY having a lot of hair on your body and face

his¹ /ɪz; *strong* hɪz/ S1 W1 *possessive adj.* [possessive form of "he"] **1** belonging to or relating to a man, boy, or male animal that has been mentioned or is known about: *His parents were born in Russia.* | *I think his name is Greg.* **2** OLD-FASHIONED used after singular PRO-

NOUNS such as "everyone," "anyone," "no one," "each" etc. to show the POSSESSIVE: *No one wants his family to be threatened.* **[Origin:** Old English] → see also THEIR

> USAGE **his or their/theirs**
> Some people still use **his** as a singular pronoun or determiner with pronouns like **everyone**, especially in formal writing: *Everyone has his own ideas about what is important.* However, it is more common now to use the plural determiner **their** or the plural pronoun **theirs** instead: *Everyone has their own ideas about what is important.* In formal English, it is best to use "his or her": *Everyone has his or her own ideas about what is important.*

his² S1 W2 *possessive pron.* [possessive form of "he"] **1** the thing or things belonging to or relating to a male person or animal that has been mentioned or is known about: *I think he has my suitcase and I have his.* | *Martin's a friend* ***of his.*** **2** OLD-FASHIONED used after singular PRONOUNS like "everyone," "anyone," "no one," "each" etc. to show the POSSESSIVE: *Everyone just wants what is his by right.* → see also THEIRS

His·pan·ic /hɪˈspænɪk/ *adj.* from or relating to a country where Spanish or Portuguese is spoken **[Origin:** 1500–1600 Latin *hispanicus*, from *Hispania* **Spain]** —**Hispanic** *n.* [C]

hiss /hɪs/ *v.* **1** [I] to make a noise which sounds like "ssss": *The cat hissed and backed away.* **2** [T] to say something quietly but in a way that shows you are angry or that it is important that someone listens to you: *"Are you crazy?" he hissed.* **3** [T +at] to make this noise when you do not like a performer or speaker **[Origin:** 1300–1400 from the sound] —**hiss** *n.* [C]

his·self /ɪˈsɛlf; *strong* hɪˈsɛlf/ *pron.* NONSTANDARD himself

his·ta·mine /ˈhɪstəˌmin/ *n.* [C] BIOLOGY MEDICINE a chemical compound that increases the flow of blood in the body and is involved in ALLERGIC reactions

his·to·gram /ˈhɪstəˌgræm/ *n.* [C] MATH a type of BAR GRAPH in which the area of each bar represents how often a value appears in a set of data

his·to·ri·an /hɪˈstɔriən/ W3 *n.* [C] someone who studies or writes about history: *art historians*

his·tor·ic /hɪˈstɔrɪk, -ˈstɑr-/ W3 *adj.* [usually before noun] **1** a historic event, time, or place is or will be remembered as part of history, because important things happened in that time or place: *a historic building* | *historic developments in Eastern Europe* | *a historic voyage* **2** historic times are the periods of time whose history has been recorded **3** TECHNICAL having happened or existed in the past, used especially in business language: *the historic cost of the item* → see also PREHISTORIC

his·tor·i·cal /hɪˈstɔrɪkəl/ S3 W3 *adj.* [usually before noun] **1** relating to the past: *a historical record* **2** relating to the study of history: *historical research* **3** historical books, movies etc. describe or are based on events in the past: *a historical novel* **4** historical events, facts, people etc. happened or existed in the past: *The legend of John Henry is based on a historical figure.* —**historically** /-kli/ *adv.*

his·to·ry /ˈhɪstəri/ S1 W1 *n. plural* **histories**
1 PAST EVENTS [U] all the things that happened in the past, especially the political, social, or economic development of a nation: *a very interesting period in history* | *Lincoln was one of the greatest U.S. presidents* ***in history.*** | ***Throughout history,*** *most societies have been governed by men.* | *The disaster was the worst* ***in recent history.*** | **human/recorded history** (=all the time since humans have written down facts about themselves) | *a city* ***steeped in history*** (=with a lot of interesting history) | ***History shows that*** *stock prices move higher more frequently than they fall.*
2 SUBJECT OF STUDY [U] the study of history, especially as a subject in school or college: *a history test* | *I have a degree in history.*
3 DEVELOPMENT OF STH [singular, U] the development of a subject, activity, institution etc. since it started: *the history of jazz* | *the first black governor in American history* | *Chernobyl was the worst accident* ***in the history of*** *nuclear power.* | **sth's 75-year/200-year etc. history** *During its 80-year history, the organization has undergone many changes.*
4 SB'S ACTIONS/EXPERIENCES [C,U] all the things that someone has done or experienced: *The doctor will ask for your* ***medical history.*** | **+of** *a man with a history of violence* | *The patient* ***has a history of*** *drug abuse* (=has done it in the past).
5 ACCOUNT [C] a book, article, program etc. about past events: **+of** *a history of World War II*
6 make history to do something important that will be recorded and remembered: *Lindbergh made history when he flew across the Atlantic in 1927.*
7 sb/sth will go down in history (as sth) used to say that something is important enough to be remembered and recorded: *He will go down in history as a great Olympic champion.*
8 sb/sth is history SPOKEN INFORMAL used to say that someone or something has or soon will fail or end: *I knew that if I didn't apologize to my boss, my job was history.*
9 ...and the rest is history used to say that everyone knows the rest of a story you have been telling
10 the history books used to talk about the way something will be remembered: *Charlie Parker's genius earned him* ***a place in the history books.***
11 that's past/ancient history SPOKEN used to say that something is not important anymore
12 history repeats itself used to say that things often happen in the same way as they happened before
[Origin: 1400–1500 Latin *historia*, from Greek, from *histor* **knowing, learned]** → see also NATURAL HISTORY, CASE HISTORY

his·tri·on·ics /ˌhɪstriˈɑnɪks/ *n.* [plural] loud extremely emotional behavior that is intended to get people's sympathy and attention —**histrionic** *adj.*

hit¹ /hɪt/ S1 W1 *v. past tense and past participle* **hit, hitting**
1 STRIKE [I,T] to touch someone or something hard and quickly with your hand, a stick etc.: *I thought she was going to hit me.* | **hit sb with sth** *She was angry at Joe for hitting the dog with a stick.* | **hit sb on the head/on the nose/in the stomach etc.** (=hit a particular part of someone's body)

> THESAURUS
> **strike** FORMAL to hit someone or something very hard: *Suddenly one of the soldiers struck her.*
> **punch** to hit someone hard with your closed hand, especially in a fight: *The other boxer punched him on the shoulder.*
> **slap** to hit someone with the flat part of your hand, especially because you are angry with them: *I felt like slapping his face.*
> **beat** to hit someone or something deliberately many times, or to hit against the surface of something continuously: *He had been robbed and beaten.* | *The wind howled and rain beat against the windows.*
> **beat sb up** to hurt someone badly by hitting them many times: *A bunch of drunks beat him up.*
> **spank** to hit a child on their bottom with your open hand, as a punishment: *Dad spanked me for lying.*
> **smack** to hit someone or something, usually with your open hand: *Rick smacked him in the face.*
> **whack** INFORMAL to hit someone or something very hard: *Edmonds whacked the ball over the fence.*
> **thump** to hit someone or something hard with your closed hand: *Harris thumped him on the back.*
> **knock** to hit a door or window with your closed hand in order to attract the attention of the people inside: *Someone was knocking on the door.*
> **bang** to make a loud noise, especially by hitting something against something hard: *The gate banged shut.*
> **bash** to hit someone or something hard, in a way that causes damage: *The police bashed the door down.*

H

tap to gently hit your fingers or foot against something: *I tapped him on the shoulder.*
pound/hammer to knock very hard, making a lot of noise: *Thomas pounded on the door with his fist.*
rap to knock quickly several times: *Tom rapped the table to get everyone's attention.*

2 CRASH INTO SB/STH [T] to fall or crash into someone or something quickly and hard: *The ball hit the rim and bounced off.* | *When it hit the ground, the plane burst into flames.* | *Our cat **got hit by** a car.*

THESAURUS

bump to hit or knock against something, especially by accident: *He fell and bumped his head.*
collide to crash violently into something or someone: *The two cars almost collided.*
bang to hit a part of your body against something by accident: *I'm always banging my hip on the desk.*
bash to hit someone or something hard, in a way that causes pain: *I bashed my head as I got into the car.*
stub to hit your foot against something and hurt it: *Eddie stubbed his toe on a rock.*

3 ACCIDENTALLY [T] to move a part of your body quickly and hard against something by accident SYN **bang**: *Careful, don't hit your head.* | **hit sth on/against etc.** *I kept hitting my knees against the table.*

H

4 AFFECT BADLY [T] to have a bad effect on someone or something: **be hard/badly/heavily hit** *Florida was hardest hit by the storm.*
5 SUDDENLY AFFECT [I,T] to suddenly start to affect someone or something: *Tiredness suddenly hit me.*
6 IN SPORTS [T] to make something such as a ball move by hitting it with a BAT, stick etc.: *You need to hit the ball harder.*
7 BULLETS/BOMBS [I,T] to attack, wound, or damage someone or something with bullets, bombs etc.: *The building was hit by a bomb.*
8 REACH STH [T] to reach a particular level or number: *The temperature hit 100 degrees today.* | **hit a record high/low** *Oil prices hit a record high last week.* | *The President's approval rating has **hit a new low**.*
9 PROBLEM/TROUBLE [T] to experience trouble, a problem etc.: *I had hit a few snags in my work.*
10 REALIZE [T] INFORMAL if a fact, idea etc. hits you, you suddenly realize its importance and feel surprised or shocked: *The horror of the situation suddenly hit her.* | ***It hit me that** Anita had been right all along.*
11 BECOME AVAILABLE [T] INFORMAL to become available for people to buy, see etc.: *the latest products to hit the market* | *I remember when that song first hit the charts.*
12 ARRIVE [T] INFORMAL to arrive somewhere: *The Bolshoi Opera will hit New York on June 25.*
13 PRESS STH [T] INFORMAL to press a part in a machine, car etc. to make it work: *Hit the brakes!* | *Oops, I hit the wrong button.*

SPOKEN PHRASES

14 DO STH [T] used in some expressions to show that you will do a particular thing: *It's time to hit the shower* (=go wash in one). | *We'll stay up north and hit Mount Rushmore* (=visit it). | *I have to **hit the books*** (=study).
15 sb hit the nail on the head used to say that what someone has said is exactly right
16 hit the spot if a food or drink hits the spot, it tastes good and is exactly what you want: *A cold beer sure would hit the spot.*
17 hit the roof/the ceiling to become extremely angry
18 hit the sack/hay to go to bed

19 hit bottom/rock-bottom INFORMAL to be as unsuccessful or unhappy as you can be: *I had to hit bottom before I decided to kick the drugs.* | *The economy has hit rock-bottom.*
20 not know what hit you INFORMAL to be so surprised or shocked by something that you cannot think clearly
21 hit sb where it hurts also **hit sb where they live** INFORMAL to do something that damages or hurts someone a lot: *She wanted to hit her ex-husband where it hurt – in his wallet.*
22 hit the road INFORMAL to leave a place, especially to start on a trip: *We have to hit the road again in the morning.*
23 hit it off INFORMAL if two people hit it off, they like each other as soon as they meet
24 hit it big also **hit the big time** INFORMAL to suddenly become very famous, successful, and rich: *Di Caprio hit it big in the movie "Titanic."*
25 hit the ground/deck/dirt INFORMAL to fall to the ground to avoid something dangerous
26 hit the ground running to start doing something successfully without any delay: *If we can hit the ground running, we'll stay ahead of the competition.*
27 hit the headlines/news to be reported a lot in the newspapers or on television: *The couple's divorce hit the headlines in May.*
28 hit the jackpot a) to win a lot of money by GAMBLING **b)** INFORMAL to be very lucky or suddenly successful: *He really hit the jackpot when he married Jo.*
29 hit the bottle INFORMAL to drink a lot of alcohol regularly
30 hit a brick wall INFORMAL to suddenly be unable to make any more progress in a situation
[**Origin:** 1000–1100 Old Norse *hitta* **to find, hit**] → see also **hit/strike home** at HOME² (5), **hit pay dirt** at PAY DIRT (1)

hit back *phr. v.* to attack or criticize a person or group that has attacked or criticized you: *The government hit back with two 500-pound bombs.* | **hit back at sb** *He hit back at his critics.*

hit on *phr. v.* **1 hit on sb** INFORMAL to talk to someone in a way that shows you are sexually attracted to them: *He's hit on every woman in the department.* **2 hit on/upon sth** to have a good idea about something, often by chance: *I think we've hit on a solution.* | *Then we **hit on the idea of** marketing it for children.* **3 hit on sth** to discover the facts about a situation, the real reason for something etc.: *I was sure I'd hit on the truth.*

hit out *phr. v.* to criticize someone or something very strongly or angrily: **+at** *It's natural to want to hit out at people who have hurt you.*

hit sb up for sth *phr. v.* SPOKEN to ask someone for something, especially money: *Did he hit you up for cash again?*

hit sb with sth *phr. v.* INFORMAL **1** to make someone experience something that is unpleasant, especially legal trouble: *The company hit us with a lawsuit.* **2** to tell someone something that is unpleasant, surprising, or shocking: *She hit me with the news that she was leaving.*

hit² S3 W3 *n.* [C]
1 SONG/MOVIE/PLAY ETC. something such as a movie, song, play etc. that is extremely popular or successful: *an album of Michael Jackson's **greatest hits*** | **a big/huge/massive/smash hit** *The song became a massive hit.* | **a hit show/record/song** *Irving Berlin wrote dozens of hit songs.* ►see THESAURUS box at **popular**
2 POPULAR to be liked very much by a person or group: **+with** *Since the museum opened, it has been a hit with the kids.*
3 HIT STH an occasion when something that is aimed at something else touches it, reaches it, or damages it: *One bomb scored a **direct hit** on the aircraft carrier.*
4 WEBSITE an occasion when someone uses a website: *Our site had 2,000 hits in the first month.*
5 SEARCH RESULT INFORMAL a result of a computer search on the Internet, a DATABASE etc.: *The question turned up thousands of hits.*
6 BASEBALL an occasion when a baseball player hits the ball and successfully runs to a BASE
7 DRUG SLANG an amount of a drug that you smoke, swallow etc.
8 MURDER SLANG a murder in which someone is paid to kill someone else

9 take a hit INFORMAL if profits, sales etc. take a hit, they become less: *The company's stock took another hit.* → see also HIT MAN

ˌhit-and-ˈmiss also **ˌhit-or-ˈmiss** *adj.* INFORMAL done in a way that gives some successes and some failures: *a hit-and-miss advertising campaign*

ˌhit-and-ˈrun *adj.* [only before noun] **1** a hit-and-run accident is one in which the driver of a car hits a person or another car and does not stop to help **2** a hit-and-run military attack is one in which the attackers arrive suddenly and leave quickly

hitch[1] /hɪtʃ/ *v.* **1** [I,T] INFORMAL to hitchhike: +**across/around/to** *They spent the summer hitching around Europe.* **2 hitch a ride a)** INFORMAL to get a ride from someone by hitchhiking: *We hitched a ride in the back of a pick-up.* **b)** SPOKEN to travel somewhere by asking someone such as a friend if you can go in their car: *I hitched a ride to school with Jamie.* **3** [T always + adv./prep.] to fasten something such as a TRAILER to the back of a car so that it can be pulled **4** [T always + adv./prep.] to tie something to something else, especially to tie a horse to something: **hitch sth to sth** *A few horses were hitched to the fence.* **5 get hitched** OLD-FASHIONED, INFORMAL to get married

hitch sth ↔ **up** *phr. v.* **1** INFORMAL to pull a piece of clothing up, especially your pants **2 hitch up a horse/wagon/team** to tie a horse to something, so that the horse can pull it

hitch[2] *n. plural* **hitches** [C] **1** a small problem that makes something difficult or delays it for a short time: *The ceremony **went off without a hitch**.* ►see THESAURUS box at **problem**[1] **2** a part on a vehicle that is used to connect it to something it is pulling: *a trailer hitch* **3** INFORMAL a period of time you spend in the Army, Navy etc. **4** a type of loosely tied knot

Hitch·cock /ˈhɪtʃkɑk/, **Sir Al·fred** /ˈælfrɪd/ (1899–1980) a British movie DIRECTOR who is famous for his THRILLERS

hitchhike

hitch·hike /ˈhɪtʃhaɪk/ *v.* [I] to travel by standing beside a road and holding out your thumb to ask for free rides from passing cars SYN **hitch** —**hitchhiker** *n.* [C]

hi-tech /ˌhaɪˈtɛk◂/ *adj.* another spelling of HIGH-TECH

hith·er /ˈhɪðɚ/ *adv.* **1** OLD USE here, to this place: **hither and thither/yon** (=here and there) *Fish darted hither and thither.* **2 a come-hither look/voice** a way of looking at someone or saying something that is meant to attract someone

hith·er·to /ˌhɪðɚˈtu, ˈhɪðɚˌtu/ *adv.* FORMAL until this time: ***a hitherto unknown** galaxy*

Hit·ler /ˈhɪtlɚ/, **A·dolf** /ˈeɪdɔlf/ (1889–1945) a German politician who was leader of the Nazi Party in Germany from 1921, and "Führer" (=leader) of Germany from the mid–1930s until his death. Hitler tried to establish a pure race of German people through a policy of ANTI-SEMITISM and started World War II by ordering his armies to enter Poland in 1939.

ˈhit list *n.* [C] INFORMAL the names of people, organizations etc. whom you would like to damage or hurt: *He **was on a** Mafia **hit list**.*

ˈhit man *n.* [C] a criminal who is employed to kill someone

ˈhit paˌrade *n.* OLD-FASHIONED **the hit parade** a list that shows which popular records or songs have sold the most copies

Hit·tite /ˈhɪtaɪt/ one of the people that lived in Turkey and Syria from the 20th century to the 11th century B.C.

HIV *n.* [U] MEDICINE **Human Immunodeficiency Virus** a type of VIRUS that enters the body through the blood or through sexual activity, and can develop into AIDS: **HIV positive/negative** (=having or not having HIV in your body)

hive /haɪv/ *n.* **1** [C] **a)** also **beehive** a place where BEES live **b)** the group of bees that live together in a hive **2 hives** [plural] MEDICINE a condition in which someone's skin swells and becomes red, usually because they are ALLERGIC to something **3 a hive of activity/industry etc.** a place that is full of people who are very busy

hi·ya /ˈhaɪyə/ *interjection* SPOKEN, INFORMAL hello

h'm, hmm /hm, hmh/ *interjection* a sound that you make to express doubt, a pause, or disagreement, or when you are thinking about what someone has said

HMO *n.* [C] **Health Maintenance Organization** a type of health insurance in which members can only go to doctors and hospitals within the organization → see also PPO

hmph /hmf/ *interjection* used especially in writing to represent the sound you make to show that you do not approve of something

H

ho /hoʊ/ *interjection* **1** also **ho ho** or **ho ho ho** used in writing to represent the sound of laughter in a low voice SYN **ha ha** **2 land/westward etc. ho** used to get someone's attention, in order to tell them that you can see land from a ship, that you are leaving to travel westward etc.

hoa·gie /ˈhoʊgi/ *n.* [C] a SUBMARINE SANDWICH

hoard[1] /hɔrd/ also **hoard up** *v.* [T] to collect, save, and sometimes hide large amounts of food, money etc., so you can use it later SYN **stock up**: *People began hoarding canned food.* —**hoarder** *n.* [C]

hoard[2] *n.* [C] a collection of things that someone hides somewhere, especially so that they can use them later SYN **stockpile**: +**of** *a hoard of weapons*

hoar·frost /ˈhɔrfrɔst/ *n.* [U] FROST

hoarse /hɔrs/ *adj.* if you are hoarse, or if your voice is hoarse, your voice sounds rough, often because you have a sore throat SYN **throaty**: *She was hoarse from yelling.* [**Origin:** Old English *has*] —**hoarsely** *adv.* —**hoarseness** *n.* [U]

hoar·y /ˈhɔri/ OLD-FASHIONED *adj.* **1** old, well-known and not very interesting or original: *a hoary old story* **2** gray or white in color, especially through age SYN **grizzled** —**hoariness** *n.* [U]

hoax[1] /hoʊks/ *n.* [C] an attempt to make people believe something that is not true SYN **trick**: *The UFO sightings were a hoax.*

hoax[2] *v.* [T] to trick someone by using a hoax —**hoaxer** *n.* [C]

hob /hɑb/ *n.* OLD-FASHIONED **play hob with sth** to do something that damages or spoils something

Hobbes /hɑbz/, **Thomas** (1588–1679) a British political PHILOSOPHER

hob·ble /ˈhɑbəl/ *v.* **1** [I] to walk with difficulty, taking small steps, usually because you are injured SYN **limp**: *Laurel hobbled into the room on crutches.* ►see THESAURUS box at **walk**[1] **2** [T] if an injury hobbles someone, it makes it difficult for them to walk **3** [T] to make it difficult for a plan, system etc. to work successfully SYN **hinder**: *Mistakes can hobble a deal from the start.* **4** [T] to loosely fasten two of an animal's legs together, to stop it from running away

hob·by /ˈhɑbi/ *n. plural* **hobbies** [C] an activity that you enjoy doing in your free time: *Write about your hobbies and interests.* —**hobbyist** *n.* [C]

hob·by·horse /ˈhɑbiˌhɔrs/ *n.* **1** [C] a child's toy like a horse's head on a stick **2** a subject that someone has strong opinions about and that they talk about too much

hob·gob·lin /ˈhɑbˌgɑblən/ *n.* [C] a GOBLIN that plays tricks on people

hob·nail /ˈhɑbneɪl/ *n.* [C] a large nail with a big flat top, fastened to the bottom part of heavy boots to make them stronger —**hobnailed** *adj.*

hob·nob /ˈhɑbnɑb/ *v.* [I] INFORMAL to spend time talking to people who are in a higher social position than you: +**with** *Benech liked to hobnob with local politicians.* [**Origin:** 1700–1800 *drink hobnob* **to take turns in drinking** (18–19 centuries), from *habnab* **in one way or another**]

ho·bo /ˈhoʊboʊ/ *n. plural* **hobos** [C] someone who travels around and has no home or regular job SYN **tramp**

Hob·son's choice /ˌhɑbsənz ˈtʃɔɪs/ *n.* [U] a situation in which there is only one thing you can do, so that you really have no choice at all [**Origin:** 1600–1700 from Thomas *Hobson* (1554–1631), who rented out horses and would only let his customers take the horse nearest the door]

Ho Chi Minh /ˌhoʊ tʃi ˈmɪn/ (1890–1969) the President of North Vietnam during the first part of the Vietnam War

ˌHo Chi Minh ˈCity a city in the southern part of Vietnam. It was formerly known as Saigon, and was the capital of South Vietnam when the country was divided.

ˌHo Chi Minh ˈTrail, the HISTORY a system of roads that were used to carry soldiers and supplies from North Vietnam to South Vietnam, through Laos and Cambodia, during the Vietnam War

hock¹ /hɑk/ *n.* **1 in hock** INFORMAL **a)** in debt **b)** something that is in hock has been sold temporarily because its owner needs money SYN **pawned** **2** [C] a piece of meat from above the foot of a pig **3** [C] BIOLOGY the middle joint of an animal's back leg

hock² *v.* [T] INFORMAL to sell something temporarily because you need some money SYN **pawn**

hock·ey /ˈhɑki/ *n.* [U] **1** also **ice hockey** a sport played on ice, in which players use long curved sticks to hit a hard flat round object into a GOAL **2** FIELD HOCKEY

hock·shop /ˈhɑkʃɑp/ *n.* [C] INFORMAL a PAWNSHOP

ho·cus-po·cus /ˌhoʊkəs ˈpoʊkəs/ *n.* [U] a word meaning "magic," used about methods or beliefs that you think are tricks or based on false ideas: *financial hocus-pocus*

hod /hɑd/ *n.* [C] a container shaped like a box with a long handle, used for carrying bricks

hodge·podge /ˈhɑdʒpɑdʒ/ *n.* [singular] INFORMAL a lot of things mixed up together in no order SYN **jumble**: +**of** *The album is a hodgepodge of folk, pop, soul, and jazz.*

hoe /hoʊ/ *n.* [C] a garden tool with a long handle, used for making the soil loose and removing WEEDS —**hoe** *v.* [I,T] → see also **a hard/tough row to hoe** at ROW¹ (5)

hoe·down /ˈhoʊdaʊn/ *n.* [C] a party where there is SQUARE DANCING

hog¹ /hɑg, hɔg/ *n.* [C] **1** BIOLOGY a large pig that is kept for its meat → see also BOAR, SOW² **2** INFORMAL someone who eats, keeps, or uses more than their share of something: *Don't be such a hog.* | *He's kind of a ball hog* (=he keeps the ball when he should pass it to someone during a game). **3 go (the) whole hog** INFORMAL to do something thoroughly **4 go hog wild** INFORMAL to suddenly do an activity in an uncontrolled and excited way —**hoggish** *adj.* → ROAD HOG

hog² *v.* **hogged**, **hogging** [T] INFORMAL to keep or use all of something when you should share it: *Mom, Pam's hogging the bathroom again!*

ho·gan /ˈhoʊgən/ *n.* [C] a traditional Navajo house made of branches covered with mud or soil

Ho·gan /ˈhoʊgən/, **Ben** /bɛn/ (1912–1997) a U.S. GOLF player

hogs·head /ˈhɑgzhɛd, ˈhɔgz-/ *n.* [C] a large BARREL

ˈhog-tie *v. past tense and past participle* **hog-tied**, **hog-tying** [T] to tie someone's hands and feet together

hog·wash /ˈhɑgwɑʃ, ˈhɔgwɔʃ/ *n.* [U] talk that you think is full of lies or is wrong SYN **nonsense**

ho ho ho /ˌhoʊ hoʊ ˈhoʊ/ *interjection* used to represent the sound of laughter

ho-hum /ˌhoʊ ˈhʌm/ *adj.* [no comparative] INFORMAL boring and ordinary: *a ho-hum performance*

hoi pol·loi /ˌhɔɪ pəˈlɔɪ/ *n.* **the hoi polloi** an insulting phrase for ordinary people

hoist¹ /hɔɪst/ also **hoist up** *v.* [T] **1** to raise, lift, or pull up something, especially using ropes SYN **raise**: *The crew hoisted the flag.* | *Fathers hoisted sons onto their shoulders.* **2 hoist a glass** to raise a glass of a drink in the air before you drink it to celebrate something **3 be hoisted by your own petard** to be harmed or embarrassed by something that you planned or said yourself

hoist² *n.* **1** [C] a piece of equipment for lifting heavy objects with ropes **2** [C usually singular] a movement that lifts something up to a higher position

hoi·ty-toi·ty /ˌhɔɪṭi ˈtɔɪṭi/ *adj.* OLD-FASHIONED behaving in a proud way, as if you are important

ho·key /ˈhoʊki/ *adj. comparative* **hokier**, *superlative* **hokiest** INFORMAL expressing emotions in a way that is too simple, old-fashioned, or silly: *a hokey song*

ho·kum /ˈhoʊkəm/ *n.* [U] something that seems to be true or impressive but is actually wrong or not sincere

Hol·bein /ˈhoʊlbaɪn/, **Hans** /hɑns/ **1 Hans Holbein the Elder** (1464?–1524) a German PAINTER who painted pictures for churches and was the father of Hans Holbein the Younger **2 Hans Holbein the Younger** (1497–1543) a German PAINTER famous for his pictures of people

hold¹ /hoʊld/ S1 W1 *v. past tense and past participle* **held** /hɛld/

1 IN YOUR HANDS/ARMS [T] to have something firmly in your hand or arms: *Hold my books for a minute, will you?* | **hold sth in your hand/arms** *I held the baby in my arms.* | *Two little girls walked by,* ***holding hands*** (=each other's hands).

THESAURUS

grip to hold something very tightly: *I gripped the rail and tried not to look down.*
clutch to hold something tightly, especially because you do not want to drop it: *She was clutching a letter in her hand.*
keep hold of sth to continue to hold something: *Keep hold of my hand as we cross the street.*
take/get/catch hold of sth to take something in your hands and hold it: *The baby caught hold of her necklace and broke it.*
grasp to take hold of something and hold it tightly: *He leaned forward and grasped my wrist.*
grab (hold of something) also **seize** FORMAL to take hold of someone or something suddenly or violently: *The boy grabbed her purse and ran.*

2 HOLD SB CLOSE [T] to put your arms around someone to comfort them, show you love them etc.: *I just wanted my mother to hold me.* | **hold sb close/tight** *Max held her close and wiped away the tears.* ►see THESAURUS box at **hug¹**

3 MOVE IN YOUR HAND [T always + adv./prep.] to move your hand or something in your hand in a particular direction: **hold sth up/toward/out etc.** *He* ***held out*** *his* ***hand*** *to help her to her feet.* | *Hold up the picture so everyone can see it.*

4 KEEP STH IN POSITION [T always + adv./prep.] to make something stay in a particular position: **hold sth down/up/open etc.** *Martin held the door open for her.* | *She held her hands out to keep from bumping into*

anything. | *Short posts will* **hold** *the rails* **in place.** | *Try to* **hold** *this* **position** *for a count of ten.*
5 HAVE SPACE FOR [T not in progressive] to have the space to contain a particular amount of something: *Each carton holds 113 oranges.* | *The tank should hold enough water to last a few days.*
6 JOB/TITLE [T] to have a particular job or position, an important one: *Less than 4% of top business jobs are held by women.* | *Birnbaum holds a doctorate in physics.* | *The president* **holds office** *for four years.*
7 TITLE/RECORD [T] to have a particular title or record, because you have won a competition, are the best at something etc.: *The program* **holds the record for** *the longest running TV series.* | *He held the world title until he lost to Holyfield.*
8 EVENT [T] to have a meeting, party etc. in a particular place or at a particular time: *The competition is held in Jackson every four years.* | *Classes were held in the auditorium.* | *In April, the President* **held talks with** *Chinese leaders.*
9 OWN STH [T] to own or possess something, especially money, land, a document etc.: *IBM holds shares in the new company.* | *a privately held company*
10 KEEP SB SOMEWHERE [T] to keep a person or animal somewhere, and not allow them to leave SYN **detain**: *Police are holding two men in connection with the shooting.* | *Nobody will be* **held against their will** (=made to stay when they do not want to). | **hold sb hostage/captive** *They were held hostage for four months.* | *The animals are held in large enclosures.*
11 KEEP STH AVAILABLE FOR SB [T] to save a place, room, ticket etc. for someone until the time when they use it SYN **reserve**: *The library will hold the book for you for two weeks.* | **hold a place/reservation/room etc.** *I've asked them to hold a table for twelve people, okay?*
12 SUPPORT STH'S WEIGHT [I,T] to be strong enough to support the weight of something SYN **bear**: *The branch held, and Nick climbed higher.* | *Will the ice* **hold your weight?**
13 KEEP/CONTAIN [T] to keep or contain something so it can be used or gotten later: *Lost items will be held for thirty days.*
14 AMOUNT/LEVEL [I,T] to continue at a particular amount, level, or rate, or to make something do this: *Traders thought gold would hold at $350 an ounce.* | *His approval rating is* **holding steady** *at 53 percent.*
15 hold sb's interest/attention to make someone continue being interested in something: *Storytellers held the children's interest.*
16 OPINION [T not in progressive, usually passive] FORMAL to have a particular opinion or belief: *Experts hold varying opinions as to the cause of the disease.* | **+that** *Buddhism holds that the state of existence is suffering.* | **be widely/generally/commonly held** *They challenged the widely held belief that losing weight improves your health.*
17 COURT [T not in progressive] if a court or judge holds that something is true, they decide that something is true: **be held to be sth** *The law was held to be unconstitutional.* | **hold that** *The judge held that the police had acted illegally.*
18 hold sb responsible/accountable/liable to consider someone to be responsible for something, so that they will be blamed if anything bad happens: **+for** *I can't be held responsible for what Floyd does.*

SPOKEN PHRASES

19 hold it! also **hold everything! a)** used to interrupt someone: *Hold it a minute! I've just had a really good idea.* **b)** used to tell someone to wait or to stop what they are doing: *Hold it! Sara just lost a contact lens.*
20 TELEPHONE [I] also **hold the line** to wait until the person you have telephoned is ready to answer: *Thank you for calling Society Bank – can you hold please?*
21 hold your horses! used to tell someone to wait or to do something more slowly and carefully
22 hold your fire! a military order used to tell soldiers to stop shooting

23 NOT CHANGE [I] to continue to be true, effective, good etc.: *What I said yesterday still holds.* | **hold true/good** *If past experience holds true, about 10% of the injured will need immediate surgery.* | **weather/luck holds (out)** *If our luck holds, we could reach the playoffs.* | *As long as the mild weather holds, you can keep planting.*
24 STOP/NOT INCLUDE [T] to not include something that is usually included, or stop doing something that is usually done: *A roast beef sandwich, please – hold the mayo.*
25 MUSIC [T] to make a musical note continue for a long time
26 ARMY [T] if an army holds a place, it controls it or defends it from attack: *The French army held the town for three days.*
27 hold the lead/advantage to be winning in competition, game etc.: *Johnson held the lead throughout the race.*
28 hold your own to defend yourself, or to succeed, in a difficult situation: *Colman held his own against Miller, one of the league's toughest players.*
29 hold fast to sth FORMAL to keep believing strongly in an idea or principle, or keep doing something in spite of difficulties: *Jackson urged the Democrats to hold fast to their traditions.*
30 be left holding the bag to become responsible for something that someone else has started, whether you want to be or not
31 hold the fort to be responsible for taking care of something, while the person usually responsible is not there: *The three of you will be holding the fort in the kitchen tonight.*
32 THE FUTURE [T] FORMAL if the future holds something, that is what may happen: *Who knows* **what the future holds?** | *Learning computer skills* **holds the promise** *of better jobs.*
33 hold sth dear to feel that something is very important: *Everything I held dear was destroyed in the war.*
34 HAVE A QUALITY [T] FORMAL to have a particular quality: **hold interest/appeal etc.** *The program held little appeal for most children.*
35 not hold water if an argument, statement etc. does not hold water, it is not true or reasonable: *His explanation just didn't hold water.*
36 hold sway to have a lot of influence or power: *Hutton's geographical theories held sway for many years.*
37 hold a conversation to have a conversation
38 hold your head up/high to show pride or confidence in a difficult situation: *I can hold my head high because I know that I am innocent.*
39 not hold a candle to sb/sth INFORMAL to be much worse than someone or something else: *Dry herbs don't hold a candle to fresh ones.*
40 hold all the cards to have a strong advantage in a situation where people are arguing or competing: *Politically, the logging industry holds all the cards.*
41 hold the road if a car holds the road well, you can drive it quickly around bends without losing control
42 can hold your alcohol/liquor to be able to drink a lot of alcohol without becoming drunk
43 there's no holding sb (back) used to say that someone is so determined to do something that you cannot prevent them from doing it: *For Casey, there was no holding back when it came to music.*
44 hold a course if an aircraft, ship, storm etc. holds a course, it continues to move in a particular direction
[**Origin:** Old English *healdan*] → see also **hold your breath** at BREATH (2), **hold court** at COURT[1] (5), **hold a grudge** at GRUDGE[1] (1), **hold your tongue** at TONGUE[1] (9)

hold sth **against** sb *phr. v.* to continue to dislike someone or not forgive them because of something bad they have done in the past: *He had been awful to her, but she didn't seem to hold it against him.*

hold back *phr. v.* **1 hold sb/sth ↔ back** to make someone or something stop moving forward: *Police in riot gear held back the demonstrators.* **2 hold sth ↔ back** to stop yourself from feeling or showing a particular emotion: *Nancy tried to* **hold back the tears.** | *They don't hold anything back when they're* *on stage.* **3 hold sb/sth ↔ back** to prevent someone or something from developing or improving: *The housing market is being held back by a weak economy.* **4 hold sb/sth ↔ back** to be slow or unwilling to do something, especially because you are being careful, or to make someone unwilling to do something: *Trading was light as many investors held back.* | *She wanted to tell him but pride held her back.* **5 hold sth ↔ back** to keep something secret SYN **withhold**: *He held back important information about his background.*

hold sb/sth **down** *phr. v.* **1 hold sb/sth ↔ back** to make someone or something stay in a position, and stop them moving away: *The edges of the tipis are held down by rocks.* | *It took three police officers to hold him down.* **2 hold sth ↔ down** to prevent the level of something such as prices from rising: *Employees are asked to help hold down costs.* **3 hold down a job** to succeed in keeping a job for a period of time: *Clarke holds down two jobs to support his family.* **4 hold sb ↔ down** to keep people under control or limit their freedom: *The treaty is meant to help people, not hold them down.*

hold forth *phr. v.* give your opinion on a subject, especially for a long time: **+on** *The speaker was holding forth on the collapse of modern society.*

hold off *phr. v.* **1 hold sth ↔ off** to delay something: **hold off (on) doing sth** *Businesses are holding off on hiring new employees.* **2 hold sb ↔ off** to prevent someone who is trying to attack you or defeat you from succeeding: *The Pittsburgh Pirates held off New York 10–8.* **3 hold sb ↔ off** to prevent someone from coming toward you or succeeding in speaking to you: *There's a crowd of reporters outside – I'll try to hold them off.* **4** if rain or snow holds off, none of it falls, although you thought it would

hold on *phr. v.* **1 hold on!** SPOKEN **a)** said when you want someone to wait or stop talking for a short time, for example during a telephone call: *Could you hold on, please, while I transfer you.* | ***Hold on a minute.*** *Let me put this in the car.* **b)** used when you have just noticed something surprising: *Hold on, who's that in the picture?* **2** to hold something tightly with your hand or arms: *Okay,* ***hold on tight!*** | **+to** *She can walk now without holding on to anything.* **3** to continue doing something when it is very difficult to do so: *How long will good teachers like her hold on?*

hold on to sb/sth *phr. v.* to keep something or someone, so that they do not leave, get lost, be sold, or get taken away: *Can you hold on to those tickets for me?* | *Schools must try to hold on to all students until graduation.*

hold out *phr. v.* **1** if something such as a supply of something holds out, there is still some left: *We stayed as long as the wine held out.* **2** to continue to defend a place that is being attacked: *For ten weeks the troops have held out against mortar attacks.* **3** to try to prevent yourself from doing something that someone is trying to force you to do: **+against** *I didn't know if I could hold out against their questioning.* **4 hold sth ↔ out** to think or say that something is possible or likely to happen, especially something good: **not hold out much hope/hold out little hope** *Authorities held out little hope of finding more survivors.* | **hold out the prospect/promise of sth** *The treatment holds out the promise of improved health.*

hold out for sth *phr. v.* to not accept anything less than what you have asked for: *Some house sellers are still holding out for higher offers.*

hold out on sb *phr. v.* INFORMAL to refuse to give someone information or an answer that they need: *Why didn't you tell me right away instead of holding out on me?*

hold over *phr. v.* **1 be held over** if a play, movie, concert etc. is held over, it is shown for longer than planned, because it is very popular **2 hold sth over sb** to threaten to do something to someone if they do not do something you want: *The company gives money to schools without* ***holding*** *anything* ***over their heads*** (=without making them promise to do anything in particular). **3 hold sth over** to do or deal with something at a later date: *The House committee plans to hold the bill over until next week.* → see also HOLDOVER

hold sb **to** sth *phr. v.* **1** to make someone do what they have promised: *"I'll ask him tomorrow." "All right, but I'm going to hold you to that."* **2** to prevent your opponent in a sports game from getting more than a particular number of points: *Louisiana Tech held the Cougars to a 3–3 tie in the first quarter.*

hold together *phr. v.* **1 hold sth together** if a group or organization holds together or you hold it together, it stays strong and does not break apart: **hold sth together** *It's love that holds this family together.* **2** to remain whole, without breaking or separating, or to make sth do this: *Stir in milk just until the dough holds together.* | **hold sth together** *Strong ropes held the raft together.*

hold up *phr. v.* **1 hold sb/sth ↔ up** to support someone or something and stop them from falling down: *The roof is held up by huge stone pillars.* **2 hold sb/sth ↔ up** to delay someone or something: *The cotton harvest has been held up by rain.* | *Sorry I'm late – I was held up at work.* **3 hold up sth** to rob or try to rob a place while using a weapon SYN **rob** SYN **stick up**: *Preston held up a jewelry store downtown.* → see also HOLDUP **4** to remain strong or in good condition: *I'm surprised by how well this car has held up.*

hold sb/sth **up as** sth *phr. v.* to use someone or something as an example: *The school has been* ***held up as a model*** *for others.*

hold² S1 W3 *n.*

1 ACTION OF HOLDING STH [singular] the action of holding something tightly with your hands SYN **grasp**: *Kara* ***tightened*** *her* ***hold*** *on the bat.* | **have/keep hold of sth** *Keep hold of my hand when we cross the road.* | **grab/seize/catch hold of sth** (=start holding something quickly and firmly) *Grab hold of the rope and pull yourself up.* | *I* ***took hold of*** (=started holding) *her hand and gently led her away.* → see also GRIP¹ (1)

2 get (a) hold of sb SPOKEN to manage to speak to someone for a particular reason: *Four-thirty would be the best time to get a hold of me.*

3 get (a) hold of sth SPOKEN to find or borrow something: *I need to get hold of a car.* | *She got hold of a copy before it was published.*

4 on hold a) if someone is on hold, they are waiting to talk to someone on the telephone: *Do you mind if I* ***put you on hold****?* **b)** if something is on hold, it is going to be done or dealt with at a later date rather than now: *The deal is on hold while lawyers look into it.* | *She has* ***put*** *her career* ***on hold*** *to help her husband campaign for president.*

5 CONTROL/POWER [singular] control, power, or influence over something or someone: *Yeltsin's hold over the Russian parliament became weaker.* | **get/keep (a) hold on/of sth** *He struggled to get hold of his emotions.* | *I keep a* ***tight hold*** *on our finances.* | *The book has always* ***had*** *a curious* ***hold over*** *me.*

6 take hold to start to have an effect: *The fever was beginning to take hold.*

7 get hold of an idea/impression/story etc. INFORMAL to learn or begin to believe something: *Where on earth did you get hold of that idea?*

8 SPORTS/FIGHT [C] a particular position that you hold an opponent in, in a fight or in a sport such as WRESTLING or JUDO

9 CLIMBING [C] somewhere you can put your hands or feet when you are climbing: *The cliff is steep and it's difficult to find a hold.*

10 SHIP [C] the part of a ship below the DECK where goods are stored

11 no holds barred used to say that there are no rules or limits in a situation: *It seems there are no holds barred when it comes to making a profit.*

hold·er /ˈhoʊldɚ/ *n.* [C] **1** someone who possesses or controls something: *credit card holders* | *the world-*

H

record holder **2** something that holds or contains something else: *a cigarette holder* | *candle holders*

hold·ing /ˈhoʊldɪŋ/ *n.* [C] ECONOMICS something that you own or rent, especially land or STOCK in a company: **land/property/stock etc. holdings** *companies with large property holdings*

ˈholding ˌcompany *n.* [C] ECONOMICS a company that controls part or all of the SHARES in another company

ˈholding ˌpattern *n.* [C usually singular] **1** the path that an aircraft follows as it flies over a place while it is waiting for permission to go down to the ground **2** a situation in which you cannot do anything more until you know the results of someone else's decision or action: *Her career has been* ***in a holding pattern****.*

hold·o·ver /ˈhoʊldˌoʊvɚ/ *n.* [C] a feeling, idea, fashion etc. from the past that has continued into the present: **+from** *Abe looks like a holdover from the 1960s.* → see also **hold over** at HOLD[1]

hold·up /ˈhoʊldʌp/ *n.* [C] **1** INFORMAL an attempt to rob a person or place, using a weapon SYN **stickup** SYN **robbery**: *a supermarket holdup* **2** INFORMAL a delay: *What's the holdup?* → see also **hold up** at HOLD[1]

hole[1] /hoʊl/ S2 W2 *n.* [C]

1 SPACE IN STH SOLID an empty space in something that should be solid or whole: **+in** *There were huge holes in the road.* | *He was* ***digging a hole*** *for the fence post.*

THESAURUS

space an empty area between two things, into which you can put something: *a space on the bookshelf*
gap an empty area between two things or two parts of something: *the gap between his two front teeth*
leak a small hole that lets liquid or gas flow into or out of something: *a leak in the pipe*
crack a very narrow space between two things or two parts of something: *the cracks in the ceiling*
crater a round hole in the ground made by a large object hitting it hard or by an explosion: *the craters of the moon*

Make a hole in something
pierce to make a small hole in or through something, using a pointed object: *An arrow pierced his shield.*
prick to make a small hole in the surface of something, using a pointed object: *The nurse pricked my finger to get a drop of blood.*
punch to make a hole in something using a metal tool or other sharp object: *He punched a hole in the bottom of the bucket.*
drill to make a hole using a special tool, often one which has a spinning part that makes the hole: *The dentist drilled a hole in my tooth to make it ready for the filling.*
bore to make a deep round hole in or through something hard: *Huge drills bored a hole eight feet into the rock.*

2 SPACE STH CAN GO THROUGH a space in something solid that allows light or things to pass through: *These socks are* ***full of holes****.* | **+in** *a bullet hole in the wall*
3 ANIMAL'S HOME the home of a small animal: *a rabbit hole*
4 WEAK PART a part of an idea, plan, story etc. that is weak or wrong: *Levitt concluded that the article was* ***full of holes****.*
5 be in the hole SPOKEN to owe money: *We're already $140 in the hole.*
6 be in a hole INFORMAL to be in a difficult situation: *By halftime, the team was deep in a hole.*
7 UNPLEASANT PLACE INFORMAL a place for living in, working in etc. that is dirty, small, or in bad condition: *I have to get out of this hole.*
8 GOLF a) a hole in the ground that you try to get the ball into in the game of GOLF **b)** one part of a GOLF COURSE with this kind of hole at one end: *the ninth hole*
9 EMPTY PLACE a place where someone or something should be, but is missing: **+in** *The Regents have a big hole in center field.*
10 hole in one an occasion when you hit the ball in GOLF from the starting place into the hole with only one hit
11 I need sth like a hole in the head SPOKEN used to say that you definitely do not need or want something: *I need a new girlfriend like I need a hole in the head.*
12 make a hole in sth INFORMAL to use a large part of an amount of money, food etc.: *The house repairs made a big hole in my savings.*
[**Origin:** Old English *hol*] → see also BLACK HOLE, WATERING HOLE, **a square peg in a round hole** at SQUARE[1] (11)

hole[2] *v.* **1 be holed** if an aircraft or ship is holed, it has a hole in it **2** [T] also **hole out** to hit the ball into the hole in GOLF

hole up *phr. v.* INFORMAL to hide or stay somewhere for a period of time: **+at/in** *Nine Cuban refugees were holed up in the embassy.*

ˌhole in the ˈheart *n.* [singular, U] a medical condition in which the two sides of someone's heart are not correctly separated

ˌhole-in-the-ˈwall *n.* [C] INFORMAL a small dark store or restaurant

hol·i·day /ˈhɑləˌdeɪ/ S2 W3 *n. plural* **holidays** [C] **1** a day set by law on which people do not have to go to work or school: *July 1 is a* ***national holiday*** *in Canada.* | *Martin Luther King Day was made into a* ***federal holiday****.* | **a Jewish/religious/Hindu etc. holiday** *Rosh Hashanah is a Jewish holiday.* ►see THESAURUS box at **vacation[1]** **2 the holiday season** also **the holidays** the period of time between Thanksgiving and New Year's Day in the U.S.: *Sales were up during the holiday season.* | *We'll get together after the holidays.* **3** BRITISH a VACATION [**Origin:** Old English *haligdæg* **holy day**]

Hol·i·day /ˈhɑləˌdeɪ/, **Bil·lie** /ˈbɪli/ (1915–1959) a JAZZ and BLUES singer, who is considered one of the greatest jazz and blues singers ever

Billie Holiday

ˌholier-than-ˈthou *adj.* DISAPPROVING showing that you think you are morally better than other people SYN **self-righteous**: *a holier-than-thou attitude*

ho·li·ness /ˈhoʊlinɪs/ *n.* **1** [U] the quality of being pure and good in a religious way SYN **sanctity** **2 Your/His Holiness** used as a title for talking to or about the Pope

ho·lis·tic /hoʊˈlɪstɪk/ *adj.* **1** considering a person or thing as a whole, rather than as separate parts: *a* ***holistic approach*** *to education* **2 holistic medicine/therapy/health etc.** medical treatment based on the belief that the whole person must be treated, not just the part of their body that has a disease —**holistically** /-kli/ *adv.*

Hol·land /ˈhɑlənd/ another name for the Netherlands

hol·lan·daise sauce /ˌhɑlənˈdeɪz ˌsɔs/ *n.* [U] a creamy SAUCE made of butter, eggs, and LEMON

hol·ler /ˈhɑlɚ/ *v.* [I,T] INFORMAL to shout loudly SYN **yell**: *If you need anything, just holler.* | **+at** *Hollering at me isn't going to find us a parking place.* ►see THESAURUS box at **shout[1]** —**holler** *n.* [C]

hol·low[1] /ˈhɑloʊ/ *adj.* **1** having an empty space inside: *The walls are made of hollow concrete blocks.* | *a hollow tree* ►see THESAURUS box at **empty[1]** **2** words, events, or people that are hollow have no real worth or value, or are not sincere: *hollow threats* | *They won, but so easily it was a* ***hollow victory****.* | *His promises had a* ***hollow ring*** (=they seemed not to be sincere). **3 hollow eyes/cheeks etc.** eyes, cheeks etc. where the skin sinks in: *prisoners of war with hollow cheeks* **4** a

H

sound that is hollow is low and clear like the sound made when you hit something empty: *He hit the ground with a hollow thump.* **5** if someone feels hollow, they feel very sad and as if nothing is important **6 hollow laugh/voice etc.** a hollow laugh or voice is one that makes a weak sound and is without emotion [**Origin:** Old English *holh* **hole, hollow place**] —**hollowly** *adv.* —**hollowness** *n.* [U]

hollow² *n.* **1** a place in something that is at a slightly lower level than its surface SYN **dip**: *Make a hollow in each cupcake and fill with jam.* **2** a small valley in an area of mountains

hollow³ *v.*

hollow sth ↔ **out** *phr. v.* to make a hole or empty space by removing the inside part of something: *The water had hollowed out caves and tunnels.*

hol·ly /ˈhɑli/ *n.* [U] a small tree with sharp dark green leaves and red berries (BERRY), or the leaves and berries of this tree used as a decoration at Christmas

Hol·ly /ˈhɑli/, **Bud·dy** /ˈbʌdi/ (1936–1959) a U.S. singer, GUITAR player, and SONGWRITER who helped to make ROCK 'N' ROLL music popular in the 1950s

hol·ly·hock /ˈhɑliˌhɑk/ *n.* [C] a tall thin garden plant with many flowers growing together

Hol·ly·wood /ˈhɑliˌwʊd/ a part of Los Angeles, California, where movies are made, often used to mean the movie industry itself: *Beatty is wise and wary about his position in Hollywood.*

H

Holmes /hoʊmz, hoʊlmz/, **Ol·i·ver Wen·dell¹** /ˈɑləvɚ ˈwɛndl/ (1809–1894) a U.S. doctor and writer

Holmes, Oliver Wendell² (1841–1935) a judge on the U.S. Supreme Court

hol·o·caust /ˈhɑləˌkɔst, ˈhoʊ-/ *n.* [C] **1** an event that kills many people and destroys many things: *a nuclear holocaust* **2 the Holocaust** the killing of millions of Jews and other people by the Nazis in World War II [**Origin:** 1200–1300 Old French *holocauste*, from Greek *holokaustos* **burnt whole**]

hol·o·gram /ˈhoʊləˌgræm, ˈhɑ-/ *n.* [C] a type of photograph made with a LASER, that looks as if it is not flat when you look at it from an angle —**holographic** /ˌhoʊləˈgræfɪk, ˌhɑ-/ *adj.* —**holography** /hoʊˈlɑgrəfi/ *n.* [U]

Holst /hoʊlst/, **Gus·tav** /ˈgʊstɑv/ (1874–1934) a British composer who wrote CLASSICAL music

Hol·stein /ˈhoʊlstin, -staɪn/ *n.* [C] a type of cow that is black and white

hol·ster /ˈhoʊlstɚ/ *n.* [C] a leather object in which a gun is carried, that is worn on a belt

ho·ly /ˈhoʊli/ S3 W3 *adj. comparative* **holier**, *superlative* **holiest** **1** relating to God and religion SYN **sacred**: *the holy city of Jerusalem* | *The Koran is the Islamic holy book.* ►see THESAURUS box at **religion** **2** very religious: *a holy man* **3 holy cow/mackerel/moly etc.** SPOKEN used to express surprise, admiration, or fear **4 a holy terror** INFORMAL a child who causes a lot trouble, especially because they are very active [**Origin:** Old English *halig*] → see also **take (holy) orders** at ORDER¹ (18)

ˌHoly ˈBible *n.* [singular] the BIBLE

ˌHoly ˈFamily *n.* **the Holy Family** Jesus Christ, his mother Mary, and her husband Joseph

ˌHoly ˈFather *n.* [singular] a phrase used when speaking to or about the Pope

ˌHoly ˈGhost *n.* [singular] the HOLY SPIRIT

holy grail /ˌhoʊli ˈgreɪl/ *n.* [singular] **1** something that you try very hard to get or achieve: *A vaccine for malaria has become something of a scientific holy grail.* **2 the Holy Grail** the cup believed to have been used by Jesus Christ before his death. In stories, especially stories about King Arthur, people search for this cup

ˈHoly ˌLand *n.* **the Holy Land** the parts of the Middle East where most of the events mentioned in the Bible happened

ˌholy of ˈholies *n.* **1** HUMOROUS a special place where only a few people are allowed to go **2 the holy of holies** the most holy part of a Jewish TEMPLE

ˌholy ˈroller *n.* [C] an insulting word for a member of a PENTECOSTAL church, whose ceremonies include a lot of singing, shouting, and clapping

ˌHoly ˈSee *n.* FORMAL **the Holy See** the authority the Pope has, and everything he is responsible for

ˌHoly ˈSpirit *n.* **the Holy Spirit** God in the form of a spirit, according to the Christian religion SYN **Holy Ghost**

ˈholy ˌwar *n.* [C] a war that is fought to defend the beliefs of a religion

ˌholy ˈwater *n.* [U] water that has been BLESSED by a priest

ˈHoly Week *n.* [singular] the week before Easter in the Christian Church

ˌHoly ˈWrit *n.* [U] **1** OLD-FASHIONED the Bible, considered as a book that is true in every detail **2** writing or instructions that people treat as if it were completely true in every detail: *Freudian theory was then holy writ.*

hom·age /ˈhɑmɪdʒ, ˈɑ-/ *n.* [U] FORMAL something that you say or do to show respect for a person or thing that you think is important: *Memorial Day is when Americans **pay homage** to those killed in the nation's wars.* [**Origin:** 1200–1300 Old French *hommage*, from *homme* **man, man who owes duty to a ruler**]

hom·bre /ˈɑmbreɪ/ *n.* [C] INFORMAL a man, especially one who is strong [**Origin:** 1800–1900 a Spanish word meaning **man**]

hom·burg /ˈhɑmbɚg/ *n.* [C] a soft hat for men, with a wide edge around it

home¹ /hoʊm/ S1 W1 *n.*

1 PLACE WHERE YOU LIVE [C,U] the house, apartment, or place where you live: *The park isn't far from our home.* | *I was **at home** watching TV.* | *Birds had **made their home** under the roof.* | **work from home/at home** *Many companies are now allowing employees to work from home.*

THESAURUS

place INFORMAL the house, apartment, or room where someone lives: *We went to Sara's place after the movie.*
residence FORMAL the place where you live: *a private residence*
house the house, apartment, or room where someone lives: *Let's go over to Dave's house.*

2 FAMILY [C,U] the place where a child and his or her family live: *I think she still **lives at home**.* | *He **left home** at 18.* | *Are you **going home** for Christmas?* | *It was the first time I'd ever been **away from home**.*

3 WHERE YOU LIVED/BELONG [C,U] the place where you lived as a child or where you usually live, especially when this is the place where you feel happy and comfortable: *She was born in Italy, but she's **made** Charleston her **home**.* | *My friends **back home** won't believe I've done this.*

4 IN YOUR COUNTRY the country where you live, as opposed to foreign countries: *Our country has plenty of problems **here at home**.* | *a speech aimed at the voters **back home***

5 be/feel at home a) to feel happy or confident about doing or using something: **+with/in** *I feel more at home in blue jeans than in a suit.* | *He is **equally at home** directing theater and opera.* **b)** to feel comfortable in a place or with a person: **+in** *I'm already feeling at home in the new apartment.* | *Helen always **makes people feel at home*** (=makes people feel comfortable by being friendly).

6 PROPERTY [C] a house, apartment etc., considered as property that you can buy or sell: *new homes for sale*

7 FOR TAKING CARE OF SB [C] a place where people who are very old or sick are taken care of, or where children who have no family are taken care of: *a children's home* | *I never wanted to put my mother in a home.* → see also NURSING HOME

8 make yourself at home SPOKEN used to tell someone

who is visiting you that they should relax: *Sit down and make yourselves at home.*
9 be the home of sth a) to be the place where something was first made, discovered, or developed: *America is the home of baseball.* **b)** to be the place where a person, animal, or plant lives
10 be home to sth a) to be the place where a person, animal, or plant lives: *Paris was home to many important artists.* **b)** to be the place where something is or where something typically happens: *North Carolina is home to the Green River Narrows.*
11 SPORTS TEAM at home if a sports team plays at home, it plays at its own sports field OPP **away**: *The Jets lost 6–3 at home to New England.*
12 GAMES/SPORTS a place in some games or sports which a player must try to reach in order to win a point or be safe from the opposing players → see also HOME PLATE
13 home away from home a place that you think is as pleasant and comfortable as your own house: *For many people, the office has become a home away from home.*
14 home sweet home used to say that you think it is very pleasant to be in your home
[**Origin:** Old English *ham* **village, home**] → see also HOME RUN

home² S1 W1 *adv.* **1** to or at the place where you live: *Is Sue home from work yet?* | *Joe had to* ***go home*** *early.* | *You should* ***stay home*** *until you're feeling better.* | **come/get home** (=arrive at your home) *What time did you get home?* | **bring/take sb/sth home** *I brought him home to meet my parents.* **2 take home $1,000 a week/month etc.** to earn a certain amount of money after tax has been taken off: *Diane takes home about $340 a week.* **3 hit/drive/hammer sth home a)** to make sure that someone understands something by saying it in an extremely direct and determined way: *an ad that drives the anti-drug message home* **b)** to hit or push something firmly into the correct position **4 bring sth home to sb** also **come home to sb** to make you realize how serious, difficult, or dangerous something is: *The pictures brought home the suffering in Sudan.* **5 hit/strike home** if a comment, situation, experience etc. hits or strikes home, it makes someone realize how serious, difficult, or dangerous something is: *The news of his death didn't really hit home until later.* **6 be home free** INFORMAL to have succeeded in doing the most difficult part of something: *He's lost a lot of weight, but he's not home free yet.* → see also **hit/strike close to home** at CLOSE³ (6), **nothing to write home about** at WRITE (10)

home³ *adj.* [only before noun] **1** done at home or intended for use in a home: *Mom's* ***home cooking*** (=food that is cooked at home) | *a home computer* **2** relating to or belonging to your home or family: **home address/number** (=the address at your house or the telephone number there) | *children who have a happy* ***home life*** → see also HOMETOWN **3** played or playing at a team's own sports field, rather than an opponent's field: *a home game* | *The* ***home team*** *took an early lead.* **4** relating to a particular country, as opposed to foreign countries SYN **domestic**: *the home market*

home⁴ *v.*
home in on (sth) *phr. v.* **1** to aim exactly at something and move directly toward it: *Sharks home in on the blood.* **2** to direct your efforts or attention to one particular thing: *The FBI is homing in on a large drug ring.*

ˈhome base *n.* **1** [C usually singular] the place that someone returns to in order to rest, learn new things, or exchange information: *the astronauts' home base at Johnson Space Center* **2** [C usually singular] a company's HEADQUARTERS **3** [U] HOME PLATE

home·bod·y /ˈhoʊmˌbɑdi/ *n. plural* **homebodies** [C] someone who enjoys being at home

home·boy /ˈhoʊmbɔɪ/ *n. plural* **homeboys** [C] SLANG a male HOMEY

ˌhome ˈbrew *n.* [U] beer made at home —**home brewed** *adj.*

home·com·ing /ˈhoʊmˌkʌmɪŋ/ *n.* **1** [C] an occasion when someone comes back to their home after a long absence **2** [C,U] a special occasion every year when former students return to their high school or college: **homecoming game/dance** (=special sports game or dance that happens at homecoming) **3 homecoming king/queen** a boy and girl who are chosen by other students to represent them at homecoming events

ˌhome-court adˈvantage also **ˌhome-field adˈvantage** *n.* [singular, U] an advantage that a sports team has because it is playing a game on its own sports field or court

ˌhome ecoˈnomics *n.* [U] the study of cooking, SEWING, and other skills used in the home, taught as a subject at school

ˈhome fries *n.* [plural] boiled potatoes that have been cut and fried in butter or oil

ˌhome ˈfront *n.* [singular] the people who stay and work in their own country while others go abroad to fight in a war: *The President also praised the families* ***on the home front.***

home·grown /ˌhoʊmˈgroʊn◂/ *adj.* **1** born, made, or produced in your own country, town etc.: *homegrown entertainment* **2** vegetables and fruit that are homegrown are grown in your own garden

home·land /ˈhoʊmlænd/ *n.* [C] **1** the country where someone was born **2** an area of land that is given to a group of people so that they can live in it: *the creation of a Jewish homeland*

home·less /ˈhoʊmlɪs/ *adj.* **1 the homeless** people who do not have a place to live, and who often live on the streets **2** without a home: *Recent floods have* ***left*** *thousands* ***homeless.*** —**homelessness** *n.* [U]

home·ly /ˈhoʊmli/ *adj. comparative* **homelier**, *superlative* **homeliest** **1** a homely person is not very attractive SYN **plain** **2** simple and ordinary: *a homely tune*

home·made /ˌhoʊmˈmeɪd◂/ *adj.* made at home rather than bought in a store: *homemade ice cream*

home·mak·er /ˈhoʊmˌmeɪkɚ/ *n.* [C] APPROVING a woman who works at home cleaning, cooking etc. and does not have another job SYN **housewife**

ˌhome ˈmovie *n.* [C] a movie you make, often of a family occasion, that is intended to be shown at home SYN **home video**

ˌhome ˈoffice *n.* [C] a room in your house that is organized so that you can do your job at home

ho·me·op·a·thy /ˌhoʊmiˈɑpəθi/ *n.* [U] a system of medicine in which a disease is treated by giving extremely small amounts of a substance that causes the disease —**homeopathic** /ˌhoʊmiəˈpæθɪk/ *adj.* —**homeopath** /ˈhoʊmiəˌpæθ/ *n.* [U]

ho·me·o·sta·sis /ˌhoʊmioʊˈsteɪsɪs/ *n.* [U] BIOLOGY the process in which a living ORGANISM or cell stays in the same state even when its environment changes

home·own·er /ˈhoʊmˌoʊnɚ/ *n.* [C] someone who owns their house

ˈhome page, homepage *n.* [C] the place on a WEBSITE that appears first when you connect to it, that tells you how to find the information you want on that WEBSITE

ˈhome plate *n.* [singular] the place where you stand to hit the ball in baseball, which is also the last place the player who is running must touch in order to get a point → see picture at BASEBALL

hom·er /ˈhoʊmɚ/ *n.* [C] INFORMAL a HOME RUN —**homer** *v.* [I]

Ho·mer /ˈhoʊmɚ/ a Greek poet who probably lived between 800 and 700 B.C. He is known for his two EPIC poems, the ILLIAD and the ODYSSEY which have had great influence on European literature —**Homeric** /hoʊˈmerɪk/ *adj.*

Homer, Wins·low /ˈwɪnzloʊ/ (1836–1910) a U.S. painter, known especially for his paintings of the sea and people connected with the sea

ˈhome room *n.* [C] a CLASSROOM where students go at the beginning of every school day, or at the beginning

H

of each SEMESTER, to get information that is given to all students

ˌhome ˈrule *n.* [U] POLITICS the right of the people in a country to control their own government and laws, after previously being controlled by another country

ˌhome ˈrun *n.* [C] a long hit in baseball that lets the player who hit the ball run around all the bases and get a point

ˈhome-school *v.* [I,T] to teach children at home instead of sending them to school —**home-school** *adj.* [only before noun] *home-school programs* —**home schooling** *n.* [U]

ˌhome ˈshopping ˌnetwork *n.* [singular] a television company that shows products that you can order and buy by telephone

home·sick /ˈhoʊmˌsɪk/ *adj.* feeling unhappy because you are a long way from your home: **+for** *Do you ever get homesick for Japan?* —**homesickness** *n.* [U]

home·spun /ˈhoʊmspʌn/ *adj.* **1** homespun ideas are simple and ordinary **2** homespun cloth is woven at home

home·stead¹ /ˈhoʊmstɛd/ *n.* [C] **1** a farm and the area of land around it **2** a piece of land, usually for farming, that was given to people by the U.S. government under the Homestead Act or by the Canadian government under the Dominion Lands Act

homestead² *v.* [I,T] to live and work on a homestead: *The McLeods homesteaded along the river in 1858.* —**homesteader** *n.* [C]

ˈHomestead ˌAct, the HISTORY a U.S. law passed in 1862 that gave 160 ACRES of land in the western U.S. to people who met certain conditions

ˌhome ˈstretch *n.* **a) the home stretch** the last part of a race where horses, runners etc. go straight to the finish **b)** the last part of an activity or trip: *New York's mayoral campaign hits the home stretch this week.*

home·town, home town /ˈhoʊmtaʊn/ *n.* [C] the place where you were born and lived when you were a child: *the hometown newspaper* | *He returned to his hometown of Cody, Wyoming.*

ˈhome ˌvisit *n.* [C] an occasion when a nurse, doctor etc. comes to see you at your home when you are sick —**home visitor** *n.* [C]

home·ward /ˈhoʊmwɚd/ *adv.* **1** toward home: *Frances made her way homeward.* **2 homeward bound** LITERARY traveling or going toward home —**homeward** *adj.*: *the homeward journey* OPP outward

home·work /ˈhoʊmwɚk/ S3 *n.* [U] **1** work for school that a student does at home → see also CLASSWORK: *She **did** her **homework** after dinner.* | **math/English/biology etc. homework** *My dad helped me with my math homework.* ►see THESAURUS box at school¹ **2** if you do your homework, you prepare for an important activity by finding out information you need SYN research: ***Do your homework** and look at the company's record before investing.*

home·y¹ /ˈhoʊmi/ *adj.* pleasant, like home: *We stayed at a homey bed and breakfast inn.*

homey² *n. plural* **homeys** [C] SLANG a friend, or someone who comes from your area or GANG

hom·i·ci·dal /ˌhɑməˈsaɪdl◂, ˌhoʊ-/ *adj.* likely to murder someone

hom·i·cide /ˈhɑməˌsaɪd/ *n.* **1** [C,U] the crime of murder ►see THESAURUS box at crime **2** [U] the police department that deals with murders [**Origin:** 1200–1300 French, Latin *homicidium*, from *homo* **man** + *caedere* **to kill**]

hom·i·ly /ˈhɑməli/ *n. plural* **homilies** [C] FORMAL **1** a short speech given as part of a Christian church ceremony → see also SERMON **2** advice about how to behave that is often unwanted

hom·ing /ˈhoʊmɪŋ/ *adj.* a bird or animal that has a homing instinct has a special ability that helps it find its way home over long distances

ˈhoming deˌvice *n.* [C usually singular] a special part of a weapon that helps it to find the place that it is aimed at

ˈhoming ˌpigeon *n.* [C] a PIGEON that is able to find its way home over long distances

hom·i·nid /ˈhɑmənɪd, ˈhoʊ-/ *n.* [C] BIOLOGY member of a group of animals which includes humans and also the animals from whom humans developed

hom·i·ny /ˈhɑməni/ *n.* [U] a food made from crushed dried corn [**Origin:** 1600–1700 Virginia Algonquian *uskatahomen*]

homo- /hoʊmoʊ, -mə, hɑmə/ *prefix* FORMAL OR TECHNICAL the same as something else: *homosexual* (=attracted to someone of the same sex) | *homographs* (=words spelled the same way)

ho·mo·ge·ne·ous /ˌhoʊməˈdʒiniəs, -nyəs/, **ho·mo·ge·nous** /həˈmɑdʒənəs/ *adj.* consisting of people or things that are all of the same kind: *an ethnically homogeneous country* → see also HETEROGENEOUS —**homogeneously** *adv.*

homoˌgeneous ˈmixture *n.* [C] CHEMISTRY a chemical substance consisting of two or more different substances that have completely combined together, so that all parts of the mixture look the same SYN solution → see also HETEROGENEOUS MIXTURE

ho·mo·ge·nize /həˈmɑdʒəˌnaɪz/ *v.* [T] to change something so that its parts become similar or the same: *American towns are being homogenized by malls and fast-food restaurants.*

hoˌmogenized ˈmilk *n.* [U] milk that has had the cream mixed with the milk

hom·o·graph /ˈhɑməɡræf, ˈhoʊ-/ *n.* [C] ENG. LANG. ARTS a word that is spelled the same as another, but is different in meaning, origin, grammar, or pronunciation. For example, the noun "record" is a homograph of the verb "record."

ho·mol·o·gous /həˈmɑləɡəs/ *adj.* **1** BIOLOGY relating to two CHROMOSOMES that have the same form and structure: *a pair of homologous chromosomes situated together during meiosis* **2** BIOLOGY relating to parts of a person's or animal's body which EVOLVED (=developed) from the same animal, and which now look different or have a different purpose: *A seal's flipper is homologous with the human arm, even though they look very different.*

hoˌmologous ˈseries *n.* [C] CHEMISTRY a group of compounds with related chemical qualities because of shared FUNCTIONAL GROUPS (=chemical structures), in which there is a regular increase in the MOLECULAR structure from each compound in the series to the next

hoˌmologous ˈstructure *n.* [C] BIOLOGY a part of a person's or animal's body which has EVOLVED (=developed) from the same animal, and which now looks different or has a different purpose

ˈhomo milk *n.* [U] CANADIAN INFORMAL another word for WHOLE MILK

hom·o·nym /ˈhɑməˌnɪm/ *n.* [C] ENG. LANG. ARTS a word that is spelled the same and sounds the same as another, but is different in meaning or origin. For example, the noun "bear" and the verb "bear" are homonyms.

ho·mo·pho·bi·a /ˌhoʊməˈfoʊbiə/ *n.* [U] hatred and fear of HOMOSEXUALS —**homophobic** *adj.*

hom·o·phone /ˈhɑməˌfoʊn, ˈhoʊ-/ *n.* [C] ENG. LANG. ARTS a word that sounds the same as another but is different in spelling, meaning, or origin. For example, the verb "knew" and the adjective "new" are homophones.

Ho·mo sa·pi·ens /ˌhoʊmoʊ ˈseɪpiənz/ *n.* [U] the type of human being that exists now

ho·mo·sex·u·al /ˌhoʊməˈsɛkʃuəl/ *adj.* if someone, especially a man, is homosexual, they are sexually attracted to people of the same sex SYN gay SYN lesbian: *a homosexual relationship* | *Her brother is homosexual.* —**homosexual** *n.* [C] —**homosexuality** /ˌhoʊməˌsɛkʃuˈælət̬i/ *n.* [U] → see also BISEXUAL

ho·mo·zy·gous /ˌhoʊmoʊˈzaɪɡəs/ *adj.* BIOLOGY relating to a homologous CHROMOSOME which contains a pair of GENES which are exactly the same → see also HETEROZYGOUS

Hon. **1** the written abbreviation of HONORABLE **2** the written abbreviation of HONORARY, used in official job titles

hon /hʌn/ *pron.* SPOKEN a short form of HONEY, used to address someone you love: *I'm sorry, hon.*

hon·cho /ˈhɑntʃoʊ/ *n.* [C] INFORMAL an important person who controls something, especially a business: *The* ***head honchos*** *are in Tokyo this week.* [**Origin:** 1900–2000 Japanese *hancho* **group leader**]

Hon·du·ras /hɑnˈdʊrəs/ a country in Central America, north of Nicaragua —**Honduran** *n., adj.*

hone /hoʊn/ *v.* [T] **1** to improve your skill at doing something, especially when you are already good at it: *He* ***honed*** *his legal* ***skills*** *as a public defender.* | ***finely honed*** *surgical techniques* **2** to make knives, swords etc. sharp SYN **sharpen** [**Origin:** 1800–1900 *hone* **stone for making things sharp** (14–19 centuries), from Old English *hon* **stone**]

hon·est /ˈɑnɪst/ S2 *adj.*
1 CHARACTER someone who is honest does not lie, cheat, or steal OPP **dishonest**: *a fair and honest businessman* | *She has an honest face.*
2 STATEMENT/ANSWER not hiding the truth or the facts about something SYN **candid**: *an honest answer* | *Do you want my honest opinion?* | *Shannon, tell me the* ***honest truth.*** | **+about** *She always been honest about her drug problems.* | **+with** *Well, at least I was honest with him.* | ***To be honest,*** *I didn't like him very much.* | ***Let's be honest;*** *he did it and he should be punished.*

THESAURUS

frank honest and direct in the way that you speak: *To be frank, I don't like him very much.*
candid telling the truth, even when the truth may be unpleasant or embarrassing: *We had a good, candid discussion.*
upfront telling the truth, even when the truth might be unpleasant or embarrassing: *Parents need to be upfront about the risks of drugs and alcohol.*
direct saying exactly what you mean in an honest and clear way: *direct criticism*
straightforward honest and not hiding what you think: *He seems like a straightforward guy.*
blunt speaking in an honest way even if it upsets people: *Jensen was blunt: "This isn't going to work."*
forthright saying honestly what you think, in a way that may seem rude: *She gave me a forthright reply.*
open not trying to hide any facts from other people: *People have become more open about their feelings.*
outspoken expressing your opinions or criticism honestly and directly, usually in public or in newspapers, on television, etc.: *an outspoken critic of the government*

3 honest mistake a mistake that you make without intending to deceive or harm anyone
4 ORDINARY/GOOD PEOPLE honest people are not famous or special, but behave in a good and socially acceptable way SYN **decent** SYN **respectable**: *They were good, honest, hard-working people.*
5 WORK honest work is done without cheating, using your own efforts: *People look down on garbage collectors, but it's honest work.* | *They made an honest effort to help her.* | *I'm just trying to* ***make an honest living.***
6 make an honest woman (out) of sb OLD-FASHIONED to marry a woman because she is going to have a baby
7 honest! SPOKEN used to try to make someone believe you: *I didn't mean to hurt him, honest!*
8 honest to God SPOKEN used to emphasize that something you say is really true: *Honest to God, I wasn't there.*
[**Origin:** 1200–1300 Old French *honeste*, from Latin *honestus*]

hon·est·ly /ˈɑnɪstli/ S3 *adv.* **1** in an honest way SYN **truthfully**: *Please answer the questions honestly.* | *He talked honestly about his drug addiction.* **2** SPOKEN used to try to make someone believe you: *It wasn't me, honestly!* **3** SPOKEN used to emphasize that what you are saying is true, even though it may seem surprising: *I honestly don't know where my dad was born.* **4** SPOKEN used when you are surprised or annoyed, or to emphasize that you are shocked that something could be true: *Oh honestly! I don't know why I even bother.*

ˌhonest-to-ˈgoodness also **ˌhonest-to-ˈGod** *adj.* [only before noun] exactly the way something is meant to be SYN **genuine**

hon·es·ty /ˈɑnəsti/ *n.* [U] **1** the quality of being honest OPP **dishonesty**: *He has a reputation for honesty and decency.* **2** the quality of being what you appear to be, so that you say what you think, show what you feel etc.: *"There's such an honesty about kids," says Eastin.* | *the honesty of the song's lyrics* **3 in all honesty** SPOKEN used to tell someone that what you are saying is what you really think: *In all honesty, it didn't go very well.*

hon·ey /ˈhʌni/ S1 *n.* [U] **1** a sweet sticky substance produced by BEES, used as food **2** also **honey bun/bunch** SPOKEN used to talk to someone you love: *Hi, honey, how was your day?* [**Origin:** Old English *hunig*]

hon·ey·bee /ˈhʌnibi/ *n.* [C] a BEE that makes honey

hon·ey·comb /ˈhʌniˌkoʊm/ *n.* [C] **1** BIOLOGY a structure made by BEES, which consists of many six-sided cells in which honey is stored **2** something that is arranged or shaped in this pattern

hon·ey·combed /ˈhʌniˌkoʊmd/ *adj.* [not before noun] filled with many holes, hollow passages etc.

hon·ey·dew mel·on /ˈhʌnidu ˌmɛlən/ *n.* [C] a type of MELON with sweet green flesh

hon·eyed /ˈhʌnid/ *adj.* **1** honeyed words or honeyed voices sound soft and pleasant, but are often insincere **2** tasting like HONEY, or covered in honey

hon·ey·moon¹ /ˈhʌniˌmun/ *n.* [C] **1** a vacation taken by two people who have just been married: *We went to Italy* ***on our honeymoon.*** | *the hotel's honeymoon suite* ►see THESAURUS box at **wedding** **2** also **honeymoon period** the period of time when a new government, leader etc. has just started and no one criticizes them: *The mayor's* ***honeymoon is over.*** [**Origin:** 1500–1600 *honey* + *moon*; because the moon appears to get smaller, like the love of some newly married people]

honeymoon² *v.* [I always + adv./prep.] to go somewhere for your honeymoon —**honeymooner** *n.* [C]

hon·ey·suck·le /ˈhʌniˌsʌkəl/ *n.* [C] a climbing plant with nice-smelling yellow or pink flowers

Hong Kong /ˌhɑŋ ˈkɑŋ◂ / an area on the south coast of China, consisting of several islands and a small part of the Chinese MAINLAND which is part of China but has its own government and financial system

Ho·ni·a·ra /ˌhoʊniˈɑrə/ the capital city of the Solomon Islands

honk¹ /hɑŋk, hɔŋk/ *n.* **1** a loud noise made by a car horn **2** a loud noise made by a GOOSE

honk² *v.* [I,T] if a car horn or a GOOSE honks, it makes a loud noise

honk·ing /ˈhɑŋkɪŋ, ˈhɔŋ-/ *adj.* SPOKEN used to emphasize that something is very large

hon·ky-tonk¹ /ˈhɑŋki tɑŋk/ *n.* [C] a cheap bar where COUNTRY MUSIC is played

honky-tonk² *adj.* [only before a noun] **1 honky-tonk music/piano** a type of piano music which is played in a loud cheerful way **2** cheap, brightly colored, and not good quality

Hon·o·lu·lu /ˌhɑnəˈlulu/ the capital and largest city of the U.S. state of Hawaii

hon·or¹ /ˈɑnɚ/ S3 W3 *n.*
1 RESPECT [U] the respect that someone or something receives from other people: **national/family/personal etc. honor** *a matter of national honor* | *His trophies hold a* ***place of honor*** *on the mantelpiece.*
2 STH THAT MAKES YOU PROUD [singular] FORMAL some-

thing that makes you feel very proud: *It is a **great honor**, something I never expected.* | **have the honor of doing sth** *I had the honor of meeting Mrs. Edelman.* | **be an honor to do sth** *It's an honor to serve your country.* | **do sb the honor of doing sth** *Sylvia has done me the honor of agreeing to be my wife.* | *I will always **count it an honor** to be his friend.*
3 MORAL PRINCIPLES [U] strong moral beliefs and standards of behavior that make people respect and trust you: *a soldier's honor* | *They were criminals, but with a **code of honor*** (=rules about how to behave). | *I know Bob to be a **man of honor**.*
4 in honor of sb/sth a) in order to show how much you admire and respect someone: *The building is named in honor of the basketball coach.* | *Beth is giving a party in his honor.* **b)** to celebrate an event: *An oak tree was planted **in honor of the occasion**.*
5 GIVEN TO SB [C] something that is given to someone to show them that people respect and admire what they have done: *He's won many honors.* | *She won a Nobel Prize, literature's **highest honor**.*
6 Your/His/Her Honor used when speaking to or about a judge
7 be an honor to sb/sth to bring admiration and respect to your country, school, family etc. because of your behavior or achievements: *They are an honor to their parents.*
8 with honors if you finish high school or college with honors, you get one of the highest grades
9 with full military honors if someone is buried with full military honors, there is a military ceremony at their funeral
10 be/feel honor bound to feel that it is your moral duty to do something: *We felt honor bound to attend their wedding.*
11 do the honors SPOKEN to pour the drinks, serve food etc. at a social occasion: *Deborah, would you do the honors?*
12 on your/my honor a) if you swear on your honor to do something, you promise very seriously to do it **b)** OLD-FASHIONED if you are on your honor to do something, you are being trusted to do it
13 your word of honor a very serious promise that what you are saying is true, or that you will do what you say: *I **gave** him my **word of honor** that I would find some way to help.*
14 SEX [U] OLD USE if a woman loses her honor, she has sex with a man she is not married to → see also **guest of honor** at GUEST[1] (1), MAID OF HONOR

honor² W3 *v.* **1 be/feel honored (to do sth)** to feel very proud and pleased: *I am **deeply honored** to be chosen.* **2** [T] FORMAL to show publicly that someone is respected and admired, especially by praising them or giving them a special title: *We remember and honor our fallen soldiers.* | **honor sb with sth** *He was honored with an award for excellence in teaching.* | **honor sb for sth** *Two firefighters have been honored for their courage.* **3 honor a contract/agreement /request etc.** to do what you have agreed to do: *We have honored the family's request to keep the details confidential.* **4** [T] to treat someone with special respect: *They treated me like an **honored guest**.* **5 honor a check/coupon/card etc.** to accept something besides CASH as payment **6 sb has decided to honor us with their presence** SPOKEN, HUMOROUS said when someone arrives late, or to someone who rarely comes to a meeting, class etc. → see also TIME-HONORED

Hon·or·a·ble /ˈɑnərəbəl/ *adj.* used when writing to or about a judge or an important person in the government: *The Honorable James A. Baker*

hon·or·a·ble /ˈɑnərəbəl/ *adj.* **1** behaving in a way that is morally correct and shows you have high moral standards: *Dunne was an honorable and conscientious public servant.* **2** an honorable action or activity deserves respect and admiration: *Military service is an honorable career choice.* **3** an honorable agreement is fair to everyone who is involved in it

ˌhonorable ˈdischarge *n.* [C] if you leave the Army with an honorable discharge, your behavior and work have been very good

ˌhonorable ˈmention *n.* [C] a special honor in a competition, for work that was of high quality but did not get a prize

hon·o·rar·i·um /ˌɑnəˈrɛriəm/ *n.* [C] FORMAL a sum of money offered to a professional for a piece of advice, a speech etc.

hon·or·ar·y /ˈɑnəˌrɛri/ *adj.* [no comparative] **1** an honorary title, rank, or college degree is given to someone as an honor, although the person did not earn the title etc. in the usual way **2** an honorary position in an organization is held without receiving any payment **3** an honorary member of a group is treated like a member of that group but does not belong to it

hon·or·if·ic /ˌɑnəˈrɪfɪk/ *n.* [C] an expression or title that is used to show respect for the person you are speaking to —**honorific** *adj.*

ˈhonor roll *n.* [C] a list of the best students in a school or college

ˈhonor ˌsystem *n.* [C] an agreement between members of a group to obey rules, although no one checks to make sure they are being followed: *Ticket buying is on the honor system.*

hon·our /ˈɑnɚ/ *n., v.* the British and Canadian spelling of HONOR

hooch, hootch /hutʃ/ *n.* [U] strong alcohol, especially alcohol that has been made illegally [**Origin:** 1800–1900 *hoochinoo* **alcoholic drink made by the Hoochinoo people of Alaska** (19–20 centuries)]

hood /hʊd/ *n.* [C]
1 CAR the metal covering over the engine on a car: *I opened up the hood to check the oil.* | *Dan got out to take a look **under the hood**.* → see picture on page A36
2 COVER FOR HEAD a) a part of a coat, SWEATSHIRT etc. that you can pull up to cover your head: *Sanders put his hood up against the cold.* **b)** a cover that goes over someone's face and head, used especially to prevent them from being recognized: *A black hood covered Gilbert's face.*
3 NEIGHBORHOOD [usually singular] also **'hood** SLANG a NEIGHBORHOOD: *Most of our relatives still live **in the hood**.*
4 EQUIPMENT a) a piece of equipment with a FAN that is used above a STOVE to remove the smell of cooking from the kitchen **b)** an enclosed area in a scientific LABORATORY with a FAN that removes dangerous gases from the room
5 CRIMINAL INFORMAL a hoodlum: *A group of hoods mugged a woman on Park Avenue in the middle of the afternoon.*
[**Origin:** (1, 2) Old English *hod*]

-hood /hʊd/ *suffix* [in nouns] **1** used to show a period of time or a state: *a happy childhood* (=time when you were a child) | *parenthood* (=state of being a parent) **2** the people who belong to a particular group: *the priesthood* (=all people who are priests)

Hood, Mount /hʊd/ a mountain in the Cascade Range that is the highest mountain in the U.S. state of Oregon

hood·ed /ˈhʊdɪd/ *adj.* having or wearing a hood: *a hooded sweatshirt*

hood·lum /ˈhudləm, ˈhʊd-/ *n.* [C] a criminal, often a young person, who does violent or illegal things [**Origin:** 1800–1900 German dialect *hudellump* **lazy useless person**]

hoo·doo /ˈhudu/ *n.* [U] a type of VOODOO (=magic)

hood·wink /ˈhʊdˌwɪŋk/ *v.* [T] to trick someone so that you can get an advantage for yourself SYN **cheat** [**Origin:** 1600–1700 *hoodwink* **to cover the eyes with a hood** (16–19 centuries), from *hood* + *wink*]

hoo·ey /ˈhui/ *n.* [U] SPOKEN stupid or untrue talk SYN **nonsense**

hoof¹ /hʊf, huf/ *n. plural* **hoofs** or **hooves** /hʊvz, huvz/ [C] the hard foot of an animal such as a horse, cow etc. → see picture at DEER

hoof² *v.* **1 hoof it** SPOKEN to run or walk, especially quickly **2** [I] INFORMAL to dance, especially in the theater as a job

hoof·er /ˈhʊfɚ/ *n.* [C] INFORMAL a dancer, especially one who works in the theater

hoo-ha /ˈhu hɑ/ *n.* [U] INFORMAL noisy talk or excitement that seems too much for the thing it is about: *election day hoo-ha*

hook¹ /hʊk/ S3 *n.* [C]
1 FOR HANGING THINGS a curved piece of metal or plastic that you use for hanging things on: *The helmet hung from a hook by the door.* | *a coat hook*
2 FISH a curved piece of thin metal with a sharp point for catching fish: *a fish hook*
3 let/get sb off the hook to allow someone or help someone to get out of a difficult situation: *I didn't want to let her off the hook too easily.*
4 leave/take the phone off the hook to leave or take the telephone RECEIVER (=the part you speak into) off the part where it is usually placed so that no one can call you
5 be ringing off the hook if your telephone is ringing off the hook, a lot of people are calling you
6 WAY OF HITTING SB a way of hitting your opponent with your elbow bent in BOXING: *a left hook*
7 by hook or by crook if you are going to do something by hook or by crook, you are determined to do it in whatever way works SYN **somehow or other**: *The police are going to get these guys, by hook or by crook.*
8 STH TO GET ATTENTION something that is attractive and gets people's attention and interest: *You have to find a hook to sell a new show.*
9 TUNE a part of the tune in a song that makes it very easy to remember
10 BALL a way of hitting or throwing a ball so that it moves in a curve, or an occasion when a ball is hit or thrown in this way
11 get your hooks into sb to succeed in taking control of someone, especially by deceiving them
12 hook, line, and sinker if someone believes something hook, line, and sinker, they believe a lie completely
[**Origin:** Old English *hoc*]

hook² S2 *v.*
1 FISH [T] to catch a fish with a hook: *I hooked a trout.*
2 FASTEN [T always + adv./prep.] to attach or hang something onto something else: *Only one strap of his overalls was hooked.* | **hook sth on/onto sth** *Buckets were hooked on long poles.*
3 INTEREST/ATTRACT [T] INFORMAL to succeed in making someone interested in something or attracted to something: *ads designed to hook teenagers*
4 ELECTRONIC EQUIPMENT [T always + adv./prep.] also **hook up** to connect a piece of electronic equipment to another piece of equipment or to an electricity supply: *The new TV isn't hooked up yet.* | **hook sth together** *All the computers in the office are hooked together.*
5 BEND YOUR FINGER/ARM ETC. [T always + adv./prep.] to bend your finger, arm, or leg, especially so that you can pull or hold something else: **hook sth in/around/through sth** *Morris hooked his thumbs in his belt.*
6 BALL [I,T] to throw or kick a ball so that it moves in a curve, or to move or curve in this way
7 RUG [T] to make a RUG or decoration using short pieces of YARN that are pulled with a special tool through a type of material with wide holes

hook up *phr. v.* **1** SLANG to start having a sexual relationship with someone **2** SPOKEN to meet someone and become friendly with them: *We first hooked up when we were playing high school basketball.* **3** INFORMAL to agree to work together with another person or organization for a particular purpose: **+with** *Poet Levine hooked up with artist Terry Allen to produce the work.* **4 hook sb ↔ up with sb/sth** to help someone meet someone or help them get something they need or want: *A friend helped hook her up with a specialist in the disease.*

hook·ah /ˈhʊkə/ *n.* [C] a pipe for smoking tobacco or drugs, that consists of a long tube and a container of water

ˌhook and ˈeye *n.* [U] a small metal hook and ring used for fastening clothes → see picture at FASTENER

ˌhook-and-ˈladder truck *n.* [C] a FIRE ENGINE with long LADDERS attached to it

hooked /hʊkt/ *adj.* **1** curved out or shaped like a hook: *a hooked nose* **2** [not before noun] INFORMAL if you are hooked on a drug, you feel a strong need for it and you cannot stop taking it SYN **addicted**: **+on** *Jane got **hooked** on cocaine.* **3** [not before noun] INFORMAL if you are hooked on something, you enjoy it very much and you want to do it as often as possible: **+on** *I saw the first show, and **got hooked** on it.*

hook·er /ˈhʊkɚ/ *n.* [C] INFORMAL a PROSTITUTE

Hooke's law /ˌhʊks ˈlɔ/ PHYSICS the scientific statement that the amount that an ELASTIC material stretches, is pressed, etc. relates directly to the amount of force that is used

ˌhook-ˈnosed *adj.* having a large nose that curves out in the middle

hook·up /ˈhʊkʌp/ *n.* [C] a temporary connection between two pieces of equipment such as computers, or between a piece of equipment and an electricity or water supply: *trailer hookups at the campsite*

hook·y /ˈhʊki/ *n.* OLD-FASHIONED **play hooky** to stay away from school without permission

hoo·li·gan /ˈhulɪgən/ *n.* [C] a noisy violent person who causes trouble by fighting, shouting etc. —**hooliganism** *n.* [U]

hoop /hup/ *n.* [C] **1** a circular piece of wood, metal, plastic etc.: *an embroidery hoop* **2 jump/go through hoops** to have to do a lot of difficult things that someone makes you do as part of a process: *We had to jump through a lot of hoops in order to get the play on stage.* **3** the ring that you have to throw the ball through to score points in basketball SYN **rim** **4 hoops** [plural] the game of basketball: *Tom's at the park **shooting hoops*** (=playing basketball). **5** an EARRING that is shaped like a ring **6** a large ring that CIRCUS animals are made to jump through, or that children used to play with in the past **7** one of the circular bands of metal or wood around a BARREL **8 hoop skirt/dress** an old-fashioned skirt or dress with a long full bottom part that is supported by metal rings → see also HULA-HOOP

hoop·la /ˈhuplɑ, ˈhʊp-/ *n.* [U] INFORMAL excitement about something that attracts a lot of public attention: *The new casino opened amid much hoopla.*

hoo·ray /hʊˈreɪ/ *interjection* shouted when you are very glad about something —**hooray** *n.* [C] → see also **hip, hip, hooray** at HIP³

hoose·gow /ˈhusgaʊ/ *n.* [C usually singular] HUMOROUS a prison

hoot¹ /hut/ *n.* [C] **1** a shout or laugh that shows you think something is funny or stupid: *Leary's speech drew hoots from the crowd.* **2 not give a hoot** also **not give two hoots** SPOKEN to not care or be interested in something: **+about** *She doesn't give a hoot about what her mother thinks.* **3 be a hoot** SPOKEN to be very funny or amusing: *I thought the movie was a hoot.* **4 not be worth a hoot** SPOKEN to be completely worthless or useless **5** the sound that an OWL makes **6** a short clear sound made by a boat or ship, as a warning

hoot² *v.* **1** [I,T] to laugh loudly because you think something is funny or stupid **2** [I] if an OWL hoots, it makes a long "oo" sound **3** [I,T] if a boat or ship hoots, it makes a loud clear noise as a warning

hoot·en·an·ny /ˈhutˀnˌæni/ *n. plural* **hootenannies** [C] an event at which musicians play FOLK MUSIC or COUNTRY MUSIC, and the people listening often sing with them or dance to the music

Hoo·ver /ˈhuvɚ/, **Her·bert** /ˈhɚbɚt/ (1874–1964) the 31st President of the U.S.

Hoover, J. Ed·gar /dʒeɪ ˈɛdgɚ/ (1895–1972) the director of the FBI from 1924 until his death

ˌHoover ˈDam, the a DAM on the Colorado River on

H

the border between the U.S. states of Arizona and Nevada

Hoo·ver·ville /ˈhuvɚˌvɪl/ *n.* [C] HISTORY a group of simple buildings or tents where unemployed people and people without homes lived during the Depression

hooves /hʊvz, huvz/ *n.* the plural of HOOF

hop¹ /hɑp/ *v.* **hopped, hopping** **1** [I] to move by jumping on one foot or by making short quick jumps on both feet: *Lorna hopped over to a bench to put on her shoes.* ►see THESAURUS box at **jump¹** **2** [I always + adv./prep.] INFORMAL to move into, onto, or out of something suddenly, especially a vehicle: **+in/out/on etc.** *Hop in – I'll give you a ride.* **3 hop a plane/bus/train etc.** INFORMAL to get on an airplane, bus, train etc., especially after suddenly deciding to do so: *Wilson hopped a plane and arrived in time for the auction.* **4** [I] if a bird, an insect, or a small animal hops, it moves by making quick short jumps **5 hop to it!** SPOKEN used to order someone to do something immediately **6 be hopping** INFORMAL very busy with a lot of activity going on: *The street was hopping with jazz musicians and tourists.* **7 hopping mad** INFORMAL very angry [**Origin:** Old English *hoppian*]

hop² *n.* **1** [C] a short jump: *The bird took another hop toward Kyle's outstretched hand.* **2** [C] a single short trip, especially by airplane: *It's just a short hop from Cleveland to Detroit.* **3 a) hops** [plural, U] parts of dried flowers used in making beer, which give the beer a bitter taste **b)** [C] the tall plant on which these flowers grow **4 a hop, skip, and a jump** INFORMAL a very short distance: *My place is just a hop, skip, and a jump from here.* **5** [C] an occasion when a ball falls on the ground, goes back into the air, and then falls again a short distance away **6** [C] OLD-FASHIONED a social event at which people dance → see also HIP-HOP

hope¹ /hoʊp/ [S1] [W1] *v.* [I,T] **1** to want something to happen or be true, and to believe it is possible: **hope (that)** *I hope everything is okay.* | *Jo was hoping that Jamal would come tonight.* | **hope to do sth** *Allison is hoping to be a high-school teacher.* | **+for** *We were hoping for good weather.* | *At this point, we'll just have to* ***hope for the best*** (=hope that things end well when a lot may go wrong). | *Daniel waited all day,* ***hoping against hope*** (=hoping for something that is unlikely to happen) *that Annie would change her mind.*

SPOKEN PHRASES

2 I hope so used to say that you hope something that has been mentioned happens or is true: *"So you're going to the Amazon?" "I hope so."* **3 I hope not** used to say that you hope something that has been mentioned does not happen or is not true: *"Is it going to rain tomorrow?" "I hope not."* **4 I hope (that) a)** used when you want to be polite and make sure that you are not interrupting, bothering, or offending someone: *I hope you don't mind if Kathy comes too.* **b)** used with negative statements to show that you do not like what someone is doing or thinking of doing: *That's not my beer you're drinking, I hope.* **5 let's hope (that)** used to tell someone that you hope something will happen or will not happen: *Let's hope he checks his voice mail.* **6 I hope to God (that)** used to say that you hope very much that something will happen or will not happen, because of the serious problems that could happen: *I just hope to God there aren't any problems.* **7 I should hope so/not** used to say that you feel very strongly that something should or should not happen: *They're good quality." "I should hope so, at that price!"*

[**Origin:** Old English *hopian*]

hope² [S3] [W2] *n.*
1 FEELING [C usually plural, U] a feeling or belief that something you want is likely to happen: **+for** *The people were full of hope for the future.* | **give/bring/offer hope to sb** *This new treatment offers hope to thousands of cancer patients.* | **give up/lose hope** *During all his time in prison, he never gave up hope.* | *We will keep searching* ***in the hope that*** *a miracle might happen.* | *Frustrated fans found* ***a glimmer of hope*** (=a little hope) *in the team's new quarterback.* | *He* ***held out*** *little* ***hope*** (=had very little hope) *that the decision would be reversed.* | *The search for survivors continues, but* ***hopes are fading*** (=people are losing hope) *fast.*
2 STH YOU HOPE FOR [C] something that you hope will happen: *Your donation can fulfill the* ***hopes and dreams*** *of a child this Christmas.* | **hopes of doing sth** *I moved to the city with hopes of finding a job.* | **sb's/the hope is to do sth** *Our hope is to resolve the dispute in a friendly way.* | ***The hope is that*** *audiences will come back to the theater.* | *Tina had* ***high hopes*** (=hopes that something will be successful) *for her team at the beginning of the season.*
3 get/build sb's hopes up to make what someone wants seem more likely to happen, or to feel that your hopes are more likely to happen: *Libby, don't get your hopes up, because you may not get the job.*
4 be sb's last/only hope to be someone's last or only chance of getting the result they want: *A bone marrow transplant is Marta's only hope for survival.*
5 CHANCE [C,U] a chance of succeeding or of something good happening [SYN] **chance**: **+of** *There was little hope of getting home before dark.* | **hope that** *Is there any hope that the patient will recover?* | *Joe* ***has no hope of*** *getting into Yale.*
6 sb's best/brightest/greatest etc. hope a person someone believes has a chance of succeeding and achieving something good for them: *the U.S. best Olympic hopes*
7 hope springs eternal LITERARY used to say that people will always hope that things will get better, even after something bad has happened
8 be beyond hope (of sth) if a situation is beyond hope, it is so bad that there is no chance of any improvement: *Some of the houses were beyond hope of repair.* → see also **dash (sb's) hopes/dreams** at DASH¹ (2), **pin your hopes on sb/sth** at PIN²

ˈhope chest *n.* [C] a large wooden box containing things needed to start a new home, such as SILVERWARE and bed sheets, which young women used to collect before getting married

hope·ful¹ /ˈhoʊpfəl/ *adj.* **1** believing that what you hope for is likely to happen [SYN] **optimistic**: **hopeful (that)** *We remain hopeful that her health will continue to improve.* | **+about** *Louise is hopeful about the future.* **2** making you feel that what you hope for is likely to happen: *The poll result is a hopeful sign that attitudes are changing.* | *a hopeful smile* —**hopefulness** *n.* [U]

hopeful² *n.* [C] someone who is hoping to be successful, especially in politics, sports etc.: *a presidential hopeful*

hope·ful·ly /ˈhoʊpfəli/ [S1] *adv.* **1** [sentence adverb] SPOKEN a word used when you are saying what you hope will happen, which some people consider incorrect: *Hopefully, I'll be home by nine tonight.* | *We're hopefully going to keep practicing once a month.* **2** in a way that shows that you are hopeful: *"But," Tim added hopefully, "there's always tomorrow."*

hope·less /ˈhoʊp-lɪs/ *adj.* **1** a hopeless situation is so bad that there is no chance of success or improvement: *Helen's condition appeared hopeless.* | ***It's hopeless*** *– I'm the only one who's really interested in getting anything done.* **2** INFORMAL very bad at doing something: *Doug was hopeless at waiting tables.* **3** feeling or showing no hope: *I had this hopeless feeling as I approached the hospital.* **4** used to say that someone's bad or foolish behavior cannot be changed: *I'm just a hopeless romantic, I guess.* **5 a hopeless case** someone who cannot be helped: *Doctors can now help people who were once considered hopeless cases.* —**hopelessness** *n.* [U]

hope·less·ly /ˈhoʊp-lɪsli/ *adv.* **1** used when emphasizing how bad a situation is, and saying that it will not get better: *We're hopelessly behind schedule.* **2 be/fall hopelessly in love** to have very strong feelings of love for someone **3** feeling that you have no hope: *"I feel like quitting," she said hopelessly.*

Ho·pi /ˈhoʊpi/ a Native American tribe from Arizona in the U.S.

ˌhopped ˈup *adj.* SLANG **1** happy and excited,

especially because of the effects of drugs: +**on** *I could tell Domingo was hopped up on speed.* **2** a hopped-up car, engine etc. has been made much more powerful: *a hopped-up Ford Mustang*

hop•per /ˈhɑpɚ/ *n.* [C] **1** a large container that is wide at the top, with a narrow opening at the bottom, in which things can be stored before being put into another container: *a grain hopper* **2 in/into the hopper** if someone's name, a proposal, an idea etc. is put or goes into the hopper, it is considered for something: *There are a couple of points I would like to* ***throw into the hopper***. **3** a box that proposals for new laws are put into before they are discussed in Congress **4** something that BOUNCES or HOPS: *Reed hit a one-hopper* (=a ball that bounces once) *to Gaetti.* → see also CLODHOPPER

Hop•per /ˈhɑpɚ/, **Ed•ward** /ˈɛdwɚd/ (1882–1967) a U.S. painter known for his REALISTIC paintings of life

hop•scotch /ˈhɑpskɑtʃ/ *n.* [U] a children's game in which each child has to jump from one numbered square to another in a pattern marked on the ground

ho•ra /ˈhɔrə/ *n.* [C usually singular] a traditional Jewish dance in which a group of people hold hands and stand in a circle

Hor•ace /ˈhɔrəs, ˈhɑr-/ (65–8 B.C.) a Roman poet whose work greatly influenced English poetry

horde /hɔrd/ *n.* [C usually plural] a large crowd moving in a noisy uncontrolled way: +**of** *hordes of tourists*

ho•ri•zon /həˈraɪzən/ *n.* **1 the horizon** the line far away where the land or ocean seems to meet the sky: *We could see a ship* ***on the horizon***. | **over/above/below etc. the horizon** *Slowly, a full moon came up over the horizon.* **2 horizons** [plural] the limits of your ideas, knowledge, and experience: *Takayo came to the U.S. to* ***broaden*** *her cultural* ***horizons***. **3 be on the horizon** to seem likely to happen in the future: *Companies don't see any improvement on the horizon.* [**Origin:** 1300–1400 Late Latin, Greek, from *horizein* **to limit**]

hor•i•zon•tal[1] /ˌhɔrəˈzɑntəl, ˌhɑr-/ *adj.* **1** flat and level, from left to right OPP vertical: *a horizontal line* | *Time is graphed along the horizontal axis.* | *horizontal layers of rock* ▸see THESAURUS box at flat[1] → see picture at VERTICAL[1] **2** between people or groups that are at the same level in an organization OPP vertical —**horizontally** *adv.* → see also DIAGONAL

horizontal[2] *n.* **1 the horizontal** TECHNICAL a horizontal position: *The ramp was angled at 12 degrees below the horizontal.* **2** [C] a horizontal line or surface

horiˌzontal consoliˈdation *n.* [U] ECONOMICS a process in which many companies in the same business or industry combine

horiˌzontal inteˈgration *n.* [U] ECONOMICS an occasion when a company obtains control of its competitors

ˌhorizontal ˈmerger *n.* [C] ECONOMICS an occasion when a company combines with one of its competitors

hor•mone /ˈhɔrmoun/ *n.* [C,U] BIOLOGY a chemical substance produced in one part of the body that causes a change or activity in another part of the body: *growth hormones* | *teenagers with* ***raging hormones*** (=changing levels of hormones, which are believed to make them act in ways that are not sensible) [**Origin:** 1900–2000 Greek *hormon*, from *horman* **to cause to move around**] —**hormonal** /hɔrˈmounl/ *adj.*

ˌhormone reˈplacement ˌtherapy *n.* [U] ABBREVIATION **HRT** MEDICINE a medical treatment for women during or after MENOPAUSE (=the time when they stop having monthly PERIODS), which involves adding hormones to the body

horn[1] /hɔrn/ *n.*

1 CAR [C] the piece of equipment in a car, bus etc. that is used to make a loud sound as a signal or warning: *Someone behind me* ***honked*** *his* ***horn*** *when the light changed.* → see picture on page A36

2 ANIMAL [C] **a)** one of the pair of hard pointed parts that grow on the heads of cows, goats, and other animals: *a bull with long horns* **b)** a part of an animal's head that stands out like a horn, for example on a DEER SYN antler

3 MUSICAL INSTRUMENT [C] **a)** ENG. LANG. ARTS one of several musical instruments that consist of a long metal tube, wide at one end, that you play by blowing: *The huntsman* ***blew*** *his* ***horn***. **b)** INFORMAL a TRUMPET **c)** a FRENCH HORN **d)** a musical instrument made from an animal's horn → see also ENGLISH HORN

4 get/be on the horn SPOKEN to use the telephone: *Su got on the horn and spoke to somebody in Design.*

5 SUBSTANCE [U] the substance that animals' horns are made of: *ivory and rhinocerous horn*

6 drinking horn/powder horn etc. a container in the shape of an animal's horn or made from an animal's horn, used in the past for drinking from, carrying GUNPOWDER etc.

7 be on the horns of a dilemma to be in a situation in which you have to choose between two bad or difficult situations

8 pull/draw in your horns to reduce the amount of money you spend: *Businesses are starting to pull in their horns.* → see also **blow your own horn** at BLOW[1] (14), **take the bull by the horns** at BULL (3), **lock horns with sb (over sth)** at LOCK[1] (8)

horn[2] *v.*

horn in *phr. v.* to interrupt or try to take part in something when you are not wanted SYN butt in: +**on** *Don't try and horn in on our fun.*

horn•bill /ˈhɔrnˌbɪl/ *n.* [C] BIOLOGY a tropical bird with a very large beak

horned /hɔrnd/ *adj.* having horns or something that looks like horns: *a horned owl*

hor•net /ˈhɔrnɪt/ *n.* [C] **1** BIOLOGY a large black and yellow insect that can sting **2 a hornet's nest** a situation in which there are a lot of problems and arguments, usually one that someone does not intend to enter: *Hersh's book* ***stirred up a hornet's nest*** (=created a lot of problems and arguments) *in the media.*

ˌhorn of ˈplenty *n.* [C] a CORNUCOPIA

horn•pipe /ˈhɔrnpaɪp/ *n.* [C] a traditional dance performed by SAILORS, or the music for this dance

ˈhorn-rimmed *adj.* horn-rimmed GLASSES have frames made of dark-colored plastic

hor•o•scope /ˈhɔrəˌskoup, ˈhɑr-/ *n.* [C] a description of your character and the things that will happen to you, based on the position of the stars and PLANETS at the time of your birth [**Origin:** 1000–1100 French, Greek *horoskopos*, from *hora* **hour** + *skopein* **to look at**] → see also ASTROLOGY

hor•ren•dous /həˈrɛndəs, hɔ-/ *adj.* **1** frightening and terrible: *a horrendous experience* **2** INFORMAL extremely unreasonable or bad: *horrendous medical costs* | *Traffic downtown is horrendous.* —**horrendously** *adv.*

hor•ri•ble /ˈhɔrəbəl, ˈhɑr-/ S1 *adj.* **1** very bad: *a horrible smell* | *The weather has been horrible all week.* ▸see THESAURUS box at bad[1], taste[1] **2** very frightening, worrying, or upsetting: *a horrible accident*

THESAURUS

Describing a horrible taste or smell
disgusting: *It tastes disgusting.*
awful: *The wine was awful.*
revolting: *the revolting stench in the bathrooms*
foul: *a pool of foul water*

Describing a horrible experience, situation, or feeling
terrible: *a terrible accident*
awful: *an awful headache*
dreadful: *a dreadful crime*
nasty: *It was a nasty situation.*

3 impolite and unfriendly: *What a horrible thing to say!* [**Origin:** 1200–1300 French, Latin *horribilis*, from *horrere*] —**horribly** *adv.*

hor•rid /ˈhɔrɪd, ˈhɑrɪd/ *adj.* **1** very bad and shocking: *The dogs were raised in horrid conditions.* **2** OLD-FASHIONED behaving in a way that is not nice at all: *a horrid little boy* —**horridly** *adv.*

H

hor•rif•ic /hɔˈrɪfɪk, hə-/ *adj.* extremely bad, especially in a way that is frightening, shocking, or upsetting: *He lost his legs in a horrific car crash.* —**horrifically** /-kli/ *adv.*

hor•ri•fied /ˈhɔrəˌfaɪd, ˈhɑ-/ *adj.* very shocked and upset or afraid: *They were horrified to think that they had caused so much trouble.*

hor•ri•fy /ˈhɔrəˌfaɪ, ˈhɑ-/ *v.* **horrifies, horrified, horrifying** [T] to make someone feel very shocked and upset or afraid: *The idea of human cloning horrified her.* —**horrifying** *adj.* —**horrifyingly** *adv.*

hor•ror /ˈhɔrɚ, ˈhɑrɚ/ *n.* **1** [U] a strong feeling of shock and fear: *They watched **in horror** as the fire swept through the house.* | *I realized, **to my horror**, that I didn't have enough money to pay the bill.* **2 the horror of sth** the quality of being frightening and very shocking: ***The full horror of** the accident soon became clear.* **3** [C] something that is very terrible, shocking, or frightening: *the horrors of war* **4** [U] the type of movies or books etc. in which shocking and frightening things happen: *horror and science fiction* **5 horror of horrors** INFORMAL, OFTEN HUMOROUS used to say how bad something is: *Horror of horrors – he saw me without my makeup!* **6 have a horror of sth** LITERARY to be very frightened of something or dislike it very much: *I had long had a horror of snakes.* **7** [C] something that is extremely ugly: *That dress is a horror.*

ˈhorror ˌmovie also **ˈhorror ˌfilm** *n.* [C] a movie in which strange and frightening things happen

ˈhorror ˌstory *n.* [C] **1** a report about bad experiences, bad conditions etc.: *You hear a lot of horror stories when you're out looking for a job.* **2** a story in which strange and frightening things happen

ˈhorror-ˌstricken also **ˈhorror-ˌstruck** *adj.* suddenly very shocked and frightened: *a horror-stricken expression*

hors d'oeu•vre /ɔr ˈdɚv/ *n.* *plural* **hors d'oeuvres** /-ˈdɚvz/ [C] food that is served in small amounts before the main part of the meal [**Origin:** 1700–1800 a French phrase meaning **outside of work**]

horse¹ /hɔrs/ S1 W2 *n.* **1** [C] BIOLOGY a large strong animal that people ride on and use for pulling heavy things: *I had never **ridden a horse** before.* | *a man **on a horse*** **2 (straight/right) from the horse's mouth** if you hear something straight from the horse's mouth, you are told it by someone who has direct knowledge of it **3 change/switch horses in midstream** to stop supporting or working with one person or set of ideas and start supporting or working with another, while you are in the middle of doing something: *It's never a good idea to change horses in midstream.* **4 a horse of a different color** something that is completely different from another thing or situation: *"I was talking about unpaid leave, not vacation time." "Well, that's a horse of a different color."* **5** [C] a piece of sports equipment in a GYMNASIUM that people jump over **6 the horses** the sport of HORSE RACING [**Origin:** Old English *hors*] → see also **put the cart before the horse** at CART¹ (4), **choke a horse** at CHOKE¹ (7), DARK HORSE, **beat/flog a dead horse** at DEAD¹ (11), **I could eat a horse** at EAT (11), **don't look a gift horse in the mouth** at GIFT¹ (5), **be/get on your high horse** at HIGH¹ (17), **hold your horses!** at HOLD¹ (21), STALKING HORSE

horse² *v.*

horse around *phr. v.* INFORMAL to play roughly: *Some kids were horsing around on the playground.*

horse•back /ˈhɔrsbæk/ *n.* **on horseback** riding a horse —**horseback** *adv.* —**horseback** *adj.*

ˈhorseback ˌriding *n.* [U] the activity of riding a horse for pleasure

ˌhorse ˈchestnut *n.* [C] **1** BIOLOGY a large tree that produces shiny brown nuts and has white and pink flowers **2** BIOLOGY a nut from this tree

ˈhorse-drawn *adj.* [only before noun] pulled by a horse: *a horse-drawn carriage*

horse•fly /ˈhɔrsflaɪ/ *n.* *plural* **horseflies** [C] a large fly that bites horses and cattle

horse•hair /ˈhɔrshɛr/ *n.* [U] the hair from a horse's MANE and tail, sometimes used to fill the inside of furniture

ˌhorseless ˈcarriage *n.* [C] a word for a car, used in the early 1900s when cars were very new and unusual

horse•man /ˈhɔrsmən/ *n.* *plural* **horsemen** /-mən/ [C] **1** someone who rides horses **2 the four horsemen of the Apocalypse** a phrase from the Christian Bible meaning war, FAMINE (=a severe lack of food), disease, and death, which the Bible says will affect the Earth just before the end of the world

horse•man•ship /ˈhɔrsmənˌʃɪp/ *n.* [U] the practice or skill of riding horses

horse•play /ˈhɔrs-pleɪ/ *n.* [U] rough noisy behavior in which children play by pushing or hitting each other for fun: *Horseplay on the school bus is not allowed.*

horse•pow•er /ˈhɔrsˌpaʊɚ/ WRITTEN ABBREVIATION **hp** *n.* *plural* **horsepower** [C,U] a unit for measuring the power of an engine

horse•puck•ey /ˈhɔrsˌpʌki/ *n.* [U] SPOKEN, OLD-FASHIONED nonsense

ˈhorse race *n.* [C] **1** a race in which people ride horses around an OVAL track **2** a competition, especially in politics, in which all the competitors seem to have equal chances of succeeding and are trying very hard to win using every possible means, so that it is difficult to guess who will win: **a one-/two-/three- etc. horse race** (=a competition or an election with only two, three etc. people in it who can win)

ˈhorse ˌracing *n.* [U] a sport in which horses with riders race against each other

horse•rad•ish /ˈhɔrsˌrædɪʃ/ *n.* [U] **1** a strong-tasting white SAUCE made from the root of a plant, which is usually eaten with meat **2** BIOLOGY the plant whose root is used in making this SAUCE

ˈhorse sense *n.* [U] OLD-FASHIONED sensible judgment gained from experience SYN **common sense**

horse•shoe /ˈhɔrʃ-ʃu, ˈhɔrs-/ *n.* **1** [C] a U-shaped piece of iron that is nailed onto the bottom of a horse's foot to protect it **2** [C] a U-shaped object which is used as a sign of good luck **3 horseshoes** [U] an outdoor game in which horseshoes are thrown at a post

ˈhorse show *n.* [C] a sports event in which people riding horses compete to show their skill in riding

ˈhorse-ˌtrading *n.* [U] DISAPPROVING the activity of discussing things and making deals in which everyone tries hard to gain advantages for their own side, especially in politics or business: *political horse-trading*

ˈhorse ˌtrailer *n.* [C] a large vehicle for carrying horses, pulled by another vehicle

horse•whip /ˈhɔrsˌwɪp/ *v.* **horsewhipped, horsewhipping** [T] to beat someone hard with a whip —**horsewhip** *n.* [C]

horse•wom•an /ˈhɔrsˌwʊmən/ *n.* *plural* **horsewomen** /-ˌwɪmɪn/ [C] a woman who rides horses

hors•ey, horsy /ˈhɔrsi/ *adj.* **1** very interested in horses and events that involve horses **2** looking like a horse

hor•ti•cul•ture /ˈhɔrt̬əˌkʌltʃɚ/ *n.* [U] the practice or science of growing flowers, fruit, and vegetables [**Origin:** 1600–1700 Latin *hortus* **garden** + English *culture*] —**horticultural** /ˌhɔrt̬əˈkʌltʃərəl/ *adj.* —**horticulturalist** *n.* [C] → see also AGRICULTURE

ho•san•na /hoʊˈzænə/ *n.* [C] a shout of praise to God —**hosanna** *interjection*

hose¹ /hoʊz/ *n.* **1** [C] a long rubber or plastic tube that can be moved and bent to put water onto fires, gardens etc. or to take air or a gas from one place to another **2** [U] PANTYHOSE **3** [U] tight-fitting pants worn by men in past times [**Origin:** Old English *hosa* **leg-covering**]

hose² *v.* [T] **1** to cover something with water using a hose: *You don't have to hose the car before washing it.* **2** SLANG to cheat or deceive someone: *Marcus tried to hose someone on a drug deal.*

hose sb /sth ↔ **down** also **hose sb/sth↔ off** *phr. v.* to use a hose to put water on something, for example in order to clean it or to make it completely wet: *Every week they hose down the floors of the prison cells.*

Ho·se·a /hoʊˈzeɪə, -ˈziə/ a book in the Old Testament of the Christian Bible

hosed /hoʊzd/ *adj.* [not before noun] SPOKEN, SLANG in a lot of trouble or in a very difficult situation: *If we don't finish this tonight, we're hosed.*

hos·er /ˈhoʊzɚ/ *n.* [C] SPOKEN, SLANG someone who you do not respect because you think they are stupid, unfashionable etc.

ho·sier·y /ˈhoʊʒəri/ *n.* [U] a word meaning clothing such as "socks" and STOCKINGS, used in stores and in the clothing industry

hos·pice /ˈhɑspɪs/ *n.* [C] a special hospital where people who are dying are taken care of

hos·pi·ta·ble /hɑˈspɪt̬əbəl, ˈhɑspɪ-/ *adj.* **1** friendly, welcoming, and generous to visitors OPP **inhospitable**: *The local people were very kind and hospitable.* ►see THESAURUS box at **friendly** **2** favorable and allowing things to grow or develop OPP **inhospitable**: *a hospitable climate* [**Origin:** 1500–1600 French *hospiter* **to receive a guest**, from Latin *hospes*] —**hospitably** *adv.*

hos·pi·tal /ˈhɑspɪt̬l/ S1 W1 *n.* [C,U] a large building where sick or injured people are taken care of and receive medical treatment: *Elena was **in the hospital** for a week.* | *He had to **go to the hospital**.* | *Ramon **was admitted to the hospital** on Tuesday.* | **take/rush sb to a/the hospital** *Victims were rushed to a local hospital.* [**Origin:** 1200–1300 Old French, Medieval Latin *hospitale* **place to stay at**, from Latin *hospitalis* **of a guest**]

> **THESAURUS**
>
> **medical center** a large hospital, or a place where a lot of doctors have offices
> **clinic** a place where medical treatment and advice is given to people who do not need to stay in a hospital, or where treatment is given at a low cost
> **hospice** a special hospital for people who are dying
> **nursing home** a place where people who are old and sick can live and be taken care of
> **convalescent home** a place where people stay when they need care from doctors and nurses, but are not sick enough to be in a hospital
>
> **Parts of a hospital**
> **ER/emergency room** the part of a hospital where people who are injured or who need urgent treatment are brought
> **operating room** a room in a hospital where operations are done
> **intensive care** the part of a hospital where people who are very seriously ill or badly injured are cared for
> **unit** part of a hospital where a particular kind of treatment is carried out: *the burns unit* (=where people with serious burns are treated)
> **ward** a large room in a hospital where people who need medical treatment stay

hos·pi·tal·i·ty /ˌhɑspəˈtæləti/ *n.* [U] **1** friendly behavior toward visitors: *Thank you for your hospitality over the past few weeks.* **2** services such as food and drink that an organization provides for customers: *the hospitality industry* → see also **corporate hospitality** at CORPORATE (1)

hos·pi·tal·ize /ˈhɑspɪtˌaɪz/ *v.* [T usually passive] to put someone in a hospital for treatment: *Roger was hospitalized after a severe asthma attack.* —**hospitalization** /ˌhɑspɪt̬l-əˈzeɪʃən/ *n.* [U]

host¹ /hoʊst/ S3 W2 *n.* [C]
1 AT A PARTY the person at a party, meal etc. who has invited the guests and who welcomes them, gives them food and drinks etc.: *Our host greeted us at the door.*
2 ON TELEVISION ENG. LANG. ARTS someone who introduces the guests on a television or radio show: *a game show host*
3 COUNTRY/ORGANIZATION a country, government, or organization that provides the necessary space, equipment etc. for a special event: **be/play host to sth** *Helsinki **was host to** the 1952 Olympics.*
4 a (whole) host of sth FORMAL a large number of things: *a host of problems*
5 ANIMAL/PLANT BIOLOGY an animal or plant on which a smaller animal or plant is living as a PARASITE
6 COMPUTER a computer that other computers are connected to and from or through which they can get information and services
7 the Host TECHNICAL the bread that is used in the Christian ceremony of Communion
[**Origin:** (1–3) 1200–1300 Old French *hoste* **host, guest**, from Latin *hospes*]

host² *v.* [T] **1** to provide the place and everything that is needed for an organized event: *Which country is going to host the next World Cup?* **2** to be the host on a television or radio show: *Smith hosts a sports show on a local radio station.* **3** to be the person who takes the role of host at a social event: *The governor hosted a dinner in Li's honor.*

hos·tage /ˈhɑstɪdʒ/ *n.* [C] **1** someone who is kept as a prisoner by an enemy so that the other side will do what the enemy demands: *Four U.S. citizens are still being **held hostage** by the guerrillas.* | *The hijackers **took** a crew member **hostage**.* ►see THESAURUS box at **prisoner** **2 be (held) hostage to sth** to be influenced or controlled by something, so that you are not free to do what you want: *The treaty was a hostage to the president's political career.*

hos·tel /ˈhɑstl/ *n.* [C] **1** a place where people, especially people who have no homes or who are working in a place far from their home, can stay and eat fairly cheaply: *He stayed at a hostel for migrant workers.* **2** a YOUTH HOSTEL

hos·tel·er /ˈhɑstələ/ *n.* [C] someone who is traveling from one YOUTH HOSTEL to another

hos·tel·ry /ˈhɑstəlri/ *n. plural* **hostelries** [C] FORMAL a hotel

host·ess /ˈhoʊstɪs/ *n.* [C] **1** the woman at a party, meal etc. who has invited all the guests and welcomes them, provides them with food and drink etc.: *Our hostess was waiting to greet us by the door.* **2** the woman who introduces the guests on a television or radio show **3** a woman who takes people to their table in a restaurant **4 the hostess with the mostest** SPOKEN, HUMOROUS a woman who gives many parties and is considered very good at it

hos·tile /ˈhɑstl, ˈhɑstaɪl/ *adj.* **1** angry and deliberately unfriendly toward someone, and ready to argue with them OPP **friendly**: *a hostile attitude* | **+to/toward** *Several of the neighbors were openly hostile to each other.* | *He warned his players to expect **a hostile reception** from local fans.* **2** opposing a plan or idea very strongly: **+to/toward** *They tend to be hostile to anything they don't understand.* **3** belonging to an enemy OPP **friendly**: *Civilians had to flee through **hostile territory**.* **4 a hostile takeover/bid/buyout** a situation in which one company starts to control a smaller one, or tries to start controlling it, because the smaller one does not have enough power or money to stop the larger company **5 hostile environment/climate/terrain etc.** conditions that are difficult to live in or exist in **6 a hostile witness** LAW someone who is asked to answer questions in a court of law, but who is considered unlikely to give answers that are favorable to the side that asked them [**Origin:** 1500–1600 French, Latin *hostilis*, from *hostis* **stranger, enemy**]

hos·til·i·ty /hɑˈstɪləti/ *n.* **1** [U] a feeling or attitude that is extremely unfriendly: *The police were greeted with open hostility.* | **+toward/to/between** *hostility toward foreigners* **2** [U] strong or angry opposition to a plan or idea: *The reform program was greeted with hostility by conservatives.* | **+to** *There is a lot of public hostility to the new tax.* **3 hostilities** [plural] FORMAL acts of fighting: *the outbreak of hostilities*

hot /hɑt/ S1 W1 *adj. comparative* **hotter**, *superlative* **hottest**
1 WEATHER/FOOD/LIQUID ETC. having a high temperature OPP **cold**: *Be careful, the water's very hot.* | *They serve both hot and cold food.* | ***It's too hot*** *to go for a bike ride.* | *a pot of hot coffee* | **boiling/scalding hot** (=used to describe liquid that is extremely hot) | *Heat waves rose off the* ***burning hot*** *desert sands.* | *Pour the sauce over the pasta and serve* ***piping hot***. | *The handle was* ***red hot*** (=very hot).

THESAURUS

warm a little hot, especially in a pleasant way: *a warm summer evening*
humid having air that feels hot and wet rather than dry: *the humid heat of the Brazilian rainforest*
boiling/baking/scorching (hot) extremely hot: *a scorching day in the middle of July*
sweltering hot in a very unpleasant, uncomfortable way: *a sweltering August day*
lukewarm a liquid that is lukewarm is only slightly warm, and not as cold or hot as it should be: *The water in the tub was only lukewarm.*
scalding a scalding liquid is extremely hot, and hot enough to burn you: *a cup of scalding coffee*
→ COLD[1], WEATHER[1]

2 BODY [not before noun] if you feel hot, your body feels warm in a way that is uncomfortable OPP **cold**: *I'm really hot. Can I get a drink of water?*
3 TASTE food that tastes hot contains pepper, CHILI etc. and has a burning taste that makes your mouth feel warm SYN **spicy** OPP **mild**: *hot salsa* ►see THESAURUS box at **taste**[1]
4 POPULAR INFORMAL popular at a particular point in time: *one of Hollywood's hottest young directors* | *This success of his last novel has made him a* ***hot property*** (=an actor, singer etc. that many companies want) *in the literary world.* | **a hot item/ticket** (=something that people want to buy or pay to go to see) | **a hot topic/issue etc.** (=something that many people are discussing and interested in)
5 CLOTHES if clothes are hot, they make you feel too hot in a way that is uncomfortable: *This sweater's too hot to wear inside.*
6 SEXUALLY EXCITING a movie, book, relationship etc. that is hot is sexually exciting: *a* ***red-hot*** *love affair* | *I've got a* ***hot date*** *tonight.*
7 SUCCESSFUL INFORMAL very successful or very lucky at doing something: *The Penguins are still hot, beating the Rangers 5–3.*
8 CAUSING TROUBLE difficult or dangerous to deal with and likely to cause problems, trouble, or arguments: *Studio bosses decided her video was* ***too hot to handle***.

SPOKEN PHRASES

9 SEXUALLY ATTRACTIVE a person who is hot is sexually attractive: *A really hot Italian guy sat down at the next table.* | *She looks really hot in that dress.* ►see THESAURUS box at **attractive**, **beautiful**
10 **not too/so/very hot** **a)** not very good or well: *"How's the sound quality of those new microphones?" "Not so hot."* | **+at** *Brian was never too hot at math.* **b)** slightly sick: *I'm not feeling too hot today.*
11 **be hot on sth** to know a lot about something: *I'm* ***not too hot on*** *sports.*
12 **(is it) hot enough for you?** HUMOROUS used to say that the weather is very hot
13 **be hot stuff** **a)** to be sexually attractive **b)** to be very good at a particular activity: *You should see Doug on the tennis court – he's really hot stuff.*
14 **be hot for sb** to be sexually attracted to someone: *Everybody is hot for the new guy at the gym.*
15 **have sth in your hot little hands** used to emphasize that you have something in your possession
16 CLOSE [not before noun] used especially in children's games to say that someone is close to finding something or guessing something OPP **cold**: *You're getting hot!*

17 **a hot temper** someone who has a hot temper becomes angry very easily → see also HOT-TEMPERED
18 **in hot pursuit** following someone quickly and closely because you want to catch them: *The cops and the dogs set out after them in hot pursuit.*
19 **be hot on sb's trail/tail/heels** to be close to and likely to catch someone you have been chasing: *He had the police hot on his trail.*
20 **come/follow hot on the heels of sth** to happen very soon after another event: *The album comes hot on the heels of her first movie.*
21 DIFFICULT SITUATION [not before noun] INFORMAL if a situation or place becomes too hot for someone, it is because other people are angry with them: *If things get too hot, I can always leave.*
22 COMPETITION competition that is hot is between people or companies that are trying very hard to win or succeed: *Competition for the best jobs is getting hotter all the time.*
23 NEWS hot news is about very recent events and therefore is interesting or exciting
24 **be hot off the presses/press** if a newspaper, report etc. is hot off the presses, it is very new and has just been printed
25 **blow/run hot and cold** to keep changing your mind about whether you like or want to do something: *She keeps running hot and cold about the wedding.*
26 **hot air** INFORMAL things someone says that sound important or impressive, but really are not: *The theory was dismissed as a lot of hot air.*
27 **a hot tip** a good piece of advice about something that not many people know about
28 **be in hot water** to be in a difficult situation because you have done something wrong: *Cabral was in hot water over his job performance.*
29 **hot under the collar** angry and ready to argue
30 **be in the hot seat** to be forced to deal with a difficult or bad situation, especially in politics
31 **a hot spot** **a)** a place where there is likely to be trouble, fighting etc.: *There are many hot spots of unrest in the area.* **b)** an area that is popular for a particular activity or type of entertainment: *We visited a few downtown hot spots.* **c)** a HOTSPOT **d)** a place where a fire can spread from
32 STOLEN SLANG goods that are hot have been stolen: *The boss's new Ferrari turned out to be hot.*
33 MUSIC having a strong exciting RHYTHM
34 **be hot and bothered** INFORMAL **a)** to be so worried and confused by something that you cannot think clearly **b)** to be sexually excited
35 **hot money** money that is frequently moved from one country, bank, account etc. to another in order to make a quick profit
36 **hot to trot** INFORMAL feeling sexually excited and interested in finding someone to have sex with
[**Origin:** Old English *hat*] → see also HOTS, RED-HOT

hot-'air bal,loon *n.* [C] a very large BALLOON made of cloth and filled with hot air with a large basket attached to the bottom, used for carrying people in the air

hot·bed /'hɑt˺bɛd/ *n.* a place where a lot of a particular type of activity, especially bad or violent activity, happens: **+of** *The troubled province is a hotbed of ethnic violence.*

,hot-'blooded *adj.* having very strong emotions such as anger or love, that are difficult to control SYN **passionate**

'hot ,button *n.* [C] a problem or subject that causes a lot of arguments or strong feelings between people: *Your letter certainly hit a hot button.* —**hot-button** *adj.*: *hot-button issues*

hot·cake /'hɑtkeɪk/ *n.* [C] **1 be selling/going like hotcakes** INFORMAL to be sold very quickly and in large amounts **2** a PANCAKE

,hot 'chocolate *n.* [C,U] a hot drink made with chocolate powder and milk or water SYN **cocoa**

,hot-cross 'bun *n.* [C] a small round sweet bread roll, with a cross-shaped mark on top, eaten just before Easter

'hot dish, **hotdish** *n.* [C,U] hot food, usually a mixture of meat and vegetables, sometimes with PASTA, cooked and served in a deep covered dish

'hot dog[1] *n.* [C] **1** a long type of SAUSAGE, cooked and eaten in a long BUN (=round piece of bread) **2** INFORMAL someone who does risky and exciting things in a sport, especially SKIING, in a way that attracts people's attention

hot 'dog[2] *interjection* OLD-FASHIONED used to express pleasure or surprise

'hot-dog *v.* [I] INFORMAL to do something in a sport, especially SKIING, in a fast, risky, and exciting way that attracts a lot of attention and admiration: *We were both hot-dogging down the hill.*

ho·tel /hoʊ'tɛl/ S2 W1 *n.* [C] a building where people pay to spend the night: *a luxury hotel* | **stay in/at a hotel** *We'll be staying in a hotel by the cathedral.* | **check into/out of a hotel** *You must check out of the hotel by noon.* [**Origin:** 1600–1700 French *hôtel*, from Old French *hostel*]

THESAURUS

motel a hotel for people traveling by car, usually with a place for the car near each room
inn a small hotel, especially one where you can have breakfast and that is not in a city
bed and breakfast (B&B) a house or a small hotel where you pay to sleep and have breakfast
campground a place where you camp in a tent

ho·te·lier /hoʊ'tɛlyɚ, ˌoʊtl'yeɪ/ *n.* [C] FORMAL someone who owns or manages a hotel

hot 'flash *n.* [C] a sudden hot feeling that women have during MENOPAUSE (=the time when they stop having monthly PERIODS)

hot·foot /'hɔt˺fʊt/ *v.* **hotfoot it** INFORMAL to walk or run quickly

hot·head /'hɑthɛd/ *n.* [C] INFORMAL someone who does things too quickly and without thinking about them before doing them —**hotheaded** *adj.*

hot·house /'hɑtˌhaʊs/ *n. plural* **hothouses** /-ˌhaʊzɪz/ [C] **1** a heated building, usually made of glass, where flowers and plants can grow → see also GREENHOUSE: *hothouse flowers* (=grown in a hothouse) **2** a place or situation where a lot of people are interested in particular ideas or activities: +**of** *The campus was once a hothouse of political protest.* **3 hothouse atmosphere/environment** a situation or place with conditions that encourage a particular activity or attitude

'hot key *n.* [C] COMPUTERS a button or set of buttons that you can press on a computer KEYBOARD as a quick way of making it do a particular job

hot·line /'hɑt-laɪn/ *n.* [C] **1** a special telephone line for people to find out about or talk about something: *a suicide hotline* **2** [usually singular] a direct telephone line between government leaders in different countries, which is only used in serious situations

'hot link *n.* [C] INFORMAL COMPUTERS a HYPERTEXT LINK

hot·ly /'hɑtli/ *adv.* **1 hotly debated/contested/disputed etc.** discussed etc. very angrily or with very strong feelings: *Increases in defense spending are always hotly contested.* **2 be hotly pursued** to be chased closely by someone: *The BMW was hotly pursued by an unmarked police car.*

'hot ˌpad *n.* [C] a small piece of thick cloth, wood, plastic etc. that you put under a hot dish or plate

'hot pants *n.* [plural] very short tight women's SHORTS

hot 'pink *n.* [U] a very bright pink color —**hot pink** *adj.*

hot·plate, hot plate /'hɑt˺pleɪt/ *n.* [C] a small piece of equipment with a flat heated top, used for cooking food

'hot pot, hotpot *n.* [C] a piece of electrical equipment with a small container, used to boil water

ˌhot po'tato *n. plural* **hot potatoes** [C usually singular] **1** a subject or problem that no one wants to deal with, because it is difficult and any decision will make people angry: *Euthanasia for terminally ill patients is a political hot potato.* **2 drop sb/sth like a hot potato** to suddenly stop being involved with someone or something: *When she said she was married, he dropped her like a hot potato.*

'hot rod *n.* [C] INFORMAL an old car into which a more powerful engine has been put, to make it go very fast —**hot rodder** *n.* [C] —**hot rodding** *n.* [U]

hots /hɑts/ *n.* **have/get the hots for sb** INFORMAL to be sexually attracted to someone: *I think he's got the hots for you, Elaine.*

'hot shot, hotshot *n.* [C] INFORMAL someone who is very successful and confident —**hotshot** *adj.*: *a hotshot lawyer*

hot·spot, hot spot /'hɑtspɑt/ *n.* [C] a part of a computer image on the screen that you can CLICK on or point to in order to make other pictures, words etc. appear → see also **hot spot** at HOT (31)

ˌhot 'spring *n.* [C] EARTH SCIENCE a place where hot water comes up naturally from the ground

ˌhot-'tempered *adj.* tending to become angry easily

hot tod·dy /ˌhɑt 'tɑdi/ *n. plural* **hot toddies** [C] a hot drink made with WHISKEY, sugar, SPICES, and hot water

'hot tub *n.* [C] a heated bathtub or large wooden container that several people can sit in → see also JACUZZI

hot·ty, hottie /'hɑṭi/ *n. plural* **hotties** [C] SLANG someone who is very sexually attractive

ˌhot-'water ˌbottle *n.* [C] a rubber container that you put hot water in, used to keep yourself warm or to make sore muscles feel better

hot-wire /'hɑt˺waɪɚ/ *v.* [T] INFORMAL to start the engine of a vehicle by using the wires of the IGNITION system, and not using the key

hound[1] /haʊnd/ *n.* [C] **1** BIOLOGY a dog used for hunting **2** BIOLOGY a dog → see also NEWS HOUND

hound[2] *v.* [T] to keep following someone and asking them questions in an annoying or threatening way: *The landlord keeps hounding me for the rent.*

hound sb **out** *phr. v.* to make things so bad for someone that they are forced to leave: **hound sb out of sth** *He should resign now rather than wait to be hounded out of office.*

H

hour /aʊɚ/ S1 W1 *n.* [C]
1 60 MINUTES a period of 60 minutes or 1/24 of a day: *They left about 4 hours ago.* | *I study* ***for two hours*** *every night.* | *You can come back for us* ***in an hour*** (=an hour from now). | *The test will* ***take*** *about three* ***hours***. | **per/an hour** *A lot of attorneys charge about $175 an hour.* | *a top speed of 120 miles per hour*
2 DISTANCE the distance you can travel in an hour: *Our house is a 20-minute walk from my sister's.* | *We're still about* ***three hours from*** *Amarillo.* | *It's only about* ***an hour's drive*** *from here.*
3 TIME OF DAY a particular period or point of time during the day or night: *We serve meals* ***24 hours a day****, seven days a week.* | *We danced until the* ***small hours*** (=between midnight and 2 or 3 o'clock) *of the morning.* | *Sir, I'm sorry to bother you* ***at this hour*** (=very late at night or early in the morning). | *My wife got me out of bed* ***at some ungodly hour*** *to go antique shopping.* | *I was getting calls* ***at all hours***. | *He was out* ***till all hours*** (=until an unreasonably late time) *last night.* | **keep late/regular etc. hours** (=go to bed and get up at late, regular etc. times) → see also **waking hours/life/day etc.** at WAKING (1)
4 PERIOD WHEN STH HAPPENS [usually plural] a certain period of time in the day when a particular activity, business etc. happens: **office/opening/business hours** (=when an office, store etc. is open) | *Nicole goes biking during her* ***lunch hour***. | *Our telephone hotline is open* ***during*** *regular* ***business hours***. | *You can come back tomorrow during* ***visiting hours*** (=when you can visit someone in a hospital). | ***After hours*** (=after an office, store etc. is closed), *callers can leave a voice mail message.* → see also RUSH HOUR, HAPPY HOUR
5 WORK hours [plural] the time that you spend doing your job: *The job's part-time and I don't get many hours.* | **put in/work long hours** *We've all been putting in long hours lately.*
6 A LONG TIME hours [plural] INFORMAL a long time or a time that seems long: *I've been trying to call you* ***for hours***. | *I could spend* ***hours and hours*** (=a very long time) *telling you all the stories.*
7 within hours of sth only a few hours after doing something or after something happened: *Tickets for the concerts sold out within hours of going on sale.*

8 O'CLOCK the time of the day when a new hour starts, for example one o'clock, two o'clock etc.: *There are news bulletins **on the hour**.* | *Carriage tours of the town depart **every hour on the hour*** (=every hour at nine o'clock, ten o'clock etc.). | **10/20/25 etc. minutes before/after the hour** *It's twelve minutes before the hour, and you're listening to Morning Edition on NPR.* | **strike/sound the hour** (=if a clock strikes or sounds the hour, it rings to show that it is one o'clock, seven o'clock etc.)
9 by the hour also **from hour to hour** if a situation is changing by the hour or from hour to hour, it is changing very quickly and very often: *The number of casualties is mounting by the hour.*
10 IMPORTANT MOMENT an important moment or period in history or in your life: *It was his **finest hour** as coach of the Detroit Lions.* | *New hope had come to the villagers **in their darkest hour**.* | *He helped others **in their hour of need**.*
11 the sth of the hour something that is very popular or famous at the present time: *World security is the **question of the hour*** (=the problem being dealt with at a particular time). | *Williams is tonight's **man of the hour**.*
12 1300/1530/1805 hours used to give the time in official or military reports and orders, and in some airports, train stations etc. The system is based on numbering the hours from 01:00 (1 a.m.) to 24:00 (12 midnight).
[**Origin:** 1100–1200 Old French *heure*, from Latin *hora*, from Greek] → see also **at the eleventh hour** at ELEVENTH[1] (2), HOURLY, ZERO HOUR

H

hour·glass /ˈaʊɚglæs/ *n.* [C] **1** a glass container for measuring time, in which sand moves slowly from the top half to the bottom in exactly one hour **2 hourglass figure** a woman who has an hourglass figure has a narrow waist in comparison with her chest and HIPS

ˈhour ˌhand *n.* [C] the shorter of the two pieces on a clock or watch that show you what time it is → see also MINUTE HAND

hour·ly /ˈaʊɚli/ *adj.* **1** happening or done every hour: *hourly bus service* ►see THESAURUS box at **regular**[1] **2 hourly pay/earnings/fees etc.** the amount you earn or charge for every hour you work —**hourly** *adv.*: *The database is updated hourly.*

house[1] /haʊs/ S1 W1 *n. plural* **houses** /ˈhaʊzɪz/
1 WHERE YOU LIVE [C] **a)** a building that you live in and is intended to be used by one family: *My parents have a five-bedroom house.* | *We met **at Alison's house**.* | *I'm not allowed to smoke **in the house**.* | *It would be nice if you'd help out **around the house**.* **b)** all the people who live in a house: *Be quiet or you'll wake the whole house!*

THESAURUS

ranch house/ranch a long narrow house built on one level
cottage a small house in the country
row house one of a row of houses that are joined together
mansion a very large house
bungalow a small house that is usually all on one level
duplex a house that is divided into two separate homes
apartment a set of rooms that is part of a bigger building
condominium/condo one apartment in a building with several apartments, each of which is owned by the people living in it
townhouse a house in a group of houses that share one or more walls
mobile home/trailer a type of house that can be pulled by a large vehicle and moved to another place

►see THESAURUS box at **home**[1]
2 GOVERNMENT [C] **a)** POLITICS one of the groups of people who make the laws of a state or country: *The bill has the backing of both houses of Congress.* **b) the House** the HOUSE OF REPRESENTATIVES
3 opera/court house etc. a large public building used for a particular purpose
4 COMPANY [C] a company, especially one that produces books, lends money, or designs clothes: *America's oldest publishing house* | *the House of Dior*
5 keep house OLD-FASHIONED to do all the cooking, cleaning etc. in a house: *His daughter keeps house for him.*
6 be on the house if drinks or food are on the house, you do not have to pay for them because they are provided free by the owner of the bar, restaurant etc.
7 house of God also **house of worship** a church
8 THEATER [C] **a)** ENG. LANG. ARTS the part of a theater where people sit: **a packed/full house** *The show has played to packed houses across the country.* | *The **house lights*** (=lights in the part where people sit) *came up, and we knew the show was finally over.* **b)** the people who have come to watch a performance SYN **audience**
9 house wine/white/red ordinary wine that is provided by a restaurant to be drunk with meals: *Dorothy ordered a glass of the house white with her fish.*
10 put/get your house in order to start behaving in a responsible way, especially by taking care of any money problems: *The U.S. needs to get its financial house in order.*
11 hen/coach/store house etc. a building in which animals, goods, equipment etc. are kept
12 MUSIC [U] ENG. LANG. ARTS HOUSE MUSIC
13 do sth like a house on fire INFORMAL to do something very well and with a lot of eagerness and enjoyment: *The two girls got along like a house on fire.*
14 the big house HUMOROUS prison
15 bring the house down to do something while performing in a play, concert etc. that the people watching enjoy a lot: *Her final song brought the house down.*
16 ROYAL FAMILY [C] an important family, especially a royal family: *the House of Windsor*
[**Origin:** Old English *hus*] → see also **eat sb out of house and home** at EAT (7), HOUSE ARREST, IN-HOUSE, OPEN HOUSE

house[2] /haʊz/ *v.* [T] **1** to provide someone with a place to live: *The refugees are being housed in schools and hospitals.* **2** if a building houses something, it is in that building: *The plush hotel once housed a casino and several restaurants.*

ˈhouse arˌrest *n.* **be under house arrest** to be told by the government that you must stay inside your house, or you will go to prison

house·boat /ˈhaʊsboʊt/ *n.* [C] a boat that you can live in

house·bound /ˈhaʊsbaʊnd/ *adj.* unable to leave your house, especially because you are sick or old

house·boy /ˈhaʊsbɔɪ/ *n. plural* **houseboys** [C] a young man who works as a servant in someone's house, especially in past times

house·break /ˈhaʊsbreɪk/ *v.* [T] to train an animal, especially a dog, not to make the house dirty with its URINE and FECES (=body waste)

house·break·er /ˈhaʊsˌbreɪkɚ/ *n.* [C] a thief who enters someone else's house by breaking locks, windows etc. SYN **burglar** —**housebreaking** *n.* [U]

house·bro·ken /ˈhaʊsˌbroʊkən/ *adj.* an animal that is housebroken has been trained not to make the house dirty with its URINE and FECES (=body waste)

ˈhouse call *n.* [C] a visit that someone, especially a doctor, makes to someone in their home as part of their job: *Where can you find a doctor who **makes house calls** nowadays?*

house·coat /ˈhaʊs-koʊt/ *n.* [C] a long loose coat made of thin material that a woman wears at home to cover her clothes or PAJAMAS

house·fly /ˈhaʊsflaɪ/ *n. plural* **houseflies** [C] a common type of fly that often lives in houses

house·ful /ˈhaʊsfʊl/ *n.* **a houseful of sth** a large number of people or things in your house: *Having a houseful of relatives can be pretty stressful.*

ˈhouse ˌguest *n.* [C] someone who is staying in your house for a short time

house·hold[1] /ˈhaʊshoʊld, ˈhaʊsoʊld/ W3 *n.* [C] all the people who live together in one house: *a two-income household*

household[2] *adj.* [only before noun] **1** relating to taking care of a house and the people in it SYN **domestic**: *household cleaning products* | *household appliances* **2 be a household name/word** to be very well known: *Apple computers became a household name in the late '80s.*

house·hold·er /ˈhaʊsˌhoʊldɚ/ *n.* [C] FORMAL someone who owns or is in charge of a house

ˈhouse ˌhusband *n.* [C] a husband who works at home doing the cooking, cleaning etc., but who does not have a job outside the house → see also HOUSEWIFE

house·keep·er /ˈhaʊsˌkipɚ/ *n.* [C] **1** someone who is employed to manage the cleaning, cooking etc. in a house or hotel **2** someone who is employed to clean your house, do the cooking etc.

house·keep·ing /ˈhaʊsˌkipɪŋ/ *n.* [U] **1** the work and organization of things that need to be done in a house, for example cooking and buying food **2** jobs that need to be done to keep a system working correctly **3** the department in a large building such as a hotel or a hospital that is RESPONSIBLE for cleaning the inside of the building

house·maid /ˈhaʊsmeɪd/ *n.* [C] OLD-FASHIONED a female servant who cleans someone's house

house·man /ˈhaʊsmən/ *n. plural* **housemen** /-mən/ [C] a man who is employed to do general work, especially cleaning work, in someone's house or in a hotel

house·mas·ter /ˈhaʊsˌmæstɚ/ *n.* [C] a male teacher who is in charge of a DORMITORY at a private school

house·moth·er /ˈhaʊsˌmʌðɚ/ *n.* [C] a woman employed to be in charge of a house or a DORMITORY where students or young people live at a private school

ˈhouse ˌmusic *n.* [U] a type of popular music played on electronic instruments, with a strong fast beat

House of Bur·gess·es, the /ˌhaʊs əv ˈbɚdʒəsɪz/ HISTORY the LEGISLATURE of the COLONY of Virginia, formed in 1619

ˌhouse of ˈcards *n.* [singular] **1** a plan that is so badly arranged that is likely to fail: *The whole thing fell apart like a house of cards.* **2** an arrangement of PLAYING CARDS built carefully but easily knocked over

ˌHouse of ˈCommons *n.* **the House of Commons** the part of the British or Canadian PARLIAMENT whose members are elected by the people

ˌHouse of ˈLords *n.* **the House of Lords** the part of the British PARLIAMENT whose members are not elected but have positions because of their rank or title

ˌHouse of Repreˈsentatives *n.* **the House of Representatives** the larger of the two parts of the U.S. Congress or of the PARLIAMENT of Australia or New Zealand → see also SENATE

ˈhouse ˌparty *n.* [C] a party in someone's house, often one where people stay for several days

ˈhouse phone *n.* [C] a telephone that can only be used to make calls within a building, especially a hotel

house·plant /ˈhaʊsplænt/ *n.* [C] a plant that you grow indoors for decoration

ˈhouse-sit, house sit *v.* **house-sat, house-sitting** [I + for] to take care of someone's house while they are away —**house-sitter** *n.* [C]

ˌhouse-to-ˈhouse *adj.* [only before noun] **house-to-house search/survey etc.** a search, SURVEY etc. made by visiting each house in a particular area SYN **door-to-door** —**house to house** *adv.*: *Police went house to house looking for the girl.*

house·top /ˈhaʊs-tɑp/ *n.* **1** [C usually plural] the ROOF of a house SYN **rooftop** **2 shout/proclaim etc. sth from the housetops** to say something publicly so that everyone will hear or know about it

ˌHouse Un-Aˌmerican Acˈtivities Comˌmittee, the HISTORY a committee in the U.S. House of Representatives, which was established in 1938 to find out who was disloyal to the country, especially to find out if people were COMMUNISTS

house·wares /ˈhaʊswɛrz/ *n.* [plural] small things used in the home, for example kitchen utensils, lamps etc., or the department of a large store that sells these things

house·warm·ing /ˈhaʊsˌwɔrmɪŋ/ also **ˈhouse-warming ˌparty** *n.* [C] a party that you give to celebrate when you have just moved into a new house: *Julie and Dean invited us to their housewarming.*

house·wife /ˈhaʊswaɪf/ *n. plural* **housewives** /-waɪvz/ [C] a married woman who works at home doing the cooking, cleaning etc. but does not have a job outside the house SYN **homemaker** —**housewifely** *adj.* → see also HOUSE HUSBAND

house·work /ˈhaʊswɚk/ *n.* [U] work that you do to take care of a house, such as washing, cleaning etc.: *Our kids always help with the housework.* → see also HOMEWORK

hous·ing /ˈhaʊzɪŋ/ S3 W2 *n.* **1** [U] the houses or conditions that people live in: *student housing near campus* | *We need more affordable housing.* | *public housing* (=provided by the government for poor people to live in) **2** [U] the work of providing houses for people to live in: *public services such as education, housing and transportation* **3** [C] a protective cover for a machine: *the engine housing*

ˈhousing devˌelopment *n.* [C] a large number of houses that have been built together in a planned way

ˈhousing ˌproject *n.* [C] a group of houses or apartments, usually built with government money, for poor people to rent

Hous·ton /ˈhyustən/ a city and port in the U.S. state of Texas

Houston, Sam /sæm/ (1793–1863) a U.S. soldier and politician who fought to make Texas independent from Mexico and was President of the Republic of Texas from 1836 until it became a state of the U.S. in 1845

hove /hoʊv/ *v.* a past tense and past participle of HEAVE

hov·el /ˈhʌvəl, ˈhɑ-/ *n.* [C] a small dirty place where someone lives, especially a very poor person

hov·er /ˈhʌvɚ/ *v.*

1 FLYING THINGS [I] if a bird, insect, or HELICOPTER hovers, it stays in one place in the air: **+over/above** *Flies hovered above the surface of the water.*

2 STAY [I] to stay nervously in the same place, especially because you are waiting for something or are uncertain what to do: **+around/over etc.** *He hovered anxiously in the doorway.*

3 NOT CHANGE [I always + adv./prep.] if something such as a price, temperature, or rate that can go up or down hovers, it remains at around a particular level for a period of time: **+around/between etc.** *Temperatures hover around 100 degrees daily.*

4 IN AN UNCERTAIN CONDITION [I always + adv./prep.] to be in a state that is not clear or certain, or that could change suddenly: **+between** *The patient is hovering between life and death.* | *She was* ***hovering on the brink*** *of tears.*

5 CLOUDS [I always + adv./prep.] if fog, clouds etc. hover somewhere, they stay in the air in or over that place for a period of time

6 COMPUTER [T] if you hover a computer MOUSE or CURSOR over an area on a computer screen, you move it so that it is over that area

hov·er·craft /ˈhʌvɚˌkræft/ *n. plural* **hovercraft, hovercrafts** [C] a vehicle that travels just above the surface of land or water using a strong current of air forced out beneath it → see also HYDROFOIL

HOV lane /ˌeɪtʃ oʊ ˈvi leɪn/ *n.* [C] **high-occupancy vehicle lane** a LANE on main roads that can only be used by vehicles carrying two or three or more passengers during the time of day when there is a lot of traffic

how /haʊ/ S1 W1 *adv., conjunction*

1 METHOD used to ask or talk about the way something is done: *How should I dress for this job interview?* | *Do you know how she spells her name?* | *How do I get to North Bend?* | **how to do sth** *Ron showed me how to use the scanner.*

H

2 SIZE/DEGREE used to ask or talk about the amount, size, degree etc. of something: *Do you know how old she is?* | ***How many** people does each cabin sleep?* | ***How much*** (=how much money) *do they charge for a haircut?*
3 HEALTH/MOOD used to ask or talk about someone's health or mood: *How are you feeling this morning?* | *I didn't tell him how I feel about it.*
4 OPINION used to ask or talk about someone's opinion of something or about their experience with something: *How was the movie?* | *I asked her **how** the test **went**.*
5 MANNER used to ask or talk about the way someone or something happens, looks, sounds, behaves, is expressed etc.: *How do I look in glasses?* | *How does American English differ from British?* | *That's how we met.*
6 EMPHASIS used before an adjective or adverb to emphasize the quality you are mentioning: *Everyone was talking about how great the workshop was.* | *He was surprised at how bitter Sabina sounded.* | *He won't buy the kids an ice cream. How mean is that!*
7 INTRODUCING A FACT used like "that" for referring to a particular fact, an event, or a situation: *It's amazing how they've managed to do the work so quickly.*

SPOKEN PHRASES

8 **how are you?** used when you meet someone, to ask if they are well: *"How are you, Fumiko?" "Fine, thank you."*
9 **how's it/sth going?** also **how are you doing?**, **how are things?** **a)** used when you meet someone, to ask if they are well, happy etc.: *"How's it going, Joyce?" "Oh, okay, I guess."* | *"How are things at work?" "Just fine."* **b)** used to ask if someone is happy with what they are doing: *Hey, John, how's your work going?*
10 **how about...?** **a)** used to make a suggestion about what to do: *How about some iced tea?* | **how about doing sth?** *How about going to see a movie?* **b)** used to introduce a new idea, fact etc. that has not yet been discussed: *"I couldn't get Missy to babysit." "How about Rebekah?"*
11 **how about you?** used to ask someone what they want or what their opinion is, after you have said what you want or what your opinion is: *I like to play tennis – how about you?*
12 **how come?** used to ask why something has happened or been said, especially when you are surprised by it: *"I didn't even eat lunch today." "Really? How come?"* | *How come you got back so early?*
13 **how's that** **a)** used to ask someone whether they like something or agree with it: *How's that? Is it comfortable?* **b)** used to ask someone to repeat what they have just said
14 **how do you mean?** used to ask someone to explain something they just said: *I have strange dreams." "How do you mean, strange?"*
15 **how do you know?** used to ask in a slightly impolite way how someone found out about something or why they are sure about something: *"I don't think she'll agree." "How do you know?"*
16 IN WHATEVER WAY in whatever way someone wants, likes etc. SYN **however**: *In your own house you can act how you want.*
17 **how can/could you...?** used when you are very surprised by something or disapprove strongly of something: *How can you say that about your own parents?* | *How could you be so rude?*
18 **how about that!** also **how do you like that!** used to ask what someone thinks of something that you think is surprising, impolite, very good etc.: *He's going to pay our mortgage for us. How about that!*
19 **how so?** used to ask someone to explain an opinion they have given: *"Paul's different from other boys." "How so?"*
20 **and how!** OLD-FASHIONED an expression meaning "yes, very much," used to strongly emphasize your reply to a question: *"Did you like your hot dog?" "And how!"*
21 **how do you do?** OLD-FASHIONED, FORMAL a polite expression used when you meet someone for the first time

[**Origin:** Old English *hu*]

how·dy /ˈhaʊdi/ *interjection* used to say hello in an informal, usually humorous, way: *Howdy, folks!*

Howe /haʊ/, **E·li·as** /ɪəˈlaɪəs/ (1819–1867) the U.S. inventor of the SEWING MACHINE

Howe, Ju·li·a Ward /ˈdʒuliə wɔrd/ (1819–1910) a U.S. writer who supported women's rights and worked against SLAVERY

how·ev·er[1] /haʊˈɛvɚ/ S2 W1 *adv.* **1** [sentence adverb] used when you are adding a fact or piece of information that seems surprising, or seems to disagree with what you have just said: *This is a cheap and simple process. However, there are dangers involved.* → see Word Choice box at BUT[1] **2** used before adjectives and adverbs to say that it makes no difference how good, bad, difficult etc. something is, or how much there is of something SYN **no matter how**: *You should report all accidents, however minor.* | *I want that car, **however much** it costs.* **3** OLD-FASHIONED used to mean how, when you want to show that you find something very surprising: *However did he get to be manager?*

however[2] *conjunction* in whatever way: *You guys can split up the driving however you want.*

how·it·zer /ˈhaʊɪtsɚ/ *n.* [C] a heavy gun that fires SHELLS high into the air so that they travel a short distance

howl[1] /haʊl/ *v.* **1** [I] if a dog, WOLF, or other animal howls, it makes a long loud sound **2** [I,T] to shout or demand something angrily: **+for** *Many citizens are howling for tougher regulations.* **3** [I] to make a long loud cry because you are unhappy, in pain, or angry: *Dave **howled in pain** as the man beat him.* **4** [I] if the wind howls, it makes a loud high sound as it blows: *Strong winds howled across the region.* **5** **howl with laughter** to laugh very loudly [**Origin:** 1200–1300 from the sound]

howl sb/sth ↔ **down** *phr. v.* to prevent someone or something from being heard by shouting loudly and angrily

howl[2] *n.* [C] **1** a long loud sound made by a dog, WOLF, or other animal **2** a loud cry of pain or anger **3** **howl of laughter** a very loud laugh **4** **howl of protest** a statement or opinion that criticizes something very strongly or protests against it: *The suggestion provoked howls of protest from Democrats.*

howl·er /ˈhaʊlɚ/ *n.* [C] INFORMAL a stupid mistake that makes people laugh

howl·ing /ˈhaʊlɪŋ/ *adj.* **1** making a long loud sound: *howling winds* **2** **a howling success** something that is very successful: *The movie has been a howling success.*

how·so·ev·er /ˌhaʊsoʊˈɛvɚ/ *adv.* LITERARY HOWEVER

ˈ**how-to** *adj.* [only before noun] a how-to book, magazine etc. gives instructions on what you need to do to make something, fix something etc. —**how-to** *n.* [C]

hox gene /ˈhɑks dʒin/ *n.* [C] BIOLOGY one of a group of GENES which control how the legs, arms, and other body parts develop in an EMBRYO (=human or animal that has just begun to develop inside the mother)

HP the abbreviation of HORSEPOWER

HQ the abbreviation of HEADQUARTERS

HR[1] *n.* [C] HUMAN RESOURCES

HR[2] the written abbreviation of HOME RUN

hr. *plural* **hrs.** the written abbreviation of HOUR

H.S. the written abbreviation of HIGH SCHOOL

HST the written abbreviation of HAWAII STANDARD TIME

HT the written abbreviation of HAWAII TIME

ht. the written abbreviation of HEIGHT

HTML *n.* [U] COMPUTERS **hypertext markup language** a computer language used to make documents that can connect to other documents and FILES even if they have very different forms. It is used especially for documents on the Internet

HTTP *n.* [U] COMPUTERS **hypertext transfer protocol** a set of standards that controls how computer DOCUMENTS written in HTML connect to each other

HUAC /ˈhyuæk/ → see HOUSE UN-AMERICAN ACTIVITIES COMMITTEE

hub /hʌb/ *n.* [C] **1** the central and most important part of an area, system etc., that all the other parts are connected to: +**of** *the commercial hub of the city* **2** an airport which is a main base in a region through which many flights connect: *Detroit is one of the airline's hubs.* **3** the central part of a wheel to which the AXLE is joined → see picture at BICYCLE[1]

hub·ba-hub·ba /ˌhʌbə ˈhʌbə/ *interjection* OLD-FASHIONED SPOKEN said when you think someone is very attractive

Hub·ble /ˈhʌbəl/, **Ed·win** /ˈɛdwɪn/ (1889–1953) a U.S. ASTRONOMER who made an important discovery that shows that the universe is EXPANDING

hub·bub /ˈhʌbʌb/ *n.* [singular, U] a mixture of loud noises, especially the noise of a lot of people talking at the same time

hub·by /ˈhʌbi/ *n. plural* **hubbies** [C] INFORMAL a husband

hub·cap /ˈhʌbkæp/ *n.* [C] a metal cover for the center of a wheel on a car or truck

hu·bris /ˈhyubrɪs/ *n.* [U] LITERARY too much pride

huck·le·ber·ry /ˈhʌkəlˌbɛri/ *n. plural* **huckleberries** [C] BIOLOGY a small dark-blue North American fruit that grows on a bush

huck·ster /ˈhʌkstɚ/ *n.* [C] **1** someone who sells things, especially in a way that seems dishonest or too direct **2** someone in past times who sold small things in the street or to people in their houses

huck·ster·ism /ˈhʌkstɚˌɪzəm/ *n.* [U] the use of very strong, direct, and sometimes dishonest methods to try to persuade someone to buy something

HUD /hʌd/ Housing and Urban Development; a U.S. government department that is responsible for providing houses for people to live in, and the way cities are developed

hud·dle[1] /ˈhʌdl/ *v.* **1** [I,T] also **huddle together/up** if a group of people huddle together, they gather closely together in a group: *They huddled up close to each other.* | +**around** *People huddled around their radios and TVs, waiting for news.* **2** [I always + adv./prep.] to lie or sit with your arms and legs close to your body, especially because you are cold or frightened: *Homeless men huddled beneath flimsy blankets on the sidewalk.* **3** [I] to meet with a small group of people in order to discuss something or make a decision privately: *The executive board huddled to discuss the issue.* **4** [I] if football players huddle, they gather around one player who tells them the plan for the next part of the game

huddle[2] *n.* [C] **1** a group of players in football who gather around one player who tells them the plan for the next part of the game **2** a group of people standing or sitting close together, especially in order to discuss something **3** a group of things that are close together: +**of** *a huddle of small houses around the harbor*

Hud·son /ˈhʌdsən/, **Henry** (?1550–1611) an English EXPLORER who was the first European to discover the Hudson River

ˌHudson ˈBay a large area of sea in northern Canada which is frozen for most of the year

ˌHudson ˈRiver, the a river in New York State in the northeastern U.S. that meets the Atlantic Ocean in New York City

hue /hyu/ *n.* [C] LITERARY a color or type of color: *The sky had turned a rosy hue.*

ˌhue and ˈcry *n.* [singular, U] angry protests about something: *The bill has raised a hue and cry from the gay community.*

huff[1] /hʌf/ *n.* **in a huff** feeling angry or in a bad mood, especially because someone has offended you: *Michelle got mad and left in a huff.*

huff[2] *v.* [I] INFORMAL **1 huff and puff** to breathe out in a noisy way, especially because you are tired: *A couple of pudgy joggers were huffing and puffing along the path.* **2** [T] to say something in a way that shows you are angry, often because you have been offended: *"You should have warned me," she huffed.*

huff·y /ˈhʌfi/ *adj. comparative* **huffier**, *superlative* **huffiest** INFORMAL in a bad mood, especially because someone has offended you: *Some customers* ***get huffy*** *when you ask them for their ID.* —**huffily** *adv.*

hug[1] /hʌg/ *v.* **hugged, hugging 1** [I,T] to put your arms around someone and hold them tightly to show love or friendship: *He picked the little girl up and hugged her.* | *They hugged and said goodbye.*

THESAURUS

embrace to put your arms around someone and hold him or her in a caring way: *Jason warmly embraced his son.*
cuddle to put your arms around someone or something as a sign of love: *She sat on a chair, cuddling her daughter.*
hold to have something firmly in your hands or arms: *She held the baby in her arms.*

2 [T] to move along the side, edge, top etc. of something, staying very close to it: *The railroad hugs the coast for about 50 miles.* **3** [T] if clothes hug your body, they fit closely: **body-/figure-hugging** *Surfers wear body-hugging wetsuits.* **4** [T] to hold something in your arms, close to your chest: *He sat up in bed, hugging his knees.*

hug[2] *n.* [C] the act of hugging someone: *Come on, Kelly,* ***give*** *Grandma* ***a hug.*** → see also BEAR HUG

huge /hyudʒ/ S1 W2 *adj.* **1** extremely large in size SYN **enormous**: *a huge dog* | *These shoes make my feet look huge.* ►see THESAURUS box at **big** **2** extremely large in number, amount, or degree SYN **enormous**: *huge debts* | *The novel was a huge success.* | *Your changes make a huge difference.* | *A huge number of people came.* [**Origin:** 1100–1200 Old French *ahuge*] —**hugely** *adv.*: *hugely successful* —**hugeness** *n.* [U]

Hughes /hyuz/, **Charles S.** (1862–1948) a CHIEF JUSTICE on the U.S. Supreme Court

Hughes, How·ard /ˈhaʊɚd/ (1905–1976) a U.S. BUSINESSMAN, aircraft designer, pilot, and film PRODUCER

Hughes, Lang·ston /ˈlæŋstən/ (1902–1967) a U.S. poet and writer

Hu·go /ˈhyugoʊ/, **Vic·tor** /ˈvɪktɚ/ (1802–1885) a French writer of poems, plays, and NOVELS

Hu·gue·nots /ˈhyugəˌnɑts/ *n.* a group of French Protestants during the 16th and 17th centuries, when Protestants were often treated very badly in France —**Huguenot** *adj.*

huh /hʌ/ *interjection* **1** said when you have not heard or understood a question: *"It should work, don't you think?" "Huh?"* **2** said at the end of a question, to ask for agreement: *Not a bad restaurant, huh?*

huh-uh /ˈhʌ ʌ/ *interjection* a sound you make that means "no" SYN **uh-uh** OPP **uh-huh**: *"Did he lose that money?" "Huh-uh."*

hu·la /ˈhulə/ *n.* [C] a Poynesian dance done by women using gentle movements of the HIPS

ˈHula-Hoop, hula hoop *n.* [C] TRADEMARK a large ring which you make swing around your waist by moving your HIPS

ˈhula skirt *n.* [C] a skirt made of many long thin pieces of material or tropical grass that are fastened together around the waist and hang loosely at the bottom

hulk /hʌlk/ *n.* [C] **1** an old ship, plane, or vehicle that is not used anymore: *The rusty hulks of old tractors sit on the hill.* **2** a large heavy person or thing

hulk·ing /ˈhʌlkɪŋ/ *adj.* [only before noun] very big and often awkward: *Two hulking guards stood at attention.*

hull[1] /hʌl/ *n.* [C] **1** the main part of a ship **2** the outer covering of seeds, rice, grain etc. **3** the hard usually green part of a fruit such as a strawberry or raspberry, where it joins the stem

hull² *v.* [T] to remove the hull of seeds, rice, grain, fruit etc.

hul·la·ba·loo /ˈhʌləbəˌlu, ˌhʌləbəˈlu/ *n.* [C usually singular, U] **1** excited talk, newspaper stories etc., especially about something surprising or shocking: *There's been a huge hullabaloo over her new book.* **2** a lot of noise, especially made by people shouting

hum¹ /hʌm/ *v.* **hummed, humming** **1** [I,T] to sing a tune by making a continuous sound with your lips closed: *Carol hummed along to the song on the radio.* **2** [I] to make a low continuous sound: *Sewing machines hummed on the factory floor.* **3** [I usually in progressive] to be very busy and full of activity: *By nine o'clock, the restaurant was humming.* [**Origin:** 1300–1400 from the sound]

hum² *n.* [singular, U] **1** a low continuous sound: *the distant hum of traffic* **2** the sound made when you hum

hu·man¹ /ˈhyumən/ S2 W1 *adj.* **1** belonging to or relating to people, especially as opposed to animals or machines: *human behavior* | *The noise he made didn't sound human.* | *No two **human beings** (=people) are exactly alike.* | *diseases of the **human body*** | *The organisms are not visible to **the human eye**.* **2** human weaknesses, emotions etc. are typical of ordinary people: *Fear is a very human emotion.* **3 sb is only human** used to say that someone should not be blamed for what they have done, because they could not have done anything more: *Judges are only human – sometimes they make mistakes.* **4** someone who seems human shows that they have the same feelings and emotions as ordinary people OPP **inhuman**: *The incident made Herman seem more human to his fans.* **5 human error** a mistake or mistakes made by people, rather than machines, computers etc.: *The accident was caused by human error.* **6 human interest** the quality in a story, news report, etc. that make people want to read it because it is about people's lives, feelings, relationships etc.: *human interest stories* **7 put a human face on sth** to make the public think differently about an event, political situation etc. by directing their attention to a particular person: *Anne Frank's diary put a human face on the Holocaust.* [**Origin:** 1300–1400 French *humain*, from Latin *humanus*]

human² W3 also **ˌhuman ˈbeing** *n.* [C] a person

ˌhuman ˈcapital also **ˌhuman ˈresource** *n.* [U] SOCIAL SCIENCE people and their skills, considered as one of the things an economic system, country, or organization needs in order to produce goods or services and make wealth

ˌhuman characterˈistic also **ˌhuman ˈfeature** *n.* [C] something that people have built in order to use, such as a city, airport, road etc. → see also PHYSICAL FEATURE: *The human characteristics of the community include its schools, parks, museums, and hospitals.*

hu·mane /hyuˈmeɪn/ *adj.* treating people or animals in a way that is kind, not cruel OPP **inhumane**: *Animals are now raised in more humane conditions.* —**humanely** *adv.*

ˌhuman-enˈvironment interˌaction *n.* [U] the way that people and their environment affect and change each other

Huˈmane Soˌciety a U.S. organization that takes care of unwanted pets, especially ones that were treated cruelly, and encourages people to treat animals better

hu·man·ism /ˈhyuməˌnɪzəm/ *n.* [U] **1** a system of beliefs that tries to solve human problems through science rather than religion **2 Humanism** HISTORY the study during the Renaissance of the ideas of the ancient Greeks and Romans —**humanist** *n.* [C] —**humanistic** /ˌhyuməˈnɪstɪk/ *adj.*

hu·man·i·tar·i·an /hyuˌmænəˈtɛriən/ *adj.* [only before noun] concerned with improving bad living conditions and preventing unfair treatment of people: **humanitarian aid/assistance/relief** *Humanitarian aid is being sent to the refugees.* | **for humanitarian reasons/on humanitarian grounds** *The prisoners were released on humanitarian grounds.* —**humanitarian** *n.* [C] —**humanitarianism** *n.* [U]

human body

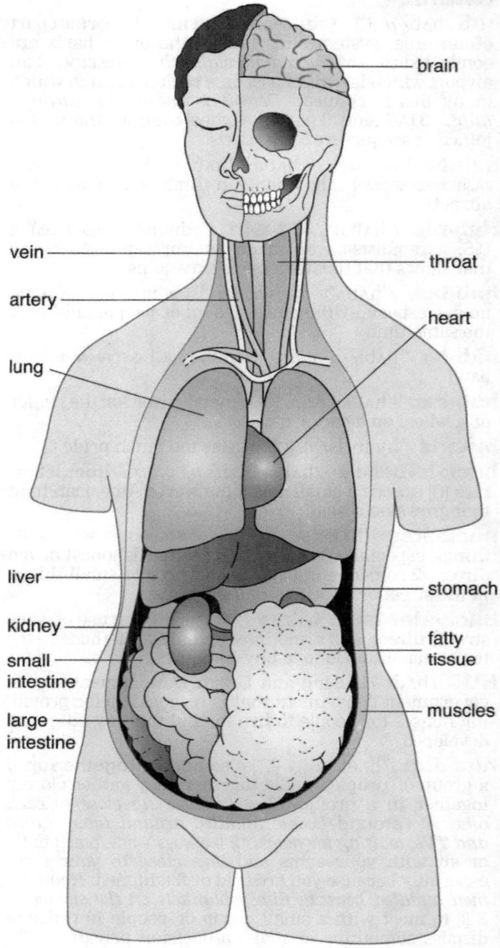

hu·man·i·ty /hyuˈmænət̬i/ *n.* **1** [U] people in general: *We want a clean environment for all humanity.* | *He described the invasion of his country as **a crime against humanity**.* **2** [U] the state of being a human being: *We must never forget **our common humanity**.* **3** [U] kindness, respect, and sympathy toward other people: *a man of deep humanity* **4 humanities** [plural] subjects of study such as literature, history, art, PHILOSOPHY etc., rather than subjects relating to science or mathematics **5** [U] the state of being human and having qualities and rights that all people have: *The medical course stresses each patient's humanity.*

hu·man·ize /ˈhyuməˌnaɪz/ *v.* [T] to make a place or system nicer or more appropriate for people: *The administration has made attempts to humanize the prison.*

hu·man·kind /ˈhyumənˌkaɪnd/ *n.* [U] people in general: *the history of humankind*

hu·man·ly /ˈhyumənli/ *adv.* **1 do everything humanly possible** as much as anyone could possibly do: *Firefighters did everything humanly possible to save lives.* **2 humanly possible** if something is humanly possible, it can be done using a great deal of effort: *It is not humanly possible to work all day without a break.* **3** relating to or similar to humans: *The poor animal's eyes seemed humanly expressive.*

ˌhuman ˈnature *n.* [U] **1** the qualities or ways of

behaving that are natural and common to most people: *What does the novel reveal about human nature?* **2 be (only/just) human nature** used to say that a particular feeling or way of behaving is normal and natural: *It's human nature to put off doing things you don't like to do.*

hu•man•oid /ˈhyuməˌnɔɪd/ *adj.* something that is humanoid has a human shape and qualities —**humanoid** *n.* [C]

ˌhuman ˈrace *n.* **the human race** all people, considered together as a single group

ˌhuman ˈresources *n.* **1** [U] ABBREVIATION **HR** the department in a company that deals with employing, training, and helping people SYN **personnel** **2** [plural] the abilities and skills of people

ˌhuman ˈrights *n.* [plural] the basic rights which every person has to be treated in a fair equal way without cruelty, especially by their government

ˌhuman ˈshield *n.* [C] someone who is taken and kept as a prisoner in order to protect a criminal from being killed, injured, or caught, or in order to stop the enemy in a war from attacking or bombing a place

hum•ble¹ /ˈhʌmbəl/ *adj.* **1** APPROVING not considering yourself or your ideas to be as important as other people's OPP **proud**: *a humble and modest man* | *Please accept my **humble apologies**.* **2** relating to a low social class or position: *a humble house on a back street* | **humble beginnings/origins** *The senator rose from humble beginnings on an Iowa farm.* **3 in my humble opinion** SPOKEN used to give your opinion about something in a slightly humorous way **4 my humble abode** HUMOROUS said when you are talking about your house to suggest it is not big, nice, or expensive: *Welcome to our humble abode.* **5** [only before noun] simple, ordinary, and not special: *Scientists say the humble potato may be the key to feeding the world's population.* **6 eat humble pie** to admit that you were wrong about something [**Origin:** 1200–1300 Old French, Latin *humilis* **low, humble**, from *humus* **earth**] —**humbly** *adv.* → see also HUMILITY

humble² *v.* **1 be humbled** if you are humbled, you realize that you are not as important, good, powerful etc. as you thought you were: *You can't help but be humbled when you walk into this magnificent cathedral.* **2** [T] to easily defeat someone who is much stronger than you are: *A band of soldiers had humbled the mighty army.* **3 humble yourself** FORMAL to show that you are not too proud to ask for something, admit you are wrong etc.: *In the end I had to humble myself and ask them to help.* —**humbling** *adj.*: *a humbling experience*

hum•bug /ˈhʌmbʌg/ *n.* **1 bah, humbug!** OLD-FASHIONED SPOKEN, HUMOROUS used when you do not believe something is true, or when you think something is insincere and silly **2** [U] OLD-FASHIONED insincere or dishonest words or behavior: *He dismissed the president's comments as humbug.* **3** [U] OLD-FASHIONED someone who pretends to be someone they are not, or to have qualities or opinions they do not have

hum•ding•er /ˌhʌmˈdɪŋɚ/ *n.* [singular] INFORMAL a very exciting or impressive game, performance, or event: *a humdinger of a party*

hum•drum /ˈhʌmdrʌm/ *adj.* boring and ordinary, and having very little variety or interest: *a humdrum job*

Hume /hyum/, **Da•vid** /ˈdeɪvɪd/ (1711–1776) a Scottish writer on PHILOSOPHY and history, known for his belief in EMPIRICISM

hu•mer•us /ˈhyumərəs/ [C] *n.* BIOLOGY the bone between your shoulder and elbow → see picture at SKELETON¹

hu•mid /ˈhyumɪd/ *adj.* weather that is humid makes you feel uncomfortable because the air feels very hot and wet: *a hot, humid afternoon* [**Origin:** 1300–1400 Latin *humidus*, from *humere* **to be slightly wet**]

ˌhumid ˌcontinental ˈclimate *n.* [C] EARTH SCIENCE a CLIMATE (=typical weather conditions in an area) with cool to hot summers and very cold winters

hu•mi•dex /ˈhyumɪˌdɛks/ *n.* [singular] CANADIAN → see HEAT INDEX

hu•mid•i•fi•er /hyuˈmɪdəˌfaɪɚ/ *n.* [C] a machine that makes the air in a room less dry

hu•mid•i•fy /hyuˈmɪdəˌfaɪ/ *v.* **humidifies**, *past tense and past participle* **humidified, humidifying** [T] to add very small drops of water to the air in a room etc. because the air is too dry

hu•mid•i•ty /hyuˈmɪdət̬i/ *n.* [U] EARTH SCIENCE the amount of water contained in the air: *Some plants need warmth and high humidity.*

hu•mi•dor /ˈhyumɪˌdɔr/ *n.* [C] OLD-FASHIONED a box that CIGARS are kept in

hu•mil•i•ate /hyuˈmɪliˌeɪt/ *v.* [T] to make someone feel ashamed and upset, especially by making them seem stupid or weak: *You humiliated me in front of my friends!* —**humiliated** *adj.* —**humiliating** *adj.*: *a humiliating defeat*

hu•mil•i•a•tion /hyuˌmɪliˈeɪʃən/ *n.* **1** [U] a feeling of shame and great embarrassment, because you have been made to look stupid or weak: *Rape is an act of violence and humiliation.* **2** [C] a situation that makes you feel humiliated

hu•mil•i•ty /hyuˈmɪlət̬i/ *n.* [U] APPROVING the quality of not being too proud about yourself: *Humility and discipline are important in the martial arts.* → see also HUMBLE¹

hum•ming•bird /ˈhʌmɪŋˌbɚd/ *n.* [C] BIOLOGY a very small brightly colored bird whose wings move very quickly

hum•mus, humus /ˈhuməs, ˈhʊ-/ *n.* [U] a type of Middle Eastern food made from a soft mixture of CHICKPEAS, oil, and GARLIC

hu•mon•gous, **humungous** /hyuˈmʌŋgəs/ *adj.* INFORMAL very large: *They have a humongous dog.*

hu•mor¹ /ˈhyumɚ/ S3 W3 *n.* **1** [U] the quality in something that makes it funny and makes people laugh: *an attempt at humor* | *She couldn't **see the humor in** the situation.* **2** [U] the ability to laugh at things and think that they are funny: *a man of great humor and charm.* | *Vicki has a really zany **sense of humor**.* **3** [U] the way that a particular person or group find certain things amusing: *Jewish humor has greatly affected American culture.* | **dry/deadpan humor** (=a way of saying something funny as if you are serious) **4** [singular, U] the mood that someone is in: **good/bad humor** *She soon recovered her good humor.* | **in a good/bad humor** *She was in a bad humor that day.* | *Walsh **took** all the teasing **in good humor**.* → see also GOOD-HUMORED **5** [C] TECHNICAL one of the liquids that is naturally present in the body **6** [C] one of the four liquids that in the past were thought to be present in the body and to influence someone's character

humor² *v.* [T] to do what someone wants so they will not become angry or upset: *Just humor me and listen.*

hu•mor•ist /ˈhyumərɪst/ *n.* [C] someone, especially a writer, who tells funny stories

hu•mor•less /ˈhyumɚlɪs/ *adj.* too serious and not able to laugh at things that are funny —**humorlessly** *adv.* —**humorlessness** *n.* [U]

hu•mor•ous /ˈhyumərəs/ *adj.* funny and enjoyable: *a humorous speech* —**humorously** *adv.*

hu•mour /ˈhyumɚ/ the British and Canadian spelling of HUMOR, also used in the word "humourless"

hump /hʌmp/ *n.* [C] **1** a large round shape that rises above the surface of the ground or a surface: *I saw the hump under the blanket and figured you were asleep.* **2 be over the hump** to have finished the most difficult part of something: *With this win, the coach feels the team is over the hump.* **3** BIOLOGY a raised part on the back of a CAMEL and some other animals **4** BIOLOGY a raised part on someone's back that is caused by an unusually curved SPINE

hump•back whale /ˌhʌmpbæk ˈweɪl/ *n.* [C] a large type of WHALE

H

humph /hʌmf, hmh, hm/ *interjection* a sound you make to show that you do not believe something or do not approve of something

hu·mus /ˈhyuməs/ *n.* [U] **1** BIOLOGY material made of decayed plants, leaves etc., which is good for growing plants **2** HUMMUS

hum·vee /ˌhʌmˈvi/ *n.* [C] TRADEMARK a large military car that can climb hills and drive through sand

Hun /hʌn/ *n.* [C] a member of a group of people from central Asia who attacked and controlled parts of Europe during the 4th and 5th centuries A.D.

hunch¹ /hʌntʃ/ *n.* [C] a feeling that something is true or that something will happen, even if you do not have any facts of proof about it: *I **had a hunch** you'd call this morning.*

hunch² *v.* [I,T] to bend forward and downward so that your back forms a curve: +**over** *Lori hunched over to keep the wind out of her face.* | *Try not to **hunch** your **shoulders** when you walk.* —**hunched** *adj.*

hunch·back /ˈhʌntʃbæk/ *n.* [C] OFFENSIVE someone who has a large raised part on their back because their SPINE curves in an unusual way

hun·dred¹ /ˈhʌndrɪd/ S2 *number* **1** 100: *a hundred years* | *two hundred miles* **2 hundreds of sth** a very large number of things or people: *Hundreds of people came to the meeting.* **3 a hundred times** SPOKEN a phrase meaning "many times," used when you are annoyed: *I've told you a hundred times to turn off the lights!* **4 a/one hundred percent** SPOKEN completely: *I'm a hundred percent sure I put it back in the cupboard.* **5 give a hundred percent** also **give a hundred and ten percent** to do everything you can in order to achieve something: *Everyone on the team gave a hundred percent.* [**Origin:** Old English]

GRAMMAR

Singular and plural forms of the number words **dozen, hundred, thousand, million,** and **billion** are all used in the same ways. When one of these words follows a word showing a number or amount, it is not put in the plural and does not have *of* after it: *a/three/several hundred years* (NOT *three hundreds of years*)| *ten million people* | *a few dozen eggs* | *about fifty thousand miles.* Where there is no other word showing a number or amount, the plural is used: *He has hundreds of books* (NOT *He has hundred of books*). | *It will cost thousands of dollars* (=I do not know how many thousand exactly).

hundred² *n.* [C] a piece of paper money worth $100

hun·dredth¹ /ˈhʌndrɪdθ/ *adj.* 100th; next after the ninety-ninth: *my great-grandmother's hundredth birthday*

hundredth² *pron.* **the hundredth** the 100th thing in a series

hundredth³ *n.* [C] 1/100; one of one hundred equal parts

hun·dred·weight /ˈhʌndrɪdˌweɪt/ WRITTEN ABBREVIATION **cwt.** *n.* [C] a unit for measuring weight equal to 100 pounds or 45.36 kilograms

ˌHundred Years' ˈWar, the HISTORY a series of wars between England and France from 1337 to 1453, which finally resulted in England losing all its French land except Calais

hung¹ /hʌŋ/ *v.* the past tense and past participle of HANG → see also **be hung up on/about sth** at HANG UP (3)

hung² *adj.* **hung jury** a JURY that cannot agree about whether someone is guilty of a crime → see also HUNG OVER

Hun·ga·ry /ˈhʌŋgəri/ a country in central Europe, east of Austria and west of Romania —**Hungarian** /hʌŋˈgɛriən/ *n., adj.*

hun·ger¹ /ˈhʌŋgɚ/ *n.* **1** [U] lack of food, especially for a long period of time, that can cause illness or death SYN **starvation**: *the problem of hunger in developing nations* | *The prisoners were weak **from hunger**.* **2** [U] the feeling that you need to eat → see also THIRST: *Have a healthy snack to **satisfy your hunger**.* **3** [C,U] a strong need or desire for something: +**for** *From birth, every child has a hunger for learning.* [**Origin:** Old English *hungor*]

hunger² *v.*

hunger for sth *phr. v.* LITERARY to want something very much: *people who are hungering for a better life*

ˈhunger strike *n.* [C] a situation in which someone refuses to eat for a long time, in order to protest about something: *In 1986, Snyder **went on a hunger strike**.* —**hunger striker** *n.* [C]

ˌhung ˈover *adj.* feeling sick because you drank too much alcohol the previous day → see also HANGOVER

hun·gri·ly /ˈhʌŋgrəli/ *adv.* **1** in a way that shows you want to eat something very much: *The two little girls ate hungrily.* **2** in a way that shows you want something very much: *Developers have been eyeing the land hungrily.*

hun·gry /ˈhʌŋgri/ S1 *adj.* *comparative* **hungrier**, *superlative* **hungriest** **1** wanting to eat something → see also THIRSTY: *I'm really hungry!* | *a hungry baby* | *There's some cold chicken in the fridge if you **get hungry**.* **2** sick or weak as a result of not having enough to eat for a long time: *Our country's children are poor and hungry.* | *Thousands of families **go hungry*** (=live in a constant state of hunger) *every day.* **3** wanting or needing something very much: +**for** *People are hungry for good music.* | **hungry to do sth** *These kids are hungry to learn.* **4 the hungry** people who never have enough food to eat: *Your money will help feed the hungry* **5 a hungry mouth to feed** someone, usually a child, who depends on you for food: *I had no job and four hungry mouths to feed.*

-hungry /hʌŋgri/ [in adjectives] **power-hungry/news-hungry etc.** wanting or needing power, news etc. very much: *money-hungry politicians* | *energy-hungry appliances*

hunk /hʌŋk/ *n.* [C] **1** a thick piece of something that has been taken from a bigger piece: +**of** *a hunk of cheese* **2** INFORMAL a sexually attractive man with a big strong body

hun·ker /ˈhʌŋkɚ/ *v.*

hunker down *phr. v.* **1** to not do things that may be risky, so that you are safe and protected: *People are hunkering down and waiting for the economy to get better.* **2** to sit on your heels with your knees bent SYN **squat**

hunk·y /ˈhʌŋki/ *adj.* *comparative* **hunkier**, *superlative* **hunkiest** a man who is hunky is sexually attractive and strong-looking

hun·ky-dor·y /ˌhʌŋki ˈdɔri/ *adj.* [not before noun] INFORMAL a situation that is hunky-dory is one in which everyone feels happy and there are no problems

hunt¹ /hʌnt/ S3 W3 *v.* **1** [I,T] to try to kill an animal to eat it, to get its skin, or for sport: *This isn't the season for hunting deer.* **2** [I] if an animal hunts, it chases other animals in order to kill and eat them: *Owls usually hunt at night.* | +**for** *The cat was hunting for mice.* **3** [I] to look for someone or something very carefully SYN **search**: +**for** *The kids were hunting for shells on the beach.* **4** [I,T] to search for and try to catch someone, especially a criminal: *Police are still hunting the killer.* | **hunt for sb** *The military has been hunting for him for years.* **5 hunt and peck** a method of typing by which you must look for every letter on the KEYBOARD before you type it [**Origin:** Old English *huntian*]

hunt sb/sth ↔ **down** *phr. v.* to find an enemy or a criminal after searching hard: *Army troops are hunting down the guerrillas.*

hunt sb/sth ↔ **out** *phr. v.* **1** to search for someone in order to catch or get rid of them: *a mission to hunt out enemy submarines* **2** to look for something that is difficult to find: *Jack hunted out a shady spot where he could sit and read.*

hunt² *n.* [C] **1** [usually singular] a careful search for someone or something that is difficult to find SYN **search**: +**for** *the hunt for the missing child* | *a hunt* *for the best person to lead the party* **2** an occasion when people look for or chase animals in order to kill them: *illegal elephant hunts*

hunt·er /ˈhʌntɚ/ *n.* **1** [C] a person or animal that hunts wild animals: *deer hunters* **2 bargain/treasure etc. hunter** someone who looks for or collects a particular type of thing → see also BOUNTY HUNTER, FORTUNE HUNTER

hunt·ing /ˈhʌntɪŋ/ *n.* [U] **1** the act of chasing and killing animals for food or for sport: *deer hunting* | *a hunting rifle* | *We drove up into the mountains to **go hunting**.* **2 job-hunting/house-hunting etc.** the activity of looking for a job, house etc.: *We're house-hunting in the suburbs right now.* —**hunting** *adj.* [only before noun] *a hunting rifle*

ˈhunting ˌground *n.* [C] **1** [usually plural] an area of land where animals are hunted: *traditional Native American hunting grounds* **2** a place where people who are interested in a particular thing can easily find what they want: *Roadsides are an ideal hunting ground for recyclable bottles and cans.*

hunt·ress /ˈhʌntrɪs/ *n.* [C] LITERARY a female hunter

hunts·man /ˈhʌntsmən/ *n. plural* **huntsmen** /-mən/ [C] LITERARY a man who hunts animals

hur·dle[1] /ˈhɚdl/ *n.* **1** [C] a problem or difficulty that you must deal with before you can achieve something: *Finding enough money for the project was the first hurdle.* | **overcome/clear a hurdle** *Just to get this far, Alison has overcome several hurdles.* **2** [C] a type of small fence that a person or horse has to jump over during a race **3 the hurdles** [plural] a race in which the runners have to jump over hurdles: *the women's 100-meter hurdles*

hurdle[2] *v.* **1** [T] to jump over something while you are running: *Barrett hurdled the fence and ran down the street.* **2** [I] to run in hurdle races —**hurdler** *n.* [C] —**hurdling** *n.* [U]

hur·dy-gur·dy /ˌhɚdi ˈgɚdi/ *n. plural* **hurdy-gurdies** [C] a small musical instrument that you operate by turning a handle

hurl /hɚl/ *v.* **1** [T always + adv./prep.] to throw something violently and with a lot of force, especially because you are angry: **hurl sth through/across/over etc. sth** *Vandals hurled rocks through the windows.* ▸see THESAURUS box at **throw**[1] **2 hurl abuse/insults/accusations etc. at sb** to shout at someone in a loud and angry way: *Fans were hurling abuse at the referee.* **3 hurl yourself at/against etc. something** to make make yourself move very quickly, sometimes through the air, with a lot of force **4** [I] SLANG to VOMIT

hur·ly-bur·ly /ˌhɚli ˈbɚli/ *n.* [U] a lot of busy noisy activity: *the hurly-burly of city life*

Hu·ron /ˈhyʊrən, -ɑn/ a group of Native American tribes who lived near the Great Lakes in North America in the 16th and 17th centuries

Huron, Lake the second largest of the five Great Lakes on the border between the U.S. and Canada

hur·ray /həˈreɪ, hʊˈreɪ/ also **hur·rah** /həˈrɑ, hʊ-/ *interjection* OLD-FASHIONED another spelling of HOORAY

hur·ri·cane /ˈhɚɪˌkeɪn, ˈhʌr-/ *n.* [C] EARCH SCIENCE a severe tropical storm that forms over the Atlantic Ocean at the end of summer and beginning of fall, with very strong winds of at least 74 miles per hour → see picture on page A30 [**Origin:** 1500–1600 Spanish *huracán*, from Taino *hurakán*] → see also CYCLONE, TORNADO, TYPHOON

ˈhurricane ˌlamp *n.* [C] a lamp that has a cover to protect the flame inside from the wind

hur·ried /ˈhɚɪd, ˈhʌrid/ *adj.* [usually before noun] done more quickly than usual SYN **rushed** OPP **leisurely**: *a hurried meeting with the lawyers* —**hurriedly** *adv.*

hur·ry[1] /ˈhɚi, ˈhʌri/ S3 *v.* **hurries, hurried, hurrying** **1** [I,T] to do something or go somewhere more quickly than usual, especially because there is not much time SYN **rush**: *If we hurry, we'll get there in time* | *I hate having to hurry a meal.* | **hurry through/along/down etc.** *My mother came hurrying down the stairs.* | **hurry after sb** *John hurried after his girlfriend.* | **hurry to do sth** *Congress hurried to enact a $151 billion highways bill.* ▸see THESAURUS box at **rush**[1] **2** [T] to make someone do something more quickly SYN **rush**: *Don't hurry me. I'm working as fast as I can.* | **hurry sb along/across/through etc.** *Their mother hurried them across the street.* | **hurry sb into (doing) sth** *I don't want to hurry you into making a decision.* **3** [T always + adv./prep.] to take someone or something quickly to a place SYN **rush**: **hurry sth to/through/across etc.** *Emergency supplies were hurried to the war zone.*

hurry up *phr. v.* **1** SPOKEN used to tell someone to do something more quickly: ***Hurry up!** We're late!* **2 hurry sb/sth up** to make someone do something more quickly or to make something happen more quickly: *See if you can hurry the process up a little.*

hurry[2] S3 *n.* **1 in a hurry** more quickly than usual: *I was in a hurry.* | **do sth in a hurry** *He needs to get that mailed off in a hurry.* | **be in a hurry to do sth** *Eva was in a hurry to get back to Albuquerque.* **2 (there's) no hurry** SPOKEN said in order to tell someone that they do not have to do something quickly or soon: *You can get it sometime when you visit – there's no hurry.* **3 be in no hurry (to do sth)** also **not be in any hurry (to do sth) a)** to be able to wait because you have a lot of time in which to do something: *Take your time – I'm not in any hurry.* **b)** to be unwilling to do something or not want to do it soon: *Jill's in no hurry to sell that house.* **4 what's/why (all) the hurry?** also **what's your hurry?** SPOKEN said when you think someone is doing something too quickly: *What's the hurry? It will still be there tomorrow.* **5 in sb's hurry to do sth** while someone is trying to do something too quickly: *In his hurry to leave, Carlos tripped over a chair.*

hurt[1] /hɚt/ S1 W2 *v. past tense and past participle* **hurt**

1 INJURE SB [T] to injure yourself or someone else SYN **injure**: *Was anyone hurt in the accident?* | *Be careful, you could hurt someone with that knife.* | **hurt sth (doing sth)** *I hurt my ankle playing football.* | **hurt yourself (doing sth)** *Don't hurt yourself lifting that box.*

THESAURUS

injure used especially to say that someone is hurt quite severely, or to say that someone is hurt in an accident
wound to hurt someone using a weapon
maim to wound or injure someone very seriously and often permanently
disable to injure someone so that a part of their body no longer works correctly
paralyze to make someone lose the ability to move part or all of their body
break to damage a bone in your body
bruise to get a dark mark on your skin after part of your body has hit against something quite hard
sprain/twist to damage a joint in your body by suddenly twisting it
strain/pull to injure one of your muscles by stretching it or using it too much
dislocate to move a bone out of its normal position in a joint
→ INJURY

2 FEEL PAIN [I,T] to feel pain in a part of your body: *My feet hurt.* | **it hurts** *It hurts when I try to move my leg.* | **sth hurts sb** *I sat down because my leg was really hurting me.*

THESAURUS

ache to feel a continuous pain: *My back was aching.*
throb if a part of your body throbs, you get a regular feeling of pain in it: *She held her throbbing hand under the cold water.*
sting to feel a sudden sharp pain in your eyes, throat, or skin, or to make someone feel this: *The antiseptic might sting a little*

H

smart to hurt with a stinging pain: *The smoke made my eyes smart.*
burn to make a part of your body feel hot and uncomfortable: *The ointment burned a little when I first put it on my skin.*
pinch if something you are wearing pinches you, it is too tight and presses painfully on your skin: *These shoes pinch my toes.*
→ PAINFUL

3 CAUSE PAIN [T] to cause pain in a part of your body: *The sun's hurting my eyes.* | *It hurts my knees to run.* | *Don't worry. It won't hurt.*
4 UPSET SB [I,T] to make someone feel very upset, unhappy, sad etc.: *I'm sure she didn't say it to hurt you.* | *Her words hurt, but I didn't get angry.* | **it hurts that** *It hurts that she never calls me.* | *Michelle, I'm sorry. I didn't mean to* ***hurt your feelings****.*
5 BAD EFFECT [T] to have a bad effect on someone or something, especially by making them less successful or powerful: *The weak economy has hurt business for many retailers.* | **be (only/just) hurting yourself** *You're only hurting yourself if you don't stay in school.*
6 be hurting a) INFORMAL to feel very upset or unhappy about something: *Martha's going through a divorce and really hurting right now.* **b)** to have problems, especially financial or economic problems: *The oil industry is hurting right now.* **c)** to not have enough of something or to need something of better quality than what is already there: **+for** *The team is hurting for quarterbacks.*
7 sth won't/doesn't/can't/wouldn't hurt SPOKEN said when you think someone should do something or that something is a good idea: *The house looks pretty good, but a fresh paint job wouldn't hurt either.* | **it won't/doesn't/can't/wouldn't hurt (sb) to do sth** *It won't hurt Kyle to clean up his room.* | *It doesn't hurt to keep a record of the transaction.*
8 it doesn't/can't/won't hurt that used to say that something is an advantage in a particular situation: *She'll convince them. It can't hurt that she's a talented lawyer.*
[**Origin:** 1100–1200 Old French *hurter* **to crash violently into**] → see also HARM

hurt² S3 *adj.* **1** [not usually before noun] suffering pain or injury SYN **injured**: *It's okay; nobody* ***got hurt****.* | **badly/seriously hurt** *She was seriously hurt in the accident.* **2** very upset or unhappy because someone has said or done something that is dishonest, unfair, or not nice: *a hurt expression* | **+that** *I was very hurt that she'd forgotten my birthday.* | *She* ***felt hurt*** *and betrayed.* | *I know you like him, but I don't want you to* ***get hurt****.*

hurt³ *n.* [C,U] a feeling of great unhappiness because someone, especially someone you trust, has treated you badly or unfairly: *She saw the hurt in his eyes.* → see also HARM

hurt·ful /ˈhɚtfəl/ *adj.* making you feel very upset or offended: *a hurtful remark* —**hurtfully** *adv.* —**hurtfulness** *n.* [U]

hur·tle /ˈhɚṭl/ *v.* [I always + adv./prep.] if something, especially something big or heavy, hurtles somewhere, it moves or falls very fast: **hurtle down/through/along etc.** *Imagine an asteroid hurtling through space toward the Earth.*

hus·band¹ /ˈhʌzbənd/ S1 W1 *n.* [C] the man that a woman is married to: *Have you met my husband Roy?* ►see THESAURUS box at **relative¹** [**Origin:** Old English *husbonda*, from Old Norse, from *hus* **house** + *bondi* **someone who lives in a house**]

husband² *v.* [T] FORMAL to be very careful in the way you use your money, supplies etc., and not waste any: *Families have been husbanding their small reserves of food.*

hus·band·ry /ˈhʌzbəndri/ *n.* **1** [U] TECHNICAL farming: *animal husbandry* **2** [U] OLD-FASHIONED careful management of money and supplies

hush¹ /hʌʃ/ *v.* SPOKEN **hush** also **hush up** said in order to tell someone to be quiet, or to comfort a child who is crying or upset: *Hush, now. Try to get to sleep.* [**Origin:** 1500–1600 *husht* **silent, hushed** (15–19 centuries), from *husht* a word used to tell people to keep quiet]
hush sth ↔ **up** *phr. v.* to prevent the public from knowing about something dishonest or immoral: *The article says the Army hushed up the theft.*

hush² *n.* [singular] a peaceful silence, especially one that happens when people are expecting something to happen: *The tension mounted as* ***a hush fell over*** *the crowd* (=everyone became quiet).

hushed /hʌʃt/ *adj.* [usually before noun] quiet because people are listening, waiting to hear something, or talking quietly: *the hushed courtroom.* | *Visitors to the museum spoke in* ***hushed tones*** (=spoke quietly).

ˌhush-ˈhush *adj.* INFORMAL very secret: *The location of the operation was very hush-hush.*

ˈhush ˌmoney *n.* [U] money that is paid to someone not to tell other people about something embarrassing

ˈhush ˌpuppy *n.* [C] a small round type of bread made of corn flour that is cooked in oil or fat, usually eaten in the southern states of the U.S.

husk¹ /hʌsk/ *n.* **1** [C,U] BIOLOGY the dry outer part of corn, some grains, nuts, etc. **2** LITERARY used to describe people who seem to have lost the qualities that made them exciting and lively

husk² *v.* [T] to remove the husks from corn, grains, seeds etc.

husk·y¹ /ˈhʌski/ *adj.* **1** a husky voice is deep, quiet, and rough-sounding, often in an attractive way **2** a husky boy or man is big and strong —**huskily** *adv.* —**huskiness** *n.* [U]

husky

husky² *n. plural* **huskies** [C] a large dog with thick hair, used in Canada and Alaska to pull SLEDs over the snow

Huss /hʌs/, **John** (?1372–1415) a Czech religious leader who criticized the Catholic Church

Hus·sein /huˈseɪn/, **Sad·dam** /sæˈdæm/ → see SADDAM HUSSEIN

hus·sy /ˈhʌsi, ˈhʌzi/ *n. plural* **hussies** [C] OLD-FASHIONED a woman who is sexually immoral

hust·ings /ˈhʌstɪŋz/ *n.* **on the hustings** if a politician is on the hustings he or she is trying to get votes by traveling around to different towns and making speeches etc.

hus·tle¹ /ˈhʌsəl/ *v.* **hustled, hustling** **1** [T] to make someone move quickly, especially by pushing them: **hustle sb out/into/through etc.** *Jackson was hustled into his car by his bodyguards.* **2** [I] INFORMAL to do something with a lot of energy and determination, especially in sports: *Cindy's not a great player, but she really hustles.* **3** [I] to hurry in doing something or going somewhere: *We need to hustle if we want to make our flight.* **4** [I,T] to sell or obtain things in an illegal or dishonest way: *Kids try to hustle tourists on the streets.* **5** [I,T] SLANG to work as a PROSTITUTE, or to be in charge of PROSTITUTES

hustle² *n.* [U] **1** busy and noisy activity: *the* ***hustle and bustle*** *of the city* **2** ways of getting money that involve cheating or deceiving people **3** INFORMAL a quick and very active way of doing something, especially in sports: *Williams brings talent and hustle to the team.*

hus·tler /ˈhʌslɚ/ *n.* [C] **1** someone who cheats or deceives people to get money **2** a PROSTITUTE

Hus·ton, John /ˈhyustən/ (1906–1987) a U.S. movie DIRECTOR, writer, and actor

hut /hʌt/ *n.* [C] a small simple building with only one or two rooms: *a wooden hut*

hutch /hʌtʃ/ *n.* [C] **1** a wooden box that small animals are kept in, especially rabbits **2** a piece of furniture used for storing and showing dishes

Hut·ter·ite /ˈhʌṭəˌraɪt, ˈhʊ-/ *n.* a member of a Christian religious group who live a simple life with strict rules, separate from other people, in Canada and the northwestern U.S.

Hux·ley, Al·dous /ˈhʌksli/, /ˈɔldəs/ (1894–1963) a British writer of NOVELS

Huxley, Thomas (1825–1895) a British BIOLOGIST who supported Darwin's ideas about EVOLUTION

hwy. *n.* the written abbreviation of HIGHWAY

hy·a·cinth /ˈhaɪəˌsɪnθ/ *n.* [C] a garden plant with blue, pink, or white bell-shaped flowers and a sweet smell [**Origin:** 1500–1600 Latin *hyacinthus* **jewel, flowering plant**, from Greek *hyakinthos*]

hy·brid /ˈhaɪbrɪd/ *n.* [C] **1** BIOLOGY an animal or plant produced from parents that are GENETICally different, usually in order to produce a stronger plant or animal: *a special corn hybrid* | *hybrid plants* | +**of** *a hybrid of two species of angelfishes* **2** something that is a mixture of two or more other things: *The new trams are a hybrid. They are something between street cars and suburban trains.* | +**of** *a unique hybrid of blues, country, and pop music* **3** a car that sometimes uses a BATTERY to run instead of the GASOLINE engine, so that it does not use as much gasoline

hy·brid·i·za·tion /ˌhaɪbrɪdəˈzeɪʃən/ *n.* [U] BIOLOGY a process in which a HYBRID plant or animal is made —**hybridize** /ˈhaɪbrəˌdaɪz/ *v.* [I,T]

hy·dra /ˈhaɪdrə/ *n.* [C] **1 Hydra** a snake in ancient Greek stories that has many heads which grow again when they are cut off **2** FORMAL a problem that is very difficult to get rid of because it keeps returning when you try to get rid of it

hy·drant /ˈhaɪdrənt/ *n.* [C] a FIRE HYDRANT

hy·drate¹ /ˈhaɪdreɪt/ *n.* [C] CHEMISTRY a chemical COMPOUND that contains MOLECULES of water

hydrate² *v.* [T usually passive] to supply someone or something with water to keep them healthy and in good condition: *a cream that protects and hydrates the skin* —**hydration** /haɪˈdreɪʃən/ *n.* [U]

hy·drau·lic /haɪˈdrɔlɪk/ *adj.* [usually before noun] PHYSICS moved or operated by the pressure of water or other liquids: *a hydraulic pump* | *hydraulic brakes* —**hydraulically** /-kli/ *adv.*

hy·drau·lics /haɪˈdrɔlɪks/ *n.* **1** [plural] parts of a machine or system that use the pressure of water or other liquids to move or lift things **2** [U] the study of how to use the pressure of water or other liquids to produce power

hy·dro /ˈhaɪdroʊ/ *n.* [U] CANADIAN, INFORMAL the supply of electricity, especially from water power

hydro- /haɪdroʊ, -drə/ *prefix* **1** relating to water, or using water: *hydroelectricity* (=produced by water power) | *hydrotherapy* (=treatment of disease using water) **2** relating to HYDROGEN, or containing it: *hydrocarbons*

hy·dro·car·bon /ˈhaɪdroʊˌkɑrbən/ *n.* [C usually plural] CHEMISTRY a chemical compound that consists only of HYDROGEN and CARBON, such as coal or NATURAL GAS

hy·dro·ceph·a·ly /ˌhaɪdroʊˈsɛfəli/ also **hy·dro·ceph·a·lus** /-ˈsɛfələs/ *n.* [U] a serious medical condition, usually happening before someone is born, in which liquid becomes trapped inside their head, causing swelling which affects the brain —**hydrocephalic** /ˌhaɪdroʊsəˈfælɪk/ *adj.*

hy·dro·chlo·ric ac·id /ˌhaɪdrəklɔrɪk ˈæsɪd/ ABBREVIATION **HCl** *n.* [U] CHEMISTRY a strong acid used especially in industry

hy·dro·cor·ti·sone /ˌhaɪdroʊˈkɔrṭɪˌsoʊn/ *n.* [U] a chemical substance that is used in skin creams and other medicines, and is also produced naturally in the body

hy·dro·e·lec·tric /ˌhaɪdroʊɪˈlɛktrɪk/ *adj.* PHYSICS using water power to produce electricity: *a hydroelectric power plant* —**hydroelectrically** /-kli/ *adv.* —**hydroelectricity** /ˌhaɪdroʊɪlɛkˈtrɪsəṭi/ *n.* [U]

hy·dro·foil /ˈhaɪdrəˌfɔɪl/ *n.* [C] a large boat that raises itself above the surface of the water when it travels at high speeds → see also HOVERCRAFT

hy·dro·gen /ˈhaɪdrədʒən/ *n.* [U] SYMBOL **H** CHEMISTRY a gas that is an ELEMENT and that is lighter than air, and that forms water when it combines with OXYGEN

hy·dro·gen·at·ed /ˈhaɪdrədʒəˌneɪṭɪd, haɪˈdrɑdʒəˌneɪṭɪd/ *adj.* hydrogenated oils or fats, such as MARGARINE, have been through a process in which HYDROGEN is added to them, so that they become harder

ˈhydrogen ˌbomb *n.* [C] an extremely powerful NUCLEAR bomb

ˌhydrogen perˈoxide *n.* [U] CHEMISTRY a chemical liquid used for killing BACTERIA and for making hair and other substances lighter in color

hy·drol·o·gy /haɪˈdrɑlədʒi/ *n.* [U] the scientific study of water —**hydrologist** *n.* [C]

hy·drol·y·sis /haɪˈdrɑləsɪs/ *n* [U] CHEMISTRY a chemical reaction in which water reacts with a compound and produces two other compounds

hy·dro·pho·bi·a /ˌhaɪdrəˈfoʊbiə/ *n.* **1** [U] MEDICINE a technical word for RABIES **2** fear of water

hy·dro·plane¹ /ˈhaɪdrəˌpleɪn/ *n.* **1** [C] an airplane that can take off from and land on water SYN **seaplane** **2** [C] a HYDROFOIL

hydroplane² *v.* [I] **1** if a car hydroplanes, it slides out of control on a wet road **2** if a boat hydroplanes, it travels very quickly, just touching the surface of the water

hy·dro·pon·ics /ˌhaɪdrəˈpɑnɪks/ *n.* [U] the practice of growing plants in special liquids, rather than in dirt —**hydroponic** *adj.* —**hydroponically** /-kli/ *adv.*

hy·dro·sphere /ˈhaɪdrəˌsfɪr/ *n.* **the hydrosphere** EARTH SCIENCE all the water on, under, and above the surface of the Earth, including water in the oceans, lakes, and rivers etc., and the clouds

hy·dro·ther·mal vent /ˌhaɪdroʊˌθɚməl ˈvɛnt/ *n.* [C] EARTH SCIENCE an opening in the ground at the bottom of the sea, from which very hot water containing a lot of MINERALS is sent out with a lot of force

hy·drox·ide /haɪˈdrɑksaɪd/ *n.* [C] CHEMISTRY a chemical compound that contains one oxygen atom combined with one HYDROGEN atom

hyˌdroxide ˈion also **hy·drox·yl** /haɪˈdrɑksɪl/ *n.* [C] CHEMISTRY a negative ION which has one oxygen atom and one HYDROGEN atom

hy·e·na /haɪˈinə/ *n.* [C] a wild animal like a dog that makes a loud sound like a laugh

hy·giene /ˈhaɪdʒin/ *n.* [U] **1** the practice of keeping yourself and the things around you clean in order to prevent diseases: *Schools should have policies to ensure good hygiene in kitchen areas.* | *dental hygiene* **2** the study and practice of preventing illness or stopping it from spreading, especially by keeping things clean: *public hygiene* [**Origin:** 1600–1700 French *hygène*, from Greek *hygieina*, from *hygies* **healthy**]

hy·gi·en·ic /haɪˈdʒɛnɪk, -ˈdʒinɪk/ *adj.* clean and likely to prevent BACTERIA, infections, or diseases from spreading: *The food was not prepared in hygienic conditions.* —**hygienically** /-kli/ *adv.*

hy·gien·ist /haɪˈdʒinɪst/ *n.* [C] a DENTAL HYGIENIST

H

hy·gro·scop·ic /ˌhaɪgrəˈskɑpɪk◂/ *adj.* CHEMISTRY hygroscopic salts and other compounds are able or likely to take in water easily from the surrounding air

hy·men /ˈhaɪmən/ *n.* [C] BIOLOGY a piece of skin that partly covers the entrance to the VAGINA of some girls or women who have not had sex

hymn /hɪm/ *n.* [C] a song of praise to God: *a hymn book* [**Origin:** 800–900 Latin *hymnus* **song of praise**, from Greek *hymnos*]

hym·nal /ˈhɪmnəl/ also **ˈhymn book** *n.* [C] a book of hymns

hype¹ /haɪp/ *n.* [U] DISAPPROVING attempts to make people think something is good or important by talking about it a lot on television, the radio etc.: *media hype about the movie* [**Origin:** 1900–2000 *hype* **deceiving, lies**]

hype² *v.* [T] also **hype sth ↔ up** to try to make people think something is good or important by talking about it a lot on television, the radio etc.: *He's using the controversy to hype his new book.* ►see THESAURUS box at **advertise**

ˌhyped ˈup *adj.* INFORMAL very excited or nervous, and unable to keep still

hy·per /ˈhaɪpɚ/ *adj.* INFORMAL extremely excited and active

hyper- /haɪpɚ/ *prefix* **1** more than usual, especially too much: *hypersensitive* (=too sensitive) | *hyperextension* (=bending something too far) | *a hyper-intelligent person* (=much smarter than normal people) **2** beyond the usual size or limits: *a hyperlink* (=from one WEBSITE to another)

hy·per·ac·tive /ˌhaɪpɚˈæktɪv/ *adj.* TECHNICAL someone, especially a child, who is hyperactive is too active, and is not able keep still or be quiet for very long —**hyperactivity** /ˌhaɪpɚækˈtɪvət̬i/ *n.* [U]

hy·per·bo·la /haɪˈpɚbələ/ *n.* [C] MATH a pair of curved lines formed by a PLANE (=flat surface) crossing two matching CONES one directly above the other and touching at the points, so that the difference of the distances between two fixed points inside the curves to any point on the curves is always the same → see also CONIC SECTION

hy·per·bo·le /hɪˈpɚbəli/ *n.* [U] ENG. LANG. ARTS a way of describing something by saying it is much bigger, smaller, worse etc. than it really is: *The article separates the facts from hyperbole.* —**hyperbolic** /ˌhaɪpɚˈbɑlɪk/ *adj.* → see also EXAGGERATE

hy·per·crit·i·cal /ˌhaɪpɚˈkrɪt̬ɪkəl◂/ *adj.* too eager to criticize other people and things, especially about small details —**hypercritically** /-kli/ *adv.*

hy·per·in·fla·tion /ˌhaɪpərɪnˈfleɪʃən/ *n.* [U] ECONOMICS a rapid rise in prices that seriously damages a country's ECONOMY

hy·per·link /ˈhaɪpɚˌlɪŋk/ *n.* [C] COMPUTERS a LINK between two computer documents

hy·per·sen·si·tive /ˌhaɪpɚˈsɛnsət̬ɪv/ *adj.* **1** if someone is hypersensitive to a drug, substance etc., their body reacts very badly to it: **+to** *Jen's doctors found that she was hypersensitive to smoke.* **2** very easily offended or upset: **+to/about** *Bill's hypersensitive to criticism.* —**hypersensitivity** /ˌhaɪpɚˌsɛnsəˈtɪvət̬i/ *n.* [U]

hy·per·ten·sion /ˌhaɪpɚˈtɛnʃən, ˈhaɪpɚˌtɛnʃən/ *n.* [U] MEDICINE a medical condition in which your BLOOD PRESSURE is too high

hy·per·text /ˈhaɪpɚˌtɛkst/ *n.* [U] COMPUTERS a way of writing computer documents that makes it possible to move from one document to another by CLICKing on words or pictures, especially on the Internet

hy·per·ton·ic /ˌhaɪpɚˈtɑnɪk/ *adj.* CHEMISTRY a hypertonic SOLUTION (=liquid with substances dissolved in it) contains more of a SOLUTE (=substance that is dissolved) than another solution that you are comparing it to → see also HYPOTONIC

hy·per·ven·ti·late /ˌhaɪpɚˈvɛntlˌeɪt/ *v.* [I] to breathe too quickly or too deeply, so that you get too much OXYGEN and feel DIZZY —**hyperventilation** /ˌhaɪpɚvɛntlˈeɪʃən/ *n.* [U]

hy·phen /ˈhaɪfən/ *n.* [C] a short written or printed line (-) that joins words or SYLLABLES [**Origin:** 1600–1700 Late Latin, Greek, from *hyph' hen* **under one**] → see also DASH

hy·phen·ate /ˈhaɪfəˌneɪt/ *v.* [T] to join words or SYLLABLES with a HYPHEN —**hyphenated** *adj.* —**hyphenation** /ˌhaɪfəˈneɪʃən/ *n.* [U]

Hyp·nos /ˈhɪpnəs, -noʊs/ in Greek MYTHOLOGY, the god of sleep

hyp·no·sis /hɪpˈnoʊsɪs/ *n.* [U] **1** a state similar to sleep, in which someone's thoughts and actions can be influenced by someone else, or in which they can remember things they cannot remember when they are awake: *He recalled details from his childhood* ***under hypnosis*** (=in this state). **2** the act of producing this state

hyp·no·ther·a·py /ˌhɪpnoʊˈθɛrəpi/ *n.* [U] the use of hypnosis to treat emotional or physical problems —**hypnotherapist** *n.* [C]

hyp·not·ic¹ /hɪpˈnɑt̬ɪk/ *adj.* **1** making you feel sleepy or unable to pay attention to anything else, especially because a sound or movement is repeated: *hypnotic music* **2** [only before noun] relating to HYPNOSIS: *a hypnotic trance* —**hypnotically** /-kli/ *adv.*

hypnotic² *n.* [C] MEDICINE a drug that helps you to sleep

hyp·no·tism /ˈhɪpnəˌtɪzəm/ *n.* [U] the practice of hypnotizing people

hyp·no·tist /ˈhɪpnətɪst/ *n.* [C] someone who hypnotizes people, especially in public for entertainment, or in order to help them

hyp·no·tize /ˈhɪpnəˌtaɪz/ *v.* [T] **1** to produce a sleep-like state in someone, so that you can ask questions about things they do not remember while they are awake, or so that you can influence their thoughts or actions: *Nazan agreed to be hypnotized to help him stop smoking.* **2** [usually passive] to be so interesting or exciting that people cannot think of anything else: *The crowd was hypnotized by Parker's effortless performance.*

hy·po /ˈhaɪpoʊ/ *n. plural* **hypos** [C] INFORMAL a HYPODERMIC needle

hypo- /haɪpoʊ, -pə/ *prefix* TECHNICAL under or below something: *hypothermia* (=condition in which your body temperature is too low) | *a hypodermic injection* (=given under the skin)

hy·po·al·ler·gen·ic /ˌhaɪpoʊˌæləˈdʒɛnɪk/ *adj.* hypoallergenic MAKEUP, jewelry, soaps etc. are made so that they do not cause an ALLERGIC reaction when they are put on your skin

hy·po·chon·dri·a /ˌhaɪpəˈkɑndriə/ *n.* [U] a condition in which someone worries that there is something wrong with their health, even when they are not sick [**Origin:** 1500–1600 Late Latin (plural), **parts of the body just below the chest** (which was thought to be where hypochondria came from), from Greek, **parts below the central bone in the chest**]

hy·po·chon·dri·ac /ˌhaɪpəˈkɑndriˌæk/ *n.* [C] someone who worries all the time about their health, even when they are not sick —**hypochondriac** *adj.*

hy·poc·ri·sy /hɪˈpɑkrəsi/ *n.* [U] DISAPPROVING behavior or statements that show someone's moral principles, beliefs, and the things they say are not sincere: *His work is terrible. It would be* ***sheer hypocrisy*** *to compliment him.* [**Origin:** 1100–1200 Old French *ypocrisie*, from Greek *hypokrisis* **act of playing a part on stage, hypocrisy**]

hyp·o·crite /ˈhɪpəˌkrɪt/ *n.* [C] DISAPPROVING someone whose behavior or statements show that their moral principles, beliefs, and the things they say are not sincere

hy·po·crit·i·cal /ˌhɪpəˈkrɪt̬ɪkəl◂/ *adj.* DISAPPROVING behaving in a way that shows your moral principles, beliefs, and the things you say are not sincere: **it is**

hypocritical (of sb) to do sth *It would be hypocritical to ban imported weapons but not U.S.-made ones.*

hy·po·der·mic¹ /ˌhaɪpəˈdɚmɪk/ *adj.* used in an INJECTION beneath the skin: *a hypodermic needle* —**hypodermically** /-kli/ *adv.*

hypodermic² *n.* [C] an instrument with a very thin hollow needle, used for putting drugs into someone's body through the skin SYN **syringe**

hy·po·gly·ce·mi·a /ˌhaɪpoʊglaɪˈsimiə/ *n.* [U] a medical condition in which someone does not have enough sugar in their blood —**hypoglycemic** *adj.*

hy·pot·e·nuse /haɪˈpɑtˀn-us/ *n.* [C] MATH the longest side in a RIGHT TRIANGLE, opposite the right angle

hy·po·thal·a·mus /ˌhaɪpoʊˈθæləməs/ *n.* [C usually singular] BIOLOGY a small part of the brain that controls body temperature and some other FUNCTIONS → see picture at BRAIN¹

hy·po·ther·mi·a /ˌhaɪpəˈθɚmiə/ *n.* [U] MEDICINE a serious medical condition in which someone's body temperature becomes very low, caused by extreme cold

hy·poth·e·sis /haɪˈpɑθəsɪs/ Ac *n.* *plural* **hypotheses** /-siz/ **1** [C] an idea that is based on what you have seen or done, that may explain something, but that has not yet been tested or proven to be true → see also THEORY: +**that** *the hypothesis that longterm unemployment causes illness* | *Our data do not* ***support this hypothesis*** (=show that it is correct). **2** [U] ideas or guesses rather than facts SYN **speculation**: *My guess is the driver was drunk, but that's pure hyposthesis.* **3** [C] MATH the idea that follows 'if' or 'unless' in a CONDITIONAL sentence (=sentence that expresses an idea, fact etc. that causes something else to be true)

hy·poth·e·size /haɪˈpɑθəˌsaɪz/ Ac *v.* [I,T] to suggest a possible explanation that has not yet been proven to be true: **hypothesize that** *Scientists hypothesized that the dinosaurs were killed by a giant meteor.*

hy·po·thet·i·cal /ˌhaɪpəˈθɛt̬ɪkəl/ Ac *adj.* based on a situation that is not real, but that might happen SYN **theoretical**: *a hypothetical question* | *a hypothetical accident at a nuclear power station* → see also IMAGINARY —**hypothetically** /-kli/ *adv.*

hy·po·ton·ic /ˌhaɪpoʊˈtɑnɪk/ *adj.* CHEMISTRY a hypotonic SOLUTION (=liquid with substances dissolved in it) contains less of a SOLUTE (=substance that is dissolved) than another solution that you are comparing it to → see also HYPERTONIC

hys·ter·ec·to·my /ˌhɪstəˈrɛktəmi/ *n.* *plural* **hysterectomies** [C] MEDICINE a medical operation to remove a woman's UTERUS

hys·ter·i·a /hɪˈstɛriə, -ˈstɪriə/ *n.* [U] **1** a situation in which a lot of people feel fear, anger, or excitement, which makes them behave in an unreasonable way: *the anti-Communist hysteria of the 1950s in the U.S.* **2** MEDICINE a medical condition in which someone suddenly feels very nervous, excited, anxious etc. and is not able to control their emotions [**Origin:** 1800–1900 *hysteric* **hysterical** (17–20 centuries), from Greek *hystera* **uterus**; because it was believed hysteria was caused by the uterus] —**hysteric** *adj.*

hys·ter·i·cal /hɪˈstɛrɪkəl/ S3 *adj.* **1** unable to control your behavior or emotions because you are very upset, afraid, excited etc.: *Hysterical parents were calling the school for details of the accident.* **2** INFORMAL extremely funny SYN **hilarious**: *It's a hysterical movie.* ▸see THESAURUS box at **funny** **3** reacting to something in a way that seems unreasonable: *the hysterical headlines in the newspapers* **4** [only before noun] MEDICINE suffering from or caused by the medical condition of hysteria —**hysterically** /-kli/ *adv.*

hys·ter·ics /hɪˈstɛrɪks/ *n.* [plural] **1** a state of being unable to control your behavior or emotions because you are very upset, afraid, excited etc.: *She* ***went into hysterics*** *when she heard about her husband.* **2 in hysterics** if someone is in hysterics, they are laughing and not able to stop: *The audience was in hysterics.*

Hz *n.* [C] PHYSICS the written abbreviation of HERTZ

H

I,i

I[1], i /aɪ/ *n. plural* **I's, i's** [C] **a)** the ninth letter of the English alphabet **b)** a sound represented by this letter

I[2] S1 W1 *pron.* used as the subject of a verb when you are the person speaking: *I saw Mike yesterday.* | *I'm going to Mexico next month.* | *I've been playing softball every week.*

I[3] **1** the abbreviation of INTERSTATE (=an important road between states in the U.S.): *We were driving on I-40 east.* **2** the number one in the system of ROMAN NUMERALS

i *number* MATH an imaginary number that is equal to the SQUARE ROOT of negative 1

-i /-i/ *suffix plural* **-is** **1** [in nouns] a person from a particular country or place, or their language: *two Pakistanis* | *speakers of Nepali* **2** [in adjectives] relating to a particular place or country: *Bengali food* | *the Israeli Army*

IA the written abbreviation of IOWA

-ial /iəl/ *suffix* [in adjectives] relating to something, or like something: *a managerial job* (=with the duties of a manager) | *financial* (=relating to money) | *colonial style furniture* (=like the style used when America was a COLONY) → see also -AL

I

i•amb /ˈaɪ-æmb/ also **i•am•bus** /aɪˈæmbəs/ *n.* [C] ENG. LANG. ARTS a unit of RHYTHM in poetry that has one short or weak beat followed by a long or strong beat, as in the word "alive" —**iambic** /aɪˈæmbɪk/ *adj.*

iˌambic penˈtameter *n.* [C,U] ENG. LANG. ARTS a common pattern of beats in English poetry, in which each line consists of five iambs, used more commonly in the past

-ian /iən/ *suffix* **1** [in adjectives and nouns] someone or something from a place, or relating to a place: *a librarian* (=someone who works in a library) | *an old Bostonian* (=someone from Boston) **2** [in adjectives and nouns] relating to the ideas of a particular person or group, or someone who follows these ideas: *Jacksonian democracy* (=the ideas of Andrew Jackson) | *a Freudian* (=someone who follows the ideas of Sigmund Freud) **3** [in adjectives] relating to or similar to a person, thing, or period of time: *the Victorian era* → see also -AN, -EAN

-iana /iænə/ *suffix* [in U nouns] a collection of objects, papers etc., relating to someone or something: *Shakespeariana* → see also -ANA

I-beam /ˈaɪ bim/ *n.* [C] a long piece of steel shaped like the letter "I," used in the CONSTRUCTION of buildings

I•be•ri•an /aɪˈbɪriən/ *adj.* relating to Spain or Portugal: *the Iberian peninsula*

i•bex /ˈaɪbɛks/ *n. plural* **ibexes** or **ibex** [C] a wild goat that lives in the mountains of Europe, Asia, and North Africa

ibid. *adv.* used in formal writing to mean from the same book, writer, or article as the one that has just been mentioned

-ibility /əbɪləṭi/ *suffix* [in nouns] used with adjectives that end in -IBLE to form nouns: *invincibility* | *flexibility* → see also -ABILITY

i•bis /ˈaɪbɪs/ *n. plural* **ibises** [C] BIOLOGY a large bird with a long beak and long legs that is related to the STORK

-ible /əbəl/ *suffix* [in adjectives] used to show that someone or something has a particular quality or condition: *visible* (=able to be seen) | *irresistible* (=difficult to resist) → see also -ABLE

IBM-com•pat•i•ble /ˌaɪ bi ɛm kəmˈpæṭəbəl/ *adj.* an IBM-compatible computer is designed to work in the same way as a type of computer made by the IBM company, and can use the same computer PROGRAMS SYN PC —**IBM-compatible** *n.* [C]

I•bo /ˈiboʊ/ another form of IGBO

Ib•sen /ˈɪbsən/, **Hen•rik** /ˈhɛnrɪk/ (1828–1906) a Norwegian writer of plays known especially for writing about MIDDLE CLASS society and criticizing social attitudes and behavior

i•bu•pro•fen /ˌaɪbyʊˈproʊfən/ *n.* [U] a drug used for reducing pain and swelling that contains no ASPIRIN

-ic /ɪk/ *suffix* **1** [in adjectives] relating to something, or similar to it: *an alcoholic drink* (=containing alcohol) | *an Islamic country* (=where the laws follow the rules of Islam) | *pelvic pain* (=in your PELVIS) | *Byronic poetry* (=similar to the poems of Byron) **2** [in nouns] someone who is affected by a particular condition, for example a mental illness: *an alcoholic* (=someone who cannot stop drinking alcohol)

-ical /ɪkəl/ *suffix* [in adjectives] another form of the SUFFIX -IC: *historical* (=relating to history) | *a satirical play* —**-ically** /-ɪkli/ *suffix* [in adverbs] *historically*

ICBM *n.* [C] **Intercontinental Ballistic Missile** a MISSILE that can travel very long distances

ice[1] /aɪs/ S1 W2 *n.* [U] **1** water that has frozen into a solid state: *Drive carefully – there's ice on the road.* **2** small squares of ice, used to make drinks cold: *There was hardly any ice in my Coke.* **3 put/keep something on ice** to do nothing about a plan or suggestion for a period of time: *Negotiations have been put on ice for now.* **4 be (skating) on thin ice** to be in a situation in which you do something risky that is likely to upset someone or cause trouble: *Legally, the company is on very thin ice.* **5** OLD-FASHIONED DIAMONDS **[Origin:** Old English *is*] → see also BLACK ICE, **break the ice** at BREAK[1] (32), **cut no ice** at CUT[1] (29), DRY ICE, ICY

ice[2] *v.* [T] **1** to cover a cake with ICING (=a mixture made of liquid and sugar) → see also FROST **2** if you ice a game, you do something to put your team in a strong position to win

ice sth ↔ **down** *phr. v.* **a)** to cover an injury in ice to stop it from swelling: *He iced down his sore shoulder.* **b)** to put something in or on ice to make it cold

ice over/up *phr. v.* to become covered with ice: *Thousands of workers were sent home early as roads iced up.*

ˈIce Age *n.* [C] **the Ice Age** HISTORY one of the long periods of time, thousands of years ago, when ice covered many northern countries

ˈice ax *n.* [C] a metal tool used by mountain climbers to cut into ice → see also ICE PICK

ˈice bag *n.* [C] a bag containing ice that is put on an injured part of your body to reduce swelling or pain

ice•berg /ˈaɪsbɚg/ *n.* [C] EARTH SCIENCE a very large mass of ice floating in the ocean, most of which is under the surface of the water → see also **the tip of the iceberg** at TIP[1] (6)

ˌiceberg ˈlettuce *n.* [C,U] a type of LETTUCE that is firm, round, and pale green

ice•bound /ˈaɪsbaʊnd/ *adj.* surrounded by ice, especially so that it is impossible to move: *Eight of the ships remain icebound.*

ice•box /ˈaɪsbɑks/ *n.* [C] **1** OLD-FASHIONED a REFRIGERATOR **2** a special cupboard in which you put ice in order to keep food cold, in past times

ice•break•er /ˈaɪsˌbreɪkɚ/ *n.* [C] **1** a ship that cuts a passage through floating ice **2** something that you say or do to make people less nervous when they first meet: *This game is an effective icebreaker for a new class.* → see also **break the ice** at BREAK[1] (32)

ˈice ˌbucket *n.* [C] **1** a container filled with ice to keep bottles of wine cold **2** a container in which pieces of ice for putting in drinks are kept

ˈice cap *n.* [C] EARTH SCIENCE an area of thick ice that permanently covers the North and South Poles

ˈice chest *n.* [C] a special box that you put ice in to keep food and drinks cold

ˌice-ˈcold *adj.* extremely cold: *ice-cold beer* | *Her hands were ice-cold.*

ˈice cream S1 *n.* **1** [U] a frozen sweet food made of milk, cream, and sugar, with fruit, nuts, chocolate etc. sometimes added to it **2** [C] a small amount of this food for one person: *Two chocolate ice creams, please.*

ˈice cream ˌcone *n.* [C] a hard thin cookie shaped like a CONE, that you put ice cream in, or one of these with ice cream in it

ˈice-cream ˌparlor *n.* [C] a restaurant that only sells ice cream

ˌice-cream ˈsocial *n.* [C] in the past, a social event where people come together to eat ice cream

ˈice cream ˌsoda *n.* [C] a mixture of ice cream, sweet SYRUP, and SODA WATER, served in a tall glass

ˈice cube *n.* [C] a small block of ice that is put in a drink to make it cold

ˌiced ˈcoffee also **ˌice ˈcoffee** *n.* [C,U] cold coffee with ice, milk, and sometimes sugar, or a glass of this drink

ˌiced ˈtea also **ˌice ˈtea** *n.* [C,U] cold tea with ice, and sometimes LEMON or sugar, or a glass of this drink

ˈice ˌfishing *n.* [U] the sport of catching fish through a hole in the ice on a lake or river

ˈice floe *n.* [C] EARTH SCIENCE an area of ice floating in the ocean, that has broken off from a larger mass

ˈice ˌhockey *n.* [U] HOCKEY

Ice•land /ˈaɪslənd, -lænd/ an island country in the Atlantic Ocean just south of the Arctic Circle

Ice•land•er /ˈaɪsləndɚ/ *n.* [C] someone from Iceland

Ice•land•ic /aɪsˈlændɪk/ *adj.* relating to Iceland, its people, or their language, or coming from there

ice•man /ˈaɪs-mɛn/ *n. plural* **icemen** /-mɛn/ [C] a man who delivered ice to people's houses in past times, so that they could keep food cold

ˈice milk *n.* [U] a frozen sweet food that is similar to ICE CREAM, but has less fat in it

ice pack

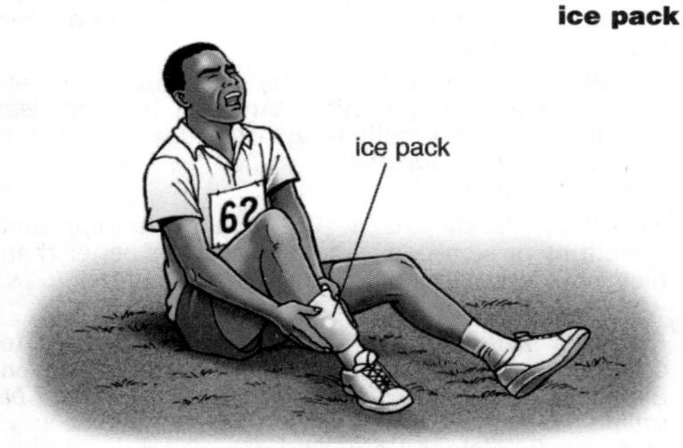

ˈice pack *n.* [C] **1** a bag containing ice that is put on an injured part of your body to reduce swelling or pain **2** EARTH SCIENCE a large area of crushed ice floating in the ocean → see also PACK ICE

ˈice pick *n.* [C] a sharp tool used for cutting or breaking ice

ˈice rink *n.* [C] a specially prepared surface of ice where you can ICE SKATE

ˈice sheet *n.* [C] EARTH SCIENCE an ICE CAP

ˈice skate[1] *n.* [C usually plural] a special boot with a metal blade on the bottom, that allows you to move quickly on ice → see also ROLLER SKATE → see picture at SKATE[1]

ice skate[2], **ice-skate** *v.* [I] to move on ice wearing ice skates —**ice skater** *n.* [C] —**ice skating** *n.* [U]

ˈice ˌwater *n.* [C,U] very cold water with pieces of ice in it, or a glass of this

-ician /ɪʃən/ *suffix* [in nouns] a skilled worker who deals with a particular thing: *a beautician* (=someone who gives beauty treatments) | *a technician* (=someone with technical or scientific skills)

i•ci•cle /ˈaɪsɪkəl/ *n.* [C] a long thin pointed stick of ice hanging from a roof or other surface

-icide /ɪsaɪd/ *suffix* [in nouns] someone or something that kills a particular person or thing, or the act of killing: *insecticide* (=chemical substance for killing insects) | *fratricide* (=act of killing your brother or sister) —**-icidal** /ɪsaɪdl/ *suffix* [in adjectives] —**-icidally** [in adverbs] → see also -CIDE

i•ci•ly /ˈaɪsəli/ *adv.* if you say something icily or look at someone icily, you do it in an angry or very unfriendly way

ic•ing /ˈaɪsɪŋ/ *n.* [U] **1** a mixture made from sugar, a liquid, and sometimes a fat such as butter, which is used to cover cakes → see also FROSTING **2 (the) icing on the cake** something that makes a good situation even better: *The raise was great, but the company car was the icing on the cake.*

ick•y /ˈɪki/ *adj.* SPOKEN very bad, especially to look at, taste, or feel SYN **disgusting**: *What's this icky black stuff on the rug?*

i•con /ˈaɪkɑn/ *n.* [C] **1** someone famous who is admired by many people and is thought to represent an important idea: *a British rock icon* **2** COMPUTERS a small sign or picture on a computer screen that is used to start a particular operation: *Click on the icon to open the program.* ►see THESAURUS box at **computer** **3** also **ikon** a picture or figure of a holy person that is used in WORSHIP in the Greek or Russian Orthodox Church [**Origin:** 1500–1600 Latin, Greek *eikon*, from *eikenai* **to be like**] —**iconic** /aɪˈkɑnɪk/ *adj.*

i•con•o•clast /aɪˈkɑnəˌklæst/ *n.* [C] someone who attacks established ideas and customs

i•con•o•clas•tic /aɪˌkɑnəˈklæstɪk/ *adj.* iconoclastic ideas, writings, or people attack established beliefs and customs

i•co•nog•ra•phy /ˌaɪkəˈnɑgrəfi/ *n.* [U] the way that a particular people, religious, or political group etc. represent ideas in pictures or images

-ics /ɪks/ *suffix* [in nouns] **1** the scientific study of a subject, or the use of our knowledge about it: *linguistics* (=the study of language) | *electronics* (=the study or making of electronic equipment) | *genetics* (=the study of GENES) **2** the actions typically done by someone with particular skills: *acrobatics* **3** used to make nouns out of words ending in -ICAL or -IC: *the acoustics* (=sound qualities) *of the hall*

ICU *n.* [C] TECHNICAL **Intensive Care Unit** a department in a hospital that gives special attention and treatment to people who are very sick or badly injured

ic•y /ˈaɪsi/ *adj. comparative* **icier**, *superlative* **iciest** **1** extremely cold: *an icy wind* **2** covered in ice: *The sidewalks were icy.* **3** an icy remark, look etc. shows that you feel annoyed with someone or feel unfriendly toward them: *Her question got an icy response from the chairman.* —**iciness** *n.* [U] → see also ICILY

I'd /aɪd/ **1** the short form of "I would": *I'd love to go out for dinner.* **2** the short form of "I had": *I'd hoped to finish everything before the trip.*

ID[1] *n.* [C,U] a document or card that shows your name, date of birth etc., usually with a photograph SYN **identification**: *Do you have any ID?* | *a fake ID*

ID[2] *v.* **ID'd, ID'ing** [T] SPOKEN to IDENTIFY a criminal or dead body: *The police were able to ID the body quickly.*

ID[3] the written abbreviation of Idaho

id /ɪd/ *n.* [singular] TECHNICAL according to Freudian PSYCHOLOGY, the part of your mind that is completely unconscious, but that has hidden desires and needs that you try to meet → see also EGO, SUPEREGO

I•da•ho /ˈaɪdəˌhoʊ/ ABBREVIATION **ID** a state in the northwestern U.S.

ID card /ˌaɪ ˈdi kɑrd/ *n.* [C] a card with your name, date of birth, photograph, SIGNATURE etc. on it, that proves who you are

-ide /aɪd/ *suffix* [in nouns] a chemical compound: *cyanide* | *sulphide*

i·de·a /aɪˈdiə/ S1 W1 *n.*

1 PLAN/SUGGESTION [C] a plan or suggestion for a possible course of action, especially one that you think of suddenly: *That's a good idea!* | **+for** *Ellen got the idea for the business ten years ago.* | *Laura always* ***has*** *great* ***ideas*** *for gifts.* | **the/sb's idea of doing sth** *I like Louis's idea of meeting on Saturday mornings.* | **it was sb's idea to do sth** *It was Pete's idea to have the wedding in December.* | *Rob* ***came up with the idea*** (=thought of the idea) *of renting out a room in our house.* | *My son* ***gave me the idea*** *for the game* (=something he said helped me think of it).

THESAURUS

thought something that you think of, think about, or remember: *It was a crazy idea, really, but he'd had the same thought.*
inspiration something or someone that encourages you to do or produce something good: *A good teacher can be a real inspiration.*

2 INFORMATION [C,U] some information or knowledge about something, that is not very exact: *Could you* ***give me an idea of*** *how bad his injuries are?* | *You must* ***have some idea*** (=have at least a little information) *of when Joyce will be home.* | *I* ***have no idea*** (=no knowledge about) *whose jacket that is.*
3 GOAL/PURPOSE [C,U] the GOAL or purpose of doing something: **the idea (of/behind sth) is to do sth** *The idea behind the advertising campaign is to get people to vote.* | *Mike's parents wanted him to go to college, but he* ***had other ideas*** (=had different plans).
4 IMAGE [C,U] an image in your mind of what something is like or should be like: **+of/about** *The two chefs have different ideas about what makes a good dessert.* | **a rough/general/vague idea** *I only have a vague idea of who she is.*
5 PRINCIPLE [C] an opinion or belief about how something is or should be: **+of/about** *the Christian idea of an eternal soul* | *Her ideas about marriage are very old-fashioned.* | **idea that** *This concept is based on Rousseau's idea that men are born morally neutral.*
6 BELIEF a belief that someone has that other people think is wrong or strange: *Somehow Ken's* ***gotten the idea that*** (=wrongly begun to believe) *I'm in love with him.* | *No, I didn't get fired.* ***Where did you get that idea?***
7 it is (not) a good idea to do sth used to give someone advice about what to do, or what not to do: *It's a good idea to drink lots of water on hot days.*

SPOKEN PHRASES

8 get the idea to begin to understand something or be able to do something: *By now I'm sure you get the idea that this survey was not scientific.*
9 get the wrong idea to think that something is true when it is not: *Don't get the wrong idea – the Dixons aren't as arrogant as they sound.*
10 that's/there's an idea! used to say that you like what someone has just suggested: *"Maybe you could do some babysitting." "Yeah, that's an idea."*
11 that's the idea a) used to tell someone who is learning to do something that they are doing it the right way, in order to encourage them: *Now try playing the three chords one after the other. That's the idea!* **b)** used to emphasize what the main point of something is, or to say that someone understands that point: *"You're going to meet them there?" "Yeah, that's the idea."*
12 have an idea (that) to be fairly sure that something is true, without being completely sure: *I* ***had a pretty good idea that*** *this was going to happen.*
13 not have the faintest/slightest/foggiest idea used to say that you have no knowledge of something: *I didn't have the faintest idea what he was talking about.*
14 the idea! OLD-FASHIONED used to express surprise or disapproval when someone has said something stupid, strange, or shocking

15 have the right idea to act or think in a way that will probably lead to the correct result: *The new superintendent has the right idea about attacking illiteracy, but the wrong method.*
16 bright idea a very smart idea, often used in a joking way to mean a very stupid idea or action: *Whose bright idea was it to give the cat a bath?*
17 sb's idea of a joke INFORMAL something that is intended to be a joke but makes you angry: *Is this your idea of a joke?*
18 sb's idea of heaven/fun/a good time etc. something that someone loves to do: *Watching golf on TV is my father's idea of heaven.* | *Mowing the lawn* ***is not my idea of a good time.***
19 put ideas into sb's head INFORMAL to make someone think of doing something that they had not thought of before, especially something stupid or impossible
[**Origin:** 1300–1400 Latin, Greek, from *idein* **to see**]

i·de·al¹ /aɪˈdiəl/ *adj.* **1** the best or most appropriate that something could be: *It seemed like an ideal opportunity to ask him.* | *The weather was ideal.* | *I realize this isn't an ideal situation.* | **ideal for sb/sth** *The game is ideal for pre-school children.* ►see THESAURUS box at perfect¹ **2** [only before noun] an ideal world, job, system etc. is one that you imagine to be perfect, but that is not likely to exist: *In an ideal world, no one would ever get sick.*

ideal² *n.* [C] **1** a principle or standard that you would like to achieve or that you want to behave according to: *a leader with high ideals* | **+of** *the ideal of a free and democratic society* **2** a perfect example of what something should be like: **+of** *the American ideal of the nuclear family*

i·de·al·ism /aɪˈdiəˌlɪzəm/ *n.* [U] **1** the belief that you should live your life according to high standards or principles, even when they are very difficult to achieve: *moral and religious idealism* | **+of** *the idealism of young people* **2** TECHNICAL a way of using art or literature to show the world as a perfect place, even though it is not → see also NATURALISM, REALISM

i·de·al·ist /aɪˈdiəlɪst/ *n.* [C] someone who tries to live according to high standards or principles, especially in a way that is not practical or possible → see also REALIST: *She's a young idealist who believes in all her students' potential.*

i·de·al·is·tic /ˌaɪdiəˈlɪstɪk/ *adj.* believing that you should live according to high standards or principles, even if they cannot really be achieved: *idealistic young doctors* | *the idealistic values of the 1960s* —**idealistically** /-kli/ *adv.*

i·de·al·ize /aɪˈdiəˌlaɪz/ *v.* [T] to imagine or represent something or someone as being perfect or better than they really are: *The movie idealizes life in the 1600s.* —**idealization** /aɪˌdiələˈzeɪʃən/ *n.* [U]

i·de·al·ly /aɪˈdiəli/ *adv.* **1** [sentence adverb] used to describe the way you would like things to be, even though this may not be possible: *Ideally, we should be saving money every month.* **2** in the best possible way: **ideally suited/placed/qualified etc.** *Robertson is ideally suited for the job.* | **ideally located/situated etc.** *The hotel is ideally located for enjoying the beauty of the beaches.*

i·den·ti·cal /aɪˈdɛntɪkəl, ɪ-/ Ac *adj.* exactly the same: *three identical statues* | **+to** *Your shoes are identical to mine.* | **+in** *The words are identical in meaning.* | **almost/nearly/virtually etc. identical** *The new models are virtually identical.* —**identically** /-kli/ *adv.*

iˌdentical ˈtwin *n.* [C usually plural] BIOLOGY one of a pair of brothers or sisters born at the same time, who develop from the same EGG and look almost exactly alike → see also FRATERNAL TWIN

i·den·ti·fi·a·ble /aɪˌdɛntəˈfaɪəbəl, ɪ-/ Ac *adj.* able to be recognized: *The fingerprint on the door was not identifiable.* | **be identifiable as sth** *The name was not identifiable as Hispanic.* | **clearly/easily/readily etc. identifiable** *The bones were easily identifiable as human.*

i·den·ti·fi·ca·tion /aɪˌdɛntəfəˈkeɪʃən/ Ac *n.* [U] **1** official papers or cards, such as your PASSPORT, that prove who you are: *You need two pieces of identification to write a check here.* | **form/proof/means etc. of**

identification *Bring some form of identification, preferably a passport.* → see also ID[1] **2** the act or process of saying officially that you know who someone is, especially a criminal or a dead person: *The bodies were brought to the hospital **for identification*** (=in order to be identified). | +**of** *Identification of the victims will be difficult.* **3** the act or process of recognizing something or discovering exactly what it is, what its nature or origin is etc.: +**of** *Correct identification of customer needs is vital.* **4** a strong feeling that you are like someone or something, and share the same qualities or feelings: +**with** *Teens feel a strong identification with the book's characters.* **5** the act of saying that two things are very closely related: **the identification of sth with sth** *the identification of sexism with the oppression of women*

i·den·ti·fy /aɪˈdɛntəˌfaɪ/ Ac S2 W1 *v.* **identifies, identified, identifying** [T] **1** to recognize and correctly name someone or something: *Can you identify the man who robbed you?* | **identify sb/sth as sb/sth** *The suspect was identified as Daniel Hargraves.* **2** to recognize something or discover exactly what it is, what its nature or origin is etc.: *We have identified a number of problems that need to be addressed.* **3** if a particular thing identifies someone, it makes it clear to other people who that person is: **identify sb as sb** *Workers wear badges to identify them as park employees.*

identify with sb/sth *phr. v.* **1 identify with sb** to be able to share or understand the feelings of someone else: *Young boys, especially, identify with the movie's hero.* **2 identify sth with sb/sth** to think or show that something has a relationship or connection with something else: *Ad agencies glamorize drinking and identify it with social status.*

i·den·ti·ty /aɪˈdɛntəṭi, ɪ-/ Ac W3 *n. plural* **identities** **1** [C,U] who someone is or the name of someone: +**of** *We don't know the identity of the other man in the picture.* | **conceal/hide/protect your identity** *She was given a false name in order to protect her identity.* | **reveal/disclose sb's identity** *The victims' identities have not been revealed yet.* | *Wong was jailed overnight in **a case of mistaken identity*** (=someone thought that Wong was someone else). **2** [U] the qualities and attitudes a person or group of people have that make them different from other people: *Some fear the community is **losing** its Hispanic **identity**.* | *Many men get their **sense of identity** from their careers.* | **national/cultural/social/corporate etc. identity** *a sense of national identity* | *The city has been suffering a kind of **identity crisis*** (=a feeling of uncertainty about what its basic qualities are and what its purpose is). **3** [U] FORMAL an exact SIMILARITY between two things [**Origin:** 1500–1600 Late Latin *identitas*, from Latin *idem* **same**]

iˈdentity ˌtheft also **iˈdentity ˌfraud** *n.* [U] any crime in which someone steals personal information about another person, for example their bank account number or the number of their driver's license, and uses this information to deceive other people and get money or goods

id·e·o·gram /ˈɪdiəˌɡræm, ˈaɪdiə-/ also **id·e·o·graph** /ˈɪdiəˌɡræf, ˈaɪdiə-/ *n.* [C] ENG. LANG. ARTS a written sign, for example in Chinese, that represents an idea or thing rather than the sound of a word

i·de·o·log·i·cal /ˌaɪdiəˈlɑdʒɪkəl, ˌɪdiə-/ Ac *adj.* based on a particular set of beliefs or ideas, especially political ideas: *ideological differences between the two political parties* | *My objections to the plan were mostly ideological.* —**ideologically** /-kli/ *adv.*

i·de·o·logue /ˈaɪdiəˌlɑɡ, -ˌlɔɡ/ *n.* [C] someone whose actions are influenced too much by an ideology

i·de·ol·o·gy /ˌaɪdiˈɑlədʒi, ˌɪdi-/ Ac *n. plural* **ideologies** [C,U] **1** a set of ideas on which a political or economic system is based: *Marxist ideology* **2** a set of ideas and attitudes that strongly influence the way people behave: *a group with a racist ideology*

ides /aɪdz/ *n.* [plural] a date or period of time around the middle of the month in the ancient Roman CALENDAR

id·i·o·cy /ˈɪdiəsi/ *n. plural* **idiocies** **1** [U] extreme stupidity or silliness **2** [C] a very stupid remark or action

id·i·o·lect /ˈɪdiəˌlɛkt/ *n.* [C,U] ENG. LANG. ARTS the way in which a particular person uses language → see also DIALECT

id·i·om /ˈɪdiəm/ *n.* ENG. LANG. ARTS **1** [C] a group of words that has a special meaning that is different from the ordinary meaning of each separate word: *"Under the weather" is an idiom that means "not feeling well".* ►see THESAURUS box at **phrase**[1] **2** [C,U] FORMAL a style of expression in writing, speech, or music, that is typical of a particular group of people [**Origin:** 1500–1600 French *idiome*, from Greek *idioma* **personal way of expressing yourself**]

id·i·o·mat·ic /ˌɪdiəˈmæṭɪk◂/ *adj.* ENG. LANG. ARTS **1 an idiomatic phrase/expression** an idiom **2** typical of the natural way in which someone using their own language speaks or writes: *Their books are translated into idiomatic English.* —**idiomatically** /-kli/ *adv.*

id·i·o·syn·cra·sy /ˌɪdiəˈsɪŋkrəsi/ *n. plural* **idiosyncrasies** [C] **1** an unusual habit or way of behaving that someone has: *Her employees don't mind her idiosyncrasies.* **2** an unusual or unexpected feature that something has: *the idiosyncrasies of English spelling* —**idiosyncratic** /ˌɪdioʊsɪŋˈkræṭɪk/ *adj.*

id·i·ot /ˈɪdiət/ S2 *n.* [C] **1** a stupid person, or someone who has done something stupid: *You idiot! What did you do that for?* **2** OLD USE a word meaning someone who is mentally ill or has a very low level of intelligence, now considered offensive [**Origin:** 1300–1400 Latin *idiota* **person who knows nothing**, from Greek *idiotes* **private person, person who knows nothing**] —**idiotic** /ˌɪdiˈɑṭɪk/ *adj.* —**idiotically** /-kli/ *adv.*

ˈidiot box *n.* [C usually singular] OLD-FASHIONED a television

ˈidiot ˌlight *n.* [C] NOT TECHNICAL one of the lights in a car that warns you when something is wrong

ˈidiot-ˌproof *adj.* HUMOROUS so easy to use or do that even stupid people will not break it or make a mistake: *idiot-proof instructions*

i·dle[1] /ˈaɪdl/ *adj.* **1** not working or being used: *The factory has been idle since May.* | **sit/stand/lie idle** *Tractors were sitting idle in the fields.* **2** having no useful purpose: *Out of **idle curiosity*** (=without any real reason or or desire to know something), *I looked in his drawer.* | **idle gossip/chatter/speculation etc.** *She never took part in the idle office gossip.* | *Haley said he'd quit, and it wasn't an **idle threat*** (=a threat he did not mean). **3** OLD-FASHIONED lazy ►see THESAURUS box at **lazy** **4 the idle rich** DISAPPROVING rich people who do not have to work —**idly** *adv.*

idle[2] *v.* **idled, idling** **1** [I,T] if an engine idles or if you idle it, it runs slowly while the vehicle, machine etc. is not moving: *My car sounds rough when it idles.* **2** [T] to stop using a factory or stop providing work for your workers, especially temporarily: *GM announced it would idle four assembly plants.* **3** [I always + adv./prep.] to spend time doing nothing

idle sth ↔ **away** *phr. v.* to spend time in a relaxed way, doing nothing: *I idled away the afternoon by the pool.*

i·dler /ˈaɪdlɚ/ *n.* [C] OLD-FASHIONED someone who is lazy and does not work

i·dol /ˈaɪdl/ *n.* [C] **1** someone or something that you love or admire very much: *Muhammad Ali was my idol when I was a boy.* **2** a picture or STATUE that is WORSHIPED as a god ►see THESAURUS box at **god** [**Origin:** 1200–1300 Old French *idole*, from Greek *eidolon* **image, idol**]

i·dol·a·try /aɪˈdɑlətri/ *n.* [U] **1** the practice of WORSHIPing IDOLS **2** too much admiration for someone or something —**idolatrous** *adj.*

i·dol·ize /ˈaɪdlˌaɪz/ *v.* [T] to admire and love someone so much that you think they are perfect: *Susan idolizes her mother.*

I

i·dyll /ˈaɪdl/ *n.* [singular] LITERARY a place or experience in which everything is peaceful and everyone is perfectly happy

i·dyl·lic /aɪˈdɪlɪk/ *adj.* very happy and peaceful, with no problems or dangers: *an idyllic vacation resort* —**idyllically** /-kli/ *adv.*

-ie /i/ *suffix* [in nouns] INFORMAL used to make a word or name less formal, and often to show that you care about someone: *Hi Eddie!* | *Come on, sweetie!* → see also -Y² (1)

i.e. FORMAL an expression written before a word or phrase that gives the exact meaning of something you have just written or said: *The film is for adults, i.e., people over 18.*

IED *n.* [C] **improvised explosive device** a bomb that has been made using whatever materials are available. IEDs are used by TERRORISTS or people who are opposed to their government rather than by official military forces.

-ier /iɚ/ *suffix* [in nouns] **1** someone who does something, or someone who is in charge of something: *a cashier* (=someone who receives and pays out money) | *a hotelier* (=someone in charge of a hotel) **2** used instead of -ER after the letter "y": *a mail carrier* | *pretty, prettier*

-iest /iɪst/ *suffix* [in adjectives] used when -EST is added to words ending in "y", and the "y" is replaced by "i": *pretty, prettiest*

if¹ /ɪf/ S1 W1 *conjunction* **1** used to introduce a phrase when something else depends on that action and situation: *We'll have to leave Monday if it snows today.* | *If you wash my car, I'll give you $5.* | *What would happen to your children if you died in an accident?* | *You can come with us **if you want**.* | *I want to get back by five o'clock **if possible*** (=if it is possible). | *Taste the soup and add salt **if necessary*** (=if it is necessary). | **if sb/sth were/was to do sth** *If I were to offer you $1,000 would you accept it?* | *I think I can fix it now. **If not**, I'll come back tomorrow.* | *Is the book available, and **if so*** (=if the answer to the question is "yes") *where?* | *We'll deal with that problem **if and when** it arises.* → see Word Choice box at UNLESS **2** used to mention a fact, situation, or event that someone asks about, or is not certain about SYN **whether**: *Do you know if we have to work on Christmas Eve?* | *I wonder if Matt's home yet.* → see Grammar box at WHETHER **3** used when you are talking about something that always happens in a particular situation: *If I drink too much coffee, I can't sleep.* | *The plastic will melt if it gets too hot.* **4** used when saying what someone's feelings are about a possible situation: *I'm sorry if I upset you.* | *I don't care if my boss fires me – I'm leaving.* **5** used when making a polite request: ***Would you mind if** I used your phone?* | ***If you can** wait a moment, I'll find your papers for you.* **6 if I were you** SPOKEN used when giving advice and telling someone what you think they should do: *If I were you, I'd sell that car.* **7 if anything** used when adding a remark that changes what you have just said or makes it stronger: *It was warm in L.A. If anything it was a little too warm.* **8 if it weren't for sth/sb** used for mentioning someone or something that prevents something from happening now: *If it weren't for my kids being sick, I'd come and help you.* **9 if it hadn't been for sth/sb** used for mentioning someone or something that prevented something from happening in the past: *If it hadn't been for her quick actions, we'd all have been killed.* **10 if only a)** used to give a reason for something, although you think it is not a good one: *Just call her, if only to say you're sorry.* **b)** used to express a strong wish, especially when you know what you want cannot happen: *If only I could be 18 again!* **11** SPOKEN used during a conversation, speech, etc. when you are trying to make a suggestion, change the subject, or interrupt someone else: *If I could just interrupt for a minute, I have a question.* **12 if ever** used for emphasizing that something is particularly true in the case you are mentioning: *If ever a family deserved some good luck, they do.* | ***If there ever was** a time when we needed help, it's now.* **13** used when you are adding that something may be even more, less, better, worse etc than you have just said: *Brian rarely, if ever, goes to bed before 3 a.m.* | *Her needs are just as important as yours, if not more so.* **14** used when adding one criticism of a person or thing that you generally like SYN **though**: *The car is beautiful and fast, if a little expensive.* **15 if sb's... (then) I'm...** SPOKEN used to say that you do not believe what someone has said about themselves: *If Harry's a professional ice skater, I'm the Pope.* [**Origin:** Old English *gif*] → see also **as if.../as though** at AS² (4), **even if** at EVEN¹ (4)

if² *n.* [C usually plural] INFORMAL **1** a possibility or condition: *There are too many ifs in this plan.* **2 no ifs, ands, or buts** SPOKEN used to say that someone is not allowed to disagree with you

if·fy /ˈɪfi/ *adj.* INFORMAL an iffy situation is one in which you do not know what will happen, but you think the result will probably not be good: *Your chances of finding a better job are iffy.*

-iform /ɪfɔrm/ *suffix* [in adjectives] TECHNICAL having a particular shape: *cruciform* (=cross-shaped)

ˌif-ˈthen ˌstatement *n.* [C] MATH a statement that says that if one thing happens or is true, then another specific thing will happen or must be true. For example, "if $x^2=4$, then $x=2$" is an if-then statement.

-ify /əfaɪ/ *suffix* [in verbs] **1** to make something be in a particular state or condition: *to purify something* (=make it pure) | *to clarify a situation* (=make it clear) | *to amplify sound* (=make it louder) **2** to make someone have a particular feeling: *Spiders terrify me* (=make me very afraid). | *to stultify someone* (=make them extremely bored) **3** INFORMAL to do something in a silly or annoying way: *to speechify* (=make annoying speeches) → see also -FY

Ig·bo /ˈɪgboʊ/ *plural* **Igbo** or **Igbos** also **I·bo** /ˈiboʊ/ *plural* **Ibo** or **Ibos** *n.* **1** [C] a member of a group of people who live in southeastern Nigeria **2** [U] the language of the Igbo

ig·loo /ˈɪglu/ *n. plural* **igloos** [C] a house made from blocks of hard snow or ice [**Origin:** 1800–1900 Inuit *iglu* **house**]

Ig·na·tius of Loy·o·la /ɪgˌneɪʃəs əv lɔɪˈoʊlə/**, St.** also **St. Ignatius Loyola** (1491–1556) a Spanish priest who started the religious ORDER of Jesuits, also called the Society of Jesus

ig·ne·ous /ˈɪgniəs/ *adj.* EARTH SCIENCE igneous rocks are formed from LAVA (=hot liquid rock)

ig·nite /ɪgˈnaɪt/ *v.* **1** [T] to start a dangerous situation, angry argument etc.: *A shortage of bread ignited the 1917 riots.* **2** [I,T] FORMAL to start burning, or to make something start burning: *Luckily, the firebomb did not ignite.* ►see THESAURUS box at **burn¹** **3** [T] to make someone suddenly have strong feelings about something, especially so that they become interested or concerned SYN **spark**: *The book ignited my interest in history.* [**Origin:** 1600–1700 Latin, past participle of *ignire* **to cause to start burning**]

ig·ni·tion /ɪgˈnɪʃən/ *n.* **1** [C, usually singular] the place in a car where you put in a key to start the engine: *Phil left his key in the ignition again.* ►see THESAURUS box at **drive¹** → see picture on page A36 **2** [singular] the electrical part of a vehicle's engine that makes it start working **3** [U] FORMAL the act of starting to burn, or of making something do this

ig·no·ble /ɪgˈnoʊbəl/ *adj.* FORMAL ignoble thoughts, feelings, or actions are ones that you should feel ashamed or embarrassed about —**ignobly** *adv.*

ig·no·min·i·ous /ˌɪgnəˈmɪniəs/ *adj.* FORMAL making you feel ashamed or embarrassed: *an ignominious defeat* —**ignominiously** *adv.*

ig·no·min·y /ˈɪgnəˌmɪni/ *n. plural* **ignominies** [C,U] FORMAL an event or situation that makes you feel ashamed or embarrassed, especially in public and usually because of defeat or failure

ig·no·ra·mus /ˌɪgnəˈreɪməs/ *n.* [C] someone who does not know about things that most people know about

ig·no·rance /ˈɪgnərəns/ Ac *n.* [U] **1** lack of knowledge or information about something: +**of** *The average American's ignorance of geography is shocking.* **2 ignorance is bliss** used to say that if you do not know about a problem, you cannot worry about it

ig·no·rant /ˈɪgnərənt/ Ac *adj.* **1** not knowing facts or information that you ought to know: *a crude and ignorant man* | +**of/about** *Many young people are ignorant of recent history.* | *I was* **blissfully ignorant** (=not worried because I did not know) *about the dangers of too much sun.* **2** caused by a lack of knowledge and understanding: *That was an ignorant joke!* **3** OLD-FASHIONED lacking any education: *ignorant peasants* → see Word Choice box at IGNORE

ig·nore /ɪgˈnɔr/ Ac S3 W2 *v.* [T] **1** to behave as if you had not heard or seen someone or something: *The phone rang, but she ignored it.* | *If you completely ignore him, he'll stop bothering you.* **2** to deliberately pay no attention to something that you have been told or that you know about: *We cannot just ignore the problem.* | **ignore sb's advice/warning** *She ignored her parents' advice.* | **ignore the fact (that)** *Politicians have ignored the fact that our schools are getting worse every year.* [**Origin:** 1600–1700 French *ignorer* **not to know**, from Latin, from *ignarus* **not knowing, unknown**]

WORD CHOICE **ignore, be ignorant of**
If you **ignore** something, you know about it, but choose not to take notice of it: *Some drivers simply ignore speed limits.* If you are **ignorant of** something, you do not know about it: *No driver can pretend to be ignorant of speed limits.*

I·gua·çu Falls /ˌigwəsu ˈfɔlz/ a very large WATERFALL on the border between Argentina and Brazil in South America

i·gua·na /ɪˈgwɑnə/ *n.* [C] a large tropical American LIZARD [**Origin:** 1500–1600 Spanish, Arawakan *iwana*]

IIRC also **iirc** a written abbreviation of "if I remember correctly," used in EMAIL, or by people communicating in CHAT ROOMS on the Internet

IL a written abbreviation of ILLINOIS

il- /ɪl/ *prefix* used instead of IN- before the letter "l"; not: *illogical* (=not logical)

il·e·um /ˈɪliəm/ *plural* **ilea** /ˈɪliə/ *n* [C] BIOLOGY the last part of the SMALL INTESTINE, used by the body in the process of DIGESTION → see picture at DIGESTIVE SYSTEM

ILGWU International Ladies' Garment Workers' Union a UNION of women in the clothing industry

ilk /ɪlk/ *n.* FORMAL **of that/his/their ilk** of that type, his type etc.: *Irving Berlin and composers of his ilk*

ill¹ /ɪl/ S1 W3 *adj.* **1** [not usually before noun] suffering from a disease or not feeling well SYN **sick**: *Several people* ***became ill*** *after eating the clams.* | *caring for* ***the mentally ill*** (=people with an illness that affects the mind) | +**with** *She is* ***seriously ill*** *with tuberculosis.* | ***terminally ill*** (=having an illness that you will die from) *patients* → see also ILLNESS ▶see THESAURUS box at **sick¹** **2** [only before noun] bad or harmful: *the* ***ill treatment*** *of animals* | *The patient seems to be suffering no* ***ill effects*** *from the treatments.* | ***Ill health*** *forced Mr. Cacitti to retire in 1980.* **3 ill at ease** nervous, uncomfortable, or embarrassed: *Brad looked ill at ease in his suit.* **4 it's an ill wind (that blows nobody any good)** used to say that every problem brings an advantage for someone **5 house/place of ill repute** a place where men can pay to have sex with PROSTITUTES [**Origin:** 1100–1200 Old Norse *illr*] → see also ILL WILL

ill² *adv.* **1** not well or not enough SYN **badly**: *We were ill-prepared to camp out in the snow.* **2** badly or cruelly: *The animals had been ill-treated by their owner.* **3 sb can ill afford (to do) sth** used to say that someone is unable to do or have something without making the situation they are in very difficult: *The senator can ill afford another scandal.* **4 think/speak ill of sb** FORMAL to think or say bad things about someone

ill³ *n.* **1** [U] FORMAL harm, evil, or bad luck: *I don't agree with him, but I don't wish him any ill.* **2 ills** [plural] problems and difficulties: *the nation's economic ills* **3 the ill** [plural] people who are seriously ill for a long time: *the terminally ill* | *the mentally ill*

I'll /aɪl/ the short form of "I will": *I'll see you later.*

ˌill-adˈvised *adj.* FORMAL not sensible or not wise and likely to cause problems in the future: *an ill-advised decision* | **be ill-advised to do sth** *You would be ill-advised to discuss your salary with colleagues.* —**ill-advisedly** *adv.*

ˌill-conˈceived *adj.* not planned well and not having an aim that is likely to be achieved: *an ill-conceived scheme*

ˌill-conˈsidered *adj.* FORMAL decisions, actions, ideas etc. that are ill-considered have not been carefully thought about: *an ill-considered business venture*

ˌill-deˈfined *adj.* FORMAL **1** not described clearly enough: *The procedures are ill-defined and untested.* **2** not clearly marked, or not having a clear shape: *an ill-defined border*

il·le·gal¹ /ɪˈligəl/ Ac S3 W2 *adj.* not allowed by the law OPP **legal**: *Gambling is illegal in some states.* | *illegal immigrants* | **it is illegal to do sth** *It's illegal to make copies of computer programs.* —**illegally** *adv.*: *The drugs were obtained illegally.*

ilˌlegal ˈalien also **ilˌlegal ˈimmigrant** or **illegal** INFORMAL *n.* [C] someone who comes into a country to live or work without official permission

il·le·gal·i·ty /ˌɪlɪˈgæləṭi/ Ac *n. plural* **illegalities** **1** [U] the state of being illegal **2** [C] an action that is illegal

il·leg·i·ble /ɪˈlɛdʒəbəl/ *adj.* difficult or impossible to read OPP **legible**: *Ron's handwriting is completely illegible.* —**illegibly** *adv.* —**illegibility** /ɪˌlɛdʒəˈbɪləṭi/ *n.* [U]

il·le·git·i·mate /ˌɪləˈdʒɪṭəmɪt/ *adj.* **1** not allowed or acceptable according to established rules or agreements SYN **legitimate**: *illegitimate insurance claims* **2** an illegitimate child is born to parents who are not married SYN **legitimate** —**illegitimately** *adv.* —**illegitimacy** *n.* [U]

ˌill-eˈquipped *adj.* FORMAL not having the necessary equipment or skills for a particular situation or activity: *Rural hospitals are ill-equipped to handle such emergencies.*

ˌill-ˈfated *adj.* LITERARY unlucky and leading to serious problems or death: *an ill-fated journey*

ˌill-ˈfavored *adj.* **1** FORMAL not lucky **2** LITERARY having an unattractive face SYN **ugly**

ˌill ˈfeeling *n.* [U] angry feelings toward someone: *There's no ill feeling toward our rivals.*

ˌill-ˈfitting *adj.* ill-fitting clothes do not fit the person who is wearing them: *an ill-fitting suit*

ˌill-ˈfounded *adj.* FORMAL based on something that is untrue: *ill-founded worries*

ˌill-ˈgotten *adj.* **ill-gotten gains/wealth etc.** ESPECIALLY HUMOROUS money that was obtained in an unfair or dishonest way

il·lib·er·al /ɪˈlɪbərəl/ *adj.* FORMAL **1** not supporting freedom of expression or of personal behavior **2** not generous

il·lic·it /ɪˈlɪsɪt/ *adj.* not allowed by laws or rules, or strongly disapproved of by society: *an illicit love affair* | *illicit drugs* —**illicitly** *adv.*

Il·li·nois /ˌɪləˈnɔɪ/ **1** WRITTEN ABBREVIATION **IL** a state in the Midwestern area of the U.S. **2** a group of Native American tribes who formerly lived in the northeastern central area of the U.S.

il·lit·er·ate /ɪˈlɪṭərɪt/ *adj.* **1** someone who is illiterate has not learned to read or write: *My grandparents were illiterate.* **2** badly written, in an uneducated way: *an illiterate composition* **3 culturally/politically etc. illiterate** knowing very little about CULTURE, politics etc. —**illiteracy** *n.* [U] —**illiterate** *n.* [C usually plural]

ˌill-ˈmannered *adj.* FORMAL not polite and behaving badly in social situations OPP **well-mannered**

ill·ness /ˈɪlnɪs/ W3 *n.* [C,U] a disease of the body or mind: *childhood illnesses* | **have an illness/suffer from an illness** *a rare illness that affects the muscles* | *There is a history of **mental illness*** (=illness of the mind) *in the family.* | *She suffers from several **chronic illnesses*** (=illness that comes back again and again). → see also DISEASE

THESAURUS

disease a particular type of illness, especially one that is spread from one person to another or that affects one part of your body: *childhood diseases such as measles and chickenpox* | *heart disease*
ill health the state of being sick or having things wrong with your health, usually for a long period of time: *He had to retire due to ill health.*
sickness usually used to refer to the state of being sick or used after a noun to refer to a particular illness: *How many working days are lost due to sickness?* | *radiation sickness*
infection a disease that is caused by bacteria or a virus: *an infection in the wound*
condition something wrong with your health that affects you permanently or for a long time: *an existing medical condition*
problem used especially after a noun to refer to something that is wrong with your health: *serious back problems* | *health problems*

il·log·i·cal /ɪˈlɑdʒɪkəl/ Ac *adj.* **1** not sensible or reasonable OPP **logical**: *illogical fears* **2** not based on the principles of LOGIC: *English has plenty of illogical spelling rules.* —**illogically** /-kli/ *adv.*

I

ˌ**ill-ˈserved** *adj.* not helped by something or not represented well: *Lee believes women have been ill-served by the medical system.*

ˌ**ill-ˈstarred** *adj.* LITERARY unlucky and likely to cause or experience a lot of problems or unhappiness SYN **ill-fated**: *his ill-starred football career*

ˌ**ill-ˈsuited** *adj.* not useful for a particular purpose: +**to** *an environment ill-suited to learning*

ˌ**ill-ˈtempered** *adj.* FORMAL **1** easily made angry or impatient SYN **bad-tempered** **2** an ill-tempered meeting, argument etc. is one in which people are angry and often impolite to each other

ˌ**ill-ˈtimed** *adj.* happening, done, or said at the wrong time: *His remarks are ill-timed and inappropriate.*

ˌ**ill-ˈtreat** *v.* [T usually passive] to treat someone in a cruel way: *Several people complained of being ill-treated by the staff.* —**ill-treatment** *n.* [U]

il·lu·mi·nate /ɪˈluməˌneɪt/ *v.* [T] **1** [usually passive] to use light to make something visible or make it shine: *The room was illuminated by candles.* **2** FORMAL to make something much clearer and easier to understand: *The artifacts may help illuminate the culture of the Aztecs.* **3** LITERARY if a smile or expression illuminates someone's face, it makes them look happy or excited

il·lu·mi·nat·ed /ɪˈluməˌneɪt̬ɪd/ *adj.* **1** lit up by lights: *an illuminated billboard* **2** illuminated books were made by hand in the Middle Ages, and have pages that are decorated with gold paint and other bright colors

il·lu·mi·nat·ing /ɪˈluməˌneɪt̬ɪŋ/ *adj.* making things much clearer and easier to understand: *The film provides illuminating insights into Chinese culture.*

il·lu·mi·na·tion /ɪˌluməˈneɪʃən/ *n.* **1** [U] FORMAL lighting provided by a lamp, light etc.: *the harsh illumination of security lights* **2** [C,U] FORMAL a clear explanation or understanding of a particular subject: *a moment of illumination* **3** [C usually plural] a picture or pattern painted on a page of a book, especially in past times

il·lu·sion /ɪˈluʒən/ *n.* [C] **1** an idea or opinion that is wrong: *Jeff's **under the illusion that*** (=believes wrongly that) *he can afford to buy a house.* | *The argument **shattered*** (=destroyed) *all my **illusions** about my family.* | *They **have no illusions about*** (=realize the unpleasant truth about) *how difficult marriage can be.* **2** something that seems to be different from the way it really is: **create/give an illusion** *A mirror gives the illusion that the room is much larger.* → see also OPTICAL ILLUSION

il·lu·sion·ist /ɪˈluʒənɪst/ *n.* [C] someone who does surprising tricks that make things seem to appear or happen

il·lu·so·ry /ɪˈlusəri, -zəri/ also **il·lu·sive** /ɪˈlusɪv/ *adj.* FORMAL false but seeming to be real or true: *Signs of economic recovery may be illusory.*

il·lus·trate /ˈɪləˌstreɪt/ Ac W3 *v.* [T] **1** to be an example that shows that something is true or that a fact exists: *America needs its allies, as recent events have illustrated.* | **illustrate how/what** *This story illustrates how important the family is in Latin American culture.* | **illustrate that** *The research illustrated that the problem still existed.* **2** to make the meaning of something clearer by giving examples or showing pictures, charts etc.: *The pictures on page 45 illustrate the process.* | *Raymond **illustrated** his **point** by playing a recording of the interview.* | **illustrate sth with sth** *Let me illustrate the problem with some real cases.* **3** [usually passive] ENG. LANG. ARTS to put pictures in a book, article etc.: *The book was illustrated by Robert May.* [**Origin:** 1500–1600 Latin, past participle of *illustrare*, from *lustrare* **to make pure or bright**]

il·lus·tra·tion /ˌɪləˈstreɪʃən/ Ac *n.* **1** [C] ENG. LANG. ARTS a picture in a book, article etc., especially one that helps you to understand it: *black and white illustrations* ►see THESAURUS box at **picture**[1] **2** [C,U] a story, event, situation, or action that shows the truth or existence of something very clearly: +**of** *a striking illustration of 19th century attitudes to women* | **give/provide an illustration** *The case provides a graphic illustration of the dangers of drunk driving.* **3** [U] the art or process of illustrating something: *magazine illustration*

il·lus·tra·tive /ɪˈlʌstrət̬ɪv, ˈɪləˌstreɪt̬ɪv/ Ac *adj.* **1** helping to explain the meaning of something: *illustrative stories* **2** having pictures, especially to help you understand something: *illustrative diagrams of home repairs* → see also ILLUSTRATE

il·lus·tra·tor /ˈɪləˌstreɪt̬ɚ/ *n.* [C] someone who draws pictures, especially for books

il·lus·tri·ous /ɪˈlʌstriəs/ *adj.* FORMAL famous and admired because of what you have achieved

ˌ**ill ˈwill** *n.* [U] a feeling of strong dislike or anger toward someone: *Jon's arrogance created a lot of ill will within the company.* | **bear/hold/harbor no ill will toward sb** (=feel no anger toward someone)

I'm /aɪm/ the short form of "I am": *I'm a lawyer.* | *Hello, I'm Donna.*

im- /ɪm/ *prefix* **1** used instead of IN- before the letters "b," "m," or "p"; not: *impossible* | *immobilize* (=not allow something to move) **2** used instead of IN- before the letters "b," "m," or "p": *to implode* (=explode inward)

im·age /ˈɪmɪdʒ/ Ac S2 W1 *n.* [C] **1** the way a person, organization, product etc. presents themselves to the public: *The company needs to improve its image among young people.* | **sb's/sth's image as sth** *his image as a strong leader* | +**of** *an image of respectability* | **a positive/negative image** *The military still has **a positive image** in Mexican society.* | *Attorneys want to **project** the best **image** possible for their clients* (=they want to make people see them in a good way). **2** a picture that you have in your mind, especially about what someone or something is like or the way they look: +**of** *People have an image of me as some kind of monster.* | *At forty-six, Burnett hardly **fits** most people's **image** of an American college student* (=he is not what you expect one to look like). **3 a)** a picture on the screen of a television, movie theater, or computer: *images of starving people on the news* **b)** a picture of an object in a mirror or in the LENS of a camera: *I stood staring at my image in the mirror.* **c)** a picture or shape of a person or thing that is copied onto paper or cut in wood or stone: *billboards showing Mickey Mouse's image* ►see THESAURUS box at **picture**[1] **4** ENG. LANG. ARTS a word, phrase, or picture that describes an idea in a poem, book, movie etc.: *The image of the tree in the story symbolizes personal growth.* **5 in the image of sb/sth** LITERARY in the same form or shape as someone or something else: *According to the Bible, man was made in the image of God.* **6** MATH a GEOMETRIC shape formed by turning, moving, changing, or REFLECTing an existing shape [**Origin:** 1100–1200 Old French *imagene*, from Latin *imago*] → see also MIRROR IMAGE, SPITTING IMAGE

ˈimage-ˌmaker, image maker *n.* [C] someone whose job is to use newspapers, television, radio etc. to change people's opinion of a product, company, or famous person so that it is favorable

im·age·ry /ˈɪmɪdʒri/ Ac *n.* [U] ENG. LANG. ARTS the use of words or pictures to describe ideas or actions in poems, books, movies etc.: *religious imagery*

i·mag·i·na·ble /ɪˈmædʒənəbəl/ *adj.* able to be imagined: **every imaginable.../every ... imaginable** *Doctors have tried every imaginable treatment for her skin disease.* | **the best/worst/coldest etc. imaginable** *We had the best vacation imaginable.*

i·mag·i·nar·y /ɪˈmædʒəˌnɛri/ *adj.* not real, but produced from pictures or ideas in your mind: *Many young children have imaginary playmates.* | *The events in the book are imaginary.* → see also IMAGINATIVE

ˌimaginary ˈnumber *n.* [C] MATH any number that can be written in the form bi, where i is the SQUARE ROOT of -1 and b is not zero → see also COMPLEX NUMBER

i·mag·i·na·tion /ɪˌmædʒəˈneɪʃən/ W3 *n.* **1** [C,U] the ability to form pictures or ideas in your mind: *The game encourages children to use their imaginations.* | *I thought her answer showed a real **lack of imagination*** | *He'd make a great children's author with his **vivid imagination*** (=strong and creative imagination). **2 sb's imagination** the ability to believe that something is real or true, when it is not: *Maybe it was just my imagination, but he seemed really hostile.* | *My fears were all **in my imagination*** (=from my imagination). **3 leave sth to sb's imagination** to deliberately not describe something because you think someone can guess or imagine it: *The production successfully leaves much of the detail to the audience's imagination.* **4 leave nothing to the imagination a)** if someone is wearing clothes that leave nothing to the imagination, the clothes are very thin or are worn in a way that shows the person's body: *Her blouse left nothing to the imagination.* **b)** if something, especially something violent or sexual, is described in a way that leaves nothing to the imagination, it is explained in too much detail: *The description of the murders left nothing to the imagination.* **5 capture/catch sb's imagination** to make people feel very interested and excited: *The story of a boy raised by monkeys caught the imagination of millions.* **6 use your imagination!** SPOKEN used to tell someone that they should be able to guess the answer to a question without help if they think hard enough → see also **a figment of sb's imagination** at FIGMENT, **by any stretch (of the imagination)** at STRETCH² (3)

i·mag·i·na·tive /ɪˈmædʒənət̬ɪv/ *adj.* **1** good at thinking of new and interesting ideas: *an imaginative novelist* **2** containing new and interesting ideas: *an imaginative Halloween costume* **3** involving the use of your imagination: *children's imaginative play* → see also IMAGINARY —**imaginatively** *adv.*

i·mag·ine /ɪˈmædʒɪn/ S1 W2 *v.* [T] **1** [not usually in progressive] to form a picture or idea in your mind about what something could be like: **imagine (that)** *Imagine that you've just won six million dollars.* | **imagine what/how/why etc.** *I can't imagine how it would feel to have so much influence.* | **imagine (sb) doing sth** *Can you imagine Becky going to the Olympics?* | *It's hard to imagine living anywhere else but here.* | **imagine sb/sth as sth** *I always imagine my great-grandmother as a kind, gentle person.* | **imagine sb in/with/without etc. sth** *Can you imagine Ted in a suit and tie?* | **it's hard/easy/difficult etc. to imagine** *It's hard to imagine him without a beard.*

THESAURUS

visualize to form a picture of someone or something in your mind: *Athletes often visualize their performance before a competition.*
picture to imagine something, especially by making an image in your mind: *I had pictured him as short and dark, but he was actually very tall.*
conceive of sth to imagine a situation or what something is like: *It's difficult to conceive of any reason why he would do something like that.*
fantasize to think about something that is pleasant or exciting, but unlikely to happen: *I'd always fantasized about being a famous actress.*
daydream to think about nice things, so that you forget what you should be doing: *She sat looking out of the window, daydreaming.*
envisage/envision to imagine something as a future possibility or think it likely: *Many colleges do not envisage any growth of total student numbers.*

2 be imagining things used to say that someone thinks that something is happening or has happened, when this is not true: *There's no one at the door. You're just imagining things.* **3 I imagine (that)** SPOKEN used to say what you think must be true, although you cannot be sure: *I imagine you're feeling pretty homesick.* **4 you can imagine** SPOKEN used to emphasize how good, bad etc. something is: *You can imagine how mad I was.* **5 (just) imagine!** OLD-FASHIONED used to show surprise, shock, or disapproval

i·mag·in·ings /ɪˈmædʒənɪŋz/ *n.* [plural] LITERARY situations or ideas that you imagine, but which are not real or true

i·m·am /ˈɪmɑm, ˈɪmæm/ *n.* [C] a Muslim religious leader or priest

im·bal·ance /ɪmˈbæləns/ *n.* [C,U] a lack of a fair or correct balance between two things, which causes problems or results in an unfair situation: *a hormonal imbalance* | **+in/between** *a trade imbalance between the two countries*

im·be·cile /ˈɪmbəsəl/ *n.* [C] **1** someone who behaves very stupidly or who you think is stupid **2** OLD USE a word meaning someone who is not intelligent, now considered offensive

im·be·cil·i·ty /ˌɪmbəˈsɪlət̬i/ *n.* [U] very stupid behavior

im·bed /ɪmˈbɛd/ *v.* **imbedded, imbedding** [T] another spelling of EMBED

im·bibe /ɪmˈbaɪb/ *v.* [I,T] FORMAL OR HUMOROUS to drink something, especially alcohol

im·bro·glio /ɪmˈbroʊlyoʊ/ *n. plural* **imbroglios** [C] FORMAL a difficult, embarrassing, or confusing situation, especially in politics or public life

im·bue /ɪmˈbyu/ *v.*
imbue sb/sth **with** sth *phr. v.* **1** to make someone feel an emotion very strongly: *He was imbued with a deep love for his country.* **2** to give something a particular quality, especially strong emotion: *His songs are imbued with romantic tenderness.*

IMF, the *n.* **the International Monetary Fund** an international organization that tries to encourage trade between countries and to help poorer countries develop economically

IMHO, imho a written abbreviation of "in my humble opinion," used in EMAIL, or by people communicating in CHAT ROOMS on the Internet when they are expressing their opinion

im·i·tate /ˈɪməˌteɪt/ *v.* [T] **1** to copy something because you think it is good: *Our methods have been imitated all over the world.* **2** to copy the way someone behaves, speaks, moves etc., especially in order to make people laugh SYN **mimic**: *"Don't talk to me like that!" he said, imitating his mother.* —**imitator** *n.* [C]

im·i·ta·tion¹ /ˌɪməˈteɪʃən/ *n.* **1** [C] an attempt to copy the way someone speaks or behaves, especially in order to be funny SYN **impression**: *Ed **does a** great*

***imitation of** Elvis.* **2** [U] the act of copying what someone else does: *Children learn through imitation.* **3** [C] a copy of something: **+of** *His first poems were imitations of his father's works.* | ***cheap imitations** of famous brand-name bags* | **a pale/poor imitation** *It's not a Matisse. It's just a poor imitation.*

imitation² *adj.* made to look and seem like something else: *imitation leather* ►see THESAURUS box at **artificial**, **fake²**

im•i•ta•tive /ˈɪməˌteɪt̬ɪv/ *adj.* FORMAL copying someone or something, especially in a way that shows you do not have any ideas of your own

im•mac•u•late /ɪˈmækyəlɪt/ *adj.* **1** very clean and neat: *an immaculate house* ►see THESAURUS box at **clean¹** **2** exactly correct or perfect in every detail: *They dance with immaculate precision.* [**Origin:** 1400–1500 Latin *immaculatus*, from *macula* **spot of dirt**] —**immaculately** *adv.*

Imˌmaculate Conˈception *n.* **the Immaculate Conception** the Catholic belief that Jesus Christ's mother Mary was born without SIN

im•ma•nent /ˈɪmənənt/ *adj.* FORMAL **1** a quality that is immanent seems to be naturally present: *Hope seems immanent in human nature.* **2** God or another spiritual power that is immanent is present everywhere —**immanence, immanency** *n.* [U] → see also EMINENT, IMMINENT

im•ma•te•ri•al /ˌɪməˈtɪriəl/ *adj.* **1** not important in a particular situation: *The difference in our ages was immaterial.* **2** FORMAL not having a real physical form

im•ma•ture /ˌɪməˈtʃʊr, -ˈtʊr/ [Ac] *adj.* **1** someone who is immature behaves or thinks in a way that is typical of someone much younger: *I think Jim's too immature to live on his own.* **2** not fully formed or developed: *an immature plant* —**immaturity** *n.* [U]

im•meas•ur•a•ble /ɪˈmɛʒərəbəl/ *adj.* FORMAL too big or too extreme to be measured: *The war has caused immeasurable suffering.* —**immeasurably** *adv.*

im•me•di•a•cy /ɪˈmidiəsi/ *n.* [U] the quality of something being important or urgent, and directly relating to what is happening now: *They approached the peace talks with a sense of immediacy.*

im•me•di•ate /ɪˈmidiɪt/ [S3] [W2] *adj.* **1** happening or done without delay: *The UN demanded the immediate release of the hostages.* | *The change in his behavior was immediate.* **2** [only before noun] happening now, and needing to be dealt with quickly: *Our immediate concern was to stop the fire from spreading.* | *We have no **immediate plans*** (=plans to do something very soon) *to change the rules.* **3** [only before noun] happening just before or just after someone or something else: *The layoffs are planned for **the immediate future**.* | *the immediate aftermath of World War II* **4** [only before noun] next to, or very near to, a particular place: *Several homes in the immediate area of the volcano were evacuated.* **5** closest to someone in a family relationship or working relationship: *members of your **immediate family*** | **sb's immediate superior/boss** (=the person who is directly in charge of someone) [**Origin:** 1300–1400 Late Latin *immediatus*, from *mediatus* **in between, separated**]

im•me•di•ate•ly /ɪˈmidiɪtli/ [S2] [W2] *adv.* **1** without delay: *He answered the phone immediately when I called.* | **not immediately available/known/clear etc.** *The victims' identities were not immediately available.*

> **THESAURUS**
>
> **instantly** immediately, used when something happens at almost the same time as something else: *He was killed instantly in the crash.*
> **right away** ESPECIALLY SPOKEN immediately, used especially when something needs to be done urgently: *Jill called him right away.*
> **at once** immediately or without waiting: *Jimmy! Come here at once!*
> **right now** SPOKEN immediately, used especially when something needs to be done urgently: *I need it right now!*

2 [+ adv./prep.] very soon before or after something: **immediately before/after etc.** *I went home immediately after I heard the news.* | **immediately upon sth** FORMAL (=as soon as something happens) **3** [+ adv./prep.] very near to something: **immediately across/above/below etc.** *Our house is immediately across from the post office.* **4** used when saying that something was able to be seen or understood quickly and easily: *I could see immediately that he was upset.* | **immediately obvious/apparent/clear** *The solution to the problem was immediately obvious to him.* **5 immediately involved/concerned/affected etc.** very closely involved etc. in a particular situation: *Ukraine was the republic immediately affected by the nuclear reactor's accident.*

im•me•mo•ri•al /ˌɪməˈmɔriəl◂/ *adj.* FORMAL starting longer ago than people can remember, or than written history shows: **from/since time immemorial** *People have been gambling since time immemorial.*

im•mense /ɪˈmɛns/ *adj.* extremely large: *an immense palace* [**Origin:** 1400–1500 French, Latin *immensus*, from *mensus* **measured**]

im•mense•ly /ɪˈmɛnsli/ *adv.* very much [SYN] **extremely**: *Counseling has helped our relationship immensely.* | *They are immensely wealthy.*

im•men•si•ty /ɪˈmɛnsət̬i/ *n.* **1** [U] the great size and seriousness of something such as a problem you have to deal with or a job you have to do: *the immensity of the budget crisis* **2** [C,U] something that is very great in size, especially something that cannot be measured: *the immensity of outer space*

im•merse /ɪˈmɚs/ *v.* [T] **1** FORMAL OR TECHNICAL to put someone or something deep into a liquid so that they are completely covered: **immerse sb/sth in sth** *Immerse a silver wire in the solution.* **2 immerse yourself in sth** to become completely involved in an activity: *Jarrod completely immersed himself in his work.* —**immersed** *adj.*

im•mer•sion /ɪˈmɚʒən/ *n.* [U] **1** the fact of being completely involved in something you are doing: **+in** *her immersion in feminist politics* **2** the action of immersing something in liquid, or the state of being immersed **3** the language teaching method in which the teacher and students use only the new language the students are learning, and not their own language: *Spanish immersion classes* **4** a type of BAPTISM (=a ceremony to show that you belong to the Christian faith) in which someone's whole body is put into water

im•mi•grant /ˈɪməgrənt/ [Ac] [W2] *n.* [C] someone who enters another country to live there permanently: *the number of **illegal immigrants** in California* | **Mexican/German/Chinese etc. immigrant** *Many Polish immigrants settled in Chicago.* | ***a wave of immigrants*** (=a large number of immigrants) *from Latin America* → see also EMIGRANT

im•mi•grate /ˈɪməˌgreɪt/ [Ac] *v.* [I] to come to a country in order to live there permanently: **+from/to** *Yatsu immigrated from Japan when he was 13.* [**Origin:** 1600–1700 Latin, past participle of *immigrare* **to go in**, from *migrare*]

> **THESAURUS**
>
> **immigrate** to enter a new country in order to live there: *Her parents had immigrated to the U.S. when Andrea was five.*
> **emigrate** to leave your own country in order to live in a different one: *My grandparents emigrated from Italy.*
> **migrate** if birds **migrate**, they go to another part of the world in the fall and in the spring

im•mi•gra•tion /ˌɪməˈgreɪʃən/ [Ac] [W2] *n.* [U] **1** the process of entering another country in order to live there permanently → see also EMIGRATION **2** the total number of people who immigrate: *Immigration fell in the 1980s.* **3** the place at an airport, border etc. where officials check the documents of everyone entering the country ▸see THESAURUS box at **airport**

Immiˌgration and ˌNaturaliˈzation ˌService, the the INS

Immiˌgration Reˌform and Conˈtrol ˌAct, the HISTORY a 1986 U.S. law that made it a crime to hire illegal IMMIGRANTS (=people who had come from other countries without permission), but also allowed many people who were already in the U.S. illegally to become citizens

im·mi·nent /ˈɪmənənt/ *adj.* an event that is imminent will happen very soon SYN **impending**: *A new trade agreement is imminent.* | **imminent danger/threat/death/disaster etc.** *There is no **imminent danger** of the hurricane hitting the coast.* | **imminent arrival/departure** *Reporters have predicted his **imminent departure** as chief of staff.* [**Origin:** 1500–1600 Latin, present participle of *imminere* **to stick out, threaten**] —**imminently** *adv.* —**imminence** *n.* [U] → see also IMMANENT

im·mis·ci·ble /ɪˈmɪsəbəl/ *adj.* CHEMISTRY immiscible liquids do not mix and combine together into one liquid OPP **miscible**: *Immiscible liquids, such as oil and water, are insoluble in each other.*

im·mo·bile /ɪˈmoʊbəl/ *adj.* **1** not moving at all SYN **motionless**: *Mrs. Knowles remained immobile.* **2** unable to move or walk normally: *The disease can leave victims immobile.* —**immobility** /ˌɪmoʊˈbɪləṭi/ *n.* [U]

im·mo·bi·lize /ɪˈmoʊbəˌlaɪz/ *v.* [T] **1** to prevent someone or something from moving: *Doctors put on a cast to immobilize her ankle.* **2** to completely stop something from working: *The virus has immobilized around 6,000 computers.* —**immobilization** /ɪˌmoʊbələˈzeɪʃən/ *n.* [U]

im·mod·er·ate /ɪˈmɑdərɪt/ *adj.* FORMAL not within reasonable and sensible limits SYN **excessive**: *immoderate drinking*

im·mod·est /ɪˈmɑdɪst/ *adj.* **1** having a very high opinion of yourself and your abilities, and not embarrassed about telling people how smart you are etc. OPP **modest**: *an immodest man* **2** behavior, especially sexual behavior, that is immodest shocks or embarrasses people SYN **shameless** **3** clothes that are immodest show too much of someone's body SYN **revealing** OPP **modest** —**immodestly** *adv.* —**immodesty** *n.* [U]

im·mo·late /ˈɪməˌleɪt/ *v.* [T] FORMAL to kill someone or destroy something by burning them —**immolation** /ˌɪməˈleɪʃən/ *n.* [U]

im·mor·al /ɪˈmɔrəl, ɪˈmɑr-/ *adj.* **1** morally wrong OPP **moral**: *a church that believes dancing is immoral* | *immoral conduct* ▸see THESAURUS box at **bad**[1] **2** not following accepted standards of sexual behavior OPP **moral** —**immorally** *adv.* —**immorality** /ˌɪməˈræləṭi/ *n.* [U] → see also AMORAL

im·mor·tal /ɪˈmɔrṭl/ *adj.* **1** an immortal line, play, song etc. is so famous that it will never be forgotten: *In the immortal words of James Brown, "I feel good!"* **2** living or continuing for ever OPP **mortal**: *Christians believe that the soul is immortal.* —**immortal** *n.* [C]

im·mor·tal·i·ty /ˌɪmɔrˈtæləṭi/ *n.* [U] the state of living forever or being remembered forever

im·mor·tal·ize /ɪˈmɔrṭlˌaɪz/ *v.* [T usually passive] to make someone or something famous for a long time, especially by writing about them, painting a picture of them etc.: *The difficulties of the famers were immortalized in Steinbeck's "The Grapes of Wrath."*

im·mov·a·ble /ɪˈmuvəbəl/ *adj.* **1** impossible to move OPP **movable**: *Always lock your bicycle to something immovable like a railing.* **2** impossible to change or persuade: *The president is immovable on this issue.*

im·mune /ɪˈmyun/ *adj.* **1** BIOLOGY someone who is immune to a particular disease cannot become sick with that disease: +**to** *The vaccine makes you immune to polio.* **2 immune response/reaction** BIOLOGY the reaction of the body's immune system to something that is harmful **3** not affected by something that happens or is done, especially not affected by criticism: +**to** *The dictatorship seems immune to economic pressures.* **4** specially protected from something bad: +**from** *The governor is popular, but not immune from criticism.* [**Origin:** 1800–1900 Latin *immunis*, from *munis* **ready for service**]

imˌmune reˈsponse also **imˌmune reˈaction** *n.* [C,U] BIOLOGY the reaction of the body's immune system to disease or infection: +**to** *the body's immune response to infection*

imˈmune ˌsystem *n.* [C usually singular] BIOLOGY the system by which your body protects itself against disease

im·mun·i·ty /ɪˈmyunəṭi/ *n.* [U] **1** the state or right of being protected from laws or bad things: +**from** *Both men were **granted immunity*** (=given immunity) *from prosecution.* **2** BIOLOGY the ability of the body not to be affected by a particular disease or diseases: *The patient's immunity is low.* | +**to/from** *The vaccine offers long-term immunity to the virus.*

im·mu·nize /ˈɪmyəˌnaɪz/ *v.* [T] MEDICINE to protect someone from a particular disease by giving them a VACCINE SYN **vaccinate** SYN **inoculate**: **immunize sb against sth** *the importance of immunizing children against measles* —**immunization** /ˌɪmyənəˈzeɪʃən/ *n.* [C,U]

im·mu·no·de·fi·cien·cy /ɪˌmyunoʊdɪˈfɪʃənsi, ˌɪmyənoʊ-/ *n.* [U] MEDICINE a medical condition in which your body is unable to fight infection in the usual way —**immunodeficient** *adj.*

im·mu·nol·o·gy /ˌɪmyəˈnɑlədʒi/ *n.* [U] MEDICINE the scientific study of the prevention of disease and how the body reacts to disease

im·mu·ta·ble /ɪˈmyuṭəbəl/ *adj.* FORMAL never changing or impossible to change OPP **mutable**: *an immutable fact* —**immutability** /ɪˌmyuṭəˈbɪləṭi/ *n.* [U]

imp /ɪmp/ *n.* [C] OLD-FASHIONED **1** a child who behaves badly, but in a way that is funny **2** a small creature in stories, who has magic powers and behaves very badly → see also IMPISH

im·pact[1] /ˈɪmpækt/ Ac W2 *n.* **1** [C] the effect or influence that an event, situation etc. has on someone or something: +**on/upon** *Piaget's work has **had** a strong **impact** on education.* | **significant/major/profound etc. impact** *The change in leadership will **have** a huge **impact** on government policy.* | *an environmental impact report* | +**of** *the impact of new technologies* **2** [C,U] the force of one object hitting another: *The aircraft was traveling at about 155 mph before impact.* **3 on impact** at the moment when one things hits another: *The car burst into flames on impact.* [**Origin:** 1600–1700 Latin, past participle of *impingere*, from *pangere* **to fasten, drive in**]

im·pact[2] /ɪmˈpækt/ Ac *v.* [I,T] **1** to have an important or noticeable effect on someone or something: *How will the new law impact health care?* | +**on** *This will impact on our profits.* **2** FORMAL to hit something with a lot of force

im·pact·ed /ɪmˈpæktɪd/ Ac *adj.* a tooth that is impacted is growing under another tooth so that it cannot develop correctly

im·pair /ɪmˈpɛr/ *v.* [T] to damage something or make it not as good as it should be SYN **weaken**: *Drinking alcohol seriously impairs your ability to drive.* [**Origin:** 1300–1400 Old French *empeirer*, from Vulgar Latin *impejorare*, from Late Latin *pejorare* **to make worse**]

im·paired /ɪmˈpɛrd/ *adj.* **1** damaged, less strong, or not as good as it should be: *impaired vision* **2 hearing/visually/speech etc. impaired** someone who is hearing impaired etc. cannot hear well

im·pair·ment /ɪmˈpɛrmənt/ *n.* [C,U] **1 mental/hearing/visual etc. impairment** a condition in which a part of a person's mind or body is damaged or does not work well **2** the condition of being damaged, or weaker or worse than usual: *an impairment of the firm's ability to borrow money*

im·pa·la /ɪm'pælə, -'pɑ-/ *n.* [C] a graceful brown African ANTELOPE

im·pale /ɪm'peɪl/ *v.* [T often passive] if someone or something is impaled, a sharp pointed object goes through them

im·pal·pa·ble /ɪm'pælpəbəl/ *adj.* FORMAL **1** impossible to touch or feel physically OPP **palpable** **2** very difficult to understand

im·pan·el, empanel /ɪm'pænl/ *v.* [T] to choose the people to serve on a JURY: *A new grand jury is to be impaneled Wednesday.*

im·part /ɪm'pɑrt/ *v.* [T] FORMAL **1** to give a particular quality to something: **impart sth to sth** *Oak barrels impart a nutty flavor to this wine.* **2** to give information, knowledge, wisdom etc. to someone: **impart values/knowledge/wisdom etc.** *She had information she couldn't wait to impart.* | **impart sth to sb** *What she knew about raising children she imparted to me by example.*

im·par·tial /ɪm'pɑrʃəl/ *adj.* not giving special approval or support to any one person or group SYN **fair** SYN **unbiased** OPP **partial** OPP **biased**: *The bureau provides impartial advice.* | *an impartial judge* —**impartially** *adv.* —**impartiality** /ɪm,pɑrʃi'æləṭi/ *n.* [U]

im·pass·a·ble /ɪm'pæsəbəl/ *adj.* impossible to travel along or through: *The flooding made many streets impassable.*

im·passe /'ɪmpæs/ *n.* [C usually singular] a situation in which it is impossible to continue with a discussion or plan because the people involved cannot agree SYN **deadlock**: *The two groups have **reached an impasse** in their talks.* | *The negotiations are **at an impasse**.*

im·pas·sioned /ɪm'pæʃənd/ *adj.* full of strong feeling and emotion SYN **passionate**: *an impassioned speech*

im·pas·sive /ɪm'pæsɪv/ *adj.* not showing or feeling any emotions: *Ramirez's face was impassive as the judge spoke.* —**impassively** *adv.* —**impassivity** /,ɪmpæ'sɪvəṭi/ *n.* [U]

im·pa·tience /ɪm'peɪʃəns/ *n.* [U] **1** annoyance at having to accept delays, other people's weaknesses etc. OPP **patience**: *the impatience in his voice* | +**with** *There is growing impatience with long trials.* **2** great eagerness for something to happen, especially something that is going to happen soon: **impatience to do sth** *Some troops expressed impatience to get home.*

im·pa·tiens /ɪm'peɪʃəns/ *n. plural* **impatiens** [C,U] a garden plant with brightly colored flowers

im·pa·tient /ɪm'peɪʃənt/ *adj.* **1** annoyed because of delays, someone else's mistakes etc. OPP **patient**: **get/become/grow impatient** *She grew impatient with all the questions.* | +**with** *Citizens are impatient with the slow pace of reform.* **2** very eager for something to happen and not wanting to wait: **be impatient to do sth** *Trent was hungry and impatient to sit down to lunch.* | +**for** *Business groups are impatient for change.* —**impatiently** *adv.*

im·peach /ɪm'pitʃ/ *v.* [T] LAW **1** POLITICS if a government official is impeached, they are formally ACCUSED of a serious crime in a special government court: *The governor was impeached for using state funds improperly.* **2** FORMAL if you impeach someone's honesty, you say that you think they are not telling the truth [**Origin:** 1300–1400 Old French *empeechier*, from Late Latin *impedicare* **to fasten the feet together**] —**impeachment** *n.* [U]

im·pec·ca·ble /ɪm'pɛkəbəl/ *adj.* completely perfect and impossible to criticize SYN **perfect** SYN **faultless**: *impeccable taste in clothes* [**Origin:** 1500–1600 Latin *impeccabilis*, from *peccare* **to do bad things**] —**impeccably** *adv.*

im·pe·cu·ni·ous /,ɪmpɪ'kyuniəs/ *adj.* FORMAL OR HUMOROUS having very little money, especially over a long period of time SYN **penniless** SYN **poor**: *a gifted but impecunious painter*

im·pe·dance /ɪm'pidns/ *n.* [singular,U] PHYSICS a measure of the power of a piece of electrical equipment to stop the flow of an ALTERNATING CURRENT

im·pede /ɪm'pid/ *v.* [T] FORMAL to make it difficult for someone or something to move forward or make progress SYN **hinder**: *Rescue attempts were impeded by the storm.* | *Poor hearing may **impede** a child's academic **progress**.*

im·ped·i·ment /ɪm'pɛdəmənt/ *n.* [C] **1** a fact or event that makes it difficult or impossible for someone or something to succeed or make progress SYN **hindrance**: +**to** *The country's debt has been an impediment to development.* **2** a physical problem that makes speaking, hearing, or moving difficult: *a speech impediment*

im·ped·i·men·ta /ɪm,pɛdə'mɛntə/ *n.* [plural] FORMAL things that you think you need to have or do, but which can slow your progress

im·pel /ɪm'pɛl/ *v.* **impelled, impelling** [T] FORMAL to make you feel very strongly that you must do something: **impel sb to do sth** *They felt impelled to help.* → see also COMPEL

im·pend·ing /ɪm'pɛndɪŋ/ *adj.* likely to happen soon SYN **imminent**: *their impending divorce* | **impending doom/death/disaster etc.** *A sense of impending doom gripped her.* [**Origin:** 1500–1600 Latin *impendere* **to hang over**, from *pendere* **to hang**]

im·pen·e·tra·ble /ɪm'pɛnətrəbəl/ *adj.* **1** impossible to get through, see through, or get into: *An impenetrable fog halted traffic.* **2** very difficult or impossible to understand: *an impenetrable 25-page report*

im·pen·i·tent /ɪm'pɛnətənt/ *adj.* FORMAL not feeling sorry for something bad or wrong that you have done SYN **unrepentant** OPP **penitent** —**impenitence** *n.* [U]

im·per·a·tive[1] /ɪm'pɛrəṭɪv/ *adj.* **1** extremely important, and needing to be done or dealt with immediately: **it is imperative that** *It's imperative that you leave immediately.* | **it is imperative (for sb) to do sth** *It is even more imperative to keep good records.* **2** ENG. LANG. ARTS an imperative verb expresses a command, for example "Stand up!" [**Origin:** 1400–1500 Late Latin *imperativus*, from Latin *imperatus*, past participle of *imperare* **to command**]

imperative[2] *n.* [C] **1** something that must be done urgently: *Reducing air pollution has become an imperative.* **2** ENG. LANG. ARTS the form of a verb that expresses a command. In the sentence "Do it now!" the verb "do" is in the imperative → see also INDICATIVE **3** FORMAL an idea, belief, or emotion that has a strong influence on people, making them behave in a particular way: *Having children is a biological imperative.*

im·per·cep·ti·ble /,ɪmpɚ'sɛptəbəl/ *adj.* impossible to see or notice OPP **perceptible**: *an **almost imperceptible** earthquake* —**imperceptibly** *adv.*

im·per·fect[1] /ɪm'pɚfɪkt/ *adj.* not completely perfect SYN **flawed** OPP **perfect**: *my imperfect Spanish* | *Democracy, no matter how imperfect, is still the best method of government.* —**imperfectly** *adv.*

imperfect[2] *n.* ENG. LANG. ARTS **the imperfect** also **the imperfect tense** the form of a verb that is used when talking about an action in the past that is not complete, and that is formed with "be" and the PAST PARTICIPLE. In the sentence "We were walking down the road," the phrase "were walking" is in the imperfect.

im,perfect compe'tition *n.* [C] ECONOMICS a situation in which only a small number of companies are producing the same product or providing the same service, and all the things that have an effect on the cost of producing the product or providing the service are different for each company OPP **perfect competition**

im·per·fec·tion /,ɪmpɚ'fɛkʃən/ *n.* [C,U] the state of being imperfect, or something that is imperfect OPP **perfection** SYN **flaw**: *human imperfection* | *There are slight imperfections in the cloth.*

im·pe·ri·al /ɪm'pɪriəl/ *adj.* **1** POLITICS relating to an EMPIRE or to the person who rules it: *History is full of attempts at imperial domination.* | *the imperial jewels* **2** [only before noun] relating to the British system of weights and measurements based on pounds, INCHES miles, gallons etc.

im·pe·ri·al·ism /ɪm'pɪriəˌlɪzəm/ *n.* [U] **1** POLITICS a political system in which one country rules a lot of other countries: *the history of British imperialism* **2** POLITICS the desire of one country to rule or control other countries **3** DISAPPROVING the way in which a rich or powerful country's way of life, CULTURE, businesses etc. influence and change a poorer country's way of life etc.: **cultural imperialism** (=bringing ideas from one country or culture into another weaker one, either deliberately or without intending to) | **economic imperialism** (=the way that one country controls another using economic methods) —**imperialist** *n.* —**imperialist** also **imperialistic** /ɪmˌpɪriə'lɪstɪk/ *adj.* → see also COLONIALISM

im·per·il /ɪm'pɛrəl/ *v.* [T] FORMAL to put something or someone in danger SYN endanger: *Putting off the surgery would imperil the girl's life.*

im·pe·ri·ous /ɪm'pɪriəs/ *adj.* giving orders and expecting to be obeyed, in a way that seems too proud: *an imperious gesture* —**imperiously** *adv.*

im·per·ish·a·ble /ɪm'pɛrɪʃəbəl/ *adj.* FORMAL existing or continuing to be in good condition for a long time or forever OPP perishable

im·per·ma·nent /ɪm'pɚmənənt/ *adj.* FORMAL not staying the same forever SYN temporary OPP permanent: *an impermanent arrangement* —**impermanence** *n.* [U]

im·per·me·a·ble /ɪm'pɚmiəbəl/ *adj.* TECHNICAL not allowing something, especially a liquid or gas, to pass through OPP permeable

im·per·mis·si·ble /ˌɪmpɚ'mɪsəbəl/ *adj.* FORMAL not allowable OPP permissable

im·per·son·al /ɪm'pɚsənəl/ *adj.* **1** not showing any feelings of sympathy, friendliness etc.: *Just signing your name on a Christmas card seems too impersonal.* **2** a place or situation that is impersonal does not make people feel that they are important: *The school was large and impersonal.* **3** ENG. LANG. ARTS an impersonal sentence or verb is one where the subject is represented by a word such as "it," as in the sentence "It rained all day." —**impersonally** *adv.* → see also PERSONAL

im·per·so·nate /ɪm'pɚsəˌneɪt/ *v.* [T] **1** to pretend to be someone else by copying their appearance, voice etc., in order to deceive people: *It is a serious offense to impersonate a police officer.* **2** to copy someone's voice and behavior, especially to make people laugh SYN mimic: *a contest for people impersonating Elvis Presley* —**impersonation** /ɪmˌpɚsə'neɪʃən/ *n.* [C,U]

im·per·son·at·or /ɪm'pɚsəˌneɪt̬ɚ/ *n.* [C] someone who copies the way that other people look, speak, and behave, as part of a performance or to deceive people → see also IMPRESSIONIST

im·per·ti·nent /ɪm'pɚt̚n-ənt/ *adj.* impolite and not respectful, especially to someone who is older or more important SYN rude SYN impudent: *an impertinent child* | *impertinent questions* —**impertinence** *n.* [U]

im·per·turb·a·ble /ˌɪmpɚ'tɚbəbəl/ *adj.* remaining calm and unworried in spite of problems or difficulties —**imperturbably** *adv.*

im·per·vi·ous /ɪm'pɚviəs/ *adj.* FORMAL **1** not affected or influenced by something and seeming not to notice it: **+to** *The college administration seemed impervious to criticism.* **2** not allowing anything to enter or pass through: **+to** *materials that are impervious to water*

im·pe·ti·go /ˌɪmpə'tigoʊ, -'taɪgoʊ/ *n.* [U] MEDICINE an infectious skin disease

im·pet·u·ous /ɪm'pɛtʃuəs/ *adj.* tending to do things very quickly and without thinking carefully first, or showing this quality SYN impulsive: *Williams was wild and impetuous.* | *an impetuous decision* —**impetuously** *adv.* —**impetuousness** *n.* [U] —**impetuosity** /ɪmˌpɛtʃu'ɑsət̬i/ *n.* [U]

im·pe·tus /'ɪmpət̬əs/ *n.* [U] **1** an influence that makes something happen, or makes it happen more quickly: **+for** *The report **provided the impetus** for changes in the way math is taught.* | **+to** *The education of black people helped **give impetus** to the Civil Rights Movement.* **2** PHYSICS the force that makes an object start moving, or keeps it moving [**Origin:** 1600–1700 Latin *impetere* **to attack**, from *petere* **to go to, look for**]

im·pi·e·ty /ɪm'paɪət̬i/ *n. plural* **impieties** FORMAL [C,U] lack of respect for religion or God, or an action that shows this SYN irreverence OPP piety

im·pinge /ɪm'pɪndʒ/ *v.*

impinge on/upon sb/sth *phr. v.* **1** FORMAL to have an effect, often a harmful or unwanted one, on someone or something: *Personal problems may impinge on a student's schoolwork.* **2** TECHNICAL if light, sound etc. impinges on something such as a surface, it hits it —**impingement** *n.*

im·pi·ous /ɪm'paɪəs, 'ɪmpiəs/ *adj.* FORMAL lacking respect for religion or God OPP pious —**impiously** *adv.*

imp·ish /'ɪmpɪʃ/ *adj.* tending to behave badly and showing a lack of respect or seriousness, but in a way that is amusing rather than annoying SYN mischievous: *an impish grin* —**impishly** *adv.*

im·plac·a·ble /ɪm'plækəbəl/ *adj.* determined to do something, especially to continue opposing someone or something: *an implacable enemy* —**implacably** *adv.* —**implacability** /ɪmˌplækə'bɪlət̬i/ *n.* [U]

im·plant¹ /ɪm'plænt/ *v.* [T] **1** to put something into someone's body by doing a medical operation: **implant sth in/into sth** *The fertilized eggs were implanted in her uterus.* **2** to establish an idea or emotion strongly in someone's mind, so that it is not easily forgotten: **implant sth in sb/sth** *She had to read it several times before it was implanted in her memory.* **3** [I] MEDICAL if an egg or EMBRYO implants, it attaches itself inside a woman's body and begins to develop normally

im·plant² /'ɪmplænt/ *n.* [C] something that has been implanted in someone's body in a medical operation: *silicone breast implants* → see also TRANSPLANT

im·plan·ta·tion /ˌɪmplæn'teɪʃən/ *n.* [U] BIOLOGY a process in which an egg that has been FERTILIZEd attaches itself to the wall of the UTERUS (=place in a woman's body where a baby develops before it is born)

im·plau·si·ble /ɪm'plɔzəbəl/ *adj.* difficult to believe and not likely to be true SYN unbelievable OPP plausible: *an implausible excuse* —**implausibly** *adv.* —**implausibility** /ɪmˌplɔzə'bɪlət̬i/ *n.* [U]

im·ple·ment¹ /'ɪmpləˌmɛnt/ Ac W2 *v.* [T] if you implement a plan, process etc., you begin to make it happen: **implement a policy/plan/program etc.** *Cost-cutting measures have been implemented in most hospitals.*

im·ple·ment² /'ɪmpləmənt/ Ac *n.* [C] a tool or instrument, especially one used in farming or building: *agricultural implements* [**Origin:** 1400–1500 Late Latin *implementum* **act of filling up**, from Latin *implere* **to fill up**]

im·ple·men·ta·tion /ˌɪmpləmən'teɪʃən/ Ac *n.* [U] the act of implementing a plan, process etc.

im·pli·cate /'ɪmplɪˌkeɪt/ Ac *v.* [T] **1** if you implicate someone, you show or claim that they are involved in something wrong or illegal: **implicate sb in sth** *The suspect implicated two other men in the robbery.* **2** if something is implicated in something bad or harmful, it is shown to be its cause: **implicate sth in sth** *The gene has been implicated in many types of cancer.* [**Origin:** 1400–1500 Latin, past participle of *implicare* **to twist together, make complicated**]

im·pli·ca·tion /ˌɪmplɪ'keɪʃən/ Ac W3 *n.* **1** [C usually plural] a possible future effect or result of a plan, action, or event: +**of** *What are the implications of these proposals?* | **important/profound/significant etc. implications** *The admissions policy could **have** serious **implications for** ethnic diversity on campus.* | **political/ethical/financial etc. implications** *The board is **considering the** financial **implications** of the changes.* **2** [C,U] something that is not directly said or shown, but that is suggested or understood: +**that** *He said it would take time, with the implication that he meant a long time.* | *The airline is among the youngest – and **by implication** the safest – in the air.* **3** [U] a situation in which it is shown or claimed that someone or something is involved in something wrong, illegal, or dangerous: +**of** *the implication of fat in heart disease* → see also IMPLICATE

im·plic·it /ɪmˈplɪsɪt/ Ac *adj.* **1** suggested or understood without being stated directly SYN **implied** OPP **explicit**: *an implicit admission of guilt* | +**in** *Implicit in the article is the idea that single mothers are responsible for poverty.* **2 be implicit in sth** FORMAL to be a central part of something without being stated: *Risk is implicit in owning a business.* **3 implicit trust/faith/belief** trust etc. that is complete and contains no doubts —**implicitly** *adv.*

im,plied 'powers *n.* [plural] POLITICS the powers given to the U.S government that are not clearly stated in the CONSTITUTION, which are accepted as necessary in order for the government to carry out its EXPRESSED POWERS (=those written down in the Constitution) → see also DELEGATED POWERS, EXPRESSED POWERS, INHERENT POWERS

im·plode /ɪmˈploʊd/ *v.* **1** [I] WRITTEN if an organization or system implodes, it fails suddenly, often because of problems that it has: *The political system is imploding, due to the government's corruption.* **2** [I,T] to explode toward the inside, or to make something do this: *The jet's engine may have imploded.* —**implosion** /ɪmˈploʊʒən/ *n.* [C,U] → see also EXPLODE

im·plore /ɪmˈplɔr/ *v.* [T] FORMAL to ask for something in an emotional way SYN **beg**: **implore sb to do sth** *The U.N. implored both groups to end the violence.* [**Origin:** 1500–1600 French *implorer*, from Latin, from *plorare* **to cry out**]

im·ply /ɪmˈplaɪ/ Ac W3 *v.* **implied, implies, implying** [T] **1** to suggest that something is true, without saying or showing it directly → see also INFER: *an implied threat* | **imply (that)** *She had not meant to imply that he was lying.* → see Word Choice box at INFER ▸see THESAURUS box at **say**[1] **2** if a fact, information, event etc. implies something, it shows that it is likely to be true: **+ (that)** *The radiation in the rocks implies that they are volcanic in origin.* **3** if one thing implies another, the second thing must exist for the first to happen: *Democracy implies a respect for freedom of speech.* **4 as the name implies** used to give more details about why something has a particular name or why the name is appropriate: *The wildlife refuge, as the name implies, is a peaceful, natural area full of animals.*

im·po·lite /ˌɪmpəˈlaɪt/ *adj.* not polite SYN **rude** OPP **polite**: **it is impolite (to do sth)** *In Japan, it is impolite to show your emotions in public.* —**impolitely** *adv.*

im·pol·i·tic /ɪmˈpɑlətɪk/ *adj.* FORMAL behaving in a way that is not careful or sensible and that may offend people OPP **politic**: *an impolitic remark about people "deserving" AIDS*

im·pon·der·a·ble /ɪmˈpɑndərəbəl/ *adj.* FORMAL something that is imponderable cannot be exactly measured, judged, or calculated —**imponderable** *n.* [C usually plural]

im·port[1] /ˈɪmpɔrt/ *n.* **1** [C,U] the action or business of bringing goods into one country from another to be sold OPP **export**: *Oil imports have risen recently.* | +**of** *The U.S. banned the import of African elephant ivory in 1989.* **2** [C] something that is brought into one country from another in order to be sold, especially a car: *Californian small-car buyers tend to buy imports.* **3** [C] something new or different that is brought to a place where it did not previously exist: *The beetle is thought to be a European import.* **4** [U] FORMAL importance or meaning: *a matter of little import*

im·port[2] /ɪmˈpɔrt/ *v.* [T] **1** to bring something from one country into another so that it can be sold there OPP **export**: **import sth from sth** *The wood had been imported from China.* **2** COMPUTERS to move computer information from one computer to the one you are using, or from one computer DOCUMENT to the one you are using OPP **export** **3** to introduce something new or different in a place where it did not previously exist: *The fish, not native to California, had been imported from Florida.* [**Origin:** 1400–1500 Latin *importare*, from *portare* **to carry**]

im·por·tance /ɪmˈpɔrt̚ns, -pɔrtn̩s/ W2 *n.* [U] **1** the quality of being important: +**of** *His story illustrates the importance of staying in school.* | *The government **attaches** great **importance to** human rights.* | *This is an issue **of** much **importance** to everyone in the region.* | **critical/vital/paramount etc. importance** *These changes are of the utmost importance.* **2** the reason why something is important SYN **significance**: *Explain the importance of the Monroe Doctrine in a 750-word essay.*

im·por·tant /ɪmˈpɔrt̚nt/ S1 W1 *adj.* **1** having a big effect or influence on people or events, or having a lot of value or meaning to someone or something OPP **unimportant**: *She asked some important questions.* | *an important meeting* | +**for** *Regular exercise is important for everyone.* | +**to** *Money and possessions aren't very important to me.* | **it is important (for sb) to do sth** *It is important to explain the treatment to the patient.* | **it is important that sb/sth does sth** *It's important that the community sees their tax dollars at work.*

THESAURUS

of great/considerable importance very important: *Friends are of great importance to your child's development.*
crucial very important: *The U.S. plays a crucial role in the region.*
vital/essential extremely important or necessary: *The computer has become an essential tool in offices.*
major very large or important, especially when compared to other things: *our major cities* | *a major problem*
significant noticeable or important: *The film upset a significant number of people.*
key very important and necessary for success or to understand something: *the team's key players* | *Do the students understand the key concepts of biology?*
paramount FORMAL more important than anything else: *Education should be a paramount concern.*
main/chief/principal/primary/central more important than all other things of the same kind: *the main aim of the expedition*
noteworthy important or interesting enough to deserve your attention: *a noteworthy accomplishment*

2 having a lot of power or influence: *a very important customer* | *J. S. Bach is the most important Baroque composer.* [**Origin:** 1400–1500 French, Old Italian *importante* **carrying a meaning, significant**, from Latin *importare*]

im·por·tant·ly /ɪmˈpɔrt̚ntli/ *adv.* **1 more/equally/less etc. importantly** [sentence adverb] used to show that the next statement or question is more, equally etc. important than what you said before it: *I enjoy my job, but more importantly, it pays the bills.* **2** in a way that shows you think that what you are saying or doing is important: *She walked importantly into the boss's office.*

im·por·ta·tion /ˌɪmpɔrˈteɪʃən/ *n.* **1** [U] the process of bringing something from one area into another, especially in order to be sold: +**of** *The law banned the importation of waste into the state.* **2** [C,U] the act of bringing something new or different to a place where it did not previously exist, or something that arrives in this way: *They are resisting American cultural importations.*

'import ˌduty *n. plural* **import duties** [C,U] a tax on goods that are brought into one country from another country

im·port·er /ɪm'pɔrṭɚ/ *n.* [C] a person, company, or country that buys goods from another country so that they can sell them in their own country → see also EXPORTER

'import ˌlicense *n.* [C] a document that gives permission for goods to be brought into one country from another country

'import ˌquota *n.* [C] ECONOMICS an official limit on the amount of a particular product or goods allowed into a country: *The federal government imposes import quotas on sugar to protect domestic beet growers.*

'import substiˌtution *n.* [U] ECONOMICS encouragement of the local production of goods to replace IMPORTS

im·por·tu·nate /ɪm'pɔrtʃənɪt, -tyʊnɪt/ *adj.* FORMAL continuously asking for things in an annoying or unreasonable way —**importunity** /ˌɪmpɚ'tunəṭi/ *n.* [U]

im·por·tune /ˌɪmpɚ'tun/ *v.* [T] FORMAL to ask someone for something continuously, in an annoying or unreasonable way SYN **beg**

im·pose /ɪm'poʊz/ Ac W2 *v.* **1** [T] if someone in authority imposes a rule, tax, punishment etc., they force people to accept it: *Troops were sent to the region to impose order.* | **impose sth on sb** *The new law imposes fines on the parents of children who break the curfew.* | **impose restrictions/sanctions/penalties etc.** *The U.N. imposed restrictions on flights over the area.* **2** [T] to force someone to have the same ideas, beliefs etc. as you: **impose sth on sb** *Teachers may not impose their religious beliefs on their students.* **3** [I] to expect or ask someone to do something for you when this is not convenient for them: *No, we'll find a motel – we don't want to impose.* | **+on/upon** *I'm sorry if I imposed on you.* **4** [T] to have a bad effect on someone or something by causing them problems: **impose a burden/hardship etc. (on sb/sth)** *A higher sales tax would impose an unfair burden on poorer Americans.* [**Origin:** 1400–1500 French *imposer*, from Latin *imponere*, from *ponere* **to put**]

im·pos·ing /ɪm'poʊzɪŋ/ Ac *adj.* large, important-looking, and impressive: *an imposing building*

im·po·si·tion /ˌɪmpə'zɪʃən/ Ac *n.* **1** [U] the introduction of something such as a rule, tax, or punishment: **+of** *the imposition of martial law* **2** [C usually singular] something that someone expects or asks you to do for them, when this is not convenient for you: *My dad seemed to feel that picking me up from school was an imposition.*

im·pos·si·ble¹ /ɪm'pɑsəbəl/ S3 W2 *adj.* **1** not able to be done or to happen OPP **possible**: *With all the noise, sleep was impossible.* | *an impossible task* | **it is impossible (for sb) to do sth** *It would be impossible to list them all.* | *I* ***found it impossible*** *to read his writing.* | **virtually/nearly/almost impossible** *Divorces were almost impossible to get.* | *a* ***seemingly impossible*** *task* | *Darkness and bad weather* ***made*** *the* ***search*** *impossible.* | *Peace now seems like* ***an impossible dream*** (=something that you hope for that is not likely to happen). **2** an impossible situation is extremely difficult to deal with: *Sometimes an abortion seems like the only way out of an impossible situation.* | *the impossible burdens society places on working parents* **3** behaving in unreasonable and annoying way: *You're impossible!* —**impossibility** /ɪmˌpɑsə'bɪləṭi/ *n.* [C,U]

impossible² *n.* **the impossible** something that cannot be easily done: **do/attempt/accomplish etc. the impossible** *To her, it seemed that he had done the impossible.*

im·pos·si·bly /ɪm'pɑsəbli/ *adv.* [+ adj./adv.] extremely, in a way that is difficult to believe: *The clothes were impossibly expensive.*

im·pos·tor, **imposter** /ɪm'pɑstɚ/ *n.* [C] someone who pretends to be someone else in order to trick people: *He said he was a police officer, but turned out to be an impostor.*

im·pos·ture /ɪm'pɑstʃɚ/ *n.* [U] FORMAL a situation in which someone tricks people by pretending to be someone else

im·po·tent /'ɪmpəṭənt/ *adj.* **1** MEDICINE a man who is impotent is unable to have sex because he cannot get an ERECTION **2** unable to take effective action because you do not have enough power, strength, or control SYN **powerless**: *The U.S. seems impotent to influence events in the region.* —**impotently** *adv.* —**impotence** *n.* [U]

im·pound /ɪm'paʊnd/ *v.* [T] LAW if the police or a court of law impounds your possessions, they take them for a period of time because you have broken a rule or law: *The documents were impounded at the beginning of the investigation.*

im·pov·er·ish /ɪm'pɑvərɪʃ/ *v.* [T] **1** [often passive] to make someone very poor: *Many patients worry that paying for medical care will impoverish them.* **2** to make something worse in quality: *Crop rotation has not impoverished the soil.* —**impoverishment** *n.* [U]

im·pov·er·ished /ɪm'pɑvərɪʃt/ *adj.* **1** very poor SYN **poverty-stricken**: *Brazil's impoverished northeast region* ▸see THESAURUS box at **poor** **2** worse in quality: *Our lives would be impoverished without music.*

im·prac·ti·ca·ble /ɪm'præktɪkəbəl/ *adj.* FORMAL impossible or very difficult to do for practical reasons OPP **practicable**: *It is an appealing plan, but completely impracticable.*

im·prac·ti·cal /ɪm'præktɪkəl/ *adj.* **1** a thing or idea that is impractical is not possible, or is not likely to be useful or effective OPP **practical**: *Tight skirts are impractical if you need to run.* | *The plan was* ***wildly impractical*** (=very impractical). | **it is impractical to do sth** *It was impractical to close the border.* **2** a person who is impractical is not good at dealing with ordinary practical matters OPP **practical** —**impracticality** /ɪmˌpræktɪ'kæləṭi/ *n.* [C,U]

im·pre·ca·tion /ˌɪmprɪ'keɪʃən/ *n.* [C] FORMAL an offensive word or phrase, used when you are very angry SYN **curse**

im·pre·cise /ˌɪmprɪ'saɪs/ Ac *adj.* not clear or exact OPP **precise** OPP **exact**: *imprecise estimates* | *His use of language is vague and imprecise.* —**imprecisely** *adv.* —**imprecision** /ˌɪmprɪ'sɪʒən/ *n.* [U]

im·preg·na·ble /ɪm'prɛgnəbəl/ *adj.* **1** a building or area that is impregnable is so strong or well defended that it cannot be entered by force: *an impregnable fortress* **2** FORMAL strong and impossible to change or influence: *The law case he builds must be impregnable.*

im·preg·nate /ɪm'prɛgˌneɪt/ *v.* [T] **1** BIOLOGY to make a woman or female animal PREGNANT **2** to make a substance spread completely through something, or to spread completely through something: **impregnate sth with sth** *The material is impregnated with insect repellent.*

im·pre·sa·ri·o /ˌɪmprə'sɑrioʊ/ *n.* [C] someone who organizes performances in theaters, concert halls etc.

im·press¹ /ɪm'prɛs/ S2 W3 *v.* **1** [I,T not in progressive] to make someone feel admiration and respect for you: *You don't need to make fancy foods to impress guests.* | *He was dressed to impress.* | **impress sb with sth** *The students impressed us with their creativity.* **2** [T] to press something into a soft surface, so that a mark or pattern appears on it [**Origin:** 1300–1400 Latin, past participle of *imprimere*, from *premere* **to press**]

impress sb **as** sth *phr. v.* to make someone think of someone as having particular qualities, because of the way they seem: *She impressed me as a quiet, serious person.*

impress sth **on/upon** sb *phr. v.* to make the importance of something clear to someone: **impress sth on/upon sb** *My parents impressed on me the value of hard work.*

im·press² /ˈɪmprɛs/ *n.* [C] FORMAL OR LITERARY a mark or pattern made by pressing something into a surface

im·pressed /ɪmˈprɛst/ *adj.* feeling admiration and respect for someone or something: **be impressed by/with** *He was impressed with the students' knowledge and insight.* | **greatly/deeply/very impressed** *We were not greatly impressed with the results.*

im·pres·sion /ɪmˈprɛʃən/ S2 W3 *n.* [C] **1** the opinion, belief, or feeling you have about someone or something because of the way they seem: +**of** *What's your impression of Hal?* | **have/get the impression (that)** *I got the impression that he wasn't very happy.* | **good/bad/favorable etc. impression** *It's important to* ***make a*** *good* ***impression*** *at your interview.* | **false/wrong impression** *The report* ***gave the*** *false* ***impression*** *that the disease had been cured.* | ***My first impression*** (=my opinion when I first saw something) *was that the car was fun to drive.* **2 be under the impression that...** to believe that something is true when it is not true: *Sorry, I was under the impression that you were the manager.* **3** the act of copying the speech or behavior of a famous person in order to make people laugh SYN **imitation**: +**of** *Sandy* ***does a*** *pretty good* ***impression*** *of Madonna.* **4** a mark left by pressing something into a soft surface: *An* ***impression*** *of a heel was* ***left*** *in the mud.* **5** all the copies of a book printed at one time → see also EDITION

im·pres·sion·a·ble /ɪmˈprɛʃənəbəl/ *adj.* someone who is impressionable is easy to influence, especially because they are young: *What kind of impact will this movie have on impressionable kids?*

im·pres·sion·ism /ɪmˈprɛʃəˌnɪzəm/ *n.* [U] ENG. LANG. ARTS **1** a style of painting used especially in France in the 19th century, which uses color instead of details of form to produce effects of light or feeling **2** a style of music or literature from the late 19th and early 20th centuries that emphasizes feelings and images —**impressionist** *adj.*: *impressionist painters*

im·pres·sion·ist /ɪmˈprɛʃənɪst/ *n.* [C] **1** ENG. LANG. ARTS someone who uses impressionism in the paintings or music that they produce **2** someone who copies the speech or behavior of famous people in order to entertain other people

im·pres·sion·is·tic /ɪmˌprɛʃəˈnɪstɪk/ *adj.* based on a general feeling of what something is like, rather than on specific facts or details: *an impressionistic picture of life in the inner city*

im·pres·sive /ɪmˈprɛsɪv/ *adj.* something that is impressive makes you admire it because it is very good, large, important etc.: *The Bruins have been impressive in their last five games.* | *an* ***impressive array*** *of authors at the book festival* —**impressively** *adv.* —**impressiveness** *n.* [U]

THESAURUS

imposing large and impressive: *He was an imposing figure.*
dazzling very impressive, exciting, or interesting: *a dazzling display of Christmas decorations*
awe-inspiring so impressive that you feel awe (=a feeling of respect and admiration): *the awe-inspiring views from the top of the mountain*
breathtaking extremely impressive, exciting, or surprising: *The coastline was breathtaking in its beauty.*
majestic looking very big and impressive: *the majestic pyramids at Giza in Egypt*

im·press·ment /ɪmˈprɛsmənt/ *n.* [U] FORMAL HISTORY the action of forcing people to serve in the military or the government, or the action of taking things for government use

im·pri·ma·tur /ˌɪmprəˈmeɪtʊr, ɪmˈprɪməˌtʊr/ *n.* [singular] FORMAL **1** approval of something, especially from an important person: *The New England Journal of Medicine put its imprimatur on the two studies.* **2** official permission to print a book, given by the Roman Catholic Church

im·print¹ /ˈɪmˌprɪnt/ *n.* [C] **1** the mark left by an object being pressed into or onto something: +**of** *a rock with a fossil imprint of algae* **2** an effect or influence that something has on a place, person, event etc.: +**on** *Simmons wants to put his own imprint on the firm.* **3** the name of a PUBLISHER as it appears on a book: *This dictionary is published under the Longman imprint.*

im·print² /ɪmˈprɪnt, ˈɪmˌprɪnt/ *v.* **1** [T usually passive] to print or press the mark of an object on something: **imprint sth with sth** *The leather was imprinted with a pattern of flowers.* | **imprint sth on sth** *Deep purple bruises were imprinted on her neck.* **2** [T] if something is imprinted on your mind or memory, you can never forget it: *The image of Helen's sad face was* ***imprinted on his mind.***

im·print·ing /ˈɪmˌprɪntɪŋ/ *n.* [U] BIOLOGY a very early learning process in animals, in which a young animal learns patterns of behavior and its connection to members of its own kind, especially its parents

im·pris·on /ɪmˈprɪzən/ *v.* [T] **1** to put someone in prison, or to keep them somewhere and prevent them from leaving SYN **incarcerate**: *If convicted, she will be imprisoned for at least six years.* **2** if a situation or feeling imprisons people, it restricts what they can do: *Many elderly people felt imprisoned in their own homes.*

im·pris·on·ment /ɪmˈprɪzənmənt/ *n.* [U] the state of being in prison, or the time someone spends there: *Corelli could face* ***life imprisonment*** (=imprisonment for the rest of his life).

im·prob·a·ble /ɪmˈprɑbəbəl/ *adj.* **1** not likely to happen or be true SYN **unlikely** OPP **probable**: **it is improbable that** *It is* ***highly improbable*** *that mining would be allowed in the national parks.* **2** surprising and slightly strange: *a dress with an improbable combination of colors* —**improbably** *adv.* —**improbability** /ɪmˌprɑbəˈbɪləṭi/ *n.* [C,U]

im·promp·tu /ɪmˈprɑmptu/ *adj.* done or said without any preparation or planning: *an impromptu performance* [**Origin:** 1600–1700 French, Latin *in promptu* **in readiness**] —**impromptu** *adv.*

im·prop·er /ɪmˈprɑpɚ/ *adj.* **1** unacceptable according to professional, moral, or social standards of behavior SYN **inappropriate** OPP **proper**: *Displaying alcohol ads at the conference was improper, in my opinion.* | **it is improper (for sb) to do sth** *It would be improper for me to discuss the case at this point.* **2** illegal or dishonest: *improper banking practices* | **improper conduct/behavior etc.** *his improper sexual conduct* **3** not correct according to certain rules OPP **proper**: *Many cases of food poisoning result from improper cooking of food.* —**improperly** *adv.*

imˌproper ˈfraction *n.* [C] MATH a FRACTION such as 107/8, in which the top number is larger than the bottom number → see also PROPER FRACTION

im·pro·pri·e·ty /ˌɪmprəˈpraɪəṭi/ *n. plural* **improprieties** [C,U] FORMAL behavior or an action that is unacceptable according to moral, social, or professional standards OPP **propriety**: *charges of financial impropriety*

im·prove /ɪmˈpruv/ S3 W1 *v.* [I,T] to become better, or to make something or yourself better: *Let's hope the weather improves before Saturday.* | *The government hopes to improve relations with the West.* | *Lifting weights will improve your muscle strength.*

improve on/upon sth *phr. v.* to do something better than before, or to make it better than before: *Lamson wants to improve on last year's third-place finish.* [**Origin:** 1500–1600 *emprowe* **to improve** (15–16 centuries), from Anglo-French *emprouer* **to make a profit**]

im·proved /ɪmˈpruvd/ *adj.* better than before: *They're the most improved team in the league.* | *a detergent with a* ***new improved*** *formula*

im·prove·ment /ɪmˈpruvmənt/ W2 *n.* **1** [C,U] an act of improving or a state of being improved: +**in** *There has been much improvement in air quality.* | +**to** *At least $2 million is needed for improvements to the arena.* | +**on/over** *It was a great improvement on the old system.* | *His condition has* ***shown*** *some* ***improvement.*** | **significant/major/dramatic etc.**

improvement *There has been a significant improvement in customer care.* | *His behavior is better, but there's still* ***room for improvement*** (=the need for more improvement). **2** [C] a change or addition that improves something: *home improvements*

im·prov·i·dent /ɪm'prɑvədənt/ *adj.* FORMAL too careless to save any money or to plan for the future

im·pro·vise /'ɪmprəˌvaɪz/ *v.* [I,T] **1** to do something without any preparation, especially because you are forced to do this by unexpected events: *I left my lesson plan at home, so I had to improvise.* **2** to make something using whatever you can find, because you do not have the equipment or materials that you need: *Use these recipes as a guideline, but feel free to improvise!* | *Kids were improvising games with a ball and some string.* **3** ENG. LANG. ARTS to perform music, sing etc. from your imagination, without planning or preparing first: *Jazz musicians are good at improvising.* | *He likes to improvise his comedy.* [**Origin:** 1800–1900 French *improviser*, from Italian, from *improvviso* **sudden**] —**improvised** *adj.* —**improvisation** /ɪmˌprɑvə'zeɪʃən/ *n.* [C,U]

im·pru·dent /ɪm'prudnt/ *adj.* FORMAL not sensible or wise OPP **prudent**: *imprudent investments* —**imprudence** *n.* [C,U]

im·pu·dent /'ɪmpyədənt/ *adj.* impolite and not showing respect SYN **impertinent** SYN **rude**: *an impudent child* —**impudence** *n.* [U]

im·pugn /ɪm'pyun/ *v.* [T] FORMAL to say something that makes people doubt someone's honesty, courage, ability etc. SYN **malign**: *His opponents impugned his patriotism.*

im·pulse /'ɪmpʌls/ *n.* **1** [C,U] a sudden strong desire to do something without thinking about the results or whether it is sensible: **an impulse to do sth** *I had a strong* ***impulse*** *to laugh.* | *Her* ***first impulse*** *was to run.* | *Children with this disorder often act* ***on impulse.*** | *You might want that cheesecake, but* ***resist the impulse.*** | *Last-minute shopping results in* ***impulse buying*** (=buying things without planning or choosing carefully). **2** [C] PHYSICS a short electrical signal sent in one direction along a wire or nerve, or through the air **3** [C] a reason, feeling, or aim that causes a particular kind of activity or behavior: *The impulse of governments all over the world is to control information.* **4** PHYSICS a measure of MOMENTUM that you get if you multiply the average value of a force by the length of time that the force acts

im·pul·sive /ɪm'pʌlsɪv/ *adj.* someone who is impulsive does things without considering the possible dangers or problems first SYN **impetuous**: *an impulsive decision* | *These children tend to be impulsive and restless.* —**impulsively** *adv.* —**impulsiveness** *n.* [U]

THESAURUS

rash done too quickly without thinking carefully first, or behaving in this way: *a rash promise*
hotheaded someone who gets angry or excited easily and does things too quickly, without thinking: *a hotheaded young man*
hasty FORMAL done in a hurry, especially with bad results: *He soon regretted his hasty decision.*

im·pu·ni·ty /ɪm'pyunəṭi/ *n.* **with impunity** without punishment or risk of punishment: *The government is corrupt, and steals from its people with impunity.*

im·pure /ɪm'pyʊr/ *adj.* **1** not pure or clean, and often consisting of a mixture of things OPP **pure**: *impure drugs* **2** OLD-FASHIONED impure thoughts, feelings etc. are morally bad, especially because they are about sex OPP **pure**

im·pu·ri·ty /ɪm'pyʊrəṭi/ *n. plural* **impurities** **1** [C usually plural] a substance that is mixed in with another substance, so that the second substance is not pure: *The water is tested for impurities.* **2** [U] the state of being impure OPP **purity** **3** [U] OLD-FASHIONED the fact that someone or something is not morally perfect

im·pute /ɪm'pyut/ *v.* FORMAL

impute sth **to** sb *phr. v.* to say, often unfairly, that someone is responsible for something bad or that they have bad intentions: *The police were not guilty of the violence imputed to them.* —**imputation** /ˌɪmpyə'teɪʃən/ *n.* [C,U]

IN the written abbreviation of INDIANA

in[1] /ɪn/ S1 W1 *prep.* **1** used with the name of a container, place, or area to show where someone or something is: *The scissors are in the top drawer.* | *I was still in bed at 11:30.* | *Bob's out working in the yard.* | *There's a hole in my sock.* | *He lived in Boston for four years.* | *Grandpa's in the hospital.* **2** from the outside to the inside of a container, a building etc. SYN **into**: *She went in the house.* | *Put your clothes in the closet.* | *He fell in the river.* **3** happening in a particular month, year, season etc.: *We bought our car in April.* | *In 1969 the first astronauts landed on the moon.* | *We use the furnace all the time in the winter.* **4** during a period of time: *We finished the whole project in a week.* **5** at the end of a period of time: *Gerry should be home in an hour.* | *I wonder if they'll still be married in a year.* **6** included as part of a book, document, film etc.: *One of the guys in the story is a doctor.* | *In the first part of the speech he talked about the environment.* **7** experiencing a particular state or situation: *I'm in a hurry.* | *You're in big trouble.* | *The castle was in ruins.* **8** used to say what situation, activity, or organization someone does: *I spent three years in the marching band.* | *He died in the war.* **9 sb has not done sth in years/months/weeks etc.** also **the first sth in years/months etc.** used to say how much time has passed since the last time something happened: *I haven't talked to him in months.* | *It was the first time I'd seen him in three years.* **10** used to say how something is done or happens: *Roger spoke in a low whisper.* | *I had to speak to him in French.* | *Do not write in pen on this test.* | *His early comedies were filmed in black and white.* | *We waited in silence.* **11** used to mention to the weather or the physical conditions somewhere: *They were out playing in the rain.* | *A couple sat in the shade of a tree.* **12** doing or affecting a particular type of job: *Wendy's in advertising.* | *reforms in education* **13** used to show what person or thing has the quality you are mentioning: *There's a hint of fall in the air.* | *She's everything I'd want in a wife.* | *He was very aggressive – I didn't realize he* ***had it in*** *him!* **14** used to talk about the shape, arrangement, or course of something or someone: *Everybody stand in a straight line.* | *He made a bowl in the shape of a heart.* | *Put the files in alphabetical order.* **15** wearing a particular color or piece of clothing: *She was dressed in black.* | *He looked very handsome in his uniform.* **16** used to show the connection or relationship between two ideas or subjects: *That dessert looks awfully high in calories.* | *an expert in nuclear physics* | *strong growth in exports* **17** used to name the substance, food, drink etc. that contains something: *Vitamin C is found in oranges and lemons.* **18** used to say what color something is or what it is made of: *The china is trimmed in blue.* | *a sculpture in white marble* **19** used before numbers or amounts to say how many people or things are involved with something, or how many there are in each group: *Mourners lined the streets in the thousands.* | *Please work in pairs.* **20 be in your 20s/30s/40s etc.** to be between the ages of 20 and 29, 30 and 39 etc.: *I'd say she's in her mid 40s.* **21** used between a smaller number and a larger number to say how common or likely something is, or what the rate of something is: *One in every ten children now suffers from asthma.* **22** used to say what feeling you have when you do something: *Lily looked at me in shock.* | *He was just teasing – it was all in fun.* **23** used before the name of someone or something when you are saying how they are regarded: *You'll always have a friend in me.* **24 in all** used when giving a total number or amount: *I think there were about 25 of us in all.* **25 in two/half/pieces/thirds etc.** used to say how many pieces something is divided into: *She ripped the sheet of paper in two.* | *a book in four parts* **26** used to say that something else happens at the same time as what you are doing, or as a result of it: *In my excitement, I forgot all about the message.* | **in doing sth** *In* *reading the story, I felt nothing but sympathy for the victims.* **27 in that** used after a statement to begin to explain in what way it is true: *She was lucky in that her cancer could be treated.* [**Origin:** Old English] → see also **the ins and outs (of sth)** at INS

in² S1 W1 *adv.* **1** from the outside to the inside of a container, building etc. OPP **out**: *She pushed the box toward me so that I could put my money in.* | *Should we wait out here, or should we go in?* | *The water looked inviting, and he dived in.* **2** inside a building, especially the building where you live or work: *Ms. Shaewitz isn't in yet this morning.* | *You're never in when I call.* **3** if a bus, train, airplane etc. gets in or is in, it arrives or has arrived at a station, airport etc.: *What time does his bus get in?* | *Her flight's not in yet.* **4** given or sent to a person or place to be read or looked at: *Your final papers have to be in by Friday.* | *Letters have been pouring in from all over the country.* **5** if you write, paint, or draw something in, you write it, paint it etc. in the correct place: *Write in your name and address at the bottom.* **6** if someone is in or is voted in, they have been elected to be part of the government: *The Republicans are in now, but for how long?* **7** if you color, paint, fill etc. in a shape or space, you cover the area inside its borders with color, paint etc.: *Can you color in this picture of a teddy bear for me?* **8** if a ball is in during a game, it is inside the area where the game is being played: *Her second serve was just in.* **9** if clothes, colors etc. are in, they are fashionable: *Long hair is in again.* **10 be in for sth** if someone is in for something bad, it is going to happen to them: *She's in for a surprise if she thinks we're going to help her pay for it.* | *You're really* ***in for it*** *now* (=you are going to be punished)*!* **11 be in on sth** to be involved in something, sometimes something secret → see also GET (SB) IN ON STH: *The movie asks questions about who was in on the plan to kill Kennedy.* | *He really ought to be in on this discussion.* **12 in joke** an in joke is one that is only understood by a small group of people **13** if the TIDE comes in or is in, the ocean water moves toward the shore, or is at its highest level **14** if you are in, you agree to take part in a plan, particular job etc.: *We need to make plans for next week, so are you in or out?* **15 sb has (got) it in for sb** INFORMAL if someone has it in for you, they do not like you and want to cause problems or difficulties for you: *I think the P.E. teacher has it in for me.* **16** if something falls or turns in, it falls or turns toward the center: *The map had started to curl in at the edges.* **17 be/get in with sb** INFORMAL to be friendly with someone, or to become friendly with them: *She's in with the theatrical crowd.*

-in /ɪn/ *suffix* [in nouns] an activity organized by a group of people as a protest against something: *a sit-in* (=where people sit in a place to prevent its usual activity)

in- /ɪn/ *prefix* **1** the opposite of something, or the lack of something → see also UN- SYN **not**: *insensitive* (=not sensitive) | *inattention* (=lack of attention) → see also IL-, IM-, IR- **2** in or into something: *income* (=money that you receive) | *inward* (=toward the inside) | *to insert something* (=put it in something else) → see also IM-

in·a·bil·i·ty /ˌɪnəˈbɪləṭi/ [singular,U] the fact of being unable to do something OPP **ability**: **inability to do sth** *An inability to concentrate affects these children's schoolwork.*

in ab·sen·tia /ˌɪn æbˈsɛnʃə/ *adv.* without being present: *The ten men were tried and convicted in absentia.*

in·ac·ces·si·ble /ˌɪnɪkˈsɛsəbəl/ Ac *adj.* **1** difficult or impossible to reach OPP **accessible**: *These mountain villages are completely inaccessible in winter.* | **+to** *The building is inaccessible to wheelchair users.* **2** difficult or impossible to understand or afford OPP **accessible**: **+to** *This textbook would be inaccessible to my students.* —**inaccessibility** /ˌɪnɪkˌsɛsəˈbɪləṭi/ *n.* [U]

in·ac·cu·ra·cy /ɪnˈækyərəsi/ Ac *n.* plural **inaccuracies** **1** [C] a mistake: *The report contained several inaccuracies.* **2** [U] a lack of correctness OPP **accuracy**: *the inaccuracy of a weather forecast*

in·ac·cu·rate /ɪnˈækyərɪt/ Ac *adj.* **1** not completely correct OPP **accurate**: *Some of the information provided was inaccurate or incomplete.* ►see THESAURUS box at **wrong¹** **2** not aimed correctly, or not reaching the place aimed for OPP **accurate**: *an inaccurate pass* —**inaccurately** *adv.*

in·ac·tion /ɪnˈækʃən/ *n.* [U] the fact that someone is not doing anything: *the government's inaction on environmental issues*

in·ac·tive /ɪnˈæktɪv/ *adj.* **1** not doing anything, not working, or not moving OPP **active**: *inacitve factories* | *Children whose parents are inactive* (=do not exercise) *are less likely to be active themselves.* **2** not taking part in something or working, especially when you used to take part or usually take part: *Haley was inactive for Saturday's game because of a knee injury.* **3** CHEMISTRY an inactive substance does not react chemically with other substances —**inactivity** /ˌɪnækˈtɪvəṭi/ *n.* [U]

in·ad·e·qua·cy /ɪnˈædəkwəsi/ Ac *n.* plural **inadequacies** **1** [U] the fact of not being good enough in quality, ability, size etc. for a particular purpose: **+of** *the inadequacy of America's health-care system* **2** [U] the feeling that you are not as good, intelligent, skilled etc. as other people: *Unemployment can cause* ***feelings of inadequacy.*** **3** [C] something that is not good enough: *Parents complained about the school's inadequacies.*

in·ad·e·quate /ɪnˈædəkwɪt/ Ac *adj.* not good enough, big enough, skilled enough etc. for a particular purpose OPP **adequate**: *an inadequate supply of water* | **+for** *The highways are inadequate for the number of cars that pass through here.* | **grossly/wholly/woefully etc. inadequate** *Some of the schools are grossly inadequate.* | *The new computer system* ***proved inadequate.*** | *Some new mothers are anxious and* ***feel inadequate.*** —**inadequately** *adv.*

in·ad·mis·si·ble /ˌɪnədˈmɪsəbəl/ *adj.* FORMAL LAW not allowed, especially in a court of law OPP **admissible**: *The results of lie detector tests are inadmissible in criminal trials.* —**inadmissibility** /ˌɪnədˌmɪsəˈbɪləṭi/ *n.* [U]

in·ad·vert·ent·ly /ˌɪnədˈvɚṭˀntli/ *adv.* without intending to do something SYN **accidentally**: *They inadvertently cut through a telephone cable.* [**Origin:** 1600–1700 Latin *advertens*, present participle of *advertere* **to turn your mind to**] —**inadvertent** *adj.*

in·ad·vis·a·ble /ˌɪnədˈvaɪzəbəl/ *adj.* an inadvisable action, decision etc. is not sensible OPP **advisable**: *Bad weather made the trip inadvisable.*

in·al·ien·a·ble /ɪnˈeɪlyənəbəl/ *adj.* FORMAL LAW an inalienable right cannot be taken away from you

in·ane /ɪˈneɪn/ *adj.* extremely stupid or without much meaning: *an inane movie* —**inanity** /ɪˈnænəṭi/ *n.* [C,U]

in·an·i·mate /ɪnˈænəmɪt/ *adj.* not living OPP **alive**: *an* ***inanimate object***

in·ap·pli·ca·ble /ɪnˈæplɪkəbəl, ˌɪnəˈplɪkəbəl/ *adj.* a description, question, or rule that is inapplicable is not appropriate, correct, or able to be used in a particular situation OPP **applicable**: **+to/in** *The death penalty is inapplicable in this case.* —**inapplicability** /ɪnˌæplɪkəˈbɪləṭi/ *n.* [U]

in·ap·pro·pri·ate /ˌɪnəˈproʊpriɪt/ Ac *adj.* not appropriate or correct for a particular purpose or situation SYN **unsuitable** OPP **appropriate**: **wholly/totally/completely etc. inappropriate** *A poster of a nude woman is wholly inappropriate for the office.* | **it is inappropriate (for sb) to do sth** *Vanalden said it would be inappropriate to comment on the report.* | **+for** *The movie is inappropriate for children.* | *swearing and other inappropriate behavior* —**inappropriately** *adv.*

in·ar·tic·u·late /ˌɪnɑrˈtɪkyəlɪt/ *adj.* **1** not able to express yourself or speak clearly OPP **articulate**: *He is a shy and inarticulate man.* | *her inarticulate despair* **2** speech that is inarticulate is not clearly expressed or pronounced: *an inarticulate cry*

in·as·much /ˌɪnəzˈmʌtʃ/ *adv.* FORMAL **inasmuch as** used when adding a statement that explains the way in which what you are saying is true: *Ann is guilty, inasmuch as she knew what the others were planning.*

in·at·ten·tion /ˌɪnəˈtɛnʃən/ *n.* [U] lack of attention OPP **attention**: +**to** *The company has been criticized for its inattention to environmental issues.*

in·at·ten·tive /ˌɪnəˈtɛntɪv◂ / *adj.* not giving enough attention to someone or something OPP **attentive**: *inattentive students* —**inattentively** *adv.* —**inattentiveness** *n.* [U]

in·au·di·ble /ɪnˈɔdəbəl/ *adj.* if something is inaudible, it is not able to be heard, usually because it is too quiet OPP **audible**: *The whistle is inaudible to most humans.* —**inaudibly** *adv.* —**inaudibility** /ɪnˌɔdəˈbɪləṭi/ *n.* [U]

in·au·gu·ral /ɪˈnɔgyərəl/ *adj.* [only before noun] **1** relating to a ceremony that inaugurates a president, GOVERNOR etc.: *Over 500 people attended the inaugural ball.* **2** an inaugural event is the first in a series: *the plane's inaugural flight*

in·au·gu·rate /ɪˈnɔgyəˌreɪt/ *v.* [T] **1** to have an official ceremony when someone starts doing an important job in the government: *The new President will be inaugurated in January.* **2** to open a new building or start a new service or public event, usually with a ceremony: *In 1960, Brazil inaugurated its new capital, Brasilia.* **3** if an event inaugurates an important change or period of time, it comes at the beginning of it: *The International Trade Agreement inaugurated a period of high economic growth.* —**inauguration** /ɪˌnɔgyəˈreɪʃən/ *n.* [C,U] *a presidential inauguration*

in·aus·pi·cious /ˌɪnɔˈspɪʃəs/ *adj.* FORMAL seeming to show that success in the future is unlikely OPP **auspicious**: *an inauspicious beginning to his career* —**inauspiciously** *adv.*

ˌin-ˈbetween *adj.* INFORMAL in the middle between two points, sizes, periods of time etc.: *She's at that in-between age, neither a girl nor a woman.*

in·board /ˈɪnbɔrd/ *adj.* inside a boat or an airplane: *an inboard motor* → see also OUTBOARD MOTOR

in·born /ˌɪnˈbɔrn◂ / *adj.* an inborn quality or ability is one that you have had naturally since birth SYN **innate**: *an inborn talent for music*

in·bound[1] /ˈɪnbaʊnd/ *adj.* an inbound flight, train etc. is coming toward the place where you are OPP **outbound**

inbound[2] *v.* [T] to return the ball to the playing area in a sport such as basketball: *The Lakers inbounded the ball.*

ˌin-ˈbounds *adv.* if the ball is in-bounds in a sport, it is in the playing area

in·box, in box /ˈɪnbɑks/ *n.* [C] **1** COMPUTERS the place on a computer email program where new messages arrive **2** a container on an office desk to hold work and letters that need to be dealt with → see also OUT BOX

in·bred /ˌɪnˈbrɛd◂ / *adj.* **1** DISAPPROVING an inbred quality or attitude develops as a natural part of someone's character, because of the beliefs or attitudes of the people they grew up with: *There is an inbred racism in some parts of the country.* **2** BIOLOGY produced by inbreeding: *an inbred genetic defect*

in·breed·ing /ˈɪnˌbridɪŋ/ *n.* [U] BIOLOGY the producing of children, animals, or new plants by SEXUAL REPRODUCTION involving closely related members of the same family

Inc. /ɪŋk, ɪnˈkɔrpəˌreɪṭɪd/ the written abbreviation of INCORPORATED: *Pizza Hut, Inc.*

In·ca /ˈɪŋkə/ *n.* one of the people who lived in and controlled a large area of the Andes mountains in South America until the 16th century —**Inca** *adj.*: *the Inca priesthood*

in·cal·cu·la·ble /ɪnˈkælkyələbəl/ *adj.* too many or too great to be measured SYN **immeasurable**: *statues of incalculable value* | *Her contributions to the department are incalculable.*

in·can·des·cent /ˌɪnkənˈdɛsənt/ *adj.* **1** PHYSICS giving a bright light when heated: *an incandescent light bulb* **2** used to describe extreme anger, hatred etc.: *his incandescent fury* **3** very impressive: *an incandescent performance* **4** LITERARY having a very bright appearance: *The light was incandescent on the mountains.* —**incandescence** *n.* [U] → see also FLUORESCENT

in·can·ta·tion /ˌɪnkænˈteɪʃən/ *n.* [C,U] a set of special words that someone uses in magic, or the act of saying these words SYN **spell**

in·ca·pa·ble /ɪnˈkeɪpəbəl/ Ac *adj.* not able to do something OPP **capable**: **incapable of doing sth** *She is physically incapable of caring for herself.* | +**of** *Is the government incapable of change?*

in·ca·pac·i·tate /ˌɪnkəˈpæsəˌteɪt/ Ac *v.* [T often passive] **1** to make someone too sick or weak to live and work normally: *She suffered a stroke that incapacitated her.* **2** to make something unable to work normally, especially by damaging it: *Severe storms incapacitated the town.* —**incapacitation** /ˌɪnkəˌpæsəˈteɪʃən/ *n.* [U]

in·ca·pac·i·ty /ˌɪnkəˈpæsəṭi/ *n.* [singular,U] lack of ability, strength, or power to do something, especially because you are sick: *mental incapacity*

in·car·cer·ate /ɪnˈkɑrsəˌreɪt/ *v.* [T usually passive] FORMAL to put someone in prison, or keep them there SYN **imprison**: *He was incarcerated for 240 days.* —**incarceration** /ɪnˌkɑrsəˈreɪʃən/ *n.* [U]

in·car·nate[1] /ɪnˈkɑrnɪt, -ˌneɪt/ *adj.* [usually after noun] **1 evil/beauty/greed etc. incarnate** used when emphasizing that someone is extremely evil, beautiful etc., so that they seem to be the human form of that quality **2** having taken human form: *Jesus, the incarnate Son of God*

in·car·nate[2] /ɪnˈkɑrˌneɪt/ *v.* [T] FORMAL **1** to represent a particular quality in a physical or human form SYN **embody**: *She incarnates innocence in the role.* **2** to make something appear in a human form

in·car·na·tion /ˌɪnkɑrˈneɪʃən/ *n.* [C] **1** the form or character that a person or thing takes at a particular time: **present/previous/latest/earlier etc. incarnation** *The building is a restaurant in its latest incarnation.* **2** the state of being alive in the form of a particular person or animal, or the period during which this happens, according to some religions: *In Hindu lore, Rama is an incarnation of the god Vishnu.* **3 be the incarnation of goodness/evil/sweetness** to perfectly represent goodness etc. in the way you live SYN **embodiment**: *She is the incarnation of femininity.* **4 the Incarnation** the act of God coming to Earth in the human form of Jesus Christ, according to the Christian religion

in·cau·tious /ɪnˈkɔʃəs/ *adj.* if someone is incautious, they do or say something without thinking carefully about the possible effects OPP **cautious**: *Incautious investors may lose money.*

in·cen·di·ar·y[1] /ɪnˈsɛndiˌɛri/ *adj.* [only before noun] **1 incendiary bomb/device etc.** a bomb, piece of equipment etc. designed to cause a fire **2** an incendiary speech or piece of writing is intended to make people angry SYN **inflammatory**

incendiary[2] *n. plural* **incendiaries** [C] a bomb designed to cause a fire

in·cense[1] /ˈɪnsɛns/ *n.* [U] a substance that has a pleasant smell when you burn it [**Origin:** 1200–1300 Old French *encens*, from Latin *incensus*, past participle of *incendere* **to cause to start burning**]

in·cense[2] /ɪnˈsɛns/ *v.* [T] to make someone extremely angry SYN **anger** SYN **infuriate**: *The parking changes incensed residents.*

in·censed /ɪnˈsɛnst/ *adj.* extremely angry SYN **furious**: +**by/at** *Perry was incensed at the accusations.* | **incensed that** *He was incensed that he had not been paid.*

in·cen·ter of a tri·an·gle /ɪnˌsɛntɚ əv ə ˈtraɪˌæŋgəl/ *n.* [singular] MATH the point where three lines drawn from the middle of each of the angles of a TRIANGLE meet in the center of the triangle

in·cen·tive /ɪnˈsɛntɪv/ Ac W3 *n.* [C,U] something that

I

encourages you to work harder, start new activities etc. SYN **inducement**: *Low prices **give** the farmers little **incentive**.* | **incentive to do sth** *The promise of a good job **provides** a clear **incentive** to work hard in school.* | **economic/financial/tax etc. incentives** *The high-tech industry was lured here by tax incentives* (=offers of reduced taxes). [**Origin:** 1600–1700 Late Latin *incentivum*, from Latin *incinere* **to set the tune**]

in·cep·tion /ɪnˈsɛpʃən/ *n.* [singular] FORMAL the start of an organization or institution SYN **beginning**: *Graham danced with the company **since its inception** in 1976.*

in·ces·sant /ɪnˈsɛsənt/ *adj.* without stopping, in an annoying way SYN **constant** SYN **ceaseless**: *the incessant buzzing of helicopters* —**incessantly** *adv.*

in·cest /ˈɪnsɛst/ *n.* [U] illegal sex between people who are closely related in a family [**Origin:** 1200–1300 Latin *incestum*, from *castus* **pure**]

in·ces·tu·ous /ɪnˈsɛstʃuəs/ *adj.* **1** involving sexual activity between people who are closely related in a family **2** relating to a small group of people or organizations who only help or spend time with each other, in a way that is unfair to other people: *an incestuous relationship among city officials*

inch¹ /ɪntʃ/ S1 W2 *n.* [C] **1 in.** a unit for measuring length, equal to 1/12 of a FOOT or 2.54 centimeters: *a six-inch nail* | **... inches long/deep/wide/thick etc.** *The paper was 10 inches long.* **2** [usually plural] a very small distance: *The next bullet missed Billy **by inches**.* | *His face was **only inches from** hers.* **3** enough rain or snow to cover an area an inch deep: *three inches of snow* **4 every inch a)** all of something or someone: +**of** *Every inch of the apartment was filled with boxes.* **b)** completely or in every way: *She **looks every inch** the high-powered businesswoman.* **5 inch by inch** very slowly or by a small amount at a time: *He moved inch by inch toward the animal.* **6 not budge/give an inch** to refuse to change your opinions at all: *Neither side would budge an inch during the discussions.* **7 give sb an inch and they'll take a mile** used to say that if you allow someone a little freedom or power, they will try to take a lot more **8 within an inch of sth** if you do something or come within an inch of something, you almost do it but do not: *I came within an inch of crying.* | *He was **beaten within an inch of his life*** (=hit so much that he almost died). [**Origin:** 1000–1100 Latin *uncia* **one twelfth**]

inch² *v.* [I always + adv./prep., T always + adv./prep.] to move or do something very slowly and carefully, or to move something in this way: +**along/toward/around etc.** *The two sides are inching toward agreement.* | *Several buses **inched their way** toward the exit.* | **inch sth along/toward etc.** *We inched our luggage forward as we waited in line.*

in·cho·ate /ɪnˈkoʊɪt/ *adj.* FORMAL inchoate ideas, plans, attitudes etc. are just starting to develop or are not well formed

in·ci·dence /ˈɪnsədəns/ Ac *n.* [C usually singular,U] FORMAL the number of times something happens, especially something bad: +**of** *There is a **higher incidence** of suicide among women than men.*

in·ci·dent¹ /ˈɪnsədənt/ Ac W2 *n.* [C] **1** an event, especially one that is unusual, serious, or violent: *The incident was reported in the local paper.* | *Unfortunately, this was not an **isolated incident*** (=one event) *of abuse.* | *Police say the **shooting incident** was gang-related.* | *The plane took off **without incident*** (=without anything unusual or bad happening). ▸see THESAURUS box at **event** **2** a serious disagreement between two countries over a particular event: **diplomatic/international incident** *His refusal to shake the leader's hand provoked an international incident.* [**Origin:** 1400–1500 French, Latin, present participle of *incidere* **to fall into**]

incident² Ac *adj.* **1** FORMAL [not before noun] happening or likely to happen as the result of something else: +**to** *injuries incident to military service* **2** TECHNICAL incident light hits a surface

in·ci·den·tal¹ /ˌɪnsəˈdɛntl◂/ *adj.* **1** happening or existing in relation to something else that is more important: +**to** *Her story is incidental to the main plot of the novel.* **2** FORMAL naturally happening or existing as a result of something you are doing, but in a way that is not planned and not the main purpose: *incidental expenses* | +**to** *The dolphin catch was incidental to the fishing operation.*

incidental² *n.* [C usually plural] something that you have to do, buy etc., which you had not planned to: *Carry some cash for cabs, tips, and other incidentals.*

in·ci·den·tally /ˌɪnsəˈdɛntli/ Ac *adv.* **1** [sentence adverb] used when adding more information to what you have said, or to introduce a new subject SYN **by the way**: *The symphony orchestra, incidentally, will perform outdoors for its final concert.* | *Incidentally, where were you born?* **2** happening or existing as a result of something else, but in a less important way or in a way that is not planned: *The moon landing was only incidentally about science.*

ˌincidental ˈmusic *n.* [U] music played during a play, movie etc. in order to give the right feeling

in·cin·er·ate /ɪnˈsɪnəˌreɪt/ *v.* [T] to burn something completely so that it is destroyed: *Infected animals are killed and incinerated.* —**incineration** /ɪnˌsɪnəˈreɪʃən/ *n.* [U]

in·cin·er·a·tor /ɪnˈsɪnəˌreɪtɚ/ *n.* [C] a machine that burns things in order to destroy them

in·cip·i·ent /ɪnˈsɪpiənt/ *adj.* [only before noun] FORMAL starting to happen or exist: *an incipient drinking problem*

in·cise /ɪnˈsaɪz/ *v.* [T] **1** FORMAL to cut a pattern or mark into a surface: +**in/into** *Someone had incised their initials in the tree.* **2** TECHNICAL to cut carefully into something with a sharp knife

in·ci·sion /ɪnˈsɪʒən/ *n.* [C,U] a neat cut made into something, especially during a medical operation, or the act of making this cut

in·ci·sive /ɪnˈsaɪsɪv/ *adj.* showing intelligence and a clear understanding of something: *an incisive critique of American politics*

in·ci·sor /ɪnˈsaɪzɚ/ *n.* [C] one of the eight teeth at the front of your mouth that have sharp edges and are used for biting food → see also CANINE TOOTH, MOLAR

in·cite /ɪnˈsaɪt/ *v.* [T] to deliberately encourage people to cause trouble, fight, argue etc.: *He was charged with **inciting a riot**.* | **incite sb to do sth** *Slave owners feared that education would incite slaves to rebel.* | **incite sb to sth** *Three men were arrested for inciting the crowd to violence.* [**Origin:** 1400–1500 French *inciter*, from Latin *citare* **to cause to start moving**] —**incitement** *n.* [U]

in·ci·vil·i·ty /ˌɪnsəˈvɪləṭi/ *n.* [U] FORMAL impolite behavior

incl. the written abbreviation of "including"

in·clem·ent /ɪnˈklɛmənt/ *adj.* FORMAL inclement weather is bad because it is cold, it is raining etc. —**inclemency** *n.* [U]

in·cli·na·tion /ˌɪnkləˈneɪʃən/ Ac *n.* **1** [C,U] a feeling that makes you want to do something: *My **natural inclination** was to say no.* | **inclination to do sth** *Neither side has shown any inclination to compromise.* **2** [C,U] a tendency to think or behave in a particular way: +**to** *his inclination to nausea during car rides* **3** [C,U] FORMAL a slope or the angle at which something slopes: *a 62-degree inclination* **4 inclination of sb's head** the movement of bending your neck so that your head is lowered

in·cline¹ /ɪnˈklaɪn/ Ac *v.* [not in progressive] **1** [T] FORMAL if a situation, fact etc. inclines you to do or think something, it influences you toward a particular action or opinion: **incline sb to do sth** *Nothing has happened that would incline us to agree to the proposal.* **2** [I,T] to slope at a particular angle or to make something do this **3** [I,T] FORMAL to think that a particular belief or opinion is most likely to be right: **incline to do sth**

I incline to trust the Harrises. **4** [I] FORMAL to tend to behave in a particular way or show a particular quality: +**to/toward** *Men who incline toward violence don't make good husbands.* **5 incline your head** to bend your neck so that your head is lowered [**Origin:** 1300–1400 French *incliner*, from Latin *clinare* **to lean**]

in·cline² /ˈɪnklaɪn/ Ac *n.* [C] a slope: *a steep incline*

in·clined /ɪnˈklaɪnd/ Ac *adj.* **1** [not before noun] wanting to do something: **inclined to do sth** *I'm not inclined to give them any more money.* | *There's dancing afterwards, for those who are* ***so inclined.*** **2 be inclined to agree/think/believe etc.** to have a particular opinion, but to not hold it very strongly: *I'm inclined to believe her story.* **3** [not before noun] likely or tending to do something: **inclined to do sth** *My mother is inclined to overreact.* | +**to** *He is inclined to self-pity.* **4 mathematically/linguistically/musically inclined** naturally interested in or good at mathematics, languages etc.: *My son is not mechanically inclined.* **5** sloping or leaning in a particular direction

in·close /ɪnˈkloʊz/ *v.* [T] another spelling of ENCLOSE

in·clos·ure /ɪnˈkloʊʒɚ/ *n.* [C,U] another spelling of ENCLOSURE

in·clude /ɪnˈklud/ S1 W1 *v.* [T] **1** [not in progressive] if a set or a group includes something or someone, it has that thing or person as one of its parts: *The price for the hotel includes breakfast.* | *His job includes some teaching.* **2** to make something or someone part of a larger set or group OPP exclude: *The book includes information on the area around Los Angeles as well.* | **include sth in/on sth** *The boys refused to include a girl in their game.* [**Origin:** 1400–1500 Latin *includere*, from *claudere* **to close**]

in·clud·ed /ɪnˈkludɪd/ *adj.* [only after noun] including someone or something: *Everyone's going to church, you included.*

in·clud·ing /ɪnˈkludɪŋ/ S3 W1 *prep.* used to show that someone or something is part of the larger group that you are talking about OPP excluding: *The price is $25.50, including shipping and handling.* | *There's about twenty of us, including the instructors.*

in·clu·sion /ɪnˈkluʒən/ *n.* **1** [C,U] the act of including someone or something in a larger group or set, or the fact of being included in one OPP exclusion: +**in/into** *photos chosen* ***for inclusion*** *in the magazine* | +**on** *his inclusion on the Olympic team* | +**of** *Madison opposed the inclusion of a Bill of Rights in the Constitution.* **2** [C] someone or something that has been included in a larger group or set

in·clu·sive /ɪnˈklusɪv/ *adj.* **1** including all types of people OPP exclusive: +**of** *Churches needed to be more inclusive of women* **2** including all the possible information, parts, numbers etc. OPP exclusive: *The list is not* ***all-inclusive.***

in·cog·ni·to /ˌɪnkɑgˈnit̬oʊ/ *adv.* if a person, especially a famous person, does something incognito, they do it without letting people know who they are [**Origin:** 1600–1700 Italian, Latin *incognitus* **unknown**]

in·co·her·ent /ˌɪnkoʊˈhɪrənt/ Ac *adj.* **1** something that is incoherent is not organized clearly, and is therefore difficult to understand OPP coherent: *Rawlings gave rambling, incoherent answers.* | *an incoherent military policy* **2** someone who is incoherent is not talking clearly or not expressing themselves clearly OPP coherent: *One man was incoherent with grief.* **3** PHYSICS relating to light waves that do not have the same FREQUENCY or travel in the same direction OPP coherent —**incoherently** *adv.* —**incoherence** *n.* [U]

in·come /ˈɪnkʌm, ˈɪŋ-/ Ac S2 W1 *n.* [C,U] the money that you earn from working or that you receive from INVESTMENTS, the government etc.: *The amount you have to pay depends on your income.* | *Try to save ten percent of your* ***annual income.*** | +**from** *income from your investments* | +**of** *He has a* ***taxable income*** (=income on which he pays tax) *of $77,500.* | *With no kids at home, they have more* ***disposable income*** (=the money you can spend on what you want, after paying all your bills and tax). | *She's* ***on a fixed income*** (=an income that cannot be made larger). | **high-/low-/middle-income** (=earning a lot of money, a little money etc.) *help for low-income families*

ˈincome distriˌbution *n.* [U] ECONOMICS the way in which the total income earned by the population of a country exists in different amounts in different areas, depending on the number of people living in each place and their level of income

ˈincome efˌfect *n.* [C,U] ECONOMICS the effect a change in the price of a product, goods, or a service has on someone's ability to buy it or on the amount he or she buys

ˈincome tax *n.* [U] ECONOMICS tax paid on the money that you earn

in·com·ing /ˈɪnˌkʌmɪŋ/ *adj.* [only before noun] **1 incoming call/letter/fax** a telephone call, letter etc. that you receive **2** arriving at or coming toward a place OPP outgoing: *incoming flights* | *the incoming tide* | *Please hold all my* ***incoming calls.*** **3** an incoming president, government, class etc. is just beginning a period of time in that position OPP outgoing: *Women made up 40% of the incoming freshman class.*

in·com·mo·di·ous /ˌɪnkəˈmoʊdiəs/ *adj.* FORMAL inconvenient, difficult, or uncomfortable

in·com·mu·ni·ca·do /ˌɪnkəˌmyunɪˈkɑdoʊ/ *adj., adv.* if you are incommunicado, you are in a place where you are not allowed to speak or write to anyone outside that place: *The opposition leader has been* ***held incommunicado*** *for two years.*

in·com·pa·ra·ble /ɪnˈkɑmpərəbəl/ *adj.* extremely good, beautiful etc., and much better than others: *His singing voice is incomparable.* | *incomparable views of the mountains*

in·com·pat·i·ble /ˌɪnkəmˈpæt̬əbəl/ Ac *adj.* **1** too different to be able to have a good relationship with each other OPP compatible: *Diane and I are completely incompatible.* **2** incompatible beliefs, statements, actions etc. are too different to exist or be accepted together: +**with** *Such violent attacks are incompatible with a civilized society.* **3** two things that are incompatible are of different types and cannot be used together OPP compatible: *incompatible blood groups* | +**with** *The software is incompatible with the operating system.* —**incompatibly** *adv.* —**incompatibility** /ˌɪnkəmˌpæt̬əˈbɪlət̬i/ *n.* [U]

in·com·pe·tence /ɪnˈkɑmpət̬əns/ *n.* [U] lack of the ability or skill to do your job correctly or well OPP competence: *Money is being wasted through governmental incompetence.* | *He was fired for incompetence.*

in·com·pe·tent /ɪnˈkɑmpət̬ənt/ *adj.* **1** not having the ability or skill to do your job correctly or well OPP competent: *Incompetent teachers should be fired.* | *Some drivers are just plain incompetent.* **2** not able to understand something, because you are very sick, have a mental illness, or are not intelligent enough OPP competent: *Price was found mentally incompetent to stand trial.* —**incompetent** *n.* [C]

in·com·plete /ˌɪnkəmˈplit◂ / *adj.* **1** not having all its parts OPP complete: *Historical records for this time are incomplete.* | *an incomplete job application* **2** not completely finished SYN unfinished OPP complete: *incomplete drawings* **3 an incomplete pass** a ball thrown in football that is not caught by the player you are throwing to —**incompletely** *adv.*

incomˌplete metaˈmorphosis *n.* [U] BIOLOGY the development process of some insects, such as CRICKETS, in which the insect goes from the first stage of development to the adult stage, without going through a stage of being a PUPA (=a stage when an insect is protected by a special cover) as most other insects do

in·com·pre·hen·si·ble /ˌɪnkɑmprɪˈhɛnsəbəl/ *adj.* difficult or impossible to understand SYN unintelligible OPP comprehensible: *incomprehensible legal documents* | +**to** *These scientific ideas are incomprehensible to many people.* —**incomprehensibly** *adv.*

I

in·com·pre·hen·sion /ɪnˌkɑmprɪˈhɛnʃən/ *n.* [U] the state of not being able to understand something OPP **comprehension**: *He stared at her with annoyed incomprehension.*

in·con·ceiv·a·ble /ˌɪnkənˈsivəbəl/ Ac *adj.* too strange or unusual to be thought real or possible SYN **unimaginable** OPP **conceivable**: **it is inconceivable that** *It is inconceivable that anyone would choose to live here.*

in·con·clu·sive /ˌɪnkənˈklusɪv/ Ac *adj.* not leading to a clear decision or result OPP **conclusive**: *inconclusive evidence* | *Studies on the benefits of year-round schools are inconclusive.* —**inconclusively** *adv.*

in·con·gru·ous /ɪnˈkɑŋgruəs/ *adj.* strange, unexpected, or not appropriate in a particular situation: **+with** *The high-tech building is incongruous with its rural surroundings.* —**incongruously** *adv.* —**incongruity** /ˌɪnkənˈgruəṭi/ *n.* [C,U]

in·con·se·quen·tial /ˌɪnkɑnsəˈkwɛnʃəl/ *adj.* not important SYN **insignificant**: *an inconsequential little lie* —**inconsequentially** *adv.*

in·con·sid·er·a·ble /ˌɪnkənˈsɪdərəbəl/ *adj.* **not/no inconsiderable** FORMAL fairly large or important OPP **considerable**: *His knowledge was not inconsiderable.*

in·con·sid·er·ate /ˌɪnkənˈsɪdərɪt/ *adj.* not caring about the feelings or needs of other people SYN **thoughtless** OPP **considerate**: **it is inconsiderate (of sb) to do sth** *It was really inconsiderate of him not to even leave a message.*

in·con·sist·en·cy /ˌɪnkənˈsɪstənsi/ Ac *n. plural* **inconsistencies** **1** [U] the quality of not doing things in the same way each time, so that what you do is not always done well and people do not know what to expect from you OPP **consistency**: *The team's inconsistency on defense has lost them three games.* **2** [C,U] a situation in which two statements, actions etc. are different and cannot both be true SYN **contradiction** OPP **consistency**: **+in** *There are some inconsistencies in the witness's statement.* | **+between** *the inconsistencies between what the management says and what it does*

in·con·sist·ent /ˌɪnkənˈsɪstənt/ Ac *adj.* **1** if two ideas, statements, or actions are inconsistent, they are not the same and cannot both be true or right: *inconsistent statements* | *The research has produced inconsistent results.* **2** not always doing something in the same way, so that sometimes it is done well and sometimes it is done badly: *a talented but inconsistent player* **3 inconsistent with sth** not right according to a particular set of principles or standards: *His conduct was inconsistent with what is expected of our leaders.* | *The law is inconsistent with the Constitutional right to free speech.*

ˌinconsistent ˈsystem *n.* [C] MATH a set of related EQUATIONS that does not have a solution → see also DEPENDENT SYSTEM

in·con·sol·a·ble /ˌɪnkənˈsoʊləbəl/ *adj.* so sad that it is impossible for anyone to comfort you: *During the funeral service, Doris was inconsolable.* —**inconsolably** *adv.*

in·con·spic·u·ous /ˌɪnkənˈspɪkyuəs/ *adj.* not easily seen or noticed: *an inconspicuous little restaurant* —**inconspicuously** *adv.*

in·con·stant /ɪnˈkɑnstənt/ *adj.* FORMAL **1** unfaithful in love or friendship OPP **constant**: *an inconstant and unreliable friend* **2** not happening all the time OPP **constant**: *inconstant winds* —**inconstancy** *n.* [U]

in·con·test·a·ble /ˌɪnkənˈtɛstəbəl/ *adj.* clearly true and impossible to disagree with SYN **indisputable**: *Proof of the harmful effects of smoking is incontestable.*

in·con·ti·nent /ɪnˈkɑntˀn-ənt, -tənənt/ *adj.* **1** unable to control the passing of liquid or solid waste from your body OPP **continent** **2** OLD USE unable to control your sexual urges OPP **continent** —**incontinence** *n.* [U]

in·con·tro·vert·i·ble /ˌɪnkɑntrəˈvəṭəbəl/ *adj.* a fact that is incontrovertible is definitely true and no one can prove it to be false SYN **indisputable**: *incontrovertible evidence* —**incontrovertibly** *adv.*

in·con·ven·ience¹ /ˌɪnkənˈvinyəns/ *n.* **1** [C] something that causes you problems or difficulty OPP **convenience**: **minor/major/small etc. inconvenience** *Having to go downtown was a major inconvenience.* | **+to** *Lane closures were an inconvenience to commuters.* **2** [U] the state of having problems or difficulty: *We apologize for any **inconvenience** the delay has **caused**.* | **+to** *The work must be done at the least cost and inconvenience to the public.*

inconvenience² *v.* [T] to cause someone problems or difficulty: *Cuts in bus services will greatly inconvenience commuters.*

in·con·ven·ient /ˌɪnkənˈvinyənt/ *adj.* causing problems or difficulty, often in a way that is annoying OPP **convenient**: *I can come tomorrow, if **it's** not **inconvenient**.* | *Computer breakdowns are annoying and inconvenient.* —**inconveniently** *adv.*

in·cor·po·rate /ɪnˈkɔrpəˌreɪt/ Ac *v.* **1** [T] to include something as part of a group, system, plan etc.: *Karate is a martial art that incorporates kicking, striking, and punching techniques.* | **incorporate sth into/in sth** *Schools are trying to incorporate ethnic foods into their menus.* **2** [I,T] ECONOMICS if a city or business incorporates or is incorporated, it becomes a CORPORATION (=a separate legal unit with rights and responsibilities): *The city was incorporated in 1873.* [**Origin:** 1300–1400 Late Latin, past participle of *incorporare*, from Latin *corpus* **body**] —**incorporation** /ɪnˌkɔrpəˈreɪʃən/ *n.* [U]

in·cor·po·rat·ed /ɪnˈkɔrpəˌreɪṭɪd/ Ac WRITTEN ABBREVIATION, **Inc.** *adj.* used after the name of a company in the U.S. to show that it has become a CORPORATION

in·cor·po·re·al /ˌɪnkɔrˈpɔriəl/ *adj.* FORMAL not existing in any physical form but only as a spirit OPP **corporeal**

in·cor·rect /ˌɪnkəˈrɛkt◂/ *adj.* **1** not correct or true SYN **wrong** OPP **correct**: *an incorrect answer* ►see THESAURUS box at **wrong¹** **2** not following the rules of polite behavior SYN **impolite** —**incorrectly** *adv.* —**incorrectness** *n.* [U]

in·cor·ri·gi·ble /ɪnˈkɔrədʒəbəl, -ˈkɑr-/ *adj.* FORMAL OR HUMOROUS someone who is incorrigible is bad in a way that cannot be changed or improved, or has bad habits that they do not change: *an incorrigible liar* —**incorrigibly** *adv.*

in·cor·rupt·i·ble /ˌɪnkəˈrʌptəbəl/ *adj.* **1** too honest to be persuaded to do anything that is illegal or morally wrong: *an incorruptible judge* **2** FORMAL material that is incorruptible will never decay: *Gold is incorruptible.* —**incorruptibly** *adv.* → see also CORRUPT¹

in·crease¹ /ɪnˈkris/ S2 W1 *v.* [I,T] to become larger in amount, number, or degree, or to make something do this OPP **decrease** OPP **reduce**: *The company has increased its workforce by 10 percent.* | **+by** *Sales have increased by 7 percent in the past six months.* | **+in** *Investments in real estate are certain to increase in value.* [**Origin:** 1300–1400 Old French *encreistre*, from Latin *increscere*, from *crescere* **to grow**]

THESAURUS

go up to increase in number, amount, or value: *Prices have gone up 2%.*
rise to increase in number, amount, quality, or value: *The price of gold rose to nearly $400 an ounce.*
grow to increase in amount, size, or degree: *The number of people working from home has grown substantially.*
double to become twice as large or twice as much, or to make something do this: *The job took double the time we had allowed for it.*
shoot up to quickly increase in number, size, or amount: *Unemployment shot up.*

in·crease² /ˈɪnkris, ˈɪŋ-/ W1 *n.* [C,U] a rise in amount, number, or degree OPP **decrease**: *wage increases* | **+in** *an increase in housing prices* | **dramatic/sharp/rapid**

etc. increase *a sharp increase in drug use* | *Hate crimes are* ***on the increase*** (=increasing) *around the nation.*

in·creased /ɪn'krist/ *adj.* larger or more than before: *an increased risk for cancer*

in·creas·ing /ɪn'krisɪŋ/ *adj.* becoming larger in size, amount, or number: *an increasing number of accidents*

in·creas·ing·ly /ɪn'krisɪŋli/ W2 *adv.* more and more all the time [+ adj./adv.] *The conflict has become increasingly violent.* [sentence adverb] *Increasingly, humans and animals are in competition for the same land.*

in,creasing ,marginal re'turns *n.* [U] ECONOMICS when the MARGINAL PRODUCT OF LABOR (=the increase in the number of goods a machine or factory produces when a business employs one additional worker) increases as the number of workers increases

in·cred·i·ble /ɪn'krɛdəbəl/ S2 *adj.* **1** extremely good, large, or impressive SYN **unbelievable**: *The pain was incredible.* | *She's an incredible dancer.* **2** too strange to be believed or very difficult to believe OPP **credible**: ***It's incredible that*** *he survived the fall.* —**incredibility** /ɪn,krɛdə'bɪləṭi/ *n.* [U]

in·cred·i·bly /ɪn'krɛdəbli/ S3 *adv.* **1** [+adj./adv.] extremely: *Raising money has been incredibly difficult.* **2** [sentence adverb] in a way that is hard to believe: *Incredibly, six men ran the 100-meter final in less than 10 seconds.*

in·cre·du·li·ty /,ɪnkrɪ'duləṭi/ *n.* [U] a feeling that you cannot believe something SYN **disbelief** OPP **credulity**: *Workers expressed incredulity and anger at being laid off.*

in·cred·u·lous /ɪn'krɛdʒələs/ *adj.* unable or unwilling to believe something, or showing this: *"You don't have a car?" asked one incredulous woman.* —**incredulously** *adv.*

in·cre·ment /'ɪnkrəmənt, 'ɪŋ-/ *n.* [C] an increase in a number, value, or amount, especially one of a series of increases: *pay increments* | *The tickets are printed in 50-cent increments* (=for example, 50 cents, $1.00, $1.50 etc.). —**incremental** /,ɪnkrə'mɛntl◂/ *adj.*

,incremental 'cost *n.* [C usually singular] ECONOMICS the additional cost of producing one more of a particular product or thing SYN **marginal cost**

in·crim·i·nate /ɪn'krɪmə,neɪt/ *v.* [T] to make someone seem guilty of a crime: **incriminate yourself** *He incriminated himself in a conversation with another prisoner.* | *incriminating documents* —**incrimination** /ɪn,krɪmə'neɪʃən/ *n.* [U]

in·crim·i·na·to·ry /ɪn'krɪmənə,tɔri/ *adj.* making someone seem to be guilty

'in-crowd *n.* **the in-crowd** a small group of people in an organization or activity who are popular and have influence, but who do not want other people to join them: *We were never part of the in-crowd in high school.*

in·crust·a·tion /,ɪnkrʌ'steɪʃən/ *n.* [C] an amount of dirt, salt etc. that forms a hard layer on a surface

in·cu·bate /'ɪŋkyə,beɪt/ *v.* [I,T] **1** BIOLOGY if an animal such as a bird incubates its eggs or if they incubate, they are kept warm under the animal's body until the young animals come out **2** MEDICINE if a disease incubates, or if you incubate it, it develops in your body until you show physical signs of it —**incubation** /,ɪŋkyə'beɪʃən/ *n.* [U]

in·cu·ba·tor /'ɪŋkyə,beɪṭə/ *n.* [C] **1** MEDICINE a piece of hospital equipment like a clear box that is used for keeping very small or weak babies alive by keeping them warm **2** a heated container for keeping eggs warm until the young birds etc. come out, and for protecting very young birds or animals **3** an organization that provides new businesses with advice and sometimes with services and equipment

in·cu·bus /'ɪŋkyəbəs/ *n.* [C] a male DEVIL that in past times was believed to have sex with a sleeping woman → see also SUCCUBUS

in·cul·cate /'ɪnkʌl,keɪt, ɪn'kʌl,keɪt/ *v.* [T] FORMAL to make someone accept an idea by repeating it to them often SYN **instill**: **inculcate sth in/into sb** *Dad had inculcated in us a strong sense of family loyalty.* | **inculcate sb with sth** *The Army inculcates its recruits with patriotism.* —**inculcation** /,ɪnkʌl'keɪʃən/ *n.* [U]

in·cum·ben·cy /ɪn'kʌmbənsi/ *n. plural* **incumbencies** [C,U] FORMAL the state of holding an official position, especially in the government, or the time when someone holds this position

in·cum·bent¹ /ɪn'kʌmbənt/ *n.* [C] FORMAL someone who has been elected to an official position, and who is doing that job at the present time: *In the election, Steiner easily beat the incumbent.*

incumbent² *adj.* FORMAL **1 the incumbent president/senator etc.** the president, governor etc. at the present time **2 it is incumbent upon sb to do sth** used to say that it is someone's duty or responsibility to do something: *It is incumbent upon parents to control what their children watch on TV.*

in·cur /ɪn'kə/ *v.* **incurred**, **incurring** [T] **1** if you incur a cost, debt, fine etc., you have to pay money because of something that you have done, or you lose money because of something that has happened: *The auto manufacturer incurred a $843.6 million loss.* **2** if you incur something unpleasant, it happens to you because of something you have done: *Crowder's comments* ***incurred the wrath*** *of the board of directors.* [**Origin:** 1400–1500 Latin *incurrere* **to run into**, from *currere* **to run**]

in·cur·a·ble /ɪn'kyʊrəbəl/ *adj.* **1** impossible to cure OPP **curable**: *an incurable disease* **2** incurable attitudes or behavior are impossible to change or stop: *Jane is an incurable gossip.* —**incurably** *adv.* —**incurable** *n.* [C]

in·cu·ri·ous /ɪn'kyʊriəs/ *adj.* FORMAL not naturally interested in finding out about the things around you OPP **curious**

in·cur·sion /ɪn'kəʒən/ *n.* [C] FORMAL **1** a sudden attack into an area of land that belongs to other people: *Government forces were able to halt the rebel incursion.* **2** the unwanted arrival of something in a place where it does not belong or has not been before: +**into** *The incursion of whiteflies into the area could damage crops.*

in·debt·ed /ɪn'dɛṭɪd/ *adj.* **1 be (greatly/deeply) indebted to sb/sth** to be very grateful to someone for the help they have given you: *We are deeply indebted to all the doctors.* **2** owing money to someone: *a* ***heavily indebted*** *hotel chain* —**indebtedness** *n.* [U]

in·de·cen·cy /ɪn'disənsi/ *n.* **1** [U] LAW behavior that is sexually offensive, especially INDECENT EXPOSURE **2** [C] FORMAL an action that is shocking or offensive

in·de·cent /ɪn'disənt/ *adj.* **1** something that is indecent is shocking and offensive, usually because it involves sex or shows parts of the body that are usually covered: *an indecent photo* | *That dress is almost indecent!* **2** completely unacceptable: *The prices they charge for this food are indecent.* —**indecently** *adv.*: *indecently dressed*

in,decent as'sault *n.* [C,U] LAW the crime of attacking someone in a sexual way, but not RAPING them (=forcing them to have sex)

in,decent ex'posure *n.* [U] LAW the crime of deliberately showing your sex organs in a public place → see also FLASHER

in·de·ci·pher·a·ble /,ɪndɪ'saɪfrəbəl/ *adj.* impossible to read or understand SYN **illegible**: *an indecipherable signature*

in·de·ci·sion /,ɪndɪ'sɪʒən/ *n.* [U] the state of being unable to decide what to do: *We finally bought the house after months of indecision.*

in·de·ci·sive /,ɪndɪ'saɪsɪv/ *adj.* **1** unable to make clear decisions or choices OPP **decisive**: *a weak and indecisive leader* **2** not having a clear result SYN **inconclusive**: *an indecisive debate* —**indecisiveness** *n.* [U]

in·dec·o·rous /ɪn'dɛkərəs/ *adj.* FORMAL behaving in a way that is not polite or socially acceptable OPP **decorous**

in·deed /ɪnˈdid/ W1 *adv.* **1** [sentence adverb] FORMAL used when adding more information to emphasize or support what you have just said: *Minorities are not well represented. Indeed, the city has only one black city council member.* **2** used to emphasize a statement or answer: *The blood tests prove that Vince is indeed the father.*

in·de·fat·i·ga·ble /ˌɪndɪˈfætɪɡəbəl/ *adj.* FORMAL determined and never becoming tired SYN **tireless**: *an indefatigable worker*

in·de·fen·si·ble /ˌɪndɪˈfɛnsəbəl/ *adj.* **1** too bad to be excused or defended SYN **inexcusable**: *It is indefensible that in such a rich country so many people are poor.* **2** impossible or very difficult to defend from military attack OPP **defensible**

in·de·fin·a·ble /ˌɪndɪˈfaɪnəbəl/ *adj.* an indefinable feeling, quality etc. is difficult to describe or explain: *She felt a sudden indefinable sadness.*

in·def·i·nite /ɪnˈdɛfənɪt/ Ac *adj.* **1** an indefinite action or period of time has no definite end arranged for it: *The refugees will be housed and fed here for an indefinite period.* **2** not clear or definite SYN **vague**: *Our traveling plans are deliberately indefinite.*

inˌdefinite ˈarticle *n.* [C] ENG. LANG. ARTS the word "a" or "an" → see also ARTICLE (4), DEFINITE ARTICLE

in·def·i·nite·ly /ɪnˈdɛfənɪtli/ Ac *adv.* for a period of time for which no definite end has been arranged: *This situation cannot continue indefinitely.*

inˌdefinite ˈpronoun *n.* [C] ENG. LANG. ARTS a word such as "some," "any," or "either" that is used instead of a noun, but that does not say exactly which person or thing is meant

I

in·del·i·ble /ɪnˈdɛləbəl/ *adj.* **1** impossible to remove or forget SYN **permanent**: *His death left an indelible impression on my life.* **2 indelible ink/markers etc.** ink, pens etc. that make a permanent mark which cannot be removed —**indelibly** *adv.*

in·del·i·cate /ɪnˈdɛlɪkɪt/ *adj.* impolite or offensive SYN **rude**: *an indelicate and tasteless comment* —**indelicacy** *n.* [U]

in·dem·ni·fy /ɪnˈdɛmnəˌfaɪ/ *v.* [T] **indemnifies, indemnified, indemnifying** LAW **1** to pay someone money if something they own is damaged or lost or if they are injured **2** to provide someone with insurance against a loss, injury, damage etc. that they might suffer —**indemnification** /ɪnˌdɛmnəfəˈkeɪʃən/ *n.* [C,U]

in·dem·ni·ty /ɪnˈdɛmnəti/ *n. plural* **indemnities** LAW **1** [U] protection against loss, damage, or injury, especially in the form of a promise to pay you for any losses, injuries etc. **2** [C] a payment for injury or the loss of money, goods etc.

in·dent /ɪnˈdɛnt/ *v.* [T] to start a line of writing closer to the middle of the page than other lines

in·den·ta·tion /ˌɪndɛnˈteɪʃən/ *n.* **1** [C] a space at the beginning of a line of writing **2** [C] a space or cut which goes into the surface or edge of something: *Make a small indentation in the center of each cookie.* **3** [U] the act of indenting

in·dent·ed /ɪnˈdɛntɪd/ *adj.* an indented edge or surface has cuts or spaces that go into the surface of it: *plants with indented leaves*

in·den·tured /ɪnˈdɛntʃɚd/ *adj.* an indentured servant or worker in past times was someone who agreed or was forced to work for their employer for a particular number of years before they could be free —**indenture** *n.* [C,U]

in·de·pend·ence /ˌɪndɪˈpɛndəns/ W3 *n.* [U] **1** POLITICS political freedom from control by the government of another country: **+from** *Algeria **won independence** from France more than thirty years ago.* | *The U.S.A. **declared independence*** (=officially stated their independence) *in 1776.* **2** the time when a country becomes politically independent: *Since independence, the country has had high unemployment.* **3** the freedom and ability to make your own decisions, without having to ask other people for permission, help, or money: *The apartments allow older people to **maintain their independence**.* | *financial independence*

Indeˈpendence ˌDay *n.* [C,U] **1** the day every year on which a country celebrates its independence from another country that controlled it in the past **2** this day in the U.S., celebrated on July 4th

in·de·pend·ent¹ /ˌɪndɪˈpɛndənt◂/ S3 W2 *adj.*
1 CONFIDENT confident and able to do things by yourself in your own way, without needing help or advice from other people OPP **dependent**: *a strong independent woman* | *Many older people are **fiercely independent** and don't like to ask for help.*
2 NOT OWNED/CONTROLLED [no comparative] existing separately and not influenced or controlled by other people, organizations, or the government: *a small independent book store* | **+of** *The research center is independent of the university.*
3 COUNTRY [no comparative] POLITICS an independent country is not governed or controlled by another country: *India became independent in 1947.*
4 NOT INVOLVED [no comparative] done or given by people who are not involved in a particular situation and who can therefore be trusted to be fair in judging it: *an independent analysis of the data* | *independent legal experts*
5 HAVING ENOUGH MONEY having enough money to live without having to ask for help from other people: *I wanted to become financially independent.*
6 NOT CONNECTED if one thing is independent of another, the two are not connected, or the second thing does not influence the first SYN **unrelated**: *two independent series of experiments* | **+of** *The two movements were entirely independent of each other.*
7 POLITICIANS an independent politician does not belong to a particular party
8 independent study/learning the process of studying on your own rather than being taught by a teacher
9 a man/woman of independent means someone who has their own income, especially so that they do not have to work or depend on anyone —**independently** *adv.*: *The two departments operate independently of each other.*

independent², Independent *n.* [C] POLITICS a politician who does not belong to a political party

ˌindependent asˈsortment *n.* [U] BIOLOGY in the process of cell division that produces egg and SPERM cells, the fact that each member of a pair of CHROMOSOMES separates independently from members of other pairs so that the GENES are RANDOMly (=by chance) spread across the new cells being formed

ˌindependent ˈclause *n.* [C] ENG. LANG. ARTS a CLAUSE that can make a sentence by itself; for example, "He woke up" in the sentence "He woke up when he heard the bell." SYN **main clause**

ˌindependent exˈecutive ˌagency *n.* [C] POLITICS an official U.S. government organization that deals with a particular area of government and reports to the president, but which is not elected or part of one of the main government departments

ˌindependent ˈregulatory comˌmission *n.* [C] POLITICS an official U.S. government organization that is not controlled by Congress or the president, but which makes rules for a particular part of the economy and makes sure that rules are followed

ˌindependent ˈsystem *n.* [C] MATH a set of related EQUATIONS that has only one possible solution → see also DEPENDENT SYSTEM

ˌindependent ˈvariable *n.* [C] **1** SCIENCE in a scientific EXPERIMENT (=test), the condition that you change, add, or remove in order to test its effect on something else involved in the experiment → see also CONTROLLED VARIABLE SYN **manipulated variable** **2** MATH in math, a VARIABLE (=mathematical quantity that is not fixed and can be any of several amounts) that can be any value and does not depend on the value chosen for another variable → see also DEPENDENT VARIABLE

ˌindependent ˈvoter *n.* [C] POLITICS someone who votes but does not support one particular political party: *Independent voters played an important role in the last election.*

'in-depth *adj.* [only before noun] **an in-depth study/report/investigation etc.** a study, report etc. of something that is thorough and complete and considers all the details

in·de·scrib·a·ble /ˌɪndɪˈskraɪbəbəl/ *adj.* too good, strange, frightening etc. to be described, or very difficult to describe: *an indescribable flavor* —**indescribably** *adv.*

in·de·struct·i·ble /ˌɪndɪˈstrʌktəbəl/ *adj.* impossible to destroy: *Diamonds are practically indestructible.* —**indestructibility** /ˌɪndɪˌstrʌktəˈbɪləṭi/ *n.* [U]

in·de·ter·min·a·ble /ˌɪndɪˈtɚmənəbəl/ *adj.* impossible to find out or calculate exactly

in·de·ter·mi·nate /ˌɪndɪˈtɚmənɪt/ *adj.* impossible to know about definitely or exactly: *an indeterminate length of time*

in·dex¹ /ˈɪndɛks/ Ac W2 *n.* plural **indices** /-dɪˌsiz/ or **indexes** [C] **1** an alphabetical list of names, subjects etc. at the back of a book, with the numbers of the pages where they can be found: +**of** *There's an index of plant names at the back.* **2** a standard by which the level of something can be judged or measured: +**of** *These figures are the best index of economic growth.* **3** TECHNICAL a system by which prices, costs etc. can be compared to those of a previous date: *the Dow Jones index* | +**of** *the government's official index of retail prices* **4** a set of cards or a DATABASE containing information, usually arranged in alphabetical order and used especially in a library SYN **catalog** **5** ALGEBRA the number written before and slightly above a RADICAL SIGN (√) showing how many times a quantity was multiplied by itself to produce the quantity after the radical sign. The index of $\sqrt[3]{5}$ is 3. [**Origin:** 1500–1600 Latin **first finger, guide,** from *indicare*]

index² Ac *v.* [T] **1** to make an index for something: *The reports are indexed by subject and location.* **2** to arrange for the level of wages, pensions etc. to increase at the same rate as the level of prices: **be indexed to sth** *Pensions are indexed to retail prices.*

in·dex·a·tion /ˌɪndɛkˈseɪʃən/ *n.* [U] TECHNICAL the practice of increasing salaries or SOCIAL SECURITY at the same rate as prices increase, according to the CONSUMER PRICE INDEX

'index card *n.* [C] a small card for writing notes and information on

'index ˌfinger *n.* [C] the finger next to your thumb SYN **forefinger**

'index ˌfossil *n.* [C] BIOLOGY a FOSSIL of a creature that is known to have lived during a particular period of time in the Earth's history, used to learn the age of rock in which it was found

In·di·a /ˈɪndiə/ a large country in south Asia —**Indian** *n., adj.*

'India ink *n.* [U] black ink used especially for Chinese or Japanese writing with a brush

In·di·an¹ /ˈɪndiən/ *n.* **1** [C] a Native American person SYN **American Indian** SYN **Native American** **2** [C] someone from India SYN **East Indian**

Indian² *adj.* **1** relating to NATIVE AMERICANS **2** from or relating to India

In·di·an·a /ˌɪndiˈænə/ WRITTEN ABBREVIATION **IN** a state in the Midwestern area of the U.S.

In·di·a·nap·o·lis /ˌɪndiəˈnæpəlɪs/ the capital city of the U.S. state of Indiana

ˌIndian 'corn *n.* [U] corn with KERNELS of different colors

'Indian ˌfile *n.* OLD-FASHIONED **move/walk etc. in Indian file** to walk as a group in a straight line in which one person walks behind another person SYN **single file**

ˌIndian 'giver *n.* [C] INFORMAL a word for someone who gives you something and then wants it back, considered offensive by many people

ˌIndian ˌNational 'Congress, the ABBREVIATION **INC** HISTORY a major political party in India that helped lead the country to independence from Great Britain

ˌIndian ˌNew 'Deal, the HISTORY the INDIAN REORGANIZATION ACT

ˌIndian 'Ocean, the the ocean between Africa and Australia

ˌIndian Re'moval ˌAct, the HISTORY a U.S. law passed in 1830, which said that Native Americans could be given land to live on in parts of the Louisiana Purchase, in exchange for their land in the east. After this law, many Native Americans were encouraged or forced to move west.

ˌIndian Reˌorgani'zation ˌAct, the also **the Indian New Deal** HISTORY a set of laws passed by Congress in 1934 designed to give Native Americans more control of their land and government

ˌIndian reser'vation *n.* [C] OLD-FASHIONED a RESERVATION

ˌIndian 'summer *n.* [C] **1** a period of warm weather in the fall **2** a happy or successful time, especially near the end of your life or CAREER

ˌIndian 'wrestling *n.* [U] a game in which you stand facing someone with your foot touching theirs, and try to push them over by pushing one of their hands

ˌindia 'rubber *n.* [U] a type of ERASER made from rubber

in·di·cate /ˈɪndəˌkeɪt/ Ac S3 W2 *v.* [T] **1** to show that a particular situation exists, or that something is likely to be true: *The study indicates a link between poverty and crime.* | **indicate that** *Reports from hospitals indicated that over 13 people died in the storm.* | *These figures* ***clearly indicate*** *that the problem is getting worse.* ►see THESAURUS box at **demonstrate** **2** to say or do something to make your wishes, intentions, meaning etc. clear: *She indicated her willingness to help.* | **indicate that** *He nodded several times to indicate that he understood.* **3** to represent something: *A dotted line indicates a road that is still under construction.* **4** to direct someone's attention to something, for example by pointing: *He indicated a point on the map with his pen.* [**Origin:** 1600–1700 Latin, past participle of *indicare*, from *dicare* **to say publicly or officially**]

in·di·ca·tion /ˌɪndəˈkeɪʃən/ Ac *n.* [C,U] a sign that something is probably happening or that something is probably true: +**of** *Dark green leaves are a good indication of healthy roots.* | **indication that** *Police said there was no indication that the two robberies were related.* | *Collier* ***gave every indication*** (=gave very clear signs) *that he was ready to compromise.* | *We are now seeing the first* ***clear indications*** *of global warming.*

in·dic·a·tive¹ /ɪnˈdɪkəṭɪv/ Ac *adj.* **1 be indicative of sth** to be a clear sign that a particular situation exists or that something is likely to be true: *Yesterday's win was indicative of the team's talent.* **2** ENG. LANG. ARTS an indicative form of a verb is in the indicative

indicative² Ac *n.* [C,U] ENG. LANG. ARTS the form of a verb that is used to make ordinary statements. For example, in the sentences "Penny passed her test," and "Michael likes cake," the verbs "passed" and "like" are in the indicative → see also IMPERATIVE, SUBJUNCTIVE

in·di·ca·tor /ˈɪndəˌkeɪṭɚ/ Ac *n.* [C] **1** something that can be regarded as a sign of something else: *High cholesterol levels may be an indicator of heart disease risk.* ►see THESAURUS box at **sign¹** **2** a POINTER on a machine that shows the temperature, speed etc.

in·di·ces /ˈɪndɪˌsiz/ *n.* a plural of INDEX

in·dict /ɪnˈdaɪt/ *v.* [I,T] LAW to officially charge someone with a crime: **indict sb for sth** *Three of the men were indicted for kidnapping.* | **indict sb on sth** *Two men were indicted on fraud charges.*

in·dict·a·ble /ɪnˈdaɪṭəbəl/ *adj.* LAW an indictable offense is one for which you can be indicted

in·dict·ment /ɪnˈdaɪt˺mənt/ *n.* **1** [U] LAW the act of officially charging someone with a crime: *Owners of the city's biggest casino are* ***under indictment*** (=charged with a crime). **2 be an indictment of sth** to show clearly that a system, method etc. is very bad or very wrong: *The results are an indictment of the educa-*

I

tion system. **3** [C] LAW an official written statement charging someone with a crime: +**for** *an indictment for murder* ▸see THESAURUS box at **accusation**

in·die /ˈɪndi/ *n.* **1** [C] a small independent company, especially one that produces popular music or movies **2** [U] also **indie music** popular music or rock music that is produced by small, indpendent companies —**indie** *adj.*: *an indie band*

in·dif·ference /ɪnˈdɪfrəns/ *n.* [U] lack of interest or concern: +**to** *public indifference to environmental problems*

in·dif·ferent /ɪnˈdɪfrənt/ *adj.* **1** not interested in someone or something, or not having any feelings or opinions about a person, thing, event etc.: +**to** *He seemed indifferent to what was happening around him.* **2** not particularly good: *The service at the restaurant was indifferent at best.* [**Origin:** 1300–1400 Old French, Latin *indifferens* **making no difference**]

in·dig·e·nous /ɪnˈdɪdʒənəs/ *adj.* **1** indigenous people, customs, CULTURES etc. are the people, customs etc. that have always been in a place, before other people or customs arrived **2** BIOLOGY indigenous animals, plants etc. have always lived or grown naturally in the place where they are, as opposed to others that were brought there: +**to** *Red foxes are indigenous to the East and Midwest parts of the U.S.* [**Origin:** 1600–1700 Late Latin *indigenus*, from Latin *indigena* **someone born in a place**]

in·di·gent /ˈɪndɪdʒənt/ *adj.* FORMAL not having much money or many possessions SYN **poor** —**indigent** *n.* [C] —**indigence** *n.* [U]

in·di·gest·i·ble /ˌɪndɪˈdʒɛstəbəl, -daɪ-/ *adj.* **1** food that is indigestible cannot easily be broken down in the stomach into substances that the body can use **2** facts that are indigestible are not easy to understand: *indigestible statistics*

in·di·ges·tion /ˌɪndɪˈdʒɛstʃən/ *n.* [U] pain that you get when it is difficult for your stomach to break down the food that you have eaten: *Spicy food always gives me indigestion.*

in·dig·nant /ɪnˈdɪgnənt/ *adj.* angry and surprised, because you feel insulted or unfairly treated: +**at/over** *Eric was indignant over being made to wait for 20 minutes.* [**Origin:** 1500–1600 Latin, present participle of *indignari*, from *indignus* **unworthy**] —**indignantly** *adv.*

in·dig·na·tion /ˌɪndɪgˈneɪʃən/ *n.* [U] feelings of anger and surprise because you feel insulted or unfairly treated: +**at/over** *She expressed indignation at the way she had been treated.* | *His voice rose* ***in indignation*** *as he talked about the beating he suffered.*

in·dig·ni·ty /ɪnˈdɪgnət̬i/ *n. plural* **indignities** [C,U] a situation that makes you feel very ashamed, unimportant, and not respected: *Many women have suffered the indignity of being sexually harassed.*

in·di·go /ˈɪndɪgoʊ/ *plural* **indigoes** or **indigos** *n.* **1** [U] a dark purple-blue color **2** [C] BIOLOGY a tropical plant used in past times for making blue DYE (=color for cloth) **3** [U] the DYE made from this plant [**Origin:** 1500–1600 Italian, Latin *indicum*, from Greek *indikos* **Indian**] —**indigo** *adj.*

in·di·rect /ˌɪndəˈrɛkt◂, -daɪ-/ *adj.* **1** not directly caused by or related to something OPP **direct**: **an indirect result/effect/benefit etc.** *There are many indirect benefits of tourism.* **2** not coming directly from a particular thing or place OPP **direct**: *indirect lighting* **3** not using the fastest, easiest, or straightest way to get to a place OPP **direct**: *an indirect route* **4** suggesting something without saying it directly OPP **direct**: *George's comments were an indirect way of blaming me.* —**indirectly** *adv.*

ˌindirect ˈdiscourse *n.* [U] ENG. LANG. ARTS → see REPORTED SPEECH

ˌindirect ˈmeasurement *n.* [U] MATH a method for measuring the size of something without using a ruler or other measuring tool. Multiplying the length and width of a shape that is almost square to find its area, or comparing one shape to a similar but bigger or smaller shape are examples of indirect measurement.

ˌindirect ˈobject *n.* [C] ENG. LANG. ARTS in grammar, the person or thing that receives something as the result of the action of the verb in a sentence. In the sentence "Ryan gave me a gift," the indirect object is "me." → see also DIRECT OBJECT

ˌindirect ˈreasoning also **ˌindirect ˈproof** *n.* [U] MATH the process of proving that a mathematical statement is true which involves first supposing that it is false, and then showing that if the statement is in fact false other mathematical statements which are known or believed to be true must also be false

ˌindirect ˈrule *n.* [U] POLITICS the governing of a COLONY or area under local laws

ˌindirect ˈspeech *n.* [U] ENG. LANG. ARTS → see REPORTED SPEECH

ˌindirect ˈtax *n.* [C] ECONOMICS a type of tax that is collected by adding it to the price of goods and services that people buy

ˌindirect taxˈation *n.* [U] ECONOMICS a system of collecting taxes by adding an amount of tax to the price of goods and services that people buy

in·dis·cern·i·ble /ˌɪndɪˈsɚnəbəl/ *adj.* very difficult to see, hear, or notice: *The crack in the windshield was almost indiscernible.*

in·dis·ci·pline /ɪnˈdɪsəplɪn/ *n.* [U] a lack of control over a group of people, so that they behave badly → see also DISCIPLINE[1] (2)

in·dis·creet /ˌɪndɪˈskrit/ *adj.* careless about what you say or do, especially by talking about things that should be kept secret —**indiscreetly** *adv.*

in·dis·cre·tion /ˌɪndɪˈskrɛʃən/ Ac *n.* [C,U] an action, remark or behavior that shows bad judgment and a lack of careful thought, and is usually considered socially or morally unacceptable: *a minor indiscretion* | *Dodd says his involvement in the racist group was just* ***youthful indiscretion***.

in·dis·crim·i·nate /ˌɪndɪˈskrɪmənɪt/ *adj.* **1** indiscriminate killing, violence, damage etc. is done without any thought about who is harmed or what is damaged: *the indiscriminate killing of civilians* **2** not thinking carefully before you make a choice —**indiscriminately** *adv.*

in·dis·pen·sa·ble /ˌɪndɪˈspɛnsəbəl/ *adj.* someone or something that is indispensable is so important or useful that it is impossible to manage without them: *Police dogs have proved indispensable in the war on drugs.* —**indispensably** *adv.* —**indispensability** /ˌɪndɪˌspɛnsəˈbɪlət̬i/ *n.* [U]

in·dis·posed /ˌɪndɪˈspoʊzd◂/ *adj.* FORMAL [not before noun] **1** sick and therefore unable to be present: *I am afraid Mr Jones is indisposed this morning.* **2 be indisposed to do sth** to not be willing to do something

in·dis·po·si·tion /ɪnˌdɪspəˈzɪʃən/ *n.* FORMAL **1** [C,U] a slight illness: *the actor's sudden indisposition* **2** [U] an unwilling attitude

in·dis·pu·ta·ble /ˌɪndɪˈspyut̬əbəl/ *adj.* an indisputable fact must be accepted because it is definitely true: *The evidence was indisputable.* —**indisputably** *adv.*

in·dis·sol·u·ble /ˌɪndɪˈsɑlyəbəl/ *adj.* FORMAL an indissoluble relationship cannot be destroyed —**indissolubility** /ˌɪndɪˌsɑlyəˈbɪlət̬i/ *n.* [U]

in·dis·tinct /ˌɪndɪˈstɪŋkt/ Ac *adj.* an indistinct sound, image, or memory cannot be seen, heard, or remembered clearly: *My memories of childhood are very indistinct.*

in·dis·tin·guish·a·ble /ˌɪndɪˈstɪŋgwɪʃəbəl/ *adj.* things that are indistinguishable are so similar that you cannot see any difference between them: +**from** *Their house was indistinguishable from all the others on the street.*

in·di·vid·u·al[1] /ˌɪndəˈvɪdʒuəl/ Ac S2 W1 *adj.* **1** [only before noun] considered separately from other people or things in the same group: *We try to address the needs of each individual customer.* **2** [only before noun] belonging to or intended for one person rather than a group:

Children get far more individual attention in small classes. | *an individual serving* **3** an individual style, way of doing things etc. is different from anyone else's: *He has his own individual method of organizing his work.* [**Origin:** 1400–1500 Medieval Latin *individualis*, from Latin *individuus* **undividable**]

individual² Ac S2 W1 *n.* [C] **1** one person, considered separately from the rest of the group or society that they live in: *the rights of the individual* | *Effects of the drug vary from individual to individual.* | *We have received donations from companies and* ***private individuals.*** **2** INFORMAL a particular person, especially one who is unusual in some way: *Mandy's a real individual.* | **a strange/talented/complex etc. individual** *He's a very talented individual.*

in·di·vid·u·al·ism /ˌɪndəˈvɪdʒuəˌlɪzəm/ Ac *n.* [U] **1** the belief that the rights and freedom of individual people are the most important rights in a society **2** the practice of allowing someone to do things in their own way, without being influenced by other people

in·di·vid·u·al·ist /ˌɪndəˈvɪdʒuəlɪst/ Ac *n.* [C] someone who does things in their own way and has different opinions from most other people —**individualistic** /ˌɪndəˌvɪdʒuəˈlɪstɪk/ *adj.*

in·di·vid·u·al·i·ty /ˌɪndəˌvɪdʒuˈæləṭi/ Ac *n.* [U] the quality that makes someone or something different from all other things or people: *Changing his hair color was his way of expressing his individuality.*

in·di·vid·u·al·ize /ˌɪndəˈvɪdʒuəˌlaɪz/ *v.* [T] to make something different so that it fits the special needs of a particular person or place: *We try to individualize the service we provide as much as possible.* —**individualized** *adj.*: *an individualized weight loss program*

in·di·vid·u·al·ly /ˌɪndəˈvɪdʒuəli, -dʒəli/ Ac *adv.* separately, not together in a group: *The children work individually or in groups.* | *Each cake is individually wrapped.*

in·di·vid·u·ate /ˌɪndəˈvɪdʒuˌeɪt/ *v.* **1** [T] to make someone or something clearly different from others of the same kind SYN **differentiate**: *Developers try to find ways to individuate the houses they build.* **2** [I] to have an idea of yourself as an independent person, separate from other people

in·di·vis·i·ble /ˌɪndəˈvɪzəbəl/ *adj.* something that is indivisible cannot be separated or divided into parts —**indivisibly** *adv.* —**indivisibility** /ˌɪndəˌvɪzəˈbɪləṭi/ *n.* [U]

Indo- /ˈɪndoʊ/ *prefix* INDIAN and something else: *Indo-European languages*

In·do·chi·na /ˌɪndoʊˈtʃaɪnə/ a former name given to part of southeast Asia by Europeans. During the 19th century, Indochina included Vietnam, Cambodia, Myanmar (Burma), Thailand, Malaysia, and Laos, but in the 20th century Indochina came to mean the countries ruled by France: Vietnam, Cambodia and Laos.

in·doc·tri·nate /ɪnˈdɑktrəˌneɪt/ *v.* [T] to train someone to accept a particular set of beliefs, especially political or religious ones, and not consider any others: *Training seminars are held to indoctrinate recruits.* —**indoctrination** /ɪnˌdɑktrəˈneɪʃən/ *n.* [U]

ˌIndo-Euroˈpean *adj.* ENG. LANG. ARTS the Indo-European family of languages includes related languages spoken in Europe and central southwest and southern Asia

in·do·lent /ˈɪndələnt/ *adj.* FORMAL lazy —**indolently** *adv.* —**indolence** *n.* [U]

in·dom·i·ta·ble /ɪnˈdɑməṭəbəl/ *adj.* having determination, courage, or other qualities that can never be defeated: *an indomitable spirit*

In·do·ne·si·a /ˌɪndəˈniʒə/ a country in the southeastern Pacific Ocean consisting of more than 13,000 islands, including Java, Sumatra, most of Borneo, Sulawesi, and Bali

In·do·ne·sian /ˌɪndəˈniʒən/ *n.* **1** [C] a person who comes from Indonesia **2** [U] the official language used in Indonesia —**Indonesian** *adj.*

in·door /ˈɪndɔr/ *adj.* [only before noun] used or happening inside a building OPP **outdoor**: *indoor lighting* | *indoor soccer*

in·doors /ˌɪnˈdɔrz/ *adv.* into or inside a building OPP **outdoors**: *Let's stay indoors where it's nice and warm.*

in·du·bi·ta·ble /ɪnˈdubɪṭəbəl/ *adj.* FORMAL definitely true without any possible doubt —**indubitably** *adv.*

in·duce /ɪnˈdus/ Ac *v.* [T] **1** to make someone decide to do something, especially something that does not seem wise: **induce sb to do sth** *I don't know what induced her to do that.* **2** FORMAL to cause a particular physical condition, feeling, or change: *She was given medicine to induce vomiting.* | **stress-induced/drug-induced/alcohol induced etc.** *a stress-induced allergy* **3** MEDICINE to make a woman give birth to her baby, by giving her a special drug: *She had to be induced because the baby was four weeks late.*

in·duced /ɪnˈdust/ *adj.* **1** PHYSICS an induced current or VOLTAGE is an electric current that is produced by a moving MAGNETIC FIELD, or by motion through a magnetic field: *The changing magnetic field produces an induced current in the coil which is sufficient to light the bulb if it is close enough.* **2** PHYSICS an induced charge is an electric CHARGE that is produced in one object by the electricity that surrounds another nearby object

in·duce·ment /ɪnˈdusmənt/ *n.* [C,U] something such as money or a gift that you are offered to persuade you to do something: *Businesses were offered inducements to move to the area.*

in·duct /ɪnˈdʌkt/ *v.* [T often passive] FORMAL **1** to give someone an important place of honor in a special ceremony: **induct sb into sth** *Rick Barry was inducted into the Basketball Hall of Fame in 1987.* **2** to officially make someone a member of a group, club, organization etc. in a special ceremony: *On Sunday, the fraternity inducts the new pledges.* **3** to officially give someone a job or position of authority, especially at a special ceremony: **induct sb to sth** *He was inducted to the post of foreign minister late last year.* **4** to take someone into a military organization such as the Army or Navy

in·duct·ee /ˌɪndʌkˈti/ *n.* [C] someone who is being taken into the Army, Navy, or another organization

in·duc·tion /ɪnˈdʌkʃən/ Ac *n.* **1** [C,U] the act of officially giving someone an official position or place of honor, or the ceremony in which this is done: **+into** *induction into the Baseball Hall of Fame* **2** [U] a process of thought that uses known facts to produce general rules or principles → see also DEDUCTION: *You can discover the rules through induction.* **3** [C,U] MEDICINE the act or process of making a woman give birth to her baby by giving her a special drug **4** [U] PHYSICS the production of electricity in one object by another nearby object that has electrical or MAGNETIC power

inˈduction ˌcoil *n.* [C] PHYSICS a piece of electrical equipment that changes a low VOLTAGE to a higher one

in·duct·ive /ɪnˈdʌktɪv/ *adj.* **1** using known facts to produce general principles: *inductive reasoning* **2** PHYSICS relating to electrical or MAGNETIC induction

inˌductive ˈreasoning *n.* [U] **1** the process by which you form a general opinion about something from known facts or patterns **2** MATH the process of forming a general mathematical principle or solving a mathematical problem using an existing pattern of specific results or facts → see also DEDUCTIVE REASONING

in·dulge /ɪnˈdʌldʒ/ *v.* **1** [I,T] to let yourself do or have something that you enjoy, especially something that is considered bad for you: **+in** *A funeral is not an appropriate time to indulge in gossip.* | **indulge yourself** *If you're dieting, indulge yourself once in a while* (=eat what you want). | **indulge your fantasy/passion/taste etc.** *I have to indulge my craving for chocolate a few times a week.* **2** [T] to let someone have or do whatever they want, even if it is bad for them: *Parents should avoid indulging their children.* **3** [I] to take part in an activity, especially an illegal or immoral one: **+in**

Women do not indulge in crime to the same extent as men.

in·dul·gence /ɪnˈdʌldʒəns/ *n.* **1** [U] the habit of eating too much, drinking too much etc. **2** [C] something that you do or have for pleasure, not because you need it: *Swiss chocolate is my only indulgence.* **3** [C,U] freedom from punishment by God, or a promise of this, which was sold by priests in the Middle Ages. **4** [U] OLD USE permission

in·dul·gent /ɪnˈdʌldʒənt/ *adj.* willing to allow someone, especially a child, to do what they want, even if this is not good for them: +**with** *Billy's parents are too indulgent with him.* —**indulgently** *adv.* → see also SELF-INDULGENT

in·dus·tri·al /ɪnˈdʌstriəl/ W2 *adj.* [only before noun] **1** relating to industry: *modern industrial practices* | *industrial waste* | *The cleaner is for **industrial use*** (=not to be used at home) *only.* **2** involving the people working in industry: *an industrial dispute* | *industrial accidents* **3** having many industries, or industries that are well developed: *an industrial nation* | **an industrial zone/area** *pollution in industrial zones* **4** of the type used in industry: *industrial cleaning products* —**industrially** *adv.* → see also INDUSTRIOUS

in,dustrial ˈarts *n.* [U] a subject taught in school about how to use tools, machinery etc.

in,dustrial ˈespionage *n.* [U] stealing secret information from one company in order to help a different company

in·dus·tri·al·ism /ɪnˈdʌstriə,lɪzəm/ *n.* [U] the system by which a society gets its wealth through industries and machinery

in·dus·tri·al·ist /ɪnˈdʌstriəlɪst/ *n.* [C] the owner or manager of a factory, industrial company etc.

in·dus·tri·al·ize /ɪnˈdʌstriə,laɪz/ *v.* [I,T] if a country or place is industrialized or if it industrializes, it develops a lot of industry —**industrialization** /ɪn,dʌstriələˈzeɪʃən/ *n.* [U]

in·dus·tri·al·ized /ɪnˈdʌstriə,laɪzd/ *adj.* having factories, mines, industrial companies etc. on a very wide scale: *industrialized nations*

in,dustrial ˈpark *n.* [C] an area of land that has offices, businesses, small factories etc. on it

in,dustrial reˈlations *n.* [plural] the relationship between workers and employers

in,dustrial revoˈlution *n.* [singular] **1 the Industrial Revolution** the period in the 18th and 19th centuries in Europe, when machines and factories began to be used to produce goods in large quantities **2** a period of time in other countries when more machines are being used to produce goods

inˈdustrial-,strength *adj.* [only before noun] very strong or effective, and appropriate for use in factories: *an industrial-strength detergent*

in·dus·tri·ous /ɪnˈdʌstriəs/ *adj.* someone who is industrious tends to work hard —**industriousness** *n.* [U] → see also INDUSTRIAL

in·dus·try /ˈɪndəstri/ S3 W1 *n. plural* **industries** **1** [U] the production of goods, especially in factories: *This type of software is widely used in industry.* | *a collaboration between **private industry** and the government* | **light/heavy industry** (=industry that produces small goods or large goods) ▸see THESAURUS box at **business** **2** [C] a particular type of trade or service: *the airline industry* | *Miami's tourist industry* **3** [U] FORMAL the energy and willingness to work very hard: *Her colleagues admired her industry, energy, and knowledge.* [**Origin:** 1400–1500 Old French *industrie* **skill, work involving skill**, from Latin *industria* **willingness to work hard**] → see also COTTAGE INDUSTRY, SERVICE INDUSTRY

ˈindustry associ,ation *n.* [C] ECONOMICS another word for a TRADE ASSOCIATION

-ine /aɪn, in/ *suffix* FORMAL OR TECHNICAL **1** relating to a particular thing: *equine* (=relating to horses) **2** made of something, or similar to it: *a crystalline substance*

in·e·bri·ate /ɪˈnibriɪt/ *n.* [C] OLD-FASHIONED someone who is often drunk —**inebriate** *adj.*

in·e·bri·at·ed /ɪˈnibri,eɪt̬ɪd/ *adj.* FORMAL drunk

in·ed·i·ble /ɪnˈɛdəbəl/ *adj.* not good enough to eat, or not appropriate for eating: *The meat had been cooked so long that it was inedible.*

in·ed·u·ca·ble /ɪnˈɛdʒəkəbəl/ *adj.* FORMAL impossible or very difficult to educate

in·ef·fa·ble /ɪnˈɛfəbəl/ *adj.* FORMAL too great to be described in words: *ineffable satisfaction* —**ineffably** *adv.*

in·ef·fec·tive /,ɪnəˈfɛktɪv/ *adj.* **1** something that is ineffective does not achieve what it is intended to achieve: *Efforts to get homeless people off the streets have been largely ineffective.* **2** someone who is ineffective is not able to deal successfully with the work they have to do: *an ineffective manager* —**ineffectively** *adv.* —**ineffectiveness** *n.* [U]

in·ef·fec·tu·al /,ɪnəˈfɛktʃuəl/ *adj.* **1** not having the ability, confidence, or personal authority to get things done SYN **ineffective**: *an ineffectual leader* **2** something that is ineffectual does not achieve what it is intended to achieve SYN **ineffective**: *ineffectual attempts to reach an agreement* —**ineffectually** *adv.*

in·ef·fi·cient /,ɪnəˈfɪʃənt/ *adj.* an inefficient worker, organization, or system does not work well and wastes time, money, or energy: *an inefficient banking system* | *The army was inefficient and poorly equipped.* —**inefficiently** *adv.* —**inefficiency** *n.* [C, U]

in·e·las·tic /,ɪnɪˈlæstɪk/ *adj.* ECONOMICS used to say that a change in one thing, such as the demand for a product, has only a small effect on another thing, such as the price of the product: *If fans still buy the same number of tickets when the prices go up, then **demand is inelastic**.*

in·el·e·gant /ɪnˈɛləgənt/ *adj.* not graceful or well done: *an inelegant turn of phrase*

in·el·i·gi·ble /ɪnˈɛlədʒəbəl/ *adj.* not allowed to do or have something: +**for** *Part-time employees are ineligible for health benefits.* | **ineligible to do sth** *People under 18 are ineligible to vote.* —**ineligibility** /ɪn,ɛlədʒəˈbɪlət̬i/ *n.* [U]

in·e·luc·ta·ble /,ɪnɪˈlʌktəbəl/ *adj.* LITERARY impossible to escape from SYN **unavoidable**

in·ept /ɪˈnɛpt/ *adj.* having no skill: *When it comes to girls, Isaac is socially inept and awkward.* —**ineptly** *adv.* —**ineptitude**, **ineptness** *n.* [U]

in·e·qual·i·ty /,ɪnɪˈkwɑlət̬i/ *n. plural* **inequalities** **1** [C,U] an unfair situation, in which some groups in society have less money, influence, or opportunity than others: +**in** *gender inequality in education* | +**of** *inequality of opportunity* | **social/sexual/racial etc. inequality** *the removal of racial inequalities* **2** [C] **a)** MATH a mathematical statement that shows that two values are not equal, using the signs < (meaning "is less than") or > (meaning "is more than") **b)** MATH the signs < or >, used to show that one value is less than or more than another value; the sign ≤, used to show that one value is less than or equal to another value; and the sign ≥ used to show that one value is more than or equal to another value

in·eq·ui·ta·ble /ɪnˈɛkwɪt̬əbəl/ *adj.* FORMAL not equally fair to everyone SYN **unjust**: *an inequitable distribution of wealth* —**inequitably** *adv.*

in·eq·ui·ty /ɪnˈɛkwət̬i/ *n. plural* **inequities** [C,U] FORMAL lack of fairness, or something that is unfair: *There are many inequities in our healthcare system.*

in·e·rad·i·ca·ble /,ɪnɪˈrædɪkəbəl◂/ *adj.* FORMAL an ineradicable fact, quality, or situation is permanent and cannot be changed: *Poverty seems an ineradicable fact of the human condition.*

in·ert /ɪˈnɚt/ *adj.* **1** CHEMISTRY not producing a chemical reaction when combined with other substances: *inert gases* **2** not moving or not having the strength or power to move: *She lay there, inert.* **3** [not before noun] very slow and unwilling to take any action: *The government was inert and inefficient.* [**Origin:** 1600–1700 Latin *iners* **unskilled, doing nothing**, from *ars* **skill, art**] —**inertly** *adv.* —**inertness** *n.* [U]

in·er·tia /ɪˈnɝʃə/ *n.* [U] **1** a tendency for a situation to stay unchanged for a long time: *the inertia and bureaucracy of large companies* **2** lack of energy and a feeling that you do not want to do anything: *a feeling of tiredness and inertia* **3** PHYSICS the force that keeps an object in the same position, or keeps it moving until it is moved or stopped by another force —**inertial** *adj.*

in·es·cap·a·ble /ˌɪnəˈskeɪpəbəl/ *adj.* impossible to avoid: *The conclusion is inescapable.* —**inescapably** *adv.*

in·es·sen·tial /ˌɪnəˈsɛnʃəl/ *adj.* FORMAL not needed SYN unnecessary: *inessential details* —**inessentials** *n.* [plural]

in·es·ti·ma·ble /ɪnˈɛstəməbəl/ *adj.* FORMAL too much or too great to be calculated: *a painting of inestimable value* —**inestimably** *adv.*

in·ev·i·ta·ble[1] /ɪˈnɛvət̬əbəl/ Ac *adj.* certain to happen and impossible to avoid: *War now seems inevitable.* | **an inevitable consequence/result** *Disease was an inevitable consequence of poor living conditions.* | **it is inevitable (that)** *It is inevitable that some mistakes will be made.* —**inevitability** /ɪˌnɛvət̬əˈbɪlət̬i/ *n.* [U]

inevitable[2] Ac *n.* **the inevitable** a situation that is certain to happen: *You have to face up to the inevitable.*

in·ev·i·ta·bly /ɪˈnɛvət̬əbli/ Ac *adv.* if something will inevitably happen, it is sure to happen and cannot be prevented: *Bad economic conditions inevitably lead to crime.*

in·ex·act /ˌɪnɪgˈzækt/ *adj.* not exact: *the inexact science of earthquake prediction* —**inexactness** *n.* [U]

in·ex·cus·a·ble /ˌɪnɪkˈskyuzəbəl/ *adj.* inexcusable behavior is too bad to be excused: *Being late for your own wedding is inexcusable.* —**inexcusably** *adv.*

in·ex·haust·i·ble /ˌɪnɪgˈzɔstəbəl/ *adj.* existing in such large amounts that it can never be finished or used up: *The group has a seemingly* ***inexhaustible supply of*** *money.* —**inexhaustibly** *adv.*

in·ex·o·ra·ble /ɪnˈɛksərəbəl/ *adj.* FORMAL an inexorable process cannot be stopped: *the inexorable progress of rain forest destruction* —**inexorably** *adv.*

in·ex·pe·di·ent /ˌɪnɪkˈspidiənt/ *adj.* FORMAL not quick or effective in helping to solve a problem —**inexpedience**, **inexpediency** *n.* [U]

in·ex·pen·sive /ˌɪnɪkˈspɛnsɪv/ *adj.* APPROVING cheap and of good quality for the price you pay: *an inexpensive meal* —**inexpensively** *adv.* ▸see THESAURUS box at cheap[1]

in·ex·pe·ri·ence /ˌɪnɪkˈspɪriəns/ *n.* [U] lack of experience or knowledge: *His political inexperience often shows.*

in·ex·pe·ri·enced /ˌɪnɪkˈspɪriənst/ *adj.* not having much experience or knowledge: *inexperienced drivers*

in·ex·pert /ɪnˈɛkspɝt/ *adj.* not having the skill to do something well —**inexpertly** *adv.*

in·ex·pli·ca·ble /ˌɪnɪkˈsplɪkəbəl/ *adj.* too unusual or strange to be explained or understood: *For some inexplicable reason, he felt depressed.* —**inexplicably** *adv.*

in·ex·press·i·ble /ˌɪnɪkˈsprɛsəbəl/ *adj.* **inexpressible joy/bitterness/grief etc.** a feeling or condition that is too strong to be described in words —**inexpressibly** *adv.*

in·ex·pres·sive /ˌɪnɪkˈsprɛsɪv◂/ *adj.* a face that is inexpressive shows no emotion at all

in·ex·tin·guish·a·ble /ˌɪnɪkˈstɪŋgwɪʃəbəl/ *adj.* LITERARY **inextinguishable hope/love/passion etc.** hope, love etc. that is so strong that it cannot be destroyed

in ex·tre·mis /ˌɪn ɪkˈstrimɪs/ *adv.* FORMAL **1** in a very difficult and urgent situation when very strong action is needed **2** at the moment of death

in·ex·tric·a·ble /ˌɪnɪkˈstrɪkəbəl, ɪnˈɛkstrɪk-/ *adj.* FORMAL two or more things that are inextricable cannot be separated from each other: *the* ***inextricable link*** *between language and culture*

in·ex·tric·a·bly /ˌɪnɪkˈstrɪkəbli/ *adv.* **be inextricably linked/connected/mixed etc.** if two or more things are inextricably LINKed, connected etc., they are very closely connected and cannot be separated: *The racism in our culture today is inextricably tied to our past.*

in·fal·li·ble /ɪnˈfæləbəl/ *adj.* **1** always right and never making mistakes: *Not even the experts are infallible.* **2** something that is infallible always works or has the intended effect: *DNA testing is an almost infallible method of identification.* —**infallibly** *adv.* —**infallibility** /ɪnˌfæləˈbɪlət̬i/ *n.* [U]

in·fa·mous /ˈɪnfəməs/ *adj.* well known for being bad or morally evil SYN notorious: *an infamous killer* | +**for** *This area is infamous for drugs and prostitution.* —**infamously** *adv.*

in·fa·my /ˈɪnfəmi/ *n.* **1** [U] the state of being evil or well known for evil things **2** [C usually plural] an evil action

in·fan·cy /ˈɪnfənsi/ *n.* [singular,U] **1** the period of a child's life before they can walk or talk: *John's twin brother died* ***in infancy*** (=during infancy). **2 in its infancy** something that is in its infancy is just starting to be developed: *Genetic engineering is still in its infancy.*

in·fant[1] /ˈɪnfənt/ W3 *n.* [C] FORMAL a baby, especially one that has not yet learned to walk or talk ▸see THESAURUS box at baby[1] [**Origin:** 1300–1400 French *enfant*, from Latin *infans* **unable to speak**, from *fari* **to speak**]

infant[2] *adj.* [only before noun] an infant company, organization etc. has just started to exist or be developed

in·fan·ti·cide /ɪnˈfæntəˌsaɪd/ *n.* [U] TECHNICAL the crime of killing a young child

in·fan·tile /ˈɪnfənˌtaɪl, -təl/ *adj.* **1** infantile behavior seems silly in an adult because it is typical of a child: *an infantile temper tantrum* **2** [only before noun] MEDICINE affecting very young children: *infantile development*

ˌinfantile paˈralysis *n.* [U] OLD-FASHIONED → see POLIO

ˌinfant morˈtality rate *n.* [C] the number of deaths of babies under one year old, expressed as the number out of each 1,000 babies born alive in a year

in·fan·try /ˈɪnfəntri/ *n.* [U] soldiers who fight on foot → see also CAVALRY

in·fan·try·man /ˈɪnfəntrimən/ *n. plural* **infantrymen** /-mən/ [C] a soldier who fights on foot

in·farc·tion /ɪnˈfɑrkʃən/ *n.* [C] MEDICINE a medical condition in which a blood VESSEL becomes blocked

in·fat·u·at·ed /ɪnˈfætʃuˌeɪt̬ɪd/ *adj.* having strong unreasonable feelings of love for someone or interest in something: +**with** *Steve was infatuated with his friend's girlfriend.*

in·fat·u·a·tion /ɪnˌfætʃuˈeɪʃən/ *n.* [C,U] strong unreasonable feelings of love for someone or interest in something: +**with** *an infatuation with motorcycles*

in·fect /ɪnˈfɛkt/ *v.* [T] **1** MEDICINE to give someone a disease: **infect sb with sth** *One patient infected 20 people with tuberculosis.* **2** to make food, water, the air etc. dangerous and able to spread disease: *A fungus had infected the fruit.* **3** if a feeling or interest that you have infects other people, it makes them begin to feel the same way: *Lucy's enthusiasm soon infected the rest of the class.* **4** COMPUTERS if a computer VIRUS infects your computer or DISKS, it changes or destroys the information in them [**Origin:** 1300–1400 Latin, past participle of *inficere* **to dip in, stain**]

in·fect·ed /ɪnˈfɛktɪd/ *adj.* **1** MEDICINE a part of your body or a wound that is infected has harmful BACTERIA in it that prevents it from HEALing: *The cut became infected.* | *an infected finger* **2** food, water etc. that is infected contains BACTERIA that spread disease: +**with** *The water here is infected with cholera.* **3** COMPUTERS if a computer or DISK is infected, the information in it has been changed or destroyed by a computer VIRUS

in·fec·tion /ɪnˈfɛkʃən/ S3 W3 *n.* [C,U] a disease caused by BACTERIA or a VIRUS that affects a particular part of your body, or the process of becoming infected with such a disease: *an ear infection* | *The antibiotic ointment will prevent infection.*

in·fec·tious /ɪnˈfɛkʃəs/ *adj.* **1** MEDICINE an infectious disease can be passed from one person to another, especially through the air you breathe: *a highly infectious virus* **2** someone who is infectious has an illness and could pass it to other people **3** infectious feelings or laughter spread quickly from one person to another: *Sheila has an infectious smile.*

in·fe·lic·i·ty /ˌɪnfɪˈlɪsət̮i/ *n. plural* **infelicities** [C,U] FORMAL **1** the quality of not being happy **2** something such as a remark, way of writing or speaking etc. that is not appropriate or not correct for a particular situation: *At best, his remark was an infelicity.* —**infelicitous** *adj.*

in·fer /ɪnˈfɚ/ Ac *v.* **inferred, inferring** [T] to form an opinion that something is probably true because of other information that you already know: **infer sth from sth** *A lot can be inferred from these statistics.* | **infer that** *Based on the evidence, we can infer that the victim knew her killer.*

> WORD CHOICE **infer, imply**
> A speaker or writer can **imply** something, and the listener or reader can **infer** it: *Jeanie implied that she was mad at me.* This means that Jeanie indirectly said that she was mad, but did not say those words specifically: *I inferrred from what Jeanie said that she was mad at me.* This means that this is what I thought she meant.

in·fer·ence /ˈɪnfərəns/ Ac *n.* **1** [C] something that you think is probably true, based on information that you already know: **make/draw an inference** *What inferences have you drawn from seeing the report?* **2** [U] the act of inferring something: *They portrayed her as the hero, and* ***by inference****, Mr. Thompson as the villain.* —**inferential** /ˌɪnfəˈrɛnʃəl◂/ *adj.* —**inferentially** *adv.*

ˌinferential ˈquestion *n.* [C] ENG. LANG. ARTS a question that asks someone what they think is true based on information that they have, especially based on information that they have read → see also EVALUATIVE QUESTION, LITERAL QUESTION

in·fe·ri·or¹ /ɪnˈfɪriɚ/ *adj.* **1** not good, or worse in quality, value, or skill than someone or something else OPP **superior**: *inferior health-care facilities* | *She always makes me* ***feel inferior****.* | **+to** *Are American wines inferior in quality to European wines?* **2** FORMAL lower in rank OPP **superior**: *an inferior court of law* [**Origin:** 1400–1500 Latin **lower**, from *inferus* **below**] —**inferiority** /ɪnˌfɪriˈɔrət̮i, -ˈɑr-/ *n.* [U] → see also SUPERIOR

inferior² *n.* [C] someone who has a lower position or rank than you in an organization OPP **superior**

inˌferior ˈcourt *n.* [C] LAW a LOWER COURT → see also SUPERIOR COURT

inˌferior ˈgood *n.* [C usually singular] ECONOMICS a product that people choose to buy less of when their income increases

inˌferiˈority ˌcomplex *n.* [C] a continuous feeling that you are much less important, smart etc. than other people

in·fer·nal /ɪnˈfɚnl/ *adj.* **1** [only before noun] OLD-FASHIONED used to express anger or annoyance about something: *I can't get this infernal machine to work.* **2** LITERARY relating to HELL and evil

in·fer·no /ɪnˈfɚnoʊ/ *n. plural* **infernos** [C] LITERARY an extremely large and dangerous fire: *High winds turned the fire into an inferno.*

in·fer·tile /ɪnˈfɚt̮l/ *adj.* **1** BIOLOGY an infertile person or animal is unable to have babies or unable to produce eggs or SPERM **2** infertile land or soil is not good enough to grow plants in —**infertility** /ˌɪnfɚˈtɪlət̮i/ *n.* [U]

in·fest /ɪnˈfɛst/ *v.* [T usually passive] if insects, rats etc. infest a place, they are there in large numbers and usually cause damage: **be infested with sth** *The kitchen was infested with cockroaches.* [**Origin:** 1500–1600 French *infester*, from Latin, from *infestus* **angry and unfriendly**] —**infestation** /ˌɪnfɛˈsteɪʃən/ *n.* [C,U]

-infested /ɪnfɛstɪd/ *suffix* [in adjectives] **1 shark-infested/rat-infested/mosquito-infested etc.** full of large numbers of harmful animals or insects: *shark-infested waters* **2 crime-infested/drug-infested etc.** full of large numbers or amounts of something bad: *crime-infested neighborhoods*

in·fi·del /ˈɪnfədl, -ˌdɛl/ *n.* [C] OLD-FASHIONED used by people from one religion to talk with strong disapproval about someone who believes in a different religion

in·fi·del·i·ty /ˌɪnfəˈdɛlət̮i/ *n. plural* **infidelities** [C,U] a situation in which one person in a couple has a sexual relationship with someone who is not their wife, husband, or partner: *a marriage destroyed by infidelity*

in·field /ˈɪnfild/ *n.* [singular] **1** the part of a baseball field inside the four bases → see picture at BASEBALL **2** the group of players who play in this part of the field —**infielder** *n.* [C] → see also OUTFIELD

in·fight·ing /ˈɪnˌfaɪt̮ɪŋ/ *n.* [U] unfriendly competition and disagreement among members of the same group or organization: *political infighting*

in·fil·trate /ɪnˈfɪlˌtreɪt, ˈɪnfɪl-/ *v.* **1** [I always + adv./prep.,T] to secretly join an organization or enter a place in order to find out information about it or to harm it: *Federal agents infiltrated a Miami drug ring.* | **+into** *Terrorists have infiltrated into the region.* **2** [T] to put people into an organization or place to find out information about it or to harm it: **infiltrate sb into sth** *They tried to infiltrate assassins into the palace.* —**infiltrator** *n.* [C] —**infiltration** /ˌɪnfɪlˈtreɪʃən/ *n.* [U]

in·fi·nite /ˈɪnfənɪt/ Ac *adj.* **1** very great in size, number, or degree: *One of Keyes' gifts is her infinite patience.* | **an infinite number/variety** *There was an infinite variety of desserts to choose from.* **2** without limits in space or time OPP **finite**: *The universe is infinite.* → see also **in sb's (infinite) wisdom** at WISDOM (4)

in·fi·nite·ly /ˈɪnfənɪtli/ Ac *adv.* [+ adj./adv.] very much: *Our new office building is infinitely better than the old one.*

in·fin·i·tes·i·mal /ˌɪnfɪnəˈtɛsəməl/ *adj.* extremely small: *The device can detect infinitesimal temperature changes.* —**infinitesimally** *adv.*

in·fin·i·tive /ɪnˈfɪnət̮ɪv/ *n.* [C] ENG. LANG. ARTS in grammar, the basic form of a verb, used with "to." In the sentence "I want to watch TV," "to watch" is an infinitive [**Origin:** 1400–1500 Late Latin *infinitivus*, from Latin *infinitus*; because the verb is not limited by person or number] → see also SPLIT INFINITIVE

in·fin·i·tude /ɪnˈfɪnəˌtud/ *n.* [singular, U] FORMAL a number or amount without limit

in·fin·i·ty /ɪnˈfɪnət̮i/ *n.* **1** [U] a space or distance without limits or an end: *the infinity of space* **2 an infinity of sth** a very large number of things: *an infinity of possible solutions* **3** [singular] MATH a number that larger than any known number

in·firm /ɪnˈfɚm/ *adj.* weak or sick, especially because you are old: *He was too infirm to hold a steady job.* —**the infirm** *n.* [plural]

in·fir·ma·ry /ɪnˈfɚməri/ *n. plural* **infirmaries** [C] **1** a room in a school or other institution where people can get medical treatment **2** a hospital, especially in the military

in·fir·mi·ty /ɪnˈfɚmət̮i/ *n. plural* **infirmities** [C,U] FORMAL bad health or a particular illness

in fla·gran·te de·lic·to /ɪn fləˌgrɑnteɪ dɪˈlɪktoʊ/ *adv.* FORMAL OR HUMOROUS during the act of having sex, especially with someone else's husband or wife

in·flame /ɪnˈfleɪm/ *v.* [T] to make someone's feelings of anger, excitement etc. much stronger: *The shooting inflamed ethnic tensions.*

in·flamed /ɪnˈfleɪmd/ *adj.* **1** an inflamed part of

your body is red and swollen, because it is hurt or infected: *an inflamed left knee* **2 inflamed with passion/jealousy/desire etc.** having very strong upsetting or exciting feelings

in·flam·ma·ble /ɪnˈflæməbəl/ *adj.* **1** inflammable materials or substances will start to burn very easily SYN **flammable** OPP **nonflammable**: *an inflammable liquid* → see Word Choice box at FLAMMABLE **2** easily becoming angry or violent, or easily making people angry or violent: *an inflammable political issue*

in·flam·ma·tion /ˌɪnfləˈmeɪʃən/ *n.* [C,U] MEDICINE swelling and soreness on or in part of your body, which is often red and feels hot: +**of** *The disease causes inflammation of the brain.*

in·flam·ma·to·ry /ɪnˈflæməˌtɔri/ *adj.* **1** an inflammatory speech, piece of writing etc. is likely to make people feel angry: *inflammatory news accounts of the trial* **2** MEDICINE an inflammatory disease, condition etc. causes inflammation

inˌflammatory reˈsponse *n.* [C,U] BIOLOGY a protective reaction by the body to damage caused by injury or infection, in which the affected part becomes red, swollen, and painful

in·flat·a·ble /ɪnˈfleɪṭəbəl/ *adj.* an inflatable object has to be filled with air before you can use it: *an inflatable life boat*

in·flate /ɪnˈfleɪt/ *v.* **1** [I,T] if you inflate something, or if it inflates, it fills with air or gas so that it becomes larger SYN **blow up** OPP **deflate**: *It only takes a minute to inflate the mattress.* | *The raft inflates automatically.* **2** [T] to make a feeling, opinion, or idea become stronger than it should OPP **deflate**: *All the attention he's had has inflated his ego.* **3** [T] to say that a number, amount, price etc. is larger than it really is, often to deceive someone SYN **exaggerate**: *It became clear that the corporation was inflating its profits.* **4** [I,T] ECONOMICS to increase in price, or to make something increase in price, often in an unfair or unreasonable way OPP **deflate**: *Hotels often inflate their prices in the summer.* [**Origin:** 1400–1500 Latin, past participle of *inflare*, from *flare* **to blow**]

inflate

in·flat·ed /ɪnˈfleɪṭɪd/ *adj.* **1** DISAPPROVING inflated prices, sums etc. are high and unreasonable: *an inflated budget estimate* **2** DISAPPROVING inflated ideas or opinions about something make it seem more important than it really is: *All this attention has given Carla an inflated opinion of herself.* **3** filled with air or gas

in·fla·tion /ɪnˈfleɪʃən/ W2 *n.* [U] **1** ECONOMICS a continuing increase in prices over time, or the rate at which prices increase: *Inflation is now running at 5%.* | *the **high inflation** of the 1970s* | *a low **inflation rate*** **2** the process of filling something with air

in·fla·tion·a·ry /ɪnˈfleɪʃəˌnɛri/ *adj.* [usually before noun] ECONOMICS relating to or causing price increases: *inflationary pressures in the economy* | *an **inflationary spiral*** (=the continuing rise in wages and prices because an increase in one causes an increase in the other)

inˈflation-proof *adj.* protected against price increases: *inflation-proof stocks*

inˈflation ˌrate also **ˌrate of inˈflation** *n.* [C] ECONOMICS the rate at which prices continue to rise over time, often expressed as a PERCENTAGE (=as if it is part of a total which is 100): *an inflation rate of 3.2 percent* | *There have been much higher rates of inflation in South America in recent years.*

in·flect /ɪnˈflɛkt/ *v.* **1** [I] ENG. LANG. ARTS if a word inflects, its form changes according to its meaning or use **2** [I,T] if your voice inflects or if you inflect it, the sound of it becomes higher or lower as you are speaking [**Origin:** 1400–1500 Latin *inflectere*, from *flectere* **to bend**]

in·flect·ed /ɪnˈflɛktɪd/ *adj.* ENG. LANG. ARTS an inflected language contains many words that change their form according to their meaning or use: *German is an inflected language.*

-inflected /ɪnflɛktɪd/ *suffix* [in adjectives] **jazz-inflected/pop-inflected/gospel-inflected etc.** influenced by jazz, pop music etc.: *a reggae-inflected album*

in·flec·tion /ɪnˈflɛkʃən/ *n.* ENG. LANG. ARTS **1** [U] the way in which a word changes its form to show difference in its meaning or use **2** [C] one of the forms of a word that changes in this way, or one of the parts that is added to it: *The inflections of "run" are "runs," "ran," and "running."* **3** [C,U] the way the sound of your voice goes up and down when you are speaking —**inflectional** *adj.*

in·flex·i·ble /ɪnˈflɛksəbəl/ Ac *adj.* **1** DISAPPROVING unwilling to make even the slightest change in your attitudes or plans etc.: *Some of his employees find him inflexible.* **2** inflexible rules, arrangements etc. are impossible to change: *The proposed law is poorly written and inflexible.* **3** inflexible material is stiff and will not bend —**inflexibility** /ɪnˌflɛksəˈbɪləṭi/ *n.* [U]

in·flict /ɪnˈflɪkt/ *v.* **1** [T] to make someone suffer something bad or painful: **inflict sth on sb/sth** *The hurricane inflicted severe damage on Florida's coast.* **2 inflict yourself on sb** HUMOROUS to visit or be with someone when they do not want you [**Origin:** 1500–1600 Latin, past participle of *infligere*, from *fligere* **to hit**] —**infliction** /ɪnˈflɪkʃən/ *n.* [U]

ˈin-flight *adj.* [only before a noun] provided or happening during an airplane flight: *in-flight movies*

in·flow /ˈɪnfloʊ/ *n.* **1** [C] the movement of people, money, goods etc. into a place OPP **outflow**: *the inflow of foreign investment* **2** [singular,U] the flow of water into a place OPP **outflow**

in·flu·ence¹ /ˈɪnfluəns/ W2 *n.* **1** [C,U] power to have an effect on the way someone or something develops, behaves, or thinks without using direct force or commands: +**on** *the influence of television on sporting events* | +**over** *the unions' influence over local politics* | **have/exert/exercise an influence** *These theories have continued to exert an influence in the scientific community.* | *Senior officials **used their influence to** prevent their own sons from being sent to war.* | *They had come **under the influence of*** (=controlled by the influence of) *a strange religious sect.* **2** [C] someone or something that has an effect on other people or things: **be a bad/good/negative etc. influence (on sb/sth)** *Ruth has been a good influence on Carol.* | *Basically, both sides want to limit any **outside influence*** (=influence from other groups or people) *on the negotiations.* | **musical/cutural/religious etc. influences** *The two regions share cultural influences.* **3 under the influence (of alcohol/drugs etc.)** drunk or feeling the effects of a drug [**Origin:** 1300–1400 French, Medieval Latin *influentia*, from Latin *fluere* **to flow**]

influence² W2 *v.* [T] to have an effect on the way someone or something develops, behaves, thinks etc. without directly forcing or commanding them: *Don't let me influence your decision.* | **strongly/heavily/greatly influence sb/sth** *His writing was greatly influenced by Henry James.* | **influence sb to do sth** *What influenced you to study philosophy?* ▸see THESAURUS box at **persuade**

ˈinfluence-ˌpeddling *n.* [U] when a politician agrees illegally to help someone, support their plans etc. in exchange for money

in·flu·en·tial /ˌɪnfluˈɛnʃəl◂/ *adj.* having a lot of influence and therefore changing the way people think and behave: *an influential book* | **influential in (doing) sth** *Chavez was influential in improving working conditions for farm workers.*

in·flu·en·za /ˌɪnfluˈɛnzə/ *n.* [U] FORMAL the FLU

in·flux /ˈɪnflʌks/ *n.* [C] the arrival of large numbers of people or large amounts of money, goods etc., especially suddenly: +**of** *a huge influx of immigrants*

in·fo /ˈɪnfoʊ/ *n.* [U] INFORMAL information

in·fo·mer·cial /ˈɪnfoʊˌməʃəl/ *n.* [C] a long television advertisement that provides a lot of information about a product and seems like a normal program

in·form /ɪnˈfɔrm/ W3 *v.* [T] **1** to formally or officially tell someone about something or give them information: *Do you think we should inform the police?* | **inform sb about/of sth** *Please inform us of any change of address.* | **inform sb (that)** *I'm sorry to inform you that your application has been rejected.* **2** [usually passive] FORMAL to influence someone's attitude, opinion, or way of doing something: *Her style is informed by the writings of Kafka and Beckett.* [**Origin:** 1300–1400 Old French *enformer*, from Latin *informare* **to give shape to**]

inform on sb *phr. v.* to tell the police information about what someone has done, especially something illegal: *He denied that he had ever informed on his neighbors.*

in·for·mal /ɪnˈfɔrməl/ *adj.* **1** relaxed and friendly without being restricted by rules of correct behavior: *The atmosphere at work is fairly informal.* | *an informal occasion* **2** not done or made officially or publicly: *informal peace talks* | *The group met* ***on an informal basis*** *until last year.* **3** informal clothes are appropriate for wearing at home or in ordinary situations SYN **casual** **4** ENG. LANG. ARTS an informal style of writing or speaking is appropriate for ordinary conversations or letters to friends: *informal speech* —**informally** *adv.* —**informality** /ˌɪnfɔrˈmæləṭi/ *n.* [U]

inˌformal aˈmendment *n.* [U] LAW POLITICS the process by which the government and judges change their understanding of the Constitution over time, without actually changing the words of the Constitution → see also FORMAL AMENDMENT

in·form·ant /ɪnˈfɔrmənt/ *n.* [C] someone who secretly tells the police, the army, the government etc. about criminal activities, especially in return for money: *an FBI informant*

in·for·ma·tion /ˌɪnfəˈmeɪʃən/ S1 W1 *n.* **1** [U] facts or details that tell you something about a situation, person, event etc.: *I need more information before I make a decision.* | +**about/on** *Do you have any information about hotels in the area?* | *I have a useful* ***piece of information*** *for you.* | **further/additional information** *For further information, call the number below.* | *Your travel agent can* ***provide*** *you with more* ***information*** *about visas.* | **gather/collect information** *Surveys are good for gathering information about your customers.* **2** [U] the telephone service that you can call to get someone's telephone number **3 for your information** ABBREVIATION **FYI** SPOKEN used when you are telling someone that they are wrong about a particular fact: *For your information, he really was sick yesterday.* **4** [U] LAW a formal statement made by a PROSECUTOR that says someone is probably guilty of a crime, which does not involve a GRAND JURY —**informational** *adj.* → see also **inside information** at INSIDE[4] (2)

inforˌmational ˈdocument *n.* [C] ENG. LANG. ARTS writing that describes or gives more information about something, such as a report, a JOURNAL, or a TRANSCRIPT → CONSUMER DOCUMENT, FUNCTIONAL DOCUMENT, PUBLIC DOCUMENT, WORKPLACE DOCUMENT

inforˈmation ˌcenter *n.* [C] a place where you can get information about an area, event etc.

inforˈmation reˌtrieval *n.* [U] COMPUTERS the process of finding stored information, especially on a computer

ˌinformation ˈscience *n.* [U] the science of collecting, arranging, storing, and sending out information

ˌinformation ˈsuperhighway *n.* **the information superhighway** OLD-FASHIONED the Internet

inforˈmation techˌnology ABBREVIATION **IT** *n.* [U] COMPUTERS the study or use of electronic processes for gathering information, storing it, and making it available, using computers

inforˈmation ˌtheory *n.* [U] MATH the mathematical principles relating to sending and storing information

in·form·a·tive /ɪnˈfɔrməṭɪv/ *adj.* providing many useful facts or ideas: *an informative lecture* —**informatively** *adv.* —**informativeness** *n.* [U]

in·formed /ɪnˈfɔrmd/ *adj.* **1** [usually before noun] having a lot of knowledge or information about a particular subject or situation: *An informed public is important for a democracy to survive.* | **well-informed/ill-informed/badly informed etc.** *well-informed sources* **2 an informed decision/choice/recommendation etc.** a decision, choice etc. that is based on knowledge of a subject or situation: *Parents must make informed choices about what their children watch on TV.* **3 keep sb informed** to give someone the latest news and details about a situation: *Please keep me fully informed of any new developments.*

in·form·er /ɪnˈfɔrmə/ *n.* [C] someone who secretly tells the police, the army etc. about criminal activities, especially in return for money SYN **informant**

in·fo·tain·ment /ˌɪnfoʊˈteɪnmənt/ *n.* [U] television programs that deal with important subjects in a way that people can enjoy

infra- /ɪnfrə/ *prefix* TECHNICAL below and beyond something in a range → see also ULTRA-: *an infrared camera* (=that can see things below red in the color range)

in·frac·tion /ɪnˈfrækʃən/ *n.* [C,U + of] FORMAL an act of breaking a rule or law

in·fra·red /ˌɪnfrəˈrɛd◂ / *adj.* infrared light gives out heat but cannot be seen → see also ULTRAVIOLET

ˌinfrared radiˈation *n.* [U] PHYSICS energy in the form of waves that you cannot see, which are longer than waves of light that we can see and shorter than radio waves: *The dark areas of the surface give off more infrared radiation.*

in·fra·son·ic /ˌɪnfrəˈsɑnɪk◂ / *adj.* PHYSICS relating to sound that is too low for humans to hear, below 20 HERTZ: *Some animals use sounds in the infrasonic range.*

in·fra·struc·ture /ˈɪnfrəˌstrʌktʃə/ Ac *n.* [C] the basic systems and structures that a country or organization needs in order to work well, for example roads, communications, and banking systems: *The country's infrastructure was badly damaged during the war.* —**infrastructural** *adj.*

in·fre·quent /ɪnˈfrikwənt/ *adj.* not happening often SYN **rare**: *Rain is infrequent in this region of the world.* —**infrequently** *adv.* —**infrequency** *n.* [U]

in·fringe /ɪnˈfrɪndʒ/ *v.* [T] to do something that is against a law or that limits someone's legal rights: *The court ruled that he had infringed the company's patent.* —**infringement** *n.* [C,U]

infringe on/upon sth *phr. v.* to limit someone's freedom in some way: *The students argued that the rule infringed on their right to free speech.*

in·fu·ri·ate /ɪnˈfyʊriˌeɪt/ *v.* [T] to make someone extremely angry: *Her racist attitudes infuriated her co-workers.* —**infuriated** *adj.*

in·fu·ri·at·ing /ɪnˈfyʊriˌeɪṭɪŋ/ *adj.* extremely annoying: *He has some infuriating habits.* —**infuriatingly** *adv.*

in·fuse /ɪnˈfyuz/ *v.* **1** [T] FORMAL to fill someone or something with a particular feeling or quality: **infuse sb/sth with sth** *The program has infused kids with new hope.* | *Her books are infused with humor and wisdom.* **2** [I,T] if you infuse tea or HERBS or if they infuse, you leave them in very hot water while their taste passes into the water

in·fu·sion /ɪnˈfyuʒən/ *n.* **1** [C,U] the act of putting a new feeling or quality into something: *What the department needs is an infusion of new ideas.* **2** [C] MEDICINE a medicine made with HERBS in hot water and usually taken as a drink **3** [C,U] MEDICINE the process of giving a patient a liquid through a tube to feed or treat them, or the liquid itself

-ing /ɪŋ/ *suffix* [added to verbs] **1** [in verbs and adjectives]

used to form the present participle of verbs: *She is laughing.* | *an interesting story* **2** [in U nouns] used to describe the action or process of doing something: *She hates swimming.* | *No parking.* **3** [in C nouns] **a)** used to describe an example of doing something: *a meeting* **b)** used to describe a product or result of doing something: *a beautiful painting* **4** [in nouns] used to describe something used for making or doing something: *a silk lining* (=fabric for the inside of clothes) | *underground piping* (=pipes used to carry water away)

Inge /ɪndʒ/, **William** (1913–1973) a U.S. writer of plays

in·ge·nious /ɪn'dʒinyəs/ *adj.* **1** an ingenious plan, idea, INVENTION etc. works well and is the result of intelligent thinking and new ideas: *an ingenious marketing strategy* **2** very good at inventing things or thinking of new ideas [**Origin:** 1400–1500 French *ingénieux*, from Latin *ingenium* **natural ability**] —**ingeniously** *adv.*

in·gé·nue /'ændʒənu, 'ɑnʒə-/ *n.* [C] a young inexperienced girl, especially in a movie or play

in·ge·nu·i·ty /ˌɪndʒə'nuəṭi/ *n.* [U] skill at inventing things and thinking of new ideas

in·gen·u·ous /ɪn'dʒɛnyuəs/ *adj.* FORMAL an ingenuous person trusts people too much and is honest, especially because they do not have experience in how badly people can behave OPP **disingenuous** —**ingenuously** *adv.* —**ingenuousness** *n.* [U]

in·gest /ɪn'dʒɛst/ *v.* [T] TECHNICAL to take food into your body —**ingestion** /ɪn'dʒɛstʃən/ *n.* [U] → see also DIGEST

in·gle·nook /'ɪŋgəlˌnʊk/ *n.* [C] a seat by the side of a large open FIREPLACE, or the space that it is in

in·glo·ri·ous /ɪn'glɔriəs/ *adj.* LITERARY causing shame and dishonor: *an inglorious defeat* —**ingloriously** *adv.*

in·got /'ɪŋgət/ *n.* [C] a LUMP of pure metal in a regular shape, usually shaped like a brick

in·grained /ɪn'greɪnd, 'ɪngreɪnd/ *adj.* **1** ingrained attitudes or behavior are firmly established and therefore difficult to change: *deeply ingrained religious beliefs* **2** ingrained dirt is under the surface of something and very difficult to remove

in·grate /'ɪngreɪt/ *n.* [C] FORMAL someone who is ungrateful

in·gra·ti·ate /ɪn'greɪʃiˌeɪt/ *v.* DISAPPROVING **ingratiate yourself (with sb)** to try hard to get someone's approval, by doing things to please them, expressing admiration etc.

in·gra·ti·at·ing /ɪn'greɪʃiˌeɪṭɪŋ/ *adj.* DISAPPROVING trying too hard to get someone's approval: *an ingratiating smile* —**ingratiatingly** *adv.*

in·grat·i·tude /ɪn'grætəˌtud/ *n.* [U] the quality of not being grateful for something: *They were shocked by her ingratitude.*

in·gre·di·ent /ɪn'gridiənt/ W3 *n.* [C] **1** one of the different types of foods that you use to make a particular dish: *The main ingredient was ground pork.* | *Add the* ***dry ingredients*** (=flour, SPICES etc.) *to the egg mixture.* **2** a quality you need to achieve something: **a key/a vital/an essential ingredient** *Imagination and hard work are the key ingredients of success.* | *Powell* ***has all the ingredients of*** *a great player.* [**Origin:** 1400–1500 Latin, present participle of *ingredi*, from *gradi* **to go**]

In·gres /'æŋgrə/, **Jean Au·guste Dom·i·nique** /ʒɑn oʊ'gust dɑmɪ'nik/ (1780–1867) a French PAINTER famous for his pictures of people

in·gress /'ɪngrɛs/ *n.* [U] LITERARY the right to enter a place, or the act of entering it OPP **egress**

'in-group *n.* [C] a small group of people in an organization or activity who are popular or have influence, and who are friendly with each other but do not want other people to join them SYN **clique** —**in-group** *adj.*

in·grown /'ɪngroʊn/ *adj.* [no comparative] an ingrown TOENAIL or FINGERNAIL grows inward, cutting into the surrounding skin

in·hab·it /ɪn'hæbɪt/ *v.* [T] if animals or people inhabit an area or place, they live there: *The site was once inhabited by the Ohlone Indians.* —**inhabitable** *adj.*

in·hab·it·ant /ɪn'hæbəṭənt/ *n.* [C] one of the people who live in a particular place: *a city of six million inhabitants*

in·ha·lant /ɪn'heɪlənt/ *n.* [C,U] MEDICINE a medicine or drug that you breathe in, for example when you have a cold or ASTHMA

in·hale /ɪn'heɪl/ *v.* [I,T] to breathe in air, smoke, or gas OPP **exhale**: *It was later determined that Burke had inhaled poisonous fumes.* | *Myra lit another cigarette and* ***inhaled deeply*** (=inhaled a lot of smoke). —**inhalation** /ˌɪnhə'leɪʃən/ *n.* [C,U]

in·hal·er /ɪn'heɪlɚ/ *n.* [C] MEDICINE a small plastic tube containing medicine that you inhale in order to make breathing easier

in·here /ɪn'hɪr/ *v.*

inhere in sth *phr. v.* LITERARY to be a natural part of something

in·her·ent /ɪn'hɪrənt, -'hɛr-/ Ac *adj.* a quality that is inherent in something is a natural part of it and cannot be separated from it: *Dance is an inherent part of the culture.* | +**in** *risks inherent in starting a small business* —**inherently** *adv.*

inˌherent 'powers *n.* [plural] POLITICS the powers given to the U.S government that are not clearly stated in the CONSTITUTION, but which are accepted as necessary in order for the United States to be a completely independent country → see also DELEGATED POWERS, EXPRESSED POWERS, IMPLIED POWERS

in·her·it /ɪn'hɛrɪt/ *v.* **1** [I,T] to receive money, property etc. from someone after they have died → see also DISINHERIT: **inherit sth from sb** *She inherited the money from her mother.* **2** [T] BIOLOGY to get a quality, type of behavior, appearance etc. from one of your parents: **inherit sth from sb** *Janice inherited her good looks from her mom.* **3** [T] to have a problem that was caused by mistakes that other people have made in the past: **inherit sth from sb** *I inherited this mess from the previous manager.* **4** [T] INFORMAL to get something from someone else who does not want it any longer: **inherit sth from sb** *We inherited the furniture from the last owners.*

in·her·i·tance /ɪn'hɛrɪṭəns/ *n.* **1** [C,U] money, property etc. that you receive from someone after they have died, or the process of receiving it: *Garth he just lives off his inheritance from his aunt.* **2** [C,U] BIOLOGY physical and mental qualities that you inherit from your family: *genetic inheritance* **3** [U] FORMAL ideas, beliefs, skills, literature, music etc. from the past that influence people in the present: *our literary inheritance*

in'heritance ˌtax *n.* [U] ECONOMICS a tax on the money or property that you receive from someone after they die

in·her·i·tor /ɪn'hɛrɪṭɚ/ *n.* [C] someone who receives money, property etc. from someone else after that person has died

in·hib·it /ɪn'hɪbɪt/ Ac *v.* [T] **1** to prevent something from growing or developing as much as it might have: *An unhappy family life may inhibit children's learning.* **2** to make someone feel embarrassed or less confident so that they cannot do or say what they want to: **inhibit sb from doing sth** *Taping the meeting might inhibit people from expressing their opinions.* **3** to make it more difficult or impossible for someone to do something: **inhibit sb from doing sth** *His handicap doesn't inhibit him from working.* [**Origin:** 1400–1500 Latin, past participle of *inhibere* **to prevent**, from *habere* **to have**]

in·hib·it·ed /ɪn'hɪbɪṭɪd/ Ac *adj.* not confident or relaxed enough to do or say what you want to: *You shouldn't* ***feel inhibited*** *about asking questions.*

in·hi·bi·tion /ˌɪnhɪ'bɪʃən, ˌɪnə-/ Ac *n.* **1** [C,U] a feeling of worry or embarrassment that stops you from doing or saying what you really want to: *People* ***lose their inhibitions*** *when they're chatting on the Internet.*

2 [singular,U] TECHNICAL the process of restricting something or preventing it from happening or developing: *the inhibition of cell growth*

in·hib·i·tor /ɪnˈhɪbɪt̬ɚ/ *n.* [C] CHEMISTRY something that stops the chemical change that would normally happen when two or more substances are mixed together, or that makes it happen more slowly

in·hos·pi·ta·ble /ˌɪnhɑˈspɪt̬əbəl/ *adj.* **1** an inhospitable place is difficult to live or stay in because of severe weather conditions or lack of shelter: *an inhospitable climate* **2** unfriendly to a visitor, especially by not welcoming them, not offering them food etc.

ˌin-ˈhouse *adj.* within a company or organization rather than outside it: *an in-house training program* **—in house** *adv.*: *All of our product design is done in house.*

in·hu·man /ɪnˈhyumən/ **1** very cruel and not showing any care about other people's suffering: *cruel and inhuman treatment* | *Torture is inhuman.* **2** lacking any human qualities in a way that seems strange or frightening: *cold, inhuman eyes*

in·hu·mane /ˌɪnhyuˈmeɪn/ *adj.* treating people or animals in a cruel and unacceptable way: *the inhumane treatment of prisoners* **—inhumanely** *adv.*

in·hu·man·i·ty /ˌɪnhyuˈmænəti/ *n.* [C usually plural,U] cruel behavior or acts of extreme cruelty: *the inhumanity of the slave trade*

in·im·i·cal /ɪˈnɪmɪkəl/ *adj.* **1** making it difficult for something to exist or happen: *a cold, inimical climate* | **+to** *Price controls are inimical to economic growth.* **2** very unfriendly or hostile

in·im·i·ta·ble /ɪˈnɪmət̬əbəl/ *adj.* too good or skillful for anyone else to copy with the same high standard: *an inimitable comedic style* → see also IMITATE

in·iq·ui·tous /ɪˈnɪkwət̬əs/ *adj.* FORMAL very unfair and morally wrong: *an iniquitous system of taxes*

in·iq·ui·ty /ɪˈnɪkwət̬i/ *n. plural* **iniquities** [C,U] FORMAL the quality of being very unfair or evil, or an action that is very unfair or evil → see also **den of iniquity** at DEN (5)

i·ni·tial¹ /ɪˈnɪʃəl/ Ac S3 W3 *adj.* [only before noun] happening at the beginning of a plan, process, situation etc. SYN **first**: *Initial sales figures have been very good.* | **the initial stage/phase/period** *the initial stages of the disease* [**Origin:** 1500–1600 Latin *initialis*, from *initium* **beginning**, from *inire* **to go in**]

initial² Ac *n.* [C] the first letter of someone's or something's name: *Nancy's initials are N.O.H.*

initial³ Ac *v.* [T] to write your initials on a document to make it official or to show that you have seen it or agree with it: *Initial any corrections you make to the form.*

in·i·tial·ly /ɪˈnɪʃəli/ Ac W3 *adv.* at the beginning of a plan, process, situation etc. SYN **at first**: *Stan initially wanted to go to medical school.*

iˌnitial ˌpublic ˌoffering *n.* [C] an IPO

iˌnitial ˈside also **ˌinitial ˌside of an ˈangle** *n.* [C] MATH the side or line from which the measurement of an angle begins → see also TERMINAL SIDE

i·ni·ti·ate¹ /ɪˈnɪʃiˌeɪt/ Ac *v.* [T] **1** FORMAL to arrange for something to start, such as an official process or a new plan: *They have initiated legal proceedings.* **2** to introduce someone to special knowledge or skills that they did not know about before: **initiate sb into sth** *My grandmother initiated me into the mysteries of quilting.* **3** to introduce someone into an organization, club, group etc., usually with a special ceremony: *Sororities and fraternities are initiating new members this week.*

i·ni·ti·ate² /ɪˈnɪʃiɪt/ Ac *n.* [C] someone who has been allowed to join a particular group and has been taught its secrets

in·i·ti·a·tion /ɪˌnɪʃiˈeɪʃən/ Ac *n.* [C,U] **1** the process of officially introducing someone into a club or group, or of introducing a young person to adult life, often with a special ceremony: **+into** *traditional initiations into manhood* | *an initiation ceremony* **2** the act of starting something such as an official process, a new plan etc.: **+of** *the initiation of criminal prosecution*

i·ni·tia·tive /ɪˈnɪʃət̬ɪv/ Ac W2 *n.* **1** [U] the ability to make decisions and take action without waiting for someone to tell you what to do: *Employers look for workers who* ***show initiative****.* | *They were* ***acting on their own initiative*** (=without being told to do it) *when they reorganized the office.* | *Don't keep asking me for advice.* ***Use your initiative****.* **2** [C] an important new plan or process that has been started in order to achieve a particular aim or to solve a particular problem: *a government initiative to help exporters* **3** [C] LAW a process by which ordinary citizens can suggest a change in the law by signing a PETITION asking for the change to be voted on **4 the initiative** if you have or take the initiative, you are able to take actions that will influence events or a situation, especially in order to change a situation or gain an advantage for yourself: *Parents at the school* ***took the initiative*** *to raise money for a music program.* | *The rebels have* ***seized the initiative*** *and launched a counterattack.*

in·ject /ɪnˈdʒɛkt/ *v.* [T] **1** MEDICINE to put liquid, especially a drug, into someone's body by using a special needle: **inject sth into sb/sth** *The drug was injected into his arm.* | **inject sb with sth** *She has to inject herself with insulin daily.* **2** to improve something by adding excitement, interest etc. to it: **inject sth into sth** *Jen has injected new energy into the office.* **3** to provide more money, equipment etc. for something: **inject sth into sth** *They will inject at least $600,000 into the local economy.* [**Origin:** 1500–1600 Latin, past participle of *inicere*, from *jacere* **to throw**]

in·jec·tion /ɪnˈdʒɛkʃən/ *n.* **1** [C,U] MEDICINE an act of giving a drug by using a special needle: *The nurse* ***gave*** *me* ***an injection*** *and some pills.* | **+of** *an injection of morphine* **2** [C,U] the act of forcing a liquid into something: *a fuel-injection engine* **3** [C] an addition of money to something in order to improve it: **+of** *an injection of public funds*

ˈin-joke *n.* [C] a joke that is only understood by a particular group of people

in·ju·di·cious /ˌɪndʒuˈdɪʃəs/ *adj.* FORMAL an injudicious action, remark etc. is not sensible and is likely to have bad results: *an injudicious investment* **—injudiciously** *adv.*

in·junc·tion /ɪnˈdʒʌŋkʃən/ *n.* [C] **1** LAW an order given by a court which forbids someone to do something: **+against** *The family is seeking an injunction against the book's publication.* **2** FORMAL a piece of advice or a command from someone in authority

in·jure /ˈɪndʒɚ/ Ac W3 *v.* [T] **1** to hurt someone or yourself, for example in an accident or an attack: *He injured his leg playing football.* | **badly/severely/critically injure** *Two men were severely injured in the accident.* ►see THESAURUS box at **hurt¹** **2 injure sb's pride/self-esteem/reputation etc.** to cause someone harm by hurting their feelings, damaging their reputation, etc. → see also WOUND

in·jured /ˈɪndʒɚd/ Ac *adj.* **1** having an injury: *an injured bird* | **badly/severely/seriously injured** *He does not seem to be badly injured.* **2 an injured look/expression etc.** LITERARY a look that shows you feel you have been treated unfairly **3 injured pride/feelings etc.** a feeling of being upset or offended because you think you have been unfairly treated **4 the injured party** FORMAL the person who has been unfairly treated in a particular situation **—the injured** *n.* [plural] *Many of the injured are still in a serious condition.*

ˈinjured list *n.* the DISABLED LIST

in·ju·ri·ous /ɪnˈdʒʊriəs/ *adj.* FORMAL causing injury, harm, or damage

in·ju·ry /ˈɪndʒəri/ Ac W2 *n. plural* **injuries** [C,U] a wound or damage to part of your body caused by an accident or attack: *Smith has missed several games because of injury.* | **+to** *an injury to the shoulder* | **a minor/serious/severe injury** *She was treated in hospital for minor injuries.* | **suffer/sustain an injury** *Ras-*

mussen sustained head and neck injuries in the crash. | *Three of the passengers have* ***internal injuries*** (=injuries inside their bodies). [**Origin:** 1300–1400 Latin *injuria*, from *jus* **right, law**] → see also **add insult to injury** at ADD (6)

THESAURUS

wound an injury, especially a deep cut made in your skin by a knife or bullet
bruise a black or blue mark on your skin that you get when you fall or get hit
cut the small wound you get if a sharp object cuts your skin
scrape a mark or slight injury caused by rubbing your skin against a rough surface
sprain an injury to a joint in your body, caused by suddenly twisting it
bump an area of skin that is swollen because you have hit it on something
fracture a crack or broken part in a bone

in·jus·tice /ɪnˈdʒʌstɪs/ *n.* **1** [C,U] a situation in which people are treated very unfairly and not given their rights: *racial injustice* **2 do sb an injustice** to treat someone or judge their character or abilities unfairly: *To call yourself a bad cook is to do yourself a great injustice.*

ink¹ /ɪŋk/ *n.* **1** [C,U] colored liquid used for writing, printing, or drawing **2** [U] BIOLOGY the black liquid in an ocean creature such as an OCTOPUS or SQUID [**Origin:** 1200–1300 Old French *enque*, from Late Latin *encaustum*, from Greek *enkaiein* **to burn in**] → see also RED INK

ink² *v.* [T] **1** to put ink on something **2** OLD-FASHIONED to write something in ink, especially your SIGNATURE on a contract etc.

ink sth **in** *phr. v.* to complete something done in pencil by drawing over it in ink

ink·blot /ˈɪŋkblɑt/ *n.* [C] a pattern made by a drop of ink on a piece of paper, especially used in PSYCHOLOGICAL tests

ˌin-kind ˈbenefit *n.* [C usually plural] **1** also **in-kind income** [U] ECONOMICS any goods or services that you receive for free or at a much lower price than normal, including things such as public schools, roads, or money a government gives to people who are poor or sick **2** also **benefit in kind** something other than money that an employer gives to a worker instead of his or her normal pay, for example a company car

ink·jet print·er /ˈɪŋkdʒɛt ˌprɪntɚ/ *n.* [C] a type of electronic PRINTER that forms letters by spraying small streams of ink on the paper

ink·ling /ˈɪŋklɪŋ/ *n.* **have an inkling** to have a slight idea about something: *I had an inkling that he would change jobs.*

ˈink pad *n.* [C] a small box containing ink on a thick piece of cloth, used for putting ink onto a STAMP that is then pressed onto paper

ink·stand /ˈɪŋkstænd/ *n.* [C] a container used for holding pens and pots of ink, kept on a desk

ink·well /ˈɪŋk-wɛl/ *n.* [C] a container that holds ink and fits into a hole in a desk, used especially in past times

ink·y /ˈɪŋki/ *adj.* *comparative* **inkier**, *superlative* **inkiest** **1** very dark: *clouds of inky black smoke* **2** marked with ink: *inky fingers*

in·laid /ˈɪnleɪd, ɪnˈleɪd/ *adj.* **1** an inlaid box, table, floor etc. has a thin layer of another material set into its surface for decoration: **+with** *a belt inlaid with diamonds and rubies* **2 +in/into** metal, stone etc. that is inlaid into the surface of another material is set into its surface as decoration

in·land¹ /ˈɪnlənd/ *adj.* [only before noun] an inland area, city etc. is not near the coast

in·land² /ɪnˈlænd, ˈɪnlænd/ *adv.* in a direction away from the coast and toward the center of a country: *The mountains are five miles inland.*

inland delta

ˌinland ˈdelta *n.* [C] EARTH SCIENCE an area of low wet land that is not near the sea, where a river spreads into many smaller rivers, streams, and lakes

ˌinland ˈsea *n.* [C] EARTH SCIENCE a sea that is completely surrounded by land

ˈin-laws *n.* [plural] INFORMAL your relatives by marriage, especially the father and mother of your husband or wife: *My in-laws are coming to visit next week.*

in·lay /ˈɪnleɪ/ *n.* **1** [C,U] a material that has been set into the surface of furniture, floors etc. for decoration, or the pattern made by this: *a box with mother-of-pearl inlay* **2** [C] a substance used by a DENTIST to fill a hole in a decayed tooth

in·let /ˈɪnlɛt, ˈɪnlət/ *n.* [C] **1** EARTH SCIENCE a narrow area of water reaching from an ocean or a lake into the land or between islands **2** the part of a machine through which liquid or gas flows in

ˌin-line ˈskate *n.* [C usually plural] a special boot with a single row of wheels attached under it → see also ROLLERBLADE, ROLLER SKATE → see picture at SKATE¹

ˌin-line ˈskating *n.* [U] the sport of using in-line skates to move quickly over roads, streets etc.

in lo·co pa·ren·tis /ɪn ˌloʊkoʊ pəˈrɛntɪs/ *adv.* LAW having the responsibilities of a parent for someone else's child

in·mate /ˈɪnmeɪt/ *n.* [C] someone who is kept in a prison or MENTAL HOSPITAL

in me·mo·ri·am /ɪn məˈmɔriəm/ *prep.* an expression meaning "in memory of," used especially on the stone above a grave

in·most /ˈɪnmoʊst/ also **in·ner·most** /ˈɪnɚmoʊst/ *adj.* [only before noun] **1** your inmost feelings, desires etc. are the ones you feel most strongly about and usually do not talk about **2** FORMAL farthest inside OPP **outermost**

inn /ɪn/ *n.* [C] **1** a word used in the names of some hotels and restaurants: *We're staying at the Ramada Inn.* **2** a small hotel, especially one in the country ▸see THESAURUS box at **hotel**

in·nards /ˈɪnɚdz/ *n.* [plural] INFORMAL **1** the parts inside your body, especially your stomach **2** the parts inside a machine

in·nate /ˌɪˈneɪt◂/ *adj.* an innate quality is part of a person's character from the time they are born: *He has an innate sense of fairness.* —**innately** *adv.*

ˌinnate beˈhavior *n.* [U] BIOLOGY the ways that an animal or person does things from the time they are first born, which they do naturally without learning to behave in this way

in·ner /ˈɪnɚ/ W3 *adj.* [only before noun]
1 INSIDE on the inside or close to the center of something OPP **outer**: *an inner room*
2 FEELINGS thoughts or feelings that you feel at a very basic level but do not always show to other people: *I've had to rely on my inner strength to weather the rumors.*

3 HIDDEN relating to things that happen or exist but are not easy to see: *the inner workings of a bank*
4 inner circle the few people in an organization, political party etc. who control it or share power with its leader: *the president's inner circle*
5 sb's inner voice thoughts or feelings that someone does not express but which seem to warn or advise them: *My inner voice told me to be cautious.*
6 sb's inner child the part of someone's character that still feels like a child even though they are an adult
7 the inner man/woman the soul
[**Origin:** Old English *innera*, from *inne* **inside**]

ˌinner 'city *n. plural* **inner cities** [C] the part of a city near the middle, where usually the buildings are in a bad condition and the people are poor —**inner-city** *adj.*: *inner-city schools*

ˌinner 'ear *n.* [C] BIOLOGY the part of your ear inside your head that you use for hearing and balance

'inner tube *n.* [C] the rubber tube filled with air that is inside a tire

'inner-ˌtubing *n.* [U] **go inner-tubing** to ride on an inner tube either on water or down a snow-covered hill

in·nie /'ɪni/ *n.* [C] INFORMAL a BELLY BUTTON that does not stick out → see also OUTIE

in·ning /'ɪnɪŋ/ *n.* [C] one of the nine playing periods in a game of baseball or SOFTBALL

inn·keep·er /'ɪnˌkipɚ/ *n.* [C] OLD USE someone who owns or manages an INN

in·no·cence /'ɪnəsəns/ *n.* [U] **1** LAW the fact of being not guilty of a crime OPP **guilt**: *He was unable to* ***prove his innocence.*** | *Both defendants* ***maintained their innocence*** (=continued to say they were not guilty). **2** the state of not having much experience of life or knowledge about evil in the world: *the innocence of childhood*

I

in·no·cent¹ /'ɪnəsənt/ *adj.* **1** LAW not guilty of a crime OPP **guilty**: *Nobody believes that she's innocent.* | **+of** *Nathan's lawyer says his client is innocent of any wrongdoing.* | *The jury* ***found*** *him* ***innocent*** *of dealing drugs.* **2 an innocent victim/bystander/person etc.** someone who gets hurt or killed in a war or as a result of a crime, though they are not involved in it **3** done or said without intending to harm or offend anyone: *an innocent mistake* **4** not having much experience of life, so that you are easily deceived SYN **naive**: *I was thirteen years old and very innocent.* [**Origin:** 1300–1400 French, Latin, from *nocens* **evil**, present participle of *nocere* **to harm**] —**innocently** *adv.*

innocent² *n.* [C] someone who does not have much experience about life or knowledge about evil in the world: *He's such an innocent; anyone can take advantage of him.*

in·noc·u·ous /ɪ'nɑkyuəs/ *adj.* not offensive, dangerous, or harmful: *an innocuous comment* —**innocuously** *adv.*

in·no·vate /'ɪnəˌveɪt/ Ac *v.* [I] to think of and begin to use new ideas, methods, or inventions: *Their ability to innovate has allowed them to compete in world markets.*

in·no·va·tion /ˌɪnə'veɪʃən/ Ac *n.* **1** [C] a new idea, method, or invention: *Anti-lock brakes were a major safety innovation.* **2** [U] the introduction of new ideas, methods, or inventions: *Innovation is one of the cornerstones of this company.*

in·no·va·tive /'ɪnəˌveɪt̬ɪv/ Ac *adj.* **1** an innovative process, method, plan etc. is new, different, and better than those that existed before **2** using or inventing good new ideas and methods: *an innovative young man*

in·no·va·tor /'ɪnəˌveɪt̬ɚ/ Ac *n.* [C] someone who introduces changes and new ideas

in·nu·en·do /ˌɪnyu'ɛndoʊ/ *n. plural* **innuendoes** or **innuendos** [C,U] a remark that suggests something sexual or unpleasant without saying it directly, or these remarks in general: *The play is full of* ***sexual innuendoes.***

In·nu·it /'ɪnuɪt/ *n.* another spelling of INUIT

in·nu·mer·a·ble /ɪ'numərəbəl/ *adj.* very many, or too many to be counted: *She has received innumerable get-well cards and flowers.*

in·nu·mer·a·cy /ɪ'numərəsi/ *n.* [U] the inability to do calculations or understand basic mathematics —**innumerate** *adj.*

in·oc·u·late /ɪ'nɑkyəˌleɪt/ *v.* [T] MEDICINE to protect someone against a disease, usually by INJECTing them with a weak form of it: **inoculate sb against sth** *None of the children had been inoculated against measles.* [**Origin:** 1400–1500 Latin, past participle of *inoculare* **to attach a bud to a plant**] —**inoculation** /ɪˌnɑkyə'leɪʃən/ *n.* [C,U] → see also IMMUNIZE, VACCINATE

in·of·fen·sive /ˌɪnə'fɛnsɪv/ *adj.* unlikely to offend anyone: *His first campaign ads were bland and inoffensive.* —**inoffensively** *adv.*

in·op·er·a·ble /ɪn'ɑpərəbəl/ *adj.* **1** MEDICINE an inoperable illness or TUMOR (=lump) cannot be treated or removed by a medical operation: *an inoperable brain tumor* **2** an inoperable system or method does not work or cannot be used because it is broken or not practical

in·op·er·a·tive /ɪn'ɑpərət̬ɪv/ *adj.* **1** an inoperative machine is not working, or is not in working condition **2** an inoperative system or a law is not working or cannot be made to work

in·op·por·tune /ɪnˌɑpɚ'tun, ˌɪnɑ-/ *adj.* happening at a time that is not appropriate or good for something: *Telemarketers always seem to call at the most inopportune times.*

in·or·di·nate /ɪn'ɔrdn-ɪt/ *adj.* much more than you expect or think is reasonable or normal: *an inordinate number of meetings* —**inordinately** *adv.*

in·or·gan·ic /ˌɪnɔr'gænɪk◂/ *adj.* **1** CHEMISTRY not containing any HYDROCARBONS, or not consisting of anything that is living **2** not produced or allowed to develop in a natural way —**inorganically** /-kli/ *adv.*

ˌinorganic 'chemistry *n.* [U] CHEMISTRY the science and study of substances that do not contain HYDROCARBONS → see also ORGANIC CHEMISTRY

in·pa·tient /'ɪnˌpeɪʃənt/ *n.* [C] someone who stays in a hospital for treatment, rather than coming in for treatment from outside → see also OUTPATIENT

in·put¹ /'ɪnpʊt/ Ac *n.* [C,U] **1** ideas, advice, money, or effort that you put into a job, meeting etc. in order to help it succeed: *We value the input of everyone who answered the questionnaire.* **2** COMPUTERS information that is put into a computer: *What happens on the screen depends on the input.* **3** electrical power that is put into a machine for it to use → see also OUTPUT

input² Ac *v.* **inputted** or **input** [T] COMPUTERS to put information into a computer

in·quest /'ɪnkwɛst/ *n.* [C] **1** LAW a legal process to find out the cause of a sudden or unexpected death, especially if there is a possibility that the death is the result of a crime: *The inquest ruled the cause of death was suicide.* **2** an unofficial discussion about the reasons for a bad situation, especially someone's failure to do something

in·qui·e·tude /ɪn'kwaɪəˌtud/ *n.* [U] LITERARY anxiety

in·quire, enquire /ɪn'kwaɪɚ/ *v.* [I,T] to ask someone for information: *"Why are you doing that?" he inquired.* | **+about** *I am writing to inquire about your advertisement.* | **+of** *"Where's the station?" she inquired of a passer-by.* | **inquire why/whether/how etc.** *It's just human nature to inquire why things went wrong.* [**Origin:** 1200–1300 Old French *enquerre*, from Latin *inquirere*, from *quaerere* **to look for**] —**inquirer** *n.* [C]

inquire after sb *phr. v.* to ask about someone's health, how they are doing etc.: *She inquired after you and Marie.*

inquire into sth *phr. v.* to ask questions in order to get more information about something or to find out why something happened: *Inspectors also inquire into nursing home residents' quality of life.*

in·quir·ing, enquiring /ɪn'kwaɪərɪŋ/ *adj.* [only before noun] **1 an inquiring mind/reader/reporter etc.** someone who has an inquiring mind or is an inquiring reader, REPORTER etc. is naturally very interested in finding out more information or gaining more knowledge **2** an inquiring look or expression shows that you want to ask about something —**inquiringly** *adv.*

in·quir·y, enquiry /ɪnˈkwaɪəri, ˈɪŋkwəri/ *n. plural* **inquiries 1** [C] a question you ask in order to get information: **+about** *Thank you for your recent inquiry about work opportunities in the U.S.* | *I've* ***made*** *some* ***inquiries*** *about air fares.* **2** [C] an official process intended to get information about something or find out why something happened: **+into** *Senior diplomats have ordered an inquiry into the shooting.* | **conduct/hold an inquiry** *Police are conducting a murder inquiry.* | *The EPA agreed to hold a* ***public inquiry****.* **3** [U] the act or process of asking questions in order to get information or find out about something: *On* ***further inquiry****, it became clear that Walters had not been involved.* **4 scientific/scholarly/intellectual etc. inquiry** a process of trying to discover facts by scientific, SCHOLARLY etc. methods

in·qui·si·tion /ˌɪnkwəˈzɪʃən/ *n.* **1 the Inquisition** the Catholic organization in past times whose purpose was to find and punish people who had unacceptable religious beliefs **2** [singular] a series of questions that someone asks you in a way that seems threatening or not nice: *The detectives have turned the investigation into an inquisition.*

in·quis·i·tive /ɪnˈkwɪzət̬ɪv/ *adj.* **1** APPROVING interested in a lot of different things and wanting to find out more about them: *a bright, inquisitive child* **2** DISAPPROVING asking too many questions and trying to find out too many details about something or someone: *Don't be so inquisitive – it makes people uncomfortable.* —**inquisitively** *adv.*

in·quis·i·tor /ɪnˈkwɪzət̬ɚ/ *n.* [C] **1** someone who asks you a lot of difficult questions and makes you feel very uncomfortable **2** an official of the INQUISITION —**inquisitorial** /ɪnˌkwɪzəˈtɔriəl/ *adj.* —**inquisitorially** *adv.*

in re /ɪn ˈri, -ˈreɪ/ *prep.* an expression used especially in business letters that means "concerning" → see also RE[1]

in·roads /ˈɪnroʊdz/ *n.* **make inroads (into/on sth) 1** to become more and more successful, powerful, or popular and so take away power, trade, votes etc. from a competitor or enemy: *Many banks have made inroads into the insurance business.* **2** to make steady progress toward achieving something difficult: *The government claims to have made inroads into the housing problem.*

INS *n.* **the INS the Immigration and Naturalization Service** a former U.S. government department whose work is now done by USCIS

ins /ɪnz/ *n.* **the ins and outs (of sth)** all of the details of something such as a system, profession etc.: *I'm still learning the ins and outs of the import business.*

in·sa·lu·bri·ous /ˌɪnsəˈlubriəs/ *adj.* FORMAL insalubrious conditions or places are dirty or not nice, and are bad for your health

in·sane /ɪnˈseɪn/ S3 *adj.* **1** INFORMAL completely stupid or crazy, often in a way that is dangerous: *The whole idea is insane.* | *Have you* ***gone insane****?* **2** someone who is insane is seriously mentally ill, so that they cannot live in normal society: *The killer was declared criminally insane.* ►see THESAURUS box at **crazy**[1] **3 drive sb insane** INFORMAL to make someone feel more and more annoyed or angry, usually over a long period of time: *The noise from the construction project is driving us insane.* —**insanely** *adv.*: *insanely jealous* —**the insane** *n.* [plural] OLD-FASHIONED: *a hospital for the insane*

in·san·i·tar·y /ɪnˈsænəˌtɛri/ *adj.* UNSANITARY

in·san·i·ty /ɪnˈsænət̬i/ *n.* [U] **1** the state of being seriously mentally ill, so that you cannot live normally in society: *Brennan blames her actions on temporary insanity.* **2** very stupid actions that may cause you serious harm: *It was sheer insanity to try to drive in all that snow.*

in·sa·tia·ble /ɪnˈseɪʃəbəl/ *adj.* always wanting more and more of something: *an insatiable appetite* —**insatiably** *adv.*

in·scribe /ɪnˈskraɪb/ *v.* [T] **1** to carefully cut, print, or write words on something, especially on the surface of a stone or coin: **inscribe sth on/in sth** *The names of the men who had died were inscribed on a plaque.* | **be inscribed with** *The silver cup had been inscribed with his name.* **2 be inscribed in sth a)** MATH if a circle is inscribed in another shape, the circle is inside the shape and each of the sides of the shape share one point with the circle **b)** MATH if a shape is inscribed in a circle, it is inside the circle and its angles are points on the circle

inˌscribed ˈangle *n.* [C] GEOMETRY an angle formed inside a circle when two lines meet at a point on the edge of the circle

inˌscribed ˈrectangle *n.* [C] MATH a RECTANGLE that fits inside a curved line or other shape and can be used to calculate the area inside the curve or shape

in·scrip·tion /ɪnˈskrɪpʃən/ *n.* [C] a piece of writing inscribed on a stone, in the front of a book etc.

in·scru·ta·ble /ɪnˈskrut̬əbəl/ *adj.* **1** someone who is inscrutable shows little emotion or reaction so that it is impossible to know what they are feeling or thinking: *an inscrutable expression* **2** impossible to know or understand —**inscrutability** /ɪnˌskrut̬əˈbɪləti/ *n.* [U]

in·seam /ˈɪnsim/ *n.* [C] a SEAM on the part of a pair of pants that covers the inside of your legs

insects

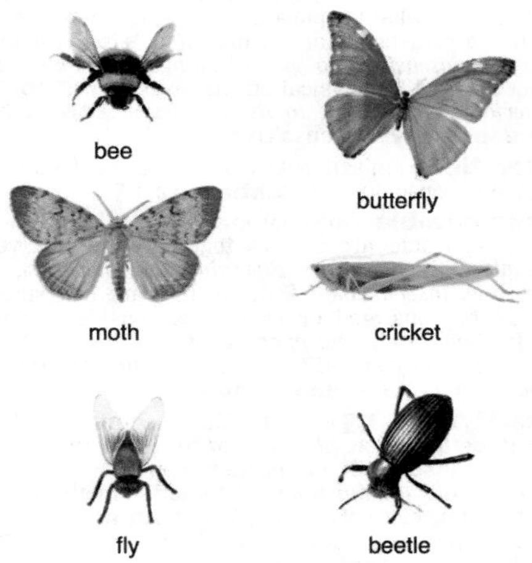

in·sect /ˈɪnsɛkt/ *n.* [C] a small creature such as a fly or ANT, that has six legs, and sometimes wings: *mosquitoes and other flying insects* [**Origin:** 1600–1700 Latin *insectum*, from *insecare* **to cut into**; because insects have a body in separate parts]

in·sec·ti·cide /ɪnˈsɛktəˌsaɪd/ *n.* [U] a chemical substance used for killing insects —**insecticidal** /ɪnˌsɛktəˈsaɪdl/ *adj.* → see also PESTICIDE

in·sec·ti·vore /ɪnˈsɛktəˌvɔr/ *n.* [C] BIOLOGY a creature that eats insects —**insectivorous** /ˌɪnsɛkˈtɪvərəs/ *adj.*

in·se·cure /ˌɪnsɪˈkyʊr/ Ac *adj.* **1** not feeling confident about yourself, your abilities, your relationships etc.: *Meeting new people always makes me feel insecure.* | **+about** *Most teenagers are insecure about their looks.*

THESAURUS

unsure of yourself not very confident about yourself: *She's nervous and unsure of herself.*
lack confidence also **be lacking in confidence** to not believe that you have the ability to do something well: *After eight years out of the workplace, she lacked the confidence to get the job she really wanted.*

2 an insecure job, situation etc. does not give you a feeling of safety, because it is likely to change or be taken away at any time: *The U.S. needs to reduce its dependence on insecure foreign oil supplies.* **3** an insecure building, system, NETWORK etc. is not locked or guarded, so that people can use it without permission: *an insecure computer connection* **4** a building or structure that is insecure is not safe, because it is likely to fall down —**insecurity** *n.* [U] —**insecurely** *adv.*

in·sem·i·nate /ɪnˈsɛməˌneɪt/ *v.* [T] BIOLOGY to put SPERM into a woman or female animal in order to make her have a baby —**insemination** /ɪnˌsɛməˈneɪʃən/ *n.* [U] → see also ARTIFICIAL INSEMINATION

in·sen·sate /ɪnˈsɛnseɪt, -sɪt/ *adj.* FORMAL **1** BIOLOGY not able to feel things **2** unreasonable and crazy: *insensate rage*

in·sen·si·bil·i·ty /ɪnˌsɛnsəˈbɪləṭi/ *n.* [U] **1** FORMAL the state of being unconscious **2** OLD USE inability to experience feelings such as love, sympathy, anger etc.

in·sen·si·ble /ɪnˈsɛnsəbəl/ *adj.* FORMAL **1** not knowing about something that could happen to you SYN **unaware**: +**of** *She remained insensible of the dangers that lay ahead.* **2** unable to feel something or be affected by it: +**to/of** *Doug seemed insensible to the cold.*

in·sen·si·tive /ɪnˈsɛnsəṭɪv/ *adj.* **1** DISAPPROVING not noticing other people's feelings, especially not realizing when something that you do upsets them: *racially insensitive remarks* | +**to** *She's totally insensitive to Jack's feelings.* **2** not paying attention to what is happening or to what people are saying, and therefore not changing your behavior because of it: +**to** *Companies that are insensitive to global change will lose sales.* **3** not affected by physical effects or changes: +**to** *The material is insensitive to light.* —**insensitively** *adv.* —**insensitivity** /ɪnˌsɛnsəˈtɪvəṭi/ *n.* [U]

in·sen·tient /ɪnˈsɛnʃənt/ *adj.* FORMAL not feeling or not being conscious —**insentience** *n.* [U]

in·sep·a·ra·ble /ɪnˈsɛpərəbəl/ *adj.* **1** people who are inseparable are always together and are very friendly with each other: *Ever since they met those two have been inseparable.* **2** things that are inseparable cannot be separated or cannot be considered separately: *Democracy and open debate are inseparable.* | +**from** *The responsibility and long hours are inseparable from the job.* —**inseparably** *adv.*

in·sert¹ /ɪnˈsɚt/ Ac *v.* [T] **1** to put something inside or into something else: *She inserted the video and pushed "play."* | **insert sth in/into/between sth** *Insert two quarters into the machine.* **2** to add something to a document or piece of writing: **insert sth in/into sth** *An extra clause was inserted into the contract.* [**Origin:** 1400–1500 Latin, past participle of *inserere*, from *serere* **to join**]

in·sert² /ˈɪnsɚt/ Ac *n.* [C] **1** a printed page that is put inside a newspaper or magazine in order to advertise something: *Look for the coupon inserts in Sunday's paper.* **2** something that is designed to be put inside something else: *A steel insert must be pushed into the end of the pipe.*

in·ser·tion /ɪnˈsɚʃən/ Ac *n.* **1** [U] the act of putting something inside something else: *the insertion of a hypodermic needle into the vein* **2** [C] something that is added to the middle of a document or piece of writing

ˌin-ˈservice *adj.* **in-service training/courses etc.** training etc. that you do while you are working in a job

in·set¹ /ˈɪnsɛt/ *n.* [C] **1** a small picture, map etc. on a page or larger picture, that shows more detail or information: *The inset on the next page shows the downtown area.* **2** something that is put into the surface of something else, especially as a decoration

in·set² /ˈɪnsɛt, ɪnˈsɛt/ *v. past tense and past participle* **inset** [T] **1** to put something in as an inset on a printed page **2 be inset with sth** if something is inset with decorations, jewels etc., it has them set in its surface

in·shore /ˌɪnˈʃɔr◂/ *adv.* near, toward, or to the shore —**inshore** *adj.*: *inshore currents*

in·side¹ /ɪnˈsaɪd, ˈɪnsaɪd/ S2 W2 also **inˈside of** *prep.*

1 CONTAINER/BUILDING in a container, building, vehicle, room, object etc. OPP **outside**: *There was a card inside the envelope.* | *We were watching **from inside** the car.* | *The ticket office is **just inside** the entrance.*

2 INTO into the inner part of a container, building, room, vehicle, object etc. OPP **out of**: *Carl stuffed the book inside his jacket.* | *They ran inside the house.*

3 COUNTRY/AREA in a country or area SYN **within** OPP **outside**: *Very little is known of events inside this mysterious country.* | *We were attacking targets **deep inside** enemy territory.*

4 ORGANIZATION within an organization or company SYN **within** OPP **outside**: *Sources inside the company said that they plan to move more factories overseas.*

5 HEAD/MIND if something happens inside you, or inside your head or mind, it is part of what you think and feel: *It's not healthy to keep your feelings all locked inside of you.* | *You never know what's going on inside Rob's head.* | *Anger bubbled up **deep inside** her.*

6 BODY in your body: *She could feel the baby kicking inside her.*

7 TIME a) if you do something inside a particular amount of time, it takes you less than that amount of time to do it: *Jonson's time of 9.3 seconds was just inside the world record.* **b)** before a particular amount of time has passed: *I should be back inside of an hour.*

inside² S2 W2 *adv.* **1** in or into something: *The box has some letters inside.* | *I opened the suitcase and looked inside.* **2** in or into a house or other building SYN **indoors** OPP **outside**: *I'm getting cold. Let's go inside.* | *Through the window I could see people inside.* | *We heard a loud crash **from inside**.* **3** if you have a feeling inside, you have the feeling but do not show it to other people: *He felt sick inside.* **4 inside and out** including every part of the inside and outside of something: *They have painted the house inside and out.* → see also **know sth inside (and) out** at KNOW¹ (20)

inside³ S2 *n.* **1 the inside** the inner part of something, which is surrounded or hidden by the outer part OPP **the outside**: *I've seen the outside of the house, but I've never seen the inside.* | +**of** *The inside of the car was dirty.* | *The apple was rotten **on the inside**.* | *The door had been locked **from the inside**.* **2 the inside** the surface of something that faces inward OPP **the outside**: +**of** *He had bruises on the inside of his arm.* | *The window was scratched **on the inside**.* **3 inside out** with the usual outside parts on the inside: *She had her shirt on inside out.* → see also **turn sth inside out** at TURN¹ (2) **4 sb's insides** INFORMAL someone's stomach and other organs: *I laughed until my insides ached.* **5 on the inside a)** someone who is on the inside is a member of a group or an organization: *To have such accurate information, they must have someone on the inside.* **b)** used to say what someone or something is really like when this is different from their appearance: *She's tough on the outside, but soft on the inside* **c)** on the part of a curved RACETRACK that is nearest the center

inside⁴ S3 *adj.* **1** on or facing the inside of something OPP **outside**: *a jacket with an inside pocket* **2** coming from or involving people within an organization: *Police believe the robbers may have had **inside information**.* | *His book tells **the inside story** of the terrorist group.* | *The theft looked like an **inside job*** (=done by people within an organization). **3** in baseball, an inside pitch is a ball thrown unfairly or illegally nearer to the batter than to the bat **4 an inside forward/left/right** games such as soccer or hockey, a player in the forward line who plays between the WINGER and the CENTER, or the position of such a player

in·sid·er /ɪnˈsaɪdɚ/ *n.* [C] someone who has a special knowledge of a particular organization because they are part of it: *a White House insider* → see also OUTSIDER

inˌsider ˈtrading *n.* [U] ECONOMICS the crime of buying and selling company STOCK at a profit using secret information known only by people who work within the company

ˌinside ˈtrack *n.* [C] **1** a position that gives someone an advantage over the people they are competing against: *Another newspaper* ***has the inside track on*** *the story.* **2** the part of a circular track for racing that is nearest to the center of the circle and is therefore shorter

in·sid·i·ous /ɪnˈsɪdiəs/ *adj.* causing serious harm, often in a way that happens slowly and is not immediately noticeable: *an insidious form of water pollution* [**Origin:** 1500–1600 Latin *insidiosus*, from *insidiae* **attack from a hiding-place**] **—insidiously** *adv.* **—insidiousness** *n.* [U]

in·sight /ˈɪnsaɪt/ Ac *n.* **1** [C,U] a very useful understanding of something that you did not have before: *a flash of insight* | +**into** *new insights into how the universe began* | +**about** *The reports provided little insight about the economy's condition.* **2** [U] the ability to understand and realize what people or situations are really like: *a woman of great insight*

ˈinsight ˌlearning *n.* [U] BIOLOGY when a person or animal uses their existing knowledge in order to do something new or deal with a new situation, rather than trying various different methods before finding the best

in·sig·ni·a /ɪnˈsɪgniə/ *n. plural* **insignia** [C] **1** a PATCH or other object that shows someone's military rank, or which group or organization they belong to **2** a sign or mark on something that shows who made it or who it belongs to

in·sig·nif·i·cant /ˌɪnsɪgˈnɪfəkənt/ Ac *adj.* too small or unimportant to consider or worry about: *an insignificant amount of money* | *Sitting alone in the vast desert can make you feel insignificant.* **—insignificantly** *adv.* **—insignificance** *n.* [U]

in·sin·cere /ˌɪnsɪnˈsɪr/ *adj.* expressing something that you do not really feel or think, especially in order to gain an advantage for yourself: *The mayor's sympathy seemed insincere.* | *an insincere smile* **—insincerely** *adv.* **—insincerity** /ˌɪnsɪnˈsɛrət̬i/ *n.* [U]

in·sin·u·ate /ɪnˈsɪnyuˌeɪt/ *v.* [T] **1** to express something negative or unkind, without saying it directly → see also IMPLY: **insinuate that** *He insinuated that Harman was lying.* **2 insinuate yourself into sth** to gradually introduce yourself into a situation, in a way that is not direct or completely honest in order to gain an advantage: *Rogers tried to insinuate herself into the wealthiest social circles.*

in·sin·u·a·tion /ɪnˌsɪnyuˈeɪʃən/ *n.* **1** [C] something that someone insinuates: *an insinuation of sexual harassment* **2** [U] the act of insinuating something

in·sip·id /ɪnˈsɪpɪd/ *adj.* **1** food or drink that is insipid does not have much taste SYN **bland** **2** not interesting, exciting, or attractive: *insipid commercials* [**Origin:** 1600–1700 French *insipide*, from Late Latin *insipidus*, from Latin *sapere* **to taste**] **—insipidly** *adv.* **—insipidness** *n.* [U]

in·sist /ɪnˈsɪst/ S3 W2 *v.* [I,T] **1** to say firmly and often that something is true, especially when other people think it may not be true: **insist (that)** *Mike insisted that he was right.* | *Experts insist there is no chance of a recession in the near future.* | **insist on sth** *She has always insisted on her innocence.* **2** to demand that something should happen and refuse to let anyone say "no": *Let me pay this time.* ***I insist*** (=used to firmly and politely offer to do something). | **insist (that)** *I'm glad my parents insisted that we speak Spanish at home.* | *Bud insisted he drive us home.* | **insist on (sb) doing sth** *He insisted on going with me.* ►see THESAURUS box at **tell** **3 if you insist** SPOKEN used when agreeing to do something that you do not really want to do: *"Let's invite them over for dinner." "OK, if you insist."* [**Origin:** 1500–1600 Latin *insistere* **to stand on, continue with determination**, from *sistere* **to stand**]

insist on (doing) sth *phr. v.* **1** to think that something is very important, and demand that you have it or do it: *The chef insists on the best and freshest ingredients.* **2** to keep doing something, especially something that is inconvenient or annoying: *Tim insists on watching those stupid action movies.*

in·sist·ence /ɪnˈsɪstəns/ *n.* [U] an act of demanding that something should happen and refusing to let anyone say no: **insistence that** *my father's insistence that I find work* | +**on** *Their insistence on a formal apology created tension between the two countries.* | ***At*** *Ms. Taylor's* ***insistence*** (=because she insisted), *an ambulance was called to the store.*

in·sist·ent /ɪnˈsɪstənt/ *adj.* **1** demanding firmly and often that something should happen or that something is true: **insistent that** *The mechanic was insistent that the car could not be repaired.* | +**on** *Grandma was always insistent on going to church on Sunday.* **2** continuing in a way that is difficult to ignore: *The sound grew louder, more insistent.* **—insistently** *adv.*

in si·tu /ɪn ˈsaɪtu, -ˈsɪtu/ *adv.* if something remains in situ, it remains in its usual place

in·so·far as, in so far as /ˌɪnsəˈfɑr əz/ *conjunction* FORMAL to the degree that: *Insofar as they could, my parents helped us with money.*

in·sole /ˈɪnsoʊl/ *n.* [C] a flat piece of cloth, leather etc. on the inside bottom of a shoe

in·so·lent /ˈɪnsələnt/ *adj.* impolite and not showing any respect: *the boy's insolent attitude* **—insolently** *adv.* **—insolence** *n.* [U]

in·sol·u·ble /ɪnˈsɑlyəbəl/ *adj.* **1** an insoluble problem is or seems impossible to solve: *At this point, the crisis appears insoluble.* **2** CHEMISTRY an insoluble substance does not become a liquid when you put it into liquid → see also DISSOLVE

in·solv·a·ble /ɪnˈsɑlvəbəl, -ˈsɔl-/ *adj.* INSOLUBLE

in·sol·vent /ɪnˈsɑlvənt/ *adj.* not having enough money to pay what you owe SYN **bankrupt**: *insolvent businesses* **—insolvency** *n.* [U]

in·som·ni·a /ɪnˈsɑmniə/ *n.* [U] the condition of not being able to sleep

in·som·ni·ac /ɪnˈsɑmniˌæk/ *n.* [C] someone who cannot sleep easily **—insomniac** *adj.*

in·so·much /ˌɪnsoʊˈmʌtʃ/ *adv.* FORMAL **1 insomuch that** to such a degree that **2** another form of the word INASMUCH

in·sou·ci·ance /ɪnˈsusiəns/ *n.* [U] a cheerful feeling of not caring or worrying about anything: *She hid her sadness behind an air of insouciance.* **—insouciant** *adj.* **—insouciantly** *adv.*

in·spect /ɪnˈspɛkt/ Ac *v.* [T] **1** to examine something carefully in order to find out more about it or check that it is satisfactory: *Customs officials inspected my luggage thoroughly.* | **inspect sth for sth** *We hired someone to inspect our roof for leaks.* ►see THESAURUS box at **check**[1] **2** to make an official visit to a building, organization etc. to check that everything is satisfactory and that rules are being obeyed: *Restaurants are inspected at least once a year by the Health Department.* | *General Allen arrived to inspect the troops.*

in·spec·tion /ɪnˈspɛkʃən/ Ac *n.* [C,U] **1** an official visit to a building or organization to check that everything is satisfactory and that rules are being obeyed: *Federal inspection is required for all meat and poultry products.* | +**of** *an annual inspection of the facility* **2** a careful examination of something to find out more about it: +**of** *an inspection of the aircraft for problems* | ***On closer inspection*** (=when she looked more closely), *she realized they were baby rats.*

in·spec·tor /ɪnˈspɛktɚ/ Ac *n.* [C] **1** an official whose job is to check that something is satisfactory and that rules are being obeyed: *the building inspectors* | *a Health Department inspector* **2** a police officer of the second highest rank: *Inspector Blake*

in·spi·ra·tion /ˌɪnspəˈreɪʃən/ *n.* **1** [C,U] a good idea or feelings of enthusiasm that help you do or create something: *Suddenly I had an inspiration!* | *Her* ***inspiration came from*** *early French films.* | *He* ***draws inspiration from*** (=gets ideas from) *scenes of everyday life.* | *When improving your home, magazines can be* ***a source of inspiration.*** | **a flash/moment of inspiration** *The idea came to me in a flash of inspiration.* | *The preacher claimed* ***divine inspiration*** (=inspiration

I

from God) *for his ministry.* ►see THESAURUS box at **idea** **2** [C,U] the place, person etc. that you get ideas from or that encourages you to do something: *My father was my main inspiration.* | **+for/behind** *His childhood in rural Alabama is the inspiration for his stories.* | *Sam Walton* ***is an inspiration to*** *business students everywhere.*

in·spi·ra·tion·al /ˌɪnspəˈreɪʃənəl◂/ *adj.* providing inspiration: *an inspirational speech*

in·spire /ɪnˈspaɪə/ W3 *v.* [T] **1** to encourage someone by making them feel confident and eager to achieve something great: *The country needs a leader who can inspire its citizens.* | **inspire sb to do sth** *My two daughters were inspired to take violin lessons when a friend played for them.* | **inspire sb to sth** *The coach inspired them to victory.* **2** to make someone have a particular feeling or react in a particular way: *Mrs. Pianto was the kind of woman who inspired kindness.* | **inspire sth in sb** *A good teacher inspires a love of learning in children.* **3** to give someone the idea for a story, painting, poem etc.: *The movie was inspired by real events.* **4** TECHNICAL to breathe in SYN **inhale** [**Origin:** 1300–1400 French *inspirer*, from Latin, from *spirare* **to breathe**]

in·spired /ɪnˈspaɪəd/ *adj.* **1** having very exciting special qualities that are better than anyone or anything else: *an inspired performer* | *Dickinson wrote some very inspired poems.* **2 -inspired** used for describing what causes something to happen or where an idea or a style comes from: *colorful 1960s-inspired designs* | *Spanish-inspired architecture* **3 an inspired choice/ guess/move** a very good or impressive choice, guess, or action, especially one that someone made because they had a sudden good idea: *In an inspired move, he hired the new younger director that day.* **4 politically/ divinely/religiously etc. inspired** started for political, divine etc. reasons: *The sergeant's court-martial was politically inspired.*

in·spir·ing /ɪnˈspaɪrɪŋ/ *adj.* giving people energy, a feeling of excitement, and a desire to do something great: *an inspiring success story*

in·sta·bil·i·ty /ˌɪnstəˈbɪləti/ Ac *n.* [U] **1** UNCERTAINTY in a situation that is caused by the possibility of sudden change OPP **stability**: *the instability of the market* | *Political instability in the region could lead to civil war.* **2** mental problems that are likely to cause sudden changes of behavior: *Her mental instability led her to drugs.*

in·stall /ɪnˈstɔl/ W3 *v.* [T] **1** to put a piece of equipment somewhere and connect it so that it is ready to be used: *Lights were installed under the upper cabinets.* | *We're* ***having*** *a new dishwasher* ***installed*** (=paying someone else to install it for you). **2** COMPUTERS to add new software to a computer so that it is ready to use OPP **uninstall**: *Would you like to install your new virus software now?* **3** [usually passive] to put someone in an important job or position, especially with a ceremony: **install sb as sth** *He was soon installed as the club's new president.* **4** to settle yourself somewhere, especially somewhere new, safe, or comfortable [**Origin:** 1400–1500 Old French *installer*, from Medieval Latin, from *stallum* **stall**]

in·stal·la·tion /ˌɪnstəˈleɪʃən/ *n.* **1** [C,U] the act of fitting a piece of equipment somewhere: *the installation of a security system* **2** [C] a place where industrial or military equipment, machinery etc. has been put: *the bombing of a military installation* **3** [C] a piece of equipment that has been fitted in its place: *electrical installations* **4** [C] ENG. LANG. ARTS a piece of modern art that can include objects, light, sound etc. not just painting or sculpture **5** [U] FORMAL the ceremony of putting someone in an important job or position: *the installation of the new government*

in·stall·ment /ɪnˈstɔlmənt/ *n.* [C] **1** one of a series of regular payments, especially ones that you make until you have paid all the money you owe: *We just paid the last installment of our car loan.* | *The club will make its annual donation* ***in two installments*** *of $2,000.* **2** one of the parts of a story that appears as a series in a magazine, newspaper, movie etc. SYN **episode**: *the fourth installment of the western movie series*

inˈstallment ˌplan *n.* [singular, U] a system of paying for goods by making a series of small regular payments

in·stance /ˈɪnstəns/ Ac S2 W2 *n.* **1 for instance** for example: *She's always late. For instance, this morning she didn't come in until 10:30.* **2** [C] an example of a particular type of situation: *The committee found many instances where police officers had lied.* | **+of** *instances of discrimination* | ***In this instance****, I have decided there is not enough evidence to bring the case to court.* **3 in the first instance a)** happening as the first thing in a series of actions: *We must act to prevent pollution in the first instance.* **b)** used when giving the first and most important reason why you think something is true: *In the first instance, I never lie to anyone, especially you.*

in·stant[1] /ˈɪnstənt/ *adj.* **1** happening or produced immediately: *The show was an instant success.* | *We live in an age of instant communication.* **2** [only before noun] instant food, coffee etc. is in the form of powder and is prepared by adding hot water [**Origin:** 1400–1500 French, Latin *instans*, present participle of *instare* **to stand on, be present**]

instant[2] *n.* **1** [C usually singular] a moment: *It took me an instant to recognize who he was.* | *In the desert, dust storms can rise up* ***in an instant*** (=immediately). | ***For an instant*** *I thought we were on the wrong plane.* **2 the instant (that)** as soon as something happens: *The instant I saw the house, I knew we'd live there.* **3 this instant** SPOKEN used when telling someone, especially a child, to do something immediately: *Come here this instant!*

in·stan·ta·ne·ous /ˌɪnstənˈteɪniəs/ *adj.* happening immediately: *Fortunately for him, his death was instantaneous.* —**instantaneously** *adv.*

in·stant·ly /ˈɪnstəntli/ *adv.* immediately: *They recognized him instantly.* | *He knew instantly something was wrong.*

ˌinstant ˈmessaging ABBREVIATION **I.M.** *n.* [U] a system that allows you to communicate with someone using the Internet, receiving messages as soon as they are written —**instant message** *n.* [C]

ˌinstant ˈreplay *n.* [C] the immediate repeating of an important moment in a sports game by showing the film or VIDEOTAPE again

in·stead /ɪnˈstɛd/ S1 W1 *adv., prep.* **1 instead of sth** if you do one thing instead of another thing, you choose to do the first and not the second: *We should do something instead of just talking about it.* | *You must have picked up my keys instead of yours.* | *Could I have tuna instead of ham?* | **instead of doing sth** *Instead of getting mad, he grinned.* **2** in place of something or someone that has just been mentioned: *If Joe can't get to the meeting, I could go instead.* | *We didn't have enough money for a movie, so we went to the park instead.* | [sentence adverb] *Cardew did not join the navy. Instead, he decided to become an actor.*

in·step /ˈɪnstɛp/ *n.* [C] **1** BIOLOGY the raised part of the bottom of your foot between your toes and your HEEL **2** the part of a shoe or sock that covers this part

in·sti·gate /ˈɪnstəˌgeɪt/ *v.* [T] **1** to start trouble by persuading someone to do something bad: *Both sides accuse each other of instigating the fighting.* **2** to start something such as a legal process or an official INQUIRY: *The mayor instigated an investigation into the charges.* —**instigator** *n.* [C]

in·sti·ga·tion /ˌɪnstəˈgeɪʃən/ *n.* [U] **1 at sb's instigation** also **at the instigation of sb** FORMAL because of someone's suggestion, request, or demand: *Shepard lied to investigators at the instigation of his direct superior officer.* **2** the act of officially starting something such as a legal process, an inquiry, or a policy: *the instigation of legal proceedings* **3** [U] the act of starting something violent by persuading other people to do it: *the instigation of genocide*

in·still /ɪnˈstɪl/ *v.* [T] to teach someone a way of thinking or behaving over a long period of time: **instill sth in**

sb *She tried to instill responsibility in her sons.* [**Origin:** 1400–1500 Latin *instillare*, from *stillare* **to fall in drops**] **—instillation** /ˌɪnstɪ'leɪʃən/ *n.* [U]

in·stinct /'ɪnstɪŋkt/ *n.* [C,U] a natural tendency or ability to think, behave, or react in a particular way, without learning it or thinking about it first: | +**for** *an animal's instinct for survival* | *a talented photographer with an instinct for a good picture* | **instinct to do sth** *a lion's instinct to hunt* | *The bees find their way back to the hive* ***by instinct.*** | ***My instincts tell me*** (=used to say that you feel something strongly without having thought about it first) *that she's not the right woman for you.* | *I decided to* ***follow my instincts*** (=do the thing that I felt was right) *and accept the job.* [**Origin:** 1400–1500 Latin *instinctus*, from *instinguere* **to make someone wish to do something**] → see also INTUITION

in·stinc·tive /ɪn'stɪŋktɪv/ *adj.* based on instinct: *an instinctive sense of style* | *My instinctive reaction was to run.* **—instinctively** *adv.*: *Fish know instinctively when a predator is nearby.*

in·stinc·tual /ɪn'stɪŋktʃuəl/ *adj.* TECHNICAL based on instinct: *an instinctual reaction*

in·sti·tute¹ /'ɪnstəˌtut/ Ac W2 *n.* [C] an organization that has a particular purpose such as scientific or educational work, or the building where this organization is based: *the Academy of Arts Institute* | *research institutes*

institute² Ac *v.* [T] FORMAL to introduce or start a system, rule, legal process etc.: **institute proceedings/reforms/a program etc.** *The governor wants to institute reforms by the end of the year.*

in·sti·tu·tion /ˌɪnstə'tuʃən/ Ac W2 *n.* [C] **1** a large establishment or organization that has a particular type of work or purpose, such as scientific, educational, or medical work: *Tokyo University is the most important educational institution in Japan.* | *a financial institution* ▸see THESAURUS box at **organization**
2 a place where people go to live when they need to be looked after, for example old people, children whose parents have died, people who are mentally ill etc.: *Most abandoned children are brought up in institutions.*
3 an established system or custom in society: *the institution of marriage* **4** the act of starting or introducing a system, rule etc.: +**of** *They approved the institution of a new law.* **5 be an institution** HUMOROUS someone or something that has been an important part of a place for a long time, and that people expect will always be there: *This place is not just a restaurant; it's an institution in this town.* **—institutional** *adj.*

in·sti·tu·tion·al·ize /ˌɪnstə'tuʃənlˌaɪz/ *v.* [T] **1** to make something a normal accepted part of a system or organization: *The trade agreement institutionalized the economic reforms.* **2** to put someone in a mental hospital or institution for old people etc.

in·sti·tu·tion·al·ized /ˌɪnstə'tuʃənlˌaɪzd/ Ac *adj.* **1** bad or negative attitudes or behavior that are institutionalized have happened for so long in an organization or society that they have become normal, accepted, and difficult to change: *institutionalized racism in the police force* **2** FORMAL someone who has become institutionalized has lived for a long time in a prison, mental hospital etc. and now cannot easily live outside one

'in-store *adj.* happening within a large store, especially a DEPARTMENT STORE or GROCERY STORE: *an in-store bakery*

in·struct /ɪn'strʌkt/ Ac *v.* [T] **1** to officially tell someone what to do: **instruct sb to do sth** *Tourists are instructed to not take pictures inside the building.* | *I filled out the forms* ***as instructed*** (=in the way I was told to do). ▸see THESAURUS box at **tell** **2** to teach or show someone how to do something: **instruct sb in sth** *In flight school, we were instructed in the basics of aerial combat.* [**Origin:** 1400–1500 Latin, past participle of *instruere*, from *struere* **to build**]

in·struc·tion /ɪn'strʌkʃən/ Ac S3 W3 *n.* **1 instructions** the printed information that tells you how to use a piece of equipment, product etc.: **instructions on how to do sth/on doing sth** *Are there any instructions on how to plant the trees?* | +**for** *Click here to download instructions for assembly and care.* | ***Follow the instructions*** (=do what they say) *on the back of the box.* **2** [C usually plural] a statement telling someone what they must do: *Her instructions were very clear.* | *A stewardess* ***gave*** *safety* ***instructions*** *in both English and Spanish.* | **instructions to do sth** *The guards had instructions to watch the prisoners carefully.* | **instruction that** *The teacher had left instructions that no one was to talk during the test.* | **strict/specific instructions** *I gave strict instrtuctions that we were not to be disturbed.* | *He failed to* ***follow*** *his commander's* ***instructions.*** | *The police were* ***under instruction to*** (=were told to) *fire if necessary.* **3** [U] FORMAL teaching that you are given in a particular skill or subject: *religious instruction* | +**in** *basic instruction in chemistry* | ***Under*** *Stewart's* ***instruction*** (=while being taught by him), *I mastered the technique.*

in·struc·tion·al /ɪn'strʌkʃənl/ *adj.* providing instruction: *an instructional videotape on how to play the guitar*

in'struction ˌmanual *n.* [C] a book that gives you instructions on how to use or take care of a machine, piece of equipment etc.

in·struc·tive /ɪn'strʌktɪv/ Ac *adj.* providing a lot of useful information: *instructive drawings*

in·struc·tor /ɪn'strʌktɚ/ Ac S3 *n.* [C] **1** someone who teaches a particular subject, sport, or skill: *ski instructors* **2** someone who teaches at a college or university and who has a rank below ASSISTANT PROFESSOR → see Word Choice box at PROFESSOR

in·stru·ment /'ɪnstrəmənt/ S3 W3 *n.* [C]
1 MUSIC an object such as a piano, horn, VIOLIN etc., used for producing musical sounds SYN **musical instrument**: *Do you* ***play*** *any* ***instruments?*** | **wind/stringed/brass/percussion instrument** (=used to show what kind of instrument)
2 TOOL a small tool used in work such as science or medicine: *surgical instruments*
3 FOR MEASURING SCIENCE a piece of equipment for measuring and showing distance, speed, temperature etc.: *The instrument measures blood pressure.*
4 METHOD [usually singular] something such as system, method, or law that is used to achieve a particular result: *The army is an instrument of the government.* | *Interest rates are an important instrument of economic policy.*
5 FOR HURTING an object that is used to hit or hurt someone: *He was struck with a blunt instrument.* | *a medieval* ***instrument of torture***
6 instrument of fate/God LITERARY someone or something that is used by God or fate to achieve a purpose
7 DOCUMENT LAW a legal document
[**Origin:** 1200–1300 Latin *instrumentum*, from *instruere*, from *struere* **to build**]

in·stru·ment·al¹ /ˌɪnstrə'mɛntl/ *adj.* **1 be instrumental in (doing) sth** to be important in making something possible: *Siegel was instrumental in creating Las Vegas as it is today.* **2** ENG. LANG. ARTS instrumental music is for instruments only, not for voices

instrumental² *n.* [C] ENG. LANG. ARTS a piece of music or a part of a piece of music where no voices are used, only instruments

in·stru·men·tal·ist /ˌɪnstrə'mɛntl-ɪst/ *n.* [C] someone who plays a musical instrument → see also VOCALIST

in·stru·men·ta·tion /ˌɪnstrəmɛn'teɪʃən/ *n.* [U] **1** the set of INSTRUMENTS used to control a machine: *high-tech instrumentation* **2** ENG. LANG. ARTS the way in which a piece of music is arranged to be played by several different instruments

'instrument ˌpanel *n.* [C] the board in front of the pilot of an aircraft, where all the INSTRUMENTS are

in·sub·or·di·na·tion /ˌɪnsəˌbɔrdn'eɪʃən/ *n.* [U] the act of refusing to obey someone who has a higher rank than you: *Shores was fired for insubordination.* **—insubordinate** /ˌɪnsə'bɔrdn-ɪt/ *adj.*

in·sub·stan·tial /ˌɪnsəbˈstænʃəl/ *adj.* FORMAL not solid, large, strong, or satisfying: *Their houses are small and insubstantial.* | *Epstein called the evidence insubstantial* (=not good enough). —**insubstantiality** /ˌɪnsəbˌstænʃiˈæləti/ *n.* [U]

in·suf·fer·a·ble /ɪnˈsʌfərəbəl/ *adj.* extremely annoying or bad: *the man's insufferable rudeness* | *The heat was insufferable.* —**insufferably** *adv.*

in·suf·fi·cient /ˌɪnsəˈfɪʃənt/ Ac *adj.* not enough: *an insufficient source of water* | *There was insufficient evidence to convict them.* —**insufficiently** *adv.* —**insufficiency** *n.* [singular,U]

in·su·lar /ˈɪnsələ/ *adj.* **1** DISAPPROVING not interested in or trusting anything except your own group, country etc.: *a small, insular community* **2** FORMAL relating to or like an island —**insularity** /ˌɪnsəˈlærəti/ *n.* [U]

in·su·late /ˈɪnsəˌleɪt/ *v.* [T] **1** to cover or protect something so that electricity, sound, heat etc. cannot get in or out: *insulated containers for cold drinks* | *Properly insulating your home can save a lot on energy bills.* **2** to protect someone from bad experiences or unwanted influences: **insulate sb/sth from sth** *Her family's money insulated her from the pressures of the real world.*

ˈinsulating ˌtape *n.* [U] narrow material used for wrapping around electric wires to insulate them

in·su·la·tion /ˌɪnsəˈleɪʃən/ *n.* [U] **1** material used to insulate something, especially a building **2** the act of insulating something or the state of being insulated: *Blankets provided insulation against the cold.*

in·su·la·tor /ˈɪnsəˌleɪtə/ *n.* [C] PHYSICS an object or material that insulates, especially one that does not allow electricity to pass through it

in·su·lin /ˈɪnsələn/ *n.* [U] BIOLOGY MEDICINE a substance produced naturally by your body that allows sugar to be used for energy [**Origin:** 1900–2000 Latin *insula* **island**; because insulin is made by body organs called the "islets of Langerhans"] → see also DIABETES

in·sult¹ /ˈɪnsʌlt/ *n.* [C] **1** an impolite or offensive remark or action: *As he spoke the crowd shouted insults at him.* | +**to** *The remark was an insult to my faith.* | *Their offer on the house was so low, I* ***took it as an insult*** (=though it was not intended as an insult). **2 be an insult to sb's intelligence** if information, a book, a movie etc. is an insult to your intelligence, it is presented in a way that treats you as if you are stupid: *Most advertising is an insult to people's intelligence.* [**Origin:** 1500–1600 French *insulter*, from Latin *insultare* **to jump on, insult**] → see also **add insult to injury** at ADD (6)

in·sult² /ɪnˈsʌlt/ *v.* [T] **1** to say or do something that offends someone by showing that you do not respect them: **insult sb by doing sth** *He insulted the delegates by refusing to shake their hands.* | **be/feel insulted** *I hope Andy won't be insulted if I don't come to dinner.* **2 insult sb's intelligence (by doing sth)** to say or do something that suggests you think someone is stupid: *I won't insult your intelligence by lying.*

in·sult·ing /ɪnˈsʌltɪŋ/ *adj.* very impolite or offensive to someone, and showing a lack of respect: *insulting language* | +**to** *It would be insulting to the local people not to accept their gifts.*

in·su·per·a·ble /ɪnˈsupərəbəl/ *adj.* FORMAL an insuperable difficulty or problem is impossible to deal with

in·sup·port·a·ble /ˌɪnsəˈpɔrtəbəl/ *adj.* FORMAL **1** not acceptable or not able to be proved needed or useful: *Staffing levels are currently insupportable.* **2** too annoying or bad for you to accept or deal with: *insupportable pain*

in·sur·ance /ɪnˈʃʊrəns/ S1 W2 *n.* **1** [U] an arrangement with a company in which you pay them money each year and they pay the costs if anything bad happens to you or your house, things etc., such as having an illness or an accident: +**on/for** *Do you have insurance on your car?* | +**against** *insurance against fire and theft* | **home/car/travel etc. insurance** *Many Americans cannot afford health insurance.* | *father* ***took out insurance*** (=bought it) *to cover the mortgage.* | *We can probably* ***claim for*** *the damage* ***on our insurance*** (=ask the insurance company to pay). → see also LIFE INSURANCE **2** [U] the money that you pay regularly to an insurance company: *Did you pay the home insurance?* | +**on/for** *My monthly insurance for two cars is $301.00* **3** [U] the business of providing insurance: *My uncle works in insurance.* | *the insurance industry* **4** [singular, U] protection against something bad happening: +**against** *An underground water supply is good insurance against drought.*

inˈsurance adˌjuster *n.* [C] someone who works for an insurance company and decides how much to pay people who have had an accident, had something stolen etc.

inˈsurance ˌagent *n.* [C] someone who arranges and sells insurance for a particular insurance company as their job

inˈsurance ˌbroker *n.* [C] someone who sells insurance by looking at many insurance companies and finding the customer the best deal

inˈsurance ˌclaim *n.* [C] a request to your insurance company that they pay for your lost, damaged, or stolen property, for care after an injury or illness, etc.

inˈsurance ˌpolicy *n.* [C] a written agreement for insurance with an insurance company

inˈsurance ˌpremium *n.* [C] the money that you pay regularly to an insurance company

in·sure /ɪnˈʃʊr/ *v.* [T] **1** to buy insurance to protect yourself against something bad happening to you, your family, your possessions etc.: *We insured all our valuables before the move.* | **insure sb/sth against sth** *Purchases made with the card are insured against theft.* | **insure sb/sth for sth** *The planes are insured for $3.1 million.* **2** to agree to provide insurance for something or someone: *No one will insure him because of his heart condition.* | **insure sb against sth** *The insurance doesn't insure us against flooding.* **3** another spelling of ENSURE

WORD CHOICE **assure, reassure, insure, ensure, make sure**

- If you **assure** someone of something, you tell them that it is really true or will happen: *Adam assured me that he would call.*
- You **reassure** someone who is worried by telling them that there is nothing to worry about: *The government needs to reassure the people that the food supply is safe.*
- You may **insure** someone or something against something bad happening to them by paying money to an insurance company: *The apartment building is insured against earthquakes.*
- If you **insure** (or, more formally, **ensure**) that something happens, you make certain or **make sure** (less formal) it does happen: *Anything that prevents surprises will help insure our success.* | *Make sure you lock the door when you leave.*

in·sured /ɪnˈʃʊrd/ *n.* **1** protected by insurance: *Is the car insured?* | +**against** *All your possessions should be insured against theft.* | +**for** *His house is insured for $1.5 million.* **2 the insured** LAW the person or people who are insured: *The insured is required to pay a portion of all medical bills.*

in·sur·er /ɪnˈʃʊrə/ *n.* [C] a person or company that provides insurance: *The full cost of storm damage will be paid by the insurer.*

in·sur·gen·cy /ɪnˈsədʒənsi/ *n. plural* **insurgencies** [C] an attempt by a large group of people to take control of their government using force and violence: *a 21-year insurgency against the national government* → see also COUNTERINSURGENCY, REBELLION

in·sur·gent /ɪnˈsədʒənt/ *n.* [C usually plural] POLITICS one of a group of people who are fighting against the government of their own country —**insurgent** *adj.*: *insurgent forces*

in·sur·mount·a·ble /ˌɪnsəˈmaʊntəbəl/ *adj.* an insurmountable difficulty or problem is too large or too difficult to deal with: *insurmountable debt* | *an insurmountable obstacle to reform*

in·sur·rec·tion /ˌɪnsəˈrɛkʃən/ *n.* [C,U] POLITICS an attempt by a large group of people within a country to take control of their government using force and violence: *Rebel members of the army* ***staged an insurrection.*** —**insurrectionist** *n.* [C]

in·tact /ɪnˈtækt/ *adj.* [not before noun] not broken, damaged, spoiled, or badly affected: *The package arrived intact.* | *Somehow his reputation survived the scandal intact.*

in·ta·glio /ɪnˈtælyoʊ, -ˈtɑl-/ *n.* [C,U] the art of cutting patterns into a hard substance, or the pattern that you get by doing this

in·take /ˈɪnteɪk/ *n.* FORMAL **1** [singular] the amount of food, FUEL etc. that is eaten by someone or put into something: **+of** *Try to reduce your intake of caffeine.* | **a high/low intake** *a high intake of fat* **2** [C] a tube, pipe, etc. through which air, gas, or liquid is taken in: *air intakes on a jet engine* **3** [singular] the number of people who join an organization, school, profession etc., especially at the same time: *the yearly intake of students* **4 an intake of breath** a sudden act of breathing in, showing that you are shocked, surprised etc.

in·tan·gi·ble /ɪnˈtændʒəbəl/ *adj.* an intangible quality or feeling cannot be clearly felt or described, although you know it exists: *an intangible hostility between the two men* —**intangible** *n.* [C]

in·te·ger /ˈɪntədʒɚ/ *n.* [C] MATH a whole number, for example 6 is an integer, but 6.4 is not

in·te·gral /ˈɪntəgrəl, ɪnˈtɛgrəl/ Ac *adj.* **1** forming a necessary part of something: *Music should be an integral part of children's education.* | **+to** *Cooperation is integral to the success of the program.* **2** MATH in mathematics, relating to an integer

in·te·grate /ˈɪntəˌgreɪt/ Ac *v.* **1** [I,T] to end the practice of separating people of different races in a place or institution, usually by making the separation illegal → see also SEGREGATE SYN **desegregate**: *Many cities have given up trying to integrate the schools.* **2** [T] to combine two or more things in order to make an effective system: *Bus and subway services have been fully integrated.* | **integrate sth with/into sth** *Using computers, students are able to integrate text with graphics.* **3** [I,T] to join in the life and customs of a group or society, or to help someone do this: *Disabled students are integrated in regular classrooms.* | **+into/with** *Some groups of immigrants find it hard to integrate into our society.* **4** [I] if machines, computers, or systems integrate, they can work together

in·te·grat·ed /ˈɪntəˌgreɪt̬ɪd/ Ac *adj.* an integrated system, institution etc. combines many different groups, ideas, or parts in a way that works well: *integrated information systems* | *a racially integrated neighborhood* → see also SEGREGATED

ˌintegrated ˈcircuit *n.* [C] PHYSICS a very small set of electronic connections printed on a single piece of SEMICONDUCTOR material instead of being made from separate parts

in·te·gra·tion /ˌɪntəˈgreɪʃən/ Ac *n.* [U] **1** the combining of two or more things so that they work together effectively: *the integration of European economies* **2** the process of making or allowing people of different races to live, work etc. together instead of separately: *Integration of the public schools is still a goal.* **3** the process by which people join in with a group or society and become accepted as members of it: **+into** *the integration of disabled people into society*

in·teg·ri·ty /ɪnˈtɛgrət̬i/ Ac *n.* [U] **1** the quality of being honest and of always having high moral principles: *a woman of great integrity* | **personal/professional integrity** *I would never question your professional integrity* **2** FORMAL the state of being united as one complete thing, rather than divided into separate parts: *the country's territorial integrity* **3** FORMAL the quality that information has of being accurate and of good quality

in·teg·u·ment /ɪnˈtɛgyəmənt/ *n.* [C] BIOLOGY something such as a shell that covers something else

in·tel·lect /ˈɪntlˌɛkt/ *n.* **1** [C,U] the ability to understand things and to think intelligently: *Schools should nurture a child's intellect.* | *his shrewd intellect* **2** [C] someone who is very intelligent: *the great scientific intellects of the twentieth century*

in·tel·lect·u·al¹ /ˌɪntlˈɛktʃuəl/ W3 *adj.* **1** relating to the ability to understand things and to think intelligently: *the intellectual development of children* | *a job that requires a large amount of intellectual effort* **2** [only before noun] relating to ideas about science, art, literature etc., which are discussed by educated intelligent people: *Her works reflect the intellectual climate of the time.* **3** an intellectual person is well educated and interested in serious ideas and subjects such as science, literature etc. ►see THESAURUS box at **intelligent** **4** involving or needing serious thinking to be understood: *an intellectual film* —**intellectually** *adv.*

intellectual² *n.* [C] someone who is intelligent and well educated, and who thinks about complicated ideas: *a group of leading right-wing intellectuals*

in·tel·lec·tu·al·ize /ˌɪntlˈɛktʃuəˌlaɪz/ *v.* [I,T] to think or talk about a problem carefully, especially in order to avoid dealing with your feelings about it

ˌintellectual ˈproperty *n.* [U] LAW something that someone has invented or has the right to make or sell, especially something protected by a PATENT, TRADEMARK, or COPYRIGHT

in·tel·li·gence /ɪnˈtɛlədʒəns/ Ac W2 *n.* [C,U] **1 a)** the ability to learn, understand, and think about things: *a test designed to measure intelligence* | **high/low intelligence** (=a strong or weak ability to learn and understand things easily) **b)** a high level of this ability: *I doubt whether he had the intelligence to be so devious.* **2** POLITICS information about the secret activities of foreign governments, the military plans of an enemy etc.: *According to our intelligence, further attacks were planned.* | ***Intelligence gathering*** (=obtaining intelligence) *is a dangerous business.* **3** POLITICS a group of people or an organization that gathers secret information for their government: *military intelligence* | *U.S. intelligence agencies*

inˈtelligence ˌquotient *n.* [C] IQ

in·tel·li·gent /ɪnˈtɛlədʒənt/ Ac S3 *adj.* **1** having a high level of ability to learn, understand, and think about things, or showing this ability: *an ambitious and intelligent young woman* | *an intelligent decision* | *a group of* ***highly intelligent*** (=very intelligent) *students*

> **THESAURUS**
>
> **smart** intelligent: *a really smart guy*
> **bright** intelligent, used especially about children and young people: *a bright kid*
> **brilliant** extremely intelligent and good at the work you do: *a brilliant scientist*
> **wise** having a lot of experience and knowledge about people and the world: *a wise grandparent*
> **clever** intelligent, especially in a way that is unusual: *She's clever and creative.*
> **cunning/crafty** good at using your intelligence to trick people: *a cunning criminal*
> **intellectual** having a lot of education and interested in learning about art, science, literature, etc.: *his intellectual interests*
> **gifted** a gifted child is much more intelligent than most other children: *special classes for gifted children*

2 an intelligent creature is able to think, understand, and communicate: *Dolphins are highly intelligent creatures.* | *Is there* ***intelligent life*** *on other planets?* **3** an intelligent computer or a machine, system etc. that contains a computer, is able to learn and use information [**Origin:** 1500–1600 Latin, present participle of *intelligere* **to understand**, from *inter-* + *legere* **to gather, choose**] —**intelligently** *adv.*

I

in,telligent de'sign *n.* [U] the belief that because living things are very complicated, then they must have been made by God and cannot be the result of natural development over a long period of time (the idea of EVOLUTION, which most scientists believe): *Some schools teach intelligent design as well as evolution.*

in·tel·li·gent·si·a /ɪn,tɛləˈdʒɛntsiə/ *n.* **the intelligentsia** the people in a society who are most highly educated and who are most interested in new ideas, especially in art, literature, or politics

in,telligent 'terminal *n.* [C] a type of computer that is connected to another computer, but which can still perform certain operations without using the other computer → see also DUMB TERMINAL

in·tel·li·gi·ble /ɪnˈtɛlədʒəbəl/ *adj.* intelligible speech, writing, or ideas can be easily understood OPP **unintelligible**: +**to** *The information is presented in a way that is intelligible to everyone.* —**intelligibly** *adv.* —**intelligibility** /ɪn,tɛlədʒəˈbɪləṭi/ *n.* [U]

in·tem·per·ate /ɪnˈtɛmpərɪt/ *adj.* DISAPPROVING FORMAL **1** showing anger and a lack of control over your feelings: *intemperate remarks* **2** regularly drinking too much alcohol —**intemperance** *n.* [U]

in·tend /ɪnˈtɛnd/ S3 W2 *v.* [T] **1** to have something in your mind as a plan or purpose: **intend to do sth** *The laws were intended to protect wildlife.* | **it was intended that** *It was never intended that Ford pay the money back.* | **intend sb/sth to do sth** *I didn't intend her to see the painting until it was finished.* | **intend on doing sth** *Kristen intends on staying in Rome for three days.* | **intend sth as sth/intend sth to be sth** *I'm sorry. I intended it as a joke* | *Miss Stein* ***fully intended*** *to make the painting a gift.* **2 be intended for sb/sth** to be provided or designed for a particular purpose or person: *The movie is intended for adults.* | *The equipment was originally intended for use by the army.* [**Origin:** 1300–1400 Old French *entendre* **to have as a purpose**, from Latin *intendere* **to stretch out, have as a purpose**]

in·tend·ed¹ /ɪnˈtɛndɪd/ *adj.* [only before noun] **1** used to refer to the person or thing that an action is intended to affect, especially when it does not actually affect them: *the killer's intended victim* | *the book's intended audience* **2** used to refer to the thing you are trying to achieve or the place you are trying to reach: *the plane's intended destination* | *The money was not used for its intended purpose.* | **sth's intended effect/result** *The tax legislation had its intended effect.*

intended² *n.* **sb's intended** OLD-FASHIONED or HUMOROUS the person that someone is going to marry

in·tense /ɪnˈtɛns/ Ac W3 *adj.* **1** having a very strong effect or felt very strongly: *the intense heat of the desert* | *The pain was so intense, I couldn't breathe.* | *The pressure on students to succeed is intense.* **2** involving a lot of effort, especially in a short time: *intense excercise* | *Nothing broke his intense concentration.* **3** very serious and having very strong feelings or opinions: *He's a little too intense for me.* **4** serious and making you feel strong emotions or opinions: *an intense conversation* —**intensely** *adv.*

in·ten·si·fi·er /ɪnˈtɛnsə,faɪɚ/ *n.* [C] ENG. LANG. ARTS word that is used to emphasize another word and make its meaning stronger. For example, the adjective "splitting" in the phrase "a splitting headache" and the adverb "badly" in the phrase "badly needed changes"

in·ten·si·fy /ɪnˈtɛnsə,faɪ/ Ac *v.* **intensifies, intensified, intensifying** [I,T] to increase in strength, size, amount etc., or to make something do this: *Winds intensified during the afternoon.* | *Police have now intensified the search for the lost child.* —**intensification** /ɪn,tɛnsəfəˈkeɪʃən/ *n.* [U]

in·ten·si·ty /ɪnˈtɛnsəṭi/ Ac *n.* [U] **1** the strength of something, how strongly it is felt, or how strong its effect is: *the intensity of the hurricane* | *the intensity of her anger* | *light intensity* **2** the quality of being serious and having very strong feelings or opinions: *He spoke with great intensity.*

in·ten·sive /ɪnˈtɛnsɪv/ Ac *adj.* involving a lot of activity, effort, or careful attention in a short period of time: *intensive instruction in English* | *intensive diplomatic efforts to gain a cease-fire* —**intensively** *adv.*

-intensive /ɪntɛnsɪv/ [in adjectives] involving the use of a lot of something: *labor-intensive work* | *an energy-intensive system*

in,tensive 'care *n.* [U] the department in a hospital that treats people who are very sick or badly injured, or the treatment that they receive there: *patients* ***in intensive care***

in,tensive 'farming also **in,tensive 'agriculture** *n.* [U] **1** farming that produces a lot of food from a small area of land, usually by using chemicals and machinery **2** farming that involves a lot of hard physical work

in·tent¹ /ɪnˈtɛnt/ *n.* [U] **1** FORMAL what you intend to do SYN **intention**: **sb's intent to do sth** *Wilder announced his intent to seek reelection.* | *The statement was cruel* ***in its intent*** (=the statement was deliberately cruel). **2** LAW the intention to do something illegal: *The gun was fired* ***with intent.*** | **intent to do sth** *possession of a gun with intent to commit robbery* **3 for/to all intents and purposes** almost completely, or very nearly: *The war was, for all intents and purposes, over.*

intent² *adj.* **1 be intent on/upon (doing) sth** to be determined to do something or achieve something: *The organization is intent on changing the rules.* | *She was intent on a career as a lawyer.* **2** paying careful attention to something so that you think about nothing else: *an intent gaze* | +**on/upon** *Intent on her work, she didn't notice him enter.* —**intently** *adv.*: *Jurors listened intently to the testimony.*

in·ten·tion /ɪnˈtɛnʃən/ W3 *n.* [C,U] **1** a plan or desire to do something: **have no intention of doing sth** *I have no intention of moving again anytime soon.* | *Perez bought the house* ***with the intention of*** *fixing it up and reselling it.* | +**that** *It was always the intention that the convention be held in Kobe.* | **sb's intention to do sth** *It was always my attention to pay you back.* | *I* ***have every intention of*** (=definitely plan on) *reporting him to the police.* **2 good intentions** also **the best (of) intentions** a desire to do something good or kind, especially when you do not succeed in doing it: *They have good intentions, but they never finish anything.* **3 what are your intentions (toward sb)?** OLD-FASHIONED or HUMOROUS used to ask someone whether or not they plan to marry someone else → see also WELL-INTENTIONED

in·ten·tion·al /ɪnˈtɛnʃənəl/ *adj.* done deliberately SYN **deliberate** OPP **unintentional**: *an intentional act of agression* | *I'm sorry I upset you, but it wasn't intentional.*

in·ten·tion·al·ly /ɪnˈtɛnʃənəli/ *adv.* in a way that is intended or planned SYN **deliberately** OPP **unintentionally**: *Employees may have intentionally broken the law.*

in·ter /ɪnˈtɚ/ *v.* **interred, interring** [T] FORMAL to bury a dead person OPP **disinter** → see also INTERMENT

inter- /ɪntɚ/ *prefix* between or among a group of things or people: *to intermarry* (=marry someone of another race, religion etc.) | *the Internet* (=connection among computers) → see also INTRA-, INTRO-

in·ter·act /,ɪntəˈrækt/ Ac *v.* [I] **1** if people interact with each other, they talk to each other, work together etc.: *Playing a game is a way for a family to interact.* | +**with** *Kate interacts well with the other children in class.* **2** if two or more things interact, or one interacts with another, they have an effect on each other: *We learned how people and their environment interact.* | +**with** *How will the drug interact with other medications?*

in·ter·ac·tion /,ɪntəˈrækʃən/ Ac S3 *n.* [C,U] **1** the activity of talking to other people, working together with them etc.: +**with/between/among** *interaction with students from other colleges* | *events that encourage interaction among residents* | *the animal's patterns of* ***social interaction*** **2** a process by which two or more things have an effect on each other, or an occasion when this happens: *a chemical interaction* | +**of** *the interaction of carbon and hydrogen* **3** PHYSICS one of the four basic ways in which PARTICLES or physical objects affect each other. These four basic forces are STRONG INTERACTION, WEAK INTERACTION, ELECTROMAGNETISM, and GRAVITATION.

in·ter·ac·tive /ˌɪntəˈræktɪv/ Ac *adj.* **1** COMPUTERS something such as a computer PROGRAM or system that is interactive does things in reaction to the actions of the person who is using it: *interactive software* | *The museum features interactive exhibits.* **2** involving talking and working together: *interactive teaching methods* —**interactivity** /ˌɪntəækˈtɪvəti/ *n.* [U]

in·ter·a·gen·cy /ˌɪntəˈeɪdʒənsi/ *adj.* between or involving different organizations or departments, especially within a government: *an interagency committee*

in·ter a·li·a /ˌɪntə ˈeɪliə, -ˈɑliə/ *adv.* FORMAL among other things: *The paper discussed, inter alia, recent political issues.*

in·ter·breed /ˌɪntəˈbrid/ *v. past tense and past participle* **interbred** /-ˈbrɛd/ [I,T] BIOLOGY to produce young animals or people from parents of different breeds or groups: +**with** *The bees are unable to interbreed with native species.* → see also CROSSBREED

in·ter·cede /ˌɪntəˈsid/ *v.* [I] **1** to talk to someone in authority in order to prevent something bad from happening to someone else: +**with** *Johnson* ***interceded*** *with the authorities* ***on*** *Kelly's* ***behalf.*** | +**for** *The priest would often intercede for prisoners.* **2** to try to help two or more people, groups etc. end a disagreement, war etc.: +**in** *Teachers are expected to intercede in student disagreements.* → see also INTERCESSION

in·ter·cept¹ /ˌɪntəˈsɛpt/ *v.* [T] **1** to stop something or someone that is going from one place to another and prevent it from getting there: *The boat carrying 653 refugees was intercepted at sea.* | *Someone has been intercepting our email messages.* **2** in sports, especially football, to catch and take possession of a ball that an opponent is throwing to someone on his or her team —**interception** /ˌɪntəˈsɛpʃən/ *n.* [C,U]

in·ter·cept² /ˈɪntəˌsɛpt/ *n.* [C] MATH the point at which a line crosses an AXIS on a GRAPH

in·ter·cep·tor /ˌɪntəˈsɛptə/ *n.* [C] **1** a light fast military aircraft **2** a MISSILE designed to intercept enemy MISSILES

in·ter·ces·sion /ˌɪntəˈsɛʃən/ *n.* **1** [U] an act of interceding **2** [C,U] a prayer asking for someone to be helped or cured

in·ter·change¹ /ˈɪntəˌtʃeɪndʒ/ *n.* **1** [C] a place where two or more HIGHWAYS or FREEWAYS meet **2** [singular, U] FORMAL an occasion when people give each other information or talk to each other SYN exchange: *a social interchange* | +**of** *the interchange of ideas*

in·ter·change² /ˌɪntəˈtʃeɪndʒ/ *v.* [I,T] to put or use each of two things in the place of the other, or to be exchanged in this way: *The two spices can be easily interchanged.*

in·ter·change·a·ble /ˌɪntəˈtʃeɪndʒəbəl/ *adj.* things that are interchangeable can be used instead of each other: *The camera has two interchangeable lenses.* | *The two terms are interchangeable.* —**interchangeably** *adv.* —**interchangeability** /ˌɪntəˌtʃeɪndʒəˈbɪləti/ *n.* [U]

in·ter·cit·y /ˌɪntəˈsɪti/ *adj.* [only before noun] going from one city to another, or happening between different cities: *intercity bus service*

in·ter·col·le·giate /ˌɪntəkəˈlidʒɪt/ *adj.* intercollegiate competitions are between members of different colleges: *an intercollegiate golf tournament*

in·ter·com /ˈɪntəˌkɑm/ *n.* [C] a communication system by which people in different parts of a building, aircraft, or ship can speak to each other or make announcements to everyone: *"Welcome to St. Petersburg," said a voice* ***over the intercom.***

intercom

in·ter·con·nect·ed /ˌɪntəkəˈnɛktɪd/ *adj.* interconnected problems, systems etc. relate to each other, influence each other, or are connected to each other: *a book with three interconnected themes* | *The movements of the Earth and its neighboring planets are closely interconnected.* —**interconnectedness** *n.* [U] —**interconnect** *v.* [I,T] —**interconnection** /ˌɪntəkəˈnɛkʃən/ *n.* [C]

in·ter·con·ti·nen·tal /ˌɪntəˌkɑntəˈnɛntl, -ˌkɑntˀnˈɛntl/ *adj.* happening between two CONTINENTS, or going from one CONTINENT to another: *an intercontinental flight* | *intercontinental trade*

in·ter·course /ˈɪntəˌkɔrs/ *n.* [U] FORMAL **1** BIOLOGY the act of having sex SYN sexual intercourse **2** any activity that involves people communicating with each other, for example conversations or trade: *ordinary social intercourse*

in·ter·cul·tur·al /ˌɪntəˈkʌltʃərəl/ *adj.* between people from different cultures or societies: *intercultural marriages* → see also MULTICULTURAL

in·ter·cut /ˌɪntəˈkʌt/ *v. past tense and past participle* **intercut**, *present participle* **intercutting** [T] if a movie, song etc. is intercut with pictures, words, sounds etc., the pictures or words appear in different places in the movie or song: *The score is intercut with bits of Mexican music.*

in·ter·de·nom·i·na·tion·al /ˌɪntədɪˌnɑməˈneɪʃənl/ *adj.* between or involving Christians from different groups or churches: *an interdenominational prayer service*

in·ter·de·part·men·tal /ˌɪntədipɑrtˀˈmɛntl/ *adj.* between or involving different departments of a company, government etc.: *the college's interdepartmental mail system*

in·ter·de·pend·ent /ˌɪntədɪˈpɛndənt/ *adj.* depending on or necessary to each other: *Ecosystems are interdependent networks of plants and animals.* —**interdependence** *n.* [U]

in·ter·dict /ˈɪntəˌdɪkt/ *n.* [C] **1** LAW an official order from a court telling someone not to do something **2** a punishment in the Catholic Church, by which a whole area or country is not allowed to take part in church ceremonies —**interdict** /ˌɪntəˈdɪkt/ *v.* [T] —**interdiction** /ˌɪntəˈdɪkʃən/ *n.* [C,U]

in·ter·dis·ci·pli·nar·y /ˌɪntəˈdɪsəplənəˌnɛri/ *adj.* involving ideas, information, or people from different subjects or areas of study: *an interdisciplinary team of researchers*

in·terest¹ /ˈɪntrɪst/ S2 W1 *n.*
1 FEELING [singular, U] a feeling that makes you want to pay attention to someone or something and find out more about them: +**in** *my interest in science* | *I'd recommend the book to anyone who* ***has an interest in*** *jazz.* | *He was looking at me* ***with interest.*** | *I watched the first few episodes and then* ***lost interest.*** | *He never* ***took an interest in*** *what the children were doing.* | *Lori has* ***shown interest in*** *learning to dance.* | *Other cities have* ***expressed an interest in*** *the school program.* | *The case* ***attracted*** *a lot of public* ***interest.***
2 ACTIVITY [C] a subject or activity that you enjoy studying or doing: *In retirement, Nelson added personal computing to his interests.* | *Ms. Walters has many* ***outside interests*** (=interests besides her work).

I

3 MONEY [U] **a)** ECONOMICS money that you must pay for borrowing money: *interest payments* | **+on** *The foundation has been **paying** 8.5% **interest** on the loan.* **b)** money that a bank pays you when you keep money there: *This savings account **earns interest** even if the balance is very low.* → see also COMPOUND INTEREST, SIMPLE INTEREST

4 QUALITY [U] a quality or feature of something that attracts your attention or makes you want to know more about it: *The red tiles **add interest** to the kitchen.* | *A sales job **holds** no **interest** for me whatsoever.* | *This report might be **of interest to** your students.* | *art galleries, museums and other **places of interest*** | *questions **of general interest*** (=that everyone wants to know about) | **of special/particular interest to sb** *Today's guest will be of particular interest to hunters.*

5 ADVANTAGE [C] the things or situations that gives someone an advantage or are favorable to them: *I don't think it **was in his best interest** to resign.* | *I've always **had** my children's **best interests at heart*** (=been concerned about what is best for them). | **protect/safeguard sb's interests** *The regulations protect the interests of local fishing communities.* | **the national/public interest** *The commission's aim is to protect the public interest.*

6 have no interest in doing sth to not want to do something: *I have no interest in continuing this conversation.*

7 SHARE IN COMPANY [C,U] ECONOMICS a share in a company, business etc.: *the company's overseas interests* | **+in** *the government's interest in the national phone company*

8 POWERFUL GROUP [C] TECHNICAL a group of people in the same business who share aims or ideas and often try to influence people in authority: *Most of Brazil's huge commercial interests support the proposal.*

9 in the interest(s) of justice/safety/efficiency etc. in order to make a situation or system fair, safe, EFFICIENT etc.: *The race was postponed in the interest of safety.*

10 (just) out of interest used to say that you are asking a question only because you are interested and not because you need to know: *Just out of interest, how much does it cost?*

11 pay sb back, with interest INFORMAL to harm or offend someone in an even worse way than they have harmed you

[**Origin:** 1400–1500 *Anglo-French interesse*, from Latin *interesse* **to be between, make a difference, concern**]

→ see also CONFLICT OF INTEREST, **human interest** at HUMAN[1] (6), SELF-INTEREST, SPECIAL INTEREST GROUP, **vested interest** at VESTED INTEREST

interest² *v.* [T] **1** to make someone want to pay attention to something and find out more about it: *Here's an article that might interest you.* | ***What interests me is** the history of these places.* | ***It may interest you to know that** Bob and Rachel are getting a divorce.* **2 could I interest you in a drink/dessert etc.?** SPOKEN used as a polite way of offering someone something, usually something to eat or to buy

in·terest·ed /ˈɪntrɪstɪd, ˈɪntəˌrɛstɪd/ S1 *adj.* **1** giving a lot of attention to something, because you want to find out more about it or because you enjoy it OPP **uninterested**: **+in** *Zack is only interested in girls and skateboarding.* | *It was great that they were interested in our opinions.* | **be interested to hear/know/see etc.** *I'd be interested to find out what really happened.*

THESAURUS

curious wanting to know more about something: *He was surrounded by a crowd of curious children.*
intrigued interested in something because it seems strange or mysterious: *I was intrigued by her story.*
fascinated very interested: *a child fascinated by machines*
absorbed/enthralled very interested in something, which is keeping your attention: *The girl was absorbed in her book.*
gripped/riveted/spellbound very interested in a story you are reading, a movie you are watching etc.: *They were spellbound, listening to his stories.*

2 eager to do or have something: *I offered to help, but they weren't interested.* | **interested in doing sth** *Michelle is interested in joining the tennis club.* | **+in** *Would you be interested in a second-hand Volvo?* **3 interested party/group** a person or group that is directly or personally concerned with a situation and is likely to be affected by its results: *All interested parties are invited to attend the meeting.* → see also DISINTERESTED → see Word Choice box at ADJECTIVE

ˌinterest-ˈfree *adj.* an interest-free LOAN has no interest charged on it: *interest-free credit*

ˈinterest ˌgroup *n.* [C] POLITICS a group of people who join together to try to influence the government in order to protect their own particular rights, advantages, concerns etc.

in·terest·ing /ˈɪntrɪstɪŋ, ˈɪntəˌrɛstɪŋ/ S1 *adj.* unusual or exciting in a way that keeps your attention or makes you think OPP **boring**: *an interesting man* | *I hope the work will be interesting.* | **it is interesting that** *It's interesting that so few men are involved in early childhood education.* | **it is interesting to see/know etc.** *It will be interesting to see how the team plays this week.* | *I **found** his talk very **interesting*** (=thought it was interesting). → see Word Choice box at ADJECTIVE

THESAURUS

fascinating very interesting: *He's had a fascinating life.*
intriguing something that is intriguing is interesting because it is unusual or mysterious, and you want to find out more: *That raises some intriguing questions.*
absorbing/enthralling interesting and keeping your attention: *The book is an absorbing read.*
compelling very interesting or exciting: *The movie is long but compelling.*
→ BORING
gripping/riveting/spellbinding used about a very interesting story, movie etc.: *Money, power, and romance combine in this riveting story.*

in·terest·ing·ly /ˈɪntrɪstɪŋli, ˈɪntəˌrɛstɪŋli/ *adv.* **1** [sentence adverb] used to introduce a fact that you think is interesting: ***Interestingly enough**, many of the writers were Vietnamese immigrants.* **2** in an interesting way

ˈinterest ˌrate W2 *n.* [C] ECONOMICS the PERCENTAGE amount that is charged by a bank etc. when you borrow money, or that is paid to you by a bank when you keep money in an account there: **high/low interest rates** *Interest rates are pretty low right now.* | **interest rates rise/fall** *If interest rates fall, people will borrow more.* | *The Federal Reserve **cut interest rates*** (=made them lower).

in·ter·face¹ /ˈɪntəˌfeɪs/ *n.* [C] **1** COMPUTERS something that helps a computer or a PROGRAM work with another program, another piece of electronic equipment, or the person who is using the computer **2** the way in which two subjects, events etc. affect each other: *the interface between labor and management* **3** TECHNICAL the surface where two things touch each other

interface² *v.* **1** [I,T + with] COMPUTERS if you interface two parts of a computer system, or if they interface, you connect them **2** [I + with] if two people or groups interface with each other, they communicate with each other and work together

in·ter·faith /ˈɪntəˌfeɪθ/ *adj.* between or involving people from different religions: *an interfaith Thanksgiving service*

in·ter·fere /ˌɪntəˈfɪr/ *v.* [I] to deliberately get involved in a situation where you are not wanted or needed SYN **meddle**: *It's not your problem — don't interfere.* | **interfere in sth** *I never interfere in other people's private* *lives.* [**Origin:** 1400–1500 Old French *entreferir* **to hit each other**, from *ferir* **to hit**]

interfere with sth/sb *phr. v.* **1** to prevent something from succeeding or from happening in the way that is normal or planned: *Aspirin interferes with the blood's ability to form clots.* **2** if something interferes with a television or radio broadcast, it spoils the sound or picture that you receive

in·ter·fer·ence /ˌɪntə-ˈfɪrəns/ *n.* [U] **1** an act of interfering: *The organization is protected from political interference.* | +**in** *her interference in the private affairs of other people* **2** unwanted noise on television, the radio, or the telephone, or problems in the television picture: *There's a lot of interference on my car radio.* **3** in some sports, the act, which is against the rules, of preventing another player from moving freely by standing in front of them or touching them **4 run interference a)** to help someone achieve something by dealing with people or problems that might cause them trouble: *Truscati's job is to run interference for troubled kids in the courts.* **b)** in football, to protect a player who has the ball by blocking players from the opposing team

ˌinterˈference ˌpattern *n.* [C] PHYSICS a pattern of waves of light, sound, or energy that forms when two or more waves arrive somewhere at the same time and combine

in·ter·fer·on /ˌɪntə-ˈfɪrɑn/ *n.* [U] BIOLOGY MEDICINE a chemical substance that is produced by your body to fight against VIRUSes that cause disease

in·ter·ga·lac·tic /ˌɪntə-gəˈlæktɪk/ *adj.* happening or existing between the galaxies (GALAXY (1) (=large groups of stars)) in space: *intergalactic travel*

in·ter·gen·er·a·tion·al /ˌɪntə-ˌdʒɛnəˈreɪʃənl/ *adj.* between or involving people from different age groups: *Intergenerational programs help both the children and retired people.*

in·ter·gov·ern·men·tal /ˌɪntə-gʌvə-ˈmɛntl/ *adj.* between or involving governments of different countries: *an intergovernmental conference*

ˌintergovernˌmental ˈrevenue *n.* [C] ECONOMICS money that one level of government gets from another level for a particular purpose or for financial support

in·ter·im[1] /ˈɪntərəm/ *adj.* [only before noun] used or accepted for a short time, until something or someone permanent or final is found SYN **provisional**: *the committee's interim chairman* | *an interim agreement*

interim[2] *n.* **in the interim** in the period of time between two events SYN **in the meantime**: *Ms. Keyes will be acting police chief in the interim.*

in·te·ri·or[1] /ɪnˈtɪriə-/ *n.* **1** [C usually singular] the inner part or inside of something OPP **exterior**: *Heat is trapped in the Earth's interior.* | +**of** *the interior of the car* **2 the interior** the part of a country or area that is farthest away from the coast or its borders: *forest fires in the Alaskan interior* **3 the Interior** in some countries, used in the name for the government department that is responsible for things that happen within the country, not things that happen between itself and other countries: *the Department of the Interior*

interior[2] *adj.* [only before noun] inside or indoors OPP **exterior**: *the interior walls of the house* [**Origin:** 1400–1500 French *intérieur*, from Latin *interior*]

inˌterior ˈangle *n.* [C] MATH an angle inside a POLYGON (=flat shape with straight sides) or other GEOMETRIC FIGURE → see also EXTERIOR ANGLE

inˌterior ˈdecorator *n.* [C] an interior designer —**interior decorating** also **inˌterior decoˈration** *n.* [U]

inˌterior deˈsigner *n.* [C] someone whose job is to plan and choose the colors, materials, furniture etc. for the inside of buildings, especially people's houses —**interior design** *n.* [U]

in·ter·ject /ˌɪntə-ˈdʒɛkt/ *v.* [I,T] to interrupt what someone else is saying with a sudden remark: *"Of course not!" Garland interjected.* [**Origin:** 1500–1600 Latin, past participle of *intericere*, from *jacere* **to throw**]

in·ter·jec·tion /ˌɪntə-ˈdʒɛkʃən/ *n.* **1** [C] ENG. LANG. ARTS a word or phrase used to express surprise, shock, pain etc. In the sentence "Ouch! That hurt!," "Ouch!" is an interjection **2** [C,U] the act of making a sudden remark while someone else is speaking, or this remark itself

in·ter·lace /ˌɪntə-ˈleɪs/ *v.* [I,T] to join things together by weaving and twisting them over and under each other, or to be joined in this way: *He sat with his fingers interlaced.*

in·ter·link /ˌɪntə-ˈlɪŋk/ *v.* [I,T] to connect or be connected with something else: *These two questions interlink in several ways.*

in·ter·lock /ˌɪntə-ˈlɑk/ *v.* [I] if two or more things interlock, they are connected by means of parts that fit firmly together: *The path is paved with interlocking stones.*

in·ter·loc·u·tor /ˌɪntə-ˈlɑkyəṭə-/ *n.* [C] FORMAL the person someone is speaking with

in·ter·lop·er /ˈɪntə-ˌloʊpə-/ *n.* [C] someone who enters a place or joins a group or activity where they are not wanted SYN **intruder**

in·ter·lude /ˈɪntə-ˌlud/ *n.* [C] **1** a short period of time, an event, an activity etc. that comes between other events, activities etc.: *the interlude of peace between the world wars* **2** a short romantic or sexual meeting or relationship: *a romantic interlude* **3** ENG. LANG. ARTS a short piece of music that comes between parts of a longer piece of music, between parts of a play etc.

in·ter·mar·ry /ˌɪntə-ˈmæri/ *v.* **intermarries, intermarried, intermarrying** [I] **1** to marry someone from a different group or race: +**with** *Spaniards and Mexicans began to intermarry with the Indians.* **2** to marry someone within your EXTENDED FAMILY: *Royal cousins sometimes intermarry.* —**intermarriage** *n.* [U]

in·ter·me·di·ar·y[1] /ˌɪntə-ˈmidiˌɛri/ *n. plural* **intermediaries** [C] **1** a person or organization that tries to help two other people or groups to agree with each other SYN **go-between**: +**between** *The Swiss foreign minister* ***acted as an intermediary*** *between the two countries.* **2** someone who represents someone else and does things for them SYN **representative**: *The King responded to the questions through an intermediary.*

intermediary[2] *adj.* **1** involving an intermediary or relating to being an intermediary: *Larsen had an intermediary role in the negotiations.* **2** coming between two other stages, levels etc.: *an intermediary step in the process*

in·ter·me·di·ate /ˌɪntə-ˈmidiɪt/ AC *adj.* **1** existing between the beginning skill level and the most advanced level, or made for someone at this level: *intermediate skiers* | *an intermediate Japanese language class* **2** existing, happening, or done between two other stages, levels etc.: *an intermediate stage in the problem-solving process* **3** existing or happening in the middle of a range of amounts, qualities etc.: *One intermediate estimate put the cost at $3,500.*

interˌmediate diˈrection *n.* [C] a direction, such as northeast or southwest, that lies between north and west, north and east, south and west, or south and east

interˌmediate ˈgoods *n.* [plural] ECONOMICS goods that are not in a finished state or materials such as steel, which are used in the production of other goods

interˈmediate ˌschool *n.* [C] a JUNIOR HIGH SCHOOL or MIDDLE SCHOOL

in·ter·ment /ɪnˈtə-mənt/ *n.* [C,U] FORMAL the act of burying a dead body → see also INTER

in·ter·mez·zo /ˌɪntə-ˈmɛtsoʊ, -ˈmɛdʒoʊ/ *n.* [C] a short piece of music, especially one that is played between the main parts of a concert, OPERA etc.

in·ter·mi·na·ble /ɪnˈtə-mənəbəl/ *adj.* very long and boring: *the professor's interminable lectures* —**interminably** *adv.*

in·ter·min·gle /ˌɪntə-ˈmɪŋgəl/ *v.* [I,T usually passive] to mix together, or to mix something with something else: *The movie intermingles danger and humor.*

in·ter·mis·sion /ˌɪntɚˈmɪʃən/ *n.* [C] a short period of time between the parts of a play, concert etc.

in·ter·mit·tent /ˌɪntɚˈmɪt̚nt/ *adj.* starting and stopping again and again: *intermittent rain* —**intermittently** *adv.*

in·ter·mix /ˌɪntɚˈmɪks/ *v.* [I,T] to mix together, or to mix things together: *Heavy rain was intermixed with snow and ice.*

in·tern¹ /ɪnˈtɚn/ *v.* **1** [T] to put someone in prison for political reasons or during a war, not because they have committed a crime: *Seven hundred men were interned in the camps.* **2** [I] to work somewhere without pay, especially while you are student, in order to get experience: *I was interning at a biotech company.* → see also INTERNMENT

in·tern² /ˈɪntɚn/ *n.* [C] **1** someone who has nearly finished training as a doctor and is working in a hospital ►see THESAURUS box at **doctor¹** **2** someone, especially a student, who works for a short time in a particular job in order to gain experience

in·ter·nal /ɪnˈtɚnl/ Ac S3 W2 *adj.* **1** within a particular country, company, organization etc., rather than outside it OPP **external**: *an internal investigation into the money transfers* | *the internal affairs of other nations* | *an internal memo* **2** inside your body OPP **external**: *internal organs such as the heart or liver* **3** [only before noun] inside something rather than outside OPP **external**: *an internal corridor* | *a computer's internal hard drive* **4** existing in your mind: *an internal dialogue with himself* [**Origin:** 1400–1500 Medieval Latin *internalis*, from Latin *internus* **inward, inside**]

inˌternal-comˈbustion ˌengine *n.* [C] an engine that produces power by burning GASOLINE

inˌternal ˈenergy *n.* PHYSICS the total amount of energy in or relating to all the atoms and MOLECULES in an object or substance

ˌinternal fertiliˈzation *n.* [U] BIOLOGY a process in which an egg cell (=cell that can become a baby) combines with SPERM (=male cells) inside a female's body → see also EXTERNAL FERTILIZATION

intˌernal fiˈnancing *n.* [U] **1** ECONOMICS money that a business makes from its normal business operations, and which it uses for particular purposes, rather than the money that a business borrows from a bank or gets by selling new STOCK **2** ECONOMICS money that a government receives in tax or through selling BONDS, and which it uses to build or improve roads, schools etc.

in·ter·nal·ize /ɪnˈtɚnlˌaɪz/ Ac *v.* [T] **1** if you internalize a particular belief, attitude, way of behaving etc. it becomes part of your character: *We encourage children to internalize adult values.* **2** if you internalize emotions, you do not express them but think about them: *Girls tend to internalize their fears, becoming sick as a result.* —**internalization** /ɪnˌtɚnələˈzeɪʃən/ *n.* [U]

in·ter·nal·ly /ɪnˈtɚnl-i/ Ac *adv.* **1** on or from the inside of something: *She was bleeding internally* (=inside her body). **2** within a particular company, country, organization etc.: *The complaint will be investigated internally.* **3** used to say that you do not express what you are feeling or thinking: *I groaned internally as she spoke.*

inˌternal ˈmedicine *n.* [U] a type of medical work in which doctors treat illnesses that do not need operations

Inˌternal ˈRevenue ˌService *n.* [singular] the IRS

in·ter·na·tion·al¹ /ˌɪntɚˈnæʃənl/ *adj.* **1** concerning more than one country, or involving people from more than one country: *The restaurant serves international cuisine.* | *international trade* | *How will **the international community** react to the attack?* **2** thinking or behaving in a way that shows that you know about other countries: *someone with an international perspective*

international² *n.* [C] **1** an international sports game **2** a company or organization that has offices in two or more countries

interˌnational ˈdate line *n.* **the international date line** an imaginary line that goes from the NORTH POLE to the SOUTH POLE in the Pacific Ocean, to the east of which the date is one day earlier than it is to the west

in·ter·na·tion·al·ism /ˌɪntɚˈnæʃənlˌɪzəm/ *n.* [U] POLITICS the belief that nations should work together and help each other —**internationalist** *n.*

in·ter·na·tion·al·ize /ˌɪntɚˈnæʃənlˌaɪz/ *v.* [T] to make something international or bring it under international control: *The crisis has become internationalized.* —**internationalization** /ɪntɚˌnæʃənl-əˈzeɪʃən/ *n.* [C]

in·ter·na·tion·al·ly /ˌɪntɚˈnæʃənl-i/ *adv.* in many different parts of the world: *The concert will be broadcast internationally.* | *internationally accepted standards* | **internationally known/famous** *Urban is an internationally known cancer surgeon.*

Interˌnational ˈMonetary ˌFund *n.* the IMF

Interˌnational ˈPEN an international organization of writers

Interˌnational Phoˈnetic ˌAlphabet *n.* [singular] the IPA

interˌnational reˈlations *n.* [plural] the political relationships between countries, or the study of this

Interˌnational ˌSystem of ˈUnits, the SCIENCE a system of standard measurements based on the METRIC SYSTEM, used for measuring distance, weight, time, temperature, electric current, amounts of a substance, and strength of light. There are seven units: the meter, kilogram, second, AMPERE, KELVIN, MOLE, and CANDELA, which are usually called SI UNITS.

in·ter·nec·ine /ˌɪntɚˈnɛsin/ *adj.* FORMAL internecine fighting, DISPUTES etc. happen between members of the same group or nation

in·tern·ee /ˌɪntɚˈni/ *n.* [C] someone who is put into prison during a war or for political reasons, usually without a TRIAL

In·ter·net /ˈɪntɚˌnɛt/ S2 W2 *n.* **the Internet** a network of computer connections that allows millions of computer users around the world to exchange information

THESAURUS

modem a piece of electronic equipment that allows information from one computer to be sent along telephone lines to another computer
broadband a system of connecting computers to the Internet and moving information at a very high speed
search engine a computer program that helps you find information on the Internet
website a place on the Internet where you can find information about a variety of subjects, including people, products, and organizations
address the set of words that you type into a computer to look at a website or send someone an email
chat room a place on the Internet where you can write messages to other people and receive messages back from them immediately, so that you can have a conversation
forum/newsgroup a group of computer users who are interested in a subject and discuss it using the Internet
blog a web page that is made up of information about a particular subject, in which the newest information is always at the top of the page
email a system that allows you to send and receive messages by computer, or a message sent this way
→ EMAIL, COMPUTER

ˈInternet caˌfé *n.* [C] a public place where anyone can pay to use a computer and the Internet

in·ter·nist /ɪnˈtɚnɪst/ *n.* [C] a doctor who treats medical problems inside your body without medical operations

in·tern·ment /ɪnˈtɚnmənt/ *n.* [C,U] the act of imprisoning someone for political reasons or during a war, not because they have committed a crime, or the period of time someone is kept this way: *a 27-year internment*

in'ternment camp *n.* [C] a place where people are kept as prisoners for political reasons

in·ter·node /'ɪntɚˌnoʊd/ *n.* [C] BIOLOGY an area between two NODES (=places where a leaf or branch grows) on the stem of a plant

in·ter·of·fice /'ɪntɚˌɔfɪs/ *adj.* between or involving different offices of the same organization or company: *interoffice mail*

in·ter·per·son·al /ˌɪntɚ'pɚsənl/ *adj.* involving relationships between people: *interpersonal communication* | *a man with poor* ***interpersonal skills*** (=a poor ability to deal with other people)

in·ter·phase /'ɪntɚˌfeɪz/ *n.* [C] BIOLOGY a period after a cell has divided into two cells and before it starts dividing again

in·ter·plan·e·tar·y /ˌɪntɚ'plænəˌtɛri/ *adj.* [only before noun] happening or existing between the PLANETS: *interplanetary exploration*

in·ter·play /'ɪntɚˌpleɪ/ *n.* [U] the way in which two people or things react to one another or affect each other: **+of/between** *the interplay of ideas in the book* | *the interplay between work and family life*

In·ter·pol /'ɪntɚˌpoʊl/ *n.* [singular] an international police organization that helps national police forces catch criminals

in·ter·po·late /ɪn'tɚpəˌleɪt/ *v.* FORMAL **1** [T] to put additional words, ideas, information etc. into something such as a piece of writing SYN **insert** **2** [T] to interrupt someone by saying something **3** [I,T] TECHNICAL to find or guess the middle of a range of amounts —**interpolation** /ɪnˌtɚpə'leɪʃən/ *n.* [C,U]

in·ter·pose /ˌɪntɚ'poʊz/ *v.* [T] FORMAL **1** to put yourself or something else between two other things **2** to introduce something between the parts of a conversation or argument: *"That might be difficult," interposed Mrs. Flavell.*

in·ter·pret /ɪn'tɚprɪt/ Ac S3 *v.* **1** [I,T] to tell someone, in their own language, what someone speaking a foreign language is saying → see also TRANSLATE: **interepret for sb** *She spoke Spanish and offered to interpret for me.* **2 interpret sth as sth** to consider someone's behavior or words or an event as having a particular meaning: *I interpreted her silence as anger.* **3** [T] to understand or explain the meaning of something: *How would you interpret this line from the song?* | *The data has not yet been interpreted.* **4** [T] ENG. LANG. ARTS to perform a part in a play, a piece of music etc. in a way that shows your feelings about it or what you think it means [**Origin:** 1300–1400 French *interpréter*, from Latin *interpretari*, from *interpres* **someone who explains or translates**]

in·ter·pre·ta·tion /ɪnˌtɚprə'teɪʃən/ Ac *n.* [C,U] **1** the way in which someone explains or understands an event, information, someone's actions etc.: *Lawyers called the police department's interpretation of the law "ridiculous."* | **open/subject to interpretation** (=able to be explained or understood in different ways) **2** ENG. LANG. ARTS the way in which someone performs a play, a piece of music etc.: *his skillful interpretation of the Mozart concerto*

in·ter·pre·ta·tive /ɪn'tɚprəˌteɪt̬ɪv/ Ac *adj.* interpretive

in·ter·pret·er /ɪn'tɚprət̬ɚ/ *n.* [C] **1** someone who has the skill or job of telling someone, in their own language, what someone speaking a foreign language is saying → see also TRANSLATOR: *Maria* ***acted as an interpreter*** *for us.* **2** COMPUTERS a computer PROGRAM that changes an instruction into a form that can be understood directly by the computer

in·ter·pre·tive /ɪn'tɚprət̬ɪv/ Ac *adj.* **1** relating to, explaining, or understanding the meaning of something: *Reading is an interpretive process.* **2** relating to how feelings are expressed through music, dance, art etc.: *interpretive dance*

inˌterpretive 'center *n.* [C] a place where tourists can receive information about the place they are visiting, for example information about its history or about the animals and plants there SYN **visitor's center**

in·ter·quar·tile range /ˌɪntɚˌkwɔrtaɪl 'reɪndʒ/ *n.* [C] MATH the difference between the first and the third QUARTILES (=the three values that divide a set of data into four equal parts) in a set of NUMERICAL data

in·ter·ra·cial /ˌɪntɚ'reɪʃəl◂ / *adj.* between different races of people: *Interracial marriage is more common today.*

in·ter·reg·num /ˌɪntə'rɛgnəm/ *n.* *plural* **interregnums, interregna** /-nə/ [C] a period of time when a country, government, organization etc. temporarily has no king, queen, leader etc.

in·ter·re·late /ˌɪntɚrɪ'leɪt/ *v.* [I,T] if two or more things interrelate, or you interrelate them, they are or become connected and have an effect on each other: *The diagram interrelates population and natural resources.*

in·ter·re·lat·ed /ˌɪntɚrɪ'leɪt̬ɪd/ *adj.* things that are interrelated are connected and have an effect on each other: *four interrelated short stories*

in·ter·re·la·tion·ship /ˌɪntɚrɪ'leɪʃənˌʃɪp/ *n.* [C,U] a connection between two things that makes them affect each other: *the economic interrelationship between the three countries*

in·ter·ro·gate /ɪn'tɛrəˌgeɪt/ *v.* [T] to ask someone a lot of questions for a long time in order to get information, sometimes in a threatening way: *His job was to interrogate prisoners of war.* —**interrogator** *n.* [C] —**interrogation** /ɪnˌtɛrə'geɪʃən/ *n.* [C,U]

in·ter·rog·a·tive[1] /ˌɪntɚ'rɑgət̬ɪv/ *adj.* ENG. LANG. ARTS an interrogative sentence, PRONOUN etc. asks a question or has the form of a question. For example, "who" and "what" are interrogative PRONOUNS. → see also DECLARATIVE, EXCLAMATORY

interrogative[2] *n.* ENG. LANG. ARTS **1 the interrogative** the form of a sentence or verb that is used for asking questions **2** [C] a word such as "who" or "what" that is used to ask questions

in·ter·rog·a·to·ry /ˌɪntɚ'rɑgəˌtɔri/ *n.* [C] LAW a formal or written question that a WITNESS must answer —**interrogatory** *adj.*

in·ter·rupt /ˌɪntɚ'rʌpt/ S3 *v.* **1** [I,T] to stop someone from continuing what they are saying or doing by suddenly saying or doing something yourself: *Can I interrupt you for a second?* | ***Sorry to interrupt*** (=used to politely interrupt), *but it's really important.* **2** [T] to make a process or activity stop for a short time: *Train service was interrupted for about ten minutes.* **3** [T] LITERARY if something interrupts a line, surface, view etc. it stops it from being continuous [**Origin:** 1300–1400 Latin, past participle of *interrumpere*, from *rumpere* **to break**]

in·ter·rup·tion /ˌɪntɚ'rʌpʃən/ *n.* [C,U] **1** something that you say or do that stops a person during what they are saying or doing: *Don't allow any phone calls or other interruptions.* **2** the act of stopping a process or activity for a short time, or the things that make it stop: *Work on the project continued without interruption.*

in·ter·scho·las·tic /ˌɪntɚskə'læstɪk/ *adj.* between or involving different schools: *interscholastic athletics*

in·ter·sect /ˌɪntɚ'sɛkt/ *v.* **1** [I,T] if two lines or roads intersect, they go across each other **2** [T usually passive] to divide an area with several lines, roads etc.: *Venus's surface is intersected by a network of ridges and valleys.* [**Origin:** 1600–1700 Latin, past participle of *intersecare*, from *secare* **to cut**]

in·ter·sec·tion /'ɪntɚˌsɛkʃən, ˌɪntɚ'sɛkʃən/ S3 *n.* **1** [C] the place where two or more roads, lines etc. meet and go across each other: *Turn left at the next intersection.* **2** [U] the act of intersecting something

in·ter·ses·sion /'ɪntɚˌsɛʃən/ *n.* [C,U] the time between two parts of a college year, when ordinary classes are not taught

in·ter·sperse /ˌɪntɚˈspɚs/ *v.* [T usually passive] to mix one group of things together with another group, or to put parts of one group between parts of the other group: **intersperse sth between/among sth** *New homes are interspersed among the older ones.* | **intersperse sth with sth** *The 12-minute program was interspersed with 30-second commercials.*

in·ter·state¹ /ˈɪntɚˌsteɪt/ *n.* [C] a wide road that goes between states, on which cars can travel very fast: *The interstate goes from North Carolina to California.* ▸see THESAURUS box at **road**

interstate² *adj.* [only before noun] between or involving different states in the U.S.: *interstate commerce* —**interstate** *adv.*

ˌInterstate ˈCommerce Comˌmission, the ABBREVIATION **ICC** the former U.S. government organization was replaced in 1995 by the Surface Transportation Board

in·ter·stel·lar /ˌɪntɚˈstɛlɚ/ *adj.* [only before noun] PHYSICS happening or existing between the stars: *interstellar gas and dust*

in·ter·stice /ɪnˈtɚstɪs/ *n.* [C usually plural] FORMAL a small space or crack in something or between things

in·ter·twined /ˌɪntɚˈtwaɪnd/ *adj.* **1** closely related: *Research and teaching are intertwined.* **2** twisted together: *intertwined arms and legs* —**interwine** *v.* [I,T]

in·ter·val /ˈɪntɚvəl/ Ac *n.* [C] **1** a period of time or distance between two events, activities etc.: *After a five-minute interval, go back and check on the baby.* | **+between** *The intervals between the passing cars increased.* **2 at intervals** with a particular amount of time or distance between things, activities etc.: **at regular/frequent intervals** *Feed your puppy at regular intervals during the day.* | *Pillars were spaced at regular intervals.* | **at intervals of 3 feet/2 minutes etc.** *Tests were given at intervals of three or six months.* | **at daily/weekly/half-hour etc. intervals** *The train runs at seven-minute intervals all day.* **3** ENG. LANG. ARTS the amount of difference in PITCH between two musical notes [**Origin:** 1300–1400 Old French *entreval*, from Latin *intervallum* **space between castle walls, interval**]

in·ter·vene /ˌɪntɚˈvin/ Ac *v.* [I] **1** to do something to try and stop an argument, war etc. or to deal with a problem, especially one that you are not directly involved in: *The UN has not yet decided whether to intervene militarily.* | **+in** *So far the court has refused to intervene in the case.* **2** if an event intervenes, it delays or interrupts something else: *The economy was doing better until the earthquake intervened.* **3** FORMAL if a period of time intervenes, it comes between two events

in·ter·ven·ing /ˌɪntɚˈvinɪŋ/ Ac *adj.* **the intervening years/months/decades etc.** FORMAL the amount of time between two events: *I hadn't seen him since 1980, and he had aged a lot in the intervening years.*

in·ter·ven·tion /ˌɪntɚˈvɛnʃən/ Ac *n.* [C,U] the act of becoming involved in a difficult situation in order to affect or change what happens: *He opposed U.S. military intervention overseas.* | ***Early intervention*** (=early medical help) *can save the lives of breast cancer patients.*

in·ter·ven·tion·ism /ˌɪntɚˈvɛnʃəˌnɪzəm/ *n.* [U] **1** the belief that a government should try to influence trade by spending government money **2** the belief that a government should try to influence what happens in foreign countries —**interventionist** *adj.*

in·ter·view¹ /ˈɪntɚˌvyu/ S2 W1 *n.* **1** [C] an occasion when a famous person is asked questions about their life, experiences, or opinions for a newspaper, magazine, television program etc.: *Julia Roberts' interview in People Magazine* | **+with** *an interview with the president* | *She rarely **gives interviews*** (=agrees to be interviewed) *to the press.* | **a newspaper/tv/radio interview** *He said in a newspaper interview that he had no plans to retire.* **2** [C,U] a formal meeting at which someone is asked questions, for example to find out if they are good enough for a job: *Can you come in for an interview?* | **+for** *He has an interview for a job at the Dallas Tribune.* | *I don't do well in **job interviews**.* [**Origin:** 1500–1600 Early *French entrevue*, from *entrevoir* **to see each other, meet**]

interview² S2 W3 *v.* **1** [T] to ask someone questions during an interview: *We interviewed 12 candidates in three days.* | *She has interviewed many famous people in her career.* **2** [I] to go to a job interview in order to try to get a job: **+with/at** *I've only interviewed with two other companies so far.*

in·ter·view·ee /ˌɪntɚvyuˈi/ *n.* [C] the person who answers the questions in an interview

in·ter·view·er /ˈɪntɚˌvyuɚ/ *n.* [C] the person who asks the questions in an interview

in·ter·weave /ˌɪntɚˈwiv/ *v.* **interwove** /-ˈwoʊv/, **interwoven** /-ˈwoʊvən/ **1** [I,T usually passive] to combine things in a complicated way: *"Poison" is three interwoven stories in one.* | **be interwoven with sth** *The modern music is interwoven with hits from the 1920s.* **2** [T usually passive] to weave two or more things together: *The silk is interwoven with gold and silver threads.*

in·tes·tate /ɪnˈtɛˌsteɪt/ *adj.* LAW **die intestate** to die without having made a WILL (=an official statement about who you want to have your property after you die)

in·tes·ti·nal /ɪnˈtɛstənl/ *adj.* **1** relating to or existing in the intestines: *intestinal disease* **2 intestinal fortitude** HUMOROUS courage and determination SYN **guts**

in·tes·tine /ɪnˈtɛstɪn/ *n.* [C usually plural] BIOLOGY the long tube, consisting of two parts, that takes food from your stomach out of your body [**Origin:** 1400–1500 French *intestin*, from Latin *intestinum*, from *intus* **inside**] → see also LARGE INTESTINE, SMALL INTESTINE

ˌin-ˈthing *n.* **be the in-thing** INFORMAL to be very fashionable and popular at the present time

in·ti·fa·da /ˌɪntəˈfɑdə/ *n.* [C] POLITICS one of two periods of violence by Palestinians in the West Bank and the Gaza Strip in protest of the Israeli presence in these areas. The first began in 1987 and the second in 2000.

in·ti·ma·cy /ˈɪntəməsi/ *n. plural* **intimacies** **1** [U] a state of having a close personal relationship with someone: *the intimacy of married couples* | **+between** *the intimacy between parent and child* **2** [C,U] the quality of a place or situation that makes you feel that you are in private with someone: *the restaurant's cozy intimacy* **3** [C usually plural] remarks or actions of a type that happen only between people who know each other very well: *the whispered intimacies of lovers* **4** [U] a word meaning "sex," used when you want to avoid saying this directly: *Intimacy took place on several occasions.*

in·ti·mate¹ /ˈɪntəmɪt/ *adj.*
1 RESTAURANT/MEAL/PLACE private and friendly, so that you feel comfortable: *an intimate dinner for two*
2 PRIVATE relating to very private or personal matters: *an intimate conversation* | *She was asked about the most **intimate details** of her life.*
3 FRIENDS having an extremely close relationship: *an intimate relationship* | *Harper **is on intimate terms with*** (=has a very close relationships with) *the band's lead singer.*
4 SEXUAL relating to sex: *The virus is transmitted through **intimate contact**.*
5 an intimate knowledge of sth very detailed knowledge of something, as a result of careful study or a lot of experience: *Goldston has an intimate knowledge of the footwear industry.*
6 CONNECTION a very close connection between two things: **intimate link/connection etc.** *the intimate connection between physical and mental health* —**intimately** *adv.*

in·ti·mate² /ˈɪntəˌmeɪt/ *v.* [T] FORMAL to make people understand what you mean without saying it directly: **intimate that** *Cuevas intimated that a compromise might be reached soon.* [**Origin:** 1500–1600 Late Latin, past participle of *intimare* **to put in, announce**, from Latin *intimus* **furthest inside**]

in·ti·mate³ /ˈɪntəmɪt/ *n.* [C] a close personal friend

ˌintimate apˈparel *n.* [U] a word for women's underwear often used in stores and advertisements

in·ti·ma·tion /ˌɪntəˈmeɪʃən/ *n.* [C,U] FORMAL an indirect or unclear sign that something is true or may happen: *the first intimations that there was a problem*

in·tim·i·date /ɪnˈtɪməˌdeɪt/ *v.* [T] **1** to frighten someone by behaving in a threatening way, especially in order to make them do what you want: *The gang had been intimidating passengers on the subway.* **2** to make someone feel worried and less confident: *Large audiences don't intimidate him.* [**Origin:** 1600–1700 Medieval Latin, past participle of *intimidare*, from Latin *timidus*] —**intimidation** /ɪnˌtɪməˈdeɪʃən/ *n.* [U]

in·tim·i·dat·ed /ɪnˈtɪməˌdeɪt̬ɪd/ *adj.* feeling worried and less confident, for example because you are in a difficult situation or other people seem better than you: *I was shy and felt intimidated by the other students.*

in·tim·i·dat·ing /ɪnˈtɪməˌdeɪt̬ɪŋ/ *adj.* making you feel worried, frighthened, and less confident: *an intimidating letter from her ex-husband's lawyer*

in·to /ˈɪntə; *before vowels* ˈɪntʊ; *strong* ˈɪntu/ S1 W1 *prep.* **1** from the outside to the inside of a container, substance, place, area etc.: *The child had fallen into the water.* | *Jeff went into the living room.* | *I'm going into town this morning to do some shopping.* **2** involved in a situation or activity: *They decided to go into business together.* | *Don't get into any trouble.* **3** from one situation or physical form to a different one: *Ellen is going into fifth grade next year.* | *Roll the cookie dough into balls.* **4** to a point where you hit something, usually causing damage: *Maggie bumped into the dessert cart and knocked it over.* | *The other car just backed into me.* **5** in a particular direction: *They rode off into the sunset.* | *Make sure you're speaking directly into the microphone.* **6 be/get into sth** SPOKEN to like and be interested in something, or to become interested in it: *I was really into ice skating when I was 10.* **7** at or until a certain time: *We talked into the night.* **8** SPOKEN used to say that a second number is divided by the first number: *Six goes into thirty five times.* | *Eight into twenty-four is three.* **9 be into sb** SLANG to owe someone money: *He's into me for $25.* **10 be/get into everything** INFORMAL if a young child is or gets into everything, he or she is curious about everything and wants to touch everything [**Origin:** Old English]

in·tol·er·a·ble /ɪnˈtɑlərəbəl/ *adj.* too difficult, bad, annoying etc. for you to accept or deal with: *Living conditions in the building were intolerable.*

in·tol·er·ant /ɪnˈtɑlərənt/ *adj.* **1** not willing to accept ways of thinking and behaving that are different from your own: *an intolerant society* | +**of** *people who are intolerant of other people's political beliefs* **2 -intolerant** not physically able to eat a particular type of food or substance in food: *Her son is gluten-intolerant* (=he cannot foods with GLUTEN in it). —**intolerance** *n.* [U] *racial intolerance*

in·to·na·tion /ˌɪntəˈneɪʃən, -toʊ-/ *n.* [C,U] **1** ENG. LANG. ARTS the way in which the level of your voice changes in order to add meaning to what you are saying, for example by going up at the end of a question **2** [U] the act of intoning something

in·tone /ɪnˈtoʊn/ *v.* [T] say something slowly and clearly without making your voice rise and fall much as you speak: *Uncle Danny intoned the prayer in Hebrew.*

in to·to /ɪn ˈtoʊtoʊ/ *adv.* as a whole SYN **totally**: *The paper reprinted the article in toto.*

in·tox·i·cant /ɪnˈtɑksəkənt/ *n.* [C] TECHNICAL something that makes you drunk, especially an alcoholic drink

in·tox·i·cat·ed /ɪnˈtɑksəˌkeɪt̬ɪd/ *adj.* **1** FORMAL having drunk too much alcohol, so that you are unable to function normally SYN **drunk**: *The driver was clearly intoxicated.* **2** happy, excited, and unable to think clearly, especially as a result of love, success, power etc.: *We were intoxicated by victory.* —**intoxicate** *v.* [T]

in·tox·i·cat·ing /ɪnˈtɑksəˌkeɪt̬ɪŋ/ *adj.* **1** intoxicating drinks can make you drunk **2** making you feel happy, excited, and unable to think clearly: *Their sudden freedom was intoxicating.*

in·tox·i·ca·tion /ɪnˌtɑksəˈkeɪʃən/ *n.* [U] the state of being drunk

intra- /ɪntrə/ *prefix* FORMAL OR TECHNICAL into, inside or within something: *intra-departmental* (=within a department) | *an intranet* (=connection for computers inside a company) | *an intravenous injection* (=into a VEIN) → see also INTER-, INTRO-

in·trac·ta·ble /ɪnˈtræktəbəl/ *adj.* FORMAL **1** an intractable problem is very difficult to deal with or solve: *intractable poverty* **2** having a strong will and difficult to control: *intractable enemies* —**intractability** /ɪnˌtræktəˈbɪləṱi/ *n.* [U]

in·tra·mu·ral /ˌɪntrəˈmyʊrəl/ *adj.* happening within one school, or intended for the students of one school: *intramural sports* → see also EXTRAMURAL

in·tra·net /ˈɪntrəˌnɛt/ *n.* [C] COMPUTERS a computer system within a company or organization that allows its computer users around the world to exchange information

in·tran·si·gent /ɪnˈtrænsədʒənt, -zə-/ *adj.* FORMAL unwilling to change your ideas or behavior in a way that seems unreasonable, or showing this quality: *intransigent attitudes* —**intransigence** *n.* [U] —**intransigently** *adv.*

in·tran·si·tive /ɪnˈtrænsət̬ɪv, -zə-/ *adj.* ENG. LANG. ARTS an intransitive verb has a subject but no object. For example, in the sentence "They arrived," "arrive" is an intransitive verb. Intransitive verbs are marked [I] in this dictionary → see also TRANSITIVE

in·tra·pre·neur /ˌɪntrəprəˈnɚ/ *n.* [C] TECHNICAL someone who helps the company they work for by working to develop new products or ways of working —**intrapreneurial** *adj.* → see also ENTREPRENEUR

in·tra·state /ˈɪntrəˌsteɪt/ *adj.* within one state in the U.S.: *intrastate phone calls* → see also INTERSTATE

in·tra·u·ter·ine /ˌɪntrəˈyut̬ərɪn, -raɪn/ *n.* [C] an IUD

in·tra·ve·nous /ˌɪntrəˈvinəs/ *adj.* **1** MEDICINE within or into a VEIN (=a tube that takes blood to your heart): *an intravenous injection* **2 intravenous drugs/fluids etc.** MEDICINE drugs, liquids etc. that are put directly into the blood in a VEIN —**intravenously** *adv.*: *The drugs were administered intravenously.*

in·trep·id /ɪnˈtrɛpɪd/ *adj.* FORMAL willing to do dangerous things or go to dangerous places: *intrepid explorers*

in·tri·ca·cy /ˈɪntrɪkəsi/ *n. plural* **intricacies** **1 the intricacies of sth** the complicated details of something: *The movie can't match the intricacies of the novel.* **2** [U] the state of containing a large number of parts or details: *the intricacy of the designs in her textiles*

in·tri·cate /ˈɪntrɪkɪt/ *adj.* containing many small parts or details: *the intricate workings of an old watch* [**Origin:** 1400–1500 Latin, past participle of *intricare* **to mix up in a complicated way**, from *tricae* **small unimportant things, things that get in your way**]

in·trigue¹ /ɪnˈtrig/ *v.* **1** [T] if something intrigues you, it interests you a lot because it is strange or mysterious: *Other people's houses always intrigue me.* | *He was intrigued by the final line of the letter.* **2** [I] LITERARY to make secret plans to harm someone or make them lose their position of power

in·trigue² /ˈɪntrig, ɪnˈtrig/ *n.* **1** [U] the act or practice of secretly planning to harm someone or make them lose their position of power: *a story of political intrigue* **2** [C] a secret plan to harm someone or make them lose their position of power

in·trigu·ing /ɪnˈtrigɪŋ/ *adj.* something that is intriguing is very interesting because it is strange, mysterious, or unexpected and makes you want to know more: *the story's intriguing characters* | *Your question is intriguing.* —**intriguingly** *adv.*

in·trin·sic /ɪnˈtrɪnzɪk, -sɪk/ Ac *adj.* being part of the nature or character of someone or something: *the*

I

intrinsic value of honesty | **+to** *Flexibility is intrinsic to good management.* —**intrinsically** /-kli/ *adv.*

in·tro /ˈɪntroʊ/ *n.* [C] INFORMAL the introduction to a song, piece of writing etc.

intro- /ɪntrə/ *prefix* inside or within something: *introspection* (=examining your own feelings and thoughts) → see also INTER-, INTRA-

in·tro·duce /ˌɪntrəˈdus/ S2 W2 *v.* [T]
1 WHEN PEOPLE MEET if you introduce someone to another person, you tell them each other's names when they meet for the first time: *Have you two been introduced?* | **introduce sb to sb** *Russell, let me introduce you to Katie.* | *I **introduced myself*** (=tell someone your name) *to the girl next to me.*
2 MAKE STH HAPPEN/EXIST to make something happen, exist, or be available for the first time: *The college wants to introduce a fairer examination system.* | **introduce reforms/a law/a tax etc.** *plans to introduce a law to ban hunting* | **introduce a product/model etc.** *We will be introducing the product onto the market in 2011.*
3 **introduce sb to sth** to show someone something or tell them about it for the first time: *My father introduced me to fishing when I was seven.*
4 BRING TO A PLACE to take or bring something to a place or put it in a place for the first time from somewhere else: **introduce sth to/into sth** *Chocolate was introduced into Europe in the 1700s.*
5 PRESENT to formally present or announce someone or something in public: *Jim will introduce tonight's speaker.*
6 LAW to formally present something such as a proposed new law or new evidence to be discussed and considered: *The evidence could not be introduced in court.* | *Several senators introduced legislation aimed at sexual harassment.*
7 BE THE START OF FORMAL if an event introduces a particular period or time or a change, it is the beginning of it: *The election has introduced a feeling of optimism here.*
8 PUT STH INTO STH TECHNICAL to put something carefully into something else: *Fuel was introduced into the jet pipe.*
[**Origin:** 1400–1500 Latin *introducere*, from *ducere* **to lead**]

in·tro·duc·tion /ˌɪntrəˈdʌkʃən/ *n.*
1 MAKING STH AVAILABLE [U] the act of making something exist, happen, or be available for the first time: *Since its introduction two years ago, the game has outsold all its competitors.* | **+of** *the introduction of new drugs to fight AIDS*
2 BOOK/SPEECH [C] a written or spoken explanation at the beginning of a book, speech etc.: *The introduction was written by Colin Powell.* | **+to** *the introduction to the article*
3 LEARN ABOUT STH [C] a book, class, article etc. which gives a simple explanation of a subject for someone studying it for the first time: **+to** *The class is an introduction to poetry.*
4 BRINGING STH TO A PLACE [C,U] **a)** the act of bringing something to a place or putting it in a place for the first time from somewhere else: **+of** *the introduction of Buddhism to China from India* **b)** something that is brought into a place for the first time from somewhere else: *The potato was a 16th-century introduction.*
5 WHEN PEOPLE MEET [C often plural] the act of formally telling two people each other's names, and often a little about who they are, when they first meet: *I'll **make the introductions**.*
6 FIRST EXPERIENCE [C] a situation in which someone experiences an activity for the first time: **+to** *Sgt. Mornay's voice in my ear was my introduction to the army.*
7 MUSIC [C] a short part at the beginning of a piece of music, before the main tune begins
8 **the introduction of sth** TECHNICAL the act of adding or putting something carefully into something else: *the introduction of foreign DNA into the cell*
9 **sb needs no introduction** SPOKEN said when introducing someone well-known to an audience: *Our next guest needs no introduction.*

in·tro·duc·to·ry /ˌɪntrəˈdʌktəri/ *adj.* [usually before noun] **1** said or written at the beginning of a book, speech etc. in order to explain what it is about: *his introductory remarks* **2** intended for people who do not know a lot about a particular subject or activity in order to give them basic information: *an introductory class called "Understanding Computers"* **3 an introductory price/rate/offer etc.** a price, rate etc. designed to encourage people to buy a new product

in·tro·spec·tion /ˌɪntrəˈspɛkʃən/ *n.* [U] the process of thinking deeply about your own thoughts and feelings to find out their real meaning

in·tro·spec·tive /ˌɪntrəˈspɛktɪv/ *adj.* tending to think deeply about your own thoughts, feelings etc.: *a quiet, introspective woman* —**introspectively** *adv.*

in·tro·vert /ˈɪntrəˌvɚt/ *n.* [C] someone who is quiet and shy, and does not enjoy being with other people OPP **extrovert** —**introvert** *adj.* —**introversion** /ˌɪntrəˈvɚʒən/ *n.* [U]

in·tro·vert·ed /ˈɪntrəˌvɚt̬ɪd/ *adj.* quiet and shy, and not enjoying being with other people OPP **extroverted**: *an introverted and serious boy*

in·trude /ɪnˈtrud/ *v.* **1** [I] to interrupt someone or become involved in their private affairs in an annoying and unwanted way: *Sorry, I didn't mean to intrude.* | **+on/upon/into** *We didn't want to intrude on the family's grief.* **2** [I] to begin to have an unwanted effect on a situation: **+on** *Worries about money began to intrude on our daily life.* [**Origin:** 1400–1500 Latin *intrudere*, from *trudere* **to push**]

in·trud·er /ɪnˈtrudɚ/ *n.* [C] **1** someone who illegally enters a building or area, usually in order to steal something: *Intruders took several of the school's computers.* **2** someone who is in a place where they are not wanted: *At first, I felt like an intruder in their family.*

in·tru·sion /ɪnˈtruʒən/ *n.* **1** [C,U] an unwanted action or person in a situation that is private: *Are you sure that my staying here won't be an intrusion?* | **+into/on/upon** *intrusions on people's privacy* | **+of** *the intrusion of the press* **2** [C,U] something that has an unwanted effect on a situation, on people's lives etc.: *Some players resent the intrusion of religion into sports.*

in·tru·sive /ɪnˈtrusɪv/ *adj.* affecting someone's private life or interrupting them in an unwanted and annoying way: *intrusive questions*

in·tu·it /ɪnˈtuɪt/ *v.* [I,T] FORMAL to understand that something is true through your feelings rather than through thinking about it

in·tu·i·tion /ˌɪntuˈɪʃən/ *n.* **1** [U] the ability to understand or know something by using your feelings rather than by carefully considering the facts SYN **instinct**: *women's intuition* | *Much of what doctors do is based on intuition.* **2** [C] an idea about what is true in a particular situation, based on strong feelings rather than facts: *People had an intuition that something was not right.* [**Origin:** 1400–1500 Late Latin *intuitio*, from Latin *intueri* **to look at, think about**]

in·tu·i·tive /ɪnˈtuət̬ɪv/ *adj.* **1** based on feelings rather than on knowledge or facts SYN **instinctive**: *Macelo's style of management is intuitive and informal.* **2** someone who is intuitive is able to understand situations using their feelings, without being told what is happening or having any proof **3** an intuitive system, piece of software etc. is easy to use without having to learn about it first —**intuitively** *adv.* —**intuitiveness** *n.* [U]

In·u·it, Innuit /ˈɪnuɪt/ *n. plural* **Inuits** or **Inuit** [C] a word often used to mean INUK [**Origin:** 1800–1900 an Aleut word that is the plural of *inuk* **person**]

I·nuk /ɪˈnuk/ *n. plural* **Inuit** [C] a member of a race of people living in the very cold northern areas of North America → see also ESKIMO

I·nuk·ti·tut /ɪˈnuktəˌtut/ *n.* [U] the language of the Inuits

in·un·date /ˈɪnənˌdeɪt/ *v.* **1 be inundated with sth** to receive so much of something that you cannot easily deal with it all SYN **swamp**: *The TV station was inun-*

dated with complaints after the show. **2** [T] FORMAL to cover an area with a large amount of water SYN **flood**: *Floodwaters regularly inundate the lowlands of the state.* [**Origin:** 1500–1600 Latin, past participle of *inundare*, from *unda* **wave**] —**inundation** /ˌɪnən'deɪʃən/ *n.* [C,U]

in•ured /ɪ'nʊrd/ *adj.* **inured to sth** so used to something bad, that you do not get upset by it anymore: *Nurses soon become inured to the sight of suffering.*

in•urn•ment /ɪ'nɚnmənt/ *n.* [C] FORMAL the act of putting a dead person's ashes into an URN in order to bury them —**inurn** *v.* [T]

in•vade /ɪn'veɪd/ *v.* **1** [I,T] to enter a country, town, or area using military force, in order to take control of it: *The Romans invaded Britain more than 2,000 years ago.* **2** [T] to go into a place in large numbers or amounts, when this is not wanted: *Every summer the town is invaded by tourists.* | *the rate at which the virus invades cells* **3** [T] to affect someone in an unwanted and annoying way: *He claims investigators* ***invaded his privacy*** *by searching his garage.* [**Origin:** 1400–1500 Latin *invadere*, from *vadere* **to go**] → see also INVASION

in•vad•er /ɪn'veɪdɚ/ *n.* [C usually plural] someone who is part of an army that enters a country or town by force in order to take control of it

in•val•id¹ /ɪn'vælɪd/ *adj.* **1** a contract, ticket, claim etc. that is invalid is not legally or officially acceptable SYN **valid**: *Do not detach the coupon or your ticket will be invalid.* **2** reasons, opinions etc. that are invalid are not based on clear thoughts or facts SYN **valid**: *Ackerman said the argument was invalid.* **3** if something you type into a computer is invalid, the computer does not recognize or accept it SYN **valid** —**invalidity** /ˌɪnvə'lɪdəṭi/ *n.* [U]

in•va•lid² /'ɪnvələd/ *n.* [C] someone who cannot take care of themselves because of illness, old age, or injury —**invalid** *adj.*: *her invalid father*

in•val•i•date /ɪn'væləˌdeɪt/ Ac *v.* [T] **1** to make a document, ticket, claim etc. not legally or officially acceptable anymore: *They invalidated his insurance policy because he hadn't payed.* **2** to show that something such as a belief or explanation is wrong: *Later findings invalidated the theory.*

in•val•ua•ble /ɪn'vælyəbəl, -yuəbəl/ *adj.* extremely useful: +**to/for** *Martin's marketing expertise has been invaluable to our project.* | **invaluable in doing sth** *Police said the information was invaluable in making the arrest.*

in•var•i•a•ble /ɪn'vɛriəbəl/ Ac *adj.* **1** always happening in the same way, at the same time etc.: *My father's invariable reply was, "We'll just see what happens."* **2** TECHNICAL never changing: *the invariable rules of mathematics*

in•var•i•a•bly /ɪn'vɛriəbli/ Ac *adv.* if something invariably happens or is invariably true, it almost always happens or is true, so that you expect it: *It invariably rains when I go on vacation.*

in•va•sion /ɪn'veɪʒən/ *n.* **1** [C,U] an occasion when one country's army enters another country by force, in order to take control of it: *the invasion of Normandy* ▸see THESAURUS box at **attack¹** **2** [C] the arrival in a place of a lot of people or things, often where they are not wanted: *an invasion of cheap imports* **3 invasion of privacy** a situation in which someone tries to find out personal details about another person's private affairs in a way that is upsetting and often illegal

in•va•sive /ɪn'veɪsɪv/ *adj.* invasive medical treatment involves cutting into someone's body OPP **non-invasive**

inˌvasive 'species *n.* [C] BIOLOGY a type of plant that does not naturally grow in an area, but which when introduced into the area grows and spreads very quickly, stopping existing plants from growing successfully

in•vec•tive /ɪn'vɛktɪv/ *n.* [U] FORMAL impolite and insulting words that someone says when they are very angry

in•veigh /ɪn'veɪ/ *v.*
inveigh against sb/sth *phr. v.* FORMAL to criticize someone or something strongly

in•vei•gle /ɪn'veɪgəl/ *v.*
inveigle sb **into** sth *phr. v.* FORMAL to persuade someone to do what you want, especially in a dishonest way

in•vent /ɪn'vɛnt/ S3 W3 *v.* [T] **1** to make or design something new for the first time: *Who invented the personal computer?* | *The children invented a new game.* **2** to think of an idea, story etc. that is not true, usually in order to deceive people SYN **make up**: *Kai invented some excuse about having a headache.* [**Origin:** 1400–1500 Latin, past participle of *invenire* **to come upon, find**, from *venire* **to come**] ▸see THESAURUS box at **lie²**

THESAURUS

create to invent or design something: *a dish created by our chef*
think up to produce an idea, plan etc. that is completely new: *Teachers constantly have to think up new ways to keep the kids interested.*
come up with sth to think of a new idea, plan, reply etc.: *I had to come up with an excuse not to go, and fast.*
devise FORMAL to plan or invent a way of doing something: *The game of basketball was devised to fill up a rainy day.*
make up sth to produce a new story, song, game etc.: *Grandpa made up stories for us at bedtime.*
dream sth up to think of a plan or idea, especially an unusual one: *The company's name was dreamed up by Harris' fifteen-year-old daughter.*

in•ven•tion /ɪn'vɛnʃən/ *n.* **1** [C] a useful machine, tool, instrument etc. that has been invented: *The dishwasher is a wonderful invention.* **2** [U] the act of inventing something: +**of** *the invention of the wheel* **3** [C,U] a story, explanation etc. that is not true: *The stories of her involvement in the crime are pure invention.* **4** [U] the ability to think of new and smart ideas: *Michelangelo had a genius for invention.*

in•ven•tive /ɪn'vɛntɪv/ *adj.* **1** able to think of new, different, or interesting ideas: *an inventive writer* **2** containing new, different, or interesting ideas: *inventive ways to cheaply redecorate your home* —**inventively** *adv.* —**inventiveness** *n.* [U]

in•ven•tor /ɪn'vɛntɚ/ *n.* [C] someone who has invented something, or whose job is to invent things

in•ven•to•ry /'ɪnvənˌtɔri/ *n. plural* **inventories** **1** [C,U] an official list of all the objects in a place, written so that you can know exactly what is there: +**of** *an inventory of everything in the apartment* | *My job was to* ***take inventory*** (=make a list of everything in a store) *every month.* **2** [U] all the goods in a store SYN **stock**: *We have the largest inventory in the mattress business.*

in•verse¹ /ɪn'vɚs, 'ɪnvɚs/ *adj.* **1** changing in the opposite way to something else, especially in position, size, or amount: ***the inverse relationship between*** *prices and interest rates* (=if one gets smaller, the other gets larger, etc.) | *The usefulness of a meeting is* ***in inverse proportion*** *to how many people attend.* (=the more people who attend, the less useful the meeting is) **2** [only before noun] FORMAL exactly opposite, especially in order or position: *The list of winners will be read* ***in inverse order***. —**inversely** *adv.*

inverse² *n.* [singular] **1** the complete opposite of something: *The song's lack of rhythm makes it the inverse of dance music.* **2** MATH a number that is related to another number because an INVERSE OPERATION has been been performed → see also ADDITIVE INVERSE, MULTIPLICATIVE INVERSE **3** ALGEBRA a LOGICAL or mathematical CONDITIONAL statement in which both parts of the statement are made negative. For example, the inverse of "If you swim, you will get wet" is "If you do not swim, you will not get wet." The inverse of a true statement is not necessarily true. → see also CONVERSE

ˌinverse ˈfunction *n.* [C] MATH the mathematical RELATION that you get by doing the opposite thing to the VARIABLE than you did in the first FUNCTION. For example, for the function y= x+2, the inverse function is x=y-2

ˌinverse opeˈration *n.* [C] MATH a mathematical operation that does the opposite of another operation. For example, addition is the inverse operation of SUBTRACTION, and subtraction is the inverse operation of addition.

ˌinverse reˈlation also **ˌconverse reˈlation** *n.* [C] ALGEBRA a relationship between a pair of numbers that is the exact opposite of another relationship. If (a,b) is a relation, then (b,a) is its inverse relation.

ˌinverse-ˈsquare ˌlaw *n.* [C] PHYSICS a principle of PHYSICS that describes how the strength of something such as a force or light changes in INVERSE (=opposite) relation to the SQUARE (=a number multiplied by itself) of the distance to the place that it comes from. Therefore, when the distance of light from its source doubles, the light is only 1/4 as strong.

ˌinverse variˈation *n.* [U] MATH a relationship between two VARIABLES (=mathematical quantities which can represent several different amounts) in which as one of the variables increases, the other decreases by the same amount or to the same degree. It can be written as xy=k, where k is a quantity which does not change. → see also DIRECT VARIATION

in·ver·sion /ɪnˈvɚʒən/ *n.* [C,U] **1** FORMAL the act of changing something so that it is the opposite of what it was before **2** also **inversion layer** EARTH SCIENCE a type of weather condition in which the air nearest the ground is cooler than the air above it

in·vert /ɪnˈvɚt/ *v.* [T] FORMAL to put something in the opposite position to the one it was in before, especially by turning it upside down —**inverted** *adj.*: *an inverted triangle*

in·ver·te·brate /ɪnˈvɚt̬əbrɪt, -ˌbreɪt/ *n.* [C] BIOLOGY an animal that does not have a BACKBONE —**invertebrate** *adj.* → see also VERTEBRATE

in·vest /ɪnˈvɛst/ Ac W2 *v.* **1** [I,T] ECONOMICS to spend money by buying something that you believe will give you a profit or a successful result in the future: *How much did you want to invest?* | **invest (sth) in sth** *The company has invested in new production technology.* | *The goverment is promising to invest more money in education.* | ***Investing in the stock market*** (=buying stocks in companies on the stock market) *is risky without professional help.* | *Many of us had* ***invested heavily*** (=invested a lot of money) *in high-tech stocks.* **2** [T] to use a lot of time, effort etc. in order to make something succeed: *Learning a new language means investing a lot of time and effort.* **3 have a lot invested in sth** used to say that someone wants something to succeed very much because they have put a lot of time and effort into it: *The kids have a lot invested in this project.* [**Origin:** 1500–1600 Italian *investire* **to dress, invest**, from Latin, **to dress**]

invest in sth *phr. v.* to buy something even though it is expensive, because you know that you need it: *We decided it was finally time to invest in a new car.*

invest sb/sth **with** sth *phr. v.* FORMAL **1** to officially give someone power to do something: *Later that year, the Congress invested the President with broader powers.* **2** to make someone or something seem to have a particular quality or character: *The glasses invested him with a new air of dignity.*

in·ves·ti·gate /ɪnˈvɛstəˌgeɪt/ Ac W3 *v.* **1** [I,T] to try to find out the truth about something such as a crime, accident, or scientific problem: *The FBI is investigating the murder.* | *I heard a noise and went downstairs to investigate.* | **investigate how/whether/why etc.** *Scientists are investigating how the bacteria live in these conditions.* **2** [T] to try to find out more about someone's character, actions etc., because you think they may have been involved in a crime: *Hunt was investigated for more than a year before he was arrested.* [**Origin:** 1500–1600 Latin, past participle of *investigare* **to follow the track of**, from *vestigium* **track**]

in·ves·ti·ga·tion /ɪnˌvɛstəˈgeɪʃən/ Ac W2 *n.* **1** [C] an official attempt to find out the reasons for something such as a crime, accident, or scientific problem: *a criminal investigation* | **+into/of** *an investigation into the accident* | *A private detective was hired to* ***conduct the investigation*** (=investigate something). | **launch/order/start an investigation** *Congress has ordered an investigation into the case.* | **a police/criminal investigation** (=an investigation into a crime) **2** [U] the act of investigating something: *The matter needs* ***further investigation*** (=more investigation). | **+of** *The investigation of identify theft is very difficult.* | *Six army generals are* ***under investigation*** (=being investigated).

in·ves·ti·ga·tive /ɪnˈvɛstəˌgeɪt̬ɪv/ Ac *adj.* **1** intended to discover new details and facts about something: *an investigative report* **2 an investigative journalist/reporter/team etc.** a journalist, team etc. whose job is to discover new facts and details about something

in·ves·ti·ga·tor /ɪnˈvɛstəˌgeɪt̬ɚ/ Ac W3 *n.* [C] someone who investigates things, especially crimes: *police investigators* | *accident investigators at the crash site*

in·ves·ti·ga·to·ry /ɪnˈvɛstəgəˌtɔri/ *adj.* relating to investigation: *investigatory techniques*

in·ves·ti·ture /ɪnˈvɛstəˌtʃʊr, -tʃɚ/ *n.* [C] FORMAL a ceremony at which someone is given an official title

in·vest·ment /ɪnˈvɛstmənt/ Ac W1 *n.* **1** [C,U] ECONOMICS the money that a person, company, organization etc. spends on something in order to get a profit or to make a business activity successful, or the process of spending this money: *We plan to buy some property as an investment.* | *cuts aimed at stimulating investment* | **+in** *a large investment in automated technology* | *An independent financial advisor can help you* ***make the best investments.*** | **short-term/long-term investment** (=one that will give you results in a short time, or only after a long time) **2** something that you buy or do because it will be useful later: *Going back to college was* ***a good investment.*** **3** [C,U] a large amount of time, energy, emotion etc. that you spend on something: *Raising kids requires a huge investment of time and energy.*

inˈvestment ˌbank *n.* [C] a bank that buys and sells securities (SECURITY) such as STOCKS or BONDS —**investment banker** *n.* [C] —**investment banking** *n.* [U]

inˈvestment ˌcapital *n.* [U] ECONOMICS money that a company spends because it hopes to gain something from it in the future

in·ves·tor /ɪnˈvɛstɚ/ Ac W1 *n.* [C] ECONOMICS someone who gives money to a company, business, or bank in order to get a profit back: *an attempt to attract foreign investors* | *The company advises* ***small investors*** (=people with small amounts to invest).

in·vet·er·ate /ɪnˈvɛt̬ərɪt/ *adj.* [only before noun] **1 an inveterate liar/smoker/gambler etc.** someone who always does something, especially something bad such as lying, smoking etc. **2 inveterate fondness/distrust/hatred etc.** an attitude or feeling that you have had for a long time and cannot change: *my inveterate distrust of any salesman* —**inveterately** *adv.*

in·vid·i·ous /ɪnˈvɪdiəs/ *adj.* unpleasant or unfair, especially because it is likely to offend people or make you unpopular: *invidious comparisons between the two schools*

in·vig·or·ate /ɪnˈvɪgəˌreɪt/ *v.* [T usually passive] **1** to make someone feel that they have more energy, enthusiasm, or strength: *The cold water invigorated me.* **2** to make something stronger and more successful: *an attempt to renew and invigorate the church*

in·vig·or·at·ed /ɪnˈvɪgəˌreɪt̬ɪd/ *adj.* [not before noun] feeling healthier and stronger, and having more energy than you did before: *A weekend in the mountains always makes me feel invigorated.*

in·vig·o·rat·ing /ɪnˈvɪgəˌreɪt̬ɪŋ/ *adj.* making you feel like you have more energy: *cold, invigorating air*

in·vin·ci·ble /ɪn'vɪnsəbəl/ *adj.* **1** too strong to be destroyed or defeated: *an invincible army* | *"Kids think they're invincible," said the school's drug counselor.* **2** an invincible belief, attitude etc. is extremely strong and cannot be changed —**invincibly** *adv.* —**invincibility** /ɪnˌvɪnsə'bɪləṭi/ *n.* [U]

in·vi·o·la·ble /ɪn'vaɪələbəl/ *adj.* FORMAL an inviolable right, law, principle etc. is extremely important and should not be gotten rid of —**inviolability** /ɪnˌvaɪələ'bɪləṭi/ *n.* [U]

in·vi·o·late /ɪn'vaɪəlɪt/ *adj.* FORMAL something that is inviolate cannot be attacked, changed, or destroyed

in·vis·i·ble /ɪn'vɪzəbəl/ Ac *adj.* **1** something that is invisible cannot be seen: *an invisible and odorless gas* | **+to** *The new plane is invisible to radar.* | *stars that are* ***invisible to the naked eye*** (=cannot be seen without the help of a special instrument) **2** not noticed, or not talked about: *There's an invisible barrier that keeps women out of top jobs.* **3** relating to money that is made from services and TOURISM rather than from products: *invisible earnings* —**invisibly** *adv.* —**invisibility** /ɪnˌvɪzə'bɪləṭi/ *n.* [U]

inˌvisible 'hand *n.* [singular] ECONOMICS used to talk about the things that strongly influence and control an economic system that does not have a lot of government controls, and which help make the system work effectively

inˌvisible 'ink *n.* [U] ink that cannot be seen on paper until it is heated, treated with chemicals etc., used for writing secret messages

in·vi·ta·tion /ˌɪnvə'teɪʃən/ S2 *n.* **1** [C] a card asking someone to attend a party, wedding, meal etc.: *a wedding invitation* | **+to** *Did you* ***get an invitation to*** *Keri's party?* | *She* ***turned down*** *my* ***invitation*** (=said "no" to it) *to dinner.* **2** [C] a formal written or spoken request to someone, asking them to go somewhere or do something: **an invitation to do sth** *Howard has* ***accepted an invitation*** *to teach at Harvard this summer.* | *The governor* ***declined an invitation*** (=did not accept an invitation) *to speak at the conference.* **3** [singular] a situation that encourages people to do something, especially something bad or that you do not want: *He* ***took*** *my silence* ***as an invitation to*** *talk.* | **be an (open) invitation for/to** *Leaving the car unlocked is just an open invitation to thieves.* **4 by invitation (only)** if attendance at an event or membership of a club is by invitation, only people who have been invited are allowed to attend or join **5 open/standing invitation** an invitation to visit someone or do something at any time: *You know you have a standing invitation to use our pool.* **6 at sb's invitation** FORMAL if you go somewhere or do something at someone's invitation, you go there or do it because they have invited you to

in·vite¹ /ɪn'vaɪt/ S1 W2 *v.* [T] **1** to ask someone to come to a party, wedding, dinner etc.: **invite sb to sth** *About a hundred people were invited to the wedding.* | **invite sb to do sth** *Let's invite her to come to dinner with us.* | **invite sb for sth** *We've been invited for drinks on Friday at Rachel's.* | **be invited** *No, I wasn't invited.* **2** to politely offer someone the chance to do something: **invite sb to do sth** *Mr. Quinn was invited to sing a song he had written.* | *I've been invited to speak at the conference.* **3** to encourage something bad to happen, but not deliberately: *This policy is bound to invite criticism.* **4** to formally say that you would like to receive something, for example applications for a job, comments, questions etc.: *The government has invited comments on its proposals.* [**Origin:** 1500–1600 French *inviter*, from Latin *invitare*]

invite sb **along** *phr. v.* to ask someone if they would like to come with you when you are going somewhere: *Why don't you invite Barbara along?*

invite sb **back** *phr. v.* **1** to ask someone to come to your home, your office etc. again: *The team was invited back to the tournament the following year.* **2** to ask someone to come to your home after you have been somewhere with them: *I invited Dean back for coffee after the show.*

invite sb **in** *phr. v.* to ask someone to come into your home: *She opened the door and invited us in.*

invite sb **out** *phr. v.* to ask someone to go somewhere with you, especially to a restaurant or movie: *Josh invited her out for Saturday night.*

invite sb **over** *phr. v.* to ask someone to come to your home for a drink, a meal, a party etc.: *We invited a bunch of people over to watch a movie.*

in·vite² /'ɪnvaɪt/ *n.* [C] SPOKEN, INFORMAL an invitation to a party, meal etc.

in·vit·ing /ɪn'vaɪṭɪŋ/ *adj.* an inviting object, place, smell, offer etc. is very attractive and makes you want to go somewhere or do something: *the inviting smell of coffee* | *The fire looked warm and inviting.* —**invitingly** *adv.*

in vi·tro fer·til·i·za·tion /ɪn ˌvitroʊ fəṭl-ə'zeɪʃən/ *n.* [U] MEDICINE a process in which a human egg is FERTILIZED outside a woman's body

in·vo·ca·tion /ˌɪnvə'keɪʃən/ *n.* LITERARY **1 the invocation** a speech or prayer at the beginning of a ceremony or meeting **2** [C,U] a request for help, especially from God or a god

in·voice¹ /'ɪnvɔɪs/ *n.* [C] a list of goods that have been supplied or work that has been done, showing how much you owe for them [**Origin:** 1500–1600 Early French *envois*, plural of *envoi* **message**] ►see THESAURUS box at **bill¹**

invoice² *v.* [T] **1** to send someone an invoice: *You will be invoiced as soon as the work is complete.* **2** to prepare an invoice for goods that have been supplied or work that has been done

in·voke /ɪn'voʊk/ Ac *v.* [T] FORMAL **1** LAW if you invoke a law, rule etc., you say that you are doing something because the law allows or forces you to: *The UN threatened to invoke economic sanctions if the talks were ended.* **2** to make a particular idea, image, or feeling appear in people's minds: *During his speech, he invoked the memory of Harry Truman.* **3** LAW to use a law, principle, or THEORY to support your views: *The judge invoked an individual's right to privacy in his writing on the matter.* **4** to ask for help from someone more powerful than you, especially God or a god: *Rev. Moran invoked a blessing.* **5** to make spirits appear by using magic

in·vol·un·tar·y /ɪn'vɑlənˌtɛri/ *adj.* an involuntary movement, sound, reaction etc. is one that you make suddenly and without intending to because you cannot control yourself: *an involuntary muscle contraction* —**involuntarily** *adv.* —**involuntariness** *n.* [U]

in·volve /ɪn'vɑlv/ Ac W1 *v.* [T] **1** to include something as a necessary part or result: *What will the job involve?* | **involve doing sth** *Running your own business usually involves working long hours.* **2** to include or affect someone or something: *accident involving a drunken driver* | *These changes will involve all members of staff.* **3** to deliberately try to include someone in an activity and encourage them to take part in it: **involve sb in sth** *The city is making an effort to involve the public in these discussions.* **4 involve yourself** to take part actively in a particular activity: **involve yourself in (doing) sth** *The U.S. has been unwilling to involve itself in the crisis.* [**Origin:** 1300–1400 Latin *involvere* **to wrap**, from *volvere* **to roll**]

in·volved /ɪn'vɑlvd/ Ac S1 *adj.* **1 be/get involved** to take part in an activity or event, or be connected with it in some way: *The show was a lot of fun for all the students involved.* | **+in** *10 vehicles were involved in the accident.* | **+with** *None of our kids has been involved with drugs.* | *I don't want to* ***get involved in*** *their argument.* | **deeply/heavily involved** (=involved very much) **2** if something is involved in an activity, event etc., it is a necessary part of it: **+in** *There's a lot of work involved in putting on a concert.* **3 be involved with sb a)** to be having a sexual relationship with someone, especially someone you should not have a relationship with: *Matt's involved with a married woman at work.* **b)** to spend time with someone that you have a relationship with: *He's a father who wants to be more involved with his family.* **4** having many different parts and therefore difficult to understand SYN **complicated**: *The movie's plot is very involved.*

in·volve·ment /ɪnˈvɑlvmənt/ Ac W3 *n.* [U] **1** the act of taking part in an activity or event, or the way in which you take part in it → see also PARTICIPATION: *School officials say they welcome parental involvement.* | +**in** *His involvement in the case was very brief.* **2** the feeling of excitement and satisfaction that you get from an activity: +**in** *his deep sense of involvement in the civil rights movement* **3** a romantic relationship between two people, especially when they are not married to each other SYN **relationship**: *He denied ever having any involvement with her.*

in·vul·ner·a·ble /ɪnˈvʌlnərəbəl/ *adj.* someone or something that is invulnerable cannot be harmed or damaged OPP **vulnerable**: +**to** *bacteria that is invulnerable to drugs* —**invulnerably** *adv.* —**invulnerability** /ɪnˌvʌlnərəˈbɪləṭi/ *n.* [U]

in·ward /ˈɪnwəd/ *adj.* **1** [only before noun] felt or experienced in your own mind but not expressed to other people OPP **outward**: *a feeling of inward satisfaction* **2** toward the inside or center of something OPP **outward**: *The middle of the car door was bent inward.* —**inwardly** *adv.*: *Inwardly, I was furious.*

ˈinward-ˌlooking *adj.* an inward-looking person or group is more interested in themselves than in other people: *an inward-looking society*

i·o·dine /ˈaɪəˌdaɪn, -ˌdɪn/ *n.* [U] SYMBOL **I** CHEMISTRY a dark red chemical substance that is an ELEMENT and is used on wounds to prevent infection

i·o·dized /ˈaɪəˌdaɪzd/ *adj.* iodized salt has had iodine added to it to help your body stay healthy

i·on /ˈaɪən, ˈaɪɑn/ *n.* [C] CHEMISTRY an atom or group of atoms that has been given a positive or negative charge by adding or taking away an ELECTRON

-ion /ən/ *suffix* [in nouns] used to make nouns that show actions, results, or states: *completion* (=act of finishing something) | *election* (=when someone is elected) | *complete exhaustion* (=state of being extremely tired)

I·o·nes·co /ˌiəˈnɛskoʊ/, **Eu·gène** /yuˈdʒin, uˈʒɛn/ (1912–1994) a French writer of plays, born in Romania

I·o·ni·an /aɪˈoʊniən/ **1** one of the people that lived in ancient Greece from the 20th century B.C. **2** one of the people from ancient Greece that lived on the northeast coast of the Mediterranean from the 10th century B.C.

Iˌonian ˈSea, the a part of the Mediterranean Sea that is between southern Italy and southern Greece

I·on·ic /aɪˈɑnɪk/ *adj.* made in the simply decorated style of ancient Greek buildings: *an Ionic column*

iˌonic ˈbond *n.* [C] CHEMISTRY a chemical BOND which results from atoms gaining and losing an ELECTRON, so that a negative ion and a positive ion are formed SYN **electrovalent bond**

iˌonic ˈcompound *n.* [C] CHEMISTRY a compound that consists of positive and negative IONS

i·on·ize /ˈaɪəˌnaɪz/ *v.* [I,T] CHEMISTRY to form ions or make them form —**ionization** /ˌaɪənəˈzeɪʃən/ *n.* [U]

i·on·iz·er /ˈaɪəˌnaɪzə/ *n.* [C] a machine used to make the air in a room more healthy by producing negative IONS

i·on·o·sphere /aɪˈɑnəˌsfɪr/ *n.* **the ionosphere** the part of the ATMOSPHERE that is used to help send radio waves around the Earth

i·o·ta /aɪˈoʊṭə/ *n.* [singular] **1 not one iota** not even a small amount: *Your eyesight has not changed one iota.* **2** the Greek letter "I"

IOU *n.* [C] INFORMAL a note that you sign to say that you owe someone some money

-ious /iəs/ *suffix* [in adjectives] used to make adjectives: *furious* (=extremely angry) | *ambitious* (=full of ambition) → see also -EOUS, -EOUS

I·o·wa¹ /ˈaɪəwə/ ABBREVIATION **IA** a state in the Midwestern area of the U.S. —**Iowan** *n., adj.*

Iowa² a Native American tribe from the northern central area of the U.S.

IPA *n.* [singular] **International Phonetic Alphabet** ENG. LANG. ARTS a system of special signs that are used to represent the sounds made in speech

IPO *n.* [C] **initial public offering** the first time that STOCK in a company is available to be bought by people in general

iPod /ˈaɪpɑd/ *n.* [C] TRADEMARK a small piece of electronic equipment for playing music, made by the Apple computer company. You can carry an iPod with you and it can store a very large amount of music which you get from the Internet.

ip·so fac·to /ˌɪpsoʊ ˈfæktoʊ/ *adv.* FORMAL used to say that something is known from or proved by the facts

IQ, I.Q. *n.* [C] **Intelligence Quotient** your level of intelligence, measured by a special test, with 100 being the average result: *a young man with a high IQ*

ir- /ɪr/ *prefix* used instead of IN- before the letter "r"; not: *irregular* (=not regular)

IRA /ˈaɪrə/ *n.* **Individual Retirement Account** a special bank account in which you can save money for your RETIREMENT without paying tax on it until later

I·ran /ɪˈræn, ɪˈrɑn/ a country in southwest Asia, east of Iraq and west of Afghanistan —**Iranian** /ɪˈreɪniən/ *n., adj.*

I·raq /ɪˈræk, ɪˈrɑk/ a country in southwest Asia, west of Iran and north of Saudi Arabia —**Iraqi** *n., adj.*

i·ras·ci·ble /ɪˈræsəbəl/ *adj.* FORMAL easily becoming angry —**irascibly** *adv.*

i·rate /ˌaɪˈreɪt◂/ *adj.* extremely angry, especially because you have been treated unfairly: *an irate customer* —**irately** *adv.*

ire /aɪə/ *n.* [U] FORMAL anger: **raise/draw sb's ire** (=make someone angry)

Ire·land /ˈaɪələnd/ a large island to the west of Great Britain, from which it is separated by the Irish Sea. It is divided politically into Northern Ireland and the Republic of Ireland. Northern Ireland is part of the U.K.

ir·i·des·cent /ˌɪrəˈdɛsənt/ *adj.* showing colors that seem to change in different lights: *an iridescent silk tie* —**iridescence** *n.* [U]

i·rid·i·um /ɪˈrɪdiəm/ *n.* [U] SYMBOL **Ir** CHEMISTRY a rare metal that is an ELEMENT and is used in medicine

i·ris /ˈaɪrɪs/ *n.* [C] **1** BIOLOGY a tall plant with long thin leaves and large purple, yellow, or white flowers **2** BIOLOGY the round colored part of your eye, that surrounds the black PUPIL → see picture at EYE¹

I·rish¹ /ˈaɪrɪʃ/ *n.* **the Irish** people from Ireland

Irish² *adj.* from or relating to Ireland

ˌIrish ˈcoffee *n.* [C,U] coffee with cream and WHISKEY added

I·rish·man /ˈaɪrɪʃmən/ *n. plural* **Irishmen** /-mən/ [C] a man from Ireland

ˌIrish ˈsetter *n.* [C] a type of large dog with long hair

I·rish·wom·an /ˈaɪrɪʃˌwʊmən/ *n. plural* **Irishwomen** /-ˌwɪmɪn/ [C] a woman from Ireland

ˈiris scan *n.* [C] an examination of someone's IRIS, the round colored part in the middle of your eye, using special computer equipment in order to tell who they are. Iris scans are done by the police and IMMIGRATION officials at some airports to check the information on someone's PASSPORT or ID card.

irk /ək/ *v.* [T] if something irks you, it makes you feel annoyed, especially because you feel you cannot change the situation: *The increased traffic noise has irked many residents.*

irk·some /ˈəksəm/ *adj.* FORMAL annoying: *an irksome habit*

iron

i·ron¹ /ˈaɪɚn/ W3 *n.* **1** [U] SYMBOL **Fe** CHEMISTRY a common hard metal that is an ELEMENT, is used to make steel, is MAGNETIC, and is found in very small quantities in food and blood: *tools made of iron* | *My doctor said I need more iron in my diet.* **2** [C] a thing used for making clothes smooth, which has a heated flat metal base **3 have several irons in the fire** to be involved in several different activities or have several plans **4** [C] a GOLF CLUB made of metal rather than wood **5 irons** [plural] LITERARY a set of chains used to prevent a prisoner from moving [**Origin:** Old English *isern, iren*] → see also **pump iron** at PUMP² (9), **rule sb/sth with an iron fist/hand** at RULE² (5), **strike while the iron is hot** at STRIKE¹ (28), **have a will of iron** at WILL² (7)

iron² *v.* [T] to make clothes smooth using an iron: *I need to iron a few shirts for my trip.* → see also IRONING

iron sth ↔ **out** *phr. v.* **1** to solve or get rid of problems or difficulties, especially small ones: *There are still a few problems we need to iron out.* **2** to remove the folds from your clothes by ironing them

iron³ *adj.* [only before noun] very firm and strong or determined: *iron discipline*

ˈIron Age **the Iron Age** HISTORY the period of time about 3000 years ago when iron was first used for making tools, weapons etc. → see also BRONZE AGE, STONE AGE

i·ron·clad /ˈaɪɚnˌklæd/ *adj.* **1** an ironclad agreement, proof, defense etc. is so strong and sure that it cannot be changed or argued against: *an ironclad guarantee* **2** covered with iron: *an ironclad battleship*

ˈIron ˈCurtain **the Iron Curtain** the name that was used for the border between the Communist countries of Eastern Europe and the rest of Europe

ˈiron-gray *adj.* iron-gray hair is a dark gray color

i·ron·ic /aɪˈrɑnɪk/ also **i·ron·i·cal** /aɪˈrɑnɪkəl/ *adj.* **1** an ironic situation is one that is unusual or amusing because something strange happens or the opposite of what is expected happens or is true: *Her car was stolen from outside the police station, which seems a little ironic.* | ***It's ironic that** professional athletes are often so unhealthy.* **2** ENG. LANG. ARTS using words that are the opposite of what you really mean, often in a joking way → see also SARCASTIC: *ironic comments*

i·ron·i·cally /aɪˈrɑnɪkli/ *adv.* **1** [sentence adverb] used to say that a situation is one in which the opposite of what you expected happens or is true: *Ironically, he had just decided to buy a burglar alarm when he was robbed.* **2** in a way that shows you really mean the opposite of what you are saying

i·ron·ing /ˈaɪɚnɪŋ/ *n.* [U] **1** the activity of making clothes smooth with an iron: *I do the laundry and Sharon **does the ironing**.* **2** clothes that are waiting to be ironed or have just been ironed: *a huge pile of ironing*

ˈironing ˌboard *n.* [C] a tall narrow table used for ironing clothes

ˌiron ˈlung *n.* [C] a large machine with a metal case that fits around your body and helps you to breathe, used especially for people who had POLIO

ˈiron-on also **ˈiron-on ˌpatch** *n.* [C] a PATCH that you can stick to your clothes using a hot iron

i·ron·stone /ˈaɪɚnˌstoʊn/ *n.* [U] a type of rock that contains a lot of iron

i·ron·ware /ˈaɪɚnˌwɛr/ *n.* [U] things made of iron, especially for cooking

i·ron·work /ˈaɪɚnˌwɚk/ *n.* [U] fences, gates etc. that are made of iron bent into attractive shapes

i·ro·ny /ˈaɪrəni/ *n.* [U] **1** ENG. LANG. ARTS the use of words that are the opposite of what you really mean, often in order to be amusing → see also SARCASM: *The teacher's irony was lost on him* (=he didn't understand it). **2** a situation that seems strange, sad, or amusing because the opposite of what is expected happens or is true: *The **tragic irony*** (=what makes the situation very sad) *is that the drug was supposed to save lives.* [**Origin:** 1500–1600 Latin *ironia*, from Greek *eironeia*, from *eiron* **person who lies**] → see also DRAMATIC IRONY

ir·ra·di·ate /ɪˈreɪdiˌeɪt/ *v.* [T] **1** TECHNICAL to treat someone or something with X-RAYS or other kinds of RADIATION **2** LITERARY to make something look bright by shining light onto it —**irradiated** *adj.*: *irradiated meat* —**irradiation** /ɪˌreɪdiˈeɪʃən/ *n.* [U]

ir·ra·tion·al /ɪˈræʃənəl/ Ac *adj.* **1** irrational behavior, feelings etc. seem strange because they are not based on clear thought or reason OPP **rational**: *an irrational fear of flying* | *His argument seemed completely irrational.* **2** someone who is irrational behaves without thinking clearly or without good reason OPP **rational**: *I knew I was being irrational, but I couldn't stop yelling.* —**irrationally** *adv.* —**irrationality** /ɪˌræʃəˈnæləṭi/ *n.* [U]

irˌrational ˈnumber *n.* [C] MATH any REAL NUMBER that cannot be written as the exact RATIO of two INTEGERS OPP **rational number**

ir·rec·on·cil·a·ble /ɪˌrɛkənˈsaɪləbəl/ *adj.* **1** irreconcilable opinions, positions etc. are so strongly opposed to each other that it is not possible for them to reach an agreement: +**with** *Fighting in a war was irreconcilable with his religious beliefs.* **2** two people or groups who are irreconcilable are unwilling to compromise or try to come to an agreement: *irreconcilable enemies* **3 irreconcilable differences** strong disagreements between two people who are married, given as a legal reason for getting a DIVORCE —**irreconcilably** *adv.*

ir·re·cov·er·a·ble /ˌɪrɪˈkʌvərəbəl/ *adj.* something that is irrecoverable is lost or has gone and you cannot get it back: *irrecoverable costs* —**irrecoverably** *adv.*

ir·re·deem·a·ble /ˌɪrɪˈdiməbəl/ *adj.* **1** FORMAL too bad to be CORRECTED or repaired **2** ECONOMICS irredeemable STOCK cannot be exchanged for money —**irredeemably** *adv.*

ir·re·duc·i·ble /ˌɪrɪˈdusəbəl/ *adj.* an irreducible sum, level etc. cannot be made smaller or simpler —**irreducibly** *adv.*

ir·re·fut·a·ble /ˌɪrɪˈfyuṭəbəl, ɪˈrɛfyəṭəbəl/ *adj.* an irrefutable statement, argument etc. cannot be disagreed with and must be accepted: *irrefutable evidence of his guilt* —**irrefutably** *adv.*

ir·re·gard·less /ˌɪrɪˈgɑrdlɪs/ *adv.* **irregardless of sth** NONSTANDARD a word meaning REGARDLESS, which many people consider incorrect

ir·reg·u·lar¹ /ɪˈrɛgyəlɚ/ *adj.* **1** having a shape, surface, pattern etc. that is not even, smooth, or balanced SYN **uneven** OPP **regular**: *a jagged, irregular coastline* **2** not happening at times that are an equal distance from each other OPP **regular**: *an irregular heartbeat* **3** not doing something or happening at the expected time every day, week etc. OPP **regular**: *Some weeks, I work long, irregular hours.* | *irregular meals* **4** FORMAL not obeying the usually accepted legal or moral rules: *a **highly irregular*** (=very unusual and possibly illegal) *business deal.* **5** ENG. LANG. ARTS an irregular verb or a form of a word does not follow the usual pattern of grammar, such as the past tense "went" of the verb "go" or the plural "deer" OPP **regular** **6** [only after noun] a word meaning CONSTIPATED (=unable to easily pass solid waste from your body), used in order to be polite OPP **regular** —**irregularly** *adv.*

irregular² *n.* [C] a soldier who is not an official member of a country's army

ir·reg·u·lar·i·ty /ɪˌrɛgyəˈlærəṭi/ *n.* *plural* **irregularities** **1** [C usually plural] a situation in which something has not been done according to rules:

I

irregularities in the voting | **financial/accounting irregularities** (=when rules for dealing with money have not been followed) **2** [C,U] a situation in which something does not happen regularly in the way it should or at the time it normally does: *irregularities in her heartbeat* | *menstrual irregularity* **3** [U] a word meaning CONSTIPATION, used in order to be polite

ir·rel·e·vance /ɪˈrɛləvəns/ Ac also **ir·rel·e·van·cy** /ɪˈrɛləvənsi/ *n.* **1** [singular] the fact that something has no real connection or importance in relation to a particular situation: **the irrelevance of sth to sth** *the irrelevance of his argument to the subject being discussed* **2** [C] someone or something that is not important in a particular situation: *She considered polite conversation an irrelevancy.*

ir·rel·e·vant /ɪˈrɛləvənt/ Ac *adj.* not useful in or not relating to a particular situation, and therefore not important: *His age is completely irrelevant if he can do the job.* | *How the problem happened is irrelevant now. We just have to fix it.* —**irrelevantly** *adv.*

ir·re·lig·ious /ˌɪrɪˈlɪdʒəs/ *adj.* FORMAL opposed to religion, or not having any religious feeling

ir·re·me·di·a·ble /ˌɪrɪˈmidiəbəl/ *adj.* FORMAL so bad that it is impossible to make it better —**irremediably** *adv.*

ir·rep·a·ra·ble /ɪˈrɛpərəbəl/ *adj.* irreparable damage, harm etc. is so bad that it can never be repaired or made better: *The shooting victim has irreparable damage to the brain.* —**irreparably** *adv.*

ir·re·place·a·ble /ˌɪrɪˈpleɪsəbəl/ *adj.* too special, valuable, or unusual for anything else to be used instead: *Several works of art were lost, many of them irreplaceable.*

I

ir·re·press·i·ble /ˌɪrɪˈprɛsəbəl/ *adj.* full of energy, confidence, and happiness, so that you never seem unhappy: *an irrepressible optimist* —**irrepressibly** *adv.*

ir·re·proach·a·ble /ˌɪrɪˈproʊtʃəbəl/ *adj.* FORMAL behavior or actions that are irreproachable are perfect or impossible to criticize —**irreproachably** *adv.*

ir·re·sist·i·ble /ˌɪrɪˈzɪstəbəl/ *adj.* **1** so attractive, desirable etc. that you cannot prevent yourself from wanting it: *The idea of starting my own business was irresistable.* | *Tax-cutting proposals could **prove irresistible to** lawmakers.* | *Men **find** Natalie **irresistible**.* **2** too strong or powerful to be stopped or prevented: *I felt an **irresistible urge** to laugh.* —**irresistibly** *adv.*

ir·res·o·lute /ɪˈrɛzəˌlut/ *adj.* FORMAL unable to decide what to do SYN **uncertain** —**irresolutely** *adv.* —**irresolution** /ɪˌrɛzəˈluʃən/ *n.* [U]

ir·re·spec·tive /ˌɪrɪˈspɛktɪv/ *adv.* **irrespective of sth** used to say that a particular fact, situation, or quality does not affect a situation: *The class is open to everyone, irrespective of age.*

ir·re·spon·si·ble /ˌɪrɪˈspɑnsəbəl/ *adj.* doing careless things without thinking or worrying about the possible bad results: *Dan is completely irresponsible with money.* | **be irresponsible (of sb) to do sth** *It was irresponsible of you to leave your sister alone.* —**irresponsibly** *adv.* —**irresponsibility** /ˌɪrɪˌspɑnsəˈbɪləṭi/ *n.* [U]

ir·re·triev·a·ble /ˌɪrɪˈtrivəbəl/ *adj.* FORMAL **1** an irretrievable situation cannot be made right again: *the irretrievable breakdown of their marriage* **2** the loss of something that you can never get back: *They told me the data was irretrievable.* —**irretrievably** *adv.*

ir·rev·er·ent /ɪˈrɛvərənt/ *adj.* showing a lack of respect for organizations, customs, beliefs etc.: *an irreverent sense of humor* —**irreverently** *adv.* —**irreverence** *n.* [U]

ir·re·vers·i·ble /ˌɪrɪˈvɚsəbəl/ Ac *adj.* unable to be changed back to how something was before, because the change is so serious or so great SYN **reversible**: *an irreversible decision* | *The process is irreversible.* —**irreversibly** *adv.*

ir·rev·o·ca·ble /ɪˈrɛvəkəbəl/ *adj.* an irrevocable decision, action etc. cannot be changed or stopped —**irrevocably** *adv.*: *Computers have irrevocably changed our society.*

ir·ri·gate /ˈɪrəˌgeɪt/ *v.* [T] **1** to supply land or crops with water: *The water is used to irrigate nearby farmland.* **2** TECHNICAL to wash a wound with a flow of liquid —**irrigation** /ˌɪrəˈgeɪʃən/ *n.* [U] *an irrigation system*

ir·ri·ta·ble /ˈɪrəṭəbəl/ *adj.* getting annoyed quickly or easily: *Mom seemed tired and irritable.* —**irritably** *adv.* —**irritability** /ˌɪrəṭəˈbɪləṭi/ *n.* [U]

ir·ri·tant /ˈɪrətənt/ *n.* [C] **1** a substance that can make a part of your body painful or sore: *an eye irritant* | **+to** *an irritant to the lining of the stomach* **2** something that makes you feel annoyed over a period of time: **+to** *The priest was a critic of and irritant to the Communist Party.*

ir·ri·tate /ˈɪrəˌteɪt/ *v.* [T] **1** to make someone feel annoyed and impatient: *His complaining started to irritate me.* **2** to make a part of your body painful and sore: *Perfumes in soap can irritate your skin.* [**Origin:** 1500–1600 Latin, past participle of *irritare* **to cause strong feelings in, excite**]

ir·ri·tat·ed /ˈɪrəˌteɪṭɪd/ *adj.* **1** feeling annoyed and impatient about something: **+about/at/with/by** *John was irritated by all the questions.* | **be irritated with/at sb (for sth)** *I was irritated at her for being late.* ►see THESAURUS box at **angry** **2** painful and sore: *irritated skin*

ir·ri·tat·ing /ˈɪrəˌteɪṭɪŋ/ *adj.* making you feel annoyed and impatient: *the dog's irritating bark* | **it's irritating (that)** *It's so irritating that she never calls me back.* | *Nate has **an irritating habit of** interrupting people.* —**irritatingly** *adv.*

ir·ri·ta·tion /ˌɪrəˈteɪʃən/ *n.* **1** [U] the feeling of being annoyed about something, especially something that happens again and again: *The heavy traffic is a constant source of irritation.* | **+about/with/at** *The Professor's irritation with the delays was obvious.* **2** [C,U] a painful sore feeling on a part of your body: *Exposure to the fertilizer can **cause irritation to** the skin or eyes.* | *a minor throat irritation* **3** [C] something that makes you annoyed

IRS *n.* **the IRS the Internal Revenue Service** the department of the U.S. government that collects national taxes

Ir·ving /ˈɚvɪŋ/, **John** (1942–) a U.S. writer of NOVELS

Irving, Washington (1783–1859) a U.S. writer known especially for his stories

is /z, s, əz; *strong* ɪz/ *v.* the third person singular of the present tense of BE

I·sa·iah /aɪˈzeɪə/ **1** (8th century B.C.) in the Jewish and Christian religions, a Hebrew PROPHET who said that God would send a MESSIAH to save the Jews. **2** a book in the OLD TESTAMENT in the Bible

ISBN *n.* **International Standard Book Number** a number that is given to every book that is PUBLISHED

ISDN *n.* [U] **Integrated Services Digital Network** COMPUTERS a special telephone network through which computers can send information much faster than usual

-ish /ɪʃ/ *suffix* **1** [in nouns] the people or language of a particular country or place: *Turkish* (=the language of Turkey). | *the British* (=people from Britain) **2** [in adjectives] relating to a particular place: *Spanish* (=from Spain) **3** [in adjectives] similar to a particular type of person or thing, or having qualities of that person or thing: *foolish* (=typical of a fool) | *childish* (=like a child) | *cartoonish* **4** [in adjectives] used in some adjectives that show disapproval: *selfish* | *childish* **5** [in adjectives] a little SYN **slightly**: *tallish* (=slightly tall) | *youngish* (=still a little young) | *reddish* **6** [in adjectives] SPOKEN about SYN **approximately**: *eightish* (=at about 8 o'clock) | *fortyish* (=about 40 years old) **7** [in adjectives and nouns] having a particular set of beliefs, or being a member of a religious group: *Jewish* | *the Amish*

I·sis /ˈaɪsɪs/ in ancient Egyptian MYTHOLOGY, the most important goddess. She was the goddess of nature and was also the wife and sister of Osiris

Is•lam /ˈɪzlɑm, ɪzˈlɑm, ˈɪslɑm/ *n.* [U] **1** the Muslim religion, which was started by Muhammad and whose holy book is the Koran **2** the people and countries that follow this religion [**Origin:** 1600–1700 Arabic *islam* **obeying (the will of God)**] —**Islamic** /ɪzˈlɑmɪk, ɪsˈlɑmɪk/ *adj.*

Is•lam•a•bad /ɪsˈlɑməˌbɑd/ the capital city of Pakistan

is•land /ˈaɪlənd/ S2 W2 *n.* [C] EARTH SCIENCE a piece of land completely surrounded by water: *the Hawaiian Islands | the relaxed routine of island life | She lives on the mainland, but works* ***on the island.*** | **the island of** *I'm from the Greek island of Thassos.* [**Origin:** Old English *igland*, from *ig* **island** + *land*] → see also DESERT ISLAND, TRAFFIC ISLAND

island

is•land•er /ˈaɪləndɚ/ *n.* [C] someone who lives on an island

isle /aɪl/ *n.* [C] a word for an island, used in poetry or in names of islands

is•let /ˈaɪlɪt/ *n.* [C] EARTH SCIENCE a very small island

ism /ˈɪzəm/ *n.* [C] INFORMAL used to describe a set of ideas or beliefs whose name ends in "ism," especially when you think that they are not reasonable or practical: *History is full of dangerous isms.*

-ism /ɪzəm/ *suffix* [in nouns] **1** a religion, political belief, or style of art based on a particular principle or the teachings of a particular person: *Buddhism | socialism | cubism* (=a style of modern art) | *Darwinism* (=based on the work of Charles Darwin) **2** the state of being like someone or something, or of having a particular quality: *heroism* (=being a HERO) | *magnetism* (=being MAGNETIC) **3** the practice of treating people unfairly because of something: *racism* (=against people of a different race) | *classism* (=against people in a different social class) **4** the action or process of doing something: *criticism* (=criticizing something) **5** an action or remark that has a particular quality: *witticisms* (=smart funny remarks) **6** illness caused by too much of something: *alcoholism*

is•n't /ˈɪzənt/ *v.* the short form of "is not": *Lisa isn't home.*

iso- /aɪsoʊ, -sə/ *prefix* TECHNICAL the same all through or in every part of something SYN **equal**: *isogon* (=many-sided shape with sides that are all equal in length)

i•so•bar /ˈaɪsəˌbɑr/ *n.* EARTH SCIENCE a line on a weather map joining places where the air pressure is the same

i•so•late /ˈaɪsəˌleɪt/ Ac *v.* [T] **1** to stop someone or something from having contact with particular people, things, or ideas: **isolate sb from sb/sth** *Elvis' early success isolated him from his friends. | Many parents try to isolate their children from problems.* **2** to separate an idea, word, problem etc., so that it can be examined or dealt with by itself: **isolate sth from sth** *Sexual issues cannot be isolated from other political issues.* **3** prevent a country, region, political group etc. from getting support or resources, so that it becomes weaker: *The army's goal was to surround and isolate the town.* **4** TECHNICAL to separate a substance, disease etc. from other substances, so that it can be studied: *They have isolated the gene that determines a person's weight.* **5** to keep someone separate from other people, especially because they have a disease: **isolate sb from sb** *Tuberculosis patients were isolated from the other patients.*

i•so•lat•ed /ˈaɪsəˌleɪt̬ɪd/ Ac *adj.* **1** an isolated place is far away from where there are other buildings, towns etc. SYN **remote**: *an isolated mountain village* | +**from** *societies that were completely isolated from the modern world* **2** an isolated action, event, example etc. happens only once or in only one place, and is not related to other things that happen: *isolated thunderstorms* | **an isolated case/incident/event etc.** *Abram believes the five recent shootings are isolated incidents.* **3** feeling alone and unable to meet or speak to other people: *During my first month here, I felt very isolated.* [**Origin:** 1700–1800 French *isolé*, from Italian *isolata*, from *isola* **island**]

i•so•la•tion /ˌaɪsəˈleɪʃən/ Ac *n.* [U] **1** a feeling of being lonely and unable to meet or speak to other people: +**from** *her isolation from her family and friends* **2** a situation in which an area, country or group has little contact with other areas, countries, or groups: *Because of its isolation, the island developed its own culture.* **3** MEDICINE the process or state of keeping a patient separate from other patients, so that infections are not passed from one patient to another: *Your father is being kept* ***in isolation*** *until we know what is wrong.* **4** the process or state of keeping a prisoner separate from other prisoners, usually as a severe punishment: *He is being held* ***in isolation*** *until his trial.* **5** the act of deliberately separating one group, person, or thing from others, or the state of being separate: +**from** *the country's isolation from the rest of the world* **6 in isolation** if you consider something in isolation from other things, you consider it separately from them: +**from** *We should not consider science in isolation from economics.* **7 splendid isolation** HUMOROUS used to say that someone or something is noticeably separated or different from other people or things: *The statue stands in splendid isolation in the middle of a busy road.*

i•so•la•tion•is•m /ˌaɪsəˈleɪʃəˌnɪzəm/ Ac *n.* [U] DISAPPROVING POLITICS beliefs or actions that are based on the political principle that your country should not be involved in the affairs of other countries —**isolationist** *n.* [C] —**isolationist** *adj.*

isoˈlation ˌperiod *n.* [C] the period of time that someone with an infectious illness needs to be kept apart from other people

i•so•mer /ˈaɪsəmɚ/ *n.* [C] CHEMISTRY one of two or more chemical compounds that have the same number of the same types of atoms but different chemical structures and qualities

ˌisometric proˈjection also **ˌisometric ˈdrawing** *n.* [C] MATH a drawing that shows the length, depth, and height of an object with all the measurements on the same scale. One corner of the object appears at the front of the drawing, and the left and right sides slope backward from it at angles of 30 degrees.

i•so•met•rics /ˌaɪsəˈmɛtrɪks/ *n.* [plural] exercises that make your muscles stronger, done by making the muscles work against each other —**isometric** *adj.*

i•som•e•try /aɪˈsɑmətri/ *n.* [C] MATH a TRANSFORMATION (=change in position, size, shape etc.) of a GEOMETRIC FIGURE in which all measurements remain the same

i•sos•ce•les trap•e•zoid /aɪˌsɑsəliz ˈtræpəˌzɔɪd/ *n.* [C] MATH a TRAPEZOID (=shape with four straight sides, two of which are parallel) in which the two angles at its base are the same size, and the two sides that are not parallel are the same length

i•sos•ce•les tri•an•gle /aɪˌsɑsəliz ˈtraɪˌæŋgəl/ *n.* [C] MATH a TRIANGLE in which two of the sides are the same length, and the two angles at its base are the same size → see also EQUILATERAL, SCALENE → see also picture at TRIANGLE

i•so•therm /ˈaɪsəˌθɚm/ *n.* [C] EARTH SCIENCE a line on a weather map joining places where the temperature is the same

i•so•ton•ic /ˌaɪsəˈtɑnɪk◂/ *adj.* BIOLOGY an isotonic SOLUTION (=liquid with substances dissolved in it) contains the same amount of SOLUTE (=substance that is dissolved) as another solution that you are comparing it to → see also HYPERTONIC

i•so•tope /ˈaɪsəˌtoʊp/ *n.* [C] PHYSICS one of two or more atoms of a chemical ELEMENT that have the same number of PROTONS but a different number of NEUTRONS

ISP *n.* [C] **Internet Service Provider** a company that you pay money to, to connect your computer to the Internet

Is•ra•el /ˈɪzriəl/ **1** a country on the eastern side of the Mediterranean Sea, north of Egypt, west of Jordan, and south of Lebanon **2** in the Bible, another name for Jacob, which is sometimes used to mean all the Jewish people —**Israeli** /ɪzˈreɪli/ *adj.*

Is·rae·li /ɪzˈreɪli/ *n.* [C] someone from Israel

Is·ra·el·ite /ˈɪzriəˌlaɪt, ˈɪzrə-/ *n.* someone who lived in the ancient KINGDOM of Israel —**Israelite** *adj.*

Is·sa·char /ˈɪsəˌkɑr/ in the Bible, the head of one of the 12 tribes of Israel

is·sue¹ /ˈɪʃu/ Ac S1 W1 *n.*

1 SUBJECT/PROBLEM [C] a problem or subject that people discuss, especially a social or political matter that affects the interests of a lot of people: *Racial discrimination is a sensitive issue.* | **the issue of sth** *the issue of illegal immigration* | *I've already **raised the issue*** (=started a discussion on a particular subject or problem) *with my teacher.* | *Taxation is the **key issue*** (=most important issue) *in the election campaign.* | *He **addressed the issue*** (=discussed or dealt with an issue) *of child abuse in his speech.* | **avoid/dodge/duck/evade the issue** (=avoid discussing a problem or subject) | **confuse/cloud the issue** (=make a problem or subject more difficult by talking about things that are not directly related to it)

2 MAGAZINE [C] a magazine or newspaper printed for a particular day, week, or month: *this week's issue of "Newsweek"* | **the current/latest issue of sth** (=the most recent one)

3 take issue with sb/sth FORMAL to disagree or argue with someone about something SYN **disagree**: *I take issue with his analysis of the problem.*

4 at issue FORMAL if something is at issue, there is disagreement about it and it is being discussed: *At issue are the moral questions raised by cloning.*

5 make an issue (out) of sth to argue about something, especially in a way that annoys other people because they do not think it is important: *Don't make an issue out of something so unimportant.*

6 be not the issue to not be the problem or subject that you are concerned about: *The price is not the issue – it's the quality of his work.*

7 be not an issue (for me) to not be important to someone: *Your age is not an issue for me.*

8 have issues (with sb/sth) INFORMAL **a)** to have problems dealing with something because of something that happened in your past: *teenagers who have issues with their bodies or weight* **b)** if you have issues with someone or something, you do not agree with or approve of them: *I have issues with Mark.*

9 ACT OF GIVING STH [U] the act of officially giving someone something to use: *the issue of a driver's license*

10 SET OF THINGS FOR SALE [C] a new set of something such as STOCKS or stamps, made available for people to buy: *a new issue of bonds*

[**Origin:** 1200–1300 Old French *issir* **to come out, go out**, from Latin *exire*, from *ire* **to go**] → see also **die without issue** at DIE¹ (16), -ISSUE

issue² Ac S3 W2 *v.* [T] **1** to officially make a statement, give an order, warning etc.: *a warning issued by the Surgeon General* | *The State Department will **issue a statement** at noon.* **2** to officially provide something for each member of a group: **issue sb sth** *Every soldier is issued a rifle.* | **issue sb with sth** *Visitors to the factory are issued with identity cards.* **3** to officially produce something such as new stamps, coins, or STOCKS and make them available for people to buy

issue forth *phr. v.* FORMAL OR LITERARY to come out of a place

issue from *phr. v.* FORMAL if something issues from a place or thing, it comes out of it: *Smoke issued from the factory chimneys.*

-issue /ɪʃu/ [in adjectives] **army-issue/military-issue/government-issue** given to someone by the military or another official government organization: *black, army-issue glasses*

-ist /ɪst/ *suffix* **1** [in nouns] someone who believes in or practices a particular religion, set of principles or ideas, or style of art: *a Baptist* | *an Impressionist painter* **2** [in adjectives] relating to a particular set of political or religious beliefs, or to the ideas of a particular person: *feminist* | *Communist* **3** [in nouns] someone who studies a particular subject, plays a particular instrument, or does a particular type of work: *a linguist* (=who studies or learns languages) | *a guitarist* (=who plays the GUITAR) | *a novelist* (=who writes NOVELS) → see also -OLOGIST **4** [in adjectives and nouns] treating people unfairly because of something, or someone who does this: *sexist* (=unfair to someone because of their sex) | *racists*

Is·tan·bul /ˈɪstænˌbʊl, -stɑn-/ the largest city in Turkey, which is at the point where Europe joins Asia

isth·mus /ˈɪsməs/ *n.* [C] EARTH SCIENCE a narrow piece of land with water on both sides, that connects two larger areas of land: *the Isthmus of Panama*

IT *n.* [U] the abbreviation of INFORMATION TECHNOLOGY

it /ɪt/ S1 W1 *pron.* [used as subject or object] **1** used to talk about the thing, situation, idea etc. that has already been mentioned or that is already known about: *Do you like my suit? It was on sale.* | *The whole room was on fire. It was so scary.* | *With the new stereo in the car, it makes a big difference.* **2** used as the subject or object of a verb when the real subject or object is later in the sentence: *It's a nice camera.* | *What's it like living in Miami?* | *It costs $12 just to get in the door.* | **it is nice/sweet/stupid etc. of sb to do sth** *It was nice of him to help.* **3** used with the verb "be" to make statements about the weather, the time, distances etc.: *It's a three-hour drive to Raleigh.* | *It was 4 o'clock and the mail still hadn't come.* | *Is it still raining?* **4** the situation that someone is in now: *I can't stand it any more. I'm resigning.* | *How's it going, man?* | *And that's the end of it?* **5** used to emphasize that one piece of information in a sentence is more important than the rest: *It was Josh who paid for lunch yesterday* (=it was Josh and not another person). | *It was lunch that Josh paid for yesterday* (=it was lunch and not something else). **6** used as the subject of "seem," "appear," "look," and "happen": *It looks like they left without us.* | *It happened to be a nice day, so we went to the beach.* **7** used as the subject of a passive sentence with verbs of saying and thinking: *It was once thought that the world was flat* (=people once thought the world was flat). | *It is believed that he is still alive.* **8** INFORMAL a particular ability, quality, or talent: *I'm sorry, but you just don't have it as a singer.* | *He hasn't lost it even though he's getting older.* **9** used to talk about a child or an animal when you do not know what sex they are

[**Origin:** Old English *hit*]

SPOKEN PHRASES

10 it's me/John etc. used to say who you are to someone who cannot see you, for example at the beginning of a telephone conversation: *Hi, Scott. It's Mark.* | *Don't worry, it's just me. Let me in.* **11 That's it a)** used to praise someone because they have done something correctly: *That's it! Just keep your eye on the ball.* **b)** used when you are angry about a situation and you do not want it to continue: *That's it! I want both of you to be quiet!* **c)** used to say that a particular situation has finished: *That's it. I guess there's nothing more we can do.* **12 this is it!** used to say that something you expected to happen is actually going to happen: *This is it – the moment we've been waiting for!* **13 be it** in children's games, if you are it, you are the person whom everyone has to escape from

I·tal·ian¹ /ɪˈtælyən/ *adj.* **1** relating to or coming from Italy **2** relating to the Italian language

Italian² *n.* **1** [U] the language used in Italy **2** [C] someone from Italy

I·tal·ian·ate /ɪˈtælyəˌneɪt, -nɪt/ *adj.* having an Italian style or appearance

i·tal·i·cize /ɪˈtæləˌsaɪz/ *v.* [T] to put or print something in italics: *I have italicized the important words.* —**italicized** *adj.*

i·tal·ics /ɪˈtælɪks, aɪ-/ *n.* [plural] TECHNICAL a type of printed letters that lean to the right, often used to emphasize particular words: **in italics** (=printed this way) [**Origin:** 1500–1600 Latin *italicus* **Italian**; because these letters were introduced by a 16th-century Italian printer, Aldus Manutius] —**italic** *adj.*: *italic script* → see also ROMAN

Italo- /ɪtæloʊ/ *prefix* Italian and something else: *the Italo-Austrian border*

It·a·ly /ˈɪt̬li/ a country in southern Europe, surrounded on three sides by the Mediterranean Sea

itch¹ /ɪtʃ/ *v.* **1** [I] if part of your body itches, you have an unpleasant feeling on your skin that makes you want to SCRATCH it: *My back itches.* **2** [I] if your clothes itch, they give you this unpleasant feeling on your skin: *These pants itch.* **3 be itching to do sth** INFORMAL to want to do something very much, as soon as possible: *Chris is itching to get back to work.* [**Origin:** Old English *giccan*]

itch² *n.* **1** [C usually singular] an uncomfortable feeling on your skin that makes you want to SCRATCH it **2** INFORMAL a strong desire to do or have something: *an itch for adventure*

itch·y /ˈɪtʃi/ *adj.* *comparative* **itchier**, *superlative* **itchiest** **1** part of your body that is itchy has an annoying feeling that makes you want to rub it with your nails: *My eyes are itchy.* **2** clothes that are itchy make you have this feeling on your skin: *an itchy sweater* **3** wanting to go somewhere new or do something different: *Tyrell was getting itchy and wanted to start his own record label.* **4 itchy feet** INFORMAL the desire to move on to a new place, country, or job **5 itchy fingers** INFORMAL someone with itchy fingers is likely to steal things **6 have an itchy trigger finger** to be likely to shoot a gun in a situation in which you are afraid or nervous —**itchiness** *n.* [U]

it'd /ˈɪt̬əd/ USUALLY SPOKEN **1** the short form of "it would": *It'd be nice if you could come.* **2** the short form of "it had": *It'd been raining since Sunday.*

-ite /aɪt/ *suffix* **1** [in nouns] a follower or supporter of a particular idea or person: *Trotskyites* (=followers of Trotsky) **2** [in adjectives] relating to a particular set of political or religious ideas, or to the ideas of a particular person: *Reaganite* (=based on the political ideas of Ronald Reagan) **3** [in nouns] someone who lives in a particular place or belongs to a particular group: *a suburbanite* (=someone who lives just outside a city) | *the Israelites* (=the people of Israel, in the Bible) **4** [in U nouns] a substance such as a mineral, a compound, or an explosive: *graphite* | *dynamite*

i·tem /ˈaɪt̬əm/ [Ac] [S2] [W2] *n.* [C] **1** FORMAL a single thing in a set, group, or list [SYN] **thing**: *very expensive items such as cars and houses* | **item of clothing/furniture/jewelry etc.** *bracelets and other items of jewelry* | *fur coats and other **luxury items*** ▸see THESAURUS box at **thing** **2** something on a list, especially a list of things to be discussed or dealt with: **an item on the agenda/list/menu** *We moved on to the next item on the agenda.* **3** a single, usually short, piece of news in a newspaper or magazine, or on TV: *a short news item on the back page* **4 be an item** OLD-FASHIONED to be having a sexual or romantic relationship [**Origin:** 1500–1600 Latin **in the same way, also** (used to introduce things in a list), from *ita* **in this way**]

i·tem·ize /ˈaɪt̬əˌmaɪz/ *v.* [T] to make a detailed list of things: *I don't need to itemize my tax deductions.* —**itemized** *adj.*: *an itemized bill*

ˈitem ˌveto *n.* [C] POLITICS a LINE ITEM VETO

it·er·ate /ˈɪt̬əˌreɪt/ *v.* [T] FORMAL to say or do something again —**iterative** /ˈɪt̬əˌreɪt̬ɪv, -rə-/ *adj.*

i·ter·a·tion /ˌɪt̬əˈreɪʃən/ *n.* [C,U] MATH an action or process of repeating an operation or calculation

it·er·a·tive /ˈɪt̬əˌreɪt̬ɪv -rə-/ *adj.* MATH repeating a mathematical process or set of instructions for a computer program until a particular result is achieved: *an iterative process*

ˈiterative ˌprocess *n.* [C] MATH a mathematical process or a set of instructions for a computer program that are repeated continuously until a particular result is achieved

i·tin·er·ant /aɪˈtɪnərənt/ *adj.* [only before noun] FORMAL traveling from place to place, especially to work: *itinerant farm workers*

i·tin·er·ar·y /aɪˈtɪnəˌrɛri/ *n.* *plural* **itineraries** [C] a plan or list of the places you will visit on a trip

-itis /aɪt̬ɪs/ *suffix* [in U nouns] a disease or INFLAMMATION that affects a particular part of the body: *tonsilitis* (=infection of the TONSILS)

it'll /ˈɪt̬l/ USUALLY SPOKEN the short form of "it will": *It'll be dark when they get back.*

its /ɪts/ [S1] [W1] *possessive adj.* [possessive form of "it"] belonging or relating to a thing, situation, person, or idea that has been mentioned or is known about: *By November the tree had lost all its leaves.* | *The city is famous for its music.* | *The apartment has **its own*** (=belonging only to that apartment) *indoor pool.*

it's /ɪts/ **1** the short form of "it is": *It's all over now.* **2** a short form of "it has": *It's been snowing all day.*

it·self /ɪtˈsɛlf/ [S1] [W1] *pron.* **1** the REFLEXIVE form of "it": *The DVD player shuts itself off when it's done.* | *The bird was looking at itself in the mirror.* **2** used for emphasizing that you are talking about a particular thing, animal, or situation rather than something else related to it: *It's plugged in, so the problem must be the computer itself.* | *There are usually speeches before the meeting itself begins.* **3 in itself** also **in and of itself** considered without other related ideas or situations: *Housework is a full-time job in itself.* **4 (all) by itself a)** alone: *Will the dog be safe left in the car by itself?* **b)** without help: *The door's not going to close by itself.* **5 (all) to itself** if something has something else to itself, it does not have to share that thing with others: *This idea deserves a chapter to itself.*

itty-bitty /ˌɪt̬i ˈbɪt̬i◂/ also **it·sy-bit·sy** /ˌɪtsi ˈbɪtsi◂/ *adj.* [only before noun] SPOKEN, HUMOROUS very small

-itude /ətud/ *suffix* [in nouns] FORMAL the state of having a particular quality: *certitude* (=being certain) | *exactitude* (=being exact) → see also -TUDE

-ity /ət̬i/ *suffix* [in nouns] the state of having a particular quality, or something that has that quality: *regularity* (=the quality of being regular). | *stupidities* (=stupid actions or remarks) → see also -TY

IUD *n.* [C] a small plastic or metal object placed inside a woman's UTERUS to prevent her from being able to have a baby → see also COIL² (4)

IV *n.* [C] the abbreviation of INTRAVENOUS; a piece of medical equipment that is used to put liquid directly into your blood

I·van IV /ˌaɪvən ðə ˈfɔrθ/ also **ˌIvan the ˈTerrible** (1530–1584) the ruler of Russia from 1547 to 1584, who made many changes to Russia's laws and system of government

-ive /ɪv/ *suffix* [in nouns and adjectives] **1** someone or something that does something or is able to do something: *a detective* | *explosive* (=that can explode) **2** able to do something: *effective* (=able to have an effect) | *creative* (=good at creating things)

I've /aɪv/ the short form of "I have": *I've seen him somewhere before.*

Ives /aɪvz/, **Charles** (1874–1954) a U.S. musician who wrote CLASSICAL music

IVF → see IN VITRO FERTILIZATION

i·vied /ˈaɪvid/ *adj.* LITERARY covered with ivy

I·vo·ri·an /aɪˈvɔriən/ *adj.* relating to or coming from the Ivory Coast —**Ivorian** *n.* [C]

i·vo·ry¹ /ˈaɪvəri/ *n.* *plural* **ivories** **1** [U] the hard smooth yellowish-white substance from the TUSKS of an ELEPHANT **2** [U] a yellowish-white color **3 the ivories** INFORMAL the KEYS (=parts you press down) of a piano → see also **tickle the ivories** at TICKLE¹ (5) **4** [C often plural] something made of ivory, especially a small figure of a person or animal **5 ivories** [plural] HUMOROUS someone's teeth

I

ivory² *adj.* **1** yellowish white in color: *an ivory wedding dress* **2** made from ivory: *an ivory figure*

ˌIvory 'Coast a country on the coast of West Africa, between Ghana and Liberia. It is sometimes called Côte d'Ivoire. —**Ivorian** /aɪˈvɔriən/ also **Ivoirian** /ɪˈvwɑriən/ *n., adj.*

ˌivory 'tower *n.* [C] a place or situation where you are separated from the difficulties of ordinary life and so are unable to understand them: *Scientists are coming out of the ivory tower and starting businesses.*

i·vy /ˈaɪvi/ *n. plural* **ivies** [C,U] a climbing plant with dark-green shiny leaves → see also POISON IVY

'Ivy ˌLeague *adj.* relating to a group of eight old respected universities in the northeastern U.S.: *an Ivy League college* —**Ivy League** *n.* [singular]

-ization /əzeɪʃən/ *suffix* [in nouns] used to make nouns from verbs that end in -IZE: *civilization* | *industrialization*

-ize /aɪz/ *suffix* [in verbs] **1** to make something have a particular quality, or more of a particular quality: *legalize* (=make legal) | *modernize* (=make more modern) **2** to become something else, or change something into something else: *crystallize* (=turn into CRYSTALS) | *liquidize* (=change into liquid) **3** to put someone or something into a particular place or condition: *hospitalize* (=put someone in a hospital) **4** to speak in a particular way: *sermonize* (=talk in a boring way about morals)

Contents

Language Notes

Full-page Illustrations

Writing Guide

You will often find that several words share a similar general meaning. But be careful – their meanings are almost always different in one way or another. When comparing two words in the dictionary, look at the definitions and examples and any Thesaurus Boxes.

The Meaning is not Exactly the Same

smart/bright Both words can mean "intelligent, and good at learning or understanding things quickly," but **bright** is usually used about young people rather than adults:

Their daughter is very ***bright****. | I like him a lot. He's* ***smart*** *and funny.*

cheap/inexpensive Both words mean "not costing a lot of money," but **cheap** also means that something did not cost as much as you expected, while **inexpensive** means that the quality of something is good.

I got a ***cheap*** *flight to New York. | The clothes are* ***inexpensive*** *and well-made.*

Sometimes the words are different in degree

furious is a stronger word than **angry**
exhausted is a stronger word than **tired**
filthy is a stronger word than **dirty**
terror is a stronger word than **fear**

Sometimes the words express a different attitude

You can say someone is **slim** if they are thin and you like the way they look. If you think they are too thin, you might say they are **skinny**, or if they are thin in a healthy-looking way, **lean**.

Words with a Similar Meaning Are Often Used in Very Different Situations

Sometimes the words have a different register

Some words have a particular register and are not usually used in ordinary situations.

stuff (INFORMAL)/**belongings**
chow down (INFORMAL)/**eat**
cop (INFORMAL)/**policeman**
seek (FORMAL)/**look for**

Sometimes the words are used by particular people

Some words are normally used by specialists, such as doctors, lawyers, or scientists. Other people will use another word for the same thing. Compare:

demise (FORMAL or LAW)/**death** **cardiac arrest** (MEDICINE)/**heart attack**

Do the words have the same grammar?

Sometimes words with a similar meaning are used in different grammatical patterns. Compare:

answer/reply You **answer** a question or **answer** somebody, or just **answer**:

You still haven't ***answered*** *my question. | He didn't* ***answer****.*

You **reply to** someone or something or simply **reply**, but you cannot **reply** a question or **reply** someone:

He ***replied*** *to her email promptly. | "Do you think he'll come?" She didn't* ***reply****.*

advise/recommend Both verbs can mean "to tell someone what you think should be done," but are followed by different verb patterns:

The doctor ***advised*** *me to stay in bed. | The doctor* ***recommended*** *that I stay in bed.*

Collocations

A collocation is a group of words which "naturally" go together through common usage. Unlike idioms, their meaning can usually be understood from the individual words. In order to speak natural English, you need to be familiar with collocations. You need to know, for example, that you say a "heavy smoker" because **heavy** (NOT **big**) collocates with **smoker**, and that you say "free of charge" because **free of** collocates with **charge** (NOT **cost**, **payment** etc.). If you do not choose the right collocation, you will probably be understood by native English speakers, but you will not sound natural. This dictionary will help you with the most common collocations.

Common Set Collocations

When you look up a word, read the examples carefully. Common collocations are shown in **bold**:

Note that you cannot change the word order in these phrases and that you cannot use other words even if they have similar meanings. We say **final exams** (NOT **tests**), **make a mistake** (NOT **do** a mistake).

ex•am /ɪɡ'zæm/ S2 *n.* [C] **1** a spoken or written test of knowledge, especially an important one at the end of a school year or course of study : *a difficult exam question* | *Only fifteen students* ***passed the exam.*** | *One of the kids cheated* ***on an exam.*** | **fail/flunk an exam** *I failed my Chemistry exam.* | *Do you have to* ***take an exam*** *today?* | *When are your* ***final exams?*** | **a history/biology/English etc. exam** *My English exam is Tuesday.* → see also TEST

These entries show you that **take an exam**, **final exams**, **follow a rule**, **obey a rule**, **break a rule**, **make a mistake**, and **common mistake** are all common collocations.

rule[1] /rul/ S1 W1 *n.*
1 OFFICIAL INSTRUCTION [C] an official instruction that says how things must be done or what is allowed, especially in a game, organization, or job: +**of** *What are the rules of the game?* | **follow/observe/obey rules** *Employees are expected to obey certain rules.* | *You can't come in if you're not a member – it's* ***against the rules.*** | *Elizabeth was expelled for* ***breaking the*** *school's* ***rules.***

Note that other examples in the entries show natural patterns of language, for example *rules of something*.

mis•take[1] /mɪ'steɪk/ S2 W2 *n.* [C]
1 INCORRECT ACTION/OPINION ETC. something that has been done in the wrong way, or an opinion or statement that is incorrect SYN error: *The attorney admitted that she had* ***made a mistake*** *in writing the contract.* | *The essay was full of* ***spelling mistakes.*** | *The teacher points out* ***common mistakes*** *that children make in their writing.*

Collocating Prepositions

When you look up a word, the entry will show you if there is a particular preposition which collocates with it. These entries show that you say:

graduate from:
She graduated from Yale.

grad•u•ate[2] /'grædʒuˌeɪt/ S2 W3 *v.* **1** [I] to obtain a DIPLOMA or a degree by completing your studies at a school, college, or university: +**from** *Ruth graduated from Princeton.*

harmful to:
Smoking is harmful to health.

harm•ful /'hɑrmfəl/ *adj.* causing harm, or likely to cause harm: *the harmful effects of smoking* | *harmful bacteria* | +**to** *Some pesticides are harmful to the environment.* —**harmfully** *adv.* —**harmfulness** *n.* [U]

▶▶ See LANGUAGE NOTES **Idioms**, **Identifying Adjectives**, ***Make*** **and** ***Do***

Make and Do

Why do you **drive** a car but **ride** a bicycle, **do** your best but **make** a mistake, **give** a performance but **play** a part? There is often no real reason except that a particular noun needs a particular verb to express what is done to it.

In order to speak or write English well, it is important to know which nouns go with which verbs. Usually these have to be learned by practice, as there are no specific rules to help you decide which verb to choose.

In choosing between when to use **make** and when to use **do**, there again is no simple rule. However, we usually use **make** to talk about producing something that did not exist before, or when something or someone is changed in some way. We usually use **do** to talk about actions.

Some Typical Uses of *Make* and *Do*

make	do
make **an accusation**	do **your best**
make **an arrangement**	do **business (with someone)**
make **an attempt**	do **the cleaning**
make **a change**	do **(some) damage**
make **a comment**	do **a dance**
make **a deal**	do **the dishes**
make **a decision**	do **your duty**
make **a demand**	do **(someone) a favor**
make **an effort**	do **harm**
make **an estimate**	do **your homework**
make **a fuss**	do **the housework**
make **a gesture**	do **the ironing**
make **an impression (on someone)**	do **a job**
make **a meal (=prepare a meal)**	do **the laundry**
make **a mistake**	do **research**
make **money**	do **(some) work**
make **a movement**	
make **a noise**	
make **an offer**	
make **progress**	
make **a promise**	
make **a recommendation**	
make **a remark**	
make **a request**	

Other Verbs Commonly Used with Particular Nouns

give	take
give **(someone) a chance**	take **action**
give **a command**	take **advantage (of something or someone)**
give **details**	take **a bath**
give **evidence**	take **a class**
give **information**	take **a guess**
give **a performance**	take **a look**
give **permission**	take **medicine**
give **an opinion**	take **a picture/photo**
give **an order**	take **a pill**
give **a talk/speech/lecture**	take **responsibility (for something)**
	take **risks**
	take **a test**
	take **a walk**

have
have **an accident**
have **a fit**
have **a headache**
have **an idea**
have **an illness** (a cold, cancer)
have **a meal** (=eat a meal)
have **an operation** (if you are sick)
have **a party**
have **a thought**

perform
perform **a duty**
perform **a function**
perform **an operation** (if you are a doctor)
perform **a piece of music**
perform **a play**
perform **a task**

play
play **cards**
play **a game**
play **a trick (on someone)**
play **a musical instrument**
play **a tune**
play **music**
play **a part**
play **a CD, cassette, tape etc.**
play **a role**

Using Different Collocating Verbs for the Same Noun

Collocating verbs such as **make**, **do**, **give**, **take** etc. are strongly linked to nouns and you cannot usually choose a different verb to express the same meaning. However, many nouns use a variety of collocating verbs to express their meanings.

Using Different Verbs with a Similar Meaning

Sometimes a noun will use several collocating verbs to express the same meaning. For example, you can **make/arrive at/come to/reach a decision**. Usually, however, the choice is limited.

Using Different Verbs for Different Actions

Different collocating verbs will usually describe different actions that are done to the noun. Compare:

You ***take*** *a test.* (if you are a student)
You ***give*** *a test.* (if you are a teacher)
You ***pass*** *a test.* (if you are successful)
You ***fail*** *a test.* (if you are not successful)
You ***drive*** *a bus.* (if you are the driver)
You ***ride/take*** *a bus.* (to travel from one place to another)
You ***catch*** *a bus.* (if you arrive on time)
You ***miss*** *a bus.* (if you are too late)

Using Different Verbs for Different Senses

If a noun has more than one sense, different collocating verbs may be used for the different senses, to help express the different meanings. Compare:

He ***played*** *a trick on his brother.* (trick = a joke)
She ***performed/did*** *some tricks at the party.* (tricks = card tricks or magic tricks)
He ***placed*** *an order for some new textbooks.* (order = a list of things to be bought)
The captain ***gave*** *orders to advance.* (orders = military commands)

When you look up a word in this dictionary, remember to read the examples!

They will often help you to choose a verb to go with a noun. Collocating verbs are shown in bold in the examples.

▶▶ See LANGUAGE NOTES **Collocations**

Intensifying Adjectives

You can use many different adjectives to talk about large physical size: **big**, **large**, **enormous**, **huge**, **tall** etc. But which adjectives can you use to intensify a noun (to express the idea of great degree or strength) when you are talking about something which is not physical?

Below are some of the most common intensifying adjectives. Note that nouns can have different intensifying adjectives without really changing their meaning:

a ***great/large*** *quantity* | *a* ***big/bitter/great*** *disappointment* |
a ***significant/major/dramatic*** *improvement*

However, the choice of adjective depends on the noun; different nouns need different adjectives to intensify them. Below, you will find some of the most common examples.

Great

Great is used in front of uncountable nouns which express feelings or qualities: *She looked at her son with* ***great pride.*** | *His handling of the problem showed* ***great sensitivity.*** With uncountable nouns, **great** can be replaced by **a lot of** which is more informal, but very common: *I have* ***a lot of admiration*** *for her.* | *It takes* ***a lot of skill*** *to pilot a plane.* When used with countable nouns, **great** is more formal than **big**: *a* ***big/great surprise***. **Great** can often be replaced by stronger adjectives, such as **enormous** and **tremendous**: **enormous enjoyment** | **tremendous admiration**. **Great** is commonly used with these nouns:

great danger
(in) great demand
in great detail
great difficulty
at great length
great effort
great enjoyment
great excitement
great happiness
(a) great honor
great importance
great joy
great strength
a great number (of sth)
great pleasure
great power
a great quantity (of sth)
great respect
(a) great disappointment
(a) great success
great understanding

Total

Total, **complete**, **absolute**, and **utter** are used more frequently than **great** in front of words which express very strong feelings (such as **ecstasy** or **amazement**), or extreme situations, happenings etc., especially bad ones (such as **chaos** or **disaster**):

She stared at him in ***utter amazement.*** | *The trip was a* ***complete disaster.***

In the examples below, **complete** and **absolute** could all be used in place of **total**:

total agony
total astonishment
a total catastrophe
total darkness
total despair
total destruction
total ecstasy
total failure
a total idiot
a total lack (of sth)
total silence
a total stranger

Big

Big is mostly used when talking about physical size, but it can also be used as an intensifying adjective. Note that it is not usually used with countable nouns:

a big decision
a big disappointment
a big eater (=someone who eats a lot)
a big improvement
a big mistake
a big spender (=someone who spends a lot)
a big surprise

Large

Large is mostly used to express physical size. It is also commonly used with nouns which are connected with numbers or measurements, as in the examples below. Note that it is not usually used with uncountable nouns:

a large amount	a large population	a large quantity
a large number (of sth)	a large proportion	a large scale

Deep/Heavy/High/Strong

Deep, **heavy**, **high**, and **strong** are also commonly used as intensifying adjectives, as in these examples:

deep

deep depression	deep distrust	(a) deep sleep
deep devotion	a deep feeling (=emotion)	in deep thought

heavy

a heavy drinker	a heavy sleeper	heavy snow
heavy rain	a heavy smoker	heavy traffic

high

high cost	a high expectation (of sth)	a high price
high density	a high level (of sth)	high quality
high energy	a high opinion (of sb/sth)	high speed

strong

strong demand	a strong opinion (about sth)	a strong taste
a strong denial	a strong sense (of humor/fun etc.)	a strong smell

Other Intensifying Adjectives

The examples above show some of the most common intensifying adjectives, but many other adjectives are used to express the idea of great degree, size, or strength. When deciding which adjective to use, remember that it usually depends on the noun. Particular nouns need particular adjectives:

a ***fierce/heated*** *argument* — *a* ***distinct/marked*** *improvement*
a ***close*** *connection* — *a* ***hard*** *worker*

Note that different adjectives are used with different meanings of a noun:

She has ***strong feelings*** *on the issue* (opinion).
He spoke with ***deep feeling*** *about conditions in the camp* (with emotion).

See LANGUAGE NOTES **Collocations**

What Is an Idiom?

An idiom is a particular group of words with a special meaning which is different from the meanings of the individual words.

Idioms usually have a set word order

Although certain small changes can be made in idiomatic expressions (see below: **Using idioms**) you cannot usually change the words, the word order, or the grammatical forms in the same way as you can change a non-idiomatic expression.

For example:

The answer's easy can be changed to *The answer's simple*. But in the expression *It's* **(as) easy as pie**, the word **simple** cannot be used.

She likes cats and dogs can be changed to *She likes dogs and cats*. But in the expression *It's* **raining cats and dogs** (=raining hard), the word order is unchangeable.

Idioms have a special meaning

Sometimes the meaning of an idiom can be guessed from the meaning of one of the words:

I could eat a horse (=used to say that you are very hungry; something to do with **eating**)

to live **in the lap of luxury** (=to have a lot of very expensive things; something to do with **luxury**)

Usually, however, the meaning of an idiom is completely different from any of the separate words:

It's not like she's **asking for the moon** (=she isn't asking for anything difficult to get).

The test was a **piece of cake** (=the test was very easy).

Sometimes an expression can have two meanings, one literal and one idiomatic. This happens most often when the idiomatic expression is based on a physical image:

a slap in the face (=a physical hit to the face; an insult or an action which seems to be aimed directly at somebody)

to **keep your head above water** (=to prevent yourself from sinking into the water; to be just barely able to live on your income, or to be just barely able to go on with life, work etc.)

Recognizing Idioms

How do you recognize an idiom? It is sometimes difficult to know whether an expression is literal or idiomatic, so it is useful to remember some of the most common types of idioms.

Pairs of words

touch-and-go | **high and dry** | **in black and white** | **the birds and the bees**

(Note that the word order in these pairs is unchangeable.)

Similes

quick as a wink | **(go) like clockwork** | **sleep like a baby**

Phrasal verbs

chicken out | **take to sth** | **dry off** | **come up with sth**

Actions which represent feelings

turn your back (on sb) (to refuse to help or support someone) | **raise eyebrows** (in surprise, doubt, displeasure, or disapproval)

These idioms can be used by themselves to express feelings even when the feeling is not stated. For example *His recent decision has raised eyebrows in City Hall* means “everyone was surprised and not sure the decision was right.”

Sayings

Many sayings are complete sentences. Remember, however, that sayings are not always given in full:

It's a difficult time for retailers, but the **silver lining** *for shoppers is that prices are coming down.*
(The speaker is saying that stores are having a difficult time selling goods, but it is good for shoppers as the prices are becoming lower.) The full saying is: **Every cloud has a silver lining.**
If she doesn't give me the money, I'll be **up a creek** *for sure.*
(The speaker is saying that he will have difficulties if she doesn't give him the money.) The full saying is: **Be up a creek without a paddle.**

Using Idioms

Before using an idiom, ask yourself the following questions:

How set is the expression?

Sometimes certain parts of an idiom can be changed.

Verbs, for example, can often be used in different forms. (Note, however, that they are rarely used in the passive form.)

He **caught** *her eye.* | **Catching** *the waiter's eye, he asked for the bill.*

In many expressions, it is possible to change the **subject pronoun**:

He *swallowed his pride.* | **They** *swallowed their pride.* | **Janet** *swallowed her pride.*

Remember, however, that most idioms are far more set than literal expressions, and many cannot be changed at all. (See the *Longman American Idioms Dictionary* for full details.)

Is the style right for the situation?

Many idiomatic expressions are informal or slang, and are only used in informal (usually spoken) language. Compare:

He said the wrong thing and *He* **put his foot in his mouth**. (INFORMAL)
She criticizes him all the time and *She's always* **on his case**. (INFORMAL)

You will find all the common English idioms in this dictionary. Look them up at the entry for the first main word in the idiom. Idioms are shown in bold, and each idiom has its own number.

▶▶ See LANGUAGE NOTES **Collocations**, **Phrasal Verbs**

Prepositions

A preposition is a word which is used to show the way in which other words are connected. Prepositions may be single words such as: **by**, **from**, **over**, or **under**, or they may be more complex and composed of several words such as: **apart from**, **in front of**, **in spite of**, **instead of**.

Where Are Prepositions Used?

Prepositions are usually followed by a noun or pronoun, a verb with **-ing**, or a **wh-** clause. In the following sentences, **in** is a preposition:

Write your name **in** *the book.*
This soup's awful. There's too much salt **in** *it.*
There's no sense **in** *putting off homework until later.*
I'm very interested **in** *what you said.*

Note that prepositions are NOT used in front of infinitives or clauses beginning with **that**:

I was astonished **at/by** *the news.*
I was astonished to hear the news/to hear what she said.
I was astonished (**by** *the fact) that she had quit her job.*

What Do Prepositions Mean?

Unlike some other languages, English uses many prepositions to express basic relationships between words. Relationships of time and place, for example, are usually expressed by the use of a preposition:

I can see you **on Monday**/**in August**/**at 8 o'clock**/**for half an hour**/**over the weekend** etc.
I'll meet you **at the bus stop**/**in Boston**/**on the corner**/**outside the theater** etc.

Prepositions are used to express many other different kinds of relationships, such as:

reason – *I did it* **because of** *my father/***for** *my mother/***out of** *a sense of duty.*
manner – *She spoke* **with** *a smile/* **in** *a soft voice.*
means – *I came* **by** *bus/***on** *foot/* **in** *a cab* etc.
reaction – *I was surprised* **at** *his attitude/* **by** *his refusal* etc.

Note that a particular preposition can often be used to express more than one kind of relationship. For example, **by** can be used for relationships of:

time – **by** *next week*
place – **by** *the window*
means – **by** *working very hard*

The entries for prepositions in this dictionary will show you which relationships they can be used to express.

Prepositions in Set Phrases

Prepositions are often part of set phrases in phrasal verbs, collocations, and idioms.

Phrasal verbs

Sometimes a combination of a verb and a preposition has its own particular meaning: **call on**, **look out for**, **send for**. In this dictionary, these combinations are treated as phrasal verbs. They are listed in a separate section at the end of the entry for the main verb.

Collocating prepositions

Some nouns, verbs, and adjectives are often followed by particular prepositions: **example (of)**, **prohibit (from)**, **afraid (of)**. The prepositions which can be used with particular words are shown at the entries for these words.

Idioms and typical collocations

Idioms are shown in bold after a sense number. Typical collocations (groups of words which "naturally" go together, through common usage) are also shown in **bold** in the dictionary entries. Idioms and collocations often show a set use of prepositions: **by the name of**, **be out of your mind**, **be on a diet**, **in safe hands**.

Word Order

In some situations it is possible for a preposition to come at the end of a clause or sentence. This happens especially with **wh-** questions, relative clauses, exclamations, passive verbs, and some infinitive clauses:

Who are you talking **to**?
Is this the book you're interested **in**?
Let me **in**!
Don't worry. He's being taken care **of**.
She's really interesting to talk **to**.

This use is very common in everyday informal English, and especially in spoken English. Some people feel that in formal English it is better to avoid putting the prepositions at the end, by using sentences such as this:

To whom *are you speaking?* | *Is this the book* **in which** *you are interested?*

However, sentences like these can sometimes sound too formal and old-fashioned, especially in spoken English.

See LANGUAGE NOTES **Collocations**, **Phrasal Verbs**, **Words Followed by Prepositions**

In English many nouns, verbs, and adjectives are commonly followed by prepositions. If you do not know whether to use a preposition with a particular word or if you are not sure which preposition to use, look up the word in this dictionary. At each entry, you will be given the prepositions that are commonly used with that word. These are printed in bold before an example showing how the word is used in context with a preposition. Note that prepositions may be followed by the **-ing** form of the verb, but cannot be followed by an infinitive.

Below are some sample entries for nouns, verbs, and adjectives.

Prepositions with Nouns

This entry tells you that **candidate** can be used with the preposition **for**.

can·di·date /ˈkændəˌdeɪt, -dɪt/ W1 *n.* [C] **1** someone who is being considered for a job or is competing to be elected: *a presidential candidate* | +**for** *There are only three candidates for the job.* **2** a person, group, or idea that is appropriate for something or likely to get something: +**for** *The school is an obvious candidate for extra funding.* | *The city is **a prime candidate** to host the next Olympics.* [**Origin:** 1600–1700 Latin *candidatus*, from *candidatus* **dressed in white**; because someone trying to get elected in ancient Rome wore white clothes]

Some words are followed by different prepositions that have the same meaning. This entry tells you that **article** can be used with either **about** or **on**. The slash between the prepositions shows that they are used with the same meaning.

ar·ti·cle /ˈɑrt̬ɪkəl/ S1 W2 *n.* [C] **1** a piece of writing about a particular subject in a newspaper, magazine etc.: *a newspaper article* | +**about/on** *Mayer **wrote an article** about the Hubble telescope.* ▸see THESAURUS box at **newspaper**

Some prepositions change the meaning of the sentence. In this entry, **bias** can be used with either **against**, **toward**, or **in favor of**. The entry shows you that **toward** and **in favor of** are similar in meaning, while **against** has a separate example because it has a different meaning. The choice of preposition will thus depend on the meaning of the sentence in which the word is used.

bi·as[1] /ˈbaɪəs/ Ac *n.* **1** [singular, U] DISAPPROVING an attitude that shows more support for one group, person, or belief than others, in a situation where fairness to all people and balanced treatment of all beliefs is important: +**against** *the newspaper's bias against women* | +**toward/in favor of** *The managment has shown a bias in favor of younger employees.*

Prepositions with Verbs

This entry tells you that in its first meaning, **slip** is used with the preposition **on**. The second example shows that you usually **slip on** something.

slip[1] /slɪp/ S2 W2 *v.* **slipped, slipping**
1 SLIDE/FALL [I] to slide a short distance accidentally, and fall or lose your balance slightly: *He slipped and fell.* | +**on** *Brenda slipped on the icy sidewalk.* ▸see THESAURUS box at **fall**[1], **slide**[1]

This entry tells you that **argue** can be used with the prepositions **with**, **about**, and **over**. The choice of preposition will depend on the meaning of the sentence in which the word is used.

ar·gue /ˈɑrgyu/ S2 W1 *v.* **1** [I] to disagree with someone in words, often in an angry way SYN **fight** SYN **quarrel**: *We could hear the neighbors arguing.* | +**with** *He was sent off the court for arguing with a referee.* | +**about/over** *They were arguing about how to spend the money.* | *The kids were arguing over which TV program to watch.*

This entry tells you that in its first meaning, **chat** can be used with either **with** or **to**. The example shows you that these two prepositions are used with the same meaning.

chat[1] /tʃæt/ *v.* **chatted, chatting** [I] **1** to talk in a friendly informal way, especially about things that are not important: *The two women chatted all evening.* | +**about** *We sat up late, chatting about life in the city.* | +**with/to** *Dad really enjoys chatting with people from other countries.*

Prepositions with Adjectives

Some words can be used with prepositions in one meaning and without them in another meaning. This entry tells you that when **confused** means "unable to understand," it can be followed by the preposition **about**. In its second meaning, however, it is used without a preposition.

con•fused /kən'fyuzd/ S2 *adj.* **1** unable to understand clearly what someone is saying or what is happening: *Now I'm totally confused. Can you say that again?* | +**about** *We're confused about what we're supposed to be doing.* | *Every time someone tries to explain the game to me, I* ***get more confused***. **2** not clear, or not easy to understand: *a lot of confused ideas* | *confused political thinking* **3** unable to remember things or think clearly: *a confused old man* [**Origin:** 1300–1400 Old French *confus*, from Latin *confusus*, past participle of *confundere* **to pour together, confuse**] —**confusedly** /kən'fyuzɪdli/ *adv.*

The prepositions used can change according to which meaning of the word is being used. This entry tells you that in its first meaning, **concerned** can be used with the prepositions **about** or **for**, but in its second meaning it is used with the prepositions **in** or **with**.

con•cerned /kən'sənd/ S2 W2 *adj.*
1 WORRIED worried about something important: *Brian didn't seem concerned at all.* | *Concerned parents were calling the school.* | +**about** *Zoo officials are concerned about the mother elephant.* | +**for** *Rescuers are concerned for the safety of two men.* | **concerned that** *The police are concerned that the protests may lead to violence.* ▶see THESAURUS box at **worried**
2 INVOLVED [not before noun] involved in something or affected by it: *Divorce is very painful, especially when children are concerned.* | +**in** *Everyone concerned in the incident was questioned by the police.* | +**with** *Businesses concerned with the oil industry do not support solar energy research.* | *The company's closure was a shock to* ***all concerned***.

Phrasal Verbs

The examples in this Language Note show words that can be used with a preposition, where the preposition does not change the basic meaning of the word itself. There are also many verbs where a word which looks like a preposition is used with a verb to form a completely new meaning, and the preposition cannot be left out without changing this meaning. Examples of this are **come across**, which means "discover," and **look into**, which means "investigate." These are considered to be phrasal verbs and are listed in this dictionary under the main verb in a separate section at the end of the entry.

▶▶ See LANGUAGE NOTES **Collocations**, **Phrasal Verbs**

In this dictionary, a verb is considered to be a phrasal verb if it consists of two or more words. One of these words is always a verb; the other may be an adverb as in **throw away**, a preposition as in **look into**, or both an adverb and a preposition as in **put up with**. The meaning of a phrasal verb is often very different from the meaning of the verb on its own. For example, **look into** (=investigate) and **look after** (=take care of) have completely different meanings from **look**. In fact, many phrasal verbs are idiomatic (see Language Notes: **Idioms**).

How Are Phrasal Verbs Listed?

Phrasal verbs are listed in alphabetical order at the end of the entry for the main verb. They are marked *phr. v*. In this sample entry, **bear out** and **bear up** are phrasal verbs listed after the entry for **bear**.

bear sb/sth out *phr. v.* if facts or information bear out a claim, story, opinion etc., they help to prove that it is true: *Silberman said more people are carrying pistols, and gun sales bear him out.*

bear up *phr. v.* to show courage or determination during a difficult or upsetting time: *People who have hope bear up better in bad circumstances.*

Sometimes the main verb of a phrasal verb is not used alone. In these cases, the verb is shown as a headword but the phrasal verb is listed immediately underneath the headword. This sample entry tells you that the verb **rely** is not used alone but only as part of the phrasal verb **rely on**.

re·ly /rɪˈlaɪ/ Ac *v.* **[Origin:** 1300–1400 Old French *relier*, from Latin *religare* **to tie back]**

rely on/upon sb/sth *phr. v.* **1** to trust someone or something to do what you need or expect them to do SYN **count on** SYN **depend on**: *Thanks for your help. I knew I could rely on you.* | **rely on sb/sth to do sth** *You can rely on me to keep this quiet.* | **rely on sb/sth for sth** *Most Americans rely on TV for news.* **2** to depend on something in order to continue to live or exist SYN **depend on**: *Sudan **relies heavily on** foreign aid.* | **rely on sb/sth for sth** *They rely on the river for their drinking water.* | **rely on sb/sth to do sth** *Most students rely on their parents to support them financially.*

With or without an Object?

As with all other verbs, some phrasal verbs are used with an object and some are not used with an object. In this dictionary, objects are shown within the structure of the phrasal verb itself. These sample entries show that **grow out of** takes the object something, but **grow up** has no object.

grow out of sth *phr. v.* **1** if a child grows out of clothes, they become too big to wear them: *Kids grow out of their shoes so quickly.* **2** if a child grows out of a habit, they stop doing it as they get older: *He sucked his thumb till he was six, but he grew out of it eventually.* **3** to develop from something small or simple into something bigger or more complicated: *The union grew out of worker dissatisfaction.*

grow up *phr. v.* **1** BIOLOGY to develop from being a child to being an adult: *I grew up in Chicago.* | *What do you want to do when you grow up?* **2** to start thinking and behaving more like an adult instead of acting foolish and irresponsible: *Some men just refuse to grow up.* **3** to start to exist and become bigger or more important: *Trading settlements grew up by the river.*

Position of the Object

When a phrasal verb takes an object, it is important to know where to put the object. Sometimes it comes after the adverb or preposition. This entry tells you that the direct object, which can be a person (sb) or a thing (sth), is always placed after the complete phrasal verb **plow into**.

> **plow into** **sb/sth** *phr. v.* to crash into something or someone, especially while driving, because you are unable to stop quickly enough: *A train derailed and plowed into two houses.*

Sometimes the direct object can appear in either position. This is shown by the use of the symbol ↔. This entry tells you that you can say **hand in** *your papers* or **hand** *your papers* **in**.

> **hand** **sth** ↔ **in** *phr. v.* to give something to a person in authority: *He handed in his essay three days late.* | ***I handed in my resignation*** (=told my employer I was going to leave my job) *yesterday.*

Note, however, that with verbs of this type, when the direct object is a pronoun it MUST be put between the verb and the adverb or preposition:

> **Hand in** *your papers* or **Hand** *your papers* **in** but only **Hand** *them* **in** (NOT "**Hand in** *them*"). *They* **knocked down** *the building* or *They* **knocked** *the building* **down** but only *They* **knocked** *it* **down** (NOT "*They* **knocked down** *it*").

Some phrasal verbs can have more than one object. The dictionary will help you decide where to put these objects. This entry tells you that **take out on** has two objects; the first always follows the verb and the second always follows **on**.

> **take** **sth** **out on** **sb** *phr. v.* to treat someone badly because you are feeling angry, tired etc.: *Don't* ***take it out on*** *me! It's not my fault.*

Finally, note that some phrasal verbs can be used with or without an object. This entry shows you that **lead off** is one of these verbs. It also tells you that when it is transitive, the direct object comes either before or after **off**.

> **lead off** *phr. v.* **lead sth** ↔ **off** to start something such as a meeting, event, or performance by saying or doing something: *I'd like to lead off by thanking Dr. Jacobs for visiting us.* | **lead off with sth** *He led off with a few jokes.*

Passives

In passive forms, phrasal verbs follow the usual pattern of word order with the grammatical subject coming in front of the main verb:

> *When's this problem* **going to be looked into**?
> *He says he's always* **being picked** *on by other kids.*
> *Papers* **must be handed in** *before the end of the week.*
> *Hackett's proposal* **was put to** *the board last week.*

▶▶ See LANGUAGE NOTES **Idioms**, **Prepositions**

Modal Verbs

Modal verbs are a small group of verbs which are used with other verbs to change their meaning in some way. The table below shows you some of the many meanings which can be expressed by the modal verbs: **can**, **could**, **may**, **might**, **must**, **have to**, **ought**, **shall**, **should**, **will**, and **would**.

prediction of future events *He'll* (=**will**) *meet you for lunch.* *I give up! It* **won't** *make any difference anyway.*	Remember that the negative form of **will** is **won't**.
personal intention, willingness, wish *I'll* (=**will**) *be back in a minute.* **Will/would** *you help me with my work?* (request) *No, I* **won't**. (refusal) *I'll* (=**will**) *help you.* (offer) **Shall I** *cook tonight?* (offer)	**Shall** can be used in questions with **I** and **we**, but is only used in statements in formal or official English.
ability *I* **can** *speak Chinese, but I* **can't** *write it.* *She* **could** *ride a bike at the age of four.*	**Could** is used to talk about ability, NOT about particular events which actually happened in the past. Other expressions such as **manage to** or **be able to** can be used for past events: *She finally* **managed to** *pass the test.* Or no other verb is needed: *She finally passed the test.*
Can/Could *you close the window, please?* (request)	Polite requests are often made with **can** and **could**.
permission **Can/may** *I have another piece of cake, Dad?* (request) *No, you* **can't**. *You'll make yourself sick.* *Do you think I* **could** *leave early tonight?* (request) *You* **can/may** *leave at 5:30 if you want.*	**Can** is commonly used to ask for or give permission. **May** is formal, but some teachers prefer it. **Could** is used to ask for (NOT to give) permission. It is more tentative than **can**.
unreality, hypothesis *I* **would** *love to travel around the world* (if I had the chance). *What* **would** *you do if you won a million dollars?* *I* **wouldn't have** *gone, if I'd known he was going to be there.* **Would** *you like some coffee?* (offer)	**Would** is commonly used in the main clause of conditional sentences to show that a situation is unreal or uncertain. Because it can express uncertainty, **would** is also used in polite invitations, offers, and requests.
possibility *She* **may/might** *(not) stay home tomorrow.* *Joe* **may have/might have** *missed the bus.* *Where* **can/could** *they be?* *Learning English* **can** *be fun* (=is sometimes fun). *Don't touch! It* **could** *be hot.* *They* **could have** *left already, I guess.*	**Could** suggests that something is less likely than **may** or **might**. **Can't**, **couldn't**, and **couldn't have** are used to show that there is no possibility. (See **certainty** below.)
probability *The meeting* **should/ought to** *be over now* (=I think it probably is). *He* **should/ought to** *be home at 5 o'clock today* (=I think he probably will be).	In this meaning, **should** and **ought to** are not as strong as **will** and **must**. (See **certainty** below.)
certainty *Joe* **must** *be at least 45* (=I'm sure he's at least 45). *No, he* **can't** *be over 40* (=I'm sure he isn't over 40). *He* **must have** *started working 20 years ago* (=I'm sure he started working 20 years ago).	**Must have** (+ past participle) is the form of **must** that is used to express certainty about things in the past. **Must** and **must have** express stronger certainty than **would** and **would have**.

We **couldn't have** *been there at the same time* (=I'm sure we weren't there at the same time). *They'***d** *be back by now* (=I'm sure they're back). *No, they* **wouldn't** *be there yet* (=I'm sure they are not there yet). *Mary* **would have** *landed already* (=I'm sure she's landed already). *No, she* **wouldn't have** *left home yet* (=I'm sure she hasn't left home yet).	**Couldn't** and **couldn't have** express stronger certainty than **wouldn't** and **wouldn't have**.
obligation, requirement *Accidents at school* **must** *be recorded in the accident book.* *Visitors* **must not** *smoke in the hospital.* (it is forbidden)	**Must** and **must not** are used mainly in formal or official writing.
I **have to** *finish this report by tomorrow.* *He* **had to** *finish the report by the next day.*	**Have to** is usually used instead of **must** in more informal writing and speech. **Had to** is the past form of **must** when it is used to express obligation.
You **don't have to** *do it until next week* (=it is not necessary). *I didn't have to go to the meeting* (=it was not required).	**Don't have to** is used to show that there is no obligation.
desirability *You* **should/ought** *to quit smoking.* (advice) *The teachers* **should have/ought to have** *been consulted* (but they were not consulted). *You* **shouldn't** *watch so much TV.*	The contracted form **oughtn't** is rarely used.

Grammatical Behavior of Modal Verbs

Grammatically, modal verbs behave in a different way from ordinary verbs.

- They have no **-s** in the third person singular.
- Most modal verbs, except for **ought**, are followed by the infinitive of other verbs without **to**.
- Modal verbs have no infinitive or **-ing** form. They can be replaced by other expressions if necessary: *She* **can** *leave work early if she wants.* | *She likes* **being able to** *leave work early.*
- They make questions and negative forms without using **do/did**: **May** *I see that?* | *You* **shouldn't** *shout.*

Note that some modal verbs appear to have past tense forms (**could**, **should**, **might**), but these are not usually used with a past meaning. One exception is **could** which, when talking about ability, is used as a past form of **can**: *I* **could** *run a long way when I was younger.*

Most modal verbs can be used in some of their meanings with another verb in the present perfect to talk about the past: *I* **may have** *seen him yesterday.* | *You* **should have** *told me last week.* (See the table for more examples.)

In past indirect speech, the following modals usually change their form:

can *"You* **can't** *leave until tomorrow."* → *They said she* **couldn't** *leave until the next day.*
have to *"You* **have to** *finish your work first."* → *"Dad said I* **had to** *finish my work first."*
may *"They* **may** *have missed the bus."* → *He suggested that they* **might** *have missed the bus.*
will *"I'***ll** *do that tomorrow."* → *She said she* **would** *do it the next day.*

Other modals usually remain the same:

*"I'***d** *like some coffee."* → *She said she* **would** *like some coffee.*
"You **ought to** *stop smoking."* → *She told me I* **ought to** *stop smoking.*

In English there are many word beginnings (prefixes) and word endings (suffixes) that can be added to a word to change its meaning or its part of speech. The most common ones are shown here, with examples of how they are used in the process of word formation. Many more are listed in the dictionary.

Verb Formation

The endings **-ize** and **-ify** can be added to many nouns and adjectives to form verbs, like this:

legal modern popular scandal	**-ize**	legalize modernize popularize scandalize	*The school wants to make its science labs more **modern**. It wants to **modernize** its science labs.*
beauty pure simple solid	**-ify**	beautify purify simplify solidify	*The explanation is not **simple** enough. You need to **simplify** the explanation.*

Adverb Formation

The ending **-ly** can be added to most adjectives to form adverbs, like this:

easy main odd quick stupid	**-ly**	easily mainly oddly quickly stupidly	*His behavior was **stupid**. He behaved **stupidly**.*

Noun Formation

The endings **-er**, **-ment**, and **-ation** can be added to many verbs to form nouns, like this:

drive zip open teach	**-er**	driver zipper opener teacher	*John **drives** a bus. He is a bus **driver**. A can **opener** is a tool for **opening** cans.*
amaze develop pay retire	**-ment**	amazement development payment retirement	*How would you like to **pay**? The **payment** can be in cash or by check.*
admire associate examine organize	**-ation**	admiration association examination organization	*The doctor **examined** me carefully. She gave me a careful **examination**.*

The endings **-ty**, **-ity**, and **-ness** can be added to many adjectives to form nouns, like this:

cruel pure stupid	**-ty** **-ity**	cruelty purity stupidity	*The water is very **pure**. the **purity** of the water*
dark deaf happy kind	**-ness**	darkness deafness happiness kindness	*It was very **dark**. We needed a flashlight to see in the **darkness**.*

Adjective Formation

The endings **-y**, **-ic**, **-ical**, **-ful**, and **-less** can be added to many nouns to form adjectives, like this:

bush dirt hair smell	**-y**	bushy dirty hairy smelly	*The dog had a lot of* **hair**. *He is a* **hairy** *dog.*
algebra atom biology mythology	**-ic** **-ical**	algebraic atomic biological mythological	*Her work involves research in* **biology**. *She does* **biological** *research.*
pain hope care	**-ful**	painful hopeful careful	*His broken leg caused him a lot of* **pain**. *It was very* **painful**.
pain hope care	**-less**	painless hopeless careless	*The operation didn't cause her any* **pain**. *It was* **painless**.

The ending **-able** can be added to many verbs to form adjectives, like this:

wash love debate break	**-able**	washable lovable debatable breakable	*You can* **wash** *this coat. It's* **washable**.

Opposites

The following prefixes can be used in front of many words to produce an opposite meaning. Note, however, that the words formed in this way are not always EXACT opposites, and may have a slightly different meaning.

un-	happy lucky wind block	unhappy unlucky unwind unblock	*I'm not a* **lucky** *person. I'm very* **unlucky**.
in- **im-** **il-** **ir-**	efficient possible literate regular	inefficient impossible illiterate irregular	*It's just not* **possible** *to do that; it's totally* **impossible**.
dis-	agree approve honest	disagree disapprove dishonest	*I don't* **agree** *with everything you said.* *I* **disagree** *with the last part.*
de-	centralize increase ascend inflate	decentralize decrease descend deflate	**Increase** *means to make or become larger in amount or number.* **Decrease** *means to make or become smaller in amount or number.*
non-	sense alcoholic violent conformist	nonsense nonalcoholic nonviolent nonconformist	*The protests were not* **violent**. *They were* **nonviolent**.

Articles

In English, it is often necessary to use an article in front of a noun. There are two kinds of article: the definite article **the**, and the indefinite article **a** or **an**. In order to speak or write English well, it is important to know how articles are used. When deciding whether or not to use an article, and which kind of article to use, you should ask the following questions:

Is the Noun Countable or Uncountable?

Singular countable nouns always need an article or another determiner such as **my**, **this** etc. Other nouns can sometimes be used alone. The chart below tells you which articles can be used with which type of noun:

the +	singular countable nouns	*the hat, the apple*
	plural countable nouns	*the hats, the apples*
	uncountable nouns	*the water, the information*
a/an +	singular countable nouns	*a hat, an apple*
no article + or **some**	plural countable nouns	*(some) hats, (some) apples*
	uncountable nouns	*(some) water, (some) information*

The dictionary shows you when nouns are countable [C] or uncountable [U]. Nouns which are labeled [C,U] can be either countable or uncountable, depending on the context. The examples below show how articles can be used with countable and uncountable nouns:

countable/ uncountable noun	examples
dog [C]	***The dog*** *is a mammal.*
	The dogs *in the park are chasing balls.*
	She wants ***a dog*** *as a pet.*
	There were ***some dogs*** *running around.*
	The park was full of people walking ***dogs****.*
pizza [C,U]	***The pizza*** [C] *we ordered was cold.*
	The pizzas [C] *were cold when they arrived.*
	The *piece of* ***pizza*** [U] *that's still in the box is cold.*
	We'd like ***a pizza*** [C] *with pepperoni and extra cheese.*
	There are still ***some pizzas*** [C] *in the freezer.*
	I'll make ***some pizza*** [U] *for supper.*
	They make really good ***pizzas*** [C] *at Gino's.*
	I could eat ***pizza*** [U] *every day.*
information [U]	***The information*** *they gave us was wrong.*
	We'd like ***some information*** *about hotels.*
	What we really need is ***information****.*

Note that most proper nouns, such as **Susan**, **Boston**, and **Canada**, do not usually have an article:

Susan's *traveling through* ***Boston*** *next week, on her way to* ***Canada****.*

However, **the** is usually used with names of rivers (**the Colorado River**), oceans (**the Pacific**), groups of mountains (**the Andes**), deserts (**the Sahara**), museums and theaters (**the Playhouse**), and hotels (**the Waldorf Hotel**). It is also used with the names of a few countries, especially those whose names contain a common countable noun, such as **the People's Republic of China**.

Are You Talking about Things or People in General?

When nouns appear in general statements, they can be used with different articles, depending on whether they are countable or uncountable.

In general statements, countable nouns can be used

in the plural without an article:

Elephants have tusks. | *I like elephants.*

in the singular with **the**:

The *elephant is a magnificent animal.* | *He is studying* **the** *elephant in its natural habitat.*

in the singular with **a/an**:

An *elephant can live for a very long time.*

Note that **a/an** can only be used in this way if the noun is the grammatical subject of the sentence.

In general statements, uncountable nouns are always used

without an article:

Basketball is a popular sport. | *She loves basketball.* | *Water is essential to life.*

Are You Talking about Particular Things or People?

Nouns are more often used with a particular meaning. Particular meanings can be **definite** or **indefinite**, and they need different articles accordingly.

Definite

Both countable and uncountable nouns are definite in meaning when the speaker and the hearer know exactly which people or things are being referred to. For example, the definite article **the** is used when the noun has already been mentioned:

I brought her some paper and a pencil, but she didn't need **the paper.** | *Here's one shoe, but where's* **the other one** (=the other shoe)?

when it is clear from the situation which noun you mean:

Can you pass me **the salt,** *please?* (=the salt on the table) | *Are you going to see the doctor about it?* (= the doctor you always go to)

when the words following the noun explain exactly which noun you mean:

I just talked to **the man from across the street** (=not just any man). | **The information that you gave me** *was wrong* (=not just any information).

when the person or thing is the only one that exists:

The earth *travels around* **the sun** (=there is only one earth and one sun).

Indefinite

Nouns can also be used with a particular meaning without being definite. For example, in the sentence *I met* **a man** *in a restaurant*, the speaker is talking about one particular man (not all men in general), but we do not know exactly which man.

Singular countable nouns with an indefinite meaning are used with the indefinite article, **a/an**:

Would you like **a cup** *of coffee?* *She's* **an engineer.**

When their meaning is indefinite, plural countable nouns and uncountable nouns are used with **some** or **any**, or sometimes with no article:

I think you owe me **some money.**	*We don't have* **any milk.**
Do you have **any money** *on you?*	*Would you like* **some coffee**?
We need **some eggs.**	*Would you like* **coffee, tea,** *or* **orange juice**?

Does the noun follow a special rule for the use of articles?

The dictionary will tell you if a noun is always used with a particular article. For example:

Nouns describing people or things which are considered to be the only ones of their kind are used with **the**.

> **ˌBig ˈApple** *n.* INFORMAL **the Big Apple** a name for New York City

Some nouns are used with different articles when they have different meanings. (The entry tells you that **left** in its second meaning is always used with **the**.)

> **left**[4] *n.* **1** [singular] the left side or direction: **on/to the left (of sth)** *The entrance is on the left.* | *To the left of the church is an old shoe factory.* | **on/to your left** *You can get tickets at the booths on your left.* | *The picture shows,* ***from left to right****, Molly, Dana, and Anne.* **2 the left/Left** also **the left wing** political parties or groups, such as Socialists and Communists, that want money and property to be divided more fairly, and generally support workers rather than employers: *He has support from the left.*

Some nouns are never used with **the**.

> **god** /gɑd/ S1 W1 *n.* **1 God** [singular, not with the] the spirit or BEING whom Christians, Jews, and Muslims believe created the universe, and to whom they pray

Nouns in some common expressions, such as **in/to the hospital**, use **the**.

> **hos·pi·tal** /ˈhɑspɪtl/ S1 W1 *n.* [C,U] a large building where sick or injured people are taken care of and receive medical treatment: *Elena was* ***in the hospital*** *for a week.* | *He had to* ***go to the hospital.*** | *Ramon was* ***admitted to the hospital*** *on Tuesday.* | **take/rush sb to a/the hospital** *Victims were rushed to a local hospital.* [**Origin:** 1200–1300 Old French, Medieval Latin *hospitale* **place to stay at**, from Latin *hospitalis* **of a guest**]

In some common expressions with prepositions, such as **on foot**, **go home**, **go to school**, **by plane**, **at noon**, **by car** the nouns do not use the article.

> **car** /kɑr/ S1 W1 *n.* [C] **1** a vehicle with four wheels and an engine, that you use to travel from one place to another: *a car parked on the side of the road* | *a car accident* | *You can* ***drive*** *my* ***car*** *today if you need to.* | *We decided to go* ***by car****.*

When you look up a word in this dictionary, check the entry and read the examples to see whether there is any special information about the use of the article.

▶▶ See GRAMMAR NOTES at **some** and **the**

United States
National capital
State capital
Secondary city
Primary road
Railroad
State border
International border
Canada
Mexico
Atlantic Ocean
Pacific Ocean
Gulf of Mexico
The Bahamas
Cuba
Havana
Ottawa
Lake Superior
Lake Michigan
Lake Huron
Lake Erie
Lake Ontario
Lake Winnipeg
Mississippi
Missouri
Ohio
Colorado
Rio Grande
Snake
Columbia
Washington D.C.
Augusta
Montpelier
Concord
Boston
Providence
Hartford
Albany
Trenton
Dover
Annapolis
Harrisburg
Richmond
Raleigh
Columbia
Atlanta
Tallahassee
Montgomery
Jackson
Baton Rouge
Nashville
Frankfort
Charleston
Columbus
Indianapolis
Lansing
Springfield
Madison
St. Paul
Des Moines
Jefferson City
Little Rock
Topeka
Lincoln
Oklahoma City
Austin
Pierre
Bismarck
Cheyenne
Denver
Santa Fe
Helena
Salt Lake City
Phoenix
Boise
Carson City
Sacramento
Salem
Olympia
Juneau
Honolulu
800 km
500 mi
45°
30°
75°
90°
105°
120°

American Business and Industry

Oil was first discovered in what is now Texas in 1543.

North Dakota has been a defense center since the establishment of several air bases in the 1960s.

Agriculture has been an important industry in most states since the country's beginnings.

Las Vegas became the entertainment and gambling capital in 1931.

Silicon Valley in California has been at the center of the computer industry since the late 1960s.

The first great steel plants were constructed in Pennsylvania in the mid-nineteenth century.

New York's first stock exchange was set up on Wall Street in 1792.

Florida has been at the heart of the American space industry since the 1950s.

The movie industry was born in Hollywood in the 1920s.

Michigan has been the center of the U.S. auto industry since 1899.

The Wright Brothers made the first successful flight in an airplane in 1903.

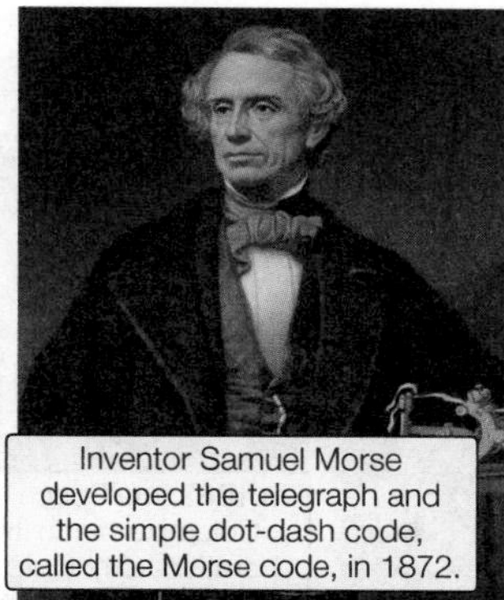

Inventor Samuel Morse developed the telegraph and the simple dot-dash code, called the Morse code, in 1872.

In 1975, Bill Gates formed the Microsoft company, which became the computer industry's leading software and operating system developer.

Scientist, politician and writer Benjamin Franklin invented bifocal eyeglasses in 1752.

Astronaut John Glenn was the first American to orbit the Earth in 1962. In 1988 he became the oldest person to travel in space.

Inventor Eli Whitney developed the cotton gin, a machine for removing the seeds from cotton, in 1793.

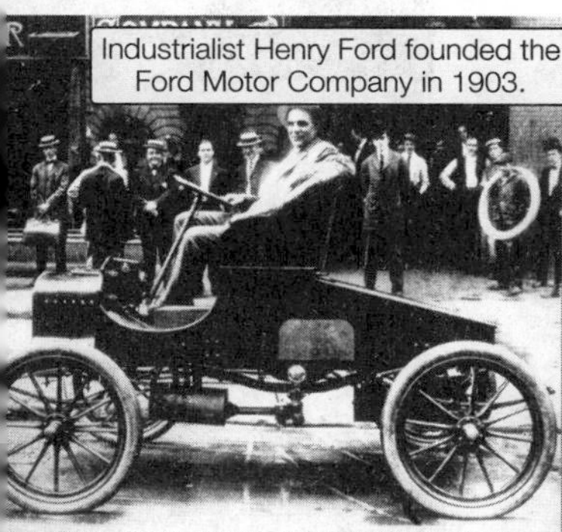

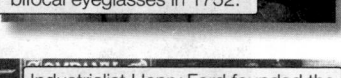

Industrialist Henry Ford founded the Ford Motor Company in 1903.

Industrialist George Eastman perfected the hand-held Kodak camera in 1888.

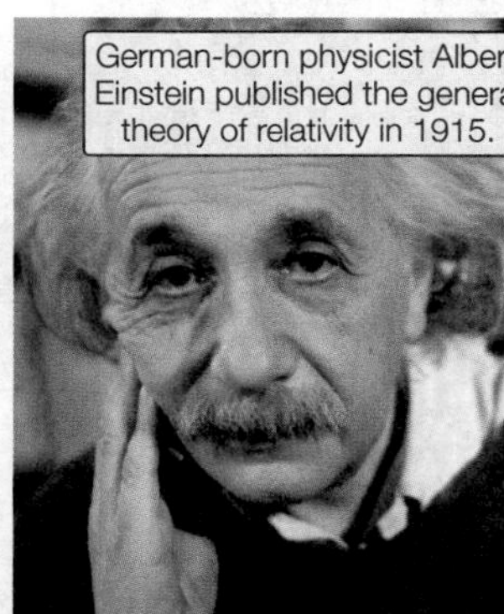

German-born physicist Albert Einstein published the general theory of relativity in 1915.

Inventor Thomas Edison patented the incandescent light bulb in 1872.

Scientist George Washington Carver announced the results of his experiments to make products from peanuts and sweet potatoes in 1914.

Scottish-born inventor Alexander Graham Bell invented the telephone in 1876.

Important Events in the Twentieth and Twenty-first Centuries

In 1906, violent earthquakes and fire devastated San Francisco, California.

In 1982, the Space Shuttle Columbia made its first operational flight into space.

In 2005, Hurricane Katrina caused devastation along the Gulf Coast and flooded the city of New Orleans.

In 1969, the spacecraft Apollo 11 landed on the moon and astronaut Neil Armstrong became the first man to walk on its surface.

In 1927, the pilot Charles Lindbergh became the first person to fly alone across the Atlantic without stopping, in his plane, The Spirit of St. Louis.

In 1968, the black religious and civil rights leader Martin Luther King was assassinated in Memphis, Tennessee.

In 1969, a huge popular music festival was held near the town of Woodstock, New York.

In 1949, The North Atlantic Treaty Organization (NATO) was established to provide mutual protection for the U.S., Canada, and Western Europe.

In 1929, The New York Stock Exchange slumped dramatically in the Wall Street Crash, causing financial chaos and worldwide economic depression.

In 2004, the rover Spirit landed on Mars as part of NASA's Mars Exploration Program.

On September 11, 2001, a terrorist attack destroyed the World Trade Center in New York.

In 1963, President John F. Kennedy was assassinated in Dallas, Texas.

American Artists

Pansy (1962) by Georgia O'Keeffe

The Nighthawks (1943) by Edward Hopper

False Start (1959) by Jasper Johns

Homage to Matisse (1954) by Mark Rothko

Campbell's Soup Cans (1965) by Andy Warhol

Lady Agnes of Lochnaw (c.1892–93) by J. S. Sargent

Number 22, 1949 (1949) by Jackson Pollock

American Gothic (1930) by Grant Wood

Did You Know?

The Sears Tower in Chicago, Illinois: the tallest habitable building (1,454 feet or 443 meters).

The New York Public Library: the biggest public library (15,634,320 books).

Arizona: the sunniest state (4,000 hours of sun per year in Yuma).

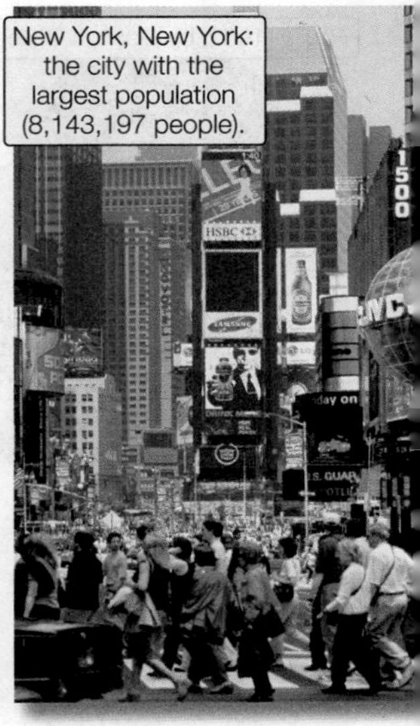

New York, New York: the city with the largest population (8,143,197 people).

The Golden Gate Bridge in San Francisco, California: the longest suspension bridge on the West Coast (4,200 feet or 1,280 meters).

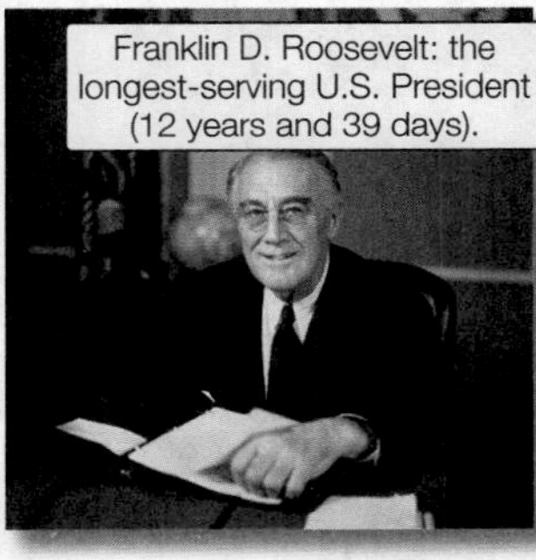

Franklin D. Roosevelt: the longest-serving U.S. President (12 years and 39 days).

Crazy Horse on Thunderhead Mountain in South Dakota: the tallest free-standing statue when completed (563 feet or 172 meters).

The MBTA in Boston, Massachusetts: the oldest subway system (constructed in 1897).

Mount McKinley (or Denali) in Alaska: the highest mountain (20,320 feet or 6,194 meters).

Crater Lake in Oregon: the deepest freshwater lake (1,932 feet or 589 meters).

Extreme Sports

bungee jumping

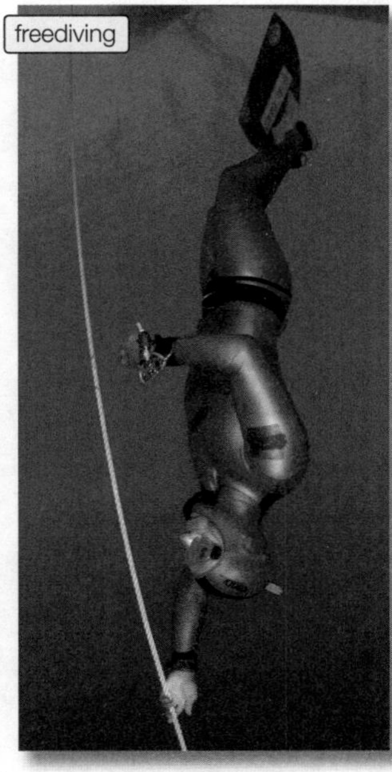

freediving

bodyboarding

kite surfing

snowboarding

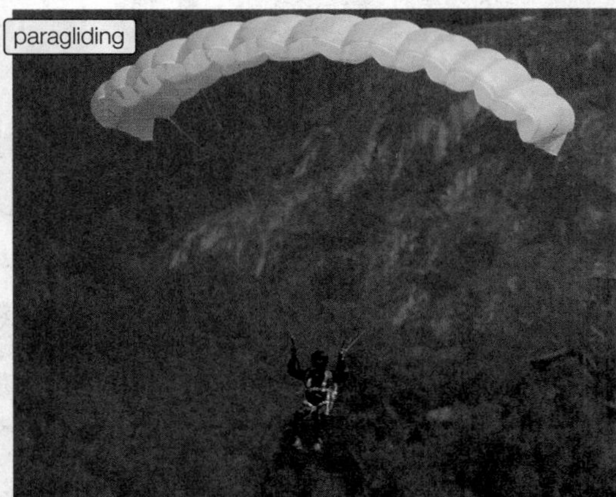

paragliding

skydiving

whitewater rafting

Severe Weather

Ice storms cause power outages in northeast.

Thick fog blankets New England.

Mudslide engulfs houses in Virginia.

Extensive flooding devastates North Dakota.

Severe thunderstorms down power lines in Wyoming.

Avalanche buries homes in Colorado.

Violent hurricane batters Gulf Coast.

High winds fuel forest fires in California.

Savage tornadoes hit Kansas.

Severe blizzard strikes upstate New York.

American Landscapes

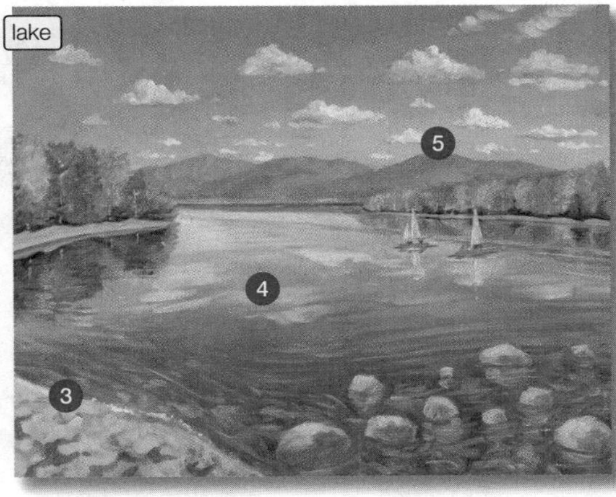

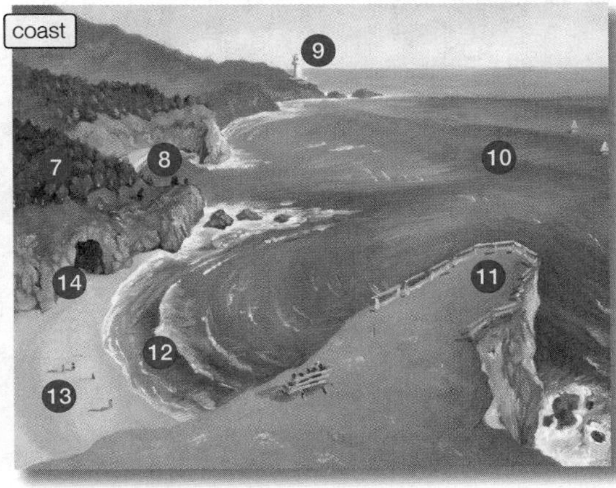

1 sand dune
2 cactus
3 shore
4 lake
5 hill
6 sequoia
7 forest
8 cove
9 lighthouse
10 ocean
11 headland
12 wave
13 beach
14 cave
15 alligator
16 swamp
17 reeds
18 egret
19 trail
20 peak
21 pass
22 summit
23 ridge
24 cliff
25 waterfall
26 river

Verbs in the Kitchen

skewer

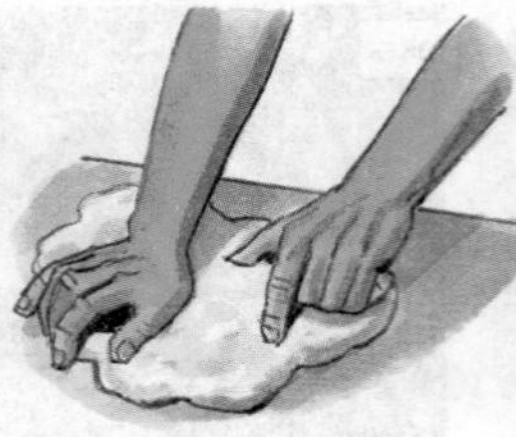
knead

mix

sprinkle

dice

mash

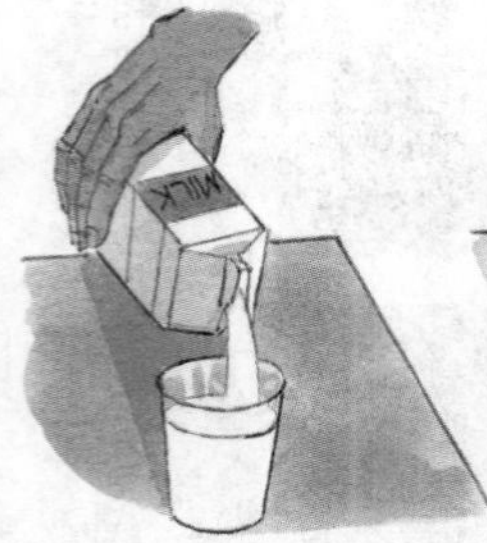

pour

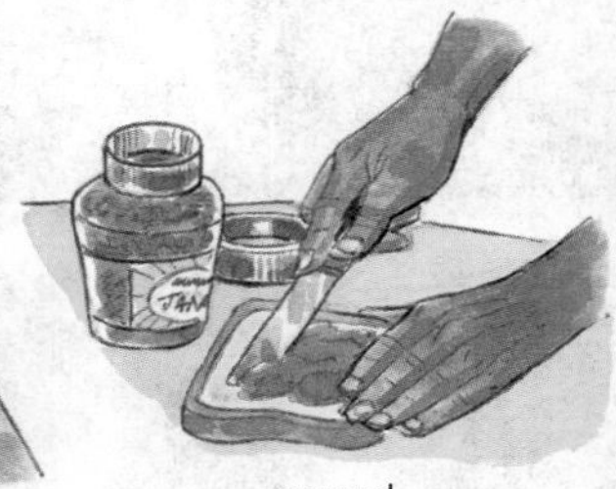
spread

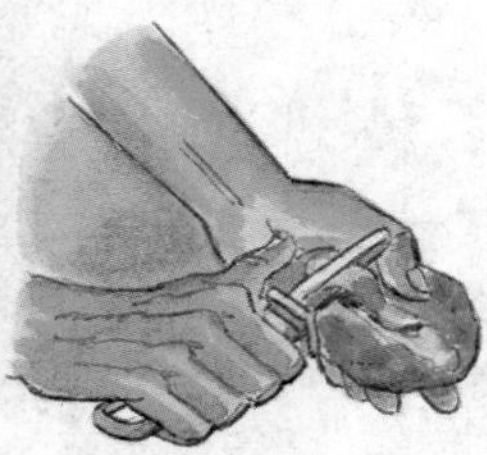
peel

squeeze

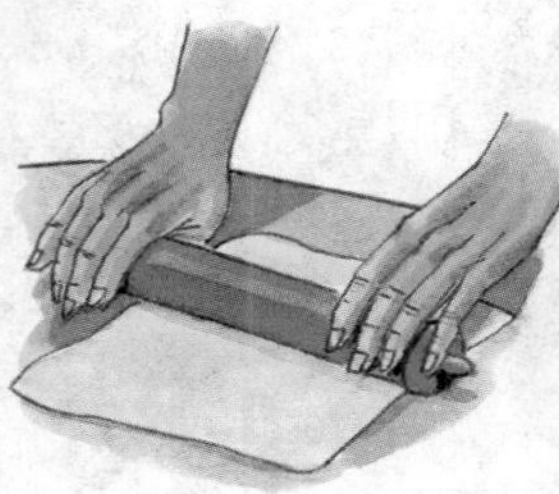
roll

grate

crush

whisk

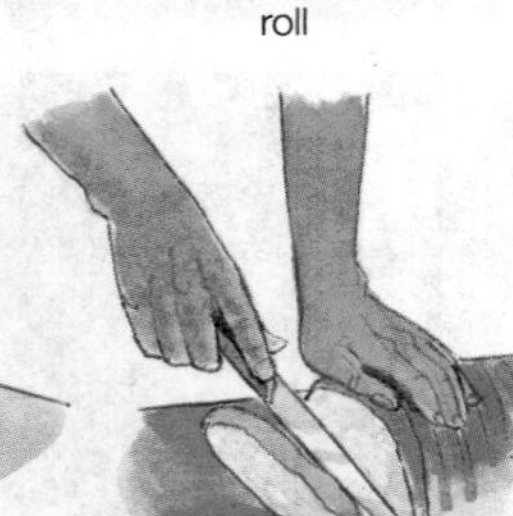
cut

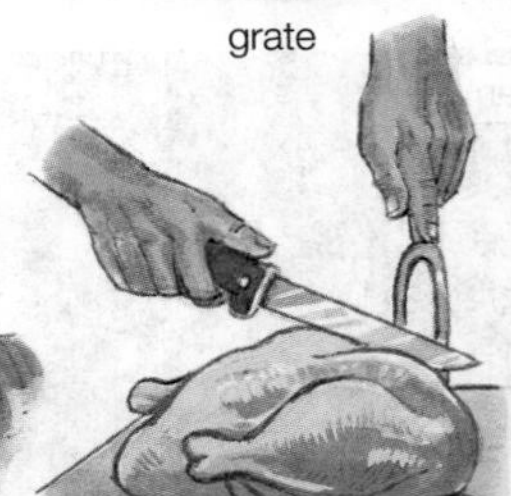
carve

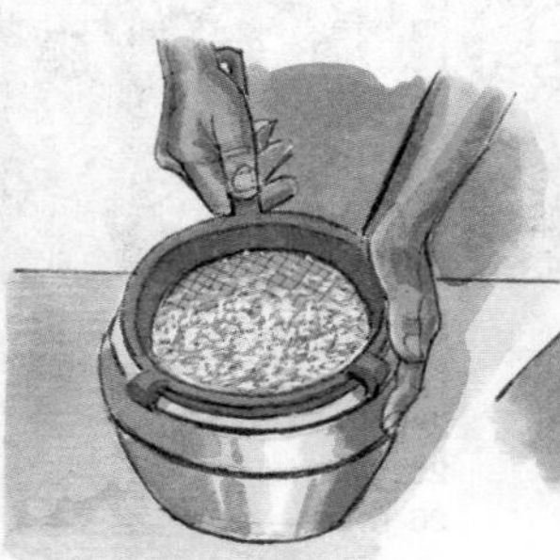
sift/sieve

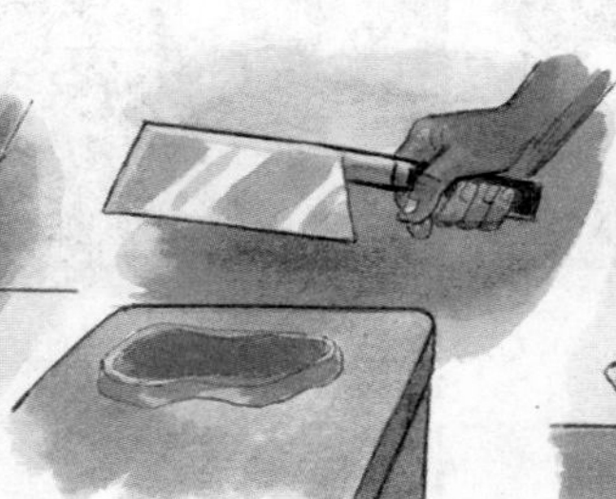
chop

dip

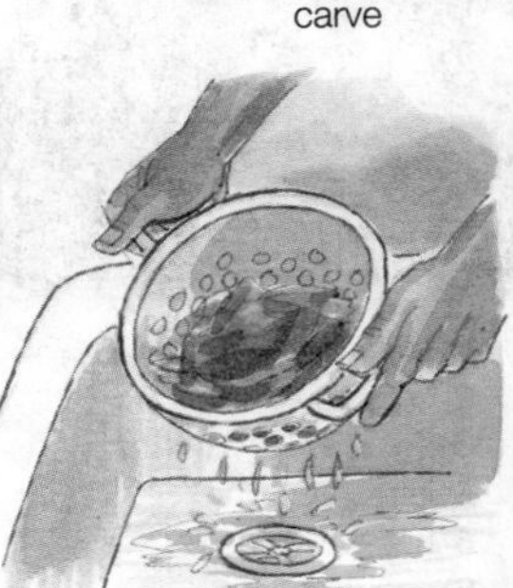
drain/strain

run

jog

scramble

jump

crawl

hop

skip

stretch

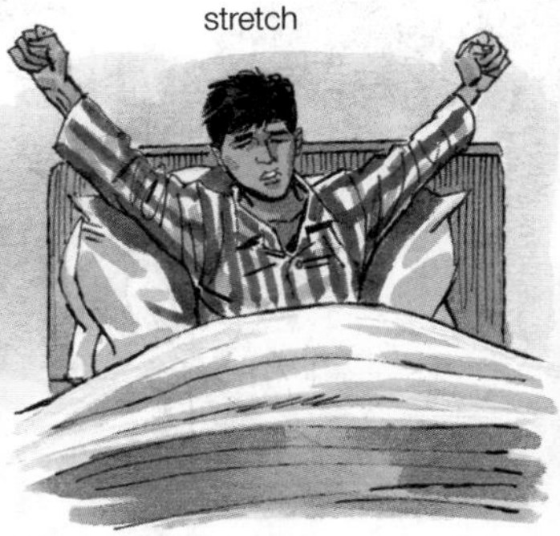

lift

bend

crouch

squat

Native Animals and Birds of America

Fruit and Vegetables

lime
oranges
cherries
lemon
apples
core
pip
kiwi fruit
coconuts
pear
papaya
stalk
figs
peaches
pineapple
raspberries
stone
watermelon
starfruit
seeds
melon
celery
artichokes
pumpkin
radish
corn on the cob
eggplant
asparagus
spinach
cucumber
green beans
cauliflower
zucchini
broccoli
cabbage
leek

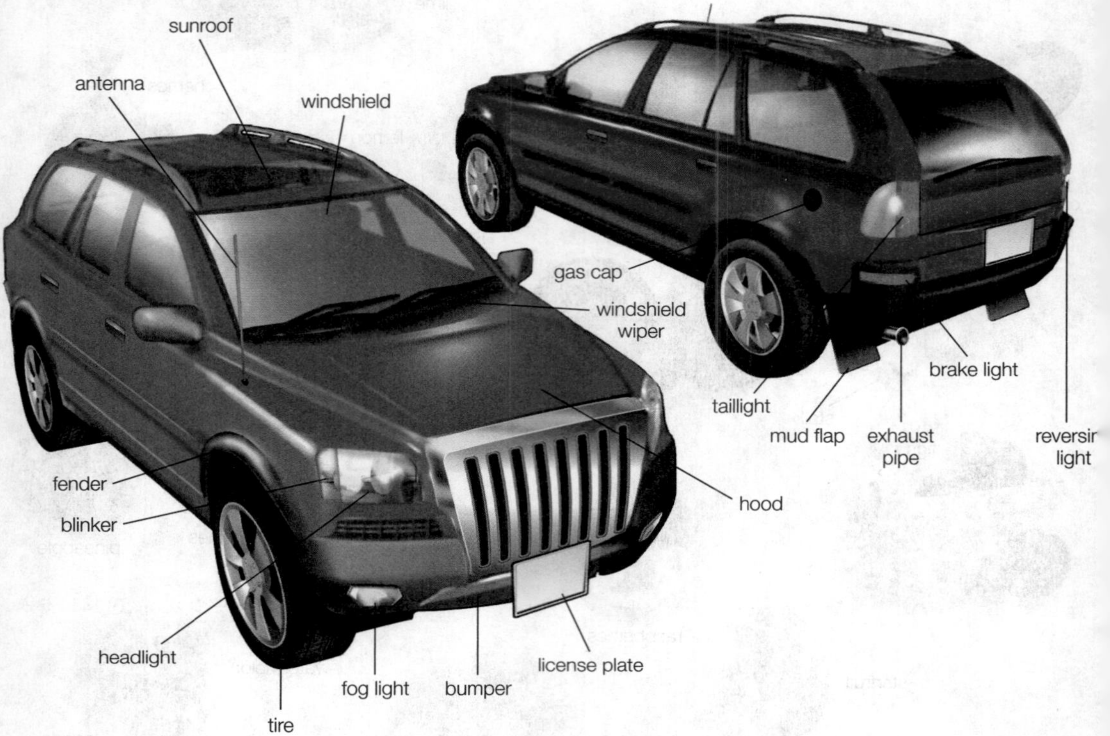
sunroof
antenna
windshield
gas cap
windshield wiper
brake light
taillight
mud flap
exhaust pipe
reversir light
fender
blinker
hood
headlight
fog light
bumper
license plate
tire

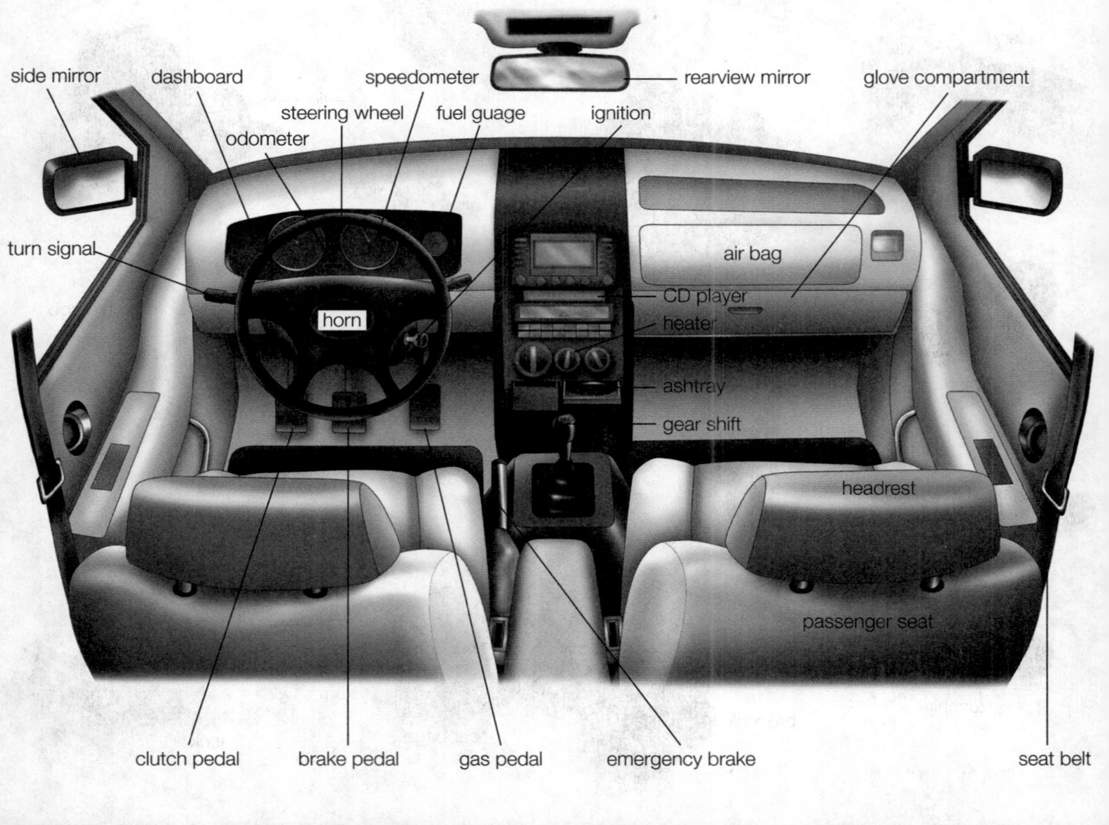
side mirror
dashboard
speedometer
rearview mirror
glove compartment
steering wheel
fuel guage
ignition
odometer
turn signal
air bag
horn
CD player
heater
ashtray
gear shift
headrest
passenger seat
clutch pedal
brake pedal
gas pedal
emergency brake
seat belt

1 Paragraphing

Successful paragraphing is essential to good writing. Do not use too many paragraphs. If paragraphs are very short, this may mean that the writer has either introduced ideas without developing them, or separated one idea over several paragraphs.

If paragraphs are very long, there is likely to be more than one idea in the same paragraph. Poor paragraphing is considered poor style and will result in a lower grade.

As a general rule, a paragraph should use a minimum of three sentences to develop an idea. It is not common to see paragraphs of more than six sentences, although there are some exceptions.

There are ten easy ways to develop an idea into a paragraph. You can select from the following:

1.1 Begin with an idea

Introduce the topic of your paragraph clearly in the first sentence.

USEFUL PHRASES

■ Introduce the main idea: ***I think that*** *more time will be needed to complete the project.* | ***Many people argue that*** *there is a strong case for capital punishment.* | ***I'd like to ask you*** *about what Adam and Angie might like as a wedding present.*

This sentence is often called the topic sentence because the main idea of the paragraph is clearly stated. Although a topic sentence can appear anywhere in the paragraph, it is often the first sentence in the paragraph.

1.2 Give more information

If something is unclear, you can give more information in the following sentence.

USEFUL PHRASES

■ Add an explanation or further information: ***I was wondering*** *whether towels would be a good present for their wedding.* | ***By*** *young people,* ***I mean*** *children under the age of 12 who are not yet completely responsible for their actions.*

1.3 Show concession

Showing concession means that you admit that there are different opinions about the point that you are making. Most arguments have two sides. Show that you understand the weaker side to the argument, but that you are not persuaded or not able to accept this idea.

USEFUL PHRASES

■ Use a word that shows concession: ***Although*** *I would be happy to help you, I am not able to volunteer until the end of this month.* | ***While*** *many people believe that teachers work short hours, this is far from the truth.* | ***Despite*** *the high levels of unemployment in that year, crime did not rise.*

1.4 Reject an idea

A strong way of making a point is to express your doubts about an argument, say what part of the argument you believe is not true, or state what is not possible.

USEFUL PHRASES

■ Say that you do not think something is true: ***I am not convinced*** *that this method of discipline works in schools.* | ***I do not believe*** *that the customer service department has dealt with this complaint in a satisfactory way.*

■ State what is not possible or point out false conclusions: ***It is not necessarily the case that*** *providing more money would make a difference.* | *Unfortunately,* ***I am not able*** *to meet with you until after February 18.*

1.5 Give evidence or examples

Giving details about what, where, or when something happens makes your ideas stronger.

USEFUL PHRASES

■ Use examples: ***There are several reasons for this, such as*** *a change in diet or a lack of exercise.* | ***A good example of this*** *is in cities which have added light rail and special bus routes to reduce traffic.*

■ Give evidence: ***According to*** *the survey, 85% of people were willing to recycle waste items to help preserve the environment.* | ***Research suggests*** *that a good diet may be more important to educational achievement than we previously thought.*

1.6 Give the reason for something

Say why something has happened or what the result of something has been.

USEFUL PHRASES

■ Give the reasons or results of something that has happened: ***This would mean that*** *many children would have even fewer chances to play outside.* | ***As a result of this****, unemployment has risen.*

■ Talk about the causes or effects of something that has happened: ***A key factor*** *is the level of education in a society.* | *The new security measures have had* ***serious implications*** *for the airlines.*

You should pay careful attention to the construction of words and phrases that show reasons and results. Some of these words are verbs and you will need to learn the grammar patterns that are used with them (*result in sth*, *cause sth to happen*, etc.); some are nouns (*a factor*, *a repercussion*); and some are conjunctions and come between clauses (*because*, *therefore*). Also, you will need to be aware that reasons and results are often expressed using the past or present perfect or using modal verbs.

1.7 Give the possible consequences of an action

Say what might happen next, or what the possible results of an action might be.

USEFUL PHRASES

■ Give consequences: ***If this is not possible, we will have to*** *change the date of the meeting.* | *We must take action now,* ***otherwise*** *it may be too late.*

You should pay careful attention to synonyms of the word "if". Not all of the words that are similar to "if" can be used in exactly the same way. You may only be able to use an expression with a positive idea (e.g. ***Provided that*** *you are photocopying the article for your own research, the copying is allowable.*), or with a negative idea (e.g. *We must act now,* ***otherwise*** *it will be too late.*).

1.8 Give additional information

Giving more than one reason, example, or result is a clear way of building a strong point.

USEFUL PHRASES

■ Give additional information: *Diamonds are used* ***not only*** *in jewelry* ***but also*** *in industry.* | ***Another good reason*** *is the time this will save.*

1.9 Make important issues clear

Some events or reasons are more important than others. Occasionally, using words or phrases that signal important points can make your ideas much clearer.

USEFUL PHRASES

■ Introduce strong arguments and ideas using words that emphasize them: ***Besides****, there is not enough money in the budget for the program.* | ***Moreover****, many people feel that this policy is unfair to the most vulnerable members of our society.* | ***To make matters worse****, the weather had become stormy and most of the passengers felt sick.*

1.10 Remind the reader of the main point of the paragraph

Say why the information in your paragraph is important, usually by emphasizing or summarizing the point. You may also want to say what might happen or what will happen because of the points you are discussing, or what the reader should do next.

USEFUL PHRASES

■ Repeat the main point: ***For this reason****, many people argue that guns should be banned.* | *I am sorry for the confusion, and I hope the information is now clear.*

■ Say what might or what will happen next: ***Please could I have your response by*** *the end of next week?* | ***This will have a significant effect on*** *the wildlife in the area.*

2 Cohesion

A paragraph is a group of sentences that are connected in terms of the ideas in them. They are also connected in terms of grammar, for example by using the same verb tense throughout the paragraph, and in terms of vocabulary, for example by consistently using formal language. This is called cohesion.

There are three effective ways of developing cohesion in your writing.

2.1 Paraphrasing

Paraphrasing means expressing the same idea, but using different words. This can be done in several ways.

USEFUL PHRASES

- You can use a different part of speech: *The number of cases of polio* ***dropped*** *considerably in that year.* ***The drop*** *was entirely due to the new vaccine.*
- You can use synonyms: *Most children have* ***arguments*** *at some time, but when their* ***squabbles*** *turn into bullying adults must intervene.*
- Use summaries: *Middle managers tend to feel under more pressure to work long hours than their superiors.* ***This tendency*** *is seen in many different sectors.*

2.2 Substitution

Substitution means writing a pronoun instead of a full name or phrase.

USEFUL PHRASES

- Use **he/they** etc.: *I saw Maria at the supermarket, and* ***she*** *said that you were meeting* ***her*** *on Friday.*
- Use **this/this + noun**: *The sales tax is set at 13%.* ***This*** *means that people pay 13 cents in tax for every dollar they spend.* | *The figures were much lower in European countries.* ***This difference*** *was largely a result of higher spending on education.*
- Use **that/those** after a comparative form: *The incidence of obesity among women in these groups was significantly lower than* ***that*** *of their poorer counterparts.* | *Students in smaller classes progressed much more quickly than* ***those*** *in larger classes.*
- Use **such** + **(a)** + noun: *The company asked customers to rate the quality of the product and service they received.* ***Such*** *surveys are used to identify problems and improve service.*
- Use an **auxiliary verb** + **so**: *We cannot continue to ignore the problem. If we* ***do so****, the effects may become impossible to reverse.*
- Change **a** to **the** after the first mention: *There was* ***a*** *rise in unemployment in that year.* ***The*** *rise was largely due to the closure of several large factories.*
- Shorten names after the first mention: ***James Watson****, Francis Crick, and Maurice Wilkins shared the Nobel Prize in 1962 for their work on the structure of DNA.* ***Watson*** *was only 34 at the time of the award.* | ***The Institute for Cancer Research (ICR)*** *has come up with a few solutions. According to scientists at the* ***ICR****, we may need to look more closely at lifestyle issues than we have before.*

2.3 Connectors

There is a wide range of connecting words and phrases available to give the reader clues about how one sentence relates to the previous one. These connectors tell us if we are about to read the reason (*because*), something surprising (*despite*), something important (*moreover*) etc. Many are already discussed in **Paragraphing** above. However, you can also build cohesion by using relative clauses, which give more details or make clear exactly which thing or person you are talking about.

USEFUL PHRASES

- Use a relative clause: *Water supplies,* ***which*** *depend on snowfall in the Sierras, may run low this year.* | *The man* ***who*** *was standing in front of me in line started to argue with her.*
- Use a present or past participle: *The factories* ***located*** *overseas were cheaper to run.* | *The people* ***sitting*** *in the back of the room couldn't hear the teacher.*

3 Complex Sentences

Good writing should have a mixture of sentence lengths. Longer sentences demonstrate control of language and are more interesting to read. Short sentences can be used to make a dramatic point.

USEFUL LANGUAGE

- Use complex noun phrases: *The* ***drop in the birth rate*** *may mean that some schools will close.* | *There have been* ***several problems with the new computer system****.*
- Use relative clauses: *Now that his injured shoulder,* ***which*** *caused him to miss several games, is healed, he will be playing in Saturday's game.* | *Many students* ***who*** *have studied abroad say it was one of the best experiences of their college years.*
- Use connectors: ***Despite*** *the many difficulties, we felt the weekend was an overall success.*
- Add description with adjectives and adverbs: *We camped in Yosemite National Park and had a* ***fantastic*** *time. The scenery is* ***spectacular****, with the* ***impressive*** *granite mountains surrounding the valley.* | *She* ***frantically*** *searched for her son.*

4 Using Your Own Language and Terms

It is never a good idea to copy phrases or expressions from the question or from any information you are given.

Copying another person's words and using them in your own work is considered to be plagiarism and will always be marked down in a test or paper. See **Term Papers** for more information on avoiding plagiarism.

Try to find ways of rewriting information so that it means the same thing, but uses different words, or use quotation marks when you need to copy someone's words exactly.

USEFUL PHRASES

- Use synonyms: *What are your* ***qualifications*** *for the* ***job****?* becomes *I believe my* ***education and previous work experience*** *make me the right choice for this* ***position****.*
- Change the word class and order of the sentence: *Levels of obesity* ***are rising*** becomes *There is* ***a rise*** *in the levels of obesity.*

5 Audience and Purpose

We always write for someone in particular and with a particular purpose. Your writing should reflect this.

USEFUL PHRASES

- Be consistent with the register of your writing: *I just wanted to find out how it all went.* (Informal) | *I am writing to inquire about the results of your recent tests.* (Formal)
- Use the formulaic phrases appropriate to your purpose and audience: *Hope to hear from you soon.* (Informal letter) | *Please do not hesitate to contact me if you need any further information.* (Formal letter)

After you have finished writing, reread your work. Would the reader be informed, persuaded, or entertained? Have you covered all the points that are essential to make your letter or writing effective? If the answer is no, you will not get a good grade, even if the writing is of a high standard.

6 Range

The quality of the language and vocabulary that you use will influence the final effect of your writing on the target reader.

USEFUL LANGUAGE

- Use an appropriate range of tenses: *We* ***have been working*** *hard to get everything finished on time.* | *By 2006, the figures* ***had fallen*** *to five million.* | *Call me on Friday –* ***I'll know*** *if* ***I've gotten*** *the job by then.*
- Try to use a variety of ways to begin your sentences: *I sent the package to you last week.* | *The package was sent last week.* | *Unfortunately, the package was sent last week.*
- Learn phrases, rather than isolated words: *The number of* ***crimes committed*** *in this area has fallen.* | *Researchers* ***carried out the experiments*** *under strictly controlled conditions.*

Sample extract from a term paper

In the past few decades, there has been concern over the effect of advertising on girls' and women's perception of their bodies. In the 1960s feminists began complaining that advertisements often portrayed women as "objects" rather than people. There is now concern that boys and men face the same pressures, as in advertisements for perfumes, underwear, and the like men are also used as objects. The purpose of this paper is to examine the effects that advertising has on self-image.

We are constantly bombarded with images in advertising that show us what our culture considers to be the ideal body type. Judging from numerous advertisements, for women this shape appears to be very slender, with quite large breasts and smaller hips and bottom. For men, the ideal appears to be wide shoulders, well-developed muscles, and a flat stomach.

Susan A. Brown argues that even when we know that the body shapes we see in advertising are unrealistic, we are still affected by them. In her article entitled "Body Image and Self-Esteem," she shows that after being shown advertising images, women and men described themselves more negatively than they did before being shown the images.[1]

[1]Brown, Susan A., "Body Image and Self-Esteem," *Journal of Health*, 63 (2006), pp. 35–37.

Sample from the original author's work

During the discussion period, the men and women in the study, who were aged from 15 to 35, all agreed with the idea that the models portrayed in advertising are not realistic, in the sense that most men and women cannot and do not look like them. They spontaneously made remarks such as "no one can be that thin without starving themselves." They also commented that our culture puts too much emphasis on appearance, and that this is detrimental to self-esteem, especially for adolescents.

Summarizing the original work

In her article, Susan A. Brown points out that people are aware that advertising does not portray people's bodies in a realistic way, and that this affects self-esteem (Brown, p. 35).

Paraphrasing the original work

Susan A. Brown's research suggests that people are aware that advertising uses models who are not representative of how most people really look. People also think our society values appearances too much, and this has a negative effect on people's self-esteem (Brown, p. 35).

Quoting directly from the original work

Brown points out that people know that "the models portrayed in advertising are not realistic" (Brown, p. 35).

There are many similarities between a college term paper and an academic discursive essay. The main differences are that a paper requires more preparation, you must read more material on the topic, and your final essay will be longer.

1 Planning Stages for a Paper

There are four main stages when writing a paper:

1 The draft thesis stage;
2 Drawing up the working bibliography and researching the theme;
3 Organizing your ideas and rewriting your thesis;
4 Writing up your work.

1.1 Writing a draft thesis

You may be given a "thesis statement" by your professor in the form of an essay title. If not, you may need to write your own.

If you have to write your own thesis statement, try to limit a fairly broad area of study to a narrower theme.

EXAMPLE

■ The topic is listening skills in language teaching – your field of study would be: *The benefits of using songs with adolescents in the classroom.*

You then need to write a draft thesis. A draft thesis is an idea that you think might be true, and which you want to investigate. Your original draft thesis is likely to change by the time you have finished your research.

EXAMPLE

■ Draft thesis statement: *Using pop songs with adolescents can improve their listening comprehension skills.*

1.2 Drawing up a bibliography and carrying out research

Once you have chosen the draft thesis, go to your class reading list, library listings, or Internet databases and websites to find titles of books, journals, or papers that may be relevant to your research topic. As a general rule, more recent titles tend to be more useful as it is fairly safe to assume that the writer is probably familiar with, and will cover, all the relevant aspects of previous research in his field.

At this stage you should not read the books in detail. Look at the themes of the chapters and the way they approach the topic to get a rough idea of what materials are available before you spend a lot of time reading in detail, because some of your material will not be useable.

When you have found enough material on the specific theme that you have chosen, begin reading the books or articles in order of relevance to your topic, taking notes on interesting points and writing down page numbers of any ideas that you think you might want to use.

Always keep notes listing the title of the book or article and journal you are using and the author's name. Note down where you can find the book again. Unless you have this information, you will not be able to use the ideas in your essay. See the notes below on plagiarism.

1.3 Organizing your ideas and rewriting your thesis statement

As you research the topic, your understanding of it will probably change and you may need to alter your original thesis statement.

Organize your notes into appropriate paragraphs. There should be some comments on the history of the topic before you begin your main essay, but these must be brief (one or two paragraphs). Most of your writing will be a selection of the most relevant ideas. An outline form can be very useful as it helps make the structure of your essay clear.

2 Writing the Paper

A college paper begins with a summary of the background to the paper, and perhaps a justification for its writing. You should include your thesis statement toward the end of the introduction, summarizing your overall conclusion and the paper's message in one sentence. See **Discursive Essays** for ideas on the introduction, body, and conclusions of essays.

Your writing should be objective, so keep your report factual. Any ideas or opinions should be supported with evidence.

USEFUL PHRASES

- Generalize if you find similar conclusions in several different places: ***Research suggests*** *that there is a link between improvements in pronunciation and the use of songs in the classroom.*
- Give an example of a research group that supports your point: ***One such study*** *was carried out by researchers at the University of California at Berkeley.*
- Quote experts who support this point: ***Brown argues*** *that there may be a need for even tighter legislation.*
- Compare and contrast experts who disagree with each other: ***This view is not supported by*** *the evidence collected by the research team at the University of Philadelphia.*

3 Plagiarism

When you begin writing your final version of the paper, you must be careful not to commit plagiarism.

STUDY NOTE

- Plagiarism means copying someone else's ideas or words without naming the original writer, or without acknowledging that you have copied their words exactly. It is taken very seriously at most universities and may result in you failing the paper, or even in you being asked to leave the university.

There are three ways to avoid committing plagiarism:

3.1 Summary

Much of your essay will summarize other people's arguments and ideas. Summarizing is reducing several sentences, paragraphs, or even an entire article into one or two sentences by explaining the author's key point. You *must* credit the idea to the original writer and add a footnote or parenthetical note to the details of the summarized work, even if you do not quote the writer's exact words. For example:

In his book The Health Link, Michael J. Brown argues that a more dynamic model is needed.[1]
1. Brown, Michael J., The Health Link, Poole: Poole University Press, 1990.

3.2 Paraphrasing

Paraphrasing is slightly less common. It means using more or less the same number of words or sentences as the original writer, but using different vocabulary and sentence structure. You *must* credit the idea to the original writer and add a footnote or parenthetical note showing where the idea was taken from. For example:

The original text says: "This is a significant issue, which the academic community has ignored."

Paraphrase: *Brown claims that this important point has not received enough attention from the academic community (Brown, p. 33).*

3.3 Direct quotation

You must be careful not to quote directly too often. When the original writer has expressed an idea so clearly that you could not rewrite it without damaging its quality, you can copy the exact words. These must be enclosed in quotation marks, with the name of the writer clearly stated and a footnote or parenthetical note that includes the page number where the words can be found. For example:

Michael J. Brown claims that "this is a significant issue, which the academic community has ignored" (Brown, p. 107).

If the quotation is a phrase (not a complete sentence) it can be included as part of your own sentence, in quotation marks. If it is a longer quotation, indent it as a separate paragraph.

STUDY NOTE

- Universities have their own requirements for referencing materials. However, as a general rule you must always include the following:

Books: The last name of the writer + the first name(s) or initials + the title of the book + the place of publication + the publisher + the year of publication
Journals: The last name of the writer + the first name(s) or initials + the title of the article + the title of the journal + the issue number and/or date of the journal + the page numbers of the article

TASK

Some states have limited or banned junk food and drinks sold in vending machines in schools, in an effort to reduce obesity in children. To what extent do you agree with this course of action?

Sample answer

Obesity in children has, in the past few years, become a major health problem. Many more children are now considered to be overweight than in previous decades. While there are many things that may contribute to this rise in obesity, such as lack of exercise, the fact that many children eat too much junk food and drink too many sugary drinks definitely is part of the problem. To combat this, many states have passed laws saying that schools should either limit or ban junk food and beverages sold in vending machines on school grounds.

In my view, banning junk food and drinks on school campuses is the right thing to do. Schools can easily offer healthy food, such as fruit, vegetables, granola bars, low-salt pretzels etc. in the vending machines if they want to keep them. I think that schools, as well as parents, should try to encourage healthy eating. It is inconsistent to teach children about which foods are good for you and which are not, and then have vending machines that only offer foods that are not good for your health, such as candy, carbonated soft drinks, and chips.

Many people will argue that schools make a lot of much-needed money from having vending machines on campus. While this is true, it is possible that they will still make money from vending machines with healthy options. If children are hungry and want a snack, they will choose from what is available rather than eat nothing. Some people will also say that parents and individual schools should have the most say over what goes into their school's vending machines, not the government. However, states have laws concerning alcohol and cigarette sales, so why not have laws controlling junk food in schools, which affect children's health just as much?

In conclusion, banning the sale of junk food in schools will not completely end the problem of obesity in children. Outside of school, what children eat will be up to them and their parents. However, children do need to develop good eating habits if they want to be healthy adults. Schools should both teach about healthy eating and provide a healthy diet. One way to do this is to offer only healthy foods in vending machines.

A discursive paper gives you the opportunity to demonstrate your ability to write an argument on a particular topic. Strong organization of ideas is essential to the success of a discursive paper.

Discursive papers may be written for general purposes, for example as a newspaper opinion piece, or for academic purposes, and there are several differences in style depending on this.

1 Introductions to General and Academic Papers

Both a general and an academic paper need to start with an introductory paragraph. The first paragraph introduces the topic, often by giving some background information on what has been happening recently to make us concerned about this topic, or the reason why we should be interested in this issue.

USEFUL PHRASES

- Point out a situation that has got worse: ***In recent years*** *obesity has become a major health problem.*
- Point out a situation that is regularly in the newspapers: ***Almost every day there's a story in the newspaper*** *about juvenile crime being on the rise.*
- Point out a change in politics: ***Most governments now*** *recognize the need to protect the environment.*
- Point out how this affects the reader: *The consequences of global warming will* ***affect us all.***
- Point out the benefits/disadvantages to the reader: ***No one wins*** *if pollution is allowed to continue unchecked.*

The introductory paragraph to an academic discursive essay may include a final statement on the conclusion that the essay will finally reach.

USEFUL PHRASES

■ Summarize your view: ***The aim of this essay is to demonstrate that*** *large corporations should not have too much influence on the government of our country.*

2 General Discursive Papers – Body and Conclusions

A general discursive paper usually has four paragraphs in total. After the introductory paragraph, the second and third paragraphs group arguments for and against the topic. You should put the paragraph with the weaker ideas before the paragraph with stronger ideas.

USEFUL PHRASES

■ Start with an opinion: ***In my view****, there are many benefits to walking as a form of exercise.* | ***On the whole****, music education has benefits even for children who will not become musicians.*

■ Add additional explanations or reasons: ***In fact****, most criminals leave prison with far fewer opportunities to earn money in an honest way than they had before they went in.*

■ Summarize what you have said at the end: ***This all suggests that*** *prison may not be the most effective form of punishment for minor crimes.* | ***The arguments in favor of*** *music education seem persuasive.*

■ Begin your second paragraph with a contrast: ***However****, the purpose of education is not solely to teach children to read and write.* | ***While I agree that*** *smoking is extremely bad for your health, I do not think sales of tobacco should be banned.*

■ Continue to build arguments in the same way as the previous paragraph: ***I believe that*** *team sports and more energetic sports have more benefits than walking.*

Your final paragraph should summarize your point of view on the topic, and perhaps recommend future action.

USEFUL PHRASES

■ Summarize what you think: ***As we have seen****, music education has benefits for all children.* | ***In the final analysis****, I believe that prison is a valid way of dealing with crime.*

■ Make a suggestion: *However, it should not be seen as the only option for reducing the amount of crime.*

3 Academic Discursive Papers – Body and Conclusions

An academic argument does not require you to list all the ideas for and against, but rather to select two or three ideas and build these into a persuasive argument. Your conclusions will be based on the strength of the evidence, rather than your own opinions. You should avoid personalizing an academic text too much, with phrases such as *I think …* , although using evidence from your own personal experience is perfectly acceptable.

USEFUL PHRASES

■ Start with an argument: ***Many experts agree*** *that watching too much television has a negative effect on the development of children.* | ***According to this research****, use of contraception goes up in poor countries when fewer babies die in infancy.*

■ Illustrate this: *There are many health problems,* ***such as*** *poor eyesight, lack of physical fitness, and obesity, which are related to spending a long time watching television.*

■ Accept that there is another argument against your point: ***Although*** *there are many good educational programs, children do not often watch them.*

■ Discuss the implications: *The health problems caused by watching television too much in childhood might be impossible to reverse.*

Continue to build arguments on the topic. These can be balanced or offer only one side of the argument, depending on the instructions you are given. You should present two or three strong ideas, again depending on the word limit and the amount of supporting evidence you can supply.

End by summarizing the findings of the evidence. You may like to make a reference to future studies or action that needs to be taken.

USEFUL LANGUAGE

- Summarize the evidence: ***The evidence suggests that*** *children should be encouraged to be more active.*
- Make a positive prediction: *The increase in the popularity of after-school activities* ***suggests that*** *more children are now choosing to do more active things.*
- Make a warning: ***Unless*** *children are encouraged to be more active, we may be facing a health crisis in the next 20 years.*
- Suggest where more research is necessary: ***More research may be needed*** *to find out if health problems created by inactivity in children can be reversed later in life.*

4 Problem-Solution Essays – Body and Conclusions

A problem-solution essay should begin in the same way, with a general statement on the topic, some background information, or some reasons why we should be interested.

You should put forward possible solutions, beginning a new paragraph for each problem. Discuss the benefits of implementing these solutions, and also the difficulties involved.

USEFUL PHRASES

- Introduce the solution: ***One possible solution would be to*** *provide incentives for people to use public transportation.*
- Suggest the benefits: ***This would help*** *reduce the problems of pollution.*
- Suggest the problems, often with a conditional: ***However, if*** *money is not invested in more reliable and frequent public transportation, people will still be unwilling to use it.*

Make sure that in the final paragraph you select the solution you think would be best.

USEFUL PHRASES

- Summarize your findings: ***As we have seen,*** *this is a complex issue with no easy solution, but some suggestions offer a possible way forward.*

TASK

The table below shows the total number of pupils enrolling each year at the Global Language Schools in four different countries from 1980 to 2005.

Write a report describing the information shown in the table.

	1980	1985	1990	1995	2000	2005
London	490	990	1500	1200	1500	1300
New York	–	200	300	610	1000	1400
Sydney	–	–	700	650	500	450
Toronto	–	–	–	310	350	500

Sample answer

The table illustrates the number of students studying in various branches of the Global Language School (GLS) around the world over a 25-year period. There are significant differences in the size of the school in the four different cities in the survey.

Numbers at the oldest school, based in London, England, remained consistently high throughout the period. There was a dramatic increase in the first five years, and the numbers doubled during this time. The numbers continued to rise significantly up to 1990, after which time they have fluctuated between 1,200 and 1,500. The biggest growth, however, has been in the New York branch. Since opening in 1985, the number of students has increased to seven times the original number. By 2005, it had become the most popular GLS in the world.

The newer branches of the GLS are considerably smaller than the other two. In Australia, despite relatively high numbers of students in the first years of opening, student enrollment dropped on a steady basis every five years. The newest branch in Toronto began with very low figures, saw a very slow improvement in the first five-year period, but rose significantly between 2000 and 2005.

In general, the first two branches to be established remain the most popular among students.

A factual description requires you to comment on numerical information that is presented in the form of a table, pie chart, or bar or line graph. It is important that you only comment on the facts that you are given, and do not speculate about reasons for any changes. In business writing there may be an opportunity for you to make recommendations on the basis of the results, but this is not the case for academic descriptions.

1 Openings

Begin by rewriting the title that you are given, but using different language, and make a general comment on the statistics.

USEFUL PHRASES

- Use synonyms: *The bar chart* ***shows*** *the number* ***of live births to girls aged 18 and under between 1995 and 2000.*** becomes *The bar chart* ***illustrates*** *the number of* ***teenage girls who had babies in the five-year period beginning in 1995.***
- Make a general comment: ***Overall,*** *the number of smokers has decreased significantly.*

2 The Main Body

Start with the most interesting point from the statistics. This is often the category that has shown the greatest increase or decrease over the period of the study, though it may also be the category that is the largest or the smallest.

USEFUL PHRASES

■ Describe a large change: ***The most significant loss*** *in the numbers of trees occurred where pollution was highest.* | ***The greatest change*** *can be seen in the figures for the United States.*
■ Describe the largest/smallest category: *The Catholic Church remains* ***by far the largest*** *denomination in the United States, with roughly 60 million members.* | *These households had* ***the highest levels*** *of domestic violence.* | ***Levels*** *of literacy* ***were lowest*** *in the African countries in the survey.*

Continue to add comments on the information in order of importance. Try to make connections between the different parts of the chart.

USEFUL PHRASES

■ Contrast results: ***This trend contrasts with*** *what is happening abroad.* | ***While*** *the amount of pollution produced by each car has diminished, the increase in the number of cars means that the amount of actual pollution has increased.* | ***There was a clear distinction*** *between the answers given by men and women.*
■ Find similarities: ***There was a similar trend*** *in Canada.* | ***A similar pattern can be observed*** *among Asian women.*

3 Ending Your Description

You should keep a general comment on the statistics for the last sentence. It is important not to speculate about the information or make suggestions, unless you are specifically asked to do so in the question.

USEFUL PHRASES

■ Conclude your findings: ***Overall,*** *there was a marked decline in manufacturing in each of the three countries.* | ***Finally,*** *we can see that there were significant differences in the results for the different socioeconomic groups.*

4 Describing Percentages

Try to generalize about percentages, rather than repeat the exact figures that you are given.

USEFUL PHRASES

■ Use fractions: ***A third*** *of the money was spent on food.* | ***Three quarters*** *of the girls said they thought they could have a happy life even if they did not marry.*
The general construction for fractions is: ***a + third + of + the + noun***. For example: ***A quarter of the people*** *had never smoked in their lives.*
Half is an exception: ***half + the + noun*** is much more common than ***a + half + of + the + noun***. For example: ***Half the states*** *prohibit strikes by teachers.* | ***A half of the states*** *prohibit strikes by teachers.*
■ Use proportions: ***Two out of three*** *divorced men did not pay enough in child support.* | ***One in four*** *people with diabetes develop foot problems.* (Instead of ***two thirds*** or ***a quarter***.)
■ If the first number is ***one***, use the preposition ***in***. If the first number is ***higher than one***, use the preposition ***out of***. For example: ***One in three*** *women drank small amounts of alcohol during pregnancy.* | ***Three out of four*** *students were working to help pay for their college expenses.*
■ Use general vocabulary to describe the size of something: ***The majority*** *of new immigrants settled in the cities.* | *He received only* ***a small minority*** *of the votes cast.*

5 Comparing between Categories

You will often have to compare the results of two different categories in the statistical information.

USEFUL PHRASES

- Use a general ***comparative adjective + than***: *The number of children going on to college was **lower than** in the other three groups.*
- Use adverbs that express differences in size or importance: *The women's salaries were **significantly** lower than the men's.* | *Levels of pollution were **slightly** better the following year.*
- We often use ***comparative adjective + than*** when the difference is expressed as a percentage: *The amount was 50% **lower than** the previous year.* | *The figures were only 20% **higher than** in Texas.*
- Use ***as + adjective + as***: *The figures were **three times as high** in California **as** in Alabama.* | *The newer model was **four times as popular as** the older version.*
- ***as + adjective + as*** is particularly useful for large changes expressed as multiples: *The figures were **twice as high as** the previous year.*

6 Describing Trends

Many factual descriptions require you to compare information over a period of time.

USEFUL PHRASES

- Describe increases: *The number of passengers using the metro system **rose significantly** in the five-year period.*
- Describe decreases: *There was a **marked drop** in the number of deaths caused by heart disease.* | *The company's stock prices **fell significantly** in that quarter.*
- Describe future predictions: *Most analysts **predict** an increase in the level of immigration.*
- If you choose to use a noun (***a fall***), your sentence should begin: There ***was + a fall in + the category***: *There was a fall in the country's population.*
- If you choose to use a verb (***a fall***), your sentence should begin: ***The category + to fall***: *The population of the country fell over this period.*

7 Identifying Categories

Often categories are written on charts, graphs, and diagrams in note form, and you will have to add words such as prepositions, articles, or even change the words themselves to use the categories from the chart in your sentences.

Consumer goods sold: televisions

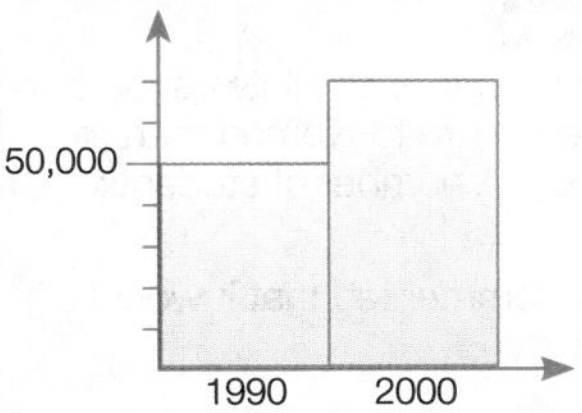

Make sure that you accurately represent the information. In the above chart, for example, write ***Sales of televisions went up***. Not, Televisions went up.

Introduce the category with the word number, amount, or level.

USEFUL PHRASES

- Use ***the + amount + of + uncountable noun + singular verb***: *The amount of pollution has increased.*
- Use ***the + number + of + plural noun + singular verb***: *The number of traffic accidents dropped sharply.*
- For human activities such as smoking use ***the + level + of + noun + singular verb***: *The level of heart disease has increased.*

TASK

You are a member of the facilities board at a community college. The college is considering converting one of its two gymnasiums into an exercise room. Use the information below, gathered from a survey of students, to complete your report. You may add any further information.

Would you exercise on campus more or less often if these changes were made?

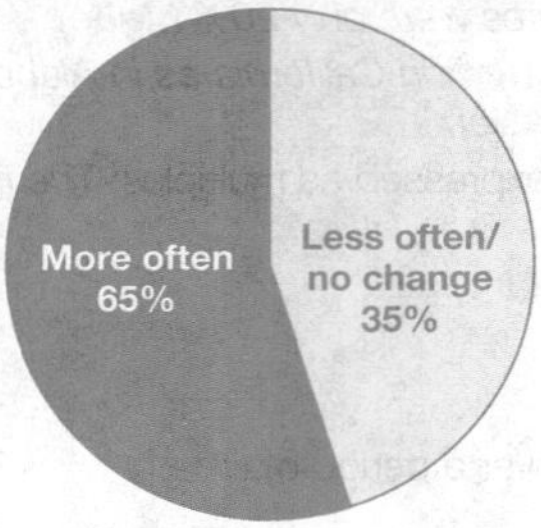

Which of these options would you prefer?

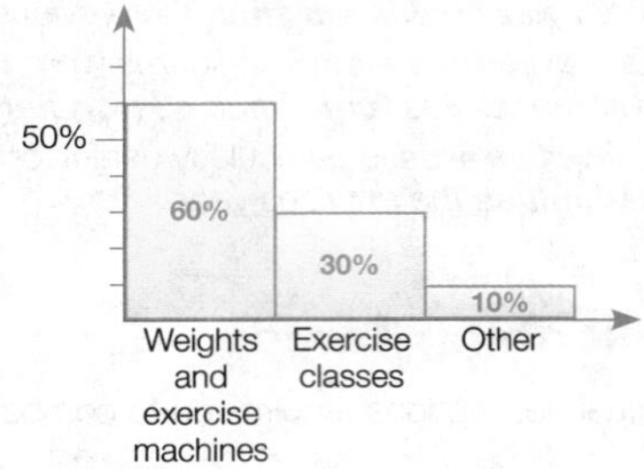

Student comments:
"I could fit exercise machines into my schedule more easily."
"I'd much rather exercise after class than drive to a health club."

Sample answer: Changing the exercise facilities

Introduction

The purpose of this report is to summarize the findings of a recent survey of students on the proposed changes to campus exercise facilities.

The data was collected by questionnaire and interviews with students. In addition, a page was set up on the college website to allow students to add their views on these changes.

General findings

In general, most students felt that they would use the exercise facilities more often if they were changed. Currently, there are two large gymnasiums that are mainly used for team sports, such as basketball, and for dance classes. During large parts of the day they are unused.

Proposals to introduce exercise classes or exercise machines

A substantial number of students felt that exercise classes such as aerobics, step, or Pilates should be offered. A key issue, however, was whether these classes would appeal more to women than to men and would thus not be used by a large proportion of the student body. A number of students suggested that some classes could be held in the remaining gymnasium.

Most students preferred the weights and exercise machine option. Many commented that it would allow them to exercise at times that suited their schedules.

Conclusion

Although the weights and exercise machine option would be more expensive to implement than the classes option, it is preferred by more students and is likely to be more heavily used. A problem that still needs to be addressed, however, is the provision of locker rooms. I conclude that a decision should be made about this issue before contacting any contractors for estimates.

A report requires clear organization and presentation. The language is formal. Often, if the report is for business purposes, a large amount of the language used is formulaic.

1 Openings

A successful report needs a title and often makes use of subheadings as well. Begin with a title that summarizes the purpose of writing the report. It may be relevant to include some comments on how the information was gathered.

USEFUL PHRASES

- Start with the purpose of the report: ***The aim of this report is*** *to assess the impact an earthquake will have on the college buildings.* | ***This report is intended to give a brief summary of the findings of our recent survey*** *on the foods teenagers eat.*
- Say how you collected the data: ***The data was collected*** *from newspaper reports and documents on the Internet.* | ***A survey was carried out*** *among members of the community.*

2 Analyzing the Findings

Group your information into logical themes.

Introduce each theme with a subtitle. A report should be objective, so try to keep your report factual.

USEFUL PHRASES

- Give general impressions of the topic: ***On the whole,*** *children who read a lot tend to spell better.* | ***The majority said that*** *the airport noise was a concern.*
- Quote other people's opinions: ***According to*** *students in the dormitories, the food is usually very good.* | ***Many of our customers*** *have complained that they are waiting too long on the telephone.*

3 Evaluating Options

A report often requires you to compare alternative projects or options, or to assess the value of something.

USEFUL PHRASES

- Compare options or systems: *Most parents* ***preferred*** *the proposal to offer breakfast.*
- Assess a problem: ***A key challenge facing us*** *is a lack of funds.*
- Assess a solution: ***This action will address some of the concerns*** *of staff members.*
- Consider the benefits: ***One of the big advantages of this proposal*** *is that much of the software is available free on the Web.*

4 Discussing Implications

You may need to consider the reasons for your decisions, or the consequences of following one course of action rather than another.

USEFUL PHRASES

- Give reasons for any suggestions: *The vending machines should be removed,* ***because*** *we want to encourage healthy eating.*
- Give the implications of the action: ***This will have an impact on*** *other departments.*

5 Conclusions

Make sure that your report has covered all the key points and achieves its purpose. End with a final evaluation and/or recommendation, or a reference to further action that is necessary.

USEFUL PHRASES

- Summarize the points so far: ***In conclusion,*** *we are not yet in a position to make a final decision.* | ***The following conclusions can be drawn:***
- Make a recommendation: ***As can be seen from the findings of this report,*** *music education should not be cut from the budget.*
- Refer to future action: ***The next stage is*** *to ask an architect for some cost estimates.*

TASK

You have recently bought a computer, but it is not working. Look at the advertisement below and the notes that you have made, and write a letter, requesting a visit from one of the company's technicians.

SPRINGBOURNE TECHNOLOGIES *"for all your computer needs"*

Springbourne the friendly way to do business

■ We offer a wide range of home computers and laptops at discount prices.

■ All our computers come with a choice of popular free software and games.

■ You can arrange for a free home visit from one of our qualified technicians, who will come to your home at a time that suits you to help you set up your computer.

■ If you experience any problems call our free hotline – we will be happy to help you!

I found the same model $150 cheaper locally.

He would only come in the morning when I had classes. He took the computer out of the box and left!

An old tennis game and a recipe organizer!

Cost me $1 per minute.

Sample answer

1842 Lakeside Road, Apt. 304 • Hoboken, NJ 07030 • Tel: (201) 555-0000 / cell: (201) 555-5555

March 5, 2006
Customer number: AF 2789

Mr. A. Fountain
Springbourne Technologies
Unit 7, Riverside Business Park
Newark, NJ 07107

Dear Mr. Fountain:

I am writing to complain about the computer that I bought from your company last week. I am not happy with the computer and the service that I have received.

In your advertisement you state that a choice of software is included in the price. I had indicated that I wanted a word-processing program and something for the Internet, but you included an outdated tennis game and a program for organizing recipes. Neither piece of software is useful for me.

I am also not pleased with the service I have received. Although you claim in your advertisement that you offer discounts, I saw the computer that I bought on sale for $150 less in a local store. I decided to pay the extra money to your company because I am not very confident with computers and I thought your company would offer me the extra technical help that I need. However, this was not the case.

I had to miss my college classes to wait for the computer to arrive, despite your claims that you would arrange a convenient time. The technician who finally came stayed for only ten minutes, just long enough to take the computer out of the box. When I had problems setting up the computer on my own, I decided to phone your hotline. I waited on hold for 15 minutes before giving up and was shocked to find the call had cost me $1 a minute!

I am still having trouble getting the computer set up and would like you to send one of your technicians to my apartment as soon as possible to fix it. I would also like a refund for the $15 phone call, which I feel I should not have to pay, and a choice of a better range of software products than the ones you have sent me.

I look forward to hearing from you in the near future, and can be contacted at any time on the cellphone number above.

Sincerely,

Chris Brown

We often write formal letters to people who we do not know very well. Polite forms are always used, even in letters of complaint. Formal letters use a lot of formulaic language, and even native speakers use the same phrases in their letters each time they write. You should try to include some of these phrases in your own work.

1 Titles and Addresses

If the letter is not written on headed paper, you should write your address and telephone number at the top of the page. This should usually appear on the left-hand side of the page, above the name and address of the person that you are writing to, with the date underneath. There may also be a reference number, for example your order number or customer account number, beneath the date.

The full name (Ms. Penny Smith) or a title (The Manager, Customer Services), and the address of the person you are writing to goes on the next line, on the left-hand side of the page.

EXAM TIP

■ Many exams do not require you to write addresses and the date at the start of your letter, so make sure that you follow any instructions carefully.

USEFUL PHRASES

■ If you know the name of the person to whom you are writing, begin your letter:
Dear Mr. *Smith:* | ***Dear Ms.*** *Brown:* Follow the name with a colon, not a comma.

■ If you do not know the name of the person you are writing to, begin your letter: ***Dear Sir:*** (if you know that you are writing to a man) | ***Dear Madam:*** (if you know that you are writing to a woman) | or ***Dear Sir or Madam:*** (if you do not know the gender)

■ If you do not know the particular company or person you are writing to, begin your letter: ***To Whom It May Concern:***

■ Only write the title and the last name, not the first name: ***~~Dear Mr. John Brown~~***.

2 Covering the Issues

A formal letter is always written in response to another letter, piece of communication, or a situation that has arisen. There are always some things that you must mention in your letter.
These are always clear from the situation.

EXAM TIP

■ There is often a prompt for a negative and/or interrogative sentence in your reply. For example, the notes may contain information such as: *No – Monday impossible*. You are expected to write a negative sentence such as: *I am sorry but I am not available next Monday.*

■ Prompts may be in the form of notes, or in the exam question itself. Make sure that you deal with any such prompts in your answer.

■ In the letter on the opposite page, there are five key points to make:
The four points in the notes (the cost, the poor software, the technician, and the price of the hotline) and the request for a visit by a technician in the first part of the question.

■ If you do not cover all the key points your letter will not receive a good grade, even if you use a wide, accurate range of language and vocabulary. In any exam, if you fail to mention a key issue, you will be heavily penalized or may automatically fail the essay task.

3 Beginning Your Letter

A formal letter can begin by referring to the previous communication, stating the relationship between the writer and the person being written to, or by summarizing the purpose of the letter.

USEFUL PHRASES

■ Begin by referring to previous communication: ***Following our telephone conversation this morning,*** *I am happy to confirm our offer of a position with Working Press.* | ***I am writing in reply to your letter dated*** *July 27.* | ***I am writing in response to your advertisement*** *for technical writers, which appeared in the Seattle Post-Intelligencer today.*

■ State the relationship between you: ***I recently bought*** *tickets from you to a concert by the Dixie Chicks, to be held on August 31.*
■ Summarize the purpose of the letter: ***I am writing to inform you of*** *some changes we have made to the conference program.* | ***I would like to be considered for*** *this position.* | ***I am writing to request more information on*** *evening classes.*

4 Ordering Ideas

Try to group your ideas into logical paragraphs. Group your paragraphs either chronologically or in order of importance.

Use connectors to help structure this order.

USEFUL PHRASES
■ Chronological order: ***When*** *I placed the order with you, I was told that it would be delivered within two weeks.* | ***Once*** *you arrive, please give your name to the receptionist.*
■ Order of importance: *I was not pleased with the way my complaint was dealt with.* ***First of all****, I was sent to three different departments before talking to someone who could help me.*

5 Range

It is important to use high-level language and vocabulary in a formal letter. A good letter will make use of some of the formulaic phrases appropriate for the style. It will also use appropriate connectors.

Another way you can show your language ability is by not repeating the exact phrases in the original communication (or exam question).

USEFUL LANGUAGE
■ Change the part of speech of a word to avoid repetition: **the instructions**: *I am happy to* ***offer*** *you the position.* **your answer**: *I am eager to accept your job* ***offer****.*
■ Use a synonym: **the instructions**: *You recently* ***bought*** *a phone from this company.* **your answer**: *I* ***purchased*** *a telephone from you a few weeks ago.*
■ Change the order of ideas: **the instructions**: *I am unable to meet with you on that day because of prior commitments.* **your answer**: *Unfortunately, prior commitments mean that I am unable to meet with you on that day.*

6 Ending the Letter

The end of your letter is as important as the beginning. You should state what you expect the other person to do next, and tell them how they can contact you.

USEFUL PHRASES
■ State the next course of action: ***I look forward to hearing from you in the near future.*** | ***I would like to request*** *a refund of the full amount.* | ***I will wait to hear from you*** *before I take any further action.*
■ Tell them how they can contact you: ***I can be contacted at the above address*** *at any time Monday to Friday.* | ***Please do not hesitate to contact me*** *if you have any further questions.*

Write the complimentary close on a new line, on the left.

USEFUL PHRASES
■ End your letter with: ***Sincerely,*** You may also use ***Yours truly,*** or ***Best regards,*** but ***Sincerely,*** is the most widely used. Always use a comma after it.

Sign your name immediately below the complimentary close and print your full name clearly on the line below.

TASK

You have received the following email from a friend in Miami. Write your reply using the information given.

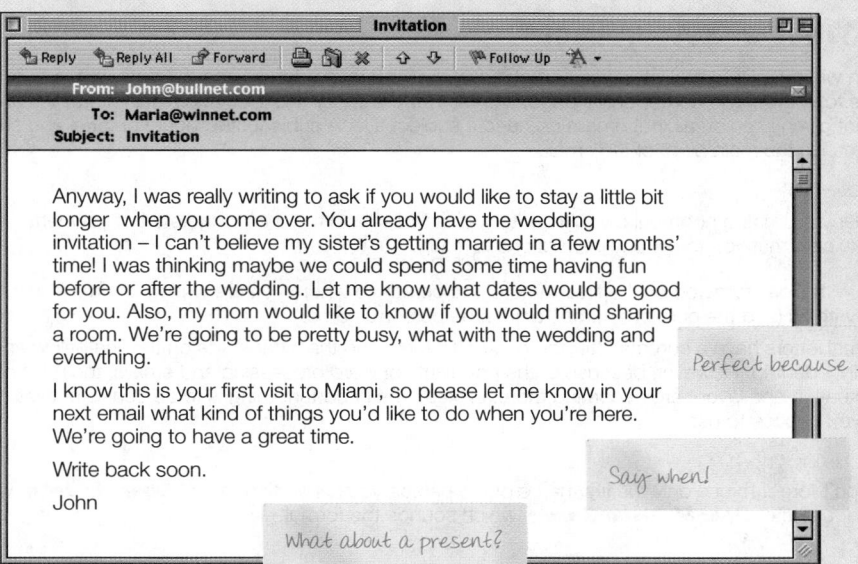

Invitation

Reply | Reply All | Forward | Follow Up

From: John@bullnet.com
To: Maria@winnet.com
Subject: Invitation

Anyway, I was really writing to ask if you would like to stay a little bit longer when you come over. You already have the wedding invitation – I can't believe my sister's getting married in a few months' time! I was thinking maybe we could spend some time having fun before or after the wedding. Let me know what dates would be good for you. Also, my mom would like to know if you would mind sharing a room. We're going to be pretty busy, what with the wedding and everything.

I know this is your first visit to Miami, so please let me know in your next email what kind of things you'd like to do when you're here. We're going to have a great time.

Write back soon.

John

Perfect because ...

Say when!

What about a present?

Sample answer

Your invitation

Reply | Reply All | Forward | Follow Up

From: Maria@winnet.com
To: John@bullnet.com
Subject: Your invitation

Dear John,

Thanks for your email. I'm glad to hear that everything is going well. Sorry I'm late replying, but I've been really busy studying for my final exams and I haven't had time to check my mail for days.

Thank you so much for inviting me to stay longer. I'd love to spend some more time with you. I'll really need a break after all this studying. My finals finish on June 15. Would it be okay if I came on Friday, June 21, and left on the 28th? If these dates sound good, let me know and I'll go ahead and get tickets for the flight.

I need to ask you a few questions about your sister's wedding. What kind of clothes should I bring? I've never been to a wedding in the States before. Also, my family really wants to get a present for Jane. What do you think about some beach towels? They could use them on their honeymoon.

Finally, you asked me what I'd like to do when I get there. Well, I guess the first few days we'll be busy getting ready for the wedding. After that though, there are one or two things I'd like to do. I'd really love to go to Disney World, of course—I hope it's not too far to drive. Do you think we could go to the beach one day, too? That would be great. Other than that, I'll leave it up to you.

Anyway, I hope to hear from you soon.

Take care,

Maria

P.S. By the way, could you please tell your mother that I don't mind about the room. Whatever is easiest for her will be fine.

An informal letter or email is usually between people who know each other fairly well. In addition to giving news, they are often used to request information, congratulate people, give advice, and ask questions. There are a lot of similarities between informal letters and conversation. Informal letters ask a lot of questions, show interest and enthusiasm, and imagine a lot of shared information.

1 Titles and Addresses

When writing an informal letter you sometimes write your own address and the date (but not your name) at the top right-hand corner of the page, then start the letter on the left-hand side. Addresses and dates are not given in an email, but emails do need a subject title. A subject title should be brief and should summarize the main point of the email.

EXAM TIP

■ Many exams do not require you to write your address and the date at the start of your letter, so make sure that you follow any instructions carefully.

Start with ***Dear*** followed by the first name of the person to whom you are writing. In emails, you can also start with ***Hi*** (and the person's name), or just the person's name.

Informal letters have a comma after the person's name, and the letter starts on the line below and is usually indented. However, because of the popularity of word processing and emails, the rules on punctuation and layout are becoming more relaxed. The important thing is to be consistent with the style that you choose to use.

STUDY NOTE

■ Don't forget to use only the first name of the person you are writing to, not ~~***Dear Mr. John***~~, which is never used, or ~~***Dear Mr. John Brown***~~, which sounds too formal.

2 Openings

When writing an informal letter, you are usually replying to another letter. You would normally start with a greeting, then acknowledge the letter to which you are replying. It is often a good idea to acknowledge some key information given in the original letter too. You can also make a comment on your own reply.

USEFUL PHRASES

■ Start with a greeting: ***How are you?*** | ***How's everything going?*** | ***I hope you are okay.***

■ Acknowledge the original letter: ***Thank you for the letter and package*** *which arrived this morning.* | ***It was great to hear from you again.*** | ***I was so surprised to hear*** *that you are getting married!*

■ Make a comment on your reply: ***I have so much to tell you.*** | ***I'm sorry I haven't written for so long.***

3 Covering All the Issues

When you have finished your opening comments, begin a new paragraph and cover all the information that you want to mention. A letter that is written accurately and with a good range of language will still not be effective unless you make sure that you say all the things you need to say.

Make sure that your reply answers any questions that you were asked in the original letter or email and takes into account any additional information that you have been told to mention.

EXAM TIP

■ In many exam questions, you will be told what to include in your reply. There will also often be additional notes which serve as prompts for your reply. It is important that you take these into account in order to get a good grade.

4 Using Informal Language

An informal letter or email is an opportunity to demonstrate informal language skills. There are a number of ways to make your language informal:

USEFUL PHRASES

- Use intensifying adjectives and adverbs to show enthusiasm: *My new English teacher is* ***fantastic.*** | *It has been an* ***absolutely horrible*** *week.*
- Use idiomatic language: *I've been* ***snowed under*** *at work.* | *It's been months since we last* ***got together.*** | ***What have you been up to*** *lately?* | ***Let me know*** *if Friday's okay.* | ***I'll tell you all about it*** *then.*
- Use question forms to make the letter read more like a conversation: ***How*** *are your classes going?* | ***When*** *can you come and visit?*
- Use informal vocabulary: use ***get*** instead of ***receive***, ***I guess*** instead of ***I think***
- Use phrasal verbs and phrases: *we* ***stopped in*** *at Uncle Dan's,* ***write back*** *soon,* ***keep in touch***
- Use contractions: ***I won't*** *have time.* | *I* ***should've*** *told you sooner.*

5 Range

It is important that you use grammatical expressions and vocabulary appropriate to the level of the exam. Even if there are no mistakes in your writing, you will not be able to get a good grade if you use only basic language and vocabulary. Even in informal writing, there is a good range of language you can use.

USEFUL LANGUAGE

- Use the present perfect progressive to give news: ***I've been working*** *hard this summer.*
- Use a future progressive for future plans: ***I'm going to be going*** *home for Christmas.*
- Use conditional sentences to make suggestions: ***If*** *you want to go, give me a call by Friday.*
- Use polite question forms for requests: ***Do you think*** *you could send me a copy of the picture?* | ***Would you mind*** *if we didn't go to Miriam's party?*
- Use tag questions to check information: *You're planning on going,* ***aren't you****?*

6 Connectors

All good writing makes use of connectors. However, many of the connectors you have learned for other styles of writing are inappropriate in an informal letter or email. For informal writing, you need to use some of the connectors that are more specific to spoken language.

USEFUL PHRASES

- To introduce a topic: ***Well,*** *you'll never guess who I bumped into yesterday.* | ***I know*** *you don't think he's a good actor, but his new movie is a lot of fun.* | ***By the way,*** *did you know that Keith is going out with Kim?*
- To go back to a previous topic: ***Anyway,*** *I didn't really like him very much.* | ***Now, where was I? Oh yes,*** *I wanted to ask you if you could come visit us this summer.* | ***As I was saying earlier,*** *Mom's having the operation next week.*
- To introduce surprising or bad news: ***I'm really sorry but*** *I can't make it.* | ***To tell you the truth,*** *I don't really like basketball.*
- To summarize what you've already said: ***Anyway,*** *we had a really nice time.* | ***Well, to cut a long story short,*** *I didn't have enough money to go.*

7 Closing Statements

The end of your letter is as important as the beginning. There are some standard ways of finishing an informal letter or email.

USEFUL PHRASES

- Give a reason why you're ending the letter: *Anyway,* ***I'd better*** *get back to work!* | *I guess* ***it's time to hit the books again.***
- Make a reference to future contact: ***Don't forget*** *to let me know when you can come.* | ***I'll try to phone you*** *on Saturday.* | ***We should get together soon.*** | ***I can't wait to hear from you.***

A closing statement, such as ***Take care, Best wishes,*** or ***Love,*** should be written on a new line. Use a comma after it. Your name then follows on another new line.

If you have forgotten something important, add it at the end, below your name, after the letters ***P.S.***

TASK

You have seen the following job advertisement in the local paper. Write a cover letter to accompany your résumé for this job.

WANTED CAMP COUNSELORS

We are looking for camp counselors to work in locations around the U.S. in the summer months. You must speak good English and preferably be able to teach a skill, either in sports or arts and crafts. Experience of working with children would be a plus.

Interviews will be held locally. Please send applications to: Sue Brown, U.S. Camps, or sbrown@uscamps.com

Sample answer

4602 Anywhere St., Apt. 203
Los Angeles, CA 90019

April 22, 2007

Sue Brown
US Camps
Austin, TX 78713

Dear Ms. Brown:

I am writing to apply for the position of camp counselor with your company. I saw your advertisement in the Los Angeles Daily News and I am very interested in working for U.S. Camps.

I believe I am the right person for the job as I already have experience working with young people. I worked at a church day camp for children aged 8–12 last summer and greatly enjoyed supervising a group of six children. I was responsible for their behavior and welfare, and my duties also included taking care of basic first aid. I found the job very rewarding and I would like to work with this age group again. Also, during my last three years in high school, I helped coach a youth soccer team. I have played soccer myself since I was five, and I would greatly enjoy teaching more young people to play. I feel that my experiences would be an asset as a camp counselor.

In addition, I am hard-working and responsible. I graduated from high school with a 2.8 grade point average, and passed the TOEFL test with a score of 560, so you can see that I have the language skills needed for this job. I also speak Spanish fluently.

I would like to work for your company as I have been impressed by what I have heard about the quality of your camps. I am interested in developing my skills in working with young people, and U.S. Camps look like a great opportunity.

I am enclosing a copy of my résumé with this letter. I would be available for an interview at any time convenient to you. Please do not hesitate to contact me if you have any further questions.

I look forward to hearing from you.

Sincerely,

Miguel Hernandez

Miguel Hernandez

There are many different ways to write a **résumé**, and expectations are different depending on the kind of work which you are applying for. However, there are some things that they all have in common.

A **cover letter** tends to be more standardized and uses a lot of formulaic language. You should try to include some of the phrases given below when you write a cover letter.

1 Résumé

A résumé should contain your personal details, and information about your education and work experience. You may also include information about any additional skills and personal interests, and the names and addresses of anyone who would be willing to give you a reference. Try to keep your résumé to one page. Future employers want a concise summary of your details.

USEFUL PHRASES

- Give personal information: ***permanent address – temporary address – home telephone number – cellphone number – email address – nationality – visa status***

In the United States, you are not expected to give information about age or marital status on your resume. It is not considered acceptable to use these as criteria in selecting people.

- Give information about your education: ***High School Diploma; University Degree – BS or BA; Master's Degree; Ph.D.***
- Say what you specialized in: *Civil Engineering*; *Dental Assistant*
- If your Grade Point Average is good, give it, and the scale it is calculated on: ***3.5 G.P.A. on a 4.0 scale | 4.8 G.P.A. on a 6.0 scale***
- Give information about any honors or special projects: ***Graduated with honors. | Phi Beta Kappa.*** | ***My final project*** *was to design a Braille keyboard.*
- Give information about your responsibilities at work: ***I was responsible*** *for checking the monthly accounts.* | ***I managed*** *a small team of three people.*
- Mention any special achievements: ***I succeeded*** *in reducing costs by 20%.* | ***I achieved*** *the highest level of sales while I was working there.* | ***I was promoted to the position*** *of supervisor.*
- Mention any additional skills: *I am* ***computer literate.*** | ***I have a working knowledge*** *of German.* | ***I am fluent*** *in English.* | ***I am a member of*** *the professional institute of accountants in my country.*
- Give the details of two people who would be willing to give you a reference: ***The following people will be happy to provide a reference.*** | ***References available on request*** (if you do not want to list the names).

Information can be given in the form of full sentences or as bullet points. If you use bullet points, you do not have to use complete sentences. This can make a résumé clearer and easier for possible employers to read:

MIGUEL HERNANDEZ

Permanent address:
4602 Anywhere St., Apt. 203
Los Angeles, CA 90019
(213) 555-5555
email: Miguel@bullnet.com

College address:
CSUN Housing
17950 Lassen St.
Northridge, CA 91330
(818) 555-5555

Education

2006 – present	California State University, Northridge. Liberal Studies major, completed first year with G.P.A. of 2.5 on 4.0 scale.
2002–2006	Los Angeles High School. Graduated with a 2.8 G.P.A. Soccer team captain, 2006. Soccer team member, 2002–2006. School council member 2003–2006.

Work Experience

Sept. 2006 – present	CSUN Food Service. Food preparation assistant.
June–August 2006	Central Church Day Camp, Los Angeles. Supervised 6 children, aged 8–12. Arranged arts and crafts. Supervised soccer, softball, kickball, and other games. Trained in first aid.
2003 – 2006	Youth Soccer coaching assistant, volunteer.

Skills and Interests	Fluent in Spanish. Good knowledge of English. Passed TOEFL with score of 560. Soccer. Model airplane building.

References upon request.

2 Cover Letter

For general guidelines on titles and addresses, and signing letters at the end, see the section **Formal Letters** in this Writing Guide. There is a fairly predictable order to the paragraphs for all cover letters.

2.1 Introductions

You should begin your letter stating your reason for writing, naming the position that you would like to apply for, and saying where you have seen the position advertised.

USEFUL PHRASES

■ State your purpose in writing, name the position and say where you saw it advertised: ***I am writing in response to the advertisement in*** *the Daily Herald for a job as a receptionist.* | ***I would like to be considered for the position of*** *sales assistant.*

■ State that you think you are the right person for the job: ***I believe that I have all the necessary skills and experience for this position.*** | ***I believe that I would be an asset to your company.***

2.2 Education, skills, and experience

Say what experiences from your past make you a good choice for the job.

USEFUL PHRASES

■ State your work experience: ***I have two years' experience*** *working in this field.* | ***I have had considerable experience working with*** *children.* | ***I have been*** *a qualified aerobics instructor* ***for five years.***

■ State your skills and education: ***I have passed the*** *TOEFL.* | ***I am skilled at using*** *Word, Excel, and PowerPoint.* | ***I graduated from college with a Grade Point Average of 4.5 (6.0 scale).***

2.3 Personal qualities and additional skills

State what personal qualities you will bring to the job. Try to give some evidence of these qualities. For example, if you say you are hard-working, mention the high grades that you got at school or college. If you say that you get along well with people, mention that you were working in a team in your last job.

USEFUL PHRASES

■ Give personal qualities: ***I enjoy working with a team.*** | ***I enjoy the challenge*** *of meeting targets.* | ***I am patient and thorough in my work.***

■ Talk about language abilities: ***I have a working knowledge of*** *French.* | ***I am fluent in*** *Spanish.*

■ Talk about computer skills: ***I am computer literate.*** | ***I have a good working knowledge of*** *Word.*

2.4 Say why you want the job

Give the reason why you would like this particular job, or why you would like to work for this company.

USEFUL PHRASES

■ Say why you want this position: ***I would like the opportunity*** *to build on my accounting experience and learn more about accounting systems internationally.* | ***I am very interested in working for your company in a position*** *that will allow me to gain experience and make a contribution in my professional field.*

■ State why you want to work for this company: *XY Systems* ***is a leader in the field*** *of cellphone technology.* | ***I would like the opportunity*** *to work for a large, international company like BY Bank.*

2.5 End the letter

It is not appropriate to ask about salary or other work conditions in a cover letter, unless you have been asked to do so. If you have been asked for salary requirements, you should provide them in a range. You should end your letter with a reference to future contact, and express your interest in hearing from them soon.

USEFUL PHRASES

■ Mention salary requirements in a range, if asked: ***I seek a starting salary of $30,000.***

■ Mention any documents you are sending with you letter: ***You will find a copy of my resume enclosed.***

■ Say that you would like to come to an interview: ***I would be happy to attend an interview at a time convenient to you.***

■ Mention possible references: ***I can send you the names and addresses of people who would be happy to provide a reference on request.***

■ Express your interest in hearing from them: ***Please do not hesitate to contact me if you require any further information.***

■ Refer to future contact: ***I hope to hear from you in the near future.*** | ***I will call you in two weeks to answer any questions you may have.***

J,j

J¹, j /dʒeɪ/ *n. plural* **J's, j's** [C] **a)** the tenth letter of the English alphabet **b)** a sound represented by this letter

J² the written abbreviation of JOULE

jab¹ /dʒæb/ *v. past tense and past participle* **jabbed, jabbing** [I,T] to push something into or towards something else with short quick movements: *My brother jabbed me with his elbow.* | **jab a finger at/in/toward etc. sth** *Ramon jabbed his finger in the umpire's face.* | **jab at sth** *She jabbed at the buttons on the remote control.*

jab² *n.* [C] **1** something you say to criticize someone or something else: *White House officials* ***took a jab at*** *the Democrats' plan.* **2** a sudden hard push or hit, especially with a pointed object or your closed hand: *I gave her a quick jab in the ribs.* | **right/left jab** (=a hit with your right or left hand)

jab·ber /ˈdʒæbɚ/ *v.* [I,T] to talk quickly and excitedly in a way that is difficult to understand: *He was* ***jabbering away*** (=he kept talking) *in Greek.* —**jabber** *n.* [singular, U]

jac·a·ran·da /ˌdʒækəˈrændə/ *n.* [C] a type of tropical American tree with purple flowers

jack¹ /dʒæk/ S3 *n.* **1** [C] a piece of equipment used to lift a heavy weight off the ground, such as a car, and support it while it is in the air: *a hydraulic jack* **2** [C] a card used in card games that has a man's picture on it and is worth less than a QUEEN and more than a ten: *the jack of hearts* **3** [C] an electronic connection for a telephone or other electric machine: *a phone jack* **4 jacks** [U] a children's game in which the players try to pick up small objects (=jacks) while bouncing (BOUNCE) and catching a ball **5** [C] a small metal or plastic object that has six points, used in the game of JACKS

jack² *v.* **be jacked (up)** SLANG to be excited and nervous, often because of taking drugs

jack sb **around** *phr. v.* SPOKEN INFORMAL to waste someone's time by deliberately making things difficult for them: *Quit jacking me around, and just tell me!*

jack sb/sth **up** *phr. v.* **1** to lift something heavy such as a car off the ground using a jack **2** INFORMAL to increase prices, sales etc. by a large amount: *Local sales tax really jacks the prices up.*

jack·al /ˈdʒækəl/ *n.* [C] a wild animal like a dog that lives in Asia and Africa and eats the remaining parts of dead animals

jack·ass /ˈdʒækæs/ *n.* [C] **1** INFORMAL an annoying or stupid person **2** a male DONKEY (=animal similar to a horse)

jack·boot /ˈdʒækbut/ *n.* [C] a boot worn by soldiers that covers their leg up to the knee —**jackbooted** *adj.*

jack·daw /ˈdʒækdɔ/ *n.* [C] a type of small European CROW

jack·et /ˈdʒækɪt/ S2 W3 *n.* [C] **1** a short light coat: *a denim jacket* | *a ski jacket* **2** the part of a SUIT that covers the top part of your body: *a jacket and tie* **3** a DUST JACKET **4** a cover that surrounds and protects some types of equipment **5** a stiff paper cover that protects a record [**Origin:** 1400–1500 French *jaquet*, from *jaque* **short coat**] → see also DINNER JACKET, LIFE JACKET, STRAITJACKET

Jack Frost /ˌdʒæk ˈfrɔst/ *n.* a name used to describe FROST as a person, especially when talking to children

jack·ham·mer /ˈdʒækˌhæmɚ/ *n.* [C] a large powerful tool used to break hard materials such as the surface of a road

ˈjack-in-the-ˌbox *n.* [C] a children's toy shaped like a box with a figure inside that jumps out when the box is opened

jack-in-the-ˈpulpit *n.* [C] a type of wild flower in the northeastern U.S.

jack·knife¹ /ˈdʒæknaɪf/ *n. plural* **jackknives** /-naɪvz/ [C] **1** a knife with a blade that folds into its handle **2** a DIVE in which you bend at the waist in the air and then make your body straight again before you go into the water

jackknife² *v.* **jackknifed, jackknifing** [I] **1** if a large vehicle with two parts jackknifes, the back part swings toward the front part: *A big-rig jackknifed on the highway.* **2** to perform a jackknife DIVE into water

jack-of-ˈall-trades *n.* [singular] someone who can do many different types of work

jack-o'-lan·tern /ˈdʒæk ɚ ˌlæntɚn/ *n.* [C] a PUMPKIN used at Halloween that has a design cut through it, usually of a face, and that usually has a light inside

jack·pot /ˈdʒækpɑt/ *n.* [C] a large amount of money that you can win in a game that is decided by chance → see also **hit the jackpot** at HIT¹ (28)

jack·rab·bit /ˈdʒækˌræbɪt/ *n.* [C] a large North American HARE (=animal like a large rabbit) with very long ears

Jack·son /ˈdʒæksən/ the capital city of the U.S. state of Mississippi

Jackson, Andrew (1767–1845) the seventh President of the U.S.

Jackson, Reg·gie /ˈrɛdʒi/ (1946–) a baseball player famous for hitting HOME RUNS, especially during the World Series

Jackson, the Reverend Jes·se /ˈdʒɛsi/ (1941–) a U.S. politician in the Democratic Party, who was a leader in the U.S. CIVIL RIGHTS movement

Jackson, Thomas "Stone·wall" /ˈtɑməs ˈstoʊnwɔl/ (1824–1863) a general in the Confederate army during the U.S. Civil War

Jack the Rip·per /ˌdʒæk ðə ˈrɪpɚ/ the name given to a British criminal who killed and cut up the bodies of several PROSTITUTES, and was never caught

JACL → see JAPANESE AMERICAN CITIZENS LEAGUE

Ja·cob /ˈdʒeɪkəb/ in the Bible, the son of Isaac whose 12 sons were the ANCESTORS of the 12 tribes of Israel

Jac·o·be·an /ˌdʒækəˈbiən◂/ *adj.* relating to or typical of the period between 1603 and 1623 in Britain, when James I was king

Ja·cuz·zi /dʒəˈkuzi/ *n.* [C] TRADEMARK a large bathtub that makes hot water move in strong currents around your body → see also HOT TUB, SPA

jade /dʒeɪd/ *n.* [U] **1** a hard, usually green, stone often used to make jewelry **2** also **jade green** the light green color of this stone [**Origin:** 1500–1600 French from early Spanish *(piedra de la) ijada* **(stone of the) lower back**; because it was believed that jade cures pain in the kidneys]

jad·ed /ˈdʒeɪdɪd/ *adj.* not interested in or excited by life anymore, because you have experienced too many things: *New York musicians are jaded and tough.*

ˈjade plant *n.* [C] a plant with thick rounded leaves that can be kept in a house or grown outside in hot places

Jag /dʒæg/ *n.* [C] SPOKEN a Jaguar car

jag /dʒæg/ *n.* [C] INFORMAL **crying/shopping/talking etc. jag** a short period of time when you suddenly do cry, shop, talk etc. without controlling how much you do it

jag·ged /ˈdʒægɪd/ *adj.* having a rough uneven edge or surface, often with sharp points on it: *jagged mountain peaks*

jag·uar /ˈdʒægwɑr/ *n.* [C] a large South American wild cat with brown and yellow fur and black spots [**Origin:** 1600–1700 Spanish *yaguar* and Portuguese *jaguar*, from Guarani *yaguara* and Tupi *jaguara*]

jai a·lai /ˈhaɪ laɪ/ *n.* [U] a game played by two, four, or six people in which players use an object like a basket on a stick to throw a ball against a wall

jail¹ /dʒeɪl/ S3 W3 *n.* [C,U] a place where criminals are kept as part of their punishment, or where people who have been charged with a crime are kept before they are judged in a court of law SYN **prison**: *a high security jail* | *a seven-year jail sentence* | *Konrad's been* ***in jail*** *for nine years.* | *He could* ***go to jail*** *for this.* | **put/throw sb in jail** *They arrested the protestors and put them in jail.* | *He was* ***sent to jail*** *for 18 months.* | **spend time/a night/14 days etc. in jail** *She spent last night in jail.* | *Carter was* ***released from jail*** *last week.* [**Origin:** 1200–1300 Old French *jaiole*, from Latin *caveola*, from *cavea* **cage**]

jail² *v.* [T] to put someone in jail: *The brothers were jailed for robbery.*

jail·bait /ˈdʒeɪlbeɪt/ *n.* [U] INFORMAL a girl who is sexually attractive but is too young to legally have sex, so that a boy or man who has sex with her can be charged with RAPE

jail·bird /ˈdʒeɪlbɚd/ *n.* [C] INFORMAL someone who has spent a lot of time in prison

jail·break /ˈdʒeɪlbreɪk/ *n.* [C] an escape or an attempt to escape from prison, especially by several people

jail·er /ˈdʒeɪlɚ/ *n.* [C] someone whose job is to guard a prison or prisoners

jail·house¹ /ˈdʒeɪlhaʊs/ *adj.* related to prisons or prisoners, or happening in a prison: *his jailhouse riot* | *the jailhouse doctor*

jail·house² *n.* [C] a building that has a jail in it

Jain /dʒaɪn, dʒeɪn/ *n.* [C] someone whose religion is Jainism —**Jain** *adj.*

Jain·ism /ˈdʒaɪˌnɪzəm/ *n.* [U] a religion from India that is against violence toward any living thing

Ja·kar·ta /dʒəˈkɑrt̬ə/ the capital and largest city of Indonesia, which is in northwest Java

J

ja·la·pe·ño /ˌhæləˈpeɪnyoʊ, ˌhɑ-/ *n. plural* **jalapeños** [C] a small very hot green PEPPER, used especially in Mexican food

ja·lop·y /dʒəˈlɑpi/ *n. plural* **jalopies** [C] INFORMAL a very old car in bad condition

jal·ou·sie /ˈdʒæləsi/ *n.* [C] a covering for a window that is made of a set of HORIZONTAL flat pieces of wood, metal, or plastic that can be moved to let in sun or air

jam¹ /dʒæm/ S3 *v.*
1 PUSH HARD [I,T] to push something somewhere using a lot of force, until it can go no further: **jam sth into/under/on sth** *Mr. Braithe jammed the letters into his pocket and left.*
2 BLOCK [T] also **jam up** if a lot of people or vehicles jam a place, they block it so that it is difficult to move: *Crowds of supporters jammed the lobby.*
3 MACHINE [I,T] also **jam up** if a machine jams or you jam it, it stops working because part of it is stuck: *The pilot reported that his controls had jammed.*
4 MUSIC [I] ENG. LANG. ARTS to play music in an informal way with others for fun, without practicing first: *We were jamming with Max's band last night.* → see also JAM SESSION
5 jam on the brakes to suddenly put your foot down hard on the BRAKE to stop a car
6 jam a switchboard if telephone calls jam a SWITCHBOARD, so many people are telephoning the same organization that its telephone system cannot work correctly
7 RADIO/TELEVISION [T] to deliberately prevent broadcasts or other electronic signals from being received, by broadcasting other signals on the same WAVELENGTH: *The electronic equipment jams enemy radar signals.*
8 sb is jamming SLANG said when someone is doing something very quickly or well → see also JAMMED

jam² S3 *n.* **1** [C,U] a thick sweet sticky substance made from boiled fruit and sugar and eaten especially on bread: *strawberry jam* **2** [C] a situation in which it is difficult or impossible to move because there are so many cars or people: *Sorry we're late. We got stuck in* ***a traffic jam.*** **3 be/get in a jam** INFORMAL to be or become involved in a difficult or uncomfortable situation: *Can you help me out? I'm kind of in a jam.* **4** a situation in which something is stuck somewhere: *a jam in the copy machine* **5** a JAM SESSION

Ja·mai·ca /dʒəˈmeɪkə/ a country which is an island in the Caribbean Sea —**Jamaican** *n., adj.*

jamb /dʒæm/ *n.* [C] a side post of a door or window

jam·ba·lay·a /ˌdʒʌmbəˈlaɪə/ *n.* [U] a dish from the southern U.S. containing rice and SEAFOOD

jam·bo·ree /ˌdʒæmbəˈri/ *n.* [C] **1** a big noisy party or celebration **2** a large meeting of SCOUTS

James /dʒeɪmz/ a book in the New Testament of the Christian Bible

James, Henry (1843–1916) an American writer of NOVELS

James, Jes·se /ˈdʒɛsi/ (1847–1882) a famous bank and train robber

James, Saint in the Bible, a brother or close relation of Jesus who was important in the early Church

James, William (1842–1910) an American PHILOSOPHER and PSYCHOLOGIST

ˌJames the ˈGreat, Saint in the Bible, one of the 12 APOSTLES, a son of Zebedee and brother of Saint John

ˌJames the ˈLess, Saint in the Bible, one of the 12 APOSTLES, son of Alpheus

James·town /ˈdʒeɪmztaʊn/ a town, established in 1607, in the U.S. state of Virginia which was the first town built by English people who went to live in North America

jammed /dʒæmd/ *adj.* **1** used to emphasize that a place is full of people, vehicles, or other things SYN **packed**: *The place was already jammed an hour before the game.* **2** [not before noun] impossible to move or use because of being stuck in a particular position: *The lock's jammed again.* **3** if phone lines are jammed with calls, so many people are calling an organization that they cannot deal with all the calls

jam·mies /ˈdʒæmiz/ *n.* [plural] INFORMAL → see PAJAMAS

jam-ˈpacked *adj.* INFORMAL full of people or things that are very close together: **+with** *Gloria's closet is jam-packed with designer clothes.*

ˈjam ˌsession *n.* [C] an occasion when JAZZ or ROCK musicians play music together in an informal way for fun

Jan. the written abbreviation of JANUARY

Jane Doe /ˌdʒeɪn ˈdoʊ/ *n.* [C,U] a name used especially by the police for a woman whose name is not known → see also JOHN DOE

jan·gle /ˈdʒæŋgəl/ *v.* **1** [I,T] if metal objects or bells jangle or if you jangle them, they make a sharp sound when they hit each other: *He kept jangling the coins in his pocket* **2 jangle sb's nerves** to make someone feel nervous or upset —**jangle** *n.* [C,U]

jan·i·tor /ˈdʒænət̬ɚ/ *n.* [C] someone whose job is to clean and take care of a large building: *the school janitor* [**Origin:** 1500–1600 Latin *janua* **door**] —**janitorial** /ˌdʒænəˈtɔriəl/ *adj.*

Jan·u·ar·y /ˈdʒænyuˌɛri/ WRITTEN ABBREVIATION **Jan.** *n.* [C,U] the first month of the year, between December and February: *She wanted to go to Texas* ***in January.*** | ***On January 19,*** *Kelley's brother came home.* | *I haven't seen Julio since* ***last January.*** | ***Next January*** *Ben will be three years old.* | *We leave* ***January 1st*** *and return* ***January 29th.*** [**Origin:** 1200–1300 Latin *Januarius*, from *Janus* ancient Roman god of doors, gates, and new beginnings]

> **GRAMMAR** **January, February, March, April etc.**
> When you use a month without a date, say "in January," "in February," etc. If you use it with a date, write "on January 9" or "on January 9th," "on February 22" or "on February 22nd" etc., but always say "on January ninth," "on February twenty-second" etc.

Ja·pan /dʒəˈpæn/ a country in East Asia consisting of four large islands, Hokkaido, Honshu, Shikoku, and Kyushu, and many smaller ones

Jap·a·nese¹ /ˌdʒæpəˈniz◂, -ˈnis◂/ *adj.* **1** relating to or coming from Japan **2** relating to the Japanese language

Japanese² *n.* **1** [U] the language used in Japan **2 the Japanese** [plural] people from Japan

ˌJapanese AˌAmerican ˈCitizens ˌLeague an organization of Japanese Americans that works to protect the rights and interests of Asian Americans

ˌJapanese ˈlantern *n.* [C] a paper decoration, usually with a light inside

jar¹ /dʒɑr/ S3 *n.* **1** [C] a round glass container with a wide lid, used for storing food: *a large, glass jar* | **a jelly/pickle/mustard etc. jar** *a honey jar* | **+of** *a jar of pickles* → see picture at CONTAINER **2** [C] the amount of food, drink etc. contained in a jar: **+of** *half a jar of peanut butter* **3** [C] a round container made of clay, stone etc. that you keep food in: *a cookie jar* **4** [singular] the shock caused by two things hitting together, or by a sudden movement [**Origin:** 1500–1600 Old Provençal *jarra*, from Arabic *jarrah* **pot for carrying water**]

jar² *v.* **jarred, jarring 1** [I,T] to shock a person or group, or make them feel nervous or upset: *The experience jarred my faith.* | **jar sb into sth** *The governor's office was jarred into investigating the situation.* **2** [I,T] to hit against another thing hard enough to cause damage or become loose, or to shake or hit something so that this happens: *Alice landed hard, jarring her ankle.* | *O'Neal jarred the ball loose from Ramirez.* **3** [I]**+with** to be different in style or appearance from something else and therefore look strange: *The modern lamp jarred with the rest of the furniture.* —**jarring** *adj.*

jar·gon /ˈdʒɑrgən/ *n.* [U] ENG. LANG. ARTS words and expressions that are used mainly by people who belong to the same professional group, and that are difficult for others to understand: *military jargon*

jas·mine /ˈdʒæzmɪn/ *n.* [C,U] a climbing plant with small sweet-smelling white or yellow flowers

jas·per /ˈdʒæspɚ/ *n.* [U] a red, yellow, or brown stone that is not very valuable

jaun·dice /ˈdʒɔndɪs, ˈdʒɑn-/ *n.* [U] MEDICINE a medical condition in which your skin and the white part of your eyes become yellow [**Origin:** 1300–1400 Old French *jaunice*, from *jaune* **yellow**]

jaun·diced /ˈdʒɔndɪst/ *adj.* **1** MEDICINE suffering from jaundice **2** thinking that people or things are bad, especially because you have had bad experiences in the past: ***a jaundiced view of** the world* | *She viewed politics and politicians **with a jaundiced eye*** (=in a jaundiced way).

jaunt /dʒɔnt, dʒɑnt/ *n.* [C] a short trip for pleasure: *a weekend jaunt* —**jaunt** *v.* [I]

jaun·ty /ˈdʒɔnti, ˈdʒɑnti/ *adj. comparative* **jauntier**, *superlative* **jauntiest** jaunty actions, clothes etc. show that you are confident and cheerful —**jauntily** *adv.*

Ja·va¹ /ˈdʒɑvə/ an island which is part of Indonesia

Ja·va² /ˈdʒɑvə, ˈdʒæ-/ *n.* [U] TRADEMARK COMPUTERS a computer language used especially to write computer programs for the Internet

ja·va /ˈdʒɑvə/ *n.* [U] INFORMAL coffee

jav·e·lin /ˈdʒævəlɪn, -vlɪn/ *n.* **1** [C] a light SPEAR for throwing, now used mostly in sports **2 the javelin** a sports event in which competitors throw a javelin to see who can throw it the farthest

jaw¹ /dʒɔ/ *n.*

1 BONES/FACE [C] BIOLOGY one of the two bones that your teeth are connected to, or the lower part of your face that covers these bones: *a broken jaw*

2 sb's jaw dropped used to say that someone looked surprised or shocked: *His jaw dropped when he saw his ex-girlfriend.*

3 set your jaw to hold your jaw in a firm position to show that you are determined

4 MOUTH jaws [plural] the mouth of a person or animal, especially a dangerous animal: *a lion's jaws*

5 TOOL jaws [plural] the two parts of a machine or tool that move together to hold something tightly

6 the jaws of death/defeat/despair LITERARY a situation in which you almost die, are almost defeated etc.: **snatch victory from the jaws of defeat** (=manage to win or succeed after you have nearly failed)

7 SHAPE OF JAW [C usually singular] the shape of someone's jaw, especially when it shows something about their character: *a strong jaw*

[**Origin:** 1300–1400 Old French *joe*] → see also JAWS OF LIFE, -JAWED

jaw² *v.* [I] INFORMAL to talk

jaw·bone /ˈdʒɔboʊn/ *n.* [C] one of the two big bones of the jaw, especially the lower jaw

jaw·break·er /ˈdʒɔˌbreɪkɚ/ *n.* [C] **1** a type of round very hard candy **2** a word that is difficult to say

-jawed /dʒɔd/ [in adjectives] **square-jawed/fine-jawed/strong-jawed etc.** having a jaw that has a particular shape or appearance → see also SLACK-JAWED

jaw·line /ˈdʒɔlaɪn/ *n.* [C usually singular] the shape of someone's JAW

ˌJaws of ˈLife *n.* [plural] TRADEMARK **the Jaws of Life** a tool used to make a hole in a vehicle after an accident, so the people inside can be taken out

jay /dʒeɪ/ *n.* [C] BIOLOGY a type of noisy bird → see also BLUEJAY

Jay /dʒeɪ/**, John** (1745–1829) the first CHIEF JUSTICE of the U.S. Supreme Court

jay·bird /ˈdʒeɪbɚd/ *n.* → see **naked as a jaybird** at NAKED (5)

Jay·cee /ˌdʒeɪˈsi/ *n.* [C] a member of the Junior Chamber of Commerce, a local organization in the U.S. that encourages useful and interesting activities for young people

ˈJay ˌTreaty HISTORY an agreement in 1794 between the U.S. and Britain in which Britain agreed to remove its soldiers from FORTS in the Northwest Territory, and rules relating to trade were established

jay·walk·ing /ˈdʒeɪˌwɔkɪŋ/ *n.* [U] the act of walking across a street in an area that is not marked for walking —**jaywalker** *n.* [C] —**jaywalk** *v.* [I]

jazz¹ /dʒæz/ *n.* [U] **1** ENG. LANG. ARTS a type of popular music that usually has a strong beat and parts for performers to play alone: *a jazz festival* **2 and all that jazz** SPOKEN and things like that: *There will be cake and all that jazz at the party.*

jazz² *v.*

jazz sth **up** *phr. v.* INFORMAL to make something more attractive or exciting: *You could jazz up that outfit with a cool belt.* —**jazzed-up** *adj.*

ˈJazz Age, the HISTORY the 1920s, especially in the U.S., when jazz became popular

jazzed /dʒæzd/ *adj.* [not before noun] SPOKEN excited

jazz·y /ˈdʒæzi/ *adj. comparative* **jazzier**, *superlative* **jazziest** INFORMAL **1** bright, colorful, and easily noticed: *a jazzy tie* **2** similar to the style of jazz music: *a jazzy version of the song*

jct. the written abbreviation of JUNCTION

jeal·ous /ˈdʒɛləs/ S3 *adj.* **1** feeling angry and unhappy because someone has a quality, thing, or ability that you wish you had: *He's jealous because I got the job and he didn't.* | **+of** *Why are you so jealous of his success?* **2** feeling angry and unhappy because someone you like or love is showing interest in another person, or another person is showing interest in them: *a jealous husband* | *She's just using him to **make** her old boyfriend **jealous**.* **3 jealous of sth** FORMAL wanting to keep or protect something that you have because you are proud of it: *a country jealous of its heritage* [**Origin:** 1200–1300 Old French *jelous*, from Late Latin *zelus*] —**jealously** *adv.*

WORD CHOICE jealous, envious

• If you feel **jealous**, you feel angry or unhappy because you cannot have something that someone else has: *Eric was jealous of his sister's success.* | *Older children can sometimes be jealous of the attention given to the new baby.*

• If you are **envious**, you want to have the things or qualities that someone else has: *Hank was envious of his neighbor's fancy new SUV.*

jeal·ous·y /ˈdʒɛləsi/ *n. plural* **jealousies** [C,U] the feeling of being jealous: *sexual jealousy* | *professional jealousy* | +**of** *her jealousy of her daughter's successful career* | *the* ***petty jealousies*** (=jealousy about unimportant things) *of small town life* → see also ENVY

jeans /dʒinz/ S2 *n.* [plural] a popular type of pants made from DENIM (=a strong, usually blue, cotton cloth): *jeans and a T-shirt* [**Origin:** 1800–1900 *jean* **strong cotton cloth** (15–21 centuries), from *Gene*, early form of the name *Genoa*, Italian city where the cloth was first made]

jeep, Jeep /dʒip/ *n.* [C] TRADEMARK a type of car made to travel over rough ground

jeer /dʒɪr/ *v.* [I,T] to laugh at someone in an unkind way, to show that you strongly disapprove of them: *About 5,000 teachers jeered the Governor.* | +**at** *Fans were jeering at the referee.* —**jeer** *n.* [C]

jeer·ing /ˈdʒɪrɪŋ/ *adj.* a jeering remark or sound is unkind and shows disapproval

jeez /dʒiz/ *interjection* used to express feelings such as surprise, anger, annoyance etc.: *Give me a break, man, jeez.*

Jef·fer·son /ˈdʒɛfɚsən/**, Thomas** (1743–1826) the third President of the U.S. and writer of most of the Declaration of Independence

ˌJefferson ˈCity the capital city of the U.S. state of Missouri

Je·ho·vah /dʒɪˈhoʊvə/ *n.* a name given to God in the OLD TESTAMENT (=first part of the Bible)

Jeˌhovah's ˈWitness *n.* [C] a member of a religious organization that believes the end of the world will happen soon and sends its members to people's houses to try to persuade them to join

J

je·june /dʒɪˈdʒun/ *adj.* FORMAL **1** ideas and behavior that are jejune are too simple or childish: *jejune political opinions* **2** writing or speech that is jejune is boring because it lacks interesting details and humor

Jek·yll and Hyde /ˌdʒɛkəl ənd ˈhaɪd/ *n.* [C] someone who is sometimes nice but at other times is nasty or violent [**Origin:** 1800–1900 The Strange Case of Dr *Jekyll* and Mr *Hyde*, a story (1886) by Robert Louis Stevenson about a man with a good character and an evil character]

jell /dʒɛl/ *v.* [I] **1** if a thought, plan etc. jells, it becomes clearer or more definite: *The idea has finally jelled in my mind.* **2** if two or more people jell, they start working well together as a group: *It took some time for the team to jell.* **3** if a liquid jells, it becomes firmer or thicker SYN **gel**

jel·lied /ˈdʒɛlid/ *adj.* [only before noun] cooked or served in GELATIN or jelly, or in the form of GELATIN or jelly: *jellied cranberry sauce*

Jell-O, jello /ˈdʒɛloʊ/ *n.* [U] TRADEMARK a soft sweet food made from GELATIN and fruit juice

jel·ly /ˈdʒɛli/ S3 *n. plural* **jellies** **1** [U] a very thick sweet substance made from boiled fruit and sugar with no pieces of fruit in it, that is usually eaten on bread: *a peanut butter and jelly sandwich* **2 feel like jelly** also **turn to jelly** if your legs, knees etc. feel like jelly, they start to shake because you are frightened or nervous: *I went into her office with my legs feeling like jelly.* **3** [C] a substance that is solid but very soft, and moves easily when you touch it: *The frogs' eggs are in a protective jelly.* **4 jellies** [plural] shoes made of clear colored plastic [**Origin:** 1300–1400 Old French *gelee*, from *geler* **to freeze**, from Latin *gelare*] → see also GELATIN, PETROLEUM JELLY

ˈjelly bean *n.* [C] a type of small soft candy that is shaped like a bean, each piece having a different color and taste

jel·ly·fish /ˈdʒɛliˌfɪʃ/ *n.* [C] a round transparent animal that lives in the ocean, that has long parts that hang down from its body

ˈjelly ˌroll *n.* [C] a long thin cake that is rolled up with JAM or cream inside

je ne sais quoi /ˌʒə nə seɪ ˈkwɑ/ *n.* OFTEN HUMOROUS a good quality that you cannot easily describe: *Being a New Yorker, she had* ***a certain je ne sais quoi.***

Jen·ner /ˈdʒɛnɚ/**, Ed·ward** /ˈɛdwɚd/ (1749–1823) a British doctor who developed the prevention of SMALLPOX by VACCINATION

jeop·ard·ize /ˈdʒɛpɚˌdaɪz/ *v.* [T] to risk losing or spoiling something important or valuable: *I would never jeopardize the safety of my children.*

jeop·ard·y /ˈdʒɛpɚdi/ *n.* **in jeopardy** in danger of being lost or harmed: *His baseball career was in jeopardy after his injury in July.* | *The killings could* ***put*** *the peace process* ***in jeopardy.*** [**Origin:** 1300–1400 Anglo-French *juparti*, from Old French *jeu parti* **divided game, uncertainty**]

jer·e·mi·ad /ˌdʒɛrəˈmaɪəd/ *n.* [C] FORMAL a long speech or piece of writing that complains about a situation or lists things that have gone wrong

Jer·e·mi·ah /ˌdʒɛrəˈmaɪə/ (6th century B.C.) in the Bible, a Hebrew PROPHET who said that God would become angry with the Jews and punish them

Jer·i·cho /ˈdʒɛrɪˌkoʊ/ a city in Israel, north of the Dead Sea, thought to be the oldest city in the world

jerk¹ /dʒɚk/ *v.* **1** [I,T] to move with a quick sudden movement, or to make something move in this way: +**back/up/forward etc.** *The bus jerked forward and gathered speed.* | *Sue jerked her thumb toward the garage.* **2** [I,T] to pull something suddenly and roughly: **jerk sth away (from sb)** *She jerked the phone away from Mark.* | **jerk at/on sth** *He jerked hard on the girl's hair.* **3** [T always + adv./prep.] to make someone move with a sudden movement so that they wake up or stop thinking deeply about something: *The sound of a car outside jerked him back to reality.* | *The doorbell* ***jerked*** *me* ***awake.*** → see also TEARJERKER

jerk sb **around** *phr. v.* INFORMAL to waste someone's time or deliberately make things difficult for them: *Consumers get jerked around by advertisers all the time.*

jerk² S3 *n.* [C] **1** INFORMAL someone, especially a man, who is stupid or who does things that annoy or hurt other people: *Ignore him. He's a total jerk.* **2** a sudden quick pulling movement: *Sherman* ***gave*** *the leash* ***a jerk*** (=pulled it hard). **3** a sudden strong movement: *The train started* ***with a jerk.*** → see also KNEE-JERK

jer·kin /ˈdʒɚkɪn/ *n.* [C] a short JACKET that covers your body but not your arms, worn in past times

jerk·wa·ter /ˈdʒɚkˌwɔt̬ɚ/ *adj.* [only before noun] SPOKEN a jerkwater town, organization etc. is small and uninteresting

jerk·y¹ /ˈdʒɚki/ *adj. comparative* **jerkier**, *superlative* **jerkiest** **1** jerky movements are rough, with many start and stops OPP **smooth**: *the jerky motion of old movies* **2** SPOKEN behaving like a jerk —**jerkily** *adv.*

jerky² *n.* [U] meat that has been cut into thin pieces and dried in the sun or with smoke [**Origin:** 1800–1900 American Spanish *charqui*, from Quechua *ch'arki*]

jerry-built /ˈdʒɛriˌbɪlt/ *adj.* [no comparative] built cheaply, quickly, and badly: *jerry-built structures*

jer·sey /ˈdʒɚzi/ *n. plural* **jerseys** **1** [C] a shirt worn as part of a sports uniform: *a basketball jersey* **2** [U] a soft material that stretches easily, used for clothing **3** [C] a shirt or SWEATER that is made out of this material

Je·ru·sa·lem /dʒəˈrusələm/ a city in Israel, which is of great historical importance to Jews, Christians, and Muslims, and is regarded by Israel as its capital city

Jeˌrusalem ˈartichoke *n.* [C] a plant that has a TUBER (=part like a root) that you can eat

jest¹ /dʒɛst/ *n.* **1 in jest** something you say in jest is intended to be funny, not serious **2** [C] OLD-FASHIONED something that you say or do to amuse people SYN **joke**

jest² *v.* [I] OLD-FASHIONED or HUMOROUS to say things that you do not really mean in order to amuse people: **Surely you jest** HUMOROUS (=said when you do not believe what someone is saying)

jest·er /ˈdʒɛstɚ/ *n.* [C] a man employed in past times by a king or ruler to entertain people with jokes, stories etc.

Jes·u·it /ˈdʒɛzuɪt, -ʒuɪt/ *n.* [C] a man who is a member of the Catholic religious Society of Jesus —**Jesuit** *adj.*

Je·sus[1] /ˈdʒizəs/ also **ˌJesus ˈChrist** the person who Christians believe was the son of God, and whose life and teaching Christianity is based on

jet[1] /dʒɛt/ W3 *n.* **1** [C] a fast airplane with a jet engine: *He has a private jet.* | *a jet fighter* ►see THESAURUS box at **plane**[1] **2** [C] a narrow stream of liquid or gas that comes quickly out of a small hole, or the hole itself: +**of** *strong jets of water* **3** [U] a hard black stone that is used for making jewelry [**Origin:** (1–2) 1600–1700 Old French *jetter, getter* **to throw** from Latin *jactare*] → see also JUMBO JET, JUMP JET

jet[2] *v.* **jetted, jetting** [I always + adv./prep.] **1** INFORMAL also **jet off** to travel by airplane, used especially when the places you go seem exciting: *They're jetting off tomorrow for a Caribbean vacation.* **2** if a liquid or gas jets from somewhere, it comes quickly out of a small hole

ˌjet-ˈblack, jet black *adj.* very dark black: *jet-black eyebrows*

ˈjet ˌengine *n.* [C] an engine that pushes out a stream of hot air and gases behind it, used in aircraft

ˈjet foil *n.* [C] a boat that rises out of the water on structures that look like legs when it is traveling fast

ˈjet lag *n.* [U] the tired and confused feeling that you can get after flying a long distance, because of the difference in time between the place you left and the place you arrived —**jet-lagged** *adj.*

ˌjet-proˈpelled *adj.* using a jet engine for power

ˌjet proˈpulsion *n.* [U] the use of a JET ENGINE for power

jet·sam /ˈdʒɛtsəm/ *n.* [U] things that are thrown from a ship and float on the ocean toward the shore → see also **flotsam and jetsam** at FLOTSAM (2)

ˈjet set *n.* **the jet set** rich and fashionable people who travel a lot —**jet-setter** *n.* [C] —**jet set** *v.* [I]

ˈjet-ski *n.* [C] a small fast vehicle on which one or two people can ride over water for fun

jet-ski

ˈjet stream *n.* [singular, U] EARTH SCIENCE a current of very strong winds high above the Earth's surface

jet·ti·son /ˈdʒɛt̬əsən, -zən/ *v.* [T] **1** to get rid of something or decide not to do something anymore: *Berger jettisoned much of the original movie plot.* **2** to throw things away, especially from a moving airplane or ship

jet·ty /ˈdʒɛt̬i/ *n. plural* **jetties** [C] **1** a wide wall built out into the water as protection against large waves **2** a PIER → see also WHARF

Jew /dʒu/ *n.* [C] a member of a group of people whose religion is Judaism, who lived in ancient times in the land of Israel, some of whom now live in the modern state of Israel and others in various countries of the world [**Origin:** 1100–1200 Old French *gyu*, from Latin *Judaeus*, from Greek *Ioudaios*, from Hebrew *Yehudhah* **Judah, Jewish kingdom**]

jew·el /ˈdʒuəl/ *n.* [C] **1** a small valuable stone, such as a DIAMOND SYN **gem** **2 jewels** [plural] jewelry or other objects made with valuable stones and worn for decoration **3** INFORMAL someone or something that is very valuable, attractive, or important: *Sarasota is* ***a jewel of a city.*** **4 the jewel in the crown** the best or most valuable part of something **5** a very small stone used in the machinery of a watch [**Origin:** 1200–1300 Old French *juel*, from *jeu* **game, play**] → see also CROWN JEWEL

jew·eled /ˈdʒuəld/ *adj.* decorated with jewels

jew·el·er /ˈdʒuələɚ/ *n.* [C] someone who buys, sells, makes, or repairs jewelry

jew·el·ry /ˈdʒuəlri/ S3 *n.* [U] decorations you wear that are usually made from gold, silver, or jewels, such as rings and NECKLACES: *a piece of jewelry* | *She wears a lot of jewelry.* → see also COSTUME JEWELRY

Jew·ess /ˈdʒuɪs/ *n.* [C] OLD-FASHIONED a word meaning a "Jewish woman," now usually considered offensive

Jew·ish /ˈdʒuɪʃ/ *adj.* relating to Jews or Judaism: *Kate's husband is Jewish.* | *the Jewish community*

ˌJewish Comˈmunity ˌCenters Associˌation an organization that provides activities for Jewish communities in sports, education, and other areas

Jew·ry /ˈdʒuri/ *n.* [U] FORMAL Jewish people as a group

jib /dʒɪb/ *n.* [C] **1** a small sail → see also MAINSAIL **2** the long part of a CRANE → see also **like the cut of sb's jib** at LIKE[2] (6)

jibe[1] /dʒaɪb/ *v.* [I] **1** if two statements, reports etc. jibe with each other, the information in them matches: **jibe with sth** *What you see in movies doesn't always jibe with reality.* **2** also **gibe** to say something unkind that criticizes someone or something or makes them seem silly

jibe[2], **gibe** *n.* [C] a remark that is not nice and is intended to make someone seem stupid or criticize them: +**at/about** *They used to* ***make jibes*** *about her clothes.*

ji·ca·ma /ˈhikəmə/ *n.* [C] a type of root that is often eaten raw in SALADS

jif·fy /ˈdʒɪfi/ also **jiff** /dʒɪf/ *n.* SPOKEN **in a jiffy** very soon: *I'll be with you in a jiffy.*

jig[1] /dʒɪg/ *n.* **1** [C] ENG. LANG. ARTS a type of quick dance, or a piece of music for this dance **2 the jig is up** used to say that someone who has been deceiving people has been found out and will have to stop

jig[2] *v.* **jigged, jigging** **1** [I] to dance a jig **2** [I always + adv./prep.] to move with short quick movements, starting and stopping often

jig·ger[1] /ˈdʒɪgɚ/ *n.* [C] a unit for measuring alcohol, equal to 1.5 OUNCES, or the small glass this is measured with

jigger[2] *v.* [T] to slightly change something for illegal or dishonest purposes

jig·gle /ˈdʒɪgəl/ *v.* **jiggled, jiggling** [I,T] to move with short small quick movements, or to make something do this: *His stomach jiggled as he laughed.*

jig·saw /ˈdʒɪgsɔ/ *n.* [C] a special SAW (=cutting tool) for cutting out shapes in thin pieces of wood

jigsaw puzzle

ˈjigsaw ˌpuzzle also **jigsaw** *n.* [C] a picture cut up into many pieces that you try to fit together for fun

ji·had /dʒɪˈhɑd/ *n.* [C] a holy struggle to defend the Muslim faith against people, organizations, governments etc. who are believed to be against Islam

jilt /dʒɪlt/ *v.* [T] to suddenly end a relationship with someone [**Origin:** 1600–1700 *jilt* **woman who ends a relationship**] —**jilted** *adj.*: *a jilted lover*

Jim Crow /ˌdʒɪm ˈkroʊ/ *n.* [singular] a system of laws and practices used in the U.S. until the 1960s, that treated African-American people unfairly and separated them from white people SYN **segregation**

jim-dan·dy /ˌdʒɪm ˈdændi/ *adj.* OLD-FASHIONED very good or of high quality

jim·my¹ /ˈdʒɪmi/ *v.* **jimmied, jimmying** [T] to force a door, window, lock etc. open by using a metal bar

jimmy² *n.* [C] a small metal bar used especially by thieves to break open doors, windows etc.

jin·gle¹ /ˈdʒɪŋgəl/ *v.* **jingled, jingling** [I,T] to shake small metal things together so that they produce a sound, or to make this sound: *The bell on the cat's neck jingled.*

jingle² *n.* **1** [C] ENG. LANG. ARTS a short song used in advertisements **2** [singular] the sound of small metal objects being shaken together **3 give sb a jingle** SPOKEN INFORMAL to call someone on the telephone

jin·go·ism /ˈdʒɪŋgoʊˌɪzəm/ *n.* [U] DISAPPROVING a strong belief that your own country is better than others [**Origin:** 1800–1900 *jingo* (17–21 centuries), used in the phrase by jingo as an exclamation in a 19th-century British song encouraging people to fight for their country] —**jingoistic** /ˌdʒɪŋgoʊˈɪstɪk/ *adj.*

jinks /dʒɪŋks/ *n.* → see HIGH JINKS

jinn /dʒɪn/ *n.* [C] a DJINN

jinx¹ /dʒɪŋks/ *n. plural* **jinxes** [C usually singular] someone or something that brings bad luck, or a period of bad luck that results from this: +**on** *I think there's a jinx on this building.*

J

jinx² *v.* [T] to make someone or something have bad luck: *Don't jinx the game by talking about it.* —**jinxed** *adj.*

jit·ter·bug /ˈdʒɪṭɚˌbʌg/ *n.* [singular] a popular fast JAZZ dance in the 1940s

jit·ters /ˈdʒɪṭɚz/ *n.* [plural] INFORMAL the feeling of being nervous and worried, especially before an important event: *Mary* ***has the jitters about*** *her new job.*

jit·ter·y /ˈdʒɪṭəri/ *adj.* INFORMAL anxious or nervous: *jittery investors*

jive¹ /dʒaɪv/ *n.* [C,U] a very fast dance, popular especially in the 1930s and 1940s, performed to fast JAZZ music

jive² *v.* **1** [I] ENG. LANG. ARTS to dance a jive **2** [T] SLANG to try to make someone believe something that is not true: *You better not be jiving me.* → see also JIBE

Joan of Arc /ˌdʒoʊn əv ˈɑrk/ also **St. Joan** (?1412–1431) the PATRON SAINT of France, who led a French army which defeated the English at Orléans. Later she was made a prisoner by the English and burned to death as a WITCH.

Job¹ /dʒoʊb/ **1** in the Bible, a man who continued to have faith in God even though God destroyed his property and his family **2** a book in the OLD TESTAMENT in the Bible

Job² *n.* **1 have the patience of Job** to be extremely patient **2 Job's comforter** someone who tries to make you feel more cheerful, but actually makes you feel worse

job /dʒɑb/ Ac S1 W1 *n.*

1 WORK [C] the regular paid work that you do for an employer: *Jennifer* ***got a job as*** *a receptionist.* | *Pat* ***took a job*** (=accepted a job) *up in Albany.* | *More than 40 workers* ***lost their jobs.*** | *I was* ***offered a job*** *at BYU, but I turned it down.* | *Twelve other people were* ***applying for*** *the same* ***job*** (=trying to get it). | *She just* ***quit her job*** *because she was having a baby.* | *Kelly wants to prove that he can* ***hold down a job*** (=keep a job). | *If we don't get this account, we'll all* ***be out of a job*** (=no longer have a job). | **a part-time/full-time job** (=a job in which you work less than 40 hours per week, or one that you work 40 hours per week) | **job security** (=the state of being sure that your job is permanent) | **job satisfaction** (=how much you like or enjoy your job) → see also JOB DESCRIPTION

THESAURUS

work employment or the activities involved in it: *I started work when I was 18.*
position/post FORMAL a job in a particular organization: *his position as CEO of the company*
occupation used mainly on official forms to mean your job: *Please give your name, age, and occupation.*
profession a job for which you need special education and training: *the legal profession*
career the work you do for most of your life: *I'm interested in a career in journalism.*
vocation a feeling that the purpose of your life is to do a particular job, or the job itself: *Teaching is often seen as a vocation, not just a job.*
→ WORK

2 on the job while doing work, or at work: *Today's my first day on the job.* | *on-the-job training*
3 DUTY [C usually singular] a particular duty or responsibility that you have SYN **responsibility**: **it's sb's job to do sth** *It's my job to make sure all the bills get paid.* | **the job of doing sth** *I was given the job of collecting the mail each day.* | *The police* ***have a difficult job to do.*** | *When the police stop you for speeding, they're* ***just doing their job.***
4 a nose/face/boob etc. job SURGERY to change the shape of a part of your body
5 STH YOU MUST DO [C] something that you have to do which involves working or making an effort: *Moving all this stuff will be a big job.* | *I've got a lot of* ***odd jobs*** (=different things) *to do on Saturday.* | *Pay attention to* ***the job at hand*** (=the work you are doing now).
6 do a good/great/bad etc. job to do something well or badly: *The vacuum does a good job on the rugs.*
7 good job SPOKEN used to tell someone they have done something well: *Good job, Carl. That looks a lot better.*
8 do the job INFORMAL to have the effect or produce the result that you want or need: *A little more glue should do the job.*
9 do a job on sb/sth INFORMAL to have a damaging effect on someone or something: *The sun does quite a job on people's skin.*
10 CRIME [C] INFORMAL a crime in which money is stolen from a bank, company etc.: *a bank job* | **an inside job** (=a crime done by a member of the organization in which it happens)
11 COMPUTER [C] an action for a computer to do: *a print job*
12 TYPE OF THING [C] also **jobby** SPOKEN used to say that something is of a particular type: *His new computer's one of those little portable jobs.* → see also PAINT JOB

ˈjob ˌaction *n.* [C] an action such as a STRIKE that does not continue for very long, done by workers who are asking for more money or better working conditions

job·ber /ˈdʒɑbɚ/ *n.* [C] **1** ECONOMICS someone whose job is buying and selling STOCKS and SHARES **2** ECONOMICS someone who buys a product from a company at a WHOLESALE price and then sells it to a customer, usually another company, at a higher price

ˈjob deˌscription *n.* [C] an official list of the work and responsibilities that you have in your job

job·less /ˈdʒɑblɪs/ *adj.* **1** for or relating to people without jobs: *the jobless rate* (=number of people who do not have jobs) **2** without a job SYN **unemployed**: *jobless workers*

ˈjob lock *n.* [C] INFORMAL a situation in which you are afraid to leave your job because you will lose your medical insurance

job ˈlot *n.* [C] a large mixed group of things that are sold together: *a job lot of furniture*

Jobs /dʒɑbz/, **Steve** /stiv/ (1955–) a U.S. computer

designer and BUSINESSMAN who, together with Steve Wozniak, designed the first personal computer and started the Apple computer company

'job-ˌsharing *n.* [U] an arrangement by which two people both work PART-TIME doing the same job —**jobshare** *n.* [C]

'job shop *n.* [C] a factory that only produces goods which have already been ordered by its customers

jock /dʒɑk/ *n.* [C] **1** INFORMAL, DISAPPROVING someone, especially a student, who plays a lot of sports and is often considered to be stupid **2** INFORMAL a JOCKSTRAP

jock·ey[1] /'dʒɑki/ *n. plural* **jockeys** [C] someone who rides horses in races [**Origin:** 1500–1600 *Jockey*, Scottish male name, from *John*] → see also COMPUTER JOCKEY, DESK JOCKEY, DISC JOCKEY

jockey[2] *v.* **jockeyed, jockeying** **1** [I always + adv./prep.] to compete strongly to get into the best position or situation, or to get the most power: *Two airlines are **jockeying for position** in the trans-Atlantic market.* **2** [I,T] to ride a horse as a jockey **3** [T] to skillfully make something move in a particular direction or fit somewhere: *Camera operators jockey the cameras around the movie set.* —**jockeying** *n.* [U]

'Jockey ˌshorts *n.* [plural] TRADEMARK a type of men's cotton underwear that fits tightly → see also BOXER SHORTS

'jock itch *n.* [U] NOT TECHNICAL a medical condition in which the skin cracks and starts to ITCH near a man's sex organs

jock·strap /'dʒɑkstræp/ *n.* [C] a piece of underwear that men wear to support their sex organs when playing sports

jo·cose /dʒə'koʊs, dʒoʊ-/ *adj.* LITERARY joking or humorous —**jocoseness** also **jocosity** /dʒə'kɑsət̬i/ *n.* [U]

joc·u·lar /'dʒɑkyələ˞/ *adj.* FORMAL joking or humorous: *a jocular tone* —**jocularity** /ˌdʒɑkyə'lærət̬i/ *n.* [C,U]

joc·und /'dʒɑkənd, 'dʒoʊ-, dʒoʊ'kʌnd/ *adj.* LITERARY cheerful and happy —**jocundly** *adv.* —**jocundity** /dʒoʊ'kʌndət̬i, dʒɑ-/ *n.* [U]

jodh·purs /'dʒɑdpə˞z/ *n.* [plural] a special type of pants that you wear when riding horses

Joe /dʒoʊ/ *n.* INFORMAL **1** [C usually singular] also **Joe Blow/Schmo** an ordinary average man: *a regular Joe* **2 Joe College/Citizen etc.** someone who is a typical example of people in a particular situation or involved in a particular activity: *Brian just looked like Joe Businessman – nothing special.* **3 Joe Six-Pack** a man who is a typical example of someone who does physical work, and who has the same political, moral etc. ideas as most people in this social class → see also JOHN Q. PUBLIC

joe /dʒoʊ/ *n.* [U] INFORMAL **a cup of joe** a cup of coffee

Jo·el /'dʒoʊəl/ a book in the Old Testament of the Christian Bible

Jof·frey /'dʒɑfri/, **Rob·ert** /'rɑbə˞t/ (1930–1988) an American dancer and CHOREOGRAPHER of modern dance and BALLET

jog[1] /dʒɑg/ *v.* **jogged, jogging** **1** [I] to run slowly and in a steady way, especially as a way of exercising: *We jog together every morning.* **2 jog sb's memory** to make someone remember something: *Maybe this picture will help jog your memory.* **3** [T] to knock or push something lightly by mistake SYN **bump**: *I accidentally jogged her elbow.*

jog[2] *n.* [singular] **1** a slow steady run, especially done as a way of exercising: *I'm **going for a jog** in the park.* **2** a light knock or push done by accident

jog·ger /'dʒɑgə˞/ *n.* [C] someone who runs slowly and in a steady way as a way of exercising

jog·ging /'dʒɑgɪŋ/ *n.* [U] the activity of running slowly and in a steady way as a way of exercising: *It was too rainy to **go jogging**.*

'jogging suit *n.* [C] loose clothes that you wear when you are running for exercise, or to keep warm after exercise → see also SWEAT SUIT

jog·gle /'dʒɑgəl/ *v.* [I,T] INFORMAL JIGGLE

Jo·han·nes·burg /dʒoʊ'hænɪsˌbə˞g, -'hɑ-/ also **Jo'burg** /'dʒoʊbə˞g/ INFORMAL the largest city in South Africa

john /dʒɑn/ *n.* [C] INFORMAL a toilet or BATHROOM → see also LONG JOHNS

John /dʒɑn/ **1** also **The Gospel according to St. John** one of the four books in the New Testament of the Christian Bible that describe the life and teaching of Jesus **2 1 John, 2 John, 3 John** three short books in the New Testament of the Christian Bible

John, King (1167–1216) a king of England, remembered especially for signing the Magna Carta which put limits on his power as king

John, Saint in the Bible, one of the 12 APOSTLES who is believed to have written several of the books of the New Testament of the Bible

ˌJohn 'Birch SoˌCiety, the a very RIGHT-WING organization started in the U.S. during the 1950s to fight Communism

John Doe /ˌdʒɑn 'doʊ/ *n.* [C,U] a name used especially by the police for a man whose name is not known → see also JANE DOE

John Han·cock /ˌdʒɑn 'hæŋkɑk/ *n.* [C] INFORMAL your SIGNATURE

John·ny-come-late·ly /ˌdʒɑni kʌm 'leɪtli/ *n.* [singular] DISAPPROVING someone who has only recently started doing something, supporting something etc.

ˌJohnny-on-the-'spot *n.* [singular] INFORMAL someone who immediately offers to help, takes an opportunity etc.

John Paul II, Pope /ˌdʒɑn pɔl ðə 'sɛkənd/ (1920–2005) a Polish priest who became the first Polish POPE

John Q. Pub·lic /ˌdʒɑn kyu 'pʌblɪk/ *n.* [C,U] INFORMAL a name that is used to mean an average person or people in general: *This is not the kind of car that John Q. Public drives* (=it is a very special or expensive type). → see also JOE

Johns /dʒɑnz/, **Jas·per** /'dʒæspə˞/ (1930–) a U.S. PAINTER famous for his paintings of ordinary things like letters, numbers, and flags, in the style of POP ART

John·son /'dʒɑnsən/, **Andrew** (1808–1875) the 17th President of the U.S.

Johnson, Ear·vin (Mag·ic) /'ə˞vɪn, 'mædʒɪk/ (1959–) a U.S. basketball player, known for his skill and for saying in 1991 that he has HIV

Johnson, Lyn·don /'lɪndən/ (1908–1973) the 36th President of the U.S.

Johnson, Samuel (1709–1784) known as Dr. Johnson, a British CRITIC and dictionary writer, famous for his "Dictionary of the English Language"

John XXIII, Pope /ˌdʒɑn ðə ˌtwɛnt̬i 'θə˞d/ (1881–1963) the POPE who called together the Second Vatican Council, a meeting of church leaders from all over the world

joie de vi·vre /ˌʒwɑ də 'vivrə/ *n.* [U] a feeling of general pleasure and excitement, especially when this is part of someone's character

join /dʒɔɪn/ S2 W1 *v.*

1 GROUP/ORGANIZATION [I,T] to become a member or part of an organization, group etc.: *He left home at 18 and joined the army.* | *Eight new members are expected to join.*

2 ACTIVITY [T] to begin to take part in an activity that other people are involved in: *It is not known if the other parties will join the peace talks.* | *She urged everyone to **join the fight** against AIDS.*

3 DO STH TOGETHER [I,T] to do something together with someone else: **join (with) sb in doing sth** *Please join with me in welcoming tonight's speaker.* | **join (with) sb to do sth** *Two Republicans joined the Democrats to pass the law.* | *Everyone is invited to **join in the fun**.*

4 GO/BE WITH SB [T] to go somewhere with someone, or to go to where they are in order to be with them: *Are you going to join us for dinner?*

J

5 CONNECT a) [T] to connect or fasten things together: *pieces of wood joined with glue* | *The island is joined to the mainland by a bridge.* **b)** [I,T] also **join up** to come together and become connected: *They met at the spot where the creek joins the river.* | *The pipes join up over here.* ►see THESAURUS box at **fasten**
6 join the club SPOKEN used to say that you and a lot of other people are in the same situation: *"I don't trust politicians." "Yeah, join the club."*
7 join hands if people join hands, they hold each other's hands
8 join a line (of people) to stand at the end of a line of people who are waiting for something and wait for your turn to get it
9 join voices to sing or speak together
10 be joined in marriage also **be joined in holy matrimony** FORMAL to be married
11 join battle FORMAL to begin fighting
[**Origin:** 1200–1300 Old French *joindre*, from Latin *jungere*] → see also **if you can't beat 'em, join 'em** at BEAT[1] (12), **join/combine forces** at FORCE[1] (9)

join in *phr. v.* to take part in an activity as part of a group of two or more people: *Steve started talking about sports, and a few other people joined in.*

join up *phr. v.* to become a member of the military: *Bobby joined up when he was 19.*

join up with sb/sth *phr. v.* INFORMAL to begin to do something with other people so that you form one group: *They joined up with Chinese researchers to develop the technology.*

join·er /ˈdʒɔɪnɚ/ *n.* [C] **1** someone who makes wooden doors, window frames etc. → see also CARPENTER **2** someone who is always eager to join different clubs or organizations in order to do things with other people

join·er·y /ˈdʒɔɪnəri/ *n.* [U] the trade and work of a joiner → see also CARPENTRY

J

joint[1] /dʒɔɪnt/ W3 *adj.* [only before noun] involving two or more people or groups, or owned or shared by them: *a joint bank account* | *a **joint effort** of NASA and the European Space Agency* | *Eight states will take **joint action** on air pollution issues.* —**jointly** *adv.*

joint

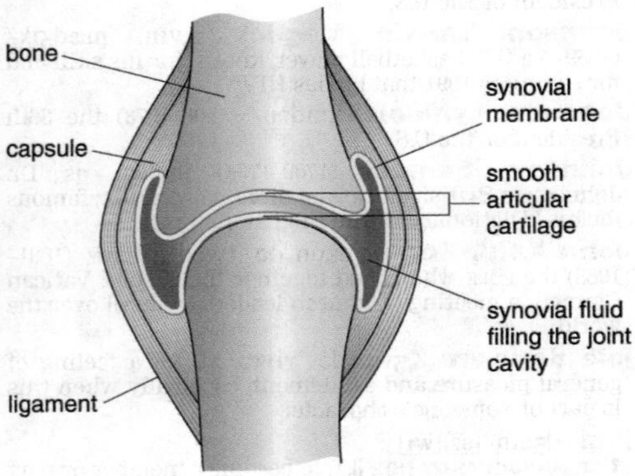

joint[2] S3 *n.*
1 [C] **BODY PART** BIOLOGY a part of the body where two bones meet and which allows one or more of the bones to move in relation to the other: *the elbow joint* | *aching joints*
2 PLACE [C] INFORMAL a place, especially a BAR, club, or restaurant: *a fast-food joint*
3 DRUGS [C] SLANG a MARIJUANA cigarette
4 JOIN TOGETHER [C] a place where two things or parts of an object are joined together: *the joints of a chair*
5 out of joint a) if a bone in your body is out of joint, it has been pushed out of its correct position SYN **dislocated b)** if a system, group etc. is out of joint, it is not working correctly: *Something is out of joint in their family.* → see also **put sb's nose out of joint** at NOSE[1] (9)
6 the joint SLANG prison
7 MEAT a large piece of meat for cooking, usually containing a bone: *a joint of beef* → see also **case the joint** at CASE[2] (2)

ˌJoint ˌChiefs of ˈStaff *n.* [plural] **the Joint Chiefs of Staff** the group consisting of the leaders of the Army, Navy, Air Force, and Marines, that gives the U.S. President advice

joint ˈcustody *n.* [U] LAW a situation in which DIVORCED parents share the responsibility for taking care of their child and share the right to spend time with their child

joint·ed /ˈdʒɔɪntɪd/ *adj.* having joints and able to move and bend: *a jointed puppet* → see also DOUBLE-JOINTED

joint ˈfamily *n.* [C] SOCIAL SCIENCE a family where members of several GENERATIONS share the family home

joint resoˈlution *n.* [C] LAW a decision or law agreed by both houses of the U.S. Congress and signed by the President

joint-ˈstock ˌcompany *n.* [C] TECHNICAL a company that is owned by all the people with STOCK in it

joint ˈventure *n.* [C] a business PROJECT begun by two or more people or companies working together

joist /dʒɔɪst/ *n.* [C] one of the beams that support a floor or ceiling

joke[1] /dʒoʊk/ S1 W3 *n.* [C]
1 STH FUNNY something that you say or do to make people laugh, especially a funny story or trick: **+about** *a good joke about salesmen* | *We stayed up **telling jokes** until 2 a.m.* | *It's not funny to **make jokes about** other people.* | *I don't think he **gets the joke*** (=understands why a joke is funny). | *She's always **cracking jokes*** (=saying something funny). | *The lady thought we were **playing a joke on her*** (=tricking her). | **dirty/sick joke** (=a joke about sex or something disgusting) | **a private/an inside joke** (=a joke that only people who know about a particular situation, subject etc. can understand) → see also IN-JOKE, PRACTICAL JOKE, **standing joke** at STANDING[1] (4)

THESAURUS
gag a short joke, especially one told by a professional entertainer
wisecrack a quick, funny, and often slightly unkind remark
one-liner a very short joke
pun an amusing use of a word or phrase that has two meanings, or of words with the same sound but different meanings: *The band is called Esso Es, a pun that to English-speakers sounds like a call for help, but in Spanish means "That's what it is."*
funny story a short story that is told to make people laugh

2 STH USELESS INFORMAL a situation or event that is so stupid, useless, or unreasonable that you do not consider it seriously: *That meeting was such a joke.*
3 take a joke to be able to laugh at a joke about yourself: *Can't you take a joke?*
4 sth is no joke used to emphasize that a situation is serious or that someone really means what they say: *These bills are no joke.*
5 make a joke (out) of sth to treat something serious as if it was intended to be funny: *My mother always makes a joke of everything.*
6 sb's idea of a joke SPOKEN a situation that someone else thinks is funny but you do not: *Is this your idea of a joke?*
7 the joke's on sb used to say that someone has made themselves seem stupid, especially when they were trying to make another person seem stupid: *They used to tease me, but in the end the joke was on them.*
[**Origin:** 1600–1700 Latin *jocus*]

joke[2] S3 *v.* [I] **1** to say things that are intended to be funny SYN **kid**: *Calm down, I was just joking!* | **joke (with sb) about sth** *I can joke with my boss about* *anything.* **2 you must be joking!** SPOKEN used to tell someone that what they are saying is so strange or stupid that you cannot believe that they are serious **3 all joking aside** SPOKEN used before you say something serious after you have been joking: *All joking aside, you did a great job tonight.* —**jokingly** *adv.*

joke around *phr. v.* INFORMAL to have fun by telling jokes, doing silly things etc.: *Sometimes we joke around to get rid of tension.*

jok·er /ˈdʒoʊkɚ/ *n.* [C] **1** SPOKEN someone who plays tricks on other people or does things that are stupid: *Some joker nailed my chair to the floor.* **2** a PLAYING CARD that has no particular value and is only used in some card games **3** someone who makes a lot of jokes

jok·ey, joky /ˈdʒoʊki/ *adj. comparative* **jokier**, *superlative* **jokiest** INFORMAL not serious and tending to make people laugh: *a jokey TV show*

Jo·li·et /ʒoʊlˈyeɪ, ˈdʒoʊliˌɛt/, **Lou·is** /ˈlui / (1645–1700) a French-Canadian EXPLORER who, with Jacques Marquette, discovered the upper Mississippi River in 1673

Jo·li·ot-Cu·rie /ˌʒoʊlyoʊ kyʊˈri/, **I·rène** /iˈrɛn/ (1897–1956) a French scientist, daughter of Pierre and Marie Curie, who discovered how to produce new RADIOACTIVE substances with her husband Frédéric Joliot-Curie (1900–1958)

jol·lies /ˈdʒɑliz/ *n.* [plural] **get your jollies** SPOKEN, DISAPPROVING to get pleasure in a way that is strange, unpleasant, or disgusting to other people

jol·li·ty /ˈdʒɑləṭi/ *n.* [U] FORMAL the state or quality of being happy and cheerful

jol·ly[1] /ˈdʒɑli/ *adj. comparative* **jollier**, *superlative* **jolliest** **1** happy and cheerful: *a jolly Santa Claus* **2** OLD-FASHIONED very pleasant and enjoyable

jolly[2] *v.* **jollied, jollying** [T] INFORMAL

jolly sb along *phr. v.* to persuade and encourage someone to do something that you want by being nice to them

jolly sb into sth *phr. v.* to gently persuade someone to do something

Jol·ly Rog·er /ˌdʒɑli ˈrɑdʒɚ/ *n.* a black flag with a picture of a SKULL and bones on it, used in past times by PIRATES → see also SKULL AND CROSSBONES (1)

jolt[1] /dʒoʊlt/ *n.* [C] **1** a sudden rough shaking movement: *Residents felt the first jolt of the earthquake at about 8 a.m.* **2** a sudden shock or surprise: *The news of his resignation* ***gave*** *even critics* ***a jolt.*** | **+to** *His death was a jolt to the whole community.* **3** a sudden burst of energy: *electric jolts* **4** something that has a sudden strong effect: *a jolt of caffeine* | **+to** *The tax laws may be a severe jolt to the economy.*

jolt[2] *v.* **1** [I,T] to move suddenly and roughly, or to make someone or something move in this way: *The train jolted and then stopped.* **2** [T] to give someone a sudden shock or surprise: *Vic was jolted awake by an explosion.* | **jolt sb into/out of sth** *The experience jolted me out of my depression.*

Jo·nah /ˈdʒoʊnə/ **1** in the Bible, a PROPHET who tried to escape from God by getting on a ship, and was then swallowed by a WHALE **2** a book in the OLD TESTAMENT of the Bible

Jones /dʒoʊnz/, **John Paul** (1747–1792) a U.S. navy officer who fought the British in the American Revolutionary War

Jones, Le·Roi /ˈlirɔɪ/ the original name of the African-American writer Amiri Baraka

Jones·es /ˈdʒoʊnzɪz/ *n.* → see **keep up with the Joneses** at KEEP UP (14)

jon·quil /ˈdʒɑŋkwəl/ *n.* [C] a small common spring flower that is bright yellow

Jonson /ˈdʒɑnsən/, **Ben** /bɛn/ (1572–1637) an English writer of plays

Jop·lin /ˈdʒɑplɪn/, **Scott** /skɑt/ (1868–1917) a U.S. JAZZ musician who played the piano and wrote RAGTIME music

Jor·dan[1] /ˈdʒɔrdn/ an Arab country in the Middle East, which is east of Israel and west of Iraq —**Jordanian** /dʒɔrˈdeɪniən/ *n.*

Jordan[2] a river in Israel and Jordan, that flows into the Dead Sea

Jordan, Mi·chael /ˈmaɪkəl/ (1963–) a U.S. basketball player who is considered the best player of the 1980s and 1990s

Michael Jordan

Jor·da·ni·an /dʒɔrˈdeɪniən/ *adj.* relating to or coming from Jordan

Jo·seph[1] /ˈdʒoʊzəf/ in the Bible, a son of Abraham who was sent to Egypt as a slave, became powerful there, and brought his people to live in Egypt

Joseph[2] in the Bible, the husband of Mary, the mother of Jesus

Joseph, Chief (?1840–1904) the chief of a Native American tribe who fought against the U.S. army in 1870

Jo·se·phine /ˈdʒoʊzəˌfin/ (1763–1814) the EMPRESS of France from 1804 to 1809 and the wife of Napoleon

josh /dʒɑʃ/ *v.* OLD-FASHIONED **josh (with) sb** to talk to someone in a gentle joking way

Josh·u·a /ˈdʒɑʃuə/ **1** in the Bible, a man who led the Jews to the "Promised Land" **2** a book in the OLD TESTAMENT of the Bible

joss stick /ˈdʒɑs ˌstɪk/ *n.* [C] a stick of INCENSE

jos·tle /ˈdʒɑsəl/ *v.* [I,T] to push or knock against someone, especially in a crowd: **jostle (sb) for sth** *Three people were hurt as the crowd jostled each other for a better view.*

jot[1] /dʒɑt/ *v. past tense and past participle* **jotted**, **jotting** [T] INFORMAL to write something quickly: *The officer was jotting notes on a pad.*

jot sth ↔ down *phr. v.* to write a short piece of information quickly: *I'll just jot down your number.*

jot[2] *n.* **not a jot** OLD-FASHIONED not at all, or none at all

jot·tings /ˈdʒɑṭɪŋz/ *n.* [plural] INFORMAL short notes, usually written to remind yourself about something

joule /dʒul, dʒaʊl/ WRITTEN ABBREVIATION **J** *n.* [C] PHYSICS a unit of energy equal to the amount of energy used to move something one meter against a force of one NEWTON

jour·nal /ˈdʒɚnl/ Ac *n.* [C] **1** a written record that you make of the things that happen to you each day SYN **diary**: *They* ***kept a journal*** (=wrote in one regularly) *of all their travels.* ►see THESAURUS box at **record**[1] **2** a serious magazine or newspaper that relates to a particular profession or area of interest: *a journal article* | *The New England Journal of Medicine* **3 Journal** used in the names of some magazines and newspapers: *The Wall Street Journal*

jour·nal·ese /ˌdʒɚnlˈiz/ *n.* [U] DISAPPROVING language that is typical of newspapers: *"Death toll" is journalese for "the number of dead people."*

jour·nal·is·m /ˈdʒɚnlˌɪzəm/ *n.* [U] **1** the job or activity of writing reports for newspapers, magazines, television, or radio: *a career in journalism* | *The hospital has been the target of* ***investigative journalism*** (=journalism that examines an event or situation in order to find out the truth about it). **2** [U] the information that is used for news reports or they way the reports are written: *The story was not particularly good journalism.* | *the history of modern journalism*

jour·nal·ist /ˈdʒɚnl-ɪst/ W3 *n.* [C] someone who writes reports for newspapers, magazines, television, or radio SYN **reporter**: *radio and television journalists* → see also REPORTER

jour·ney[1] /ˈdʒɚni/ W3 *n. plural* **journeys** [C] **1** a trip from one place to another, especially a long one

SYN trip: **+to/from/through/across etc.** *a three-month journey through China* | *My ancestors* ***made*** *the long* ***journey*** *across the Atlantic in 1744.* ►see THESAURUS box at trip[1] **2** a long and often difficult process in which you experience new things from which you learn and develop: *an alcoholic's journey to recovery* **3 a journey into the past/mind/truth etc.** an experience from which you learn more about the past, the mind etc. [**Origin:** 1100–1200 Old French *journee* **day's journey**, from *jour* **day**, from Latin *diurnus*]

journey[2] *v.* **journeyed, journeying** [I always + adv./prep.] LITERARY to travel

jour·ney·man /ˈdʒɚnimən/ *n.* [C] **1** [only before noun] used to describe an experienced worker whose work is acceptable but not excellent: *a journeyman actor* **2** OLD-FASHIONED a trained worker who works for the person who owns the business

joust·ing /ˈdʒaʊstɪŋ/ *n.* [U] **1** fighting or arguing: *verbal jousting* **2** the activity of fighting with LANCES (=long sticks) while riding a horse —**joust** *v.* [I] —**joust** *n.* [C]

Jove /dʒoʊv/ *n.* **by Jove!** OLD-FASHIONED used to express surprise or to emphasize something

jo·vi·al /ˈdʒoʊviəl/ *adj.* friendly and cheerful: *a jovial personality* [**Origin:** 1500–1600 French, Late Latin *jovialis* **of the god Jove or Jupiter**; because people born under the influence of the planet Jupiter were thought likely to be happy] —**joviality** /ˌdʒoʊviˈæləṭi/ *n.* [U]

jowl /dʒaʊl/ *n.* [C, usually plural] loose or unattractive skin on someone's lower jaw: *a man with heavy jowls* → see also **cheek by jowl** at CHEEK (5) —**jowled** *adj.*: *his jowled face*

joy[1] /dʒɔɪ/ W3 *n. plural* **joys** **1** [U] great happiness and pleasure: *the look of joy on her face* | **with/for joy** *The kids yelled for joy when they saw the ocean.* | **+at** *his joy at seeing his family again* **2** [C] something or someone that gives you happiness and pleasure: *Having my own home was a sheer joy.* | **+of** *the joy of travel* | **be a joy to read/watch/use etc.** *His stories are always a joy to read.* [**Origin:** 1100–1200 Old French *joie*, from Latin *gaudia*] → see also **jump for joy** at JUMP[1] (14)

joy[2] *v.* **joyed, joying**

joy in sth *phr. v.* LITERARY to be happy because of something

Joyce /dʒɔɪs/, **James** (1882–1941) an Irish writer of NOVELS, famous for his use of unusual and invented words, and new styles of writing

joy·ful /ˈdʒɔɪfəl/ *adj.* very happy, or making people very happy: *a joyful celebration* —**joyfully** *adv.*

joy·less /ˈdʒɔɪlɪs/ *adj.* without any happiness or pleasure at all: *a joyless task*

Joy·ner /ˈdʒɔɪnɚ/, **Flor·ence Grif·fith** /ˈflɔrəns, ˈflɑ-, ˈgrɪfɪθ/ (1955–1998) an American runner who won three GOLD MEDALS at the Olympic Games in 1988

joy·ous /ˈdʒɔɪəs/ *adj.* LITERARY very happy, or making people very happy: *a joyous occasion* —**joyously** *adv.*

joy·rid·ing /ˈdʒɔɪˌraɪdɪŋ/ *n.* [U] the crime of stealing a car and driving it in a fast and dangerous way for fun —**joyride** *v.* [I] —**joyrider** *n.* [C]

joy·stick /ˈdʒɔɪˌstɪk/ *n.* [C] an upright handle that you use to control something such as an aircraft or a computer game

J.P. *n.* [C] a JUSTICE OF THE PEACE

JPEG, JPG /ˈdʒeɪ pɛg/ *n.* [C] COMPUTERS **Joint Photographic Experts Group** a type of computer FILE used on the Internet that contains pictures, photographs, or other images

Jr. the written abbreviation of JUNIOR; used after the name of a man who has the same name as his father: *Donald McGee, Jr.*

Juan Car·los /wɑn ˈkɑrloʊs/ (1938–) the King of Spain since 1975, who had an important part in helping Spain to become a DEMOCRATIC country after Franco's DICTATORSHIP

Juá·rez /ˈwɑrɛz/, **Be·ni·to** /beɪˈnitoʊ/ (1806–1872) a Mexican politician who was President of Mexico, introduced changes that gave more people wealth and political power, and tried to stop foreign countries having influence over Mexico

ju·bi·lant /ˈdʒubələnt/ *adj.* extremely happy and pleased, or showing this emotion: *a jubilant smile* —**jubilantly** *adv.*

ju·bi·la·tion /ˌdʒubəˈleɪʃən/ *n.* [U] FORMAL extreme happiness and pleasure: *Shouts of jubilation rose from the crowd.*

ju·bi·lee /ˌdʒubəˈli, ˈdʒubəli/ *n.* [C] a date that is celebrated because it is exactly 25 years, 50 years etc. after the beginning of something

Ju·dah /ˈdʒudə/ in the Bible, one of Jacob's sons

Ju·da·ism /ˈdʒudiˌɪzəm, -deɪ-, -də-/ *n.* [U] the Jewish religion based on the Old Testament of the Bible, the Talmud, and the later teachings of the RABBIS —**Judaic** /dʒuˈdeɪ-ɪk/ *adj.*

Ju·das[1] /ˈdʒudəs/ also **Judas Is·car·i·ot** /-ɪˈskæriət/ in the Bible, one of the 12 APOSTLES, who BETRAYed Jesus to the Jewish authorities

Judas[2] *n.* [C] someone who is disloyal to a friend SYN traitor

Jude /dʒud/ **1** in the Bible, one of the 12 APOSTLES, also called Thaddeus **2** a book in the New Testament of the Bible

judge[1] /dʒʌdʒ/ S2 W1 *n.* [C] **1** LAW the official in control of a court who decides how criminals should be punished: *Judge Pamela Gifford* | *the judge's controversial decision* | **federal judge/high court judge etc.** (=a judge in a particular court) | **appear/come/go etc. before a judge** (=to come to a court of law because you have been charged with committing a crime) ►see THESAURUS box at court[1] **2** someone who decides on the result of a competition: *the judges in the national essay competition* | *The* ***panel of judges*** (=group of judges) *included several well-known writers.* **3 a good/bad judge of sth** someone whose opinion on something is usually right or wrong: *Sarah's not a very good judge of character.* **4 be the judge (of sth)** to be the person who decides what to do about something, or what action is correct: *Which one is right for you? Only you can be the judge.* | **let me be the judge of that!/I'll be the judge of that!** SPOKEN (=used to tell someone angrily that you will decide about something and you do not need their advice) [**Origin:** 1100–1200 Old French *juge*, from Latin *judex*]

judge[2] S3 W3 *v.* **judged, judging**

1 OPINION [I,T] to form or give an opinion about someone or something according to what you know, see, hear etc. about them: *He seems like a nice guy, but it's too early to judge.* | **judge sb/sth by sth** *You shouldn't judge a person by their past.* | **judge sb/sth on sth** *A public library is judged on how well it serves people.* | **judge sb/sth (to be) sth** *We believe the experiment will be judged a success.* | *I'd say she's pretty rich,* ***judging from*** (=after looking at) *her clothes.* | **judge who/whether/what etc.** *It was hard to judge whether he was telling the truth.* | *Come and see the play and* ***judge for yourself*** (=form your own opinion).

THESAURUS

evaluate FORMAL to judge how good, useful, or successful someone or something is: *Most colleges have a system in which students can evaluate their professors.*
assess to judge a person or situation after thinking carefully about it: *Psychologists will assess the child's behavior.*
appraise to judge how valuable, effective, or successful someone or something is: *The company regularly appraises the performance of its employees.*
gauge to judge what someone is likely to do or how she or he feels: *She was silent, and he could not gauge the impact of what he was saying on her.*

2 COMPETITION [I,T] to decide on the result of a competi-

tion: *Who's judging the talent contest?* | **judge sb on sth** *The gymnasts are judged on skill and strength.*
3 CRITICIZE [I,T] to form an opinion about someone in an unfair or criticizing way: *I try not to judge other people.*
4 LAW [T] LAW to decide whether someone is guilty of a crime in court: **judge sb guilty/innocent** *If he's judged guilty, he will go to jail for at least 4 years.*
5 GUESS [I,T] to guess an amount, distance, height, weight etc. SYN **estimate**: *I have a hard time judging ages, but the baby looked about six months old.*
6 don't judge a book by its cover used to say that you should not form an opinion based only on the way someone or something looks
7 it's not for sb to judge also **who is sb to judge?** used to say that you do not think someone has the right to give their opinion about something: *I don't think it was right, but who am I to judge?*

Judg·es /ˈdʒʌdʒɪz/ a book in the Old Testament of the Christian Bible

judg·ment W3, **judgement** /ˈdʒʌdʒmənt/ *n.*
1 OPINION [C,U] an opinion that you form, especially after thinking carefully about something: *They* ***made a judgment*** *without knowing all the facts.* | ***In our judgment*** (=according to our opinion), *the very poor would benefit most from the program.* | *I'm not* ***passing judgment on*** *any lifestyle* (=giving an opinion about it or criticizing it). | **suspend/reserve judgment** FORMAL (=to not make a decision about something until you know more about it)
2 ABILITY TO DECIDE [U] the ability to make sensible decisions about situations or people: *I trust your judgment.* | **good/sound/bad/poor judgment** *It was a decision based on sound* (=good) *judgment.* | **professional/personal/moral etc. judgment** *Don't let your private life affect your professional judgment.* | **use/exercise your judgment** *If I'm not there, just use your own judgment.* | **cloud/impair sb's judgment** (=make someone's judgment less effective)
3 LAW [C,U] an official decision given by a judge or a court of law: *The court did not alter the $2,500 judgment.*
4 a judgment call INFORMAL a decision you have to make yourself because there are no certain rules in a situation
5 against sb's better judgment even though someone does not think something is the right or best thing to do: *I lent her the money against my better judgment.*
6 sit in judgment (over sb) DISAPPROVING to criticize someone's behavior, especially unfairly
7 a judgment (on sb) something bad that happens to someone and seems like a punishment from God → see also LAST JUDGMENT, VALUE JUDGMENT

judg·ment·al /dʒʌdʒˈmɛntl/ *adj.* too quick and willing to criticize people: *You're being too judgmental.*

ˈjudgment day *n.* [singular] also **the ˌday of ˈjudgment** the time after death when everyone is judged by God for what they have done in life, according to some religions, such as Christianity

ju·di·ca·ture /ˈdʒudɪkətʃɚ/ *n.* **the judicature** FORMAL judges and the organization, power etc. of the law

ju·di·cial /dʒuˈdɪʃəl/ *adj.* [only before noun] **1** LAW relating to a court of law, judges, or their decisions: *the judicial system* | *a judicial decision* **2** LAW relating to the way judges are meant to behave, especially in being sensible and fair

juˌdicial ˈactivism *n.* [U] LAW when judges become actively involved in the process of making or changing laws, often by making new decisions that are different from decisions made by other judges in the past → see also JUDICIAL RESTRAINT

juˌdicial ˈbranch *n.* [singular] **the judicial branch** the part of a government that decides whether laws are good and whether people have disobeyed these laws → see also **the executive branch** at EXECUTIVE² (3), **the legislative branch** at LEGISLATIVE (2)

juˌdicial reˈstraint *n.* [U] LAW when judges do not try to become involved in the process of making or changing laws → see also JUDICIAL ACTIVISM

juˌdicial reˈview *n.* [U] LAW a court's examination of a law, a decision by a lower court, or an action by a government official to decide if it is right or CONSTITUTIONAL

ju·di·ci·ar·y /dʒuˈdɪʃiˌɛri, -ʃəri/ *n.* **the judiciary** FORMAL all the judges in a country who, as a group, form part of the system of government

ju·di·cious /dʒuˈdɪʃəs/ *adj.* FORMAL sensible and careful: *a judicious use of time and resources* —**judiciously** *adv.*

Ju·dith /ˈdʒudɪθ/ a book in the Apocrypha of the Protestant Bible and in the Old Testament of the Catholic Bible

ju·do /ˈdʒudoʊ/ *n.* [U] a Japanese method of defending yourself, in which you try to throw your opponent onto the ground, usually done as a sport [**Origin:** 1800–1900 a Japanese word meaning **gentle way**]

jug /dʒʌg/ *n.* [C] **1** a large deep container for liquids that has a narrow opening and a handle: *a two-gallon jug* → see also PITCHER **2** also **jugful** the amount of liquid that a jug will hold: *a two-gallon jug of wine*

jug-eared /ˈdʒʌg ɪrd/ *adj.* having large ears that stick out

jug·ger·naut /ˈdʒʌgɚˌnɔt, -ˌnɑt/ *n.* [C] a very powerful force, organization etc. whose effect or influence cannot be stopped: *the juggernaut of advancing technology* [**Origin:** 1800–1900 Hindi *Jagannath*, title of the god Vishnu; from the belief that people who worshiped him threw themselves under the wheels of a large carriage with his image on it]

juggle

jug·gle /ˈdʒʌgəl/ *v.* **1** [I,T] to keep three or more objects moving through the air by throwing and catching them very quickly **2** [I,T] to try to fit two or more jobs, activities etc. into your life, especially when this is difficult: *It's hard trying to juggle a job, kids, and housework.* **3** [T] to arrange numbers, information etc. in the way that you want in order to make someone believe something that is not true: *Newspapers sometimes juggle the statistics a little.* **4** [T] to change things and arrange them in the way you want, so that it is possible for you to do something: *I can juggle a few appointments, and get you in to see the doctor.* **5** [T] to hold or carry several things without dropping any of them, especially with difficulty: *Waiters came by, juggling trays of drinks and food.* [**Origin:** 1300–1400 *juggler* (11–21 centuries), from Old French *jogleour*, from Latin *joculari* **to make fun**] —**juggler** *n.* [C] —**juggling** *n.* [U] → see also **balancing/juggling act** at ACT¹ (10)

jug·u·lar /ˈdʒʌgyəlɚ/ *n.* [C] **1** a jugular vein **2 go for the jugular** INFORMAL to criticize or attack someone very strongly, especially in order to harm them

ˈjugular ˌvein *n.* [C usually singular] the large VEIN (=tube) in your neck that takes blood from your head back to your heart

juice¹ /dʒus/ S1 W3 *n.* **1** [C,U] the liquid that comes from fruit and vegetables, or a drink that is made from this: *Would you like some juice?* | **orange/apple/tomato etc. juice** *grape juice* **2** [U] the liquid that comes out of meat when it is cooked **3 gastric/digestive juice(s)** the liquid inside your stomach that helps you to DIGEST food **4** [U] INFORMAL something that produces power, such as electricity or gasoline: *Give it a little more juice.* [**Origin:** 1200–1300 Old French *jus*, from Latin] → see also **stew (in your own juices)** at STEW² (2)

juice² *v.* [T] to get the juice out of fruit or vegetables SYN **squeeze**
juice sth **up** *phr. v.* INFORMAL to make something more interesting or exciting

ˈjuice box *n.* [C] a small box filled with enough juice for one person, that comes with a STRAW to drink from

J

juiced /dʒust/ *adj.* [not before noun] **1** also **juiced up** INFORMAL excited **2** OLD-FASHIONED drunk

juic·er /ˈdʒusɚ/ *n.* [C] a small kitchen tool used for getting juice out of fruit, or an electric machine for doing this

juic·y /ˈdʒusi/ *adj. comparative* **juicier**, *superlative* **juiciest** **1** containing a lot of juice: *a juicy steak* **2 juicy gossip/details/stories etc.** INFORMAL interesting or shocking information, especially about people's sexual behavior **3** INFORMAL giving you work that will lead to a feeling of satisfaction: *a juicy role in the play* **4** INFORMAL involving a lot of money: *a big juicy contract* —**juiciness** *n.* [U]

ju·jit·su /ˌdʒuˈdʒɪtsu/ *n.* [U] a Japanese method of defending yourself, in which you hold, throw, and hit your opponent [**Origin:** 1800–1900 Japanese *jujutsu* **gentle art**]

ju·ju /ˈdʒudʒu/ *n.* [C,U] a type of West African magic involving objects with special powers, or one of these objects

ju·jub·e /ˈdʒudʒuˌbi/ *n.* [C] a small soft CHEWY candy that tastes like fruit

juke /dʒuk/ *v.* [I,T] INFORMAL to trick an opponent in a game such as football by changing directions as you run

ˈjuke box *n.* [C] a machine in restaurants, BARS etc. that plays music when you put money in it

ˈjuke joint *n.* [C] INFORMAL a place, popular in the middle 20th century, where people could eat inexpensive food, drink alcohol, and dance

ju·lep /ˈdʒuləp/ *n.* → see MINT JULEP

ju·li·enne /ˌdʒuliˈɛn/ *adj.* cut in very thin pieces: *julienne strips of ham* —**julienne** *v.* [T]

Ju·ly /dʒʊˈlaɪ, dʒə-/ WRITTEN ABBREVIATION **Jul.** *n.* [C,U] the seventh month of the year, between June and August: *"When do you go to Greece?" "In July."* | *She was born* ***on July 14th***. | ***Last July*** *my parents drove to Santa Fe.* | *I hope to finish this project by* ***next July***. | *A ceremony was held* ***July 7*** *to honor veterans.* [**Origin:** 1100–1200 Latin *Julius*, from Gaius *Julius* Caesar who was born in this month] → see Grammar box at JANUARY

J

jum·ble¹ /ˈdʒʌmbəl/ *n.* [singular] a mixture of things that are in no particular order, giving a feeling of confusion: +**of** *Downtown is a crowded jumble of shops and restaurants.* | *Inside, she was a jumble of emotions.*

jumble² also **jumble up** *v.* [T often passive] to mix things together so that they are not in a neat order: *Jewelry, belts, and scarves were* ***jumbled up together*** *in the bottom drawer.*

jum·bo /ˈdʒʌmboʊ/ *adj.* [only before noun] INFORMAL larger than other things of the same type: *jumbo shrimp* → see also MUMBO-JUMBO

ˈjumbo jet also **jumbo** *n.* [C] a very large aircraft for carrying passengers

Jum·bo·Tron /ˈdʒʌmboʊˌtrɑn/ *n.* [C] TRADEMARK a very large screen similar to a television screen, which is used at sports STADIUMS for showing points, VIDEOS, pictures etc.

jump¹ /dʒʌmp/ S1 W2 *v.*

1 UPWARD [I] to push yourself suddenly up in the air using your legs: *How high can you jump?* | +**on/in/across etc.** *He jumped over a low wall.* | *I'd love to jump in the pool right now.* | **jump 4 feet/2 meters etc.** *Lewis jumped 27 feet in the Olympics.* | *Fans were* ***jumping up and down*** *and cheering.*

THESAURUS

skip to move forward with little jumps between your steps
hop to move around by jumping on one leg, or with both your legs together, without going very high in the air
leap to jump high into the air or over something
dive to jump into water with your head and arms first
vault to jump over something in one movement, using your hands or a pole to help you

2 OVER/ACROSS [T] to go over or across something by jumping: *A kid could easily jump that fence.*
3 DOWNWARD [I] to let yourself drop from a place that is above the ground by pushing your body into the air with your legs: +**out/down etc.** *The worst moment was jumping out of the plane.* | *He fell in the pool and she jumped in after him.*
4 MOVE FAST [I always + adv./prep.] to move quickly or suddenly in a particular direction,: +**out/away/up etc.** *Joe jumped up to answer the telephone.* | *Flames jumped across treetops, setting roofs on fire.*
5 MOVE INTO/OUT OF STH [I always + adv./prep.] to get into or out of a vehicle or other enclosed space, especially quickly: *We all jumped in a taxi and headed downtown.* | *I'm about to jump in the shower.*
6 IN FEAR/SURPRISE [I] to make a sudden movement because you are surprised or frightened: *Sorry, I didn't mean to* ***make you jump***. | *She just about* ***jumped out of her skin*** (=she moved suddenly because she was very surprised).
7 INCREASE [I] to increase suddenly and by a large amount: **jump (from sth) to sth** *Profits have jumped to over $200 million.* | *The team jumped from ninth to third place in the league.*
8 KEEP CHANGING to change quickly from one place, position, idea etc. to another, often missing something that comes in between SYN **skip**: **jump (from sth) to sth** *The conversation jumped from one topic to another.* | *The movie suddenly* ***jumped ahead*** *to 40 years from now.*
9 jump down sb's throat also **jump all over sb** INFORMAL to suddenly speak very angrily to someone: *I just asked a question, and she jumped down my throat!*
10 jump to conclusions to form an opinion about something before you have all the facts: *There may be a simple explanation. Let's not jump to conclusions.*
11 jump the gun to start doing something too soon, especially without thinking about it carefully: *The editors jumped the gun and published the story without checking facts.*
12 ATTACK [T] INFORMAL to attack someone suddenly: *Somebody jumped her from an alley.*
13 CAR [T] INFORMAL to JUMP-START a car
14 jump for joy to be extremely happy and pleased
15 jump through hoops to do a series of things that are difficult or annoying in order to achieve something: *They'll have to jump through a lot of hoops to prove we can trust them.*
16 jump rope to jump over a rope as you swing it over your head and under your feet, as a game or for exercise
17 jump bail to leave a town, city, or country where a court of law has ordered you to stay until your TRIAL
18 jump to your feet to stand up quickly
19 OBEY [I] INFORMAL to immediately do what someone tells you to do SYN **obey**: *If an officer gives you an order, you jump.*
20 be jumping INFORMAL if a place is jumping, it is full of activity
21 jump to it! SPOKEN used to order someone to do something immediately
22 (go) jump in the lake! SPOKEN used to tell someone in an impolite way to go away
23 jump the tracks if a train jumps the tracks, it falls off its tracks
24 jump ship a) INFORMAL to leave an organization that you are working for, especially in order to join a different organization **b)** to leave a ship on which you are working as a sailor, without permission
25 jump in line to join a line of people by moving in front of others who were already waiting SYN **cut**
26 jump a train to travel on a train, especially a train carrying goods, without paying
27 jump a claim an expression meaning "to claim someone else's land as your own," used especially in the 19th century in the U.S.

jump at sth *phr. v.* to eagerly accept an opportunity to do something: *Michael* ***jumped at the chance to*** *teach in Barcelona.*

jump in *phr. v.* **1** to interrupt someone or suddenly join a conversation: *I was trying to talk to her, but Ted* *kept jumping in.* **2** to suddenly start to be involved in something, in order to take an opportunity or get an advantage: *Small businesses have to jump in before the opportunity is lost.* **3** to stop people who are fighting or arguing: *The teacher jumped in to break up the fight.* **4 jump in with both feet** to quickly become deeply involved in a situation without first thinking about it carefully: *Jumping in with both feet, he spent large sums of money on equipment.*

jump on sb *phr. v.* INFORMAL to criticize or punish someone, especially unfairly: **jump on sb for sth** *Dad jumps on Jeff for every little mistake.*

jump out at sb *phr. v.* if something jumps out at you, it is extremely easy to notice: *The spelling mistakes jumped out at me.*

jump² S3 *n.* **1** [C] a sudden large increase, improvement, or advance in something: +**in** *a jump in real estate prices* | *a jump in quality* | **a jump from sth to sth** *He's made the jump from college football to the professional game.* **2** [C] an act of pushing yourself suddenly up into the air using your legs: *his best jump of the competition* **3** [C] an act of letting yourself drop from a place that is above the ground: *a parachute jump* **4 get a jump on sb/sth** INFORMAL to gain an advantage by doing something earlier than usual or earlier than someone else: *I want to get a jump on my Christmas shopping.* **5 stay/keep etc. one jump ahead (of sb)** INFORMAL to keep your advantage over the people you are competing with by always being the first to do or know something new: *A successful company stays one jump ahead of the competition.* **6** [C] a fence, gate, or wall for jumping over in a race or competition → see also HIGH JUMP, **a hop, skip, and a jump** at HOP² (4), LONG JUMP, RUNNING JUMP, SKI JUMP

'jump ball *n.* [C] the act of throwing the ball up in a game of basketball, so that one player from each team can try to gain control of it

jump·er /'dʒʌmpɚ/ *n.* [C] **1** a dress without SLEEVES, usually worn over a shirt **2** a person or animal that jumps **3** a JUMP SHOT

'jumper ˌcables *n.* [plural] thick wires used to connect the batteries (BATTERY) of two cars in order to start one that has lost power

'jumping bean *n.* [C] a MEXICAN JUMPING BEAN

ˌjumping 'gene *n.* [C] INFORMAL BIOLOGY a GENE (=piece of DNA) that can move from one position on a CHROMOSOME to another position on the same chromosome or a different chromosome SYN **transposon**

ˌjumping 'jack *n.* [C usually plural] a jump in which you start from a standing position and then move your arms and legs out to the side

ˌjumping-'off ˌpoint *n.* [C] a place to start from, especially at the beginning of a trip: *The town is the jumping-off point for hikers.*

'jump jet *n.* [C] an aircraft that can take off and land by going straight up and down

'jump rope *n.* [C] a long piece of rope that you hold with one end in each hand and pass over your head and under your feet as you jump, either as a game or for exercise —**jump rope** *v.* [I]

'jump seat *n.* [C] a small seat in a car, airplane etc. that folds down

'jump shot *n.* [C] an action in basketball in which you throw the ball toward the basket as you jump in the air

'jump-start *v.* [T] **1** to start a car whose BATTERY has lost power by connecting it to the battery of another car **2** to help a process or activity start or become more successful: *Congress hopes the tax cut will jump-start the economy.* —**jump start** *n.* [C]

jump·suit /'dʒʌmpsut/ *n.* [C] a single piece of clothing like a shirt attached to a pair of pants, worn especially by women

jump·y /'dʒʌmpi/ *adj. comparative* **jumpier**, *superlative* **jumpiest** worried, nervous, or excited, especially because you are expecting something bad to happen: *People still feel jumpy after last month's violence.*

junc·tion /'dʒʌŋkʃən/ *n.* [C] a place where one road, railroad track etc. joins another: *a railroad junction* [**Origin:** 1700–1800 Latin *junctio*, from *jungere*]

junc·ture /'dʒʌŋktʃɚ/ *n.* FORMAL **1** a particular point in an activity or period of time: ***At this juncture**, I'd like to suggest we take a short break.* | *"We stand **at a critical juncture** in our history," Baker said.* **2** [C] a place where two things join: *the juncture of the Mississippi and Arkansas rivers*

June /dʒun/ WRITTEN ABBREVIATION **Jun.** *n.* [C,U] the sixth month of the year, between May and July: ***In June**, we're going on vacation.* | *We get paid **on June 24th**.* | *Tim and Debra got divorced **last June**.* | *I hope to move to California **next June**.* | *His birthday's **June 21**.* [**Origin:** 1200–1300 French *juin*, from Latin *Junius*] → see Grammar box at JANUARY

Ju·neau /'dʒunoʊ/ the capital city of the U.S. state of Alaska

June·teenth /ˌdʒun'tinθ/ *n.* [singular] an African-American celebration on June 19 that celebrates the time when slaves in Texas learned that they had been set free

Jung /yʊŋ/, **Carl Gus·tav** /kɑrl 'gʊstɑf/ (1875–1961) a Swiss PSYCHIATRIST who studied the importance of dreams and religion in problems of the mind, and developed the idea of the COLLECTIVE UNCONSCIOUS —**Jungian** *adj.*

jun·gle /'dʒʌŋgəl/ *n.* **1** [C,U] EARTH SCIENCE a thick tropical forest with many large plants growing very close together: *the Amazon jungle* ►see THESAURUS box at **forest**, **tree** **2** [singular] a situation or place in which it is difficult to succeed or get what you want, because people are competing with each other: *workers in the corporate jungle* **3** [singular] something that is very messy, complicated, and confusing: *a jungle of freeways and highways* **4** [singular] a place, especially a city, that is dangerous and frightening because there is a lot of violent crime and people do not feel safe: *the urban jungle* [**Origin:** 1700–1800 Hindi *jangal* **forest**, from Sanskrit *jangala*] → see also CONCRETE JUNGLE, **the law of the jungle** at LAW (8)

'jungle ˌgym *n.* [C] a large frame made of metal bars for children to climb on

Jun·ior /'dʒunyɚ/ *n.* [singular] **1** → see JR **2** SPOKEN, HUMOROUS a name used when speaking to or about a boy or younger man, especially your son: *Where's Junior?*

jun·ior¹ /'dʒunyɚ/ S2 *adj.* [only before noun] younger or of a lower rank: *a junior partner* → see also SENIOR ►see THESAURUS box at **position¹**, **rank¹** [**Origin:** 1200–1300 Latin **younger**, from *juvenis* **young**]

junior² *n.* **1** [C] a student in the third year of HIGH SCHOOL or college → see also FRESHMAN, SENIOR² (1), SOPHOMORE **2 be two/five/ten etc. years sb's junior** to be two, five, ten etc. years younger than someone: *She married a man seven years her junior.* **3** [C,U] also **junior miss** a range of clothing sizes for girls and young women **4** [C] someone who has a low rank in an organization or profession → see also SENIOR¹

junior 'college *n.* [C,U] a college where students take a course of study that continues for two years SYN **community college**

junior 'high school also **ˌjunior 'high** *n.* [C,U] a school in the U.S. and Canada for students aged between 12 and 14 or 15 → see also MIDDLE SCHOOL

junior 'varsity *n.* [C,U] JV

ju·ni·per /'dʒunəpɚ/ *n.* [C,U] a small bush that produces berries and has leaves that are green all year

junk¹ /dʒʌŋk/ S2 *n.* **1** [U] old or unwanted objects that have no use or value: *a garage filled with junk* **2** [U] things that are of very low quality, or that you have no respect for: *There's so much junk on TV these days.* **3** [U] SPOKEN JUNK FOOD **4** [C] a Chinese sailing boat **5** [U] SLANG a dangerous drug, especially HEROIN [**Origin:** (4) 1500–1600 Portuguese *junco*, from Javanese *jon*]

junk² *v.* [T] to get rid of something because it is old or useless: *We couldn't afford to fix the car, so we junked it.*

'junk bond *n.* [C] ECONOMICS a BOND that has a high risk and is often sold to pay for a TAKEOVER

junk·er /'dʒʌŋkɚ/ *n.* [C] INFORMAL an old car in bad condition

J

jun·ket /ˈdʒʌŋkɪt/ *n.* [C] a free trip that is paid for by government money or by a business that hopes to gain some advantage by paying for people to go on this trip —**junket** *v.* [I]

ˈjunk food *n.* [U] INFORMAL food that is not healthy because it contains a lot of oil or sugar: *a diet of junk food and soft drinks*

junk·ie, junky /ˈdʒʌŋki/ *n.* [C] SLANG **1** someone who takes dangerous drugs and is physically dependent on them **2** HUMOROUS someone who likes something so much that they seem to be dependent on it: *My dad's a TV junkie.*

ˈjunk mail *n.* [U] letters that advertisers send to people

ˈjunk shop *n.* [C] a small store that buys and sells old things

ˈjunk yard *n.* [C] a place where you can take your old car, furniture etc., so that the parts or the metal can be sold → see also DUMP

Ju·no /ˈdʒunoʊ/ the Roman name for the goddess Hera

jun·ta /ˈhʊntə, ˈdʒʌntə/ *n.* [C] POLITICS a military government that has gained power by using force [**Origin:** 1600–1700 Spanish *junto* **joined**, from Latin *jungere*]

Ju·pi·ter /ˈdʒupɪt̬ɚ/ **1** PHYSICS the largest PLANET, fifth in order from the sun → see picture at SOLAR SYSTEM **2** the Roman name for the god Zeus

ju·rid·i·cal /dʒʊˈrɪdɪkəl/ *adj.* FORMAL LAW relating to judges or the law

jur·is·dic·tion /ˌdʒʊrɪsˈdɪkʃən/ *n.* [C,U] LAW the official right or power to make legal decisions, or the area where this right exists: **have jurisdiction over sb/sth** *The U.S. has no legal jurisdiction over crimes committed outside the country.* | **within/outside sb's jurisdiction** (=part of or not part of someone's rights or powers)

ju·ris·pru·dence /ˌdʒʊrɪsˈprudns/ *n.* [U] LAW the science or study of law

ju·rist /ˈdʒʊrɪst/ *n.* [C] LAW someone who has a very detailed knowledge of law

ju·ror /ˈdʒʊrɚ/ W3 *n.* [C] a member of a jury: *Two of the jurors were dismissed.*

ju·ry /ˈdʒʊri/ W2 *n. plural* **juries** [C] **1** LAW a group of twelve people who listen to details of a case in court and decide whether someone is guilty or not: *a trial by jury* | *members of the jury* | *People with criminal records may not* ***sit on a jury*** (=be part of a jury). ►see THESAURUS box at court[1] **2** a group of people chosen to judge a competition **3 the jury is out on sth** used to say that it is not yet certain whether something is a good or bad thing [**Origin:** 1300–1400 Anglo-French *juree*, from Old French *jurer* **to swear**] → see also GRAND JURY, **hung jury** at HUNG[2]

ˈjury box *n.* [C usually singular] the place where the jury sits in a court

ˈjury ˌduty *n.* [U] a period of time during which you must be ready to be part of a jury if necessary

ˈjury-rig *v.* **jury-rigged, jury-rigging** [T] INFORMAL to put something together quickly for temporary use, using whatever is available: *We jury-rigged a shower from water bottles.* —**jury-rigged** *adj.*

jus san·gui·nis /ˌyus ˈsæŋgwɪnɪs/ *n.* [U] LAW the right to be a citizen of a particular country if your parents were citizens of that country → see also JUS SOLI

jus so·li /ˌyus ˈsoʊlaɪ/ *n.* [U] LAW the right to be a citizen of a particular country if you were born in that country → see also JUS SANGUINIS

just[1] /dʒʌst/ S1 W1 *adv.* **1** exactly: *Thank you! That's just what I wanted.* | *My brother looks* ***just like*** *my dad.* | *You got the sauce* ***just right***. | ***Just then*** *my mom walked in and saw us.* | **just as/when** *Just as the season was starting, we lost our best player.* **2** only: *She's not dating Zack – they're just friends.* | *He's just a kid. Don't be so hard on him.* | *Can you wait five minutes? I just have to iron this* (=it is the last thing I have to do). | *"Can I help you?" "No thanks,* ***I'm just looking*** (=said when someone asks if you need help in a store)." **3** only a short time ago: *I just got off the phone with Mrs. Kravitz.* | *Myra just saw him yesterday.* ►see THESAURUS box at recently **4 just about** almost: *It's just about time to leave.* | *I'm just about finished.* **5** used to emphasize a statement: *She just kept eating and eating.* | *I just can't believe it.* **6** at this moment or at that moment: **be just about to do sth** *I was just about to say the same thing.* | **be just doing sth** *I'm just finishing my homework.* | *We're leaving, but* ***not just yet*** (=not now, but very soon). | *I saw it on TV* ***just now*** (=a very short time ago). **7** only by a small amount: **+before/after/over etc.** *I got there just before Aaron.* | *Coby's just over two months old now.* **8 just as good/strong/nice etc. (as sth)** equally as good, strong etc. as something else: *The $250 TV is just as good as the $300 one.* **9** if something just happens or is just possible, it does happen or is possible, but it almost did not happen or almost was not possible: *She had* ***just enough*** (=enough but not more) *money to live on.* | *We got to the bus stop* ***just in time*** (=almost too late, but not). | *Kurt* ***only just*** *made it home before dinner* (=he made it but almost did not). | **might/could just** *This is a game that we might just win, with a little luck.* **10 just around the corner a)** very near: *I live just around the corner.* **b)** used to say that something will happen or arrive soon: *Summer is just around the corner.*

SPOKEN PHRASES

11 used when politely asking something or telling someone to do something: *Could I just use your phone for a minute?* **12** used when firmly telling someone to do something: *Just sit down and shut up!* **13 a) just a minute/second/moment** used to ask someone to wait for a short time while you do something: *Just a minute. Let me see if he's here.* **b)** used to interrupt someone in order to ask them something, disagree with them etc.: *Just a minute, that's not fair!* **14 it's just that** used when explaining the reason for something, especially when someone thinks there is a different reason: *He's very cute. It's just that he's too short for me.* **15 just like that** suddenly, unexpectedly, and without any good reason or explanation: *You can't quit your job just like that!* **16 I can just see/hear...** used to say that you can easily imagine seeing or hearing something: *I can just hear Will saying something crazy like that.* **17 would just as soon** used to say in a polite way that you would prefer to do something: *I'd just as soon ride with you, if that's okay.* **18 it's just as well** used to say that it is lucky that something has happened in the way it did, because there might have been problems if it had happened another way: *It's just as well you didn't go to the party. It was boring.* **19 not just any/anyone etc.** used to emphasize that you are talking about things or people that are especially good or important: *I love chocolate, but not just any chocolate. It has to be dark chocolate.* **20 just the same** used to say that one fact or argument does not change a situation or your opinion SYN anyway: *I know they say it's safe, but we should be careful just the same.* **21 just because... doesn't mean** used to say that although one thing is true, another thing is not necessarily true: *Just because you're older doesn't mean you can tell me what to do.* **22 just because** said when you do not want to explain your reasons for something: *"Why do you want to leave?" "Just because."* **23 may/might just** used to say what you might do, especially when it is unusual or shocking: *I might just ask for next week off and take a trip.* **24 just think/look/listen** used for directing someone's attention to an idea, a sight, a sound etc.: *Just think – in a couple of hours we'll be home.* **25 just the same** used to say that one fact or argument does not change a situation or your opinion: *It doesn't matter what kind of bike it is – they'll steal it just the same.* **26 just testing** said when you have made a mistake, to pretend that you only did it to see if someone would notice: *"He's from Idaho, not Iowa." "I know – just testing."* **27 just checking** used to tell someone not to be offended when you ask if they have done something yet: *"Did you lock the door?" "Yes." "OK, just checking."* **28 just the thing** exactly the right thing in this situation: *A warm fire would be just the thing right now.* **29 just so** with everything arranged very neatly: *Her house always has to be just so.*

→ see also **just kidding** at KID[2] (1), **just my luck!** at LUCK[1] (9), **might (just) as well** at MIGHT[1] (5)

GRAMMAR **just, already, yet**
In formal or written English, these words are usually used with the present perfect tense: *He's just gotten here.* | *I've already read it.* | *Have you eaten yet?* However, in speech and less formal writing, we often use these words, especially **just**, with the simple past tense: *He just got here.* | *I already read it.* | *Did you eat yet?*

just[2] *adj.* **1** morally right and fair OPP **unjust**: *a just reward* ▸see THESAURUS box at **fair**[1] **2 just deserts** the punishment that other people think you deserve: *The defendant got his just deserts.* [**Origin:** 1300–1400 French *juste*, from Latin *justus*, from *jus* **right, law**] —**justly** *adv.*

jus·tice /ˈdʒʌstɪs/ W2 *n.*
1 FAIRNESS [U] fairness in the way people are treated OPP **injustice**: *We demand justice and equal rights for all U.S. citizens.* | *promises on human rights and* ***social justice*** (=fairness for all the people who belong to a society) → see also POETIC JUSTICE
2 SYSTEM OF JUDGMENT [U] LAW the system by which people are judged in courts of law and criminals are punished: *the criminal justice system*
3 LEGAL PROCESS [U] LAW the process of reaching a fair decision in a court of law to punish someone who has been found guilty of a crime: *We will* ***bring*** *the killers* ***to justice*** (=make sure they are put on trial). | *war criminals who* ***escape justice*** (=avoid being caught and given a trial) | **justice has been done/served** (=used to say that someone has been treated fairly and punished fairly if they are guilty)
4 do justice to sb/sth also **do sb/sth justice** to treat or represent someone or something in a way that is fair and shows their best qualities: *The picture on TV didn't do him justice.*
5 JUDGE [C] LAW a judge in a law court, for example in the Federal Supreme Court of the U.S.
6 BEING RIGHT [U] the quality of being right and reasonable: *No one doubts the justice of our cause.*
7 do yourself justice to do something such as a test or contest well enough to show your real ability: *She panicked and didn't do herself justice on the test.* → see also **rough justice** at ROUGH[1] (15)

ˌJustice of the ˈPeace WRITTEN ABBREVIATION **J.P.** *n.* [C] LAW someone who judges less serious cases in small law courts and can perform marriage ceremonies

jus·ti·fi·a·ble /ˌdʒʌstəˈfaɪəbəl/ Ac *adj.* justifiable actions, reactions, decisions etc. are done for good reasons and should not be criticized: *justifiable anger* —**justifiably** *adv.*

ˌjustifiable ˈhomicide *n.* [U] LAW a situation in which you are not punished for killing someone, usually because you did it to defend yourself

jus·ti·fi·ca·tion /ˌdʒʌstəfəˈkeɪʃən/ Ac *n.* [C,U] a good and acceptable reason for doing something: *There is no justification for holding her in jail.*

jus·ti·fied /ˈdʒʌstəˌfaɪd/ Ac *adj.* **1** having an acceptable explanation or reason: *A few of his complaints were justified.* | **justified in doing sth** *Do you think I'm justified in refusing?* **2** TECHNICAL printed material that is justified has the edge of the lines on the left or right forming a straight line down the page: **right-justified/left-justified** (=with the straight edge on the left or the right)

jus·ti·fy /ˈdʒʌstəˌfaɪ/ Ac *v.* **justified, justifying** [T] **1** to give an acceptable explanation for something that other people think is unreasonable: *The university has tried to justify its decision.* | **justify doing sth** *How can you justify spending so much money on shoes?* **2** to be a good and acceptable reason for something: *Nothing justifies murdering another human being.* **3 justify yourself (to sb)** to prove that what you are doing is reasonable: *I don't have to justify myself to you or anyone.* **4** to type or print TEXT so that the words form a straight line on the right and left sides of the page

jut /dʒʌt/ *v.* **jutted, jutting** [I always + adv./prep.] also **jut out** something that juts in a particular direction sticks up or out further than the other things around it: *Jagged rocks jutted out over the beach.*

jute /dʒut/ *n.* [U] a natural substance that is used for making rope and rough cloth

ju·ve·nile /ˈdʒuvənl, -ˌnaɪl/ *adj.* **1** [only before noun] LAW relating to young people who are not yet adults: *juvenile crime* **2** silly and typical of a child rather than an adult SYN **childish**: *a juvenile sense of humor* —**juvenile** *n.* [C]

ˌjuvenile deˈlinquent *n.* [C] a child or young person who behaves in a criminal way —**juvenile delinquency** *n.* [U]

jux·ta·pose /ˈdʒʌkstəˌpoʊz, ˌdʒʌkstəˈpoʊz/ *v.* [T] FORMAL to put things together, especially things that are not normally together, in order to compare them or make something new: **juxtapose sth with/and sth** *The design juxtaposes antiques with modern furniture.* —**juxtaposition** /ˌdʒʌkstəpəˈzɪʃən/ *n.* [C,U]

JV *n.* [U] SPOKEN **junior varsity** the younger and less experienced of two teams of sports players who represent a school or college → see also VARSITY

K,k

K¹, k /keɪ/ *n.* [C] *plural* **K's, k's a)** the eleventh letter of the alphabet **b)** the sound represented by this letter

K², k 1 INFORMAL an abbreviation for one thousand, especially one thousand dollars: *He makes 60k a year.* **2 k** PHYSICS an abbreviation of KILOBYTE (=a measurement of computer information) **3 K** PHYSICS an abbreviation of KELVIN (=a measurement of temperature) **4 k** an abbreviation of KILOMETER: *a 10k race*

K–12 /ˌkeɪ ˈtwɛlv/ *adj.* [only before noun] relating to education in schools from KINDERGARTEN through twelfth grade: *K–12 teachers*

K2 /keɪ ˈtu/ also **Mount Goodwin Austen** a mountain in the Himalayas, on the border between Kashmir and China, that is the second highest mountain in the world

Kaa·ba /ˈkɑbə/ a small SHRINE (=holy building) in Mecca, Saudi Arabia, that Muslims turn toward when they pray

ka·bob, kebab /kəˈbɑb/ *n.* [C] small pieces of meat and vegetables cooked on a stick

ka·boom /kəˈbum/ *interjection* INFORMAL used to represent the sound of an explosion: *Then, kaboom, the car burst into flames.*

kabuki

ka·bu·ki /kəˈbuki/ *n.* [U] a traditional type of Japanese theater plays in which men wear decorated clothes and use strictly controlled movements and dances

Ka·bul /ˈkɑbəl, kəˈbʊl/ the capital and largest city of Afghanistan

Kad·dish /ˈkɑdɪʃ/ *n.* [singular, U] a Jewish prayer for the dead

kaf·fee·klatsch /ˈkɔfiˌklætʃ/ *n.* [C] another spelling of COFFEE KLATCH

Kaf·ka /ˈkɑfkə/**, Franz** /frɑnz/ (1883–1924) a Czech writer who wrote in German, known for his NOVELS and stories about ordinary people trying to deal with large organizations and strange events

Kaf·ka·esque /ˌkɑfkəˈɛsk/ *adj.* a Kafkaesque situation is one that is very complicated, confusing, and strange, especially because there are complicated rules that prevent you from doing what you want, similar to situations found in the writing of Franz Kafka

kaf·tan /ˈkæftæn/ *n.* [C] another spelling of CAFTAN

Kah·lo /ˈkɑloʊ/**, Fri·da** /ˈfridə/ (1907–1954) a Mexican PAINTER famous for her paintings of herself that express strong feelings in the style of SURREALISM

ka·hu·na /kəˈhunə/ *n.* **1 the big kahuna** SPOKEN, HUMOROUS someone who has a very important powerful position **2** [C usually singular] a traditional priest or leader from Hawaii

Kai·ser, kaiser /ˈkaɪzɚ/ *n.* [C] HISTORY a ruler of Germany or Austria before 1918, especially Wilhelm II, who ruled Germany during World War I

Ka·lash·ni·kov /kəˈlɑʃnɪˌkɔf/ *n.* [C] a type of RIFLE (=long gun) that can fire very quickly

kale /keɪl/ *n.* [U] a dark green vegetable with curled leaves

ka·lei·do·scope /kəˈlaɪdəˌskoʊp/ *n.* [C] **1** a pattern, situation, or scene that is always changing and has many details or bright colors: **+of** *a kaleidoscope of cultures* **2** a tube with mirrors and pieces of colored glass at one end, that shows colored patterns when you look into the tube and turn it [**Origin:** 1800–1900 Greek *kalos* **beautiful** + *eidos* **form** + English *-scope* (as in telescope)]

ka·lei·do·scop·ic /kəˌlaɪdəˈskɑpɪk/ *adj.* kaleidoscopic scenes, colors, or patterns change often and quickly

ka·mi·ka·ze¹ /ˌkɑmɪˈkɑzi/ *n.* [C] **1** a pilot, especially one from Japan during World War II, who deliberately crashes his airplane on enemy camps, ships etc., knowing he will be killed **2** a strong alcoholic drink containing VODKA and LIME juice [**Origin:** 1800–1900 a Japanese word meaning **wind of god**]

kamikaze² *adj.* [only before noun] **1** willing to take great risks, without caring about your safety, especially when you risk being killed: *kamikaze taxi drivers* **2** relating to kamikazes or their attacks: *a kamikaze pilot*

Kam·pa·la /kɑmˈpɑlə/ the capital and largest city of Uganda, on Lake Victoria

ka·na /ˈkɑnə/ *n.* [U] ENG. LANG. ARTS SYMBOLS representing SYLLABLES, used when writing Japanese

Kan·din·sky /kænˈdɪnski/**, Was·si·ly** /ˈvɑsili/ (1866–1944) a Russian PAINTER famous for his ABSTRACT paintings

kangaroo

kan·ga·roo /ˌkæŋgəˈru/ *n.* *plural* **kangaroos** [C] an Australian animal that has strong back legs for jumping and carries its babies in a POUCH (=a special pocket of skin) on its stomach [**Origin:** 1700–1800 from an Australian Aboriginal language]

ˌkangaroo ˈcourt *n.* [C] an unofficial court that punishes people unfairly

Ka·no ˈEi·to·ku /ˌkɑnoʊ ˈeɪtoʊku/ (1543–1590) a Japanese PAINTER who was the best artist of the Kano family of Japanese court painters, and introduced many important new ideas into Japanese art

Kan·sas /ˈkænzəs/ ABBREVIATION **KS** a state in the Great Plains area of the central U.S. —**Kansan** *n., adj.*

ˌKansas ˈCity ABBREVIATION **KC** a city and port on the Mississippi River in the U.S. state of Missouri

Kant /kɑnt/**, Im·man·u·el** /ɪˈmænyuəl/ (1724–1804) a German PHILOSOPHER who believed that moral decisions must be based on reason

ka·o·lin /ˈkeɪəlɪn/ *n.* [U] a type of white clay used for making cups, plates etc., and also in medicine and beauty products [**Origin:** 1700–1800 French *Gaoling*, name of a hill in China where it was originally obtained]

ka·put /kəˈpʊt/ *adj.* [not before noun] SPOKEN broken: *All three phones were kaput.* [**Origin:** 1800–1900 German, French *capot* **having lost in a card game**]

Ka·ra·ko·ram Range, the /ˌkærəˈkɔrəm ˌreɪndʒ/ a system of mountain RANGES that runs from northern Pakistan through India to southwest China and includes K2, the world's second highest mountain

kar·a·o·ke /ˌkæriˈoʊki/ *n.* [U] the activity of singing to specially recorded music for fun [**Origin:** 1900–2000

Japanese *kara* **empty** + *oke* (from *okesutora* **orchestra**, from English *orchestra*)]

kar·at /ˈkærət/ *n.* [C] a measurement used for showing how pure gold is, on a scale from 1 to 24, which is pure gold → see also CARAT

ka·ra·te /kəˈrɑṭi/ *n.* [U] a Japanese fighting sport, in which you use your hands and feet to hit and kick [**Origin:** 1900–2000 a Japanese word meaning **empty hand**]

kar·ma /ˈkɑrmə/ *n.* [U] **1** according to the Hindu and Buddhist religions, the force that is produced by the things you do in your life and that will influence you in the future or in future lives **2** INFORMAL luck resulting from your actions SYN **fate** **3** INFORMAL the feeling that you get from a person, place, or action: **good/bad karma** *The house had a lot of bad karma.* [**Origin:** 1800–1900 a Sanskrit word meaning **work**] —**karmic** *adj.*

Kar·ok /kəˈrɑk/ a Native American tribe from the southwestern area of the U.S.

Kas·hmir /ˈkæʃmɪr, kæʃˈmɪr/ an area in the northern part of the Indian SUBCONTINENT that is claimed by India, Pakistan, and China

Kas·kas·ki·a /kæsˈkæskiə/ a Native American tribe from the northeastern central area of the U.S.

Kath·man·du, **Katmandu** /ˌkætmænˈdu, ˌkɑtmɑn-/ the capital and largest city of Nepal

ka·ty·did /ˈkeɪṭiˌdɪd/ *n.* [C] a type of large GRASSHOPPER (=insect) that makes a noise like the sound of the words "katy did"

Kau·ai /ˈkaʊi/ an island in the Pacific Ocean that is part of the U.S. state of Hawaii

kay·ak[1] /ˈkaɪæk/ *n.* [C] a type of light boat usually for one person, that has a hole in the top for that person to sit in, and that is moved using a PADDLE [**Origin:** 1700–1800 Inuit *qajaq*]

kayak[2] *v.* [I] to travel in a kayak —**kayaking** *n.* [U] —**kayaker** *n.* [C]

Ka·zakh·stan /ˈkæzækˌstæn, ˈkɑzɑkˌstɑn/ a country in central Asia, between Russia and China, which was part of the former Soviet Union, and is now an independent country —**Kazakh** *n., adj.*

Ka·zan /kəˈzæn/, **E·lia** /ˈilyə/ (1909–2003) an American movie and theater DIRECTOR, who helped to start the Actors' Studio in New York City

ka·zoo /kəˈzu/ *n.* [C] a simple musical instrument that you play by holding it to your lips and making sounds into it

Kb an abbreviation of KILOBYTE

kcal *n.* [C] PHYSICS a written abbreviation of KILOCALORIE

Keats /kits/, **John** (1795–1821) a British poet and a leading figure in the Romantic movement

ke·bab /kəˈbɑb/ *n.* [C] another spelling of KABOB → see also SHISH KEBAB

keel[1] /kil/ *n.* [C] **1** a bar along the bottom of a boat that keeps it steady in the water **2 on an even keel** working normally or feeling normal without sudden changes, especially when you have dealt with a difficult situation: *We're hoping to get the company back on an even keel as soon as possible.*

keel[2] *v.*

keel over *phr. v.* to fall over sideways: *Several soldiers keeled over in the hot sun.*

keel·haul /ˈkilhɔl/ *v.* [T] to pull someone under the keel of a ship with a rope as a punishment

keen /kin/ *adj.*

1 INTERESTED/EAGER very interested in something or very eager to do it: *a keen interest in science* | *keen golfers* | **not be keen on sth** *Margaret wasn't keen on moving so far away.* | **keen to do sth** *Airlines will be keen to lease more aircraft in coming years.*

2 INTELLIGENT intelligent and quick to understand things: *Greg has a keen mind.* | *a keen understanding of finance*

3 GOOD SIGHT/SMELL/HEARING a keen sense of smell, sight, or hearing etc. is an extremely good ability to smell etc.: *Dogs have a very keen sense of smell.* | *a keen eye for detail*

4 STRONG FEELING feeling something strongly: *When she died he felt a keen sense of loss.*

5 keen competition a situation in which people compete strongly: *We won the contest in the face of keen competition.*

6 SHARP LITERARY a keen knife or blade is extremely sharp —**keenness** *n.* [U]

keen·er /ˈkinɚ/ *n.* [C] *Canadian* INFORMAL someone who BROWN-NOSES

keen·ly /ˈkinli/ *adj.* **keenly aware/interested/felt etc.** extremely or strongly AWARE, interested etc.

keep[1] /kip/ S1 W1 *v. past tense and past participle* **kept** /kɛpt/

1 NOT CHANGE/MOVE [I linking verb] to continue to be in a particular state, condition, or place and not change or move SYN **stay**: *We sat around the fire to keep warm.* | *I ride my bike to keep in shape.* | **keep right/left** *Slower traffic should keep right.*

2 MAKE SB/STH NOT CHANGE [T] to make someone or something continue being in a particular state or situation: *My job keeps me really busy.* | *It's hard to keep the house clean with three kids.* | **keep sb/sth doing sth** *They kept us waiting for more than an hour!* | *Don't **keep** me **in suspense** – tell me!*

3 NOT GET RID OF STH [T] to continue to have something and not lose it or get rid of it: *We decided to keep our old car.* | *I kept his letters for years.* | *In spite of the difficulties, Rob's kept his sense of humor.* | **keep sth for yourself** *Keep some of the money for yourself.*

THESAURUS

store to put things away and keep them there until you need them: *We stored the boxes in the basement.*
save to keep something so that you can use or enjoy it in the future: *I'm saving this bottle of champagne for a special occasion.*
reserve to keep something separate so that it can be used for a particular purpose: *Reserve two tablespoons of the orange juice for the frosting.*
file to store papers or information in a particular order or a particular place: *All the contracts are filed alphabetically.*
collect to get and keep objects of the same type because you think they are attractive or interesting: *She collects teddy bears.*

4 NOT GIVE BACK [T] to have something and not give it back to the person who had it before: *You can keep that pen – I have another one.*

5 CONTINUE/REPEAT [T] to continue doing an activity or repeat the same action several times SYN **keep on**: **keep doing sth** *I keep making the same mistake over and over.* | *Don just kept talking like nothing happened.*

6 MAKE SB STAY IN A PLACE [T always + adv./prep.] to make someone stay in a place: *They want to keep him in the hospital overnight.* | **keep sb prisoner/hostage** *She was kept prisoner in the castle.* | *The teacher **kept** me **after school** for an hour.*

7 STORE STH [T always + adv./prep.] to leave something in one particular place so that you can find it easily: **keep sth in/on/under etc. sth** *Keep the money in a safe place.*

8 DELAY SB [T] to delay someone or stop someone from doing something: *Mac should be here by now. What's keeping him?* | *Don't let me keep you.*

9 keep a record/account/diary etc. to regularly write down information in a particular place: *Keep a record of the food you eat for one week.*

10 keep your promise/word etc. to do what you have promised to do: *You can rely on Kurt – he always keeps his word.*

11 keep sb posted/informed to continue to tell someone the most recent news about someone or something: *Keep me posted – I'd like to know of any changes.*

12 keep guard/watch to guard a place or watch around you all the time

13 keep order/discipline/the peace to control a situa-

tion so that people behave well and do not fight each other: *Police were sent in to keep order.*
14 FRESH FOOD [I] if food keeps, it stays fresh enough to be eaten: *Potato salad doesn't keep very well in the summertime.*
15 ANIMALS [T] to own and take care of animals: *We keep chickens and a couple of pigs.*
16 PROVIDE FOOD/CLOTHES ETC. [T] to provide someone with money, food etc.: **keep sb in sth** *It costs hundreds of dollars a year just to keep the kids in shoes.*
17 **keep going** **a)** to continue to move: *Keep going until you come to the big intersection.* **b)** to continue doing something difficult or tiring: *Keep going! There's not much left.* **c)** to have enough hope and emotional strength to continue living and doing things in spite of a difficult situation
18 **keep sb going** **a)** to give someone the necessary hope or energy they need to continue living or doing something: *Her letters were the only things that kept me going while I was a prisoner.* **b)** if something keeps you going, it is enough to satisfy your needs while you are waiting to get something bigger or better: *The loan should keep us going for another few months.*
19 **keep sth going** if you keep something going, such as a business, institution, or regular event, you keep it open or make it continue to happen
20 SPOKEN **keep the change** used when paying someone, to tell them they can keep the additional amount of money you have given them: *"That's $18." "Here's $20. Keep the change."*
21 **keep your shirt/hair on!** SPOKEN used to tell someone to be more calm, patient etc.
22 **it'll keep** SPOKEN used to say that you can tell someone something or do something later: *"I don't have time to listen now." "Don't worry, it'll keep."*
23 **you can keep sth** SPOKEN used for telling someone that you do not want something, or do not want to be involved in something: *You can keep the job – I don't want it anyway.*
24 GOD [T] FORMAL to guard or protect someone: *May the Lord bless you and keep you.*
25 CELEBRATE [T] OLD-FASHIONED to do the things that are traditionally done to celebrate something such as Christmas
[**Origin:** Old English *cepan*] → see also **keep/lose your head** at HEAD[1] (14), **keep house** at HOUSE[1] (5), **keep pace (with sb/sth)** at PACE[1] (4), **keep (sth) quiet/keep quiet about sth** at QUIET[1] (6), **keep track of sb/sth** at TRACK[1] (1)

keep at *phr. v.* **1 keep at sth** to continue working hard at something: ***Keep at it!*** *You're almost done.* **2 keep at sb** SPOKEN to continue asking, attacking etc. someone, so that they become less determined or stop opposing you: *We kept at them and finally wore them down.*

keep away *phr. v.* **1** to not go near someone or something: +**from** *Keep away from the fire.* **2 keep sb/sth ↔ away** to prevent someone or something from coming near: **keep sb/sth away from sb/sth** *His work keeps him away from his family.* → see also KEEP-AWAY

keep back *phr. v.* **1** to not go forward or near someone or something: *Police told us to keep back.* **2 keep sb/sth ↔ back** to prevent someone or something from going forward or near someone or something SYN **hold back**: *We piled sandbags to keep back the rising water.* **3 keep sth ↔ back** to not tell someone something that you know SYN **hold back**: *I suspected he was keeping something back.* **4 keep sb back** to prevent someone from being as successful as someone else SYN **hold back**: *The attitudes of men have kept women back for centuries.*

keep down *phr. v.* **1 keep sth ↔ down** to control something in order to prevent it from increasing: *The new regulations should help keep rents down.* **2** to stay near the ground, for example in order not to be seen or in order not to get shot: *Keep down! He's got a gun.* **3 keep sth ↔ down** to succeed in keeping food in your stomach, without VOMITING: *I just couldn't keep anything down yesterday.* **4 keep sb ↔ down** to prevent someone from achieving something, usually by not letting them do things other people are allowed to do: *One way to keep slaves down was to refuse them an education.* **5 keep sth ↔ down** to control sound so that it is not too loud: ***Keep it down*** *– I'm trying to sleep.*

keep from sth/sb *phr. v.* **1 keep sth from sb** to not tell someone something that you know: *You won't be able to keep the truth from Emily.* **2 keep sb/sth from (doing) sth** to prevent someone from doing something or prevent something from happening: *Lower the heat to keep the cake from burning.* **3 keep (yourself) from doing sth** to prevent yourself from doing something: *She had to cover her mouth to keep from laughing.*

keep off *phr. v.* **1 keep off sth** to not go on an area or object: *Keep off the grass.* **2 keep sb/sth ↔ off, keep sb/sth off sth** to prevent someone or something from going onto an area or object: *How can I keep cats and dogs off my lawn?* **3 keep sth ↔ off, keep sth off sth** to prevent something from touching, affecting, or damaging something else: *Spray pesticide to keep the fungus off new leaves.* **4 keep sth off** if you keep weight off, you do not get heavier again after you lose weight **5 keep your hands/paws/mitts off sth** SPOKEN to not touch or take someone or something: *Keep your hands off my lunch.*

keep on *phr. v.* **1 keep on (doing sth)** to continue doing an activity or repeat the same action several times: *Why do you keep on calling Brad?* **2 keep sb on** to continue to employ someone: *They might keep me on until next summer.*

keep out *phr. v.* **1** to not enter a place or building: *Danger. Keep out!* **2 keep sth sth ↔ out** to prevent someone or something from getting into a place: *You ought to close the lid to keep the ants out.*

keep out of *phr. v.* **1 keep out of sth** to try not to become involved in something: *You should keep out of other people's business.* **2 keep sb/sth out of sth** to prevent someone or something from becoming involved in something: *The injury will keep him out of Saturday's game.*

keep to sth *phr. v.* **1 keep to sth** to stay on a particular road, course, piece of ground etc.: *It's best to keep to the paved roads.* **2 keep to sth** to continue to do or use something, and not change: *Mullin kept to the same strategy through most of the game.* **3 keep to sth** to do what you have promised or agreed to do or what the rules say: *Keep strictly to the terms of the contract.* **4 keep sth to yourself** to not tell other people about something: *Nobody else knows about this, so keep it to yourself.* **5 keep to the point/subject etc.** to talk or write only about the subject you are supposed to be talking about **6 keep to yourself** to live a very quiet private life and not do many things that involve other people **7 keep sth to sth** to prevent an amount, degree, or level from going higher than it should: *Can you please keep costs to a minimum?*

keep up *phr. v.*
1 STAY AT HIGH LEVEL **keep sth ↔ up** to prevent something from falling or going to a lower level: *The shortage of supplies is keeping the price up.*
2 CONTINUE **keep sth ↔ up** to continue doing something, or to make something continue: *Keep up the good work!* | *It's unlikely either runner will be able to keep this quick pace up.*
3 MOVE AS FAST to move as fast as someone else: *Slow down – Davey can't keep up.* | +**with** *Janir struggled to keep up with the bigger kids.*
4 DO AS WELL to manage to do as much or as well as other people: +**with** *I'm having trouble keeping up with the rest of the class.*
5 CHANGE AS QUICKLY to increase, develop, or change at the same rate as something else: +**with** *It's difficult to produce enough to keep up with demand.*
6 CONTINUE DEALING WITH STH to manage to continue dealing with something that is changing or happening again and again: +**with** *She was finding it hard to keep up with her rent.*

7 STOP FROM SLEEPING **keep sb up** to prevent someone from going to sleep: *The baby kept us up all night.*
8 CONTINUE TO PRACTICE **keep sth ↔ up** to continue to practice a skill or subject that you learned in the past so that you do not forget it: *I wanted to keep up the French that I'd learned.*
9 CONTINUE TO READ/LEARN to continue to read and learn about a particular subject: **+with/on** *I read the newspaper to keep up with current events.*
10 KEEP STH IN GOOD CONDITION **keep sth ↔ up** to continue to pay the money that is needed to keep something in good condition or to keep it working → see also UPKEEP
11 TALK/WRITE TO FRIEND to continue to talk or write to someone, especially a friend, so that know what they are doing: **+with** *I haven't kept up with Jodi since college.*
12 keep your spirits/strength/morale etc. up to try to stay happy, strong, confident etc.: *We sang to keep our spirits up.*
13 keep up appearances to pretend that everything in your life is normal and happy even though you are in trouble, especially financial trouble
14 keep up with the Joneses to try to have all the possessions that your friends or NEIGHBORS have, because you want people to think that you are as good as they are

keep² [S3] *n.* **1 for keeps** INFORMAL forever: *Marriage ought to be for keeps.* **2** [U] all the things such as food, clothing etc. that you need to keep you alive, or the cost of providing this: *It's time you got a job and started **earning your keep*** (=making money to help buy your food, clothing etc.). **3** [C] a large strong tower, usually in the middle of a castle

'keep-ˌaway *n.* [U] a children's game in which you try to catch a ball that is being thrown between two other people

keep·er /'kipɚ/ *n.* [C] **1** someone who cares for or protects animals: *the zoo's head gorilla keeper* → see also GAMEKEEPER **2** someone whose job is to take care of a particular place or thing: *a lighthouse keeper* | **+of** *the keeper of the museum's coins* → see also STOREKEEPER, GROUNDSKEEPER **3** [usually singular] INFORMAL something you have found or caught, especially a fish, that is worth keeping: *This one's a keeper.* **4 I am not sb's keeper** SPOKEN used to say that you are not responsible for someone else's actions: *I'm not Janey's keeper.* **5 the keeper of the flame** someone who considers it their duty to continue supporting an idea, belief etc. **6** a GOALKEEPER in SOCCER

keep·ing /'kipɪŋ/ *n.* [U] **1 in keeping with sth** appropriate for a particular occasion or purpose [OPP] **out of keeping with sth**: *In keeping with tradition, everyone wore black.* **2 in sb's keeping** being taken care of or guarded by someone → see also SAFEKEEPING

keep·sake /'kipseɪk/ *n.* [C] a small object that reminds you of someone or something

keg /kɛg/ *n.* [C] a large round container, used especially for storing beer: **+of** *a keg of beer*

keg·ger /'kɛgɚ/ also **'keg ˌparty** *n.* [C] INFORMAL a big party, usually outside, where beer is served from KEGS

keis·ter /'kistɚ, 'kaɪstɚ/ *n.* [C] SPOKEN your BUTTOCKS (=part of your body that you sit on)

Kel·ler /'kɛlɚ/, **Hel·en** /'hɛlən/ (1880–1968) a U.S. writer known especially for the way she learned to speak and write after becoming blind and DEAF as a baby

Kel·logg /'kɛlɑg, -lɔg/, **Will K.** /wɪl keɪ/ (1860–1951) a U.S. maker of CEREALS who started the Kellogg Company

Kel·ly /'kɛli/, **Gene** /dʒin/ (1912–1996) a U.S. dancer, singer, actor, and DIRECTOR who appeared in many movies that were MUSICALS

kelp /kɛlp/ *n.* [U] a type of large brown SEAWEED (=plant that grows in the ocean)

kel·vin /'kɛlvɪn/ WRITTEN ABBREVIATION **K** *n.* [U] PHYSICS a unit for measuring temperature that shows the temperature of something above ABSOLUTE ZERO. The size of one unit is the same as the size of one degree CELSIUS.

Kel·vin /'kɛlvɪn/, **William** (1824–1907) a British scientist who discovered the second law of THERMODYNAMICS and invented the Kelvin scale for measuring temperature

'Kelvin ˌscale *n.* [singular] PHYSICS a system for measuring temperature in which ABSOLUTE ZERO (=the lowest temperature that is possible) is represented as 0 K, water freezes at 273.15 K, and water boils at 373.15 K

Kem·pis /'kɛmpɪs/, **Thom·as à** /'tɑməs ə/ (1380?–1471) a German MONK who is believed to be the writer of a book, THE IMITATION OF CHRIST, which has influenced many Christians

ken /kɛn/ *n.* **beyond sb's ken** OLD-FASHIONED outside someone's knowledge or understanding

Ken·ne·dy /'kɛnədi/, **Jack·ie** /'dʒæki/ → see ONASSIS, JACQUELINE KENNEDY

J.F. Kennedy

Kennedy, John Fitzger·ald /dʒɑn fɪtz'dʒɛrəld/ (1917–1963) the 35th President of the U.S., who was shot in Dallas, Texas, in 1963

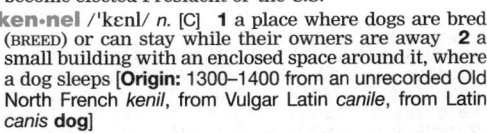

Kennedy, Joseph (1888–1969) an American businessman and government official who was the father of President Kennedy

Kennedy, Rob·ert Fran·cis (Bob·by) /'rɑbɚt 'frænsɪs, 'bɑbi/ (1925–1968) a U.S. politician in the Democratic Party who was the brother of John F. Kennedy. He was shot in 1968, when he was trying to become elected President of the U.S.

ken·nel /'kɛnl/ *n.* [C] **1** a place where dogs are bred (BREED) or can stay while their owners are away **2** a small building with an enclosed space around it, where a dog sleeps [**Origin:** 1300–1400 from an unrecorded Old North French *kenil*, from Vulgar Latin *canile*, from Latin *canis* **dog**]

ke·no /'kinoʊ/ *n.* [U] a game, played especially in CASINOS, in which you try to guess which numbers a computer will choose

Ken·tuck·y /kən'tʌki/ ABBREVIATION **KY** a state in the south-central U.S.

Ken·ya /'kɛnyə, 'ki-/ a country in east Africa which is south of Ethiopia and north of Tanzania —**Kenyan** *n., adj.*

Kenya, Mount a mountain in Kenya that is the second highest mountain in Africa

Kep·ler /'kɛplɚ/, **Jo·han·nes** /yoʊ'hɑnəs/ (1571–1630) a German ASTRONOMER who discovered how the PLANETS move around the sun

kept¹ /kɛpt/ *v.* the past tense and past participle of KEEP

kept² *adj.* **a kept woman** OLD-FASHIONED a woman who is given a place to live, money, and clothes by a man who visits her regularly for sex

ker·a·tin /'kɛrətɪn/ *n.* [U] BIOLOGY a type of PROTEIN that exists in hair, skin, and the NAILS on your fingers and toes

kerb /kɚb/ *n.* the British spelling of CURB

ker·chief /'kɚtʃɪf/ *n.* [C] **1** a square piece of cloth, worn especially by women in past times around their head or neck **2** OLD-FASHIONED a HANDKERCHIEF

Ke·ren·sky /kə'rɛnski/, **A·lek·san·dr** /ˌælɪg'zændɚ/ (1881–1970) a leader of the Russian government after the Russian Revolution, who was removed from power by the Bolsheviks

ker·nel /'kɚnl/ *n.* [C] **1** BIOLOGY one of the small yellow parts that you eat on an EAR of corn **2** BIOLOGY the center part of a nut or seed, usually the part you can eat **3** something that forms a small but important

K

part of a statement, idea, plan etc.: *This history story contains a* ***kernel of truth****.*

ker·o·sene /ˈkɛrəˌsin, ˌkɛrəˈsin/ *n.* [U] a type of oil that is burned for heat and used in lamps for lighting

Ker·ou·ac /ˈkɛruˌæk/, **Jack** /dʒæk/ (1922–1969) a U.S. writer famous as one of the 1950s beat GENERATION

Jack Kerouac

kes·trel /ˈkɛstrəl/ *n.* [C] a type of small FALCON

ketch /kɛtʃ/ *n.* [C] a small sailing ship with two MASTS (=poles)

ketch·up /ˈkɛtʃəp, ˈkæ-/ *n.* [U] a thick red SAUCE made from TOMATOes, eaten with food [**Origin:** 1600–1700 Malay *kechap* **hot-tasting fish sauce**]

ket·tle /ˈkɛṭl/ *n.* [C] **1** a special metal pot with a handle and SPOUT, used for boiling and pouring water SYN **teakettle**: *The kettle's boiling.* **2** a large pot, used especially for making soup **3 a different/another kettle of fish** INFORMAL used to say that a situation is very different from one that you have just mentioned

ket·tle·drum /ˈkɛṭlˌdrʌm/ *n.* [C] a large metal drum with a round bottom, used in an ORCHESTRA → see also TIMPANI

Kev·lar /ˈkɛvlɑr/ *n.* [U] TRADEMARK an extremely strong material used in clothing that protects people from being shot

kew·pie doll /ˈkyupi ˌdɑl/ also **kewpie** *n.* [C] a type of plastic DOLL with a fat body and a curl of hair on its head

key¹ /ki/ S1 W2 *n. plural* **keys** [C]
1 LOCK a small specially shaped piece of metal that you put into a lock and turn in order to lock or unlock a door, start a car etc.: **+to** *the key to the safe* | **car/house keys** *Do you know where my car keys are?*
2 the key the part of a plan, action, etc., that everything else depends on: **+to** *Hard work is the key to success.* | *This witness could* ***hold the key to*** *the whole case.*
3 MACHINE/MUSICAL INSTRUMENT the part of a machine, computer, or musical instrument that you press with your fingers to make it work: *Press the ESCAPE key to exit.* | *piano keys*
4 MUSICAL NOTES ENG. LANG. ARTS a set of musical notes with a particular base note, or the quality of sound that they have: *a minor key* | *The song is played* ***in the key of*** *G.* → see also OFF-KEY
5 MAP/DRAWING the part of a map, technical drawing etc. that explains the signs or SYMBOLS on it
6 TEST ANSWERS the printed answers to a test or to the questions in a TEXTBOOK that are used to check your work SYN **answer key**
7 ISLAND EARTH SCIENCE a small flat island, especially one near the coast of Florida: *the Florida Keys* → see also LOW-KEY

key² W2 *adj.* [no comparative] very important and necessary for success or to understand something: *the area's key businesses* | *Confidence is a key factor in any sport.* | **+to** *Your support is key to the plan's success.* | **a key point/question/issue etc.** *the key points of her speech* | **a key role/position** *He played a key role in the team's victory.* | **a key person/player/figure etc.** (=the most important person in achieving a result, change etc.) [**Origin:** Old English *cæg*] ▸see THESAURUS box at **important**

key³ *v.* [T] **1** to pull a key along the side of a car to SCRATCH it because you are angry at its owner: *Somebody keyed my car.* **2** INFORMAL if you key a win for your team, you help your team win a game by playing better than anyone else: *Rollins keyed a 98–89 victory for the Hawks.* → see also KEYED UP

key sth ↔ **in** *phr. v.* to put information into a computer by using a KEYBOARD

key (in) on sth *phr. v.* INFORMAL to direct your energy or attention toward one particular thing: *Reporters immediately keyed on the last sentence of the report.*

key sth **to** sth *phr. v.* **1** if something is keyed to something else in a system or plan, a change in one thing is designed to directly affect the other: *Pension adjustments are keyed to the rate of inflation.* **2** to make or change a system so that it works well with something else: *The daycare hours are keyed to the needs of working parents.*

keyboards

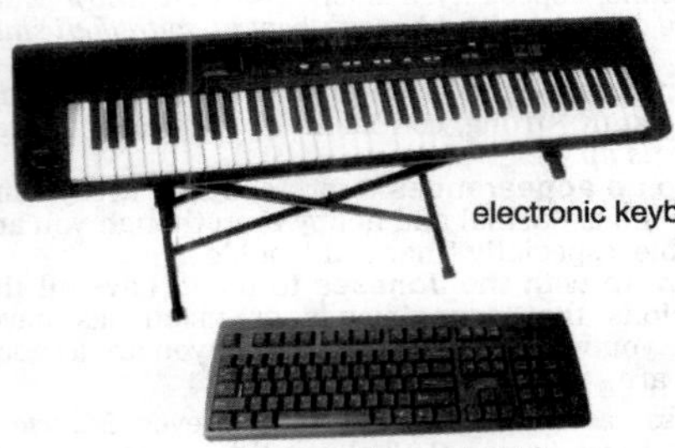

electronic keyboard

computer keyboard

key·board¹ /ˈkibɔrd/ *n.* [C] **1** COMPUTERS a row or several rows of keys on a musical instrument such as a piano or a machine such as a computer: *a computer keyboard* → see picture at COMPUTER **2** ENG. LANG. ARTS an electronic musical instrument with a keyboard similar to a piano, that can sound like a piano, drums etc.

keyboard² *v.* [I] to put information into a computer using a KEYBOARD —**keyboarder** *n.* [C] —**keyboarding** *n.* [U]

ˈkey card *n.* [C] a special plastic card that you put in an electronic lock to open a door, gate etc.

ˈkey chain *n.* [C] a KEY RING with some type of decoration attached to it

ˌkeyed ˈup *adj.* [not before noun] INFORMAL worried or excited: **+about** *Mike's really keyed up about the tournament.*

key·hole /ˈkihoʊl/ *n.* [C] the hole that you put a key in to open a lock

Keynes /keɪnz/, **John May·nard** /dʒɑn ˈmeɪnɑrd/ (1883–1946) a British ECONOMIST whose ideas greatly influenced economic thinking in the 20th century, and who believed that governments should use public money to control the level of employment —**Keynesian** *adj.*

ˌKeynesian Ecoˈnomics *n.* ECONOMICS a set of economic beliefs and actions based on the ideas of John Maynard Keynes. One of the central ideas of Keynesian Economics is that a government should take action to help limit high unemployment or continuous rises in the price of goods by increasing or decreasing the amount of money the government spends and by reducing taxes. Keynes also believed that a government control the cost of borrowing money by raising or lowering interest rates.

key·note¹ /ˈkinoʊt/ *n.* [C] the main point in a piece of writing, system of beliefs, activity etc., that influences everything else: **+of** *Creating jobs was the keynote of his campaign.*

keynote² *adj.* **1 a keynote address/speech/lecture** the most important speech at an official event **2 a keynote speaker** the person who gives the most important speech at an official event

keynote³ *v.* [T] to give a keynote speech at a ceremony, meeting etc.: *Mr. Graham is expected to keynote the conference.*

key·pad /ˈkipæd/ *n.* [C] **1** a small KEYBOARD on a piece of electronic equipment such as a CALCULATOR **2** COMPUTERS the part of a computer KEYBOARD that has the number and command keys on it

key·punch /ˈkipʌntʃ/ *n.* [C] a machine that puts holes in special cards which are read by computers

ˈkey ring *n.* [C] a metal ring that you keep keys on

key ring

ˈkey ˌsignature *n.* [C] a set of marks at the beginning of a line of written music to show which KEY it is in

key·stone /ˈkistoun/ *n.* [C usually singular] **1** the large central stone in an ARCH that keeps the other stones in position **2** the most important part of an idea, belief, event, etc., often one that other parts depend on: **+of** *Low interest rates are the keystone of the government's economic policy.*

key·stroke /ˈkistrouk/ *n.* [C] the action of pressing a key on a TYPEWRITER or computer KEYBOARD

kg the written abbreviation of KILOGRAM

KGB, the *n.* the secret police of the former U.S.S.R.

kha·ki /ˈkæki/ *n.* [U] **1** a dull brown or green-brown color **2** strong cloth of this color, especially when worn by soldiers **3 khakis** [plural] pants made of strong cotton cloth, usually dull brown in color [**Origin:** 1800–1900 Hindi **dust-colored**, from *khak* **dust**] —**khaki** *adj.*

khan /kɑn/ *n.* [C] a ruler or official in India or central Asia, or their title

Khar·toum /kɑrˈtum/ the capital and largest city of Sudan

Khmer Em·pire, the /kəˌmɛr ˈɛmpaɪə/ HISTORY an EMPIRE from about the 9th to 15th centuries that included at different times parts of the areas that are now Cambodia, Laos, Thailand, and Vietnam

Khmer Rouge, the /kəˌmɛr ˈruʒ/ HISTORY a Communist organization that controlled Cambodia from 1975 to 1979 and was responsible for the killing of millions of Cambodians

Khru·shchev /ˈkrustʃɔf, -tʃɛf/, **Ni·ki·ta** /nɪˈkitə/ (1894–1971) a Russian politician who was leader of the former Soviet Union from 1953 to 1964, and publicly criticized Stalin and his policies after Stalin's death in 1953

kHz the written abbreviation of KILOHERTZ

KIA *n.* [C] **killed in action** a soldier who is killed in a battle → see also MIA

kib·ble /ˈkɪbəl/ *n.* [U] small round pieces of dry food for dogs or cats

kib·butz /kɪˈbʊts/ *n. plural* **kibbutzes** or **kibbutzim** /ˌkɪbʊtˈsim/ [C] a type of farm in Israel where many people live and work together [**Origin:** 1900–2000 Hebrew *qibbus*, from Hebrew, **gathering**]

kib·itz /ˈkɪbɪts/ *v.* [I] INFORMAL **1** to make unhelpful remarks while someone is doing something **2** to talk in an informal way about things that are not important —**kibitzer** *n.* [C]

ki·bosh /ˈkaɪbɑʃ, kɪˈbɑʃ/ *n.* **put the kibosh on sth** INFORMAL to stop a plan, idea etc. from developing

kick[1] /kɪk/ S1 W3 *v.*

1 HIT WITH YOUR FOOT [I,T] to hit someone or something with your foot: *Stop kicking!* | *The kid behind me kept kicking the back of my seat.* | **kick sth in/down/over etc.** *Billy was kicking a ball around the yard.* | **kick sb in the head/face/stomach etc.** *Murray kicked him in the face.* | *He went to the nearest door and* ***kicked*** *it* ***open****.* | *Lewis* ***kicked*** *the winning* ***goal****.*

2 MOVE YOUR LEGS [I,T] to move your legs as if you were kicking something: *One boy lay on the floor, kicking and screaming.* | **kick your legs/feet** *Casey was waving her arms and kicking her feet in the air.*

3 kick yourself said when you are annoyed with yourself because you realize that you have made a mistake or missed a chance: *I* ***could have kicked*** *myself for getting her name wrong.*

4 to stop doing something, such as smoking or taking drugs, that is a harmful habit: *After nearly 60 years, it's hard to* ***kick the habit*** (=stop smoking).

5 kick sb when they are down to criticize or attack someone who is already in a weak position or having difficulties: *The newspapers cannot resist kicking a man when he is down.*

6 kicking and screaming protesting violently or being very unwilling to do something: *The company was dragged kicking and screaming into the 21st century.*

7 kick sb in the teeth/stomach/pants etc. INFORMAL to disappoint or upset someone very much, especially when they need support or hope

8 be kicking (it) SPOKEN to be relaxing and having a good time

9 kick sb upstairs to move someone to a job that seems to be more important than their present one, but that actually has less influence or power

10 kick the bucket HUMOROUS to die

kick around *phr. v.* INFORMAL **1 kick sb ↔ around** to treat someone badly and unfairly: *Don't let your sister kick you around like that!* **2 kick sth ↔ around** to think about something a lot or ask other people's opinions about it before making a decision: *Mom's been kicking around the idea of moving to Florida.* **3 kick around sth** to move around a place without having a plan of what to do or where to go: *We kicked around downtown all morning.*

kick back *phr. v.* INFORMAL **1** to relax and not worry about your problems: *I'm just going to kick back and wait for the end of the semester.* **2 kick sth ↔ back** to secretly or illegally pay someone part of the money you get from a deal because they have helped you to make the deal in some way

kick sth ↔ **down** *phr. v.* to cause a door or other structure to break and fall down by kicking it

kick in *phr. v.* **1** INFORMAL to begin to have an effect or come into operation: *Around noon, my cold medicine kicked in.* **2 kick in sth** INFORMAL to join with others in giving money or help SYN **contribute**: *Our company kicked in $5,000 for the school's music program.* **3 kick sb's face/head/teeth in** INFORMAL to severely hurt someone by kicking them in the face, head etc.: *If Jared says one more thing, I'm going to kick his head in.* **4 kick sth ↔ in** to kick something such as a door so hard that it breaks open: *Firemen kicked in the door and rescued three children.*

kick off *phr. v.* **1** INFORMAL when a game of football kicks off, it starts: *The Jets-Lions game kicks off at 1 o'clock.* **2 kick sth ↔ off** INFORMAL if you kick off a meeting, event etc., or if it kicks off, it starts: **+with** *Our annual conference kicked off with a speech from the President.* | *The Poetry Center kicks off its fall reading series at 8 p.m. Wednesday.* **3 kick your shoes off** also **kick off your shoes** to remove your shoes by shaking them off your feet **4 kick sb off sth** to force someone to leave a group, or leave a place: *Joe was kicked off the team.* **5** SPOKEN to die: *It's only been about a month since Joe kicked off.*

kick sb **out** *phr. v.* to make someone leave or dismiss them: *I can't believe that Glen's wife kicked him out.* | **kick sb out of sth** *What did you do to get kicked out of the restaurant?*

kick up *phr. v.* **1 kick up a fuss/controversy/debate etc.** to cause people to start complaining or arguing about something: *Mom kicked up a fuss when Dad told her how much the car cost.* **2 kick up your heels** to dance with a lot of energy and enjoyment **3 kick sth ↔ up** to make something, especially dust, go up into the air by walking or moving: *The bulldozers kicked up so much dust that you could hardly see.* **4 kick sth ↔ up** INFORMAL to increase something: *Saudi Arabia is kicking up its oil production.*

kick[2] S2 *n.* [C] **1** an act of hitting someone or something with your foot: *If the door won't open, just* ***give it a good kick****.* **2** an act of kicking a ball in a sports game, or the ball that is kicked and the direction in which it goes: *Bahr's kick went just to the left of the goal post.* **3 a kick in the teeth/stomach/pants etc.** INFORMAL something that is very disappointing or upsetting, especially when you need support or hope: *Finding out that Roger lied to me was a real kick in the pants.* **4 a**

K

kick in the pants/rear etc. INFORMAL criticism or strong words of encouragement that make someone start doing something they should do, work faster etc.: *Somebody needs to **give** the staff **a** good, swift **kick in the pants**.* **5** [singular] INFORMAL a feeling of excitement you get from doing something enjoyable: *I **get a** real **kick out of** watching my two cats play.* **6 do sth (just) for kicks** also **get your kicks (from) doing sth** INFORMAL to do something, especially something dangerous or harmful, in order to get a feeling of excitement: *Kent blew up things just for kicks.* **7** [singular] INFORMAL the strong effect of a drug or an alcoholic drink, or the strong SPICY taste of food: *The sauce has a real kick to it.* **8 be on a health/decorating/dieting etc. kick** INFORMAL to have a strong new interest in something **9 sth is better than a kick in the pants/teeth etc.** INFORMAL HUMOROUS used to say that something is good or acceptable, even if it is not perfect

Kick·a·poo /ˈkɪkəˌpu/ a Native American tribe from the northeastern central area of the U.S.

kick·back /ˈkɪkbæk/ *n.* [C usually plural] money that you pay someone for secretly or dishonestly helping you to make money, especially by using their political or professional influence: *Top executives received millions of dollars in kickbacks.*

kick·ball /ˈkɪkbɔl/ *n.* [U] a children's game, similar to baseball, in which you kick a large rubber ball that is rolled along the ground

kick·box·ing /ˈkɪkˌbɑksɪŋ/ *n.* [U] a form of BOXING in which you kick as well as hit —**kickboxer** *n.* [C]

kickboxing

kick·off /ˈkɪk-ɔf/ *n.* [C usually singular] **1** the time when a game of football starts, or the first kick in a SOCCER game: *Kickoff is at 3:00.* **2** the beginning of a new activity: *a kickoff for the governor's reelection campaign*

kick·stand /ˈkɪkstænd/ *n.* [C] a piece of metal on the bottom of a bicycle or MOTORCYCLE that supports it in an upright position when it is not moving

ˈkick start *n.* **1** [C] also **ˈkick ˌstarter** the part of a MOTORCYCLE that you press with your foot to start it **2** [singular] something that helps a process or activity to start or develop more quickly: *The deal is likely to **give** the business **a kick start**.*

ˈkick-ˌstart *v.* [T] **1** to start a MOTORCYCLE using your foot **2** to do something to help a process or activity start or develop more quickly: *Interest rates were lowered to kick-start the economy.*

kid[1] /kɪd/ S1 W1 *n.* **1** [C] a child: *Some kids were playing in the street.* ►see THESAURUS box at **child** **2** [C] a son or daughter: *He's married with three kids.* **3** [C] a TEENAGER or young adult: *college kids* **4 kid stuff** also **kids' stuff** INFORMAL something that is very easy, boring, or not very serious: *Baseball cards aren't just kid stuff anymore – there's serious money involved.* **5** [C] BIOLOGY a young goat **6** [U] leather made from the skin of a young goat **7 treat/handle someone with kid gloves** to treat someone very carefully because they easily become upset [**Origin:** 1100–1200 Old Norse *kith*] → see also **the new kid on the block** at NEW (14)

kid[2] S1 *v.* **kidded, kidding** INFORMAL **1** [I,T] to say something that is not true, especially as a joke: *You've got to be kidding me.* | *"Did you really go to China?" "No, I'm **just kidding**."* | *"A movie there costs $15." "**You're kidding**, right?"* **2** [T] to make jokes about someone, but not in an unpleasant way: **kid sb about sth** *Uncle Gene always kids me about my long hair.* **3 kid yourself** to make yourself believe something that is not true or not likely: ***You're kidding yourself** if you think the test's going to be easy.* **4 no kidding** SPOKEN **a)** used when you do not completely believe someone, or are surprised by what they say: *No kidding? You mean Becky's actually going to Princeton?* **b)** used to agree with what someone has said: *"Man, physics class is hard!" "No kidding!"* **5 I kid you not** SPOKEN, HUMOROUS used to emphasize that you are telling the truth **6 who is sb trying to kid?** SPOKEN INFORMAL used to say that no one believes what someone says: *He claims he's 29 – who is he trying to kid?* —**kidder** *n.* [C] —**kidding** *n.* [U]

kid around *phr. v.* to behave in a silly way: *Hey, don't get mad! I was just kidding around.*

kid[3] S2 *adj.* **sb's kid sister/brother** INFORMAL your sister or brother who is younger than you

Kidd /kɪd/, **William** (1645?–1701) a British PIRATE

kid·die[1] /ˈkɪdi/ *n.* [C] INFORMAL a young child

kiddie[2], kiddy *adj.* [only before noun] made or intended for young children: *a kiddie pool*

kid·do /ˈkɪdoʊ/ *n.* [C usually singular] SPOKEN said when talking to a child or friend: *Cheer up, kiddo – there'll be other games.*

kid·nap /ˈkɪdnæp/ *v.* **kidnapped**, **kidnapping** also **kidnaped**, **kidnaping** [T] to take someone away illegally, usually by force, and demand money for returning them: *Terrorists have kidnapped a French officer.* —**kidnapper** *n.* [C]

kid·nap·ping /ˈkɪdnæpɪŋ/ also **kidnap** [C,U] the crime of kidnapping someone: *the recent series of kidnappings* | *a kidnap attempt*

kid·ney /ˈkɪdni/ *n. plural* **kidneys** **1** [C] BIOLOGY one of the two organs in your lower back that separate waste liquid from your blood and make URINE **2** [C,U] one or more of these organs from an animal, used as food

ˈkidney bean *n.* [C] a dark red bean that has a wide curved shape slightly like the letter "C"

ˈkidney-shaped *adj.* [usually before noun] having a wide curved shape that looks slightly like the letter "C"

ˈkidney stone *n.* [C] a small hard piece of minerals that can form in your KIDNEY, causing a lot of pain

kiel·ba·sa /kɪlˈbɑsə/ *n.* [U] a type of SAUSAGE from Poland that is eaten hot

Kier·ke·gaard /ˈkɪrkəˌgɑrd/, **Sör·en Aa·bye** /ˈsɔ·ən ˈɑbi/ (1813–1855) a Danish PHILOSOPHER

Ki·ev /ˈkiɛv, -ɛf/ the capital city of Ukraine

Ki·ga·li /kɪˈgɑli/ the capital city of Rwanda

Ki·ku·yu /kɪˈkuyu/ *plural* **Kikuyu** or **Kikuyus** also **Gi·ku·yu** /gɪˈkuyu/ *plural* **Gikuyu** or **Gikuyus** *n.* **1** [C] a member of a group of people who live in central and southern Kenya **2** [U] the language of the Kikuyu

Kil·i·man·ja·ro /ˌkɪlɪmənˈdʒɑroʊ/ also **Mount Kilimanjaro** a mountain in Tanzania that is the highest mountain in Africa

kill[1] /kɪl/ S1 W1 *v.*

1 MAKE SB/STH DIE [I,T] to make a person or living thing die: *She was accused of killing her husband.* | *You'll kill your plants if you water them too much.* | *Smoking kills.* | **kill yourself** *What made Alan kill himself?* | *The driver was **killed instantly**.*

THESAURUS

murder to deliberately kill someone
commit manslaughter to kill someone without intending to
commit suicide to deliberately cause your own death
assassinate to deliberately kill an important person, especially a politician
slaughter/massacre to kill a large number of people in a violent way
execute sb/put sb to death to kill someone as a punishment for a crime
→ CRIME

2 MAKE STH STOP/FAIL [T] to make something stop or fail, or to turn off the power to something: *Could you give me something to kill the pain?* | *Quick! Kill the lights.*

3 sb will kill sb INFORMAL used to say that someone is

very angry with someone else: *Carrie will kill me if I forget her birthday.*
4 ANNOYED/SAD [T] INFORMAL to make someone feel extremely unhappy, tired, angry etc.: *Work is killing me.* | **it kills sb to do sth** *It kills her to have to be nice to Randy.*
5 kill time/an hour etc. to do something that is not very useful or interesting while you are waiting for something to happen

SPOKEN PHRASES

6 my head/back etc. is killing me used to say that a part of your body is hurting a lot: *I can't go with you tonight. My head is killing me.*
7 it won't/wouldn't kill sb (to do something) used when saying that someone could easily do something, and ought to do it: *It wouldn't kill you to do the dishes.*
8 MAKE SB LAUGH [T] to make someone laugh a lot at something: *Alan wore a dress to the party? That kills me!*
9 (even) if it kills me said when you want to show that you are determined to do something, even if it is very difficult: *I'm going to finish this even if it kills me.*
10 kill a beer/a bottle of wine etc. to drink something quickly or to finish what is left of a drink: *Let's kill these beers and go.*

11 kill yourself to do sth to work very hard to achieve something, but in a way that is likely to make you sick or very tired: *He's been killing himself to make the business go.*
12 kill two birds (with one stone) to achieve two things with one action: *I need to go and see Annie so I thought I'd kill two birds and visit you on the way.*
13 kill the goose that lays the golden egg to destroy the thing that brings you profit or success
14 kill sb with kindness to be too kind to someone who does not like or approve of you → see also **dressed to kill** at DRESSED (5), **if looks could kill** at LOOK² (7)

kill sb/sth ↔ off *phr. v.* **1** to cause the death of a lot of living things: *Some scientists think an asteroid killed off the dinosaurs.* **2** used to say that the writer of a story has a character in a story die or be killed: *The main character's wife **gets killed off** in the first chapter.* **3** to stop something completely or cause it to fail completely: *Deregulation had killed off a lot of small airlines.*

kill² *n.* **1** [C usually singular] the act of killing a hunted animal: *Shoot only if you are confident of a kill.* **2 move/go/close in for the kill** to come nearer to something and prepare to kill, defeat, or destroy it: *Enemy submarines were moving in for the kill.* **3** [singular] an animal killed by another animal, especially for food **4** [C] the act of gaining a point by hitting the ball very hard down to the ground in VOLLEYBALL

kill·deer /ˈkɪlˌdɪr/ *n.* [C] BIOLOGY a type of bird with two black rings across its breast

kill·er¹ /ˈkɪlɚ/ W3 *n.* [C] **1** a person, animal, or thing that kills: *Police are still searching for the killer.* | *Heart disease is America's number one killer.* → see also **serial killer** at SERIAL¹ (1) **2** something that is very difficult and tiring, or very boring: *Tracy's schedule is a real killer.* → see also LADY-KILLER

killer² *adj.* **1** SPOKEN very attractive or very good: *The concert was killer.* **2** [only before noun] very harmful or likely to kill you: *a killer cyclone* **3 a killer instinct** a desire to succeed that is so strong that you are willing to harm other people

killer app /ˈkɪlɚ ˌæp/ also **ˈkiller appliˌcation** *n.* [C] a piece of computer SOFTWARE that many people want to buy, especially one that works so well on a particular type of machine that people also want to buy the machine

ˈkiller whale *n.* [C] a black and white WHALE that eats meat SYN orca

kill·ing /ˈkɪlɪŋ/ *n.* [C] **1** a murder: *a gang-related killing* **2 make a killing** to make a lot of money in a short time: *Adams made a killing in the stock market.*

killer whale

kill·joy /ˈkɪldʒɔɪ/ *n. plural* **killjoys** [C] someone who spoils other people's pleasure

ˈkill switch *n.* [C] a part of a machine or piece of electrical equipment that immediately stops the flow of electricity so that the machine stops working

kiln /kɪln/ *n.* [C] a special OVEN for baking clay pots, bricks etc. [**Origin:** 700–800 Latin *culina* **kitchen**, from *coquere* **to cook**]

ki·lo /ˈkiloʊ/ *n. plural* **kilos** [C] a KILOGRAM, used especially when talking about illegal drugs: *275 kilos of cocaine*

kilo- /kɪlə/ *prefix* 1,000 times a particular unit of measurement: *a kilogram* (=1,000 grams)

ki·lo·byte /ˈkɪləˌbaɪt/ ABBREVIATION **K** *n.* [C] COMPUTERS a unit for measuring computer information, equal to 1,024 BYTES

kil·o·cal·o·rie /ˈkɪləˌkæləri/ WRITTEN ABBREVIATION **Kcal** *n.* [C] PHYSICS a unit of heat. It equals the amount of heat needed to increase the temperature of one KILOGRAM of water by 1°C.

kil·o·gram /ˈkɪləˌgræm/ WRITTEN ABBREVIATION **kg** *n.* [C] PHYSICS a unit for measuring weight and MASS, equal to 1,000 grams or 2.2046 pounds

kil·o·hertz /ˈkɪləˌhɚts/ WRITTEN ABBREVIATION **kHz** *n.* [C] a unit for measuring wave lengths, especially of radio signals, equal to 1,000 HERTZ

ki·lom·e·ter /kɪˈlɑmət̬ɚ, ˈkɪləˌmit̬ɚ/ WRITTEN ABBREVIATION **km** *n.* [C] a unit for measuring length, equal to 1,000 meters

ki·lom·e·tre /kɪˈlɑmət̬ɚ, ˈkɪləˌmit̬ɚ/ the British and Canadian spelling of kilometer

kil·o·ton /ˈkɪləˌtʌn/ *n.* [C] **1** a unit of weight equal to 1,000 TONS **2** the force of an explosion equal to that of 1,000 TONS of TNT

kil·o·watt /ˈkɪləˌwɑt/ WRITTEN ABBREVIATION **kW** *n.* [C] PHYSICS a unit for measuring electrical power, equal to 1,000 WATTS

ˌkilowatt ˈhour WRITTEN ABBREVIATION **kWh** *n.* [C] a unit for measuring electrical power, equal to the amount of work produced by a KILOWATT in one hour

kilt /kɪlt/ *n.* [C] a type of wool skirt with a pattern of lines and squares on it, traditionally worn by Scottish men

kil·ter /ˈkɪltɚ/ *n.* **out of kilter** if something is out of kilter, it is not working the way it should be or not doing what it should: *The district's budget was $9 million out of kilter.* → see also OFF-KILTER

kim·chee, kimchi /ˈkɪmtʃi/ *n.* [U] a SPICY Korean food made from CABBAGE in sour-tasting liquid

ki·mo·no /kəˈmoʊnoʊ/ *n. plural* **kimonos** [C] **1** a traditional piece of Japanese clothing like a long coat, that is worn at special ceremonies **2** a long loose piece of clothing like a ROBE worn indoors, especially by women [**Origin:** 1800–1900 a Japanese word meaning **clothes**]

kin /kɪn/ also **kinfolk** *n.* [plural] OLD-FASHIONED your family, including your grandparents, AUNTS, UNCLES, COUSINS etc. → see also KITH AND KIN, NEXT OF KIN

K

kind¹ /kaɪnd/ S1 W1 *n.*
1 TYPE [C] a type or sort of person or thing SYN **type** SYN **sort**: **+of** *What kind of car is that?* | *Are you and your brother in* ***some kind of*** *trouble?* | ***All kinds of*** *people live here.* | *Disasters* ***of this kind*** *take everyone by surprise.* | **the biggest/best etc. of its kind** *It's the best sports shoe of its kind.* | **be the kind (of person/man etc.) to do sth** *Martha's not the kind of woman to make quick decisions.* | **of some/any kind** *She doesn't eat meat of any kind.* | **the right/wrong/best etc. kind** *They had lots of bags in the store, but they weren't the right kind.* | **of the worst/best etc. kind** *hypocrisy of the worst kind* | *Ben's not* ***the marrying kind*** (=he is unlikely to want to get married). ►see THESAURUS box at **type¹**

SPOKEN PHRASES

2 kind of also **kinda a)** slightly or in some ways SYN **sort of**: *I think he's kind of cute.* **b)** used when you are explaining something and want to avoid being exact or giving details SYN **sort of**: *I kind of borrowed the money from your wallet.* ►see THESAURUS box at **rather**
3 a kind of (a) used to say that your description of something is not exact: *a kind of reddish-brown color*
4 something of that/the kind something similar to what has been mentioned: *"Did your principal really say that he was sorry?" "Yeah, something of that kind."*

5 nothing of the kind also **not anything of the kind** used to emphasize that what has been said is not true: *I never said anything of the kind.*
6 GROUP [singular] people or things that are similar in some way or belong to the same group: *New immigrants tend to cling to* ***their own kind*** (=people who are like them).
7 two/three etc. of a kind two or three people or things that are of the same type: *Three of a kind* (=three playing cards with the same number on them) *beats two pairs.*
8 one of a kind the only one of a particular type of something: *This Persian carpet is one of a kind.* → see also ONE-OF-A-KIND
9 of a kind used to say that something is not as good as it should be: *Elections of a kind are held, but there is only one party to vote for.*
10 in kind reacting by doing the same thing as someone else has just done: *Other airlines* ***responded in kind*** *to United's lowering of prices.* → see also **payment in kind** at PAYMENT (4)
[**Origin:** Old English *cynd*]

USAGE **kind of, sort of**
Kind of and **sort of** are used in informal contexts, mainly before adjectives and verbs, to mean that something is uncertain or partly true: *I kind of like getting up early.* | *"Did you enjoy the movie?" "Sort of* (=not as much as I hoped)."

GRAMMAR
Kind of and **sort of** are regularly used in the singular before singular and uncountable nouns: *one kind of flower/person/bread.* The plural forms **kinds of/sorts of** are used before plural nouns in more informal English: *these kinds of flowers/programs/people* (but NOT *this kind/sort of programs,* though you can more formally say *programs of this kind/sort*).

kind² *adj.* **1** saying or doing things that show that you care about other people and want to help them or make them happy OPP **unkind**: *That was such a kind thing to say.* | *a kind woman* | **+to** *Mr. Linam has been very kind to me.* | **it is kind of sb to do sth** *It's so kind of them to let us borrow their car.*

THESAURUS
nice friendly and kind: *That was really nice of him.*
considerate thinking about other people's feelings: *How considerate of her, I thought, to leave a light on for me.*
thoughtful thinking of things you can do to make other people happy: *It was a really thoughtful gift.*
caring kind to someone and willing to help him or her: *a caring father*
soft-hearted likely to feel sympathy for and be kind to someone with problems: *His grandmother and aunts were too soft-hearted to punish him.*
→ NICE

2 would you be so kind as to do sth also **would you be enough to do sth** FORMAL used to make a polite request: *I wonder if you would be so kind as to check these figures for me.* **3** not bad or not causing harm or suffering OPP **unkind**: **+to** *Life has been kind to me.* → see also KINDLY¹, KINDNESS → and see Word Choice box at KINDLY¹

kind·a /ˈkaɪndə/ SPOKEN a short form of "kind of": *I'm kinda tired.*

kin·der·gar·ten /ˈkɪndəˌgɑrtˀn, -ˌgɑrdn/ *n.* [C,U] a school or class for young children, usually aged five to six, that prepares them for later school years [**Origin:** 1800–1900 a German word meaning **children's garden**] → see also NURSERY SCHOOL

kin·der·gart·ner /ˈkɪndəˌgɑrtˀnə, -ˌgɑrd-/ *n.* [C] a child who is in kindergarten

ˌkind-ˈhearted *adj.* kind and generous —**kind-heartedly** *adv.* —**kind-heartedness** *n.* [U]

kin·dle /ˈkɪndl/ *v.* **1** [T] to make something start burning **2 kindle interest/excitement etc.** to make someone interested, excited etc.: *Recent events have kindled hope for an end to the violence.* → see also REKINDLE

kin·dling /ˈkɪndlɪŋ/ *n.* [U] small pieces of dry wood, leaves etc. that you use for starting a fire

kind·ly¹ /ˈkaɪndli/ *adv.* **1** in a kind way SYN **generously**: *Jason kindly offered to give me a ride home.* **2 not take kindly to sth** to be annoyed or upset by something that someone does or says: *Nancy's mother didn't take kindly to being corrected.* **3 to put it kindly** used to say that the way you are describing something or someone may not seem very nice, but it is more favorable than the situation really is: *Her report was, to put it kindly, complete gibberish.* **4 look kindly on/upon sb/sth** to approve of someone or something: *The leaders did not look kindly on those who spoke out for freedom.* **5** SPOKEN, FORMAL a word meaning "please," which is sometimes used when you are annoyed: ***Would you kindly*** *stop kicking the back of my seat?* **6 think kindly of sb** FORMAL to remember how nice someone was: *I hope people will think kindly of me when I die.*

USAGE
A request like **would you kindly...?** or **kindly shut the door!** is formal and polite as well as old-fashioned. In informal contexts, it sounds as though you are annoyed. It is more common to say **could you please...?**

WORD CHOICE **kind, kindly**
• **Kindly** is either the adverb of **kind:** *He kindly opened the door for me,* or a much less common adjective which describes a person's general character: *She is a kindly person.*
• It is more common to use the adjective **kind** to describe a person's general character or their behavior at one particular moment: *Betsy is a kind person.* | *It was kind of you to help me.* | *She's often kind to me* (NOT *kindly*).

kindly² *adj.* OLD-FASHIONED kind and caring for other people: *Mr. Bonnett was a kindly old man.* —**kindliness** *n.* [C]

kind·ness /ˈkaɪndnɪs/ *n.* **1** [U] kind behavior toward someone: *We were overwhelmed by the kindness of the people there.* **2** [C usually singular] FORMAL a kind action: *It would be* ***doing him a kindness*** *to tell him the truth.*

kin·dred¹ /ˈkɪndrɪd/ *adj.* [only before noun] FORMAL **1 a kindred spirit/soul** someone who thinks and feels the way you do **2** belonging to the same group or family

kindred² *n.* [U + with] LITERARY a family relationship SYN kinship

ki·net·ic /kɪˈnɛt̬ɪk/ *adj.* **1** PHYSICS relating to movement **2 kinetic art/sculpture etc.** ENG. LANG. ARTS art that has moving parts

ki,netic ˈenergy *n.* [U] PHYSICS the energy that something moving has as a result of its own movement.: *A rock rolling down a hill contains kinetic energy.* → see also POTENTIAL ENERGY

ki·net·ics /kɪˈnɛt̬ɪks/ *n.* [U] PHYSICS the science that studies the action or force of movement

ki,netic ˈtheory *n.* [U] PHYSICS a scientific THEORY used to describe and explain the behavior and properties of gases, based on the idea that all matter consists of PARTICLES which are continuously moving around very quickly and that energy and MOMENTUM (=the force that makes a moving object keep moving) are produced when particles hit each other

kin·folk /ˈkɪnfoʊk/ *n.* [plural] OLD-FASHIONED your KIN

king /kɪŋ/ S3 W3 *n.* [C]
1 RULER a man who is the ruler of a country because he is from a royal family → see also QUEEN: *King George VI* | **+of** *the king of Norway*

THESAURUS

queen the female ruler of a country, or the wife of a king
monarch a king or queen
ruler someone such as a king, who has official power over a country and its people
emperor the ruler of an empire (=group of countries)
sovereign FORMAL a king or queen

2 THE BEST a) someone who is considered to be the most important or best member of a group: **+of** *Elvis is still called the king of Rock 'n' Roll.* **b)** something that is the best of its type: **+of** *the king of luxury cars*
3 CHESS the most important piece in CHESS
4 CARDS a playing card with a picture of a king on it
5 be king if something is king at a particular time, it has a big influence on people: *During the mid-1800s, cotton was king in the South.*
6 the king of the jungle/beasts a lion
7 a king's ransom a very large amount of money
8 live like a king to have a very good quality of life
9 the King of Kings a name used for Jesus Christ
[**Origin:** Old English *cyning*] → see also **fit for a king** at FIT³ (1)

King /kɪŋ/, **B.B.** (1925–) a U.S. JAZZ musician and singer who plays the GUITAR

King, Bil·lie Jean /ˈbɪli dʒin/ (1943–) a U.S. tennis player famous for winning many women's tennis CHAMPIONSHIPS

King, Mar·tin Lu·ther /ˌmɑrtˀn ˈluθɚ/ (1929–1968) an African-American religious leader who became the most important leader of the CIVIL RIGHTS movement and worked hard to achieve social changes for African-Americans

M. Luther King

king·dom /ˈkɪŋdəm/ *n.* [C] **1** POLITICS a country governed by a king or queen: *the kingdom of Jordan* **2** something that someone controls completely: *His office was his own private kingdom.* **3 the kingdom of God/heaven** heaven **4 the animal/plant/mineral kingdom** BIOLOGY one of the three parts into which the natural world is divided **5** BIOLOGY the largest group into which scientists divide plants and animals **6 blow sb/sth to kingdom come** INFORMAL to completely destroy someone or something **7 till kingdom come** INFORMAL forever

king·fish·er /ˈkɪŋˌfɪʃɚ/ *n.* [C] BIOLOGY a small brightly colored bird with a blue body that eats fish in rivers

king·ly /ˈkɪŋli/ *adj.* good enough for a king, or typical of a king: *a kingly sum of money*

king·mak·er /ˈkɪŋˌmeɪkɚ/ *n.* [C] someone who chooses people for important jobs, or who influences the choice of people for important jobs

King ˌPhilip's ˈWar HISTORY a war in 1675–1676, between English COLONISTS in America and Native Americans, in which the Native Americans were defeated

king·pin /ˈkɪŋˌpɪn/ *n.* [C] the most important person or thing in a group: **a drug/cocaine etc. kingpin** (=someone who has a lot of power related to selling illegal drugs)

Kings /kɪŋz/ **1 Kings, 2 Kings** two books in the Old Testament of the Christian Bible

king·ship /ˈkɪŋʃɪp/ *n.* [U] the official position or condition of being a king

ˈking-size also **ˈking-sized** *adj.* **1** very large, and usually the largest size of something: *a king-size bed* **2** INFORMAL very big or strong: *a king-size thirst*

King·ston /ˈkɪŋstən/ the capital and largest city of Jamaica

Kings·town /ˈkɪŋztaʊn/ the capital city of St. Vincent and the Grenadines

kink

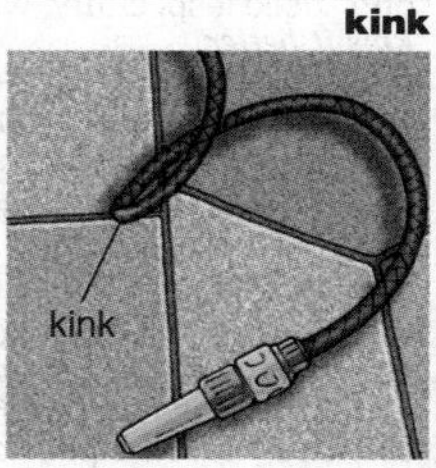

kink¹ /kɪŋk/ *n.* [C] **1** a twist or uneven part in something that is normally straight or smooth: **+in** *a kink in the hose* **2** a problem or something you do not agree about: **+in** *We expected a few kinks in the process.* **3 work/iron out the kinks** to solve all the problems in a plan, situation etc.: *We just need a few more rehearsals to iron out the kinks.* **4** a painful tight place in a muscle, especially in your neck or back: *I've got a kink in my neck.* **5** something strange or dangerous in your character

kink² *v.* [I,T] to bend or twist something that should be straight, or to become bent or twisted in this way

kink·y /ˈkɪŋki/ *adj. comparative* **kinkier**, *superlative* **kinkiest** **1** INFORMAL someone who is kinky, or does kinky things, has strange ways of getting sexual excitement **2** kinky hair has a lot of tight curls —**kinkily** *adv.* —**kinkiness** *n.* [U]

Kin·sey /ˈkɪnzi/, **Al·fred Charles** /ˈælfrɪd tʃɑrlz/ (1894–1956) a U.S. scientist who studied human sexual behavior

Kin·sha·sa /kɪnˈʃɑsə/ the capital and largest city of the Democratic Republic of Congo

kin·ship /ˈkɪnʃɪp/ *n.* **1** [U] LITERARY a family relationship: *the ties of kinship* **2** [singular, U] a strong relationship between people who are not part of the same family: **+with/for** *We felt a strong kinship with the people of China.*

kins·man /ˈkɪnzmən/ *n. plural* **kinsmen** /-mən/ [C] OLD USE a male relative

kins·wo·man /ˈkɪnzˌwʊmən/ *n. plural* **kinswomen** /-ˌwɪmɪn/ [C] OLD USE a female relative

ki·osk /ˈkiɑsk/ *n.* [C] a small building near a street where newspapers, candy etc. are sold [**Origin:** 1800–1900 French *kiosque*, from Turkish *kösk* **small building for sitting in**]

Ki·o·wa /ˈkaɪəwɑ, -ˌweɪ/ a Native American tribe from the southern central area of the U.S.

ˌKiowa Aˈpache a Native American group that lived as part of the Kiowa tribe but had a different language

Kip·ling /ˈkɪplɪŋ/, **Rud·yard** /ˈrʌdyɚd/ (1865–1936) a British writer born in India, known for his NOVELS, poems, and short stories set in that country

kip·per /ˈkɪpɚ/ *n.* [C] a type of fish that has been preserved using smoke and salt [**Origin:** 1300–1400 Old English *cypera* **male salmon**]

Kir·i·bati /ˈkɪrəˌbæs, -ˌbɑs/ a country in the Pacific Ocean consisting of 33 islands

kirsch /kɪrʃ/ *n.* [U] a strong alcoholic drink made from CHERRY juice [**Origin:** 1800–1900 German *kirschwasser* **cherry water**]

Ki·shi·nev /ˈkɪʃəˌnɛf, -ˌnɛv/ → see CHISINAU

kis·met /ˈkɪsmɛt/ *n.* [U] LITERARY the things that will happen to you in your life SYN fate

kiss¹ /kɪs/ S2 W3 *v.*
1 SHOW LOVE/GREETING [I,T] to touch someone with your lips as a greeting or to show them that you love them or have romantic feelings for them: *They kissed briefly, and then he left.* | *Did you* ***kiss*** *Daddy* ***goodnight?*** | **kiss sb on the lips/cheek etc.** *He kissed her gently on the cheek.*
2 SHOW RESPECT [T] to touch something with your lips as a sign of respect: *Each person knelt before the Pope and kissed his ring.*
3 kiss sth goodbye INFORMAL used when you think it is certain that someone will lose their chance of getting or doing something: *After that mistake, you can kiss your promotion goodbye.*
4 kiss sth away/better SPOKEN an expression meaning to take away the pain of something by kissing someone, used especially with children: *Here, let Mommy kiss it better.*
5 SUN/RAIN ETC. [T] LITERARY if the sun, rain etc. kisses something, it gently touches or moves it
[**Origin:** Old English *cyssan*]
kiss up to sb *phr. v.* SPOKEN to try to please someone in order to get them to do something for you: *Chuck's always kissing up to the teacher.*

kiss² S3 *n.* [C] **1** an act of kissing: *Do you remember your first kiss?* | *I leaned over and* ***gave*** *her* ***a kiss.*** | +**on** *a kiss on the forehead* | **a long/passionate kiss** *The two shared a passionate kiss.* **2 the kiss of death** HUMOROUS something that makes a plan, activity, business etc. fail: *An "NC–17" rating can be the kiss of death for a movie.* → see also AIR KISS, **blow sb a kiss** at BLOW¹ (6), FRENCH KISS

ˌkiss-and-ˈtell *adj.* INFORMAL a kiss-and-tell story, book etc. is one in which someone publicly tells the secret details of a romantic or business relationship: *kiss-and-tell memoirs*

kiss·er /ˈkɪsɚ/ *n.* [C usually singular] INFORMAL your mouth: *Janice* ***hit him right in the kisser.***

ˌkissing ˈcousin *n.* [C] OLD-FASHIONED a relative you are not closely related to, but whom you know well

kiss-off /ˈkɪsɔf/ *n.* [C] SLANG **give sb the kissoff** to suddenly end a romantic relationship with someone, without caring about their feelings

kit /kɪt/ S3 *n.* **1 shaving/sewing/repair etc. kit** a set of tools, equipment etc. that you use for a particular purpose or activity **2** [C] something that you buy in parts and put together yourself: *a model airplane kit* **3 the whole kit and caboodle** OLD-FASHIONED everything [**Origin:** 1300–1400 Dutch *kitte* **container for liquid**] → see also FIRST-AID KIT, TOOL KIT

kitch·en /ˈkɪtʃən/ S1 W2 *n.* [C] **1** the room where you prepare and cook food: *Jay's in the kitchen washing the dishes.* | *the kitchen table* **2 everything but the kitchen sink** HUMOROUS a phrase meaning "everything": *As usual, Joan packed everything but the kitchen sink.* [**Origin:** Old English *cycene*]

kitch·en·ette /ˌkɪtʃəˈnɛt/ *n.* [C] a small area, especially in a hotel room or office building, where you can cook food

kitch·en·ware /ˈkɪtʃənˌwɛr/ *n.* [U] pots, pans, and other things used for cooking

kite¹ /kaɪt/ *n.* [C] **1** a toy that you fly in the air on the end of a long string, made from a light frame covered in paper or plastic **2** BIOLOGY a type of HAWK (=bird that eats small animals) **3** INFORMAL an illegal CHECK that someone writes dishonestly to obtain money **4** MATH a GEOMETRIC shape with four sides of two different lengths. The pairs of sides of the same length are next to each other, and the sides opposite each other are of different lengths. → see also **go fly a kite** at FLY¹ (20), **fly a kite** at FLY¹ (21)

kite² *v.* [I,T] INFORMAL to obtain money using an illegal check → see also CHECK-KITING

kith and kin /ˌkɪθ ən ˈkɪn/ *n.* [plural] OLD-FASHIONED family and friends

kitsch /kɪtʃ/ *n.* [U] **1** decorations, movies etc. that seem to be cheap and unfashionable, and often amuse people because of this: *tourist kitsch* **2** the quality of being cheap and unfashionable, and often amusing because of this [**Origin:** 1900–2000 German *kitschen* **to put together roughly or carelessly**] —**kitsch, kitschy** *adj.*

kit·ten /ˈkɪtˀn/ S3 *n.* [C] a young cat [**Origin:** 1300–1400 from an unrecorded Old North French *caton*, from *cat* **cat**, from Late Latin *cattus*] → see also SEX KITTEN

kit·ten·ish /ˈkɪtˀn-ɪʃ/ *adj.* OLD-FASHIONED a kittenish woman behaves in a silly way in order to attract men

kit·ty /ˈkɪţi/ S2 *n. plural* **kitties** [C] **1** a word for a cat, used especially by children or when calling the cat: *Here, kitty, nice kitty.* **2** [usually singular] the money that people have collected for a particular purpose: *The funds go into the kitty, to be used for special school projects.* **3** [usually singular] the money that all the players in a game of cards have BET, which is given to the winner

ˈkitty-ˌcorner *adv.* **kitty-corner from sth** on the other side of a street from a particular place, and slightly to the left or right SYN catty-corner from SYN diagonally across from: *The drugstore is kitty-corner from the bank.*

ˈKitty ˌLitter, kitty litter *n.* [U] TRADEMARK small grains of a special substance that people put into an open container where a pet cat gets rid of its body wastes

ki·va /ˈkivə/ *n.* [C] a large round room, often underground, in a Pueblo village, used mainly for religious ceremonies

Ki·wa·nis /kəˈwɑnɪs/ an organization of business people in a town who work together to raise money for people who are poor or sick, or to help the town

ki·wi /ˈkiwi/ *n.* [C] **1** also **ˈkiwi fruit** BIOLOGY a soft green fruit with small black seeds and a thin brown skin covered in many short hairs → see picture at FRUIT¹ **2** BIOLOGY a New Zealand bird that has very short wings and cannot fly **3 Kiwi** INFORMAL someone from New Zealand

KKK *n.* the abbreviation of KU KLUX KLAN

Klam·ath /ˈklæməθ/ a Native American tribe from the western area of the U.S.

klans·man /ˈklænzmən/ *n.* [C] a member of the Ku Klux Klan

klax·on /ˈklæksən/ *n.* [C] a loud horn that was attached to police cars and other official vehicles in past times

Klee /kleɪ, kli/, **Paul** (1879–1940) a Swiss PAINTER famous for his ABSTRACT paintings

Kleen·ex /ˈklinɛks/ *n.* [C,U] TRADEMARK a paper TISSUE

klep·to·ma·ni·a /ˌklɛptəˈmeɪniə/ *n.* [U] a mental illness in which you have a desire to steal things

klep·to·ma·ni·ac /ˌklɛptəˈmeɪniˌæk/ also **klep·to** /ˈklɛptoʊ/ *n.* [C] INFORMAL someone who suffers from kleptomania

klez·mer /ˈklɛzmɚ/ *adj.* **klezmer music/band/orchestra etc.** a type of traditional Jewish music or group that plays this music

Klimt /klɪmt/, **Gus·tav** /ˈgʊstɑv/ (1862–1918) an Austrian PAINTER famous for his work in the ART NOUVEAU style

Klon·dike, the /ˈklɑndaɪk/ an area in northwest Canada, in the Yukon, where gold was discovered in the 1890s

kluge /kludʒ/ *adj.* SLANG a kluge solution to a computer problem is not a good or intelligent solution

klutz /klʌts/ *n.* [C] INFORMAL someone who often drops things and falls easily [**Origin:** 1900–2000 Yiddish *klotz, klutz*, from German *klotz* **large piece of wood**] —**klutzy** *adj.*

km *n.* the written abbreviation of KILOMETER

knack /næk/ *n.* [singular] INFORMAL **1** a natural skill or ability that you have to do something well: **a knack for (doing) sth** *a knack for languages* | *Keller* ***has a knack for*** *explaining technical concepts simply.* ▶see THESAURUS box at **ability** **2** a particular way of doing something that you have to learn: *There's a knack to finding the crabs.*

knap·sack /ˈnæpsæk/ *n.* [C] a small bag that you carry on your shoulders SYN **backpack** [**Origin:** 1600–1700 Low German *knappsack* or Dutch *knapzak* **food bag**]

knave /neɪv/ *n.* [C] OLD USE a dishonest boy or man —**knavish** *adj.*

knav·er·y /ˈneɪvəri/ *n.* [U] OLD USE dishonest behavior

knead /nid/ *v.* [T] **1** to press DOUGH (=a mixture of flour, water, and fat for making bread etc.) many times with your hands ▶see THESAURUS box at **cooking**[1] → see picture on page A32 **2** to press, rub, and SQUEEZE something many times with your fingers or hands: *He began kneading my sore shoulder muscles.*

knee[1] /ni/ S2 W2 *n.* [C]
1 BODY PART BIOLOGY the joint that bends in the middle of your leg: *When you are skiing, you have to keep your knees bent.* | *a knee injury* | *Sarah was* ***on her knees****, weeding the garden.* | *The kids were crawling around* ***on their hands and knees.***
2 CLOTHES the part of your clothes that covers your knee: *Billy's jeans had holes in both knees.*
3 on sb's knee on the top part of your legs when you are sitting down: *I used to sit on Grandpa's knee and ask him read to me.*
4 at sb's knee if you learn something at someone's knee, you learn it directly from them when you are young: *I learned Polish at my mother's knee.*
5 bring sb/sth to their knees a) to defeat a country or group of people in a war **b)** to have such a bad effect on an organization, activity etc. that it cannot continue: *The recession has brought many companies to their knees.*
6 on your knees in a way that shows you have no power but want or need something very much: *Eric was on his knees asking for forgiveness.* | *What do you want me to do?* ***Get down on*** *my* ***knees*** *and beg?*
7 drop/fall to your knees to quickly move to a position where your body is resting on your knees
8 get/go down on one knee to kneel on one knee, especially when asking someone to marry you
9 put/take sb over your knee OLD-FASHIONED to punish a child by hitting them on their BUTTOCKS
[**Origin:** Old English *cneow*] → see also **be the bee's knees** at BEE (4), **on bended knee** at BEND[1] (7), **knee/elbow/shoulder pad** at PAD[1] (1), **weak at the knees** at WEAK[1] (13)

knee[2] *v.* [T] to hit someone with your knee: *I kneed him in the groin.*

knee·cap /ˈnikæp/ *n.* [C] the bone at the front of your knee → see picture at SKELETON[1]

ˌknee-ˈdeep *adj.* **1 a)** deep enough to reach your knees **b)** in something that is deep enough to reach your knees: +**in** *knee-deep in water* **2 knee-deep in sth** INFORMAL very involved in something, or greatly affected by something you cannot avoid: *We ended up knee-deep in debt.*

ˈknee-high[1] *adj.* **1** tall enough to reach your knees: *knee-high grass* **2 when sb was knee-high to a grasshopper** OLD-FASHIONED used when talking about the past to say that someone was a very small child then

knee-high[2] *n.* [C usually plural] a sock that ends just below your knee

ˈknee-jerk *adj.* [only before noun] a knee-jerk reaction, opinion etc. is what you feel or say about a situation from habit, without thinking about it

kneel /nil/ also **kneel down** *v. past tense and past participle* **knelt** /nɛlt/ also **kneeled** [I] to be in or move into a position where your body is resting on your knees: *Tom knelt down and patted the dog.*

ˈknee-length *adj.* long enough to reach your knees: *a knee-length skirt*

knell /nɛl/ *n.* [C] LITERARY the sound of a bell being rung slowly because someone has died → see also DEATH KNELL

knelt /nɛlt/ *v.* a past tense and past participle of KNEEL

knew /nu/ *v.* the past tense of KNOW

knick·er·bock·ers /ˈnɪkɚˌbɑkɚz/ *n.* [plural] OLD-FASHIONED knickers

knick·ers /ˈnɪkɚz/ *n.* [plural] short loose pants that fit tightly at your knees, worn especially in the past [**Origin:** 1800–1900 *knickerbockers*]

knick·knack /ˈnɪkˌnæk/ *n.* [C usually plural] a small object used as a decoration in the home

knife[1] /naɪf/ S2 *n. plural* **knives** /naɪvz/ [C] **1** a tool used for cutting or as a weapon, consisting of a metal blade attached to a handle: *a knife and fork* | **kitchen/bread/vegetable etc. knife** (=a knife used in the kitchen, for cutting bread etc.) **2 you could cut the atmosphere/air/tension etc. with a knife** used to say that you felt the people in a room were angry with each other **3 go under the knife** HUMOROUS to have a medical operation **4 pull a knife (on sb)** to take a knife out of your clothes, where it had been hidden, and threaten someone with it: *Lyons claimed that Bessemer pulled a knife on him.* **5 like a (hot) knife through butter** INFORMAL used to say that something moves, happens, or is done very easily, without any problem. **6 twist/turn the knife** to say something that makes someone more upset about a subject they are already unhappy about [**Origin:** Old English *cnif*]

knife[2] *v.* [T + in] to put a knife into someone's body SYN **stab**

knight[1] /naɪt/ *n.* [C] **1** a European man with a high rank in past times, who was trained to fight while riding a horse → see also WHITE KNIGHT **2** the CHESS piece with a horse's head on it **3** a man who has received a knighthood and has the title "Sir" before his name **4 a knight in shining armor** a brave man who saves someone from a dangerous situation

knight[2] *v.* [T usually passive] to give someone the rank of knight

knight·hood /ˈnaɪthʊd/ *n.* [C,U] a special rank or

K

title that is given to someone by the British king or queen

knight·ly /ˈnaɪtli/ *adj.* LITERARY relating to being a knight or typical of a knight, especially by behaving with courage and honor

ˌKnights of Coˈlumbus, the an organization of Catholic men in a town who work together to raise money for people who are poor or sick, or to help the town

ˌKnights of ˈLabor, the POLITICS a U.S. LABOR UNION started in 1869 to protect the rights of ordinary workers

knit¹ /nɪt/ *v. past tense and past participle* **knit** or **knitted, knitting** **1** [I,T] to make clothing, blankets etc. out of thread or YARN (=thick thread) using two KNITTING NEEDLES or a special machine → see also CROCHET: **knit sb sth** *Mom knit me a pair of socks.* **2 knit your brows** LITERARY to show you are worried, thinking hard etc. by moving your EYEBROWS together **3** [I] a bone that knits after being broken grows into one piece again: +**together** *A pin holds the bones in place while they knit together.* **4** [I] TECHNICAL to use a PLAIN (=basic) knitting stitch → see also PURL [**Origin:** Old English *cnyttan*] —**knitter** *n.* [C] → see also CLOSE-KNIT, LOOSE-KNIT, TIGHT-KNIT

knit together *phr. v.* **knit sb/sth ↔ together** if something knits people, things, or ideas together, or if they knit together, they join together or become more closely related: *Worries about the future knit the family more closely together.*

knit² *adj.* [only before noun] **1** also **knitted** made by knitting: *a black knit cap* **2 closely/tightly/loosely knit** joined together as a group in a particular way: *a closely knit community*

knit³ *n.* [C] a type of cloth made by knitting, or clothing made by knitting

knit·ting /ˈnɪtɪŋ/ *n.* [U] **1** the action or activity of making clothes, blankets etc. out of thread or YARN using knitting needles **2** something that is being knitted: *Penny sat down with her knitting.*

ˈknitting ˌneedle *n.* [C] one of the two long sticks with round ends that you use to knit something

knit·wear /ˈnɪt˺wɛr/ *n.* [U] clothing made by knitting

knives /naɪvz/ *n.* the plural of KNIFE

knob /nɑb/ *n.* [C] a round handle or thing that you turn to open a door, turn on a radio etc.

knob·by /ˈnɑbi/ *adj.* with hard parts that stick out from under the surface of something: *knobby knees*

knock¹ /nɑk/ S2 W3 *v.*

1 DOOR [I] to hit a door or window with your closed hand to attract the attention of the people inside → see also TAP: *You should knock before you come in.* | +**at/on** *I think somebody's knocking at the door.* ►see THESAURUS box at **hit¹**

2 HIT/MAKE STH MOVE [I always + adv./prep., T always + adv./prep.] to hit something with a short quick action, so that it moves, falls down etc.: **knock sth down/over/aside etc.** *I accidentally knocked over the pitcher of water.* | **knock sth off/out of/from sth** *When he turned, he knocked a picture off the wall.* | **knock (sth) against/into sth** *Stewart's car knocked into a pole.* | *Huge boulders were* ***knocked loose*** *by the earthquake.*

3 HIT SB HARD a) knock sb to the ground also **knock sb on their rear etc.** to hit someone so hard that they fall down: *Everyone panicked and I got knocked to the ground.* **b) knock sb unconscious/senseless/silly** to hit someone so hard that they become unconscious: *The blast from the explosion knocked him unconscious.* **c) knock the living daylights out of sb** INFORMAL to hit someone many times or very hard **d) knock the wind out of sb** to hit someone in the stomach so that they cannot breathe for a moment

4 HURT YOURSELF to hurt yourself by accidentally causing part of your body to hit something: **knock sth on/against sth** *She knocked her head on a rock.*

SPOKEN PHRASES

5 knock on wood an expression that is used after a statement about something good, in order to prevent your luck from becoming bad: *I haven't had a cold all winter, knock on wood.*

6 knock some sense into sb/sb's head INFORMAL to make someone learn to behave in a more sensible way: *Maybe getting arrested will knock some sense into him.*

7 knock sb's socks off also **knock 'em dead** to surprise and someone very much by being very impressive: *The performance knocked my socks off!*

8 knock sb's block off to hit someone hard in the head or face: *If you touch it, I'll knock your block off!*

9 knock (sb's) heads together to shout at or punish people who are arguing or behaving stupidly in order to make them stop

10 CRITICIZE [T] to criticize someone or their work, especially in an unfair or annoying way: *Some reviewers seem to knock every movie they see.* | *"I'd never eat sushi." "Hey,* ***don't knock it till you've tried it."***

11 knock a hole in/through sth to make a hole in something, especially a wall, by hitting it hard: *You'll need to knock a hole through the wall.*

12 knock a nail in/through/into sth to push a nail into a surface by hitting it SYN **pound**

13 MAKE A NOISE [I] if an engine or pipes etc. knock, they make a noise like something hard being hit, usually because something is wrong with them: *Cheap gasoline will make your engine knock.*

14 knock the bottom out of sth to make something such as a price much lower or weaker: *A recession would knock the bottom out of corporate profits.*

[**Origin:** Old English *cnocian*] → see also **knock/throw sb for a loop** at LOOP¹ (2)

knock around *phr. v.* INFORMAL **1 knock sb around** to hit someone several times SYN **beat**: *Maggie's ex-husband used to knock her around.* **2 knock sth ↔ around** to discuss and think about an idea, plan etc. with other people SYN **discuss**: *We knocked a few possibilities around.* **3 knock around sth** to spend time in one place, or traveling to different places, without doing anything very serious or important: *We spent the day just knocking around the house.* **4 knock sth around** if people knock a ball around, they play a ball game such as SOCCER or tennis in a very informal, relaxed way

knock sth **↔ back** *phr. v.* INFORMAL to drink a large amount of alcohol very quickly: *Grace knocked back three shots of whiskey before dinner.*

knock down *phr. v.* **1 knock sb ↔ down** to hit or push someone so that they fall to the ground: *The mugger knocked her down.* | *I* ***got knocked down*** *by the crowd at the concert.* **2 knock sth ↔ down** to destroy a building or part of a building: *They knocked down my elementary school to build a mall.* **3 knock sth ↔ down** if a court knocks down a law, RULING etc., it says that it is not correct or acceptable and cannot continue **4 knock sth ↔ down** INFORMAL to reduce the price of something by a large amount: *The price of the sofa was knocked down to $300.* → see also KNOCKDOWN

knock off *phr. v.* INFORMAL **1 knock it off** used to tell someone to stop doing something, because it is annoying you: *You kids, knock it off in there!* **2 knock off sth** to stop working at the end of the day: *I'm going to* ***knock off early*** *today.* | *What time do you* ***knock off work****?* **3 knock sth ↔ off (sth)** to reduce the price of something by a particular amount: *We finally got the car dealer to knock a hundred dollars off the price.* **4 knock sth ↔ off sth** to reduce a total by a particular amount: *Taking the freeway knocks 15 minutes off my commute.* **5 knock sth ↔ off** to produce something quickly and easily: *Could you knock off a couple of copies of the report?* **6 knock sth ↔ off** to copy something, especially unfairly or illegally → see also KNOCKOFF **7 knock sb ↔ off** INFORMAL to murder someone

knock out *phr. v.* **1 out** to make someone become unconscious: *He knocked out his opponent in the first round of the fight.* → see also KNOCKOUT[1] (1) **2 knock sb ↔ out** if a team or player is knocked out of a competition, they cannot take part anymore, especially because they were defeated: **knock sb out of sth** *The Bulls knocked Boston out of the playoffs.* → see also KNOCKOUT[1] (3) **3 knock sth ↔ out** to stop the supply of electricity to an area: *Lightning knocked out power in the North Chicago area.* **4 knock sth ↔ out** INFORMAL to produce something easily and quickly, especially so that it is not of very good quality: *The factory can knock out 400 cars a week.* **5 knock sb out** INFORMAL to make you feel surprised and full of admiration: *I was knocked out the first time I heard the song.* **6 knock yourself out** INFORMAL **a)** to work very hard in order to do something well, especially so that you are very tired when you finish **b)** used to tell someone they can do something if they want to: *"I thought I'd clean the garage." "Knock yourself out."*

knock over *phr. v.* **1 knock sb/sth ↔ over** to hit or push someone or something so that it falls to the ground: *Who knocked over the vase?* **2 knock sth ↔ over** INFORMAL to rob a place such as a store or bank and threaten or attack the people who work there **3 you could have knocked me/us over with a feather** SPOKEN OLD-FASHIONED used to emphasize how surprised you were by something

knock sb ↔ up *phr. v.* INFORMAL to make a woman PREGNANT

knock² *n.* [C] **1** the sound of something hard hitting a hard surface: *a loud knock at the door* **2** the action of something hard hitting your body: **+on** *She got a knock on the head.* **3** a repeated noise that an engine or a machine makes when something is wrong with it: *a knock in the engine* **4** a criticism of someone or something: *The only knock against Whitney is his defensive playing.* **5 take/have a knock** INFORMAL to have some bad luck or trouble: *Kathy's **had a few hard knocks** in her lifetime.* → see also **the school of hard knocks** at SCHOOL[1] (10)

knock·down /ˈnɑkdaʊn/ *adj.* [only before noun] a knockdown price is very cheap → see also **knock down** at KNOCK[1]

ˌknock-down-ˈdrag-out *adj.* [only before noun] a knock-down-drag-out argument or fight is an extremely angry or violent one

knock·er /ˈnɑkɚ/ *n.* [C] a piece of metal on an outside door that you use to knock loudly

ˌknock-ˈkneed *adj.* having knees that point in slightly → see also BOW-LEGGED

ˌknock-ˈknock ˌjoke *n.* [C] a type of joke that begins with one person saying, "Knock knock," and another person asking, "Who's there?"

knock·off /ˈnɑk-ɔf/ *n.* [C] a cheap copy of something expensive

knock·out¹ /ˈnɑk-aʊt/ *n.* [C] **1** an act of hitting your opponent in BOXING so hard that he falls down and cannot get up again **2** INFORMAL someone or something that is very attractive or exciting: *Leslie's a real knockout.* **3** a defeat in a competition, in which winning players or teams continue playing until there is only one winner

knockout² *adj.* **1 knockout pills/drops etc.** PILLS etc. that make someone unconscious **2 a knockout punch/blow a)** a hard hit that causes someone to fall down and be unable to get up again → see also **knock out** at KNOCK[1] **b)** an action or event that causes defeat or failure: *High interest rates have been a knockout blow to the business.*

knoll /noʊl/ *n.* [C] EARTH SCIENCE a small round hill

knot¹ /nɑt/ *n.* [C]

1 TIED STRING a place where two ends or pieces of rope, string etc. have been tied together: **+in** *There's a knot in my shoelace.* | *Next, **tie a knot** with the two threads.* | *I can't **get** this **knot undone** (=untie it).*

2 TWISTED HAIR/THREADS many hairs, threads etc. that are accidentally twisted together: *I can't get the knots out of my hair.*

3 HAIR STYLE a way of arranging your hair into a tight round shape at the back of your head

4 WOOD a hard round place in a piece of wood where a branch once joined the tree

5 STOMACH a tight uncomfortable feeling in your stomach etc., caused by a strong emotion such as fear or anger: *My stomach was **in knots** before I got the results.* | *Tara felt **a knot in her stomach** as she waited to go on stage.*

6 MUSCLE a tight painful place in a muscle: **+in** *a knot in my shoulder muscle*

7 SHIP'S SPEED a measure of speed used for ships and aircraft that is about 1853 meters per hour

8 PEOPLE a small group of people standing close together: **+of** *A knot of reporters stood to one side of the entrance.*

9 SWOLLEN SKIN an area of skin that is swollen because you have hit it on something: *He had a knot on his forehead.*

[**Origin:** Old English *cnotta*] → see also GORDIAN KNOT, **tie the knot** at TIE[1] (5), **tie yourself (up) in knots** at TIE[1] (6)

knot² *v. past tense and past participle* **knotted, knotting 1** [T] to tie together two ends of rope, cloth, string etc. **2** [I] if hair or threads knot, they become twisted together **3** [I,T] if a muscle or other part of your body knots or is knotted, it feels hard and uncomfortable: *Fear and anxiety knotted her stomach.*

knot·hole /ˈnɑthoʊl/ *n.* [C] a hole in a piece of wood that is caused by a knot that fell out when the wood was cut

knot·ted /ˈnɑtɪd/ *adj.* **1** containing a lot of knots, or tied with a knot: *pieces of knotted string* **2** if a muscle or other part of your body is knotted, it feels hard and uncomfortable: *knotted shoulder muscles* **3** if the SCORE of a game is knotted, both teams or players have the same number of points: *At halftime, Iowa and Kansas were knotted at 21–21.* **4** knotted hands or fingers are twisted because of old age or too much work

knot·ty /ˈnɑti/ *adj.* **1** difficult to solve: *a knotty problem* **2** knotty wood contains a lot of knots

K

know¹ /noʊ/ S1 W1 *v. past tense and past participle* **knew** /nu/ *past participle* **known** /noʊn/ [not in progressive]

1 HAVE INFORMATION [I,T] to have information about something: *Who knows the answer?* | *"What time's the next bus?" "I don't know."* | **+about** *I didn't know about the problem till you told me.* | **know (that)** *We didn't know that Martin was coming.* | **know what/where/when etc.** *I don't know what I'm supposed to be doing.* | *Solly **knows all about** (=has a lot of information about) Jewish history.* | ***Everyone knows** that San Francisco is in California.* | *Mom **wants to know** (=wants to be told) who broke the vase.* | ***How did** he **know** (=how did he find information about) our names?*

2 BE CERTAIN [I,T] to be sure about something: *"Are you going home for Christmas?" "I don't know yet."* | **know (that)** *I knew they wouldn't get along.* | **know what/how/who etc.** *Mark knew exactly what he wanted.* | **know if/whether** *They didn't know if they could do it.* | **know sth for sure/certain** *I think it starts at 8, but I don't know for sure.* | ***How do you know** it won't happen again?* | ***All I know** is nobody likes her.*

3 BE FAMILIAR WITH [T] to be familiar with a person, place, system etc.: *Carol doesn't know the city very well yet.* | **know sb from sth** *We know each other from church.* | **know sb as sth** *I had first known Ann as a little girl.* | *Working here, you really **get to know** your customers.* | *The new laws promise to end welfare **as we know it**.* | *Kelly is one of the few candidates who **knows** the issues **backward and forward*** (=knows them very well).

4 REALIZE [I,T] to realize that something exists or is true, or to understand something: *Just take the money. Nobody will ever know.* | *She's very pretty, and she knows it.* | **know how/what/why etc.** *I know exactly what you mean.* | **know (that)** *Suddenly he knew that something was wrong.* | **know (all) about sth** *We knew* *all about the affair.* | **know to do sth** *Will people know to return the forms?* | *Wayne snuck out of the house* ***without*** *his parents* ***knowing.*** | **know full well/know perfectly well/know all too well** *He knew full well that he was breaking the law.* | *You* ***should have known*** *he'd forget the bread.* | ***I might have known*** *you'd do something like this.* | *I didn't say that,* ***and you know it!*** | ***If I had known*** *you were so sick, I would have asked somebody else to help.*

5 RECOGNIZE [T] to be able to recognize someone or something: *She had changed so much that I hardly knew her.* | **know sb by sth** *He looked very different, but I knew him by his walk.* | *I don't recognize the name, but I'd* ***know*** *him* ***by sight*** (=recognize him if I saw him).

6 HAVE LEARNED [T] to have learned a lot about something or be skillful and experienced at doing something: *Eric really know his job well.* | **know how to do sth** *Some of the kids don't know how to read yet.* | **+about** *You should talk to someone who knows about antiques.* | **know something/nothing etc. about sth** *I don't know anything about football.* | *She* ***knows from experience*** *that they won't want to hear the truth.* | *Are you sure* ***you know what you're doing*** (=have enough skill and experience to deal with something properly)? | *You listen to Aunt Kate; she* ***knows what*** *she's* ***talking about.*** | *She* ***knows all there is to know about*** *the subject.*

7 LANGUAGE to be able to speak and understand a foreign language: *I know a little Indonesian.*

8 SONG/TUNE/POEM ETC. to be able to sing a song, play a tune, say a poem etc. because you have learned it: *Do you know all the words to "The Star-Spangled Banner?"* | *Gabriela* ***knew*** *the whole piece* ***by heart*** (=had learned it and could play it from memory).

9 EXPERIENCE [I,T] to have experience with a particular feeling or situation: *I don't think he ever knew true happiness.* | **know (all) about sth** *I know all about being poor.*

10 let sb know to tell someone about something: *If you need any help, just let me know.*

11 before you know it used for saying that something happens very quickly or very soon: *You'll be home before you know it.*

12 know your way around (sth) a) to be familiar with a place, organization, system etc. so that you can use it effectively: *Most 7-year-olds know their way around a computer screen.* **b)** to be familiar with a place, city etc., so that you can easily move from one place to another and know where buildings, restaurants etc. are: *She already knows her way around the campus.*

13 know the/your way to know how to get to a place: **+to** *Does she know the way to our house?*

14 know sth from sth to understand the difference between one thing and another: *I don't know a French wine from a California wine.*

15 know otherwise/different INFORMAL to know that the opposite of something is true: *They thought he was honest, but I knew otherwise.*

16 know a thing or two (about sth) INFORMAL to have a lot of useful information gained from experience: *Coach Anderson knows a thing or two about winning.*

17 not know what to do with yourself to have nothing to do, for example because you cannot decide what work or activity you want to do: *After college, I didn't know what to do with myself.*

18 know better a) to be wise or experienced enough to avoid making mistakes: *How can you say that? You should know better.* **b)** to know that what someone else says or thinks is wrong because you know more than they do: *The man said it was a diamond, but Dina knew better.*

19 not know any better to do something because you do not realize it is wrong or stupid: *Don't be mad at him – he doesn't know any better.*

20 know sth inside (and) out to know something in great detail: *Kirstie knows marketing inside out.*

21 sb knows best used to say that someone should be obeyed or that their way of doing things should be accepted because they are experienced

22 not know the meaning of sth to lack any experience or understanding of a particular emotion or type of behavior: *He's a man who doesn't know the meaning of the word fear.*

23 know the ropes INFORMAL to know all the things you need to know in order to do a job or deal with a system: *Nathan knows the ropes – he's been with the company for ten years.*

24 know the score INFORMAL to know the real facts of a situation, including any unfavorable ones: *I knew the score before I started the job.*

25 know your own mind to be certain about what you like or what you want

26 not know what hit you INFORMAL to be so surprised or shocked by something that you cannot think clearly

27 not know where to turn to be in a very difficult and upsetting situation without knowing where to find help

28 sb has been known to do sth used to say that someone does something sometimes, especially something unusual: *She has been known to eat an entire box of cookies by herself.*

29 be known to be/do sth used to say that people know that something is a fact or there is information that proves it: *She is known to be a close friend of the president.* | *This species is not known to be vicious.*

30 know something/nothing/little etc. of sth ESPECIALLY WRITTEN used to say how much someone knows about something: *Little is known of his early life.*

31 know your place OFTEN HUMOROUS to behave in a way that shows that you know which people are more important than you: *I'll get back to the kitchen then – I know my place!*

32 not know your own strength to not realize how strong you are

33 know no bounds FORMAL if someone's honesty, kindness etc. knows no BOUNDS, they are extremely honest, kind etc.: *Paul's love for her knew no bounds.*

34 you will be delighted/pleased/happy etc. to know that FORMAL used before you give someone information that they will be happy to hear: *You will be pleased to know that we have accepted your offer.*

35 not know sb from Adam INFORMAL to not know who someone is at all

36 not know whether you're coming or going INFORMAL to feel very confused, especially because you have too much to do → see also YOU-KNOW-WHAT, YOU-KNOW-WHO

[**Origin:** Old English *cnawan*]

SPOKEN PHRASES

37 you know a) said when you cannot think of what you want to say next but you want to keep talking: *So I, you know, spent some time cleaning up afterward.* **b)** said when you are giving more information in order to explain which person or thing you are referring to: *We saw Nick, you know, Melissa's husband, downtown.* **c)** said when you want someone to understand the situation or feelings that you are telling them about: *I felt very upset, you know.* **d)** said in a conversation to make someone listen to something that you are going to tell them: *You know, sometimes I think we shouldn't be together.* **e)** said to emphasize a statement: *There's no reason to be so nasty, you know.*

38 I know a) used to agree with someone or to say that you feel the same way: *"It's cold out here." "I know. I'm freezing."* **b)** said when you suddenly have an idea or think of the answer to a problem: *I know! Let's turn the couch this way and then the table will fit.* **c)** used for showing that you realize what someone's criticisms or OBJECTIONS may be before they can make them: *It sounds silly, I know, but I'll explain.*

39 I don't know a) used to say that you do not have the answer to a question: *"Where's the nearest restroom?" "I don't know."* **b)** used to show that you disagree slightly with what has just been said: *"I couldn't live there." "Oh, I don't know. It might not be so bad."* **c)** used when you are not sure about something, or it does not matter to you: *"What time will we meet?" "Oh, I don't know. How about four o'clock?"*

SPOKEN PHRASES

40 **I don't know about sth** said for gently refusing to give someone permission to do something or to say that you have not decided whether to give permission yet: *"Can we come too?" "I don't know about that."*
41 **you know what/something?** **a)** used to introduce new information in a conversation: *You know what? George finally got a job.* **b)** used to emphasize what you are about to say: *They're talking about layoffs again. And you know something? I don't even care.*
42 **as far as I know** said when you think something is true, but you are not sure: *As far as I know, those dishes have never been used.*
43 **you never know** used to say that you are not sure what will happen: *He might say yes. You never know.*
44 **as you know** used when saying something that you and your listener already know: *As you know, sales have not been good this year.*
45 **you know sb/sth?** used to start talking about someone or something: *You know your cousin? You'll never guess what she did!*
46 **(you) know what I'm saying?** INFORMAL said to check that someone has understood what you are saying: *You shouldn't try to control other people – know what I'm saying?*
47 **(do) you know what I mean?** also **if you know what I mean** used when checking that someone has understood what you are saying: *People in this town are so weird, you know what I mean?*
48 **I know what you mean** used to tell someone that you understand what they are talking about, because you have had the same experience yourself: *He's cute, but I know what you mean about his personality.*
49 **I don't know about you, but...** used to give an opinion, suggestion, or decision of your own that might be different from that of the person listening: *I don't know about you, but I'm getting tired of this band.*
50 **for all I know** used to emphasize that you do not know anything about a particular subject: *It cost millions. It could be billions for all I know.*
51 **I don't know how/why etc.** used when criticizing someone, to say that you cannot understand their behavior or attitude because it is so bad: *I don't know how she can yell at her kids like that.*
52 **who knows!** also **Heaven/goodness (only) knows!** **a)** used to say that you do not have any idea what an answer might be, and do not expect to know: *"What's Roger going to do once he gets there?" "Who knows?"* **b)** used to emphasize a statement: *I haven't seen her for goodness knows how long.*
53 **wouldn't you know (it)** used to say that something bad or funny that has happened is not unexpected at all: *"He showed up late again." "Wouldn't you know it."*
54 **you don't know** used to emphasize how strong your feelings are about what you are saying: *You don't know how long I've waited to hear you say that!*
55 **I don't know how to thank you/repay you** FORMAL used to emphasize that you are very grateful to someone for doing something for you
56 **I wouldn't know** used to say that you do not know and you are not the person who should be asked: *"When's he coming back?" "I wouldn't know."*
57 **how should/would I know?** also **how do I know?** used to say that it is not reasonable to expect that you should know something: *How should I know where she lives? I just met her.*
58 **what does sb know?** used to angrily say that you do not think someone else's opinion is important or correct: *I'm not going to listen to Martha. What does she know?*
59 **knowing sb...** used to say that you expect someone to behave in a particular way because you know what they are like: *Knowing Michelle, she'll probably make her father pay for it.*

SPOKEN PHRASES

60 **knowing my luck...** used for saying that you expect something bad will happen because you are usually unlucky: *Knowing my luck, the train will be late.*

61 **(well,) what do you know!** used to express surprise: *Well, what do you know – look who's here!*
62 **I've never known sb/sth to do sth** used to say that you do not think someone or something has ever behaved in a particular way: *I've never known him to make any kind of trouble.*
63 **know your stuff** to be good at and know all you should know about a job or subject: *When it comes to math, he really knows his stuff.*
64 **if you know what's good for you** used to tell someone that they should do something, or you will harm them in some way: *You'll just keep your mouth shut if you know what's good for you!*
65 **sb ought to know** also **sb should know** used to emphasize that you expect someone to know about something because of their experience with it: *He says working with children is difficult, and, as a teacher, he should know.*
66 **how did/could I know?** also **how was I to know?** used to say that something is not your fault because you could not have known about it: *Don't get mad at me – how could I know the train would leave early?*
67 **it takes one to know one** used to rudely tell someone that they are the same kind of person as the one they are criticizing

know of sb/sth *phr. v.* **1** to have been told or to have read about someone or something, but not know much about them: *I only know of him – I've never actually met him.* **2** to know that someone or something exists, used especially when asking for or giving advice: *Do you know of any good restaurants in Chinatown?* | *I know of one or two people who could help you with this.* **3 not that I know of** SPOKEN used when answering a question to say that you believe that the answer is "no," but there may be facts that you do not know about: *"Did anyone call for me?" "Not that I know of."*

know[2] *n.* **in the know** INFORMAL having more information about something than most people: *People in the know say Silver will get the job.*

'know-how *n.* [U] INFORMAL knowledge, practical ability, or skill to do something: *technical know-how* | *We have the know-how to prevent some of theses accidents.*

know·ing /ˈnoʊɪŋ/ *adj.* showing that you know all about something, even if it has not been discussed directly: *a knowing smile*

know·ing·ly /ˈnoʊɪŋli/ *adv.* **1** deliberately: *He would never knowingly upset people.* **2** in a way that shows you know about something secret or embarrassing: *J.D. laughed softly and knowingly.*

'know-it-all *n.* [C] INFORMAL, DISAPPROVING someone who behaves as if they know everything: *a twelve-year-old know-it-all*

knowl·edge /ˈnɑlɪdʒ/ S2 W1 *n.* [U] **1** the information and understanding that you have gained through learning or experience: *scientific knowledge* | **+of** *She has impressed people with her knowledge of art.* | **+about** *Most young people lack a basic knowledge about politics.* **2** information that you have about a particular situation, event etc.: **+of/about** *the lawyer's knowledge of the case* | ***To the best of our knowledge*** (=we think this is true although we may not have all the facts)*, the young men are not part of a gang.* | *She opened an account in my name **without** my **knowledge*** (=without my knowing about it). | *"Is he planning to leave?" "**Not to my knowledge*** (=I do not think this is true, based on what I know)*."* | *Nelson **denied any knowledge of** the bribe.* | *The agency had approved the contract **with full knowledge of** its terms* (=knowing all the details about them). | *They sold the food **in the***

K

knowledge that it was not safe to eat. → see also **common knowledge** at COMMON[1] (7), GENERAL KNOWLEDGE, **a working knowledge (of sth)** at WORKING[1] (6)

knowl·edge·a·ble /ˈnɑlɪdʒəbəl/ *adj.* knowing a lot: *Our knowledgeable staff are always here to help you.* | **+about** *Mike's quite knowledgeable about jazz.* —**knowledgeably** *adv.*

known[1] /noʊn/ *v.* the past participle of KNOW

known[2] *adj.* [only before noun] **1** known about, especially by many people: *a known drug dealer* | **+to** *The actress is not known to many people outside Britain.* **2 a known quantity** someone or something that you are sure will behave in the way you expect them to → see also WELL-KNOWN

Knox /nɑks/, **John** (?1505–1572) a Scottish Protestant religious leader, who started the Presbyterian religion in Scotland, and established the Church of Scotland

knuck·le[1] /ˈnʌkəl/ *n.* [C] **1** BIOLOGY one of the joints in your fingers, including the ones where your fingers join your hands **2** a piece of meat around the lowest leg joint: *a knuckle of pork* **3 give sb a knuckle sandwich** SPOKEN to hit someone with your FIST [**Origin:** 1300–1400 Middle Low German *knökel* **small bone, knuckle**] → see also **a rap on/over the knuckles** at RAP[1] (7), BRASS KNUCKLES

knuckle[2] *v.*

knuckle down *phr. v.* INFORMAL to start working or studying hard: *You're going to have to knuckle down if you want to pass.*

knuckle under *phr. v.* INFORMAL to accept someone's authority or orders without wanting to: **+to** *She refused to knuckle under to company dress code.*

ˈknuckle ball *n.* [C] a ball in baseball that is thrown so that it moves slowly and slightly up and down

knuck·le·head /ˈnʌkəlˌhɛd/ *n.* [C] SPOKEN, INFORMAL a word for someone who has done something stupid, used when you are not very angry with them

KO[1] /keɪ ˈoʊ, ˈkeɪ oʊ/ *v. past tense and past participle* **KO'd, KO'ing** [T] **knock out** to make someone become unconscious by hitting them: *Joe Louis KO'd Billy Conn in the eighth round.*

K

KO[2] *n.* the abbreviation of KNOCKOUT

ko·a·la /koʊˈɑlə/ also **koˈala bear** *n.* [C] an Australian animal like a small bear with no tail that climbs trees and eats leaves

Ko·dak mo·ment /ˈkoʊdæk ˌmoʊmənt/ *n.* [C] TRADEMARK a special time when you want to take a photograph so that you can remember the situation later, used humorously

kohl /koʊl/ *n.* [U] a black pencil used to draw around women's eyes to make them more attractive

Kohl /koʊl/, **Hel·mut** /ˈhɛlmʊt/ (1930–) a German politician who was Chancellor of West Germany from 1982 to 1990 and was elected Chancellor of the united Germany in 1990 until 1998

kook /kuk/ *n.* [C] INFORMAL someone who is silly or crazy: *Some kook at the post office makes you sing for your packages.* —**kooky** *adj.*

Ko·ran /kəˈræn, -ˈrɑn/ *n.* **1 the Koran** the holy book of the Muslims **2** [C] a copy of this book [**Origin:** 1600–1700 Arabic *qur'an*, from *qara'a* **to read**] —**Koranic** *adj.*

Ko·re·a /kəˈriə/ a country in East Asia which, in 1948, was divided into two countries, North Korea and South Korea —**Korean** *n., adj.*

KoˌreanˈWar, the HISTORY a war between Chinese and North Korean forces on one side and UN and South Korean forces on the other. The war began in 1950 and ended in 1953, with neither side having won.

Kor·or /ˈkɔrɔr/ the capital city of Palau

ko·sher /ˈkoʊʃɚ/ *adj.* **1** kosher food is prepared according to Jewish law: *kosher meats* **2** kosher stores, restaurants, or kitchens obey Jewish food laws and sell or prepare kosher food **3 keep kosher** obey Jewish food laws **4** INFORMAL honest and legal, or socially acceptable: *This deal doesn't sound quite kosher to me.* [**Origin:** 1800–1900 Yiddish, Hebrew *kasher* **fit, suitable**]

ˈkosher salt *n.* [U] a type of salt that is in large grains and is prepared according to Jewish law

kow·tow[1] /ˈkaʊtaʊ/ *v.* [I] **1** DISAPPROVING to be too eager to obey or be polite to someone who has more power than you or who has something you want: **+to** *Members of Congress shouldn't be kowtowing to special interest groups.* **2** to perform a kowtow [**Origin:** 1800–1900 Chinese *ke tou* **to hit your head**; because when you bow very low you hit your head on the floor]

kowtow[2] *n.* [C] a low bow that was done in the past to show respect for the Chinese EMPEROR

KP *n.* [U] work that soldiers or children at a camp have to do in a kitchen, such as cleaning or cooking

kph the written abbreviation of "kilometers per hour"

Kra·ka·tau, Krakatoa /ˌkrækəˈtoʊə/ an island in Indonesia that is an active VOLCANO

Krem·lin /ˈkrɛmlɪn/ *n.* **the Kremlin a)** the government of Russia and the former U.S.S.R. **b)** the buildings in Moscow where this government's offices are

krill /krɪl/ *n.* [U] small SHELLFISH → see picture at FOOD CHAIN

Kris Krin·gle, Kriss Kringle /ˌkrɪs ˈkrɪŋgəl/ *n.* another name for SANTA CLAUS

Kris·tall·nacht /ˈkrɪstəlˌnɑkt/ HISTORY the night of November 9, 1938, when Nazis attacked Jews and Jewish homes, businesses etc. in Germany and Austria

kro·na /ˈkroʊnə/ *n. plural* **kronor** or **kronur** /-nɔr, -nɚ/ [C] the standard unit of money in Sweden and Iceland

kro·ne /ˈkroʊnə/ *n. plural* **kroner** /-nɚ/ [C] the standard unit of money in Denmark and Norway

Kru·ger·rand /ˈkrugəˌrænd, -ˌrɑnd/ *n.* [C] a South African gold coin

kryp·ton /ˈkrɪptɑn/ *n.* [U] SYMBOL **Kr** CHEMISTRY a gas that is an ELEMENT, found in very small quantities in the air

KS the written abbreviation of KANSAS

kt the written abbreviation of KNOT

Kua·la Lum·pur /ˌkwɑlə lʊmˈpʊr/ the capital and largest city of Malaysia

Ku·blai Khan /ˌkublə ˈkɑn/ (1212–1294) a Mongol emperor from China from 1259 until his death, who moved the capital of China to Peking

Ku·brick /ˈkubrɪk/, **Stan·ley** /ˈstænli/ (1928–1999) a U.S. movie DIRECTOR, PRODUCER, and writer

ku·dos /ˈkudoʊs, -doʊz/ *n.* [U] admiration and respect that you get for being important or for doing something important: **+for** *They have won kudos for their support of the arts.*

kud·zu /ˈkʊdzu, ˈkʌd-/ *n.* [U] a type of VINE used for animal food that grows very quickly and is common in the Southern U.S.

Ku Klux Klan /ˌku klʌks ˈklæn, ˌklu-/ ABBREVIATION **KKK** *n.* **the Ku Klux Klan** a U.S. political organization whose members are Protestant white people, and who believe that people of other races or religions should not have any power or influence in American society

ku·lak /kuˈlæk/ *n.* [C] HISTORY a rich land-owning farmer in Russia in the early 20th century

kum·quat /ˈkʌmˌkwɑt/ *n.* [C,U] BIOLOGY a fruit that looks like a very small orange, or the tree on which this fruit grows [**Origin:** 1600–1700 Chinese *kam kwat* **gold orange**]

kung fu /ˌkʌŋ ˈfu/ *n.* [U] an ancient Chinese fighting art in which you attack people with your hands and feet [**Origin:** 1800–1900 a Chinese word meaning **principles of boxing**]

Kun·lun Moun·tains /ˈkunlun ˌmaʊntˀnz/ also **Kunlun Shan** /ˈkunlun ʃɑn/ a RANGE of high mountains in western China, north of Tibet

Kuo·min·tang, the /ˌkwoʊmɪnˈtɑŋ/ ABBREVIATION **KMT** also **Guomindang, the** POLITICS the Nationalist Party of China that was formed in 1911 and ruled

China from 1928 to 1947, when it was defeated by the Communist Party. It is now active in Taiwan.

Kurd /kɚd/ *n.* [C] a member of a group of people that live in Iran, Iraq, Turkey etc. and speak a Kurdish language —**Kurdish** *adj.*

Ku·ro·sa·wa /ˌkʊrəˈsaʊə/, **A·ki·ra** /æˈkɪrə/ (1910–1998) a Japanese movie DIRECTOR

Ku·wait /kʊˈweɪt/ a country in the Middle East, north of Saudi Arabia and south of Iraq —**Kuwaiti** *n., adj.*

Ku,wait 'City the capital city of Kuwait

kvetch /kvɛtʃ, kfɛtʃ/ *v.* [I] INFORMAL to keep complaining about something [**Origin:** 1900–2000 Yiddish *kvetshn* **to press firmly, complain**] —**kvetch** *n.* [C]

kW the written abbreviation of KILOWATT

Kwa·ki·u·tl /ˌkwɑkiˈyuṭl/ a Native American tribe from western Canada

Kwan·zaa also **Kwanza** /ˈkwɑnzə/ *n.* [C,U] a holiday celebrated by some African-Americans between December 26 and January 1

kWh the written abbreviation of KILOWATT HOUR

KY the written abbreviation of KENTUCKY

K-Y also **ˌK-Y 'Jelly** *n.* [U] TRADEMARK a type of LUBRICANT for your body

Ky·o·to /kiˈoʊṭoʊ/ a CULTURALLY important city in central Japan which was Japan's capital city from 794 to 1868

Ky,oto A'greement, the also **Ky,oto 'Protocol, the** HISTORY an international agreement in which countries promise to reduce the amount of GREENHOUSE GASes they produce

Kyr·gy·zstan /ˈkɪrgɪˌstæn, -ˌstɑn/ a country in central Asia that is west of China and east of Uzbekistan —**Kyrgyz** /kɪrˈgɪz/ *n., adj.*

K

L,l

L¹, l /ɛl/ *n. plural* **L's, l's** [C] **a)** the twelfth letter of the English alphabet **b)** the sound represented by this letter

L² /ɛl/ **1** the number 50 in the system of ROMAN NUMERALS **2** used to warn people that a television show uses words that may offend some people

L. the written abbreviation of LAKE, used especially on maps

l **1** the written abbreviation of LITER **2** the written abbreviation of "line"

L1 /ˌɛl 'wʌn/ *n.* [C usually singular] TECHNICAL someone's first language

L2 /ˌɛl 'tu/ *n.* [C usually singular] TECHNICAL someone's second language, or another language that they are learning

LA **1** the written abbreviation of LOUISIANA **2** also **L.A.** the abbreviation of Los Angeles

la /lɑ/ *n.* [singular] the sixth note in a musical SCALE, according to the SOL-FA system

lab /læb/ S2 *n.* [C] **1** INFORMAL a LABORATORY **2** INFORMAL a Labrador

labels

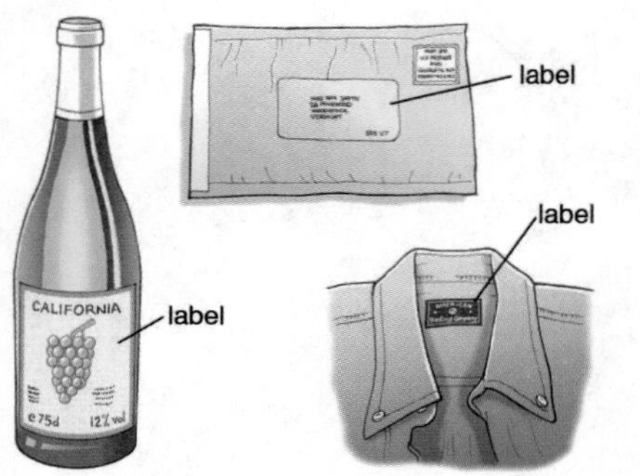

la·bel¹ /'leɪbəl/ Ac S2 W3 *n.* [C] **1** a piece of paper or other material that is attached to something and has information about that thing printed on it → see also STICKER: *He picked up the bottle and read the label.* | +**on** *the label on the box* | *It says "wash in warm water"* ***on the label.*** **2** also **record label** a company that produces records: *The group's next album will be on the Warner label.* **3** a company that designs and makes clothes, especially expensive ones, or a piece of the clothing that they make: *a designer label* **4** a word or phrase that is used to describe a person, group, or thing, but that is often unfair or not correct: *He was given the label "communist" for his opposition to the Vietnam war.* [**Origin:** 1200–1300 Old French **long narrow piece of cloth**]

label² Ac *v.* **labeled, labeling** also **labelled, labelling** [T] **1** to attach a label to something or write information on something: *Label the diagram clearly.* | **label sth sth** *The file was labeled "Top Secret."* | **label sth with sth** *She labeled each jar with its contents and the date.* **2** to use a particular word or phrase to describe someone or something, often unfairly or in an incorrect way: **label sb/sth (as) sth** *His teachers had labeled him a troublemaker.* ►see THESAURUS box at **call¹**

la·bi·a /'leɪbiə/ *n.* [plural] TECHNICAL the outer folds of the female sex organ

la·bi·al /'leɪbiəl/ *adj.* **1** TECHNICAL a labial speech sound is made using one or both lips **2** FORMAL relating to the lips —**labial** *n.* [C] → see also BILABIAL

la·bor¹ /'leɪbɚ/ Ac S2 W1 *n.* **1** [U] work, especially work using a lot of physical effort: *The garage charges $50 an hour for labor.* | *The job involves a lot of* ***manual labor*** (=physical work, especially using your hands). | *You don't look like you could do* ***physical labor.*** → see also HARD LABOR **2** [U] all the people who work for a company or in a country: *Much of the senator's support comes from* ***organized labor.*** | *a shortage of* ***skilled labor*** | *a labor dispute* | ***Labor costs*** (=the amount of money you must pay workers) *are increasing very slowly all over the country.* | *Companies have gone around the world in search of* ***cheap labor*** (=people who are paid low wages). | **child/slave labor** *The laws are designed to prevent child labor.* → see also LABOR FORCE **3** [singular, U] the process in which a baby is born by being pushed from its mother's body, or the period of time during which this happens: *Meg was* ***in labor*** *for 18 hours.* | *Doreen* ***went into labor*** *at 5:30.* | *The* ***labor pains*** *were incredible.* **4 a labor of love** something that is hard work but that you do because you want to very much **5 sb's labors** FORMAL a period of hard work: *Their labors produced a fabulous evening of entertainment.*

labor² Ac *v.* [I] **1** to work very hard, especially with your hands: **labor to do sth** *Villagers labored for five years to build the bridge.* **2** to work at doing something that is difficult: +**over** *He labored over the report all morning.* | **labor to do sth** *She labored to explain the reason for her actions.* **3 labor under a delusion/misconception/misapprehension etc.** to believe something that is not true while you do something: *We were laboring under the impression that we could make a difference.* **4** if a car, train, engine, person etc. labors, they work or move slowly and with difficulty: *The train labored up the steep hill.*

lab·ora·to·ry /'læbrəˌtɔri/ W3 *n. plural* **laboratories** [C] **1** a special room or building in which scientists do tests and RESEARCH: *The blood sample will be sent to a laboratory for analysis.* **2** part of a science course, especially at a college or university, that involves working in a laboratory [**Origin:** 1600–1700 Medieval Latin *laboratorium*, from Latin *laborare* **to work**] → see also LANGUAGE LABORATORY

'labor camp *n.* [C] a prison camp where prisoners have to do hard physical work

'Labor Day *n.* a public holiday in the U.S. and Canada on the first Monday in September

la·bored /'leɪbɚd/ Ac *adj.* showing signs of effort and difficulty: *the patient's labored breathing*

la·bor·er /'leɪbərɚ/ *n.* [C] someone whose job involves a lot of physical work: *a farm laborer*

'labor force *n.* **the labor force** all the people who work for a company or in a country

ˌlabor-in'tensive *adj.* a labor-intensive industry, type of work, or product needs a lot of workers or a lot of work: *The project is extremely labor-intensive.* → see also CAPITAL-INTENSIVE

la·bo·ri·ous /lə'bɔriəs/ *adj.* needing to be done slowly with a lot of effort, and often boring: *For Perry, writing is a laborious process.* —**laboriously** *adv.*

'labor ˌmarket *n.* [C] the combination of the workers available and the jobs available in one place at one time: *More married women are re-entering the labor market.*

'labor ˌmovement *n.* **the labor movement** the organizations, political parties etc. that represent working people

'labor reˌlations *n.* [plural] the relationship between employers and workers

'labor-ˌsaving *adj.* [only before noun] **a labor-saving device/gadget etc.** something that makes it easier for you to do a particular job

'labor ˌunion *n.* [C] an organization that represents the ordinary workers in a particular trade or profession, especially in meetings with employers

la·bour /ˈleɪbɚ/ Ac the British spelling of LABOR

Lab·ra·dor /ˈlæbrəˌdɔr/ also **ˌlabrador reˈtriever** *n.* [C] a large dog with fairly short black or yellow hair, often used in hunting wild animals and birds, or for guiding blind people

lab·y·rinth /ˈlæbəˌrɪnθ/ *n.* [C] **1** a large network of paths or passages that cross each other, making it very difficult to find your way SYN **maze**: +**of** *a labyrinth of underground tunnels* **2** something that is very complicated and difficult to understand: *a bureaucratic labyrinth* —**labyrinthine** /ˌlæbəˈrɪnθən, -ˈrɪnθaɪn/ *adj.*

lace¹ /leɪs/ *n.* **1** [U] a type of fine cloth made with patterns of very small holes: *a lace wedding veil* → see also LACY **2** [C usually plural] a string that is pulled through special holes in shoes or clothing and tied, in order to pull the edges together and fasten them → see also SHOELACE → see picture at SHOE¹ [**Origin:** 1100–1200 Old French *laz* **net, string**, from Latin *laqueus* **trap**]

lace² *v.* **1** [T] to pass a string or lace through holes in something such as a pair of shoes **2** [I,T] also **lace up** to pull something together or fasten something by tying a lace, or to be pulled together or fastened in this way: *Dave laced his running shoes and ran off.* | *The shirt laces up the back.* **3** to add a small amount of something such as alcohol, a SPICE, a drug, or poison to a drink or food: **lace sth with sth** *Someone had laced her drink with rat poison.* **4 be laced with sth** if a book, lesson, speech etc. is laced with something, it has a lot of a particular quality all through it: *Their conversations are laced with swearing.* **5** to weave or twist something together: *Hannah laced her fingers together.*

lac·er·ate /ˈlæsəˌreɪt/ *v.* [T] to badly cut or tear the skin or flesh: *The rope lacerated his forehead and scalp.*

lac·er·a·tion /ˌlæsəˈreɪʃən/ *n.* [C,U] TECHNICAL a serious cut in your skin or flesh: +**to** *multiple lacerations to the upper arms*

ˈlace-up *adj.* lace-up shoes are fastened with LACES —**lace-up** *n.* [C usually plural]

lace·work /ˈleɪswɚk/ *n.* [U] **1** something that is made out of lace **2** something that forms a complicated pattern: *the delicate lacework of feathers*

lach·ry·mal /ˈlækrəməl/ *adj.* TECHNICAL relating to tears: *lachrymal glands*

lach·ry·mose /ˈlækrəˌmoʊs/ *adj.* FORMAL **1** making you feel sad: *a lachrymose drama* **2** often crying

lack¹ /læk/ W2 *n.* **1** [singular, U] the state of not having something, or of not having enough of it: +**of** *a lack of affordable housing* | *Robbery charges were dropped **for lack of** evidence* (=because there was not enough). | **a total/complete/distinct etc. lack of sth** *a total lack of interest* | *There's **no lack of** holiday spirit around the high school* (=there is a lot of it). **2 for lack of a better word/phrase/term etc.** SPOKEN said when you are using a word or expression that you do not think is completely appropriate: *It was, for lack of a better word, fate.*

lack² W2 *v.* **1** [T] to not have something, or to not have enough of it: *Kevin lacks confidence.* **2 not lack for sth** to have a lot of something: *The resistance movement will not lack for funds.* [**Origin:** 1200–1300 Middle Dutch *laken*]

lack·a·dai·si·cal /ˌlækəˈdeɪzɪkəl/ *adj.* not showing enough interest in something or not putting enough effort into it: *a lackadaisical approach to security* [**Origin:** 1700–1800 *lackaday* expression of sadness (17–19 centuries), from *alack the day*]

lack·ey /ˈlæki/ *n. plural* **lackeys** [C] DISAPPROVING someone who is always too eager and willing to do what someone in authority wants them to do

lack·ing /ˈlækɪŋ/ *adj.* [not before noun] **1** not having enough of a particular quality, skill etc.: *His performance was lacking.* | +**in** *She certainly is not lacking in determination.* | **sadly/sorely lacking** *Support for the team has been sadly lacking this year.* **2** not existing or available: *Financial backing for the project is still lacking.*

lack·lus·ter /ˈlækˌlʌstɚ/ *adj.* not very exciting, impressive etc. SYN **dull**: *lackluster economic growth*

la·con·ic /ləˈkɑnɪk/ *adj.* FORMAL tending to use only a few words when you talk [**Origin:** 1500–1600 Latin *laconicus* **of Sparta**, from Greek *lakonikos*; because the people of ancient Sparta were famous for not using many words]

lac·quer¹ /ˈlækɚ/ *n.* [U] a clear liquid painted onto metal or wood to form a hard shiny surface [**Origin:** 1500–1600 Portuguese *lacré* **substance for keeping a letter or document closed**, from *laca* **hard substance produced by an insect**]

lacquer² *v.* [T] to cover something with lacquer: *The furniture had been lacquered.*

la·crosse /ləˈkrɔs/ *n.* [U] a game played on a field by two teams of ten players, in which each player has a long stick with a net on the end of it and uses this to throw, catch, and carry a small ball [**Origin:** 1700–1800 Canadian French *la crosse* **the crosier** (= long stick with a curved end carried by a Christian priest)]

lac·tate /ˈlækteɪt/ *v.* [I] BIOLOGY if a woman or female

laboratory

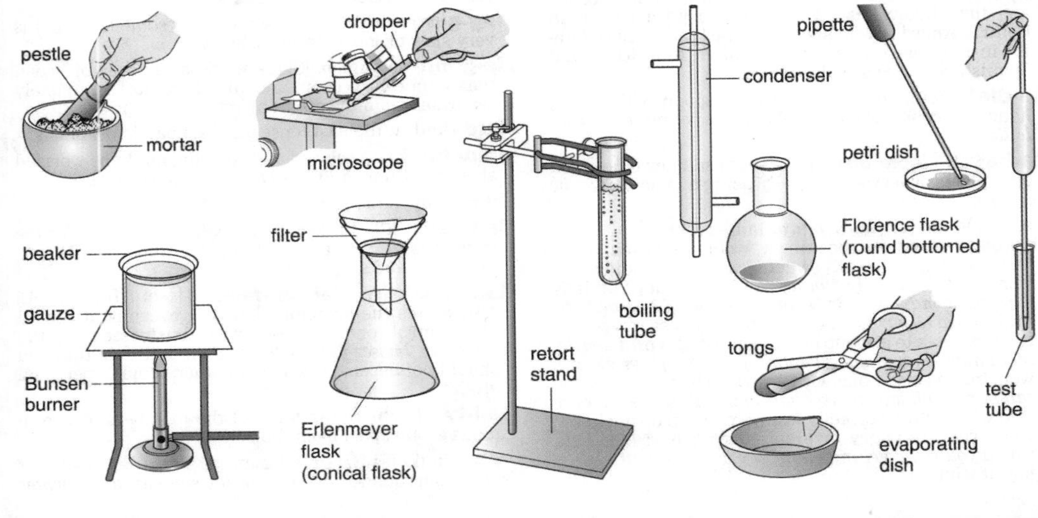

animal lactates, milk is produced in her breasts or comes out of her breasts —**lactation** /læk'teɪʃən/ *n.* [U]

lac·tic /'læktɪk/ *adj.* TECHNICAL relating to milk

,lactic 'acid *n.* [U] BIOLOGY an acid produced by muscles after exercising or found in sour milk, wine, and some other foods

lac·tose /'læktoʊs/ *n.* [U] CHEMISTRY a type of sugar found in milk

la·cu·na /lə'kunə/ *n. plural* **lacunae** /-ni/ or **lacunas** [C] FORMAL an empty space where something is missing, especially in a piece of writing

lac·y /'leɪsi/ *adj. comparative* **lacier**, *superlative* **laciest** made of LACE, or looking like LACE: *lacy underwear* | *trees with lacy leaves*

lad /læd/ *n.* [C] OLD-FASHIONED a boy or young man → see also LASS

lad·der /'lædɚ/ S3 *n.* [C] **1** a piece of equipment used for climbing up to high places, consisting of two long pieces of wood, metal, or rope, joined to each other by RUNGS (=steps): *She **climbed the ladder** to the roof.* → see also ROPE LADDER, STEPLADDER **2** a series of activities or jobs you have to do in order to gradually become more powerful or important: **the corporate/career/social ladder** *Stevens worked his way to the top of the corporate ladder.* [**Origin:** Old English *hlæder*]

lad·en /'leɪdn/ *adj.* **1** LITERARY heavily loaded with something, or containing a lot of something: **+with** *cakes and pastries laden with cream* **2 laden with sth** having a lot of a particular quality, thing etc.: *She was laden with doubts about the affair.*

-laden /leɪdn/ [in adjectives] **1** LITERARY heavily loaded with something, or containing a lot of something: *snow-laden branches* **2 debt-laden/detail-laden/value-laden etc.** having a lot of a particular quality, thing etc.: *a debt-laden company*

la·di·da¹, lah-di-dah /ˌlɑ di 'dɑ◂ / *adj., adv.* INFORMAL talking and behaving as if you think you are better than other people: *a la-di-da attitude*

la·di·da², lah-di-dah *interjection* INFORMAL said when you think someone else is trying to make themselves seem more important or impressive than they really are: *"I'm going to the opera tonight." "Well, la-di-da."*

L

'ladies' man *n.* [C] a man who likes to spend time with women and thinks they enjoy being with him

'ladies' room *n.* [C] a RESTROOM (=room with a toilet) for women in a public place

lad·ing /'leɪdɪŋ/ *n.* [C,U] → see BILL OF LADING

La·di·no /lə'dinoʊ/ *n.* **1** [U] a language related to Spanish that is spoken by Jews in southeastern Europe and the Middle East **2** also **ladino** [C] a person in Central America who speaks Spanish and whose family in the past was a mix of Native Americans and Spanish people → see also MESTIZO

la·dle¹ /'leɪdl/ *n.* [C] a large deep spoon with a long handle, used for lifting liquid out of a container: *a soup ladle*

ladle² also **ladle out** *v.* [T] to serve soup or other food onto plates or bowls, especially using a ladle: *Ladle the soup over rice.*

la·dy /'leɪdi/ S1 W2 *n. plural* **ladies** [C]

1 WOMAN a) a word meaning a "woman", used in order to be polite, especially when you do not know the woman: *Tell the lady "thank you."* | **a young/old lady** *The young lady behind the counter asked if I needed any help.* → see also CLEANING LADY **b) ladies** SPOKEN FORMAL used to speak to a group of women: ***Ladies and gentlemen**, may I have your attention please?* **c)** APPROVING a woman, especially one with a strong character: *Sharon can be a tough lady to negotiate with.* **d)** SPOKEN, IMPOLITE said when talking directly to a woman you do not know, when you are angry or annoyed with her: *Hey, lady, would you mind getting out of my way?* ▸see THESAURUS box at **woman**

2 POLITE WOMAN a woman who behaves in a polite and formal way: *Sheila always tries to be a lady.*

3 a/sb's lady friend OFTEN HUMOROUS a woman that a man is having a romantic relationship with SYN **girlfriend**: *Henry's new lady friend*

4 Lady the wife or daughter of a British NOBLEMAN or the wife of a KNIGHT, also used as a title: *Lady Macbeth* | *lords and ladies*

5 a lady of the evening a polite expression meaning a PROSTITUTE, used to avoid saying this directly

6 the lady of the house OLD-FASHIONED the most important woman in a house, usually the mother of a family

7 a lady of leisure OFTEN HUMOROUS a woman who does not work and has a lot of free time: *So you're a lady of leisure now that the kids are at school?*

8 WIFE/GIRLFRIEND OLD-FASHIONED a man's wife or female friend: *the captain and his lady*

[**Origin:** Old English *hlæfdige*, from *hlaf* **bread** + *-dige* **one who kneads**] → see also BAG LADY, FIRST LADY, OLD LADY, OUR LADY

la·dy·bug /'leɪdiˌbʌg/ *n.* [C] a small round BEETLE (=a type of insect) that is usually red with black spots

la·dy·fin·ger /'leɪdiˌfɪŋgɚ/ *n.* [C] a small cake shaped like a finger, used in some DESSERTS

,lady-in-'waiting *n.* [C] a woman who takes care of and serves a queen or PRINCESS

'lady-ˌkiller *n.* [C] INFORMAL a man who is very attractive to women and uses it to his advantage

la·dy·like /'leɪdiˌlaɪk/ *adj.* OLD-FASHIONED behaving in the polite, quiet way that was once believed to be typical of or appropriate for women: *It's not ladylike to swear.*

la·dy·ship /'leɪdiˌʃɪp/ *n.* **your/her ladyship** used as a way of speaking to or talking about a woman with the title of Lady

La·fa·yette /ˌlɑfeɪ'ɛt/, **Mar·quis de** /mɑr'ki də/ (1757–1834) a French politician who supported the Americans in the American Revolutionary War and was active as a MODERATE in the French Revolution

La·fitte /lə'fit/, **Jean** /ʒɑn/ (?1780–?1826) a French PIRATE

la Fon·taine /lɑ fɑn'tɛn/, **Jean de** /ʒɑn də/ (1621–1695) a French poet

lag¹ /læg/ *v.* **lagged, lagging** [I] to move or develop more slowly than other things, people, situations etc.: *This year, private fund-raising for the museum has lagged.* | **+behind** *Some of the younger children were lagging behind.*

lag² *n.* [C] a delay or period of waiting between one event and a second event → see also JET LAG

la·ger /'lɑgɚ/ *n.* [U] a type of light-colored beer [**Origin:** 1800–1900 German *lagerbier* **beer made to be stored**, from *lager* **storehouse** + *bier* **beer**]

lag·gard /'lægɚd/ *n.* [C] someone or something that is very slow or late —**laggardly** *adj.*

la·goon /lə'gun/ *n.* [C] EARTH SCIENCE an area of ocean that is not very deep, and that is almost completely separated from the ocean by rocks, sand, or CORAL

laid /leɪd/ *v.* the past tense and past participle of LAY

,laid-'back *adj.* relaxed and seeming not to be worried about anything: *a laid-back attitude toward work*

lain /leɪn/ *v.* the past participle of LIE

lair /lɛr/ *n.* [C] **1** a secret place where you can hide: *the smugglers' lair* **2** BIOLOGY the place where a wild animal hides and sleeps

lais·sez-faire, laisser-faire /ˌlɛseɪ 'fɛr/ *n.* [U] **1** ECONOMICS the principle that the government should not control or INTERFERE with businesses or the ECONOMY: *laissez-faire policies* **2** the attitude that you should not become involved in other people's personal affairs

la·i·ty /'leɪəṭi/ *n.* **the laity** all the members of a religious group apart from the priests

lake /leɪk/ S2 W3 *n.* [C] EARTH SCIENCE a large area of water surrounded by land: *In the summer, we go water* *skiing on the lake.* | *Lake Erie* [**Origin:** 1200–1300 Old French *lac*, from Latin *lacus*] → see picture on page A31

lake·bed /ˈleɪkbɛd/ *n.* [C] the bottom of a lake

lake·front /ˈleɪkfrʌnt/ *n.* [singular] the land along the edge of a lake: *a cabin on the lakefront* | *lakefront property*

lake·side /ˈleɪksaɪd/ also **lake·shore** /ˈleɪkʃɔr/ *n.* [singular] the land beside a lake: *a lakeside resort*

La·lique, Re·né /lɑˈlik, rəˈneɪ/ (1860–1945) a French designer famous for his jewelry and glass objects in the ART NOUVEAU style

lam /læm/ *n.* **on the lam** INFORMAL escaping or hiding from someone, especially the police: *He's on the lam in Mexico, I think.*

la·ma /ˈlɑmə/ *n.* [C] a Buddhist priest in Tibet or Mongolia

La·ma·ism /ˈlɑməˌɪzəm/ *n.* [U] a form of the Buddhist religion common in Tibet or Mongolia

La·marck, Jean /ləˈmɑrk, ʒɑn/ (1744–1829) a French scientist who developed a system of ideas about EVOLUTION

La·maze /ləˈmeɪz/ *n.* [U] a method of controlling pain by breathing in a special way, used by women who want to give birth to a baby without using drugs

lamb¹ /læm/ *n.* **1** [C] BIOLOGY a young sheep **2** [U] the meat of a young sheep: *roast lamb* **3** [C] SPOKEN someone gentle and lovable, especially a child: *Oh, he's asleep now, the little lamb.* **4 like a lamb** quietly and without any argument: *Suzie went off to school like a lamb today.* **5 like a lamb to the slaughter** used when someone goes quietly and willingly to do something dangerous because they do not realize it or have no choice [**Origin:** Old English]

lamb² *v.* [I] to give birth to lambs: *The ewes are lambing this week.*

lam·ba·da /lɑmˈbɑdə/ *n.* [singular, U] a DISCO dance from Brazil in which two people hold each other closely and move their bodies at the same time [**Origin:** 1900–2000 Brazilian Portuguese **beating**]

lam·baste, lambast /læmˈbeɪst, ˈlæmbeɪst/ *v.* [T] to attack or criticize someone very strongly, usually in public: *Critics lambasted the president for his failure to act quickly.*

lamb·skin /ˈlæmˌskɪn/ *n.* **1** [C,U] the skin of a lamb, with the wool still on it: *a lambskin jacket* **2** [U] leather made from the skin of lambs

lambs·wool, lamb's wool /ˈlæmzˌwʊl/ *n.* [U] very soft wool that comes from lambs: *a lambswool sweater*

lame¹ /leɪm/ *adj.* **1** unable to walk well because your leg or foot is injured or weak: *a lame dog* **2** INFORMAL a lame explanation or excuse does not sound very believable: *I don't want to hear any of your lame excuses for being late.* → see also LAMELY **3** SLANG boring or not very good: *The party was lame.* —**lameness** *n.* [U]

lame² *v.* [T usually passive] to make a person or animal unable to walk well

la·mé /lɑˈmeɪ, læ-/ *n.* [U] cloth containing gold or silver threads: *a gold lamé dress*

lame·brain /ˈleɪmbreɪn/ *n.* [C] INFORMAL someone you think is stupid —**lamebrained** *adj.*

ˌlame ˈduck *n.* [C] **lame duck president/governor/legislature etc.** a president, governor, legislature etc. with no real power because their period in office will soon end

lame·ly /ˈleɪmli/ *adv.* if you say something lamely, you do not sound confident and other people find it difficult to believe you: *"It wasn't my responsibility," he added lamely.*

la·ment¹ /ləˈmɛnt/ *v.* [I,T] **1** to express annoyance or disappointment about something you think is unsatisfactory or unfair: *Teachers often **lament the fact that** students lack motivation.* **2** FORMAL to express feelings of sadness about something: *The couple are still lamenting the loss of their daughter.*

lament² *n.* [C] **1** ENG. LANG. ARTS a song, poem, or something that you say, that expresses a feeling of sadness: *A lone piper played a lament.* **2** a complaint about something

la·ment·a·ble /ləˈmɛntəbəl, æmən-/ *adj.* FORMAL very unsatisfactory or disappointing: *The policy has been a lamentable failure.* —**lamentably** *adv.*

lam·en·ta·tion /ˌlæmənˈteɪʃən/ *n.* [C,U] FORMAL **1** a complaint about something, especially something that used to be better in the past: *lamentation about the state of American democracy* **2** something you say or do which expresses sadness about death or loss

Lam·en·ta·tions /ˌlæmənˈteɪʃənz/ a book in the Old Testament of the Christian Bible

lame-o /ˈleɪm oʊ/ *n.* [C] SLANG someone who is boring and not very good at doing anything

lam·i·nate /ˈlæməˌneɪt, -nɪt/ *n.* [C,U] laminated material

lam·i·nat·ed /ˈlæməˌneɪtɪd/ *adj.* **1** covered with a layer of thin plastic: *a laminated ID card* **2** laminated material has several thin sheets joined on top of each other: *a laminated wood table top* —**laminate** /ˈlæməˌneɪt/ *v.* [T]

lamps

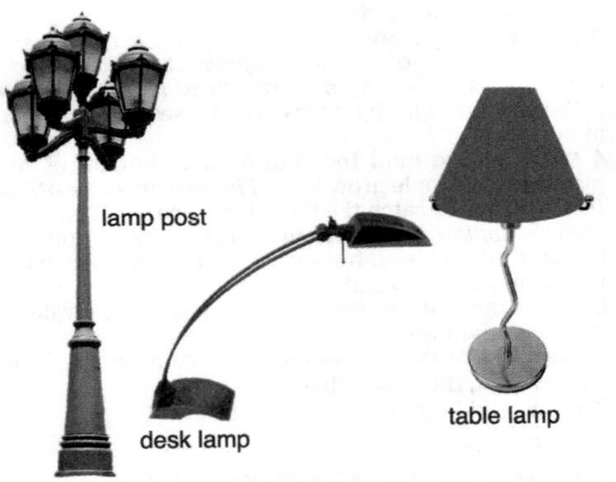

lamp /læmp/ S3 *n.* [C] **1** an object that produces light by using electricity, oil, or gas: *a desk lamp* → see also FLOOR LAMP, SAFETY LAMP **2** a piece of electrical equipment used to provide a special type of heat, especially as a medical treatment: *an infrared lamp* [**Origin:** 1100–1200 Old French *lampe*, from Latin *lampas*, from Greek *lampein* **to shine**] → see also SUNLAMP

lamp·black /ˈlæmpˌblæk/ *n.* [U] a fine black substance made from SOOT (=the black powder made by burning something) that is used in making matches, bombs etc. and in coloring things

lamp·light /ˈlæmp-laɪt/ *n.* [U] the soft light produced by a lamp

lamp·light·er /ˈlæmpˌlaɪtɚ/ *n.* [C] someone in the past whose job was to light lamps in the street

lam·poon /læmˈpun/ *v.* [T] to criticize someone such as a politician in a humorous way that makes them seem stupid or silly, in a piece of writing, a play etc. SYN **satirize**: *The senator was lampooned by the press.* [**Origin:** 1600–1700 French *lampon*] —**lampoon** *n.* [C]

lamp·post, lamp post /ˈlæmp-poʊst/ *n.* [C] a pole supporting a light over a street: *He tied the dog to the lamppost and went inside.* → see also STREETLIGHT

lam·prey /ˈlæmpri, -preɪ/ *n.* [C] BIOLOGY a type of small fish that attaches itself to larger fish

lamp·shade /ˈlæmpʃeɪd/ *n.* [C] a cover put over a lamp to reduce or direct its light

LAN /læn, ˌɛl eɪ ˈɛn/ *n.* [C] **local area network** COMPUTERS a small NETWORK of computers linked together within the same building or small area

lance¹ /læns/ *n.* [C] a long thin pointed weapon that was used in the past by soldiers riding on horses

L

lance² *v.* [T] to cut a small hole in someone's flesh with a sharp instrument to let out PUS (=yellow liquid produced by infection): *Lance the boil with a sterilized needle.*

ˌlance ˈcorporal *n.* [C] a low rank in the Marines, or someone who has this rank

Lan·ce·lot, Sir /ˈlænsəˌlɑt/ in old European stories, the most famous of King Arthur's knights, who had a romantic relationship with Arthur's wife, Guinevere

lan·cet /ˈlænsɪt/ *n.* [C] **1** a small very sharp pointed knife with two cutting edges, used by doctors to cut flesh **2 lancet arch/window** TECHNICAL a tall narrow ARCH or window that is pointed at the top

land¹ /lænd/ S2 W1 *n.*
1 GROUND [U] an area of ground, especially when used for farming or building: *A mall is being built on the land near the lake.* | *500 acres of land* | *high land prices* | **a piece/plot of land** *He bought a small plot of land and built a house.* ▸see THESAURUS box at **ground¹**
2 NOT OCEAN [U] the solid dry part of the Earth's surface, not the ocean or other water: *Frogs live **on land** and in water.* | *Troops arrived by sea and **by land**.* | *I was relieved to be back **on dry land**.* ▸see THESAURUS box at **earth**
3 COUNTRY [C] LITERARY a country or place: *a journey to foreign lands* | +**of** *a land of opportunity* | *the land of the cowboys* | *He longed to return to his **native land*** (=the country where he was born). ▸see THESAURUS box at **country¹**
4 NOT CITY the land the countryside thought of as a place where people grow food: *The peasants **live off the land*** (=grow or catch the food they need). | *About 4% of the U.S. population **works the land*** (=grows crops).
5 a land of milk and honey an imaginary place where life is easy and pleasant
6 in the land of the living SPOKEN, HUMOROUS awake, or not sick anymore
7 the land of nod OLD-FASHIONED if someone is in the land of nod, they are asleep
[**Origin:** Old English]

land² S3 W2 *v.*
1 ARRIVE BY BOAT/PLANE [I] to arrive somewhere in an airplane, boat etc.: *What time do we land?* | +**on/in/at etc.** *In 1969, the first men landed on the moon.* ▸see THESAURUS box at **arrive**
2 AIRPLANE [I,T] if an airplane lands or if a pilot lands it, it moves down onto the ground: *The pilot couldn't land the plane because of the fog.*
3 FALL/COME DOWN [I always + adv./prep.] to come down through the air onto something: +**in/on/under etc.** *A large branch landed on car.* | *He fell over and landed in a puddle.*
4 JOB/CONTRACT ETC. [T] INFORMAL to succeed in getting a job, contract etc. that was difficult to get: *Donna managed to land a great job with a law firm.* | **land yourself sth** *Bill just landed himself a part in a Broadway show.*
5 land sb in trouble/court/debt etc. to do something that causes someone to have serious problems or be in a difficult situation: *Elaine's reckless driving landed her in the hospital.*
6 BIRDS/INSECTS [I] to come onto the ground, a tree, etc. after being in the air: *The bird landed on top of the statue.*
7 FISH [T] to catch a fish: *We landed over 200 fish that day.*
8 land on your feet to get into a good situation again, after having problems: *He's having a tough time, but I'm sure he'll land on his feet.*
9 land a punch/blow etc. to succeed in hitting someone: *She managed to land one good blow to the side of his head.*
10 land on sb's desk if something lands on someone's desk, it is given to them to do or deal with, especially when it is difficult or unexpected: *The contract landed on my desk yesterday.*
11 GOODS/PEOPLE [T] to put something or someone on land from an airplane or boat: *They plan to land 3,000 troops in the region.*

Land /lænd/, **Ed·win Her·bert** /ˈɛdwɪn ˈhɚbɚt/ (1909–1991) a U.S. scientist who invented the Polaroid treatment of glass and the Polaroid camera

ˈland bridge *n.* [C] a narrow piece of land that connects two large areas of land: *Thousands of years ago, people crossed the land bridge between Asia and North America.*

land·ed /ˈlændɪd/ *adj.* [only before noun] OLD-FASHIONED **1** having owned a lot of land for a long time: *the landed aristocracy* **2** including a lot of land: *landed estates*

land·fall /ˈlændfɔl/ *n.* [C usually singular] the act of reaching land again after a trip by ocean or air: *We **made landfall*** (=arrived) *that night.*

land·fill /ˈlændfɪl/ *n.* **1** [C] a place where waste is buried under the ground **2** [U] the practice of burying waste under the ground, or the waste buried in this way

land·form /ˈlændfɔrm/ *n.* [C] a natural shape or type of land on the Earth's surface

ˈland grab *n.* [C] the act of someone powerful, such as the government, taking land, especially in an unfair or illegal way

land·hold·er /ˈlændˌhoʊldɚ/ *n.* [C] the person who owns a particular piece of land

ˈland ˌholdings, landholdings *n.* [plural] the land that is owned by someone

land·ing /ˈlændɪŋ/ *n.* [C] **1** the action of arriving on land, or of making something such as an airplane or boat come onto land → see also TAKEOFF: *the first landing of settlers in America* | **crash/emergency landing** (=a sudden landing made by an airplane because it is having trouble) **2** the floor at the top of a set of stairs or between two sets of stairs

ˈlanding charge *n.* [C] TECHNICAL money that you have to pay when goods are unloaded at a port

ˈlanding ˌcraft *n.* [C] a flat-bottomed boat that opens at one end to allow soldiers and equipment to come directly onto a shore

ˈlanding gear *n.* [U] an aircraft's wheels and wheel supports

ˈlanding pad *n.* [C] a special area where a HELICOPTER can come down

ˈlanding strip *n.* [C] a level piece of ground that has been prepared for airplanes to use

land·la·dy /ˈlændˌleɪdi/ *n.* *plural* **landladies** [C] the woman who rents you a room, building etc.

land·less /ˈlændlɪs/ *adj.* owning no land —**landless** *n.* [plural]

land·line /ˈlændlaɪn/ *n.* [C] an ordinary telephone line that people have in their homes, which is connected to the telephone system by a wire, rather than the system of electronic signals that are used by CELL PHONES

land·locked /ˈlændlɑkt/ *adj.* a landlocked country, state etc. is surrounded by other countries, states etc. and has no coast

land·lord /ˈlændlɔrd/ *n.* [C] someone who rents you a room, building etc.

land·lub·ber /ˈlændˌlʌbɚ/ *n.* [C] OLD-FASHIONED someone who does not have much experience with the ocean or ships

land·mark /ˈlændmɑrk/ *n.* [C] **1** something that is easy to recognize, such as a tall tree or building, and that helps you know where you are: *The Washington Monument is a popular historical landmark.* **2** one of the most important events, changes, or discoveries that influences someone or something: *a landmark in the history of medicine* | *a landmark court victory*

land·mass /ˈlændmæs/ *n.* [C] EARTH SCIENCE a large area of land

land·mine /ˈlændmaɪn/ *n.* [C] a type of bomb hidden in the ground that explodes when someone walks or drives over it

ˈland ˌoffice *n.* [C] **1** POLITICS a government office in the U.S. that records the sales of all public land **2 do (a) land-office business** to be very busy and make a lot of money

land·own·er /ˈlændˌoʊnɚ/ *n.* [C] someone who owns land, especially a large amount —**landowning** *adj.* —**landownership** *n.* [U]

ˈland redistriˌbution *n.* [U] ECONOMICS when land is taken away from people who own large farms and given to people who do not have any land at all or have very little land

ˈland reˌform *n.* [C,U] HISTORY measures that are taken, especially by a government, to divide up farm land so that more people own some of it

Lan·dry /ˈlændri/, **Tom** /tɑm/ (1924–2000) a U.S. football COACH

land·scape¹ /ˈlændskeɪp/ W3 *n.* **1** [C] an area of COUNTRYSIDE or land, considered in terms of how attractive it is to look at: *the rugged landscape of the West* ►see THESAURUS box at **country¹** **2** [C] a photograph or painting showing an area of COUNTRYSIDE or land: *I paint mostly landscapes.* **3** [U] the practice of painting or drawing landscapes in art: *Landscape is her main skill.* **4 the political/intellectual etc. landscape** the general situation in which a particular activity takes place: *The topic dominated the cultural landscape.* **5** [U] LANDSCAPE MODE

landscape² *v.* [T often passive] to make a park, garden etc. look attractive and interesting by planting trees, bushes, flowers etc. —**landscaping** *n.* [U]

ˌlandscape ˈarchitecture *n.* [U] the profession or art of planning the way an area of land looks, including the roads, buildings, and planted areas —**landscape architect** *n.* [C]

ˌlandscape ˈgardening *n.* [U] the profession or art of arranging gardens and parks so that they look attractive —**landscape gardener** *n.* [C]

ˈlandscape ˌmode *n.* [C] a way of printing a document or picture so that the longer edges are at the top and bottom → see also PORTRAIT MODE

land·scap·er /ˈlændˌskeɪpɚ/ *n.* [C] someone whose job is to arrange plants, paths etc. in gardens and parks

land·slide /ˈlændslaɪd/ *n.* [C] **1** EARTH SCIENCE the sudden falling of a lot of earth or rocks down the side of a hill: *Heavy rains caused serious landslides.* **2** POLITICS a victory in an election in which one person or party gets a lot more votes than all the others: *a landslide election victory* | *Lang won* ***by a landslide***.

Land·stei·ner /ˈlændˌstaɪnɚ/, **Karl** /kɑrl/ (1868–1943) a U.S. scientist who discovered the four main human BLOOD TYPES

land·ward /ˈlændwɚd/ *adj.* facing toward the land and away from the ocean: *the landward side of the hill* —**landward** *adv.*

lane /leɪn/ S3 *n.* [C] **1** one of the parts of a main road that are divided by painted lines to keep traffic apart: *That idiot* ***changed lanes*** *without signaling.* | *Cars in* ***the fast lane*** *were traveling at over 80 miles an hour.* ►see THESAURUS box at **road** **2** one of the narrow parallel areas marked for each competitor in a running or swimming race: *You must stay in your lane.* **3** a line or course along which ships or aircraft regularly travel between ports or airports: *busy shipping lanes* **4** a wooden path on which a BOWLING BALL is rolled in a BOWLING ALLEY **5** a narrow road between fields or houses, especially in the COUNTRYSIDE **6** used in street names: *Park Lane* [**Origin:** Old English *lanu*] → see also **a walk/trip down memory lane** at MEMORY (9)

Lange /lændʒ/, **Dor·o·the·a** /ˌdɔrəˈθiə/ (1895–1965) a U.S. PHOTOGRAPHER

Lang·ley /ˈlæŋli/, **Samuel** (1834–1906) a U.S. scientist who built the first model aircraft that could fly successfully

lan·guage /ˈlæŋgwɪdʒ/ S1 W1 *n.*
1 ENGLISH/FRENCH/ARABIC ETC. [C,U] a system of communication by written or spoken words which is used by the people of a particular country or area: *the Japanese language* | *How many* ***languages*** *do you* ***speak?*** | **sb's first/native language** *Kim's native language is Korean.* | *He speaks English as a* ***second language***. | *Every student has to study at least one* ***foreign language***. | *The* ***official language*** *of many African countries is English.* | *Latin is a* ***dead language*** (=language that is no longer spoken).

THESAURUS

dialect a form of a language that is spoken in one area, which is different from the way it is spoken in other areas: *Cantonese is only one of many Chinese dialects.*
accent a way of pronouncing words that someone has because of where she or he was born or lives: *a New Jersey accent*
tongue a particular language: *Winnie started school knowing only her native tongue.*
slang very informal and sometimes offensive language, used especially by people who belong to a particular group: *Soldiers have their own slang.*
jargon technical words and phrases used by people in a particular profession: *computer jargon*
terminology FORMAL the technical words or expressions that are used in a particular subject: *the basic terminology used by geologists*

2 COMMUNICATION [U] the use of written or spoken words to communicate: *the origin of language* | *language skills*
3 COMPUTERS [C,U] COMPUTERS a system of instructions and commands for operating a computer: *a programming language*
4 STYLE/TYPE OF WORDS [U] the type of words and the style used in a particular type of writing or by people in a particular job or activity: *poetic language* | +**of** *the language of science*
5 SWEARING [U] INFORMAL words that most people think are offensive: *You never heard such language! It was disgusting.* | *Ben!* ***Watch your language*** (=stop swearing)*!*
6 strong language a) angry words used to tell people exactly what you mean **b)** words that most people think are offensive SYN **swearing**
7 speak the same language if two people speak the same language, they have similar attitudes and opinions
8 SOUNDS/SIGNS/ACTIONS [U] signs, movements, or sounds that express ideas or feelings: +**of** *the language of music*
[**Origin:** 1200–1300 Old French *langue* **tongue, language**, from Latin *lingua*] → see also BODY LANGUAGE, SIGN LANGUAGE

ˈlanguage ˌlaboratory also **ˈlanguage ˌlab** INFORMAL *n.* [C] a room in a school or college where you can learn to speak a foreign language by listening to TAPES and recording your own voice

lan·guid /ˈlæŋgwɪd/ *adj.* **1** moving slowly and involving very little energy: *a languid motion* **2** slow and peaceful: *a languid summer afternoon by the pool* —**languidly** *adv.*

lan·guish /ˈlæŋgwɪʃ/ *v.* [I] FORMAL **1** to remain in a bad condition without improving or developing: *The housing market continues to languish.* **2** to be forced to stay somewhere that makes you unhappy: +**in** *Tran spent five long years languishing in refugee camps.* **3** LITERARY to become unhappy or sick because you want someone or something very much

lan·guor /ˈlæŋgɚ/ *n.* LITERARY **1** [C,U] a pleasant feeling of tiredness or lack of strength **2** [U] pleasant or heavy stillness of the air: *the languor of a hot afternoon* —**languorous** *adj.* —**languorously** *adv.*

lank /læŋk/ *adj.* **1** lank hair is thin, straight, and unattractive ►see THESAURUS box at **hair** **2** lanky

lank·y /ˈlæŋki/ *adj.* tall and thin in an awkward way: *a tall lanky young man* —**lankiness** *n.* [U]

lan·o·lin /ˈlænl-ɪn/ *n.* [U] an oil that is in sheep's wool and is used in skin creams

Lan·sing /ˈlænsɪŋ/ the capital city of the U.S. state of Michigan

lan·tern /ˈlæntɚn/ *n.* [C] **1** a lamp that you can carry,

L

consisting of a metal or glass container surrounding a flame or light **2** TECHNICAL a structure at the top of a tower or LIGHTHOUSE that has windows on all sides [**Origin:** 1200–1300 French *lanterne*, from Latin, from Greek *lampter*, from *lampein* **to shine**] → see also CHINESE LANTERN, MAGIC LANTERN

ˈlantern-jawed *adj.* having a long narrow jaw and cheeks that sink in

lan·yard /ˈlænyəd/ *n.* [C] **1** a short piece of rope or steel, used on a ship to tie things **2** a thick string that you can hang around your neck to carry something on, such as a WHISTLE

La·os /laʊs, ˈlɑoʊs, ˈleɪɑs/ a country in southeastern Asia that is south of China and north of Cambodia

La·o·tian /leɪˈoʊʃən, ˈlaʊʃən/ *adj.* **1** relating to or coming from Laos **2** relating to the language of Laos —**Laotian** *n.* [C]

Lao-tzu /laʊ ˈdzʌ/ (6th century B.C.) a Chinese religious leader who is believed to have started Taoism

lap¹ /læp/ S3 *n.* [C] **1** BIOLOGY the upper part of your legs when you are sitting down: *Teddy sat **on** his mother's **lap**.* | *She sat with her hands **in her lap**.* **2** a single trip around a race track or between the two ends of a pool: *Every morning she swims fifty laps in the pool.* | *After the race, he took a **victory lap*** (=a lap to celebrate winning). **3 drop/dump sth in sb's lap** SPOKEN to make someone else deal with something difficult that is your responsibility: *My boss just dumps these problems in my lap and expects me to deal with them.* **4 drop/fall into sb's lap** also **land in sb's lap** if something drops into your lap, it suddenly happens to you or is given to you without you having to make any effort **5 in the lap of luxury** having a very easy and comfortable life with a lot of money, expensive possessions etc. [**Origin:** (1, 3–5) Old English *Pæppa*]

lap² *v.* **lapped, lapping** **1** [I,T] if water laps something or laps against something such as the shore or a boat, it moves against it or hits it in small waves: **+at/over/against etc.** *We sat on the shore and let the warm water lap over our feet.* **2** [I,T] if an animal laps something, it drinks it by making small tongue movements SYN **lap up** **3 a)** [T] to pass a competitor in a race after having completed a whole lap more than they have: *Schumacher lapped everyone in the Grand Prix.* **b)** [I,T] to make a single trip around a track, race course etc. in a particular time **4** [I,T] TECHNICAL if one thing laps another, a part of one covers part of the other SYN **overlap** **5** [T always + adv./prep.] LITERARY to fold or wrap something around something else —**lapping** *n.* [U]

lap sth ↔ **up** *phr. v.* **1** to enjoy or believe something without criticizing or doubting it at all: *The children lapped up their grandfather's stories.* **2** if an animal laps something up, it drinks it by making small tongue movements **3** to drink all of something eagerly

lap·a·ro·scope /ˈlæpərəˌskoʊp/ *n.* [C] TECHNICAL a piece of equipment like a tube with a light on it that a doctor can use to look inside someone's body, or that the doctor can pass a small knife down to do an operation

lap·a·ros·cop·y /ˌlæpəˈrɑskəpi/ *n.* [C,U] TECHNICAL an examination or medical operation done using a laparoscope —**laparoscopic** /ˌlæpərəˈskɑpɪk/ *adj.*

La Paz /lə ˈpɑz/ the capital and largest city of Bolivia

ˈlap belt *n.* [C] a type of safety belt that fits across your waist when you are sitting in the back of a car → see also SEAT BELT

ˈlap ˌdancer *n.* [C] a dancer in a bar who sits on customers' laps and moves in a sexually exciting way as part of their performance —**lap dancing** *n.* [U]

lap·dog, lap dog /ˈlæpdɔg/ *n.* [C] **1** a small pet dog **2** someone who is completely under the control of someone else and will do anything they say

la·pel /ləˈpɛl/ *n.* [C] the part of the front of a coat or JACKET that is joined to the collar and folded back on each side

lap·i·dar·y¹ /ˈlæpəˌdɛri/ *adj.* [only before noun] TECHNICAL relating to the cutting or polishing of valuable stones or jewels

lapidary² *n.* [C] TECHNICAL someone who is skilled at cutting and polishing jewels and valuable stones

lap·is laz·u·li /ˌlæpɪs ˈlæzəli/ *n.* [C,U] a valuable bright blue stone

La·place /ləˈplɑs/, **Pierre Si·mon de** /pyɛr siˈmoʊn də/ (1749–1827) a French ASTRONOMER who did important work on GRAVITY and the SOLAR SYSTEM

ˈlap robe *n.* [C] a small thick BLANKET used to cover your legs when you are sitting

lapse¹ /læps/ *n.* [C] **1** a short time when you forget something, do not pay attention, or fail to do something you should: **+in** *lapses in security* | **+of** *a lapse of concentration* | *After taking the drug, several patients suffered **memory lapses*** (=they were unable to remember some things for short periods of time). | *Children shouldn't be harshly punished for a **lapse of judgment*** (=a time when they chose the wrong thing to do). **2** [usually singular] a period of time between two events: **+of** *There is a lapse of five seconds before the flash goes off.* **3** a failure to do something you should do, especially a failure to behave correctly: *He didn't offer Darren a drink, and Marie did not appear to notice the lapse.* [**Origin:** 1300–1400 Latin *lapsus*, from *labi* **to slip**]

lapse² *v.* [I] **1** if a contract, agreement, legal right etc. lapses, it comes to an end, for example because an agreed time limit has passed: *Catherine had allowed the insurance policy to lapse.* **2** to gradually come to an end or to stop for a period of time: *The conversation lapsed.*

lapse into sth *phr. v.* **1 lapse into silence/a coma/sleep etc.** to go into a quiet or less active state: *He lapsed into a coma and died two days later.* **2** to return to behaving or speaking in a way that you did before, especially a way that is less good or acceptable: *Gerhardt frequently lapses into German.* **3** to get into a worse state: *Following his death, the Empire lapsed into chaos.*

lapsed /læpst/ *adj.* [only before noun] **1** no longer having the beliefs you used to have, especially religious beliefs: *a lapsed Catholic* **2** LAW not used anymore

lap·top /ˈlæptɑp/ *n.* [C] a small computer that you can carry with you SYN **notebook** —**lap-top** *adj.*

laptop

lar·board /ˈlɑrbəd/ *n.* [U] OLD-FASHIONED the left side of a ship SYN **port**

lar·ce·nist /ˈlɑrsənɪst/ *n.* [C] LAW a thief

lar·ce·ny /ˈlɑrsəni/ *n.* *plural* **larcenies** [C,U] LAW the crime of stealing —**larcenous** *adj.* → see also PETTY LARCENY

larch /lɑrtʃ/ *n.* [C,U] a tree that looks like a PINE tree but drops its leaves in winter

lard¹ /lɑrd/ *n.* [U] white fat from pigs that is used in cooking

lard² *v.* [T] to put small pieces of BACON onto meat before cooking it

lard sth **with** sth *phr. v.* to include a lot of something, especially something that is not necessary, in a speech, piece of writing, plan etc.: *Lawmakers had larded the bill with pet spending projects.*

lar·der /ˈlɑrdə/ *n.* [C] a PANTRY

large /lɑrdʒ/ S1 W1 *adj.*
1 BIG bigger or more than usual in number, amount, or size SYN **big** OPP **small**: *large sums of money* | *the largest city in the U.S.* | *What size shirt do you wear? Medium or Large?* | **a large number/amount of sth** *people who drink large amounts of coffee* ▸see THESAURUS box at **big**

2 PERSON a large person is tall and often fat: *Aunt Betsy was a very large woman.* ►see THESAURUS box at fat[1]
3 be at large if a dangerous person or animal is at large, they have escaped from somewhere and may cause harm or damage: *Two of the escaped prisoners are still at large.*
4 the world/country/public etc. at large people in general: *Society at large has become more mobile.*
5 larger than life a) someone who is larger than life attracts a lot of attention because they are more amusing, attractive, or exciting than most people: *one of the larger-than-life legends of the rock era* **b)** much larger and easier to notice than usual
6 in large part/measure FORMAL mostly: *The research is based in large part on newspaper records.*
7 the larger issues/picture/view the important general facts and questions about a situation, problem etc.: *Let's focus our discussion on the larger issues first.*
[**Origin:** 1100–1200 Old French, Latin *largus*] —**largeness** *n.* [U] → see also **by and large** at BY[2] (4), **loom large** at LOOM[1] (3), **writ large** at WRIT[2] → see Word Choice box at WIDE[1]

ˌlarge inˈtestine *n.* [singular] BIOLOGY the lower part of the INTESTINES, in which water is removed from waste food as it passes through → see also SMALL INTESTINE → see picture at DIGESTIVE SYSTEM

large•ly /ˈlɑrdʒli/ W2 *adv.* mostly or mainly: *The state of Nevada is largely desert.* | *It was a tiring day, largely because of all the waiting.*

ˌlarge-ˈscale *adj.* [only before noun] **1** using or involving a lot of effort, people, supplies etc., or happening over a large area OPP **small-scale**: *a large-scale rescue operation* | *large-scale unemployment* **2** a large-scale map, model etc. is drawn or made bigger than usual, so that more details can be shown

lar•gesse, largess /lɑrˈdʒɛs, -ˈʒɛs/ *n.* [U] FORMAL the quality or act of being generous and giving money or gifts to people who have less than you, or the money or gifts that you give → see also GENEROSITY

larg•ish /ˈlɑrdʒɪʃ/ *adj.* INFORMAL fairly big

lar•go /ˈlɑrgoʊ/ *adj., adv.* TECHNICAL played or sung slowly and seriously —**largo** *n.* [C]

lar•i•at /ˈlæriət/ *n.* [C] a LASSO

lark /lɑrk/ *n.* [C] **1** INFORMAL something that you do to amuse yourself or as a joke: **on/as/for a lark** *Grisham began writing novels as a lark.* **2** BIOLOGY a small brown singing bird with long pointed wings SYN **skylark** → see also **as happy as a lark** at HAPPY (10)

lark•spur /ˈlɑrkspɚ/ *n.* [C] a type of tall flower

lar•va /ˈlɑrvə/ *n. plural* **larvae** /-vi/ [C] BIOLOGY a stage in the life of some animals such as insects or FROGS, when they look completely different from the adult that they will become. For example a CATERPILLAR becomes a BUTTERFLY, and a TADPOLE becomes a frog. —**larval** *adj.* → see picture at FOOD WEB

lar•yn•gi•tis /ˌlærənˈdʒaɪt̬ɪs/ *n.* [U] MEDICINE an illness which makes talking difficult because your larynx and throat are swollen

lar•ynx /ˈlærɪŋks/ *n.* [C] BIOLOGY the part of the throat which produces sound → see picture at LUNG

la•sa•gna, lasagne /ləˈzɑnyə/ *n.* [C,U] a type of Italian food made with layers of flat PASTA, meat or vegetables, and cheese [**Origin:** 1800–1900 Italian, Latin *lasanum* **cooking pot**]

las•civ•i•ous /ləˈsɪviəs/ *adj.* DISAPPROVING showing strong sexual desire, or making someone feel this way: *a lascivious wink* —**lasciviousness** *n.* [U]

la•ser /ˈleɪzɚ/ S2 *n.* [C] **1** SCIENCE a piece of equipment that produces a powerful narrow beam of light which can be used in medical operations, to cut metals etc.: *laser surgery* **2** a beam of light produced by this machine [**Origin:** 1900–2000 from "*light amplification by stimulated emission of radiation*"]

ˈlaser disc, laser disk *n.* [C] a flat round object like a CD that can be read by laser light, used in computers or to watch movies

ˈlaser ˌprinter *n.* [C] a machine connected to a computer system, that prints by using laser light

lash[1] /læʃ/ *v.*
1 TIE [T always + adv./prep.] to tie something tightly to something else with a rope, so that it does not move at all: **lash sth to/onto sth** *Our luggage was lashed to the car's roof.* | **lash sth together** *They lashed trees together to make a raft.*
2 WIND/RAIN ETC. [I always + adv./prep.,T] to hit against something with violent force: *Giant waves were lashing the shore.* | **lash against/down/across etc. sth** *The rain lashed violently against the door.*
3 HIT [T] to hit someone very hard with a whip, stick etc.: *Two men were lashed for falling asleep on guard duty.*
4 TAIL [I,T] if an animal lashes its tail or its tail lashes, it moves it from side to side quickly and strongly, especially because it is angry
5 CRITICIZE [I,T] a word meaning "to criticize someone angrily," used especially in newspapers: *politicians being lashed by the media*
lash back *phr. v.* to angrily reply to someone who has criticized you: **lash back at sb** *He lashed back at those who accused him of corruption.*
lash out *phr. v.* **1** to suddenly speak angrily to someone: **+at** *Judge Atkins lashed out at the attorneys for talking to the press.* **2** to try to hit someone, with a series of violent, uncontrolled movements: *In its panic, the bear started to lash out.*

lash[2] *n.* [C] **1** [usually plural] one of the hairs that grow around the edge of your eyes SYN **eyelash**: *the boy's thick lashes* **2** a sudden or violent movement like that of a whip: *With a lash of its tail, the lion sprang.* **3** a hit with a whip, given especially as a punishment **4** the thin piece of leather at the end of a whip

lash•ing /ˈlæʃɪŋ/ *n.* [C] **1** a punishment of hitting someone with a whip **2** a rope that fastens something tightly to something else

lass /læs/ also **las•sie** /ˈlæsi/ *n.* [C] OLD-FASHIONED a girl or young woman → see also LAD

Las•sen Peak /ˌlæsən ˈpik/ a mountain in the Cascade Range that is in the U.S. state of California and is an active VOLCANO

las•si•tude /ˈlæsɪˌtud/ *n.* [U] FORMAL tiredness and lack of energy or interest: *a feeling of lassitude amongst voters*

lasso

las•so[1] /ˈlæsoʊ/ *n. plural* **lassos** [C] a rope with one end tied in a circle, used to catch cattle and horses, especially in the western U.S.

lasso[2] *v.* [T] to catch an animal using a lasso

last[1] /læst/ S1 W1 *determiner, adj.* **1** most recent, or the nearest one to the present time → see also NEXT: *What was his last job?* | *Who did you go out with last night?* | *The **last time** I ate there, I got sick.* | *He hasn't been feeling good **for the last few days/weeks*** (=during the days/weeks before and up to now).

THESAURUS

previous happening or existing before the particular event, time, or thing mentioned: *See the diagram in the previous chapter.*
former happening or existing before, but not now: *the former owner of the property*

2 happening or existing at the end, after everything and everyone else: *the last page of the book* | *the last week in June* | *the last thing he said before he died* | *It's the last house on the left.* **3** remaining after all others have gone, been used etc.: *I took the last piece of cake.* | *We were the last ones to leave the party.* | **sb's last chance** *Tomorrow is your last chance to get tickets.* **4 the last minute/moment** the latest possible time before something happens: *We got to the airport at the last minute.* **5 the last person/thing** used for emphasizing that a particular person or thing etc. is much less likely, appropriate, or desirable than all others: *The last thing we wanted was to go into debt.* | *Chad's the last person I would ask for advice.* **6 if it's the last thing I/we do** SPOKEN used to emphasize that you are determined to do something: *I'm going to buy that dress if it's the last thing I do.* **7 last thing (at night)** at the very end of the day: *Take the pills last thing at night.* **8 the last straw** the final thing in a series of annoying things that makes a person very angry: *Then she lied to me. That was the last straw.* **9 have the last laugh** to finally be successful or prove that you were right after other people have defeated you or said you were wrong **10 the last word a)** the final statement or action that ends an argument or causes you to win something: *Erin always has to have the last word!* | *We refuse to give the terrorists the last word.* **b)** the final decision on something: *The manager has the last word on any price.* **11 on its last legs** INFORMAL old or in bad condition, and likely to stop working soon: *Your car sounds like it's on its last legs.* **12 on your last legs** INFORMAL **a)** very tired **b)** very sick and likely to die soon **13 last hurrah** a final effort, event etc. at the end of a long period of work, a CAREER, a life etc.: *"Star Trek – Generations" was the original cast's last hurrah.* **14 sb's last will and testament** OLD-FASHIONED a WILL **15 be the last word in sth** to be the best, most modern, or most comfortable example of something: *It's the last word in luxury resorts.* → see also **every last drop/bit/scrap etc.** at EVERY (1)

last² S2 W3 *adv.* **1** most recently before now: *When I saw her last, she was pregnant.* **2** after everything or everyone else: *I was told I'll be speaking last.* | *Connect the black wires last.* | *My horse finished* ***second to last*** (=just before the last horse). | *Your name is* ***next to last*** (=just before the last name) *on the list.* **3 last of all** used when giving a final point or statement: *Last of all, I'd like to say that everyone has done a wonderful job.* **4 last but not least** used when mentioning the last person or thing in a list, to emphasize that they are still important: *Last but not least, I would like to thank my wife for her support.*

last³ S2 W2 *n., pron.* **1** the person or thing that comes after all the others: *Their third child was their last.* | **the last of sth** *Joel was the last of nine kids.* | **the last to do sth** *Who was the last to leave?* **2** the most recent thing or person before the present one: *Her new movie is even better than her last.* **3 the day/week/year etc. before last** the day, week etc. before the one that has just finished: *We got our new car the week before last.* **4 save/keep/leave sth for last** to delay dealing with or using something until after you have dealt with or used all the others: *I'm saving the chocolate cake for last.* **5 at (long) last** if something happens at last, it happens after you have waited a long time: *At last, we were able to afford a house.* **6 the last of sth a)** the remaining part of something: *Dennis ate the last of the bread at lunchtime.* **b)** the thing that represents the end of something, after which nothing else happens, is done etc.: *That was the last I saw of him* (=I never saw him again). **7 haven't heard the last of sb/sth** used to say that someone or something may cause more problems in the future: *I'll leave now, but you haven't heard the last of this.* **8 the last I/we...** SPOKEN used to tell someone the most recent news that you know about a person or situation: *The last I heard, Paul was in Cuba.* | *The last we talked to Shelly, she seemed fine.* **9 to the last** FORMAL until the end of an event or the end of someone's life: *Brown died, insisting to the last he was innocent.*

last⁴ S2 W2 *v.* **1** [I always + adv./prep., linking verb] to continue for a particular length of time: *Her operation lasted around three hours.* | *The ceasefire didn't last long.* | **+for/until/through etc.** *The rainy season lasts until March.* | *The ceasefire did* ***not last long.*** **2** [I,T always + adv./prep] to continue to be effective, useful, or in good condition for someone to use for a period of time: **last (sb) for/until/through etc.** *Most batteries last for about 8 hours.* | **last (sb) a week/month year** *We have enough money to last us the rest of the month.* **3** [I] to continue to exist for a long time without changing, failing, etc.: *These cars are built to last.* | **not/never last** *We all said their marriage wouldn't last.* **4** [I,T] to continue being able to do something in a situation, in spite of problems: *The new manager only lasted six months.* | *They won't last the night* (=live through the night) *without water.*

last⁵ *n.* [C] a piece of wood or metal shaped like a human foot, used by someone who makes or repairs shoes

ˌlast ˈcall *n.* [U] the time when the person who is in charge of a bar tells customers they can order just one more set of drinks because the bar is going to close

ˈlast-ditch *adj.* **a last-ditch attempt/effort etc.** a final attempt to achieve something before it is too late: *a last-ditch effort to save the company*

last·ing /ˈlæstɪŋ/ *adj.* strong enough, well enough planned etc. to continue for a very long time: *The committee's decision could have a lasting effect on the community.* | *a lasting peace settlement* | *Our first meeting* ***left a lasting impression*** *on me.*

ˌLast ˈJudgment *n.* **the Last Judgment** the time after the end of the world when everyone is judged by God for what they have done in life, according to Christian, Jewish, and Muslim beliefs SYN **judgment day**

last·ly /ˈlæstli/ *adv.* [sentence adverb] used when telling someone the last thing at the end of a list or series of statements: *Lastly, the course trains students to think logically.*

THESAURUS

lastly/finally used to introduce the last point, action, or instruction in a list: *Lastly, there is the question of legality.* | *Add flour, salt, and finally the milk.*
finally/eventually used to say that something happens after a long time: *Finally, we managed to get the car started.* | *She eventually apologized.*
at last used to emphasize that you are glad when something happens, because you have been waiting a long time for it: *I felt we were making progress at last.*
in the end/finally used when something happens after a long period of time: *In the end, he turned out to be a liar.*
→ FIRST

ˈlast-minute *adj.* [only before noun] happening or done as late as possible within a process, event, or activity: *a last-minute decision*

ˈlast name S2 *n.* [C] your family's name, which in English comes after your other names: **sb's last name** *Could you spell your last name, please?* → see also FIRST NAME

ˌlast ˈrites *n.* [plural] the religious ceremony performed, especially in Catholicism, for people who are dying

Las Ve·gas /lɑs ˈveɪgəs/ a city in the desert of the U.S. state of Nevada

lat. the written abbreviation of LATITUDE

latch¹ /lætʃ/ *n.* [C] a small metal or plastic object used to keep doors, gates, windows etc. closed

latch

latch² *v.* [T] to fasten a door, window etc. with a latch

latch onto sb/sth *phr. v.* INFORMAL **1** to decide that an idea or practice that someone else is using is very good, and start using it or doing it yourself: *A few doctors have latched onto the idea of using natural medicines.* **2** to follow someone and keep trying to get their attention, especially someone who would prefer to be left alone: *He latched onto me at the party.* **3** to pay a lot of attention to someone or something, because you think they are important or interesting: *The press latches onto any story about the British royal family.* **4** to bite or suck and not let go of someone or something

latch·key /ˈlætʃki/ *n.* [C] a key that opens a lock on an outside door of a house or apartment

ˈlatchkey kid also **ˈlatchkey child** *n.* [C] a child whose parents both work and who spends time alone in the house after school

late¹ /leɪt/ S1 W1 *adj.*
1 AFTER EXPECTED TIME arriving, happening, or done after the time that was expected, agreed, or arranged OPP early: *Sorry I'm late – I overslept.* | *The bus is late again.* | **+for** *Peggy was late for school.* | **ten minutes/two hours etc. late** *You're half an hour late!*

THESAURUS
overdue not done or happening when expected: *an overdue library book*
be behind with sth to be late or slow in doing something: *They were three months behind with the rent.*
be delayed to make someone or something late: *The flight was delayed by bad weather.*
be held up to be late because of something that has happened: *I was held up in traffic.*
tardy late: *At school, he was always tardy.*
belated used about something that arrives or happens late: *a belated birthday card*

2 too late after the time when something could or should have been done: *He shouted a warning, but it was too late.* | **too late to do sth** *Are we too late to get tickets?*
3 NEAR THE END [only before noun] near the end of a period of time OPP early: *a house built in the late 19th century* | *Paul's in his late forties.*
4 AFTER USUAL TIME happening or done after the usual or normal time OPP early: *a late breakfast* | *The harvest was late this year.* | *I had* ***a late night*** (=night when I stayed awake after the normal time) *last night.*
5 EVENING [only before noun] near the end of the day, especially at night when most people are asleep OPP early: *the late movie on TV* | **it's (getting) late** *It's late. We should go to bed.*
6 PAYMENTS ETC. a) paid, given back etc. after the arranged time: *Oh, no, my library books are late.* **b) be late with sth** to pay something, bring something back etc. after the arranged time: *I've never been late with a payment before.*
7 DEAD [only before noun] FORMAL dead: *Mrs. Moody's late husband* ▸see THESAURUS box at dead¹
8 a late bloomer/developer a) a child who develops socially, emotionally, or physically at a later age than other children **b)** someone who does not become successful until later in life
9 WOMEN if a woman is late, she has not had her PERIOD (=the monthly flow of blood) when she expected it
10 late of sth FORMAL having lived in a place, worked in a place etc. until fairly recently: *Julia Loukyanov, late of Moscow*
11 late in the day at a late stage in a process or in the development of something, especially when it is too late to change something: *It's a little late in the day to say you're sorry!*
[**Origin:** Old English *læt*] → see also LATER², LATEST¹

late² S2 W3 *adv.* **1** after or later than the usual time: *All the stores in the mall are open late tonight.* | *I stayed late at work last night.* | *I usually sleep late on Sundays.* **2** after the arranged or expected time OPP early: *I arrived at the interview late.* | **ten minutes/two hours etc. late** *The bus came ten minutes late.* **3** near to the end of a period of time or an event OPP early: **+in** *late in the afternoon* | *We took a walk* ***late at night.*** **4 as late as** used to express surprise that something considered old-fashioned was still happening so recently: *As late as the 1960s, about 20 states had laws against interracial marriage.* **5 of late** FORMAL recently: *He's taken to mountain climbing of late.* **6 late in life** if you do something late in life, you do it at an older age than most people do it **7 better late than never** used to say that you are glad someone has done something, or that they should do something, even though they are late **8 too late** after the time when something could or should have been done: *We got there too late to see the first act.* → see also LATER¹, **run late/early/on time** at RUN¹ (9)

ˈlate-ˌbreaking *adj.* late-breaking news concerns events that happen just before a news broadcast or just before a newspaper is printed

late·com·er /ˈleɪtˀˌkʌmɚ/ *n.* [C] someone who arrives late

late·ly /ˈleɪtli/ S2 *adv.* recently: *I've been really tired lately.* | *Lately, we've been listening to more jazz.*

GRAMMAR **lately, recently**
Use both these words with the present perfect tenses to talk about something that began in the recent past and continues until now: *Lately I've been thinking about changing jobs.* | *You've been going to a lot of parties recently.* You can also use **recently** (but NOT *lately*) with the past tense to talk about a particular action in the recent past: *She got married recently* (NOT *lately*).

ˈlate-night *adj.* [only before noun] happening late at night: *a late-night TV talk show*

la·tent /ˈleɪtˀnt/ *adj.* something that is latent is present but hidden, and may develop or become more noticeable in the future: *The virus remains latent in the body for many years.* → see also DORMANT —**latency** *n.* [U]

ˌlatent ˈheat *n.* [U] CHEMISTRY the additional heat necessary to change a solid into a liquid, or a liquid into a gas

lat·er¹ /ˈleɪtɚ/ S1 W1 *adv.* **1** after the present time or a time you are talking about: *I'll tell you about it later.* | **two years/three weeks etc. later** *A few days later, I received another call.* | **later that day/morning/week etc.** *Later that night the house burned to the ground.* | **later in the day/week/year etc.** *We'll have the house painted later in the summer.* ▸see THESAURUS box at after³ **2 see/talk to you later, later** SPOKEN used to say goodbye to someone you will see or talk to again soon: *All right. I'll see you later.* | *Later, Wayne.* **3 later on** at some time later or in the future: *She took notes so she could remember it all later on.* **4 no/not later than** used to say that something must be done by a particular time in the future: *Applications are due no later than April 21.* → see Word Choice box at AFTER¹

later² *adj.* [only before noun] **1** coming in the future or after something else: *You'll find that information in a later chapter.* | *The weapons will be destroyed* ***at a later date.***

THESAURUS
next coming after the present one, or after the one you have been talking about: *The next bus wouldn't come for twenty minutes.*
following coming after the one you have been talking about: *He resigned the following year.*

L

the ... after (that) coming after the one you have been talking about: *The first day Mark arrived on time, but the day after that he was late.*
future likely to happen or exist at some time in the future: *You need to plan for your future career.*
subsequent FORMAL happening or coming after something else: *a subsequent decision by the Supreme Court*
succeeding used about all the times or things that happen or come after something else: *succeeding generations*

►see THESAURUS box at **next**[1] **2** more recent: *We traded in our old VW for a later model.* | *a later version of the software* **3 in sb's later years** also **in later life** when someone is older: *In later life he published two novels.*

lat·er·al[1] /ˈlæt̬ərəl/ *adj.* **1** FORMAL relating to the sides of something or movement to or from the side: *a lateral pass* (=of a ball) **2 a lateral move** a change of jobs within a company or between companies in which you stay at a similar level or rank **3** ENG. LANG. ARTS a lateral speech sound is made by using the sides of the tongue —**laterally** *adv.*

lateral[2] *n.* [C] TECHNICAL **1** something that is at the side or comes from the side **2** a lateral speech sound

ˌlateral ˈarea *n.* [C] MATH the sum of the areas of all the lateral faces of a PRISM or a PYRAMID, or the area of the curved surface of a CONE or CYLINDER

ˌlateral ˈbud *n.* [C] BIOLOGY a BUD on the side of the stem of a plant in the angle formed by a leaf and the stem

ˌlateral ˈface *n.* [C] MATH one of the flat sides of a GEOMETRIC shape that has many sides, such as a PRISM or a PYRAMID, but not the base

ˌlateral ˈline also **ˌlateral ˈline ˌsystem** *n.* [C] BIOLOGY a series of sense organs in a line along the head and body of fish, through which they are able to sense movements in the water and to feel changes in its force or direction

lat·est[1] /ˈleɪt̬ɪst/ *adj.* [only before noun] **1** the most recent or the newest: *Have you heard the latest news?* | *the latest fashions* ►see THESAURUS box at **new** **2** last possible: *The latest date for applications is Friday the 23rd.*

latest[2] *n.* **1 the latest a)** the most recent news or information: **+on** *What's the latest on the war?* **b)** the last possible time: *Tomorrow is the latest I can accept your papers.* | **at the latest** *I should be back by 11 o'clock at the latest.* **c)** the most recent thing: *the latest in a series of meetings* **2 the latest in sth** the most modern or advanced thing in a particular field: *Every hospital wants the latest in high-tech equipment.*

L

la·tex /ˈleɪtɛks/ *n.* [U] **1** a thick whitish liquid produced by some plants, especially the rubber tree **2** a rubber substance made from latex, or an artificial rubber similar to this, which stretches and changes shape easily: *latex gloves*

lath /læθ/ *n.* [C] a long flat narrow piece of wood used in building to support PLASTER (=material used to cover walls)

lathe /leɪð/ *n.* [C] a machine that shapes wood or metal, by turning it around and around against a sharp tool

lath·er[1] /ˈlæðɚ/ *n.* [singular, U] **1** a white mass of BUBBLES produced by mixing soap in water **2** a white mass that forms on a horse's skin when it has been SWEATING **3 in a lather** INFORMAL very anxious or upset —**lathery** *adv.*

lather[2] also **lather up** *v.* **1** [I] to produce a lather: *This soap lathers really well.* **2** [I,T] to cover something, especially your body, with lather: *He lathered his face to shave.*

Lat·in[1] /ˈlætˀn/ *n.* **1** [U] the language of the ancient Romans, now used mostly for legal, scientific, or medical words **2** [C] someone from a country that speaks a language such as Italian, Spanish, or Portuguese, that developed from Latin, especially someone from Latin America

Latin[2] *adj.* **1** relating to or coming from a nation that speaks a language such as Italian, Spanish, or Portuguese, that developed from Latin: *Latin music* **2** relating to the Latin language: *a Latin inscription*

La·ti·na /ləˈtinə/ *n.* [C] a woman in the U.S. whose family comes from a country in Latin America

ˌLatin Aˈmerica *n.* the land including Mexico, Central America, and South America —**Latin American** *adj.*

La·ti·no /ləˈtinoʊ/ *n. plural* **Latinos** [C] a man in the U.S. whose family comes from a country in Latin America. In the plural, Latinos can mean a group of men and women, or just men. —**Latino** *adj.*: *Latino culture*

lat·i·tude /ˈlæt̬əˌtud/ *n.* **1** [C,U] TECHNICAL the distance north or south of the EQUATOR (=the imaginary line around the middle of the world) measured in degrees → see also LONGITUDE → see picture at GLOBE **2** [U] FORMAL freedom to choose what you do or say: *Students are **given latitude** in deciding what they want to study.* **3 latitudes** [plural] GEOGRAPHY an area at a particular latitude: *the planet's southernmost latitudes* —**latitudinal** /ˌlæt̬əˈtudn-əl/ *adj.*

la·trine /ləˈtrin/ *n.* [C] a toilet that is outdoors in a camp or military area [**Origin:** 1200–1300 French, Latin *latrina*, from *lavatrina*, from *lavare* **to wash**]

lat·te /ˈlɑteɪ/ *n.* [C,U] ESPRESSO coffee with a lot of STEAMed milk in it, or a cup of this [**Origin:** 1900–2000 Italian *caffè latte* **milk coffee**]

lat·ter[1] /ˈlæt̬ɚ/ *n.* **the latter** FORMAL the second of two people or things just mentioned OPP **former**: *The choice was to spend money or save: he chose the latter.* | **the latter of sth/sb** *It is the latter of these two questions that I am trying to answer.*

latter[2] *adj.* [only before noun] FORMAL **1** being the second of two people or things, or the last in a list just mentioned: *The latter method would be simpler.* **2** the latter part of a period of time is nearest to the end of it: *Crandall served in Italy during the latter part of the war.*

ˈlatter-day *adj.* [only before noun] **a latter-day Versailles/Czar etc.** something or someone that exists now but is like a famous thing or person that existed in the past: *Romer portrayed himself as a latter-day Robin Hood.*

ˌLatter-Day ˈSaints *n.* [plural] the MORMONS

lat·tice /ˈlætɪs/ *n.* [C] **1** also **lat·tice·work** a pattern or structure made of long flat narrow pieces of wood, plastic etc. that are arranged so that they cross each other and the spaces between them are shaped like DIAMONDS: *cherry pie with a lattice crust* **2** TECHNICAL a regular arrangement of objects over an area or in space: *a crystal lattice*

Lat·vi·a /ˈlætviə/ a country in northeastern Europe on the Baltic Sea, that is south of Estonia and north of Lithuania —**Latvian** *n., adj.*

laud /lɔd/ *v.* [T] FORMAL to praise someone or something OPP **deride**: *Honig lauded his wife's charity work.*

laud·a·ble /ˈlɔdəbəl/ *adj.* FORMAL deserving praise or admiration, even if not completely successful: *Preserving the environment is a laudable goal.* —**laudably** *adv.*

lau·da·num /ˈlɔdn-əm, -nəm/ *n.* [U] a substance containing the drug OPIUM, used in the past to control pain and help people to sleep

laud·a·to·ry /ˈlɔdəˌtɔri/ *adj.* FORMAL expressing praise or admiration: *a laudatory book review*

laugh[1] /læf/ S1 W1 *v.*
1 MAKE SOUND [I] to make sounds with your voice, usually while you are smiling, because you think something is funny: *We were **laughing so hard** (=laughing so much) we couldn't stop.* | **+at/about** *Everybody laughed at the joke.* | *When we saw what had happened we **burst out laughing** (=suddenly started laughing).* | *When I first heard the idea, I almost **laughed out loud** (=laughed so that other people could hear).* | *Joe's probably outside someplace **laughing his head off** (=laughing a lot).*

THESAURUS

giggle to laugh quickly in a high voice, especially because you think something is very funny or because you are nervous or embarrassed
chuckle to laugh quietly
cackle to laugh in an unpleasant loud way
snicker to laugh quietly in an unkind way
titter to laugh quickly in a high voice, in a nervous or embarrassed way
guffaw to laugh loudly
(be) in stitches to be laughing so much that you cannot stop
roar with laughter to laugh very loudly

2 [I] to show that you think an idea or suggestion is very silly, and should not be considered seriously: *When I told them my plan they just* ***laughed in my face****.*
3 no laughing matter something serious that should not be joked about: *Age discrimination is no laughing matter.*
4 don't make me laugh SPOKEN used when someone has just told you something that is completely untrue, has asked for something impossible etc.: *"Could you finish this by tomorrow?" "Don't make me laugh."*
5 be laughing all the way to the bank INFORMAL to be in a good situation because you have made a lot of money without making much effort
6 not know whether to laugh or cry to feel upset or annoyed by something bad or unlucky that has happened, but to also be able to see that there is something funny about it: *When the whole cake fell off the table, I didn't know whether to laugh or cry.*
7 be laughed out of court/town etc. if a person or idea is laughed out of a place, the idea is not accepted because people there think it is completely stupid: *We can't ask for more money again. We'd be laughed out of court!*
8 SPEAK [T] to say something in a voice that shows you are amused: *"Don't be ridiculous," Sabina laughed.*
9 you have to laugh SPOKEN used to say that, even though a situation is annoying or disappointing, you can also see that there is something funny about it
10 laugh up your sleeve to be secretly happy, especially because you have played a trick on someone or criticized them without their knowing
11 sb will be laughing out of the other side of their mouth SPOKEN used to say that although someone is happy or confident now, they will be in trouble later
[**Origin:** Old English *hliehhan*]

laugh at *phr. v.* **1 laugh at sb** to make unkind or funny remarks about someone SYN **make fun of**: *The other kids laughed at him.* | *He's the kind of person who* ***laughs at people behind their backs*** (=is unkind about someone when they are not there). **2 laugh at sb/sth** to show that you think an idea or suggestion is very silly, and should not be considered in a serious way SYN **ridicule**: *People laugh at the idea of life on Mars, but it's possible.* **3 laugh at yourself** to not be too serious about yourself and the things you do, and to understand that other people might think you are funny **4** to seem not to care about something that most people would worry about: *Criminals just laugh at the gun control laws.*

laugh sth ↔ **off** *phr. v.* to pretend that something is less serious than it really is by laughing or joking about it: *After she fell, she tried to laugh it off.*

laugh² W3 *n.* [C] **1** an act of laughing, or the sound you make when you laugh: *a nervous laugh* | *"I guess I'm a comedian at heart," she said* ***with a laugh****.* | *He'll do anything to* ***get a laugh*** (=make people laugh). **2 that's a laugh!** SPOKEN INFORMAL used to say that you do not believe something: *"She says she'll be here early." "That's a laugh."* **3 be a laugh riot** also **be a laugh a minute** INFORMAL to be very funny, amusing, and enjoyable **4 for laughs a)** if you do something for laughs, you do it in a particular way so that other people will laugh: *Williams plays the part for laughs.* **b)** for fun: *We took the helicopter ride just for laughs.* **5 get a laugh out of sth** to enjoy something and think it is funny: *The ads are fun to do; we get a laugh out of the whole thing.* → see also **have the last laugh** at LAST¹ (9)

laugh·a·ble /ˈlæfəbəl/ *adj.* impossible to be treated seriously because of being so silly, bad, or difficult to believe: *The price of the house was laughable.* —**laughably** *adv.*

ˈlaughing gas *n.* [U] INFORMAL a gas that is sometimes used to stop you from feeling pain during an operation

laugh·ing·ly /ˈlæfɪŋli/ *adv.* **1** if you do something laughingly, you are laughing while you do it: *Several other women laughingly agreed.* **2** if something is laughingly described in a particular way, it is done in a joking, often unkind, way: *Critics laughingly called CNN "Chicken Noodle News."*

ˈlaughing ˌstock *n.* [C] someone who has done something so silly or stupid that people laugh at them in a way that is not nice: **the laughing stock of sth** *He has become the laughing stock of the school.*

ˈlaugh lines *n.* [plural] lines on your skin around your eyes that are made when you laugh

laugh·ter /ˈlæftɚ/ *n.* [U] the action of laughing or sound of people laughing: *We heard laughter coming from the next room.* | *The audience* ***roared with laughter****.*

ˈlaugh track *n.* [C] recorded laughter that is used during a humorous television show to make it sound as if people are laughing during the performance

launch¹ /lɔntʃ, lɑntʃ/ W2 *v.* [T]
1 START STH to start an important activity or a serious attempt to achieve something: *The book launched his career as a novelist.* | *The city launched a campaign to change public opinion.* | *Rebels launched another attack late Sunday.*
2 INTO SPACE to send a weapon or SPACECRAFT into the sky or into space: *NASA will launch the space shuttle on Sunday.*
3 PRODUCT/SERVICE to make a new product, book etc. available for sale for the first time: *The magazine was launched last month.*
4 COMPUTER COMPUTERS to make a computer program start SYN **open**
5 BOAT to put a boat or ship into the water
6 THROW [always + adv./prep.] INFORMAL to throw something into the air with a lot of force SYN **hurl**
7 launch yourself forward/up/from etc. to move somewhere very suddenly and with force
[**Origin:** 1300–1400 Old North French *lancher*, from Late Latin *lanceare* **to throw a lance**]

launch into sth *phr. v.* to suddenly start doing or saying something with a lot of energy or excitement: *Powell launched into a ten-minute summary of the plan.*

launch² *n.* [C] **1** an act of launching something: +**of** *the launch of nuclear weapons* | *the launch date for his new clothing line* **2** an event at which a company, organization etc. announces that it is starting to do or sell something **3** a large boat with a motor

launch·er /ˈlɔntʃɚ, ˈlɑn-/ *n.* [C] a structure from which a weapon, ROCKET, or SPACECRAFT is sent into the sky

ˈlaunch pad also **ˈlaunching ˌpad** *n.* [C] a special place from which a ROCKET or MISSILE is sent up into the sky

laun·der /ˈlɔndɚ, ˈlɑn-/ *v.* [T] **1** to put money that has been obtained illegally into legal businesses and bank accounts, so that you can hide it or use it: *He was jailed for laundering drug money.* **2** FORMAL to wash and sometimes IRON clothes, sheets etc. [**Origin:** 1500–1600 *launder* **someone who washes clothes** (14–17 centuries), from French *lavandier*, from Latin *lavare* **to wash**] —**laundered** *adj.*

Laun·dro·mat, **laundromat** /ˈlɔndrəˌmæt/ *n.* [C] TRADEMARK a place where you pay money to wash your clothes in machines SYN **launderette**

laun·dry /ˈlɔndri/ S2 *n. plural* **laundries** **1** [U] clothes, sheets etc. that need to be washed or have just

L

been washed: *My dad was folding laundry.* | *I have to pack and* ***do the laundry*** (=wash clothes, sheets etc.). **2** [C] a place or business where clothes etc. are washed and IRONED

'laundry ˌbasket *n.* [C] a basket used for carrying clothes that have been washed or need to be washed → see picture at BASKET

'laundry list *n.* [C] INFORMAL a long list of things, often problems: *a laundry list of complaints*

'laundry room *n.* [C] a room in a house or apartment building where there are machines for washing and drying clothes, sheets etc.

lau•re•ate /ˈlɔriɪt, ˈlɑr-/ *n.* [C] someone who has been given an important prize or honor: *a Nobel laureate* → see also POET LAUREATE

lau•rel /ˈlɔrəl, ˈlɑr-/ *n.* **1** [C,U] BIOLOGY a small tree with smooth shiny dark green leaves that do not fall off in winter **2 laurels** [plural] something you receive that recognizes and rewards your achievements: *academic laurels* **3 rest/sit on your laurels** to be satisfied with what you have achieved and therefore stop trying to achieve anything new **4 look to your laurels** to work hard in order not to lose the success that you have achieved

la•va /ˈlɑvə, ˈlævə/ *n.* [U] EARTH SCIENCE **1** hot liquid rock that flows from a VOLCANO → see picture at VOLCANO **2** the rock that forms when liquid lava is cold

'lava ˌlamp *n.* [C] a type of lamp with a colored liquid substance inside that moves up and down, used as a decoration

lav•a•to•ry /ˈlævəˌtɔri/ *n. plural* **lavatories** [C] FORMAL a room containing a toilet, especially in a airplane, hospital etc. [**Origin:** 1300–1400 Medieval Latin *lavatorium* **bowl for washing in**, from Latin *lavare* **to wash**]

lav•en•der /ˈlævəndɚ/ *n.* **1** [C,U] BIOLOGY a plant that has purple flowers with a nice smell **2** [U] the dried flowers of this plant, often used to make things smell nice **3** [U] a pale purple color [**Origin:** 1300–1400 Anglo-French *lavendre*, from Medieval Latin *lavandula*]

lav•ish¹ /ˈlævɪʃ/ *adj.* **1** [usually before noun] large, generous, or expensive: *lavish gifts* | *a lavish party* **2 be lavish with/in sth** to give something very generously: *He is always lavish with his praise.* [**Origin:** 1400–1500 *lavish* **too great quantity** (15–16 centuries), from Old French *lavasse* **heavy rain**] —**lavishly** *adv.*: *a lavishly illustrated book* —**lavishness** *n.* [U]

lavish² *v.* [T] to give someone a lot of something such as expensive presents, love, or praise: **lavish sth on/upon sb** *The teachers lavished praise on the winners.* | **lavish sb with sth** *His followers lavished him with riches.*

La•voi•si•er /ləˌvwɑziˈeɪ/, **An•toine** /ɑnˈtwɑn/ (1743–1794) a French scientist whose work is considered to be the beginning of modern chemistry

law /lɔ/ S1 W1 *n.*

1 SYSTEM OF RULES [singular, U] the system of rules that citizens of a country, city, state etc. must obey: *Public drunkenness is* ***against the law*** (=is illegal) *in Mexico.* | **it is against the law to do sth** *It is against the law to sell cigarettes to minors.* | *Traders who* ***break the law*** (=do something illegal) *will be prosecuted.* | *Many companies are refusing to* ***obey the law.*** | *The bill will* ***become law*** (=be officially made a law) *next month.* | *Candidates are required* ***by law*** *to file financial reports.* | *The court has ruled that the adult theater was operating* ***within the law*** (=not doing anything illegal). | **tax/divorce/libel etc. law** (=all the laws relating to tax etc.) | **state/federal/international law** *An armed attack would violate international law.* | *The new government is slowly bringing back* ***law and order*** (=a situation in which people respect the law, and crime is controlled). → see also CRIMINAL, LAW FIRM ►see THESAURUS box at **rule¹**

2 A RULE [C] a rule that people in a particular country, city, state etc. must obey: ***Under*** *the new* ***law,*** *all drivers over the age of 18 are required to have insurance.* | **+against** *severe laws against drug use* | **+on** *the law on prescription drug advertising* | **an immigration/environmental/tax etc. law** *the fight for tougher environmental laws* | *Five people were arrested* ***under*** (=as a result of) *anti-terrorism* ***laws.*** | *The state* ***passed a law*** (=approved it) *banning casino gambling.*

3 STUDY/PROFESSION [U] the study of law, or the profession involving law: *She practices law in New York.*

4 the law INFORMAL the police: *He's in trouble with the law again.*

5 DESCRIPTION/EXPLANATION [C] a statement that describes and explains how something works: *the economic law of supply and demand* | *the law of gravity*

6 RELIGIOUS RULES [U] a system of rules that a particular religion has: **under Jewish/Islamic law** *The practice is not allowed under Jewish law.*

7 SPORTS [C] one of the rules that say how a sport should be played

8 the law of the jungle a) the idea that people should only take care of themselves and not care about other people, if they want to succeed **b)** the principle that only the strongest creatures will stay alive

9 take the law into your own hands to do something illegal in order to correct something that you think is not fair or not being dealt with by the police: *He took the law into his own hands and shot the man.*

10 have the law on your side to be legally right in what you are doing

11 the law of averages the PROBABILITY that one result will happen as often as another if you try something often enough: *The law of averages says we're due for a win.*

12 there ought to be a law (against sth) OFTEN HUMOROUS used to say that you think something should not be allowed

13 be a law unto yourself to do only what you want to do and not follow the rules of behavior that other people follow

[**Origin:** Old English *lagu*] → see also CIVIL LAW, COMMON LAW, **lay down the law** at LAY DOWN (4), MURPHY'S LAW, ROMAN LAW, **unwritten law** at UNWRITTEN (1)

'law-aˌbiding *adj.* respectful of the law and obeying it: *a law-abiding citizen*

law•break•er /ˈlɔˌbreɪkɚ/ *n.* [C] someone who does something illegal —**law-breaking** *n.* [U]

'law enˌforcement *n.* [U] the job of making sure that the law is obeyed

'law enˌforcement ˌagent *n.* [C] a police officer

'law firm *n.* [C] a company that provides legal services and employs many lawyers

law•ful /ˈlɔfəl/ *adj.* FORMAL OR LAW allowed or officially accepted by the law: *a lawful marriage* | *lawful demonstrations* —**lawfully** *adv.*

law•less /ˈlɔlɪs/ *adj.* not obeying the law, or not controlled by the law: *lawless terrorists* | *a lawless war zone* —**lawlessness** *n.* [U]

law•mak•er /ˈlɔˌmeɪkɚ/ W3 *n.* [C] any elected official responsible for making laws SYN **legislator**: *state lawmakers* | *Republican lawmakers*

law•man /ˈlɔmən/ *n. plural* **lawmen** /-mən/ [C] INFORMAL any officer who is responsible for making sure that the law is obeyed

lawn /lɔn/ S2 *n.* **1** [C] an area of ground in a yard or park, that is covered with short grass: *a well-kept front lawn* | *The boy next door* ***mows the lawn*** (=cuts the grass) *for us.* **2** [U] a fine cloth made from cotton or LINEN [**Origin:** (1) 1500–1600 Old French *launde* **open space between woods**]

'lawn ˌbowling *n.* [U] an outdoor game played on grass in which you try to roll a big ball as near as possible to a smaller ball

'lawn chair *n.* [C] a light chair that you use outside, especially one that folds up

'lawn ˌmower *n.* [C] a machine that you use to cut grass

'lawn ˌparty *n.* [C] a formal party held outside in the afternoon, especially in a large yard

ˌlawn 'tennis *n.* [U] FORMAL → see TENNIS

ˌlaw of comˌparative adˈvantage *n.* [singular] **the law of comparative advantage** ECONOMICS an idea which states that a country will be more successful and wealthy if it only produces products that it is good at making, and brings into the country products that other countries are better at making

ˌlaw of conserˌvation of ˌangular ˈmovement *n.* [singular] PHYSICS a principle of PHYSICS that states that if no outside force affects an object that is spinning around, it will continue to spin at the same speed → see also PLANCK'S CONSTANT

ˌlaw of conserˌvation of ˈenergy *n.* [singular] **the law of conservation of energy** PHYSICS a scientific principle that states that energy cannot be made or destroyed in a closed system, it can only be changed from one form into another

ˌlaw of conserˌvation of ˈmass *n.* [singular] **the law of conservation of mass** PHYSICS a scientific principle that states that MASS is not gained or lost in a chemical reaction

ˌlaw of conserˌvation of moˈmentum *n.* [singular] PHYSICS a principle of PHYSICS that states that if no outside force affects an object, the MOMENTUM of the object will not change

ˌlaw of deˈmand *n.* [singular] **the law of demand** ECONOMICS the idea that people will buy more of a product when its price decreases and buy less of a product when its price increases

ˌlaw of disˈorder *n.* [singular] **the law of disorder** PHYSICS a scientific principle, based on the SECOND LAW OF THERMODYNAMICS, which says that all systems tend to move towards a state of being in the most disorder → see also ENTROPY

ˌlaw of inˈertia *n.* [singular] **the law of inertia** PHYSICS another name for NEWTON'S FIRST LAW

ˌlaw of reˈflection *n.* [singular] PHYSICS a principle of PHYSICS that states that when a RAY of light strikes a surface and then REFLECTS off a surface, the angle between the light and the surface is the same when it hits as when it reflects off

ˌlaw of supˈply *n.* [singular] **the law of supply** ECONOMICS an idea which states that businesses will try to sell people more of a product when the price of the product increases → see also LAW OF DEMAND

Law•rence /ˈlɔrəns, ˈlɑr-/, **D.H.** (1885–1930) a British writer of NOVELS

Lawrence, Jacob (1917–) a U.S. PAINTER and educator, famous for his paintings of people and events from African-American history

ˈlaw school *n.* [C,U] a part of a university or a special school where you study to become a lawyer after you get your BACHELOR'S DEGREE

law•suit /ˈlɔsut/ W3 *n.* [C] a problem or complaint that someone brings to a court of law to be settled: *Neighbors have* ***filed a lawsuit*** *to stop development.* | **+against** *a lawsuit against the government*

law•yer /ˈlɔyɚ/ S2 W1 *n.* [C] someone whose job is to advise people about laws, write formal agreements, or represent people in court: *a defense lawyer* | **hire/get a lawyer** *I think you should get a lawyer.* → see also ATTORNEY, COUNSEL[1]

lax /læks/ *adj.* **1** not strict or careful about standards of behavior, work, safety etc. SYN **slack**: *lax security at the airport* | **be lax in (doing) sth** *He was lax in his duties.* **2** not firm, stiff, or tight [**Origin:** 1300–1400 Latin *laxus* **loose**] —**laxly** *adv.* —**laxity, laxness** *n.* [U]

lax•a•tive /ˈlæksət̮ɪv/ *n.* [C] a medicine or something that you eat that makes your BOWELS empty easily —**laxative** *adj.*

lay[1] /leɪ/ S1 W2 *v.* **lays, laid, laying**

1 PUT SB/STH DOWN [T always + adv./prep.] to put someone or something down carefully into a flat position: **lay sth/sb down** *Nancy laid the baby down.* | **lay sth in/on/under etc. sth** *He laid his gloves on the table.* | *Lay the map* ***flat*** *on the floor.*

2 EGGS [I,T] BIOLOGY if an animal, insect etc. lays eggs, it produces them from its body: *Turtles lay their eggs on the beach at night.*

3 lay bricks/carpet/cables/pipes etc. to put or attach something in the correct place, especially onto something flat or under the ground: *Workers were laying carpet in the new building.*

4 LIE NONSTANDARD [I] to LIE

5 lay a finger/hand on sb to touch someone, or to hurt them, especially by hitting them: *Don't you lay a finger on my child!*

6 lay (the) blame on sb also **lay the blame at sb's feet/doorstep** to blame someone for something: *The President is laying the blame on Congress.*

7 lay sth to rest to stop arguing about, worrying about, or discussing something, or to make people stop doing this: *He is anxious to lay all the rumors to rest.*

8 lay waste (to sth) to destroy or damage everything in a place, especially in a war: *The fire laid waste to the area.*

9 lay sth on the line to risk losing your life, your job etc., especially in order to help someone: *soldiers who lay their lives on the line*

10 lay it on the line to state something, especially a threat, demand, or criticism, in a very clear way: *I'm going to lay it on the line, now. This has to stop!*

11 lay your hands on sth to find or get something: *As a child, I read any book I could lay my hands on.*

12 PREPARE [T] to carefully prepare something, especially something that will harm someone else: *Local leaders laid plans to raise money for the stadium.* | **lay the foundation/groundwork for sth** (=do what is necessary for something to develop successfully) | **even the best-laid plans...** (=used to say that even if you plan carefully, you may still have problems)

13 lay sb open to blame/criticism/ridicule etc. FORMAL to do something that makes it possible for other people to blame you, criticize you etc.: *Such behavior could lay her open to criticism.*

14 lay claim to sth to state that you have the right to own or be something or that you possess a particular ability: *Two families laid claim to the property.* | *He lays claim to the title "greatest athlete of all time."*

15 lay your case before sb to give your side of an argument in an official or public way: *Moyers laid his case before the public.*

16 lay a trap a) to do something to prepare to catch someone: *Authorities had laid a trap for the drug smugglers.* **b)** to prepare a piece of equipment for catching animals: *The farmer was laying traps for rabbits.*

17 lay sb to rest to bury someone, used especially when talking about funeral ceremonies

18 lay sth at sb's door to say that something is someone's fault

19 lay sth ↔ bare a) to remove what covers, hides, or shelters something: *After weeks of work, the old foundations were laid bare.* **b)** to stop hiding something, or to show what the truth about something really is: *Krushchev laid bare Stalin's crimes.*

20 lay an egg INFORMAL to fail or be unsuccessful: *The first episode of the series laid an egg.*

21 RISK MONEY [T] to risk an amount of money on the result of a race, sports game etc.: *She* ***laid a bet*** *on Golden Boy* (=a horse).

22 lay hands (on sb) to pray for someone while touching them

23 lay sb/sth flat to hit someone or something and knock them down

24 lay sb low a) to make someone very ill and unable to do their normal activities for a period of time **b)** LITERARY to hit someone and knock them down

25 lay a table OLD-FASHIONED to put plates, knives, forks etc. on a table, ready for a meal; set the table → see also **put/lay your cards on the table** at CARD[1] (12), **get/lay your hands on sth** at HAND[1] (20)

WORD CHOICE lay, lie, lie

• **Lay** means "to put something in a particular position": *Just lay the papers on the desk.* The other forms of this verb are **laid**, **laid**, **laying**, and **lays**.

• **Lie** has two different meanings. Use one meaning of **lie** to talk about someone or something that is flat on a surface: *He was lying face down on the bathroom floor.* | *Don't leave your stuff lying all over the house.* The

L

other forms of this verb are **lay**, **lain**, **lying**, and **lies**. In spoken English you will also sometimes hear things like: *I need to lay down* (instead of *I need to lie down*) but this is generally considered incorrect.
• The other meaning of **lie** is "to say something that is not true": *Are you lying to me?* The other forms of this verb are **lied**, **lying**, and **lies**.

lay sth ↔ **aside** *phr. v.* **1** to stop using, doing, or preparing something, especially to do something else: *Yolanda laid her book aside.* **2** to stop behaving in a particular way, or stop showing particular feelings, especially so you can achieve something: *We must lay aside our personal differences in the interest of national defense.* **3** to save something, usually money, to use in the future: *I've laid aside a little money for next summer.*

lay back *phr. v.* NONSTANDARD to take no action when action is needed SYN **sit back**: *We're not going to lay back and let them close our business.*

lay sth ↔ **down** *phr. v.* **1 lay down your weapons/arms etc.** to stop fighting in a war, battle etc. when you realize that you cannot win: *The Prime Minister urged the rebels to lay down their arms.* **2** to state something officially or firmly, for example a rule or a set of principles: *The law lays down the rules for the treatment of prisoners.* **3 lay down your life** FORMAL to lose your life, for example in a war, in order to help other people **4 lay down the law** to tell someone very firmly how they should behave, usually in a way that annoys them: *I finally laid down the law and limited my son's TV-watching time.* **5** to store something, especially wine, to use in the future

lay sth ↔ **in** *phr. v.* FORMAL to obtain and store a large supply of something to use in the future SYN **stock up**: *Squirrels laid in plenty of nuts for the winter.*

lay into sb *phr. v.* to attack someone physically or with words: *As soon as he got home, she laid into him.*

lay off *phr. v.* **1 lay sb ↔ off** to stop employing a worker, because there is no work for them to do: *The company closed and laid off 40 employees.* **2 lay off sth** INFORMAL to stop doing, having, or using something: *I think you should lay off coffee for a while.* **3 lay off sb** to stop annoying someone: *Lay off him. He's just a kid.*

L

lay on *phr. v.* **1** SPOKEN, INFORMAL **lay sth on sb** to give someone something such as a responsibility or problem that is difficult to deal with: *Sorry to lay this on you now, but we need the report by Friday.* **2 lay it on thick** INFORMAL to do or say something in a way that makes something seem better, more amusing, bigger etc. than it really is SYN **exaggerate**: *She was flattering him, really laying it on thick. He loved it!*

lay out *phr. v.*
1 SPREAD **lay sth ↔ out** to put something on or over a surface, especially in a neat or organized way: *I laid out my clothes for the next day.*
2 ARRANGE **lay sth ↔ out** to arrange or plan a building, town, garden etc.: *May's home is laid out in a U-shape.*
3 DESCRIBE **lay sth ↔ out** to officially tell about or describe a plan, idea etc.: *The letter laid out the administration's plans for economic reform.*
4 LIE SPOKEN, NONSTANDARD to lie in the sun in order to make your skin brown: *We're going to the park to lay out.*
5 SPEND **lay sth ↔ out** INFORMAL to spend money, usually a lot of money: **lay out sth on sth** *We had to lay out $800 on car repairs.* → see also OUTLAY
6 HIT **lay sb ↔ out** to knock someone down, especially hard enough to make them unconscious
7 BODY **lay sb ↔ out** FORMAL to prepare a dead body so that it can be buried

lay over *phr. v.* to stay somewhere for a short time before continuing your trip: *We laid over in Chicago for a few hours.*

lay sb/sth ↔ **up** *phr. v.* if an injury or illness lays you up, you have to stay in bed: **be laid up with sth** *Jeff is laid up with a broken leg.*

lay² *v.* the past tense of LIE

lay³ *n.* [C] **1 the lay of the land a)** the situation that exists at a particular time: *Get the lay of the land before you make any decisions.* **b)** the general shape of an area of land and the positions of features such as hills, rivers, etc. **2** ENG. LANG. ARTS a poem or song

lay⁴ *adj.* [only before noun] **1** belonging to a Christian church but not officially employed by it as a priest: *a lay minister* **2** not trained or knowing much about a particular profession or subject: *It is difficult for a lay person to understand these technical reports.* [**Origin:** 1300–1400 Old French *lai*, from Late Latin *laicus*, from Greek *laikos* **of the people**] → see also LAYPERSON

lay·a·way /ˈleɪəˌweɪ/ *n.* [U] a method of buying goods in which you give the seller a small amount of money to keep the goods until you can pay the full price: *a layaway plan* | *I* ***put*** *the dress* ***on layaway.***

lay·er¹ /ˈleɪɚ/ Ac W3 *n.* [C] **1** an amount or piece of a material or substance that covers a surface or that is between two other things: **+of** *There was a thin layer of ice on the road* | *Several layers of clothing are warmer than one thick layer.* | *a layer of volcanic rock* **2** one of several different levels or parts in an organization, system, set of ideas etc.: **+of** *There are many layers of meaning to be discovered in the poem.* | *layers of bureaucracy* **3** pieces of someone's hair that are cut shorter than the pieces under them → see also -LAYERED, OZONE LAYER

layer² Ac *v.* [T] **1** to make a layer of something, or to put something down in layers: **layer sth with sth** *slices of bread layered with ham and cheese* **2** to cut someone's hair in layers of different length rather than all the same length

-layered /leɪɚd/ *suffix* [in adjectives] **multi-layered/single-layered etc.** having a lot of layers, one layer etc.

lay·ette /leɪˈɛt/ *n.* [C] a complete set of clothing and other things that a new baby needs

lay·man /ˈleɪmən/ *n. plural* **laymen** /-mən/ [C] **1** a LAYPERSON who is a man **2** a man who is not a priest but is a member of a church

lay·off /ˈleɪ-ɔf/ *n.* [C] the act of stopping a worker's employment because there is not enough work: *Some of the layoffs were caused by the weak economy.* → see also **lay off** at LAY¹

lay·out /ˈleɪaʊt/ *n.* [C] **1** the way in which something such as a town or building is arranged: **+of** *He wasn't familiar with the layout of the building.* **2** the way in which writing and pictures are arranged on a page: **+of** *the layout of text on the page* → see also **lay out** at LAY¹

lay·o·ver /ˈleɪˌoʊvɚ/ *n.* [C] a short stay somewhere between parts of a trip, especially a long airplane trip

lay·per·son /ˈleɪˌpɚsən/ *n. plural* **laypeople** /-ˌpipəl/ [C] **1** someone who is not trained in a particular subject or type of work, especially when they are being compared with someone who is OPP **expert**: *a layperson's guide to medicine* | *The report was readable and understandable to* ***the layperson*** (=laypeople in general). **2** someone who is not a priest but is a member of a church

ˌlay ˈreader *n.* [C] someone in the Episcopal or Catholic church who is not a priest but who has been given authority to read part of the religious service

lay·up /ˈleɪʌp/ *n.* [C] a throw in basketball made from very close to the basket or from under it

lay·wom·an /ˈleɪˌwʊmən/ *n.* [C] **1** a LAYPERSON who is a woman **2** a woman who is not a priest but is a member of a church

Laz·a·rus /ˈlæzərəs/, **Em·ma** /ˈɛmə/ (1849–1887) a U.S. writer famous for her poem that is written at the base of the Statue of Liberty

laze /leɪz/ *v.* [I always + adv./prep.] to relax and enjoy yourself in a lazy way: *I'm just going to laze around and watch TV.* —**laze** *n.* [singular]

la·zy /ˈleɪzi/ S3 *adj. comparative* **lazier**, *superlative* **laziest** **1** disliking work and physical activity, and never making any effort: *He's too lazy to cook himself dinner.* | *She's the laziest girl I know.*

THESAURUS

idle OLD-FASHIONED lazy and wasting time when there is work to do: *In the story, Jack is an idle boy who would rather play than work.*
indolent FORMAL lazy and living a comfortable life: *He wasn't indolent or lacking in ambition, but he never seemed to get very far.*
shiftless lazy and not at all interested in working: *her shiftless husband*
slack lazy and not taking enough care to do things correctly: *Some of the students were slack, not bothering to even turn in their homework.*

2 a lazy period of time is spent doing nothing except relaxing: *a lazy afternoon* **3** moving slowly: *a lazy river* —**lazily** *adv.* —**laziness** *n.* [U]

la·zy·bones /ˈleɪziˌbounz/ *n.* [C] INFORMAL a word for a lazy person, often used in a friendly way to someone you like: *Come on, lazybones! Get out of bed.*

ˈlazy eye *n.* [singular] NOT TECHNICAL a medical condition in which one eye does not move with the other one

lazy Su·san /ˌleɪzi ˈsuzən/ *n.* [C] a shelf or TRAY for food, that turns around in a circle

lb. *plural* **lbs.** the written abbreviation of POUND [**Origin:** 1300–1400 Latin *libra* **pound**]

LCD *n.* [C] **Liquid Crystal Display** the part of a WATCH, CALCULATOR, or small computer where numbers and letters are shown by means of an electric current that is passed through a special liquid

lea /li/ *n.* [C] POETIC an area of land with grass

leach /litʃ/ also **leach out** *v.* [I,T] EARTH SCIENCE if a substance leaches or is leached from a larger mass such as the soil, it is removed from it by water passing through the larger mass: *Nitrates from fertilizers leached into the rivers.*

lead[1] /lid/ S2 W1 *v.* **led** /lɛd/
1 GUIDE [T always + adv./prep.] to take someone to a place by going with them or in front of them, or by pulling them gently: **lead sb through/to/along etc. sth** *Dale led us down a dirt path to the farmhouse.* | *We led the horses along the river.* | *Firemen* ***led*** *the families* ***to safety.*** | *Mr. Adams* ***led the way*** (=walked in front) *to the library.*

THESAURUS

guide to take someone to a place and show him or her interesting things there: *She guides tourists around the White House.*
direct FORMAL to explain to someone how to get somewhere: *Can you direct me to the Student Union building?*
point to show someone which direction to go: *a sign pointing the way*
show to take someone somewhere, especially when it is hard for him or her to find the way: *Mr. Mason showed him to my office.*
escort to take someone somewhere, protecting them, guarding them, or showing them the way: *The president was escorted by security guards.*
usher to show someone the way to somewhere nearby, usually into or out of a room or building: *His housekeeper ushered us into the living room.*

2 GO IN FRONT [I,T] to go in front of a group of people or vehicles: *The high school band is leading the parade.*
3 BE IN CHARGE OF [T] to be in charge of something such as an important activity, a group of people, or an organization, and therefore influence what people do: *Who is leading the investigation?* | *She became the first woman to lead the country.* | *The rebels were led by a former army colonel.* | *The best managers* ***lead by example*** (=show others what to do by doing it yourself).
4 ROAD/WIRE [I, T always + adv./prep.] if a path, pipe, wire etc. leads somewhere or leads in a particular direction, it goes there or goes in that direction: **lead (sb) down/into/toward etc.** *The road led down to a small lake.* | *The wire led to the surveillance cameras.* | **lead sb to sth** *The path leads visitors to a small chapel.*
5 DOOR **lead (sb) to/into sth** if a door or passage leads to a particular room or place, you can get there by going through it: *The officer opened the door that led to the jury room.*
6 WIN [I,T] to be winning a game or competition: *With two minutes to play, the Pistons are leading.* | **lead (sb/sth) by sth** *At halftime the Cowboys were leading by 19 points.* | *The Mayor leads his opponent by 28 points.*
7 MAKE SB DO STH [T] to be the thing that makes someone decide to do something: **lead sb to do sth** *Several factors led us to sell our business.* | *Our research* ***led us to the conclusion*** (=caused us to believe) *that the present system is unfair.*
8 lead sb to believe/expect/understand to make someone think something is true, especially when it is not: *He led me to believe that he'd never been married before.*
9 LIFE [T] if you lead a particular kind of life, that is what your life is like: **lead a normal/exciting/dull etc. life** *You kids have led such an easy life.* | **lead a life of luxury/poverty etc.** *Marie imagined leading a life of luxury.* | *She had no idea that her husband had been* ***leading a double life*** (=keeping important parts of your life secret from family, friends etc.).
10 SUCCESS [I,T] to be more successful than other people, companies, or countries in a particular activity or area of business or study: **lead (sb/sth) in sth** *Japan leads the world in life expectancy.* | *His new movie* ***led the field*** (=was most successful in a particular group) *with seven Oscar nominations.*
11 [I,T] to be the first to do something which sets an example for others to follow: *Singapore has always led in this market.* | *When political change began, it was women who* ***led the way.***
12 CONVERSATION [I,T] to direct a conversation or discussion, especially so that it develops in the way you want: *Debbie always leads the conversation back to herself.*
13 lead nowhere/not lead anywhere to produce no useful result or bring no useful opportunities: *The police investigation seems to have led nowhere.*
14 lead sb astray to encourage or make someone to make bad choices or do bad things that they would not normally do: *Kids can be easily led astray by their friends.*
15 lead sb by the nose INFORMAL to make someone do anything you want them to
16 you can lead a horse to water (but you can't make him drink) used to say that you cannot force anyone to do what they do not want to do
17 this leads me/us to... SPOKEN used in a speech or discussion to introduce a new subject and connect it with what you have just said: *This leads me to our sales targets for next year.*
18 lead sb down the garden/primrose path INFORMAL to deceive someone
19 CARDS [I,T] to play a particular card as your first card in one part of a game of cards: **lead (with) sth** *He led with the eight of hearts.*
20 DANCING [I,T] to be the one of two people that are dancing together who decides which direction they will move: *Juan led her slowly around the dance floor.*
[**Origin:** Old English *lædan*]

lead into sth *phr. v.* if one thing leads into another, the second one follows naturally from the first because there is a clear relationship between them: *The history lesson can lead nicely into a discussion of modern-day issues.*

lead off *phr. v.* **lead sth ↔ off** to start something such as a meeting, event, or performance by saying or doing something: *I'd like to lead off by thanking Dr. Jacobs for visiting us.* | **lead off with sth** *He led off with a few jokes.*

lead sb **↔ on** *phr. v.* to deceive someone, especially by making them think that you are romantically interested in them when you really are not: *I don't want to lead her on.*

lead to sth *phr. v.* to make something happen or exist as a result of something else: *information leading to the man's arrest* | ***One thing led to another, and*** (=a

L

series of events happened with the result that) *we got into a big fight.*

lead up to sth *phr. v.* **1** to come before something, often causing it to happen: *the events leading up to the war* | *the last few days leading up to the election* **2** to gradually introduce a subject into a conversation, especially a subject that may be embarrassing or upsetting: *What I'm leading up to is that we need to rewrite the proposal.*

lead with sth *phr. v.* **1** if a newspaper or television program leads with a particular story, that story is the main one **2 lead with your left/right** to hit someone mainly with your left or right hand in BOXING

lead² S2 W2 *n.*
1 RACES the lead the position or situation of being in front of or better than everyone else in a race or competition: *Lewis is still **in the lead**.* | *Kent **took the lead*** (=went ahead of others) *in the fifth lap.*
2 ACTION [singular] an action that other people copy, often something that is intended to make other people copy you: *The French are **following** Germany's **lead** on this issue.* | *It was young people who **took the lead*** (=were the first to start) *in organizing a peace movement.*
3 WINNING AMOUNT [singular] the distance, number of points etc. by which one competitor is ahead of another: +**over** *Virginia holds a 12-game lead over Kentucky.* | +**of** *In March the Republican candidate had a lead of 35%.*
4 INFORMATION [C] a piece of information that may help you to make a discovery or help find the answer to a problem: *The police have no leads in the murder investigation.* | *Detectives are **following up*** (=doing something as a result of) *a number of **leads**.*
5 ACTING ROLE [C] ENG. LANG. ARTS the main acting part in a play, movie etc.: *Who's **playing the lead in** the school play?*
6 ACTOR [C] ENG. LANG. ARTS the main actor in a movie or play: **male/female lead** *They haven't chosen their male lead.*
7 NEWS [C] the first or most important story in a television news program, newspaper etc., or the first part of such a story
8 be sb's lead the right, in a game of cards, to play your card first
9 FOR DOG [C] a LEASH
10 ELECTRIC WIRE [C] TECHNICAL a wire that is used to connect parts of a piece of electrical equipment

lead³ /lɛd/ *n.* **1** [U] SYMBOL **Pb** CHEMISTRY a soft heavy gray metal which is an ELEMENT that melts easily, is poisonous, and was used in the past in paints and to make things such as pipes: *high levels of lead in the soil* **2** [C,U] the gray part of a pencil that makes the marks **3 feel like lead** if your legs or arms feel like lead, they feel very heavy because you are tired or ill **4 a lead foot** if someone has a lead foot, they always drive their car very fast **5 get the lead out** SPOKEN INFORMAL used to tell someone to do something faster **6 go down like a lead balloon** if a suggestion or joke goes down like a lead BALLOON, people do not like it at all **7** [U] OLD-FASHIONED bullets

lead⁴ /lid/ *adj.* [only before noun] **1 lead guitarist/singer/attorney etc.** the first or most important person in a group **2 lead role/part** the main acting part in a movie or play: *Nicole Kidman was cast in the lead role.* **3 lead story/editorial** the article that is given the first or most important place in a newspaper **4 lead runner/car etc.** the person, car etc. that is in front of a group in a race

lead·ed gas /ˌlɛdɪd 'gæs/ also **ˌleaded gaso'line** *n.* [U] gasoline containing LEAD

lead·en /'lɛdn/ *adj.* **1** LITERARY dark gray: *leaden skies* **2** without happiness, excitement, or energy: *a leaden speaking style*

lead·er /'lidɚ/ S2 W1 *n.* [C] **1** the person who directs or controls a team, organization, country etc., or someone who has the ability to do this: *our national political leaders* | *a Boy Scout leader* | +**of** *The leader of the revolt was Antonio Miranda.* | **a religious/military/community etc. leader** (=with an important position in a particular group) | **a natural/born leader** (=someone who naturally has the qualities needed to be a leader) **2** the person, organization etc. that is in front of all the others in a race or competition: *She was ten feet behind the leader.* **3** the product or company that is the best or most successful in a particular area: +**in** *a leader in the field of genetic research* → see also MARKET LEADER

lead·er·ship /'lidɚˌʃɪp/ S3 W2 *n.* **1** [U] the position of being the leader of a team, organization etc.: +**of** *leadership of the team* | ***Under his leadership*** (=with him as the leader), *China became a major economic power.* | *Myers' important **leadership role** in the company* **2** [U] the quality of being good at leading a team, organization, country etc.: *leadership skills* | *a woman with vision and leadership* **3** [C] all the people who lead a group, organization, country etc.: *the Korean leadership* **4** [U] the position of being better than your competitors: +**in** *the company's leadership in robot technology*

lead-free /ˌlɛd 'fri◂ / *adj.* containing no LEAD SYN **unleaded**

lead-in /'lid ɪn/ *n.* [C] **1** something that is said or written to introduce a new subject or a new part of an argument, idea etc.: +**to** *This sentence is a good lead-in to the next paragraph.* **2** remarks made by someone to introduce a television or radio show

lead·ing¹ /'lidɪŋ/ *adj.* [only before noun] **1** best, most important, or most successful: *the leading scorer in college basketball* | *the leading industrial nations* **2 leading edge a)** the part of an activity in which the most modern and advanced equipment and methods are used: *To survive, companies must stay on the leading edge of technology.* → see also LEADING-EDGE **b)** TECHNICAL the part of something that is at the front of it when it moves: *the leading edge of a plane's wing* **3 leading light** a respected person who leads a group or organization, or is important in a particular area of knowledge or activity **4 a leading question** a question that deliberately tricks someone into giving the answer you want **5 leading lady/man** the woman or man who acts the most important female or male part in a movie, play etc.

lead·ing² /'lɛdɪŋ/ *n.* [U] TECHNICAL **1** the space left between lines of print on a page **2** LEAD used for window frames

leading-edge /ˌlidɪŋ 'ɛdʒ/ *adj.* [only before noun] leading-edge machines, systems etc. are the most modern and advanced ones that exist: *leading-edge communication devices*

ˌleading 'indicators *n.* [plural] ECONOMICS a list of important economic things that are likely to change over time, printed every month by the U.S. government and used as a sign of what is likely to happen to the U.S. ECONOMY in the near future

lead-off /'lid ɔf/ *adj.* happening or going first or before others: *the lead-off witness*

lead time /'lid taɪm/ *n.* [C] the time it takes to prepare, make, and deliver something to someone who has ordered it

leaf¹ /lif/ S2 W3 *n. plural* **leaves** /livz/ **1** [C] BIOLOGY one of the usually flat and thin parts of a plant that grow out of its stem or branches. Leaves use the energy from light to make food for the plant by PHOTOSYNTHESIS.: *a few fresh basil leaves* | +**of** *the leaves of a maple tree* | +**on** *the leaves on the trees* | **be in leaf/come into leaf** (=grow leaves in the spring) **2** [C] a part of the top of a table that can be taken out to make the table smaller **3** [U] metal, especially gold or silver, in a very thin sheet **4** [C] TECHNICAL a thin sheet of paper, especially a page in a book [**Origin:** Old English] → see also LOOSE-LEAF, **turn over a new leaf** at TURN OVER (5)

leaf² *v.*

leaf through sth *phr. v.* to turn the pages of a book quickly, without reading it thoroughly: *She leafed aimlessly through magazines.*

leaf·let¹ /'liflɪt/ *n.* [C] a piece of printed paper with information, political statements, or advertising on it:

pass/hand out leaflets (=give them to people in a public place)

leaflet² *v.* [I,T] to give leaflets to people in a particular area, usually a public place

'leaf mold *n.* [U] dead decaying leaves that form a rich surface on soil

leaf·y /'lifi/ *adj. comparative* **leafier**, *superlative* **leafiest** **1** having a lot of leaves **2** having a lot of trees and plants: *leafy suburbs*

league¹ /lig/ W3 *n.* [C] **1** a group of sports teams or players who compete against each other → see also CONFERENCE: *the National Football League* **2 not in the same league (as sb/sth)** not nearly as good or important as someone or something else: *It's a good movie, but it's not in the same league as "The Matrix."* **3 in a different league** very different from someone or something else: *This car is in a different league from others in this price range.* **4 in a league of your own** much different, usually better, than other people or things **5 out of your league** to not be experienced or skillful enough to do something: *Kendall's out of his league when it comes to marketing.* **6 be in league (with sb)** to be working together secretly, especially for a bad purpose: *politicians in league with the Mafia* **7** a group of people or countries who have joined together because they have similar aims, political beliefs etc.: *the Arab League* **8** an old unit for measuring, equal to about five kilometers [**Origin:** (1–7) 1400–1500 French *ligue* **agreement to act together**, from Old Italian *liga*, from *ligare* **to tie**]

league² *v.* [I,T] FORMAL to join together with other people, especially in order to fight for or against something

,League of 'Nations, the HISTORY an association of countries that was formed in 1920 with the aim of preventing wars and achieving things together. It was replaced in 1946 by the United Nations.

,League of ,Women 'Voters a U.S. organization that encourages women to vote, and makes sure that laws or government plans that affect women are properly discussed and thought about

leak¹ /lik/ S3 *v.* **1** [I,T] if a container, pipe, roof etc. leaks, or if it leaks gas, liquid etc., there is a small hole or crack in it that lets the gas or liquid flow out or through: *The roof leaks when it rains.* | *The pipe was leaking chlorine.* ►see THESAURUS box at flow¹ **2** [I] if a gas or liquid leaks, it gets in, out, or through a hole in something: **+into/through/from etc.** *Water was leaking out of the radiator.* ►see THESAURUS box at pour **3** [T] to deliberately give secret information to a newspaper, television company etc.: **leak sth to sb** *Details of the contract were leaked to the press.* [**Origin:** 1400–1500 Old Norse *leka*]

leak

leak out *phr. v.* if secret information leaks out, a lot of people find out about it: *News of the deal leaked out three weeks ago.*

leak² *n.* [C] **1** a small hole that lets liquid or gas flow into or out of something: **+in** *a leak in the cooling system* ►see THESAURUS box at hole¹ **2 a gas/oil/water leak** an escape of gas or liquid through a hole in something **3** a situation in which secret information is deliberately given to a newspaper, television company etc.: *He denied he was the source of the leak.* **4 take a leak** SPOKEN INFORMAL to URINATE → see also **spring a leak** at SPRING² (7)

leak·age /'likɪdʒ/ *n.* **1** [C,U] an occasion when gas, water etc. leaks, or the amount of gas or liquid that has leaked **2** [U] the deliberate spreading of information that should be kept secret

leak·y /'liki/ *adj. comparative* **leakier**, *superlative* **leakiest** a container, roof etc. that is leaky has a hole, crack etc. in it, so that liquid or gas passes through it: *a leaky faucet* —**leakiness** *n.* [U]

lean¹ /lin/ S3 W2 *v.* **1** [I always + adv./prep.] to move or bend your body in a particular direction: **+forward/back/over etc.** *Celia leaned forward.* | *Then he leaned over and kissed his wife.* **2** [I always + adv./prep., T always + adv./prep.] to support yourself or be supported against a wall or other surface, or to put something in a sloping position in which it is supported: **+on/against** *Lou leaned against the wall as he talked.* | *Don't lean on the mirror.* | **lean sth on/against sth** *Dad leaned the ladder against the house.*

lean

THESAURUS

stand to put something in an almost upright position: *He stood the Christmas tree against the wall.*
rest to support an object by putting it on or against something: *I rested my head on the back of the chair.*
prop to support something or keep it in a particular position: *He propped his bike against the fence.*

3 [I] to slope or bend from an upright position: *The tower leans slightly to the left.* **4** [I] to be likely to make a particular decision or support a particular set of opinions, beliefs etc.: *The polls can show which way voters are leaning.* | **lean toward sth** *I'm leaning toward not going back to school in the fall.* [**Origin:** Old English *hleonian*]

lean on sb/sth *phr. v.* **1** to depend on someone or something for support or help, especially at a difficult time: *The sisters lean on each other for support.* **2** INFORMAL to try to influence someone, especially by threatening them: **lean on sb to do sth** *Apparently Roberts leaned on the family to give him money.*

lean² *adj.* **1** thin in a healthy and attractive way: *a lean and athletic man* ►see THESAURUS box at thin¹ **2** lean meat does not have much fat on it: *Try to choose lean cuts of meat.* **3** a lean organization, company etc. uses only as much money and as many people as it needs, so that nothing is wasted: *a **lean and mean** (=very competitive) corporation* **4** a lean period is a very difficult time because there is not enough money, business etc.: *a lean year for business* —**leanness** *n.* [U]

lean³ *n.* [U] OLD-FASHIONED the part of meat that you eat, but not the bone or fat

lean·ing /'linɪŋ/ *n.* [C usually plural] a tendency to prefer or agree with a particular set of beliefs, opinions etc.: **sb's political/conservative/ideological etc. leanings** *his radical political leanings* | **+toward** *a leaning toward the Left* —**leaning** *adj.*: *the conservative-leaning court*

'lean-to *n.* [C] **1** a small simple outdoor shelter that stands alone and has a sloping roof **2** a part of a building that has been added onto it, with a sloping roof.

leap¹ /lip/ *v.* **leapt** /lɛpt/ or **leaped** **1 a)** [I always + adv./prep.] to jump high into the air, or to jump in order to land in a different place: *The squirrels leap easily from tree to tree.* | **+over/across** *A deer leapt over the fence.* **b)** [T] to jump over something: *Brenda leaped the gate and ran across the field.* ►see THESAURUS box at jump¹ **2** [I always + adv./prep.] to move very quickly and with a lot of energy: **+up/out/into etc.** *I leapt out of bed, in a panic.* | *Fraser **leaped to his feet** (=quickly stood up) and protested.* **3** [I] to increase quickly and by

L

a large amount OPP **fall** OPP **tumble**: *The price of gas leapt 15% overnight.* | **leap to sth** *Profits leaped to $360 million.* **4 sth leaps out at you** if something you are looking at leaps out at you, it is very easy for you to notice because it is unusual or unexpected **5 leap to sb's defense/assistance** quickly defend or help someone: *When they accused him of lying, his girlfirend leaped to his defense.* **6 sb's heart/spirts leap** LITERARY to feel sudden happiness or excitement: *My heart leaped when I saw Paul at the airport.* **7 leap into action** to start doing something suddenly because of something else that has happened: *Members of the parent-teacher organization leaped into action, raising $10,000.* **8 leap off the page (at sb)** if a word, phrase, etc. leaps off the page at you, it makes you pay close attention to it when you are reading: *The photograph seemed to leap off the page at her.* [**Origin:** Old English *hleapan*] → see also **look before you leap** at LOOK[1] (6)

leap at sth *phr. v.* to accept a chance, opportunity, or offer very eagerly: *I leapt at the chance of going to India.*

leap out at sb *phr. v.* if something. leaps out at you, it is hard not to notice it: *The trees are lit up so they really leap out at you as you drive by.*

leap[2] *n.* [C] **1** a big jump: *Jordan won with a leap of 27 feet, 10 inches.* | *He **took a flying leap*** (=made a long jump) *and got to the other side of the stream.* **2 by leaps and bounds** if someone or something increases, develops, grows etc. by leaps and BOUNDS, they do it very quickly: *The Hispanic population of the county has grown by leaps and bounds.* **3** a sudden large increase in the number or amount of something OPP **drop** OPP **plunge**: **+in** *a leap in prices* **4** a sudden large improvement in something: **+in** *a significant leap in military technology* | **a quantum/giant/huge leap** *The moon-landing represented a quantum leap to the scientific community.* | *the huge economic **leap forward** that took place in the 1980s* **5** a big change in the way that you behave or think or in the way that something happens, often a change that involves some uncertainty or risk: *Opening my own business was a big leap for me.* | *She hasn't yet **made the leap from** TV to movies.* | *It takes quite **a leap of the imagination** to see John as a teacher* (=it is hard to imagine him as a teacher). **6 a leap of faith** something you do even though it involves a risk, hoping that it will have a good result: *It was a huge leap of faith to open the restaurant during a slow economy.* **7 a leap in the dark** something you do, or a risk that you take, without knowing what will happen as a result

leap·frog[1] /ˈlipfrɑg/ *n.* [U] a children's game in which someone bends over and someone else jumps over them

leapfrog[2] *v.* [I,T] to achieve something more quickly than usual, especially by missing some of the usual stages: *The win leapfrogged them into second place.*

leapt /lɛpt/ *v.* a past tense and past participle of LEAP

ˈleap year *n.* [C] a year when February has 29 days instead of 28, which happens every four years

Lear·jet /ˈlɪrdʒɛt/ *n.* [C] TRADEMARK a type of airplane that is fast and comfortable

learn /lɚn/ S1 W1 *v.*

1 SUBJECT/SKILL [I,T] to gain knowledge of a subject or skill in an activity, by experience, by studying it, or by being taught → see also TEACH: *When did you start learning Spanish?* | *a student who is eager to learn* | **learn (how) to do sth** *Didn't you learn to drive when you were 16?* | **learn about sth** *We're learning about the Civil War.* | **learn sth from sb** *I learned a lot from my teachers.* → see KNOW[1]

THESAURUS

study to spend time going to classes, reading, etc. to learn about a subject: *Many students use computers to help them study.*
pick sth up to learn something without much effort, by watching or listening to other people: *I picked up some Korean when I was in the army.*
get the hang of sth to learn how to do something, especially by practicing it: *I couldn't get the hang of the game.*
master to learn something so well that you understand it completely and have no difficulty with it: *I had finally mastered Chopin's Nocturne No. 2.*

2 FIND OUT [I,T] FORMAL to find out information, news etc. by hearing it from someone else: **+of/about** *I learned of her death yesterday.* | **learn (that)** *Several months ago McNaughtan learned that he had cancer.* | **learn who/what/whether etc.** *Will we ever learn what really happened?*

3 REMEMBER [T] to get to know something so well that you can easily remember it SYN **memorize**: *As an actor, she always had trouble learning her lines.* | *As kids, we had to **learn** a lot of poetry **by heart*** (=learn it so that you can say it exactly without reading).

4 CHANGE YOUR BEHAVIOR [I,T] to gradually understand a situation and start behaving in the way that you should: *You just never learn, do you?* | **learn to do sth** *We've learned to treat each other with respect.* | **learn (that)** *I soon learned that it was best to keep quiet.* | *She was stupid to believe him, but she's **learned** her **lesson*** (=she won't do it again, because something bad happened). | **learn from your mistakes** (=improve the way you do things because of mistakes you have made) | *I **learned the hard way*** (=learned from my mistakes) *that drugs weren't the answer to my problems.*

5 that'll learn sb! SPOKEN NONSTANDARD used to say in an unkind way that a bad experience someone has had should change the way they behave in the future

[**Origin:** Old English *leornian*] → see also **live and learn** at LIVE[1] (28)

learn·ed /ˈlɚnɪd/ *adj.* FORMAL **1** having a lot of knowledge because you have read and studied a lot: *a learned professor* **2 learned books/works etc.** books or other materials that are written by people who have a lot of knowledge —**learnedly** *adv.*

learn·er /ˈlɚnɚ/ *n.* [C] someone who is learning to do something: **slow/quick/fast learner** *Jill's a very quick learner.* | **+of** *a grammar book for learners of English*

ˈlearner's ˌpermit *n.* [C] an official document that gives you permission to learn to drive

learn·ing /ˈlɚnɪŋ/ W2 *n.* [U] **1** knowledge gained through reading and study: *a woman of great learning* **2** BIOLOGY small changes in behavior that result from experience or training → see also CONDITIONING

ˈlearning curve *n.* [C] the rate at which you learn a new skill

ˈlearning disaˌbility *n.* [C] a mental problem that affects someone's ability to learn

ˈlearning efˌfect *n.* [singular] ECONOMICS the idea that education can have a positive effect on business because people who are well educated work more effectively, produce more goods etc., and earn higher wages

learnt /lɚnt/ *v.* OLD-FASHIONED a past tense and past participle of LEARN

leas·a·ble /ˈlisəbəl/ *adj.* available to be leased: *leasable office space*

lease[1] /lis/ *n.* [C] **1** LAW a legal agreement that allows you to use a car, building etc. for a period of time, in return for rent: *a six-month lease on an apartment* | *I decided to **take out a lease*** (=get one) *on a BMW.* **2 give sb/sth a new lease on life a)** to make someone feel healthy, active, or happy again after being weak, sick, or tired: *Changing jobs has given me a new lease on life.* **b)** to change or improve a thing or a situation so that something will continue to work longer: *Rising oil prices could give atomic energy a new lease on life.*

lease[2] *v.* [T] **1** also **lease out** to use or let someone use buildings, property etc. on a lease: **lease sth to sb** *They decided to lease the building to another company.* **2** to pay to use expensive machinery or equipment for a long period, instead of buying it: *We lease all our computers.*

lease·back /ˈlisbæk/ *n.* [C,U] TECHNICAL an arrangement in which you sell or give something to someone, but continue to use it by paying them rent

lease·hold /ˈlishoʊld/ *n.* [C] LAW an agreement by which you lease a building or piece of land for a particular, usually long, period of time

lease·hold·er /ˈlisˌhoʊldɚ/ *n.* [C] LAW someone who has leased a building or piece of land

leash¹ /liʃ/ [S3] *n.* [C] **1** a piece of rope, leather etc. attached to a dog's collar in order to control it: *All dogs must be kept* ***on a leash*** *at all times in the park.* **2 have sb on a leash** HUMOROUS to be able to control someone

leash² *v.* [T] to put a leash on a dog —**leashed** *adj.*

least¹ /list/ [S1] [W1] *quantifier* **1 at least a)** not less than a particular number or amount → see also AT MOST: *At least fifty people were there.* | *It will take a year* ***at the very least*** (=used to emphasize that it is likely to be much more than a year) *to build the stadium.* **b)** even if nothing else is true, or even if nothing else happens: *At least you should listen to his explanation.* | *His parents should at least go to his graduation.* **c)** used when you are mentioning an advantage that makes particular problems or disadvantages seem less serious: *The food was terrible, but at least we had a nice view.* **d)** used when you are correcting or changing something that you have just said: *His name is Kevin. At least that's what he told me.* | *The law has changed, at least as far as I know.* **2 the least** the smallest in number, amount, or importance [OPP] **the most**: *Which jacket costs the least?* | *$10,000 is the least we'll need to repair the roof.* **3 least of all** especially not a particular person or thing: *Dave doesn't take anything seriously, least of all himself.* **4 the least sb could do** used when saying what you think someone should or could do to help someone else: *The least he could do is help you with the housework.* **5 not in the least** also **not the least (bit)** used to emphasize that you mean none at all, or not at all: *Neither of them is adventurous in the least.* | *She didn't seem the least bit worried.* **6 to say the least** used to emphasize that something is worse or more serious than you are actually saying: *Mrs. Russell was upset, to say the least.* **7 the least of your worries** something you are not worried about because there are other more important problems: *Figuring out where to go eat is the least of my worries right now.* **8 not least** FORMAL used to emphasize that something is more important than other things [SYN] **mainly** [SYN] **especially**: *She's very famous, not least because she's very rich.*

least² *adv.* less than anything or anyone else → see also MOST: *Car problems happen when you least expect them.* | *The tax hits those who can least afford it.* | *I was* ***the least*** (=used before adjectives) *experienced member of the expedition.*

ˌleast ˌcommon deˈnominator *n.* [C] MATH the smallest positive INTEGER (=1, 2, 3, 4 etc.) that can be divided exactly by all the DENOMINATORS in a set of FRACTIONS

ˌleast ˌcommon ˈmultiple *n.* [C] MATH the smallest positive INTEGER (=1, 2, 3, 4 etc.) that each of a set of numbers divides into exactly → see also GREATEST COMMON FACTOR

least·wise /ˈlistwaɪz/ also **least·ways** /ˈlistweɪz/ *adv.* SPOKEN INFORMAL at least [SYN] **anyway**

leath·er /ˈlɛðɚ/ [S3] *n.* **1** [U] animal skin, especially from cows, that has been treated to preserve it, and is used for making shoes, bags etc.: *a belt made of leather* | *a pair of leather gloves* **2 leathers** [plural] special leather clothes worn for protection by someone riding a MOTORCYCLE [**Origin:** Old English *lether*]

Leath·er·ette /ˌlɛθɚˈɛt/ *n.* [U] TRADEMARK a cheap material made to look like leather

leath·er·neck /ˈlɛðɚˌnɛk/ *n.* [C] SLANG a U.S. Marine

leath·er·y /ˈlɛðəri/ *adj.* thick and stiff like leather rather than soft or smooth: *leathery skin*

leave¹ /liv/ [S1] [W1] *v. past tense and past participle* **left** /lɛft/

1 GO AWAY [I,T] to go away from a place or a person: *What time did you leave the office?* | *The bus leaves at 8:30.* | *We* ***left home*** (=leave your house temporarily) *at about 10:00.* | **+for** *We're leaving for Tokyo next week.* | **leave to do sth** *I left to pick up the kids at school.* | *Just a few more questions, then we'll* ***leave you in peace*** (=stop bothering you). | *I'll* ***leave you two alone*** (=leave someone so they can be alone) *now.* | **leave sb to their work/reading etc** (=leave so that someone can work, read etc.) ►see THESAURUS box at **give¹**

2 LET STH STAY WHEN YOU GO [T always + adv./prep.] to let something or someone stay where they are when you go away: *I'll leave my bike here until we get back.* | *We're leaving the kids with Debbie tonight.* | *The box was too heavy, so we* ***left it behind.***

3 REMAIN a) be left if an amount or number of something is left, that amount or number remains after everything else has been taken away or used: *Is there any coffee left?* | *By 5 o'clock there was hardly anyone left in the office.* | **have sth left** *I still have three chapters left to read.* | *If there's any money* ***left over*** (=remaining), *you can keep it.* → see also LEFTOVER **b) that leaves sth** used to say that one thing remains after all other things have been used or tried: *I didn't do it, and neither did Dave, so that leaves you.*

4 FOR SB TO FIND [T] to put or deliver something in a place where someone else can find it when they come back: *I'll leave the report on your desk.* | *Please* ***leave your name and number*** (=said on a recorded phone message) *and I'll get back to you.* | **leave sth for sb** *We left $10 on the table for the waitress.* | **leave sb sth** *If I'm not home,* ***leave*** *me* ***a message*** (=a recorded phone message).

5 IN A CONDITION/STATE [T] **a)** to make or let something stay in a particular state or position: *You left the door open again.* | *The trial left a lot of questions unanswered.* | **leave sth on/off/out etc.** *Leave the kitchen light on when you go out.* | **leave sth doing sth** *Don't leave the water running while you brush your teeth.* **b)** if something leaves you in a particular condition or state, you are in that condition as a result of it: *The tornado left many people homeless.* | **leave sb doing sth** *Carla's narrow escape left her shaking with terror.* **c) leave yourself open to blame/criticism/ridicule etc.** to do something that makes it possible that you will be blamed, criticized, ridiculed etc.: *Expressing your true opinions can leave you open to criticism.*

6 FORGET STH [T always + adv./prep.] to forget to take something with you when you leave a place: **leave sth in/on/at etc.** *I think I left my umbrella at the store.*

7 NOT EAT/USE [T] to not eat or use all of something: *If you don't like the meat, just leave it.* | **leave sb sth/leave sth for sb** *Did you leave any hot water for me?*

8 LET SB DECIDE/TAKE RESPONSIBILITY [T] to let someone decide something or take responsibility for something: **leave (doing) sth to sb** *I've always left financial decisions to my wife.* | **leave it (up) to sb to do sth** *Don't leave it up to Ryan to do the cooking.*

9 HUSBAND/WIFE ETC. [I,T] to stop living with someone you had a close relationship with: *It was the constant arguing that made Pam leave.* | *I'm surprised that Kent left her.* | **leave sb for sb** *Jan's husband left her for another woman.*

10 COUNTRY/PLACE [I,T] to stop living in a country, town etc. and go somewhere else: *They're leaving Minneapolis to live in Santa Fe.*

11 JOB/GROUP [I,T] to stop working for a company, or stop being a member of a group: *After 30 years, Paige is leaving the company.*

12 HOME/SCHOOL ETC. [I,T] to stop living at your parents' home, stop going to school etc.: *Brian's parents talked him out of leaving college.* | *I* ***left home*** *when I was 14.*

13 TRAIN/SHIP ETC. [T] to get off a train, ship etc.

14 DELAY [T] to not do something until later: *Let's leave the ironing until tomorrow.* | *Don't* ***leave*** *the decision* ***until the last minute*** (=until just before it must be done). | *Let's* ***leave it at that*** (=not do any more of a job) *for today.*

15 WHEN YOU DIE [T] **a)** to give something to someone after you die: **leave sb sth** *Uncle Gene left us his house.* | **leave sth to sb/sth** *He had left all his money to*

L

charity. **b)** FORMAL to have members of your family still alive when you die: *Collins leaves a wife and three children.*
16 leave something/nothing to chance to take no action and wait to see what happens, or to make sure you have done everything to make something happen the way you want: *The producers of the show left nothing to chance.*
17 leave sb with no choice/option etc. to force someone to do something because there is nothing else they can do: *I was left with no alternative other than to take out a loan.*
18 leave a mark/stain/scar etc. to make a mark that cannot be removed: *The cut left a scar on my left hand.* | *Red wine can leave terrible stains on clothes.*
19 leave a space/gap etc. to deliberately make a space or room for something: *Leave two spaces between each sentence.* | ***Leave room** in the trunk for my suitcase.*
20 leave sb in the lurch also **leave sb high and dry** to leave someone without the help and support they need or were promised: *Electricity workers went on strike, leaving thousands of customers in the lurch.*
21 leave well (enough) alone to not try to change a situation because you might make it worse than it was before
22 leave something/a lot/much to be desired to be very unsatisfactory: *Your grades leave a lot to be desired.*
23 leave sb cold to not interest or excite someone at all: *Opera leaves me cold.*

SPOKEN PHRASES

24 leave sb alone to stop annoying or upsetting someone: *Just leave me alone and stop asking me questions.*
25 leave sth alone to stop touching something: *Leave it alone or you'll break it.*
26 leave it at that used to say that you do not want to say or do any more about something: *We're not moving, so let's leave it at that.*
27 leave it to sb used to say that you are not surprised that someone does something, because it is typical of them: *Leave it to you to have your whole year planned already!*
28 leave sb/sth be OLD-FASHIONED to not annoy or interrupt someone, or not touch or move something

29 not leave sb's side to always be with someone and take care of them: *Walter never left his wife's side in the hospital.*
30 leave sb to themselves to go away from someone so that they are alone
31 leave sb to their own devices to not tell someone what to do or offer them help, but let them do what they decide to do
32 leave sb in the dust to be more successful, smarter, better etc. than someone else, especially someone you are competing with: *When it came to math, Kate left him in the dust.*
33 leave sth/sb hanging to fail to finish something, or not to tell someone your decision about something: *The investigation should not be left hanging.*
34 leave a bad taste in your mouth if an experience leaves a bad taste in your mouth, remembering it upsets you or makes you feel uncomfortable
35 leave no stone unturned to do everything that you can in order to find something or solve a problem
[**Origin:** Old English *læfan*] → see also **take it or leave it** at TAKE[1] (28)

leave sth ↔ **aside** *phr. v.* to not think about or consider something for a time, so that you can think about something else SYN **ignore** SYN **disregard**: *Leaving aside the question of cost, is this plan really going to work?*

leave sb/sth **behind** *phr. v.* **1** to make progress much more quickly than someone or something else: *U.S. manufacturers were leaving Europe behind.* | **be/get left behind** *You'll have to work harder if you don't want to get left behind.* **2** to not take something or someone with you when you leave a place or go somewhere: *The enemy retreated, leaving their equipment behind.* | **be/get left behind** *I was young, so I always got left behind when everyone else went to the movies.* **3 leave sb behind** to move far ahead of someone who cannot run, walk, or drive as fast as you can: *Slow down, we're leaving Jim behind.* | **leave sb far/way behind** (=move very far ahead of someone) **4 leave sb/sth ↔ behind** to stop being involved with a place, person, or situation, or stop being affected by them: *I really wanted to leave my old life behind me.*

leave off *phr. v.* INFORMAL **1 take up/pick up/continue etc. (sth) where sb left off** to continue something that stopped, or that someone else stopped doing, from the place or point where it stopped: *Let's start again from where Justin left off.* **2 leave sb/sth off sth** to not include someone or something in a group, list, activity etc.: *Why was my name left off the list?*

leave sb/sth ↔ **out** *phr. v.* **1** to not include someone or something: *Tell me everything. Don't leave anything out.* | **leave sb/sth out of sth** *My wife was not involved. Leave her out of this.* **2 be/feel left out** to feel as if you are not accepted or welcome in a social group: *Kids who aren't on the team often feel left out.*

leave² S3 *n.* **1** [U] time that you are allowed to spend away from your work, especially in the military or for a particular reason: *I **took** a couple of days' **leave** when my dad died.* | *Carter is in charge of the office while I'm **on leave**.* | **sick/maternity/disability etc. leave** (=leave that you take because you are sick, having a baby, disabled etc.) | **leave of absence** (=a period that you are allowed to spend away from work to study, for personal reasons etc.) ►see THESAURUS box at **vacation**[1] **2 take leave of your senses** OLD-FASHIONED to suddenly start behaving in a crazy way **3 take leave of sb** also **take your leave** OLD-FASHIONED to say goodbye to someone **4 by your leave** OLD USE used when asking permission to do something

leav·en¹ /ˈlɛvən/ *v.* [T] **1** FORMAL to make something less boring and more interesting or cheerful **2** OLD-FASHIONED to add leavening to a mixture of flour and water → see also UNLEAVENED

leaven² also **leavening** *n.* **1** [C,U] LITERARY a small amount of a quality that makes an event or situation less boring and more interesting or cheerful **2** [U] another word for LEAVENING

leav·en·ing /ˈlɛvənɪŋ/ also **ˈleavening ˌagent** *n.* [U] a substance such as YEAST that is added to a mixture of flour and water so that it will swell and can be baked into bread

leaves /livz/ *n.* the plural of LEAF

ˈleave-ˌtaking *n.* [C] LITERARY an act of saying goodbye when you go away

leav·ings /ˈlivɪŋz/ *n.* [plural] OLD-FASHIONED things that are left because they are not wanted, especially food → see also LEFTOVERS

Leb·a·non /ˈlɛbəˌnɑn, -nən/ a country in the Middle East on the Mediterranean Sea, that is north of Israel and west of Syria —**Lebanese** /ˌlɛbəˈniz◂/ *adj.*

lech·er /ˈlɛtʃɚ/ also **lech** /lɛtʃ/ *n.* [C] DISAPPROVING a man who is always thinking about sex or trying to get sexual pleasure —**lecherous** *adj.* —**lecherously** *adv.*

lech·er·y /ˈlɛtʃəri/ *n.* [U] too much interest in or desire for sex

Le Cor·bu·si·er /lə ˌkɔrbuˈzyeɪ/ (1887–1965) a French ARCHITECT who built many important modern buildings, and planned the city of Chandigarh in India

lec·tern /ˈlɛktɚn/ *n.* [C] a piece of furniture that you stand behind when giving a speech, teaching a class etc., that is like a tall desk with a sloping surface for putting a book or notes on

lec·ture¹ /ˈlɛktʃɚ/ Ac S3 *n.* [C] **1** a long talk given to a group of people on a particular subject, especially as a method of teaching in colleges or universities → see also SPEECH: **+on/about** *We went to a lecture on economics.* | **give/deliver a lecture** *Professor Dunn will give a lecture on medieval art.* | *I'll give you my **lecture***

notes (=notes taken in a lecture). | **the lecture circuit** (=a set of places that someone goes to to give lectures) ►see THESAURUS box at **speech**, **university** **2** an act of criticizing someone or warning them about something in a long, serious talk, in a way that they think is unfair or unnecessary: **+on/about** *I don't need lectures on how to use my own camera.* | *Mom* ***gave me a lecture*** *for coming home late.* [**Origin:** 1200–1300 Late Latin *lectura* **act of reading**, from Latin *legere* **to read**]

lecture² Ac *v.* **1** [T] to talk seriously or angrily to someone in order to criticize or warn them, in a way that they think is unfair or unnecessary: *I wish you'd stop lecturing me!* | **lecture sb about/on sth** *He lectured us about making too much noise.* **2** [I] to talk to a group of people on a particular subject, especially as a method of teaching at a college or university

lec·tur·er /ˈlɛktʃərɚ/ Ac *n.* [C] **1** someone who gives a lecture **2** someone who teaches at a college or university, who has a rank below that of an ASSISTANT PROFESSOR ►see THESAURUS box at **teacher**

LED *n.* [C] TECHNICAL **Light Emitting Diode** a small piece of equipment on a watch, computer screen etc. that produces light when electricity passes through it

led /lɛd/ *v.* the past tense and past participle of LEAD

-led /lɛd/ *suffix* [in adjectives] having a particular thing as the most important or effective cause, influence etc.: *an export-led economic recovery*

ledge /lɛdʒ/ *n.* [C] **1** a flat narrow shelf or surface that sticks out from a building or wall on the outside: *Flags hung from the* ***window ledges.*** **2** a flat narrow surface of rock that is parallel to the ground

ledg·er /ˈlɛdʒɚ/ *n.* [C] **1** ECONOMICS a book recording the money received and spent by a business, bank etc. ►see THESAURUS box at **record¹** **2** a ledger line

ˈledger line *n.* [C] a line on which you write musical notes that are too high or low to be recorded on a STAFF

lee /li/ *n.* **1 the lee of sth** the side of something that is away from the wind or provides shelter from it: *a cabin in the lee of the hills* **2 the lees** [plural] the substance that collects at the bottom of a bottle of wine → see also DREGS

Lee /li/, **Har·per** /ˈhɑrpɚ/ (1926–) a U.S. writer famous for her NOVEL "To Kill a Mockingbird"

Lee, Rob·ert E. /ˈrɑbɚt i/ (1807–1870) a general in the Confederate army during the U.S. Civil War

leech /litʃ/ *n.* [C] **1** BIOLOGY a small soft creature that attaches itself to the skin of animals in order to drink their blood → see picture at FOOD WEB **2** someone who takes advantage of other people, usually by taking their money, food etc. **3** OLD USE a doctor

leek /lik/ *n.* [C] a vegetable with a long white stem and long flat green leaves, which tastes a little like an onion [**Origin:** Old English *leac*] → see picture on page A35

leer /lɪr/ *v.* [I] to look at someone in a way that upsets or offends them because it shows that you find them sexually attractive: **+at** *The man leered at her from the bar.* —**leer** *n.* [C] *a disgusting leer*

leer·y /ˈlɪri/ *adj.* [not before noun] INFORMAL careful in the way that you deal with something or someone, because you are worried something bad may happen SYN **wary**: **+of** *Landlords are often leery of renting to large families.*

ˌlee ˈshore *n.* [singular] TECHNICAL a shore which the wind from the ocean is blowing onto

Leeu·wen·hoek /ˈleɪvənˌhʊk/, **An·ton van** /ˈæntɑn væn/ (1632–1723) a Dutch scientist who developed MICROSCOPES with which he could see blood cells and BACTERIA

lee·ward /ˈliwɚd, ˈluɚd/ *adj.* TECHNICAL **1** the leeward side of something is the side that is sheltered from the wind OPP **windward** **2** a leeward direction is the same direction as the wind is blowing OPP **windward** —**leeward** *adv.*

Lee·ward Is·lands, the /ˌliwɚd ˈaɪləndz/ a group of islands in the Caribbean Sea, between Puerto Rico and Martinique, which includes the islands of Antigua, Montserrat, and Guadeloupe, and the Virgin Islands

lee·way /ˈliweɪ/ *n.* [U] **1** freedom to do things in the way you want to: *States now have more leeway to restrict the sale of guns.* **2** TECHNICAL the sideways movement of a ship, caused by strong wind

left¹ /lɛft/ S1 *v.* the past tense and past participle of LEAVE [**Origin:** Old English **weak**]

left² S2 W2 *adj.* [only before noun] **1** on the side of your body that contains your heart OPP **right**: *my left foot* **2** on, by, or in the direction of your left side SYN **left-hand** OPP **right**: *the left side of the page* | *a left turn* **3 have two left feet** INFORMAL to be very awkward in the way you move, especially when dancing **4 the left hand doesn't know what the right hand is doing** used to say that a group or organization is not organized because the people in one part do not know what is happening in the other parts of it → see also **be left** at LEAVE¹ (3), LEFT-OF-CENTER

left³ S2 *adv.* **1** toward the left side OPP **right**: *Turn left at the stop sign.* **2 left and right** very often, especially in a way that is wrong or not fair: *We're losing good teachers left and right.*

left⁴ *n.* **1** [singular] the left side or direction: **on/to the left (of sth)** *The entrance is on the left.* | *To the left of the church is an old shoe factory.* | **on/to your left** *You can get tickets at the booths on your left.* | *The picture shows,* ***from left to right,*** *Molly, Dana, and Anne.* **2 the left/Left** also **the left wing** political parties or groups, such as Socialists and Communists, that want money and property to be divided more fairly, and generally support workers rather than employers: *He has support from the left.* **3** [singular] a turn to the left when walking, driving etc.: **take/hang a left (at sth)** *Take a left at the next light.* | **the next/first etc. left** *The road is the second left off Main St.* **4** [C] a hit made with your left hand

ˈleft-click *v.* [I,T] to press the left button on a computer MOUSE once in order to choose something from the screen that you want the computer to do

ˈleft field *n.* **1** [singular] a position in baseball in the left side of the OUTFIELD **2 be (way) out in left field** INFORMAL strange or unusual: *Some of his ideas are way out in left field.* **3 come (from) out of left field** INFORMAL to be very surprising or unexpected

left ˈfielder *n.* [C] a baseball player who plays in left field

ˌleft-ˈhand *adj.* [only before noun] **1** on the left side of something OPP **right-hand**: *the left-hand page* | *a left-hand turn* | ***the left-hand side of*** *the street* **2** using your left hand to do a particular thing OPP **right-hand**: *a left-hand piano concerto*

ˌleft-ˈhanded *adj.* **1** someone who is left-handed uses their left hand for most things, especially writing **2** done with the left hand OPP **right-handed**: *a left-handed punch* **3** made to be used by left-handed people OPP **right-handed**: *left-handed scissors* **4 a left-handed compliment** a remark that seems to express praise or admiration, but in fact is insulting SYN **backhanded compliment** —**left-handed** *adv.* —**left-handedness** *n.* [U]

ˌleft-ˈhander *n.* [C] someone who uses their left hand, especially for throwing a ball OPP **right-hander**

left·ie /ˈlɛfti/ *n.* another spelling of LEFTY

left·ist /ˈlɛftɪst/ *adj.* POLITICS supporting LEFT-WING politics, groups, or ideas: *leftist views* | *a leftist organization* —**leftism** *n.* [U] —**leftist** *n.* [C]

ˈleft-of-ˌcenter *adj.* having ideas or opinions that agree more with the LEFT in politics than with the RIGHT, but not being extreme in those ideas

left·o·ver /ˈlɛftˌoʊvɚ/ *adj.* [only before noun] remaining after all the rest has been used, eaten etc.: *There's some leftover soup.*

left·o·vers /ˈlɛftˌoʊvɚz/ *n.* [plural] food that has not been eaten at the end of a meal, and that was not on

L

anyone's plate: *You can have the leftovers for lunch tomorrow.*

left·ward /ˈlɛftwərd/ *adj., adv.* **1** tending to support the LEFT in politics OPP **rightward**: *a major leftward swing in the party* **2** on or toward the left OPP **rightward**: *a leftward bend*

ˌleft ˈwing *n.* [singular] **1** a group of people whose ideas are more left-wing than those of other members of the same political group: *the left wing of the Democratic Party* **2** the left side of a playing area in sports such as SOCCER and HOCKEY, or a player who plays on this side

ˌleft-ˈwing *adj.* POLITICS supporting the political aims of groups such as Socialists and Communists, such as the idea that money and property should be divided more fairly OPP **right-wing**: *a left-wing newspaper* —**left-winger** *n.* [C]

left·y, leftie /ˈlɛfti/ *n.* [C] INFORMAL someone who uses their left hand to write, throw etc.

leg /lɛg/ S1 W2 *n.*

1 BODY PART [C] BIOLOGY either of the two long parts of your body that your feet are joined to and that you use for walking, or a similar part on an animal or insect: *Angie broke her leg skiing.* | *leg muscles* | *A spider has eight legs.*

2 FURNITURE [C] one of the upright parts that supports a piece of furniture: *a table leg*

3 PANTS [C usually plural] a part of your pants or other piece of clothing that covers your leg: *Pull up your pant legs.*

4 FOOD [C,U] the leg of an animal when eaten as food: *roast leg of lamb*

5 TRIP/RACE ETC. [C] a part of a long trip, race, process etc. that is done one part at a time: *the second leg of the band's U.S. tour*

6 leg room space in which to put your legs comfortably when you are sitting in a car, aircraft etc.: *There isn't enough leg room for me.*

7 a leg up an advantage over a person or group of people: *This new technology should **give** the company **a leg up on** their competition.*

8 sth is on its last legs INFORMAL used to say that something is in very bad condition and about to stop working: *Our printer is on its last legs.*

9 not have a leg to stand on INFORMAL to be in a situation where you cannot prove or legally support what you say: *If you didn't sign a contract, you don't have a leg to stand on.*

10 sth has legs INFORMAL if a movie, television show, piece of news etc. has legs, people continue to be interested in it

11 MATH [C] the two CONGRUENT (=same length) sides of a RIGHT TRIANGLE, that meet and form an angle of 90°; or the two congruent sides of an ISOSCELES TRIANGLE, that meet at the VERTEX (=top); or the two congruent sides of a TRAPEZOID, that are not parallel

[**Origin:** 1200–1300 Old Norse *leggr*] → see also **break a leg!** at BREAK[1] (21), -LEGGED, PEG LEG, **pull sb's leg** at PULL[1] (18), SEA LEGS, **shake a leg** at SHAKE[1] (13), **stretch your legs** at STRETCH[1] (12)

leg·a·cy /ˈlɛgəsi/ *n. plural* **legacies** [C] **1** a situation that exists as a result of things that happened at an earlier time: *Her rich musical legacy lives on in her recordings.* | **+of** *Racial tension is a legacy of slavery.* **2** money or property that you receive from someone after they die: *The house was a legacy from her aunt.* **3** someone who joins an organization or attends a college or university that someone in their family used to belong to or attend [**Origin:** 1300–1400 Old French *legacie* **position of a legate**, from Latin *legatus*]

le·gal /ˈligəl/ Ac S2 W1 *adj.* **1** allowed, ordered, or approved by law OPP **illegal**: *The students' actions were perfectly legal.* | *Carrying identity cards will become a legal requirement.* | **the legal maximum/limit/minimum** *His blood alcohol level was five times the legal limit.* | **make sth legal** *In 2004 gay marriage was made legal in Massachusetts.* **2** [only before noun] relating to the law: *the legal system* | *free legal advice* | *a long legal battle* | *Citizens' groups are **taking legal action** to prevent the expansion of the freeway* (=using the legal system to try to stop this). **3 make it legal** INFORMAL to get married: *When are you two going to make it legal?* [**Origin:** 1400–1500 French, Latin *legalis*, from *lex* **law**] → see also LEGALLY

ˌlegal ˈage *n.* **1** [U] the age at which a person is legally considered an adult, usually 18 or 21: *Since your daughter's **of legal age**, she can marry anyone she wants.* **2** [singular] the age at which someone is legally allowed to do something: **+for** *The legal age for gambling in Nevada is 21.* | **the legal driving/drinking/voting age** (=when someone is allowed drive a car, buy alcoholic drinks, or vote)

ˌlegal ˈaid *n.* [U] legal help that is given free to people who cannot pay for it

ˈlegal ˌcode *n.* [C] LAW a set of written laws that are used in all the courts within an individual country

ˌlegal eˈquality *n.* [U] ECONOMICS a situation in which every person has the same legal rights as everyone else

le·gal·ese /ˌligəˈliz/ *n.* [U] INFORMAL language used by lawyers that is difficult for most people to understand

ˌlegal ˈholiday *n.* [C] a holiday that the government has established and on which most government offices and banks are closed

le·gal·is·tic /ˌligəˈlɪstɪk◂/ *adj.* too concerned about small rules or details, and not concerned enough about what is really important —**legalistically** /-kli/ *adv.* —**legalism** /ˈligəˌlɪzəm/ *n.* [U]

le·gal·i·ty /lɪˈgæləṭi/ Ac *n.* **1** [U] the fact of being allowed by law: **+of** *The legality of testing employees for drugs is questionable.* **2 the legalities** [plural] the formal, legal parts of an agreement: *We don't need to talk about all the legalities here.*

le·gal·ize /ˈligəˌlaɪz/ *v.* [T] to make a law that allows people to do something that was not allowed before: *Gambling has recently been legalized in three towns in Colorado.* —**legalization** /ˌligələˈzeɪʃən/ *n.* [U]

le·gal·ly /ˈligəli/ Ac *adv.* according to the law: *They are still legally married.* | *You are **legally responsible** for your child.* | **legally blind/dead/drunk etc.** (=declared to be in a particular condition according to the law) | *The contract is **legally binding*** (=it is illegal not to obey it).

ˈlegal pad *n.* [C] a long PAD of yellow writing paper with lines on it

ˈlegal proˌfession *n.* **the legal profession** lawyers, judges, and other people who work in courts of law or advise people about legal problems

ˈlegal-size *adj.* legal-size paper is 14 INCHES long and 8 inches wide

ˈlegal ˌsystem *n.* [C] the laws and the way they work through the police, courts etc. in a particular country

ˌlegal ˈtender *n.* [U] coins or paper money that are officially allowed to be used as money

leg·ate /ˈlɛgət/ *n.* [C] an important official representative, especially one sent by the POPE

leg·a·tee /ˌlɛgəˈti/ *n.* [C] LAW someone who has received money or property from someone who has died because they were mentioned in that person's WILL

le·ga·tion /lɪˈgeɪʃən/ *n.* [C] **1** POLITICS an office that represents a government in a foreign country but that is lower in rank than an EMBASSY: *the Cuban legation* **2** POLITICS the people who work in this office

le·ga·to /lɪˈgɑṭoʊ/ *adj., adv.* ENG. LANG. ARTS played or sung so that each note connects to the next one without pauses between them → see also STACCATO

le·ga·tor /lɪˈgeɪṭər/ *n.* [C] LAW someone who gives money or property to someone else after they die by making a WILL

leg·end /ˈlɛdʒənd/ *n.* **1** [C,U] an old, well-known story, often about brave people, adventures, or magical events, or all stories of this kind: *The Legend of Prince Valiant* | ***Legend has it that** an ape-like man lives in the woods around here.* | ***According to legend,** he escaped by leaping into the sea.* | *Dr. John's music is **the stuff of legend*** (=so good that stories are told about it). ▸see THESAURUS box at **story** **2** [C] someone who is

L

famous and admired for being extremely good at doing something: *the rock and roll legend Elvis Presley* → see also **living legend** at LIVING[1] (6) **3** [C usually singular] the words that explain a picture, map etc., or that explain the SYMBOLS used on a map, CHART etc. SYN **key** **4** LITERARY words that have been written somewhere, for example on a sign: *a T-shirt with the legend "save the whales"* [**Origin:** 1300–1400 French *légende*, from Latin *legere* **to gather, choose, read**] → see also URBAN LEGEND

leg·end·ar·y /ˈlɛdʒənˌdɛri/ *adj.* **1** famous and admired: *the legendary guitarist Jimi Hendrix* ►see THESAURUS box at **famous** **2** talked or read about in legends → see also MYTHICAL: *the legendary palace of Kublai Khan*

Lé·ger /leɪˈʒeɪ/, **Fer·nand** /fɛrˈnɑn/ (1881–1955) a French PAINTER famous for his work in the style of Cubism

leg·er·de·main /ˌlɛdʒɚdəˈmeɪn/ *n.* [U] OLD-FASHIONED skillful use of your hands when performing tricks

-legged /lɛgɪd/ *suffix* [in adjectives] **four-legged/two-legged/long-legged etc.** having four legs, two legs, long legs etc.: *a four-legged animal* → see also BOW-LEGGED, CROSS-LEGGED

leg·gings /ˈlɛgɪŋz/ *n.* **1** [plural] women's tight pants that stretch to fit the shape of the body, and that have no ZIPPER **2** [C usually plural] a piece of clothing worn to protect your legs, especially the lower part of your legs

leg·gy /ˈlɛgi/ *adj. comparative* **leggier**, *superlative* **leggiest** a woman or child who is leggy has long legs: *a leggy blonde* —**legginess** *n.* [U]

leg·i·ble /ˈlɛdʒəbəl/ *adj.* written or printed clearly enough for you to read OPP **illegible**: *The letter was torn but still legible.* —**legibly** *adv.* —**legibility** /ˌlɛdʒəˈbɪləṭi/ *n.* [U]

le·gion[1] /ˈlidʒən/ *n.* [C] **1** a large group of soldiers, especially in the army of ancient Rome **2** LITERARY a large number of people

legion[2] *adj.* LITERARY **be legion** to be very many in number SYN **numerous**

le·gion·ar·y /ˈlidʒəˌnɛri/ *n.* [C] a member of a legion

le·gion·naire /ˌlidʒəˈnɛr/ *n.* [C] a member of a legion, especially the French Foreign Legion

ˌlegion'naire's disˌease *n.* [U] MEDICINE a serious lung disease

'leg irons *n.* [plural] metal circles or chains that are put around a prisoner's legs

leg·is·late /ˈlɛdʒəˌsleɪt/ Ac *v.* [I,T] **1** to make a law about something: *Congress failed to legislate effective handgun controls.* | **legislate against sth** *It's useless to try to legislate against something that people want to do.* **2 legislate from the bench** DISAPPROVING if a judge or court of law legislates from the BENCH, they make an official decision that has the effect of a new law

leg·is·la·tion /ˌlɛdʒəˈsleɪʃən/ Ac W2 *n.* [U] **1** a law or set of laws: *civil rights legislation* | *an important* ***piece of legislation*** | +**on** *legislation on the sale of alcohol* | **pass/approve/enact legislation** (=to accept a particular piece of legislation and to make it become law) | *She* ***introduced legislation*** *that would boost spending on research.* **2** the act or process of making laws

leg·is·la·tive /ˈlɛdʒəˌsleɪṭɪv/ Ac W3 *adj.* **1** relating to laws or to making laws: *the legislative process* | *legislative powers* **2** a legislative institution has the power to make laws: *a legislative committee* | ***the legislative branch*** *of government* → see also THE EXECUTIVE BRANCH, **the judicial branch** at JUDICIAL BRANCH

leg·is·la·tor /ˈlɛdʒəˌsleɪṭɚ/ Ac *n.* [C] someone who has the power to make laws or who belongs to an institution that makes laws, and has usually been elected: *state legislators*

leg·is·la·ture /ˈlɛdʒəˌsleɪtʃɚ/ Ac W3 *n.* [C] POLITICS an institution that has the power to make or change laws, and whose members are usually elected: **the state/national/federal etc. legislature** *the Florida State Legislature* → see also CONGRESS

leg·it /lɪˈdʒɪt/ *adj.* [not before noun] SPOKEN **1** legal or following official rules SYN **legitimate**: *The win was strictly legit.* | *The mafia boss says he has* ***gone legit*** (=become legit). **2** honest and not trying to deceive people: *Are you sure he's legit?*

le·git·i·mate /lɪˈdʒɪṭəmɪt/ *adj.* **1** correct, allowable, or operating according to the law OPP **illegitimate**: *legitimate business operations* | *The legitimate government was overthrown in a coup.* **2** fair, correct, or reasonable according to accepted standards of behavior: *Safety is an obvious and legitimate concern.* | *He had a legitimate reason for being late.* **3** LAW legitimate children are born to parents who are legally married to each other OPP **illegitimate** —**legitimately** *adv.* —**legitimacy** *n.* [U]

le·git·i·mize /lɪˈdʒɪṭəˌmaɪz/ *v.* [T] **1** to make something, especially something that is unfair or morally wrong, seem acceptable and right: *The media helped to legitimize the use of force by government troops.* **2** to make something official or legal that had not been before: *Elections will be held to legitimize the current regime.* **3** LAW to make a child LEGITIMATE

leg·man /ˈlɛgmæn/ *n. plural* **legmen** /-mɛn/ [C] someone who works for someone else and does things for them such as collecting information which involves a lot of walking or traveling around

Leg·o /ˈlɛgoʊ/ *n. plural* **Legos** [C usually plural] TRADEMARK a toy consisting of plastic pieces of various sizes that can be put together to build things

'leg room *n.* [U] space for your legs in front of the seats in a car, theater etc.

leg·ume /ˈlɛgyum, lɪˈgyum/ *n.* [C] **1** BIOLOGY a plant from the family that includes beans, PEAS, LENTILS etc. that has seeds in a POD (=a long thin case) **2** BIOLOGY a bean, seed, or POD from one of these plants that people eat —**leguminous** /lɪˈgyumɪnəs/ *adj.*

'leg ˌwarmer *n.* [C usually plural] a cover for the lower part of your leg, usually worn by dancers while practicing

leg·work /ˈlɛgwɚk/ *n.* [U] work, such as collecting information for a PROJECT, which involves a lot of walking or traveling around

lei /leɪ/ *n.* [C] a circle made of flowers that you put around someone's neck as a greeting, especially in Hawaii

Leib·niz /ˈlaɪbnɪts/, **Gott·fried Wil·helm, Baron von** /ˈgɑtfrid ˈvɪlhɛlm/ (1646–1716) a German PHILOSOPHER and mathematician

lei·sure /ˈliʒɚ/ *n.* [U] **1** time when you are not working or studying, and can relax and do things you enjoy: *leisure activities* | *People have less* ***leisure time*** *these days.* **2 at sb's leisure** whenever you want to do something, even if it takes a long time: *Return the forms to me at your leisure.* **3 at leisure** not working, and having time to relax: *James spent the summer at leisure.* **4 a gentleman/lady of leisure** HUMOROUS someone who does not have to work [**Origin:** 1200–1300 Old French *leisir*, from *leisir* **to be allowed**, from Latin *licere*]

lei·sured /ˈliʒɚd/ *adj.* **1** [only before noun] not needing to work and having a lot of leisure time, especially because you are rich: *the leisured classes* **2** leisurely

lei·sure·ly /ˈliʒɚli/ *adj.* done slowly because you feel relaxed and are enjoying yourself: *a leisurely drive in the country* | *a leisurely pace* —**leisurely** *adv.*: *He moved leisurely across the room.*

'leisure suit *n.* [C] an informal suit popular during the 1970s, consisting of a shirt-like JACKET and pants made of the same material

'leisure wear *n.* [U] a word meaning clothes that are made to be worn when relaxing or playing sports, used especially by companies that make or sell these clothes

leit·mo·tif, leitmotiv /ˈlaɪtmoʊˌtif/ *n.* [C] **1** ENG. LANG. ARTS a musical phrase that is played at various times during an OPERA or similar musical work to represent a particular character or idea → see also MOTIF **2** ENG. LANG. ARTS a feature that appears often in something such as a book, a speech, or an artist's work

lem·ming /ˈlɛmɪŋ/ *n.* [C] **1** BIOLOGY a small rat-like animal that many people believe kills itself by following other lemmings and jumping into the ocean in large numbers **2 like lemmings** if people do something like lemmings, a large number of them copy other people's actions and ideas without thinking about it

lem·on /ˈlɛmən/ S3 *n.* **1** [C,U] BIOLOGY a fruit with hard yellow skin and sour juice: *a slice of lemon* | *lemon juice* → see picture at FRUIT[1] **2** [U] also **lemon yellow** a bright yellow color **3** [C] something, especially a car, that is useless because it fails to work correctly [**Origin:** 1300–1400 French *limon*, from Medieval Latin *limo*, from Arabic *laymun*]

lem·on·ade /ˌlɛməˈneɪd/ *n.* [U] a drink made from lemon juice, sugar, and water

Le·Mond /ləˈmɑnd/, **Greg** /grɛg/ (1961–) a U.S. bicycle racer who was the first American to win the Tour de France bicycle race

ˈlemon ˌgrass, lemongrass *n.* [U] a tropical grass that is used in cooking to give food a taste similar to lemons

ˈlemon law *n.* [C] a law that forces companies to give money to people who have bought a car that does not work from them, or to repair the car so that it works

ˌlemon ˈsole *n.* [C,U] BIOLOGY a flat fish, or the meat of this fish

lem·on·y /ˈlɛməni/ *adj.* tasting, smelling, or looking like lemon: *a lemony flavor*

ˌlemon ˈyellow *n.* [U] a bright yellow color

le·mur /ˈlimɚ/ *n.* [C] a small animal like a monkey with large eyes and a long tail, that lives mainly in Madagascar

lend

I borrowed $10.
Sue lent me $10.
I paid Sue back the next day.

lend /lɛnd/ W3 *v. past tense and past participle* **lent** /lɛnt/

1 BANK [I,T] if a bank or financial institution lends money, it lets someone borrow it if they pay it back with an additional amount of money: **+to** *I doubt they'll lend to us, with our credit histories.* | **lend sth to sb** *U.S. banks lent billions of dollars to the country.* | **lend sb sth** *The bank agreed to lend me the money at 4.4% interest.*

2 LET SB BORROW [T] to let someone borrow money from you or use something that you own, which they will give back later: **lend sb sth** *Could you lend me $5 until tomorrow?* | **lend sth to sb** *"Where'd you get the car, Mimi?" "A friend lent it to me."* ►see THESAURUS box at **borrow**

3 lend (sb) a hand to help someone do something, especially something that needs physical effort: *Lend me a hand with this box.*

4 sth lends itself to sth used to say that something is appropriate to be used in a particular way: *Fish does not lend itself well to reheating.*

5 GIVE A QUALITY [T] FORMAL to give an event or situation a particular quality that it would not normally have had: **lend sth to sth** *Whisky lends an interesting flavor to the sauce.*

6 lend an ear to listen to someone in a sympathetic way

7 lend support/assistance to support or help someone

8 lend weight/credibility/credence to sth to make an opinion, belief etc. seem more acceptable or likely to be correct: *The new evidence lends weight to the prosecution's case.*

9 lend your name to sth to allow your name to be used to support something, sell something etc.

[**Origin:** Old English *lænan*, from *læn*] **—lender** *n.* [C]

ˈlending ˌlibrary *n.* [C] a library that lends books, records etc. for people to use at home → see also REFERENCE LIBRARY

ˈlending rate *n.* [C] ECONOMICS the rate of INTEREST that you have to pay to a bank or other financial institution when you borrow money from them

ˈlend-lease, Lend-Lease HISTORY an arrangement in which the U.S. provided military equipment, etc. to the countries fighting Germany in World War II. The Lend-Lease Act, allowing such an arrangement, was passed in 1941.

L'En·fant /ˈlɑnfɑn/, **Pierre** /pyɛr/ (1754–1825) a French-American ARCHITECT famous for designing the plans for the city of Washington, D.C.

length /lɛŋkθ, lɛnθ/ S2 W2 *n.*

1 SIZE [C,U] the measurement of something from one end to the other → see also BREADTH: **the length of sth** *I like the length of this skirt.* | **a length of 3 feet/6 inches/40 meters etc.** *The leaves reach a length of about 4 inches.* | **3 feet/6 inches/40 meters etc. in length** *Each board measures 5 feet in length.* → WIDTH (1)

2 TIME [C,U] the amount of time that you spend doing something, or that something continues for → see also DURATION: **the length of sth** *the length of the average news broadcast* | *The boy wasn't alone* ***for any length of time*** (=for more than a short time).

3 WHOLE DISTANCE the length of sth the whole distance that something covers from end to end: *The road extends the length of the island.*

4 BOOKS/WRITING ETC. [C,U] the amount of writing in a book, article etc.: **the length of sth** *Greene's book is less than half the length of most novels.* | **500 words/2 pages etc. in length** *The paper should be 2,000 words in length.*

5 go to great/any lengths to do sth to try very hard to do whatever is necessary to achieve something, sometimes when what you do is wrong or illegal: *Most companies go to great lengths to avoid controversy.*

6 at length a) also **at some/great length** for a long time: *She spoke at great length about her travels.* **b)** WRITTEN after a long time SYN **eventually**: *"Yes," she answered at length.*

7 PIECE [C] a piece of something long and thin: *a length of rope*

8 CLOTH [C] a piece of material, cloth etc.: *a length of striped cotton canvas*

9 IN RACES [C] the measurement from one end of a horse, boat etc. to the other, used when saying how far one is ahead of another: *Aksar won by three lengths.*

10 SWIMMING [C] the distance from one end of a swimming pool to the other: *Ron swims 25 lengths every morning.* → see also **at arm's length** at ARM[1] (8), FULL-LENGTH, SHOULDER-LENGTH

length·en /ˈlɛŋkθən/ *v.* [I,T] **1** to make something longer, or to become longer OPP **shorten**: *Can you lengthen these pants for me?* | *The shadows lengthened as the sun went down.* **2** to make something last longer, or to last longer OPP **shorten**: *Military service has been lengthened from 15 to 18 months.* | *It was May, and the days were lengthening.* ►see THESAURUS box at **prolong**

length·wise /ˈlɛŋkθwaɪz/ *adv.* in the direction or position of the longest side: *Slice each banana lengthwise.* **—lengthwise** *adj.* [only before noun] *a lengthwise cut* → see also CROSSWISE

length·y /ˈlɛŋkθi/ *adj. comparative* **lengthier**, *superlative* **lengthiest** **1** continuing for a long time, often too long: *a lengthy period in the hospital* ►see THESAURUS box at long[1] **2** a speech, piece of writing etc. that is lengthy is long and often contains too many details: *a lengthy two-volume book*

le·ni·ent /ˈliniənt, ˈlinyənt/ *adj.* not strict in the way you punish someone or control their behavior: *His parents are too lenient with him.* | *a very lenient jail sentence* [**Origin:** 1600–1700 Latin, present participle of *lenire* **to soften**] —**leniency** also **lenience** *n.* [U] *Ross asked the judge for leniency in his sentencing.* —**leniently** *adv.*

Len·in /ˈlɛnɪn/, **Vlad·i·mir Il·yich** /ˈvlædɪmɪr ˈɪlɪtʃ/ (1870–1924) a Russian Marxist REVOLUTIONARY and writer who was leader of the Bolshevik party and first leader of the Soviet Union

lens /lɛnz/ *n.* [C] **1** SCIENCE a piece of curved glass or plastic which makes things look bigger or smaller, for example in a pair of GLASSES or in a TELESCOPE: *glasses with thick lenses* **2** the part of a camera through which the light travels before it reaches the film: *a 115mm zoom lens* **3** BIOLOGY the clear part behind the eye that changes shape to help the eye FOCUS in order to see clearly → see picture at EYE[1] **4** a CONTACT LENS [**Origin:** 1600–1700 Latin **lentil**; because of its shape]

Lent /lɛnt/ *n.* [U] the 40 days before Easter when some Christians stop eating particular things or stop particular habits [**Origin:** 1200–1300 *Lenten* **springtime, Lent** (11–17 centuries), from Old English *lengten*; because the days get longer in spring] —**Lenten** *adj.* [only before noun]

lent /lɛnt/ *v.* the past tense and past participle of LEND

len·til /ˈlɛntl/ *n.* [C usually plural] a small round seed like a bean, which has been dried and can be cooked

Le·o /ˈlioʊ/ *n.* **1** [U] the fifth sign of the ZODIAC, represented by a lion, and believed to affect the character and life of people born between July 23 and August 22 **2** [C] someone who was born between July 23 and August 22

Le·o·nar·do da Vin·ci /liəˌnɑrdoʊ də ˈvɪntʃi, leɪə-/ (1452–1519) an Italian painter, inventor, and scientist of the Renaissance period, who is generally regarded as one of the greatest artists and GENIUSES who ever lived

le·o·nine /ˈliəˌnaɪn/ *adj.* LITERARY relating to lions, or like a lion in character or appearance

leop·ard /ˈlɛpəd/ *n.* [C] **1** BIOLOGY a large animal of the cat family, with yellow fur and black spots, which lives in Africa and South Asia **2 a leopard can't change its spots** used to say that people cannot change their character [**Origin:** 1200–1300 Old French *leupart*, from Late Latin *leopardus*, from Greek, from *leon* **lion** + *pardos* **leopard**]

le·o·tard /ˈliəˌtɑrd/ *n.* [C] a tight-fitting piece of women's clothing that covers your body from your neck to the top of your legs, and is worn for exercise or dancing [**Origin:** 1800–1900 Jules *Léotard* (1830–1870), French trapeze artist who invented it]

lep·er /ˈlɛpɚ/ *n.* [C] **1** MEDICINE someone who has leprosy **2** someone that people avoid because they have done something that people disapprove of: *They treated me like some kind of leper.*

lep·re·chaun /ˈlɛprəˌkɑn/ *n.* [C] an imaginary creature in the form of a little man, in old Irish stories, who will show hidden gold to anyone who can catch him [**Origin:** 1600–1700 Irish Gaelic *leipreachan*, from Middle Irish *luchorpan* **small body**]

lep·ro·sy /ˈlɛprəsi/ *n.* [U] MEDICINE an infectious disease in which someone's skin and nerves are gradually destroyed —**leprous** *adj.*

Ler·ner /ˈlənɚ/, **A·lan Jay** /ˈælən dʒeɪ/ (1918–1986) a U.S. SONGWRITER famous for writing MUSICALS with Frederick Loewe

les·bi·an /ˈlɛzbiən/ *n.* [C] a woman who is sexually attracted to other women [**Origin:** 1800–1900 *Lesbian* **of the Greek island Lesbos** (17–21 centuries), home of the 7th-century B.C. female poet Sappho, who was said to be homosexual] —**lesbian** *adj.* —**lesbianism** *n.* [U] → see also GAY

le·sion /ˈliʒən/ *n.* [C] **1** MEDICINE a wound or injury: *multiple lesions to the skin* **2** MEDICINE a sore red area on the skin, caused by an infection or disease **3** MEDICINE a dangerous change in part of someone's body such as their lungs or brain, caused by injury or illness: *a spinal cord lesion*

Le·so·tho /ləˈsoʊtoʊ/ a country in southern Africa that is completely surrounded by the Republic of South Africa —**Sotho** *adj.*

less[1] /lɛs/ S2 W1 *quantifier, pron.* [the comparative of "little"] **a)** [with uncountable nouns] a smaller amount: *Skim milk has less fat than whole milk.* | **less than sb/sth** *I can finish it in less than an hour.* | *She knows less about it than I do.* | *He said he would accept $30,000 and* **no less**. | **less of sth** *She spends less of her time at home.* | *She only has $5 and I have* **even less**. | ***Less and less of*** (=a decreasing amount of) *this money reaches poor people.* **b)** NONSTANDARD used to mean "fewer" or "not as many," but often considered incorrect in this meaning: *There were less people there than we expected.* → see also **the less...the better** at BETTER[1] (5)

> **GRAMMAR** **less, fewer**
> Use **less** before an uncountable noun: *We've had a lot less rain this year than last year.* Use **fewer** before a countable noun: *There are fewer kids in our neighborhood now.*

less[2] S1 W1 *adv.* [the comparative of "little"] **1** not so much, or to a smaller degree OPP **more**: *I drive less and walk more often.* | *Tickets were less expensive than I expected.* | *We go to movies less often than we used to.* **2 less and less** gradually becoming smaller in amount or degree: *The fighting has become less and less frequent.* **3 no less than** used to emphasize that an amount or number is large: *No less than six people claim to have written the song.* **4 no less** used to emphasize that the person or thing you are talking about is very important or impressive: *Our awards were presented by the mayor, no less.* → see also **I/he/they etc. couldn't care less** at CARE[2] (6), **much less** at MUCH[1] (4), **be nothing less than** at NOTHING[2] (2), **think less/badly of sb (for doing sth)** at THINK (19)

less[3] *adj.* [not before noun] **less than helpful/perfect/friendly etc.** not helpful, perfect, friendly etc. at all: *The public was less than enthusiastic about our newest product.*

less[4] *prep.* taking away or not counting a particular amount: *He gave us our money back, less the $2 service charge.*

-less /lɪs/ *suffix* [in adjectives] **1** not having something SYN **without**: *childless* | *shirtless* **2** never doing something: *ceaseless* (=that never ends) | *harmless* (=that will not harm you) **3** unable to be treated in a particular way, or never becoming a particular way: *countless* (=too many to be counted) | *tireless* (=never getting tired)

ˌless deˌveloped ˈcountry *n.* [C] ECONOMICS a poor country whose economic system is developing slowly and is less successful than most other countries

les·see /lɛˈsi/ *n.* [C] LAW someone who is legally allowed to use a house, building, land etc. for a particular period of time in return for payment to the owner → see also LESSOR

less·en /ˈlɛsən/ *v.* [I,T] to become smaller in size, amount, importance, or value, or to make something do this: *Exercise lessens the risk of heart disease.* | *By Thursday, smoke in the valley had considerably lessened.*

less·er /ˈlɛsɚ/ *adj.* **1** [only before noun] FORMAL not as large, as important, or as much as something else: *They settled for the lesser sum of $3.5 million.* | *The movie was popular in New York, and* **to a lesser extent**, *in L.A.* | **a lesser woman/man/person** (=someone who is not as strong or courageous as the person being mentioned) **2 the lesser of two evils** the less bad or harmful of two bad choices **3 lesser-known** not well known, or not as well known as others: *a lesser-known French poet* **4** BIOLOGY used in the names of some types of animal, bird, or plant that are slightly smaller than the main type

les·son /ˈlɛsən/ S2 W2 *n.* [C]
1 LEARNING A SKILL a period of time in which someone is taught a particular skill, for example how to play a musical instrument or drive a car: **+in/on** *lessons in fire safety* | **piano/swimming/riding etc. lessons** *Ben is **taking** violin **lessons**.*
2 WARNING an experience, especially a bad one, that makes you more careful in the future: *He had **learned a lesson** that he would never forget.* | *This tragic accident should **be a lesson to*** (=act as a warning to) *all parents.*
3 BOOK a part of a book that is used for learning a particular subject, especially in school: *Turn to lesson 25.*
4 CHURCH a short piece that is read from the Bible during a Christian religious ceremony
5 IN SCHOOL OLD-FASHIONED a period of time in which students in a school are taught a particular subject SYN **class**
[**Origin:** 1100–1200 Old French *leçon*, from Latin *lectio* **act of reading**] → see also **learn your lesson** at LEARN (4), **teach sb a lesson** at TEACH (6)

les·sor /ˈlɛsɔr, lɛˈsɔr/ *n.* [C] LAW someone who allows someone else to use their house, building, land etc. for a period of time for payment → see also LESSEE

lest /lɛst/ *conjunction* **1 afraid/anxious/worried etc. lest sb do sth** LITERARY afraid or worried that a particular thing might happen SYN **in case**: *I was afraid lest I say too much.* **2** OLD USE in order to make sure that something will not happen: *Hide, lest anyone see us!*

let /lɛt/ S1 W1 *v. past tense and past participle* **let**, **letting**
1 ALLOW [T not in passive] **a)** to give someone permission to do something: *I want to go out, but my parents won't let me.* | **let sb do sth** *His wife won't let him watch football on TV.* | *Let me show you how to do it.* **b)** to not prevent something from happening, or to make it possible for something to happen: *It'll drive you crazy if you let it.* | *How can you let him treat you like that?* | **let sth do sth** *Don't let the door slam shut.* | **don't let sb do sth** *Don't let me forget to call Pam.* ►see THESAURUS box at **allow**
2 let go a) to stop holding someone or something: *Just let go and jump.* | **+of** *Let go of my arm!* **b)** to stop worrying or thinking about a person or a problem: *My kids are grown up now, and I have to let go.*
3 let sb go a) to allow a person or animal to leave a place where they have been kept: *The police let her go after a night in jail.* **b)** a phrase meaning "to dismiss someone from their job," used to avoid saying this directly: *We've had to let three people go this month.*
4 let sb know to tell someone some information: *Could you let me know by Thursday?* | **let sb know if/whether** *Let us know if you need anything else.* | **let sb know what/when/where etc.** *Let me know what time your plane gets in.*
5 let sb have sth to give or sell something to someone: *I can let you have both chairs for $75.* | *Could you let me have the report this afternoon?*
6 let alone used after a negative statement to say that the next thing you mention is even less likely: *I wouldn't work with my mom, let alone my whole family.*
7 let sth go/pass to decide not to react to something bad or annoying that someone has done or said: *I'll let it go this time, but don't let it happen again.*
8 let there be no doubt/mistake used for saying in a firm or determined way that what you are saying is true: *Let there be no doubt. This is a serious problem.*
9 let sb/sth be also **let sb/sth alone** to stop annoying someone, or asking questions, or trying to change things: *Kate, let your sister be.*
10 let yourself go a) to allow yourself to relax completely in a social situation, and not worry about what other people think **b)** to take less care of your appearance than usual
11 let sth drop/rest to stop discussing something or trying to deal with something that has been annoying you or worrying you: *The newspapers are not going to let the matter drop.*
12 let sth go for $2/$25 etc. INFORMAL to sell something at a low price
13 WISH LITERARY used to express a wish that something will happen or will not happen: *Let him come home safely, she prayed.*
14 let us do sth FORMAL **a)** used to suggest to a group of people that you all do something together: *Let us pray.* **b)** used to ask a reader or listener to do something, as a way of helping them understand what you are talking about: *Let us consider a few examples of the problem.*
15 let sth be/equal/represent sth FORMAL used in mathematics or science to mean that one thing can be imagined as representing another: *Let c equal 6.*
16 let sb have it INFORMAL **a)** to shout at someone because you are angry with them: *Mrs. Kramer really let him have it for spilling the paint.* **b)** to attack or punish someone severely
17 ROOM/BUILDING [T] BRITISH to allow someone to use a room or building in return for money every week or month SYN **rent**

SPOKEN PHRASES

18 let me see/think said when pausing to think of some information or think what to do next: *He said he was going to the store, and, let me see...where else...?*
19 let me do sth a) used to politely offer to do something for someone: *Here, let me get the door for you.* **b)** used to tell someone politely what will do next, before you can help them, talk to them, etc.: *Let me take this phone call, and then I can help you.*
20 let sb (do sth) a) used to say that you do not care whether someone does something or not: *Well, if he wants to throw away his life, let him.* **b)** used to say that someone else should do something instead of you: *Let them clean up the mess – they made it.*
21 let me tell you (something) used to emphasize a statement: *It was pretty early in the morning too, let me tell you!*
22 I'll/we'll let it go at that used to tell someone that you will not punish or criticize them anymore for something bad they have done: *If you give me $25, we'll just let it go at that.*

[**Origin:** Old English *lætan*] → see also **let the cat out of the bag** at CAT (2), **let fly** at FLY[1] (18), LET'S, **live and let live** at LIVE[1] (24), **let sth ride** at RIDE[1] (6), **let her/it rip** at RIP[1] (5), **let (it) slip that** at SLIP[1] (13), **never let it be said (that)** at NEVER (1), **let/get sb off the hook** at HOOK[1] (3), **let/blow off steam** at STEAM[1] (4)

let down *phr. v.* **1 let sb ↔ down** to make someone feel disappointed because you have not behaved well or not done what you promised: *I trust you – don't let me down!* | **feel let down (by sb)** *These people feel let down by the legal system.* **2 let sth ↔ down** to give something to someone who is in a lower position, or to move something that is on a string, rope etc. down: *Let the basket down gently.* **3 let sb/sth ↔ down** to make someone less successful or impressive than they should be, by not achieving a high enough standard: *McKenzie's judgment rarely lets him down.* | *Work hard this year and don't **let yourself down*** (=do not fail to achieve what you know you are able to). **4 let your guard/defenses down** to show feelings or thoughts that you have been hiding from someone because you felt they would try to gain an advantage over you: *I never felt I could let my guard down and be relaxed with him.* **5 let your hair down** INFORMAL to relax and enjoy yourself, especially after working hard **6 let sb down easy/gently** to give someone bad news in a way that will not upset them too much **7** to make a piece of clothing longer

let in *phr. v.* **1 let sb ↔ in** to open the door of a room, building etc. so that someone can come in: *I unlocked the door and let him in.* | *If I'm not there, just let yourself in.* **2 let sth ↔ in** to allow light, water, air etc. to enter a place: *These curtains let in too much light.* **3 let sb in on sth** to tell someone about a secret plan, idea etc., and trust them not to tell other people: *I'm going to let you in on a little secret.* **4 let yourself in for sth** INFORMAL to do something or become involved with something that will cause you trouble later: *I don't think Jamie knows what he's letting himself in for.*

let sb/sth **into** sth *phr. v.* to allow someone to come into a room or building: *Maria wouldn't let Billy into her house.*

let off *phr. v.* **1 let sb off** to not punish someone, or to not make them do something they should do: **let sb off sth** *I'll let you off cleaning your room this weekend.* | **let sb off with sth** *The judge let her off with a fine of $50.* | *You're lucky that he* ***let*** *you* ***off*** *so* ***easy****.* **2 let sb off** to allow someone to get out of a car, off an airplane etc.: *You can let me off at the next corner.* **3 let sb off** to allow someone to leave work: *They let me off work to come to this class.* **4** to produce something such as heat, light, or sound: *The ship let off a huge blast of its foghorn.*

let on *phr. v.* INFORMAL to tell someone something that was meant to be a secret: *He's letting on what he knows.* | **let on (that)** *Don't let on that I told you.*

let out *phr. v.* **1 let sb ↔ out** to allow someone to leave a room, building etc.: *Who let the cat out?* | **let sb out of sth** *My brother wouldn't let me out of my room.* **2** if a school, college, movie etc. lets out, it ends, so that the people attending it can leave: *School lets out at 3:15.* **3 let sth ↔ out** to allow light, water, air etc. to leave a place: *Close the door – you're letting all the heat out.* | **let sth out of sth** *Someone had let the air out of my tires.* **4 let sth ↔ out** to express strong feelings in order to get rid of them: *It's better to let your anger out.* | *Sometimes it's good to cry and* ***let it all out****.* **5 let out a scream/cry/roar etc.** to make a sound, especially a loud sound: *Anita let out a sob.* **6 let sth ↔ out** to make a piece of clothing wider or looser, especially because the person it belongs to has become fatter

let sb/sth **through** *phr. v.* to allow someone or something to pass through a place to somewhere: *The guards at the border refused to let us through.* | **let sb/sth through sth** *A camera crew was let through the barrier.*

let up *phr. v.* **1** if something, such as bad weather or a bad situation, lets up, it stops or becomes less serious: *I wish this rain would let up.* | *The economic crisis* ***shows no signs of letting up****.* **2 not let up** to refuse to stop doing something, especially something that annoys or frightens people: *They kept banging on the door and they wouldn't let up.* | **+on** *America must not let up on its criticism of the dictatorship.*

-let /lɪt/ *suffix* [in nouns] **1** a smaller type of something: *booklet* (=small book with a thin cover) | *piglet* (=young pig) **2** a band worn on a particular part of your body: *anklet*

letch /lɛtʃ/ *n.* [C] another spelling of LECH

let·down /ˈlɛtdaʊn/ *n.* [singular] INFORMAL something that makes you feel disappointed because it is not as good as you expected SYN **disappointment**: *It will be a major letdown if we lose the game to Kansas.* → see also **let down** at LET

le·thal /ˈliθəl/ *adj.* **1** causing death, or able to cause death: *a lethal dose of heroin* **2** HUMOROUS likely to be powerful, dangerous, or dangerously effective: *That cocktail looks pretty lethal.* [**Origin:** 1500–1600 Latin *lethalis*, from *lethum* **death**]

le·thar·gic /ləˈθɑrdʒɪk/ *adj.* feeling as if you have no energy and no interest in doing anything: *The heat made us lethargic.* [**Origin:** 1300–1400 Latin *lethargicus*, from Greek, from *lethargos* **forgetful, lazy**] —**lethargy** /ˈlɛθɚdʒi/ *n.* [U]

let's /lɛts/ SPOKEN **1** the short form of "let us," used to suggest to someone or a group of people that you all do something together: *I'm hungry. Let's eat!* | *Let's buy a present for Grandma together.* | ***Let's not*** *talk about work tonight.* **2 let's see a)** said when you are going to try to do something: **let's see if/whether** *Let's see if I can get this window open.* **b)** said when pausing because you cannot remember or find something: *Now, let's see, where did I leave my glass?* **c)** used to ask someone to show you something: *"I got some new shoes." "Really? Let's see."* **3 let's say** said to ask someone to imagine something in order to discuss it or understand it better: *If you found some money on the street — let's say $100 — what would you do?* | **let's say (that)** *Okay, let's say he comes. Will you be happy to see him?* **4 let's hope (that)** said when you hope something is true or will happen: *Let's hope they remembered to bring the tickets.* **5 let's just say** used to say that you are not going to tell someone all the details about something: *"So who was she with?" "Let's just say it wasn't Ted."* **6 let's face it/let's be honest** used to say that you must accept a fact that is difficult or unfavorable: *Let's be honest – she's boring!*

let·ter¹ /ˈlɛt̬ɚ/ S1 W1 *n.* [C] **1** a written or printed message that is usually put in an envelope and sent through the mail: *Jim* ***wrote a letter to*** *his Congressman.* | *Could you* ***mail*** *these* ***letters*** *for me?* | *I* ***got a letter from*** *Mike today.* | **+to** *a letter to my father* | *Don't forget to send* ***a thank-you letter****.* | **a letter of complaint/apology/resignation etc.** (=one in which you complain, apologize etc.) ►see THESAURUS box at **mail¹** **2** ENG. LANG. ARTS any of the signs in writing or printing that represent a speech sound: *the letter "A"* | *Her name was written in big red letters.* → see also CAPITAL, LOWER CASE **3 to the letter** if you follow instructions or rules to the letter, you do exactly what you are told to do SYN **exactly** **4 the letter of the law** the exact words of a law or agreement, rather than the intended or general meaning **5** a large cloth letter that you sew onto a JACKET, given as a reward for playing on a school or college sports team **6 English/American/German etc. letters** FORMAL the study of the literature of a particular country or language [**Origin:** 1200–1300 Old French *lettre*, from Latin *littera*] → see also CHAIN LETTER, COVER LETTER, DEAR JOHN LETTER, MAN OF LETTERS, OPEN LETTER

letter² *v.* [I,T] to write, draw, or paint letters or words on something: **badly/beautifully/carefully etc. lettered** *a plainly lettered sign* → see also HAND-LETTERED, LETTERED

letter in sth *phr. v.* to earn a LETTER in a sport in school or college

ˈletter ˌbomb *n.* [C] a small bomb hidden in a package and sent to someone in order to hurt or kill them

let·ter·box /ˈlɛt̬ɚˌbɑks/ *n.* **1** also **letterbox format** [U] a way of showing movies on television in which the picture looks narrower from top to bottom, so that the whole width of the picture can be shown **2** [C] BRITISH a MAILBOX

ˈletter ˌcarrier *n.* [C] a MAIL CARRIER

let·tered /ˈlɛt̬ɚd/ *adj.* FORMAL well educated

let·ter·head /ˈlɛt̬ɚˌhɛd/ *n.* **1** [U] paper that has the name and address of a person or business printed at the top of it: *the company's letterhead* **2** [C] the name and address of a person or business printed at the top of a sheet of paper

let·ter·ing /ˈlɛt̬ərɪŋ/ *n.* [U] **1** written or drawn letters, especially of a special type, size, color etc.: *two scrolls in Chinese lettering* **2** ENG. LANG. ARTS the art of writing or drawing letters or words

let·ter·man /ˈlɛt̬ɚmən/ *n.* [C] OLD-FASHIONED someone who earns a LETTER in sports in high school or college

ˌletter of ˈcredit *n.* [C] an official letter from a bank allowing a particular person to take money from another bank

ˌletter of inˈtent *n.* [C] an official document that says what someone plans to do, such as join a sports team, buy a company etc.

ˌletter-ˈperfect *adj.* correct in every detail

ˈletter-ˌquality *adj.* used to describe print or a PRINTER that is good enough to be used for business letters, reports etc.

ˈletter-size *adj.* letter-size paper is 8½ inches wide and 11 inches long and is the standard size used in the U.S.

let·tuce /ˈlɛt̬ɪs/ S3 *n.* [C,U] a vegetable with thin green

L

leaves which are used raw in SALADS: *a head of lettuce* [**Origin:** 1200–1300 Old French *laitues*, plural of *laitue*, from Latin *lactuca*, from *lac* **milk**; because of its milky juice]

let·up /ˈlɛṭʌp/ *n.* [singular, U] a pause or a reduction in a difficult, dangerous, or tiring activity: *There is no sign of a letup in the crisis.* → see also **let up** at LET

leu·ke·mi·a /luˈkimiə/ *n.* [U] MEDICINE a type of CANCER in which the blood contains too many WHITE BLOOD CELLS, causing weakness and sometimes death [**Origin:** 1800–1900 Greek *leukos* **white** + *-aimia* (from *haima* **blood**)]

leu·ko·cyte /ˈlukəˌsaɪt/ *n.* [C] BIOLOGY one of the cells in your blood which fight against infection SYN **white blood cell**

lev·ee /ˈlɛvi/ *n.* [C] EARTH SCIENCE a special wall built to stop a river from flooding

lev·ée /ˈlɛvi, ləˈveɪ/ *n.* [C] HISTORY an occasion when a king or other person of high rank, especially Louis XIV of France, would receive visitors just after getting up in the morning

level

The parking garage has four levels.

lev·el¹ /ˈlɛvəl/ S1 W1 *n.* [C]

1 AMOUNT the amount, degree, or number of something, as compared to another amount, degree, or number: **+of** *There was a **low level** of interest in the conference.* | *Temperatures will stay **at these levels** until Friday.* | *Stock prices were at their **highest level** since June.* | **stress/noise/tension etc. levels** *The noise level in the room was unbearable.*

2 HEIGHT the height or position of something in relation to the ground or to another thing: *Check the water level in the car radiator.* | *Your arms should be at the same level as your desk.* | *Do not raise the weight above shoulder level.* | *Her face was **on a level with*** (=at the same level as) *his.* → see also EYE LEVEL, SEA LEVEL

3 STANDARD a particular standard of skill or ability in a subject, sport etc.: *higher-level math courses* | **+of** *a high level of fluency in English* | **at a/the level** *Few athletes can compete at the international level.*

4 FLOOR/GROUND a floor or piece of ground, especially when considered in relation to another floor or piece of ground that is higher or lower: *Didn't we park the car on Level 2?*

5 POSITION/RANK a particular position in a system that has different ranks: *Training is offered at every level in the company.* | **at local/state/national etc. level** *No research was being done at the federal level.* | **at junior/low/senior/high etc. levels** *The decision was made at senior levels.* | *high-level talks* (=discussions between important people)

6 WAY OF UNDERSTANDING a way of considering or understanding something: *We can find meaning in the story **on** many different **levels**.* | **on a practical/personal etc. level** *They never got along on either a personal or a professional level.*

7 TOOL a tool used for checking that a surface is flat

8 be on the level INFORMAL to be honest: *Do you think his offer is on the level?*

9 descend/sink/stoop to sb's level to lower your standards, so that you become as bad as the person or thing mentioned: *I would never stoop to your level.*

[**Origin:** 1300–1400 Old French *livel*, from Latin *libella*, from *libra* **weight, balance**]

level² *adj.*

1 a level surface is flat and does not slope in any direction: *level ground* | *The floor isn't level.* ►see THESAURUS box at **flat¹**

2 be level a) two things that are level are at the same height as each other SYN **even**: *Keep your shoulders level.* | **+with** *Your eyes should be level with the top of the computer screen.* **b)** if two or more people or things are level, none of them is behind or in front of the others SYN **even**: **+with** *He stayed level with me, riding on the path to my right.* | *The red boat **drew level** with us.*

3 a level playing field a situation in which different companies, countries etc. can all compete fairly with each other because no one has special advantages: *We just want our exports to compete on a level playing field.*

4 CALM a voice, expression, etc. that is level is calm and determined: *Her cool, level gaze was disturbing.* → see also **a clear/cool/level head** at HEAD¹ (12)

5 do your level best to try as hard as possible to do something: *I'll do my level best to help you.*

6 level spoonful/teaspoon etc. an amount of a substance, that is just enough to fill a spoon, used as a measure in cooking

level³ S3 *v.* [T] **1** to knock down or completely destroy a building or area: *The storm leveled hundreds of houses.* **2 level a charge/accusation/criticism etc.** [usually passive] to publicly criticize someone or say they are responsible for a crime, mistake etc.: **+at/against** *Similar accusations of corruption have been leveled at other organizations.* **3** to make something flat and even: *Workers leveled the wet concrete with a piece of wood.* **4 level the playing field** to make a situation fairer, so that different companies, countries, or people can all compete without anyone having special advantages: *The Internet helps level the playing field by making information widely available.*

level sth **at** sb *phr. v.* to point something, such as a weapon, at someone: *A gun was leveled at Ron's head.*

level off/out *phr. v.* **1** to stop going up or down, and continue at the same height or amount: *The plane climbed to 20,000 feet, then leveled off.* | *The city's murder rate has begun to level off.* **2 level sth ↔ off/out** to make something flat and smooth

level with sb *phr. v.* INFORMAL to speak honestly to someone, after hiding some facts from them for a period of time: *I wish the President would level with the American people.*

lev·el·er /ˈlɛvələ/ *n.* [C] something that makes all people seem the same, because it affects everyone in the same way: *Public school was viewed an important leveler.* | *Death is the great leveler.*

ˌlevel-ˈheaded *adj.* calm and sensible in making judgments or decisions, or showing this quality: *a level-headed solution*

lev·er /ˈlɛvə, ˈli-/ *n.* [C] **1** a stick or handle attached to a machine, that you move to make the machine work: *Pull this lever to activate the brake.* **2** a long thin piece of metal, wood etc. that you use to lift something heavy by putting one end under the object and pushing the other end down **3** something that you use to influence a situation in order to get the result that you want: *The White House used the threat of sanctions as a lever.* [**Origin:** 1200–1300 Old French *levier*, from *lever* **to raise**] —**lever** *v.* [T] *He levered up a few floorboards.*

lev·er·age¹ /ˈlɛvərɪdʒ, ˈli-/ *n.* [U] **1** influence that you can use to make people do what you want: **political/economic/diplomatic etc. leverage** *Europe will try to use its economic leverage to end the dispute.* **2** the amount of force that something or someone has in relation to their ability to make something else move: *A longer stick will give you better leverage.*

3 borrowed money that is used to INVEST or buy something such as a company

leverage² *v.* [T] TECHNICAL **1** ECONOMICS to make money available to someone in order to INVEST or buy something such as a company: *the use of public funds to leverage private investment* **2** to use the things a business owns or the people it employs in new ways, in order to achieve success in the best way possible: *We need to leverage our biggest asset – the people who work for us.*

ˌleveraged ˈbuyout *n.* [C] TECHNICAL a situation in which someone gets a LOAN to buy most or all of the STOCK in a company by promising to pay the bank back by selling the company's ASSETS if they cannot pay back the money they borrowed

Le·vi /ˈlivaɪ/ in the Bible, the head of one of the 12 tribes of Israel

le·vi·a·than /lɪˈvaɪəθən/ *n.* [C] **1** something very large and strong: *a leviathan of a ship* **2** LITERARY any very large and frightening sea animal, especially a WHALE [**Origin:** 1300–1400 *Leviathan* a very large sea animal in the Bible, from Late Latin, from Hebrew *liwyathan*]

Lé·vi-Strauss /ˌlɛvi ˈstraʊs, ˌleɪ-/, **Claude** /kloʊd/ (1908–) a French teacher and writer in the area of ANTHROPOLOGY who helped to develop important ideas in STRUCTURALISM

lev·i·tate /ˈlɛvəˌteɪt/ *v.* [I,T] to rise and float in the air as if by magic, or to make someone do this —**levitation** /ˌlɛvəˈteɪʃən/ *n.* [U]

Le·vit·i·cus /ləˈvɪt̬ɪkəs/ a book in the Old Testament of the Christian Bible

lev·i·ty /ˈlɛvət̬i/ *n.* [U] FORMAL a quality in someone's behavior which is not serious and involves joking and having fun: *a moment of levity in a very serious situation*

lev·y¹ /ˈlɛvi/ Ac *v. past tense and past participle* **levied** [T] **levy a tax/charge etc. (on sth)** ECONOMICS to officially make someone pay a tax etc.

levy² Ac *n. plural* **levies** [C] ECONOMICS an additional sum of money, usually paid as a tax

lewd /lud/ *adj.* using OBSCENE words or behaving in a way that makes someone think of sex: *a lewd gesture* | **lewd and lascivious behavior/acts/conduct etc.** LAW (=sexual behavior that is illegal and morally unacceptable) [**Origin:** Old English *læwede* **not a priest, knowing nothing**] —**lewdly** *adv.* —**lewdness** *n.* [U]

Lew·is /ˈluɪs/, **Carl** /kɑrl/ (1961–) a U.S. ATHLETE who won several GOLD MEDALS in the Olympic Games for the LONG JUMP and for running races

Lewis, C.S. (1898–1963) a British writer and university professor, known especially for his children's stories with a SPIRITUAL meaning

Lewis, Sin·clair /sɪnˈklɛr/ (1885–1951) a U.S. writer of NOVELS, known for writing about life in small U.S. towns

lex·i·cal /ˈlɛksɪkəl/ *adj.* ENG. LANG. ARTS dealing with words, or related to words

lex·i·cog·ra·phy /ˌlɛksɪˈkɑɡrəfi/ *n.* [U] ENG. LANG. ARTS the skill, practice, or profession of writing dictionaries —**lexicographer** *n.* [C] —**lexicographical** /ˌlɛksɪkəˈɡræfɪkəl/ *adj.*

lex·i·con /ˈlɛksɪˌkɑn/ *n.* [C] **1** ENG. LANG. ARTS all the words used in a language, a particular group, a particular profession etc.: *the political lexicon* **2** a book containing lists of words with their meanings [**Origin:** 1600–1700 Late Greek *lexikon*, from *lexikos* **of words**, from Greek *lexis* **word, speech**]

lex·is /ˈlɛksɪs/ *n.* [U] ENG. LANG. ARTS all the words in a language

lg. the written abbreviation of LARGE

li·a·bil·i·ty /ˌlaɪəˈbɪlət̬i/ *n. plural* **liabilities** **1** [U] legal responsibility for something, especially for paying money that is owed, or for damage or injury: **accept/admit liability (for sth)** *The company did not admit any liability for the accident.* **2** **liabilities** [plural] TECHNICAL the amount of debt that a company owes → see also ASSET **3** [C] someone or something that is likely to cause problems for someone: **+to** *She was becoming a liability to the Democratic party.* **4** [U] a situation in which someone has to pay tax → see also ASSET, LIMITED LIABILITY

li·a·ble /ˈlaɪəbəl/ *adj.* **1** **be liable to do sth** to be likely to do something, behave in a particular way, or be treated in a particular way: *She's liable to start crying if you mention Mike.* | *Refugees are liable to be shot if they return.* **2** [not before noun] LAW legally responsible for something, especially for the cost of something: **+for** *The company can* ***hold*** *parents* ***liable for*** *their children's actions.* **3** [not before noun] likely to be affected by a particular kind of problem, illness etc.: **+to** *You're more liable to illness when you don't exercise.* **4** if someone is liable for tax or liable to a fine, they have to pay it **5** if an amount of money or other BENEFIT is liable to tax, you have to pay tax on it

li·aise /liˈeɪz/ *v.*

liaise with sb *phr. v.* to exchange information with someone who works in another organization or department, so that you can work effectively together: *Part of his job is to liaise with teachers.*

liaise between sb/sth *phr. v.* to help other people to exchange information, so that they can be more effective: *a co-ordinator who liaises between the different groups*

li·ai·son /liˈeɪˌzɑn/ *n.* **1** [C] also **liaison officer** someone whose job is to liaise between groups: **+between** *Turner serves as a liaison between management and staff.* **2** [C] a sexual relationship between two people who are not married **3** [U] a working relationship between two groups, companies etc. [**Origin:** 1600–1700 French *lier* **to tie**]

li·ar /ˈlaɪɚ/ *n.* [C] someone who tells lies: *Are you calling me a liar?* | **congenital/compulsive/pathological liar** (=someone who cannot stop lying)

lib /lɪb/ *n.* → see AD-LIB, WOMEN'S LIB

li·ba·tion /laɪˈbeɪʃən/ *n.* [C] **1** HUMOROUS an alcoholic drink **2** LITERARY a gift of wine to a god

lib·ber /ˈlɪbɚ/ *n.* **women's libber** —see WOMEN'S LIB

li·bel¹ /ˈlaɪbəl/ *n.* [C,U] the crime of writing or printing an untrue statement about someone, with the result that other people are likely to have a bad opinion of them: *Holt* ***sued*** *the newspaper* ***for libel.*** | *a libel suit* (=a court case against someone for libel) ►see THESAURUS box at lie³ [**Origin:** 1300–1400 Old French, Latin *libellus*, from *liber* **book**] → see also SLANDER

libel² *v.* [T] **libel sb** to write or print libelous statements about someone

li·bel·ous /ˈlaɪbələs/ *adj.* containing untrue written statements about someone which are illegal because they could make other people have a bad opinion of them: *libelous gossip*

lib·eral¹ /ˈlɪbrəl, -bərəl/ Ac W3 *adj.* **1** willing to understand or respect the different behavior, ideas etc. of other people → see also CONSERVATIVE: *a liberal view of homosexuality* **2** POLITICS supporting LEFT-WING political ideas that include more government involvement in business and in people's lives, more taxes, and a willingness to accept people's differences and changes in society → see also CONSERVATIVE: *liberal Democrats* **3** supporting or allowing changes in political, social, or religious systems that give people more freedom: *liberal immigration policies* **4** generous, or given in large amounts: *a liberal supply of drinks* **5** not exact: *a liberal interpretation of the original play* **6** **liberal education** a type of education that encourages you to develop a large range of interests and knowledge and respect for other people's opinions, rather than learning specific technical skills

liberal² Ac *n.* [C] POLITICS someone with liberal opinions or principles → see also CONSERVATIVE

ˌliberal ˈarts *n.* [plural] the areas of learning which develop someone's ability to think and increase their

L

general knowledge, rather than developing technical skills: *a liberal arts college*

ˌliberal deˈmocracy *n.* [C,U] a political system in which everyone can vote to elect the government, and in which people have a lot of freedom and the government does not influence trade very much

lib·eral·is·m /ˈlɪbrəˌlɪzəm/ Ac *n.* [U] POLITICS LIBERAL opinions and principles, especially on social and political subjects → see also CONSERVATISM

lib·er·al·i·ty /ˌlɪbəˈræləṭi/ *n.* [U] FORMAL **1** understanding of, and respect for, other people's opinions: *a spirit of liberality and fairness* **2** the quality of being generous

lib·eral·ize /ˈlɪbrəˌlaɪz/ Ac *v.* [T] to make a system, laws, or moral attitudes less strict: *Spain liberalized its immigration policies.* —**liberalization** /ˌlɪbrələˈzeɪʃən/ *n.* [U]

lib·eral·ly /ˈlɪbrəli/ Ac *adv.* **1** in large amounts: *Apply sunscreen liberally.* **2** in a way that is not limited or restricted: *The teachers interpreted the rules fairly liberally* (=they were not too strict). **3** willing to accept different beliefs, systems, and behavior

ˈliberal ˌstudies *n.* [plural] a subject of study at a college or university that includes many different subjects such as history, literature, and politics → see also LIBERAL ARTS

lib·er·ate /ˈlɪbəˌreɪt/ Ac *v.* [T] **1** to free someone from feelings or conditions that make their life unhappy or difficult SYN **free**: **liberate sb from sth** *Electricity liberated farmers from many hard chores.* **2** to free prisoners, a city, a country etc. from someone's control SYN **free**: *The city was liberated by the Allies in 1944.* **3** to allow something to develop or happen freely, especially someone's imagination, knowledge, etc. SYN **free**: *Music can liberate your imagination.* —**liberating** *adj.*: *a liberating experience* —**liberator** *n.* [C]

lib·er·at·ed /ˈlɪbəˌreɪṭɪd/ Ac *adj.* free from feelings or rules which force you to behave in a particular way: *I felt liberated after telling my secret.*

lib·er·a·tion /ˌlɪbəˈreɪʃən/ Ac *n.* [U] **1** the act of freeing prisoners, a city, a country etc.: +**of** *the liberation of prisoners* **2** the state of being liberated: *sexual liberation*

libeˈration theˌology *n.* [U] a modern form of Christian teaching and activity, mainly in the Roman Catholic Church, that is based on the idea that the Church should work to change bad social, political, and economic conditions

Li·be·ri·a /laɪˈbɪriə/ a country in west Africa on the Atlantic Ocean, to the southeast of Sierra Leone —**Liberian** *n., adj.*

lib·er·tar·i·an /ˌlɪbəˈtɛriən/ *n.* [C] someone who believes strongly that people should be free to live with little or no government involvement in their lives —**libertarian** *adj.*

lib·er·tine /ˈlɪbəˌtin/ *n.* [C] someone who leads an immoral life and always looks for pleasure, especially sexual pleasure —**libertine** *adj.*

lib·er·ty /ˈlɪbəṭi/ *n. plural* **liberties**

1 FREEDOM [U] the freedom and the right to do whatever you want without asking permission or being afraid of authority: *The Constitution promises liberty and justice to all citizens.* | **political/religious liberty** (=freedom to hold any political or religious beliefs you want)

2 LEGAL RIGHT [C usually plural] a particular legal right: *liberties such as the freedom of speech* → see also CIVIL LIBERTY

3 take the liberty of doing sth to do something without asking permission because you do not think it will upset or offend anyone: *I took the liberty of taking a piece of cake.*

4 be at liberty to do sth FORMAL to have the right or permission to do something: *We are not at liberty to discuss our hiring practices.*

5 take liberties with sth to make unreasonable changes in something such as a piece of writing: *The media seems too willing to take liberties with facts.*

6 FREEDOM FROM PRISON [U] freedom for someone who has been in prison: **give sb their liberty** (=let someone leave prison) | **at liberty** FORMAL (=out of prison)

7 take liberties with sb OLD-FASHIONED to treat someone without respect by being too friendly too quickly, especially in a sexual way

[**Origin:** 1300–1400 French *liberté*, from Latin *libertas*, from *liber* **free**]

ˈLiberty ˌBond *n.* [C] HISTORY a BOND sold by the U.S. government to obtain money to support the Allies during World War I

ˈLiberty ˌship, liberty ship *n.* [C] HISTORY one of a large number of CARGO ships built in World War II in the U.S.

li·bi·do /lɪˈbidoʊ/ *n. plural* **libidos** [C,U] TECHNICAL someone's desire to have sex [**Origin:** 1900–2000 Latin **desire**, from *libere* **to please**] —**libidinous** /lɪˈbɪdn-əs/ *adj.*

Li·bra /ˈlibrə/ *n.* **1** [U] the seventh sign of the ZODIAC, represented by a pair of SCALES, and believed to affect the character and life of people born between September 23 and October 23 **2** [C] someone who was born between September 23 and October 23

li·brar·i·an /laɪˈbrɛriən/ *n.* [C] someone who works in a library —**librarianship** *n.* [U]

li·brar·y /ˈlaɪˌbrɛri/ S2 W2 *n. plural* **libraries** [C] **1** a room or building containing books that you can read there or borrow → see also BOOKSTORE: *a public library* | *library books* **2** a group of books, records etc., collected by one person: *his personal record library* **3** a set of books, records etc. that are produced by the same company and have the same general appearance: *a library of modern classics* **4** a room in a large house where most of the books are kept [**Origin:** 1300–1400 Medieval Latin *librarium*, from Latin *liber* **book**]

ˈlibrary ˌscience *n.* [U] the study of the skills that are necessary to organize and work in a library

li·bret·tist /lɪˈbrɛṭɪst/ *n.* [C] someone who writes librettos

li·bret·to /lɪˈbrɛṭoʊ/ *n. plural* **librettos** [C] the words of an OPERA or musical play

Li·bre·ville /ˈlibrəvɪl/ the capital city of Gabon

Lib·y·a /ˈlɪbiə/ a country in north Africa on the Mediterranean Sea, that is east of Algeria and west of Egypt —**Libyan** *n., adj.*

lice /laɪs/ *n.* the plural of LOUSE

li·cense[1] /ˈlaɪsəns/ Ac S2 *n.* **1** [C] an official document giving you permission to own something or do something for a period of time: *How much does a driver's license cost?* | *a fishing license* | *You can apply for a business license online.* **2 lose your license** to have your driver's license taken by the police as punishment **3** [U] freedom to do or say whatever you think is best: *Teachers should be given greater license in the classroom.* **4 artistic/poetic/creative license** the way in which a writer or painter changes the facts of the real world to make their story, description, or picture of events more interesting or more beautiful **5** [C,U] the right to behave in a way that is wrong, disgusting, or immoral: *Being old does not give someone license to be rude.* **6 under license** if something is sold, made etc. under license, it is sold, made etc. with the official permission of a company or organization **7 a license to print money** INFORMAL an officially approved plan in which there is no control over how much money is spent

license[2] Ac *v.* [T usually passive] to give official permission for someone to do something or for an activity to take place: **license sb to do sth** *He is licensed to carry a gun.*

li·censed /ˈlaɪsənst/ Ac *adj.* **1** having been given official permission to do something: *a licensed private investigator* | *licensed drivers* **2** a licensed car, gun etc. is one that someone has official permission to own or use

L

ˌlicensed ˌpractical ˈnurse ABBREVIATION **LPN** *n.* [C] someone who has been trained and is officially allowed to work as a nurse if a doctor or REGISTERED NURSE works with them

ˌlicensed voˌcational ˈnurse ABBREVIATION **LVN** *n.* [C] a licensed practical nurse in California or Texas

li·cen·see /ˌlaɪsənˈsi/ *n.* [C] someone who has official permission to do something

ˈlicense plate *n.* [C] one of the signs with numbers and letters on it at the front and back of a car → see picture on page A36

li·cen·tious /laɪˈsɛnʃəs/ *adj.* LITERARY sexually immoral or uncontrolled: *licentious behavior* —**licentiousness** *n.* [U]

li·chen /ˈlaɪkən/ *n.* [C,U] BIOLOGY a gray, green, or yellow combination of FUNGUS and ALGAE that spreads over the surface of stones and trees → see also MOSS

Roy Lichtenstein

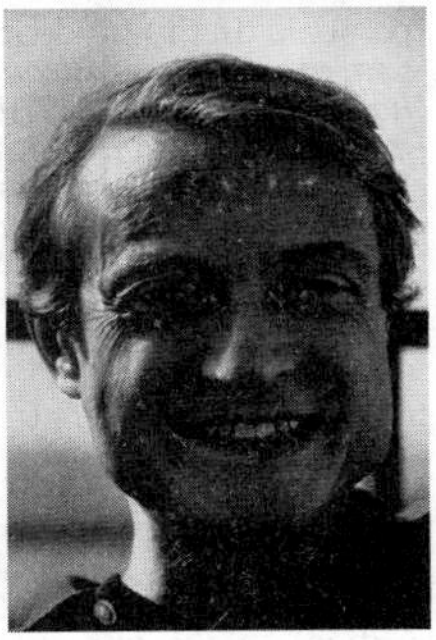

Lich·ten·stein /ˈlɪktənˌstaɪn, -ˌstin/, **Roy** /rɔɪ/ (1923–1997) a U.S. PAINTER and SCULPTOR famous for his work in POP ART, especially paintings in the style of COMIC STRIPS

lic·it /ˈlɪsɪt/ *adj.* FORMAL legal OPP illicit

lick[1] /lɪk/ S3 *v.*
1 TONGUE [T] to move your tongue across something in order to eat it, clean it etc.: *The cat licked itself.*
2 DEFEAT [T] INFORMAL to defeat an opponent or solve a problem: *We have to lick this thing before it gets worse.*
3 FLAMES/WAVES [I,T] LITERARY also **lick at** if flames or waves lick something, they touch it again and again with quick movements: *Flames licked at the ceiling.*
4 lick your lips/chops INFORMAL to feel eager and excited because you are expecting something good
5 lick your wounds to quietly think about a defeat or disappointing experience that has just happened to you: *Defeated conservatives were still licking their wounds.*
6 lick sb's boots DISAPPROVING to obey someone completely or do things to please them
[**Origin:** Old English *liccian*]

lick sth ↔ **up** *phr. v.* to drink or eat something by licking it: *The dog licked up the melting ice cream.*

lick[2] *n.* **1** [C usually singular] an act of licking something with your tongue: *Can I have a lick of your ice cream cone?* **2 not a lick of sth** SPOKEN INFORMAL not even a small amount of something: *Those kids don't have a lick of common sense.* **3** [C] INFORMAL an act of hitting someone: *I got a few good licks in.* **4 give sth a lick and a promise** to do a job, especially cleaning something, quickly and carelessly

lick·e·ty-split /ˌlɪkəṭi ˈsplɪt/ *adv.* OLD-FASHIONED very quickly

lick·ing /ˈlɪkɪŋ/ *n.* [singular] INFORMAL **1** a severe beating as a punishment **2** a defeat in a sports competition

lic·o·rice /ˈlɪkərɪʃ/ *n.* [U] **1** a type of strong-tasting black candy **2** a strong-tasting sweet black substance from the root of a plant, used in candy and medicine [**Origin:** 1100–1200 Old French, Late Latin *liquiritia*, from Latin *glycyrrhiza*, from Greek, from *glykys* **sweet** + *rhiza* **root**]

lid /lɪd/ S3 *n.* [C]
1 COVER a cover for the open part of a pot, box, or other container: *Put a lid on the pot.* | **the lid to/for sth** *Where's the lid to this jar?* ►see THESAURUS box at **cover**[2] → see picture at PAN
2 keep a lid on sth to control a situation or to keep something secret, especially so that the situation does not become worse: *The slow economy kept a lid on inflation last month.* | *Company officials are* ***keeping a tight lid on*** *their plans.*
3 EYE an EYELID
4 put a lid on sth to do something that stops a bad situation from getting worse: *New laws could put a lid on the rising cost of insurance.*
5 take the lid off sth/lift the lid on sth to let people know the true facts about a bad or shocking situation
[**Origin:** Old English *hlid*]

lid·ded /ˈlɪdɪd/ *adj.* a lidded container, pot etc. has a lid → see also HEAVY-LIDDED

lie[1] /laɪ/ S2 W1 *v. past tense* **lay** /leɪ/ *past participle* **lain** /leɪn/, **lying**
1 FLAT POSITION [I always + adv./prep.] **a)** to be in a position in which your body is flat on the floor, on a bed etc.: **+on/in/there etc.** *We lay on the beach all day.* | *For a few minutes he just lay there.* | *The dog was lying dead on the floor.* | *I* ***lie awake*** (=stay awake when you want to be asleep) *at night worrying about her.* | *I* ***lay still,*** *pretending to be asleep.* **b)** also **lie down** to put yourself in a position in which your body is flat on the floor, on a bed etc.: **+on/in/there etc.** *Lie flat on the floor.* | *She lay back against the pillows.* **c)** to be in a flat position on a surface: **+on/in/there etc.** *A thick layer of snow lay on the ground.* | *Her suitcase was lying near the door.* → see Word Choice at LAY[1]
2 PLACE [I always + adv./prep.] if a town, city, etc. lies in a particular place, it is in that place: **+in/on/below etc.** *The town lies in a small valley.* | *Several poorer districts lie between here and the capital.*
3 EXIST [I always + adv./prep.] used to talk about where an idea, number, quality, etc. exists or is present: **+in/within/outside etc.** *The solution lies in alternative sources of power.* | *China's* ***future lies with*** *the world community* (=it will be an important part of China's future). | *Not all the patients wanted to take part in the study. And* ***therein lies the problem*** (=used to say that a problem, answer etc. exists in what you are talking about).
4 BE IN A CONDITION [I] to be or remain in a particular condition or position: *Now the town lay in ruins.* | *His diary lay open on the desk.*
5 lie low to remain hidden because someone is trying to find you or catch you: *Brown seems to be lying low until the controversy passes.*
6 FUTURE [I] if something lies ahead, lies in your future, etc. it is going to happen in the future: *What lies in the future for her?* | **lie ahead/lie in store** *It's clear to us that many difficult tasks still lie ahead.* | *So many new possibilities* ***lay before*** *him.*
7 INTEREST [I] if your interest lies in something, you are interested in it: **lie in sth** *His main interst lies in genetic research.*
8 sb's loyalties/sympathies lie with sb/sth used to say that someone supports someone or something, for example one side in a political or personal argument: *Her sympathies clearly lie with the nationalists.*
9 lie at the heart/root of sth to be the most important part of something: *Oil and tourism lie at the heart of the dispute between the two nations.*
10 lie in wait (for sb/sth) a) to remain hidden in a place and wait for someone so that you can attack them **b)** if something bad lies in wait for you, it is going to happen to you
11 lie heavy on sb FORMAL if problems, duties etc. lie heavy on you, they make you feel unhappy, often because you have a lot of responsibility
12 DEAD PERSON [I always + adv./prep.] FORMAL if someone lies in a particular place, they are buried there: *The saint's body lies in the crypt.* | ***Here lies*** (=written on a grave) *Edgar Fuller, 1834–1912.*
13 lie in state FORMAL if an important person who has died lies in state, their body is put in a public place so that people can go and show their respect for them → see also **let sleeping dogs lie** at SLEEP[1] (7)

lie around *phr. v.* **1** to be left out of the correct place, so that things look messy or get lost: *You shouldn't* ***leave*** *your keys* ***lying around*** *like that.* | **lie around sth** *Books and papers were lying around the office.*

L

2 to spend time being lazy and not doing anything useful: *You can't just lie around all day!* | **lie around sth** *When I got home, he was still lying around the house.*

lie behind sth *phr. v.* to be the true reason for an action, decision etc.: *It is still unclear what lay behind the sudden resignation of the two officials.*

lie down *phr. v.* **1** to put yourself in a position in which your body is flat on the floor or on a bed: *I'm going to go lie down for a little while.* **2 take sth lying down** INFORMAL to accept bad treatment without complaining: *We are not going to take this verdict lying down.* **3 lie down on the job** to be lazy at work and not work as hard as you should

lie with sb *phr. v.* **1** if a power, duty etc. lies with someone, they are responsible for it: *Much of the responsibility for the city's current problems lies with the mayor.* **2** OLD USE OR BIBLICAL to have sex with someone

lie² S1 *v. past tense and past participle* **lied**, **lying** **1** [I] to deliberately tell someone something that is not true: *I could tell that Tom was lying.* | **lie to sb** *Don't lie to me!* | **+about** *I was pretty sure she was lying about her age.* | *Don't listen to him. He's* ***lying through his teeth*** (=deliberately saying something that is completely untrue).

THESAURUS

make sth up to invent a story, explanation, etc. in order to deceive someone: *"What'll you tell your mother?" "I'll make something up."*
tell (sb) a lie to lie: *Did he make a mistake, or did he tell a lie?*
invent to think of an idea, story, etc. that is not true: *If I can't find a reason, I'll invent one.*
mislead to make someone believe something that is not true by giving him or her false or incomplete information: *Had the senator misled Congress?*
deceive to make someone believe something that is not true: *She still found it hard to believe that he had deceived and betrayed her.*
perjure yourself/commit perjury to tell a lie in a court of law: *Company executives may have perjured themselves in sworn testimony.*

L

2 [I not in progressive] if a picture, numbers etc. lie, they do not show the true facts or the true situation: *Statistics can often lie.* | *The camera doesn't lie.*

lie³ W3 *n.* **1** [C] something that you say or write that you know is untrue: *Tina got in trouble for* ***telling lies.*** | *White calls her accusations "****a pack of lies****"* (=a set of statements that are lies). | *I knew it was* ***a bald-faced lie*** (=a clear and shocking lie).

THESAURUS

fib INFORMAL a small unimportant lie
white lie a small lie that you tell someone, usually to avoid hurting his or her feelings
slander LAW something untrue that is said about someone which could harm the opinion people have of him or her
libel LAW something untrue that is written about someone which could harm the opinion people have of him or her

2 give the lie to sth FORMAL to show that something is untrue: *Their success gives the lie to predictions of the city's economic doom.* → see also **live a lie** at LIVE¹ (7), WHITE LIE

Liech·ten·stein /ˈlɪktənˌʃtaɪn, -ˌstaɪn/ a very small country in Europe that is west of Austria and east of Switzerland —**Liechtensteiner** *n.*

ˈlie deˌtector *n.* [C] a piece of equipment used to check whether someone is lying, by measuring sudden changes in their heart rate

lien /lin, ˈliən/ *n.* [C + against/on] LAW the legal right to keep something that belongs to someone who owes you money, until the debt has been paid

lieu /lu/ *n.* **in lieu (of sth) a)** FORMAL instead of something else: *Employees may be given extra vacation days in lieu of payment.* **b)** LAW if you are held in lieu of a particular amount of money, you will be kept in prison until someone pays that money to the police: *She was being held in lieu of $40,000 bail.*

lieu·ten·ant /luˈtɛnənt/ *n.* **1** WRITTEN ABBREVIATION **Lt.** [C] an officer who has a middle rank in the Army, Navy, Air Force, Marines, police etc. **2 lieutenant colonel/general etc.** an officer with the rank below COLONEL, GENERAL etc. **3** [C] someone who does work for, or in place of, someone in a higher position SYN **deputy**: *the CEO's top lieutenant* [**Origin:** 1300–1400 French *lieu* **place** + *tenant* **holding**]

lieuˌtenant ˈgovernor *n.* [C] POLITICS the person with the rank just below the GOVERNOR of a U.S. state, who is responsible for the Governor's duties if he or she is unable to do them

life /laɪf/ S1 W1 *n. plural* **lives** /laɪvz/
1 PERIOD OF BEING ALIVE [C,U] the period between a person's birth and death, during which they are alive: *Learning goes on throughout life.* | *My mother worked hard* ***all her life.*** | *This is one of the happiest days* ***of my life.*** | *I'd only seen her maybe three times* ***in my life.*** | *He deserves to* ***spend his life*** *in prison for what he's done.* | *The accident left him crippled* ***for life*** (=for the rest of his life). | *It is hard to get reliable information about St. Catherine's* ***early life*** (=when she was young). | *Arlene's father took up painting* ***in later life*** (=when he was older). | *She didn't have children until relatively* ***late in life*** (=when she was fairly old).
2 STATE OF BEING ALIVE [C,U] the state of being alive: *a baby's first moments of life* | *A heart transplant could* ***save his life.*** | *Chuen* ***risked his life*** (=did something during which he could have been killed) *to save Sammler.* | *Over 2,000 Americans* ***lost their lives*** (=died) *in the attack.* | *Failure to follow safety rules could result in needless* ***loss of life.*** | *Anna* ***took her own life*** (=killed herself) *when she was 23.* | *She felt his neck for* ***signs of life*** (=signs that he was alive). | *I can't* ***bring*** *my child* ***back to life****, but I need to know how he died.* | *Every time you cross this highway you* ***take your life in your hands*** (=put yourself in a dangerous situation). | *My mother was in the hospital* ***fighting for her life*** (=struggling to stay alive). | *The president survived two* ***attempts on his life*** (=attempts to kill him). | **give your life/lay down your life** (=die willingly in order to save other people, or because of a strong belief)
3 LIVING THINGS [U] **a)** the quality that people, animals, and plants have that rocks, machines, dead bodies etc. do not have **b)** BIOLOGY living things, such as people, animals, or plants: *Do you think there is life on other planets?* | **animal/plant/bird life** (=living animals, plants, or birds) | **life forms/forms of life** *All forms of life on earth depend on oxygen.*
4 WAY OF LIVING [C,U] all the experiences and activities that are typical of a particular way of living: *Life in L.A. is exciting.* | *He started his* ***working life*** *as an urban planner.* | ***Married life*** *isn't everything we expected.* | *the American* ***way of life*** | **sb's life as sth** *The book tells about her life as a singer.* | ***This is the life*** (=what we are doing is the most enjoyable way to live)*!*
5 EXPERIENCES [C usually singular] the type of experience that someone has during their life: *Having children changes your life.* | *an account of* ***daily life*** *in ancient Egypt* | **lead/live/have a ... life** *He hasn't had an easy life, you know.* | **a life of crime/luxury/poverty etc.** *We all have dreams of a life of luxury.* | **start/build/make a new life** *They moved to Australia to start a new life.* | *The* ***pace of life*** (=how fast events in life happen and how busy you are) *was slower in the South.* | *Our* ***quality of life*** *is more important than money.* | *She* ***lived life to the full*** (=used every opportunity to do exciting or interesting things). → see also LIFE STORY
6 PART OF LIVING [C usually singular] a particular part of someone's life and the activities that relate to it: *her busy social life* | **home/family life** *We had a happy home life.* | **private/personal life** *I never discuss my personal life.* | *How's your* ***love life*** (=used about both romantic and sexual relationships) *these days?*

7 HUMAN EXISTENCE [U] human existence, considered as all the experiences that humans can have or have had: *Life can be hard sometimes.* | *Cindy still doesn't know much about life.*
8 real life what really happens as opposed to what happens in people's imaginations or in stories: *a real-life drama* | ***In real life** it's not so easy to catch a criminal.*
9 PRISON [U] also **life imprisonment** the punishment of being put in prison for the rest of your life: *Pratt was **sentenced to life** for the 1968 murder.* → see also LIFE SENTENCE
10 INTEREST/EXCITEMENT [U] the quality of being interesting or exciting: *There wasn't much life in her performance.* | *A good teacher can **bring** literature **to life** for students.* | *The place **came to life*** (=became exciting) *when Sarah walked in.*
11 ENERGY [U] a quality of energy and happiness in the way someone lives: *She always seemed so happy and **full of life**.*
12 the life of sth the period of time during which something happens, exists, or has a use: *What's the average life of a passenger airplane?* → see also SHELF LIFE
13 MOVING/WORKING [U] the state in which a machine or piece of equipment is active or working: *Suddenly the engine **came to life*** (=started working).
14 be sb's (whole) life to be the most important thing or person in someone's life: *Music is Laura's life.*
15 be the life of the party someone who is fun and exciting to be with at social occasions
16 make life difficult/easier etc. to make it difficult, easier etc. to do something: *It would make life easier for me if the two of you would cooperate.*
17 a life of its own used to say that something seems to move, work, or develop in a way that you cannot control: *Suddenly the ball seemed to take on a life of its own.*
18 the race/surprise/game etc. of sb's life the best race someone has ever run, the biggest surprise they have ever had etc. → see also **have the time of your life** at TIME[1] (21)
19 the woman/man in your life the woman or man with whom you have a sexual or romantic relationship
20 IN A GAME [C] a chance in a game, for example a computer game, to continue playing even after you have done something that defeats your player: *I'm at level five with three lives left.*
21 BOOK/MOVIE [C] the story of someone's life SYN **biography**: *"The Life of Christopher Columbus"*
22 paint/draw from life to paint or draw something that you are looking at directly, not from another picture
23 the next life/the life to come a continued existence that is expected after death

SPOKEN PHRASES

24 that's life used when you are disappointed or upset that something has happened, but realize that you must accept it: *Oh well, that's life!*
25 how's life (treating you)? used as an informal greeting: *Hi Jim! How's life?*
26 life is too short (to do sth) said when telling someone that something is not important enough to worry about: *Life's too short to worry about every little detail.*
27 Get a life! used to tell someone you think they are boring
28 life goes on used to say that you must continue living as usual even when something sad or disappointing happens
29 for the life of me said when you cannot do something, even when you try very hard: *I can't remember her name for the life of me!*
30 not on your life! used to say that you definitely will not do something

[**Origin:** Old English *lif*] → see also **for dear life** at DEAR[3] (3), HIGH LIFE, **larger than life** at LARGE (5), **give sb/sth a new lease on life** at LEASE[1] (2), LOW LIFE, **sth is a matter of life and death** at MATTER[1] (17), **can't do sth to save your life** at SAVE[1] (11)

GRAMMAR

When talking about **life** [U] in general, do not use *the*: *Life is full of surprises* (NOT *The life...*).

'life-af,firming *adj.* giving you a positive and happy attitude about life: *a life-affirming experience*

'life belt *n.* [C] a special belt you wear in the water to prevent you from sinking

life·blood, life-blood /ˈlaɪfblʌd/ *n.* [U] **1** [singular] the most important thing needed by an organization, relationship etc. for it to continue to exist or develop successfully: *Advertising is the lifeblood of newspapers.* **2** BIOLOGY your blood

life·boat /ˈlaɪfboʊt/ *n.* [C] **1** a small boat carried by ships in order to save people if the ship sinks **2** a boat that is sent out to help people who are in danger on the ocean

'life ,buoy *n.* [C] a large ring made of material that floats that you throw to someone who has fallen in the water, to prevent them from DROWNING

'life coach *n.* [C] someone who you pay to give you advice on how to improve your life, especially to make you happier or more successful

'life ,cycle *n.* [C] **1** BIOLOGY all the different stages of development that an animal or plant goes through during its life **2** the length of time for which a product is expected to last or be useful: *The vehicle has a life cycle of about 30 years.*

,life ex'pectancy *n.* [C] **1** the length of time that a person or animal is expected to live: *an animal with an average life expectancy of four years* **2** the length of time that something is expected to continue to work, be useful etc.: *CDs have a life expectancy of at least 20 years.* **3** TECHNICAL the age that someone will probably live to, based on things such as current age, whether or not someone smokes cigarettes, the type of job they do etc., used by insurance companies to work out the risk of insuring someone

'life form *n.* [C] a living thing such as a plant or animal

'life guard *n.* [C] someone who works at a beach or swimming pool to help swimmers who are in danger

'life ,history *n.* [C] all the events and changes that happen during the life of a living thing

'life in,surance *n.* [U] a type of insurance that someone makes regular payments into so that when they die their family will receive money

'life ,jacket *n.* [C] a piece of clothing that you wear around your upper body to prevent you from sinking in the water

life·less /ˈlaɪflɪs/ *adj.* **1** LITERARY dead or appearing to be dead: *his lifeless body* ▸see THESAURUS box at **dead**[1] **2** lacking the positive qualities that make something or someone interesting, exciting, or active: *a lifeless performance* **3** not living, or not having living things on it: *The surface of the moon is dry and lifeless.* —**lifelessly** *adv.* —**lifelessness** *n.* [U]

life·like /ˈlaɪflaɪk/ *adj.* a lifelike picture, model etc. looks exactly like a real person or thing: *a lifelike doll*

life·line /ˈlaɪflaɪn/ *n.* [C] **1** something that someone depends on completely: *Because I work at home, the telephone is like a lifeline to me.* **2** a rope used for saving people in danger, especially on the ocean

life·long /ˈlaɪflɔŋ/ *adj.* [usually before noun] continuing or existing all through your life: *a lifelong relationship* | *a lifelong friend*

'life pre,server *n.* [C] something such as a LIFE BELT or LIFE JACKET that can be worn in the water to prevent you from sinking

lif·er /ˈlaɪfɚ/ *n.* [C] INFORMAL **1** someone who has been sent to prison for the rest of their life **2** someone who spends their whole working life in the military or in a profession

'life raft *n.* [C] a small rubber boat that can be filled with air and used by passengers on a sinking ship

life·sav·er /ˈlaɪfˌseɪvɚ/ *n.* [C] **1** someone or something that helps you avoid a difficult or bad situation: *The company's day care service is a lifesaver for many parents.* **2** someone or something that prevents you from dying: *The seat belt is the biggest single lifesaver in cars.*

'life-ˌsaving also **lifesaving** *adj.* [only before noun] a life-saving drug, action, piece of equipment etc. has saved someone's life, or makes it possible to save people's lives: *a life-saving operation*

life·sav·ing /ˈlaɪfˌseɪvɪŋ/ *n.* [U] the skills necessary to save a person from DROWNING

ˌlife 'sciences *n.* [plural] subjects such as BIOLOGY that are concerned with the study of humans, plants, and animals

ˌlife 'sentence *n.* [C] the punishment of sending someone to prison for the rest of their life

'life-size also **'life-sized** *adj.* a picture or model of something or someone that is life-size is the same size as they really are: *a life-sized statue of Elvis*

life·span /ˈlaɪfspæn/ *n.* [C] the average length of time that someone will live or that something will continue to work: *Men have a shorter lifespan than women.* → see also LIFE EXPECTANCY

'life ˌstory *n.* [C] the story of someone's whole life: *Karinna can't resist **telling her life story** to anyone who will listen.*

life·style /ˈlaɪfstaɪl/ *n.* [C] the way someone lives, including the place they live in, the things they own, the type of job they have, and the activities they enjoy: *an urban lifestyle* | *a healthy lifestyle* | *My parents disapprove of my lifestyle.*

'life ˌsupport *n.* [U] machines or methods that keep someone alive when they are extremely sick or in conditions where they would not normally be able to live, such as in space: *She spent 12 days **on life support** in the hospital.* | *the **life support systems** of the space shuttle*

'life-ˌthreatening *adj.* a life-threatening situation or injury could cause a person to die

life·time /ˈlaɪftaɪm/ W3 *n.* [C usually singular] **1** the period of time during which someone is alive or something exists: *In our lifetime, ordinary people will travel to the moon.* | +**of** *a lifetime of achievement* | *This kind of opportunity only comes **once in a lifetime**.* **2 the chance/experience etc. of a lifetime** the best opportunity, experience etc. that you will ever have → see also LIFESPAN

'life vest *n.* [C] a LIFE JACKET

life·work /laɪfˈwɚk/ *n.* [U] the main work that someone does during their life, especially work that is very important to them

lift¹ /lɪft/ S2 W2 *v.*

1 MOVE STH UPWARD [I,T] to move to a higher position, or to make something do this: *She slowly lifted the lid.* | **lift (sth) up/off/onto etc.** *Brendan lifted Gilbert out of the wheelchair.* | *The wind lifted the roof right off.* | *The balloon lifted up just beyond his reach.*

2 PART OF THE BODY [I,T] also **lift up** if a part of your body lifts, or you lift it, it moves to a higher position: *I'm so tired I can't even lift up my arms.*

3 HEAD/EYES [T] to move your head or eyes up so that you can look at someone or something: *He lifted his head to see who was at the door.* | **lift sth from sth** *He never once lifted his head from his book.*

4 CONTROLS/LAWS [T] to remove a rule or a law that says that something is not allowed: **lift a ban/embargo/sanction etc.** *The government plans to lift its ban on cigar imports.*

5 CLOUDS/MIST [I] if cloud or mist lifts, it disappears

6 not lift a finger INFORMAL to do nothing to help: *He never even lifted a finger to help me with the kids.*

7 lift sb's spirits to make someone feel more cheerful and hopeful

8 INCREASE [T] ESPECIALLY WRITTEN to increase the amount or level of something: *Lower prices should eventually lift corporate profits.*

9 be lifted into/to/from etc. if people or things are lifted somewhere, they are taken there by plane: *More troops are being lifted into the area.*

10 like sth lifted from your shoulders happier because something that was worrying you or causing you problems has ended: *They were safe, and suddenly it was like a giant weight was lifted from my shoulders.*

11 lift sb out of sth LITERARY to take someone out of a bad situation: *Hard work is not enough to lift these people out of poverty.*

12 be lifted from sth if words, ideas, music etc. are lifted from something, they are copied from someone else's work without stating where they came from: *The movie's ending was lifted from Frankenheimer's "Black Sunday."*

13 STEAL [T] INFORMAL to steal something

14 lift (up) your voice LITERARY to speak, shout, or sing more loudly

[**Origin:** 1100–1200 Old Norse *lypta*]

lift off *phr. v.* if a space vehicle lifts off, it leaves the ground and rises into the air

lift² *n.* **1** [C usually singular] a ride in someone's car to a place you want to go SYN **ride**: *Sheri **gave me a lift** home.* | *I **got a lift from** David.* **2 give sb/sth a lift a)** to make someone feel more cheerful and hopeful: *If I'm feeling down, shopping gives me a lift.* **b)** to make something such as a business, the ECONOMY etc. operate better: *Interest rates cuts were supposed to give the economy a lift.* **3** [C] a piece of equipment used to lift heavy objects, especially one for helping injured or DISABLED people go up stairs **4** [U] PHYSICS the pressure of air that keeps something up in the air or lifts it higher **5** [C] INFORMAL a CHAIRLIFT → see also SKI LIFT **6** [C] BRITISH an ELEVATOR

'lift-off *n.* [C,U] the moment when a vehicle that is about to travel in space leaves the ground: *Lift-off is set for 10:55 a.m.* → see also TAKEOFF

lig·a·ment /ˈlɪgəmənt/ *n.* [C] BIOLOGY a band of strong white TISSUE that holds bones together at a joint [**Origin:** 1300–1400 Latin *ligamentum*, from *ligare* **to tie**] → see picture at JOINT

light¹ /laɪt/ S1 W1 *n.*

1 BRIGHTNESS [U, singular] brightness from the sun, or from something such as a lamp or flame, that allows you to see things: *a bright light* | *We could see light coming from under the door.* | *The morning light shone through the window.* | *Lincoln studied **by the light of*** (=using light produced by) *a fire.* | *Come **into the light*** (=out of the shadows to a place with more light) *where I can see you.* | **a beam/ray/shaft of light** (=a thin line of light shining from the sun, a lamp etc.) | **soft/warm light** (=light that is not too strong) | **blinding/dazzling light** (=extremely bright light) | *They started searching **at first light*** (=when the sun first begins to shine). → see also NORTHERN LIGHTS

2 LAMP/ELECTRIC LIGHT ETC. [C] an electric piece of equipment that produces light: *the lights of the city at night* | **a light is on/off** *All the lights were on in the house.* | *Is the porch light off?* | **turn the light on/off** *Please turn on the light.* | **switch on/off the light** *Could you switch off all the lights?* | *Suddenly all **the lights** in the house **went out*** (=stopped shining). | *The lights **came on*** (=started shining) *a few minutes later.* | *The police officer **shined** her **light** into the bushes.* | **turn the lights down/dim the lights** (=make lights less bright) → see also **the bright lights (of sth)** at BRIGHT (8)

3 TRAFFIC CONTROL [C] one of a set of red, green, and yellow lights used for controlling traffic, or the whole set considered as one: *Turn right at the next light.* | **the light turns red/green/yellow** (=the light becomes red, green, yellow) | *We waited for the **lights to change**.* | *I can't believe you just **ran a red light*** (=drove past a red light). → see also GREEN LIGHT, TRAFFIC LIGHTS

4 ON A VEHICLE [C usually plural] one of the lights on a car, bicycle etc., especially the HEADLIGHTS: *You left your lights on.* → see also BRAKE LIGHT, PARKING LIGHT

5 be/stand in sb's light to prevent someone from getting all the light they need to see or do something: *Could you move over? You're standing in my light.*

6 in a new/different/bad etc. light if someone or something is seen or shown in a new, different etc. light, a particular part of their character becomes clear and this affects your opinion of them: *Baltz is trying present the sales figures in a positive light.*

7 in light of sth if you do or decide something in light of a new situation or new information, you do it because of that situation or information: *In light of recent events, we have canceled our celebration.*

8 come to light also **be brought to light** if new information comes to light, it becomes known: *It eventually came to light that the CIA had information about the security problem.*
9 throw/shed/cast light on sth to provide new information that makes a difficult subject or problem easier to understand: *Newly found Aztec artifacts may shed some light on their mysterious culture.*
10 FOR A CIGARETTE a light a match or CIGARETTE LIGHTER to light a cigarette: *Do you have a light?*
11 see the light of day a) if an object sees the light of day, it is taken from the place where it has been hidden, and becomes publicly known: *Business contracts go through armies of lawyers before they see the light of day.* **b)** if a law, decision etc. sees the light of day, it begins to exist
12 light at the end of the tunnel something that gives you hope for the future after a long and difficult period: *After a year of declining profits, there's finally a light at the end of the tunnel.*
13 see the light a) OFTEN HUMOROUS to suddenly understand something: *Danny finally saw the light and bought me flowers on Valentine's Day.* **b)** INFORMAL to begin to believe in a religion very strongly
14 go/be out like a light INFORMAL to go to sleep very quickly because you are very tired: *She was out like a light, as soon as we put her in bed.*
15 the light of sb's life the person whom someone loves the most: *We have a four-year-old son who is the light of my life.*
16 IN YOUR EYES [singular] LITERARY an expression in your eyes that shows an emotion or intention
17 have your name in lights INFORMAL to be successful and famous in the theater or movies
18 a leading light in/of sth INFORMAL someone who is important in a particular group: *a leading light in the local drama society*
19 the lights are on, but nobody's home SPOKEN, HUMOROUS used to say that someone is stupid or not paying attention
20 ART [U] areas of lighter color in paintings, drawings, and photographs
21 WINDOW [C] TECHNICAL a window or other opening in a roof or wall that allows light into a room
[**Origin:** Old English *leoht*] → see also **in the cold light of day** at COLD[1] (15), **be all sweetness and light** at SWEETNESS (6)

light[2] S1 W2 *adj.*
1 COLOR a light color or light skin is pale and not dark: *a light blue shirt* | *She has light brown hair.* → see also DARK, DEEP[1] (5)

THESAURUS
pale a pale color has more white in it than usual: *a dress made of pale yellow silk*
pastel having a soft light color: *a baby blanket in pastel blue*
faded having lost color, for example by being washed many times or by being left out in the sun: *a pair of faded jeans*

►see THESAURUS box at **color**[1]
2 WEIGHT not weighing very much, or weighing less than you expect OPP **heavy**: *Why is your suitcase lighter than mine?* | *You can carry this – it's light.* | **as light as air/as light as a feather** (=extremely light) → see also LIGHTEN, LIGHTWEIGHT[2]
3 CLOTHES light clothes are thin and not very warm OPP **thick**: *You'll need at least a light jacket.*
4 it is/gets light used to say that there is enough natural light outside to see by, or that the light outside increases because the sun rises: *It gets light before 6 a.m.*
5 ROOM a room that is light has plenty of light in it, especially from the sun OPP **dark**: *The studio was light and spacious.*
6 WIND blowing without much force OPP **strong**: *a light breeze*
7 TOUCH very gentle and soft: *She gave him a light kiss on the cheek.* → see also LIGHTLY
8 small in amount, or less than you expected: *The traffic's much lighter than usual.* | **a light meal/lunch etc.** (=a meal in which you only eat a small amount) → see also HEAVY
9 a) not containing much fat or having fewer CALORIES: *light yogurt* → see also LITE **b)** food or an alcoholic drink that is light either does not have a strong taste or is easy to DIGEST: *a light white wine* | *a light dessert*
10 PUNISHMENT not very severe OPP **harsh**: *Jones received only a light punishment.*
11 WORK/EXERCISE not very tiring: *I try to have a light workout every day.*
12 a light smoker/drinker/eater etc. someone who does not smoke, drink, eat etc. very much
13 SLEEP used to describe sleep from which you wake up very easily OPP **deep**: *I fell into a light sleep.* | **a light sleeper** (=someone who wakes up easily)
14 NOT SERIOUS not serious in meaning, style, or manner: *an evening of light entertainment* | *a show that takes a look at* ***the lighter side of*** *working in a hospital* | *I picked up a novel for some* ***light reading*** *on the flight.* | *In her book, Rose handles these difficult questions with* ***a light touch*** (=a relaxed and pleasant style). | **on a lighter note/in a lighter vein** (=used to introduce a joke, funny story etc. after you have been speaking about something serious) | *It is shocking that anyone could* ***make light of*** (=make a joke of) *child abuse.* → see also LIGHTLY
15 be light on your feet to be able to move quickly and gracefully
16 make light work of sth to finish a job quickly and easily
17 SOIL easy to break into small pieces OPP **heavy**
18 HEART LITERARY someone who has a light heart feels happy and not worried → see also LIGHT-HEADED, LIGHT-HEARTED —**lightness** *n.* [U]

light[3] S2 W2 *v. past tense and past participle* **lit** /lɪt/ or **lighted 1** [I,T] to start to burn, or to deliberately make something start to burn: *The old man lit a cigarette and took a puff.* | *The fire won't light.* ►see THESAURUS box at **burn**[1] **2** [T usually passive] to give light to something: *a Christmas display lit by 30,000 colored bulbs.* | **well/poorly lit** *a well lit room* → see also LIGHTEN **3 light sb's way** to provide light for someone while they are going somewhere
light on/upon sth *phr. v.* **1** to fly to something and sit on it: *The dragonfly had lighted on her arm.* **2** LITERARY to suddenly notice, find, or discover something by chance: *His eye lit on the wedding ring on her finger.* | *Then we lit on a new idea.*
light out *phr. v.* INFORMAL to go or run somewhere as quickly as you can: *The boys lit out for home.*
light up *phr. v.* **1 light sth ↔ up** to give light to a place or to shine light on something: *Fireworks lit up the sky.* **2** if someone's face or eyes light up or something lights them up, they show pleasure, excitement etc.: *Sue's face lit up when Sean walked in.* | **+with** *The boy's face lit up with delight.* | **light sth ↔ up** *Suddenly a smile lit up her face.* **3** to become bright with light or color: *All the buttons on his phone lit up.* **4** INFORMAL to light a cigarette **5** to make a place or situation seem happier, more pleasant, or more exciting: *Her smile lights up the whole room.*

light[4] *adv.* → see **travel light** at TRAVEL[1] (1)

ˌlight ˈaircraft *n.* [C] a small airplane

ˈlight bulb *n.* [C] the glass object inside a lamp that produces light

light·en /ˈlaɪtˀn/ *v.* **1** [T] to reduce the amount of work, worry, debt etc. that someone has: *The school is looking at ways to lighten teachers' workloads.* **2** [I,T] to become brighter or less dark, or to make something brighter etc. OPP **darken**: *As the sky lightened, we could see the distant mountains.* **3** [I,T] to reduce the weight of something or become less heavy **4 lighten up!** SPOKEN used to tell someone not to be so serious about something: *Lighten up, man! We don't need to argue.* **5** [I] if someone's face, expression, or voice lightens, they begin to look or sound more cheerful

light·er /ˈlaɪt̬ɚ/ *n.* [C] a small object that produces a flame for lighting cigarettes etc.

ˌlight-ˈfingered *adj.* **1** likely to steal things **2** able to move your fingers easily and quickly, especially when you play a musical instrument

ˌlight-ˈfooted *adj.* able to move quickly and gracefully

ˌlight-ˈheaded *adj.* [not before noun] unable to think clearly or move steadily because you are sick or have drunk alcohol SYN **dizzy** —**light-headedness** *n.* [U]

ˌlight-ˈhearted *adj.* **1** not intended to be serious: *a light-hearted comedy* **2** cheerful and not worried about anything: *a happy, light-hearted girl* —**light-heartedly** *adv.* —**light-heartedness** *n.* [U]

ˌlight ˈheavyweight *n.* [C] a BOXER who weighs between 160 and 175 pounds (72.5 and 79.5 kilograms) —**light heavyweight** *adj.*

lighthouse

light·house /ˈlaɪthaʊs/ *n.* [C] a tower with a powerful flashing light that guides ships away from danger near the shore

ˌlight ˈindustry *n.* [U] the part of industry that produces small goods, such as things used in the house

light·ing /ˈlaɪṭɪŋ/ *n.* [U] the lights that light a room, building, or street, or the quality of the light produced: *The lighting isn't good for reading.*

light·ly /ˈlaɪtli/ *adv.* **1** with only a small amount of weight or force SYN **gently**: *I knocked lightly on the door.* **2** using or having only a small amount of something: *a lightly greased pan* | *lightly armed soldiers* **3 take/treat/approach sth lightly** to do something without serious thought: *We don't take any bomb threat lightly.* **4** if you sleep lightly, you wake up very easily if there is even a quiet noise **5 get off lightly** also **be let off lightly** to be punished in a way that is less severe than you deserve: *I'm letting you off lightly this time.* **6** without worrying, or without appearing to be worried: *"Things will be fine," he said lightly.*

ˈlight ˌmeter *n.* [C] an instrument used by a photographer to measure how much light there is

L

light·ning¹ /ˈlaɪtˀnɪŋ/ *n.* [U] **1** a powerful flash of light in the sky caused by electricity and usually followed by THUNDER: *Two farmworkers were **struck by lightning*** (=hit by lightning). **2 like lightning** extremely quickly: *The cat ran up the tree like lightning.*

lightning² *adj., adv.* [only before noun] very fast, and often without warning: *a **lightning quick*** (=very fast) *start* | **at/with lightning speed** (=extremely quickly)

ˈlightning bug *n.* [C] an insect with a tail that shines in the dark SYN **firefly**

ˈlightning ˌrod *n.* [C] **1** a metal ROD or wire on a building or structure that gives lightning a direct path to the ground, so that it does not cause damage **2 a lightning rod (for sth)** someone or something who gets most of the criticism, blame, or public attention when there is a problem, although they may not be responsible for it: *Mr. Daniels has become a lightning rod for criticism.*

ˈlightning strike *n.* [C] a situation in which LIGHTNING hits something

light ˈopera *n.* [C,U] an OPERETTA, or this type of entertainment

ˈlight pen *n.* [C] COMPUTERS a piece of equipment like a pen, used to draw or write on a computer screen

light ˈrail *n.* [C] an electric railroad system that uses light trains and usually carries only passengers, not goods —**light-rail** *adj.*

light·ship /ˈlaɪtˌʃɪp/ *n.* [C] a small ship that stays near a dangerous place in the ocean and guides other ships using a powerful flashing light

ˈlight show *n.* [C] a type of entertainment that uses a series of moving colored lights, especially at a POP concert

ˈlights-out *n.* [U] the time at night when a group of people who are in a school, the army etc. must turn the lights off and go to sleep

light·stick /ˈlaɪtˌstɪk/ *n.* [C] a small plastic tube containing liquid chemicals that mix together and make light when you break the end of the tube SYN **glowstick**: *People at the concert were dancing and waving lightsticks.*

light·weight¹ /ˈlaɪtˀweɪt/ *adj.* **1** weighing less than average: *a lightweight computer* **2** lightweight clothing or material is thin enough to be worn in warm weather: *a lightweight jacket* **3** showing a lack of serious thought: *lightweight novels*

lightweight² *n.* [C] **1** DISAPPROVING someone who you do not think has the ability to think about serious or difficult subjects: *Call me a lightweight, but I like movies with happy endings.* **2** DISAPPROVING someone who has no importance or influence: *a political lightweight* **3** a BOXER who weighs between 126 and 135 pounds (59 and 61 kilograms)

ˈlight year *n.* [C] **1** PHYSICS the distance that light travels in one year, about 9,500,000,000,000 kilometers (5.88 trillion miles), used for measuring distances between stars **2 light years ahead/better etc. than sth** INFORMAL much more advanced, much better etc. than someone or something else: *The show was light years ahead of its competition.* **3 light years ago** a long time ago

lig·nin /ˈlɪgnɪn/ *n.* [U] BIOLOGY a substance that makes the sides of plant cells stiff and is the main substance in wood

lig·nite /ˈlɪgnaɪt/ *n.* [U] EARTH SCIENCE a soft substance such as coal, used as FUEL

lik·a·ble, likeable /ˈlaɪkəbəl/ *adj.* likable people are nice and easy to like

like¹ /laɪk/ S1 W1 *prep.*

1 SIMILAR similar in some way to something else: *The lamp was round, like a ball.* | *You two are behaving like children.* | **look/sound/taste/smell like sth** *Ken looks like his brother.* | *This candy tastes like peppermint.* | *I have some shoes **just like*** (=exactly like) *yours.* | *A new paint job made the car look **like new**.* | *She looks **nothing like*** (=not similar at all) *her sister.* | *Is your new job **anything like*** (=used in questions and negative statements to compare things) *your old one?* ►see THESAURUS box at **similar**

2 like this/so SPOKEN said when you are showing someone how to do something: *Cut the paper diagonally, like this.*

3 TYPICAL typical of a particular person: **it's not like sb to do sth** *It's not like Emily to lie.* | ***It's just like*** (=it's very typical of) *her to leave me here by myself.*

4 what is sb/sth like? used when asking someone to describe or give their opinion of a person or thing: *What's the new teacher like?* | *What's it like living in Spain?*

5 SUCH AS a word meaning "such as" or "for example", used only in informal speech: *Fruits like oranges and kiwis have lots of vitamin C.* | *They make purses and wallets and **things like that**.*

6 something like a) not much more or less than a particular amount SYN **about** SYN **roughly**: *The project will take us something like three weeks.* **b)** used in comparisons to say that one thing is fairly similar to another: *The animal looks something like a gopher.*

7 more like used when giving an amount or number that you think is more correct than one that has been mentioned: *Brian said he'll be here at 7, but it'll probably be more like 8 or 9.*

8 there's nothing like SPOKEN used to say that something is the best: *There's nothing like Mom's chicken soup.*

9 that's more like it SPOKEN used to tell someone that what they are doing or suggesting is more satisfactory than what they did or suggested before: *"I said 400, but I meant 200." "Oh OK, that's more like it."*

[**Origin:** 1300–1400 Old English *gelic*]

like² S1 W1 *v.* [T not usually in progressive]

1 LIKE STH to enjoy something or think that it is nice or good OPP **dislike**: *I like your new car.* | *My daughter doesn't like peas.* | **like doing sth** *My mother likes* *working in her vegetable garden.* | **like to do sth** *I like to go mountain biking on the weekends.* | **like sth about sb/sth** *She's very independent – I like that about her.* | *I **like** the blue one **best*** (=prefer it). | *Linda doesn't **like it** when we talk about politics.* | ***How do you like** living in London?* | *I don't think I'll ever **get to like** flying.* | **like the idea/thought of (doing) sth** *Paul doesn't like the idea of borrowing money.* | ***I like the way*** (=I think it is good that) *everyone's ideas are listened to.* ►see THESAURUS box at **enjoy**

2 LIKE SB to think that someone is nice or enjoy being with them: *You should meet my brother. You'll like him.*

3 PREFER to prefer that something is done in one particular way: ***How do you like** your steak cooked?* | **like to do sth** *I like to put lots of ketchup on my fries.*

4 THINK STH IS GOOD TO DO to think that it is good to do something, so that you do it regularly or so that you want other people to do it regularly: **like to do sth** *I like to try to eat well and keep myself healthy.* | **like sb to do sth** *They like their children to be involved in sports.*

5 not like to do sth also **not like doing sth** to not want to do something because you do not feel it is polite, fair, nice etc.: *I don't like calling her at work.*

6 like the cut of sb's jib HUMOROUS OR OLD-FASHIONED to like the way someone appears or behaves: *I guess Pauline's father didn't like the cut of my jib.*

SPOKEN PHRASES

7 would you like...? also **how would you/he etc. like...?** used to ask someone if they want something: *Would you like a glass of wine?* | **would you like to do sth?** *How would you like to go shopping with me?* | **would you like sb to do sth?** *Would you like me to babysit for you?*

8 would like used to express politely what you want to happen or do: *I'd like a vanilla milkshake.* | **would like to do sth** *I'd like to know how much it'll cost.* | **would like sb to do sth** *Grandma would like you to be there if you can.* | **would like (to have) sth done** *I'd like to have the report finished by tomorrow.* | **would like it if** *I'd like it if you could stay a little longer.*

9 if you'd like also **if you like** **a)** used to suggest or offer something politely: *If you'd like, I'll do the dishes.* **b)** used to agree to something politely, even if it is not what you want yourself: *"Can we have spaghetti tonight?" "If you'd like."*

10 whatever/anything etc. you like whatever you want: *You can wear whatever you like.*

11 how would you like ...? used to try to make someone feel sympathy for someone who is having trouble, by asking them to imagine having the same trouble themselves: ***How would you like it if** someone made fun of you?* | **how would you like sb doing sth?** *How would you like your boss calling you an idiot?*

12 how do you like that? said when you are annoyed by something that just happened, or that you just heard about: *Well, how do you like that? He didn't even say thank you.*

13 (whether you) like it or not used to emphasize that something bad is true or will happen and cannot be changed: *You're going to the dentist, whether you like it or not.*

14 I'd like to see sb do sth used to say that you do not believe someone can do something: *I'd like to see you run that fast.*

15 I'd like to think/believe (that) **a)** used to say that you wish or hope something is true, when you are not sure that it is: *I'd like to believe that he's telling the truth.* **b)** used to say that you think you do something well, especially when you want to be MODEST: *I'd like to think I know a little about airplanes.*

16 like it or lump it used to say that someone must accept a situation or decision they do not like because it cannot be changed

[**Origin:** Old English *lician*]

like³ S1 *adv.* SPOKEN, NONSTANDARD **1 I'm/he's/she's like ... a)** used in order to tell someone the exact words someone used: *I asked him if he thought Liz was cute, and he's like, yeah, definitely.* **b)** used to describe an event, feeling, or person, when it is difficult to describe or when you use a noise instead of a word: *We were like, oh no* (=we realized something was wrong)*!* **2** said when you do not know what to say, or you cannot be exact: *Do you think you could, like, not tell anyone what happened?* **3** said in order to give an example: *That is a scary intersection. Like yesterday I saw two cars go straight through a red light.*

like⁴ *n.* **1 likes and dislikes** all the things you like and do not like: *Don't let your personal likes and dislikes get in the way of the job.* **2 and the like** and similar things: *gold chains, bracelets, rings and the like.* **3 the like(s) of sb/sth** also **sb's/sth's like** something similar to someone or to a particular person or thing, or of equal importance or value: *Our country enjoys wealth **the likes of which** no civilization has ever seen.* | *Arlins is a lying politician, and we have seen his like before.* **4 the likes of him/her/us etc.** SPOKEN **a)** used to talk about someone you do not like: *I'd never vote for the likes of him!* **b)** used to talk about people of a particular type or social class: *Those expensive restaurants with fancy food aren't for the likes of us.*

like⁵ S1 W3 *conjunction* SPOKEN INFORMAL **1** as if: *He acted like he owned the place.* **2 like I say/said** used when you are repeating something that you have already said: *Like I said, I really appreciate your help.* **3 it's not like** used to say that something definitely is not true: *It's not like he's an expert.* **4** in the same way as: *Don't let him treat you like Jim treated you.*

like⁶ *adj.* [only before noun] FORMAL similar in some way: *I glad we're **of like minds about** the project.*

-like /laɪk/ *suffix* [in adjectives] like something, typical of something, or appropriate for something: *a jelly-like substance* | *childlike simplicity*

like·a·ble /ˈlaɪkəbəl/ *adj.* another spelling of LIKABLE

like·li·hood /ˈlaɪkliˌhʊd/ *n.* [U] **1** the degree to which something can reasonably be expected to happen SYN **probability**: *We need to reduce the likelihood of another attack.* | *They must face **the likelihood that** the newspaper might go bankrupt.* **2 in all likelihood** almost certainly: *In all likelihood, he will win the race.*

like·ly¹ /ˈlaɪkli/ W1 *adj. comparative* **likelier**, *superlative* **likeliest** **1** something that is likely will probably happen or is probably true: *Rain is likely in the afternoon.* | **likely to do/be sth** *She's not likely to change her mind.* | ***It is likely that** the girl knew her killer.* | *It is **more than likely*** (=almost certain) *the votes will have to be counted again.* | **more/most/very likely** *He'll most likely drop out of school.* **2** [only before noun] appropriate, or almost certain to produce good results: *a list of likely candidates* | *I found the earrings in the **least likely** place* (=place where you would not expect to find them).

likely² S3 *adv.* probably: **most/very likely** *I'd most likely have done the same thing in your situation.*

ˌlike-ˈminded *adj.* having similar interests and opinions —**like-mindedness** *n.* [U]

lik·en /ˈlaɪkən/ *v.*

liken sb/sth to sb/sth *phr. v.* FORMAL to describe something or someone as being similar to another person or thing: *Critics have likened the new theater to a barn.*

like·ness /ˈlaɪknɪs/ *n.* **1** [C] the image of someone in a painting or photograph: **+of** *The red pins **bore the likeness of*** (=show the likeness of) *Lenin.* **2** [C,U] the quality of being similar in appearance to someone or something else SYN **resemblance**: **+to** *Phillip's likeness to his father*

ˌlike ˈradicals *n.* [plural] MATH RADICALS that have the same INDEX and the same RADICAND

ˌlike ˈterms *n.* [plural] MATH mathematical expressions which have the same VARIABLES raised to the same INDEX. For example, $3x^2$ and $5x^2$ are like terms.

like·wise /ˈlaɪk-waɪz/ AC *adv.* **1** FORMAL in the same way SYN **similarly**: *I put on my life jacket and told the children to **do likewise**.* | [sentence adverb] *The clams were delicious. Likewise, the eggplant was excellent.* **2** SPOKEN used to return someone's greeting or polite remark: *"It's great to see you." "Likewise."*

L

lik·ing /ˈlaɪkɪŋ/ *n.* **1 liking for sb/sth** FORMAL the feeling when you like someone or something: *She'd tried to hide her liking for him.* | *I'd **developed a liking for** afternoon talk shows.* **2 take a liking to sb/sth** to begin to like someone or something: *He immediately took a liking to the town.* **3 to your liking** FORMAL being just what you wanted: *I hope everything in the suite was to your liking, sir.*

li·lac /ˈlaɪlɑk, -læk, -lək/ *n.* **1** [C] BIOLOGY a small tree with pale purple or white flowers **2** [U] a pale purple color [**Origin:** 1600–1700 Early French, from Arabic *lilak*, from Persian *nilak* **bluish**] —**lilac** *adj.*: *a lilac dress*

lil·li·pu·tian /ˌlɪləˈpyuʃən◂/ *adj.* extremely small compared to normal things [**Origin:** 1700–1800 *Lilliput*, an imaginary country full of very small people in the book Gulliver's Travels (1726) by Jonathan Swift]

Li·long·we /lɪˈlɔŋweɪ/ the capital and largest city of Malawi

lilt /lɪlt/ *n.* [singular] a pleasant pattern of rising and falling sound in someone's voice or in music: *her soothing Southern lilt* —**lilting** *adj.*: *a lilting melody*

lil·y /ˈlɪli/ *n. plural* **lilies** [C] one of several types of plant with large bell-shaped flowers of various colors, especially white → see also **gild the lily** at GILD (3), WATER LILY

ˌlily-ˈlivered *adj.* OLD-FASHIONED lacking courage

ˌlily of the ˈvalley *n.* [C] a plant with several small white bell-shaped flowers

ˈlily pad *n.* [C] the round leaf of the WATER LILY, that you can see on the surface of the water

ˌlily-ˈwhite *adj.* **1** LITERARY pure white: *lily-white skin* **2** INFORMAL morally perfect: *You're not so lily-white yourself!*

Li·ma /ˈlimə/ the capital and largest city of Peru

li·ma bean /ˈlaɪmə ˌbin/ *n.* [C] a flat bean that grows in tropical America, or the plant that produces it

limb /lɪm/ *n.* [C] **1** BIOLOGY a large branch of a tree: *the limbs of a dead tree* **2 go/be out on a limb** to do something risky or uncertain: *He went out on a limb to help us.* **3** BIOLOGY an arm or leg: *artificial limbs* [**Origin:** Old English *lim*] → see also **risk life and limb** at RISK² (1), **tear sb limb from limb** at TEAR² (6)

L

-limbed /lɪmd/ *suffix* [in adjectives] **strong-limbed/long-limbed etc.** having strong, long etc. arms and legs

lim·ber¹ /ˈlɪmbɚ/ *v.*

limber up *phr. v.* to do gentle exercises in order to make your muscles stretch and move easily, especially when preparing to race, exercise etc. SYN **warm up**

limber² *adj.* able to move and bend easily: *I'm not even limber enough to touch my toes.*

lim·bo /ˈlɪmboʊ/ *n.* **1 be in limbo** to be in an uncertain situation in which it is difficult to know what to do: *I'm in limbo, until I know I've gotten the job.* **2 the limbo** a Caribbean dance in which people bend backward and go under a stick that is moved lower as the dance continues

lime¹ /laɪm/ *n.* **1** [C] BIOLOGY a small juicy green fruit with a sour taste, or the tree this fruit grows on → see picture at FRUIT¹ **2** [U] a white substance used for making CEMENT, marking sports fields etc. **3** [C] BIOLOGY a LINDEN tree [**Origin:** (1) 1600–1700 French provençal *limo*, from Arabic *lim*; (2) Old English *lind*]

lime² *v.* [T] TECHNICAL to add lime to soil to control acid

lime·ade /ˌlaɪmˈeɪd, ˈlaɪmeɪd/ *n.* [U] a drink made from the juice of limes

ˌlime ˈgreen *n.* [U] a light yellowish green color —**lime-green** *adj.*

lime·light /ˈlaɪmlaɪt/ *n.* **the limelight** the attention someone gets from newspapers and television: *"I'm not used to being **in the limelight**"* (=having lots of attention), *Hargrove told reporters.* [**Origin:** 1800–1900 *lime* + *light*; because originally the light was produced by burning lime]

lim·er·ick /ˈlɪmərɪk/ *n.* [C] ENG. LANG. ARTS a humorous short poem, with two long lines, two short lines, and then one more long line

lime·stone /ˈlaɪmstoʊn/ *n.* [U] EARTH SCIENCE a type of rock that contains CALCIUM, often used to make buildings

li·mey /ˈlaɪmi/ *n.* [C] OLD-FASHIONED an insulting word for a British person [**Origin:** 1800–1900 *lime-juicer* **British sailor** (19–20 centuries); because lime juice was drunk to prevent the disease scurvy in the British navy]

lim·it¹ /ˈlɪmɪt/ S2 W2 *n.* [C]

1 GREATEST/LEAST ALLOWED the greatest or least amount, number, speed etc. that is allowed: *$50 is my limit.* | **+to/on** *There's a limit on the time you have to take the test.* | *My wife and I **set a limit on** how much we spend on clothes.* | **a speed/time/age etc. limit** *The speed limit is 65 mph.* | **go over/exceed a limit** *His blood alcohol level exceeded the legal limit.* | **the lower/upper limit** *The upper limit on the budget is revised each year.*

2 GREATEST AMOUNT POSSIBLE also **limits** [plural] the greatest possible amount or degree of something that can exist or be obtained: **+of** *the limits of human knowledge* | *Our finances are **stretched to the limit*** (=we do not have any extra money). | ***There's no limit** to what you can do if you try.*

3 PLACE also **limits** [plural] the furthest point or edge of a place, that must not be passed: *No one is allowed within a 2-mile limit of the missile site.* | *a house on the **city limits***

4 within limits within the time, level, amount etc. considered acceptable: *You can decorate the apartment yourself – within limits, of course.*

5 off limits a) beyond the area where someone is allowed to go: *The basement was always off limits to us kids.* **b)** if something is off limits, you are not allowed to know about it or talk about it: *His private life is off limits to the press.*

6 be over the limit to have drunk more alcohol than is legal or safe for driving

7 have your limits INFORMAL to have a set of ideas about what is reasonable to do and to behave according to them: *Even the biggest spenders have their limits.*

8 know your limits INFORMAL to know what you are good at doing and what you are not good at

[**Origin:** 1300–1400 French *limite*, from Latin *limes* **edge, boundary**]

limit² S2 W1 *v.* [T] **1** to stop an amount or number from increasing beyond a particular point: *The higher toll should limit the number of cars on the bridge.* | **limit sth to sth** *Seating is limited to 500.* **2** to prevent someone from doing what they want or from developing and improving in a satisfactory way: *Lack of education often limits people in ways they do not realize.* **3** to prevent something from being as good, effective etc. as it should be: *Alcohol limits the effectiveness of some drugs.* **4 limit yourself to sth** to allow yourself to have or do only a particular amount of something: *I limit myself to two cups of coffee a day.* **5 be limited to sth** to exist or happen only in a particular place, group, or area of activity: *The damage was limited to the roof.*

lim·i·ta·tion /ˌlɪməˈteɪʃən/ *n.* **1** [C usually plural] a weakness that someone or something has, which stops it from being as good as it could be: *Computers definitely **have their limitations**.* **2** [C] a rule or limit which stops something from increasing beyond a certain point: **+on/to** *a limitation on the number of hours children can work* **3** [U] the act or process of limiting something: *a nuclear limitation treaty* → see also STATUTE OF LIMITATIONS

lim·it·ed /ˈlɪmɪt̬ɪd/ *adj.* **1** not very great in amount, number, ability etc.: *A limited number of tickets are available.* | *My knowledge of the subject is very limited.* **2** a limited train or bus only makes a few stops **3** restricted by law in what you are allowed to do or what you are responsible for: *limited immunity from lawsuits* **4 Limited** WRITTEN ABBREVIATION **Ltd.** used after the name of British or Canadian companies that have limited LIABILITY → see also INCORPORATED

ˌlimited eˈdition *n.* [C] a small number of special copies of a book, picture etc. which are produced at one time only —**limited-edition** *adj.*

ˌlimited ˈgovernment *n.* [U] POLITICS a principle of the U.S. CONSTITUTION which states that the only powers that the government should have are those which it is given by the Constitution: *the core conservative ideals of limited government and a balanced budget*

ˌlimited liaˈbility *n.* [U] LAW the legal position of being responsible for paying only a limited amount of debt if something bad happens to yourself or your company

ˌlimited liaˈbility ˌpartnership WRITTEN ABBREVIATION **LLP** *n.* [C] ECONOMICS a PARTNERSHIP (=business owned by two or more partners who share the profits and losses) in which all of the partners are responsible for a limited amount of the partnership's debts, not all of the debts → see also GENERAL PARTNERSHIP

ˌlimited ˈmonarchy *n.* [C,U] POLITICS a system of government in which a king's or queen's powers are limited by a CONSTITUTION or other rules

ˌlimited ˈpartner *n.* [C] ECONOMICS in a LIMITED PARTNERSHIP, a partner who has limited involvement in managing the business and who is responsible for some of the partnership's debts, but only up to the amount they INVESTED when they first joined the partnership → see also GENERAL PARTNER

ˌlimited ˈpartnership WRITTEN ABBREVIATION **LP** *n.* [C] ECONOMICS a PARTNERSHIP (=business owned by two or more partners who share the profits and losses) in which only one of the partners has to be a GENERAL PARTNER (=one who is responsible for a partnership's debts, without any limit). The other partners are responsible for some of the partnership's debts, but only up to the amount they INVESTED when they first joined the partnership. → see also GENERAL PARTNERSHIP

ˌlimited point of ˈview *n.* [C] ENG. LANG. ARTS the style of telling a story in which the NARRATOR is not a character in the story but tells what only one character or a limited number of characters experience, think, and feel → see also OMNISCIENT POINT OF VIEW

lim·it·ing /ˈlɪmɪṭɪŋ/ *adj.* **1** preventing any improvement or increase in something: *Transportation has always been* ***a limiting factor*** *on trade in this area.* **2** INFORMAL preventing someone from developing and doing what they are interested in: *I found staying at home with the kids very limiting.*

lim·it·less /ˈlɪmɪtlɪs/ *adj.* without a limit or end: *limitless possibilities* —**limitlessly** *adv.* —**limitlessness** *n.* [U]

lim·o /ˈlɪmoʊ/ *n. plural* **limos** [C] INFORMAL a limousine

lim·ou·sine /ˈlɪməˌzin, ˌlɪməˈzin/ *n.* [C] **1** a very large, expensive, and comfortable car, driven by someone who is paid to drive ▸see THESAURUS box at **car** **2** a small bus that people take to and from airports in the U.S. [**Origin:** 1900–2000 French **covering for the driver of a horse-drawn vehicle (as worn in Limousin)**, from *Limousin* area of France]

limp¹ /lɪmp/ *adj.* something that is limp is soft or weak when it should be firm or strong: *a limp handshake* —**limply** *adv.* —**limpness** *n.* [U]

limp² *v.* [I] **1** to walk slowly and with difficulty because one leg is hurt or injured ▸see THESAURUS box at **walk¹** **2** if a vehicle, airplane etc. limps somewhere, it goes there slowly, because it has been damaged

limp along *phr. v.* if a company, vehicle, process etc. limps along, it does not work well at all: *The team is limping along in fifth place.*

limp³ *n.* [C] the way someone walks when they are limping: *She walks with a limp.*

lim·pet /ˈlɪmpɪt/ *n.* [C] a small sea animal with a shell shaped like a CONE, which usually attaches itself to a rock

lim·pid /ˈlɪmpɪd/ *adj.* LITERARY clear or transparent: *limpid blue eyes* —**limpidly** *adv.* —**limpidness** *n.* [U] —**limpidity** /lɪmˈpɪdəṭi/ *n.* [U]

lin·age /ˈlaɪnɪdʒ/ *n.* [U] another spelling of LINEAGE

linch·pin /ˈlɪntʃˌpɪn/ *n.* **the linchpin of sth** the person or thing in a group, system etc. that is most important, because everything depends on them: *My mother had always been the linchpin of our family.*

Lin·coln /ˈlɪŋkən/ the capital city of the U.S. state of Nebraska

Lincoln, Abraham (1809–1865) the 16th President of the U.S., famous especially for the Emancipation Proclamation in 1863 by which all SLAVES in the U.S. became free people, and for his speech known as the Gettysburg Address

Abraham Lincoln

Lincoln-Doug·las De·bates, the /ˌlɪŋkən ˈdʌgləs dɪˌbeɪts/ HISTORY a series of seven public discussions in 1858 between Senate CANDIDATES Abraham Lincoln and Stephen A. Douglas, mainly about SLAVERY

Lind·bergh /ˈlɪndbɚg/, **Charles** (1902–1974) a U.S. pilot who in 1927 became the first person to fly alone across the Atlantic Ocean without stopping

lin·den /ˈlɪndən/ *n.* [C,U] a tree which has leaves shaped like hearts and light yellow flowers, or the wood of this tree

Lind·say /ˈlɪnzi/, **Va·chel** /ˈveɪtʃəl, ˈvæ-/ (1879–1931) a U.S. poet

line¹ /laɪn/ S1 W1 *n.*

1 LONG THIN MARK [C] a long thin, usually continuous mark on a surface: *a straight line* | ***Draw a line*** *five inches long.* | *Sign your name on the* ***dotted line*** (=a broken straight line drawn or printed on paper).

THESAURUS

stripe a long narrow line of color: *a tie with thin blue and white stripes*
streak a colored line or thin mark, especially one that is not straight or has been made accidentally: *His hair was black with streaks of gray.*
band a narrow area of color that is different from the areas around it: *The fish has a black band on its fin.*

2 LIMIT/END [C] a long thin mark used to show a limit or end of something: *The ball had clearly gone over the line.* → see also FINISH LINE

3 ATTITUDE/BELIEF [C usually singular] an attitude or belief, especially one that is stated publicly SYN **stance** SYN **position**: +**on** *What's the candidate's line on abortion?* | *There is a fear of expressing views contrary to* ***the party line*** (=the official opinion of a political party or other group). | ***The official line*** *is that all the committee members agree.*

4 along the lines of sth also **along the same/similar etc. lines, along these/those lines** used to say that something is similar to or done in a similar way to what you are talking about: *They're planning a trip to the beach or* ***something along those lines*** (=something like that).

5 take a firm/hard/strict etc. line on sth to have a very strict attitude toward something: *The governor has taken a hard line on illegal immigration.*

6 DIFFERENCE [C usually singular] the difference between one type of thing and another type, or the point at which one type of thing becomes another type when it changes slightly: *Her comments really* ***crossed the line*** *of good taste.* | *families living below* ***the poverty line*** | **a thin/fine line between sth and sth** *There's a fine line between patriotism and nationalism.*

7 PEOPLE WAITING [C,U] a row of people or cars that are waiting one behind the other: +**of** *There was a line of people halfway down the block.* | **be/stand/wait in (a)**

line *I waited in line for over an hour to get my license.* | *He'd tried to* ***cut in line.***
8 a line of action/thought/reasoning etc. a way or method of doing something or thinking about something: *the lawyer's unusual line of questioning*
9 TELEPHONE [C] a telephone wire, or the wires that connect a system of telephones: *We're thinking about getting a second line installed.* | *The* ***lines were down*** (=they were not working) *for days after the storm.* | *There's a lot of static* ***on the line.*** ►see THESAURUS box at **phone**[1]
10 along religious/party/ethnic etc. lines a) used to say that people make a decision according to the beliefs of the religion, political party, ETHNIC group etc. that they belong to: *The vote went almost strictly along party lines.* **b)** organized according to a particular method or idea: *The party was re-formed along socialist lines.*
11 WORDS [C] a line of words on a page from a poem, story, song etc.: *Read the first two lines of the poem.*
12 PEOPLE/THINGS [C] a row of people or things next to each other: **+of** *a line of bushes* | *The toys were arranged* ***in a line*** *on the shelf.*
13 REMARK [C] INFORMAL something that someone says, especially something you think is insincere or dishonest: *She* ***gave me a line*** *about her mother being sick.*
14 ON SB'S FACE [C] a line on the skin of someone's face or skin SYN **wrinkle**: *I'm getting little lines around my eyes.*
15 SHAPE [C usually plural] the outer shape of something long or tall: *the car's smooth elegant lines*
16 LAND [C] a border or imaginary line, that shows the limits of an area of land: *lines of longitude* | **a state/county line** *a small town just across the state line*
17 ROPE/STRING [C] a piece of string or rope that you hang wet clothes on outside in order to dry them SYN **clothesline**: *Towels hung on* ***the line.***
18 FISHING [C] a strong thin string with a hook on the end, used for catching fish
19 ACTOR'S SPEECH [C usually plural] the words of a play or performance that an actor learns: *After 30 years on the stage, I still forget my lines.*
20 RAILROAD [C] a track that a train travels along: *A train had broken down further along the line.* | **the Richmond/Freemont etc. line** (=the line that goes to Richmond, Freemont etc.)
21 DIRECTION [C usually singular] the direction or the imaginary line along which something travels between two points in space: *Light travels* ***in a straight line.*** | **a line of fire/attack/movement etc.** (=the direction in which someone shoots, attacks, moves etc.)
22 sb's line of vision in the area that someone can see at a particular time: *He stood still, trying to stay out of Sabine's line of vision.*
23 JOB [C usually singular] the kind of work someone does: *What* ***line of work*** *are you in?*
24 in the line of duty if something happens in the line of duty, it happens while you are doing your job: *Officer Choi was killed in the line of duty.*
25 in line a) happening according to particular rules, laws, plans etc.: **+with** *In line with expectations, the economy has grown by 1.5% this year.* | **bring/keep sth in line (with sth)** *Construction companies are trying to keep their costs in line.* **b)** behaving in the right way, or according to the way other people behave: *She was tough enough to* ***keep*** *the teenagers* ***in line.***
26 into line into a situation where someone or something starts to behave similarly to other people or things or do what they are supposed or expected to do: **fall/come into line** *Eventually all the Republicans fell into line and voted yes.* | **bring/pull drag sb/sth into line (with sb/sth)** *State laws will have to be brought into line with the Supreme Court's ruling.*
27 out of line a) if someone's behavior is out of line, it is not appropriate in a particular situation: *I thought what Kenny said* ***was way out of line.*** **b)** not obeying someone, or doing something that you should not do: **get/step out of line** *Anybody who steps out of line will be in deep trouble.* **c)** not fair or correct in size or amount when compared with other similar things: **+with** *The CEO's pay is way out of line with profits.* **d)** not forming the desired straight line with each other, or with other people or things
28 WAR [C usually plural] a row of military defenses in front of the area that an army controls during a war: *The base was stationed inside* ***enemy lines.*** | *They were sent to the* ***front lines*** *to fight.*
29 be in line for sth to be very likely to get or be given something: *Claire's in line for a promotion.* | **be first/second/next etc. in line for sth** (=to be the first, second, next etc. person to be likely to get something)
30 on the line if something important such as your job or your life is on the line, there is a risk that you might lose it or something bad could happen to it: *With the game on the line, Kansas City scored two touchdowns in five minutes.* | *I've already* ***put myself on the line*** *for you once.*
31 down/along the line SPOKEN later, after an activity or situation has been continuing for a period of time: ***Somewhere along the line,*** *we just stopped talking to each other.*
32 PRODUCT [C] a type of goods for sale in a store: *a new line of clothes for winter* | *The company has* ***discontinued its line of*** (=stopped selling) *sports equipment.*
33 COMPANY [C] a company that provides a system for moving goods by sea, air, road etc.: *a shipping line*
34 be in the line of fire also **be on the firing line a)** to be one of the people who could be criticized or blamed for something: *She's already on the firing line for her earlier comments.* **b)** to be in a place where a bullet etc. might hit you
35 SPORTS [C] a row of players in a game such as football or RUGBY that is formed when they move into position before play starts again
36 the first/last/next etc. in a line of sth used to talk about a series of things: *the latest in a long line of political scandals*
37 get a line on sb/sth INFORMAL to get information about someone or something: *Have we got any kind of line on that guy Marston?*
38 IN A COMPANY/ORGANIZATION the line [singular] the series of levels of authority within an organization: *The information was slowly passed down the line.*
39 DRUG [C] INFORMAL an amount of an illegal drug in powder form, arranged in a line before it is taken: **+of** *a line of coke*
40 FAMILY [singular] the people that came or existed before you in your family: *She* ***comes from a long line of*** *actors.*
[**Origin:** 1200–1300 Partly from Old French *ligne*, from Latin *linum* **flax**; partly from Old English *line*] → see also **draw the line (at sth)** at DRAW[1] (6), **hook, line, and sinker** at HOOK[1] (12), **lay sth on the line** at LAY[1] (9), ONLINE, **picket line** at PICKET[1] (1), **read between the lines** at READ[1] (12)

line[2] S2 W2 *v.* **1** [T] to form a layer that covers the inside or inner surface of something, or to make something do this: *Leaves line the nest.* | *Use wax paper to line the baking pan.* | **line sth with sth** *The jacket is lined with fur.* **2** [T] to form rows along something, especially along the edge of something: *Crowds lined the route to watch the parade.* | **be lined with sth** *The street is lined with shops and boutiques.* **3 line your own pockets** to make yourself richer by doing something dishonest **4** [I,T] to hit a ball straight with a lot of force in baseball

line up *phr. v.* **1 line sb/sth ↔ up** to form a row or arrange people or things in a row: *Hundreds of customers lined up in front of the store.* | *The teacher lined the students up to go to the playground.* **2 line sb/sth ↔ up** to make arrangements so that something will happen or that someone will be available for an event: *I've already lined up a job for January.* **3 line sth ↔ up** to put things in the correct position in relation to each other: *Make sure you line up the edges.* **4 be lining up to do sth** if people are lining up to do something, many people are very eager to do it → see also LINE-UP

line up against sb/sth *phr. v.* if people line up against someone or something, they all oppose that person or thing: *Democrats quickly lined up against the tax cuts.*

line up behind sb *phr. v.* if people line up behind someone, many people support that person

lin·e·age¹ /ˈlɪniɪdʒ/ *n.* [C,U] FORMAL the way in which members of a family are DESCENDed from other members: *He can trace his lineage back to the 14th century.*

line·age² also **linage** /ˈlaɪnɪdʒ/ *n.* [U] the number of printed lines in a newspaper, magazine etc. or a particular part of a newspaper etc., used as a measurement of space: *the journal's advertising lineage*

lin·e·al /ˈlɪniəl/ *adj.* **1** FORMAL related directly to someone who lived a long time before you: *lineal descendants* **2** another form of LINEAR —**lineally** *adv.*

lin·e·a·ment /ˈlɪniəmənt/ *n.* [C usually plural] FORMAL **1** the basic shape of the physical features of a person or GEOGRAPHICAL area **2** a typical quality or feature that makes someone or something different from others of the same kind

lin·e·ar /ˈlɪniɚ/ *adj.* **1** consisting of lines, or in the form of a straight line: *a linear diagram* **2** [only before noun] concerning length: *linear measurements* **3** if something changes in a linear way, it changes in a steady, regular way that can be shown as a straight line on a GRAPH → see also EXPONENTIAL **4** involving a series of directly connected events, ideas etc. → see also LATERAL: *linear thinking* —**linearly** *adv.* —**linearity** /ˌlɪniˈærət̬i/ *n.* [U]

ˌlinear acˈcelerator *n.* [C] TECHNICAL a piece of equipment that makes PARTICLES (=small pieces of atoms) travel in a straight line at increasing speed

ˌlinear eˈquation *n.* [C] MATH an EQUATION that appears as a straight line when it is represented on a GRAPH

ˌlinear ˈfunction *n.* [C] MATH a mathematical FUNCTION in which the VARIABLES are multiplied only by CONSTANTS and not by themselves, and are combined only by addition and SUBTRACTION. A linear function can be represented by a linear equation.

ˌlinear ˈprogramming *n.* [U] MATH a mathematical method used to find the highest and lowest possible values of a LINEAR FUNCTION with VARIABLES that are somehow limited

line·back·er /ˈlaɪnˌbækɚ/ *n.* [C] a player in football who tries to TACKLE the member of the other team who has the ball

lined /laɪnd/ *adj.* **1** a lined coat, skirt etc. has a piece of thin material covering the inside: *cashmere-lined gloves* **2** lined paper has straight lines printed or drawn across it **3** lined skin has WRINKLES on it

ˈline dance *n.* [C] a dance that is done, especially to COUNTRY MUSIC, by a group of people standing together in a line —**line dance** *v.* [I] —**line dancing** *n.* [U]

ˈline ˌdrawing *n.* [C] a DRAWING consisting only of lines

ˈline drive *n.* [C] a BASEBALL hit with great force in a straight line fairly near the ground

ˈline-item ˌveto *n.* [C] POLITICS the power of a president, GOVERNOR etc. to refuse to accept some parts of a bill that a LEGISLATURE has passed without refusing to accept the whole bill

line·man /ˈlaɪnmən/ *n. plural* **linemen** /-mən/ [C] **1** a player who plays in the front line of a football team **2** someone whose job is to take care of railroad lines or telephone wires

lin·en /ˈlɪnən/ *n.* [U] **1** sheets, TABLECLOTHS etc.: *bed linen* | *table linen* **2** cloth made from the FLAX plant, used to make high quality clothes, home decorations etc.: *a linen jacket* **3** OLD USE underwear

ˈlinen ˌcloset *n.* [C] a special CLOSET in which sheets, TOWELS etc. are kept

ˌline of best ˈfit *n.* [singular] MATH the straight line that passes as closely as possible to the most points that are spread out on a SCATTER DIAGRAM

ˌline of ˈscrimmage *n.* [C] a line in American football where the ball is placed at the beginning of a particular PLAY

lin·er /ˈlaɪnɚ/ *n.* **1** [C] a piece of material used inside something in order to protect it: *a trash can liner* **2** [C] a large passenger ship, especially one of several owned by a company: *an ocean liner* → see also AIRLINER, CRUISE LINER ►see THESAURUS box at **ship¹** **3** [C,U] → see EYELINER

ˈliner ˌnotes *n.* [plural] printed information about the music or musicians that comes with a CD or record

lines·man /ˈlaɪnzmən/ *n. plural* **linesmen** /-mən/ [C] an official in a sport who decides when a ball has gone out of the playing area

ˈline ˌsymmetry *n.* [U] MATH REFLECTIONAL SYMMETRY

ˈline-up *n.* [C usually singular] **1** the players in a sports team who play in a particular game: *Cordell may not be in the line-up for tonight's game.* | **the starting line-up** (=the players who begin the game) **2** all the competitors who are going to take part in a race **3** a group of people, especially performers, who have agreed to be involved in an event: *The line-up of stars includes Tom Cruise.* **4** a set of events or programs arranged to follow each other: *CBS has a great Wednesday night line-up.* **5** a row of people examined by a WITNESS to a crime in order to try to recognize a criminal **6** all the products that a company produces

-ling /lɪŋ/ *suffix* [in nouns] a smaller, younger, or less important type of something: *a duckling* (=young duck)

lin·ger /ˈlɪŋgɚ/ *v.* [I] **1** also **linger on** to continue to exist for a long time: *The taste of the sauce lingers in your mouth.* | *Summer weather has lingered on longer than usual.* **2** also **linger on** to stay somewhere a little longer, especially because you do not want to leave: *The crowd lingered on, hoping for more entertainment.* | +**over** *We lingered over drinks in a small cafe.* **3** [always + adv./prep.] to continue looking at or dealing with something for longer than is usual: +**on/over etc.** *The camera lingered over the man's old wrinkled face.* **4** also **linger on** to stay alive for a long time although you are extremely weak: *Uncle Gene lingered on a year longer than doctors expected.* [**Origin:** 1200–1300 *leng* **to lengthen, delay** (11–16 centuries), from Old English *lengan*] —**lingerer** *n.* [C]

lin·ge·rie /ˌlɑnʒəˈreɪ, ˌlɑndʒə-/ *n.* [U] women's underwear [**Origin:** 1800–1900 French *linge* **linen**]

lin·ger·ing /ˈlɪŋgərɪŋ/ *adj.* slow to finish or disappear: *lingering effects of radiation treatment* | *lingering doubts* | **a lingering death** (=a slow and often painful death) —**lingeringly** *adv.*

lin·go /ˈlɪŋgoʊ/ *n.* [C usually singular] INFORMAL **1** words used only by a group of people who do a particular job or activity SYN **jargon** **2** SPOKEN OLD-FASHIONED INFORMAL a language, especially a foreign one

lin·gua fran·ca /ˌlɪŋgwə ˈfræŋkə/ *n.* [C] a language used between people whose main languages are different: *Swahili is the lingua franca of East Africa.*

lin·gual /ˈlɪŋgwəl/ *adj.* TECHNICAL related to the tongue or sounds that are made with the tongue → see also BILINGUAL

lin·gui·ni /lɪŋˈgwini/ *n.* [U] long thin flat pieces of PASTA

lin·guist /ˈlɪŋgwɪst/ *n.* [C] **1** someone who studies and is good at foreign languages **2** someone who studies or teaches linguistics

lin·guis·tic /lɪŋˈgwɪstɪk/ *adj.* related to language, words, or linguistics: *linguistic skills* —**linguistically** /-kli/ *adv.*

lin·guis·tics /lɪŋˈgwɪstɪks/ *n.* [U] ENG. LANG. ARTS the study of language in general and of particular languages, their structure, grammar, and history → see also PHILOLOGY

lin·i·ment /ˈlɪnəmənt/ *n.* [U] a liquid containing oil, that you rub on your skin to cure soreness and stiffness

lin·ing /ˈlaɪnɪŋ/ *n.* [C,U] a piece of material covering the inside of a box, piece of clothing etc.: *The coat has a silk lining.*

link¹ /lɪŋk/ Ac W2 *v.* [T] **1 be linked** if two things are linked, they are related, often because one strongly affects or causes the other: *I think that the two problems are linked.* | +**to/with** *Some*

L

birth defects are linked to smoking during pregnancy. | **be closely/directly/strongly linked** *Skin cancer is directly linked to sun exposure and damage.*
2 MAKE CONNECTION to make or prove a connection between people, groups, situations etc.: *A love of nature links the two poets.* | **link sb to/with sth** *The new evidence clearly links Runnels to the crime.*
3 MAKE STH DEPEND ON STH to make one action or situation dependent on another action or situation: **link sth to sth** *They're going to link pay increases with performance.*
4 COMPUTERS also **link up** to connect computers, broadcast systems etc., so that electronic messages can be sent between them: **link sth to/with sth** *Each terminal is linked to the central computer.*
5 JOIN also **link up** to physically join or form a connection between two or more things, people, or places: *The Brooklyn Bridge links Brooklyn and Manhattan.* | **link sb/sth with sth** *The pipe must be linked to the cold water supply.* | **link sb/sth together** *The climbers were linked together by ropes.*
6 link arms to bend your arm and put it through someone else's bent arm
7 PUT TOGETHER to connect two or more things by putting them through or around each other, such as pieces of a chain

link up *phr. v.* **1 link sth ↔ up** if things link up or someone or something links them up, they join or connect together: **link (sth) up with/to sth** *This line links up with the main East Coast line.* | *They're planning to link this road up to the highway.* **2 link sth ↔ up** COMPUTERS to connect computers, broadcast systems etc., so that electronic messages can be sent between them: **link sth up with/to sth** *All these PCs are linked up to the network.* **3** to join together in order to do something: *The two companies linked up to form the largest computer software company in the world.* | **+with** *The UPS strategy has been to buy or link up with foreign companies.* **4** if people link up, they can communicate with each other using computers and electronic messages → see also LINKUP

link² Ac W3 *n.* [C]
1 THINGS OR IDEAS a relationship between two things or ideas, in which one is caused or affected by the other: **+between** *the link between drug use and crime*
2 PEOPLE, COUNTRIES ETC. a relationship or connection between two or more people, countries, organizations etc.: **+with/between** *Schools are looking to find new ways to forge links with families.*
3 THING THAT CONNECTS a person or thing that makes possible a relationship or connection with someone or something else: **+with** *The telephone was my only link with home.*
4 a satellite/telephone/rail etc. link something that makes communication or travel between two places possible
5 COMPUTER DOCUMENT a special picture or word in a computer document that you CLICK on to move quickly to another part of the document or another place on the Internet, or the connection that makes this possible: *The Web page includes a list of related links.*
6 COMPUTERS a connection between different computers which allows them to operate as a network: *We can set up a computer link between the two colleges.*
7 CHAIN one of the rings in a chain
8 SAUSAGE also **link sausage** a small SAUSAGE in the shape of a tube → see also PATTY
9 a link in the chain one of a series of things, facts, people involved in a process: *This was the first link in a chain of events that led eventually to his death.*
10 links [plural] a GOLF COURSE SYN **golf links**
[**Origin:** (1–9) 1300–1400 Old Norse *hlekkr*] → see also CUFF LINK, MISSING LINK, **a/the weak link** at WEAK¹ (16)

link·age /ˈlɪŋkɪdʒ/ Ac *n.* **1** [singular, U] a relationship or connection between two people or things SYN **link** **2** [C,U] a condition in a political or business agreement, by which one country or company agrees to do something, only if the other promises to do something in return **3** [C] a system of links or connections **4** [C,U] a connection between different computers that allows people to use information that is stored on other computers

ˈlinking ˌverb *n.* [C] ENG. LANG. ARTS a verb that connects the subject of a sentence to a word or phrase that describes it. In the sentence, "She seems friendly," "seems" is the linking verb.

link·up /ˈlɪŋk-ʌp/ *n.* [C] a connection between computers, broadcasting systems etc. that sends electronic messages between them

Lin·nae·us /lɪˈniəs, -ˈneɪ-/, **Ca·rol·us** /ˈkærələs/ (1707–1778) a Swedish BOTANIST who invented the Linnean System, by which plants and animals are put into groups according to their GENUS (=general type) and SPECIES (=particular type)

li·no·cut /ˈlaɪnoʊˌkʌt/ *n.* **1** [U] ENG. LANG. ARTS the art of cutting a pattern on a block of linoleum **2** [C] ENG. LANG. ARTS a picture printed from such a block

li·no·le·um /lɪˈnoʊliəm/ *n.* [U] smooth shiny material in flat sheets used to cover a floor

Li·no·type /ˈlaɪnəˌtaɪp/ *n.* [U] TRADEMARK a system for arranging TYPE in the form of solid metal lines

lin·seed /ˈlɪnsid/ *n.* [U] the seed of the FLAX plant

ˌlinseed ˈoil *n.* [U] the oil from linseed used in some paints, inks etc.

lint /lɪnt/ *n.* [U] soft light pieces of thread or wool that come off cotton, wool, or other material

lin·tel /ˈlɪntl/ *n.* [C] a piece of stone or wood across the top of a window or door, forming part of the frame

li·on /ˈlaɪən/ *n.* [C] **1** BIOLOGY a large animal of the cat family that lives in Africa and parts of southern Asia. Lions have gold-colored fur and the male has a MANE (=hair around his neck): **a pride of lions** (=a group of lions) → see also LIONESS **2 the lion's share (of sth)** the largest part of something: *One family owns the lion's share of the county's farmland.* **3** ESPECIALLY LITERARY someone who is very important, powerful, or famous **4 in the lion's den** among people who are your enemies **5 be thrown/tossed to the lions** to be put in a dangerous or difficult situation [**Origin:** 1200–1300 Old French, Latin *leo*, from Greek *leon*]

li·on·ess /ˈlaɪənɪs/ *n.* [C] a female lion

li·on·heart·ed /ˈlaɪənˌhɑrt̬ɪd/ *adj.* LITERARY very brave

li·on·ize /ˈlaɪəˌnaɪz/ *v.* [T] to treat someone as being important or famous —**lionization** /ˌlaɪənəˈzeɪʃən/ *n.* [U]

ˈLions Club *n.* an international organization whose members work together to help their local areas by doing CHARITY work

lip /lɪp/ S2 W2 *n.* **1** [C] BIOLOGY one of the two edges of your mouth where your skin is redder or darker: *dry lips* | **sb's upper/lower/top/bottom lip** *Her lower lip was red and swollen.* | *Marty* ***kissed*** *me right* ***on the lips!*** | *Stephen* ***pursed*** *his* ***lips*** (=brought them together tightly) *with distaste.* **2** [U] INFORMAL talk that is not polite or respectful: *Don't* ***give*** *me any of your* ***lip!*** **3** [C usually singular] the top edge of something that is used to hold or pour liquid: **+of** *the lip of the glass* **4** [C] the edge of a hollow or deep place in the land: **+of** *the lip of the canyon* **5 my lips are sealed** SPOKEN used to say that you are not going to tell anyone about a secret **6 on everyone's lips** being talked about by everyone: *News of the divorce seems to be on everyone's lips.* [**Origin:** Old English *lippa*] → see also **lick your lips/chops** at LICK¹ (4), **thin-lipped/full-lipped etc.** at -LIPPED, **never/not pass sb's lips** at PASS¹ (28), **pay lip service to sth** at PAY¹ (15), **read sb's lips** at READ¹ (14), **keep a stiff upper lip** at STIFF¹ (9)

ˈlip balm *n.* [C,U] a substance used to protect dry lips

ˈlip gloss *n.* [C,U] a substance used to make lips look shiny

lip·id /ˈlɪpɪd/ *n.* [C] BIOLOGY one of several types of FATTY substance in living things, such as fat, oil, or WAX

lip·id bi·lay·er /ˌlɪpɪd ˈbaɪˌleɪɚ/ *n.* [C] BIOLOGY a structure formed by lipids, consisting of two layers of MOLECULES, which is the main material in cell MEMBRANES

lip·o·suc·tion /ˈlɪpoʊˌsʌkʃən/ *n.* [U] a type of medical operation in which fat is removed from someone's body using SUCTION

-lipped /lɪpt/ [in adjectives] **thin-lipped/full-lipped etc.** with lips that are thin, round etc.

lip-read /ˈlɪp rid/ *v.* **lip-read** /-rɛd/ [I,T] to understand what someone is saying by watching the way their lips move, especially because you cannot hear —**lip-reading** *n.* [U]

lip·stick /ˈlɪpˌstɪk/ *n.* [C,U] a piece of a substance shaped like a small stick, used for adding color to your lips → see picture at MAKEUP

lip synch /ˈlɪpˌsɪŋk/ *n.* [U] the action of moving your lips at the same time as a recording is being played, to give the appearance that you are singing —**lip-synch** *v.* [I]

liq·ue·fy /ˈlɪkwəˌfaɪ/ *v.* **liquefies, liquefied, liquefying** [I,T] FORMAL to become liquid, or make something become liquid —**liquefaction** /ˌlɪkwəˈfækʃən/ *n.* [U]

li·queur /lɪˈkɚ, lɪˈkʊɚ/ *n.* [C,U] a sweet and very strong alcoholic drink, drunk in small quantities after a meal → see also LIQUOR

liq·uid¹ /ˈlɪkwɪd/ *n.* **1** [C,U] PHYSICS a substance that is not a solid or a gas, and which flows, is wet, and has no particular shape but has a fixed VOLUME: *Add a little more liquid to the sauce.* **2** [C] TECHNICAL either of the CONSONANT sounds /l/ or /r/ → see also DISHWASHING LIQUID

liquid² *adj.* **1** [only before noun] in the form of a liquid instead of a gas or solid: *liquid soap* | *liquid nitrogen* | *The medicine is available* ***in liquid form****.* **2** easily exchanged or sold to pay debts: *Certificates of deposit are not as liquid as money in a savings account.* → see also LIQUID ASSETS **3 liquid refreshment** HUMOROUS something you drink, especially alcoholic drink **4 a liquid lunch** HUMOROUS a LUNCH in which you mainly have alcoholic drinks rather than eating food **5** clear and shiny, like water: *liquid green eyes* **6** LITERARY liquid sounds are very clear [**Origin:** 1300–1400 French *liquide*, from Latin *liquidus*, from *liquere* **to flow as a liquid**]

ˌliquid ˈassets *n.* [plural] TECHNICAL the money that a company or person has, and the property they can easily exchange for money

liq·ui·date /ˈlɪkwəˌdeɪt/ *v.* **1** [I,T] ECONOMICS to close a business or company in order to pay its debts by selling everything, especially at very low prices **2** [T] ECONOMICS to pay a debt: *The stock will be sold to liquidate the loan.* **3** [T] INFORMAL to kill someone

liq·ui·da·tion /ˌlɪkwəˈdeɪʃən/ *n.* [C,U] **1** ECONOMICS the act of closing down a company in order to pay its debts by selling its ASSETS: *The department chain has* ***gone into liquidation****.* **2** ECONOMICS the act of paying a debt

liq·ui·da·tor /ˈlɪkwəˌdeɪtɚ/ *n.* [C] ECONOMICS a person or company that sells everything that another company owns, so that its debts can be paid

li·quid·i·ty /lɪˈkwɪdət̬i/ *n.* [U] TECHNICAL **1** ECONOMICS a situation in which a business or a person has money or goods that can be sold to pay debts **2** the state of being LIQUID

liq·ui·dize /ˈlɪkwəˌdaɪz/ *v.* [T] to turn something into liquid by crushing or melting it

ˈliquid ˌmeasure *n.* [U] the system of measuring the VOLUME of liquids

ˌLiquid ˈPaper *n.* [U] TRADEMARK white liquid that is used to cover mistakes in writing, typing etc.

liq·uor /ˈlɪkɚ/ *n.* [U] a strong alcoholic drink, such as WHISKEY → see also LIQUEUR [**Origin:** 1200–1300 Old French *licour*, from Latin *liquor*, from *liquere* **to flow as a liquid**]

ˈliquor store *n.* [C] a store where alcohol is sold

li·ra /ˈlɪrə/ *n. plural* **lire** /ˈlɪreɪ/ or **liras** [C] the standard unit of money in various countries including Turkey, and in Italy before the EURO

Lis·bon /ˈlɪzbən/ the capital and largest city of Portugal

lisle /laɪl/ *n.* [U] cotton material, used in the past for GLOVES and STOCKINGS

lisp¹ /lɪsp/ *v.* [I,T] to pronounce "s" sounds as "th" when you are speaking

lisp² *n.* [C usually singular] if someone has a lisp, they lisp when they speak: *She speaks with a slight lisp.*

lis·som, lissome /ˈlɪsəm/ *adj.* LITERARY a body that is lissom is thin and graceful: *the girl's lissom figure*

list¹ /lɪst/ S1 W1 *n.* [C] **1** a set of words, numbers etc. written one below the other, so that you can remember them or keep them in order: *So who's* ***on the*** *guest* ***list****?* | **+of** *an alphabetical list of students* | **make/compile/write etc. a list** *Make a list of the things you have to do.* **2 at the top/bottom of the/sb's list** also **high/low on the/sb's list** considered the most or least important: *Taking care of his family is at the top of his list.* [**Origin:** 1500–1600 French *liste*, from Italian *lista*] → see also HIT LIST, MAILING LIST, SHORT LIST, WAITING LIST

list² S2 W2 *v.* **1** [T] to write a list, or mention things one after the other: *The guide lists more than 100 budget hotels.* **2** [T] to record or state something officially: **list sb/sth as sth** *The airline is listed as the nation's largest.* | **list sb in fair/stable/critical etc. condition** *Two of the injured passengers were listed in stable condition.* **3** [I] if a ship lists, it leans to one side

ˌlisted seˈcurity *n.* [C] TECHNICAL a BOND or STOCK in a large company that you can buy or sell on the STOCK EXCHANGE

lis·ten /ˈlɪsən/ S1 W1 *v.* [I] **1** to pay attention to what someone is saying or to a sound that you can hear: *I'm sorry. I wasn't listening.* | **+to** *I like listening to the radio.* | **listen carefully/intently** *Listen carefully to what I'm about to say.* | *You have to* ***listen hard*** (=try to hear something that is quiet) *to hear what he's saying.* → see Word Choice box at HEAR **2** SPOKEN used to tell someone to pay attention to what you are about to say: *Listen, I have an idea.* | *Now* ***listen here*** (=used to emphasize, especially when you are angry), *you two. You know the rules.* **3** to consider carefully what someone says to you: *I told him not to go, but he wouldn't listen.* | **+to** *I wish I'd listened to your advice.* | *She refuses to* ***listen to reason****.* [**Origin:** Old English *hlysnan*]

listen for sb/sth *phr. v.* to listen carefully so that you will notice a particular sound: *Tom was listening for the phone.*

listen in *phr. v.* to listen to someone's conversation without them knowing it: **+on** *The FBI had been listening in on their conversations for months.*

listen up *phr. v.* SPOKEN used to get people's attention so they can hear what you are going to say: *Listen up! Pat has an announcement.*

GRAMMAR

Remember you can only **listen to** (or sometimes **for**) something: *He's listening to music* (NOT *He's listening music*).

lis·ten·a·ble /ˈlɪsənəbəl/ *adj.* INFORMAL pleasant to hear

lis·ten·er /ˈlɪsənɚ/ *n.* [C] **1** someone who listens, especially to the radio → see also VIEWER: *a new program for younger listeners* **2 a good/sympathetic/ready listener** someone who listens patiently and sympathetically to other people

ˈlistening deˌvice *n.* [C] a piece of equipment that allows you to listen secretly to other people's conversations SYN **bug** → see also HEARING AID

Lis·ter /ˈlɪstɚ/, **Joseph** (1827–1912) a British doctor who was the first person to use ANTISEPTICS during operations

lis·te·ri·a /lɪˈstɪriə/ *n.* [U] MEDICINE a type of BACTERIA that makes you sick

list·ing /ˈlɪstɪŋ/ *n.* **1** [C] something that is on a printed, official, or public list, or the list itself: *a business listing in the phone book* **2 listings** [plural] lists of films, plays, and other events with the times and places

L

at which they will happen: *Check your local listings for times.*

list·less /ˈlɪstlɪs/ *adj.* feeling tired and not interested in things: *The heat was making me listless.* [**Origin:** 1400–1500 *list* **pleasure, desire** (13–19 centuries) (from Old English *lystan* **to please, wish**) + *-less*] —**listlessly** *adv.* —**listlessness** *n.* [U]

ˈlist price *n.* [C] a price that is suggested for a product by the people who make it

list·serv /ˈlɪstˌsɚv/ *n.* [C] COMPUTERS a computer program that allows a group of people to send and receive EMAIL from each other about a particular subject

Liszt /lɪst/, **Franz** /frɑnz/ (1811–1886) a Hungarian musician who wrote CLASSICAL music and was considered the greatest PIANIST of the 19th century

lit /lɪt/ the past tense and past participle of LIGHT

lit. an abbreviation of LITERATURE or LITERARY

lit·a·ny /ˈlɪtˀn-i/ *n. plural* **litanies** [C] **1** a long prayer in the Christian church in which the priest says a sentence and the people reply **2** something that takes a long time to say, that repeats phrases, or sounds like a list: *an endless litany of rules*

li·tchi /ˈlitʃi/ *n.* [C] another spelling of LYCHEE

lite /laɪt/ *adj.* used in the names of some food and drink products to mean that they have fewer CALORIES or less fat than normal food or drinks: *lite beer* | *lite sour cream*

li·ter /ˈliṭɚ/ *n.* [C] **1** the basic unit for measuring an amount of liquid, in the METRIC system, equal to 2.12 PINTS or 0.26 GALLONS **2 1.3/2.4 etc. liter engine** a measurement that shows the size and power of a vehicle's engine [**Origin:** 1700–1800 French *litre*, from Medieval Latin *litra*, a measure, from Greek, a weight]

lit·er·a·cy /ˈlɪṭərəsi/ *n.* [U] the state of being able to read and write: *The program aims to increase literacy in the community.* | *a rise in the* ***literacy rate*** → see also LITERATE

ˈliteracy ˌrate *n.* [C] the number of people in a country over the age of 15 who can read and write, considered in relation to all the people over the age of 15 living in the country: *Sweden has a very high literacy rate* (=a lot of people over the age of 15 can read and write).

L

lit·er·al /ˈlɪṭərəl/ *adj.* **1** the literal meaning of a word or expression is its basic or original meaning → see also FIGURATIVE: *A trade war is not a war in the literal sense.* **2 a literal translation** a translation from one language to another that gives a single word for each original word instead of giving the meaning of the whole sentence in a natural way **3** also **literal-minded** understanding ideas in a basic way that does not show much imagination [**Origin:** 1300–1400 French, Medieval Latin *literalis*, from Latin *littera*] —**literalness** *n.* [U]

ˌliteral eˈquation *n.* [C] MATH an EQUATION that uses letters instead of numbers and usually contains two or more VARIABLES

lit·er·al·ly /ˈlɪṭərəli/ S2 W3 *adv.* **1** according to the most basic or original meaning of a word or expression → see also FIGURATIVELY: *I know I said I felt like quitting, but I didn't* ***mean it literally*** (=mean exactly what you say). **2** used to emphasize that something is actually true: *Literally thousands of people had their money stolen.* **3 take sb/sth literally** to only understand the most basic meaning of words, phrases etc., often with the result that you do not understand what someone really means: *Kids tend to take fairy tales literally.* **4** SPOKEN used to emphasize something you say that is already expressed strongly: *Jan and I have literally nothing in common.*

ˌliteral ˈquestion *n.* [C] ENG. LANG. ARTS a question that asks for a fact, detail, event etc., especially a fact, detail etc. that is stated directly in a piece of writing → see also EVALUATIVE QUESTION, INFERENTIAL QUESTION

lit·er·ar·y /ˈlɪṭəˌrɛri/ W3 *adj.* ENG. LANG. ARTS **1** relating to LITERATURE: *a literary prize* | *literary criticism* **2** typical of the style of writing used in literature rather than in ordinary writing and talking: *a very literary style of writing* **3** liking literature very much, and studying or producing it: *a literary woman* —**literariness** *n.* [U]

ˈliterary ˌelement *n.* [C] ENG. LANG. ARTS one of the features of the story in a book, play etc., such as the characters, the PLOT (=what happens), the SETTING (=where the story happens) etc.

lit·er·ate /ˈlɪṭərɪt/ *adj.* **1** able to read and write → see also NUMERATE OPP **illiterate**: *a literate workforce* **2 culturally/musically/technologically etc. literate** having enough knowledge about a particular subject **3** well educated → see also COMPUTER LITERATE, LITERACY —**literately** *adv.* —**literateness** *n.* [U]

lit·er·a·ti /ˌlɪṭəˈrɑṭi/ *n.* **the literati** [plural] FORMAL a small group of people in a society who know a lot about literature

lit·er·a·ture /ˈlɪṭərətʃɚ, ˈlɪtrə-/ S3 W3 *n.* [U] **1** ENG. LANG. ARTS books, plays, poems etc. that people think have value, or the study of these works: *modern literature* | **American/Japanese/German etc. literature** *"The Sun Also Rises" is a classic of American literature.* ►see THESAURUS box at **book**[1] **2** books, articles etc. on a particular subject: *medical literature* **3** printed information produced by organizations that want to sell something or tell people about something: *sales literature* [**Origin:** 1300–1400 Old French, Latin *litteratura*, from *litteratus*]

lithe /laɪð/ *adj.* having a body that moves easily and gracefully: *the dancer's lithe body* —**lithely** *adv.*

lith·i·um /ˈlɪθiəm/ *n.* [U] SYMBOL **Li** **1** CHEMISTRY a soft silvery ELEMENT that is the lightest known metal **2** MEDICINE a substance used in making a medicine for people with the mental illness MANIC DEPRESSION

lith·o·graph[1] /ˈlɪθəˌgræf/ *n.* [C] a printed picture made by lithography

lithograph[2] *v.* [T] to print a picture by lithography

li·thog·ra·phy /lɪˈθɑgrəfi/ *n.* [U] a process for printing patterns, pictures etc. from something that has been cut into a piece of stone or metal —**lithographic** /ˌlɪθəˈgræfɪk◂/ *adj.*

lith·o·sphere /ˈlɪθəˌsfɪr/ *n.* [C] EARTH SCIENCE the solid surface of the Earth, including the CRUST (=the outer layer of rocks, soil etc.) and the upper MANTLE (=the layer directly below the Earth's crust)

Lith·u·a·ni·a /ˌlɪθəˈweɪniə/ a country in northeastern Europe on the Baltic Sea, which is south of Latvia and north of Poland —**Lithuanian** *n., adj.*

lit·i·gant /ˈlɪṭəgənt/ *n.* [C] LAW someone who is making a claim against someone or defending themselves against a claim in a court of law

lit·i·gate /ˈlɪṭəˌgeɪt/ *v.* [I,T] LAW to take a claim or complaint against someone to a court of law

lit·i·ga·tion /ˌlɪṭəˈgeɪʃən/ *n.* [U] LAW the process of taking claims to a court of law, in cases that do not involve crimes

li·ti·gious /lɪˈtɪdʒəs/ *adj.* FORMAL LAW very willing to take any disagreements to a court of law —**litigiousness** *n.* [U]

lit·mus /ˈlɪtˀməs/ *n.* [U] CHEMISTRY a chemical that turns red when touched by acid, and blue when touched by an ALKALI

ˈlitmus ˌpaper *n.* [U] CHEMISTRY paper containing litmus used to test whether a chemical is an acid or an ALKALI

ˈlitmus ˌtest *n.* **1** [singular] something that makes it clear what someone's attitude, intentions etc. are: +**for** *Personal loyalty seems to be the litmus test for the mayor's new appointees.* **2** [C] CHEMISTRY a test using litmus paper

li·to·tes /ˈlaɪṭəˌtiz, ˈlɪ-, laɪˈtoʊtiz/ *n.* [U] ENG. LANG. ARTS a way of expressing your meaning by using a word that has the opposite meaning with a negative word such as "not," for example by saying "not bad" when you mean "good"

li·tre /ˈliṭɚ/ *n.* [C] the British and Canadian spelling of LITER

lit·ter[1] /ˈlɪt̬ɚ/ *n.*
1 WASTE [U] waste paper, containers etc. that people have thrown away and left on the ground in a public place: *The streets are full of litter.* → see also TRASH[1] (1) ►see THESAURUS box at **garbage**
2 BABY ANIMALS [C] BIOLOGY a group of baby animals such as dogs or cats which one mother gives birth to at the same time: +**of** *a litter of puppies* ►see THESAURUS box at **group**[1]
3 FOREST [U] BIOLOGY dead leaves and other decaying plants on the ground in a forest
4 CAT'S TOILET [U] small grains of a dry substance that is put in a container that a cat uses as a toilet indoors SYN **cat litter**
5 a litter of sth a group of things arranged in a messy way: *a litter of notes, papers, and textbooks*
6 BED [C] a chair or bed for carrying important people on, used in past times
7 FOR ANIMAL'S BED [U] a substance such as STRAW that a farm animal sleeps on
[**Origin:** 1300–1400 Old French *litiere*, from *lit* **bed**]

litter[2] *v.* **1** also **litter up** [T] if things litter an area, there are a lot of them in that place, scattered in a messy way: *Dirty plates littered the kitchen.* | **be littered with sth** *The streets were littered with glass.* **2** [I,T] to leave pieces of waste paper etc. on the ground in a public place: *Please do not litter.* **3 be littered with sth** if something is littered with things, there are a lot of those things in it: *The guide book is littered with bits of wisdom and humor.* **4** [I] BIOLOGY if an animal such as a dog or cat litters, it gives birth to babies

ˈlitter bag *n.* [C] a small bag used to put waste in, especially kept in a car

lit·ter·bug /ˈlɪt̬ɚˌbʌg/ *n.* [C] INFORMAL someone who leaves waste on the ground in public places

lit·tle[1] /ˈlɪtl/ S1 W1 *adj.*
1 SIZE small in size: *a little farm on the hill* | *I always bring Maggie **a little something*** (=a small present) *when I come back from business trips.* | **little tiny/tiny little** *a little tiny bug* ►see THESAURUS box at **small**[1]
2 a little bit a) a small amount SYN **a little**: *Just give me a little bit – I'm not that hungry.* | +**of** *I'm going to give you a little bit of advice.* **b)** to a small degree, or by a small amount SYN **a little**: *Try a little bit harder.*
3 TIME/DISTANCE [only before noun] short in time or distance: *a little nap* | *We walked a little way along this path.* | *I waited **a little while*** (=a short period of time) *before I called back.*
4 YOUNG little children are young: *I loved playing with blocks when I was little.* | **a little boy/girl** (=a young boy or girl) | **sb's little boy/girl** (=someone's son or daughter who is still a child) | **sb's little brother/sister** (=a younger brother or sister who is still a child) ►see THESAURUS box at **young**[1]
5 USED TO EMPHASIZE used between an adjective and the noun it describes to emphasize that you like or dislike something small or unimportant [only before noun]: **a cute/pretty/nice little sth** *a pretty little house* | **a stupid/silly little sth** *another of Todd's stupid little jokes* | *a **poor little** bird*
6 UNIMPORTANT a) not important: *There isn't time to discuss every little detail.* **b)** used humorously when you really think that something is important: *There's just **that little matter of** the $5,000 you owe me.*
7 SLIGHT done in a way that is not very strong or noticeable SYN **slight**: *a little laugh*
8 a little bird told me SPOKEN, HUMOROUS used to say that someone who you are not going to name has told you something about another person: *A little bird told me there's a new man in your life.*
9 the little woman OLD-FASHIONED INFORMAL an expression meaning someone's wife, considered offensive by many people
10 quite the little sth used to describe someone's character or abilities in a way that does not show respect: *She was quite the little rebel in those days.*
[**Origin:** Old English *lytel*] → see also LITTLE FINGER, LITTLE PEOPLE, LITTLE TOE

WORD CHOICE little, small
• **Little** usually expresses an emotional attitude you have about someone or something such as whether you like or dislike someone or something: *We rented a cozy little cottage in the mountains.* | *Shawn's little laugh is getting on my nerves.*
• **Small** generally describes the size of something: *This jacket's too small for me.* | *He packed his things into a small bag.*

little[2] S1 W1 *quantifier, pron., n.* **1** only a small amount or hardly any of something: *We know little about his past.* | +**of** *Little of the money is left.* | **very/so/too little sth** *Scott has very little time these days.* | *The government **does little** to help single working mothers.* | ***Little or no** attention is paid to the rights of victims.* | *He knew **little or nothing** about fixing cars.* | *I've spent my life doing **as little as possible*** (=the smallest amount that I have to do). | *I've had **precious little*** (=very little) *help from my parents.* | *You can buy an original painting for **as little as $100**.* → see also LEAST[1], LESS[1] → see Word Choice box at FEW **2 a little** a small amount SYN **a little bit**: *If you'd like more coffee, there's a little left.* | *I know only a little Korean.* | +**of** *Spend a little of your time just relaxing.* | *Would you like **a little more** cake?* **3 what little** also **the little (that)** the small amount that there is, that is possible etc.: *I gave him what little money I had.* **4 a little (sth) goes a long way** SPOKEN used to say you do not need much of something: *A little ketchup goes a long way.*

little[3] S2 W1 *adv.* **1 a little** to a small degree, or by a small amount SYN **a little bit**: *She seems a little upset.* | *You'll feel better if you rest a little.* | *Move the table a little closer to the wall.* | **a little more/less/over/under** *Use a little more salt.* **2** *comparative* **less**, *superlative* **least** not much or only slightly: *The town has changed little since I was a boy.* | **little known/understood** *a little known part of the country* | *There are **little more than** three minutes left in the game.* | *His health has improved **very little**.* | *I tried to disturb him **as little as possible**.* **3 little did sb know/think/realize** used to mean that someone did not know, think, realize etc. that something was true: *Little did she know that her life was about to change.* **4 little by little** gradually: *Little by little I became more fluent in German.* → see also **think little of sb/sth** at THINK (15)

Little Big·horn, the /ˌlɪtl ˈbɪghɔrn/ a river in the U.S. state of Montana, where General Custer fought against and was killed by Native Americans led by Sitting Bull and Crazy Horse in the Battle of the Little Bighorn

ˌLittle ˈDipper *n.* **the Little Dipper** a group of stars which is thought to look like a bowl with a handle, seen in the sky near the BIG DIPPER

ˌlittle ˈfinger *n.* [C] the smallest finger on your hand

ˈLittle ˌLeague *n.* a baseball LEAGUE for children

ˈlittle ˌpeople *n.* [plural] **1 (the) little people** all the people in a country or organization who have no power: *The real victims of the bank failure will be the little people.* **2** [singular] **little person** people who do not grow to average size because of GENETIC or medical conditions → see also DWARF, MIDGET **3 the little people** imaginary people with magical powers, especially LEPRECHAUNS

ˈLittle Rock the capital and largest city of the U.S. state of Arkansas

ˌlittle ˈtoe *n.* [C] the smallest toe on your foot

lit·to·ral /ˈlɪtərəl, ˌlɪt̬əˈræl, -ˈrɑl/ *n.* [C] EARTH SCIENCE an area of land near the coast —**littoral** *adj.*

li·tur·gi·cal /lɪˈtɚdʒɪkəl/ *adj.* [only before noun] related to church services and ceremonies —**liturgically** /-kli/ *adv.*

lit·ur·gy /ˈlɪt̬ɚdʒi/ *n. plural* **liturgies** **1** [C,U] a way of praying in a religious service using a particular order of words, prayers etc. **2 the Liturgy** the written form of these services

liv·a·bil·i·ty /ˌlɪvəˈbɪləti/ *n.* [U] the degree to which a

L

place is comfortable, attractive, and easy to live in: *the livability of our urban environments*

liv·a·ble /ˈlɪvəbəl/ *adj.* **1 a)** good enough to live in, but not very good SYN **habitable**: *The area is poor, but livable.* **b)** nice to live in: *the country's most livable cities* **2 a livable wage/salary** an amount of money that you are paid for work that is enough to buy the necessary things for life, such as food and housing **3** a livable situation is satisfactory, but not very good: *livable working conditions*

live¹ /lɪv/ S1 W1 *v.*

1 BE/STAY ALIVE [I] to be alive or continue to stay alive: *Plants can't live without water.* | *St. Patrick probably lived in the 5th century.* | **live to be 70/85/99 etc.** *Why do some people live to be 100?* | *They never thought they'd* ***live to see*** *their grandchildren graduate from college.* | *The doctors only* ***give*** *him a year* ***to live*** (=they only expect him to live a year).

2 IN A PLACE/HOME [I always + adv./prep.] to have your home in a particular place: *Where do you live?* | **+in/at/near etc.** *My parents live in Cleveland.* | *Boston is a great* ***place to live****.* | *Kate still* ***lives at home*** (=lives with her parents). | *He prefers to* ***live alone****.*

3 LIVE IN A PARTICULAR WAY [I always + adv./prep.,T] to have a particular type of life, or live in a particular way: *I couldn't live like that.* | *The number of children* ***living in poverty*** *is increasing.* | *Villagers* ***lived in fear of*** *another attack.* | *They earn enough money to* ***live well*** (=have a comfortable life). | *People with the disease can* ***live*** *normal productive* ***lives****.* | *Keenan has* ***lived the life of*** *a nomad.*

4 live from day to day to deal with each day as it comes without making plans

5 live by doing sth to keep yourself alive by doing a particular thing: *He lived by selling things he found on the street.*

6 live by your wits to get money by being smart or dishonest, and not by doing an ordinary job: *The city's homeless live completely by their wits.*

7 live a lie to pretend all the time that you feel or believe something when actually you do not: *He announced he was gay because didn't want to go on living a lie.*

8 STILL HAVE INFLUENCE [I] if someone's idea or work lives, it continues to influence people SYN **live on**: *Elvis lives.* | *His name will* ***live forever****.*

9 live happily ever after a phrase that means to live a happy life until you die, used especially at the end of children's stories

10 live out of a suitcase to travel a lot, especially as part of your work

11 live beyond your means to spend more money than you earn

12 live within your means to not spend more money than you earn and not be in debt

13 live in a dream/fantasy/imaginary world also **live in a world of your own** to have strange ideas about life that are not practical or are not like those of other people: *She's a sweet woman, but she lives in a dream world.*

14 the best/greatest/worst... that ever lived someone who was better, greater etc. at doing something than anyone else in the past or present: *Olivier was one of the greatest actors that ever lived.*

15 EXCITING LIFE [I] to have an exciting life: *You need to get out there and* ***live a little****.*

16 live in sin OLD-FASHIONED, DISAPPROVING to live together and have a sexual relationship without being married

17 live from hand to mouth to have very little money and never be sure if you will have enough to eat

18 live and breathe sth to enjoy doing something so much that you spend most of your time on it: *Residents of the city live and breathe high school football.*

19 be living on borrowed time a) to be still alive after the time that you were expected to die **b)** to be expected to fail and end soon

20 live in the past a) to think too much about the past: *You've got to stop living in the past.* **b)** to have old-fashioned ideas and attitudes

21 sb will live to regret sth used to say that someone will wish that they had not done something: *If she marries him, she'll live to regret it.*

22 live to fight/see another day to continue to live or work after a failure or after you have dealt with a difficult situation

SPOKEN PHRASES

23 as long as I live used to emphasize that you will always do or feel something: *I'll never forget this day as long as I live.*

24 live and let live used to say that you should accept other people's behavior, even if it seems strange

25 live high on the hog INFORMAL to enjoy expensive food, clothes etc. without worrying about the cost

26 you haven't lived if/until... used for emphasizing that someone should experience something because it is very good: *You haven't lived until you've tried my mom's apple pie.*

27 sb'll live used to say that you do not think someone should get too upset about something: *"Dad's going to be mad we're late." "He'll live."*

28 (you) live and learn used to say that you have learned something from a bad experience you have had and you will not make the same mistake again

29 as I live and breathe OLD-FASHIONED said to show surprise

[**Origin:** Old English *libban*] → see also **long live sb/sth** at LONG² (10)

live by sth *phr. v.* to always behave according to a particular set of rules or ideas: *My daughters are going to live by my rules, or else.*

live down *phr. v.* **never live sth down** to not be able to make people forget about something bad or embarrassing you have done: *You'll never live this evening down.*

live for sb/sth *phr. v.* **1** to consider someone or something very important, or the most important thing in your life: *Some men seem to live for football.* **2 live for the day when...** to want something to happen very much: *Lilly lives for the day when she can have an apartment of her own.* **3 live for today/the moment** to do good and exciting things now and every day, instead of simply planning to do them in the future **4 something/nothing/everything to live for** something, nothing, or many things that make life seem good and worth living: *Her promises gave him something to live for.*

live off (of) *phr. v.* **1 live off (of) sb** DISAPPROVING to get the money that you need to live from someone else, especially instead of earning it yourself: *Dave's been living off his girlfriend for a year.* **2 live off (of) sth** to eat only or mainly a particular type of food: *I was living off bagels and TV dinners.* **3 live off (of) sth** to get money or food from something and use it in order to live: *They planned to farm and* ***live off the land****.*

live on *phr. v.* **1 live on sth** to eat only or mainly a particular type of food: *These chickens from Peru live on ants.* **2 live on sth** to buy your food, pay bills etc. with a particular amount of money, especially a small amount: *The whole family lives on just $900 a month.* **3** to continue to exist SYN **live**: *She will live on in our memories.*

live out *phr. v.* **1 live out a dream/fantasy/ambition etc.** to experience or do something that you have planned or hoped for: *The adult sports league gives people a chance to live out their childhood dreams.* **2 live out your life/days** to continue to live in a particular way or place until you die: *She lived out the rest of her life in the countryside.*

live through *phr. v.* **1 live through sth** to still be alive after experiencing difficult or dangerous conditions, during which you thought you might die SYN **survive**: *Don didn't expect to live through the war.* **2 live through sb** to do nothing interesting or exciting yourself, but get pleasure from hearing about the interesting or exciting things that someone else does: *You've got to stop living through your children.*

live together *phr. v.* to live in the same house or apartment with another person in a sexual relationship, without being married: *Lori and her boyfriend have been living together for two years.*

live up *phr. v.* **live it up** INFORMAL to do things that you enjoy and spend a lot of money: *Lisa was living it up like she didn't have a care in the world.*

live up to sth *phr. v.* to be as good as people expect, hope, or need: *The movie didn't really* ***live up to*** *my* ***expectations.***

live with *phr. v.* **1 live with sb** to live in the same house, apartment etc. with someone you are having a sexual relationship with but are not married to: *Tim is living with his girlfriend.* **2 live with sb** to share a house or apartment with other people: *She lives with some friends from college.* **3 live with sth** to accept a difficult situation that is likely to continue for a long time: *She's had to learn to live with the pain.*

live[2] /laɪv/ S3 W3 *adj.*
1 LIVING [only before noun] not dead or artificial SYN **living**: *experiments on live animals* → see also DEAD, **real live...** at REAL[1] (1)
2 performed for people who are watching, rather than for a movie, record etc.: *The bar has* ***live music*** *every Saturday.* | *Weber released a* ***live recording*** (=a recording made of a live performance) *of his New York concert.* | *The show is filmed before a* ***live studio audience*** (=people who are watching a live performance).
3 a live broadcast/report etc. a concert, sports event etc. that is seen or heard on television or radio at the same time as it is happening: ***live coverage*** *of the president's speech* → DELAYED BROADCAST
4 ELECTRIC PHYSICS live equipment or wires have electricity flowing through them → see also LIVE WIRE
5 BULLETS/BOMBS a live bullet, bomb etc. still has the power to explode because it has not been used: *live ammunition*
6 a live ball a ball that is being played with inside the area allowed by the rules of some sports OPP **dead**
7 live coals pieces of coal or other material that are burning
8 a live issue/concern an ISSUE that still interests or worries people OPP **dead**

live[3] /laɪv/ *adv.* **1 broadcast/show/carry etc. sth live** to broadcast something such as a concert, speech etc. at the same time as it actually happens: *We'll be broadcasting the program live from Washington.* **2** in front of an AUDIENCE (=group of people): **peform/play live** *The band has never performed live before.* | *The show is* ***recorded live*** *before a studio audience.* **3 go live** to start being used after being planned and discussed for a long time: *The Website goes live next week.*

live·a·ble /ˈlɪvəbəl/ *adj.* another spelling of LIVABLE

ˈlived-in *adj.* a place that looks lived-in has been used often by people, so that it does not seem too new or neat: *Sally's apartment* ***had that*** *comfortable* ***lived-in look.***

live-in /ˈlɪv ɪn/ *adj.* [only before noun] **1 a live-in maid/nanny etc.** a worker who lives in the house belonging to the family they work for **2 a live-in lover/boyfriend etc.** someone who lives with their sexual partner without being married to them

live·li·hood /ˈlaɪvliˌhʊd/ *n.* [C,U] the way you earn money in order to live: *Farmers depend on the weather for their livelihood.*

live·long /ˈlɪvlɔŋ/ *adj.* **all the livelong day** OLD-FASHIONED a phrase meaning "all day," used when this seems like a long time to you

live·ly[1] /ˈlaɪvli/ *adj.* *comparative* **livelier**, *superlative* **liveliest**
1 PEOPLE very active, full of energy, and cheerful: *a lively child*
2 PLACE/SITUATION a lively place or situation is exciting because a lot of things are happening: *the city's lively nightlife*
3 MOVEMENTS/MUSIC involving a lot of quick movement and therefore exciting or enjoyable: *a lively dance*
4 DISCUSSION/CONVERSATION ETC. exciting because people are speaking quickly, have a lot of interesting ideas etc.: *a lively debate*
5 MUSIC fast, cheerful, and exciting: *lively Latin rhythms*
6 a lively imagination someone with a lively imagination often invents stories, descriptions etc. that are not true
7 TASTE strong but pleasant: *The wine has a lively, fruity flavor.*
8 MIND/THOUGHTS someone who has a lively mind or shows a lively interest is intelligent and wants to learn about them: *a lively curiosity*
9 COLOR very bright: *a lively combination of colors* —**liveliness** *n.* [U]

lively[2] *adv.* **Step lively!** SPOKEN, HUMOROUS used to tell someone to hurry

li·ven /ˈlaɪvən/ *v.*
liven up *phr. v.* **1 liven sth ↔ up** to become more exciting, or to make an event become more exciting: *Better music might liven the party up.* **2 liven sth ↔ up** to make something look, taste etc. more interesting or colorful: *A colorful shawl can liven up a trench coat.* **3 liven sb ↔ up** to become more interested or excited, or to make someone feel like this: *After a few drinks, she livened up a little.*

liv·er /ˈlɪvɚ/ *n.* **1** [C] BIOLOGY a large organ in the body which produces BILE and cleans the blood → see picture at DIGESTIVE SYSTEM **2** [U] the liver of an animal, used as food

liv·er·ied /ˈlɪvərid/ *adj.* wearing LIVERY: *a liveried servant*

ˈliver spot *n.* [C usually plural] a small round brown spot that appears on someone's skin, especially their hands, as they get older

liv·er·wurst /ˈlɪvɚˌwɚst/ *n.* [U] a type of cooked soft SAUSAGE, made mainly of LIVER

liv·er·y /ˈlɪvəri/ *n. plural* **liveries** **1** [C,U] a type of old-fashioned uniform for servants **2** [C] a company that rents out vehicles, or drives people where they want to go for money: *a livery cab* **3** [U] the business of keeping and taking care of horses for money, especially in the past **4** [C] a livery stable → see also LIVERIED

ˈlivery ˌstable *n.* [C] a place where people pay to have their horses kept, fed etc. or where horses can be rented, especially in the past

lives /laɪvz/ the plural of LIFE

live·stock /ˈlaɪvstɑk/ *n.* [plural, U] the animals that are kept on a farm

live wire /ˌlaɪv ˈwaɪɚ/ *n.* [C] **1** INFORMAL someone who is very active and has a lot of energy **2** PHYSICS a wire that has electricity passing through it

liv·id /ˈlɪvɪd/ *adj.* **1** extremely angry SYN **furious**: *I was so livid I just ripped up the letter.* ►see THESAURUS box at **angry** **2** a mark on your skin that is livid is dark blue and gray: *livid bruises* **3** LITERARY a face that is livid is very pale [**Origin:** 1400–1500 French *livide*, from Latin *lividus*, from *livere* **to be blue**]

liv·ing[1] /ˈlɪvɪŋ/ *adj.* **1** [only before noun] alive now: *one of the greatest living composers* | *Ecology is the study of how* ***living things*** (=plants, animals, and people) *relate to their environment.* **2** [only before noun] relating to where or how people live: *improved living conditions* **3 living proof** if someone is living proof of a particular fact, they are a good example of how true it is: *I'm living proof that people can make their dreams come true.* **4 in/within living memory** for as long as anyone can remember: *The famine is worse than any disaster in living memory.* **5 a living language** a language that is still spoken today **6 a living legend** someone who is famous for being extremely good at something: *one of the living legends of rhythm and blues* **7 a living wage** money that you earn from your work that is enough to allow you to buy the things that you need to live **8 a living hell** a situation that causes you a lot of suffering for a long time **9 a living death** a life that is so bad that it would seem better to be dead → see also **beat/knock/pound the (living) daylights out of sb/sth** at DAYLIGHT (4), **scare/frighten the (living) daylights out of sb** at DAYLIGHT (3)

living[2] *n.* **1** [C usually singular] the way that you earn

L

money, or the money that you earn: *So what do you **do for a living**?* | *It's not a great job, but **it's a living**.* | *I want to **make a living*** (=earn enough money to live) *being creative.* **2 the living** [plural] all the people who are alive as opposed to dead people: *Funerals are really for the living.* **3** [U] the way in which someone lives their life: *the harsh realities of city living* → see also COST OF LIVING, **in the land of the living** at LAND¹ (6), STANDARD OF LIVING

'living ,quarters *n.* [plural] the part of an army or industrial camp etc. or a large official building where the soldiers or workers live and sleep

'living room *n.* [C] the main room in a house where people relax, watch television etc. → see also FAMILY ROOM

'living ,standard *n.* [C usually plural] ECONOMICS the level of comfort and wealth that people have SYN **standard of living**: *a decline in the country's living standards*

Liv·ing·stone /'lɪvɪŋstən/, **Dr. Da·vid** /'deɪvɪd/ (1813–1873) a Scottish MISSIONARY and EXPLORER of Africa, who was the first European to see the Zambezi River and the Victoria Falls

,living 'will *n.* [C] LAW a document explaining what medical or legal decisions should be made if you become so sick that you cannot make those decisions yourself

Liv·y /'lɪvi/ (59 B.C.–A.D. 17) a Roman HISTORIAN known for his history of Rome, which greatly influenced historical writing. His Latin name was Titus Livius.

liz·ard /'lɪzɚd/ *n.* [C] a type of REPTILE that has four legs and a long tail [**Origin:** 1300–1400 Old French *lesard*, from Latin *lacerta*]

Ljub·lja·na /,lyubli'ɑnə/ the capital and largest city of Slovenia

'll /əl, l/ *v.* the short form of "will": *She'll be gone until Wednesday.*

lla·ma /'lɑmə/ *n.* [C] a South American animal with thick hair like wool and a long neck [**Origin:** 1600–1700 Spanish, Quechua]

lla·no /'lɑnoʊ/ *n. plural* **llanos** [C] EARTH SCIENCE a large area of flat dry land with grass growing on it, found especially in the western and southern U.S. and parts of South America

L

LL.B. *n.* [C] **Bachelor of Laws** a first college or university degree in law

LL.D. *n.* [C] **Doctor of Laws** a DOCTORATE in law

LL.M. *n.* [C] **Master of Laws** a MASTER'S DEGREE in law

LLP *n.* [C] ECONOMICS the abbreviation for LIMITED LIABILITY PARTNERSHIP

Ln. the written abbreviation of LANE

lo /loʊ/ *interjection* **lo and behold** HUMOROUS said before mentioning something funny or surprising that has happened: *Lo and behold, Dave was sitting sitting there when we arrived.*

load¹ /loʊd/ S3 *n.* [C]
1 AMOUNT OF STH a large quantity of something that is carried by a person, a vehicle etc.: **+of** *The first load of supplies will arrive at the camp next week.* | **a truckload/carload/busload etc. (of sth)** (=the largest amount or number of something that a car, truck etc. can carry)
2 WORK the amount of work that a person or machine has to do SYN **workload**: *Leslie has a **light** teaching **load*** (=not much work) *this semester.*
3 WASHING CLOTHES a quantity of clothes that are washed together in a washing machine: *I did two **loads of laundry** this morning.*
4 WORRY a responsibility or worry that is difficult to deal with SYN **burden**: *a $1.2 billion debt load* | *Working three jobs is a **heavy load to bear**.*
5 WEIGHT the amount of weight that the frame of a building or structure can support: *the load on the vehicle's wheels* | *a load-bearing wall*
6 MONEY TECHNICAL an amount of money that someone pays a company in order to let them INVEST (=put their money) in a particular FUND: *a no-load mutual fund*
7 ELECTRICITY TECHNICAL an amount of electrical power that is produced by a GENERATOR or a POWER PLANT: *Load demand can exceed 66% during peak periods.* → see also **be a load/weight off your mind** at MIND¹ (20)

SPOKEN PHRASES
8 a load of sth also **loads of sth** a lot of something: *We got a load of complaints about the music.*
9 get a load of sb/sth used to tell someone to look at or listen to something surprising or funny: *Get a load of Ted's new haircut!*
10 a load of bull IMPOLITE used to say that something is untrue, wrong, or stupid
11 take a load off (your feet) used to invite someone to sit down

[**Origin:** Old English *lad* **support, carrying**]

load² S2 W3 *v.* **1** [I,T] to put a load of something on or into a vehicle SYN **load up**: *We should finish loading soon.* | *It took an hour to load the van.* | **load sth with sth** *Two men were loading a truck with crates.* | **load sth into/onto sth** *Emma loaded all the groceries into the car.* **2** [T] to put a necessary part into something so that it will work, such as bullets into a gun, film into a camera etc.: *You are taught how to load and fire a gun.* **3** [I,T] COMPUTERS to put a program into a computer, or to be put into a computer: *This program takes a while to load.* **4 load the bases** to get players in a baseball game on all the BASES, so that they are in a position to be able to gain points

load sb/sth ↔ **down** *phr. v.* to make someone or something carry too many things or do too much work: *If you load down the car, it won't go as fast.* | **load sb/sth ↔ down with sth** *They've loaded me down with work again.*

load up *phr. v.* **load sth ↔ up** to put a load of something on or into a vehicle SYN **load**: **load (sth ↔) up with sth** *She loaded up the car with camping gear.*

load up on sth *phr. v.* to get a lot of something, so that you are sure that you will have enough available: *People were loading up on bottled water.*

load sb **(up) with** sth *phr. v.* to give someone a lot of things to carry: *I see Dick's loaded you up with boxes.*

load·ed /'loʊdɪd/ *adj.*
1 GUN/CAMERA ETC. containing bullets, film etc.: *That gun's not loaded, is it?* | *a loaded camera*
2 FULL VEHICLE carrying a load of something: **+with** *The truck was loaded with bananas.*
3 RICH [not before noun] INFORMAL very rich: *Carter's family is loaded.*
4 WORD/STATEMENT having more meanings than you first think, or having a strong emotional effect: *a loaded question* | *politically loaded words*
5 be loaded with sth INFORMAL to be full of a particular quality, or containing a lot of something: *The library is loaded with interesting books.* | *Linda's fruitcake is loaded with fruit and nuts.*
6 DRUNK INFORMAL very drunk
7 loaded dice DICE that have weights in them so that they always fall with the same side on top, used to influence games in an unfair way
8 BASEBALL if the BASES are loaded, there are players on all three bases so that they are in a position to be able to gain points

'loading dock *n.* [C] a structure from which goods are taken off or put onto trucks, trains etc.

load·mas·ter /'loʊd,mæstɚ/ *n.* [C] someone who is responsible for loading heavy equipment, weapons etc. on or off an aircraft

loaf¹ /loʊf/ *n. plural* **loaves** /loʊvz/ [C] **1** bread that is shaped and baked in one piece and can be cut into SLICES: *a **loaf of bread*** → see picture at BREAD¹ **2** food that has been cut into very small pieces, pressed together, and baked in the shape of a loaf of bread: *a nut loaf* → see also MEATLOAF [**Origin:** Old English *hlaf*]

loaf² *v.* **loafs, loafed, loafing** [I] also **loaf around** to waste time in a lazy way when you should be working: *He spent all summer loafing around the house.*

loaf·er /ˈloʊfɚ/ *n.* [C] **1** also **Loafer** TRADEMARK a flat leather shoe without LACES that you slide onto your foot **2** DISAPPROVING someone who wastes time in a lazy way when they should be working

loam /loʊm/ *n.* [U] EARTH SCIENCE good-quality soil consisting of sand, clay, and decayed plants —**loamy** *adj.*

loan¹ /loʊn/ S3 W2 *n.* **1** [C] an amount of money that you borrow from a bank, financial institution etc.: *a $2 million loan* | +**of** *a loan of $175,000* | *I had to* ***take out a loan*** (=borrow money) *to buy my car.* | *The company* ***makes loans*** *to small businesses.* | *You pay a fixed rate of interest on some* ***bank loans*** (=from a bank). | **repay/pay off/pay back a loan** *Krebs needed more time to pay back the loan.* | **a student/personal/business etc. loan** (=a loan for a student, a person for private use etc.) | **a car/home loan** (=a loan to buy a car or a house) **2 on loan** if something such as a painting or book is on loan, someone is borrowing it: +**from** *The gems in the display are on loan from the Academy of Science.* **3** [U] the act of lending something: +**of** *Thanks for the loan of your camera.* [**Origin:** 1100–1200 Old Norse *lan*]

loan² *v.* [T] **1** to let someone borrow something SYN **lend**: **loan sb sth** *Jeff loaned us his car for the weekend.* ▶see THESAURUS box at **borrow** **2** if a bank or other institution loans money, they lend it to someone and charge INTEREST SYN **lend**: **loan sth to sb/sth** *Large sums of money were loaned to developing countries.* **3** to lend something valuable, such as a painting, to an organization: *The family loaned their collection of paintings for the exhibition.*

ˈloan ˌcapital *n.* [U] the part of a company's money that was borrowed to help start it

loan·er /ˈloʊnɚ/ *n.* [C] INFORMAL something such as a car, piece of equipment etc. that someone is allowed to use while theirs is being repaired

ˈloan shark *n.* [C] DISAPPROVING someone who lends money at a very high rate of INTEREST and will often use threats or violence to get the money back —**loansharking** *n.* [U]

ˈloan word, loanword *n.* [C] a word taken into one language from another and sometimes changed to fit the rules of the new language

loath /loʊθ, loʊð/ *adj.* **be loath to do sth** FORMAL to be unwilling to do something: *He seemed loath to raise the subject.*

loathe /loʊð/ *v.* [T not in progressive] FORMAL to hate someone or something very much SYN **detest**: *Judy loathes her ex-husband.* [**Origin:** Old English *lathian*, from *lath*]

loath·ing /ˈloʊðɪŋ/ *n.* [singular, U] FORMAL a very strong feeling of hatred: +**for** *She had a loathing for men who called her "Honey."*

loath·some /ˈloʊθsəm, ˈloʊð-/ *adj.* FORMAL very bad or cruel: *a loathsome little man*

loaves /loʊvz/ the plural of LOAF

lob /lɑb/ *v.* **lobbed, lobbing** [T] **1** to throw something somewhere in a high curve, especially over a wall, fence etc.: **lob sth into/at/over etc. sth** *About 40 demonstrators lobbed eggs over the wall.* **2** to throw or hit a ball in a slow high curve, especially in a game of tennis: *Sampras lobbed the ball high over Chang's head.* —**lob** *n.* [C]

lob·by¹ /ˈlɑbi/ *n. plural* **lobbies** [C] **1** a wide area or large hall just inside the entrance to a public building → see also FOYER: *a hotel lobby* **2** POLITICS a group of people or companies who try to persuade the government or someone with political power to change a law so that it is more favorable to them: *The law has the support of the gun-control lobby.* [**Origin:** 1500–1600 Medieval Latin *lobium* **covered way for walking**]

lobby² *v.* **lobbies, lobbied, lobbying** [I,T] POLITICS to try to persuade the government or someone with political power to change a law to make it more favorable to you: +**for/against** *Price lobbied hard for passage of the helmet law.* | **lobby sb to do sth** *Alquist is lobbying the governor to sign the controversial bill.*

lob·by·ing /ˈlɑbiɪŋ/ *n.* [U] the activity of trying to persuade the government or someone with political power to change a law so that it is more favorable to you

lob·by·ist /ˈlɑbiɪst/ *n.* [C] POLITICS someone whose job involves trying to persuade the government or someone with political power to change a law so that it is more favorable to the particular group of people they represent

lobe /loʊb/ *n.* [C] **1** BIOLOGY the soft piece of flesh at the bottom of your ear SYN **ear lobe** **2** BIOLOGY a round part of an organ in your body, especially in your brain or lungs

lo·bot·o·my /ləˈbɑt̬əmi, loʊ-/ *n. plural* **lobotomies** [C] a medical operation to remove part of someone's brain in order to treat mental problems, which was done more commonly in the past —**lobotomize** *v.* [T]

lob·ster /ˈlɑbstɚ/ S3 *n.* **1** [C] an ocean animal with eight legs, a shell, and two large CLAWS → see picture at CRUSTACEAN **2** [U] the meat of this animal [**Origin:** Old English *loppestre*]

lob·ster·man /ˈlɑbstɚmən/ *n.* [C] someone whose job is to catch lobsters

ˈlobster ˌpot *n.* [C] a trap shaped like a basket, in which lobsters are caught

lo-cal /ˌloʊ ˈkæl◂ / *adj.* INFORMAL another spelling of LOW-CAL

lo·cal¹ /ˈloʊkəl/ S2 W1 *adj.* **1** connected with a particular place or area, especially the place you live in: **local people/residents/community etc.** *Local residents oppose the new highway.* | **a local store/school/library etc.** *You can find all these books in your local library.* | **local newspaper/radio/television** *The fire was reported in the local newspaper.* ▶see THESAURUS box at **near³** **2 a local train/bus** a train or bus that stops at all regular stopping places → see also EXPRESS TRAIN/BUS **3** MEDICINE affecting or limited to one part of your body → see also GENERAL: *a local anesthetic* [**Origin:** 1300–1400 French, Late Latin *localis*, from Latin *locus* **place**]

local² *n.* [C] **1** [usually plural] someone who lives in the place where you are, or the place that you are talking about: *I asked one of the locals for directions.* **2** a branch of a UNION: *Local 54 of the Hotel Employees' Union* **3** a bus, train etc. that stops at all regular stopping places → see also EXPRESS

ˌlocal ˌarea ˈnetwork *n.* [C] COMPUTERS a LAN

ˈlocal ˌcall *n.* [C] a telephone call to someone in a place near you → see also LONG-DISTANCE CALL

ˌlocal ˈcolor *n.* [U] the unusual or additional details about a place or in a story that give you a better idea of what it is like, and that make it special or interesting: *His stories are full of local color.*

lo·cale /loʊˈkæl/ *n.* [C] the place where an event happens, or where the action takes place in a book or a movie: *Malta is the perfect locale for the conference.*

ˌlocal ˈgovernment *n.* [C,U] the government of cities, towns etc. rather than of a whole state or country

ˌlocal ˈhistory *n.* [U] the history of a particular area in a country, state etc. —**ˌlocal hisˈtorian** *n.* [C]

lo·cal·i·ty /loʊˈkæləti/ *n. plural* **localities** [C] a small area of a country, city etc.: *In some localities house prices have risen by more than 50%.*

lo·cal·ize /ˈloʊkəˌlaɪz/ *v.* [T] FORMAL **1** to limit the effect that something has, or the size of area it covers, or to be limited in this way: *Croft plans to localize his campaign to each state.* **2** to find out exactly where something is —**localization** /ˌloʊkələˈzeɪʃən/ *n.* [U]

lo·cal·ized /ˈloʊkəˌlaɪzd/ *adj.* FORMAL only within a small area: *localized flooding* | *localized cancer*

lo·cal·ly /ˈloʊkəli/ *adv.* **1** in or near the area where you are or the area you are talking about: *The company employs 1,300 workers locally.*

L

THESAURUS

nearby not far away: *Do you live nearby?*
close by/close to here not far away: *My folks live close by.*
around here in or near a place: *Is there a bank around here?*
in the neighborhood in a small area of the town, where you are: *Are there good schools in the neighborhood?*
in/around these parts in the particular area you are in: *There aren't any foxes in these parts.*
→ NEAR[1]

2 in particular small areas: *locally elected governments*

ˌlocal ˈpaper *n.* [C] a newspaper that contains local news in addition to national and international news

ˈlocal time *n.* [U] the time of day in a particular part of the world: *We'll arrive in Boston at 4:00 local time.*

lo·cate /ˈloʊkeɪt/ Ac S3 W2 *v.* **1** [T] to find the exact position of someone or something: *Divers have located the shipwreck.* ►see THESAURUS box at **find**[1] **2 be located** to be in a particular place or position SYN **be situated**: *Where exactly is the tumor located?* | **+in/at/near etc.** *The theater is located in the center of town.* **3** [I always + adv./prep.,T always+ adv./prep.] to come to a place and start a business, company etc. there, or to bring a business, company etc. somewhere and start it: **located (sth) in/at etc. sth** *Several discount stores have located in nearby communities.* [**Origin:** 1500–1600 Latin, past participle of *locare* **to place**, from *locus*]

lo·ca·tion /loʊˈkeɪʃən/ Ac S3 W3 *n.* **1** [C] a particular place or position, especially in relation to other areas, buildings etc.: *His apartment is in a really good location.* | **+of** *The map shows the location of the crash.* ►see THESAURUS box at **place**[1] **2** [C,U] a place where a movie is filmed, away from the STUDIO: *The film was shot **on location** in Hungary.* **3 the location of sb/sth** the act of finding the exact position of someone or something: *techniques for the location of tumors*

loch /lɑk/ *n.* [C] a word meaning a lake or a part of the ocean partly enclosed by land, used in Scotland: *Loch Ness*

lo·ci /ˈloʊsaɪ, -ki/ *n.* the plural of LOCUS

L

lock[1] /lɑk/ S1 W2 *v.*
1 FASTEN [I,T] to fasten something using a key, or to be fastened using a key OPP **unlock**: *Lock the door when you leave.* | *I can't get this drawer to lock.*
2 IN A SAFE PLACE [T always + adv./prep.] to put something in a safe place and lock the door, lid etc., or to attach it to something using a lock: **lock sth in/to sth** *Always lock valuables in the trunk of your car while shopping.* | *We locked our bikes to the fence.*
3 FIXED POSITION [I,T] to become set in one position and impossible to move, or to set a wheel, a part of a machine etc. in this way SYN **lock up**: *The brakes locked and we skidded.* | *Lock the brakes before you take him out of the stroller.*
4 COMPUTERS [T] to prevent information on a computer from being changed or looked at by someone who is not allowed to change or look at it: *These files have all been locked.*
5 BODY PART [I,T] to be held in one position and not move, or to make a body part do this: *He locked his hands around my throat.* | *Their **eyes locked** (=they stared at each other) for an instant.*
6 be locked in an embrace if two people are locked in an EMBRACE, they are holding each other very tightly
7 lock arms to join your arms tightly together with someone else by putting your arm through the bend in their arm: *Fifty students locked arms to block the entrance to the building.*
8 lock horns with sb (over sth) to argue, fight, or compete with someone —**lockable** *adj.*

lock away *phr. v.* **1 lock sth ↔ away** to put something in a safe place and lock the door, lid etc.: *He locked his money away in the safe.* **2 lock sb ↔ away** to put someone in prison or an institution for people who are mentally ill **3 lock yourself away** to keep yourself separate from other people by staying in your room, office etc.

lock in *phr. v.* **1 lock sb/sth in (sth)** also **lock sb/sth inside (sth)** to prevent a person or animal from entering a place by locking the door, a lid etc.: *Prisoners are only locked in at night.* | *She locked herself inside her room.* **2 lock sth ↔ in** to do something so that a price, offer, agreement etc. cannot be changed: *Sell your stocks now to lock in some of the gains of recent months.* **3 be locked in sth** to be in situation that continues for a long time and is hard to get out of: *Some families are locked in a cycle of poverty.* | **be locked in a battle/combat/dispute etc.** *The two firms have been locked in a legal battle for months.* **4 lock sth ↔ in** to make the taste, liquid etc. remain in something: *This method of cooking locks in the meat's flavor.*

lock sb **into** sth *phr. v.* to make someone behave according to an agreement or promise without changing it: *The company is locked into a three-year contract with PARCO.*

lock onto sth *phr. v.* f a something such as a MISSILE or SATELLITE locks onto a TARGET or signal, it finds it and follows it closely

lock sb **↔ out** *phr. v.* **1** to prevent someone from entering a place by locking the door: *If you come home drunk again, I'll lock you out.* | **lock sb/sth out of sth** *I accidentally locked myself out of the house.* **2** if employers lock workers out, they do not let them enter their place of work until they accept the employers' conditions for settling a disagreement → see also LOCKOUT

lock up *phr. v.* **1 lock sb ↔ up** INFORMAL to put someone in prison or in a place that they cannot escape from: *He was repeatedly locked up for drug dealing.* | *They ought to **lock him up and throw away the key*** (=put him in prison permanently)*!* **2 lock sth ↔ up** to make a building safe by locking the doors, especially at night: *I have to lock up and turn on the alarm before I go.* **3 lock sth ↔ up** to put something in a safe place and lock the door, lid etc., or to attach it to something using a lock: *I have all my stuff locked up downstairs.* **4** if a wheel, a part of a machine, body part etc. locks up, it becomes set in one position and impossible to move SYN **lock**: *The steering wheel locked up and we drove into a ditch.* **5 be locked up (in sth)** if your money is locked up, you have put it into a business, INVESTMENT etc. and cannot easily move it or change it into CASH

lock[2] S3 *n.* [C]
1 ON A DOOR/CHAIN ETC. a thing that keeps a door, drawer, chain etc. fastened or shut and is usually opened with a key: *the sound of a key in the lock* | *a bike lock* | **+on** *There's no lock on the door.* | *Kelly **picked the lock** on the desk drawer* (=he used something such as a pin to open it).
2 ON A VEHICLE/MACHINE a piece of equipment on a vehicle, machine etc., that prevents someone from moving, using, or stealing something it: *Put the lock on the stroller wheels before you put the baby in.*
3 lock, stock, and barrel including every part of something: *They sold everything lock, stock, and barrel.*
4 under lock and key a) kept safely in something that is locked: *All patient files are kept under lock and key.* **b)** kept in a place such as a prison
5 HAIR a) a small number of hairs on your head that grow and hang together: *a lock of hair* **b) locks** [plural] POETIC someone's hair: *long flowing locks*
6 ON A RIVER a part of a CANAL or river that is closed off by gates on either end so that the water level can be increased or decreased to raise or lower boats
7 IN A FIGHT a HOLD that a WRESTLER uses to prevent their opponent from moving: *a head lock*
8 GUN the part of a gun that makes the bullet explode out of the gun
9 CONTROL complete control of someone or something that makes the result you want certain: *Parker **has a lock on** the Republican nomination.*

Locke /lɑk/, **John** (1632–1704) an English PHILOSOPHER who developed the idea of EMPIRICISM and believed that a government received the right to rule from the people

lock·er /ˈlɑkɚ/ *n.* [C] **1** a type of large box or container attached to a wall, that can be locked so that you can leave your books, clothes etc. there while you do something else **2** a very cold room used for storing food in a restaurant or factory: *a meat locker*

ˈlocker room *n.* [C] a room where people change their clothes and leave them in lockers, especially in places where they are playing sports

ˈlocker-room ˌhumor *n.* [U] impolite jokes that men tell, especially about sex

lock·et /ˈlɑkɪt/ *n.* [C] a piece of jewelry that you wear around your neck on a chain, with a small metal case in which you can put a picture, a piece of hair etc. [**Origin:** 1300–1400 Old French *locquet*, from Middle Dutch *loke* **latch**]

lock·jaw /ˈlɑkdʒɔ/ *n.* [U] MEDICINE the disease TETANUS

lock·out /ˈlɑk-aʊt/ *n.* [C] a period of time when a company does not allow workers to go back to work, especially in a factory, until they accept its working conditions → see also **lock out** at LOCK¹, STRIKE

lock·smith /ˈlɑkˌsmɪθ/ *n.* [C] someone who makes and repairs locks

lock·step /ˈlɑkstɛp/ *n.* **in lockstep** agreeing with someone completely, or doing something in exactly the same way as them, often without thinking: +**with** *She feels no obligation to vote in lockstep with other Democrats.*

lock·up /ˈlɑk-ʌp/ *n.* [C] **1** a small prison where a criminal can be kept for a short time **2** a situation in which a wheel, part of a machine, body part etc. becomes set in one position and is impossible to move **3** an act of locking someone in prison or in a place they cannot escape from

Lock·wood /ˈlɑkwʊd/, **Bel·va** /ˈbɛlvə/ (1830–1917) a U.S. lawyer who supported women's rights and was the first woman lawyer to appear before the U.S. Supreme Court

lo·co /ˈloʊkoʊ/ *adj.* INFORMAL crazy → see also IN LOCO PARENTIS

lo·co·mo·tion /ˌloʊkəˈmoʊʃən/ *n.* [U] FORMAL OR TECHNICAL movement or the ability to move

lo·co·mo·tive¹ /ˌloʊkəˈmoʊtɪv/ *n.* [C] **1** a train engine **2** a powerful force that makes other things happen or succeed: *The U.S. is usually seen as the locomotive of the world economy.*

locomotive² *adj.* TECHNICAL relating to movement

lo·co·weed /ˈloʊkoʊˌwid/ *n.* [C] a plant that makes animals very sick if they eat it

lo·cus /ˈloʊkəs/ *n. plural* **loci** /ˈloʊkaɪ, -ki/ [C] **1** FORMAL a place or position where something is particularly known to exist or happen: +**of** *Southeast Asia is a major locus of economic growth.* **2** MATH the set of all points given by a particular rule in mathematics

lo·cust /ˈloʊkəst/ *n.* [C] an insect similar to a GRASSHOPPER that flies in large groups and often destroys crops: *a swarm of locusts*

lo·cu·tion /loʊˈkyuʃən/ *n.* **1** [U] ENG. LANG. ARTS a style of speaking **2** [C] ENG. LANG. ARTS a phrase, especially one used in a particular area or by a particular group of people: *a Yiddish locution*

lode /loʊd/ *n.* [C usually singular] an amount of ORE (=metal in its natural form) found in a layer between stones → see also MOTHER LODE (1)

lodge¹ /lɑdʒ/ *n.* [C] **1** a building or hotel in the country or in the mountains where people can stay for a short time, especially to do a particular activity: *a ski lodge* | *Lake Star Lodge has rooms for a reasonable price.* **2** a local meeting place for some organizations, or the group of people who belong to one of these organizations: *a Masonic lodge* **3** a traditional structure such as a LONGHOUSE or a WIGWAM that Native Americans live in, or the group of people that live in it **4** the home of a BEAVER

lodge² *v.* **1** [I always + adv./prep.,T usually passive] to become firmly stuck somewhere, or make something become stuck OPP **dislodge**: +**in/down etc.** *A piece of meat lodged in her throat.* | **be lodged in/down etc. sth** *The bullet is still lodged in his chest.* **2 lodge a complaint/protest/appeal etc.** to make a formal or official complaint, protest etc.: *Several former patients lodged a complaint against the doctor.* **3** [T] to give or find someone a place to stay for a short time: *This building was used to lodge prisoners of war.* | **lodge sb in/at etc. sth** *The refugees were lodged in old army barracks.* **4** [I always + adv./prep.] to live somewhere for a short time, especially by paying someone to stay in their home: *Kim lodged with a local family the summer she studied in Paris.*

lodg·er /ˈlɑdʒɚ/ *n.* [C] OLD-FASHIONED someone who pays to live in a room or rooms in someone else's house

lodg·ing /ˈlɑdʒɪŋ/ *n.* [C,U] a place to stay: *The tourist office will send you information on lodging.*

lo·ess /ˈloʊəs, lɛs/ *n.* [U] EARTH SCIENCE a type of soil consisting of sand, clay, MINERALS, and other materials pressed loosely together. Loess is carried by the wind and is found especially in northern China and the central parts of the northern U.S.

Loewe /loʊ/, **Fred·erick** /ˈfrɛdrɪk/ (1904–1988) a U.S. COMPOSER famous for writing MUSICALS with Alan Jay Lerner

loft¹ /lɔft/ *n.* [C] **1 a)** a raised area above the main part of a room, usually used for sleeping **b)** an apartment with this type of loft **2** a space above a business, factory etc. that was once used for storing goods, but has been changed into living space or work space for artists: *Marris lives in a loft in lower Manhattan.* **3** a raised area in a BARN used for storing HAY or other crops: *a hay loft* **4** the raised place in a church where the ORGAN or CHOIR is: *the choir loft* **5** a set of CAGES used to keep PIGEONS in [**Origin:** 900–1000 Old Norse *lopt* **air, upstairs room**]

loft² *v.* [T] to hit, kick, or throw a ball in a high gentle curve, especially in some sports such as GOLF

loft·y /ˈlɔfti/ *adj. comparative* **loftier**, *superlative* **loftiest** **1** lofty ideas, beliefs, attitudes etc. show high standards or high moral qualities: *lofty ideals of equality and social justice* **2** LITERARY lofty mountains, buildings etc. are very high **3** DISAPPROVING seeming to think you are better than other people, or showing this quality —**loftily** *adv.*

log¹ /lɔg, lɑg/ *n.* [C] **1** a thick piece of wood cut from a tree: *Can you put another log on the fire?* **2** also **log book** an official recorded or written record of something, especially a trip in a ship or airplane: *The captain always* ***keeps a log.*** **3** MATH a LOGARITHM → see also **it's as easy as falling off a log** at EASY¹ (15), **sleep like a log** at SLEEP¹ (2)

log² *v.* **logged, logging** **1** [T] to make an official record of events, facts etc.: *All phone calls are logged.* **2** [T] to travel a particular distance or to work for a particular length of time, especially in an airplane or ship: *The pilot had logged over 1,200 hours of flying time.* **3** [I,T] to cut down large numbers of trees to be sold

log in/on *phr. v.* to enter a computer system by typing (TYPE) a special word or giving it a particular command: *You have to log in with your password.*

log into sth *phr. v.* to enter a computer system by typing (TYPE) a special word or giving it a particular command

log off/out *phr. v.* to stop using a computer system by giving it a particular command or typing (TYPE) a special word: *Don't forget to log off when you're done.*

-log /lɔg, lɑg/ *suffix* [in nouns] something that is written or spoken: *a sportswear catalog* (=a book with pictures and information) → see also -LOGUE

Lo·gan, Mount /ˈloʊgən/ the highest mountain in Canada

lo·gan·ber·ry /ˈloʊgənˌbɛri/ *n. plural* **loganberries** [C] a soft dark red berry, similar to a RASPBERRY [**Origin:** 1800–1900 James H. *Logan* (1841–1928), U.S. lawyer who developed it + *berry*]

log·a·rithm /ˈlɑgəˌrɪðəm/ also **log** *n.* [C] MATH the number of times a number must be multiplied by itself to equal another number

log·a·rith·mic func·tion /ˌlɑgərɪðmɪk ˈfʌŋkʃən/ *n.* [C] MATH a mathematical FUNCTION that involves a logarithm, and is the INVERSE of an EXPONENTIAL FUNCTION

ˈlog book *n.* [C] a LOG

ˌlog ˈcabin *n.* [C] a small house made of LOGS

log·ger /ˈlɔgɚ, ˈlɑ-/ *n.* [C] someone whose job is to cut down trees

log·ger·heads /ˈlɔgɚˌhɛdz, ˈlɑ-/ *n.* **be at loggerheads** if two people are at loggerheads they disagree very strongly with each other about something: **+over** *Officials are at loggerheads over energy policy.* [**Origin:** 1800–1900 *loggerhead* **stupid person, large head, type of heavy tool** (16–20 centuries), from *logger* **block of wood** (16–18 centuries) + *head*]

log·ging /ˈlɔgɪŋ/ *n.* [U] the work of cutting down trees in a forest: *the logging industry*

log·ic /ˈlɑdʒɪk/ Ac *n.* **1** [singular, U] a set of sensible and correct reasons, or reasonable thinking: *It's easy to understand their logic.* | **+of** *the logic of his argument* | **+in/to** *There is a certain logic in their approach to the problem.* | **+behind** *We just don't see the logic behind the decision.* **2** [U] the science or study of careful REASONING using formal methods **3** [U] TECHNICAL a set of choices that a computer uses to solve a problem → see also FUZZY LOGIC [**Origin:** 1300–1400 French *logique*, from Latin *logica*, from Greek *logos* **speech, word, reason**]

log·i·cal /ˈlɑdʒɪkəl/ Ac *adj.* **1** seeming reasonable and sensible OPP **illogical**: *a logical explanation* | *Taking the job seemed like **the logical thing to do** at the time.* **2** good at thinking in a very careful, clear, and organized way OPP **illogical**: *Joe's always very logical.* **3** using a series of connected steps to form an opinion, argument, or decision, in which if one thing is true, then another thing is therefore true: *a logical error* | **a logical step/conclusion/extension etc.** *The next logical step would be to open your own business.* —**logically** /-kli/ *adv.*

lo·gi·cian /loʊˈdʒɪʃən/ Ac *n.* [C] someone who studies or is skilled in logic

-logist /lədʒɪst/ *suffix* [in nouns] someone who studies or does work in a particular type of science: *a biologist* (=who studies biology) | *a genealogist* (=who studies the history of families) → see also -OLOGIST

lo·gis·tics /loʊˈdʒɪstɪks, lə-/ *n.* **1 the logistics (of doing sth)** the practical arrangements that are needed in order to make a plan or activity successful: *The logistics of traveling with small children involve making frequent stops.* **2** [U] the study or skill of moving soldiers, supplying them with food etc. —**logistical** also **logistic** *adj.* —**logistically** /-kli/ *adv.*

log·jam /ˈlɔgdʒæm/ *n.* [C] **1** a lot of problems that are preventing something from being done: *If we don't **break the** budget **logjam** soon* (=solve the problems), *Congress won't accomplish anything this session.* **2** a tightly packed mass of floating LOGS on a river

lo·go /ˈloʊgoʊ/ *n. plural* **logos** [C] a small design or way of writing a name that is the official sign of a company or organization

log·roll·ing /ˈlɔgˌroʊlɪŋ/ *n.* [U] **1** POLITICS the practice in the U.S. Congress of helping a member to pass a BILL, so that they will do the same for you later **2** INFORMAL the practice of praising or helping someone, so that they will do the same for you later **3** a sport in which two people stand on a LOG floating on water and roll it, each person trying to make the other fall off

-logue /lɑg, lɔg/ *suffix* [in nouns] something that is written or spoken: *a monologue* (=speech by one person) | *the book's prologue* (=the introduction to it)

-logy /lədʒi/ *suffix* [in nouns] a spelling of -OLOGY used if there is already a sound like "a" or "o" before this SUFFIX: *mineralogy* (=the study of minerals) | *geology* (=the study of rocks and the Earth)

loin /lɔɪn/ *n.* **1 loins** [plural] LITERARY the part of your body below your waist and above your legs, which includes your sexual organs **2** [C,U] a piece of meat from the lower part of an animal's back → see also **the fruit of sb's loins** at FRUIT[1] (5), **gird (up) your loins** at GIRD (2)

loin·cloth /ˈlɔɪnklɔθ/ *n.* [C] a piece of cloth that men in some hot countries wear around their loins

Loire, the /lwɑr/ a river in central France that flows into the Bay of Biscay

loi·ter /ˈlɔɪtɚ/ *v.* [I] **1** to stand or wait somewhere, especially in a public place, without any clear reason: **+in/around etc.** *Teens were loitering in the parking lot.* **2** to move or do something slowly, or to keep stopping when you should keep moving: **+over** *No one has time to loiter over a meal these days.* —**loiterer** *n.* [C]

loi·ter·ing /ˈlɔɪtərɪŋ/ *n.* [U] the crime of staying in a place for a long time without having any reason to be there, so that it seems as if you are going to do something illegal

LOL, lol a written abbreviation of "laughing out loud," used by people communicating in EMAIL, in CHAT ROOMS on the Internet, etc. to say that they are laughing at something that someone else has written

loll /lɑl/ *v.* **1** [I] also **loll around** to sit or lie in a very lazy and relaxed way: *He lolled around in the Florida sunshine.* **2** [I,T] if your head or tongue lolls or if you loll your head, you allow it to hang in a relaxed uncontrolled way

lol·li·pop, lollypop /ˈlɑliˌpɑp/ *n.* [C] a hard candy made of boiled sugar on the end of a stick

lol·lop /ˈlɑləp/ *v.* [I + around/across/about] to run with long awkward steps

lol·ly·gag /ˈlɑliˌgæg/ *v.* [I] INFORMAL to waste time, or move or work very slowly: *Quit lollygagging and get back to work!*

lol·ly·pop /ˈlɑliˌpɑp/ another spelling of LOLLIPOP

Lom·bar·di /ləmˈbɑrdi/, **Vince** /vɪns/ (1913–1970) a U.S. COACH whose team won the first two Super Bowls in 1967 and 1968

Lo·mé /loʊˈmeɪ/ the capital and largest city of Togo

Lon·don /ˈlʌndən/ the capital and largest city of the U.K.

London, Jack /dʒæk/ (1876–1916) a U.S. writer of adventure NOVELS

Jack London

ˈLondon broil *n.* [C,U] BEEF that is cooked under direct heat and cut into thin pieces

lone /loʊn/ *adj.* [only before noun] LITERARY being the only person or thing in a place, or the only person or thing that does something: *the lone "no" vote* | *A lone figure came toward me.* [**Origin:** 1300–1400 *alone*] → see Word Choice box at ALONE

lone·ly /ˈloʊnli/ *adj. comparative* **lonelier**, *superlative* **loneliest** **1** unhappy because you are alone and feel that you do not have anyone to talk to, or making you feel this way SYN **lonesome**: *She felt lonely with all her friends gone.* | *a lonely childhood* **2** ESPECIALLY LITERARY a lonely place is a long way from where people live and very few people go there SYN **lonesome**: *a lonely stretch of highway* —**loneliness** *n.* [U] → see also ALONE (5) → see Word Choice box at ALONE

ˌlonely ˈhearts *n.* **a lonely hearts club/page/column** a club or an advertisement page of a newspaper that is used by people who want to meet a romantic partner

lon·er /ˈloʊnɚ/ *n.* [C] someone who prefers to be alone or someone who has no friends

lone·some¹ /ˈloʊnsəm/ *adj.* **1** very unhappy because you are alone or have no friends, or making you feel this way SYN **lonely**: *Beth is lonesome without the kids around.* | *a lonesome song* **2** a lonesome place is a long way from where people live and very few people go there SYN **lonely**: *a lonesome patch of desert* → see Word Choice box at ALONE

lonesome² *n.* **on/by your lonesome** INFORMAL alone SYN **on your own**: *Are you by your lonesome this weekend?*

ˌlone ˈwolf *n.* [C] a LONER

long¹ /lɔŋ/ S1 W1 *adj.*
1 GREAT LENGTH/DISTANCE measuring a great length or distance, or a greater length or distance than usual, from one end to the other OPP **short**: *long hair* | *a long line of people* | *She has long legs.* | **a long walk/trip/drive etc.** *a long drive in the country* | *Springfield is* ***a long way from*** *Chicago.* ►see THESAURUS box at **hair**
2 LARGE AMOUNT OF TIME continuing for a large amount of time, or for a larger amount of time than usual OPP **short**: *The meeting was too long.* | *a long illness* | *She's been gone* ***a long time.*** | *Writing a novel* ***takes a long time.*** | *It took me* ***the longest time*** (=a very long time) *to figure out how to open the windows.* | *I can't wait for the days to start* ***getting longer.***

THESAURUS

lengthy/protracted continuing for a long time, often too long: *protracted negotiations*
interminable very long and boring: *an interminable lecture*
long-drawn-out continuing for a longer time than is wanted or necessary: *a long-drawn-out explanation*
endless seeming never to end: *endless discussions about politics*
marathon continuing for a long time and needing a lot of energy, patience, or determination: *a marathon practice session*
lasting/enduring strong enough, great enough, or good enough to continue for a very long time: *I wanted a lasting relationship.*

3 A PARTICULAR LENGTH/TIME used for asking about a particular length, distance, or period of time: *The rope is not quite long enough.* | ***How long*** *is the movie?* | **two hours/three inches/12 miles etc. long** *The sofa is six feet long.*
4 BOOK/LIST/NAME ETC. containing a lot of words, letters, ITEMS, or pages OPP **short**: *a long novel* | *He has a long last name that nobody can pronounce.*
5 SEEMING LONG INFORMAL seeming to continue for a longer time or distance than is usual, especially because you are bored, tired etc.: *It's been* ***a long day.***
6 long hours a) if you work long hours, you work for more time than is usual: *The worst thing about this job is the long hours.* **b)** a large amount of time: *He spent long hours just thinking.*
7 a long weekend three or more days, including Saturday and Sunday, when you do not have to go to work or school
8 in the long run when something is finished, or at a later time: *All our hard work will be worth it in the long run.* → see also IN THE SHORT RUN
9 CLOTHING long dresses, pants, SLEEVES etc. cover all of your arms or legs OPP **short**: *a long ballgown*
10 at long last after a long period of time SYN **finally**: *At long last, change may be coming.*
11 (to make a) long story short SPOKEN said when you want to finish a story quickly: *To make a long story short, I didn't get the job.*
12 it's a long story SPOKEN used for saying that something will take a long time to explain: *It's a long story – I'll tell you later.*
13 long time, no see SPOKEN used to say hello when you have not seen someone for a long time
14 long odds if there are long ODDS against something happening, it is very unlikely that it will happen
15 take the long view (of sth) to think about the effect that something will have in the future rather than what happens now
16 have come a long way to have developed or changed a lot: *Psychiatry has come a long way since the 1920s.*
17 be a long way from (doing) sth to be very different from what is true or very different from a particular level of development: *We're still a long way from making a decision.*
18 go a long way toward doing sth to help greatly in achieving something: *Your contributions will go a long way toward helping children in need.*
19 a long face an expression on someone's face that shows they are unhappy or worried
20 not long for this world likely to die or stop existing soon: *The old corner drugstore is not long for this world.*
21 a long memory an ability to remember things that happened a long time ago
22 the long arm of sth WRITTEN the power and influence of someone or something in authority, especially the power to catch and punish someone: *He won't escape the long arm of the law.*
23 be long on sth to have a lot of a particular quality or feature: *The candidate is long on promises and short on action.*
24 VOWEL ENG. LANG. ARTS a long vowel in a word is pronounced for a longer time than a short vowel with the same sound, or it is pronounced as part of a DIPHTHONG
25 BALL in sports, a long ball is one that travels a long distance
26 long in the tooth INFORMAL too old: *She's a little long in tooth to be wearing miniskirts.*
[**Origin:** Old English *long, lang*] → see also **as long as your arm** at ARM¹ (10), **a long/short haul** at HAUL² (2), **a little (of sth) goes a long way** at LITTLE² (4), LONG SHOT, **a hard/good/close/long etc. look (at sth)** at LOOK² (2), **in the long/short/near etc. term** at TERM¹ (7), **have a (long) way to go** at WAY¹ (33)

long² S1 W1 *adv.* **1** for a long time: *I haven't been waiting long.* | *The peaceful atmosphere* ***didn't last long.*** | *It* ***didn't take*** *him* ***long*** *to solve the problem.* **2** used for asking and talking about particular amounts of time: ***How long*** *were they here?* | *It* ***took*** *me* ***longer*** *to finish than I thought.* | *We'll stay* ***as long as*** *you want.* **3** much earlier or later than a particular point in time: *We met again* ***long after*** *she had gotten married.* | *My grandfather died* ***long before*** *I was born.* | *Life was different* ***long ago.*** | ***It wasn't long before*** (=a short time later) *everyone was laughing and having a good time.* **4 all day/year/summer etc. long** during all of the day, year etc. **5 as/so long as a)** used to say that one thing can happen or be true only if another thing happens or is true: *You can go as long as you're home for dinner.* **b)** used to say one thing can continue happening for the same amount of time that another thing is happening or is true: *Pam stayed awake as long as she could.* **c)** used to say that because one thing is true, something else can or should happen or be true: *As long as you're just sitting there, come help me with the groceries.* **6 no longer** also **not any longer** FORMAL used when something used to happen or exist in the past but does not happen or exist now: *The company is no longer in business.* **7 so long** SPOKEN goodbye **8 sb/sth won't be long** SPOKEN used to say that someone or something will be ready, will be back, will happen etc. soon: *Wait here. I won't be long.* | *Dinner won't be long – we'll eat in five minutes.* **9 long since** if

L

something has long since happened, it happened a long time ago: *I've long since stopped caring about him.* **10 long live sb/sth** used to show support for a person, idea, principle, or nation: *Long live the King!*

long[3] *n.* **1 for long** [usually in questions and negatives] for a long time: *Have you known the Garretts for very long?* | *She's smiling now, but **not for long*** (=she'll soon stop). **2 before long** soon: *The school year will be over before long.* **3 the long and (the) short of it** the most important part or main idea of something: *The long and the short of it is, he doesn't work hard enough.* **4** used in the sizes of clothing for men who are taller than average: **38/42/44 etc. long** *I think Jim wears a 44 long.*

long[4] *v.* [I] FORMAL to want something very much, especially when it seems unlikely to happen soon: **+for** *We longed for a bed after several days of camping.* | **long to do/have sth** *Kyoto is a city I have always longed to visit.* —**longed-for** *adj.* [only before noun] → see also LONGING, LONGINGLY

long. the written abbreviation of LONGITUDE

ˌlong-aˈwaited *adj.* [only before noun] a long-awaited event, moment etc. is one that you have been waiting for a long time: *the long-awaited sequel*

long·bow /ˈlɔŋboʊ/ *n.* [C] a large BOW made from a long thin curved piece of wood, used in the past for hunting or fighting

ˈlong-day ˌplant *n.* [C] BIOLOGY a plant that produces flowers during the times of the year when the light from the sun shines for many hours each day → see also SHORT-DAY PLANT

ˈlong-ˌdistance *adj.* [only before noun] **1** traveling over a long distance: *a long-distance flight* | *long-distance truck drivers* **2** relating to communication, especially telephone calls, between people who are in places which are far away from each other → see also LOCAL CALL: *a long-distance phone call* **3** happening between people in places which are far away from each other: *a long-distance relationship* —**ˌlong-ˈdistance** *adv.*

ˌlong diˈvision *n.* [C,U] MATH a method of dividing one large number by another

ˌlong-drawn-ˈout *adj.* [only before noun] continuing for a longer time than necessary: *a long-drawn-out court battle*

lon·gev·i·ty /lɑnˈdʒɛvət̬i, lɔn-/ *n.* [U] **1** FORMAL long life: *The inhabitants enjoy good health and longevity.* **2** TECHNICAL the length of a person or animal's life

ˌlong-exˈpected *adj.* [only before noun] a long-expected event, moment etc. is one that you have been expecting for a long time: *a long-expected announcement*

Long·fel·low /ˈlɔŋˌfɛloʊ/, **Hen·ry Wads·worth** /ˈhɛnri ˈwɑdzwɚθ/ (1807–1882) a U.S. poet

long·hair /ˈlɔŋhɛr/ *n.* [C] INFORMAL someone with long hair, especially a HIPPIE

long·hand /ˈlɔŋhænd/ *n.* [U] writing full words by hand rather than using a machine such as a computer → see also SHORTHAND

ˈlong-haul *adj.* a long-haul aircraft or flight goes a very long distance without stopping OPP **short-haul** → see also **the long/short haul** at HAUL[2] (2)

long·horn /ˈlɔŋhɔrn/ *n.* **1** [C] BIOLOGY a type of cow with long horns that is raised for meat **2** [U] a type of CHEDDAR cheese

long·house /ˈlɔŋhaʊs/ *n.* [C] a type of house, about 100 feet long, that was used by some Native American tribes

long·ing /ˈlɔŋɪŋ/ *n.* [singular, U] a strong feeling of wanting something or someone: **+for** *a longing for home*

long·ing·ly /ˈlɔŋɪŋli/ *adv.* in a way that shows that you want someone or something very much: *Jack looked longingly at the cookies.* —**longing** *adj.*

long·ish /ˈlɔŋɪʃ/ *adj.* INFORMAL fairly long: *longish red hair*

ˈLong ˌIsland an island in the U.S. that contains the New York City BOROUGHS of Queens and Brooklyn, and many other towns

lon·gi·tude /ˈlɑndʒəˌtud/ *n.* [C,U] a position on the Earth that is measured in degrees east or west of a MERIDIAN (=an imaginary line drawn from the top of the Earth to the bottom) → see also LATITUDE: *The town is at longitude 21° east.* → see picture at GLOBE

lon·gi·tu·di·nal /ˌlɑndʒəˈtudn-əl◂/ *adj.* **1** FORMAL relating to the development of something over a period of time: *a longitudinal study of unemployed workers* **2** going from top to bottom, not across: *longitudinal muscles* **3** TECHNICAL measured according to longitude —**longitudinally** *adv.*

ˈlong johns *n.* [plural] warm underwear that covers your legs

ˈlong jump *n.* **the long jump** a sport in which each competitor tries to jump as far as possible —**long jumper** *n.* [C]

ˌlong-ˈlasting *adj.* existing or continuing to work for a long time: *The impact of divorce on children can be long-lasting.* | *long-lasting batteries*

ˌlong-ˈlife *adj.* long-life batteries (BATTERY), LIGHT BULBS etc. are made so that they continue working for a long time

long-lived /ˌlɔŋ ˈlɪvd◂/ *adj.* living or existing a long time OPP **short-lived**: *the band's long-lived appeal*

ˌlong-ˈlost *adj.* [only before noun] lost or not seen for a long time: *long-lost treasures* | *a long-lost uncle*

ˌLong ˈMarch, the HISTORY the 6,000-mile (9,660-kilometer) march of the Chinese COMMUNISTS from southeastern China to northwestern China in 1934–35, during which Mao Zedong became leader of the Communist Party

ˌlong-playing ˈrecord *n.* [C] an LP

ˌlong-ˈrange *adj.* [usually before noun] **1** relating to a time that continues far into the future: *the city's long-range development plans* **2** a long-range missile, bomb etc. is able to hit something that is a long way away

ˌlong-ˈrunning *adj.* [usually before noun] a long-running battle, show etc. has been happening for a long time: *a long-running FBI investigation*

long·shore·man /ˌlɔŋˈʃɔrmən, ˈlɔŋˌʃɔrmən/ *n.* [C] someone whose job is to load and unload ships at a DOCK

ˈlong shot *n.* [C] INFORMAL **1** someone or something with very little chance of success: *Murphy is a long shot for the position.* **2 not by a long shot** not at all, or not nearly: *This isn't over – not by a long shot.*

ˌlong-ˈstanding *adj.* having continued or existed for a long time: *a long-standing agreement between the two countries*

ˌlong-ˈsuffering *adj.* [usually before noun] patient in spite of problems, other people's annoying behavior, or unhappiness: *a long-suffering wife*

ˈlong-term W2 *adj., adv.* continuing for a long period of time into the future, or relating to what will happen in the distant future OPP **short-term**: *long-term investments* | *People need to think long-term.* → see also **in the long/short/near etc. term** at TERM[1] (7)

long·time, long-time /ˈlɔŋtaɪm/ *adj.* [only before noun] having existed or continued to be a particular thing for a long time: *a longtime friend of the family*

ˈlong ˌwave WRITTEN ABBREVIATION **LW** *n.* [U] radio broadcasting or receiving on waves of 1,000 meters or more in length → see also MEDIUM WAVE

long·ways /ˈlɔŋweɪz/ *adv.* LONGWISE

ˌlong-ˈwearing *adj.* long-wearing clothes, shoes etc. remain in good condition for a long time even when they are used a lot

ˌlong-ˈwinded *adj.* continuing to talk for too long or using too many words in a way that is boring: *long-winded politicians*

L

long·wise /ˈlɔŋwaɪz/ *adv.* in the direction of the longest side SYN **lengthwise**: *Cut the cucumber in half longwise.*

loo·fah, loofa /ˈlufə/ *n.* [C] a rough type of SPONGE for washing your body, made from the dried inner part of a tropical fruit

loo·gie /ˈlugi/ *n.* [C] SLANG PHLEGM (=thick sticky liquid from your throat) that you SPIT out of your mouth → see also **hawk a loogie** at HAWK² (2)

look¹ /lʊk/ S1 W1 *v.*

1 SEE [I] to deliberately turn your eyes so that you can see something: *He took a cookie when she wasn't looking.* | **+at** *She turned to look at me.* | **+through/toward/across etc.** *The children looked sadly through the locked gates.* | **look away/up/down etc.** *She smiled sadly then looked away.*

THESAURUS

glance to look at someone or something for a short time and then look quickly away: *Kevin glanced at the clock.*
peek/peep to quickly look at something, especially something you are not supposed to see: *I caught him peeking around the corner.*
peer to look very carefully, especially because you cannot see something well: *Hansen peered through the windshield at the street signs.*
stare to look at someone or something for a long time, especially without blinking your eyes: *She was staring out the window.*
gaze to look at someone or something for a long time, often without realizing that you are doing it: *He gazed on the baby as she slept.*
gape to look at something for a long time, usually with your mouth open, because you are very shocked or surprised: *She backed away as the children gaped at her.*
regard FORMAL to look at someone or something, especially in a particular way: *He regarded her steadily.*

2 SEARCH [I] to try and find someone or something that is hidden or lost, using your eyes: *I've looked everywhere, but I can't find my gloves.* | *Did you look under the bed?* | **+for** *Could you help me look for my notebook?*

THESAURUS

search to look carefully for someone or something: *Rescue parties are searching for the missing boys.*
hunt for sb/sth to look in a lot of places for someone or something: *I always seem to be hunting for my keys.*
try to find sb/sth to look for someone or something, especially when this is difficult: *He's been trying to find a job for several months.*
seek FORMAL to try to find someone or something: *teenagers seeking information about careers*
go through sth to examine something very thoroughly when looking for something: *Security officers went through our bags.*
have a look for sb/sth SPOKEN to look quickly for someone or something: *I don't think we carry that book, but let me have a look.*

3 SEEM [linking verb] to seem to be something, especially by having a particular appearance: *You look tired.* | *Do these jeans make me look fat?* | **+like** *I don't look much like my sister.* | **look as if/though** *This car looks as if it could cost more.* | *With all the commotion **it looked as if** the circus had come to town.* ►see THESAURUS box at **seem**
4 look over your shoulder to be nervous or worried that something bad is going to happen to you: *Since half of the staff was laid off, we're all looking over our shoulders.*
5 be looking to do sth INFORMAL to be planning or expecting to do something: *We're not just looking to make money.*
6 look before you leap used to say that it is wise to think about possible dangers or difficulties before doing something
7 look the other way a) to deliberately ignore a problem or something bad that someone else is doing: *Politicians have looked the other way while children go hungry.* **b)** to turn your head and look in the opposite direction, especially to avoid looking at someone or something
8 look no further used for telling someone that something is available that is exactly what they have been trying to find: *If you're looking for a good family car, look no further.*

SPOKEN PHRASES

9 look a) used to tell someone to look at something that you think is interesting, surprising etc.: *Look! There's a bluejay!* | **+at** *Look at me, Mommy!* | **look what/how/where etc.** *Look how tall he's gotten!* **b)** said to get someone's attention so that you can tell them something, or to emphasize what you are saying when you are annoyed: *Look, I'm very serious about this.*
10 (I'm/We're) just looking used when you are in a store, to say that you are only looking at things, and do not intend to buy anything now: *"Do you need help with anything?" "No thanks. We're just looking."*
11 it looks like... used to say that it is likely that someone will do something or something will happen: *If this rain keeps up, it looks like we'll have to cancel the picnic.*
12 look sb in the eye/face to look directly at someone when you are speaking to them, especially to show that you are not afraid of them or that you are telling the truth: *Look me in the eye and tell me you didn't take that money.*
13 look who's here! said when someone arrives without being expected
14 don't look now used when you see someone you want to avoid: *Don't look now – here comes Kristen.*
15 look what you've done! used to angrily tell someone to look at the result of a mistake they have made or something bad they have done: *Now look what you've done! You'll have to clean it up.*
16 lookin' good! SLANG used to tell someone that they look attractive
17 not be looking yourself to appear tired, unhappy, sick etc., when you are not this way usually: *Are you okay? You haven't been looking yourself lately.*
18 look what the cat dragged in! said when someone comes into a room or building late or in a worse than normal condition
19 look here OLD-FASHIONED used to get someone's attention in order to tell them something, especially when you are annoyed with them

20 look sb up and down to look at someone, examining them carefully from their head to their feet, as if you are judging their appearance
21 look down your nose at sb/sth INFORMAL to think that you are better than someone else or that something is not very good: *People in the club look down their noses at people like us.*
22 FACE A DIRECTION [I always + adv./prep.] if a building looks in a particular direction, it faces that direction SYN **face**: *Most of the rooms look south.*
[**Origin:** Old English *locian*] → see also, **don't/never look a gift horse in the mouth** at GIFT¹ (5), **look kindly on/upon sb/sth** at KINDLY¹ (4), OVERLOOK¹

look after *phr. v.* **1 look after sb** to take care of someone by helping them, giving them what they need, or keeping them safe SYN **take care of**: *Who looks after the kids while you're at work?* | **look after yourself** *She's old enough to look after herself.* **2 look after sth** to be responsible for dealing with something and making sure nothing bad happens to it: *Clayton has a manager who **looks after** his business **interests**.*

look ahead *phr. v.* to plan future situations, events etc., or to think about the future: **+to** *The company is looking ahead to next year.*

look around *phr. v.* **1 look around sth** to look at what is in a place such as a building, store, town etc.,

L

especially when you are walking: *We have about three hours to look around the downtown.* **2** to search for something: **+for** *I began to look around for a place to live.*

look at *phr. v.* **1 look at sth** to read something quickly, but not thoroughly: *I haven't had a chance to look at the report yet.* **2 look at sth** to examine something, especially in order to try to find out what is wrong with it: *You should get the doctor to look at that cut.* **3 look at sth** to study and consider something, especially in order to decide what to do: *Wildlife experts are looking at ways to protect the animals.* **4 look at sb/sth** to have a particular opinion about someone or something or consider them in a particular way: *The incident changed the way I looked at my parents.* **5 look at sb/sth** SPOKEN **a)** used to show surprise at how good someone or something looks: *Look at you! You're filthy!* **b)** used to show that you do not like the way someone or something looks or is behaving: *Look at him, walking around as if he owns the place!* **c)** used to give an example of something: *Look at Eric. He didn't go to college, and he's doing all right.* **6 not much to look at** INFORMAL if someone is not much to look at, they are not attractive

look back *phr. v.* **1** to think about something that happened in the past: **+on/to/at** *The program looks back at the events leading up to the war.* | ***Looking back on it,*** *I'm glad I didn't get the job.* **2 never look back** to not think about what has happened in the past, especially because you are very successful and are thinking about the future: *He left his acting acreer and never looked back.*

look down on sb/sth *phr. v.* to think that you are better than someone else or that something is not very good: *Many looked down on the new immigrants.*

look for sb/sth *phr. v.* **1** to try to find someone or something by looking in several places or asking several people: *Brad was looking for you last night.* **2** to want a particular type of person or thing for a particular purpose: *How long have you been looking for a job?* | *Leslie, you're* ***just the person I'm looking for****! Come help me with this.* **3 be looking for trouble** INFORMAL to be behaving in a way that makes it likely that problems will happen

look forward to sth *phr. v.* to be excited and pleased about something that is going to happen: *I'm really looking forward to our vacation.* | **look forward to doing sth** *We're looking forward to meeting Don.*

L

look in *phr. v.* INFORMAL to make a short visit to someone, while you are going somewhere else, especially if they are sick or need help: **+on** *I promised to look in on Dad.*

look into sth *phr. v.* **1** to try to find out the truth about a problem, crime etc. in order to solve it SYN **investigate**: *A special investigator will look into the murders.* **2** to try to find out more information about something: *That sounds like a good idea. I'll look into it.*

look on *phr. v.* **1** to watch something happening, without being involved in it or trying to stop it: *The crowd looked on as the two men fought.* → see also ONLOOKER **2 look on/upon sth** to consider something in a particular way, or as a particular thing: **look on/upon sth as sth** *My family looks on divorce as a sin.* | **look on/upon sth with sth** *Townspeople looked upon them with contempt.*

look out *phr. v.* **look out!** used to tell someone to pay attention or warn them that they are in danger: *Look out! You almost hit that cat!*

look out for sb/sth *phr. v.* **1** to pay attention so that you will notice someone or something, or you will be prepared for anything dangerous that might happen: *In this region, you have to look out for snakes.* **2** to try to protect someone or something from anything bad that might happen, or to try to give them advantages: *My older brother always looked out for me.* **3 look out for yourself** also **look out for number one** to think only about what will bring you an advantage, and not think about other people

look out on sth *phr. v.* to face a particular direction, so that you can see things in that direction: *My apartment window looks out on the park.*

look sth/sb ↔ **over** *phr. v.* to examine something quickly, without paying much attention to detail: *Can you look this letter over before I send it?*

look through *phr. v.* **1 look through sth** to look for something among a pile of papers, in a drawer, in someone's pockets etc.: *I caught my mother looking through my stuff.* **2 look through sth** to read something quickly and not very carefully: *I'll look through my notes again.* **3 look through sb** to not notice someone or pretend that you do not see them: *I said hello to Paige, but she just* ***looked right through*** *me.*

look to/toward sb/sth *phr. v.* **1** to depend on someone to provide help, advice etc.: **+for** *Cities are looking to state governments for aid.* **2** to think about something in the future and plan for it, instead of thinking about the past: *The ballet company is looking toward the 21st century.*

look up *phr. v.* **1 look sth ↔ up** to try to find information in a book, on a computer etc.: *If you don't know the word, look it up in the dictionary.* **2** if a situation is looking up, it is improving: ***Things are looking up*** *for downtown businesses.* **3 look ↔ sb up** to visit someone you know, especially when you have come to the place where they live for a different reason: *If you ever get to Nashville, look me up.*

look up to sb *phr. v.* to admire or respect someone: *Kids need role models to look up to.*

look² S1 W1 *n.*

1 LOOKING AT STH [C usually singular] an act of looking at something: *Wow!* ***Take a look at*** *that moon. It's huge!* | **take a good/close look (at sb/sth)** *Take a good look at the picture.* | *I'm not sure. I didn't* ***get a look at*** *his face.* | ***Take a look around*** *and see if you like the place.*

2 CONSIDERING STH [C] an act of reading something quickly or considering it, especially in order to decide what to do: *Have you* ***taken a look at*** *my proposal yet?* | **a hard/good/close/long etc. look (at sth)** *We need to* ***take a long hard look*** *at how the office is organized.*

3 EXPRESSION [C] an expression that you make with your eyes or face to show how you feel: *Heather* ***gave*** *him* ***an*** *angry* ***look****.* | *She keeps* ***giving me dirty looks*** (=unfriendly looks).

4 APPEARANCE [C usually singular] the appearance of something or someone: *The blue walls give the room a cold look.* | *I* ***don't like the look of*** *those storm clouds.* | ***By the looks of*** *it, the furniture was very old.*

5 DESCRIPTION [C] a short explanation or description of something: **+at** *Here's a brief look at today's news.*

6 looks [plural] someone's physical attractiveness: *She was afraid of* ***losing*** *her* ***looks*** (=becoming less attractive). | *He gets his* ***good looks*** (=attractive appearance) *from his father.*

7 if looks could kill (sb would be dead) used to say that someone looked at someone else in a very angry way

8 STYLE [singular] a particular style in clothes, hair, furniture etc.: *He's trying for a '70s disco look.*

ˈlook-aˌlike, lookalike *n.* [C] INFORMAL someone who looks very similar to someone else, especially someone famous: *an Elvis look-alike*

look·er /ˈlʊkɚ/ *n.* [C] INFORMAL someone who is attractive, usually a woman

ˌlooker-ˈon *n. plural* **lookers-on** [C] an ONLOOKER

-looking /lʊkɪŋ/ *suffix* [in adjectives] having a particular type of appearance: **strange-looking/good-looking/smooth-looking etc.** *a funny-looking dog*

ˈlooking glass *n.* [C] OLD-FASHIONED a MIRROR

look·it /ˈlʊkɪt/ *interjection* NONSTANDARD **1** used to get someone's attention so that you can tell them something, especially when you are annoyed: *Lookit, there are only three of us, so we all have to help.* **2** used to tell someone to look at something that you think is interesting, surprising etc.

look·out /ˈlʊk-aʊt/ *n.* **1 be on the lookout for sth** to continuously watch a place or pay attention in order to find something you want or to be ready for problems or opportunities: *You've got to be on the lookout for snakes* *around here.* **2 keep a lookout** to keep watching carefully for something or someone, especially for danger: *Soldiers kept a lookout for enemy planes through the night.* **3** [C] someone whose duty is to watch carefully for something, especially danger **4** [C] a place for a lookout to watch from

ˌlook-'see *n.* [C] INFORMAL a quick look at something: *We moved in closer for a look-see.*

loom¹ /lum/ *v.* [I] **1** also **loom up** [always + adv./prep.] to appear as a large, unclear shape, especially in a threatening way: *The mountain loomed in front of us.* **2** if a problem or difficulty looms, it is likely to happen very soon: *Many economists warned that a crisis was looming.* **3 loom large** to seem important, worrying, and difficult to avoid: *Economic issues loomed large in the election.*

loom² *n.* [C] a frame or machine on which thread is woven into cloth

loon /lun/ *n.* [C] **1** BIOLOGY a large North American bird that eats fish and that makes a long wild sound **2** a silly or strange person → see also **crazy as a loon** at CRAZY¹ (8)

loon·y¹ /'luni/ *n. plural* **loonies** [C] **1** SPOKEN someone who behaves in a crazy or silly way ▸see THESAURUS box at crazy¹ **2** CANADIAN also **loonie** a Canadian one-dollar coin

loony² also **'loony tunes** *adj. comparative* **loonier**, *superlative* **looniest** INFORMAL silly, crazy, or strange: *a loony idea*

loop¹ /lup/ *n.* [C]
1 SHAPE OR LINE a shape like a curve or a circle made by a line curving back toward itself, or a piece of wire, string etc. that has this shape: *A loop of wire held the gate shut.* | ***belt loops*** (=cloth loops used for holding a belt on pants)
2 knock/throw sb for a loop INFORMAL to surprise and upset someone: *His response was so unexpected that it really threw me for a loop.*
3 be out of the loop to not be part of a group of people that makes decisions or gets information: *Being out of the loop is the biggest problem for someone working from home.*
4 in the loop part of a group of people that makes decisions or gets information: *Keep me in the loop as you make plans.*
5 COMPUTER COMPUTERS a set of operations in a computer PROGRAM that repeats continuously
6 FILM/TAPE a film or TAPE loop contains images or sounds that are repeated again and again
7 PLANE also **loop-the-loop** a pattern like a circle made by an airplane flying up, upside down, and then down

loop² *v.* **1** [I,T] to form a loop, or to make something into a loop: *A man in the next car was looping a tie around his neck.* **2** [I,T] to move in a curve that forms the shape of a loop, or to make something move in this way: *The space probe looped toward Jupiter.* **3 loop the loop** to fly an airplane in a loop

loop·hole /'luphoul/ *n.* [C] a small mistake in a law that makes it possible to avoid doing something that the law is supposed to make you do: *tax loopholes* [**Origin:** 1500–1600 *loop* **hole in a wall for shooting through** (14–19 centuries) + *hole*]

loop·y /'lupi/ *adj. comparative* **loopier**, *superlative* **loopiest** INFORMAL crazy or strange

loose¹ /lus/ S2 W3 *adj.*
1 NOT FASTENED not firmly attached or fastened in place: *a loose screw* | *One of Sean's front teeth is loose.* | *One of my buttons* ***came loose.***
2 NOT TIED TIGHTLY not tied or fastened very tightly: *My shoelaces are loose.* | *a loose knot*
3 CLOTHES loose clothes are big and do not fit your body tightly: *a loose sweatshirt* ▸see THESAURUS box at clothes
4 FREE free from being controlled or held in a CAGE, prison, or institution: *A 34-year-old inmate* ***broke loose*** *from the sheriff's office Saturday.* | *In 1882 pigs were* ***turned loose*** *on the streets of New York City to eat garbage.* | *Don't* ***let*** *your dog* ***loose*** *on the beach.*
5 NOT ATTACHED not tied together, fastened to anything else etc.: *loose papers* | *The boat* ***broke loose*** *from the dock.*
6 CLOTH woven in a way that is not tight, so that there are small holes between the threads: *linen cloth with a loose weave*
7 NOT EXACT [usually before noun] not exact or thoroughly done: *The title is a loose translation of the Korean original.* | *a loose interpretation of the law*
8 NOT CONTROLLED [only before noun] not strictly controlled or organized: *a loose group of local organizations*
9 loose change coins that you have in your bag or pocket
10 loose cannon someone who cannot be trusted because they say or do things you do not want them to
11 loose ends parts of something that have not been completed or correctly done: *His new movie will* ***tie up*** *some of the* ***loose ends*** *from the last one.*
12 cut loose INFORMAL to start enjoying yourself in a happy, noisy way after a period of controlled behavior: *I'm ready to cut loose and enjoy the weekend.*
13 let loose (sth) to relax and speak or behave in an uncontrolled way: *She let loose a string of four-letter words that shocked everyone.*
14 be at loose ends to have nothing to do
15 loose bowels/stools NOT TECHNICAL having a problem in which the waste from your BOWELS has too much liquid in it
16 turn sb loose on sth to allow someone to deal with something in the way they want to: *He had a lot of ability, so his boss decided to turn him loose on the project.*
17 turn sb loose on sb to get someone to argue, fight, criticize etc. someone else for you: *Shapiro turned his assistant loose on his critics.*
18 hang/stay loose SPOKEN used to tell someone to stay calm, or not to worry about something
19 TALK OLD-FASHIONED not careful about what you say or who is listening
20 IMMORAL OLD-FASHIONED behaving in a way that is considered to be sexually immoral: *a loose woman*
21 loose lips sink ships OLD-FASHIONED used to say that if you tell other people's secrets you will cause problems for them
[**Origin:** 1100–1200 Old Norse *lauss*] —**loosely** *adv.*: *A towel was loosely wrapped around his neck.* | *The film is loosely based on the novel.* —**looseness** *n.* [U]

L

loose² *v.* [T] **1** to untie someone or something, especially an animal SYN **release**: *Police fired tear gas and loosed police dogs.* **2** to make something bad or negative begin to happen SYN **unleash**: *The recent court case has loosed a number of racist attacks.* **3** to let a substance escape or flow out of something SYN **release** **4** LITERARY to shoot an ARROW, a bullet from a gun etc.

loose sth **on/upon** sb/sth *phr. v.* LITERARY to allow something dangerous or harmful to begin to affect a situation or other people: *A deadly disease had been loosed upon the public.*

loose³ *n.* **be on the loose** if a criminal or dangerous animal is on the loose, they have escaped from prison or from their CAGE

loose⁴ *adv.* NONSTANDARD loosely → see also **play fast and loose with sb/sth** at PLAY¹ (32)

ˌloose con'struction *n.* [singular] LAW the belief that the government can do anything that the Constitution does not forbid

ˌloose-'fitting *adj.* loose-fitting clothes are big and do not fit your body closely, so that they are comfortable

'loose-knit *adj.* [only before noun] a loose-knit group of people are not closely related to each other: *a loose-knit coalition of human rights groups*

loose-leaf /'luslif/ *adj.* [only before noun] having pages that can be put in and removed easily: *a loose-leaf binder*

loos·en /ˈluːsən/ *v.* **1** [I,T] to make something less tight or less firmly fastened, or to become less tight or less firmly fastened OPP **tighten**: *After dinner we all had to loosen our belts.* | *The screws in this shelf have loosened.* **2** [T] to make laws, rules etc. less strict SYN **relax** OPP **tighten**: *Congress has loosened some of the restrictions on immigration.* **3 loosen your grip/hold a)** to reduce the control or power you have over someone or something: **+on** *The government has loosened its hold on the media considerably.* **b)** to start holding someone less tightly than you were before: *He loosened his grip on David's arm.* **4 loosen sb's tongue** to make someone talk more than usual, especially about things they should not talk about: *The whiskey loosened his tongue.*

loosen up *phr. v.* **1 loosen sb ↔ up** to become more relaxed and feel less worried or serious, or make someone do this: *We used to fight a lot, but Dad has loosened up a little lately.* **2 loosen sth ↔ up** if your muscles loosen up, or if you loosen them up, they stop feeling stiff

loos·ey-goos·ey /ˌlusi ˈgusi/ *adj.* SPOKEN, INFORMAL very relaxed, informal, and not well organized

loot¹ /lut/ *v.* [I,T] to steal things, especially from stores or homes that have been left empty because of a war, a NATURAL DISASTER etc.: *Rioters looted stores and set fires.* —**looter** *n.* [C] —**looting** *n.* [U]

loot² *n.* [U] **1** INFORMAL goods or money that have been stolen **2** goods taken by soldiers from a place where they have won a battle **3** HUMOROUS things that you have bought or been given in large amounts: *Jodie came home from the mall with bags of loot.* **4** SPOKEN INFORMAL money

lop /lɑp/ *v.* **lopped, lopping** [T] to cut branches from a tree, especially with a single strong movement

lop sth **off** *phr. v.* **1** to cut a part of something off **2** to remove a particular amount from a price or charge: *The judge lopped $1.1 million off the $4.2 million award.*

lope /loʊp/ *v.* [I always + adv./prep.] to run easily with long steps: **+along/across/up etc.** *Karen loped up two flights of stairs.* —**lope** *n.* [singular]

ˌlop-ˈeared *adj.* a lop-eared animal, for example a lop-eared rabbit, has long ears that hang down instead of sticking up

L

lop·sid·ed /ˈlɑpˌsaɪdɪd/ *adj.* **1** having one side that is lower, larger, or heavier than the other: *a lopsided grin* **2** unequal or uneven: *a lopsided 10–0 win* (=one team won by a large amount)

lo·qua·cious /loʊˈkweɪʃəs/ *adj.* FORMAL liking to talk a lot, sometimes too much —**loquaciousness** also **loquacity** /loʊˈkwæsət̬i/ *n.* [U]

Lord /lɔrd/ *n.* **1** a title of God or Jesus Christ, used when praying to or talking about God: *Thank you, Lord, for your blessings.* | ***The Lord** helps and guides us.* | ***our Lord,** Jesus Christ* **2 the Lord's Day** Sunday, considered as the holy day of the Christian religion

SPOKEN PHRASES

3 Lord knows a) used to emphasize that something is true: *Lord knows I tried my best.* **b)** also **Lord only knows** used to say strongly that you do not know something: *Lord knows where I left my keys.* **4 (Good) Lord!/Oh Lord!** said when you are suddenly surprised, annoyed, or worried about something: *Good Lord, Tom! What are you doing?* **5 Lord willing** OLD-FASHIONED used to say that you hope nothing will prevent something from happening

lord¹ /lɔrd/ *n.* [C] **1** also **Lord** a man who has a particular position in the ARISTOCRACY, especially in Britain, or his title → see also LADY: *Lord Tennyson* **2** HISTORY a man in MEDIEVAL Europe who was very powerful and owned a lot of land: *the feudal lords* **3 sb's lord and master** HUMOROUS someone who must be obeyed because they have power over someone else [**Origin:** Old English *hlaford*, from *hlaf* **bread** + *weard* **keeper**]

lord² *v.* **lord it over sb** to behave in a way that shows you think you are better or more powerful than someone else: *He tries to lord it over the younger kids.*

lord·ly /ˈlɔrdli/ *adj.* **1** behaving in a way that shows you think you are better or more important than other people: *a lordly disdain* **2** very grand or impressive: *a lordly feast*

ˌLord's ˈPrayer *n.* **the Lord's Prayer** the most important prayer of the Christian religion

Lor·dy, lordy /ˈlɔrdi/ *interjection* SPOKEN, OLD-FASHIONED used when you are suddenly surprised, annoyed, or worried about something: *Lordy, look at that hat!*

lore /lɔr/ *n.* [U] knowledge or information about a subject, for example nature or magic, that is not written down but that one person tells to another person: *According to local lore, a the castle is haunted.*

lor·gnette /lɔrˈnyɛt/ *n.* [C] a pair of GLASSES with a long handle at the side that you hold in front of your eyes

lor·ry /ˈlɔri, ˈlɑri/ *n. plural* **lorries** [C] BRITISH a TRUCK

Los Al·a·mos /lɔs ˈæləmoʊs, lɑs-/ a town in the U.S. state of New Mexico where the first ATOM bomb and HYDROGEN BOMB were developed

Los An·ge·les /lɔs ˈændʒəlɪs, -liz/ the largest city in the U.S. state of California

lose /luz/ S1 W1 *v. past tense and past participle* **lost** /lɔst/

1 NOT HAVE ANYMORE [T] if you lose something, you stop having it, especially because it has been taken from you or destroyed OPP **gain**: *Michelle lost her job again.* | *Tim **lost everything** in the earthquake.*

2 CANNOT FIND [T] to be unable to find someone or something: *Stephen keeps losing his gloves.* | *Oh there you are – I thought I'd lost you.*

3 NOT WIN [I,T] to not win a game, argument, war etc. OPP **win**: *I'm not playing tennis with her any more – I always lose.* | *Noel lost the argument.* | **lose (sth) to/against sb** *The Vikings lost to the Packers 27–7.* | *We lost the game to Birmingham.* | **lose (sth) by sth** *Mr. Ewing lost by at least 39,000 votes.* | *Penn State lost the game by only one basket.*

4 QUALITY/ABILITY [T] to stop having a particular quality, belief, attitude, or ability either permanently or temporarily: *She's lost a lot of confidence* | *The driver **lost control of** the vehicle.* | *The kids were **losing interest** in the game.* | **lose your sight/hearing/memory** (=permanently lose the ability to see, hear, etc.) | **lose your voice/balance/footing** (=temporarily lose the ability to speak, balance your body etc.) | **lose your sense of time/direction/reality etc.** *It's easy to lose your sense of direction in the dark.* | *He was going to go talk to her, but he **lost his nerve*** (=stopped being confident). | ***Don't lose heart*** (=become disappointed and unhappy) – *you'll do better next time.* | *He **lost his head*** (=stopped being calm) *and in a state of panic started running.* | *I finally **lost patience with** her and yelled at her.* | *Her latest show proves that she hasn't **lost her** comic **touch*** (=lost her special ability). | **lose your temper/cool** (=to become angry)

5 MONEY [T] if you lose money, you do not get as much money back from your business, INVESTMENT etc. as you put into it: *Investors lost several million dollars.* | **lose (sth) on sth** *He lost the money on a game of blackjack.* | *If the project fails, the company **stands to lose*** (=risks losing) *millions.* | *I **lost the bet,** so I had to pay him.*

6 WEIGHT [T] if you lose weight, your body becomes lighter and you usually become thinner: *I need to lose 10 pounds before the wedding.* | *You look different. Have you **lost weight?***

7 DISADVANTAGE [I,T] to be in a situation in which you have a disadvantage: *You don't lose anything by asking a question.* | *Whatever the result is, we **can't lose*** (=we will have an advantage in any situation). | *You should apply for the job – you **have nothing to lose*** (=will not make the situation worse by trying).

8 lose sleep (over sth) to worry a lot about something: *It's a problem, but I wouldn't lose sleep over it.*

9 lose an arm/leg etc. to have an arm, leg etc. cut off

after an injury in an accident or in a war: *He lost his right arm in a motorcycle accident.*
10 lose sb sth to make someone stop having something that is important, or to make them not win a game, argument etc.: *Allegations of corruption lost Wilson the election.*
11 lose sb a) INFORMAL to confuse someone when you are trying to explain something to them: *You've lost me. Can you repeat that?* **b)** used to say that someone has died, especially when you do not want to upset anyone by saying it directly: *Fern lost her husband six years ago.* | *Oh, I didn't know she'd **lost the baby*** (=the baby died before being born). **c)** to escape from someone who is chasing or following you: *Whew! I think we lost him.* **d)** to stop being able to follow someone: *He tried to follow her but lost her in the crowd.*
12 lose your life to die: *Over 100 soldiers lost their lives.*
13 WASTE [T] to waste time or opportunities etc.: *We lose time whenever we make changes in the plan.* | *Sorry, you lost your chance.* | *Hurry – **there's no time to lose*** (=we have to be quick). | *Johnson **lost no time in** applying for the grant* (=she did it immediately).
14 lose touch (with sb/sth) a) to not speak to, write to, or see a friend or family member for a long time, so that you do not know where they are: *Over the years we just lost touch with each other.* **b)** if you lose touch with a situation or subject, you stop being involved in it and so you do not know about it or understand it: *A lot of producers have lost touch with what makes good music.* | *Sometimes I think Joe has **lost touch with reality**.*
15 lose track of sb/sth to stop paying attention to someone or something so that you do not know where they are or what is happening to them: *I've lost track of where Ian is living.* | *It's easy to **lose track of time*** (=forget to check the time) *when you're working hard.* → see also TRACK
16 lose count (of sth) a) to not be able to say how many of something there are, because there are too many: *I've lost count of the boyfriends she's had.* **b)** to forget the total while you are counting: *Is this the third or fourth game? I've lost count.*
17 lose it SPOKEN **a)** to suddenly start shouting, laughing, crying etc. a lot because you think something is very bad, funny, or wrong: *Brad must have said something bad, because she totally lost it.* **b)** to become crazy: *After her parents died, Ginny just seemed to lose it.*
18 lose sight of sb/sth a) to stop being able to see someone or something: *He lost sight of the car as it went around the curve.* **b)** to forget about the most important part of something you are doing: *We can't lose sight of our goals.*
19 lose your way/bearings a) to not know where you are or which direction you should go: *I completely lose my bearings when I go outside the city.* **b)** to not know what you should do or what you believe in: *When my wife left me, I lost my bearings for a while.*
20 lose your mind also **lose your marbles** to become crazy or to stop behaving in a sensible way: *What are you doing on the roof? Have you lost your mind?*
21 lose your heart to sb to start to love someone very much
22 CLOCK/WATCH [T] if a clock or watch loses time, it works too slowly [OPP] **gain**: *That clock loses about two minutes a day.*
23 sth loses sth in (the) translation used to say that something is not exactly the same when it is done in a new or different way or when it is said in a different language: *The joke loses something in the translation.*
24 lose yourself in sth to be so involved in something that you do not notice anything else: *The boy could lose himself in his imaginary world for hours.*
25 lose face to not be trusted or respected anymore, especially in a public situation, because of something you have done
26 lose altitude if an aircraft loses ALTITUDE it drops to a lower height in the sky
[**Origin:** Old English *losian* **to destroy or be destroyed, to lose**]

lose out *phr. v.* to not win or get something that would be an advantage to you, because someone else gets it instead: **lose out to sb** *Tierney lost out to Joan Crawford at the Oscars.* | **lose out on sth** *Hurry, or you'll lose out on the low interest rates.*

WORD CHOICE lose, miss, lost, missing, disappear
- Use **lose** if you cannot find something: *I lost my favorite pen.*
- Use **miss** if you do not attend a class, meeting etc. that you regularly go to or that you intended to go to: *You've been missing a lot of school lately.*
- Use **lost** to describe someone who does not know where they are: *We have a lost little boy at the customer service desk.*
- Use **missing** to describe someone or something that you have been looking for, especially when the situation is serious: *a missing Rembrandt* | *Police continue to search for the missing children.*
- Use **disappear** when the way in which someone or something has been lost seems very strange: *Five planes disappeared off the coast of Florida.* | *The seven-year-old girl disappeared on her way home from school* (But don't say: *the disappeared planes* or *the disappeared girl*).

los·er /ˈluzɚ/ *n.* [C] **1** someone who has lost a competition or game [OPP] **winner**: *My dad taught us to be **good losers*** (=someone who behaves well after losing). | **a bad/sore/poor loser** (=someone who behaves badly after losing) **2** someone who is never successful in life, work, or relationships [OPP] **winner**: *The man is **a born loser*** (=someone who has always been one and always will be one). **3** someone who is in a worse situation than they were, because of something that has happened [OPP] **winner**: *Who does the law benefit and who are the losers?*

loss /lɔs/ [W1] *n.*
1 NO LONGER HAVING STH [C,U] the fact of not having something anymore that you used to have, or the action of losing something: **+of** *his loss of confidence* | *the effects of loss of sleep* | *Depression can lead to **loss of appetite**.* | *About 35,000 **job losses** are expected.* | ***Weight loss** should be gradual.* | **hearing/memory loss** *She has some short-term memory loss.*
2 MONEY [C,U] money that a business, organization, or person loses, because they earn less money than they spend [OPP] **profit**: **+of** *The company reported losses of $82 million last quarter.* | *We **made a loss** in the first half of this year.* | *She had to **sell** her house **at a loss*** (=sell it for less money than she paid for it). | **run/operate at a loss** (=earn less money from something you sell than it costs you to produce it)
3 GAME [C] an occasion when you do not win a game or a competition; [SYN] **defeat** [OPP] **win**: **+to** *a 52–14 loss to Georgia Tech* | *three wins and four losses*
4 DEATH [C,U] the death of someone: *I was sorry to hear about the loss of your mother.* | *U.S. forces withdrew after **suffering heavy losses*** (=many soldiers were killed). | *The war has led to a tragic **loss of life**.*
5 FEELING [U] a feeling of being sad or lonely because someone or something is not there anymore: *feelings of loss and grief* | *He looks back on his youth with a huge **sense of loss**.*
6 at a loss a) confused and uncertain about what to do or say: **at a loss to do sth** *Police were at a loss to explain the boy's death.* | *When she won the award, she seemed **at a loss for words*** (=she could not think of what to say). **b)** not having enough of something: **at a loss for sth** *I was never at a loss for female companionship.*
7 PROBLEM [singular] a disadvantage caused by someone or something leaving or being removed: *His retirement is **a great loss** to the entire community.* | **+to** *The loss to the environment is impossible to calulate.*
8 that's/it's sb's loss SPOKEN said when you think someone is stupid for not taking a good opportunity: *Well, if he doesn't want to come it's his loss.* → see also **cut your losses** at CUT[1] (11)

ˈloss ˌleader *n.* [C] something that is sold at a very low price to make people go into a store

L

lost¹ /lɔst/ S2 W3 *adj.*
1 CANNOT FIND YOUR WAY not knowing where you are or which way to go: *A couple of tourists who were lost asked for directions.* | *We **got lost** driving around the city.*
2 CANNOT BE FOUND something that is lost is something you had but cannot now find SYN **missing**: *a lost dog* | *The invitation must have **gotten lost** in the mail.*
3 WASTED lost time or opportunities have not been used in the way that would have given you the greatest advantage SYN **wasted**: *It'll be impossible to make up the lost time.* | *Several good business opportunities have been lost.*
4 not feeling confident or knowing what to do or how to behave: *She'd come to the party alone and looked a little lost.* | **feel lost** *He felt completely lost when his wife died.* | *I'd **be lost without** all your help.*
5 DESTROYED/KILLED destroyed, ruined, or killed: *Several ships were **lost at sea** in the storm.* | *More than 250 troops were **lost in battle*** (=killed in the war).
6 be lost on sb if something is lost on someone, they do not understand or do not want to accept it: *The joke was lost on Chris.* | *All my warnings were completely lost on Beth.*
7 Get lost! SPOKEN used to tell someone in an impolite way to go away or stop annoying you
8 a lost cause something that has no chance of succeeding: *Trying to make it to the playoffs at this point is a lost cause.*
9 NOT WON a lost game, battle etc. was not won
10 NOT NOTICING [not before noun] thinking so hard about something or being so interested in something that you do not notice what is happening around you: **+in** *Amy lay on her bed totally lost in her book.* | *For a moment she seemed **lost in thought**.*
11 get lost (in sth) to be forgotten or not noticed in a complicated process or busy time: *It's easy for your main points to get lost in the middle of a long essay.* | **lost in the crowd/shuffle** (=not noticed in a large group or busy situation)
12 CONFUSED completely confused by a complicated explanation: *"Did you understand him?" "No, I'm completely lost."*
13 NOT EXISTING not existing or owned anymore: *the lost dreams of her youth*
14 lost soul OFTEN HUMOROUS someone who does not seem to know what they should do → see also **give sb up for dead/lost etc.** at GIVE UP (7), **there is no love lost between sb and sb** at LOVE² (9), **make up for lost time** at MAKE UP FOR STH (2) → see Word Choice box at LOSE

lost² *v.* the past tense and past participle of LOSE

ˌlost-and-ˈfound *n.* **the lost-and-found** a place where things that are lost are kept until someone comes to claim them

ˌLost Genеˈration, the ENG. LANG. ARTS a group of American writers such as F. Scott Fitzgerald and Ernest Hemingway who felt upset after World War I and did not like the importance Americans put on money and possessions. Many of this group went to live in Europe.

lot¹ /lɑt/ S1 W1 *quantifier, pron.* INFORMAL **1 a lot** also **lots a)** a large amount, quantity, or number: *I ate a lot last night.* | *"How many songs have you downloaded?" "Lots."* | **a lot of sth/lots of sth** *A hundred dollars was a lot of money in 1901.* | *You'll save lots of time doing it this way.* | **a lot to do/see/eat etc.** *I still have a lot to learn.* | **lots to do/see/eat etc.** *There's lots to see in the city.* | *There were **lots and lots*** (=very many) *of plants for sale.* | *There's **an awful lot*** (=a very large amount) *of cake left.* | ***A lot of times*** (=usually or very often) *we just sat around and talked.* **b)** [+ comparative] much: *You'll get there a lot quicker if you drive.* | *This is a lot more work than I thought it would be.* **c)** very often: *He gets drunk a lot with his friends.* **2 have a lot on your mind** to have a lot of problems that you are worried about: *Don't bother him now. He's got a lot on his mind.* **3 have a lot on your plate** INFORMAL to have many problems to deal with or work to do: *Can someone else do the report? I have a lot on my plate right now.* **4 have a lot of explaining to do** to be responsible for a bad situation, or thought to be responsible: *Jacobs has a lot of explaining to do for the company's losses.* → see also **a fat lot of good/use** at FAT¹ (9), **have a lot/so much etc. going for you** at GO FOR (6), **thanks a lot** at THANKS¹ (2) → see Grammar box at MUCH¹

lot² S1 *n.* [C]
1 LAND an area of land used for building on or for another particular purpose: *We used to play baseball in the vacant lot.* | *a used-car lot* → see also PARKING LOT
2 SB'S LOT the kind of life you have, for example the work, responsibilities, social position etc. that you have, especially when they could be better: *She seems happy enough with her lot in life.*
3 MOVIE ENG. LANG. ARTS a building and the land surrounding it where movies are made: *the Universal Studios lot*
4 TO BE SOLD something that is sold, especially at an AUCTION: *Lot fifteen was a box of old books.*
5 throw in your lot with sb also **cast your lot with sb** to join or support someone, so that what happens to you depends on what happens to them: *The new government has cast its lot with the West.*
6 by lot if someone or something is decided on by lot, it is decided on by choosing one piece of paper, object etc. from among many
[**Origin:** Old English *hlot* **object used for making a choice by chance**] → see also **draw lots** at DRAW¹ (26)

loth /loʊθ/ *adj.* another spelling of LOATH

lo·tion /ˈloʊʃən/ *n.* [C,U] a liquid mixture that you put on your skin to make it soft or protect it: *suntan lotion*
[**Origin:** 1300–1400 Latin *lotio* **act of washing**, from *lavare* **to wash**]

lots /lɑts/ S1 *quantifier, pron.* INFORMAL → see LOT¹ (1)

lot·sa /ˈlɑtsə/ *quantifier, pron.* a way of writing "lots of" to show how it sounds when it is spoken

lot·ter·y /ˈlɑt̬əri/ *n. plural* **lotteries** **1** [C] a game used to make money for a state or a CHARITY in which people buy tickets with numbers, so that if their number is picked by chance, they win money or a prize → see also RAFFLE: *a lottery ticket* | *Well, if I **win the lottery** I'll buy it for you.* **2** [C,U] a system of choosing who will get something by choosing people's names by chance: *the NFL draft lottery* | *The State Department issues 55,000 visas each year **by lottery*** (=using a lottery system). **3** [singular] a situation in which what happens depends on chance: *A baby's sex is a genetic lottery.* → DRAWING (3)

lo·tus /ˈloʊt̬əs/ *n.* [C] **1** BIOLOGY a flower that grows on the surface of lakes in Asia, or the shape of this flower used in decorations **2** a fruit that gives you a pleasant dreamy feeling after you eat it, according to ancient Greek stories

loud¹ /laʊd/ S2 W3 *adj.* **1** making a lot of noise OPP **quiet**: *a loud explosion* | *The TV's too loud.* | *"Who's that?" said Colleen **in a loud voice**.*

THESAURUS
noisy making a lot of noise, or full of noise: *a classroom full of noisy kids* | *a noisy washing machine*
rowdy behaving in a noisy and uncontrolled way: *rowdy football fans*
thunderous extremely loud: *thunderous applause*
deafening very loud, so that you cannot hear anything else: *the deafening blast of the guns*
ear-splitting painfully loud: *The car stopped with an ear-splitting screech.*
shrill a shrill sound is high and unpleasant: *a shrill voice*
raucous unpleasantly loud: *raucous laughter*
resounding used to describe a loud noise that seems to continue for a few seconds: *a resounding cheer*
→ QUIET

2 DISAPPROVING someone who is loud talks too loudly and confidently: *Bloom is loud and aggressive.* **3** loud clothes are too bright or have too many bright patterns

SYN garish: *a loud purple jacket* **4 loud and clear** very easily understood: *The play's message is loud and clear.* **5 be loud in your praise/opposition etc.** to express your approval, disapproval etc. very strongly: *The local business community was loud in its support for the plan.* [**Origin:** Old English *hlud*] —**loudly** *adv.* —**loudness** *n.* [U]

loud[2] S3 *adv.* SPOKEN in a way that makes a lot of noise SYN loudly: *Could you speak a little louder?* | *The band was so loud, we couldn't hear each other.* → see also **actions speak louder than words** at ACTION (14), **for crying out loud** at CRY[1] (3), **out loud** at OUT[1] (14), **think out loud** at THINK (13)

loud·mouth /ˈlaʊdmaʊθ/ *n.* [C] someone who talks too much and says offensive or stupid things —**loudmouthed** *adj.*

loud·speak·er /ˈlaʊdˌspikɚ/ *n.* [C] **1** a piece of equipment used to make sounds louder: *The voice over the loudspeaker said the flight was delayed.* **2** a SPEAKER

Lou Geh·rig's dis·ease /ˌlu ˈgɛrɪgz dɪˌziz/ *n.* [U] NOT TECHNICAL a serious disease in which your muscles become weaker and weaker until you cannot move anymore

Lou·is /ˈluɪs/**, Joe** /dʒoʊ/ (1914–1981) a U.S. BOXER famous for being the world HEAVYWEIGHT CHAMPION for 11 years, the longest time that any BOXER held this title

Lou·i·si·a·na /luˌiziˈænə/ WRITTEN ABBREVIATION **LA** a state in the southern U.S.

Louˌisiana ˈPurchase, the also **the Louˌisiana ˈTerritory** HISTORY the area of land which the U.S. bought from France in 1803, that covered the land between the Mississippi River and the Rocky Mountains and between Canada and the Gulf of Mexico

Lou·is·ville /ˈluivɪl/ the largest city in the U.S. state of Kentucky

Lou·is XIV, King /ˌlui ðə fɔrˈtinθ/ (1638–1715) a king of France who was called the "Sun King," built the PALACE at Versailles, and supported important artists and writers

Louis XV, King /ˌlui ðə fɪfˈtinθ/ (1710–1774) the king of France at the time when it lost power in Canada to England

Louis XVI, King /ˌlui ðə sɪksˈtinθ/ (1754–1793) the king of France from 1774 to 1792. He and his wife Marie Antoinette were put in prison and killed during the French Revolution.

lounge[1] /laʊndʒ/ *n.* [C] **1** a public room in a hotel, airport, or other building where people can relax, sit down, or drink: *the airport's departure lounge* **2** a COCKTAIL LOUNGE

lounge[2] *v.* [I] [always + adv./prep.] to stand, sit, or lie in a lazy way: +**in/on etc.** *We spent the weekend lounging on the beach.*

lounge around *phr. v.* to spend time doing nothing: **lounge around sth** *James doesn't do anything but lounge around the apartment.*

ˈlounge chair *n.* [C] a comfortable chair made for relaxing in → see picture at CHAIR[1]

ˈlounge ˌlizard *n.* [C] OLD-FASHIONED DISAPPROVING a man who spends a lot of his time at COCKTAIL LOUNGES, drinks too much, and thinks he is stylish and attractive to women

ˈlounge ˌmusic *n.* [U] a relaxed style of music from the 1940s and 1950s, usually songs, piano music, or JAZZ

louse[1] /laʊs/ *n.* [C] **1** *plural* **lice** /laɪs/ BIOLOGY a small wingless insect that lives on people's or animals' skin and hair **2** *plural* **louses** INFORMAL someone who is mean and treats people very badly

louse[2] *v.*

louse up *phr. v.* INFORMAL **1 louse sth ↔ up** to make something that is good become worse SYN spoil: *I don't want to louse things up in our relationship.* **2** to do something badly: +**on** *Chris really loused up on his finals.* | **louse sth ↔ up** *You really loused the whole thing up.*

lous·y /ˈlaʊzi/ *adj.* *comparative* **lousier**, *superlative* **lousiest** **1** ESPECIALLY SPOKEN very bad: *What lousy weather!* | *I feel lousy.* ▸see THESAURUS box at bad[1] **2** SPOKEN not large enough in number or amount: *He left me a lousy fifty cent tip.* | *The pay is lousy.* **3** SPOKEN not very good at doing something: +**at/with** *I'm lousy at tennis.* | *Brenda's lousy with kids.* **4 be lousy with sth** a place that is lousy with people of a particular kind is too full of them **5 be lousy with money** DISAPPROVING to be very rich **6** covered with lice (LOUSE)

lout /laʊt/ *n.* [C] FORMAL a man who is very impolite or offensive

lou·ver /ˈluvɚ/ *n.* [C] a narrow piece of wood, glass etc., in a door or window, that slopes out to let some light in and keep rain or strong sun out —**louvered** *adj.*: *a louvered window*

lov·a·ble /ˈlʌvəbəl/ *adj.* friendly and attractive: *a sweet lovable child*

love[1] /lʌv/ S1 W1 *v.* [T, not in progressive]
1 CARE ABOUT to care very much about someone, especially a member of your family or a close friend OPP hate: *It was wonderful to be surrounded by people who loved me.* | *I love you, Mom.* | *a much-loved colleague* | *The group was founded to help cancer patients and their* ***loved ones*** (=people they love).

THESAURUS

be infatuated with sb to have unreasonably strong feelings of love for someone: *He was as infatuated with me as I was with him.*
have a crush on sb to have a strong feeling of romantic love for someone you are not having a relationship with, often when this continues for only a short time: *Carrie has a crush on her brother's best friend.*
be crazy about sb INFORMAL to love someone very much, especially in a way that you cannot control: *He says he's crazy about me.*
be devoted to sb to love someone very much and give them a lot of attention: *He has always been devoted to his wife.*
adore sb to love and admire someone very much: *She adores her grandchildren.*
→ HATE

2 ROMANTIC ATTRACTION to have a strong feeling of caring for and liking someone, combined with sexual attraction: *I love you, Betty.* | *Tom was the only man she had ever loved.*
3 LIKE/ENJOY [not in passive] to like something very much or enjoy doing something very much OPP hate: **love doing sth** *Katie loves playing tennis.* | **love sth** *I love chocolate.* | *Don't you just love the way she dresses?* | **love to do sth** *We all love to talk about ourselves.* ▸see THESAURUS box at enjoy
4 LOYALTY to have a strong feeling of loyalty to your country, an institution etc.: *Dad's always loved the Navy.*
5 WANT would love (to do) sth used to say that you want to do something very much, or want something very much: *"Would you like to go out to dinner?" "I'd love to."* | *He'd love to have a big family.* | *I'd love to know what she's really thinking.*

SPOKEN PHRASES

6 I love it! also **don't you just love it?** used when you are amused by something, especially by someone else's mistake or bad luck: *"So then Susan had to explain how the dishes got broken." "Oh, I love it!"*
7 she's/he's etc. going to love sth used to say that someone will enjoy something you are about to say or be amused by it: *Listen guys, you're going to love this.*
8 you (have) got to love sth used to say that you are amused by something because it is so bad, good, or unusual that it is funny: *You've got to love the way he tries to pick up older women.*

→ see also LOVER

love[2] S1 W1 *n.*
1 FOR FAMILY/FRIENDS [U] a strong feeling of caring about someone, especially a member of your family or

L

a close friend OPP hate: *What these kids need is love and support.* | **+for** *a mother's love for her child*
2 ROMANTIC [U] a strong feeling of liking and caring about someone, especially combined with sexual attraction: *a love song* | *He **was in love with** Mary.* | *We **fell in love** on our first date.* | *When you met your husband, was it **love at first sight*** (=when you love someone the first time you see them)? | *Teenage girls dream of finding **true love*** (=strong romantic love that remains for ever). | *The movie is **a love story*** (=a book or movie about love). → see also **head over heels in love** at HEAD[1] (34), **madly in love (with sb)** at MADLY (1)
3 PERSON YOU LOVE [C] someone that you feel a strong romantic and sexual attraction to: *Jack was her first love.* | *I think of her as **the love of my life*** (=the person that you feel or felt the most love for).
4 PLEASURE/ENJOYMENT a) [singular,U] a strong feeling of pleasure and enjoyment that something gives you: **+of/for** *Jerrod has a love for the game of chess.* **b)** [C] something that gives you a lot of pleasure and enjoyment: *Sailing was her great love.*
5 make love (to/with sb) a) to have sex with someone that you love **b)** OLD USE to say loving things to someone, to kiss them etc.
6 send your love (to sb) to ask someone to give your loving greetings to someone else when they see them, write to them etc.: *Aunt Mary sends her love.*
7 give my love to sb SPOKEN used to ask someone to give your loving greetings to someone else: *Bye! Give my love to Jackie.*
8 love also **lots of love** used at the end of a letter to a friend, a member of your family, or someone you love: *See you soon. Lots of love, Clare.*
9 there is no love lost between sb and sb used to say that two people dislike each other
10 TENNIS [U] an expression meaning "no points," used in the game of tennis
11 not for love nor money INFORMAL if you cannot get something or do something for love or money, it is impossible to obtain or to do: *I can't get a hold of that book for love nor money.*
12 for the love of God/Mike/Pete etc. SPOKEN used to show that you are extremely angry, disappointed etc.
13 love nest HUMOROUS a place where two people who are having a romantic relationship live or go to see each other
[**Origin:** Old English *lufu*] → see also **a labor of love** at LABOR[1] (4)

L

ˈlove afˌfair *n.* [C] **1** a romantic sexual relationship, usually between two people who are not married to each other SYN **affair** **2** a strong enjoyment of something: *America's love affair with the automobile*

love·bird /ˈlʌvbɚd/ *n.* [C] **1 lovebirds** [plural] HUMOROUS two people who show by their behavior that they love each other very much **2** BIOLOGY a small brightly colored PARROT

love·child /ˈlʌvtʃaɪld/ *n.* [C] a word meaning a child whose parents are not married, used especially in newspapers

love·fest /ˈlʌvˌfɛst/ *n.* [C] INFORMAL, HUMOROUS a situation in which everyone is very friendly, says nice things to each other etc.

ˈlove ˌinterest *n.* [C] the character in a movie, book, or play that the main character loves

love·less /ˈlʌvlɪs/ *adj.* without love: *a loveless marriage*

ˈlove ˌletter *n.* [C] a letter that someone writes to tell someone else how much they love them

ˈlove life *n.* [C,U] the part of your life that involves your romantic relationships, especially sexual ones

love·lorn /ˈlʌvlɔrn/ *adj.* LITERARY sad because the person you love does not love you

love·ly /ˈlʌvli/ S2 *adj. comparative* **lovelier**, *superlative* **loveliest** **1** beautiful or attractive: *What a lovely baby!* | *Her hair's a lovely shade of red.* | *You **look lovely** in blue.* **2** SPOKEN very pleasant, enjoyable, or good: *Thank you for a lovely evening.* **3** INFORMAL friendly and pleasant: *Rita's a lovely young girl.* —**loveliness** *n.* [U]

love·mak·ing /ˈlʌvˌmeɪkɪŋ/ *n.* [U] the act of having sex → see also **make love (to/with sb)** at LOVE[2] (5)

lov·er /ˈlʌvɚ/ S3 W3 *n.* [C] **1** someone who has a sexual relationship with someone they are not married to: *Arabella has had many lovers.* **2** someone who enjoys doing a particular thing very much or is very interested in it: *an opera lover*

ˈlove scene *n.* [C] a part of a movie or play in which two people show their love for each other, usually when this involves kissing or sex

love·seat /ˈlʌvsit/ *n.* [C] a small SOFA for two people

love·sick /ˈlʌvˌsɪk/ *adj.* spending all your time thinking about someone you love, especially someone who does not love you

ˈlove ˌtriangle *n.* [C] INFORMAL a situation in which one person is having a romantic relationship with two other people

lov·ey-dov·ey /ˌlʌvi ˈdʌvi◂/ *adj.* INFORMAL behavior that is lovey-dovey is too romantic: *The newlyweds were acting all lovey-dovey.*

lov·ing /ˈlʌvɪŋ/ *adj.* [only before noun] behaving in a way that shows you love someone: *a loving husband* —**lovingly** *adv.*: *He kissed her lovingly.* → see also **tender loving care** at TENDER[1] (5)

-loving /lʌvɪŋ/ [in adjectives] **peace-loving/fun-loving etc.** thinking that peace, having fun etc. is very important: *a peace-loving nation* | *a music-loving family*

ˈloving cup *n.* [C] a very large cup with two handles that was passed around at formal meals in past times

low

a low wall

shallow water

low[1] /loʊ/ S1 W1 *adj.*
1 HEIGHT a) having a top that is not far above the ground: *a low fence* | *a long low building* **b)** at a point that is not far above the ground: *low clouds* | *I'm going to trim some of the low branches.* **c)** below the usual height: *a low ceiling* | *The river's water level has been low for weeks now.* OPP **high**
2 AMOUNT a) small, or smaller than usual, in amount, value etc.: *a low income* | *low-cost housing* | *The price of oil is at its lowest in 10 years.* **b)** having less than the usual amount of a substance or chemical: **low-fat/low-cholesterol/low-sodium etc.** *a low-salt diet* | **low in fat/calories/alcohol etc.** *foods that are low in cholesterol* OPP **high**

3 **NUMBER** **in the low 20s/30s/40s etc.** a number, temperature etc. in the low 20s, 30s etc. is no higher than 23, 33 etc. → see also HIGH: *Tonight's temperatures will be in the low 50s.*
4 **LEVEL/DEGREE** less in level or degree than usual OPP **high**: *a low-risk investment* | *Morale has been low since the latest round of job-cuts.* | *teachers with* ***low expectations for*** (=who do not expect much from) *their students* | *She* ***has a very low opinion of*** *her brother-in-law.*
5 **STANDARDS/QUALITY** bad, or below an acceptable or usual level or quality OPP **high**: *low quality goods* | *My class's scores on the test were quite low.*
6 **SUPPLY** if a supply of something is low, you have used almost all of it: **be/get/run low (on sth)** *We're running low on gas.* | *The medical supplies were getting low.*
7 **SOUND** a low voice, sound etc. is quiet or deep: *The volume is too low.* | *You could hear low voices from the other room.* ►see THESAURUS box at **quiet**[1]
8 **LIGHT** a light that is low is not bright, especially so that it makes a room feel more relaxing: *The lights in the restaurant were low.*
9 **HEAT** if you cook something on a low heat, you use only a small amount of heat OPP **high**
10 **NOTES** near the bottom of the range of sounds that humans can hear OPP **high**: *She played a low note on the piano.*
11 **UNHAPPY** unhappy and without much hope for the future: *I've been feeling pretty low since he left.* | *Carol looks like she's* ***in low spirits*** (=unhappy and not hopeful) *today.* ►see THESAURUS box at **sad**
12 **BATTERY** a BATTERY that is low does not have much power left in it
13 **DISHONEST** behavior that is low is unfair or not nice: *I can't believe you said that.* ***That's a low blow*** (=that is an unfair or mean thing to say)*!*
14 **of low birth/breeding** OLD-FASHIONED not from a high social class
[**Origin:** 1100–1200 Old Norse *lagr*] —**lowness** *n.* [U] → see also **be at a low ebb** at EBB[1] (2), LOW GEAR

low[2] W1 *adv.* **1** in or to a low position or level that is closer to the ground than usual OPP **high**: *The sun sank low in the sky.* | *That plane's flying too low.* **2** at or to a level that is not loud or bright OPP **high**: *Turn the volume down low.* **3** at or to a low value, cost, amount, rank etc. OPP **high**: *Stock prices are expected to fall even lower.* **4** if you play or sing musical notes low, you play or sing them with deep notes: *Can you sing an octave lower?* **5** to an unfair, unkind, or dishonest level: *I can't believe you would* ***stoop so low*** (=behave in such a surprisingly bad way) *as to lie.* **6 be brought low** OLD-FASHIONED to become much less rich or important → see also **look/search high and low** at HIGH[2] (5), **lay sb low** at LAY[1] (24), **lie low** at LIE[1] (5), LOWLY

low[3] *n.* [C] **1** the smallest or least amount or level that has happened at a particular time OPP **high**: **fall/hit/reach a low** *The company's stock fell to a low of $2.2.* | **a new/record/all-time low** *The dollar has* ***fallen to a new low*** (=is worth less than ever before) *against the euro.* | *Prices on homes have dropped to* ***an all-time low*** (=much lower than ever before). **2** a very difficult time or situation for a person, organization, country etc.: *The 1920s marked* ***an all-time low*** (=the worst situation that had happened) *in the U.S. economy.* | ***the highs and lows*** (=good times and bad times) *of parenting* **3** the lowest point that the temperature reaches during a particular time OPP **high**: *The overnight low will be 25° F.* **4** EARTH SCIENCE a large area of air where there is very little pressure, which affects the weather in a particular area OPP **high**: *A low is making its way over the Mid-Atlantic states.*
5 the lowest of the low INFORMAL **a)** someone you think is completely unfair, cruel, immoral etc. **b)** someone from a low social class

low[4] *v.* [I] LITERARY if cattle low, they make a deep sound

'low beam *n.* **1 low beams** [plural] the regular HEADLIGHTS of a vehicle, as opposed to the brighter HIGH BEAMS **2 on low beam** if your car lights are on low beam, they are shining at the normal level of brightness → see also ON HIGH BEAM

low·born /ˌloʊˈbɔrn◂/ *adj.* OLD-FASHIONED coming from a low social class

low·brow, low-brow /ˈloʊbraʊ/ *adj.* entertainment, books, newspapers etc. that are easy for everyone to understand and do not deal with serious ideas OPP **highbrow**

low-cal /ˌloʊ ˈkæl◂/ *adj.* INFORMAL low-cal food or drink does not contain many CALORIES

ˌlow-ˈclass *adj.* INFORMAL DISAPPROVING **1** of poor quality and not desirable or attractive OPP **high-class**: *a low-class street in the downtown area* **2** not having a lot of money and behaving in a way that is not socially acceptable OPP **high-class**: *a low-class woman*

ˈLow ˌCountries, the an area of northwest Europe that includes Belgium, Luxembourg, and the Netherlands, and is also known as Benelux

ˌlow-ˈcut *adj.* a low-cut dress, BLOUSE etc. is shaped so that it shows a woman's neck and the top of her chest

ˈlow-down *adj.* [only before noun] INFORMAL dishonest and not nice: *a low-down, dirty trick*

low·down /ˈloʊdaʊn/ *n.* **the lowdown (on sth)** INFORMAL the most important facts about something or someone: *Ryan called and* ***gave me the lowdown on*** *the merger.*

Low·ell /ˈloʊəl/, **A·my** /ˈeɪmi/ (1874–1925) a U.S. poet

Lowell, James Rus·sell /dʒeɪmz ˈrʌsəl/ (1819–1891) a U.S. poet and newspaper EDITOR

Lowell, Rob·ert /ˈrɑbɚt/ (1917–1977) a U.S. poet and writer of plays

ˈlow-end *adj.* [usually before noun] relating to products or services that are less expensive and of lower quality than other products of the same type OPP **high-end**: *low-end electronics*

low·er[1] /ˈloʊɚ/ S2 W3 *adj.* [only before noun] **1** below something else, especially beneath something of the same type OPP **upper**: *your lower lip* | *muscles of the lower leg* **2** at or near the bottom of something OPP **upper**: *the lower deck of the stadium* **3** [only before noun] less important than something else of the same type OPP **upper**: *the lower levels of the organization* **4 the lower forty-eight (states)** all the states of the U.S. except for Alaska and Hawaii **5 the lower animals/organisms/mammals etc.** animals etc. that do not have an advanced biological structure or brain

lower[2] W2 *v.* **1** [I,T] to reduce something in amount, degree, strength etc., or to become less SYN **reduce** SYN **drop** OPP **raise**: *We're lowering prices on all of our trucks.* | *Housing has lowered in value recently.* | *Graham* ***lowered his voice*** (=made it quieter) *to a near whisper.* ►see THESAURUS box at **reduce** **2** [T] to move something down from a higher position OPP **raise**: *The flags were lowered to half-mast.* | *We had our kitchen cabinets lowered.* | **lower sth down/into/between etc. sth** *The workers lowered the box onto the cart.* | *He* ***lowered himself*** *slowly into an armchair.*
3 lower yourself (to sb's level) [usually in negatives] to behave in a way that makes people respect you less
4 lower your eyes/head to look down, especially because you are embarrassed, ashamed, or shy: *He lowered his head and blushed.* —**lowered** *adj.*

lower[3] *v.* [I] **1** when the sky or the weather lowers, it becomes dark because there is going to be a storm SYN **darken**: *lowering clouds* **2** LITERARY to look threatening or annoyed SYN **frown**

ˈlower case *n.* [U] letters in their small forms, such as a, b, c etc. OPP **upper case** —**lower case** *adj.* → see also CAPITAL

ˌlower ˈchamber *n.* [C usually singular] the LOWER HOUSE

ˌlower ˈclass *n.* [C] OLD-FASHIONED also **the lower classes** [plural] the social class that has less money, power, or education than anyone else —**lower-class** *adj.* → see also MIDDLE CLASS, WORKING CLASS

ˌlower ˈcourt *n.* [C] LAW any court whose decisions can be considered and changed by a higher court SYN **inferior court**: *The Supreme Court overruled the decision of the lower courts.*

ˈlower-end *adj.* [usually before noun] LOW-END

ˌlower ˈhouse *n.* [C usually singular] the larger of two elected groups of government officials that make laws, usually more REPRESENTATIVE and made up of less experienced officials than the smaller group → see also UPPER HOUSE

ˌlower ˈorders *n.* OLD-FASHIONED **the lower orders** an expression meaning "people of a low social CLASS," used especially by people who consider themselves to be more important

ˌLower ˈSouth, the the U.S. states of Texas, Louisiana, Mississippi, Alabama, Florida, Georgia, and South Carolina

ˌlowest ˌcommon deˈnominator *n.* [U] **1** DISAPPROVING the biggest possible number of people, including people who are willing to accept low standards: *The band's vulgar lyrics appeal to the lowest common denominator.* **2** MATH the smallest number that the bottom numbers of a group of FRACTIONS can be divided into exactly

ˌlow-ˈfat *adj.* containing or using only a small amount of fat: *low-fat cottage cheese*

ˌlow-ˈflying *adj.* flying close to the ground

ˌlow ˈfrequency *n.* [U] a radio FREQUENCY in the range of 30 to 300 KILOHERTZ —**low-frequency** *adj.*: *a low-frequency radio antenna* → see also HIGH FREQUENCY

ˌlow ˈgear *n.* [C,U] one of a vehicle's GEARS that you use when you are driving at a slow speed

ˈlow-grade *adj.* [only before noun] **1** not very good in quality: *inexpensive low-grade paper* **2** a low-grade medical condition is not very serious: *a low-grade fever*

ˈlow-ˌincome *adj.* [only before noun] not earning very much money compared with the rest of a society: *low-income familes*

ˌlow ˈisland *n.* [C] EARTH SCIENCE an island that is formed by CORAL rising out of the ocean → see also HIGH ISLAND

ˌlow-ˈkey *adj.* having a style that is quiet and calm rather than one that is exciting or likely to attract attention: *This year's campaign was low-key.* | *a low-key approach to management*

low·lands /ˈloʊləndz/ *n.* [plural] an area of land that is lower than the land around it: *the Bolivian lowlands* —**lowland** *adj.* [only before noun] —**lowlander** *n.* [C] → see also HIGHLANDS

ˌlow ˈlatitudes *n.* [plural] TECHNICAL the area between the Tropic of Cancer and the Tropic of Capricorn → see also HIGH LATITUDES

ˌlow-ˈlevel *adj.* **1** not in a powerful position or job, or involving people who are not in powerful positions or jobs OPP **high-level**: *a low-level manager* | *low-level positions in the company* **2** at a low degree or strength: *a low-level tension headache* **3** COMPUTERS a low-level computer language is used to give instructions to a computer and is similar to the language that the computer operates in

ˈlow life *n.* **1** [C] also **lowlife** INFORMAL someone who is involved in crime or who is dishonest: *Venuto is a lowlife who can't be trusted.* **2** [U] criminals and their activities —**low-life** *adj.* INFORMAL

low·ly /ˈloʊli/ *adj.* not high in rank, importance, or social class: *a lowly trainee* —**lowliness** *n.* [U]

ˌlow-ˈlying *adj.* **1** low-lying land is not far above the level of the ocean **2** below the usual level: *low-lying fog*

ˌlow-ˈpaid *adj.* providing or earning only a small amount of money: *low-paid workers*

ˈlow-paying *adj.* providing only a small amount of money: *low-paying jobs*

ˌlow-ˈpitched *adj.* **1** a low-pitched musical note or sound is deep: *her familiar low-pitched voice* **2** a low-pitched roof is not steep

ˈlow point *n.* [C usually singular] the worst moment of a situation or activity OPP **high point**: *Being arrested was the low point of my life.* | **reach/hit/mark a low point** *At that time the negotiations had reached a low point.*

ˌlow-ˈpowered also **ˌlow-ˈpower** *adj.* a low-powered machine, vehicle, or piece of equipment is not very powerful OPP **high-powered**: *a low-powered telescope*

ˌlow ˈpressure *n.* [U] EARTH SCIENCE a type of air pressure that covers a large area and that usually causes wet weather

low·rid·er /ˈloʊˌraɪdɚ/ *n.* [C] **1** a big car that has its bottom very close to the ground **2** a young man who drives this type of car

ˈlow-rise *adj.* [only before noun] a low-rise building does not have many stories (STORY)

ˌlow-ˈrisk *adj.* [only before noun] likely to be safe or without difficulties: *a low-risk investment*

ˌlow-ˈslung *adj.* built or made to be closer to the ground than usual: *a low-slung gray Chevy*

ˌlow-ˈspirited *adj.* unhappy or DEPRESSED

low-tech /ˌloʊ ˈtɛk◂/ *adj.* not using the most modern machines or methods in business or industry OPP **high-tech**: *a low-tech solution to the problem*

ˌlow ˈtide *n.* [C,U] EARTH SCIENCE the time when ocean water is at its lowest level OPP **high tide**: *You can walk across to the island **at low tide**.*

ˌlow ˈwater *n.* [U] the time when the water in a river, lake etc. is at its lowest level

ˌlow ˈwater ˌmark *n.* [C] EARTH SCIENCE a mark showing the lowest level reached by a river or other area of water

lox /lɑks/ *n.* [U] SALMON that has been treated with smoke in order to preserve it

loy·al /ˈlɔɪəl/ *adj.* always supporting your friends, principles, country etc., and never changing your feelings about them: *loyal customers* | +**to** *Most corporate executives do not feel loyal to their firms.* | **remain loyal (to sb/sth)** *My mother remained loyal to the Catholic church.* [**Origin:** 1500–1600 Old French *leial*, *leel*, from Latin *legalis*, from *lex* **law**] —**loyally** *adv.*

loy·al·ist /ˈlɔɪəlɪst/ *n.* [C] **1** POLITICS someone who continues to support a government or country, when a lot of people want to change it **2 Loyalist** HISTORY an American who supported the British during the Revolutionary War SYN **Tory**

loy·al·ty /ˈlɔɪəlti/ *n. plural* **loyalties** **1** [singular, U] the quality of remaining faithful to your friends, principles, country etc.: *a family with a strong sense of loyalty* | +**to/toward** *Readers feel a strong loyalty to their local newspaper.* **2** [C usually plural] a feeling of support for someone or something: *political loyalties* | *During World War II, many families in the region had **divided loyalties*** (=loyalty to two different or opposing people, groups etc.). | **sb's loyalties lie/are with sth** *As a lawyer, my loyalties are with my client.*

Loy·o·la /lɔɪˈoʊlə/, **St. Ignatius (of)** /ɪgˈneɪʃəs/ → see IGNATIUS OF LOYOLA, ST.

loz·enge /ˈlɑzəndʒ/ *n.* [C] **1** a small flat candy, especially one that contains medicine: *a cough lozenge* **2** MATH a shape similar to a square, with two angles of less than 90° opposite each other and two angles of more than 90° opposite each other

LP *n.* [C] **1** ECONOMICS the abbreviation for LIMITED PARTNERSHIP **2 long playing record** a record that turns 33 times per minute, and usually plays for between 20 and 25 minutes on each side SYN **album**

LPN *n.* [C] a LICENSED PRACTICAL NURSE

LSAT /ˈɛlsæt/ *n.* [C] TRADEMARK **Law School Admission Test** an examination taken by students who have completed a first degree and want to go to LAW SCHOOL

LSD *n.* [U] an illegal drug that makes you see things as more beautiful, strange, frightening etc. than usual, or see things that do not exist

Lt. the written abbreviation of LIEUTENANT

Ltd. the written abbreviation of LIMITED, used after the names of British companies or businesses → see also INC.

Lu·an·da /luˈɑndə/ the capital city of Angola

lu·au /ˈluaʊ/ *n.* [C] an outdoor party at which Hawaiian food is cooked and served outdoors, and Hawaiian decorations are used

lube /lub/ *n.* INFORMAL **1** [singular] also **ˈlube job** [C] the service of lubricating the parts of a car's engine **2** [C,U] INFORMAL a lubricant —**lube** *v.* [T]

lu·bri·cant /ˈlubrəkənt/ *n.* [C,U] a substance such as oil that you put on surfaces that rub together, for example machine parts, in order to make them move smoothly and easily

lu·bri·cate /ˈlubrəˌkeɪt/ *v.* [T] to put a lubricant on something in order to make it move more smoothly: *Lubricate all moving parts with grease.* [**Origin:** 1600–1700 Latin, past participle of *lubricare*, from *lubricus* **slippery**] —**lubrication** /ˌlubrəˈkeɪʃən/ *n.* [U]

lu·bri·cious /luˈbrɪʃəs/ *adj.* FORMAL too interested in sex, in a way that seems unacceptable —**lubriciously** *adv.*

Luce /lus/**, Henry** (1898–1967) a U.S. EDITOR and PUBLISHER who started "Time" magazine

lu·cid /ˈlusɪd/ *adj.* **1** expressed in a way that is clear and easy to understand: *a lucid analysis of the situation* **2** a word meaning "able to understand and think clearly," used about someone who is not always able to do this: *At the moment, Peter is lucid, but his condition is becoming worse.* —**lucidly** *adv.* —**lucidity** /luˈsɪdət̬i/ *n.* [U]

Lu·ci·fer /ˈlusɪfɚ/ *n.* the DEVIL

luck¹ /lʌk/ S2 W3 *n.* [U]

1 CHANCE a force or influence that makes good or bad things happen to people for no reason or in spite of what they do: *There's no skill in a game of roulette – it's all luck.* | *It was* ***good luck*** (=good things that happen by chance) *that we met you when we did!* | *It was just* ***bad luck*** (=bad things that happen by chance) *that she was sick that day.* | **have good/bad luck** *I hope you have better luck next year.* | *I've had nothing but bad luck since I moved here.* | *The company's had* ***a run of*** *bad* ***luck*** (=a series of good or bad things that happen) *this year.* | *It was* ***sheer luck*** (=used to emphasize that something happened only by luck) *that we happened to find each other again.* | *We could have died, but* ***luck was on our side*** (=we had good luck). | ***As luck would have it*** (=used to say that something happened by chance), *there were two seats left on the flight.*

2 SUCCESS the good things that happen to someone by chance, not through their work or effort: *Let's hope our luck continues.* | *We're not* ***having*** *much* ***luck*** *today.* | **have the luck to do sth** *I had the luck to be chosen for special training.* | **have luck with sth** *He's never had much luck with girls.* | *Mom came over to* ***wish*** *me* ***luck*** (=wish someone success) *before the race.* | *It was* ***a stroke of luck*** (=something unexpected and good) *that she happened to be staying in the same hotel as me.* | *People touch the statue* ***for luck*** (=to bring success). | *He thinks that wearing the shirt* ***brings*** *him* ***luck*** (=causes success). | *We* ***couldn't believe*** *our* ***luck*** *when they took us to the front of the line.* | *The team's* ***luck*** *was beginning to* ***run out*** (=their success was ending). | *The program is for motivated people who are temporarily* ***down on*** *their* ***luck*** (=not being very successful).

3 it's good/bad luck to do sth used to say that doing, seeing, finding etc. something makes good or bad things happen to someone: *It's bad luck to walk under a ladder.*

4 be in luck INFORMAL to be able to do or get something, especially when you did not expect to: *You're in luck. There's one ticket left.*

5 be out of luck INFORMAL to be prevented from getting or doing something by bad luck: *We're out of luck. The store's closed.*

SPOKEN PHRASES

6 Good luck! used to tell someone that you hope they will be successful in something they are about to do: *Good luck in the interview!*

7 any/no luck used in questions and negatives to say whether or not someone has been able to do something: *Did you have any luck getting into the show?* | *"Any luck?" "Yes, I got a flight on Friday."* | *I'm having no luck reaching Julie at home.* | *"No luck?"* (=said when you think someone has not been able to do something) *"No, the guy said they left yesterday."*

8 no such luck! used to say you are disappointed, because something good that could have happened did not happen: *I was hoping for a good night's sleep, but no such luck.*

9 just my luck! used to say that you are not surprised something bad has happened to you, because you are not usually lucky: *Just my luck! They've already gone home.*

10 with/knowing sb's luck used to say that you expect something bad will happen to someone because bad things often do happen to them: *Knowing his luck, he'll get hit with a golf ball or something.*

11 some people/guys/girls have all the luck! used to say that you wish you had what someone else has

12 better luck next time! used to say that you hope someone will be more successful the next time they try to do something

13 (one) for luck used when you take, add, or do something for no particular reason, or in order to say that you hope good things happen: *You get three kisses for your birthday, and one for luck.*

14 with any luck also **with a little luck** INFORMAL used to say that you hope something will happen in a particular way SYN **hopefully**: *With any luck, the old music hall will never be torn down.*

15 the luck of the draw the result of chance rather than something you can control: *It was by the luck of the draw that I got a corner office.*

[**Origin:** 1400–1500 Middle Dutch *luk*] → see also **beginner's luck** at BEGINNER (2), **hard-luck story** at HARD¹ (20), **push your luck** at PUSH¹ (15), **tough luck** at TOUGH¹ (6), **trust sth to luck/chance/fate etc.** at TRUST² (5), **try your luck** at TRY¹ (9)

WORD CHOICE **luck, lucky**

- Use the noun **luck** without an adjective to mean the good things that happen to you by chance: *It was just luck that there were two seats left.* | *With luck, you'll find the right job.* You can use the verb "have" with the word **luck**, but only if a word such as an adjective or determiner comes before **luck**: *Ted's had a lot of bad luck recently.* | *Did you have any luck* (NOT "did you have luck") *reaching Tina on the phone?*
- Use **lucky** to describe a situation that is good by chance, or someone who has good luck: *You're lucky you didn't lose any money in Frank's business venture.*

luck² *v.* INFORMAL

luck into sth *phr. v.* to manage to get something good by chance: *We lucked into great seats near the stage.*

luck out *phr. v.* to be lucky: *We lucked out and found someone who spoke English.*

luck·i·ly /ˈlʌkəli/ *adv.* as a result of good luck SYN **fortunately**: [sentence adverb] *Luckily, no one was injured in the accident.* | **+for** *Luckily for me, I had loving parents.*

luck·less /ˈlʌklɪs/ *adj.* LITERARY having no good luck in something you are trying to do: *a luckless explorer who died alone in the wilderness*

luck·y /ˈlʌki/ S2 W3 *adj. comparative* **luckier**, *superlative* **luckiest** **1** having good luck SYN **fortunate** OPP **unlucky**: **be lucky to do/be sth** *He's lucky to be alive.* | *We were lucky to find a parking spot.* | *John was*

lucky enough to** be selected for the team.* | **lucky (that)** *Janet's lucky the car didn't hit her.* | **+with** *We've been very lucky with the weather* | *We **got lucky (=achieved something because we were lucky) *and won a few races.* | **consider/count yourself lucky** *William considered himself lucky to have married Leonora.* **2** resulting from good luck: *Then the Red Wings scored a very lucky goal.* | *That was just **a lucky guess**. I had no idea what the answer was.* **3** bringing good luck: *a lucky rabbit's foot*

SPOKEN PHRASES

4 lucky you/me etc.! used to say that someone is fortunate to be able to do something: *"I've got free tickets to the game!" "Lucky you."* **5 be sb's lucky day** used to say that something good and often unexpected has happened to someone: *"Look at the size of the fish I caught!" "It must be your lucky day!"* **6 I'll be lucky if...** used to say that you think something is very unlikely: *I'll be lucky if I get even half of my money back.* **7 I/you should be so lucky!** used to say that someone wants something that is not likely to happen, especially because it is unreasonable: *Sleep past 6 a.m.? I should be so lucky!* **8 (you) lucky dog!** used to say that someone is very lucky and that you wish you had what they have: *You didn't have to pay for the tickets? You lucky dog!*

→ see also **thank your lucky stars** at THANK (4) → see Word Choice box at LUCK[1]

lu·cra·tive /ˈlukrət̬ɪv/ *adj.* a job or activity that is lucrative lets you earn a lot of money SYN **profitable**: *a lucrative business* [**Origin:** 1400–1500 Latin *lucrativus*, from *lucrari* **to gain**]

lu·cre /ˈlukɚ/ *n.* [U] DISAPPROVING money or wealth

Lud·dite /ˈlʌdaɪt/ *n.* [C] DISAPPROVING someone who is strongly opposed to using modern machines and methods SYN **technophobe**

lude /lud/ *n.* [C] SLANG A QUAALUDE

lu·di·crous /ˈludɪkrəs/ *adj.* completely unreasonable, stupid, or wrong SYN **ridiculous**: *They want two million dollars for the house? That's ludicrous!* [**Origin:** 1600–1700 Latin *ludicrus* **playful**, from *ludus* **play**] —**ludicrously** *adv.*: *The test was ludicrously easy.* —**ludicrousness** *n.* [U]

L

lug[1] /lʌg/ *v.* **lugged, lugging** [T] to pull or carry something heavy with difficulty: **lug sth up/down/around etc. sth** *We had to lug our suitcases up four flights of stairs.* ►see THESAURUS box at **carry**[1]

lug[2] *n.* [C] a big stupid slow-moving man: *I can't figure out why she's so attracted to that **big lug**.*

luge /luʒ/ *n.* [C] a vehicle with blades instead of wheels, on which you slide down a track made of ice

lug·gage /ˈlʌgɪdʒ/ *n.* [U] the suitcases, bags etc. carried by someone who is traveling [**Origin:** 1500–1600 *lug* + *-age* (as in baggage)]

ˈluggage rack *n.* [C] **1** a special frame on top of a car that you tie luggage, boxes etc. onto **2** a shelf in a train, bus etc. for putting luggage on

ˈlug nut *n.* [C] a small rounded NUT that is screwed onto a BOLT

lu·gu·bri·ous /ləˈgubriəs/ *adj.* LITERARY OR HUMOROUS very sad and serious: *a lugubrious voice* —**lugubriously** *adv.* —**lugubriousness** *n.* [U]

Luke /luk/ also **the Gospel according to St. Luke** one of the four books in the New Testament of the Christian Bible that describe the life and teaching of Jesus

Luke, Saint in the Bible, one of the 12 APOSTLES, who is believed to have written the Gospel according to St. Luke

luke·warm /ˌlukˈwɔrm◂/ *adj.* **1** food, liquid etc. that is lukewarm is slightly warm, often when it should be hot: *a lukewarm bath* | *The meal was only lukewarm.* ►see THESAURUS box at **hot** **2** not showing much interest or excitement: *The movie received a lukewarm reaction from critics.*

lull[1] /lʌl/ *v.* [T] **1** to make someone feel calm or sleepy: *The soft music lulled me to sleep.* **2** to make someone feel safe and confident so that they are completely surprised when something bad happens: **lull sb into (doing) sth** *The tests have lulled the public into believing the water is safe to drink.* | *The disease is not common, but tourists should not be **lulled into a false sense of security*** (=made to think they are safe when they are not).

lull[2] *n.* [C] **1** a short period of time when there is less activity or less noise than usual: **+in** *a brief lull in the conversation* | *a lull in the fighting* **2 the lull before the storm** a short period of time when things are calm that is followed by a lot of activity, noise, or trouble

lul·la·by /ˈlʌləˌbaɪ/ *n. plural* **lullabies** [C] a slow quiet song sung to children to make them go to sleep [**Origin:** 1500–1600 *lulla* word used to make a child calm or sleepy (15–18 centuries) + *bye* word used to make a child sleepy (15–20 centuries)]

lu·lu /ˈlulu/ *n.* [C] INFORMAL **1** something very good or exciting: *The roller coaster at Magic Mountain is **a real lulu**.* **2** something extremely stupid, bad, embarrassing etc.: *She's said some stupid things in her life, but that one was a lulu!*

lum·ba·go /lʌmˈbeɪgoʊ/ *n.* [U] OLD-FASHIONED pain in the lower part of the back

lum·bar /ˈlʌmbɑr, -bɚ/ *adj.* BIOLOGY relating to the lower part of the back: *The seats have built-in lumbar supports.*

lum·ber[1] /ˈlʌmbɚ/ *v.* [I] **1** [always + adv./prep.] to move in a slow, awkward way: **lumber after/into/along etc. sth** *The bear lumbered over to our campsite.* **2** to cut down trees in a large area and prepare them to be sold **3** [always + adv./prep.] to operate slowly and not effectively: **lumber along/through etc. sth** *The company lumbered through the 1990s until it was taken over in 2004.*

lumber[2] *n.* [U] pieces of wood used for building, that have been cut to specific lengths and widths → see also TIMBER: *stacks of lumber* | *lumber companies* ►see THESAURUS box at **tree**

lum·ber·jack /ˈlʌmbɚˌdʒæk/ *n.* [C] OLD-FASHIONED someone whose job is cutting down trees for wood

lum·ber·man /ˈlʌmbɚmən/ *n.* [C] someone in the business of cutting down large areas of trees and selling them for wood

lum·ber·yard /ˈlʌmbɚˌyɑrd/ *n.* [C] a place where wood is kept before it is sold

lu·mi·nar·y /ˈluməˌnɛri/ *n. plural* **luminaries** [C] someone who is very famous or highly respected for their skill at doing something or their knowledge of a particular subject: *Jazz luminary Oscar Peterson*

lu·mi·nous /ˈlumənəs/ *adj.* **1** made of a substance or material that shines in the dark: *luminous paint* | *luminous road signs* **2** very brightly colored, especially in green, pink, or yellow: *luminous socks* **3** LITERARY bright or full of light in a way that is beautiful SYN **shining** SYN **radiant**: *her luminous eyes* **4** FORMAL writing, music etc. that is luminous is very powerful because it explains or describes something in a strong, clear way **5** TECHNICAL producing light: *a star that is 500 times as luminous as the sun* —**luminously** *adv.* —**luminosity** /ˌluməˈnɑsət̬i/ *n.* [U]

lum·mox /ˈlʌməks/ *n.* [C] LITERARY a large stupid slow-moving man

lump[1] /lʌmp/ *n.* [C] **1** a small piece of something solid, that does not have a definite shape: *Stir the batter until all the lumps are gone.* | **+of** *a lump of clay* ►see THESAURUS box at **piece**[1] **2** a small hard swollen area that sticks out from someone's skin or grows in their body, usually because of an illness: *The lump in Kay's breast was cancerous.* **3 bring a lump to sb's throat** to make someone feel as if they want to cry: *Martin's speech at the funeral brought a lump to my throat.* **4** also **sugar lump** a small square block of sugar, used to make coffee or tea sweet **5 take your lumps** INFOR-

MAL to accept the bad things that happen to you and not let them affect you: *If the critics don't like the book, I'll have to take my lumps.*

lump² *v.* [T] DISAPPROVING [always + adv./prep.] to consider two or more different people together as a single group, rather than treating them separately: **lump sth together** *The statistics lump all minority students together.* | **lump sth (in) with sth** *Marijuana is often lumped in with more dangerous drugs.*

lump·ec·to·my /lʌm'pɛktəmi/ *n.* [C] an operation in which a TUMOR is removed from someone's body, especially from a woman's breast

lum·pen /'lʌmpən, 'lʊm-/ *adj.* [only before noun] unintelligent and rude

lump·ish /'lʌmpɪʃ/ *adj.* **1** awkward or stupid: *lumpish dialogue* **2** like a lump: *lumpish food*

ˌlump 'sum *n.* [C] an amount of money given in a single payment: *At retirement, your pension money can be taken out as a lump sum.*

lump·y /'lʌmpi/ *adj. comparative* **lumpier**, *superlative* **lumpiest** DISAPPROVING covered with or containing small solid pieces OPP **smooth**: *lumpy mashed potatoes* | *a lumpy mattress*

lu·na·cy /'lunəsi/ *n.* [U] **1** a situation or behavior that is completely crazy: *It would be* ***sheer lunacy*** *to turn down a great offer like that.* **2** OLD-FASHIONED mental illness → see also LUNATIC

lu·nar /'lunɚ/ *adj.* relating to the moon or with travel to the moon: *the lunar landscape*

ˌlunar e'clipse *n.* [C] an occasion when the sun and the moon are on the opposite sides of the Earth, so that the moon is hidden by the Earth's shadow for a short time

ˌlunar 'month *n.* [C] a period of 28 or 29 days between one NEW MOON and the next

lu·na·tic /'lunəˌtɪk/ *n.* [C] **1** someone who behaves in a crazy or very stupid way: *Some lunatic came into the store and shot him.* **2** OLD-FASHIONED TECHNICAL someone who is mentally ill **3 the lunatic fringe** the people in a political group or organization who have the most extreme opinions or ideas [**Origin:** 1200–1300 Old French *lunatique*, from Latin *luna* **moon**; because people thought mental illness was caused by the moon] —**lunatic** *adj.*

'lunatic aˌsylum *n.* [C] OLD-FASHIONED a word for a hospital where people who are mentally ill are cared for, now considered offensive

lunch¹ /lʌntʃ/ S1 W2 *n.* [C,U] **1** a meal eaten in the middle of the day, or the period during the day when you eat this meal: *We've already* ***had lunch.*** | *I'm starved. Let's* ***have some lunch.*** | *What did you bring* ***for lunch?*** | *Let's talk about this* ***over lunch*** (=during lunch). | *She's* ***at lunch*** (=away from her work, eating lunch) *right now, can I help you?* | *She came last week and* ***took*** *my parents* ***out to lunch*** (=paid for their lunch at a restaurant). | *What time are we going to* ***go to lunch*** (=go somewhere to eat lunch)*?* | *The restaurant's atmosphere is well-suited for a* ***working lunch*** (=a lunch during which you discuss business). | **bag/sack lunch** (=food, usually sandwiches, that you take with you to work, school etc.) ►see THESAURUS box at **meal** **2 sb's out to lunch** INFORMAL used to say that someone behaves or talks in a strange or confused way [**Origin:** 1800–1900 *luncheon*] → see also **there's no free lunch** at FREE¹ (15)

lunch² *v.* FORMAL [I] to eat lunch

lunch·box /'lʌntʃbɑks/ *n.* [C] a box in which food is carried to school, work etc.

'lunch break *n.* [C] the time in the middle of the day when people at work stop working to eat lunch

'lunch ˌcounter *n.* [C] a place in a building or store in the past that served quick, simple meals for lunch, or a small restaurant that was open only for lunch

lunch·eon /'lʌntʃən/ *n.* [C,U] FORMAL lunch

lunch·eon·ette /ˌlʌntʃə'nɛt/ *n.* [C] a place in a building or store in the past that served quick, simple food for lunch

'lunch meat also **'luncheon meat** *n.* [U] meat that has been cooked and sold in SLICES SYN **cold cuts**

'lunch pail *n.* [C] a PAIL (=metal container) that children or workers carried their lunch in in past times

lunch·room /'lʌntʃrum/ *n.* [C] a large room in a school or office where people can eat → see also CAFETERIA

lunch·time /'lʌntʃtaɪm/ *n.* [U] the time in the middle of the day when people usually eat their lunch

lungs

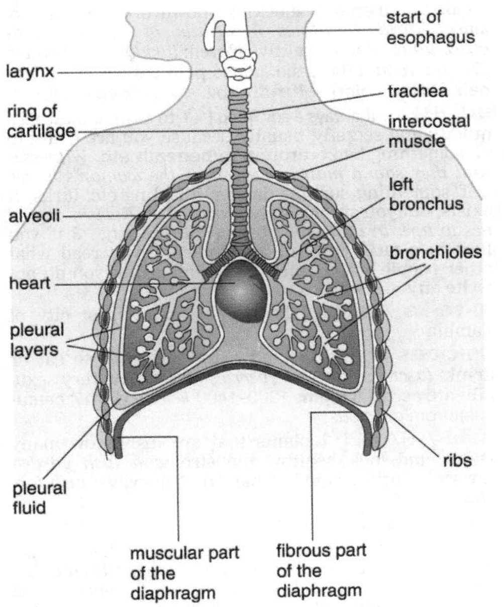

lung /lʌŋ/ S3 *n.* [C] BIOLOGY one of the two organs in your body that you breathe with: *Take a deep breath and really fill your lungs.* | *lung cancer* [**Origin:** Old English] → see also IRON LUNG, **sing/shout/yell etc. at the top of your lungs** at TOP¹ (14)

lunge /lʌndʒ/ *v.* [I] to make a sudden forceful movement toward someone or something, for example to attack them: **+at** *The man lunged at them with a knife.* | **+forward/toward etc.** *Turner lunged toward the goal line.* [**Origin:** 1700–1800 French *allonger* **to make longer, put (your arm) out**] —**lunge** *n.* [C]

lunk·head /'lʌŋkhɛd/ *n.* [C] INFORMAL someone who is very stupid

lu·pine /'lupən/ *n.* [C] a plant with a tall stem and many small flowers

lu·pus /'lupəs/ *n.* [U] any of several diseases that affect the skin and joints [**Origin:** 1500–1600 Latin **wolf**; because people with the disease were thought to look as if they had been attacked by a wolf]

lurch¹ /lɚtʃ/ *v.* [I] **1** to walk or move suddenly in an uncontrolled or unsteady way: **+across/into/along etc.** *Jill lurched into me drunkenly.* **2 your heart/stomach lurches** used to say that your heart or stomach seems to move suddenly because you feel shocked, frightened etc. **3 lurch from sth to sth** to have one serious problem after another and seem to have no plan and no control over what you are doing: *The country's economy seemed to lurch from one disaster to another.*

lurch² *n.* [C] **1** a sudden movement: *The train made a violent lurch forward.* **2 leave sb in the lurch** to leave someone at a time when they need your help: *The pager company shut down Tuesday, leaving 2,000 customers in the lurch.*

lure¹ /lʊr/ *n.* [C] **1** [usually singular] something that attracts people, so that they want something or want to do something, or the quality of attracting people in this way → see also TEMPTATION: *The promise of gambling is a lure for tourists.* | +**of** *the lure of power and money* **2** an object used to attract animals or fish so that they can be caught → see also DECOY

lure² *v.* [T] to persuade someone to do something, often something wrong or dangerous, by making it seem attractive or exciting: *People can be lured into buying products they don't need by smart advertising.*

lu·rid /ˈlʊrɪd/ *adj.* **1** a description, story etc. that is lurid is deliberately shocking and involves sex or violence: *lurid headlines* | *details of lurid sexual misconduct* **2** too brightly colored: *lurid red nail polish* [**Origin:** 1600–1700 Latin *luridus* **pale yellow**, from *luror* **pale yellow color**] —**luridly** *adv.* —**luridness** *n.* [U]

lurk /lɚk/ *v.* [I always +adv./prep.] **1** to wait somewhere quietly and secretly, usually because you are going to do something bad: +**around/in/beneath etc.** *Witnesses said they saw a man lurking near the woman's home.* **2** if something such as danger, a feeling etc. lurks, it exists, but you are not fully AWARE of it: *Racism continues to lurk in the heart of American society.* **3** if you lurk in a CHAT ROOM on the Internet, you read what other people are writing to each other but you do not write any messages yourself

Lu·sa·ka /luˈsɑkə/ the capital and largest city of Zambia

lus·cious /ˈlʌʃəs/ *adj.* **1** extremely good to eat or drink: *luscious ripe strawberries* **2** INFORMAL very sexually attractive [**Origin:** 1300–1400 *licious* (14–17 centuries), from *delicious*]

lush¹ /lʌʃ/ *adj.* **1** plants that are lush grow many leaves and look healthy and strong: *a lush garden* **2** very beautiful, comfortable, and expensive: *lush fabrics*

lush² *n.* [C] INFORMAL an ALCOHOLIC

lust¹ /lʌst/ *n.* **1** [C,U] very strong sexual desire, especially when it does not include liking or love: *Their affair was based on lust not love.* **2** [singular, U] a very strong desire to have something, usually power or money: +**for** *Stalin's unbridled lust for power* **3 (a) lust for life** a strong determination to enjoy life as much as possible

lust² *v.*

lust after sb/sth *phr. v.* INFORMAL, OFTEN HUMOROUS **1** to be strongly sexually attracted to someone, and think about having sex with them: *Andy's been lusting after Marla for years.* **2** to want something very much, especially something that you do not really need: *I had always lusted after the 1957 Chevy Bel Air in the window.*

lus·ter /ˈlʌstɚ/ *n.* [singular, U] **1** the quality that makes something interesting or exciting: *Beverly Hills has not **lost its luster**.* | **add/give luster to sth** *A celebrity guest will add luster to the occasion.* **2** an attractive shiny appearance: *the natural luster of the animal's fur*

lust·ful /ˈlʌstfəl/ *adj.* feeling or showing strong sexual desire —**lustfully** *adv.*

lus·trous /ˈlʌstrəs/ *adj.* shining in a soft, gentle way: *lustrous black hair*

lust·y /ˈlʌsti/ *adj.* *comparative* **lustier**, *superlative* **lustiest** strong and healthy SYN **powerful**: *The baby gave a lusty cry.* | *lusty young men* —**lustily** *adv.* —**lustiness** *n.* [U]

lute /lut/ *n.* [C] a musical instrument similar to a GUITAR with a round body, played especially in past times

Lu·ther /ˈluθɚ/, **Mar·tin** /ˈmɑrtˀn/ (1483–1546) a German religious leader whose ideas helped to start the Reformation, and who translated the Bible from Latin into German

Lu·ther·an /ˈluθərən/ *n.* [C] a member of a Protestant Christian church that follows the teachings and ideas of Martin Luther —**Lutheran** *adj.*

Lux·em·bourg /ˈlʌksəmˌbɚg/ **1** a small country in western Europe, between Germany and France **2** the capital city of Luxembourg —**Luxembourger** *n.*

Lux·em·burg /ˈlʌksəmˌbɚg/, **Ro·sa** /ˈroʊzə/ (1871–1919) a German SOCIALIST leader, born in Poland

lux·u·ri·ant /lʌgˈʒʊriənt, lʌkˈʃʊ-/ *adj.* **1** growing strongly and thickly: *a luxuriant black beard* | *luxuriant vegetation* **2** beautiful and pleasing to your senses: *luxuriant prose* —**luxuriantly** *adv.* —**luxuriance** *n.* [U]

lux·u·ri·ate /lʌgˈʒʊriˌeɪt/ *v.* [I usually + adv./prep.] to relax and deliberately try to enjoy something: *She luxuriated in the bathtub for an hour.*

lux·u·ri·ous /lʌgˈʒʊriəs/ *adj.* very expensive, beautiful, and comfortable: *a luxurious brown leather sofa* | *The hotel was old and luxurious.* —**luxuriously** *adv.* —**luxuriousness** *n.* [C]

lux·u·ry /ˈlʌkʃəri, ˈlʌgʒəri/ *n.* *plural* **luxuries** **1** [U] very great comfort and pleasure, such as you get from expensive food, beautiful things etc.: *Champagne and caviar are symbols of luxury* | *We traveled **in luxury** on a friend's yacht.* | **a luxury home/vacation/car etc.** (=expensive and of the highest standard) | *They led **a life of luxury**, in a huge house in the country.* **2** [C] something pleasant or good that you are not always able to have or experience, or that you would like to have but cannot: *A night alone felt like a luxury.* | *This was the first time I'd ever **had the luxury of** a regular paycheck.* **3** [C] something expensive that you do not need, but that you buy for pleasure and enjoyment → see also NECESSITY: *We can't afford luxuries like piano lessons any more.* [**Origin:** 1300–1400 Old French *luxurie*, from Latin *luxuria* **too great quantity**] → see also **in the lap of luxury** at LAP¹ (5)

LVN *n.* [C] a LICENSED VOCATIONAL NURSE

LW the written abbreviation of LONG WAVE

-ly /li/ *suffix* **1** [in adverbs] in a particular way: *slowly* | *secretly* **2** [in adverbs] considered in a particular way: *politically* (=considered in terms of politics) | *financially* (=considered in relation to money) **3** [in adjectives and adverbs] happening at regular periods of time: *hourly* (=done every hour) | *monthly* (=once a month) **4** [in adjectives] like a particular thing or person in manner, type, or appearance: *motherly* (=showing the love, kindness etc. of a mother)

ly·ce·um /laɪˈsiəm, -ˈseɪəm/ *n.* [C] OLD-FASHIONED a building used for public meetings, concerts, speeches etc.

ly·chee /ˈlitʃi/ *n.* [C] BIOLOGY a small round fruit with a rough pink-brown shell and sweet white flesh [**Origin:** 1500–1600 Chinese *lizhi*]

Ly·cra /ˈlaɪkrə/ *n.* [U] TRADEMARK a material that stretches, used especially for making tight-fitting sports clothes

lye /laɪ/ *n.* [U] a substance using for making soap in past times

ly·ing /ˈlaɪ-ɪŋ/ *v.* the present participle of LIE

ˌlying-ˈin *n.* [singular] OLD-FASHIONED the period of time during which a woman stays in bed before and after the birth of a child

Lyme dis·ease /ˈlaɪm dɪˌziz/ *n.* [U] MEDICINE a serious illness that is caused by a bite from a TICK

lymph /lɪmf/ *n.* [U] BIOLOGY a clear liquid that is formed in your body and passes into your blood, which contains cells that help to fight against infection [**Origin:** 1600–1700 Latin *lympha* **water goddess, water**, from Greek *nymphe*] —**lymphatic** /lɪmˈfæt̬ɪk/ *adj.*

ˈlymph node also **ˈlymph gland** *n.* [C] BIOLOGY a small rounded GLAND in your body through which lymph passes for the removal of BACTERIA before entering your blood system

lym·pho·cyte /ˈlɪmfəˌsaɪt/ *n.* [C] BIOLOGY a kind of white blood cell that produces ANTIBODIES to fight disease

lynch /lɪntʃ/ *v.* [T] if a crowd of people lynches someone, they kill them, especially by HANGing them, without using the usual legal process: *One of the city leaders was nearly lynched by the mob.* [**Origin:** 1800–1900 William *Lynch* (1724–1820), U.S. citizen who organized illegal trials in Virginia] —**lynching** *n.* [C]

ˈlynch mob *n.* [C] a group of people that kills someone by HANGing them, without a legal TRIAL

lynch·pin /ˈlɪntʃˌpɪn/ *n.* [C] another spelling of LINCHPIN

Lynn /lɪn/, **Lo·ret·ta** /ləˈrɛt̬ə/ (1935–) a U.S. COUNTRY AND WESTERN singer

lynx /lɪŋks/ *n.* [C] a large wild cat that has no tail and lives in forests

lyre /laɪɚ/ *n.* [C] a musical instrument with strings across a U-shaped frame, used especially in ancient Greece

lyr·ic¹ /ˈlɪrɪk/ *n.* ENG. LANG. ARTS **1** [C] a poem, usually a short one, written in a lyric style **2 lyrics** [plural] the words of a song, especially a modern popular song: *the brilliance of Sondheim's lyrics* [**Origin:** 1500–1600 French *lyrique* **of a lyre**, from Latin, from Greek, from *lyra*]

lyric² *adj.* [only before noun] **1** expressing strong personal emotions such as love, in a way that is similar to music in its sounds and RHYTHM: *lyric poetry* **2** ENG. LANG. ARTS a lyric singing voice is high and not very loud: *a lyric soprano*

lyr·i·cal /ˈlɪrɪkəl/ *adj.* **1** ENG. LANG. ARTS beautifully expressed in words, poetry, or music: *her lyrical first novel* **2 wax lyrical** to talk about and praise something in a very eager way: *The coach waxed lyrical on his team's winning effort.* —**lyrically** /-kli/ *adv.*

lyr·i·cism /ˈlɪrəˌsɪzəm/ *n.* [U] the romantic or song-like expression of something in writing or music

lyr·i·cist /ˈlɪrəsɪst/ *n.* [C] someone who writes the words for songs, especially modern popular songs

ly·so·gen·ic in·fec·tion /ˌlaɪsədʒɛnɪk ɪnˈfɛkʃən/ *n.* [C,U] BIOLOGY a process of infection in which a VIRUS enters a cell bringing together its DNA and the cell's DNA, so that when the DNA copies itself, the virus is copied and spreads in this way

ly·tic in·fec·tion /ˌlɪt̬ɪk ɪnˈfɛkʃən/ *n.* [C,U] BIOLOGY the normal process of infection of a cell in which a VIRUS enters a cell, makes a copy of itself, and causes the cell to burst

L

M,m

M¹, m /ɛm/ *n. plural* **M's, m's** **1** [C] **a)** the 13th letter of the English alphabet **b)** the sound represented by this letter **2 M0/M1/M2/M3 etc.** [singular, U] TECHNICAL different measures of a country's supply of money

M² **1** the number 1,000 in the system of ROMAN NUMERALS **2** the written abbreviation of MALE **3** the written abbreviation of MEDIUM, used on clothes to show the size **4** the written abbreviation of MILLION: *$300M* (=$300,000,000)

m **1** the written abbreviation for METER **2** PHYSICS the abbreviation for MASS, when written in ITALICS

m. **1** the written abbreviation of MILE **2** the written abbreviation of "married"

MA the written abbreviation of MASSACHUSETTS

Ma, ma /mɑ/ *n.* [C] INFORMAL **1** mother: *Hey Ma, can I go out with Billy?* **2** OLD-FASHIONED a word meaning "Mrs.," used in some country areas of the U.S.: *old Ma Harris*

M.A. *n.* [C] **Master of Arts** a university degree in a subject such as history or literature that you can get after you have your first degree: *Mrs. Wilding has an M.A. in education.* → see also M.S.

ma'am /mæm/ *n.* SPOKEN **1** used to address a woman in order to be polite or show respect: *Can I help you today, ma'am?* **2** used to get the attention of a woman whose name you do not know: *Excuse me ma'am, are these keys yours?* → see also MADAM, SIR

Mac /mæk/ *n.* **1** [C] COMPUTERS **Macintosh** a type of PERSONAL COMPUTER: *My roommate just got a Mac.* **2** SPOKEN, IMPOLITE used to talk to a man whose name you do not know: *Hey, Mac, get out of the way.*

ma·ca·bre /məˈkɑbrə, məˈkɑb/ *adj.* very strange and unpleasant, and relating to death, serious accidents etc.: *a macabre sense of humor* | *a macabre tale of murder* [**Origin:** 1400–1500 French *(danse) macabre* **dance of death**, from earlier *(danse de) Macabré*]

mac·ad·am /məˈkædəm/ *n.* [U] a road surface made of layers of broken stones and TAR or ASPHALT

mac·a·da·mi·a /ˌmækəˈdeɪmiə/ *n.* [C] **1** also **maca'damia nut** a sweet nut that grows on a tropical tree **2** a tree that produces this type of nut [**Origin:** 1900–2000 John *Macadam* (1827–1865), Australian scientist]

Ma·cao, Macau /məˈkaʊ/ a small area in southeast China, which was a Portuguese PROVINCE but became part of China in 1999

mac·a·ro·ni /ˌmækəˈroʊni◂/ *n.* [U] a type of PASTA in the shape of small tubes, which is cooked in boiling water: *a good recipe for* ***macaroni and cheese*** (=macaroni baked with a cheese sauce) [**Origin:** 1500–1600 Italian *maccheroni*, from Italian dialect *maccarone*]

mac·a·roon /ˌmækəˈrun/ *n.* [C] a small round cookie made of sugar, eggs, and crushed ALMONDS or COCONUT [**Origin:** 1500–1600 French *macaron*, from Italian dialect *maccarone*]

Mac·Ar·thur /məˈkɑrθɚ/, **Doug·las** /ˈdʌgləs/ (1880–1964) the leader of the U.S. Army in the Pacific area during World War II

ma·caw /məˈkɔ/ *n.* [C] BIOLOGY a large brightly colored bird like a PARROT, with a long tail

Mac·ca·bees /ˈmækəˌbiz/ **1 Maccabees, 2 Maccabees** two books in the Apocrypha of the Protestant Bible and in the Old Testament of the Catholic Bible

Mace /meɪs/ *n.* [U] TRADEMARK a chemical that makes your eyes and skin sting painfully, which some women carry to defend themselves

mace /meɪs/ *n.* **1** [U] powder made from the dried shell of a NUTMEG, used to give food a special taste **2** [C] a heavy ball with sharp points that is attached to a short metal stick, used in past times as a weapon **3** [C] a decorated stick that is carried by an official in some ceremonies as a sign of power

Ma·ce·do·nia /ˌmæsɪˈdoʊnyə/ **1** a country in southeast Europe, north of Greece and south of Serbia, that was formerly part of Yugoslavia and is officially called the Former Yugoslav Republic of Macedonia (FYROM) **2** a PROVINCE of northern Greece —**Macedonian** *n., adj.*

mac·er·ate /ˈmæsəˌreɪt/ *v.* [I,T] TECHNICAL to make something soft by leaving it in water, or to become soft in this way —**maceration** /ˌmæsəˈreɪʃən/ *n.* [U]

Mach, mach /mɑk/ *n.* [U] a unit for measuring speed, especially of an aircraft, in relation to the speed of sound, in which Mach 1 is the speed of sound, Mach 2 is twice the speed of sound etc.

ma·che·te /məˈʃɛṭi, -ˈtʃɛ-/ *n.* [C] a large knife with a broad heavy blade, used as a weapon or a tool

Mach·i·a·vel·li /ˌmækiəˈvɛli/, **Nic·co·lò** /ˈnɪkəloʊ/ (1469–1527) an Italian political PHILOSOPHER famous for his book "The Prince," in which he explains how political leaders can gain power and keep it

Mach·i·a·vel·li·an /ˌmækiəˈvɛliən/ *adj.* using smart but immoral methods to get what you want: *a Machiavellian conspiracy*

mach·i·na·tions /ˌmækəˈneɪʃənz, ˌmæʃə-/ *n.* [plural] secret and often complicated plans, usually to get a result that gives you an advantage: *political machinations*

ma·chine¹ /məˈʃin/ S1 W1 *n.* [C] **1** a piece of equipment that uses power such as electricity to do a particular job: *Just hit that button to stop the machine.* | *Our soft-serve ice cream machine isn't working.* | *Can you show me how to* ***operate the machine?*** | **turn/switch a machine on/off** *Turn the machine off before removing the cover.* | **sewing/washing etc. machine** (=a machine that can sew, wash clothes etc.) | **a copy/fax etc. machine** (=a machine that makes copies, sends faxes etc.)

> **THESAURUS**
>
> **appliance** a machine that is used in the home: *kitchen appliances such as refrigerators*
> **device** a piece of equipment that is usually small and usually electronic, that does a special job: *A seismograph is a device that measures earthquake activity.*
> **gadget** a small piece of equipment that makes a particular job easier to do: *a gadget that tells you exactly where you are on the map*

2 a computer: *Her new machine's much faster.* **3** INFORMAL an ANSWERING MACHINE: *I left a message for you on your machine.* **4** POLITICS a group of people who control an organization, especially a political party: *the Republican party machine* | *the government's propaganda machine* **5** a person or animal that does something very well or without having to think about it: *The tiger is the perfect hunting machine.* **6** someone who does something without stopping, or who seems to have no feelings or independent thoughts: *He's like an eating machine.* **7 like a well-oiled machine** working very smoothly and effectively [**Origin:** 1500–1600 Old French, Latin *machina*, from Greek *mechane*, from *mechos* **way of doing things**] → see also CASH MACHINE, SLOT MACHINE, TIME MACHINE

machine² *v.* [T] **1** to fasten pieces of cloth together using a SEWING MACHINE **2** to make or shape something using a machine

ma'chine ˌcode *n.* [C,U] COMPUTERS instructions in the form of numbers that are understood by a computer

ma'chine gun *n.* [C] a gun that fires a lot of bullets very quickly —**machinegun** *v.* [T]

M

ma'chine ˌlanguage *n.* [C,U] instructions in a form such as numbers that can be used by a computer

ma'chine-made *adj.* made using a machine: *machine-made candles* → see also HANDMADE

maˌchine 'readable *adj.* in a form that can be understood and used by a computer

ma·chin·er·y /mə'ʃinəri/ *n.* [U] **1** machines, especially large ones: *farm machinery* | *labor-saving machinery* | *a license to operate* ***heavy machinery*** (=large machines or vehicles) **2** the parts inside a machine that make it work: *Loose clothing can easily get caught in the machinery.* **3** POLITICS system or set of processes for doing something: +**of** *the machinery of government* | +**machinery for (doing) sth** *The company has no effective machinery for resolving disputes.*

ma'chine ˌshop *n.* [C] a company, or a part of a company that makes products, especially out of metal, using machines to cut and shape them

ma'chine ˌtool *n.* [C] a tool used for cutting and shaping metal, wood etc., usually run by electricity

ma'chine transˌlation *n.* [U] translation done by a computer

maˌchine-'washable *adj.* able to be washed in a WASHING MACHINE, rather than washed by a person —**machine wash** *v.* [T usually passive]

ma·chin·ist /mə'ʃinɪst/ *n.* [C] someone who operates a machine, especially in a factory

ma·chis·mo /mɑ'tʃɪzmoʊ/ *n.* [U] traditional male behavior that emphasizes how brave, strong, and sexually attractive a man is

ma·cho /'mɑtʃoʊ/ *adj.* INFORMAL macho behavior emphasizes a man's physical strength, lack of sensitive feelings, and other qualities considered to be typical of men: *a car with a macho image* | *He always plays the tough* ***macho man*** *in movies.* [**Origin:** 1900–2000 Spanish **male**, from Latin *masculus*]

Mac·ken·zie /mə'kɛnzi/**, Alexander** (1764–1820) a Scottish EXPLORER who discovered the Mackenzie River in Canada and was the first European to cross the North American CONTINENT

mack·er·el /'mækərəl/ *n. plural* **mackerel** [C] BIOLOGY an ocean fish that has oily flesh and a strong taste

mack·in·tosh /'mækɪnˌtɑʃ/ *n.* [C] OLD-FASHIONED a RAINCOAT [**Origin:** 1800–1900 Charles *Macintosh* (1766–1843), Scottish scientist who invented a way of preventing liquid from getting through cloth]

Mack truck /'mæk trʌk/ *n.* [C] TRADEMARK a type of large truck used to carry goods

mac·ra·mé /ˌmækrə'meɪ/ *n.* [U] the art of knotting string together in patterns for decoration

mac·ro /'mækroʊ/ *n. plural* **macros** [C] COMPUTERS a set of instructions for a computer, stored and used as a unit

macro- /mækroʊ, -krə/ *prefix* TECHNICAL dealing with large systems as a single unit, rather than with the particular parts of them: *macroeconomics* (=the study of large money systems) → see also MICRO-

mac·ro·bi·ot·ic /ˌmækroʊbaɪ'ɑtɪk/ *adj.* macrobiotic food consists mainly of grains and vegetables, with no added chemicals

mac·ro·cosm /'mækrəˌkɑzəm/ *n.* [C] a large complicated system such as the whole universe or a society, considered as a single unit → see also MICROCOSM

mac·ro·ec·o·nom·ics /ˌmækroʊˌɛkə'nɑmɪks/ *n.* [U] ECONOMICS the study of large economic systems such as those of a whole country or area of the world —**macroeconomic** *adj.* → see also MICROECONOMICS

mac·ro·ev·o·lu·tion /ˌmækroʊˌɛvə'luʃən/ *n.* [U] BIOLOGY very large and important changes to the way in which whole groups of plants, animals etc. develop over a long period of time, especially at the level of a KINGDOM (=one of the largest groups into which plants, animals etc. are placed in a scientific system) —**macroevolutionary** *adj.*: *Macroevolutionary processes occur above the level of species.*

mac·ro·mol·e·cule /ˌmækroʊ'mɑləˌkyul/ *n.* [C] CHEMISTRY a large MOLECULE such as a PROTEIN

mac·ro·nu·cle·us /ˌmækroʊ'nukliəs/ *n. plural* **macronuclei** /-kliaɪ/ [C] BIOLOGY the larger of the two nuclei (NUCLEUS) in a simple living creature that has only one cell, which is involved in the activities of the cell that are not related to REPRODUCTION, for example feeding and taking in energy from food → see also MICRONUCLEUS

mac·ro·scop·ic /ˌmækrə'skɑpɪk/ *adj.* SCIENCE large enough to be seen or examined without using equipment such as a MICROSCOPE or a TELESCOPE [OPP] **microscopic**: *The organism can induce fever and microscopic lung lesions but not the macroscopic changes of pneumonia.*

mad /mæd/ [S1] [W3] *adj. comparative* **madder**, *superlative* **maddest**

1 ANGRY [not before noun] angry: *Was he mad?* | +**about** *Mom was really mad about my grades.* | **mad at sb** *Why are you so mad at me? I didn't do anything.* | *Cara* ***got*** *really* ***mad.*** | **hopping/boiling mad** (=very angry) ▸see THESAURUS box at **angry**

2 do sth like mad INFORMAL to do something as quickly or as well as you can: *I ran like mad to catch up to his car.*

3 WILD/UNCONTROLLED behaving in a wild uncontrolled way, without thinking about what you are doing [SYN] **crazy**

4 MENTALLY ILL OLD-FASHIONED or LITERARY mentally ill [SYN] **insane**: *a mad gleam in his eye* | *He looked at me as if I had* ***gone mad.***

5 be mad about sb/sth OLD-FASHIONED to love someone or be extremely interested in something, in a strong uncontrolled way

6 CRAZY BRITISH crazy or silly

[**Origin:** Old English *gemæd*]

-mad /mæd/ [in adjectives] **power-mad/money-mad/sex-mad etc.** only interested in power, money etc.: *This country is publicity-mad.*

Mad·a·gas·car /ˌmædə'gæskɚ/ an island in the Indian Ocean near the coast of southeast Africa that is an independent country —**Madagascan** *n., adj.*

mad·am /'mædəm/ *n.* **1 Madam President/Ambassador etc.** used to address a woman who has an important official position **2 Dear Madam** used at the beginning of a business letter to a woman whose name you do not know **3** [C] a woman who is in charge of a BROTHEL (=place where women are paid to have sex with men) **4** OLD-FASHIONED used to address a woman in order to be polite, especially someone you do not know [**Origin:** 1200–1300 Old French *ma dame* **my lady**]

Ma·dame /mə'dɑm, mɑ-/ *n. plural* **Mesdames** /meɪ'dɑm/ [C] a title used to address a woman who speaks French, especially a married one: *Madame Lefèvre*

mad·cap /'mædkæp/ *adj.* [no comparative] done or behaving in a wild or silly way that is often amusing or entertaining: *a madcap adventure*

ˌmad 'cow disˌease *n.* [U] NOT TECHNICAL → see BSE

mad·den /'mædn/ *v.* [T usually passive] to make someone extremely angry or annoyed

mad·den·ing /'mædn-ɪŋ, 'mædnɪŋ/ *adj.* extremely annoying: *maddening delays* —**maddeningly** *adv.*

made /meɪd/ *v.* **1** the past tense and past participle of MAKE **2 sb has (got) it made** INFORMAL to have everything that you need for a happy life or to be successful: *You have a nice house, good job, beautiful family – you've got it made!* **3 be made (for life)** INFORMAL to be so rich that you will never have to work again **4** someone who is made has been accepted as a member of a MAFIA family

Ma·dei·ra /mə'dɪrə, -'dɛr-/ *n.* [U] a strong sweet wine [**Origin:** 1500–1600 *Madeira*, Portuguese island in the Atlantic, where the wine is made]

Mad·e·moi·selle /ˌmædəmwə'zɛl/ *n. plural* **Mesdemoiselles** /ˌmeɪdəmwə'zɛl/ [C] a title used to

M

address a young unmarried woman who speaks French: *Mademoiselle Dubois*

ˌmade-to-ˈmeasure *adj.* made-to-measure clothes are specially made to fit you

ˌmade-to-ˈorder *adj.* [only before noun] made specially for one particular customer: *Try our made-to-order omelets.* —**made to order** *adv.*: *I got a rug made to order at a good price.*

ˈmade-up *adj.* **1** something that is made-up is not true or real: *a made-up name* **2** wearing MAKEUP on your face, especially so that it is noticeable: *Do I look too made-up?*

mad·house /ˈmædhaʊs/ *n.* [C] **1** a place with a lot of people, noise, and activity: *The police station is a madhouse most of the time.* **2** OLD USE a MENTAL HOSPITAL

Mad·i·son /ˈmædɪsən/ the capital city of the U.S. state of Wisconsin

Madison, James (1751–1836) the fourth President of the U.S.

mad·ly /ˈmædli/ *adv.* **1 madly in love (with sb)** very much in love with someone **2** in a wild uncontrolled way

mad·man /ˈmædmæn, -mən/ *n. plural* **madmen** /-mɛn, -mən/ [C] **1** NOT TECHNICAL a man who is mentally ill **2 like a madman** used to say that a man does something in a wild uncontrolled way: *He drives like a madman.*

ˈmad ˌmoney *n.* [U] INFORMAL money that you have saved in order to spend it when you suddenly see something you want

mad·ness /ˈmædnɪs/ *n.* [U] **1** NOT TECHNICAL serious mental illness **2** stupid or uncontrolled behavior, especially behavior that could be dangerous: *the madness and violence of war* | *the annual Christmas shopping madness* → see also **there's a method to sb's madness** at METHOD (3)

Ma·don·na /məˈdɑnə/ *n.* **1 the Madonna** Mary, the mother of Jesus Christ, in the Christian religion **2** [C] a picture or figure of Mary

mad·ras /ˈmædrəs, məˈdræs/ *n.* [U] a type of cotton cloth with a brightly colored PLAID pattern

Ma·drid /məˈdrɪd/ the capital and largest city of Spain

mad·ri·gal /ˈmædrɪgəl/ *n.* [C] a song for several singers without musical instruments, popular in the 16th and 17th centuries

mad·wom·an /ˈmædˌwʊmən/ *n. plural* **madwomen** /-ˌwɪmɪn/ [C] NOT TECHNICAL **1** a woman who is mentally ill **2 like a madwoman** used to say that a woman does something in a wild uncontrolled way: *I've been working like a madwoman lately.*

mael·strom /ˈmeɪlstrəm/ *n.* [C] **1** a situation full of activity, confusion, or violence: **+of** *a maelstrom of criticism* **2** EARTH SCIENCE a violent storm

mae·stro /ˈmaɪstroʊ/ *n. plural* **maestros** [C] someone who can do something very well, especially a musician or CONDUCTOR

ma·fi·a /ˈmɑfiə/ *n.* [singular] **1 the Mafia** a large organized group of criminals who control many illegal activities, especially in Italy and the U.S. **2** a powerful group of people within an organization or profession who support and protect each other: *the legal mafia* [**Origin:** 1800–1900 Italian, Italian dialect, **great confidence, proud talk**]

ma·fi·o·so /ˌmɑfiˈoʊsoʊ/ *n. plural* **mafiosi** /-si/ [C] a member of the Mafia

mag /mæg/ *n.* [C] INFORMAL a magazine

mag·a·zine /ˌmægəˈzin, ˈmægəˌzin/ S1 W1 *n.* [C] **1** a large thin book with a paper cover that contains news stories, articles, photographs etc., and is sold weekly or monthly: *Her face was on the cover of "Newsweek" magazine.* | *an article **in a magazine*** | **travel/fashion/computer etc. magazine** *He writes for a travel magazine* | **a women's/men's/children's etc. magazine** *the editor of a popular women's magazine* **2** the part of a gun that holds the bullets **3** the container that holds the film in a camera or PROJECTOR **4** a room or building for storing weapons, explosives etc. [**Origin:** 1500–1600 Early French, **building where things are stored**, from Old Provençal, from Arabic *makhazin*, plural of *makhzan* **storehouse**]

Ma·gel·lan /məˈdʒɛlən/, **Fer·di·nand** /ˈfɚdnˌænd/ (?1480–1521) a Portuguese sailor who led the first EXPEDITION to sail around the world

ma·gen·ta /məˈdʒɛntə/ *n.* [U] a bright purple-red color [**Origin:** 1800–1900 *Magenta*, town in Italy where the substance the color is made from was discovered] —**magenta** *adj.*

mag·got /ˈmægət/ *n.* [C] a small creature like a WORM that is the young form of a FLY and lives in decaying food, flesh etc.

Ma·gi /ˈmædʒaɪ/ *n.* [plural] **the Magi** the three wise men who brought gifts to the baby Jesus Christ, according to the Christian religion

mag·ic¹ /ˈmædʒɪk/ S3 W3 *n.* **1** [U] a secret power used to control events or do impossible things, by saying special words or performing special actions: *Do you believe in magic?* → see also BLACK MAGIC, WHITE MAGIC

THESAURUS

witchcraft the use of magic, usually to do bad things: *Hundreds of women were accused of witchcraft in the 1600s.*
spell a piece of magic that someone does, or the special words or ceremonies used in making it happen: *An evil witch cast a spell on him, turning him into a beast.*
curse magic words that bring someone bad luck: *People believed the pharaoh would put a curse on anyone who broke into the tomb.*
hex magic words that make something bad happen to someone: *She believed her former husband had put a hex on her.*
charm a phrase or action believed to have special magical powers: *a charm that turned the prince into a frog*
the occult the knowledge and study of magic and spirits: *stories that deal with the occult*
voodoo magical beliefs and practices used as a form of religion: *a voodoo curse*

2 [U] a special, attractive, or exciting quality: *The city has a special magic.* | **+of** *the magic of travel* | *The band's guitars **worked their magic** on the crowd.* **3** [U] the skill of doing tricks to entertain people that is used by MAGICIANS, for example making something disappear, or the tricks a magician does → see also BLACK MAGIC **4 like magic** also **as if by magic** in a surprising way that seems impossible to explain: *The cats vanished from the roof like magic.* **5 work like magic** to be very effective: *His law enforcement methods have worked like magic.* [**Origin:** 1300–1400 French *magique*, from Latin *magice*, from Greek *magos* **person with magic powers**]

magic² S3 *adj.* **1** [only before noun] having special powers that are not normal or natural, so that you can do impossible things: **magic spell/charm/hat etc.** (=something that lets you do things which seem impossible) **2** relating to the tricks or performance of a magician: *The kids will learn how to perform **magic tricks**.* | *a magic act* **3** very special, attractive, or exciting: *When I was a kid and television arrived, it was magic.* **4** having an especially powerful effect: *The Maharishi's followers say that 7,000 is a **magic number**.* **5 a magic formula** a way that will suddenly make you have the results you want, without you having to do very much yourself: *Young people are looking for a magic formula for success.* **6 magic bullet** INFORMAL a quick painless cure for illness, or something that solves a difficult problem in an easy way: *There is no magic bullet for reducing cholesterol.* **7 the magic touch** a special ability to make things work well or to make people happy: *She has the magic touch with babies.*

8 the magic word SPOKEN the word "please," said to remind a child to be polite: ***What's the magic word?***

mag·i·cal /ˈmædʒɪkəl/ *adj.* **1** very enjoyable, exciting, or romantic, in a strange or special way: *A room lit with candles has a magical quality.* **2** containing magic, or done using magic [SYN] **magic**: *Some people think garlic has magical powers.* —**magically** /-kli/ *adv.*

ˌmagical ˈrealism also **ˌmagic ˈrealism** *n.* [U] a style in literature that combines REALISM with magic, imagination, dreams etc.

ˌmagic ˈcarpet *n.* [C] a CARPET that people use to travel through the air, according to children's stories

ma·gi·cian /məˈdʒɪʃən/ *n.* [C] **1** someone in stories who can use magic **2** an entertainer who performs magic tricks

ˌmagic ˈlantern *n.* [C] a piece of equipment used in past times to make pictures shine onto a white wall or surface

ˌMagic ˈMarker *n.* [C] TRADEMARK a large pen with a thick soft point

ˌmagic ˈmushroom *n.* [C] INFORMAL a type of MUSHROOM that has an effect like some drugs, and makes you see things that are not really there

ˌmagic ˈwand *n.* [C] **1** a small stick used by a MAGICIAN **2 wave a magic wand** to solve problems or difficulties immediately: *We can't wave a magic wand and make taxes disappear.*

mag·is·te·ri·al /ˌmædʒəˈstɪriəl/ *adj.* **1** a magisterial way of behaving or speaking shows that you think you have authority: *the teacher's magisterial manner* **2** a magisterial book is written by someone who has a very great knowledge about a subject **3** LAW relating to or done by a magistrate: *magisterial permission* —**magisterially** *adv.*

mag·is·tra·cy /ˈmædʒəstrəsi/ *n.* [U] LAW **1** the official position of a magistrate, or the time during which someone has this position **2 the magistracy** magistrates considered together as a group

ma·gis·trate /ˈmædʒɪˌstreɪt, -strɪt/ *n.* [C] LAW someone who judges less serious crimes in a court of law [**Origin:** 1300–1400 Latin *magistratus*, from *magister* **master**]

ˈmagistrates' court *n.* [C] a court of law that deals with less serious crimes

mag·ma /ˈmægmə/ *n.* [U] EARTH SCIENCE hot melted rock below the surface of the Earth. When it cools, it becomes IGNEOUS rock.

Mag·na Car·ta /ˌmægnə ˈkɑrṭə/ HISTORY a document that established the rights of NOBLES, the church, and free citizens and that limited the power of the king, which King John of England signed in 1215

mag·na cum lau·de /ˌmægnə kʊm ˈlaʊdeɪ, -də, -ˈlɔ-/ *adj., adv.* with high honor, used to show that you have finished high school or college at the second of the three highest levels of achievement that students can reach → see also CUM LAUDE, SUMMA CUM LAUDE

mag·nan·i·mous /mægˈnænəməs/ *adj.* kind and generous toward other people, especially people who are not in as good a position as you are: *a magnanimous gesture* —**magnanimously** *adv.* —**magnanimity** /ˌmægnəˈnɪməṭi/ *n.* [U]

mag·nate /ˈmægneɪt, -nɪt/ *n.* [C] a rich and powerful person in a particular industry: *newspaper magnate William Randolph Hearst*

mag·ne·sia /mægˈniʒə/ *n.* [U] a light white powder used in medicine and in industry [**Origin:** 1300–1400 Modern Latin *magnes carneus* **flesh magnet**, used of a white powder that stuck to the lips] → see also MILK OF MAGNESIA

mag·ne·si·um /mægˈniziəm, -ʒəm/ *n.* [U] SYMBOL **Mg** CHEMISTRY a common silver-white metal that is an ELEMENT and that burns with a bright yellow light

mag·net /ˈmægnɪt/ *n.* [C] **1** PHYSICS a piece of iron or steel that can make other metal objects move toward it **2** a person or place that attracts many other people or things: +**for** *The city was a magnet for painters and writers.* | **attract/draw sb like a magnet** *Isabella attracts men like a magnet.* **3** a MAGNET SCHOOL [**Origin:** 1400–1500 Old French *magnete*, from Latin *magnes*, from Greek *magnes (lithos)* **(stone) of Magnesia**, ancient city in Turkey]

mag·net·ic /mægˈnɛṭɪk/ *adj.* **1** relating to or produced by MAGNETISM: *A compass needle points to the magnetic North Pole.* | *magnetic forces* **2 magnetic personality** a quality that someone has that makes other people feel strongly attracted toward them **3** having the power of a magnet: *a magnetic bulletin board* —**magnetically** /-kli/ *adv.*

magˌnetic ˈfield *n.* [U] PHYSICS an area around an object that has magnetic power: *the Earth's magnetic field*

magˌnetic ˈhead *n.* [C] **1** the part of a computer that reads and writes DATA **2** the part of a TAPE RECORDER that the tape is pulled across, and that records sound

magˌnetic ˈmedia *n.* [plural, U] COMPUTERS magnetic methods of storing information for computers, for example FLOPPY DISKS or MAGNETIC TAPE

magˌnetic ˈnorth *n.* [U] the northern direction shown by the needle on a COMPASS → see also TRUE NORTH

magˌnetic ˈpole *n.* [C] **1** EARTH SCIENCE one of the two points near the North and South Poles of the Earth, toward which the needle on a COMPASS points **2** a POLE

magˌnetic ˈresonance ˌimaging *n.* [U] → see MRI

magˌnetic reˈversal also **ˌpolar reˈversal** *n.* [C,U] SCIENCE a complete change in the Earth's MAGNETIC FIELD, so that the needle of a COMPASS begins to point in the opposite direction. Scientists believe this last happened about 780,000 years ago and that it has happened many times during the Earth's history, but they do not know what causes it.

magˌnetic ˈtape *n.* [U] a type of TAPE on which sound, pictures, or computer information can be recorded using magnetism

mag·net·ism /ˈmægnəˌtɪzəm/ *n.* [U] **1** a quality that makes other people feel attracted to you: *his **animal magnetism*** (=his physical attractiveness) **2** PHYSICS the physical force by which a MAGNET attracts metal, or which is produced when an electric current is passed through iron or steel

mag·net·ize /ˈmægnəˌtaɪz/ *v.* [T] **1** PHYSICS to make iron or steel able to attract other pieces of metal **2** to have a powerful effect on people, so that they feel strongly attracted to you

mag·ne·to /mægˈniṭoʊ/ *n.* [C] PHYSICS a piece of equipment containing one or more MAGNETS that is used for producing electricity

ˈmagnet ˌschool *n.* [C] a school that has more or better classes in a particular subject than usual, or special equipment to teach that subject, and so attracts students from a wide area: *a math magnet school*

mag·ni·fi·ca·tion /ˌmægnəfəˈkeɪʃən/ *n.* PHYSICS **1** [U] the act of magnifying: *High-power magnification is needed to see the crystals.* **2** [C] the degree to which something is able to magnify things: *The mirror has triple magnification and a light.*

mag·nif·i·cent /mægˈnɪfəsənt/ *adj.* extremely impressive because of being very beautiful or beautifully done: *Wolves are magnificent and beautiful animals.* | *a magnificent art deco building* | *a magnificent performance* [**Origin:** 1400–1500 Latin *magnificus* **very impressive, excellent**, from *magnus* **great**] —**magnificently** *adv.* —**magnificence** *n.* [U]

mag·ni·fy /ˈmægnəˌfaɪ/ *v.* **magnifies, magnified, magnifying** [T] **1** to make something look bigger than it is, especially using special equipment: *Her eyes were magnified by her thick glasses.* | *Binoculars magnify far-off objects.* **2** to make something such as a problem have a much greater effect or power: *Our lack of information magnified our mistakes.* **3** to make something

M

seem greater or more important than it really is SYN **exaggerate**: *This report tends to magnify the risks involved.* **4** BIBLICAL to praise God —**magnifier** *n.* [C]

ˈmagnifying ˌglass *n.* [C] a round piece of glass with a handle, used to make objects or print look bigger

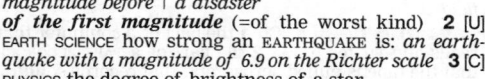

magnifying glass

mag·ni·tude /ˈmægnəˌtud/ *n.* **1** [U] greatness of size or importance: **+of** *They didn't seem to understand the magnitude of their mistake.* | **sth of this/such magnitude** *We've never dealt with a problem of this magnitude before* | *a disaster **of the first magnitude*** (=of the worst kind) **2** [U] EARTH SCIENCE how strong an EARTHQUAKE is: *an earthquake with a magnitude of 6.9 on the Richter scale* **3** [C] PHYSICS the degree of brightness of a star

mag·no·lia /mægˈnoʊlyə/ *n.* [C] a tree with large white, pink, yellow, or purple flowers that smell sweet [**Origin:** 1700–1800 Pierre *Magnol* (1638–1715), French plant scientist]

mag·num /ˈmægnəm/ *n.* [C] **1** a large bottle containing about 1.5 liters of wine, CHAMPAGNE etc. **2** a type of large PISTOL (=hand-held gun): *a .44 magnum*

ˌmagnum ˈopus *n.* [singular] the most important piece of work by a writer or artist

mag·pie /ˈmægpaɪ/ *n.* [C] **1** BIOLOGY a bird with black and white feathers and a long tail **2** INFORMAL someone who talks a lot [**Origin:** 1500–1600 *Mag* female name (from *Margaret*) + *pie* **magpie** (13–20 centuries) (from Old French, from Latin *pica*)]

Ma·gritte /məˈgrit/, **Re·né** /rəˈneɪ/ (1898–1967) a Belgian PAINTER famous for his pictures in the style of SURREALISM that combine familiar objects that are not usually seen together

Ma·ha·bha·ra·ta, the /ˌmɑhəˈbɑrət̬ə/ an ancient EPIC poem (=very long poem) that is written in Sanskrit and contains many of the basic ideas of Hinduism

ma·ha·ra·jah, **maharaja** /ˌmɑhəˈrɑdʒə/ *n.* [C] an Indian PRINCE or king

ma·ha·ra·ni, maharanee /ˌmɑhəˈrɑni/ *n.* [C] an Indian PRINCESS or queen

ma·ha·ri·shi /ˌmɑhəˈriʃi/ *n.* [C] a HINDU holy teacher

Ma·ha·ya·na Bud·dhism /ˌmɑhəyɑnə ˈbudɪzəm/ *n.* [U] one of the two main forms of Buddhism, and the main religion in China, Tibet, and Japan. It emphasizes that everyone can reach the perfect state of understanding and wisdom through faith. → see also THERAVADA BUDDHISM

Ma·hi·can, Mohican /məˈhikən/ a Native American tribe that formerly lived in the northeastern area of the U.S.

mah-jong, **mahjongg** /ˈmɑʒɑŋ, mɑˈʒɑŋ/ *n.* [U] a Chinese game played with small pieces of wood or bone with pictures on them [**Origin:** 1900–2000 Chinese *maque* **sparrows**]

Mah·ler /ˈmɑlɚ/, **Gus·tav** /ˈgʊstɑv/ (1860–1911) an Austrian musician who wrote CLASSICAL music

ma·hog·a·ny /məˈhɑgəni/ *n.* **1** [C,U] BIOLOGY a type of hard reddish-brown wood used for making furniture, or the tree that produces this wood **2** [U] a dark reddish-brown color [**Origin:** 1600–1700 Early Spanish *mahogani*] —**mahogany** *adj.*

maid /meɪd/ *n.* [C] **1** a woman who cleans houses or hotel rooms as their job → see also CLEANER **2** a female servant, especially in a large house: *a kitchen maid* **3** LITERARY a woman or girl who is not married → see also OLD MAID

maid·en¹ /ˈmeɪdn/ *n.* [C] LITERARY a girl who is not married

maiden² *adj.* **maiden flight/voyage** the first trip that an airplane or ship makes

ˌmaiden ˈaunt *n.* [C] an AUNT who has never married

maid·en·hair /ˈmeɪdnˌhɛr/ *n.* [U] a type of FERN

maid·en·head /ˈmeɪdnˌhɛd/ *n.* LITERARY **1** [U] the state of being a female VIRGIN **2** [C] a HYMEN

maid·en·ly /ˈmeɪdnli/ *adj.* LITERARY typical of a girl or young woman who is not sexually experienced: *maidenly modesty*

ˈmaiden name *n.* [C] the family name that a woman had before she got married

ˌmaid of ˈhonor *n.* [C] **1** the main BRIDESMAID at a wedding ▸see THESAURUS box at **wedding** **2** an unmarried lady who serves a queen or a PRINCESS

maid·ser·vant /ˈmeɪdˌsɚvənt/ *n.* [C] OLD USE a female servant → see also MANSERVANT

mail¹ /meɪl/ S1 W2 *n.* [singular, U] **1** the letters, packages etc. that are delivered to a particular person or at a particular time: *Is that all the mail that came today?* | *Sarah brought your mail over.* | *My parents are **forwarding** my **mail** to my new address.* | *She gets bags of **fan mail*** (=mail from people who are fans of hers) *every day.* | *The judge received **hate mail*** (=mail filled with messages of hate) *and death threats.* → see also JUNK MAIL

THESAURUS

letter a written or printed message that you put in an envelope and send to someone
postcard a card that can be sent without an envelope, especially one with a picture on it
package/parcel something wrapped or in a box so that it can be sent in the mail
junk mail a disapproving expression for letters, especially advertisements, that are sent by organizations to large numbers of people
mailman/letter carrier the person who delivers your mail
courier a person or company that is paid to take packages somewhere
post office a place where you can buy stamps, send letters and packages etc.
mailbox a box in a public place, into which you put letters that you want to send, or a special box outside your house where letters and packages are delivered to you

2 the system of collecting and delivering letters, packages etc.: *The mail here is really slow.* | *I'll put the check **in the mail** today.* | *Did you send the document **by mail**?* | *a birthday present sent **through the mail*** | **express/first-class/second-class etc. mail** (=used to show the speed of mail service, from fastest to slowest) → see also ELECTRONIC MAIL, SNAIL MAIL **3** [U] COMPUTERS messages sent by email SYN **email**: *I just want to check my mail.* | *incoming mail* **4** [U] ARMOR made of metal, worn in the Middle Ages [**Origin:** (1-3) 1200–1300 Old French *male* **bag**]

mail² S2 W3 *v.* [T] **1** to send a letter, package etc. to someone: **mail sb sth** *They're going to mail me the contract.* | **mail sth to sb** *We'll just mail the flyers to all the people on the list.* **2** COMPUTERS to send a message, document etc. to someone by email SYN **email**

mail sth ↔ **out** *phr. v.* to send letters, packages etc. to a lot of people at the same time SYN **send out**: *The department has just mailed out 300,000 notices.*

mail·bag /ˈmeɪlbæg/ *n.* [C] **1** a large, strong bag used for carrying mail by train, truck etc. **2** a bag used by mail carriers to deliver letters to people's houses **3** all the letters sent to a television show, magazine, government official etc.: *This week's mailbag was full of letters of complaint.*

mail·box /ˈmeɪlbɑks/ *n.* [C] **1** a box, usually outside a house, where someone's letters are delivered or picked up ▸see THESAURUS box at **mail¹** **2** a special box in the street or at a POST OFFICE where you mail letters **3** COMPUTERS the part of a computer's memory where email messages are stored: *There were 102 messages in my mailbox this morning.* → see also P.O. BOX

'mail ˌcarrier *n.* [C] someone who delivers mail to people's houses

'mail drop *n.* [C] **1** an address where someone's mail is delivered, but which is not where they live **2** a box in a post office where your mail can be left

mail·er /'meɪlɚ/ *n.* [C] a container or envelope used for sending something small by mail

'mailing list *n.* [C] **1** a list of names and addresses kept by an organization, so that it can send information or advertising material by mail: *We have millions of customers* ***on our mailing list.*** **2** COMPUTERS a list of names and email addresses kept on a computer so that you can send the same message to the same group of people at the same time

mail·man /'meɪlmæn, -mən/ *n. plural* **mailmen** /-mɛn, -mən/ [C] a man who delivers mail to people's houses

ˌmail 'order *n.* [U] a method of buying and selling in which the buyer chooses goods at home and orders them from a company that sends them by mail: *Our software is available* ***by mail order.*** **—mail-order** *adj.*: *a mail-order catalog*

'mail train *n.* [C] a train that carries mail

maim /meɪm/ *v.* [T] to wound or injure someone very seriously and often permanently: *A five-year-old girl was maimed in the bombing.*

Mai·mon·i·des /maɪ'mɑnəˌdiz/ (1135–1204) a Jewish PHILOSOPHER

main¹ /meɪn/ S1 W2 *adj.* [only before noun] **1** bigger or more important than all other things, ideas, influences etc. of the same kind: *the main entrance of the building | the main character in the book | a summary of the main points from the meeting | Our main concern was "What did we do wrong?"* | **the main reason/purpose/aim/goal etc.** *The main reason I was calling was to invite you to dinner.* ►see THESAURUS box at **important** **2 the main thing** SPOKEN used to say what is the most important thing in a situation: *Saving the peace plan is the main thing right now. | The main thing is that you didn't get hurt.* [**Origin:** Old English *mægen-*, from *mægen* **strength**]

main² *n.* **1** [C] a large pipe or wire carrying the public supply of water, electricity, or gas: *a broken water main* **2 in the main** mostly: *The people here are, in the main, illiterate.*

ˌmain 'clause *n.* [C] ENG. LANG. ARTS in grammar, a CLAUSE that can form a sentence on its own

ˌmain 'course also **ˌmain 'dish** *n.* [C] the largest part of a meal: *We just had a main course and dessert.*

ˌmain 'drag *n.* INFORMAL **the main drag** the most important street in a town or city, where big stores and businesses are: *We found a bar right there on the main drag.*

Maine /meɪn/ ABBREVIATION **ME** a state in the northeastern U.S. next to the Atlantic coast

main·frame /'meɪnfreɪm/ *n.* [C] COMPUTERS a large computer that can work very fast and that a lot of people can use at the same time

main·land /'meɪnlænd, -lənd/ *n.* **the mainland** the main area of land that forms a country, as compared to islands near it that are also part of that country: *Young people leave the island to find work on the mainland.* **—mainland** *adj.*: *mainland China*

main·line¹ /'meɪnlaɪn/ *adj.* [only before noun] belonging to the normal accepted part of a group, business, tradition etc., and therefore having a position that is fairly important SYN **mainstream**: *mainline Protestant churches*

mainline² *v.* [I,T] SLANG to INJECT illegal drugs into your blood

main·ly /'meɪnli/ S3 W3 *adv.* as the largest or most important reason, thing, part of something etc. SYN **mostly**: *Our customers are mainly young people. | I joined the club* ***mainly because*** *it has a basketball court. | The virus is spread mainly through contact with infected blood. | We cater mainly to small businesses.*

THESAURUS

chiefly mainly: *Small businesses are chiefly responsible for new jobs in the U.S.*
principally firstly and most importantly: *Foreign aid was sent principally to the south of the region.*
largely mainly, and because of a particular reason: *The school is in a largely black neighborhood.*
primarily mainly because of one reason or situation, which is more important than any other: *The animal is endangered, primarily because of a loss of its habitat.*

main·mast /'meɪnmæst, -məst/ *n.* [C] the largest or most important of the MASTS that hold up the sails on a ship

main·sail /'meɪnseɪl, -səl/ *n.* [C] NOT TECHNICAL the largest and most important sail on a ship

main·spring /'meɪnsprɪŋ/ *n.* **1** [C] the most important spring in a watch or clock **2 the mainspring of sth** FORMAL the most important reason or influence that makes something happen: *His religious faith was the mainspring of Peter's life.*

main·stay /'meɪnsteɪ/ *n. plural* **mainstays** [C] **1** an important part of something that makes it possible for it to work correctly or continue to exist: +**of** *Shopping has become a mainstay of American culture.* **2** someone whom a group or organization depends on to do important work: +**of** *She was the mainstay of the team.*

main·stream¹ /'meɪnstrim/ *n.* **the mainstream** ideas, methods, or people that are considered the most usual or normal in a society: *the integration of minorities into the mainstream* | +**of** *Tamayo brought Mexican themes into the mainstream of international art.* **—mainstream** *adj.*: *mainstream American politics*

mainstream² *v.* [T] to include a child with physical or mental problems in an ordinary class

main·stream·ing /'meɪnˌstrimɪŋ/ *n.* [U] the practice of placing a child with physical or mental problems in a school where they have lessons with ordinary children

'Main Street *n.* **1** [C] the most important street in many small towns in the U.S., with many stores and businesses on it. **2** [U] ordinary people who believe in traditional American values: *The President's new tax hikes won't be too popular on Main Street.*

main·tain /meɪn'teɪn/ Ac S3 W1 *v.*

1 MAKE STH CONTINUE [T] to make something continue in the same way or at the same level or standard as before SYN **keep**: *Our main wish is to help maintain world peace. | Dieters should try to reach and maintain a reasonable weight. | Our company has maintained close business ties with China for over 20 years. | King lives in Chicago but maintains an apartment in New York.*

2 TAKE CARE OF STH [T] to take care of something so that it stays in good condition: *His first job was installing and maintaining computers. | It's hard to do this job and still maintain a marriage. | The house has been* ***well maintained.*** | **poorly/badly maintained** *a poorly maintained factory*

3 SAY [T] to strongly express your belief that something is true: **maintain (that)** *He maintains that the authorities were not involved in the killings. | During their trial, the brothers* ***maintained their innocence*** (=continued to say they were not guilty).

4 SUPPORT LIFE to provide someone with the things they need to live, such as food or money: *the basic costs of maintaining a family | The goal is to build a space station that can* ***maintain life*** *on Mars.*

5 NOT LOSE CONTROL [I] SPOKEN to deal with a difficult situation without losing control: *Cox said he and his wife, Chrissy, were "trying to just maintain."*

[**Origin:** 1200–1300 Old French *maintenir*, from Latin *manu tenere* **to hold in the hand**]

main·te·nance /'meɪnt⁼n-əns/ Ac *n.* [U] **1** the repairs, painting etc. that are necessary to keep something in good condition: *the cost of repairs and*

M

maintenance | *essential maintenance work on the railroad tracks* | +**of** *the maintenance of public roads* | *The crack was discovered during* ***routine maintenance*** (=the usual regular maintenance). | **home/car/building etc. maintenance** *the state's highway maintenance department* | **maintenance man/worker/person** (=someone who looks after buildings and equipment for a school or company) **2 the maintenance of sth** the act of making a state or situation continue: *Our primary concern is the maintenance of discipline in the school.*

'maintenance fee *n.* [C] money that you pay for your share of the cleaning and repairs of the building that your CONDOMINIUM is in

maî·tre d' /ˌmeɪtrə 'di, ˌmɛ-, ˌmeɪtə-/ also **maître d'hô·tel** /-doʊ'tɛl/ *n.* [C] someone who is in charge of a restaurant, and who welcomes guests, gives orders to the WAITERS etc.

maize /meɪz/ *n.* [U] CORN [**Origin:** 1500–1600 Spanish *maíz*, from Taino *mahiz*]

Maj. the written abbreviation of MAJOR

ma·jes·tic /mə'dʒɛstɪk/ *adj.* very big, impressive, and beautiful: *the majestic coast around Big Sur* —**majestically** /-kli/ *adv.*

maj·es·ty /'mædʒəsti/ *n.* **1** [U] the quality that something big has of being impressive, powerful, and beautiful: *the majesty of the Rocky Mountains* **2 Your/Her/His Majesty** used when talking to or about a king or queen: *His Majesty, King Juan Carlos I* | *How do you like the White House, Your Majesty?*

ma·jor[1] /'meɪdʒə/ Ac S1 W1 *adj.* [no comparative] **1** [usually before noun] very large, serious, or important, when compared to other things or people of a similar kind OPP **minor**: *Confidence is a major part of leadership.* | *a major road* | *Most major credit cards are accepted.* | *There were no major problems during the project.* ▸see THESAURUS box at **important** **2** [not before noun] SPOKEN used to emphasize that something is very large, important, bad etc.: *I have to go on a major shopping trip before I start this job.* **3** ENG. LANG. ARTS a major KEY is based on a musical SCALE in which there are HALF STEPS between the third and fourth and the seventh and eighth notes: *the key of A major* [**Origin:** 1200–1300 Latin **larger, greater**, from *magnus* **large, great**] → see also MINOR

major[2] Ac S3 *n.* [C] **1** also **Major** a rank in the Army, Marines, or Air Force, or someone who has this rank: *Major John Franks* → see also DRUM MAJOR **2** the main subject that a student studies at a college or university: *I'm changing my major to political science.* ▸see THESAURUS box at **university** → see also MINOR **3 an English/biology/business etc. major** someone studying a particular subject as their main subject at a college or university: *Greg is a philosophy major.* **4 the majors** the group of teams that make up the highest level of American professional baseball SYN **the Major Leagues**: *his first season in the majors*

major[3] Ac *v.*

major in sth *phr. v.* to study something as your main subject at a college or university: *I'm majoring in English.* → see also MINOR

ˌmajor 'arc *n.* [C] MATH a curved line that is greater than half of a circle → see also MINOR ARC

ma·jor·do·mo /ˌmeɪdʒə'doʊmoʊ/ *n.* [C] OLD-FASHIONED a man who is in charge of the servants in a large house

ma·jor·ette /ˌmeɪdʒə'rɛt/ *n.* [C] a girl who spins a BATON while marching with a band

ˌmajor 'general, Major General *n.* [C] a high rank in the Army or the Air Force, or someone who has this rank

ma·jor·i·ty /mə'dʒɔrəṭi, -'dʒɑr-/ Ac W1 *n. plural* **majorities** **1 a/the majority** most of the people or things in a particular group OPP **minority**: +**of** *A majority of Americans support the law.* | *The Muslim population is* ***in the majority*** (=forms the largest group) *here.* | **the great/vast/overwhelming etc. majority of sth** (=almost all of a group) | **a majority decision/ruling** (=a decision made by more people voting for it than against it) | **Republican/Democratic etc. majority** *the Republican majority in Congress* **2** [C] POLITICS the difference between the number of votes gained by the winning party or person in an election and the number of votes gained by other parties or people OPP **minority**: *A two-thirds majority is needed to override a veto.* | **a small/narrow/tiny majority** *The resolution was passed by a narrow majority.* **3** [U] LAW the age when someone legally becomes a responsible adult

ma'jority ˌleader *n.* [C] POLITICS the person who organizes the members of the political party that has the most people elected, in either the House of Representatives or the Senate → see also MINORITY LEADER

'major league, major-league *adj.* [usually before noun] **1** relating to the Major Leagues: *a major league pitcher* **2** important, large, or having a lot of influence: *The wines come with major-league price tags.*

ˌMajor 'Leagues *n.* [plural] **the Major Leagues** the group of teams that make up the highest level of American professional baseball —**major leaguer** *n.* [C] → see also MINOR LEAGUE

Ma·ju·ro /mə'dʒʊroʊ/ the island that is the capital of the Marshall Islands

make[1] /meɪk/ S1 W1 *v. past tense and past participle* **made** /meɪd/

1 PRODUCE STH [T] to produce something by working or doing something: *Carol's making carrot cake for dessert.* | *Did you make that dress yourself?* | *a car made in Japan* | *He made two small holes in the wood.* | *Mark made a video of his daughter's wedding.* | **make sth out of sth** *You can make some bookcases out of those crates.* | **make sth from sth** *We made a shelter from leaves and branches.* | *Paper is made from wood.* | **be made of sth** *a shirt made of silk* | *The table is made of mahogany.* | **make sb sth** *Can you make me a copy of those receipts?* | **make sth for sb** *I'm making a cake for my sister.* | **make breakfast/lunch/dinner etc.** *My father makes breakfast on the weekends.* ▸see THESAURUS box at **cook**[1]

> **THESAURUS**
> **produce** to make something to be bought, used, or enjoyed by someone or by people in general
> **create** to make a new thing or type of thing exist
> **manufacture** to use machines to make goods or materials, usually in large numbers or amounts
> **mass-produce** to use machines to make goods in large numbers
> **develop** to design or make a new idea, product, system etc. over a period of time
> → BUILD

2 DO STH [T] used with some nouns to say that you do the actions relating to the noun: *We will* ***make a decision*** *by Friday.* | *Can I use your cell phone to* ***make a call***? | **make a mistake/error** *I made a mistake in the last math problem.* | *Can I* ***make a suggestion***? | *Did you* ***make an appointment*** *to see the doctor?* | *You need to* ***make reservations*** *at least six weeks in advance.* | *People have to* ***make a commitment*** *to be in the program.* | *We're* ***making progress*** *on the house painting, but it's slow.* | **make a sound/noise** *My car's making that weird noise again.* | **make a speech/statement** *He refused to make a statement to the press.* | **make a contribution/donation etc.** (=give money for a particular purpose) | **make an appearance/entrance etc.** (=to suddenly appear somewhere, enter a room etc.)

3 CAUSE STH [T] to cause a particular state or situation, or cause something to happen: *You made a mess in the kitchen* | **make sb/sth do sth** *This cold medicine makes me fall asleep.* | *Drink this – it'll* ***make you feel better***. | **make sb happy/sad/mad etc.** *Stop staring! You're making me nervous.* | *He's* ***making himself sick*** *worrying about the trial.* | **make sth difficult/easy/interesting etc.** *Pictures make the book look more interesting.* | **make it easy/possible/necessary etc. (for sb) to do sth** *Computers have made it possible for* people to work from home. | **make sb/sth sth** *The movie made him a star.* | *ways of making the world a better place* | **make sth the best/worst/most expensive etc.** *What makes humans the most successful animal species on earth?* | *Earlier this year, Reid* ***made it known*** *that he was thinking of retiring.* ►see THESAURUS box at cause[2]

4 FORCE [T] to force someone to do something, or force something to happen: **make sb do sth** *Mom made him wear a hat.* | *You can't make someone stop smoking. They have to want to do it.* ►see THESAURUS box at force[2]

5 EARN MONEY [T] to earn or get money: *They say he makes seven million dollars a year.* | *Do you* ***make*** *good* ***money*** *in that line of work?* | *Betty* ***makes a living*** (=makes enough money to buy the things she needs) *growing organic vegetables.* | *They could sell CDs for three bucks each and still* ***make a profit*** (=earn money in a trade or business). ►see THESAURUS box at earn

6 make it a) INFORMAL to succeed in arriving somewhere when this is difficult, or by a particular time: *It's only ten till seven – we'll make it.* | *Did she make it home last night?* | **make it to sth** *We just made it to the hospital before the baby arrived.* **b)** INFORMAL to manage to continue doing something difficult until it is finished: **make it to sth** *Three of my students didn't make it to the midterm.* | **make it through sth** *I'm so tired, I'm not sure I can make it through the 11 o'clock news.* **c)** SPOKEN to be at an event, meeting etc. that has been arranged, when there was a possibility that you might not be: *I'm glad you could make it, Nancy.* | **make it to sth** *Eric won't be able to make it to the meeting tomorrow.* **d)** INFORMAL to live after a serious illness or accident, or manage to deal with a difficult experience: *Children with the disease rarely make it past their tenth birthday.* | **make it through sth** *Would $50 help you to make it through the rest of the week?* | *New antifreeze will help the car make it through the winter.* **e)** INFORMAL to be successful in a particular activity or profession, when this is difficult: *He was starting to wonder if he would ever make it in the Major Leagues.* | *We had two flop records before we* ***made it big*** (=became very successful).

7 make the meeting/the party/Tuesday etc. to be able to go to something that has been arranged for a particular date or time, even though you are busy: *I can make 8:30 on Tuesday.* | *Will you be able to make the next meeting?*

8 make a deadline/target/rate to succeed in doing something by a particular time, producing a particular amount etc.: *We'll never make the deadline.*

9 HAVE A QUALITY [linking verb] to have the qualities, character etc. necessary for a particular job, use, or purpose: *Cooper's going to make a good doctor one day.* | *Don't they make a cute couple?* | *An old cardboard box makes a comfortable bed for a kitten.*

10 make way (for sb/sth) a) to move to one side so that someone or something can pass: *She made way for him, pushing back her chair.* **b)** to remove something so that something newer or better can be used or made instead: *Stores are clearing winter goods to make way for spring merchandise.*

11 make your way (to/through/back etc.) a) to move toward something, especially slowly or with difficulty: *They eventually made their way to Canada and settled there.* **b)** to work toward a particular aim, or toward general success in life: *the new energy bill now making its way through Congress*

12 make the papers/headlines/front page to be interesting or important enough to be printed in the newspaper: *Stories about the couple's split continue to make the papers.*

13 make the team/squad etc. to be good enough to be chosen to play on a sports team: *Heidi is sure to make the varsity basketball team.*

14 make the bed to pull the sheets and covers over a bed so that it is neat after someone has slept in it

15 make time (for sb/sth) to find enough time to do something, even though you are busy: *We always made time to see Sam when we were in San Francisco.*

16 ADDING NUMBERS [linking verb] if two or more numbers make another number, they equal a particular amount when added together: *Two plus two makes four.* | *There are nine people coming, plus me, which makes ten.*

17 make it quick/snappy used to tell someone to do something as quickly as possible: *Okay, have a Coke, but make it quick.*

18 make that/it used when correcting something you have just said: *And an order of onion rings. No, better make it two orders.* | *His employees think he's a hero. Make that a god.*

19 make it 10/20/100 etc. [T] to decide that a particular amount, especially an amount of money, is acceptable, even if it is not the exact amount owed or needed: *I think it was $19.50, but let's just make it an even $20.*

20 that makes two of us used to agree with someone's opinion or to say that something that happened to them has also happened to you: *"I'd like to work in Hawaii." "That makes two of us."*

21 make it up to sb to do something good for someone because you feel responsible for something bad or disappointing that happened to them: *I'm sorry I can't get away from work. I'll make it up to you this weekend.*

22 make do (with/without sth) INFORMAL to manage with or without something, even though this is not completely satisfactory: *Until our furniture arrives we're making do with a folding table and a mattress.*

23 make sb captain/leader etc. to give someone a new job or position in a group, organization etc., that is higher than the one they had before: *She's just been made a full partner.*

24 make or break sb/sth to cause either great success or complete failure: *A review in the Times can make or break a show on Broadway.*

25 make believe to pretend that something is true or exists: *You can't go on making believe that nothing is wrong.* → see also MAKE-BELIEVE

26 make as if to do sth to move in such a way that it seems that you are going to do something, although you do not do it: *Hardin made as if to rise from his seat.*

27 MAKE STH PERFECT [T] INFORMAL to provide the qualities that make something complete or successful: *The hat really makes the outfit.* | *Your letter really* ***made my day*** (=made the day seem good)*!*

28 make it with sb OLD-FASHIONED to have sex with someone

29 ARRIVE AT A PLACE [T] OLD-FASHIONED to arrive at a particular place after a long or difficult trip: *We'll never make town before nightfall.*

[**Origin:** Old English *macian*] → see also **make the best of sth** at BEST[3] (6), **make certain** at CERTAIN[2] (3), **make a (big) difference** at DIFFERENCE (3), **make friends** at FRIEND (2), **make good on a debt/promise/threat etc.** at GOOD[2] (11), **make love (to/with sb)** at LOVE[2] (5), MADE, **make sense** at SENSE[1] (3), **make sure** at SURE[1] (3)

make away with sb/sth *phr. v.* INFORMAL to steal something and take it away from a place: *Thieves made away with over $20,000 in yesterday's robbery.*

make for sth *phr. v.* **1** to move toward something, or move in a particular direction: *Sue made for the snack bar while Brian bought tickets.* **2** to be likely to have a particular result or make something possible: *The stormy weather made for a very bumpy landing.* **3 be made for each other** INFORMAL if two people, groups, organizations etc. were made for each other, they are completely appropriate for each other: *I'd like to see them get married. They're made for each other.*

make sb/sth **into** sth *phr. v.* **1** to change something so that it has a different form or purpose SYN **turn into**: *We made Jason's room into a guest bedroom.* **2** to change someone's character, job, or position in society: *Good new players have made the Steelers into a great team.*

make sth **of** sb/sth *phr. v.* **1** to understand something in a particular way, or have a particular opinion about something SYN **think of**: *He smiled, not quite sure what to make of my comments.* | ***What do you make of him?*** **2** to use the chances, opportunities etc. you have in a way that achieves a good result: *I want to* ***make something of myself*** (=be successful or famous). | *Danville* ***makes the most of*** *the snow by*

M

holding an annual winter carnival (=they do something really good with the situation). **3 make (too) much of sth** to treat something as if it is more important than it really is: *Much is being made of the number of women serving in the army.* **4 make a day/night/evening of it** to decide to spend a whole day, night etc. doing something: *Why don't you make a day of it and have lunch with us?* **5 do you want to make sth (out) of it?** SPOKEN used in an angry way to say that you are willing to have a fight or argument with someone **6 what sb is (really) made of** INFORMAL the qualities that someone shows when they are in a very difficult situation: *We'll see what the team is made of if they get to the finals!* **7 I'm/We're not made of money** SPOKEN used to say that you cannot afford to buy whatever you want

make off *phr. v.* to leave quickly, especially in order to escape SYN **take off**: *They made off when the police arrived.*

make off with sth *phr. v.* to take something SYN **steal**: *Someone made off with the barber shop's striped pole.*

make out *phr. v.* **1 make sth ↔ out** to just be able to hear, see, or understand something: *Many people in the crowd could hardly make out what he was saying.* | *I could just make out a shape in the dim light.* **2 make out a check (to sb)** to write a check: *Who do I make the check out to?* **3 make sb ↔ out** INFORMAL to understand someone or something, especially the reason why something has happened, or what someone's character is like: *I couldn't make him out at all.* | ***As far as I can make out*** (=I guess from the information I have that), *he's never been married.* **4** INFORMAL to claim or pretend that something is true when it is not: **make out that** *We tried to make out that we didn't speak English.* | **make sb out to be sth** *Norm's not the bad guy that some people make him out to be.* **5** to succeed or progress in a particular way: *How did your parents make out in Las Vegas?* **6** INFORMAL to kiss and touch someone in a sexual way: *A couple was making out in the hallway.* **7 make out like a bandit** INFORMAL to get a lot of money or gifts, win a lot etc.

make sth **↔ over** *phr. v.* to change someone or something so that they look different or have a different use or role: *Zellwegger made herself over completely for the movie role.* → see also MAKEOVER

make toward sth *phr. v.* to move toward something: *a group of soldiers making toward the trees*

make up *phr. v.*

1 EXCUSE/EXPLANATION make sth ↔ up to invent a story, explanation etc. in order to deceive someone: *She made up the whole story.* → see also MADE-UP (1)

2 SONG/POEM make sth ↔ up to invent the words or music for a new song, story, poem etc.: *My daughter made up all the words for the song.*

3 FORM/BE make sth ↔ up to combine together to form a particular system, group, result etc.: *Minority groups make up more than two-thirds of the city's population.* | **be made up of sth** *Protons and neutrons are made up of smaller components called quarks.*

4 make sth up as you go along to decide how to do something while you are doing it instead of planning it before: *I've given so many of these speeches, I just make them up as I go along now.*

5 PREPARE/ARRANGE make sth ↔ up to prepare or arrange something by putting things together: *Why don't you make up a list of what things to buy.* | *I made up a bottle of formula for the baby.*

6 SB'S FACE make sb ↔ up to put special paints or colors on someone's face, especially in order to completely change the way they look: **make sb up to do/be sth** *They made him up to look like he was dead.* → see also MADE-UP (2), MAKEUP (1)

7 TIME/WORK make sth ↔ up to work at times when you do not usually work, so that you do all the work that you should have done: *I'm trying to make up the time I lost while I was sick.* | *Is it OK if I make the work up next week?*

8 FRIENDS to become friendly with someone again after you have had an argument: *I'm glad to see you've made up* | **make up with sb** *Have you made up with her yet?*

9 make up sth to complete an amount or number to the level that is needed: *If you don't have enough money we can* ***make up the difference*** (=give you the amount you do not have).

10 FROM CLOTH make sth ↔ up to produce something from cloth by cutting and sewing: **make sth up into sth** *I'm going to make that material up into a dress.* → see also **make up your mind** at MIND[1] (3)

make up for sth *phr. v.* **1** to make a bad situation seem better, by providing something nice SYN **compensate**: *What the airline lacks in frills it makes up for in service.* | *The good days* ***more than make up for*** *the bad ones* (=are so good that the bad ones do not matter). **2 make up for lost time a)** to work more quickly, or at times when you do not usually work, because something has prevented you from working before: *The bus driver was speeding to make up for lost time.* **b)** to become involved in an activity very eagerly, because you wish you could have done it earlier in your life: *He went to a boys' school, and now he's making up for lost time by dating every girl in sight.* **3** to have so much of one quality that it does not matter that you do not have enough of something else: *She's not particularly bright, but she's so nice that that makes up for it.*

> **WORD CHOICE make or do**
>
> There is no simple rule for when to use **make** or **do**. Generally, we tend to use **make** to talk about producing things that did not exist before: *I made a blueberry pie.* | *John made a good point.* | *You're making a mess there.* We also use **make** when someone or something is changed in some way: *That should make him happy.* | *You'll have to make the picture bigger.* | *They've really made a name for themselves.*
>
> We usually use **do** to talk about actions: *My kids don't have to do chores in the summer.* | *Could you do a favor for me?* | *Have you done your homework?*

make² *n.* **1** a particular type of product, made by one company: *What make is your car?* | **+of** *They use a different make of computer.* ►see THESAURUS box at **type**[1] **2 be on the make** INFORMAL **a)** to be always trying to get an advantage for yourself **b)** to be trying to have a sexual relationship with someone

ˈmake-beˌlieve *adj.* not real, but imagined or pretended: *Many small children have make-believe friends.* —**make-believe** *n.* [U]

ˌmake-or-ˈbreak *adj.* causing either great success or complete failure: *The last couple of games were make-or-break.*

make·o·ver /ˈmeɪkˌoʊvɚ/ *n.* [C] **1** a process in which you make someone look more attractive by giving them new clothes, a new HAIRSTYLE, MAKEUP etc.: *He picks a guest from the audience and gives them a makeover on TV.* **2** a process in which you improve the way a place looks, usually making it more a fashionable and useful space: *a kitchen makeover*

mak·er /ˈmeɪkɚ/ S3 W2 *n.* [C] **1** a person or company that makes or produces something: **+of** *a well-known maker of sporting goods* | **car/movie/shoe etc. maker** *California wine makers* **2 a decision/policy/peace etc. maker** someone who does something or makes something happen: *U.S. policy makers must address a number of tough issues.* **3 ice cream/popcorn/coffee etc. maker** a machine used to make a particular thing → see also **meet your maker** at MEET[1] (24), TROUBLEMAKER

make·shift /ˈmeɪkˌʃɪft/ *adj.* [only before noun] made for temporary use from available materials when you need something and there is nothing better available: *Thousands have tried to flee in makeshift boats.* [**Origin:** 1500–1600 *make shift* **to make efforts, try all methods, manage to do something** (15–19 centuries)]

makeup

make·up, make-up /'meɪk-ʌp/ *n.* **1** [U] substances such as powders, creams, and LIPSTICK that people, especially women or actors, put on their faces to improve or change their appearance: *eye makeup* | *She never **wears makeup**.* | *a woman wearing **heavy makeup*** (=a lot of makeup) | *Give me a minute to **put on my makeup**.* → see also **make up** at MAKE¹, PANCAKE MAKEUP **2** [singular] a particular combination of people or things that form a group or whole: +**of** *the multicultural makeup of the area* **3 sb's makeup** the qualities that form someone's character: *It's not in her makeup to give up.* **4** [C] also **makeup test/exam** a test taken in school because you were not able to take a previous test

'make-work *adj.* [only before noun] make-work jobs or positions are not important but are given to people to keep them busy —**make-work** *n.* [U]

mak·ing /'meɪkɪŋ/ *n.* **1** [U] the process or business of producing something: **the making of sth** *Eleanor Coppola wrote a book about the making of "Apocalypse Now."* | **cheese/wine/rug etc. making** *a group famous for its quilt making* | **decision/policy making** *She was involved in decision making in the Clinton administration.* **2 sth in the making** a person or thing that will develop into something: *This is not just news – this is history in the making.* | *a young movie star in the making* **3 have the makings of sth** to have the qualities or skills needed to become a particular kind of person or thing: *We've got the makings of a winning team.* **4 of your own making** problems or difficulties that are of your own making have been caused by you and no one else: *He found himself caught in a dilemma of his own making.* **5 be the making of sb/sth** to be the situation that makes a person or thing much better or more successful: *The trip could be the making of him.*

mal- /mæl/ *prefix* bad or badly: *malodorous* (=that smells bad) | *malfunction* (=when something does not work properly)

Mal·a·bo /mɑ'lɑboʊ/ the capital city of Equatorial Guinea

Mal·a·chi /'mæləˌkaɪ/ a book in the Old Testament of the Christian Bible

mal·ad·just·ed /ˌmælə'dʒʌstɪd◂/ *adj.* unable to form good relationships with people because of problems in your character and attitudes —**maladjustment** *n.* [U]

mal·ad·min·is·tra·tion /ˌmæləd̩ˌmɪnə'streɪʃən/ *n.* [U] FORMAL careless or dishonest management

mal·a·droit /ˌmælə'drɔɪt/ *adj.* FORMAL not good at dealing with people or problems —**maladroitly** *adv.* —**maladroitness** *n.* [U]

mal·a·dy /'mælədi/ *n. plural* **maladies** [C,U] FORMAL **1** something that is wrong with a system or organization: *The airline suffers from a common malady – lack of cash.* **2** ESPECIALLY WRITTEN an illness

mal·aise /mæ'leɪz/ *n.* [singular, U] **1** a feeling of anxiety, DISSATISFACTION, and lack of confidence within a group of people that is not clearly expressed or understood: *There is a restlessness, a malaise, among the workers.* | *economic malaise* **2** a feeling of being slightly sick that usually does not continue for very long

M

Mal·a·mud /'mæləˌmʌd/, **Ber·nard** /bɚ'nɑrd/ (1914–1986) a U.S. writer of NOVELS

mal·a·prop·ism /'mæləˌprɑpɪzəm/ *n.* [C] an amusing mistake that is made when someone uses a word that sounds similar to the word they intended to say, but that means something completely different [**Origin:** 1800–1900 Mrs. *Malaprop*, character who uses words wrongly in the play "The Rivals" (1775) by Richard Sheridan, from French *mal à propos* **not appropriate**]

ma·lar·i·a /mə'lɛriə/ *n.* [U] MEDICINE a disease common in hot countries that is caused when an infected MOSQUITO bites you [**Origin:** 1700–1800 Italian *mala aria* **bad air**; because it was believed that the disease came from gases rising from wet land] —**malarial** *adj.*: *malarial fever*

ma·lar·key /mə'lɑrki/ *n.* [U] INFORMAL things that you think are silly or untrue SYN **nonsense**: *Don't give me that malarkey. Tell me the truth.*

Ma·la·wi /mə'lɑwi/ a country in east Africa between Zambia and Mozambique —**Malawian** *n., adj.*

Ma·lay¹ /mə'leɪ, 'meɪleɪ/ *n.* **1** [C] someone from the largest population group in Malaysia **2** [U] the language of these people

Malay² *adj.* relating to Malaysia: *the Malay peninsula*

Ma·lay·si·a /mə'leɪʒə/ a country in Southeast Asia made up of 13 states on the Malay PENINSULA and on the island of Borneo —**Malaysian** *n., adj.*

Malcolm X

Mal·colm X /ˌmælkəm 'ɛks/ (1925–1965) an African-American political leader who worked to improve the social and economic position of African Americans

mal·con·tent /ˌmælkən'tɛnt/ *n.* [C] FORMAL someone who is likely to cause trouble because they are not satisfied with the way things are done or organized: *political malcontents*

Mal·dives, the /'mɔldaɪvz/ a country that consists of a group of small islands in the Indian Ocean southwest of Sri Lanka —**Maldivian** /mɔl'dɪviən/ *n., adj.*

male¹ /meɪl/ S2 W2 *adj.* **1** BIOLOGY belonging to the sex that cannot have babies OPP **female**: *A rooster is a male chicken.* | *All the texts are written by male philosophers.* **2** BIOLOGY typical of or relating to this sex OPP **female**: *male sexuality* | *a survey of male and female attitudes* **3 male plant/flower etc.** BIOLOGY a plant, flower etc. that cannot produce fruit **4** TECHNICAL a male PLUG fits into a hole or SOCKET [**Origin:** 1300–1400 Old French *masle*, *male*, from Latin *masculus*] —**maleness** *n.* [U] → see Word Choice box at MASCULINE

male² S3 W3 *n.* [C] BIOLOGY **1** a male animal OPP **female**: *The male uses its light to find receptive female fireflies.* **2** a man, especially a typical man OPP **female**: *Males under 25 have a higher accident rate.* ▸see THESAURUS box at **man¹**

Ma·lé /'mɑli, -leɪ/ the capital city of the Maldives

ˌmale 'bonding *n.* [U] OFTEN HUMOROUS the forming of strong friendship between men: *They went away over the weekend to do some male bonding.*

male chau·vin·ist /ˌmeɪl 'ʃoʊvənɪst/ *n.* [C] a man who believes that men are better than women and who

M

has strict traditional ideas about the way men and women should behave and is not willing to change his ideas: *Joe's the biggest **male chauvinist pig** I've ever met.*

mal·e·dic·tion /ˌmælə'dɪkʃən/ *n.* [C] FORMAL a wish or prayer that something bad will happen to someone [SYN] **curse**

mal·e·fac·tor /'mæləˌfæktɚ/ *n.* [C] FORMAL someone who does evil things

ma·lef·i·cent /mə'lɛfəsənt/ *adj.* FORMAL doing evil things, or able to do them —**maleficence** *n.* [U]

ˌmale 'menopause *n.* [singular] HUMOROUS a period in the middle of a man's life when he feels anxious and unhappy → see also MIDLIFE CRISIS

ma·lev·o·lent /mə'lɛvələnt/ *adj.* showing a desire to harm other people [SYN] **evil** [OPP] **benevolent**: *He gave me a malevolent look.* —**malevolence** *n.* [U] —**malevolently** *adv.*

mal·fea·sance /mæl'fizəns/ *n.* [U] LAW illegal activity, especially by a government official

mal·for·ma·tion /ˌmælfɔr'meɪʃən/ *n.* [C,U] a part of the body that is badly formed, or the state of being badly formed: *a malformation in the brain* | *organ malformation*

mal·formed /ˌmæl'fɔrmd◂/ *adj.* used about parts of the body that are badly formed: *a malformed spinal cord*

mal·func·tion /mæl'fʌŋkʃən/ *n.* [C] a fault in the way a machine, computer, or part of someone's body operates: *a malfunction in one of the engines* —**malfunction** *v.* [I]

Ma·li /'mɑli/ a large country in west Africa, south of Algeria —**Malian** *n., adj.*

mal·ice /'mælɪs/ *n.* **1** [U] the desire or intention to deliberately harm someone: *His voice was filled with malice as he spoke.* | ***I bore no malice*** (=felt no malice) *against this man whatsoever.* **2 with malice aforethought** LAW a criminal act that is done with malice aforethought is done in a carefully planned and deliberate way

ma·li·cious /mə'lɪʃəs/ *adj.* showing a desire to harm or hurt someone: *malicious rumors* —**maliciously** *adv.* —**maliciousness** *n.* [U]

ma·lign¹ /mə'laɪn/ *v.* [T usually passive] to say or write bad things about someone that are untrue: *She has been maligned by politicians and newspapers.* | **much-maligned/oft-maligned/often-maligned** (=criticized by a lot of people, often unfairly)

malign² *adj.* FORMAL harmful: *malign spirits* —**malignly** *adv.* —**malignity** /mə'lɪgnəṭi/ *n.* [U]

ma·lig·nan·cy /mə'lɪgnənsi/ *n. plural* **malignancies** **1** [C] MEDICINE a TUMOR **2** [U] FORMAL feelings of great hatred

ma·lig·nant /mə'lɪgnənt/ *adj.* **1** MEDICINE a malignant TUMOR, disease etc. is one that develops quickly and cannot be easily controlled and is likely to cause death [OPP] **benign**: *malignant cells* **2** FORMAL showing hatred and a strong desire to harm someone [OPP] **benign**: *malignant thoughts* [**Origin:** 1500–1600 Late Latin, present participle of *malignari*, from Latin *malignus*, from *male* **badly** + *gigni* **to be born**] —**malignantly** *adv.*

ma·lin·ger /mə'lɪŋgɚ/ *v.* [I] to avoid work by pretending to be sick [**Origin:** 1700–1800 French *malingre* **sick**, from Old French *mal* **badly** + *haingre* **thin, weak**] —**malingerer** *n.* [C]

mall /mɔl/ [S2] *n.* [C] a very large building with a lot of stores in it [SYN] **shopping mall**: *Let's meet at the mall and go see a movie.* [**Origin:** 1700–1800 *mall* **long path used for playing a game called "pall-mall"** (17–19 centuries)] → see also STRIP MALL

mal·lard /'mælɚd/ *n.* [C] a type of wild duck

Mal·lar·mé /ˌmælɑr'meɪ/, **Sté·phane** /stɛ'fɑn/ (1842–1898) a French poet

mal·le·a·ble /'mæliəbəl, -ləbəl/ *adj.* **1** something that is malleable is able to be pressed or pulled into a new shape: *malleable steel* **2** someone who is malleable is easily influenced, changed, or trained: *malleable young people* —**malleability** /ˌmæliə'bɪləṭi/ *n.* [U]

mal·let /'mælɪt/ *n.* [C] **1** a wooden hammer with a large end: *Use a mallet to hammer in the tent pegs.* **2** a wooden hammer with a long handle used when playing CROQUET or POLO

mal·low /'mæloʊ/ *n.* [C,U] a plant with pink or purple flowers and long stems → see also MARSHMALLOW

mal·nour·ished /ˌmæl'nɚɪʃt, -'nʌrɪʃt/ *adj.* sick or weak because of not having enough food to eat, or because of not eating good food: *a pale malnourished child*

mal·nu·tri·tion /ˌmælnu'trɪʃən/ *n.* [U] sickness or weakness caused by not having enough food to eat, or by not eating good food

mal·o·dor·ous /mæl'oʊdərəs/ *adj.* LITERARY smelling bad

mal·prac·tice /ˌmæl'præktɪs/ *n.* [C,U] LAW the act of failing to do a professional duty correctly, or of making a mistake while doing it: *Hospitals are always concerned about **malpractice suits**.*

Mal·raux /mæl'roʊ/, **An·dré** /ɑn'dreɪ/ (1901–1976) a French politician and writer of NOVELS

malt¹ /mɔlt/ *n.* **1** [U] grain, usually BARLEY, that has been kept in water for a time and then dried, used for making beer, WHISKEY etc. **2** [C] a drink made from milk, malt, and ICE CREAM, that usually has something else such as chocolate added **3** [C,U] also **malt whiskey** a type of high-quality WHISKEY from Scotland

malt² *v.* [T] to make grain into malt

Mal·ta /'mɔltə/ a country which consists of a group of small islands in the Mediterranean Sea —**Maltese** /ˌmɔl'tiz◂/ *n., adj.*

malt·ed /'mɔltɪd/ also **ˌmalted 'milk** *n.* [C] a MALT

Maltese Cross /ˌmɔltiz 'krɔs/ *n.* [C] a cross with four pieces that become wider as they go out from the center

Mal·thus /'mælθəs/, **Thomas** (1766–1834) a British ECONOMIST who studied population growth —**Malthusian** /mæl'θuʒən, -ziən/ *adj.*

ˌmalt 'liquor *n.* [U] a type of beer

mal·treat /mæl'trit/ *v.* [T] to treat a person or animal cruelly, especially by hurting them physically: *Several of the prisoners had been maltreated.* —**maltreatment** *n.* [U]

ma·ma [S2], **mamma**, **momma** /'mɑmə/ *n.* [C] a word meaning "mother," used by or to children [**Origin:** 1500–1600 from the sounds made by a baby]

'mama's ˌboy *n.* [C] a man or boy who people think is weak, because his mother protects him too much and because he always does what his mother says

mam·ba /'mɑmbə, 'mæmbə/ *n.* [C] BIOLOGY a poisonous African snake

Mam·et /'mæmɪt/, **Da·vid** /'deɪvɪd/ (1947–) a U.S. writer of plays, and writer and director of movies

mam·ma /'mɑmə/ *n.* [C] another spelling of MAMA

mam·mal /'mæməl/ *n.* [C] BIOLOGY one of the class of animals that drinks milk from its mother's body when it is young [**Origin:** 1800–1900 Late Latin *mammalis* **of the breast**, from Latin *mamma* **breast**] —**mammalian** /mə'meɪliən/ *adj.*

mam·ma·ry /'mæməri/ *adj.* [only before noun] BIOLOGY relating to the breasts

M

ˈmammary ˌgland *n.* [C] BIOLOGY the part of a woman's breast that produces milk, or a similar part of a female animal

mam·mo·gram /ˈmæməˌgræm/ *n.* [C] an X-RAY picture of a woman's breast, used to check for CANCER: *Women over the age of fifty should* ***have yearly mammograms****.* —**mammography** /mæˈmɑgrəfi/ *n.* [U]

mam·mon /ˈmæmən/ *n.* [U] FORMAL, DISAPPROVING money, wealth, and profit, regarded as something that people want or think about too much

mam·moth¹ /ˈmæməθ/ *adj.* [only before noun] extremely large: *This country has a mammoth drug problem.* | *a mammoth corporation*

mammoth

mammoth² *n.* [C] a large hairy ELEPHANT that lived on Earth thousands of years ago

mam·my /ˈmæmi/ *n. plural* **mammies** [C] OLD-FASHIONED a mother

man¹ /mæn/ S1 W1 *n. plural* **men** /mɛn/

1 MALE PERSON [C] an adult male person: *He's a smart man.* | *There were two men in the car.* | *a man's watch* → see also WOMAN

THESAURUS

guy INFORMAL a man: *One of the guys at work is from Mexico.*
gentleman a polite word for a man, often used in formal situations: *Good evening, ladies and gentlemen.*
boy a young male person, usually a child or a teenager: *A couple of boys were playing soccer in the park.*
youth a teenage boy or young man: *He teaches at a school for troubled youths in San Diego.*
male FORMAL a man, used especially by researchers or the police: *The suspect is a young white male.*
→ WOMAN

2 ALL PEOPLE a) [U] all people, both male and female, considered as a group SYN **humans** SYN **humankind**: *the evolution of man* | *one of the worst diseases* ***known to man*** **b)** [C usually plural] OLD-FASHIONED a person, either male or female SYN **person**: *All men are equal in the eyes of the law.*

3 WORKER [C] **a) gas/milk/delivery man etc.** a man who comes to your house to do a job for you **b)** OLD-FASHIONED [usually plural] a worker, soldier, SAILOR, police officer etc. who has a low rank

4 GAME [C] one of the pieces you use in a game such as CHESS

5 STRONG/BRAVE MAN [C usually singular] a man who has the qualities that people think a man should have, such as being brave, strong etc.: *Would you* ***be man enough to*** (=be strong or brave enough) *stand up for your beliefs?* | *The Army will* ***make a man of*** *him* (=make a young man start having these qualities).

6 WHAT SB LIKES [C] a man who likes, or likes doing, a particular thing: *He's a meat-and-potatoes man.* | *I'm not a gambling man.*

7 MAN FROM PARTICULAR PLACE/WORK ETC. [C] a man who belongs to a particular organization, comes from a particular place, does a particular type of work etc.: *Bush was a Yale man* (=he went to Yale University).

SPOKEN PHRASES

8 USED TO SPEAK TO SB [singular] used in order to speak to someone, especially an adult male: *Hey, what's happening, man?*

9 the man a) used to talk about a particular man in a negative or insulting way: *I can't stand the man.* | *The man weighs over three hundred pounds!* **b) The Man** OLD-FASHIONED someone who has authority over you, especially a white man or police officer

10 you the/da man! also **you're the man!** INFORMAL used to praise someone for having done something well

11 my man used by some men when talking to a male friend

12 sb's your/our/the man used to say that a man is the best person for a particular job, situation etc.: *If you need financial help, I'm your man.*

13 a man OLD-FASHIONED used by a man to mean himself: *Can't a man read his paper in peace?*

14 HUSBAND/PARTNER [C] INFORMAL a woman's husband, or the man she is having a romantic relationship with: *Tania was at the party with her new man.*

15 take sth like a man to accept a difficult situation or bad treatment without showing any emotion: *Stop whining and take it like a man.*

16 the man on the street OLD-FASHIONED the average man or the average person, who represents the opinion of many people: *He remains a hero to the man on the street.*

17 a man of his word a man you can trust, who will do what he has promised to do

18 a man of few words a man who does not talk very much

19 a man of the people a man who understands and expresses the views and opinions of ordinary people

20 be your own man to behave and think independently without worrying about what other people think: *Do you want to be your own man and run your own business?*

21 it's every man for himself INFORMAL used to say that in a particular situation people do not tend to help each other: *In journalism it's every man for himself.*

22 a man of God a religious man, especially a priest or minister

23 man about town a rich man who spends a lot of time at parties, restaurants, theaters etc.

24 man's best friend a dog or dogs in general

25 a man's man a man who other men admire and like, because he is strong and likes the kinds of activities that men usually do

26 to a man also **to the last man** used to say that all the men in a group do something or have a particular quality: *To a man, they all credit their success to an influential teacher.*

27 be/become man and wife FORMAL to be or become married: *I now pronounce you man and wife* (=said by the person who marries a man and woman).

28 live as man and wife to live together as though you are married, although you are not

29 SERVANT [C] OLD-FASHIONED a male servant

[**Origin:** Old English] → see also BEST MAN, LADIES' MAN, MAN OF LETTERS, MAN-TO-MAN, OLD MAN, **a man/woman of the world** at WORLD¹ (24)

WORD CHOICE

• **Man** can mean "people in general": *Man has always tried to understand the stars.*
• **Mankind** means "all people, considered as a group": *the darkest time in the history of mankind*
• Some people think that using **man** and **mankind** in this way seems to not include women. To avoid this problem, you can use **people** to mean "people in general" and **humankind** instead of **mankind**: *People have always tried to understand the stars.* | *the darkest time in the history of humankind*

man² *v.* **manned, manning** [T] to use or operate a vehicle, system, piece of equipment etc.: *The booths are*

M

manned by customs officials. | *the first manned spacecraft*

man³ S1 *interjection* **1** used to emphasize what you are saying: *Man, your car is noisy!* **2 oh, man** used when you are disappointed, annoyed, or surprised, in order to emphasize what you are saying: *Oh, man, it's snowing.*

man·a·cle /ˈmænəkəl/ *n.* [C usually plural] an iron ring on a chain that is put around the hands or feet of prisoners —**manacled** *adj.*

man·age /ˈmænɪdʒ/ S2 W1 *v.*

1 DO STH DIFFICULT [I,T] to succeed in doing something or dealing with a situation, especially when it is difficult: **manage to do sth** *Did you manage to get any sleep on the plane?* | *He managed to arrange a loan through a finance company.* | *It was a long hike to the top, but we* ***managed it****.*

2 BUSINESS [T] to organize and control a business, department, team etc. and the people who work in it: *Turpin manages a staff of six employees.* | *a badly managed company* ▸see THESAURUS box at **control¹**

3 LIVING WITH PROBLEMS [I] to succeed in living in a difficult situation, without having enough money or other things that can help: *It's hard to see sometimes how single parents manage.* | **+without** *How do you manage without a phone?* | **+with** *We are trying to manage with a very limited budget.* | **manage on sth** *Some families manage on $50 a week.*

4 NOT NEED HELP [I,T] SPOKEN to be able to do something or carry something without help: *"Can I help you with that?" "That's OK, I can manage."*

5 CONTROL/ORGANIZE [T] to control or organize something: *My office manages the college's admissions process.* | *The teacher could not manage such a huge class.* → see also MANAGEABLE

6 PROPERTY/LAND [T] to be responsible for organizing the way something is done or taken care of, often including the financial matters connected with it: *The Forestry Service manages all the land in the area.* | *We manage people's financial portfolios.* | **manage your time/money** (=use your time or money effectively, without wasting them)

7 DEAL WITH EMOTION to deal with strong emotions such as STRESS or anger: *ways of managing stress*

8 BE STRONG ENOUGH [T] to be able to do something because you are strong enough or healthy enough: *I could only manage three sit-ups.*

9 EAT/DRINK [T] SPOKEN to be able to eat or drink something: *I think I could manage another glass of wine.*

10 manage a smile/a few words etc. to make yourself say or do something when you do not really want to: *Smith managed a smile after her defeat.*

11 CAUSE PROBLEMS [T] SPOKEN to do something that is annoying or that seems silly: **manage to do sth** *The kids managed to spill paint all over the carpet.*

12 sb can manage (to do) sth SPOKEN used to say that someone has enough time or money to do something, or to ask if they do, even though it is difficult: *Can you manage a few extra hours' work next week?*

[**Origin:** 1500–1600 Italian *maneggiare*, from *mano* **hand**, from Latin *manus*]

man·age·a·ble /ˈmænɪdʒəbəl/ *adj.* easy to control or deal with OPP **unmanageable**: *My hair's more manageable since I had it cut.* —**manageability** /ˌmænɪdʒəˈbɪləṭi/ *n.* [U]

ˌmanaged ˈcare *n.* [U] a system of health care in which people have health insurance that allows them only to use particular doctors or hospitals

man·age·ment /ˈmænɪdʒmənt/ S3 W1 *n.* **1** [U] the act or process of controlling and organizing the work of a company or organization and the people who work for it: *a management consulting firm* | *a class in management skills* | **+of** *He won praise for his management of the Winter Olympics.* | **good/bad/poor management** *The mill closed because of bad management.* **2** [C,U] the people who are in charge of a company or organization: *The management felt this was the right decision.* | *a management team* | *The restaurant is* ***under new management*** (=being managed by different people). | *Miller spent 27 years* ***in management*** *at a pharmaceutical company.* | **senior/upper management** (=people at the highest levels in a company) | *Many* ***middle management*** (=people in charge of small groups within a company) *jobs have been cut.* **3** [U] the act or process of dealing with a situation that needs to be controlled in some way: *traffic management* | **+of** *the administration's management of the economy* | *the skills of* ***crisis management*** (=when you deal with an unusual and very difficult situation at work) **4 anger/stress management** the activity of dealing with anger and STRESS, so that you do not become very angry or upset

ˌmanagement ˈbuyout *n.* [C] an occasion when the management of a company buys a lot of STOCK in that company so that they control it

ˈmanagement conˌsultant *n.* [C] someone who is paid to advise the management of a company about how to improve their organization and working methods

man·ag·er /ˈmænɪdʒɚ/ S2 W1 *n.* [C] **1** someone whose job is to manage part or all of a company or other organization: *the store manager* | *I'd like to speak to the manager, please.* **2** someone who is in charge of the business affairs of a singer, an actor etc. **3** someone who is in charge of training and organizing a sports team

man·a·ge·ri·al /ˌmænəˈdʒɪriəl/ *adj.* relating to the job of a manager: *a managerial decision*

ˌmanaging diˈrector *n.* [C] someone who is in charge of a large company or organization, or of a part of a large company

Ma·nag·ua /məˈnɑgwə/ the capital and largest city of Nicaragua

Ma·na·ma /məˈnæmə/ the capital city of Bahrain

ma·ña·na /mənˈyɑnə, mɑn-/ *adv., adj.* a Spanish word meaning "tomorrow," used in English when talking about someone who delays doing things: *a mañana attitude*

Ma·nas·seh /məˈnæsə/ in the Bible, the head of one of the 12 tribes of Israel

man·a·tee /ˈmænəˌti/ *n.* [C] a large plant-eating sea animal with FLIPPERS and a large flat tail

Man·chu·ri·a /mænˈtʃʊriə/ an area of northeast China that is south of Russia and west of Japan

man·da·la /ˈmændələ/ *n.* [C] a picture of a circle around a square, that represents the universe in Hindu and Buddhist religions

Man·dan /ˈmændæn, -dən/ a Native American tribe from the northern central area of the U.S.

Man·da·rin /ˈmændərɪn/ *n.* [U] the official language of China, spoken by most educated Chinese people

man·da·rin /ˈmændərɪn/ *n.* [C] **1** also **ˈmandarin ˌorange** a type of small orange with skin that is easy to remove **2** an important official in an organization or government **3** HISTORY an important government official in the former Chinese EMPIRE [**Origin:** (2–3) 1500–1600 Portuguese *mandarim*, from Malay *menteri*, from Sanskrit *mantrin* **adviser**]

man·date¹ /ˈmændeɪt/ *n.* **1** [C] an official command given to a person or organization to do something: **mandate to do sth** *She was hired as editor with a mandate to change the newspaper's coverage.* **2** [C] POLITICS the right and power that a government or elected official has to do something, as a result of winning an election or vote: **mandate to do sth** *The organization's leadership was* ***given a mandate*** *to pursue its eco-policies.* **3** [C,U] POLITICS the power given to one country to govern another country, or the country that is being governed: *Lebanon became a French mandate after World War I.* [**Origin:** 1500–1600 Latin *mandatum*, from *mandare* **to give into someone's hand, command**]

mandate² *v.* [T] **1** to give an official command that something must be done: *The state mandates that high school students take three years of English.* **2** [often passive] to give someone the right or power to do something: *Is a doctor mandated to stop life-sustaining treatment at the patient's request?*

man·dat·ed /ˈmænˌdeɪt̬ɪd/ *adj.* POLITICS a mandated country or area has been placed under the control of another country

ˌMandate of ˈHeaven, the the Chinese political belief in the past that heaven gives rulers the right to rule and that people must obey the rulers as long as they rule fairly → see also DIVINE RIGHT

man·da·to·ry /ˈmændəˌtɔri/ *adj.* something that is mandatory must be done, especially because a law or rule says it must be done SYN **compulsory**: *Wearing a helmet when riding a motorcycle is mandatory.* | *The mandatory retirement age is 65.*

ˌmandatory ˈspending *n.* [singular] ECONOMICS money that the U.S. government has to spend on programs and plans approved by existing laws, and which is not controlled by Congress

Man·del·a /mænˈdɛlə/, **Nelson** (1918–) the first black President of South Africa

man·di·ble /ˈmændəbəl/ *n.* [C] BIOLOGY **1** the jaw of an animal or fish, especially the lower jaw **2** the upper or lower part of a bird's beak **3** a part like a jaw at the front of an insect's mouth

man·do·lin /ˌmændəˈlɪn, ˈmændl-ən/ *n.* [C] a musical instrument with eight metal strings and a rounded back

mane /meɪn/ *n.* [C] **1** BIOLOGY the long hair on the back of a horse's neck, or around the face and neck of a lion **2** INFORMAL a person's long thick hair

ˈman-eater *n.* [C] an animal that eats human flesh —**man-eating** *adj.*: *a man-eating tiger*

Ma·net /mæˈneɪ/, **Éd·ouard** /ɛˈdwɑr/ (1832–1883) a French PAINTER who greatly influenced the development of the style of IMPRESSIONISM

ma·neu·ver¹ /məˈnuvɚ/ *n.* **1** [C] a complicated movement that you make with skill and care, and which often involves several actions which are done in a particular order: *basic skiing maneuvers* **2** [C,U] a skillful or carefully planned action intended to achieve something or avoid something: **a political/legal maneuver** *The defense has tried a number of legal maneuvers to reduce the charges.* **3 room for maneuver** the possibility of changing your plans or decisions in order to achieve an aim: *The guidelines are written in a way that gives managers room for maneuver.* **4 maneuvers** [plural] a military exercise like a battle used for training soldiers: *Two ships are* ***on maneuvers*** *in the Atlantic.* → see also HEIMLICH MANEUVER

maneuver² *v.* [I,T] **1** to move or turn skillfully or to move or turn something skillfully, especially something large and heavy: **maneuver (sth) along/into/through etc.** *The driver maneuvered the limo through the heavy traffic.* | *The aircraft could not maneuver into the space.* **2** to use carefully planned and often dishonest methods to get what you want: *a plan to maneuver the company president out of office*

ma·neu·ver·a·ble /məˈnuvərəbəl/ *adj.* easy to move or turn within small spaces: *a small maneuverable car* —**maneuverability** /məˌnuvərəˈbɪlət̬i/ *n.* [U]

ma·neu·ver·ing /məˈnuvərɪŋ/ *n.* [C,U] the use of carefully planned and sometimes dishonest methods to get what you want: *diplomatic maneuverings*

man·ful·ly /ˈmænfəli/ *adv.* in a brave and determined way —**manful** *adj.*

man·ga /ˈmɑŋgə/ *n.* [U] a Japanese COMIC BOOK for adults → see also ANIME

man·ga·nese /ˈmæŋgəˌniz/ *n.* [U] **Mn** SYMBOL CHEMISTRY a grayish-white metal that is an ELEMENT and is used for making glass, steel etc.

mange /meɪndʒ/ *n.* [U] a skin disease that some animals get which makes them lose small areas of fur

man·ger /ˈmeɪndʒɚ/ *n.* [C] a long open container that horses, cattle etc. eat from → see also **dog in the manger** at DOG¹ (11)

man·gle¹ /ˈmæŋgəl/ *v.* [T] **1** [often passive] to damage or injure something badly by crushing or twisting it: *A mangled bicycle lay by the railroad tracks.* **2** to spoil something, especially what someone has said or written: *his ability to mangle the English language* [**Origin:** 1300–1400 Anglo-French *mangler*, from Old French *maynier*]

mangle² *n.* [C] a machine with two ROLLERS, used in the past to remove water from washed clothes

man·go /ˈmæŋgoʊ/ *n. plural* **mangoes** or **mangos** [C] BIOLOGY a tropical fruit with a thin skin, sweet yellow flesh, and a large seed [**Origin:** 1500–1600 Portuguese *manga*, from Tamil *man-kay*]

man·grove /ˈmæŋgroʊv/ *n.* [C] a tropical tree that grows in or near water and grows new roots from its branches: *a mangrove swamp*

mang·y /ˈmeɪndʒi/ *adj. comparative* **mangier**, *superlative* **mangiest** **1** suffering from MANGE **2** looking old, dirty, and in bad condition: *He wore a mangy fur hat and a ragged coat.*

man·han·dle /ˈmænˌhændl/ *v.* [T] **1** to push or move someone roughly, using force: *Rivera claimed he was kicked and manhandled by police.* **2** to move a heavy object using force

Manhattan

Man·hat·tan /mænˈhætˀn/ a BOROUGH of New York City that is an island between the Hudson River and the East River

Manˈhattan ˌProject, the HISTORY the secret American program during World War II in which scientists developed the first ATOMIC BOMB

man·hole /ˈmænhoʊl/ *n.* [C] a hole in the road covered by a lid that people go down to examine pipes, wires etc.

man·hood /ˈmænhʊd/ *n.* **1** [U] qualities such as strength, courage, and especially sexual power, that people think a man should have **2** [U] the state of being a man and not a boy anymore: *the time when a boy reaches manhood* **3** [singular] LITERARY or HUMOROUS a PENIS **4** [U] LITERARY all the men of a particular nation → see also WOMANHOOD

ˈman-hour *n.* [C] the amount of work done by one person in one hour, used as a measurement

man·hunt /ˈmænhʌnt/ *n.* [C] an organized search, especially for a criminal or a prisoner who has escaped

ma·ni·a /ˈmeɪniə/ *n.* [C,U] **1** a very strong desire for something or interest in something, especially one that affects a lot of people at the same time: *baseball mania* | +**for** *the modern mania for diets* **2** MEDICINE a serious mental illness

ma·ni·ac /ˈmeɪniˌæk/ *n.* [C] **1** INFORMAL someone who behaves in a stupid or dangerous way: *He drives like a maniac.* **2 a religious/sex/computer etc. maniac** INFORMAL someone who thinks about religion, sex etc. all the time **3** OLD-FASHIONED someone who is mentally ill: *a* ***homicidal maniac*** (=a mentally ill person who kills people) [**Origin:** 1500–1600 Late Latin *maniacus*, from Greek *mania*, from *mainesthai* **to be mentally ill**]

ma·ni·a·cal /məˈnaɪəkəl/ *adj.* behaving as if you are crazy: *maniacal laughter* —**maniacally** /-kli/ *adv.*

man·ic /ˈmænɪk/ *adj.* **1** INFORMAL behaving in a very anxious or excited way: *Williams is a comedian with a lot of manic energy.* **2** MEDICINE relating to the feeling of great happiness and excitement that is part of manic depression

ˌmanic deˈpression *n.* [U] MEDICINE a mental illness that makes people sometimes feel extremely happy and excited and sometimes extremely sad and hopeless

ˌmanic deˈpressive *n.* [C] someone who suffers from manic depression —**manic-depressive** *adj.*

man·i·cure /ˈmænɪˌkyʊr/ *n.* [C,U] a treatment for the hands and FINGERNAILS that includes cutting, cleaning, polishing etc. [**Origin:** 1800–1900 French, Latin *manus* **hand** + *cura* **care**] —**manicure** *v.* [T] —**manicurist** *n.* [C]

man·i·cured /ˈmænɪˌkyʊrd/ *adj.* **1** manicured hands have FINGERNAILS that are neatly cut and polished **2** manicured gardens or LAWNS are very neat, and the grass is cut very short

man·i·fest¹ /ˈmænəˌfɛst/ *v.* [T] FORMAL to clearly show a feeling, attitude, disease etc., so that it is easy to see: **be manifested in/through/as sth** *The sickness is usually manifested as headache and tiredness.* | *The stress of her job often* ***manifests itself*** *as anger.*

manifest² *adj.* [no comparative] FORMAL **1** able to be clearly and easily understood SYN **obvious**: *The educational system is a manifest failure.* | *The event's full importance only* ***became manifest*** *much later.* **2 manifest destiny** the idea in the 19th century that the U.S. was clearly intended by God to have all the land between the Atlantic and Pacific Oceans [**Origin:** 1300–1400 Latin *manifestus* **seized by the hand**] —**manifestly** *adv.*: *The statement is manifestly untrue.*

manifest³ *n.* [C] a list of all the goods or people carried on a ship, airplane, or train: *the flight's passenger manifest*

man·i·fes·ta·tion /ˌmænəfəˈsteɪʃən/ *n.* FORMAL **1** [C] a very clear sign that a particular situation or feeling exists: +**of** *The riots are a clear manifestation of growing discontent.* **2** [U] the act of appearing or becoming clear: +**of** *Manifestation of the disease often does not occur until middle age.* **3** [C] the appearance of a GHOST

man·i·fes·to /ˌmænəˈfɛstoʊ/ *n. plural* **manifestoes** or **manifestos** [C] POLITICS a written statement by a group, especially a political group, saying what they believe in and what they intend to do: *the Communist manifesto*

man·i·fold¹ /ˈmænəˌfoʊld/ *adj.* FORMAL many and of different kinds: *the manifold possibilities in life*

manifold² *n.* [C] TECHNICAL an arrangement of pipes through which gases enter or leave a car engine

Ma·nil·a /məˈnɪlə/ the capital and largest city of the Philippines

ma·nil·a /məˈnɪlə/ *adj.* made of a strong brown paper: *a manila envelope*

man·i·oc /ˈmæniˌɑk/ *n.* [U] CASSAVA

ma·nip·u·late /məˈnɪpyəˌleɪt/ Ac *v.* [T] **1** DISAPPROVING to make someone do what you want by deceiving or influencing them: *Conner used bribes and threats to manipulate her employees.* | **manipulate sb into (doing) sth** *He abused her and then tried to manipulate her into keeping quiet.* **2** DISAPPROVING to dishonestly change information or influence an event or situation: *It became clear that the police had manipulated evidence.* **3** to work with or change information, systems etc. to achieve the result that you want: *The images can be manipulated and stored on disk.* **4** to make something move or turn in the way that you want, especially using your hands: *Babies investigate their world by manipulating objects.* **5** TECHNICAL to skillfully move and press a joint or bone into the correct position [**Origin:** 1800–1900 *manipulation* (18–21 centuries), from French, from *manipule* **handful**, from Latin *manipulus*] —**manipulation** /məˌnɪpyəˈleɪʃən/ *n.* [U]

maˌnipulated ˈvariable *n.* [C] SCIENCE an INDEPENDENT VARIABLE in a scientific EXPERIMENT

ma·nip·u·la·tive /məˈnɪpyələt̬ɪv, -ˌleɪt̬ɪv/ Ac *adj.* **1** DISAPPROVING good at controlling or deceiving people to get what you want: *She was charming and manipulative.* **2** TECHNICAL relating to the skill of moving bones and joints into the correct position: *manipulative treatment* **3** TECHNICAL relating to the ability to handle objects in a skillful way: *manipulative techniques* —**manipulatively** *adv.*

ma·nip·u·la·tor /məˈnɪpyəˌleɪt̬ɚ/ *n.* [C] DISAPPROVING someone who is good at controlling or deceiving other people in order to get what they want

Man·i·to·ba /ˌmænɪˈtoʊbə/ a PROVINCE in central Canada

man·kind /ˌmænˈkaɪnd/ *n.* [U] all humans considered as a group SYN **humankind**: *His work had a great influence on the history of mankind.* → see also WOMANKIND → see Word Choice box at MAN

man·ly /ˈmænli/ *adj.* having qualities that people expect and admire in a man, such as being brave and strong: *a manly name* —**manliness** *n.* [U]

man-made

a man-made pond

a natural lake

ˌman-ˈmade, manmade *adj.* **1** made of substances such as plastic that are not natural: *man-made fibers* **2** made by people, rather than by natural processes: *a man-made lake* ▸see THESAURUS box at **artificial** → see also ARTIFICIAL

Mann /mɑn/, **Thomas** (1875–1955) a German writer of NOVELS

man·na /ˈmænə/ *n.* **1 manna from heaven** something that you need, which you suddenly get or are given **2** [U] the food which, according to the Bible, was provided by God for the Israelites in the desert after their escape from Egypt

man·ne·quin /ˈmænɪkən/ *n.* [C] **1** a model of the human body used for showing clothes in stores **2** OLD-FASHIONED a woman whose job is to wear fashionable clothes and show them to people SYN **model**

man·ner /ˈmænɚ/ W2 *n.*

1 WAY OF BEHAVING/SPEAKING [singular] the way in which someone behaves toward or talks to other people: *She has a very pleasant manner.* | +**toward** *Dean's manner toward me had changed.* | *Greet the customer* ***in a*** *friendly and courteous* ***manner***. | ***The manner in which*** *she asked the question was very aggressive.* ▸see THESAURUS box at **behavior**

2 manners [plural] **a)** polite ways of behaving in social situations: *Her kids have such* ***good manners***. | *Jack,* ***mind your manners*** (=used to tell a child to behave politely). | ***It's bad manners to*** *chew with your mouth open.* | *John's* ***table manners*** (=accepted ways of eating politely) *are terrible.* **b)** FORMAL the customs of a particular group of people: *the life and manners of Victorian London*

3 WAY [singular] FORMAL the way in which something is done or happens: *The issue should be resolved* ***in a manner*** *that is fair to both parties.* | ***The manner in which*** *the investigation was conducted was very odd.* |

M

the manner of sth *The police were unable to determine the manner of Allen's death.*
4 in a manner of speaking in some ways, though not exactly: *I guess I am in charge, in a manner of speaking.*
5 (as if) to the manner born if you do something new as if to the manner born, you do it in a natural and confident way as if you have done it many times before
6 all manner of sth FORMAL many different kinds of things or people: *All manner of people have been involved on the project.*
7 [singular] in the style that is typical of a particular person or thing: *The house is built **in the** Victorian **manner**.* | *a painting **in the manner of** the early Impressionists*
8 what manner of... LITERARY what kind of: *She soon discovered what manner of man she married.*
[**Origin:** 1100–1200 Old French *maniere* **way of acting, way of handling**, from Latin *manuarius* **of the hand**] → see also **a comedy of manners** at COMEDY (4), -MANNERED

man·nered /ˈmænɚd/ *adj.* DISAPPROVING a mannered way of speaking or behaving seems too formal and not very natural

-mannered /mænɚd/ [in adjectives] behaving in a particular way in social situations: *well-mannered* (=having good manners) | **bad-/ill-mannered** *He was ill-mannered and arrogant.* → see also MILD-MANNERED

man·ner·ism /ˈmænəˌrɪzəm/ *n.* **1** [C,U] a way of speaking or moving that is typical of a particular person: *He has the same mannerisms as his father.* **2** [U] the use of a style in art that does not look natural

man·ni·kin, **manikin** /ˈmænɪkən/ *n.* [C] another spelling of MANNEQUIN

man·nish /ˈmænɪʃ/ *adj.* used for describing women or women's clothes that have the typical qualities of men or men's clothes, often when this is considered unattractive: *a mannish jacket* —**mannishly** *adv.*

ˌman of ˈletters *n.* [C] a male writer, especially one who writes NOVELS or writes about literature

ˌman-of-ˈwar, **man-o'-war** /ˌmænə ˈwɔr/ *n. plural* **men-of-war** [C] OLD USE a fighting ship in the Navy

man·or /ˈmænɚ/ *n.* [C] **1** also **ˈmanor house** a large house in the COUNTRYSIDE, especially in Europe, with a large area of land around it **2** HISTORY the land that belonged to an important man, under the FEUDAL system —**manorial** /məˈnɔriəl/ *adj.*

man·pow·er /ˈmænˌpaʊɚ/ *n.* [U] all the workers available to do a particular kind of work: *skilled manpower* | *a reduction in manpower*

man·qué /mɑŋˈkeɪ/ *adj.* **artist/actor/teacher manqué** someone who could have been successful as an artist etc., but never became one

man·sard roof /ˈmænsɑrd ˌruf/ also **mansard** *n.* [C] a roof whose lower part slopes more steeply than its upper part

manse /mæns/ *n.* [C] a house that the minister of certain Christian churches lives in

man·ser·vant /ˈmænˌsɚvənt/ *n.* [C] OLD-FASHIONED a male servant, especially a man's personal servant

-manship /mənʃɪp/ *suffix* [in U nouns] a particular skill or art: *horsemanship* (=skill at horse riding) | *salesmanship* (=the ability to sell things to people) → see also -SHIP (2)

man·sion /ˈmænʃən/ *n.* [C] a very large house

ˈman-sized also **ˈman-size** *adj.* [only before noun] **1** large and considered appropriate for, or typical of, a man: *man-sized bites of a sandwich* **2** about the same size as a man: *a man-sized box*

man·slaugh·ter /ˈmænˌslɔtɚ/ *n.* [U] LAW the crime of killing someone illegally but not deliberately → see also MURDER

manta ray /ˈmæntə ˌreɪ/ *n.* [C] BIOLOGY a type of ocean fish with a flat body and two FINS that look like wings

man·tel /ˈmæntl/ also **man·tel·piece** /ˈmæntlˌpis/ *n.* [C] a frame surrounding a FIREPLACE, especially the top part that can be used as a shelf

man·til·la /mænˈtiyə, -ˈtɪlə/ *n.* [C] a piece of thin pretty material that covers the head and shoulders, traditionally worn by Spanish women

man·tis /ˈmæntɪs/ *n.* [C] a PRAYING MANTIS

man·tle¹ /ˈmæntl/ *n.* [C] **1 take on/assume/inherit etc. the mantle of sb** FORMAL to accept or have a particular duty or responsibility: *The Vice President will assume her boss's mantle, temporarily.* **2 a mantle of snow/darkness etc.** LITERARY something such as snow or darkness that covers a surface or area **3** EARTH SCIENCE the part of the Earth around the central CORE → see picture at GLOBE **4** a loose piece of outer clothing without SLEEVES, worn in past times **5** a cover put over the flame of a gas or oil lamp to make it shine more brightly **6** BIOLOGY a fold in the layer of skin around the body of a sea or land animal with a soft body and hard outer shell, which contains GLANDS that produce the substance that becomes the shell

mantle² *v.* [T] LITERARY to cover the surface of something

Man·tle /ˈmæntl/, **Mick·ey** /ˈmɪki/ (1931–1995) a baseball player, known especially for his skill as a BATTER

ˈman-to-man *adj.* [only before noun] INFORMAL **1** playing a game, especially basketball, in such a way that one person on your team tries to stay near one person on the other team: *man-to-man defense* **2** if two men have a man-to-man talk or discussion, they discuss something in an honest direct way —**ˌman-to-ˈman** *adv.*

man·tra /ˈmæntrə/ *n.* [C] **1** a repeated word or sound used as a prayer or to help people MEDITATE **2** INFORMAL a frequently used word or phrase that represents a rule or principle that someone believes is important: *Politicians continually repeat the mantra that they will not raise taxes.* **3** a piece of holy writing in the Hindu religion

man·u·al¹ /ˈmænyuəl/ Ac *adj.* **1** manual work involves using physical skill or strength rather than your mind: *manual labor* **2 manual laborer/worker** someone who does manual work **3** operated or done by a person and not by electricity, a computer etc. OPP **automatic**: *a manual typewriter* | *The car has a five-speed manual transmission.* **4 manual dexterity** the ability of being able to use your hands and fingers skillfully, or how well you can do this [**Origin:** 1400–1500 French *manuel*, from Latin *manualis*, from *manus* **hand**] —**manually** *adv.*

manual² Ac *n.* [C] **1** a book that gives instructions about how to use a machine SYN **handbook**: *an instruction manual* **2** a setting on a machine that allows it only to be operated using your hands and not by AUTOMATIC means: *The dial was set on manual.*

man·u·fac·ture¹ /ˌmænyəˈfæktʃɚ/ *v.* [T] **1** to use machines to make goods or materials, usually in large numbers or amounts: *The car was manufactured in Germany until 1961.* ▶ see THESAURUS box at **make¹** **2** to invent an untrue story, excuse etc. SYN **invent**: *If the media can manufacture stories like this, then who should we believe?* **3** if your body manufactures a particular substance, it produces it SYN **produce**: *Bile is manufactured by the liver.*

manufacture² *n.* **1** [U] the process of making goods using machines, usually in large numbers: **+of** *Local clay was used in the manufacture of bricks.* **2 manufactures** [plural] TECHNICAL goods that are produced in large quantities using machinery **3** [U] the process of producing a particular substance in your body SYN **production**: **+of** *the manufacture of hormones* [**Origin:** 1500–1600 French, Latin *manu factus* **made by hand**]

man·u·fac·tur·er /ˌmænyəˈfæktʃərɚ/ W3 *n.* [C] a company or industry that makes large quantities of goods SYN **maker**: *a drug manufacturer* | **+of** *the manufacturer of your washing machine*

man·u·fac·tur·ing /ˌmænyəˈfæktʃərɪŋ/ W3 *n.* [U] the process or business of making goods in factories: *Thousands of jobs were lost in manufacturing.*

M

man·u·mis·sion /ˌmænyəˈmɪʃən/ *n.* [U] the act of allowing a SLAVE or SERVANT to become free —**manumit** /ˌmænyəˈmɪt/ *v.* [T]

ma·nure /məˈnʊɚ/ *n.* [U] waste matter from animals that is put into the soil to produce better crops [**Origin:** 1300–1400 Old French *manouvrer* **to work with the hands**, from Latin *manu operare*] —**manure** *v.* [T]

man·u·script /ˈmænyəˌskrɪpt/ *n.* [C] **1** a book or piece of writing before it is printed: *the author's unpublished manuscripts* **2** a book or document written by hand before printing was invented: *ancient manuscripts* [**Origin:** 1500–1600 Latin *manu scriptus* **written by hand**]

Manx /mæŋks/ *adj.* **1** a Manx cat is a type of cat that has no tail **2** related to the Isle of Man

man·y /ˈmɛni/ S1 W1 *quantifier, pron.* **1** a large number of people or things OPP **few**: *Many animals do not eat meat.* | *Does she have many friends?* | *"Have another donut." "No thanks, I've eaten* ***too many*** *already* (=more than I should)*!* | *We were behind by* ***so many*** *points I thought there was no chance of winning.* | *There* ***aren't many*** (=are not many) *tickets left.* | ***Many of*** *these old baseball cards are worth a lot of money.* | ***Many of*** *them do not speak any English.* | ***For many,*** *these have been very difficult years.* | ***The many*** *illustrations in the book are a delight.* | **a good many/a great many/very many** (=a large number) → see also LOT

THESAURUS

a large number: *A large number of people attended the meeting.*
a lot/lots a large amount, quantity, or number of something: *There are lots of books to choose from.* | *He has a lot of money.*
plenty a large amount that is enough or more than enough: *Make sure you eat plenty of fruits and vegetables.*

2 used for asking or talking about what number of people or things there are: ***How many*** (=what number of) *people are coming to the party?* | *There weren't* ***as many*** *people at the meeting* ***as*** *we had hoped* (=there weren't the number that we had hoped for). | *Print* ***as many as*** (=the same number that) *you think you'll need.* | *He made four free throws* ***in as many*** *attempts* (=he tried four times and made it four times). | **twice as many/three times as many etc.** *The company now employs four times as many women as men.* **3 have had one too many** INFORMAL to be drunk: *Ron looked like he'd had one too many.* **4 many thanks** used in letters or in a formal speech to thank someone for something: *Many thanks for your letter.* **5 the many** FORMAL used to mean a large group of people who all have a particular disadvantage, usually to compare it with a smaller group who do not OPP **the few**: *We have to measure the needs of the many against the needs of the few.* **6 many a time/many's the time** SPOKEN often: *Many a time, we sat in that bar discussing the world.* **7 many a sth** a large number of people or things: *Many a young writer has made the same mistake.* [**Origin:** Old English *manig*] → see also MORE, MUCH², **in so many words** at WORD¹ (23) → see Grammar box at MUCH²

ˈman-year *n.* [C] the amount of work done by one person in one year, used as a measurement

ˌmany-ˈsided *adj.* **1** consisting of many different qualities or features: *Johnson had a many-sided personality.* **2** having many sides

Mao·ism /ˈmaʊˌɪzəm/ *n.* [U] the system of political thinking invented by Mao Zedong —**Maoist** *n., adj.*

Mao·ri /ˈmaʊri/ *n.* **1** [C] someone who belongs to the race of people that first lived in New Zealand **2** [U] the language of the Maori people —**Maori** *adj.*: *a Maori tradition*

Mao Ze·dong /ˌmaʊ dzɪ ˈdʊŋ, -tsɪ ˈtʊŋ/ also **Chairman Mao** (1893–1976) a Chinese politician who helped to start the Chinese Communist Party in 1921 and became its leader in 1935. In 1949 he gained control of the government and established the People's Republic of China.

map¹ /mæp/ S2 W3 *n.* [C] **1** a drawing of an area of country showing rivers, roads, mountains, towns etc., or of a whole country or several countries: +**of** *a map of Texas* | *Let me show you how to get there* ***on the map.*** | *I'm no good at* ***reading maps*** (=understanding maps). | **a road/street map** (=a map that shows roads or streets rather than features of the land) **2** a drawing of an area that shows a particular feature such as the rocks, weather, population etc.: *a weather map* | +**of** *an archeological map of the town* **3** the structure of a political, social etc. system and the way the parts relate to each other: *Germany's political map changed completely.* **4 put sth on the map** to make a place, person, organization etc. famous, so that everyone knows it and talks about it: *It was Ray Kroc that really put McDonald's restaurants on the map.* [**Origin:** 1500–1600 Medieval Latin *mappa*, from Latin, **cloth, towel**] → see also **wipe sth off the map** at WIPE¹ (8)

map² *v.* **mapped, mapping** [T] **1** to make a map of a particular area: *The spacecraft mapped the surface of Venus.* **2** also **map sth ↔ out** to carefully plan how something will happen: *Polk has already mapped out a 20-city tour for the band.* **3** BIOLOGY to find and record information about where a particular type of GENETIC information is on a CHROMOSOME

ma·ple /ˈmeɪpəl/ *n.* BIOLOGY **1** [C] a tree that grows in northern countries, that has pointed leaves that turn red or yellow in the fall **2** [U] the wood from this tree

ˌmaple ˈsugar *n.* [U] a type of sugar made by boiling maple syrup, used to make candy

ˌmaple ˈsyrup *n.* [U] a sweet sticky liquid eaten especially on PANCAKES, obtained from some kinds of maple trees

map·ping /ˈmæpɪŋ/ *n.* **1** [U] the act or process of making a map **2** [C] TECHNICAL a relationship between two mathematical sets in which a member of the first set is matched by a member of the second

ˈmap proˌjection *n.* [C] the way in which an image of the earth is shown on a flat map SYN **projection**

ˈmap-ˌreading *n.* [U] the practice of using a map to find which way you should go: *map-reading skills* —**map-reader** *n.* [C]

Ma·pu·to /mɑˈputoʊ/ the capital and largest city of Mozambique

ma·qui·la·do·ra /ˌmɑkilɑˈdoʊrə/ *n.* [C] ECONOMICS a kind of factory in Mexico where local workers make goods out of parts from other countries. The goods are then sold in other countries rather than in Mexico.

Mar. *n.* the written abbreviation of March

mar /mɑr/ *v.* **marred, marring** [T often passive] to make something less attractive or enjoyable SYN **spoil**: *The celebrations were marred by violence.*

mar·a·bou /ˈmærəˌbu/ *n.* [C] BIOLOGY a large African STORK (=a long-legged bird)

ma·ra·cas /məˈrɑkəz/ *n.* [plural] a PERCUSSION instrument consisting of a pair of hollow balls, filled with small objects such as stones, that are shaken

mar·a·schi·no /ˌmærəˈʃinoʊ, -ˈski-/ *n.* [U] a sweet alcoholic drink made from a type of CHERRY

ˌmaraschino ˈcherry *n.* [C] a CHERRY that has been colored bright red and kept in sweet liquid, and that is used for decorating cakes, drinks etc.

Ma·rat /məˈrɑ/, **Jean Paul** /ʒɑn pɔl/ (1743–1793) a political leader and writer in the French Revolution

mar·a·thon¹ /ˈmærəˌθɑn/ *n.* [C] **1** a long race in which competitors run 26 miles and 385 yards: *the Boston Marathon* | *Garcia* ***ran the marathon*** *in just under three hours.* **2** a series of activities or competitions that are planned to continue for a very long time and demand a lot of effort and determination to finish: *the movie theater's annual horror film marathon* | *a soccer marathon that benefits charity* **3** a situation that continues for too long or much longer that usual: *The meeting was a real marathon.* [**Origin:** 1800–1900 *Mara-*

thon, place in Greece; from the story that in 490 B.C. a Greek soldier ran about 25 miles from the battlefield of Marathon to Athens, to bring news of the Athenian victory over the Persians]

marathon² *adj.* [only before noun] continuing for a very long time: *a marathon game of Monopoly* ►see THESAURUS box at **long¹**

mar·a·thon·er /ˈmærəˌθɑnɚ/ *n.* [C] someone who runs in a marathon

ma·raud·ing /məˈrɔdɪŋ/ *adj.* [only before noun] a marauding person or animal moves around looking for something to destroy or kill: *a marauding gang of youths* —**marauder** *n.* [C]

mar·ble /ˈmɑrbəl/ *n.* **1** [U] EARTH SCIENCE a type of hard rock that becomes smooth when polished, and is used for making buildings, STATUES etc.: *The columns were made of white marble.* | *a marble statue* **2** [C] a small colored glass ball that children roll along the ground as part of a game **3 lose your marbles** INFORMAL to start behaving in a crazy way **4** [C] ENG. LANG. ARTS a STATUE or SCULPTURE made of marble **5 marbles** [U] a children's game played with marbles [**Origin:** 1100–1200 Old French *marbre*, from Latin *marmor*]

ˈmarble cake *n.* [C] a cake made with two different colors of BATTER that form curved lines in the cake

mar·bled /ˈmɑrbəld/ *adj.* **1** having an irregular pattern of lines and colors: *a marbled silk scarf* **2** made of marble: *a marbled floor* **3** marbled meat contains lines of fat

March /mɑrtʃ/ WRITTEN ABBREVIATION **Mar.** *n.* [C,U] the third month of the year, between February and April [**Origin:** 1200–1300 Old French, Latin *martius*, from *martius* **of Mars, god of war**] → see Grammar box at JANUARY

march¹ /mɑrtʃ/ *v.* **1** [I] to walk quickly and with firm, regular steps like a soldier: *The 555th Battalion marched in the parade.* | +**across/along/through** *The Union Army marched through Georgia.* ►see THESAURUS box at **walk¹** **2** [I] to walk somewhere in a large group to protest about something: *Several hundred students marched across campus to protest.* | **march on sth** *Outraged citizens marched on City Hall, demanding the police chief's resignation.* | **march for/against sth** *The suffragettes marched for women's right to vote.* ►see THESAURUS box at **protest²** **3** [I always + adv./prep.] to walk somewhere quickly and with determination, often because you are angry: +**down/off etc.** *One angry woman marched out of the auditorium.* **4** [T always + adv./prep.] to force someone to walk somewhere with you, often pushing or pulling them roughly: *The prisoners of war were marched around the compound.* **5 marching orders** the instructions someone has been given by the people who have authority over them: *The department heads have their marching orders: cut the budget, now.* [**Origin:** 1300–1400 Old French *marchier* **to step heavily**] —**marcher** *n.* [C]

march² S2 *n.* [C] **1** an organized event in which many people walk together to protest about something: **protest/peace/civil rights etc. march** *a Civil Rights march in Washington* **2** the act of walking with firm regular steps, as soldiers do, from one place to another: *The soldiers did a march around the parade ground.* | **a day's march/two weeks' march etc.** (=the distance a group of soldiers can march in a particular period of time) **3** ENG. LANG. ARTS a piece of music with a regular beat for soldiers to march to: *a military march* **4 on the march a)** an army that is on the march is marching somewhere **b)** a belief, idea etc. that is on the march is becoming stronger and more popular: *Fascism is on the march again in some parts of Europe.* **5 the march of time/history/events etc.** FORMAL the way that things happen or change over time and cannot be stopped: *Too many trees are being lost in the constant march of development.* → see also **steal a march on sb** at STEAL¹ (10)

ˈmarching ˌband *n.* [C] a group of musicians who march while they play musical instruments

ˌMarch of ˈDimes, the a U.S. CHARITY organization that collects money for children, especially those with serious mental or physical disabilities (DISABILITY)

ˌMarch on ˈWashington, the HISTORY a large protest march in Washington, D.C. in 1963 in support of CIVIL RIGHTS for African-Americans. People on the march demanded "Jobs and Freedom," and Martin Luther King gave his famous speech that included the words "I have a dream."

Mar·ci·a·no /ˌmɑrsiˈɑnoʊ/, **Rock·y** /ˈrɑki/ (1923–1969) a BOXER who was world HEAVYWEIGHT CHAMPION from 1952 to 1956

Mar·co·ni /mɑrˈkoʊni/, **Gu·gliel·mo** /gʊˈlyɛl moʊ/ (1874–1937) an Italian electrical engineer who invented the first method of sending messages by radio

Mar·cus Au·re·li·us /ˌmɑrkəs ɔˈriliəs/ (121–180) a Roman EMPEROR and PHILOSOPHER

Mar·cu·se /mɑrˈkuzə/, **Her·bert** /ˈhɚbɚt/ (1898–1979) a U.S. PHILOSOPHER and writer on politics

Mar·di Gras /ˈmɑrdi ˌgrɑ, -ˌgrɔ/ *n.* [C,U] the day before Lent, or the music, dancing etc. that celebrate this day

mare /mɛr/ *n.* [C] a female horse or DONKEY → see also STALLION

mar·ga·rine /ˈmɑrdʒərɪn/ *n.* [U] a yellow substance that is similar to butter but is made from oil, which you eat with bread or use for cooking [**Origin:** 1800–1900 French, Greek *margaron* **pearl**]

mar·ga·ri·ta /ˌmɑrgəˈriṭə/ *n.* [C] an alcoholic drink made with TEQUILA and LIME juice

mar·gin /ˈmɑrdʒɪn/ Ac W3 *n.* [C] **1** the empty space at the side of a printed page: *two-inch margins* | *There were some penciled notes* ***in the margin***. ►see THESAURUS box at **edge¹** **2** the difference in the number of votes, points etc. that exists between the winner and the loser of an election or competition: *an eight-goal margin of defeat* | **by a wide/narrow margin** *The mayor was voted out of office by a wide* (=large) *margin.* | **by a margin of ten points/100 votes etc.** *The bill was approved by a margin of 55 votes.* **3** the difference between what a business pays for something and what they sell it for SYN **profit margin** **4** an additional amount of something such as time, money, or space that you include in order to make sure that you are successful in achieving something: *The design has safety margins built in.* | +**for** *There is no* ***margin for error*** (=even a small error would mean you fail). **5 margin of error** the degree to which a calculation can be wrong without affecting the final results: *The poll has a margin of error of three percent.* **6 on the margin(s) of** a person on the margins of a situation or group is one of the least important, powerful, or typical parts of that situation or group: *Many mentally ill people have been forced to live* ***on the margins of society***. **7** the edge of something, especially an area of land [**Origin:** 1300–1400 Latin *margo* **border**]

mar·gin·al /ˈmɑrdʒənl/ Ac *adj.* **1** a marginal change or difference is too small to be important: *a marginal increase in sales* ►see THESAURUS box at **unimportant** **2** marginal people, things etc. are the least powerful, important, or typical ones in a particular group or situation: *poor and socially marginal groups* **3** TECHNICAL relating to a change in cost, value etc. when one more thing is produced, one more dollar is earned etc.: *marginal revenue* **4 marginal land** land that cannot produce good crops **5** written in a margin: *marginal notes* —**marginality** /ˌmɑrdʒəˈnæləṭi/ *n.* [U] → see also MARGINALLY

ˌmarginal ˈbenefit *n.* [C,U] ECONOMICS the additional advantage or satisfaction that results from a small increase in the use of a good or service SYN **marginal utility**

ˌmarginal ˈcost *n.* [C usually singular] ECONOMICS the additional cost of producing one more of a particular product or thing SYN **incremental cost**

mar·gin·al·ize /ˈmɑrdʒənəˌlaɪz/ *v.* [T] to make a group of people unimportant and powerless: *Our*

M

society marginalizes people with handicaps. —**marginalized** *adj.* —**marginalization** /ˌmɑrdʒənələˈzeɪʃən/ *n.* [U]

mar·gin·al·ly /ˈmɑrdʒənl-i/ Ac *adv.* not enough to make an important difference SYN **slightly**: *Stock prices rose marginally in early trading today.* | [+ adj./adv.] *The new system was only marginally better.*

ˌmarginal ˌproduct of ˈlabor *n.* [singular] ECONOMICS the small increase in the number of goods a machine or factory produces when a business employs one additional worker

ˌmarginal ˈrevenue *n.* [U] also **marginal revenues** [plural] ECONOMICS the additional money a business earns from selling one more of a particular product. This amount is sometimes equal to the price of the product sold.

ˌmarginal uˈtility *n.* [C,U] ECONOMICS the additional advantage or satisfaction that results from using one additional unit of a good or service

ˈmargin ˌbuying *n.* [U] ECONOMICS the buying of shares and other INVESTMENTS with borrowed money

ma·ri·a·chi /ˌmɑriˈɑtʃi/ *n.* [U] a type of Mexican dance music

Mar·i·an·as Trench, the /ˌmæriˈænəs ˌtrɛntʃ, -ˈɑnəs-/ a very deep part of the western Pacific Ocean that is the deepest part of all the oceans in the world

Ma·rie An·toi·nette /məˌri æntwɑˈnɛt/ (1755–1793) the Queen of France from 1774 to 1792, and the wife of Louis XVI. She and Louis XVI were killed in the French Revolution.

mar·i·gold /ˈmærəˌgoʊld, ˈmɛr-/ *n.* [C] a plant with golden-yellow or orange flowers [**Origin:** 1300–1400 *Mary*, mother of Jesus + *gold*]

mar·i·jua·na, **marihuana** /ˌmærəˈwɑnə/ *n.* [U] an illegal drug in the form of dried leaves that people smoke [**Origin:** 1800–1900 Mexican Spanish *mariguana*, *marihuana*]

ma·rim·ba /məˈrɪmbə/ *n.* [C] a musical instrument like a XYLOPHONE

ma·ri·na /məˈrinə/ *n.* [C] a small area of water where people keep boats that are used for pleasure

mar·i·nade /ˌmærəˈneɪd/ *n.* [C,U] a mixture of oil, wine, and SPICES in which meat or fish is put before it is cooked [**Origin:** 1700–1800 French, Spanish *marinada*, from *marinar* **to preserve in salt**, from Latin *marinus*]

mar·i·nate /ˈmærəˌneɪt/ also **mar·i·nade** /ˈmærəˌneɪd/ *v.* [I,T] to leave meat or fish in a marinade, or to be left in a marinade for a period of time

ma·rine /məˈrin/ *adj.* [only before noun] **1** EARTH SCIENCE relating to the ocean and the animals and plants that live there: *marine biology* | *marine life* **2** relating to ships or the Navy [**Origin:** 1300–1400 Latin *marinus*, from *mare* **sea**]

mar·i·ner /ˈmærənɚ/ *n.* [C] LITERARY a SAILOR

Ma·rines /məˈrinz/ *n.* **1 the Marines** also **the Maˈrine Corps** the military organization of the U.S. consisting of soldiers who work from ships **2 tell it to the Marines!** SPOKEN used to say that you do not believe what someone has told you, see also AIR FORCE → ARMY, NAVY[1] (1)

maˌrine ˌwest coast ˈclimate *n.* [C] EARTH SCIENCE a CLIMATE (=typical weather conditions in an area) with a lot of rain and temperatures that are not extreme, which is found on the west coast of land areas next to an ocean

Ma·ri·no /məˈrinoʊ/, **Dan** /dæn/ (1961–) a U.S. football player who is considered one of the best QUARTERBACKS in the NFL

mar·i·o·nette /ˌmæriəˈnɛt/ *n.* [C] a toy that looks like a person, animal etc., that is moved by pulling strings attached to its body → see also PUPPET

Mar·is /ˈmærɪs/, **Ro·ger** /ˈrɑdʒɚ/ (1934–1985) a U.S. baseball player famous for hitting 61 HOME RUNS in 1961, which broke the record of Babe Ruth

mar·i·tal /ˈmærətl/ *adj.* relating to marriage: *marital problems* | *What is your* ***marital status*** (=are you married or unmarried)*?* [**Origin:** 1400–1500 Latin *maritalis*, from *maritus* **husband**]

mar·i·time /ˈmærəˌtaɪm/ *adj.* **1** relating to ships that sail on the ocean **2** EARTH SCIENCE near the ocean: *the Canadian maritime provinces* [**Origin:** 1500–1600 Latin *maritimus*, from *mare* **sea**]

mar·jo·ram /ˈmɑrdʒərəm/ *n.* [U] an HERB that smells sweet and is used in cooking

Mark /mɑrk/ also **The Gospel according to St. Mark** one of the four books in the New Testament of the Christian Bible that describe the life and teaching of Jesus Christ

mark[1] /mɑrk/ S2 W2 *v.*

1 WRITE ON STH [T] to make a sign, shape, or word using a pen or pencil: *I'll just mark the one I want in the catalog.* | **mark sth with sth** *Joe's boxes were marked with a blue triangle.* | **mark sth on sth** *She's marked the date on the calendar.* | **mark sth personal/fragile/urgent etc.** *The letter was marked "personal."*

2 SHOW POSITION [T] to show where something is or was: *He had marked the route* ***in red*** (=using red ink). | **mark sth with sth** *Troop positions were marked with colored pins.* | *I folded the page to* ***mark my place.***

3 SHOW A CHANGE [T] to show that an important change has happened, or show the beginning of a new period in the development of something: *The album marks a change in the band's musical style.* | **mark the end/beginning of sth** *These elections mark the end of an era.*

4 QUALITY/FEATURE [T often passive] if a particular quality or feature marks something, it is a typical or important part of that thing SYN **characterize**: *The meeting was marked by bitter exchanges between the two sides.*

5 CELEBRATE to celebrate an important event in a particular way: **mark sth with sth** *The last day of the holidays is marked with a feast.*

6 YEAR/MONTH/WEEK if a particular year, month, or week marks an important event, the event happens during that time: *This year marks the company's 50th anniversary.*

7 SPOIL STH [I,T] to make a mark on something in a way that spoils its appearance or damages it, or to become spoiled in this way: *Her shoes marked the floor.* | *The linoleum marks easily.*

8 STUDENT'S WORK [T] to grade a student's work ►see THESAURUS box at **sign**[1]

9 mark time a) INFORMAL to spend time doing very little because you are waiting for something else to happen: *Investors are marking time, waiting for the market to improve.* **b)** if soldiers mark time, they move their legs as if they were marching, but remain in the same place

10 (you) mark my words! OLD-FASHIONED used to tell someone that they should pay attention to what you are saying: *Mark my words, that relationship won't last.*

[**Origin:** (1–9) Old English *mearc* **border, edge, sigh**] → see also MARKED

mark sth **as** sth *phr. v.* if a quality or feature marks someone or something as something, it shows that they are that type of person or thing: *Expensive cameras mark you as a tourist.*

mark sb/sth ↔ **down** *phr. v.* **1** to reduce the price of things that are being sold SYN **reduce**: *All our merchandise has been marked down by at least 30%!* **2** to give a student a lower grade on a test, paper etc. because they have made mistakes: *You'll be marked down five points for each spelling mistake.* **3** to write something down, especially in order to keep a record SYN **write down**

mark sb/sth ↔ **off** *phr. v.* **1** to make an area separate by drawing a line around it, putting a rope around it etc.: *Police marked off the area with white lines.* **2** to make a mark on something such as a list to show that something has been done or completed: *We marked off the days on the calendar.*

mark sb/sth ↔ **out** *phr. v.* **1** to show the shape or position of something by drawing lines around it: *A volleyball court had been marked out on the grass.* **2** to make someone or something seem different from or better than other similar people or things: **mark sb/sth out as sth** *This victory marked her out as the best horse of the year.*

mark sb/sth ↔ **up** *phr. v.* **1** to increase the price of something, so that you sell it for more than you paid for it: *The retailers mark up the goods by three to ten percent.* → see also MARK-UP **2** to write notes or instructions on a piece of writing, music etc.: *Someone had already marked up the alto part.*

mark² S2 W2 *n.* [C]

1 DIRT a spot or small dirty area on something that spoils its appearance: *I can't get these marks off the wall.* | **leave/make a mark** *The tape left a mark on the paint.*

THESAURUS

Types of dirty marks

stain a mark that is difficult to remove: *an ink stain on the shirt pocket*

spot a small mark: *a grease spot on his shirt*

smudge a dirty mark, made when something is rubbed against a surface: *a smudge of paint on her cheek*

smear a mark that is left when a substance is spread on a surface: *a smear of ketchup on his face*

Types of marks on someone's skin

blemish a mark on your skin that spoils its appearance

bruise a purple or brown mark on your skin that you get because you have fallen or been hit

scar a permanent mark on your skin, caused by a cut or by something that burns you

pimple a small raised red mark or lump on your skin that teenagers often have

zit INFORMAL a pimple

wart a small hard raised mark on your skin caused by a virus (=a living thing that causes an infectious illness)

blister a small area of skin that is swollen and full of liquid because it has been rubbed or burned

freckle one of several small light brown marks on someone's skin

mole a small usually brown mark on the skin that is often slightly higher than the skin around it

2 WRITING a written shape or sign: *Put a check mark beside each person's name as they come in.* | *Rose* ***made a mark*** *on the map to show where her house was.*
3 DAMAGED AREA a cut, hole, or other small damaged area: **burn/bite/scratch/teeth etc. marks** *Check the power cord for any burn marks.*
4 LEVEL/NUMBER a particular level, number, amount, or time: *The city's population has* ***passed the*** *million* ***mark***. | *The temperature is expected to* ***reach the*** *100 degree* ***mark*** *in the next few days.*
5 make/leave your mark to become successful or famous: **+as** *Ivins made her mark as the managing editor of the "Texas Observer".* | **+in** *He made his mark in Hollywood as an action hero.* | **+on** *Babe Ruth has left his mark on baseball history.*
6 be off the mark also **be wide of the mark** to be incorrect: *Our estimate was* ***way off the mark***.
7 hit the mark a) to be correct and exact, or to have the effect that you intended: *Their economic predictions hit the mark.* | *Most of the acting in her latest movie hits the mark.* **b)** to hit the thing that you were aiming at OPP **miss the mark**
8 a mark of sth something that shows that a particular quality exists in a person, thing, or situation: *The ability to perform under pressure is the mark of a true champion.* | *Everyone brought gifts as* ***a mark of respect*** *for the old man.*
9 leave/make its mark on sb to affect someone or something so that they change in a permanent or very noticeable way: *Growing up during the Depression left its mark on Schreier.*
10 be quick/slow/first etc. off the mark INFORMAL to be quick, slow, first etc. to understand things or react to situations: *The country has been slow off the mark with its reforms.*
11 on your mark(s), get set, go! SPOKEN said in order to start a race
12 STUDENT'S WORK BRITISH a GRADE
13 CRIME someone that a criminal has chosen to steal from or trick
14 Mark 1/2/3 etc. used to show the type or VERSION of a car, machine etc.: *the Lincoln Mark 5*
15 MONEY the standard unit of money used in Germany before the Euro
16 SIGNATURE OLD USE a sign in the form of an "X" used by someone who is not able to write their name → see also BIRTHMARK, **a black mark (against sb)** at BLACK¹ (6), **halfway point/mark** at HALFWAY (1), MARKING, PUNCTUATION MARK, QUESTION MARK, QUOTATION MARK

Mark /mɑrk/**, Saint** one of Jesus Christ's DISCIPLES. He is believed to have written "The Gospel according to St. Mark," which describes the life and teaching of Jesus Christ.

mark·down /ˈmɑrkdaʊn/ *n.* [C] a reduction in the price of something: **+of** *a markdown of 20%*

marked /mɑrkt/ *adj.* **1** very easy to notice SYN **noticeable**: *a marked improvement in the patient's condition* | *The blue-green office tower is* ***in marked contrast to*** *the city's traditional brick buildings.* **2 a marked man/woman** someone who is in danger because someone wants to harm him or her —**markedly** /ˈmɑrkɪdli/ *adv.*: *They have a markedly different approach to the problem.*

mark·er /ˈmɑrkɚ/ *n.* [C] **1** an object, sign etc. that shows the position of something: *A granite marker shows where the battle took place.* **2** a large pen with a thick point, used for marking or drawing things: *a red marker* **3 put/lay/set down a marker** to say or do something that clearly shows what you will do in the future

mar·ket¹ /ˈmɑrkɪt/ S1 W1 *n.*

1 PLACE TO BUY THINGS [C] **a)** a place where people buy and sell goods, food etc., especially an outside area or a large building: *I went down to the flower market to get these – aren't they gorgeous?* | *Every Sunday there's a* ***farmers' market*** *in the park.* **b)** a GROCERY STORE
2 the market a) the STOCK MARKET: *Most analysts think the market will continue to rise.* | *Investors are currently reluctant to* ***play the market*** (=risk money on the stock market). | *A sharp decline in the Dow Jones average rocked* ***the markets*** (=all the stock markets in the world) *Friday.* **b)** the total amount of trade in a particular kind of goods: *They've captured about 60% of the market.* | *There have been dramatic changes in the real estate market.* | **+in** *the world market in aluminum* **c)** the economic system in which all prices and pay depend on what goods people want to buy, how many they buy etc.: *Capitalism is based on a belief in the market.*
3 BUYING AND SELLING [C] ECONOMICS **a)** the activity of buying and selling goods or services: *competitive global markets* **b)** the activity of buying and selling STOCKS and BONDS: *the world's* ***financial markets*** | **bond/stock/currency etc. market**
4 on the market available for people to buy: *There are thousands of different computer games on the market.* | *The Paynes are* ***putting their house on the market*** (=offering it for sale). | *A clean-burning diesel fuel* ***came onto the market*** (=began being sold) *in 1993.* | *Handguns are freely available* ***on the open market*** (=for anyone to buy).
5 COUNTRY/AREA [C] a particular country or area where a company sells its goods or where a particular type of goods is sold: *Japanese cars account for about 30% of the U.S. car market.* | **+for** *The main market for computer software is still the U.S.* | *Some major* ***overseas markets*** (=markets in other countries) *have been having economic problems.*
6 PEOPLE WHO BUY [singular] the number of people who want to buy something, or the kind of people who want to buy it: **+for** *a growth in the urban market for dairy products* | ***There is a*** *major* ***market for*** *Californian designs in Asia.*
7 be in the market for sth to be interested in buying

M

something: *If you're in the market for a mobile home, this is a good time to buy.*
8 the job/labor market the people looking for work, and the number of jobs that are available: *Half of the teenagers **entering the job market** in Los Angeles are Latino.* | **competitive/tough/tight job market** (=one in which many people are looking for the same jobs)
9 a buyer's/seller's market a time that is better for buyers because prices are low, or better for sellers because prices are high
[**Origin:** 1100–1200 Old North French, Latin *mercatus* **buying and selling, marketplace**, from *mercari* **to buy and sell**, from *merx* **things to sell**] → see also BLACK MARKET, **corner the market** at CORNER² (2), FLEA MARKET, FREE MARKET, **price yourself out of the market** at PRICE² (4)

market² W3 *v.* [T] **1** to try to persuade people to buy a product by advertising it in a particular way, using attractive packages etc.: *The toy is marketed for children aged two to six.* | **market sth as sth** *The noodles are being marketed as a health food.* ►see THESAURUS box at **advertise** **2** to make a product available in stores: *Most turkeys are marketed at a young age.*

mar·ket·a·ble /ˈmɑrkɪṭəbəl/ *adj.* marketable goods, skills etc. can be sold easily because people want them: *Too many graduates lack marketable skills.* —**marketability** /ˌmɑrkɪṭəˈbɪləṭi/ *n.* [U]

ˈmarket ˌbasket *n.* [C] ECONOMICS a collection of different goods that appear on lists, such as the CONSUMER PRICE INDEX, that record the changes in price of certain products over a particular period of time. These lists are considered to be an important sign of what is likely to happen to the U.S. ECONOMY in the future.

ˌmarket ˈclearing ˌprice *n.* [C] ECONOMICS a price at which the amount of a good or service that people are willing to buy equals the amount that is produced or supplied SYN **equilibrium price**

ˌmarket deˈmand ˌcurve → see DEMAND CURVE

ˌmarket deˈmand ˌschedule → see DEMAND SCHEDULE

ˈmarket-ˌdriven *adj.* ECONOMICS market-driven activities, products, developments etc. are a result of public demand for a particular product, service, or skill

ˌmarket eˈconomy *n.* [C] ECONOMICS an economic system in which companies are not controlled by the government, but decide what they want to produce or sell, based on what they believe will give them a profit

mar·ket·eer /ˌmɑrkəˈtɪr/ *n.* [C] someone who sells goods or services into a MARKET —**marketeering** *n.* [U] → see also BLACK MARKETEER, FREE MARKETEER

ˈmarket ˌfailure *n.* [C,U] ECONOMICS a situation in which a MARKET does not work successfully or well, for example when the people who are buying a product do not have all the information they need to make decisions, or when machinery or materials are not used effectively

ˌmarket ˈforces *n.* [plural] ECONOMICS the free operation of business and trade without any government controls, which decides the level of prices and pay at a particular time

mar·ket·ing /ˈmɑrkɪṭɪŋ/ S3 W2 *n.* [U] **1** the activity of deciding how to advertise a product, what price to charge for it etc., or the type of job in which you do this: *Car safety is a hot marketing topic.* | *a job in marketing* **2 do the marketing** OLD-FASHIONED to go to the store to buy food

ˌmarket ˈleader *n.* [C] the company that sells the most of a particular kind of product, or the product that is the most successful one of its kind: +**in** *the U.S. market leader in sporting goods*

ˈmarket-led *adj.* MARKET-DRIVEN

ˈmarket ˌmaker *n.* [C] TECHNICAL someone who works on the STOCK MARKET buying and selling STOCKS and SHARES

mar·ket·place /ˈmɑrkɪt˺ˌpleɪs/ *n.* **1 the marketplace** the part of business activities that is concerned with buying and selling goods in competition with other companies: *the company's strong position in the marketplace* **2** [C] an open area in a town where a MARKET is held

ˈmarket ˌpower *n.* [U] ECONOMICS a company's ability to set the price of their product or service, or to control how much of a product they will produce and supply

ˈmarket price *n.* [singular] the price of something on a MARKET at a particular time

ˌmarket ˈresearch *n.* [U] a business activity that involves collecting information about what goods people buy and why they buy them

ˌmarket revoˈlution *n.* [C usually singular] ECONOMICS a change from an economic system where people grow, farm, find, or make the things they need to one based on buying and selling goods for money

ˈmarket share *n.* [C,U] the PERCENTAGE (=amount measured as parts out of 100) of sales in a MARKET that a company or product has: *We'd like to double our market share.*

ˌmarket supˈply ˌcurve → see SUPPLY CURVE

ˌmarket supˈply ˌschedule → see SUPPLY SCHEDULE

ˌmarket ˈvalue *n.* [C,U] **1** the value of a product, building etc. based on the price that people are willing to pay for it rather than the cost of producing it or building it **2** ECONOMICS the total value of all the SHARES on a STOCK MARKET, or the value of the STOCK of a particular company

mark·ing /ˈmɑrkɪŋ/ *n.* [C usually plural, U] **1** things written or painted on something, especially something such as an aircraft, road, vehicle etc.: *The markings on the road are unclear.* | *a black box with no markings* **2** the colored patterns and shapes on an animal's fur, on leaves etc.: *a cow with black and white markings*

mark·ka /ˈmɑrkɑ/ *n.* [C] the basic unit of money in Finland

marks·man /ˈmɑrksmən/ *n. plural* **marksmen** /-mən/ [C] someone who can shoot very well

marks·man·ship /ˈmɑrksmənˌʃɪp/ *n.* [U] the ability to shoot very well

ˈmark-up *n.* [C] an increase in the price of something, especially from the price a store pays for something to the price it sells it for: *The retailer's mark-up is 50%.*

Mar·ley /ˈmɑrli/**, Bob** /bɑb/ (1945–1981) a Jamaican singer and SONGWRITER who helped to make REGGAE music popular

mar·lin /ˈmɑrlɪn/ *n. plural* **marlin** [C] BIOLOGY a large ocean fish with a long sharp nose, which people hunt as a sport

Mar·lowe /ˈmɑrloʊ/**, Christopher** (1564–1593) an English poet and writer of plays

mar·ma·lade /ˈmɑrməˌleɪd/ *n.* [U] a JAM made from fruit such as oranges, usually eaten at breakfast [**Origin:** 1400–1500 Portuguese *marmelada* **jam made from quinces**, from *marmelo* **quince**]

mar·mo·re·al /mɑrˈmɔriəl/ *adj.* LITERARY like MARBLE

mar·mo·set /ˈmɑrməˌsɛt, -ˌzɛt/ *n.* [C] a type of small monkey with long hair and large eyes that lives in Central and South America [**Origin:** 1300–1400 Old French *marmouset* **strangely ugly figure**]

mar·mot /ˈmɑrmət/ *n.* [C] a small animal with a short furry tail that lives in northern areas, especially in the mountains

ma·roon¹ /məˈrun/ *n.* [U] a very dark red-brown color [**Origin:** 1700–1800 French *marron* **chestnut**] —**maroon** *adj.*

maroon² *v.* [T usually passive] to be left in a place where there are no other people or from which you cannot escape: *The car broke down and left us marooned in the middle of the desert.* [**Origin:** 1600–1700 *maroon* **runaway black slave** (17–19 centuries), from American Spanish *cimarrón* **wild**]

mar·quee¹ /mɑrˈki/ *n.* [C] a large sign on a theater that gives the name of the play or movie

M

marquee² *adj.* a marquee player, actor etc. is someone who people want to see because they are good or famous

Mar·quette /mɑrˈkɛt/, **Jacques** /ʒɑk/ (1637–1675) a French MISSIONARY and EXPLORER in North America. He and Louis Joliet were the first Europeans to discover the Mississippi River.

mar·quis /ˈmɑrkwəs, mɑrˈki/ *n.* [C] a man who, in the British system of NOBLE titles, has a rank between DUKE and EARL

mar·riage /ˈmærɪdʒ/ S2 W1 *n.* **1** [C] the relationship between two people who are married: *One in three marriages ends in divorce.* | **have a long/good/bad etc. marriage** *My parents had a long and happy marriage.* | +**to** *his marriage to Marilyn Monroe* | *The two women are related* ***by marriage*** (=because one is married to someone in the other's family). **2** [U] the state of being married: *Many people still disapprove of sex before marriage.* **3** [C] the ceremony in which two people get married SYN **wedding**: *The marriage took place at our church.* **4** [C] a close relationship between two ideas, things, or groups: +**between** *The film is the ideal marriage between pictures and words.*

mar·riage·a·ble /ˈmærɪdʒəbəl/ *adj.* OLD-FASHIONED appropriate for marriage: *a young woman of marriageable age* —**marriageability** /ˌmærɪdʒəˈbɪləṭi/ *n.* [U]

ˈmarriage cerˌtificate *n.* [C] an official document that proves that two people are married

ˈmarriage ˌlicense *n.* [C] an official written document saying that two people are allowed to marry

ˌmarriage of conˈvenience *n.* [C] a marriage that is made for political or economic reasons, not for love

ˈmarriage ˌvows *n.* [plural] the promises that you make during the marriage ceremony

mar·ried /ˈmærid/ S2 W2 *adj.* **1** having a husband or a wife: *Are you married or single?* | *a happily married man* | *Tony* ***is married to*** *my sister.* | *We're* ***getting married*** *next month.* | *Newlyweds often started* ***married life*** *by living with one set of in-laws.* | *The sign on the car said* ***"Just Married."*** → see also MARRY

THESAURUS

single not married
engaged having formally agreed to marry someone in the future
fiancée/fiancé a woman or man who is engaged
separated no longer living with your husband or wife because of problems in your marriage
estranged FORMAL an estranged husband or wife is one who is no longer living with his or her partner, but who is not yet divorced
divorced no longer married because you have officially ended your marriage
divorcee someone who is divorced
widowed no longer married because your husband or wife has died
widow/widower a woman or man who is widowed
living together in a romantic relationship and sharing a home together, though not married
partner one of two people who are living together or who are married
spouse FORMAL a husband or wife
→ WEDDING

2 be married to sth to give most of your time and attention to a job or an activity

mar·row /ˈmæroʊ/ *n.* **1** [U] BIOLOGY the soft substance in the hollow center of bones **2 chilled/frozen/shocked etc. to the marrow** extremely cold, shocked etc.

mar·ry /ˈmæri/ S1 W2 *v.* **marries, married, marrying** **1** [I,T] to become someone's husband or wife: *He converted to Catholicism so he could marry her.* | *She married three times.* | *I'm going to ask her to marry me.* | *Tina* ***married young*** (=she was young when she got married). | *She always said she'd* ***marry money*** (=marry someone who is rich). | *My brother says he's* ***not the marrying kind*** (=not the type of person who wants to marry). → see also MARRIED **2** [I] if two people marry, they become husband and wife to each other: *My father said we were too young to marry.* **3** [T] to perform the ceremony at which two people get married: *Rabbi Feingold will marry us.* **4** [T] to make your son or daughter marry a particular person: **marry sb to sb** *Her family wanted to marry her to a doctor.* **5** [T] FORMAL to combine two different ideas, styles, tastes etc. together: **marry sth with/and sth** *The design marries traditional styles with modern materials.*

marry into sth *phr. v.* to join a family or social group by marrying someone who belongs to it: *He married into a wealthy family.* [**Origin:** 1200–1300 French *marier*, from Latin *maritare*, from *maritus* **husband**]

marry sb ↔ **off** *phr. v.* if parents marry off their son or daughter, they find a husband or wife for them: **marry sb off to sb** *Calla was married off to a prosperous local farmer.*

USAGE

Get married is more informal and more common in spoken English than **marry**: *Ann is getting married to Chris next week* (compare *Ann is marrying Chris next week*). In spoken English, speakers often avoid using the word *to* with **married** by saying, for example: *Chris and Ann got married/are married.*

Mars /mɑrz/ *n.* **1** PHYSICS the small red PLANET that is fourth in order from the sun and is the first planet outside the Earth's orbit → see picture at SOLAR SYSTEM **2** the Roman name for the god ARES

Mar·seil·laise /ˌmɑrseɪˈɛz/ *n.* [singular] the national song of France

marsh /mɑrʃ/ *n.* [C,U] EARTH SCIENCE an area of low wet ground, often between the ocean and land, in which grasses or bushes may grow → see also BOG —**marshy** *adj.*: *marshy ground*

mar·shal¹ /ˈmɑrʃəl/ *n.* [C] **1** a police officer in the U.S. employed by the national or city government to make sure people do what a COURT ORDER says they must do: *a federal marshal* **2** the officer in charge of a fire-fighting department in the U.S.: *the fire marshal* **3** an officer of the highest rank in an Army or Air Force **4** someone famous who is chosen to lead a PARADE: *the grand marshal of the Thanksgiving parade*

marshal² *v.* **marshaled, marshaling** [T] **1** to organize all the people and things that you need in order to be ready for a battle, election etc.: *Raia is a city police officer who* ***marshaled support for*** *the bill.* | *The party* ***is marshaling its forces*** *for the election.* **2** to organize your arguments, ideas etc. so that they are effective or easy to understand: **marshal your thoughts/arguments** *He paused for a moment to marshal his thoughts.* | **marshal the facts/evidence** *The prosecution is marshaling evidence against them.*

Mar·shall /ˈmɑrʃəl/, **George** (1880–1959) a general in the U.S. Army during World War II who later organized the Marshall Plan by which the U.S. helped Europe after the war

Marshall, John (1755–1835) a CHIEF JUSTICE on the U.S. Supreme Court

Marshall, Thur·good /ˈθɚgʊd/ (1908–1993) a U.S. lawyer who became the first African-American member of the Supreme Court in 1967

ˈMarshall ˌIslands, the a country consisting of a group of islands in the central Pacific Ocean

ˈMarshall ˌPlan, the HISTORY a program of economic help for Europe after World War II, provided by the U.S. between 1948 and 1952. It was organized by General George Marshall.

ˈmarsh gas *n.* [U] gas formed from decaying plants under water in a MARSH SYN **methane**

marsh·land /ˈmɑrʃlænd/ *n.* [U] EARTH SCIENCE an area of land where there is a lot of MARSH

marsh·mal·low /ˈmɑrʃˌmɛloʊ/ *n.* [C,U] a very soft light white candy that is made of sugar and EGG WHITES [**Origin:** 1800–1900 *marshmallow* type of plant whose root contains a sweet substance once used in candy (11–21 centuries), from Old English *merscmealwe*]

mar·su·pi·al /mɑr'supiəl/ *n.* [C] BIOLOGY a type of animal that carries its young in a POUCH on the front of its body while the young animal is still growing

Mart, -Mart /mɑrt/ *n.* [C] used in the names of stores, markets, or MALLS → see also MINI-MART

mar·ten /'mɑrt̚n/ *n.* [C] a small flesh-eating animal that lives mainly in trees

mar·tial /'mɑrʃəl/ *adj.* [only before noun] relating to war and fighting: *martial music* [**Origin:** 1300–1400 Latin *martialis* **of Mars**, from *Mars* **Mars, god of war**]

ˌmartial 'art *n.* [C usually plural] a sport such as JUDO or KARATE, in which you fight with your hands and feet, and which was developed in Eastern countries

ˌmartial 'law *n.* [U] POLITICS a situation in which the army takes direct control of an area and many citizens' rights are taken away, especially because of fighting against the government: *According to media reports, the country is now* ***under martial law****.*

Mar·tian /'mɑrʃən/ *n.* [C] an imaginary creature from the PLANET Mars —**Martian** *adj.*

mar·tin /'mɑrt̚n/ *n.* [C] BIOLOGY a small bird like a SWALLOW

mar·ti·net /ˌmɑrt̚n'ɛt/ *n.* [C] FORMAL someone who is very strict and makes people obey rules exactly

mar·ti·ni /mɑr'tini/ *n. plural* **martinis** [C,U] an alcoholic drink made by mixing GIN or VODKA with VERMOUTH

Mar·ti·nique /ˌmɑrtɪ'nik, -tn'ik/ an island in the Caribbean Sea that is controlled by France

Mar·tin Lu·ther King Day /ˌmɑrt̚n ˌluθɚ 'kɪŋ ˌdeɪ/ *n.* an American holiday on the third Monday in January to remember the day that Martin Luther King Jr. was born

mar·tyr¹ /'mɑrt̬ɚ/ *n.* [C] **1** someone who dies for their religious or political beliefs, and whose death makes people believe more strongly in those beliefs **2** someone who tries to get other people's sympathy by talking about how hard their life is: *Don't be such a martyr!* —**martyred** *adj.* [only before noun]

martyr² *v.* **be martyred** to become a martyr by dying for your religious or political beliefs

mar·tyr·dom /'mɑrt̬ɚdəm/ *n.* [U] the death or suffering of a martyr

mar·vel¹ /'mɑrvəl/ *v.* **marveled, marveling** [I,T] to feel great surprise or admiration for the quality of something: **marvel at sth** *I marveled at my mother's ability to remain calm in a crisis.* | **marvel that** *We sat there marveling that anyone could be so stupid.*

marvel² *n.* [C] something or someone that is extremely impressive: *The bridge is an engineering marvel.* | ***the marvels of*** *modern technology*

mar·vel·lous /'mɑrvələs/ the British and Canadian spelling of MARVELOUS

mar·vel·ous /'mɑrvələs/ *adj.* extremely good, enjoyable, or impressive SYN **great** SYN **fantastic**: *The food was absolutely marvelous.* | *It's really a marvelous place.* —**marvelously** *adv.*

Marx /mɑrks/, **Karl** /kɑrl/ (1818–1883) a German writer and political PHILOSOPHER who established the principles of COMMUNISM with Friedrich Engels

'Marx ˌBrothers, the three American actors, Groucho Marx (1890–1977), Harpo Marx (1888–1964) and Chico Marx (1891–1961), famous for performing in many humorous movies

Marx·is·m /'mɑrkˌsɪzəm/ *n.* [U] POLITICS a political system based on Karl Marx's ideas, that explains changes in history as the result of a struggle between social classes —**Marxist** *n.* [C]

Mar·y /'mɛri/ also **the ˌVirgin 'Mary** in the Christian religion, the mother of Jesus Christ, and the most important of all the saints

Mar·y·land /'mɛrələnd/ WRITTEN ABBREVIATION **MD** a state on the east coast of the U.S.

ˌMaryland ˌAct of Tole'ration, the also **the ˌMaryland Tole'ration Act** HISTORY a 1649 law that allowed religious freedom for all Christian groups in Maryland

Mary Mag·da·lene, Saint /ˌmɛri 'mægdələn, -lin/ in the Bible, a woman who was the first person to see Jesus Christ when he returned to life after his death

mar·zi·pan /'mɑrzɪˌpæn, 'mɑrtsəˌpɑn/ *n.* [U] a sweet food made from ALMONDS, sugar, and eggs, used in candies, cakes etc. [**Origin:** 1400–1500 German, Italian *marzapane* **medieval coin, marzipan**, from Arabic *mawthaban* **medieval coin**]

Ma·sai /mɑ'saɪ/ *n. plural* **Masai, Masais** **1** [C] a member of a group of people who live in Kenya and parts of Tanzania **2** [U] the language of the Masai

masc. the written abbreviation of MASCULINE

mas·car·a /mæ'skærə/ *n.* [U] a dark substance that you use to color your EYELASHES and make them look thicker [**Origin:** 1800–1900 Italian *maschera* **mask**]

mas·cot /'mæskɑt/ *n.* [C] an animal, toy etc. that represents a team or organization, and is thought to bring them good luck: *The school's mascot is a lion.* [**Origin:** 1800–1900 French *mascotte*, from Provençal *mascoto*, from *masco* **woman with magic powers**]

mas·cu·line /'mæskyəlɪn/ *adj.* **1** having qualities that are considered to be typical of men or of what men do: *a deep masculine voice* | *masculine aggression* **2** if a woman's appearance or voice is masculine, it is like a man's **3** ENG. LANG. ARTS in English grammar, a masculine noun or PRONOUN has a form that means it REFERS to a male, such as "widower": *The word for "book" is masculine in French.* → see also FEMININE

> **WORD CHOICE** **masculine, feminine, male, female**
> • Use **masculine** to talk about things that people think are typical of men: *a masculine voice*
> • Use **feminine** to talk about things that people think are typical of women: *a feminine voice*
> • Use **male** and **female** to describe the sex of a person or animal: *a female rabbit*

mas·cu·lin·i·ty /ˌmæskyə'lɪnət̬i/ *n.* [U] the qualities that are considered to be typical of men: *Children's ideas of masculinity tend to come from their fathers.* → see also FEMININITY

ma·ser /'meɪzɚ/ *n.* [C] a piece of equipment that produces a very powerful electric force → see also LASER

Mas·er·u /'mæsəˌru/ the capital and largest city of Lesotho

mash¹ /mæʃ/ also **mash up** *v.* [T] to crush something, especially a food that has been cooked, until it is soft and smooth: *Mash the banana and add it to the batter.* → see picture on page A32 —**masher** *n.* [C] ►see THESAURUS box at **press¹**

mash² *n.* [U] **1** a mixture of grain cooked with water to make a food for animals **2** a mixture of MALT or crushed grain and hot water, used to make beer or WHISKEY → see also MISHMASH

ˌmashed po'tatoes also **mashed potato** *n.* [U] potatoes that have been boiled and then mashed with butter and milk

'mash note *n.* [C] OLD-FASHIONED a note to someone of the opposite sex in which you tell them that you like them and think they are attractive

mask¹ /mæsk/ S3 *n.* [C] **1** something that covers all or part of your face, to protect or to hide it: *a surgical face mask* **2** something that covers your face, and has another face painted on it which is used for ceremonies, in the theater, or special occasions: *a Halloween* *mask* **3** [usually singular] an expression or way of behaving that hides your real emotions or character: *her mask of confidence* **4** also **masque** a substance that you put on your face and leave there for a short time to clean the skin or make it softer: *a facial mask* [**Origin:** 1500–1600 French *masque*, from Old Italian *maschera*] → see also DEATH MASK, GAS MASK

mask² *v.* [T] **1** to hide the truth about a situation, about how you feel etc.: *Children find it hard to mask their emotions.* | *His public image masked a history of drug problems.* ►see THESAURUS box at **hide¹** **2** to make a noise, strong taste or smell etc. less noticeable by making a different noise, introducing other tastes or smells etc.: *Liz turned on the radio to mask the noise.* **3** to cover something so that it cannot be clearly seen: *The house was masked by trees.*

masked /mæskt/ *adj.* wearing a mask: *a masked gunman*

ˌmasked 'ball *n.* [C] a formal dance at which everyone wears masks

'masking tape *n.* [U] narrow paper-like material that is sticky on one side, used especially for protecting the edge of something that you are painting

mas•och•ism /'mæsəˌkɪzəm/ *n.* [U] **1** sexual behavior in which you gain pleasure from being hurt **2** the enjoyment of something that most people think is unpleasant or painful: *Walking to work in the snow sounds like pure masochism to me.* [**Origin:** 1800–1900 Leopold von Sacher-*Masoch* (1836–1895), Austrian writer who described such sexual behavior] —**masochist** *n.* [C] —**masochistic** /ˌmæsə'kɪstɪk/ *adj.* → see also SADISM

ma•son /'meɪsən/ *n.* [C] **1** someone who builds walls, buildings etc. with bricks, stones etc. **2 Mason** someone who belongs to a secret society, in which each member helps the other members to become successful

Ma•son–Dix•on line /ˌmeɪsən 'dɪksən ˌlaɪn/ *n.* **the Mason–Dixon line** HISTORY the border between the states of Pennsylvania and Maryland, considered to be the dividing line between the northern and southern U.S.

Ma•son•ic /mə'sɑnɪk/ *adj.* relating to Masons: *a Masonic temple*

'Mason jar *n.* [C] a glass container with a tight lid used for preserving fruit and vegetables

ma•son•ry /'meɪsənri/ *n.* [U] **1** brick or stone from which a building, wall etc. is made **2** the skill of building with stone **3** the system and practices of MASONS

masque /mæsk/ *n.* [C] **1** another spelling of MASK **2** a play written in poetry and including music, dancing, and songs, written and performed mainly in the 16th and 17th centuries

mas•quer•ade¹ /ˌmæskə'reɪd/ *n.* **1** [C] also **masquerade ball** a formal dance or party where people wear MASKS and unusual clothes **2** [C,U] a way of behaving or speaking that hides your true thoughts or feelings SYN **pretense**: *She didn't love him, but she kept up the masquerade for her children.*

masquerade² *v.* [I] to pretend to be something or someone different: **masquerade as sth** *Some of these breakfast foods are really candy masquerading as cereal.*

mass¹ /mæs/ S3 W2 *n.* **1 a mass of sth a)** a large amount or quantity of something: *The room was decorated with masses of brilliant orange flowers.* | *Scientists have collected a huge mass of data.* **b)** a large amount of a substance, liquid, or gas that does not have a definite or regular shape: *a mass of thick black smoke* **2 a mass of sb** a large crowd: *A mass of people marched past the White House.* ►see THESAURUS box at **group¹** **3 the mass of people/workers/the population etc.** most of the people in a group or society SYN **the majority**: *The mass of the American people are with us on this issue.* **4 the masses** [plural] all the ordinary people in society who do not have power or influence: *Henry Ford made automobiles affordable to the masses.* **5** also **Mass a)** [C,U] the main ceremony in some Christian churches, especially the Catholic Church: *We **go to Mass** in the morning.* | **say/celebrate Mass** (=perform this ceremony as a priest) **b)** [C] a piece of music written to be played at this ceremony: *Mozart's Mass in C Minor* **6 be a mass of sth** if someone's skin or another surface is a mass of something, it is covered with a lot of that thing: *Her skin was a mass of wrinkles.* **7** [U] PHYSICS the amount of matter that a physical object contains. An object's mass relates to its weight, and how easily it changes its speed, direction etc. when it is affected by a force such as GRAVITY: *Carbon, nitrogen, and oxygen make up more than half of the mass of the planet.* [**Origin:** (1–4, 6, 7) 1300–1400 French *masse*, from Latin *massa*, from Greek *maza*] → see also CRITICAL MASS

mass² W3 *adj.* [only before noun] involving or intended for a very large number of people: *mass communications* | *a mass grave* | *mass destruction*

mass³ *v.* [I,T] to come together in a large group, or to make people or things come together in a large group: *Huge crowds massed outside the U.S. embassy.* | *Both countries massed troops at the border.*

Mas•sa•chu•sett, Massachuset /ˌmæsə'tʃusɪt/ a Native American tribe who formerly lived in the northeastern area of the U.S.

Mas•sa•chu•setts /ˌmæsə'tʃusɪts/ ABBREVIATION **MA** a state on the northeast coast of the U.S.

mas•sa•cre¹ /'mæsəkə/ *v.* [T] **1** to kill a lot of people, especially people who cannot defend themselves: *A family of eight was massacred by unidentified gunmen.* ►see THESAURUS box at **kill¹** **2** INFORMAL to defeat the opposing team, player etc. very easily in a game, competition etc. **3** INFORMAL to completely spoil a piece of music, a part in a play etc. by performing it very badly

massacre² *n.* **1** [C,U] the killing of a lot of people, especially people who cannot defend themselves: *the massacre of innocent women and children* **2** INFORMAL a very bad defeat in a game or competition when one team or player has many more points than the other

mas•sage¹ /mə'sɑʒ, -'sɑdʒ/ S3 *n.* [C,U] the action of pressing and rubbing someone's body with your hands, to help them relax or to reduce pain in their muscles: *Massage can help relieve stress.* | *He **gave** me a gentle back **massage**.* [**Origin:** 1800–1900 French *masser* **to massage**, from Arabic *massa* **to stroke**]

massage² *v.* [T] **1** to press and rub someone's body with your hands, to help them relax or to reduce pain in their muscles: *Helen massaged the back of my neck.* **2** to change official numbers or information in order to make them seem better than they are: *Speech writers had massaged the facts to be presented.* **3 massage sb's ego** to try to make someone feel that they are important, attractive, intelligent etc., so that they feel better about themselves: *This organization spends more time massaging egos than developing new products.*

massage sth **into** sth *phr. v.* to rub something into your skin or hair: *Gently massage the lotion into your skin.*

mas'sage ˌparlor *n.* [C] **1** a word meaning a BROTHEL (=place where people pay to have sex), used to pretend that it is not a brothel **2** a place where you pay to have a MASSAGE

mas'sage ˌtherapist *n.* [C] someone who has studied MASSAGE and whose job is to give massages —**massage therapy** *n.*

Mas•sa•soit /ˌmæsə'sɔɪt/ (?1580–1661) a Wampanoag chief who helped the Pilgrim Fathers after they landed in America

mas•se /mɑs/ → see EN MASSE

mas•seur /mæ'sə, mə-/ *n.* [C] a man who gives MASSAGES

mas•seuse /mæ'suz, mə-/ *n.* [C] a woman who gives MASSAGES

ˌmass ex'tinction *n.* [C,U] BIOLOGY a situation in which a very large number of animals or plants stops existing at the same time, caused by a natural event

M

that completely changes an environment: *At the end of the Permian, many forms of life suffered mass extinctions.*

mas·sif /mæˈsif/ *n.* [C] EARTH SCIENCE a group of mountains forming one large solid shape

mas·sive /ˈmæsɪv/ W3 *adj.* **1** very large, solid, and heavy: *The bell is massive, weighing over 40 tons.* | *the castle's massive walls* ►see THESAURUS box at **big** **2** unusually large, powerful, or damaging: *a massive tax bill* | **a massive stroke/heart attack etc.** *He suffered a massive hemorrhage.*

ˈmass-ˌmarket *adj.* [only before noun] designed for sale to as wide a range of people as possible: *mass-market paperbacks* —**mass market** *n.* [C]

ˌmass ˈmedia *n.* [used with singular or plural verb] all the organizations, such as television, radio, and newspapers, that provide news and information for large numbers of people in a society

ˌmass ˈmurderer *n.* [C] someone who has murdered a lot of people —**mass murder** *n.*

ˈmass ˌnumber *n.* [C] CHEMISTRY the total number of PROTONS and NEUTRONS in the NUCLEUS (=central part) of an atom

ˌmass-proˈduced *adj.* produced in large numbers using machinery, so that each object is the same and can be sold cheaply: *mass-produced furniture* —**mass-produce** *v.* [T] —**mass production** *n.* [U]

ˌmass ˈtransit *n.* [U] a system of TRANSPORTATION in a city which includes buses, SUBWAYS etc.: *Today, Los Angeles has virtually no mass transit.* —**mass-transit** *adj.*

mast /mæst/ *n.* [C] **1** a tall pole on which the sails or flags on a ship are hung **2** a tall pole on which a flag is hung SYN **pole** → see also HALF-MAST

mas·tec·to·my /mæˈstɛktəmi/ *n. plural* **mastectomies** [C] a medical operation to remove a breast, usually done to remove CANCER

mas·ter¹ /ˈmæstɚ/ S2 W2 *n.* [C]
1 SKILLED someone who is very skilled at something: *a work of art by a true master* | **+of** *Hitchcock was the master of suspense movies.* | **+at** *Aunt Sonia is a master at cooking everything from lobster to salmon.* | *She's* ***a past master*** *at making people feel sorry for her* (=she's been good at doing this for a long time).
2 FAMOUS ARTIST a famous artist, especially a painter, who produced great work: *the great Italian master, Caravaggio*
3 AUTHORITY a) a man who has control or authority over other people or groups of people, for example servants, SLAVES, or workers: *Slaves ate separately from their masters.* **b)** a wise person whose teachings others accept and follow, especially in some religions: *a Zen master*
4 ORIGINAL a document, record etc. from which copies are made: *I gave him the master to copy.*
5 be master of your own fate to be in complete control of a situation: *If Maura is to become master of her own fate, she has got to start making her own decisions.*
6 be your own master to be in control of your own life or work: *As a writer you are your own master.*
7 DOG OWNER OLD-FASHIONED the owner of a dog
8 SHIP someone who commands a ship
[**Origin:** 1000–1100 Old French *maistre* and the word it came from, Latin *magister* **chief**] → see also GRAND MASTER, M.A., MASTER'S DEGREE, M.S., OLD MASTER, WEBMASTER

master² *v.* [T] **1** to learn a skill or a language so well that you understand it completely and have no difficulty with it: *Nguyen helps Vietnamese students who haven't mastered English.* | *I never quite* ***mastered the art of*** *walking in high heels* (=developed the ability to do it well). ►see THESAURUS box at **learn** **2 master your fear/weakness etc.** to manage to control a strong emotion: *I finally mastered the fear of failure and went for an audition.*

master³ *adj.* [only before noun] **1 master list/tape etc.** the original list, recording etc. from which copies are made: *the master list of telephone numbers* **2 master craftsman/mechanic/chef etc.** someone who is very skilled at a particular job, especially a job that involves making or fixing things with your hands **3** most important or main: *All the information is gathered in the master file.*

ˌmaster-at-ˈarms *n.* [C] an officer with police duties on a ship

ˈmaster ˌbedroom *n.* [C] the largest BEDROOM in a house or apartment, that usually has its own BATHROOM

ˈmaster ˌclass *n.* [C] a lesson, especially in music, given to a group of very skillful students by someone famous

mas·ter·ful /ˈmæstɚfəl/ *adj.* **1** controlling people or situations in a skillful and confident way: *The prosecutor's closing argument was masterful.* | **be masterful at doing sth** *He was masterful at maintaining order in meetings.* **2** done with great skill and understanding: *the painter's masterful contrast of light and darkness* —**masterfully** *adv.*

ˈmaster key *n.* [C] a key that will open all the door locks in a building

mas·ter·ly /ˈmæstɚli/ *adj.* done or made very skillfully: *a masterly performance*

mas·ter·mind¹ /ˈmæstɚˌmaɪnd/ *n.* [C usually singular] someone who plans and organizes a complicated operation, especially a criminal operation: **the mastermind of/behind sth** *the terrorist mastermind behind the kidnappings*

mastermind² *v.* [T] to think of, plan, and organize a large, important, and difficult operation: *Manson was convicted of masterminding the murder of Tate and six others.*

ˌMaster of ˈArts *n.* [C] an M.A.

ˌmaster of ˈceremonies *n.* [C] someone who introduces speakers or performers at a social or public occasion

ˌMaster of ˈScience *n.* [C] an M.S.

mas·ter·piece /ˈmæstɚˌpis/ *n.* [C] a work of art, piece of writing, or music etc. that is of very high quality or that is the best that a particular artist, writer etc. has produced: *Orson Welles's masterpiece "Citizen Kane"* | *The painting is one of the great masterpieces of Western art.*

ˈmaster plan *n.* [C usually singular] a detailed plan for controlling everything that happens in a complicated situation: *The state recently unveiled its master plan for higher education.*

mas·ter's /ˈmæstɚz/ *n.* [C] INFORMAL a MASTER'S DEGREE: **+in** *Eve has a master's in English.*

Mas·ters and John·son /ˌmæstɚz ən ˈdʒɑnsən/ two U.S. scientists, William Howell Masters (1915–) and Virginia Eshelman Johnson (1925–), who have studied and written about human sexual behavior

ˈmaster's deˌgree *n.* [C] a university degree that you get by studying for one or two years after your first degree; an M.A. or M.S.

mas·ter·stroke /ˈmæstɚˌstroʊk/ *n.* [C] a very intelligent, skillful, and often unexpected action that is completely successful: *Politically, it was a masterstroke.*

ˈmaster ˌswitch *n.* [C] the SWITCH that controls the supply of electricity to the whole of a building or area

mas·ter·work /ˈmæstɚˌwɚk/ *n.* [C] a painting, SCULPTURE, piece of music etc. that is the best that someone has done SYN **masterpiece**

mas·ter·y /ˈmæstəri/ *n.* [U] **1** complete control or power over someone or something: **+of/over** *humankind's mastery of the environment* **2** thorough understanding or great skill: **+of/over** *her mastery of the gymnastic skills required to win*

mast·head /ˈmæsthɛd/ *n.* [C] **1** the name of a newspaper, magazine etc. printed in a special design at the top of the first page **2** the top of a MAST on a ship

M

mas·tic /ˈmæstɪk/ *n.* [U] a type of glue that does not crack or break when it is bent

mas·ti·cate /ˈmæstəˌkeɪt/ *v.* [I,T] TECHNICAL to CHEW (=crush food between the teeth) —**mastication** /ˌmæstəˈkeɪʃən/ *n.* [U]

mas·tiff /ˈmæstɪf/ *n.* [C] a large strong dog often used to guard houses

mas·tur·bate /ˈmæstɚˌbeɪt/ *v.* [I,T] to make yourself or someone else sexually excited by touching or rubbing sexual organs —**masturbation** /ˌmæstɚˈbeɪʃən/ *n.* [U]

mat[1] /mæt/ *n.* [C] **1** a small piece of thick rough material that covers part of a floor: *The men knelt on their **prayer mats**.* | *You can leave the key under the **door mat*** (=one by a door to clean your feet on). **2** a small flat piece of wood, cloth etc. that protects a surface, especially on a table: *a computer mouse mat* | **a table/place mat** (=one that you put under a dish to protect the table) **3** a piece of rubber, used for exercise, or for falling down on in some indoor sports: *an exercise mat* | *a gymnastics mat* **4** a piece of thick paper that is put around a picture inside a frame **5 a mat of hair/fur/grass etc.** a thick mass of pieces of hair, fur etc. that are stuck together → see also MATTING

mat[2] *adj.* another spelling of MATTE

mat·a·dor /ˈmæṭəˌdɔr/ *n.* [C] a man who fights and kills BULLS during a BULLFIGHT [**Origin:** 1600–1700 Spanish *matar* **to kill**]

Ma·ta Ha·ri /ˌmɑṭə ˈhɑri/ (1876–1917) a Dutch dancer famous for being a SPY for the Germans during World War I

match[1] /mætʃ/ S3 W2 *n.*
1 FIRE [C] a small wooden or paper stick with a special substance at the top, used to light a fire, cigarette etc.: *a box of matches* | **light/strike a match** (=rub a match against a surface to make it burn) → see also MATCHBOOK
2 GAME [C] an organized sports event between two teams or people: *a tennis match* | *Eric scored the only goal in the match against Albany.*
3 A GOOD COMBINATION [singular] something that works or combines well with something else, so that the two things make a good combination: **+for** *I'm looking for a match for this material.* | **a good/perfect match** *Sauvignon blanc is a perfect match for oysters.*
4 STH THE SAME/SIMILAR [C] something that looks exactly the same or is extremely similar to something else: **+for** *Doctors failed to find a match for the bone marrow transplant.* | *Stores will mix paints so you can get **an exact match**.*
5 TWO PEOPLE [singular] a combination of people, especially people who get married or live together as a couple: **be/make a good/perfect match** *Kim and Peter are a good match.* | *The two of them are not really a **match made in heaven*** (=they are not a very good combination).
6 be no match for sb to be much less strong, skilled, intelligent etc. than an opponent: *Their primitive weapons were no match for guns.*
7 be more than a match for sb to be much stronger, smarter etc. than an opponent
8 a shouting match a loud angry argument in which two people insult each other
[**Origin:** (1) Old English *mæcca*] → see also **meet your match** at MEET[1] (16), **mix and match** at MIX[1] (7)

match[2] S2 W3 *v.*
1 LOOK GOOD TOGETHER [I,T] if one thing matches another, or if two or more things match, they look attractive together because they have a similar color, pattern etc. OPP **clash**: *This lipstick matches your blouse exactly.* | *Everything in the baby's room matches.* → see also MATCHING
2 SEEM THE SAME [I,T] if two or more things or pieces of information match, or if one matches the other, there is no important difference between them: *The man matched the description provided by the witness.* | *She checked the signatures to see if they matched.*
3 BE PART OF A PAIR [I,T] if two socks, shoes etc. match, they look the same and belong together because they are a pair: *Your socks don't match.*
4 CONNECT [T] to put two people or things together because they are similar to each other, or because they are connected in some way: **match sb/sth with sb/sth** *The college tries to match students with companies that will hire them.* | *Match the words on the left with the pictures on the right.* | **match sb/sth to sb/sth** *I look for qualities that match the actor to the character.*
5 BE APPROPRIATE [T] to be suitable or appropriate for a particular person, thing, or situation: *I want to earn a salary that matches my expertise.* | *Teaching materials should **match the needs of** the students.* | **well-matched/ill-matched** *The two companies are ill-matched* (=badly matched) *for a merger.*
6 BE EQUAL TO STH [T] to equal something in value, size, amount, quality etc.: *His skill was matched by his intelligence.* | **be equally/evenly matched** *The teams were evenly matched.*
7 DO STH TO EQUAL STH [T] to do something that is equal in value, amount, size, quality etc. to something else: *No one has ever matched his record.*
8 GIVE MONEY [T] to give a sum of money equal to a sum given by someone else: *Anderson will receive a bonus that matches his base salary.*

match sb **against** sb *phr. v.* if you are matched against someone else in a game or competition, you are competing against them: *He will be matched against Federer in the men's final.*

match up *phr. v.* **1** if two things match up, they seem the same or similar, without any important differences: *The two witnesses' accounts don't match up.* **2 match sb/sth ↔ up** to bring together people or things that seem suitable for each other: **match sb/sth up with sb/sth** *It's my job to match up the right horse with the right owner.* **3 match up to your hopes/expectations/ideals etc.** to be as good as you expected, hoped etc.

match up with sb *phr. v.* to be of a similar level or of similar quality as something else: *I'm embarrassed that we didn't match up with Nebraska. They're good!*

match·book /ˈmætʃbʊk/ *n.* [C] a small folded piece of thick paper containing paper matches

match·box /ˈmætʃbɑks/ *n.* [C] a small box containing matches

match·ing /ˈmætʃɪŋ/ *adj.* [only before noun] having the same color, style, or pattern as something else: *a striped tie with a matching pocket handkerchief*

match·less /ˈmætʃlɪs/ *adj.* FORMAL more intelligent, beautiful etc. than anyone or anything else: *the matchless beauty of Antarctica*

match·mak·er /ˈmætʃˌmeɪkɚ/ *n.* [C] someone who tries to find the right person for someone else to marry —**matchmaking** *n.* [U]

ˌmatch ˈpoint *n.* **1** [U] a situation in tennis when the person who wins the next point will win the match **2** [C] the point that a player must win in order to win the match → see also GAME POINT

match·stick /ˈmætʃˌstɪk/ *n.* [C] a wooden MATCH

mate[1] /meɪt/ W3 *n.*
1 office/band/locker etc. mate someone you do or share something with: *Myra and I were locker mates in high school.* → see also ROOMMATE, RUNNING MATE, SOUL MATE, TEAMMATE
2 ANIMAL [C] BIOLOGY the sexual partner of an animal
3 HUSBAND/WIFE [C usually singular] a word meaning your "husband" or "wife," used especially in magazines: *How does your mate score on a scale of 1 to 10?*
4 PAIR OF OBJECTS [C] one of a pair of objects: *What happened to this sock's mate?*
5 SAILOR [C] a ship's officer who is one rank below the CAPTAIN: *the first mate*
6 NAVY OFFICER [C] a U.S. Navy PETTY OFFICER
7 FRIEND [C] BRITISH a male friend, or a friendly way of speaking to a man you do not know
[**Origin:** 1300–1400 Middle Low German *mat*]

mate[2] *v.* **1** [I + with] BIOLOGY if animals mate, they have sex to produce babies **2** [T] BIOLOGY to put animals together so that they will have sex and produce babies

3 [T] to achieve the CHECKMATE of your opponent in CHESS

ma·te·ri·al¹ /mə'tɪriəl/ S1 W1 *n.* **1** [C,U] cloth used for making clothes, curtains etc. SYN **fabric**: *I bought some material to make curtains.* → see Word Choice box at CLOTH **2** [C usually plural, U] SCIENCE a substance that can be used to make something or that has a particular quality: *The chairs are made of recycled material.* | *the basic* ***genetic material*** *that all plants and animals are made of* | **toxic/harmful/dangerous materials** *companies dumping toxic materials into the river* | **building/construction material(s)** (=things, such as bricks and wood, used to build buildings) → see also RAW MATERIALS **3** [U] also **materials** [plural] the objects that are used for doing something: *art material* | **teaching/writing/reading material(s)** *a basket containing writing materials* **4** [U] information or ideas used in books, movies etc.: *The album contains a lot of new material.* | +**for** *She finds raw material for her stories in her home life.* **5 officer/executive/husband etc. material** someone who is good enough for a particular job or position

material² *adj.* [usually before noun] **1** relating to people's money, possessions, living conditions etc., rather than the needs of their mind or soul OPP **spiritual**: *Matt had little desire for* ***material possessions.*** | *Many people lack* ***material comforts.*** **2** relating to the real world and physical objects: *the material world* **3** LAW important and needing to be considered when making a decision: *a material witness* | +**to** *Are these facts material to the investigation?* **4** FORMAL important and having a noticeable effect: *material changes to the schedule* [**Origin:** 1300–1400 Late Latin *materialis*, from Latin *materia* **matter, substance**] → see also MATERIALLY, RAW MATERIALS

ma·te·ri·al·ism /mə'tɪriə,lɪzəm/ *n.* [U] **1** DISAPPROVING the belief that money and possessions are more important than art, religion, morals etc. **2** TECHNICAL the belief that only physical things really exist —**materialist** *adj., n.* [C]

ma·te·ri·al·is·tic /mə,tɪriə'lɪstɪk/ *adj.* DISAPPROVING caring only about money and possessions rather than things relating to the mind and soul, such as art or religion: *a materialistic person* —**materialistically** /-kli/ *adv.*

ma·te·ri·al·ize /mə'tɪriə,laɪz/ *v.* [I] **1** to happen or appear in the way that you planned or expected: **fail to materialize/never materialize** *The money we had been promised failed to materialize.* **2** to appear in an unexpected and strange way: *A row of huts materialized out of the fog as we approached.* —**materialization** /mə,tɪriələ'zeɪʃən/ *n.* [U]

ma·te·ri·al·ly /mə'tɪriəli/ *adv.* **1** in a big enough or strong enough way to change a situation: *The situation would materially affect U.S. security.* **2** in a way that concerns possessions and money, rather than the needs of a person's mind or soul: *Materially, we are better off than ever before.*

ma·té·ri·el, materiel /mə,tɪri'ɛl/ *n.* [U] supplies of weapons used by an army

ma·ter·nal /mə'tɚnl/ *adj.* **1** typical of the way a good mother behaves or feels: *maternal love* | *Gertrude lacks any* ***maternal instinct*** (=desire to have and take care of babies). **2** [only before noun] BIOLOGY relating to being a mother: *the maternal fatality rate* **3 maternal grandfather/aunt etc.** your mother's father, sister etc. → see also PATERNAL —**maternally** *adv.*

ma,ternal mor'tality *n.* [U] the number of women who die during the time they have an unborn baby growing inside their body or when the baby is being born, in every 100,000 babies who are born alive

ma·ter·ni·ty¹ /mə'tɚnət̬i/ *adj.* [only before noun] relating to a woman who is PREGNANT, or who has had a baby, or to the time when she is PREGNANT: *maternity clothes* | *a maternity hospital*

maternity² *n.* [U] the state of being a mother

ma'ternity ,leave *n.* [U] time that a mother is allowed to spend away from work when she has a baby

ma'ternity ,ward *n.* [C] a department in a hospital where women who are having babies are cared for

math /mæθ/ S2 W3 *n.* [U] **1** MATH mathematics: *a math test* | *I don't think Jim should major in math.* **2 do the math a)** to work with numbers and calculate amounts: *I've done the math, and I know we're losing money.* **b)** SPOKEN used to tell someone to consider the details of a situation, especially numbers, and guess their meaning: *She got married five months ago and just had a baby – you do the math.*

math·e·mat·i·cal /mæθ'mæt̬ɪkəl/ *adj.* **1** MATH relating to or using mathematics: *a mathematical formula* | *mathematical calculations* **2** calculating things in a careful exact way: *The whole trip was planned with mathematical precision.* **3 a mathematical certainty** something that is completely certain to happen **4 there is a mathematical chance (of sth)** used to say that there is a very small chance that something will happen, but that it is very unlikely —**mathematically** /-kli/ *adv.*

math·e·ma·ti·cian /,mæθmə'tɪʃən/ *n.* [C] someone who has special knowledge and training in mathematics

math·e·mat·ics /,mæθ'mæt̬ɪks, ,mæθə-/ *n.* [U] **1** the study or science of numbers and of the structure and measurement of shapes, including ALGEBRA, GEOMETRY, and ARITHMETIC **2 the mathematics of sth** the way something is calculated [**Origin:** 1500–1600 Latin *mathematicus*, from Greek, from *mathema* **learning, mathematics**]

Math·er /'mæðɚ/, **Cot·ton** /'kɑt˺n/ (1663–1728) an American religious leader who was a PURITAN

Mather, In·crease /'ɪŋkris/ (1639–1723) an American political and religious leader who was the first president of Harvard University

mat·i·nee /,mæt˺n'eɪ/ *n.* [C] a performance of a play or movie in the afternoon

mati'nee ,idol *n.* [C] OLD-FASHIONED a movie actor who is very popular with women

mat·ing /'meɪt̬ɪŋ/ *n.* [U] sex between animals: *the mating season*

mat·ins /'mæt˺nz/ *n.* [U] the first prayers of the day in the Christian religion

Ma·tisse /mæ'tis/, **Hen·ri** /ɑn'ri/ (1869–1954) a French PAINTER and SCULPTOR famous for his paintings of ordinary places and objects that use pure bright colors and black lines

matri- /meɪtri, mætrə/ *prefix* **1** relating to mothers: *matricide* (=killing one's mother) **2** relating to women: *a matriarchal society* (=controlled by women) → see also PATRI-

ma·tri·arch /'meɪtri,ɑrk/ *n.* [C] a woman, especially an older woman, who controls a family or a social group → see also PATRIARCH

ma·tri·ar·chal /,meɪtri'ɑrkəl◂/ *adj.* **1** ruled or controlled by women: *a matriarchal society* **2** relating to or typical of a matriarch → see also PATRIARCHAL

ma·tri·ar·chy /'meɪtri,ɑrki/ *n. plural* **matriarchies** [C,U] **1** a social system in which the oldest woman controls a family and its possessions **2** a society that is led or controlled by women → see also PATRIARCHY

mat·ri·cide /'mætrə,saɪd/ *n.* [U] FORMAL the crime of murdering your mother → see also PARRICIDE, PATRICIDE

ma·tric·u·late /mə'trɪkyə,leɪt/ *v.* [I] FORMAL to officially begin studying at a school or college —**matriculation** /mə,trɪkyə'leɪʃən/ *n.* [U]

mat·ri·lin·e·al /,mætrə'lɪniəl/ *adj.* a matrilineal society is one in which connections between the mothers and daughters in a family are regarded as the most important → see also PATRILINEAL

mat·ri·mo·ny /'mætrə,moʊni/ *n.* [U] FORMAL the state of being married SYN **marriage**: *They were joined in* ***holy matrimony.*** [**Origin:** 1200–1300 Old French *matremoine*, from Latin *matrimonium* **being a mother, marriage**] —**matrimonial** /,mætrə'moʊniəl/ *adj.*

ma·trix /ˈmeɪtrɪks/ *n. plural* **matrices** /-trəsiz/ or **matrixes** [C] TECHNICAL **1** MATH an arrangement of numbers, letters, or signs on a GRID (=a background of regular crossed lines) used in mathematics, science etc. **2** a situation from which a person or society can grow and develop: *the cultural matrix* **3** BIOLOGY a living part in which something is formed or developed, such as the substance out of which the FINGERNAILS grow **4** a MOLD into which melted metal, plastic etc. is poured to form a shape **5** EARTH SCIENCE the rock in which hard stones or jewels have formed → see also DOT-MATRIX PRINTER

ˈmatrix ˌelement *n.* [C] MATH any of the signs, letters, or numbers appearing in a MATRIX

ˈmatrix eˌquation *n.* [C] MATH an equation in which a matrix appears on either side of the equal sign

ma·tron /ˈmeɪtrən/ *n.* [C] **1** LITERARY an older married woman **2** a woman who is in charge of women and children in a school or prison

ma·tron·ly /ˈmeɪtrənli/ *adj.* a word to describe a woman who is fairly fat and not young anymore, used to avoid saying this directly

ˌmatron of ˈhonor *n.* [C] a married woman who helps the BRIDE on her wedding day and stands beside her during the wedding ceremony → see also MAID OF HONOR

matte, mat /mæt/ *adj.* matte paint, color, or photographs have a dull surface, not shiny [**Origin:** 1600–1700 French *mat*, from Old French, **defeated**, from Latin *mattus* **drunk**] → see also GLOSS

mat·ted /ˈmæt̬ɪd/ *adj.* twisted or stuck together in a thick mass: +**with** *Her hair was matted with blood.*

mat·ter[1] /ˈmæt̬ɚ/ S1 W1 *n.*
1 SUBJECT/SITUATION [C] a subject or situation that you have to think about or deal with: *We should discuss the matter ourselves.* | *The* ***subject matter*** *is fairly difficult.* | **religious/financial/political etc. matters** *Rick wasn't particularly interested in financial matters.* | *Wilson always consulted Landers on* ***matters of importance****.* | *The safety of Americans abroad is a* ***matter of*** *serious* ***concern****.* | **personal/private matter** *He doesn't discuss personal matters at the office.* | *I think that's* ***a matter for*** *the voters to decide.* | *Woodbury had decided to* ***let the matter drop*** (=stop worrying about something). | *He steered the conversation back to* ***the matter at hand****.* | *People make jokes about snorers, but it's* ***no laughing matter*** (=it is a serious situation).
2 SITUATION NOW matters [plural] a situation that you are in or have been describing: *Herrera still hoped to settle matters peaceably.* | *It* ***didn't help matters*** *when the books failed to arrive.* | ***To make matters worse****, it was raining.* | ***To complicate matters further*** (=to make the situation more complicated), *the law has recently been changed.*
3 SUBSTANCE [U] **a)** PHYSICS anything in the universe that has MASS, including solids, liquids, and gases SYN substance **b) waste/solid/organic/vegetable etc. matter** a substance that consists of waste material, solid material etc. **c)** a yellow or white substance that is found in wounds or next to your eye
4 a matter of sth used when what happens or what you do involves or depends on something else: ***As a matter of*** *policy* (=because of a rule), *the department refuses to comment on the investigation.* | *It's nothing to do with money;* ***it's a matter of principle*** (=the money isn't important because I'm doing something I firmly believe in). | **a matter of course/routine** *We have spoken to the police as a matter of course* (=because it is what we do in this type of situation). | *Today, family size is a matter of choice, not luck.* | *The type of vacation you prefer is a matter of taste.* | *Beauty is all a* ***matter of opinion*** (=different people will have different opinions).
5 be a matter of (doing) sth used to say that you only have to do a particular thing, or do something in a particular way, in order to be successful: *A lot of things in life are* ***just a matter of*** *believing it's going to happen.* | *Installing a new modem isn't always a* ***simple matter of*** *replacement.*

SPOKEN PHRASES

6 the matter used in several phrases to ask or talk about why someone seems worried, unhappy, or ill, why something about a situation seems wrong, or why a machine seems not to be working correctly: ***What's the matter****, Sue? You look like you've been crying.* | ***What's the matter with*** *your eye? It looks red.* | ***What's the matter with*** *the telephone?* | *Don't be so rude!* ***What's the matter with you*** (=used when you are surprised or angry about what someone has said or done)*?* | **is (there) something/anything the matter?** (=used to ask someone why they are upset or angry, or if they are not feeling well) *You look upset. Is something the matter?* | *Tom's been acting really strange – I think there must be* ***something the matter****.* | ***There's something the matter with*** *the washing machine.* | *Stop pretending that* ***nothing's the matter*** *and tell me what's wrong.* | *The doctor said* ***there was nothing the matter with*** *him* (=he was not sick or injured).
7 as a matter of fact used when giving a surprising or unexpected answer that adds more detail to a question or statement: *I met her last week – as a matter of fact, I have her phone number right here.*
8 no matter how/where/what etc. used to say that something is always the same whatever happens, or in spite of someone's efforts to change it: *Vince tends to wake up at the same time, no matter what time he goes to bed.* | *No matter how hot it is outside, it's always cool in here.*
9 no matter what (happens) used to say that you will definitely do something: *I decided to leave at the end of six months, no matter what.*
10 no matter used to say that something you have asked about or said is not important: *No matter, I'll pick up the clothes at the cleaners tomorrow.* | *He wanted to swim,* ***no matter that*** *the water was icy.*
11 or... for that matter used to say that what you are saying about one thing is also true about something else: *I've never seen the place this quiet on a Friday night, or any other night for that matter.*
12 the fact/truth of the matter (is) used to say what you think is really true: *The fact of the matter is we have a crisis on our hands.*
13 that's the end of the matter used to tell someone that you do not want to talk about something anymore: *You're not going out tonight, and that's the end of the matter.*

14 be a different matter used to say that one situation or problem is very different from the one you have just mentioned, and may not be as easy, nice etc.: *Saying you'll do something is one thing, but actually doing it can be an entirely different matter.*
15 the little/small matter of sth an expression meaning something that is not important or not difficult, used in a joking way to when something really is important or difficult: *Calder faces suspension, and* ***there's that little matter of*** *the bar fight in Houston.*
16 sth is only/just a matter of time used to say that something will definitely happen at some time in the future: +**until/before** *It's just a matter of time before someone gets seriously hurt.*
17 sth is a matter of life and death used to say that a situation is extremely serious or dangerous and something must be done immediately: *Call the police immediately – this is a matter of life and death.*
18 a matter of days/hours/months etc. only a few days, hours etc.: *His whole life had come apart in a matter of days.*
19 reading/printed matter things that are written for people to read
20 as a matter of urgency FORMAL done as quickly as possible because it is very important
[**Origin:** 1100–1200 Old French *matere*, from Latin *materia* **matter, substance**, from *mater* **mother**] → see also GRAY MATTER, **mind over matter** at MIND[1] (48)

M

GRAMMAR

We use **the matter** to mean "trouble" or "a problem" only in questions or negative sentences: *What's the matter, Audrey?* | *There's nothing the matter with it.*

matter² S1 W2 *v.* [I] **1** [not in progressive] to be important, especially to be important to you personally, or to have a big effect on what happens: ***Does it matter** what he thinks?* | **+to** *Do you think what I say will matter to him?* | *It calls for brown sugar, but **it doesn't matter** – you can use white.* | **it does/doesn't matter who/why/what etc.** *It doesn't matter how much suntan lotion I put on, I still burn.* | *We seldom talk about the things that **really matter**.* | **matter most/much/little/less** *What will matter most to the voters?* | *As long as it serves the community, that's **all that matters**.* | *That's **the only thing that matters** to them – money.* | ***What matters is** how the food tastes, not how it looks.* | *She was with the man she loved and **nothing else mattered**.* | *At that time, **it hardly mattered** that some workers couldn't read. Now it does.* **2 it doesn't matter** SPOKEN **a)** used to say that you do not care which one of two things you have: *"Do you want white or dark meat?" "Oh, it doesn't matter."* **b)** used to tell someone that you are not angry or upset about something, especially something that they have done: *"I think I taped over your show." "It doesn't matter."* **3 what does it matter?** SPOKEN used to say that something is not very important: *We'll do it tomorrow or the next day. What does it matter?*

Mat·ter·horn, the /ˈmætə̬ˌhɔrn/ a high mountain in the Alps near the border between Italy and Switzerland

ˌmatter-of-ˈfact *adj.* showing no emotion when you are talking about something exciting, frightening, upsetting etc.: *She spoke of death in a calm matter-of-fact way.* —**matter-of-factly** *adv.* —**matter-of-factness** *n.* [U]

THESAURUS

detached not reacting to something in an emotional way: *Throughout the funeral I was detached and controlled.*
impassive not showing any emotions: *The witness remained impassive during questioning.*
cold without friendly feelings: *a cold and distant man*

Mat·thew /ˈmæθyu/ also **The Gospel according to St. Matthew** one of the four books in the New Testament of the Christian Bible that describe the life and teaching of Jesus Christ

Matthew, Saint one of Jesus Christ's DISCIPLES, who is believed to have written "The Gospel according to St. Matthew," which describes the life and teaching of Jesus Christ

mat·ting /ˈmæt̬ɪŋ/ *n.* [U] strong rough material, used for making MATS

mat·tress /ˈmætrɪs/ *n.* [C] the soft part of a bed that you lie on: *a good **firm mattress*** [**Origin:** 1200–1300 Old French *materas*, from Arabic *matrah* **place where something is thrown**]

mat·u·ra·tion /ˌmætʃəˈreɪʃən/ Ac *n.* [U] FORMAL the period during which something grows and develops

ma·ture¹ /məˈtʃʊr, məˈtʊr/ Ac *adj.*
1 SENSIBLE someone, especially a child or young person, who is mature behaves in a sensible and reasonable way, as you would expect an adult to behave OPP **immature**: *High school students are mature enough to understand this policy.* | *Laura is **very mature for** her **age**.*
2 FULLY GROWN fully grown and developed: *a mature apple tree* | **emotionally/physically/sexually mature** *Eagles aren't sexually mature until age five.* | *The human brain is not **fully mature** until about age 25.*
3 OLDER a polite or humorous way of describing someone who is not young anymore SYN **middle-aged**: *wedding dresses for the mature bride*
4 NOVEL/PAINTING ETC. a mature piece of work by a writer or an artist is usually done when they are older and shows a high level of understanding or skill
5 FINANCIAL ECONOMICS a mature financial arrangement, such as a BOND or POLICY, is ready to be paid
6 mature market/industry ECONOMICS a mature industry or market is one where growth is low and there are fewer competitors than before
7 WINE/CHEESE/FOOD mature cheese, wine etc. has a good strong taste which has developed during a long period of time
[**Origin:** 1300–1400 Latin *maturus*] —**maturely** *adv.*

mature² Ac *v.* **1** [I] to become sensible and start to behave like an adult: *John's really matured in the last two years.* **2** [I] to become fully grown or developed: *Corn needs longer to mature than soybeans.* **3** [I,T] if a cheese, wine, WHISKEY etc. matures or is matured, it develops a good strong taste over a period of time **4** [I] ECONOMICS if a financial arrangement such as a BOND or POLICY matures, it becomes ready to be paid

ma·tur·i·ty /məˈtʃʊrət̬i, -ˈtʊr-/ Ac *n.* [U] **1** the quality of behaving in a sensible way and like an adult OPP **immaturity**: *There's a real difference in maturity between a 13- and a 15-year-old.* **2** the time or state when a person, animal, or plant is fully grown or developed: ***At maturity**, a gray whale will reach a length of 40 feet.* | **sexual/emotional/physical maturity** *These animals **reach physical maturity** at about a year.* **3** ECONOMICS the time when a financial arrangement such as a BOND or POLICY becomes ready to be paid

mat·zo, matzoh /ˈmɑtsə/ *n.* [C,U] a type of thin flat bread, eaten by Jewish people during PASSOVER, or the type of flour used to make this bread

maud·lin /ˈmɔdlɪn/ *adj.* **1** a maudlin song, story, movie etc. tries too hard to make people cry or feel emotions such as love or sadness so that it seems silly SYN **sentimental**: *a song that is tender without being maudlin* **2** someone who is maudlin is talking or behaving in a sad, silly, and emotional way, especially because they are drunk [**Origin:** 1500–1600 *Maudlin* **Mary Magdalen** (14–16 centuries), from Latin *Magdalena*; because she was shown in pictures as crying]

Maugham /mɔm/**, Som·er·set** /ˈsʌməˌsɛt/ (1874–1965) a British writer of NOVELS and short stories

Mau·i /ˈmaʊi/ an island in the Pacific Ocean that is part of the U.S. state of Hawaii

maul /mɔl/ *v.* [T] **1** if an animal mauls someone, it injures them badly by tearing their flesh: *A six-year-old boy was mauled by a mountain lion.* **2** to badly defeat someone in a game or competition: *Cincinnati mauled the Oilers Monday night.* **3** to severely criticize someone or something: *election ads that mauled his opponent* **4** to touch someone in a rough sexual way

Mau·na Ke·a /ˌmaʊnə ˈkeɪə, ˌmɔ-/ a mountain on the island of Hawaii that is an active VOLCANO

Mauna Lo·a /ˌmaʊnə ˈloʊə, ˌmɔ-/ a mountain on the island of Hawaii that is an active VOLCANO

maun·der /ˈmɔndə, ˈmɑn-/ *v.* [I] LITERARY to talk or move in a way that has no particular purpose

Maun·dy Thurs·day /ˌmɔndi ˈθəzdi, ˌmɑn-/ *n.* [U] the Thursday before Easter [**Origin:** 1200–1300 *maundy* Christian ceremony of washing poor people's feet, from Latin *mandatum* **command**]

Mau·pas·sant /ˌmoʊpæˈsɑn/**, Guy de** /gi də/ (1850–1893) a French writer of short stories

Mau·riac /mɔriˈɑk/**, Fran·çois** /frɑnˈswɑ/ (1885–1970) a French writer of NOVELS

Mau·ri·ta·nia /ˌmɔrəˈteɪnyə/ a country in northwest Africa on the Atlantic coast and west of Mali —**Mauritanian** *n., adj.*

Mau·ri·tius /mɔˈrɪʃəs, -ʃiəs/ a country which is an island in the Indian Ocean —**Mauritian** *n., adj.*

mau·so·le·um /ˌmɔsəˈliəm, -zə-/ *n.* [C] **1** a large stone building containing many graves or built over a grave **2** a large building that seems very dark and empty and makes you feel sad [**Origin:** 1400–1500 Latin,

M

Greek, from *Mausolos* king of Caria in ancient Turkey, for whom such a building was made]

mauve /moʊv/ *n.* [U] a pale purple color —**mauve** *adj.*

ma•ven /ˈmeɪvən/ *n.* [C] someone who knows a lot about a particular subject: **food/fashion/media etc. maven** *Food maven Rebecca Cook edited the restaurant guide.* [**Origin:** 1900–2000 Yiddish *meyvn*, from Hebrew *l'havin* **to understand**]

mav•er•ick /ˈmævərɪk/ *n.* [C] someone who does not follow accepted rules of behavior or ways of doing things, and who is confident and often successful: *a political maverick* [**Origin:** 1800–1900 Samuel A. *Maverick* (1803–1870), U.S. cattle owner who did not mark some of his young cattle] —**maverick** *adj.*: *a maverick cop*

maw /mɔ/ *n.* [C] LITERARY **1** something that seems to take control over or use up things or people completely: *They were about to enter the maw of the criminal justice system.* **2** BIOLOGY an animal's mouth or throat

mawk•ish /ˈmɔkɪʃ/ *adj.* showing too much emotion in a way that is embarrassing SYN **sentimental**: *The movie is set to a mawkish score.* —**mawkishly** *adv.* —**mawkishness** *n.* [U]

max¹ /mæks/ Ac *n.* [U] INFORMAL **1** an abbreviation of MAXIMUM: *Five people will fit in the car, but that's the max.* **2 to the max** to the greatest degree possible: *We had the air conditioner turned up to the max.* —**max** *adj., adv.*: *Let's say two hours to get there, max.*

max² Ac *v.* INFORMAL

max out *phr. v.* **1 max sth ↔ out** to use something such as money or supplies so that there is none left: *He maxed out his credit card.* **2** to do too much, eat too much etc.: +**on** *Not turkey again – I maxed out on it at Thanksgiving.* **3** to do something with as much effort and determination as you can: *Erickson has been maxing out every game.* —**maxed out** *adj.*

max•im /ˈmæksɪm/ *n.* [C] ENG. LANG. ARTS a well-known phrase or saying, especially one that gives a rule for sensible behavior SYN **proverb** SYN **saying**

max•i•mal /ˈmæksɪməl/ *adj.* TECHNICAL as much or as large as possible: *a maximal increase in profits* —**maximally** *adv.*

max•i•mize /ˈmæksəˌmaɪz/ Ac *v.* [T] **1** to increase something as much as possible for the best results OPP **minimize**: *Every firm wants to **maximize** its **profits**.* | *Diamonds are cut to maximize the stone's beauty.* | **maximize your chances/potential/influence etc.** *Wolves choose weak animals to maximize their chances of making a kill.* **2** COMPUTERS to CLICK on a special part of a WINDOW on a computer screen so that it becomes as big as the screen OPP **minimize** —**maximization** /ˌmæksəməˈzeɪʃən/ *n.* [U] → see also MINIMIZE

max•i•mum¹ /ˈmæksəməm/ Ac *adj.* [only before noun] the maximum amount, quantity, speed etc. is the largest that is possible or allowed OPP **minimum**: *The car has a maximum speed of 120 mph.* | *Let's try to make maximum use of this opportunity.* | **maximum amount/number etc.** *You should save the maximum amount allowed in your retirement account.* | **maximum fine/penalty/sentence/punishment etc.** *a felony that carries a maximum penalty of ten years in prison* | *She was posed and photographed for **maximum effect**.* —**maximum** *adv.*

maximum² Ac *n.* [C usually singular] the largest number or amount that is possible or is allowed: +**of** *He's facing a maximum of ten years in prison.* | *It'll take 45 minutes – that's **the maximum**.* | *You can take **up to a maximum of** five capsules daily.* [**Origin:** 1500–1600 Latin *maximus* **greatest**, from *magnus* **great**]

May /meɪ/ *n.* [C,U] the fifth month of the year, between April and June: *Memorial Day is always **in May**.* | ***On May 8** I have a doctor's appointment.* | *My grandmother died **last May**.* | *Brian plans to move to San Francisco **next May**.* | *His court date is **May 31**.* [**Origin:** 1100–1200 Old French *mai*, from Latin *Maius*, from *Maia* Roman goddess] → see Grammar box at JANUARY

may /meɪ/ S1 W1 *modal verb*
1 POSSIBILITY if something may happen or may be true, there is a possibility that it will happen or be true but this is not certain SYN **might**: *Well, I may have been wrong.* | *Seven thirty may be too late.* | *It may make a big difference.* | ***There may** not **be** enough money to pay for the repairs.* | *They may have called while you were out.* | ***It may be that** we'll never know exactly what happened.* | *He **may well** (=it is likely but not certain) change his mind.* → see also MIGHT
2 may I...? **a)** SPOKEN used to ask politely if you can do something: *Hi, may I speak to Valerie, please?* | *Thank you for calling, how may I help you?* | *May I have a cookie?* **b) may I say/ask/suggest etc.** FORMAL used to say, ask, or suggest something politely: *May I suggest you start again?* → see also CAN
3 ALLOWED FORMAL used to say that someone is allowed to do something SYN **can**: *You may now kiss the bride.* | *These books may not be removed from the library.*
4 POSSIBLE TO DO STH FORMAL if something may be done, completed etc. in a particular way, that is how it is possible to do it SYN **can**: *The Commission may then take one of three actions.* | *The problem may be solved in several different ways.*
5 ALTHOUGH used to say that although one thing is true, something else which seems very different is also true: *I **may** be slow, **but** I don't make stupid mistakes.* | *Strange as it may seem, the story is true.* → see also MIGHT
6 may as well SPOKEN **a)** used for suggesting that someone should do something because there is no good reason to do anything else: *If you're tired, you may as well go to bed.* **b)** also **may just as well** used for saying that the situation is the same as if something were true: *Even though my grandparents' farm was only a hundred miles away, at that time it may as well have been a million.*
7 may you/he/they etc. do sth LITERARY used to say that you hope that a particular thing will happen to someone: *May we never have to fight another war.* | ***Long may** he live!*
8 PURPOSE FORMAL used for introducing a reason or purpose after phrases such as "so that" or "in order that": *The king has ordered a festival so that his son may select a bride.*
9 be that as it may FORMAL in spite of something that has just been said: *"He never meant it to happen." "Be that as it may, it did happen."*
[**Origin:** Old English *mæg*]

Ma•ya /ˈmaɪə/ also **Ma•yan** /ˈmaɪən/ one of the tribes of the Yucatan area in Central America, who had a very advanced society in the 4th–10th centuries A.D. —**Maya**, **Mayan** *adj.*

may•be /ˈmeɪbi/ S1 W1 *adv.* [sentence adverb] **1** used to say that something may happen or may be true, but you are not certain SYN **perhaps**: *Maybe I'll buy myself a new dress.* | *Maybe this wasn't such a good idea.* | *"It's not necessary." "Well, **maybe not**, but I want to help anyway."* | *It's supposed to rain, **maybe even** thunder.* **2** SPOKEN used to reply to a suggestion or idea when either you are not sure if you agree with it, or you do not want to say "yes" or "no": *"Mom, can I go to Kelly's after dinner?" "Maybe."* | *"I think she'd be really good as the manager." "Maybe."* **3** used to show that you are not sure of an amount or number: *Kovitsky earns maybe $45,000.* **4** SPOKEN used to make a suggestion you are not very sure about: *I thought maybe you should give them another call.*

USAGE

Maybe and **perhaps** mean the same thing, but **maybe** is more informal. To a friend you might say or write: *Maybe you could help, Joe.* In a report or a story you could write: *It was a large office containing perhaps twenty desks.*

ˈMay Day *n.* [C,U] the first day of May when people traditionally celebrate the arrival of spring

M

may·day /ˈmeɪdeɪ/ *n.* [C usually singular] a radio signal used to ask for help when a ship or an airplane is in serious danger [**Origin:** 1900–2000 French *m'aider* **help me**] → see also SOS

May·er /ˈmeɪɚ/, **Louis B.** /ˈluɪs bi/ (1885–1957) a U.S. movie PRODUCER, born in Russia, who started the company that became MGM with Samuel Goldwyn

may·est /ˈmeɪəst/ *v.* OLD USE **thou mayest** you may

May·flow·er, the /ˈmeɪˌflaʊɚ/ HISTORY the ship in which the Pilgrims (=a group of English people) sailed from England to America in 1620 to establish a COLONY

ˈMayflower ˌCompact, the HISTORY an agreement signed in 1620 by the Pilgrims (=a group of English people who had come to live in America), which established a government for their COLONY in Plymouth, Massachusetts

may·fly /ˈmeɪflaɪ/ *n. plural* **mayflies** [C] a small insect that lives near water, and only lives for a short time [**Origin:** 1600–1700 *May + fly*; because it was believed it only lived in May]

may·hem /ˈmeɪhɛm/ *n.* [U] an extremely confused situation in which people are very frightened or excited SYN **chaos**: *The new rules are meant to prevent mayhem on school enrollment days.* [**Origin:** 1400–1500 Anglo-French *mahaime* **crime of cutting off someone's arm or leg**, from Old French *maynier*]

May·o /ˈmeɪoʊ/ a COUNTY in the west of the Republic of Ireland

may·o /ˈmeɪoʊ/ *n.* [U] SPOKEN mayonnaise

Mayo, Charles (1865–1939) a U.S. doctor who started the Mayo Clinic with his brother William Mayo (1861–1939)

ˈMayo ˌClinic, the a medical institution and hospital in Rochester, Minnesota, famous for its modern equipment and successful treatments

may·on·naise /ˈmeɪəˌneɪz, ˌmeɪəˈneɪz/ *n.* [U] a thick white SAUCE made of egg and oil, often eaten on SANDWICHES [**Origin:** 1800–1900 French]

may·or /ˈmeɪɚ, mɛr/ W2 *n.* [C] someone who is elected to lead the government of a town or city —**mayoral** *adj.*: *mayoral candidates*

may·or·al·ty /ˈmeɪərəlti, ˈmɛrəlti/ *n.* [U] FORMAL the position of mayor, or the period when someone is mayor

ˌMayor-ˈcouncil ˌgovernment *n.* [C,U] POLITICS the most common type of city government in the U.S., consisting of an an elected MAYOR and an elected council which make laws

may·pole /ˈmeɪpoʊl/ *n.* [C] a tall decorated pole around which people danced on May Day in past times

Mays /meɪz/, **Wil·lie** /ˈwɪli/ (1931–) a U.S. baseball player who is considered one of the greatest players ever

mayst /meɪst/ *v.* OLD USE **thou mayst** you may

may've /ˈmeɪəv/ *v.* the short form of "may have": *She may've already phoned him.*

maze /meɪz/ *n.* [C] **1** a complicated and confusing arrangement of streets etc. that it is difficult to find your way through SYN **labyrinth**: **maze of streets/paths/wires etc.** *a maze of narrow streets* | *She led me* ***through the maze*** *of corridors to his office.* **2** a large number of rules, instructions etc. that are complicated and difficult to understand: **maze of rules/regulations etc.** *the maze of American tax laws* | *Students have to find their way* ***through a maze*** *of training programs.* **3** a game on paper in which you try to draw a line through a complicated pattern of lines without crossing any of them, played especially by children **4** a specially designed system of paths, usually surrounded by tall plants and made in a park or public garden, that is difficult to find your way through [**Origin:** 1200–1300 *maze* **to confuse**]

ma·zur·ka /məˈzɚkə/ *n.* [C] a fast Polish dance, or the music for this dance

Mb the written abbreviation of MEGABYTE

M.B.A. *n.* [C] **1 Master of Business Administration** a university degree in the skills needed to be in charge of a business, that you do after your first degree **2** a person who has this degree: *Rick is a 32-year-old M.B.A. from Harvard.*

Mba·ba·ne /əmbɑˈbɑneɪ, -ˈbɑn/ the capital and largest town of Swaziland

MC **1** the abbreviation of MASTER OF CEREMONIES → see also EMCEE **2** the person in a RAP group who holds the MICROPHONE and says the words to the songs

MCAT /ˈɛmkæt/ *n.* [C] TRADEMARK **Medical College Admission Test** an examination taken by students who have completed a first degree and want to go to MEDICAL SCHOOL

McCain /məˈkeɪn/, **John** (1936–) a U.S. politician who was a CANDIDATE for U.S. President in 2000

Mc·Car·thy /məˈkɑrθi/, **Joseph** (1909–1957) a U.S. politician famous for saying officially that many important people were COMMUNISTS, and therefore enemies of the U.S.

Mc·Car·thy·ism /məˈkɑrθiˌɪzəm/ *n.* [U] HISTORY the practice of saying that people are COMMUNISTS and therefore dangerous or disloyal. The word comes from the name of Senator Joseph McCarthy, who was very active in trying to stop the influence of Communism in the U.S. in the 1950s → see also HOUSE UN-AMERICAN ACTIVITIES COMMITTEE —**McCarthyite** *n.* [C] —**McCarthyite** *adj.*

Mc·Cor·mick /məˈkɔrmɪk/, **Cy·rus** /ˈsaɪrəs/ (1809–1884) the U.S. inventor of a machine to REAP crops

Mc·Coy /məˈkɔɪ/ *n.* **the real McCoy** INFORMAL something that is real and is not a copy, especially something valuable: *"Is it a Rolex watch?" "Yes, it's the real McCoy."*

Mc·Kin·ley, Mount /məˈkɪnli/ → see DENALI

McKinley, William (1843–1901) the 25th President of the U.S.

McVeigh /məkˈveɪ/, **Tim·o·thy** /ˈtɪməθi/ (1968–2001) a U.S. TERRORIST who was EXECUTED for making and exploding a bomb in Oklahoma City which killed 167 people

MD the written abbreviation of MARYLAND

M.D. **1** the written abbreviation of "Doctor of Medicine" **2** the abbreviation of MUSCULAR DYSTROPHY

MDT the abbreviation of MOUNTAIN DAYLIGHT TIME

ME the written abbreviation of MAINE

me /mi/ S1 W1 *pron.* **1** used by the person speaking or writing to refer to himself or herself; the object form of "I": *You guys go without me.* | *Judy, will you bring me that book?* | *She's about two years older than me.* | *Bud was sitting across from me.* | *Ken gave it to me for Christmas.* | *That's me, standing on the left.* **2 me too** SPOKEN said when you agree with someone, are in a similar situation, or are going to do the same thing as they are: *"I'm hungry." "Me too."* **3 me neither** SPOKEN also **me either** NONSTANDARD said when you agree with a negative statement someone has just made: *"I can't believe he's fifty." "Me neither."* [**Origin:** Old English]

me·a cul·pa /ˌmeɪə ˈkʊlpə/ *n.* [C] FORMAL a phrase used to admit that something is your fault

mead /mid/ *n.* **1** [U] an alcoholic drink made from HONEY **2** [C] POETIC a meadow

Mead, Lake /mid/ the largest RESERVOIR in the U.S. on the Colorado River behind the Hoover Dam

Mead, Mar·ga·ret /ˈmɑrgrɪt/ (1901–1978) a U.S. ANTHROPOLOGIST who studied the ways in which parents on the islands of Samoa, Bali, and New Guinea taught their children

Margaret Mead

mead·ow /ˈmɛdoʊ/ *n.* [C] a field with wild grass and flowers

mead·ow·lark /ˈmɛdoʊˌlɑrk/ *n.* [C] BIOLOGY a brown North American bird with a yellow front

mea·ger /ˈmigɚ/ *adj.* a meager amount of food, money etc. is too small and is much less than you need SYN inadequate: *schools with **meager resources*** | **meager income/funds/earnings etc.** *The industry expects only meager profits this year.* [**Origin:** 1300–1400 French *maigre*, from Latin *macer* **thin**] —**meagerly** *adv.* —**meagerness** *n.* [U]

meal /mil/ S2 W2 *n.* **1** [C] an occasion when you eat food, for example breakfast or dinner: *The price includes the hotel and two meals a day.* | *We **have a meal** together in the evening.* | *We'll stop on the way **for a meal**.* | *Try to stop snacking **between meals**.* | *The family sat down for their **evening meal**.*

THESAURUS

Types of meals
breakfast a meal that you eat in the morning
lunch a meal that you eat in the middle of the day
brunch a meal that you eat in the late morning, instead of breakfast or lunch
dinner/supper a meal that you eat in the evening
picnic a meal that you eat outdoors, consisting of food that you cook or prepare earlier
barbecue a meal that you cook and eat outdoors

Parts of a large meal
appetizer the small first part of a meal
hors d'oeuvre small pieces of food that you eat before a meal
main course/entrée the main part of a meal
side dish food eaten with the main course
dessert sweet food eaten at the end of a meal

2 [C] the food that you eat on a particular occasion: *Did you enjoy your meal?* | *a gourmet meal* | *I was looking forward to a **hot meal**.* | *The cinnamon roll has as many calories as a **full meal**.* | *After years of **cooking** three **meals** a day, I'm bored with preparing food.* | *She **ate** her **meal** in silence.* → see also **square meal** at SQUARE¹ (5) **3** [U] grain that has been crushed into a powder, used for making flour or animal food → see also BONE MEAL, CORNMEAL [**Origin:** (1, 2) Old English *mæl* **time, meal**]

ˈmeal ˌticket *n.* [C] **1** INFORMAL something or someone that you depend on to give you money or food **2** a card that you buy and use to get meals at school or work

meal·time /ˈmiltaɪm/ *n.* [C,U] a time during the day when you have a meal: *Some days the only time I see the kids is **at mealtimes**.*

meal·y /ˈmili/ *adj.* **1** fruit or vegetables that are mealy are dry and do not taste good: *mealy apples* **2** containing MEAL

mealy-mouthed /ˌmili ˈmaʊðd◂/ *adj.* DISAPPROVING not brave enough or honest enough to say clearly and directly what you really think

mean¹ /min/ S1 W1 *v.* *past tense and past participle* **meant** /mɛnt/ [T]

1 HAVE A PARTICULAR MEANING [not in progressive] to have or represent a particular meaning: ***What does** "patronizing" **mean?*** | **mean (that)** *This triangle means that there's a campsite there.* | *A red light means stop.* | ***What is meant by** "essential" in this case?* ▶ see THESAURUS box at **demonstrate**

2 INTEND TO SAY STH [not in progressive] to intend a particular meaning when you say something: **mean (that)** *Oh, I meant that I wasn't going to go.* | *You may want to ask her later **what** she **meant by** that.* | *Oh, **I see what you mean*** (=I now understand what you said) *about Jane's accent being strong.* | *I want to buy her something really special, **know what I mean*** (=used to check that someone understands you)*?* | *"I thought the final was really hard." "**I know what you mean*** (=I understand and have had the same experience)*; it was a lot tougher than the midterm."* | ***What I mean is,*** (=used to explain more about what you have said) *we don't really need the money.* | **(do) you mean** (=used to check that you have understood what someone intended to say) *You mean I could make money off this?* | *Straight? **How do you mean*** (=used to ask someone to explain what they have said)*, straight?*

3 INTEND TO DO STH to intend to do something or intend that someone else should do something: **mean to do sth** *Sorry, I didn't mean to pull your hair.* | *I've been meaning to ask you about this bill.* | *I'm sure she **didn't mean it*** (=did not intend to upset or hurt you)*; she's just tired.* | *The doctor **meant well*** (=intended to be helpful or kind)*, but he should have checked the drug's side effects.* | *He had **meant no harm*** (=not intended to hurt or upset anyone)*; he was only doing his job.* | **mean for sb to do sth** *I didn't mean for Tina to get hurt.* → see also **mean no harm** at HARM¹ (2)

4 RESULT IN STH [not in progressive] to have a particular result or involve something: *Does this mean I can't go?* | **mean (that)** *The curfews meant that about 250,000 people were confined to their homes.* | **mean doing sth** *My new job will mean traveling all over the world.* | *A lack of discipline in a child's life can **mean trouble*** (=result in problems) *later on.*

5 SAY STH SERIOUSLY [not in progressive] to have a serious purpose in something you say or write: *With children, if you say "no," you have to **mean it**.* | *Jordan, stop that. I **meant what I said** before.* | *You don't **really mean** that, do you?*

SPOKEN PHRASES

6 I mean a) used when explaining or giving an example of something, or when pausing to think about what you are going to say next: *You'd better do it. I mean, you've done it before.* | *I mean, he was nice and everything, but I just didn't find him attractive.* **b)** used to quickly correct something you have just said: *I just bought some apricots, no, I mean peaches.*

7 that's what I mean used when someone is saying the same thing that you were trying to say earlier: *"We might not have enough money." "That's what I mean. We have to find out the price first."*

8 what do you mean...? a) used when you do not understand what someone is trying to say: *What do you mean by "better"? Better for whom?* | *What do you mean by that?* **b)** used when you are very surprised or annoyed by what someone has just said: *I got there first! What do you mean I lost?* **c)** OLD-FASHIONED used when you are annoyed by what someone has just done: **what do you mean by doing sth?** *What do you mean by coming here and frightening the animals?*

9 see what I mean? used when something that happens proves what you said before: *See what I mean? Every time she phones she wants me to do something for her.*

10 SAY WHICH PERSON/THING [not in progressive] used to say that a particular person or thing is the one that you are talking about, pointing to etc.: *Oh, you mean the blue shorts.* | *What's her name, I mean the lady over there?*

11 SHOW STH IS TRUE/WILL HAPPEN [not in progressive] to be a sign that something is true or will happen: *Finding a lump does not necessarily mean you have cancer.* | *Clear skies mean a cold night.* | *For heaven's sake, just because we went out for coffee **doesn't mean** we're getting married.*

12 HOW IMPORTANT SB/STH IS used to say something is

very important to someone: **mean sth to sb** *I know how much your work means to you.* | *It **means a lot** to me to do a good job.* | *The farm **meant everything** to Dad.* | *Her son **means the world** to her.* | *Democracy **means nothing*** (=is not important) *to those who do not have enough to eat.* | **mean something/anything** *You say you love me, but you act like I don't mean anything to you.*

13 sb means business to be determined to succeed in getting the result you want: *The decision is a sign that the administration means business.*

14 mean something/anything/nothing to sb if a name, word, idea etc. means something to you, you are familiar with it: *Does the name Blackman mean anything to you?* | *Then, phrases like "ozone layer" meant nothing to most Americans.*

15 be meant to do sth a) to be intended to do something: *Christmas time is meant to bring people together.* **b)** if you are meant to do something, you should do it, especially because someone has told you to or because it is your responsibility SYN **be supposed to be**: *Come on, Ellie, you're meant to be helping me.*

16 be meant for sb/sth to be intended for a particular person or purpose: *a book meant for children*

17 be meant to do/be sth to have the appropriate qualities to do a particular job or activity: *Perhaps she is meant to be a teacher.*

18 be meant for each other if two people are meant for each other, they are very good partners for each other: *Judith and Eric were meant for each other.*

19 sth was meant to be used to say that you think a situation was certain to happen and that no one had any power to prevent it: *"He hasn't called yet." "Maybe it just wasn't meant to be."*

20 know/understand/see what it means to be sth to have experienced a particular situation, so that you know what it is like: *I know what it means to be alone.*

[**Origin:** Old English *mænan*] → see also WELL-MEANING, WELL-MEANT

mean² S3 *adj.*

1 NOT NICE cruel or not nice: *There's no reason to be mean.* | *That was a mean trick.* | **+to** *Mom, Laverne is being mean to me.* | *She has a **mean streak*** (=a tendency to be mean). | *Clay **doesn't have a mean bone in his body*** (=he's not mean at all).

> **THESAURUS**
>
> **cruel** deliberately making someone suffer or feel unhappy: *Kids can be very cruel to each other.*
> **unkind** treating people in a way that makes them unhappy or hurts their feelings: *She said some very unkind things.*
> **nasty** not kind and not pleasant, often deliberately: *Their neighbors were really nasty.*
> **thoughtless** not thinking about the needs and feelings of other people: *How could you have been so thoughtless, when you knew she was already upset?*

►see THESAURUS box at **unkind**

2 no mean feat/trick/achievement etc. something that is very difficult to do, so that someone who does it deserves to be admired: *Charlie found a notepad, no mean feat given the state of his desk.*

3 no mean performer/player etc. someone who is very good at doing something: *The competition was judged by William Styron, no mean novelist himself.*

4 a mean sth INFORMAL used to say that something is very good or someone is very skillful at doing something: *Stritch plays a mean piano.*

5 AVERAGE [only before noun] MATH average: *The mean length of stay in the hospital is 11 days.*

6 POOR [only before noun] LITERARY poor or looking poor: *His photos captured forever the **mean streets** of New York.*

[**Origin:** (1–4, 6) Old English *gemæne*] **—meanly** *adv.* **—meanness** *n.* [U]

mean³ *n.* [C] **1** also **arithmetic mean** MATH the average of two or more numbers, amounts, or values, calculated by adding the numbers together and dividing the result by how many numbers there are: *The mean of 3, 8, and 10 is 7, because 3+8+10=21, and 21 divided by 3 is 7.* → see also MEDIAN, MODE **2 the/a mean between sth and sth** a method or way of doing something that is between two very different methods, and better than either of them: *It's a case of finding the mean between firmness and compassion.* → see also MEANS

me·an·der /mi'ændɚ/ *v.* [I] **1** if a river, stream, road etc. meanders, it has a lot of curves in it: *The trail meanders eastward into Sunol Park.* **2** [always + adv./prep.] to walk in a slow, relaxed way, and not go in any particular direction SYN **stroll**: *We meandered around the shops in Innsbruck.* **3** also **meander on** if a conversation, book, movie etc. meanders or meanders on, it is too long and has no purpose or structure: *The movie's plot meanders on and on.* [**Origin:** 1500–1600 Latin *maeander*, from Greek, from *Maiandros* (now Menderes), river in Turkey] **—meanderings** *n.* [plural] **—meander** *n.* [C]

mean·ie, meany /'mini/ *n. plural* **meanies** [C] SPOKEN a word meaning a person who is cruel or not nice, used especially by children: *You meany!*

mean·ing /'minɪŋ/ S2 W2 *n.*

1 OF A WORD/SIGN ETC. [C,U] the thing or idea that a word, expression, or sign represents: *The same symbol can have more than one meaning.* | **+of** *Use the examples to figure out the **meaning of the word**.*

2 IDEAS IN SPEECH/BOOK/MOVIE ETC. [C,U] the thoughts or ideas that someone intends to express when they say something, write a book, make a movie etc.: *His meaning was clear – we'd lost our jobs.* | **+of** *When I first read it, I didn't **get the meaning** of the poem.* | *the **deeper meaning** of the story*

3 what's the meaning of this? SPOKEN used to demand an explanation: *What's the meaning of this? I asked you to be here an hour ago!*

4 PURPOSE/SPECIAL QUALITY [U] the quality that makes life, work etc. seem to have a purpose and value: *I want my life to **have meaning**.* | *Taking care of her family **gave meaning to** Bessy's life.* | *Life seemed to have **lost** its **meaning** since her husband's death.* | *Her education **had no meaning** for her anymore.* | *For many people, it is religion that **gives meaning to** their lives.*

5 TRUE NATURE [U] the true nature and importance of something: **+of** *We want children to remember the **true meaning** of Christmas.*

6 (not) know the meaning of sth to have experience and understanding of a particular situation or feeling, or to not have this: *He's the sort of guy who doesn't know the meaning of fear.*

mean·ing·ful /'minɪŋfəl/ *adj.* **1** serious, important, or useful and having a purpose or value: *They want a chance to do **meaningful work**.* | *She longs for a **meaningful relationship**.* | *a meaningful conversation* | *We try to celebrate Christmas in a **meaningful way**.* **2** having a meaning that is easy to understand and makes sense: *Without more data we can't make a meaningful comparison of the two systems.* | *The statistics weren't presented in any **meaningful way**.* | **+to** *Rules must be put in a context that is meaningful to the children.* **3 a meaningful look/glance/smile etc.** a look that clearly expresses the way someone feels, even though nothing is said: *Sam and Barbara exchanged a meaningful glance.* **—meaningfully** *adv.*

mean·ing·less /'minɪŋlɪs/ *adj.* **1** something that is meaningless has no purpose or importance and does not seem worth doing or having: *a brief meaningless affair* | *a meaningless ritual* | **utterly/entirely/absolutely meaningless** *a statistic that is absolutely meaningless* **2** not having a meaning that you can understand or explain: *If he can't read it, then it will be meaningless to him.* **—meaninglessness** *n.* [U]

means /minz/ W2 *n.*

1 METHOD [C] a method, system, object etc. that you use as a way of achieving a result: **+of** *a new means of financing highways* | *Bicycles are an environmentally friendly **means of transportation**.* | *Bird songs are a **means of communication**.* | **a means of doing sth** *The only effective means of controlling this disease is vaccination.* | *They entered the store by **illegal means**.* |

They were told to **use any means** *possible to achieve their task.* | *Critics were silenced* **by means of** (=using the method of) *imprisonment.*
2 MONEY [plural] the money or income that you have: **means to do sth** *The school does not* **have the means** *to pay for music lessons.* | *Houses in this area are* **beyond the means** (=cost more money than you have) *of most people.* | *We're struggling to* **live within** *our* **means** (=only spend the money we have, and no more). | **a man/woman of means** (=someone who is rich)
3 by all means SPOKEN used to mean "of course" when politely allowing someone to do something or agreeing with a suggestion: *If you have binoculars, by all means take them along.*
4 by no means also **not by any means** not at all: *The game is by no means over.* | *She's not a bad kid, by any means.*
5 a means to an end something that you do only to achieve a result, not because you want to do it: *Technology is not a magic wand, but only a means to an end.*
6 the means of production TECHNICAL the materials, tools, and equipment that are used in the production of goods → see also **by fair means or foul** at FAIR[1] (18), **ways and means** at WAY[1] (47)

ˌmean-ˈspirited *adj.* not generous or sympathetic

ˈmeans test *n.* [C] POLITICS an official check in order to find out whether someone is poor enough to need money from the government —**means-tested** *adj.*: *means-tested programs* —**means testing** *n.* [U]

meant /mɛnt/ *v.* the past tense and past participle of MEAN

mean·time /ˈmintaɪm/ *adv.* **1** usually **in the meantime** in the period of time between now and a future event, or between two events in the past [SYN] **meanwhile**: *The doctor will be here soon. In the meantime, try and relax.* | *I didn't see Laura for five years, and in the meantime she had gotten married.* | *Faulk and several others, meantime, have played excellent basketball.* **2 for the meantime** for the present time, until something happens: *The power supply should be back soon – for the meantime we'll have to use candles.*

mean·while /ˈminwaɪl/ [W2] *adv.* [sentence adverb] **1** also **in the meanwhile** in the period of time between two events: *The flight will be announced soon. Meanwhile, please remain seated.* | *I wouldn't get my test results for several weeks, and I wasn't sure what to do in the meanwhile.* **2** while something else is happening: *Jim went to answer the phone. Meanwhile, Pete started to prepare lunch.* **3** used to compare two things that are happening at the same time: *The incomes of male professionals went up by almost 80%. Meanwhile, part-time women workers saw their earnings fall.*

mean·y /ˈmini/ *n.* [C] another spelling of MEANIE

mea·sles /ˈmizəlz/ also **the measles** *n.* [U] MEDICINE an infectious illness in which you have a fever and small red spots on your face and body → see also GERMAN MEASLES

mea·sly /ˈmizli/ *adj.* [only before noun] INFORMAL very small and disappointing in size, quantity, or value: *a measly little paycheck*

meas·ur·a·ble /ˈmɛʒərəbəl/ *adj.* **1** large or important enough to have a definite effect [SYN] **noticeable**: *There has been no measurable progress toward peace.* **2** able to be measured: *measurable rainfall* —**measurably** *adv.*

meas·ure[1] /ˈmɛʒɚ/ [W1] *n.*
1 OFFICIAL ACTION [C] an official action that is intended to deal with a particular problem: ***Measures** are being* **taken** *to reduce crime in the city.* | **security/safety measure** *New security measures will soon be in place.* | *The aid was seen as a* **temporary measure**. | **preventative** *health care* **measures**, *such as flu shots* | **drastic/extreme measure** *Nothing will change unless drastic measures are taken.* | **Half measures** (=actions that are not effective or firm enough) *will not fix America's health care problems.* ▶see THESAURUS box at **action**
2 LAW POLITICS a written proposal for a new state or local law, that people vote on in elections: *Voters in Montana rejected a measure to increase cigarette tax.* | *a successful* **ballot measure** *for transportation funding*
3 SIGN/PROOF be a measure of sth to be a sign of the importance, strength etc. of something: +**of** *The flowers and tears at the funeral were a measure of the people's love for her.*
4 WAY OF JUDGING STH a way of testing or judging something: +**of** *Test scores are not always a* **true measure** *of a student's abilities.* | *Profits are often used as a measure of a company's success.*
5 AMOUNT a measure of sth an amount of something good or something that you want: *Jones simply wanted a measure of respect from her co-workers.* | **some/a small/a large etc. measure of sth** *This gives the children some measure of control over their own money.*
6 UNIT OF MEASUREMENT [C,U] an amount or unit in a measuring system, or the system for measuring amount, size, weight etc.: *An inch is a measure of length.* | *a table of U.S. standard weights and measures*
7 for good measure in addition to what you have already done or given: *I threw in a little more chili, for good measure.*
8 in large/no small/some measure to a great degree or to some degree: *Parents were in large measure responsible for getting the school a new library.*
9 beyond measure FORMAL very great or very much: *They had suffered beyond measure.*
10 in equal measure used when the amount of one thing is the same as the amount of another thing: *I was angry and embarrassed in equal measure.*
11 take the measure of sth to become familiar with something, so that you can control it or deal with it: *He thought he had taken the measure of the market, but then it had done something unexpected.*
12 ALCOHOL a standard amount of an alcoholic drink: *a measure of bourbon*
13 the full measure of sth FORMAL the whole of something: *His poetry expresses the full measure of God's glory.*
14 in full measure if someone gives something back in full measure, they give back as much as they received
15 THING USED FOR MEASURING [C] something used for measuring, such as a piece of wood or a container → see also TAPE MEASURE
16 MUSIC [C] one of a group of notes and RESTS, separated by VERTICAL lines, into which a line of written music is divided [SYN] **bar** → see also MADE-TO-MEASURE

measure[2] [S2] [W2] *v.* **1** [T] to find the size, length, or amount of something using standard units such as INCHES, METERS etc.: *Measure the wall area before buying the paint.* | **measure sb for sth** *She was measured for her wedding dress.* | **measure sth in sth** *Drinks are measured in liquid ounces.* **2** [T] to judge the importance, value, or true nature of something [SYN] **assess**: *It is too early to measure the effectiveness of the drug.* | **measure sth by sth** *Education cannot only be measured by test scores.* **3** [linking verb] to be a particular size, length, or amount: *When full grown, the blue whale measures 110 feet in length.* | *The earthquake measured 6.5 on the Richter scale.* **4** [T] if a piece of equipment measures something, it shows or records a particular type of measurement: *An odometer measures the number of miles your car travels.*

measure sb/sth **against** sth *phr. v.* to judge someone or something by comparing them with another person or thing: *Measured against our whole budget last year, $2.7 million seems a small amount.*

measure sth ↔ **off** *phr. v.* to measure a particular length or distance, and make a mark so that you can see the beginning and end: *He measured off three yards of rope.*

measure sth ↔ **out** *phr. v.* to take a particular amount of liquid, powder etc. from a larger amount: *Measure out 1¾ cups of flour.*

measure up *phr. v.* **1** to be good enough to do a particular job or to reach a particular standard: *Teachers who don't measure up must be fired.* | +**to** *How will the Secretary General measure up to his new responsibilities?* **2 measure sth** ↔ **up** to measure

M

something: *I'd better measure up before I start laying the carpet.*

meas·ured /ˈmɛʒɚd/ *adj.* careful and slow or steady: *a calm and measured response* | *She spoke* ***in measured tones*** (=a slow deliberate way of speaking).

meas·ure·less /ˈmɛʒɚlɪs/ *adj.* LITERARY too big or too much to be measured

meas·ure·ment /ˈmɛʒɚmənt/ *n.* **1** [C usually plural] the length, height, weight, speed etc. of something, that can be measured using units such as yards, pounds etc.: *What are his measurements?* | **take/make measurements of sth** *Take measurements of the room first.* | **take sb's measurements** *The tailor took his measurements for a new suit.* | **precise/accurate measurements** *Precise measurements are important in baking.* **2** [U] the act of measuring something: *a system of performance measurement* | +**of** *the accurate measurement of time*

ˌmeasure of ˌcentral ˈtendency also **ˌmeasure of ˈcenter** *n.* [C] MATH one of the three units of measurement used to show the degree to which STATISTICAL data groups around a particular point. They are the MEAN (=used to show the average quantity), the MODE (=used to show the most frequent quantity), and the MEDIAN (=used to show the middle quantity).

ˌmeasure of ˈspread also **ˌmeasure of ˌvariaˈbility, ˌmeasure of ˌvariˈation** *n.* [C] MATH one of the measurements used to show how STATISTICAL data is spread out, including the RANGE and STANDARD DEVIATION

ˌmeasures ˈof center *n.* [plural] MATH three standard units of measurement used when examining and describing data. The units are called the MEAN (=used to show the average quantity), the MODE (=used to show the most frequent quantity), and the MEDIAN (=used to show the middle quantity).

ˌmeasures of ˌvariˈation *n.* [plural] MATH measurements for showing the range of difference from the smallest to the greatest quantity in a set of data

ˈmeasuring ˌcup *n.* [C] a special cup used for measuring food or liquid when cooking

ˈmeasuring ˌtape *n.* [C] a TAPE MEASURE

meat /mit/ S1 W2 *n.* **1** [C,U] the flesh of animals and birds eaten as food: *I stopped eating meat when I was 14.* | *spaghetti with a meat sauce* | *cold meats* | **red meat** (=a dark-colored meat such as BEEF) | **white meat** (=meat that is pale in color, for example some parts of a CHICKEN) → see also DELI MEAT, LUNCH MEAT

THESAURUS

Types of meat
beef the meat from a cow
veal the meat from a young cow
pork the meat from a pig
ham meat from a pig, that has been preserved with salt or smoke
bacon long thin pieces of meat from the back or sides of a pig, that have been preserved with salt or smoke
The meat from lamb, birds, or fish is called by the name of the animal: *We had chicken for dinner.* | *roast lamb* | *salmon steaks in tomato sauce*
mutton a word for meat from a sheep, which is not used much now
poultry meat from birds such as chickens and ducks
venison meat from a deer
game meat from wild animals and birds

2 [U] the main or most important part of a talk, book etc.: *Finally we got down to the real meat of the debate.* | *There's* ***no meat to*** *their arguments.* **3 meat and potatoes** INFORMAL the most important or basic parts of a discussion, decision, piece of work etc.: +**of** *Parks, crime, and traffic are the meat and potatoes of council elections.* → see also MEAT-AND-POTATOES **4 be dead meat** if someone is dead meat, someone is going to be angry at them, or they cannot succeed at what they are doing: *He was widely considered to be political dead meat.* **5 need some (more) meat on your bones** INFORMAL used to say that someone looks too thin **6 be meat and drink to sb** to be something that someone enjoys doing or finds easy to do: *Most people hate the stress of the job, but it seems to be meat and drink to Brian.* **7 one man's meat is another man's poison** used to say that something that one person likes may not be liked by someone else [**Origin:** Old English *mete* **food**] → see also MEAT MARKET

ˌmeat-and-poˈtatoes *adj.* [only before noun] **1** basic, simple, and ordinary: *meat-and-potatoes language* | *meat-and-potatoes voters* **2** a meat-and-potatoes person likes to eat basic meals that consist of traditional foods such as meat and vegetables

meat·ball /ˈmitˀbɔl/ *n.* [C] a small round ball made from very small pieces of meat, and usually egg and HERBS, pressed together

ˈmeat ˌgrinder *n.* [C] a machine that cuts meat into very small pieces by forcing it through small holes

meat·less /ˈmitlɪs/ *adj.* food that is meatless contains no meat: *The menu has several meatless options.*

meat·loaf /ˈmitloʊf/ *n.* [C,U] a dish made from GROUND meat (=meat cut into very small pieces) mixed with egg and bread, and then baked in the shape of a LOAF

ˈmeat ˌmarket *n.* [C] **1 be a meat market** INFORMAL used about a situation or place in which people are only interested in finding someone to have sex with **2** a place, often outside, where people go to sell or buy meat

ˈmeat-ˌpacking *n.* [U] the preparation of animals that have been killed so that they can be sold as meat: *the meat-packing industry* —**meat-packer** *n.* [C]

meat·y /ˈmit̬i/ *adj. comparative* **meatier**, *superlative* **meatiest** **1** containing a lot of meat or having a strong meat taste: *big meaty barbecued ribs* **2** INFORMAL big and fat, with a lot of flesh: *ripe meaty tomatoes* | *his meaty forearms* **3** INFORMAL a meaty part in a play, movie etc. is an interesting or important one: *"Joan of Arc" was her first* ***meaty role*** *as an actress.* **4** containing a lot of interesting ideas or information: *a meaty issue of the magazine* **5** having a strong pleasant taste: *a meaty red wine*

mec·ca /ˈmɛkə/ **1 Mecca** a city in Saudi Arabia that many Muslims visit because it is the holiest city of Islam where the Prophet Muhammad was born **2** [C usually singular] a place that many people want to visit for a particular reason SYN **magnet**: +**for** *Florida is a mecca for students during spring break.*

me·chan·ic /mɪˈkænɪk/ *n.* **1** [C] someone who is skilled at repairing motor vehicles and machinery **2 mechanics** the way in which something works or is done: **the mechanics of (doing) sth** *He had little interest in the mechanics of government.* **3 mechanics** [U] PHYSICS the science that deals with the effects of forces on objects → see also QUANTUM MECHANICS

me·chan·i·cal /mɪˈkænɪkəl/ *adj.* **1** affecting or involving a machine: *The flight has been canceled due to* ***mechanical failure.*** | *the space shuttle's mechanical arm* **2** using power from an engine or machine to do a particular type of work: *He was breathing with the aid of a* ***mechanical device.*** **3** a mechanical action, reply etc. is done without thinking, and has been done many times before: *He was asked the same question so many times that the answer became mechanical.* **4** INFORMAL someone who is mechanical understands how machines work **5** PHYSICS relating to or produced by physical forces: *the mechanical properties of solids* —**mechanically** /-kli/ *adv.*

meˌchanical adˈvantage *n.* [U] PHYSICS the amount by which a machine increases the effort that you put into it, so that more work is done using the same amount of effort

meˌchanical engiˈneering *n.* [U] the study of the design and production of machines and tools —**mechanical engineer** *n.* [C]

meˌchanical ˈpencil *n.* [C] a pencil made of metal or

plastic, with a thin piece of LEAD (=the part that you write with) inside that comes out when you press a button on the pencil

me,chanical 'weathering *n.* [U] EARTH SCIENCE a process by which rocks and stones etc. are gradually broken down by the roots of plants or by natural forces such as ice and wind

mech·a·nism /ˈmɛkəˌnɪzəm/ Ac *n.* [C] **1** part of a machine, or a set of parts, that does a particular job: *the locking mechanism on the car door* **2** a system that is intended to achieve something or deal with a problem: **mechanism to do sth** *The Army has set up mechanisms to help jobless ex-soldiers get work.* | **+for** *The law sets out the mechanism for establishing tax rates.* **3** the way that something works: *the mechanism of the brain* **4 defense/survival/escape mechanism** a way of behaving that helps a living thing to avoid or protect itself from something that is difficult or dangerous: *The odor is part of the skunk's defense mechanism.*

mech·a·nis·tic /ˌmɛkəˈnɪstɪk◂/ *adj.* tending to explain the actions and behavior of living things as if they were machines: *a **mechanistic view** of nature* —**mechanistically** /-kli/ *adj.*

mech·a·nized /ˈmɛkəˌnaɪzd/ *adj.* **1** a mechanized system or process has been changed so that it uses machines instead of people or animals to do the work: *a highly mechanized factory* | *mechanized farming* **2** a mechanized army uses TANKS and other ARMORED vehicles (=protected military vehicles) —**mechanize** *v.* [I,T] —**mechanization** /ˌmɛkənəˈzeɪʃən/ *n.* [U]

med·al /ˈmɛdl/ W3 *n.* [C] a flat piece of metal, usually shaped like a coin, that is given to someone who has won a competition or who has done something brave: **gold/silver/bronze medal** *She **won a** gold **medal** in the last Olympics.* | *the bronze **medal winner*** | *He was **awarded a medal** for bravery.* [**Origin:** 1500–1600 French *médaille*, from Old Italian *medaglia* **coin of half value, medal**] → see also **sb deserves a medal** at DESERVE (4)

med·al·ist /ˈmɛdl-ɪst/ *n.* [C] someone who has won a medal in a competition: **gold/silver/bronze medalist** *an Olympic silver medalist*

me·dal·lion /məˈdælyən/ *n.* [C] a piece of metal shaped like a large coin, worn as jewelry on a chain around the neck

,Medal of 'Honor *n.* [C] the most important medal given by Congress to a soldier, sailor etc. who has done something extremely brave

med·dle /ˈmɛdl/ *v.* [I] to deliberately try to influence or change a situation that does not concern you, or that you do not understand fully SYN **interfere**: **+in** *He accused the U.S. of **meddling in** China's **internal affairs**.* | **+with** *Why meddle with the Constitution? It has served us well all these years.* [**Origin:** 1200–1300 Old French *mesler*, *medler*, from Latin *miscere* **to mix**] —**meddler** *n.* [C] —**meddling** *n.* [U] —**meddling** *adj.* [only before noun]

med·dle·some /ˈmɛdlsəm/ *adj.* a meddlesome person becomes involved in situations that do not concern them, in a way that annoys people: *meddlesome neighbors*

Med·e·vac /ˈmɛdɪˌvæk/ *n.* [C,U] air TRANSPORTATION that is used to take injured or very sick people to a hospital

Med·fly, medfly /ˈmɛdflaɪ/ *n. plural* **medflies** [C] a type of fly that destroys CITRUS fruit trees

me·di·a /ˈmidiə/ Ac W2 *n.* **1** [used with singular or plural verb] all the organizations, such as television, radio, and newspapers, that provide news and information for the public, or the people who report the news stories: ***The media** have reported two more arrests.* | *The story was picked up by international **news media**.* | *There are not enough positive images of black males **in the media**.* | **media attention/coverage/interest** *The case received massive amounts of media coverage* (=there were a lot of stories about the case). | *The Superbowl is the NFL **media event*** (=an event the media give a lot of attention to) *of the year!* **2** the plural of MEDIUM → see also MASS MEDIA, MULTIMEDIA

me·di·an[1] /ˈmidiən/ *n.* [C] **1** also **'median ,strip** a narrow piece of land or a fence that divides a road or HIGHWAY **2** MATH the middle number or value in a set of values that are arranged in order of size: *The median of 3, 9, 11, 13, and 14 is 11.* → see also MEAN, MODE **3** TECHNICAL MATH **a)** a line passing from one of the points of a TRIANGLE to the middle of the opposite side **b)** a line connecting the MIDPOINTS of the two sides of a TRAPEZOID that are not parallel to each other SYN **midsegment**

median[2] *adj.* [only before noun] TECHNICAL **1** MATH being the middle number or measurement in a set of numbers of measurements that have been arranged in order SYN **average**: *The median age for marriage for women is 24.5.* **2** in or passing through the middle of something **3** MATH relating to the median of a TRIANGLE or TRAPEZOID

'media ,studies *n.* [U] a subject that you study at college, that deals with how newspapers, television, radio etc. communicate and how they affect society

me·di·ate /ˈmidiˌeɪt/ Ac *v.* **1** [I,T] to help people, groups, countries etc. try to end an argument and reach an agreement: *Former President Jimmy Carter agreed to mediate the peace talks.* | **+between** *U.N. officials mediated between the rebel fighters and the government.* **2** [T] to change the effect or influence of something, especially to make the effect less bad: *Exercise may mediate the effects of a bad diet.* —**mediation** /ˌmidiˈeɪʃən/ *n.* [U]

me·di·a·tor /ˈmidiˌeɪtɚ/ *n.* [C] someone who helps people, groups, countries etc. to end an argument and reach an agreement

med·ic /ˈmɛdɪk/ *n.* [C] someone who is trained to give medical treatment, but who is not a doctor, especially someone in the army → see also PARAMEDIC

Med·i·caid /ˈmɛdɪˌkeɪd/ *n.* [U] a system in the U.S. by which the government helps to pay the cost of medical treatment for poor people → see also MEDICARE

med·i·cal /ˈmɛdɪkəl/ Ac S2 W1 *adj.* relating to the treatment of disease or injury: *a lack of medical care* | *medical insurance* | *He has a lot of medical problems.* | *a patient's **medical history*** (=the illnesses they have had) | *Is there still sexism within **the medical profession*** (=all the people who work as doctors, nurses etc.)*?* [**Origin:** 1600–1700 French *médical*, from Late Latin *medicalis*, from Latin *medicus* **doctor**] —**medically** /-kli/ *adv.*

'medical cer,tificate *n.* [C] an official piece of paper signed by a doctor saying that you are too sick to work or that you are completely healthy

,medical ex'aminer *n.* [C] a doctor who examines dead people's bodies in order to find out how they died, especially if they died in a sudden or unusual way

'medical school *n.* [C,U] a part of a university where people study to become doctors

'medical ,student *n.* [C] someone who is studying to become a doctor

me·dic·a·ment /mɪˈdɪkəmənt, ˈmɛdɪ-/ *n.* [C] MEDICINE a substance used on or in the body to treat a disease SYN **medicine**

Med·i·care /ˈmɛdɪˌkɛr/ *n.* [U] a system by which the U.S. government helps to pay for the medical treatment of old people → see also MEDICAID

med·i·cate /ˈmɛdɪˌkeɪt/ *v.* [T] FORMAL to treat someone by giving them medicine or drugs

med·i·cat·ed /ˈmɛdɪˌkeɪtɪd/ *adj.* medicated products such as soap, powder, or SHAMPOO contain a small amount of medicine to treat medical problems of your skin that are not serious

med·i·ca·tion /ˌmɛdɪˈkeɪʃən/ S3 *n.* [C,U] MEDICINE medicine or drugs given to people who are sick: **be on medication (for sth)** *He's on medication for high blood pressure.*

M

Med·i·ci, the /ˈmɛdɪtʃi/ a rich and powerful Italian family of bankers who ruled Florence, Italy, from the 15th to the 18th century, and spent much of their money on art and on providing financial support to artists

me·dic·i·nal /məˈdɪsənl/ *adj.* MEDICINE a medicinal substance is used for treating illness or disease: *Garlic is believed to have* ***medicinal properties***. | *Marijuana was legalized* ***for medicinal purposes*** (=for use as a medicine). → see also MEDICAL —**medicinally** *adv.*

med·i·cine /ˈmɛdəsən/ S2 W2 *n.* **1** [C,U] a substance used for treating illness SYN **medication**: *Medicines should be kept out of children's reach.* | *Have you been* ***taking*** *your* ***medicine***?

THESAURUS

pill/tablet a small hard piece of medicine that you swallow
capsule a small tube-shaped container with medicine inside that you swallow whole
caplet a small smooth pill that is slightly longer than it is wide
eye/ear drops liquid medicine that you put into your eye or ear
drug a medicine or a substance for making medicines: *a new drug in the treatment of breast cancer*
dosage the amount of medicine that you should take: *The usual dosage is 25 to 50 mg.*

2 [U] the treatment and study of illnesses and injuries: *a professor of medicine* | *Chinese herbal medicine* **3 the best medicine** the best way of making you feel better when you are sad: *Laughter is the best medicine.* **4 give someone a taste/dose of their own medicine** to treat someone as badly as they have treated you: *Just ignore him, Judy. That'll give him a taste of his own medicine.* **5 take your medicine** to accept a bad situation or a punishment that you deserve, without complaining → see also ALTERNATIVE MEDICINE, **strong medicine** at STRONG (30)

ˈmedicine chest *n.* [C] a small cupboard used to store medicines, usually in the BATHROOM

ˈmedicine man *n.* [C] a man in a Native American tribe who is considered to have the ability to cure illness and disease

ˈmedicine ˌwoman *n.* [C] a woman in a Native American tribe who is considered to have the ability to cure illness and disease

me·die·val /mɪˈdivəl, mɛ-, mi-/ *adj.* **1** [usually before noun] relating to the Middle Ages (=the period between about A.D. 1100 and 1400): *medieval art* **2** old-fashioned and not acceptable or not useful: *a medieval attitude toward women* [**Origin:** 1800–1900 Modern Latin *medium aevum* **middle age**]

me·di·na /mɪˈdinə/ *n.* [C] an old part of many North African towns and cities, where Arab people traditionally live, and which usually has a MOSQUE (=building in which Muslims worship)

me·di·o·cre /ˌmidiˈoʊkɚ◂/ *adj.* not very good: *the team's mediocre performance* [**Origin:** 1500–1600 French, Latin *mediocris* **halfway up a mountain**] —**mediocrity** /ˌmidiˈɑkrət̬i/ *n.* [U]

med·i·tate /ˈmɛdəˌteɪt/ *v.* **1** [I] to spend time sitting in a silent calm state, in order to relax completely or for religious purposes: *I try to meditate every day.* **2** [I] to think seriously and deeply about something SYN **contemplate**: +**on/upon** *She sat quietly, meditating on the day's events.* **3** [T] FORMAL to plan to do something, usually something bad: *Silently she meditated revenge.*

med·i·ta·tion /ˌmɛdəˈteɪʃən/ *n.* **1** [U] the practice of emptying your mind of thoughts and feelings, in order to relax completely or for religious reasons: *Yoga involves breathing exercises, stretching, and meditation.* | *He spent hours* ***in meditation***. | *If you* ***practice*** *Zen* ***meditation***, *you concentrate on your breathing.* **2** [C usually plural, U] the act of thinking deeply and seriously about something SYN **contemplation**: *Priests perform daily meditations at the temple.* | *a peaceful place for quiet meditation* **3** [C usually plural] serious thoughts or writing about a particular subject: +**on** *meditations on death and loss*

med·i·ta·tive /ˈmɛdəˌteɪt̬ɪv/ *adj.* **1** thinking deeply and seriously about something SYN **contemplative**: *He looked at the picture in meditative silence.* **2** relating to meditation: *meditative techniques* —**meditatively** *adv.*

Med·i·ter·ra·ne·an¹ /ˌmɛdətəˈreɪniən/ *n.* **the Mediterranean a)** the sea that is surrounded by the countries of southern Europe, North Africa, and the Middle East **b)** the area of southern Europe that surrounds this sea

Mediterranean² *adj.* relating to or coming from the Mediterranean Sea, or typical of the area of Southern Europe around it: *a cruise along the Mediterranean coast*

me·di·um¹ /ˈmidiəm/ Ac S2 *adj.* **1** of middle size, level, or amount: *What size shirt does he wear – medium or large?* | *two medium potatoes* | **medium height/length/build etc.** *a man with a medium build* | *medium length brown hair* | *Fry the onions over* ***medium heat*** (=a temperature that is not too hot or cold). → see also AVERAGE **2** also **ˌmedium ˈrare** meat that is medium or medium rare is partly cooked but still slightly pink inside → see also RARE **3** if a food or drink is medium hot, sweet, dry etc., it is not as hot, sweet etc. as some similar foods, but it is more hot or sweet than others : *medium salsa* → see also MILD **4 medium brown/blue etc.** a color that is neither light nor dark: *a medium gray sweater*

medium² Ac *n. plural* **media** /-diə/, **mediums** [C] **1** ENG. LANG. ARTS a particular way of communicating information and news to people, such as a newspaper, television broadcast etc: *Advertising is a powerful medium.* | +**of** *Politicians prefer to use the medium of television.* | *They used English as a medium of communication.* → see also MEDIA **2** a way of expressing your ideas, especially as a writer or an artist: +**for** *The novel has always been an excellent medium for satire.* | *the visual media* (=painting, movies etc.) **3** an object on which information is printed, stored etc.: *DVDs have quickly become a popular medium.* **4** *plural* **mediums** someone who claims to have the power to receive messages from the spirits of the dead **5 medium of exchange** money or other ways of paying for things **6** *plural* **mediums** something of medium size, especially a piece of clothing: *I* ***take a medium*** (=I wear that size). **7** TECHNICAL a substance or material in which things grow or exist **8** PHYSICS a substance through which a force travels → see also **a happy medium** at HAPPY (7), MAGNETIC MEDIA

ˈmedium-sized also **ˈmedium-size** *adj.* not small, but not large either: *a medium-sized business*

ˈmedium ˌterm *n.* [singular] the period of time that is a few weeks, months, or years ahead of the present: *The company's prospects look good* ***in the medium term***. —**medium-term** *adj.* → see also SHORT-TERM

ˈmedium ˌwave WRITTEN ABBREVIATION **MW** *n.* [U] a system of radio broadcasting that uses radio WAVES that are between 100 and 1,000 meters in length

med·ley /ˈmɛdli/ *n. plural* **medleys** [C] **1** ENG. LANG. ARTS a group of songs or tunes sung or played one after the other as a single piece of music: +**of** *a medley of Christmas carols* **2** a swimming race in which the competitors swim using four different STROKES **3** [usually singular] a mixture of different types of something, which produces an interesting or unusual effect: +**of** *a medley of vegetables*

med school /ˈmɛd skul/ *n.* [C] INFORMAL a MEDICAL SCHOOL

med stu·dent /ˈmɛd ˌstudnt/ *n.* [C] INFORMAL a MEDICAL STUDENT

me·dul·la ob·lon·ga·ta /məˌdʌlə ɑblɔŋˈgɑt̬ə/ *n.* [singular] BIOLOGY the lowest part of your brain, where it connects with your SPINAL CORD. The medulla oblongata controls your breathing and the flow of blood to and from your heart. → see picture at BRAIN[1]

meek /mik/ *adj.* very quiet and gentle and unwilling to argue or express an opinion: *a shy meek child* —**meekly** *adv.*: *She smiled meekly.* —**meekness** *n.* [U]

meet[1] /mit/ S1 W1 *v. past tense and past participle* **met** /mɛt/

1 SEE SB AT AN ARRANGED PLACE [I, T not in passive] to come to the same place as someone else because you have arranged to find them there: *We're going to meet at 11:00.* | *Why don't I meet you guys downtown?* | **meet (sb) for sth** *Kerry and I are meeting for lunch today.*

THESAURUS

get together to meet with someone or with a group of people: *Why don't we all get together and go out for a drink?*
gather if people gather somewhere, or if someone gathers them, they come together in the same place: *Fans have started to gather outside the stadium.*
assemble if you assemble people, or if people assemble, they are brought together in the same place: *If the fire alarm rings, please assemble in the parking lot.*
come together if people come together, they meet in order to discuss things, exchange ideas etc.: *The family came together to help when Julie got sick.*

2 SEE SB BY CHANCE [I, T not in passive] to see someone you know by chance and talk to them: *Guess who I met at the grocery store!*
3 SB YOU DO NOT KNOW [I, T not in passive] to see and talk to someone for the first time, or be introduced to them: *Did you ever meet her boyfriend?* | *Jim and I met at NYU.* | *I met this really nice lady on the bus yesterday.*
4 nice/pleased/good to meet you SPOKEN **a)** a polite phrase used to greet someone when you meet them for the first time, especially when another person has introduced you: *"This is my friend Betty." "Hi. Nice to meet you."* **b)** used when you are about to stop talking with someone you have just met: *Well, it was good to finally meet you, Joan.*
5 (it was) nice/good meeting you SPOKEN a polite phrase used when you say goodbye to someone you have met for the first time: *Nice meeting you, Karla.*
6 AIRPORT/STATION ETC. [T] to be waiting for someone at an airport, station etc. when they arrive: *Dad said he'd meet our flight.* | *I was met by a company representative.*
7 COMMITTEE/GROUP ETC. [I] to be together in the same place, usually in order to discuss something: *Officials of both sides have agreed to meet in North Korea's capital.* | *The committee meets once a month.*
8 OPPONENT [I, T not in passive] to play against another person or team in a competition, or to fight another army in a war: *The Yankees and the Orioles will meet next week to fight for the American League pennant.*
9 RIVERS/ROADS/LINES ETC. [I, T not in passive] to join together at a particular place: *There's a stop sign where the two roads meet.*
10 EXPERIENCE A PROBLEM/SITUATION [T] to experience a problem, attitude, or situation SYN **encounter**: *Wherever she went she met hostility and prejudice.*
11 meet a problem/challenge etc. to deal with a problem or something difficult that you have to do: *The school hired specialist teachers to meet this new challenge.*
12 meet a need/demand/condition etc. to do something that someone wants, needs, or expects you to do or be as good as they need, expect etc.: *Customers who meet certain conditions will be given a 20% discount.*
13 meet a goal/target/aim etc. to achieve an aim etc.: *The Red Cross met their goal of raising $1.6 million for food supplies.* | *We are still hoping to* ***meet*** *the November* ***deadline*** (=achieve something on time).
14 meet debts/costs/expenses etc. to make a payment that needs to be made: *The group may not be able to meet its costs this year.*
15 there's more to sb/sth than meets the eye used to say that someone or something is more interesting, intelligent etc. than they seem to be
16 meet your match to have an opponent who is as strong or as skillful as you are and therefore might be able to defeat you: *It seems Connoly's finally met her political match.*
17 meet sb halfway to do or give some of the things that someone wants or needs, in order to reach an agreement with them
18 meet (sth) head-on if you meet a problem head-on, you deal with it directly without trying to avoid it: *The company intends to meet the competition head-on.*
19 our/their eyes meet if two people's eyes meet, they look at each other, because they are attracted to each other or because they are thinking the same thing: *Their eyes met, and Nina smiled.*
20 meet sb's eye(s)/gaze/glance etc. to look directly at someone who is looking at you: *Ruth looked down, unable to meet his eye.*
21 meet your eye(s) if something meets your eyes, you see it: *A horrific scene met our eyes.*
22 TOUCH/HIT [I,T] to touch, join, or hit another object: *Their hands met under the table.*
23 meet your death/end/fate/destiny to die in a particular way: *Two brothers met their tragic fate in the icy waters.*
24 meet your maker HUMOROUS to die
[**Origin:** Old English *metan*] → see also **make ends meet** at END[1] (8)

meet up *phr. v.* to meet someone in an informal way in order to do something together: *Why don't we meet up for dinner in the city?* | **+with** *Molly's going to meet up with us after basketball practice.*

meet with sb/sth *phr. v.* **1** to have a meeting with someone: *Dodd will fly to Washington, D.C., to meet with the Secretary of State.* **2** to get a particular reaction or result: **meet with approval/disapproval/criticism** *The company's decision was met with sharp criticism.* | **meet with success/failure** *Their efforts to save the theater have met with little success.* **3 meet with danger/death/disaster etc.** FORMAL to experience something by chance, usually something bad: *Five teens met with disaster when their stolen vehicle crashed into a wall.*

meet[2] *n.* [C] a sports competition, especially a competition between people who are racing: *a swim meet*

meet[3] *adj.* OLD USE right or appropriate SYN **suitable**

meet·ing /ˈmitɪŋ/ S1 W2 *n.* [C] **1** an organized event at which people gather to talk and decide things: *Over a hundred people* ***attended the meeting.*** | *She's* ***in a meeting*** *right now.* | *A* ***meeting*** *was* ***held*** *to discuss global warming.* | **+with** *I* ***have a meeting*** *with her teacher at 3 o'clock.* | **+about/on** *a* ***public meeting*** *on the issue* | **+between** *a meeting between representatives from the two countries* | **+of** *a meeting of the board of trustees* **2 the meeting** FORMAL all the people who attend a meeting: *The meeting was asked to discuss the problem of unemployment.* **3** [usually singular] an occasion when two or more people meet each other by chance or because they have arranged to do this: *I fell in love with her at our first meeting.* **4** a game that is part of a larger competition in a particular sport: *San Diego won their first meeting this season 21–13.* **5 meeting of (the) minds** a situation in which two people agree with each other: *There is still no meeting of the minds between Congress and the White House.* **6** an event at which a group of Quakers (=a Christian religious group) worship together

ˈmeeting-house *n.* [C] a building where Quakers WORSHIP

mega- /mɛgə/ *prefix* **1** a million times a particular unit of something: *a 100-megaton bomb* **2** INFORMAL much larger than usual in amount, importance, or size: *Hollywood megastars* | *a megarich new boyfriend*

meg·a·bit /ˈmɛgəˌbɪt/ *n.* [C] TECHNICAL a million BITS

meg·a·bucks /ˈmɛgəˌbʌks/ *n.* [plural] INFORMAL a very large amount of money

meg·a·byte /ˈmɛgəˌbaɪt/ WRITTEN ABBREVIATION **Mb** *n.* [C] COMPUTERS a unit for measuring the amount of infor-

M

mation a computer can use, equal to 1,024 KILOBYTES, or about a million BYTES

meg·a·hertz /ˈmɛgəˌhɚts/ WRITTEN ABBREVIATION **MHz** *n.* [U] a unit for measuring FREQUENCY especially of radio signals, equal to one million HERTZ

meg·a·lith /ˈmɛgəˌlɪθ/ *n.* [C] **1** a very large company or business **2** a tall stone put outside in an open place, by people in ancient times —**megalithic** /ˌmɛgəˈlɪθɪk/ *adj.*

meg·a·lo·ma·ni·a /ˌmɛgəlouˈmeɪniə/ *n.* [U] the belief that you are extremely important and powerful, which makes you want to control other people's lives. This is often a type of mental illness.

meg·a·lo·ma·ni·ac /ˌmɛgəlouˈmeɪniˌæk/ *n.* [C] someone who believes they are extremely important or powerful and tries to control other people's lives —**megalomaniac** *adj.*

meg·a·lop·o·lis /ˌmɛgəˈlɑpəlɪs/ *n.* [C] a very large city, or a very large URBAN area that is made up of several cities and towns that are very near each other

meg·a·phone /ˈmɛgəˌfoun/ *n.* [C] a piece of equipment like a large horn, that you talk through to make your voice sound louder when you are speaking to a crowd

meg·a·plex /ˈmɛgəˌplɛks/ *n.* [C] a building with a very large number of movie theaters in it

meg·a·star /ˈmɛgəˌstɑr/ *n.* [C] INFORMAL a very famous singer or actor

meg·a·ton /ˈmɛgəˌtʌn/ *n.* [C] a unit for measuring the power of an explosive, equal to the power of a million TONS of TNT (=a powerful explosive)

mei·o·sis /maɪˈousɪs/ *n.* [U] BIOLOGY the process by which a cell divides to become two cells, in which the new cells have only half the number of CHROMOSOMES as the original cell. The new cells that are formed are called GAMETES in animals and SPORES in plants and can combine with another cell during REPRODUCTIVE activity to make a new plant or animal.: *The chromosomes failed to separate during meiosis.* → see also MITOSIS

Me·ir /mɛˈɪr/, **Gol·da** /ˈgouldə/ (1898–1978) an Israeli politician who was Israel's first female Prime Minister, from 1969 to 1974

Me·kong, the /ˈmeɪkɑŋ, -kɔŋ/ a river in southeast Asia that flows from Tibet through Cambodia and Laos to Vietnam

mel·a·mine /ˈmɛləˌmin/ *n.* [U] a material like plastic used to make hard smooth surfaces on tables and shelves

mel·an·cho·li·a /ˌmɛlənˈkouliə/ *n.* [U] OLD-FASHIONED a feeling of great sadness and lack of energy, often caused by mental illness SYN **depression**

mel·an·chol·ic /ˌmɛlənˈkɑlɪk◂/ *adj.* FORMAL suffering from melancholia, or expressing great sadness and lack of hope

mel·an·chol·y[1] /ˈmɛlənˌkɑli/ *adj.* sad or making you feel sad: *a melancholy man* | *the melancholy tone of the poem*

melancholy[2] *n.* [U] FORMAL a feeling of sadness

me·lange /meɪˈlɑnʒ/ *n.* [singular] a mixture of different things: +**of** *a melange of different cultures*

mel·a·nin /ˈmɛlənɪn/ *n.* [U] BIOLOGY a natural dark brown color in skin, hair, and eyes

mel·a·no·ma /ˌmɛləˈnoumə/ *n.* [C] MEDICINE a TUMOR on the skin which causes CANCER

mel·a·to·nin /ˌmɛləˈtounɪn/ *n.* [U] BIOLOGY a HORMONE that is sometimes used as a drug to help you sleep, especially because of JET LAG

Mel·ba toast /ˈmɛlbə ˌtoust/ *n.* [U] a type of thin hard TOAST that breaks easily into small pieces [**Origin:** 1900–2000 Nellie *Melba* (1861–1931), Australian singer; because she was given it when she was ill]

Mel·bourne /ˈmɛlbɚn/ the capital city of the state of Victoria in Australia

me·lée /ˈmeɪleɪ, meɪˈleɪ/ *n.* [usually singular] a situation in which people rush around in a confused way, and often fight SYN **fracas**: *No one was hurt in the melée.*

mel·lif·lu·ous /məˈlɪfluəs/ *adj.* FORMAL having a pleasant smooth musical sound: *a mellifluous voice* —**mellifluously** *adv.*

Mel·lon /ˈmɛlən/, **An·drew** /ˈændru/ (1855–1937) a U.S. FINANCIER who was Secretary of the Treasury for 11 years and gave the National Gallery of Art in Washington, D.C. to the nation

mel·low[1] /ˈmɛlou/ *adj.* **1** gentle, calm, and sympathetic because of age or experience: *She seems a little more mellow now that she's gotten married.* ▶see THESAURUS box at **calm**[1] **2** friendly and relaxed, or feeling friendly and relaxed: *He's a totally mellow guy.* | *After a few drinks, everyone was pretty mellow.* **3** a mellow sound is pleasant and smooth: *the mellow sound of a trombone* **4** a mellow color or light looks soft, warm, and not too bright: *the mellow golden light of autumn sunsets* **5** a food or drink that is mellow has a smooth taste that is not too strong: *a rich mellow blend of coffee* —**mellowness** *n.* [U]

mellow[2] *v.* [I,T] **1** to become gentle, wise, and not criticize other people as much, because of your age or experience: *Parenthood had mellowed him.* | **mellow with age/time etc.** *My father has mellowed* ***over the years.*** **2** [I,T] also **mellow (sb) out** to become friendly, relaxed, and calm, or make someone feel this way: *Stop yelling! You need to mellow out.* **3** if colors mellow or are mellowed, they begin to look warm and soft **4** if a food or drink mellows, or if it is mellowed, it gets a smoother taste that is not as strong

me·lod·ic /məˈlɑdɪk/ *adj.* **1** ENG. LANG. ARTS relating to the main tune in a piece of music: *the melodic structure of Beethoven's symphonies* **2** having a pleasant tune or a pleasant sound like music: *a sweet melodic voice*

me·lo·di·ous /məˈloudiəs/ *adj.* FORMAL having a pleasant tune or a pleasant sound like music SYN **tuneful**: *melodious temple bells* —**melodiously** *adv.* —**melodiousness** *n.* [U]

mel·o·dra·ma /ˈmɛləˌdrɑmə/ *n.* [C,U] **1** a story or play in which many sudden exciting events happen, the characters are very good or very bad, and the emotions are too strong or simple to seem real, or this style of writing **2** a situation in which people become more angry or upset than is really necessary: *Why does she have to turn everything into a melodrama?*

mel·o·dra·mat·ic /ˌmɛlədrəˈmæt̬ɪk/ *adj.* **1** having or showing emotions that are very strong or not appropriate for the situation: *a melodramatic musical score* | *It sounds melodramatic, but I felt like someone was watching me.* **2** relating to melodrama —**melodramatically** /-kli/ *adv.*

mel·o·dy /ˈmɛlədi/ *n. plural* **melodies** ENG. LANG. ARTS **1** [C,U] a song or tune: *a sad haunting melody* ▶see THESAURUS box at **music** **2** [C] the main tune in a complicated piece of music **3** [U] the arrangement of musical notes in a way that is pleasant to listen to [**Origin:** 1100–1200 Old French *melodie*, from Late Latin, from Greek *meloidia* **music**]

mel·on /ˈmɛlən/ *n.* [C,U] BIOLOGY one of several types of large round fruits with hard skins and sweet juicy flesh [**Origin:** 1300–1400 French, Late Latin *melo*, from Latin *melopepo*, from Greek, from *melon* **apple** + *pepo* **gourd**] → see picture at FRUIT[1]

melt[1] /mɛlt/ S2 *v.* [I,T] **1** if something solid melts or if heat melts it, it becomes liquid: *The snow was beginning to melt.* | *Melt the butter in a frying pan.* ▶see THESAURUS box at **cooking**[1] → see also FREEZE **2** to feel or to make someone feel more love, sympathy etc. than before: *I just melt whenever I see him.* | *Just seeing those little kids smile would* ***melt your heart*** (=make you suddenly feel very sympathetic). **3** **melt in your mouth** if food melts in your mouth, it is soft and tastes good [**Origin:** Old English *meltan*]

M

melt away *phr. v.* **1 melt sth ↔ away** to disappear gradually, or to make something do this: *Exercise will help those pounds melt away.* **2** if a crowd of people melts away, the people gradually leave

melt sth ↔ **down** *phr. v.* to heat a metal object until it becomes a liquid, especially so that you can use the metal again: *The metal from the weapons will be melted down.*

melt (sth) **into** sth *phr. v.* **1** to gradually become a part of something or change into something else, so that there is no difference any more: *Some ethnic groups quickly melted into the general American population.* **2** to gradually become hidden by something: *Sam melted into the woods.*

melt² *n.* [C] **1** a type of SANDWICH that has melted cheese on it: **patty/tuna/veggie melt** *a turkey melt and French fries* **2** the water that flows out of an area as snow melts, or the time when this happens

melt·down /ˈmɛltdaʊn/ *n.* [C,U] **1** PHYSICS a very dangerous situation in which the material in a NUCLEAR REACTOR melts and burns through its container, allowing RADIOACTIVITY to escape **2** a situation in which an important system, process, way of living etc. fails completely: *a global financial meltdown*

ˈmelting point *n.* [C,U] CHEMISTRY the temperature at which a solid substance becomes a liquid

ˈmelting pot *n.* [C usually singular] **1** a place where people from different races, countries, or social classes come to live together: *the American melting pot* **2** a situation or place in which many different ideas, styles etc. exist: *Paris remains a melting pot for fashion.*

Mel·ville /ˈmɛlvɪl/, **Her·man** /ˈhɚmən/ (1819–1891) a U.S. writer famous for his book "Moby Dick", one of the most famous American NOVELS

mem·ber /ˈmɛmbɚ/ S1 W1 *n.* [C] **1** someone who has joined a particular club, group, or organization: *The club is hoping to attract new members.* | +**of** *members of the church* | *You have to be 18 to* ***become a member***. | **club/party/committee etc. members** *Two gang members were arrested.* | **member states/countries/organizations etc.** (=the states etc. that have joined a particular group) **2** one of a particular group of people or things: +**of** *Dogs and wolves are both members of the same species.* | *A* ***staff member*** (=worker at a particular company) *will return your call as soon as possible.* | *Only* ***family members*** *are allowed to visit.* **3** TECHNICAL or HUMOROUS the male sex organ SYN **penis** **4** BIOLOGY a part of the body, especially an arm or leg [**Origin:** 1300–1400 Old French *membre*, from Latin *membrum*]

ˈmember ˌbank *n.* [C] ECONOMICS a bank that is a member of the FEDERAL RESERVE SYSTEM

ˌMember of ˈParliament *n.* [C] an MP

mem·ber·ship /ˈmɛmbɚˌʃɪp/ S2 *n.* **1** [U] the state of being a member of a club, group, organization, or system, and receiving the advantages of belonging to that group: *To qualify for membership, you must be 55 or older.* | +**in** *Membership in the club is free to all local residents.* | *Present your* ***membership card*** *at the door.* | *The annual* ***membership fee*** (=money you must pay to be a member) *is $55.* **2** [C usually singular] all the members of a club, group, or organization: +**of** *The entire membership of the club voted to accept the changes.* **3** [singular, U] the number of people who belong to a club, group, or organization: *Membership has dropped by 500,000.*

mem·brane /ˈmɛmbreɪn/ *n.* [C,U] **1** BIOLOGY a very thin piece of skin that covers or connects parts of the body or of a plant cell: *the outer membrane of the cell* **2** a very thin piece of material that covers or connects something [**Origin:** 1400–1500 Latin *membrana* **skin**, from *membrum*] —**membranous** /ˈmɛmbrənəs/ *adj.*

me·men·to /məˈmɛntoʊ/ *n. plural* **mementos** [C] a small thing that you keep to remind you of someone or something: +**of** *I kept the bottle as a memento of my time in Spain.*

mem·o /ˈmɛmoʊ/ *n. plural* **memos** [C] a short official note to another person in the same company or organization: +**from/to** *a memo from the CEO to all department heads* | *I* ***sent*** *him a* ***memo*** *telling him about the meeting.*

mem·oir /ˈmɛmwɑr/ *n.* **1 sb's memoirs** [plural] a book written by a famous person about their life and experiences: *He is planning to write his memoirs next year.* **2** [C] FORMAL a short piece of writing about someone or something that you know well

mem·o·ra·bil·i·a /ˌmɛmərəˈbɪliə, -ˈbil-/ *n.* [plural] things that you keep or collect because they relate to a famous person, event, or time: *Civil War memorabilia*

mem·ora·ble /ˈmɛmrəbəl/ *adj.* very good, enjoyable, or unusual, and worth remembering: *We want to make this a truly memorable day for the kids.* —**memorably** *adv.*

mem·o·ran·dum /ˌmɛməˈrændəm/ *n. plural* **memoranda** /-də/ or **memorandums** [C] **1** FORMAL a MEMO **2** LAW a short legal document recording the conditions of an agreement

me·mo·ri·al¹ /məˈmɔriəl/ *adj.* [only before noun] made, happening, or done in order to remind people of someone who has died: *Jackson Memorial Hospital* | *A* ***memorial service*** *will be held at the Presbyterian Church.* | **a memorial prize/scholarship/fund etc.** *the Nobel Memorial Prize in Economic Science*

memorial² *n.* [C] something, especially something made of stone with writing on it, to remind people of someone who has died: *the Lincoln Memorial in Washington, D.C.* | +**to** *a memorial to black Americans who fought in the Civil War* → see also WAR MEMORIAL

Meˈmorial ˌDay *n.* [U] a U.S. national holiday on the last Monday in May, to remember soldiers killed in wars

me·mo·ri·a·lize /məˈmɔriəˌlaɪz/ *v.* [T] to do something in order to remind people of someone who has died: *The sculpture memorializes the fall of the Berlin Wall.*

mem·o·rize /ˈmɛməˌraɪz/ *v.* [T] to learn and remember words, music, or other information in detail: *Have you memorized your speech?* —**memorization** /ˌmɛmərəˈzeɪʃən/ *n.* [U]

mem·o·ry /ˈmɛmri, -məri/ S2 W2 *n. plural* **memories**

1 ABILITY TO REMEMBER [C,U] the ability to remember things, places, experiences etc.: *My memory's not as good as it once was.* | *memory loss* | **have a good/bad/terrible etc. memory (for sth)** *I have a terrible memory for birthdays.* | *The pianist played the whole piece* ***from memory*** (=without using anything written to help). | *The image has remained* ***in my memory*** *ever since.* | **sb's long-term/short-term memory** (=someone's ability to remember things that happened recently or a long time ago)

2 STH YOU REMEMBER [C usually plural] something that you remember from the past about a person, place, or experience: +**of** *memories of her years at college* | **happy/good/bad etc. memories** *He has lots of happy memories of his stay in Japan.* | *Being here* ***brings back*** *bad* ***memories***. | *Doug recalls* ***childhood memories*** *of long summers spent outside.*

3 COMPUTER a) [C] COMPUTERS the part of a computer in which information can be stored: *a memory chip* **b)** [U] the amount of space that can be used for storing information on a computer or DISK: *16 megabytes of memory*

4 in recent memory during the recent past: *It's certainly our best team in recent memory.*

5 in memory of sb also **in sb's memory** for the purpose of remembering someone and reminding other people of them after they have died: *The group lit candles in memory of Laura and her brother.*

6 sb's memory also **the memory of sb** the way you think about someone who has died, who you love, respect, or admire: *a rose garden dedicated* ***to his memory*** | *Her intention was to honor the memory of her mother.*

M

7 sb's memory lives on used to say that people still remember someone after they have died or gone away
8 if memory serves also **if my memory serves me well/right/correctly** used when you are almost sure that you have remembered something correctly: *If memory serves, he joined the company in 1999.*
9 a walk/trip down memory lane an occasion when you spend time remembering the past
[**Origin:** 1200–1300 Old French *memorie*, from Latin *memor* **remembering**] → see also **commit sth to memory** at COMMIT (6), **jog sb's memory** at JOG¹ (2), **in/within living memory** at LIVING¹ (4), **lose your memory/sight/voice etc.** at LOSE (4), **a photographic memory** at PHOTOGRAPHIC (2), **refresh sb's memory/recollection** at REFRESH (2)

ˈmemory bank *n.* [C] the part of a large computer system that stores information

ˈmemory hog *n.* [C] COMPUTERS **1** a computer program that uses a lot of MEMORY **2** someone who uses computer programs that use a lot of the power available on a network, so that other people have trouble using their programs on the same network —**memory-hogging** *adj.* [only before noun]

Mem·phis /ˈmɛmfɪs/ the largest city in the U.S. state of Tennessee

men /mɛn/ *n.* the plural of MAN

men·ace¹ /ˈmɛnɪs/ *n.* **1** [C] something or someone that is dangerous: *Drivers like that are a menace.* | +**of** *the menace of illegal drugs* | +**to** *a menace to society* **2** [C] a person, especially a child, that is annoying or causes trouble **3** [U] a threatening quality or manner: *His eyes blazed with menace.* [**Origin:** 1300–1400 French, Latin *minacia*, from *minari* **to threaten**]

menace² *v.* [T] FORMAL to threaten someone or something

men·ac·ing /ˈmɛnɪsɪŋ/ *adj.* making you expect something bad SYN **threatening**: *a dark menacing sky* —**menacingly** *adv.*

mé·nage /meɪˈnɑʒ/ *n.* [C] FORMAL or HUMOROUS all the people who live in a particular house SYN **household**

ménage à trois /meɪˌnɑʒ ɑ ˈtrwɑ/ *n.* [singular] a sexual relationship involving three people who live together

me·nag·er·ie /məˈnædʒəri, -ʒə-/ *n.* [C] **1** BIOLOGY a collection of wild animals kept privately or for the public to see **2** a group of people or characters that seems strange because they are all very different

Men·ci·us /ˈmɛnʃiəs, -ʃəs/ also **Meng·zi** /ˈmʌŋzi/ (?371–?289 B.C.) a Chinese PHILOSOPHER

Menck·en /ˈmɛŋkɪn/, **H.L.** (1880–1956) a U.S. JOURNALIST famous for his criticism of the American MIDDLE CLASS

mend¹ /mɛnd/ *v.*
1 REPAIR [T] to repair a hole or tear, especially in a piece of clothing: *I need to get my sleeve mended.* ►see THESAURUS box at **repair¹**
2 MAKE/BECOME HEALTHY [I,T] to make a broken bone become whole and healthy again, or to become better after a bone injury: *Leg fractures can take months to mend.*
3 mend your ways to improve the way you behave after behaving badly for a long time: *If he doesn't mend his ways, he'll be asked to leave.*
4 mend (your) fences to talk to someone you have offended or argued with, and try to persuade them to be friendly with you again
5 mend relations/ties/differences etc. if two people or groups mend their relations, ties etc., they start to be friendly with each other again: *Whether they can mend their relationship is still uncertain.*
6 END A PROBLEM [T] to end a problem by dealing with its causes: *Mending this problem will take more than money.*
[**Origin:** 1100–1200 *amend*]

mend² *n.* [C] **be on the mend** to be getting better after an illness or after a difficult period: *He had the flu, but he's on the mend now.* | *There are signs that the economy is on the mend.*

men·da·cious /mɛnˈdeɪʃəs/ *adj.* FORMAL not truthful: *a secretive and mendacious government* —**mendaciously** *adv.*

men·dac·i·ty /mɛnˈdæsət̬i/ *n.* [U] FORMAL the quality of being false or not truthful

Men·del /ˈmɛndl/, **Greg·or Jo·hann** /ˈgrɛgər ˈyoʊhɑn/ (1822–1884) an Austrian MONK whose studies of plants later provided some of the basic ideas of the new science of GENETICS

Men·de·ley·ev /ˌmɛndəˈleɪəf/, **Dmi·tri** /dəˈmitri/ (1834–1907) a Russian scientist who discovered the rules about the structure of ELEMENTS that made possible the PERIODIC TABLE

Men·dels·sohn /ˈmɛndlsən/, **Fe·lix** /ˈfilɪks/ (1809–1847) a German musician who wrote CLASSICAL music

men·di·cant /ˈmɛndɪkənt/ *n.* [C] FORMAL someone who asks people for money in order to live, usually for religious reasons —**mendicant** *adj.*: *mendicant monks*

mend·ing /ˈmɛndɪŋ/ *n.* [U] clothes that need to be mended

men·folk /ˈmɛnfoʊk/ *n.* [plural] OLD-FASHIONED a word for men, especially the male relatives of a family

me·ni·al¹ /ˈminiəl, -nyəl/ *adj.* menial work is boring and needs no skill, and is usually done using your hands rather than your mind: *a menial job* [**Origin:** 1300–1400 Anglo-French *meiniee* **household**, from Latin *mansio*] —**menially** *adv.*

menial² *n.* [C] OLD-FASHIONED a servant who works in a house

me·nin·ges /məˈnɪndʒiz/ *n.* [plural] BIOLOGY MEMBRANES (=substance like very thin skin) that completely cover and protect the brain and the SPINAL CORD

men·in·gi·tis /ˌmɛnənˈdʒaɪt̬ɪs/ *n.* [U] MEDICINE a serious illness in which the outer part of the brain becomes swollen

Men·non·ites /ˈmɛnəˌnaɪts/ a Protestant religious group that refuses to join the armed forces or to hold official public positions, and does not BAPTIZE its children —**Mennonite** *adj.*

Men·no Si·mons /ˌmɛnoʊ ˈsimoʊnz, ˈsaɪ-/ (1496–1561) a Dutch religious leader who started the Mennonite religious group of Protestants

Me·nom·i·nee /məˈnɑməˌni/ a Native American tribe from the northeastern central area of the U.S.

men·o·pause /ˈmɛnəˌpɔz/ *n.* [U] BIOLOGY the time when a woman stops menstruating (MENSTRUATE), which usually happens around age 50 —**menopausal** /ˌmɛnəˈpɔzəl/ *adj.*

me·no·rah /məˈnɔrə/ *n.* [C] a special CANDLESTICK that holds seven CANDLES, used in Jewish ceremonies

MENSA /ˈmɛnsə/ an international organization for people who are very intelligent

mensch /mɛnʃ/ *n.* [C] SPOKEN someone that you like and admire, especially because they have done something good for you: *You've been a real mensch.* [**Origin:** 1900–2000 Yiddish *mensh*, from German *Mensch* **human**]

men·ses /ˈmɛnsiz/ *n.* [plural] BIOLOGY the blood that flows out of a woman's body each month

ˈmen's room *n.* [C] a room in a public place with toilets for men

men·stru·al /ˈmɛnstruəl, -strəl/ *adj.* BIOLOGY relating to the time each month when a woman MENSTRUATES: *the menstrual cycle*

ˌmenstrual ˈcycle *n.* [C] BIOLOGY the regular monthly cycle in the bodies of women and some female animals, during which an egg is sent out from an OVARY, material builds up in the UTERUS (=organ where a baby develops) to make it ready to receive a FERTILIZED egg, and if the egg is not fertilized, the material from the uterus flows from the female's body

ˌmenstrual 'period *n.* [C] BIOLOGY the time each month when a woman menstruates SYN **period**

men·stru·ate /ˈmɛnstruˌeɪt, -streɪt/ *v.* [I] BIOLOGY when a woman menstruates, blood flows from her body during her monthly menstrual period [**Origin:** 1800–1900 Late Latin, past participle of *menstruari*, from Latin *menstruus* **monthly**] —**menstruation** /ˌmɛnstruˈeɪʃən, mɛnˈstreɪ-/ *n.* [C,U]

mens·wear /ˈmɛnzwɛr/ *n.* [U] a word meaning "clothing for men," used especially in stores: *the menswear department*

-ment /mənt/ *suffix* [in nouns] used to form nouns that show actions, the people who do them, and their results: *entertainment* (=activity of entertaining people) | *management* (=people who manage a company) | *an arrangement* (=result of arranging something) —**-mental** /məntl/ *suffix* [in adjectives] *governmental*

men·tal /ˈmɛntl/ Ac S3 W2 *adj.* **1** affecting the mind or happening in the mind: *a child's mental development* | *What was his **mental state** at the time?* | **a mental picture/image** (=a picture that you form in your mind) **2** [only before noun] relating to illnesses of the mind, or to treating illnesses of the mind: *mental health* | *a mental breakdown* | *Violent **mental patients** are kept in a separate ward.* | **mental illness/disorder/problem** *His wife has a history of mental illness.* → see also MENTAL HOSPITAL **3 make a mental note** to make a special effort to remember something: *She made a mental note to call Marcia when she got home.* **4** INFORMAL crazy: *That guy's mental!* [**Origin:** 1400–1500 French, Late Latin *mentalis*, from Latin *mens* **mind**] —**mentally** *adv.*: *mentally ill*

ˌmental 'age *n.* [C] a measure of someone's ability to think, obtained by comparing their ability with the average ability of children at various ages: *She was 12, but she had a mental age of two.*

ˌmental a'rithmetic *n.* [U] the act of adding numbers together, multiplying them etc. in your mind, without writing them down

ˌmental 'block *n.* [C] a difficulty in remembering something or in understanding something: *I have a complete mental block when it comes to computers.*

'mental ˌhospital also **'mental instiˌtution** *n.* [C] a hospital where people with mental illnesses are treated SYN **psychiatric hospital**

men·tal·i·ty /mɛnˈtæləti/ Ac *n. plural* **mentalities** [C] a particular type of attitude or way of thinking, often one that you think is wrong or stupid: *the get-rich-quick mentality*

ˌmentally 'handicapped *adj.* a mentally handicapped person has a problem with their brain, often from the time they are born, that affects their ability to think or control their body movements —**the mentally handicapped** *n.* [plural]

men·thol /ˈmɛnθɔl, -θɑl/ *n.* [U] a substance that has a strong MINT smell and taste, used in cough medicines and cigarettes to give them a special taste

men·tho·lat·ed /ˈmɛnθəˌleɪtɪd/ *adj.* containing menthol

men·tion[1] /ˈmɛnʃən/ S1 W2 *v.* [T] **1** to talk about something or someone in a conversation, piece of writing etc., especially without saying very much or giving details: *They didn't mention anything about money.* | *As I mentioned earlier, there have been a lot of changes.* | **mention sth to sb** *Don't mention this to Larry, but I'm thinking of quitting my job.* | **mention (that)** *Sue mentioned that you might be moving to Florida.* | ***It's worth mentioning that*** (=this is a useful or important piece of information) *only 20% of all applicants are accepted each year.* | ***Now you mention it***, *I haven't seen her lately.* | **fail/neglect to mention sth** *She neglected to mention that she was bringing a guest.* | **mentioned above/below** (=mentioned earlier in a piece of writing) | *The statistics are from **the above-mentioned** report.*

THESAURUS

refer to sth to mention or speak about someone or something: *Palmer was referring to an article in "the Times."*
raise to begin to talk or write about something that you want someone to consider: *You need to raise the issue with him directly.*
allude to sth to mention something in a way that is not direct: *Many stories and poems allude to this myth.*
bring sth up to start to talk about a particular subject or person: *She got really mad, and I was sorry I'd ever brought the subject up.*
touch on sth to say a small amount about something: *This problem has already been touched on in Chapter 4.*
cite to mention something as an example or proof of something else: *Collins cited the document as evidence that something had gone wrong.*
▸see THESAURUS box at **say**[1]

2 not to mention used to introduce an additional thing that makes a situation even more difficult, surprising, interesting etc.: *I do all the housework, not to mention the gardening.* **3 don't mention it** SPOKEN used to say politely that there is no need for someone to thank you for helping them: *"Thanks for the ride home!" "Don't mention it."* → see also **mention/say/note sth in passing** at PASSING[2] (1)

mention[2] *n.* [C usually singular, U] the act of mentioning something or someone in a conversation, piece of writing etc.: *He **made no mention of** his wife's illness.* | ***There was no mention of** this fact in the report.* | *Joe gets anxious **at the mention of*** (=when people talk about) *flying.* | *I didn't even **get a mention*** (=I was not mentioned) *in the list of contributors.* [**Origin:** 1300–1400 Old French, Latin *mentio*, from *mens* **mind**] → see also HONORABLE MENTION

men·tor /ˈmɛntɔr, -tɚ/ *n.* [C] an experienced person who advises, encourages, and helps a less experienced person [**Origin:** 1700–1800 *Mentor*, adviser of Odysseus's son Telemachus in the ancient Greek "Odyssey" by Homer]

mentoring /ˈmɛntərɪŋ/ *n.* [U] a system of using people with a lot of experience, knowledge etc. to advise other people and give them encouragement to succeed at school or work: *mentoring programs for students at community colleges*

men·u /ˈmɛnyu/ S2 *n.* [C] **1** a list of all the types of food that are available for a meal, especially in a restaurant: *Could we have the menu, please?* | *There are several pasta dishes **on the menu**.* ▸see THESAURUS box at **restaurant** **2** COMPUTERS a list of things that you can choose from or ask a computer to do, that is shown on the computer screen: *Go back to the main menu.* | **a pull-down/drop-down menu** (=a list of choices which appears when you click on a place on the screen) ▸see THESAURUS box at **computer** [**Origin:** 1800–1900 French *menu* **small, full of details**, from Latin *minutus*, from *minuere* **to make smaller**]

me·ow /miˈaʊ/ *n.* [C] the crying sound that a cat makes —**meow** *v.* [I]

Meph·i·stoph·e·les /ˌmɛfɪˈstɑfəliz/ another name for the DEVIL, especially in the story of Faust —**Mephistophelean** /ˌmɛfɪstəˈfiliən, ˌmɛfɪˌstɑfəˈliən/ *adj.*

mer·can·tile /ˈmɚkənˌtil, -ˌtaɪl/ *adj.* [only before noun] FORMAL relating to trade SYN **commercial**: *mercantile law*

mer·can·til·ism /ˈmɚkəntilˌɪzəm/ *n.* [U] ECONOMICS the idea, held especially in 17th- and 18th-century Europe, that trade produces wealth, so EXPORTS should be encouraged and IMPORTS should be restricted

mer·ce·nar·y[1] /ˈmɚsəˌnɛri/ *n. plural* **mercenaries** [C] a soldier who fights for any country or group that pays him or her: *an army of foreign mercenaries*

M

mercenary² *adj.* DISAPPROVING only interested in money, and not caring about whether your actions are right or wrong or about the effect of your actions on other people: *a mercenary attitude*

mer·cer·ized /ˈmɚsəˌraɪzd/ *adj.* mercerized thread or cotton has been treated with chemicals to make it shiny and strong

mer·chan·dise¹ /ˈmɚtʃənˌdaɪz, -ˌdaɪs/ *n.* [U] goods that are produced in order to be sold, especially goods that are shown in a store for people to buy: *Customers are not allowed to handle the merchandise.*

merchandise² *v.* [T] to try to sell goods or services using methods such as advertising: *If the product is properly merchandised, it should sell very well.*

ˈmerchandise ˌmix *n.* [C] TECHNICAL the number and type of different products sold by a particular store

mer·chan·dis·ing /ˈmɚtʃənˌdaɪzɪŋ/ *n.* [U] **1** the business of trying to sell products or services by using methods such as advertising **2** toys, clothes, and other products that are sold which relate to a popular movie, sports team, singer etc.: *"Star Wars" merchandising*

mer·chant /ˈmɚtʃənt/ *n.* [C] a person or store that buys and sells goods in large quantities: *Local merchants are stocking up for Christmas.* | **a wine/diamond/coffee etc. merchant** *a family of Belgian diamond merchants*

ˌmerchant ˈbank *n.* [C] ECONOMICS a bank that provides banking services for business

ˌmerchant maˈrine *n.* **the merchant marine** all of a country's ships that are used for trade, not war, and the people who work on these ships

ˌmerchant ˈseaman *n.* [C] a sailor in the merchant marine

mer·ci·ful /ˈmɚsɪfəl/ *adj.* **1** being kind to people and forgiving them rather than punishing them or being cruel: +**to** *The prisoners begged their captors to be merciful to them.* **2 a merciful death/end/release** something that seems fortunate because it ends someone's suffering or difficulty: *With the Giants leading 28–7, half-time came as a merciful relief.*

mer·ci·ful·ly /ˈmɚsɪfəli/ *adv.* fortunately or luckily, because a situation could have been much worse: *Mercifully, the screaming ended.*

mer·ci·less /ˈmɚsɪlɪs/ *adj.* cruel and showing no kindness or forgiveness: *a merciless killer* —**mercilessly** *adv.* —**mercilessness** *n.* [U]

mer·cu·ri·al /mɚˈkyʊriəl/ *adj.* **1** LITERARY changing mood suddenly: *the actress's infamous mercurial nature* **2** LITERARY quick and lively: *her mercurial wit* **3** containing mercury

Mer·cu·ry /ˈmɚkyəri/ the Roman name for the god HERMES

mer·cu·ry /ˈmɚkyəri/ *n.* **1 Mercury** PHYSICS the PLANET that is nearest the sun → see picture at SOLAR SYSTEM **2** [U] SYMBOL **Hg** CHEMISTRY a heavy silver-white metal that is an ELEMENT, is liquid at ordinary temperatures, and is used in THERMOMETERS **3 the mercury** the temperature outside: *The mercury dropped to 24° Thursday.*

mer·cy¹ /ˈmɚsi/ *n.* **1** [U] kindness, pity, and a willingness to forgive, which you show toward someone that you have power over: *The terrorists* ***showed no mercy*** *to the hostages.* | **beg/plead for mercy** *At his trial he begged for mercy.* | *May God* ***have mercy on*** *their souls.* **2 at the mercy of sb/sth** unable to do anything to protect yourself from someone or something: *We were lost, and at the mercy of the weather.* **3 leave sb to sb's (tender) mercies** OFTEN HUMOROUS to let someone be dealt with by another person, who may treat them very badly or strictly **4 a mercy flight/mission etc.** a trip taken to bring help to people: *a mercy mission to help the refugees* **5 throw yourself on the mercy of sb** to BEG someone to help you or not to punish you [**Origin:** 1100–1200 Old French *merci*, from Latin *merces* **price paid, payment for work**]

mercy² also **ˌmercy ˈme** *interjection* OLD-FASHIONED used to show strong emotions, especially when you are shocked, surprised, or frightened

ˈmercy ˌkilling *n.* [C,U] INFORMAL the act of killing someone who is very sick or old so that they do not have to suffer anymore SYN **euthanasia**

mere¹ /mɪr/ W3 *adj.* [only before noun, no comparative] **1** used to emphasize how small or unimportant someone or something is: *She lost the election by a mere 20 votes.* **2 the mere/merest** used when something small or unimportant has a big effect: *The mere thought of food made her feel sick.* [**Origin:** 1300–1400 Latin *merus* **pure, unmixed**]

mere² *n.* [C] LITERARY a lake

mere·ly /ˈmɪrli/ W2 *adv.* FORMAL used to emphasize that an action, person, or thing is very small, simple, or unimportant, especially when compared to what it could be SYN **only** SYN **just**: *He was merely a boy when it happened.* | *Instead of getting angry, she merely smiled.*

me·ren·gue /məˈrɛŋgeɪ/ *n.* [C,U] a type of fast dance from Haiti and the Dominican Republic, or the music played for this dance

mer·e·tri·cious /ˌmɛrəˈtrɪʃəs◂/ *adj.* FORMAL seeming attractive, interesting, or believable, but having no real value or not based on the truth: *a meretricious argument* —**meretriciously** *adv.* —**meretriciousness** *n.* [U]

merge /mɚdʒ/ *v.* **1** [I,T] to combine or join together to form one thing, or to make two or more things do this: *Some of the district's high schools will be merged to cut costs.* | **merge (sth) with sth** *The company merged with a German firm.* | **merge sth into sth** *The government wants to merge all three departments into one.* **2** [I] if two things merge, you can no longer clearly see them, hear them etc. as separate things: +**with** *Memories seemed to merge with reality.* | +**into** *She avoided reporters by merging into the crowd.* **3** [I] if traffic merges, the cars from two roads come together onto the same road: *Expect delays where freeway traffic merges.* [**Origin:** 1600–1700 Latin *mergere* **to dive**]

merg·er /ˈmɚdʒɚ/ W3 *n.* [C] the act of joining together two or more companies or organizations to form one larger one: +**between** *the merger between AOL and Time-Warner* | +**with** *the company's planned merger with a French firm*

me·rid·i·an /məˈrɪdiən/ *n.* **1** [C] an imaginary line drawn from the North Pole to the South Pole over the surface of the Earth, used to show the position of places on a map **2 the meridian** TECHNICAL the highest point reached by the sun or another star, when seen from a point on the Earth's surface

me·ringue /məˈræŋ/ *n.* [C,U] a light sweet food made by baking a mixture of sugar and the white part of eggs: *lemon meringue pie*

me·ri·no /məˈrinoʊ/ *n.* **1** [C] a type of sheep with long wool, or cloth made from this wool **2** [U] wool from this type of sheep, or cloth made from this wool

mer·i·stem /ˈmerɪˌstɛm/ *n.* [C] BIOLOGY groups of cells that divide to produce new growth at either the end of a plant stem or at the root

mer·it¹ /ˈmɛrɪt/ *n.* **1** [C usually plural] one of the good features of something such as a plan or system OPP **demerit**: *Each of these approaches has its merits.* | +**of** *The committee will discuss the merits of the plan.* **2** [U] FORMAL a good quality that makes something deserve praise or admiration: *a merit scholarship* | **artistic/literary merit** *The film lacks any kind of artistic merit.* | **of outstanding/considerable/some etc. merit** *She is a writer of considerable merit.* | *Promotions are based entirely* ***on merit.*** **3 judge/decide/accept sth on its (own) merits** to judge something only by how good it is, without considering anything else: *Each application will be judged solely on its own merits.* [**Origin:** 1100–1200 Old French *merite*, from Latin *meritum*, from *merere* **to deserve, earn**]

merit² *v.* [T not in progressive] FORMAL to deserve something SYN **deserve**: *The story didn't merit all the attention it received in the press.*

mer·i·toc·ra·cy /ˌmɛrəˈtɑkrəsi/ *n. plural* **meritocracies** POLITICS **1** [C] a social system that gives the greatest power and highest social positions to people with the most ability **2 the meritocracy** [singular] the people who have power in this type of system

mer·i·to·ri·ous /ˌmɛrəˈtɔriəs/ *adj.* FORMAL very good and deserving praise —**meritoriously** *adv.*

Mer·lin /ˈmɚlɪn/ in old stories, a MAGICIAN who helped King Arthur

mer·lot /mɚˈloʊ/ *n.* [U] a type of red wine

mer·maid /ˈmɚmeɪd/ *n.* [C] in stories, a woman who has a fish's tail instead of legs

mer·man /ˈmɚmæn, -mən/ *n.* [C] in stories, a man who has a fish's tail instead of legs

mer·ri·ment /ˈmɛrɪmənt/ *n.* [U] FORMAL laughter, fun, and enjoyment: *Sounds of merriment were coming from the bar.*

mer·ry /ˈmɛri/ *adj. comparative* **merrier**, *superlative* **merriest** **1 Merry Christmas!** used to say that you hope someone will have a happy time at CHRISTMAS **2** OLD-FASHIONED cheerful and happy: *She smiled, her eyes bright and merry.* **3 the more the merrier** SPOKEN used to tell someone that you will be happy if they join you in something you are doing: *"Do you mind if I bring Tony?" "Nah, the more the merrier."* **4 make merry** LITERARY to enjoy yourself by drinking, singing etc. **5** OLD USE pleasant: *the merry month of June* —**merrily** *adv.* —**merriness** *n.* [U]

merry-go-round

ˈmerry-go-ˌround *n.* **1** [C] a machine that children ride on for fun, which turns around and around and has seats in the shape of animals **2** [singular] a series of related events that happen very quickly one after another: *the endless Washington merry-go-round of parties and socializing*

ˈmerry-ˌmaking *n.* [U] LITERARY fun and enjoyment, especially drinking, dancing, and singing

me·sa /ˈmeɪsə/ *n.* [C] a hill with a flat top and steep sides, in the southwestern U.S.

mes·cal /mɛsˈkæl/ *n.* [U] an alcoholic drink made from a type of CACTUS

mes·ca·line /ˈmɛskəlin/ *n.* [U] an illegal drug made from a CACTUS plant that makes people imagine that they can see things that do not really exist

mesh¹ /mɛʃ/ *n.* [C,U] **1** a piece of material made of threads or wires that have been woven together like a net: *wire-mesh screens* **2** a combination of people, ideas, or things: +**of** *a mesh of intrigue and corruption*

mesh² *v.* **1** [I] if two ideas or qualities mesh, they go well together and are appropriate for each other: +**with** *His own ideas did not mesh with the views of the party.* **2** [T] if someone meshes two different ideas, qualities, or other parts of something, they use them together: **mesh sth with sth** *The band meshes Celtic folk music with punk rock.* **3** [I] if people or organizations mesh, they get along well with each other and can work well or have a good relationship: *After a few weeks together, the team was starting to mesh.* **4** [I] if two parts of an engine or machine mesh, they fit or connect correctly

mes·mer·ize /ˈmɛzməˌraɪz/ *v.* [T often passive] to make someone feel that they cannot stop watching or listening to something or someone, because they are so interested in it or attracted by it: *He was mesmerized by her beauty.* [**Origin:** 1800–1900 Franz *Mesmer* (1734–1815), Austrian doctor who developed hypnotism] —**mesmerizing** *adj.*

mes·o·derm /ˈmɛzəˌdɚm/ *n.* [singular, U] BIOLOGY the middle layer of cells of an EMBRYO from which structures like bone and muscle develop → see also ECTODERM

mes·o·phyll /ˈmɛzəˌfɪl/ *n.* [C,U] BIOLOGY a material inside the leaves of green plants. It contains CHLOROPHYLL that reacts with light from the sun during PHOTOSYNTHESIS to produce the food the plant needs.

Mes·o·zo·ic /ˌmɛzəˈzoʊɪk◂ / *n.* **the Mesozoic** EARTH SCIENCE the ERA (=long period of time in the history of the Earth) from about 250 million years ago to about 65 million years ago, when DINOSAURS, birds, and plants with flowers started to exist → see also CENOZOIC —**Mesozoic** *adj.*: *the Mesozoic era*

mes·quite /mɛˈskit/ *n.* [C,U] a tree or bush from the northwest U.S., or the outer covering of this tree, used when cooking food on a BARBECUE to give it a special taste [**Origin:** 1700–1800 Spanish, Nahuatl *mizquitl*]

mess¹ /mɛs/ S2 *n.*
1 DIRTY/DISORGANIZED [singular, U] a place or group of things that looks dirty, or not neatly arranged: *Eric! Get in here and clean up this mess!* | *The house is a total mess.* | *My hair's a mess.* | *I hope the kids aren't* ***making a mess*** *in the living room.*
2 PROBLEMS/DIFFICULTIES [singular] INFORMAL a situation in which there are a lot of problems and difficulties, especially as a result of mistakes or people not being careful: *Dave's life was a mess.* | *The economy is* ***in a*** *terrible* ***mess.*** | *How did we* ***get in this mess?***
3 make a mess of sth INFORMAL to do something badly and make a lot of mistakes: *I guess I've really* ***made a mess of things*** *this time.*
4 be a mess to be in a bad emotional or mental state: *She's a mess when she drinks.*
5 a mess of sth INFORMAL a lot of something: *a mess of fresh fish*
6 ARMY/NAVY [C] a room in which members of the army, navy etc. eat and drink together
7 WASTE MATTER [C] solid waste material from a baby or animal: *If the dog makes a mess, you clean it up!*
[**Origin:** 1200–1300 Old French *mes* **food**, from Late Latin *missus* **course at a meal**]

mess² S1 *v.* [I] **1** to make something look dirty or messy SYN **mess up**: *Don't mess my hair.* **2** [always + adv./prep.] if an animal messes somewhere where it shouldn't, it URINATES or DEFECATES there **3** to have meals in a room where members of the army, navy etc. eat together

mess around *phr. v.* INFORMAL **1** to play or do silly things instead of working or paying attention SYN **fool around**: *Stop messing around and get ready for school.* **2** to have a sexual relationship with someone whom you should not have a sexual relationship with SYN **fool around**: +**with** *Sam's wife was caught messing around with another man.*

mess around with *phr. v.* **1 mess around with sth** to use something or make small changes to it, especially in a way that annoys someone else SYN **mess with**: *Who's been messing around with my computer?* **2 mess around with sb/sth** to get involved with someone or something that may cause problems or be dangerous SYN **mess with**: *Don't mess around with drugs.* **3 mess around with sth** to spend time play-

M

ing with something, repairing it etc.: *Dave likes messing around with old cars.*

mess up *phr. v.* INFORMAL **1 mess sth ↔ up** to spoil or ruin something, especially something important or something that has been carefully planned: *His flight was canceled, which messed everybody's schedule up.* **2 mess sth ↔ up** to make something dirty or messy SYN **mess**: *Stop it! You'll mess up my hair!* **3 mess sth ↔ up** to make a mistake and do something badly SYN **screw up**: *Don't worry if you mess it up the first time – just keep on practicing.* | +**on** *I think I messed up on the last question.* **4 mess sb ↔ up** to make someone have emotional or mental problems SYN **screw up**: *A childhood like that would mess anyone up.* **5 mess sb ↔ up** to badly injure someone, especially by hitting them → see also MESSED UP

mess with *phr. v.* **1 mess with sth** to use something or make small changes to it, especially in a way that annoys someone else SYN **mess around with**: *Don't mess with my stuff.* **2 mess with sb** to deliberately cause trouble for someone: *You mess with me, and I'll rip your head off.* **3 mess with sb/sth** to try to deceive or confuse someone: *He did all sorts of things to **mess with** her **mind**.* **4 mess with sb/sth** to get involved with someone or something that may cause problems or be dangerous SYN **mess around with**: *She started messing with the wrong group of kids at school.*

mes·sage /ˈmɛsɪdʒ/ S1 W1 *n.* [C] **1** a spoken or written piece of information that you send to another person: *Did you get my message?* | +**for/from** *There's an urgent message for you from your mother.* | *Sarah called and **left a message** for you on the answering machine.* | *He's not at his desk. **Can I take a message** for him* (=used on the telephone when offering to give a message to someone)*?* **2** the main or most important idea that someone is trying to tell people: *The campaign **sends a** clear **message** that women do not have to tolerate violence.* **3** a piece of written information that appears on a computer screen to tell the user about something, especially a problem: *an error message* **4 get the message** INFORMAL to understand what someone means or what they want you to do: *Hopefully he'll get the message and leave me alone.* **5 on/off message** if a politician is on or off message, he or she either says only the official party opinion, or says things that are not the official party position [**Origin:** 1200–1300 Old French, Medieval Latin *missaticum*, from Latin *mittere* **to send**]

message[2] *v.* [T] to send a message using electronic equipment, for example EMAIL or a CELL PHONE

mes·sag·ing /ˈmɛsɪdʒɪŋ/ *n.* [U] the system or process of sending messages using electronic equipment: *automated messaging*

ˌmessed ˈup *adj.* **1** INFORMAL very unhappy and having mental problems because of bad experiences: *Steve was pretty messed up in high school.* **2** INFORMAL spoiled or ruined, or not working correctly: *This computer program is all messed up.* **3** INFORMAL messy: *messed up papers* **4** INFORMAL badly injured: *His face was messed up.* **5** SLANG strange, upsetting, and unacceptable: *"Bob's friends did it, but he has to go to jail." "Man, that is messed up."*

mes·sen·ger /ˈmɛsəndʒɚ/ *n.* [C] **1** someone who takes messages to people **2 blame/shoot the messenger** to be angry with someone for telling you about something bad that has happened → see also BIKE MESSENGER

ˌmessenger RNˈA WRITTEN ABBREVIATION **mRNA** *n.* [U] BIOLOGY a form of RNA which copies GENETIC information from DNA and brings that information to RIBOSOMES

ˈmess hall *n.* [C] a large room where soldiers eat

mes·si·ah /məˈsaɪə/ *n.* [singular] **1 the Messiah a)** Jesus Christ, who is believed by Christians to be sent by God to save the world **b)** a great religious leader who, according to Jewish belief, will be sent by God to save the world **2** someone who people believe will save them from great social or economic problems: *The media made him out to be a political messiah.*

mes·si·an·ic /ˌmɛsiˈænɪk◂/ *adj.* FORMAL **1** someone who has messianic beliefs or feelings wants to make very big social or political changes: *environmentalists' messianic zeal* **2** relating to the Messiah

Messrs. /ˈmɛsɚz/ FORMAL the plural of MR.: *Messrs. Jacobs and Bates*

mess·y /ˈmɛsi/ *adj. comparative* **messier**, *superlative* **messiest 1** dirty, not organized, or not neatly arranged OPP **neat**: *Mom yells if my room is messy.* | *Does my hair look messy?* **2** INFORMAL a messy situation is complicated and not nice to deal with: *a messy divorce* **3** making someone or something dirty: *messy jobs around the house* —**messily** *adv.* —**messiness** *n.* [U]

mes·ti·zo /mɛˈstizoʊ/ *n. plural* **mestizos** [C] someone who has one Hispanic parent and one Native American parent

met /mɛt/ *v.* the past tense and past participle of MEET

meta- /mɛt̬ə/ *prefix* TECHNICAL beyond the ordinary or usual: *metaphysical* (=beyond ordinary physical things)

me·tab·o·lism /məˈtæbəˌlɪzəm/ *n.* [C,U] BIOLOGY the physical and chemical processes that take place in an ORGANISM to produce energy from food: *The drug speeds up your metabolism.* [**Origin:** 1800–1900 Greek *metabole* **change**] —**metabolic** /ˌmɛt̬əˈbɑlɪk/ *adj.*

me·tab·ol·ize /məˈtæbəˌlaɪz/ *v.* [T] BIOLOGY to change food into energy in the body by chemical activity

met·a·car·pals /ˌmɛt̬əˈkɑrpəlz/ *n.* [plural] BIOLOGY the five bones that stretch from the wrist to the fingers → see picture at SKELETON[1]

met·al /ˈmɛt̬l/ S2 W2 *n.* [C, U] **1** CHEMISTRY a hard, usually shiny substance such as iron, gold, or steel. Metals are usually good at allowing heat or electric current through them: *The frame is made of metal.* | *metal pipes* | *Jewels and **precious metals*** (=expensive metals such as gold and silver) *decorated the tombs.* | *The old trucks were sold as **scrap metal**.* **2** INFORMAL HEAVY METAL music [**Origin:** 1200–1300 Old French, Latin *metallum* **mine, metal**, from Greek *metallon*] → see also METALLIC

met·a·lan·guage /ˈmɛt̬əˌlæŋgwɪdʒ/ *n.* [C,U] ENG. LANG. ARTS words used for talking about or describing language

ˈmetal deˌtector *n.* [C] **1** a special frame that you walk through at an airport, used to check for weapons made of metal **2** a machine used to find pieces of metal that are buried under the ground

ˈmetal faˌtigue *n.* [U] a weakness in metal that makes it likely to break

me·tal·lic /məˈtælɪk/ *adj.* **1** like metal in color, appearance, or taste: *metallic paint* **2** a metallic noise sounds like pieces of metal hitting each other: *a metallic click* **3** made of or containing metal: *metallic minerals*

met·al·loid[1] /ˈmɛt̬lˌɔɪd/ *n.* [C] CHEMISTRY a chemical ELEMENT, such as SILICON or ARSENIC, that is not a metal but has some of the qualities of a metal

metalloid[2] *adj.* CHEMISTRY **1** relating to or being a metalloid **2** similar to a metal

met·al·lur·gy /ˈmɛt̬lˌɚdʒi/ *n.* [U] SCIENCE the scientific study of metals and their uses —**metallurgist** *n.* [C] —**metallurgical** /ˌmɛt̬lˈɚdʒɪkəl/ *adj.*

met·al·work /ˈmɛt̬lˌwɚk/ *n.* [U] **1** the activity or skill of making metal objects: *a course in metalwork* **2** objects made by shaping metal: *Art Nouveau metalwork* —**metalworker** *n.* [C]

met·a·mor·phism /ˌmɛt̬əˈmɔrˌfɪzəm/ *n.* [U] SCIENCE changes in the structure of rock, caused by the continuous effects of pressure, heat, or water: *If the pressure and temperatures are high enough, the rocks can undergo metamorphism.*

metamorphosis

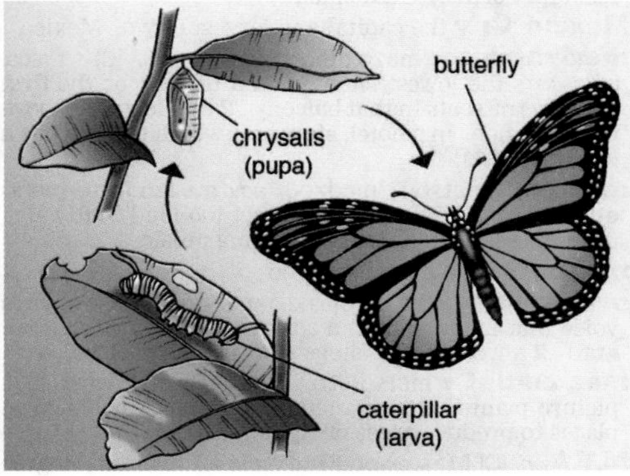

met·a·mor·pho·sis /ˌmɛt̬əˈmɔrfəsɪs/ *n. plural* **metamorphoses** /-siz/ [C,U] **1** FORMAL a process in which something changes completely into something very different SYN **transformation**: *Lewis has gradually* ***undergone a metamorphosis*** *into the state's best basketball player.* **2** BIOLOGY a process in which a young insect, FROG etc. changes into another stage in its development —**metamorphose** /ˌmɛt̬əˈmɔrfouz/ *v.* [I,T]

met·a·phase /ˈmɛt̬əˌfeɪz/ *n.* [U] BIOLOGY the second stage of the process that takes place when a cell divides, during which CHROMOSOMES get into a line and prepare to separate → see also ANAPHASE, PROPHASE, TELOPHASE

met·a·phor /ˈmɛt̬əˌfɔr/ *n.* [C,U] **1** ENG. LANG. ARTS a way of describing something by comparing it to something else that has similar qualities, without using the words "like" or "as" : *the use of metaphor in poetry* → see also SIMILE **2 a mixed metaphor** the use of two different metaphors at the same time to describe something, especially in a way that seems silly or funny **3** [C] something in a book, painting, movie etc. that is intended to represent a more general idea or quality: +**for** *Their relationship is a metaphor for the failure of communication in the modern world.*

met·a·phor·i·cal /ˌmɛt̬əˈfɔrɪkəl/ *adj.* ENG. LANG. ARTS using words to mean something different from their ordinary meaning when describing something in order to achieve a particular effect —**metaphorically** /-kli/ *adv.*: *I was,* ***metaphorically speaking****, pushed over the edge.*

met·a·phys·i·cal /ˌmɛt̬əˈfɪzɪkəl/ *adj.* **1** relating to the study of metaphysics **2** using words or ideas that are very complicated and difficult to understand —**metaphysically** /-kli/ *adv.*

met·a·phys·ics /ˌmɛt̬əˈfɪzɪks/ *n.* [U] the part of the study of PHILOSOPHY that tries to explain the nature of REALITY (=what is real) and discusses whether ideas, space, life, the world etc. really exist

met·a·tar·sals /ˌmɛt̬əˈtɑrsəlz/ *n.* [plural] BIOLOGY the five bones that stretch from the heel to the toes → see picture at SKELETON[1]

mete /mit/ *v.*

mete sth ↔ **out** *phr. v.* FORMAL to give someone a punishment: *Judges are meting out increasingly harsh sentences for car theft.*

me·te·or /ˈmit̬iɚ/ *n.* [C] PHYSICS a piece of rock or metal that floats in space, and makes a bright line in the night sky when it falls down to Earth → see also METEORITE

me·te·or·ic /ˌmit̬iˈɔrɪk, -ˈɑr-/ *adj.* **1** happening very suddenly and quickly: **a meteoric rise/career** *his meteoric rise in politics* **2** PHYSICS from a METEOR —**meteorically** /-kli/ *adv.*

me·te·or·ite /ˈmit̬iəˌraɪt/ *n.* [C] PHYSICS a piece of rock or metal that has come from space and landed on Earth → see also METEOR

meteorite

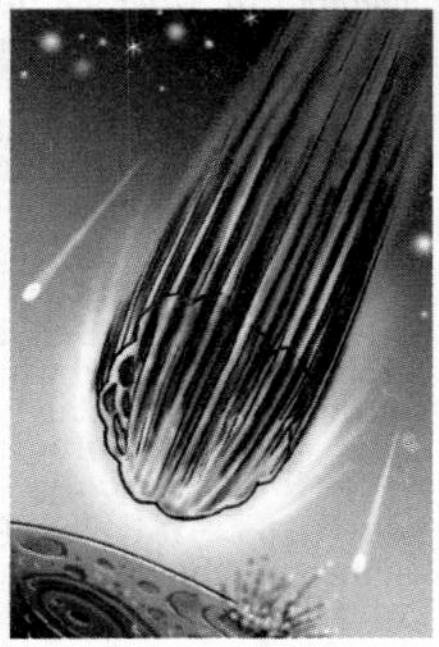

me·te·o·roid /ˈmit̬iəˌrɔɪd/ *n.* [C] PHYSICS a piece of rock or dust in space. When it enters the ATMOSPHERE of the Earth, it becomes a meteor, and if it reaches the surface of the Earth it is called a meteorite.

me·te·or·ol·o·gist /ˌmit̬iəˈrɑlədʒɪst/ *n.* [C] **1** someone who studies meteorology **2** someone on television or the radio who tells you what the weather will be like SYN **weather forecaster**

me·te·or·ol·o·gy /ˌmit̬iəˈrɑlədʒi/ *n.* [U] the scientific study of weather conditions —**meteorological** /ˌmit̬iərəˈlɑdʒɪkəl/ *adj.*

meter[1] /ˈmit̬ɚ/ S3 W3 *n.* **1** [C] a machine that measures and shows the amount of something you have used or the amount of money that you must pay: *the taxi meter* | *A man came to* ***read*** *the gas* ***meter****.* **2** a PARKING METER: *I need some change for the meter.* **3** [C] WRITTEN ABBREVIATION **m** the basic unit for measuring length in the METRIC SYSTEM equal to 39.37 inches: *The plants grow to one meter in height.* **4** a machine that measures the level of something: *a sound level meter* **5 the meter is running (on sth)** used to say that money is being spent continuously while you wait for something to happen: *The meter is running on bank reform.* **6** [C,U] the arrangement of sounds in poetry into patterns of strong and weak beats [**Origin:** (1–5) 1800–1900 French *mètre*, from Greek *metron* **measure**] → see also RHYTHM

meter[2] *v.* [T usually passive] to measure something with a meter, or to supply gas, water, electricity etc. through a meter: *Water use is metered in most Sacramento homes.*

-meter /mət̬ɚ, mit̬ɚ/ *suffix* [in nouns] **1** part of a meter, or a particular number of meters: *a millimeter* (=1/1000th of a meter) | *a kilometer* (=1,000 meters) **2** an instrument for measuring something: *an altimeter* (=measures the height at which an aircraft is flying)

ˈmeter maid *n.* [C] OLD-FASHIONED a woman whose job is to make sure that cars are not parked illegally

meth /mɛθ/ *n.* [U] INFORMAL METHAMPHETAMINE

meth·a·done /ˈmɛθəˌdoun/ *n.* [U] a drug that is often given to people who are trying to stop taking HEROIN

meth·am·phet·a·mine /ˌmɛθæmˈfɛt̬əˌmin/ *n.* [U] an illegal drug that makes you feel like you have more energy

meth·ane /ˈmɛθeɪn/ *n.* [U] CHEMISTRY a colorless gas with no smell that can be burned to give heat

meth·a·nol /ˈmɛθəˌnɔl, -ˌnoul/ *n.* [U] CHEMISTRY a poisonous alcohol that can be made from wood

me·thinks /mɪˈθɪŋks/ *v.* OLD USE or HUMOROUS I think

meth·od /ˈmɛθəd/ Ac S3 W2 *n.* **1** [C] a planned way of doing something, especially one that a lot of people know about and use: *I think we should try again using a different method.* | *traditional teaching methods* | +**of** *The pill is one of the safest methods of birth control.* | +**for** *a new method for the early detection of cancer* **2** [U] FORMAL a reasonable and effective way of planning something: *He didn't seem to have any method in the way he approached the problem.* **3 there's a method to sb's madness, there is method in sb's madness** used to say that even though someone seems to be behaving strangely, there is a sensible reason for what they are doing [**Origin:** 1400–1500 Latin *methodus*, from Greek *methodos*, from *meta-* + *hodos* **way**] → see also SCIENTIFIC METHOD

me·thod·i·cal /məˈθɑdɪkəl/ Ac *adj.* **1** always doing

M

things carefully, using an ordered system: *a cautious methodical killer* **2** done in a careful and well organized way: *methodical research* ►see THESAURUS box at careful **—methodically** /-kli/ *adv.*

Meth·od·ist /'mɛθədɪst/ *n.* [C] someone who belongs to a Christian religious group that follows the teachings of John Wesley **—Methodist** *adj.* **—Methodism** *n.* [U]

meth·od·ol·o·gy /ˌmɛθə'dɑlədʒi/ Ac *n. plural* **methodologies** [C,U] the set of methods and principles that are used when studying a particular subject or doing a particular type of work: *scientific methodology* **—methodological** /ˌmɛθədə'lɑdʒɪkəl/ *adj.* **—methodologically** /-kli/ *adv.*

Me·thu·se·lah /mə'θuzələ/ *n.* **1** a name used for someone who is extremely old **2** in the Bible, a man who lived for 969 years

meth·yl al·co·hol /ˌmɛθəl 'ælkəhɔl/ *n.* [U] TECHNICAL → see also ETHYL ALCOHOL, METHANOL

me·tic·u·lous /mə'tɪkyələs/ *adj.* very careful about small details, and always making sure that everything is done correctly: *The book describes the journey in meticulous detail.* | +**in/about** *He was meticulous in his use of words.* [**Origin:** 1800–1900 Latin *meticulosus* **afraid**, from *metus* **fear**] **—meticulously** *adv.* **—meticulousness** *n.* [U]

me·tier /mɛ'tyeɪ, 'mɛtyeɪ/ *n.* [C usually singular] FORMAL a type of work or activity that you enjoy doing because you have a natural ability to do it well

me·tre /'mit̬ɚ/ *n.* [C,U] the British and Canadian spelling of METER

-metre /mit̬ɚ, mɪt̬ɚ/ *suffix* [in nouns] the British and Canadian spelling of -METER

met·ric /'mɛtrɪk/ *adj.* MATH using or relating to the METRIC SYSTEM of weights and measures: *2.3 metric tons* → see also IMPERIAL

met·ri·cal /'mɛtrɪkəl/ *adj.* ENG. LANG. ARTS written in the form of poetry, with regular beats **—metrically** /-kli/ *adv.*

'metric ˌsystem *n.* **the metric system** the system of weights and measures that is based on the meter and the kilogram → see also AVOIRDUPOIS

ˌmetric 'ton *n.* [C] a unit for measuring weight, equal to 1,000 kilograms or about 2,205 pounds

me·tro¹ /'mɛtroʊ/ *n.* [C] a railroad system that runs under the ground below a city SYN **subway**: *the Paris Metro*

metro² *adj.* [only before noun] INFORMAL METROPOLITAN: *metro Dallas*

met·ro·nome /'mɛtrəˌnoʊm/ *n.* [C] a piece of equipment that shows the speed at which music should be played, by making a short repeated sound

me·trop·o·lis /mə'trɑpəlɪs/ *n.* [C] a very large city that is the most important city in a country or area

met·ro·pol·i·tan /ˌmɛtrə'pɑlət¬n/ *adj.* relating or belonging to a very large city: *the Miami metropolitan area*

met·tle /'mɛt̬l/ *n.* [U] courage and determination to do something even when it is very difficult: **prove/show your mettle** *He soon proved his mettle as a tough manager.* | **test sb's mettle** *The crisis has tested the governor's mettle.*

mew /myu/ also **mewl** /myul/ *v.* [I] to MEOW **—mew** *n.*

Mex·i·can¹ /'mɛksɪkən/ *adj.* from or relating to Mexico

Mexican² *n.* [C] someone from Mexico

ˌMexican 'jumping bean *n.* [C] a seed of particular Mexican plants that has the LARVA (=young form) of a MOTH (=flying insect) inside it which makes the seed move

ˌMexican 'War, the HISTORY a war between the U.S. and Mexico from 1846 to 1848, which resulted in the U.S. taking control of an area from Mexico that now forms some of the southwestern states

Mex·i·co /'mɛksɪˌkoʊ/ a country that is south of the U.S. and north of Guatemala

ˌMexico 'City the capital and largest city of Mexico

mez·za·nine /'mɛzəˌnin, ˌmɛzə'nin/ *n.* [C] **1** ENG. LANG. ARTS the lowest BALCONY in a theater, or the first few rows of seats in that balcony **2** the floor just above the main floor in a hotel, store etc., which usually has a low ceiling

mez·zo¹ /'mɛtsoʊ, 'mɛdzoʊ/ *adv.* **mezzo forte/piano etc.** TECHNICAL a word meaning not too loud, softly etc., used in instructions for performing music

mezzo² *n.* [C] a mezzo-soprano

ˌmezzo-so'prano *n.* [C] ENG. LANG. ARTS **1** a woman's voice that is lower than a SOPRANO but higher than an ALTO **2** a woman who sings with this kind of voice

mez·zo·tint /'mɛtsoʊˌtɪnt/ *n.* [C,U] OLD-FASHIONED a picture printed from a metal plate that is polished in places to produce areas of light and shade

M.F.A. *n.* [C] **Master of Fine Arts** a university degree in a subject such as painting or SCULPTURE that you do after your first degree

mfg. the written abbreviation of MANUFACTURING

mfr. the written abbreviation of MANUFACTURER

mg the written abbreviation of MILLIGRAM

mgr. *n.* the written abbreviation of "manager"

MHz the written abbreviation of MEGAHERTZ

MI **1** the written abbreviation of MICHIGAN **2** also **M.I.** the written abbreviation of middle INITIAL (=first letter of your middle name), usually written on forms

mi /mi/ *n.* [singular] the third note in a musical SCALE according to the SOL-FA system

MIA *n. plural* **MIA's** [C] **missing in action** a soldier who has disappeared in a battle and who may still be alive **—MIA** *adj.*

Mi·am·i /maɪ'æmi/ **1** a city in the southeast of the U.S. state of Florida **2** a Native American tribe from the northeastern central area of the U.S.

mi·as·ma /mi'æzmə, maɪ-/ *n.* [singular, U] LITERARY **1** thick dirty air or an unpleasant mist that smells bad: *a toxic miasma from the sewage plant* **2** a bad influence or feeling: *The miasma of defeat hung over them.*

mi·ca /'maɪkə/ *n.* [U] EARTH SCIENCE a mineral that separates easily into small flat transparent pieces of rock, often used to make electrical instruments

Mi·cah /'maɪkə/ a book in the Old Testament of the Christian Bible

mice /maɪs/ *n.* the plural of mouse

Mi·chel·an·ge·lo /ˌmaɪkəl'ændʒəˌloʊ/ (1475–1564) an Italian painter, SCULPTOR, and ARCHITECT of the Renaissance period

Mich·i·gan /'mɪʃɪgən/ WRITTEN ABBREVIATION **MI** **1** a state in the north of the U.S. **2 Lake Michigan** a large lake in the north of the U.S., which is one of the Great Lakes

mick·ey /'mɪki/ also **Mickey Finn** /ˌmɪki 'fɪn/ *n.* [C] OLD-FASHIONED, INFORMAL a type of drug that you secretly put into someone's drink in order to make them unconscious: **slip/give sb a mickey** (=to secretly put a drug into someone's drink)

'Mickey Mouse *adj.* [only before noun] **1 a Mickey Mouse operation/organization/outfit** a company or organization that is usually very small and that does not do things well **2** something that people do not take seriously, especially because it is too easy or simple: *He had some Mickey Mouse excuse for being late.*

Mic·mac /'mɪkmæk/ a Native American tribe from eastern Canada

micro- /maɪkroʊ, -krə/ *prefix* **1** extremely small compared with others of the same type: *a microcomputer* | *microelectronics* (=using extremely small electrical parts) **2** dealing with the smaller parts that make up a large unit: *microeconomics* (=the study of all of the parts of a national economy) → see also MACRO-

mi·crobe /'maɪkroʊb/ *n.* [C] BIOLOGY an extremely small living creature that cannot be seen without a

MICROSCOPE, and that can sometimes cause diseases —**microbial** *adj.*

mi·cro·bi·ol·o·gy /ˌmaɪkroʊbaɪˈɑlədʒi/ *n.* [U] BIOLOGY the scientific study of very small living things such as BACTERIA —**microbiologist** *n.* [C] —**microbiological** /ˌmaɪkroʊˌbaɪəˈlɑdʒɪkəl/ *adj.*

mi·cro·brew /ˈmaɪkroʊˌbru/ *n.* [C] a type of beer that is produced only in small quantities

mi·cro·brew·er·y /ˈmaɪkroʊˌbruəri/ *n. plural* **microbreweries** [C] a small company that makes only a small amount of beer to sell, and often has a restaurant where its beer is served

mi·cro·chip /ˈmaɪkroʊˌtʃɪp/ *n.* [C] COMPUTERS a computer CHIP

mi·cro·cli·mate /ˈmaɪkroʊˌklaɪmɪt/ *n.* [C] EARTH SCIENCE the CLIMATE in a small area, when this is different from the climate in the surrounding area

mi·cro·com·put·er /ˈmaɪkroʊkəmˌpyuṭɚ/ *n.* [C] COMPUTERS a small computer SYN **PC**

mi·cro·cosm /ˈmaɪkrəˌkɑzəm/ *n.* [C,U] a small group, society etc. that has the same qualities as a much larger one: +**of** *New York's mix of people is a microcosm of America.* | *Harris' production company is starting to look like an empire* ***in microcosm.*** —**microcosmic** /ˌmaɪkrəˈkɑzmɪk/ *adj.* → see also MACROCOSM

mi·cro·dot /ˈmaɪkroʊˌdɑt, -krə-/ *n.* [C] a secret photograph of something such as a document, that is made as small as a DOT so that it can easily be hidden

mi·cro·ec·o·nom·ics /ˌmaɪkroʊɛkəˈnɑmɪks/ *n.* [U] the study of small economic systems that are part of national or international systems, such as those of particular companies, families etc. —**microeconomic** *adj.* → see also MACROECONOMICS

mi·cro·e·lec·tron·ics /ˌmaɪkroʊɪlɛkˈtrɑnɪks/ *n.* [U] the practice or study of designing very small PRINTED CIRCUITS that are used in computers —**microelectronic** *adj.*

mi·cro·fiche /ˈmaɪkroʊˌfiʃ/ *n.* [C,U] a small sheet of microfilm that can be read using a special machine, especially in a library

mi·cro·film /ˈmaɪkrəˌfɪlm/ *n.* [C,U] a special type of film used for making very small photographs of important documents, newspapers, maps etc., or a roll of this film —**microfilm** *v.* [T]

mi·cro·fos·sil /ˈmaɪkroʊˌfɑsəl/ *n.* [C] BIOLOGY a very small FOSSIL, for example of BACTERIA, that can only be seen with a MICROSCOPE

mi·cro·light /ˈmaɪkroʊˌlaɪt/ *n.* [C] a very light small airplane for one or two people —**microlight** *adj.* [only before noun]

mi·cro·man·age /ˈmaɪkroʊˌmænɪdʒ/ *v.* [T] to organize and control all the details of other people's work in a way that they find annoying: *She micromanaged every aspect of her children's lives.* —**micromanagement** *n.* [U]

mi·crom·e·ter /maɪˈkrɑməṭɚ/ *n.* [C] **1** an instrument for measuring very small distances **2** one millionth of a meter

mi·cron /ˈmaɪkrɑn/ *n.* [C] a MICROMETER

Mi·cro·ne·si·a /ˌmaɪkrəˈniʒə/ a group of more than 2000 small islands in the western Pacific Ocean, including the Caroline Islands, the Marshall Islands, and Kiribati —**Micronesian** *n., adj.*

mi·cro·nu·cle·us /ˈmaɪkroʊˌnukliəs/ *n. plural* **micronuclei** /-kliaɪ/ [C] BIOLOGY the smaller of the two nuclei (NUCLEUS) in a simple living creature that has only one cell, which contains GENETIC material and is involved in sexual REPRODUCTION → see also MACRONUCLEUS

mi·cro·or·ga·nism /ˌmaɪkroʊˈɔrgəˌnɪzəm/ *n.* [C] BIOLOGY a living thing that is so small that it cannot be seen without a microscope

mi·cro·phone /ˈmaɪkrəˌfoʊn/ *n.* [C] a piece of equipment that you hold in front of your mouth when you are singing, giving a speech etc. in order to make your voice sound louder or to record your voice SYN **mike**

mi·cro·proc·es·sor /ˌmaɪkroʊˈprɑsɛsɚ/ *n.* [C] COMPUTERS the central CHIP in a computer, that controls most of its operations

microscope

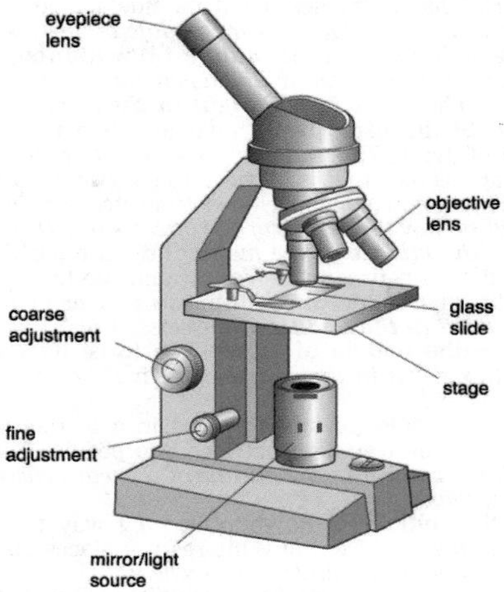

mi·cro·scope /ˈmaɪkrəˌskoʊp/ *n.* [C] **1** SCIENCE a scientific instrument that makes extremely small things appear large enough to be seen: **under/through a microscope** *You can see the cancer cells quite easily under a microscope.* → see also ELECTRON MICROSCOPE **2 under the microscope** being examined very closely and carefully: *The school district's finances were* ***put under the microscope.***

mi·cro·scop·ic /ˌmaɪkrəˈskɑpɪk◂/ *adj.* **1** extremely small and therefore very difficult to see; used especially to describe things that can be seen only by using a microscope: *microscopic particles* **2** [only before noun] SCIENCE using a microscope: *microscopic analysis* —**microscopically** /-kli/ *adv.*

mi·cro·sec·ond /ˈmaɪkroʊˌsɛkənd/ *n.* [C] one millionth of a second

mi·cro·sur·ger·y /ˈmaɪkroʊˌsɚdʒəri/ *n.* [U] medical treatment in which very small instruments and LASERS are used

mi·cro·wave[1] /ˈmaɪkrəˌweɪv/ S2 *n.* [C] **1** also **microwave oven** a type of OVEN that cooks food very quickly by using electric waves instead of heat: *I'll heat it up* ***in the microwave.*** **2** PHYSICS a very short electric wave that is used in cooking food, sending messages by radio, and in RADAR

microwave[2] *v.* [T] to cook something in a microwave oven ►see THESAURUS box at **cook**[1] —**microwaveable, microwavable** /ˌmaɪkrəˈweɪvəbəl/ *adj.*

mid- /mɪd/ *prefix* in the middle of something: *She's in her mid-20s* (=about 25 years old). | *in mid-July* | *a cold midwinter night*

mid·air /ˌmɪdˈɛr◂ / *n.* **in midair** in the air or the sky, away from the ground: *These aircraft are able to refuel in midair.* —**midair** *adj.* [only before noun] *a midair collision*

Mi·das touch /ˈmaɪdəs ˌtʌtʃ/ *n.* **the Midas touch** if someone has the Midas touch, everything they do is successful and makes money for them [**Origin:** 1800–1900 *Midas* king of Phrygia in ancient times who was given the magic power of turning everything he touched into gold]

ˌmid-Atˈlantic *adj.* **1 the mid-Atlantic states/region** the U.S. states New York, New Jersey, Pennsylvania, Maryland, and Delaware, which are on the east coast but are not considered part of New England or the South **2** a mid-Atlantic ACCENT is one that uses a mixture of British and American sounds and words

M

mid·day /ˈmɪd-deɪ/ *n.* [U] the middle of the day, around 12:00 NOON SYN **noon**: *Lunch is **at midday**.* → see also MIDNIGHT

mid·dle¹ /ˈmɪdl/ S1 W2 *n.*
1 the middle a) the center part of a thing, place, or position that is farthest from its sides or edges: **+of** *Janet was on her knees in the middle of the floor.* | *a cookie with a hole **in the middle*** | **down/through the middle (of sth)** *Draw a line down the middle of the page.* | *The arrow landed **right in the middle of** the target.* **b)** the inside part of an object such as a ball, or piece of fruit: *The pastries have cream **in the middle**.* **c)** the part that is between the beginning and the end of an event, story, period of time etc.: **+of** *The rain should stop by the middle of the afternoon.* | *He walked out **in the middle of** the meeting.* **d)** the position or rank that is between the highest and the lowest position in a list of people or things: *In terms of ability, she's about **in the middle of** the class.*
2 be in the middle of (doing) sth to be busy doing something: *I'm in the middle of fixing dinner – can I call you back?*
3 in the middle (of sth) involved in a bad situation, especially an argument between two people: *Innocent people are **caught in the middle** of the war between the two factions.*
4 in the middle of nowhere a long way from the nearest town or from any interesting places: *Michael lives way out in the middle of nowhere.*
5 divide/split sth down the middle to divide something into equal halves or groups: *The vote was split right down the middle.*
6 BODY [C usually singular] INFORMAL the waist and the part of the body around the stomach

WORD CHOICE **middle, center**
Use both of these words to talk about where something is. The **middle** of something is the area or part that is farthest away from the sides or edges: *His clothes were in a heap in the middle of the floor.* The **center** of something is exactly in the middle: *Put the vase in the center of the table.*

middle² S2 W2 *adj.* [only before noun]
1 CENTER nearest to the center of something: *It's in the middle drawer of the file cabinet.* | *I always drive in the middle lane.*
2 TIME/EVENT between the beginning and end of an event or period of time: *I missed the middle part of the movie.*
3 SCALE/RANGE between the highest and the lowest position in a list of people or things: *We're looking for a car priced in the middle range.* | **a middle brother/child/daughter etc.** (=the brother, child etc. who is between the oldest and the youngest)
4 a middle course/way/path etc. a way of dealing with something that is between two opposite and often extreme ways: *Schoenfeld is **steering a middle course** between restoration and modernization of the building.*
5 Middle English/French etc. an old form of English, French etc., used in the Middle Ages
[**Origin:** Old English *middel*] → see also MIDDLE FINGER, MIDDLE NAME

ˌmiddle ˈage *n.* [U] the period of your life when you are not young anymore but are not yet old, from about age 40 to age 65: *He began to reevaluate his life at middle age.*

ˌmiddle-ˈaged *adj.* **1** not young anymore but not yet old, usually between the ages of around 40 and 65: *a middle-aged businessman* **2 middle-aged spread** an area of fat that many people develop around their waist as they grow older

ˌMiddle ˈAges *n.* [plural] **the Middle Ages** the period in European history between the 5th and 15th centuries A.D.

ˌMiddle Aˈmerica *n.* [U] **1** the central part of the U.S.: *the small towns of Middle America.* **2** the part of American society that is neither rich nor poor, usually with traditional ideas and beliefs: *His policies appealed to Middle America.* **3** Central America and Mexico —**middle American** *adj.*

mid·dle·brow, middle-brow /ˈmɪdlˌbraʊ/ *adj.* DISAPPROVING liked by ordinary people and not difficult to understand: *a middlebrow newspaper* → see also HIGHBROW

ˌmiddle ˈC *n.* [singular] the musical note C which is at the middle point of a piano KEYBOARD

ˌmiddle ˈclass *n.* **the middle class** also **the middle classes a)** the social class that includes people who are neither rich nor poor: *Tuition increases will hit the middle class especially hard.* **b)** HISTORY the social class in Europe in the past between NOBLES (=rich royal people who owned land) and PEASANTS (=poor farmers), which included people who made and traded things → see also LOWER CLASS

ˌmiddle-ˈclass *adj.* **1** belonging to or typical of the middle class: *middle-class neighborhoods* | *a typical middle-class family* **2** middle-class attitudes, values etc. are typical of middle-class people and are often concerned with work, education, and possessions: *a middle-class view of life*

ˌMiddle ˈColonies, the HISTORY four of the English colonies (COLONY) in America: New York, New Jersey, Pennsylvania, and Delaware

ˌmiddle ˈdistance *n.* **the middle distance** the part of a picture or a view that is between the nearest part and the part that is farthest away

ˈmiddle-ˌdistance *adj.* [only before noun] a middle-distance race is neither very short nor very long, and a middle-distance runner is someone who runs those races

ˌmiddle ˈear *n.* [singular] BIOLOGY the central part of the ear, between the outside part and the EARDRUM

ˌMiddle ˈEast also **Mideast** *n.* **the Middle East** the part of Asia between the Mediterranean Sea and the Arabian Sea, including countries such as Turkey, Saudi Arabia, and Iran —**Middle Eastern**, **Mideast** *adj.* → see also FAR EAST

ˌmiddle ˈfinger *n.* [C] the longest finger, which is the middle one of the four fingers and thumb on your hand

ˌmiddle ˈground *n.* [singular, U] something that two opposing groups can both agree about: *The two sides have shown no willingness to **find a middle ground**.*

ˌmiddle ˈlatitudes *n.* [plural] EARTH SCIENCE the areas between the Arctic Circle and the Tropic of Cancer and the Tropic of Capricorn and the Antarctic Circle → see also HIGH LATITUDES, LOW LATITUDES

mid·dle·man /ˈmɪdlˌmæn/ *n. plural* **middlemen** /-ˌmɛn/ [C] someone who buys things in order to make a profit by selling them to someone else, or who helps to arrange business deals for other people: *He worked as a middleman for U.S. companies who wanted to do business in the region.* | *Manufacturers are **cutting out the middleman** (=not using a middleman) and selling directly to customers.*

ˌmiddle ˈmanagement *n.* [U] managers who are in charge of small groups of people but do not make the most important decisions —**middle manager** *n.* [C]

ˌmiddle ˈname *n.* [C] **1** the name that, in English, comes between your first name and your family name ▸see THESAURUS box at **name¹** **2 sth is sb's middle name** INFORMAL used to say that someone has a lot of a particular personal quality: *You can trust him – loyalty is his middle name.* → see also FIRST NAME

ˌmiddle-of-the-ˈroad *adj.* middle-of-the-road ideas, opinions etc. are not extreme, so many people agree with them: *middle-of-the-road voters*

ˈmiddle school *n.* [C,U] a school in the U.S. for children between the ages of about 11 and 14, usually including grades 6 through 8

ˌmiddle-ˈsized *adj.* neither very large nor very small: *middle-sized cities*

mid·dle·weight /ˈmɪdlˌweɪt/ *n.* [C] a BOXER who weighs between 147 and 160 pounds (67–73 kilograms) → see also HEAVYWEIGHT, LIGHTWEIGHT

ˌMiddle ˈWest *n.* **the Middle West** the Midwest

mid·dling /ˈmɪdlɪŋ/ *adj.* INFORMAL not very good or bad, not very big or small etc. SYN **average**: *They've had only middling success.* | *Jonathan considers himself a* ***fair to middling*** (=not very good) *cook.*

Mid·east /ˌmɪdˈist/ *n.* **the Mideast** the Middle East

mid·field /ˈmɪdfild/ *n.* **1** [U] the middle part of the area where a game such as football or SOCCER is played **2** [singular] the group of players on a football or SOCCER team who play in the midfield

mid·field·er /ˈmɪdˌfildɚ/ *n.* [C] a football or SOCCER player who usually plays in the midfield

midge /mɪdʒ/ *n.* [C] a small flying insect that bites people

midg·et[1] /ˈmɪdʒɪt/ *n.* [C] **1** OFFENSIVE a very small person who will never grow tall → see also LITTLE PEOPLE **2** someone or something that is very small: *The skyscraper is a midget by today's standards.*

midget[2] *adj.* **a midget car/camera etc.** a very small car etc.

MIDI /ˈmɪdi/ *n.* [C] **musical instrument digital interface** COMPUTERS a system that allows computers to communicate with electronic musical instruments

mid·i /ˈmɪdi/ *adj.* **a midi skirt/dress/coat** a skirt, dress etc. that comes to the middle of the lower leg

mid·life cri·sis /ˌmɪdlaɪf ˈkraɪsɪs/ *n.* [C] a period of worry and lack of confidence that some people feel when they are about 40 or 50 years old: *He bought a sportscar during his midlife crisis.*

mid·night /ˈmɪdnaɪt/ S3 *n.* [U] 12:00 at night: *It's already midnight – we should be going.* | *The boat leaves* ***at midnight.*** | **after/before/by midnight** *I'm supposed to be home by midnight.* → see also **burn the midnight oil** at BURN[1] (15), MIDDAY

ˌmidnight ˈjudge *n.* [C] HISTORY a judge with FEDERALIST beliefs who was given an official position by President John Adams just before Thomas Jefferson became President. Midnight judges kept their positions after Adams stopped being President, and opposed some of Jefferson's Republican plans.

ˌmidnight ˈsun *n.* **the midnight sun** the sun, seen in the middle of the night in summer in the far north or south of the world

mid·point /ˈmɪdpɔɪnt/ *n.* [C usually singular] **1** a point that is HALFWAY through or along something: *Thomas was leading at the midpoint of the race.* **2** MATH a point that divides a part of a line exactly in half: *the midpoint of a segment*

ˌmidpoint of a ˈsegment *n.* [C] MATH a point that is in the middle of a SEGMENT (=line connecting two points), so that the segment is divided into two parts of equal length

mid·riff /ˈmɪdrɪf/ *n.* [C] the part of the body between your chest and your waist

mid·sec·tion /ˈmɪdˌsɛkʃən/ *n.* [C usually singular] the middle part of something or of someone's body: *There are 24 missiles in the submarine's midsection.*

mid·seg·ment /ˈmɪdˌsɛgmənt/ *n.* [C] MATH **1** a line connecting the MIDPOINTS of two side of a TRIANGLE **2** a line connecting the MIDPOINTS of the two sides of a TRAPEZOID that are not parallel to each other SYN **median**

mid·ship·man /mɪdˈʃɪpmən/ *n.* *plural* **midshipmen** /-mən/ [C] someone who is training to become an officer in the Navy

mid·size /ˈmɪdsaɪz/ *adj.* [only before noun] neither very large nor very small: *a midsize car*

midst /mɪdst/ *n.* **1 in the midst of sth a)** in the middle of a period, situation, or event: *Deb's in the midst of a messy divorce.* **b)** in the middle of a place or a group of things: *We stood in the midst of thousands of people.* **2 in sb's midst** FORMAL in a particular group of people: *They believe there are angels in our midst.*

mid·stream /ˌmɪdˈstrim◂/ *n.* [U] **1 in midstream** while something is happening or being done: *The employees found it difficult to adjust to changes in midstream.* → see also **change/switch horses in midstream** at HORSE[1] (3) **2** the middle of a river or STREAM

mid·sum·mer /ˌmɪdˈsʌmɚ◂/ *n.* [U] the middle of summer: *the long evenings of midsummer* —**midsummer** *adj.* [only before noun]

mid·term[1], **mid-term** /ˈmɪdtɚm/ *n.* **1** [C] a test that students take in the middle of a SEMESTER or QUARTER: *Alison has a history midterm next week.* ►see THESAURUS box at **university** **2** [U] POLITICS the middle of the period when elected government officials are in power: *The chairman resigned in midterm.*

midterm[2] *adj.* [only before noun] during or in the middle of a SEMESTER or QUARTER: *midterm exams* | *a midterm paper*

ˌmidterm eˈlection *n.* [C] POLITICS an election to choose members of the SENATE and the HOUSE OF REPRESENTATIVES held in one of the years between elections for the American president SYN **off-year election**

mid·town /ˈmɪdtaʊn/ *adj., adv.* in the area of a city that is near the center but is not the main business area: *a restaurant in midtown Manhattan* —**midtown** *n.* [U] → see also DOWNTOWN

mid·way[1] /ˌmɪdˈweɪ◂/ *adv.* **1** in the middle of a period of time or event: +**through** *Smith scored midway through the first quarter.* **2** at the middle point between two places or along a line: +**between/along** *The town is midway between Joliet and Chicago.*

mid·way[2] /ˈmɪdweɪ/ *n.* [C usually singular] the place where games, shows, and food are at a FAIR

Mid·way A·toll /ˌmɪdweɪ ˈætɔl, -toʊl/ two small islands in the Pacific Ocean northwest of Honolulu that are controlled by the U.S. and used as a U.S. military base

mid·week /ˌmɪdˈwik◂/ *adj., adv.* on one of the middle days of the week, such as Tuesday, Wednesday, or Thursday: *Many resorts offer midweek discounts.* | *A meeting is scheduled for midweek.*

Mid·west /ˌmɪdˈwɛst/ *n.* **the Midwest** the north-central area of the U.S., including states such as Iowa, Illinois, and Minnesota —**Midwestern** *adj.*

mid·wife /ˈmɪdwaɪf/ *n.* *plural* **midwives** /-waɪvz/ [C] a specially trained nurse, usually a woman, whose job is to help women when they are having a baby [**Origin:** 1200–1300 *mid* **with** (11–14 centuries) (from Old English) + *wife* **woman**]

mid·wife·ry /ˈmɪdˌwaɪfəri, ˌmɪdˈwaɪ-/ *n.* [U] the skill or work of a midwife

mid·win·ter /ˌmɪdˈwɪntɚ◂/ *n.* [U] the middle of winter: *They crossed the mountains in midwinter.* —**midwinter** *adj.* [only before noun] *a midwinter festival*

mid·year /ˈmɪdyɪr/ *n.* [U] the middle of the year: *Sales had improved by midyear.* —**midyear** *adj.* [only before noun] *a midyear review*

mien /min/ *n.* [singular, U] LITERARY someone's typical expression or way of behaving: *a young man with a solemn mien*

Mies van der Ro·he /ˌmis væn də ˈroʊə, ˌmiz-/, **Lud·wig** /ˈlʊdwɪg/ (1886–1969) a U.S. architect, born in Germany, famous for his steel and glass buildings

miffed /mɪft/ *adj.* INFORMAL slightly annoyed or upset: +**at/by** *She was miffed at being left out.*

might[1] /maɪt/ S1 W1 *modal verb*

1 POSSIBILITY used in order to talk about what is or was possible, when you cannot be certain SYN **may**: *Carrie might not be able to go.* | *This might help the pain a little bit.* | ***There might be*** *some truth in what she says.* | **might have done/been sth** *They might have made a mistake.* | *He might have been outside.* | **might not/never** *We might never know the truth.*

2 REPORTED SPEECH used instead of "may" when reporting what someone said or thought: *I thought it might rain, so I brought an umbrella.* | *She said she might be late.*

3 might have done/been sth used to say that something was a possibility in the past but did not actually happen: *We might have been killed.* | *She would cry herself to sleep thinking of* ***what might have been.***

M

SPOKEN PHRASES

4 ADVICE/SUGGESTION used to politely give advice or make a suggestion: *You might try calling the store.* | *You **might want to** get your blood pressure checked.*
5 might (just) as well a) used for suggesting that someone should do something because there is no good reason to do anything else: *You might as well come along if you're not busy.* **b)** used to say that the situation is the same as if something were true: *I might as well have been talking to a brick wall.*
6 might I say/ask/add etc. also **I might say/add etc.** used to politely give more information, ask a question, interrupt etc.: *Whose underwear is that, might I ask?*
7 ANNOYED used when you are angry or surprised when someone did not do something that you think they should have done: *You might have at least said thank you.*
8 as you might expect/imagine/guess used to show that you realize that what you are saying is not surprising: *They were not happy, as you might imagine.*
9 I might have known/guessed etc. used to say that you are not surprised at a situation: *I might have known you'd never finish.*
10 PERMISSION OLD-FASHIONED used to ask politely if you can do something [SYN] **could**: *Might I come in?*
11 who/where/what etc. might sb/sth do? OLD-FASHIONED, HUMOROUS used to politely ask for information: *And who might you be, young man?*

12 might well a) also **might easily** if something might well or easily happen or be true, you think it is fairly likely to happen or be true: *The project might well fail.* **b)** used to say that a statement, question, reaction, or feeling is reasonable: *He might well be described as the world's greatest player.*
13 ALTHOUGH used for saying that although one thing is true, something different or more important is also true: *He **might** be very smart, **but** he doesn't understand women.* | **strange/surprising as it might seem** *Strange as it might seem, some people like the cold weather.* → see also **try as sb might** at TRY[1] (6)
14 REASON/PURPOSE LITERARY used to say why something happens or the reason why someone does something: *I moved forward so that I might have a better view.*
[**Origin:** Old English *meahte, mihte*] → see also MAY

might² *n.* [U] LITERARY **1** strength and power: *America's military might* | *She tried **with all** her **might** to push him away.* **2 might makes right** used to say that powerful people and countries can do whatever they want

might-have-beens /ˈmaɪt̬əˌbɪnz, -t̬əv-/ *n.* [plural] things that you wish had happened in the past but which never did

might·i·ly /ˈmaɪt̬əli/ *adv.* **1** [+ adj./adv.] very: *I was **mightily impressed** with their performance.* **2** a lot or to a great degree: *The country has changed mightily in recent years.* **3** using great strength and determination: *Taylor has struggled mightily to help her daughter.*

might·n't /ˈmaɪtˀnt/ *v.* OLD-FASHIONED the short form of "might not": *He mightn't like it.*

might·y¹ /ˈmaɪt̬i/ *adj. comparative* **mightier**, *superlative* **mightiest** ESPECIALLY LITERARY **1** very strong and powerful, or very big and impressive: *the mighty Mississippi River* | *mighty warriors* **2** done with a lot of force: *a mighty crash* → see also **high and mighty** at HIGH[1] (18)

mighty² *adv.* [+ adj./adv.] SPOKEN very: *That's a mighty big fish.*

mi·graine /ˈmaɪgreɪn/ *n.* [C] MEDICINE an extremely bad HEADACHE, during which you feel sick and have pain behind your eyes [**Origin:** 1300–1400 French, Late Latin *hemicrania* **pain in one side of the head**]

mi·grant /ˈmaɪgrənt/ [Ac] *n.* [C] **1** someone who goes to another area or country, especially in order to find work : *Historically, California has welcomed migrants from other states and nations.* | ***Migrant workers** still live in poor quality housing.* | *Officials said they did not know whether the people were **economic migrants*** (=people who go to another country to find better jobs and living conditions) *or political refugees.* → see also EMIGRANT **2** BIOLOGY a bird or animal that travels from one part of the world to another, especially in the fall and spring

mi·grate /ˈmaɪgreɪt/ [Ac] *v.* [I] **1** BIOLOGY if birds or animals migrate, they travel from one part of the world to another, especially in the fall and spring: *The birds migrate south in the winter.* ►see THESAURUS box at **immigrate** **2** to go to another area or country, usually in order to find a place to live or work: *People migrated north in search of work.*

mi·gra·tion /maɪˈgreɪʃən/ [Ac] *n.* [C,U] the movement from one place to another of a large group of people, birds, animals etc.: *the yearly migration of geese*

Mik·a·su·ki, Miccosukee /ˌmɪkəˈsuki/ a Native American tribe from the southwestern area of the U.S.

mike¹ /maɪk/ *n.* [C] INFORMAL a MICROPHONE → see also OPEN MIKE

mike² *v.* [T] to attach a MICROPHONE to someone or something: *All the instruments are miked.*

mi·la·dy /mɪˈleɪdi/ *n.* [singular] OLD USE a way of politely speaking to a woman who is of a higher social class

mild /maɪld/ *adj.*
1 SMALL EFFECT not having a serious, strong, or severe effect [OPP] **strong**: *a mild swear word* | *a mild feeling of irritation* | *The painkiller is quite mild.* | *a mild earthquake* | *The doctor thinks Geri has a mild concussion.* | *Steve had a **mild case of** food poisoning.*
2 FOOD/TASTE not very strong-tasting or SPICY: *mild salsa* | *Lentils have a mild nutty flavor.* ►see THESAURUS box at **taste¹** → see also MEDIUM
3 WEATHER not too cold, stormy, or wet: *It was a very mild winter.* | *mild temperatures* | *a mild climate*
4 PUNISHMENT/CRITICISM not severe or strict [SYN] **harsh**: *a mild rebuke*
5 SOAP ETC. soft and gentle to your skin [SYN] **gentle** [OPP] **harsh**: *a mild detergent*
6 CHARACTER/MANNER OLD-FASHIONED having a gentle character and not easily getting angry: *Joe was a mild man who rarely raised his voice.* → see also MILDLY

mil·dew /ˈmɪldu/ *n.* [U] a white or gray FUNGUS (=simple type of living thing like a plant without leaves) that grows on walls, leather, or other surfaces in warm, slightly wet places [**Origin:** Old English *meledeaw* **sweet sticky substance from plants**] —**mildewed** *adj.*

mild·ly /ˈmaɪldli/ *adv.* **1** slightly: *McKee was only mildly interested.* **2 to put it mildly** SPOKEN used to say that you could use much stronger words to describe something: *His proposals were unpopular, to put it mildly.* **3** in a gentle way without being angry: *"Perhaps," she answered mildly.*

ˌmild-ˈmannered *adj.* gentle and polite: *a mild-mannered, kind man*

mile /maɪl/ [S1] [W1] *n.* [C] **1** a unit for measuring distance or length, equal to 1,760 yards or 1,609 meters: *Dane's father lives about a mile from here.* | *Mark jogs as least five miles a day.* | **2/10/25 etc. miles long/wide/high** *The bridge is nearly two miles long.* | **20/40/60 etc. miles per/an hour** *I was driving at 50 miles per hour.* | **25/30/35 etc. miles to the gallon** also **25/30/35 etc. miles per gallon** (=used to talk about the amount of gas a car uses) **2 miles** INFORMAL a very long distance: *The traffic was backed up **for miles*** (=for a very long distance). | *The bus stop is **miles away**.* | *They finally found him, wandering around **miles from** home.* | **miles from anywhere/nowhere** *The campsite is miles from anywhere.* **3 a mile a minute** SPOKEN if you talk or do something a mile a minute, you do it very quickly without stopping: *The two of them were talking a mile a minute.* **4 go the extra mile** to try a little harder in order to achieve something, after you have already used a lot of effort: *The President vowed to go the extra mile for peace in the region.* **5 by a mile** by a very large amount: *This one's the best by a mile.* **6 the mile** a race that is a mile in length: *He's the world record holder in the mile.* **7 see/spot/tell etc. sth from a mile away** also **see/spot/tell etc. sth a mile off** to be able to see, notice, or recognize something very easily:

You could tell he was a policeman from a mile away. [**Origin:** Old English *mil*, from Latin *milia passum* **thousands of paces**] → see also NAUTICAL MILE

mile·age /ˈmaɪlɪdʒ/ *n.* [U] **1** the number of miles a vehicle has traveled since it was made or since another particular time: *Always check the mileage before buying a used car.* | *The rental car costs $35 a day, with unlimited mileage.* | **low/high mileage** *a used car with low mileage* **2** also **gas mileage** the number of miles a vehicle can travel using each GALLON of gasoline: *My car **gets** pretty **good mileage**.* **3** the advantage or use that you get from something: *The newspapers want to **get** as much **mileage out of** the story as they can.* **4** an amount of money paid for each mile that is traveled by someone using a car for work: *I get paid for mileage.* | *a mileage allowance* **5** a distance in miles that is covered by something: *the city's square mileage*

mile·post /ˈmaɪlpoʊst/ *n.* [C] **1** a small sign next to a road that marks distances by miles **2** a MILESTONE

mil·er /ˈmaɪlɚ/ *n.* [C] a person or horse that competes in one-mile races

mile·stone /ˈmaɪlstoʊn/ *n.* [C] **1** a very important event in the development of something: **+in** *The promotion was an important milestone in her career.* **2** a stone next to a road that shows the distance in miles to another town

mi·lieu /milˈyu, mɪlˈyʊ/ *n.* [C] FORMAL the things and people that surround you and influence the way you live and think: *His novels reflect his own social and cultural milieu.*

mil·i·tant /ˈmɪlətənt/ *adj.* a militant organization or person is willing to use extreme methods in order to achieve political or social change: *a group of militant nationalists* | *The organization has gradually become more militant.* —**militant** *n.* [C] —**militancy** *n.* [U] —**militantly** *adv.*

mil·i·ta·ris·m /ˈmɪlɪt̬əˌrɪzəm/ *n.* [U] the belief that a country should increase its military forces and use them to get what it wants, or the practice of increasing and using a country's military force in this way —**militarist** *n.* [C] —**militaristic** /ˌmɪlɪt̬əˈrɪstɪk/ *adj.*

mil·i·ta·rized /ˈmɪlɪt̬əˌraɪzd/ *adj.* a militarized area is one that has a lot of soldiers and weapons in it → see also DEMILITARIZE

mil·i·tar·y¹ /ˈmɪləˌtɛri/ Ac S3 W1 *adj.* [only before noun, no comparative] **1** relating to or used by the army, navy, air force, Marine Corps, or Coast Guard, or relating to war: *a military leader* | *the country's military power* | **military force/action** *The government has warned of possible military action.* | *an attack by U.S. **military forces*** (=the army, navy etc.) | **a military school/academy** *We are going to send our 15-year-old son to military school.* | **a military coup** (=a situation in which the military takes over the government) **2** typical of or similar to someone who is a member of the military or what is expected in the military: *School trips have to be planned with **military precision**.* [**Origin:** 1400–1500 French *militaire*, from Latin *militaris*, from *miles* **soldier**] —**militarily** *adv.*

military² Ac *n.* **the military** the military organizations of a country, such as the army and navy: *The military took over when police were unable to stop the rioting.* | *The country does not allow women **in the military**.*

ˌmilitary-inˈdustrial ˌcomplex *n.* [singular] ECONOMICS a country's military and the industries that produce weapons and other things for the military, especially in the U.S., considered as having economic and political influence

ˌmilitary inˈtelligence *n.* [U] information about what another country's military forces plan to do, which is usually obtained secretly

ˌmilitary poˈlice *n.* [plural] a police force in the military forces whose job is to deal with members of the army etc. who break the rules → see also MP (1)

mil·i·tate /ˈmɪləˌteɪt/ *v.*

militate against sth *phr. v.* FORMAL to prevent something or make it less likely to happen: *Environmental factors militate against developments in this area.*

militate for sth *phr. v.* FORMAL to make something possible or more likely to happen

mi·li·tia /məˈlɪʃə/ *n.* [C] **1** a group of people trained as soldiers, who are not part of the permanent army but can be called to join the army if needed **2** a group of people who are armed and can fight like soldiers but are not controlled by a government and may oppose a government

mi·li·tia·man /məˈlɪʃəmən/ *n. plural* **militiamen** /-mən/ [C] a member of a militia

milk¹ /mɪlk/ S1 W3 *n.* [U] **1** a white liquid that people drink, usually produced by cows, goats, or sheep: *a glass of milk* | *We need more milk.*

THESAURUS

Types of milk

skim milk milk that has had all the fat removed from it

low-fat/2% milk milk that has had some of the fat removed from it

whole milk milk that has not had any fat removed from it

buttermilk the liquid that remains after butter has been made, used for drinking or cooking

half-and-half a mixture of milk and cream, used in coffee

2 a white liquid produced by female animals and women for feeding their babies: *breast milk* **3** a liquid or juice produced by certain plants, especially the COCONUT: *coconut milk* **4 the milk of human kindness** LITERARY ordinary kindness and sympathy for other people **5** a thin white liquid that you put on your skin to clean it or make it feel softer [**Origin:** Old English *meolc, milc*] → see also **cry over spilled milk** at CRY¹ (6), EVAPORATED MILK, **land of milk and honey** at LAND¹ (5), SKIM MILK

milk² *v.* [T] **1** to take milk from a cow or goat **2** INFORMAL to get all the money or advantages etc. that you can from a situation, person, or thing: **milk sb for sth** *He seemed to be milking me for information.* | *It was a good idea, and he **milked it for all it was worth**.* **3** to take the poison from a snake

ˌmilk ˈchocolate *n.* [U] chocolate made with milk and sugar

ˈmilk cow *n.* [C] a cow kept to give milk rather than for meat

ˈmilking maˌchine *n.* [C] a machine used for taking milk from cows

ˈmilking ˌparlor *n.* [C] a building on a farm where milk is taken from the cows

milk·maid /ˈmɪlkmeɪd/ *n.* [C] OLD USE a woman who gets milk from cows on a farm

milk·man /ˈmɪlkmæn/ *n. plural* **milkmen** /-mɛn/ [C] OLD-FASHIONED someone who delivers milk to houses each morning

ˌmilk of magˈnesia *n.* [U] a thick white liquid medicine used for stomach problems and CONSTIPATION

ˈmilk run *n.* [C] INFORMAL a train trip or regular airplane flight that stops in many places

milk·shake /ˈmɪlkʃeɪk/ *n.* [C] a drink made of milk, ICE CREAM, and fruit or chocolate

milk·sop /ˈmɪlksɑp/ *n.* [C] OLD-FASHIONED a boy or man who is too gentle and weak, and who is afraid to do anything dangerous

milk·weed /ˈmɪlkwid/ *n.* [U] a common North American plant that produces a bitter white substance when its stem is broken

milk·y /ˈmɪlki/ *adj.* **1** water or other liquids that are milky are not clear and look like milk: *The tree has a milky sap.* **2** a drink that is milky contains a lot of milk: *milky coffee* **3** milky skin is white and smooth —**milkiness** *n.* [U]

ˌMilky ˈWay *n.* **the Milky Way** PHYSICS the pale white band of light that you can see across the sky at night,

M

that consists of a large number of stars which are a very long way away

mill¹ /mɪl/ W3 *n.* [C]
1 FACTORY a factory where materials such as paper, steel, or cotton cloth are made: *a lumber mill*
2 GRAIN a building containing a large machine for crushing grain into flour, or the machine itself: *an old mill with a ruined water-wheel*
3 a coffee/pepper mill a small machine or tool for crushing coffee or pepper
4 have been through the mill to have gone through a time when you experience a lot of difficulties and problems, or to make someone go through such a time: *Baker has been through the mill with these federal investigators.*
5 put sb through the mill to make someone answer a lot of difficult questions or do a lot of difficult things in order to test them: *Candidates are put through the mill by the Senate.*
6 MILLION SPOKEN a short form of "million": *The movie has earned almost $2 mill in the first weekend.*
7 MONEY TECHNICAL a unit of money equal to 1/10 of a cent, used in setting taxes and for other financial purposes
[**Origin:** (1–5) Old English *mylen* from Latin *mola* **mill, millstone**] → see also **grist for the mill** at GRIST, **the rumor mill** at RUMOR (2), RUN-OF-THE-MILL

mill² *v.* [T] **1** [always + adv./prep.] if a lot of people are milling somewhere, they move around a place in different directions without any particular purpose: *A crowd of reporters were milling outside his house.* | +**around/about** *Shoppers were milling around the parking lot waiting for the mall to open.* **2** to produce flour by crushing grain in a mill **3** to press, roll, or shape metal in a machine **4** TECHNICAL to mark the edge of a coin with regular lines

Mill /mɪl/, **John Stu·art** /dʒɑn ˈstuɚt/ (1806–1873) a British PHILOSOPHER and ECONOMIST

Mil·lay /mɪˈleɪ/, **Ed·na St. Vin·cent** /ˈɛdnə seɪnt ˈvɪnsənt/ (1892–1950) a U.S. poet

mil·len·ni·um /məˈlɛniəm/ *n. plural* **millennia** /-niə/ **1** [C] a period of 1000 years **2** [C usually singular] the time when a new 1000-year period begins, for example on January 1, 2000: *What did you do to celebrate the millennium?* **3 the millennium** the time in the future when Christians believe that Jesus Christ will return and rule on Earth for 1000 years —**millennial** *adj.*

mill·er /ˈmɪlɚ/ *n.* [C] OLD USE someone who owns or operates a mill that makes flour

Mil·ler /ˈmɪlɚ/, **Arthur** (1915–2005) a U.S. writer of plays that deal with political or moral problems

Miller, Henry (1891–1980) a U.S. writer of NOVELS

mil·let /ˈmɪlət/ *n.* [U] a plant similar to grass, with small seeds that are used as food

milli- /mɪlə/ *prefix* 1/1000th part of a particular unit: *a milliliter* (=1/1000th of a liter)

mil·li·bar /ˈmɪləˌbɑr/ *n.* [C] TECHNICAL a unit for measuring the pressure of air

mil·li·gram /ˈmɪləˌgræm/ WRITTEN ABBREVIATION **mg** *n.* [C] a unit for measuring weight, equal to 1/1000th of a gram

mil·li·li·ter /ˈmɪləˌliṭɚ/ WRITTEN ABBREVIATION **ml** *n.* [C] a unit for measuring the amount of a liquid, equal to 1/1000th of a liter

mil·li·me·ter /ˈmɪləˌmiṭɚ/ WRITTEN ABBREVIATION **mm** *n.* [C] a unit for measuring length, equal to 1/1000th of a meter

mil·li·ner /ˈmɪlənɚ/ *n.* [C] someone who makes and sells women's hats [**Origin:** 1500–1600 *Milan* city in Italy from which women's clothing was bought in the 16th century]

mil·li·ner·y /ˈmɪləˌnɛri/ *n.* [U] **1** a word meaning "hats," used in stores and in the fashion industry **2** the activity of making women's hats

mil·lion /ˈmɪlyən/ *plural* **million** or **millions** *number, quantifier* **1** 1,000,000: *three million dollars* | *a population of 12 million people* **2 millions** [plural] several million people or things: *Millions of people will be affected by the tax changes.* | *He made millions* (=several million dollars) *on that deal.* **3 a million sth** also **millions of sth** an extremely large number of people or things: *I've heard that excuse a million times.* | *She seems to have millions of friends.* **4 not/never in a million years** SPOKEN said in order to emphasize how impossible or unlikely something is: *I never would have guessed in a million years!* **5 in a million** INFORMAL **a)** used to emphasize that someone or something is the best possible: *She's **one in a million** – always helping people.* **b)** used to show how unlikely something is: *a chance in a million* **6 feel/look like a million bucks/dollars** INFORMAL to look very attractive or feel very happy and healthy: *I felt like a million bucks in that tux.* [**Origin:** 1300–1400 French, Old Italian *milione*, from *mille* **thousand**] —**millionth** *adj., pron., n.* → see Grammar box at HUNDRED¹

mil·lion·aire /ˌmɪlyəˈnɛr/ *n.* [C] someone who is very rich and has at least one million dollars

mil·lion·air·ess /ˌmɪlyəˈnɛrɪs/ *n.* [C] OLD-FASHIONED a woman who is very rich and has at least one million dollars

mil·li·pede /ˈmɪləˌpid/ *n.* [C] a long thin insect with a lot of legs

mill·pond /ˈmɪlpɑnd/ *n.* [C] a very small lake that supplies water to turn the wheel of a WATER MILL

mill·stone /ˈmɪlstoʊn/ *n.* [C] **1** one of the two large circular stones that crush grain into flour in a MILL **2 a millstone (around your neck)** something that causes you a lot of problems and prevents you from doing what you would like to do: *The president's past has become a millstone around his neck.*

Milne /mɪln/, **A. A.** (1882–1956) a British writer best known for his books for children

milque·toast /ˈmɪlktoʊst/ *n.* [C] OLD-FASHIONED, HUMOROUS a weak quiet man with no courage SYN **wimp**

Mil·ton /ˈmɪltˀn/, **John** (1608–1674) an English poet who is best known for his EPIC poem "Paradise Lost"

Mil·wau·kee /mɪlˈwɔki/ the largest city in the U.S. state of Wisconsin

mime¹ /maɪm/ *n.* ENG. LANG. ARTS **1** [U] the use of actions or movements to express what you want to say without using words: *Clark has studied mime and dance.* **2** [C,U] an actor who performs without using words **3** [C] a performance in which no words are used: *One performer did a silly mime during the overture.*

mime² *v.* [I,T] to perform something using actions and movements without any words: *They mimed a tug of war.*

mim·e·o·graph /ˈmɪmiəˌgræf/ *v.* [T] to copy a letter, paper etc. on an old-fashioned machine, using a special ink —**mimeographed** *adj.* —**mimeograph** also **mimeograph machine** *n.* [C]

mi·met·ic /mɪˈmɛṭɪk/ *adj.* TECHNICAL copying the movements or appearance of someone or something else

mim·ic¹ /ˈmɪmɪk/ *v.* **mimicked**, **mimicking** [T] **1** to copy the way someone speaks, moves, or behaves, especially in order to make people laugh SYN **imitate**: *Jackson mimicked a foreign accent to tell the joke.* **2** to behave or operate in exactly the same way as someone or something else: *The taste and texture mimic that of ice cream.* **3** BIOLOGY if an animal mimics something, it tries to look or sound like something in order to protect itself: *The insect mimics the appearance of a wasp.* —**mimicry** *n.* [U]

mimic² *n.* [C] a person or animal that is good at copying the movements, sound, or appearance of someone or something else: *Parrots are excellent mimics.*

mi·mo·sa /mɪˈmoʊsə/ *n.* [C,U] **1** a drink that is a mixture of CHAMPAGNE and orange juice **2** BIOLOGY a small tree that grows in hot countries and has small yellow flowers

min. *n.* **1** the written abbreviation of MINIMUM **2** the written abbreviation of "minute" or "minutes"

min·a·ret /ˌmɪnəˈrɛt, ˈmɪnərɛt/ *n.* [C] a tall thin tower on a MOSQUE from which Muslims are called to prayer

min·a·to·ry /ˈmɪnəˌtɔri/ *adj.* FORMAL threatening

mince /mɪns/ *v.* **1** [T] to cut food into extremely small pieces: *Mince the garlic and add to the sauce.* **2 not mince words** to say exactly what you think, even if this may offend people: *If Sara doesn't like somebody, she doesn't mince words.* **3** [I always + adv./prep.] to walk with very quick short steps in a way that looks unnatural or silly: +**across/down/along etc.** *She always minced around the office in her high heels.*

mince·meat /ˈmɪnsmit/ *n.* [U] **1** a mixture of apples, dried fruit, and SPICES, but no meat, used in PIES **2 make mincemeat (out) of sb** INFORMAL to completely defeat someone in an argument, fight, or game: *He'd make mincemeat of you in a fight.*

mind[1] /maɪnd/ S1 W1 *n.*
1 ABILITY TO THINK AND IMAGINE [C,U] your thoughts, or your ability to think, feel, and imagine things: *Grandma's mind is as sharp as ever.* | *Mind and body are closely related.* | *The way **the human mind** works has been compared to computer programs.* | *I would love to know what's going on **in** his **mind** right now.*
2 change your mind to change your opinion or decision about something: *Use a pencil so you can erase it if you change your mind.* | +**about/on** *Garcia changed his mind about going.*
3 make up your mind a) to decide something, especially after thinking for a long time about your choices SYN **decide**: *I wish he'd hurry up and make up his mind.* | +**about/on** *He hasn't made up his mind about running for Congress.* | +**whether/which/what** *Have you made up your mind which college you want to go to?* **b)** to become very determined to do something, so that you will not change your decision: *I made up my mind I was going to retire.* | **make up your mind to do sth** *Once she made her mind up to go, there was no stopping her.* | +**that** *We made up our minds that, if business didn't get better by June, we'd sell the store.* **c)** to decide what your opinion is about someone or something: +**about** *You're old enough to make up your own mind about smoking.*
4 have sth/sb in mind to be thinking about or considering a particular person, plan etc. for a particular purpose: *It's nice, but it's not exactly **what I had in mind**.* | *She wanted to do something useful, and the work she had in mind was nursing.*
5 keep/bear sb/sth in mind to remember a fact, piece of information, or particular person when you are doing something: *It's a good idea – I'll keep it in mind.* | +**that** *Bear in mind that April 15 is the tax deadline.* | *Always keep the reader in mind when writing a report.*
6 with sth/sb in mind considering someone or something when doing something, and taking the appropriate action: *The hospital was designed with children in mind.*
7 on your mind a) if something is on your mind, you keep thinking about it and worrying about it: *You look worried, Sarah. Is there **something on your mind**?* | *He just found out his 15-year-old daughter is pregnant, so he **has a lot on his mind*** (=has a lot of problems to worry about). | *Her husband's illness was **weighing on her mind*** (=making her worry). **b)** if something is on your mind, that is what you are thinking about: *She just says what's on her mind.*
8 go out of your mind also **lose your mind** INFORMAL to start to become mentally ill or very worried, bored etc.: *She looked at me like I'd gone out of my mind.* | *Did I do that? I must be losing my mind.*
9 come/spring/leap to mind [not in progressive] if something comes or springs to mind, you think of it suddenly or immediately: *To describe this hotel, the word that comes to mind is "luxurious."*
10 bring/call sth to mind to remind you of something: *Each ornament on their Christmas tree brings to mind the friend or relative that gave it.*
11 cross/enter your mind (that) [not in progressive] if something crosses or enters your mind, you have a particular thought or idea, especially for a short time: *Thoughts of suicide crossed her mind.* | ***It** didn't **enter** my **mind** to ask for it.* | ***The thought** that he might not help never **crossed** my **mind**.*
12 go/run/flash etc. through sb's mind if something goes through your mind, you have a thought, especially for a short time: *All kinds of questions ran through my mind.* | *I wish I knew what was going through his mind.*
13 in your right mind sensible and making good decisions: ***Who in their right mind** would want to rock climb without a rope?* | *The place is falling apart – **no one in** their **right mind** would want to live here.*
14 INTELLIGENCE [C usually singular] intelligence and ability to think rather than emotions SYN **intellect**: *He has an incredibly good mind.* | *I don't really have a scientific mind.* | +**for** *Sandra has a good mind for numbers.*
15 INTELLIGENT PERSON [C] someone who is very intelligent, especially in a particular area of study or activity: *Cuomo is one of our foremost political minds.* | *Some of the finest minds in the country are working on the project.*
16 CHARACTER [C] used to talk about the way that someone thinks and the type of thoughts they have: *O'Rourke has a very devious mind.*
17 keep your mind on sth to keep paying attention to something even if it is boring or if you want to think about something else: *His mind didn't seem to be on the game at all.*
18 sb's mind is not on sth to not be thinking about what you are doing, because you are thinking or worrying about something else: *I was trying to study, but my mind just wasn't on it.*
19 take/get/keep your mind off sth to make someone stop thinking and worrying about something: *How about a game? It might help **take your mind off things**.*
20 be a load/weight off your mind to be something that you do not need to worry about anymore: *"**It's a** huge **weight off** my **mind**," said Hughes after the court judgment.*
21 weigh/prey on sb's mind if something is weighing or preying on your mind, you are thinking and worrying about it: *The lawsuit is weighing on her mind.*
22 sb's mind is racing if your mind is racing, you are thinking very quickly about something because you are excited, frightened etc.: *As Robinson left, Jim's mind was racing.*
23 get/push/block sb/sth out of your mind to stop thinking about someone or something, or try to forget them: *I just can't get him out of my mind.* | *Cary says he's trying to put the rumors out of his mind.*
24 be the last thing on sb's mind to be the thing that someone is least likely to be thinking about: *Marriage is the last thing on my mind right now.*
25 your mind goes blank if your mind goes blank, you suddenly cannot remember something: *As soon as Mr. Dixon asked me the question, my mind just went blank.*

SPOKEN PHRASES

26 be out of your mind to behave in a way that is crazy or stupid: *You'd be out of your mind to sell it now.* | *Are you out of your mind?*
27 bored out of your mind INFORMAL extremely bored: *The kids were bored out of their minds this summer.*
28 stoned/drunk etc. out of your mind affected by drugs or alcohol so that you do not really know what you are doing
29 there's no doubt/question in my mind used when you are very sure about something: *There's no doubt in my mind that she'll win.*
30 great minds think alike used to say in a joking way that you and someone else must be very intelligent because you both agree about something or you have both thought of something
31 have half a mind to do sth also **have a good mind to do sth a)** used to say that you might do something to show that you disapprove of something someone has done: *I have a good mind to ground you for a week.* **b)** used when you are considering doing something, but are not sure you will do it: *I have half a mind to just go home.*
32 in/to my mind used when you are giving your opinion about something SYN **in my opinion**: *In my mind, his actions amount to criminal fraud.*

33 at/in the back of your mind if something is at the back of your mind, you keep remembering it or feeling it, but you do not think about it directly: *I guess at the back of my mind I always knew she'd leave.*
34 state/frame of mind the way someone is thinking and feeling at a particular time, such as how happy or sad they are: *What was his state of mind on the day of the shooting?* | **in a good/bad/positive etc. frame of mind** *He went off to work in an optimistic frame of mind.*
35 keep/have an open mind (about sth) also **do sth with an open mind** to be willing to think about and accept new ideas or ways of doing things: *The new assemblyman has an open mind on the subject of marijuana legalization.* → see also OPEN-MINDED
36 have a mind of your own **a)** to have strong opinions and make your own decisions: *Joey's only two, but he has a mind of his own.* **b)** if an object has a mind of its own, it seems to control itself and does not work or move in the way you want it to: *My hair seems to have a mind of its own today.*
37 be of two minds about sth to be unable to make a decision about something, or to not be sure what you think of something: *Americans are of two minds about the proposed health care changes.*
38 be of sound mind LAW to have the ability to think clearly and be responsible for your actions
39 put/set sb's mind at ease/rest to make someone feel less worried or anxious: *Call your mom and tell her you're here, just to set her mind at rest.*
40 go/turn over sth in your mind to keep thinking about something because you are trying to understand it or solve a problem: *Tony turned over the suggestion in his mind.*
41 stick/stay in sb's mind if a name, fact, event etc. sticks in your mind, you remember it for a long time: *For some reason, the name stuck in my mind.*
42 sth is all/just in sb's mind used to tell someone that they have imagined something and it does not really exist: *At first, doctors said the illness was all in her mind.*
43 your mind wanders if your mind WANDERS, you stop paying attention to something, especially because you are bored
44 be of one/the same/like mind FORMAL to agree with someone about something: *I think we're of one mind that the service should be maintained.* | **+on/about** *The seven European leaders are not of the same mind on the issue of trade.*
45 have a closed mind (about sth) to refuse to think about or accept new ideas or ways of doing things
46 know your own mind to be very clear about what your opinions or beliefs are and not be influenced by what other people think
47 in your mind's eye if you see something in your mind's eye, you imagine or remember clearly what it looks like: *I can still see him standing there, in my mind's eye.*
48 mind over matter an expression used when someone uses their intelligence to control a difficult situation
49 have it in mind to do sth to intend to do something: *Bill said he had it in mind to drop out of school and see the world.*
50 put you in mind of sb/sth [not in progressive] to remind you of a person or thing SYN **remind**: *The girl put me in mind of my own daughter.*
51 put/set your mind to sth to decide to do something, and use a lot of effort in order to succeed: *You can do anything if you just set your mind to it.*
52 pay sb/sth no mind OLD-FASHIONED to not pay any attention to someone or something or not care about what they are saying or doing: *Most people paid no mind to the marchers.*
[**Origin:** Old English *gemynd*] → see also **sth blows your mind** at BLOW[1] (8), **the mind boggles** at BOGGLE (1), **sb/sth drives sb out of their mind** at DRIVE[1] (10), **meeting of (the) minds** at MEETING (5), -MINDED, ONE-TRACK MIND, **peace of mind** at PEACE (3), **give sb a piece of your mind** at PIECE[1] (9), PRESENCE OF MIND, **read sb's mind/thoughts** at READ[1] (9), **out of sight, out of mind** at SIGHT[1] (14), **slip your mind** at SLIP[1] (8), **speak your mind** at SPEAK (8)

mind² S1 W2 *v.*
1 FEEL ANNOYED [I, T not in progressive or passive, usually in questions and negatives] to feel annoyed, worried, or angry about something: *Are you sure your mother doesn't mind?* | *Of course* ***I don't mind*** *if you bring a few friends over.* | ***I don't mind*** *the winter – I like snow.* | **mind doing sth** *Do you mind being away from home so much?* | **mind sb doing sth** *I don't mind them coming as long as they behave.* | **mind that** *David says his parents don't mind that he spends so much time on his computer.*

SPOKEN PHRASES

2 never mind **a)** used to tell someone that something was not important, that you do not want to say something again, or that they should ignore what you said: *"What did you say?" "Oh, never mind."* | *Oh, Dad, never mind, Cheryl's got them.* | *"I was already planning to have chicken tonight." "Oh, never mind, it was just an idea."* **b)** used to tell someone not to be upset about something or not to worry about something, because it is not important: *Never mind. At least we tried.* | *Never mind about the car. You're safe, and that's the main thing.* **c)** used to tell someone that it is not important to do or consider something now, often because something else is more important: *Never mind the dishes – I'll do them later.* | *I'll take it, never mind the cost!* | **+about** *Never mind about baseball and football, say fans of soccer.* **d)** used to emphasize that something is not possible or likely, because something that should be easier or better is not possible: *He was ashamed to tell his family, never mind a stranger.* | *I didn't think I could walk that far, never mind run.*
3 would/do you mind used to ask someone something politely: **would/do you mind doing sth** *Would you mind opening the window, please?* | **would/do you mind if** *Do you mind if I call my mom?*
4 not mind (doing sth) to be willing to do something: *I don't mind driving if you're tired.* | *"We'll have to walk." "I don't mind. I like walking."*
5 I wouldn't mind (doing) sth used to say that you would like something: *I wouldn't mind a drink myself.* | *I wouldn't mind just sitting here all day listening to the birds.*
6 if you don't mind used when checking that someone is willing to do something or let you do something: *I'd like to ask you a few questions, if you don't mind.*
7 if you don't mind my saying so also **if you don't mind me asking** used when you are saying or asking something that you think might offend someone: *You look tired, if you don't mind my saying so.*
8 I don't mind telling you/admitting/saying etc. used to emphasize what you are saying, especially when it could make you seem silly: *I don't mind telling you, it really worries me, my daughter going out with someone so much older.*
9 mind your own business/beeswax to not get involved in or ask questions about other people's lives or personal details: *Mom, mind your own beeswax.*
10 be minding your own business to be doing something ordinary on your own when something unexpected happens to you: *I was just standing there minding my own business and this kid comes up and hits me!*
11 don't mind me used to tell someone not to pay any attention to you: *Oh, don't mind me, I was just thinking out loud.*
12 do you mind! used when you are annoyed at something that someone has done: *Do you mind! I just washed that floor!*
13 mind you used to say something that emphasizes what you are talking about: *It wasn't excellent, mind you, but it was a definite improvement.*
14 (I) don't mind if I do HUMOROUS used when politely accepting something such as food or drink that has been offered to you: *"Would you like another piece of cake?" "Thanks – don't mind if I do."*

15 mind your manners/p's and q's to be careful about how you behave so that you do not offend anyone: *Corey,*

M

mind your manners. | *If I want federal funding I'd better mind my p's and q's.*
16 OBEY [I, T not in progressive] to obey someone's instructions or advice: *Some dogs will mind instructions better than others.* | *Mind your mother, Sam!*
17 mind the store to be in charge of something, especially while the person who is usually in charge is not there: *Congressmen, embarrassed that they had not been minding the store, moved to prevent future scandals.*
18 TAKE CARE OF [T] OLD-FASHIONED to take care of a child, especially for someone else [SYN] watch: *He spends as much time as his wife minding the children.*

'mind-ˌbending *adj.* INFORMAL **1** strange and difficult to understand: *a page of mind-bending tax charts* **2** mind-bending drugs have a strong effect on your mind and make you have strange feelings and experiences

'mind-ˌblowing *adj.* INFORMAL very exciting, shocking, or strange: *a mind-blowing experience* → see also **sth blows your mind** at BLOW[1] (8)

mind-bog·gling /'maɪndˌbɑgəlɪŋ/ *adj.* INFORMAL difficult to imagine and very big, strange, or complicated: *The statistics were mind-boggling.*

-minded /maɪndɪd/ [in adjectives] **1 safety-minded/career-minded etc.** believing in the importance of safety etc.: *a budget-minded traveler* **2 serious-minded/evil-minded etc.** having a particular attitude or way of thinking: *an independent-minded little girl* → see also ABSENT-MINDED, NARROW-MINDED, OPEN-MINDED, SIMPLEMINDED, SINGLE-MINDED

mind·ful /'maɪndfəl/ *adj.* FORMAL doing things in a way that shows you remember a rule or fact: +**of** *Officials must be mindful of the neighborhood's needs.*

'mind games *n.* [plural] words and actions that are intended to make someone feel confused, less confident, and unhappy: *He **plays mind games with** his opponents.*

mind·less /'maɪndlɪs/ *adj.* **1** if something is mindless, you can do it or watch it without thinking or using your mind: *Stuffing envelopes is mindless work.* **2** completely stupid and without any purpose [SYN] senseless: *mindless violence* —**mindlessly** *adv.* —**mindlessness** *n.* [U]

'mind ˌreader *n.* [C] OFTEN HUMOROUS someone who knows what someone else is thinking without being told

mind·set /'maɪndsɛt/ *n.* [C usually singular] someone's way of thinking about things, which is often difficult to change

mine[1] /maɪn/ [S1] [W3] *possessive pron.* [possessive form of "I"] the thing or things belonging or relating to the person who is speaking: *"Whose coat is this?" "It's mine."* | *Louisa didn't have a pencil, so I let her borrow mine.* | *Tom's a good friend **of mine**.*

mine[2] [W3] *n.* [C] **1** a type of bomb that is hidden below the surface of the ground or the water, which explodes when someone or something touches it: *a ban on the production of **land mines*** | *The tank **hit a mine**.* **2** a deep hole or series of holes in the ground from which coal, gold etc. is dug: *an old gold mine* → see also QUARRY, STRIP MINE **3 a mine of information/gossip etc.** someone or something that can give you a lot of information about a particular subject: *The letters are a mine of information about the period.* **4** TECHNICAL a passage dug beneath the place where an enemy army is

mine[3] *v.* **1** [I,T] to dig into the ground in order to get gold, coal etc.: +**for** *Thousands came to mine for gold.* **2** [T often passive] to hide bombs in the ocean or under the ground: *The border is heavily mined.* **3** [T] to get information, ideas etc. from something: *Simon mines his childhood experiences for his plays.*

mine[4] *determiner* OLD USE a way of saying "my," before a vowel sound or "h," or after a noun: *mine host*

mine·field /'maɪnfild/ *n.* [C] **1** an area of land that has mines hidden on it **2** [usually singular] a situation in which there are a lot of dangers or difficulties, and it is difficult to make the right decision: +**of** *Businesses have to pick their way **through a minefield** of legislation.* | **political/legal/ethical etc. minefield** *The subject of abortion is a political minefield.*

min·er /'maɪnɚ/ *n.* [C] someone who works in a mine, digging out coal, gold etc.: *a coal miner*

min·er·al /'mɪnərəl/ *n.* [C] **1** EARTH SCIENCE a substance that is formed naturally in the earth, especially a solid substance such as coal, salt, stone, or gold: *an area rich in minerals* **2** CHEMISTRY an INORGANIC substance such as CALCIUM or iron that is present in some foods and that is important for good health: *Fish is a rich source of vitamins and minerals.*

min·er·al·o·gy /ˌmɪnə'rɑlədʒi/ *n.* [U] EARTH SCIENCE the scientific study of minerals —**mineralogist** *n.* [C]

'mineral oil *n.* [U] a clear oil that is made from PETROLEUM and can be used on wooden furniture, on your skin, or taken as a LAXATIVE

'mineral ˌwater *n.* [U] water that comes from under the ground and contains minerals

min·e·stro·ne /ˌmɪnə'strouni/ *n.* [U] an Italian soup containing vegetables and small pieces of PASTA

mine·sweep·er /'maɪnˌswipɚ/ *n.* [C] a ship that has equipment for removing bombs from under water —**minesweeping** *n.* [U]

min·gle /'mɪŋgəl/ *v.* **1** [I,T] if two or more feelings, sounds, smells etc. mingle or are mingled, they combine with each other [SYN] mix: +**with** *Their curiosity was mingled with fear.* **2** [I] to meet and talk with a lot of different people at a social event: +**with** *The cast came out to mingle with the audience.* —**mingled** *adj.*

min·i /'mɪni/ *n.* [C] a very short skirt or dress

mini- /mɪni/ *prefix* very small compared with others of the same type: *a miniskirt* (=very short skirt) | *a minimarket* (=a small food store) → see also MICRO-

min·i·a·ture[1] /'mɪniətʃɚ, 'mɪnɪtʃɚ/ *adj.* much smaller than normal: *a miniature train*

miniature[2] *n.* **1** [C] something that is much smaller than the usual thing of its type: *a miniature of the airplane* **2** [C] ENG. LANG. ARTS a very small painting, usually of a person **3 in miniature** exactly like something or someone but much smaller: *She is her mother in miniature.* [**Origin:** 1500–1600 Italian *miniatura* **art of drawing small pictures in a book**, from Latin *miniare* **to color with minium**]

ˌminiature 'golf *n.* [U] a GOLF game, played for fun outdoors, in which you hit a small ball through passages, over small bridges and hills etc.

min·i·a·tur·ist /'mɪniətʃərɪst, 'mɪnɪ-/ *n.* [C] someone who paints very small pictures, or makes very small objects

min·i·a·tur·ize /'mɪniətʃəˌraɪz, 'mɪnɪ-/ *v.* [T usually passive] to make something in a very small size —**miniaturized** *adj.* —**miniaturization** /ˌmɪniətʃərə'zeɪʃən/ *n.* [U]

min·i·bar /'mɪniˌbɑr/ *n.* [C] a small REFRIGERATOR in a hotel room in which there are alcoholic drinks, juice etc.

min·i·bike /'mɪniˌbaɪk/ *n.* [C] a small MOTORCYCLE

min·i·bus /'mɪniˌbʌs/ *n.* [C] a small bus with seats for six to 12 people

min·i·cam /'mɪniˌkæm/ *n.* [C] a small movie camera, used especially by news programs

min·i·com·put·er /'mɪnikəmˌpyuṭɚ/ *n.* [C] COMPUTERS a computer that is larger than a PERSONAL COMPUTER and smaller than a MAINFRAME, used by businesses and other large organizations

mini·golf /'mɪniˌgɑlf/ *n.* [U] MINIATURE GOLF

min·i·mal /'mɪnəməl/ [Ac] *adj.* very small in degree or amount: *Desert plants will stay healthy even with minimal watering.* | *The cost to taxpayers will be minimal.* —**minimally** *adv.*

min·i·mal·ism /'mɪnəməˌlɪzəm/ *n.* [U] a style of art, music etc. that uses only a very few simple ideas or patterns —**minimalist** *n.* [C] —**minimalist** *adj.*

M

min·i·mart /ˈmɪniˌmɑrt/ also **ˈmini-ˌmarket** *n.* [C] a small store that stays open very late and that sells food, cigarettes, etc. and sometimes gasoline

min·i·mize /ˈmɪnəˌmaɪz/ Ac *v.* [T] **1** to reduce something that is difficult or unpleasant to the smallest possible amount or degree SYN lessen OPP maximize: *plans to minimize traffic problems* **2** to make something seem less serious or important than it really is SYN play down: *White House officials sought to minimize the importance of the meeting.* **3** COMPUTERS to make a document or program on your computer very small, when you are not using it but still want to keep it on screen OPP maximize → see also MAXIMIZE

min·i·mum¹ /ˈmɪnəməm/ Ac S3 W3 *adj.* [only before noun] the minimum number, amount or degree is the smallest that is possible, allowed, or needed SYN least OPP maximum: *The minimum order is 500 business cards.* | *The minimum age for buying cigarettes is 18.*

minimum² Ac *n.* [C usually singular] the smallest amount, number, or degree of something that is possible, allowed, or needed: **+of** *Get to the airport a minimum of two hours before your flight.* | *A lot of the students are just doing **the bare minimum*** (=the least amount they can) *of work.* | *Staffing levels are down to an **absolute minimum**.* | ***At a minimum**, we require employees to have two years' training.* | **keep/reduce sth to a minimum** (=limit something to the smallest amount possible) *Development in the hills has been kept to a minimum.* [**Origin:** 1600–1700 Latin *minimus* **smallest**]

ˌminimum ˈbalance *n.* [singular] ECONOMICS the smallest amount of money that you need to have in your bank account to avoid paying charges or to receive INTEREST payments: *The bank provides a free checking service to customers who maintain a minimum balance of $100 in their NOW account.*

ˌminimum-seˈcurity ˌprison *n.* [C] a prison that does not restrict prisoners' freedom as much as ordinary prisons

ˌminimum ˈwage *n.* [C usually singular] the lowest amount of money that an employer can legally pay per hour to a worker —**minimum-wage** *adj.*: *a minimum-wage job*

min·ing /ˈmaɪnɪŋ/ *n.* [U] EARTH SCIENCE the work or industry of getting metals and minerals out of the earth

min·ion /ˈmɪnyən/ *n.* [C] a very unimportant person in an organization, who just obeys other people's orders [**Origin:** 1500–1600 French *mignon* word for a much-loved person]

min·i·se·ries /ˈmɪniˌsɪriz/ *n.* [C] a television DRAMA that is divided into several parts and shown every night for one or two weeks

min·i·skirt /ˈmɪniˌskɚt/ *n.* [C] a very short skirt

min·is·ter¹ /ˈmɪnəstɚ/ *n.* [C] **1** a religious leader in some Christian churches SYN clergyman → see also PASTOR **2** a politician who is in charge of a government department in some countries: *the Russian foreign minister* → see also PRIME MINISTER **3** someone whose job is to represent their country in another country, but who is lower in rank than an AMBASSADOR [**Origin:** 1200–1300 Old French *ministre*, from Latin *minister* **servant**]

minister² *v.* [I] to be a minister: *Rev. Wilson spent 20 years ministering in a poor area of New York.*

minister to sb/sth *phr. v.* FORMAL to give help to someone or something who needs it: *Volunteers minister to the poor and sick.*

min·is·te·ri·al /ˌmɪnəˈstɪriəl/ Ac *adj.* relating to a minister, or done by a minister: *ministerial committees*

min·is·tra·tions /ˌmɪnəˈstreɪʃənz/ *n.* [plural] FORMAL the giving of help and service, especially to people who are sick or who need the help of a priest

min·is·try /ˈmɪnəstri/ Ac *n. plural* **ministries** **1 the ministry** the profession of being a church leader, especially in the Protestant church: *He felt **called to the ministry**.* **2** [C] POLITICS a government department in some countries: *the Ministry of Agriculture* **3** [U] the work done by a priest or other religious person: *the ministry of Jesus*

min·i·van /ˈmɪniˌvæn/ *n.* [C] a large vehicle with seats for six to eight people

mink /mɪŋk/ *n. plural* **mink** **1** [C,U] BIOLOGY a small animal with soft brown fur, or the valuable fur from this animal: *a mink coat* **2** [C] a coat made of mink fur

Min·ne·ap·o·lis /ˌmɪniˈæpəlɪs/ a city in the U.S. state of Minnesota, which is a port on the Mississippi River. The city Saint Paul is across the river, and together, Minneapolis and Saint Paul are known as the Twin Cities.

Min·ne·so·ta /ˌmɪnəˈsoʊt̬ə/ ABBREVIATION **MN** a state in the northern central part of the U.S. —**Minnesotan** *n., adj.*

min·now /ˈmɪnoʊ/ *n.* [C] a very small fish that lives in rivers, lakes etc.

Min·o·an /mɪˈnoʊən/ *adj.* of or about the civilization of ancient Crete (3000–1100 B.C.)

mi·nor¹ /ˈmaɪnɚ/ Ac S3 W3 *adj.* **1** small and not very important or serious, especially when compared with other things OPP major: *Most of the problems have been very minor.* | *a minor traffic violation* | *minor injuries* ►see THESAURUS box at unimportant **2** ENG. LANG. ARTS based on a musical SCALE in which the third note of the related MAJOR scale has been lowered by a half step: *a minor key* | *a symphony in D minor* [**Origin:** 1200–1300 Latin **smaller**] → see also MAJOR

minor² Ac *n.* [C] **1** LAW someone who is below the age at which they become legally responsible for their actions: *Thomas pleaded guilty to buying alcohol for a minor.* ►see THESAURUS box at child **2** the second main subject that you study in college for your degree: *"What's your minor?" "History."* ►see THESAURUS box at university → see also MAJOR **3 the minors** the MINOR LEAGUES

minor³ Ac *v.*

minor in sth *phr. v.* to study a second main subject as part of your college degree: *Nguyen minored in theater studies.* → see also MAJOR

ˌminor ˈarc *n.* [C] MATH a curved line that is less than half of a circle → see also MAJOR ARC

mi·nor·i·ty /məˈnɔrət̬i, maɪ-, -ˈnɑr-/ Ac W2 *n. plural* **minorities** **1** [C usually plural] **a)** POLITICS a group of people of a different race or religion than most people in a country: *Both republics have sizable Serbian minorities.* | *minority students* | *children from many different **minority groups*** | **ethnic/racial minority** *The project leaders came from different religions and ethnic minorities.* **b)** someone in one of these groups: *The law prevents job discrimination against minorities and women.* | *minority-owned businesses* **2** [singular] a small group of people or things within a much larger group: *Gaelic is still spoken in Ireland by a tiny minority.* | **+of** *A minority of teenagers drink excessively.* | **a small/large/tiny/significant etc. minority** *A small minority of the students need extra help.* **3 be in the minority** to form less than half of a group: *Male teachers are in the minority in elementary schools.* **4 a minority of one** the only person in a group who has a particular opinion: *On policy votes, Marshall is often a minority of one.* **5** [U] LAW the period of time when someone is below the age at which they become legally responsible for their actions OPP majority

miˈnority ˌleader *n.* [C usually singular] POLITICS the leader of the political party that has fewer politicians in Congress than the leading party → see also MAJORITY LEADER

ˌminor ˈleague *n.* **1 the Minor Leagues** [plural] the groups of teams that form the lower levels of American professional baseball → see also MAJOR LEAGUES **2** [C] small businesses and organizations, rather than large powerful ones —**minor leaguer** *n.* [C]

ˈminor-league *adj.* [only before noun] **1** relating to the minor leagues in sports: *a minor-league catcher* **2** not very important, or large: *minor-league crooks*

Minsk /mɪnsk/ the capital and largest city of Belarus

min·strel /ˈmɪnstrəl/ *n.* [C] **1** HISTORY a singer or musician in the Middle Ages **2** a white singer or dancer who pretended to be an African-American person and who performed in shows in the early part of the 20th century

mint¹ /mɪnt/ *n.* **1** [C,U] a candy that tastes like PEPPERMINT (=a type of mint with a strong taste) **2** [U] BIOLOGY a small plant with leaves that have a strong fresh smell and taste and are used in cooking and making medicine → see also PEPPERMINT, SPEARMINT **3 a mint** a large amount of money SYN **fortune**: *Many young MBAs dream of* ***making a mint*** *on Wall Street.* **4** [C] a place where coins are officially made

mint² *v.* [T] **1** to make a coin **2** to invent new words, phrases, or ideas **3 newly/freshly minted** recently invented or produced: *a newly minted engineering graduate*

mint³ *adj.* **in mint condition** looking new and in perfect condition: *a 1968 Mustang car in mint condition*

mint ju·lep /ˌmɪnt˺ ˈdʒuləp/ *n.* [C] a drink in which alcohol and sugar are mixed with ice and mint leaves are added

mint·y /ˈmɪnti/ *adj.* tasting or smelling like mint

min·u·et /ˌmɪnyuˈɛt/ *n.* [C] a slow graceful dance of the 17th and 18th century, or a piece of music for this dance

mi·nus¹ /ˈmaɪnəs/ S3 *prep.* **1** used in mathematics when you SUBTRACT one number from another OPP **plus**: *17 minus 5 is 12 (17 – 5 = 12)* ►see THESAURUS box at **calculate** **2** without something that would normally be there: *He came back from the fight minus a couple of front teeth.*

minus² *n.* [C] **1** MATH a minus sign **2** something that is a disadvantage because it makes a situation bad SYN **drawback** OPP **plus**: *There are both* ***pluses and minuses*** *to living in a big city.*

minus³ *adj.* **1 minus 5/20/30 etc.** MATH less than zero, especially less than 0° in temperature: *At night the temperature can go as low as minus 30.* **2 A minus, B minus etc.** a grade used in a system of judging students' work. A minus is lower than A, but higher than B plus. OPP **plus**

min·us·cule /ˈmɪnəˌskyul/ *adj.* extremely small SYN **minute**: *The chances of getting the disease are minuscule.* | *a minuscule amount of food*

ˈminus ˌsign *n.* [C] MATH a sign (–) showing that a number is less than zero, or that the second of two numbers is to be SUBTRACTED from the first → see also PLUS SIGN

min·ute¹ /ˈmɪnɪt/ S1 W1 *n.* [C]

1 TIME a period of time equal to 60 seconds: *The power went out for about 15 minutes.* | ***It takes*** *me about ten* ***minutes*** *to walk to school.* | **+to/after** *It's five minutes after two.* | **+a one-/two-/ten- etc. minute sth** *a 20-minute bus ride*

2 last minute the last possible time, just before it is too late: *There were a few last-minute changes to the program.* | *Ellen got some extra tickets* ***at the last minute.*** | *Many voters are waiting* ***until the last minute*** *to make a decision.* → see also LAST-MINUTE

3 love/enjoy/hate etc. every minute (of sth) INFORMAL to love, enjoy etc. all of something: *"I hear John is in Alaska." "Yes, and loving every minute of it."*

4 by the minute also **minute by minute** more and more as time passes: *Medical technology changes almost by the minute.*

5 within minutes very soon after something has happened: *Police responded to the alarm within minutes.* | **+of** *We were met by our guide within minutes of our arrival.*

SPOKEN PHRASES

6 a minute a very short period of time SYN **moment**: *Stay here a minute.* | *Hold still. This won't* ***take a minute*** (=it won't take very long). | *I just have to sit* ***for a minute*** *and rest.*

7 in a minute a) very soon: *Tell him we'll be there in a minute.* | *I have a meeting with Liz in a minute.* | *Your waiter will be here* ***in just a minute.*** **b)** used to say that you would do something without stopping to think about it: *I would have married her in a minute.*

8 wait/just a minute also **hold on a minute a)** used to tell someone you want them to wait for a short time while you do or say something else: *Just a minute, Margaret, I want to introduce you to Betty.* | *Wait a minute, let me see if I understand this correctly.* **b)** used to tell someone to stop speaking or doing something for a short time because they have said or done something wrong: *Hey, wait a minute, she wasn't supposed to tell you.*

9 any minute (now) used to say that something will happen extremely soon: *Oh, they're going to be here any minute!*

10 do you have a minute? used to ask someone if you may talk to them for a short time: *Do you have a minute? I have a couple of questions.*

11 one minute a) used to say that a situation suddenly changes: *How can you guys be so nice one minute, and then so mean the next?* **b)** used to ask someone to wait for a short time while you do something else: *One minute – I'll put your call through.*

12 the minute (that) sb does sth as soon as someone does something: *Tell him I need to see him the minute he arrives.*

13 not think/believe etc. for one minute used to say that you certainly do not think something, believe something etc.: *I never for one minute thought he'd do it.*

14 this minute right now SYN **immediately**: *You don't have to tell me right this minute.* | *Go to your room this minute* (=used when you are angry)*!*

15 every minute used to emphasize that something involves all of a particular period of time: *I enjoyed every minute of it.*

16 not a minute too soon if something happens or you do something not a minute too soon, it happens almost too late

17 the next minute immediately afterward: *He was standing right next to me, and the next minute he was gone.*

18 NOTES **minutes** [plural] an official written record of what is said and decided at a meeting: *The school board must* ***keep minutes*** *of these discussions.* | *Who's going to* ***take the minutes*** (=write them down)*?*

19 MATHEMATICS MATH one of the 60 parts into which a degree of angle is divided. It can be shown as a symbol after a number. For example, 78° 52' means 78 degrees 52 minutes.

[**Origin:** 1300–1400 Old French, Medieval Latin *minuta*, from *pars minuta prima* **first small part, one sixtieth of a unit**] → see also UP-TO-THE-MINUTE → see Word Choice box at MOMENT

mi·nute² /maɪˈnut/ *adj.* **1** extremely small SYN **minuscule**: *minute living organisms* | *The print was minute!* ►see THESAURUS box at **small¹** **2** paying careful attention to the smallest details: *a minute examination of the surface* | *He explained it all* ***in minute detail.*** —**minutely** *adv.* —**minuteness** *n.* [U]

minute hand /ˈmɪnɪt ˌhænd/ *n.* [C] the long thin piece of metal that points to the minutes on a clock or watch → see also HOUR HAND

min·ute·man /ˈmɪnɪtˌmæn/ *n. plural* **minutemen** /-ˌmɛn/ [C] one of a group of men who were not official soldiers but who were ready to fight at any time during the Revolutionary War in the U.S.

mi·nu·ti·ae /maɪˈnuʃə, mə-/ *n.* [plural] very small and exact details

M

minx /mɪŋks/ *n.* [C] OLD-FASHIONED an attractive young woman who FLIRTS with men, is confident, and who does not show respect to older people

mips /mɪps/ *n.* [plural] **millions of instructions per second** COMPUTERS a way of measuring how fast a computer works

mir·a·cle /ˈmɪrəkəl/ *n.* [C] **1** something very good or lucky that happens when you did not expect it to happen or did not think it was possible: ***It will be a miracle** if we get to the airport in time.* | *the **economic miracle** in Singapore* | **minor/small miracle** (=something good or lucky but not very important) *The fact that we got it done on time was a minor miracle.* **2** something that you admire very much and that is a good example of a particular quality or skill: *Genetic testing is indeed a scientific miracle.* | +**of** *The Golden Gate bridge is a miracle of engineering.* **3** an action or event believed to be caused by God, because it is impossible according to the ordinary laws of nature: *The saint **performed** many **miracles**.* **4 work/perform miracles** to have a very good effect or result: *Try yoga – it worked miracles for me.* **5 miracle cure/drug a)** a very effective medical treatment that cures even serious diseases **b)** something that solves a very difficult problem: *a miracle cure for the educational crisis*

mi·rac·u·lous /mɪˈrækyələs/ *adj.* **1** very good, completely unexpected, and often very lucky: *a miraculous recovery from her injuries* **2** a miraculous action or event is believed to be caused by God, and is impossible according to the ordinary laws of nature: *the saint's miraculous powers of healing* —**miraculously** *adv.*

mi·rage /mɪˈrɑʒ/ *n.* [C] **1** a strange effect caused by hot air in a desert, in which you think you can see objects when they are not actually there **2** a dream, hope, or wish that cannot come true SYN **illusion**

Mi·ran·da rule, the /mɪˈrændə ˌrul/ LAW the rule that the police must inform a person they have ARRESTED of his or her legal rights

mire¹ /maɪɚ/ *n.* [U] **1** deep mud **2** a bad or difficult situation that you cannot seem to escape from SYN **quagmire**: *people stuck **in the mire** of debt and poverty*

mire² *v.* **1 be mired (down) in sth** to be in a bad situation where you are unable to get out or make progress: *a country mired in civil war* **2 be mired in sth** to be stuck in deep mud: *The plane was mired in mud and snow at the end of the runway.*

Mi·ró /miˈroʊ/, **Jo·an** /ʒʊˈɑn/ (1893–1983) a Spanish PAINTER famous for his use of bright color and ABSTRACT shapes in the style of SURREALISM

mir·ror¹ /ˈmɪrɚ/ S2 W3 *n.* [C] **1** a piece of special glass that you can look at and see yourself or see what is behind you: *I examined my face **in the mirror**.* | *When I **looked in the mirror**, I could hardly believe it.* | *a full-length mirror* **2 a mirror of sth** something that gives a clear idea of what something else is like: *The polls are an accurate mirror of public opinion.* [**Origin:** 1200–1300 Old French *mirour*, from *mirer* **to look at**, from Latin *mirare*] → see also ONE-WAY MIRROR, REARVIEW MIRROR

mirror² *v.* [T] to be very similar to something or a copy of it: *Victor's surprised expression mirrored her own.*

ˈmirror ˌimage *n.* [C] **1** an image of something in which the right side appears on the left, and the left side appears on the right **2** something that is either very similar to something else or is the complete opposite of it: *The situation is a mirror image of the one Republicans faced 25 years ago.*

ˈmirror site *n.* [C] a copy of a popular website that is on a different SERVER from the original website, so that more people can look at it more quickly

mirth /mɚθ/ *n.* [U] LITERARY happiness and laughter —**mirthful** *adj.* —**mirthfully** *adv.*

mirth·less /ˈmɚθlɪs/ *adj.* LITERARY mirthless laughter or a mirthless smile does not seem to be caused by real amusement or happiness —**mirthlessly** *adv.*

mis- /mɪs/ *prefix* **1** bad or badly: *misfortune* (=bad luck) | *He's been misbehaving* (=behaving badly). **2** wrong or wrongly: *a miscalculation* | *I misunderstood what you said.* **3** used to show an opposite or the lack of something: *I mistrust him* (=I don't trust him).

mis·ad·ven·ture /ˌmɪsədˈvɛntʃɚ/ *n.* [C,U] bad luck or an accident

mis·al·li·ance /ˌmɪsəˈlaɪəns/ *n.* [C] FORMAL a situation in which two people or organizations have agreed to work together, marry each other etc., but are not appropriate for each other

mis·an·thrope /ˈmɪsənˌθroʊp, ˈmɪz-/ also **mis·an·thro·pist** /mɪsˈænθrəpɪst/ *n.* [C] FORMAL someone who does not like other people and prefers to be alone —**misanthropic** /ˌmɪsənˈθrɑpɪk/ *adj.* —**misanthropy** /mɪsˈænθrəpi/ *n.* [U]

mis·ap·ply /ˌmɪsəˈplaɪ/ *v.* **misapplies**, *past tense and past participle* **misapplied**, **misapplying** [T] to use a principle, rule, money etc. in an incorrect way or for a wrong purpose: *Ross was charged with misapplying public money.* —**misapplication** /ˌmɪsæpləˈkeɪʃən/ *n.* [U]

mis·ap·pre·hen·sion /mɪsˌæprɪˈhɛnʃən/ *n.* [C] a belief that is not correct or that is based on a wrong understanding of something: *He was **under the misapprehension** that Wilson was rich.* —**misapprehend** *v.* [T]

mis·ap·pro·pri·ate /ˌmɪsəˈproʊpriˌeɪt/ *v.* [T] FORMAL to dishonestly take something that you have been trusted to keep safe, for example to take money that belongs to your employer SYN **steal**: *One professor had misappropriated research funds.* —**misappropriation** /ˌmɪsəˌproʊpriˈeɪʃən/ *n.* [U]

mis·be·got·ten /ˌmɪsbɪˈgɑtˀn◂ / *adj.* [only before noun] **1** a misbegotten plan, idea etc. is not likely to succeed because it is badly planned or not sensible: *a misbegotten diplomatic mission* **2** FORMAL OR HUMOROUS a misbegotten person is completely stupid or useless

mis·be·have /ˌmɪsbɪˈheɪv/ *v.* [I] to behave badly, and cause trouble or annoy people OPP **behave**: *Sam had been misbehaving in class.*

mis·be·hav·ior /ˌmɪsbɪˈheɪvyɚ/ *n.* [U] behavior that is not acceptable to other people SYN **misconduct**: *Yelling does little to stop children's misbehavior.*

mis·cal·cu·late /ˌmɪsˈkælkyəˌleɪt/ *v.* [I,T] **1** to make a mistake when deciding how long something will take to do, how much money you will need etc.: *He had miscalculated the bill.* **2** to make a wrong judgment about a situation: *The politicians may have miscalculated regarding the public's reaction.*

mis·cal·cu·la·tion /mɪsˌkælkyəˈleɪʃən/ *n.* [C] **1** a mistake made in deciding how long something will take to do, how much money you will need etc. **2** a wrong judgment about a situation

mis·car·riage /ˈmɪsˌkærɪdʒ, ˌmɪsˈkærɪdʒ/ *n.* [C,U] BIOLOGY the act of accidentally giving birth too early for the baby to live: *She **had a miscarriage** a year ago.* → see also ABORTION

misˌcarriage of ˈjustice *n.* [C,U] LAW a situation in which someone is wrongly punished by a court of law for something they did not do

mis·car·ry /ˌmɪsˈkæri/ *v.* **miscarries**, **miscarried**, **miscarrying** [I] **1** BIOLOGY to give birth to a baby too early for it to live → see also ABORT **2** FORMAL if a plan miscarries, it is not successful

mis·cast /ˌmɪsˈkæst/ *v. past tense and past participle* **miscast** [T usually passive] to choose an actor who is not appropriate to play a particular character in a play or movie

mis·cel·la·ne·ous /ˌmɪsəˈleɪniəs/ *adj.* [usually before noun] including many different things or people who do not seem to be related to each other: *a list of your miscellaneous expenses* | *It was in a box labeled "miscellaneous."*

mis·cel·la·ny /ˈmɪsəˌleɪni/ *n. plural* **miscellanies** [C] a group or collection of different things: *a miscellany of travel writing*

mis·chance /ˌmɪsˈtʃæns/ *n.* [C,U] LITERARY bad luck, or a situation that results from bad luck

mis·chief /ˈmɪstʃɪf/ *n.* [U] **1** bad behavior, especially by children, that causes trouble or damage, but no serious harm: *He's always* ***getting into mischief.*** | *Fred just loves to* ***make mischief.*** **2** enjoyment of playing tricks on people or embarrassing them: *Ann's light brown* ***eyes*** *glimmered with* ***mischief.*** | *a child who was* ***full of mischief*** **3** LAW damage or harm that may or may not have been intended: *criminal mischief* [**Origin:** 1200–1300 Old French *meschief* **something bad that happens**]

ˈmischief-ˌmaker *n.* [C] OLD-FASHIONED someone who deliberately causes trouble or arguments

mis·chie·vous /ˈmɪstʃəvəs/ *adj.* **1** liking to have fun, especially by playing tricks on people or doing things to annoy or embarrass them: *a lively mischievous boy* | *Gabby looked at me with a* ***mischievous grin.*** **2** causing trouble or arguments deliberately: *a mischievous remark* **—mischievously** *adv.* **—mischievousness** *n.* [U]

mis·ci·ble /ˈmɪsəbəl/ *adj.* CHEMISTRY miscible liquids are able to mix and combine together completely into one liquid OPP **immiscible**

mis·con·ceived /ˌmɪskənˈsivd◂/ *adj.* a misconceived idea, plan, or program is not a good one, because it has not been carefully thought about or is based on a wrong understanding of something

mis·con·cep·tion /ˌmɪskənˈsɛpʃən/ *n.* [C,U] an idea that is wrong or untrue, but that people believe because they do not understand the subject correctly: **misconception that** *It's a misconception that red meat cannot be part of a healthy diet.* | +**about** *a number of* ***popular misconceptions*** *about the causes of the disease*

mis·con·duct /ˌmɪsˈkɑndʌkt/ *n.* [U] FORMAL bad or dishonest behavior by someone in a position of authority or trust: *a doctor who has been accused of* ***professional misconduct*** | *allegations of sexual misconduct*

mis·con·struc·tion /ˌmɪskənˈstrʌkʃən/ *n.* [C,U] FORMAL an incorrect understanding of something

mis·con·strue /ˌmɪskənˈstru/ *v.* [T] FORMAL to understand in the wrong way something that someone has said or done SYN **misinterpret**: *His actions could easily be misconstrued.*

mis·count /ˌmɪsˈkaʊnt/ *v.* [I,T] to count wrongly: *They claim some ballots were miscounted.*

mis·cre·ant /ˈmɪskriənt/ *n.* [C] FORMAL a bad person who causes trouble, hurts people etc. **—miscreant** *adj.*

mis·cue /mɪsˈkyu/ *n.* [C] a mistake or MISUNDERSTANDING **—miscue** *v.* [I,T]

mis·deed /ˌmɪsˈdid/ *n.* [C] FORMAL a wrong or illegal action: *the congressman's misdeeds*

mis·de·mean·or /ˌmɪsdɪˈminɚ/ *n.* [C] LAW a crime that is not very serious → see also FELONY

mis·di·ag·nose /ˌmɪsdaɪəgˈnoʊs/ *v.* [T usually passive] to give an incorrect explanation of an illness, a problem in a machine etc.: **misdiagnose sth as sth** *Roy's heart condition was originally misdiagnosed as pneumonia.* **—misdiagnosis** *n.* [C]

mis·di·rect /ˌmɪsdəˈrɛkt/ *v.* [T usually passive] **1** FORMAL to use your efforts, energy, or abilities on doing the wrong thing: *Their criticism has been misdirected.* **2** FORMAL to send someone or something to the wrong place: *Our mail was misdirected to the wrong street.* **3** LAW if a judge misdirects a JURY, he or she gives them incorrect information about the law **—misdirection** /ˌmɪsdəˈrɛkʃən/ *n.* [U]

mise-en-scène /ˌmiz ɑn ˈsɛn, -ˈseɪn/ *n.* [C] **1** TECHNICAL the arrangement of furniture and other objects used on the stage in a play **2** FORMAL the environment in which an event takes place

mi·ser /ˈmaɪzɚ/ *n.* [C] someone who is not generous and hates spending money SYN **skinflint**

mis·er·a·ble /ˈmɪzərəbəl/ S3 *adj.* **1** extremely unhappy, for example because you feel lonely, sick, or badly treated: *Pete had a miserable childhood.* | *Dana looked miserable.* | *She* ***made life miserable*** *for anyone who crossed her.* ►see THESAURUS box at **sad** **2** [usually before noun] a miserable situation or event makes you feel very unhappy, uncomfortable etc.: *The weather has been miserable.* | *I had a miserable time at school.* **3** [only before noun] very small in amount, or very bad in quality: *The poor live in miserable conditions.* | *All that work for this miserable paycheck!* [**Origin:** 1400–1500 Old French, Latin *miserabilis*] **—miserably** *adv.*

mi·ser·ly /ˈmaɪzɚli/ *adj.* **1** a miserly amount, salary etc. is one that is much too small **2** a miserly person is not generous and hates spending money SYN **stingy** **—miserliness** *n.* [U]

mis·er·y /ˈmɪzəri/ *n. plural* **miseries** **1** [C,U] great suffering, caused for example by being very poor or very sick: *It started with a sore throat and became a week of total misery.* | *the stories of* ***human misery*** *in the drought-stricken areas* | +**of** *the miseries of war* **2** [C,U] great unhappiness: *Her face was a picture of misery.* **3 put sth/sb out of their misery** to kill a person or an animal that is sick or wounded in order to end their suffering

mis·fea·sance /mɪsˈfizəns/ *n.* [U] LAW a situation in which someone does not do something that the law says they are responsible for doing

mis·fire /ˌmɪsˈfaɪɚ/ *v.* [I] **1** if a plan or joke misfires, it does not have the result that you intended **2** if a gun misfires, the bullet does not come out **3** if an engine misfires, the gas mixture does not burn at the right time **—misfire** /ˈmɪsˌfaɪɚ, mɪsˈfaɪɚ/, **misfiring** /ˌmɪsˈfaɪərɪŋ/ *n.* [C]

mis·fit /ˈmɪsˌfɪt/ *n.* [C] someone who does not seem to belong in a group of people, and who is not accepted by them, because he or she is very different from the other people in the group: *I was a* ***social misfit*** *at school.*

mis·for·tune /mɪsˈfɔrtʃən/ *n.* [C,U] very bad luck, or something that happens to you as a result of bad luck: *The banks profit from farmers' misfortunes.* | *President Hoover* ***had the misfortune*** *to take office in 1929, when the stock market crashed.*

mis·giv·ing /mɪsˈgɪvɪŋ/ *n.* [C usually plural, U] a feeling of doubt or fear about what might happen or about whether something is right SYN **doubt**: +**about** *He* ***had misgivings*** *about changing careers.* | **grave/deep/serious misgivings** *She expressed grave misgivings about using the materials in schools.*

mis·guid·ed /mɪsˈgaɪdɪd/ *adj.* **1** intended to be helpful but in fact making a situation worse: *a misguided effort to help the poor* **2** a misguided idea or opinion is wrong because it is based on a wrong understanding of a situation: *Coleman was acting out of misguided jealousy.* **—misguidedly** *adv.*

mis·han·dle /ˌmɪsˈhændl/ *v.* [T] **1** to deal with a situation badly, because of a lack of skill or care: *The investigation had been mishandled.* **2** to treat something roughly or not in the correct way, often causing damage: *mishandled baggage* **3** to use an amount of money in a way in which you are not allowed: *He was arrested on suspicion of mishandling public funds.* **—mishandling** *n.* [U]

mis·hap /ˈmɪshæp/ *n.* [C,U] a small accident or mistake that does not have very serious results: *The launch of the space shuttle proceeded* ***without mishap.***

mis·hear /ˌmɪsˈhɪr/ *v. past tense and past participle* **misheard** /-ˈhɚd/ [I,T] to not hear correctly what someone says, so that you think they said something different: *It seemed like a strange question; I wondered if I had misheard.*

mish·mash /ˈmɪʃmæʃ/ *n.* [singular] a mixture of things, ideas, styles etc. that are not in any particular order and are not similar to one another SYN **hodgepodge**: *a mishmash of building styles*

mis·in·form /ˌmɪsɪnˈfɔrm/ *v.* [T usually passive] to give someone information that is incorrect or untrue: *Did the President misinform the nation?*

mis·in·for·ma·tion /ˌmɪsɪnfɚˈmeɪʃən/ *n.* [U] incorrect information, especially information that is deliberately intended to deceive people → see also DISINFORMATION

mis·in·ter·pret /ˌmɪsɪnˈtɚprɪt/ Ac *v.* [T] to not understand the correct meaning of something that someone says or does, or of facts that you are considering SYN **misconstrue**: *The study's findings have been widely misinterpreted.* —**misinterpretation** /ˌmɪsɪnˌtɚprəˈteɪʃən/ *n.* [C,U]

mis·judge /ˌmɪsˈdʒʌdʒ/ *v.* [T] **1** to form a wrong or unfair opinion about a person or situation: *They had badly misjudged the mood of the voters.* **2** to guess an amount, distance etc. wrongly: *I misjudged the distance and turned too soon.* —**misjudgment** *n.* [C,U]

mis·lay /mɪsˈleɪ/ *v.* **mislays**, *past tense and past participle* **mislaid**, **mislaying** [T] **1** to put something somewhere, then forget where you put it SYN **misplace**: *He's always mislaying his glasses.* **2** to lay or place something wrongly: *mislaid linoleum*

mis·lead /mɪsˈlid/ *v. past tense and past participle* **misled** /-ˈlɛd/ [T] to make someone believe something that is not true by giving them false or incomplete information: **mislead sb about sth** *They may have misled the public about the true cost of the program.* | **be misled by sth** *Don't be misled by the word "natural" on the label – it doesn't mean it's good for you.* | **mislead sb into doing sth** *They misled customers into buying the wrong type of insurance.*

mis·lead·ing /mɪsˈlidɪŋ/ *adj.* likely to make someone believe something that is not true: **highly/grossly/seriously etc. misleading** *The article was highly misleading.* —**misleadingly** *adv.*

mis·led /mɪsˈlɛd/ *v.* the past tense and past participle of MISLEAD

mis·man·age /ˌmɪsˈmænɪdʒ/ *v.* [T] if someone mismanages something they are in charge of, they deal with it badly: *The youth program had been mismanaged.* —**mismanagement** *n.* [U]

mis·match /ˈmɪsmætʃ/ *n.* [C] a combination of things or people that do not work well together or are not appropriate for each other: *The disease occurs when there is a mismatch between the mother's blood type and the baby's.* —**mismatched** /ˌmɪsˈmætʃt◂/ *adj.*: *mismatched socks*

mis·no·mer /ˌmɪsˈnoʊmɚ/ *n.* [C] a name that is wrong or not appropriate: *"Silent movie" is a misnomer since the movies usually had a musical accompaniment.*

mi·sog·y·nist·ic /mɪˌsɑdʒəˈnɪstɪk/ also **mi·sog·y·nist** /mɪˈsɑdʒənɪst/ *adj.* showing hate, strong dislike, or a complete lack of respect for women: *misogynistic rap lyrics*

mi·sog·y·ny /mɪˈsɑdʒəni/ *n.* [U] hate, strong dislike, or complete lack of respect for women —**misogynist** *n.*

mis·place /ˌmɪsˈpleɪs/ *v.* [T] to lose something for a short time by putting it in the wrong place SYN **mislay**: *Oh dear, I seem to have misplaced that letter.*

mis·placed /ˌmɪsˈpleɪst◂/ *adj.* misplaced feelings of trust, love etc. are wrong and not appropriate, because the person that you have these feelings for does not deserve them: *Children must be warned against a misplaced trust of strangers.*

mis·print /ˈmɪsˌprɪnt/ *n.* [C] a mistake, especially a spelling mistake, in a book, magazine etc.

mis·pro·nounce /ˌmɪsprəˈnaʊns/ *v.* [T] to pronounce a word or name wrongly —**mispronunciation** /ˌmɪsprəˌnʌnsiˈeɪʃən/ *n.* [C,U]

mis·quote /ˌmɪsˈkwoʊt/ *v.* [T] to make a mistake in reporting what someone else has said —**misquote** /ˈmɪskwoʊt/ also **misquotation** /ˌmɪskwoʊˈteɪʃən/ *n.* [C]

mis·read /ˌmɪsˈrid/ *v. past tense and past participle* **misread** /-ˈrɛd/ [T] **1** to make a wrong judgment about a person or situation SYN **misinterpret**: *We misread the level of interest in the campaign.* **2** to read something in an incorrect way —**misreading** *n.* [C,U]

mis·re·port /ˌmɪsrɪˈpɔrt/ *v.* [T usually passive] to give an incorrect or untrue account of an event or situation: *The facts of the story have been misreported.*

mis·rep·re·sent /ˌmɪsrɛprɪˈzɛnt/ *v.* [T] to deliberately give a wrong description of someone's opinions or of a situation: *Some sellers will attempt to misrepresent the condition of a house to buyers.* —**misrepresentation** /mɪsˌrɛprɪzɛnˈteɪʃən/ *n.* [C,U]

mis·rule /ˌmɪsˈrul/ *n.* [U] FORMAL bad government

miss

Sue missed the train. James misses his girlfriend.

miss[1] /mɪs/ S1 W1 *v.*

1 NOT GO/DO [T] to not go somewhere or do something, especially when you want to but cannot: *He missed a whole month of school.* | *You missed all the excitement!* | **miss doing sth** *I had to miss seeing her that night, because of work.*

2 NOT HIT/CATCH [I,T] to not hit something or catch something: *Darrow fired several shots but missed.* | *McCoy missed two free throws.*

3 FEEL SAD ABOUT SB [T] to feel sad because someone you love is not with you: *I miss Mom, don't you?* | *John will be* ***sorely missed*** *by his family and friends.*

4 FEEL SAD ABOUT STH [T] to feel sad because you do not have something or cannot do something you had or did before: *I can think of so many things I'll really miss when I leave.* | **miss doing sth** *Michelle's going to miss living in New York.*

5 AVOID STH [T] to avoid something bad or unpleasant: *If we leave now, we should miss the traffic.* | **miss doing sth** *As he crossed the street, a bus just missed hitting him.* | *They* ***narrowly missed*** *being killed in the fire.*

6 miss a chance/opportunity to fail to use an opportunity to do something: *It would be unforgivable to miss this opportunity to travel.*

7 TOO LATE [T] to be too late for something OPP **catch**: *We missed the beginning of the movie.* | *I think I've missed the last bus.*

8 NOT SEE/HEAR [T] to not see, hear, or notice something, especially when it is difficult to notice: *What did he say? I missed it.* | *Two inspections missed the fault in the engine that led to the crash.*

9 sth is not to be missed used to say that someone should do something while they have the opportunity: *A visit to the ancient ruins is not to be missed.*

10 miss the point to not understand the main point of what someone is saying: *You're both missing the point, which is to get more people to use public transportation.*

11 you can't miss it/him etc. SPOKEN used to say that it

is very easy to notice or recognize someone or something: *It's the house with the green windows – you can't miss it.*
12 miss the boat INFORMAL to fail to take an opportunity that will give you an advantage: *Customers were worried about missing the boat by not buying any stocks.*
13 I wouldn't miss it for the world SPOKEN used to say that you really want to go to an event, see something etc.
14 sb doesn't miss a trick used to say that someone notices every opportunity to do something or get an advantage: *Filmmaker Joe Ruben doesn't miss a trick in his new thriller.*
15 NOTICE STH ISN'T THERE [T] to notice that something or someone is not in the place you expect them to be: *It tastes so great, you won't miss the fat.*
16 without missing a beat also **not miss a beat** if you do something without missing a beat, you do it without showing that you are surprised or shocked: *She answered the reporters' questions without missing a beat.*
17 sb's heart misses a beat used to say that someone is very excited, surprised, or frightened: *When Caroline smiled at Eddie, his heart missed a beat.*
18 ENGINE [I] if an engine misses, it stops working for a very short time and then starts again
[**Origin:** Old English *missan*] → see Word Choice box at LOSE

miss out *phr. v.* to not have the chance to do something that you enjoy: *Sticking to a healthy diet always makes you feel that you're missing out.* | +**on** *I feel I'm missing out on having fun with my kids.*

miss² S2 W2 *n.*
1 Miss Smith/Davis etc. used in front of the family name of a woman who is not married to speak to her politely, to write to her, or to talk about her → see also MRS. → see Usage note at MR
2 YOUNG WOMAN used as a polite way of speaking to a young woman when you do not know her name → see also MA'AM: *Excuse me, miss, could I have another glass of water?*
3 Miss Italy/Ohio/World etc. used before the name of a country, city etc. that a woman represents in a beauty competition
4 NOT HIT/CATCH [C] a failed attempt to hit, catch, or hold something: *Murphy scored 78 consecutive foul shots without a miss.*
5 a miss is as good as a mile used to say that although someone failed by only a small amount to do something, they were still unsuccessful → see also HIT-AND-MISS

mis·sal /ˈmɪsəl/ *n.* [C] a book containing all the prayers said during each Mass for a whole year in the Catholic church

mis·shap·en /ˌmɪsˈʃeɪpən, ˌmɪˈʃeɪ-/ *adj.* not the normal or natural shape SYN **deformed**: *Ballerinas often have blunted misshapen toes.*

mis·sile /ˈmɪsəl/ W3 *n.* [C] **1** a weapon that can fly over long distances and that explodes when it hits the thing it has been aimed at: *a nuclear missile* **2** an object that is thrown at someone in order to hurt them

miss·ing /ˈmɪsɪŋ/ *adj.* **1** something that is missing is not in its usual place, so that you cannot find it: *There's a screw missing.* | *the missing piece of the jigsaw* | +**from** *Three buttons were missing from his shirt.* **2** something that is missing should exist but does not, or should have been included but was not: *The baby was born with a finger missing.* | *Fill in the missing words.* | +**from** *Your name is missing from the list.* **3** if part of something is missing, it is no longer attached or has been destroyed: *her missing front teeth* | *The last page was missing.* **4** someone who is missing has disappeared, and no one knows where they are: *Two crew members survived, but two are still missing.* | *The girl has been **reported missing**.* **5 missing in action** a soldier who is missing in action has not returned after a battle and their body has not been found → see Word Choice box at LOSE

ˌmissing ˈlink *n.* [C] **1** a piece of information that you need in order to solve a problem: *The police are continuing to look for missing links in the murder case.* **2 the missing link** an animal which was a stage in the development of humans from APES, whose bones have not yet been found

ˌmissing ˈperson *n. plural* **missing persons** [C] **1** someone who has disappeared and whose family has asked the police to try to find them **2 Missing Persons** the part of the police department responsible for trying to find people who have disappeared

mis·sion /ˈmɪʃən/ W2 *n.* [C]
1 AIR FORCE/ARMY ETC. an important job that involves traveling somewhere, done by a member of the Air Force, Army etc.: *He flew over two hundred missions.* | *troops taking part in a **peacekeeping mission***
2 JOB an important job that someone has been given to do, especially when they are sent to another place: *Her mission is to improve employee morale.* | *scientists **on a mission** to the rainforest, to study medicinal uses of plants* | **rescue/diplomatic/fact-finding etc. mission** *a rescue mission to the doomed submarine*
3 GOVERNMENT GROUP a group of important people who are sent by their government to another country to discuss something or collect information: ***a trade mission** to India*
4 PURPOSE the purpose or the most important aim of an organization: *The mission of International House is to enable students of different cultures to live together in friendship.*
5 DUTY a duty or service that you have chosen to do and be responsible for SYN **calling** SYN **vocation**: *My new **mission in life** is to help educate others.*
6 SPACE a special trip made by a space vehicle: *the Galileo mission to Mars*
7 RELIGION a) the work of a religious leader or organization that has gone to a foreign country in order to teach people about Christianity or to help poor people: *Longobardi headed up the Jesuit mission to China.* **b)** a building where this type of work is done
8 PLACE FOR HELP a place that gives food, medical help etc. to people who need it: *The food missions in Pittsburgh usually serve 750 people per day.*
9 mission accomplished used when you have successfully achieved something that you were trying to do
10 man/woman on a mission HUMOROUS someone who is very determined to achieve what they are trying to do
[**Origin:** 1500–1600 Latin *missio* **act of sending**, from *mittere* **to send, throw**]

mis·sion·ar·y /ˈmɪʃəˌnɛri/ *n. plural* **missionaries** [C] someone who has been sent to a foreign country to teach people about Christianity and persuade them to become Christians

ˈmissionary poˌsition *n.* [singular] the sexual position in which the woman lies on her back with the man on top of her and facing her

ˈmission conˌtrol *n.* [singular, not with "the"] the people on Earth who communicate with and guide a spacecraft

ˈmission ˌcreep *n.* [U] a series of gradual changes in the aim of a group of people, with the result that they do something different from what they planned to do at the beginning

ˈmission ˌstatement *n.* [C] a clear statement about the aims of a company or organization

Mis·sis·sip·pi /ˌmɪsəˈsɪpi/ **1** ABBREVIATION **MS** a state in the southeastern U.S. **2 the Mississippi** the longest river in the U.S., which flows from Minnesota to the Gulf of Mexico

mis·sive /ˈmɪsɪv/ *n.* [C] FORMAL a letter

Mis·sou·ri /mɪˈzʊri/ **1** ABBREVIATION **MO** a state in the central U.S. **2 the Missouri** a long river in the U.S., which flows from the Rocky Mountains to join the Mississippi at St. Louis

mis·spell /ˌmɪsˈspɛl/ *v.* [T] to spell a word wrongly —**misspelling** *n.* [C,U]

mis·spend /ˌmɪsˈspɛnd/ *v. past tense and past participle* **misspent** /-ˈspɛnt/ [T] **1** to use time, money etc.

M

badly or wrongly SYN **squander**: *Their business manager misspent millions of the couple's money.* **2 misspent youth** HUMOROUS someone who had a misspent youth wasted their time or behaved badly when they were young

mis·step /ˈmɪs-stɛp/ *n.* [C] a mistake, especially one that is caused by not understanding a situation correctly: *A misstep here could cost millions of dollars.*

mis·sus /ˈmɪsɪz/ *n.* [singular] SPOKEN, HUMOROUS a man's wife: *How's the missus?*

mist¹ /mɪst/ *n.* **1** [C,U] a light cloud low over the ground that makes it difficult for you to see very far → see also FOG: *the early morning mist* **2** [singular] air that is filled with very small drops of a particular liquid: *a mist of fine spray from the waterfall* **3 lost in the mists of time** if something such as a fact or secret is lost in the mists of time, no one remembers it because it happened so long ago

mist² *v.* [T] to cover something with very small drops of liquid in order to keep it wet: *Mist the plant daily.*

mist over/up *phr. v.* if someone's eyes mist over, they become filled with tears: *Dorothy's eyes misted over as she spoke of her son.*

mis·take¹ /mɪˈsteɪk/ S2 W2 *n.* [C]

1 INCORRECT ACTION/OPINION ETC. something that has been done in the wrong way, or an opinion or statement that is incorrect SYN **error**: *The attorney admitted that she had* ***made a mistake*** *in writing the contract.* | *The essay was full of* ***spelling mistakes.*** | *The teacher points out* ***common mistakes*** *that children make in their writing.* | *This can't be the right hotel – **there must be some mistake**.* | *We'd better start* ***learning from our mistakes*** (=understanding what we have done wrong and not do this again) *or this team will never win.* | **a major/bad/serious/grave etc. mistake** *Not having the website ready was a major mistake.* ▸see THESAURUS box at **fault¹**

2 STUPID ACTION something stupid or not sensible that someone does, which they are sorry about later: *It seemed like a great idea, but now I can see it was a mistake.* | *Well, go ahead, but you're **making a big mistake**.* | **big/terrible/bad etc. mistake** *Marrying him was the biggest mistake she had ever made.* | *He won't **make the same mistake** twice.* | **make the mistake of doing sth** *I made the mistake of giving him my phone number.* | **it is a mistake to do sth** *It is a mistake to rely on foreign supplies of oil.*

3 by mistake if you do something by mistake, you do it without intending to SYN **accidentally** OPP **deliberately** OPP **on purpose**: *Jodie opened the letter by mistake*

SPOKEN PHRASES

4 we all make mistakes used when telling someone not to be worried because they have made a mistake
5 make no mistake (about it) also **let there be no mistake (about it)** used to emphasize that you are very certain about what you are saying, especially when you are warning someone about something: *Make no mistake about it – I am not going to put up with this anymore.*

mistake² *past tense* **mistook** /-ˈstʊk/, *past participle* **mistaken** /-ˈsteɪkən/ *v.* [T] **1** to understand something wrongly: *Krauss mistook her silence, thinking she was angry.* **2 there is no mistaking sb/sth** used to say that you are certain about something: *There was no mistaking the threat in his voice.* **3 you can't mistake sb/sth** used to say that someone or something is very easy to recognize: *You can't mistake her – she looks just like her mother.* [**Origin:** 1300–1400 Old Norse *mistaka*]

mistake sb/sth **for** sb/sth *phr. v.* to wrongly think that one person or thing is someone or something else: *Lyme Disease is often mistaken for arthritis.*

mis·tak·en /mɪˈsteɪkən/ *adj.* **1** [not before noun] if you are mistaken, you are wrong about something you thought you knew or saw: *He couldn't have been there. You must be mistaken.* | *I had thought the job was done, but I was **sadly mistaken**.* | *There's mint in this sauce, **if I'm not mistaken**.* ▸see THESAURUS box at **wrong¹** **2 mistaken idea/belief/impression etc.** a mistaken idea, belief etc. is not correct or is based on bad judgment: *There is a mistaken idea that marijuana is not harmful.* **3 a case of mistaken identity** a situation in which someone believes that they have seen a particular person, especially taking part in a crime, when in fact it was someone else: *Lang was shot to death, apparently in a case of mistaken identity.* —**mistakenly** *adv.*

mis·ter /ˈmɪstɚ/ *n.* **1 Mister** the full form of Mr. **2** SPOKEN, OLD-FASHIONED used to speak to a man whose name you do not know: *You don't have any change, do you, mister?* **3** used by a parent, teacher etc. to address a boy they know well: *Come on, mister, it's time to go.* **4 mister macho/busy/personality etc.** used with a word that describes what someone's character or actions are like → see also SIR

mis·time /ˌmɪsˈtaɪm/ *v.* [T usually passive] to do something at the wrong time or at a time that is not appropriate: *a mistimed pregnancy*

mis·tle·toe /ˈmɪsəlˌtoʊ/ *n.* [U] a plant with small white berries, which grows over other trees and is often used as a decoration at Christmas

mis·took /mɪˈstʊk/ *v.* the past tense of MISTAKE

mis·tress /ˈmɪstrɪs/ *n.* [C] **1** a woman that a man has a sexual relationship with, even though he is married to someone else: *Harris claims she was the millionaire's mistress.* **2** OLD-FASHIONED the female employer of a servant **3 be mistress of sth** OLD-FASHIONED if a woman is mistress of something she is in control of it, highly skilled at it etc.: *It was evident that she was mistress of her subject.* **4** OLD-FASHIONED the female owner of a dog, horse etc. **5 Mistress** OLD USE used with a woman's family name as a polite way of addressing her → see also MASTER

mis·tri·al /ˈmɪstraɪl/ *n.* [C] LAW a TRIAL during which a mistake in the law is made, so that a new trial has to be held: *Judge Garcia was forced to **declare a mistrial**.*

mis·trust¹ /mɪsˈtrʌst/ *n.* [U] the feeling that you cannot trust someone, especially because you think they may treat you unfairly or dishonestly SYN **distrust**: **+of** *She showed a great mistrust of doctors.*

mistrust² *v.* [T] to not trust someone, especially because you think they may treat you unfairly or dishonestly: *As a small child she learned to mistrust adults.* —**mistrustful** *adj.* —**mistrustfully** *adv.* → see also DISTRUST

mist·y /ˈmɪsti/ *adj. comparative* **mistier**, *superlative* **mistiest** **1** misty weather is weather with a lot of mist: *a cold misty morning* **2** LITERARY if your eyes are misty, they are full of tears, especially because you are remembering a time in the past: *He paused, his eyes growing misty.* | *A few people at the wedding got **misty-eyed**.* **3** not clear or bright: *Misty people in overcoats stood against the wall.*

mis·un·der·stand /ˌmɪsʌndɚˈstænd/ *v. past tense and past participle* **misunderstood** /-ˈstʊd/ [I,T] to fail to understand correctly: *Oh, I must have misunderstood. I thought we were going to meet at 11:00.* | *She had misunderstood the question.*

mis·un·der·stand·ing /ˌmɪsʌndɚˈstændɪŋ/ *n.* **1** [C,U] a problem caused by someone not understanding a question, situation, or instruction correctly: *Listening carefully reduces misunderstandings.* | **+of** *a misunderstanding of the issue* **2** [C] an argument or disagreement that is not very serious: *There was a misunderstanding about how much Jerry owed him.*

mis·un·der·stood /ˌmɪsʌndɚˈstʊd/ *adj.* used to describe someone who is not liked by other people in a way that is unfair, because the other people do not understand his or her behavior

mis·use¹ /ˌmɪsˈyuz/ *v.* [T] **1** to use something in the wrong way or for the wrong purpose: *He misused public funds.* **2** to treat someone badly or unfairly

mis·use² /ˌmɪsˈyus/ *n.* [C,U] the use of something in the wrong way or for the wrong purpose SYN **abuse**: *a politician's misuse of power*

M

mite /maɪt/ *n.* **1** [C] BIOLOGY a very small insect that lives in plants, CARPETS etc. **2 a mite** a little SYN **slightly**: [+ adj./adv.] *Diane looked a mite tired.* | *It's a mite too big for the box.* **3** [C] OLD-FASHIONED a small child, especially one that you feel sorry for

mi·ter /ˈmaɪt̬ɚ/ *n.* [C] a tall pointed hat worn by BISHOPS and ARCHBISHOPS

mit·i·gate /ˈmɪt̬əˌgeɪt/ *v.* [T] FORMAL to make a situation or the effects of something less bad, harmful, or serious SYN **alleviate**: *an attempt to mitigate the effects on the environment* [**Origin:** 1400–1500 Latin, past participle of *mitigare* **to soften**]

mit·i·gat·ing /ˈmɪt̬əˌgeɪt̬ɪŋ/ *adj.* **mitigating circumstances/factors etc.** facts about a situation that make a crime or bad mistake seem less serious SYN **extenuating**

mit·i·ga·tion /ˌmɪt̬əˈgeɪʃən/ *n.* [U] **1** FORMAL a reduction in how bad, harmful, or serious a situation is **2 in mitigation** LAW if you say something in mitigation, you say something that makes someone's crime or mistake seem less serious or that shows that they were not completely responsible

mi·to·chon·dri·on /ˌmaɪt̬əˈkɑndriən/ *n. plural* **mitochondria** /-driə/ [C] BIOLOGY a very small part of a cell in a plant, animal, or FUNGUS, which changes ORGANIC MATTER into energy

mi·to·sis /maɪˈtoʊsɪs/ *n.* [U] BIOLOGY the process by which a cell divides to become two cells, each new cell having the same number of CHROMOSOMES as the parent cell → see also MEIOSIS

mi·tral valve /ˈmaɪtrəl ˌvælv/ *n.* [C] MEDICINE BIOLOGY a small part on your heart between the left ATRIUM and the left VENTRICLE. It opens and closes to allow blood to flow from the atrium into the ventricle, and to prevent blood from flowing back into the atrium. → see picture at HEART

mitt /mɪt/ *n.* [C] **1** a GLOVE made of thick material, worn to protect your hand: *an oven mitt* | *boxing mitts* → see picture at GLOVE **2** a type of leather GLOVE used to catch a ball in baseball **3** INFORMAL someone's hand

mit·ten /ˈmɪt˺n/ *n.* [C] a type of GLOVE that does not have separate parts for each finger

mix¹ /mɪks/ S2 W2 *v.*
1 COMBINE SUBSTANCES [I,T] if you mix two or more substances or if they mix, they combine to become a single substance, and they cannot be easily separated: *In a large bowl mix the butter and flour.* | *Oil and water don't mix.* | **mix sth together/in etc. (sth)** *Mix the cheese into the spinach.* | **mix sth with sth** *Mix the beans thoroughly with the sauce.* → see picture on page A32

> **THESAURUS**
> **combine** to join two or more things together, or to be joined together with another thing: *Combine flour, cocoa, and baking powder, and stir into the egg mixture.*
> **stir** to mix a liquid or food by moving a spoon around in it: *Cook, stirring frequently, until the oatmeal has thickened.*
> **blend** to mix together soft or liquid substances to form a single smooth substance: *Blend the yogurt with fresh fruit for a wonderful drink.*
> **beat** to mix food together quickly and thoroughly using a fork or kitchen tool: *Beat the eggs and add to the sugar mixture.*
> ▸see THESAURUS box at **cooking¹**

2 COMBINE IDEAS/ACTIVITIES ETC. [T] to combine two or more different activities, ideas, groups of things etc., or to be combined in this way: *Keillor enjoys mixing high and low culture.* | **mix sth with sth** *His books mix historical fact with fantasy.* | *I don't like to* ***mix business with pleasure*** (=do business and social activities at the same time).
3 not mix if two different ideas, activities etc. do not mix, there are problems when they are combined: *Safety and alcohol do not mix.*
4 PREPARE BY MIXING [T] to prepare something, especially food or drink, by mixing things together: *At the bar, she mixed a double scotch and water.*
5 MEET PEOPLE [I] to meet, talk, and spend time with other people, especially people you do not know very well SYN **socialize**: **+with** *Charlie doesn't mix well with the other kids.*
6 SOUND [T] ENG. LANG. ARTS to control the balance of sounds in a record or movie
7 mix and match to put different things, or parts of things, together from a range of possibilities: *You can mix and match this home-office furniture to fit your needs.*
[**Origin:** 1400–1500 *mixte* **mixed** (13–17 centuries), from Latin *mixtus*, past participle of *miscere* **to mix**] —**mix-and-match** *adj.*: *mix-and-match clothing* → see also MIXED UP, MIX-UP

mix up *phr. v.* **1 mix sb/sth ↔ up** to make the mistake of thinking that someone or something is another person or thing SYN **confuse**: *I think you've got the dates mixed up, dear.* | **+with** *I keep mixing up Tom with his brother – they look a lot alike.* **2 mix sb up** to make someone feel confused: *That's just going to mix everybody up.* **3 mix sth ↔ up** to change the way things have been arranged, often by mistake, so that they are not in the same order anymore: *My papers got all mixed up.* **4 mix sth ↔ up** to prepare something by mixing things together: *The machine mixes up the cement.* **5 mix it up with sb** to argue or threaten to fight with someone: *The fans like it when they see a player mixing it up with the umpire.*

mix² S3 W3 *n.* **1** [singular] the particular combination of things or people that form a group: *There's a real ethnic mix in the city.* | **+of** *Between them, they have a good mix of skills.* **2** [C,U] a combination of substances that you mix together to make something such as a cake SYN **mixture**: *What cake mix did you use?* | *lemonade mix* **3** [C] a particular arrangement of sounds, voices, or different pieces of music used on a recording: *the dance mix*

mixed /mɪkst/ *adj.* **1** [only before noun] consisting of many different types of things or people: *a salad of mixed greens* | *A fairly mixed group attended the lecture.* **2 mixed reaction/response/reviews etc.** if something gets a mixed reaction etc., some people say they like it or agree with it, but others dislike it or disagree with it: *Bailey's play opened to mixed reviews in New York.* **3 have mixed emotions/feelings about sth** to not be sure about whether you like or agree with something or someone: *I had mixed feelings about moving.* **4 mixed messages** two statements or opinions about the same subject that are very different from each other: *We give mixed messages to young girls, by being embarrassed to talk about sex while movies, ads, and music constantly represent it.* **5 a mixed blessing** something that is good in some ways but bad in others: *Staying at home with the baby has been something of a mixed blessing for Pam.* **6 a mixed bag** INFORMAL **a)** something that has both good and bad points: *All people are mixed bags – you just have to accept yourself as you are.* **b)** a group of things that are all very different from each other: **+of** *The show is a mixed bag of songs and dances.* **7 in mixed company** when you are with people of both sexes: *It's not the kind of joke you'd tell in mixed company.*

ˌmixed-ˈcrop farm *n.* [C] a farm that grows several different types of crops

ˌmixed ˈdoubles *n.* [U] a game in a sport such as tennis in which a man and a woman play against another man and woman

ˌmixed eˈconomy *n.* [C] ECONOMICS an economic system in which some industries are owned by the government and some are owned by private companies

ˌmixed ˈmarriage *n.* [C,U] a marriage between two people from different races or religions

ˌmixed ˈmedia *n.* [U] a combination of substances or materials that are used in a painting, SCULPTURE etc.

M

ˌmixed ˈrace *n.* [U] someone who is of mixed race has parents of different races

ˌmixed ˈup *adj.* **1** [not before noun] confused, for example because you have too many different details to remember or think about: *I got mixed up and sent in the wrong form.* **2 be/get mixed up with sb** to be involved with someone who has a bad influence on you: *He got mixed up with a bad set of friends.* **3 be/get mixed up in sth** to be involved in an illegal or dishonest activity: *I'd have to be crazy to get mixed up in something like that.* **4** INFORMAL confused and suffering from emotional problems: *a mixed up kid* → see also **mix up** at MIX[1], MIX-UP

mix·er /ˈmɪksɚ/ *n.* [C] **1** a piece of equipment used to mix things together: *Beat eggs and sugar with an electric mixer.* | *a cement mixer* **2** ENG. LANG. ARTS a piece of equipment or computer software which is used to control the sound levels or picture quality of a recording or movie, or a person whose job is to use this equipment **3** a drink that can be mixed with alcohol, for example orange juice or TONIC water **4** OLD-FASHIONED a party held so that people who have just met can get to know each other better

ˈmixing bowl *n.* [C] a large bowl used for mixing things such as flour and sugar for making cakes

mix·tape /ˈmɪksˌteɪp/ *n.* [C] a piece of music that is produced by mixing different voices or musical instruments that have already been recorded: *dance music mixtapes*

Mix·tec /ˈmistɛk/ a Native American tribe who lived in southern Mexico until they were defeated by the Aztecs in the 16th century

mix·ture /ˈmɪkstʃɚ/ W3 *n.* **1** [C,U] a liquid or other substance made by mixing several substances together: *Put the chicken in a mixture of olive oil, lemon juice, and spices.*

THESAURUS

combination two or more different things, substances etc. that are used or put together: *an unusual combination of flavors*
blend a mixture of two or more things: *All-purpose flour is a blend of hard and soft types of wheat.*
compound a chemical compound is a substance that consists of two or more different substances: *Carbon dioxide is a common compound found in the air.*
solution a liquid mixed with a solid or a gas: *a weak sugar solution*

2 [C] a combination of two or more people, things, feelings, or ideas that are different: **+of** *His work is a mixture of photography and painting.* | *She felt a mixture of concern and anger.* **3** [C] CHEMISTRY a combination of substances that are put together but do not mix with each other → see also COMPOUND **4** [U] FORMAL the action of mixing things or the state of being mixed

ˈmix-up *n.* [C] INFORMAL a mistake that causes confusion about details or arrangements: *A patient received the wrong drugs because of a hospital mix-up.*

ml the written abbreviation of MILLILITER

mm[1] /m/ *interjection* used when someone else is speaking and you want to show that you are listening or that you agree with them: *Mm, yeah, I see what you mean.*

mm[2] the written abbreviation of MILLIMETER

MN the written abbreviation of Minnesota

mne·mon·ic /nɪˈmɑnɪk/ *n.* [C] ENG. LANG. ARTS something, such as a poem or a sentence, that you use to help you remember a rule, a name etc. [**Origin:** 1700–1800 Greek *mnemonikos*, from *mimneskesthai* **to remember**] —**mnemonic** *adj.* —**mnemonically** /-kli/ *adv.*

MO the written abbreviation of MISSOURI

M.O. *n.* [singular] **modus operandi** a way of doing something that is typical of one person or a group of people

mo. the written abbreviation of MONTH

moan[1] /moʊn/ *v.* [I] **1** to make a long low sound expressing pain, unhappiness, or sexual pleasure: *I lay in bed, moaning in pain.* **2** to complain in an annoying way, especially in an unhappy voice: *"But, Mom, there's nothing to do here," moaned Josh.* | *It's easy to* ***moan and groan*** *about salaries.* **3** LITERARY if the wind moans, it makes a long low sound —**moaner** *n.* [C]

moan[2] *n.* [C] **1** a long low sound expressing pain, unhappiness, or sexual pleasure: *He* ***gave a*** *terrible* ***moan*** *of pain.* | *The announcement drew moans from the audience.* **2** LITERARY a low sound made by the wind

moat /moʊt/ *n.* [C] **1** a deep wide hole, usually filled with water, that was built around a castle as a defense **2** a deep wide hole dug around an area used for animals in a zoo to stop them from escaping —**moated** *adj.*

mob[1] /mɑb/ *n.* [C] **1** a large noisy crowd, especially one that is angry and violent: **+of** *Police officers fired at mobs of unruly protesters.* ▶see THESAURUS box at group[1] **2** a group of people of the same type: **+of** *A mob of reporters surrounded the quarterback.* **3 the Mob** the MAFIA (=a powerful organization of criminals) **4 the mob** OLD USE an insulting expression meaning all the poorest and least educated people in society → see also LYNCH MOB

mob[2] *v.* **mobbed, mobbing** [T usually passive] to form a crowd around someone in order to express admiration or to attack them: *The star was mobbed by photographers.*

mobbed /mɑbd/ *adj.* [not before noun] INFORMAL if a place is mobbed, there is a big crowd of people there

ˈmob cap *n.* [C] a light cotton hat worn by women in the 18th and 19th centuries

Mo·bile /ˈmoʊbil, moʊˈbil/ a city in the U.S. state of Alabama

mo·bile[1] /ˈmoʊbəl/ *adj.* **1** able to move or travel easily OPP **immobile**: *It's important to keep the patient mobile during recovery.* | *Alligators are really mobile animals.* **2** easy to move and use in different places SYN **movable**: *a mobile air conditioner* **3** moving or able to move from one job, place, or social class to another: *The population of the U.S. is geographically and socially mobile.* **4 mobile clinic/classroom/library etc.** a clinic etc. that is kept in a vehicle and driven from place to place: *a mobile medical van that treats homeless people* **5 mobile face/features** a face that can change its expression quickly [**Origin:** 1400–1500 French, Latin *mobilis*, from *movere* **to move**] → see also IMMOBILE, PORTABLE, UPWARDLY MOBILE

mo·bile[2] /ˈmoʊbil, moʊˈbil/ *n.* [C] a decoration made of small objects tied to wires or string and hung up so that the objects move when air blows around them

ˌmobile ˈhome *n.* [C] a type of house made of metal that can be pulled by a large vehicle and moved to another place SYN **trailer**

ˌmobile ˈphone *n.* [C] a CELLULAR PHONE

mo·bil·i·ty /moʊˈbɪləti/ *n.* [U] **1** the ability to move easily from one job, place to live, or social class to another: *Higher education increases* ***social mobility***. | *New jobs would provide opportunities for* ***upward mobility***. **2** the ability to move easily from place to place: *The exercise improves the mobility of your joints.* | *the army's mobility*

mo·bi·lize /ˈmoʊbəˌlaɪz/ *v.* **1** [I,T] if the armed forces mobilize or a country mobilizes its armed forces, it prepares to fight a war: *Troops were mobilized to protect the country's borders.* **2** to encourage people to support an idea or course of action in an active way, especially in politics or public life: *We need to* ***mobilize public support*** *to get results.* **3** [T] to bring people together so that they can all work to achieve something: *Many people were* ***mobilized into*** *political* ***action*** *by the assassination of Martin Luther King.* → see also DEMOBILIZE —**mobilization** /ˌmoʊbələˈzeɪʃən/ *n.* [C,U]

mob·ster /ˈmɑbstɚ/ *n.* [C] a member of an organized criminal group, especially the Mafia

moc·ca·sin /ˈmɑkəsɪn/ *n.* [C] a flat comfortable shoe

made of soft leather [**Origin:** 1600–1700 Virginia Algonquian *mockasin*]

mo·cha /ˈmoʊkə/ *n.* [U] **1** a type of coffee **2** a combination of coffee and chocolate [**Origin:** 1700–1800 *Mocha*, port in Arabia]

mock¹ /mɑk/ *v.* [I,T] FORMAL to show that you think that someone or something seems stupid or amusing, by laughing at them, making jokes about them etc. in an unkind way SYN **make fun of**: *They accused him of openly mocking their religion.* | *The other boys started mocking his accent* (=copying it in a way that makes it seem funny). —**mockingly** *adv.* → see also **make fun of sb/sth** at FUN¹ (2)

mock² *adj.* [only before noun] **1** not real, but intended to be very similar to a real situation, substance etc.: *a mock combat mission* | *A mock interview gives students practice.* **2 mock surprise/seriousness/horror/indignation etc.** surprise, seriousness etc. that you pretend to feel, especially as a joke: *"Who are these people?" he asked in mock despair.*

mock- /mɑk/ *prefix* pretending to be or feel something: *Sarah had a mock-serious expression on her face* (=she was only pretending to be serious).

mock·er·y /ˈmɑkəri/ *n.* **1** something that is completely stupid, useless, or ineffective: *The trial had been a mockery.* | *If we stop fighting now, it will* ***make a mockery of*** *all our efforts up to now* (=make our efforts seem stupid and useless). **2** [U] unkind behavior or remarks intended to make someone or something seem stupid, for example laughing at them or copying them: *His mockery of my family made me furious.*

mock·ing·bird /ˈmɑkɪŋˌbɚd/ *n.* [C] BIOLOGY a gray and white bird found in the southern and eastern U.S. that copies the songs of other birds → see picture on page A34

ˌmock ˈturtleneck *n.* [C] a close-fitting shirt or SWEATER that covers the lower part of your neck

ˈmock-up *n.* [C] a full-size model of a building or object which is used to test or study it, or to show how it will look: *a mock-up of the space station*

mo·dal¹ /ˈmoʊdl/ *n.* [C] ENG. LANG. ARTS a modal verb

modal² *adj.* [only before noun] ENG. LANG. ARTS relating to the MOOD of a verb —**modally** *adv.*

ˌmodal auxˈiliary *n.* [C] ENG. LANG. ARTS a modal verb

ˌmodal ˈverb also **modal** *n.* [C] ENG. LANG. ARTS in grammar, a verb that is used with other verbs to change their meaning by expressing ideas such as possibility, permission, or intention. Some examples of commonly used modals in American English: can, could, may, might, should, will, would, must, ought to, used to, and need → see also AUXILIARY VERB

mode /moʊd/ Ac *n.* [C] **1** FORMAL a particular way or style of behaving, living, or doing something SYN **way**: +**of** *the most efficient mode of transporation* **2 in work/survival/teaching etc. mode** INFORMAL thinking or behaving in a particular way at a particular time: *When I'm in work mode, I hate to be interrupted.* **3** TECHNICAL a particular way in which a machine operates when it is doing a particular job: *Put the VCR in record mode.* **4** FORMAL a fashion that is popular at a particular time: *Long skirts* ***were the mode*** (=were fashionable) *then.* **5** MATH the quantity or object that appears most frequently in a set of data → see also MEAN, MEDIAN → see also À LA MODE

mod·el¹ /ˈmɑdl/ S2 W1 *n.* [C]
1 SMALL COPY a small copy of a building, vehicle, machine etc., especially one that can be put together from separate parts: *As children build models they learn about design and construction.* | +**of** *He has a shelf full of models of airplanes that never got built.*
2 FASHION someone whose job is to show clothes, hair styles etc. by wearing them and being photographed: *a top fashion model* → see also SUPERMODEL
3 TYPE OF CAR ETC. a particular type or design of a vehicle or machine: *We also have a deluxe model for $125.* | *Ford Motor Co. will offer new features and new models this year.* ►see THESAURUS box at **type¹**
4 ART ENG. LANG. ARTS someone who is employed by an artist or photographer to be painted or photographed
5 GOOD/SPECIAL PERSON someone who has good qualities or behavior that you should copy: +**of** *As a politician, she was a model of integrity and decency.* | *Brando's a* ***role model*** *for everybody in the business.*
6 GOOD/SUCCESSFUL THING a way of doing something that is successful or useful and therefore worth copying: +**of/for** *The college is a recognized model of higher education.* | *IBM has long served as the model for American companies in Japan.*
7 DESCRIPTION a simple description of a system or structure that is used to help people understand similar systems or structures: *Civil society is a classical economist's model of the free market.*
[**Origin:** 1500–1600 French *modèle*, from Old Italian *modello*, from Latin *modulus* **small measure, rhythm**]

model² *adj.* **1 model airplane/train/car etc.** a small copy of an airplane, train etc., especially one that a child can play with or put together from separate parts **2 model wife/employee/student etc.** someone who behaves like a perfect wife, employee etc.: *We always thought she came from a model family.* **3 model city/school/farm etc.** a city, school etc. that has been specially designed or organized to be as good as possible, so that other cities, schools etc. can learn from them

model³ *v.* **1** [I,T] to wear clothes in order to show them to possible buyers: *Here we have a Kenar T-shirt modeled by Linda Evangelista.* **2** [I,T] ENG. LANG. ARTS to be employed by an artist or photographer to be painted or photographed: *She made a living modeling for art classes.* **3 model yourself after sb** to try to be like someone else because you admire them: *Byron says he models himself after Philadelphia player Charles Barkley.* **4 be modeled on sth** to be designed in a way that copies another system or way of doing something: *Mrs. Mingott's house is modeled on the private hotels of Paris.* **5** [T] to make small objects from materials such as wood or clay

mod·el·ing /ˈmɑdl-ɪŋ/ *n.* [U] **1** the work of a MODEL: *Johnson's looks got him modeling assignments.* **2** the activity of making model ships, airplanes, figures etc.

ˌModel ˈParliament, the HISTORY a group of representatives of the NOBLES, the church, and people of towns that met to advise the king of England, Edward I, in 1295

mo·dem /ˈmoʊdəm/ *n.* [C] COMPUTERS a piece of electronic equipment that allows information from one computer to be sent along telephone lines to another computer

mod·er·ate¹ /ˈmɑdərɪt/ *adj.* **1** neither very big nor very small, very hot nor very cold, very fast nor very slow etc.: *The store suffered moderate damage.* | *moderate temperatures* | *I'd rate the degree of difficulty as moderate.* **2** POLITICS having opinions or beliefs, especially about politics, that are not extreme and that most people consider reasonable or sensible: *her moderate views on social issues* | *a group of moderate Republican senators* **3** staying within reasonable or sensible limits: *The doctor recommended moderate exercise.* | *Trading on the stock exchange was moderate Friday.* | *a moderate drinker* (=someone who does not drink too much alcohol) → see also MODERATELY

mod·er·ate² /ˈmɑdəˌreɪt/ *v.* **1** [T] to control a discussion or argument and to help people reach an agreement: *A Babson College professor will moderate the debate.* **2** [I,T] FORMAL to make something less extreme or violent, or to become less extreme or violent: *Bloom has since moderated his position on low-income housing.* **3** [T] to watch a conversation in a CHATROOM in order to make sure that there is no bad language, no illegal or inappropriate things written etc.

mod·er·ate³ /ˈmɑdərɪt/ *n.* [C] POLITICS someone whose opinions or beliefs, especially about politics, are not extreme and are considered reasonable by most people OPP **hardliner**: +**on** *She's a moderate on fiscal issues.* → see also EXTREMIST

M

mod·er·ate·ly /ˈmɑdərɪtli/ *adv.* **1** fairly but not very: *a moderately successful movie* **2 moderately priced** not too expensive: *moderately priced homes*

mod·er·a·tion /ˌmɑdəˈreɪʃən/ *n.* **1 in moderation** if you do something that could be bad for you in moderation, you do not do it too much: *Drinking alcohol is fine, as long as you do it in moderation.* **2** [U] FORMAL control of your behavior, so that you keep your actions, feelings, habits etc. within reasonable or sensible limits OPP **excess**: +**in** *Matsuyama's secret to a long life is moderation in eating.* **3** [C,U] FORMAL reduction in force, degree, speed etc.: +**in/of** *a need for moderation in labor costs* | *a recent moderation in prices*

mod·e·ra·to /ˌmɑdəˈrɑt̬oʊ/ *adj., adv.* a word meaning "at an average speed," used as an instruction on how fast to play a piece of music

mod·er·at·or /ˈmɑdəˌreɪt̬ɚ/ *n.* [C] **1** someone whose job is to control a discussion or argument and to help people reach an agreement **2** someone who asks questions and keeps the marks of competing teams in a spoken game or competition **3** someone whose job is to watch the conversations in a CHATROOM in order to make sure that there is no bad language, no inappropriate or illegal things written etc.

mod·ern /ˈmɑdɚn/ S3 W1 *adj.* **1** [only before noun] belonging to the present time or most recent time SYN **contemporary**: *modern European history* | *a culture that rejected* ***the modern world*** | *It was one of the worst disasters* ***in modern times.*** | **the modern age/era** *Her views on marriage seem strange in the modern age.* | **modern society/life etc.** *Smaller families are a feature of modern society.* | **Modern Greek/Hebrew/English etc.** (=the form of the Greek, Hebrew etc. language that is used today) **2** using or willing to use the most recent methods, ideas, or fashions OPP **old-fashioned**: *modern surgical techniques* | *a bright modern office building* | **modern technology/medicine/design etc.** *Modern medicine has made huge steps toward eradicating the disease.*

THESAURUS

the latest the most modern: *the very latest cell phones*
up-to-date used about modern equipment or methods: *an up-to-date security system*
advanced used about modern weapons, machines, systems, methods etc.: *an advanced game system*
sophisticated used about modern machines, systems, methods etc. that have been carefully developed and are usually complicated: *sophisticated listening devices*
high-tech/hi-tech using very modern electronic equipment and technology, especially computers: *high-tech industries*
state-of-the-art using the newest methods, materials, or knowledge: *state-of-the-art technology*
cutting-edge extremely modern: *cutting-edge research*
→ NEW

3 [only before noun] modern art, music, literature etc. uses styles that have been recently developed and are very different from traditional styles SYN **contemporary**: *a modern dance group* [**Origin:** 1500–1600 Late Latin *modernus*, from Latin *modo* **just now**]

ˈmodern-day *adj.* [only before noun] existing in the present time, but considered in relation to someone or something else in the past: *The movie is a modern-day fairy tale.*

mod·ern·ism /ˈmɑdɚˌnɪzəm/ *n.* [U] a style of art, building etc. that was popular especially from the 1940s to the 1960s, in which artists used simple shapes and modern artificial materials —**modernist** *adj.* —**modernist** *n.* [C] → see also POSTMODERNISM

mod·ern·is·tic /ˌmɑdɚˈnɪstɪk◂/ *adj.* designed in a way that looks very modern and very different from previous styles: *modernistic furniture*

mo·der·ni·ty /mɑˈdɚnət̬i, mə-/ *n.* [U] FORMAL the quality of being modern: *the modernity of the car's design*

mod·ern·i·za·tion /ˌmɑdɚnəˈzeɪʃən/ *n.* **1** [C,U] the process or act of modernizing something: *the modernization of the railroads* **2** [C,U] ECONOMICS the process by which a country becomes more developed through new TECHNOLOGY, social change, and better government **3** [C] something that has been modernized

mod·ern·ize /ˈmɑdɚˌnaɪz/ *v.* [I,T] if something modernizes or you modernize it, it begins to use modern methods and equipment instead of older ones: *He pledged to modernize Mexico when he was elected.* | *The business will lose money if it doesn't modernize.*

ˌmodern penˈtathlon *n.* [singular] a sports competition that involves running, swimming, riding horses, FENCING, and shooting guns

mod·est /ˈmɑdɪst/ W3 *adj.* **1** APPROVING unwilling to talk proudly about your abilities and achievements OPP **immodest**: *a sincere and modest man* | *Don't be so modest!* | +**about** *Jason, a scholarship winner, is modest about his achievements.* **2** not very big, expensive etc., especially less big, expensive etc. than you would expect: *This is a terrific wine at a modest price.* | *Elliot's home is modest, but surrounded by beautiful forests.* **3** shy about showing your body or attracting sexual interest, because you are easily embarrassed OPP **immodest** **4** modest clothing covers the body in a way that does not attract sexual interest OPP **immodest**: *They're actually very modest bathing suits.* [**Origin:** 1500–1600 Latin *modestus*] —**modestly** *adv.*

mod·es·ty /ˈmɑdəsti/ *n.* [U] **1** APPROVING a way of behaving or talking about your achievements that is not proud: *He answers with modesty when asked about his role in the war.* **2 in all modesty** used to say that you do not want to seem too proud of something you have done, when in fact you are: *In all modesty, I think I've matured quite a bit since those days.* **3** the feeling of shyness about showing your body or doing anything that may attract sexual interest → see also **false modesty** at FALSE (4)

mod·i·cum /ˈmɑdɪkəm/ *n.* **a modicum of sth** FORMAL a small amount of something, especially a good quality: *Sometimes there is a modicum of truth in a cliché.*

mod·i·fi·ca·tion /ˌmɑdəfəˈkeɪʃən/ Ac *n.* **1** [C] a small change made in something such as a design, plan, or system: +**to** *We made modifications to the car to ensure passenger safety.* | **slight/minor modifications** *There have a few minor modifications to the original design.* **2** [U] the act of modifying something, or the process of being modified: *The equipment can be used without modification.* | +**of** *the modification of our business plan*

mod·i·fi·er /ˈmɑdəˌfaɪɚ/ *n.* [C] ENG. LANG. ARTS a word or group of words that give additional information about another word. Modifiers can be adjectives (such as "fierce" in "the fierce dog"), adverbs (such as "loudly" in "the dog barked loudly"), or phrases (such as "with a short tail" in "the dog with a short tail").

mod·i·fy /ˈmɑdəˌfaɪ/ Ac *v.* **modifies, modified, modifying** [T] **1** to make small changes to something in order to improve it and make it more appropriate or effective: *The feedback will be used to modify the teaching system for next year.* | **modify sth to do sth** *I modified the handlebars on my bike to make it more comfortable.* ▸see THESAURUS box at **change**[1] **2** ENG. LANG. ARTS if an adjective, adverb etc. modifies another word, it describes it or limits its meaning. In the phrase "walk slowly," the adverb "slowly" modifies the verb "walk."

Mo·di·glia·ni /ˌmoʊdilˈyɑni/, **Am·e·de·o** /ˌɑməˈdeɪoʊ/ (1884–1920) an Italian PAINTER and SCULPTOR known especially for his pictures of people in which the bodies and faces are much longer than in real life

Mo·doc /ˈmoʊdɑk/ a Native American tribe from the western U.S.

M

mod·u·lar /ˈmɑdʒələ/ *adj.* based on modules or made using modules: *a modular storage system* | *modular furniture* | *a modular education program*

mod·u·late /ˈmɑdʒəˌleɪt/ *v.* [T] **1** if your voice modulates or you modulate it, you change the sound of it: **modulate to/from/into sth** *Her voice modulated to a harsher tone.* **2** TECHNICAL to change the form of a sound wave or radio signal so that it is clearer **3** FORMAL to change a process or activity in order to make it more controlled, slower, less strong etc.: *Enzymes in the body modulate our moods.* **4** ENG. LANG. ARTS to move from one key to another in a piece of music using a series of related CHORDS —**modulation** /ˌmɑdʒəˈleɪʃən/ *n.* [C]

mod·ule /ˈmɑdʒul/ *n.* [C] **1** a part of a SPACECRAFT that can be separated from the main part and used for a particular purpose **2** COMPUTERS one of several parts of a piece of computer SOFTWARE that does a particular job: *a word processor module* **3** one of several separate parts that can be combined to form a larger object or system: *The instruction modules on our website can be combined in many different ways.* [**Origin:** 1500–1600 Latin *modulus* **small measure, rhythm**]

mo·dus op·er·an·di /ˌmoʊdəs ˌɑpəˈrændi/ *n.* [singular] FORMAL see M.O.

modus vi·ven·di /ˌmoʊdəs vɪˈvɛndi/ *n.* [singular] FORMAL an arrangement between people, groups, countries etc. with very different opinions or habits that allows them to live or work together without arguing

Mog·a·dish·u /ˌmoʊgəˈdɪʃu, ˌmɑ-/ the capital and largest city in Somalia

Mo·gul /ˈmoʊgəl/ see MUGHAL

mo·gul /ˈmoʊgəl/ *n.* **1 a movie/newspaper/record etc. mogul** someone who has great power and influence in a particular industry or activity SYN **magnate** **2** [C] a pile of hard snow on a SKI SLOPE [**Origin:** 1600–1700 *Mogul* **member of a Muslim group that ruled India in former times** (16–21 centuries), from Persian *Mughul*, from Mongolian *Mongol*]

mo·hair /ˈmoʊhɛr/ *n.* [U] expensive wool made from the hair of the ANGORA goat: *a mohair sweater*

Mo·ham·med /moʊˈhæməd/ → see MUHAMMAD

Mo·ham·med·an /moʊˈhæmədən/ → see MUHAMMADAN

Mo·ha·ve, Mojave /moʊˈhɑvi/ a Native American tribe from the southwestern area of the U.S.

Mo·hawk /ˈmoʊhɔk/ a Native American tribe from the northeast region of the U.S.

Mo·he·gan /moʊˈhigən/ a Native American tribe from the northeastern area of the U.S.

moi·e·ty /ˈmɔɪəṭi/ *n. plural* **moieties** [C + of] FORMAL a half of something

moi·ré /mwɑˈreɪ/ *n.* [U] a type of silk with a pattern that looks like waves: *a moiré bow*

moist /mɔɪst/ *adj. comparative* **moister**, *superlative* **moistest** slightly wet but not very wet, especially in a way that seems nice: *a moist chocolate cake* | *Make sure the soil is moist before planting the seeds.* | **+with** *Her hands were moist with sweat.* [**Origin:** 1300–1400 Old French *moiste*, from Latin *mucidus* **wet and slippery**] —**moistness** *n.* [U]

moist·en /ˈmɔɪsən/ *v.* [I,T] to become slightly wet, or to make something slightly wet: *My eyes moistened at the thought of my family.* | *She* ***moistened her lips*** (=with her tongue) *and began speaking.*

mois·ture /ˈmɔɪstʃə/ *n.* [U] small amounts of water that are present in the air, in a substance, or on a surface: *Dew forms from moisture in the air.* | *Plants use their roots to* ***absorb moisture*** *from the soil.*

mois·tur·ize /ˈmɔɪstʃəˌraɪz/ *v.* [T] **1** to keep your skin soft by using a special liquid or cream **2 moisturizing cream/lotion/oil** cream, oil etc. that you put on your skin to keep it soft

mois·tur·iz·er /ˈmɔɪstʃəˌraɪzə/ *n.* [C,U] a liquid or cream that you put on your skin to keep it soft

mois·tur·i·zing /ˈmɔɪstʃəˌraɪzɪŋ/ *adj.* [only before noun] intended to keep or make your skin or hair soft and less dry: *moisturizing cream*

Mo·ja·ve Des·ert, the /moʊˌhɑvi ˈdɛzət/ also **the Mohave Desert** a large desert in southern California

mok·sha /ˈmɑkʃə/ *n.* [U] in Hinduism, freedom from having to experience REINCARNATION (=coming back to earth in a different form after death)

mol /moʊl/ CHEMISTRY another spelling of MOLE

mo·lar /ˈmoʊlə/ *n.* [C] BIOLOGY one of the large teeth at the back of the mouth used for crushing food [**Origin:** 1300–1400 Latin *molaris* **crushing like a mill**, from *mola*] → see also INCISOR —**molar** *adj.*

mo·las·ses /məˈlæsɪz/ *n.* [U] a thick dark sweet liquid that is obtained from raw sugar plants when they are being made into sugar

mold[1] /moʊld/ *n.* **1** [U] a soft green or black substance that grows on food which has been kept too long, and on objects that are in warm wet air: *bread covered in mold* **2** [C] a hollow container that you pour liquid into, so that when the liquid becomes solid, it takes the shape of the container: *Cool the cake in the mold before serving.* **3** [singular] the combination qualities that are typical of a certain type of person: *In a lot of ways he doesn't* ***fit the mold of*** (=have the qualities of) *a typical politician.* | **in the classic/traditional/heroic etc. mold** *a horror movie in the classic mold* **4 break the mold** to change a situation completely, by doing something that has not been done before: *He urged educators to break the mold and find new ways of teaching.*

mold[2] *v.* **1** [T] to shape a soft substance by pressing or rolling it or by putting it into a mold: *toys made of molded rubber* | **mold sth into sth** *The cheeses are molded into distinctive shapes.* **2** [T] to influence the way someone's character or attitudes develop: *an attempt to mold public opinion* | **mold sb into sth** *He takes young athletes and molds them into team players.* **3** [I,T] to fit closely to the shape of something, or make something do this: **mold (sth) to sth** *The boot will mold itself to the shape of your foot.*

mol·der /ˈmoʊldə/ also **molder away** *v.* [I] to decay slowly and gradually: *Old medical supplies moldered in the warehouses.*

mold·ing /ˈmoʊldɪŋ/ *n.* **1** [C,U] a thin line of stone, wood, plastic etc. used as decoration around the edge of something such as a wall, car, or piece of furniture **2** [C] an object produced from a MOLD

Mol·do·va /mɑlˈdoʊvə/ a country in eastern Europe between Romania and the Ukraine, which used to be part of the former Soviet Union —**Moldovan** *n., adj.*

mold·y /ˈmoʊldi/ *adj. comparative* **moldier**, *superlative* **moldiest** covered with MOLD: *moldy cheese* —**moldiness** *n.* [U]

mole[1] /moʊl/ *n.* [C] **1** MEDICINE a small dark brown mark on the skin that is often slightly higher than the skin around it ►see THESAURUS box at **mark**[2] **2** BIOLOGY a small animal with brown fur that cannot see very well and usually lives in holes under the ground **3** someone who works for an organization, especially a government, while secretly giving information to its enemy: *FBI moles were looking for evidence of fraud.* **4** also **mol** CHEMISTRY an amount of a substance that contains 6.0225×10^{23} atoms, MOLECULES etc. This number, called AVOGADRO'S NUMBER, is equal to the number of atoms in 12 grams of CARBON 12.

mo·le[2] /ˈmoʊleɪ/ *n.* [U] a SPICY Mexican sauce with COCOA in it that you eat with meat

moˌlecular ˈcompound *n.* [C] CHEMISTRY a chemical compound that consists of MOLECULES

moˌlecular ˈformula *n.* [C] CHEMISTRY a series of numbers and letters that represent the type and exact number of atoms present in a MOLECULE → see also EMPIRICAL FORMULA

mol·e·cule /ˈmɑləˌkyul/ *n.* [C] CHEMISTRY the smallest unit into which any substance can be divided without losing its chemical properties, usually consisting of two or more atoms: *a nitrogen molecule* [**Origin:** 1700–

1800 French *molécule*, from Latin *moles* **mass**] **—molecular** /məˈlɛkyələ/ *adj.*

mole·hill /ˈmoʊlˌhɪl/ *n.* [C] a small pile of earth made by a MOLE → see also **make a mountain out of a molehill** at MOUNTAIN (3)

mole·skin /ˈmoʊlˌskɪn/ *n.* [U] **1** a soft thick material that you put on your feet to protect them from rubbing against your shoes **2** thick cloth that feels like SUEDE **3** the skin of a MOLE

mo·lest /məˈlɛst/ *v.* [T] **1** to attack or harm someone, especially a child, by touching them in a sexual way or trying to have sex with them → see also ABUSE: *The boy told officers he had been molested several times.* **2** OLD-FASHIONED to attack and physically harm someone [**Origin:** 1300–1400 Old French *molester*, from Latin *molestare*, from *molestus* **heavy, annoying**] **—molester** *n.* [C] **—molestation** /ˌmɑləˈsteɪʃən, ˌmoʊ-, -lɛ-/ *n.* [U]

Mo·lière /moʊlˈyɛr/ (1622–1673) a French actor and writer of humorous plays whose real name was Jean-Baptiste Poquelin

moll /moʊl, mɑl/ *n.* [C] OLD-FASHIONED, SLANG a criminal's GIRLFRIEND

mol·li·fy /ˈmɑləˌfaɪ/ *v.* **mollifies, mollified, mollifying** [T] to make someone feel less angry and upset about something: *Mel seemed slightly mollified by my explanation.* **—mollification** /ˌmɑləfəˈkeɪʃən/ *n.* [U]

mol·lusk /ˈmɑləsk/ *n.* [C] a type of sea or land animal that has a soft body covered by a hard shell

mol·ly·cod·dle /ˈmɑliˌkɑdl/ *v.* [T] to treat someone too kindly: *Stop mollycoddling those kids!*

Mo·lo·kai /ˌmɑləˈkaɪ, moʊ-/ an island in the Pacific Ocean that is part of the U.S. state of Hawaii

Mo·lo·tov cock·tail /ˌmɑlətɔf ˈkɑkteɪl, ˌmɔl-/ *n.* [C] a simple bomb consisting of a bottle filled with gasoline, with a piece of cloth at the end that you light

molt /moʊlt/ *v.* [I] when a bird or animal molts, it loses hair, feathers, or skin so that new ones can grow

mol·ten /ˈmoʊltˀn/ *adj.* [usually before noun] EARTH SCIENCE molten metal or rock has been made into a liquid by being heated to a very high temperature: *molten lava*

molt·ing /ˈmoʊltɪŋ/ *n.* [U] BIOLOGY a process in which a bird or animal loses its hair, feathers, skin, or shell so that new ones can grow

mol·to /ˈmoʊltoʊ/ *adv.* a word used in music meaning "very"

mol·y /ˈmoʊli/ → see **holy cow/mackerel/moly etc.** at HOLY (3)

mo·lyb·de·num /məˈlɪbdənəm/ *n.* [U] SYMBOL **Mo** CHEMISTRY a pale-colored metal that is an ELEMENT and is used especially to strengthen steel

mom /mɑm/ [S1] [W2] *n.* [C] INFORMAL mother: *Mom, can I go over to Barbara's house?* | *My mom says I have to stay home tonight.*

ˌmom-and-ˈpop *adj.* [only before noun] INFORMAL a mom-and-pop business is owned and operated by a family or a husband and wife: *a mom-and-pop restaurant*

mo·ment /ˈmoʊmənt/ [S1] [W1] *n.*

1 SHORT TIME [C] a very short period of time: *He was here a moment ago.* | *It only took a few moments to finish.* | ***Just a moment*** (=used to tell someone to wait a short time) – *I'll see if Ms. Marciano is free.* | *We'll come to some examples of this **in a moment*** (=very soon). | *Could you hold the line **for a moment?*** | ***One moment**, please* (=used to tell someone to wait a short time, especially on the telephone). | *Arthur, **do you have a moment*** (=used to ask someone if they have time to speak to you or do something for you)*?*

2 POINT IN TIME [C] a particular point in time: *I was just waiting for the right moment to tell her.* | ***From the** first **moment** I got on the ice I knew this wasn't the sport for me.* | ***At that moment*** (=used to emphasize when something happened) *she started to cry.*

3 at the moment used to say what the situation is now: *We're really busy at the moment.*

4 at this moment (in time) also **at the present moment** FORMAL used to emphasize what the situation is now, especially when things could change: *At this moment, we do not know what caused the fire.*

5 for the moment used to say that something is happening now but that it is likely to change: *We're planning to stay in this house for the moment.*

6 the sb/sth of the moment the job, person, event etc. of the moment is the one that is most important or famous at the present time: *The question of the moment is, will she run for the Senate again?*

7 OPPORTUNITY [C usually singular] a particular period of time when you have a chance to do something: *It was Tara's **big moment*** (=her chance to show her skill)*; she breathed deeply and began to play.*

8 have its/your moments a) to have periods of being good or interesting: *The White Sox had their moments, but they still lost.* **b)** to have periods of causing problems: *Generally it's an easy job, but it does have its moments.*

9 at a moment's notice without being given much time to prepare: *The soldiers must be ready to leave at a moment's notice.*

10 not a moment too soon so late that it is almost too late: *The extra money came not a moment too soon.*

11 the moment of truth the time when you will find out if something will work correctly, be successful etc.: *The moment of truth came when I tasted the sauce.*

12 a moment of weakness a time when you can be persuaded more easily than usual: *He convinced me, in a moment of weakness, to lend him money.*

13 of great moment LITERARY important: *matters of great moment*

[**Origin:** 1300–1400 French, Latin *momentum*, from *movere* **to move**]

> WORD CHOICE **moment, minute, second**
> **Moment, minute**, and **second** are used in many of the same phrases to mean exactly the same thing. **Minute** is probably the most commonly used word in these types of phrases. For example, you can say: *She'll call you the minute she gets home, She'll call you the moment she gets home,* or *She'll call you the second she gets home.*

mo·men·tar·i·ly /ˌmoʊmənˈtɛrəli/ *adv.* **1** FORMAL for a very short time [SYN] **briefly**: *The Governor paused momentarily to speak with reporters.* **2** SPOKEN very soon: *I'll be with you momentarily.*

mo·men·tar·y /ˈmoʊmənˌtɛri/ *adj.* [usually before noun] continuing for a very short time: *After a momentary pause, he continued.*

mo·men·tous /moʊˈmɛntəs, mə-/ *adj.* a momentous event, occasion, decision etc. is very important, especially because of the effects it will have in the future: *a momentous change in policy* | *I'd like to welcome you here on this momentous occasion.*

mo·men·tum /moʊˈmɛntəm, mə-/ *n.* [U] **1** the ability to keep increasing, developing, or being more successful: *She won the first match, then seemed to **lose momentum*** (=become weaker or stop being successful). | *The economic recovery is expected to **gain momentum*** (=become stronger or more successful) *soon.* | *We're playing better in this half, but we have to **keep the momentum going**.* **2** the force that makes a moving object keep moving: *the momentum of the avalanche* | *The hill got steeper and the sled **gained momentum*** (=moved faster). | *The train **loses momentum*** (=moves more slowly) *as it comes to the top of the hill.* **3** PHYSICS the force or power contained in a moving object calculated by multiplying its weight by its speed [**Origin:** 1600–1700 Latin **movement, moment**, from *movere* **to move**]

mom·ma /ˈmɑmə/ *n.* [C] another spelling of MAMA

mom·my [S1], **mommie** /ˈmɑmi/ *n. plural* **mommies** [C] a word meaning "mother," used by or to young children

M

ˈmommy ˌtrack *n.* [C] INFORMAL a situation in which women with children have less opportunity to make large amounts of money or become very successful at their jobs, for example because they are not able to work as many hours as other people

Mon. the written abbreviation of MONDAY

Mon·a·co /ˈmɑnəˌkoʊ/ a small PRINCIPALITY (=country ruled by a prince) on the Mediterranean coast between France and Italy —**Monacan** /ˈmɑnəkən, məˈnɑkən/ also **Monégasque** /ˌmɑneɪˈgæsk/ *n., adj.*

Monaco-Ville /ˌmɑnəkoʊ ˈvil/ the capital city of Monaco

mon·arch /ˈmɑnɚk, ˈmɑnɑrk/ *n.* [C] FORMAL a king or queen [**Origin:** 1400–1500 Late Latin *monarcha*, from Greek, from *mono-* + *-archos* (from *archein* **to rule**)] —**monarchic** /məˈnɑrkɪk/ also **monarchical** *adj.*: *monarchic rule*

mon·ar·chist /ˈmɑnɚkɪst/ *n.* [C] POLITICS someone who supports the idea that their country should be ruled by a king or queen

mon·ar·chy /ˈmɑnɚki/ *n. plural* **monarchies** POLITICS **1** [C,U] the system in which a country is ruled by a king or queen: *the European monarchies of the 18th century* ►see THESAURUS box at **government** **2 the monarchy** [singular] the king or queen and their family in a particular country → see also REPUBLIC

mon·as·ter·y /ˈmɑnəˌstɛri/ *n. plural* **monasteries** [C] a building or group of buildings where MONKS live [**Origin:** 1300–1400 Late Latin *monasterium*, from Greek, from *monazein* **to live alone**] → see also CONVENT

mo·nas·tic /məˈnæstɪk/ *adj.* **1** concerning or relating to MONKS or monasteries: *a monastic order* **2** someone who has a monastic way of life lives alone and very simply —**monastically** /-kli/ *adv.* —**monasticism** /məˈnæstəˌsɪzəm/ *n.* [U]

Mon·day /ˈmʌndi, -deɪ/ WRITTEN ABBREVIATION **Mon.** *n. plural* **Mondays** [C,U] the second day of the week, between Sunday and Tuesday: *Steve said he'd arrive Monday.* | *It was raining* ***on Monday***. | *Jo had a doctor's appointment* ***last Monday***. | *I'll see you* ***next Monday***. | *The concert's going to be on the radio* ***this Monday*** (=the next Monday that is coming). | *The restaurant is usually closed* ***on Mondays*** (=each Monday). | *Labor Day is always on* ***a Monday***. | **Monday morning/afternoon/night etc.** *I have a date Monday night.* [**Origin:** from Old English *monandæg*, from a translation of Latin *lunae dies* **day of the moon**] → see Grammar box at SUNDAY

ˌMonday morning ˈquarterback *n.* [C] INFORMAL, DISAPPROVING someone who criticizes something or gives advice about it only after it has happened, when it is easy to see what the problems were —**Monday morning quarterbacking** *n.* [U]

mon·do /ˈmɑndoʊ/ *adj., adv.* [only before noun] SPOKEN, INFORMAL very large in size or degree: *He has some mondo speakers in his car.*

Mon·dri·an /ˌmɔndriˈɑn/, **Piet** /pit/ (1872–1944) a Dutch painter famous for his ABSTRACT work

Mon·é·gasque /ˌmɑneɪˈgæsk/ *adj.* relating to or coming from Monaco —**Monégasque** *n.* [C]

Mon·et /moʊˈneɪ/, **Claude** /kloʊd, klɔd/ (1840–1926) a French painter who helped to start the IMPRESSIONIST movement

mon·e·ta·rism /ˈmɑnət̬əˌrɪzəm/ *n.* [U] ECONOMICS the belief that the best way to manage and control a country's economic system is to limit the amount of money that is available and being used —**monetarist** *adj., n.* [C]

mon·e·tar·y /ˈmɑnəˌtɛri/ *adj.* [usually before noun] relating to money, especially all the money in a particular country: *How does their monetary policy work?* | *the monetary value of gold* | *I'm not doing this for* ***monetary reward*** (=payment).

ˌmonetary ˈpolicy *n.* [C usually singular] ECONOMICS actions taken by the FEDERAL RESERVE SYSTEM to influence the growth and development of the U.S. ECONOMY and prevent INFLATION (=a continuing increase in prices, or the rate at which prices increase). The actions include controlling all the money that exists in the economy at any particular time and raising or lowering INTEREST RATES.

mon·e·tize /ˈmɑnəˌtaɪz/ *v.* [T] TECHNICAL to change government BONDS and debts into money —**monetization** /ˌmɑnət̬əˈzeɪʃən/ *n.* [U]

mon·ey /ˈmʌni/ [S1] [W1] *n.* [U] **1** what you earn by working and use in order to buy things, usually in the form of coins or pieces of paper with their value printed on them: *Leon dropped all his money on the floor.* | *$450 is a lot of money to pay for shoes.* | *Houses in this area* ***cost*** *a lot of* ***money***. | *Do you* ***have*** *enough* ***money*** (=have money in the form coins or paper) *to pay for the sandwiches?* | *Ann really wanted to go to Yellowstone with us, but she didn't* ***have the money*** (=she had not saved enough). | *Asa's* ***making*** *a lot of* ***money****, but he's working eighteen-hour days.* | *Lynn's dad worked two jobs to* ***earn*** *extra* ***money***. | *All the* ***money was spent*** *on special effects.* | *They never turn the heat on; I guess they're trying to* ***save money*** (=spend less). | *Young people don't usually think about* ***saving money*** (=putting it in a bank or investment for the future). | *The restaurant is* ***losing money*** (=spending more money than it earns). | *Lawyers* ***charge*** *far too much* ***money*** *for their services.* | *I didn't really want to have to* ***borrow money*** *to go to grad school.* | *The church is trying to* ***raise money*** *for a new carpet.* | *She's making about $60,000 a year, which is pretty* ***good money*** (=a good salary for your work). | **invest money in sth/put money into sth** *The state needs to put more money into schools.* | **refund money/give money back** *Take it back to the store, and they'll give you your money back.*

> **THESAURUS**
>
> **Types of money**
> **bill** paper money: *a $20 bill*
> **coin** metal money: *old coins*
> **penny** a coin worth 1 cent
> **nickel** a coin worth 5 cents
> **dime** a coin worth 10 cents
> **quarter** a coin worth 25 cents
> **cash** money in the form of coins and bills: *I didn't have enough cash, so I paid by check.*
> **change** money in the form of coins: *I need some change for the coffee machine.*
> **currency** the money used in a particular country: *He had $500 worth of Japanese currency.*

2 all the money that a person, organization, or country owns [SYN] **wealth**: *Money isn't everything.* | *In 1929, hundreds of rich men* ***lost all their money*** *when the stock market crashed.* | *He* ***made his money*** *in a successful computer business.* **3 get your money's worth** to get something worth the price that you paid: *Some publishers feel they haven't been getting their money's worth from the show.* **4 French/Japanese/Turkish etc. money** the money that is used in a particular country [SYN] **currency**: *I still have $10 in Canadian money left.* **5 the money** INFORMAL the amount of money that you earn for doing a particular job: ***"What's the money like?*** (=Does the job pay well?)*" "It's pretty good."* **6 money to burn** INFORMAL money to spend on expensive things, especially things that other people think are unnecessary or silly: *older Americans with money to burn* | *People who buy these cars usually* ***have money to burn***. **7 money is no object** used to say that you can spend as much money as you want to on something: *If money were no object, what kind of house would you want?* **8 there's money (to be made) in sth** used to say that you can get a lot of money from a particular activity or from buying and selling something: *There is plenty of money to be made in the casino business.* **9 marry (into) money** to marry someone whose family is rich **10 money pit** something such as a boat or house that causes you to spend

M

a lot of money very often in order to keep it working or repaired

SPOKEN PHRASES

11 that kind of money a phrase meaning "a lot of money," used when you think something costs too much, when someone earns a lot more than other people etc.: *If I had that kind of money, I guess I'd splurge too.* | *He wanted $5000 for the truck, and I just **don't have that kind of money**.* **12 pay good money for sth** to spend a lot of money on something: *I paid good money for that sofa, so it should last.* **13 be (right) on the money** used when something is perfect or exactly right for the situation: *He was right on the money when he said people are tired of big-shot politicians.* **14 for my money** used when giving your opinion about something, to emphasize that you believe it strongly: *For my money, it's one of the most beautiful places in Hawaii.* **15 money talks** used to say that money is powerful, and people who have money can get what they want: *Money talks, and poor working people are ignored.* **16 my money's on sb/sth, the smart money is on sb/sth** used to say what you think is very likely to happen in a situation: *The smart money is on the A's to win the series.* **17 put your money where your mouth is** to show by your actions that what you promised in the past will happen: *It's time for the governor to put his money where his mouth is.* **18 I'd put money on it** used to emphasize that you are completely sure about something: *We're not going to lose. I'd put money on it.* **19 I'm not made of money** used to say that you do not have a lot of money when someone asks you for some **20 money doesn't grow on trees** used to tell someone that they should not waste money, or that there is not enough money to buy something expensive **21 be in the money** to have a lot of money, especially suddenly or when you did not expect to

[**Origin:** 1200–1300 Old French *moneie*, from Latin *moneta* **mint, money**, from *Moneta*, name given to Juno, the goddess in whose temple the ancient Romans produced money] → see also BLOOD MONEY, HUSH MONEY, POCKET MONEY, **give sb a (good) run for their money** at RUN[2] (15), **smart money** at SMART[1] (4), **throw money at sb/sth** at THROW AT (3)

mon·ey·bags /ˈmʌniˌbægz/ *n.* [singular] INFORMAL someone who has a lot of money

ˈmoney ˌbelt *n.* [C] a special belt that you can carry money in while you are traveling

ˈmoney ˌchanger *n.* [C] someone whose business is to exchange one country's money for money from another country, sometimes without official approval

ˈmoney creˌation *n.* [U] ECONOMICS the process by which money that did not exist in the past is used for the first time and is passed from one person, business etc. to another

ˈmoney eˌconomy *n.* [C] ECONOMICS an economic system in which things are paid for using money, rather than by exchanging goods

mon·eyed, monied /ˈmʌnid/ *adj.* [only before noun] FORMAL rich: *a resort for moneyed Floridians*

money-grub·bing /ˈmʌniˌgrʌbɪŋ/ *adj.* [only before noun] INFORMAL determined to get money, even by unfair or dishonest methods: *money-grubbing land developers* —**moneygrubber** *n.* [C]

mon·ey·lend·er, money lender /ˈmʌniˌlɛndɚ/ *n.* [C] someone whose business is to lend money to people, especially at very high rates of INTEREST

mon·ey·mak·er, money-maker /ˈmʌniˌmeɪkɚ/ *n.* [C] a product or business that earns a lot of money

ˈmoney ˌmarket *n.* [C] ECONOMICS **1** a market for lending and borrowing money, in which money is lent for periods of less than one year **2** all the banks and other financial institutions that buy and sell foreign money for profit

ˈmoney ˌmarket ˌfund also **ˌmoney ˌmarket ˈmutual fund** *n.* [C] ECONOMICS a FUND (=an arrangement with a company that is experienced in buying and selling stock etc. on behalf of many people) for buying and selling BONDS or government BILLS etc. on which money is lent for less than one year

ˈmoney ˌorder *n.* [C] a special type of check that you buy and send to someone so that they can exchange it for money

ˈmoney supˌply *n.* [singular] ECONOMICS all the money that exists in a country's ECONOMY at a particular time, and the speed at which it is used

-monger /mʌŋgɚ, mɑŋgɚ/ *suffix* [in nouns] **1** someone who says things that are not nice or encourages activities that are immoral or not nice: *rumor mongers* (=people who say untrue things about other people) | *warmongers* (=people who are eager to start wars) **2** OLD-FASHIONED someone who sells a particular thing: *a fishmonger*

Mon·gol /ˈmɑŋgəl, -goʊl/ **1** one of the people who live in Mongolia **2** one of the people from several related groups who live in central Asia

Mon·go·li·a /mɑŋˈgoʊliə/ a country in north central Asia between Russia and China —**Mongolian** *n., adj.*

mon·goose /ˈmɑŋgus/ *n. plural* **mongooses** [C] a small furry tropical animal that kills snakes and rats

mon·grel /ˈmɑŋgrəl, ˈmʌŋ-/ *n.* [C] a dog that is a mix of several different breeds → see also MUTT

mon·ied /ˈmʌnid/ *adj.* another spelling of MONEYED

mon·ies /ˈmʌniz/ *n.* [plural] LAW money: *federal monies*

mon·i·ker /ˈmɑnɪkɚ/ *n.* [C] INFORMAL someone's name, SIGNATURE, or NICKNAME: *her stage moniker* (=the one she uses when she acts in a play)

mon·i·tor[1] /ˈmɑnəṭɚ/ Ac *n.* [C] **1** COMPUTERS the part of a computer that looks like a television and that shows information → see also SCREEN: *a flat-screen monitor* **2** a television that shows a picture of what is happening in a particular place: *A security guard was watching a row of monitors.* **3** a piece of equipment that receives and shows information about what is happening inside someone's body: *a monitor that shows the baby's heartbeat* **4** someone whose job is to check that something is being done correctly or fairly: *U.N. election monitors* **5** someone whose job is to listen to news, messages etc. from foreign radio stations and report on them

monitor[2] Ac W2 *v.* [T] **1** to carefully watch, listen to, or examine something over a period of time, to check for any changes or developments: *U.N. peacekeepers will be sent to monitor the ceasefire.* | *Nurses constantly monitor the patients' condition.* ►see THESAURUS box at **check[1]** **2** to secretly listen to other people's telephone calls, foreign radio broadcasts etc.: *Army intelligence has been monitoring the enemy's radio broadcasts.* [**Origin:** 1500–1600 Latin *monere* **to warn**]

monk /mʌŋk/ *n.* [C] a man who is a member of a group of religious men who live together in a MONASTERY —**monkish** *adj.*: *a monkish silence* → see also NUN

Monk /mʌŋk/, **The·lo·ni·ous** /θəˈloʊniəs/ (1917–1982) a JAZZ musician who played the piano

mon·key[1] /ˈmʌŋki/ S3 *n. plural* **monkeys** [C]
1 ANIMAL BIOLOGY a small animal with a long tail, which uses its hands to climb trees and lives in hot countries
2 CHILD INFORMAL a small child who is very active and likes to play tricks: *Stop that, you little monkey!*
3 monkey business dishonest or bad behavior: *political monkey business*
4 a monkey on your back INFORMAL a serious problem that makes your life very difficult, especially being dependent on drugs or losing a lot of sports competitions
5 get a/the monkey off your back to get rid of or end a serious problem that has been making your life very difficult: *The win finally gets the monkey off our backs.*
6 I'll be a monkey's uncle! OLD-FASHIONED, SPOKEN said when you are very surprised about something
7 make a monkey (out) of sb to make someone seem stupid

8 monkey see, monkey do SPOKEN used to say that people will often do what they see other people doing, even if it is silly or stupid → see also GREASE MONKEY

monkey² *v.* **monkeys, monkeyed, monkeying**

monkey around *phr. v.* INFORMAL to behave in a silly, stupid, or careless way: *I'm tired of monkeying around. We need to get to work!*

monkey (around) with sth *phr. v.* to touch or use something, usually when you do not know how to do it correctly: *Stop monkeying around with my iPod!*

'monkey bars *n.* [plural] a structure of metal bars for children to climb and play on

mon·key·shines /ˈmʌŋkiˌʃaɪnz/ *n.* [plural] OLD-FASHIONED tricks or jokes

'monkey suit *n.* [C] OLD-FASHIONED, HUMOROUS a TUXEDO

'monkey wrench *n.* [C] a tool that is used for holding and turning things of different widths, especially NUTS → see also **throw a (monkey) wrench in sth** at WRENCH¹ (2)

mon·o¹ /ˈmɑnoʊ/ *n.* [U] INFORMAL **1** MEDICINE an infectious illness that makes your GLANDS swell and makes you feel weak and tired for a long time **2** a system of recording or broadcasting sound, in which the sound comes from only one direction

mono² *adj.* using a system of recording or broadcasting sound in which all the sound comes from only one direction: *a mono recording* → see also STEREO

mono- /mɑnoʊ, -nə/ *prefix* one SYN **single**: *a monosyllabic word* (=a word that has only one SYLLABLE) | *a monolingual dictionary* (=dealing with only one language)

mon·o·chro·mat·ic /ˌmɑnəkroʊˈmæt̬ɪk/ *adj.* **1** having only one color: *If you like simplicity, try a monochromatic or one-color garden.* **2** PHYSICS monochromatic light has only one WAVELENGTH

mon·o·chrome /ˈmɑnəˌkroʊm/ *adj.* **1** in shades of only one color, especially shades of gray: *a monochrome color scheme for the room* **2** a monochrome computer MONITOR uses one color as a background and only one other color for the letters on the screen

mon·o·cle /ˈmɑnəkəl/ *n.* [C] a single LENS (=round piece of glass) that you hold in front of one eye to help you to see better

mon·o·cul·ture /ˈmɑnoʊˌkʌltʃɚ/ *n.* [C,U] BIOLOGY the practice of growing the same crop on an area of land every year, which can be harmful to the soil

mo·nog·a·my /məˈnɑgəmi/ *n.* [U] the custom or practice of being married to only one person at a time —**monogamous** *adj.* —**monogamously** *adv.* → see also BIGAMY, POLYGAMY

mon·o·gram /ˈmɑnəˌgræm/ *n.* [C] a design made from the first letters of someone's names, that is put on things such as shirts or writing paper —**monogrammed** *adj.*: *monogrammed towels*

mon·o·graph /ˈmɑnəˌgræf/ *n.* [C + on] a serious article or short book about a subject

mon·o·lin·gual /ˌmɑnəˈlɪŋgwəl/ *adj.* TECHNICAL speaking, using, or dealing with only one language: *a monolingual dictionary* → see also BILINGUAL, MULTILINGUAL

mon·o·lith /ˈmɑnlˌɪθ/ *n.* [C] **1** an organization, government etc. that is very large and powerful and difficult to change: *the collapse of the Communist monolith in Eastern Europe* **2** a very large tall building that looks very solid and impressive: *a chocolate-colored brick monolith on 42nd Street* **3** a large tall block of stone, especially one that was put in place in ancient times, possibly for religious reasons

mon·o·lith·ic /ˌmɑnlˈɪθɪk/ *adj.* **1** a monolithic organization, political system etc. is very large and powerful and difficult to change: *monolithic corporations* **2** very large, solid, and impressive: *monolithic office buildings*

mon·o·logue /ˈmɑnlˌɔg, -ˌɑg/ *n.* [C] **1** ENG. LANG. ARTS a long speech by one character in a play, movie, or television show → see also DIALOGUE, SOLILOQUY **2** a set of jokes and stories told by a COMEDIAN SYN **routine** **3** ENG. LANG. ARTS a play that only uses one actor **4** a long period in a conversation when only one person talks, often in way that is boring and prevents other people from taking part: *her rambling monologue*

mon·o·ma·ni·a /ˌmɑnoʊˈmeɪniə/ *n.* [U] TECHNICAL an unusually strong interest in a particular idea or subject —**monomaniac** *adj.*, *n.* [C]

mon·o·mer /ˈmɑnəmɚ/ *n.* [C] CHEMISTRY a MOLECULE with a simple chemical structure, which can combine with other molecules to form a POLYMER

mo·no·mi·al /mɑˈnoʊmiəl/ *n.* [C] MATH an algebraic expression consisting of only a single group of numbers, letters, or INDEXes. For example, an expression such as y, 5x, or $5x^2y$ is a monomial, but 2x + 9y is not. —**monomial** *adj.* → see also POLYNOMIAL

mon·o·nu·cle·o·sis /ˌmɑnoʊˌnukliˈoʊsɪs/ *n.* [U] TECHNICAL → see MONO (1)

mon·o·plane /ˈmɑnəpleɪn, -noʊ-/ *n.* [C] TECHNICAL an airplane with only one wing on each side, like most modern airplanes → see also BIPLANE

mo·nop·o·lis·tic /məˌnɑpəˈlɪstɪk◂/ *adj.* controlling or trying to control something completely, especially an industry or business activity: *monopolistic corporations*

mo·nop·o·lize /məˈnɑpəˌlaɪz/ *v.* [T] **1** to have complete control over a type of business, so that other companies cannot get involved: *One firm monopolizes the whole market.* **2** to have complete control over something so that other people cannot share it or take part in it: *The Patriots monopolized the ball in the third period.* **3** to demand or need a lot of someone's time and attention: *Susan's children monopolize her time and energy.* —**monopolization** /məˌnɑpələˈzeɪʃən/ *n.* [U]

mo·nop·o·ly /məˈnɑpəli/ *n.* *plural* **monopolies** **1** [C,U] the control of all or most of a business activity by a single company or by a government: **+on/of** *At the time, the company had a monopoly on telephone services.* **2** [C] a company that controls all or most of a business activity: *a government-owned monopoly* **3 have a monopoly on sth** to be the only person or group to have or feel something: *Working mothers do* ***not have a monopoly on*** *guilt.*

mon·o·rail /ˈmɑnəˌreɪl/ *n.* **1** [U] a type of railroad that uses a single RAIL, usually high above the ground **2** [C] a train that travels on this type of railroad

mon·o·sac·cha·ride /ˌmɑnoʊˈsækəˌraɪd/ *n.* [C] CHEMISTRY a type of natural sugar, such as GLUCOSE, that has a very simple chemical structure SYN **simple sugar** → see also POLYSACCHARIDE

mon·o·so·di·um glu·ta·mate /ˌmɑnəˌsoʊdiəm ˈglut̬əˌmeɪt/ *n.* [U] TECHNICAL → see MSG

mon·o·syl·lab·ic /ˌmɑnəsɪˈlæbɪk◂/ *adj.* **1** someone who is monosyllabic or makes monosyllabic remarks seems impolite because they do not say much: *He grunted monosyllabic responses to questions.* **2** ENG. LANG. ARTS a monosyllabic word has only one SYLLABLE

mon·o·syl·la·ble /ˈmɑnəˌsɪləbəl/ *n.* [C] TECHNICAL a word with one SYLLABLE

mon·o·the·ism /ˈmɑnəθiˌɪzəm/ *n.* [U] TECHNICAL the belief that there is only one God —**monotheist** *n.* [C] —**monotheistic** /ˌmɑnəθiˈɪstɪk/ *adj.* → see also POLYTHEISM

mon·o·tone /ˈmɑnəˌtoʊn/ *n.* [singular] a sound or way of speaking or singing that continues on the same note without getting any louder or softer, and therefore sounds very boring: *In a barely audible monotone, she gave her evidence.*

mo·not·o·nous /məˈnɑtˀn-əs/ *adj.* boring because there is no variety: *My job is monotonous, but at least I'm working.* | *a monotonous voice* —**monotonously** *adv.*

mo·not·o·ny /məˈnɑtˀn-i/ *n.* [U] a lack of variety that makes you feel bored: *the monotony of the prairie highways*

mon·o·treme /ˈmɑnətrim/ *n.* [C] BIOLOGY a type of animal that passes the waste from its body through the

M

same opening it uses to lay its eggs. A PLATYPUS is an example of a monotreme.

mon·o·un·sat·u·rat·ed /ˌmɑnoʊʌn'sætʃəˌreɪt̮ɪd/ *adj.* monounsaturated fats, such as OLIVE OIL, do not cause the body to create CHOLESTEROL and therefore are healthier than other types of fats, such as butter

mon·ox·ide /mə'nɑksaɪd/ *n.* [C,U] CHEMISTRY a chemical compound containing one atom of oxygen to every atom of another substance: *carbon monoxide*

Mon·roe /mʌn'roʊ/**, James** (1758–1831) the fifth President of the U.S.

Monroe, Mar·i·lyn /'mærəlɪn/ (1926–1962) a U.S. movie actress and singer, whose real name was Norma Jean Baker

Monˌroe 'Doctrine, the HISTORY the principle, stated by U.S. President Monroe in 1823, that European countries should not attempt to gain control of any part of North, Central, or South America or involve themselves in an American country's affairs

Mon·ro·vi·a /mən'roʊviə/ the capital and largest city of Liberia

Mon·si·gnor /mɑn'sinyɚ/ *n.* [C] a way of addressing a priest of high rank in the Catholic Church

mon·soon /mɑn'sun/ *n.* [C] EARTH SCIENCE **1** [usually singular] the season, from about April to October, when it rains a lot in India and other southern Asian countries **2** the rain that falls during this season, or the wind that comes from the south or southwest and brings the rain **3** any wind system that affects the CLIMATE (=weather system) of a large area and changes direction according to the season [**Origin:** 1500–1600 Early Dutch *monssoen*, from Portuguese *monçao*, from Arabic *mawsim* **time, season**]

mon·ster¹ /'mɑnstɚ/ *n.* [C]
1 IN STORIES an imaginary large ugly frightening creature: *a sea monster*
2 CRUEL PERSON someone who is very cruel and evil
3 CHILD OFTEN HUMOROUS a small child, especially one who is behaving badly: *Stop it, you little monster!*
4 STH LARGE INFORMAL an object, animal etc. that is unusually large: *The pumpkin was a monster.*
5 DANGEROUS PROBLEM a dangerous or threatening problem, especially one that develops gradually: *The legislation will* ***create a monster*** *that will take years to correct.*
[**Origin:** 1200–1300 French *monstre*, from Latin *monstrum* **warning, monster**]

monster² *adj.* [only before noun] SPOKEN, INFORMAL unusually large: *That's a monster tree!* | *a monster truck rally*

mon·stros·i·ty /mɑn'strɑsət̮i/ *n. plural* **monstrosities** [C] something large that is very ugly, especially a building: *a 275-room brick monstrosity*

mon·strous /'mɑnstrəs/ *adj.* **1** very wrong, immoral, or unfair: *a monstrous lie* **2** unusually large, and often frightening: *a monstrous tidal wave* —**monstrously** *adv.*

mon·tage /mɑn'tɑʒ, moʊn-/ *n.* ENG. LANG. ARTS **1** [U] an art form in which a picture, movie, piece of writing etc. is made from parts of different pictures etc., that are combined to form a whole **2** [C] something made using this process: *a photo montage*

Mon·taigne /mɑn'teɪn/**, Mi·chel Ey·quem de** /mi'ʃɛl i'kɛm də/ (1533–1592) a French writer of ESSAYS

Mon·ta·na /mɑn'tænə/ ABBREVIATION **MT** a state in the northwestern U.S.

Mon·tauk /'mɑntɔk/ a Native American tribe from the northeastern area of the U.S.

Mont Blanc /mɔn 'blɑŋ/ a mountain in the Alps on the border between France and Italy which is the highest mountain in western Europe

Mon·te·ne·gro /ˌmɑntɪ'nigroʊ, -'nɛ-/ a country in Eastern Europe. From 1992 it was part of the Federal Republic of Yugoslavia, along with Serbia, and became independent in 2006.

Mon·tes·quieu /ˌmɑntəs'kyu/**, Charles, Baron de** (1689–1755) a French political PHILOSOPHER whose ideas about the separation of powers in government influenced the U.S. Constitution

Mon·tes·so·ri /ˌmɑntɪ'sɔri/**, Ma·ri·a** /mə'riə/ (1870–1952) an Italian teacher and writer who developed a new way of teaching young children, which is used in children's schools in many countries

Mon·te·vi·de·o /ˌmɑnt̮əvɪ'deɪoʊ/ the capital and largest city of Uruguay

Mon·te·zu·ma /ˌmɑnt̮ə'zumə/ (1466–1520) the last Aztec ruler of Mexico, who was taken prisoner by the Spaniards under Cortés, and later killed by his own people

ˌMontezuma's re'venge *n.* [U] HUMOROUS DIARRHEA that you get from drinking water or eating food that is not very clean while traveling

Mont·gol·fier /mɑnt'gɑlfiɚ, -fiˌeɪ/**, Jo·seph Mi·chel** /'ʒoʊzɛf mi'ʃɛl/ (1740–1810) a French inventor who made the first HOT-AIR BALLOON with his brother Jacques Etienne Montgolfier (1745–1799)

Mont·gom·er·y /mənt'gʌməri/ the capital city of the U.S. state of Alabama

month /mʌnθ/ S1 W1 *n.* [C] **1** one of the 12 periods of time that a year is divided into: *She'll be 13* ***this month.*** | *Phil is coming home for a visit* ***next month.*** | *I earn about $3,500* ***a month*** (=each month). | **the month of June/July etc.** *It snowed heavily during the month of January.* | **once/twice etc. a month** *The magazine is published once a month.* | **the beginning/middle/end of the month** *I'll be done by the end of the month.* **2** a period of about four weeks: *Tammy has an eight-month-old daughter.* | *I bought the computer a couple of months ago.* | *She was in the hospital* ***for a month.*** | *He'll be back* ***a month from*** *Friday.* | *I've been to my parents' twice in* ***the past month.*** **3 months** a long time, especially several months: *Redecorating the kitchen took months.* | *I haven't seen Sarah* ***in months.*** | ***It was months*** *before the construction work started again.* **4 month after month** used to emphasize that something happens regularly or continuously for several months: *Month after month, our salaries were not paid.* **5 month by month** used when you are talking about a situation that develops over several months: *Unemployment figures are rising month by month.* **6 a month of Sundays** [usually with a negative] OLD-FASHIONED a very long time [**Origin:** Old English *monath*] → see also **that time of the month** at TIME¹ (36)

month·ly¹ /'mʌnθli/ *adj.* [only before noun] **1** happening or produced once a month: *a monthly magazine* | *a monthly meeting* | *a monthly credit card payment* ►see THESAURUS box at **regular¹** **2** used to talk about the total amount of something that is received, paid etc. in a month: *a monthly income of $3,750* | *a monthly rainfall of four inches* **3** a monthly ticket, pass etc. can be used for a period of one month —**monthly** *adv.*: *The committee meets monthly.*

monthly² *n. plural* **monthlies** [C] a magazine that is printed once a month

Mon·ti·cel·lo /ˌmɑnt̮ə'tʃɛloʊ/ a large house and ESTATE in the U.S. state of Virginia that was designed and lived in by U.S. President Thomas Jefferson

Mont·pel·ier /mɑnt'pilyɚ/ the capital city of the U.S. state of Vermont

Mon·tre·al /ˌmɑntri'ɔl/ a city in the PROVINCE of Quebec in eastern Canada

mon·u·ment /'mɑnyəmənt/ *n.* [C] **1** a building or other large structure that is built to remind people of an important event or famous person: *a 90-foot bronze monument* | **+to** *a moving monument to the soldiers killed in the war* **2** a building or place that is important, especially for historical reasons: *Ellis Island is preserved as a historic monument.* **3 be a monument to sth** to be a very clear example of what can happen as a result of a particular quality: *The empty office buildings are a monument to bad planning.* [**Origin:** 1200–1300 Latin *monumentum*, from *monere* **to remind**]

mon·u·men·tal /ˌmɑnyəˈmɛntl◂/ *adj.* **1** [only before noun] extremely large, bad, good, impressive etc.: *a monumental task* | *The concert was a monumental embarrassment.* **2** [usually before noun] a monumental achievement, piece of work etc. is very important, and it is usually based on many years of work: *Darwin published his monumental work on evolution in 1859.* **3** [only before noun] appearing on a monument, or built as a monument: *a monumental temple*

mon·u·ment·al·ly /ˌmɑnyəˈmɛntl-i/ *adv.* extremely: *It was a monumentally stupid thing to do.*

moo /mu/ *n.* [C] the sound that a cow makes —**moo** *v.* [I]

mooch /mutʃ/ *v.* INFORMAL [T] to get something by asking someone to give it to you, instead of paying for it yourself: *Mom got sick of him mooching food off us.*

mooch around *phr. v.* to move in a lazy way without any purpose and doing very little: **mooch around (sth)** *We just mooched around the house all day.*

mood /mud/ S2 W3 *n.*
1 WAY YOU FEEL [C] the way you feel at a particular time: *What kind of mood is she in today?* | **in a good/bad/terrible etc. mood** *Sorry – I'm just in a really bad mood today.* | *The traffic* ***put me in a*** *lousy* ***mood*** (=made me feel annoyed or angry). | **the party/festive/holiday mood** *I'm just not in the party mood.*
2 be/feel in the mood (for sth) to want to do something or feel that you would enjoy doing something: *I'm not really in the mood for Mexican food.*
3 WAY PEOPLE FEEL [singular] the way a group of people feels about something or about life in general: *Back at the Fernandez house, the mood was glum.* | **+of** *The bill appeals to the anti-government mood of the voters.*
4 be in no mood for sth also **be in no mood to do sth** to not want to do something, or be determined not to do something: *The boss is in no mood for compromise on this point.* | *La Russo was in no mood to discuss the incident.*
5 IN A PLACE/BOOK ETC. [C usually singular] the way that a place, book, movie etc. makes you feel: *The restaurant's decor aims at a romantic mood.*
6 GRAMMAR [C,U] ENG. LANG. ARTS one of the sets of verb forms in grammar such as the INDICATIVE (=expressing a fact or action), the IMPERATIVE (=expressing a command), or the SUBJUNCTIVE (=expressing a doubt or wish)
[**Origin:** (1–5) Old English *mod* **mind, courage**]

ˈmood ˌmusic *n.* [U] music that is supposed to make you feel particular emotions, especially romantic feelings

ˈmood swing *n.* [C] an occasion when someone's feelings change very suddenly from one extreme to another: *He has occasional mood swings.*

mood·y /ˈmudi/ *adj. comparative* **moodier**, *superlative* **moodiest** **1** often changing quickly from being in a good temper to being in a bad temper: *She's been really moody and emotional.* | *a moody teenager* **2** annoyed or unhappy: *Keith had seemed moody all morning.* **3** moody places, movies, pictures, and music make you feel slightly sad, lonely, or sometimes frightened —**moodily** *adv.* —**moodiness** *n.* [U]

moo·lah, moola /ˈmulə/ *n.* [U] SPOKEN, INFORMAL money

moon¹ /mun/ S2 W2 *n.* **1 the moon** also **the Moon** the round object that you can see shining in the sky at night, and that moves around the Earth every 28 days: *craters on the surface of the moon* → see picture at SOLAR SYSTEM **2** [singular] the appearance or shape of this object at a particular time: *a clear night sky with a bright moon* | *There's no moon tonight* (=you cannot see it). | *a* ***full moon*** (=the moon appearing as a full circle) → see also HALF MOON, NEW MOON **3** [C] a round object that moves around PLANETS other than the Earth: *the moons of Saturn* ►see THESAURUS box at **space¹** **4 be asking for the moon** INFORMAL to ask for something that is difficult or impossible to obtain: *I don't think the employees are asking for the moon.* **5 many moons ago** POETIC or HUMOROUS a long time ago [**Origin:** Old English *mona*] → see also **once in a blue moon** at ONCE¹ (15), **promise (sb) the moon/world** at PROMISE¹ (5)

moon² *v.* [T] INFORMAL to bend over and show someone your BARE BUTTOCKS as a joke or as a way of insulting someone

moon over sb/sth *phr. v.* OLD-FASHIONED to spend your time thinking and dreaming about someone or something that you love: *As a boy, he used to sit mooning over Doris Day.*

moon·beam /ˈmunbim/ *n.* [C] a beam of light from the moon

ˈmoon boot *n.* [C usually plural] a thick warm cloth or plastic boot worn in snow and cold weather

moon cycle

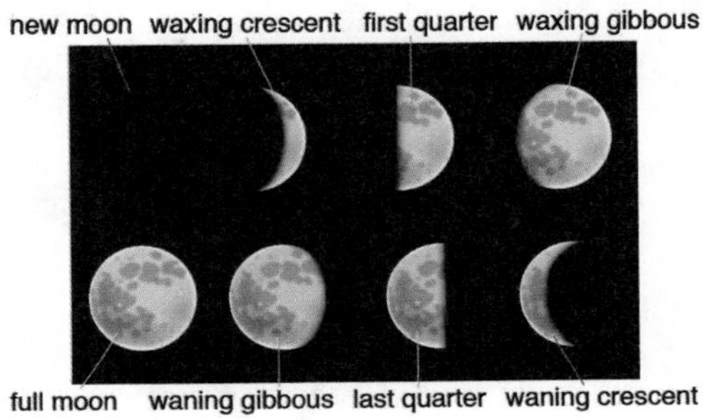

ˈmoon ˌcycle *n.* [singular] SCIENCE the changes in the appearance of the moon throughout a month, starting as a NEW MOON, becoming a FULL MOON, and then becoming a NEW MOON again

ˈmoon-ˌfaced *adj.* having a round face

Moon·ie /ˈmuni/ *n.* [C] a member of a religious group started by the Korean businessman Sun Myung Moon

ˈmoon ˌlanding *n.* [C] an occasion when humans land a vehicle on the moon

moon·less /ˈmunlɪs/ *adj.* a moonless sky or night is one in which the moon cannot be seen: *a cloudy moonless night*

moon·light¹ /ˈmunlaɪt/ *n.* [U] the light of the moon: *The trees looked silver* ***in the pale moonlight.*** | *We traveled silently* ***by moonlight*** (=with the moon providing light).

moonlight² *v.* **moonlighted** [I] to have a second job in addition to your main job: *Some officers were moonlighting as security guards.* —**moonlighter** *n.* [C] —**moonlighting** *n.* [U] *I'm moonlighting as a pizza delivery man at the moment.*

moon·lit /ˈmunˌlɪt/ *adj.* [only before noun] made brighter by the light of the moon: *a moonlit garden*

moon·roof /ˈmunruf/ *n.* [C] a small window in the roof of a car that lets in light and can be opened a small amount → see also SUNROOF

moon·scape /ˈmunskeɪp/ *n.* [C] an empty area of land that looks like the surface of the moon

moon·shine /ˈmunʃaɪn/ *n.* [U] INFORMAL strong alcohol that is produced illegally

ˈmoon ˌshot, moonshot *n.* [C] OLD-FASHIONED a SPACECRAFT flight to the moon

moon·stone /ˈmunstoʊn/ *n.* [C,U] a milky-white stone used in making jewelry

moon·struck /ˈmunstrʌk/ *adj.* INFORMAL slightly crazy

Moor /mʊr/ one of the Muslim people from North Africa who entered Spain in the 8th century and ruled the southern part of the country until 1492

moor¹ /mʊr/ *v.* [I,T] if a boat or ship moors somewhere or someone moors it, it is fastened to the land or to the bottom of the sea with ropes or an ANCHOR: *Two battleships were moored to the east of Ford Island.*

moor² *n.* [C] usually **moors** [plural] a wild open area of high land, covered with rough grass or low bushes, especially in Great Britain

M

Moore /mɔr/, **Henry** (1898–1986) a British SCULPTOR who is considered by many people to be the most important British sculptor of the 20th century

Moore, Mar·i·anne /ˈmɛriˌæn/ (1887–1972) a U.S. poet and CRITIC

moor·ing /ˈmʊrɪŋ/ *n.* [C] **1** the place where a ship or boat is moored: *a temporary mooring* **2** [usually plural] the ropes, chains, ANCHORS etc. used to moor a ship or boat: *Several ships had broken their moorings during the storm.*

Moor·ish /ˈmʊrɪʃ/ *adj.* relating to the Moors: *Moorish architecture in Spain*

moose

moose /mus/ *n. plural* **moose** [C] a large wild brown animal that has very large flat ANTLERS and a head like a horse, that lives in North America, northern Europe, and also in parts of Asia

moot[1] /mut/ *adj.* **1** an problem, decision, result etc. that is moot does not matter anymore because the situation has changed SYN **irrelevant**: *The decision has been made, so whether it was the right decision is now moot.* **2** a question or point that is moot is one that has not yet been decided, and about which people have different opinions SYN **arguable**: *Whether these controls will really reduce violent crime is **a moot point**.*

moot[2] *v.* [T] **be mooted** FORMAL to be suggested for people to consider: *Once the trip was mooted, it took weeks to decide who would go.*

ˈmoot court *n.* [C,U] a court in which law students practice holding TRIALS

mop[1] /mɑp/ *n.* [C] **1** a thing used for washing floors, made of a long stick with threads of thick string or a SPONGE fastened to one end **2** also **mop of hair** [usually singular] INFORMAL a large amount of thick, often messy hair

mop[2] *v.* **mopped, mopping** **1** [I,T] to wash a floor with a wet mop: *I just mopped the kitchen floor.* ►see THESAURUS box at **clean**[2] **2** [T] to remove liquid from a surface, especially from your face, by rubbing it with a cloth: *She mopped the sweat from her face.* **3 mop the floor with sb** INFORMAL to completely defeat someone, for example in a game or argument

mop up *phr. v.* **1** to remove a large amount of liquid from something by ABSORBING it with something: *The city is mopping up after more than a week of floods.* | **mop sth ↔ up** *I mopped up the spilled milk with a sponge.* **2 mop sth ↔ up** to remove or deal with something which you think is undesirable or dangerous, so that it is no longer a problem: *Firefighters mopped up the few hot spots left from Saturday's brush fire.* **3 mop sth ↔ up** to use all or a lot of something which is available in large amounts: *The program will mop up the rest of our budget.*

mope /moʊp/ also **mope around** *v.* [I] to pity yourself and feel sad, without making any effort to be more cheerful: *She's just been sitting there moping all day.*

mo·ped /ˈmoʊpɛd/ *n.* [C] a small two-wheeled vehicle with an engine, which can also be PEDALed like a bicycle → see also MOTORCYCLE

mop·pet /ˈmɑpɪt/ *n.* [C] INFORMAL a small child

mo·raine /məˈreɪn/ *n.* [C,U] EARTH SCIENCE rock, sand, clay etc. that is pushed along in front of a GLACIER when it moves forward, and that forms into a high area of land when the glacier moves back: *Finding its way blocked by moraine, the river is forced to turn west.* | *glacial moraine*

mor·al[1] /ˈmɔrəl, ˈmɑrəl/ W2 *adj.*

1 ABOUT RIGHT AND WRONG [only before noun] relating to the principles of what is right and wrong, and with the difference between good and evil: *Parents must give their children moral guidance.* | *the company's strict moral and ethical principles* | *the **moral dilemma** of a doctor who must make a decision about whether a patient lives or dies*

2 BASED ON WHAT IS RIGHT [only before noun] based on your ideas about what is right, rather than on what is legal or practical: **a moral duty/obligation/responsibility** *Public schools have a moral responsibility to accept all children.* | *Does the U.S. have the **moral authority*** (=influence that you have because people accept that your beliefs are right) *to demand free elections in other countries?* | *Protesting against the war was an act of **moral courage*** (=the courage to do what you believe is right).

3 moral support encouragement that you give by expressing approval or interest, rather than by giving practical help: *Steve went with her to provide moral support.*

4 take/claim/seize etc. the moral high ground USUALLY DISAPPROVING to be the only one who does what is morally right in a situation, with the intention of being noticed and considered morally good by the public: *The company seized the moral high ground, and stopped doing business in countries with oppressive military regimes.*

5 moral victory a situation in which you show that your beliefs are right and fair, even if you do not win the argument: *The protesters have won at least a moral victory.*

6 PERSON always behaving in a way that is based on strong principles about what is right and wrong: *As moral people, we cannot accept that so many children grow up in poverty.*

7 STORY a moral story, play etc. is one that teaches or shows good behavior

[**Origin:** 1300–1400 Latin *moralis*, from *mos* **what people usually or traditionally do**] → see also AMORAL, MORALLY

moral[2] *n.* **1** [C] a practical lesson about what to do or how to behave, that you learn from a story or from something that happens to you: ***The moral of the story is** be careful when you're offered something for nothing.* **2 morals** [plural] principles or standards of good behavior, especially in matters of sex: *The novel reflects the morals and customs of the time.* | *the corruption of **public morals*** (=the standards of behavior, especially sexual behavior, expected by society) | *My parents were shocked at what they called her **"loose morals"*** (=low standards of sexual behavior).

THESAURUS

ethics moral rules or principles of behavior for deciding what is right and wrong: *Corporations should learn to care about ethics as much as profit.*
standards moral principles about what kind of behavior and attitudes are acceptable: *Standards of behavior seemed to have plunged in the last twenty years.*
values your beliefs about what is right and wrong, or about what is important in life: *Children should learn values from their parents.*
principles a set of rules or ideas about what is right and wrong that influences how you behave: *During the Civil Rights era, he faced a jail term for trying to stick to his principles.*
scruples a belief about what is right and wrong that prevents you from doing something bad: *No one should set aside their moral scruples when they go to work.*
morality morals

mo·rale /məˈræl/ *n.* [U] the level of confidence and positive feelings that people have, especially people who work together, who belong to the same team etc.:

low/high morale *Morale in the sales division is high.* | **improve/boost/raise/build morale** *Anytime someone important comes over here, it really boosts the troops' morale.* | **keep up/maintain morale** *They sang songs to keep morale up.*

mor·al·ist /ˈmɔrəlɪst/ *n.* [C] **1** USUALLY DISAPPROVING someone who has very strong beliefs about what is right and wrong, especially someone who disapproves strongly when other people do not behave according to these beliefs **2** a teacher of moral principles

mor·al·ist·ic /ˌmɔrəˈlɪstɪk/ *adj.* USUALLY DISAPPROVING having strong beliefs about what is right and wrong and how people should behave: *It's difficult to talk to teenagers about drugs without sounding too moralistic.* —**moralistically** /-kli/ *adv.*

mo·ral·i·ty /məˈræləṭi/ *n. plural* **moralities** **1** [U] beliefs or ideas about what is right and wrong and about how people should behave, and behavior based on these ideas: *the decline in standards of morality* | *sexual morality* | **public/private/personal morality** *The authorities are protectors of public morality.* ▸see THESAURUS box at **moral**[2] **2 the morality of sth** the degree to which something is right or acceptable: *a discussion on the morality of abortion* **3** [C,U] a particular set of beliefs or ideas about what is right and wrong: *Christian morality*

mor·al·ize /ˈmɔrəˌlaɪz, ˈmɑr-/ *v.* [I] to tell other people your ideas about what is right and wrong and how people should behave, especially when they have not asked for your opinion SYN **preach**: +**about/on** *It is not my job as a journalist to moralize about other people's lifestyles.* —**moralizer** *n.* [C] —**moralizing** *n.* [U]

mor·al·ly /ˈmɔrəli/ *adv.* **1** according to moral principles about what is right and wrong: *He was morally opposed to the war.* | **morally right/wrong** *What you did wasn't illegal, but it was morally wrong.* **2** in a way which is good or right: **act/behave morally** *It is often difficult to behave morally.*

ˌMoral Maˈjority *n.* **1 the Moral Majority** POLITICS a U.S. CHRISTIAN organization started in 1979 and which was active in the 1980s. It gave help to politicians who supported its RIGHT-WING ideas about subjects such as ABORTION, and it actively opposed politicians who did not agree with their ideas. **2** [C usually singular] a general name for CHRISTIANS who have strong traditional ideas about sexual behavior, family values etc., and who also have right-wing political ideas

mo·rass /məˈræs/ *n.* **1** [singular] a complicated and confusing situation that is very difficult to get out of: *the state's budget morass* **2** [singular] a complicated amount of information: +**of** *a morass of detail* **3** [C] ESPECIALLY LITERARY a dangerous area of soft wet ground

mor·a·to·ri·um /ˌmɔrəˈtɔriəm, ˌmɑr-/ *n. plural* **moratoriums, moratoria** [C usually singular] **1** an official announcement stopping an activity for a period of time: +**on** *a moratorium on offshore drilling for oil* **2** a law or an agreement that gives people more time to pay their debts: *a one-year moratorium on interest payments*

mo·ray eel /ˌmɔreɪ ˈil/ *n.* [C] BIOLOGY a type of EEL (=fish like a snake) that lives in the ocean in tropical areas

mor·bid /ˈmɔrbɪd/ *adj.* **1** having a strong and unhealthy interest in disgusting subjects, especially death: *People have a morbid fascination with murder.* **2** MEDICINE relating to or caused by a disease: *a morbid gene* [**Origin:** 1600–1700 Latin *morbidus* **diseased**, from *morbus* **illness**] —**morbidly** *adv.*

mor·bid·i·ty /mɔrˈbɪdəṭi/ *n.* [U] **1** TECHNICAL the rate at which a disease or diseases affect a population **2** the quality of being MORBID

mor·dant /ˈmɔrdnt/ *adj.* **mordant humor/wit/insights etc.** FORMAL humor etc. that criticizes or insults someone or something

more[1] /mɔr/ S1 W1 *adv.* **1** used before many adjectives and adverbs that have two or more SYLLABLES in order to make the COMPARATIVE form, which shows that something has a particular quality to a greater degree than something else OPP **less**: *Can it be done more quickly?* | *It was a lot **more** expensive **than** I had expected.* | *Try to be **a little more** patient.* | **much more/far more/a lot more** *Many children feel much more confident if they work in groups.* | *She became **more and more** suspicious* (=more suspicious in a way that increased over time) | *She's **even more*** (=used for emphasis) *intelligent than her mother was.* **2** happening a greater number of times or for longer OPP **less**: *I promised Mom I'd help more with the housework.* | *I find myself thinking about it **more and more*** (=happening increasingly often). | *We'd like to see our granddaughter **more than** we do.* | **much more/far more/a lot more** *He goes out a lot more now that he has a car.* | *I need to study the report **some more*** (=for an additional amount of time). **3** used with verbs to say that something is true or happens to a greater degree: *I like him more now that I know him better.* | *She cares **more** for her dogs **than** she does for me.* | **much more/far more/a lot more** *We enjoyed the trip much more the second time.* | **even more/all the more** *This news made us worry all the more.* **4 more or less a)** almost: *This report says more or less the same thing as the previous one.* **b)** APPROXIMATELY: *There were 50 people there, more or less.* **5 more often than not** used to say that something usually happens: *Cheap movies on video are, more often than not, of very poor quality.* **6 the more...the more/better/less etc....** used to say that one thing changes in a particular way depending on what another thing does: *The more I thought about it, the less I liked the idea.* | *The more you sleep, the better you'll feel.* **7 more...than...** used for saying that one description or explanation is more correct than another: *I feel more disappointed than embarrassed.* | *It was more a worry than a pleasure.* **8 more than...** used to emphasize an adjective: *I'd be more than happy to sit down and discuss this with you.* | *It's more than likely that they'll lose the game.* **9 more than a little...** used before adjectives to mean "very": *I'm more than a little concerned about Corey's behavior.* **10 no more...than...** used for saying that one thing or person does not have a greater amount of a particular quality than another or than before: *He's no more capable of killing someone than a fly.* **11 no more than a)** also **little more than** used to say that someone or something is less important than they seem: *It was little more than a scratch.* **b)** used to say that something is needed or appropriate: *It's no more than you deserve.* **12 no more** LITERARY used in order to show that something that used to happen or be true does not happen or is not true now: *The little lost girl was lost no more.* → see also ANYMORE, **once more/again** at ONCE[1] (5), **(and) what's more** at WHAT[1] (25)

> **GRAMMAR**
>
> Use **more** as the opposite of both "less" and "fewer": *I think I'll need more money.* | *There were more people there today.* Don't use the "-er" form of the adjective with **more**: *He is richer than his brother* (NOT *He is more richer than his brother*).

more[2] S1 W1 *quantifier* [the comparative of "many" and "much"] **1** a greater amount or number: *There were **more** accidents on the highways this year **than** last year.* | *Today, **more and more** people commute long distances.* | ***A lot more** people have given up smoking.* | **many/far/lots more** *We've received many more letters than usual.* | *She has lots more experience than I do.* | **a little (bit) more** *A little more care is needed with the delicate plants.* | +**of** *Did Cara download some more songs?* **2** an additional number or amount: *You'll have to pay more for a double room.* | *Can you tell me more about your previous job?* | *I need to get two more tickets.* | *It will be five minutes more before dinner's ready.* | *Can I have a little more time to finish?* | +**of** *There are more of those cinnamon rolls if you want one.* | *Is there **any more** coffee?* | *There's **no more** gas left.* | *Aaron will finally be earning **some more** money.* | *I'll just make **a few more** phone calls.* | *There must have been 200 people **or more*** (=possibly more) *waiting outside.*

M

THESAURUS

another something in addition to a particular amount, distance, period of time etc.: *Do you want another cup of coffee?*
extra more than the usual or standard amount of something: *I always carry an extra key, in case I lose my other one.*
additional more than you already have, or more than was agreed or expected: *Students who find reading difficult receive additional help.*
further more, used especially when something happens again or is done again: *Further research is needed.*

3 more and more an increasing number of things or people: *More and more people are taking early retirement.* **4 not/no more than sth** used to say that a price, distance etc. is only a particular number or amount: *The house is no more than ten minutes from the beach.* | *The insurance covers not more than five days in the hospital.*

More /mɔr/, **Sir Thomas** (1478–1535) an English politician and writer, famous for his book "Utopia", which describes his idea of a perfect society

more·o·ver /mɔrˈoʊvɚ/ W3 *adv.* [sentence adverb] FORMAL a word meaning "in addition to this," that is used to add information to something that has just been said SYN **furthermore**: *The technology is expensive. Moreover, there have been problems with the system.*

USAGE

• **Moreover** is very formal: *News programs are cheaper to produce than dramas. Moreover, they can attract more money from commercials.*
• **Also** is a less formal way of adding a reason or idea. It can be used at the beginning of a sentence to link it to the previous one: *You can stay at our house. Also, I can give you a ride home tomorrow.* Or it can be used within a sentence: *I can also give you a ride home tomorrow.*
• **Besides (that)** is more informal and used especially to add a reason. *I've heard it's not a very good movie. Besides, I'd rather stay home tonight.*

mo·res /ˈmɔreɪz/ *n.* [plural] FORMAL the customs, social behavior, and moral values of a particular group: *middle-class mores*

Mor·gan /ˈmɔrgən/, **John Pier·point** /dʒɑn ˈpɪrpɔɪnt/ (1837–1913) a very powerful U.S. FINANCIER who collected art and gave money to hospitals and churches

morgue /mɔrg/ *n.* [C] **1** a building or room where dead bodies are kept until they are buried or burned **2 like a morgue** HUMOROUS a place that is like a morgue is quiet and boring [**Origin:** 1800–1900 French *Morgue*, name of a morgue in Paris]

mor·i·bund /ˈmɔrəˌbʌnd, ˈmɑr-/ *adj.* **1** a moribund industry, institution, custom etc. is not active or effective anymore: *the moribund economy* **2** LITERARY slowly dying

Mor·mon /ˈmɔrmən/ *adj.* relating to a religious organization formed in 1830 in the U.S., officially called The Church of Jesus Christ of Latter-Day Saints, which has strict moral rules [**Origin:** 1800–1900 *Mormon* supposed writer of the Book of Mormon, holy book of the Mormons] —**Mormon** *n.* [C] —**Mormonism** *n.* [U]

morn /mɔrn/ *n.* [C usually singular] POETIC morning

morn·ing¹ /ˈmɔrnɪŋ/ S1 W1 *n.* [C,U] **1** the early part of the day, from when the sun rises until the middle of the day: *a sunny morning* | *the morning paper* | **(on) Monday/Tuesday etc. morning** *I'll bring your book back Friday morning.* | *Liz picks me up on her way to work* ***in the morning***. | *I talked to her* ***this morning***. | *Do you have time to meet* ***tomorrow morning***? | **early/late morning** *I run in the early morning before work.* **2** the part of the day from MIDNIGHT until the middle of the day: **one/two/three etc. in the morning** *The phone rang at three in the morning.* | **the early/wee/small hours of the morning** (=very early before the sun rises) **3 in the morning** tomorrow morning: *Grandma and Grandpa will be here in the morning.* **4 mornings** during the morning each day: *Linda just works mornings, but it helps.* **5 morning, noon, and night** used to emphasize that something happens a lot or continuously: *I've been going to meetings morning, noon, and night lately.* [**Origin:** 1200–1300 *morn* + *-ing* (as in evening)]

morning² S2 *interjection* **(Good) morning** said in order to greet someone in the morning: *Morning, Dave. How are you?*

ˌmorning-ˈafter pill *n.* [C] NOT TECHNICAL MEDICINE a drug that a woman can take after having sex to prevent her from having a baby

ˈmorning coat *n.* [C] a formal black coat with a long back that men wear at formal ceremonies during the day

ˌmorning ˈglory *n.* [C,U] a plant that has white, blue, or pink flowers that open in the morning and close in late afternoon

ˈmorning ˌsickness *n.* [U] MEDICINE a feeling of sickness that some women have when they are PREGNANT

ˌmorning ˈstar *n.* **the morning star** a bright PLANET, usually Venus, that you can see in the eastern sky when the sun rises → see also EVENING STAR

ˈmorning suit *n.* [C] a special man's suit that is worn at formal ceremonies during the day

Mo·roc·co /məˈrɑkoʊ/ a country in northwest Africa on the coast where the Mediterranean Sea meets the Atlantic Ocean —**Moroccan** *n., adj.*

mo·roc·co /məˈrɑkoʊ/ *n.* [U] fine soft leather used especially for covering books

mo·ron /ˈmɔrɑn/ *n.* [C] INFORMAL an insulting word for someone who is very stupid [**Origin:** 1900–2000 Greek *moros* **of low intelligence**] —**moronic** /məˈrɑnɪk, mɔ-/ *adj.* —**moronically** /-kli/ *adv.*

Mo·ro·ni /mɔˈroʊni/ the capital city of Comoros

mo·rose /məˈroʊs/ *adj.* bad-tempered or unhappy, and saying very little: *her morose husband* —**morosely** *adv.* —**moroseness** *n.* [U]

morph /mɔrf/ *v.* [I,T] **1** to develop or change into something else, or make something develop or change in this way: **morph (sth) into sth** *The old building is morphing into a $1 billion business center.* | *The writers morphed the thriller into a love story.* **2** if one computer image morphs into another or you morph it, it changes to a new appearance in a smooth gradual process: *You can play around with the graphics and morph images.* | **morph (sth) into sth** *My character morphed into an alien.* → see also MORPHING

mor·pheme /ˈmɔrfim/ *n.* [C] ENG. LANG. ARTS the smallest meaningful unit of language, consisting of a word or part of a word that cannot be divided without losing its meaning. For example, "gun" contains one morpheme, but "gunfighter" contains three: "gun," "fight," and "-er".

mor·phi·a /ˈmɔrfiə/ *n.* [U] OLD-FASHIONED morphine

mor·phine /ˈmɔrfin/ *n.* [U] MEDICINE a powerful and ADDICTIVE drug used for stopping pain [**Origin:** 1800–1900 French *Morpheus* ancient Roman god of sleep]

morph·ing /ˈmɔrfɪŋ/ *n.* [U] COMPUTERS a computer method that is used to make one image gradually change into a different one → see also MORPH

mor·phol·o·gy /mɔrˈfɑlədʒi/ *n.* TECHNICAL **1** [U] ENG. LANG. ARTS the study of the MORPHEMES of a language and of the way in which they are joined together to make words → see also SYNTAX **2** [U] BIOLOGY the scientific study of how animals, plants, and their parts are formed **3** [C,U] the structure of an object or system or the way it was formed —**morphological** /ˌmɔrfəˈlɑdʒɪkəl/ *adj.*

mor·row /ˈmɑroʊ, ˈmɔr-/ *n.* LITERARY **the morrow a)** the next day **b)** the future: *What will the morrow bring?*

M

Morse /mɔrs/, **Samuel** (1791–1872) a U.S. inventor who developed the first TELEGRAPH system → see picture on page A25

ˈMorse code *n.* [U] a system of sending messages in which the alphabet is represented by short and long signals of sound or light

mor·sel /ˈmɔrsəl/ *n.* [C] **1** a small piece of food: *milk chocolate morsels* | +**of** *a morsel of bread* **2** a small amount of something such as information: +**of** *My editors wanted every morsel of Hollywood gossip.*

mor·tal¹ /ˈmɔrtl/ *adj.* **1** not living forever OPP **immortal**: *We are all mortal.* **2 mortal blow/injuries/danger etc.** causing death or likely to cause death: *a mortal wound* | *enemies in* ***mortal combat*** (=fighting until one person kills the other) → see also LETHAL **3 mortal enemy/foe** an enemy that you hate very much and always will hate **4 mortal fear/terror/dread** extreme fear **5 deal/strike a mortal blow (to sth)** to be something that completely destroys a plan, process, system, organization etc.: *Has photography dealt a mortal blow to art?* **6 sb's mortal remains** FORMAL someone's body after they die **7** POETIC belonging to a human: *a sight as yet unseen by mortal eyes* [**Origin:** 1300–1400 Old French, Latin *mortalis*, from *mors* **death**] → see also MORTALLY

mortal² *n.* [C] **1 mere/ordinary/lesser mortal** HUMOROUS ordinary people, as compared with people who are more important or more powerful: *In Hollywood you can stay forever young, unlike us mere mortals.* **2** LITERARY a word meaning a "human," used especially when comparing humans with gods, spirits etc.: *Jupiter disguised himself as a mortal and came down to earth.*

mor·tal·i·ty /mɔrˈtæləti/ *n.* [U] **1** also **mortality rate** the number of deaths during a certain period of time among a particular group of people or from a particular cause: *mortality from cancer* | ***Infant mortality*** (=the rate at which babies die) *has been on the increase in certain areas.* **2** the condition of being human and having to die OPP **immortality**: *Doctors are reminded of their mortality every day.*

mor·tal·ly /ˈmɔrtl-i/ *adv.* **1** in a way that will cause death: *Lincoln was shot and* ***mortally wounded*** *by Booth.* **2** FORMAL extremely or greatly: *My uncle was mortally offended.*

ˌmortal ˈsin *n.* [C] something that you do that is so bad, according to the Catholic Church, that it will bring punishment to your soul forever after death unless you ask to be forgiven

mor·tar /ˈmɔrtɚ/ *n.* **1** [U] a mixture used in building to hold bricks or stones together, made of LIME, sand, and water **2** [C] a heavy gun that fires bombs or SHELLS in a high curve **3** [C] a stone bowl in which substances are crushed with a PESTLE (=tool with a heavy round end) into very small pieces or powder

mor·tar·board /ˈmɔrtɚˌbɔrd/ *n.* [C] a cap with a flat square top, that you wear when you GRADUATE from high school or college → see picture at HAT

mort·gage¹ /ˈmɔrgɪdʒ/ W3 *n.* [C] a legal arrangement in which you borrow money from a bank in order to buy a house, and pay back the money over a period of years: +**on** *We still* ***have a $180,000 mortgage on*** *the house.* | *The* ***mortgage payment*** *will be around a thousand dollars a month.* | *Barb and Joe have* ***taken out a mortgage*** *on their first house.* | *We* ***paid off our mortgage*** (=finished paying for the mortgage) *last September.* [**Origin:** 1300–1400 Old French *mort* **dead** + *gage* **promise**] → see also SECOND MORTGAGE

mortgage² *v.* [T] **1** ECONOMICS if you mortgage your home, land, or property, you borrow money, usually from a bank, and give the bank the right to own your property if you do not pay the money back: *We mortgaged our house to start Paul's business.* | *Everything I own is* ***mortgaged to the hilt*** (=the total amount that can be borrowed has been borrowed). **2 mortgage sb's future** to do something that will make things very difficult for someone in the future: *Our lack of respect for the environment is mortgaging our children's future.*

mor·ti·cian /mɔrˈtɪʃən/ *n.* [C] OLD-FASHIONED a FUNERAL DIRECTOR

mor·ti·fied /ˈmɔrtəfaɪd/ *adj.* extremely ashamed or embarrassed: *She was mortified to find that her daughter had been lying.*

mor·ti·fy /ˈmɔrtəˌfaɪ/ *v.* **mortifies, mortified, mortifying** [T] **1** to cause someone to feel extremely embarrassed or ashamed: *As a teenager, I was mortified by my parents.* **2 mortify the flesh** also **mortify yourself** LITERARY to try to control your natural physical desires and needs by making your body suffer pain —**mortification** /ˌmɔrtəfəˈkeɪʃən/ *n.* [U]

mor·ti·fy·ing /ˈmɔrtəˌfaɪ-ɪŋ/ *adj.* extremely embarrassing: *a mortifying mistake*

mor·tise /ˈmɔrtɪs/ *n.* [C] TECHNICAL a hole cut in a piece of wood or stone to receive the TENON (=the shaped end) of another piece and form a joint

mor·tu·ar·y¹ /ˈmɔrtʃuˌɛri/ *n. plural* **mortuaries** [C] a place where a body is kept before a funeral and where the funeral is sometimes held

mortuary² *adj.* [only before noun] FORMAL relating to death or funerals: *a mortuary urn*

mo·sa·ic /moʊˈzeɪ-ɪk/ *n.* **1** [C,U] ENG. LANG. ARTS a pattern or picture made by fitting together small pieces of colored stone, glass, paper etc.: *a Roman stone mosaic floor* **2** [C usually singular] a group of various things that are seen or considered together as a pattern: +**of** *Planted last fall, the garden is a mosaic of colors.*

Mos·cow /ˈmɑskoʊ, -kaʊ/ the capital and largest city in Russia

Mo·ses /ˈmoʊzɪz/ in the Bible, a leader of the Jewish people who brought them out of Egypt and received the Ten Commandments from God

Moses, Ed·win /ˈɛdwɪn/ (1955–) a U.S. ATHLETE who set a world record for the 400 meters HURDLES in 1977, set a new record three times, and was not beaten in any race until 1988

Moses, Grandma also **Anna Mary Moses** (1860–1961) a U.S. PAINTER famous for her pictures of American country life painted in a very simple style

mo·sey /ˈmoʊzi/ *v.* **moseys, moseyed, moseying** [I always + adv./prep.] INFORMAL, HUMOROUS to walk somewhere in a slow relaxed way: +**around/down etc.** *I had time to mosey around town on my own.*

mosey along *phr. v.* to leave a place: *I guess I'd better mosey along – it's getting late.*

mosh /mɑʃ/ *v.* [I] SLANG to dance very violently at a concert with loud ROCK or PUNK music —**moshing** *n.* [U]

ˈmosh pit *n.* [C] an area in front of the stage at a ROCK or PUNK concert where people dance very violently

Mos·lem /ˈmɑzləm, ˈmɑs-/ *n.* [C] *adj.* another spelling of MUSLIM, which is unacceptable to some Muslims

mosque /mɑsk/ *n.* [C] a building in which Muslims WORSHIP [**Origin:** 1400–1500 Old French *mosquee*, from Old Spanish *mezquita*, from Arabic *sajada* **to lie face downward**]

mos·qui·to /məˈskitoʊ/ *n. plural* **mosquitoes** or **mosquitos** [C] a small flying insect that sucks the blood of people and animals, making you ITCH and sometimes spreading diseases: *a mosquito bite* [**Origin:** 1500–1600 Spanish *mosca* **fly**, from Latin *musca*]

mosˈquito net *n.* [C] a net placed over a bed as a protection against mosquitoes

moss /mɔs/ *n.* [C,U] a small flat green or yellow plant that looks like fur and grows on trees and rocks —**mossy** *adj.* → see also LICHEN

most¹ /moʊst/ S1 W1 *adv.* **1** [+ adj./adv.] used before many adjectives and adverbs that have two or more SYLLABLES in order to make the SUPERLATIVE OPP **least**: *It's most comfortable if I sit with my legs up.* | *That's the most important part!* | *This style of management is most frequently used in Japan.* | **easily the most/by far the most** (=used for emphasis) *She's easily the most intelligent student in the class.* | *Blue is by far the most popular color.* **2** also **the most** more than anything else OPP **least**: *I guess the food I eat most is pasta.* | *She*

M

liked the dark beer the most. | *They gave us help when we most needed it.* | ***Most of all,*** *I just felt sad that it was over.* **3** SPOKEN, NONSTANDARD almost: *We eat out* ***most*** ***every*** *weekend.* **4** [+ adj./adv.] FORMAL very: *I was most surprised to hear of your engagement.* | *It was a most interesting experience.*

GRAMMAR

• **Most** meaning "almost all" is followed by a noun when you are talking about something in general: *Most cheese contains a lot of fat* (NOT *most of cheese*). | *Most Americans own cars.*
• You use **most of the** when you are talking about almost all of a particular thing, group etc.: *Most of the champagne we bought was drunk that night.* | *Most of the Americans we talked to owned cars.*
• Use **the most** in comparisons before an adjective: *Donna is the most beautiful of the girls.* Don't use the "-est" form of the adjective with **most**: *He's one of the richest men in the world* (NOT *the most rich* or *the most richest*).

most² S1 W1 *quantifier* [the superlative of "many" and "much"] **1** almost all of a particular group of people or things: *Most places have air conditioning in Albuquerque.* | *I think most people hate hospitals.* | *The speed limit is 35 miles an hour in most areas.* | *Of the money donated, most is spent directly on the refugees.* | +**of** *We get most of our snow in February.* | *Sara does most of the cooking.* **2** also **the most** more than anyone or anything else: *Apparently, BMWs are stolen most.* | *Who has the most kids?* | *I'd say that in our family, Kelly talks the most.* **3** also **the most** the largest number or amount possible: *Television commercials reach most people; newspaper ads reach fewer.* | +**of** [not with "the"] *He spends most of his time in New York.* | *I think two or three minutes might be the most you can expect* **4 at (the) most** used to say that a number or amount will not be larger than you say: *It'll take fifteen minutes at the most.* | *The child was eight years old* ***at the very most*** (=used to emphasize that the age was very likely much younger). → see also AT (THE) VERY LEAST **5 for the most part** used when a statement or fact is generally true, but not completely true: *For the most part, people seemed pretty friendly.* **6 get the most from sb/sth** also **get the most out of sb/sth** to use something in the best possible way, in order to get the most use or advantage from it: *We're not getting the most out of the engine.* **7 make the most of sth** to get the most advantage that is possible from a situation: *The nice weather won't last long, so make the most of it.*

-most /moʊst/ *suffix* [in adjectives] nearest to something, or at the greatest extreme: *westernmost* (=being the farthest west) | *uppermost* (=being the farthest up or the most important)

most-ˌfavored-ˈnation ˌstatus *adj.* [C,U] official permission given by one country to another, which allows the second country to buy and sell goods and services without high taxes from the first country

most·ly /ˈmoʊstli/ S2 W2 *adv.* **1** in most cases or most of the time SYN **usually**: *I do mostly secretarial-type work.* | *Mostly, we talk about the kids.* **2** used to say what is true of most people in a group, or most parts of something SYN **mainly**: *The people at the theater were mostly college students.* **3** to a greater degree than anything else SYN **mainly**: *Mostly, I blame my dad.* | *I was mad,* ***mostly because*** *I knew he was lying.* | *He resigned* ***mostly for*** *personal reasons.*

GRAMMAR

With "all/everyone/every etc.," use **almost** rather than **mostly**: *Almost everyone seems to have a cold.*

mote /moʊt/ *n.* [C] OLD-FASHIONED a very small piece of dust

mo·tel /moʊˈtɛl/ *n.* [C] a hotel for people traveling by car, with a space for the car near each room

mo·tet /moʊˈtɛt/ *n.* [C] a piece of music on a religious subject

moth /mɔθ/ *n.* [C] an insect similar to a BUTTERFLY that usually flies at night, especially toward lights

moth·ball¹ /ˈmɔθbɔl/ *n.* [C usually plural] **1** a small white ball made of a strong-smelling chemical, used for keeping moths away from clothes **2 in mothballs** if a building, plan etc. is in mothballs, it is not being used now, although you might use it in the future **3 bring/take sth out of mothballs** to begin to use something that has not been used for a long time: *Four ships were brought out of mothballs starting in 2002.*

mothball² *v.* [T] to close a factory or to decide not to use plans or machinery for a long time: *The Defense Department plans to mothball a munitions plant.*

ˈmoth-ˌeaten *adj.* cloth that is moth-eaten has holes eaten in it by moths: *a moth-eaten sweater*

moth·er¹ /ˈmʌðɚ/ S1 W1 *n.*

1 PARENT [C] a female parent of a child or animal: *My mother says I have to be home by 9 o'clock.* | *Mother just loved crossword puzzles.* | *a mother hen and her chicks* | *a young* ***mother of two*** (=of two children) ▶see THESAURUS box at **relative¹**

2 BIG [singular] SPOKEN, INFORMAL something that is very large, difficult, impressive etc.: *That's* ***a mother of a*** *car.*

3 the mother of all sth INFORMAL something that is a very good or very bad example of its type: *I woke up with the mother of all hangovers.* | *the mother of all battles*

4 the mother of sth the origin or cause of something: *Necessity is the mother of invention.*

5 be (like) a mother to sb to care for someone as if you were their mother

6 mother hen someone who tries to protect her children too much and worries about them all the time

7 learn sth at your mother's knee to learn something as a very young child: *She had learned to flirt at her mother's knee.*

8 Mother used to address the woman who is head of a CONVENT

9 every mother's son OLD-FASHIONED an expression meaning "every man," used to emphasize something

[**Origin:** Old English *modor*]

mother² *v.* [T] to take care of and protect something in the way that a mother does: *Brenda just tries to mother everyone.*

moth·er·board /ˈmʌðɚˌbɔrd/ *n.* [C] COMPUTERS the main CIRCUIT BOARD inside a computer → see picture at COMPUTER

ˈmother ˌcountry *n.* [C usually singular] the country where you were born

ˌMother ˈEarth *n.* [U] the world, considered as the place or thing from which all life comes → see also EARTH MOTHER

moth·er·hood /ˈmʌðɚˌhʊd/ *n.* [U] the state of being a mother: *teenage motherhood* | *She's enjoying motherhood.*

ˈmother-in-ˌlaw *n. plural* **mothers-in-law** [C] the mother of your wife or husband

moth·er·land /ˈmʌðɚˌlænd/ *n.* [C usually singular] the country where you were born or that you feel you belong to → see also FATHERLAND, MOTHER COUNTRY

moth·er·less /ˈmʌðɚlɪs/ *adj.* a motherless child is one whose mother has died

ˈmother lode *n.* [C usually singular] **1** EARTH SCIENCE a mine that is full of gold, silver etc. **2** a big supply of something, or a place where you can find a big supply: *While searching the house they found the mother lode of evidence.*

moth·er·ly /ˈmʌðɚli/ *adj.* typical of a kind or concerned mother: *a kind motherly woman* | *motherly advice* —**motherliness** *n.* [U] → see also MATERNAL

ˌMother ˈNature *n.* [U] an expression used to talk about nature, especially when it is thought of as a force that affects people, living things, and the world: *After floods and a drought, what else can Mother Nature do to us?*

ˌMother of ˈGod *n.* [singular] a title for Mary, the mother of Jesus Christ, used in the Catholic Church

M

ˌ**mother-of-'pearl** *n.* [U] a pale-colored hard smooth shiny substance on the inside of some SHELLS, used for making buttons, jewelry etc.

'**Mother's Day** *n.* [C,U] a holiday in honor of mothers, on which people give cards and presents to their mother, celebrated in the U.S. and Canada on the second Sunday in May

'**mother ship** *n.* [C usually singular] a large ship or SPACECRAFT from which smaller boats or spacecraft are sent out

ˌ**Mother Su'perior** *n.* [C usually singular] the woman who is the leader of a CONVENT

Mother Te•re•sa /ˌmʌðɚ təˈrisə/ (1910–1997) an Albanian Catholic NUN who worked to help the poor and the sick in the city of Calcutta in India

ˌ**mother-to-'be** *n. plural* **mothers-to-be** [C] a woman who is PREGNANT

ˌ**mother 'tongue** *n.* [C] LITERARY the first and main language that you learn as a child SYN **native language**: *Spanish is the mother tongue of more than one-fifth of the population.*

mo•tif /moʊˈtif/ *n.* [C] ENG. LANG. ARTS **1** an idea, subject, or pattern that is regularly repeated and developed in a book, movie, work of art etc.: *an action movie with a revenge motif* **2** a small picture or pattern used to decorate something: *plates with a floral motif* ►see THESAURUS box at **pattern**[1] **3** a tune that is often repeated in a musical work

mo•tion[1] /ˈmoʊʃən/ S2 W2 *n.*
1 MOVEMENT [U] the process of moving or the way that someone or something moves: *the rocking motion of the ship*
2 MOVEMENT OF THE BODY [C] a single movement of your body, especially your hand or head: *a smooth throwing motion* | *a motion of his hand*
3 SUGGESTION AT A MEETING [C] POLITICS a proposal that is made formally at a meeting and then decided on by voting: **motion to do sth** *Is there a motion to continue?* | *I* ***make a motion that*** *we continue the hearing next week.* | *I* ***second the motion*** (=be the second person to make a proposal). | *A two-thirds majority vote was required to* ***pass the motion.*** | *Judge Lupo* ***denied*** *Smith's* ***motion*** *to dismiss charges against him.*
4 in motion a) moving from one place or position to another: *a photograph of a frog in motion* **b)** if a process or plan is in motion, it has started happening or has started being carried out: *The plans were already in motion.* | *The discovery* ***set in motion*** (=started the process of) *two days of searching for the bodies.*
5 go through the motions to do something because you have to do it, without being very interested in it: *The players seemed to be just going through the motions.*
[**Origin:** 1300–1400 Old French, Latin *motio* **movement**, from *movere*] → see also SLOW MOTION, TIME AND MOTION STUDY

motion[2] *v.* [I,T] to give someone directions or instructions by moving your head, hands etc.: **motion (for) sb to do sth** *Evans motioned for Guzman to throw.* | **motion to sb (to do sth)** *He motioned to her to be quiet.* | **motion sb in/out etc.** *A policeman motioned me through.*

'**motion deˌtector** *n.* [C] a piece of equipment that notices movement, used in systems such as BURGLAR ALARMS

mo•tion•less /ˈmoʊʃənlɪs/ *adj.* not moving at all: *Fuller sat motionless as the verdict was read.* —**motionlessly** *adv.*

ˌ**motion 'picture** *n.* [C] a movie: *a major motion picture from Tri-Star*

'**motion ˌsensor** *n.* [C] a MOTION DETECTOR

'**motion ˌsickness** *n.* [U] a feeling of sickness that some people get when traveling in cars, airplanes, boats etc.

mo•ti•vate /ˈmoʊt̬əˌveɪt/ Ac *v.* [T] **1** to make someone want to achieve something and make them willing to work hard in order to do it: *What can we do to motivate the players?* | **motivate sb to do sth** *The plan is designed to motivate staff to work harder.* **2** [often passive] to be the reason why someone does something: *The attack was motivated by revenge.* | **motivate sb to do sth** *What motivated you to sell the house?* —**motivating** *adj.*: *Money is a powerful motivating factor.*

mo•ti•vat•ed /ˈmoʊt̬əˌveɪt̬ɪd/ Ac *adj.* **1** very eager to do or achieve something, especially because you find it interesting or exciting: *Older students are often* ***highly motivated.*** **2 politically/financially/racially etc. motivated** done for political, financial etc. reasons: *a politically motivated decision*

mo•ti•va•tion /ˌmoʊt̬əˈveɪʃən/ Ac *n.* **1** [U] eagerness and willingness to do something: *Jack's an intelligent student, but he* ***lacks motivation.*** **2** [C] the reason why you want to do something: **+for/behind** *The motivation for the crime was greed.*

mo•ti•va•tor /ˈmoʊt̬əˌveɪt̬ɚ/ *n.* [C] something or someone that makes you want to do or achieve something: *Our coach is a great motivator.*

mo•tive[1] /ˈmoʊt̬ɪv/ Ac *n.* [C] **1** the reason that makes someone do something, especially when this reason is kept hidden: **+for** *The motive for the murder was jealousy.* | **+behind** *What do you think the motive behind their decision was?* | *He's just being nice. I don't think he has any* ***ulterior motives*** (=secret or hidden reasons for doing something). ►see THESAURUS box at **reason**[1] **2** a MOTIF [**Origin:** 1500–1600 Old French *motif*, from *motif* **moving**] —**motiveless** *adj.*

motive[2] Ac *adj.* [only before noun] TECHNICAL a motive power or force is one that causes movement

mot juste /ˌmoʊ ˈʒust/ *n. plural* **mots justes** /ˌmoʊ ˈʒust/ [C] FORMAL exactly the right word or phrase

mot•ley /ˈmɑtli/ *adj.* [only before noun] **1 a motley crew/bunch/crowd etc.** a group of people who do not seem to belong together, especially people you do not approve of: *a motley crew of street musicians* **2** a motley group of things contains objects that are all different in shape, size etc. and that do not seem to belong together: *a motley fleet of aircraft* **3** LITERARY motley clothes have many different colors on them

mo•to•cross /ˈmoʊt̬oʊˌkrɔs/ *n.* [U] the sport of racing MOTORCYCLES over rough land, up hills, through streams etc.

mo•tor[1] /ˈmoʊt̬ɚ/ *n.* [C] **1** the part of a machine that makes it work or move, by changing power into movement: *The fan's motor made a funny popping sound.* **2** an engine, especially a small one: *I got out of the car but left the motor running.*

motor[2] *adj.* [only before noun] **1** relating to cars or other vehicles with engines: *motor oil* **2** using power provided by an engine: *a motor vehicle* **3** BIOLOGY relating to a nerve that makes a muscle move: *The disease results in impaired motor function.*

motor[3] *v.* [I] to drive a vehicle with an engine: *I motored out to deeper water.*

mo•tor•bike /ˈmoʊt̬ɚˌbaɪk/ *n.* [C] a MOTORCYCLE, especially a small one

mo•tor•boat /ˈmoʊt̬ɚˌboʊt/ *n.* [C] a small fast boat with an engine

mo•tor•cade /ˈmoʊt̬ɚˌkeɪd/ *n.* [C] a group of cars and other vehicles that travel together and surround a very important person's car: *the President's motorcade*

'**motor car** *n.* [C] OLD-FASHIONED a car

motorcycle

mo·tor·cy·cle /ˈmoʊt̬ɚˌsaɪkəl/ *n.* [C] a fast, usually large, two-wheeled vehicle with an engine

ˈmotor home *n.* [C] a large vehicle with beds, a kitchen etc. in it, used for traveling

mo·tor·ing /ˈmoʊt̬ərɪŋ/ *n.* [U] OLD-FASHIONED the activity of driving a car

ˈmotor inn *n.* [C] a MOTEL

mo·tor·ist /ˈmoʊt̬ərɪst/ *n.* [C] FORMAL someone who drives a car: *Many motorists are failing to wear seatbelts.*

mo·tor·ized /ˈmoʊt̬əˌraɪzd/ *adj.* [only before noun] **1** having an engine, especially when most similar things do not usually have an engine: *a motorized wheelchair* **2** a motorized army or group of soldiers is one that uses motor vehicles **—motorize** *v.* [T]

ˈmotor lodge *n.* [C] FORMAL a MOTEL

mo·tor·man /ˈmoʊt̬ɚmən/ *n. plural* **motormen** /-mən/ [C] a man who drives a SUBWAY train, CABLE CAR etc.

mo·tor·mouth /ˈmoʊt̬ɚˌmaʊθ/ *n.* [C] INFORMAL someone who talks too much and too loudly

ˌmotor ˈneuron disˌease *n.* [U] MEDICINE a disease that causes a gradual loss of control over the muscles and nerves of the body, resulting in death

ˈmotor pool *n.* [C] a group of cars, trucks, and other vehicles that are available for people in a particular part of the government or military to use

ˈmotor ˌracing *n.* [U] the sport of racing fast cars on a special track

ˈmotor ˌscooter *n.* [C] a SCOOTER

ˈmotor ˌvehicle *n.* [C] FORMAL a car, bus, truck etc.: *This road is closed to motor vehicles.*

Mott /mɑt/**, Lu·cre·tia** /luˈkriʃə/ (1793–1880) a U.S. woman who supported women's rights and worked against SLAVERY

mot·tled /ˈmɑt̬ld/ *adj.* covered with patterns of light and dark colors of different shapes: *a mottled gray-and-white whale*

mot·to /ˈmɑt̬oʊ/ *n. plural* **mottos, mottoes** [C] a short statement that expresses the aims or beliefs of a person, school, organization etc.: *"Be prepared" is the motto of the Boy Scouts.*

mould /moʊld/ the British and Canadian spelling of MOLD

mound /maʊnd/ *n.* [C] **1** a pile of dirt, sand, stones etc. that looks like a small hill: *a burial mound* | **+of** *a mound of dirt* ►see THESAURUS box at **pile**[1] **2** a large pile of something: **+of** *There's a mound of papers on my desk.* **3** the small hill that the PITCHER stands on in the game of baseball → see picture at BASEBALL

mount[1] /maʊnt/ [W3] *v.*
1 INCREASE [I] if something bad mounts, it increases gradually in size, amount, strength etc.: *The death toll has already mounted to 5,000.* | **pressure/excitement/tension is mounting** *Tension is mounting, as we await the final result.* → see also MOUNTING[1]
2 EVENT/PROCESS [T] to plan, organize, and begin an event or a process: **mount a campaign/search** *The city government is mounting a recycling campaign.* | **mount an attack/a challenge** *Guerrillas have mounted an attack on the capital.* | *The museum* ***mounted an exhibition*** *of African art.*
3 CLIMB STH [T] FORMAL to go up something such as a set of stairs: *The Olympic medalists mounted the podium.*
4 ATTACH [T] to attach one thing firmly to another larger thing that supports it: **mount sth on sth** *A stuffed deer's head was mounted on the wall.*
5 PICTURE [T] to fasten a picture or photograph to a larger piece of stiff paper: **mount sth on sth** *Entries to the photography competition should be mounted on white paper.*
6 HORSE/BICYCLE [I,T] to get on a horse, bicycle etc. [OPP] **dismount**: *She mounted her horse and rode off.*
7 SEX [T] TECHNICAL if a male animal mounts a female animal, he gets up onto her back to have sex
[**Origin:** 1200–1300 Old French *monter* **to go up**, from Latin *mons*]

mount up *phr. v.* to increase and become larger in size or number: *Costs on the project have been mounting up steadily.*

mount[2] *n.* [C] **1 Mount** WRITTEN ABBREVIATION **Mt.** used in the names of mountains: *Mount Everest* **2** LITERARY an animal, especially a horse, that you ride on **3** stiff paper that is put behind or around a picture or photograph, so that it looks more attractive **4** OLD USE a mountain

Moun·tain /ˈmaʊntˀn/ *n.* **1** SPOKEN a short form of Mountain Time **2** the TIME ZONE in the west-central part of the U.S.

moun·tain /ˈmaʊntˀn/ [S1] [W1] *n.* [C] **1** a very high hill: *the Rocky Mountains* | *Mt. Fuji is the tallest mountain in Japan.* | *We went hiking* ***in the mountains.*** | **the top/bottom of the mountain** *We climbed to the top of the mountain.* | *a mountain climber* **2 a mountain of sth** also **mountains of sth** INFORMAL a very large pile or amount of something: *We get mountains of junk mail every day.* **3 make a mountain out of a molehill** to treat a problem as if it was very serious when in fact it is not

ˌmountain ˈash *n.* [C] a type of tree with red or orange-red berries

ˈmountain ˌbike *n.* [C] a strong bicycle with a lot of GEARS and wide thick tires, designed for riding up hills and on rough ground

ˌMountain ˈDaylight ˌTime ABBREVIATION **MDT** *n.* [U] the time that is used in the west-central part of the U.S. for over half the year, including the summer, when clocks are one hour ahead of Mountain Standard Time

moun·tain·eer /ˌmaʊntˀnˈɪr/ *n.* [C] someone who climbs mountains as a sport

moun·tain·eer·ing /ˌmaʊntˀnˈɪrɪŋ/ *n.* [U] the sport of climbing mountains

ˈmountain goat *n.* [C] an animal that looks like a goat with thick white fur and lives in the western mountains of North America

ˈmountain ˌlaurel *n.* [C] a bush with shiny leaves and pink or white flowers that grows in North America

ˈmountain ˌlion *n.* [C] a COUGAR

moun·tain·ous /ˈmaʊntˀn-əs/ *adj.* **1** having a lot of mountains: *a mountainous region of Turkey* **2** very large in amount or size: *mountainous debt*

ˈmountain range *n.* [C] a long row of mountains that covers a large area

moun·tain·side /ˈmaʊntˀnˌsaɪd/ *n.* [C] the side of a mountain: *a little cabin on the mountainside*

ˌMountain ˈStandard Time ABBREVIATION **MST** *n.* [U] the time that is used in the west-central part of the U.S. for almost half the year, including the winter → see also MOUNTAIN DAYLIGHT TIME

ˈMountain Time ABBREVIATION **MT** *n.* [U] the time that is used in the west-central part of the U.S.

M

moun·tain·top /ˈmaʊntˀn,tɑp/ *n.* [C] the top part of a mountain: *snow on the mountaintops*

moun·te·bank /ˈmaʊntɪ,bæŋk/ *n.* [C] LITERARY a dishonest person who tricks and deceives people

mount·ed /ˈmaʊntɪd/ *adj.* mounted soldiers or police officers ride on horses

Mount·ie /ˈmaʊnti/ *n.* [C] INFORMAL a member of the Royal Canadian Mounted Police

mount·ing¹ /ˈmaʊntɪŋ/ *adj.* [only before noun] increasing and getting more serious or worse: *There was mounting pressure on him to resign.* | *the nation's mounting foreign debt*

mounting² *n.* [C] an object to which other things, especially parts of a machine or jewels, are fastened to keep them in place: *The engine is supported by four rubberized mountings.*

Mount St. Hel·ens /,maʊnt seɪnt ˈhɛlənz/ a VOLCANO in Washington State in the northwestern U.S.

Mount Ver·non /maʊnt ˈvɚnən/ the home of George Washington between 1747 and 1799 and the place where he is buried. It is in the U.S. state of Virginia.

mourn /mɔrn/ *v.* [I,T] **1** to feel very sad because someone has died, and show this in the way you behave: +**for** *Hundreds of people gathered to mourn for the flood victims.* | *She still* ***mourns*** *her son's* ***death.*** **2** to feel very sad because something does not exist anymore or is not as good as it used to be: *Many people mourn the loss of the old theater building.* [**Origin:** Old English *murnan*]

mourn·er /ˈmɔrnɚ/ *n.* [C] someone who attends a funeral

mourn·ful /ˈmɔrnfəl/ *adj.* very sad: *slow mournful music* —**mournfully** *adj.* —**mournfulness** *n.* [U]

mourn·ing /ˈmɔrnɪŋ/ *n.* [U] **1** great sadness because someone has died and behavior that shows you remember them: *a national day of mourning* | *The family is* ***in mourning*** (=feeling great sadness). **2** black clothes worn to show that you are very sad that someone has died, especially in past times

mouse /maʊs/ S2 W3 *n.* [C] **1** *plural* **mice** /maɪs/ BIOLOGY a small animal like a rat with a long tail, smooth fur, and a pointed nose that lives in houses or fields: *My cat caught a mouse.* **2** *plural* **mouses** COMPUTERS a small object connected to a computer by a wire, that you move with your hand and press to give commands to the computer: *Click once with the mouse.* ▸see THESAURUS box at **computer** → see picture at COMPUTER **3** [usually singular] DISAPPROVING a quiet shy person [**Origin:** Old English *mus*] → see also **cat and mouse** at CAT (3)

mous·er /ˈmaʊsɚ/ *n.* [C] a cat that catches mice

mouse·trap /ˈmaʊs-træp/ *n.* [C] a trap for catching mice

mousse /mus/ *n.* [C,U] **1** a sweet food made from a mixture of cream, eggs, and fruit or chocolate, that is eaten when it is cold: *chocolate mousse* **2** a white slightly sticky substance that you put in your hair to make it look thicker or to hold it in place **3** a food that is mixed and cooked with cream or eggs so that it is very light: *salmon mousse* [**Origin:** 1800–1900 French **moss, froth**]

mous·tache /ˈmʌstæʃ, məˈstæʃ/ *n.* [C] another spelling of MUSTACHE

mous·y /ˈmaʊsi, -zi/ *adj.* **1** a mousy person, especially a woman, is quiet, shy, and unattractive **2** mousy hair is a dull brown color —**mousiness** *n.* [U]

mouth¹ /maʊθ/ S1 W2 *n. plural* **mouths** /maʊðz/ [C] **1** FACE BIOLOGY the part of your face that you put food into, or that you use for speaking, or the open area inside your head where you CHEW food: *Babies put everything into their mouths.* | *Don't talk with your mouth full!* | *The lion opened its mouth in a huge yawn.* | *I burned the* ***roof of*** *my* ***mouth*** (=the top part of the inside of your mouth). → see picture at DIGESTIVE SYSTEM

2 keep your mouth shut INFORMAL **a)** to not say anything because you might make a mistake, or annoy someone or upset them: *He just doesn't know when to keep his mouth shut.* **b)** to not tell other people about a secret: *You'd better keep your mouth shut about this.*

3 open your mouth to prepare or start to speak, especially in a situation where you feel you should not say anything: *"I'll go," Travis said quickly before she could open her mouth.* | *I shouldn't have* ***opened*** *my* ***big mouth*** (=said something I should not have). → see also **shut your mouth** at SHUT¹ (3)

4 come out of sb's mouth SPOKEN to be said by someone: *You just never know what's going to come out of her mouth.*

5 RIVER EARTH SCIENCE the part of a river where it joins the ocean: +**of** *the mouth of the river*

6 OPENING **a)** the open part at the top of a bottle or container **b)** the entrance to a large hole or CAVE

7 make sb's mouth water if food makes your mouth water, it looks so good you want to eat it immediately → see also MOUTH-WATERING

8 a mouth to feed someone who you must provide food for, especially one of your children: *We just couldn't afford another mouth to feed.*

9 out of the mouths of babes HUMOROUS used when a small child has just said something intelligent or interesting

[**Origin:** Old English *muth*] → see also **big mouth** at BIG (12), BIGMOUTH, **be down in the dumps/mouth** at DOWN² (1), **foam at the mouth** at FOAM² (2), **put your foot in your mouth** at FOOT¹ (13), **have a foul mouth** at FOUL¹ (3), HAND TO MOUTH, LOUDMOUTH, -MOUTHED, **shoot your mouth off** at SHOOT¹ (17), **shut your mouth/trap/face!** at SHUT¹ (3), **by word of mouth** at WORD¹ (30)

mouth² /maʊð/ *v.* [T] **1** to move your lips as if you are saying words, but without making any sound: *Dana mouthed, "I'm bored," from across the classroom.* **2** to say things that you do not really believe or that you do not understand: *The men spent years mouthing the Communist party line.*

mouth off *phr. v.* INFORMAL to speak in an angry or impolite way to someone: +**to/at** *She was suspended for mouthing off to teachers.*

-mouthed /maʊðd, maʊθt/ [in adjectives] **1 open-mouthed/dry-mouthed etc.** with an open, dry etc. mouth: *She stared at him open-mouthed.* **2 wide-mouthed/narrow-mouthed etc.** with a wide or narrow mouth or opening: *a wide-mouthed bottle* → see also CLOSE-MOUTHED, FOUL-MOUTHED, LOUDMOUTH, MEALY-MOUTHED, OPEN-MOUTHED

mouth·ful /ˈmaʊθfʊl/ *n.* [C] **1** an amount of food or drink that you put into your mouth at one time: +**of** *a mouthful of cookies* **2 a mouthful of sth** something that fills your mouth: *a mouthful of sharp teeth* **3 be a mouthful** INFORMAL to be long and difficult to say: *Her last name is quite a mouthful.* **4 say a mouthful** INFORMAL to say a lot of true and important things about something in a few words

ˈmouth ,organ *n.* [C] OLD-FASHIONED a HARMONICA

mouth·piece /ˈmaʊθpis/ *n.* [C] **1** the part of a musical instrument, telephone etc. that you put in your mouth or next to your mouth **2** [usually singular] DISAPPROVING a person, newspaper etc. that expresses the opinions of a government or a political organization, especially without ever criticizing these opinions: *He was just a mouthpiece of the government.*

,mouth-to-mouth resusciˈtation also **,mouth to ˈmouth** *n.* [U] a method used to make someone start breathing again by blowing air into their mouth

mouth·wash /ˈmaʊθwɑʃ/ *n.* [C,U] a liquid used to make your mouth smell fresh or to get rid of an infection in your mouth

ˈmouth-,watering *adj.* mouth-watering food looks or smells extremely good: *the mouth-watering smell of freshly baked bread*

M

mouth·y /ˈmaʊθi, -ði/ *adj.* DISAPPROVING INFORMAL someone who is mouthy talks a lot and says what they want to even when it is not polite: *a mouthy 13-year-old girl*

mov·a·ble[1], **moveable** /ˈmuvəbəl/ *adj.* able to be moved, rather than being fastened in one place or position: *a teddy bear with movable arms and legs*

movable[2], **moveable** *n.* [C usually plural] LAW a personal possession such as a piece of furniture

move[1] /muv/ S1 W1 *v.*
1 CHANGE PLACE/POSITION [I,T] to change from one place or position to another, or to make something do this: *The train started to move.* | *It took three men to move the piano.* | *My fingers were so cold I couldn't move them.* | **+around** *There was an animal moving around in the bushes.* | **+away/out/down etc.** *Move out of the way, Denise.* | *Laura yelled that she* ***couldn't move***. | ***Don't move*** *– there's a bee on your shoulder.* | *The bar was so crowded* ***you could hardly move***. ►see THESAURUS box at **action**
2 NEW HOUSE/TOWN [I,T] to go to live in a different place, or to make or help someone do this: *The neighbors are moving.* | **+around** *Dad was in the army, so we moved around a lot.* | **+to/from** *When did you move to Albuquerque?* | **move (sb) into sth** *They moved their mother into a nursing home.*
3 COMPANY [I,T] if a company moves, all of its workers and equipment go to a new place to work: *The company is moving its sales center downtown.* | **+into** *We're moving into new offices across town.*
4 CHANGE JOB/CLASS ETC. [I,T] to change to a different job, class etc., or to make someone do this: **move (sb) to/into sth** *She's been moved to a different department.* | **move from sth to sth** *He's always moving from one job to another.*
5 FEEL EMOTION [T often passive] to make someone feel a strong emotion, especially of sadness or sympathy: *I was* ***deeply moved*** *by what I heard.* | *Many in the room were* ***moved to tears*** *by the film.* → see also MOVING
6 be/feel moved to do sth to want to do something as a result of an experience or a strong emotion: *As I learned more about the situation, I felt moved to get involved.*
7 PROGRESS [I] to make progress, often in a particular way or at a particular rate: *Things moved quickly once the contract was signed.* | *The negotiations seem to be* ***moving in the right direction***. | *Our job is to* ***keep*** *the talks* ***moving***.
8 get moving also **move it** SPOKEN used in order to say that someone needs to hurry: *We'd better get moving if we don't want to miss the start of the movie.*
9 START DOING STH [I] to start doing something, especially in order to achieve something or deal with a problem: **+on/against etc.** *The administration is not moving on the issue.* | *The justices said they would* ***move quickly*** *to rule on the case.* | *You'll need to* ***move fast*** *if you want tickets.*
10 BODY [I] to move your body in a particular way, for example when you are walking or dancing: *He watched the way she moved on the dance floor.*
11 CHANGE YOUR OPINION a) [I] to change from one opinion or way of thinking to another SYN **shift**: *Neither side is willing to move on this issue.* | **+toward/away from** *The government is moving toward democratization.* | *We need to move away from the idea that violence can solve anything.* **b)** [T] to persuade someone to change their opinion SYN **shift**: *Once she's made up her mind, you can't move her.*
12 CHANGE SUBJECT/ACTIVITY [I] to change from one subject or activity to another: **+onto** *Let's move onto something else.* | **+off/away from** *We seem to have moved off the subject.* → see also **move on** at MOVE[1]
13 CHANGE ARRANGEMENTS [T] to change the time or order of something: **move sth to/from sth** *Could we move the meeting to Thursday?*
14 GAMES [I,T] to change the position of one of the pieces used to play a game such as CHESS
15 AT A MEETING [I,T] FORMAL to officially make a proposal at a meeting: **move that** *The chairman moved that the meeting be adjourned.* | **move to do sth** *I move to approve the minutes.*
16 GO FAST [I] INFORMAL to travel very fast: *That truck was really moving!*
17 SELL STH [I,T] INFORMAL if goods move or you move them, people buy them: *I've got three crates of this stuff to move.*
18 not move a muscle to stay completely still: *I was so scared, I couldn't move a muscle.*
19 move in a society/world/circle to spend a lot of time with a particular type of people and know them well: *Celia moves in different circles than I do.*
20 move with the times to change the way you think and behave, as society changes around you
[**Origin:** 1200–1300 Old French *mouvoir*, from Latin *movere*] → see also **move heaven and earth** at HEAVEN (11), **move/go/close in for the kill** at KILL[2] (2), **when/as the spirit moves you** at SPIRIT[1] (15)

move along *phr. v.* **1 move sth along** if something such as a process, story, or situation moves along or someone or something moves it along, it develops or makes progress: *After this delay, we really need to* ***move things along*** *now.* **2** used especially by the police to ask someone to leave a place and go somewhere else: *Move along, folks. There's nothing to see.*

move away *phr. v.* to go to live in a different area: *My best friend moved away when I was in sixth grade.*

move in *phr. v.* **1** to start living in a new house: *We just moved in yesterday.* **2** to start living with someone in the same house: **+with** *She's moving in with her boyfriend.* **3** to go toward a place or group of people, especially in order to attack them or take control of them: *U.N. peacekeepers moved in to calm the situation.* | **+on** *Police began moving in on the rioters.* **4** to start being involved in or gaining an advantage in an activity that someone else has always had control of: *Big companies moved in and pushed up prices.*

move into sth *phr. v.* **1** to go into a place in large numbers in order to deal with a situation or take control: *U.S. troops have moved into the region.* **2** to start to become involved in a particular type of business: *We decided to move into computers.* **3** to enter a new period of time SYN **enter**: *The strike was moving into its eighth week.*

move off *phr. v.* if a vehicle or group of people moves off, they start to leave a place

move on *phr. v.* **1** to leave the place where you have been staying in order to continue on a trip: *After three days we decided it was time to move on.* **2** to forget the unpleasant events of the past and start to consider or plan the future: *The breakup was two years ago – it's time to move on.* **3 a)** to develop in your life and gain more experience as you become older: *I enjoyed the job, but it was time to move on.* **b)** to progress, improve, or become more modern as time passes: *The business has moved on since we opened our first bakery.* **4** to leave your present job, class, or activity and start doing another one: *When you stop enjoying the job, it's time to move on.* | **+to** *Move on to the next exercise.* **5** to start talking about a new subject in a discussion, book etc.: *Then the conversation moved on to happier topics.* **6** if time moves on, the year moves on etc., the time passes

move out *phr. v.* **1** to leave the house where you are living now in order to go and live somewhere else: *The landlord wants me to move out by the 14th.* | **+of** *Lola moved out of her parents' house when she was 18.* **2** if a group of soldiers moves out, they leave a place **3** SPOKEN to leave: *Is everything ready? Then let's move out.*

move over *phr. v.* **1** to change position so that there is more space for someone else: *Move over a little, so I can sit down.* **2** to change to a different system, opinion, group of people etc.: **+to** *Most companies have moved over to computer-aided design systems.* **3** to change jobs, especially within the same organization or industry **4 move over, sb/sth** INFORMAL used when saying that one thing that has existed for a long time is not as popular as something new: *Move over, VCRs – digital recording is the future.*

move up *phr. v.* **1** to get a better job than the one you had before: *To move up, you'll need the right training.* **2** to improve your position or the quality of something you own: **+to** *Texas A&M moved up to the No. 2 position.* **3 move up in the world** also **move up the ladder** to get a better job or social position

move² S2 W2 *n.* [C]

1 DECISION something that you decide to do in order to achieve something or make progress: *What will his next move be?* | **a move to do sth** *Three board members opposed the move to raise rates.* | **a smart/wise move** *Doing some research before the trip is a smart move.* | *I think it was **a good move*** (=a good decision). | *The company has **made a move** to speed up production.* | *The authorities have **made no move** to resolve the conflict.*

2 CHANGE a change, especially one that improves a situation: **+toward/away from** *the country's move toward democracy* | *This decision is definitely **a move in the right direction**.*

3 MOVEMENT an action in which someone moves their body in a particular direction: *dance moves* | *Grodin **made a move** toward the door.* | *They watched, and **made no move** to stop us.*

4 on the move a) changing and developing a lot, especially in a way that improves things: *The economy is finally on the move.* **b)** going or traveling to another place: *With her job, she spends most of her time on the move.* **c)** busy and active: *Those kids are always on the move.*

5 get a move on SPOKEN used to tell someone to hurry: *Get a move on or we'll be late!*

6 GOING TO A NEW PLACE the process of leaving one house, office etc., and going to live or work in a different one: *The move took three days.*

7 GAMES an act of changing the position of one of the objects in a game such as CHESS, or the time when a particular player does this: *It's your move.*

8 make the first move to do something first, especially in order to end an argument or start a relationship: *Neither side is willing to make the first move in the trade talks.*

9 watch/follow sb's every move to carefully watch everything that someone does, especially because you think they are doing something illegal: *The CIA was watching our every move.*

10 put/make a move on sb INFORMAL to try to start sexual activity or a sexual relationship with someone

move·a·ble /ˈmuvəbəl/ another spelling of MOVABLE

ˌmoveable ˈtype *n.* [U] small blocks used for printing letters, numbers etc. whose positions can be easily changed to form different words etc.

move·ment /ˈmuvmənt/ S2 W1 *n.*

1 PEOPLE WORKING TOGETHER [C] a group of people who share the same ideas or beliefs and work together to achieve a particular aim: **the civil rights/peace/feminist etc. movement** *the labor movement* | **a political/religious/artistic/revolutionary etc. movement** *She was active in a number of political movements.*

2 CHANGE OF POSITION [C,U] a change in the position of something, especially a person's or animal's body: *a dancer's graceful movements* | *We watched for signs of movement in the trees.* | **+of** *a small movement of his head*

3 CHANGE OF PLACE [C,U] an act of moving things or people from one place to another: **+of** *the movement of goods across state borders*

4 CHANGE/DEVELOPMENT [C,U] a change or development in a situation or in people's attitudes: *There's been no movement in the dispute since Thursday.* | **+toward/away from etc.** *There is a growing movement among consumers away from buying processed foods.*

5 MILITARY [C,U] a planned change in the position of a group of soldiers: *Soldiers were sent into the area to report on the enemy's movements.*

6 sb's movements all of a person's activities over a certain period: *Police are trying to trace Carter's movements.*

7 MUSIC [C] one of the main parts into which some pieces of CLASSICAL music are divided: *the first movement of Bach's Violin Concerto*

8 CLOCK/WATCH [C] the moving parts of a piece of machinery, especially a clock or watch

9 BODY WASTE [C] FORMAL an act of getting rid of waste matter from the BOWELS

mov·er /ˈmuvɚ/ *n.* [C] **1** someone whose job is to help people move from one house to another **2 a mover and a shaker** POLITICS an important person who has power and influence over what happens in a situation: *one of the movers and shakers in Florida politics* **3** someone or something that moves in a particular way: *Pluto is the slowest mover of all the planets.* **4** a STOCK that people are buying and selling a lot of → see also **key mover/player etc.** at KEY² (1), PRIME MOVER

mov·ie /ˈmuvi/ S1 W1 *n.* **1** [C] ENG. LANG. ARTS a story that is told using moving pictures on film and sound SYN **film**: *a Hollywood movie* | *Have you **seen** the new Tom Hanks **movie**?* | *"What did you do last weekend?" "We **went to a movie**."* | **a movie is playing/showing** *What time is the movie playing?* | *He **starred in** 15 hit **movies**.* | **a TV movie/a made-for-TV movie** *She's appeared in a number of made-for-TV movies.*

THESAURUS

Types of movies
feature film a movie made to be shown in movie theaters
comedy a movie intended to make people laugh
romantic comedy a movie about love that is intended to make the people who watch it feel happy
thriller an exciting movie about murder or serious crimes
western a movie with cowboys in it
action movie a movie that has lots of fighting, explosions etc.
horror movie a frightening movie about ghosts, murders etc.
science fiction movie a movie about imaginary events in the future or in outer space
animated movie/cartoon a movie with characters that are drawn or made using a computer
flick INFORMAL a movie: *an action flick*
film a movie, especially one that people think is very good or important: *a foreign film*
motion picture FORMAL a movie

People who make movies
actor a man or woman who acts in a movie
actress a woman who acts in a movie
star a famous actor or actress
director the person who tells the actors and actresses in a movie what to do
producer the person who makes the arrangements for a movie to be made and controls the movie's budget (=the money available to make the movie)
film/movie crew the people operating the camera, lights etc. who help the director make a movie
►see THESAURUS box at **television**

2 the movies a) the place where you go to watch a movie: *Do you want to **go to the movies** on Saturday?* | *"Where were you this afternoon?" "We were **at the movies**."* **b)** movies in general and the events in them: *Car chases have always been popular in the movies.* **c)** the business of producing movies: *a career in the movies*

mov·ie·go·er /ˈmuviˌgouɚ/ *n.* [C] someone who goes to see movies, especially regularly

mov·ie·mak·er /ˈmuviˌmeɪkɚ/ *n.* [C] someone who DIRECTS or does other things in order to make movies —**moviemaking** *n.* [U]

ˈmovie star *n.* [C] a famous movie actor or actress

ˈmovie ˌtheater *n.* [C] a place where you go to watch a movie

mov·ing /ˈmuvɪŋ/ *adj.* **1** making you feel strong emotions, especially sadness or sympathy: *The occasion was deeply moving.* | *a moving farewell speech* ►see THESAURUS box at **emotional** **2** [only before noun] changing from one position to another: *a moving stage* | *These boats are not for use in **fast-moving** water.* **3 a**

moving target a) something that you are trying to hit, for example with a gun, which is moving **b)** something that is changing continuously, so that it is very difficult to criticize it or compete against it **4 the moving spirit/force** someone who makes something start to happen: *She has been the project's moving force since the start.* —**movingly** *adv.*

ˌmoving ˈpart *n.* [C] a part of a machine that moves when it is operating: *Keep the moving parts well oiled.*

ˌmoving ˈpicture *n.* [C] OLD-FASHIONED a movie

ˈmoving ˌvan *n.* [C] a large vehicle used for moving furniture from one house to another

mow /moʊ/ *v. past tense* **mowed**, *past participle* **mowed** or **mown** /moʊn/ [I,T] **1** to cut grass using a special machine or tool: *The boy next door mows the lawn for us.* ►see THESAURUS box at **cut**[1] **2 new-mown hay/grass etc.** recently cut hay, grass etc.

mow sb/sth ↔ **down** *phr. v.* **1** to kill large numbers of people at the same time, especially by shooting them: *Machine guns mowed down retreating soldiers.* **2** to knock someone or something down: *The car went up on the sidewalk and mowed down two children.*

mow·er /ˈmoʊɚ/ *n.* [C] **1** a machine or tool used for cutting grass SYN **lawn mower** **2** OLD USE someone who mows

mox·ie /ˈmɑksi/ *n.* [U] INFORMAL courage and determination: *Campanis makes up for her small size with plenty of moxie.*

Mo·zam·bique /ˌmoʊzəmˈbik, -zæm-/ a country in southeast Africa, between Tanzania and South Africa —**Mozambiquean** *n., adj.*

Mo·zart /ˈmoʊtsɑrt/, **Wolf·gang Am·a·de·us** /ˈwʊlfgɑŋ æməˈdeɪəs/ (1756–1791) an Austrian musician who wrote CLASSICAL music

moz·za·rel·la /ˌmɑtsəˈrɛlə/ *n.* [U] a white Italian cheese that is often used on PIZZA [**Origin:** 1900–2000 Italian *mozzare* **to cut off**]

MP *n.* [C] **1** a member of the MILITARY POLICE **2 Member of Parliament** POLITICS someone who has been elected to represent the people in a government that has a PARLIAMENT

MP3 *n.* [C] a type of computer FILE containing recorded music that is very small: *an MP3 player*

MPEG /ˈɛmpɛg/ *n.* [C] COMPUTERS a type of computer FILE that contains sound and VIDEO

mpg the abbreviation of "miles per gallon," used to describe the amount of gasoline used by a car: *a car that gets 45 mpg*

mph the abbreviation of "miles per hour," used to describe the speed of a vehicle: *He was going 100 mph.*

Mr. /ˈmɪstɚ/ **1** used in front of the full or family name of a man to speak to him politely, to write to him, or to talk about him: *Mr. John Smith* **2** a title used when speaking to a man in an official position: *Mr. President* → see also MADAM **3 Mr. Right** a man who would be the perfect husband for a particular woman: *She thinks she's found Mr. Right.* **4 no more Mr. Nice Guy!** used to say that you will stop trying to behave honestly and fairly **5 Mr. Clean** INFORMAL someone who is honest and always obeys the law: *He has a reputation as Mr. Clean.* **6 Mr. Big** INFORMAL the leader or most important person in a group, especially a criminal group **7** SPOKEN, HUMOROUS used before a noun or adjective that describes a personal quality to say that someone has this quality or behaves in this way: *We don't need any comments from Mr. Sarcasm here.*

USAGE

Mr., Mrs., Miss, and **Ms.** are used with family names or people's full names: *Hello, Mr. Gray.* | *Mrs. Betty Schwarz, 610 Murdock Rd.* Do not use **Mr., Mrs., Miss,** or **Ms.** with a first name alone, or with someone's job. For example, do not say *Please, Miss teacher* or *Good morning, Mr. Jerry*.
When you are talking or writing to someone directly, you do not usually use their full name. For example, say *Hello, Mr. Smith* not *Hello, Mr. Alan Smith*. If you do not know the name of the person you are writing to, address the letter *Dear Sir* or *Dear Madam*, not *Dear Mr.* or *Dear Mrs.* Many women, especially younger women, prefer to be addressed as **Ms.** rather than **Miss** or **Mrs.**, because **Ms.** does not draw attention to whether or not the woman is married.

MRI *n.* MEDICINE **1** [C] a picture of the inside of someone's body produced with MAGNETIC RESONANCE IMAGING equipment **2** [U] **magnetic resonance imaging** the process of using strong MAGNETIC FIELDS to make an image of the inside of the body

mRNA *n.* [U] BIOLOGY the abbreviation of MESSENGER RNA

Mrs. /ˈmɪsɪz/ **1** used in front of the family name of a married woman in order to speak to her politely, to write to her, or to talk about her: *Mrs. Monahan is secretary to the Chairman.* | *Dear Mrs. Wright,...* → see also MISS → see Usage note at MR **2** SPOKEN used before the name of a personal quality or type of behavior as a humorous name for a married woman who has that quality: *Here comes Mrs. Efficiency – everybody get back to work!*

M.S. *n.* [C] **Master of Science** a college degree in science that you do after your first degree → see also M.A.

MS **1** the written abbreviation of Mississippi **2** [U] MULTIPLE SCLEROSIS

Ms. /mɪz/ used in front of the full or family name of a woman who does not want to be called "Mrs." or "Miss," or when you do not know whether she is married or not: *Ms. Ramirez called this morning.* → see also MISS → see Usage note at MR

ms *n. plural* **mss** [C] the written abbreviation of MANUSCRIPT

MS-DOS /ˌɛm ɛs ˈdɔs, -ˈdɑs/ *n.* [U] TRADEMARK a common OPERATING SYSTEM for computers

MSG *n.* [U] **monosodium glutamate** a chemical compound added to food to make it taste better

MST the written abbreviation of MOUNTAIN STANDARD TIME

MT **1** the written abbreviation of MONTANA **2** the written abbreviation of MOUNTAIN TIME

Mt. the written abbreviation of MOUNT: *Mt. Everest*

MTV TRADEMARK **Music Television** a television company that broadcasts popular music and VIDEOS of the musicians

much[1] /mʌtʃ/ S1 W1 *adv.* **1** used especially before COMPARATIVES and SUPERLATIVES to say whether something is different, bigger, better etc. by a large amount: *It was much easier writing the letter on the computer.* | *Wayne looks much older now.* | *These shoes are much more comfortable.* | *Paul earns much more than I do.* | *I feel **so much** better.* | *He was driving **much too** fast.* **2** used to say or ask whether something happens or is true to a great degree: *Has the town changed much?* | *I didn't much care for him.* | *He loves you **very much**.* | *He worries **too much** about what other people think.* | ***Thank you very much** for all your help.* | *I don't respect her **as much as** I used to.* | *It's amazing **how much** the children have grown.* | *We're looking forward to it **so much**.* **3** [usually in negatives and questions] used to say or ask how often someone does something or how much time they spend doing it: *She doesn't complain much.* | *Do you travel much?* | *She doesn't smile **as much as** she used to.* | *He talks **too much**.* | *We don't use the car **very much**.* **4 much less** used to say that one thing is even less true or less possible than another: *I've never seen the report, much less read it.* **5 (as) much as sb does sth** used to mean that although one thing is true, something else is also true: *Much as I would like to have been there, it just wasn't possible.* **6 much to sb's surprise/disgust etc.** FORMAL used to say that someone was very surprised, very DISGUSTED etc.: *Much to my relief, she didn't see me.* **7 not be much good/use** to not be useful or skillful: *I'm not much good at tennis.* **8 much loved/praised/criticized etc.** used to describe someone or something that is loved, praised, criticized etc. a lot or by many people: *a much loved book* **9** used to say that something is very similar to something else: *We know pretty much what happened.* | *We are in* ***much the same*** *situation.* | **much like/as sth** *The taste is much like butter.* → see also **sb/sth is not so much...as...** at SO[1] (15), **so much the better** at SO[1] (12), **not think much of sb/sth** at THINK (9)

GRAMMAR **much, very, a lot, many**

• Use **much** with adjectives that come from the past participle of verbs: *Her work is much admired.*
• **Very** is used in the same way with ordinary adjectives: *The painting is very beautiful.*
• In negative sentences and in questions, use **much** with uncountable nouns and use **many** with countable nouns: *These plants aren't getting much sunlight.* | *How much money does it cost?* | *There weren't many cars on the road.*
• In affirmative statements with countable nouns, use **a lot**: *She knows a lot of people.*

much[2] S1 W1 *quantifier, pron.* **1** [usually in negatives and questions] a lot of something: *Was there much traffic?* | *I didn't spend much money.* | *There is still much work to be done.* | +**of** *The storm will bring rain to much of the state.* **2** used to talk about how large an amount of something is, or what it costs: ***How much*** *time do you think it will take?* | **how much is sth?/how much does sth cost?** *How much is this jacket?* | *I have* ***too much*** *work and not enough time.* | *There's* ***so much*** *to learn.* | **this/that/so much** *I didn't think the repairs would cost this much.* | *Eat* ***as much as*** *you want.* | *Some TV programs have* ***far too much*** *sex and violence in them.* | **as much as 10%/$1,000 etc.** *Top lawyers earn as much as $3 million a year.* **3 not/nothing much** used to say that something is not important, interesting, serious etc.: *"Anything happening?" "Not much."* | *There was nothing much I could do to help.* **4 be too much for sb** to be too difficult for someone to do: *Climbing the stairs is too much for her.* **5 think/say/suspect etc. as much** used to say that someone thought or said the fact or idea that has just been mentioned: *"Max was lying all the time." "I thought as much."* **6 not be much of a sth** to not be a very good, big, serious etc. example of something: *I'm not much of a dancer.* **7 not be much to look at** to be unattractive: *Her husband's not much to look at.* **8 be a bit much** used to say that something is too extreme or unacceptable: *The explosion at the end of the movie was a bit much.* **9 that/as much again** an additional amount that is equal to the amount that already exists: *The car only cost $2,500 but the insurance cost as much again.* **10 I'll say this/that much for sb/sth** used to say something positive about someone who has been criticized: *I'll say this much for him – he was consistent until the end.* **11 make much of sb/sth** FORMAL to treat information, a situation etc. as though you think it is very important or serious: *The press made much of the discovery.* → see also MANY, **that's not saying much** at SAY[1] (33), **not/without so much as sth** at SO[1] (9), **so much for sb/sth** at SO[1] (23)

ˌmuch-ˈheralded *adj.* [only before noun] talked about a lot before it actually appears: *much-heralded welfare reforms*

ˌmuch-ˈvaunted *adj.* [only before noun] a much-vaunted achievement, plan, quality etc. is one that people often say is very good, important etc., especially with too much pride → see also VAUNTED

muck[1] /mʌk/ *n.* [U] INFORMAL something such as dirt, mud, or another sticky substance that makes something dirty

muck[2] *v.*

muck sth ↔ **up** *phr. v.* to spoil something, especially an arrangement or plan: *The bad weather mucked up our picnic plans.*

muckety-muck /ˈmʌkət̬i ˌmʌk/ *n.* [C] INFORMAL a word meaning someone who is important and powerful, used when you want to show that you do not feel respect for their power: *a dinner with some Washington muckety-mucks*

muck·rak·ing /ˈmʌkˌreɪkɪŋ/ *n.* [U] the practice in newspapers, magazines etc. of telling the public about bad things that important or famous people have done or are said to have done —**muckraking** *adj.*: *muckraking journalists* —**muckraker** *n.* [C]

muck·y /ˈmʌki/ *adj.* INFORMAL dirty or MUDDY

mu·cous mem·brane /ˈmyukəs ˌmɛmbreɪn/ *n.* [C] BIOLOGY the thin surface that covers some inner parts of the body, such as the inside of the nose, and produces mucus

mu·cus /ˈmyukəs/ *n.* [U] BIOLOGY a thick liquid produced in parts of your body such as your nose —**mucous** *adj.*

mud /mʌd/ *n.* [U] **1** wet earth that has become soft and sticky: *Her boots were covered in mud.* ►see THESAURUS box at **ground**[1] **2** earth used for building: *a mud hut* **3 here's mud in your eye** SPOKEN, OLD-FASHIONED used for expressing good wishes when having an alcoholic drink with someone → see also **as clear as mud** at CLEAR[1] (14), **drag sb's name through the mud** at DRAG[1] (11), **sb's name is mud** at NAME[1] (12)

mud·bath /ˈmʌdbæθ/ *n.* [C] a health treatment in which heated mud is put onto your body, used especially to reduce pain

mud·dle[1] /ˈmʌdl/ *v.* [T]

muddle along/on *phr. v.* INFORMAL to continue doing something without having any clear plan: *The bureaucracy just seems to muddle along.*

muddle through *phr. v.* INFORMAL **muddle through sth** to manage to complete something with difficulty, but not in a very satisfactory way: *The team managed to muddle through another season.*

muddle[2] *n.* [C usually singular] a state of confusion or a lack of order: *a legal muddle*

mud·dled /ˈmʌdld/ *adj.* INFORMAL confused and difficult to understand: *a muddled policy*

mud·dy /ˈmʌdi/ *adj. comparative* **muddier**, *superlative* **muddiest** **1** covered with mud or containing mud: *muddy water* | *Are your shoes muddy?* ►see THESAURUS box at **dirty**[1] **2** confused and not clear: *The party's stance on the issue is muddy.* **3** colors that are muddy are dull and brownish: *muddy brown* **4** sounds that are muddy are not clear —**muddiness** *n.* [U]

muddy[2] *v.* **muddies, muddied, muddying** [T] **1** to make something dirty with mud: *The storm muddied the fields.* **2** to make things more complicated or confusing in a situation that was simple before: **muddy the waters/issue** *These new studies merely muddy the waters.*

ˈmud flap *n.* [C] a piece of rubber that hangs behind the wheel of a vehicle to prevent mud from flying up → see picture on page A36

mud·flat /ˈmʌdflæt/ *n.* [C often plural] **1** an area of muddy land, covered by the ocean when it comes up at HIGH TIDE and uncovered when it goes down at LOW TIDE **2** the muddy bottom of a dry lake

mud·pack /ˈmʌdpæk/ *n.* [C] a soft mixture containing clay that you spread over your face and leave there for a short time to improve your skin

ˌmud ˈpie *n.* [C] **1** a little ball of wet mud made by children as a game **2** a DESSERT made of ice cream and chocolate

mud·slide /ˈmʌdslaɪd/ *n.* [C] EARTH SCIENCE the sudden falling of a lot of wet earth down the side of a hill → see picture on page A30

mud·sling·ing /ˈmʌdˌslɪŋɪŋ/ *n.* [U] the practice of saying bad and often untrue things about someone in order to make other people have a bad opinion of them: *political mudslinging* —**mudslinger** *n.* [C]

ˈmud-ˌwrestling *n.* [U] a sport in which people WRESTLE in a box filled with mud —**mud-wrestle** *v.* [I]

Muen·ster /ˈmʌnstɚ/ *n.* [U] a fairly soft and mild-tasting cheese

mues·li /ˈmyusli, ˈmyuz-/ *n.* [U] a mixture of grains, nuts, and dried fruit that is eaten with milk or yogurt for breakfast [**Origin:** 1900–2000 Swiss German, German *mus* **soft food**]

M

mu·ez·zin /mu'ɛzən, 'mwɛzən/ *n.* [C] a man who calls Muslims to prayer from a MOSQUE

muff¹ /mʌf/ *n.* [C] **1** a short tube of thick cloth or fur that you can put your hands into to keep them warm in cold weather **2** a mistake in a sport, such as failing to catch a ball → see also EARMUFFS

muff² *v.* [T] INFORMAL **1** also **muff sth ↔ up** to make a mistake or do something badly **2** to fail to catch or hold a ball in a game or sport: *Clark muffed a routine groundball.*

muf·fin /'mʌfən/ *n.* [C] a small, slightly sweet type of bread that often has fruit in it: *blueberry muffins*

muf·fle /'mʌfəl/ *v.* [T] **1** to make a sound less loud and clear: *The falling snow muffled all sounds.* **2** [T usually passive] also **muffle sb ↔ up** to cover yourself with something thick and warm: *The children were muffled up in thick coats.*

muf·fled /'mʌfəld/ *adj.* muffled sounds or voices cannot be heard clearly, for example because they come from behind or under something: *the muffled yells of children at play*

muf·fler /'mʌflɚ/ *n.* [C] **1** a piece of equipment on a vehicle that makes the noise from the engine quieter **2** a thick long piece of cloth worn to keep your neck warm

muf·ti /'mʌfti/ *n.* [C] someone who officially explains Muslim law

mug¹ /mʌg/ *n.* [C] **1** a large cup with straight sides used for drinking coffee, tea etc. **2** a large glass with straight sides and a handle, used especially for drinking beer **3** also **mugful** the amount of liquid in a mug: *a mug of cocoa* **4** OLD-FASHIONED a face

mug² *v.* **mugged**, **mugging** **1** [T] to attack someone and rob them in a public place: *She **got mugged** on her way home from work.* ►see THESAURUS box at **steal¹** **2** [I] INFORMAL to make silly expressions with your face or behave in a silly way, especially in a photograph or a play: *Kids were **mugging for the camera**.*

mug·ger /'mʌgɚ/ *n.* [C] someone who attacks people and robs them in a public place

mug·ging /'mʌgɪŋ/ *n.* [C,U] an attack on someone in which they are robbed in a public place: *Robberies and muggings are common in the area.*

mug·gy /'mʌgi/ *adj.* *comparative* **muggier**, *superlative* **muggiest** INFORMAL muggy weather is not nice because it is too warm and the air seems wet: *a hot muggy summer day* —**mugginess** *n.* [U]

Mu·ghal /mu'gʌl/ *n.* [C] HISTORY a member of a Muslim DYNASTY of rulers who ruled large parts of India from 1526 to 1857 —**Mughal** *adj.*

'mug shot *n.* [C] INFORMAL a photograph of a criminal's face, taken by the police

Mu·ham·mad /mu'hæməd/ also **Mo·ham·med** /moʊ'hæmd/ (?570–632) an Arab religious leader, born in Mecca, who started the religion of Islam and is its most important PROPHET. According to Islam, God told him many things which were later written down to form the holy book called the Koran.

Muhammad, El·i·jah /ɪ'laɪdʒə/ (1897–1975) the leader of the Black Muslims from the late 1930s until his death

Mu·ham·mad·an /mu'hæmədən, -'hɑ-/ *n.*, *adj.* OLD-FASHIONED a word meaning "Muslim," now usually considered offensive —**Muhammadan** *adj.* —**Muhammadanism** *n.* [U]

Muir /myʊr/, **John** (1834–1914) a U.S. NATURALIST born in Scotland who encouraged the development of national parks

mu·ja·he·ddin /mu,dʒɑhɪ'din/ *n.* [plural] Muslim soldiers with strong religious beliefs

muk·luks /'mʌklʌks/ *n.* [plural] boots made of animal skin that have a thick bottom, used for walking in snow

mu·lat·to /mə'lɑtoʊ/ *n.* *plural* **mulattoes** [C] OLD-FASHIONED a word for someone with one black parent and one white parent, now considered offensive

mul·ber·ry /'mʌl,bɛri/ *n.* *plural* **mulberries** **1** [C] BIOLOGY a dark purple fruit that can be eaten, or the tree on which this fruit grows **2** [U] the dark purple color of these fruit

mulch¹ /mʌltʃ/ *n.* [singular, U] decaying leaves that you put on the soil to improve its quality, to protect the roots of plants, and to stop WEEDS from growing

mulch² *v.* [T] to cover the ground with a mulch

mule /myul/ *n.* [C] **1** BIOLOGY an animal that has a DONKEY and a horse as parents **2** [usually plural] a shoe or SLIPPER without a back, that has a piece of material across the toes to hold it on your foot → see picture at SHOE¹ **3** SLANG someone who brings illegal drugs into a country by hiding them on or in their body [**Origin:** (2) 1500–1600 French, Latin *mulleus* type of red shoe worn by certain officials] → see also **as stubborn as a mule** at STUBBORN (1)

mu·le·teer /,myulə'tɪr/ also **mule·skin·ner** /'myul,skɪnɚ/ *n.* [C] someone who leads mules

mul·ish /'myulɪʃ/ *adj.* refusing to do something or agree to something in an unreasonable way SYN **stubborn**: *mulish obstinacy* —**mulishly** *adv.* —**mulishness** *n.* [U]

mull /mʌl/ *v.* [T] **1** to heat wine or beer with sugar and SPICES **2** also **mull sth ↔ over** to think about a problem, plan etc. and consider it for a long time: *He's mulling over the job offer.*

mul·lah /'mʌlə/ *n.* [C] a Muslim teacher of law and religion

,mulled 'wine *n.* [U] wine that has been heated with sugar and SPICES

mul·let /'mʌlɪt/ *n.* [C] **1** a hairstyle for men in which the hair on the sides and top of the head is short and the hair on the back of the head is long **2** BIOLOGY a fairly small ocean fish that can be eaten

mul·li·gan stew /,mʌlɪgən 'stu/ *n.* [U] a type of STEW that is made of anything that you have in the house

mul·li·ga·taw·ny /,mʌlɪgə'tɔni, -'tɑni◂/ *n.* [U] a soup that tastes hot because it contains hot SPICES

multi- /mʌlti, -tɪ, -taɪ/ *prefix* more than one SYN **many**: *a multicolored bird* (=with many colors) | *a multiracial society* (=having people of many races)

mul·ti·cel·lu·lar /,mʌltɪ'sɛlyəlɚ/ *adj.* BIOLOGY having many cells: *Most animals and plants are multicellular.*

mul·ti·col·ored /'mʌltɪ,kʌlɚd/ *adj.* having many different colors: *a multicolored sweatshirt*

mul·ti·cul·tur·al /,mʌlti'kʌltʃərəl/ *adj.* involving people or ideas from many different countries, races, or religions: *The radio station serves a multicultural community.*

mul·ti·cul·tu·ral·is·m /,mʌlti'kʌltʃərə,lɪzəm/ *n.* [U] POLITICS the belief that it is important and good to include people or ideas from many different countries, races, or religions, and that the different races, religions, customs etc. within a country should all be respected —**multiculturalist** *n.* [C]

mul·ti·eth·nic /,mʌlti'ɛθnɪk/ *adj.* containing many different groups of people of different races, religions, customs etc.: *The U.S. is a multiethnic society.*

mul·ti·fac·et·ed /,mʌlti'fæsɪṭɪd/ *adj.* having many parts or sides: *The situation is complex and multifaceted.*

'multi-faith *adj.* [only before noun] including or involving people from several different religious groups: *a multi-faith service of thanksgiving*

mul·ti·fam·i·ly /,mʌlti'fæmli◂/ *adj.* multifamily housing is houses that have separate areas for more than one family: *large multifamily dwellings*

mul·ti·far·i·ous /,mʌltɪ'fɛriəs/ *adj.* of very many different kinds: *her multifarious business activities* —**multifariously** *adv.* —**multifariousness** *n.* [U]

mul·ti·lat·er·al /,mʌltɪ'læṭərəl/ *adj.* involving several different countries, companies etc.: *multilateral* *trade negotiations* —**multilaterally** *adv.* → see also BILATERAL, UNILATERAL

mul·ti·lin·gual /ˌmʌltɪˈlɪŋgwəl◂/ *adj.* ENG. LANG. ARTS **1** able to speak several different languages: *The hotel has a multilingual staff.* **2** written in several different languages: *a multilingual phrasebook* —**multilingualism** *n.* [U] → see also BILINGUAL, MONOLINGUAL

mul·ti·me·di·a /ˌmʌltɪˈmidiə, -ti-/ *adj.* [only before noun] **1** COMPUTERS relating to computers and computer programs that use a mixture of sound, pictures, VIDEO, and writing to give information **2** ENG. LANG. ARTS using several different methods of showing or advertising information, for example television, newspapers, books, and computers —**multimedia** *n.* [U]

mul·ti·mil·lion /ˌmʌltiˈmɪlyən◂/ *adj.* worth or costing many millions of dollars, pounds etc.: *a multimillion-dollar deal*

mul·ti·mil·lio·naire /ˌmʌltiˌmɪlyəˈnɛr, -ˈmɪlyəˌnɛr/ *n.* [C] an extremely rich person, who has many millions of dollars

mul·ti·na·tion·al[1] /ˌmʌltɪˈnæʃənl/ *adj.* **1** a multinational company has factories, offices, and business activities in many different countries: *a multinational manufacturer* ►see THESAURUS box at **company** **2** involving people from several different countries: *a multinational peacekeeping force* —**multinationally** *adv.*

multinational[2] *n.* [C] a large company that has offices, factories etc. in many different countries: *a huge multinational*

mul·ti·par·ty /ˈmʌltɪˌplaɪ/ *adj.* involving or including more than one political party: *the nation's first multi-party elections*

mul·ti·par·ty sys·tem /ˌmʌltipɑrt̬i ˈsɪstəm/ *n.* [C] POLITICS a political system in which three or more political parties compete against each other in elections → see also TWO-PARTY SYSTEM

mul·ti·ple[1] /ˈmʌltəpəl/ S3 *adj.* including or involving many parts, people, events etc.: *Nakamura received multiple job offers.* | *He suffered multiple stab wounds.* [**Origin:** 1600–1700 French, Latin *multiplex*]

multiple[2] *n.* [C] MATH a number that contains a smaller number an exact number of times: *20 is a multiple of 5.*

ˌmultiple ˈchoice *adj.* a multiple choice test or question shows several possible answers and you have to choose the correct one

ˌmultiple personˈality disˌorder *n.* [U] a PSYCHOLOGICAL condition in which a person has two or more completely separate personalities (PERSONALITY) and ways of behaving

multiple scle·ro·sis /ˌmʌltəpəl skləˈroʊsɪs/ ABBREVIATION **MS** *n.* [U] MEDICINE a serious illness that gradually destroys your nerves, making you weak and unable to walk

ˌmultiple tier ˈtimeline *n.* [C] TECHNICAL a TIMELINE (=a line showing the order in which events happened over a particular period of time) with two or more rows of events, each representing a different subject, activity etc.: *a multiple tier timeline of the 19th century, with separate rows for political, social, military, and technological developments*

mul·ti·plex /ˈmʌltɪˌplɛks/ *n.* [C] a building with several movie theaters in it —**multiplex** *adj.*: *a multiplex cinema*

mul·ti·plex·ing /ˈmʌltɪˌplɛksɪŋ/ *n.* [U] TECHNICAL a system used to send several electrical signals using only one connection, used especially with MODEMS —**multiplexer** *n.* [C] —**multiplex** *v.* [I,T]

mul·ti·pli·ca·tion /ˌmʌltəpləˈkeɪʃən/ *n.* [U] **1** MATH a method of calculating in which you add the same number to itself a particular number of times → see also DIVISION **2** a large increase in the size, amount, or number of something: *The drug slows the multiplication of cancer cells.*

ˌmultipliˈcation sign *n.* [C] MATH a sign (×) showing that one number is multiplied by another

ˌmultipliˈcation ˌtable *n.* [C usually plural] MATH a list showing the result of numbers between one and twelve that have been multiplied together, used by children in schools

mul·ti·pli·ca·tive in·verse /ˌmʌltəplɪˌkeɪt̬ɪv ˈɪnvɚs, ˌmʌltəplɪkət̬ɪv-/ *n.* [C] also **reciprocal** MATH a number that is related to another number because when they are multiplied together the product is 1. For example, the multiplicative inverse of 4 is ¼ or 0.25, because 0.25 × 4 = 1. → see also ADDITIVE INVERSE, NEGATIVE RECIPROCAL

mul·ti·plic·i·ty /ˌmʌltəˈplɪsət̬i/ *n.* [U] a large number or great variety of things: +**of** *a multiplicity of opinions*

ˈmultiplier efˌfect *n.* [singular] ECONOMICS an idea which says that every small increase in the money spent to improve a country's economic system will produce a bigger increase in economic activity and wealth

mul·ti·ply /ˈmʌltəˌplaɪ/ *v.* **multiplies, multiplied, multiplying** **1** [I,T] to increase greatly, or to make something increase greatly: *Environmental laws have multiplied.* | *Smoking multiplies your risk of getting cancer.* **2** [I,T] MATH to do a calculation in which you add a number to itself a particular number of times: **multiply sth by sth** *If you multiply 3 by 10, you get 30.* | *What is 25 multiplied by 5?* ►see THESAURUS box at **calculate** → see also DIVIDE **3** [I] to breed and increase in number quickly: *The germs multiply quickly in the heat.*

mul·ti·pur·pose /ˌmʌltɪˈpɚpəs◂, -ti-/ *adj.* having many different uses or purposes: *a multipurpose room*

mul·ti·ra·cial /ˌmʌltɪˈreɪʃəl◂, -ti-/ *adj.* including or involving many different races of people: *a multiracial society*

mul·ti·task·ing /ˈmʌltiˌtæskɪŋ/ *n.* [U] **1** COMPUTERS a computer's ability to do more than one job at a time **2** the practice of doing different types of work at your job at the same time

mul·ti·tude /ˈmʌltəˌtud/ *n.* [C] **1 a multitude of sth** a very large number of people or things: *The forest is home to a multitude of birds.* **2 the multitude(s)** LITERARY a very large number of ordinary people in a particular place or situation: *The news was greeted with cheers by the multitude outside.* **3 cover/hide a multitude of sins** HUMOROUS to make faults or problems seem less clear or noticeable: *Patterned carpet can hide a multitude of sins.*

mul·ti·tu·di·nous /ˌmʌltəˈtudn-əs◂/ *adj.* FORMAL very many

mul·ti·var·i·ate /ˌmʌltɪˈvɛriɪt/ *adj.* MATH having more than one VARIABLE (=mathematical quantity that is not fixed and can be any of several amounts): *a multivariate analysis of the survey data* → see also BIVARIATE, UNIVARIATE

mul·ti·vi·ta·min /ˈmʌltɪˌvaɪt̬əmɪn/ *n.* [C,U] a PILL or liquid containing many different VITAMINS

mum[1] /mʌm/ *n.* **1 mum's the word** used to tell someone that they must not tell other people about a secret **2** [C] BRITISH, CANADIAN a MOM

mum[2] *adj.* INFORMAL not telling anyone about a secret: *Hammer knew about the decision, but* ***kept mum****.*

mum·ble /ˈmʌmbəl/ *v.* [I,T] to say something too quietly and not clearly enough, so that other people cannot understand you: *Stop mumbling!* | *He mumbled something about being late.* ►see THESAURUS box at **say**[1] —**mumbler** *n.* [C] —**mumble** *n.* [C]

mum·bo-jum·bo /ˌmʌmboʊ ˈdʒʌmboʊ/ *n.* [U] something that is difficult to understand or that makes no sense: *legal mumbo-jumbo* [**Origin:** 1700–1800 *Mumbo Jumbo* name of a supposed African god]

mum·mi·fy /ˈmʌməˌfaɪ/ *v.* **mummifies, mummified, mummifying** [T] to preserve a dead body as a mummy —**mummified** /ˈmʌməˌfaɪd/ *adj.*: *a mummified body* —**mummification** /ˌmʌməfəˈkeɪʃən/ *n.* [U]

M

mum·my /ˈmʌmi/ *n. plural* **mummies** [C] a dead body that has been preserved and often wrapped in cloth, especially in ancient Egypt [**Origin:** 1600–1700 Old French *momie*, from Medieval Latin *mumia*, from Arabic *mumiyah*, from Persian *mum* **wax**]

mumps /mʌmps/ also **the mumps** *n.* [U] MEDICINE an infectious illness in which your throat swells and becomes painful [**Origin:** 1500–1600 *mump* **expression made by twisting the mouth** (16–17 centuries)]

munch /mʌntʃ/ *v.* [I,T] to eat something, especially in a way that makes a lot of noise: *The kids munched popcorn while they watched the movie.* | **+on** *He was munching on a sandwich.*

Munch /mʊŋk/**, Ed·vard** /ˈɛdvɑrd/ (1863–1944) a Norwegian painter

munch·ies /ˈmʌntʃiz/ *n.* [plural] INFORMAL **1** food such as cookies or POTATO CHIPS, especially eaten at a party: *There will be munchies and plenty to drink.* **2 have the munchies** to feel hungry and want to eat unhealthy food

munch·kin /ˈmʌntʃˌkɪn/ *n.* [C] INFORMAL someone who is small, especially a child

mun·dane /mʌnˈdeɪn/ *adj.* **1** ordinary and not interesting or exciting SYN **boring**: *mundane daily routines* **2** FORMAL relating to ordinary daily life rather than religious matters [**Origin:** 1400–1500 French *mondain*, from Latin *mundus* **world**] —**mundaneness** *n.* [U] —**mundanely** *adv.*

mung bean /ˈmʌŋ ˌbin/ *n.* [C] a small green bean, usually eaten as a BEAN SPROUT

Mu·nich /ˈmyunɪk/ the capital of the state of Bavaria in southern Germany

ˌMunich Aˈgreement, the HISTORY an agreement signed in 1938 between Germany, Italy, France, and the United Kingdom, which gave part of Czechoslovakia to Germany. The leaders of France and the United Kingdom hoped that this would stop Germany attacking other countries, but Germany attacked Poland in 1939 and World War II started as a result.

mu·nic·i·pal /myuˈnɪsəpəl/ *adj.* POLITICS relating to or belonging to the government of a town or city: *municipal elections* —**municipally** *adv.*

muˌnicipal ˈbond *n.* [C] ECONOMICS a BOND sold by a state or local government. The authorities do this as a way of borrowing money to build or make improvements to roads, schools, and other state buildings and property.

mu·nic·i·pal·i·ty /myuˌnɪsəˈpæləti/ *n. plural* **municipalities** [C] **1** POLITICS a town, city, or other small area, which has its own government that makes decisions about local affairs: *the municipality of Knoxville* **2** POLITICS the government of a town, city etc., which makes decisions about local affairs

mu·nif·i·cent /myuˈnɪfəsənt/ *adj.* FORMAL very generous: *a munificent gift* —**munificence** *n.* [U] —**munificently** *adv.*

mu·ni·tions /myuˈnɪʃənz/ *n.* [plural] military supplies such as bombs and large guns: *the manufacture of munitions* | *a munitions dump* (=a place where old military supplies are left)

mu·ral /ˈmyʊrəl/ also **ˌmural ˈpainting** *n.* [C] a painting that is painted on a wall, either inside or outside a building: *A mural was painted on the outside of the building.* → see also FRESCO —**muralist** *n.* [C]

mur·der¹ /ˈmɚdɚ/ W2 *n.* [C,U] **1** the crime of deliberately killing someone: *She was found guilty of murder.* | *a series of brutal murders* | *Curtis's husband has been charged with her murder.* | **+of** *the murder of an 80-year-old woman* | *The* ***murder was committed*** *some time between 12:00 and 3:00.* | *a murder trial* | *The murder weapon has not been found.* ►see THESAURUS box at **crime** → see also MANSLAUGHTER **2 get away with murder** INFORMAL to not be punished for doing something wrong, or to be allowed to do anything you want, even bad things: *She lets those kids get away with murder.* **3 be murder** SPOKEN to be very difficult or unpleasant: *Traffic was murder this morning.* **4 be murder on sb/sth** SPOKEN to be harmful, damaging, or painful to someone or something: *High heels might look good but they're murder on your feet.* **5 murder-for-hire** the crime of killing someone because you have been paid to do it [**Origin:** partly from Old English *morthor*, partly from Old French *murdre*]

murder² W3 *v.* [T] **1** to kill someone deliberately and illegally: *He was convicted of murdering his former boss.* | *the murdered man* ►see THESAURUS box at **kill¹** **2** INFORMAL to completely defeat someone in a game, match, competition etc.: *They murdered us in the finals.* **3** INFORMAL to spoil a song, play etc. completely by performing it very badly: *It's a good song, but they murdered it.* **4 sb will murder sb** SPOKEN, INFORMAL used to say that someone will be very angry with someone else: *Your dad'll murder you when he hears about it.*

mur·der·er /ˈmɚdərɚ/ *n.* [C] someone who murders another person: *a convicted murderer*

mur·der·ous /ˈmɚdərəs/ *adj.* **1** very dangerous or violent and likely to kill someone: *a murderous tyrant* | *a murderous attack* **2 a murderous glance/stare/expression** an expression that shows that someone is very angry —**murderously** *adv.* —**murderousness** *n.* [U]

murk /mɚk/ *n.* [U] LITERARY darkness caused by smoke, dirt, or clouds

murk·y /ˈmɚki/ *adj. comparative* **murkier**, *superlative* **murkiest** **1** dark and difficult to see through: *murky water* **2** complicated and difficult to understand: *The committee is still working on a number of murky issues.* **3** involving dishonest or illegal activities that are kept secret: *the murky world of drug smuggling* —**murkily** *adv.* —**murkiness** *n.* [U]

mur·mur¹ /ˈmɚmɚ/ *v.* **1** [I,T] to say something in a soft quiet voice that is difficult to hear clearly: *I murmured a prayer of thanks.* ►see THESAURUS box at **say¹** **2** [I] to make a soft low sound: *The wind murmured through the trees.* **3** [I] to complain to friends and people you work with, but not officially: *He didn't murmur a single word of protest.* —**murmuring** *n.* [C,U]

murmur² *n.* [C] **1** a soft low sound made by people speaking quietly or from a long way away: *The man spoke in a low murmur.* | **+of** *a murmur of voices down the hallway* | **a murmur of agreement/surprise/disapproval etc.** *There was a murmur of agreement from the crowd.* **2** a complaint, but not a strong or official complaint: **+of** *There have been murmurs of discontent over the new rules.* **3** [singular] the soft low sound made by a stream, the wind etc.: *the murmur of the little brook* **4** [usually singular] an unusual sound made by the heart that shows there may be something wrong with it: *a heart murmur* **5** something that is talked about but is not official: **+of/about** *There have been murmurs of an international boycott.* **6 do sth without a murmur** to do something without complaining, especially when this is surprising: *Students paid their tuition fees* ***without a murmur***, *despite the raise.*

Mur·phy bed /ˈmɚfi ˌbɛd/ *n.* [C] a type of bed that can be stored upright in a large cupboard when it is not being used

Mur·phy's law /ˌmɚfiz ˈlɔ/ *n.* [singular] HUMOROUS an informal rule that says that anything bad that can happen will happen [**Origin:** 1900–2000 Edward *Murphy* (born 1917), U.S. engineer who first thought of it]

Mur·row /ˈmɚoʊ, ˈmʌroʊ/**, Ed·ward R.** /ˈɛdwɚd ɑr/ (1908–1965) a U.S. television news reporter known for dealing with political subjects

Mus·cat /ˈmʌskæt/ the capital and largest city of Oman

mus·ca·tel /ˌmʌskəˈtɛl◂/ *n.* [C,U] a sweet light-colored wine, or the type of GRAPE that is used to make it

M

mus·cle[1] /ˈmʌsəl/ S2 W3 *n.* **1** [C,U] BIOLOGY one of the pieces of flesh inside your body that join bones together and make your body move: *Regular exercise will help to strengthen your muscles.* | *Muscle weighs more than fat.* | **arm/chest/stomach etc. muscles** *My leg muscles hurt the next day.* | *Weight lifting will improve your* ***muscle tone*** (=will make you stronger). | *I think I just* ***pulled a muscle*** (=injured a muscle). | *muscle tissue* **2** [U] military, political, or financial power or influence: **military/financial/political muscle** *The unions have a lot of political muscle.* | *The large stores are* ***using*** *their* ***muscle*** *to get their share of the market.* **3** [U] physical strength and power: *It* ***takes some muscle*** *to paddle a canoe.* **4** [U] SLANG strong men who are paid to protect or attack someone, especially by criminals [**Origin:** 1300–1400 French, Latin *musculus* **little mouse, muscle, mussel**, from *mus* **mouse**; because a muscle moving looks like a mouse under the skin] → see also **flex your muscles** at FLEX (2), **not move a muscle** at MOVE[1] (18)

muscle[2] *v.* [I,T] to use your strength to go somewhere: *Two police officers* ***muscled*** *their* ***way*** *through the crowd.*

muscle in *phr. v.* DISAPPROVING to use your strength or power to control or influence someone else's business: +**on** *A rival company was trying to muscle in on his business.*

mus·cle·bound /ˈmʌsəlˌbaʊnd/ *adj.* having large stiff muscles because of too much physical exercise: *musclebound weightlifters*

mus·cle·man /ˈmʌsəlˌmæn/ *n. plural* **musclemen** /-ˌmɛn/ [C] **1** a man who has developed big strong muscles by doing exercises **2** a strong man who is employed to protect someone, usually a criminal

Mus·co·vite /ˈmʌskəˌvaɪt/ *n.* [C] someone from Moscow, Russia

mus·cu·lar /ˈmʌskyələ˞/ *adj.* **1** having a lot of big muscles: *a tall muscular man* | *She's gotten really muscular.* **2** BIOLOGY relating to or affecting the muscles: *muscular pain* —**muscularly** *adv.* —**muscularity** /ˌmʌskyəˈlærət̬i/ *n.* [U]

muscular dys·tro·phy /ˌmʌskyələ˞ ˈdɪstrəfi/ *n.* [U] MEDICINE a serious illness in which the muscles become weaker over a period of time

muse[1] /myuz/ *v.* **1** [I] to think carefully about something for a long time: +**on/about/over** *He mused on how different his life might have been.* **2** [T] to say something in a way that shows you are thinking about it carefully: *"I wonder why she was killed," mused Poirot.* —**musingly** *adv.*

muse[2] *n.* [C] **1** ENG. LANG. ARTS an artist's, musician's etc. muse is the force or person that makes them want to write, paint, or make music, and helps them to have good ideas: *Rossetti's wife and creative muse* **2 the Muses** a group of ancient Greek GODDESSES, each of whom represented a particular art or a science

mu·se·um /myuˈziəm/ S2 W2 *n.* [C] a building where important CULTURAL, historical, or scientific objects are kept and shown to the public: *the Museum of Natural History* | **a science/natural history/folk etc. museum** *There's a good art museum downtown.* [**Origin:** 1600–1700 Latin, Greek *Mouseion*, from *Mousa*]

mu'seum ˌpiece *n.* [C] **1** a very old-fashioned piece of equipment or person: *The car she drives is a museum piece.* **2** an object that is so valuable or interesting that it should be in a museum: *These chairs were built to be used, not to be museum pieces.*

mush[1] /mʌʃ/ *n.* **1** [singular, U] a disgusting soft mass of a substance, especially food, which is partly liquid and partly solid: *Cook the squash until it's soft, but not mush.* | *The parking lot had* ***turned to mush*** *in the rain.* **2 turn/go to mush** if your brain turns to mush, you cannot think clearly or sensibly: *If you watch too much TV, your brains will turn to mush.* **3** [U] a thick soft food made from CORNMEAL (=a powder-like substance made from crushed corn) SYN **porridge** **4** [U] a book, movie etc. that contains too many silly expressions of love

mush[2] *v.* **1** also **mush sth ↔ up** *phr. v.* [T] to crush something, especially food, so that it becomes a soft wet mass: *He won't eat his food unless I mush it all up first.* **2** [I,T] to travel over snow in a SLED that is pulled by a team of dogs, or to drive a sled like this

mush[3] *interjection* used to tell a team of dogs that pull a SLED over snow to start moving

mush·er /ˈmʌʃə˞/ *n.* [C] someone who drives a SLED over snow, controlling the dogs that pull it

mush·room[1] /ˈmʌʃrum/ S3 *n.* [C] **1** one of several kinds of FUNGUS with stems and round tops, some of which can be eaten and some of which are poisonous: *wild mushrooms* | *mushroom soup* **2** also **magic mushroom** [usually plural] a type of mushroom that has an effect like some drugs, and makes you see things that are not really there [**Origin:** 1400–1500 French *mousseron*, from Latin *mussirio*] → see also TOADSTOOL

mushroom[2] *v.* [I] **1** to grow and develop very quickly: *New housing developments mushroomed on the edge of town.* **2** [+ adv./prep.] to spread up into the air in the shape of a mushroom

ˈmushroom ˌcloud *n.* [C usually singular] a large cloud shaped like a mushroom, which is caused by a NUCLEAR explosion

mush·y /ˈmʌʃi/ *adj. comparative* **mushier**, *superlative* **mushiest** **1** soft and wet, and feeling disgusting: *a mushy banana* ▸see THESAURUS box at **soft** **2** expressing love in a silly way: *Dave gets all mushy when he's around Gina.* —**mushiness** *n.* [U]

Mu·si·al /ˈmyuziəl/**, Stan** /stæn/ (1920–) a baseball player known for his skill at hitting the ball

mu·sic /ˈmyuzɪk/ S1 W1 *n.* [U] **1** ENG. LANG. ARTS the arrangement of sounds made by instruments or voices in a way that is pleasant or exciting: *Let's listen to some music on the radio.* | *What kind of music does your band play?* | *a wonderful* ***piece of music*** *by Handel* | *Chuck* ***wrote the music*** *for the song.* | **classical/pop/country/folk etc. music** *Do you like pop music?* | **set/put sth to music** (=to write music so that the words of a poem, play etc. can be sung)

THESAURUS

tune a series of musical notes that are nice to listen to: *Suzy was humming a tune.*
melody a song or tune: *a lovely melody*
song a short piece of music with words: *pop songs*
arrangement a piece of music that has been written or changed for a particular instrument: *a jazz arrangement of "My Favorite Things"*
composition a piece of music or art, or a poem: *one of Schubert's early compositions*
number a piece of popular music, a song, a dance etc. that forms part of a larger performance: *Each band performed a couple of numbers.*
piece a piece of music: *This is a piece I'm learning for my piano recital.*
track one of the songs or pieces of music on a CD: *The first track is my favorite.*

2 ENG. LANG. ARTS the art of writing or playing music: *My daughter teaches music.* | *Lincoln High has a good music program.* **3** ENG. LANG. ARTS a set of written marks representing music, or paper with the written marks on it: *He arranged his music on the stand.* | *McCartney never learned to* ***read music***. → see also SHEET MUSIC **4 be music to sb's ears** if someone's words are music to your ears, they make you very happy or pleased: *His offer was music to our ears.* [**Origin:** 1200–1300 Old French *musique*, from Latin, from Greek *mousike* **art of the Muses**] → see also **face the music** at FACE[2] (7)

musical notations

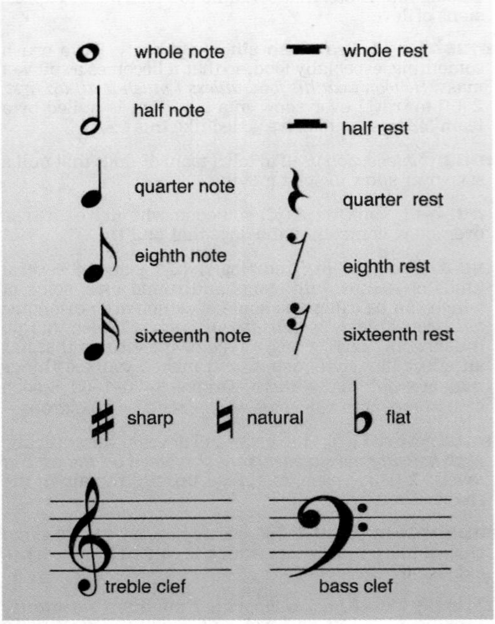

mu·si·cal[1] /ˈmyuzɪkəl/ *adj.* **1** [only before noun] ENG. LANG. ARTS relating to music, or consisting of music: *amazing musical ability* | *Her musical tastes have changed considerably.* **2** good at or interested in playing or singing music: *Amanda is very musical and loves to sing.* **3** APPROVING having a pleasant sound like music: *a musical voice* → see also MUSICALLY

musical[2] *n.* [C] a play or movie that uses singing and dancing to tell a story: *a Broadway musical* (=one that has been performed on Broadway, a famous street in New York) ►see THESAURUS box at **theater**

ˌmusical ˈchairs *n.* [U] **1** a children's game in which all the players must sit down when the music stops, but there is always one chair less than the number of people playing **2** a situation in which people change positions, jobs etc., for no good reason or with no useful result

ˌmusical ˈinstrument *n.* [C] something that you use for playing music, such as a piano or GUITAR

mu·si·cal·ly /ˈmyuzɪkli/ *adv.* **1** ENG. LANG. ARTS in a way that is related to music: *musically gifted students* **2** in a way that sounds like music: *The birds twittered musically outside.*

ˈmusic ˌbox *n.* [C] a box that plays a musical tune when you open it

mu·si·cian /myuˈzɪʃən/ *n.* [C] someone who plays a musical instrument, especially very well or as a job: *a talented young musician*

mu·si·cian·ship /myuˈzɪʃənʃɪp/ *n.* [U] skill in playing music

mu·si·col·o·gy /ˌmyuzɪˈkɑlədʒi/ *n.* [U] the study of music, especially the history of different types of music —**musicologist** *n.* [C] —**musicological** /ˌmyuzɪkəˈlɑdʒɪkəl/ *adj.*

ˈmusic stand *n.* [C] a metal or wooden object used for holding written music, so that you can read it while playing an instrument or singing

ˌMusic ˈTelevision → see MTV

ˈmusic ˌvideo *n.* [C] a VIDEO

musk /mʌsk/ *n.* [U] **1** a strong-smelling substance used to make PERFUME **2** a strong smell, especially the way a person smells

mus·ket /ˈmʌskɪt/ *n.* [C] a type of gun used in the past

mus·ket·eer /ˌmʌskəˈtɪr/ *n.* [C] a soldier in the past who used a musket

musk·mel·on /ˈmʌskˌmɛlən/ *n.* [C] a type of sweet MELON with orange-colored flesh inside SYN **cantaloupe**

ˈmusk ox *n. plural* **musk oxen** [C] a large animal with long brown or black hair and curved horns, that lives in northern Canada and Greenland

musk·rat /ˈmʌskræt/ *n.* [C] an animal that lives in water in North America and is hunted for its fur

musk·y /ˈmʌski/ *adj.* like MUSK: *a musky scent* —**muskiness** *n.* [U]

Mus·lim /ˈmʌzləm, ˈmʊz-, ˈmʊs-/ *n.* [C] someone whose religion is Islam [**Origin:** 1600–1700 an Arabic word meaning **someone who surrenders (to God)**] —**Muslim** *adj.*

ˌMuslim ˈLeague, the HISTORY a Muslim political organization in India that helped form Pakistan from India

mus·lin /ˈmʌzlən/ *n.* [U] a type of strong cotton cloth used for making clothing, bed sheets, and curtains

muss[1] /mʌs/ *v.* [T] INFORMAL also **muss ↔ sth up** *phr. v.* to make something messy, especially someone's hair: *A warm breeze mussed up her wispy hair.*

muss[2] *n.* **no muss, no fuss** also **no fuss, no muss** HUMOROUS used to say that something is done easily and without problems: *It works every time, no muss, no fuss.*

mus·sel /ˈmʌsəl/ *n.* [C] a small sea animal, with a soft body that can be eaten and a black shell that is divided into two parts → see picture at SEAFOOD

Mus·so·li·ni /ˌmusəˈlini/, **Be·ni·to** /bɛˈnitoʊ/ (1883–1945) an Italian leader who established the system of FASCISM and ruled Italy as a DICTATOR from 1925–1943

Mus·sorg·sky /məˈzɔrgski/, **Mo·dest** /moʊˈdɛst/ (1839–1881) a Russian musician who wrote CLASSICAL music

must[1] /məst; *strong* mʌst/ S1 W1 *modal verb negative short form* **mustn't** **1** used to say that something is necessary because the situation forces you to do it, because of a rule or law, or because you feel that you should do it → see also HAVE TO: *All passengers must wear seat belts.* | *We must make every effort towards peace.* | *Production costs must not exceed $400,000.* | *The book* ***must not*** *be removed from the library* (=it definitely should not be done). **2** used in order to say that something is very likely to be true or have happened: *Elsa must be furious with her.* | *This stereo must have cost a lot of money.* | *He must not want the job, or he'd be here.* | *Cox must have forgotten all about our appointment.* **3** SPOKEN, FORMAL used to suggest that someone do something, especially because you think they will enjoy it very much or you think it is a very good idea: *You must come and visit us in Houston.* **4 I must say/admit/confess (that)** SPOKEN used to emphasize that the statement you are making is an honest one: *I must admit I don't really like his music.* **5 it must be remembered/noted (that)** WRITTEN used to emphasize a particular piece of information: *It must be remembered that there were no computers at that time.* **6 I must do sth** used when you want to do something and hope to do it soon: *I must stop by sometime and thank her for all her help.* **7 if you must (do sth)** used to tell someone that they are allowed to do something, but that you do not approve or agree with it: *All right, come with us, if you must.* | *"Who was that girl?" "Well,* ***if you must know****, her name is Mabel."* [**Origin:** Old English *moste*, from *motan* **to be allowed to, have to**]

must[2] /mʌst/ *n.* **1** [C usually singular] something that you must do or must have: *Goggles are a must for skiing while it's snowing.* **2** [U] TECHNICAL the liquid made by crushing GRAPES from which wine is made

mus·tache, moustache /ˈmʌstæʃ, məˈstæʃ/ *n.* [C] hair that grows on a man's upper lip [**Origin:** 1500–1600 French *moustache*, from Italian *mustaccio*, from Medieval Greek *moustaki*]

mus•ta•chioed, **moustachioed** /mə'stæʃi,oʊd/ *adj.* HUMOROUS having a MUSTACHE

mus•tang /'mʌstæŋ/ *n.* [C] a small wild horse

mus•tard /'mʌstəd/ S3 *n.* [U] **1** a yellow SAUCE with a strong taste, eaten especially with meat **2** BIOLOGY a plant with yellow flowers whose seeds can be used to make the powder used to make mustard SAUCE **3 not cut the mustard** to not be good enough for a particular job: *If he can't cut the mustard, he should resign.* **4** a yellow-brown color [**Origin:** 1100–1200 Old French *moustarde*, from *moust* **new wine**, from Latin *mustum*]

'mustard gas *n.* [U] a poisonous gas that burns the skin, which was used during World War I

mus•ter¹ /'mʌstə/ *v.* **1 muster (up) courage/support/energy etc.** to find as much courage, support etc. as you can in order to do something difficult: *Finally I mustered up the courage to ask her out.* **2** [T] to work to get the support that you need for something: *The senator has been trying to **muster support** for his proposals.* **3** [I,T] to gather a group of people, especially soldiers, together in one place, or to come together as a group: *The captain mustered the crew on deck.*

muster² *n.* [C] LITERARY a group of people, especially soldiers, that have been gathered together → see also **pass muster** at PASS¹ (25)

must•n't /'mʌsənt/ *v.* the short form of "must not": *You mustn't touch the paintings.*

,must-'see *n.* [C] INFORMAL something that is so exciting, interesting etc. that you think people should see it or visit: *His latest movie is a real must-see.* —**must-see** *adj.* [only before noun] *must-see television*

must•y /'mʌsti/ *adj.* a musty room, house, or object has a bad wet smell, because it is old and has not had any fresh air for a long time: *a musty motel room* —**mustiness** *n.* [U]

mu•ta•ble /'myuṭəbəl/ *adj.* FORMAL able or likely to change OPP **immutable** —**mutability** /,myuṭə'bɪləṭi/ *n.* [U]

mu•ta•gen /'myuṭədʒən/ *n.* [C] TECHNICAL a substance that causes a living thing to MUTATE

mu•tant /'myut˺nt/ *n.* [C] an animal or plant that is different in some way from others of the same type, because of a change in its GENETIC structure —**mutant** *adj.*

mu•tate /'myuteɪt/ *v.* **1** [I,T] BIOLOGY if a plant or animal mutates or something mutates it, it develops a feature that makes it different from other plants or animals of the same kind, because of a change in its GENETIC structure: *Bacteria mutate rapidly.* **2** [I] to change and develop a new form: **mutate into sth** *His interest has mutated into an obsession.*

mu•ta•tion /myu'teɪʃən/ *n.* [C,U] **1** BIOLOGY a change in the GENETIC structure of an animal or plant that makes it different from others of the same type **2** TECHNICAL a change in a speech sound, especially a vowel, because of the sound of the one next to it

mute¹ /myut/ *adj.* **1** not speaking, or refusing to speak: *The kid stared at me in a state of mute fear.* **2** OLD-FASHIONED unable to speak **3** ENG. LANG. ARTS not pronounced SYN **silent**: *a mute "e"* —**mutely** *adv.* —**muteness** *n.* [U]

mute² *v.* [T] **1** to reduce the level or degree of a feeling or activity: *The senator's remarks have muted public criticism.* **2** to make a sound quieter, or make it disappear completely: *I usually mute the TV during the commercials.* **3** ENG. LANG. ARTS to make a musical instrument sound softer

mute³ *n.* [C] **1** ENG. LANG. ARTS something that is placed over or into a musical instrument to make it sound softer **2** OLD-FASHIONED someone who cannot speak → see also DEAF-MUTE

mut•ed /'myuṭɪd/ *adj.* **1 muted criticism/support/response etc.** criticism, support etc. that is not expressed strongly: *The atmosphere was one of muted optimism.* **2** quieter than usual: *He was awakened by a muted buzzer.* **3** a muted color is soft and gentle, not bright: *muted blues and purples*

mu•ti•late /'myuṭl,eɪt/ *v.* [T often passive] **1** to severely and violently damage someone's body, especially by removing part of it: *Police discovered her mutilated body.* **2** to damage or change something so much that it is completely spoiled or ruined —**mutilation** /,myuṭl'eɪʃən/ *n.* [C,U]

mu•ti•neer /,myut˺n'ɪr/ *n.* [C] someone who is involved in a MUTINY

mu•ti•nous /'myut˺n-əs/ *adj.* **1** behaving in a way that shows you do not want to obey someone SYN **rebellious**: *There was a mutinous look in Rosie's eyes.* **2** involved in a mutiny: *mutinous soldiers* —**mutinously** *adv.*

mu•ti•ny /'myut˺n-i/ *n.* *plural* **mutinies** [C,U] a situation in which people, especially SAILORS or soldiers, refuse to obey the person who is in charge of them, and try to take control for themselves: *Captain Feener suspected the crew was planning a mutiny.* —**mutiny** *v.* [I]

mutt /mʌt/ *n.* [C] INFORMAL a dog that does not belong to any particular breed

mut•ter /'mʌṭə/ *v.* **1** [I,T] to speak quietly or in a low voice, usually because you are annoyed about something, or because you do not want people to hear you: *Karen muttered something I couldn't hear.* | **+about** *What are you two muttering about?* | *"I shouldn't have come," she **muttered under** her **breath**.* ►see THESAURUS box at **say¹** **2** [I] to complain about something or express doubts about it, but without saying clearly and openly what you think: **+about** *Some residents are muttering about the design of the building.* —**mutter** *n.* [C] —**mutterer** *n.* [C] —**muttering** *n.* [C,U]

mut•ton /'mʌt˺n/ *n.* [U] the meat from an adult sheep [**Origin:** 1200–1300 Old French *moton* **(male) sheep**] → see also LAMB

'mutton ,chop *n.* [C] **1** a piece of meat containing a bone, that has been cut from the RIBS of a sheep **2 mutton chops** also **mutton-chop sideburns** hair that grows only on the sides of a man's cheeks, not on his chin, in a style that was popular in the 19th century and again in the 1970s

mu•tu•al /'myutʃuəl/ Ac W3 *adj.* [usually before noun] **1** mutual feelings or support are felt by two or more people toward one another or given to one another: *The group meets once a week for friendship and mutual support.* | **mutual respect/trust/understanding etc.** *We have mutual respect for each other's work.* → see also RECIPROCAL **2** a mutual agreement, decision etc. is one that is made by all the people involved in the situation: *It was a mutual decision.* | **by mutual agreement/consent** *The contract was ended by mutual consent.* **3** shared by two or more people: *They met years ago through a **mutual friend*** (=someone they both know). **4 a mutual admiration society** HUMOROUS a situation in which two people praise each other a lot [**Origin:** 1400–1500 French *mutuel*, from Latin *mutuus* **lent, borrowed, mutual**] —**mutuality** /,myutʃu'æləṭi/ *n.* [U] → see also **the feeling is mutual** at FEELING¹ (9), MUTUALLY

,mutual 'aid so,ciety *n.* [C] a group of people, especially people with health problems or other problems, who provide help and support for each other

'mutual fund *n.* [C] ECONOMICS an arrangement with a company that is experienced in buying and selling STOCK, through which the general public can buy stock in many different businesses

mu•tu•al•ly /'myutʃuəli, -tʃəli/ Ac *adv.* **1** done or experienced equally by two people: *a mutually agreed upon price* | *a mutually beneficial business arrangement* **2 mutually exclusive/contradictory/incompatible** two ideas or beliefs that are mutually exclusive cannot both exist or be true at the same time: *Being a mother and having a career are not mutually exclusive.*

,mutually ex,clusive e'vents *n.* [plural] MATH two things that cannot happen together at the same time. For example, a ball cannot be both in the air and on the ground at the same time, nor can someone be both 25 and 26 years old. → see also DEPENDENT EVENTS

M

muu-muu /ˈmu mu/ *n.* [C] a long loose dress, originally from Hawaii

Mu·zak /ˈmyuzæk/ *n.* [U] TRADEMARK recorded music that is played continuously in airports, stores, hotels etc.

muz·zle¹ /ˈmʌzəl/ *n.* [C] **1** BIOLOGY the nose and mouth of an animal such as a dog or horse **2** something that you put over a dog's mouth to stop it from biting people **3** the end of the BARREL of a gun

muzzle² *v.* [T] **1** to put a muzzle over a dog's mouth so that it cannot bite people **2** to prevent someone from speaking freely or expressing their opinions: *Frequently, employees are muzzled or fired.*

MVP *n.* [C] **most valuable player** the player on a sports team who is chosen to receive an honor because they did the most to help the team win games

my¹ /maɪ/ S1 W1 *possessive adj.* [possessive form of "I"] **1** relating to or belonging to the person who is speaking: *Those are my keys.* | *You're hurting my arm.* | *Even **my own** family didn't believe me.* | *I'd like an apartment **of my own**.* | *I prefer living **on my own*** (=alone or without help). **2** used when you are shocked or angry about something: *Oh **my goodness**! What happened to your face?* **3** used when talking to or about someone who you love or like a lot: *All right, my dear, I'll see you tomorrow.*

my² *interjection* used when you are surprised about something: *My! You've certainly grown!* | ***Oh my**! What a mess!*

Myan·mar /ˈmyɑnmɑr/ a country in southeast Asia, to the east of India and Bangladesh, and to the west of China and Thailand. It was called Burma until 1989.

my·e·lin sheath /ˌmaɪəlɪn ˈʃiθ/ *n.* [C] BIOLOGY in a nerve cell, a MEMBRANE (=material like a very thin piece of skin) that covers and protects the AXON (=part that carries messages to muscles and other parts of the body)

My·lar /ˈmaɪlɑr/ *n.* [U] TRADEMARK a thin strong shiny plastic-like material, used to cover windows, and many other things

my·nah bird /ˈmaɪnə ˌbɚd/ also **mynah** *n.* [C] BIOLOGY a large dark Asian bird that can copy human speech

my·o·car·di·al in·farc·tion /maɪoʊˌkɑrdiəl ɪnˈfɑrkʃən/ *n.* [C] MEDICINE a HEART ATTACK

my·o·car·di·um /ˌmaɪoʊˈkɑrdiəm/ *n. plural* **myocardia** /-diə/ [C usually singular, U] BIOLOGY the layer of muscle in the heart wall: *thinning of the myocardium* | *Diabetic patients may have a damaged myocardium.*

my·o·pi·a /maɪˈoʊpiə/ *n.* [U] **1** the lack of ability to imagine what the results of your actions will be or how they will affect other people SYN **shortsightedness** **2** MEDICINE the lack of ability to see things clearly that are far away SYN **nearsightedness**

my·op·ic /maɪˈɑpɪk, -ˈoʊ-/ *adj.* **1** unwilling or unable to think about the future results of your actions SYN **shortsighted**: *the government's myopic attitude to environmental issues* **2** MEDICINE unable to see things clearly that are far away SYN **nearsighted** —**myopically** /-kli/ *adv.*

my·o·sin /ˈmaɪəsɪn/ *n.* [U] BIOLOGY a PROTEIN in muscle cells, which makes the muscle become tighter or relaxed

myr·i·ad¹ /ˈmɪriəd/ *adj.* [only before noun] LITERARY very many SYN **countless**: *the myriad causes of homelessness*

myriad² *n.* **a myriad of sth** LITERARY a very large number of things: *There are a myriad of ways we can save money.*

myrrh /mɚ/ *n.* [U] a sticky brown substance that is used for making PERFUME and INCENSE

myr·tle /ˈmɚtl/ *n.* [C] a small tree with shiny green leaves and sweet-smelling white flowers

my·self /maɪˈsɛlf/ S1 W1 *pron.* **1** [reflexive form of "me"] used to show that the person speaking is affected by his or her own action: *I looked at myself in the mirror.* | *I might make myself a sandwich.* | *Oh, I hurt myself.* **2** the strong form of "me," used to emphasize the subject or object of a sentence: *I myself would not recommend that restaurant.* | *I'll be attending the meeting myself.* | *I'm not a very musical person myself.* **3** NONSTANDARD used sometimes instead of "me" to sound polite, but many teachers think this is incorrect: *Our party included Ann, Barbara, and myself.* **4 (all) by myself a)** alone: *I live by myself.* **b)** without help from anyone else: *I ate a whole gallon of ice cream by myself.* **5 have sth (all) to myself** to not have to share something with anyone: *I had a whole lane in the swimming pool to myself.* **6 not feel/look/seem like myself** to not feel or behave in the way you usually do because you are nervous, upset, or sick: *I finally started to feel like myself again last night.* → see also YOURSELF

mys·te·ri·ous /mɪˈstɪriəs/ *adj.* **1** mysterious events, behavior, or situations are difficult to explain or understand: *There's something mysterious going on.* | *a woman with a mysterious past* | *Five of his cows died under **mysterious circumstances**.* ►see THESAURUS box at **strange¹** **2** a mysterious person is someone who you know very little about and who seems strange or interesting: *a mysterious stranger* **3** saying very little about what you are doing SYN **secretive**: *a mysterious smile* | +**about** *Helen's being very mysterious about her plans.* **4 God works/moves in mysterious ways** also **the Lord works/moves in mysterious ways** used to say that humans cannot understand why God does things —**mysteriously** *adv.* —**mysteriousness** *n.* [U]

mys·ter·y¹ /ˈmɪstəri/ W3 *n. plural* **mysteries** **1** [C] something that is not understood or cannot be explained, or about which little is known: *"Why did he do it?" "I don't know. It's a complete mystery."* | *The police never **solved the mystery** of Gray's disappearance.* | *Twenty years later, the cause of his death **remains a mystery**.* | *How he got the job is **one of life's little mysteries**.* **2** [C] a story, movie, or play in which crimes or strange events are only explained at the end: *a murder mystery* | **a mystery story/movie/novel etc.** *She writes mainly mystery novels.* **3** [U] a quality that makes someone or something seem strange, secret, or difficult to explain: *Her dark glasses gave her **an air of mystery**.* | *Even the origin of the name is **shrouded in mystery**.* **4 it's a mystery to me** SPOKEN used to say that you cannot understand something at all: *It's a mystery to me how you keep score in this game.* **5** [C] FORMAL a quality that something has that cannot be explained in any practical or scientific way, especially because it is related to God and religion: +**of** *the mystery of Creation* **6** [C usually plural] information about a subject, activity etc. that is very complicated, secret, or difficult to understand, and that people want to learn about: *his introduction to **the mysteries of** the perfume business* [**Origin:** 1300–1400 Latin *mysterium*, from Greek, from *mystos* **keeping silent**]

mystery² *adj.* [only before noun] used to describe someone or something that people do not recognize or know anything about, especially when this causes great interest: *The mystery disease has so far killed 60 people.* | *We have **a mystery guest** on this week's show.* | **a mystery man/woman** *Who was the mystery man I saw you with?*

ˈmystery play *n.* [C] a religious play from the Middle Ages based on a story from the Bible

mys·tic /ˈmɪstɪk/ *n.* [C] someone who practices MYSTICISM

mys·ti·cal /ˈmɪstɪkəl/ also **mystic** *adj.* **1** involving religious or magical powers that people cannot understand: *a powerful mystical experience* **2** relating to mysticism: *the mystical traditions of different faiths* —**mystically** /-kli/ *adv.*

mys·ti·cism /ˈmɪstəˌsɪzəm/ *n.* [U] a religious practice in which people try to get knowledge of truth and to become united with God through prayer and MEDITATION

mys·ti·fy /ˈmɪstəˌfaɪ/ *v.* **mystifies, mystified, mystifying** [T] if something mystifies you, it is so strange or

M

confusing that you cannot understand or explain it SYN **baffle**: *Her disappearance has mystified her friends and neighbors.* —**mystifying** *adj.* —**mystification** /ˌmɪstəfəˈkeɪʃən/ *n.* [U]

mys·tique /mɪˈstik/ *n.* [singular, U] a quality that makes someone or something seem different, mysterious, or special: *Her Parisian fashions gave her a certain mystique.*

myth /mɪθ/ W3 *n.* [C,U] **1** an idea or story that many people believe, but which is not true: *Is global warming just a myth?* | +**of** *the myth of male superiority* | ***It's a myth that** good wines have to be expensive.* | **dispel/debunk/explode a myth** (=prove that a myth is not true) **2** an ancient story, especially one invented in order to explain natural or historical events, or this type of story in general: *the Greek myths* | *Opera combines myth, music, and drama.* [**Origin:** 1800–1900 Greek *mythos* **story, speech, myth**] ►see THESAURUS box at **story**

myth·ic /ˈmɪθɪk/ *adj.* **1** relating to or existing only in ancient myths: *mythic creatures* **2** very great or famous, especially in a way that seems unreal: *a mythic figure of the investment world* **3 of mythic proportions** very great in size or importance: *a feat of mythic proportions*

myth·i·cal /ˈmɪθɪkəl/ *adj.* **1** relating to or only existing in an ancient story: *the mythical hero Hercules* **2** imagined or invented: *They forged checks from their mythical client.*

my·thol·o·gy /mɪˈθɑlədʒi/ *n. plural* **mythologies** [C,U] **1** ancient myths in general, and the beliefs they represent: *Roman mythology* **2** ideas or opinions that many people believe, but that are wrong or not true: *According to popular mythology, school days are the best days of your life.* —**mythologist** *n.* [C] —**mythological** /ˌmɪθəˈlɑdʒɪkəl/ *adj.*

N,n

N

N, n /ɛn/ *n. plural* **N's, n's** [C] **a)** the 14th letter of the English alphabet **b)** the sound represented by this letter

N. the written abbreviation of NORTH or NORTHERN

n. the written abbreviation of NOUN

'n' /n, ən/ INFORMAL a short form of "and": *rock 'n' roll*

N/A **1 not applicable** written on a form to show that you do not need to answer a question **2 not available** used on order forms, in CATALOGS etc. to say that a particular type of product is not available

NAACP *n.* **the NAACP the National Association for the Advancement of Colored People** an organization that works for the rights of African-American people

nab /næb/ *v.* **nabbed, nabbing** [T] INFORMAL **1** to catch someone who has done or is doing something illegal or wrong: **nab sb for (doing) sth** *The police nabbed him for speeding.* **2** to take someone or something quickly: *She nabbed the last cookie from the jar.*

na·bob /ˈneɪbɑb/ *n.* [C] a rich, important, or powerful person

Na·bo·kov /nəˈbɔkɔf, -kəf/, **Vlad·i·mir** /ˈvlædɪmɪr/ (1899–1977) a U.S. writer of NOVELS, who was born in Russia

na·cho /ˈnɑtʃoʊ/ *n. plural* **nachos** [C usually plural] a small piece of TORTILLA usually covered with cheese, CHILIS etc.

ˈnacho ˌcheese *n.* [U] a type of cheese with SPICES and CHILIS added

Na·der /ˈneɪdɚ/, **Ralph** /rælf/ (1934–) a U.S. lawyer known for criticizing the government and big companies, and who has run for President

na·dir /ˈneɪdɚ/ *n.* [singular] LITERARY the time when a situation is at its worst, or when something is at its lowest level OPP **zenith**: *The personal savings rate* ***reached a nadir*** *of less than three percent.*

NAFTA /ˈnæftə/ **North American Free Trade Agreement** an agreement between the U.S., Canada, and Mexico to remove restrictions and taxes on trade between them

nag¹ /næg/ *v.* **nagged, nagging** [I,T] **1** to keep complaining to someone about their behavior or asking them to do something, in a way that is very annoying: *I hate to nag, but have you cleaned your room?* | **nag (at) sb about sth** *Mom keeps nagging me about my homework.* | **nag sb to do sth** *He was always nagging his son to get a job.* ▸see THESAURUS box at **ask** **2** to make someone feel continuously worried or uncomfortable: *Whelson has been nagged by injuries all season.* | **+at** *One problem continued to nag at me.*

nag² *n.* [C] INFORMAL **1** a person who nags continuously: *I don't want to be a nag but have you finished yet?* **2** a horse, especially one that is old or in bad condition

nag·ging /ˈnægɪŋ/ *adj.* [only before noun] **1** making you worry or feel pain all the time: *a few nagging doubts* | *nagging back pain* **2** a nagging person is always complaining, criticizing, or asking someone to do something, in an annoying way

Na·hum /ˈneɪəm/ a book in the Old Testament of the Christian Bible

nai·ad /ˈnaɪæd/ *n.* [C] a female spirit who, according to ancient Greek stories, lived in a lake, stream, or river

na·if, naïf /nɑˈif/ *n.* [C] LITERARY someone who does not have much experience of how complicated life is, so they trust people too much and believe that good things will always happen

nail¹ /neɪl/ S2 *n.* [C] **1** a thin pointed piece of metal that you force into a piece of wood with a hammer to fasten the wood to something else: **pound/hammer a nail into sth** *The workmen were busy hammering nails into the floor.* **2** BIOLOGY the hard smooth layer on the ends of your fingers and toes: *She scratched his face with her nails.* | **long/short nails** *The girl had long red nails.* | **cut/trim/file your nails** *I need to cut my nails.* | *Don't* ***bite your nails.*** | *Oh no. I* ***broke a nail.*** **3 a nail in sb's/sth's coffin** something bad that will help to destroy someone's success or hopes: *The report is another nail in the coffin for the tobacco industry.* **4 as tough/hard as nails** extremely determined or strict: *Jewson's lawyers are as tough as nails.* [**Origin:** Old English *nægl*] → see also **you've hit the nail on the head** at HIT¹ (15)

nail² *v.* [T] **1** to fasten something to something else with a nail or nails: *Someone* ***nailed*** *the windows* ***shut.*** | **nail sth to sth** *He nailed the sign to a tree.* **2** INFORMAL to catch someone and prove that they are guilty of a crime or something bad: **nail sb for sth** *Williams was nailed for fraud.* **3** INFORMAL to do something exactly right, or to be exactly correct: *She nailed a superb jump.* **4 nail sb to the wall/cross** to punish someone severely

nail down INFORMAL **1 nail sth ↔ down** to reach a final and definite decision about something: *They finally managed to nail down an agreement.* **2 nail sth ↔ down** to fasten something so that it cannot move, by forcing nails into it: *They nailed down the lid.* **3 nail sb down** to make someone say clearly what they want or what they intend to do: *I still haven't nailed him down on a definite price.*

ˈnail-ˌbiting *adj.* [only before noun] extremely exciting because you do not know what is going to happen next: *a nail-biting finish to the race* —**nail-biter** *n.* [C]

nail·brush /ˈneɪlbrʌʃ/ *n.* [C] a small stiff brush for cleaning the nails on your fingers → see picture at BRUSH¹

ˈnail ˌclippers *n.* [plural] a small object with two sharp blades, used for cutting the nails on your fingers and toes

ˈnail file *n.* [C] a thin piece of metal with a rough surface used for making the nails on your fingers a nice shape

ˈnail ˌpolish also **ˈnail eˌnamel** *n.* [U] colored or transparent liquid that women paint on the nails of their fingers or toes to make them look attractive

ˈnail ˌscissors *n.* [plural] a small pair of scissors for cutting the nails on your fingers or toes

Nai·ro·bi /naɪˈroʊbi/ the capital city of Kenya

Nai·smith /ˈneɪsmɪθ/, **James** (1861–1939) a Canadian sports teacher who invented the game of basketball

na·ive, naïve /nɑˈiv/ *adj.* **1** not having much experience of how complicated life is, so that you trust people too much and believe that good things will always happen: *a naive young girl* | **+about** *He was surprisingly naive about business.* **2** [only before noun] used about a style of painting that deliberately uses a very simple style [**Origin:** 1600–1700 French *naïve*, feminine of *naïf*, from Latin *natus*, past participle of *nasci* **to be born**] —**naively** *adv.* —**naiveté** /nɑˌivˈteɪ/ *n.* [U]

na·ked /ˈneɪkɪd/ S2 *adj.* **1** not wearing clothes or not covered by clothes SYN **nude**: *a naked body* | *Claire walks around* ***half naked*** (=not fully dressed) *all the time.* | **stark/buck naked** (=completely naked)

THESAURUS

nude not wearing any clothes, used especially when talking about people in paintings, movies etc.: *a drawing of a nude woman*

undressed not wearing any clothes, especially because you have just taken them off in order to go to bed, take a bath etc.: *Rachel got undressed and ready for bed.*

bare not covered by clothes: *the cold floor under her bare feet*
have nothing on also **not have anything on**: *He didn't have anything on except a towel.*

2 sth can be seen with the naked eye also **sth is visible to the naked eye** used to say that you can see something without using anything to help you such as a TELESCOPE or MICROSCOPE: *The comet is visible to the naked eye in the night sky.* **3 naked truth/self-interest/aggression etc.** truth, self-interest, aggression etc. that is not hidden and is shocking: *On his face was a look of naked terror.* **4 a naked light/flame etc.** a light, flame etc. that is not enclosed by a cover **5 naked as a jaybird** OLD-FASHIONED, INFORMAL completely naked [**Origin:** Old English *nacod*] —**nakedly** *adv.* —**nakedness** *n.* [U]

Na·math /ˈneɪməθ/, **Joe** /dʒoʊ/ (1943–) a U.S. football player famous for his skill as a QUARTERBACK

nam·by-pam·by /ˌnæmbi ˈpæmbi◂/ *adj.* INFORMAL, DISAPPROVING too weak, gentle, and lacking determination: *a bunch of namby-pamby liberals* —**namby-pamby** *n.* [C]

name¹ /neɪm/ S1 W1 *n.*
1 WORD SB/STH IS KNOWN BY [C] the word that someone or something is called or known by: *Her name was Lisa.* | *What's your name?* | *The company changed its name to Britco.* | *I can't remember **the name of** the island.* | **+for** *That's a great name for a rock band.* | **sb's first/middle/last/full name** *How do you spell your last name?* | **give/leave your name** *The caller didn't give his name.* | *I heard someone **call** my **name**.* | *O'Connor did not mention any politicians **by name**.* | *I just got off the phone with a guy **by the name of*** (=whose name is) *Tom Kaser.* | *Police say the suspect may **go by the name of*** (=call himself a name that may not be his real one) *Anthony.* | *She wrote **under the name*** (=using a name different from her real name) *of George Eliot.*

THESAURUS

Types of names
first name/given name for example "Bret" in the name Bret Stern
last name/family name/surname for example "Potter" in the name Harry Potter
middle name the name between your first and last names
full name your complete name
maiden name a woman's family name before she got married and changed it
nickname a name your friends and family use for you, not your real name
stage name the name an actor uses that is not his or her real name
pen name/pseudonym a name a writer uses that is not his or her real name
assumed name/alias a false name, often one used by a criminal

2 a big/famous/household name INFORMAL a famous person, company, or product whose name is familiar to many people: **+in** *Some of the biggest names in show business will be there.*
3 OPINION [singular] the opinion that people have about a person or organization SYN **reputation**: *This kind of behavior **gives** hockey **a bad name*** (=makes people have a bad opinion of it). | *I just want the opportunity to restore my **good name**.* | *He spent the rest of his life trying to **clear** his **name*** (=show that he had not done anything wrong, so that people should have a good opinion of him). | **make a name for yourself** *He made a name for himself* (=became known and admired) *in low-budget Westerns.*
4 in sb's name if an official document, a hotel room etc. is in someone's name, it officially belongs to them or is for them: *Walters reserved the boat ticket in Greenleaf's name.* | *The house is in my wife's name* (=she owns it legally).
5 do sth in the name of science/religion etc. to use science, religion etc. as the reason for doing something, even if it is wrong: *The cruel experiments were done in the name of science.*
6 in the name of sb doing something as someone else's representative: *He claimed the island in the name of the King of Spain.*
7 call sb names to say something insulting to someone
8 the name of the game INFORMAL the most important thing or quality needed for a particular activity: *Popularity is the name of the game in television.*
9 have sth to your name to have or own something: *I had only a few dollars to my name.*
10 in name only used when something is not true or a situation does not exist, even though it is officially said to exist: *He's the president in name only.*
11 or my name's not... also **or my name isn't...** SPOKEN used to emphasize that you believe something is definitely true: *I will do it, or my name isn't Blake Ide.*
12 sb's name is mud INFORMAL used to say that people are angry with someone because of something he or she has done
13 take the name of the Lord in vain also **take the Lord's name in vain** OLD-FASHIONED or BIBLICAL to swear using the words "God," "Jesus" etc.
14 give/lend your name to sth if you give your name to something, you allow your name to be used in connection with it, in a way that shows that you approve of it
15 in all but name if a situation exists in all but name, it is the real situation but has not been officially recognized: *She was his wife in all but name.*
16 I can't put a name to sb/sth SPOKEN used when you cannot remember what someone or something is called: *I know the song, but I can't put a name to it.*
[**Origin:** Old English *nama*] → see also **clear sb's name** at CLEAR² (3), PEN NAME, **not have a penny to your name** at PENNY (6)

name² S1 W1 *v.* [T]
1 GIVE SB A NAME to give someone or something a particular name: **a boy/woman/dog etc. named sth** *Ron has a cat named Ginger.* | **name sb sth** *We named our daughter Carol.* | **name sb/sth after sb** *We named the baby Sarah, after her grandmother.* | **name sb/sth for sb** *The King School is named for Martin Luther King.*
2 SAY SB'S/STH'S NAME to say what the name of someone or something is: *Can you name this song?* | *He would not name his clients.* | ***I could name** several people who would like to see her fired.*
3 name names to give the names of people who are involved in something, especially something wrong or something they want to hide: *She's threatening to go the police and start naming names.*
4 CHOOSE SB to officially choose someone or something: **name sb (as) sth** *The movie was named as Best Foreign Film.* | **name sb to sth** *The President named him to the Supreme Court.*
5 to name (but) a few used after a short list of things or people to say that there are many more you could mention: *The whole area is filled with fruit trees – cherries, plums, peaches, to name a few.*
6 you name it SPOKEN used after a list of things to mean that there are many more you could mention: *Clothes, furniture, books – you name it, they have it!*
7 name your price SPOKEN used to mean that you can decide how much money you want to buy or sell something for

ˈname brand *n.* [C] a popular and well-known product name —**name-brand** *adj.* [only before noun] → see also BRAND NAME

ˈname-ˌcalling *n.* [U] the act of calling someone rude names: *At school he suffered teasing and name-calling.*

ˈname day *n.* [C] the day each year when the Christian church gives honor to the particular SAINT (=holy person) who has the same name as someone

name·drop /ˈneɪmdrɑp/ *v.* **namedropped, namedropping** [I] INFORMAL to mention famous or important people's names to make it seem that you know them personally —**namedropping** *n.* [U]

N

name·less /ˈneɪmlɪs/ *adj.* **1 sb/sth who/that/which shall remain nameless** SPOKEN used when you want to say that someone has done something wrong, but without mentioning their name: *A certain person, who shall remain nameless, forgot to lock the front door.* **2** not known by name: *nameless victims* **3** having no name: *a nameless backroad* **4 a)** [only before noun] LITERARY difficult to describe: *Nameless fears made her tremble.* **b)** too terrible to name or describe: *nameless crimes*

name·ly /ˈneɪmli/ *adv.* [sentence adverb] used to introduce additional information that makes it clear exactly who or what you are talking about: *Jody has her own source of information, namely her sister.*

name·plate /ˈneɪmpleɪt/ *n.* [C] a piece of metal or plastic that is attached to something, showing the name of the owner or maker, or the person who lives or works in a place

name·sake /ˈneɪmseɪk/ *n.* [C] **sb's/sth's namesake** someone or something that has the same name as someone or something else: *Unlike its Italian namesake, the city is ugly.*

ˈname tag *n.* [C] a small sign with your name on it that you wear

Na·mib·i·a /nəˈmɪbiə/ a country in southwest Africa, west of Botswana and north of South Africa —**Namibian** *n., adj.*

Na·nak, Guru /ˈnɑnək/ (1469–?1539) an Indian religious leader who started the Sikh religion

nan·ny /ˈnæni/ *n. plural* **nannies** [C] a woman whose job is to take care of the children in a family, usually in the children's own home [**Origin:** 1700–1800 from the female name *Ann*]

ˈnanny goat *n.* [C] a female goat

nano- /nænoʊ/ *prefix* one BILLIONth (=1/1,000,000,000) of a particular unit: *a nanometer* (=one billionth of a meter)

nan·o·sec·ond /ˈnænoʊˌsɛkənd/ *n.* [C] a unit for measuring time. There are one BILLION nanoseconds in a second.

nap[1] /næp/ S3 *n.* **1** [C] a short sleep, especially during the day: *Why don't you lie down and* ***take a nap?*** **2** [singular] the soft surface on some cloth and leather, made by brushing the short fine threads or hairs in one direction → see also PILE [**Origin:** (1) 1300–1400 Old English *hnappian*]

nap[2] *v.* **napped, napping** **1** [I] to sleep for a short time during the day **2 be caught napping** INFORMAL to not be ready to deal with something when it happens, although you should be ready for it

na·palm /ˈneɪpɑm/ *n.* [U] a thick liquid made from GASOLINE, that is used in bombs

nape /neɪp/ *n.* [singular] the back of your neck: *He tickled* ***the nape of her neck.***

Naph·ta·li /ˈnæftəˌlaɪ/ in the Bible, the head of one of the 12 tribes of Israel

naph·tha /ˈnæfθə/ *n.* [U] a chemical compound similar to GASOLINE

nap·kin /ˈnæpkɪn/ S2 *n.* [C] **1** a square piece of cloth or paper used for protecting your clothes and for cleaning your hands and lips during a meal **2** a SANITARY NAPKIN [**Origin:** 1600–1700 *nape* **cloth** (1400–1500), from Old French, from Latin *mappa* **cloth, towel**]

ˈnapkin ˌring *n.* [C] a small ring in which a napkin is put for someone to use at a meal

Na·po·le·on /nəˈpoʊliən/ also **Napoleon Bo·na·parte** /ˈboʊnəˌpɑrt/ (1769–1821) the EMPEROR of France, 1804–1815. His armies took control of many European countries, but he failed in his attack on Russia in 1812, and was finally defeated at the Battle of Waterloo in 1815.

Na·po·le·on·ic Code, the /nəˌpoʊliɑnɪk ˈkoʊd/ also **the ˌCode Naˈpoleon** HISTORY a set of CIVIL LAWS that were made in France in 1804

nap·py /ˈnæpi/ *adj.* INFORMAL nappy hair is short and has very tight curls, such as black people's hair

narc[1] /nɑrk/ *n.* [C] SLANG a police officer who deals with the problem of illegal drugs

narc[2] *v.* [I + on] SLANG to secretly tell the police about someone else's criminal activities, especially activities involving illegal drugs

nar·cis·sism /ˈnɑrsəˌsɪzəm/ *n.* [U] DISAPPROVING a tendency to admire your own physical appearance or abilities [**Origin:** 1800–1900 *Narcissus*, beautiful young man in an ancient Greek story who loved to look at his face reflected in water and was turned into a flower] —**narcissist** *n.* [C] —**narcissistic** /ˌnɑrsəˈsɪstɪk/ *adj.*

nar·cis·sus /nɑrˈsɪsəs/ *plural* **narcissi** /-saɪ, -si/ *n.* [C] a white or yellow spring flower with a cup-shaped central part

nar·co·lep·sy /ˈnɑrkəˌlɛpsi/ *n.* [U] MEDICINE an illness which makes you suddenly fall asleep for short periods of time during the day —**narcoleptic** /ˌnɑrkəˈlɛptɪk/ *adj.*

nar·co·sis /nɑrˈkoʊsɪs/ *n.* [C usually singular, U] TECHNICAL a condition in which you cannot think, speak, or see clearly, usually because of drugs

nar·cot·ic[1] /nɑrˈkɑṭɪk/ *n.* [C] **1** [usually plural] MEDICINE a type of drug that takes away pain and makes you feel sleepy, which may be used in hospitals but is usually illegal: *an overdose of narcotics* | **a narcotics agent/officer** (=a police officer who deals with the problems of illegal drugs) **2** something that gives a lot of pleasure and seems like a powerful drug [**Origin:** 1300–1400 French *narcotique*, from Greek *narkotikos*, from *narkoun* **to make numb**]

narcotic[2] *adj.* **1** [only before noun] relating to illegal drugs: *narcotic addiction* **2** MEDICINE a narcotic drug takes away pain or makes you sleep

Nar·ra·gan·sett, **Narraganset** /ˌnærəˈgænsɪt/ a Native American tribe from the northeastern area of the U.S.

nar·rate /ˈnæreɪt, næˈreɪt/ *v.* [T] **1** to describe or explain what is happening during a movie, play etc.: *The documentary is narrated by Morgan Freeman.* **2** FORMAL to tell a story by describing all the events in order [**Origin:** 1600–1700 Latin, past participle of *narrare*, from *gnarus* **knowing**]

nar·ra·tion /næˈreɪʃən/ *n.* [C,U] ENG. LANG. ARTS **1** a spoken description or explanation that someone gives during a movie, play etc.: *Gerson did the narration for Disney's "Cinderella."* **2** the act of telling a story: *The book is a narration of past events.* **3** [U] a type of writing or speech that tells a story or tells what happened → see also DESCRIPTION, EXPOSITION, PERSUASION

nar·ra·tive /ˈnærəṭɪv/ *n.* ENG. LANG. ARTS **1** [C,U] FORMAL something that is told as a story: *Several times in the narrative the two characters almost meet.* **2** [U] the art or process of telling a story —**narrative** *adj.*: *a narrative poem*

nar·ra·tor /ˈnæˌreɪṭɚ/ *n.* [C] ENG. LANG. ARTS **1** a character or person outside a story who tells what happens in a book or story **2** someone whose voice explains what is happening in a television program, play, or movie

nar·row[1] /ˈnæroʊ/ W3 *adj.*

1 NOT WIDE only measuring a small distance from side to side OPP **wide** OPP **broad**: *a narrow black tie* | *The bed was much too narrow.* | *a narrow gap in the fence* | **a narrow street/path/alley etc.** *the narrow streets of Italian cities*

2 a narrow victory/defeat/majority etc. a win etc. that is just barely achieved or happens by only a small amount: *The American golfer has a narrow lead.*

3 by a narrow margin if you win or lose by a narrow margin, you do it by only a small amount

4 LIMITED limited in range: *We discussed a narrow range of topics.*

5 IDEAS/ATTITUDES DISAPPROVING a narrow attitude or way of looking at a situation is too limited and strict and does not consider enough possibilities: *Some teachers have a narrow vision of what art is.* | *Their interpre-*

tation of spirituality is narrow and limiting. → see also NARROW-MINDED
6 a narrow escape a situation in which you just barely avoid danger, difficulties, or trouble: *The family managed a narrow escape as fire consumed their apartment.*
7 CAREFUL FORMAL careful and thorough: *a narrow examination of events*
[**Origin:** Old English *nearu*] → see also NARROWLY, NARROWS, **the straight and narrow** at STRAIGHT³ (2) —**narrowness** *n.* [U]

WORD CHOICE narrow, thin
- **Thin** means "not thick" and is used for objects if the distance through them from one side to the other is not very big: *a thin cookie* | *thin curtains* | *a thin book.*
- **Narrow** is usually used to describe a hole or something flat that is not very wide from side to side: *a narrow road* | *a narrow doorway* | *narrow shoulders.* But sometimes, especially when something is both long and narrow, **thin** can also be used with this meaning: *a thin stripe.*

narrow² *v.* [I,T] **1** to become narrower, or to make something narrower: *She narrowed her eyes and stared at him.* | *The river narrows at this point.* **2** to become less, or to make something less in range, difference etc.: *The difference between the parties has narrowed.* | *Attempts to* ***narrow the gap*** *between rich and poor have been largely unsuccessful.*
narrow sth ↔ **down** *phr. v.* to reduce the number of things included in a range: *The police have narrowed down their list of suspects.*

'narrow-gauge *adj.* **narrow-gauge railroad/train/track etc.** a railroad, train, track etc. that is narrower than the standard width

nar·row·ly /ˈnæroʊli/ *adv.* **1** only by a small amount: *The bullet narrowly missed her.* | **narrowly escape/avoid sth** *They narrowly escaped death.* | *He was* ***narrowly defeated*** *in the last election.* **2** looking at or considering only a small part of something: *A lot of workers have very narrowly focused job skills.* **3** FORMAL in a thorough way, exact, or limited way: *The law is being interpreted too narrowly.*

'narrow-ˌminded *adj.* DISAPPROVING unwilling to accept or understand new or different ideas or customs OPP **broad-minded**: *a rather narrow-minded view of the world* —**narrow-mindedly** *adv.* —**narrow-mindedness** *n.* [U] → see also OPEN-MINDED

nar·rows /ˈnæroʊz/ *n. plural* **narrows** [C] EARTH SCIENCE **1** also **Narrows** a narrow passage of water between two pieces of land that connects two larger areas of water **2** a narrow part of a river, lake etc.

nar·whal /ˈnɑrwəl/ *n.* [C] a type of WHALE that lives in cold northern oceans, the male of which has a long TUSK (=tooth-like part) on its head

nar·y /ˈnɛri/ *adv.* **nary a sth** LITERARY not even one thing: *He said nary a word.*

NASA /ˈnæsə/ *n.* **National Aeronautics and Space Administration** a U.S. government organization that controls space travel and the scientific study of space

na·sal¹ /ˈneɪzəl/ *adj.* **1** BIOLOGY relating to the nose: *clogged nasal passages* **2** a nasal sound or voice comes mainly through your nose: *a nasal country twang* **3** ENG. LANG. ARTS a nasal CONSONANT or vowel such as /n/ or /m/ is one that is produced wholly or partly through your nose —**nasally** *adv.*

nasal² *n.* [C] ENG. LANG. ARTS a particular speech sound, such as /m/ or /n/ that is made through your nose

nas·cent /ˈnæsənt, ˈneɪ-/ *adj.* [only before noun] FORMAL coming into existence or starting to develop: *nascent nationalism*

Nasdaq, NASDAQ /ˈnæzdæk/ *n.* [singular] TRADEMARK ECONOMICS **National Association of Securities Dealers Automated Quotations** a system of providing people with information about the price of STOCK in small and new U.S. companies bought and sold on the OTC MARKET (=a market where stock is bought and sold using computers connected to the Internet), not on an organized STOCK EXCHANGE such as the New York Stock Exchange: *the Nasdaq Stock Market* | *stock listed on Nasdaq*

Nash /næʃ/, **Og·den** /ˈɑgdən, ˈɔg-/ (1902–1971) a U.S. writer famous for his humorous poems

Nash·ville /ˈnæʃvɪl/ the capital city of the U.S. state of Tennessee

Nas·sau /ˈnæsɔ/ the capital city of the Bahamas

Nas·ser, Lake /ˈnæsɚ/ the RESERVOIR of water formed by the Aswan High Dam in Egypt

nas·tur·tium /nəˈstɚʃəm/ *n.* [C] a garden plant with orange, yellow, or red flowers and circular leaves

nas·ty /ˈnæsti/ S2 *adj. comparative* **nastier**, *superlative* **nastiest**
1 VERY UNKIND cruel and not nice: *a nasty old man* | *a nasty rumor* | **+to** *Don't be so nasty to your sister.* ►see THESAURUS box at **mean³**
2 TASTE/SMELL/APPEARANCE SPOKEN having a bad appearance, smell, taste etc.: *There's a nasty smell in here.* | *This coffee tastes nasty!*
3 EXPERIENCE/FEELING/SITUATION bad and not enjoyable at all: *Their marriage ended in a nasty divorce.* | *She got a nasty surprise when she looked in the mirror.* ►see THESAURUS box at **horrible**
4 ACCIDENT/ILLNESS/INJURY INFORMAL very severe, painful, or bad: *a nasty case of poison oak*
5 WEATHER unpleasant with wind and rain or snow: *The weather's been really nasty all week.*
6 MORALLY BAD morally bad or offensive: *You've got a nasty mind.*
7 VIOLENT violent: ***Things got nasty****, and one of the men pulled out a knife.* —**nastily** *adv.* —**nastiness** *n.* [U]

na·tal /ˈneɪtl/ *adj.* FORMAL or TECHNICAL relating to birth → see also POSTNATAL, PRENATAL

natch /nætʃ/ *adv.* [sentence adverb] SPOKEN, INFORMAL a short form of "naturally," used to say that something is exactly as you would expect: *Most of his clients are in Southern California, natch.*

Natch·ez /ˈnætʃɪz/ a Native American tribe who formerly lived in the southeastern area of the U.S.

na·tion /ˈneɪʃən/ S3 W1 *n.* [C] **1** POLITICS a country with an independent government, considered especially in relation to its people and its social or economic structure: *industrialized nations* ►see THESAURUS box at **country¹**, **race¹** **2 the nation** all the people who live in a country, considered as a single group: *The President will speak to the nation tonight.* **3** a large group of people of the same race and language: *the Cherokee nation* [**Origin:** 1200–1300 French, Latin *natio*, from *natus*, past participle of *nasci* **to be born**]

WORD CHOICE nation, country
- **Nation** is a more formal word than **country** and is usually used when talking about the political or economic structures of a country: *Bolivia is a developing nation with a growing economy.* | *the member nations of NATO.*
- Use **country** to talk about the place where a person comes from, lives in etc.: *What part of the country are you from?* | *He had left his country at the age of ten.*

Na·tion /ˈneɪʃən/, **Car·ry** /ˈkæri/ (1846–1911) a U.S. woman who tried to stop people from drinking alcohol by going into many bars and damaging them

na·tion·al¹ /ˈnæʃənl/ S2 W1 *adj.* **1** relating to a whole nation, rather than to part of it: *The game was shown on national television.* | *national elections* | *the national government* | *The unemployment rate here is higher than the national average.* | **a national emergency/crisis/disaster** *The President declared a national emergency.* | *In Argentina, he is* ***a national hero.*** **2** relating to a particular nation, rather than other nations: *our national defense* | *national and international news* **3** [only before noun] POLITICS owned or controlled by the central government of a country: *Sabena is Belgium's national airline.* | *national forests* | *Yosemite National Park* **4** very popular in or typical of a particular country: *Kimchi is **the Korean national dish**.* → see also NATIONALLY

national² *n.* [C] FORMAL someone who is a citizen of a particular country, especially a citizen who lives in another country: *foreign nationals in the U.S.* → see also ALIEN

N

ˌnational ˈanthem *n.* [C] the official song of a nation, that is sung or played on public occasions

ˌNational Associˌation for the Adˌvancement of ˈColored ˌPeople → see NAACP

ˌnational ˈbank *n.* [C] ECONOMICS a bank that operates in many cities and states in the U.S., rather than in one city or state. National banks must be given permission to operate by a special government official who is responsible for controlling the activities of national banks, and the banks must be members of the FEDERAL RESERVE SYSTEM.

ˌNational ˈBasketball Associˌation, the → see NBA

ˌNational conˈvention *n.* [C] POLITICS a large meeting of either the REPUBLICAN PARTY or the DEMOCRATIC PARTY, at which the party's CANDIDATES for president and VICE-PRESIDENT are chosen

ˌnational ˈdebt *n.* [C] ECONOMICS the total amount of money owed by the government of a country

ˌNational Enˌdowment for the ˈArts, the a U.S. government organization which provides money for artists

ˌNational Enˌdowment for the Huˈmanities, the a U.S. government organization which provides money for writers and other people working in the HUMANITIES to help them with their work

ˌNational Geoˈgraphic a U.S. monthly magazine produced by the National Geographic Society which is known for its photographs, maps, and articles about nature, wild animals, and people from different societies all over the world

ˌNational Geoˈgraphic Soˌciety, the an organization that supports RESEARCH and education in GEOGRAPHY

ˌNational ˈGuard *n.* **the National Guard** a military force in each U.S. state, that can be used when it is needed by the state or the U.S. government

ˌNational ˌInstitutes of ˈHealth, the a U.S. government organization that supports medical RESEARCH and gives information to doctors

na·tion·al·ism /ˈnæʃənlˌɪzəm/ *n.* [U] POLITICS **1** the desire by a group of people of the same race, origin, language etc. to form an independent country: *Irish nationalism* **2** DISAPPROVING a strong love for your own country and the belief that it is better than any other country: *the dangers of militant nationalism*

na·tion·al·ist¹ /ˈnæʃənl-ɪst/ *adj.* [only before noun] **1** POLITICS a nationalist organization, party etc. wants to get or keep political independence for their country and people **2** NATIONALISTIC

nationalist² *n.* [C] **1** someone who strongly supports their own country and believes it is better and more important than all other countries **2** POLITICS someone who is involved in trying to gain or keep political independence for their country or people: *Scottish nationalists*

na·tion·al·is·tic /ˌnæʃnəˈlɪstɪk/ *adj.* DISAPPROVING believing that your country is better than other countries, and often having no respect for people from other countries —**nationalistically** /-kli/ *adv.* → see also PATRIOTIC

na·tion·al·i·ty /ˌnæʃəˈnæləṭi/ *n. plural* **nationalities** **1** [C,U] POLITICS the legal right of belonging to a particular country SYN citizenship: *What nationality are you?* | **American/British etc. nationality** *His wife has French nationality.* **2** [C] a large group of people with the same race, origin, language etc.: *Russia contains many nationalities.*

na·tion·al·ize /ˈnæʃənəˌlaɪz/ *v.* [T] POLITICS if a government nationalizes a very large industry or service such as water, gas or electricity, it buys or takes control of it: *Mexico's vast oil reserves were nationalized in 1938.* —**nationalization** /ˌnæʃnələˈzeɪʃən, -ʃənl-ə-/ *n.* [C,U] → see also PRIVATIZE

ˌNational ˌLabor Reˈlations ˈAct, the POLITICS a law passed in 1935 that protects American workers from unfair employment practices

ˌNational ˈLeague *n.* [singular] one of the two groups that professional baseball teams in the U.S. and Canada are divided into → see also AMERICAN LEAGUE

ˌNational Libeˈration ˌFront *n.* **1** [C usually singular] a group that fights or takes other action to gain INDEPENDENCE for its country or change the government of its country **2 the National Liberation Front** HISTORY a political organization formed in 1960 by the Viet Cong

na·tion·al·ly /ˈnæʃənl-i/ *adv.* by or to everyone in the nation: *Saturday's game will be nationally televised.* | *a nationally known writer*

ˌnational ˈmonument *n.* [C] a building, special feature of the land etc. that is kept and protected by a national government for people to visit

ˌNational Organiˌzation for ˈWomen, the → see NOW

ˌNational ˈPark ˌService, the a U.S. government organization that manages the national PARKS in the U.S.

ˌNational ˈRifle Associˌation, the a U.S. organization that supports people's rights to buy and keep guns, and opposes attempts to change the laws and introduce more strict controls on guns

ˌnational seˈcurity *n.* [U] the idea that a country must keep its secrets safe and its army strong in order to protect its citizens: *a threat to national security*

ˌNational Seˈcurity Adˌvisor *n.* [C] POLITICS the person whose job is to give advice to the U.S. president about national security

ˌNational Seˈcurity ˌCouncil, the ABBREVIATION **NSC** *n.* [singular] POLITICS a U.S. government committee that makes decisions about military and foreign matters. It consists of the President, the VICE PRESIDENT, the SECRETARY OF STATE, the DEFENSE SECRETARY, and the NATIONAL SECURITY ADVISOR.

ˌNational ˈWildlife Fedeˌration, the an organization that works to protect wild animals, birds etc. and the environment

ˌNation of ˈIslam *n.* [singular] a Muslim group in the U.S. for African-American people who want to help and support people of their own race and want to be separate and independent from other races

ˌnation-ˈstate *n.* [C] a nation that is a politically independent country and whose citizens share the same language, origin etc.

na·tion·wide /ˌneɪʃənˈwaɪd◂/ W3 *adj., adv.* happening or existing in every part of the country: *The case got nationwide attention.* | *We have 350 stores nationwide.*

na·tive¹ /ˈneɪṭɪv/ S2 W3 *adj.*
1 COUNTRY [only before noun] your native country, town etc. is the place where you were born: *Domingo has homes in Monte Carlo and in his native Madrid.* | *After a few years, she was sent back to her **native country**.*
2 a native New Yorker/Californian etc. a person who has always lived in New York, California etc.
3 sb's native language/tongue the language you spoke when you first learned to speak: *English is not his native language.*
4 the native inhabitants/people (of sth) BIOLOGY people who were the first people to live in a place, as opposed to other people who have arrived more recently: *the native inhabitants of North America*
5 PLANT/ANIMAL growing, living, produced etc. in one particular place: *the region's native birds* | **+to** *Chilis are native to the New World.*
6 ART/CUSTOM [only before noun] relating to the people of a country who were the earliest people to live there: **native traditions/culture/customs** *a blend of native culture and Christianity*

7 native intelligence/wit etc. a quality that you have naturally from birth: *Mozart's native genius for music*
8 native son/daughter someone who was originally born in a place, especially someone who becomes famous
9 go native HUMOROUS to behave, dress, or speak like the people who live in the country where you have come to stay or work: *Austen has been living in Papua New Guinea so long he's gone native.*

native² *n.* [C] **1** someone who was born in a particular place: *a California native* | **+of** *He is a native of Texas.* **2** someone who lives in a place all the time or has lived there a long time: *It was easy to tell the natives from the tourists.* **3 the natives** [plural] a phrase used by white people in past times to mean one of the people who lived in America, Africa, southern Asia etc. before Europeans arrived, now considered offensive **4** BIOLOGY a plant or animal that grows or lives naturally in a place: **+of** *The koala is a native of Australia.* **5 the natives are (getting) restless** HUMOROUS used to say that a group of people are becoming impatient or angry

ˌNative Aˈmerican *n.* [C] someone from one of the races that lived in North, South, and Central America before Europeans arrived —**Native American** *adj.*

ˈnative-born *adj.* [only before noun] born in a particular place: *a native-born New Yorker*

ˌnative ˈspeaker *n.* [C] someone who has learned a particular language as their first language, rather than as a foreign language: **+of** *a native speaker of English*

na·tiv·ism /ˈneɪt̬ɪvˌɪzəm/ *n.* [U] POLITICS the idea that people who were born in a country should get more opportunities, better treatment etc. than people who came to live there from somewhere else

Na·tiv·i·ty, nativity /nəˈtɪvət̬i/ *n.* **1 the Nativity** the birth of Jesus Christ **2** also **naˈtivity scene** [C] a set of STATUES, a painting etc. that shows Jesus, his parents, and others just after his birth → see also CRÈCHE

nat'l a written abbreviation of NATIONAL

NATO /ˈneɪt̬oʊ/ *n.* [U] **North Atlantic Treaty Organization** POLITICS a group of countries including the U.S. and several European countries, which give military help to each other

nat·ter /ˈnæt̬ɚ/ *v.* [I] OLD-FASHIONED to talk continuously about unimportant things

nat·ty /ˈnæt̬i/ *adj.* INFORMAL very neat and fashionable in appearance: *a natty tweed suit* —**nattily** *adv.*

nat·u·ral¹ /ˈnætʃərəl/ S1 W2 *adj.*
1 RELATING TO NATURE relating to nature or found in nature: *They wanted to preserve the forest in its natural state.* | *a scientific understanding of **the natural world*** | *a chance to see gorillas in their **natural habitat*** | **a natural phenomenon/disaster** (=an event that is caused by nature, such as a flood or an earthquake)

THESAURUS

Describing things that are natural
wild used about flowers, plants, and animals that are not controlled by people: *meadows full of wild flowers*
pure used about food or drink that has not had anything added to it: *pure orange juice*
organic used about fruit, vegetables, meat etc. that is produced without using chemicals: *More people are buying organic food.*
→ ARTIFICIAL

2 NORMAL normal or usual, and what you would expect in a particular situation or at a particular time OPP **unnatural**: *a natural reaction* | ***It's only natural** to feel that way.* | **it is natural for sb to do sth** *It's natural for brothers to fight sometimes.* | **perfectly/completely natural** *I'm sure there's a perfectly natural explanation for his behavior.*
3 NOT ARTIFICIAL not caused, made, or controlled by people OPP **artificial**: *natural fibers such as wool or cotton* | *Her natural hair color is brown.* | *natural flavors* | *all-natural snacks* | *a natural cold remedy*
4 TENDENCY/ABILITY a) a natural tendency or type of behavior is part of your character when you are born, rather than one that you learn later: *With her natural grace, she could be a dancer.* | *The puppy's **natural instinct** is to bark at strangers.* **b)** [only before noun] having a particular quality or skill without needing to be taught and without needing to try hard: *Walsh was a natural leader.* | *a natural athlete*
5 RELAXED behaving in a way that is normal and shows you are relaxed and not trying to pretend: *Just try to act natural.* | *a natural smile*
6 of/from natural causes if someone dies of natural causes, they die because they were old or sick, not because they were killed by another person or in an accident etc.
7 sb's natural father/mother/parent a child's parent through birth rather than through ADOPTION
8 QUALITY [only before noun] used about something that is part of the basic way that something is: *The fabric has a natural tendency to shrink.*
9 NOT MAGIC not relating to gods, magic, or spirits OPP **supernatural**: *I think we are dealing with a natural phenomenon here, not witchcraft.*
10 MUSIC ENG. LANG. ARTS a musical note that is natural has been raised from a FLAT by one HALF STEP or lowered from a SHARP by one half step —**naturalness** *n.* [U]

natural² *n.* [C] **1 be a natural** to be good at doing something without having to try hard or practice: *She's a natural on TV.* **2** ENG. LANG. ARTS **a)** a musical note that has been changed from a FLAT to a HALF STEP higher, or from a SHARP to a half step lower → see also FLAT **b)** the sign (♮) in written music that shows this

ˈnatural-born *adj.* **a natural-born singer/storyteller etc.** INFORMAL someone who has always had a particular quality or skill without having to try hard

ˌnatural ˈchildbirth *n.* [U] BIOLOGY a method of giving birth to a baby in which a woman chooses not to use drugs

ˌnatural diˈsaster *n.* [C] a sudden event that causes great damage or suffering, such as an EARTHQUAKE or flood

ˌnatural ˈenemy *n.* [C] an animal's natural enemy is another type of animal that eats animals of its type: *The whitefly has few natural enemies.*

ˌnatural ˈgas *n.* [U] EARTH SCIENCE gas used for heating and lighting, taken from under the earth or under the ocean → see also COAL GAS

ˌnatural ˈhistory *n.* [U] BIOLOGY the study of plants, animals, and minerals

nat·u·ral·ism /ˈnætʃərəˌlɪzəm, ˈnætʃrə-/ *n.* [U] a style of art or literature that tries to show the world and people exactly as they are → see also REALISM

nat·u·ral·ist /ˈnætʃərəlɪst/ *n.* [C] **1** BIOLOGY someone who studies plants or animals, especially outdoors **2** someone who believes in naturalism in art or literature → see also NATURIST

nat·u·ral·is·tic /ˌnætʃərəˈlɪstɪk◂/ also **naturalist** *adj.* painted, written etc. according to the ideas of naturalism —**naturalistically** /-kli/ *adv.*

nat·u·ral·ize /ˈnætʃərəˌlaɪz/ *v.* [T usually passive] POLITICS to offically make someone who was born outside a particular country a legal citizen of that country —**naturalized** *adj.*: *naturalized U.S. citizens* —**naturalization** /ˌnætʃərələˈzeɪʃən/ *n.* [U]

ˌnatural ˈlaw *n.* [C,U] a rule for moral behavior, or a set of these rules, which people naturally believe in, as opposed to laws made by governments or religious laws

nat·u·ral·ly /ˈnætʃərəli/ S3 W3 *adv.*
1 AS EXPECTED [sentence adverb] used to mean that the fact you are mentioning is exactly what you would have expected: *Naturally, we wanted our team to win.* | *His thoughts naturally turned to food.*
2 AS A NATURAL PART as a natural feature or quality, not changed artificially or learned: *Her hair is naturally curly.* | *Teaching seemed to **come naturally to** him* (=he could do it without being taught).

3 IN A RELAXED WAY in a relaxed manner, without trying to look or sound different from usual: *She embraced me as naturally as if we were family.*
4 IN NATURE found in nature, and not made artificially: *a naturally occurring substance*
5 OF COURSE SPOKEN used in order to agree with what someone has said, or to answer "of course" to a question: *"Did you accept her offer?" "Naturally!"* ▶see THESAURUS box at **certainly**

ˌnatural moˈnopoly *n.* [C] ECONOMICS an area of business in which only one company produces or supplies all of a product or service, and this is the most effective system. Natural monopolies are typically operated by companies that provide people with a service, such as supplying them with gas or electricity: *Some services are natural monopolies because, for example, it is not efficient to lay several different sets of gas lines into a city.*

ˌnatural ˈnumber *n.* [C] MATH a WHOLE NUMBER (=number that is not a fraction) that is greater than 0, for example, 1, 2, 3, 4 etc.

ˌnatural phiˈlosophy *n.* [U] OLD USE science

ˌnatural ˈresource *n.* [C usually plural] something such as land, a mineral, natural energy etc. that exists in a country

ˌnatural ˈright *n.* [C] a right that every person naturally has, as opposed to rights given to them by the laws of a country

ˌnatural ˈscience *n.* [C,U] chemistry, BIOLOGY, and PHYSICS considered together as subjects for study, or one of these subjects

ˌnatural seˈlection *n.* [U] BIOLOGY the process by which only plants and animals that are naturally suitable for life in their environment will be able to live there and REPRODUCE themselves

na·ture /ˈneɪtʃɚ/ S2 W1 *n.*
1 PLANTS/ANIMALS ETC. [U] BIOLOGY everything in the physical world that is not controlled by humans, such as wild plants and animals, earth and rocks, and the weather: *the wonders of nature* | *a deep love of nature* | **the laws/forces of nature** *Flying in airplanes seems to go against the laws of nature.* | *All these materials are found **in nature**.* → see also MOTHER NATURE
2 SB'S CHARACTER [C,U] someone's character or particular qualities: *She has a very gentle nature.* | *It's **human nature*** (=the feelings and natural qualities that everyone has) *to get upset when things go wrong.* | *I'm an optomist **by nature**.* | *It's not **in his nature** to tell lies.* | *We tried appealing to his **better nature*** (=feelings of kindness), *but he still wouldn't lend us the money.*
3 CHARACTER OF STH [C,U] a particular combination of qualities that makes something what it is and makes it different from other things: *Computers have changed **the nature of** work.* | *Fireworks **by their very nature** are dangerous.* | **the exact/precise/true etc. nature of sth** *The exact nature of the problem is not well understood.* | **the changing/complex/unique etc. nature of sth** *The incident revealed the fragile nature of their relationship.*
4 TYPE [singular] a particular type of thing: **of a personal/political/scientific etc. nature** *arrangements of a legal nature* | *He denies that any conversation **of that nature** ever occurred.* | *This article is more **in the nature of*** (=similar to) *a personal attack than anything else.*
5 in the nature of things according to the natural way things happen: *In the nature of things, a shrinking economy means less job security.*
6 let nature take its course to allow events to happen without doing anything to change the results: *With a cold, it's better to just let nature take its course.*
7 nature or/versus nurture used to talk about which has the greater effect: the CHARACTERISTICS that someone is born with, or how they are treated as they grow up
8 get/go back to nature to start living in a simpler style, without many modern machines, and spending a lot of time outdoors
9 sth is the nature of the beast used to say that the qualities that something has can make it difficult to deal with but are to be expected: *Running a business is exhausting, but that's just the nature of the beast.*
10 sth is nature's way of doing sth used to say that something is a natural process that achieves a particular result: *Disease is nature's way of keeping the population down.*
11 in a state of nature in a natural state, not having been affected by the modern world
[**Origin:** 1200–1300 French, Latin *natura*, from *natus*, past participle of *nasci* **to be born**] → see also **the call of nature** at CALL² (12), SECOND NATURE

ˈNature Conˌservancy, the an organization that preserves and protects areas of the natural environment

ˈnature reˌserve *n.* [C] an area of land in which animals and plants, especially rare ones, are protected

na·tur·ist /ˈneɪtʃərɪst/ *n.* [C] FORMAL someone who enjoys not wearing any clothes because they believe it is natural and healthy SYN **nudist** —**naturism** *n.* [U]

na·tur·o·path /ˈneɪtʃərəˌpæθ/ *n.* [C] someone who tries to cure illness using natural things such as plants, rather than drugs —**naturopathy** /ˌneɪtʃəˈrɑpəθi/ *n.* [U] —**naturopathic** /ˌneɪtʃərəˈpæθɪk/ *adj.*

Nau·ga·hyde /ˈnɔgəˌhaɪd, ˈnɑ-/ *n.* [U] TRADEMARK a type of material with plastic on one side that is made to look like leather: *a Naugahyde chair*

naught /nɔt/ *n.* [U] LITERARY nothing: *It appears all this work has been **for naught**.* | *His plans **came to naught*** (=did not happen or work).

naugh·ty /ˈnɔṭi/ *adj. comparative* **naughtier**, *superlative* **naughtiest** **1** a naughty child behaves badly, is impolite, and does not obey adults: *a naughty little girl* **2** naughty behavior, language etc. is slightly offensive or inappropriate and is often related to sex: *Betsy said a naughty word, Mom.* —**naughtily** *adv.* —**naughtiness** *n.* [U]

Na·u·ru /nɑˈuru/ an island in the southwestern Pacific Ocean near the Equator that is an independent REPUBLIC

nau·se·a /ˈnɔziə, ˈnɔʒə, ˈnɔʃə/ *n.* [U] FORMAL the feeling that you have when you think you are going to VOMIT (=bring food up from your stomach through your mouth): *The drug can cause nausea and headaches.* → see also AD NAUSEAM

nau·se·ate /ˈnɔziˌeɪt, -ʒi-/ *v.* [T] **1** FORMAL to make someone feel nausea: *Alcohol nauseates him, so he never drinks.* **2** to make someone feel very angry and upset or offended: *His crimes nauseated the public.*

nau·se·at·ed /ˈnɔziˌeɪṭɪd/ *adj.* feeling nausea: *He felt dizzy and nauseated from the fumes.*

nau·se·at·ing /ˈnɔziˌeɪṭɪŋ/ *adj.* **1** making you feel nausea: *nauseating odors from the sewer* **2** making you feel angry and upset or offended: *It's almost nauseating to think this could be true.* —**nauseatingly** *adv.* → see also DISGUSTING

nau·seous /ˈnɔʃəs, -ziəs/ *adj.* **1** feeling NAUSEA SYN **nauseated**: *I'm a little nauseous from the medication.* **2** LITERARY making you feel NAUSEA, DISGUSTING: *a nauseous potion* —**nauseously** *adv.* —**nauseousness** *n.* [U]

nau·ti·cal /ˈnɔṭɪkəl/ *adj.* relating to ships or sailing [**Origin:** 1500–1600 Latin *nauticus*, from Greek, from *nautes* **sailor**] —**nautically** /-kli/ *adv.*

ˌnautical ˈmile *n.* [C] a measure of distance used on the ocean, equal to 1,853 meters SYN **sea mile**

Nav·a·jo /ˈnævəˌhoʊ, ˈnɑ-/ *n.* **the Navajo** [plural] a Native American tribe from the southwest region of the U.S. —**Navajo** *adj.*

na·val /ˈneɪvəl/ *adj.* [only before noun] relating to or used by the navy: *a naval officer* | *a naval base*

nave /neɪv/ *n.* [C] the long central part of a church

na·vel /ˈneɪvəl/ *n.* [C] **1** BIOLOGY the small hollow or raised place in the middle of your stomach SYN **belly button** **2 contemplate your navel** also **gaze at your**

navel DISAPPROVING, HUMOROUS to spend too much time thinking about your own problems

'navel ˌgazing *n.* [U] DISAPPROVING, HUMOROUS the act of spending too much time thinking about your own problems

'navel ˌorange *n.* [C] a type of orange with few or no seeds, and a small hole at the top

nav·i·ga·ble /'nævɪgəbəl/ *adj.* a navigable river, lake etc. is deep and wide enough for ships to travel on —**navigability** /ˌnævɪgə'bɪləṱi/ *n.* [U]

nav·i·gate /'nævəˌgeɪt/ *v.* **1** [I,T] to find the way to or through a place, especially by using maps: *This time I'll drive and you navigate.* | **navigate your way to/through/around sth** *We managed to navigate our way through the forest.* **2** [I,T] to plan or direct the course of a ship or airplane: **navigate by the stars/sun** (=use them to guide you) **3** [I,T] to find your way through a complicated system, set of rules etc.: *A lawyer can help you navigate the complex legal system.* **4** [I,T] to find your way around on a particular WEBSITE, or to move from one Website to another: *The magazine's website is easy to navigate.* **5** [T] FORMAL to sail along or across an area of water: *The Elbe River is not as easy to navigate as the Rhine.* [**Origin:** 1500–1600 Latin, past participle of *navigare*, from *navis* **ship**]

nav·i·ga·tion /ˌnævə'geɪʃən/ *n.* [U] **1** the science of planning the way along which you travel from one place to another: *a satellite-based system of navigation* **2** the act of sailing a ship or flying an airplane along a particular line of travel: *Navigation is more difficult further up the river.* **3** the movement of ships or aircraft: *The channel is now open to navigation.* —**navigational** *adj.*

ˌNavi'gation Acts, the HISTORY a set of English laws that were in force in the 1650s to control trade between England and the countries that it ruled

nav·i·ga·tor /'nævəˌgeɪṱə/ *n.* [C] an officer on a ship or aircraft who plans the way along which it is traveling

Nav·ra·ti·lo·va /ˌnævrætɪ'loʊvə/, **Mar·ti·na** /mɑr'tinə/ (1956–) a U.S. tennis player, born in the former Czechoslovakia, who is regarded as one of the best players ever

na·vy[1] /'neɪvi/ *n. plural* **navies** **1** [C usually singular] also **Navy** the part of a country's military forces that is organized for fighting a war on the ocean: *a Navy fighter pilot* | *Bruce* ***joined the Navy*** *straight out of high school.* | *Koester served* ***in the Navy*** *for eight years.* → see also AIR FORCE **2** [C] the war ships belonging to a country: *Their navies are no match for ours.* **3** [U] also **navy blue** a very dark blue color [**Origin:** 1300–1400 Old French *navie* **group of ships**, from Latin *navigia* **ships**]

navy[2] also **'navy blue** *adj.* very dark blue: *a navy blue suit*

'navy ˌbean *n.* [C] a small white bean which is cooked and eaten, especially in BAKED BEANS

nay[1] /neɪ/ *adv.* **1** [sentence adverb] LITERARY used when you are adding something to emphasize what you have just said: *There were hundreds, nay thousands, like them.* **2** OLD USE no

nay[2] *n.* [C] a vote against something, or someone who votes against an idea, plan, etc. OPP aye OPP yea

nay·say·er /'neɪˌseɪə/ *n.* [C] FORMAL someone who says that something cannot be done or that a plan will fail —**naysaying** *n.* [U]

Na·zi /'nɑtsi/ *n. plural* **Nazis** [C] **1** HISTORY a member of the National Socialist Party of Adolf Hitler, which controlled Germany from 1933 to 1945 **2** SPOKEN someone who uses their authority in a way people think is cruel, unfair, or too strict —**Nazi** *adj.* —**Nazism** *n.* [U]

n.b., N.B. LITERARY used in formal writing to tell a reader to pay attention to an important piece of information

NBA **National Basketball Association** the organization that arranges professional basketball games

NBC **National Broadcasting Company** one of the main U.S. television networks

NC the written abbreviation of NORTH CAROLINA

NC-17 /ˌɛn si sɛvən'tin/ used to show that no one aged 17 or younger is allowed to see a particular movie → see also G, PG, PG-13, R^3, X (8)

NCO *n.* [C] **non-commissioned officer** a military officer of low rank, such as a CORPORAL or SERGEANT

ND the written abbreviation of NORTH DAKOTA

-nd /nd/ *suffix* used with the number 2 to form ORDINAL numbers: *the 2nd* (=second) *of March* | *her 22nd birthday*

N'dja·mé·na /ˌɛndʒə'meɪnə/ the capital and largest city of Chad

N.E., NE the written abbreviation of NORTHEAST: *N.E. Missouri*

NE the written abbreviation of NEBRASKA

NEA → see NATIONAL ENDOWMENT FOR THE ARTS

ne·an·der·thal /ni'ændəˌθɔl, -ˌtɔl, -ˌtɑl/ *n.* [C] **1** also **Neanderthal** a Neanderthal man **2** HUMOROUS a big ugly stupid man **3** DISAPPROVING someone who opposes all change without even thinking about it [**Origin:** 1800–1900 *Neanderthal*, valley of the Neander river in Germany, where bones of Neanderthal man were found in 1856] —**Neanderthal** *adj.*

Ne'anderthal ˌman *n.* [singular] an early type of human being who lived in Europe during the STONE AGE

Ne·a·pol·i·tan /ˌniə'pɑlɪt˺n/ *adj.* **1** relating to or coming from Naples, Italy: *a Neapolitan fisherman* **2** Neapolitan ICE CREAM has layers of different colors and tastes, usually chocolate, VANILLA, and STRAWBERRY

neap tide /'nip taɪd/ *n.* [C] EARTH SCIENCE a TIDE that takes place every two weeks when the moon is between a new moon and a full moon. The rise and fall of the tide are smaller than usual. → see also SPRING TIDE

near[1] /nɪr/ S2 W1 also **'near to** *prep.* **1** only a short distance from a person or thing: *He was standing near the window.* | *a small town near Boston* | *Their new home is nearer to the school.* | *the boy nearest me* | **go/come/get etc. near sb/sth** *Don't come near me.* **2** close in time to a particular time or event, especially soon before it: *It was near midnight when we got home.* | **near the end/beginning** *There's a pretty violent scene near the end of the movie.* | *They should send us more details of the concert* ***nearer the time.*** **3** to almost do something or almost be in a particular condition: *Larry seemed to know he was near death.* | **come/be near to doing sth** *I came near to losing my temper.* | *The woman was* ***near tears.*** **4** similar to someone or something in quality, size etc., or close to a particular number, age etc.: *The color is nearer to blue than to purple.* | *He's nearer my age than yours.*

near[2] *adv.* **1** only a short distance from a person or thing: *She could hear the sound of voices very near.* | **come/draw near** *Don't come any nearer.* | *People came* ***from near and far*** *to see the show.* **2** a short time away in the future: *The day of the election was* ***drawing near.*** **3 near perfect/impossible etc.** almost perfect, impossible etc.: *Road and rail travel are near impossible in winter.* **4 near to sb/sth** see NEAR **5 not anywhere near** also **nowhere near** used to say something is hardly true at all or has hardly happened at all: *A hundred dollars is nowhere near enough!* → see also NEARLY

near[3] W3 *adj. comparative* **nearer**, *superlative* **nearest** **1** NOT FAR only a short distance away from someone or something: *The nearest hospital is 20 miles away.* | *Which is nearer, your house or mine?*

THESAURUS

close not far from someone or something: *the closest planet to Earth*
not far (away) not a long distance away: *The fort is not far from the town of La Junta, Colorado.*

N

nearby near here or near a particular place: *a couple sitting at a nearby table*
local used about stores, schools etc. that are in the area where you live: *We try to use local businesses as much as possible.*
neighboring used about towns, countries etc. that are very near a particular place: *a football game against a school from a neighboring town*
within walking distance (of sth) easy to walk to from somewhere: *The beach is within walking distance of the hotel.*
→ LOCALLY

2 ALMOST [only before noun] very close to having a particular quality or being a particular thing: *Victory seemed a near certainty.* | *The concert was a near sellout.* | *She's **the nearest thing to** a mother I've got.*
3 a near miss a) a situation in which something almost hits something else: *For every serious accident there are dozens of near misses.* **b)** a situation in which something almost happens, or someone almost achieves something: *Nolte's performance was a near miss for the Oscar.*
4 in the near future soon: *I don't anticipate that happening in the near future.*
5 a near-death experience a situation in which you come close to dying because you are very sick, in an accident etc., but do not actually die
6 to the nearest $10/hundred etc. an amount to the nearest $10, hundred etc. is the number nearest to it that can be divided by $10, a hundred etc.: *Amounts are rounded to the nearest dollar.*
7 sb's nearest and dearest HUMOROUS someone's family
8 be near and dear to sb's heart also **be near and dear to sb** to be very important or special to someone
9 CLOSEST SIDE [only before noun, no comparative] used to describe the side of something that is closest to where you are: *the near bank of the river*
10 FAMILY RELATIONSHIP [only before noun] closely related to you: *Please list your nearest relative on the form.* —**nearness** *n.* [U]

near[4] *v.* **1** [T] to come closer to a particular place, time, or state: *Work is nearing completion.* | *Nevins is nearing 40 but still looks boyish.* **2** [I] FORMAL if a time nears, it gets closer and will come soon: *As the deadline neared, both sides agreed to continue talking.*

ˈnear beer *n.* [U] INFORMAL a drink that tastes similar to beer, but which contains almost no alcohol

near·by /ˈnɪrbaɪ/ W3 *adj.* [only before noun] not far away: *Dinah lives in a nearby cottage.* ►see THESAURUS box at **locally**, **near**[3] —**nearby** /ˌnɪrˈbaɪ◂/ *adv.*: *Gabby stood nearby.*

ˌNear ˈEast *n.* **the Near East** the Middle East —**Near Eastern** *adj.*

near·ly /ˈnɪrli/ S3 W1 *adv.* **1** almost, but not completely or exactly: *He's nearly six feet tall.* | *Oh, my goodness, it's nearly 12:30.* | *I nearly died from food poisoning.* | **not nearly as nice/good/tall etc.** *The food's not nearly as good as it used to be.* → see Word Choice box at ALMOST **2** used to say that you came close to doing something, but changed your mind: *I was so angry I nearly canceled the whole thing.*

near·sight·ed /ˈnɪrˌsaɪt̬ɪd/ *adj.* unable to see things clearly unless they are close to you OPP **farsighted** —**nearsightedly** *adv.* —**nearsightedness** *n.* [U] → see also SHORTSIGHTED

neat /nit/ S1 *adj.* **1** SPOKEN very good, enjoyable, interesting etc.: *What a neat idea!* | *I met some really neat people at the conference.* **2** carefully arranged and not messy: *neat handwriting* | *She folded the clothes in a neat pile.* | *Their apartment was always **neat and clean**.* **3** someone who is neat does not like their things or house to be messy: *Neither of my sons is neat by nature.* **4** simple and effective: *a neat solution* **5** neat alcoholic drinks have no ice or water or any other liquid added SYN **straight** [**Origin:** 1500–1600 French *net*, from Latin *nitidus* **bright, neat**] —**neatly** *adv.* —**neatness** *n.* [U]

neat·en /ˈnitˀn/ *v.* [T] to make something neater and more organized

ˈneat freak *n.* [C] SPOKEN someone who always wants their things and their house to be neat and clean, in a way that other people find annoying

ˈneath /niθ/ *prep.* POETIC below: *'neath the stars*

Ne·bras·ka /nəˈbræskə/ WRITTEN ABBREVIATION **NE** a state in the central U.S. —**Nebraskan** *n., adj.*

neb·u·la /ˈnɛbyələ/ *n. plural* **nebulas** or **nebulae** /-li/ [C] PHYSICS **1** a mass of gas and dust among the stars, often appearing as a bright cloud in the sky at night **2** a GALAXY (=mass of stars) that has this appearance —**nebular** *adj.*

neb·u·lous /ˈnɛbyələs/ *adj.* FORMAL **1** not clear or exact at all SYN **vague**: *a nebulous concept* **2** a nebulous shape cannot be seen clearly and has no definite edges —**nebulously** *adv.* —**nebulousness** *n.* [U]

nec·es·sar·ies /ˈnɛsəˌsɛriz/ *n.* [plural] things that you need, such as food or money, especially for a trip

nec·es·sar·i·ly /ˌnɛsəˈsɛrəli/ S2 W3 *adv.* **1 not necessarily** used to say that something is not certain, even if it might be reasonable to expect it to be: *Bigger is not necessarily better.* | *"Is it always so difficult?" "Not necessarily."* **2** FORMAL in a way that cannot be different or be avoided: *Income tax laws are necessarily complicated.*

nec·es·sar·y /ˈnɛsəˌsɛri/ S2 W1 *adj.* **1** needed in order for you to do something or have something SYN **essential**: *You'll find all the necessary information in this booklet.* | +**for** *Calcium is necessary for strong teeth and bones.* | **be necessary (for sb) to do sth** *It's not necessary for you to stay.* | **make it necessary (for sb) to do sth** *The bad weather made it necessary for us to change our plans.* | *Add more salt and pepper **if necessary**.* | *Don't call me unless it's **absolutely necessary*** (=completely necessary).

THESAURUS

essential important and necessary: *the nutrients that are essential for healthy growth*
vital extremely important and necessary: *Vital information was not given to the decision makers.*
mandatory if something is mandatory, it must be done because of a rule or law: *Parents do not want school uniform to become mandatory.*
compulsory if something is compulsory, you must do it: *Public schools may not have compulsory daily prayers.*

2 a necessary evil something bad that you have to accept in order to achieve what you want: *I consider yard work to be a necessary evil.* [**Origin:** 1300–1400 Latin *necessarius*, from *necesse* **necessary**, from *ne-* **not** + *cedere* **to give up**] → see also NECESSARIES

ne·ces·si·tate /nəˈsɛsəˌteɪt/ *v.* [T] FORMAL to make it necessary for you to do something: *The extra costs may necessitate a rise in prices.* | **necessitate doing sth** *The street party will necessitate closing Pine Avenue.*

ne·ces·si·ty /nəˈsɛsət̬i/ *n. plural* **necessities** **1** [C] something that you need to have OPP **luxury**: *food, clothing, and other necessities* | *A car is an absolute necessity in this town.* | **basic/bare necessities** *We could only afford the bare necessities.* **2** [U] the fact of something being necessary SYN **need**: +**for** *He stressed the necessity for change.* | **the necessity of doing sth** *Everyone agreed about the necessity of repaving the street.* | **a necessity to do sth** *There's no necessity to buy tickets in advance.* | *I learned to cook **out of necessity*** (=because I needed to). **3** [C] something that must happen, even if it is bad or not wanted: *Taxes are a regrettable necessity.* **4** [U] the condition of urgently needing something important, such as money or food: *The decision to sell the car was fueled by necessity.* **5 necessity is the mother of invention** used to say that if someone really needs to do something they will find a way of doing it **6 of necessity** FORMAL used when something happens in a particular way because that is the only possible way it can happen: *Many of the jobs are, of necessity, temporary.*

neck¹ /nɛk/ S2 W2 *n.*

neck and neck

1 PART OF THE BODY [C] BIOLOGY the part of your body that joins your head to your shoulders: *My neck is so sore.* | *Bud wrapped a scarf* ***around*** *his* ***neck****.* → see also THROAT
2 CLOTHING [C] the part of a piece of clothing that goes around your neck: *a blouse with a low neck* → see also CREW NECK, SCOOP NECK, TURTLENECK, V-NECK
3 BOTTLE/INSTRUMENT [C] the narrow part of something that gets narrower at the top, such as a bottle or a musical instrument: *the neck of a bottle*
4 be up to your neck in sth to be in a difficult situation with a lot of problems, or to be very busy doing something: *We're up to our necks in debt.*
5 (hanging) around your neck if a problem or difficult situation is hanging around your neck, you are responsible for it, and this makes you worry → see also **an albatross (around your neck)** at ALBATROSS (2), **a millstone (around your neck)** at MILLSTONE (2)
6 in this/sb's neck of the woods INFORMAL in this area or part of the country, or in the area where someone lives: *What are you doing in this neck of the woods?*
7 neck and neck INFORMAL if two things or people are neck and neck in a competition or race, they each have an equal chance of winning
8 by a neck INFORMAL if a race is won by a neck, the winner is only a very short distance in front: *Our horse won by a neck.*
9 LAND [C] EARTH SCIENCE a narrow piece of land that comes out of a wider part
[**Origin:** Old English *hnecca*] → see also **be breathing down sb's neck** at BREATHE (4), -NECKED, **be a pain (in the neck)** at PAIN¹ (3), **stick your neck out** at STICK OUT (7), **I'll wring sb's neck** at WRING (3)

neck² *v.* [I] INFORMAL if two people neck, they kiss for a long time in a sexual way —**necking** *n.* [U]

-necked /nɛkt/ [in adjectives] **V-necked/open-necked etc.** also **V-neck/open-neck etc.** if a piece of clothing is V-necked, open-necked etc., it has that type of neck: *a V-necked sweater*

neck·er·chief /ˈnɛkɚtʃɪf, -tʃif/ *n.* [C] a square piece of cloth that is folded and worn tied around the neck

neck·lace /ˈnɛk-lɪs/ S3 *n.* [C] a piece of jewelry that hangs around your neck: *a pearl necklace*

neck·line /ˈnɛk-laɪn/ *n.* [C usually singular] the shape made by the edge of a woman's dress, shirt etc. around or below the neck: *a black dress with a low neckline*

neck·tie /ˈnɛktaɪ/ *n.* [C] a TIE

nec·ro·man·cy /ˈnɛkrəˌmænsi/ *n.* [U] LITERARY **1** magic, especially evil magic **2** the practice of claiming to talk with the dead —**necromancer** *n.* [C]

nec·ro·phil·i·a /ˌnɛkrəˈfɪliə/ *n.* [U] sexual interest in dead bodies

nec·tar /ˈnɛktɚ/ *n.* [U] **1** thick juice made from some fruits: *apricot nectar* **2** BIOLOGY the sweet liquid that BEES and some birds eat from flowers **3** the drink of the gods, in the stories of ancient Greece

nec·ta·rine /ˌnɛktəˈrin/ *n.* [C] BIOLOGY a round juicy yellow-red fruit that has a large rough seed and smooth skin, or the tree that produces this fruit

née /neɪ/ *adj.* OLD-FASHIONED used in order to show the family name that a woman had before she was married: *Mrs. Carol Cook, née Williams*

need¹ /nid/ S1 W1 *v.* [T not in progressive]
1 to have to have someone or something because you cannot do something or continue to exist without them, or to feel that you must have them SYN **require**: *Plants need light in order to survive.* | *I need a cup of coffee.* | *Do you need any help?* | *I don't need these old books anymore.* | **need to do sth** *Does anybody need to go to the bathroom?* | **need sth for (doing) sth** *I need glasses for reading.* | **need sb to do sth** *Peter needs you to take him to the airport.* | **need sth badly/desperately/urgently** *The people desperately need food and shelter.*

THESAURUS
could use sth/could do with sth SPOKEN to need or want something: *Let's stop. I could use a rest.* | *I could do with a cup of coffee.*
be desperate for sth to need something urgently: *a little boy who is desperate for attention*
can't do without sth to be unable to manage without something: *You can't do without sleep for very long.*
be dependent on sth/sb to be unable to live or continue normally without something or someone: *The refugees are dependent on outside food supplies.*
require FORMAL to need something: *This sport requires a lot of skill and strength.*

2 need to do sth to have to do something because you feel you should do it or because it is necessary SYN **have to do sth**: *Do I need to wear a tie?* | *You need to improve your spelling.* | *Something needs to be done about this problem.* | *The pie doesn't need to be refrigerated.*
3 LACK STH IMPORTANT to be without something that is necessary, or to lack something that would improve a situation SYN **require**: *The ceiling needs a coat of paint.* | *I think Brad's car needs new tires.* | **need cleaning/painting/replacing etc.** *My new watch never needs winding.* | **need to be cleaned/painted etc.** *The engine will need to be checked.* | *Rapid transit in the area is* ***badly needed****.*
4 PUNISHMENT/WARNING used to say that someone should be punished or warned: *People need to be warned about the dangers of using drugs.*
5 sb/sth need not do/be sth FORMAL used to say that it is not necessary for someone to do something or for something to happen: *As it turns out, he need not have worried.* | *Expenses under $50 need not be itemized.*
6 if a job or activity needs a particular quality, you must have that quality in order to do it well SYN **require**: *The job needs a lot of patience.*
7 sb does not need sth SPOKEN used in order to say that something is making someone's life more difficult: *She doesn't need any more trouble right now.*
8 who needs it/them? SPOKEN used to say that you do not think someone or something is important or interesting
9 need I say more/ask/add etc.? HUMOROUS used to say that it is not necessary to say more or ask about something, because the rest is clear: *She's lazy, slow, and stubborn. Need I say more?*
10 need sth like a hole in the head INFORMAL used to say that you definitely do not need something
11 on a need-to-know basis if information is given to people on a need-to-know basis, they are given only the details that they need at the time when they need them

need² S2 W1 *n.*
1 STH THAT IS NECESSARY [singular, U] a situation in which something must be done, especially to improve the situation: **+for** *There is a need for stricter safety regulations.* | **the need (for sb) to do sth** *We recognize the need to improve teaching standards.* | *We'll work all night,* ***if need be*** (=if it is necessary). | *We can hire more people as* ***the need arises*** (=when it is necessary). | **an urgent/desperate need** *There is an urgent need for more nurses.*
2 STRONG DESIRE [C,U] a strong feeling that you want something, that you want to do something, or that you must have something: **+for** *a need for excitement* | *Don't you sometimes* ***feel the need to*** *take a vacation?*
3 be in need of sth a) to need help, advice, money etc., because you are in a difficult situation: *He is seriously ill and in need of care.* **b)** to need to be cleaned,

repaired, or given attention in some way: *Some of the buildings are **badly in need of** repair.*
4 WHAT YOU NEED [C usually plural] what someone needs to have in order to live a normal healthy life: +**of** *the medical needs of senior citizens* | **meet/satisfy/address/serve the needs of sb** *Schools were failing to meet the needs of their students.* | *Children are dependent on adults for all their **basic needs**.* | **sb's every need** *Our staff will take care of your every need.*
5 NO MONEY [U] the state of not having enough food or money: *We must care for those most **in need**.*
6 there's no need (for sb) to do sth a) used to say that someone does not have to do something: *There was no need for me to stay there.* **b)** SPOKEN used to tell someone to stop doing something: *There's no need to shout – I'm not deaf!*
7 have need of sth FORMAL to need someone or something
[**Origin:** Old English *nied*, *ned*] → see also **in your hour of need** at HOUR (10)

need·ful /ˈnidfəl/ *adj.* FORMAL **needful of sth** needing things, help etc.

nee·dle¹ /ˈnidl/ [S3] *n.* [C]
1 SEWING a small thin piece of steel used for sewing, that has a point at one end and a hole in the other end: *a needle and thread*
2 MEDICINE the sharp hollow metal part on the end of a SYRINGE, which is pushed into your skin to put a drug or medicine into your body or to take out blood: *The doctor stuck a needle in my arm.*
3 TREE BIOLOGY a small thin pointed leaf, especially from a PINE or FIR tree: *pine needles*
4 KNITTING a long thin stick used in KNITting
5 ACUPUNCTURE a short metal stick that is put into particular parts of the body as a part of ACUPUNCTURE
6 TOOL a long thin piece of metal on a scientific instrument, that moves backward and forward and points to numbers or directions: *a compass needle*
7 RECORDS the very small, pointed part in a RECORD PLAYER that picks up sound from the records: *There must be some dust on the needle.*
8 it's like looking for a needle in a haystack INFORMAL used to say that something is almost impossible to find
[**Origin:** Old English *nædl*]

needle² *v.* [T] to deliberately annoy someone by continuously making remarks that are not nice, or stupid jokes: *Paula kept needling him about getting a job.*

nee·dle·point /ˈnidlˌpɔɪnt/ *n.* [U] a method of making pictures by covering a piece of material with small stitches of colored thread, or something made in this way: *a needlepoint pillow*

need·less /ˈnid-lɪs/ *adj.* **1 needless to say** used when you are telling someone something that they probably already know or expect: *Needless to say, I was very pleased to hear the news.* **2** not necessary, and often easily avoided: *Why take needless risks?* —**needlessly** *adv.*: *Thousands of women die needlessly every year because of poor medical care.*

nee·dle·work /ˈnidlˌwɚk/ *n.* [U] the activity or art of sewing or decorating things using thread, or things made by sewing

need·n't /ˈnidnt/ *v.* the short form of "need not": *He needn't have worried.*

need·y /ˈnidi/ *adj.* *comparative* **needier**, *superlative* **neediest** **1** having very little food or money: *a needy family* ►see THESAURUS box at **poor** **2** someone who is needy has emotional problems in which they want people to love them and help them —**neediness** *n.* [U] —**the needy** *n.* [plural] *money to help the needy*

ne'er /nɛr/ *adv.* POETIC never

ne'er-do-well /ˈnɛr du ˌwɛl/ *n.* [C] OLD-FASHIONED a lazy person who never works

ne·far·i·ous /nɪˈfɛriəs, -ˈfær-/ *adj.* FORMAL evil or criminal: *murder, blackmail, and other nefarious activities* —**nefariously** *adv.* —**nefariousness** *n.* [U]

neg. the written abbreviation of NEGATIVE

ne·gate /nɪˈgeɪt/ [Ac] *v.* [T] FORMAL **1** to prevent something from having any effect: *The drug's side-effects negate any possible benefit to the patient.* **2** to show that something does not exist or is not true: *The witness's testimony negated what the defendant had claimed.* [**Origin:** 1600–1700 Latin, past participle of *negare* **to say no**] —**negation** /nɪˈgeɪʃən/ *n.* [U]

neg·a·tive¹ /ˈnɛgət̬ɪv/ [Ac] [S2] [W2] *adj.*
1 BAD/HARMFUL harmful, unpleasant, or unwanted [OPP] **positive**: *negative publicity* | *the negative aspects of capitalism* | **a negative effect/impact/consequence** *His drinking was starting to have a negative effect on his work.*
2 BAD ATTITUDE considering only the bad qualities of a situation, person etc. and not the good ones [OPP] **positive**: *Tanya has a really negative self-image.* | *The reviews of her new book were mostly negative.* | +**about** *Rick's hard to be with because he's so negative about everything.*
3 SHOWING ONLY BAD showing only the bad features of someone or something, in a way that seems unfair [OPP] **positive**: *negative ads* | *The media is responsible in part for the governor's **negative image** among voters.* | *Minorities are often shown **in a negative light**.*
4 NO/NOT a) saying or meaning "no" [OPP] **affirmative**: *Our request received a negative reply.* **b)** a negative word or sentence contains one of the words "no," "not," "nothing," "never" etc. For example, "cannot" or "can't" are negative forms of "can."
5 MEDICAL/SCIENTIFIC TEST not showing any sign of the chemical or medical condition that was being looked for [OPP] **positive**: *Anne's pregnancy test was negative.* | *Her husband **tested negative for** HIV.*
6 NUMBER/QUANTITY MATH less than zero: *negative numbers* | *There has been a negative return on our investment* (=we lost money).
7 ELECTRICITY PHYSICS having the type of electrical charge that is carried by ELECTRONS, shown by (–) on a BATTERY [OPP] **positive**
8 BLOOD TECHNICAL not having RHESUS FACTOR in your blood [OPP] **positive**: *His blood type is O negative.* —**negatively** *adv.*

negative² [Ac] *n.* **1** [C] a piece of film that shows dark areas as light and light areas as dark, from which a photograph is printed ►see THESAURUS box at **camera** **2** [C] a quality or feature of something that is not good or not useful [OPP] **positive**: *Another negative was the increase in unemployment.* **3** [C,U] ENG. LANG. ARTS a statement or expression that means "no" [OPP] **affirmative**: *Griese responded **in the negative** to both requests.* **4** [C] a negative result from a chemical or scientific test [OPP] **positive**

ˌnegative correˈlation *n.* [C] MATH a relationship between two VARIABLES in which an increase in one variable always happens together with a decrease in the other [OPP] **positive correlation**

ˌnegative reˈciprocal *n.* [C] MATH a number that is related to another number, because when they are multiplied together the product is –1. For example, the negative reciprocal of 2 is –0.5, because 2 ×–0.5 = –1. → see also ADDITIVE INVERSE, MULTIPLICATIVE INVERSE

ˌnegative square ˈroot *n.* [C] MATH a negative number that is the SQUARE ROOT of another number. For example the negative square root of 49 is –7, because –7 × –7 = 49.

ne·glect¹ /nɪˈglɛkt/ *v.* [T] **1** to not take care of someone or something very well: *She denied neglecting her children.* **2** to not pay enough attention to someone or something: *I've been neglecting my friends lately.* **3** to not do something or forget to do it, often because you are lazy or careless: **neglect to do sth** *He neglected to mention one important fact.* [**Origin:** 1500–1600 Latin, past participle of *neglegere*, *negligere*, from *neg-* **not** + *legere* **to gather**]

neglect² *n.* [U] **1** failure to take care of someone or something well: *cases of child abuse and neglect* **2** the condition that someone or something is in when they have not been taken care of: *The inner cities are in a state of neglect.* **3** the act of not doing or paying attention to something that you are supposed to do or pay attention to: *neglect of duty*

ne·glect·ful /nɪˈglɛktfəl/ *adj.* FORMAL not taking care of someone or something very well, or not giving it enough attention: *neglectful parents*

neg·li·gee, negligée /ˌnɛglɪˈʒeɪ, ˈnɛglɪˌʒeɪ/ *n.* [C] a very thin pretty long JACKET, worn over a NIGHTGOWN

neg·li·gence /ˈnɛglɪdʒəns/ *n.* [U] failure to do something that you are responsible for in a careful enough way, so that something bad happens or could happen: *The jury found Dr. Cornwell guilty of **gross negligence*** (=serious negligence).

neg·li·gent /ˈnɛglɪdʒənt/ *adj.* **1** not doing something that you are responsible for in a careful enough way, so that something bad happens or could happen: *a negligent lawyer* | +**in** *The doctor was negligent in his examination of the patient.* **2** LITERARY careless, but in a pleasantly relaxed way: *a negligent wave of the hand* —**negligently** *adv.*

neg·li·gi·ble /ˈnɛglɪdʒəbəl/ *adj.* too slight or unimportant to have any effect: *The risk of being caught was negligible.* —**negligibly** *adv.*

ne·go·tia·ble /nɪˈgoʊʃəbəl/ *adj.* **1** negotiable prices, agreements etc. can be discussed and changed before being agreed on: *The price is not negotiable.* **2** a negotiable road, path etc. is in a good enough condition to be traveled along: *The road is only negotiable in the dry season.* **3** ECONOMICS a negotiable check, BOND etc. can be exchanged for money → see also NON-NEGOTIABLE

ne·go·ti·ate /nɪˈgoʊʃiˌeɪt/ W3 *v.* **1** [I,T] to discuss something in order to reach an agreement, especially in business or politics: *We have always been willing to negotiate.* | *The U.N. has been trying to negotiate a peace settlement.* | +**with** *The company is negotiating with potential buyers.* **2** [T] to succeed in getting past or over a difficult place on a path, road etc.: *Drivers have to negotiate high mountain roads with narrow bends.* **3 the negotiating table** a situation in which people meet for official discussions to settle a disagreement: *Both sides are ready to sit down at the negotiating table.* [**Origin:** 1500–1600 Latin, past participle of *negotiari* **to do business**] —**negotiator** *n.* [C]

ne·go·ti·a·tion /nɪˌgoʊʃiˈeɪʃən/ W2 *n.* [C usually plural, U] official discussions between two or more groups who are trying to agree on something, or the process of having these discussions: *peace negotiations* | +**between/among** *Negotiations between the two countries are continuing.* | +**on/over** *negotiations on arms reduction* | *Trade representatives have said the issue is **open to negotiation*** (=can be negotiated). | *The company has **entered into negotiations*** (=start negotiations) *with the union.* | *His contract is **under negotiation**.*

né·gri·tude /ˈnigrəˌtud, ˈnɛg-/ a literary movement that began in former French colonies (COLONY) in the 1930s, which emphasized the importance of black people and their achievements all over the world

Ne·gro /ˈnigroʊ/ *n. plural* **Negroes** [C] OLD-FASHIONED a word used in the past for a black person, now considered offensive [**Origin:** 1500–1600 Spanish, Portuguese, from *negro* **black**, from Latin *niger*] —**negro** *adj.*

Ne·groid /ˈnigrɔɪd/ *adj.* OLD-FASHIONED, TECHNICAL having the physical features of a black person from Africa

NEH → see NATIONAL ENDOWMENT FOR THE HUMANITIES

Ne·he·mi·ah /ˌniəˈmaɪə/ a book in the Old Testament of the Protestant Bible

Neh·ru /ˈneɪru, ˈnɛru/, **Ja·wa·har·lal** /dʒəˈwɑhɚˌlɑl/ (1889–1964) an Indian politician who was one of the leaders of India's fight for independence from the U.K. and became India's first Prime Minister from 1947 to 1964

neigh /neɪ/ *v.* [I] to make the long loud sound that a horse makes —**neigh** *n.* [C]

neigh·bor /ˈneɪbɚ/ S2 W2 *n.* [C] **1** someone who lives in the house or apartment next to you or near you: *The neighbors invited us over for dinner.* | *neighbor kids* | *I still haven't met my **next-door neighbor*** (=neighbor who lives next to me). **2** a country's neighbors are the countries that share a border with it: *the U.S. and its neighbor to the south, Mexico* **3** someone who is standing or sitting next to you: *Don't look at your neighbor's work during the test.* [**Origin:** Old English *neahgebur*]

neigh·bor·hood /ˈneɪbɚˌhʊd/ S2 W2 *n.* [C] **1** a small area of a town, or the people who live there: *a quiet residential neighborhood* | *a neighborhood school* | *Are there any good restaurants **in the neighborhood**?* | ***The whole neighborhood** knew what they were doing.* ▸see THESAURUS box at **area** **2 in the neighborhood of 5,000/$100 etc.** a little more or a little less than a particular amount: *The company's profits are in the neighborhood of $200 million.* **3 there goes the neighborhood** HUMOROUS used when something has happened that will make other people have a bad opinion of the place where you live

ˌneighborhood ˈwatch *n.* [C] a system organized by the police, in which neighbors watch each other's houses to prevent crimes

neigh·bor·ing /ˈneɪbərɪŋ/ *adj.* [only before noun] near the place where you are or the place you are talking about: *Her parents live in a neighboring town.*

neigh·bor·ly /ˈneɪbɚli/ *adj.* friendly and helpful toward your neighbors —**neighborliness** *n.* [U]

neigh·bour /ˈneɪbɚ/ *n.* [C] the British and Canadian spelling of NEIGHBOR

nei·ther[1] /ˈniðɚ, ˈnaɪ-/ S3 W3 *determiner, pron.* not one nor the other of two people or things: *Neither team played well.* | *We saw a couple of houses, but neither was really what we wanted.* | *We asked both children, but **neither one** was interested.* | +**of** *Neither of us wanted to go.* → see also EITHER, NONE[1]

neither[2] *adv.* used in order to agree with a negative statement that someone has just made, or to add a negative statement to one that has just been made: **neither am I/neither does she/neither have we etc.** *"I don't like herb tea." "Neither do I."* | *Mary can't swim and neither can her sister.* | *"I haven't seen Greg in a long time." "**Me neither**"* (=I haven't either)." → see also EITHER

neither[3] W2 *conjunction* **1 neither...nor...** used when mentioning two statements, facts, actions etc. that are not true or possible: *Neither she nor her mother spoke English.* | *The equipment is neither accurate nor safe.* → see Word Choice box at ALSO **2 be neither here nor there** used when saying that something is not important because it does not affect or change a fact or situation: *What I think about him is neither here nor there.* **3** FORMAL used in order to emphasize or add information to a negative statement: *I could not afford to stay there, but neither could I afford to return home.*

Nel·son /ˈnɛlsən/, **Ho·ra·ti·o** /həˈreɪʃiˌoʊ/ (1758–1805) a famous leader of the British navy

nem·a·tode /ˈnɛməˌtoʊd/ *n.* [C] a type of small worm that can destroy crops

nem·e·sis /ˈnɛməsɪs/ *n.* [singular] **1** an opponent or enemy that it is very difficult for you to defeat: *In the final he will meet his old nemesis, Pete Sampras.* **2** LITERARY a punishment that is deserved and cannot be avoided [**Origin:** 1500–1600 Latin *Nemesis* goddess of destruction, from Greek, from *nemein* **to give out**]

neo- /nioʊ, niə/ *prefix* [in nouns and adjectives] new, or more recent than something similar: *a neophyte* (=someone who has just started learning something) | *neonatal* (=relating to newly born babies)

ne·o·clas·si·cal /ˌnioʊˈklæsɪkəl/ *adj.* neoclassical art and ARCHITECTURE copy the style of ancient Greece or Rome

ne·o·co·lo·ni·al·ism /ˌnioʊkəˈloʊniəˌlɪzəm/ *n.* [U] POLITICS the economic and political influence that a powerful country uses to control another country —**neocolonialist** *adj.* → see also COLONIALISM

ne·o·con·ser·va·tive /ˌnioʊkənˈsɚvətɪv/ *adj.* [usually before noun] supporting political ideas that include strict moral behavior and the importance of being responsible for your own actions and not being dependent on the government —**neoconservative** *n.* [C]

Ne•o•lith•ic /ˌniəˈlɪθɪk◂ / *adj.* HISTORY relating to the latest period of the STONE AGE, about 10,000 years ago, when people began to live together in small groups and make stone tools and weapons

N

ne•o•lo•gism /niˈɑləˌdʒɪzəm/ *n.* [C] ENG. LANG. ARTS a new word or expression, or a word used with a new meaning

ne•on¹ /ˈniɑn/ *n.* [U] SYMBOL **Ne** CHEMISTRY a gas that is an ELEMENT and that produces a bright light when electricity goes through it

neon² *adj.* [only before noun] **1** neon lights or signs use neon in glass tubes to produce brightly colored letters or pictures **2** neon colors are very bright: *neon pink shorts*

ne•o•na•tal /ˌnioʊˈneɪtl◂ / *adj.* [only before noun] TECHNICAL relating to babies that have just been born: *the hospital's neonatal intensive care unit*

ˌneo-ˈNazi *n.* [C] a member of a group that supports the ideas of Adolf Hitler and expresses hatred of people who are not white or who come from other countries —**neo-Nazi** *adj.*

ne•o•phyte /ˈniəˌfaɪt/ *n.* [C] **1** someone who has just started to learn a particular skill, art, job etc.: *a political neophyte* **2** LITERARY a new member of a religious group —**neophyte** *adj.* [only before noun] *neophyte wine enthusiasts*

ne•o•prene /ˈniəˌprin/ *n.* [U] a type of artificial rubber

NEP HISTORY the abbreviation of the NEW ECONOMIC POLICY

Ne•pal /nəˈpɔl/ a country in south Asia, in the Himalaya mountains, north of India and south of China —**Nepalese** /ˌnɛpəˈliz◂ , -ˈlis◂ / *adj.*

neph•ew /ˈnɛfyu/ [S3] *n.* [C] the son of your brother or sister, or the son of your husband's or wife's brother or sister [**Origin:** 1200–1300 Old French *neveu*, from Latin *nepos* **grandson, nephew**]

neph•ron /ˈnɛfrɑn/ *n.* [C] BIOLOGY one of the many small tubes in the KIDNEYS of VERTEBRATES (=creatures with backbones) that remove waste materials from the blood and produce URINE

nep•o•tism /ˈnɛpəˌtɪzəm/ *n.* [U] the practice of unfairly giving the best jobs to members of your family when you are in a position of power → see also CRONYISM

Nep•tune¹ /ˈnɛptun/ *n.* PHYSICS the eighth PLANET from the sun → see picture at SOLAR SYSTEM

Neptune² the Roman name for the god Poseidon

nerd /nɚd/ *n.* [C] INFORMAL **1** someone who seems boring and not fashionable, and does not know how to act in social situations **2** someone who seems only interested in computers and other technical things: *a computer nerd* —**nerdy** *adj.*

Nerf /nɚf/ *adj.* TRADEMARK Nerf balls and other toys are made of a soft FOAM RUBBER material

Ne•ro /ˈnɪroʊ/ (A.D. 37–68) a Roman EMPEROR, said to have killed his mother, his wives, and many other people

Ne•ru•da /neɪˈrudə/, **Pab•lo** /ˈpɑbloʊ/ (1904–1973) a Chilean poet

nerve¹ /nɚv/ [S3] *n.*

1 COURAGE/CONFIDENCE [U] courage and confidence in a dangerous, difficult, or frightening situation: **have the nerve to do sth** *I didn't have the nerve to ask her for a date.* | *He **lost** his **nerve** at the last minute.* | *She finally **found the nerve** to ask for a divorce.* | *Standing up to your boss **takes a lot of nerve**.* ►see THESAURUS box at courage

2 IN THE BODY [C] BIOLOGY a long thin thread-like part of your body, along which feelings and messages are sent to the brain: *the optic nerve*

3 nerves [plural] **a)** the feeling of being nervous because you are worried or a little frightened: *A lot of people suffer from nerves before interviews.* | **calm/steady your nerves** *Carey had a drink to calm his nerves.* **b)** OLD-FASHIONED a mental condition in which you are unable to deal with normal life because you are too nervous

4 get on sb's nerves to annoy someone, especially by doing something again and again: *Nick's whining is really starting to get on my nerves.*

5 strike/touch/hit a (raw) nerve to mention something that people feel strongly about or that upsets people: *I think I hit a nerve when I mentioned her ex-husband.*

6 LACK OF RESPECT INFORMAL lack of respect for other people, which causes you to do impolite things: *You invited yourself? You **have some nerve**!* | **have the nerve to do sth** *Mary had the nerve to take credit for my work.*

7 sb's nerves are frayed/shot/in tatters/on edge used to say that someone feels very nervous, worried, or upset

8 have nerves of steel to be able to be brave and calm in a dangerous or difficult situation

9 a battle/war of nerves a situation in which two people or opposing groups, countries etc. wait in order to see which one will give in under pressure

[**Origin:** 1300–1400 Latin *nervus*]

nerve² *v.* [T] **nerve yourself** LITERARY to prepare yourself to be brave enough to do something difficult or dangerous

ˈnerve cell *n.* [C] a NEURON

ˈnerve ˌcenter *n.* [C] the place from which a system, activity, organization etc. is controlled

ˈnerve ˌendings *n.* [plural] the places in your skin and inside your body where your nerves receive information about temperature, pain etc.

ˈnerve gas *n.* [C,U] a poisonous gas used in war, that damages your CENTRAL NERVOUS SYSTEM

nerve-rack•ing, **nerve-wracking** /ˈnɚv ˌrækɪŋ/ *adj.* a nerve-racking situation makes you feel very nervous because it is difficult or frightening: *The wait was nerve-racking.*

nerv•ous /ˈnɚvəs/ [S2] [W3] *adj.* **1** worried or afraid about something, and unable to relax: *Don't be nervous. You'll be fine!* | *A doctor was trying to reassure his nervous patient.* | **+about** *I was really nervous about working with him.* | **+(that)** *Her mother was nervous that something might go wrong.* | *Job cuts are **making** auto workers very **nervous** about the future.* | *Chris **gets nervous** before speaking in public.* | **a nervous smile/laugh/look** *He managed a nervous smile as he walked on stage.* | *I have **a nervous habit*** (=something you do when you are nervous) *of playing with my hair.* ►see THESAURUS box at worried **2** not very relaxed and easily becoming worried or afraid: *a thin nervous woman* | *The stress is making him into a **nervous wreck*** (=making him very worried and affecting his health and confidence). **3** BIOLOGY relating to the nerves in your body: *a nervous disorder* **4 nervous exhaustion** OLD-FASHIONED a mental condition in which you feel very tired, usually caused by working too hard or a difficult emotional problem —**nervously** *adv.* —**nervousness** *n.* [U] ►see THESAURUS box at worried

ˌnervous ˈbreakdown *n.* [C] NOT TECHNICAL a mental illness in which someone becomes extremely anxious and tired, and cannot deal with the things they usually do: **have/suffer a nervous breakdown** *Yvonne had a nervous breakdown last winter.*

ˈnervous ˌsystem *n.* [C] BIOLOGY your nerves, brain, and SPINAL CORD, through which your body feels pain, heat etc. and controls your movements

ˈnervous ˌtissue *n.* [U] BIOLOGY TISSUE (=matter in the body made from many cells) that is made up of NEURONS (=cells that send messages to parts of the body and the brain)

ner•vy /ˈnɚvi/ *adj.* showing a surprising amount of confidence and lack of fear: *Asking the chairman for a raise was pretty nervy.*

-ness /nɪs/ *suffix* [in nouns] used to form nouns from

adjectives and PARTICIPLES: *loudness* | *sadness* | *warm-heartedness* (=quality of being friendly and nice)

nest¹ /nɛst/ *n.* [C] **1** BIOLOGY a hollow place made or chosen by a bird to lay its eggs in and to live in: *a blackbird's nest* | **build/make a nest** *The birds had built a nest in the bush.* **2** BIOLOGY a place where insects or small animals live: *a field mouse's nest* | *an ant's nest* **3 leave/fly the nest a)** when baby birds leave the nest, they leave it because they are old enough to fly and live independently **b)** to leave your parents' home and start living somewhere else when you become an adult **4 a nest of spies/criminals/vice etc.** a place where there are many bad people or evil activities **5 a nest of sth** a small neat pile of something: *Arrange the meat in a nest of spinach leaves.* [**Origin:** Old English] → see also **empty nest** at EMPTY¹ (7), **feather your nest/bed** at FEATHER² (2), **a hornet's nest** at HORNET (2), **love nest** at LOVE² (13)

nest

nest² *v.* [I] to build or use a nest: *The birds stop briefly to nest and feed.*

'nest egg *n.* [C] an amount of money that you have saved: *our retirement nest egg*

nes·ting /ˈnɛstɪŋ/ *n.* [U] **1** the activity of making a nest: *a good spot for nesting* | *a nesting site for water birds* | *the birds' nesting instincts* **2 nesting instinct** INFORMAL a strong desire to have children that humans, especially women, may feel

nes·tle /ˈnɛsəl/ *v.* **1** [I always + adv./prep., T always + adv./prep.] to move into a comfortable position, pressing your head or body against someone or against something soft: **nestle against/beside/by etc.** *The baby nestled against her mother's neck.* **2** [I always + adv./prep., T always passive] LITERARY to be in a position that is protected from wind, rain etc.: **nestle among/between/in etc. sth** *Pink and blue houses nestle under the cliffs.* | **be nestled among/between/in etc. sth** *The lake was nestled amongst the hills.*

nest·ling /ˈnɛstlɪŋ/ *n.* [C] a very young bird

net¹ /nɛt/ *n.* **1 the Net** also **the net** COMPUTERS the Internet: *I order most of my clothes **on the Net*** (=using the Net). | *I found some really good sites **on the Net*** (=located on the Net). | *Are you **on the Net*** (=do you have a connection to it) *at home?* | *He spends most evenings **surfing the Net*** (=looking at different websites). | *You can **download** music **from the Net**.* **2** [C,U] a material made of strings, threads, or wires woven across each other with regular spaces between them, or something made from this material: *a fishing net* **3** [usually singular] **a)** a long net used in games such as tennis that the players must hit the ball over **b)** a net used as a GOAL in some games such as basketball, SOCCER, or HOCKEY: *The puck went straight into the net.* **4** [U] very thin material made from fine threads woven together with very small spaces between the threads: *The bride wore a veil made of ivory net.* **5** [C] material used for keeping things off something, especially insects or birds: *a mosquito net* **6** [C] COMPUTERS a communications or computer network → see also INTRANET [**Origin:** Old English *nett*] → see also **cast your net wide** at CAST¹ (15), HAIRNET, SAFETY NET

net² W3 *adj.* [only before noun] **1** ECONOMICS relating to the final amount or number that remains when all the gains and losses that affect the total have been calculated: **net profits/assets/income etc.** (=what remains after taxes, costs etc. have been taken away) | *The company's **net worth** is over $8 billion.* | *The Democrats had **a net gain of** 20 seats.* | *There was a **net loss** of 164,000 jobs.* → see also GROSS **2 net result/effect (of sth)** the final result of something: *The net result of the plan will be higher costs to the consumer.* → see also NET PRICE, NET WEIGHT

net³ *v.* **netted, netting** [T] **1** ECONOMICS to earn a particular amount of money as a profit after taxes have been paid: *I was netting around $64,000 a year.* **2** to succeed in getting something, especially by using your skill: *The police raid netted 22 suspects.* | *The Democrats netted 58 percent of the vote.* **3** to catch a fish in a net **4** INFORMAL to hit or kick the ball into the net in sport

neth·er /ˈnɛðɚ/ *adj.* [only before noun] LITERARY or HUMOROUS lower: *One of his songs did hit **the nether regions of*** (=the lower positions on) *the charts.*

Neth·er·lands, the /ˈnɛðɚləndz/ a country in northwest Europe that is north of Belgium and east of Germany

neth·er·most /ˈnɛðɚˌmoʊst/ *adj.* LITERARY lowest: *the nethermost fiery pit of hell*

neth·er·world, **nether world** /ˈnɛðɚˌwɚld/ *n.* [C usually singular] LITERARY **1** the part of society that includes people who are involved in illegal activities SYN **underworld** **2** HELL

Net·i·quette /ˈnɛt̬ɪkɪt/ *n.* [U] INFORMAL the commonly accepted rules for polite behavior when communicating with other people on the Internet [**Origin:** 1900–2000 *Net* + *etiquette*]

ˌnet ˈprice *n.* [C] the price of something, that cannot be reduced anymore

net·ting /ˈnɛt̬ɪŋ/ *n.* [U] material consisting of string, wire etc. that has been woven into a net: *The crab traps are covered in wire netting.*

net·tle¹ /ˈnɛt̬l/ *n.* [C] a wild plant with rough leaves that sting you

nettle² *v.* [T] LITERARY to annoy someone, especially so that they cannot stop thinking about something: *His remarks had obviously nettled her.*

net·tle·some /ˈnɛt̬lsəm/ *adj.* difficult or annoying SYN **thorny**: *nettlesome questions*

ˌnet ˈweight *n.* [C usually singular] the weight of a product without its container

net·work¹ /ˈnɛtˀwɚk/ Ac S3 W1 *n.* [C] **1** ENG. LANG. ARTS a group of radio or television stations, which broadcast many of the same programs in different parts of the country: *the four biggest TV networks* | *a 24-hour news network* | *network executives* **2** a system of lines, tubes, wires, roads etc. that cross each other and are connected to each other: *the freeway network* | **+of** *the network of blood vessels in the body* **3** COMPUTERS a set of computers that are connected to each other so that they can share information: *You need a password to log on to the network.* **4** a group of people, organizations etc. that communicate with each other and can help each other, for example because they do the same type of work: **+of** *Tricia has built up a good network of professional contacts.* | *Single parents need **a** good **support network*** (=people who can help them when they need it).

network² Ac *v.* **1** [I,T] COMPUTERS to connect several computers together so that they can share information: **network with sth** *This card enables your PC to network with other machines.* **2** [I] to meet other people who do the same type of work in order to share information, help each other etc.: *Conferences can be a great opportunity to network.*

net·work·ing /ˈnɛtˀˌwɚkɪŋ/ Ac *n.* [U] **1** the practice of meeting other people involved in the same type of work, in order to share information, support each other etc. **2** the design, building, and use of computer networks

ˌnet ˈworth *n.* [U] ECONOMICS the value of a company or business, calculated by taking away all the company's debts from all the things that the company owns which can be sold to pay its debts

neur- /nʊr/ *prefix* BIOLOGY relating to the nerves: *neuropathy* (=a disease of the nervous system)

neu·ral /ˈnʊrəl/ *adj.* BIOLOGY relating to a nerve or the NERVOUS SYSTEM: *signs of neural activity*

neu·ral·gia /nʊˈrældʒə/ *n.* [U] MEDICINE a sharp pain along the length of a nerve —**neuralgic** *adj.*

neuro- /nʊroʊ, -rə/ *prefix* BIOLOGY relating to the nerves: *a neurosurgeon* (=who treats the body's nervous system)

neu·rol·o·gy /nʊˈrɑlədʒi/ *n.* [U] BIOLOGY the scientific study of the NERVOUS SYSTEM and its diseases —**neurologist** *n.* [C] —**neurological** /ˌnʊrəˈlɑdʒɪkəl/ *adj.*

N

neur·o·mus·cu·lar junc·tion /ˌnʊroʊˌmʌskyələ ˈdʒʌŋkʃən/ *n.* [C] BIOLOGY the point where a nerve cell and a muscle connect, and where the nerve can send a message that causes the muscle to become tighter and ready for action or to become relaxed

neu·ron /ˈnʊrɑn/ *n.* [C] BIOLOGY a type of cell in the NERVOUS SYSTEM that sends messages to muscles and other parts of the body, and sends messages in the brain about feelings, sights, smells etc. SYN **nerve cell**

neu·ro·sis /nʊˈroʊsɪs/ *n. plural* **neuroses** /-siz/ [C,U] MEDICINE a mental illness that makes someone very worried or afraid when they have no reason to be

neu·rot·ic /nʊˈrɑṭɪk/ *adj.* **1** tending to worry in an unreasonable way: *I got really neurotic about money.* **2** MEDICINE relating to or affected by neurosis: *neurotic disorders* —**neurotic** *n.* [C] —**neurotically** /-kli/ *adv.*

neu·ro·trans·mit·ter /ˌnʊroʊˈtrænzmɪṭə/ *n.* [C] BIOLOGY a chemical in the NERVOUS SYSTEM that carries messages from one nerve cell to another

neu·ru·la·tion /ˌnʊrəˈleɪʃən/ *n.* [U] BIOLOGY the process in which the NERVOUS SYSTEM forms in the early EMBRYO

neu·ter[1] /ˈnuṭə/ *v.* [T] BIOLOGY to remove part of the sex organs of an animal so that it cannot produce babies: *a neutered tomcat* [**Origin:** 1300–1400 Latin **neither**, from *ne-* **not** + *uter* **which of two**] → see also SPAY

neuter[2] *adj.* **1** ENG. LANG. ARTS in English grammar, a neuter PRONOUN such as "it" REFERS to something that is neither male nor female, or does not show the sex of the person or animal that it refers to **2** plants or animals that are neuter have undeveloped sex organs or no sex organs

neu·tral[1] /ˈnutrəl/ Ac *adj.*

1 IN AN ARGUMENT ETC. not supporting any of the people or groups involved in an argument or disagreement: *neutral observers of the election* | **+on/about** *The government* ***remains*** *officially* ***neutral*** *on this topic.* | **take a neutral position/stance** *The newspaper decided to take a neutral stance on the election.*

2 neutral ground/territory if two opposing teams or representatives are on neutral ground, they are in a place that is not favorable to either of them: *The talks will be held on neutral territory.* | *The Super Bowl is always played on neutral ground.*

3 IN A WAR POLITICS a country that is neutral does not support any of the countries involved in a war: *During World War II, Sweden was neutral.* | **neutral territory/ground/waters** (=land or ocean that is not controlled by any of the countries involved in a war)

4 LANGUAGE language, words, subjects etc. that are neutral are deliberately chosen to avoid expressing any strong opinion or feeling: *She describes her boyfriend with the neutral term "friend."* | *Try to choose neutral topics, like the weather.*

5 COLOR a neutral color is not very strong or bright, for example gray or light brown: *a dress in a neutral fabric*

6 WIRE PHYSICS a neutral wire has no electrical CHARGE

7 CHEMICAL CHEMISTRY a neutral substance is neither acid nor ALKALINE and has a PH value of 7: *The bush grows best in neutral soil.* —**neutrally** *adv.*

neutral[2] Ac *n.* **1** [U] the position of the GEARS of a car or machine in which no power is being sent from the engine to the wheels or other moving parts → see also PARK: *Start the car* ***in neutral.*** **2** [C] POLITICS a country or person that is not fighting for or helping any of the countries involved in a war **3** [C usually plural] a neutral color, such as gray or light brown: *a room decorated in reds and neutrals*

neu·tral·ist /ˈnutrəlɪst/ *adj.* tending not to support either side in a war, argument etc. —**neutralist** *n.* [C]

neu·tral·i·ty /nuˈtræləṭi/ Ac *n.* [U] the state of not supporting either side in an argument or war: *After Pearl Harbor, U.S. neutrality ended.*

Neu'trality ˌActs, the HISTORY laws passed in the U.S. in the 1930s to stop the country from getting involved in foreign wars

neu·tral·ize /ˈnutrəˌlaɪz/ Ac *v.* [T] **1** to prevent something from having any effect: *The Oilers managed to neutralize the other team's defenses.* **2** CHEMISTRY to make a substance chemically NEUTRAL: *This fertilizer neutralizes the salts in the soil.* **3** to destroy something or kill someone dangerous to you in a war: *Government forces neutralized the rebels.* **4** POLITICS to make a country or population NEUTRAL in war —**neutralization** /ˌnutrələˈzeɪʃən/ *n.* [U]

neu·tri·no /nuˈtrinoʊ/ *n. plural* **neutrinos** [C] a SUBATOMIC PARTICLE (=piece of matter that is smaller than an atom) that has little or no mass and a NEUTRAL electrical charge

neu·tron /ˈnutrɑn/ *n.* [C] PHYSICS a PARTICLE that exists in the NUCLEUS (=central part) of an atom, and that has no electrical charge → see also ELECTRON, PROTON → see picture at ATOM

'neutron ˌbomb *n.* [C] a type of NUCLEAR bomb which kills people but which does not cause much damage to buildings, roads etc.

Ne·va·da /nəˈvædə, -ˈvɑ-/ ABBREVIATION **NV** a state in the western U.S. —**Nevadan** *n., adj.*

nev·er /ˈnɛvə/ S1 W1 *adv.*

1 NOT AT ANY TIME not at any time, or not once: *I've never been to Hawaii.* | *They never had any children.* | *It never gets this hot in Vancouver.* | *I'll* ***never*** *make that mistake* ***again.*** | *She has* ***never*** *been on a plane* ***before*** (=never until the time being talked about). | *I've* ***never ever*** (=used for emphasis) *heard Nina swear.* | ***I never once*** (=used to emphasize that something has never happened) *lied to you.* | *It* ***never*** *occurred to me* ***for one minute*** (=used for emphasis) *that he was guilty.*

THESAURUS

never ever SPOKEN used to emphasize that you mean never: *I'll never ever forgive him.*
not in a million years SPOKEN used to say that something is completely impossible: *She wouldn't go without me – not in a million years!*
not once used to show that you are surprised or annoyed, or to emphasize something: *He hadn't smiled, not once.*
→ OFTEN, RARELY, SOMETIMES

SPOKEN PHRASES

2 never mind a) used to tell someone that something is not important or serious, so that there is no need to worry or feel sorry: *"I forgot to bring your clothes back." "Oh, never mind, I'll get them later."* **b)** used in order to say that you do not want to repeat something that you have said, or do not want to finish what you are saying: *I was thinking...Oh, never mind.*
3 you never know used to say that something that seems unlikely could happen: *You never know, Paul might love it.*
4 I never knew/realized (that) used to mean that you did not know something until now: *I never knew you played the guitar!*
5 well, I never! OLD-FASHIONED used to say that you are very surprised
6 never fear OLD-FASHIONED used to tell someone not to worry

7 never so much as an expression meaning "not even," used to emphasize what you are saying: *He's never so much as made me a cup of coffee in ten years of marriage.*
8 like never before more than at any time in the past: *The president is under pressure like never before.*
9 never say never INFORMAL used to say that you should not say that you will never do something, because there is always a small possibility that you might do it: *"My teaching days are over!" "Never say never!"*
10 never say die INFORMAL used to encourage someone not to give up: *athletes with a never-say-die attitude* (=who refuse to give up) → see also **never fail (to do sth)** at FAIL[1] (8)
[**Origin:** Old English *næfre*, from *ne-* **not** + *æfre* **ever**]

GRAMMAR

Don't use **never** with negative words such as "nobody," "no one," or "nothing." Instead, use **ever**: *Nobody will ever find me here.* You can use **never** with words such as "anybody," "anything," and "anywhere": *I never told anyone this before.* **Never** usually comes before the main verb: *I never go there.* If there is a modal or auxiliary verb (such as "have", "will", "should" etc.), **never** comes after this verb and before the main verb: *You should never talk to strangers.*

ˌnever-ˈending, neverending *adj.* seeming to continue for a very long time: *The climb to the top of the hill was never-ending.*

nev•er•more /ˌnɛvɚˈmɔr/ *adv.* POETIC never again

ˌnever-ˈnever land *n.* [singular, U] INFORMAL a place where everything is perfect that only exists in someone's mind

nev•er•the•less /ˌnɛvɚðəˈlɛs◂/ Ac W3 *adv.* [sentence adverb] FORMAL in spite of what you have just mentioned: *What she said was true. Nevertheless, it was very unkind.* | *The Sharks played with two men in the penalty box, but scored nevertheless.*

new /nu/ S1 W1 *adj.*

1 RECENTLY MADE recently made, built, invented, written etc. OPP **old**: *Can the new drugs help her?* | *Have you tried that new restaurant on Fourth Street?* | *We want to put a new bathroom in.* | *the new issue of "Time" magazine*

THESAURUS

recent used about something that was new or that happened a short time ago: *an article in the recent issue of "Newsweek"*
modern used about things that are different from earlier things of the same kind: *Due to modern medicine, death in childbirth is now uncommon.*
original completely new and different from anything that has been done or thought of before: *original ideas*
fresh used about food that was made, picked etc. only a short time ago: *fresh bread*
latest used about a film, book, fashion etc. that is the newest one: *Irving's latest novel*
→ MODERN, OLD

2 RECENTLY BOUGHT recently bought OPP **old**: *I like your jacket – is it new?* | *I had to buy a new refrigerator.*
3 NOT USED BEFORE [no comparative] not used or owned by anyone before OPP **used** OPP **secondhand**: *They sell both new and secondhand books.* | *Denny just bought a* ***brand new*** (=completely new) *SUV.*
4 RECENTLY ARRIVED having recently arrived in a place, or started a different job or activity: *Margo and Ray just had a new baby.* | *I'd like to welcome all our new students.* | **+to** *I'm new to the area, and I still get lost sometimes.*
5 RECENTLY CHANGED recently changed, and replacing something that was there previously: *Have you met Keith's new girlfriend?* | *Do you have Christy's new address?* | *They just moved to a new apartment*
6 NOT THERE BEFORE having recently developed: *new leaves on the trees* | *It's a new idea, and it just may work.* | *The drug offers new hope to cancer patients.* | *Suddenly there was* ***a whole new*** (=used for emphasis) *set of problems.* | **a new way/method of doing sth** *new ways of treating asthma* | **a new breed/generation of sth** (=a group of people who are different in their attitudes to previous groups)
7 UNFAMILIAR not recognized or not experienced before: *Learning a new language is more difficult for adults.* | *a completely new experience* | *Why not try something new for your vacation this year?* | **+to** *The idea of home computers was very new to us then.*
8 RECENTLY DISCOVERED recently discovered: *the discovery of a new planet* | *new oilfields in Alaska* | *works from new artists*
9 what's new? SPOKEN used as a friendly greeting to ask what is happening in someone's life
10 like new also **as good as new** in excellent condition: *After cleaning, your pillows will be as good as new.* | *He's managed to keep the car* ***looking like new*** *for years.*
11 a new man/woman someone who feels much healthier and has a lot more energy than before, or who has a different attitude than before: *I lost 19 pounds and* ***felt like a new man.***
12 new life/day/era etc. a period of time that is just beginning and seems to offer better opportunities: *They came to America to start a new life.* | *The agreement marks a new day for the national parks.*
13 new blood new members of a group or organization who will bring new ideas and be full of energy: *Every election brings a supply of new blood to the legislature.*
14 the new kid on the block the newest person in a job, school, place etc.: *I was the new kid on the block, and Ray helped me a lot.*
15 a new arrival a) someone who has just arrived in a place: *There are 6,000 new arrivals to the city every month.* **b)** a baby that has just been born: *Attached are some pictures of the new arrival.*
16 sth is the new... used to say that something is thought to be the new fashion that will replace an existing one: *This fall, brown is the new black.*
17 there's nothing new under the sun used to say that everything that happens now has happened before
18 new-made/new-formed etc. recently made, formed etc.
19 a new broom (sweeps clean) used about someone who has just become the leader or manager of an organization and is eager to make changes
20 the new unfamiliar ideas or changes in society: *a fear of the new*
[**Origin:** Old English *niwe*] —**newness** *n.* [U] → see also **give sb/sth a new lease on life** at LEASE[1] (2), **turn over a new leaf** at TURN OVER (5)

ˌNew ˈAge *n.* [U] **1** a set of beliefs about religion, medicine, and ways of life that are not part of traditional Western society or religions **2** a type of music that is meant to help you relax and feel calm —**New Age** *adj.*

New•ark /ˈnuɚk/ a large city in the U.S. state of New Jersey

new•bie /ˈnubi/ *n.* [C] SPOKEN, INFORMAL someone who has just started doing something and therefore is not as skilled as others with more experience

new•born /ˈnubɔrn/ *adj.* **newborn child/baby/son etc.** a child that has just been born —**newborn** *n.* [C] *a young mother with a newborn*

New Bruns•wick /nu ˈbrʌnzwɪk/ a PROVINCE on the coast of western Canada

new•com•er /ˈnuˌkʌmɚ/ *n.* [C] **1** someone that has recently arrived somewhere or recently started a particular activity: *an award for the best newcomer in the film industry* | **+to** *The Johnsons were newcomers to town.* **2** a new product or company that did not exist before: *a promising newcomer on the winemaking scene* | **+to** *the most glamorous newcomer to the Volkswagen range*

ˌNew ˈDeal, the HISTORY President Franklin D. Roosevelt's program of social and economic changes in the 1930s, which tried to provide work and money for people and to end the Depression

New Del•hi /nu ˈdɛli/ the capital city of India

ˌNew ˌEconomic ˈPolicy, the HISTORY an economic program in the Soviet Union from 1921 to 1928, in which some companies were allowed to be privately owned, rather than owned by the government

New Eng•land /nu ˈɪŋglənd/ *n.* [U] the northeastern part of the U.S. that includes the states of Maine, New Hampshire, Vermont, Massachusetts, Connecticut, and Rhode Island

new•fan•gled /ˈnuˌfæŋgəld/ *adj.* DISAPPROVING newfangled ideas, machines etc. have been recently invented but seem complicated or unnecessary: *a newfangled video telephone*

ˈnew-found *adj.* [only before noun] having only recently been gained: *Her new-found fame was difficult to deal with.*

N

New·found·land /ˈnufənd,lænd, -lənd/ a PROVINCE of eastern Canada consisting of the island of Newfoundland and the coast of Labrador

New Hamp·shire /nu ˈhæmpʃɚ/ WRITTEN ABBREVIATION **NH** a state in the northeastern U.S.

,new 'issue ,market *n.* [C] ECONOMICS PRIMARY MARKET

New Jer·sey /nu ˈdʒɚzi/ WRITTEN ABBREVIATION **NJ** a state in the northeastern U.S.

,New 'Left, the HISTORY LEFT-WING people in the 1960s, especially students, who wanted social, economic, and political change

'new-look *adj.* [only before noun] different from before, especially more modern or more attractive: *the company's new-look logo*

new·ly /ˈnuli/ [W3] *adv.* very recently [SYN] **recently**: [+past participle] *a newly built home* | *newly fallen snow* | *the newly appointed director*

,newly in,dustrialized 'country *n.* [C] → see NIC

new·ly·weds /ˈnuli,wɛdz/ *n.* [plural] a man and a woman who have recently gotten married —**newlywed** *adj.*

New Mex·i·co /nu ˈmɛksɪ,koʊ/ WRITTEN ABBREVIATION **NM** a state in the southwestern U.S.

,new 'money *n.* [U] **1** people who have become rich by working, rather than by getting money from their families [OPP] **old money**: *In Chinatown, new money and old poverty live side by side.* **2** a large amount of money that someone has recently received or earned which makes them very rich

,new 'moon *n.* **1** [C usually singular] the moon when it first appears in the sky as a thin CRESCENT [SYN] **crescent moon** **2** [C usually singular, U] the time of the month at which this is first seen **3** [C usually singular] TECHNICAL the time when the moon is between the Earth and the sun, and cannot be seen → see also FULL MOON, HALF MOON

New Or·le·ans /nu ˈɔrliənz, -lənz, ,nu ɔrˈlinz/ a city in the U.S. state of Louisiana, which is regarded as the place where JAZZ music was originally developed. Much of the city was destroyed by a very strong hurricane (Hurricane Katrina) in 2005.

,new po'tato *n.* [C] a small potato from one of the first crops of a year

,new 'rich *n.* **the new rich** people who have recently or suddenly become very rich

,New 'Right, the HISTORY a RIGHT-WING political MOVEMENT (=group of people who want to achieve an aim) in the U.S. that formed between the 1960s and the 1980s and that emphasizes social and moral matters

news /nuz/ [S2] [W1] *n.* [U] **1** information about something that has happened recently: *I hope we'll have more news for you soon.* | **+about/of/on** *By the end of 1848, news about California gold reached South America.* | *What's **the latest news*** (=the most recent news) *on that job you applied for?* | **+that** *Brooks is thrilled at the news that his wife is pregnant.* | **good/great/bad/worrying etc. news** *The cancer seems to be gone, so that's great news.* | *I'm afraid I have some bad news for you.* | *The report **has** good **news for** middle-class renters.* | *Have you **heard the news** that the dairy company is closing?* | *The space agency decision was a welcome **piece of news**.* | **give/tell sb the news** *I wanted to give them the news as soon as possible.* | *Simmons **broke the news*** (=told the bad news) *to his 600 employees in a letter.* | ***News** of the tragedy **spread** quickly around the town.* **2** reports of recent events in the newspapers or on television or the radio: **+of/about** *There has been news of fighting in the area.* | **local/state/national/international news** *The Gazette covers mainly local news.* | *Walsh won an award for her **news story** on bilingual education.* | *What was the President's response to **the latest news*** (=the most recent reports) *on unemployment?* | *Twenty years ago, environmental issues rarely **made the news*** (=were reported in newspapers etc.). | *The singer has **been in the news*** (=been reported in newspapers etc.) *again this week.* | *Wallace's resignation was **front-page news*** (=was important enough to be on the front page of a newspaper). | *The President was on vacation when **the news broke*** (=when an important news story was first reported). **3 the news** a regular television or radio program that gives you reports of recent events: *We usually watch the evening news on NBC.* | *The teachers' strike was **on the news**.* | *The story has **been all over the news*** (=reported about frequently) *lately.* **4 be good/bad news for sb** used to say that a particular fact is likely to make life better or worse for someone: *House prices are very low, which is good news for first-time buyers.* **5 sb/sth is big news** used to say that people are interested in someone or something at the moment and want to know about them: *The young designer's clothes are big news right now.* **6 sb/sth is bad news** INFORMAL used to say that someone or something is likely to cause trouble: *Stay away from him. He's bad news!*

SPOKEN PHRASES

7 I've got news for sb used to say that you are going to tell someone the facts about something, which they will probably not like to hear: *You think you're so smart, but I've got news for you. You don't know anything!* **8 that's/it's news to me!** said when you are surprised or annoyed because you have not been told something earlier: *The meeting's been canceled? That's news to me.* **9 no news is good news** used when you have not received any news about someone or something and you hope this means that nothing bad has happened

'news ,agency *n.* [C] a company that supplies information to newspapers, radio, and television

'news ,blackout *n.* [C] a period of time when particular pieces of news are not allowed to be reported

'news ,bulletin *n.* [C] a short news announcement about something important that has just happened, that is broadcast suddenly in the middle of a television or radio program

news·cast /ˈnuzkæst/ *n.* [C] a news program on television

news·cast·er /ˈnuz,kæstɚ/ *n.* [C] someone who reads the news on television [SYN] **anchor**

'news ,conference *n.* [C] a meeting at which someone, especially someone famous or important, makes official statements to people who write news reports: [SYN] **press conference**: **have/hold/call a news conference** | *A news conference was held to announce the deal.*

news·group /ˈnuzgrup/ *n.* [C] a FORUM on the Internet

news·hawk /ˈnuzhɔk/ *n.* [C] INFORMAL a news hound

'news hound *n.* [C] INFORMAL someone who writes for a newspaper

news·let·ter /ˈnuz,lɛt̬ɚ/ [S3] *n.* [C] a short written report of news about a club, organization, or particular subject that is sent regularly to people: *the church newsletter* | *They publish seven newsletters on investments.*

news·mak·er /ˈnuz,meɪkɚ/ *n.* [C] someone important, whose activities are reported in newspapers and on television

news·man /ˈnuzmæn/ *n. plural* **newsmen** /-mɛn/ [C] a man who writes or reports news for a newspaper or for a television or radio broadcast

news·pa·per /ˈnuz,peɪpɚ/ [S2] [W1] *n.* **1** [C] a set of large folded sheets of paper containing news, articles, pictures, advertisements etc. that is printed and sold daily or weekly: *a local newspaper* | *newspaper articles about real estate* | *The story was **in all the newspapers**.*

THESAURUS

Newspapers in general
the papers, **the press**, **the media** (=newspapers, TV, radio etc.)
tabloid a newspaper that has small pages, a lot of photographs, short stories, and not much serious news

broadsheet a serious newspaper printed on large sheets of paper
Parts of a newspaper
front page
sports/entertainment/food etc. section the set of pages in a newspaper dealing with sports, entertainment etc.
the comics page/the funnies the part of a newspaper with many diffferent cartoons
editorial/opinion/op-ed page the page or pages of a newspaper in which the editor of a newspaper and other people express their opinions about the news, rather than just giving facts
headlines the titles of newspaper articles, printed in large letters above the article, and which usually show the most important pieces of news
article a piece of writing about a particular subject
report a piece of writing in a newspaper about an event
story a report in a newspaper about a recent event
column an article on a particular subject or by a particular writer that appears regularly
People who write newspapers
editor the person who is in charge of a newspaper, magazine etc. and decides what should be included in it, or the person who prepares an article for printing by deciding what to include and checking for mistakes
reporter someone whose job is to report on events for a newspaper or magazine, or on television or the radio
journalist someone who writes reports for newspapers and magazines
correspondent someone whose job is to report news from a distant area or about a particular subject
columnist someone who writes articles, especially about a particular subject, that appear regularly

2 [U] sheets of paper from old newspapers: *Wrap the plates in newspaper to stop them from breaking.* **3** [C] a company that produces a newspaper: *Hearst owned several newspapers.*

news·pa·per·man /ˈnuzpeɪpɚˌmæn/ *n. plural* **newspapermen** /-ˌmɛn/ [C] a man who writes or reports news for a newspaper

ˈnewspaper ˌstand *n.* [C] a NEWSSTAND

news·pa·per·wom·an /ˈnuzpeɪpɚˌwʊmən/ *n. plural* **newspaperwomen** /-ˌwɪmɪn/ [C] a woman who writes or reports news for a newspaper

news·print /ˈnuzˌprɪnt/ *n.* [U] TECHNICAL cheap paper used mostly for printing newspapers

news·reel /ˈnuzril/ *n.* [C] a short movie containing news reports, seen in movie theaters in past times

ˈnews reˌlease *n.* [C] a PRESS RELEASE

news·room /ˈnuzrum/ *n.* [C] the office in a newspaper or broadcasting company where news is received and news reports are written

news·stand /ˈnuzstænd/ *n.* [C] a place on a street where newspapers and magazines are sold

ˈnews ˌvendor *n.* [C] someone who sells newspapers

news·wom·an /ˈnuzˌwʊmən/ *n. plural* **newswomen** /-ˌwɪmɪn/ [C] a woman who writes or reports news for a newspaper or for a television or radio broadcast

news·wor·thy /ˈnuzˌwɚði/ *adj.* important or interesting enough to be reported as news: *Very little that was newsworthy was said at the conference.*

news·writ·er /ˈnuzˌraɪt̬ɚ/ *n.* [C] someone who writes news stories, especially to be read on television or radio news broadcasts

new·sy /ˈnuzi/ *adj.* a newsy letter is from a friend or relative and contains a lot of news about them

newt /nut/ *n.* [C] a small animal that lives in water and has a long body, four legs, and a tail [**Origin:** 1400–1500 *an ewt*, mistaken for *a newt*; *ewt* **newt** from Old English *efete*]

ˌNew ˈTestament *n.* **the New Testament** the part of the Bible that is about the life of Jesus Christ and what he taught → see also OLD TESTAMENT

new·ton /ˈnutˀn/ WRITTEN ABBREVIATION **N** *n.* [C] PHYSICS a unit for measuring force in the METRIC SYSTEM equal to the force that produces an ACCELERATION of one meter per second on a mass of one kilogram

New·ton /ˈnutˀn/, **Sir I·saac** /ˈaɪzək/ (1642–1727) a British PHYSICIST and MATHEMATICIAN who is best known for discovering GRAVITY and is considered one of the most important scientists who ever lived

Isaac Newton

New·to·ni·an /nuˈtoʊniən/ *adj.* PHYSICS relating to the laws of PHYSICS that were discovered by the scientist Isaac Newton: *Newtonian mechanics*

ˌNewton's ˌfirst ˈlaw also **ˌNewton's ˌfirst law of ˈmotion** PHYSICS a principle of PHYSICS that states that an object that is not moving will continue not to move unless a force acts on it. It also says that an object moving in a straight line at a steady speed will continue to do so unless a force acts on it. SYN law of inertia

ˌNewton's ˌlaw of ˈcooling PHYSICS a principle of PHYSICS that states that the rate at which an object becomes cooler depends on the difference between its temperature and the temperature of whatever surrounds it

ˌNewton's ˌsecond ˈlaw also **ˌNewton's ˌsecond law of ˈmotion** PHYSICS a principle of PHYSICS that states that the ACCELERATION of an object depends on the strength of the force acting on it, that the object moves in the direction of the force, and that the acceleration increases at the same rate as the MASS of the object decreases

ˌNewton's ˌthird ˈlaw also **ˌNewton's ˌthird law of ˈmotion** PHYSICS a principle of PHYSICS that states that whenever one object puts a force on another object, the second object puts an equal force in the opposite direction on the first object

ˌnew ˈwave *n.* **1** [C usually singular, U] new ideas or styles in music, movies, art, politics etc.: **+of/in** *the new wave of American fiction* **2** [C usually singular] a group of people who use new ideas or styles in music, movies, art, politics etc.: **+of** *the new wave of directors from Hong Kong* **3** [U] also **New Wave** a type of music that was popular in the late 1970s and the early 1980s, which uses SYNTHESIZERS and a strong beat, and in which the words are sung without much emotion —**new wave** *adj.*

ˈNew World **1 the New World** North, Central, and South America, especially as considered by Europeans when they first discovered them: *Chili peppers are native to the New World.* **2 the New World** in wine-making, non-European countries such as South Africa, New Zealand, and the United States —**New World** *adj.*: *New World civilizations* → see also OLD WORLD

ˌNew ˈYear *n.* **1 New Year** also **New Year's** the time when you celebrate the beginning of the year: *We're spending New Year's at my parents' house.* | *I'm just writing to* ***wish you a happy New Year!*** | *Have you made any* ***New Year's resolutions*** (=promises to improve yourself in the new year)*?* | **welcome/ring in the New Year** (=to celebrate the beginning of the year at midnight on December 31) **2 the new year** the year after the present year, especially the first few months of it: *The company plans to open several new stores* ***in the new year.***

ˌNew Year's ˈDay *n.* a holiday on January 1, the first day of the year in Western countries

ˌNew Year's ˈEve *n.* December 31, the last day of the

year, when many people have parties to celebrate the beginning of the next year

New York /nu 'yɔrk/ **1** → see NEW YORK CITY **2** also **New York State** WRITTEN ABBREVIATION **NY** a state in the northeastern U.S.

N

ˌNew York 'City also **New York** WRITTEN ABBREVIATION **NYC** the largest city in the U.S., which is divided into five BOROUGHS; Manhattan, the Bronx, Brooklyn, Queens, and Staten Island —**New Yorker** *n.* [C]

ˌNew York 'Stock Exˌchange WRITTEN ABBREVIATION **NYSE** *n.* [singular] the main STOCK MARKET in the U.S., where STOCKS in large U.S. companies are bought and sold

New Zea·land /nu 'zilənd/ a country consisting of two main islands, North Island and South Island, and several smaller ones, in the Pacific Ocean southeast of Australia —**New Zealander** *n.*

next¹ /nɛkst/ S1 W1 *determiner, adj.* **1** the next day, time, event etc. is the one that happens after the present one: *His next job was in a hotel.* | ***The next** flight leaves in 45 minutes.* | *I'm going to be studying Spanish intensively for **the next** three months.* | *They went back to St. Louis **the next day**.* | ***Next time** (=when this happens again), be more careful.* | **next Monday/Tuesday etc.** *I'll see you next Monday.* | **next week/month/year etc.** *Jill and I are going to Mom's next weekend.* | **the next two days/three months/five years etc.** *The next few months went by slowly.* → see also LAST ►see THESAURUS box at **later²**

THESAURUS

following immediately after: *There will be a reception following the wedding.*
subsequent FORMAL coming after or following something else: *This will be explained in more detail in subsequent chapters.*
succeeding coming after something else: *succeeding generations*
later coming in the future, or after something else: *The benefits will not become clear until a later date.*

2 the next place is the one closest to where you are now: *Turn left at the next corner.* | *We could hear everything from the next room.* **3** coming after the present one in a series or order: *The letter continues on the next page.* | *Who's next in line?* | *Read the next two chapters before Friday.* | *Do they have **the next size up** (=a slightly bigger size)?* **4 the next thing you know** SPOKEN used when talking about something that happened suddenly or was a surprise: *The next thing I knew he was trying to kiss me!* → see also NEXT OF KIN

next² S1 W2 *adv.* **1** immediately after: *What do I do next?* | *Heat the chocolate until it melts. Next, pour it into the molds and leave to cool.* ►see THESAURUS box at **after³** **2 next to sb/sth a)** very close to someone or something, with nothing in between: *There was a little girl sitting next to him.* | *Put it in the closet next to the bathroom.* **b)** used to say what is first of a list of things you like or prefer: *Next to volleyball, basketball is the sport I enjoy most.* **3 the next biggest/oldest/fastest etc. sth (after sb/sth)** the thing or person that is closest in size, age, speed etc. to the one you are talking about, but less than it: *the next most powerful person in the organization* | *The next biggest group after English speakers is Spanish speakers.* **4 next to nothing** very little: *Phil earns next to nothing.* **5 next to impossible** very difficult: *It's next to impossible to get tickets to the game.* **6 the next best thing** the thing or situation that is almost as good as the one you really want: *If we can't be together, talking on the phone is the next best thing.* **7** LITERARY the next time: *When I next saw Sylvia, she completely ignored me.*

next³ S3 *pron.* **1** the person or thing in a list, series etc. that comes after the person or thing you are dealing with now: *Jamie was next in line.* | *What's next on the shopping list?* **2 the day/week etc. after next** the day, week etc. that follows the next one: *Joanie and her husband are coming to visit the week after next.* **3 the next to last** the one before the last one: *Stewart was assured of the championship in the next to last race of the year.* **4 next (please)** SPOKEN used to tell someone that it is now their turn to do something, especially someone who is waiting in line for something **5 be next in line** to be the next person to become king, a leader etc.: *Prince Charles is next in line to become king of England.*

'next-door *adj.* relating to the room, building etc. that is next to yours: *Our **next-door neighbors** will take care of the cat for us.*

ˌnext 'door S2 *adv.* in the house, room etc. next to yours or someone else's: *The boy next door cuts our grass for us.* | *Deanna's office is right next door.* | *The Garcias bought the house **next door to** my mother's.*

ˌnext of 'kin *n.* [U] your most closely related family, including your husband or wife, who would be the first people to be told if you were injured or dead: *the victim's next of kin*

nex·us /'nɛksəs/ *n. plural* **nexus, nexuses** [C] a connection or network of connections between a number of people, things, or ideas: *a nexus of social relationships* | *the education-employment nexus*

Nez Perce, Nez Percé /ˌnɛz 'pɚs/ a Native American tribe from the northwestern area of the U.S.

NFC *n.* **National Football Conference** a group of teams that forms one of the two DIVISIONS (=parts) in the NFL → see also AFC

NFL *n.* **National Football League** the organization that is in charge of professional football in the U.S.

n-gon /'ɛn gɑn/ *n.* [C] MATH a POLYGON (=flat shape with many sides) that has n sides, where n represents a number

NH the written abbreviation of New Hampshire

NHL *n.* **National Hockey League** the organization that is in charge of professional HOCKEY in the U.S. and Canada

ni·a·cin /'naɪəsɪn/ *n.* [U] BIOLOGY a type of VITAMIN

Niagara Falls

Ni·ag·ara Falls /naɪˌægrə 'fɔlz/ two very large WATERFALLS on the border between Canada and the U.S.

Ni'agara ˌMovement, the HISTORY a group of African Americans, formed in 1905, whose aim was to gain equal rights for people of all races in the U.S.

Ni·a·mey /ni'ɑmeɪ/ the capital and largest city of Niger

nib /nɪb/ *n.* [C] the pointed metal part at the end of a pen

nib·ble¹ /'nɪbəl/ *v.* [I,T] **a)** to eat small amounts of food by taking very small bites: *We put out nuts for the squirrels to nibble.* | **+at/on** *Guests were nibbling on hors d'oeuvres.* **b)** to gently bite something, as a sign of sexual attraction

nibble

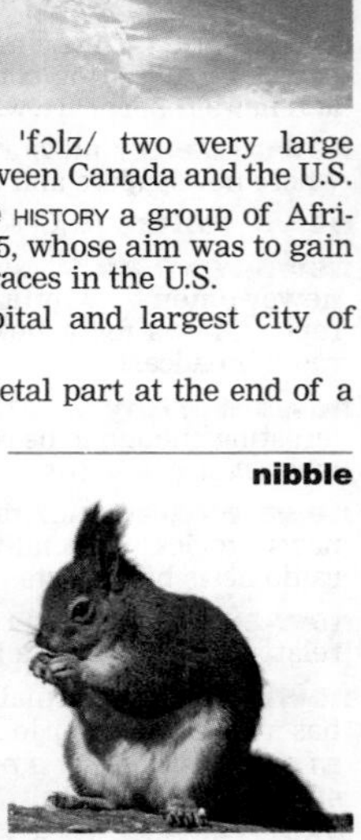

nibble (away) at sth *phr. v.* **1** to keep reducing something by taking smaller amounts from it SYN **eat**

into: *House expenses are nibbling away at our savings.* **2** to begin to deal with something in a small way: *A few studies have begun to nibble at the issue of health-care costs.*

nibble² *n.* **1** [C] a small bite of something: *One of the kids tried a nibble of the bread.* **2 nibbles** [plural] small things to eat, especially at a party: *a selection of cocktail nibbles* **3** [C] an expression of slight interest in an offer or suggestion: *We've had a few nibbles from potential buyers.*

NIC *n.* [C] ECONOMICS **Newly Industrialized Country** a country in which the economic system has recently changed from one based on farming to one based on industry, and the country is developing and improving

Nic·a·rag·ua /ˌnɪkəˈrɑgwə/ **1** a country in Central America between the Caribbean Sea and the Pacific Ocean, and south of Honduras and north of Costa Rica **2 Lake Nicaragua** the largest lake in Central America —**Nicaraguan** *n., adj.*

nice /naɪs/ S1 W2 *adj.*

1 GOOD good, pleasant, attractive, or enjoyable OPP **terrible** OPP **awful** OPP **horrible** OPP **nasty**: *That's a nice dress.* | *Did you have a nice time?* | *That wasn't a nice thing to say!* | *You **look nice** today.* | ***It's really nice to** see you again.* | **a nice big/new/long etc. sth** *a nice new car* | *I took a nice hot shower.* | *I got a nice long email from Sarah.* | **nice and cool/warm/big/soft etc.** *Their house is always so nice and neat.* | *Come back inside where it's nice and warm.*

THESAURUS

enjoyable used for describing something that gives you pleasure because it is interesting, exciting etc.: *an enjoyable game*
pleasant used for describing something that you like, especially something that is peaceful or relaxing: *It had been a pleasant evening.*
great/fantastic/wonderful used for describing something that you like very much: *"How was your vacation?" "Wonderful!"*
delightful very nice and pleasant: *a delightful story*
→ HORRIBLE

2 FRIENDLY friendly or kind: *Dave's a really nice guy.* | *He had a lot of nice things to say about you.* | *Katherine! **Be nice to** the cat!* | *Thanks. **It was nice of you to** help.* ▶see THESAURUS box at **friendly, kind²**

3 WEATHER nice weather is warm and sunny: *What a nice day!* | ***It's really nice out** today.*

SPOKEN PHRASES

4 it/that is nice also **it/that would be nice** said when you think something is good or when you would like to do something: *It's so nice to sit down and rest for a while.* | *"Let's find a place to eat outside." "That would be nice!"*
5 have a nice day! used to say goodbye to someone, especially to customers in stores and restaurants when they are leaving
6 nice try used to say that what someone has done or guessed is very good, but not completely correct: *"I'd say you're about 35." "Nice try. I'm only 29."*
7 Nice going/move! **a)** said as a joke when someone makes a mistake or does something wrong: *"Aargh, I just spilled my coffee!" "Nice move."* **b)** said when someone does something very well, especially when it is difficult: *I hear you got the job. Nice going!*
8 it's nice to know (that) used to mean that you feel happier when you know something: *Well, it's nice to know the ad is working.*

9 RESPECTABLE OLD-FASHIONED having high standards of moral and social behavior: *It's the kind of place nice people don't go to.* | ***Nice girls** don't go out dressed like that.*

10 DETAIL FORMAL involving a very small difference or detail: *a nice point of law*

[**Origin:** 1200–1300 Old French **stupid**, from Latin *nescius* **lacking knowledge**] —**niceness** *n.* [U] → see also **nice/pleased/good to meet you** at MEET¹ (4), **(it was) nice/good meeting you** at MEET¹ (5), **no more Mr. Nice Guy!** at MR (4)

GRAMMAR

Nice is often used in two-part adjectival phrases such as *nice and quiet* or *nice and clean*. These phrases are always placed after the noun they modify, and usually follow a linking verb such as "is", "seem" etc.: *Your new house looks nice and big.* Do not use "and" after **nice** when it comes in front of a noun: *This is a nice big house!*

USAGE

Use **nice** in spoken English in order to show that you like someone or something: *We had a nice time at the party.* However, many teachers think it is better to use a more specific adjective in formal and written English: *They have a beautiful house.* | *She's a very thoughtful person.*

ˌnice-ˈlooking *adj.* fairly attractive: *Ramon's a nice-looking boy.* | *a nice-looking salad*

nice·ly /ˈnaɪsli/ S3 *adv.* **1** in a pleasing or attractive way: *Ann dresses her children nicely.* | *Cook the pork until it is nicely browned.* **2** in a satisfactory way: *His arm is healing nicely.* **3** in a pleasant, polite, or friendly way: *If you ask Daddy nicely, I'm sure he'll give you some.* **4** FORMAL exactly or carefully: *a nicely calculated distance*

ni·ce·ty /ˈnaɪsət̬i/ *n. plural* **niceties** **1** [C] FORMAL a small detail, especially one that is usually considered to be part of the correct way of doing something: *a legal nicety* | *social niceties* **2 niceties** [plural] something that is pleasant but not necessary: *The car includes such niceties as a DVD player and heated seats.*

niche¹ /nɪtʃ/ *n.* [C] **1** a job or activity that is perfect for the skills, abilities, and character that you have: *Rodgers **found his niche** as a high school baseball coach.* **2** also **niche market, market niche** a part of the population that buys a particular product or uses a particular service, or is likely to do so: *Consumers of organic food are a growing niche market.* **3** a small hollow place in a wall, often made to hold a STATUE **4** BIOLOGY the environmental conditions in which a particular animal, plant etc. lives, the way it lives in these conditions, and the relationship it has with other animals, plants etc. living around it: *An osprey primarily preys upon fish, therefore its niche is near water.* [**Origin:** 1600–1700 French, Old French *nicher* **to nest**, from Latin *nidus* **nest**]

niche² *adj.* [only before noun] relating to selling goods to a particular small group of people who have similar needs, interests etc.: *niche publishing* | *niche marketing*

Nich·o·las /ˈnɪkələs/, **St.** a Christian BISHOP who lived in western Asia in the 4th century A.D. He became connected with the custom of giving gifts to children at Christmas and the imaginary character Santa Claus is based on stories about him. He is also the PATRON SAINT of Russia.

Nicholas II /ˌnɪkələs ðə ˈsɛkənd/ (1868–1918) the CZAR of Russia before the Russian Revolution of 1917, in which he was forced to ABDICATE and he and his family were killed

nick¹ /nɪk/ *n.* **1 (just) in the nick of time** just before it is too late or just before something bad happens: *The money came through just in the nick of time.* **2** [C] a very small cut made on the edge or surface of something

nick² *v.* [T] to make a small cut in the surface or edge of something, usually by accident: *I nicked myself shaving this morning.*

nick·el /ˈnɪkəl/ *n.* **1** [C] a coin that is worth five cents, used in the U.S. or Canada ▶see THESAURUS box at **money** **2** [U] SYMBOL **Ni** CHEMISTRY a hard silver-white metal that is an ELEMENT and is used in making other metals [**Origin:** 1700–1800 German *kupfernickel* substance containing nickel, from *kupfer* **copper** + *nickel*

spirit that plays tricks; because the substance contains no copper, even though it looks like copper]

ˈnickel-and-dime[1] *v.* [T] DISAPPROVING to gradually ruin something or hurt someone financially by spending too little money on them, or by making them pay lots of small amounts of money: *"Banks are trying to nickel-and-dime their customers with fees," said Cohn, an analyst.*

nickel-and-dime[2] *adj.* [only before noun] INFORMAL not large, important, or effective enough, especially not involving enough money SYN **cheap**: *We face big problems that can't be solved with nickel-and-dime solutions.*

Nick·laus /ˈnɪkləs/, **Jack** /dʒæk/ (1940–) a U.S. GOLFER

nick·name /ˈnɪkneɪm/ *n.* [C] a silly name or a shorter form of someone's real name, usually given by friends or family: *Johnson earned the nickname "Magic" in high school.* [**Origin:** 1400–1500 *an ekename*, mistaken for *a nekename*, from *eke* **also** (11–19 centuries) (from Old English *eac*) + *name*] —**nickname** *v.* [T] *Montefusco was nicknamed "The Count" in his playing days.* ►see THESAURUS box at **name**[1]

Nic·o·si·a /ˌnɪkəˈsiə/ the capital and largest city of Cyprus

nic·o·tine /ˈnɪkəˌtin/ *n.* [U] BIOLOGY a substance in tobacco that makes it difficult for people to stop smoking, and that increases their heart rate and blood pressure [**Origin:** 1800–1900 Jean *Nicot* (1530–1604), French diplomat who first brought tobacco into France]

ˈnicotine ˌpatch *n.* [C] a small piece of material containing nicotine, that you stick on your skin to help you stop smoking

nic·ti·tat·ing mem·brane /ˌnɪktəteɪṭɪŋ ˈmɛmbreɪn/ *n.* [C] BIOLOGY a thin transparent layer of skin that is closer to the eye than an EYELID, and that can move across the eyes of birds, REPTILES, and some other animals to protect the eye SYN **third eyelid**

niece /nis/ *n.* [C] the daughter of your brother or sister, or the daughter of your wife's or husband's brother or sister [**Origin:** 1200–1300 Old French, Late Latin *neptia* **granddaughter, niece**] → see also NEPHEW

Nie·tzsche /ˈnitʃi, -tʃə/, **Fried·rich** /ˈfridrɪk/ (1844–1900) a German PHILOSOPHER —**Nietzschean** *adj.*

nif·ty /ˈnɪfti/ *adj. comparative* **niftier**, *superlative* **niftiest** INFORMAL very good, fast, effective, or attractive: *It's a nifty computer game that teaches math skills.* | *a nifty new bike*

Ni·ger /ˈnaɪdʒɚ/ **1** a large country in west Africa, south of Algeria and north of Nigeria **2 the Niger** the third longest river in Africa, flowing through Mali, Niger, and Nigeria —**Nigerois** /ˌnɪʒɛrˈwɑ/ *n., adj.*

Ni·ge·ri·a /naɪˈdʒɪriə/ a country in west Africa, east of Benin and west of Cameroon —**Nigerian** *n., adj.*

nig·gard·ly /ˈnɪgɚdli/ *adj.* FORMAL **1** unwilling to spend money or be generous SYN **stingy**: *Banks have been niggardly in approving loans.* **2** a niggardly gift, amount, salary etc. is not worth very much and is not given willingly: *niggardly wages* —**niggardliness** *n.* [U]

nig·gle /ˈnɪgəl/ *v.* [I] to argue or make criticisms about small unimportant details SYN **quibble**: *She niggled over every detail of the bill.*

nig·gling /ˈnɪglɪŋ/ *adj.* [only before noun] fairly unimportant, but continuing to annoy someone: *a niggling doubt*

nigh /naɪ/ *adv.* LITERARY **1** near: *Winter is **drawing nigh*** (=coming soon). **2** also **nigh on** almost SYN **well-nigh**: *It was nigh impossible to ignore him.*

night /naɪt/ S1 W1 *n.*

1 WHEN IT IS DARK [C,U] the dark part of each 24-hour period, when the sun cannot be seen: *a cold night* | *You can see the stars really clearly here **at night**.* | *The desert is summer by day and freezing winter **by night**.* | *I stayed up **all night** to finish my paper.* | *As **night fell*** (=it became dark), *the Olympic flame was lit.*

2 EVENING [C,U] the time during the evening until you go to bed: *I saw it on the news a couple of nights ago.* | *I talked to Pat **last night**.* | *The plane leaves at 7:30 **at night**.* | *Are you going to be home **tomorrow night**?* | *I had dinner with Clay **the other night*** (=a few evenings ago). | *The kids are normally in bed by eight on **week nights*** (=the evenings during the week, not weekends). | *I was tired after my **late night*** (=when I went to sleep late). | *I don't want you walking home by yourself **late at night**.* | *Young people strolled with their dates on a **night out*** (=a night when you go to a party, restaurant etc.). | **Tuesday/Wednesday etc. night** *The school's open house is Thursday night.* | *He sat up **night after night*** (=every night for a long period of time) *to finish the book.*

3 WHEN YOU SLEEP the time when most people are sleeping: *I didn't sleep very well **last night*** (=the night just before this morning). | *A lot of people work **at night**.* | *The baby cried **all night**.* | *We had to get up **in the middle of the night** to get to the airport.* | *All you need is **a good night's sleep*** (=to sleep well at night). | *Katie still gets up **in the night*** (=during the night) *sometimes.* | *We'll **spend the night*** (=sleep) *at my parents' and come back Sunday.* | *I don't think she planned on **staying the night*** (=sleeping at someone's house).

4 nights if you do something nights, you do it regularly or often at night: *Mom lies awake nights worrying about her.* | *Juan has been **working nights**.*

SPOKEN PHRASES

5 night! used to say goodbye to someone when it is late in the evening or when they are going to bed: *Night! Thanks again for dinner.*

6 night night! also **nighty night!** used to say goodbye to a child, when he or she is going to bed SYN **good night**

7 at this time of night used when you are surprised because something happens late at night: *Who on earth could be calling at this time of night?*

8 like night and day used to say that two things, people, or situations are completely different: *He was so different from my first husband. It was like night and day.* → see also LATE-NIGHT

9 last thing at night just before you go to bed: *Lock the doors and turn off the lights last thing at night.*

10 first night also **opening night** the first performance of a play or show

[**Origin:** Old English *niht*] → see also **day and night** at DAY (2), NIGHTLY

night·cap /ˈnaɪt˺kæp/ *n.* [C] **1** an alcoholic drink that you have just before you go to bed **2** a soft cap that people in past times used to wear in bed

night·clothes /ˈnaɪt˺kloʊz/ *n.* [plural] FORMAL clothes that you wear in bed

night·club /ˈnaɪt˺klʌb/ *n.* [C] a place where people can drink alcohol and dance, that is open late at night

night·crawl·er /ˈnaɪt˺ˌkrɔlɚ/ *n.* [C] a type of worm that comes out of the ground at night, often used for fishing

ˈnight deˌpository *n.* [C] a special hole in the outside wall of a bank, where a customer can put money or documents when the bank is closed

night·dress /ˈnaɪt˺drɛs/ *n.* [C] a nightgown

night·fall /ˈnaɪtfɔl/ *n.* [U] the time in the evening when it begins to get darker SYN **dusk**: *By nightfall, the winds had grown stronger.*

night·gown /ˈnaɪt˺gaʊn/ *n.* [C] a piece of loose clothing, like a dress, that women wear in bed

night·hawk /ˈnaɪthɔk/ *n.* [C] OLD-FASHIONED a NIGHT OWL

night·ie /ˈnaɪṭi/ *n.* [C] INFORMAL a NIGHTGOWN

night·in·gale /ˈnaɪt˺nˌgeɪl, ˈnaɪṭɪŋ-/ *n.* [C] BIOLOGY a small wild European bird that sings very beautifully, especially at night

Night·in·gale /ˈnaɪt˺nˌgeɪl, ˈnaɪṭɪŋ-/, **Flor·ence** /ˈflɔrəns/ (1820–1910) an English nurse who set up a hospital for soldiers during the Crimean War, and a school for nurses

night·life /ˈnaɪt˺laɪf/ *n.* [U] entertainment that you can go to and places where you can drink, dance etc. in the evening: *I loved the nightlife in New York.*

ˈnight light *n.* [C] a very small electric light that you turn on in a child's room at night

night·long /ˈnaɪt˺lɔŋ/ *adj.* [only before noun] LITERARY continuing all night: *The protesters held a nightlong vigil.*

night·ly /ˈnaɪtli/ *adv.* every night: *The band performs nightly.* **—nightly** *adj.*: *nightly news broadcasts*

night·mare /ˈnaɪt˺mɛr/ *n.* [C] **1** a very frightening dream: *During the trial, she* ***had nightmares***. | **+about** *He still has nightmares about being in the hospital.* | *As a child I had* ***a recurring nightmare*** (=one that you have many times). **2** a person, thing, situation etc. that is very bad or very difficult to deal with: *It was a nightmare driving home in the snow.* | **+for** *The whole experience has been a nightmare for me and my family.* | **the nightmare of (doing) sth** *the nightmare of divorce* | *The winds are a firefighter's* ***worst nightmare***. **3** something terrible that you are afraid may happen in the future: **+of** *the nightmare of cancer* | *The government fears a* ***nightmare scenario*** (=the worst situation you can imagine) *of nuclear or chemical warfare.* **—nightmarish** *adj.*

ˈnight owl *n.* [C] INFORMAL someone who enjoys staying awake late at night

ˈnight school *n.* [U] classes taught in the evening, for adults who work during the day: *I was working two jobs and going to night school.*

night·shade /ˈnaɪt˺ʃeɪd/ *n.* [U] a type of plant that has poisonous leaves

ˈnight shift *n.* [C usually singular] **1** a period of time at night during which people regularly work: *Kim's working the night shift at the hospital.* **2** the group of people who work at this time: *The night shift was just arriving.*

night·shirt /ˈnaɪt˺ʃɚt/ *n.* [C] a long loose shirt that people wear in bed

ˈnight spot *n.* [C] a place people go to at night for entertainment, such as drinking or dancing: *a popular Manhattan night spot*

night·stand /ˈnaɪtstænd/ *n.* [C] a small table beside a bed

night·stick /ˈnaɪtstɪk/ *n.* [C] a type of stick carried as a weapon by police officers

ˈnight ˌtable *n.* [C] a nightstand

night·time /ˈnaɪt-taɪm/ *n.* [U] the time during the night when the sky is dark OPP **daytime**: *Nighttime temperatures dipped below freezing.*

ˌnight ˈwatchman *n.* [C] someone whose job is to guard a building at night **—night watch** *n.* [singular, U]

night·wear /ˈnaɪt˺wɛr/ *n.* [U] FORMAL clothes that people wear in bed at night

ni·hil·ism /ˈniəˌlɪzəm, ˈnaɪ-/ *n.* [U] the belief that nothing in life has any meaning or value, and that there are no moral principles or social institutions that are worth respecting or keeping **—nihilist** *n.* [C] **—nihilistic** /ˌniəˈlɪstɪk◂ / *adj.*

Ni·jin·sky /nɪˈdʒɪnski/, **Vas·lav** /ˈvɑtslɑf/ (1890–1950) a Russian dancer and CHOREOGRAPHER of BALLET

-nik /nɪk/ *suffix* [in nouns] INFORMAL used with nouns to mean someone who supports a particular group of people or a particular idea, especially an idea that is disapproved of: *healthniks* (=people who are too concerned with their health) | *peaceniks* (=people who think war is never right)

nil /nɪl/ *n.* [U] nothing or zero: **almost/virtually nil** *The chances of that happening are almost nil.*

Nile, the /naɪl/ a river in northeast Africa that is the longest river in the world

nim·ble /ˈnɪmbəl/ *adj.* **1** able to move quickly, easily, and skillfully: *nimble fingers* **2** able to think, change, or make decisions quickly: *a small nimble company* | *a nimble speechwriter* **3 a nimble mind/wit etc.** an ability to think quickly, understand things easily, or make intelligent and funny remarks [**Origin:** Old English *numol* **holding a lot**, from *niman* **to take**] **—nimbly** *adv.* **—nimbleness** *n.* [U]

nim·bus /ˈnɪmbəs/ *n.* **1** [C,U] EARTH SCIENCE a type of dark cloud that may bring rain or snow **2** [C] LITERARY a HALO

NIMBY /ˈnɪmbi/ *n. plural* **NIMBYs** [C] **not in my back yard** someone who does not want a particular activity or building near their home **—nimby** *adj.*

Nim·itz /ˈnɪmɪts/, **Ches·ter** /ˈtʃɛstɚ/ (1885–1966) the leader of the U.S. Navy in the Pacific area during World War II

nim·rod /ˈnɪmrɑd/ *n.* [C] SPOKEN a stupid person

nin·com·poop /ˈnɪŋkəmˌpup/ *n.* [C] OLD-FASHIONED a stupid person

nine /naɪn/ *number* **1** 9 **2** 9 o'clock: *I have a dentist's appointment* ***at nine***. **3 nine times out of ten** almost always: *Nine times out of ten we beat them.* **4 have nine lives** to have a lot of lucky escapes from difficult or dangerous situations [**Origin:** Old English *nigon*] → see also **be on cloud nine** at CLOUD[1] (5), **dressed to the nines** at DRESSED (6)

nine·teen /ˌnaɪnˈtin◂ / *number* 19

nine·teenth¹ /ˌnaɪnˈtinθ◂ / *adj.* 19th; next after the eighteenth: *the nineteenth century*

nineteenth² *pron.* **the nineteenth** the 19th thing in a series: *Let's have dinner on the nineteenth* (=the 19th day of the month).

ˌNineteenth Aˈmendment, the HISTORY a written change to the U.S. CONSTITUTION, which gives women the right to vote. The Nineteenth Amendment was made in 1920.

nine·ti·eth¹ /ˈnaɪntiɪθ/ *adj.* 90th; next after the eighty-ninth: *It's my grandmother's ninetieth birthday tomorrow.*

nine·ti·eth² *pron.* **the ninetieth** the 90th thing in a series

ˌnine-to-ˈfive *adv.* from 9:00 a.m. until 5:00 p.m.; the hours that most people work in an office: *Derek usually works nine-to-five, unless there's a crisis.* **—nine-to-five** *adj.*: *a nine-to-five job*

nine·ty /ˈnaɪnti/ *number* **1** 90 **2 the nineties** also **the '90s** the years from 1990 through 1999 **3 sb's nineties** the time when someone is 90 to 99 years old: **in your early/mid/late nineties** *My grandfather was in his mid nineties when he died.* **4 in the nineties** if the temperature is in the nineties, it is between 90° and 99° Fahrenheit: **in the high/low nineties** *It was hot – in the high nineties – most of the week.*

nin·ja /ˈnɪndʒə/ *n. plural* **ninja, ninjas** [C] a member of a Japanese class of professional killers in past times: *a ninja warrior*

nin·ny /ˈnɪni/ *n. plural* **ninnies** [C] OLD-FASHIONED a silly person

ninth¹ /naɪnθ/ *adj.* 9th; next after the eighth: *Sam is in ninth grade.*

ninth² *pron.* **the ninth** the 9th thing in a series: *Let's have dinner on the ninth* (=the 9th day of the month).

ninth³ *n.* [C] ⅑; one of nine equal parts

nip¹ /nɪp/ *v.* **nipped, nipping** **1** [I,T] to bite someone or something with small sharp bites, or to try to do this: *When I took the hamster out of his cage, he nipped me.* | **+at** *The dog kept nipping at my ankles.* **2 nip sth in the bud** to prevent something from becoming a problem by stopping it as soon as it starts: *The idea is to nip minor school problems in the bud.* **3 be nipping at sb's heels** to be very close to defeating someone, or causing problems for them: *Creditors are nipping at the company's heels.* **4** [T] LITERARY if cold weather nips something, it makes it very cold or damages it

nip sth ↔ in *phr. v.* if a piece of clothing is nipped in at a particular place on the body, it fits more tightly there

nip sth ↔ off *phr. v.* to remove a small part of something, especially a plant, by pressing it tightly between your finger and thumb

nip² *n.* [C] **1** a small sharp bite, or the action of biting someone or something: *The dog gave me a playful nip.* **2 nip and tuck** INFORMAL **a)** equally likely to happen or not happen, or to succeed or fail: *I made it to the airport before the plane left, but **it was nip and tuck**.* **b)** if two competitors are nip and tuck in a race or competition, they are doing equally well **3** a small amount of a strong alcoholic drink: +**of** *a nip of whiskey* **4 a nip in the air** coldness in the air

nip·per /ˈnɪpɚ/ *n.* [C] OLD-FASHIONED a child, especially a small boy

nip·ple /ˈnɪpəl/ *n.* [C] **1** BIOLOGY the small dark raised circle on a woman's breast, that a baby sucks in order to get milk **2** one of the two small dark raised circles on a man's chest **3** the rubber part on a baby's bottle that a baby sucks milk through **4** something shaped like a nipple, for example on a machine

nip·py /ˈnɪpi/ *adj.* INFORMAL weather that is nippy is cold enough that you need a coat

nir·va·na, Nirvana /nɚˈvɑnə, nɪr-/ *n.* **1** [singular, U] a condition or place of great happiness: *This mountainous region is nirvana for geologists.* **2** [U] a state of knowledge or being that is beyond life and death, suffering, and change, and is the aim of believers in Buddhism [**Origin:** 1800–1900 Sanskrit *nis-* **out** + *vati* **it blows**]

Ni·sei /ˈniseɪ/ *n. plural* **Nisei** [C] someone who is born in the U.S., but whose parents were born in Japan

nit /nɪt/ *n.* [C] an egg of a LOUSE (=a small insect), that is sometimes found in people's hair

nite /naɪt/ *n.* [C] INFORMAL an informal spelling of "night," used especially on signs

nit·pick·ing /ˈnɪtˌpɪkɪŋ/ *n.* [U] INFORMAL, DISAPPROVING the act of arguing about or criticizing unimportant details, especially in someone's work **—nitpick** *v.* [I] **—nitpicker** *n.* [C] **—nitpicking** *adj.*

ni·trate /ˈnaɪtreɪt/ *n.* [C,U] CHEMISTRY a chemical compound that is mainly used to improve the soil that crops are grown in

ni·tric ac·id /ˌnaɪtrɪk ˈæsɪd/ *n.* [U] CHEMISTRY a powerful acid that is used in explosives and other chemical products

ni·trite /ˈnaɪtraɪt/ *n.* [C,U] a chemical compound that is mainly used to preserve food, especially meat, and that may be harmful to people's health

ni·tro·gen /ˈnaɪtrədʒən/ *n.* [U] SYMBOL **N** CHEMISTRY a gas that is an ELEMENT, has no color or smell, and is the main part of the Earth's air

ˈnitrogen ˌcycle *n.* [singular] the process by which nitrogen from the atmosphere passes through various stages before being released back into the atmosphere

ˈnitrogen fixˌation *n.* [U] BIOLOGY the natural process that happens when BACTERIA in the soil take in NITROGEN from the air and return it to the soil as substances that plants can use

ni·tro·glyc·er·in, nitroglycerine /ˌnaɪtroʊˈglɪsərɪn/ *n.* [U] a chemical compound that is used in explosives, and as a medicine to prevent HEART ATTACKS

ni·trous ox·ide /ˌnaɪtrəs ˈɑksaɪd/ *n.* [U] a type of gas used by DENTISTS to reduce pain SYN **laughing gas**

nit·ty-grit·ty /ˈnɪṭi ˌgrɪṭi, ˌnɪṭi ˈgrɪṭi/ *n.* **the nitty-gritty** INFORMAL the basic and practical facts of an agreement or activity: *It's time to **get down to the nitty-gritty** of how much this will cost.* **—nitty-gritty** *adj.*: *nitty-gritty contract talks*

nit·wit /ˈnɪtˀˌwɪt/ *n.* [C] INFORMAL a stupid or silly person

nix¹ /nɪks/ *v.* [T] INFORMAL to answer no or FORBID something: *The proposal was nixed by council members.*

nix² *adv.* OLD-FASHIONED no

Nix·on /ˈnɪksən/, **Richard** (1913–1994) the 37th President of the U.S.

nitrogen cycle

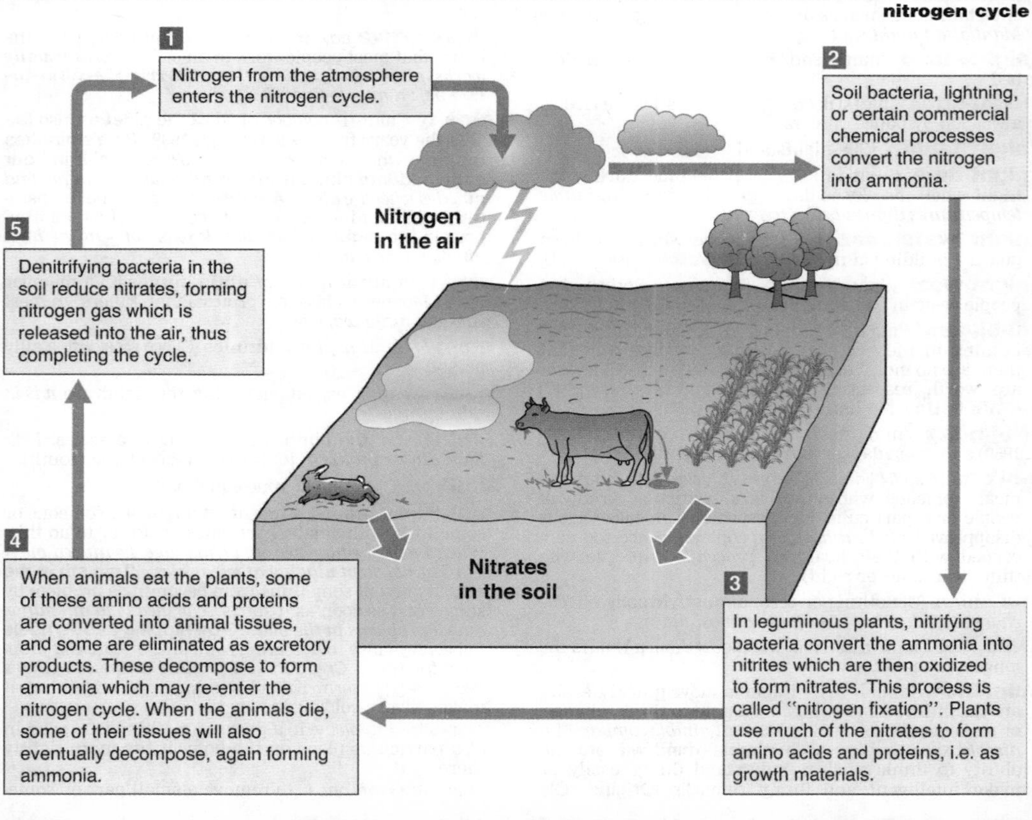

1
Nitrogen from the atmosphere enters the nitrogen cycle.
2
Soil bacteria, lightning, or certain commercial chemical processes convert the nitrogen into ammonia.
Nitrogen in the air
5
Denitrifying bacteria in the soil reduce nitrates, forming nitrogen gas which is released into the air, thus completing the cycle.
Nitrates in the soil
4
When animals eat the plants, some of these amino acids and proteins are converted into animal tissues, and some are eliminated as excretory products. These decompose to form ammonia which may re-enter the nitrogen cycle. When the animals die, some of their tissues will also eventually decompose, again forming ammonia.
3
In leguminous plants, nitrifying bacteria convert the ammonia into nitrites which are then oxidized to form nitrates. This process is called "nitrogen fixation". Plants use much of the nitrates to form amino acids and proteins, i.e. as growth materials.

NJ the written abbreviation of NEW JERSEY

NM the written abbreviation of NEW MEXICO

no¹ /noʊ/ S1 W1 *adv.* **1** used to give a negative reply to a question, offer, or request OPP yes: *"Is Cindy married?" "No, she's not."* | *"Do you want a ride home?" "**No, thanks**, I have my car."* | *Neumann said he voted no because the management misled him.* | *I asked Dad if I could have a dog, but he **said no**.*

SPOKEN PHRASES

2 used when you disagree with a statement: *"Ben's so weird." "No, he's just shy."* **3** said when you do not want someone to do something: *No, Jimmy, don't touch that.* **4** said to agree with a negative statement: *"Steve should never have left his job." "No, he shouldn't have."* **5** used to show that you are shocked, surprised, annoyed, or disappointed by what someone has just told you, or by what has just happened: *She's 45? No, you've got to be kidding!* | ***Oh no**, I forgot to put the baking powder in!* **6 no can do** INFORMAL used to say that something is not possible: *"Can't you just let us in?" "Sorry, no can do."* **7** used for adding a remark, usually a SARCASTIC remark, that emphasizes a negative statement: *He didn't even offer to help. No, that would have been too much like work.*

8 sb won't take no for an answer if someone won't take no for an answer, they keep trying to do something or to get you to do something **9 no better/more/less etc.** not better, not more etc.: *No more than three people were allowed in the room at one time.* **10** FORMAL used when you mean the opposite of what you are saying: *Linda played no small part in the orchestra's success* (=she was very important in making it succeed). [**Origin:** Old English *na*, from *ne* **not** + *a* **always**]

GRAMMAR

Use **no** before nouns to mean "not any": *It's no problem, really.* Use **not** in order to make a verb negative: *I decided not to go camping.* When the subject of a sentence is the word "all" or a word like "everyone," "everything," etc., use **not** to make the subject negative: *Not all of the students handed their papers in on time.* | *Not everyone likes horror movies.*

no² S1 W1 *determiner* **1** not any, or not at all: *There are no tickets available.* | *He has no control over his children.* | *There's no more milk.* | ***There's no reason** to get in an argument about this.* | **no good/use/help etc.** *The food's no good there.* | *These instructions were no use whatsoever.* **2** used on a sign to say that something is not allowed: *No parking.* | *No smoking.* **3 be no expert/scientist/idiot etc.** to not have a particular skill or quality: *I'm no expert, but global warming seems real to me.* **4 there's no sth like sth** used to emphasize that something is very good or very bad: *There's no cooking like Mom's cooking.* **5 there's no telling/knowing etc.** SPOKEN used to say that it is impossible to guess what will happen or what is true: *There's just no telling what Sam'll do when he's mad.*

no³ W2 *n. plural* **noes** [C] **1** a negative answer or decision OPP yes: *LeeAnn's answer was a definite no.* **2** [usually plural] POLITICS votes against a proposal in a meeting OPP aye: *The noes have it* (=the noes win).

no. *plural* **nos.** the written abbreviation of NUMBER: *The album entered the national charts at no. 1.*

ˈno-acˌcount *adj.* INFORMAL, OLD-FASHIONED lazy and not achieving anything in life: *a no-account drifter*

No·ah /ˈnoʊə/ in the Bible, a man chosen by God to build an ARK (=a large boat) so that he could save his family and every kind of animal from the flood which covered the Earth

No·bel /noʊˈbɛl/, **Al·fred** /ˈælfrɪd/ (1833–1896) a Swedish engineer and chemist who invented DYNAMITE and left all his money to establish the Nobel Prizes

No·bel Prize /ˌnoʊbɛl ˈpraɪz/ *n.* [C usually singular] a prize given in Sweden each year to people from any country for important work in science, medicine, literature, economics, or work toward world peace

no·bil·i·ty /noʊˈbɪləṭi/ *n.* **1 the nobility** the group of people in some countries who belong to the highest social class and use special titles with their names: *the Russian nobility* → see also ARISTOCRACY **2** [U] the quality of being noble in character or appearance: *the nobility of working with one's hands*

no·ble¹ /ˈnoʊbəl/ *adj.* **1** morally good or generous in a way that should be admired: *None of the characters in the book are good or noble.* | *a noble purpose* **2** belonging to the nobility: *a man of noble birth* **3** something that is noble is very impressive and beautiful: *The Siberian tiger is a noble creature.* **4 noble savage** used in past times to mean someone who comes from a society that is less developed than Western ones and is thought to be morally better than Westerners because of this

noble² *n.* [C] FORMAL a member of the highest social class in some countries, especially in past times: *a gathering of kings and nobles* → see also COMMONER

ˌnoble ˈgas *n.* [C] a gas, such as NEON or ARGON, that is an ELEMENT and which only combines with a small number of other substances

no·ble·man /ˈnoʊbəlmən/ *n. plural* **noblemen** /-mən/ [C] a man who is a member of the NOBILITY

no·blesse o·blige /noʊˌblɛs əˈbliʒ/ *n.* FORMAL a phrase meaning that people who belong to a high social class should be generous and behave with honor

no·ble·wom·an /ˈnoʊbəlˌwʊmən/ *n. plural* **noblewomen** /-ˌwɪmɪn/ [C] a woman who is a member of the NOBILITY

no·bly /ˈnoʊbli/ *adv.* **1** in a morally good or generous way that should be admired: *Foreman sacrificed nobly for what he believed was right.* **2 nobly born** LITERARY having parents who are members of the NOBILITY

no·bod·y¹ /ˈnoʊˌbʌdi, -ˌbɑdi/ S1 W2 *pron.* **1** no one, or not one person SYN no one: *There's nobody home.* | *"Who was on the phone?" "Nobody you know."* | ***Nobody else** (=no other person) knows about this.* **2 like nobody's business** SPOKEN very well, very much, or very fast: *The book is selling like nobody's business.* → see also **be no fool/be nobody's fool** at FOOL¹ (4)

nobody² *n. plural* **nobodies** [C] someone who is not important, successful, or famous: *She's from a rich family and I'm just a nobody.*

ˈno-ˌbrainer *n.* [C usually singular] INFORMAL something that you do not need to think about, because it is easy to understand or do: *The test was a complete no-brainer.* | *It seems like a no-brainer to me – you should accept the job.*

no-ˈconfidence ˌvote *n.* [C] a VOTE OF NO CONFIDENCE

ˈno-count *adj.* INFORMAL, OLD-FASHIONED another spelling of NO-ACCOUNT

noc·tur·nal /nɑkˈtɚnl/ *adj.* **1** BIOLOGY an animal that is nocturnal is active at night: *Raccoons are nocturnal creatures.* **2** FORMAL happening at night: *a nocturnal stroll* —**nocturnally** *adv.*

noc·turne /ˈnɑktɚn/ *n.* [C] a soft beautiful piece of music, especially for the piano

nod¹ /nɑd/ W3 *v.* **nodded, nodding** **1** [I,T] to move your head up and down, especially in order to show that you agree with or understand something: *I asked her if she was OK, and she nodded.* | *When asked if he would come, he **nodded yes**.* | **nod (your head) in agreement/approval/sympathy etc.** *Several women nodded in approval as Marion spoke.* | *Casey was **nodding his head** in agreement.* **2** [I,T] to move your head up and down once toward someone or something, for example to greet them, to tell them to do something, or to show who or what you are talking about: **+at/to/toward etc.** *I nodded to the waiter and asked for the check.* | *"She's in her room," Hans said, nodding his head toward the door.* | *He **nodded in the direction of** (=toward) the trees.* **3 have a nodding acquaintance (with sb/sth)** to know someone slightly or know a little about a subject: *I had only a nodding acquaintance with* *the admiral.* **4** [I] LITERARY if a tall plant nods, its top part moves up and down when the wind blows it

nod off *phr. v.* to begin to sleep, when you do not intend to: *I kept nodding off during the lecture.*

nod² *n.* [C usually singular] **1** an act of nodding: *Carlyle gave an approving **nod**.* **2 the nod** approval of something or someone: *"Charlie and the Chocolate Factory" was one novel that **got the nod** from children.* | *The plan has **been given the nod** by local officials.* **3 a nod to/toward sth** a sign that shows you recognize that something is important or worth recognizing: *The Chinese music in the background was a nod to Beijing's sponsorship of the event.* → see also **the land of nod** at LAND¹ (7)

node /noʊd/ *n.* [C] **1** TECHNICAL a place where lines in a network, GRAPH etc. meet or join **2** BIOLOGY the place on the stem of a plant from which a leaf grows **3** a LYMPH NODE **4** COMPUTERS a computer that is part of a network **5** PHYSICS a point on a STANDING WAVE where there is little or no change or VIBRATION —**nodal** *adj.*

nod·ule /ˈnɑdʒul/ *n.* [C] a small round raised part, especially a small swelling on a plant or someone's body —**nodular** *adj.*

No·el, Noël /noʊˈɛl/ *n.* [U] a word used in songs, on cards etc. meaning Christmas

noes /noʊz/ *n.* the plural of NO

ˌno-ˈfault *adj.* [only before noun] **1** no-fault car insurance will pay for the damage done in an accident, even if you caused the accident **2** a no-fault DIVORCE does not blame either the husband or the wife

no-ˈfly ˌzone *n.* [C] **1** an area that no airplane is allowed to enter, and in which it would be attacked if it did enter **2** HISTORY the no-fly zone over northern Iraq from 1992–2003 that was made by the U.S., U.K., and France to protect the Kurds

ˌno-ˈfrills *adj.* [only before noun] without any additional features that are not completely necessary SYN **basic**: *a no-frills airline*

nog·gin /ˈnɑgən/ *n.* [C] OLD-FASHIONED, INFORMAL your head or brain

ˌno-ˈgo *n.* **sth is (a) no-go** INFORMAL used to say that something does not work or does not happen: *Trying to make a deal with this guy was a no-go.*

ˈno-ˌgood *adj.* INFORMAL a no-good person causes trouble and does not behave in the way society expects them to: *her no-good husband*

ˌno-ˈhitter *n.* [C] a baseball game in which one PITCHER (=player who throws the ball) prevents the other team from successfully hitting the ball through the whole game

ˌno-holds-ˈbarred *adj.* [only before noun] a no-holds-barred discussion, situation etc. is one in which there are no rules or limits: *Viewers were promised a no-holds-barred interview with the actor.*

no·how, no how /ˈnoʊhaʊ/ *adv.* SPOKEN, NONSTANDARD not in any way or in any situation: *I won't do it! No way, nohow.*

noise /nɔɪz/ S1 W3 *n.* **1** [C,U] a sound or sounds, especially ones that are very loud, annoying, or unexpected: *the noise of the traffic* | *What was that clunking noise?* | **+of** *The noise of the drill was deafening.* | **make (a) noise** *Something was making a grunting noise in the bushes.* | *The kids were making too much noise.* | *She tried not to make any noise as she climbed the stairs.* | *Music is often used as **background noise** (=sounds that you can hear but are not the main sounds you listen to) in stores and restaurants.* **2 noises** the things someone says that suggest what their opinion or attitude is without saying it directly or definitely: *There were some **encouraging noises** (=that show he approves) from the Governor.* | **make noises about (doing) sth** *He made noises about leaving the band in 2005.* **3 make (a) noise about sth** to talk or complain about something a lot, so that people will notice it: *They made a lot of noise about having improved graphics.* **4** [U] PHYSICS unwanted signals produced by an electrical CIRCUIT **5** [U] large amounts of unwanted information that stop you from finding the exact information you want, because it takes too long to look through everything [**Origin:** 1200–1300 Old French **quarreling, noise**, from Latin *nausea*]

> WORD CHOICE **noise, sound**
>
> • Use **sound** to talk about something that you hear: *I love the sound of the ocean.* | *The sound of voices came from the next room.*
>
> • A **noise** is usually a loud unpleasant sound: *They had to shout to make themselves heard above the noise of the machines.* | *Tell the kids to stop making so much noise.*

noise·less·ly /ˈnɔɪzlɪsli/ *adv.* without making any sound: *We crept noiselessly down the hall.* —**noiseless** *adj.* —**noiselessness** *n.* [U]

noise·mak·er /ˈnɔɪzˌmeɪkɚ/ *n.* [C] something that you can use to make a loud noise, especially in order to celebrate something

ˈnoise polˌlution *n.* [U] very loud or continuous loud noise in the environment that is harmful to people

noi·some /ˈnɔɪsəm/ *adj.* LITERARY extremely bad, ugly etc.

nois·y /ˈnɔɪzi/ S3 *adj.* *comparative* **noisier**, *superlative* **noisiest** making a lot of noise, or full of noise: *a noisy crowd* | *Bars are too smoky and noisy.* —**noisily** *adv.* —**noisiness** *n.* [U]

no-ˈload *adj.* **no-load fund/stock etc.** a FUND, STOCK etc. that does not charge people an additional amount of money when they INVEST in it

no·lo con·ten·de·re /ˌnoʊloʊ kənˈtɛndəri/ *n.* [U] LAW a statement by someone in a court of law that says that they will not admit that they are guilty but will also not fight against any punishment given by the court

no·mad /ˈnoʊmæd/ *n.* [C] **1** a member of a tribe that travels from place to place, especially to find fields for their animals: *the desert nomads* **2** someone who often travels from place to place or who changes jobs, homes etc. often —**nomadic** /noʊˈmædɪk/ *adj.*: *nomadic tribes*

ˈno-man's-ˌland *n.* [singular, U] **1** an area of land that no one owns or controls, especially an area between two borders or opposing armies **2** an uncertain subject, situation etc. that does not clearly fit into a particular type because it is a combination of two or more types: *the no-man's-land between painting and photography*

nom de guerre /ˌnɑm də ˈgɛr/ *n.* *plural* **noms de guerre** /ˌnɑm-/ [C] LITERARY a name that someone uses instead of their real name, especially because they are fighting in a war

nom de plume /ˌnɑm də ˈplum/ *n.* *plural* **noms de plume** /ˌnɑm-/ [C] LITERARY a name used by a writer instead of their real name SYN **pseudonym**

no·men·cla·ture /ˈnoʊmənˌkleɪtʃɚ/ *n.* [C,U] FORMAL SCIENCE a system of naming things, especially in science: *medical nomenclature*

nom·i·nal /ˈnɑmənl/ *adj.* **1** officially having authority, a right, or a title, but not having the powers or freedoms that usually come with it: *Her authority as director was purely nominal* (=she had no real power). | *The country was given nominal independence, but its citizens were not free.* **2 nominal fee/price/sum etc.** a small amount of money, especially when compared with the usual amount that would be paid for something: *Most golf courses will rent clubs for a nominal fee.* **3** ENG. LANG. ARTS relating to nouns or used as a noun: *a nominal phrase* **4** TECHNICAL a nominal value, rate etc. does not show what something is really worth or really costs, because it does not take into account changes in the price of other goods and services: *nominal interest rates*

nom·i·nal·ly /ˈnɑmənl-i/ *adv.* officially described as something, when this may not be really true: *Eighty percent of the population is nominally Hindu.*

nom·i·nate /ˈnɑməˌneɪt/ *v.* [T] **1** to officially choose someone or something to be one of the competitors in an election, competition etc.: *The series has never won an Emmy, though it has been nominated repeatedly.* | **nominate sb for/as sth** *Ferraro was the first woman to be nominated for Vice President.* **2** to choose someone for a particular job, especially when there is a vote later to make the choice official: **nominate sb sth** *Meg was nominated club president.* | **nominate sb as sth** *Reagan nominated him as CIA director in 1987.* | **nominate sb to sth** *Roberts was nominated to the Supreme Court.* | **nominate sb to do sth** *He was nominated to represent the company at the conference.*

nom·i·na·tion /ˌnɑməˈneɪʃən/ W2 *n.* [C,U] the act of suggesting someone or something for an important job, position, or prize, or the fact of being suggested: *The movie received several Oscar nominations.* | +**for** *Who will get the Republican nomination for President?* | *The nominations for the Academy Awards were announced Tuesday.* | +**to** *O'Connor's nomination to the Supreme Court* | +**as** *her nomination as chairman*

nom·i·na·tive /ˈnɑmənətɪv, ˈnɑmnə-/ *n.* [singular] ENG. LANG. ARTS a particular form of a noun in some languages, such as Latin and German, which shows that the noun is the SUBJECT of a verb —**nominative** *adj.*

nom·i·nee /ˌnɑməˈni/ W3 *n.* [C] someone who has been suggested for a prize, duty, or honor: *the Democratic presidential nominee*

non- /nɑn/ *prefix* **1** [in adjectives and nouns] used to say that something does not have or do something: *nonalcoholic* (=without alcohol in it) | *a nonsmoker* (=someone who does not smoke) | *nonstick* (=that food does not stick to) **2** [in nouns] INFORMAL used to say that something does not deserve a particular name: *a non-event* (=something too boring to be an event)

non·a·ge·nar·i·an /ˌnɑnədʒəˈnɛriən, ˌnoʊn-/ *n.* [C] someone between 90 and 99 years old

ˌnon-agˈgression *n.* [U] the state of not fighting or attacking: *a commitment to non-aggression* | **a non-aggression pact/treaty/agreement** (=a promise not to attack another country)

non·a·gon /ˈnɑnəˌgɑn/ *n.* [C] MATH a POLYGON (=flat shape with many sides) that has nine sides

non·al·co·hol·ic, non-alcoholic /ˌnɑnælkəˈhɔlɪk/ *adj.* a drink that is nonalcoholic does not contain alcohol: *a nonalcoholic wine*

ˌnon-aˈligned, nonaligned *adj.* POLITICS a non-aligned country does not support, or is not dependent on, any of the powerful countries in the world —**non-alignment** *n.* [U]

ˈno-name *adj.* [only before noun] not famous, or not having a BRAND NAME: *a no-name personal computer*

non·bind·ing /ˌnɑnˈbaɪndɪŋ◂/ *adj.* a nonbinding vote, agreement, decision etc. expresses an opinion but does not have to be obeyed: *a nonbinding resolution*

nonce[1] /nɑns/ *n.* LITERARY **for the nonce** for the present time

nonce[2] *adj.* TECHNICAL **nonce word/phrase** a word or phrase that is invented and used only once for a particular occasion

non·cha·lant /ˌnɑnʃəˈlɑnt/ *adj.* behaving calmly and not seeming interested in anything or worried about anything: *Perkins was nonchalant about being chosen.* [**Origin:** 1700–1800 French, Old French *nonchaloir* **to pay no attention to**, from Latin *calere* **to be warm**] —**nonchalance** *n.* [U] *He reacted to her anger with surprising nonchalance.* —**nonchalantly** *adv.*

non·com /ˈnɑnkɑm/ *n.* [C] INFORMAL an NCO

non·com·bat /nɑnˈkɑmbæt/ *adj.* [only before noun] belonging to the military, but not directly involved in fighting: *soldiers in* ***noncombat roles***

non·com·bat·ant /ˌnɑnkəmˈbætˀnt, -ˈkɑmbətˀnt/ *n.* [C] someone who is in the military during a war but does not actually fight, for example a doctor —**noncombatant** *adj.*

ˌnon-commissioned ˈofficer *n.* [C] an NCO

non·com·mit·tal /ˌnɑnkəˈmɪtl◂/ *adj.* not giving a definite answer, or not willing to express your opinions: *a noncommittal reply* | +**about/on** *She was noncommittal about her plans for the future.*

non·com·pet·i·tive /ˌnɑnkəmˈpɛtət̮ɪv/ *adj.* **1** not involving competition, or not liking competition: *noncompetitive activities* | *a noncompetitive person* **2** noncompetitive pay for a particular job is lower than in other similar jobs: *Teachers in the city are still paid noncompetitive salaries.* **3** TECHNICAL noncompetitive prices, rates, business activities etc. are unfair and intended to restrict free competition between businesses: *noncompetitive mergers*

non·com·pli·ance /ˌnɑnkəmˈplaɪəns/ *n.* [U] FORMAL failure or refusal to do what you are officially supposed to do: +**with** *Noncompliance with these rules is a violation of federal law.*

non com·pos men·tis /ˌnɑn ˌkɑmpəs ˈmɛntɪs/ *adj.* [not before noun] LAW unable to think clearly or be responsible for your actions

non·con·form·ist /ˌnɑnkənˈfɔrmɪst/ Ac *n.* [C] someone who deliberately does not accept the beliefs and ways of behaving that most people in a society accept: *a political nonconformist* —**nonconformist** *adj.* —**nonconformity** *n.* [U]

non·co·op·er·a·tion /ˌnɑnkoʊˌɑpəˈreɪʃən/ *n.* [U] the refusal or failure to do something that you officially have to, especially as a protest: *the noncooperation of witnesses in the case*

non·count noun /nɑnˈkaʊnt ˌnaʊn/ *n.* [C] an UNCOUNTABLE noun

non·cus·to·di·al /ˌnɑnkəˈstoʊdiəl◂/ *adj.* a noncustodial parent does not have CUSTODY of his or her children (=his or her children do not live with him or her)

ˌnon-ˈdairy *adj.* containing no milk, and used instead of a product that contains milk: *non-dairy whipped topping*

non·de·duct·i·ble /ˌnɑndɪˈdʌktəbəl/ *adj.* an amount of money that is nondeductible cannot be subtracted from the amount of money you must pay taxes on: *nondeductible entertainment expenses*

non·de·nom·i·na·tion·al /ˌnɑndɪˌnɑməˈneɪʃənl/ *adj.* not relating to a particular religion or religious group: *a nondenominational chapel*

non·de·script /ˌnɑndɪˈskrɪpt◂/ *adj.* not having any special or interesting qualities: *a nondescript gray suit*

non·dis·clo·sure /ˌnɑndɪsˈkloʊʒɚ/ *n.* [U] **nondisclosure agreement/law etc.** an agreement, law etc. in which someone promises not to tell certain secret information to anyone else

non·dur·a·ble goods /nɑnˌdʊrəbəl ˈgʊdz/ *n.* [plural] ECONOMICS goods such as food or clothing that people replace after a short period of time SYN **non-durables** → see also DURABLE GOODS

non·dur·a·bles /nɑnˈdʊrəbəlz/ *n.* [plural] ECONOMICS NONDURABLE GOODS

none[1] /nʌn/ S1 W2 *pron., quantifier* **1** not any of something: *"Can I have some more pie?" "Sorry, there's none left."* | +**of** *She had inherited none of her mother's beauty.* | *"Was there any mail?" "No,* ***none at all.****"* **2** not one thing or person: *Even an old car is better than none.* | *"How many students passed the test?" "None."* | +**of** *None of her friends came to see her.* | *Luckily none of the furniture was damaged.* | *Any kind of decision is better than* ***none at all.*** **3 none other than sb/sth** used when the person mentioned is surprising, often because it is someone very famous or impressive: *a message from none other than the President himself* **4 sb will have none of sth** OLD-FASHIONED to not allow someone to do something, or to not allow someone to behave in a particular way: *The school wanted Sarah to skip a grade, but her parents would have none of that.* **5 none but sb/sth** LITERARY only someone or something: *None but God knows all her pain.* [**Origin:** Old English *nan*, from *ne-* **not** + *an* **one**] → see also **bar none** at BAR[3] (1), NONETHELESS, **be second to none** at SECOND[1] (9)

GRAMMAR

In spoken English, if **none of** is followed by a plural noun or pronoun, you can use a plural verb: *None of the packages were for me.* In written English, it is better to use a singular verb: *None of my friends has a car.*

N

none² *adv.* **1 none the worse/better etc.** not any worse, better etc. than before: *She seems none the worse for her experience.* | *I've read the instructions, but I'm still **none the wiser*** (=I don't know any more than I did before). | *The boat was **none the worse for wear** after the storm* (=the storm did not damage it). **2 none too soon/happy/likely etc.** not soon, happy etc. at all: *The salad was none too fresh.* | *Harden's cousin was none too bright.*

non·e·lec·tro·lyte /ˌnɑnɪˈlɛktrəˌlaɪt/ *n.* [C] CHEMISTRY a chemical compound that does not allow electricity to travel through it when it is DISSOLVED in liquid

non·en·ti·ty /nɑnˈɛntəṭi/ *n. plural* **nonentities** [C] someone who has no importance, power, or ability: *He's famous in Europe, but a nonentity in the U.S.*

non·es·sen·tial /ˌnɑnɪˈsɛnʃəl◂/ *adj.* not completely necessary: *nonessential personnel at the embassy*

none·the·less /ˌnʌnðəˈlɛs◂/ Ac W3 *adv.* [sentence adverb] FORMAL in spite of what has just been mentioned SYN **nevertheless**: *The paintings are complex, but they're appealing nonetheless.* | *The substance may not affect humans. Nonetheless, the FDA is examining it closely.*

non·e·vent /ˈnɑnɪˌvɛnt, ˌnɑnɪˈvɛnt/ *n.* [C usually singular] an event that is much less interesting and exciting than you expected: *Carver's testimony turned out to be a non-event.*

non·ex·ist·ent /ˌnɑnɪgˈzɪstənt◂/ *adj.* not existing at all, or not present in a particular place: *My memory of the event was nonexistent.* | **almost/practically/virtually nonexistent** *Crime is almost nonexistent in the area.* —**nonexistence** *n.* [U]

non·fat /ˌnɑnˈfæt◂/ *adj.* nonfat milk, YOGURT etc. has no fat in it

non·fic·tion /ˌnɑnˈfɪkʃən/ *n.* [U] books, articles etc. about real facts or events, not imagined ones —**nonfiction** *adj.* ►see THESAURUS box at **book¹** → see also FICTION

ˌnon-ˈfinite *adj.* ENG. LANG. ARTS a non-finite verb is not marked to show a particular sense or subject, and is either the INFINITIVE or the PARTICIPLE form of the verb, for example "go" in the sentence "Do you want to go home?"

non·flam·ma·ble /ˌnɑnˈflæməbəl/ *adj.* nonflammable materials or substances do not burn easily or do not burn at all OPP **flammable**

non·gov·ern·men·tal /ˌnɑngʌvənˈmɛntl/ *adj.* [only before noun] a nongovernmental organization is independent and not controlled by a government: *nongovernmental aid agencies*

non·im·mi·grant /ˌnɑnˈɪməgrənt/ *n.* [C] someone who is living in or visiting a foreign country, but is not planning to live there permanently —**nonimmigrant** *adj.*: *a nonimmigrant student visa*

ˌnon-interˈvention *n.* [U] POLITICS the refusal of a government to become involved in the affairs of other countries: *a policy of non-intervention*

non·judg·ment·al /ˌnɑndʒʌdʒˈmɛntl/ *adj.* not using your own standards or beliefs to judge or criticize other people: *Express your concerns in a nonjudgmental way.*

non·lin·e·ar pro·gres·sion /nɑnˌlɪniə prəˈgrɛʃən/ also **nonˌlinear ˈsequence** *n.* [C] MATH a series of numbers, for example 1, 3, 4, 8, with different increases between them. If you showed them on a GRAPH, they would not form a straight line. → see also ARITHMETIC SEQUENCE, GEOMETRIC SEQUENCE

non·met·al /ˌnɑnˈmɛṭl/ *n.* [C] CHEMISTRY a chemical ELEMENT, such as SULFUR, oxygen, or NITROGEN, that does not have the typical properties of a metal

ˌnon-ˈnative *adj.* **1** non-native plants, animals, or fish do not originally come from the area they are growing or living in: *The tree is a non-native species in the U.S.* **2** someone who is a non-native speaker of a language did not learn it as their first language as a child: *a dictionary for non-native speakers* **3** someone who is non-native was not born in the place they are living in: *Guam recently elected its first non-native governor.*

ˌnon-neˈgotiable *adj.* **1** not able to be discussed or changed: *The price is non-negotiable.* **2** ECONOMICS a check, BOND etc. that is non-negotiable can only be exchanged for money by the person whose name is on it

ˈno-no *n. plural* **no-nos** [C] INFORMAL something that is not allowed, or is not socially acceptable: *the magazine's list of fashion no-nos*

ˌno-ˈnonsense *adj.* [only before noun] **1** very practical, direct, and unwilling to waste time: *The nurse had a strict no-nonsense approach.* **2** very practical: *no-nonsense work boots*

non·pa·reil /ˌnɑnpəˈrɛl/ *n.* **1** [singular] LITERARY someone or something that is much better than all the others: *a ballet dancer nonpareil* **2 nonpareils** [plural] very small balls of colored sugar used to decorate cakes, cookies etc. **3** [C] a chocolate candy covered with nonpareils —**nonpareil** *adj.*

non·par·ti·san /nɑnˈpɑrṭəzən, -sən/ *adj.* not supporting the ideas of any political party or group: *The Council is a nonpartisan educational organization.*

non·pay·ment /ˌnɑnˈpeɪmənt/ *n.* [U] failure to pay bills, taxes, or debts: +**of** *The family was evicted for nonpayment of rent.*

non·plussed /ˌnɑnˈplʌst/ *adj.* so surprised that you do not know what to say or do: *She looked completely nonplussed.*

non·pre·scrip·tion /ˌnɑnprɪˈskrɪpʃən◂/ *adj.* a nonprescription drug is one that you can buy in a store without a PRESCRIPTION (=written order) from a doctor SYN **over-the-counter**

non·price com·pe·ti·tion /ˌnɑnpraɪs kɑmpəˈtɪʃən/ *n.* [U] ECONOMICS ways of selling your product or service to more people, that do not involve lowering the price. Advertising a product or having a store in a particular place are typical examples of nonprice competition.

non·prof·it /ˌnɑnˈprɑfɪt◂/ *adj.* a nonprofit organization, school, hospital etc. uses the money it earns to help people instead of making a profit, and therefore does not have to pay taxes —**nonprofit** *n.* [C] *I work for a nonprofit.*

ˌnon-proˌliferˈation *n.* [U] POLITICS the act of limiting the number of NUCLEAR or chemical weapons that are being made around the world: *the nuclear non-proliferation treaty*

non·re·fund·a·ble /ˌnɑnrɪˈfʌndəbəl/ *adj.* if something you buy is nonrefundable, you cannot get your money back after you have paid for it: *nonrefundable airline tickets*

non·re·new·a·ble /ˌnɑnrɪˈnuəbəl/ *adj.* nonrenewable types of energy such as coal or gas cannot be replaced after they have been used: *The fibers are made from oil – a nonrenewable resource.*

ˌnonreˌnewable ˈresource *n.* [C] EARTH SCIENCE a RESOURCE (=something from nature that people use), such as oil or a mineral, that is gone after it is used and cannot be replaced → see also FLOW RESOURCE, RENEWABLE RESOURCE

non·res·i·dent /ˌnɑnˈrɛzədənt/ *n.* [C] someone who does not live permanently in a particular place or country: *Montana charges nonresidents more for hunting licenses.* —**nonresident** *adj.*

non·res·i·den·tial /ˌnɑnrɛzəˈdɛnʃəl◂/ *adj.* not relating to homes: *nonresidential buildings*

ˌnon-reˈstrictive *adj.* ENG. LANG. ARTS a non-restrictive RELATIVE CLAUSE gives additional information about a particular person or thing rather than saying which person or thing is being mentioned. For example, in the sentence "Perry, who is 22, was arrested yesterday," the phrase "who is 22" is a non-restrictive clause.

non·sec·tar·i·an /ˌnɑnsɛkˈtɛriən/ *adj.* not relating

to a particular religion or religious group: *a nonsectarian charity*

non·sense /ˈnɑnsɛns, -səns/ *n.* [U] **1** [U] ideas, opinions, statements etc. that are not true or that seem very stupid: *Busch dismissed the accusations as nonsense.* | *You're just* ***talking nonsense.*** **2** behavior that is stupid and annoying: *No one should have to put up with that kind of nonsense.* | *She* ***won't take any nonsense*** *from the kids in her class.* **3** speech or writing that has no meaning or cannot be understood: *nonsense words* **4 nonsense poems/verse** poetry that is humorous because it does not have a normal sensible meaning

non·sen·si·cal /nɑnˈsɛnsɪkəl/ *adj.* not reasonable or sensible: *nonsensical ideas* —**nonsensically** /-kli/ *adv.*

non se·qui·tur /ˌnɑn ˈsɛkwɪt̬ɚ/ *n.* [C] a statement that does not seem to be related to what was said before

non·smok·er, non-smoker /ˌnɑnˈsmoʊkɚ/ *n.* [C] someone who does not smoke

non·smok·ing /ˌnɑnˈsmoʊkɪŋ/ *adj.* a nonsmoking area, building etc. is one where people are not allowed to smoke

non·spe·cif·ic /ˌnɑnspəˈsɪfɪk◂ / *adj.* **1** TECHNICAL a nonspecific medical condition could have one of several possible causes **2** not relating to or caused by one particular thing [SYN] **general**: *nonspecific fears* **3** TECHNICAL affecting more than one part of your body: *nonspecific painkillers*

non·stan·dard /ˌnɑnˈstændɚd/ *adj.* **1** not the usual size or type: *a nonstandard disk size* **2** TECHNICAL nonstandard words, expressions, or pronunciations are usually considered incorrect by educated speakers of a language → see also STANDARD

non·start·er /ˌnɑnˈstɑrt̬ɚ/ *n.* [C usually singular] INFORMAL a person, idea, or plan that has no chance of success

non·stick, non-stick /ˌnɑnˈstɪk◂ / *adj.* nonstick pans have a special inside surface that food will not stick to

non·stop /ˌnɑnˈstɑp◂ / *adj., adv.* without stopping: *She talked nonstop for over an hour.* | *a nonstop flight to Los Angeles*

non·threat·en·ing /ˌnɑnˈθrɛtˀn-ɪŋ/ *adj.* not intended to threaten someone or cause them to feel afraid: *Conference time should be as nonthreatening to the student as possible.*

non·tox·ic, non-toxic /ˌnɑnˈtɑksɪk/ *adj.* not poisonous or harmful to your health: *All the paints are nontoxic and safe for children.*

non·tra·di·tion·al /ˌnɑntrəˈdɪʃənl/ *adj.* different from the way something happened or from what was considered typical in the past: *During the 1970s, older nontraditional students fueled the growth of community colleges.*

non·un·ion, non-union /ˌnɑnˈyunyən◂ / *adj.* [usually before noun] **1** not belonging to a UNION (=official organization for workers): *nonunion public employees* **2** not officially accepting UNIONS, or not employing their members: *nonunion factories* —**non-unionized** *adj.*

non·ver·bal, non-verbal /ˌnɑnˈvɚbəl◂ / *adj.* not using words: *Nonverbal signals form an important part of communication.* —**nonverbally** *adv.*

non·vi·o·lence, non-violence /ˌnɑnˈvaɪələns/ *n.* [U] the practice of opposing a government without fighting, for example by not obeying laws

non·vi·o·lent /ˌnɑnˈvaɪələnt/ *adj.* not using or not involving violence: *nonviolent protests* —**nonviolently** *adv.*

nonˌviolent reˈsistance *n.* [U] the practice of using methods that do not involve fighting or physical violence to oppose an enemy or in order to make social change happen: *a campaign of nonviolent resistance to laws that are unjust and repressive*

non·white, non-white /ˌnɑnˈwaɪt◂ / *n.* [C] someone who does not belong to a white race —**nonwhite** *adj.*

noo·dle¹ /ˈnudl/ *n.* **1** [C usually plural] a long thin piece of soft food made from flour, water, and usually eggs, that is cooked in boiling water: *chicken noodle soup* **2** [C] OLD-FASHIONED your head or brain: *Just use your noodle.*

noodle² *v.* [I always + adv./prep.] INFORMAL **noodle (around) on sth** to play music without planning the notes before

noo·gie /ˈnugi/ *n.* [C] INFORMAL the act of rubbing your KNUCKLES on someone's head while holding their head under your arm, usually as a joke

nook /nʊk/ *n.* [C] **1** a small space in a corner of a room: *a breakfast nook* **2 nook and cranny** small parts of a place: *We searched* ***every nook and cranny.*** **3** a small quiet place that is sheltered by a rock, a big tree etc.: *a shady nook*

noon /nun/ [S2] *n.* [U] 12 o'clock in the middle of the day: *Danny hardly ever gets up before noon.* | *The gallery is open from noon to 6 p.m.* | *the noon meal* | *Lunch will be* ***at noon.*** | *It is* ***12 noon*** (=exactly noon) *and 108 degrees in the shade.* [**Origin:** Old English *non* **ninth hour from sunrise**, from Latin *nonus* **ninth**] → see also **morning, noon, and night** at MORNING¹ (5)

noon·day /ˈnundeɪ/ *adj.* [only before noun] LITERARY happening or appearing at noon: *the noonday sun*

ˈno one [S1] [W1] *pron.* not anyone [SYN] **nobody**: *I tried calling last night, but no one was home.* | *No one could remember her name.*

noose /nus/ *n.* **1** [C] a circle of rope that becomes tighter as it is pulled, used especially for killing someone by hanging → see also LASSO **2** [singular] an action that punishes or makes things difficult for a person, country etc.: *The U.S. tightened the economic noose around the dictatorship.* **3 the noose** punishment by hanging: *The outlaws managed to escape the hangman's noose.*

Noot·ka /ˈnʊtkə/ a Native American tribe from western Canada and the northwestern U.S.

nope /noʊp/ [S1] *adv.* SPOKEN, INFORMAL no: *"Hungry?" "Nope, I just ate."*

ˈno place *adv.* INFORMAL not any place [SYN] **nowhere**: *I had no place else to go.*

nor /nɔr, nɚ/ [W1] *conjunction* FORMAL used after a negative statement, especially to add information, and meaning "and not," "or not," "neither," or "not either": *Worrall was not at the meeting, nor was he at work yesterday.* | *I am not, nor have I ever been, a Communist.* → see also **neither... nor...** at NEITHER³ (1)

Nor·dic /ˈnɔrdɪk/ *adj.* from or relating to the Northern European countries of Denmark, Norway, Sweden, Iceland, and Finland: *sailing in Nordic waters*

ˌNordic ˈskiing *n.* [U] CROSS-COUNTRY SKIING

nor'east·er /ˌnɔrˈistɚ/ *n.* [C] a strong wind or storm coming from the northeast

norm /nɔrm/ [Ac] *n.* **1** [C usually singular] the usual way of doing something etc.: *Working at home* ***is*** *becoming* ***the norm*** *for many employees.* | *Joyce's style of writing was a striking* ***departure from the*** (=was very different from the) *literary* ***norm.*** **2** [C usually plural] a generally accepted way of behaving in society: *Traditional sexual norms were called into question.*

nor·mal¹ /ˈnɔrməl/ [Ac] [S2] [W2] *adj.* **1** usual, typical, or expected: *A normal work week is 40–50 hours.* | **be normal for sb/sth** *High temperatures are normal for this time of year.* | **be normal (for sb) to do sth** *It's normal to feel nervous before an interview.* | *Everything you are feeling is* ***perfectly normal*** (=used to emphasize that something is normal).

THESAURUS

ordinary not special or unusual: *a really good meal made out of ordinary ingredients*
average typical of a normal person or thing: *the average family*
standard used about products or methods that are the most usual type: *shoes in standard sizes*
routine used about something that is done regularly and is part of a normal system: *a routine check of the plane*
conventional used when comparing a piece of equipment, method etc. that has been used for a

long time with something that is new and different: *nuclear and conventional weapons*
→ NATURAL

2 a normal person, especially a child, is physically and mentally healthy and does not behave strangely: *a normal healthy baby* | *Jerry seems like a* ***perfectly normal*** *guy, funny and nice.* [**Origin:** 1400–1500 Latin *normalis*, from *norma*] → see also ABNORMAL

normal² Ac *n.* [U] the usual level, amount, number etc. SYN **usual**: *His heart rate was* ***back to normal*** *by the time he reached the hospital.* | **higher/lower/longer etc. than normal** *The rivers were about a foot higher than normal.* | **above/below normal** *His temperature was just slightly above normal.*

ˌnormal distriˈbution *n.* [C] MATH a bell-shaped curve on a GRAPH that shows that the most frequent scores or values are in the middle of the range

ˌnormal ˈforce *n.* [C,U] PHYSICS the force that a HORIZONTAL surface puts on an object that is resting on top of it

ˌnormal ˈgood *n.* [singular] ECONOMICS a product or service that people buy more of as their income increases

nor·mal·i·ty /nɔrˈmæləṭi/ Ac also **nor·mal·cy** /ˈnɔrməlsi/ *n.* [U] a situation in which things happen in the usual or expected way: *The war-torn area is returning to normality.*

nor·mal·ize /ˈnɔrməˌlaɪz/ Ac *v.* [I,T] **1** to become normal again, or to make a situation become normal again: *Some people lose weight when they normalize their eating.* **2 normalize relations** if one country normalizes relations with another country, the countries become friendly after a period of disagreement —**normalization** /ˌnɔrmələˈzeɪʃən/ *n.* [U]

nor·mal·ly /ˈnɔrməli/ Ac S2 W3 *adv.* **1** usually, or under normal conditions: *The flu normally lasts about a week.* [sentence adverb] *Normally, I'm at work early.* **2** in the usual expected way OPP **abnormally**: *Try to breathe normally.*

nor·ma·tive /ˈnɔrməṭɪv/ *adj.* FORMAL describing or establishing a set of rules or standards of behavior: *normative societal values*

Nor·plant /ˈnɔrplænt/ *n.* [singular] TRADEMARK a CONTRACEPTIVE (=way of keeping a woman from having babies) that is put under a woman's skin

Norse /nɔrs/ *adj.* relating to the people of ancient Scandinavia or their language: *Norse legends*

Norse·man /ˈnɔrsmən/ *n. plural* **Norsemen** /-mən/ [C] LITERARY a VIKING

north¹ S3 W1, **North** /nɔrθ/ *n.* [singular, U] **1 N.** the direction toward the top of a map of the world. It is on the left if you are facing the rising sun: *Which way is north?* | *A strong wind was blowing* ***from the north.*** | *The town is* ***to the north of*** *the lake.* **2 the north a)** the northern part of a country, state etc.: +**of** *My relatives live in the north of the state.* **b)** the richer countries of the world, especially Europe and North America **3 the North** the part of the U.S. that is east of the Mississippi River and north of Washington, D.C., especially the states that fought against the South in the U.S. Civil War **4 up North** in or to the north of a particular country, state etc.: *Brad's from somewhere up North.* → see also DOWN SOUTH

WORD CHOICE

- Use **north/south/east/west of** as a phrase to describe where a place is in relation to another place: *Chicago is south of Milwaukee.*
- Use **in the north/south/east/west of** as a noun phrase to say which part of a place you are talking about: *The mountains are in the north of the state.*
- You use **northern, southern, eastern,** or **western** with the name of a place: *They have a cabin in northern Ontario.*

north² *adj.* [only before noun] **1** WRITTEN ABBREVIATION **N.** in, to, or facing north: *the north side of the building* **2** a north wind comes from the north

north³ S2 W3 *adv.* toward the north: *The birds fly north in summer.* | *The window faces north.* | +**of** *The inn is about 20 miles north of Salem.* [**Origin:** Old English]

North ˈAfrica the part of Africa that is on the coast of the Mediterranean Sea and west of Egypt, consisting of Morocco, Algeria, Tunisia, and Libya

ˌNorth Aˈmerica *n.* one of the seven CONTINENTS, that includes land between the Arctic Ocean and the Caribbean Sea —**North American** *n., adj.*

north·bound /ˈnɔrθbaʊnd/ *adj.* traveling or leading toward the north: *northbound traffic* —**northbound** *adv.*

North Car·o·li·na /ˌnɔrθ kærəˈlaɪnə/ WRITTEN ABBREVIATION **N.C.** a state on the eastern coast of the U.S.

North Da·ko·ta /ˌnɔrθ dəˈkoʊṭə/ WRITTEN ABBREVIATION **N.D.** a state in the northern central U.S. on the border with Canada

north·east¹ /ˌnɔrθˈist◂ / *n.* [U] **1** WRITTEN ABBREVIATION **N.E.** the direction that is exactly between north and east **2 the Northeast a)** the northeastern part of a country, state etc. **b)** the area of the U.S. that is usually considered to include New England and the states of New Jersey, New York, and Pennsylvania

northeast² *adj.* [only before noun] **1** WRITTEN ABBREVIATION **N.E.** in or from the northeast: *the northeast suburbs* **2** a northeast wind comes from the northeast

northeast³ *adv.* toward the northeast: *The plane was traveling northeast.*

north·east·er /ˌnɔrθˈistɚ/ *n.* [C] a NOR'EASTER

north·east·er·ly /ˌnɔrθˈistɚli / *adj.* **1** in or toward the northeast **2** a northeasterly wind comes from the northeast

north·east·ern /ˌnɔrθˈistɚn◂ / WRITTEN ABBREVIATION **N.E.** *adj.* in or from the northeast part of a country, state etc.: *the northeastern states*

ˌNortheast ˈPassage, the a way by sea between the Atlantic and Pacific Oceans, going along the northern coasts of Europe and Asia

north·east·ward /ˌnɔrθˈistwɚd/ also **northeastwards** *adv.* toward the northeast —**northeastward** *adj.*

north·er·ly /ˈnɔrðɚli/ *adj.* **1** in or toward the north **2** a northerly wind comes from the north

north·ern /ˈnɔrðɚn/ S3 W2 *adj.* in or from the north part of a country, state etc.: *northern Maryland*

north·ern·er, Northerner /ˈnɔrðɚnɚ/ *n.* [C] someone from the northern part of a country

ˌnorthern ˈhemisphere *n.* **the northern hemisphere** the half of the world that is north of the EQUATOR

Northern Ire·land /ˌnɔrðɚn ˈaɪɚlənd/ the northern part of the island of Ireland, which is politically part of the United Kingdom

ˌNorthern ˈLights *n.* [plural] **the Northern Lights** bands of colored light that are seen in the night sky in the most northern parts of the world SYN **aurora borealis**

Northern Mar·i·an·a Islands, the /ˌnɔrðɚn mæriˌænə ˈaɪləndz, -ˌɑnə-/ a U.S. TERRITORY with its own government that consists of all the Mariana Islands in the western Pacific Ocean except Guam

north·ern·most /ˈnɔrðɚnˌmoʊst/ *adj.* [only before noun] farthest north: *the northernmost tip of the island*

North Ko·re·a /ˌnɔrθ kəˈriə/ a country in East Asia, west of Japan and east of China, which is officially called the Democratic People's Republic of Korea —**North Korean** *n., adj.*

ˌNorth ˈPole *n.* **the North Pole** the most northern point on the surface of the Earth, or the area around it → see also SOUTH POLE → see picture at GLOBE

ˌNorth ˈSea, the part of the Atlantic Ocean that is between Great Britain and northwest Europe

ˌNorth ˈStar *n.* **the North Star** a star that is almost directly over the North Pole and that can be seen from the northern part of the world

north·ward /ˈnɔrθwəd/ also **northwards** *adv.* toward the north: *We drove northward.* —**northward** *adj.*

north·west¹ /ˌnɔrθˈwɛst◂ / *n.* [U] **1** WRITTEN ABBREVIATION **N.W.** the direction that is exactly between north and west **2 the Northwest a)** the northwestern part of a country, state etc. **b)** the area of the U.S. that is usually considered to include the states of Idaho, Oregon, and Washington

northwest² *adj.* [only before noun] **1** WRITTEN ABBREVIATION **N.W.** in or from the northwest: *the northwest suburbs of the city* **2** a northwest wind comes from the northwest

northwest³ *adv.* toward the northwest: *We drove northwest.*

north·west·er /ˌnɔrθˈwɛstə/ *n.* [C] EARTH SCIENCE a strong wind or storm coming from the northwest

north·west·er·ly /ˌnɔrθˈwɛstəli/ *adj.* **1** in or toward the northwest **2** a northwesterly wind comes from the northwest

north·west·ern /ˌnɔrθˈwɛstən◂ / *adj.* in or from the northwest part of a country, state etc.: *northwestern Canada*

ˌNorthwest ˈPassage, the a way by sea between the Atlantic and Pacific Oceans, going along the northern coast of North America

ˌNorthwest ˈTerritories, the a very large area in northwest Canada east of the Yukon, whose capital is Yellowknife

ˌNorthwest ˈTerritory, the an area of the northern central U.S. that reaches from the Ohio River and Mississippi River to the Great Lakes, and includes the states of Ohio, Indiana, Illinois, Michigan, and Wisconsin

north·west·ward /ˌnɔrθˈwɛstwəd/ also **northwestwards** *adv.* going or leading toward the northwest —**northwestward** *adj.*

Nor·way /ˈnɔrweɪ/ a country in northern Europe that is west of Sweden and is part of Scandinavia —**Norwegian** /nɔrˈwidʒən/ *n., adj.*

nos. the written abbreviation of "numbers": *nos. 17–33*

nose¹ /noʊz/ S1 W2 *n.*

1 ON YOUR FACE [C] BIOLOGY the part of a person's or animal's face used for smelling or breathing: *He broke his nose playing football.* | *the guy with the big nose* | *Here's a Kleenex – **blow your nose*** (=clear it by blowing). | *Robin has a sore throat and a **runny nose*** (=liquid is coming out of her nose because she has a cold). | *Davey, don't **pick your nose*** (=clean it with your finger)*!* | *Her eyes were red and her **nose was running*** (=liquid was coming out of it).

2 (right) under sb's nose so close to someone that they should notice, but do not: *The drugs were smuggled in under the noses of customs officers.*

3 stick/poke your nose into sth to show too much interest in private matters that do not concern you: *No one wants the government sticking its nose into the personal business of citizens.* → see also NOSY

4 turn your nose up (at sth) INFORMAL to refuse to accept something because you do not think it is good enough for you: *He turns his nose up at television.*

5 on the nose INFORMAL exactly SYN **precisely**: *He arrived at 6 on the nose.*

6 have your nose in a book INFORMAL to be reading: *Celia always has her nose in a book.*

7 keep your nose to the grindstone INFORMAL to work very hard, without stopping to rest

8 by a nose if someone wins something by a nose, they win by only a very small amount

9 put sb's nose out of joint INFORMAL to annoy someone, especially by attracting everyone's attention away from them

10 AIRPLANE [C] the pointed front end of an airplane, ROCKET etc.

11 have a (good) nose a) to be naturally good at finding and recognizing something: **+for** *Some people have a nose for news.* **b)** to be good at recognizing smells: *Our dog has a very good nose.*

12 keep your nose clean INFORMAL to make sure you do not get into trouble or do anything wrong or illegal

13 keep your nose out (of sth) SPOKEN to stop showing too much interest in private matters that do not concern you: *Keep your nose out of my business!*

14 with your nose in the air behaving as if you are more important than other people and not talking to them: *She just walked past with her nose in the air.*

[**Origin:** Old English *nosu*] → see also BROWN-NOSE, **cut off your nose to spite your face** at CUT OFF (10), **follow your nose** at FOLLOW (19), HARD-NOSED, **look down your nose at sb/sth** at LOOK¹ (21), NOSE JOB, **pay through the nose (for sth)** at PAY¹ (14), **powder your nose** at POWDER² (2), **thumb your nose at sb/sth** at THUMB² (1)

nose² *v.* [I always + adv./prep., T always + adv./prep.] if a vehicle, boat etc. noses forward, or if you nose it forward, it moves forward slowly: *The boat nosed out into the lake.*

nose around *phr. v.* INFORMAL to try to find out private information about someone or something: *A few reporters were nosing around.*

nose·bleed /ˈnoʊzblid/ *n.* **1** [C] blood that is coming out of your nose: *Chuck **has a nosebleed**.* **2 nosebleed seats/section** the seats or areas of a sports STADIUM or ARENA that are the highest and farthest away from the field or court

nose·cone /ˈnoʊzkoʊn/ *n.* [C] the pointed front part of a MISSILE or ROCKET

-nosed /noʊzd/ [in adjectives] **red-nosed/long-nosed etc.** having a nose that is red, long etc.

nose·dive¹ /ˈnoʊzdaɪv/ *n.* [C] **1** a sudden drop in amount, price, rate etc.: *The dollar **took a nosedive** early in trading today.* **2** a sudden steep drop made by an airplane, with its front end pointing toward the ground: *The plane suddenly **went into a nosedive**.*

nosedive² *v.* [I] **1** if a price, rate, amount etc. nosedives, it becomes smaller or reduces in value suddenly SYN **plummet**: *Sales have nosedived since January.* **2** if an airplane nosedives, it drops suddenly and steeply with its front end pointing toward the ground

nose·gay /ˈnoʊzgeɪ/ *n.* [C] OLD-FASHIONED a small arrangement of flowers

ˈnose job *n.* [C] INFORMAL a medical operation on someone's nose to improve its appearance

nos·ey /ˈnoʊzi/ *adj.* another spelling of NOSY

nosh¹ /nɑʃ/ *n.* [U] INFORMAL food, especially a small amount of food eaten between meals SYN **snack**

nosh² *v.* [I] INFORMAL to eat SYN **snack** [**Origin:** 1900–2000 Yiddish *nashn*, from Middle High German *naschen* **to eat secretly**]

ˌno-ˈshow *n.* [C] someone who does not arrive somewhere they were expected to go, for example at a restaurant or for an airplane flight

nos·tal·gia /nɑˈstældʒə, nə-/ *n.* [U] a feeling that a time in the past was good, or the activity of remembering a good time in the past and wishing that things had not changed: *She remembers her first trip to Europe **with warm nostalgia**.* | **+for** ***A wave of nostalgia** for family Christmases swept over me.* [**Origin:** 1700–1800 Modern Latin, Greek *nostos* **returning home** + *algos* **pain**]

nos·tal·gic /nɑˈstældʒɪk, nə-/ *adj.* if you feel nostalgic about a time in the past, you feel happy when you remember it, and in some ways you wish that things had not changed: *a nostalgic look at the 1940s* | **+for** *old photos that made her **feel nostalgic** for happier times* —**nostalgically** /-kli/ *adv.*

nos·tril /ˈnɑstrəl/ *n.* [C] one of the two holes at the end of your nose, through which you breathe and smell things [**Origin:** Old English *nosthyrl* **nose-hole**]

nos·trum /ˈnɑstrəm/ *n.* [C] **1** FORMAL an idea that someone thinks will solve a problem easily, but probably will not help at all: *an economic nostrum* **2** OLD-FASHIONED a medicine that is probably not effective and is not given by a doctor

nos·y /ˈnoʊzi/ *adj. comparative* **nosier**, *superlative* **nosiest** always trying to find out about things that do not concern you, especially other people's private lives: *Stop being so nosy!* | *a nosy neighbor* —**nosiness** *n.* [U]

not /nɑt/ S1 W1 *adv.* **1** used to make a word, statement, or question negative: *Most of the stores do not open until 10 a.m.* | *I don't smoke.* | *She's not a very nice person.* | *Is anyone else not going?* | **not at all/not...at all** (=used to emphasize what you are saying) *The changes were not at all surprising.* | *I do not like his attitude at all.* → see also NO, -N'T **2** used in order to make a word or expression have the opposite meaning: *Des Moines isn't far now.* | *The food is **not very** good there.* | **not much/many/a lot etc.** *Not much is known about the disease.* | *Not many people have read it.* | *Most of the hotels are **not that** cheap* (=they are slightly expensive). **3** used instead of a whole phrase, to mean the opposite of what has been mentioned before it: *No one knows if the story is true **or not**.* | *I should be home, but **if not**, leave me a message.* | *"Is Mark still sick?" "I **hope not**."* → see also SO **4 not only...(but) also/as well/too etc.** in addition to being or doing something: *Shakespeare was not only a writer but also an actor.* | **not only do/will/can etc.** *Not only do they want a pay increase, they want reduced hours as well.* **5 not a** also **not one** not any person or thing: *Not one of the students knew the answer.* | *There wasn't a cloud in the sky.* | ***Not a single** person said thank you.* | *He had no criminal record, **not even a** parking ticket.* **6 not that...** used before a sentence or phrase to mean the opposite of what follows it, and to make the previous sentence seem less important: *Sarah has a new boyfriend – not that I care* (=I do not care). | *Janice had lost some weight, not that it mattered* (=it did not matter). **7 ...not!** SPOKEN, SLANG used, especially by young people, to say that you really mean the opposite of what you have just said: *She's really pretty – not!* → see also **this/that is not to say** at SAY[1] (13)

USAGE

In spoken English and informal writing, **not** is usually shortened to **n't**: *Don't worry, it will be all right.* | *I won't go without you.* Don't use another negative word, for example "nothing," "nobody," or "nowhere," in the same sentence as **not**. Use "anything," "anybody," "anywhere" etc. instead: *We didn't see anything.* | *Tom doesn't know anybody there.*

no·ta·ble /ˈnoʊt̬əbəl/ *adj.* [usually before noun] important, interesting, excellent, or unusual enough to be noticed SYN **noteworthy**: *a notable achievement* | **+for** *The music is notable for its complexity.* | **notable example/case/feature** *a notable example of this painter's work*

no·ta·bles /ˈnoʊt̬əbəlz/ *n.* [plural] important or famous people

no·ta·bly /ˈnoʊt̬əbli/ *adv.* **1** used to say that a person or thing is a typical example or the most important example of something SYN **especially** SYN **particularly**: *Some early doctors, notably Hippocrates, thought that diet was important.* **2** FORMAL in a way that is clearly different, important, or unusual: *The project has been notably successful.*

no·ta·rize /ˈnoʊt̬əˌraɪz/ *v.* [T often passive] if a notary public notarizes a document, they make it official by putting an official stamp on it: *a notarized copy of your birth certificate*

no·ta·ry pub·lic /ˌnoʊt̬əri ˈpʌblɪk/ also **notary** *n.* [C] someone who has the legal power to make a signed statement or document official

no·ta·tion /noʊˈteɪʃən/ *n.* [C,U] a system of written marks or signs used for representing subjects such as music, mathematics, or scientific ideas

notch[1] /nɑtʃ/ *n.* [C] **1** a V-shaped cut or hole in a surface or edge SYN **nick**: *Cut a notch near one end of the stick.* **2** a level on a scale that measures something, for example quality or achievement: **rise/go up/fall/go down/drop etc. a notch** *The team has moved up a notch in the rankings.* | *The Spartans **turned it up a notch*** (=increased the amount of effort they were using) *in the second half.* **3** EARTH SCIENCE a passage between two mountains or hills → see also TOP-NOTCH

notch[2] *v.* [T] **1** also **notch up** to achieve something, especially a victory or a particular total or SCORE: *The Astros have notched up another win.* **2** to cut a V-shaped mark into something, especially as a way of showing the number of times something has been done SYN **nick**

note[1] /noʊt/ S1 W2 *n.*

1 SHORT LETTER [C] a short informal letter: **+to** *I **wrote a note** to Jim's teacher.* | *Mom **left a note** on the counter about dinner.* | *The kids are old enough to write their own **thank-you notes*** (=a note to thank someone for a present etc.).

2 TO REMIND YOU [C] something that you write down to remind you of something: *There were notes written on the report.* | *Marina spoke without using any notes.* | *Tina **made a note of** their new address.* | *I **made a mental note*** (=decided that I must remember to do something) *to check on it.*

3 MUSIC [C] ENG. LANG. ARTS **a)** a particular musical sound or PITCH: **high/low note** *She couldn't **hit** the high **notes**.* **b)** a sign in written music that represents this

4 notes [plural] information that a student writes down during a class, from a book etc., so they will remember it: *Can I borrow your **lecture notes**?* | *I read the first three chapters and **took notes*** (=wrote notes).

5 VOICE [singular] if there is a particular note in someone's voice, they show what they are thinking or feeling by the way their voice sounds: *There was a strained **note in** Fischer's **voice**.* | **+of** *"Can you help me?" she asked, a note of hope in her voice.*

6 PARTICULAR QUALITY [singular] something that adds a particular quality to a situation, statement, or event: **on a...note** *She ended her speech on a **personal note**.* | **+of** *He brought a note of realism to the debate.* | **strike/hit a note** *Burke struck a pessimistic note, saying the deadline may not be met.* | **the right/wrong note** (=an appropriate or inappropriate quality for a particular occasion) *The speech hit just the right notes of outrage and grief.*

7 take note to pay careful attention to something SYN **notice**: *His performance made the music world take note.* | **+of** *Take note of how much water you're using.*

8 ADDITIONAL INFORMATION [C] a short piece of writing at the bottom of a page or at the end of a book, that gives more information about something written in the main part: *Additional sources are listed in the notes at the back of the book.* → see also FOOTNOTE (1)

9 sb/sth of note someone or something that is important, interesting, or famous: *The school has produced several architects of note.*

10 worthy/deserving of note important or interesting and deserving to be noticed SYN **noteworthy**: *Three novels are especially worthy of note.*

11 GOVERNMENT LETTER [C] TECHNICAL a formal letter between governments: *a diplomatic note*

12 MONEY [C] a piece of paper money worth a particular amount SYN **bill**

[**Origin:** 1200–1300 Latin *nota* **mark, character, written note**] → see also **compare notes (with sb)** at COMPARE[1] (4)

note down

note[2] W1 *v.* [T] FORMAL **1** to notice or pay careful attention to something SYN **notice**: *Note the painter's use of shadow.* | **note that** *Please note that the museum is closed on Mondays.* | **note who/what/how etc.** *Russell noted how animal research had led directly to some vaccines.* **2** to mention something because it is important or interesting: *The report noted a complete disregard for safety regulations.* | **note that** *The judge noted that Miller had no previous criminal record.* **3** also **note down** to write something down so that you will remember it: *Stuart noted the telephone number on a business card.*

note·book /ˈnoʊt˺bʊk/ S3 *n.* [C] **1** a book of plain

paper in which you can write notes **2** also **notebook computer** a small computer that you can carry with you

not·ed /ˈnoʊt̬ɪd/ *adj.* well known or famous, especially because of some special quality or ability SYN **famous**: *a noted author* | **+for** *The area is noted for its beauty.*

note·pad /ˈnoʊt˺pæd/ *n.* [C] **1** a group of sheets of paper fastened together at the top, used for writing notes **2** a simple computer program on which you can write notes

note·pa·per /ˈnoʊt˺ˌpeɪpɚ/ *n.* [U] paper used for writing letters or notes

note·wor·thy /ˈnoʊt˺ˌwɚði/ *adj.* important or interesting enough to deserve your attention SYN **notable**: *a noteworthy achievement*

ˌnot-for-ˈprofit *adj.* NONPROFIT

ˈnoth·er /ˈnʌðɚ/ → see **a whole ˈnother sth** at WHOLE[3] (2)

noth·ing[1] /ˈnʌθɪŋ/ S1 W1 *pron.* **1** not anything or no thing: *There's nothing in this box.* | *No, there's nothing wrong, I'm all right.* | *The kids were complaining there was nothing to do.* | *She had on socks and* ***nothing else****!* | *I have* ***nothing more*** *to say.* | *I* ***have nothing against*** *New York, I just wouldn't want to live there.* | *There is* ***absolutely nothing*** *to worry about.* **2** not anything that you consider important or interesting: *Nothing ever happens around here.* | *I have nothing to wear to the wedding.* | *There's nothing on TV tonight.* | *"What did you say?" "Oh, nothing."* | *It's nothing, just a scratch.* | *"What did you do last weekend?" "Oh,* ***nothing much****."* **3** zero: *We beat them ten to nothing.* ▸see THESAURUS box at **zero[1]** **4 for nothing a)** without paying for something or being paid for something: *My dad said he'd fix it for nothing.* | *You can't* ***get something for nothing****.* **b)** if you do something for nothing, you make an effort but do not get the result you wanted: *We drove all the way down there for nothing.* **5** no money or payment at all: *This service will cost you nothing.* **6 have nothing to do with sb/sth** [not in progressive] **a)** if something has nothing to do with a fact or situation, it is not related to that fact or situation: *Race should have nothing to do with who gets hired.* **b)** if someone has nothing to do with a situation or person, he or she is not involved in it or with them: *I don't know why she's so worried; it has nothing to do with her.* **7 have/want nothing to do with sth** to not be involved in a situation or with a person, especially because you disapprove: *Joey wanted nothing to do with the whole idea.* **8 nothing but sth** FORMAL only: *They'd had nothing but bad luck.* **9 if nothing else** used to emphasize one good quality or feature that someone or something has, while suggesting that it might be the only good one: *If nothing else, the report points out the need for better math education.* **10 nothing special** having no very good or unusual qualities: *The food there is nothing special.* **11 better than nothing** used to say that although an amount or action is small, it is more acceptable than none at all: *I guess $5 is better than nothing.* **12 not for nothing** for very good reasons: *Not for nothing was the American West described as the Big Empty.* **13 there's nothing like sth** INFORMAL used to say that something is very good: *There's nothing like a nice hot bath.* **14 sb has nothing to lose** used to say that someone should try to do something because the situation will not be worse if they fail: *You might as well apply for the job – you've got nothing to lose.*

SPOKEN PHRASES

15 (there's) nothing to it/sth used to say that something is easy to do: *Anyone can use a computer. There's nothing to it!* **16** [used with a negative] NONSTANDARD anything: *I never said nothing about taking you swimming.* **17 it was nothing** OLD-FASHIONED said, when someone thanks you, in order to say that you did not mind helping: *"Thanks a lot!" "It was nothing."* **18 nothing doing** OLD-FASHIONED used to refuse to do something: *Lend you $500? Nothing doing!*

19 be nothing if not sth used to emphasize a particular quality that someone or something has: *Well, he's nothing if not stubborn.* **20 come to nothing** if a plan or action comes to nothing, it does not continue or does not achieve anything **21 nothing of the sort/kind** used to emphasize that something is not true or that something will not happen: *They lived as man and wife when they were nothing of the kind.* **22 there is nothing to/in sth** used to say that what people are saying is not true: *An administration spokesman said there was nothing to the rumors.* [**Origin:** Old English *nan thing*, *nathing* **no thing**] → see also **nothing/nowhere etc. on earth** at EARTH (4), **to say nothing of sth** at SAY[1] (14), **sweet nothings** at SWEET[1] (11), **think nothing of (doing sth)** at THINK (8)

nothing[2] S3 *adv.* **1 be/seem/look etc. nothing like sb/sth** to have no qualities or features that are similar to someone or something else: *She looks nothing like her sister.* **2 be nothing less than sth** also **be nothing short of sth** used to emphasize that something or someone has a particular quality or seems to be something: *The country's economic recovery was seen as nothing less than a miracle.*

noth·ing·ness /ˈnʌθɪŋnɪs/ *n.* [U] **1** empty space, or the absence of anything: *He stared into nothingness.* **2** the state of not existing: *Is there only nothingness after death?*

no·tice[1] /ˈnoʊt̬ɪs/ S1 W2 *v.* [I, T not in progressive] **1** to see, hear, or feel someone or something: *I waved, but she didn't notice.* | *He hadn't noticed any smoke.* | **notice (that)** *The lifeguard didn't notice that a boy was having trouble in the pool.* | **notice who/what/how etc.** *Have you noticed how often he interrupts people?* | **notice sb/sth doing sth** *Did you notice him leaving?* ▸see THESAURUS box at **see[1]** **2 be/get noticed** to get attention from someone: *The résumé helped me get noticed.* **3 sb can't help noticing sth** also **sb can't help but notice sth** used to say that someone realizes that something exists or is happening even though they are not deliberately trying to pay attention to it: *I couldn't help noticing the bruises on her arm.*

notice[2] S3 *n.*

1 ATTENTION [U] the act of paying attention to something or someone: *When she won, people finally started to* ***take notice****.* | *The movie's popularity made industry executives* ***sit up and take notice*** (=pay more attention). | *Many employers* ***took no notice of*** (=paid no attention to) *the court decision.* | *It was the first time the problem had* ***come to my notice****.* | *I wondered how this could have* ***escaped*** *my* ***notice****.* | *The letter* ***brought*** *the matter* ***to*** *Mr. Pearson's* ***notice****.*

2 WARNING/TIME TO PREPARE [U] information or a warning about something that will happen: *Prices are subject to change* ***without notice****.* | **give/serve (sb) notice** *Employees were given* ***advance notice*** *of the layoffs.* | *Rescue workers must respond* ***on short notice*** (=without being given much warning). | *We were ready to leave* ***at a moment's notice*** (=without being given much warning). | **+of** *Teachers must be given notice of the changes.* | *He has been* ***put on notice*** *that further delays will not be acceptable.*

3 ON PAPER [C] a written or printed statement that gives information or a warning to people SYN **sign**: *a notice on the wall*

4 give notice also **hand in your notice** to inform your employer that you will be leaving your job soon, especially by writing a formal letter: *Ross gave notice yesterday.*

5 until further notice from now until another change is announced: *The museum will be closed until further notice.*

6 BOOK/PLAY ETC. [C usually plural] ENG. LANG. ARTS a statement of opinion, especially one written for a newspaper or magazine, about a new play, book, movie etc. SYN **review**: *The new play got* ***mixed notices*** (=some good, some bad) *in the newspapers.*

[**Origin:** 1400–1500 Old French, Latin *notitia* **knowledge, familiarity**, from *notus* **known**]

no·tice·a·ble /ˈnoʊt̬ɪsəbəl/ *adj.* easy to notice: *Alcohol has a noticeable effect on the body.* | *The stain was hardly noticeable.* —**noticeably** *adv.*

THESAURUS

clear impossible to doubt or make a mistake about: *clear evidence of his guilt*
obvious easy to notice: *an obvious mistake*
conspicuous very noticeable, especially because something is different from other things: *He was tall and blond, and felt conspicuous in Japan.*
striking unusual or interesting enough to be noticed: *Her beauty was striking.*
eye-catching noticeable and attractive: *an eye-catching advertisement*

no·ti·fi·ca·tion /ˌnoʊt̬əfəˈkeɪʃən/ *n.* [C,U] FORMAL an act of officially informing someone about something: **+of** *You should **receive notification** of the results within a week.*

no·ti·fy /ˈnoʊt̬əˌfaɪ/ *v.* **notifies, notified, notifying** [T] to formally or officially tell someone about something SYN **inform**: *Have you notified the police?* | **notify sb of sth** *The security company notified residents about the changes.*

no·tion /ˈnoʊʃən/ Ac S3 W2 *n.* [C usually singular] **1** an idea, belief, or opinion about something, especially one that you think is wrong: **+of** *an unrealistic notion of what teachers do* | **notion that** *We're trying to dispel the notion that it's cool to smoke.* **2** a sudden desire to do something SYN **whim**: **notion to do sth** *She had a sudden notion to go swimming.* **3 notions** [plural] small things, such as thread and buttons, used for sewing

no·tion·al /ˈnoʊʃənl/ *adj.* existing only in the mind as an idea or plan, and not existing in reality: *Their calculations were based on a notional $3.50 per share.*

no·to·ri·e·ty /ˌnoʊt̬əˈraɪət̬i/ *n.* [U] the state of being famous or well-known for doing something that is bad or that people do not approve of SYN **infamy**: **gain/earn/achieve notoriety** *Her love affairs gained her **a measure of notoriety**.*

no·to·ri·ous /noʊˈtɔriəs/ *adj.* famous or well known for something bad SYN **infamous**: *the notorious flaw in the Hubble Space Telescope* | **+for** *The company was notorious for paying its employees poorly.* —**notoriously** *adv.*: *The tests are notoriously unreliable.* ▸see THESAURUS box at **famous**[1]

not·with·stand·ing /ˌnɑtˈwɪθˈstændɪŋ/ Ac *prep.* FORMAL if something is true notwithstanding something else, it is true even though the other thing is true or has happened SYN **despite**: *Manufacturing exports are up this year, notwithstanding the recession.* —**notwithstanding** *adv.*

Nou·ak·chott /nʊˈɑkʃɑt/ the capital and largest city of Mauritania

nou·gat /ˈnugət/ *n.* [U] a type of sticky soft candy with nuts and sometimes fruit

nought /nɔt, nɑt/ *n.* [U] OLD-FASHIONED nothing: *All my efforts were **for nought**.*

noun /naʊn/ *n.* [C] ENG. LANG. ARTS a word or group of words that represent a person, place, thing, quality, action, or idea. Nouns can be used as the subject or object of a verb, for example in "The teacher arrived" or "We like the teacher," or as the object of a PREPOSITION, for example in "He is good at football." [**Origin:** 1300–1400 Anglo-French **name, noun**, from Old French *nom*, from Latin *nomen*] → see also COMMON NOUN, COUNT NOUN, PROPER NOUN, UNCOUNT NOUN

nour·ish /ˈnɚɪʃ, ˈnʌrɪʃ/ *v.* [T] **1** to give a person, plant, or animal the food or other substances they need to live, grow, and stay healthy SYN **feed**: *The roses are nourished by the rain.* | ***well-nourished** children* → see also UNDERNOURISHED **2** LITERARY to keep a feeling, idea, or belief strong or help it to grow stronger: *The Bill of Rights nourishes our freedom.*

nour·ish·ing /ˈnɚɪʃɪŋ/ *adj.* **1** food that is nourishing makes you strong and healthy SYN **nutritious** **2** BIOLOGY if an idea, place, person etc. is nourishing, it helps you develop your emotions, intelligence, or spirit

nour·ish·ment /ˈnɚɪʃmənt/ *n.* [U] FORMAL **1** food or other substances that people and living things need to live, grow, and stay healthy: *The program provides basic nourishment to low-income families.* **2** something that helps a feeling, idea, or belief to grow stronger: **spiritual/intelluctual/emotional nourishment** *The Bible is a source of spiritual nourishment.*

nou·veau riche /ˌnuvoʊ ˈriʃ/ *n. plural* **nouveaux riches** /-voʊ ˈriʃ/ [C] someone who has only recently become rich and who spends a lot of money, hoping that other people will notice and admire them —**nouveau riche** *adj.*

nou·velle cui·sine /ˌnuvɛl kwɪˈzin/ *n.* [U] a style of cooking from France that uses fresh fruit and vegetables cooked in a simple way and served attractively

Nov. the written abbreviation of NOVEMBER

no·va /ˈnoʊvə/ *n.* [C] PHYSICS a star that explodes and suddenly becomes much brighter for a short time → see also SUPERNOVA

No·va Sco·tia /ˌnoʊvə ˈskoʊʃə/ a PROVINCE of southeast Canada

nov·el[1] /ˈnɑvəl/ W2 *n.* [C] ENG. LANG. ARTS a long book in which the story and characters are usually imaginary: *a novel by John Irving* | **mystery/historical/romance etc. novel** *one of Cornwell's crime novels* [**Origin:** 1500–1600 Italian *novella*, from *storia novella* **new story**] ▸see THESAURUS box at **book**[1]

novel[2] *adj.* new, different, and unusual: **novel idea/approach/method etc.** *a novel approach to the problem*

nov·el·ist /ˈnɑvəlɪst/ *n.* [C] someone who writes novels SYN **author** SYN **writer**

nov·el·i·za·tion /ˌnɑvələˈzeɪʃən/ *n.* [C] a story that was first written as a movie or television program before being written as a book

no·vel·la /noʊˈvɛlə/ *n.* [C] ENG. LANG. ARTS a story that is shorter than a novel, but longer than a SHORT STORY

nov·el·ty /ˈnɑvəlti/ *n. plural* **novelties** **1** [C] something new and unusual that attracts people's attention and interest: *Then, the Internet was still a novelty.* **2** [C often plural] an unusual, small, cheap object, often given as a present: *a selection of novelties and T-shirts* | *a novelty key ring* **3** [U] the quality of being new, unusual, and interesting: *Modern art thrives on novelty.* | *The **novelty** of the game **had worn off*** (=it no longer seemed new and interesting).

No·vem·ber /noʊˈvɛmbɚ, nə-/ WRITTEN ABBREVIATION **Nov.** *n.* [C,U] the eleventh month of the year, between October and December [**Origin:** 1200–1300 Old French *Novembre*, from Latin *November*, from *novem* **nine**; because it was the ninth month of the ancient Roman year] → see Grammar box at JANUARY

nov·ice /ˈnɑvɪs/ *n.* [C] **1** someone who has only begun learning a skill or activity SYN **beginner**: *The computer program is easy for even a novice to master.* | *a novice skier* **2** someone who has recently joined a religious group to become a MONK or NUN

no·vi·tiate /noʊˈvɪʃət, nə-, -ʃiət/ *n.* [C] TECHNICAL the period of being a novice

No·vo·cain /ˈnoʊvəˌkeɪn/ *n.* [U] TRADEMARK a drug used for stopping pain during a small operation or treatment, especially on your teeth

NOW /naʊ/ **National Organization for Women** an organization that works for legal, economic, and social equality between women and men

now[1] /naʊ/ S1 W1 *adv.* **1** at the present time: *The town is now a major center of industry.* | ***Right now*** (=exactly now) *the weather is pretty hot.* | *Judy should be at work **by now*** (=before now). | *I want you home by 9:00 **from now on*** (=starting now and continuing into the future). | *Just leave it on the table **for now*** (=for a short time). | *Multiple sclerosis, **as of now*** (=at the present time), *is an incurable disease.* | *I never really understood what she meant **until now**.* → see Word Choice box at ACTUALLY

THESAURUS

at the moment now: *Both men are in jail at the moment.*

N

for the moment happening now but likely to change in the future: *Raskin decided, for the moment, not to sign the contract.*
at present/at the present time happening or existing now: *At present, little is known about the disease.*
currently happening or existing now: *The Canadian dollar is currently worth abut 75 cents in American money.*
presently FORMAL at this time: *The company presently employs over 1,000 people.*

2 immediately: *Come on, Dave, if we don't leave now we'll be late.* | *Time's up – stop writing now.* | *Call her **right now**, before she leaves.*

SPOKEN PHRASES

3 said when you want to get someone's attention: *Now, how many people want cake?* | *Okay, now, watch me.* **4** said when you want some information: *Now, who was Kathleen married to?* | *Let's see, now, he would have been about seven then?* **5** said when you pause because you are thinking about what to say next: *Okay, now, how about next Friday?* **6 now then** said to get someone's attention before telling them to do something or asking them a question: *Now then, you'll be 84 in August – is that right?* **7** said when you are trying to comfort someone who is upset: *Don't cry, now, it'll be all right.* **8** used when you know or understand something because of something you have just seen, just been told etc.: *"I just went to see Jim." "So, now do you see why I'm worried about him?"* **9 now you tell me!** said when you are annoyed because someone has just told you something they should have told you before: *"Mom, I need to bring cookies to school tomorrow." "Now you tell me!"* **10** said when telling or reminding someone to do something: *Call me when you get home – don't forget now!* **11 well now** said when giving your opinion or asking someone to tell you something: *Well now, do you agree or not?* **12 not now** said when you do not want to talk to someone or do something now, because you are busy, tired etc.: *"Tell me a story." "Not now, Daddy's working."* **13 now what? a)** used when an attempt to do something has failed and you do not know what to do next: *I can't reach. Now what?* **b)** also **what now?** used when it seems like the next in a series of bad things is going to happen, or when the next in a series of interruptions is happening: *Now what? Are you sick again?* **14 it's now or never** used to say that if someone does not do something now, they will not get another chance to do it **15 now's the time** used to say that someone should do something now, because it is the right time to do it: **now's the time (for sb) to do sth** *Now's the time to buy a suit, while they're on sale.* **16 what is it now?** said when you are annoyed because someone keeps interrupting you or asking you things **17 now you're talking** used to tell someone that you agree very much with what they are saying: *"How about a beer?" "Now you're talking!"* **18 now for sth** used when saying what you are going to do next: *Okay, now for the main point behind this meeting.* **19 and now** used when introducing the next activity, performer etc.: *And now, live from New York, it's "Saturday Night!"* **20 now, now** OLD-FASHIONED **a)** said in order to try to make someone feel better when they are sad, upset, hurt etc.: *"Let me look at your leg." "Ow!" "Now, now, it's not that bad."* **b)** used when someone has just said something you think is not very nice: *"Peter's such an idiot sometimes." "Now, now." "It's true!"*

21 three weeks/two years etc. now starting three weeks, two years etc. ago and continuing into the present: *They've been going out together for a long time now.* | *It's been over five years now since I started working here.* **22 any day/minute etc. now** very soon: *Peggy should get here any minute now.* **23 (every) now and then, now and again** used in order to say that something happens sometimes but not always: *I see Wanda every now and then at church.* **24 now... now...** LITERARY used to say that at one moment someone does one thing and immediately after, they do something else: *The eagle glided through the sky, now rising, now swooping.* [**Origin:** Old English *nu*]

now[2] S2 also **'now that** *conjunction* because of something or as a result of something: *The kids are getting along better now that they're older.* | *I'm going to relax now the school year is over.*

NOW ac·count /ˈnaʊ əˌkaʊnt/ *n.* [C] a CHECKING ACCOUNT that pays INTEREST on the money you have in it

now·a·days /ˈnaʊəˌdeɪz/ *adv.* in the present, compared with what happened in the past: *People are taller nowadays.*

no·where /ˈnoʊwɛr/ S3 *adv.* **1** also **no place** not in any place or to any place: **nowhere (for sb) to do sth** *There was nowhere to sit but the bed.* | *There was **nowhere else** for them to go.* **2 get/go nowhere** to have no success or make no progress: *She's been looking for a job but has gotten nowhere.* | **get sb nowhere** *Threats will get you nowhere.* | **+with** *Police were getting nowhere with the case.* | *The negotiations are **going nowhere fast**.* **3 be nowhere to be found/seen** also **be nowhere in sight** to not be in a place, or not be seen or found there: *When her parents came home, Emma was nowhere to be found.* **4 nowhere (near) a)** far from a particular place: *Mac was nowhere near her apartment that night.* **b)** not at all: *She's **nowhere near as** pretty as you.* | *They had nowhere near the number of people needed.* | *It's nowhere near ready.* **5 out of nowhere** also **from nowhere** happening or appearing suddenly and without warning: *Owens came out of nowhere to block the shot.* | *Cinderella's fairy godmother appeared from nowhere.* → see also **in the middle of nowhere** at MIDDLE[1] (4)

no-'win *adj.* [only before noun] relating to a situation that will end badly whatever you decide to do: *Politically, it's a **no-win situation**.* → see also WIN-WIN

no·wise /ˈnoʊwaɪz/ *adv.* OLD USE not at all

nox·ious /ˈnɑkʃəs/ *adj.* FORMAL harmful or poisonous SYN **toxic**: *noxious fumes* [**Origin:** 1400–1500 Latin *noxius*, from *noxa* **harm**]

noz·zle /ˈnɑzəl/ *n.* [C] a short tube fitted to the end of a HOSE, pipe etc. to direct and control the liquid or gas pouring out

NPR *n.* **National Public Radio** a national organization of radio stations in the U.S. that broadcasts without advertisements

NR *adj.* **Not Rated** used to show that a particular movie has not been given an official rating and so only people older than 17 may see it

NRA → see NATIONAL RIFLE ASSOCIATION

NRC → see NUCLEAR REGULATORY COMMISSION

NSC → see NATIONAL SECURITY COUNCIL

-n't /ənt/ the short form of "not": *Sorry, I wasn't listening.* | *She didn't see me.*

nth /ɛnθ/ *adj.* **1 to the nth degree** INFORMAL extremely, or as much as possible: *It was boring to the nth degree.* **2** [only before noun] INFORMAL the most recent of a long series of similar things that have happened: *Even after I'd reminded him for the nth time, he forgot.* [**Origin:** 1800–1900 *n* mathematical sign for a number of unknown value + *-th*]

nu·ance /ˈnuɑns/ *n.* [C,U] a very slight hardly noticeable difference in manner, color, meaning etc.: *He was aware of every nuance in her voice.* | **+of** *subtle nuances of meaning* [**Origin:** 1700–1800 French, Old French *nuer* **to make shades of color**, from *nue* **cloud**] **—nuanced** *adj.*

nub /nʌb/ *n.* [C] **1** the central or main part of something: **the nub of the matter/argument/problem etc.** *The nub of the matter is that these children are too young to decide for themselves.* **2** a small rounded piece of something, especially a piece that is left after the main part has been eaten, used etc.

Nu·bi·a /ˈnubiə/ HISTORY an area of ancient northeast Africa around the Nile, from Aswan in Egypt to Khartoum in Sudan

N

nu·bile /ˈnubaɪl, -bəl/ *adj.* FORMAL a woman who is nubile is young and sexually attractive [**Origin:** 1600–1700 French **worth marrying**, from Latin *nubilis*, from *nubere* **to marry**]

nu·cle·ar /ˈnukliə/ Ac W2 *adj.* **1** PHYSICS using or relating to the energy produced when the NUCLEUS of an atom is either split or joined with the nucleus of another atom: *a nuclear power station* | *a nuclear-powered submarine* **2** PHYSICS relating to the NUCLEUS of an atom: *nuclear fission* **3** relating to or involving the use of NUCLEAR WEAPONS: *a nuclear testing area* | *the threat of nuclear war* [**Origin:** 1800–1900 *nucleus*]

ˌnuclear deˈterrence *n.* [U] the threat of using NUCLEAR WEAPONS as a way to prevent an enemy from attacking

ˌnuclear disˈarmament *n.* [U] the process or activity of getting rid of NUCLEAR WEAPONS

ˌnuclear ˈenergy *n.* [U] the powerful force that is produced when the NUCLEUS (=central part) of an atom is either split or joined to another atom

ˌnuclear ˈenvelope also **ˌnuclear ˈmembrane** *n.* [C] BIOLOGY a MEMBRANE (=very thin piece of tissue) with two layers that encloses the NUCLEUS of a cell

ˌnuclear ˈfamily *n.* [C] a family unit that consists only of husband, wife, and children → see also EXTENDED FAMILY

ˌnuclear ˈfission *n.* [U] PHYSICS the splitting of the NUCLEUS of an atom, that results in a lot of power being produced

ˌnuclear-ˈfree *adj.* places that are nuclear-free do not allow NUCLEAR materials to be carried, stored, or used in that area: *a nuclear-free zone*

ˌnuclear ˈfusion *n.* [U] PHYSICS a NUCLEAR reaction in which the NUCLEI (=central parts) of light atoms join with the nuclei of heavier atoms, which produces power without producing any waste

ˌnuclear ˈphysics *n.* [U] PHYSICS the area of PHYSICS that is concerned with the structure and features of the NUCLEUS of atoms

ˌnuclear ˈpower *n.* [U] power, usually in the form of electricity, from NUCLEAR ENERGY

ˌnuclear reˈaction *n.* [C] PHYSICS a process in which the parts of the NUCLEUS of an atom become arranged in a different way to form new substances

ˌnuclear reˈactor *n.* [C] a large machine that produces NUCLEAR ENERGY, especially as a means of producing electricity

ˌNuclear ˈRegulatory Comˌmission, the a U.S. government organization that checks on the safety of nuclear power PLANTS

ˌnuclear ˈwaste *n.* [U] waste material from NUCLEAR REACTORS, which is RADIOACTIVE

ˌnuclear ˈweapon *n.* [C] a very powerful weapon that uses NUCLEAR ENERGY to destroy large areas

nu·cle·ic ac·id /nuˌkliɪk ˈæsɪd, -ˌkleɪ-/ *n.* [C,U] CHEMISTRY one of the two acids, DNA and RNA, that carry GENETIC information

nu·cle·oid /ˈnukliˌɔɪd/ *n.* [C] BIOLOGY the area of a cell in BACTERIA that contains the DNA → see picture at BACTERIUM

nu·cle·o·lus /nuˈkliələs/ *n. plural* **nucleoli** /-laɪ/ [C] BIOLOGY a small round body of PROTEIN and RNA (=an important chemical that exists in all living things) contained in the NUCLEUS of most cells. It is involved in making proteins.

nu·cle·on /ˈnukliɑn/ *n.* [C] PHYSICS a PROTON or a NEUTRON

nu·cle·o·tide /ˈnukliəˌtaɪd/ *n.* [C] CHEMISTRY one of the small MOLECULES that NUCLEIC acids such as RNA and DNA are built from. A nucleotide consists of a NITROGEN base, a sugar, and a PHOSPHATE.

nu·cle·us /ˈnukliəs/ *n. plural* **nuclei** /-kliaɪ/ [C] **1** PHYSICS the central part of an atom, consisting of NEUTRONS, PROTONS, and other ELEMENTARY PARTICLES **2** BIOLOGY the central part of almost all living cells, that contains the DNA **3** [usually singular] a small important group at the center of a larger group or organization: +**of** *The team has a solid nucleus of young talent.*

nude[1] /nud/ *adj.* **1** not wearing any clothes SYN **naked** ►see THESAURUS box at **naked** **2** done by or involving people who are not wearing any clothes: *a nude scene in the movie* | *nude photos*

nude[2] *n.* **1** [C] ENG. LANG. ARTS a painting, STATUE etc. of someone not wearing clothes **2 in the nude** not wearing any clothes SYN **in the buff**: *He likes to swim in the nude.*

nudge /nʌdʒ/ *v.* **1** [T] to push someone gently, usually with your elbow, in order to get their attention: *Tom nudged her when her name was called.* ►see THESAURUS box at **push**[1] **2** [T always + adv./prep.] to move something or someone a short distance by gently pushing: *He nudged the boat into the boathouse.* **3** [I always + adv./prep., T] to move forward slowly by pushing gently: *An old woman **nudged her way** through the crowd.* **4** [T always + adv./prep.] to gently persuade or encourage someone to make a particular decision or do a particular thing: **nudge sb into/toward sth** *When should you nudge a child toward something more challenging?* **5** [T usually in progressive] to almost reach a particular level or amount: *Temperatures were nudging into the '80s.* —**nudge** *n.* [C]

nud·ie /ˈnudi/ *adj.* [only before noun] INFORMAL involving people without any clothes on: *nudie magazines*

nu·dist /ˈnudɪst/ *n.* [C] someone who enjoys not wearing any clothes because they believe it is natural and healthy —**nudist** *adj.*: *a nudist camp* —**nudism** *n.* [U]

nu·di·ty /ˈnudət̮i/ *n.* [U] the state of not wearing any clothes SYN **nakedness**: *The movie is rated R for nudity and violence.*

ˈnuff /nʌf/ *adj.* NONSTANDARD, SLANG a way of writing ENOUGH that represents the way it can sound in informal spoken language

nug·get /ˈnʌgɪt/ *n.* [C] **1** EARTH SCIENCE a small rough piece of a valuable metal found in the earth: *gold nuggets* **2** a small round piece of food: *chicken nuggets* **3 nugget of information/wisdom etc.** a piece of interesting, good, or useful information, advice etc.: *What he's saying contains a nugget of truth.*

nui·sance /ˈnusəns/ *n.* **1** [C usually singular] a person, thing, or situation that annoys you or causes problems: *Rabbits can be a nuisance to gardeners.* | ***It's a nuisance** having to get up so early.* | *Billy **made such a nuisance of himself** at the party.* **2** [C,U] LAW the use of a place or property in a way that causes public annoyance: *The overgrown vacant lot was declared a **public nuisance**.* [**Origin:** 1400–1500 Anglo-French *nusaunce*, from Old French *nuisir* **to harm**]

nuke[1] /nuk/ *v.* [T] INFORMAL **1** to attack a place using NUCLEAR WEAPONS **2** to cook food in a MICROWAVE OVEN: *Nuke it for two minutes.*

nuke[2] *n.* [C] INFORMAL a NUCLEAR WEAPON

Nu·ku·ˈa·lo·fa /ˌnukuɑˈlɔfə/ the capital city of Tonga

null /nʌl/ *adj.* **1 null and void** LAW an agreement, contract etc. that is null and void has no legal effect SYN **invalid**: *The elections were **declared null and void**.* **2 null result/effect etc.** TECHNICAL a result etc. that is zero or nothing

nul·li·fy /ˈnʌləˌfaɪ/ *v.* **nullifies, nullified, nullifying** [T] **1** LAW to officially state that an agreement, contract etc. has no legal effect: *The judge nullified the sale of the property.* **2** FORMAL to make something lose its effect or value: *Inflation could nullify the economic growth of the last few years.* —**nullification** /ˌnʌləfəˈkeɪʃən/ *n.* [U]

nul·li·ty /ˈnʌlət̮i/ *n.* [U] LAW the fact that an agreement, contract etc. does not have any legal force anymore

ˌnull ˈset *n.* [C] TECHNICAL a mathematical set with no members, usually written { }

numb¹ /nʌm/ *adj.* **1** a part of your body that is numb is unable to feel anything, for example because you are very cold: *They gave me an injection to make my mouth **go numb**.* | **+with** *My fingers were **numb with cold**.* **2** unable to think, feel, or react in a normal way: *I **went numb**. I didn't know what to feel.* —**numbly** *adv.* —**numbness** *n.* [U]

numb² *v.* [T] **1** to make someone unable to feel pain or feel things they are touching: *The cold wind numbed my face and hands.* **2** to make someone unable to think, feel, or react in a normal way: *The prisoners were numbed by their years in jail.*

num·ber¹ /ˈnʌmbɚ/ S1 W1 *n.*
1 NUMBER [C] MATH a word or sign that represents an amount or a quantity: *Pick a number between one and ten.* | **an even number** (=2, 4, 6, 8, 10 etc.) | **an odd number** (=1, 3, 5, 7, 9, 11 etc.) | *In **round numbers*** (=numbers ending in 0, such as 10, 200 etc.)*, a grand piano costs close to $10,000.* → see also CARDINAL NUMBER, ORDINAL NUMBER, PRIME NUMBER, WHOLE NUMBER
2 TELEPHONE [C] a set of numbers used to call someone on the telephone: *Ann's **phone number** is 555-3234.* | *We tried Phil's number but there was no answer.* | **sb's home/office/work number** *That's my home number.* | *I'm sorry, I think I **have the wrong number**.*
3 IN A SET/LIST [C] a number used to show the position of something in an ordered set or list: *Take a look at question number three.* → see also NUMBER ONE¹ (2)
4 FOR RECOGNIZING SB/STH [C] a set of numbers used to name or recognize someone or something: *your Social Security number* | *your house number* → see also PIN, SERIAL NUMBER
5 AMOUNT [C,U] an amount of something that can be counted SYN **quantity**: **+of** *This year **the number of** houses for sale went up by 20%.* | *I've been to Greece **a number of*** (=several) *times.* | **vast/huge/large/increasing etc. numbers** *Rebels have amassed large numbers of weapons.* | *a **high number** of entries in the competition* | *Expansion will **bring the number** of major league teams **to*** (=make the number rise to) *30.* | *Hospital staff will be increased **in number** by 28%.* | *We've gotten **a good number of** new members.* | *There could be **any number of** reasons why she's late.*
6 MUSIC [C] ENG. LANG. ARTS a piece of popular music, a song, a dance etc. that forms part of a larger performance: *a new dance number* → see also PRODUCTION NUMBER ▸see THESAURUS box at **music**
7 the numbers [plural] **a)** information about something that is shown using numbers: *Get Charlie to look at the numbers.* **b)** an illegal game in which people risk money on the appearance of a combination of numbers in a newspaper: *playing the numbers*
8 numbers [plural] how many people there are, especially people attending an event or doing an activity together: *Student numbers have gone down.*
9 do a number on sb/sth INFORMAL to hurt or damage someone or something badly: *Danny did a real number on the car.*
10 have sb's number INFORMAL to understand something about someone that helps you deal with them: *I think Cara has his number.*
11 red/sexy etc. little number INFORMAL a red, sexy etc. dress or suit, especially a woman's: *She appeared in a hot little sequined number.*
12 sb's number comes up someone has the winning number in a competition
13 sb's number is up also **sb's number has come up** INFORMAL **a)** someone will stop being lucky or successful: *This could be the year a lot of politicians find their number is up.* **b)** HUMOROUS to die: *When my number is up, I want it to be quick.*
14 GROUP OF PEOPLE [U] FORMAL one, some etc. of a group of people: **one/some/20 etc. of sb's number** *The tribe says 400 of their number were killed.*
15 beyond/without number LITERARY if things are beyond number, there are so many of them that no one could count them all
16 GRAMMAR [U] ENG. LANG. ARTS the form of a word, depending on whether one thing or more than one thing is being talked about. "Cats" is plural in number, "cat" is singular.
[**Origin:** 1200–1300 Old French *nombre*, from Latin *numerus*]

number² *v.* **1** [T] to give a number to something that is part of an ordered set or list: *This function numbers all the pages in a document.* | *The streets in the Bronx are numbered.* | **number sth (from) 1 to 10/100 etc.** *Number the questions 1 to 25.* **2** [linking verb] if people or things number a particular amount, that is how many there are: *The elephant population then numbered 65,000.* **3 sb's/sth's days are numbered** used to say that someone or something cannot live or continue much longer: *His days at the firm are numbered.* **4 number among sth** FORMAL to be included as one of a particular group: *Numbered among the guests were models and movie stars.* **5** [T] LITERARY to count: *Who can number the stars?*

ˈnumber ˌcruncher, number-cruncher *n.* [C] INFORMAL **1** someone whose job involves working with numbers, such as an ACCOUNTANT **2** a computer program designed to work with numbers and calculate results

ˈnumber ˌcrunching, number-crunching *n.* [U] INFORMAL the process of working with numbers and calculating results —**number-crunching** *adj.* → see also **crunch the numbers** at CRUNCH² (3)

num·ber·less /ˈnʌmbɚlɪs/ *adj.* too many to be counted SYN **innumerable** SYN **countless**: *numberless fish*

ˌnumber ˈone¹ *n.* **1** [singular] the best, most important, or most successful person or thing in a group: *Diana's children were always number one in her life.* | *The company is number one in the market.* **2** [singular] the musical record that is the most popular at a particular time: *The song is number one on the charts.* **3 look out for number one** INFORMAL to make sure that you get all the advantages, things etc. you want, and not worry about other people **4** [U] SPOKEN, INFORMAL a word meaning URINE, used especially with children to avoid saying this directly → see also NUMBER TWO

number one² *adj.* **1** most important or successful in a particular situation: *Safety is our number one concern.* | *California is the number one travel destination in the U.S.* **2** first on a list of several things to be considered, done etc.: *Number one – always lock doors and windows.*

Num·bers /ˈnʌmbɚz/ a book in the Old Testament of the Christian Bible

ˌnumber ˈtwo *n.* [U] SPOKEN, INFORMAL a word meaning solid waste from your BOWELS, used especially with children to avoid saying this directly → see also NUMBER ONE

numb·skull /ˈnʌmskʌl/ *n.* [C] another spelling of NUMSKULL

nu·mer·al /ˈnumərəl/ *n.* [C] MATH a written sign, such as 1, 2, or 3, that represents a number —**numeral** *adj.*

nu·mer·ate /ˈnumərət/ *adj.* able to do calculations and understand simple mathematics —**numeracy** *n.* [U] → see also LITERATE

nu·mer·a·tion /ˌnuməˈreɪʃən/ *n.* [C,U] TECHNICAL a system of counting or the process of counting

nu·mer·a·tor /ˈnuməˌreɪtɚ/ *n.* [C] MATH the number above the line in a FRACTION, for example 5 is the numerator in ⅚ → see also DENOMINATOR

nu·mer·i·cal /nuˈmɛrɪkəl/ *adj.* expressed or considered in numbers: *numerical information* | *an army with numerical superiority* (=they had more people) —**numerically** /-kli/ *adv.*

nu·mer·ol·o·gy /ˌnuməˈrɑlədʒi/ *n.* [U] the study of numbers and the belief that they have influence on people and events

nu·mer·ous /ˈnumərəs/ W3 *adj.* FORMAL many: *The advantages of the plan are numerous.* | *I've worked with Ron on **numerous occasions**.*

N

nu·mi·nous /ˈnumɪnəs/ *adj.* LITERARY having a mysterious and holy quality, which makes you feel that God is present

nu·mis·mat·ics /ˌnumɪzˈmæṭɪks/ *n.* [U] TECHNICAL the activity of collecting and studying coins and MEDALS —**numismatic** *adj.* —**numismatist** /nuˈmɪzməṭɪst/ *n.* [C]

num·skull, numbskull /ˈnʌmskʌl/ *n.* [C] INFORMAL a very stupid person SYN **idiot** SYN **dope**

nun /nʌn/ *n.* [C] someone who is a member of group of Christian women who live together in a CONVENT SYN **sister** → see also MONK

nun·ci·o /ˈnʌnsioʊ, ˈnʊn-/ *n. plural* **nuncios** [C] a representative of the Pope in a foreign country

nun·ne·ry /ˈnʌnəri/ *n.* [C] LITERARY a CONVENT

nup·tial /ˈnʌpʃəl/ *adj.* FORMAL relating to marriage or the marriage ceremony: *nuptial vows* | *nuptial bliss*

nup·tials /ˈnʌpʃəlz/ *n.* [plural] FORMAL a wedding

Nu·rem·berg Tri·als, the /ˌnʊrəmbəg ˈtraɪəlz/ HISTORY a series of TRIALS in 1945–1946 in Nuremberg, Germany, at which Nazi leaders went to a court of law for war crimes

Nu·re·yev /nʊˈreɪyəf/, **Ru·dolf** /ˈrudɔlf/ (1938–1993) a Russian ballet dancer who is regarded as one of the greatest male dancers ever

nurse¹ /nəs/ S2 W3 *n.* [C] **1** someone who is trained to take care of people who are sick or injured, usually in a hospital: *A nurse began to change his dressing.* | *I told the* ***charge nurse*** (=the nurse who is responsible for the other nurses in part of a hospital) *about the problem.* | *Jo is a* ***registered nurse.*** **2** OLD-FASHIONED a woman employed to take care of a young child SYN **nanny** [**Origin:** 1200–1300 Old French *nurice*, from Latin *nutricius*] → see also WET NURSE

nurse² *v.*

1 SICK PEOPLE a) [T] to take care of someone who is sick or injured: *Martha nursed Ted herself.* | *Cindy* ***nursed*** *the two puppies* ***back to health.*** **b)** [I usually in progressive] to work as a nurse: *She spent several years nursing in a military hospital.*

2 YOUR ILLNESS/INJURY [T not in passive] to rest when you have an illness or injury so that it will get better: *Shaw has been nursing a sore ankle.*

3 FEED A BABY a) [I,T] BIOLOGY if a woman nurses a baby, she feeds it with milk from her breasts → see also BREAST-FEED **b)** [I] if a baby nurses, it sucks milk from its mother's breast

4 YOUR FEELINGS [T not in passive] to secretly have a feeling or idea in your mind for a long time, especially an angry feeling: **nurse a grudge/grievance/ambition etc.** *I stayed at home, nursing my indignation.*

5 DRINK [T] if you nurse a drink, especially an alcoholic one, you drink it very slowly

6 HOLD [T] to hold something carefully in your hands or arms close to your body: *a child nursing a kitten*

7 TAKE CARE OF STH [T] to take special care of something, especially during a difficult situation: **nurse sth through/along etc.** *He nursed the hotel through the Depression.*

[**Origin:** 1500–1600 *nursh* **to nourish** (14–16 centuries), from *nourish*]

nurse·maid /ˈnəsmeɪd/ *n.* [C] OLD-FASHIONED a woman employed to take care of young children

ˌnurse pracˈtitioner *n.* [C] a NURSE who has additional training so that she or he is able to do some of the work that is usually done by a doctor, for example to PRESCRIBE medicine

nurs·er·y /ˈnəsəri/ *n. plural* **nurseries** [C] **1** a place where plants and trees are grown and sold **2** a place where young children are taken care of during the day while their parents are at work, shopping etc. → see also DAY CARE CENTER **3** a room in a hospital where babies that have just been born or who have medical problems are taken care of **4** OLD-FASHIONED a baby's BEDROOM or a room where young children play

nurs·er·y·man /ˈnəsərimən/ *n. plural* **nurserymen** /-mən/ [C] someone who grows plants and trees in a nursery

ˈnursery rhyme *n.* [C] ENG. LANG. ARTS a short traditional song or poem for children

ˈnursery ˌschool *n.* [C] a school for children from three to five years old → see also KINDERGARTEN

nurs·ing /ˈnəsɪŋ/ *n.* [U] the job or skill of taking care of people who are sick, injured, or old: *the nursing program at the college*

ˈnursing home *n.* [C] a place where people who are old or sick can live and be taken care of → see also RETIREMENT HOME

ˌnursing ˈmother *n.* [C] a mother who is feeding her baby from her breast

nur·tur·ance /ˈnətʃərəns/ *n.* [U] FORMAL loving care and attention that you give to someone —**nurturant** *adj.*

nur·ture¹ /ˈnətʃə/ *v.* [T often passive] FORMAL **1** to help a plan, idea, feeling etc. to develop: *Reading aloud to children nurtures a love of books.* **2** to feed and take care of a child or a plant while it is growing

nurture² *n.* [U] FORMAL the education and care that you are given as a child, and the way it affects your later development and attitudes

nuts

nut /nʌt/ S2 *n.* [C]

1 FOOD BIOLOGY a dry brown fruit inside a hard shell, that grows on a tree: *a selection of nuts* | *a cashew nut*

2 TOOL a small piece of metal with a hole through the middle, which is screwed onto a BOLT to fasten things together: *Use a wrench to tighten the nuts.*

3 CRAZY PERSON INFORMAL someone who is crazy or behaves strangely: *Oh, don't be such a nut.*

4 a golf/opera etc. nut INFORMAL someone who is very interested in GOLF etc. SYN **fanatic**: *Tina is a real health nut.*

5 the nuts and bolts of sth INFORMAL the practical details of a subject or job: *the nuts and bolts of the banking system*

6 a hard/tough nut (to crack) INFORMAL a difficult problem or situation, or a difficult person to deal with: *The judge was known to be a tough nut to crack.*

[**Origin:** Old English *hnutu*] → see also NUTS¹

nut·case /ˈnʌtˀkeɪs/ *n.* [C] INFORMAL someone who behaves in a crazy way SYN **nut**

nut·crack·er /ˈnʌtˀˌkrækə/ *n.* [C] a tool for cracking the shells of nuts

nut·house /ˈnʌthaʊs/ *n.* [C] INFORMAL **1** an expression meaning a hospital for people who are mentally ill, that is usually considered offensive **2** a place that is loud, unpleasant, and not organized

nut·meg /ˈnʌtˀmɛg/ *n.* **1** [U] a brown powder used as a SPICE to give a particular taste to food **2** [C] the seed of a tropical tree from which this powder is made [**Origin:** 1200–1300 Old Provençal *noz muscada* **musky nut**]

nu·tri·ent /ˈnutriənt/ *n.* [C] BIOLOGY nutrients are substances that provide what is needed for all living ORGANISMS to live and grow: *Plants absorb nutrients from the soil.* [**Origin:** 1600–1700 Latin, present participle of *nutrire* **to feed, nourish**] —**nutrient** *adj.*

nu·tri·ment /ˈnutrəmənt/ *n.* [C,U] FORMAL a substance

that gives plants and animals what they need in order to live and grow

nu·tri·tion /nuˈtrɪʃən/ *n.* [U] the process of giving or getting the right type of food for good health and growth: **good/poor/adequate nutrition** *the foods essential for good nutrition* —**nutritional** *adj.* —**nutritionally** *adv.* → see also MALNUTRITION

nu·tri·tious /nuˈtrɪʃəs/ *adj.* food that is nutritious is full of the natural substances that your body needs to stay healthy or to grow well: *Nuts and fruit make nutritious snacks.*

nu·tri·tive /ˈnutrət̬ɪv/ *adj.* **1** [no comparative] BIOLOGY relating to nutrition **2** FORMAL nutritious

nuts[1] /nʌts/ *adj.* [not before noun] INFORMAL **1** crazy: *Are you nuts or something?* | *His uncle **went nuts*** (=became crazy) *in his twenties.* ►see THESAURUS box at crazy[1] **2 go nuts** SPOKEN **a)** to become very excited because something good has just happened: *The crowd went nuts after the third touchdown.* **b)** to become very angry about something: *Mom's going to go nuts if you don't clean this up.* **3 drive sb nuts** INFORMAL to annoy someone a lot: *The constant noise drives me nuts.* **4 be nuts about/over sth** OLD-FASHIONED to like someone or something very much: *The girls are nuts about him.*

nuts[2] *interjection* OLD-FASHIONED **1** used when you are angrily refusing to listen to someone or do something: *"**Nuts to that,**" he said, and left.* **2** used to emphasize that something bad or annoying has happened: *Nuts! Now we'll be late.*

nut·shell /ˈnʌtˀʃɛl/ *n.* [C] **1 in a nutshell** INFORMAL used when you are stating the main facts about something in a short, clear way: *To **put it in a nutshell,** he's too old for you.* **2** BIOLOGY the hard outer part of a nut

nut·ty /ˈnʌt̬i/ *adj.* *comparative* **nuttier**, *superlative* **nuttiest** **1** tasting like or containing nuts: *The rice has a nutty taste.* **2** INFORMAL crazy: *a nutty idea* —**nuttiness** *n.* [C]

Nuuk /nuk/ the capital city of Greenland

nuz·zle /ˈnʌzəl/ *v.* [I always + adv./prep., T] to gently rub or press your nose or head against someone to show you like them: *The kitten nuzzled her chin.*

NV the written abbreviation of NEVADA

N.W. also **NW** the written abbreviation of NORTHWEST

NY the written abbreviation of NEW YORK

ny·lon /ˈnaɪlɑn/ *n.* **1** [U] a strong artificial material that is used for making plastic, clothes, rope etc.: *a nylon backpack* | *nylon thread* **2 nylons** [plural] a piece of women's clothing made of very thin nylon material, that fits tightly over the feet and legs and goes up to the waist SYN pantyhose **[Origin:** 1900–2000 invented word]

nymph /nɪmf/ *n.* [C] **1** one of the spirits of nature who, according to ancient Greek and Roman stories, appeared as young girls living in trees, mountains, streams etc. **2** POETIC a girl or young woman **3** BIOLOGY the LARVA (=young adult) of some insects, that looks like the adult but without full wings, and that develops directly into the adult without passing through any other stages

nym·phet /nɪmˈfɛt/ *n.* [C] a young girl who is very sexually attractive

nym·pho·ma·ni·ac /ˌnɪmfəˈmeɪniˌæk/ also **nym·pho** /ˈnɪmfoʊ/ INFORMAL *n.* [C] a woman who wants to have sex often, usually with a lot of different men —**nymphomaniac** *adj.* —**nymphomania** /ˌnɪmfəˈmeɪniə/ *n.* [U]

NYSE *n.* [singular] the abbreviation of NEW YORK STOCK EXCHANGE

N.Z. also **NZ** the written abbreviation of NEW ZEALAND

N

O,o

O

O¹ /oʊ/ *n. plural* **O's** **1** also **o** *plural* **o's** [C] **a)** the 15th letter of the English alphabet **b)** a sound represented by this letter **2** [U] MATH a zero **3** [U] a common type of blood

O² *interjection* **1** POETIC used to show respect when speaking to someone or something, for example when praying: *O Lord, hear our prayer.* **2** another form of OH

o' /ə/ *prep.* NONSTANDARD a way of writing "of" as it is sometimes said in informal speech: *a cup o' coffee*

oaf /oʊf/ *n.* [C] a stupid awkward man or boy —**oafish** *adj.*

O·a·hu /oʊ'ɑhu/ an island in the Pacific Ocean that is part of the U.S. state of Hawaii and contains its capital city, Honolulu

oak /oʊk/ S3 *n.* [C,U] a large tree that is common in northern countries, or the hard wood of this tree: *The room had oak floors.* [**Origin:** Old English *ac*] → see also POISON OAK

oak·en /'oʊkən/ *adj.* ESPECIALLY LITERARY made of oak: *an oaken table*

Oak·ley /'oʊkli/, **An·nie** /'æni/ (1860–1926) a U.S. woman who was very skilled at shooting, and who performed in BUFFALO BILL's Wild West show

oa·kum /'oʊkəm/ *n.* [U] small pieces of old rope used for filling up small holes in the sides of wooden ships

oar /ɔr/ *n.* [C] a long pole with a wide flat blade at one end, used for rowing a boat [**Origin:** Old English *ar*] → see also PADDLE

oar·lock /'ɔrlɑk/ *n.* [C] one of the U-shaped pieces of metal on a ROWBOAT that holds the oars

oars·man /'ɔrzmən/ *n. plural* **oarsmen** /-mən/ [C] someone who rows a boat, especially in races

oars·wom·an /'ɔrz,wʊmən/ *n. plural* **oarswomen** /-,wɪmɪn/ [C] a woman who rows a boat, especially in races

OAS, the **the Organization of American States** an organization whose members include the U.S. and Canada and most of the countries of Central and South America. Its aims are to preserve peace and to help the economic development of the area.

o·a·sis /oʊ'eɪsɪs/ *n. plural* **oases** /-siz/ [C] **1** EARTH SCIENCE a place with water and trees in a desert **2** a peaceful or pleasant place that is very different from everything around it SYN **haven**: *The restaurant is a little oasis in the middle of Los Angeles.*

oath /oʊθ/ *n. plural* **oaths** /oʊðz, oʊθs/ **1** [C] a formal and very serious promise, especially a promise to be loyal to someone SYN **pledge**: **swear/take an oath** *He* ***swore an oath to*** *defend the Constitution.* | *The new President took the* ***oath of office*** (=promised to do his job well because of loyalty to the country). | **oath of loyalty/allegiance/fidelity etc.** *They raised their right hands to take the oath of allegiance.* **2** [singular] LAW a formal promise to tell the truth in a court: *The evidence was given* ***under oath.*** | *Witnesses must* ***take the oath*** (=make this promise). **3** [C] an offensive word or phrase that expresses anger, surprise, shock etc. SYN **swear word**: *He shouted oaths and curses as they took him away.* [**Origin:** Old English *ath*]

,oath of 'office *n. plural* **oaths of office** [C usually singular] POLITICS a formal promise made by each U.S. President to perform all the duties of the President's office and to preserve, protect, and defend the American CONSTITUTION: *Abraham Lincoln* ***took*** *his second* ***oath of office*** *while the Civil War was coming to an end.* | *President Bush stepped forward to recite the oath of office.*

oat·meal /'oʊtˀmil/ *n.* [U] crushed oats that are boiled and eaten for breakfast, or used in cooking

oats /oʊts/ *n.* [plural] **1** a grain that is eaten by people and animals **2** oatmeal → see also **sow your wild oats** at sow¹ (3)

O·ba·di·ah /,oʊbə'daɪə/ a book in the Old Testament of the Christian Bible

ob·du·rate /'ɑbdərət/ *adj.* FORMAL very determined not to change your beliefs or feelings, in a way that seems unreasonable SYN **stubborn**: *She remained obdurate despite their pleas.* —**obduracy** *n.* [U]

o·be·di·ence /ə'bidiəns, oʊ-/ *n.* [U] the act of doing what you are told to do, or what a law, rule etc. says you must do OPP **disobedience**: +**to** *a life lived* ***in obedience*** *to God* | **blind/absolute/unquestioning obedience** *I followed his commands with blind obedience.*

o·be·di·ent /ə'bidiənt, oʊ-/ *adj.* **1** always doing what you are told to do, or what the law, a rule etc. says you must do OPP **disobedient**: *an obedient dog* | +**to** *a belief that wives should be obedient to their husbands* **2 your obedient servant** OLD USE used to end a very formal letter —**obediently** *adv.*

o·bei·sance /oʊ'beɪsəns/ *n.* [C,U] FORMAL an act of showing respect and obedience, often shown by bending your head or the upper part of your body: *Worshippers* ***paid obeisance*** *to the gods.*

ob·e·lisk /'ɑbəlɪsk/ *n.* [C] **1** a tall pointed stone PILLAR, built to remind people of an event or of someone who has died **2** a DAGGER sign used in printing

o·bese /oʊ'bis/ *adj.* very fat in a way that is unhealthy: *At least 25% of Americans are considered obese.* [**Origin:** 1600–1700 Latin *obesus*, past participle of *obedere* **to eat up**] ►see THESAURUS box at **fat**¹

o·be·si·ty /oʊ'bisət̬i/ *n.* [U] MEDICINE the condition of being very fat in a way that is dangerous to your health

obey

o·bey /ə'beɪ, oʊ-/ *v.* [I,T] to do what someone in a position of authority tells you to do, or to do what a law or rule says you must do OPP **disobey**: *"Come here." She obeyed.* | *Teach the dog to obey you promptly.* | **obey the law/rules** *Many people refused to obey the new law.* | **obey an order/command** *A soldier must obey orders.* [**Origin:** 1200–1300 Old French *obeir*, from Latin *oboedire*, from *audire* **to hear**]

THESAURUS

do what sb says: *If you do what I say you'll be perfectly safe.*
do what you are told/do as you are told: *Why won't you just do as you're told – then we wouldn't have all this trouble.*
follow sb's orders/instructions: *Follow the manufacturer's instructions.* | *You must follow your doctor's orders.*

ob·fus·cate /'ɑbfə,skeɪt/ *v.* [T] FORMAL to deliberately make something unclear or difficult to understand:

Politicians have once again obfuscated the issue. —**obfuscation** /ˌɑbfəˈskeɪʃən/ *n.* [U]

ob/gyn, ob-gyn /ˌoʊ bi ˌdʒi waɪ ˈɛn/ *n.* **1** [U] the part of medical science that deals with OBSTETRICS and GYNECOLOGY **2** [C] a doctor who works in this part of medical science

o•bit /ˈoʊbɪt/ *n.* [C] INFORMAL an obituary

o•bit•u•ar•y /əˈbɪtʃuˌɛri, oʊ-/ *n. plural* **obituaries** [C] a report in a newspaper about the life of someone who has just died [**Origin:** 1700–1800 Medieval Latin *obituarium*, from Latin *obitus* **death**]

ob•ject¹ /ˈɑbdʒɪkt, ˈɑbdʒɛkt/ S2 W2 *n.* [C]
1 THING a thing that you can hold, touch, or see, which is usually small, and is not alive: *a small metal object* | *The baby is then able to follow a moving object with its eyes.* ►see THESAURUS box at **thing**
2 PURPOSE [usually singular] the purpose of a plan, action, or activity SYN **goal** SYN **aim**: +**of** *The object of the game is to improve children's math skills.* | *The customer will benefit, and that is* ***the object of the exercise*** (=the purpose of what you are doing).
3 an object of pity/desire/contempt etc. someone or something that is pitied, desired etc.: *He became an object of hatred and ridicule.* → see also SEX OBJECT
4 money/expense/cost is no object used to say that it does not matter to you if something cost a lot of money: *If money is no object, you could choose a luxury cruise.*
5 GRAMMAR ENG. LANG. ARTS a noun, noun phrase, or pronoun representing **a)** the person or thing that is directly affected by the action of a verb in a sentence. In the sentence "Sheila closed the door," "door" is a DIRECT OBJECT. **b)** the person or thing that is affected by an action in an indirect way. In the sentence "She gave Tom the book," "Tom" is an INDIRECT OBJECT. **c)** the person or thing that is joined by a preposition to another word or phrase. In the sentence "He sat on the bench," "bench" is the object of the preposition. → see also SUBJECT
6 an object lesson an event or story that shows you the best or worst way of doing something: *The disappearance of the buffalo was* ***an object lesson in*** *the need for animal protection.*
7 COMPUTER [C] COMPUTERS a combination of written information on a computer and instructions that act on the information, for example in the form of a document or a picture: *multimedia data objects*
[**Origin:** 1300–1400 Medieval Latin *objectum*, from Latin *obicere*]

ob•ject² /əbˈdʒɛkt/ W3 *v.* **1** [I,T] to complain or protest about something, or to feel or say that you oppose it or disapprove of it: *If no one objects, I would like my wife to be present.* | *"My name's not Sonny," the child objected.* | +**to** *He objected to the terms of the contract.* | **object to (sb) doing sth** *Be aware that some people may object to being photographed.* | +**that** *A delegate rose to object that the vote was meaningless.* ►see THESAURUS box at **complain** **2 I object** SPOKEN, FORMAL used in very formal meetings, discussions etc. to say that you disagree with what someone has said: *Mr. Chairman, I object. That is an unfair allegation.* —**objector** *n.* [C] → see also CONSCIENTIOUS OBJECTOR

ˈobject ˌcode *n.* [U] MACHINE CODE

ob•jec•tion /əbˈdʒɛkʃən/ *n.* [C] **1** a reason that you have for opposing or disapproving of something, or the feeling of opposing or disapproving of it: +**to** *Her biggest objection to pets is that they're dirty.* | *The group has* ***strong objections*** *to the death penalty.* | **raise/voice an objection** (=state an objection) *Lawyers have raised several objections to the plan.* | *Beckler* ***had no objection*** *to the plan* (=was not annoyed or upset by it). ►see THESAURUS box at **opposition** **2 objection!** SPOKEN said by lawyers to a judge in a court when they think that what another lawyer has just said should not be allowed

ob•jec•tion•a•ble /əbˈdʒɛkʃənəbəl/ *adj.* likely to offend people SYN **offensive**: *rock songs with objectionable words*

ob•jec•tive¹ /əbˈdʒɛktɪv/ Ac S3 W3 *n.* [C] **1** something that you are working hard to achieve: SYN **goal**: +**of** *What is the objective of the policy?* | **main/primary/principal objective** *The program* ***has*** *two main* ***objectives.*** | **achieve/accomplish/meet an objective** *Several of the projects failed to achieve their objectives.* ►see THESAURUS box at **purpose¹** **2** a place that you are trying to reach, especially in a military attack: *The 4th Division's objective was a town 20 miles to the east.*

objective² Ac *adj.* **1** based on facts, or making a decision based on facts rather than on personal feelings OPP **subjective**: *It's hard to give an objective opinion about your own children.* | *Scientists need to be objective when doing research.* **2** FORMAL existing outside the mind as something real, rather than as just an idea SYN **real**: *The world has an objective reality.* **3** TECHNICAL relating to an OBJECT of a sentence: *the objective case* —**objectivity** /ˌɑbdʒɛkˈtɪvət̬i/ *n.* [U]

obˌjective ˈfunction *n.* [C] MATH the highest and lowest value that you want to find when you use LINEAR PROGRAMMING

ob•jec•tive•ly /əbˈdʒɛktɪvli/ Ac *adv.* if you consider something objectively, you try to think about the facts, without being influenced by your own feelings or opinions: *Try to look at your situation objectively.*

ob•jet d'art /ˌɑbʒeɪ ˈdɑr, ˌɔb-/ *n. plural* **objets d'art** /ˌɑbʒeɪ ˈdɑr, ˌɔb-/ [C] a small object, used for decoration, that has some value as art

ob•li•gate /ˈɑbləˌgeɪt/ *v.* [T usually passive] **1** to make someone have to do something because it is the law, their duty, or the right thing to do SYN **oblige**: **be obligated to do sth** *Tenants are obligated to pay their rent on time.* **2 be/feel obligated** to feel that you have to do something because someone has done something for you: **be/feel obligated to do sth** *I felt obligated to help.* | **feel obligated to sb** *She felt obligated to Mr. Walters for the loan.*

ob•li•ga•tion /ˌɑbləˈgeɪʃən/ *n.* [C,U] a moral or legal duty to do something: **an obligation to do sth** *I* ***feel an obligation*** *to tell the truth.* | +**to** *We* ***have an obligation*** *to our customers.* | *The firm said it would continue to* ***meet*** *any legal* ***obligations*** (=do what it should do) *to the men.* | *You* ***are under no obligation to*** (=do not have to) *answer these questions.* | *I felt a* ***sense of obligation*** (=feeling that I should do something for someone, especially because they have done something for me) *to my teachers.*

o•blig•a•to•ry /əˈblɪgəˌtɔri/ *adj.* **1** FORMAL something that is obligatory must be done because of a law, a rule etc. SYN **mandatory** SYN **compulsory**: *Voting is obligatory for Brazilians aged 18 to 69.* **2 the obligatory hat/jokes/photo etc.** HUMOROUS used to describe something that is always done, worn, or included in a particular type of situation: *Who could enjoy a barbecue without the obligatory bottle of beer?*

o•blige /əˈblaɪdʒ/ *v.* FORMAL **1** [T usually passive] if you are obliged to do something, you have to do it because the situation, the law, a duty etc. makes it necessary SYN **obligate**: **oblige sb to do sth** *The law obliges drivers to wear seat belts.* | *The boat had sailed, so I was obliged to spend another week in the town.* | *The job demanded a lot of overtime, and she* ***felt obliged*** *to do it.* **2** [I,T] to do something that someone has asked you to do: *They wanted to talk about the contract, and I obliged them.* | *If you need a ride home, I'd* ***be happy to oblige.*** **3 I/we would be obliged if** used in formal letters to ask someone to do something for you: *I would be obliged if you could send me a copy.* **4 (I'm/we're) much obliged** SPOKEN, OLD-FASHIONED used to thank someone very politely [**Origin:** 1200–1300 Old French *obliger*, from Latin *obligare*, from *ligare* **to tie**]

o•blig•ing /əˈblaɪdʒɪŋ/ *adj.* willing and eager to help: *an obliging sales clerk* —**obligingly** *adv.*

o•blique /əˈblik, oʊ-/ *adj.* **1** not expressed in a direct way SYN **indirect**: *She made an* ***oblique reference*** *to his drinking problem.* **2** not looking, pointing etc. directly at someone or something: *She gave him an oblique look.* **3** not straight or direct: *a crater caused by the oblique impact of a meteor* **4** sloping: *an oblique line* —**obliquely** *adv.* —**oblique** *n.* [C]

ob'lique ˌangle *n.* [C] MATH an angle that is not 90°, 180°, or 270°

ob·lit·er·ate /əˈblɪt̬əˌreɪt/ *v.* [T] **1** to destroy something so completely that almost nothing remains: *Large areas of the city were obliterated during World War II.* **2** to cover something completely so that it cannot be seen: *The fog came down, obliterating everything.* **3** to remove a thought, feeling, or memory from someone's mind: *Nothing could obliterate the memory of those tragic events.* [**Origin:** 1500–1600 Latin, past participle of *obliterare*, from *litera* **letter**] —**obliteration** /əˌblɪt̬əˈreɪʃən/ *n.* [U]

O

ob·liv·i·on /əˈblɪviən/ *n.* [U] **1** the state of being completely forgotten: **slip/fade/drift into oblivion** *a singer who does not deserve to slip into oblivion* **2** the state of being unconscious or of not noticing what is happening: *He drank himself* ***into oblivion***. [**Origin:** 1300–1400 Old French, Latin *oblivio*, from *oblivisci* **to forget**]

ob·liv·i·ous /əˈblɪviəs/ *adj.* [not before noun] not knowing about or not noticing something that is happening around you SYN **unaware**: **+to/of** *He seemed oblivious to the danger he was in.* —**obliviousness** *n.* [U]

ob·long /ˈɑblɔŋ/ *adj.* an oblong shape is much longer than it is wide: *an oblong pan* [**Origin:** 1400–1500 Latin *oblongus*, from *ob-* **toward** + *longus* **long**] —**oblong** *n.* [C]

ob·lo·quy /ˈɑbləkwi/ *n. plural* **obloquies** [U] FORMAL **1** very strong offensive criticism **2** loss of respect and honor

ob·nox·ious /əbˈnɑkʃəs/ *adj.* **1** very offensive or not nice: *a loud, obnoxious man* **2** extremely bad: *obnoxious sewage smells* [**Origin:** 1500–1600 Latin *obnoxius*, from *noxa* **harm**] —**obnoxiously** *adv.* —**obnoxiousness** *n.* [U]

o·boe /ˈoʊboʊ/ *n.* [C] a wooden musical instrument, shaped like a narrow tube, which you play by blowing air through a REED [**Origin:** 1600–1700 Italian, French *hautbois*, from *haut* **high** + *bois* **wood**]

o·bo·ist /ˈoʊboʊɪst/ *n.* [C] someone who plays the oboe

ob·scene /əbˈsin, ɑb-/ *adj.* **1** relating to sex in a shocking and offensive way: *obscene photographs* | *The driver made an* ***obscene gesture***. | *She received several* ***obscene phone calls*** (=calls from an unknown person saying obscene things). **2** extremely immoral and unfair in a way that makes you angry: *a company earning obscene profits* **3** SPOKEN extremely ugly in a way that shocks you: *She was so fat it was almost obscene!* —**obscenely** *adv.*

ob·scen·i·ty /əbˈsɛnət̬i/ *n. plural* **obscenities** **1** [C usually plural] a sexually offensive word or action SYN **swear word**: *Protesters screamed obscenities.* **2** [U] sexually offensive language or behavior, especially in a book, play, movie etc.: *laws against obscenity*

ob·scur·ant·is·m /ɑbˈskyʊrənˌtɪzəm/ *n.* [U] FORMAL the practice of deliberately stopping ideas and facts from being known —**obscurantist** *adj.*

ob·scure[1] /əbˈskyʊr/ *adj.* **1** not well known at all, and usually not very important: *an obscure painter* | *The details of his life* ***remain obscure***. **2** difficult to understand: *an article full of obscure references*

obscure[2] *v.* [T] **1** to make something difficult to know or understand: *Recent successes* ***obscure the fact that*** *the company is still in trouble.* **2** to prevent something from being seen or heard clearly: *The view was obscured by fog.*

ob·scur·i·ty /əbˈskyʊrət̬i/ *n. plural* **obscurities** **1** [U] the state of not being known or remembered: *He died* ***in*** *relative* ***obscurity***. | **fade/slide/sink into obscurity** *After this hit song, the band faded into obscurity.* **2** [C,U] something that is difficult to understand, or the quality of being difficult to understand: *obscurities in the text* **3** [U] LITERARY darkness

ob·se·quies /ˈɑbsəkwiz/ *n.* [plural] FORMAL a funeral ceremony

ob·se·qui·ous /əbˈsikwiəs/ *adj.* too eager to please people and agree with them SYN **servile**: *the salesman's obsequious manner* —**obsequiously** *adv.*

ob·serv·a·ble /əbˈzɚvəbəl/ *adj.* able to be seen or noticed: *the observable universe* —**observably** *adv.*

ob·serv·ance /əbˈzɚvəns/ *n.* **1** [C,U] a celebration of a religious or national event: *Most businesses are closed* ***in observance of*** *Christmas.* | *Veterans Day observances* **2** [U] the practice of obeying a law or a rule: **+of** *the observance of human rights*

ob·serv·ant /əbˈzɚvənt/ *adj.* **1** good or quick at noticing things: *Police are trained to be observant.* **2** obeying laws, religious rules etc.: *observant Muslims*

ob·ser·va·tion /ˌɑbzɚˈveɪʃən, -sɚ-/ *n.* **1** [C,U] the process of watching something or someone carefully for a period of time in order to obtain information about them: *a long-term observation of the solar system* | *The whale was* ***under observation*** (=being watched) *all night.* | *She will remain in the hospital* ***for observation***. **2** [C] a spoken or written remark about something you have noticed: **+on** *the book's observations on good and bad management styles* | *The Mayor* ***made*** *some humorous* ***observations*** *about local politics.* **3 powers of observation** your natural ability to notice what is happening around you **4** [U] the act of obeying a law, rule etc. SYN **observance** —**observational** *adj.*

ˌobser'vation ˌpost *n.* [C] a position from which an enemy can be watched

ˌobser'vation ˌtower *n.* [C] a tall structure built so that you can see a long way, used for example to watch prisoners, look for forest fires etc.

ob·serv·a·to·ry /əbˈzɚvəˌtɔri/ *n. plural* **observatories** [C] a special building from which scientists watch the moon, stars, weather etc.

ob·serve /əbˈzɚv/ S3 W2 *v.* [T] **1** to watch something or someone carefully in order to find out something about them: *He spent a lot of time with horses, observing their behavior.* | **observe what/how/where** *Researchers are eager to observe how the change takes place.* ►see THESAURUS box at **eye**[2] **2** [not in progressive] FORMAL to see and notice something: **observe sb doing sth** *Officers observed Cox driving on the wrong side of the road.* | **observe that** *Doctors observed that the disease mostly occurs in women over 50.* | **observe sth** *The car I had observed earlier was no longer there.* **3** to do what you are supposed to do according to a law, agreement etc.: *Rebels continue to observe the truce.* **4** FORMAL to take part in or celebrate a holiday, religious or national event etc.: *Muslims are currently observing the holy month of Ramadan.* **5** FORMAL to say what you have noticed about a situation: **observe that** *He once observed that "cooking without herbs is not really cooking at all."* **6 observe a moment/minute of silence** if a group of people observe a moment of silence, they are silent for a short period of time to show respect for someone, especially someone who has died [**Origin:** 1300–1400 Old French *observer*, from Latin *observare* **to guard, watch**]

ob·serv·er /əbˈzɚvɚ/ W3 *n.* [C] **1** someone who regularly watches or pays attention to things relating to a particular subject, especially as part of their job, so that they know a lot about it: *Political observers say Ball could still win the election.* | **+of** *an observer of nature* | ***Outside observers*** (=independent ones who are not directly involved in the situation) *agree that the changes are good ones.* ►see THESAURUS box at **watch**[1] **2** someone who is sent to a place to check what is happening and report any problems, changes, illegal actions etc. SYN **monitor**: *International observers criticized the use of military force in the region.* | *I was invited to attend the meeting as* ***an impartial observer*** (=someone who is not on either side). **3** someone who sees or notices something: *To* ***the casual observer*** (=someone who does not look carefully) *it doesn't look as if anything has changed.*

ob·sess /əbˈsɛs/ *v.* **1** [T usually passive] if something or someone obsesses you, you think about them all the time and you cannot think of anything else: **be**

obsessed with sb/sth *Why are you so obsessed with your hair?* | *Jody has been obsessed with this guy for months.* **2** INFORMAL **obsess about/over sth** to think about something or someone much more than is necessary or sensible: *Stop obsessing about your weight. You look fine.* [**Origin:** 1500–1600 Latin, past participle of *obsidere* **to besiege**]

ob·ses·sion /əbˈsɛʃən/ *n.* [C,U] an extreme unhealthy interest in something, or worry about something, which stops you from thinking about anything else: *Freeing the hostages became his obsession.* | **+with/about** *an obsession with sex* | *Gambling* ***became an obsession****, and he lost everything.* | *Soccer is* ***a national obsession*** *in most European countries.* —**obsessional** *adj.*

ob·ses·sive /əbˈsɛsɪv/ *adj.* **1** thinking or worrying too much about someone or something so that you do not think about other things enough, or showing this quality: *She has an obsessive need to control everything.* | **obsessive about (doing) sth** *I tend to be a little obsessive about cleaning.* **2** tending to develop obsessions about people or things: *an obsessive personality* —**obsessively** *adv.*

obˌsessive-comˈpulsive *adj.* TECHNICAL tending to think and worry too much, or repeat particular actions again and again as a result of strong anxiety, fear etc. —**obsessive-compulsive** *n.* [C]

ob·sid·i·an /əbˈsɪdiən/ *n.* [U] a type of dark rock which looks like glass

ob·so·les·cence /ˌɑbsəˈlɛsəns/ *n.* [U] **1** the state of becoming old-fashioned and not useful anymore, because something else that is newer and better has been invented **2 planned/built-in obsolescence** the practice of making a product in such a way that it will soon become unfashionable or impossible to use

ob·so·les·cent /ˌɑbsəˈlɛsənt/ *adj.* becoming obsolete: *an obsolescent skill*

ob·so·lete /ˌɑbsəˈlit◂ / *adj.* not useful anymore because something newer and better has been invented: *obsolete technology* | *New computer developments have* ***rendered*** *our system* ***obsolete****.* [**Origin:** 1500–1600 Latin, past participle of *obsolescere* **to grow old, become disused**]

ob·sta·cle /ˈɑbstɪkəl/ *n.* [C] **1** something that makes it difficult for you to succeed: *Lack of money was a major obstacle.* | **+to** *Fear of change is an obstacle to progress.* | ***an obstacle in the way of*** *economic recovery* | *She has had to* ***overcome*** *many* ***obstacles*** *in her career.* **2** an object which blocks your way, so that you must go around it: *an obstacle in the road* [**Origin:** 1300–1400 Old French, Latin *obstaculum*, from *obstare* **to stand in the way, stand in front of**]

ˈobstacle course *n.* [C] **1** a line of objects that runners have to jump over, go under, climb through etc. in a race or as part of military training **2** a series of difficulties which must be dealt with to achieve a particular aim

ob·ste·tri·cian /ˌɑbstəˈtrɪʃən/ *n.* [C] MEDICINE a doctor who has special training in obstetrics

ob·stet·rics /əbˈstɛtrɪks, ɑb-/ *n.* [U] MEDICINE the part of medical science that deals with the birth of children —**obstetric** *adj.*

ob·sti·nate /ˈɑbstənɪt/ *adj.* DISAPPROVING determined not to change your opinions, ideas, behavior etc., or showing this quality SYN **stubborn**: *You're being obstinate again.* | *an obstinate refusal to face facts* —**obstinately** *adv.* —**obstinacy** *n.* [U]

ob·strep·er·ous /əbˈstrɛpərəs/ *adj.* noisy and refusing to agree or to do what someone else tells you to do, or showing this quality: *an obstreperous patient*

ob·struct /əbˈstrʌkt/ *v.* [T] **1** to block a road, passage etc. SYN **block**: *The truck was on its side, obstructing two lanes of traffic.* | *A crowd of people in front of me were* ***obstructing my view****.* **2** to deliberately make it difficult or impossible for someone to do something, or for something to happen: *Terrorists are trying to obstruct the peace process.* [**Origin:** 1600–1700 Latin, past participle of *obstruere* **to build in the way**]

obstruction

ob·struc·tion /əbˈstrʌkʃən/ *n.* **1** [C,U] something that blocks a road, passage, tube etc., or the act of doing this: *an obstruction in the artery leading to his brain* | *unlawful obstruction of the highway* **2** [U] the act of trying to prevent or delay something from happening, especially a legal or political process: **+of** *Kane could be charged with* ***obstruction of justice*** (=the crime of doing this) *for refusing to cooperate with authorities.* **3** [U] an offense in SOCCER, HOCKEY etc. in which a player gets between an opponent and the ball

ob·struc·tion·ism /əbˈstrʌkʃəˌnɪzəm/ *n.* [U] the practice of trying to prevent or delay a legal or political process —**obstructionist** *n.* [C]

ob·struc·tive /əbˈstrʌktɪv/ *adj.* **1** trying to prevent someone from doing something by deliberately making it difficult for them: *obstructive tactics* **2** blocking a tube, passage etc.

ob·tain /əbˈteɪn/ Ac W2 *v.* FORMAL **1** [T] to get something that you want, especially through your own effort, skill, or work: *Weisner is hoping to obtain funding for a follow-up study.* | **obtain sth from sb/sth** *Pepper is obtained from the dried berries of the pepper plant.* | *You will need to* ***obtain permission*** *from your parents.* ►see THESAURUS box at **get** **2** [I not in progressive] if a situation, system, or rule obtains, it continues to exist SYN **apply**: *These conditions no longer obtain.* [**Origin:** 1400–1500 Old French *obtenir*, from Latin *obtinere* **to hold on to, own, obtain**]

ob·tain·a·ble /əbˈteɪnəbəl/ Ac *adj.* able to be obtained: *Radon gas can be detected using an easily obtainable device.*

ob·trude /əbˈtrud/ *v.* [I,T] FORMAL if something obtrudes, or if you obtrude something, it becomes noticed where it is not wanted: **obtrude into/upon/on sth** *The author's personal taste is likely to obtrude into a book about wine.*

ob·tru·sive /əbˈtrusɪv/ *adj.* noticeable in a way that is not nice: *ugly and obtrusive roadside signs* | *Our waitress was friendly, but never obtrusive.*

ob·tuse /əbˈtus, ɑb-/ *adj.* slow or unwilling to understand things, in a way that is annoying: *Maybe I'm being obtuse, but I don't understand what you're so upset about.* | **deliberately/willfully obtuse** *She was being sulky and deliberately obtuse.*

obˌtuse ˈangle *n.* [C] MATH an angle between 90 and 180 degrees → see picture at ANGLE[1]

obˌtuse ˈtriangle *n.* [C] MATH a TRIANGLE with one angle that is between 90 and 180 degrees

ob·verse /ˈɑbvɚs/ *n.* FORMAL **1 the obverse (of sth)** the opposite of something else SYN **opposite**: *She was the obverse of the devoted wife and mother.* **2 the obverse** TECHNICAL the side of a coin with the head or more important design on it OPP **reverse** [**Origin:** 1600–1700 Latin *obversus*, from *obvertere* **to turn toward**] —**obverse** *adj.*

ob·vi·ate /ˈɑbviˌeɪt/ *v.* [T] FORMAL to remove a difficulty: *New technologies have* ***obviated the need for*** *surgery.*

O

ob·vi·ous /ˈɑbviəs/ Ac S2 W2 *adj.* **1** clear and easy to notice or understand: *an obvious mistake* | *The quality of his work is* ***immediately obvious.*** | **it is obvious (to sb) that** *It's obvious to everyone that he's unhappy.* | **glaringly/painfully/perfectly obvious** (=extremely obvious) | *She was* ***making it*** *painfully* ***obvious that*** (=behaving in a way that shows clearly that) *she liked him.* | *It is not easy,* ***for obvious reasons,*** *to study volcanic eruptions.* | *At the risk of* ***stating the obvious*** (=saying something that is already very clear), *I'd like to say that managers must manage better.* ►see THESAURUS box at **clear¹**, **noticeable** **2** natural, reasonable, or expected in a particular situation: *There was no obvious reason for their behavior.* | *She is* ***the obvious choice*** (=the person who everyone would choose) *for team captain.* | ***The obvious question*** *is, does his invention work?* | ***The obvious thing to do*** *would be to call the police.* **3 be obvious about sth** to behave in a way that clearly shows that you want something to happen very much: *I want to go, but I don't want to be too obvious about it.* **4** not original and lacking imagination: *The movie's story was boring and obvious.* [**Origin:** 1500–1600 Latin *obvius*, from *obviam* **in the way**]

ob·vi·ous·ly /ˈɑbviəsli/ Ac S1 W2 *adv.* used to mean that a fact can easily be noticed or understood: *He obviously likes you.* | *Obviously, I don't want to upset anyone.* | *The barber was obviously drunk.* → see also APPARENTLY, EVIDENTLY ►see THESAURUS box at **certainly**

oc·a·ri·na /ˌɑkəˈrinə/ *n.* [C] a small musical instrument shaped like an egg, that you blow through to play

O'Ca·sey /oʊˈkeɪsi/, **Sean** /ʃɔn/ (1884–1964) an Irish writer of plays

oc·ca·sion¹ /əˈkeɪʒən/ S3 W3 *n.* **1** [C] a time when something happens: *I've met with him* ***on*** *several* ***occasions.*** | **on this/that occasion** *On this occasion, she was right.* **2** [C] an important celebration, event, or ceremony: *I went out and bought a new dress just for the occasion.* | *We're saving the champagne for* ***a special occasion.*** | *Hundreds of people gathered at the stadium to* ***mark the occasion*** (=celebrate it). | *a poem written* ***on the occasion of*** *the Emperor's marriage* **3** [singular, U] a good or appropriate time, reason or opportunity to do something: **+for** *The summit is an occasion for different countries to exchange views.* | *I've never* ***had occasion to*** *dial 911.* **4 on occasion** sometimes but not often: *On occasion, prisoners were allowed visits.* **5 if/when the occasion arises** if or when a particular action ever becomes necessary: *He could also be a tough negotiator when the occasion arose.* [**Origin:** 1300–1400 French, Latin *occasio*, from *occidere* **to fall down**] → see also **rise to the occasion/challenge** at RISE TO (1), **a sense of occasion** at SENSE¹ (18)

occasion² *v.* [T] FORMAL to cause something: *His mismanagement of the company occasioned the loss of thousands of jobs.*

oc·ca·sion·al /əˈkeɪʒənl/ W3 *adj.* **1** happening sometimes but not often: *She still has occasional headaches.* | **the/an occasional sth** *I drink the occasional glass of wine, but not much else.* **2** doing something sometimes but not often: *an occasional smoker* **3** FORMAL written or intended for a special occasion: *occasional poems*

oc·ca·sion·al·ly /əˈkeɪʒənl-i/ S3 W3 *adv.* sometimes, but not regularly and not often: *He still occasionally goes out with Sam.* | *We only see each other* ***very occasionally*** (=rarely).

oc'casional ˌtable *n.* [C] a small light table that can be easily moved

Oc·ci·dent /ˈɑksədənt, -dɛnt/ *n.* **the Occident** LITERARY the western part of the world, especially Europe and the Americas → see also ORIENT

oc·ci·den·tal /ˌɑksəˈdɛntl◂/ *n.* [C] FORMAL someone from the western part of the world → see also ORIENTAL —**occidental** *adj.*

oc·clude /əˈklud/ *v.* [T] FORMAL to block or cover something: *occluded arteries* —**occlusion** /əˈkluʒən/ *n.* [C,U]

oc·cult¹ /əˈkʌlt/ *n.* **the occult** mysterious practices and powers involving magic and spirits —**occultist** *n.* [C]

occult² *adj.* mysterious and relating to magic and spirits: *occult beliefs*

oc·cu·pan·cy /ˈɑkyəpənsi/ Ac *n.* [U] FORMAL **1** someone's use of a building, piece of land, or other space, for living or working in, or the period during which they live or work there: *The new apartments are ready for occupancy.* | *The firm will* ***take occupancy of*** *the building October 1.* **2** the number of people allowed to stay, work, live etc. in a room or building at the same time: *The maximum occupancy of this elevator is 20 persons.* | **single/double/multiple occupancy** (=for one/two/many people)

oc·cu·pant /ˈɑkyəpənt/ Ac *n.* [C] FORMAL **1** someone who lives in a house, room etc.: *The letter was addressed to "Current Occupant."* **2** someone who is in a room, vehicle etc. at a particular time: *Neither of the car's two occupants was injured.*

oc·cu·pa·tion /ˌɑkyəˈpeɪʃən/ Ac S3 *n.* **1** [C] a job or profession: *The occupation of the third suspect is not known.* ►see THESAURUS box at **job** **2** [U] the act of entering a place in a large group and taking control of it, especially by military force: *occupation forces* | **+of** *the German occupation of France* | *The region has been* ***under*** *military* ***occupation*** *for over a year.* **3** [C] FORMAL a way of spending your time SYN **pastime**: *One of my childhood occupations was collecting baseball cards.* **4** [U] the act of living or staying in a building or place: *There was little evidence of human occupation in the area.*

oc·cu·pa·tion·al /ˌɑkyəˈpeɪʃənl/ Ac *adj.* [only before noun] **1** relating to your job: *occupational training* **2 an occupational hazard** a risk that always exists in a particular job: *Colds are an occupational hazard for doctors who deal with children.*

ˌoccupational ˈtherapy *n.* [U] a form of treatment that helps people with physical or emotional problems do different activities —**occupational therapist** *n.* [U]

oc·cu·pied /ˈɑkyəˌpaɪd/ *adj.* **1** [not before noun] busy doing something: **keep sb occupied** *The kids had computer games to keep them occupied.* | *I took a book to keep myself occupied on the trip.* | **+with** *It was obvious that his mind was occupied with something else.* **2** if a room, seat, or bed is occupied, someone is in it or using it: *All the seats were occupied.* **3** [only before noun] an occupied place is controlled by an army from another country: *occupied France*

oc·cu·pi·er /ˈɑkyəˌpaɪɚ/ Ac *n.* [C] **1** someone who enters a place in a large group and takes control of it, especially by military force: *a military occupier and oppressor* **2** FORMAL the person who lives, works etc. in a particular building: *the previous occupier of the apartment*

oc·cu·py /ˈɑkyəˌpaɪ/ Ac W3 *v.* **occupies, occupied, occupying** [T]

1 STAY IN A PLACE ESPECIALLY WRITTEN to live in or use a room, building, bed etc. for a period of time: *The same family had occupied the house for 35 years.* | *The upstairs offices are occupied by a software company.*

2 BUSY if you occupy someone, or occupy their time, you make them busy, especially so that they will not get bored: *How am I going to occupy all these visitors and go to work too?* | *After my husband died, I learned to* ***occupy myself.***

3 FILL TIME if something occupies you or your time, you are busy doing it: *Fishing occupies most of my spare time.* | **occupy your time with (doing) sth** *Eisemann's time was occupied with ordering computer parts.*

4 SEIZE AND CONTROL to enter a place, city, country etc. in a large group and take control of it, especially by military force: *Students occupied Sofia University on Monday.* | *an occupying army*

5 FILL SPACE to fill a particular amount of space: *Family photos occupied almost the entire wall.*

6 occupy sb's mind/thoughts/attention if something occupies your mind, thoughts etc., you think about that

thing more than anything else: *While she waited, she tried to occupy her mind with thoughts of the vacation.*
7 occupy a place/position etc. (in sth) if someone or something occupies a particular place or position in people's minds, it is thought of in a particular way, especially a good way: *Mandela occupies a unique place in the history of South Africa.*
8 OFFICIAL POSITION to have an official position or job: *All of the men* **occupied** *key supervisory* **positions** *for the state lottery.*
[**Origin:** 1300–1400 French *occuper*, from Latin *occupare*]

oc·cu·py·ing /ˈɑkyəˌpaɪ-ɪŋ/ *adj.* [only before noun] an occupying army, force etc. has entered a country, area etc. using military force to take control of its government and people

oc·cur /əˈkɚ/ Ac S2 W1 *v.* **occurred, occurring** [I] FORMAL **1** to happen SYN **take place**: *The explosion occurred at 9:00 a.m.* | *Giraldes claims he was with his wife when the killings occurred.* ►see THESAURUS box at **happen** **2** [always + adv./prep.] to happen or exist in a particular place or situation: **+in/among etc.** *Whooping cough occurs mainly in young children.* [**Origin:** 1500–1600 Latin *occurrere*, from *currere* **to run**]

occur to sb *phr. v.* if an idea or thought occurs to you, it suddenly comes into your mind: **it occurs to sb to do sth** *I washed it in hot water – it never occurred to me to check the label.* | **it occurs to sb that** *It occurred to me that she might be lying.*

oc·cur·rence /əˈkɚəns, -ˈkʌr-/ Ac *n.* **1** [C] something that happens: **a common/frequent/regular occurrence** *Rashes are a common occurrence among children.* | **a rare/unusual occurrence** (=something that does not happen often) | **an everyday/a daily occurence** *Terrorist attacks have become almost an everyday occurrence.* ►see THESAURUS box at **event** **2** [U] the fact that something happens or exists: **+of** *You can reduce the occurrence of migraine headaches with aspirin.*

o·cean /ˈoʊʃən/ S3 W2 *n.* **1 the ocean** EARTH SCIENCE the great mass of salt water that covers most of the Earth's surface: *She stood on the beach, gazing at the ocean.* | *He lives* **by the ocean**. | **on/at the bottom of the ocean** *The huge ship lies at the bottom of the ocean.* | *creatures living on the* **ocean floor** (=the bottom of the ocean) → see picture on page A31 **2** [C] EARTH SCIENCE one of the very large areas of water on the Earth's surface: *the Pacific Ocean* **3 oceans of sth** a great mass or amount of something: *oceans of collected data* [**Origin:** 1200–1300 Latin *oceanus*, from Greek *Okeanos* name of a river believed to flow around the world] —**oceanic** /ˌoʊʃiˈænɪk◂/ *adj.* → see also **a drop in the bucket/ocean** at DROP² (7)

o·cean·front /ˈoʊʃənˌfrʌnt/ *n.* [singular] **the oceanfront** the land along the edge of an ocean —**oceanfront** *adj.* [only before noun]: *oceanfront properties*

o·cean·go·ing /ˈoʊʃənˌgoʊɪŋ/ *adj.* an oceangoing ship is designed to sail across the ocean: *an oceangoing tanker*

o·cean·og·ra·phy /ˌoʊʃəˈnɑgrəfi/ *n.* [U] the scientific study of the ocean —**oceanographer** *n.* [C]

ˌocean ˈtrench *n.* [C] EARTH SCIENCE a long narrow valley in the ground beneath the ocean

oc·e·lot /ˈɑsəˌlɑt/ *n.* [C] a large American wild cat that has a pattern of spots on its back

o·cher, ochre /ˈoʊkɚ/ *n.* [U] **1** a reddish-yellow soil used in paints **2** the color of ocher —**ochre** *adj.*

o'clock /əˈklɑk/ S2 *adv.* **one/two/three etc. o'clock** one of the times when the clock shows the exact hour as a number from 1 to 12: *"It's already five o'clock."* [**Origin:** 1400–1500 *of the clock*]

O'Con·nor /oʊˈkɑnɚ/, **Flan·ne·ry** /ˈflænəri/ (1925–1964) a U.S. writer of NOVELS

O'Connor, San·dra Day /ˈsændrə deɪ/ (1930–) a U.S. judge who became the first woman member of the SUPREME COURT in 1981

-ocracy /ɑkrəsi/ *suffix* [in nouns] a spelling of -CRACY used after CONSONANT sounds: *meritocracy* (=government by people with the most ability)

-ocrat /əkræt/ *suffix* [in nouns] a spelling of -CRAT used after CONSONANT sounds: *a technocrat* (=scientist who controls an organization or country) —**-ocratic** /əkræt̬ɪk/ *suffix* —**-ocratically** /əkræt̬ɪkli/ *suffix*

Oct. the written abbreviation of OCTOBER

oc·ta·gon /ˈɑktəˌgɑn/ *n.* [C] MATH a flat shape with eight sides —**octagonal** /ɑkˈtægənl/ *adj.*: *an octagonal room* → see picture at SHAPE¹

oc·tane /ˈɑkteɪn/ *n.* [U] CHEMISTRY a type of HYDROCARBON found in FUEL that is used as a measure of its quality: *high-octane gasoline*

oc·tave /ˈɑktəv/ *n.* [C] ENG. LANG. ARTS **1** the range of musical notes between the first note of a musical SCALE and the last one **2** the first and last notes of a musical SCALE played together [**Origin:** 1300–1400 Medieval Latin *octava*, from Latin *octo* **eight**; because there are eight notes in the range]

oc·tet /ɑkˈtɛt/ *n.* [C] ENG. LANG. ARTS **1** eight singers or musicians performing together **2** a piece of music for an octet

Oc·to·ber /ɑkˈtoʊbɚ/ WRITTEN ABBREVIATION **Oct.** *n.* [C,U] the tenth month of the year, between September and November [**Origin:** 1000–1100 Old French *Octobre*, from Latin *October*, from *octo* **eight**; because it was the eighth month of the ancient Roman year] → see Grammar box at JANUARY

oc·to·ge·nar·i·an /ˌɑktədʒəˈnɛriən/ *n.* [C] a person who is between 80 and 89 years old

oc·to·pus /ˈɑktəpəs/ *n. plural* **octopuses** or **octopi** /-paɪ/ [C] an animal that lives in the ocean with eight TENTACLES (=arms) [**Origin:** 1700–1800 Modern Latin, Greek *oktopous* **scorpion**, from *okto* **eight** + *pous* **foot**]

oc·u·lar /ˈɑkyəlɚ/ *adj.* TECHNICAL relating to the eyes: *ocular movement*

oc·u·list /ˈɑkyəlɪst/ *n.* [C] OLD-FASHIONED a doctor who examines and treats people's eyes

OD /ˌoʊ ˈdi/ *v.* **OD'd, OD'ing** [I] SPOKEN, INFORMAL **1** to take too much of a dangerous drug SYN **overdose**: **+on** *"How did she die?" "She OD'd on heroin."* **2** to see, hear etc. too much of something —**OD** *n.* [C]

o·da·lisque /ˈoʊdl-ɪsk/ *n.* [C] LITERARY a beautiful female slave in former times

odd /ɑd/ Ac S2 W3 *adj.*
1 STRANGE different from what is normal or expected SYN **weird** SYN **strange**: *Timber? That's kind of an odd name for a kid.* | *an odd combination of guests at the party* | **it is odd (that)** *It's odd that she can't remember his name.* | **odd-looking/sounding** *an odd-looking solar car* | *Didn't it* **strike you as odd** (=seem odd to you) *that he never answered your calls?* ►see THESAURUS box at **strange¹**
2 the odd sth a) used to talk about something that does not happen often or regularly SYN **occasional**: *We still see each other on the odd occasion.* **b)** used to say that there are just a few of something: *I stopped writing down what he said, except for the odd phrase.*
3 VARIOUS [only before noun] not specially chosen or collected: *Any odd scrap of paper will do.* | *The boys are earning money doing* **odd jobs** (=many different small pieces of work) *for neighbors.*
4 NOT IN A PAIR/SET [only before noun] separated from its pair or set: *an odd sock*
5 NUMBER an odd number cannot be divided exactly by two, for example 1, 3, 5, 7 OPP **even**
6 20-odd/30-odd etc. SPOKEN a little more than 20, 30 etc.: *None of the 30-odd passengers complained.*
7 the odd man/one out someone or something that is different or that is not included in the rest of a group: *I was always the odd man out in my class at school.*
[**Origin:** 1300–1400 Old Norse *oddi* **point of land, triangle, odd number**] → see also ODDLY —**oddness** *n.* [U]

odd·ball /ˈɑdbɔl/ *n.* [C] INFORMAL someone who behaves in a strange or unusual way —**oddball** *adj.*: *an oddball comedian*

ˈOdd ˌFellows an organization that gives its members help with medical costs, living in RETIREMENT, educating children etc.

odd·i·ty /ˈɑdət̬i/ *n. plural* **oddities** **1** [C] a strange or unusual person or thing: *A white buffalo is an animal oddity.* **2** [U] the quality of being strange or unusual: *The oddity of the situation didn't seem to bother her at all.* **3** [C] a strange quality in someone or something

O

ˈodd jobs *n.* [plural] small or temporary jobs of different types, especially cleaning or repairing things: *He does odd jobs around the house for my parents.*

odd ˈlot *n.* [C] an amount of something to be sold that is less than normal or usual, especially an amount of STOCK that is less than the standard 100 shares

odd·ly /ˈɑdli/ *adv.* **1** in a strange or unusual way: *an oddly dressed woman* | *Brenda's response was oddly reassuring.* | **oddly matched/assorted** (=used about pairs or groups of things or people that seem strange together because they are very different from each other) **2** also **oddly enough** [sentence adverb] used to say that something seems strange or surprising: *Oddly enough, some of the best things about the broadcast were the commercials.*

odd·ments /ˈɑdmənts/ *n.* [plural] small things of no value, or pieces of a material that were not used when something was made

odds /ɑdz/ Ac *n.* [plural] **1 the odds** how likely it is that something will or will not happen, especially when this can be stated in numbers: **the odds of (sb) doing sth** *I knew that the odds of me getting the position were not very good.* | **(the) odds are (that)** *The odds are he will commit another crime.* | **the odds are against sth** *The odds are heavily against her winning again.* | **the odds are in favor of sth** *The odds are in favor of a Russian win.* | ***The odds are** pretty **good** that he'll be well enough to play.* | ***The odds are stacked against** the Democratic party candidate* (=there is a very low likelihood of the Democrat winning). **2 be at odds a)** to disagree with someone: **+with** *He often found himself at odds with his colleagues.* | **+over/on** *State lawmakers are at odds over which experts to believe.* **b)** if two statements, descriptions, actions etc. are at odds with each other, they are different although they should be the same: **+with** *His latest evidence is at odds with his earlier statements.* **3** difficulties that make a good result seem very unlikely: *Our team won **against all odds*** (=despite many difficulties). | **overcome/defy/beat the odds** (=succeed, when success seems very unlikely) **4** the calculations and numbers that are used to figure out how much money you will win when you BET on the result of a game, competition, horse race etc.: *I bet $10 on Broadway Flyer with the **odds at** 6–1.* | *I wouldn't **lay odds on*** (=be willing to risk your money on) *the outcome of that race.* | **long/short odds** (=odds based on a high or low risk of losing) | **set/offer (sb) odds** (=to officially say what the odds for a competition are)

ˌodds and ˈends *n.* [plural] small things of various kinds, without much value: *There were a few odds and ends left in his desk drawer.*

odds·mak·er /ˈɑdzˌmeɪkɚ/ *n.* [C] someone who decides what the chance of someone winning a race or game is, so that people can BET on it, especially in sports such as horse racing

ˌodds-ˈon *adj.* **the odds-on favorite** the competitor that is most likely to win a race, election, competition etc.

ode /oʊd/ *n.* [C] a poem or song that is written in order to praise a person or thing: *Keat's poem "Ode to a Nightingale"*

O·dets /oʊˈdɛts/, **Clif·ford** /ˈklɪfɚd/ (1903–1963) a U.S. writer of plays

O·din /ˈoʊdn/ in Norse MYTHOLOGY, the king of the gods

o·di·ous /ˈoʊdiəs/ *adj.* FORMAL making you feel strong dislike or DISGUST: *an odious crime* | *the odious task of scrubbing floors* —**odiously** *adv.*

o·dom·e·ter /oʊˈdɑmət̬ɚ/ *n.* [C] an instrument in a vehicle that records the distance it has traveled → see picture on page A36

o·dor /ˈoʊdɚ/ *n.* [C] a smell, especially a bad one: *Neighbors noticed a foul odor coming from the apartment.* | **+of** *a **faint odor*** (=slight smell) *of sweat in the room* → see also BODY ODOR ▶see THESAURUS box at smell[1]

o·dor·if·er·ous /ˌoʊdəˈrɪfərəs/ *adj.* LITERARY or HUMOROUS odorous

o·dor·less /ˈoʊdɚlɪs/ *adj.* having no smell: *an odorless gas*

o·dor·ous /ˈoʊdərəs/ *adj.* LITERARY having a smell, especially a pleasant one → see also MALODOROUS

O·dys·se·us /oʊˈdɪsiəs/ in ancient Greek stories, the King of Ithaca and husband of Penelope, whose trip home after the Trojan War is described in the poem "The Odyssey" by Homer

od·ys·sey /ˈɑdəsi/ *n. plural* **odysseys** [C] **1** FORMAL a long trip with many adventures or difficulties SYN **journey**: *Clarke's cross-country odyssey began in South Carolina.* **2** a series of experiences that teach you something about yourself or about life in general SYN **journey**: *a spiritual odyssey*

OECD *n.* **the OECD the Organization for Economic Cooperation and Development** a group of rich countries who work together to develop trade and economic growth

oed·i·pal /ˈɛdəpəl/ *adj.* related to an Oedipus complex: *oedipal longings*

Oed·i·pus /ˈɛdəpəs/ in ancient Greek stories, a man who did not know who his parents were, and killed his father and married his mother

ˈOedipus ˌcomplex *n.* [C] an unconscious sexual desire that a son feels for his mother, combined with a hatred for his father, according to Freudian PSYCHOLOGY → see also ELECTRA COMPLEX

o'er /ɔr/ *adv., prep.* POETIC over

oeu·vre /ˈʊvrə/ *n.* [C] LITERARY all the works of an artist, such as a painter or writer, considered as a whole

of /əv, ə; *strong* ʌv/ S1 W1 *prep.* **1** used to show a feature or quality that something has: *the brightness of the sun* | *the smell of roses* | *the length of the driveway* **2** used to show that something is part of something else: *the first chapter of the book* | *I had a pain in the back of my leg* | *the ground floor of the building* | *all the details of the agreement* **3** used to show who something or someone belongs to or has a connection with: *a cousin of mine* | *a friend of the family* | *a car of his own* **4** used to talk about a group or collection of people or things: *a flock of birds* | *a pack of cigarettes* | *a bunch of grapes* **5** used to talk about an amount or measurement of something: *a gallon of milk* | *ten pounds of cheese* | *a teaspoonful of baking soda* | *a cup of coffee* **6** used to talk about a particular person or thing from a larger group of the same people or things: *a member of the rock group* | *most of the students* | *That's one of her best poems.* **7** used in dates, before the name of the month: *the 12th of October* **8** used for saying when something happens or is done, especially for giving the date: *the Presidential election of 1960* | *the events of the past week* **9** used when giving the name of something or being more specific about something that is very general: *the game of chess* | *at the age of fifty* | *the city of New Orleans* **10 a)** used after nouns describing actions, to show who the action is done to: *the hiring of new workers* (=when new workers are hired) | *the introduction of a minimum wage* **b)** used after nouns describing actions, to show who does the action: *We could hear the barking of dogs.* **11** used to say which particular subject, person, thing etc. another subject, person, or thing is related to or deals with: *the president of the company* | *the difficulties of buying your own home* | *the decision of the city council* **12** used to describe a person or thing, showing what their main qualities or features are: *a woman of great determination* (=a very determined woman) | *The ring was an object of great beauty.* | *weapons of mass destruction* **13** used for stating the type of activity or situation that continues for a particular period of time: *several hours of hard work* | *five years of war* **14 a) the day/year etc. of sth** the day, year etc. that something happened: *the day of the accident* | *the week of the carnival* **b) ...of the day/year etc.** the best or most important person or thing during a particular period: *The Yankee's shortstop was voted Player of the Month.* **15** SPOKEN used in giving the time, to mean "before": **a quarter of seven/eight/nine etc.** (=6:45, 7:45, 8:45 etc.) **16** used for saying what someone's age is: *a boy of twelve and a girl of fifteen* **17** FORMAL used to say what substance or material something is made of: *a crown of gold and silver* | *The bride wore a dress* ***made of*** *white silk.* **18** used to show that something is the result of something else: *He died of cancer.* | *the effects of overeating* **19** used to show where something is or how far it is from something else: **north/south etc. of sth** *a small town to the west of Kansas City* | **to the left/right of sth** *The table is to the left of the door.* **20** used to say who writes a play, who paints a painting etc.: *the writings of a lunatic* | *the work of professional thieves* **21** used to show what a picture, story etc. is about or who is in it: *a map of the world* | *a photograph of my grandmother* | *a history of modern China* **22** about: *Have you ever heard of the poet T. S. Eliot?* | *News of Kirkland's arrest was soon all over town.* **23** used to say where someone comes from: *the people of Malaysia* | *Jesus of Nazareth* **24 it is kind/stupid/careless etc. of sb to do sth** used to say that something that someone has done shows that they are kind, stupid etc.: *It was smart of you to bring extra food to the picnic.* [**Origin:** Old English] → see also **of course** at COURSE[1] (1)

GRAMMAR

- When you want to say that something belongs to a particular person, you usually use **'s** or plural **s'** rather than **of**: *her boyfriend's car* | *my parents' house*. But you use **of** to say that something belongs to or is part of something else: *the corner of the street* | *the top of the mountain*.
- You also use **'s** and **s'** to talk about periods of time, for example: *a day's work* | *three weeks' vacation*. **'s** can also be used with the names of places, especially in newspapers: *America's most popular amusement park* | *China's recent history*.
- When you use words like "a", "some", "the", "this" etc. with the word for something that belongs to someone, or the person you are talking about in connection with them, you can use both **of** and **'s** together: *an old boyfriend of Sarah's*.

of 'course *adv.* → see **of course** at COURSE[1] (1)

off[1] /ɔf/ S1 W1 *adv.* **1** away or from where something is: *She drove off at top speed.* | *We turned off onto a side road.* | *I saw him hurrying off to catch his plane.* | ***We're off*** (=we are leaving). | *It happened while his wife was off on a business trip.* **2** out of a bus, train, car etc.: *I'll get off at the next stop.* | *We need to stop off and get gas soon.* **3** removed or not fastened to something anymore OPP **on**: *Can anyone get this lid off?* | *Take off your shoes.* **4** a machine, piece of equipment etc. that is off is not working or operating OPP **on**: *All the lights were off when I got home.* | *Don't forget to turn off the oven.* **5** not at work, school etc. because you are sick or on vacation: *Carol is off for the whole week.* | *I'm going to* ***take*** *Thursday* ***off*** *to go to the dentist.* | *Do you get Christmas Eve off?* **6** lower in price by a particular amount: *Get 15% off on all winter coats.* **7** an arranged event that is off will not happen OPP **on**: *I'm afraid the wedding's off.* | *Union leaders were asked to* ***call off*** *the strike* (=arrange for it not to happen). **8** a particular distance away, or a particular amount of time away in the future: *Polly's wedding was still about six weeks off* (=it would happen six weeks in the future). | *I could see snow-capped mountains* ***way off*** *in the distance.* **9 off and on** also **on and off** for short periods but not regularly, over a long period of time: *Rachel and Alan have been dating off and on for five years.* **10** used in stage directions to mean that a sound or voice is not on the stage but still able to be heard in the theater SYN **offstage**: *noises off* → see also BETTER OFF, WELL-OFF

off[2] S1 W1 *prep.* **1** not on something or someone, or not touching something or someone OPP **on**: *Get your feet off my couch.* | *The lids were off the paint cans.* **2** out of a bus, train, airplane etc. OPP **on**: *I got off the bus in Cleveland.* **3** no longer held or supported by something: *A girl had fallen off her horse.* | *I finally took his picture off the wall.* **4** no longer connected or fastened to something: *My badge fell off my jacket.* | *Cut a slice off the loaf.* **5 a)** away from a particular place: *Three players were sent off the field.* | *The truck forced my car off the road.* **b)** near and connected to a path or road: *Oak Hills? Isn't that off Route 290?* | *a room* ***just off*** (=connected to) *the Oval office* **c)** in a body of water but near the land: *a boat ten miles off Cape Cod* | *an island off the coast of West Africa* **6** no longer taking something such as medicine or drugs: *He says he's been off cocaine for five months.* **7** taken or obtained from someone or something: *I bought the shirt off a street vendor.* | *What will you live off while you're studying?* **8** not in a particular building, area etc.: *Our club had to meet off school grounds.* → see also OFF GUARD, **get/be/stay off the subject** at SUBJECT[1] (1)

off[3] S3 *adj.* **1** [not before noun] not as good as usual: *Sales figures are a little off this quarter.* | *Our performance is* ***way off*** (=much worse than usual). **2** [not before noun] not exactly right or completely correct: *Our calculations were off.* | *Johnson's free throw shooting was* ***way off*** (=completely incorrect). **3** [not before noun] TECHNICAL used to show that the STOCK EXCHANGE has fallen in value by a particular amount: *At the close of trading, the Dow Jones Index was off 28 points.* **4** SPOKEN strange or unusual: *There was something slightly off about the way he answered.* **5 an off day/week etc.** INFORMAL a day, week etc. when you are not doing something as well as you usually do it: *Everyone has an off day every now and then.* → see also OFF-SEASON

off[4] *v.* [T] SLANG to kill someone

of·fal /'ɔfəl, 'ɑ-/ *n.* [U] the inside organs of an animal, for example its heart, LIVER, and KIDNEYS, used as food

,off-'balance *adj.* **1** not prepared for something, so that it surprises you and you do not know what to do: **catch/throw sb off-balance** *News of the merger caught us all off-balance.* **2** in an unsteady position so that you are likely to fall: **throw/knock/push sb off-balance** (=make someone fall or almost fall)

off·beat /,ɔf'bit◂/ *adj.* INFORMAL unusual and not what people normally expect, but in an interesting way: *an offbeat romance novel*

'off-brand *adj.* [only before noun] an off-brand product is made by a company that is not well known: *off-brand television sets* —**off-brand** *n.* [C] → see also NAME BRAND

,off-'Broadway *adj., adv.* an off-Broadway play is one that is performed outside the Broadway entertainment area in New York City and does not involve as much money as the famous plays on Broadway

off-'campus *adj.* not on the CAMPUS (=the land and buildings) of a college or university: *off-campus housing for students*

off-'center *adj.* **1** not exactly in the center of something: *The picture is slightly off-center.* **2** INFORMAL different from other people, especially in a strange way: *Thompson's sense of humor was a little off-center.*

'off-chance *n.* **on the off-chance** hoping that something will happen, although it is unlikely: *I called on the off-chance that Patty might be home.*

off-'color *adj.* referring to sex in a way that is not considered acceptable: *off-color jokes*

,off-'duty *adj.* someone such as a police officer, nurse, or soldier is off-duty during the hours when they are not working: *an off-duty fire-fighter* | *Sorry, I'm off-duty now.*

of·fence /əˈfɛns/ the British and Canadian spelling of OFFENSE

of·fend /əˈfɛnd/ S3 *v.* **1** [T] to make someone feel angry and upset, by doing or saying something that insults them personally or shows a lack of respect for them: *I hope I haven't offended anybody.* | *The remarks **deeply offended** many in the African-American community.* **2** [I] FORMAL to do something that is a crime: *The parole board felt that Harris was unlikely to offend again.* **3** [I,T] FORMAL to go against ideas or rules about what is good, appropriate, or morally right, with the result that people feel unhappy or shocked: *Some people are offended by swearing on television.* | **offend against sth** *Broadcasters should not offend against good taste and decency.* | *The pictures may **offend** some readers' **sensibilities**.* [**Origin:** 1300–1400 Old French *offendre*, from Latin *offendere* **to strike against, offend**]

of·fend·ed /əˈfɛndɪd/ *adj.* very angry and upset by someone's behavior or remarks: *My mother is very **easily offended**.* | +**at** *I was offended at the suggestion that I had lied.* | +**that** *I hope you're not offended that we didn't invite you.*

of·fend·er /əˈfɛndɚ/ *n.* [C] **1** someone who is guilty of a crime: *drug offenders* | *a program aimed at reducing the number of **repeat offenders*** (=people who commit crimes after they have been in jail). | **first-time offender** (=someone who has done a criminal action for the first time) → see also SEX OFFENDER ►see THESAURUS box at **criminal**[2] **2** someone or something that is responsible for something bad that happens: **the worst/biggest/main offender** *Among the causes of heart disease, smoking and high-fat foods are the worst offenders.*

of·fend·ing /əˈfɛndɪŋ/ *adj.* **1 the offending** OFTEN HUMOROUS the thing that is causing a problem: *I had the offending tooth removed.* **2** causing people to feel angry or insulted: *his offending behavior*

of·fense[1] /əˈfɛns/ W3 *n.* **1** [C] an illegal action or a crime: *a parking offense* | *Jones had **committed** two previous burglary **offenses**.* | *Legislation was passed to **make** smoking in restaurants **an offense**.* | *The bill would make it **a criminal offense** for minors to possess cigarettes.* | *The man in custody has not yet been **charged with an offense**.* | +**against** *The military has committed numerous offenses against civilians.* | **first offense** (=the first illegal thing that someone has done) | **capital offense** (=a crime for which death is the punishment) | **federal offense** (=a very serious crime which the national government punishes) | **serious/minor offense** (=one that is serious or not serious) **2** [U] hurt or angry feelings: *Briggs regrets that the book has **caused offense*** (=offended someone). | *Censorship laws ban anything that might **give offense*** (=offend someone). | *She **took offense at*** (=became offended by) *my remarks.* | *Rogers said he **meant no offense*** (=had no intention of offending) *to women.* **3 no offense** SPOKEN used to tell someone that you do not want to offend them by what you are about to say: *No offense, but could you put your shoes back on, please?*

of·fense[2] /ˈɔfɛns/ *n.* [U] **1** the part of a game such as football concerned with getting points, or the group of players who do this OPP **defense**: *the best offense in the league* | *The Lions need to be more aggressive **on offense**.* **2** FORMAL the act of attacking OPP **defense**: *a weapon of offense*

of·fen·sive[1] /əˈfɛnsɪv/ *adj.* **1** very impolite or insulting, and likely to make people angry and upset OPP **inoffensive**: *Some viewers found the show offensive.* | +**to** *The jokes are likely to be offensive to women.* | *Your behavior was **deeply offensive*** (=very offensive) *to me.* ►see THESAURUS box at **rude** **2** FORMAL unpleasant in every way SYN **disgusting**: *an offensive smell* **3** [only before noun] related to the aim of getting points and winning a game, as opposed to stopping the other team from getting points OPP **defensive**: *the offensive player of the year* | *the Jets' offensive strategy* **4** [only before noun] for attacking OPP **defensive**: *offensive weapons* | *Government troops took up offensive positions.* —**offensively** *adv.*: *The weapons will not be used offensively.* | *Rick's jokes were offensively sexist.* —**offensiveness** *n.* [U]

offensive[2] *n.* [C] **1** a planned military attack involving large forces over a long period: +**on/against** *an offensive against rebels in the north* | **a military/ground/air etc. offensive** *The land offensive began again the next day.* | **launch/mount an offensive** (=start one) **2 be on the offensive** to be ready to attack or criticize people **3 take the offensive** also **go on the offensive** to be the first to make an attack or strong criticism: *He decided to go on the offensive before she could ask another question.* **4 sales/PR/diplomatic offensive** a planned set of actions intended to influence a lot of people

of·fer[1] /ˈɔfɚ, ˈɑfɚ/ S1 W1 *v.* **1** [T] to ask someone if they would like to have something, or to hold something out to them so that they can take it: **offer sb sth** *They've offered me the job!* | *He offered Sue his handkerchief.* | **offer sth to sb** *She was making a drink and offered one to me.* **2** [T] to say that you are willing to pay a particular amount of money in exchange for something: *How much are they offering?* | **offer (sb) sth for sth** *Someone offered me $300 for the bike.* | *Robin is offering a reward for the return of her necklace.* **3** [I,T] to say that you are willing to do something for someone: *I don't need any help, but thanks for offering.* | **offer sb sth** *Rob offered her a ride to the store.* | **offer to do sth** *Amy has offered to babysit this Friday.* **4** [T] to provide something that people need or want, such as information or services SYN **provide**: *The company offers a wide range of services.* | **offer sth to sb** *Both airlines offer a discount to travelers over 60.* **5** [T] to make it possible for someone to have something, especially an opportunity, a good feeling etc. SYN **provide**: **offer (sb) the opportunity/chance/possibility** *The school offers students the opportunity to study in the U.S.* | *The new treatment **offers hope** to thousands of cancer patients.* | *The shelter **offered** some **protection** from the wind.* **6** [T] to express an idea or feeling for someone to consider: **offer sb sth** *The doctor **offered** me some **advice** on diet.* | *He **offered** no **explanation** for his actions.* | *Monica's husband rarely **offers an opinion** on anything.* **7** [T] to make something available to be bought: **offer sth at $10/$2,500 etc.** *The stock is being offered at $3.40 a share.* | *The used aircraft will be **offered for sale** by the military.* **8 have much/plenty/a lot to offer** to have many qualities that people are likely to want or enjoy OPP **have nothing to offer**: *Mexico has a lot to offer in the way of great low-cost vacations.* **9 offer (up) a prayer/sacrifice etc.** to pray to God or give something to God **10 offer your hand to sb** to hold out your hand in order to shake hands with someone [**Origin:** 1200–1300 Old French *offrir*, from Latin *offerre*, from *ferre* **to carry**]

offer[2] S3 W2 *n.* [C] **1** a statement that you are willing to give someone something or do something for them: *Have you had any **job offers**?* | +**of** *an offer of employment* | **offer to do sth** *his offer to help* | **accept/take up an offer** *She gladly accepted their offer of assistance.* | **turn down/reject/refuse an offer** (=say "no" to an offer) **2** an amount of money that you are willing to pay for something: *You won't get a better offer than this.* | **make (sb) an offer (of sth)** *Brannon made an offer of $43.5 million for the two properties.* | *I've decided to **accept** their **offer** on the apartment.* **3** a reduction for a short time in the price of something that is for sale in a store: +**on** *This **special offer** on our SUVs is good for 30 days only.* **4 make sb an offer they can't refuse** to make someone a very good offer, for example of a job or a price, so that they feel they must do it **5 on offer** available to be bought or used: *There wasn't much on offer that we wanted to buy.*

of·fer·ing /ˈɔfərɪŋ, ˈɑf-/ *n.* [C] **1** something that has been produced for people to buy, see, read etc.: *the latest offering from Pixar studios* | *the vegetarian offerings on the menu* **2** an occasion when STOCKS are made available for people to buy: *an offering of two million shares of common stock* | *The **offering price*** (=the amount that a particular stock will cost) *is expected to be* *around $12 per share.* **3 the offering** money that is collected during a Christian religious service, or the part of a service when money is collected SYN **collection** **4** something that is given to God or as a present to please someone → see also PEACE OFFERING

of·fer·to·ry /ˈɔfɚˌtɔri, ˈɑ-/ *n.* [C] **1** the act of giving offerings to God in a Christian religious service **2** the music played in a Christian religious service while the offering is being collected

ˌoff ˈguard *adj.* **catch/throw/take sb off guard** to surprise someone by doing something they are not expecting and are not prepared to deal with: *The brief snow storm caught everyone off guard.*

off·hand¹ /ˌɔfˈhænd◂ / *adj.* **1** said or done without thinking or planning: *an offhand remark* **2** not caring or seeming not to care about something or someone: *his offhand manner* —**offhandedness** *n.* [U]

offhand² *adv.* immediately, without time to think about it or find out about something: *I can't think offhand of the name of the book.*

of·fice /ˈɔfɪs, ˈɑ-/ S1 W1 *n.*

1 BUILDING **a)** [C] the building that belongs to a company or organization, with a lot of rooms where people work at desks: *I never really enjoyed working in an office.* | *office equipment* | *office politics* | **main/head office** (=the most important office in a company) **b) the office** the office where you work: *Someone from the office called.* | *I must have left my keys* ***at the office***. | *Did you go to* ***the office*** (=the office where you work) *today?*

THESAURUS

In an office
desk a table, usually with drawers, where you can work
cubicle/cube a small, partly enclosed part of a room, where one person works in an office where there are many of these areas
workstation a desk and computer etc., where you work
lunchroom/cafeteria a room in which you can eat and sometimes buy lunch
Office equipment
computer/PC
printer
photocopier also **Xerox machine** TRADEMARK
fax (machine)
file cabinets/filing cabinets

2 ROOM [C] a room where you do work that involves writing, calculating, or talking to people: *the supervisor's office* | *My office is at the end of the hall.* | *Frank* ***shares an office with*** *Shirley* (=they both work in the same room).
3 DOCTOR [C] the place where a doctor or DENTIST examines or treats people: *My kids love going to the dentist's office* .
4 **information/ticket etc. office** a room or building where people go to ask for information, buy tickets etc.: *the local tourist information office* → see also BOX OFFICE, POST OFFICE
5 IMPORTANT JOB [C,U] an important job or position with power, especially in government: *the office of mayor* | *She remained* ***in office*** *until her death in 2005.* | *Mr. Christopher previously* ***held office*** (=had an important job) *as Secretary of State.* | *When she* ***took office*** (=started working in an important position), *the unemployment rate stood at 11.1 percent.* | **the office of mayor/president etc.** *He ran for the office of governor in 2000.*
6 **office hours** **a)** the time between about nine in the morning and five in the afternoon, when the people in offices are working: *Call me back tomorrow during office hours.* **b)** the time during the day or week when students can meet with their teacher in the teacher's office: *Professor Lee* ***has office hours*** *this afternoon from 2–4.*
7 **Office** used in the names of some government departments: *the District Attorney's Office*
8 **sb's good offices** FORMAL help given by someone who has authority or can influence people: *The U.N.'s good offices will be necessary in finding a peaceful solution to the crisis.*
[**Origin:** 1200–1300 Old French, Latin *officium* **service, duty, office**, from *opus* **work** + *facere* **to do**]

ˈoffice ˌbuilding *n.* [C] a large building with many offices in it

ˈoffice ˌholder *n.* [C] someone who has an important official position, especially in the government

ˌOffice of ˌManagement and ˈBudget, the ABBREVIATION **OMB** a U.S. government organization that provides help for the President in organizing the work of government departments and especially in preparing the BUDGET

ˌoffice ˈparty *n.* [C] a party in the office of a company, government department etc. for the people who work there

of·fi·cer /ˈɔfəsɚ, ˈɑ-/ S2 W1 *n.* [C] **1** someone who is in a position of authority in the army, navy etc.: +**in** *an officer in the Marines* | **an army/naval/military etc. officer** *a retired naval officer* | *Who is the* ***commanding officer*** (=officer in charge) *here?* **2** a police officer: *We need more officers on the streets.* | *The investigation will be led by Officer Murdoch.* | *Excuse me, officer. Could you help us?* **3** someone who has an important position in an organization, such as a company or a government department: *the chief financial officer* | *the government contracting officer*

WORD CHOICE **officer, official**
An **officer** is someone in the police force or the military: *an army officer*. An **official** is someone in a government or business organization, in a position of authority: *Airline officials refused to comment to reporters while negotiations were continuing.*

of·fi·cial¹ /əˈfɪʃəl/ S3 W2 *adj.* **1** approved of or done by someone in authority, especially the government: *an official investigation* | *You'll need official approval for that.* | **the official language/religion etc.** *Islam is the official religion of Saudi Arabia.* **2** done as part of your job and not for your own private purposes: *Senator Blake is here on official business.* | **an official visit/tour/engagement etc.** *The First Lady will make an official visit to Haiti.* **3** used about information, reasons etc. that are given publicly by the authorities or people in charge, when you doubt that they are true: *The official explanation for the crash was pilot error.* **4 sth is official** used to say that something has been formally announced and is definitely true or is definitely going to happen: *It's official: they're getting married.* | *The letter confirming the offer came, making it all official.* **5** [only before noun] chosen to represent a person or organization: *one of the official sponsors of the Winter Olympics* | *the company's official logo* **6** [only before noun] an official event is a formal public event: *the official opening of the new clinic*

official² W1 *n.* [C] **1** someone who has a responsible position in an organization: *a union official* | **a senior/high-ranking official** *a senior government official* **2** a REFEREE → see Word Choice box at OFFICER

of·fi·cial·dom /əˈfɪʃəldəm/ *n.* [U] government departments or the people who work in them, especially when they are annoying because they are slow, have too many rules, processes etc. → see also BUREAUCRACY

of·fi·cial·ly /əˈfɪʃəli/ *adv.* **1** publicly and formally: *Nothing has yet been officially announced.* | *Britain and Germany were still officially at war.* **2** [sentence adverb] according to what you say publicly, even though this may not be true: *Officially, he resigned, but everyone knows he was fired.*

of·fi·ci·ate /əˈfɪʃiˌeɪt/ *v.* [I + at] to do official duties, especially at a religious ceremony

of·fi·cious /əˈfɪʃəs/ *adj.* too eager to tell people what to do: *an officious security guard* —**officiously** *adv.* —**officiousness** *n.* [U]

off·ing /ˈɔfɪŋ/ *n.* **be in the offing** to be about to happen or to be possible: *Tighter airport security is in the offing.*

ˌoff-ˈkey *adj.* music that is off-key does not sound good because it is played slightly above or below the correct PITCH —**off-key** *adv.*: *Harold always sings off-key.*

ˌoff-ˈkilter *adj.* **1** not completely straight or correctly balanced: *The mirror was slightly off-kilter.* **2** unusual, in a strange or interesting way: *her off-kilter sense of humor*

O

ˌoff ˈlimits *adj.* **be off limits a)** if a place is off limits, you are not allowed to go there: **+to** *The land is strictly off-limits to commercial developers.* **b)** if something is off limits, you are not allowed to do it, change it, talk about it etc.: **+to** *The subject of his private life is off-limits to the press.*

off·line /ˌɔfˈlaɪn◂/ *adv.* COMPUTERS **1** if your computer is offline, it is not connected to the Internet OPP **online** **2** if a piece of computer equipment is offline, it is not directly connected to the computer OPP **online** —**offline** *adj.*

off·load /ˌɔfˈloʊd/ *v.* **1** [I,T] if a truck or ship offloads or someone offloads it, the goods on it are taken off: *a tanker offloading its oil* **2** [T] to get rid of something that you do not need by giving it or selling it to someone else: **offload sth onto sb** *They just want to offload the nuclear waste onto someone else.*

ˌoff-off-ˈBroadway *adj.* [only before noun] *adv.* off-off-Broadway plays, theater, events etc. are modern and often strange plays that do not cost a lot of money to make and are performed in New York City in places like churches and COFFEE HOUSES → see also OFF-BROADWAY

ˈoff-peak *adj.* **1** off-peak hours or periods are times when fewer people want to do something or use something: *Work on the highway will be done only during off-peak hours.* **2** off-peak travel is cheaper because it is done or used at these times

ˌoff-ˈpiste *adj.* not on a normal SKI SLOPE: *off-piste skiing* —**off-piste** *adv.*

off·print /ˈɔfprɪnt/ *n.* [C] an article from a magazine that is printed and sold separately

ˈoff-ramp *n.* [C] a small road that leads from a HIGHWAY or FREEWAY to a street → see also ON-RAMP

ˌoff-road ˈvehicle *n.* [C] a vehicle that is built to be very strong so that it can be used on rough ground

ˌoff-ˈscreen *adv.* when a movie actor is not acting: *Off-screen, he is a down-to-earth kind of guy.* —**off-screen** *adj.*: *off-screen romances*

ˈoff-ˌseason *n.* **the off-season a)** the time of the year when there is not much work or activity, especially in the tourist industry **b)** the time in sports between the end of one SEASON and the start of another, when teams do not play any games —**off-season** *adj., adv.*: *off-season discounts*

off·set[1] /ˌɔfˈsɛt, ˈɔfsɛt/ Ac *v.* **offset, offsetting** [T] **1** if something such as a cost or amount offsets another cost or amount or you offset them, the two things have an opposite effect and so the situation remains the same: *Rising costs for jet fuel were partially offset by higher air fares.* | **offset sth against sth** *You can offset your travel expenses against your taxes.* **2** to cause balance in a situation by having the opposite effect to something else: *Maria's sense of humor offsets her serious nature.*

off·shoot /ˈɔfʃut/ *n.* [C] **1** an organization, system of beliefs etc. which has developed from a larger or earlier one: **+of** *The Samaritan religion is an offshoot of Judaism.* **2** BIOLOGY a new stem or branch on a plant

off·shore /ˌɔfˈʃɔr◂/ *adj.* **1** in the ocean, away from the shore: *offshore fishing* | *offshore oil reserves* **2 offshore bank/company/investment etc.** a bank etc. that is based abroad, in a country where you pay less tax than in your home country **3 offshore wind/current etc.** a wind etc. that is blowing or moving away from the land → see also INSHORE, ONSHORE —**offshore** *adv.*: *The ship was anchored half a mile offshore.*

off·side /ˌɔfˈsaɪd◂/ *adj., adv.* in a position where you are not allowed to play the ball in sports such as SOCCER

ˌoff-ˈsite *adj., adv.* happening away from a particular place, especially the place where someone works: *an off-site meeting*

off·spring /ˈɔfˌsprɪŋ/ *n. plural* **offspring** [C] **1** BIOLOGY an animal's baby or babies **2** HUMOROUS someone's child or children [**Origin:** Old English *ofspring*, from *of* **off** + *springan* **to move suddenly**]

off·stage /ˌɔfˈsteɪdʒ◂/ *adv.* **1** ENG. LANG. ARTS just behind or to the side of a stage in a theater, where the people watching a play cannot see: *There was a loud crash offstage.* **2** when an actor is not acting: *Offstage, Peter was shy.* —**offstage** *adj.*

ˈoff-street *adj.* **off-street parking** places for parking that are not on main streets

ˌoff-the-ˈcuff *adj.* [usually before noun] an off-the-cuff remark, reply etc. is one that you make without thinking about it first —**off-the-cuff** *adv.*

ˌoff-the-ˈrack *adj.* off-the-rack clothes are not specially made to fit one particular person, but are made in standard sizes → see also MADE-TO-MEASURE, MADE-TO-ORDER —**off the rack** *adv.*: *I'm tall, so I have problems buying clothes off the rack.*

ˌoff-the-ˈrecord *adv.* if you say something off-the-record, you are saying things that are not official and are not supposed to be made public: *We were told off-the-record that the highway project would be canceled.* —**off-the-record** *adj.*: *an off-the-record briefing*

ˌoff-the-ˈshelf *adj., adv.* already made and available in stores, not specially made for a particular customer: *off-the-shelf database software*

ˌoff-the-ˈwall *adj.* INFORMAL a little strange or unusual, often in an amusing way: *an off-the-wall idea* | *his off-the-wall sense of humor*

off·track /ˌɔfˈtræk◂/ *adj.* away from a place where horses race: *offtrack betting*

ˌoff-ˈwhite *n.* [U] a color that is very close to white, but is not pure white —**off-white** *adj.*: *an off-white blouse*

ˈoff-year *n.* [C usually singular] **1** a year when something is not as successful as usual: **+for** *an off-year for car sales* **2** POLITICS a year in which no elections happen

ˌoff-year ˈelection, off year election *n.* [C] POLITICS an election to choose members of the SENATE and the HOUSE OF REPRESENTATIVES held in one of the years between elections for the American President SYN **midterm election**

oft /ɔft/ *adv.* POETIC OR FORMAL often: *an oft-quoted author*

of·ten /ˈɔfən, ˈɔftən/ S1 W1 *adv.* **1** if something happens often, or you do something often, it happens regularly or many times: *She often works on weekends.* | *If you wash your hair too often, it can get very dry.* | ***How often** do you go out to dinner?* | *We see my family **fairly often**.* | *I'm **not** home **very often** these days.* | ***It's not often that** a job like this comes along.*

THESAURUS

a lot INFORMAL: *He plays basketball a lot.*
frequently very often: *He's frequently late for work.*
regularly often and at regular times, for example every day, every week, or every month: *You should exercise regularly.*
repeatedly use this to emphasize that someone did something many times: *I asked him repeatedly to tell me what was wrong.*
constantly very often over a long period of time: *He seems to eat constantly.*
continuously without stopping: *A permanent resident is someone who has lived in the state continuously for a period of one year.*
again and again/over and over (again) many times, and more often than you would expect: *Fans of the show go to see it again and again.* | *I get bored doing the same thing over and over again.*
→ NEVER, RARELY, SOMETIMES

2 [sentence adverb] if something happens often, it happens in many situations or cases: *Headaches are often* *caused by stress.* | ***Very often*** *children who have trouble at school have problems at home.* **3 all too often** also **only too often** used to say that something sad, disappointing, or annoying happens too much: *This type of accident happens all too often.* **4 every so often** sometimes: *Every so often we go down to the beach.* **5 more often than not** also **as often as not** usually: *More often than not, she brings her kids along.* [**Origin:** 1200–1300 *oft*]

of·ten·times /ˈɔfənˌtaɪmz/ *adv.* often: *Oftentimes I have to wait more than twenty minutes for a bus.*

o·gle /ˈoʊgəl/ *v.* [I,T] to look at someone in an offensive way that shows you think they are sexually attractive

o·gre /ˈoʊgɚ/ *n.* [C] **1** a large ugly creature in children's stories who eats people **2** someone who seems cruel and frightening

OH the written abbreviation of OHIO

oh /oʊ/ *interjection* **1** used to express a strong emotion or to emphasize what you think about something: *Oh, what a great idea!* | *Oh, be quiet!* | ***Oh, no!*** *My purse is gone!* **2** used to make a slight pause, especially before replying to a question or giving your opinion about something: *"Nick's kind of weird." "Oh, I don't know. I think he's really nice."* | *She's worked there for, oh, around twelve years.* **3** used to get or keep someone's attention so that you can ask them a question or continue what you are saying: *Oh, and don't forget to turn off the lights.* **4 oh, did he?/are you?/was she?/really? etc.** used to show that you did not previously know what someone has just told you: *"Did you hear that Kay and Mike are dating?" "Oh, really?"* **5 oh well** used to express that you accept something bad that has happened: *Oh well, I guess we can try to have our picnic next weekend.* **6** another form of O

O·hi·o /oʊˈhaɪoʊ/ **1** WRITTEN ABBREVIATION **OH** a state in the Midwest of the U.S. **2 the Ohio** a long river in the central U.S.

ohm /oʊm/ *n.* [C] PHYSICS a unit of ELECTRICAL RESISTANCE, used to measure how easily an electric current flows through a material

Ohm's law /ˌoʊmz ˈlɔ/ PHYSICS a principle in PHYSICS that states that the VOLTAGE in an electric current can be calculated by multiplying the RESISTANCE by the current

-oid /ɔɪd/ *suffix* [in adjectives] TECHNICAL similar to something, or shaped like something: *humanoid* (=similar to humans) | *ovoid* (=egg shaped)

oil¹ /ɔɪl/ S1 W1 *n.* **1** [U] a smooth thick mineral liquid that is burned to produce heat, or used to make machines run easily: *Have the oil in your car changed regularly.* | *an oil-burning heating system* **2** [U] EARTH SCIENCE the thick dark liquid from under the ground from which oil and gasoline are produced SYN **petroleum**: *Oil prices rose significantly last month.* **3** [C,U] a smooth thick liquid made from plants or animals, used in cooking or for making beauty products: *Fry the chicken in a little oil.* | *Rub the oil gently into the skin.* | **vegetable/olive/peanut etc. oil** *a bottle of olive oil* **4 oils** [plural] ENG. LANG. ARTS paints that contain oil, used by artists SYN **oil paint**: *Mostly I paint* ***in oils.*** **5** [C] ENG. LANG. ARTS a painting done in oils [**Origin:** 1100–1200 Old French *oile*, from Latin *oleum* **olive oil**] → see also **burn the midnight oil** at BURN¹ (15)

oil² *v.* [T] to put oil into or onto something, such as a machine, in order to make it work more smoothly: *I oiled the hinges on the door.*

ˈoil-based *adj.* made with oil as the main substance: *oil-based paint*

ˈoil-ˌbearing *adj.* EARTH SCIENCE oil-bearing rock contains oil

oil·cloth /ˈɔɪlklɔθ/ *n.* [U] cloth treated with oil to give it a smooth surface

oiled /ɔɪld/ *adj.* covered with oil: *an oiled frying pan* → see also WELL-OILED

oil·field /ˈɔɪlfild/ *n.* [C] EARTH SCIENCE an area of land or water under which there is oil

ˈoil-fired *adj.* an oil-fired heating system burns oil to produce heat

oil·man /ˈɔɪlmən/ *n. plural* **oilmen** /-mən/ [C] someone who owns an oil company or works in the oil industry

ˈoil paint *n.* [C,U] paint that contains oil, used by artists

ˈoil ˌpainting *n.* ENG. LANG. ARTS **1** [C] a picture painted with oil paint **2** [U] the art of painting with oil paint

ˈoil pan *n.* [C] a part of an engine that holds the supply of oil

ˈoil ˌplatform *n.* [C] an oil rig

ˈoil rig *n.* [C] a large structure used for getting oil from under the ground or ocean

oil·skin /ˈɔɪl-skɪn/ *n.* **1** [U] cloth treated with oil so that water will not pass through it **2 oilskins** [plural] a coat and pants made of oilskin

ˈoil slick *n.* [C] a layer of oil floating on water, usually caused when oil accidentally pours out of a ship

ˈoil strike *n.* [C] a discovery of oil under the ground

ˈoil ˌtanker *n.* [C] a ship that has large containers for carrying oil

ˈoil well *n.* [C] a hole that is dug in the ground to obtain oil

oil·y /ˈɔɪli/ *adj. comparative* **oilier**, *superlative* **oiliest** **1** covered with oil or containing a lot of oil: *oily skin* | *oily fish* **2** looking or feeling like oil: *an oily liquid* **3** someone who is oily is polite and confident, but seems very insincere —**oiliness** *n.* [U]

oink /ɔɪŋk/ *interjection* used to represent the sound that a pig makes —**oink** *n.* [C]

oint·ment /ˈɔɪntˀmənt/ *n.* [C,U] a soft substance made of solid oil that you rub into your skin, especially as a medical treatment: *an ointment for burns* → see also **a fly in the ointment** at FLY² (8)

OJ *n.* [U] SPOKEN orange juice

O·jib·wa, Ojibway /oʊˈdʒɪbweɪ/ → CHIPPEWA

OK¹, okay /oʊˈkeɪ/ *adj.* SPOKEN **1** [not before noun] not sick, injured, unhappy etc.: *Are you OK?* | *Is your stomach OK?* **2** acceptable or satisfactory: *Are these clothes OK for the opera?* | *"I couldn't find the shampoo you wanted."* ***"That's okay."*** **3 (is it) OK...?** also **it's OK** used to ask if you can do something or to tell someone they can do it: *Is it OK if I borrow your umbrella?* | **it is OK for sb to do sth** *I don't know why it's OK for Ben to stay out late, but not for me.* | **it is OK with/by sb** *It's OK with me if we just stay home tonight.* **4** [not before noun] fairly good, but not extremely good: *The movie was OK, but the book was better.* **5** nice, helpful, honest etc.: *Dwight's OK. You can trust him.* —**OK** *adv.*: *I'm doing OK now.* | *Is your car running OK?*

OK², okay *interjection* **1** used when you start talking about something else, or when you pause before continuing: *OK, let's begin chapter six.* **2** used to express agreement or give permission: *"Do you want to go to the mall later?" "OK."* **3** used when you want to stop someone from arguing with you, saying angry things to you, or saying too much too quickly: *OK, so I made a mistake. I'm sorry.* **4** used as a question, to make sure that someone has understood you or that they agree with you: *Just don't tell anyone, OK?*

OK³, okay *v.* **OK's, OK'd, OK'ing** or **okays, okayed, okaying** [T] INFORMAL to say officially that you will agree to something or allow it to happen: *The plans have been okayed, so let's get started.*

OK⁴, okay *n.* **give (sb) the okay/get the okay** INFORMAL to give or get permission to do something: *We just got the OK to buy new books.*

OK⁵ the written abbreviation of OKLAHOMA

O'Keeffe /oʊˈkif/, **Geor·gia** /ˈdʒɔrdʒə/ (1887–1986) a U.S. artist known especially for her paintings of flowers and animal bones

O·ke·fe·no·kee /ˌoʊkɪfəˈnoʊki/ a large area of SWAMP land in the U.S. states of Georgia and Florida

o·key-doke /ˌoʊki ˈdoʊk/ also **okey-do·key** /-ˈdoʊki/ *adj., adv.* SPOKEN used like "okay" to express agreement

o·kie /ˈoʊki/ *n.* [C] **a)** INFORMAL a person from Oklahoma **b)** OLD-FASHIONED an offensive word for someone from Oklahoma who moved to California during the 1930s to try to find work

O

O·kla·ho·ma /ˌoʊkləˈhoʊmə/ WRITTEN ABBREVIATION **OK** a state in the central part of the U.S.

ˌOklahoma ˈCity the capital and largest city of the U.S. state of Oklahoma

o·kra /ˈoʊkrə/ *n.* [U] a green vegetable used in cooking, especially in Asia and the southern U.S.

old /oʊld/ S1 W1 *adj. comparative* **older**, *superlative* **oldest**

1 NOT NEW having existed for a long time, or having been used a lot before OPP **new**: *a pair of old shoes* | *a beat-up old car* | *As the building* ***got older****, the concrete became stained.* | **(as) old as the hills** (=extremely old)

THESAURUS

ancient used about buildings, cities, languages etc. that existed long ago: *ancient history* | *ancient cultures*
antique used about furniture, jewelry etc. that is old and valuable: *an antique chair*
vintage used about things that are old but of high quality: *vintage cars*
classic used about movies, books, television programs, and cars that are old but of very good quality: *Lumet's classic film "12 Angry Men"*
secondhand used about cars, books, clothes etc. that were owned by someone else and then sold: *secondhand textbooks*
used used about cars or other products which are being sold that are not new: *a used car dealer*
stale used about bread, cakes etc. that are no longer fresh: *The bread was stale.*
rotten used about food, especially fruit or eggs, that is no longer good to eat: *a rotten apple*
→ NEW, YOUNG

2 NOT YOUNG having lived for a long time OPP **young**: *an old woman* | *a beautiful old oak tree* | *I have two brothers, both older than me.* | **grow/get old** (=become old)

THESAURUS

elderly FORMAL used about old people, in order to be polite: *an elderly lady*
the elderly old people, used in order to be polite: *the care that is available for the elderly*
senior citizen someone who is more than 60 or 65 years old: *a discount for senior citizens*
the aged very old people: *health care for the aged*
old-timer INFORMAL an old person, especially a man: *A few old-timers sat watching the game.*

3 AGE used to talk about how long a person or thing has lived or existed: ***How old** is your cat?* | *Michelle is **older than** you.* | **too old (to do sth)** *She wanted to have a baby before she was too old.* | **old enough (to do sth)** *She's old enough to go to school on her own now.* | **3 months/two years/65 years etc. old** *Our house is about 90 years old.* | **four-day-old/six-week-old/50-year-old etc. sth** *a 30-year-old woman with short blonde hair* | *a six-week-old kitten*
4 FORMER [only before noun] used, known, or existing before, but not anymore: *our old car* | *We all liked the old teacher better.*
5 WELL KNOWN [only before noun] familiar and well known to you: *It was good to be back to the old routine.* | **an old friend/enemy** (=a friend or enemy you have known for a long time)
6 the old old people SYN **seniors** SYN **the elderly**
7 old flame someone with whom you used to have a romantic relationship

SPOKEN PHRASES

8 good/poor/silly etc. old sb used to talk to or about someone you like: *Good old Debbie! She always brings cookies.* | *The poor old cat didn't like it when we moved.*
9 good/big etc. old used with some adjectives, such as "big" and "old", to emphasize them: *We had a big old barbecue last weekend.*
10 the old... used to talk about something that you often use or are very familiar with: *I'll just turn off the old computer, and then I'll be ready.*
11 you old... used to show that you are surprised or amused by what someone has said or done: *Well you old devil! I didn't know you were dating her!*
12 a good old sth used to talk about something you enjoy: *We had a good old time at the reunion.*
13 any old thing/hat/place etc. used to say that it does not matter which thing, place etc. you choose: *Any old restaurant will do.* | *Oh, just wear any old thing.*
14 any old way/how any way: *You can wrap the presents any old way you want.*

15 be an old hand (at sth) to have a lot of experience of something: *Helms is an old hand at backroom politics.*
16 the old country the country that you were born in but do not live in anymore, used especially to mean Europe
17 sb is old enough to know better used to say that you think someone should have behaved more sensibly
18 for old times' sake if you do something for old times' sake, you do it to remind yourself of a happy time in the past
19 sb's old enough to be your father/mother DISAPPROVING used to say that someone is too old for someone to have a sexual relationship with
20 old wives' tale a belief based on old ideas that are now considered to be untrue
21 be old before your time to look or behave like someone much older than you
22 of old LITERARY from a long ago in the past: *heroes and kings of old*
23 Old English/Icelandic etc. an early form of the English, Icelandic etc. language
[**Origin:** Old English *eald*] → see also **the (good) old days** at DAY (5), **the old guard** at GUARD[1] (9), **the same old person/place/thing** at SAME[1] (2), **of/from the old school** at SCHOOL[1] (9), **it's the same old story** at STORY (9)

WORD CHOICE **older, elder**

You can use **older** to describe either people or things. **Elder** *(adj.)* is a more formal word that means the same thing, but it is only used to talk about people and is used in more formal writing: *As the verdict was read, the defendant's elder brother stared silently ahead.* **Older** can be used with **than**, but **elder** cannot: *Shane is older than Mark* (NOT *elder than*).

ˌold ˈage *n.* [U] the part of your life when you are old: *She's a little forgetful, but that comes with old age.* | *Even **in his old age**, Grandpa used to ride his bike.*

old-ˈboy ˌnetwork *n.* **the old-boy network** USUALLY DISAPPROVING the system by which men from rich families, men who went to the same school, belong to the same club etc., use their influence to help each other

old·e /ˈoʊldi/ *adj.* an old-fashioned spelling of old, used in the names of shops, products etc. to make them seem traditional: *ye olde tea shoppe*

old·en /ˈoʊldən/ *adj.* **in (the) olden days** also **in olden times** a long time ago: *People didn't travel so much in the olden days.*

Ol·den·burg /ˈoʊldnˌbɚg/**, Claes** /klɔs/ (1929–) a U.S. SCULPTOR, born in Sweden, famous for his large

SCULPTURES of ordinary objects, often made of soft materials

ˌOld English 'Sheepdog *n.* [C] a large dog with long thick gray and white hair

ˌold-'fashioned *adj.* **1** not modern, and not considered fashionable or interesting: *old-fashioned clothes* | *old-fashioned ideas about sex* | *Most of the students found the textbooks boring and old-fashioned.* **2** an old-fashioned machine, object, method etc. is one that is not generally used anymore because it has been replaced by something newer: *old-fashioned farming methods*

THESAURUS

outdated/out-of-date no longer useful or modern: *The equipment at the school is hopelessly outdated.* | *Because laws change constantly, the textbook may be out-of-date very quickly.*
dated looking old-fashioned: *The styles all looked somewhat dated.*

3 someone who is old-fashioned believes in ways of doing things that are not usual anymore: *her strict old-fashioned father* **4** not modern anymore, but in a way that people like because it is of good quality or it reminds them of the past: *Betty still bakes her own bread* ***the old-fashioned way.*** | *Her latest book is a* ***good old-fashioned*** *murder mystery.*

old fo•gey /ˌoʊld 'foʊgi/ *n. plural* **old fogeys** [C] INFORMAL someone who is boring and has old-fashioned ideas, especially someone old

'old ˌfolks *n.* [plural] INFORMAL an expression meaning "old people"

ˌold 'folks' ˌhome *n.* [C] INFORMAL a word for a RETIREMENT HOME or a NURSING HOME that may now be considered insulting by some older people

ˌOld 'Glory *n.* [U] the flag of the U.S.

ˌold 'hat *adj.* [not before noun] familiar or old-fashioned, and therefore boring: *The movie's special effects will be old hat to today's audience.*

old•ie /'oʊldi/ *n.* [C] INFORMAL someone or something that is old, especially an old movie or an old song or record → see also GOLDEN OLDIE

ˌold 'lady *n.* SPOKEN **sb's old lady a)** an expression for someone's wife or GIRLFRIEND, which many women think is offensive **b)** an expression for someone's mother, which some women may find offensive

ˌold 'maid *n.* [C] an insulting expression meaning a woman who has never married and is not young anymore

ˌold 'man *n.* [C] SPOKEN **sb's old man a)** someone's father **b)** someone's husband or BOYFRIEND

Old 'Master *n.* [C] a famous painter, especially from the 15th to 18th century, or a painting by one of these painters: *a priceless collection of Old Masters*

'old ˌmoney *n.* [U] money that has been in a family for years and that gives a family a high social position, or the families that have this type of money: *His wife comes from old money.* **—old-money** *adj.* → see also NOUVEAU RICHE

ˌOld 'Testament *n.* **the Old Testament** the first part of the Christian Bible, containing ancient Hebrew writings about the time before the birth of Jesus Christ → see also NEW TESTAMENT

ˌold 'timer *n.* [C] INFORMAL **1** someone who has been in a particular job, place etc. for a long time and knows a lot about it **2** an old man

ˌOld 'World *n.* **the Old World** the Eastern Hemisphere, especially Europe, Asia, and Africa → see also NEW WORLD

'old-world *adj.* [only before noun] an old-world place or quality is attractive because it is old or reminds you of the past: *the city's old-world charm*

ole /oʊl/ *adj.* a way of writing the word "old" to represent the way some people say it: *How's my ole friend Billy?*

o•le•ag•i•nous /ˌoʊli'ædʒənəs/ *adj.* **1** TECHNICAL containing, producing, or like oil **2** FORMAL behaving in an extremely polite or friendly way that is very insincere

o•le•an•der /'oʊliˌændɚ/ *n.* [C,U] a green bush with white, red, or pink flowers

ol•fac•to•ry /ɑl'fæktəri, oʊl-/ *adj.* BIOLOGY relating to the sense of smell

ol•i•gar•chy /'ɑləgɑrki/ *n. plural* **oligarchies** **1** [U] POLITICS government or control by a small group of people **2** [C usually singular] POLITICS a state governed by a small group of people, or the group who govern such a state **—oligarch** *n.* [C]

O

ol•i•gop•o•ly /ˌɑlə'gɑpəli/ *n.* [C] TECHNICAL the control of all or most of a business activity by very few companies, so that other organizations cannot easily compete with them

ol•ive /'ɑlɪv/ *n.* **1** [C] BIOLOGY a small bitter egg-shaped black or green fruit, used as food and for making oil: *Greek black olives* **2** [C] BIOLOGY a tree that produces this fruit, grown especially in Mediterranean countries **3** [U] a deep yellowish green color **4 olive skin/complexion** skin color that is typical in Mediterranean countries such as Greece, Italy, and Turkey **5 extend/present/offer etc. an olive branch** to do something to show that you want to end an argument **—olive** *adj.*

'Olive Branch Peˌtition, the HISTORY a letter written in 1775 by COLONISTS in America to the British king, George III, asking him to stop British forces fighting them so that disagreements between them and Britain could be dealt with peacefully

'olive drab *n.* [U] a grayish green color, used especially in military uniforms **—olive drab** *adj.*

ˌolive 'oil S3 *n.* [U] a pale yellow or green oil obtained from olives and used in cooking: *a vinegar and olive oil salad dressing*

O•liv•i•er /ə'lɪviˌeɪ/, **Laur•ence** /'lɔrəns/ (1907–1989) a British actor famous for directing and acting in movies of plays by Shakespeare

Ol•mec /'oʊlmɛk/ one of the people that lived in southeast Mexico from the 15th to the 10th century B.C.

-ologist /ɑlədʒɪst/ *suffix* [in nouns] a person who studies a particular science or subject: *a psychologist* | *a pathologist* (=who studies diseases) → see also -IST

-ology /ɑlədʒi/ *suffix* [in nouns] **1** the study of something, especially something scientific: *climatology* (=the study of CLIMATE) | *Egyptology* (=the study of ancient Egypt) **2** something that is being studied or described: *phraseology* (=the way someone uses words) | *a chronology* (=describing when, and in what order, things happened) **—-ological** /əlɑdʒɪkəl/ *suffix* [in adjectives] **—-ologically** /əlɑdʒɪkli/ *suffix* [in adverbs] → see also -LOGY

O•lym•pi•a /ə'lɪmpiə/ **1** the capital city of the U.S. state of Washington **2** an area of land and an ancient religious center in Greece, where the Olympic Games were held in ancient times

O•lym•pi•ad /ə'lɪmpiˌæd, oʊ-/ *n.* [C] **1** a particular occasion of the modern Olympic Games: *the 25th Olympiad* **2** an occasion when students compete against each other in subjects such as science, math, and knowledge: *the National Science Olympiad*

O•lym•pi•an¹ /ə'lɪmpiən/ *n.* [C] **1** someone who takes part in the Olympic Games: *former U.S. Olympian Pablo Morales* **2** one of the ancient Greek Gods

Olympian² *adj.* **1** like a god, especially by being calm or not concerned about ordinary things: *an Olympian figure* **2** relating to the ancient Greek gods

O•lym•pic /ə'lɪmpɪk/ *adj.* [only before noun] relating to or taking part in the Olympic Games: *the German Olympic team* | *the Olympic flag*

OˌIympic 'Games also **Olympics** *n.* [plural] **1** an international sports event held every four years in different countries **2** a sports event in ancient times, which was held at Olympia in Greece every four years

O·lym·pus /əˈlɪmpəs/ also **Mount Olympus** the highest mountain in Greece and, in Greek MYTHOLOGY, the place where the gods lived

O·ma·ha¹ /ˈoʊməˌhɑ, -ˌhɔ/ a city in the U.S. state of Nebraska

Omaha² a Native American tribe from the central area of the U.S.

O·man /oʊˈmɑn/ a country in the Middle East, southeast of Saudi Arabia and northeast of Yemen —**Omani** *n., adj.*

O·mar Khay·yám /ˌoʊmɑr kaɪˈyɑm / (?1048–?1123) a Persian mathematician and poet, famous in the West for his poem, the "Rubaiyat"

OMB → see OFFICE OF MANAGEMENT AND BUDGET

om·buds·man /ˈɑmbʊdzmən/ *n.* [C] someone who deals with complaints made by people against the government, banks, universities etc. [**Origin:** 1900–2000 Swedish **representative**, from Old Norse *umbothsmathr*, from *umboth* **commission** + *mathr* **man**]

o·me·ga /oʊˈmigə, -ˈmeɪgə/ *n.* [C] the last letter of the Greek alphabet

ome·let, omelette /ˈɑmlɪt/ *n.* [C] eggs mixed together and cooked in a pan, and then folded over cheese, vegetables etc.: *a cheese and mushroom omelet* [**Origin:** 1600–1700 French *omelette*, from Latin *lamella* **thin plate**]

o·men /ˈoʊmən/ *n.* [C] a sign of what will happen in the future: **a good/bad/ill etc. omen (for)** *The fog seemed like a bad omen to Sara.* | +**for** *a good omen for the future*

om·i·nous /ˈɑmənəs/ *adj.* making you feel that something bad is going to happen: *an ominous silence* —**ominously** *adv.*: *The sky looked ominously dark.*

o·mis·sion /oʊˈmɪʃən, ə-/ *n.* **1** [U] the act of not including or not doing something: **the omission of sth (from sth)** *The omission of her name from the list was accidental.* **2** [C] something that has been omitted: **a serious/major/notable omission** *There is one notable omission in the index.* | **a glaring omission** (=one that is very bad and easily noticed)

o·mit /oʊˈmɪt, ə-/ *v.* **omitted, omitting** [T] **1** to not include someone or something, either deliberately or because you forget to do it SYN **leave out**: *He omitted many details in his presentation.* | **omit sth from sth** *My daughter's name had been omitted from the list of honor students.* **2 omit to do sth** FORMAL to not do something, either because you forgot or deliberately: *Whittier omitted to mention exactly where he "found" the money.*

omni- /ɑmni/ *prefix* [in nouns and adjectives] every possible thing or place SYN **all**: *omniscient* (=knowing everything) | *omnivore* (=something that eats all kinds of food)

om·ni·bus¹ /ˈɑmnɪbəs/ *adj.* [only before noun] LAW an omnibus law contains several different laws collected together: *an omnibus civil rights bill*

omnibus² *n.* [C] **1** ENG. LANG. ARTS a book containing several stories, especially by one writer, which have already been printed separately **2** OLD USE a bus

om·nip·o·tent /ɑmˈnɪpətənt/ *adj.* able to do everything —**omnipotence** *n.* [U]: *God's omnipotence*

om·ni·pres·ent /ˌɑmnɪˈprɛzənt◂/ *adj.* present or seeming to be present everywhere at all times: *Police were virtually omnipresent on the city streets.* —**omnipresence** *n.* [U]

om·ni·scient /ɑmˈnɪʃənt/ *adj.* knowing or seeming to know everything: *the book's omniscient narrator* —**omniscience** *n.* [U]

omˌniscient point of ˈview *n.* [U] ENG. LANG. ARTS the style of telling a story in which the NARRATOR is not a character in the story but knows everything that happens and what all the characters experience, think, and feel → see also LIMITED POINT OF VIEW

om·ni·vore /ˈɑmnɪˌvɔr/ *n.* [C] BIOLOGY an animal that eats both plants and other animals

om·niv·o·rous /ɑmˈnɪvərəs/ *adj.* **1** BIOLOGY an animal that is omnivorous eats both meat and plants **2** FORMAL interested in everything and trying to gather all kinds of information: *an omnivorous reporter*

on¹ /ɔn, ɑn/ S1 W1 *prep.* **1** touching or supported by a particular surface OPP **off**: *Harry's the guy sitting on the sofa.* | *You've got some tomato sauce on your shirt.* | *Don't put your feet on my desk!* ►see THESAURUS box at **about¹** **2** printed, written, or somehow forming part of a page or other surface: *The answers are on page 350* | *a label with her name on it* | *Her picture is on the back of the book.* **3** hanging from, supported by, or attached to a particular thing: *Pictures of the family hung on the wall.* | *He hung his jacket on a hook.* | *It's not easy to skate on one foot.* **4** in a particular place, building, area of land etc.: *Our office is on the third floor.* | *Didn't Jim grow up on a farm?* **5** in a particular road or street: *Stephen lives on Crescent Drive.* | *a store on Main Street* **6** next to the side of something such as a road, river, or border SYN **by**: *a small town on the Mississippi* | *a hotel on the highway* **7** affecting or relating to someone or something: *a tax on gasoline* | *his influence on young people* **8** used to show the day or date when something happens: *On Thursday, I'll go on vacation.* | *My birthday's on April 29.* **9** in a particular position or direction in relation to something: *The school is on your left.* **10** about a particular subject SYN **about** SYN **concerning** SYN **regarding**: *a book on China* | *Could you give some advice on what to wear?* **11** in or into a large vehicle such as a bus, train, ship, or plane: *the passengers on the bus* | *I got on the first flight to Chicago.* → see also **on foot** at FOOT¹ (3) **12** in or into a position of riding a horse, bicycle, or MOTORCYCLES: *police officers on motorcycles* | *She jumped on her horse.* → see also **on horseback** at HORSEBACK (1) **13** used to say what object has caused injury or damage: *I cut my hand on a piece of glass.* **14** used to say what part of someone or something is hit or touched: *Matt kissed her on the cheek.* **15** included in a list: *My name wasn't on the list.* **16** used to talk about the expression that someone shows with their face: *She had a big smile on her face.* **17** used to say that the piece of equipment that someone uses to do something: *Did you make these graphs on a computer?* | *The kids spend hours on the Internet.* | *We talk* ***on the phone*** *every day.* **18** used to say in what form information, music etc. is stored or recorded: *The movie is now available on video and DVD.* | *She has the interview on tape.* **19** used to say what food someone eats in order to live, what FUEL something uses in order to operate etc.: *They live mainly on beans and rice.* | *Most buses run on diesel.* **20** regularly taking a particular drug or medicine: *I'm now on a different antibiotic.* **21** using a particular amount of money or money from a particular person or thing for buying the things that you need in order to live: *No one can live on $10 a week.* | *The family is now on welfare.* **22** being broadcast by television or radio, or made available on the Internet: *The movie is on Channel 9.* | **on TV/television** *We've seen him on TV.* | *We heard the news* ***on the radio.*** | *The photograph has been posted* ***on the Internet.*** **23** during a trip, vacation etc., or while you are doing an activity: *We met on a tour of Europe.* | *Could you stop by the store on your way home?* | *I never drink when I'm on duty.* **24** used to say that someone is a member of a team, organization etc.: *Hal's on the swim team this year.* **25** used to talk about the point that has been reached in a process: *I stopped reading on page 53.* **26** looking or pointing toward someone or something: *His eyes were on the stranger in the doorway.* **27** FORMAL immediately after something has happened or after someone has done something SYN **upon**: *On arrival at reception, guests are greeted with champagne.* | **on doing sth** *What was your reaction on seeing him?* **28** playing a musical instrument: *He played a short piece on the piano.* **29 have/carry etc. sth on you** INFORMAL to have a particular thing in your pocket, your bag etc.: *Do you have a pen on you?* **30** used to show how you spend, save, make, or lose money: *We saved $10 on the price by booking early.* | *How much do you spend* *on food?* **31** SPOKEN used to say that someone will pay for something such as a drink or a meal: *Dinner's on me tonight.* **32** as a result of someone's order, request, or advice: *I accepted the offer on the advice of my lawyer.* **33** INFORMAL used to show that someone or something causes you problems, for example if a machine stops working while you are using it: *Then the phone just went dead on me.* **34 what is sb on?** SPOKEN, INFORMAL used to say that you think someone is behaving in a strange or silly way: *"She thinks he loves her." "What is she on?"* [**Origin:** Old English]

on² S1 W1 *adj., adv.* [not before noun] **1** used to show that someone continues to do something or something continues to happen: *I decided to read on until the end of the chapter.* | **go/carry on** *Go on. I'm listening.* | **go/keep/carry on doing sth** *The dog just kept on barking.* | *We can't go on spending money we don't have.* | *He talked **on and on** in that dull boring voice.* **2** if you walk, drive etc. on, you continue on your trip or go toward a particular place: *We drove on toward Chicago.* | *I sent Dan on ahead to find us seats at the theater.* **3** used to say that something happens at a time that is before or after another time: **earlier/later on** *He didn't realize how this would affect him later on in life.* | ***From then on**, things have improved.* | ***From that day on**, we've never been apart.* | ***From now on**, I want you to call if you're going to be late.* **4** if you have something on, you are wearing it: *Rick was standing there with nothing on.* | ***Put** your shoes **on**, and let's go.* **5** a machine, piece of equipment etc. that is on is working or operating OPP **off**: *OK, who left the lights on?* | ***Turn on** the radio. I want to hear the sports scores.* **6** in or into a bus, train, aircraft etc.: *The driver wouldn't let me on.* **7** in or into a position of riding a horse, bicycle, or MOTORCYCLE: *Get on and I'll give you a ride home.* **8** in or into a position of covering something or being on top of it OPP **off**: *Put the lid back on.* **9** if a movie, TV program etc. is on, it is being broadcast or shown at a theater: *There's a good comedy on at eight.* **10** if an event is on, it has been arranged and it is happening or will happen: *As far as we know, the game is still on for tomorrow.* | *You should visit Chicago while the festival is on.* **11 on and off** also **off and on** for short periods but not regularly, over a long period of time: *It rained on and off for the whole afternoon.* **12 you're on!** SPOKEN, INFORMAL used to accept something such as a BET or an offer: *"I bet you $20 he won't come." "You're on!"* **13** if an actor is on, they are performing, especially on a stage: *You're on in two minutes.* **14** used to say when someone is working, or when they start to work: *not on again until two tomorrow.* → see also HEAD-ON, ONTO

ˈon-air *adj.* [only before noun] broadcast while actually happening: *an on-air interview*

O·nas·sis /oʊˈnæsɪs/, **Jac·que·line Ken·ne·dy** /ˈdʒækəlɪn ˈkɛnədi/ (1929–1994) the wife of President John Kennedy, and later of Aristotle Onassis, known for being very beautiful and fashionable

on·board /ˌɔnˈbɔrd◂ / *adj.* [only before noun] carried on a ship, in a car etc.: *an onboard motor* —**onboard** *adv.*

once¹ /wʌns/ S1 W1 *adv.*
1 ONE TIME on one occasion, or at one time: *I've only worn this dress once.* | *They'd met **once before** at a party.* | *He's threatened me **more than once**.*
2 once a week/month/year etc. one time every week, month etc. as a regular activity: *Staff meetings take place once a week.*
3 once every three weeks/two months/five years etc. one time in every period of three weeks, two months etc. as a regular activity or event: *She sends a bill once every six months.*
4 (every) once in a while sometimes, but not often: *I only see her every once in a while at school.*
5 once more/again a) one more time SYN **again**: *He kissed her once more and moved toward the door.* **b)** used to say that a situation changes back to its previous state SYN **again**: *Everyone had left and the house was quiet once again.* **c)** FORMAL used before you repeat something that you said before: *Once again, I'd like to thank everyone for coming tonight.*
6 at once a) at the same time, together: *I can't do two things at once!* | *We were angry, ashamed, and afraid all at once.* **b)** FORMAL immediately, or without delay: *Come here at once!*
7 IN THE PAST at some time in the past, but not now: *They had once been close friends.* | **once-great/once-beautiful/once-powerful etc.** *The once-elegant city was now a war zone.*
8 EVER used with negatives, in questions, and after "if" to mean "ever" or "at all": *I never once saw him get angry or upset.*
9 for once used to say that something which is happening is rare or unusual, especially if you think it should happen more often: *Just for once, let me make my own decision.* | *For once I agree with him.*
10 once and for all definitely and finally: *Let's settle this matter once and for all.*
11 (just) this once SPOKEN used to emphasize that this is the only time you will let someone do something, ask someone to do something etc.: *OK, you can stay up till 11, but just this once.*
12 all at once suddenly: *All at once the trailer started shaking.*
13 once upon a time a) a phrase meaning "a long time ago," used at the beginning of children's stories **b)** at a time in the past that you think was much better than now: *Once upon a time children did what they were told.*
14 once or twice a few times, but not often: *The same thing had happened once or twice before.*
15 once in a blue moon INFORMAL very rarely: *We go out to eat once in a blue moon.*
16 do sth once too often to do something until you make someone angry or until you are finally caught, hurt etc.: *He tried that trick once too often.*
17 once is enough SPOKEN used to say that after you have done something one time you do not need or want to do it again
18 once a..., always a... SPOKEN used to say that people stay the same and cannot change the way they behave and think: *Once a thief, always a thief.*
19 once bitten, twice shy used to say that people will not do something again if it has been a bad experience

once² S1 W3 *conjunction* just after something happens, or from the moment that something happens: *I called Lara once he'd left.*

ˈonce-over *n.* **give sb/sth a/the once-over** to look at someone or something quickly to check who they are or what they are like: *Give your car the once-over before you leave on your trip.*

on·col·o·gy /ɑŋˈkɑlədʒi/ *n.* [U] the part of medical science that deals with TUMORS and CANCER [**Origin:** 1800–1900 Greek *onkos* **mass**] —**oncologist** *n.* [C]

on·com·ing /ˈɔnˌkʌmɪŋ/ *adj.* [only before noun] coming toward you: *oncoming traffic*

on-ˈdeck ˌcircle *n.* [C] the place where a baseball player stands when he or she is the next person who is going to try to hit the ball

one¹ /wʌn/ S1 W1 *number* **1** 1 **2** one o'clock: *I have a meeting **at one**.* **3 one or two** INFORMAL a small number of people or things: *There are one or two things to do before I leave.* **4 a thousand/million and one things** INFORMAL a large number of things **5 one-armed/one-eyed/one-legged etc.** having only one arm, eye, leg etc.

one² S1 W1 *pron.* **1** used to talk about a person or thing of a type that has already been mentioned or is known about: *If you don't have a camera, buy one.* | *We missed the bus and had to take a later one.* | *one large room and two smaller ones* **2** used to talk about a specific person or thing in a group: *The houses are all pretty similar, but one is a little bigger.* | **+of** *This is one of my favorite books.* | **one of the best/biggest/most important etc.** *It was one of the best experiences of my life.* | *I've spoken to **every one of** them.* | **this/that one** *I like all the pictures except this one.* | *Jane's **the one** with red hair.* **3** used to talk about a single person or thing: *She ate three cupcakes, but I ate **only one**.* | *We need **one more** to make up a team.* | ***Not one** of them escaped.* **4** used to talk about a person of a particular type: **a**

smart/cool/cruel etc. one *She's a nasty one – watch out.* | **the lucky/guilty/quiet etc. ones** *I was one of the lucky ones.* **5 one by one** first one person or thing, then another, then another, and so on, separately, rather than all together: *One by one, the children were lifted onto the truck.* **6 one after the other** also **one after another** if events or actions happen one after the other, they happen without much time between them: *The problems came one after the other.* **7 (all) in one** if someone or something is many different things all in one, they are all of those things: *It's a TV, radio, and DVD player all in one.* **8 one of these days** at some time in the future: *One of these days I'm going to clean out the garage.* **9 sb is the one** SPOKEN used to say that someone is the person that you will marry: *I know I just met him, but I think he's the one.* **10 sb/sth is the one** SPOKEN used to say that someone or something is the best, the winner, or the most appropriate **11** FORMAL used to mean people in general, including yourself: *One can never be too careful.* **12 I, for one,...** used to emphasize that you are doing something, believe something etc. and hope others will do the same: *I, for one, am proud of the team's effort.* **13 ...for one** used to give an example of someone or something: *"Who's going to help you clean up?" "Well, you for one."* **14** SPOKEN a joke or humorous story: *That's **a good one**.* | *Did you hear **the one about** the two-headed sailor?* **15 one up (on sb)** in a position of having an advantage over someone → see also ONE-UPMANSHIP **16 the one that got away** someone or something good that you almost had or that almost happened, but did not **17 be/feel at one with sb/sth** to feel very calm or relaxed in the situation or environment you are in: *A spiritual journey helps you be at one with life.* **18 have had one too many** INFORMAL to have drunk too much alcohol **19 have one for the road** INFORMAL to have a last alcoholic drink before you leave a place **20 as one** if many people do something as one, they all do it at the same time: *The whole team stood up as one.* **21 a hard one/an easy one etc.** a particular kind of problem or question: *213 divided by 12? That's a tricky one.* **22 one for the books** INFORMAL something very unusual, surprising, or special **23 one and the same** the same person or thing: *These two theories are in fact one and the same.* **24 not/never be one to do sth** INFORMAL to never do a particular thing, because it is not part of your character to do it: *Tom is not one to show his emotions.* **25 not/never be one for sth** INFORMAL to not enjoy a particular activity, subject etc.: *I've never really been one for lying around on beaches.* **26 one of the family** someone who is accepted as a member of a particular group of people: *I always felt like one of the family.* **27 one of us** SPOKEN used to say that someone belongs to the same group as you, or has the same ideas, beliefs etc.: *You can trust him – he's one of us.* **28 one of the boys/girls** INFORMAL someone who is accepted and treated as one of an all-male or all-female group **29 one and all** OLD-FASHIONED everyone: *Come and join us, one and all!* **30 the little/young ones** OLD-FASHIONED children, especially young children → see also **it takes one to know one** at KNOW[1] (67), ONE-ON-ONE, ONE-TO-ONE

USAGE

In informal spoken English, people often say **these ones** or **those ones**: *Give me those ones back, and I'll give you these ones.* But in more formal or written English, it is better not to use **ones**: *Give me those back, and I'll give you these.*

GRAMMAR

When **one** is the subject of the sentence, the verb is singular, even when a plural noun comes just before the verb: *One of the girls wants to be a doctor* (NOT *One of the girls want to be a doctor*).

one³ S1 *determiner* **1** used before a noun to emphasize a particular person or thing: *If there's one thing I hate, it's rudeness.* **2 one day/afternoon etc. a)** a particular day, afternoon etc. in the past: *It happened one day last summer.* **b)** any day, afternoon etc. in the future: *One day I hope to return the favor.* **3** used to talk about one person or thing in comparison with similar people or things: *A method that works for one person may not work for another.* | ***It's one thing to** see the plans on paper, **but it's another thing to** see the buildings completed.* **4 for one thing** INFORMAL used to introduce the first of several reasons: *We didn't buy it. For one thing, it was too expensive.* **5** SPOKEN used to emphasize your description of someone or something: *That is one cute kid!* **6** FORMAL used before the name of someone who you do not know well: *The car belongs to one Joseph Nelson.* [**Origin:** Old English *an*]

one⁴ *adj.* [only before noun] **1** used to emphasize that there are no others SYN **only**: *You're the one person I can trust.* | *My one worry is that she'll decide to leave college.* **2** used to talk about a particular single person or thing: *We won't all be able to fit in the one car.* **3 one and only a)** used to emphasize that someone is very special or admired: ***the one and only** Frank Sinatra* **b)** used to emphasize that something is the only one of its kind: *the architect's one and only significant achievement*

one⁵ *n.* [C] **1** a piece of paper money worth $1: *Do you have any ones?* **2 in ones and twos** if people do something in ones and twos, they do it on their own or in small groups: *Guests arrived in ones and twos.*

ˌone anˈother *pron.* used to show that each of two or more people does something to the other or others: *Many witnesses contradicted one another.* → see Word Choice box at EACH OTHER

ˌone-armed ˈbandit *n.* [C] a machine with a long handle, into which you put money in order to try to win more money SYN **slot machine**

ˌone-diˈmensional *adj.* **1** DISAPPROVING too simple and not considering or showing all the parts of something: *the novel's boring one-dimensional characters* **2** TECHNICAL in math, existing in only one DIMENSION

ˈone-horse *adj.* **1 a one-horse town** INFORMAL a small and boring town **2** pulled by one horse: *a one-horse carriage*

O·nei·da /oʊˈnaɪdə/ a Native American tribe from the northeastern area of the U.S.

O'Neill /oʊˈnil/, **Eu·gene** /yuˈdʒin/ (1888–1953) a U.S. writer of plays

ˌone-ˈliner *n.* [C] a very short joke or humorous remark

ˈone-man *adj.* [only before noun] performed, operated, done etc. by one man: *a one-man show* | *a one-man crusade to ban the film*

ˌone-man ˈband *n.* [C] **1** ENG. LANG. ARTS a street musician who plays several instruments at the same time **2** INFORMAL an organization in which one person does everything

one·ness /ˈwʌn-nɪs/ *n.* [U] a peaceful feeling of being part of a whole: +**with** *oneness with nature*

ˌone-night ˈstand *n.* [C] **1** INFORMAL **a)** an occasion when two people have sex, but do not intend to meet each other again **b)** a person that you have sex with once and do not see again **2** a performance that is given only once in a particular place

ˌone-of-a-ˈkind *adj.* very special because there is nothing or no one else similar: *one-of-a-kind handmade carpets*

ˌone-on-ˈone *adj.* between only two people: *Kids need one-on-one attention.* —**one-on-one** *adv.*: *He was speaking one-on-one with a member of the press.*

ˌone-parent ˈfamily *n.* [C] a family in which there is only one parent who takes care of the children

ˌone-party ˈsystem *n.* [C] POLITICS the political system in a country where there is only one political party

ˈone percent ˌmilk *n.* [U] milk that has had cream removed so that 1% of what remains is fat → see also SKIM MILK, TWO PERCENT MILK, WHOLE MILK

ˈone-piece *adj.* [only before noun] consisting of only one piece, not separate parts: *a one-piece bathing suit*

ˌone-resource eˈconomy *n.* [C] ECONOMICS the economic system of a country that gets money mainly from selling one substance or crop

on·er·ous /ˈɑnərəs, ˈoʊ-/ *adj.* FORMAL onerous work or responsibilities are difficult and worrying or make you tired: *an onerous but necessary task*

one·self /wʌnˈsɛlf/ *pron.* FORMAL **1** [relexive form of "one"] used for showing that, when you are speaking about people in general, an action affects the person who does it: *Mandel stresses the importance of being able to defend oneself.* **2** used to say that a person does something without anyone else helping or being involved, when the subject is "one": *One can usually manage to do simple jobs oneself.*

ˈone-shot *adj.* [only before noun] happening or done only once: *This is a* ***one-shot deal.***

ˌone-ˈsided *adj.* **1** considering or showing only one side of a question, subject etc. in a way that is unfair: *one-sided views* **2** a one-sided activity or competition is one in which one person or team is much stronger than the other: *a one-sided victory* **3** a one-sided relationship is one in which one person shows more love or does more work than the other —**one-sidedness** *n.* [U] —**one-sidedly** *adv.*

ˌone-size-fits-ˈall *adj.* **1** one-size-fits-all clothing is designed so that people of many different sizes can wear it: *one-size-fits-all dresses* **2** designed to please or be appropriate for many different people, sometimes with the result that it is good for no one: *a one-size-fits-all public education program*

ˈone-stop *adj.* **1 one-stop shopping** a situation in which you can buy many different products and do many different activities all in one place **2 a one-stop store/center etc.** a place where you can buy many different things, get many kinds of information etc.

one·time, onetime /ˈwʌntaɪm/ *adj.* [only before noun] **1** former: *the onetime owner of the club* **2** happening only once: *a onetime fee of $5*

ˌone-to-ˈone *adj.* [only before noun] **1** between only two people: *one-to-one counseling* **2** matching each other exactly: *The two currencies were exchanged* ***on a one-to-one basis.***

ˌone-track ˈmind *n.* **have a one-track mind** to be continuously thinking about one particular thing, especially sex: *That guy has a one-track mind.*

ˌone-ˈtwo also **ˌone-ˈtwo ˌpunch** *n.* [C] **1** a movement in which a BOXER hits his opponent with one hand and then quickly with the other **2** a combination of two bad things happening one after the other

one-ˈup *v.* [T] INFORMAL to try to make yourself seem better than someone else: *The two sisters were always trying to one-up each other.*

one-up·man·ship /ˌwʌn ˈʌpmənˌʃɪp/ *n.* [U] attempts to make yourself seem better than other people, no matter what they do

ˌone-ˈway *adj.* [usually before noun] **1** moving or allowing movement in only one direction: *one-way traffic* | *a one-way street* **2** a one-way ticket is for traveling from one place to another but not back again → see also ROUND-TRIP **3** a one-way process, relationship etc. is one in which only one person makes any effort

ˌone-way ˈmirror *n.* [C] a mirror that can be used as a window by people secretly watching from the other side of it

ˈone-ˌwoman *adj.* [only before a noun] performed, operated, done etc. by only one woman: *a one-woman show*

on·go·ing /ˈɔnˌgoʊɪŋ/ Ac *adj.* [usually before noun] continuing, or continuing to develop: *ongoing negotiations* → see also **go on** at GO[1]

on·ion /ˈʌnyən/ S2 W3 *n.* [C,U] a round vegetable with brownish or reddish skin and many white layers inside, which has a strong taste and smell [**Origin:** 1100–1200 Old French *oignon*, from Latin *unio*]

ˈonion dome *n.* [C] a round pointed roof that is shaped like an onion, which is common on Russian churches

ˈonion ring *n.* [C] a piece of onion in the form of a ring that is covered in BATTER and fried (FRY)

on·line, on-line /ˌɔnˈlaɪn◂/ *adj.* COMPUTERS **1** connected to other computers through the Internet, or available through the Internet: *All the city's schools will be online by the end of the year.* | *online banking* **2** using the Internet: *Are you online? I want to look something up.* **3** directly connected to or controlled by a computer: *an online printer* —**online** *adv.*: *The reports are not available online yet.* → see also OFFLINE

on·look·er /ˈɔnˌlʊkɚ/ *n.* [C] someone who watches something happening without being involved in it: *A crowd of onlookers gathered at the scene of the accident.*

on·ly[1] /ˈoʊnli/ S1 W1 *adv.* **1** used to emphasize that a particular amount, number, distance etc. is small: *Becky was only three when she started to read.* | *We need five chairs, but we only have three.* **2** nothing or no one except the thing or person mentioned: *Of course you're cold. You're only wearing a T-shirt.* | *Only Denny got all six answers right.* | *The restrooms are for customers only.* | **men-only/women-only etc.** *a women-only health club* **3** in one place, situation, or way and no other, or for one reason and no other: *These flowers grow only in Hawaii.* | *She'll lend us the car,* ***but only if*** *I drive.* | *I* ***only*** *did it* ***because*** *I thought you wanted me to.* **4** not better, worse, or more important than someone or something: *He's only a beginner.* | *I was only joking.* **5** no earlier than a particular time: *I only got here last night.* | *It was* ***only then*** (=at that moment and not before) *that I realized he was lying.* **6 only just** a very short time ago: *We've* ***only just begun*** *to understand how serious the situation is.* **7 if only a)** used to give a reason for something, although you think it is not a good one: *Just call her, if only to say you're sorry.* **b)** used to express a strong wish: *If only I could be 15 again!* **8 only too well/happy/willing etc.** very or completely well, happy etc.: *Scott was only too happy to tell the story.* **9 only to find/learn/discover etc.** used to say that someone did something, with a disappointing or surprising result: *We arrived at the airport only to find that the plane had already left.*

SPOKEN PHRASES

10 I only wish/hope used to express a strong wish or hope: *I only wish I knew how I could help.* **11 only so many/much** used to say that there is a limited amount or quantity of something: *There's only so much one person can do alone.* **12 sb'll/sth'll only do sth** used to talk about the bad effect of something: *Don't interfere – you'll only make things worse.* **13 you only have to read sth/look at sth etc.** used to say that it is easy to realize that something is true because you can see or hear things that prove it: *Of course she's in love. You only have to look at her face.* **14 I can only assume/suppose etc.** used to say that you can think of one explanation for something surprising or disappointing and no other: *I can only assume that it was a mistake.*

→ see also **only have eyes for sb** at EYE[1] (37), **not only...but (also)** at NOT (4)

GRAMMAR

The meaning of a sentence can change depending on where you use **only**. To make the meaning of your sentence clear, it is best to put **only** directly before the word it describes: *Only Paul saw the lion* (=no one except Paul saw it). | *Paul only saw the lion* (=he saw it, but he did not do anything else to it, such as touch it). | *Paul saw only the lion* (=the lion was the only animal he saw).

only[2] S1 W1 *adj.* [only before noun] **1 the/sb's only** used to say that there is one person, thing, or group in a particular situation and no others: *I was the only woman in the room.* | *The only food in the house was a box of crackers.* | *My only reason for leaving was boredom.* | *That book was* ***the only one*** *she wrote.* **2 the only** used to say that someone or something is the best and you would not choose any other: *She's the only person for this job.* | *Flying is really the only way to go.* **3 an only child** a child who has no brother or sisters **4 the only thing is...** SPOKEN used when you are going to mention a problem or disadvantage about something:

It's a great apartment. The only thing is it's a little expensive. → see also **one and only** at ONE[4] (3)

only[3] S3 *conjunction* INFORMAL used like "but" to introduce the reason why something is not possible: *I'd offer to help, only I'm kind of busy right now.*

on·o·mat·o·poe·ia /ˌɑnəmɑt̬əˈpiə/ *n.* [U] ENG. LANG. ARTS the use of words that sound like the thing that they are describing, like "hiss" or "boom" —**onomatopoeic** *adj.*

O

On·on·da·ga /ˌɑnənˈdɑgə, -ˈdɔgə/ a Native American tribe from the northeastern area of the U.S.

ˈon-ramp *n.* [C] a road for driving onto a HIGHWAY or FREEWAY → see also OFF-RAMP

on·rush /ˈɔnrʌʃ/ *n.* [singular] **1** a strong fast movement forward: **+of** *an onrush of people* **2** the sudden development of something —**onrushing** *adj.*

ˌon-ˈscreen, onscreen *adj.* **1** appearing, happening etc. in a movie or on television, rather than in real life: *her on-screen husband* **2** COMPUTERS appearing on the screen of a computer or television: *an on-screen menu* —**on-screen** *adv.*

on·set /ˈɔnsɛt/ *n.* **1 the onset of sth** the beginning of something, especially something bad: *the onset of winter* | *symptoms **at the onset of** the infection* **2** [C] ENG. LANG. ARTS the CONSONANT sound or sounds that come before a vowel in a SYLLABLE, for example "tr" in "track"

on·shore /ˌɔnˈʃɔr◂/ *adj.* [only before noun] **1** on or near the land rather than in the ocean: *onshore oil reserves* **2** moving toward the land: *strong onshore winds* —**onshore** *adv.*

ˈon-ˌsite, on·site *adj.* [only before noun] done at the place where something happens: *on-site parking* → see also **on site** at SITE[1] (4)

on·slaught /ˈɑnslɔt/ *n.* [C] **1** a very strong attack: **+on/against** *The rebels launched a full-scale onslaught on the capital.* **2** a lot of criticism, opposition etc. all at one time, which causes great problems for someone: *a massive propaganda onslaught* | **+of** *The president faced an onslaught of accusations.* **3** the forceful effect of extreme weather [**Origin:** 1600–1700 Dutch *aanslag* **act of striking**; influenced by *slaught* **slaughter** (13–17 centuries)]

on·stage /ˌɔnˈsteɪdʒ◂/ *adj., adv.* happening or performing on a stage in front of a group of people: *I get nervous whenever I **go onstage**.*

ˌon-ˈstream *adv.* in operation or ready to begin operation: *Another reactor is scheduled to go on-stream in January.* —**on-stream** *adj.*

On·ta·ri·o /ɑnˈtɛriˌoʊ/ a PROVINCE in the east of central Canada

Ontario, Lake the smallest of the five Great Lakes on the border between the U.S. and Canada

ˈon-the-job *adj.* [only before noun] while working, or at work: *on-the-job training*

ˈon-the-spot *adj.* [only before noun] happening or done where someone is at the time they are there: *on-the-spot repairs to the car* → see also **on the spot** at SPOT[1] (6)

on·to, on to /ˈɔnt̬ə, ˈɑn-; *strong* ˈɔntu, ˈɑn-/ S2 W2 *prep.* **1** used to show movement to a position of being on a surface, area, or object: *The cat jumped onto my knee.* | *Sara stepped carefully onto the ice.* **2** used to say that someone or something is added to form part of something: *She was voted onto the committee.* | *How did my name get onto your list?* **3** used to say that something is attached to something else: *The board had been screwed onto the wall.* **4 be onto sb** INFORMAL to know who did something wrong or illegal: *He's scared. He knows we're onto him.* **5 be onto something** also **be onto a good thing, be onto a winner** INFORMAL to have produced or discovered something interesting or unusual that will give you many advantages: *We knew we were onto something big.* **6 look/open etc. onto sth** used to say that a room, door, or window faces toward a place or allows you to get to a place: *The dining room looks out onto a pretty garden.* → see also ON

on·tog·e·ny /ɑnˈtɑdʒəni/ *n.* [U] BIOLOGY the development of a single living thing from the FERTILIZED egg to the adult, especially compared to the development of a SPECIES or other group over a long period of time → see also PHYLOGENY

on·tol·o·gy /ɑnˈtɑlədʒi/ *n.* [U] a subject of study in PHILOSOPHY that is concerned with the nature of existence —**ontological** /ˌɑnt̬əˈlɑdʒɪkəl/ *adj.*

o·nus /ˈoʊnəs/ *n.* **the onus** the responsibility for something: **the onus is on sb (to do sth)** *The onus is on consumers to pay for these services.* [**Origin:** 1600–1700 Latin **load**]

on·ward[1] /ˈɔnwəd/ also **onwards** *adv.* **1 from...onward** beginning at a particular time and continuing from then: *Farmers expect good crops from April onward.* **2** forward: *The ship sailed onward through the fog.* **3 onward and upward** used to describe a situation in which someone continues to succeed

onward[2] *adj.* [only before noun] **1** moving forward or continuing: *tickets for onward travel* **2** developing over a period of time: *the onward march of scientific progress*

on·yx /ˈɑnɪks/ *n.* [U] EARTH SCIENCE a stone with lines of different colors in it, often used in jewelry

oo·dles /ˈudlz/ *n.* [plural] INFORMAL a large amount of something: **+of** *They've got oodles of money.*

oof /uf/ *interjection* the sound that you make when you have been hit, especially in the stomach

ooh[1] /u/ *interjection* said when you think something is very beautiful, bad, surprising etc.: *Ooh. Nice dress, Carol.*

ooh[2] *v.* [I] INFORMAL to make the sound "ooh" when you think something is beautiful, surprising etc.: *The crowd **oohed and aahed** at the fireworks.* —**ooh** *n.* [C usually plural]: *oohs and ahs*

ooh la la /ˌu lɑ ˈlɑ/ *interjection* HUMOROUS said when you think that something or someone is surprising, unusual, or sexually attractive

oomph /ʊmf/ *n.* [U] INFORMAL energy or excitement

oops /ʊps, ups/ *interjection* said when you have fallen, dropped something, or made a small mistake: *Oops. I hit the wrong button.*

ˈoops-a-ˌdaisy *interjection* said when someone has fallen, especially a child

ooze[1] /uz/ *v.* **1** [I always + adv./prep., T] if a liquid oozes from something or if something oozes a liquid, the liquid flows out very slowly: *The cut was oozing blood.* | **+from/out of/through** *Melted cheese oozed from the ravioli.* ▸see THESAURUS box at **flow**[1], **pour** **2** [I,T] to clearly show a particular quality or feeling, so that it is very easy to notice: *He oozes charm.* | **+from/out of** *Confidence just oozed out of her.*

ooze[2] *n.* **1** [U] very soft mud, especially at the bottom of a lake or the ocean **2** [singular] a very slow flow of liquid

ooz·y /ˈuzi/ *adj.* INFORMAL soft and wet like mud

Op. the written abbreviation of OPUS

o·pac·i·ty /oʊˈpæsət̬i/ *n.* [U] **1** the quality of being difficult to understand **2** the quality of being difficult to see through → see also OPAQUE

o·pal /ˈoʊpəl/ *n.* [C,U] EARTH SCIENCE a type of white stone with changing colors in it, or a piece of this stone used in jewelry

o·pal·es·cent /ˌoʊpəˈlɛsənt/ *adj.* having colors that shine and seem to change: *an opalescent blue-green* —**opalescence** *n.* [U]

o·paque /oʊˈpeɪk/ *adj.* **1** opaque glass, liquid, or other substances are too thick or too dark to see through: *huge opaque clouds* **2** opaqe speech or writing is difficult to understand [**Origin:** 1400–1500 Latin *opacus* **dark**] → see also OPACITY, TRANSLUCENT, TRANSPARENT (1) —**opaqueness** *n.* [U]

op art /ˈɑp ɑrt/ *n.* [U] a form of art using patterns that seem to move or to produce other shapes as you look at them

op. cit. /ˌɑp ˈsɪt/ an abbreviation used in formal writing to REFER to a book that has been mentioned already

OPEC /ˈoʊpɛk/ *n.* [U] **Organization of Petroleum Exporting Countries** an organization of countries that produce and sell oil, which sets the price of the oil

op-ed /ˌɑp ˈɛd/ *adj.* [only before noun] relating to the page in a newspaper that has articles containing opinions on various interesting subjects: *the op-ed page*

o·pen¹ /ˈoʊpən/ S1 W1 *adj.*
1 DOOR/CONTAINER a) not closed, so that things, people, air etc. can go in and out or be put in and out OPP **closed** OPP **shut**: *an open window* | *Why is that drawer open?* | *She left the door **wide open*** (=completely open). | **fly/blow/burst etc. open** *The door flew open and Harry rushed in.* | **push/slide/force etc. sth open** *In the end, the police had to force the door open.* | **tear/rip sth open** *Mac took the envelope and tore it open.* **b)** not locked SYN **unlocked** OPP **locked**: *Come on in – the door's open.* ►see THESAURUS box at **honest**
2 EYES/MOUTH not closed: *The nurse held the child's mouth open.* | *She stared at the man with her eyes **wide open**.*
3 STORE/BANK ETC. [not before noun] if a place is open, for example a store, bank, school, park etc. visitors, customers etc. can come in OPP **closed**: *What hours is the bank open?* | *The restaurant has been open for a few weeks now.* | *The corner store **stays open** till midnight.* | *The store was **open for business** again the day after the robbery.*
4 AVAILABLE TO ALL available to everyone in a particular group, so that they can all take part: *open admission to the college* | **+to** *Few jobs were open to women then.* | *All conference events are **open to the public*** (=anyone can attend). | *He **threw** the meeting **open to** his colleagues for questions and comments.*
5 NOT BLOCKED if a road, border, line of communication etc. is open, it is not blocked and it can be used: *The border is now open again.* | *The highway remained open, despite all the snow.*
6 NOT ENCLOSED [only before noun] not enclosed or restricted by buildings, walls etc.: *an open staircase* | *He grew up in the **wide open spaces** of Australia.* | *They spent the day out driving **on the open road**.* | *The play will be performed **in the open air*** (=outdoors). | **the open sea** (=part of the ocean that is far from any land) → see also **in the open** at OPEN³, OPEN-AIR, OPEN SPACE
7 NOT COVERED without a roof or cover: *an open carriage* | *an open sewer* | **open to the sky/elements** (=without a roof)
8 an open wound/sore etc. a wound that has not HEALed and is not covered
9 SPREAD APART spread apart instead of closed, curled over, folded etc.: *A book lay open on the table.* | *At night the flowers were open.* | *Johnson raised an open hand.*
10 CLOTHES not fastened: *His shirt was open at the collar.*
11 CLEARLY SHOWN [only before noun] open actions, feelings, intentions etc. are not hidden or secret: *There was open hostility between the two families.* → see also OPEN SECRET
12 HONEST honest and not wanting to hide any facts from other people: *frank and open discussions* | **+with** *She was very open with me.*
13 NOT SECRET not hiding information from the public: *the need for more open government* | *Some of the memos were shown **in open court*** (=in a court of law where everything is public).
14 NOT YET DECIDED needing more discussion or thought before a decision can be made: *The matter remains an **open question**.* | **open to discussion/negotiation/interpretation etc.** *The price is open to negotiation.* → see also **keep/leave your options open** at OPTION (2)
15 NOT FINISHED if a case, investigation etc. is still open, it has not yet been settled or finished OPP **closed**: *The police say they are keeping the case open.*
16 COMPETITION if a competition or race is open, it is not certain who will win it: *The men's 100-meter race is **wide open**.*
17 be open to suggestions/help/offers etc. to be ready to consider people's suggestions, help, or offers: *We are always open to suggestions for improvements.*
18 have/keep an open mind to deliberately not make a decision or form a definite opinion about something
19 open to criticism/blame/suspicion etc. likely to be criticized, blamed etc.: *By accepting the money Bass has **left himself wide open to** criticism.*
20 be open to question/doubt if something is open to question or doubt, you are not sure if it is good, true, likely to succeed etc.: *The authenticity of the relics is open to doubt.*
21 OPPORTUNITY if an opportunity or possible action is open to someone, they have the chance to do it: **+to** *She has a right to know about all the options open to her.*
22 JOB [not before noun] a job that is open is available: *Is the position still open?*
23 be an open book to not have any secrets and be easily understood: *I'd always thought of Jeff as an open book.*
24 keep your eyes/ears open to keep looking or listening so that you will notice anything that is important, dangerous etc.
25 TIME [not before noun] if a time is open, nothing has been planned for that time: *I'm sorry, but the doctor doesn't have anything open this afternoon.*
26 an open marriage/relationship a marriage or relationship in which both partners have agreed that they are free to have sexual relationships with other people
27 welcome/greet sb with open arms to show that you are very pleased to see someone
28 be (wide) open for/to sth to be ready for a particular activity or willing to accept it: *Siberia is wide open for development.*
29 SPORTS not guarded or blocked by someone else so that you can easily catch a ball that is thrown to you
30 an open invitation a) an invitation to visit someone whenever you like **b)** something that makes it easier for someone to do something illegal or bad: *An unlocked car is an open invitation to thieves.*
31 open weave/texture cloth with an open weave or TEXTURE has wide spaces between the threads
[**Origin:** Old English] → see also **keep an eye open/peeled** at EYE¹ (7), OPEN-EYED

open

The back door opened onto the patio.

open² S1 W1 *v.*
1 DOOR/WINDOW ETC. [I,T] to move a door, window etc. so that people, things, air etc. can pass through, or to be moved in this way OPP **close** OPP **shut**: *Will you open the door for me?* | *I can't get this drawer to open.*
2 CONTAINER/PACKAGE [I,T] to unfasten or remove the lid, top, or cover of a container, package etc., or to be unfastened, uncovered etc. in this way: *Should I open another bottle of wine?* | *The children were opening their presents.* | *The suitcase wouldn't open.*

THESAURUS

unlock to open a door, drawer, box etc. with a key
unscrew to open a lid on a bottle, container etc. by turning it
unwrap to open a package by removing the paper that covers it
unfasten/undo to make something no longer fastened or tied, for example a seat belt or a piece of clothing

O

3 EYES a) [I,T] if you open your eyes or your eyes open, your EYELIDS rise so that you can see **b) open sb's eyes (to sth)** to make someone realize something that they had not realized before: *The project has opened teachers' eyes to this problem.*
4 MOUTH [I,T] if you open your mouth or your mouth opens, your lips move apart
5 BUSINESS TIME [I] if a store, bank, public building etc. opens at a particular time, it begins to let customers or visitors come in at that time OPP **close**: *What time does the bank open?*
6 START A BUSINESS [I,T] if a new business such as a store or restaurant opens or is opened, it starts operating SYN **open up** OPP **close**: *The pool will open again in the spring.* | *Runyan plans to open a casino.*
7 START AN ACTIVITY a) [I,T] to start an event, series of actions etc., or to be started in a particular way: *Tonight's concert opens a two-week festival.* | +**with** *The story opens with the family's arrival in Boston.* **b) open an inquiry/investigation** to start a process of collecting information about something: *The police have opened an investigation into the causes of his death.*
8 SPREAD/UNFOLD [I,T] to spread something out, or to become spread out: *Open your books to page 63.* | *How do you open this umbrella?* | *The rosebuds are starting to open.*
9 COMPUTER [T] to make a document or computer PROGRAM ready to use: *Click on this icon to open your File Manager.*
10 OPEN A WAY THROUGH [T] to make it possible for cars, goods etc. to pass through a place OPP **close**: *They're plowing the snow to open the road to Aspen.* | *The two countries opened their borders again after the war.*
11 MOVIE/PLAY ETC. [I] to start being shown to people: *The movie opens locally on Friday.*
12 open fire (on sb) to start shooting at someone or something
13 open sth to the public to let people come and visit a house, park etc.: *Glenn plans to open the museum to the public later this year.*
14 open an account to start an account at a bank or other financial organization by putting money into it
15 OFFICIAL CEREMONY [T] to perform a ceremony in which you officially state that a building is ready to be used: *The new airport will be officially opened by the mayor himself.*
16 open your arms a) to stretch your arms wide apart, especially to show that you want to hold someone **b)** to welcome someone or treat them very kindly: *Local people opened their arms to the earthquake victims.*
17 open the door to sth also **open the way for sth** to provide an opportunity for something to happen: *Today's ruling could open the way to a large number of new lawsuits.*
18 open doors (for/to sb) to give someone an opportunity to do something: *A college education can really open doors for you.*
19 open your mind to sth to be ready to consider or accept new ideas
20 open your heart (to sb) to tell someone your real thoughts and feelings because you trust them
21 open old wounds to remind someone of bad things that happened in the past: *Seeing my ex-boyfriend opened some old wounds.*
22 the heavens/skies open used to say that it starts to rain heavily → see also **open the floodgates** at FLOODGATE (1)

open onto/into sth *phr. v.* if a room, door etc. opens onto or into another place, you can enter the other place directly through it: *The kitchen opens onto a patio.*

open out *phr. v.* if a road, river, valley etc. opens out, it becomes wider

open up *phr. v.*
1 OPPORTUNITY open sth ↔ up to become available or possible, or to make something available or possible: *New opportunities are opening up all the time.* | *Education opens up all kinds of career choices.*
2 LAND open sth ↔ up if someone opens up a country or area of land, or if it opens up, it becomes easier to reach and ready for development, trade etc.: *China continues to open up to the West.* | *The new ferry service has opened the island up to tourism.*
3 TALK open yourself up to stop being shy, and talk freely about your thoughts or feelings: +**to** *It took Martha several weeks to open up to her therapist.*
4 START A BUSINESS open sth ↔ up if a store, restaurant etc. opens up or is opened up, someone starts it: *There's a new supermarket opening up in our neighborhood.*
5 DOOR/ROOM/CONTAINER open sth ↔ up to open a door or something such as a box or case: *Open up, we know you're in there.* | *Could you open up the suitcase, please?*
6 START A DISAGREEMENT open sth up if you open up a disagreement or DIVISION between people, or if it opens up, it begins: *The affair has opened up a rift between the two countries.*
7 MEDICAL OPERATION open sb up INFORMAL to cut open someone's body to perform a medical operation
8 open up a debate/discussion etc. to start a discussion
9 open yourself up to attack/criticism etc. to do something that makes it possible for other people to attack you, criticize you etc.
10 HOLE/CRACK if a hole or crack opens up, it appears and becomes wider
11 WITH A GUN to start shooting

open[3] S3 *n.* **1 in the open a)** outdoors without any shelter or protection: *We slept out in the open.* **b)** not hidden or secret: *By now the whole affair was in the open.* | *The argument **brought** a lot of problems **out into the open.*** **2** [C usually singular] a sports competition that both professional players and AMATEURS can compete in: *the U.S. Open*

ˌopen-ˈair *adj.* [only before noun] happening or existing outdoors, not in a building: *an open-air market*

ˌopen-and-shut ˈcase *n.* [C usually singular] something such as a law CASE that is very easy to prove and will not take long to solve

ˌopen ˈbar *n.* [C] a bar at an occasion such as a wedding, where drinks are served free

ˌopen ˈcirculatory ˌsystem *n.* [C] BIOLOGY a system in which blood in the body is not contained in blood VESSELS, but instead empties from vessels into a connected system of SINUSES (=spaces surrounding an organ) so that the body TISSUES receive oxygen and NUTRIENTS directly → see also CLOSED CIRCULATORY SYSTEM

ˌopen ˈdoor ˌpolicy *n.* [C] **1** the principle of allowing people and goods to move freely into your country **2** the principle of allowing anyone to come and talk to you while you are working **3 Open Door Policy** HISTORY the American principle of allowing equal trading rights in China among the U.S., Japan, and European countries at the end of the 19th century

ˌopen-ˈended *adj.* **1** without a definite ending: *an open-ended commitment* **2** not having a single, definite answer, result etc.: *an open-ended question*

o·pen·er /ˈoʊpənɚ/ *n.* [C] **1** a tool or machine used to open letters, bottles, or cans: *an electric can opener* **2** the first of a series of things such as sports competitions: *the team's season opener* **3 for openers** INFORMAL **a)** as a beginning or first stage **b)** used to give one reason, explanation, or idea, although there are others you might mention later SYN **for starters** → see also EYE-OPENER

ˌopen-ˈeyed *adj., adv.* **1** awake, or with your eyes open **2** accepting or taking notice of all the facts of a situation: *clear open-eyed reasoning*

ˌopen-faced ˈsandwich *n.* [C] a single piece of bread with meat, cheese etc. on top

ˌopen-ˈhanded *adj.* **1** done with an open hand: *an open-handed slap* **2** generous and friendly OPP tight-fisted —**openhandedness** *n.* [U]

ˌopen-ˈhearted *adj.* kind and sympathetic

ˌopen-heart ˈsurgery *n.* [U] a medical operation in which doctors operate on someone's heart, while a special machine keeps the person's blood flowing

ˌopen ˈhouse *n.* [C] **1** an occasion when a college, factory, or organization allows the public to come in and see the work that is done there **2** an occasion on which someone who is selling their house lets everyone who is interested in buying it come to see it **3** a party at someone's house that you can come to or leave at any time during a particular period

o·pen·ing[1] /ˈoʊpənɪŋ/ *n.* **1** [C] an occasion when a new business, building, road etc. starts working or being used: +**of** *the opening of the new library* | *Tonight's* ***the grand opening.*** **2** [C] a hole or space in something through which air, light, objects etc. can pass: +**in** *a narrow opening in the fence* **3** [C] a job or position that is available: +**for** *The department has two openings for accountants.* **4** [C usually singular] the beginning or first part of something: *the play's exciting opening* | +**of** *the opening of the trial* **5** [C] a good chance for someone to do or say something: **an opening to do sth** *I waited for an opening to give my opinion.* **6** [U] the act of opening something: +**of** *the opening of Christmas presents*

opening[2] *adj.* [only before noun] first or beginning: *the opening round of the tournament*

ˈopening ˌhours *n.* [plural] the hours during which a store, office etc. is open to the public

ˌopening ˈnight *n.* [C] the first night that a new play, movie etc. is shown to the public

ˈopening time *n.* [C] the time when a store, office etc. opens to the public

ˌopen ˈletter *n.* [C] a letter to an important person, which is printed in a newspaper or magazine so that everyone can read it, usually in order to protest about something

o·pen·ly /ˈoʊpənli/ *adv.* in a way that does not hide your feelings, opinions, or the facts: *Sarah talked openly about her problems.* | *He was openly critical of his colleagues.*

ˌopen ˈmarket *n.* **1** [C usually singular] a type of economic system in which there are few laws and controls restricting the buying and selling of goods with other countries **2 on the open market** available for sale publicly, not privately or secretly: *The buildings will be sold on the open market.* **3** [C] an outdoor area in a city where things can be bought and sold by anyone —**open-market** *adj.*: *the open-market price*

ˌopen ˈmike *n.* [U] a time when anyone is allowed to tell jokes, sing etc. in a bar or NIGHTCLUB —**open-mike** *adj.* [only after noun] *open-mike night*

ˌopen-ˈminded *adj.* APPROVING willing to consider and accept other people's ideas, opinions etc. OPP closed-minded: *an open-minded attitude* —**openmindedly** *adv.* —**openmindedness** *n.* [U] → see also NARROW-MINDED

ˌopen-ˈmouthed *adj., adv.* with your mouth open, especially because you are very surprised or shocked: *The taxi driver stared at him open-mouthed.*

ˌopen-ˈnecked *adj.* an open-necked shirt is one on which the top button has not been fastened

o·pen·ness /ˈoʊpən-nɪs/ *n.* [U] **1** the quality of being honest and not keeping things secret: *a relationship based on trust and openness* **2** the quality of being willing to accept new ideas or people: +**to** *openness to change* **3** the quality of being open and not enclosed: +**of** *the openness of the city's downtown area*

ˌopen-ˈplan *adj.* an open-plan office, school etc. does not have walls dividing it into separate rooms

ˌopen ˈprimary *n.* [C] POLITICS in the U.S., a PRIMARY election in which voters can vote for CANDIDATES from one party only, but the voters do not have to be members of any party → see also BLANKET PRIMARY

ˈopen ˌseason *n.* [singular] **1** the period of time each year when it is legal to kill certain animals or fish as a sport: +**for/on** *open season for ducks* **2 open season (on sb)** a time when a lot of people take the opportunity to criticize someone: *In the press, it seems to be open season on the administration.*

ˌopen ˈsecret *n.* [C] something that is supposed to be a secret but is actually known by everyone

ˌopen ˈsentence *n.* [C] MATH an EQUATION containing one or more VARIABLES. It is called "open" because until its variables are given values, it cannot be proved true or false.

ˌopen ˈsesame *n.* [singular] a fast way to achieve something that is very difficult: +**to** *He discovered that having wealth wasn't an open sesame to gaining respect.*

ˌopen ˈshop *n.* [C] a business such as a factory where EMPLOYEES do not have to be members of a UNION in order to work there → see also CLOSED SHOP

ˌopen ˈspace *n.* [C,U] land on which people are not allowed to build houses, buildings etc. because it is officially protected by a government, especially so that people can use it for outdoor activities

ˈopen ˌsystem *n.* [C] COMPUTERS a computer system that is made so that it can be connected with similar computer systems or parts made by other companies —**open-system** *adj.*

ˌopen-ˈtoed *adj.* **open-toed sandals/shoes** shoes that do not cover the top or end of your toes

ˌopen ˈvowel *n.* [C] ENG. LANG. ARTS a vowel that is pronounced with your tongue flat on the bottom of your mouth

op·era /ˈɑprə, ˈɑpərə/ S3 *n.* ENG. LANG. ARTS **1** [C] a musical play in which the words are sung rather than spoken: *an Italian opera* | *We try to* ***go to the opera*** (=go to a performance of an opera) *a few times a year.* ►see THESAURUS box at **theater** **2** [U] these plays considered as a form of art: *Do you enjoy opera?* **3** [C] a group that performs opera, or the building in which they perform: *the Metropolitan Opera* [**Origin:** 1600–1700 Italian, Latin, **works**, plural of *opus*] —**operatic** /ˌɑpəˈræṭɪk/ *adj.* —**operatically** /-kli/ *adv.* → see also COMIC OPERA, GRAND OPERA, OPERETTA, SOAP OPERA

op·er·a·ble /ˈɑprəbəl/ *adj.* an operable medical condition can be treated by an operation OPP inoperable

ˈopera ˌglasses *n.* [plural] a pair of special small BINOCULARS used at the theater so that you can see the stage more clearly

ˈopera house *n.* [C] a theater where operas are performed

op·e·rant con·di·tion·ing /ˈɑpərənt kənˌdɪʃənɪŋ/ *n.* [U] BIOLOGY a way of changing or improving behavior, in which a particular type of behavior is either encouraged by a reward or not encouraged using a negative experience each time it takes place

op·er·ate /ˈɑpəˌreɪt/ S2 W1 *v.*
1 MACHINES a) [T] to use and control a machine or piece of equipment: *A team of three men operate the dam.* | *Do you know how to operate the air conditioning?* **b)** [I always + adv./prep.] if a machine operates in a particular way, it works in that way SYN work SYN function: *Our generator doesn't operate well in cold weather.*
2 BUSINESS [I,T] to organize a business, service, or activity, or to carry out your business or activities in a particular way: *The company operates fast-food restaurants in over 60 countries.* | +**as** *The company will operate as a subsidiary of IBM.*
3 DO SURGERY [I] MEDICINE to cut open someone's body in order to remove or repair a part that is damaged: *Doctors had to operate to remove the bullet.* | +**on** *The surgeon operated on Taylor's knee.*
4 SYSTEM [I] if a system or process operates in a particular way, it works in that way and has particular results

O

SYN work SYN function: *The system is now operating much more efficiently.*
5 DO YOUR JOB [I always + adv./prep.] to do your job or try to achieve things in a particular way SYN work SYN function: *Alice operates on her own time schedule.*
6 POLICE/MILITARY ETC. [I] if people, such as soldiers, police, criminals etc., are operating in an area, they are working in that area
7 HAVE AN EFFECT [I] FORMAL to have an effect on something
[**Origin:** 1600–1700 Latin, past participle of *operari* **to work**]

O

'operating ˌbudget *n.* [C] ECONOMICS money spent on the general running of a business, rather than the money spent on producing goods or providing a service

'operating ˌcost *n.* [C usually plural] ECONOMICS the money a business spends regularly in order to operate a machine, factory, business, or store SYN running cost

'operating exˌpenses *n.* [plural] the money that you have to spend to keep a business going, such as paying for rent and office supplies

'operating room ABBREVIATION **OR** *n.* [C] a room in a hospital where operations are done

'operating ˌsystem ABBREVIATION **OS** *n.* [C] COMPUTERS a system in a computer that helps all the programs in it work together

'operating ˌtable *n.* [C] a special table that you lie on to have a medical operation

op·er·a·tion /ˌɑpəˈreɪʃən/ S3 W1 *n.*
1 MEDICAL [C] MEDICINE the process of cutting into someone's body to repair or remove a part that is damaged: *a throat operation* | **have/undergo an operation (on sth)** *Dan had an operation on his left hip.* | *It took three hours for doctors to* ***perform the operation***.
2 BUSINESS a) [C] a business, company, or organization, especially one with many parts: *a profitable data storage operation* **b)** [C,U] the work or activities done by a business, organization etc., or the process of doing this work: *Many small businesses fail in the first year of operation.* | *the company's day-to-day operations* | *The chain has over 200 stores* ***in operation***.
3 ORGANIZED ACTIONS [C] a set of planned actions, especially done by a large group of people, to achieve a particular purpose: *a rescue operation* | *a U.N. peacekeeping operation* | *an* ***undercover FBI operation***
4 MACHINE/EQUIPMENT [U] the way the parts of a machine or piece of equipment work together, or the process of making a machine work: *The device has a single button, allowing for easy operation.* | *Only seven of the 17 furnaces are* ***in operation*** (=working).
5 PRINCIPLE/LAW/PLAN ETC. [U] the way that something such as a law, system, or process works and has an effect: *the operation of the laws of gravity* | *New immigration controls will be* ***in operation*** *by next January.* | *The U.S. Parcel Post system first* ***went into operation*** (=started operating) *in 1913.*
6 COMPUTERS [C] an action done by a computer: *The new chip can process millions of operations per second.*
7 operations [plural] the part of a business or organization that controls the planning and practical running of its work: *the director of operations*

op·er·a·tion·al /ˌɑpəˈreɪʃənl/ *adj.* **1** [usually after noun] working and ready to be used: *The new airport is now* ***fully operational***. **2** [only before noun] POLITICS related to the operation of a business, government etc.: *an increase in operational efficiency* —**operationally** *adv.*

ˌOperation 'Overlord HISTORY the secret name given by the ALLIES to the World War II military operation that began on D-DAY (=the day when American, British, and other armies landed in France, on June 6, 1944)

op·er·a·tive¹ /ˈɑpərət̬ɪv/ *adj.* **1 the operative word** used when you repeat a word from a previous statement to emphasize its importance: *The new system offers fast solutions. "Fast" being the operative word.* **2** working and having an effect OPP inoperative: *Old trading restrictions are no longer operative.*

operative² *n.* [C] **1** POLITICS someone who does secret work, especially for a government organization: *a CIA operative* **2** TECHNICAL a worker, especially one who has a practical skill: *factory workers and similar operatives*

op·er·a·tor /ˈɑpəˌreɪt̬ɚ/ S3 W3 *n.* [C] **1** someone who works on a telephone SWITCHBOARD, who you can call to get information or to get help: *Dial "0" to get the operator.* **2** someone who operates a machine or piece of equipment: *an elevator operator* **3** a person or company that operates a particular business: *a tour operator* **4** DISAPPROVING someone who is good at getting what they want by persuading people: *a political operator* | *The former governor is seen* ***a smooth operator*** *who does favors for his friends.*

op·e·ret·ta /ˌɑpəˈrɛt̬ə/ *n.* [C] a short or romantic musical play in which some of the words are spoken and some are sung → see also MUSICAL, OPERA

op·e·ron /ˈɑpəˌrɑn/ *n.* [C] BIOLOGY a group of GENES found only in BACTERIA that operate together to control the production of a specific PROTEIN and decide its structure

oph·thal·mi·a /ɑfˈθælmiə, ɑp-/ *n.* [U] TECHNICAL a disease that affects the eyes and makes them red and swollen

oph·thal·mic /ɑfˈθælmɪk, ɑp-/ *adj.* [only before noun] MEDICINE related to the eyes and the diseases that affect them: *an ophthalmic surgeon*

oph·thal·mol·o·gist /ˌɑfθəlˈmɑlədʒɪst/ *n.* [C] TECHNICAL a doctor who treats people's eyes and does operations on them → see also OPTOMETRIST

oph·thal·mol·o·gy /ˌɑfθəlˈmɑlədʒi/ *n.* [U] MEDICINE the study of the eyes and diseases that affect them

o·pi·ate /ˈoʊpiət, -eɪt/ *n.* [C] a type of drug that contains OPIUM and makes you sleepy

o·pine /oʊˈpaɪn/ *v.* [T + that] FORMAL to express your opinion

o·pin·ion /əˈpɪnyən/ S2 W1 *n.* **1** [C] your ideas or beliefs about a particular subject: +**about/on** *I'd love to hear her opinion on all this.* | +**of** *My opinion of him has changed over the years.* | **give/express/offer an opinion** (=say what you think about something) | *We* ***asked*** *people their* ***opinion*** *about marriage.*

THESAURUS

view your opinion about something: *You cannot punish someone for expressing their views on a controversial subject.*
point of view a particular way of thinking about or judging something: *The story is told from the man's point-of-view.*
position used especially about the opinion of a government or organization: *The president has made his position perfectly clear.*
attitude your opinions and feelings about something: *a disrespectful attitude toward authority*

2 [U] the general ideas or beliefs that a group of people have about something: *The general opinion is that she's guilty.* | **public/popular opinion** *Politicians should listen more to public opinion.* **3** [C] judgment or advice from a professional person about something: *an expert opinion* | *We got* ***a second opinion*** (=advice from a second person to make sure the first was right) *before we replaced our furnace.* **4 have a high/low/bad etc. opinion of sb/sth** to think that someone or something is very good or very bad: *I've always had a good opinion of Rick's artwork.* **5 in my opinion** also **if you want my opinion** used to firmly tell someone what you think about a particular subject: *In my opinion, taxes are far too low.* **6 be of the opinion (that)** FORMAL to think that something is true: *We were all of the opinion that her treatment was unfair.* [**Origin:** 1300–1400 French, Latin *opinio*] → see also **difference of opinion** at DIFFERENCE (5), **sth is a matter of opinion** at MATTER¹ (4)

o·pin·ion·at·ed /əˈpɪnyəˌneɪt̬ɪd/ *adj.* expressing very strong opinions, and sure that your opinions are always right: *an opinionated young man*

o'pinion-ˌmakers *n.* [plural] people who have great influence over the way the public thinks

o'pinion ˌpoll *n.* [C] POLITICS a POLL

o·pi·um /'oʊpiəm/ *n.* [U] a powerful illegal drug made from POPPY seeds, that used to be used legally to stop pain, and that is used for making HEROIN

o·pos·sum /ə'pɑsəm/ also **possum** *n.* [C] one of various small animals from America and Australia that has fur and climbs trees and often pretends it is dead when it is in danger

opp. the written abbreviation of OPPOSITE

Op·pen·hei·mer /'ɑpənˌhaɪmɚ/, **J. Robert** /dʒeɪ 'rɑbɚt/ (1904–1967) a U.S. PHYSICIST who led the Manhattan Project to develop the first ATOMIC BOMB

op·po·nent /ə'poʊnənt/ W2 *n.* [C] **1** a person or group who tries to defeat another person or group in a competition, game, fight, election etc.: *Carson is Seymour's main opponent for the Senate seat.* **2** someone who disagrees with a plan, idea etc., and wants to try and stop it: +**of** *an outspoken opponent of the death penalty*

op·por·tune /ˌɑpɚ'tun/ *adj.* FORMAL **1 an opportune moment/time/place etc.** a time that is very appropriate for doing something OPP **inopportune**: *I was waiting for an opportune moment to tell her the news.* **2** done or said at a very appropriate time OPP **inopportune**: *her opportune arrival* —**opportunely** *adv.*

op·por·tun·ism /ˌɑpɚ'tunɪzəm/ *n.* [U] DISAPPROVING the practice of using every chance to gain power or advantages for yourself, without caring if you have to use dishonest methods: *His support for minority rights looks like political opportunism.*

op·por·tun·ist /ˌɑpɚ'tunɪst/ *n.* [C] DISAPPROVING someone who uses every chance to gain power or advantages, even if they have to use dishonest methods: *an unethical opportunist* —**opportunist** *adj.*: *the union's opportunist leadership*

op·por·tun·is·tic /ˌɑpɚtu'nɪstɪk/ *adj.* **1** typical of an opportunist: *an opportunistic change of loyalties* **2 an opportunistic infection/disease/virus** MEDICINE an illness that affects your body when it is weak and cannot fight diseases —**opportunistically** /-kli/ *adv.*

op·por·tu·ni·ty /ˌɑpɚ'tunəṭi/ S2 W1 *n. plural* **opportunities** **1** [C] a chance to do something, or an occasion when it is easy for you to do something SYN **chance**: *investment opportunities in China* | **an opportunity to do sth** *I hope we have an opportunity to discuss this later.* | +**for** *It seemed like a great opportunity for making money.* | *The party* ***gave*** *him* ***the opportunity*** *to see Donna again.* | *I'd like to* ***take this opportunity to*** (=use this chance to) *thank my staff for their hard work.* | *Drama classes* ***provide an opportunity*** *for children to express themselves.* | *His children seem to get into trouble* ***at every opportunity*** (=whenever they have the chance to do it). | **at the first/earliest opportunity** (=as soon as possible) **2** [U] chances to do something, in general: **opportunity to do sth** *There will be plenty of opportunity to ask questions after the talk.* | **ample/little opportunity** *She had had little opportunity to rest.* **3** [C] a chance to get a job: *career opportunities* | +**for** *There are fewer opportunities for new graduates this year.* → see also **equal opportunities** at EQUAL[1] (3) **4 opportunity knocks** used to say that someone gets the chance to do something → see also **window of opportunity** at WINDOW (3)

oppor'tunity ˌcost *n.* [U] ECONOMICS the cost to a business that results from a decision to do something or produce something. For example, if a company has to close a factory in one town in order to pay for a bigger factory in a different town, the opportunity cost is the value of what would be produced by the factory that has closed.

opˌposable 'thumb *n.* [C] BIOLOGY a thumb like that of people or MONKEYS, that can be used for holding things

op·pose /ə'poʊz/ S2 W2 *v.* [T] **1** to disagree with something such as a plan or idea and try to prevent it from happening or succeeding OPP **support**: *Many people opposed the new law.* **2** [usually passive] to fight or compete against another person or group in a battle, competition, or election: *He will be opposed by two other candidates.* [**Origin:** 1300–1400 French *opposer*, from Latin *opponere*]

op·posed /ə'poʊzd/ *adj.* [not before noun] **1 be opposed to sth** disagreeing with a plan, a type of behavior etc., or feeling that it is wrong: *I'm opposed to the death penalty.* | **strongly/firmly/bitterly etc. opposed** *He was strongly opposed to the legalization of marijuana.* **2 as opposed to sth** used to compare two different things and show that you mean one and not the other: *Students discuss ideas, as opposed to just copying from books.* → see also **diametrically opposed/opposite** at DIAMETRICALLY

op·pos·ing /ə'poʊzɪŋ/ *adj.* [only before noun] **1** opposing teams, groups, forces etc. are competing, arguing, or fighting against each other: *The group has split into two opposing factions.* **2** opposing ideas, opinions etc. are completely different from each other: *Bobbie and Jo have opposing views on marriage.*

op·po·site[1] /'ɑpəzɪt, -sɪt/ W3 *adj.* **1** as different as possible from something else: *two words with opposite meanings* | *We thought the medicine would make him sleep, but it had the opposite effect.* | +**to** *Everything turned out opposite to the way I planned.* **2** on the other side of the same area, often directly across from it: *I think our hotel is* ***on the opposite side of*** *the street.* | *We work* ***at opposite ends of*** *the building.* **3** the opposite direction, way etc. is directly away from someone or something: *She turned and ran* ***in the opposite direction.*** **4 the opposite sex** people of the other sex: *attraction to the opposite sex* **5 sb's opposite number** someone who has the same job in another similar organization

opposite[2] *prep.* **1** if one thing or person is opposite another, they are facing each other: *Put the piano opposite the sofa.* **2 play/star/appear opposite sb** to act with another person in a movie or play as one of the main characters

opposite[3] *n.* [C] **1** a person or thing that is as different as possible from someone or something else: *The two sisters are complete opposites.* | **the opposite (of sb/sth)** *The results were the opposite of what we expected.* | *Eileen's parents are very formal, but mine are* ***just the opposite.*** **2 opposites attract** said to explain the romantic attraction between two people who are very different from each other **3** MATH one of a pair of positive and negative numbers that are the same distance away from zero, but in the opposite direction. For example, +8 and –8 are opposites. The sum of opposite numbers is zero. → see also ADDITIVE INVERSE

opposite[4] *adv.* in a position on the other side of the same area: *My cousin was sitting opposite.*

op·po·si·tion /ˌɑpə'zɪʃən/ W2 *n.* [U] **1** strong disagreement with, or protest against, something such as a plan, law, or official decision: +**to** *There was a great deal of opposition to the war.* | **strong/fierce/stiff opposition** *The proposal faces strong opposition in Congress.* | **meet with/encounter opposition** *Plans to turn the site into a leisure complex have met with stiff opposition.* | **in opposition (to sth)** *Restaurant owners protested in opposition to the new regulations.*

THESAURUS

objection a reason you give for not approving of an idea or plan: *Lawyers raised no objections to the plan.*
antagonism strong opposition to or hatred of someone else: *the antagonism between the two men*
antipathy FORMAL a feeling of strong dislike or opposition: *her growing antipathy toward her stepmother*

2 the people who you are competing against, especially in a sports game: *We've outscored the opposition in our last three games.* **3** FORMAL a situation in which two things are completely different from each other:

+**between** *the opposition between capitalism and socialism* **4 the opposition** in some countries, the main political party that is represented in PARLIAMENT but that is not part of the government: *opposition parties*

op·press /ə'prɛs/ *v.* [T often passive] **1** to treat a group of people unfairly or cruelly, and prevent them from having the same rights and opportunities as other people: *The colonists oppressed the native peoples for centuries.* **2** WRITTEN to make someone feel unhappy by restricting their freedom in some way: *The loneliness of her little apartment oppressed her.*

op·pressed /ə'prɛst/ *adj.* **1** an oppressed group of people is treated unfairly or cruelly and prevented from having the same rights and opportunities as other people: *oppressed minorities* **2** someone who is oppressed feels their freedom has been restricted —**the oppressed** *n.* [plural]

op·pres·sion /ə'prɛʃən/ *n.* [U] the act of oppressing a group of people, or the state of being oppressed: *the oppression of women*

op·pres·sive /ə'prɛsɪv/ *adj.* **1** powerful, cruel, and unfair: *an oppressive dictatorship* **2** oppressive weather is very hot with no movement of air, which makes you feel uncomfortable: *Summers in Houston can be oppressive.* **3** an oppressive situation makes you feel too uncomfortable to do or say anything: *The silence in the meeting was becoming oppressive.* —**oppressively** *adv.* —**oppressiveness** *n.* [U]

op·pres·sor /ə'prɛsɚ/ *n.* [C] a person, group, or country that OPPRESSES people: *The people rose against their oppressors.*

op·pro·bri·ous /ə'proʊbriəs/ *adj.* FORMAL showing great disrespect —**opprobriously** *adv.*

op·pro·bri·um /ə'proʊbriəm/ *n.* [U] FORMAL strong public criticism or disapproval

opt /ɑpt/ *v.* [I] to choose one thing or one course of action instead of another: +**for** *Some 700 students have opted for a major in engineering.* | **opt to do sth** *While Jan went sailing, I opted to bike into town.*

opt in *phr. v.* to decide to join a group, system etc. that other people are involved in

opt into sth *phr. v.* to decide to join a group, system etc. that other people are involved in: *Employees can opt into the insurance plan.*

opt out *phr. v.* **1** to choose not to do something, or not to become involved in something that other people are doing: +**of** *You can't just opt out of all responsibility for your own child!* **2** to decide not to join a group, system, or action: +**of** *Miller opted out of military service for religious reasons.*

op·tic /'ɑptɪk/ *adj.* [only before noun] BIOLOGY concerning the eyes: *optic nerves* → see picture at EYE[1]

optical instruments

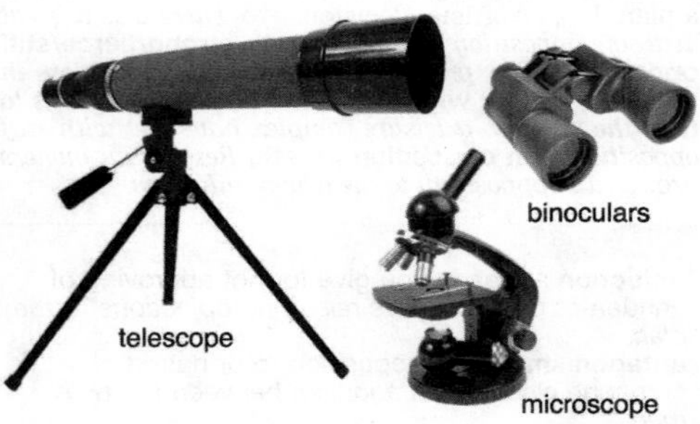

op·ti·cal /'ɑptɪkəl/ *adj.* [only before noun] **1** used for seeing images and light: *optical equipment such as cameras and telescopes* **2** relating to the way light is seen: *optical distortions* **3** PHYSICS using light as a means of sending or storing information, especially for use in a computer system: *optical transmission* —**optically** /-kli/ *adv.*

ˌoptical 'fiber *n.* [U] a thread-like material made of glass which is used for sending information, for example in a telephone or computer system

ˌoptical il'lusion *n.* [C] a picture or image that tricks your eyes and makes you see something that is not actually there

op·ti·cian /ɑp'tɪʃən/ *n.* [C] someone who makes and sells LENSES for GLASSES → see also OPTOMETRIST

op·tics /'ɑptɪks/ *n.* [U] PHYSICS the scientific study of light

op·ti·mal /'ɑptəməl/ *adj.* FORMAL the best or most appropriate SYN **optimum**

op·ti·mism /'ɑptəˌmɪzəm/ *n.* [U] a tendency to believe that good things will always happen and the future will be good OPP **pessimism**: *the optimism of the postwar years*

op·ti·mist /'ɑptəˌmɪst/ *n.* [C] someone who is always hopeful and always believes that good things will happen OPP **pessimist**: *Jim, the* ***eternal optimist****, was already making new plans.*

op·ti·mis·tic /ˌɑptə'mɪstɪk/ *adj.* **1** believing that good things will happen in the future, or feeling confident that you will succeed OPP **pessimistic**: **optimistic (that)** *Authorities are optimistic the killer will be caught.* | +**about** *I'm pretty optimistic about our chances of winning.* **2** thinking and believing that things will be better, easier, or more successful than is actually possible: *She said she could be here by 7:30, but I think that's a little optimistic.* —**optimistically** /-kli/ *adv.* → see also OVER-OPTIMISTIC

op·ti·mize /'ɑptəˌmaɪz/ *v.* [T] to make the way that something operates as effective and successful as possible —**optimization** /ˌɑptəmə'zeɪʃən/ *n.* [U]

op·ti·mum /'ɑptəməm/ *adj.* [only before noun] the best or most appropriate that is possible SYN **optimal**: *This design makes optimum use of the available space.*

op·tion /'ɑpʃən/ Ac S2 W2 *n.* [C]

1 A CHOICE something that you can choose to do, have, or use in a particular situation: *Joining the army seemed like the best option at the time.* | **the option of doing sth** *We were given the option of canceling our insurance policy.* | +**for** *What are the options for cutting costs?* | **one/another/the only option is to do sth** *My only option was to call the police.* | *Many teenage mothers* ***have no option but to*** *live with their parents.*

2 keep/leave your options open to wait and consider all possibilities before making a decision: *Many young people want to keep their options open.*

3 STH THAT IS ADDITIONAL something that is offered in addition to the standard equipment when you buy something new, especially a car: *Leather seats are an option on this model.*

4 COMPUTERS one of the possible choices you can make when using a computer program: *Press "P" to select the print option.*

5 RIGHT TO BUY/SELL ECONOMICS the right to buy or sell something in the future: +**on** *All employees are given an option on 100 shares of stock.*

6 (the) first option the chance to buy or get something before anyone else: *Local farmers will get first option to buy the government land.*

[**Origin:** 1500–1600 French, Latin *optio* **free choice**]

op·tion·al /'ɑpʃənl/ Ac W1 *adj.* if something is optional, you do not have to do it or use it, but you can choose to if you want to OPP **mandatory** OPP **required**: *Attendance at the meeting is optional.*

op·tom·e·trist /ɑp'tɑmətrɪst/ *n.* [C] someone who tests people's eyes and orders GLASSES for them

THESAURUS

optician someone who makes and sells lenses for glasses
ophthalmologist a doctor who treats people's eyes and does operations on them

op·u·lence /'ɑpyələns/ *n.* [U] wealth and LUXURY: *the opulence of Monte Carlo*

op·u·lent /'ɑpyələnt/ *adj.* **1** very beautiful, highly decorated, and made from expensive materials SYN **luxurious**: *an opulent hotel* **2** very rich and spending a lot of money: *an opulent lifestyle*

o·pus /ˈoʊpəs/ *n.* [usually singular] ENG. LANG. ARTS **1** a piece of music by a great musician, numbered according to when it was written **2** a piece of work by a well-known writer, painter etc.: *His latest opus is a romantic comedy.* → see also MAGNUM OPUS

OR **1** the written abbreviation of OREGON **2** the abbreviation of OPERATING ROOM

or /ɚ, ɔr/ S1 W1 [conjunction] **1** used between two words or phrases to show that either of two things is possible, or used before the last in a list of possibilities or choices : *Should we go see a movie or stay home?* | *You can have ham, cheese, or tuna.* | *Which color do you prefer? Yellow or white?* | *You can have* **either** *cherry* **or** *apple pie for dessert.* | *I don't care* **whether** *she stays* **or** *goes.* | *We could take the train to Paris* **or else** *fly there.* → see also EITHER **2** used after a negative verb when you mean not one thing and also not another thing: *Jody doesn't eat meat or dairy products.* | *I've never been to Africa or Asia.* **3 or anything/or something** SPOKEN similar to what you have just mentioned: *Jeff plays the bongo drums or something.* | *Does it have chili peppers or anything in it?* **4** used to warn or advise someone that if they do not do something, something bad will happen: *Hurry up or you'll miss your flight.* | *Put down your gun or I'll shoot.* | *Get me my money by next week* **or else** (=used as a threat). **5 or so** used with an amount, number, distance etc. to show that it is not exact: *There's a gas station a mile or so down the road.* **6** used to show that an amount or number is not exact: *He left a minute or two ago.* | *It costs only three or four dollars.* **7** used to explain why something happens or to show that something must be true: *They must not be home, or their car would be there.* | *It must be important,* **or else** *he wouldn't have called at 3 a.m.* **8** used to correct something that you have said or to give more specific information: *There'll be snow tomorrow, or that's what the forecast says.* | *We've cleaned up the mess,* **or at least** *most of it.* | *John picked us up in his car,* **or rather** *his dad's car.* [**Origin:** Old English *oththe*]

-or /ɚ/ *suffix* [in nouns] someone who does something: *an actor* (=someone who acts) | *an inventor* (=someone who invents things) → see also -ER

or·a·cle /ˈɔrəkəl, ˈɑr-/ *n.* [C] **1** HISTORY someone the ancient Greeks believed could communicate with the gods, who gave advice to people or told them what would happen in the future **2** the holy place where an oracle could be found **3** a message given by an oracle

o·rac·u·lar /ɔˈrækyələ, ə-/ *adj.* **1** said by an oracle **2** difficult to understand

o·ral[1] /ˈɔrəl/ *adj.* **1** spoken, not written: *an oral report* **2** BIOLOGY concerned with or involving the mouth: *oral cancer* | *oral hygiene* [**Origin:** 1600–1700 Late Latin *oralis*, from Latin *os* **mouth**] **—orally** *adv.*

oral[2] *n.* [C] a test in which questions and answers are spoken, rather than written

ˌoral contraˈceptive *n.* [C] TECHNICAL a drug that a woman takes by mouth, so that she can have sex without having a baby SYN **the pill**

ˈoral exˌam *n.* [C] an ORAL

ˌoral ˈhistory *n.* [C,U] spoken accounts of things that happened in the past, especially events experienced by the person speaking, or one of these spoken accounts

ˌoral ˈsex *n.* [U] touching someone's sex organs with the lips and tongue to give sexual pleasure

ˈoral ˌsurgeon *n.* [C] a DENTIST who performs operations in the mouth

ˌoral traˈdition *n.* **1** [singular, U] the way that older people pass on stories and customs to younger people by speaking to them, rather than by using books or formal education: *The oral tradition lived on into the 20th century.* **2** [C] a story or custom that has been passed on by speaking to younger people

or·ange /ˈɔrɪndʒ, ˈɑr-/ S1 W3 *n.* **1** [C] BIOLOGY a round fruit that has a thick orange skin and is divided into parts inside: *Slice the orange in half.* | *orange juice* → see picture at FRUIT[1] **2** [U] a color that is between red and yellow: *The sun was a deep fiery orange.* [**Origin:** 1200–1300 Old French, Arabic *naranj*, from Sanskrit *naranga* **orange tree**] **—orange** *adj.*: *an orange cotton sweater*

or·ange·ade /ˌɔrəndʒˈeɪd, ˌɑr-/ *n.* [U] a drink that tastes like oranges

or·ange·ry /ˈɔrəndʒri, ˈɑr-/ *n.* [C] a place where orange trees are grown

o·rang·u·tang, orangutan /əˈræŋəˌtæŋ/ *n.* [C] a large APE with long arms and long reddish-brown hair [**Origin:** 1600–1700 Malay *orang hutan* **man of the forest**]

o·ra·tion /əˈreɪʃən, ɔ-/ *n.* [C] a formal public speech

or·a·tor /ˈɔrət̬ɚ, ˈɑr-/ *n.* [C] someone who is good at making speeches that can influence the way people think and feel

or·a·to·ri·o /ˌɔrəˈtɔrioʊ, ˌɑr-/ *n.* [C] a long piece of music for singers and an ORCHESTRA, in which there are parts for SOLO singers

or·at·o·ry /ˈɔrəˌtɔri, ˈɑr-/ *n.* **1** [U] the skill of making powerful speeches that persuade others to believe you or do what you ask them **2** [C] a small building or part of a church where people can go to pray **—oratorical** /ˌɔrəˈtɔrɪkəl, ˌɑr-/ *adj.*: *oratorical skills* **—oratorically** /-kli/ *adv.*

orb /ɔrb/ *n.* [C] LITERARY a bright ball-shaped object, especially the sun or the moon: *The moon was a bright orb on the horizon.*

or·bit[1] /ˈɔrbɪt/ *n.* [C] **1** PHYSICS the path traveled in space by an object which is moving around another much larger object, such as the Earth moving around the sun: +**around** *the Moon's orbit around the Earth* | **in orbit** *a space station in orbit around Earth* | *Two more satellites were* **put into orbit** (=put into space to travel in an orbit). | +**of** *the orbit of the meteor* **2 in/within sb's orbit** within someone's area of power and influence

orbit[2] *v.* [I,T] PHYSICS to travel in a circle in space around a much larger object, such as the Earth or the sun: *Venus orbits the sun once every 225 Earth days.* [**Origin:** 1500–1600 Latin *orbita* **wheel-track**]

or·bit·al /ˈɔrbɪt̬l/ *adj.* concerned with the orbit of one object around another: *Mars' orbital path*

or·chard /ˈɔrtʃɚd/ *n.* [C] a place where fruit trees are grown: *a peach orchard*

or·ches·tra /ˈɔrkɪstrə/ *n.* [C] a large group of musicians playing many different kinds of instruments, usually CLASSICAL MUSIC, and led by a CONDUCTOR: *the Chicago Symphony Orchestra*

THESAURUS

Sections of an orchestra
the woodwind/wind section also **the winds** the instruments made mostly of wood that you blow through
the strings/the string section the instruments that have strings
the brass (section) the instruments made of metal that you blow through
the percussion (section) the instruments such as drums

People in an orchestra
conductor the person who directs the music and musicians
cellist a person who plays the cello
flutist a person who plays the flute
violinist a person who plays the violin
percussionist a person who plays percussion

or·ches·tral /ɔrˈkɛstrəl/ *adj.* concerned with or written for an orchestra: *orchestral music*

ˈorchestra pit *n.* [C] the space below the stage in a theater where the musicians sit

or·ches·trate /ˈɔrkɪˌstreɪt/ *v.* [T] **1** to carefully organize an event or a complicated plan, especially secretly:

Police believe Casey orchestrated the kidnapping. **2** ENG. LANG. ARTS to arrange a piece of music so that it can be played by an orchestra —**orchestrated** *adj.* —**orchestration** /ˌɔrkɪˈstreɪʃən/ *n.* [C,U]

or·chid /ˈɔrkɪd/ *n.* [C] a plant that has flowers with three parts, the middle one being shaped like a lip [**Origin:** 1800–1900 Modern Latin *orchis*, from Greek, **testicle, orchid**; because of the shape of its roots]

O

or·dain /ɔrˈdeɪn/ *v.* [T usually passive] **1** to officially make someone a priest or religious leader: **be ordained (as) sth** *She is the first woman to be ordained as a bishop.* → see also ORDINATION **2** FORMAL to make the decision that something should happen: **ordain that** *People believed that God had ordained that the King should rule them.*

or·deal /ɔrˈdil/ *n.* [C] a very bad or frightening experience: *the hostages' terrifying six-week ordeal* | **the ordeal of doing sth** *She had to suffer the ordeal of giving evidence about the rape.* [**Origin:** Old English *ordal* **trial, judgment**]

or·der[1] /ˈɔrdɚ/ S1 W1 *n.*

1 ARRANGEMENT [C,U] the way that several things, events etc. are arranged or put on a list, showing whether something is first, second, third etc. SYN **sequence**: *The program shows the order of events.* | *Check that all the names are* ***in order*** (=in the correct order). | **in...order** *Make sure the files are in the right order.* | *The pictures can be looked at in any order.* | *Some of the pages were* ***out of order*** (=in the wrong order). | **in order of sth** *Characters are listed in order of appearance.* | **in chronological/alphabetical/numerical order** *The names of contributing authors are listed in alphabetical order.* | **in reverse order** (=in the opposite order to what is usual) | **in ascending/descending order** (=starting with the lowest or highest number)

2 FOR A PURPOSE **a) in order (for sb) to do sth** for the purpose of doing something: *They need to raise $5 million in order to pay for the repairs.* | *In order for you to graduate this year, you'll need to go to summer school.* **b) in order that** FORMAL so that something can happen: *The research is necessary in order that new treatments can be developed.*

3 WELL-ORGANIZED CONDITION [U] a situation in which everything is well organized and correctly arranged: *You have some good ideas here, but you need to give them some order.* | *I have to* ***get*** *my finances* ***in order*** (=organize them properly).

4 NO TROUBLE OR CRIME [U] a situation in which rules and laws are obeyed, and authority is respected: *Neighborhood leaders are working with police to maintain* ***law and order***. | **keep/maintain order** *The military was called in to maintain* ***public order*** *in the capital.* | *It took the police an hour to* ***restore order***. | **call sb to order** (=order someone in a formal meeting or court of law to obey the rules) | **Order (in the court)!** (=used in court to tell people to be quiet and obey the rules)

5 CUSTOMER'S REQUEST [C] **a)** a request made by a customer, for example a request for goods to be supplied or for a meal in a restaurant: *May I* ***take your order*** *now* (=used to ask what a customer in a restaurant wants)? | *I* ***placed an order*** (=made an order) *for some curtains last week.* | *I'm afraid we never* ***received the order***. | *You can* ***cancel the order*** *at any time until it is shipped.* | *Kepler's has 50 copies of the book* ***on order*** (=ordered but not yet received). | *The carpet we wanted is* ***on back order*** (=not currently available from the company who you are buying from). | *There aren't many stores left that* ***make*** *suits* ***to order*** (=make them especially for a particular customer). → see also MADE-TO-ORDER **b)** what a customer has asked for, such as a meal or a type of goods: *We'll call you when your order is ready.* | **+of** *She returned with my order of fries* → see also SIDE ORDER

6 COMMAND [C] **a)** also **orders** a command given by someone in authority: *Military people are trained to* ***obey orders***. | *Margaret thinks she can just* ***give*** *everyone* ***orders***. | *General Marshall* ***gave the order to*** *bomb the city.* | *It's hard to* ***take orders from*** (=obey) *someone you don't respect.* | *The families were moved out of their building* ***by order of*** (=because of an order from) *the mayor.* | *U.S. customs officials* ***have orders to*** (=have been told to) *seize all imported tobacco.* | *The guards were* ***under orders to*** (=commanded to) *shoot to kill.* **b)** an official statement from a court of law which says that something must be done SYN **court order**: *The court has issued an order blocking the sale of this drug.* | *The documents were made public Wednesday,* ***by order of the court***.

7 be out of order **a)** if a machine or piece of equipment is out of order, it is not working: *Oh no, the copy machine's out of order.* **b)** to be breaking the rules in a court, committee, CONGRESS etc.: *Sit down, Mr. Phillips! You're out of order.*

8 be in order **a)** if an official document is in order, it is legal and correct: *Your work visa seems to be in order.* **b)** FORMAL to be an appropriate thing to do or say on a particular occasion: *I think a brief summary of the situation may be in order.*

9 in (good) working/running order if a vehicle or machine is in good working or running order, it is working well

10 POLITICAL/ECONOMIC SITUATION [singular] the political, social, or economic situation at a particular time: ***the new order*** (=the new situation, following important changes) *in American politics* | **the existing/established order** *The rich and powerful families wanted to maintain the existing order.*

11 first/main/next etc. order of business the first, most important etc. thing that needs to be done or discussed: *The main order of business is to select the site for the next convention.*

12 of the highest/the first/a high order of the best kind or of a very good kind: *The situation requires diplomatic skills of the highest order.*

13 be the order of the day **a)** to be a very common or typical feature of a particular time, place etc.: *Smaller families are now the order of the day.* **b)** to be appropriate for a particular occasion or situation: *Casual clothes will be the order of the day.*

14 the (natural) order of things the way that life and the world are organized and intended to be: *Death is part of the natural order of things.*

15 on the order of sth a little more or a little less than a particular amount SYN **approximately**: *an increase in profits on the order of $20 million*

16 LEGAL DOCUMENT [C] a legal document that says what a person must or must not do: *a demolition order* (=one saying that a building must be destroyed)

17 RELIGIOUS GROUP [C] a society of MONKS or NUNS (=people who live a holy life according to religious rules): *the Benedictine Order* | **+of** *the Order of St. Agnes*

18 take (holy) orders to become a priest

19 CLUB/SOCIETY [C] an organization or society whose members have the same profession, interests etc.: *The Fraternal Order of Police*

20 OFFICIAL HONOR [C] **a)** a group of people who have received a special honor from a king, president etc. for their services or achievements: *the National Order of Loyal Knights* **b)** a special piece of metal, silk etc. that members of the order wear at ceremonies

21 OF ANIMALS/PLANTS [C] TECHNICAL one of the groups into which scientists divide animals and plants. An order is larger than a FAMILY, but smaller than a CLASS.

22 COMPUTER [C] TECHNICAL a list of jobs that a computer has to do in a particular order

[**Origin:** 1200–1300 Old French *ordre*, from Latin *ordo* **arrangement, group**] → see also **marching orders** at MARCH[1] (5), MONEY ORDER, PECKING ORDER, **in short order** at SHORT[1] (15), **standing order** at STANDING[1] (2), **be a tall order** at TALL (3)

order[2] S1 W2 *v.* **1** [I,T] to ask for food, goods, or services to be given to you: **order sth** *We ordered a pizza.* | *Saudi Arabia has ordered 15 of the planes.* | **order sb sth** *Maybe we should order John a drink too.* | **order sth for sb/sth** *They've ordered a new carpet for the bedroom.* | **order sth from sb/sth** *I ordered a new computer from a discount electronics site.* | *Are you ready to order?* (=used to ask if someone is ready to request their food in a restaurant) ►see THESAURUS box at ask, restaurant **2** [T] to tell someone to do something, using your authority or power: *"Put your hands up!" the officer ordered.* | **order sb to do sth** *Health officials may order the hospital to close.* | **order sth** *The President ordered an immediate attack.* | **order sb in/out/back etc** *He ordered us off his land.* | **+that** *The court ordered that the professor be given his job back.* ▶see THESAURUS box at tell **3** [T usually passive] to arrange something in a particular order: *Order the names alphabetically.* **4** [T] OLD USE to organize things neatly or effectively

order sb **around** *phr. v.* to continuously give someone orders in an annoying or threatening way: *Stop ordering me around!*

order out *phr. v.* **1** to order food to be delivered to your home or office: *Let's order out tonight.* | **order out for sth** *We ordered out for pizza.* **2 order sb out** to order soldiers or police to go somewhere to stop violent behavior by a crowd: *The Governor had to order out the National Guard.*

> **WORD CHOICE order, command**
> • Use **order** for most situations when someone in a position of authority tells other people to do something: *All foreigners were ordered to leave the city.*
> • Use **command** when it is someone in the military who is telling other people to do something: *General Gaines commanded his men to fire.*

or·dered /ˈɔrdɚd/ also **ˌwell-ˈordered** *adj.* well arranged or controlled SYN **orderly**: *a well-ordered society* | *an ordered house* → see also DISORDERED

ˌordered ˈpair *n.* [C] MATH two numbers that are used to represent a point on a GRID. The first number relates to the horizontal line of the grid, and the second number relates to the vertical line.

ˈorder form *n.* [C] a special piece of paper for writing orders on: *Have you **filled out the order form** (=completed it)?*

or·der·ly¹ /ˈɔrdɚli/ *adj.* **1** arranged or organized in a sensible or neat way OPP **disorderly**: *The tools were arranged in orderly rows.* **2** peaceful or well-behaved OPP **disorderly**: *an orderly crowd* —**orderliness** *n.* [U]

orderly² *n.* [C] someone who does unskilled jobs in a hospital

or·di·nal /ˈɔrdn-əl, -nəl/ *adj.* showing a position in a set of numbers

ˈordinal ˌnumber also **ordinal** *n.* [C] MATH a number such as first, second, third etc. which shows the order of things → see also CARDINAL NUMBER

or·di·nance /ˈɔrdn-əns/ *n.* [C] LAW a law, usually of a city or town, that forbids or restricts an activity

ˈOrdinance ˌPowers *n.* [plural] POLITICS the official powers the American President has to make decisions or pass laws. These powers are given to the President by CONGRESS and are in the CONSTITUTION. → see also RESERVED POWERS

or·di·nar·i·ly /ˌɔrdnˈɛrəli/ *adv.* **1** [sentence adverb] usually or in most cases: *Counseling ordinarily costs about $100 a session.* | *Ordinarily, it takes six weeks for applications to be processed.* **2** in a way that is normal and not different or special in any way: *The day began ordinarily enough.* | *an ordinarily quiet neighborhood*

or·di·nar·y /ˈɔrdnˌɛri/ W2 *adj.* **1** average or usual, and not different or special in any way: *Housing prices in Manhattan are out of reach for ordinary people.* | *ordinary household items* | *an ordinary workday* ▶see THESAURUS box at normal¹ **2 out of the ordinary** very different from what is usual: *Did you notice anything out of the ordinary in Julie's behavior?* **3 sb/sth is no ordinary sth** used to say that someone or something is very special and unusual: *As soon as you listen, you know this is no ordinary radio station.* **4** not very good, interesting, or impressive: *a pretty ordinary performance* [**Origin:** 1300–1400 Latin *ordinarius*, from *ordo* **arrangement, group**] —**ordinariness** *n.* [U] → see also EXTRAORDINARY

ˌordinary ˈshares *n.* [plural] ECONOMICS the largest part of a company's CAPITAL, which is owned by people who have the right to vote at meetings and to receive part of the company's profits

or·di·na·tion /ˌɔrdnˈeɪʃən/ *n.* [C,U] the act or ceremony of making someone a priest: *the ordination of women*

ord·nance /ˈɔrdnəns/ *n.* [U] **1** large guns with wheels SYN **artillery** **2** weapons, explosives, and vehicles used in fighting

or·dure /ˈɔrdʒɚ/ *n.* [U] FORMAL solid waste matter from a person's or animal's body SYN **feces**

ore /ɔr/ *n.* [C,U] EARTH SCIENCE rock or earth from which metal can be obtained: *uranium ore* | *ore deposits*

o·reg·a·no /əˈrɛgəˌnoʊ/ *n.* [U] an HERB used in cooking, especially in Italian and Greek cooking

Or·e·gon /ˈɔrɪgən/ WRITTEN ABBREVIATION **OR** a state in the northwestern U.S.

ˈOregon ˌTrail, the one of the main paths across the U.S. to the western part of the country, used by PIONEERS in the mid–19th century. The Trail crossed the Great Plains and the Rocky Mountains before turning toward Idaho, Washington, and Oregon.

org /ɔrg/ the abbreviation of ORGANIZATION, used in U.S. Internet addresses

organs

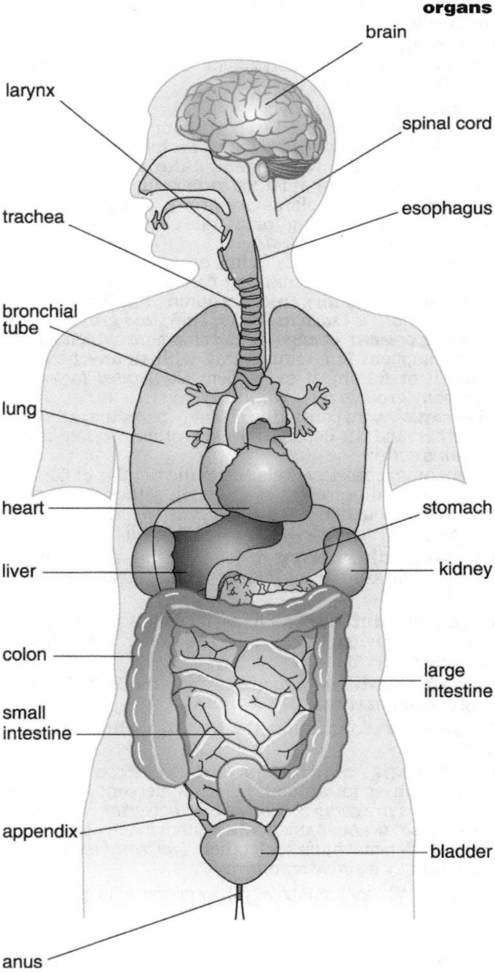

or·gan /ˈɔrgən/ *n.* [C]
1 BODY PART BIOLOGY a part of the body, such as the heart or lungs, that has a particular purpose: *internal*

organs | *an organ transplant* | *the liver, heart, and other* ***internal organs*** | *Fortunately, the bullet missed all the* ***vital organs*** (=the ones that are essential for you to live).
2 MUSICAL INSTRUMENT ENG. LANG. ARTS a large musical instrument used especially in churches, with one or more KEYBOARDS and large pipes out of which the sound comes: *organ music*
3 ORGANIZATION an organization that is part of a larger organization, especially part of a government: **+of** *The bank is an organ of the central government.*
4 NEWSPAPER/MAGAZINE FORMAL a newspaper or magazine which gives information, news etc. for an organization: **+of** *the official organ of the Communist Party*
5 PLANT BIOLOGY a structure such as an eye, heart, or leaf consisting of a group of TISSUES that carry out a particular function in an ORGANISM
[**Origin:** 1200–1300 Old French *organe*, from Latin, from Greek *organon* **tool, instrument**]

or·gan·die, organdy /ˈɔrgəndi/ *n.* [U] very thin stiff cotton, used to make dresses

ˈorgan ˌdonor *n.* [C] someone who allows doctors to use one of their organs to replace a sick person's organ

or·ga·nelle /ˌɔrgəˈnɛl/ *n.* [C] BIOLOGY one of several structures in a cell that has a particular purpose, as the different organs have in the body. The NUCLEUS is one organelle.

ˈorgan ˌgrinder *n.* [C] a musician who plays a BARREL ORGAN (=a musical instrument played by turning a handle) in the street

or·gan·ic /ɔrˈgænɪk/ *adj.*
1 FOOD grown or produced without using artificial chemicals: *organic vegetables* | *Is the milk organic?* ►see THESAURUS box at **environment, natural**[1]
2 FARMING using or relating to farming or gardening methods in which plants are grown and animals are raised without using artificial chemicals: *organic farmers* | *organic gardening*
3 LIVING/NATURAL BIOLOGY living, or produced by or from living things, and containing CARBON in one form or another OPP **inorganic**: **organic matter/material** *organic material such as leaves, bark, and grass*
4 DEVELOPMENT change or development which is organic happens in a natural way, without anyone planning it or forcing it to happen: *He wanted to let the company grow in an organic way.*
5 RELATED PARTS consisting of many parts that all work together and all depend on each other: *Society is an organic entity.*
6 BIOLOGICAL TECHNICAL relating to the regular biological and chemical processes of the body, rather than influences from outside the body: *a possible organic explanation for the disease* —**organically** /-kli/ *adv.*

orˌganic ˈchemistry *n.* [U] CHEMISTRY the study of compounds containing CARBON → see also INORGANIC CHEMISTRY

orˌganic ˈmatter *n.* [U] material consisting of plants and other living things that are going through the process of decaying

or·gan·i·sa·tion /ˌɔrgənəˈzeɪʃən/ the British spelling of ORGANIZATION

or·gan·ise /ˈɔrgəˌnaɪz/ the British spelling of ORGANIZE

or·ga·nism /ˈɔrgəˌnɪzəm/ *n.* [C] **1** BIOLOGY a living thing such as an animal, plant, or person: *All living organisms are composed of cells.* | *bacterial organisms* → see also MICROORGANISM **2** a system made up of parts that are dependent on each other: *The world economy is increasingly a single organism.*

or·gan·ist /ˈɔrgənɪst/ *n.* [C] someone who plays the ORGAN

or·ga·ni·za·tion /ˌɔrgənəˈzeɪʃən/ S2 W1 *n.* **1** [C] a group of people, such as a club, a business, or a political party, which has formed for a particular purpose: *a non-profit environmental organization* | *international organizations such as the U.N.* | *a dangerous terrorist organization*

THESAURUS

institution a large important organization such as a bank, church, or university
association an organization for people who do the same kind of work or have the same interests
(political) party an organization of people with the same political aims
club/society an organization for people who share an interest
union an organization formed by workers in order to protect their rights

2 [U] the act or process of planning and arranging things effectively: *A big wedding involves a lot of organization.* | *The problems were the result of poor organization.* | **+of** *the organization of the museum's exhibitions* **3** [U] the way in which the different parts of something are arranged and work together: *The essay lacks organization and clarity.* | **+of** *the social organization of early human cultures* —**organizational** *adj.*: *organizational ability* —**organizationally** *adv.*

ˌorganiˈzation ˌchart also **ˌorganiˈzational ˌchart** *n.* [C] a chart that shows the names of all the people in a business or other organization, and shows what they are responsible for and how they are related to each other

Organiˌzation of ˌAfrican ˈUnity, the ABBREVIATION **OAU** POLITICS an organization of independent African countries from 1963 to 2002 whose purpose was to help all African countries become independent and work together. It was replaced in 2002 by the African Union.

Organiˌzation of Aˌmerican ˈStates, the → see OAS, THE

or·ga·nize /ˈɔrgəˌnaɪz/ S2 W2 *v.* **1** [T] to make the necessary arrangements so that an activity can happen: *I agreed to help organize the company picnic.* | *A search for the missing girl was quickly organized.* **2** [T] to put things or people into an order or system, especially one that has a clear structure or purpose: *You will be taught how to organize information effectively.* | **organize sth around sth** *Our science curriculum is organized around the central theme of the Earth.* | **organize sth into/in sth** *The children are organized into groups according to ability.* **3** [I,T] to form a TRADE UNION (=an organization that protects workers' rights) or persuade people to join one SYN **unionize**

or·ga·nized /ˈɔrgəˌnaɪzd/ S3 *adj.* **1** achieving aims in an effective, ordered, and sensible way OPP **disorganized**: *Barbara's a very organized person.* | *a* ***well-organized*** *trip* | *a* ***poorly organized*** *attempt to overthrow the government* | *I'll need at least thirty minutes to* ***get organized*** *for the presentation.* | *a* ***highly organized*** (=very well organized) *radical student group*

THESAURUS

efficient working well, without wasting time or energy: *an energy efficient refrigerator* | *efficient workers*
well-run organized efficiently: *a neat and well-run home*
businesslike sensible and practical in the way you do things: *He spoke again in a businesslike tone.*

2 an organized place is arranged neatly and in a well-planned way OPP **disorganized**: *an organized filing cabinet* | **well/carefully/neatly organized** *her neatly organized desk* **3** an organized activity is arranged for and done by many people: *organized hockey* | *organized religion* **4** organized workers are workers who have formed or joined a union SYN **unionized**: *the industry's battle with* ***organized labor***

ˌorganized ˈcrime *n.* [U] illegal activity involving powerful well-organized groups of criminals

or·gasm /ˈɔrˌgæzəm/ *n.* [C,U] the greatest point of sexual pleasure —**orgasmic** /ɔrˈgæzmɪk/ *adj.*

org chart /ˈɔrg tʃɑrt/ *n.* [C] INFORMAL an ORGANIZATION CHART

or·gy /ˈɔrdʒi/ *n. plural* **orgies** [C] **1** a wild party with a lot of eating, drinking, and especially sexual activity **2** an occasion when a group of people have sex with each other **3 an orgy of sth** an occasion or time when something is done in a way that is extreme and not controlled: *an orgy of violence and looting* —**orgiastic** *adj.*

o·ri·ent[1] /ˈɔriˌɛnt/ Ac *v.* [T] **1 be oriented to/toward** to have as its main purpose or area of interest: *a curriculum oriented toward science and math* → see also -ORIENTED **2 orient yourself a)** to get used to a new situation, and become familiar with it, for example when you have moved to a new place, a new job etc.: **+to** *It takes students a few weeks to orient themselves to college life.* **b)** to find out where you are by looking around you, using a map etc.: *The climbers stopped to orient themselves.* **3** to position something in a particular direction: *The palace's courtyards are oriented toward the mountains.* [**Origin:** 1700–1800 French *orienter*, from Old French *orient*, present participle of *oriri* **to rise**]

o·ri·ent[2] /ˈɔriənt, -ˌɛnt/ Ac *n.* **the Orient** OLD-FASHIONED the eastern part of the world, especially China and Japan and the countries near them → see also THE EAST, OCCIDENT

o·ri·en·tal[1] /ˌɔriˈɛntl◂/ *adj.* from or related to the eastern part of the world, especially China or Japan: *oriental religions* | *a beautiful oriental carpet*

oriental[2] *n.* [C] OLD-FASHIONED a word for someone from the eastern part of the world, now considered offensive → see also OCCIDENTAL

or·i·en·tate /ˈɔriənˌteɪt/ Ac *v.* [T] another form of the word ORIENT

o·ri·en·ta·tion /ˌɔriənˈteɪʃən/ Ac *n.* **1** [C,U] the type of activity or subject that a person, organization etc. is most interested in and gives most attention to: **+toward/to** *The local economy has a strong orientation toward tourism.* **2** [C,U] the political views or religious beliefs that a person or organization has: *the party's liberal orientation* | **sb's political/religious orientation** *The meeting is open to everyone, whatever their political orientation.* **3** [U] a short period of training and preparation for a new job or activity: *This is orientation week for the new students.* **4** [C] MATH the angle or position of an object or shape in relation to another object or shape → see also SEXUAL ORIENTATION

-oriented /ɔriɛntɪd/ [in adjectives] **work-oriented/family-oriented etc.** mainly concerned with or paying attention to work, family etc.: *an export-oriented company* | *family-oriented entertainment*

o·ri·en·teer·ing /ˌɔriənˈtɪrɪŋ/ *n.* [U] a sport in which people have to find their way quickly across unknown country using a map and a COMPASS

or·i·fice /ˈɔrəfəs, ˈɑr-/ *n.* [C] FORMAL **1** BIOLOGY one of the holes in your body, such as your mouth, nose etc. **2** a hole or opening in something such as a tube or pipe

o·ri·ga·mi /ˌɔrəˈɡɑmi/ *n.* [U] the Japanese art of folding paper to make attractive objects [**Origin:** 1900–2000 a Japanese word meaning **fold paper**]

or·i·gin /ˈɔrədʒɪn, ˈɑr-/ S3 W3 *n.* **1** [U] also **origins** [plural] the situation, place, cause etc. from which something begins: **+of** *The origin of the infection is still unknown.* | *Valentine's Day* ***has its origins in*** (=began in) *third-century Rome.* | *This recipe is Spanish* ***in origin*** (=it was first made in Spain). | *a poem* ***of unknown origin*** **2** [U] also **origins** [plural] the country, race, or class from which a person or their family comes: *Kennedy's Irish-Catholic origins* | **of European/Indian/Asian etc. origin** *Nine percent of the city's population is of Hispanic origin.* **3** [C] MATH the point where two axes (AXIS) cross on a GRAPH [**Origin:** 1500–1600 French *origine*, from Latin *origo*, from *oriri* **to rise**]

o·rig·i·nal[1] /əˈrɪdʒənl/ S2 W2 *adj.* **1** [only before noun] existing or happening first, before being changed or replaced by something or someone else: *The original plan was to fly out to New York, not drive.* | **original owner/member etc.** *Barnes was one of the three original board members.* **2** new and different from anything that has been thought of before, especially in an interesting way: *She has a lot of original ideas.* | *His books are always funny and* ***highly original*** (=very original). ►see THESAURUS box at **new** **3** an original writer, thinker etc. writes stories, thinks of ideas etc. that are new, interesting, and different from anything else: *one of the most original political thinkers in America* **4** [only before noun] an original work of art is one that was made by the artist and is not a copy: *an original screenplay*

original[2] *n.* **1** [C] a painting, document etc. that is not a copy, but is the one that was produced first: *I'll keep the copies and give you the originals.* | *Are you sure the painting is an original?* **2 in the original** in the language that a book, play etc. was first written in, before it was translated: *Tim has read Homer in the original.* **3** [C usually singular] INFORMAL an unusual person who thinks or behaves very differently from other people: *Jack is a true original.*

o·rig·i·nal·i·ty /əˌrɪdʒəˈnæləṭi/ *n.* [U] **1** the quality of being completely new and different from anything that anyone has thought of before: *The play lacked originality.* **2** the quality someone has when they are able to think of or make something new, interesting, and different: *a writer of great imagination and originality*

oˌriginal jurisˈdiction *n.* [U] LAW the official authority of a U.S. court to judge a case before it is sent to a higher court → see also APPELLATE JURISDICTION

o·rig·i·nal·ly /əˈrɪdʒənl-i/ S2 W3 *adv.* in the beginning, before other things happened or changed: *Her family originally came from Malaysia.* | [sentence adverb] *Originally, we had hoped to be finished by May.*

oˌriginal ˈsin *n.* [U] the tendency to do bad or evil things, which people are born with according to some Christian teaching

o·rig·i·nate /əˈrɪdʒəˌneɪt/ *v.* **1** [I always + adv./prep., not in progressive] FORMAL to start to develop in a particular place or from a particular situation: **+originate in sth** *Buddhism originated in India.* | *The virus originates in pigs.* | **+originate with/from sb** *The idea originated with a U.S. environmental group.* **2** [T] to have the idea for something and start it: *The rumor was probably originated by one of the President's aides.* —**origination** /əˌrɪdʒəˈneɪʃən/ *n.* [U]

o·rig·i·na·tor /əˈrɪdʒəˌneɪṭɚ/ *n.* [C] the person who first has the idea for something and starts it: **+of** *Caesar Cardini was the originator of the Caesar salad.*

O·ri·no·co, the /ˌɔrɪˈnoʊkoʊ/ a river in the northern part of South America, that flows eastward through Venezuela to the Atlantic Ocean

o·ri·ole /ˈɔriˌoʊl, ˈɔriəl/ *n.* [C] BIOLOGY **1** a North American bird that is black with a red and yellow STRIPE on each wing **2** a European bird with black wings and a yellow body

or·mo·lu /ˈɔrməˌlu/ *n.* [U] a gold-colored mixture of metals, not containing real gold

or·na·ment[1] /ˈɔrnəmənt/ *n.* **1** [C] an object that you use for decoration because it is beautiful rather than useful: *Christmas ornaments* **2** [U] decoration that is added to something: *The towers are square and completely without ornament.* **3 be an ornament to sth** FORMAL to add honor, importance, or beauty to something: *He is a world-class scientist, and a real ornament to MIT.*

or·na·ment[2] /ˈɔrnəˌmɛnt/ *v.* **be ornamented with sth** to be decorated with something: *a dress ornamented with beads and pearls*

or·na·men·tal /ˌɔrnəˈmɛntl/ *adj.* designed to decorate something: *ornamental vases*

or·na·men·ta·tion /ˌɔrnəmənˈteɪʃən/ *n.* [U] decoration: *elaborate ornamentation, typical of the Victorian style*

or·nate /ɔrˈneɪt/ *adj.* with a lot of decoration, especially with many complicated details: *the ornate 18th-century Royal Palace* [**Origin:** 1500–1600 Latin, past participle of *ornare* **to decorate**] —**ornately** *adv.* —**ornateness** *n.* [U]

or·ne·ry /ˈɔrnəri/ *adj.* behaving in an unreasonable and angry way, especially by doing the opposite of what people expect you to do: *an ornery ten-year-old*

or·ni·thol·o·gy /ˌɔrnəˈθɑlədʒi/ *n.* [U] BIOLOGY the scientific study of birds —**ornithologist** *n.* [C] —**ornithological** /ˌɔrnəθəˈlɑdʒɪkəl/ *adj.*

O

o·ro·tund /ˈɔrəˌtʌnd, ˈɑr-/ *adj.* FORMAL **1** DISAPPROVING orotund speech or writing contains very formal complicated language that is intended to sound important and impressive SYN **pompous** **2** an orotund sound or voice is strong and clear SYN **sonorous**

O·roz·co /oʊˈroʊskoʊ/, **Jo·sé** /hoʊˈzeɪ/ (1883–1949) a Mexican PAINTER famous for his wall paintings of political and social subjects

or·phan¹ /ˈɔrfən/ *n.* [C] a child whose parents are both dead

orphan² *v.* **be orphaned** to become an orphan: *Thousands of children were orphaned in the war.*

or·phan·age /ˈɔrfənɪdʒ/ *n.* [C] a place where orphans live and are taken care of

Orr /ɔr/, **Bob·by** /ˈbɑbi/ (1948–) a Canadian HOCKEY player, who was the most successful player of the 1970s

or·tho·don·tics /ˌɔrθəˈdɑntɪks/ *n.* [U] the practice or skill of making teeth move into the right position when they have not been growing correctly —**orthodontic** *adj.*: *orthodontic braces*

or·tho·don·tist /ˌɔrθəˈdɑntɪst/ *n.* [C] a DENTIST who makes teeth straight when they have not been growing correctly

or·tho·dox /ˈɔrθəˌdɑks/ *adj.* **1** orthodox ideas or methods are generally accepted as being normal or correct OPP **unorthodox**: *orthodox methods of treating disease* | *orthodox views on education* **2** accepting as true and following all the traditional beliefs and laws of a religion: *an orthodox Jew* ►see THESAURUS box at **religious** **3** believing in or practicing the usual form of a particular set of ideas or methods: *orthodox communism* | *His views were in conflict with more orthodox psychologists.* [**Origin:** 1500–1600 French *orthodoxe*, from Late Latin, from Late Greek *orthodoxos*, from Greek *ortho-* (from *orthos* **straight, correct**) + *doxa* **opinion**]

ˌOrthodox ˈChurch *n.* **the Orthodox Church** one of the Christian churches in eastern Europe and parts of Asia

or·tho·dox·y /ˈɔrθəˌdɑksi/ *n. plural* **orthodoxies** **1** [C,U] an idea or set of ideas that is generally accepted as normal or correct: *He challenged the political orthodoxy of his time.* **2** [U] the traditional ideas and beliefs of a group or religion, or the practice of following these strictly: *Ratzinger was seen as the "guardian of Catholic orthodoxy."*

or·thog·o·nal pro·jec·tion /ɔrˌθɑgənl prəˈdʒɛkʃən/ also **ˌorthographic proˈjection**, **orˌthogonal ˈdrawing** *n.* [C] MATH a drawing that shows what a THREE-DIMENSIONAL object looks like when you look at it directly from different directions (usually the top, the front, and one side), or a drawing that shows a collection of such views of the different sides

or·thog·ra·phy /ɔrˈθɑgrəfi/ *n.* [U] TECHNICAL **1** the system for spelling words in a language **2** correct spelling —**orthographic** /ˌɔrθəˈgræfɪk◂/ *adj.*

or·tho·pe·dic, **orthopaedic** /ˌɔrθəˈpidɪk◂/ *adj.* **1** related to or providing medical treatment for problems affecting bones, muscles etc.: *an orthopedic surgeon* **2 an orthopedic bed/chair/shoe etc.** a bed, chair etc. that is designed to cure or prevent medical problems affecting your bones, muscles etc.

or·tho·pe·dics, **orthopaedics** /ˌɔrθəˈpidɪks/ *n.* [U] the area of medical science or treatment that deals with problems, diseases, or injuries of bones, muscles etc. —**orthopedist** *n.* [C]

Or·well /ˈɔrwɛl/, **George** (1903–1950) a British writer known for his NOVELS about political systems in which people are completely controlled by the government

Or·well·i·an /ɔrˈwɛliən/ *adj.* typical of the political systems described in the novels of George Orwell, in which the state controls everything and ordinary people have no power: *an Orwellian attempt to rewrite history*

-ory /ɔri, əri/ *suffix* **1** [in nouns] a place or thing used for doing something: *an observatory* (=where people look at the sky and stars) | *a directory* (=book giving lists of information) **2** [in adjectives] doing a particular thing: *explanatory* (=giving an explanation) | *congratulatory* (=giving) CONGRATULATIONS

or·zo /ˈɔrzoʊ/ *n.* [U] a type of PASTA in the shape of very small round balls

O·sage /ˈoʊseɪdʒ, oʊˈseɪdʒ/ a Native American tribe from the central area of the U.S.

Os·borne /ˈɑzbɔrn/, **John** (1929–1994) a British writer of plays

Os·car /ˈɑskɚ/ *n.* [C] TRADEMARK the usual name for an ACADEMY AWARD, a prize given each year, in the form of a small gold STATUE, to the best movies, actors etc. in the movie industry: *the Oscar for best director*

Os·ce·o·la /ˌɑsiˈoʊlə/ (?1804–1838) a Seminole chief who tried to stop U.S. soldiers from making his tribe leave Florida

os·cil·late /ˈɑsəˌleɪt/ *v.* [I] **1** FORMAL to keep changing between two extreme amounts or limits SYN **fluctuate**: *For several days the stock market oscillated wildly.* **2 oscillate between sth and sth** FORMAL to keep changing between two very different feelings, attitudes, situations etc. SYN **vacillate** **3** TECHNICAL to keep moving regularly from side to side, between two limits: *an oscillating fan* **4** PHYSICS if an electric current, light wave, or sound wave oscillates, it changes frequently in size, strength, direction etc. —**oscillation** /ˌɑsəˈleɪʃən/ *n.* [C,U] —**oscillatory** /ˈɑsələˌtɔri/ *adj.*

os·cil·la·tor /ˈɑsəˌleɪtɚ/ *n.* [C] PHYSICS a machine that produces electrical oscillations

-ose /oʊs/ *suffix* **1** [in adjectives] full of something, or involving too much of something: *verbose* (=using too many words) **2** [in nouns] used to name sugars, CARBOHYDRATES, and substances formed from PROTEINS: *sucrose* (=common type of sugar) | *lactose* (=from milk)

-oses /oʊsiz/ *suffix* the plural form of -OSIS

OSHA /ˈoʊʃə/ *n.* **the Occupational Safety and Health Administration** a U.S. government organization that makes rules about the safety and health of people at work

O·si·ris /oʊˈsaɪrɪs/ in ancient Egyptian MYTHOLOGY, the god of the dead, who was the husband and brother of ISIS

-osis /oʊsɪs/ *suffix plural* **-oses** /-oʊsiz/ [in nouns] **1** TECHNICAL a diseased condition: *tuberculosis* (=a lung disease) | *neuroses* (=mental illnesses) **2** a state or process: *a metamorphosis* (=a change from one state to another) | *hypnosis* (=state that is like sleep) —**-otic** /ɑt̬ɪk/ *suffix* [in adjectives] *neurotic* —**-otically** /ɑt̬ɪkli/ *suffix* [in adverbs]

Os·lo /ˈɑzloʊ/ the capital and largest city of Norway

os·mo·sis /ɑzˈmoʊsɪs, ɑs-/ *n.* [U] **1 by/through osmosis** if you learn something or receive ideas by osmosis, you gradually learn them by hearing them often: *Jose seemed to learn English by osmosis.* **2** PHYSICS the gradual process of liquid passing through a MEMBRANE —**osmotic** *adj.*

os·prey /ˈɑspri, -preɪ/ *n.* [C] BIOLOGY a large HAWK (=type of bird) that eats fish

os·si·fy /ˈɑsəˌfaɪ/ *v.* **ossifies**, **ossified**, **ossifying** [I,T] **1** FORMAL to gradually become unwilling or unable to change, or to make something do this: *an ossifying economic system* **2** [I,T] BIOLOGY to change into bone or to make CARTILAGE change into bone —**ossification** /ˌɑsəfəˈkeɪʃən/ *n.* [U]

os·ten·si·ble /ɑˈstɛnsəbəl/ *adj.* [only before noun] the ostensible purpose or reason for something is the one which appears to be true or is said to be true, but which may hide the real or reason: *The ostensible reason for his resignation was poor health.*

os·ten·si·bly /ɑˈstɛnsəbli/ *adv.* pretending to do something for one reason, but having another purpose or reason which is the real one: *A stranger came to the door, ostensibly to ask for directions.*

os·ten·ta·tion /ˌɑstənˈteɪʃən/ *n.* [U] a deliberate show of wealth or knowledge intended to make people admire you: *the ostentation of the building's architecture*

os·ten·ta·tious /ˌɑstənˈteɪʃəs/ *adj.* DISAPPROVING **1** something that is ostentatious is large, looks expensive, and is designed to make people think that its owner must be very rich: *an ostentatious engagement ring* | *I wanted a car that was fast but not ostentatious.* **2** trying to IMPRESS people by showing them how rich you are: *an ostentatious lifestyle* —**ostentatiously** *adv.*

osteo- /ɑstioʊ, -tiə/ *prefix* TECHNICAL relating to bones: *osteoporosis* (=disease of the bones)

os·te·o·ar·thri·tis /ˌɑstioʊɑrˈθraɪt̬ɪs/ *n.* [U] MEDICINE a serious condition which makes your knees and other joints stiff and painful

os·te·o·path /ˈɑstiəˌpæθ/ *n.* [C] someone trained in osteopathy

os·te·op·a·thy /ˌɑstiˈɑpəθi/ *n.* [U] MEDICINE the practice or skill of treating physical problems such as back pain by moving and pressing muscles and bones

os·te·o·po·ro·sis /ˌɑstioʊpəˈroʊsɪs/ *n.* [U] MEDICINE a disease in which the bones become very weak and break easily

os·tra·cism /ˈɑstrəˌsɪzəm/ *n.* [U] **1** the action or result of ostracizing someone from a group **2** HISTORY the process in ancient Greece by which citizens could vote to send another citizen away from their society temporarily → see also BANISHMENT

os·tra·cize /ˈɑstrəˌsaɪz/ *v.* [T] **1** if a group of people ostracize someone, they stop accepting them as a member of the group: *After her husband's arrest, she was ostracized by her neighbors.* **2** to send someone away from a society through, ostracism as in ancient Greece [**Origin:** 1800–1900 Greek *ostrakizein* **to send away by voting with broken pieces of pot**, from *ostrakon* **broken piece of pot**] → see also BANISH

os·trich /ˈɑstrɪtʃ, ˈɔs-/ *n.* [C] **1** BIOLOGY a very large African bird with long legs, that can run fast but cannot fly **2** INFORMAL someone who refuses to accept that problems exist, instead of trying to deal with them [**Origin:** (2) because ostriches were believed to bury their heads in sand so that their hunters could not see them]

ostrich

Os·tro·goth /ˈɑstrəˌɡɑθ/ one of a tribe of Goths that ruled Italy in the sixth century A.D.

Os·wald /ˈɑzwɔld/, **Lee Har·vey** /li ˈhɑrvi/ (1939–1963) the man who is believed to have shot and killed the U.S. President John F. Kennedy in 1963

OT **1** the written abbreviation of OLD TESTAMENT **2** the abbreviation of OVERTIME

OTC the abbreviation of OVER-THE-COUNTER

OT'C ˌmarket *n.* [C] ECONOMICS **over-the-counter market** a market for buying and selling STOCK in new and small companies that are not on the list of an organized STOCK EXCHANGE, using computers that are connected to each other and to the Internet

oth·er¹ /ˈʌðɚ/ S1 W1 *determiner, adj.* **1** used to talk about all the people or things in a group except for the one or ones already mentioned or known about: **the other sth** *I could do it, but none of the other boys could.* | *Add the flour and the other ingredients.* | **sb's other sth** *None of my other friends agreed.* | **these/those other sth** *We need those other chairs too.* **2** used to talk about the second of two people or things, which is not the one you already have or the one you have already mentioned: **the other sth** *The other man said nothing.* | **sb's other sth** *I can't find my other pants.* | **this/that other** *The other girl saw what happened.* | *Here's one sock, but where's* ***the other one****?* **3** used for talking about additional people or things of the same kind: *Max was thrown into a cell with three other men.* | *The other good news is that Jan is pregnant.* | *I'm busy now – could we talk* ***some other*** *time?* | *Do you have* ***any other*** *questions?* | **many/several etc. other sth** *There are many other places to visit.* **4 the other day/morning etc.** SPOKEN on a recent day, morning etc.: *I saw Mark the other day.* **5 the other side/end etc.** the part of a road, room, place etc. that is opposite where you are or furthest away from where you are: *the other side of the street* | *She drove off in the other direction.* **6 the other way/direction etc.** in a different direction, especially in the opposite direction: *The pickup turned and started back in the other direction.* **7 in other words** said when you are going to express an idea or opinion in a different way, especially one that is easier to understand: *These are people with incomes over $1 million – in other words, the very rich.* **8 other than a)** except for something SYN **except**: *There's nothing we can do other than hope she comes back.* | *The music was a little loud, but* ***other than that*** *it was a great concert.* **b)** in addition to something SYN **besides**: *Did you go anywhere other than Cairo?* → see also **none other than sb/sth** at NONE¹ (3) **9 the other way around** if the situation, process etc. is the other way around, it is actually the opposite of how you thought it was: *Students translate from French to English and the other way around.* **10 the other woman** a woman with whom a man is having a sexual relationship, even though he already has a wife or partner: *He left his wife and moved in with the other woman.* [**Origin:** Old English] → see also EACH OTHER, **every other day/week/one etc.** at EVERY (6), **(on the one hand...) on the other hand** at HAND¹ (3)

other² S1 W1 *pron.* **1** used to talk about all the people or things in a group except for the one or ones already mentioned or known about: *We ate one pizza and froze* ***the other****.* | *You pass out these forms and I'll do* ***the others****.* | *We found one letter, but there weren't* ***any others*** *in the drawer.* **2 others** [plural] additional people or things: *I love this painting. Do you have others like it?* | **any/some/no etc. others** *We found one letter, but there weren't any others in the drawer.* | **many/several etc. others** *songs by the Beatles, the Rolling Stones, and various others* | *The guests included,* ***among others****, Elizabeth Taylor and Michael Jackson* (=used to say that these were just a few of the other people). **3 others** [plural] different people or things from the one or ones already mentioned, or already known about: *Many people seemed offended, while others just laughed.* | **some...others** *Some people can do more than others.* | *Some trees lose their leaves in winter, while others stay green.* **4 some...or other** used when you are not being specific about which thing, person etc. you mean, often because you do not know or you cannot remember: *For some reason or other, she doesn't believe me.* | **someone/something or other** *She heard a rumor from someone or other.* | **somewhere/somehow etc. or other** *a foreign diplomat from somewhere or other* → see also **one after the other** at ONE² (6)

oth·er·ness /ˈʌðɚnɪs/ *n.* [U] the quality of being strange, different, or separate: *Many immigrants experience a sense of otherness.*

oth·er·wise /ˈʌðɚˌwaɪz/ S1 W2 *adv.* **1** used to say that a bad result will happen if something is not done [sentence adverb] *I'll type it; otherwise, they won't be able to read it.* **2** except for what has just been mentioned: [sentence adverb] *The sleeves are a little long, but otherwise it fits fine.* | [adj./adv.] *one excellent performance in an otherwise boring show* **3** used to say what would have happened, or what might have happened, if something else had not happened: *We were stuck at the* airport. Otherwise we would have been here by lunch.* **4 say/think/decide etc. otherwise** to say, think etc. something different from what has been mentioned: *He says he has quit politics, but his recent activities suggest otherwise.* **5 or otherwise** in another way, or of another type: *I can't see any advantage in buying a new house – financially or otherwise.* | *We welcome comments from viewers, favorable or otherwise.* **6 otherwise known as** also called: *Global warming is otherwise known as the greenhouse effect.* **7 be otherwise engaged/occupied** FORMAL to be busy doing something else **8 it cannot be otherwise** also **how can it be otherwise** FORMAL used to mean that it is impossible for something to be different from the way it is

O

oth·er·world·ly /ˌʌðɚˈwɚldli◂/ *adj.* seeming to belong to a different or more SPIRITUAL world rather than to the real world: *The humpback whales make otherworldly sounds.*

-otic /ɑt̬ɪk/ *suffix* → see -OSIS

Ot·ta·wa¹ /ˈɑt̬əwə/ the capital city of Canada

Ottawa² a Native American tribe from the Great Lakes area of North America

ot·ter /ˈɑt̬ɚ/ *n.* [C] BIOLOGY a small animal that can swim, has brown fur, and eats fish

ot·to·man /ˈɑt̬əmən/ *n.* [C] **1** a soft piece of furniture shaped like a box that you rest your feet on when you are sitting down **2** a piece of furniture like a SOFA without arms or a back

Ot·to·man Em·pire, the /ˌɑt̬əmən ˈɛmpaɪɚ/ HISTORY a large EMPIRE, based in Turkey and with its capital in Istanbul, which also included large parts of Eastern Europe, Asia, and North Africa. It continued from the 13th century until after World War I, but was most powerful in the 16th century.

Oua·ga·dou·gou /ˌwɑgəˈdugu/ the capital and largest city of Burkina

ouch /aʊtʃ/ *interjection* a sound that you make when you feel sudden pain: *Ouch! That hurt!*

ought·a /ˈɔt̬ə/ *modal verb* NONSTANDARD the spoken short form of "ought to": *He oughta know.*

ought·n't /ˈɔtˀnt/ *v.* OLD-FASHIONED the short form of "ought not": *She oughtn't to have said that.*

ought to /ˈɔt̬ə; *strong* ˈɔt̬u/ S1 W2 *modal verb* **1** used to say that someone should do something or something should happen because it is the best, most sensible, or the right or fair thing to do: *Maybe we ought to call the doctor.* | *Don't you think you ought to email or call her and say you're sorry?* | *That kind of behavior ought to be illegal.* | *I* ***ought to have*** (=should have) *listened to your advice.* | *You* ***ought not to have*** (=should not have) *taken the car without asking.* **2** used to say that you think something will probably happen, probably be true etc.: *This ought to be easy.* | *They ought to have left the house by now.* | *Just one more screw – there,* ***that ought to do it*** (=used to say that something you have been working on is finished or enough). **3** used to suggest something that you think is good: *You ought to try sailing. You'd like it.* [**Origin:** Old English *ahte*, past tense of *agan*] → see also OUGHTA, SHOULD

Oui·ja board /ˈwidʒi ˌbɔrd, -dʒə/ *n.* [C] TRADEMARK a board with letters and signs on it, used to try to receive messages from the spirits of dead people

ounce /aʊns/ S3 W3 *n.* **1** [C] WRITTEN ABBREVIATION **oz.** a unit for measuring weight, equal to 1/16 of a pound or 28.35 grams: *The baby weighed 8 pounds and 13 ounces.* | **+of** *12 ounces of butter* → see also FLUID OUNCE **2 an ounce of sense/truth/decency etc.** a very small amount of a particular quality: *There isn't an ounce of truth in what he says.* **3 every (last) ounce of courage/energy/strength etc.** all the courage, energy etc. that you have: *I gave every ounce of energy that I had to the job.* **4 not have an ounce of fat on you** used to say that someone is thin and healthy looking **5 an ounce of prevention is worth a pound of cure** OLD-FASHIONED used to say that it is better to avoid a problem than to try to solve it after it has happened [**Origin:** 1300–1400 Old French *unce*, from Latin *uncia* **twelfth part, ounce**]

our /ɑr; *strong* aʊɚ/ S1 W1 *possessive adj.* [possessive form of "we"] belonging or relating to the person who is speaking and one or more other people: *You can stay at our house.* | *It is important that we preserve our natural resources.* | *Even* ***our own*** (=used to emphasize something) *children criticized us.* | *We'd like a house* ***of our own*** *some day.* [**Origin:** Old English *ure*] → see also OURS

Our ˈFather *n.* [singular] another name for the LORD'S PRAYER

ˌOur ˈLady *n.* [singular, not with "the"] a name used by some Christians for Mary, the mother of Jesus Christ

ˌOur ˈLord *n.* [singular, not with "the"] a name used by Christians for Jesus Christ

ours /aʊɚz, ɑrz/ S2 *possessive pron.* [possessive form of "we"] the thing or things belonging or relating to the person who is speaking and one or more other people: *Their car is bigger than ours.* | *Ed is a good friend* ***of ours.***

our·selves /aʊɚˈsɛlvz, ɑr-/ S2 W2 *pron.* **1** the REFLEXIVE form of "we": *We prepared ourselves for the hike.* | *We kept some of the food for ourselves.* **2** the strong form of "we," used to emphasize the subject or object of a sentence: *We started this business ourselves.* | ***We ourselves*** *were unaware of what was about to happen.* **3** also **(all) by ourselves** without help from anyone else: *We built the porch ourselves.* **4 (all) by ourselves** alone: *This year we wanted to take a vacation by ourselves.* **5 (all) to ourselves** not having to share something with any other people: *When Sarah goes to college we'll finally have the house to ourselves.* **6** used instead of "us" after some prepositions, for example "as," "about," and "of," when "we" is used earlier in the sentence: *We live among people who have the same opinions as ourselves.* **7 be ourselves** to feel or behave in the way you usually do, or in the way you want to do: *We all want a relationship in which we can be ourselves.* → see also YOURSELF

-ous /əs/ *suffix* [in adjectives] having a particular quality: *dangerous* (=full of danger) | *nervous* (=worried or afraid about something) → see also -EOUS, -IOUS

oust /aʊst/ *v.* [T] to force someone out of a position of power, especially so that you can take their place: **oust sb from sth** *The next month he was ousted from the board of directors.*

oust·er /ˈaʊstɚ/ *n.* [C usually singular] **sb's ouster** also **the ouster of sb** an act of removing someone from a position of power: *Her ouster came as a shock to everybody.*

out¹ /aʊt/ S1 W1 *adv., adj.* [adv. only after verb, adj. not before noun]
1 FROM INSIDE STH away from the inside of a place or container: *Gwen reached in the drawer and pulled out a knife.* | *We opened the window to let all the smoke out.* | **+of** *My keys fell out of my pocket.* | *Sit down, and I'll get a couple of beers out of the cooler.* ▸see THESAURUS box at outside²
2 LEAVE A PLACE from the inside part of a building, vehicle etc., to the outside: *Watch the step on your way out.* | **+of** *I saw him come out of the hotel.* | **out came/jumped/walked etc.** *The plane door opened, and out stepped the President.*
3 OUTSIDE not inside a building SYN **outside**: *children playing out in the snow* | *In the summer, we sometimes sleep out in the yard.*
4 NOT THERE away from the place where you usually are, especially for a short time: *Ms. Nichols is out this morning. Can I take a message?* | *Do you know how long he'll be out?*
5 SOCIAL ACTIVITY to or in a place that is not your home, in order to enjoy yourself or meet people: *I always go out on Saturday nights.* | | *We* ***eat out*** (=eat in restaurants) *all the time.* | *He finally* ***asked me out*** (=invited me to go somewhere). | *My parents* ***took me out*** *to dinner.*
6 DISTANT PLACE in or to a place that is far away from city centers, or difficult to get to: *a little hotel out in the desert* | *a farm way out on the prairie*

7 AWAY FROM THE EDGE moving away or sticking out from the main part or edge of something: *I swam out into the middle of the lake.* | *The small peninsula juts out into the sea.* | **out of sth** *There were tree stumps sticking out of the ground.*
8 WESTERN U.S. toward the West in the U.S.: *We moved out to California when I was little.*
9 COMPLETELY/CAREFULLY completely or carefully: *I got the kids to clean out the garage for me.* | *Poor Steve – the job is just wearing him out* (=making him extremely tired). | *It's a nice idea, but I don't think they've really thought it out* (=considered it carefully and thoroughly).
10 NOT WORKING power, electricity, a piece of equipment etc. that is out is not working: *I think the electricity went out again last night.* → see also **out of order** at ORDER[1]
11 FIRE/LIGHT a fire or light that is out is not burning or shining anymore: *The lights are out – I don't think anybody's home.* | *I put out my cigarette and went back inside.*
12 NOT IN POWER a politician or political party that is out does not have power or authority any longer: *The only way to lower taxes is to vote the Democrats out.* | *He may face prosecution once he is **out of office**.*
13 APPEAR used to say that someone or something has appeared: *It looks like the sun's finally going to come out.* | *It was spring and the leaves were finally out.*
14 **read/shout etc. sth out (loud)** to say something in a voice that is loud enough for others to hear: *"See you later," she called out.* | *What does it say? Read it out loud.*
15 GIVEN TO MANY PEOPLE used to say that something is given to many people: *She got a job handing out pamphlets.* | *I'll send out the invitations tomorrow.*
16 GET RID OF STH used to say that something does not exist anymore or is getting rid of something: *Can I throw out the corn? Nobody's going to eat it.* | **+of** *How can I get this wine stain out of my blouse?*
17 NOT INCLUDED not included in a team, group etc.: *Ramirez has an ankle injury, and could be out for several weeks.* | **+of** *Why did she get kicked out of the club?*
18 NOT POSSIBLE/ALLOWED INFORMAL not possible or not allowed: *Skiing's out because I don't have any money.* | *I'm training for the marathon, so things like alcohol and rich foods are out.*
19 ORIGIN used to say where someone or something comes from: *The burning complex poured out smoke.* | **+of** *one of the most talented players to come out of Europe* | *New product research is financed out of company profits.*
20 **out of wood/metal/glass etc.** used to say what substance a particular thing is made of: *People were living in shacks made out of metal sheets.*
21 AVAILABLE a product that is out is available to be bought: *Is her new book out yet?* | *I heard there's a cheaper model coming out this fall.*
22 CHOOSE used to say that one person or thing is chosen or taken from a larger group: *You can pick out whatever you want.* | *Why was Kenny singled out for punishment?*
23 **be out for sth** also **be out to do sth** INFORMAL to have a particular intention: *He's convinced that his colleagues are out to cheat him.* | *Andre's just out for a good time.*
24 **be out to get sb** to want to punish or do something bad to someone because they have done something bad to you: *He thinks everyone is out to get him.*
25 NOT AWAKE **a)** asleep: **be/go out like a light** *Billy was out like a light by 8:00 p.m.* **b)** not conscious: *I felt dizzy and almost passed out.* | *He must have hit his head pretty hard. He's **out cold**.*
26 SPORTS/GAMES **a)** a player or team that is out is not allowed to play anymore, or has lost one of their chances to get a point: *If the ball hits you, you're out.* | *Hingis went out in the second round, beaten by an almost unknown Australian.* **b)** a ball that is out in a game such as tennis or basketball is not in the area of play
27 NOT FASHIONABLE clothes or styles that are out are not fashionable anymore: *Don't you know tight jeans are out?*
28 NOT SECRET not secret anymore: *The secret's out.* | *Somehow **word** of Beasley's arrest **got out**.*
29 FREE not in prison or kept in a place against your will anymore: *How did the dog get out?* | **+of** *Dutton has been out of prison since 1976.*
30 FINISHED/USED **be/run/sell etc. out** to not have something because you have used it all, sold it all etc.: *Tickets for the show sold out immediately.* | **+of** *I didn't finish because I ran out of time.* | *We're almost out of gas.*
31 HOMOSEXUAL if a HOMOSEXUAL person is out or comes out, they tell everyone that they are homosexual: *The congressman has been out for several years now.*
32 REASON FOR DOING STH **out of sth** if you do something out of interest, kindness, or some other feeling, you do it because you are interested, kind etc.: *Out of respect for the dead woman's family, there were no journalists at the funeral.* | *Why did I go? Just out of curiosity, I guess.*
33 **out there** **a)** in a place that could be anywhere except here: *My real father is out there and one day I plan to find him.* **b)** where something or someone can be noticed by many people: *He was out there all the time raising money for disabled kids.* **c)** SPOKEN, INFORMAL used to say that an idea or person seems very strange: *Sheila's ideas can be way out there sometimes.*
34 OCEAN if the TIDE is out, the ocean is at its lowest level
35 **be out of control/danger etc.** used to say that someone or something is not in a particular condition or situation anymore: *Strong winds sent the boat out of control.* | *Kids are more out of shape than they used to be.*
36 **watch/look out** SPOKEN used to tell someone to be careful: *Look out! There's a van coming.*
37 **a)** **be/feel out of it** INFORMAL to be unable to think clearly because you are very tired, drunk etc.: *I was so out of it, I didn't really understand what he was saying.* **b)** to not feel completely involved in an activity or situation: *Shelly felt out of it her first week back at work.*
38 **out with it!** SPOKEN used to tell someone to say something that they are having difficulty saying: *OK, out with it! What really happened?*
39 **out (you go)!** SPOKEN used to order someone to leave a room
40 **be out of work** also **out of a job** to not have a job: *Ramos has been out of work for over six months.*
41 **get out from under sb/sth** to not be controlled by someone anymore, or to not suffer because of a bad situation anymore: *We need to do something to get out from under this debt.*
42 **9 out of 10** also **3 out of 5 etc.** used to show a percent or the relationship in size of one group to another: *Almost five out of ten marriages end in divorce.*
43 **out front** **a)** in front of something, especially a building, where everyone can see you: *There's a station wagon waiting out front.* **b)** taking a leading position: *As a civil rights leader, he was always out front.*
44 **out back** in a back yard or behind a building: *I think there's an old wheelbarrow out back.* → see also OUTBACK
45 **out and about** going from one place, house etc. to another, especially for social activities: *Most teenagers would rather be out and about with their friends.*
46 **out of earshot/sight** so far away from someone that they cannot hear you or see you: *They only use those expressions when their parents are out of earshot.*
47 **before the day/year etc. is out** before the day, year etc. has ended: *Derry signed the contract and was performing onstage before the week was out.*
[**Origin:** Old English *ut*] → see also **out of the blue** at BLUE[2] (4), **go out of your mind** at MIND[1] (8), OUT-OF-THE-WAY, **out of place** at PLACE[1] (14), **be out of the question** at QUESTION[1] (7), **out of sight** at SIGHT[1] (8), **out of sorts** at SORT[1] (5), **be out of this world** at WORLD[1] (20)

out[2] S1 W3 *prep.* from inside to the outside of something: *Karen looked out the window at the back yard.* | **+of** *Grass grows out small holes in the side of the pot.*

O

out³ *v.* **1** [T usually passive] to publicly say that someone is HOMOSEXUAL, especially when that person wants it to be a secret: *John knew that he might be outed if he decided to run for office.* **2 truth/murder etc. will out!** used to say that it is difficult to hide the truth, a murder etc.

out⁴ *n.* **1** [singular] INFORMAL an excuse for not doing something, or a chance to avoid a difficult situation: *I'm busy Sunday, so that* ***gives me an out****.* **2** [C] an act of making a player in baseball lose the chance to get a point **3 on the outs (with sb)** INFORMAL arguing or not agreeing with someone → see also **the ins and outs (of sth)** at INS

out- /aʊt/ *prefix* **1** used to form nouns and adjectives from verbs that are followed by "out": *outbreak* (=from "break out") | *outspoken* (=from "speak out") **2** [in nouns and adjectives] outside or beyond something: *an outhouse* (=a toilet outside a house) | *outlying* (=far from the center of the something) **3** [in verbs] being bigger, further, greater etc. than someone or something else: *outlive* (=live longer) | *outgrow* (=become too big for something) **4** [in verbs] doing better than someone else, so that you defeat them: *outrun* (=run faster)

out·age /ˈaʊt̬ɪdʒ/ *n.* [C] a period when a service such as the electricity supply is not provided: *a power outage*

ˌout-and-ˈout *adj.* [only before noun] having all the qualities of a particular kind of person or thing, especially someone or something bad: *out-and-out lies* | *The guy is an out-and-out conman.*

out·back /ˈaʊt˺bæk/ *n.* **the outback** the Australian COUNTRYSIDE far away from cities, where few people live

out·bal·ance /aʊt˺ˈbæləns/ *v.* [T] to be more important or valuable than something else SYN **outweigh**

out·bid /aʊt˺ˈbɪd/ *v.* **outbid, outbidding** [T] to offer a higher price than someone else, especially at an AUCTION: *Shue outbid three competitors for the painting.*

out·board mo·tor /ˌaʊt˺bɔrd ˈmoʊt̬ɚ/ *n.* [C] a motor fastened to the back end of a small boat

out·bound /ˈaʊt˺baʊnd/ *adj.* moving away from you or away from a town, country etc.: *outbound planes*

ˈout box, outbox *n.* [C] **1** a container on an office desk used to hold work and letters which are ready to be sent out or put away **2** a place on a computer where the email messages that you are going to send or sending are shown → see also IN BOX

out·break /ˈaʊt˺breɪk/ *n.* [C] the sudden appearance or start of war, fighting, or serious disease: *a cholera outbreak* | **+of** *the outbreak of World War II* → see also **break out** at BREAK¹

out·build·ing /ˈaʊt˺ˌbɪldɪŋ/ *n.* [C] a building such as a BARN or SHED near a main building

out·burst /ˈaʊt˺bɚst/ *n.* [C] **1** a sudden powerful expression of strong emotion, especially anger: *I was embarrassed by my husband's outburst.* | **+of** *outbursts of anger* **2** a sudden temporary increase in activity: *a fresh outburst of violence in the region*

out·cast /ˈaʊt˺kæst/ *n.* [C] someone who is not accepted by the people they live among, or has been forced out of their home: *Smokers are often treated as social outcasts.* —**outcast** *adj.*

out·class /aʊt˺ˈklæs/ *v.* [T] to be much better than someone at doing something, or to be much better than something else: *De Niro completely outclasses the other members of the cast.*

out·come /ˈaʊt˺kʌm/ Ac W3 *n.* [C] **1** the final result of a meeting, process, series of events etc., especially when no one knows what it will be until it actually happens: *Both sides are hoping for a positive outcome.* | **+of** *factors that influenced the outcome of the war* ▸see THESAURUS box at **result¹** **2** MATH one of the things that happens as a result of a test done to find out how likely it is that particular things will happen. For example, in a test of rolling a dice, one outcome would be rolling a six. → see also EVENT

out·crop·ping /ˈaʊt˺ˌkrɑpɪŋ/ also **out·crop** /ˈaʊt˺ˌkrɑp/ *n.* [C] a rock or group of rocks above the surface of the ground

out·cry /ˈaʊt˺kraɪ/ *n.* [C] an angry protest by a lot of people: *The killings by the military have caused an international outcry.* | **+against** *a* ***public outcry*** *against the new rule*

out·dat·ed /ˌaʊtˈdeɪt̬ɪd◂/ *adj.* **1** not useful or modern anymore: *outdated equipment* | *teaching methods that were hopelessly outdated* ▸see THESAURUS box at **old-fashioned** **2** an outdated document cannot be used because the period of time for which it was effective has passed SYN **out-of-date**: *an outdated passport* **3** information is not recent and may no longer be correct SYN **out-of-date**: *This estimate was based on outdated numbers.* → see also OUT-OF-DATE

out·did /aʊtˈdɪd/ *v.* the past tense of OUTDO

out·dis·tance /aʊtˈdɪstəns/ *v.* [T] to run, ride etc. faster than other people, especially in a race, so that you are far ahead: *Turner easily outdistanced the other competitors.*

out·do /aʊtˈdu/ *v. past tense* **outdid** /-ˈdɪd/ *past participle* **outdone** /-ˈdʌn/ [T] **1** to be better or more successful than someone else at doing something: *Kwan outdid Bobek to win the finals.* | **outdo sb in (doing) sth** *The skaters try to outdo each other in grace and speed.* **2 outdo yourself** to do something extremely well: *The costumes are great. You've really outdone yourself this time.* **3 not to be outdone** in order not to let someone else do better than you: *Not to be outdone by the girls, the boys' team also won its second team title.*

out·door /ˈaʊtdɔr/ *adj.* **1** [only before noun] existing, happening, or used outside, not inside a building OPP **indoor**: *outdoor sports* | *an outdoor concert in the park* | *outdoor furniture* **2 outdoor type** a person who enjoys camping, and other outdoor activities such as walking, climbing etc.

out·doors¹ /aʊtˈdɔrz/ *adv.* outside, not inside a building OPP **indoors** SYN **out of doors**: *It's warm enough to eat outdoors.* ▸see THESAURUS box at **outside²**

outdoors² *n.* **the (great) outdoors** the open lands, mountains, rivers etc. far away from buildings and cities: *a love of the great outdoors*

out·door·sy /aʊtˈdɔrzi/ *adj.* INFORMAL enjoying outdoor activities: *Jeff is really outdoorsy.*

out·draw /aʊtˈdrɔ/ *v. past tense* **outdrew** /-ˈdru/ *past participle* **outdrawn** /-ˈdrɔn/ [T] to pull a gun out faster than someone else

out·er /ˈaʊt̬ɚ/ *adj.* [only before noun] **1** on the outside of something OPP **inner**: *Remove the tough outer leaves before cooking.* | **the outer layer/surface/edge etc.** *outer layer of the Earth* **2** away from the center of something, when there are other similar things that are closer to the center OPP **inner**: *the outer suburbs* **3** relating to someone's appearance or the behavior they show to others, as opposed to the private feelings they have OPP **inner**: *For all her outer toughness, she is emotionally fragile.*

out·er·most /ˈaʊt̬ɚˌmoʊst/ *adj.* [only before noun] farthest outside or farthest from the middle OPP **inmost** OPP **innermost**: *the outermost petals of the flower*

ˌouter ˈspace *n.* [U] the space outside the Earth's air, where the PLANETS and stars are

out·er·wear /ˈaʊt̬ɚˌwɛr/ *n.* [U] clothes, such as coats, that are worn over ordinary clothes

out·fall /ˈaʊtfɔl/ *n.* [C] a place where water flows out, especially from a DRAIN or river: *a sewage outfall*

out·field /ˈaʊtfild/ *n.* **the outfield 1** the part of a baseball field farthest from the player who is batting (BAT) **2** the players in this part of the field —**outfielder** *n.* [C] → see also INFIELD → see picture at BASEBALL

out·fit¹ /ˈaʊtˌfɪt/ S2 *n.* [C] **1** a set of clothes worn together: *I love your outfit!* | *a cowboy outfit* **2** a group of people who work together as a team or organization: *an outfit of 120 engineers* | *a five-piece jazz outfit* **3** a set of tools or equipment that you need for a particular purpose or job

outfit² *v.* **outfitted, outfitting** [T] to provide someone with a set of clothes or equipment for a special purpose: **outfit sb/sth with sth** *Police had been outfitted* *with protective riot gear.* | **outfit sb in sth** *The groom was outfitted in a beautifully cut tuxedo.*

out·fit·ter /ˈaʊtˌfɪtɚ/ *n.* [C] a store that sells equipment for outdoor activities such as camping

out·flank /aʊtˈflæŋk/ *v.* [T] **1** to gain an advantage over an opponent, especially in politics or business: *Republicans sought to outflank Democrats on the tax bill.* **2** to go around the side of an enemy during a battle and attack them from behind: *To the west, the army was outflanked by a huge number of British forces.*

out·flow /ˈaʊtfloʊ/ *n.* [C,U] **1** ECONOMICS a process in which money, goods, people etc. leave a place: +**of** *large outflows of investment funds* **2** a flow of liquid or air from something OPP **inflow**: *chemical outflow into the bay* | *outflow pipes*

out·fox /aʊtˈfɑks/ *v.* [T] to gain an advantage over someone by being more intelligent than they are SYN **outwit** SYN **outsmart**: *So far Hutchinson has managed to outfox police.*

out·go·ing /ˈaʊt˺ˌgoʊɪŋ/ *adj.* **1** liking to meet and talk to new people: *a friendly outgoing woman* | *his outgoing personality* ▶see THESAURUS box at **sociable** **2 the outgoing president/CEO etc.** someone who will soon be finishing a job as a president etc. OPP **incoming** **3** [only before noun] going out or leaving a place OPP **incoming**: *outgoing phone calls*

out·grow /aʊt˺ˈgroʊ/ *v.* *past tense* **outgrew** /-ˈgru/ *past participle* **outgrown** /-ˈgroʊn/ [T] **1** to grow too big for something SYN **grow out of**: *Kara's already outgrown her shoes.* **2** to not do something or enjoy something anymore, because you have grown older and changed: *Most children outgrow the need for an afternoon nap.* **3** to grow or increase faster than someone or something else: *The female population outgrew the male population in most of the experiments.*

out·growth /ˈaʊt˺groʊθ/ *n.* [C] **1** something that develops from something else, as a natural result: +**of** *Crime is often an outgrowth of poverty.* **2** TECHNICAL something that grows out of something else

out·guess /aʊt˺ˈgɛs/ *v.* [T] to guess what someone or something is going to do before they do it: *Too many investors try to outguess the stock market.*

out·gun /aʊt˺ˈgʌn/ *v.* **outgunned**, **outgunning** [T usually passive] **1** to defeat someone in a competition, argument etc. because you have more skills, are better prepared etc.: *The prosecution was outgunned by high-priced defense lawyers.* **2** to defeat another group or army because you have more or better weapons than they do

out·house /ˈaʊthaʊs/ *n.* [C] a small building which is used as a toilet, found in places such as camping areas, and in the past behind houses SYN **privy**

out·ie /ˈaʊt̬i/ *n.* [C] INFORMAL a BELLY BUTTON that sticks out → see also INNIE

out·ing /ˈaʊt̬ɪŋ/ *n.* **1** [C] a short enjoyable trip for a group of people: *a family outing* | +**to** *an outing to the beach* | *The class was* ***on an outing*** *to the local museum.* **2** [C,U] the practice of publicly naming people as HOMOSEXUALS, when they do not want anyone to know this, or an occasion when this is done

out·land·ish /aʊtˈlændɪʃ/ *adj.* very strange and unusual: *outlandish costumes*

out·last /aʊtˈlæst/ *v.* [T] to continue to exist, work etc. for a longer time than someone or something else: *Shien's has outlasted every other restaurant in the neighborhood.* → see also OUTLIVE

out·law¹ /ˈaʊt˺lɔ, aʊt˺ˈlɔ/ *v.* [T] to make something illegal SYN **ban**: *The bill would have outlawed several types of guns.*

outlaw² /ˈaʊt˺lɔ/ *n.* [C] a word meaning a "criminal," often one who is hiding from the police, used especially in past times

outlaw³ *adj.* [only before noun] not obeying the law or accepted rules: *an outlaw regime*

out·lay /ˈaʊt˺leɪ/ *n.* *plural* **outlays** [C,U] the amount of money that you have to spend in order to start a new business, activity etc.: +**on/for** *There'll be* ***an initial outlay*** *of $2,500 for tools and equipment.*

out·let /ˈaʊt˺lɛt, -lɪt/ S3 *n.* [C] **1** PHYSICS a place on a wall where you can connect electrical equipment to the supply of electricity: *an electrical outlet* → see picture at PLUG² **2** a store, company, organization etc. through which products are sold: *car-rental outlets* | *one of the largest* ***retail outlets*** (=stores that sell products to the public) *in the world* | *an interview published in various* ***media outlets*** (=company or organization that broadcasts news, produces newspapers etc.) **3** a way of expressing or getting rid of strong feelings: +**for** *Children need a physical outlet for their energy.* **4** a pipe or a hole through which something such as a liquid or gas can flow out

ˈoutlet ˌmall *n.* [C] a large building or set of buildings where many stores sell their products at DISCOUNT (=lower) prices than their normal stores do

out·li·er /ˈaʊtˌlaɪɚ/ *n.* [C] MATH a value that is a lot higher or a lot lower than all of the other values in a set of data

out·line¹ /ˈaʊt˺laɪn/ *n.* [C] **1** the main ideas or facts about something, without all the details: *In a short statement, Wilson gave an outline of his plans.* | *an outline agreement* | *The events are familiar, at least* ***in outline****, to most of the students.* | **a broad/rough/general outline** (=a very general outline) **2** a plan for a piece of writing in which each new idea is separately written down: +**of/for** *The professor wants an outline of our papers by Friday.* **3** a line around the edge of something which shows its shape but no details: *She drew an outline around the shape.*

outline² *v.* [T] **1** ENG. LANG. ARTS to describe something in a general way, giving the main points but not the details: **outline a plan/proposal/program etc.** *The Republican candidate outlined his plans to improve education.* **2** to draw or put a line around the edge of something to show its shape: **outline sth in sth** *a map with our town outlined in red* **3 be outlined against/by sth** if something is outlined against another thing, its edge or shape is clearly shown against that background: *He could see the huge ship outlined against the sky.*

out·live /aʊt˺ˈlɪv/ *v.* [T] **1** to live longer than someone else: *Women usually outlive their husbands.* **2** to continue to live or exist after something else has ended or disappeared SYN **outlast**: *Great art usually outlives anyone who wants to ban it.* **3 outlive your usefulness** to become no longer useful: *The old docks have outlived their usefulness.* → see also OUTLAST

out·look /ˈaʊt˺lʊk/ *n.* **1** [singular] your general attitude to life and the world: +**on** *Nels has a very positive outlook on life.* | *There are major differences* ***in outlook*** *between the two candidates.* **2** [singular] what is expected to happen in the future: +**for** *The outlook for the housing market is improving.* **3** [C] a place from which something such as an area of land can be seen, or the view from that place

out·ly·ing /ˈaʊt˺ˌlaɪ-ɪŋ/ *adj.* [only before noun] far from a city, town etc. or its center, or far from a main building: *outlying farm communities*

out·man /aʊt˺ˈmæn/ *v.* **outmanned**, **outmanning** [T usually passive] to have more people in your group than in your opponent's group SYN **outnumber**: *The Mexicans were outmanned by three to one.*

out·ma·neu·ver /ˌaʊt˺məˈnuvɚ/ *v.* [T] to gain an advantage over an opponent by using better or more skillful methods: *The President found himself consistently outmaneuvered by his rivals in Congress.*

out·mod·ed /aʊt˺ˈmoʊdɪd/ *adj.* not fashionable or useful anymore SYN **outdated**: *outmoded economic policies*

out·num·ber /aʊt˺ˈnʌmbɚ/ *v.* [T] to be more in number than another group: *In nursing, women still outnumber men by four to one.* | *Spanish speakers far outnumber speakers of other foreign languages in the U.S.*

ˌout-of-ˈbody *adj.* **an out-of-body experience** the feeling that you are outside your body and looking down on it from above, which people sometimes have when they are close to death

ˌout of ˈbounds *adj.* **1** not inside the official playing area in a sports game [OPP] **in bounds**: *The ball was out of bounds.* **2** not allowed or acceptable: +**for** *Certain topics, such as sex, were out of bounds for discussion.* **3** if a place is out of bounds, you are not allowed to go there [SYN] **off-limits**: +**for** *All of the kids in my family knew that the railroad tracks were out of bounds.* —**out of bounds** *adv.*: *Stark knocked the ball out of bounds.*

O

ˌout-of-ˈcourt *adj.* **an out-of-court settlement** an agreement to settle a legal argument, in which one side agrees to pay money to the other so that the problem is not brought to court

ˌout-of-ˈdate, out of date *adj.* not useful, correct, or fashionable anymore [SYN] **outdated**: *out-of-date theories on education* | *The new manuals are already out of date.*

ˌout of ˈdoors *adv.* outside, not in a building [SYN] **outdoors**

ˌout-of-ˈpocket *adj.* **out-of-pocket expenses/costs etc.** costs that you have to pay yourself, rather than costs that someone else, such as your employer, pays

ˌout-of-ˈsight, out of sight *adj.* an amount of money that is out of sight is extremely large: *out-of-sight housing prices* → see also **out of sight** at SIGHT[1] (8), **out of sight, out of mind** at SIGHT[1] (14)

ˌout-of-ˈstate *adj.* from, to, or in another state: *out-of-state license plates* —**out of state** *adv.*: *She may go to college out of state.*

ˌout-of-the-ˈway *adj.* far from other people or towns, or in a place that is difficult to find: *He spent the summer in an out-of-the-way village.* → see also **out of the way** at WAY[1] (19)

ˌout of ˈtouch *adj.* **1** not realizing what a situation is really like, how other people live or think etc.: +**with** *The party has grown increasingly out of touch with ordinary people.* **2** someone who is out of touch with someone else has not spoken, written etc. to them for a long time: *Over the years we just sort of fell out of touch.*

ˈout-of-town *adj.* [only before noun] to, from, or in another town: *The museum attracts a lot of out-of-town visitors.*

ˌout-of-ˈwork *adj.* unemployed: *out-of-work actors*

out·pace /aʊt̚ˈpeɪs/ *v.* [T] to go faster, perform better, or develop more quickly than someone or something else: *Home computer sales were outpacing business orders.*

out·pa·tient /ˈaʊt̚ˌpeɪʃənt/ *n.* [C] someone who goes to a hospital for treatment but does not stay there → see also INPATIENT

out·per·form /ˌaʊt̚pɚˈfɔrm/ *v.* [T] to perform better or be more successful than someone or something else: *Spanish students outperformed U.S. students in science.*

out·place·ment /ˈaʊt̚ˌpleɪsmənt/ *n.* [C,U] a service that a company provides to help its workers find other jobs when it cannot continue to employ them —**outplace** *v.* [T]

out·play /aʊt̚ˈpleɪ/ *v.* [T] to beat an opponent in a game by playing with more skill than they do

out·poll /aʊt̚ˈpoʊl/ *v.* [T] to defeat an opponent by receiving more votes than they do: *Bond outpolled three other Republicans to win the primary.*

out·post /ˈaʊt̚poʊst/ *n.* [C] a small town or group of buildings in a place far from city or towns, usually established as a military camp or a place for trade: *The city began its life as a remote border outpost.*

out·pour·ing /ˈaʊt̚pɔrɪŋ/ *n.* [C] **1** an expression of strong feelings by a large number of people: +**of** *Her death provoked an outpouring of sadness and sympathy.* **2** a lot of something, especially ideas, writings etc., that is produced suddenly: +**of** *an outpouring of creative energy*

out·put /ˈaʊt̚pʊt/ [Ac] [W3] *n.* **1** [C,U] the amount of goods or work produced by a person, machine, factory etc.: *Output is up 20% from last year.* | +**of** *the company's annual output of 300,000 cars* | **manufacturing/industrial/agricultural etc. output** *Korea's total annual agricultural output* **2** [U] COMPUTERS the information produced by a computer, and shown on the screen or printed onto paper **3** [C,U] PHYSICS the amount of electricity produced by a piece of equipment or an engine —**output** *v.* [T] → see also INPUT

out·rage¹ /ˈaʊt̚reɪdʒ/ *n.* **1** [U] a feeling of great anger or shock: *Several parents wrote to the school to express their outrage.* | +**at/over** *environmentalists' outrage at plans to develop the coastline* | **cause/spark/provoke/prompt etc. outrage** *The case prompted a lot of public outrage.* **2** [C] something that causes this feeling: *The prices they charge are an outrage!* [**Origin:** 1200–1300 Old French **too great quantity**, from *outre* **beyond, too much**; influenced in meaning by rage]

outrage² *v.* [T usually passive] to make someone feel very angry and shocked: **be outraged at/by sth** *Customers were outraged by the price increases.*

out·ra·geous /aʊt̚ˈreɪdʒəs/ *adj.* **1** so unfair or offensive as to be shocking: *outrageous prices* | *outrageous lies* | ***It's outrageous that** company executives get such high salaries.* **2** extremely unusual, amusing, or shocking: *an outrageous hairstyle* | *Almodovar's outrageous new movie*

out·ran /aʊt̚ˈræn/ *v.* the past tense of OUTRUN

out·rank /aʊt̚ˈræŋk/ *v.* [T] **1** to have a higher rank or position than someone else in the same group **2** to be more important than something else: *The survey shows that humor and shared activities outrank sex as features of a good relationship.*

ou·tré /uˈtreɪ/ *adj.* FORMAL strange, unusual, and slightly shocking: *a slightly outré theater production*

out·reach /ˈaʊt̚ritʃ/ *n.* [U] the practice of providing help, advice, or other services to people in an area who have particular problems: *a youth outreach program* | *outreach and education for homeless people*

out·ride /aʊt̚ˈraɪd/ *v. past tense* **outrode** /-ˈroʊd/, *past participle* **outridden** /-ˈrɪdn/ [T] to ride faster or farther than someone or something else

out·rid·er /ˈaʊt̚ˌraɪdɚ/ *n.* [C] a guard or police officer who rides on a MOTORCYCLE or horse beside or in front of a vehicle in which an important person is traveling

out·rig·ger /ˈaʊt̚ˌrɪgɚ/ *n.* [C] **1** a piece of wood shaped like a small narrow boat which is fastened to the side of a boat, especially a CANOE, to prevent it from turning over in the water **2** a boat that has one of these

out·right¹ /ˈaʊt̚raɪt/ *adj.* [only before noun] **1** complete or definite, with no doubt about the result: *The Republicans won **an outright victory**.* | *The party failed to win **an outright majority** in the Parliament.* | *They want an **outright ban** on hunting.* | *There were no **outright winners** or losers in the election.* **2** clear, direct, and with no attempt to hide what you think: *outright racism* | *his outright opposition to the proposal* | *The report contains several **outright lies**.*

outright² /ˈaʊt̚raɪt, aʊt̚ˈraɪt/ *adv.* **1** without trying to hide your feelings or intentions: *They laughed outright at my suggestion.* **2** completely or definitely: *Kahn needs 50% plus one vote to win the primary outright.* | **reject/refuse sth outright** *Most of the lawmakers rejected the idea outright.* **3 buy/own sth outright** to own something such as a house completely because you have paid the full price with your own money

out·rode /aʊt̚ˈroʊd/ *v.* the past tense of OUTRIDE

out·run /aʊt̚ˈrʌn/ *v. past tense* **outran** /-ˈræn/, *past participle* **outrun, outrunning** [T] **1** to run faster or farther than someone or something: *The fire was moving so fast you couldn't outrun it.* **2** to develop more quickly than something else: *The company's spending was outrunning its income.*

out·sell /aʊtˈsɛl/ *v. past tense and past participle* **outsold** /-ˈsoʊld/ [T] **1** to be sold in larger quantities than something else: *This book may outsell his previous novels.* **2** to sell more goods or products than a competitor: *Australia now outsells the U.S. in wines.*

out·set /ˈaʊtsɛt/ *n.* **at/from the outset** at or from the beginning of an event or process: *It was clear from the outset that there were going to be problems.* | **+of** *an incident that occurred at the outset of the hostilities*

out·shine /aʊtˈʃaɪn/ *v. past tense and past participle* **outshone** /-ˈʃoʊn/ or **outshined** [T] **1** to be clearly better than someone or something else: *Kelly outshone every other player on the field.* **2** to shine more brightly than something else

out·shoot /aʊtˈʃut/ *v. past tense and past participle* **outshot** /-ˈʃɑt/ [T] to get more points than an opponent in HOCKEY, basketball etc.

out·side¹ /ˌaʊtˈsaɪd, ˈaʊtsaɪd/ [S2] [W2] also **outside of** *prep.* **1** not inside a building, vehicle, an area etc. but still close to it [OPP] **inside**: *the crowd outside the courtroom* | *a town a few miles outside of the city* | *The hotel is **just outside*** (=very close, but not inside) *the park.* **2** not within a building or place [OPP] **inside** [OPP] **within**: *Store all chemicals outside of the house.* | *The company has offices outside of the United States.* **3** used about movement from inside a building or area to another place: *Don't go outside the yard.* | *These people never travel outside of Washington.* **4** beyond the limits or range of a situation, activity, group etc. [SYN] **beyond**: *Teachers can't control what students do outside of school.* | *a problem outside my experience* | *Try not to worry about things that are **outside your control*** (=that you cannot control). | *a subject **outside the scope** of this discussion* **5** someone who is outside a group of people or an organization, does not belong to it: *Experts were brought in from outside the company.* **6 outside of sth/sb** except for something or someone [SYN] **except for**: *Outside of a trip to the movie theater, we didn't go anywhere.*

outside² [S1] [W2] *adv.* **1** not inside a building, but in the open air [OPP] **inside**: *It's cold outside.*

> **THESAURUS**
>
> **out** away from a building, especially from the place where you live or work: *Let's go out for dinner.* | *I'm sorry, Mr. Hartman is out of the office.*
> **outside** not inside a room or building, but usually close to it: *You have to go outside if you want to smoke.*
> **outdoors** away from buildings and in the open air: *kids playing outdoors*
> **out of doors** FORMAL away from buildings and in the open air: *He was tanned from so much time spent out of doors.*

2 not in a room or building, but close to it [OPP] **inside**: *Would you wait outside please?* | *There were a couple of guards standing outside.* **3** from a place indoors to a place outdoors [OPP] **inside**: *Jenny, take the dog outside.* | *I opened the door and looked outside.* **4** on the outer surface [OPP] **inside**: *The house is beautiful outside, and filthy inside.*

outside³ [S3] [W3] *adj.* [only before noun] **1** not inside a building [SYN] **outdoor** [OPP] **inside**: *The apartment is reached by an outside stairway.* | *an outside toilet* → OUTER **2** from or involving people who do not belong to the same group or organization as you [SYN] **external** [OPP] **internal**: *We plan to hire an outside design team to produce our brochures.* | *outside influences on children's behavior* **3 the outside world** the rest of the world, which you do not know much about because you have no communication with it, you are not involved in it etc.: *Since the attack the city has been cut off from the outside world.* **4 outside interests/experiences etc.** interests, experiences etc. that are separate from those that you have in your job or at your school: *Greene plans to retire and enjoy some of his outside interests.* **5 an outside chance/possibility** a very small possibility that something will happen: *We still have an outside chance of getting into the playoffs.* **6 outside line/call etc.** a telephone line or telephone call that is to or from someone who is not inside a building or organization **7 an outside figure/estimate etc.** a number or amount that is the largest something could possibly be

outside⁴ [S2] *n.* **1 the outside** the outer part or surface of something [SYN] **exterior** [OPP] **inside**: **+of** *They painted the outside of the house green.* | *a note **on the outside** of the envelope* **2 the outside** the area around something such as a building, vehicle etc. [OPP] **the inside**: **+of** *We took a walk around the outside of the castle.* | *The house is a lot bigger than it looks **from the outside**.* **3 the outside** the position of not being involved in something, or of not belonging to a group [OPP] **the inside**: *People **on the outside** don't understand how we feel.* | *The situation looks different **from the outside**.* **4 on the outside a)** used to describe the way someone appears to be or to behave [OPP] **on the inside**: *On the outside she appeared perfectly calm, but she was furious.* **b)** not in prison [OPP] **on the inside**: *Life on the outside was not as easy as he'd first thought.* **5 at the outside** used to say that a number or amount is the largest something could possibly be, and it might be less: *It's only a 20-minute walk, half an hour at the outside.*

out·sid·er /aʊtˈsaɪdɚ/ *n.* [C] **1** someone who is not accepted as a member of a particular social group [OPP] **insider**: *Italian residents don't like to discuss the matter with outsiders.* **2** someone who does not belong to a particular company or organization, is not involved in a particular activity etc. [OPP] **insider**: *We don't want outsiders to tell us how to run the business.* **3** someone who does not seem to have much chance of winning a race or competition

out·sized /ˈaʊtsaɪzd/ also **out·size** /-saɪz/ *adj.* [only before noun] **1** larger than normal: *an outsized pair of glasses* **2** made for people who are very large: *outsized clothes*

out·skirts /ˈaʊtskɚts/ *n.* **the outskirts** the parts of a town or city that are farthest from the center: *We stayed **on the outskirts of** the capital.*

out·smart /aʊtˈsmɑrt/ *v.* [T] to gain an advantage over someone using tricks or using your intelligence [SYN] **outwit**: *The older kids can easily outsmart the younger ones.*

out·sold /aʊtˈsoʊld/ *v.* the past tense and past participle of OUTSELL

out·sourc·ing /ˈaʊtˌsɔrsɪŋ/ *n.* [U] the practice of using workers from outside a company, or of buying supplies, parts etc. from another company instead of producing them yourself

out·spend /aʊtˈspɛnd/ *v. past tense and past participle* **outspent** /-ˈspɛnt/ [T] to spend more money than another person or organization: *Gregg had consistently outspent rival candidates.*

out·spo·ken /ˌaʊtˈspoʊkən◂/ *adj.* expressing your opinions honestly, even when it is not popular to do so: *outspoken views* | *She's **an outspoken critic of** U.S. policy.* —**outspokenness** *n.* [U]

out·spread /ˌaʊtˈsprɛd◂/ *adj.* spread out flat or completely: *He was lying on the beach with arms outspread.*

out·stand·ing /aʊtˈstændɪŋ/ *adj.* **1** extremely good: *an outstanding football player* | *Her performance was outstanding.* | *an outstanding achievement* ▶see THESAURUS box at **good¹** **2** not yet dealt with, solved, or paid: *Two of the lawsuits are still outstanding.* | *an outstanding debt* —**outstandingly** *adv.*

out·stay /aʊtˈsteɪ/ *v.* [T] to stay somewhere longer than someone else → see also **overstay/outstay your welcome** at WELCOME³ (3)

out·stretched /ˌaʊtˈstrɛtʃt◂/ *adj.* stretched out to full length: *The birds rose with outstretched wings.*

out·strip /aʊtˈstrɪp/ *v.* **outstripped, outstripping** [T] **1** to be greater in quantity than something else: *Demand for energy is outstripping the supply.* **2** to do something better than someone else **3** to run or move faster than someone or something else

out·ta /ˈaʊt̬ə/ *prep.* NONSTANDARD used in writing to represent the spoken form of "out of": *I've got to get outta here.*

out·take /ˈaʊtˌteɪk/ *n.* [C] a piece of a movie or television show that is removed before it is broadcast, especially because it contains a mistake

O

out·vote /aʊt'voʊt/ *v.* [T usually passive] politics **1** to defeat someone or something by having a larger number of votes: *France was outvoted on that issue.* **2** to vote in larger numbers than someone else: *In the election the poor outvoted the rich.*

out·ward¹ /'aʊt˺wɚd/ *adj.* [only before noun] **1** relating to how a person or situation seems to be, rather than how it really is SYN external OPP inward: *My parents showed no **outward signs of** affection.* | ***To all outward appearances*** (=as much as can be judged by the way things seem) *Jodie seemed like a normal 12-year-old.* **2** directed toward the outside, or away from a place OPP inward: *the outward flow of oil* | *The outward flight was very uncomfortable.*

outward² also **outwards** *adv.* toward the outside or away from the center of something OPP inward: *The door opens outward into the street.* | +**from** *Fragments flew outward from the burning plane.*

out·ward·ly /'aʊt˺wɚdli/ *adv.* according to how people, things etc. seem, rather than how they are OPP inwardly: *Amy was outwardly calm, but actually very tense.* | [sentence adverb] *Outwardly, nothing seemed to have changed.*

out·weigh /aʊt˺'weɪ/ *v.* [T] to be more important or valuable than something else: *Benefits of the surgery far outweigh the risk.*

out·wit /aʊt˺'wɪt/ *v.* **outwitted, outwitting** [T] to gain an advantage over someone using tricks or using your intelligence SYN outsmart: *Speeders can outwit police radar with a variety of devices.*

out·worn /ˌaʊt'wɔrn◂ / *adj.* old-fashioned, and not useful or important anymore : *outworn traditions* → see also WORN OUT

ou·zo /'uzoʊ/ *n.* [U] a Greek alcoholic drink with a strong taste, usually drunk with water

o·va /'oʊvə/ *n.* the plural form of OVUM

o·val /'oʊvəl/ *n.* [C] a shape like a circle, but longer than it is wide [**Origin:** 1500–1600 Medieval Latin *ovalis*, from Latin *ovum* **egg**] —**oval** *adj.* ►see THESAURUS box at shape¹

ˌOval 'Office *n.* **the Oval Office** the office of the U.S. President, in the White House in Washington, D.C.

o·var·i·an /oʊ'vɛriən/ *adj.* [only before noun] relating to the ovaries: *ovarian cancer*

o·va·ry /'oʊvəri/ *n. plural* **ovaries** [C] BIOLOGY **1** one of the two parts in the body of a woman or a female MAMMAL that produces eggs **2** the part of a flower that produces seeds → see picture at FLOWER¹

o·va·tion /oʊ'veɪʃən/ *n.* [C] FORMAL if a group of people give someone an ovation, they CLAP their hands to show approval: *The President received **a standing ovation*** (=everyone stood up to give it) *as he entered.*

ov·en /'ʌvən/ S3 W3 *n.* [C] **1** a piece of equipment that food is cooked inside, shaped like a metal box with a door on it: *There were cookies baking in the oven.* | **set/preheat the oven (to sth)** *Set the oven to 400 degrees.* **2 like an oven** INFORMAL if a place is like an oven, it is so hot that you are uncomfortable [**Origin:** Old English *ofen*]

ov·en·proof /'ʌvənˌpruf/ *adj.* ovenproof dishes, plates etc. will not be harmed by the high temperatures in an oven

ov·en·ware /'ʌvənˌwɛr/ *n.* [U] cooking pots that can be put in a hot oven without cracking

o·ver¹ /'oʊvɚ/ S1 W1 *prep.* **1** above or higher than something, without touching it SYN above OPP under: *A thick layer of smoke hung over the city.* | *a sign over the door* | *Leaning over her desk, she grabbed the phone.* → see also ACROSS **2** on something, so that it is covered OPP under: *I put another blanket over the baby.* | *He wore a jacket over his sweater.* | *He spilled wine **all over*** (=covering a large area of) *my new carpet.* **3** from one side of something to the other side: *the road over the mountain* | *One of the men jumped over the counter and grabbed the money.* | *Their house has a view over the bay.* **4** moving across the space above something or someone: *A helicopter was flying over the beach.* **5** more than a particular number, level, age etc.: *It cost over $20,000.* | *She lost over 80 pounds.* | *a game for children over six years old* | **the over-30s/the over-40s etc.** (=people who are more than a particular age) **6** during: *Did you go anywhere over New Year's?* | *Let's discuss the contract over lunch.* | **over the years/months/weeks etc.** (=during a period of years, months etc.) **7 over on** on the opposite side of something from where you already are: *Bill lives over on 32nd Avenue* (=on the other side of a city). **8** down from the edge of something: *The car plunged over the cliff.* **9** making a sound louder than another sound SYN above: *I had to shout over the noise of the engine.* **10** hanging from: *He had a towel over his arm.* **11** in or to many parts of a place: *I've traveled over most of Europe.* | *Scientists **from all over*** (=from every part) *of the world.* | *There were kids running **all over the place*** (=in many places). **12 be/get over sth** to feel better after being sick or upset: *Susan's mad at me, but she'll get over it.* | *Are you over your cold now?* **13 be/get over sb** to no longer love someone after a period of being upset about the end of your relationship with them: *She soon got over him.* **14 over the Internet/phone/radio etc.** using a telephone, the Internet, or other system for communicating information SYN via: *Most of their business is done over the Internet.* **15** about a particular subject, person, or thing SYN concerning: *a dispute over payment* **16 trip/fall/stumble over sth** to hit your foot against something so that lose your balance and fall or almost fall: *I tripped over the cat.* **17** used for saying that one person, group, or thing is more successful than another or is winning against another: *Can the Red Sox maintain their lead over the Yankees?* **18** if one thing is chosen or preferred over another, it is chosen rather than the other: *What made you choose the Chianti over the other wines?* **19** in control of someone or having authority to give orders to someone OPP under: *He ruled over a large kingdom.* **20 over and above** more than a certain amount: *He will receive a $10,000 bonus over and above his normal salary.* [**Origin:** Old English *ofer*] → see also **all over** at ALL² (3), **sb can't/couldn't get over sth** at GET OVER (5)

over² S1 W1 *adv.* **1** falling down from an upright position: *Don't knock the candle over.* | *I got so dizzy that I almost fell over.* **2** to, from, or in a particular place: +**to/from/in** *We drove over to Grandma's after lunch.* | *They came over from Sweden for the conference.* | *The fax machine is over in the corner.* | *Come **over here*** (=in or to the place where you are, from somewhere else)*!* | *Let's go **over there*** (=in or to another place) *and see what's happening.* **3** in or into a position of being bent or folded in the middle: *Dan bent over to pick up the keys.* | *Fold the piece of paper over.* **4** toward one side: *Move over. I don't have any room.* **5** so that the side or bottom of someone or something can now be seen: *Turn the box over and open it at that end.* | *Josh rolled over and went back to sleep.* **6 and/or over** more or higher than a particular amount, number, or age OPP under: *a puzzle for kids aged ten and over* | *a store for women who are size 14 or over* **7** from one person or group to another: *The men handed over the stolen money to the authorities.* **8** from one thing or person to another: *The guards change over at midnight.* **9 read/think/talk sth over** to read something, think about something etc. very carefully before deciding what to do: *I'll need to read this contract over before I sign it.* **10 start over** also **do sth over** to start or do something again: *I got mixed up and had to start over.* **11 over and over (again)** repeatedly: *They kept playing the same songs over and over.* **12** completely covered with a particular substance or material: *The sky had clouded over.* | +**with** *The door had been painted over with a bright red varnish.* **13** above someone or something: *Two planes flew over.* **14 twice over/three times over etc.** used for saying how many times the same thing happens: *He sings each song twice over.* **15 over to sb** used to say that it is now someone else's turn to do something, to speak etc.: *Now over to Bob who's live at the scene of the crime.* **16 over!** SPOKEN used by pilots, soldiers etc. when speaking to each other with a radio, to say that they are finished speaking so that another person can speak: **over and out** (=used to say that a radio conversation is finished) → see also **all over** at ALL[2] (3), **left over** at LEAVE[1] (3)

over[3] *adj.* [not before noun] if an event or period of time is over, it has finished: *Is the game over yet?* | *I'm so glad that my exams* ***are over and done with*** (=used to emphasize that something bad is finished). ►see THESAURUS box at **done**[2] → see also **get sth over with** at GET

over- /oʊvɚ/ *prefix* **1** too much, too many, or to too great a degree: *overcrowded* (=with too many people in it) | *overcooked* → see also OVER[1] **2** above, beyond, or across: *overhanging* (=hanging above and across something) **3** outside or covering something: *an overcoat* **4** in addition: *overtime* (=hours of work which extend past the usual time)

o·ver·a·chiev·er, over-achiever /ˌoʊvɚəˈtʃivɚ/ *n.* [C] someone who works very hard to be successful, and is very unhappy if they do not achieve everything they want to —**over-achieve** *v.* [I] → see also UNDERACHIEVER

o·ver·act /ˌoʊvɚˈækt/ *v.* [I,T] to act a part in a play with too much emotion or too much movement

o·ver·ac·tive /ˌoʊvɚˈæktɪv◂/ *adj.* too active, in a way that causes problems: *an overactive thyroid gland* | *Jan* ***has an overactive imagination*** (=often imagines things that are untrue).

ˌover-ˈage *adj.* too old for a particular purpose or activity → see also UNDERAGE

o·ver·all[1] /ˌoʊvɚˈɔl◂/ Ac *adj.* [only before noun] including or considering everything: *The overall cost of the trip is $500.* | *I left the building with the* ***overall impression*** *of a very well-run business.*

overall[2] Ac *adv.* **1** [sentence adverb] generally: *Overall, it's been a good year.* **2** considering or including everything: *The budget is around $25 million overall.*

o·ver·alls /ˈoʊvɚˌɔlz/ *n.* [plural] heavy cotton pants that have a piece covering your chest and are held up by pieces of cloth that go over your shoulders

o·ver·arch·ing /ˌoʊvɚˈɑrtʃɪŋ◂/ *adj.* [only before noun] **1** including or influencing every part of something: *Economic growth is the overarching priority.* **2** forming a curved shape over something: *the overarching sky*

o·ver·awe /ˌoʊvɚˈɔ/ *v.* [T usually passive] to make someone feel so impressed that they are nervous or unable to say or do anything

o·ver·bear·ing /ˌoʊvɚˈbɛrɪŋ/ *adj.* always trying to control other people without considering their wishes or feelings SYN **domineering**: *an overbearing teacher*

o·ver·bid /ˌoʊvɚˈbɪd/ *v.* **1** [I + for] to offer too high a price for something, especially at an AUCTION **2** [I,T] to offer more than the value of your cards in a card game such as BRIDGE

o·ver·bite /ˈoʊvɚˌbaɪt/ *n.* [C] a condition in which someone's upper jaw is too far forward beyond their lower jaw

o·ver·blown /ˌoʊvɚˈbloʊn◂/ *adj.* FORMAL something that is overblown is made to seem more important or impressive than it really is SYN **exaggerated**

o·ver·board /ˈoʊvɚˌbɔrd/ *adv.* **1 go overboard (with/on sth)** INFORMAL to do or say something that is too extreme for a particular situation: *Don't you think you went a little overboard with the decorations?* **2** over the side of a ship or boat into the water: *One of the crew* ***fell overboard.*** | *Man overboard!* (=said when someone falls off a boat) **3 throw sb/sth overboard** to get rid of someone or something because they have become a disadvantage to you: *All his prinicples were thrown overboard in an effort to get elected.*

o·ver·book /ˌoʊvɚˈbʊk/ [I,T] to sell more tickets for a theater, airplane etc. than there are seats available

o·ver·bur·den /ˌoʊvɚˈbɚdn/ *v.* [T usually passive] to give a person, organization, or system too much work or too many problems to deal with: *Public health systems are already overburdened by patients with no insurance.* —**overburdened** *adj.*: *the overburdened court system*

o·ver·came /ˌoʊvɚˈkeɪm/ *v.* the past tense of OVERCOME

o·ver·ca·pac·i·ty /ˌoʊvɚkəˈpæsəṭi/ *n.* [singular, U] when a factory or business is able to make more products than people will buy

o·ver·cast /ˈoʊvɚˌkæst/ *adj.* dark with clouds: *The afternoon will be overcast.* | *an overcast sky*

o·ver·charge /ˌoʊvɚˈtʃɑrdʒ/ *v.* **1** [I,T] to charge someone too much money for something OPP **undercharge**: *The taxi driver overcharged us by about $20.* **2** [T] to put too much power into a BATTERY or electrical system

o·ver·coat /ˈoʊvɚˌkoʊt/ *n.* [C] a long thick warm coat worn over other clothes in cold weather

o·ver·come /ˌoʊvɚˈkʌm/ S3 W3 *v. past tense* **overcame** /-ˈkeɪm/ *past participle* **overcome** [T] **1** to successfully deal with a feeling or problem that prevents you from achieving something SYN **conquer**: *He struggled to overcome his shyness.* | *She finally overcame the difficulties of her childhood.* **2** [usually passive] if smoke or gas overcomes someone, they become extremely sick or unconscious because they breathe it: *Five employees were overcome by smoke.* **3** if an emotion overcomes someone, they cannot behave normally because they feel the emotion so strongly SYN **overwhelm**: *I was overcome with an irresistible urge to hit him.* **4** to fight and win against someone or something SYN **beat**

o·ver·com·pen·sate /ˌoʊvɚˈkɑmpənˌseɪt/ *v.* [I] to try to correct a weakness or mistake by doing too much of the opposite thing: +**for** *Zoe overcompensates for her shyness by talking a lot.* —**overcompensation** /ˌoʊvɚˌkɑmpənˈseɪʃən/ *n.* [U]

o·ver·cook /ˌoʊvɚˈkʊk/ *v.* [T] to cook food for too long, so that it does not taste good —**overcooked** *adj.*: *overcooked vegetables*

o·ver·crowd·ed /ˌoʊvɚˈkraʊdɪd◂/ *adj.* filled with too many people or things: *overcrowded prisons*

o·ver·crowd·ing /ˌoʊvɚˈkraʊdɪŋ/ *n.* [U] the condition of being or living too close together, with too many people in a small space: *overcrowding on the subways*

o·ver·de·vel·oped /ˌoʊvɚdɪˈvɛləpt◂/ *adj.* DISAPPROVING **1** too great or large: *Ryan has an overdeveloped sense of his own importance.* | *overdeveloped muscles* **2** if a city or area is overdeveloped, too many houses, buildings, roads etc. have been built there

o·ver·do /ˌoʊvɚˈdu/ *v. past tense* **overdid** /-ˈdɪd/, *past participle* **overdone** /-ˈdʌn/ [T] **1** to do something more than is appropriate or natural: *Don't overdo the praise. She wasn't that good.* **2 overdo it a)** to work too hard or be too active, so that you become tired: *She's been overdoing it lately.* **b)** to do or use something too much or in an extreme way: *Use a few drawings and photos, but don't overdo it.* | *I think I overdid the salt.*

o·ver·done /ˌoʊvɚˈdʌn/ *adj.* **1** cooked too much OPP **underdone**: *As usual, the fish was overdone.* **2** doing, saying, or using too much of something: *Be careful that your makeup is not overdone.*

overdose[1] /ˈoʊvɚˌdoʊs/ *n.* **1** [C] too much of a drug taken at one time: +**of** *He died of a massive overdose of heroin.* **2** [singular] INFORMAL a situation in which you do, see, eat etc. too much of one thing: +**of** *an overdose of soap operas*

o·ver·dose[2] ABBREVIATION **OD** *v.* [I] **1** to take too much of a drug: +**on** *He overdosed on heroin.* **2** to do or have too much of something so that you do not want to do or have any more: +**on** *I think I overdosed on reality TV shows.*

o·ver·draft /ˈoʊvɚˌdræft/ *n.* [C] the amount of money you owe to a bank when you have taken out more money than you had in your bank account

o·ver·drawn /ˌoʊvɚˈdrɔn/ *adj.* if your bank account is overdrawn, you have spent more than is in it and you owe the bank money: *If you are overdrawn, there's a $25 fee.* | *The account was* ***overdrawn by*** *$700.*

overdressed

o·ver·dressed /ˌoʊvɚˈdrɛst◂/ *adj.* dressed in clothes that are too formal for the occasion: *We were completely overdressed for the party.* —**overdress** *v.* [I]

o·ver·drive /ˈoʊvɚˌdraɪv/ *n.* [U] **1** an additional GEAR which allows a car to go fast while its engine produces the least power necessary **2 go/move/shift etc. into overdrive** to quickly become very excited, exciting, or active: *About halfway through, the movie shifts into overdrive.*

o·ver·due /ˌoʊvɚˈdu◂/ *adj.* **1** a payment that is overdue should have been paid earlier: *overdue mortgage payments* | **one week/two months etc. overdue** *The rent is three weeks overdue.* ►see THESAURUS box at **late**[1] **2** something that is overdue should have happened or been done a long time ago: +**for** *Our house is overdue for a paint job.* | *Tougher laws on air pollution are **long overdue**.* **3** a library book that is overdue was not returned to the library when it should have been **4** [not before noun] a baby that is overdue has not been born yet, even though the date it was expected has passed: *The baby is two weeks overdue.*

ˌover-ˈeasy *adj., adv.* eggs that are over-easy are cooked in a pan and turned over to cook on the other side for only a moment so that the YOLK is still liquid

o·ver·eat /ˌoʊvɚˈit/ *v. past tense* **overate** /-ˈeɪt/ *past participle* **overeaten** /-ˈitˀn/ [I] to eat too much, or eat more than is healthy

o·ver·em·pha·size /ˌoʊvɚˈɛmfəˌsaɪz/ *v.* [T] to emphasize something too much or give it too much importance: *The need for better car safety regulations **cannot be overemphasized*** (=used to say that something is very important). —**overemphasis** /ˌoʊvɚˈɛmfəsɪs/ *n.*: *an overemphasis on money*

o·ver·es·ti·mate[1] /ˌoʊvɚˈɛstəˌmeɪt/ Ac *v.* **1** [T] to think that someone or something is better, larger, more important etc. than they really are OPP **underestimate**: *The generals had overestimated the strength of the enemy forces.* | *The significance of these changes **cannot be overestimated*** (=they are extremely important). **2** [I,T] to wrongly guess an amount, price, or number by making the total too high OPP **underestimate**: *We overestimated how long the trip would take.*

o·ver·es·ti·mate[2] /ˌoʊvɚˈɛstəmɪt/ Ac *n.* [C] a calculation, judgment, or guess that is too large

o·ver·ex·cit·ed /ˌoʊvɚɪkˈsaɪṭɪd◂/ *adj.* too excited to behave in a sensible way: *overexcited children*

o·ver·ex·pose /ˌoʊvɚɪkˈspoʊz/ *v.* [T] **1** to allow too much light to reach the film when taking or developing a photograph OPP **underexpose** **2 be overexposed** someone who is overexposed has appeared too many times on television, in the newspapers etc. and people have become bored by them OPP **underexpose** **3** to allow too much sunlight to reach something such as your skin or body so that you suffer harm

o·ver·ex·po·sure, **over-exposure** /ˌoʊvɚɪkˈspoʊʒɚ/ *n.* [U] **1** the state of having received too much sunlight, RADIATION etc., that is harmful to someone's skin, film etc. **2** the fact of being overexposed

o·ver·ex·tend /ˌoʊvɚɪkˈstɛnd/ [T] **overextend yourself a)** to try to do or use too much of something so that problems, illness, or damage result: *Be careful not to overextend yourself. You've been sick.* **b)** to spend more money than you actually have —**overextended** *adj.*: *loans to overextended consumers*

o·ver·flow[1] /ˌoʊvɚˈfloʊ/ *v.* [I,T] **1** if a river, lake, or container overflows or overflows its edges, it is so full that the liquid or material inside it flows over its edges: *Turn off the water so the sink doesn't overflow.* | *Shoal Creek overflowed its banks Friday.* | +**with** *The trash can overflowed with beer bottles.* **2** if something inside a container, river, lake etc. overflows, there is too much of it, so that it flows over the edges of the container, river etc.: *The drainage system flooded, and water overflowed down the streets.* **3** if a place overflows with people or if people overflow a place, there are too many of them to fit into it: +**with** *The hospitals are overflowing with victims of the hurricane.* **4 overflowing (with sth)** completely full: *Her little room was overflowing stuffed animals.* **5 overflow with love/gratitude etc.** to have a very strong feeling of love etc.: *Hampton overflows with enthusiasm when he talks about jazz.*

o·ver·flow[2] /ˈoʊvɚˌfloʊ/ *n.* **1** [C usually singular] the additional people or things that cannot be contained in a place because it is already full: *Two temporary parking lots were set up to handle the overflow.* | +**of** *an overflow of students* **2** [U] an act of overflowing something: +**of** *an overflow of water from the lake* **3** [C] a pipe through which water flows out of a container when it becomes too full —**overflow** *adj.*: *The overflow crowd stood in the back of the theater.*

o·ver·fly /ˌoʊvɚˈflaɪ/ *v. past tense* **overflew** /-ˈflu/, *past participle* **overflown** /-ˈfloʊn/ [T] to fly over an area or country in an aircraft

o·ver·graz·ing /ˌoʊvɚˈgreɪzɪŋ/ *n.* [U] a situation in which animals are allowed to eat too much of the grass in an area, with the result that the land becomes damaged

o·ver·grown /ˌoʊvɚˈgroʊn◂/ *adj.* **1** BIOLOGY covered with plants that have grown in a wild way: *an overgrown field* | +**with** *Both sides of the road were overgrown with weeds.* **2 overgrown child/kid/etc.** DISAPPROVING an adult who behaves like a child: *They were fooling around like a bunch of overgrown kids.*

o·ver·growth /ˈoʊvɚˌgroʊθ/ *n.* [U] plants and branches of trees growing above your head, usually in a forest

o·ver·hand /ˈoʊvɚˌhænd/ *adj., adv.* an overhand throw in a sport is when you throw the ball with your arm above the level of your shoulder OPP **underhand** —**overhand** *adv.*

o·ver·hang[1] /ˌoʊvɚˈhæŋ/ *v. past tense and past participle* **overhung** /-ˈhʌŋ/ [I,T] to hang over something or stick out above it: *a branch overhanging the water*

o·ver·hang[2] /ˈoʊvɚˌhæŋ/ *n.* [C usually singular] **1** a rock, roof etc. that hangs over something else: *We stood under the overhang while it rained.* **2** the amount by which something hangs over something else: *The roof has a five-foot overhang.* **3** a quantity of something that has not been sold, which has a bad influence on prices, markets etc.: *a huge overhang of crude oil*

o·ver·haul[1] /ˌoʊvɚˈhɔl, ˈoʊvɚˌhɔl/ *v.* [T] to repair or improve a machine, system etc., by checking it thoroughly and fixing anything that does not work well: *They promised to overhaul the whole welfare system.* | *An engineer is coming in to overhaul the air conditioning.*

o·ver·haul[2] /ˈoʊvɚˌhɔl/ *n.* [C] a process of making necessary changes or repairs to a machine or system: *The Chevy needs a complete overhaul.* | *an overhaul of the election process*

o·ver·head[1] /ˌoʊvɚˈhɛd◂/ *adv.* above your head: *Helicopter gunships hovered overhead.* —**overhead** *adj.*: *Their bags fit in the overhead compartment.*

o·ver·head[2] /ˈoʊvɚˌhɛd/ S3 *n.* **1** [U] money spent regularly on rent, insurance, electricity, and other things that are needed to keep a business operating: *We're trying to lower our overhead.* | *overhead costs*

2 [C] a piece of transparent material used with an overhead projector to show words, pictures etc.

ˌoverhead proˈjector *n.* [C] a piece of electrical equipment used by teachers, trainers etc. which makes words and images look larger by showing them on a wall or large screen

o·ver·hear /ˌoʊvɚˈhɪr/ *v. past tense and past participle* **overheard** /-ˈhɚd/ [I,T] to accidentally hear what other people are saying, when they do not know that you have heard: *She overheard an argument between her parents.* | **overhear sb doing sth** *Two U.S. soldiers were overheard discussing the invasion plans.* | **overhear sb say/saying (that)** *We overheard the teacher say there would be a pop quiz today.* → see also EAVESDROP

o·ver·heat /ˌoʊvɚˈhit/ *v.* [I,T] **1** to become too hot, or to make something too hot: *If the fan doesn't work, the engine could overheat.* **2** if a country's ECONOMY overheats or if something overheats it, it grows too fast and this leads to increases in prices, salaries, interest rates etc.

o·ver·heat·ed /ˌoʊvɚˈhit̮ɪd◂/ *adj.* **1** too hot: *an overheated waiting room* **2** ECONOMICS an overheated economic system is growing too fast, and this leads to increases in prices, salaries, interest rates etc. **3** full of angry feelings: *an overheated debate*

o·ver·hung /ˌoʊvɚˈhʌŋ/ *v.* the past tense and past participle of OVERHANG

o·ver·in·dulge /ˌoʊvɚɪnˈdʌldʒ/ *v.* **1** [I] to eat or drink too much: **overindulge in sth** *I always overindulge in desserts during the holidays.* **2** [T] to let someone have everything they want, or always let them do what they want: *Sam's parents overindulge him.* —**overindulgence** *n.* [U]

o·ver·joyed /ˌoʊvɚˈdʒɔɪd/ *adj.* [usually after noun] extremely happy about something: **be overjoyed (that)** *Mom was overjoyed that I got the job.* | **overjoyed to hear/find/see sth** *We were overjoyed to see them safely back home.* | +**at** ***I wasn't overjoyed*** (=used to emphasize that you do not like something) *at the thought of taking care of two babies.*

o·ver·kill /ˈoʊvɚˌkɪl/ *n.* [U] **1** more of something than is needed or wanted: *The coverage of the trial is a clear example of media overkill.* **2** more than enough weapons, especially NUCLEAR weapons, to kill everyone in a country

o·ver·land /ˈoʊvɚˌlænd/ *adv.* across land, not by sea or air: *We decided not to travel overland to Oaxaca.* —**overland** *adj.*: *an overland route*

o·ver·lap¹ /ˌoʊvɚˈlæp/ Ac *v.* **overlapped, overlapping** [I,T] **1** if two or more things overlap or if one thing overlaps another, part of one thing covers part of the other: *The tiles on the roof overlap.* | *One of her front teeth overlaps the other.* **2** if two subjects, ideas etc. overlap or one overlaps the other, they each include some but not all of the same features: *The responsibilities of the two departments overlap in certain areas.* | **overlap with sth** *The study of sociology overlaps with the study of economics.* **3** if two events or activities overlap, the first one finishes after the second one starts: **overlap with sth** *My vacation overlaps with yours.*

o·ver·lap² /ˈoʊvɚˌlæp/ Ac *n.* [C,U] the degree to which two things, activities etc. overlap: *Allow an overlap of about two centimeters.* | +**between** *We're working to reduce overlap between jobs.*

o·ver·lay¹ /ˌoʊvɚˈleɪ/ *v. past tense and past participle* **overlaid** [T] **1** to thinly cover something with a substance, especially as a decoration: **overlay sth with sth** *semi-precious stones overlaid with gold* **2** to be added to an existing idea, quality, feeling etc., especially by becoming stronger or more noticeable than it: *Here Buddhism overlays even older folk beliefs.* | +**with** *The rich bass rhythms are overlaid with delicate melodies.* **3** if something overlays something else, it lies on top of it so that both can be seen: *A new menu will appear on the screen, overlaying the main page.*

o·ver·lay² /ˈoʊvɚˌleɪ/ *n.* [C] **1** something laid over something else **2** a transparent sheet with a picture or drawing on it which is put on top of another picture to change it **3** an additional quality or feeling

o·ver·leaf /ˈoʊvɚˌlif/ *adv.* on the other side of the page: *See the diagram overleaf.*

o·ver·lie /ˌoʊvɚˈlaɪ/ [T] TECHNICAL **1** to lie over something SYN **cover**: *A layer of limestone overlies older rocks.* **2** if a parent animal overlies its young it kills them by lying on them

o·ver·load /ˌoʊvɚˈloʊd/ *v.* [T] **1** to fill something with too many things or people: *Don't overload the washing machine.* **2** to put too much electricity through an electrical system or piece of equipment: *Plugging in too many appliances will overload the outlet.* **3** to give someone too much work: +**with** *Employees are overloaded with work.* —**overload** /ˈoʊvɚˌloʊd/ *n.* [C,U]

o·ver·long /ˌoʊvɚˈlɔŋ◂/ *adj.* continuing for too long: *an overlong romantic melodrama*

o·ver·look¹ /ˌoʊvɚˈlʊk/ *v.* [T] **1** to not notice or do something because you have not been careful enough SYN **miss**: *They found some important evidence that the police had overlooked.* **2** [usually passive] to not consider someone or something or recognize their importance, success, or value: *Women's contributions have been largely overlooked in history books.* **3** if a building, room, or window overlooks a place, you can look down on that place from it: *Thaden's house overlooks an alpine valley.* **4** to ignore and forgive someone's mistake, bad behavior etc.

o·ver·look² /ˈoʊvɚˌlʊk/ *n.* [C] a high place from which you can see the land below it

o·ver·lord /ˈoʊvɚˌlɔrd/ *n.* [C often plural] someone who has great power over a large number of people, especially in the past

o·ver·ly /ˈoʊvɚli/ *adv.* [often in negatives] too or very: *We weren't overly impressed with the movie.* | *I think you're being overly critical.*

o·ver·manned /ˌoʊvɚˈmænd/ *adj.* OVERSTAFFED

o·ver·much /ˌoʊvɚˈmʌtʃ/ LITERARY too much

o·ver·night¹ /ˌoʊvɚˈnaɪt/ *adv.* **1** for or during the night: *The paint should dry overnight.* | **stay overnight** *Higgins was not required to stay overnight at the hospital.* **2** quickly or suddenly, in a way that is surprising: *He became a millionaire overnight.*

o·ver·night² /ˈoʊvɚˌnaɪt/ *adj.* [only before noun] **1** continuing all night: *an overnight flight to Seoul* **2** done in one night: *an overnight delivery service* **3 an overnight success** something that suddenly becomes very popular or successful: *The show was an overnight success on Broadway.*

ˌover-optiˈmistic *adj.* expecting that things will be better than is possible or likely: *over-optimistic forecasts of the company's earnings*

o·ver·paid /ˌoʊvɚˈpeɪd◂/ *adj.* [not before noun] given more money for a job than you deserve: *overpaid athletes*

o·ver·pass /ˈoʊvɚˌpæs/ *n.* [C] a structure like a bridge that allows one road to go over another road

o·ver·pay /ˌoʊvɚˈpeɪ/ *v.* **overpays**, *past tense and past participle* **overpaid, overpaying** **1** [I,T] to pay too much money for something: *We overpaid our taxes this year.* **2** [T] to pay someone more money than they deserve: *Most big companies continue to overpay their top executives.* —**overpayment** *n.* [C,U]

o·ver·play /ˌoʊvɚˈpleɪ/ *v.* **overplays, overplayed, overplaying** [T] **1** to make something seem more important or more exciting than it is OPP **underplay**: *The press overplays these disagreements among Cabinet members.* **2** to play a piece of music, show something on television etc. too often **3 overplay your hand** to behave too confidently, and try to gain more advantage than you can reasonably expect: *The gun lobby overplayed its hand, and failed to get what it wanted.*

o·ver·pop·u·lat·ed /ˌoʊvɚˈpɑpyəˌleɪt̮ɪd/ *adj.* an overpopulated city, country etc. has too many people: *overpopulated areas* —**overpopulation** /ˌoʊvɚˌpɑpyəˈleɪʃən/ *n.* [U]

o·ver·pow·er /ˌoʊvɚˈpaʊɚ/ *v.* [T] **1** to defeat someone, especially by taking hold of them, because you are stronger than they are: *Three inmates overpowered guards at the county jail in Madison.* **2** if a smell or taste or an emotion overpowers someone or something, it has bad effects because it is too strong: *The wine is light enough not to overpower the fish.*

O

o·ver·pow·er·ing /ˌoʊvɚˈpaʊərɪŋ/ *adj.* **1** very strong SYN **intense**: *Her loneliness was overpowering.* | *an overpowering smell* **2** someone who is overpowering has such a strong character that they make other people feel uncomfortable or afraid

o·ver·priced /ˌoʊvɚˈpraɪst◂/ *adj.* something that is overpriced is much more expensive than it should be: *overpriced Italian restaurants* —**overprice** *v.* [I,T]

o·ver·print /ˌoʊvɚˈprɪnt/ *v.* [T + with/on] to print additional words over a document, stamp etc. that already has printing on it

o·ver·pro·duc·tion /ˌoʊvɚprəˈdʌkʃən/ *n.* [U] the act of producing more of something than people need or want: *the overproduction of crude oil* —**overproduce** /ˌoʊvɚprəˈdus/ *v.* [I,T]

o·ver·pro·tec·tive /ˌoʊvɚprəˈtɛktɪv◂/ *adj.* so anxious to protect someone from harm, danger etc. that you restrict their freedom: *overprotective parents*

o·ver·qual·i·fied /ˌoʊvɚˈkwɑləˌfaɪd◂/ *adj.* having so much education, experience, or training that people do not want to employ you for particular jobs that do not need much skill or knowledge: +**for** *He's overqualified for this position.*

o·ver·ran /ˌoʊvəˈræn/ *v.* the past tense of OVERRUN

o·ver·rat·ed /ˌoʊvɚˈreɪt̬ɪd◂/ *adj.* not as good or important as some people think or claim OPP **underrated**: *the most overrated film of the year* —**overrate** *v.* [T]

o·ver·reach /ˌoʊvɚˈritʃ/ *v.* [I,T] to try to do more than you have the power, ability, or money to do: *Critics say the commissioner* ***overreached his authority***. | **overreach yourself** *The company had overreached itself, and got into debt.*

o·ver·re·act /ˌoʊvɚriˈækt/ *v.* [I] to react to something that happens by showing too much emotion or by doing something that is not really necessary: *I think you're overreacting a little. I'm only ten minutes late.* | +**to** *You always overreact to criticism.* —**overreaction** /ˌoʊvɚriˈækʃən/ *n.* [C,U]

o·ver·ride¹ /ˌoʊvɚˈraɪd/ *v.* *past tense* **overrode** /-ˈroʊd/, *past participle* **overridden** /-ˈrɪdn/ [T] **1** to change someone's official decision by using your power or authority to do so: *City council members voted to override the mayor's veto.* **2** to be regarded as more important than something else: *Should the opinions of experts override the wishes of the people?* **3** to change a process that is normally AUTOMATIC: *Pilots tried to manually override the plane's computer control.*

o·ver·ride² /ˈoʊvɚˌraɪd/ *n.* [C] **1** an act of overriding an official decision: *Congress' override of the President's veto* **2** a system or piece of equipment that allows you to change a process that is usually AUTOMATIC: *a manual override*

o·ver·rid·ing /ˌoʊvɚˈraɪdɪŋ/ *adj.* [only before noun] more important than anything else: *a question of overriding importance* | **an overriding need/concern** *an overriding concern about safety*

o·ver·ripe /ˌoʊvɚˈraɪp◂/ *adj.* overripe fruit and vegetables are past the point of being fully grown and ready to eat: *overripe bananas*

o·ver·rule /ˌoʊvɚˈrul/ *v.* [T] **1** to change an order or decision that you think is wrong, using your official power: *The Supreme Court overruled the lower court's decision.* **2 (objection) overruled** LAW used by a judge in a court of law to say that someone was not right to object to another person's statement → see also SUSTAIN

o·ver·run¹ /ˌoʊvɚˈrʌn/ *v.* *past tense* **overran** /-ˈræn/, *past participle* **overrun**, **overrunning** **1** [T] if something unwanted overruns a place or area, it spreads all over it in large quantities: **be overrun by/with sth** *an apartment building overrun by gangs and drugs* | *The trees and bushes were overrun with vines.* **2** [I,T] if a river overruns its banks, it is so full that the water flows over its edges **3** [T] to defeat a place or an area and take control of it: *Soviet troops overran the nation in 1940.* → see also **run over** at RUN¹

o·ver·run² /ˈoʊvɚˌrʌn/ *n.* [C] an act of spending more money on a program of work, a product etc. than had been planned or agreed: ***cost overruns*** *of $7.2 million*

o·ver·seas¹ /ˌoʊvɚˈsiz/ Ac *adv.* to or in a foreign country that is across the ocean: *Lara plans to study overseas.* | *Most of the applications came from overseas.*

o·ver·seas² /ˈoʊvɚˌsiz/ Ac *adj.* [only before noun] coming from, existing, or happening abroad: *overseas travel* | *overseas bank accounts*

o·ver·see /ˌoʊvɚˈsi/ *past tense* **oversaw** /-ˈsɔ/ *past participle* **overseen** /-ˈsin/ *v.* [T] to be in charge of a program of work or a group of workers, and check that everything is done correctly SYN **supervise**: *Somers oversaw construction of the water treatment plant.*

o·ver·se·er /ˈoʊvɚˌsiɚ/ *n.* [C] someone in charge of a group of workers, who checks that their work is done correctly, especially in past times

o·ver·sell /ˌoʊvɚˈsɛl/ *past tense and past participle* **oversold** /-ˈsoʊld/ *v.* [T] **1** to praise someone or something too much, or make claims about them that may not be true: *The movie was oversold and ended up disappointing everyone.* **2** to sell more tickets, seats etc. than are actually available

o·ver·sen·si·tive /ˌoʊvɚˈsɛnsət̬ɪv◂/ *adj.* very easily upset or offended

o·ver·sexed /ˌoʊvɚˈsɛkst◂/ *adj.* having too much interest in or desire for sex

o·ver·shad·ow /ˌoʊvɚˈʃædoʊ/ *v.* [T] **1** [usually passive] to make someone or something else seem less important, especially by being more successful than them: *Tim felt constantly overshadowed by his older brother.* **2** to make an occasion, period, event etc. seem less enjoyable by making people feel sad or worried: *The scandal in Washington overshadowed the President's inauguration ceremony.* **3** if a tall building, mountain etc. overshadows a building, place etc., it is very close to it and much taller than it

o·ver·shoe /ˈoʊvɚˌʃu/ *n.* [C] a rubber shoe that you wear over an ordinary shoe to keep your feet dry

o·ver·shoot /ˌoʊvɚˈʃut/ *v.* *past tense and past participle* **overshot** /-ˈʃɑt/ [T] **1** to miss a place where you wanted to stop or turn, by going too far past it: *A small commuter plane overshot the runway.* **2** to go beyond an intended limit or level: *The department is likely to overshoot its cash limit.* | *They* ***overshot the mark*** *in estimating what consumers would pay* (=they people would pay more than they actually did).

o·ver·sight /ˈoʊvɚˌsaɪt/ *n.* **1** [C,U] a mistake that you make by not noticing something or by forgetting to do something: *They sent a letter of apology for the oversight.* **2** [U] the situation of being in charge of a piece of work and checking that it is satisfactory: *a school oversight committee*

ˈoversight ˌfunction *n.* [C] POLITICS an official examination by a special government committee of the decisions taken by the EXECUTIVE BRANCH of the U.S. government (=the part that is responsible for approving decisions and making laws) to make certain that the government acted legally and correctly

o·ver·sim·pli·fy /ˌoʊvɚˈsɪmpləˌfaɪ/ *v.* **oversimplifies**, **oversimplified**, **oversimplifying** [I,T] to make a situation or problem seem less complicated than it really is, by ignoring important facts: *The article oversimplifies the causes of the current crisis.* —**oversimplification** /ˌoʊvɚˌsɪmpləfəˈkeɪʃən/ *n.* [C,U]

o·ver·sized /ˌoʊvɚˈsaɪzd◂ / also **o·ver·size** /-ˈsaɪz◂ / *adj.* bigger than usual or too big: *oversized pants*

o·ver·sleep /ˌoʊvɚˈslip/ *v. past tense and past participle* **overslept** /-ˈslɛpt/ [I] to sleep for longer than you intended: *Sorry I'm late. I overslept.* → see also **sleep over** at SLEEP[1], SLEEP IN

o·ver·spend /ˌoʊvɚˈspɛnd/ *v. past tense and past participle* **overspent** /-ˈspɛnt/ [I,T] to spend more money than you can afford: *Too many people overspend during the holidays.* | **overspend sth by sth** *The city has overspent its budget by 10%.*

o·ver·staffed /ˌoʊvɚˈstæft◂ / *adj.* an overstaffed company, organization etc. has more workers than it needs OPP **understaffed**

o·ver·state /ˌoʊvɚˈsteɪt/ *v.* [T] to talk about something in a way that makes it seem more important, serious etc. than it really is SYN **exaggerate** OPP **understate**: *Our opponents say we are overstating the seriousness of the problem.* | *They're calling it a revolutionary change in television, which may be* ***overstating the case.*** | *The importance of a child's early years* ***cannot be overstated*** (=they are very important). —**overstatement** *n.* [C,U]

o·ver·stay /ˌoʊvɚˈsteɪ/ *v.* **overstays, overstayed, overstaying** [T] to stay somewhere longer than you intended or longer than you should: *tourists who have overstayed their visas* → see also **overstay/outstay your welcome** at WELCOME[3] (3)

o·ver·step /ˌoʊvɚˈstɛp/ *v.* **overstepped, overstepping** [T] **overstep the bounds/rules/limits etc.** to do something that goes beyond what is acceptable or what is allowed by the rules: *Lawmakers appear to be overstepping their authority this time.*

o·ver·stock /ˌoʊvɚˈstɑk/ *v.* [I,T] to obtain more of something than is needed for a store, hotel etc.

o·ver·stuffed /ˌoʊvɚˈstʌft◂ / *adj.* **1** an overstuffed chair is filled with thick PADDING **2** filled with too much of something or too many things: *overstuffed lockers*

o·ver·sub·scribe /ˌoʊvɚsəbˈskraɪb/ *v.* [T] **be oversubscribed** if an activity, service etc. is oversubscribed, too many people want to do it or use it: *Most publicly funded clinics are oversubscribed.*

o·ver·sup·ply /ˈoʊvɚsəˌplaɪ/ *n. plural* **oversupplies** [C,U] the state of having more of a particular product than you need or can sell: *an oversupply of steel*

o·vert /oʊˈvɚt, ˈoʊvɚt/ *adj.* FORMAL overt actions or feelings are done or shown publicly, without trying to hide anything OPP **covert**: *an overt attempt to force landowners to sell* | *overt racism* [**Origin:** 1300–1400 Old French, past participle of *ovrir* **to open**] —**overtly** *adv.*

o·ver·take /ˌoʊvɚˈteɪk/ *v. past tense* **overtook** /-ˈtʊk/, *past participle* **overtaken** /-ˈteɪkən/ [T] **1** to become bigger, more advanced, more successful etc. than someone or something that you are competing with: *By 1970 the U.S. had overtaken the Soviet Union in space technology.* **2** to go past someone or something because you are going faster than them: *A large wave came up and overtook the people on the beach, knocking them down.* **3** if a bad feeling or bad event overtakes you, it happens to you suddenly and prevents you from doing what you had planned: *He was overtaken by exhaustion.* **4 be overtaken by events** if you are overtaken by events, the situation changes so that your plans or ideas are not useful or appropriate anymore

o·ver·tax /ˌoʊvɚˈtæks/ *v.* [T] **1** to make someone or something do more than they are really able to do: *He's 85. He shouldn't overtax himself like that.* **2** ECONOMICS to make people pay too much tax —**overtaxed** *adj.*

ˈover-the-ˌcounter *adj.* [only before noun] **1** over-the-counter drugs can be obtained without a PRESCRIPTION (=a written order from a doctor) **2** ABBREVIATION **OTC** ECONOMICS over-the-counter business shares are ones that do not appear on an official STOCK EXCHANGE list —**over the counter** *adv.*: *The medicine is available over the counter.*

ˌover-the-ˈtop *adj.* INFORMAL an over-the-top remark, performance, type of behavior etc. is so EXAGGERATED that it seems slightly silly or extreme: *her over-the-top satirical comedy*

o·ver·throw[1] /ˌoʊvɚˈθroʊ/ *v. past tense* **overthrew** /-ˈθru/, *past participle* **overthrown** /-ˈθroʊn/ [T] **1** POLITICS to remove a leader or government from a position of power by force SYN **oust**: *an attempt by the military to overthrow the government* **2** to cause a complete change by getting rid of the existing rules, ideas etc.: *a discovery that could overthrow conventional ideas about computing* **3** to throw a football or baseball too far for someone to catch it

o·ver·throw[2] /ˈoʊvɚˌθroʊ/ *n.* [U] **1** POLITICS the defeat and removal from power of a leader or government, especially by force: +**of** *the overthrow of a hated dictator* **2** the act of completely changing or getting rid of a set of rules or ideas, or a social system: +**of** *an organization whose aim is the overthrow of capitalism*

o·ver·time /ˈoʊvɚˌtaɪm/ *n.* [U] **1** time that you spend working in your job in addition to your normal working hours: *overtime pay* | *I had to* ***work overtime*** *three days last week.* | *Workers will* ***be on overtime*** *until Christmas.* **2** the money that you are paid for working more hours than usual: *a salary of $45,000 plus overtime* | *I don't mind working weekends as long as they* ***pay me overtime.*** **3** a period of time added to the end of a sports game to give one of the two teams a chance to win: *Miller scored 9 of his 23 points* ***in overtime.*** | *If a game is tied, it* ***goes into overtime.*** **4 sth is working overtime** INFORMAL used to say that your brain, imagination etc. is very active: *Price's wit and sarcasm are working overtime in this production.*

o·ver·tone /ˈoʊvɚˌtoʊn/ *n.* [C] **1** [usually plural] signs of an emotion or attitude that is not expressed directly: **racial/political/religious etc. overtones** *The defeat of the city's first black mayor had racial overtones.* **2** ENG. LANG. ARTS a higher musical note that sounds together with the main note → see also UNDERTONE

o·ver·took /ˌoʊvɚˈtʊk/ *v.* the past tense of OVERTAKE

o·ver·ture /ˈoʊvɚtʃɚ, -ˌtʃʊr/ *n.* [C] **1** ENG. LANG. ARTS a short piece of music written as an introduction to a longer piece, especially to an OPERA **2** [usually plural] an attempt to begin a friendly relationship with a person, country, or organization etc.: *U.S. business chiefs were beginning to* ***make overtures to*** *the leadership in Beijing.* **3 be an overture to sth** if an event is an overture to a more important event, it happens just before the important event and leads to it: *The beating incident was a disturbing overture to the riots that followed.*

o·ver·turn /ˌoʊvɚˈtɚn/ *v.* **1** [T] to change an official decision or result so that it becomes the opposite of what it was before: *Today's ruling overturns the lower court's decision.* **2** [I,T] if you overturn something or if it overturns, it turns upside down or falls over on its side: *Demonstrators overturned several cars and set fire to them.* | *His vehicle overturned, trapping him inside.* **3** [T] to suddenly remove a government from power, especially by using violence SYN **overthrow**

o·ver·use /ˌoʊvɚˈyuz/ *v.* [T] to use something too much, or more than is necessary OPP **underuse**: *People tend to overuse words like "really" and "totally."* —**overuse** /ˌoʊvɚˈyus/ *n.* [U]

o·ver·val·ue /ˌoʊvɚˈvælyu/ *v.* [T] to believe or say that something is more valuable or more important than it really is: *Analysts overvalued the company's inventories.* —**overvalued** *adj.*: *overvalued currency* —**overvaluation** /ˌoʊvɚˌvælyuˈeɪʃən/ *n.* [U]

o·ver·view /ˈoʊvɚˌvyu/ *n.* [C usually singular] a short description of a subject or situation that gives the main ideas without all the details: *The exhibition begins with a historical overview.* | +**of** *an overview of the issues involved in the debate*

o·ver·ween·ing /ˌoʊvɚˈwinɪŋ◂ / *adj.* [only before noun] FORMAL **1** an overweening personal quality is unpleasant and extreme, especially as the result of too much confidence: *overweening ambition* **2** an overweening person or organization is too proud and confident

o·ver·weight /ˌoʊvɚˈweɪt◂ / *adj.* **1** BIOLOGY too heavy or too fat OPP **underweight**: **10 pounds/50 pounds/30 kilos etc. overweight** *I'm 15 pounds overweight.* | **grossly/seriously/dangerously/severely overweight** *a camp for seriously overweight children* ►see THESAURUS box at **fat**[1] **2** something such as a package that is overweight weighs more than it is supposed to weigh OPP **underweight**: *overweight luggage*

O

o·ver·whelm /ˌoʊvɚˈwɛlm/ *v.* [T] **1** [often passive] if an emotion, experience, or problem overwhelms you, it affects you so strongly that you cannot think clearly: *I was overwhelmed by their generosity.* | *Deep frustration overwhelmed her, and she started to cry.* | *Local police were* ***completely overwhelmed*** *by the rise in crime.* **2** if a color, smell, taste etc. overwhelms another color, taste etc., it is much stronger and more noticeable: *Most preparations overwhelm the flavor of good oysters.* **3** to defeat an opponent or army completely **4** LITERARY if water overwhelms an area of land, it covers it completely and suddenly

o·ver·whelm·ing /ˌoʊvɚˈwɛlmɪŋ/ *adj.* **1** large enough in size, number, or amount to be very impressive or to have a strong effect: *The evidence against them is overwhelming.* | *An* ***overwhelming majority*** (=a very large majority) *of the members are women.* | *He faced* ***overwhelming odds*** (=situation in which he was very likely to be hurt or killed) *and survived.* **2** an overwhelming situation or emotion affects you so strongly that it is difficult to deal with or fight against: *She had an overwhelming urge to call him back.* | *an overwhelming experience* —**overwhelmingly** *adv.*: *Congress voted overwhelmingly in favor of the bill.*

o·ver·work[1] /ˌoʊvɚˈwɚk/ *v.* [I,T] to work too much, or to make someone work too much: *The company has been overworking its employees.*

o·ver·work[2] /ˈoʊvɚˌwɚk/ *n.* [U] too much hard work

o·ver·worked /ˌoʊvɚˈwɚkt◂ / *adj.* **1** working too hard and for too long: *overworked teachers* **2** a word or phrase that is overworked is used too much and has become less effective: *overworked metaphors*

o·ver·write /ˌoʊvɚˈraɪt/ *v. past tense* **overwrote** /-ˈroʊt/, *past participle* **overwritten** /-ˈrɪtn/ **1** [T] to enter new information in a computer file or document, so that it replaces the existing information, which is lost: *I overwrote the file by mistake.* **2** [I,T] to write something in a style that is too emotional or uses too many unnecessary or difficult words

o·ver·wrought /ˌoʊvɚˈrɔt◂ / *adj.* **1** very upset, nervous, and worried **2** written, acted etc. in a way that is too careful and seems awkward: *an overwrought performance*

o·ver·zeal·ous /ˌoʊvɚˈzɛləs◂ / *adj.* too eager about something you feel strongly about: *overzealous fans* | *an overzealous tax inspector*

Ov·id /ˈɑvɪd/ (43 B.C.–A.D. 17) a Roman poet whose Roman name was Publius Ovidius Naso

o·vi·duct /ˈoʊvɪˌdʌkt/ *n.* [C] BIOLOGY one of the two tubes in a female through which eggs pass to the UTERUS

o·vip·a·rous /oʊˈvɪpərəs/ *adj.* BIOLOGY MAMMALS and other animals that are oviparous produce babies which develop inside an egg that is outside the mother's body

o·void /ˈoʊvɔɪd/ *adj.* TECHNICAL having a shape like an egg —**ovoid** *n.* [C]

o·vo·vi·vip·a·rous /ˌoʊvoʊvaɪˈvɪpərəs/ *adj.* BIOLOGY MAMMALS and other animals that are ovoviviparous produce babies which develop inside an egg in the mother's body → see also VIVIPAROUS

o·vu·late /ˈɑvyəˌleɪt/ *v.* [I] BIOLOGY when a woman or female animal ovulates, eggs move out of her OVARY (=place in her body where they are formed) toward the WOMB —**ovulation** /ˌɑvyəˈleɪʃən/ *n.* [U]

ov·ule /ˈavyul/ *n.* [C] BIOLOGY a very small structure in plants that have seeds that develops into a seed after the plant has been FERTILIZED

o·vum /ˈoʊvəm/ *n. plural* **ova** /ˈoʊvə/ [C] BIOLOGY an egg, especially one that develops inside a woman or female animal's body

ow /aʊ/ *interjection* said to show that something hurts you: *Ow! That hurt!*

owe /oʊ/ S2 W3 *v.* [T] **1** to have to pay someone for something that they have done for you or sold to you, or to have to give someone back money that they have lent you: *How much do you owe?* | **owe sb $10/$500 etc.** *Chris owes me $20.* | **owe sth to sb** *The country owes billions of dollars to the World Bank.* | **owe sb for sth** *I still owe him for gas.*

THESAURUS

be in debt to owe an amount of money
be overdrawn to owe money to your bank, as a result of spending more money than you have in your bank account
be in the red to have spent more money than you have

2 to feel that you should do something for someone or give something to someone, because they have done something for you or given something to you: *Joanne will watch the kids – she* ***owes me a favor***. | *Thanks, Mandy. I really* ***owe you one*** (=used to thank someone for helping you). | **owe sb dinner/a drink etc.** *Let's go to the bar. I owe you a drink, anyway.* **3 owe sb an apology/explanation** to feel that you should say sorry to someone or explain to them why you did something **4 a)** to have something valuable or important as a result of a particular person, quality etc.: **owe sth to sb/sth** *About one million Americans owe their jobs to foreign tourism.* | **owe sb sth** *We owe those firefighters our lives.* **b)** to feel that someone's help has been important to you in achieving something: *I owe my parents a lot for everything they've done for me.* | *I can cook now, but I* ***owe it all to*** *my mother.* | *The nation* ***owes a debt of gratitude to*** *its brave veterans.* **5 owe it to sb to do sth** to feel you should do something for someone because it is what they deserve or it will be good for them: *We owe it to our children to clean up the environment.* | *You* ***owe it to yourself*** *to take a vacation.* **6 owe allegiance to sb/sth** to have a duty to obey someone or be loyal to them: *People with dual nationality owe allegiance to more than one country.* **7 How much do I owe you?** also **What do I owe you?** used to ask someone you are buying something from how much you need to pay for something: *How much do I owe you for the books?* [**Origin:** Old English *agan*]

Ow·ens /ˈoʊənz/, **Jes·se** /ˈdʒɛsi/ (1913–1980) a very successful African-American ATHLETE, who won four GOLD MEDALS at the 1936 Olympic Games in Berlin

Jesse Owens

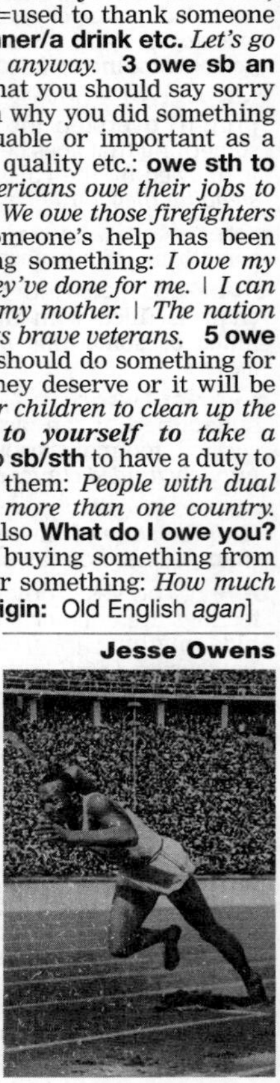

ow·ie /ˈaʊi/ *n.* [C] SPOKEN a word meaning a small injury, used by or to children

ow·ing /ˈoʊɪŋ/ *adj.* [not before noun] if money is owing, it has not yet been paid to the person who should receive it: *How much is still owing?*

ˈowing to *prep.* because of SYN **due to**: *The event was canceled owing to bad weather.*

owl /aʊl/ *n.* [C] BIOLOGY a bird that hunts at night and has a large head, eyes that face forward, and a loud call

owl·ish /ˈaʊlɪʃ/ *adj.* looking like an owl and seeming serious and intelligent: *his owlish looks*

own[1] /oʊn/ S1 W1 *adj., pron.* **1** belonging to a particular person and no one else: *Ben wants his own room.* | *This is my newspaper. Go get your own.* | *Now I've got* ***my very own*** (=used for emphasis) *credit card.* | **(all) of its/his/her etc. own** *He recently started a* *business of his own.* | *Every city has a character all of its own.* **2** done or made without the help or influence of someone else: *I'm old enough to make my own decisions.* | *It's* ***his own fault*** (=used to emphasize that someone is responsible for a mistake) *for leaving it there.* **3 (all) on your own a)** alone: *Will you be OK here on your own?* **b)** without help: *Did you build this all on your own?* → see Word Choice box at ALONE **4 its own** used to emphasize that something includes something else: *Every room has its own balcony.* **5** used when comparing two situations to emphasize that someone or something else also has something: *She couldn't think them. She had her own problems to worry about.* | *Our children all have children* ***of their own*** *now.* **6 make sth your own** to change something that used to belong to someone else, so that it seems to be typical of you and seems to belong to you: *It's taken years, but it feels like we've finally made this house our own.* **7 be your own man/woman** to have strong opinions and intentions which are not influenced by other people → see also **in sb's own backyard** at BACKYARD (2), **come into your own** at COME INTO STH (6), **hold your own** at HOLD[1] (28), **too nice/clever/fast etc. for your own good** at TOO (5), **in sb's own way** at WAY[1] (37)

GRAMMAR

Use **own** only after possessive words like *my, Carol's, the company's* etc.: *Becky has her own office.* You can also use **very** to emphasize **own**, especially in informal spoken English: *I love her like my very own child.*

own² S2 W1 *v.* [T not in progressive] **1** to legally have something because you have bought it, been given it etc.: *They own a small electronics company.* | *The horse is owned by a Saudi businessman.*

THESAURUS

possess FORMAL to own or have something: *Jefferson possessed slaves.*
have to own something: *How many students have a cell phone?*
belong to sb if something belongs to you, you own it: *The ring belonged to my grandmother.*

2 do sth like you own the place INFORMAL to behave in a way that is too confident and annoys other people: *He walks around here like he owns the place!* **3 own (that)** OLD USE to admit that something is true [**Origin:** Old English *agnian*, from *agen* **own**]

own up *phr. v.* to admit something embarrassing or something bad that you have done: **+to** *Chuck wouldn't own up to the fact that he'd been drinking.*

own·er /ˈoʊnɚ/ S3 W1 *n.* [C] someone who owns something: *We took the cat back to its owner.* | **+of** *the owner of the restaurant* | *Scheer is* ***the proud owner of*** *a copy of the Declaration of Independence.* | *I bought the car from* ***the original owner*** (=the first person to own it). | **a restaurant/store/business etc. owner** *a small-business owner* → see also HOMEOWNER

ˌowner-ˈoccupied *adj.* owner-occupied houses, apartments etc. are lived in by the people who own them —**owner-occupier** *n.* [C]

ˌowner-ˈoperator *n.* [C] someone who owns a small business and runs it

own·er·ship /ˈoʊnɚˌʃɪp/ *n.* [U] **1** the fact or state of owning something: *vehicle ownership* | **+of** *a dispute over ownership of the land* | **public/private ownership** *The agency was transferred from public to private ownership.* **2** the person or group that owns something: *the team's new ownership* | *The ship was then* ***under*** *Scandinavian* ***ownership.*** **3 take ownership of sth** to accept the responsibility for something: *The course teaches you to take ownership of your mistakes.*

ˌown ˈgoal *n.* [C] a GOAL that you accidentally SCORE against your own team without intending to in a game of SOCCER, HOCKEY etc.

ox /ɑks/ *n. plural* **oxen** /ˈɑksən/ [C] BIOLOGY **1** a BULL whose sex organs have been removed, often used for working on farms **2** a large cow, BULL etc.

ox·bow /ˈɑksboʊ/ *n.* [C] a U-shaped bend in a river

ˈox cart, oxcart *n.* [C] a vehicle pulled by oxen

ox·eye /ˈɑksaɪ/ *n.* [C] a yellow flower like a DAISY

ox·ford /ˈɑksfɚd/ *n.* **1** [U] also **oxford cloth** a type of thick cotton cloth used for making shirts **2** [C] also **oxford shirt** a shirt made of this cloth **3** [C] a type of leather shoe that fastens with SHOELACES

O

ox·i·da·tion /ˌɑksəˈdeɪʃən/ *n.* [U] CHEMISTRY the process in which a chemical combines with oxygen, losing one or more ELECTRONS

ˌoxidation-reˈduction reˌaction also **redox reaction** *n.* [C] CHEMISTRY a chemical reaction in which one or more ELECTRONS are moved from one atom or MOLECULE to another

ox·ide /ˈɑksaɪd/ *n.* [C,U] CHEMISTRY a chemical compound in which another substance is combined with oxygen: *iron oxide*

ox·i·dize /ˈɑksəˌdaɪz/ *v.* [I,T] CHEMISTRY **1** to combine with oxygen, or make something combine with oxygen, for example in the process that causes a metal to RUST **2** to lose ELECTRONS, or make another chemical compound lose electrons → see also REDUCE

ˈoxidizing ˌagent *n.* [C] CHEMISTRY a chemical substance that oxidizes another substance and gives up oxygen or gains ELECTRONS in the process → see also REDUCING AGENT

ox·tail /ˈɑks-teɪl/ *n.* [U] the meat from the tails of cattle, used especially in soup

ox·y·a·cet·y·lene /ˌɑksiəˈsɛtl̩ˌin◂, -ˈsɛtl̩-ən◂/ *n.* [U] CHEMISTRY a mixture of oxygen and ACETYLENE that produces a hot white flame that can cut steel

ox·y·gen /ˈɑksɪdʒən/ *n.* [U] SYMBOL **O** CHEMISTRY a gas that is an ELEMENT, has no color, smell, or taste, is present in the air, and is necessary for animals and plants to live [**Origin:** 1700–1800 French *oxygène*, from Greek *oxys* **sharp, acid** + French *-gène* **forming**; because it was believed that oxygen forms part of all acids]

ox·y·gen·ate /ˈɑksɪdʒəˌneɪt/ *v.* [T] CHEMISTRY to add oxygen to something —**oxygenated** *adj.* —**oxygenation** /ˌɑksɪdʒəˈneɪʃən/ *n.* [U]

ˈoxygen mask *n.* [C] a piece of equipment that fits over someone's mouth and nose to provide them with oxygen

ˈoxygen tent *n.* [C] a piece of equipment shaped like a tent that is put around someone who is very sick in a hospital, to provide them with oxygen

ox·y·mo·ron /ˌɑksiˈmɔrɑn/ *n.* [C] ENG. LANG. ARTS a combination of two words that seem to mean the opposite of each other, such as "new classics"

o·yez /oʊˈyɛz, -ˈyeɪ, ˈoʊ-/ *interjection* a word used by law officials or by TOWN CRIERS in the past to get people's attention

oys·ter /ˈɔɪstɚ/ *n.* [C,U] a small ocean animal that has a shell and can produce a jewel called a PEARL, or the inside part of this animal, which can be eaten raw or cooked → see also **the world is sb's oyster** at WORLD[1] (32) → see picture at SEAFOOD

ˈoyster bed *n.* [C] an area at the bottom of the ocean where oysters live

oz. the written abbreviation of OUNCE or ounces

O·zarks, the /ˈoʊzɑrks/ an area of high land covered by forests in the southern central U.S. states of Missouri and Arkansas

o·zone /ˈoʊzoʊn/ *n.* [U] **1** CHEMISTRY a blue gas that is a type of oxygen **2** clean fresh air, especially near the ocean [**Origin:** 1800–1900 German *ozon*, from Greek, from *ozein* **to smell**]

ˌozone-ˈfriendly *adj.* not containing chemicals that damage the ozone layer: *ozone-friendly hair spray*

ˈozone ˌlayer *n.* [singular] **the ozone layer** EARTH SCIENCE a layer of the gas ozone in the top part of the air surrounding the Earth which prevents harmful RADIATION from the sun from reaching the Earth

P,p

P

P, p /pi/ *n. plural* **P's, p's** [C] **1** the 16th letter of the English alphabet **2** the sound represented by this letter → see also **mind your manners/p's and q's** at MIND² (15)

p the written abbreviation of "piano," used in written music to show that a part should be played or sung quietly

p. **1** *plural* **pp.** the written abbreviation of PAGE **2** the written abbreviation of PARTICIPLE

PA¹ a written abbreviation of Pennsylvania

PA² *n.* [C usually singular] a PA SYSTEM

Pa CHEMISTRY a written abbreviation of PASCAL

pa /pɑ/ *n.* [C] OLD-FASHIONED a word meaning "father," used by or to children

pab·lum /ˈpæbləm/ *n.* [U] FORMAL books, speeches, movies etc. that are very simple or boring, and contain no new or original ideas

PAC /pæk/ *n.* [C] **Political Action Committee** an organization that tries to influence politicians so that they support the group's aims, for example by voting a particular way

pace¹ /peɪs/ W3 *n.*

1 SPEED OF EVENTS/CHANGES [singular] the rate or speed at which something happens or is done: +**of** *The pace of change in our lives is becoming faster.* | *Here in Bermuda, **the pace of life** is very slow* (=people do not try to do things too quickly). | *She's been working so hard. I doubt she can **keep up this pace*** (=continue working at this rate). | *The Senator says he does not intend to **force the pace*** (=make something happen more quickly than is normal) *of the legislation.* | *Professor Morrey lets us study **at our own pace**.* | **at a slow/rapid/steady etc. pace** (=slowly, quickly etc.) | **pick/speed/step up the pace** (=do something more quickly or cause something to happen more quickly)

2 SPEED OF WALKING [singular] the speed at which you walk, run, or move: **at a brisk/steady/leisurely etc. pace** *The women walked by **at a brisk pace*** (=quick).

3 A STEP [C] a single step when you are running or walking, or the distance moved in one step: *About 20 paces from the house is an old oak tree.* | +**from/behind** *Eddie walked a few paces behind his mother.*

4 keep pace (with sb/sth) to move or change as fast as someone or something else: *Funding for the program is unlikely to keep pace with the community's needs.*

5 a change of pace a change in the way something is done, the speed at which it is done etc.: *This year's smaller festival is a welcome change of pace from last year's.*

6 set the pace a) to establish a rate of development, a level of quality etc. that other people or organizations try to copy: *For the last few years we have been setting the pace in wireless technology.* **b)** to run at a speed that other runners try to follow

7 put sb/sth through their/its paces to make a person, machine etc. show how well they can do something

8 HORSE [C] one of the ways that a horse walks or runs [**Origin:** 1200–1300 Old French *pas* **step**, from Latin *passus*]

pace² *v.* **1** [I always + adv./prep., T] to walk first in one direction and then in another, again and again, when you are waiting for something or worried about something: *Stewart was **pacing the floor** as he watched the game on TV.* | *When I get nervous I start **pacing back and forth**.* **2 pace yourself** to do something at a steady speed so that you do not get tired quickly: *It's a long climb, so pace yourself.* **3 pace sb** to set the speed or level of activity for someone in a race, playing in a sports competition etc.: *I need someone to pace me or I fall too far behind.* **4** also **pace off, pace out** [T] to measure a distance by taking steps of an equal length: *He paced off the distance just to make sure.* **5** [T] to make the story in a book, movie, play etc. develop at a particular speed: *She paces the book well.* → see also PACING

-paced /peɪst/ [in adjectives] **slow-paced/fast-paced/lightning-paced etc.** moving, happening, or developing slowly, quickly etc.: *a fast-paced adventure movie*

pace·mak·er /ˈpeɪsˌmeɪkɚ/ *n.* [C] **1** MEDICINE a very small machine that is attached to someone's heart to help it beat regularly **2** a PACESETTER **3** BIOLOGY a part of the muscle in the right ATRIUM of the heart which sends out a regular pattern of electrical signals that make the heart beat regularly

pace·set·ter /ˈpeɪsˌsɛt̬ɚ/ *n.* [C] **1** someone or something that establishes a level of quality or achievement which others try to copy: *The French TGV is the pacesetter for high-speed trains.* **2** a team that is ahead of others in a competition **3** someone who runs at the front at the beginning of a race and sets the speed at which others must run

Pa·chel·bel /ˈpɑkəlˌbɛl/, **Jo·hann** /ˈyoʊhɑn/ (1653?–1706) a German musician who wrote CLASSICAL music

pach·y·derm /ˈpækɪˌdɚm/ *n.* [C] TECHNICAL a thick-skinned animal such as an ELEPHANT or a RHINOCEROS

Pa·cif·ic /pəˈsɪfɪk/ *n.* **1 the Pacific** the Pacific Ocean: *a huge storm over the Pacific* **2** [U] SPOKEN a short form of Pacific Time, the TIME ZONE in the western part of the U.S.

pa·cif·ic /pəˈsɪfɪk/ *adj.* LITERARY **1** peaceful or loving peace: *a pacific community* **2** helping to cause peace

Paˌcific ˈDaylight Time ABBREVIATION **PDT** *n.* [U] the time that is used in the western part of the U.S. for just over half the year, during the summer months, when clocks are one hour ahead of Pacific Standard Time

Paˌcific Northˈwest *n.* [U] **the Pacific Northwest** the area of the U.S. that includes the states of Oregon and Washington, and can include the southwestern part of British Columbia, Canada

Paˌcific ˈOcean, the also **the Pacific** /pəˈsɪfɪk/ the ocean between the continents of North and South America to the east and Asia and Australia to the west

Paˌcific ˈRim *n.* **the Pacific Rim (countries)** the countries or parts of countries that border the Pacific Ocean, such as Japan, Australia, and the west coast of the U.S., often considered as an economic group

Paˌcific ˈStandard Time ABBREVIATION **PST** *n.* [U] the time that is used in the western part of the U.S. for almost half the year, during the winter months → see also PACIFIC DAYLIGHT TIME

Paˈcific Time ABBREVIATION **PT** *n.* [U] the time that is used in the western part of the U.S.

pac·i·fi·er /ˈpæsəˌfaɪɚ/ *n.* [C] **1** a specially shaped rubber object that you give a baby to suck so that it does not cry **2** something that makes people calm

pac·i·fism /ˈpæsəˌfɪzəm/ *n.* [U] the belief that all wars and all forms of violence are wrong

pac·i·fist /ˈpæsəfɪst/ *n.* [C] someone who believes that all wars are wrong and who refuses to use violence

pac·i·fy /ˈpæsəˌfaɪ/ *v.* **pacifies, pacified, pacifying** [T] **1** to make someone calm, quiet, and satisfied after they have been angry or upset: *"You're right," she said to try to pacify him.* **2** to bring peace to an area or to end war in a place —**pacification** /ˌpæsəfəˈkeɪʃən/ *n.* [U]

pac·ing /ˈpeɪsɪŋ/ *n.* [U] **1** the rate at which events develop in a book, movie etc. **2** the action of walking first in one direction and then in another, again and again, when you are waiting for something or worried about something

pack¹ /pæk/ S2 W2 *v.*

1 BOXES/SUITCASES ETC. [I,T] **a)** to fill a suitcase, box etc. with things: *Why do you always pack at the last minute?* | **pack a bag/suitcase** *She packed a bag quickly and left.* **b)** to put objects, clothes etc. in boxes,

suitcases etc.: *Don't forget to pack your bathing suit.* | *I'll pack a lunch for the kids.* | **pack sth in/into sth** *We packed all the books into boxes.*
2 LARGE CROWD [I always + adv./prep., T] to go in large numbers into a space that is not big enough, or to make a lot of people or things do this: *Tourists pack the ferries to visit the islands.* | *The sheep had all been packed into a tiny truck.* | **pack into/onto sth** *More than 50,000 fans packed into the stadium.*
3 SNOW/SOIL ETC. [T] to press soil, snow etc. down firmly: **pack sth into/down etc.** *Pack soil around the roots of the plant.* | *Kenny packed the snow into a perfect snowball.*
4 PROTECT STH [T] to cover, fill, or surround something closely with material to protect it: **pack sth in/with sth** *Pack the crystal in tissue paper.* | *Pack the knee with ice to reduce swelling.*
5 FOOD [T] to prepare food, especially meat, and put it into containers for preserving or selling: *The tuna is packed in oil.* | *a meat packing factory*
6 pack your bags INFORMAL to leave a place and not return, especially because of a disagreement
7 pack a committee/jury/court etc. to secretly and dishonestly arrange for a group to be filled with people who support you
8 pack a gun/piece also **pack heat** SPOKEN, INFORMAL to carry a gun
9 pack a punch/wallop INFORMAL **a)** to have a strong effect: *The beer packs quite a punch.* **b)** to be able to hit another person hard in a fight
[**Origin:** (1–5) 1300–1400 Low German, Dutch *pak*] → see also **send sb packing** at SEND (11)

pack sth ↔ **away** *phr. v.* to put something back in a box, case etc. where it is usually kept: *I packed the tools carefully away.*

pack sb/sth **in** *phr. v.* **1 pack them in** INFORMAL to attract a lot of people: *Any movie with Tom Cruise in it will pack them in.* **2 pack sb/sth ↔ in** to fit a lot of people, things, activities etc. into a limited space or a limited period of time: *It was a very short vacation, but we packed a lot in.*

pack sth **into** sth *phr. v.* to fit a lot of something into a limited space, place, or period of time: *We packed a lot of sightseeing into two weeks.*

pack sb **off** *phr. v.* INFORMAL to send someone away quickly because you want to get rid of them: +**to** *Our folks used to pack us off to camp every summer.*

pack up *phr. v.* to put things into boxes, suitcases, bags etc. in order to take or store them somewhere: *When I got home, Sally and the kids were packing up.* | **pack sth ↔ up** *Shannon packed up her belongings and left.*

pack² S2 W3 *n.* [C]
1 SMALL CONTAINER a small container made of paper, CARDBOARD etc., with a set of things in it, especially things that are sold together in this way: *Susan took a mint out of the pack.* | +**of** *a pack of cigarettes* → see picture at CONTAINER
2 GROUP OF ANIMALS BIOLOGY a group of wild animals that live and hunt together, or a group of dogs trained together for hunting: *a wolf pack* | +**of** *a pack of hounds* ►see THESAURUS box at **group¹**, **package¹**
3 GROUP OF PEOPLE DISAPPROVING a group of people who do something together: +**of** *A pack of reporters and photographers was following her.*
4 THINGS WRAPPED TOGETHER several things wrapped or tied together or put in a case, to make them easy to carry, sell, or give to someone: *a video gift pack* | +**of** *a six-pack of beer*
5 IN A RACE the main group of runners or competitors following behind the leader in a race or competition
6 BAG a BACKPACK → see also FANNY PACK
7 CARDS also **pack of cards** a complete set of playing cards SYN **deck**
8 be a pack of lies INFORMAL to be completely untrue
9 MILITARY a group of aircraft, SUBMARINES etc. that fight the enemy together
10 ON A WOUND MEDICINE a thick mass of soft cloth that you press on a wound to stop the flow of blood → see also ICE PACK, MUDPACK

pack·age¹ /ˈpækɪdʒ/ S2 W2 *n.* [C]
1 FOR FOOD the box, bag, or other container that food is put in to be sold: *The cooking instructions are on the package.* | +**of** *a package of frozen spinach*

THESAURUS
packet a small envelope containing a substance or group of small things: *a packet of seeds*
pack a small box, bag, or covering that things are sold in: *a pack of cigarettes*
packaging the container or material that a product is sold in, which protects it or makes it attractive or easily recognizable: *Instructions for use are printed on the packaging.*
packing material material used for packing things so that they can be sent somewhere: *Popcorn is sometimes used as a packing material.*

2 IN MAIL something packed together firmly or packed in a box and wrapped in paper, especially for mailing: *The mailman left a package for you at our house.* ►see THESAURUS box at **mail¹**
3 FOR COMPUTER a set of related programs sold together for use on a computer: *a new software package*
4 IDEAS a set of ideas, measures, or services that are suggested or offered all together as a group for dealing with something: +**of** *a package of measures to assist the flooded areas* | **an aid/a financial/an economic etc. package** *Congress passed the aid package Thursday.*
5 FOR EMPLOYEE pay, health insurance, and other BENEFITS considered as a unit that an employer offers an employee: *They're giving me a pretty good package.* | *a benefits package*
6 VACATION a completely planned vacation arranged by a company at a particular price, which includes travel, hotels, meals etc.: *The seven-night package includes breakfast and dinners daily.*

package² *v.* [T] **1** to put something in a special package, especially to be sent or sold: *The code tells us where and when a product was packaged.* | **package sth in sth** *We do not package any of our products in plastic.* **2** to sell two or more things together as a single product: | **package sth with sth** *The CD will be packaged with a documentary video.* **3** to try to make a person, idea, or product seem interesting or attractive so that people will like them or want them: *His manager had packaged him to appeal to teenage girls.*

ˈpackage deal *n.* [C] an offer or agreement that includes several things that must all be accepted together

ˈpackage store *n.* [C] a word used in some parts of the U.S., meaning a store where alcohol is sold

ˈpackage tour *n.* [C] a completely planned vacation arranged by a company at a particular price, which includes travel, hotels, meals etc.

pack·ag·ing /ˈpækɪdʒɪŋ/ *n.* [U] **1** bags, boxes, and all the other materials that contain a product that is sold in a store: *Remove the plastic packaging* **2** a way of making a person, idea etc. seem interesting, attractive, or better than they are: *the packaging of the company image* **3** the process of wrapping food or other products for sale: *The stamp shows the date of packaging.*

ˈpack ˌanimal *n.* [C] an animal such as a horse used for carrying heavy loads

packed /pækt/ *adj.* **1** extremely full of people: *The subway was packed today.* | +**with** *The hotels were packed with tourists.* | **packed to the rafters/roof/gills** (=used to emphasize that a place is very full) **2** containing a lot of a particular kind of thing: +**with** *The new tourist guide is packed with useful information* **3** [not before noun] also **packed up** if you are packed, you have put everything you need into bags, suitcases etc. before going somewhere: *Are you packed yet?* | *By the time we **got packed** it was almost noon.* **4** put or pressed together: *packed snow* | *Use half a cup of **loosely packed** basil leaves.* | *a **tightly packed** football crowd*

P

pack·er /ˈpækɚ/ *n.* [C] someone who works in a factory, preparing food and putting it into containers

pack·et /ˈpækɪt/ S3 *n.* [C] **1** a small envelope containing a substance or a group of things: *a packet of carrot seeds* ►see THESAURUS box at **package**[1] → see picture at CONTAINER **2** a set of documents wrapped together, giving information about something: *We received our membership packets in the mail.* **3** COMPUTERS a quantity of information that is sent as a single unit from one computer to another on a network or on the Internet

ˈpack ice *n.* [U] EARTH SCIENCE a large mass of ice floating in the sea, formed by ICEBERGS joining together when the sea is very cold

pack·ing /ˈpækɪŋ/ *n.* [U] **1** the act of putting things into suitcases or boxes so that you can send or take them somewhere: *I usually **do my packing** the night before I leave.* **2** the act of putting goods into containers so that they can be sent somewhere and sold: *food processing and packing*

ˈpacking crate *n.* [C] a large strong wooden box in which things are packed to be sent somewhere or stored

ˈpacking maˌterial *n.* [U] paper, plastic, cloth etc. that is put around things you are packing to protect them

ˈpack rat *n.* [C] INFORMAL someone who collects and stores things that they do not really need

ˈpack trip *n.* [C] a trip through the countryside on horses, for fun or as a sport

pact /pækt/ *n.* [C] **1** POLITICS a formal agreement between two groups, nations, or people, especially to help each other or fight together against an enemy: +**with/between** *a pact between the government and the rebels* | *The two countries **signed a** non-aggression **pact**.* **2** an agreement between two people to help each other in some way: *We **made a pact** always to help each other.* [**Origin:** 1400–1500 French *pacte*, from Latin *pactum*, from *pacisci* **to agree**] → see also SUICIDE PACT

pad[1] /pæd/ S3 *n.* [C]
1 SOFT MATERIAL something made of or filled with soft material that is used to protect something, clean something, or make something more comfortable: *Clean the wound with a cotton pad.* | *I had to sleep on a foam pad on the floor.* | **knee/elbow/shoulder pad** (=a pad sewn into someone's clothes to protect their knee, elbow etc. or make them look bigger)
2 PAPER many sheets of paper fastened together, used for writing letters, drawing pictures etc.: +**of** *a pad of paper* | **a note/message/sketch pad** *simple drawings on a sketch pad*
3 FOR WOMEN a piece of soft material that a woman puts in her underwear during her PERIOD to take up the blood
4 HOME OLD-FASHIONED a house, room, or apartment where someone lives: *a bachelor pad*
5 ANIMAL'S FOOT BIOLOGY the flesh on the bottom of the foot of a cat, dog etc.
6 FOR INK a piece of material that has been made wet with ink and is used for covering a STAMP with ink SYN **ink pad**
7 WATER PLANT the large floating leaf of some water plants such as the WATER LILY: *a lily pad*
8 a LAUNCH PAD
9 a HELICOPTER PAD

pad[2] *v.* **padded, padding** **1** [I always + adv./prep.] to walk softly and quietly: *The cat padded silently across the room.* **2** [T] to protect something, make it more comfortable, or change its shape by covering or filling it with soft material: **pad sth with sth** *The jacket is padded with a soft cotton filling.* **3** [T] also **pad sth ↔ out** to make a speech or piece of writing longer, by adding unnecessary words or details: **pad sth (out) with sth** *His autobiography is padded with boring anecdotes.* **4** [T] to dishonestly make bills more expensive than they should be: *They realized their lawyer was padding the court fees.* **5** [T] to add to your points in a game that you are already winning: *The A's padded their lead with two more runs.*

pad·ded /ˈpædɪd/ *adj.* something that is padded is filled or covered with a soft material to make it thicker or more comfortable: *chairs with padded headrests* | *a padded bra*

ˌpadded ˈcell *n.* [C] a special room with thick soft walls in a MENTAL HOSPITAL, used to stop people who are being violent from hurting themselves

pad·ding /ˈpædɪŋ/ *n.* [U] **1** soft material used to fill or cover something to make it softer or more comfortable **2** unnecessary words or details that are added to make a sentence, speech etc. longer

pad·dle[1] /ˈpædl/ *n.* [C] **1** a short pole that is wide and flat at one end or both ends, used for moving a small boat along → see also OAR **2** a flat round object with a short handle, used for hitting the ball in PING-PONG **3** a piece of wood with a handle, used for hitting a child to punish them **4** one of the wide blades on the wheel of a PADDLE STEAMER **5** a tool like a flat spoon, used for mixing food → see also DOG PADDLE

paddle[2] *v.* **paddled, paddling** **1** [I,T] to move a small light boat through water, using one or more paddles: *Sam paddled the canoe down the creek.* | +**along/upstream/toward** *We got in the kayaks and paddled upstream.* → see also ROW **2** [I] to swim by moving your hands and feet up and down → see also DOG PADDLE **3** [T] to hit a child with a piece of wood as a punishment

ˈpaddle boat *n.* [C] **1** a small boat that one or two people move by turning PEDALS with their feet **2** a PADDLE WHEELER

ˈpaddle wheel *n.* [C] a large wheel on a boat, which has many boards attached to it that push the boat through the water

ˈpaddle ˌwheeler *n.* [C] a STEAMBOAT (=large boat driven by steam) which is pushed forward by one or more paddle wheels

pad·dock /ˈpædək/ *n.* [C] **1** a place where horses are brought together before a race so that people can look at them **2** a small field near a house or STABLE in which horses are kept or exercised

pad·dy, padi /ˈpædi/ also **ˈpaddy field** *n. plural* **paddies** [C] a field in which rice is grown in water

ˈpaddy ˌwagon *n.* [C] INFORMAL a covered truck or VAN used by the police to carry prisoners

pad·i /ˈpædi/ *n.* another spelling of PADDY

pad·lock /ˈpædlɑk/ *n.* [C] a small metal lock with a rounded bar that you can attach to a door, bicycle etc. —**padlock** *v.* [T]

pa·dre /ˈpɑdreɪ, -dri/ *n.* [C] SPOKEN, INFORMAL a priest, especially one in the army

pae·an /ˈpiən/ *n.* [C] LITERARY a piece of writing, music etc. expressing praise or happiness

pa·el·la /pɑˈɛlə, -ˈeɪyə/ *n.* [U] a Spanish dish of rice cooked with pieces of meat, fish, and vegetables [**Origin:** 1800–1900 Catalan **pot, pan**, from Latin *patella*]

pa·gan[1] /ˈpeɪgən/ *adj.* **1** relating to or believing in a religion that is not one of the main religions of the world, especially one from a time before these religions developed: *ancient pagan beliefs and rituals* | *pagan Germanic tribes* **2** not religious

pagan[2] *n.* [C] **1** someone who believes in a pagan religion **2** HUMOROUS someone who has few or no religious beliefs [**Origin:** 1300–1400 Late Latin *paganus*, from Latin, **someone who lives in the country**] —**paganism** *n.* [U]

page[1] /peɪdʒ/ S1 W1 *n.* [C]
1 PAPER one side of a sheet of paper in a book, newspaper etc., or the sheet of paper itself: *How many pages are we supposed to read?* | *a ten-page handwritten letter* | **on page 1/10/12 etc.** *The address is given on page 15.* | **at the top/bottom of the page** *You'll find the answers at the bottom of the page.* | *Look at the diagram **on the opposite page**.* | *Did you see **the front page** of the newspaper this morning?* | *Alex **turned the pages** of the book slowly.* | **the sports pages/the fashion page etc.** (=part of a newspaper dealing with

sports, fashion etc.) | **flip/flick through the pages of sth** (=turn the pages quickly without reading carefully) ▸see THESAURUS box at **wedding**
2 YOUNG WORKER a young person who works in the U.S. CONGRESS for a short time to gain experience
3 COMPUTER COMPUTERS all the writing that can be seen at one time on a computer screen: *How do I go back to the previous page?* | *a well-designed **web page*** (=single screen on a website)
4 a page in history an important event or period in a country's or organization's history: *a new page in American religious history*
5 BOY a) HISTORY a boy who served a KNIGHT during the Middle Ages as part of his training **b)** a PAGE-BOY **c)** OLD USE a boy who is a servant to a person of high rank
[**Origin:** (1, 3) 1500–1600 French, Latin *pagina*] → see also **be on the same page** at SAME[1] (6)

page² S2 *v.* [T] **1** to call someone by sending a message to their PAGER (=a small machine they carry that receives signals): *Don't page me after 10 o'clock.* **2** to call someone's name out in a public place, especially using a LOUDSPEAKER, in order to find them: *I couldn't find Jenny at the airport, so I **had** her **paged**.*

page down *phr. v.* to press a key on a computer that makes the screen show the page after the one you are reading

page through sth *phr. v.* to quickly look at a book, magazine etc., by turning the pages: *Her son paged through a toy catalog on the floor.*

page up *phr. v.* to press a key on a computer that makes the screen show the page before the one you are reading

pag·eant /ˈpædʒənt/ *n.* **1** [C] a public competition for young women in which their appearance and other qualities are compared and judged **2** [C] a public show or ceremony where people dress in beautifully decorated clothes and perform historical or traditional scenes **3** [singular] LITERARY a continuous series of historical events that are interesting and impressive: *the pageant of African history*

pag·eant·ry /ˈpædʒəntri/ *n.* [U] impressive ceremonies or events, involving many people wearing special clothes

page·boy /ˈpeɪdʒbɔɪ/ *n.* [C] **1** a style of cutting women's hair in which the hair is cut fairly short and has its ends turned under **2** OLD-FASHIONED a boy or young man employed in a hotel, club, theater etc. to deliver messages, carry bags etc.

pag·er /ˈpeɪdʒɚ/ *n.* [C] a small electronic machine that you carry or wear, that makes a high noise or VIBRATES to tell you to call someone

pag·i·na·tion /ˌpædʒəˈneɪʃən/ *n.* [U] FORMAL the process of giving a number to each page of a book, magazine etc. —**paginate** /ˈpædʒəˌneɪt/ *v.* [T] FORMAL

pa·go·da /pəˈgoʊdə/ *n.* [C] a TEMPLE of a type that is common in China, Japan, and other Asian countries, that has several levels with a decorated roof at each level [**Origin:** 1500–1600 Portuguese *pagode*]

Pa·go Pa·go /ˌpɑŋgoʊ ˈpɑŋgoʊ/ the capital city of the U.S. TERRITORY of American Samoa

paid /peɪd/ *v.* the past tense and past participle of PAY

Paige /peɪdʒ/, **Satch·ell** /ˈsætʃəl/ (1906–1982) a U.S. baseball player, famous as a PITCHER, who became one of the first African-American players in the Major Leagues in 1948

pail /peɪl/ *n.* [C] **1** a container with a handle used for holding or carrying liquids, or used by children playing with sand SYN **bucket**: *a milk pail* | *a diaper pail* **2** also **pail·ful** the amount a pail will hold: *a pail of water*

pain¹ /peɪn/ S2 W2 *n.* [C,U]
1 IN YOUR BODY the feeling you have when part of your body hurts: *a pain in my right shoulder* | *A month after surgery she was still **in pain*** (=feeling pain). | *He was tired and **felt** some **pain** in his left leg.* | **relieve/ease pain** *Her drugs don't do much to relieve the pain.* | *They gave me something to **kill the pain*** (=stop it). | *Injuries to the major joints can cause **severe pain**.* | *We had minor **aches and pains** for days after the game.* | *Suddenly I felt **a sharp pain*** (=one that you feel very severely, usually for a short time) *in my neck.* | *patients who suffer from **chronic pain*** (=constant pain or pain that comes regularly) | *Joe felt **a dull pain** in his arm after the shot.* | *Julie woke up about 5 a.m. with **labor pains*** (=pain felt by women beginning to have a baby). | *What did the doctor prescribe for **pain relief**?* → see also GROWING PAINS
2 IN YOUR MIND the feeling of unhappiness you have when you are sad, upset etc.: *the joys and pains of being in love* | *The scandal has **caused** me and my family great **pain**.* | *She turned to drugs to **ease the pain** of her family life.*
3 be a pain (in the neck) SPOKEN used to say that someone or something is very annoying: *It's such a pain to have to drive downtown.*
4 no pain, no gain INFORMAL used to say that you have to use a lot of effort or deal with a lot of unpleasant things, if you want to achieve something
5 on/under pain of death/punishment etc. at the risk of being killed, punished etc.: *Members were sworn to keep the secret, on pain of death.*
6 take pains to do sth also **go to (great) pains to do sth** to try hard to do something, or to be very careful in doing something: *He took pains to avoid racist language in the speech.*
7 be at pains to do sth to make a special effort to do something, because you think it is very important: *My boss was at pains to explain that it wasn't my fault.*
8 for sb's pains as a reward for making an effort to do something, used especially when the award is unfair or not a reward at all: *He works there his whole life, and then he gets fired for his pains!*
[**Origin:** 1200–1300 Old French *peine*, from Latin *poena*, from Greek *poine* **payment, punishment**]

pain² *v.* [T] **1 it pains sb to do sth** FORMAL it is very difficult and upsetting for someone to have to do something: *It pained her to see how much older Bill was looking.* **2** OLD USE if a part of your body pains you, it hurts

Paine /peɪn/, **Thomas** (1737–1809) a U.S. PHILOSOPHER and writer, born in England, who supported the American states in their fight to become independent of Great Britain

pained /peɪnd/ *adj.* worried, upset, or offended: *a **pained expression** on her face*

pain·ful /ˈpeɪnfəl/ W3 *adj.* **1** making you feel very unhappy or upset: *events from her painful and troubled past* | ***Painful memories** are never easy to forget.* | *The car manufacturer made the **painful decision** to lay off 3,000 workers.* | **it is painful for sb (to do sth)** *It's still painful for him to talk about the divorce.* **2** causing physical pain: *painful surgery* | *a slow painful death*

> **THESAURUS**
> **tender** a tender part of your body is painful if someone touches it: *Her arm was still too tender to touch.*
> **stiff** if a part of your body is stiff, your muscles hurt and it is difficult to move, usually because you have exercised too much or you are sick: *My legs are so stiff!*
> **sore** painful as a result of a wound, infection, or too much exercise: *a sore throat and fever*
> → HURT[1]

3 very bad and embarrassing for other people to watch, hear etc.: *His total humiliation was painful to watch.* | *painful shyness* **4** if part of your body is painful, you feel pain in it: *painful, swollen knee-joints* —**painfulness** *n.* [U]

pain·ful·ly /ˈpeɪnfəli/ *adv.* **1** very: *He is painfully thin.* | *I am **painfully aware** of the criticism that has been directed at me.* | **painfully obvious/clear/evident etc.** *It was painfully obvious that he didn't like her.* **2** with pain: *Muriel watched her father die painfully of*

P

cancer. **3** involving a lot of effort or trouble: *a painfully slow process*

pain·kill·er /ˈpeɪnˌkɪlɚ/ *n.* [C] a medicine which reduces or removes pain

pain·less /ˈpeɪnlɪs/ *adj.* **1** causing no pain: *a painless trip to the dentist* **2** INFORMAL needing no effort or hard work: *a painless way to learn a foreign language* —**painlessly** *adv.*

pains·tak·ing /ˈpeɪnzˌteɪkɪŋ/ *adj.* very careful and thorough: *painstaking research* —**painstakingly** *adv.*

paint¹ /peɪnt/ S2 *n.* **1** [U] a liquid that you put on a surface to make it a particular color: *a can of blue paint* | *Careful, the paint is still wet.* | *This room needs* ***a fresh coat of paint.*** **2** [singular] the layer of dried paint on a surface: *The paint was starting to peel off.* **3** [U] OLD-FASHIONED → see MAKEUP **4 paints** [plural] ENG. LANG. ARTS a set of small tubes or dry blocks of paint, used for painting pictures

paint² S1 W2 *v.* **1** [I,T] to put paint on a surface: *We really need to paint the bedroom.* | *Don't wear that shirt when you're painting.* | **paint sth red/green/blue etc.** *Sarah painted the table blue.* | **paint sth in sth** *The trucks were painted in bright colors.* **2 a)** [I,T] to make a picture, design etc. using paint: *My neighbor painted that picture.* | **paint in oils/watercolors/acrylic etc.** (=paint using a particular kind of paint) **b)** [T] to make a picture of someone or something using paint: *an artist who painted my brother* **3 paint sb/sth as sth** to describe someone or something in a particular way: *Her lawyers paint her as an innocent victim.* **4 paint a picture of sb/sth** also **paint a portrait of sb/sth** to describe someone or something in a particular way: *She doesn't* ***paint a very flattering portrait*** *of her first husband.* | **paint a grim/rosy/gloomy etc. picture of sth** *Officials paint a bleak picture of the country's economy.* **5** [T] to put a colored substance on part of your face or body to make it more attractive: *She painted her nails red.* **6 paint yourself into a corner** to put yourself in a difficult situation in which you do not have any good choices about what to do next **7 paint the town (red)** INFORMAL to go out to bars, clubs etc. to enjoy yourself or celebrate something [**Origin:** 1100–1200 Old French *peint*, past participle of *peindre* **to paint**, from Latin *pingere*] → see also **paint/tar (sb/sth) with a broad brush** at BROAD¹ (7)

paint sth ↔ **in** *phr. v.* to fill a space in a picture or add more to it using paint

paint sth ↔ **out** *phr. v.* to remove a design, figure etc. from a picture or surface by covering it with more paint

paint sth ↔ **over** *phr. v.* to cover a picture or surface with new paint: *Don't just paint over grease and dirt.*

paint·brush /ˈpeɪntˀbrʌʃ/ *n.* [C] a brush for spreading paint on a surface → see picture at BRUSH¹

ˌPainted ˈDesert, the a desert area in Arizona in the southwestern U.S. east of the Little Colorado River

paint·er /ˈpeɪntɚ/ *n.* [C] **1** ENG. LANG. ARTS someone who paints pictures SYN **artist**: *a landscape painter* ►see THESAURUS box at **artist** **2** someone whose job is painting houses, rooms etc.: *a house painter*

paint·er·ly /ˈpeɪntɚli/ *adj.* LITERARY typical of painters or painting: *painterly images*

paint·ing /ˈpeɪntɪŋ/ *n.* **1** [C] ENG. LANG. ARTS a painted picture: *a painting by Matisse* | +**of** *an oil painting of Columbus* ►see THESAURUS box at **picture¹** **2** [U] ENG. LANG. ARTS the skill or process of making a picture using paint: *a class in drawing and painting* ►see THESAURUS box at **art¹** **3** [U] the act of covering a wall, house etc. with paint: *painting and decorating*

ˈpaint job *n.* [C] the way a car, house, building etc. is painted, or the work done to achieve this: *This place needs a paint job.*

ˈpaint ˌstripper *n.* [U] a substance used to remove paint from walls, doors etc.

ˈpaint ˌthinner *n.* [U] a liquid that you add to paint to make it less thick

paint·work /ˈpeɪntˀwɚk/ *n.* [U] paint on a car, wall etc.

pair¹ /pɛr/ S2 W3 *n. plural* **pairs** or **pair** [C]
1 SHOES/GLOVES ETC. two things of the same kind that are used together: +**of** *a pair of socks* | *a pair of earrings* | *She felt as if every pair of eyes in the room was looking at her.*
2 PANTS/SCISSORS ETC. a single thing made of two similar parts that are joined together: *I broke my glasses and I don't have a spare pair.* | +**of** *a new pair of jeans*
3 TWO PEOPLE two people who are standing or doing something together, or who have some type of connection: *Stein and his business partner are a rather unusual pair.* | +**of** *a pair of dancers*
4 TWO THINGS two of the same type of thing: +**of** *We have five pairs of tickets to give away.*
5 in pairs in groups of two: *Alexander advises women to travel in pairs or groups.*
6 TWO ANIMALS two animals, one male and one female, that come together to have sex: +**of** *a pair of blue jays*
7 an extra/another pair of hands SPOKEN additional help from someone when you are busy: *If you need an extra pair of hands, just let me know.*
8 CARDS two PLAYING CARDS which have the same value: *I've got three pairs.* | +**of** *a pair of queens*
[**Origin:** 1200–1300 Old French *paire*, from Latin *paria* **equal things**] → see Word Choice box at COUPLE¹

pair² *v.* [T usually passive] to put people together in groups of two: **be paired with sb/sth** *Each Russian student will be paired with an American at the camp.*

pair off *phr. v.* **pair sb** ↔ **off** to come together or bring two people together to have a romantic relationship: *Toward the end of the evening everyone at the party started to pair off.*

pair up *phr. v.* **1** to join together with someone to do something SYN **team up**: *Nunn and Lloyd Webber paired up to create "Cats."* **2 pair sb** ↔ **up** to form groups of two, or to put people into groups of two: **pair sb** ↔ **up with sb** *She pairs up students who are doing well with those who are struggling.*

pais·ley /ˈpeɪzli/ *adj.* made from cloth that is covered with a pattern of shapes that look like curved drops of rain: *a paisley tie* —**paisley** *n.* [U]

Pai·ute /ˈpaɪyut/ a Native American tribe from the southwestern region of the U.S. —**Paiute** *adj.*

pa·ja·ma /pəˈdʒɑmə, -ˈdʒæ-/ *adj.* [only before noun] **1 a pajama top/bottoms** the shirt or pants of a set of PAJAMAS **2 a pajama party** a SLUMBER PARTY

pa·ja·mas /pəˈdʒɑməz, -ˈdʒæ-/ *n.* [plural] a soft loose pair of pants and a top that you wear in bed [**Origin:** 1800–1900 Hindi *pajama* (singular), from Persian *pa* **leg** + *jama* **piece of clothing**]

Pak·i·stan /ˈpækɪˌstæn/ a country in Asia, west of India and east of Afghanistan and Iran

Pak·i·stan·i /ˌpækɪˈstæni◂/ *adj.* relating to or coming from Pakistan —**Pakistani** *n.* [C]

pal¹ /pæl/ *n.* [C] **1** OLD-FASHIONED, INFORMAL a close friend: *They'd been pals since childhood.* **2** SPOKEN used to address a man in an unfriendly way: *Listen, pal, you're not welcome around here.* [**Origin:** 1600–1700 Romany *phral*, *phal* **brother, friend**, from Sanskrit *bhratr* **brother**] → see also PEN PAL

pal² *v.* **palled, palling**

pal around *phr. v.* INFORMAL to go places and do things with someone as a friend: +**with** *He was palling around with some of the other neighborhood kids.*

pal·ace /ˈpælɪs/ *n.* [C] **1** often **Palace** the large official home of a person of very high rank, especially a king or queen: *Buckingham Palace* **2** a large beautifully decorated house: *the splendid palaces of Florence* | *Their house* ***is like a palace*** *compared to ours.* **3** a large public building, such as a MUSEUM or movie theater: *the Palace of Justice* [**Origin:** 1200–1300 Old French *palais*, from Latin *palatium*, from *Palatium* the Palatine Hill in Rome where the ruler's palace was]

ˈpalace guard *n.* **1** [C] someone whose job is to protect the king, queen etc. in a palace, or a group of these people **2** [singular] a small group of people who support and give advice to a powerful person

pal·a·din /ˈpælədɪn/ *n.* [C] **1** HISTORY a KNIGHT (=a soldier of high rank) in the Middle Ages who fought loyally for his prince **2** FORMAL a respected person who strongly supports a particular action or opinion

pal·at·a·ble /ˈpælət̬əbəl/ *adj.* **1** a palatable idea, suggestion, feature etc. is acceptable or sounds good OPP **unpalatable**: *We made several compromises to **make** the plan **more palatable to** voters.* **2** FORMAL having a pleasant or acceptable taste OPP **unpalatable**: *a palatable wine*

pal·a·tal /ˈpælət̬l/ *n.* [C] TECHNICAL a CONSONANT sound such as /tʃ/ in the word "chin" made by putting your tongue against or near your HARD PALATE —**palatal** *adj.*

pal·ate /ˈpælɪt/ *n.* **1** [C,U] the sense of taste: *The cheese is extremely pleasing to the palate.* **2** [C] BIOLOGY the ROOF (=top inside part) of the mouth → see also **a cleft lip/palate** at CLEFT[2] (2), HARD PALATE, SOFT PALATE

pa·la·tial /pəˈleɪʃəl/ *adj.* very large and beautifully decorated, like a PALACE: *a palatial Beverly Hills estate*

Pa·lau /pəˈlaʊ/ a country consisting of a group of islands in the western Pacific Ocean

pa·lav·er /pəˈlævɚ, -ˈlɑ-/ *n.* [U] WRITTEN a lot of talk about something, especially when the talking does not produce anything useful [**Origin:** 1700–1800 Portuguese *palavra* **word, speech**, from Late Latin *parabola*]

pale[1] /peɪl/ *adj.* **1** having a much whiter skin color than usual, especially because you are sick, worried, frightened etc.: *You look kind of pale. Are you feeling okay?* | *a pale complexion* **2** lighter than the usual color OPP **dark**: *pale blue eyes* → DEEP[1] (5), LIGHT[2] (1) ►see THESAURUS box at **color[1]**, **light[2]** **3** pale light is not bright: *the pale light of early morning* **4 a pale imitation/copy/shadow etc. (of sth)** an unimpressive or bad-quality copy of an earlier performance, movie, event etc.: *The cheese is a pale imitation of real Parmesan.* [**Origin:** 1300–1400 Old French, Latin *pallidus*] —**paleness** *n.* [U]

pale[2] *v.* [I] **1** to seem much less important, much less big or serious, or much less good when compared to something else: *Today's economic problems **pale in comparison** with those of the 1930s.* | *The education budget **pales into insignificance** when compared to the defense budget.* **2** LITERARY if your face pales, it becomes much whiter than usual because you have had a shock

pale[3] *n.* **beyond the pale** unacceptable, unreasonable, and often offensive: *His remarks **went** completely **beyond the pale**.*

pale·face /ˈpeɪlfeɪs/ *n.* [C] an insulting word for a white person used by Native Americans in old movies

paleo- /peɪlioʊ, peɪliə/ *prefix* TECHNICAL extremely ancient, or relating to things that happened before historical times: *paleobotany* (=study of ancient plants)

pa·le·o·lith·ic, Paleolithic /ˌpeɪliəˈlɪθɪk/ *adj.* relating to the earliest period of the STONE AGE (=the period many thousands of years ago when people made stone tools and weapons): *the Paleolithic era* → see also NEOLITHIC

pa·le·on·tol·o·gy /ˌpeɪliənˈtɑləd͡ʒi, -liɑn-/ *n.* [U] SCIENCE the study of FOSSILS (=ancient animals and plants that have been preserved in rock) —**paleontologist** *n.* [C]

Pa·le·o·zo·ic /ˌpeɪliəˈzoʊɪk/ *n.* **the Paleozoic** EARTH SCIENCE the ERA (=long period of time in the history of the Earth) from about 570 million years ago to about 250 million years ago, when fish, insects, REPTILES, and some plants first started to exist → see also CENOZOIC —**Paleozoic** *adj.*: *the Paleozoic creatures*

Pal·es·tine /ˈpæləˌstaɪn/ an area of land which is now part of the country of Israel

ˌPalestine Libeˈration Organiˌzation, the POLITICS the PLO

Pal·es·tin·i·an /ˌpæləˈstɪniən/ *adj.* **1** relating to or coming from the area between the Jordan River and the Mediterranean Sea, which used to be called Palestine **2** relating to the Arab people who come from or live in this area —**Palestinian** *n.* [C]

pal·ette /ˈpælɪt/ *n.* [C] **1** ENG. LANG. ARTS a board with a curved edge and a hole for the thumb, on which a painter mixes colors **2** [usually singular] the range of colors, tastes, or qualities that are included in things such as pictures, food, and music: +**of** *the reds and blues of the artist's palette* **3** COMPUTERS the choice of colors or shapes that are available in a computer program [**Origin:** 1700–1800 French, Old French *pale* **spade**]

ˈpalette knife *n.* [C] a thin knife that bends easily and has a rounded end, used by painters for mixing paint

Pa·li·kir /ˌpɑlɪˈkɪr/ the capital city of Micronesia

pal·i·mo·ny /ˈpæləˌmoʊni/ *n.* [U] money that someone is ordered to pay regularly to a former partner, when they lived together without being married → see also ALIMONY

pal·imp·sest /ˈpæləmpˌsɛst/ *n.* [C] HISTORY an ancient written document which has had its original writing rubbed out, not always completely, and has been written on again

pal·in·drome /ˈpælənˌdroʊm/ *n.* [C] ENG. LANG. ARTS a word or phrase such as "deed" or "level," which is the same when you read it backward

pal·ing /ˈpeɪlɪŋ/ *n.* [C usually plural] a pointed piece of wood used with other pointed pieces in making a fence

pal·i·sade /ˌpæləˈseɪd/ *n.* [C] **1** a fence made of strong pointed poles, used for defense in past times **2 palisades** [plural] EARTH SCIENCE a line of high straight cliffs, especially along a river or beside the ocean

pall[1] /pɔl/ *n.* **1 cast a pall over/on sth** to spoil an event or occasion that should have been happy and enjoyable: *Injuries cast a pall over the team's victory.* **2** [singular] a low dark cloud of smoke, dust etc.: +**of** *A huge pall of smoke hangs over the city.* **3** [C] a large piece of cloth spread over a CASKET (=box in which a dead body is carried) **4** [C] OLD USE a CASKET with a body inside

pall[2] *v.* [I] to gradually become uninteresting or unenjoyable: *Gradually, the novelty of city life began to pall.*

pal·la·di·um /pəˈleɪdiəm/ *n.* [U] a type of shiny soft whitish metal

pall·bear·er /ˈpɔlˌbɛrɚ/ *n.* [C] someone who walks beside a CASKET (=a box with a dead body inside) or helps to carry it at a funeral

pal·let /ˈpælɪt/ *n.* [C] **1** a large metal plate or flat wooden frame on which heavy goods can be lifted, stored, or moved **2** OLD-FASHIONED a temporary bed, or a cloth bag filled with STRAW for someone to sleep on

pal·li·ate /ˈpæliˌeɪt/ *v.* [T] FORMAL **1** to reduce the bad effects of illness, pain etc. without curing them **2** to make a bad situation seem better than it really is, for example by explaining it in a positive way —**palliation** /ˌpæliˈeɪʃən/ *n.* [U]

pal·lia·tive /ˈpælyət̬ɪv, -liˌeɪt̬ɪv/ *n.* [C] FORMAL **1** an action taken to make a bad situation seem better, but which does not solve the problem: *Promises of reform are mere palliatives.* **2** a medical treatment that will not cure an illness but will reduce the pain —**palliative** *adj.*: *palliative therapy*

pal·lid /ˈpælɪd/ *adj.* **1** MEDICINE unusually pale, or pale in an unhealthy way: *Paul looked pallid and sick.* **2** boring, without any excitement: *a pallid performance* —**pallidness** *n.* [U]

pal·lor /ˈpælɚ/ *n.* [singular, U] unhealthy paleness of the skin or face: *Her skin had a deathly pallor.*

palm[1] /pɑm/ *n.* [C] **1** BIOLOGY the inside surface of your hand, between the base of your fingers and your wrist: *She had an ink stain on her palm.* | *He held the pebble in **the palm of** his **hand**.* **2** BIOLOGY a PALM TREE **3 hold/have sb in the palm of your hand** to have a strong influence on someone, so that they do what you want them to do: *She's got the whole committee in the palm of her hand.* **4 read sb's palm** to tell someone what is going to happen to them by looking at their hand **5** INFORMAL a PALMTOP → see also **grease sb's palm** at GREASE² (2)

palm² *v.* [T] to hide something in the palm of your hand, especially when performing a magic trick or stealing something

palm sth ↔ **off** *phr. v.* to persuade someone to accept or buy something bad or unwanted, especially by deceiving them: **palm sth off as sth** *Plenty of dealers try to palm off fakes as works of art.* | **palm sth off on/onto sb** *He wants to palm off his old car on his younger brother.*

P

Palm·er /ˈpɑmɚ/, **Ar·nold** /ˈɑrnəld/ (1929–) a U.S. GOLFER who was one of the most successful players of the 1950s and 1960s

pal·met·to /pɑˈmɛt̬oʊ/ *n. plural* **palmettos** or **palmettoes** [C] a small PALM TREE that grows in the southeastern U.S.

palm·is·try /ˈpɑməstri/ *n.* [U] the activity of looking at the PALM of someone's hand to tell them what is going to happen to them in the future SYN **palm reading** —**palmist** *n.* [C]

ˈ**palm oil** *n.* [U] the oil obtained from the nut of an African PALM TREE

ˈ**palm ˌreader** *n.* [C] someone who claims they can tell what a person is like or what will happen to them in the future, by looking at the PALM of their hand —**palm reading** *n.* [U] → see also FORTUNE TELLER

ˌ**Palm ˈSunday** *n.* the Sunday before Easter in the Christian religion

palm·top /ˈpɑmtɑp/ *n.* [C] a very small computer that you can hold in your hand

ˈ**palm tree** also **palm** *n.* [C] a tropical tree which typically grows near beaches or in deserts, with a long straight trunk and large pointed leaves at the top

palm·y /ˈpɑmi/ *adj.* **1** covered with palm trees **2** used to describe a period of time when people have money and life is good

pal·o·mi·no /ˌpæləˈminoʊ◂/ *n. plural* **palominos** [C] a horse of a golden or cream color, with a white MANE and tail [**Origin:** 1900–2000 American Spanish, Spanish, **like a dove**, from Latin *palumbes* **dove**]

pal·pa·ble /ˈpælpəbəl/ *adj.* **1** FORMAL easily and clearly noticed SYN **obvious** OPP **impalpable**: *There was a palpable sense of relief among the crowd.* **2** FORMAL able to be touched or physically felt SYN **tangible** OPP **impalpable**: *A palpable chill shot through his limbs.* **3** TECHNICAL able to be felt by palpating —**palpably** *adv.*

pal·pate /ˈpælpeɪt/ *v.* [T] TECHNICAL to touch and press someone's body during a medical examination —**palpation** /pælˈpeɪʃən/ *n.* [C,U]

pal·pi·tate /ˈpælpəˌteɪt/ *v.* [I] **1** BIOLOGY if your heart palpitates, it beats quickly and in an irregular way **2** LITERARY to shake, especially because of fear, excitement etc.: **+with** *We were palpitating with excitement.*

pal·pi·ta·tions /ˌpælpəˈteɪʃənz/ *n.* [plural] irregular or extremely fast beating of your heart, caused by illness or too much effort

pal·sied /ˈpɔlzid/ *adj.* NOT TECHNICAL suffering from an illness that makes your arms and legs shake because you cannot control your muscles

pal·sy /ˈpɔlzi/ *n.* [U] MEDICINE **1** an illness that makes your arms and legs shake because you cannot control your muscles **2** PARALYSIS → see also CEREBRAL PALSY

pal·try /ˈpɔltri/ *adj.* [usually before noun] **1** a paltry amount of something such as money is too small to be useful or important: *a paltry 1.2% growth rate* **2** worthless and silly: *paltry excuses*

pam·pas /ˈpæmpəz, -pəs/ *n.* **the pampas** the large wide flat areas of land covered with grass in some parts of South America [**Origin:** 1700–1800 American Spanish, plural of *pampa*, from Quechua and Aymara, **plain**]

ˈ**pampas grass** *n.* [U] a type of tall grass with silver-white feathery flowers

pam·per /ˈpæmpɚ/ *v.* [T] to take care of someone very kindly, for example by giving them the things that they want and making them feel warm and comfortable: **pamper yourself** *Pamper yourself with a stay in one of our luxury hotels.* —**pampered** *adj.*

pam·phlet /ˈpæmflɪt/ *n.* [C] a very thin book with paper covers, giving information about something: **+on** *a pamphlet on healthy eating* [**Origin:** 1300–1400 *Pamphilus seu De Amore* **Pamphilus or On Love**, popular Latin love poem of the 12th century]

pam·phlet·eer /ˌpæmfləˈtɪr/ *n.* [C] someone who writes pamphlets giving political opinions

pans

pan¹ /pæn/ S3 W3 *n.* [C] **1** a round metal container used for cooking, usually with one long handle and sometimes a lid: *a frying pan* | *pots and pans* **2** a metal container for baking things in, or the food that this contains: *a cake pan* | **+of** *a pan of rolls* **3** a container with low sides, used for holding liquids: *an oil pan* **4** a container used to separate gold from other substances, by washing them in water **5** one of the two dishes on a pair of SCALES (=a small weighing machine) **6** a metal drum that is played in a STEEL BAND [**Origin:** Old English *panne*] → see also BEDPAN, **a flash in the pan** at FLASH² (5), FRYING PAN, SAUCEPAN, WARMING PAN

pan² *v.* **panned, panning** **1** [T] to strongly criticize a movie, play etc. in a newspaper or on television or radio: *Critics panned the movie.* ►see THESAURUS box at **criticize** **2** ENG. LANG. ARTS **a)** [I always + adv./prep., T] if a movie or television camera pans in a particular direction, it moves slowly while taking a picture: *The camera panned slowly across the crowd.* **b)** [I always + adv./prep.,T] to move a camera in this way **3** [I,T] to wash soil in a pan, especially to separate gold from it: **+for** *Henkins moved to the Sierras to pan for gold.*

pan out *phr. v.* SPOKEN **1** to happen or develop in the way you expected or hoped: *None of the job possibilities have panned out.* **2** to happen or develop in a particular way: *They're waiting to see how the negotiations pan out.*

pan-, **Pan-** /pæn/ *prefix* including all of something: *the Pan-American highway* | *Pan-Arabism* (=political union of all Arabs)

pan·a·ce·a /ˌpænəˈsiə/ *n.* [C] **1** something that people think will make everything better and solve all their problems SYN **cure-all**: **+for** *There is no panacea for the country's economic problems.* **2** a medicine or form of treatment that is supposed to cure any illness

pa·nache /pəˈnæʃ, -ˈnɑʃ/ *n.* [U] a confident way of doing things with style that makes them seem easy, and makes other people admire you: *He conducted the symphony* ***with great panache***.

Pan-ˈAfricanism, **pan-Africanism** *n.* [U] POLITICS the belief that all Africans or African countries should work together to improve their situation, or be united politically

Pan·a·ma /ˈpænəˌmɑ/ a country on a narrow piece of land connecting Central and South America, between Costa Rica and Colombia

pan·a·ma /ˈpænəˌmɑ/ also **ˌpanama ˈhat** *n.* [C] a light hat for men, made from STRAW

ˌPanama Caˈnal, the a long narrow CANAL that was built across Panama in 1914 in order to allow ships to sail between the Atlantic and Pacific Oceans

ˌPanama ˈCity the capital city of Panama

Pan·a·ma·ni·an /ˌpænəˈmeɪniən/ *adj.* relating to or coming from Panama —**Panamanian** *n.* [C]

ˌPan Aˈmerican *adj.* relating to or including all of the countries in North, Central, and South America: *the Pan American Games*

ˌPan-ˈArabism, pan-Arabism *n.* [U] POLITICS the belief that all Arab people or Arab countries should work together to improve their situation, or be united politically

pan·a·tel·la /ˌpænəˈtɛlə/ *n.* [C] a long thin CIGAR

pan·cake /ˈpænkeɪk/ S3 *n.* [C] a thick round flat cake made from flour, milk, and eggs that has been cooked in a flat pan and is eaten for breakfast, often with SYRUP

ˌpancake ˈlanding *n.* [C] an act of bringing an aircraft down to the ground in such a way that it drops flat from a low height

ˈpancake ˌmakeup *n.* [U] very thick MAKEUP for the face

pan·cre·as /ˈpæŋkriəs/ *n.* [C] BIOLOGY a GLAND inside the body, near the stomach, that produces INSULIN and a liquid that helps the body to process food —**pancreatic** /ˌpæŋkriˈætɪk/ *adj.* → see picture at DIGESTIVE SYSTEM

pan·da /ˈpændə/ also **ˈpanda bear** *n.* [C] a large black and white animal similar to a bear that lives in the mountains of China

pan·dem·ic /pænˈdɛmɪk/ *n.* [C] MEDICINE an illness or disease that affects the population of a very large area —**pandemic** *adj.* → see also ENDEMIC

pan·de·mo·ni·um /ˌpændəˈmoʊniəm/ *n.* [U] a situation in which there is a lot of noise because people are angry, confused, or frightened: *When the verdict was read,* ***pandemonium broke out*** *in the courtroom.* [**Origin:** 1600–1700 *Pandaemonium* city of evil spirits in the poem "Paradise Lost" (1667) by John Milton, from Greek *pan-* + *daimon* **evil spirit**]

pan·der /ˈpændɚ/ *v.* [**Origin:** 1600–1700 *pander* **someone who finds lovers for others** (14–20 centuries), from *Pandarus* man in an ancient Greek story who acted as a messenger between lovers]

pander to sb/sth *phr. v.* DISAPPROVING to try to please people by doing or saying what they want you to do, even though you know this is wrong: *Liberals charge that the senator is pandering to racist voters.*

pan·der·ing /ˈpændərɪŋ/ *n.* [U] **1** DISAPPROVING the action of trying to please people by doing or saying what they want you to do, even though you know this is wrong **2** the crime of finding customers for PROSTITUTES: *McFadden was arrested for pimping and pandering.* → see also PIMP

P and L state·ment /ˌpi ənd ˈɛl ˌsteɪtˀmənt/ *n.* [C] a document that shows the profits and losses (LOSS) of a business

Pan·do·ra's box /pænˌdɔrəz ˈbɑks/ *n.* **open (up) a Pandora's box** to do something that causes a lot of problems that did not exist before, without meaning to [**Origin:** 1500–1600 *Pandora* woman in an ancient Greek story who opened a box and let all evils out into the world]

pane /peɪn/ *n.* [C] a sheet of glass used in a window or door → see also WINDOWPANE

pan·e·gyr·ic /ˌpænəˈdʒɪrɪk/ *n.* [C] FORMAL a speech or piece of writing that praises someone or something very highly

pan·el¹ /ˈpænl/ Ac S3 W2 *n.* [C]
1 GROUP OF PEOPLE a) a group of people with skills or special knowledge who have been chosen to give advice or opinions on a particular subject: *the Senate ethics panel* | +**of** *a panel of experts* | *There will be at least three senior doctors* ***on the panel.*** **b)** a group of well-known people who discuss a subject or answer questions in front of an AUDIENCE (=group of people), especially on a television or radio program: *Let me introduce tonight's panel.* | *a panel discussion on sexual harassment* → see also PANELIST **c)** a group of people who are chosen to listen to a case in a court of law and to decide the result SYN **jury**: *The panel spent 14 hours going over the evidence.*
2 PART a) a flat piece of wood, glass etc. with straight sides, which forms part of a door, wall, fence etc.: *a carved-wood panel* **b)** a piece of metal that forms part of the outer structure of a vehicle: *a door panel* **c)** a piece of material that forms part of a piece of clothing
3 instrument/control panel the place in a car, airplane, boat etc. where the controls are
4 PICTURE ENG. LANG. ARTS a thin board on which a picture is painted, or the picture and board together
5 DRAWING ENG. LANG. ARTS one of the drawings in a series in a COMIC STRIP that tell a story
[**Origin:** 1300–1400 Old French **piece of cloth, piece,** from Latin *pannus*] → see also SOLAR PANEL

panel² Ac *v.* **paneled, paneling** [T usually passive] to cover or decorate a room, wall, door etc. with flat pieces of wood, glass etc.: *They're still paneling the basement.*

pan·el·ing /ˈpænl-ɪŋ/ *n.* [U] wood, especially in long or square pieces, used to decorate walls, doors etc.: *oak paneling*

pan·el·ist /ˈpænl-ɪst/ *n.* [C] one of a group of well-known people who discuss a subject or answer questions in front of an AUDIENCE (=group of people), especially on a television or radio program

ˈpanel truck *n.* [C] a motor vehicle used for delivering goods, which has doors on the sides that slide up and down

pang /pæŋ/ *n.* [C] a sudden feeling of pain, sadness etc.: *hunger pangs* | +**of** *a pang of guilt*

pan·han·dle¹ /ˈpænˌhændl/ *v.* [I] to ask for money in the streets or public places: *Large numbers of the homeless panhandle on the eastern edge of the park.* —**panhandler** *n.* [C] —**panhandling** *n.* [U]

panhandle² *n.* [C] EARTH SCIENCE a thin piece of land that is joined to a larger area like the handle of a pan: *the Oklahoma panhandle*

pan·ic¹ /ˈpænɪk/ *n.* **1** [singular, U] a sudden strong feeling of fear or nervousness that makes you unable to think clearly or behave sensibly: *She was gripped by a feeling of panic.* | *People fled* ***in panic.*** | **throw/send sb into a panic** *Rumors of a food shortage could send the population into a panic.* | +**over/about** *widespread panic over the threat of invasion* | *Small business owners* ***are in a panic*** *over whether they will survive.* | **go/get into a panic** *Toby went into a panic when he couldn't find his passport.* ►see THESAURUS box at **fear¹**
2 [C usually singular, U] a situation in which people are suddenly made very anxious, and make quick decisions without thinking carefully: *A bomb hoax caused a panic on the subway today.* | *Amid the panic and confusion, the police had to maintain order.* **3** [singular] a situation in which there is a lot to do and not much time to do it in: *a last-minute panic of Christmas shoppers* **4 press/push/hit the panic button** to do something quickly without thinking enough about it, because something bad has suddenly happened and made you very anxious: *Even though stock prices have dropped, I wouldn't hit the panic button just yet.* [**Origin:** 1600–1700 French *panique* **caused by panic,** from Greek *panikos,* from *Pan* ancient Greek god of nature, who caused great fear]

panic² *v. past tense and past participle* **panicked, panicking** [I,T] to suddenly become so frightened that you cannot think clearly or behave sensibly, or to make someone do this: *A week before the exam I started to panic.* | +**about** *She was panicking about the tickets.* | **Don't panic!** (=used to tell people to stay calm) | **panic**

sb into (doing) sth *Don't let them panic you into making a quick decision.*

ˈpanic atˌtack *n.* [C] a very sudden strong feeling of fear or anxiety that makes it difficult for you to breathe or behave sensibly

ˈpanic ˌbuying *n.* [U] a situation in which many people buy all or most of the supply of a product or products at one time because they are afraid there will be none left soon: *Panic buying stripped stores bare before the hurricane.*

pan·ick·y /ˈpænɪki/ *adj.* INFORMAL very nervous or anxious: *I get panicky before a performance.*

P

ˈpanic ˌselling *n.* [U] a situation in which someone sells all of something they have, especially STOCK because they are afraid the price will go down soon

ˈpanic-ˌstricken *adj.* so frightened that you cannot think clearly or behave sensibly: *Panic-stricken passengers were rushing for the exits.*

pan·ni·er /ˈpæniɚ/ *n.* [C] **1** one of a pair of baskets or bags carried one on each side of an animal or a bicycle **2** a basket used to carry a load on someone's back

pan·o·ply /ˈpænəpli/ *n.* [U] **1** FORMAL a large number and variety of people or things: +**of** *the panoply of gods in Greek mythology* **2** an impressive show of special clothes, decorations etc., especially at an important ceremony: +**of** *the whole panoply of a royal wedding*

pan·o·ram·a /ˌpænəˈræmə, -ˈrɑ-/ *n.* [C usually singular] **1** an impressive view of a wide area of land: *a stunning mountain panorama* | +**of** *a gorgeous panorama of the Gobi Desert* **2** all the events or things included in a historical period, a type of art etc., or a description of them: +**of** *a panorama of modern India* **3** ENG. LANG. ARTS a picture that shows a very wide view of a place —**panoramic** /ˌpænəˈræmɪk/ *adj.*: *a panoramic view of the valley* —**panoramically** /-kli/ *adv.*

pan·pipes /ˈpænpaɪps/ *n.* [plural] a simple musical instrument made of several short wooden pipes of different lengths, that are played by blowing across their open ends

pan·sy /ˈpænzi/ *n. plural* **pansies** [C] a small garden plant with flat brightly colored flowers [**Origin:** 1400–1500 French *pensée*, from *pensée* **thought**]

pant[1] /pænt/ *v.* **1** [I] to breathe quickly with short noisy breaths because you have been running, climbing etc. or because it is very hot: *He was still panting after his run.* | *After five minutes I was* ***panting for breath.*** ▸see THESAURUS box at **breathe** **2** [T] to say something while panting: *"Go on without me," Mike panted.* **3** to want something very much: +**for** *He left his fans panting for more.* | **pant to do sth** *I'm not exactly panting to get married.* [**Origin:** 1400–1500 Old French *pantaisier*, from Vulgar Latin *phantasiare* **to see things which are not there**]

pant[2] *adj.* relating to or part of PANTS: *my left pant leg*

pan·ta·loons /ˌpæntəˈlunz/ *n.* [plural] long pants with wide legs, which are narrow at the ANKLES

pan·the·ism /ˈpænθiˌɪzəm/ *n.* [U] the religious idea that God and the universe are the same thing and that God is present in all natural things —**pantheist** *n.* [C] —**pantheistic** /ˌpænθiˈɪstɪk/ *adj.*

pan·the·on /ˈpænθiɑn/ *n.* [C] **1** a group of famous and important people in a particular area of work, sports etc.: +**of** *the pantheon of 20th-century artists* **2** all the gods of a particular people or nation: *the Roman pantheon* **3** a TEMPLE built in honor of all gods

pan·ther /ˈpænθɚ/ *n.* [C] BIOLOGY **1** a COUGAR **2** a black LEOPARD

pant·ies /ˈpæntiz/ *n.* [plural] a piece of women's underwear that covers the area between the waist and the top of the legs: *a pair of silk panties*

pan·to·mime /ˈpæntəˌmaɪm/ *n.* [C,U] a method of performing using only actions and not words, or a play performed using this method SYN **mime**

pan·try /ˈpæntri/ *n. plural* **pantries** [C] a very small room in a house where food is kept

pants /pænts/ S2 *n.* [plural] **1** a piece of clothing that covers you from your waist to your feet and has a separate part for each leg: *She was wearing red pants and a white shirt.* | *Jason needs a new* ***pair of pants*** *for school.* **2 scare/bore/shock/charm etc. the pants off sb** INFORMAL to make someone feel very frightened, very bored etc.: *That movie scared the pants off Heidi.* **3 sb puts their pants on one leg at a time** SPOKEN used to say that someone who is famous is really just like everyone else [**Origin:** 1800–1900 *pantaloons*] → see also **beat the pants off sb/sth** at BEAT[1] (1), **do sth by the seat of your pants** at SEAT[1] (11), **wear the pants** at WEAR[1] (9)

pant·suit /ˈpæntsut/ *n.* [C] a woman's suit consisting of a JACKET and matching pants

pan·ty·hose /ˈpæntiˌhoʊz/ *n.* [plural] a very thin piece of women's clothing that covers their legs from the toes to the waist and is usually worn with dresses or skirts

pan·ty·lin·er /ˈpæntiˌlaɪnɚ/ *n.* [C] a very thin SANITARY NAPKIN

ˈpanty raid *n.* [C] INFORMAL an occasion when young men go into women's rooms to steal their underwear as a joke, especially done at college in the past

pap /pæp/ *n.* [U] **1** DISAPPROVING books, television programs etc. that people read or watch for entertainment but which have no serious value: *boring sentimental pap* **2** OLD-FASHIONED very soft food eaten by babies or sick people → see also PAP SMEAR

pa·pa /ˈpɑpə/ *n.* [C] INFORMAL a word meaning "father," especially used by children

pa·pa·cy /ˈpeɪpəsi/ *n.* **1 the papacy** the position and authority of the POPE **2** [U] the time during which a particular POPE is in power

Pa·pa·go /ˈpɑpəˌgoʊ/ a Native American tribe from the southern U.S. and northern Mexico

pa·pal /ˈpeɪpəl/ *adj.* [only before noun] relating or belonging to the POPE: *papal authority*

ˌpapal ˈbull *n.* [C] an official statement from the POPE

pa·pa·raz·zi /ˌpɑpəˈrɑtsi/ *n.* [plural] newspaper photographers who follow famous people [**Origin:** 1900–2000 Italian, from the name of a character in the film "La Dolce Vita" (1960)]

pa·pa·ya /pəˈpaɪə/ *n.* [C] BIOLOGY a large yellow-green tropical fruit

pa·per[1] /ˈpeɪpɚ/ S1 W1 *n.*

1 FOR WRITING ON [U] material in the form of thin sheets that is used for writing on, wrapping things etc.: **a piece/sheet of paper** *Joe handed me a piece of paper with a list of the winners.* | *The glasses were wrapped in white paper.* | **writing/wrapping/drawing paper** *Do you have any writing paper I could borrow?*

2 NEWSPAPER [C] **a)** a newspaper: *Today's paper is over on the coffee table.* | *Why don't you put an ad in the paper?* | **a daily/weekly/Sunday paper** *I like to read the Sunday paper in bed.* | **a local/national paper** *Our local paper doesn't have much international news.* **b)** a company that produces a newspaper: *a reporter with the local paper*

3 papers [plural] **a)** pieces of paper with writing on them that you use in your work, at meetings etc.: *Kim left some important papers in her briefcase.* **b)** official legal documents: *court papers* | *She received the* ***divorce papers*** *yesterday.*

4 sb's papers [plural] **a)** documents and letters concerning someone's private or public life: *The letter was found among the president's* ***private papers.*** **b)** someone's official documents such as their PASSPORT, ID etc.: *After checking our papers, the border guards let us through.*

5 on paper a) if you put ideas or information on paper, you write them down: **get/put sth down on paper** *Try to get your ideas down on paper.* **b)** something that seems to be good or true on paper may not be good or true in a real or practical situation: *The idea looks good on paper.* | *On paper, the family is worth over $5 billion.*

6 SCHOOL WORK [C] a piece of writing that is done as part of a course at a school or college: *When is your*

sociology paper due? | **+on** *a paper on the American Revolution*
7 SPEECH/PIECE OF WRITING [C] a piece of writing or a talk by someone who has made a study of a particular subject: **present/give a paper (on sth)** *We're presenting a paper on bilingualism at the conference.*
8 FOR WALLS [C,U] paper for covering walls SYN wallpaper
9 sth is not worth the paper it is written/printed on if something such as a contract is not worth the paper it is written on, it has no value because whatever is promised in it will not happen
[**Origin:** 1300–1400 Old French *papier*, from Latin *papyrus*] → see also **put/set pen to paper** at PEN[1] (3), TOILET PAPER, WASTE PAPER, WHITE PAPER, WORKING PAPERS

paper² *adj.* [only before noun] **1** made of paper: *a paper bag* **2** existing only as an idea but not having any real value: *paper profits*

paper³ *v.* [T] **1** to decorate the walls of a room by covering them with special paper **2** to cover an object or wall with lots of different pieces of paper, with things written or drawn on them **3 paper over the cracks/a problem etc.** to try to hide disagreements or difficulties

pa·per·back /ˈpeɪpɚˌbæk/ *n.* **1** [C] a book with a stiff paper cover: *a shelf full of paperbacks* ►see THESAURUS box at book¹ **2 in paperback** produced with a stiff paper cover: *The book is now available in paperback.* → see also HARDCOVER

pa·per·board /ˈpeɪpɚˌbɔrd/ *n.* [U] a type of stiff CARDBOARD made of lots of layers of thick paper

pa·per·boy /ˈpeɪpɚˌbɔɪ/ *n.* [C] a boy who delivers newspapers to people's houses

ˈpaper chase *n.* [C] INFORMAL an attempt to do something that involves writing and reading a lot of documents, and takes a very long time

ˈpaper clip *n.* [C] a small piece of curved wire used for holding sheets of paper together —**paper-clip** *v.* [T] *The documents were paper-clipped, not stapled.*

ˈpaper doll *n.* [C] a piece of stiff paper cut in the shape of a person

ˈpaper girl *n.* [C] a girl who delivers newspapers to people's houses

pa·per·hang·er /ˈpeɪpɚˌhæŋɚ/ *n.* [C] someone whose job is to decorate rooms with WALLPAPER

pa·per·less /ˈpeɪpɚlɪs/ *adj.* [usually before noun] using electronic ways of storing, recording, and sending information, documents etc., without writing or printing anything on paper: *a paperless office* | *paperless bank statements*

ˌpaper ˈmoney *n.* [U] money consisting of small sheets of paper, not coins

ˈpaper-ˌpusher *n.* [C] someone whose job is doing unimportant office work

ˈpaper route *n.* [C] the job of delivering newspapers to a group of homes, or the group of homes you have to deliver newspapers to

ˌpaper-ˈthin *adj.* very thin: *paper-thin walls*

ˌpaper ˈtiger *n.* [C] an enemy or opponent who seems powerful but actually is not

ˌpaper ˈtowel *n.* [C] a sheet of soft thick paper that you use to clean up small amounts of liquid, food etc. or to dry your hands

ˈpaper ˌtrail *n.* [C usually singular] documents and records that show what someone has done, especially when they prove that someone is guilty of a crime: *The paper trail led investigators straight to the White House.*

pa·per·weight /ˈpeɪpɚˌweɪt/ *n.* [C] a small heavy object used to hold pieces of paper in place

pa·per·work /ˈpeɪpɚˌwɚk/ S2 *n.* [U] **1** work such as writing letters or reports, which must be done but is not very interesting: *My job involves a lot of paperwork.* **2** the documents that you need for a business deal, a trip etc.: *The car dealer will give you the necessary paperwork.*

pa·per·y /ˈpeɪpəri/ *adj.* papery things such as skin or leaves are very dry and thin and a little stiff: *the papery outer skin of an onion*

pa·pier-mâ·ché also **papermâché** /ˌpeɪpɚməˈʃeɪ/ *n.* [U] a soft substance made from a mixture of paper, water, and glue, which becomes hard when it dries and is used for making boxes, pots etc.

pa·poose /pæˈpus/ *n.* [C] **1** a type of bag fastened to a frame, used to carry a baby on your back **2** OLD USE a Native American baby or young child

pap·py /ˈpæpi/ *n.* [C] OLD-FASHIONED a word meaning "father"

pa·pri·ka /pəˈprikə, pæ-/ *n.* [U] a red powder made from a type of sweet PEPPER, used to give a strong taste to food

P

Pap smear /ˈpæp smɪr/ also **ˈPap test** *n.* [C] a medical test that takes cells from a woman's CERVIX and examines them for signs of CANCER

Pap·u·a New Guin·ea /ˌpæpyuə nu ˈgɪni/ a country in the southwestern Pacific Ocean, north of Australia, which includes the eastern half of the island of New Guinea and several small islands —**Papuan** *n., adj.*

pa·py·rus /pəˈpaɪrəs/ *n. plural* **papyruses** or **papyri** /-raɪ/ **1** [U] BIOLOGY a plant like grass that grows in water **2** [C,U] a type of paper made from this plant and used in ancient Egypt, or a piece of this paper

par /pɑr/ *n.* **1 on (a) par (with sb/sth)** at the same level or standard: *The new pay deal puts us on a par with other workers in the industry.* **2 be below/under par** also **not be up to par a)** to feel a little sick or lacking in energy: *I haven't been up to par since the operation.* **b)** to be less good than usual or below the appropriate standard: *Economic growth has been below par.* **3** [C,U] the number of STROKES a player should take to hit the ball into a hole in the game of GOLF: *Woods finished his third round on four under par.* **4 be par for the course** to be the same as you would normally expect, especially to be as bad as you expect: *It rained all week, but I guess that's par for the course in Ireland.* **5** [U] also **par value** ECONOMICS the value of a STOCK or BOND that is printed on it when it is first sold → see also PAR EXCELLENCE

par. the written abbreviation of PARAGRAPH

para- /pærə/ *prefix* **1** beyond something: *the paranormal* (=strange events that go beyond what normally happens) **2** connected with a profession, and helping more highly trained people: *a paramedic* (=who gives medical help before a doctor does) | *a paralegal* (=someone who helps a lawyer) **3** very similar to something: *a paramilitary group* **4** relating to PARACHUTES: *a paratrooper*

par·a·ble /ˈpærəbəl/ *n.* [C] a short simple story that teaches a moral or religious lesson, especially one of the stories told by Jesus Christ in the Bible

pa·rab·o·la /pəˈræbələ/ *n.* [C] MATH a curved shape formed by a PLANE (=flat surface) crossing through the side of a CONE, so that the distance from the curve to a fixed point inside the curve and the distance from the curve to the DIRECTRIX (=line outside the curve) are always the same. A parabola looks like the curve that a ball makes when it is thrown high in the air and comes down a short distance away. —**parabolic** /ˌpærəˈbɑlɪk◂/ *adj.*: *a parabolic curve* → see also CONIC SECTION

par·a·chute¹ /ˈpærəˌʃut/ *n.* [C] a large piece of cloth fastened to the back of people who jump out of airplanes, which opens and makes them fall slowly and safely to the ground: *It is vitally important to fold the parachute properly.*

parachute² *v.* **1** [I always + adv./prep.] to jump from an airplane using a parachute: **+into/in/onto etc.** *Troops parachuted into enemy territory overnight.* **2** [T always + adv./prep.] to drop someone or something from an airplane with a parachute: **parachute sth to/into sth** *Emergency supplies were parachuted into the region.* —**parachuting** *n.* [C]

par·a·chut·ist /ˈpærəˌʃutɪst/ *n.* [C] someone who jumps from an airplane with a parachute

pa·rade¹ /pəˈreɪd/ *n.* [C] **1** a public celebration when musical bands, brightly decorated vehicles etc. move down the street: *Macy's Thanksgiving Day Parade* | *The city has a parade every 4th of July.* **2** a military ceremony in which soldiers stand or march together so that important people can examine them: **be on parade** (=be standing or marching in a parade) **3** a series of many people, events etc. coming one after another: +**of** *There was an endless parade of taxis to and from the station.* [**Origin:** 1600–1700 French, Old French *parer* **to prepare**] → see also HIT PARADE

P

parade² *v.* **1** [I always + adv./prep.] to walk or march together to celebrate or protest about something: +**around/past etc.** *The demonstrators paraded through the capital.* **2** [I always + adv./prep.] to walk around, especially in a way that shows that you want people to notice and admire you: +**around/past etc.** *Michelle was parading around in her new bikini.* **3** [T always + adv./prep.] to proudly show someone or something to other people, because you want to look impressive to them or prove how powerful, rich, good etc. you are: *The captured pilots were paraded through the town.* | *He talked loudly, eager to parade his knowledge.* **4** [I,T] if soldiers parade or if an officer parades them, they march together so that an important person can watch them: +**around/down/past etc.** *The President stood as a battalion of soldiers paraded past him.*

parade as *phr. v.* DISAPPROVING **1 parade as sth** if one thing parades as another better thing, people are pretending that it is the better thing: *It's just old-fashioned racism parading as scientific research.* **2 parade sb/sth as sth** to state or claim that something or someone is a particular thing, when they are not

paˈrade ˌground *n.* [C] a large flat area where soldiers practice marching or standing together in rows

par·a·digm /ˈpærəˌdaɪm/ Ac *n.* [C] **1** a particular way of doing something or thinking about something, which is generally accepted or copied: *changing paradigms in the business world* | +**for** *a new education paradigm for the 21st century* **2** FORMAL a very clear or typical example of something: +**of** *The policy is not exactly a paradigm of logic.* **3** TECHNICAL an example or pattern of a word, showing all its forms in grammar, like "child, child's, children, children's" —**paradigmatic** /ˌpærədɪgˈmætɪk/ *adj.* —**paradigmatically** /-kli/ *adv.*

par·a·dise /ˈpærəˌdaɪs, -ˌdaɪz/ *n.* **1** [U] a place or situation that is extremely pleasant, beautiful, or enjoyable: *a tropical island paradise* | *The hotel felt like paradise after two weeks of camping.* **2** [C] a place that is perfect for a particular type of person or activity, because it has everything you need: *The market is a bargain-hunter's paradise.* | +**for** *San Felipe is paradise for seafood lovers.* **3 Paradise** [singular] **a)** Heaven, thought of as the place where God lives and where there is no illness, death, or evil **b)** the garden where Adam and Eve lived (=the first humans, according to the Bible) [**Origin:** 1100–1200 Old French, Late Latin, from Greek *paradeisos* **enclosed park**] → see also BIRD OF PARADISE, **be living in a fool's paradise** at FOOL¹ (9)

par·a·dox /ˈpærəˌdɑks/ *n.* **1** [C] a situation that seems strange because it involves two ideas or qualities that are opposite or very different: *It's a paradox that in such a rich country there is so much poverty.* **2** [C] a statement that seems impossible because it contains two opposing ideas that are both true **3** [U] the use of such statements in writing or speech —**paradoxical** /ˌpærəˈdɑksɪkəl/ *adj.*

par·a·dox·i·cal·ly /ˌpærəˈdɑksɪkli/ *adv.* [sentence adverb] in a way that is surprising because it is the opposite of what you would expect: *Paradoxically, the problem of loneliness is most acute in big cities.*

par·af·fin /ˈpærəfɪn/ *n.* [U] a soft white substance used for making CANDLES, made from PETROLEUM or coal [**Origin:** 1800–1900 German, from Latin *parum* **too little** + *affinis* **related**, because it does not easily make compounds with other substances]

par·a·glid·ing /ˈpærəˌglaɪdɪŋ/ *n.* [U] a sport in which you jump off a hill or out of an aircraft and use a special type of PARACHUTE to fly through the air and float back down to the ground

par·a·gon /ˈpærəˌgɑn/ *n.* [C] OFTEN HUMOROUS someone or something that is perfect or is extremely brave, good etc.: +**of** *a paragon of virtue*

par·a·graph /ˈpærəˌgræf/ Ac S2 *n.* [C] ENG. LANG. ARTS a group of several sentences in a piece of writing, the first sentence of which starts on a new line: *The first paragraph of the essay should grab your readers' attention.* [**Origin:** 1400–1500 Old French, Medieval Latin, from Greek, from *paragraphein* **to write beside**] —**paragraph** *v.* [T]

Par·a·guay /ˈpærəˌgwaɪ/ a country in South America between Brazil and Argentina —**Paraguayan** /ˌpærəˈgwaɪən◂ / *n., adj.*

par·a·keet /ˈpærəˌkit/ *n.* [C] BIOLOGY a small brightly colored bird with a long tail [**Origin:** 1500–1600 Spanish *periquito*, from Old French *perroquet*]

par·a·le·gal /ˌpærəˈligəl/ *n.* [C] someone whose job is to help a lawyer do his or her work

par·al·lel¹ /ˈpærəˌlɛl/ Ac *n.* **1** [C] a relationship or similarity between two things, especially things that exist or happen in different places or at different times: +**between** *There are many parallels between politics and acting.* | +**with** *When looking at Mozart's life, the parallels with "Hamlet" are astonishing.* | *The article **draws a parallel between** (=shows that two things are similar) the political situation now and that in the 1930s.* **2 in parallel (with sb/sth)** together with and at the same time as something else: *The CIA is working in parallel with the FBI to solve the case.* **3** [C] an imaginary line drawn on a map of the Earth, that is parallel to the EQUATOR: *The 42nd parallel is the northern border of Pennsylvania.* **4** [C] something that is similar to something else: *Our system has parallels in most Western countries.* | **have no parallel/be without parallel** *His achievement was without parallel in Olympic history.* **5 be in parallel** TECHNICAL if two electrical CIRCUITS (=complete circular paths) are in parallel, they are connected so that any electric current is divided equally between them

parallel² Ac *adj.* **1** MATH parallel lines, paths etc. are the same distance apart along their whole length: *The airport's two parallel runways are only 750 feet apart.* | +**to/with** *Place the boards parallel with each other, six inches apart.* | *The road **runs parallel to** (=is parallel to) the river.* **2** FORMAL similar and happening at the same time: *The film attempts to follow two parallel story lines.* **3** TECHNICAL parallel structures in writing or poetry are of the same style or GRAMMATICAL type: *The items in the list should be parallel.* **4 a parallel universe a)** a universe that is extremely similar to our own, and exists at the same time **b)** used when someone or something seems very strange and unusual, and different or separate from your normal experience **5** TECHNICAL parallel computers, systems etc. perform several operations at the same time

parallel³ Ac *v.* [T] FORMAL **1** to be the same as or similar to something else: *Political events in the state closely parallel what's happening nationally.* **2** to happen at the same time as something else: *The development of online job services has paralleled the evolution of the Internet itself.* **3** to be in a position that is parallel with something else: *The railroad tracks paralleled the stream for several miles.*

ˌparallel ˈbars *n.* [plural] two wooden bars that are held parallel to each other on a set of posts, used in GYMNASTICS

par·al·lel·ism /ˈpærəlɛˌlɪzəm/ *n.* FORMAL **1** [U] the state of being similar or related to something **2** [C] a similarity **3** [U] the use of similar structures in poetry and writing

par·al·lel·o·gram /ˌpærəˈlɛləˌgræm/ *n.* [C] MATH a flat shape with four sides in which each side is parallel to the side opposite to it, but not necessarily the same length → see picture at SHAPE[1]

ˌparallel ˈparking *n.* [U] **1** a way of parking a car so that it is parallel to the SIDEWALK **2** spaces that are arranged so that you can park a car in this way

ˌparallel ˈport *n.* [C] COMPUTERS part of a computer that sends or receives information through more than one wire at once, connected to something such as a printer

ˌparallel ˈprocessing *n.* [U] COMPUTERS the use of several computers to work on a single problem at one time, or the process by which a single computer can perform several operations at the same time

ˌparallel ˈstructure *n.* [U] ENG. LANG. ARTS a way of writing or speaking in which ideas of equal importance are expressed using the same types of GRAMMATICAL structure

pa·ral·y·sis /pəˈræləsɪs/ *n.* [U] **1** MEDICINE the loss of the ability to move all or part of your body or to experience any feeling in it: *Such injuries can cause permanent paralysis.* **2** a state of being unable to take action, make decisions, or operate normally: *a long period of political paralysis* → see also INFANTILE PARALYSIS

par·a·lyt·ic[1] /ˌpærəˈlɪt̬ɪk◂/ *adj.* [only before noun] suffering from paralysis —**paralytically** /-kli/ *adv.*

paralytic[2] *n.* [C] someone who is paralyzed

par·a·lyze /ˈpærəˌlaɪz/ *v.* [T] **1** to make a person or animal lose the ability to move part or all of their body, or to feel anything in it: *The spider uses a poison to paralyze its victim.* ►see THESAURUS box at **hurt**[1] **2** to make something or someone unable to operate normally: *Strikes have paralyzed the country's transportation network.* | *Fear paralyzed him, just as he was about to jump.*

par·a·lyzed /ˈpærəˌlaɪzd/ *adj.* **1** unable to move part or all of your body or feel things in it: *She was paralyzed from the neck down.* **2** unable to think clearly or operate normally: *Trade in the country is virtually paralyzed.* | +**with/by** *They were both paralyzed with fear.*

Par·a·mar·i·bo /ˌpærəˈmærəˌboʊ/ the capital city of Suriname

par·a·med·ic /ˌpærəˈmɛdɪk/ *n.* [C] someone who has been trained to help people who are hurt or to do medical work, but who is not a doctor or nurse

par·a·med·i·cal /ˌpærəˈmɛdɪkəl◂/ *adj.* [usually before noun] helping or supporting doctors, nurses, or hospitals: *paramedical staff*

pa·ram·et·er /pəˈræmət̬ɚ/ Ac *n.* [C usually plural] a set of agreed limits that control the way that something should be done: **within/outside parameters** *The system operates within fairly rigid parameters.* | **establish/set/lay down parameters** *The committee's job is to establish new parameters for allocating public housing.*

par·a·mil·i·tar·y /ˌpærəˈmɪləˌtɛri/ *adj.* [usually before noun] **1** a paramilitary organization is an illegal military force that uses violence to achieve its political aims: *extremist paramilitary groups* **2** relating to or helping a military organization: *paramilitary operations* —**paramilitary** *n.* [C]

par·a·mount /ˈpærəˌmaʊnt/ *adj.* more important than anything else: *At times like these, secrecy is paramount.* | *Our customers' concerns are* ***of paramount importance*** *to us.*

par·a·mour /ˈpærəˌmʊr/ *n.* [C] LITERARY someone who has a romantic or sexual relationship with another person who they are not married to SYN **lover**

Pa·ra·ná Riv·er /ˌpærəˈnɑ ˌrɪvɚ/ a river in central South America that flows south through Brazil and Paraguay to the Atlantic Ocean on the coast of Argentina

par·a·noi·a /ˌpærəˈnɔɪə/ *n.* [U] **1** an unreasonable belief that you cannot trust other people, or that they are trying to harm you: +**about** *some people's paranoia about government conspiracies* **2** MEDICINE a serious mental illness that makes someone believe that people hate them and treat them badly

par·a·noid /ˈpærəˌnɔɪd/ also **par·a·noi·ac** /ˌpærəˈnɔɪæk/ *adj.* **1** believing that you cannot trust other people, that other people want to harm you, or that you are always in danger: *I get a little paranoid around big dogs.* | +**about** *He's alway paranoid about catching a cold.* **2** TECHNICAL suffering from a mental illness that makes you believe that other people are trying to harm you —**paranoid** also **paranoiac** *n.* [C]

par·a·nor·mal /ˌpærəˈnɔrməl◂/ *adj.* **1** paranormal events cannot be explained by science and seem strange and mysterious: *ESP and other paranormal phenomena* **2 the paranormal** these events in general → see also SUPERNATURAL

par·a·pet /ˈpærəpət, -pɛt/ *n.* [C] **1** a low wall at the edge of a high roof, bridge etc. **2** a protective wall of earth or stone built in front of a TRENCH in a war

par·a·pher·na·lia /ˌpærəfɚˈneɪlyə, -fəˈneɪl-/ *n.* [U] a lot of small things that belong to someone or are needed for a particular activity: *drug paraphernalia* [**Origin:** 1600–1700 Medieval Latin, Greek *parapherna* **things brought to a marriage by a woman apart from the agreed amount of money**]

par·a·phrase[1] /ˈpærəˌfreɪz/ *v.* [T] ENG. LANG. ARTS to express in a shorter or clearer way what someone has written or said: *The article only paraphrased his comments; it didn't quote him directly.*

paraphrase[2] *n.* [C] ENG. LANG. ARTS a statement that expresses something that someone has said or written in a shorter, clearer, or different way

par·a·ple·gi·a /ˌpærəˈplidʒiə, -dʒə/ *n.* [U] MEDICINE the inability to move your legs and the lower part of your body

par·a·ple·gic /ˌpærəˈplidʒɪk/ *n.* [C] MEDICINE someone who is unable to move the lower part of their body including their legs ►see THESAURUS box at **disabled** —**paraplegic** *adj.*

par·a·psy·chol·o·gy /ˌpærəsaɪˈkɑlədʒi/ *n.* [U] the scientific study of mysterious abilities that some people claim to have, such as knowing what will happen in the future

par·a·sail·ing /ˈpærəˌseɪlɪŋ/ *n.* [U] a sport in which you wear a PARACHUTE and are pulled behind a motor boat so that you sail through the air

par·a·site /ˈpærəˌsaɪt/ *n.* [C] **1** BIOLOGY a plant or animal that lives on or in another plant or animal and gets food and protection from it without giving anything to the other plant or animal **2** DISAPPROVING a lazy person who does not work but depends on other people: *Her brother's a lazy free-loading parasite.*

par·a·sit·ic /ˌpærəˈsɪt̬ɪk/ also **par·a·sit·i·cal** /ˌpærəˈsɪt̬ɪkəl/ *adj.* **1** BIOLOGY living in or on another plant or animal and getting food from them: *parasitic worms in the intestine* **2** DISAPPROVING a parasitic person is lazy, does no work, and depends on other people **3** MEDICINE a parasitic disease is caused by parasites —**parasitically** /-kli/ *adv.*

par·a·sit·ism /ˈpærəsɪˌtɪzəm/ *n.* [U] BIOLOGY the relationship between a PARASITE and the animal or plant that it lives on

par·a·sol /ˈpærəˌsɔl, -ˌsɑl/ *n.* [U] a type of UMBRELLA used to provide shade from the sun

par·a·troop·er /ˈpærəˌtrupɚ/ *n.* [C] a soldier who is trained to jump out of an airplane using a PARACHUTE

par·a·troops /ˈpærəˌtrups/ *n.* [plural] a group of paratroopers that fight together as a military unit

par·boil /ˈpɑrbɔɪl/ *v.* [T] to boil something until it is partly cooked

par·cel[1] /ˈpɑrsəl/ *n.* [C] **1** something wrapped so it can be sent by mail SYN **package** ►see THESAURUS box at **mail**[1] **2** an area of land that is part of a larger area which has been divided up: *a parcel of farmland* → see also **be part and parcel of sth** at PART[1] (22)

parcel[2] *v.* **parceled, parceling**

parcel sth ↔ **off** *phr. v.* to divide something into

small parts so that it can be sold: *The new owner has parceled off many of the company's assets.*

parcel sth ↔ **out** *phr. v.* to divide or share something among several people: *It's Clare's job to parcel out the work to members of the team.*

'parcel post *n.* [U] the slowest and cheapest system of sending packages by mail in the U.S.

parch /partʃ/ *v.* [T] if sun or wind parches land, plants etc., it makes them very dry

parched /partʃt/ *adj.* **1** very dry, especially because of hot weather: *a parched desert* **2** [not before noun] INFORMAL to be very THIRSTY

P

parch•ment /'partʃmənt/ *n.* **1** [U] a material used in the past for writing on, made from the skin of a sheep or a goat **2** [U] thick yellow-white writing paper, sometimes used for official documents **3** [C] a document written on this paper or material

pard•ner /'pardnɚ/ *n.* SPOKEN, HUMOROUS a word used when speaking to someone you know well, thought to be typical of the way COWBOYS speak: *Howdy, pardner!*

par•don¹ /'pardn/ S3 *v.* [T] **1** LAW to officially allow someone to be free without being punished, although a court has decided they are guilty of a crime: *The President pardoned dozens of political prisoners.* **2** [not in progressive] to forgive someone for doing something wrong: **pardon sb for sth** *He could never pardon her for saying those things.*

SPOKEN PHRASES

3 pardon me a) used when you did not hear what someone said and you ask them politely to repeat it SYN **excuse me**: *Pardon me. What did you say?* **b)** used to politely say you are sorry when you do something rude, for example interrupt someone or make a rude sound SYN **excuse me**: *Oh, pardon me. Did I interrupt?* **c)** used before you politely correct someone or disagree with them SYN **excuse me**: *Pardon me, but that's not exactly what happened.* **d)** used to politely get someone's attention in order to ask them a question SYN **excuse me**: *Pardon me, can you tell me how to get to the library?* **e)** used politely when you want to move past someone in a small space SYN **excuse me**: *Pardon me, I just need to reach that shelf.* → see also PARDON³ → see Word Choice box at EXCUSE¹ **4 pardon me for interrupting/asking/saying** used to politely ask if you can interrupt someone, ask something etc.: *Pardon me for asking, but where did you buy your shoes?* **5 if you'll pardon the expression** used when you are saying sorry for using a slightly impolite phrase **6 pardon my French** HUMOROUS used to say sorry after you have said an impolite word **7 pardon my ignorance/rudeness etc.** used when you think that you may seem not to know enough, not to be polite enough etc.: *Pardon my ignorance, but what does OPEC stand for?* **8 pardon me for living/breathing** used when you are annoyed because you think someone has answered you angrily for no good reason

pardon² *n.* **1** [C] LAW an official order allowing someone to be free without being punished, although a court has decided they are guilty of a crime: **grant/give sb a pardon** *The governor was persuaded to give him a pardon.* **2** [U] OLD-FASHIONED the act of forgiving someone: **ask/beg sb's pardon (for)** *Walter begged her pardon for all the pain he had caused her.* [**Origin:** 1200–1300 Old French *pardoner*, from Late Latin *perdonare* **to give freely**] → see also **I beg your pardon** at BEG (4) → see Word Choice box at EXCUSE¹

pardon³ S2 *interjection* used when you want someone to repeat something because you did not hear it SYN **pardon me**: *"We're leaving at eight." "Pardon?"*

par•don•a•ble /'pardn-əbəl/ *adj.* FORMAL pardonable behavior or mistakes are not very bad and can be forgiven —**pardonably** *adv.*

pare /pɛr/ *v.* [T] **1** to cut off the thin outer part of a fruit or vegetable using a sharp knife: *First pare the apples.* **2** to reduce an amount or number, especially by making a series of small reductions: **pare sth from sth** *$600,000 has been pared from next year's budget.*

pare sth ↔ **down** *phr. v.* to gradually reduce an amount or number: *The Navy has pared its carrier fleet down to nine ships from 14.* —**pared-down** *adj.*

par•ent /'pɛrənt, 'pær-/ S1 W1 *n.* [C] **1** the father or mother of a person or animal: *I'd like you to meet my parents sometime.* | *What's it like to be a parent?* | +**of** *the parents of teenagers* **2** a larger company or organization that owns a particular organization: *The airline's parent lost $115 million in the first nine months.* [**Origin:** 1400–1500 Old French, Latin, present participle of *parere* **to give birth to**] → see also PARENT COMPANY, SINGLE PARENT

par•ent•age /'pɛrəntɪdʒ/ *n.* [U] someone's parents and the country or social class they are from: *children of French-Canadian parentage*

pa•ren•tal /pə'rɛntl/ *adj.* [usually before noun] related to a child's parent or parents: *parental responsibilities*

pa,rental 'leave *n.* [U] time that a parent is allowed to spend away from work with his or her baby → see also MATERNITY LEAVE

'parent ,company *n.* [C] a company that controls a smaller company or organization

'parent ,function *n.* [C] MATH in a group of FUNCTIONS that have common features, the parent function is the simplest function with these features → see also RELATED FUNCTION

pa•ren•the•sis /pə'rɛnθəsɪs/ *n. plural* **parentheses** /-siz/ [usually plural] ENG. LANG. ARTS one of the marks ( ), used in writing to separate additional information from the main information: *Ratings of the movies are shown **in parentheses**.*

par•en•thet•i•cal /,pærən'θɛṭɪkəl/ *adj.* ENG. LANG. ARTS said or written as an additional, usually less important, piece of information: *a parenthetical comment* —**parenthetically** /-kli/ *adv.*

par•ent•hood /'pɛrənt,hʊd/ *n.* [U] the state of being a parent: *They didn't feel ready for parenthood.*

par•ent•ing /'pɛrəntɪŋ/ *n.* [U] the skill or activity of taking care of children as a parent

,Parent-'Teacher Associ,ation *n.* → see PTA

par ex•cel•lence /,par ɛksə'lans/ *adj.* [only after noun] of the best possible kind: *an entertainer par excellence*

par•fait /par'feɪ/ *n.* [U] a sweet food made of layers of ICE CREAM and fruit

pa•ri•ah /pə'raɪə/ *n.* [C] **1** a person, organization, country etc. that is hated and avoided by others: *a social pariah* | *The country was viewed by the U.S. State Department as a **pariah state**.* **2** OLD USE a member of a very low social class in India [**Origin:** 1600–1700 Tamil *paraiyan* **drummer**]

par•i•mu•tu•el /,pæri'myutʃuəl/ *n.* **1** [U] a system in which the money that people have risked on a horse race is shared between the people who have won **2** [C] a machine used to calculate the amount of money people can win by risking it on horse races

'paring knife *n.* [C] a small knife used for cutting vegetables and fruit

par•ings /'pɛrɪŋz/ *n.* [plural] thin pieces of something that have been cut off

Par•is /'pærɪs/ the capital and largest city of France

par•ish /'pærɪʃ/ *n.* [C] **1** the area that a priest in some Christian churches is responsible for: *a parish priest* **2** POLITICS an area in the state of Louisiana that contains several towns that are governed together **3 the parish** the people who live in a particular area, especially those who go to church

pa•rish•ion•er /pə'rɪʃənɚ/ *n.* [C] someone who lives in a parish, especially someone who regularly goes to the church there

Pa•ris•i•an /pə'riʒən/ *adj.* coming from or connected with Paris —**Parisian** *n.* [C]

ˌParis ˈpeace talks, the HISTORY talks held in Paris between the U.S., South Vietnam, and North Vietnam, during the Vietnam War. The talks began in 1968 and led to an agreement which was signed in January 1973, after which all American soldiers left Vietnam

par·i·ty /ˈpærət̬i/ *n.* [U] **1** the state of being equal, especially having equal pay, rights, or power: **+between/with** *Women workers are demanding parity with their male colleagues.* **2** ECONOMICS equality between the units of money from two different countries: *The currency was recently set* ***at parity with*** *the U.S. dollar.*

park[1] /pɑrk/ S2 W1 *n.* [C] **1** a large open area with grass and trees, especially in a city, where people can walk, play games etc.: *Let's go for a walk in the park.* | *Central Park* | *a park bench* **2** a large area of land in the country that has been kept in its natural state to protect the trees, plants, and animals in it, where people can visit, go CAMPing etc.: **a national/state/county park** (=one that is controlled by the national, state etc. government) **3** the field where a game of BASEBALL is played ▸see THESAURUS box at **sport**[1] [**Origin:** 1200–1300 Old French *parc*, from Medieval Latin *parricus*] → see also AMUSEMENT PARK, BALLPARK, BUSINESS PARK, SCIENCE PARK, THEME PARK, TRAILER PARK

park[2] S1 *v.* **1 a)** [I,T] to put a car or other vehicle in a particular place for a period of time: *I couldn't find a place to park.* | *Where did you park your car?* **b)** [I] if a vehicle parks somewhere, it stops there and remains there for a period of time: *Taxis aren't allowed to park here.* → see also PARKED ▸see THESAURUS box at **drive**[1] **2 park yourself** INFORMAL to sit or stand in a particular place: *He came home and parked himself in front of the TV.* **3** [T always + adv./prep.] SPOKEN to put something in a place and leave it there, especially in a way that is annoying: **park sth in/on/here etc.** *Hey, don't park those bags down there.*

par·ka /ˈpɑrkə/ *n.* [C] a thick warm JACKET with a HOOD [**Origin:** 1700–1800 Aleut **skin, outer clothing**, from Russian, **animal skin and fur**, from Yurak]

ˌpark and ˈride *n.* [U] a system in which you leave your car in a PARKING LOT on the edge of a city, and then take a special bus, train, or SUBWAY to the center of the city

parked /pɑrkt/ *adj.* **1** a parked vehicle is not moving but has been left in a place for a period of time: *a row of parked cars* **2 be parked** to have stopped your vehicle in order to leave it for a period of time: *Where are you parked?*

Par·ker /ˈpɑrkɚ/, **Bon·nie** /ˈbɑni/ (1911–1934) a young criminal who stole money from banks and businesses with Clyde Barrow

Par·ker, Char·lie /ˈtʃɑrli/ (1920–1955) a JAZZ musician who played the SAXOPHONE and invented the BEBOP style of jazz with Dizzy Gillespie

Parker, Dor·o·thy /ˈdɔrəθi/ (1893–1967) a U.S. writer and JOURNALIST, famous for her many clever and funny sayings

park·ing /ˈpɑrkɪŋ/ S3 *n.* [U] **1** the act of parking a car or other vehicle: *The sign said "No Parking."* | *a parking fine* | *We found* ***a parking space*** *near the exit.* **2** spaces in which you can leave a car or other vehicle: *Parking is available on Lamay Street.*

ˈparking ˌbrake *n.* [C] a piece of equipment in a car that prevents it from moving when it is parked

ˈparking gaˌrage *n.* [C] an enclosed building in a public place for cars to be parked in

ˈparking ˌlight *n.* [C] one of two small lights next to the main front lights on a car

ˈparking lot *n.* [C] an open area for cars to park in

ˈparking ˌmeter *n.* [C] a machine which you put money into when you park your car next to it

ˈparking ˌticket *n.* [C] an official notice fastened to a vehicle, saying that you have to pay money because you have parked your car in the wrong place or for too long

Par·kin·son's dis·ease /ˈpɑrkənsənz dɪˌziz/ also **Parkinson's** *n.* [U] MEDICINE a serious illness in which your muscles become very weak and your arms and legs shake

park·land /ˈpɑrk-lænd/ *n.* [U] land with grass and trees, which is used as a park

ˈpark ˌranger *n.* [C] a RANGER

Rosa Parks

Parks /pɑrks/, **Ro·sa** /ˈroʊzə/ (1913–2005) an African-American woman who became famous in 1955 because she refused to give her seat on a bus to a white man, which was an important event in the CIVIL RIGHTS movement

park·way /ˈpɑrkweɪ/ *n. plural* **parkways** [C,U] a wide road with an area of grass and trees in the middle or along the sides

par·lance /ˈpɑrləns/ *n.* **in common/medical/advertising etc. parlance** expressed in words that most people, or a particular group of people, would use: *"Sexual assault" is referred to in common parlance as "rape".*

par·lay /ˈpɑrleɪ, -li/ *v.* **parlays, parlayed, parlaying** [T] to use advantages that you already have, such as your skills, experience, or money, and increase their value by using all your opportunities well: **parlay sth into sth** *He parlayed a $1,000 investment into the nation's largest sandwich chain.*

par·ley /ˈpɑrli/ *n.* [C] OLD-FASHIONED a discussion in which enemies try to achieve peace —**parley** *v.* [I]

par·lia·ment /ˈpɑrləmənt/ *n.* [C] POLITICS **1** the group of people in some countries who are elected to make the country's laws and discuss important national affairs: *the Russian parliament* **2 Parliament** the main law-making institution in some countries, such as the United Kingdom **3** the period during which this institution meets: *The prime minister has* ***dissolved parliament*** *and called new elections.* [**Origin:** 1200–1300 Old French *parlement*, from *parler* **to speak**]

par·lia·men·tar·i·an /ˌpɑrləmənˈtɛriən/ *n.* [C] POLITICS an experienced member of a parliament

par·lia·men·ta·ry /ˌpɑrləˈmɛntri◂ , -ˈmɛntəri◂ / *adj.* [only before noun] POLITICS relating to or governed by a parliament: *parliamentary elections* | *a parliamentary debate*

ˌparliamentary deˈmocracy *n.* [C,U] POLITICS a system of government in which the citizens vote to elect representatives to a Parliament, or a country that has this system

ˌparliamentary ˈgovernment *n.* [C,U] POLITICS a system of government in which decisions and laws are approved by a PRIME MINISTER and his or her CABINET, usually after they are discussed in Parliament → see also REPUBLIC

par·lor /ˈpɑrlɚ/ *n.* [C] **1 an ice cream/a massage/a funeral etc. parlor** a store or type of business that provides a particular service **2** OLD-FASHIONED a room in a house which has comfortable chairs and is used for meeting guests

ˈparlor game *n.* [C] OLD-FASHIONED a game that can be played indoors, such as a guessing game or a word game

par·lous /ˈpɑrləs/ *adj.* FORMAL in a very bad or dangerous condition: *the parlous state of the country's economy*

Par·me·san /ˈpɑrməˌzɑn, -ˌʒɑn/ also **ˈParmesan ˌcheese** *n.* [U] a hard Italian cheese with a strong taste

pa·ro·chi·al /pəˈroʊkiəl/ *adj.* **1** only interested in the things that affect you and your local area, and not interested in more important matters: *Local newspapers tend to be very parochial.* **2** [only before noun] relating to a particular church —**parochialism** *n.* [U] —**parochially** *adv.*

pa'rochial ˌschool *n.* [C] a private school which is run by or connected with a church

par·o·dy[1] /ˈpærədi/ *n. plural* **parodies** **1** [C] ENG. LANG. ARTS a song, piece of writing, television show etc. that copies a particular well-known style in an amusing way, to make fun of it or show its faults: +**of** *a parody of a disaster movie* **2** [U] ENG. LANG. ARTS the method of copying a well-known style of writing, singing, TV program etc. in an amusing way, to make fun of it or show its faults: *Her act contains a strong element of **self-parody*** (=when someone makes fun of their own style). **3** [C] a very bad or unacceptable copy of something: *The trial was an outrageous **parody of justice*** (=a very unfair trial).

parody[2] *v.* **parodies, parodied, parodying** [T] to copy someone's style or attitude, especially in an amusing way, to make fun of it or show its faults: *The book parodies traditional detective novels.* —**parodist** *n.* [C]

pa·role[1] /pəˈroʊl/ *n.* [U] permission for someone to leave prison before the end of their sentence, on the condition that they behave well and report regularly to the police or other authority. People who break the conditions of their parole are sent back to prison to serve the rest of their sentence: *Hicks was released **on parole** May 17.* | *Police arrested Ramos for **violating parole*** (=not behaving as he was supposed to while on parole). | *She is appearing before the **parole board*** (=the official group that can give a prisoner parole) *next week.* [**Origin:** 1400–1500 French **speech, word, word of honor**, from Late Latin *parabola*]

parole[2] *v.* [T usually passive] to allow someone to leave prison on the condition that they promise to behave well and report regularly to the police or other authority

pa·rol·ee /pəˌroʊˈli/ *n.* [C] someone who is on parole

par·ox·ys·m /ˈpærəkˌsɪzəm, pəˈrɑk-/ *n.* [C] **1 a paroxysm of rage/laughter/excitement etc.** a sudden expression of strong feeling that you cannot control **2** a sudden short attack of pain, coughing, shaking etc.: +**of** *paroxysms of coughing*

par·quet /pɑrˈkeɪ, ˈpɑrkeɪ/ *n.* [U] small flat blocks of wood fitted together in a pattern, which cover the floor of a room: *a parquet floor*

par·ri·cide /ˈpærəˌsaɪd/ *n.* [U] FORMAL the crime of killing your father, mother, or any other close relative → see also MATRICIDE, PATRICIDE

par·rot[1] /ˈpærət/ *n.* [C] BIOLOGY a tropical bird with a curved beak and brightly colored feathers, which can be taught to copy human speech

parrot[2] *v.* [T] to repeat someone else's words or ideas without really understanding what you are saying

par·ry /ˈpæri/ *v.* **parries, parried, parrying** [T] **1** to avoid directly answering a difficult question: *Robins repeatedly parried questions from reporters on his personal finances.* **2** to defend yourself against someone who is attacking you by pushing their weapon or hand to one side —**parry** *n.* [C]

parse /pɑrs/ *v.* [T] ENG. LANG. ARTS to examine each part of a word, phrase, or sentence in order to explain its use, form, or meaning

Par·see, Parsi /ˈpɑrsi, pɑrˈsi/ *n.* [C] a member of an ancient Persian religious group in India SYN Zoroastrian —**Parsee** *adj.*

par·si·mo·ni·ous /ˌpɑrsəˈmoʊniəs◂/ *adj.* FORMAL extremely unwilling to spend money —**parsimoniously** *adv.* —**parsimony** /ˈpɑrsəˌmoʊni/ *n.* [U]

pars·ley /ˈpɑrsli/ *n.* [U] a small plant with curly leaves that have a strong taste, used in cooking or as decoration on food

pars·nip /ˈpɑrsnɪp/ *n.* [C,U] a plant with a thick white or yellowish root that is eaten as a vegetable

par·son /ˈpɑrsən/ *n.* [C] OLD-FASHIONED a Christian priest or minister responsible for a small area

par·son·age /ˈpɑrsənɪdʒ/ *n.* [C] the house where a priest or minister lives

part[1] /pɑrt/ S1 W1 *n.*

1 PIECE OF STH [C,U] one of the pieces or features of something, for example of an object, place, event, or period of time: *Fill in the form, and keep the top part.* | +**of** *Which part of town do you live in?* | *This is the widest part of the river.* | *I spent a month in Austin **as part of** my training.* | **be/form (a) part of sth** *These cells form a part of the body's immune system.* | *Falling over is part of learning how to ski.* | **the later/early part of sth** *She spent the early part of her life in Barcelona.* | **an important/vital/essential/crucial part** *an important part of the nation's economy* | **the best/worst part (of sth)** *The best part of the movie was when she slapped him.* | **the hard/easy/nice etc. part** *The hardest part of my job is making sure that everyone is happy.*

THESAURUS

piece one of several different parts that you join together to make something: *One of the pieces of the jigsaw puzzle was missing.*
section one of several parts that something is divided into: *the sports section of the newspaper*
chapter one of the parts that a book is divided into: *Read Chapter 3 for homework.*
scene one of the parts that a play or movie is divided into: *a love scene*
department one part of a large organization, which is responsible for a particular kind of work: *the marketing department*
→ STAGE[1]

2 NOT ALL [C,U] some but not all of a particular thing or group of things: +**of** *I stayed for only part of the day.* | *Parts of New England got two to three inches of snow Tuesday night.* | **a good/large part of sth** *A large part of the money will go to charity.* | **the greater/major part of sth** *I spend the greater part of my time in front of a computer screen.* | *The film is very violent **in parts**.* | **(only) part of the problem/explanation/reason etc.** *Bad housing conditions are only part of the problem.*

3 MACHINE/EQUIPMENT [C] one of the separate pieces that something such as a machine or piece of equipment is made of: *Where does this part go?* | *Check inside the box to see if all the parts are there.* → see also SPARE PART

4 take part (in sth) to be involved in an activity, sport, event etc. together with other people: *About 400 students took part in the protest.* | *John has **taken an active part in** organizing the festival.*

5 play/have a part (in sth) if someone or something plays a part in something, they are involved in it and have a lot of influence on the way it happens or develops: *They've certainly worked very hard, but luck has played a part too.* | **play a big/important part in sth** *The local church plays an important part in people's lives.* | *I **had no part in** the plan.*

6 (a) part of a group/team/family etc. a member of a group, team etc.: *I enjoy being part of a team.* | *It takes a long time for people to accept you as part of their community.*

7 the better/best part of sth almost all of something: *I spent the better part of the afternoon fixing the carburetor on my car.*

8 for the most part also **in large/good part** mostly or in most places: *Success was due in large part to the team's hard work.* | *For the most part, she's a fair person.*

9 in part to some degree, but not completely: *It's my fault, at least in part.*

10 sb's part in sth what a particular person did in an activity that was shared by several people, especially something bad: *Larkin went to jail for his part in the robbery.*

11 want no part of sth to not want to be involved in something, because you do not agree with or approve

of it: *Matthews said he wanted no part of anything illegal.*
12 HAIR [C usually singular] the line on your head formed by dividing your hair with a comb
13 QUANTITY [C] a particular quantity of a substance used when measuring different substances together into a mixture: *Mix one part milk with two parts flour and stir.*
14 ACTING [C] ENG. LANG. ARTS the words and actions of a particular character in a play, movie etc., performed by an actor SYN role: *Have you learned your part yet?* | *He* ***played the part of*** *Romeo in the movie.*
15 look/act/dress etc. the part to look, act etc. like a typical person of a particular type: *In his expensive suit, he certainly looks the part.*
16 BOOK/TV ETC. ENG. LANG. ARTS a piece of a book, story, television series, play etc.: *The book was adapted for TV in six parts.* | **the first/last/final etc. part (of sth)** *The final part of the story is in tomorrow's paper.* | **Part One/Two/Three etc.** *Part One of the series*
17 MUSIC [C] ENG. LANG. ARTS a tune that a particular type of instrument or voice within a group plays or sings: *I'll sing the bass part if you want.*
18 in/around these parts in the particular area, part of a country etc. that you are in: *I'm not from around these parts.*
19 on sb's part also **on the part of sb** used to say what someone does or feels: *There has never been any jealousy on my part.* | *It was probably just a mistake on her part.*
20 part of sb used when someone has many different feelings or thoughts about something, so it is difficult to decide what they feel or what they should do: *Part of him wanted to stay.*
21 for sb's part used to say what someone thinks about something, especially when you are comparing this with someone else's opinion: *For my part, I can't see what the problem is.*
22 be part and parcel of sth to be included in something else, as a necessary feature: *Occasional unemployment is part and parcel of being an actor.*
23 part of the furniture someone who you see often but do not really notice because they do not do anything new or interesting
[**Origin:** 1200–1300 Old French, Latin *pars*]

part² S3 *v.* **1** [I,T] to pull the two sides of something apart, or to move apart in this way, making a space in the middle: *The crowd parted to let them through.* | *He parted the curtains and looked out.* | *Ralph's lips parted into a smile.* **2** [I] FORMAL to separate from someone, or end a relationship with them: *Sharon and I parted on friendly terms.* | *With a brief hug, they parted.* **3** [T] FORMAL if something parts people, it separates them so that they cannot be with each other: *Fate had parted them forever.* | **be parted (from sb)** *He hates being parted from his children.* **4** [T] if you part your hair, you separate it into two parts with a comb so that it looks neat: *Jen's black hair was parted down the middle.* **5 part company a)** also **part ways** to separate from someone, or end a relationship with them: *She and her husband have since parted ways.* | **+with** *He parted company with the band in 2004.* **b)** to not agree with someone anymore or think the same as they do: *This is where different economists part company.*

part with sth *phr. v.* to spend, give away, or get rid of something although you do not want to: *We finally had to part with our old station wagon.*

part³ *adv.* **be part sth, part sth** to consist of two different things: *The medical exams are part written, part practical.*

par·take /pɑrˈteɪk/ *v. past tense* **partook** /-ˈtʊk/, *past participle* **partaken** /-ˈteɪkən/ [I] OLD-FASHIONED, FORMAL **1** to eat or drink something: **+of** *Would you like to partake of a little red wine?* **2** to take part in an activity or event SYN participate: **+in** *Residents are encouraged to partake in all activities.*

partake of sth *phr. v.* FORMAL to have a certain amount of a particular quality

par·the·no·gen·e·sis /ˌpɑrθənoʊˈdʒɛnəsɪs/ *n.* [U] BIOLOGY the production of a new plant or animal from a female without the sexual involvement of the male

par·tial /ˈpɑrʃəl/ *adj.* **1** not complete: *a partial solution to the problem* | *partial disability* **2 be partial to sth** FORMAL to like something very much: *Tom's quite partial to ice cream.* **3** unfairly supporting one person or one side against another OPP impartial: *She wished she had a less partial judge.*

par·ti·al·i·ty /ˌpɑrʃiˈæləṭi/ *n.* [U] **1** unfair support of one person or one side against another SYN bias: *The chairman must avoid any appearance of partiality.* **2 a partiality for sth** FORMAL a special liking for something: *Chris has a partiality for fast cars.*

par·tial·ly /ˈpɑrʃəli/ *adv.* not completely SYN partly: *Food shortages were partially responsible for riots.* | *A stroke left her partially paralyzed.*

ˌpartial ˈpressure *n.* [C] PHYSICS the pressure of one particular gas in a mixture of gases considered as a part of the total pressure of the mixture

par·tic·i·pant /pɑrˈtɪsəpənt, pɚ-/ Ac S3 W3 *n.* [C] someone who is taking part in an activity or event: **+in** *Participants in the 10K run will receive a T-shirt.*

par·tic·i·pate /pɑrˈtɪsəˌpeɪt, pɚ-/ Ac S2 W2 *v.* [I] FORMAL to take part in an activity or event: *About 1,000 protesters are expected to participate.* | **+in** *All students are expected to participate in class discussions.*

par·ti·ci·pa·tion /pɑrˌtɪsəˈpeɪʃən, pɚ-/ Ac W3 *n.* [U] the act of taking part in an activity or event: *Voter participation has declined by 5%.* | **+in** *the country's participation in the U.N. peace-keeping mission* | *The show involves a lot of* ***audience participation.***

par·tic·i·pa·to·ry /pɑrˈtɪsəpəˌtɔri, pɚ-/ Ac *adj.* [usually before noun] FORMAL a participatory way of organizing something, making decisions etc. is one that involves everyone who is affected by such decisions: *a participatory management style*

par·ti·cip·i·al /ˌpɑrṭəˈsɪpiəl/ *adj.* ENG. LANG. ARTS using a participle, or having the form of a participle: *a participial phrase*

par·ti·ci·ple /ˈpɑrṭəˌsɪpəl/ *n.* [C] ENG. LANG. ARTS the form of a verb, usually ending in "-ing" or "-ed," which is used to make compound forms of the verb (such as "She is singing") or used as an adjective (such as "annoying" or "annoyed") → see also PAST PARTICIPLE, PRESENT PARTICIPLE

par·ti·cle /ˈpɑrṭɪkəl/ *n.* [C] **1** a very small piece of something: **+of** *tiny particles of dust in the air* **2** PHYSICS one of the very small pieces of matter that an atom consists of: *subatomic particles such as protons* **3 not a particle of sth** not even a small amount of a particular quality: *There wasn't a particle of truth in what he said.* **4** ENG. LANG. ARTS an ADVERB or PREPOSITION that combines with a verb to form a PHRASAL VERB

ˈparticle acˌcelerator *n.* [C] PHYSICS a machine used in scientific studies which makes particles (=the pieces that atoms are made of) move at very high speeds

ˈparticle ˌphysics *n.* [U] PHYSICS the scientific study of the way particles (=the pieces that atoms are made of) develop and behave

par·tic·u·lar¹ /pɚˈtɪkyəlɚ/ S2 W1 *adj.* **1** [only before noun] a particular thing or person is the one that you are talking about, and not any other SYN specific: *This particular part of Idaho is especially beautiful.* | *Most students choose one particular area for research.* **2** [only before noun] special or important enough to mention separately: *You should pay particular attention to spelling.* | *Was there any particular reason why he quit?* | **of particular interest/concern/importance etc.** *The building is of particular interest to historians.* **3** [not before noun] very careful about choosing exactly what you like and not easily satisfied: **+about** *He's very particular about cleanliness.* **4 any particular time/place etc.?** SPOKEN used when you are asking someone which time, place etc. is good for them, when you are arranging to meet them, go somewhere with them etc.: *"Let's meet for lunch." "Any particular time?"* **5** belonging or relating to just one person or group and different from other people's SYN peculiar: **+to** *problems that are particular to one country* **6 I'm not (too) particular**

SPOKEN used to say that you do not care what is decided [**Origin:** 1300–1400 Old French, Late Latin *particularis*, from Latin *particula*]

particular² S3 *n.* **1 in particular** especially: *There was one incident in particular that made us suspicious.* | **anything/anyone/anywhere in particular** *Is there anyone in particular you have in mind for the job?* | **nothing/no one/nowhere in particular** *There's nothing in particular I want for my birthday.* **2 particulars** [plural] the facts and details about something: +**of** *I can't discuss the particulars of the case.* **3 in every particular/in all particulars** FORMAL in every detail: *Hann's analysis is right in almost all particulars.* **4 sb's particulars** [plural] details of someone's name, address, age, profession etc.

P

par·tic·u·lar·i·ty /pɚˌtɪkyəˈlærət̬i/ *n. plural* **particularities** FORMAL **1** [U] the quality of being exact and paying attention to details **2** [C] a detail

par·tic·u·lar·ize /pɚˈtɪkyələˌraɪz/ *v.* [I,T] FORMAL to give the details of something SYN **itemize**

par·tic·u·lar·ly /pɚˈtɪkyələ̸li, -ˈtɪkyəli/ S2 W1 *adv.* **1** more than usual or more than others SYN **especially**: *a particularly difficult question* | *Exercise reduces the risk of cancer, particularly colon cancer.* **2 not particularly a)** not very: *Jon isn't particularly worried about money.* **b)** SPOKEN not very much: *"Do you want to come to the party?" "Not particularly."*

par·tic·u·late¹ /pɚˈtɪkyəlɪt, pɑr-, -ˌleɪt/ *n.* [C usually plural, U] very small separate pieces of a substance, especially a substance in the air that comes from car engines and can damage your health: *toxic particulates*

particulate² *adj.* [only before noun] consisting of very small separate pieces: *particulate matter*

part·ing¹ /ˈpɑrt̬ɪŋ/ *n.* **1** [C,U] an occasion when two people leave each other or end a relationship: *an emotional parting at the airport* **2 parting of the ways** a situation in which two people or organizations decide to separate: *They called Smith's leaving an "amicable parting of the ways."* **3** [U] an act of separating two things or of making two things separate: *the parting of clouds*

parting² *adj.* **1 a parting kiss/gift/glance etc.** a kiss, gift etc. that you give someone as you leave **2 a parting shot** a cruel or severe remark that you make just as you are leaving, especially at the end of an argument: *At the door, she could not resist a parting shot.*

par·ti·san¹ /ˈpɑrt̬əzən, -sən/ *adj.* POLITICS strongly supporting one particular party, plan, leader etc., and not liking all others: *Gore was speaking before a partisan crowd of about 500 Democrats.* → see also BIPARTISAN, NONPARTISAN

partisan² *n.* [C] POLITICS someone who supports a particular political party, plan, or leader: +**of** *a well-known partisan of the democratic movement in China*

par·ti·san·ship /ˈpɑrt̬əzənˌʃɪp/ *n.* [U] when someone shows their strong support for a particular political party, plan, or leader

par·ti·tion¹ /pɑrˈtɪʃən, pɚ-/ *n.* **1** [C] a thin wall that separates one part of a room from another **2** [U] POLITICS the act of dividing a country into two or more independent countries: +**of** *the partition of Cyprus* **3** TECHNICAL a part into which computer memory can be divided

partition² *v.* [T + adv./prep.] **1** to divide a country, building, or room into two or more parts: *Korea was partitioned at the 38th parallel after World War II.* **2** TECHNICAL to divide computer memory into separate parts

partition sth ↔ **off** *phr. v.* to divide part of a room from the rest by using a partition: *The rest of the room had been partitioned off into smaller offices.*

par·ti·tive /ˈpɑrt̬ət̬ɪv/ *n.* ENG. LANG. ARTS a word that shows that part of something is being described, not the whole of it, for example the word "some" in the phrase "some of the money" —**partitive** *adj.*

part·ly /ˈpɑrtli/ W3 *adv.* to some degree, but not completely: *He quit his job partly because of health problems.* | *Driver error was partly to blame for the accident.* | *Skies were* ***partly cloudy*** *across much of Texas today.*

part·ner¹ /ˈpɑrt˺nɚ/ Ac S2 W1 *n.* [C]
1 IN BUSINESS one of the owners of a business, who share the profits and losses: *a business partner* | **a senior/junior partner** *He's the senior partner at a law firm.*
2 MARRIAGE ETC. one of two people who are married or who live together and have a sexual relationship. This word is used especially when both people are of the same sex: *Are we allowed to bring our partners to the staff party?* → see also DOMESTIC PARTNER ▸see THESAURUS box at **married**
3 SEX a person that someone has sex with: *The chance of infection increases with each partner.*
4 DANCING/GAMES ETC. someone you do a particular activity with, for example dancing or playing a game against two other people: *Jeff's my tennis partner.*
5 COUNTRY/ORGANIZATION a country or organization that has an agreement with another country or organization: *Japan is a major trading partner of the U.S.*
6 sb's partner in crime OFTEN HUMOROUS one of two people who have planned and done something together, either something illegal or something that annoys other people
[**Origin:** 1300–1400 Anglo-French *parcener* **heir sharing half**, from Old French *parçon* **share**; influenced by *part*]

partner² Ac *v.* [T usually passive] to be someone's partner in a dance, game, or other activity: *She was brilliantly partnered by pianist Kramer.*

partner up *phr. v.* to join with someone as their partner: +**with** *I'd like you all to partner up with someone for the square dance.*

partner with sb/sth *phr. v.* to join with another organization in order to do something: *The company plans to partner with other microchip manufacturers.*

part·ner·ship /ˈpɑrt˺nɚˌʃɪp/ Ac W3 *n.* **1** [U] the state of being a partner and working with someone else, for example in a business or other shared activity: *Police and community leaders need to work together in a spirit of partnership.* | **be/work in partnership (with sb)** *At that time, Tannen was in partnership with Jack Baker in the automobile business.* | *Eleven years ago, the sisters* ***went into partnership with each other***. **2** [C] a relationship between two people, organizations, or countries that work together regularly: *The YMCA and other youth agencies have set up a partnership to reach the city's poor children.* | *the great movie partnership of De Niro and Scorsese* **3** [C] ECONOMICS a business owned by two or more partners who share the duties, responsibilities, and decisions involved in running the business, and also share the profits and losses: *The law firm is run as a partnership.*

ˌpart of ˈspeech *n.* [C] ENG. LANG. ARTS one of the types into which words are divided in grammar according to their use, such as noun, verb, or adjective

par·took /pɑrˈtʊk/ *v.* the past tense of PARTAKE

par·tridge /ˈpɑrtrɪdʒ/ *n.* [C] BIOLOGY a fat brown bird with a short tail, which some people shoot as a sport or for food

ˌpart-ˈtime *adj.* **1** [only before noun] a part-time worker works regularly in a job, but only for part of the usual working time: *She's a part-time bartender.* **2** a part-time job involves only part of the working time of a usual job: *The job is only part-time.* | *They said they would hire me* ***on a part-time basis***. → see also FULL-TIME —**part-time** *adv.*: *Brenda teaches math part-time.* —**part-timer** *n.* [C] INFORMAL: *A part-timer helps us out in the mornings.*

par·tu·ri·tion /ˌpɑrtʃəˈrɪʃən/ *n.* [U] TECHNICAL the act or process of giving birth to a baby

part·way, part way /ˌpɑrt˺ˈweɪ◂ / *adv.* **1** after part of a distance has been traveled, or after part of a period of time has passed: +**in/through/down etc.** *A fire alarm went off partway through the meeting.* | *Jose got stuck after climbing partway up the cliff.* **2** in part, not completely: *Cyril opened his eyes partway.*

par·ty[1] /ˈpɑrṭi/ S1 W1 *n. plural* **parties** [C]
1 FOR FUN an occasion when people meet together, to enjoy themselves by eating, drinking, dancing etc.: *Were you invited to the party?* | *I'm* ***going to a party*** *tonight.* | *We met* ***at a party***. | **give/throw/have a party** *We're having a party for Maria to celebrate her graduation.* | **a birthday/surprise/farewell/Chirstmas etc. party** *Olivia's fourth birthday party* | **a party dress/hat** (=worn at a party) | *Do you remember that* ***party game*** (=played at a party) *called Telephone?* → see also COCKTAIL PARTY, DINNER PARTY

THESAURUS
get-together a small informal party
bash INFORMAL a party
dinner party a party where people are invited to someone's house for an evening meal
birthday party a party to celebrate someone's birthday, especially a child's
costume party a party at which people wear special clothes, for example dressing like a cowboy or an animal
house-warming party a party that you have when you move into a new house
cocktail party a party that people go to in order to talk and drink together for a few hours
bachelor party a social event that is just for men, which happens before a wedding
baby/wedding/bridal shower an event at which people give presents to a woman who is going to have a baby or get married
reception a large formal party, for example after a wedding
celebration a party that is organized in order to celebrate something

2 POLITICS an organization of people with the same political beliefs and aims, which you can vote for in elections: *political parties* | *the Republican Party* | *Do you* ***belong to a*** *political* ***party?*** | **a party leader/member** *Party leaders met to discuss their housing policy.* | *Morris continues to have deep support among the* ***party faithful*** (=a party's most loyal members). → see also PARTY LINE
3 GROUP OF PEOPLE a group of people that has come together in order to go somewhere or do something in an organized way: *a search party* | +**of** *a party of tourists* | *Foster, party of six, your table is ready.* ►see THESAURUS box at **group**[1]
4 CONTRACT/ARGUMENT LAW one of the people or groups involved in an argument, agreement etc., especially a legal one: *Both parties will meet to discuss the contract.* | *Mrs. Blake is really the* ***injured party*** *here* (=the person who has been unfairly treated). → see also THIRD PARTY
5 the guilty party FORMAL the person who has done something illegal or wrong
6 be (a) party to sth FORMAL to be involved in or have your name connected with an activity, especially something bad or illegal: *I refuse to be a party to anything so dishonest.*
7 a party girl/boy INFORMAL a young attractive woman or man who is not very serious about life and likes to go to parties
8 party foul! SPOKEN, HUMOROUS said when someone does something embarrassing at a party or does something that interrupts the good feelings at a party
[**Origin:** 1200–1300 Old French *partie* **part, party**, from *partir* **to divide**]

party[2] *v.* **parties, partied, partying** [I] **1** INFORMAL also **party down** to enjoy yourself, especially by drinking alcohol, eating, dancing etc.: *I just got paid and I'm ready to party.* **2** SLANG to use illegal drugs

ˈparty ˌanimal *n.* [C] INFORMAL someone who enjoys parties very much

ˌparty ˈcaucus *n.* also **ˌparty ˈconference** [C] POLITICS a meeting of either the REPUBLICAN PARTY or the DEMOCRATIC PARTY in the HOUSE OF REPRESENTATIVES or the SENATE, that only members of the party organizing the meeting can attend

ˈparty ˌfavor *n.* [C usually plural] **1** a small gift such as a paper hat or toy given to children at a party **2** SLANG illegal drugs

ˈparty line *n.* **1 the party line** POLITICS the official opinion of a political party, which its members are expected to agree with and support: *Few party members were willing to go against the party line.* **2** [C] a telephone line that is shared by more than one person

ˌparty ˈpolitics *n.* [U] POLITICS political activity that is concerned more with getting advantage for a particular party than with doing things to improve the situation in a country

party poop·er /ˈpɑrṭi ˌpupɚ/ *n.* [C] INFORMAL someone who spoils other people's fun and does not want people to enjoy themselves

ˈparty school *n.* [C] INFORMAL a college or university where the students are not serious about studying and have lots of parties

ˌparty ˈwall *n.* [C] a dividing wall between two buildings, apartments etc. which belongs to both owners

ˈpar ˌvalue *n.* [C,U] ECONOMICS the value that a BOND or a STOCK will be worth when it becomes ready to be paid, written on the bond or stock when it is sold for the first time. Bonds and stock are usually sold for less than the par value, which is then used to calculate the amount of profit to the buyer.

par·ve·nu /ˈpɑrvəˌnu/ *n.* [C] OLD-FASHIONED, FORMAL an insulting word for someone from a low social class who suddenly becomes rich or powerful —**parvenu** *adj.*

PASCAL /pæˈskæl/ *n.* TECHNICAL [U] a computer language that works well on small computer systems and is used especially in teaching computer science

pas·cal /pæˈskæl/ WRITTEN ABBREVIATION **Pa** *n.* [C] PHYSICS a unit of pressure equal to a force of one NEWTON in an area of one meter squared

Pas·cal /pæˈskæl/, **Blaise** /bleɪz/ (1623–1662) a French PHILOSOPHER, MATHEMATICIAN, and PHYSICIST, known for writing about religion, and for his scientific discoveries

pas·chal /ˈpæskəl/ *adj.* **1** relating to the Jewish holiday of Passover **2** relating to the Christian holiday of Easter

pas de deux /ˌpɑ də ˈdu/ *n.* [C] a dance in BALLET performed by a man and a woman

pas·ha /ˈpɑʃə/ *n.* [C] HISTORY the governor of an area or another official of high rank in the Ottoman Empire

pass[1] /pæs/ S1 W1 *v.*
1 GO PAST [I,T] **a)** to come up to a particular point or object and go past it SYN **go by**: *They kept quiet until the soldiers had passed.* | *I pass her house every day on my way to work.* **b)** to move toward another vehicle from behind and then continue going beyond it SYN **go by**: *A police car passed us doing 90 miles an hour.* ►see THESAURUS box at **approve**
2 MOVE/GO [I always + adv./prep.] to go or travel along or through a place: +**through/into/from etc.** *We heard the sound of helicopters passing overhead.* | *They passed through the castle gates.* | *I'm* ***just passing through*** (=traveling through a place) *on my way to Tulsa.*
3 ROAD/RIVER ETC. [I always + adv./prep., T] a road, river, or railroad line that passes through a place goes through or near the place: *The railroad passes north of town.*
4 PUT [T always + adv./prep.] to move or put something across, through, around etc. something else: **pass sth around/across/through etc.** *He passed the rope through the hole.*
5 TIME a) [I] if time passes, it goes by: *The days passed slowly.* | *Twenty-five years have passed since the civil war.* | *She became more frustrated* ***with every passing day*** (=as each day passed). | ***Hardly a day passed without*** *Carver's face being on the front page of the newspaper* (=it was there almost every day). **b)** [T] if you pass a period of time in a particular way, you spend it in that way SYN **spend**: *Lewis and Clark passed the winter with the Indians of the Mandan*

P

tribe. | *I read to* ***pass the time*** (=keep from being bored).

6 GIVE [T] to take something in your hand and give it to someone else, especially because they cannot reach it: *Pass the butter, please.* | **pass sb sth** *Could you pass me that pen over there?* | **pass sth to sb** *Just a minute. I'll pass the phone to Bob.* ►see THESAURUS box at **give**[1]

7 GIVE INFORMATION [T always + adv./prep.] to give someone information, especially so that they can deal with something: **pass sth (on/over/back) to sb** *Details of the attack had been passed to enemy agents.* | *I'll pass the information on to the sales department.*

8 TEST a) [I,T] to succeed on a test OPP **fail**: *Do you think you'll pass?* | *Dan's worried he won't pass calculus.* | *Kerry* ***passed*** *her finals* ***with flying colors*** (=got very high grades). **b)** [T] to officially decide that someone has passed a test: *The driving examiner passed me even though I made a few mistakes.*

9 SPORTS [I,T] to kick, throw, or hit a ball etc. to a member of your own team: **pass (sth) to sb** *Miller passed to Rison for a 24-yard touchdown.* | *Hey, pass me the ball!* ►see THESAURUS box at **throw**[1]

10 LAW/PROPOSAL POLITICS **a)** [T] to officially accept a law or proposal, especially by voting: **pass a law/motion/resolution etc.** *The city council passed a resolution banning smoking in restaurants.* | *Several Southern states* ***passed*** *similar* ***legislation***. **b)** [I,T] if a law or proposal passes an official group, it is officially accepted by that group: *The bill failed to pass the House of Representatives.*

11 let sth pass to deliberately not react when someone says or does something that you do not like: *When she started criticizing my parents, I couldn't let it pass.*

12 NUMBER to become more than a particular number or amount, as a total gradually increases: *Around 1800, the world population* ***passed the*** *one billion* ***mark***.

13 SAY/COMMUNICATE [I always + adv./prep.] if words, looks, or signs pass between two or more people, they exchange them with one another: **+between** *Not many words passed between us during the trip home.*

14 pass the time of day (with sb) to talk to someone for a short time in order to be friendly

15 END [I] to gradually come to an end: *The pain should pass in a day or two.* | *The storm soon passed.*

16 NOT ACCEPT [I] SPOKEN to not accept an invitation or offer: *"Do you want to go fishing Saturday?" "Sorry, I'll have to pass this time."*

17 GIVE NO ANSWER [I] to say that you do not know the answer to a question, especially in a competition: *"What's the capital of Albania?" "Pass."* | **+on** *I had to pass on the last question.*

18 pass judgment (on sb) to give your opinion about someone's behavior, especially in order to criticize them

19 pass (a) sentence (on sb) to officially decide how a criminal will be punished, and to announce what the punishment will be

20 CHANGE OF OWNERSHIP [I,T] FORMAL to go from one person's control or possession to someone else's: **+from/to** *The title passes from father to son.* | **pass sth to sb** *Last week's election passed control of Congress to the Republicans.*

21 pass the hat (around) to collect money from a group of people, especially after a performance or for a particular purpose: *Employees passed the hat and raised $500 to help with the boy's medical costs.*

22 pass unnoticed to happen without anyone noticing or saying anything

23 pass the torch (to sb) if someone passes the torch to someone else, they give their position or work to them

24 CHANGE [I] FORMAL if a substance passes from one state or condition into another, it changes into another state or condition: **+from/to** *When water freezes, it passes from a liquid to a solid state.*

25 pass muster to be accepted as good enough for a particular job: *Only if a paper passes muster is it accepted for publication.*

26 pass the buck to try to blame someone else or make them responsible for something that you should deal with: *a bunch of politicians all trying to pass the buck*

27 FALSE MONEY [T] to use false money to pay for something: *The two men were arrested for passing a counterfeit 100-dollar bill at a gas station.*

28 never/not pass sb's lips a) used to say that you will not talk about something that is secret: *Don't worry, not a word of this will pass my lips!* **b)** used to say that you have not eaten or drunk a particular thing, especially alcoholic drinks or something that is not healthy: *Junk food has never passed his lips.*

29 DIE INFORMAL a word meaning "to die," used when you want to avoid saying this directly

30 BODY WASTE TECHNICAL to send out something as waste material or in waste material from your BLADDER or BOWELS: **pass urine/blood etc.** *See your doctor immediately if you pass any blood.* | **pass gas** (=a polite way of saying to allow air to come out from your bowels) | **pass water** (=send out URINE)

31 DIFFERENT RACE ETC. [I] DISAPPROVING if someone who is not white or who is HOMOSEXUAL passes, they look and behave in a way that makes other people think they are white or HETEROSEXUAL

32 come to pass LITERARY or BIBLICAL to happen

[**Origin:** 1200–1300 Old French *passer*, from Vulgar Latin *passare*, from Latin *passus* **step**]

pass sth ↔ **around** *phr. v.* to give something to one person in a group, who then gives it to the person next to them, and so on: *The soldiers passed a bottle around.* | *She passed around a few pictures of her grandchildren.*

pass as sb/sth *phr. v.* → see **pass for sb/sth**

pass away *phr. v.* **1** an expression meaning "to die," used because you want to avoid upsetting someone by saying this directly: *It's been over a year since Dad passed away.* **2** if time or a feeling passes away, it gradually comes to an end: *The summer passed away and autumn approached.*

pass by *phr. v.* **1** to move past or go past a person, place, vehicle etc. on your way to another place: *I was just passing by so I thought I'd stop for a visit.* | **pass by sb/sth** *People glanced at Ron as they passed by our table.* → see also PASSERBY **2 pass sb by** if something passes you by, it is there or happens but you are not involved in it: *She felt that life was passing her by.*

pass sth ↔ **down** *phr. v.* to give something or teach something to people who are younger than you or live after you: **pass sth down (from sb) to sb** *The tradition has been passed down from generation to generation.*

pass for sb/sth *phr. v.* if someone or something passes for something else, they are so similar to that thing that people think that is what they are SYN **be accepted as**: *Shawn's only 17, but he's so big he could pass for 21.* | *It's amazing* ***what passes for*** *entertainment on TV* (=what bad quality things people will accept as entertainment).

pass sb/sth **off** *phr. v.* to try to make people think that something or someone is another thing or person: **pass sb/sth off as sth** *They tried to pass the crystals off as diamonds.* | *He* ***passed himself off*** *as a doctor.*

pass on *phr. v.* **1 pass sth ↔ on** to tell someone a piece of information that someone else has told you: **pass sth on to sb** *I'll pass your suggestion on to the committee.* **2 pass sth on** to give something to someone else, usually after another person has given it to you: *Take one copy and pass the rest on to the next person.* **3 pass sth ↔ on a)** to give someone a slight illness that you have: *I don't want to pass on my cold to the baby.* **b)** to give something, especially a disease, to your children through your GENES **4 pass sth on** to make someone else pay the cost of something: **pass sth on to sb** *Any increase in wage costs is bound to be passed on to the consumer.* **5** an expression meaning "to die," used when you want to avoid saying this directly: *David's father passed on last year.*

pass out *phr. v.* **1** to become unconscious SYN **faint**: *It was so hot in there I thought I was going to pass out.* **2 pass sth ↔ out** to give something to each one of a group of people SYN **hand out**: *Could you help me pass out the worksheets?*

pass sb/sth **over** *phr. v.* **pass sb ↔ over** if you pass over someone for a job, you give the job to someone else who is younger or lower in the organization than they are: *This is the second time he's been* ***passed over for a promotion.***

pass sth ↔ **up** *phr. v.* to not make use of an invitation, opportunity, offer etc.: *I couldn't pass up dessert.* | **pass up a chance/opportunity/offer etc.** *You shouldn't pass up the opportunity to visit Florence while in Italy.* | **too good/tempting/cheap etc. to pass up** *The salary was too good to pass up.*

WORD CHOICE **pass, passed, past**

- Remember that **passed** is the past tense and past participle of the verb **pass**: *I think we just passed Rick's house a second ago.*
- **Past** is used as a preposition or an adverb: *She walked right past us without even saying hello.* | *Just then, Mike drove past in his new Jeep.* **Past** can also be an adjective: *the past few weeks*, or a noun: *In the past, people didn't have as much free time.*

pass[2] S2 W2 *n.* [C]
1 DOCUMENT/TICKET an official paper or ticket which shows that you are allowed to enter or leave a building, travel on a bus or train etc.: *The guard checked our passes.* | *Students need a* ***hall pass*** *to go to the library during class time.* | **movie/zoo/museum etc. pass** (=a pass that allows you to enter a movie, zoo etc., without paying each time you go) *You can buy a zoo pass for $150 per family.* | *We won* ***free passes*** *to Disneyland!*
2 SPORTS a single act of kicking, throwing, or hitting a ball etc. to another member of your team: *Davis scored on a 40-yard pass from Elway.*
3 MOUNTAIN ROAD a road or path that goes between mountains to the other side: *a narrow mountain pass*
4 SEX an attempt to kiss or touch another person with the intention of starting a sexual relationship with them: **+at** *Her boss* ***made a pass*** *at her.*
5 MOVEMENT PAST a movement in which an aircraft, SATELLITE etc. flies once over or through a place: *They scored a direct hit of the target on their second pass.* | *the comet's pass through our solar system*
6 TEST/CLASS if you receive a pass on a test or in a class, you are successful: **receive/get a pass** *Students who received low passes were assigned to College Skills.*
7 STAGE one part of a process that involves dealing with the whole of something several times: **first/next/final etc. pass** *This will be our final editing pass before the brochure is printed.*

pass·a·ble /ˈpæsəbəl/ *adj.* **1** fairly good, but not excellent SYN **acceptable**: *Linda speaks passable Arabic.* **2** [not before noun] a road or river that is passable is not blocked, so you can travel along or across it OPP **impassable** —**passably** *adv.*

pas·sage /ˈpæsɪdʒ/ W3 *n.*
1 NARROW WAY [C] also **passageway** a long narrow area with walls on either side, which connects one room or place to another: *an underground passage*
2 OF A LAW [U] POLITICS the process of discussing and accepting a new law, for example in Congress: **passage of a bill/law/measure etc.** *There is a Senate vote in March, but passage of the bill is far from certain.*
3 WAY THROUGH [C usually singular] a way through or to something: *The refugees risked crossing the dangerous ocean passage to Florida.*
4 FROM A BOOK ETC. [C] ENG. LANG. ARTS a short part of a book, poem, speech, piece of music etc.: *He read a passage from the Bible.*
5 MOVEMENT [U] FORMAL the movement of people, vehicles, or animals along a road or river or across an area of land: *The steamboat made steady passage up the Ohio River.* | *Both sides agreed to allow the* ***free passage*** *of medical supplies into the area.* | *He was guaranteed* ***safe passage*** *out of the country.*
6 TIME [U] the passing of time: **+of** *Despite the passage of half a century, tension still exists between the two countries.*
7 INSIDE A BODY [C] BIOLOGY a tube in your body that air or liquid can pass through: *your nasal passages*
8 TRIP [C usually singular] OLD-FASHIONED a trip on a ship: **+to** *My parents couldn't afford the passage to America.* → see also **rite of passage** at RITE OF PASSAGE

pas·sage·way /ˈpæsɪdʒˌweɪ/ *n.* [C] a PASSAGE

Pas·sa·ma·quod·dy /ˌpæsəməˈkwɑdi/ a Native American tribe from the northeastern area of the U.S.

pass·book /ˈpæsbʊk/ *n.* [C] a book in which a record is kept of the money you put into and take out of a SAVINGS ACCOUNT

pas·sé /pæˈseɪ/ *adj.* not modern or fashionable any more SYN **outmoded**: *a style which is already passé*

pas·sel /ˈpæsəl/ *n.* [C usually singular] OLD-FASHIONED a group of people or things SYN **bunch**: **+of** *a whole passel of kids*

pas·sen·ger /ˈpæsəndʒɚ/ W2 *n.* [C] someone who is traveling in a vehicle, airplane, boat etc., but is not driving it or working on it: *About 70 of the train's 500 passengers were injured in the crash.* | **passenger train/car/ship** (=for people, not for goods)

ˈpassenger ˌseat *n.* [C] the seat in the front of a vehicle next to the driver → see picture on page A36

pass·er·by /ˌpæsɚˈbaɪ/ *n. plural* **passersby** [C] someone who is walking past a place: *The robbery was witnessed by several passersby.*

pass·ing[1] /ˈpæsɪŋ/ *adj.* [only before noun] **1** going past: *noise from passing traffic* **2** continuing only a short time and not very serious SYN **brief**: *a passing glance* | *passing fashions* | *He didn't even give the matter a* ***passing thought.*** ▸see THESAURUS box at **short**[1] **3 with each passing day/week etc.** continuously as time passes: *The costs of medical insurance seem to increase with each passing year.* **4** only a small amount SYN **slight**: *She* ***bore a passing resemblance*** (=she looked slightly like) *to her cousin.* | *a passing knowledge of Spanish* **5** a passing remark is one you make while you are talking or writing about something else: *He made a passing reference to cutting the nation's debt.*

passing[2] *n.* [U] **1 in passing** if you say something in passing, you mention it while you are mainly talking about something else: **mention/say/note sth in passing** *The issue was mentioned, but only in passing.* **2** the fact of something ending or gradually stopping: *the passing of the Cold War* **3** the act or skill of throwing or kicking the ball to another member of your team: *They lost the game partly because of ineffective passing.* **4 the passing of time/the years** the process of time going by: *The passing of the years has not weakened his artistic ability.* **5 sb's passing** an expression meaning someone's death, used when you want to avoid saying this directly: *There was no one to mourn his passing.*

pas·sion /ˈpæʃən/ W3 *n.* **1** [C,U] a very strong feeling of sexual love SYN **desire**: *He was trembling with passion.* | **+for** *her passion for a married man* **2** [C,U] a very strong belief or feeling about something: *a sermon full of passion and inspiration* | *He plays* ***with passion*** *and has a great attitude.* **3** [C] a very strong liking for something: *Acting is his passion.* | **+for** *The two boys* ***had a passion*** *for basketball.* **4 the Passion** FORMAL the suffering and death of Jesus Christ —**passionless** *adj.* → see also **a crime of passion** at CRIME (6)

pas·sion·ate /ˈpæʃənɪt/ *adj.* **1** having or involving very strong feelings of sexual love: *His kiss was passionate.* | *a passionate love affair* **2** having or expressing a very strong feeling, especially a strong belief in an idea or principle: *He is a passionate defender of the poor.* | *a passionate speech* **3** having a very strong interest in or liking for something SYN **intense**: *Her father indulged her* ***passionate interest*** *in horses.* | **+about** *Brian is passionate about football.* —**passionately** *adv.*: *He was passionately committed to the ideal of non-violence.*

pas·sion·fruit, passion fruit /ˈpæʃənˌfrut/ *n.* [C,U] BIOLOGY a small fruit that has dry brown skin and many seeds inside

P

'Passion play *n.* [C] a play telling the story of the suffering and death of Jesus Christ

pas·sive¹ /'pæsɪv/ Ac *adj.* **1** someone who is passive tends to accept things that happen to them or things that people say to them, without taking any action: *a passive role in their relationship* | *She is a quiet passive woman.* **2** not actively involved or taking part: *The student's role in a traditional classroom is largely passive.* | *passive watchers of television* **3** ENG. LANG. ARTS a passive verb or sentence has as its subject the person or thing to which an action is done, as in "Two men were injured in the fire.": *a paragraph written in **the passive voice*** (=written using passive verbs and sentences) → see also ACTIVE **4 passive vocabulary/knowledge** words or knowledge that you can recognize or understand, but cannot think of or use on your own: *Her passive vocabulary in French is fairly good.* —**passively** *adv.* —**passiveness** also **passivity** /pæ'sɪvəṭi/ *n.* [U]

passive² Ac *n.* **the passive** TECHNICAL the passive form of a verb, for example "was destroyed" in the sentence "The building was destroyed by a bomb." → see also ACTIVE

ˌpassive im'munity *n.* [U] BIOLOGY the state of being IMMUNE to a disease because you already have ANTIBODIES to that disease, either obtained naturally from your mother before you were born or artificially because of an INJECTION

ˌpassive re'sistance *n.* [U] a way of opposing someone or protesting against something without using violence

ˌpassive re'straint also **ˌpassive re'straint ˌsystem** *n.* [C] TECHNICAL a safety system such as an AIR BAG which protects someone in a car accident, without that person having to fasten anything

ˌpassive 'smoking *n.* [U] the act of breathing in smoke that is in the air from someone else's cigarette, PIPE etc., which can damage your health → see also SECONDHAND SMOKE

pass·key /'pæsˌki/ *n.* [C] a key that will open several different locks in a building

Pass·o·ver /'pæsˌoʊvɚ/ *n.* [U] an important Jewish religious holiday when people remember the escape of the Jews from Egypt [**Origin:** 1500–1600 translation of Hebrew *pesah* **to pass without affecting**; because, according to the Bible, God did not kill Jewish children when he killed children of other races]

pass·port /'pæspɔrt/ *n.* [C] **1** a small official document that a citizen gets from the government, which proves who that person is and which they need in order to leave the country and enter other countries: **American/Canadian/Japanese passport** *He was born in Kenya and has a British passport.* | **have/hold a passport** *Do you have a valid passport?* | *He entered the country **on a false passport**.* **2 passport to success/romance/happiness etc.** something that makes success, romance etc. possible and likely: *Dad believed education was a passport to a better life.*

pass·word /'pæswɚd/ *n.* [C] **1** COMPUTERS a secret group of letters or numbers that you must type into a computer before you can use a system or program **2** a secret word or phrase that someone has to say before they are allowed to enter a place such as a military camp

past¹ /pæst/ S2 W1 *adj.*

1 BEFORE NOW [only before noun] happening, done, or existing before the present time: *From past experience she knew that it was no use arguing with him.* | *The problems we face now are a result of past decisions.*

2 RECENT [only before noun] a little earlier than the present, or in the period up until now: *the terrible events of the past year* | **in the past 24 hours/few weeks/year etc.** *Weather conditions have worsened in the past 48 hours.* | **for the past 24 hours/few weeks/year etc.** *For the past 18 years, Robbins has been the editor of the magazine.*

3 FORMER [only before noun] having achieved something in the past, or having held a particular important position in the past: **past President/champion/heroes etc.** *Bruce Jenner, a past Olympic champion* | *Past and present members have been invited.*

4 FINISHED finished or having come to an end: *Winter is past and spring has come at last.* | *The divorce is all part of Jenny's **past life**.* | *The time for resolving these problems is already **long past**.*

5 GRAMMAR [only before noun] ENG. LANG. ARTS being the form of a verb that is used to show a past action or state: *the past tense*

[**Origin:** 1200–1300 old past participle of *pass*] → see Word Choice box at PASS¹

past² S2 W2 *prep.* **1** further than a particular place: *The library is a block past the main intersection.* | *There's a movie theater **just past*** (=a little farther away than) *the bank.* **2** up to and beyond a person or place, without stopping: *You drive past the stadium on your way to work, don't you?* | **right/straight past** *I was so deep in thought I almost walked right past Jerry.* **3** later than a particular time: *It's ten past nine.* | *Come on Annie, it's past your bedtime.* **4** beyond or no longer at a particular point or stage: *These roses are past their best now.* | *a baseball player who is **past** his **prime*** (=not as good as he was when he was younger) | *When we arrived, I was so sick I was way **past caring*** (=I did not care any more) *where I slept.* **5 I wouldn't put it past sb (to do sth)** SPOKEN used to say that you would not be surprised if someone did something bad or unusual because it is typical of them to do that type of thing: *I wouldn't put it past Colin to lie to his wife.* **6 be past due** something that is past due has not been paid or done by the time it should have been: *Their rent is three months past due.*

past³ S2 W2 *n.* **1 the past a)** the time that existed before the present: *Historians study the events of the past.* | *Barker had tried **in the past** to commit suicide.* | *Good manners seem to have become **a thing of the past*** (=something that does not exist anymore). | *You have to stop **living in the past*** (=thinking only about past events). **b)** the PAST TENSE of a verb **2 it's all in the past** SPOKEN used to say that a bad experience has ended and you can now forget about it: *Don't worry about what he said. It's all in the past now.* **3** [C usually singular] all the things that have happened to someone or something in the time before now: *She'd like to forget her past and start over.* | *At some time in its past the church had been rebuilt.* | *a woman with **a shady past***

past⁴ *adv.* **1** up to and beyond a particular place: *A car drove past at high speed.* **2 go past** if a period of time goes past, it passes: *Weeks went past without any news.* | *The summer seemed to fly past.*

pas·ta /'pɑstə/ S3 *n.* [U] an Italian food made from flour, eggs, and water and cut into various shapes, which you then cook in water. Pasta is usually eaten with a SAUCE: SYN **noodles** [**Origin:** 1800–1900 Italian, Late Latin]

paste¹ /peɪst/ *n.* **1** [U] a soft mixture made from crushed solid food that is used in cooking or is spread on bread: *tomato paste* **2** [U] a type of glue that is used for sticking paper onto things SYN **adhesive**: *wallpaper paste* **3** [C,U] a soft thick mixture that can easily be shaped or spread: *Mix the powder with water to make a smooth paste.* **4** [U] pieces of glass that are used in jewelry to look like DIAMONDS or other valuable stones

paste² *v.* **1** [T always + adv./prep.] to stick paper to a surface using paste: **paste sth on/over/across etc.** *Newspaper was pasted over the windows.* | *She pasted the picture into her scrapbook.* **2** [I,T] COMPUTERS to make words that you have removed or copied appear in a new place on a computer screen **3** [T] INFORMAL to defeat someone easily in a game or other competition SYN **clobber**: *Florida State pasted South Carolina 59–0.* → see also PASTING

paste·board /'peɪstbɔrd/ *n.* [U] flat stiff CARDBOARD made by sticking sheets of paper together

pas·tel¹ /pæ'stɛl/ *n.* **1** ENG. LANG. ARTS **a)** [C,U] a small colored stick used for drawing pictures, made of a substance like CHALK **b)** [C] a picture drawn with pastels: *a pastel portrait* **2** [C usually plural] a soft light color, such as pale blue or pink

pastel² *adj.* [only before noun] **1** a pastel color is pale and light: *pastel blue* ►see THESAURUS box at **color¹**, **light²** **2** ENG. LANG. ARTS drawn using pastels: *the child's pastel drawing*

Pas·ter·nak /ˈpæstɚˌnæk/, **Bor·is** /ˈbɔrɪs/ (1890–1960) a Russian poet and writer, best known for his NOVEL about the Russian revolution "Doctor Zhivago"

Pas·teur /pæˈstɚ/, **Lou·is** /ˈlui/ (1822–1895) a French SCIENTIST who established the study of MICROBIOLOGY, and proved that disease can be caused by GERMS

Louis Pasteur

pas·teur·ized /ˈpæstʃəˌraɪzd, -stə-/ *adj.* a liquid, usually milk, that is pasteurized is heated using a special process that kills any BACTERIA in it —**pasteurize** *v.* [T] —**pasteurization** /ˌpæstʃərəˈzeɪʃən/ *n.* [U]

pas·tiche /pæˈstiʃ/ *n.* ENG. LANG. ARTS **1** [C] a work of art that consists of a variety of different styles put together: +**of** *a novel that is a pastiche of journals, letters, and interviews* **2** [C + of] a piece of writing, music etc. that is deliberately made in the style of another artist **3** [U] the style or practice of making works of art in either of these ways

pas·time /ˈpæs-taɪm/ *n.* [C] something that you do in your free time because you find it enjoyable or interesting: *Reading was her favorite pastime.* [**Origin:** 1400–1500 translation of French *passe-temps* **pass time**]

past·ing /ˈpeɪstɪŋ/ *n.* **1** [singular] INFORMAL an easy defeat of an opponent in a game or other competition **2** [U] COMPUTERS the act of moving words from one place to another on a computer screen: *cutting and pasting*

ˌpast ˈmaster *n.* [C] someone who is very skilled at doing something, and has done it many times before: +**at** *Duvall is a past master at playing cowboy roles.*

pas·tor /ˈpæstɚ/ *n.* [C] a Christian priest in some Protestant churches: *the pastor of Central Lutheran Church* | *Pastor Glenn Hetland* [**Origin:** 1300–1400 Old French *pastour*, from Latin *pastor* **someone who takes care of sheep**] ►see THESAURUS box at **priest**

pas·tor·al /ˈpæstərəl/ *adj.* **1** [usually before noun] relating to the duties of a priest, minister etc. toward the members of their religious group: *his pastoral work among the congregation* **2** LITERARY typical of the simple peaceful life in the country: *a pastoral landscape*

ˌpast ˈparticiple *n.* [C] ENG. LANG. ARTS the form of a verb used with the verb "to have" in PERFECT tenses (for example "eaten" in "I have eaten") or with the verb "to be" in the PASSIVE tense (for example "changed" in "it was changed"), or sometimes as an adjective (for example "broken" in "a broken leg")

ˌpast ˈperfect *n.* **the past perfect** ENG. LANG. ARTS the form of a verb that shows that the action described by the verb was completed before a particular time in the past, formed in English with "had" and a past participle, for example "I had already met her" —**past perfect** *adj.*

pas·tra·mi /pəˈstrɑmi/ *n.* [U] smoked BEEF that contains a lot of SPICES

pas·try /ˈpeɪstri/ *n. plural* **pastries** **1** [U] a mixture of flour, fat, and milk or water, used to make the outer part of baked foods such as PIES **2** [C] a small sweet cake, made using this substance: *a Danish pastry*

ˌpast ˈtense *n.* **the past tense** ENG. LANG. ARTS the form of a verb that shows that something happened or existed before the present time, for example "walked" in "I walked away"

pas·tur·age /ˈpæstʃərɪdʒ/ *n.* [U] pasture

pas·ture¹ /ˈpæstʃɚ/ *n.* [C,U] **1** a field or area of land that is covered with grass and is used for cattle, sheep etc. to eat: *a cow pasture* **2 put sth out to pasture** to move cattle, horses etc. into a field to feed on the grass **3 put sb out to pasture** INFORMAL to make someone leave their job because you think they are too old to do it well **4 greener pastures** a new job, place, or activity, which you think will be better or more exciting: *Butler decided to head off for greener pastures in Los Angeles.*

pasture² *v.* [T] to put animals outside in a field to feed on the grass

pas·ture·land /ˈpæstʃɚˌlænd/ *n.* [U] pasture

past·y /ˈpeɪsti/ *adj.* a pasty face looks very pale and unhealthy

P

ˌpasty-ˈfaced *adj.* having a very pale face that looks unhealthy

PA sys·tem /pi ˈeɪ ˌsɪstəm/ also **ˌpublic-adˈdress ˌsystem** *n.* [C] an electrical system used to make a person's voice loud enough for large numbers of people to hear it

pat¹ /pæt/ *v.* **patted, patting** [T] **1** to touch someone or something lightly with your hand flat, usually repeating this movement quickly several times: *He patted the dog affectionately.* | **pat sb on the arm/head/back etc.** *She patted him on the shoulder and smiled.* | **pat sb's hand/shoulder etc.** *He reached down and patted the boy's head.* ►see THESAURUS box at **touch¹** **2 pat sth dry** to dry something by touching it lightly with a cloth or paper **3 pat sb/yourself on the back** to praise someone or feel pleased with yourself for doing something well: *She should pat herself on the back and take a well-earned break.* **4** to touch something with your hand flat in order to shape it: **pat sth into/down** *Pat the dough into a nine-inch square.*

pat sb **down** *phr. v.* to search someone for hidden weapons, drugs etc. by feeling their body with your hands

pat² *n.* [C] **1** a friendly act of touching someone with your hand flat: **a pat on the back/shoulder etc.** *Coach Brown* ***gave*** *him* ***a pat*** *on the shoulder.* **2 a pat of butter** a small flat piece of butter **3 a pat on the back** INFORMAL praise for something that you have done well: *I think you all deserve a pat on the back for your hard work.*

pat³ *adj.* a pat answer or explanation seems too quick and too simple, and sounds as if it has been used before: *There are no pat answers or simple solutions to this.*

pat⁴ *adv.* **1 have sth down pat** to know something thoroughly so that you can say it, perform it etc. immediately without thinking about it **2 stand pat** to refuse to change your opinion or decision

Pat·a·go·nia /ˌpæt̬əˈgoʊnyə/ a large area in southern Argentina, which has a small population and many sheep farms

patch¹ /pætʃ/ *n.* [C]

1 PART OF AN AREA a part of an area that is different from the parts that surround it: *There were some darker patches on the carpet.* | **patch of dirt/grease/ice etc.** *Patches of weeds had grown up all around the yard.* | **patch of light/sky** *A small patch of sky was visible through the clouds.* | *a bald patch right at the top of his head*

2 OVER A HOLE a small piece of material used to cover a hole in something: *Both knees of his jeans had patches on them.*

3 FRUITS/VEGETABLES a small area of ground used for growing fruit or vegetables: *a pumpkin patch*

4 EYE a piece of material that you wear over your eye to protect it when it has been hurt

5 TIME a particular period of time, especially one when you are experiencing a lot of problems: **a rough/bad patch** *Morris is going through one of the roughest patches of his presidency.*

6 DECORATION a small piece of cloth with words or pictures on it that you can sew onto clothes

7 COMPUTER COMPUTERS a small computer program that is added to another program to make it work better
8 SKIN MEDICINE a small piece of material you stick to your skin that sends medicine into your body: *a nicotine patch*

patch[2] *v.* [T] to repair a hole in something by putting a piece of material over it, for example in a piece of clothing

patch sth ↔ **together** *phr. v.* to make something quickly or carelessly from a number of different pieces or ideas: *He patched together the financing for the project.*

patch sth/sb ↔ **up** *phr. v.* **1** to end an argument because you want to stay friendly with someone: *They made an effort to patch up their marriage.* | *Do you think you two can* ***patch things up****?* **2** to repair a hole in something by putting a piece of material over it or filling it in: *Road crews are working overtime to patch up potholes.* **3** to give quick and basic medical treatment to someone who is hurt: *Soldiers with minor injuries were patched up and sent back into battle.*

pa·tchou·li /pəˈtʃuli/ *n.* [U] a type of PERFUME made from the leaves of an Asian bush.

ˌpatch ˈpocket *n.* [C] a pocket made by sewing a square piece of cloth onto a piece of clothing

patch·work /ˈpætʃwɚk/ *n.* [U] **1** a type of sewing in which many colored squares of cloth are sewn together to make one large piece: *a* ***patchwork quilt*** **2** something that is made up of a combination of many different things: **+of** *a patchwork of architectural styles* **3 a patchwork of fields/hills etc.** a pattern that fields, hills etc. seem to make when you see them from above

patchwork

a patchwork hat

patch·y /ˈpætʃi/ *adj.* **1** happening or existing in some areas but not in others: *patchy fog* | *The grass looked pretty patchy.* **2** not complete enough to be useful: *His knowledge of French remained pretty patchy.* | *patchy evidence* —**patchiness** *n.* [U]

pate /peɪt/ *n.* [C] OLD USE the top of your head: *his bald pate*

pâ·té /pɑˈteɪ, pæ-/ *n.* [U] a smooth soft substance made from meat or fish, that can be spread on bread

pa·tel·la /pəˈtɛlə/ *n.* [C] BIOLOGY your KNEECAP → see picture at SKELETON[1]

pa·tent[1] /ˈpætˀnt/ *n.* [C] ECONOMICS the right to make or sell a new INVENTION or product that no one else is allowed to copy for a set period of time, or the official document which gives you this right: **+on/for** *He was* ***granted a patent*** *on a new type of bicycle.* | **take out a patent/file a patent** *The researchers have recently taken out a patent on the product.* | *These drugs are still protected by patent.*

patent[2] *adj.* [only before noun] **patent lie/impossibility/nonsense etc.** FORMAL used to emphasize that something is clearly a lie, clearly impossible etc. SYN **obvious** → see also PATENTLY

patent[3] *v.* [T] to officially obtain a patent for something such as a new invention or product

ˌpatent ˈleather *n.* [U] thin shiny leather, usually black: *patent leather shoes*

pa·tent·ly /ˈpætˀntli/ *adv.* FORMAL very clearly: *a patently offensive remark* | **patently false/unfair/ridiculous etc.** *a patently false accusation*

ˌpatent ˈpending TECHNICAL a phrase written on a product to show that a patent for that product is in the process of being considered

pa·ter·fa·mil·i·as /ˌpɑtɚfəˈmiliəs, ˌpæ-, ˌpeɪ-/ *n.* [C] FORMAL a father or a man who is the head of a family

pa·ter·nal /pəˈtɚnl/ *adj.* **1** paternal feelings or behavior are like those of a father for his children SYN **fatherly**: *his paternal authority* **2 paternal grandmother/uncle/grandfather etc.** your father's mother, brother etc. [**Origin:** 1400–1500 Latin *paternus* **of a father**, from *pater* **father**] —**paternally** *adv.* → see also MATERNAL

pa·ter·nal·ism /pəˈtɚnl̩ˌɪzəm/ *n.* [U] a way of controlling people or organizations, in which people are protected and their needs are satisfied, but they do not have any freedom or responsibility

pa·ter·nal·is·tic /pəˌtɚnlˈɪstɪk/ *adj.* a paternalistic person, government, company etc. takes good care of the people it is responsible for, but also limits their freedom and makes all the important decisions for them: *a paternalistic employer*

pa·ter·ni·ty /pəˈtɚnət̬i/ *n.* [U] LAW the fact of being the father of a particular child, or the question of who the child's father is: *The test will establish the child's paternity.*

paˈternity ˌleave *n.* [U] a period of time that a father of a new baby is allowed away from work → see also MATERNITY LEAVE

paˈternity ˌsuit *n.* [C] LAW a legal action in which a mother asks a court of law to say officially that a particular man is the father of her child

path /pæθ/ S3 W2 *n.* *plural* **paths** /pæðz, pæθs/ [C]
1 TRACK a track that people walk along over an area of ground SYN **footpath**: *a path through the woods* | *Students had* ***worn a path*** *across the courtyard.* | **along/down/up a path** *They walked along the path arm in arm.*
2 WAY THROUGH the space ahead of you as you move forward: *Workers found their* ***path was blocked*** *by protesters.* | **+through** *Police* ***cleared a path*** *through the crowd.*
3 DIRECTION the direction or line along which someone or something moves SYN **route**: *The tornado destroyed everything in its path.* | *the Earth's path around the sun* | *the plane's* ***flight path***
4 PLAN a plan or series of actions that helps you to achieve something, especially over a long period of time: *a career path* | *He and his brother had* ***followed*** *very different* ***paths****.* | **+to** *our country's path to economic recovery*
5 sbs' paths cross if two people's paths cross, they meet by chance
6 the path of least resistance a set of actions that are the easiest thing to do in a particular situation
[**Origin:** Old English *pæth*] → see also **beat a path (to sb's door)** at BEAT[1] (25), FLIGHT PATH, **lead sb down the garden/primrose path** at LEAD[1] (18)

pa·thet·ic /pəˈθɛt̬ɪk/ *adj.* **1** something or someone that is pathetic is so useless, unsuccessful, or badly done that they annoy you: *The movie's special effects are pathetic.* | *You're pathetic! Here, let me do it.* | *a pathetic attempt at escape* **2** making you feel pity or sympathy: *pathetic images of half-starved children* —**pathetically** /-kli/ *adv.*

path·find·er /ˈpæθˌfaɪndɚ/ *n.* [C] **1** someone who goes ahead of a group and finds the best way through unknown land **2** someone who discovers new ways of doing things SYN **trailblazer**

path·o·gen /ˈpæθədʒən/ *n.* [C] MEDICINE an ORGANISM that causes disease —**pathogenic** /ˌpæθəˈdʒɛnɪk◂/ *adj.*

path·o·log·i·cal /ˌpæθəˈlɑdʒɪkəl/ *adj.* **1** pathological behavior or feelings are bad or unreasonable, and also impossible to control: *his pathological gambling* | *Kern was a pathological liar.* **2** MEDICINE a mental or physical condition that is pathological is caused by disease **3** MEDICINE relating to pathology —**pathologically** /-kli/ *adv.*: *pathologically shy*

pa·thol·o·gy /pəˈθɑlədʒi, pæ-/ *n.* [U] MEDICINE the study of the causes and effects of illnesses —**pathologist** *n.* [C]

pa·thos /ˈpeɪθoʊs, -θɑs, ˈpæ-/ *n.* [U] FORMAL the quality that a person, situation, or work of art has that makes you feel pity and sadness: *the novel's mix of comedy and pathos*

path•way /ˈpæθweɪ/ *n. plural* **pathways** [C] **1** a path **2** a plan or series of actions that will help you achieve something, especially over a long period of time: +**to** *the pathway to peace* **3** a series of nerves that pass information to each other: *the pain pathway*

pa•tience /ˈpeɪʃəns/ *n.* [U] **1** the ability to continue waiting or doing something for a long time, without becoming angry or anxious OPP **impatience**: *This type of research requires enormous patience.* | *I wouldn't **have the patience** to sit sewing all day.* **2** the ability to accept trouble and other people's annoying behavior without complaining or becoming angry: *Parents need a lot of patience.* | **have no/little patience with/for sth** *I have little patience for people who don't work hard.* | *Teachers soon **lost their patience*** (=stopped being patient and got angry) *with her behavior.* | *Her constant questions were beginning to **try my patience*** (=make me angry). **3 the patience of a saint** a very large amount of patience → see also **have the patience of Job** at JOB² (1)

pa•tient¹ /ˈpeɪʃənt/ S3 W1 *n.* [C] someone receiving medical treatment from a doctor or in a hospital

patient² W3 *adj.* able to wait calmly for a long time or to accept difficulties, people's annoying behavior etc. without becoming angry or anxious OPP **impatient**: *You're just going to have to **be patient**, Katie.* | +**with** *You have to be very patient with young learners.* [**Origin:** 1300–1400 French, Latin, present participle of *pati* **to suffer**] —**patiently** *adv.*

pat•i•na /pəˈtinə, pæ-/ *n.* [singular, U] **1** a greenish layer that forms naturally on the surface of COPPER or BRONZE **2** a smooth shiny surface that gradually develops on wood, leather, metal etc. **3 a patina of wealth/success/authority etc.** FORMAL the appearance of wealth, success etc. that someone or something has

pat•i•o /ˈpæti̦ˌoʊ/ *n. plural* **patios** [C] a flat area with a hard floor next to a house, where people sit outside [**Origin:** 1800–1900 Spanish]

ˈpatio door *n.* [C usually plural] a glass door that you open by sliding it to one side, and that goes from a living room onto a patio

pa•tis•se•rie /pəˈtisəri/ *n.* [C] a store that sells cakes and PIES, especially French ones, or the cakes that it sells

pat•ois /ˈpætwɑ/ *n. plural* **patois** /-wɑz/ [C,U] ENG. LANG. ARTS a spoken form of a language used by the people of a small area or by a certain group that is different from the national or standard language → see also CREOLE, DIALECT

pat. pend. TECHNICAL the written abbreviation of PATENT PENDING

patri- /peɪtrə, pætrə/ *prefix* **1** relating to fathers: *patricide* (=killing one's father) **2** relating to men: *a patriarchal society* (=controlled by men) → see also MATRI-

pa•tri•arch /ˈpeɪtriˌɑrk/ *n.* [C] **1** an old man who is respected as the head of a family or tribe → see also MATRIARCH **2** a BISHOP in the early Christian church **3** a chief BISHOP of the Orthodox Christian churches

pa•tri•arch•al /ˌpeɪtriˈɑrkəl/ *adj.* **1** ruled or controlled only by men: *a patriarchal society* **2** relating to being a patriarch, or typical of a patriarch: *patriarchal authority* → see also MATRIARCHAL

pa•tri•arch•y /ˈpeɪtriˌɑrki/ *n. plural* **patriarchies** [C,U] **1** a social system in which men have all the power **2** a social system in which the oldest man rules his family and passes power and possessions on to his sons → see also MATRIARCHY

pa•tri•cian /pəˈtrɪʃən/ *adj.* **1** having the appearance, manners, way of speaking etc. that is typical of people from the highest social class SYN **aristocratic**: *his patrician background* **2** belonging to the high class of people who governed in ancient Rome → see also PLEBEIAN —**patrician** *n.* [C]

pat•ri•cide /ˈpætrəˌsaɪd/ *n.* [U] FORMAL the crime of murdering your father → see also MATRICIDE, PARRICIDE

Pat•rick, Saint /ˈpætrɪk/ (A.D. ?389–?461) the PATRON SAINT of Ireland, who helped to spread the Christian religion there

pat•ri•lin•e•al /ˌpætrəˈlɪniəl/ *adj.* a patrilineal society is one in which connections between the fathers and sons in a family are regarded as the most important → see also MATRILINEAL

pat•ri•mo•ny /ˈpætrəˌmoʊni/ *n.* [U] **1** the art, natural RESOURCES, valuable objects etc. of a country: *the national patrimony of Canada* **2** LAW property given to you after the death of your father, which was given to him by your grandfather etc. SYN **inheritance** —**patrimonial** /ˌpætrəˈmoʊniəl/ *adj.*

pa•tri•ot /ˈpeɪtriət/ *n.* [C] APPROVING someone who loves their country and is willing to defend it

pa•tri•ot•ic /ˌpeɪtriˈɑtɪk/ *adj.* APPROVING having or expressing a great love of your country: *patriotic songs* | *He was a deeply patriotic man.* —**patriotism** /ˈpeɪtriəˌtɪzəm/ *n.* [U] → see also NATIONALISTIC

pa•trol¹ /pəˈtroʊl/ *v.* **patrolled, patrolling** [I always + adv./prep., T] **1** to go around the different parts of an area or building at regular times to check that there is no trouble or danger: *Guards patrolled the hotel.* **2** to drive or walk again and again around an area in a threatening way: *Gangs of young men patrolled the street at night.* [**Origin:** 1600–1700 French *patrouiller*, from *patte* **animal's foot**]

patrol² *n.* **1** [C,U] the act of going around different parts of an area at regular times to check that there is no trouble or danger: *Police have increased patrols in some neighborhoods.* | *Navy ships **on patrol** in the Atlantic* **2** [C] a group of police, soldiers, airplanes etc. sent to patrol a particular area: *the U.S. border patrol* | **patrol boat/car/helicopter etc.** (=used by the military or police) **3** [C] a small group of BOY SCOUTS → see also HIGHWAY PATROL

paˈtrol ˌcar *n.* [C] a police car that drives around the streets of a city

pa•trol•man /pəˈtroʊlmən/ *n. plural* **patrolmen** /-mən/ [C] a police officer who regularly walks or drives around a particular area to prevent crime from happening

pa•tron /ˈpeɪtrən/ W3 *n.* [C] **1** someone who supports a person, organization, or activity, especially by giving money: *a wealthy patron* | +**of** *a great patron of the arts* **2** FORMAL someone who uses a particular store, restaurant, or hotel → see also CUSTOMER

pa•tron•age /ˈpeɪtrənɪdʒ, ˈpæ-/ *n.* [U] **1** FORMAL the fact of being a customer of a particular store, restaurant, or hotel: *Thank you for your patronage.* **2** the support, especially financial support, that is given by a patron to a person, activity, or organization: *a patron of the museum* **3** a system by which someone in a powerful position gives people help or important jobs in return for their support

pa•tron•ize /ˈpeɪtrəˌnaɪz, ˈpæ-/ *v.* [T] **1** to talk to someone or treat someone in a way that seems friendly but shows that you think they are not as intelligent or important as you SYN **condescend**: *Don't patronize me!* | *The program focuses on kids' interests without patronizing them.* **2** FORMAL to use or visit a store, restaurant etc.: *a little restaurant which is mostly patronized by local residents* **3** to support or give money to an organization or activity

pa•tron•iz•ing /ˈpeɪtrəˌnaɪzɪŋ/ *adj.* talking to someone or treating someone in a way that shows you think they are not as intelligent or as important as you SYN **condescending**: *It is patronizing to assume that men cannot nurture their children.* | **patronizing attitude/manner/tone etc.** *the senator's patronizing attitude*

ˌpatron ˈsaint *n.* [C] a Christian SAINT (=very holy person) who people believe gives special protection to a particular place, activity, or person: +**of** *St. Christopher, the patron saint of travelers*

pat•sy /ˈpætsi/ *n. plural* **patsies** [C] INFORMAL someone who is easily tricked or deceived, especially so that they take the blame for someone else's crime

pat·ter¹ /ˈpætɚ/ *v.* [I] if something, especially water, patters, it makes quiet sounds as it keeps hitting a surface lightly and quickly: +**on** *Rain pattered on windows.*

patter² *n.* **1** [singular] the sound made by something as it keeps hitting a surface lightly and quickly: +**of** *the patter of raindrops* **2** [U, singular] fast, continuous, and often amusing talk, used for example by someone telling jokes or trying to sell something SYN **spiel**: *a comedian's patter | his sales patter* **3 the patter of tiny feet** HUMOROUS used to mean that someone is going to have a baby soon: *Are we going to hear the patter of tiny feet?*

P

pat·tern¹ /ˈpætɚn/ S2 W2 *n.* [C]
1 OF EVENTS the regular way in which something happens, develops, or is done: *Weather patterns have changed in recent years. |* +**of** *a normal pattern of development |* +**in** *Researchers noticed patterns in the data. |* **follow/fit a pattern** *Romantic novels tend to follow a **set pattern**.*
2 DESIGN a regularly repeated arrangement of shapes, colors, or lines on a surface, usually intended as decoration SYN **design**: *a floral pattern |* +**of** *a pattern of light and dark bands*

THESAURUS

design a pattern used for decorating something: *curtains with a floral design*
markings the colored patterns and shapes on an animal's fur, feathers, or skin: *the tiger's black and orange markings*
motif a pattern that is regularly repeated: *a shirt with a Hawaiian motif*

3 SOUNDS/WORDS a regularly repeated arrangement of sounds or words: *A sonnet has a fixed rhyming pattern.*
4 GOOD EXAMPLE [usually singular] a thing, idea, or person that is a very good example to copy: +**for** *This deal will be the pattern for future investments. | Their work set the pattern for many other conservation projects.*
5 MAKING THINGS a shape used as a guide for making something, especially a thin piece of paper used when cutting material to make clothing: *a skirt pattern*
[**Origin:** 1300–1400 Old French *patron*, from Medieval Latin *patronus* from *pater* **father**]

pattern² *v.* [T usually passive] to design or make something in a way that is copied from something else: **pattern sth after/on sb/sth** *The TV ratings are patterned after the movie ones.*

pat·terned /ˈpætɚnd/ *adj.* decorated with a pattern: *patterned sheets |* +**with** *shirts patterned with bright flowers*

pat·tern·ing /ˈpætɚnɪŋ/ *n.* [U] **1** TECHNICAL the development of particular ways of behaving, thinking, doing things etc. as a result of copying and repeating actions, language etc.: *cultural patterning* **2** patterns of a particular kind, especially on an animal's skin

pat·ty /ˈpæti/ *n. plural* **patties** [C] a round flat piece of meat or other food: *a hamburger patty*

ˈpatty ˌmelt *n.* [C] a flat round piece of HAMBURGER that is cooked with cheese on top and served on bread

pau·ci·ty /ˈpɔsəti/ *n.* **a/the paucity of sth** FORMAL less of something than is needed SYN **scarcity**: *a paucity of information*

Paul, Saint /pɔl/ (A.D. ?3–?68) a Christian APOSTLE who wrote many of the Epistles in the New Testament of the Bible

Pau·ling /ˈpɔlɪŋ/, **Li·nus** /ˈlaɪnəs/ (1901–1994) a U.S. scientist who studied how atoms join together and form larger structures, and who strongly opposed the use of NUCLEAR WEAPONS

paunch /pɔntʃ, pɑntʃ/ *n.* [C] OFTEN HUMOROUS a man's fat stomach —**paunchy** *adj.*

pau·per /ˈpɔpɚ/ *n.* [C] OLD-FASHIONED someone who is very poor

pause¹ /pɔz/ W3 *v.* [I] **1** to stop speaking or doing something for a short time before starting again: *He paused at the door to straighten his tie. |* +**for** *Jill **paused for a moment** to look at her notes. | He stopped, **pausing for breath**. |* **pause to do sth** *John paused to think.* ►see THESAURUS box at **stop¹** **2** [I,T] to push a button on a tape player, CD PLAYER, computer etc. in order to make a tape, CD etc. stop playing for a short time

pause² *n.* [C] **1** a short time during which someone stops speaking or doing something before starting again: **a long/brief/short etc. pause** *After a brief pause, Sharon said, "You're right." |* +**in** *an awkward pause in the conversation* **2** also **pause button** a button that allows you to stop a CD PLAYER, VCR etc. for a short time and start it again: *She **hit the pause button** and pointed at the screen.* **3 give sb pause (for thought)** to make someone stop and consider carefully what they are doing: *High house prices have given potential buyers pause.* **4** ENG. LANG. ARTS a mark (𝄐) over a musical note, showing that the note is to be played or sung longer than usual [**Origin:** 1400–1500 Latin *pausa*, from Greek *pausis*, from *pauein* **to stop**]

pave /peɪv/ *v.* [T usually passive] **1** to cover a path, road, area etc. with a hard level surface: *The road through the valley was only paved last year.* **2 pave the way for sb/sth** to make a later event or development possible by producing the right conditions: *Galileo's achievements paved the way for Newton's scientific discoveries.* —**paved** *adj.*: *a paved courtyard* → see also **the road to hell is paved with good intentions** at ROAD (8)

pave·ment /ˈpeɪvmənt/ *n.* **1** [U] the hard surface of a road **2** [C,U] a paved surface or area of any kind SYN **paving**: *The saint is buried beneath the pavement of a little chapel.* **3 pound/hit the pavement** to work very hard to get something, especially a job, by going to a lot of different places: *For months, Garcia pounded the pavement for jobs.*

pa·vil·ion /pəˈvɪlyən/ *n.* [C] **1** a large building with big open areas, used for sports or other public events **2** a temporary building or tent which is used for public entertainment or EXHIBITIONS and is often large with a lot of space and light: *There will be a live band at the dance pavilion.*

pav·ing /ˈpeɪvɪŋ/ *n.* [U] **1** material used to form a hard level surface on a path, road, area etc. **2** an area that is PAVED

ˈpaving stone *n.* [C] one of the flat usually square pieces of stone that are used to make a hard surface to walk on

Pav·lov /ˈpævlɑv, ˈpɑvlɔf/, **I·van Pet·ro·vich** /ˈaɪvən ˈpɛtrəvɪtʃ/ (1849–1936) a Russian scientist known especially for his work with dogs, which proved the existence of CONDITIONED REFLEX —**Pavlovian** /pævˈloʊviən/ *adj.*

Pav·lo·va /pɑvˈloʊvə/, **An·na** /ˈɑnə/ (1885–1931) a Russian BALLET dancer who is considered by many to have been the world's greatest ballet dancer

paw¹ /pɔ/ *n.* [C] **1** BIOLOGY an animal's foot that has nails or CLAWS: *The cat licked its paws.* **2** INFORMAL someone's hand: *Keep your paws to yourself!* [**Origin:** 1200–1300 Old French *poue*]

paw² *v.* **1** [I,T] if an animal paws a surface, it touches or rubs one place several times with its paw: +**at** *The dog's pawing at the door again.* **2** [I,T] INFORMAL to feel or touch someone in a rough or sexual way that is offensive: *He'd had too much to drink and started pawing me.* **3** [I always + adv./prep.] to touch a lot of things, especially when you are looking for something: +**through/over/around** *She pawed through the wastebasket, searching for the letter.*

pawn¹ /pɔn/ *n.* [C] **1** one of the eight smallest and least valuable pieces which each player has in the game of CHESS **2** someone who is used by a more powerful person or group and has no control of the situation: +**in** *The children became pawns in their parents' divorce battle.*

pawn² *v.* [T] to leave something valuable with a pawnbroker in order to borrow money from them SYN **hock**

pawn sth ↔ **off** *phr. v.* **1 pawn sth ↔ off on sb** INFORMAL to persuade someone to buy or accept something that you want to get rid of, especially something of low quality: *They tried to pawn off out-of-date medicines on Third World countries.* **2 pawn sb/sth ↔ off as sth** to present something in a dishonest way: *The program pawns off gossip and trivia as real news.*

pawn·bro·ker /ˈpɔnˌbroʊkɚ/ *n.* [C] someone whose business is to lend people money in exchange for valuable objects. If the money is not paid back, the pawnbroker can sell the object.

Paw·nee /ˌpɔˈni/ a Native American tribe from the midwestern region of the U.S. —**Pawnee** *adj.*

pawn·shop /ˈpɔnʃɑp/ *n.* [C] a pawnbroker's shop

Pax Ro·ma·na, the /ˌpæks roʊˈmɑnə/ HISTORY the long period of peace in the Roman Empire

pay¹ /peɪ/ S1 W1 *v.* **pays, paid**
1 BUY STH [I,T] to give someone money for something you are buying: *They ran off without paying.* | +**for** *Let me pay for dinner this time.* | **pay $10/$75 etc. for sth** *They paid over $100 each for the tickets.* | **pay sb for sth** *Did he ever pay you for your guitar?* | **pay (in) cash** *You get a discount for paying cash.* | **pay by check/by credit card** *If you pay by credit card there's a small extra charge.*
2 DEBT/BILL/TAX [T] to pay money that you owe to a person, organization, or government: *Have you paid the rent yet?* | *I forgot to* ***pay*** *the electricity* ***bill***. | *If you earn below $6,000, you pay no income tax.*
3 JOB/SERVICE [I,T] to give someone money for the job they do, or for doing something for you: *How much do they pay?* | *Bartending can pay pretty well.* | *a job that pays the minimum wage* | **pay sb $8 an hour/$3,500 a month etc.** *Some lawyers* ***get paid*** *over $400 an hour.* | **pay sb to do sth** *I paid a neighborhood boy to wash the car.* | **pay sb for (doing) sth** *They still haven't paid me for mowing their lawn.* | **be well/badly/poorly paid** *Many women work in poorly paid positions.*
4 pay attention (to sb/sth) to watch, listen to, or think about someone or something carefully: *I don't think she was paying any attention to what I was saying.* | *They* ***paid no attention to*** (=ignored) *him.*
5 pay a visit to sb/sth also **pay sb/sth a visit** to visit someone or a place: *I think it's time I paid my grandparents a visit.* | *You should try to pay a visit to the Smithsonian when you're in Washington.*
6 GOOD RESULT [I] if a particular action pays, it brings a good result or advantage for you: *Crime doesn't pay.* | **it pays to do sth** *In my experience, it doesn't pay to argue with her.* | **it would/it might pay to do sth** *It might pay to get your roof fixed before winter comes.* | *Taking care of your customers* ***pays*** *big* ***dividends*** (=brings a lot of advantages) *in the long run.*
7 PROFIT a) [I] if a store or business pays, it makes a profit: *Although both of them worked hard, they couldn't make the business pay.* **b)** [T] to provide a certain amount as profit or in INTEREST SYN **yield**: *Our fixed rate savings account currently pays 6.5% interest.*
8 SAY STH GOOD [T] to say something good or polite about someone or to someone: *I was just trying to* ***pay*** *her* ***a compliment***. | *Staff and friends gathered to* ***pay tribute to*** *Professor Collins.* | *Celebrities turned out in large numbers yesterday to* ***pay their last respects*** (=go to someone's funeral).
9 pay for itself if something you buy pays for itself, it helps you to save as much money as you paid for it: *Installing solar film on the windows will pay for itself.*
10 pay the penalty/price to experience something bad because you have done something wrong, made a mistake etc.: *She makes plenty of money, but there's a high price to pay in terms of long hours.* | **pay the price/penalty for (doing) sth** *I'm now paying the penalty for not saving enough money for retirement.*
11 BE PUNISHED [I] to suffer or be punished for something you have done wrong: *I'll* ***make*** *him* ***pay***! | +**for** *He* ***paid dearly*** *for his mistakes.*
12 sb has paid their debt to society used to say that someone who has done something illegal has been fully punished for it
13 pay your way to pay for everything that you need without having to depend on anyone else for money: *Tim worked his way through college.*
14 pay through the nose (for sth) INFORMAL to pay far too much for something
15 pay lip service to sth to say that you support or agree with something without doing anything to prove your support: *City leaders are just paying lip service to affordable housing.*
16 pay your dues if you pay your dues, you work at the lowest levels of a profession or organization in order to earn the right to move up to a better position: *Now a news anchorman, Shaw paid his dues as a reporter.*
17 pay a call on sb also **pay sb a call** OLD-FASHIONED to visit someone
18 pay court to sb OLD-FASHIONED to treat someone, especially a woman, with great respect and admiration
[**Origin:** 1100–1200 Old French *paier*, from Latin *pacere* **to make calm or peaceful**]

pay sb/sth ↔ **back** *phr. v.* **1** to give someone the money that you owe them SYN **repay**: *Bob said he would pay me back on Wednesday.* | *You still have to pay back your student loans, don't you?* | **pay sb back (for) sth** *Did you pay Alice back for lunch?* **2** to make someone suffer for doing something wrong or bad to you: **pay sb back for sth** *I want to pay him back for the way he embarrassed me at the party.*

pay sth ↔ **in** also **pay sth into sth** *phr. v.* to put money in your bank account, a RETIREMENT account etc.: *If you have a pension fund, consider increasing the amount you pay in each month.* | *The check for $250 was paid into your account on Friday.*

pay off *phr. v.* **1 pay sth ↔ off** to pay someone all the money you owe them: *We paid off our mortgage last year.* | *He worked overtime to* ***pay off*** *all his* ***debts***. **2** if something you do pays off, it brings success, especially after a lot of effort or after a long time: *My persistence finally paid off when they called me in for an interview.* **3 pay sb ↔ off** to pay someone to keep quiet about something illegal or dishonest → see also PAYOFF

pay out *phr. v.* **1 pay sth ↔ out** to pay a lot of money for something: *Our company pays out a huge amount in health benefits.* | *If you have kids, you're always paying out.* **2 pay sth ↔ out** if a company or organization pays out, it gives someone money as a result of an insurance claim, INVESTMENT etc.: *Insurance companies were slow to pay out on claims for flood damage.* **3 pay sth ↔ out** to allow a piece of rope to unwind → see also PAYOUT

pay sth ↔ **over** *phr. v.* to make an official payment of money: **pay sth over to sb** *His share of the inheritance had been paid over to him.*

pay up *phr. v.* to pay money that you owe, especially when you do not want to or you are late: *He lost the bet, but refused to pay up.*

pay² S2 W2 *n.* [U] **1** money that you are given for doing your job SYN **salary** SYN **wages**: *The pay is around $8 an hour.* | **a pay raise/increase/cut etc.** *Workers say they haven't had a pay raise in two years.* | *The* ***base pay*** (=the amount you normally earn) *is low, but you can get a lot of overtime.* | *Women fought for* ***equal pay*** *for equal work.*

THESAURUS

income money that you receive from working, investments etc.: *families on a low income*
salary the pay that professional people such as teachers or lawyers earn every year: *a salary of $65,000 a year*
wages the pay that someone earns every hour or every week: *Her wages barely cover the rent.*
bonus money added to someone's pay, as a reward for good work or as a reward when the company does well: *The company pays an attendance bonus – if you go thirty days without being late or absent, you get the bonus.*

P

earnings all the money that you earn by working: *In a good year, a bonus can double an executive's earnings.*

2 in the pay of sb someone who is in someone else's pay is working for them, often secretly or illegally: *Several cops were in the pay of the Mafia.*

pay·a·ble /ˈpeɪəbəl/ *adj.* [not before noun] **1** a bill, debt etc. that is payable must be paid: *A lab fee of $25 is payable during the first week of class.* | +**in** *The bill is payable in quarterly installments.* **2 payable to sb** a check that is payable to someone has that person's name written on it and should be paid to them: *Checks should be **made payable to** the "Refugee Relief Fund."*

P

pay·back /ˈpeɪbæk/ *n.* **1** [U] INFORMAL an action that harms or punishes someone who has defeated you or done something bad to you SYN **revenge**: *Now the Knicks want payback for their defeat a month ago.* | *For many voters, this election is **payback time** for the people who raised their taxes.* **2** [C] the money or advantage that you get from a business, project, or something you have done: *The paybacks from these investments are potentially large.* **3 payback period/schedule a)** the period of time during which you pay back money you have borrowed **b)** the period of time in which you will make a profit on an INVESTMENT

pay·check /ˈpeɪtʃɛk/ *n.* [C] **1** a check that someone receives as payment for their job: *a weekly paycheck* **2** the amount of money someone earns: *a baseball player's annual paycheck*

pay·day /ˈpeɪdeɪ/ *n.* [U] the day on which you get the money you have earned from your job

ˈpay dirt, paydirt *n.* [U] **hit/strike pay dirt** to make a valuable or useful discovery: *a group of scientists who struck pay dirt*

pay·ee /peɪˈi/ *n.* [C] TECHNICAL the person to whom money, especially a check, should be paid

pay·er /ˈpeɪɚ/ *n.* [C] TECHNICAL someone who pays for something

pay·load /ˈpeɪloʊd/ *n.* [C] **1** the amount of goods or passengers carried by a vehicle, aircraft, or SPACECRAFT, or the goods that it is carrying: *The helicopter can carry a payload of 2,640 pounds.* | *The shuttle's main payload will be a satellite.* **2** the amount of explosive that a MISSILE can carry

pay·mas·ter /ˈpeɪˌmæstɚ/ *n.* [C] **1** someone who is responsible for giving people their pay, for example in the army or a factory **2** a powerful person or organization that secretly pays someone else to do something, especially something illegal: *The assassin's paymasters were never identified.*

pay·ment /ˈpeɪmənt/ S2 W2 *n.* **1** [C] an amount of money that has been paid or must be paid: *Flood victims received a one-time payment of $2,000 from the government.* | **house/car/mortgage/insurance etc. payment** *He lost his job and couldn't **make** the house **payments**.* | *The country cannot **meet the payments** on its foreign debt.* | +**on** *a monthly payment on the car* | +**to** *a cut in Medicare payments to doctors* | +**for** *payments for services such as electricity and water* **2** [U] the act of paying for something: +**of** *penalties for late payment of taxes* | +**in** *Most hotels here only accept payment in dollars.* | ***Payment** can be **made** by check or credit card.* | *Doctors expect immediate **payment in full*** (=paying the entire amount of money). **3** [U] someone's reward for doing something: +**for** *The only payment I got for my effort was insults.* **4 payment in kind** a way of paying for something with goods or services instead of money → see also DOWN PAYMENT

pay·off /ˈpeɪɔf/ *n.* [C] **1** an advantage or profit that you get as a result of doing something: *For most people, staying in education has an economic payoff.* **2** a payment that is made to someone, often illegally, in order to stop them from causing you trouble: *Corrupt policemen received payoffs from drug bosses.* **3** a payment made to someone when they are forced to leave their job → see also **pay off** at PAY[1]

pay·o·la /peɪˈoʊlə/ *n.* [U] INFORMAL **1** the illegal practice of paying someone to use their influence to encourage people to buy what your company is selling, used especially about payments to radio DISC JOCKEYS in the past so that they would play particular records → see also BRIBE **2** the money that is paid to someone to use their influence

pay·out /ˈpeɪ-aʊt/ *n.* [C] a large payment of money to someone, for example from an insurance claim or from winning a competition, or the act of making this payment: *payouts to shareholders* → see also **pay out** at PAY[1]

ˌpay-per-ˈview *adj.* [only before noun] a pay-per-view television CHANNEL makes people pay for each program they watch —**pay-per-view** *n.* [U]

ˈpay phone *n.* [C] a public telephone that you can use when you put in coins or a CREDIT CARD

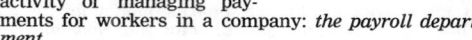

pay phone

ˈpay raise *n.* [C] an increase in the amount of money you are paid for doing your job: *a 4% pay raise*

pay·roll /ˈpeɪroʊl/ *n.* **1** [C] **on the payroll** if someone is on the payroll of a company, they are employed by that company: *a company with 350 people on the payroll* **2** [singular] the total amount that a particular company pays to all the people who work for it **3** [singular] the activity of managing payments for workers in a company: *the payroll department*

ˈpayroll ˌtax *n.* [C,U] ECONOMICS a tax that an employer must take from the money its workers earn and pay directly to the government

ˌpayroll withˈholding ˌstatement *n.* [C] ECONOMICS a document that is attached to someone's PAYCHECK, showing the various amounts of money that have been taken away from the total, such as, for example, the amount paid in tax

ˈpay stub *n.* [C] a piece of paper that an employed person gets every time they are paid, which shows how much money they have earned and how much has been taken away for tax, insurance etc.

ˌpay ˈtelephone *n.* [C] a PAY PHONE

ˈpay ˌtoilet *n.* [C] a toilet that you must pay to use

ˌpay TˈV also **ˌpay ˈtelevision** *n.* [U] television CHANNELS you must pay to watch

Paz /pɑz, pɑs/, **Oc·ta·vi·o** /ɑkˈtɑvioʊ/ (1914–1998) a Mexican poet

PBS *n.* [U] **Public Broadcasting System** a company in the U.S. that broadcasts television programs without advertisements

PC[1] *n.* [C] **personal computer** COMPUTERS the most common type of computer, which is used by one person at a time, either at home or at work

PC[2] *adj.* the abbreviation of POLITICALLY CORRECT

PCB *n.* [C] one of a group of chemicals that was used in the past in industry but that are very harmful to the environment

PCP *n.* **1** [U] an ANESTHETIC that is also taken as an illegal drug **2** [U] PNEUMOCYSTIS **3** [C] a PRIMARY CARE PHYSICIAN

PCS *n.* [U] **personal communications service** a system that allows CELLULAR PHONES to communicate with each other

pct. a written abbreviation of PERCENT

pd. the written abbreviation of "paid"

pdq /ˌpi di ˈkyu/ *adv.* SPOKEN, INFORMAL **pretty damn quick** used to say that something should be done immediately: *I told her to get back here pdq.*

PDT the abbreviation of PACIFIC DAYLIGHT TIME

P.E. *n.* [U] **physical education** sports and physical activity taught as a school subject

pea /pi/ *n.* [C] **1** a round green seed that is cooked and eaten as a vegetable: *pea soup* | *frozen peas* **2** a plant that produces long green PODS that contain these seeds **3 the size of a pea/pea-sized** small in size: *a pea-sized gland at the base of the brain* **4 pea-brained** INFORMAL a stupid creature or person **5 like two peas in a pod** INFORMAL exactly the same in appearance, behavior etc. [**Origin:** 1600–1700 *pease* **pea** (11–19 centuries) (mistaken as plural), from Latin *pisa*, plural of *pisum*, from Greek *pison*] → see also SPLIT PEA, SWEET PEA

Pea·bod·y /ˈpiˌbɑdi, -bədi/, **Elizabeth** (1804–1894) a U.S. educator who started the first KINDERGARTEN in the U.S.

peace /pis/ S3 W1 *n.*
1 NO WAR a) [U] the situation in which there is no war or fighting: *Some of these children have never known a time of peace.* | *a threat to* ***world peace*** | *The country is* ***at peace with*** *its neighbors for the first time in years.* | *a city where Christians and Muslims* ***live together in peace*** | *efforts to* ***bring peace*** *to the region* | +**between** *a lasting peace between the two sides* | *the Middle East* ***peace process*** (=series of talks etc. to end fighting) | **peace talks/agreements/treaties** (=discussions, agreements etc. to end or prevent wars) | *The rival armies are now involved in peace negotiations.* | **peace movement/campaign/vigil etc.** (=organized efforts to prevent war) **b)** [singular] a period of time in which there is no war: *a lasting peace* | *An* ***uneasy peace*** (=a time when there is no fighting, but when people are still disagreeing) *continued until 1939.*
2 NO NOISE [U] a situation that is very calm, quiet, and pleasant, and in which you are not interrupted: *All I want is some* ***peace and quiet.*** | *Let me read the paper* ***in peace!*** | *Luckily, she* ***left me in peace.***
3 CALMNESS [U] the feeling of being calm, happy, and not worried: *the search for inner peace* | *Saving for the future will help give you* ***peace of mind.*** | *Lying beside her, he felt* ***at peace.*** | *She seems more* ***at peace with herself*** *now.*
4 keep the peace to stop people from fighting, arguing, or causing trouble: *U.N. troops have been sent to keep the peace.* | *Parents who want to keep the peace in the car should try story tapes.*
5 make (your) peace to end an argument or disagreement with a person or a group, especially by telling them you are sorry: +**with** *Laurie wanted to make peace with her father before he died.*
6 DOCUMENT [singular] a formal agreement that ends a war: *In 1648 the Peace of Westphalia ended the 30 Years War.*
7 keep/hold your peace FORMAL to keep quiet even though there is something you would like to say: *She wanted to disagree, but held her peace.*
8 at peace an expression meaning "dead," used when you want to say this in a gentle way
9 rest in peace words that are said during a funeral service for someone who has died, or written on a GRAVESTONE
[**Origin:** 1100–1200 Old French *pais*, from Latin *pax*] → see also **disturb the peace** at DISTURB (4)

peace·a·ble /ˈpisəbəl/ *adj.* **1** someone who is peaceable does not like fighting or arguing OPP **violent** OPP **aggressive**: *A peaceable and orderly crowd staged a protest outside the city hall.* **2** a peaceable situation or way of doing something is calm, without any violence or fighting: *a peaceable end to the dispute* —**peaceably** *adv.*

ˈPeace Corps *n.* **the Peace Corps** a U.S. government organization that helps poorer countries by sending VOLUNTEERS (=people who work without payment), especially young people, to teach skills in education, health, farming etc.

ˈpeace ˌdividend *n.* [singular] the money that is saved on weapons and available for other purposes, when a government reduces its military strength because the risk of war has been reduced

peace·ful /ˈpisfəl/ *adj.* **1** a peaceful time, place, or situation is quiet and calm without any worry or excitement SYN **tranquil**: *It's peaceful out here in the woods.* ▸see THESAURUS box at **quiet**[1] **2** without war, fighting, or violence: *a peaceful protest* | *the use of nuclear power for peaceful purposes* | **peaceful solution/conclusion/settlement** *Everyone hoped a peaceful solution might be found.* | *Will the two groups ever live in* ***peaceful coexistence*** (=exist together without fighting)? **3** peaceful people do not like violence and do not behave in a violent way: *a noisy but peaceful group of demonstrators* —**peacefully** *adv.* —**peacefulness** *n.* [U]

peace·keep·ing /ˈpisˌkipɪŋ/ *adj.* **peacekeeping force/troops etc.** a group of soldiers who are sent to a place in order to stop opposing groups from fighting each other —**peacekeeper** *n.* [C]

P

ˈpeace-ˌloving *adj.* believing strongly in peace rather than war: *peace-loving nations*

peace·mak·er /ˈpisˌmeɪkɚ/ *n.* [C] someone who tries to persuade other people or countries to stop fighting: *The U.S. wants to be a peacemaker in the region.*

ˈpeace march *n.* [C] a march by people who are protesting against violence or military activities

ˈpeace ˌoffering *n.* [C] something you give to someone to show them that you are sorry and want to be friendly, after you have annoyed or upset them: *Mike brought in some doughnuts – I think they were a sort of peace offering.*

ˈpeace pipe *n.* [C] a pipe which Native Americans use to smoke tobacco, which is shared in a ceremony as a sign of peace

peace·time /ˈpis-taɪm/ *n.* [U] a period of time when a nation is not fighting a war OPP **wartime**

peach /pitʃ/ S3 *n.* **1** [C] BIOLOGY a round juicy fruit with a soft yellow-red skin and a large hard seed in the center, or the tree that it grows on → see picture at FRUIT[1] **2** [U] a pale pinkish-orange color **3** [C usually singular] OLD-FASHIONED someone or something that you like very much or think is attractive: *Jan's a real peach.* **4 a peaches-and-cream complexion** smooth skin with an attractive pink color [**Origin:** 1200–1300 Old French *peche* from Latin *persicus* **Persian**]

ˈpeach fuzz *n.* [U] INFORMAL soft light body hair, especially hair that grows on a boy's face before he becomes a man

peach·y /ˈpitʃi/ *adj.* **1** tasting or looking like a peach **2** SPOKEN, OLD-FASHIONED very good or pleasant: *Everything here's just peachy.*

ˈpea coat *n.* [C] a short DOUBLE-BREASTED coat made with heavy wool, which used to be worn especially by SAILORS

peacock

pea·cock /ˈpikɑk/ *n.* [C] BIOLOGY a large bird, the male of which has long shiny blue and green tail feathers that it can lift up and spread out

ˌpeacock ˈblue *n.* [U] a deep greenish-blue color —**peacock blue** *adj.*

ˌpea ˈgreen *n.* [U] a light green color, like that of a PEA —**pea-green** *adj.*

ˈpea ˌjacket *n.* [C] a PEA COAT

peak[1] /pik/ W3 *n.* [C] **1** [usually singular] the time or point at which something is biggest, most successful, or best: *Oil production is* ***down from its peak*** *several years ago.* | *He is* ***at the peak of*** *his career.* | *As a tennis player, she's* ***past*** *her* ***peak.*** | **reach/hit a peak** *The city's population reached its peak a decade ago.* **2** the sharply pointed top of a mountain, or the whole mountain: *the Alps' snow-covered peaks* → see picture on page A31 → see also SUMMIT **3** a part that forms a point above a surface or at the top of something: *Whisk the egg whites until they form stiff peaks.* → see also WIDOW'S PEAK

peak[2] *v.* [I] to reach the highest point or level: *Sales* *peaked in August, then fell sharply.* | **+at** *Wind speeds peaked at 105 mph yesterday.*

peak³ *adj.* **1** used to talk about the best, highest, or greatest level or amount of something: *athletes who are in peak condition* | **peak level/rate/value etc.** *Gasoline prices are 14% below the peak level they hit in November.* **2** a peak time or period is when the largest number of people are doing the same thing, using the same service etc.: *Traffic increases during* ***peak hours***. → see also OFF-PEAK

peak·ed¹ /ˈpikɪd/ *adj.* pale and looking sick: *You're* ***looking*** *a little* ***peaked*** *this morning.*

P

peaked² /pikt, ˈpikɪd/ *adj.* **1** having a point at the top: *a peaked roof* **2** a peaked cap has a flat curved part at the front above the eyes

peal¹ /pil/ *n.* [C] **1** a sudden loud sound of laughter: **+of** *They burst into* ***peals of laughter***. **2** a loud ringing sound made by a bell or set of bells: **+of** ***a peal of*** *church* ***bells*** **3** a loud sound of THUNDER **4** TECHNICAL **a)** a musical pattern made by ringing a number of bells one after the other **b)** a set of bells

peal² also **peal out** *v.* [I] **1** ENG. LANG. ARTS if bells peal, they ring loudly **2** LITERARY to make a loud sound of laughter or THUNDER

Peale /pil/, **Charles** (1741–1827) a U.S. PAINTER famous for his pictures of people

Peale, Nor·man Vin·cent /ˈnɔrmən ˈvɪnsənt/ (1898–1993) a U.S. Protestant minister and SELF-HELP writer

pea·nut /ˈpinʌt/ S3 *n.* [C] a pale brown nut in a thin soft shell that grows under the ground, or the plant this nut grows on: *salted peanuts*

ˈpeanut ˌbrittle *n.* [U] a type of hard candy with peanuts in it

ˈpeanut ˌbutter *n.* [U] a soft substance made from crushed peanuts, usually eaten on bread: *a peanut butter and jelly sandwich*

ˈpeanut ˌgallery *n.* [C] HUMOROUS the cheap rows of seats at the back of a theater, or the people sitting there

pea·nuts /ˈpinʌts/ *n.* [U] INFORMAL a very small amount of money: *I'm tired of* ***working for peanuts***.

pear /pɛr/ *n.* [C] BIOLOGY a sweet juicy fruit that has a round wide bottom and becomes thinner on top near the stem, or the tree that it grows on [**Origin:** 1000–1100 Latin *pirum*] → see also PRICKLY PEAR

pearl /pɚl/ *n.*

1 JEWEL [C] **a)** a small white round object that is formed inside the shell of an OYSTER, and is considered valuable and used in jewelry: *a string of pearls* **b)** an artificial copy of this jewel

2 HARD SUBSTANCE [U] a hard shiny substance of various colors formed inside some SHELLFISH, which is used for decorating objects SYN **mother-of-pearl**: *pearl buttons*

3 pearls of wisdom an expression meaning "wise remarks," often used jokingly to mean slightly stupid remarks: *Do you have any other pearls of wisdom for us?*

4 LIQUID [C] LITERARY a small round drop of liquid: *Pearls of dew sparkled on the grass.*

5 EXCELLENT THING/PERSON [C usually singular] OLD-FASHIONED someone or something that is especially good or valuable: *a pearl of a wife* → see also **cast pearls before swine** at CAST¹ (19)

ˈpearl ˌdiver *n.* [C] someone who swims under the water in the ocean, looking for shells that contain pearls

ˌPearl ˈHarbor an important U.S. Navy base in Hawaii, which was attacked by Japanese planes in December 1941 without any warning. This made the U.S. start fighting in World War II.

ˈpearl ˌonion *n.* [C] a type of small white onion

pearl·y /ˈpɚli/ *adj.* pale in color and shiny, like a pearl: *a pearly white fish*

ˌpearly ˈgates *n.* [plural] **the pearly gates** HUMOROUS the entrance to heaven

ˌpearly ˈwhites *n.* [plural] INFORMAL, HUMOROUS your teeth

ˈpear-shaped *adj.* someone, especially a woman, who is pear-shaped is larger around the waist and HIPS than around the chest

Pea·ry /ˈpɪri/, **Rob·ert** /ˈrɑbɚt/ (1856–1920) a U.S. EXPLORER who was leader of the first group to reach the North Pole

peas·ant /ˈpɛzənt/ *n.* [C] **1** a poor farmer who owns or rents a small amount of land, either in past times or in poor countries: *the peasants who worked the land* **2** INFORMAL a stupid uneducated person who does not have good manners

peas·ant·ry /ˈpɛzəntri/ *n.* [U] **the peasantry** all the peasants of a particular country

pea·shoot·er /ˈpiˌʃuṭɚ/ *n.* [C] a small tube used by children to blow small objects, especially dried PEAS, at someone or something

peat /pit/ *n.* [U] EARTH SCIENCE a substance formed from decaying plants under the surface of the ground in some areas, which can be burned instead of coal, or mixed with earth to help plants grow well —**peaty** *adj.*

ˈpeat moss *n.* [U] **1** a type of MOSS (=soft green plant) that grows in wet areas **2** pieces of this plant used to help other plants grow

peb·ble /ˈpɛbəl/ *n.* [C] a small smooth stone found on the beach or on the bottom of a river —**pebbly** *adj.*

pe·can /pəˈkɑn, -ˈkæn/ *n.* [C] a long thin sweet nut with a dark shell, or the tree that it grows on, common in the southern states of the U.S.: *pecan pie* [**Origin:** 1700–1800 French *pacane*, from an Algonquian language]

pec·ca·dil·lo /ˌpɛkəˈdɪloʊ/ *n. plural* **peccadilloes, peccadillos** [C] something bad which someone does, especially involving sex, which is not regarded as very serious or important: *The public is willing to forgive him for his peccadillos.* [**Origin:** 1500–1600 Spanish *pecadillo*, from *pecado* **evil act**, from Latin *peccare* **to do evil**]

pec·ca·ry /ˈpɛkəri/ *n. plural* **peccaries** [C] a wild animal like a pig that lives in Central and South America

peck¹ /pɛk/ *v.* **1** [I,T] if a bird pecks something or pecks at something, it quickly and repeatedly moves its beak to try to eat it, make a hole in it etc.: **+at** *Chickens pecked at the corn on the ground.* **2 peck sb on the cheek/forehead etc.** to kiss someone quickly and lightly → see also HENPECKED, **hunt and peck** at HUNT¹ (5)

peck at sth *phr. v.* to eat only a little bit of a meal because you are not interested in it or not hungry: *She just pecked at her food.*

peck² *n.* [C] **1** a quick light kiss: *He* ***gave me a peck on the cheek***. **2** an action in which a bird pecks at something with its beak **3** a unit used for measuring dry substances such as fruit or grain, equal to 8 QUARTS or 8.81 liters

ˈpecking ˌorder *n.* [C] a social system within a particular group of people or animals, in which each one knows who is more important and less important than themselves: *He was once a star, but now he's* ***at the bottom of the*** *Hollywood* ***pecking order***.

Pe·cos Bill /ˌpeɪkɑs ˈbɪl/ a very strong COWBOY in old American stories

pecs /pɛks/ *n.* [plural] INFORMAL PECTORALS

pec·tin /ˈpɛktɪn/ *n.* [U] a chemical substance like sugar that is found in some fruits and that is added to JAM and JELL-O to make them more solid —**pectic** *adj.*

pec·to·ral /ˈpɛktərəl/ *adj.* relating to your chest: *pectoral muscles*

ˌpectoral ˈfin *n.* [C] BIOLOGY the FIN that is on the side of a fish's head and helps it to control the direction it swims in → see picture at FISH¹

pec·to·rals /ˈpɛktərəlz/ *n.* [plural] BIOLOGY your chest muscles: *bulging pectorals*

pe·cu·liar /pɪˈkyulyə/ *adj.* **1** strange, unfamiliar, or a little surprising, especially in a way that is not good SYN **strange** SYN **odd**: *This cheese has a peculiar smell.* | **it is peculiar that** *It seemed peculiar that no one noticed Tammy leaving.* ▸see THESAURUS box at **strange**[1] **2 be peculiar to sb/sth** to be a quality that only one particular person, place, or thing has SYN **be unique to**: *The problem of racism is not peculiar to this country.* **3** behaving in a strange and slightly crazy way SYN **strange** SYN **odd**: *Martha has been a little peculiar lately.* [**Origin:** 1400–1500 Latin *peculiaris* **of private property, special**, from *peculium* **private property**]

pe·cu·li·ar·i·ty /pɪˌkyuliˈærət̬i/ *n. plural* **peculiarities 1** [C] something that is a feature of only one particular place, person, situation etc.: +**of** *the peculiarities of his handwriting* **2** [C] a strange or unusual habit, quality etc. SYN **idiosyncrasy**: *Margaret regarded her mother's peculiarities with a fond tolerance.* **3** [U] the quality of being strange or unfamiliar

pe·cu·liar·ly /pɪˈkyulyəli/ *adv.* **1 peculiarly American/female/middle-class etc.** something that is peculiarly American, female etc. is a typical feature only of Americans, only of women etc.: *a peculiarly Japanese institution* **2** in a strange or unusual way: *John and Sylvia looked at me peculiarly.* **3** FORMAL especially or extremely: *a peculiarly difficult question*

pe·cu·ni·ar·y /pɪˈkyuniˌɛri/ *adj.* FORMAL relating to or consisting of money: *pecuniary losses*

ped·a·go·gi·cal /ˌpɛdəˈgɑdʒɪkəl/ *adj.* FORMAL relating to methods of teaching or the practice of teaching: *current pedagogical practices* —**pedagogically** /-kli/ *adv.*

ped·a·go·gy /ˈpɛdəˌgoʊdʒi, -ˌgɑ-/ *n.* [U] FORMAL the practice of teaching, or the study of teaching

ped·al[1] /ˈpɛdl/ *n.* [C] **1** one of the two parts of a bicycle that you push with your feet to make the bicycle go forward → see picture at BICYCLE[1] **2** a part in a car or on a machine that you press with your foot to control it: *the gas pedal* **3** ENG. LANG. ARTS a part on a piano or organ that you press with your foot to change the quality of the sound **4 put/push the pedal to the metal** to drive a car, truck etc. very fast [**Origin:** 1600–1700 French *pedale*, from Italian, from Latin *pedalis* **of the foot**]

pedal[2] *v.* [I,T] to ride a bicycle or other machine that has pedals → see also BACKPEDAL, SOFT-PEDAL

ˈpedal ˌpushers *n.* [plural] a type of pants worn by women, which reach the middle of the lower leg

ped·ant /ˈpɛdnt/ *n.* [C] DISAPPROVING someone who pays too much attention to rules or to small unimportant details —**pedantry** *n.* [U]

pe·dan·tic /pəˈdæntɪk/ *adj.* paying too much attention to rules or to small unimportant details: *Her book is informative and scholarly, but never pedantic.* —**pedantically** /-kli/ *adv.*

ped·dle /ˈpɛdl/ *v.* [T] **1** to sell something on the street, or by traveling from place to place: *Farmers come to Seoul to peddle rice.* ▸see THESAURUS box at **sell**[1] **2** to sell goods that people disapprove of because they are of low quality or dangerous, illegal etc.: *She now peddles cheap jewelry on TV.* **3** to try to get people to accept opinions, false information etc.: *The newspaper accused him of peddling lies to voters.* → see also INFLUENCE-PEDDLING

ped·dler /ˈpɛdlə/ *n.* [C] **1** someone who sells small things either in the street or going from place to place: *Smithson had been a rose peddler in Portland.* **2** a person who sells things, especially when they are illegal or of low quality: *arms peddlers* → see also PUSHER

ped·er·ast /ˈpɛdəˌræst/ *n.* [C] a man who has sex with a boy —**pederasty** *n.* [U]

ped·es·tal /ˈpɛdəstl/ *n.* [C] **1** the base on which a PILLAR or STATUE stands **2 put/place sb on a pedestal** to admire or love someone so much that you treat them or talk about them as though they are perfect, especially in a way that is annoying: *My last boyfriend put me on a pedestal.* **3 a pedestal table/sink etc.** a table, SINK etc. that is supported by a single COLUMN [**Origin:** 1500–1600 French *piédestal*, from Old Italian *piedestallo*, from *pie di stallo* **foot of the stall**]

pe·des·tri·an[1] /pəˈdɛstriən/ *n.* [C] someone who is walking, especially on a city street, as opposed to driving a car, riding a bicycle etc.

pedestrian[2] *adj.* **1** [only before noun] relating to pedestrians or used by pedestrians: *pedestrian traffic* **2** ordinary, uninteresting, and without any imagination: *The food was fairly pedestrian.*

peˌdestrian ˈcrossing *n.* [C] a CROSSWALK

pe·des·tri·an·ize /pəˈdɛstriəˌnaɪz/ *v.* [T] to change a street or shopping area into a place where vehicles are not allowed —**pedestrianization** /pəˌdɛstriənəˈzeɪʃən/ *n.* [U]

peˌdestrian ˈmall *n.* [C] a shopping area in the center of a city where cars, trucks etc. cannot go

pe·di·a·tri·cian /ˌpidiəˈtrɪʃən/ *n.* [C] a doctor who treats children

pe·di·at·rics /ˌpidiˈætrɪks/ *n.* [U] the area of medicine that deals with children and their illnesses —**pediatric** *adj.*: *a pediatric hospital*

ped·i·cure /ˈpɛdɪˌkyʊr/ *n.* [C,U] a treatment for the feet and TOENAILS, to make them more comfortable or beautiful —**pedicurist** *n.* [C] → see also MANICURE

ped·i·gree /ˈpɛdəˌgri/ *n.* **1** [C,U] the history and achievements of something or someone, especially when they are good and should be admired SYN **background**: *her strong academic pedigree* **2** [C,U] BIOLOGY the parents and other past family members of an animal, or an official written record of this: *a horse with a good pedigree* **3** [C] BIOLOGY an animal whose parents, grandparents etc. were all of the same breed **4** [C,U] someone's parents and the family members that came before them, especially in families of a high social class: *an impressive family pedigree* [**Origin:** 1400–1500 Anglo-French *pe de gru* **crane's foot**; because the lines connecting related people can look like the bird's foot]

ped·i·greed /ˈpɛdəˌgrid/ also **pedigree** *adj.* a pedigreed animal comes from a family that has been recorded for a long time and is considered to be of a very good breed: *pedigreed dogs* → see also PUREBRED, THOROUGHBRED

ped·i·ment /ˈpɛdəmənt/ *n.* [C] a three-sided piece of stone or other material placed above the entrance to a building, especially in the buildings of ancient Greece

pe·dom·e·ter /pəˈdɑmət̬ə/ *n.* [C] an instrument for measuring distance that has to be pushed by someone walking

ped·o·phile /ˈpɛdəˌfaɪl, ˈpi-/ *n.* [C] an adult who is sexually attracted to young children

pee[1] /pi/ S3 *v.* [I] INFORMAL to pass liquid waste from your body SYN **urinate**: *It smells like the cat peed in there.* | *I have to* ***go pee***. [**Origin:** 1700–1800 from the first letter of *piss*]

pee[2] *n.* [U] INFORMAL liquid waste passed from your body SYN **urine**

peek[1] /pik/ *v.* [I] **1** to look quickly at something, especially something that you are not supposed to see: *OK, don't look. No peeking!* | **peek out/in/into etc.** *Billy peeked out from under his blanket.* ▸see THESAURUS box at **look**[1] **2 peek out (from sth)** WRITTEN to appear slightly from behind or under something: *The moon peeked out from behind a cloud.* → see also PEEP

peek[2] *n.* [C] a quick look at something: ***Take a peek*** *and see if the cake's done.*

peek·a·boo /ˈpikəˌbu/ *interjection*, *n.* [U] a game played to amuse babies and young children, in which you hide your face and then show it again, saying "peekaboo!"

peel[1] /pil/ S3 *v.* **1** [T] to remove the skin from fruit or vegetables: *Could you peel an orange for me?* ▸see THESAURUS box at **cut**[1] → see picture on page A32 **2** [T always

+ adv./prep.] to remove something from the surface of something else, especially something that is stuck to it or fits tightly to it: **peel sth ↔ off** *Peel the label off and wash the bottle.* | **peel sth off/from sth** *I was trying to peel the sticker off the box.* | **peel sth ↔ away/back** *When the paint is dry, peel away the masking tape.* **3** [I] if skin, paper, or paint peels, it comes off, usually in small pieces: *I got sunburned, and now my face* (=the skin on my face) *is peeling.* [**Origin:** 1200–1300 Latin *pilare* **to remove the hair from**, from *pilus* **hair**] → see also **keep your eyes open/peeled** at EYE[1] (7)

peel off *phr. v.* **1** if something peels off, small pieces of it start to come off or become separated from the surface it is covering: *The wallpaper was starting to peel off.* **2 peel sth ↔ off** to take your clothes off, especially if they are wet or tight: *She peeled off her jeans.* **3** to leave a moving group of vehicles, aircraft etc. and go in a different direction: *The last two motorcycles peeled off to the left.* **4 peel off ↔ sth** to take a piece of paper money off the top of a pile of paper money, to give it to someone: *He peeled off a hundred dollar bill and gave it to me.*

peel out *phr. v.* to suddenly make a car start moving very quickly so that it makes a loud noise: +**of** *He peeled out of the driveway.*

peel[2] *n.* [C,U] the thick skin of some fruits and vegetables, especially the ones that you peel before eating: *a banana peel*

peel·er /ˈpilɚ/ *n.* [C] a special type of knife for removing the skin from fruit or vegetables

peel·ings /ˈpilɪŋz/ *n.* [plural] pieces of skin that have been removed from fruit or vegetables: *carrot peelings*

peep[1] /pip/ *v.* [I] **1** to look at something quickly and secretly, especially through a hole or opening: **peep into/through etc. sth** *A reporter once peeped through her bedroom window.* ►see THESAURUS box at **look**[1] **2** [always + adv./prep.] if something peeps from somewhere, it is just possible to see it: +**through/from etc.** *The wreck of an old car was peeping from the weeds.* → see also PEEK **3** [I] to make a short quiet high sound like the sound a young bird makes: *The chicks were peeping in the barn.*

peep[2] *n.* [C] **1 not a peep** INFORMAL used to say that someone does not or should not make a sound, communicate, complain etc.: *The baby didn't make a peep all night.* | *We **haven't heard a peep** from our daughter for weeks.* **2** a quick or secret look at something: *He got a peep at her face before she slammed the door.* **3** a short weak high sound like the sound a young bird makes: *the peep of the baby robins*

peep·ers /ˈpipɚz/ *n.* [plural] OLD-FASHIONED your eyes

ˈpeep-hole *n.* [C] a small hole in a door or wall that you can see through

peep·ing Tom /ˌpipɪŋ ˈtɑm/ *n.* [C] INFORMAL someone who secretly watches people, especially when they are undressing, having sex etc.

ˈpeep-show *n.* [C] **1** a type of show in which a man pays for a woman to take her clothes off while he watches through a window **2** a box containing moving pictures that you look at through a small hole or LENS

peer[1] /pɪr/ *n.* [C] **1** someone who is the same age as you, or has the same type of job, rank etc.: *She is highly respected by her peers.* → see also PEER GROUP, PEER PRESSURE **2** a member of the British NOBILITY

peer[2] *v.* [I always + adv./prep.] to look very carefully or hard, especially because you cannot see something well: **peer at/across/through etc. (sth)** *I realized he was peering at me over his glasses.* | *The door opened and a woman peered out.* ►see THESAURUS box at **look**[1]

ˈpeer group *n.* [C] a group of people who are the same age, are from the same social class, or have the same type of job etc.: *As children reach adolescence, peer groups become a more significant influence.*

peer·less /ˈpɪrlɪs/ *adj.* better than anyone or anything else: *B.B. King's peerless blues guitar playing*

ˈpeer ˌpressure *n.* [C] a strong feeling that you must do the same things as other people of your age if you want them to like you: *A lot of kids start drinking because of peer pressure.*

peeve /piv/ *n.* [C] INFORMAL something that annoys you: *One of my **pet peeves** (=things that annoy me most) is pointless meetings that go on forever.*

peeved /pivd/ *adj.* INFORMAL annoyed: *She was peeved that Murray hadn't remembered her birthday.*

pee·vish /ˈpivɪʃ/ *adj.* easily annoyed by small and unimportant things, or showing this: *The kids were peevish after the long car ride.* —**peevishness** *n.* [U]

pee·wee /ˈpiwi/ *n.* [C] INFORMAL a small child, or a very small adult —**peewee** *adj.*: *a peewee football game* (=for young children)

peg[1] /pɛg/ *n.* [C] **1** a short piece of wood, metal etc. that fits into a hole or is fastened to a wall, used especially for hanging things on, or instead of nails for fastening things together: *Samantha hung her hat on a peg.* **2 take/bring/knock sb down a peg (or two)** to make someone realize that they are not as important or as good at something as they think they are: *He deserved to be taken down a peg or two.* **3** ENG. LANG. ARTS a wooden screw used to tighten or loosen the strings of a VIOLIN, GUITAR etc. **4** also **tent peg** a pointed piece of wood or metal that you push into the ground in order to keep a tent in the correct position SYN **stake** **5** a fact or opinion that is used as a reason for doing something: *The fact that loans are available becomes **a peg on which to hang** a college career.* (=a reason to go to college) → see also **a square peg in a round hole** at SQUARE[1] (11)

peg[2] *v.* **pegged, pegging** [T] **1** ECONOMICS to set prices, values, salaries etc. at a particular level, or set them in relation to something else: **peg sth to sth** *In the past, most countries pegged their currencies to gold.* | **peg sth at sth** *Rents are pegged at market rates.* **2 peg sb/sth as sth** to believe or say that someone has a particular type of character, or that a situation has particular qualities: *Initial reports pegged the crime as drug-related.* | *I didn't **have** her **pegged as** a troublemaker.* **3** to fasten something somewhere with a peg

peg·board /ˈpɛgbɔrd/ *n.* **1** [C,U] thin board with holes in it, into which you can put pegs or hooks to hang things on, or a piece of this **2** [C] a small piece of board with holes in it, used to record the players' points in some games, especially card games

ˈpeg leg *n.* [C] INFORMAL an artificial leg without a foot, used especially in past times

Pei /peɪ/, **I. M.** (1917–) a Chinese-American ARCHITECT

Peirce /pɚs, pɪrs/, **Charles San·ders** /tʃɑrlz ˈsændɚz/ (1839–1914) a U.S. PHILOSOPHER

pe·jor·a·tive /pɪˈdʒɔrət̬ɪv, -ˈdʒɑr-/ *adj.* FORMAL a pejorative word or expression is used to show disapproval or to insult someone: *For the far right, the word "liberal" became a pejorative term.* —**pejoratively** *adv.* —**pejorative** *n.* [C]

Pe·king /ˌpiˈkɪŋ◂, ˌpeɪ-/ a name for the city of Beijing that was formerly used in English

Pe·king·ese, **Pekinese** /ˌpikəˈniz◂/ *n.* [C] a very small dog with a short flat nose and long silky hair

pe·lag·ic /pəˈlædʒɪk/ *adj.* BIOLOGY relating to or living in the ocean, far from shore: *a pelagic shark*

Pe·lé /pɛˈleɪ, ˈpeɪleɪ/ (1940–) a Brazilian SOCCER player, considered the best player ever by many people

pel·i·can /ˈpɛlɪkən/ *n.* [C] BIOLOGY a large water bird that catches fish for food and stores them in a deep bag of skin under its beak [**Origin:** 1000–1100 Late Latin *pelecanus*, from Greek]

pel·lag·ra /pəˈlægrə, -ˈleɪ, -ˈlɑ-/ *n.* [U] MEDICINE a disease caused by a lack of a type of B VITAMIN, that makes you feel tired and causes problems with your skin and CENTRAL NERVOUS SYSTEM

pel·let /ˈpɛlɪt/ *n.* [C] **1** a small hard ball made from ice, paper, food etc. **2** a small ball of metal made to be fired from a gun

pell-mell /ˌpɛl ˈmɛl◂/ *adv.* running or moving in a

fast uncontrolled way: *Rioters were rushing pell-mell through the streets.* —**pell-mell** *adj.*

pel·lu·cid /pəˈlusɪd/ *adj.* LITERARY **1** very clear in a way that can be seen through easily → see also TRANSLUCENT: *a pellucid stream* **2** very clear in meaning or style: *the book's pellucid prose*

Pel·o·pon·ne·sian War, the /ˌpɛləpəniʒən ˈwɔr/ HISTORY the war from 431–404 B.C. between groups of Greek states led by Athens and Sparta, which ended with the defeat of Athens

pelt¹ /pɛlt/ *v.* **1** [T] to attack someone or something by throwing a lot of things at them: **pelt sb/sth with sth** *Angry residents pelted Baker's car with tomatoes.* **2** [I,T] if rain or snow pelts a place or person, or if it pelts down, it is raining or snowing very heavily: *the cold rain that pelts this region in March* **3** [I always + adv./prep.] INFORMAL to run somewhere very fast: *Joey pelted down the street.*

pelt² *n.* [C] **1** the skin of a dead animal, especially with the fur or hair still on it: *mink pelts* **2** BIOLOGY the fur or hair of a living animal

pel·vic /ˈpɛlvɪk/ *adj.* BIOLOGY within or relating to your pelvis: *a pelvic exam*

pel·vis /ˈpɛlvɪs/ *n.* [C] BIOLOGY the set of large wide curved bones at the base of your SPINE, to which your legs are joined [**Origin:** 1600–1700 Latin **basin**] → see picture at SKELETON¹

Pen., pen. a written abbreviation of PENINSULA

pen¹ /pɛn/ S1 *n.* [C] **1** an instrument for writing or drawing with ink: *a ballpoint pen* | *a felt-tip pen* | *Write your papers* ***in pen*** (=using a pen) *not pencil.* **2** a small piece of land enclosed by a fence, where farm animals are kept → see also PIGPEN, PLAYPEN **3 put/set pen to paper** to begin to write **4 the pen** INFORMAL a PENITENTIARY SYN **prison** [**Origin:** (1) 1200–1300 Old French *penne* **feather, pen** from Latin *penna* **feather**]

pen² *v.* **penned, penning** [T] **1** FORMAL to write something such as a letter or article, especially with a pen: *a song penned by Kurt Cobain* **2** also **pen sth ↔ in/up** to shut an animal in a small enclosed area: *The cattle are penned up at night.* **3 be penned in/up** to be restricted or forced to remain in a small place SYN **be cooped up**: *She felt restless and penned in.*

pe·nal /ˈpinl/ *adj.* [only before noun] relating to the legal punishment of criminals: *the penal system* | *penal reform* | **a penal colony** (=a place far away from any other city where prisoners were kept, especially in past times)

ˈpenal ˌcode *n.* [C] LAW a set of laws and the punishments for not obeying these laws

pe·nal·ize /ˈpinlˌaɪz, ˈpɛn-/ *v.* [T] **1** to punish someone or treat them unfairly: *The proposed tax penalizes people living in rural areas.* | **penalize sb for (doing) sth** *Employees are not penalized for taking days off for child care.* **2** to punish a team or player in sports by giving an advantage to the other team: **penalize sb for (doing) sth** *Wallace was penalized twice for false starts.* —**penalization** /ˌpinl-əˈzeɪʃən/ *n.* [U]

pen·al·ty /ˈpɛnlti/ W3 *n. plural* **penalties** [C] **1** LAW a punishment for not obeying a law, rule, or legal agreement: **+for** *The penalty for a first offense is a fine.* | **+of** *a penalty of $100,000* | *a maximum penalty of one year in jail* | **a stiff/heavy/severe penalty** *The U.S. has stiff penalties for drug violations.* | *Murder* ***carries a*** *minimum* ***penalty of*** (=results in a penalty of) *15 years to life in prison.* | *They* ***imposed*** *stricter* ***penalties on*** (=give stricter penalites to) *those who commit crimes with guns.* → see also DEATH PENALTY ►see THESAURUS box at **punishment** **2** a disadvantage in sports given to a player or team for not obeying a rule: *A ten-yard penalty was given to the offense.* **3** a chance to kick the ball or hit the PUCK into the GOAL in a game of SOCCER, HOCKEY etc. given because the other team has not obeyed a rule **4** something bad that happens to you because of a bad decision you made in the past or because of the situation you are in: *If you don't do the job right, you'll* ***pay the penalty*** (=have problems) *later.* | *One of* ***the penalties of*** *being famous is the loss of privacy.*

ˈpenalty ˌarea *n.* [C] the area in front of the GOAL in SOCCER, in which the team opposing you is given a PENALTY if you do not obey a rule there

ˈpenalty ˌbox *n.* [C] **1** an area off the ice where a player in HOCKEY must wait after not obeying a rule **2** a penalty area

ˈpenalty ˌclause *n.* [C] part of a contract which says what someone will have to pay or do if they do not obey the agreement, for example if they fail to complete work on time

ˈpenalty ˌkick *n.* [C] a PENALTY in the game of SOCCER

pen·ance /ˈpɛnəns/ *n.* [C,U] punishment or suffering that you accept or give to yourself, especially for religious reasons, to show you are sorry for having behaved badly: *time spent in prayer and penance*

ˌpen-and-ˈink *adj.* [only before noun] a pen-and-ink drawing is drawn with a pen instead of a pencil

pen·chant /ˈpɛntʃənt/ *n.* [singular] **a penchant for sth** something you like doing or having very much and try to do or have often: *a penchant for gambling* | *the party's penchant for tax cuts*

pen·cil¹ /ˈpɛnsəl/ S3 *n.* [C,U] a narrow pointed wooden instrument, used for writing or drawing, containing a thin stick of a black or colored substance: *a sharp pencil* | *colored pencils* | *pencil drawings* | *a note written* ***in pencil*** (=using a pencil) [**Origin:** 1300–1400 Old French *pincel* **paintbrush**, from Latin *penicillus* **little tail**] → see also EYEBROW PENCIL, MECHANICAL PENCIL

pencil² *v.* **penciled, penciling** [T] to write something with a pencil or make a mark with a pencil: *a name penciled inside the back cover of the book* —**penciled** *adj.*

pencil in *phr. v.* **1 pencil sb/sth ↔ in** to make an arrangement for a meeting or other event, knowing that it might have to be changed later: *Let's pencil in a meeting for next Wednesday.* **2 pencil sth ↔ in** to draw or write something using a pencil, especially to add something to something that has already been written or drawn

ˈpencil ˌpusher *n.* [C] INFORMAL someone who has a boring unimportant job in an office

ˈpencil ˌsharpener *n.* [C] a small piece of equipment with a blade inside, used for making pencils sharp

ˌpencil-ˈthin *adj.* very thin: *a pencil-thin mustache* | *pencil-thin models*

pen·dant, pendent /ˈpɛndənt/ *n.* [C] a jewel or small decoration that hangs from a chain that you wear around your neck: *a diamond pendant*

pen·dent /ˈpɛndənt/ *adj.* **1** hanging from something: *a pendent lamp* **2** sticking out beyond a surface: *pendent ledges of rocks*

pend·ing¹ /ˈpɛndɪŋ/ *prep.* FORMAL while waiting for something, or until something happens: *Sales of the drug have been stopped, pending further research.*

pending² *adj.* FORMAL **1** not yet decided, agreed on, or finished: *Funeral arrangements are pending.* **2** something that is pending is going to happen soon: *the pending election*

pen·du·lous /ˈpɛndʒələs/ *adj.* LITERARY hanging down loosely and swinging freely: *pendulous breasts* —**pendulously** *adv.*

pen·du·lum /ˈpɛndʒələm/ *n. plural* **pendulums** [C] **1** a long stick or string with a weight at the bottom that swings regularly from side to side, and controls the operation of a large clock **2 the pendulum** used to talk about the tendency of ideas, beliefs etc. to change regularly from one position to an opposite one: *Today, the fashion pendulum is swinging back to more severe tailored styles.*

Pe·nel·o·pe /pəˈnɛləpi/ in ancient Greek stories, the wife of ODYSSEUS, who remained faithful to him while he was away from home for over 20 years

pen·e·trate /ˈpɛnəˌtreɪt/ *v.*
1 ENTER/GO THROUGH [I,T] to enter something or pass through it, especially when this is difficult: *The bullets*

penetrated the thick armor. | **penetrate into sth** *Oil had penetrated into the concrete.* | **penetrate through sth** *Light does not penetrate through water as easily as through air.*
2 SPREAD THROUGH [I,T] to spread through an area, group of people, society etc. and have an effect: *The fall weather outside penetrated the room.* | **penetrate into sth** *Islam has penetrated into vast parts of Africa and Asia.*
3 MOVE INTO AREA [I,T] to move into a place or area when someone is trying to stop you: *An American plane had penetrated deep into Russian defenses.* | **penetrate into sth** *The soldiers penetrated deep into enemy-held territory.*
4 BUSINESS [T] to succeed in selling your products in an area or country, especially when this is difficult: *Few U.S. companies have successfully penetrated the Japanese electronics market.*
5 ORGANIZATION [T] to join and be accepted into a group or an organization in order to find out their secrets: *Spies had penetrated the highest ranks of both governments.*
6 SEE THROUGH [T] to see into or through something even though it is difficult: *My eyes couldn't penetrate the gloom.*
7 UNDERSTAND [T] FORMAL to succeed in understanding something very difficult: *Scientists are attempting to penetrate the mysteries of deep space.* → see also IMPENETRABLE —**penetrable** /ˈpɛnətrəbəl/ *adj.* —**penetrability** /ˌpɛnətrəˈbɪləṭi/ *n.* [U]

pen·e·trat·ing /ˈpɛnəˌtreɪṭɪŋ/ *adj.* **1** showing a special ability to understand things very clearly and completely: *The book has several penetrating insights into teenage behavior.* | *a penetrating question* **2** a penetrating sound is loud, high, and often annoying: *a penetrating whistle* **3** penetrating looks or eyes make you feel uncomfortable and seem to see inside your mind: *her penetrating stare* **4** spreading and reaching everywhere: *penetrating cold*

pen·e·tra·tion /ˌpɛnəˈtreɪʃən/ *n.* **1** [C,U] the act of entering something or passing through it, especially when this is difficult: *Protect the wood against water penetration.* **2** [C,U] the act of moving into an area, especially when other people are trying to stop you: *enemy penetrations of U.S. airspace* **3** [U] the degree to which a product is available or is sold in an area: **+of** *The company is aiming to increase its penetration of overseas markets.* **4** [U] FORMAL the act or process of an idea or system of beliefs entering and becoming accepted by a society or group of people: **the penetration of sth into sth** *the penetration of Marxism into Latin America* **5** [U] the act of joining and being accepted by an organization, business etc. to find out secret information: *foreign penetration of the British secret service*

pen·e·tra·tive /ˈpɛnəˌtreɪṭɪv/ *adj.* showing a special ability to understand things very clearly and completely: *a penetrative thinker*

pen·guin /ˈpɛŋgwɪn/ *n.* [C] BIOLOGY a large black and white Antarctic sea bird, which cannot fly but uses its wings for swimming → see picture at FOOD CHAIN

pen·i·cil·lin /ˌpɛnəˈsɪlən/ *n.* [U] MEDICINE a substance used as a medicine to destroy BACTERIA

pe·nile /ˈpinaɪl/ *adj.* TECHNICAL relating to the penis

pe·nin·su·la /pəˈnɪnsələ/ *n.* [C] EARTH SCIENCE a piece of land almost completely surrounded by water but joined to a large mass of land: *the San Francisco peninsula* —**peninsular** *adj.*

pe·nin·su·lar /pəˈnɪnsələ˞/ *n.* [C usually plural] HISTORY someone in one of the Spanish colonies (COLONY) of Latin America from the 16th century through the early 19th century who had been born in Spain and therefore belonged to the highest social class

pe·nis /ˈpinɪs/ *n.* [C] BIOLOGY the sex organ of men and male animals, used in sexual activity and for getting rid of URINE from the body

ˈpenis ˌenvy *n.* [U] the desire of a girl or woman to have a penis, according to the ideas of Sigmund Freud

pen·i·tent¹ /ˈpɛnətənt/ *adj.* FORMAL feeling sorry because you have done something bad, and showing you do not intend to do it again: *Phil tried hard to look penitent.* —**penitently** *adv.* —**penitence** *n.* [U]

penitent² *n.* [C] someone who is doing religious PENANCE

pen·i·ten·tial /ˌpɛnəˈtɛnʃəl◂/ *adj.* FORMAL relating to being sorry for having done something wrong: *a penitential journey to a holy shrine*

pen·i·ten·tia·ry /ˌpɛnəˈtɛnʃəri/ *n.* [C] *plural* **penitentiaries** another word for a prison, used especially in names: *the North Carolina State Penitentiary*

pen·knife /ˈpɛn-naɪf/ *n. plural* **penknives** /-naɪvz/ [C] a small knife with blades that fold into the handle, usually carried in your pocket

pen·light /ˈpɛnlaɪt/ *n.* [C] a small thin FLASHLIGHT that is about the size of a pen

pen·man·ship /ˈpɛnmənˌʃɪp/ *n.* [U] the art of writing by hand, or skill in this art: *penmanship exercises*

Penn /pɛn/, **William** (1644–1718) an English religious leader who went to North America and established Pennsylvania as a place of religious freedom

ˈpen name *n.* [C] a name used by a writer instead of their real name

pen·nant /ˈpɛnənt/ *n.* [C] **1** a long narrow pointed flag used on ships or by schools, sports teams etc. **2 the pennant** the prize given to the best team in the American League and National League baseball competitions

Pen·ney /ˈpɛni/, **James** (1875–1971) a U.S. businessman who started the J. C. Penney chain of stores

pen·ni·less /ˈpɛnɪlɪs/ *adj.* having no money SYN **broke**: *a penniless student*

pen·non /ˈpɛnən/ *n.* [C] HISTORY a long narrow pointed flag, especially one carried on the end of a long pole by soldiers on horses in the Middle Ages

Penn·syl·va·nia /ˌpɛnsəlˈveɪnyə/ ABBREVIATION **PA** a state in the northeastern U.S. —**Pennsylvanian** *n.* [C]

pen·ny /ˈpɛni/ *n. plural* **pennies** [C]
1 U.S. COIN a coin that is worth one cent (1/100th of a dollar), used in the U.S. and Canada: *Do you have three pennies?* ▸see THESAURUS box at **money**
2 not a penny no money at all: *It wouldn't cost him a penny to go to college here.*
3 every penny all of an amount of money: *He's* ***worth every penny*** *they paid him.* | *It's all gone.* ***Every last penny*** (=used to emphasize that you mean "all") *of it.*
4 a penny saved is a penny earned SPOKEN used to say that it is a good idea to save money
5 the/your last penny the only money that is left: *They took everything she had, down to the last penny.*
6 not have a penny to your name to not have any money at all
7 a penny for your thoughts SPOKEN used to ask someone what they are thinking about when they are silent
8 in for a penny, in for a pound used to mean that if something has been started, it should be finished, whatever the cost may be
9 penny wise, pound foolish used to say that someone saves money on small things but spends too much on large things
10 BRITISH COIN [plural] **pence** a British coin that is worth 1/100th of a pound, or the value of this coin → see also **a bad penny** at BAD¹ (27), **cost a pretty penny** at PRETTY² (8)

ˈpenny ˌante *adj.* INFORMAL involving very small sums of money, and therefore not important: *penny-ante criminal activity* | *penny-ante investors*

ˈpenny ˌcandy *n.* [C,U] OLD-FASHIONED candy that costs one cent for a piece

ˈpenny-ˌpinching *adj.* unwilling to spend or give money: *a penny-pinching husband* —**penny pinching** *n.* [U] —**penny pincher** *n.* [C]

penny·weight /ˈpɛniˌweɪt/ *n.* [C] WRITTEN ABBREVIATION

dwt a unit for measuring weight, equal to 1/20 of an OUNCE (about 1.555 grams)

ˌpenny ˈwhistle *n.* [C] a simple musical instrument shaped like a tube with holes, which you blow down

pen·ny·worth /ˈpɛniˌwɚθ/ *n.* [singular + of] OLD USE as much as you can buy with a PENNY

Pe·nob·scot /pəˈnɑbskət, -skɑt/ a Native American tribe from the northeastern area of the U.S.

pe·nol·o·gy /pɪˈnɑlədʒi/ *n.* [U] the study of the punishment of criminals and the operation of prisons —**penologist** *n.* [C]

ˈpen pal *n.* [C] someone you make friends with by writing letters, especially someone in another country whom you have never met

pen·sion /ˈpɛnʃən/ *n.* [C] **1** the money that a company or organization pays regularly to someone who used to work there, after that person RETIRES (=stops working): *Howe **draws a** yearly **pension** of $22,000.* **2** a house like a small hotel where you can get a room and meals in France and some other European countries

pen·sion·er /ˈpɛnʃənɚ/ *n.* [C] someone who is receiving a pension

ˈpension fund *n.* [C] ECONOMICS a large amount of money that a company or organization etc. INVESTS and uses to pay PENSIONS

ˈpension plan *n.* [C] ECONOMICS a system organized by a company for paying PENSIONS to its workers when they become too old to work → see also RETIREMENT PLAN

pen·sive /ˈpɛnsɪv/ *adj.* thinking about something a lot, especially when this makes you seem worried or a little sad: *She was in a pensive mood.* —**pensively** *adv.*

penta- /pɛntə/ *prefix* five: *a pentagon* (=shape with five sides)

Pen·ta·gon /ˈpɛntəˌgɑn/ *n.* **the Pentagon** the U.S. government building from which the Army, Navy etc. are controlled, or the military officers who work in this building

pen·ta·gon /ˈpɛntəˌgɑn/ *n.* [C] MATH a flat shape with five sides —**pentagonal** /pɛnˈtægənl/ *adj.* → see picture at SHAPE[1]

pen·ta·gram /ˈpɛntəˌgræm/ *n.* [C] a five-pointed star, especially one used as a magic sign

pen·tam·e·ter /pɛnˈtæmət̬ɚ/ *n.* [C] ENG. LANG. ARTS a line of poetry with five main beats → see also IAMBIC PENTAMETER

pen·tath·lon /pɛnˈtæθlən, -lɑn/ *n.* [singular] a sports competition involving five different events SYN modern pentathlon

Pen·te·cost /ˈpɛntɪˌkɑst/ *n.* [C,U] **1** the seventh Sunday after Easter, when Christians celebrate the time when the Holy Spirit came from Heaven to Jesus Christ's followers **2** a Jewish religious holiday 50 days after Passover, celebrating the time when Moses received the Ten Commandments from God [**Origin:** 1000–1100 Late Latin *pentecoste*, from Greek, from *pentekostos* **fiftieth**]

Pen·te·cos·tal /ˌpɛntɪˈkɑstl◂/ *adj.* **1** relating to Christian churches whose members pray in special languages and believe that the Holy Spirit can help them to cure diseases **2** relating to the holiday of Pentecost —**Pentecostal** *n.* [C]

ˌPentecostal ˈchurches a group of Christian churches that are especially interested in the gifts of the HOLY SPIRIT

Pen·te·cos·tal·ist /ˌpɛntɪˈkɑstl-ɪst/ *n.* [C] someone who belongs to a Pentecostal church —**Pentecostalist** *adj.* —**Pentecostalism** *n.* [U]

pent·house /ˈpɛnthaʊs/ *n.* [C] a very expensive and comfortable apartment or set of rooms on the top floor of a building: *a penthouse apartment above Central Park*

ˈpent-up *adj.* **1** pent-up emotions are prevented from being freely expressed for a long time: *pent-up anger and frustration* **2 pent-up demand** a situation in which people want to buy something but have not been able to, for example because it has not been available: *a pent-up demand for consumer goods*

pe·nul·ti·mate /pɪˈnʌltəmɪt/ *adj.* [only before noun] FORMAL next to the last: *the penultimate game of the season*

pe·num·bra /pəˈnʌmbrə/ *n.* [C] TECHNICAL a slightly dark area between full darkness and full light

pe·nu·ri·ous /pəˈnʊriəs/ *adj.* FORMAL very poor

pen·u·ry /ˈpɛnyəri/ *n.* [U] FORMAL the state of being very poor SYN poverty: *Over two-thirds of the population lives **in penury**.*

pe·on /ˈpiɑn/ *n.* [C] **1** INFORMAL someone who works at a boring or physically hard job for low pay **2** someone in Mexico or South America who works as a kind of slave to pay his debts

pe·on·age /ˈpiənɪdʒ/ *n.* [U] HISTORY a system used especially in the past by which someone has to work for someone else to pay back a debt

pe·o·ny /ˈpiəni/ *n. plural* **peonies** [C] a garden plant with large round flowers that are dark red, white, or pink

peo·ple¹ /ˈpipəl/ S1 W1 *n.*

1 PERSONS [plural] used as the plural of "person" to mean men, women, and children: *How many people were at the concert?* | *I like the people I work with.*

2 PEOPLE IN GENERAL [plural] people in general, or people other than yourself: *People sometimes make fun of my name.* | *The advertising is aimed at young people.* | **business/theater etc. people** *Computer people seem to speak a language of their own.*

THESAURUS

the public ordinary people, not people who work for the government or other special organizations: *The building will be open to the public on weekends.*

society all the people who live in a country: *Volunteer groups make a huge contribution to society.*

the human race/mankind/humankind all the people in the world, considered as a group: *the origins of the human race*

population the number of people or animals living in a particular area, country etc.: *What's the population of Los Angeles?*

→ GROUP

3 the people [plural] all the ordinary people in a country who do not belong to the government or ruling class: *The mayor should remember that he was elected to serve the people.* | *Rice was the main food of **the common people*** (=ordinary people). | *Supporters viewed him as **a man of the people*** (=a politician who understands ordinary people).

4 NATION [C] the people who belong to a particular country, race, or area: *the diverse peoples of the world* | **the American/Japanese/Brazilian etc. people** *the history of the Iraqi people* | **+of** *The Statue of Liberty was a gift from the people of France.* | **native/indigenous/aboriginal people** (=race of people who have always lived in a country, as opposed to people who settled there from other places) ▸see THESAURUS box at race[1]

5 the People used in the names of court cases in which the U.S. government or a state government officially says that someone is guilty of a crime: *The People versus Thomas Stanton*

6 of all people SPOKEN used to say that someone is the one person who you would not have expected to do something: *You of all people should have realized the risks.*

7 you people SPOKEN used to talk about a group of people when you are annoyed with them: *Do you people have any idea how much trouble you've caused?*

8 a people person a person who is good at dealing with other people and likes to be or work with people, especially as part of their job

9 sb's people [plural] **a)** INFORMAL the people who work for a person or organization: *Your people have done a*

great job on this! **b)** the people that a king or leader rules or leads: *The rebel leader has urged his people to refrain from violence.* **c)** OLD-FASHIONED your family, especially your parents, grandparents etc.
10 TO GET ATTENTION SPOKEN, INFORMAL used to get the attention of a group of people: *Listen up, people!*
[**Origin:** 1200–1300 Old French *peuple*, from Latin *populus* **people**] → see also LITTLE PEOPLE, PERSON

people² *v.* [T usually passive] **1** FORMAL to be filled with people of a particular type: *The cafés downtown are peopled with college students.* **2** [T] to live in a place SYN **inhabit**: *The region has traditionally been peopled by Armenians.*

ˈpeople-ˌwatching *n.* [U] the act of watching different kinds of people who you do not know in a public place because you are interested in people and what they do: *Sunday afternoons on this street are great for people-watching.*

Pe·or·i·a /piˈɔriə/ a Native American tribe from the northeastern central area of the U.S.

pep¹ /pɛp/ *v.* **pepped**, **pepping**
pep sb/sth ↔ **up** *phr. v.* INFORMAL to make something or someone more active, interesting, or full of energy: *I had an espresso to pep myself up.* | *Interest rates are being lowered to pep up the economy.*

pep² *n.* [U] INFORMAL physical energy —**peppy** *adj.* → see also PEP BAND, PEP PILL, PEP RALLY, PEP SQUAD, PEP TALK

ˈpep band *n.* [C] a band that plays at sports events at a school or at a PEP RALLY

pep·per¹ /ˈpɛpɚ/ S2 W3 *n.* **1** [U] a powder that is usually black or gray which is used to add a slightly strong taste to food: *Pass the salt and pepper, please.* → see also BLACK PEPPER, WHITE PEPPER **2** a red powder like this, especially CAYENNE PEPPER or PAPRIKA **3** [C] BIOLOGY a hollow red, green, or yellow fruit with a sweet or SPICY taste that is eaten as a vegetable or added to other foods [**Origin:** Old English *pipor*, from Latin *piper*, from Greek *peperi*] → see also BELL PEPPER

pepper² *v.* [T] **1** to scatter things all over or all through something: **pepper sth with sth** *Her speech was peppered with jokes.* **2** to hit something with many bullets in a very short time: **pepper sth with sth** *Rebel forces peppered the parliament building with gunfire.* **3 pepper sb with questions** to ask someone many questions, one after the other: *At every stop, reporters peppered Davis with questions.* **4** to add pepper to food

ˌpepper-and-ˈsalt *adj.* SALT-AND-PEPPER

pep·per·corn /ˈpɛpɚˌkɔrn/ *n.* [C] the small dried fruit from a tropical plant which is crushed to make pepper

ˈpepper mill *n.* [C] a small piece of kitchen equipment which is used to crush peppercorns into pepper

pep·per·mint /ˈpɛpɚˌmɪnt/ *n.* **1** [U] BIOLOGY a MINT plant with strong-tasting leaves, which is often used in candy, tea, and medicine **2** [U] the taste of this plant: *peppermint candy* **3** [C] a candy with this taste

pep·pe·ro·ni /ˌpɛpəˈroʊni/ *n.* [C,U] a strong-tasting red Italian SAUSAGE: *pepperoni pizza*

ˈpepper ˌshaker *n.* [C] a small container with little holes in the top used for shaking pepper onto food

ˈpepper ˌspray *n.* [C,U] a substance, used especially by the police for controlling people, containing red pepper that can be SPRAYed in people's eyes to make them blind for a short time

pep·per·y /ˈpɛpəri/ *adj.* **1** having the taste of pepper: *a peppery sauce* **2** easily annoyed or made angry

ˈpep pill *n.* [C] a PILL containing a drug that gives you more energy for a short time

ˈpep ˌrally *n.* [C] a meeting of all the students at a school before a sports event, when CHEERLEADERS lead students in encouraging their team to win

pep·sin /ˈpɛpsən/ *n.* [U] BIOLOGY a liquid in your stomach that changes food into a form that can be used by your body

ˈpep squad *n.* [C] a group of CHEERLEADERS who perform at school sports events or pep rallies

ˈpep talk *n.* [C] INFORMAL a short speech that is intended to encourage you to work harder, win a game etc.: *a pre-game pep talk from the coach*

pep·tic ul·cer /ˌpɛptɪk ˈʌlsɚ/ *n.* [C] MEDICINE a sore painful place inside the stomach caused by the action of pepsin

pep·tide /ˈpɛptaɪd/ *n.* [C] CHEMISTRY an ORGANIC compound consisting of two or more AMINO ACIDS joined together in a chain. PROTEINS are formed when many peptides are connected to each other.

Pepys /pips/, **Samuel** (1633–1703) an English writer famous for his DIARY which describes his personal life and the important events of the time

Pe·quot /ˈpikwɑt/ a Native American tribe from the northeastern area of the U.S.

ˌPequot ˈWar, the HISTORY a war in 1637 between English SETTLERS in America and the Pequot tribe, in which the Pequot tribe was defeated

per /pɚ/ S1 W1 *prep.* **1** for each: *Oranges are 39 cents per pound.* | *My car gets about 30 miles per gallon* (=for each gallon of gasoline). | *Entry costs $55* ***per head*** (=for each person). **2 per hour/day/week etc.** during each hour, day etc.: *City buses carry about 20,000 passengers per day.* | *The speed limit is 65* ***miles per hour***. **3** FORMAL according to what has been agreed or what you have been asked to do: *I purchased a one-way ticket* ***as per*** *your instructions.* **4 as per usual** SPOKEN used when something annoying happens which has often happened before: *Alicia was late, as per usual.* **5 as per normal** SPOKEN used to say that something happens in the way it usually happens: *Life continued as per normal.* [**Origin:** 1300–1400 Latin **through, by**] → see also PER ANNUM, PER CAPITA

per·am·bu·late /pəˈræmbyəˌleɪt/ *v.* [I,T] OLD-FASHIONED to walk around or along a place without hurrying —**perambulation** /pəˌræmbyəˈleɪʃən/ *n.* [C,U]

per an·num /pɚ ˈænəm/ WRITTEN ABBREVIATION **p.a.** *adv.* for or in each year: *an inflation rate of about 4% per annum*

per·cale /pɚˈkeɪl, -ˈkæl/ *n.* [U] a type of cotton cloth, used especially for making bed sheets

per cap·i·ta /pɚ ˈkæpət̬ə/ *adj., adv.* TECHNICAL for or by each person in a particular place: *Per capita income rose by 1.2% last year.*

per·ceive /pɚˈsiv/ Ac W3 *v.* [T not in progressive] **1** to understand or think of something or someone in a particular way: **perceive sb/sth as sb/sth** *The tax system was* ***widely perceived*** (=perceived by many people) *as unfair.* | **perceive sb/sth to be sth** *High-tech industries are perceived to be crucial to the country's economic growth.* | **perceive that** *Many students perceive that on-the-job training is more important than college.* **2** FORMAL to notice something, especially something that is difficult to notice: *Emma perceived a slight bitterness in his tone.* **3** TECHNICAL to be able to see something: *Cats are not able to perceive color.* → see also PERCEPTION

per·ceived /pɚˈsivd/ Ac *adj.* a perceived situation or possibility is one which people believe exists, even though it may not exist or even though it may be different from what people believe: *the perceived threat to national security*

percent¹ /pɚˈsɛnt/ Ac S1 W2 *n. plural* **percent** [C] an amount equal to a particular number of parts in every 100 parts. The sign for this word is %: *The money was divided up and they each got 25%.* | **+of** *More than 70 percent of the country's population is younger than 25.*

percent² Ac W1 *adj., adv.* **1** equal to a particular number of parts in every 100 parts. The sign for this word is %: *Our "Gold" credit card only charges 8.5 percent interest.* | *You're supposed to leave a 15% tip* (=15 cents for every dollar you have spent on a meal). **2 a/one hundred percent** completely SYN **totally**: *I agree with you a hundred percent.*

per·cent·age /pɚˈsɛntɪdʒ/ Ac S3 W2 *n.* **1** [C,U] MATH an amount or number that is part of a total amount, when the total is thought of as having 100 parts: **+of** *The percentage of students over 35 has increased.* | **a high/low/large/small etc. percentage** *A growing percentage of women are choosing not to get married.* | *Prices have fallen by three* ***percentage points*** *this month.* **2** [C usually singular] a share of profits equal to a particular amount of every dollar: *He gets a percentage for every book that is sold.* **3 there is no percentage in (doing) sth** INFORMAL used to say that there is no advantage or profit in doing something

GRAMMAR

Percentage is singular, but if the noun that follows **a percentage of** is plural, use a plural verb: *A high percentage of shoppers downtown are tourists.*

per·cen·tile /pɚˈsɛnˌtaɪl/ *n.* [C usually singular] MATH one of 100 equal-sized groups that a set of data is divided into: *Dumont third-graders scored* ***in the 87th percentile*** *in reading* (=they did better than 87 percent of other students).

per·cep·ti·ble /pɚˈsɛptəbəl/ *adj.* FORMAL able to be noticed or seen OPP **imperceptible**: *a* ***barely perceptible*** *change* —**perceptibly** *adv.*

per·cep·tion /pɚˈsɛpʃən/ Ac W3 *n.* **1** [C] the way you understand or think of something and your beliefs about what it is like: **+about** *a false perception about the dangers of nuclear power* | **+of** *children's perceptions of the world* | **+that** *There's a perception that all lawyers are overpaid.* **2** [U] the way that you notice things with your senses: **+of** *Part of the brain controls our perception of pain.* **3** [U] a natural ability to understand or notice things that are not easy to notice: *Ross shows unusual perception for a boy of his age.* [**Origin:** 1300–1400 Latin *perceptio*, from *percipere*]

per·cep·tive /pɚˈsɛptɪv/ *adj.* APPROVING good at noticing and understanding what is happening or what other people are thinking or feeling: *a perceptive observer of the political scene* | *perceptive comments* —**perceptively** *adv.* —**perceptiveness** *n.* [U]

per·cep·tu·al /pɚˈsɛptʃuəl/ *adj.* FORMAL relating to the way you see things, hear things, understand things etc.: *children's perceptual abilities*

perch¹ /pɚtʃ/ *n.* **1** [C] a branch, stick etc. where a bird sits, especially in a CAGE **2** [C] a high place or position, especially one where you sit and watch something: *She watched the parade from her perch on her father's shoulders.* **3** [C,U] BIOLOGY a type of fish that lives in lakes, rivers etc., or the meat of this fish

perch² *v.* **1** [I] if a bird perches on something, it sits on it: **+in/on** *Birds like to perch in nearby trees.* **2** to place something on top of, or on the edge of something else, especially not firmly: *She perched the tray on her knees.* **3 be perched on/upon/over etc. sth** if a building or other object is perched on something, it is in a position on top of or on the edge of something: *The castle is perched on top of a cliff.* **4 perch (yourself) on sth** to sit on top of, or on the edge of, something: *He had perched himself on a tall wooden stool.*

per·chance /pɚˈtʃæns/ *adv.* OLD USE or LITERARY **1** perhaps **2** by chance

per·cip·i·ent /pɚˈsɪpiənt/ *adj.* FORMAL quick to notice and understand things SYN **perceptive** —**percipience** *n.* [U]

per·co·late /ˈpɚkəˌleɪt/ *v.* **1** [I,T] if coffee percolates, or if you percolate it, you make coffee by passing hot water through crushed coffee beans in a special pot **2** [I] if an idea, feeling, piece of information etc. percolates, it gradually develops or spreads: *She already has an idea percolating for her next novel.* | **percolate (down) through sth** *The message has begun to percolate through the school.* **3** [I always + adv./prep.] if liquid, air, or light percolates somewhere, it passes slowly through a surface that has very small holes in it: **percolate through/down/into sth** *Rainwater percolates down through the rock.* —**percolation** /ˌpɚkəˈleɪʃən/ *n.* [C,U]

per·co·la·tor /ˈpɚkəˌleɪtɚ/ *n.* [C] a pot in which coffee is percolated

per·cus·sion /pɚˈkʌʃən/ *n.* [U] **1 the percussion** ENG. LANG. ARTS the part of an ORCHESTRA or band that consists of drums and other instruments that are played by being hit with an object such as a stick or hammer **2** ENG. LANG. ARTS these instruments in general, considered as a group: *percussion instruments* **3** the sound or effect of two things hitting each other with great force

per·cus·sion·ist /pɚˈkʌʃənɪst/ *n.* [C] someone who plays percussion instruments

per di·em¹ /pɚ ˈdiəm/ *n.* [C] an amount of money that an employer gives a worker each day or allows them to spend each day for additional things while doing their job, especially when they are on a business trip

per diem² *adv.* FORMAL for or in each day: *Our consultants receive $500 per diem plus expenses.*

per·di·tion /pɚˈdɪʃən/ *n.* [U] LITERARY complete destruction or failure

per·e·gri·na·tion /ˌpɛrəgrəˈneɪʃən/ *n.* [C usually plural] LITERARY a long trip, especially in foreign countries

per·e·grine fal·con /ˌpɛrəgrən ˈfælkən/ also **peregrine** *n.* [C] BIOLOGY a hunting bird with a black and white spotted front

pe·remp·to·ry /pəˈrɛmptəri/ *adj.* FORMAL **1** peremptory behavior, speech etc. is not polite or friendly and shows that the person speaking does not want to be argued with: *a peremptory tone of voice* **2 a peremptory challenge** LAW an opportunity for a lawyer to have someone removed from a JURY without giving a reason —**peremptorily** *adv.*

per·en·ni·al¹ /pəˈrɛniəl/ *adj.* **1** happening again and again, or existing for a long time: *Mickey Mouse remains a perennial favorite.* | *perennial problems of the local economy* **2** BIOLOGY relating to plants that live for more than two years —**perennially** *adv.*

perennial² *n.* [C] BIOLOGY a plant that lives for more than two years → see also ANNUAL² (1), BIENNIAL (2)

perˌennial irriˈgation *n.* [U] a system for supplying land or crops with water all through the year

per·e·stroi·ka /ˌpɛrəˈstrɔɪkə/ *n.* [U] HISTORY the policies (POLICY) of social, political, and economic change that happened in the U.S.S.R. in the 1980s just before the end of the COMMUNIST government

per·fect¹ /ˈpɚfɪkt/ S1 W2 *adj.* **1** of the best possible type or standard, without any faults or mistakes: *We had perfect weather the whole trip.* | *Michiko's English is perfect.* | *The quilt is* ***in almost perfect condition.*** **2** exactly right for a particular purpose, situation, or person SYN **ideal**: *That's a perfect example of the problems we're having.* | **+for** *It's a perfect frame for that picture.* | *I think he'd be perfect for you.* | **the perfect place/opportunity/time etc. to do sth** *It was the perfect place to have a picnic.*

THESAURUS

ideal being the best that something could possibly be: *It's an ideal vacation spot for families.*
just right being the best or most appropriate for something: *The weather was just right for a day at the beach.*

3 [only before noun] complete or total: *He doesn't mind asking perfect strangers for help.* | *Cindy's been a perfect angel all morning.* | *You* ***have a perfect right to*** (=it is completely reasonable for you to) *be angry.* | *His explanation* ***made perfect sense*** (=was completely reasonable) *to me.* **4 nobody's perfect** SPOKEN said when you are answering someone who has criticized you or someone else: *OK, so he made some mistakes – nobody's perfect.* **5 the perfect gentleman/student/host etc.** someone who behaves exactly as a gentleman, student etc. ought to behave [**Origin:** 1200–1300 Old French *parfit*, from Latin *perfectus*, past participle of *perficere* **to do completely, finish**] → see also **the perfect crime** at

CRIME (7), PERFECTLY, **practice makes perfect** at PRACTICE[1] (7)

per·fect² /pɚˈfɛkt/ *v.* [T] to make something perfect or as good as you are able to: *I spent three years in Mexico City perfecting my Spanish.*

per·fect³ /ˈpɚfɪkt/ *n.* TECHNICAL **the perfect** perfect tenses are formed using a form of the verb "have" with a PAST PARTICIPLE → see also FUTURE PERFECT, PAST PERFECT, PRESENT PERFECT

ˌperfect compeˈtition also **ˌpure compeˈtition** *n.* [U] ECONOMICS a situation in which a lot of companies are producing the same product or providing the same service, and all the things that have an effect on the cost of producing the product or providing the service are the same for every company

P

per·fect·i·ble /pɚˈfɛktəbəl/ *adj.* able to be improved or made perfect

per·fec·tion /pɚˈfɛkʃən/ *n.* [U] **1** the state of being perfect: *Our father expected perfection from all of us.* | *The bacon was cooked **to perfection*** (=perfectly). **2** the process of making something perfect: *He spent years in the perfection of his beer-brewing techniques.* **3** a perfect example of something: *The sushi was pure perfection.*

per·fec·tion·ist /pɚˈfɛkʃənɪst/ *n.* [C] someone who is not satisfied with anything unless it is perfect —**perfectionist** *adj.* —**perfectionism** *n.* [U]

per·fect·ly /ˈpɚfɪktli/ S2 W3 *adv.* **1** used to emphasize that you mean "completely": *The boy stood perfectly still.* | *He's not welcome here. We made that perfectly clear.* | *They were throwing out a **perfectly good** DVD player* (=one that was in perfect condition). **2** in a perfect way: *The plan worked perfectly*

ˌperfect ˈparticiple *n.* [C] ENG. LANG. ARTS a PAST PARTICIPLE

ˌperfect ˈpitch *n.* [U] the ability to correctly name any musical note that you hear, or to sing any note at the correct PITCH without the help of an instrument

ˌperfect ˈsquare *n.* [C] MATH a number whose SQUARE ROOT is a WHOLE NUMBER. For example, 25 is a perfect square whose square root is 5.

per·fid·i·ous /pɚˈfɪdiəs/ *adj.* LITERARY disloyal and not able to be trusted: *a perfidious scheme* —**perfidy** /ˈpɚfədi/ *n.* [U]

per·fo·rat·ed /ˈpɚfəˌreɪt̬ɪd/ *adj.* **1** paper that is perforated has a line of small holes in it so that part of it can be torn off easily: *a perforated sheet of stamps* **2** something that is perforated, especially a part of the body, has had a hole or holes cut in it or torn in it: *a perforated eardrum* | *Use a perforated spatula to stir the mixture.* —**perforate** *v.* [T] FORMAL

per·fo·ra·tion /ˌpɚfəˈreɪʃən/ *n.* **1** [C] a small hole in something, or a line of holes made in a piece of paper so that it can be torn easily **2** [U] the action or process of making a hole or holes in something

per·form /pɚˈfɔrm/ S3 W1 *v.* **1** [I,T] ENG. LANG. ARTS to do something to entertain people, for example by acting in a play or playing a piece of music: *The opera was performed in over 100 cities.* | *Griffin loves performing in front of a live audience.* | **perform in sth** *Perez is currently performing in "The Nutcracker."* **2** [T] to do something, especially something difficult or something useful: *Surgery was performed Friday to correct the heart defects.* | **perform a task/duty/service** *Rubin says he will resign when he is no longer able to perform his duties.* | **perform a function/role** *These sharks peform a useful function by cleaning the ocean floor.* | **perform an experiment/study/analysis** *The experiments were performed on rats.* | *The priest from our church will **perform the ceremony*** (=lead a wedding ceremony). | *You can't expect me to **perform miracles*** (=do things that seem impossible). **3** [I] to work or do something in a successful or unsuccessful way: *A child's home life will affect how he or she performs in school.* | **perform well/badly/poorly etc.** *All systems on the space shuttle appear to be performing well.* | *The electronics industry continues to perform poorly.* **[Origin:** 1300–1400 Anglo-French *performer*, from Old French *perfournir*, from *fournir* **to complete]**

per·form·ance /pɚˈfɔrməns/ S2 W1 *n.* **1** [C] ENG. LANG. ARTS an act of performing a play, piece of music etc., or an occasion when it is performed: *It was the band's last performance together.* | **+of** *The festival opens with a performance of Mozart's "Requiem."* | *Nicole Kidman **gives a** moving **performance** as the mother.* | *Their recordings are not as good as their **live performances*** (=one that takes place in front of an audience). **2** [U] how well or badly you do a particular job or activity: *the company's economic performance* | **poor/good performance** *His performance at school was better this year.* **3** [U] how well a car or other machine works: *Its performance on mountain roads was impressive.* | *a **high-performance** car* (=very powerful car) **4** [U] how much money a product, business etc. makes: **+of** *the disappointing performance of the bond market* **5** [U] the act of doing a piece of work, duty etc.: **+of** *The police failed in the performance of their duties.* **6 a performance** SPOKEN, DISAPPROVING something that someone does in a very noticeable way, especially in order to attract a lot of attention to themselves: *Then she burst into tears. It was quite a performance.*

perˈformance ˌart *n.* [U] a type of art that can combine acting, dance, painting, film etc. to express an idea —**performance artist** *n.* [C]

perˈformance-enˌhancing *adj.* [only before noun] a performance-enhancing drug or substance is used illegally by people competing in sports events to improve their performance

perˈformance-reˌlated *adj.* [only before noun] performance-related pay, BENEFITS etc. increase when your work improves and decrease if the opposite happens

perˈformance reˌview also **perˈformance evaluˌation** *n.* [C] a meeting between a worker and a manager to discuss how the worker is doing in his or her job, what might happen in the future etc.

per·form·er /pɚˈfɔrmɚ/ *n.* [C] **1** ENG. LANG. ARTS an actor, musician etc., who performs to entertain people: *a group of talented young performers* | *The city is full of street performers.* **2** a person, product, business etc. that is good or successful, or bad or unsuccessful: *children who are poor performers at school* | **the star/top/outstanding performer** *This product has been an outstanding performer.* | *the team's star performer*

perˌforming ˈarts *n.* **the performing arts** arts such as dance, music, and DRAMA, which are performed to entertain people

per·fume¹ /ˈpɚfyum, pɚˈfyum/ *n.* [C,U] **1** a liquid that has a strong pleasant smell, that women put on their skin or clothing to make themselves smell nice: *She **wears** too much **perfume**.* → see also COLOGNE **2** a sweet or pleasant smell: *the rose's heady perfume* ▸see THESAURUS box at **smell**[1] **[Origin:** 1500–1600 French *parfum***]**

per·fume² /pɚˈfyum/ *v.* [T] **1** LITERARY to fill something with a sweet pleasant smell: *The sweet scent of sagebrush perfumed the air.* **2** to add perfume or something else to make something smell nice —**perfumed** *adj.*: *a perfumed envelope*

per·fum·er·y /pɚˈfyuməri/ *n. plural* **perfumeries** **1** [C] a place where perfumes are made or sold **2** [U] the process of making perfumes

per·func·to·ry /pɚˈfʌŋktəri/ *adj.* FORMAL a perfunctory action is done quickly or without interest, and only because people expect it: *a perfunctory apology* —**perfunctorily** *adv.*

per·go·la /ˈpɚɡələ/ *n.* [C] a structure made of posts built for plants to grow over in a garden

per·haps /pɚˈhæps/ S2 W1 *adv.* FORMAL **1** possibly SYN **maybe**: *I wonder if perhaps I offended him somehow.* **2** used to give your opinion, when you do not want to be too definite SYN **maybe**: *This is, perhaps, her finest novel yet.* **3** used to say that a number is only a guess SYN **maybe**: *It was a big space, perhaps*

60 by 80 feet. **4** SPOKEN, FORMAL used to politely say, ask, or suggest something SYN **maybe**: *Perhaps you'd like to speak to my supervisor.* [**Origin:** 1400–1500 *per* + *haps*, plural of *hap* **chance**]

per·i·car·di·um /ˌperiˈkardiəm/ *n.* *plural* **pericardia** /-diə/ [C] TECHNICAL the MEMBRANE that is filled with liquid that surrounds the heart

per·i·gee /ˈperədʒi/ *n.* [C] PHYSICS the point where the moon, a SATELLITE, or other object that is traveling in a curved path through space around the Earth is nearest the Earth OPP **apogee**

per·il /ˈperəl/ *n.* FORMAL **1** [U] great danger, especially of being harmed or killed: *They put their own lives **in peril** to rescue us.* **2 perils** [plural] the dangers or problems relating to a particular activity or situation: *the perils that lie ahead in life* | **the perils of sth** *The men survived the perils of ice, snow, and storms.* **3 do sth at your peril** to do something that is very dangerous or could cause very serious problems for you: *We destroy the rainforests at our peril.*

per·il·ous /ˈperələs/ *adj.* LITERARY very dangerous: *a perilous mountain road* —**perilously** *adv.*: *We came to a stop perilously close to the edge.*

pe·rim·e·ter /pəˈrɪmət̬ɚ/ *n.* [C] **1** the border around an enclosed area of land: *the perimeter of the airfield* | *a perimeter fence* **2** MATH the whole length of the border around an area or shape → see also CIRCUMFERENCE

per·i·na·tal /ˌperəˈneɪt̬l◂/ *adj.* BIOLOGY at or around the time when a woman gives birth: *perinatal health care*

pe·ri·od¹ /ˈpɪriəd/ Ac S1 W1 *n.* [C]
1 LENGTH OF TIME a length of time with a beginning and an end: *Both his parents died within a short period.* | **a three-month/two-year etc. period** *The loan has to be repaid over a 15-month period.* | **+of** *Cleve went through several periods of depression.* | *The new taxes will be introduced over a **period of time**.* | *You can get the magazine for **a trial period*** (=period to try something to see if it is good or works).
2 HISTORY a particular time in history: *the Civil War period* | **a period of/in history** *an extremely violent period in the country's history*
3 IN DEVELOPMENT a) a particular time during someone's life, relationship SYN **time**: *It was one of the happiest periods in my life.* **b)** a particular time during the development of someone's artistic style: *Picasso's Cubist period* | **sb's early/late period** *a work from Storni's early period*
4 WOMEN sb's period BIOLOGY the monthly flow of blood from a woman's UTERUS: *I'm going to get my **period** soon.*
5 DOT ENG. LANG. ARTS the mark (.) used in writing that shows the end of a sentence or of an ABBREVIATION ▸see THESAURUS box at **punctuation mark**
6 SCHOOL one of the equal parts that the school day is divided into, during which students study a particular subject: *Mike has Spanish second period.* ▸see THESAURUS box at **school¹**
7 SPORTS one of the equal parts that a game is divided into in a sport such as HOCKEY
8 UNIT OF TIME BIOLOGY a period of time into which an ERA is divided, in the scientific study of rocks, soil, and minerals, and the way they have changed since the Earth was formed
9 period! SPOKEN used to emphasize that a decision has been made and there is nothing more to discuss: *I'm not giving them any more money, period!*
10 MATH MATH the space between regularly repeated values of a mathematical FUNCTION
[**Origin:** 1300–1400 French *période*, from Latin, from Greek, from *peri-* + *hodos* **way**]

period² Ac *adj.* **period costume/furniture etc.** clothes, furniture etc. in the style of a particular time in history: *actors dressed in period costume* → see also PERIOD PIECE

pe·ri·od·ic /ˌpɪriˈɑdɪk◂/ Ac also **periodical** *adj.* [only before noun] happening many times over a long period, usually at regular times: *periodic crop failures* —**periodically** /-kli/ *adv.*: *The information on our website is updated periodically.*

pe·ri·od·i·cal /ˌpɪriˈɑdɪkəl/ Ac *n.* [C] a magazine, especially one about a serious or technical subject, that comes out at regular times such as once a month

ˌperiodic ˈfunction *n.* [C] MATH a mathematical FUNCTION (=quantity that changes according to how another quantity changes) whose values are repeated again and again in a regular pattern → see also PERIOD OF FUNCTION

ˌperiodic ˈtable *n.* **the periodic table** CHEMISTRY a list of ELEMENTS arranged according to their ATOMIC structure

ˌperiod of ˈfunction *n.* [C] MATH the smallest length of the X-AXIS that a periodic function goes over before repeating

per·i·o·don·tal /ˌperioʊˈdɑntl/ *adj.* TECHNICAL relating to the part of the mouth at the base of the teeth: *periodontal disease*

ˈperiod piece *n.* [C] **1** a movie or play whose story takes place during a particular period in history: *a Victorian period piece* **2** something such as a piece of furniture or work of art that comes from a particular period in history

per·i·os·te·um /ˌperiˈɑstiəm/ *n.* [U] BIOLOGY a thick layer of TISSUE (=matter in the body made of many cells) that covers the surface of all bones except for the joints, and to which muscles and TENDONS are attached

per·i·pa·tet·ic /ˌperəpəˈtet̬ɪk◂/ *adj.* FORMAL traveling from place to place, especially in order to do your job: *peripatetic priests* | *a peripatetic lifestyle*

pe·riph·e·ral¹ /pəˈrɪfərəl/ *adj.* **1** not as important as other things or people in a particular activity, situation etc.: *He had only a peripheral role in the negotiations.* | **+to** *Their love story is peripheral to the main plot.* ▸see THESAURUS box at **unimportant** **2** in the outer area of something, or relating to this area: *the peripheral nervous system* **3** COMPUTERS peripheral equipment can be connected to a computer and used with it —**peripherally** *adv.*

peripheral² *n.* [C] COMPUTERS a piece of equipment that is connected to a computer and used with it, such as a screen or a PRINTER

peˌripheral ˈvision *n.* [U] your ability to see things to the side of you when you are looking straight ahead

pe·riph·er·y /pəˈrɪfəri/ *n.* **1** [C usually singular] the outer area or edge that surrounds a place SYN **edge**: **on the periphery of sth** *stores on the periphery of downtown* **2 on/at the periphery (of sth)** only slightly involved in a group or activity: *beggars on the periphery of society*

pe·riph·ra·sis /pəˈrɪfrəsɪs/ *n.* *plural* **periphrases** /-siz/ [C,U] FORMAL ENG. LANG. ARTS the unnecessary use of long words or phrases or unclear expressions —**periphrastic** /ˌperəˈfræstɪk/ *adj.*

per·i·scope /ˈperəˌskoʊp/ *n.* [C] a long tube with mirrors inside it, used to look over the top of something, especially to see out of a SUBMARINE

per·ish /ˈperɪʃ/ *v.* **1** [I] LITERARY to die, especially in a terrible or sudden way: *Sanchez perished in a mudslide in 1985.* **2** [I] LITERARY to stop existing or be destroyed: *We must make sure that democracy does not perish.* **3 Perish the thought!** SPOKEN used to say that an unacceptable idea that has just been mentioned would never happen, and often used in a joking way to say that something is actually likely to happen: *I'm not trying to criticize his judgment – perish the thought!* → see also **publish or perish** at PUBLISH (5)

per·ish·a·ble /ˈperɪʃəbəl/ *adj.* perishable food is likely to decay if it is not kept in the correct conditions: *perishable crops like fruits and vegetables* —**perishables** *n.* [plural]

per·i·stal·sis /ˌperəˈstɔlsɪs, -ˈstæl-/ *n.* *plural* **peristalses** /-siz/ [C] BIOLOGY a series of movements of muscles in the DIGESTIVE TRACT, stomach, or INTESTINE that act in waves to push food, waste etc. along through the body

per·i·to·ni·tis /ˌperət̚nˈaɪt̬ɪs/ *n.* [U] MEDICINE a poisoned and sore condition of the inside wall of your ABDOMEN (=part around and below your stomach)

per·i·win·kle /ˈpɛrɪˌwɪŋkəl/ *n.* **1** [C] BIOLOGY a small plant with light blue or white flowers that grows close to the ground **2** [C] BIOLOGY a small ocean animal that lives in a shell and can be eaten **3** [U] a light blue color

per·jure /ˈpɚdʒɚ/ *v.* [I] **perjure yourself** to tell a lie after promising to tell the truth in a court of law —**perjurer** *n.* [C]

per·jured /ˈpɚdʒɚd/ *adj.* **perjured statements/testimony** lies that someone tells after promising to tell the truth in a court of law

P

per·ju·ry /ˈpɚdʒəri/ *n.* [U] LAW the crime of telling a lie after promising to tell the truth in a court of law, or a lie told in this way

perk¹ /pɚk/ *n.* [C usually plural] money, goods, or other advantages that you get from your job in addition to the money you are paid: +**of** *One of the perks of the job is the use of a company car.*

perk² *v.* [I,T] INFORMAL to make coffee using a PERCOLATOR

perk up *phr. v.* INFORMAL **1 perk sb ↔ up** to become more cheerful, active, and interested in what is happening around you, or to make someone feel this way: *The dogs always perk up when we come home.* | *She was taking some herbal energy pills to perk herself up.* **2 perk sth ↔ up** to become more active, more interesting, more attractive etc., or to make something do this: *Congress is hoping the economy will perk up soon.* | *You can perk up the sauce with some fresh lime juice.*

Per·kins /ˈpɚkənz/, **Fran·ces** /ˈfrænsɪs/ (1882–1965) a U.S. social REFORMER who was the first woman to hold a CABINET position in the U.S. government

perk·y /ˈpɚki/ *adj. comparative* **perkier**, *superlative* **perkiest** INFORMAL confidently cheerful and active —**perkiness** *n.* [U]

perm¹ /pɚm/ *n.* [C] a process of putting curls into straight hair, by chemical treatment: *Did you get a new perm?*

perm² *v.* [T] to put curls into straight hair by means of a chemical treatment

per·ma·frost /ˈpɚməˌfrɔst/ *n.* [U] EARTH SCIENCE a thick layer of permanently frozen ground just below the top layer of soil in countries where it is very cold for most of the year

per·ma·nence /ˈpɚmənəns/ also **per·ma·nen·cy** /ˈpɚmənənsi/ *n.* [U] the state of being permanent: *our desire for a feeling of permanence in our lives* | *the permanence of a parent's love*

per·ma·nent¹ /ˈpɚmənənt/ S3 W3 *adj.* **1** continuing to exist for a long time or for all future time OPP **temporary**: *Mr. Lo has applied for permanent residence in the U.S.* | *Alex seems to have become **a permanent fixture*** (=someone or something that is always there) *around here.* **2** relating to work or jobs that is certain to last for a long time, or having a job or position of this kind OPP **temporary**: *a permanent job* | *Only five of the firm's employees are permanent.* [**Origin:** 1400–1500 Latin, present participle of *permanere* **to stay till the end**]

permanent² *n.* [C] a PERM

per·ma·nent·ly /ˈpɚmənəntli/ *adv.* always, or for a very long time: *The accident left him permanently paralyzed.* | *I came to this city intending to live here permanently.*

ˌpermanent ˈpress *n.* [U] a process of treating cloth so that it does not WRINKLE easily, or cloth that has been treated in this way

ˌpermanent ˈwave *n.* [C] OLD-FASHIONED a PERM

per·me·a·ble /ˈpɚmiəbəl/ *adj.* TECHNICAL material that is permeable allows water, gas etc. to pass through it OPP **impermeable**: *a permeable membrane* —**permeability** /ˌpɚmiəˈbɪləṭi/ *n.* [U]

per·me·ate /ˈpɚmiˌeɪt/ *v.* **1** [T] if ideas, beliefs, emotions etc. permeate something, they are present in every part and have an effect on all of it: *Racism permeates the entire organization.* **2** [I always + adv./prep., T] if liquid, gas etc. permeates something, it enters it and spreads through every part of it: *The smell of smoke permeated the house.* | **permeate through/into sth** *Toxic vapors can permeate into the plaster and wood.* —**permeation** /ˌpɚmiˈeɪʃən/ *n.* [U]

per·mis·si·ble /pɚˈmɪsəbəl/ *adj.* FORMAL allowed by law or by the rules SYN **allowable**: *permissible levels of radiation*

per·mis·sion /pɚˈmɪʃən/ S2 *n.* [U] an act of allowing someone to do something, especially in an official or formal way: **permission to do sth** *Producers did not **have permission** to use the song.* | **ask/get (sb's) permission** *You have to ask permission before you take the car.* | *They **gave** us **permission** to use the pool.* | **refuse/deny permission** *The organizers were refused permission to hold the demonstration.*

per·mis·sive /pɚˈmɪsɪv/ *adj.* not strict, and allowing behavior, especially sexual behavior, that many other people disapprove of: *permissive divorce laws* | *He had very permissive parents.* —**permissiveness** *n.* [U] *sexual permissiveness*

per·mit¹ /pɚˈmɪt/ W2 *v.* **permitted, permitting** [T usually passive] **1** FORMAL to allow something to happen, especially by an official decision, a rule, or a law: *Horseback riding is not permitted in the park.* | **permit sb to do sth** *No one is permitted to pick the flowers.* | **permit sth in/near etc. sb/sth** *No one under 17 will be permitted in the theater.* | **permit sb sth** *Workers are permitted five sick days per year.* ►see THESAURUS box at **allow** **2** [I, T] to make it possible for something to happen: *The new system permits greater flexibility.* | **permit sb/sth to do sth** *Different package sizes permit consumers to buy exactly as much as they need.* | *We're going to the beach this weekend, **weather permitting*** (=if the weather is good). | ***If time permits*** (=if there is enough time), *you can repeat the process.* [**Origin:** 1400–1500 Latin *permittere* **to let through, allow**]

permit of sth *phr. v.* FORMAL to make something possible: *The facts permit of no other explanation.*

per·mit² /ˈpɚmɪt/ *n.* [C] an official written statement giving you the right to do something: +**for** *Do you have a permit for that gun?* | **a permit to do sth** *Farmers must apply for permits to use the new chemicals.* | **a travel/work/export etc. permit** (=an official document allowing you to travel, work etc.) | **a parking/fishing/hiking etc. permit** (=one that allows you to leave your car somewhere, catch fish etc.) → see also WORK PERMIT

per·mu·ta·tion /ˌpɚmyʊˈteɪʃən/ *n.* [C] **1** one of the different ways in which a set of things can be arranged, combined, or put in order: *The dinners on the menu are mostly permutations of beef, chicken, noodles, and rice.* **2** MATH in mathematics and other sciences, an ordered arrangement of the numbers, TERMS etc. of a set into specific groups —**permute** /pɚˈmyut/ *v.* [T] → see also COMBINATION

per·ni·cious /pɚˈnɪʃəs/ *adj.* FORMAL very harmful or evil, but often in a way that is difficult to notice: *the pernicious effects of advertising* | *a pernicious lie* —**perniciously** *adv.*

perˌnicious aˈnemia *n.* [U] MEDICINE a form of severe ANEMIA that will kill someone if it is not treated

Pe·rón /pəˈroʊn, peɪ-/, **E·va** /ˈeɪvə/ also **E·vi·ta** /ɛˈvitə/ (1919–1952) the first wife of the Argentinian President Juan Perón

Perón, Juan Do·min·go /wɑn dəˈmɪŋgoʊ/ (1895–1974) the President of Argentina from 1946 to 1955 and again in 1973–1974

per·o·ra·tion /ˌpɛrəˈreɪʃən/ *n.* [C] FORMAL **1** ENG. LANG. ARTS the last part of a speech, especially a part in which the main points are repeated **2** a long speech that sounds impressive but does not have much meaning

per·ox·ide /pəˈrɑkˌsaɪd/ *n.* [U] a chemical liquid used to make dark hair lighter or to kill BACTERIA

perˌoxide ˈblonde *n.* [C] OLD-FASHIONED a woman who has changed the color of her hair to very light yellow by using peroxide

per·pen·dic·u·lar[1] /ˌpɚpən'dɪkyələr/ *adj.* **1** if one line is perpendicular to another line, they form an angle of 90 degrees where they cross: *perpendicular lines* | **+to** *First Street is perpendicular to Main Street.* **2** not leaning to one side or the other but exactly upright SYN **vertical**: *a perpendicular pole* **3 Perpendicular** in the style of 14th- and 15th-century English churches which are decorated with straight upright lines —**perpendicularly** *adv.*

perpendicular[2] *n.* MATH **1 the perpendicular** an exactly upright position or line: *at an angle to the perpendicular* **2** [C] a line that is perpendicular to another line

ˌperpendicular 'bisector *n.* [C] MATH a line that crosses a line segment at 90 degrees and divides it into two equal parts

ˌperpendicular 'lines *n.* [plural] MATH two lines that cross and form a 90 degree angle

per·pe·trate /'pɚpəˌtreɪt/ *v.* [T] FORMAL to do something that is seriously wrong or criminal: *groups that perpetrate bombings and other acts of terror* | **perpetrate sth against sb** *Many abuses have been perpetrated against farm workers.* [**Origin:** 1500–1600 Latin, past participle of *perpetrare* **to achieve something**] —**perpetration** /ˌpɚpə'treɪʃən/ *n.* [U]

per·pe·tra·tor /'pɚpəˌtreɪtɚ/ *n.* [C] someone who does something that is seriously wrong or criminal: **+of** *the perpetrator of a sex crime*

per·pet·u·al /pɚ'pɛtʃuəl/ *adj.* **1** continuing all the time without changing SYN **constant**: *These deep sea creatures live in perpetual darkness.* **2** repeated many times in a way that annoys you SYN **constant**: *perpetual interruptions during the meeting* —**perpetually** *adv.*

perˌpetual 'motion *n.* [U] **1** the idea that a machine would be able to continue moving forever without getting energy from anywhere else, which is not considered possible **2 be in perpetual motion** INFORMAL to be very active for a long time without stopping: *She seemed to be in perpetual motion, never stopping to relax.*

per·pet·u·ate /pɚ'pɛtʃuˌeɪt/ *v.* [T] to make a situation, attitude etc., especially a bad one, continue to exist: *We have an education system that perpetuates the problems in our society.* —**perpetuation** /pɚˌpɛtʃu'eɪʃən/ *n.* [U]

per·pe·tu·i·ty /ˌpɚpə'tuət̬i/ *n.* **in perpetuity** LAW for all future time

per·plex /pɚ'plɛks/ *v.* [T] to be difficult to understand in a way that makes you feel worried and confused SYN **puzzle**: *Shea's symptoms perplexed the doctors.* —**perplexing** *adj.*: *perplexing questions*

per·plexed /pɚ'plɛkst/ *adj.* confused and worried by something that you cannot understand SYN **puzzled**: **+by/about** *He seemed rather perplexed by these criticisms.*

per·plex·i·ty /pɚ'plɛksət̬i/ *n. plural* **perplexities** **1** [C usually plural] something that is complicated or difficult to understand: *moral perplexities* **2** [U] the feeling of being confused or worried by something you cannot understand

per·qui·site /'pɚkwəzɪt/ *n.* [C] FORMAL a PERK

Per·ry /'pɛri/, **Matthew** (1794–1858) the U.S. Navy officer who made the agreement with Japan that started trade between Japan and the U.S.

per se /ˌpɚ 'seɪ/ *adv.* used to say that something is being considered alone, apart from anything else: *We're not against the changes per se, it's the speed of change which is a problem.*

per·se·cute /'pɚsɪˌkyut/ *v.* [T] **1** to treat someone cruelly or unfairly, especially because of their religious or political beliefs: *Christians were often persecuted under Communism.* | **persecute sb for sth** *He was persecuted for his beliefs.* **2** to deliberately cause trouble for someone by annoying them often, asking them too many questions etc. SYN **harass**: *He says he is being persecuted by a hostile media.* [**Origin:** 1400–1500 French *persécuter*, from Latin *persecutus*, past participle of *persequi* **to pursue, follow**] —**persecutor** *n.* [C]

per·se·cu·tion /ˌpɚsɪ'kyuʃən/ *n.* [C,U] the act of persecuting someone: **+of** *the persecution of journalists who criticized the government* | *Thousands of people left to* **escape** *religious* **persecution**.

perse'cution ˌcomplex *n.* [C] MEDICINE a mental illness in which someone believes that other people are always trying to harm them

Per·seph·o·ne /pɚ'sɛfəni/ in Greek MYTHOLOGY, the goddess of the spring, who returns to Earth each year after spending the winter months in the UNDERWORLD

per·se·ver·ance /ˌpɚsə'vɪrəns/ *n.* [U] APPROVING determination to keep trying to achieve something in spite of difficulties: *Her perseverance paid off and she eventually became world champion.*

per·se·vere /ˌpɚsə'vɪr/ *v.* [I] APPROVING to continue trying to do something in a very determined way, in spite of difficulties: **persevere in/with sth** *U.S. leaders have encouraged Adams to persevere in his efforts to bring peace.* —**persevering** *adj.*

Per·shing /'pɚʃɪŋ/, **John** (1860–1948) the leader of the U.S. Army Expeditionary Force in Europe during World War I

Per·sian[1] /'pɚʒən/ *n.* **1** [U] the language of Iran SYN **Farsi** **2** [C] OLD-FASHIONED someone from Iran, especially in the time when it was called Persia

Persian[2] *adj.* relating to or coming from Iran, especially from the time when it was called Persia: *a Persian carpet*

ˌPersian 'cat *n.* [C] a type of cat with long silky hair

ˌPersian 'Gulf, the a part of the Indian Ocean between Iran and Saudi Arabia

ˌPersian Gulf 'War, the HISTORY see GULF WAR, THE

per·sim·mon /pɚ'sɪmən/ *n.* [C] BIOLOGY a soft orange-colored fruit that grows in hot countries

per·sist /pɚ'sɪst/ Ac *v.* [I] **1** to continue doing something in a determined way, even though you do not immediately get the result that you want: *He persisted and finally someone came to the door.* | **persist in/with sth** *Anna persisted with her studies in spite of money problems.* **2 persist in (doing) sth** to continue to do something, even though it is unreasonable or annoying to others: *Why does she persist in believing she doesn't need help?* **3** to continue to exist or happen: *If the pain persists, call a doctor.* [**Origin:** 1500–1600 French *persister*, from Latin *persistere*, from *sistere* **to stand firm**]

per·sist·ence /pɚ'sɪstəns/ Ac *n.* [U] **1** determination to do something even though it is difficult or other people oppose it: *Their persistence was rewarded with a touchdown in the last minute of the game.* **2** the state of continuing to exist or happen, especially for longer than is usual or desirable: *the persistence of inequalities*

per·sist·ent /pɚ'sɪstənt/ Ac *adj.* **1** continuing to exist or happen, especially for longer than is usual or desirable: *Unemployment has been a persistent problem.* | *persistent headaches* **2** continuing to do something even though it is difficult or other people oppose it: *If she hadn't been so persistent, she wouldn't have gotten the job.* | *persistent efforts to bring the warring factions together* —**persistently** *adv.*

per·snick·e·ty /pɚ'snɪkət̬i/ *adj.* INFORMAL **1** worrying too much about small and unimportant things SYN **picky**: *She's persnickety about her clothes.* **2** difficult to do or use because you have to deal with a lot of small details: *a persnickety task*

per·son /'pɚsən/ S1 W1 *n.* **1** [C] *plural* **people** /'pipəl/ a man, woman, or child, especially considered as someone with their own character: *The person who finishes first gets a special prize.* | *Kevin's not an easy person to get to know.* | **kind/type/sort of person** *So, what kind of person is he?* | *She's a great actor, but what's she like* **as a person?** | **a morning/computer/cat/city etc. person** (=someone who likes a particular thing or activity) → see also PEOPLE[1] **2 in person** doing

P

something yourself, without asking another person to do it, or using the phone, a letter etc. to do it: *You have to sign for the package in person.* **3 businessperson/salesperson etc.** someone who works in business, who sells things etc. → see also CHAIRPERSON, SPOKESPERSON **4** [C] *plural* **persons** FORMAL or LAW someone who is not known or not named: *This elevator can hold up to 12 persons.* | *No person under 21 allowed.* **5** [C] *plural* **persons** FORMAL in someone's pockets or hidden in their clothes: *Hide your passport securely* ***on your person.*** **6 in the person of sb** FORMAL used before someone's name to emphasize that this is the person that you are talking about in relation to a larger group or organization that you have mentioned: *I was met by the police in the person of Sergeant Black.* [**Origin:** 1100–1200 Old French *persone*, from Latin *persona* **actor's mask, character in a play, person**] → see also FIRST PERSON, MISSING PERSON, PERSON-TO-PERSON, SECOND PERSON, THIRD PERSON

P

GRAMMAR

• **Person** means one man, woman, or child: *Will is the smartest person I know.* **Persons** is one possible plural form of **person**, but this is only used in very official language: *Unauthorized persons will be escorted from the premises.*

• When talking about more than one **person**, use **people** as the plural: *There were at least 30 people at the party.* **People** can also sometimes be a countable noun, meaning a particular race or group that lives in a country or area. With this meaning, its plural is **peoples**: *the peoples of Central Asia.*

per·so·na /pɚˈsoʊnə/ *n.* [C] **1** *plural* **personas, personae** /-ni/ the way you behave when you are with other people or in a particular situation, which may be different from other situations: *Green's on-screen persona* (=the way she behaves when acting in movies) *is cute and innocent.* **2** *plural* **personae** /-ni/ ENG. LANG. ARTS **a)** the character or voice that represents the NARRATOR in a book, play etc.: *The author used the persona of a teenage girl to tell the story.* **b)** any of the characters in a book, play etc. → see also PERSONA NON GRATA

per·son·a·ble /ˈpɚsənəbəl/ *adj.* having an attractive appearance and a pleasant polite way of talking and behaving: *a very personable young man*

per·son·age /ˈpɚsənɪdʒ/ *n.* [C] FORMAL **1** a famous or important person: *notable personages* **2** a character in history or in a NOVEL, play etc.

per·son·al /ˈpɚsənəl/ S2 W1 *adj.*

1 RELATING TO YOU [only before noun] used to emphasize that something is done, known, experienced, felt etc. by you: *My personal opinion is that we should offer him the job.* | *The President made a direct personal appeal to the terrorists.* | *She has the* ***personal qualities*** *needed to be successful in business.* | *I know* ***from personal experience*** *how difficult this kind of work is.* | *Her gifts always have a* ***personal touch*** (=something personal you do that makes something special).

2 PRIVATE concerning only you, especially the private areas of your life: *Beth had a lot of personal problems at that time.* | *Can I ask you a personal question?* | *I'm sorry I can't give you* ***personal information*** *about our customers* (=about where they live, how old they are etc.). | *I don't answer questions about my* ***personal life.*** ▶see THESAURUS box at private[1]

3 BELONGING TO YOU [only before noun] used to emphasize that something belongs only to you, or someone works only for you: *I've got my own personal web site.* | *a personal fitness trainer* | *After Alan's death, his mother received his* ***personal effects*** (=small possessions, clothing, documents etc. of someone who has died). | **personal possessions/property/belongings** (=things belonging only to you)

4 DONE BY HUMANS involving direct communication between people, or done by people rather than by machines or in writing: *Internet classes don't give you any personal contact with the teacher.*

5 CRITICISM involving rude or upsetting criticism of someone: *a bitter personal attack on the Senator* | *It's unprofessional to make such* ***personal remarks*** (=unkind remarks about someone's appearance or behavior). | ***Nothing personal*** (=I am not criticizing you)*, but I'd like to be alone right now.*

6 a personal friend someone that you know well, especially a famous or important person: *David is* ***a close personal friend of*** *Bill and Hillary.*

7 NOT WORK not relating to your work, business, or official duties: *We're not allowed to make personal phone calls at work.*

8 YOUR BODY [only before noun] relating to your body or the way you look: *a manufacturer of personal care products* | *personal hygiene*

9 personal development the improvements in your character that come from your experiences in life

ˈpersonal ˌad *n.* [C] a short advertisement put in a newspaper or magazine by someone who wants a romantic relationship or friendship → see also PERSONALS

ˌpersonal asˈsistant *n.* [C] someone who works for one person and helps them do their job

ˌpersonal ˈbest *n.* [C] a result of a race, competition etc. that is better than anything you have done before —**personal-best** *adj.*

ˌpersonal ˈcheck *n.* [C] a CHECK (=piece of paper you sign and use instead of money) that is written by an ordinary person rather than a company or bank

ˌpersonal comˈputer *n.* [C] COMPUTERS a PC; the usual type of computer that is used by one person for business or at home

ˌpersonal elecˌtronic deˈvice *n.* [C] FORMAL a piece of electronic equipment, such as a LAPTOP computer or CELL PHONE, that is small and easy to carry

ˌpersonal exˈemption *n.* [C] a specific part of the total amount of money that you earn in a year, on which you do not have to pay INCOME TAX

ˌpersonal identifiˈcation ˌnumber also **PIN** *n.* [C] a number that you use when you put your plastic bank card into a machine in order to get money out of your bank account

per·son·al·i·ty /ˌpɚsəˈnæləṭi/ S2 W3 *n.* *plural* **personalities 1** [C,U] someone's character, especially the way they behave toward other people: *A 17-year-old with a lively personality.* | *My personality is very different from my brother's.* | *His temper is one of his least attractive* ***personality traits.*** | **a personality clash/conflict** (=a situation in which two people do not live or work well together because their personalities are very different) **2** [C] someone who is very well known and often in the newspapers, on television etc., especially an entertainer or sports person: **a TV/radio/sports etc. personality** *Barnes is a local radio personality.* **3** [U] qualities of character that make someone interesting or enjoyable to be with: *The Senator is a good reliable man, but he lacks personality.* **4** [U] the qualities that make a place or thing special and different: *Each of the three islands has a distinct personality.*

personˈality ˌcult also **ˌcult of personˈality** *n.* [C] the officially encouraged practice of giving too much admiration, praise, love etc. to a leader, especially a political leader

per·son·al·ize /ˈpɚsənəˌlaɪz/ *v.* [T] **1** to put someone's name or INITIALS on something: *You can ask the author to personalize the book with your child's name.* **2** to design, make, or change something so that it is useful or appropriate for a particular person's needs, wishes, or personality: *We try to personalize our presentation for each client.* | *Let's do something to personalize your office a little more.* **3** if someone or something personalizes a situation, it makes people pay attention to specific people involved in the situation, rather than thinking about the situation in general: *The President has personalized the debate by attacking his opponents by name.* | *Meeting someone with AIDS personalizes the disease for many people.* —**personalized** *adj.*: *personalized stationery* —**personalization** /ˌpɚsənələˈzeɪʃən/ *n.* [U]

ˌpersonalized ˈlicense plate *n.* [C] a VANITY PLATE

per·son·al·ly /ˈpɚsənəli/ S2 W3 *adv.* **1** [sentence

adverb] ESPECIALLY SPOKEN used to emphasize that you are only giving your own opinion about something: *Personally, I don't care how you do it.* | *Most of our customers like French wine, though I personally prefer Californian.* **2** doing something yourself, or affecting you yourself rather than someone else: *It's best to write about things you have experienced personally.* | *Maureen is **personally responsible** for all the arrangements.* **3 take sth personally** to let yourself get upset or hurt by the things other people say or do: *Please don't take it personally – he doesn't want to see anyone.* **4 not know sb personally** used to say that you do not know someone at all or not very well: *I don't know him personally, but I love his music.* **5** in a way that unfairly criticizes someone's character or appearance: *Members of the Senate rarely attack each other personally.*

personal organizers

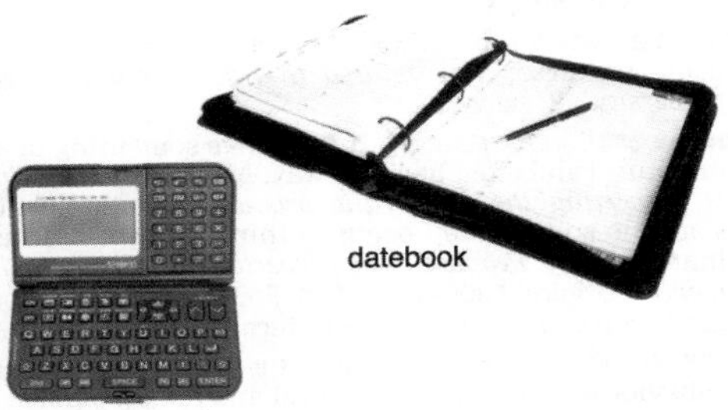

ˌpersonal 'organizer *n.* [C] **1** a small book in which you write addresses, things you must do etc., with loose pages so that you can add more **2** COMPUTERS a very small computer used for the same purpose → see also DATEBOOK

ˌpersonal 'pronoun *n.* [C] ENG. LANG. ARTS a PRONOUN used for the person who is speaking, being spoken to, or being spoken about, such as "I," "you," or "they"

ˌpersonal 'property *n.* [U] money, property, jewelry etc. that belongs to one particular person, rather than to several people or to people in general

per·so·nals /'pɚsənəlz/ *n.* **the personals** a part of a newspaper in which people can have private or personal messages printed

ˌpersonal 'shopper *n.* [C] someone whose job is to help other people decide what to buy or to go shopping for them

ˌpersonal 'space *n.* [U] the distance that you like to keep between you and other people in order to feel comfortable, for example when you are talking to someone

ˌpersonal 'stereo *n.* [C] a small radio or CD player that you carry around with you and listen to through small HEADPHONES

ˌpersonal 'trainer *n.* [C] someone whose job is to help people decide what type of exercise is best for them and show them how to do it

persona non gra·ta /pɚˌsoʊnə nɑn 'grɑt̬ə/ *n.* [U] **1** FORMAL someone who is not welcome in a particular place or in a particular group: *After the court case, he found himself persona non grata in the business community.* **2** a DIPLOMAT (=government representative) who has been ordered to go home from the country where he or she has been sent to work

per·son·i·fi·ca·tion /pɚˌsɑnəfə'keɪʃən/ *n.* **1 the personification of sth** someone who is a perfect example of a quality because they have a lot of it: *That woman is the personification of evil!* **2** [C,U] the representation of a thing or a quality as a person, in literature or art: *the poem's personification of the moon*

per·son·i·fy /pɚ'sɑnəˌfaɪ/ *v.* **personifies, personified, personifying** [T] **1** to perfectly represent a particular quality or idea, by having a lot of that quality or being a typical example of it: *Carter personifies the values of self-reliance and hard work.* | *She will be remembered as kindness personified.* **2** to think of or represent a quality or thing as a person: *The new year is sometimes personified as a baby.*

per·son·nel /ˌpɚsə'nɛl/ [W3] *n.* **1** [plural] the people who work in a company, organization, or military force [SYN] staff: *hospital personnel* | *All personnel must attend the meeting.* **2** [U] the department in an organization that chooses people for jobs and deals with their complaints, problems etc. [SYN] human resources

ˌperson-to-'person *adj.* **1 a person-to-person call** a telephone call that is made to one particular person and does not have to be paid for if they are not there **2** involving direct communication between people: *person-to-person counseling*

per·spec·tive /pɚ'spɛktɪv/ [Ac] [S2] [W3] *n.* **1** [C] a way of thinking about something, which is influenced by the kind of person you are or by your experiences: +**on** *Students have a unique perspective on matters of school policy.* | *The story is told **from the perspective** of an ordinary soldier.* | *We need to view the current crisis **from a** historical **perspective**.* | *Let's try to look at the situation from **a broader perspective*** (=a way of thinking that includes more people, more countries etc.). **2** [C,U] a sensible way of thinking about, judging, and comparing situations, so that you do not imagine that something is more serious or important than it really is: *Despite all his problems, Tony hasn't **lost** his **sense of perspective**.* | *We're trying to **keep** the team's recent losses **in perspective*** (=not get too worried about them). | *If we compare this to other droughts, it helps us to **put it into perspective*** (=not make the problem seem too serious). **3** [U] ENG. LANG. ARTS a method of drawing a picture that makes objects look solid and shows distance and depth, or the effect this method produces in a picture **4** [C] a view, especially one that stretches into the distance

per·spi·ca·cious /ˌpɚspɪ'keɪʃəs◂/ *adj.* FORMAL good at judging and understanding people and situations, or showing this quality: *a perspicacious critic* —**perspicaciously** *adv.* —**perspicacity** /ˌpɚspɪ'kæsət̬i/ *n.* [U]

per·spi·ra·tion /ˌpɚspə'reɪʃən/ *n.* [U] BIOLOGY **1** liquid that appears on your skin when you are hot or nervous [SYN] sweat **2** the process of perspiring

per·spire /pɚ'spaɪɚ/ *v.* [I] to become wet on parts of your body, especially because you are hot or nervous [SYN] sweat [**Origin:** 1600–1700 French *perspirer*, from Latin *spirare* **to breathe**]

per·suade /pɚ'sweɪd/ [W3] *v.* [T] **1** to make someone decide to do something, especially by giving them reasons why they should do it, or asking them many times to do it: **persuade sb to do sth** *I tried to persuade Freddie to see her.* | **persuade sb** *Leo wouldn't agree, despite our efforts to persuade him.*

THESAURUS

talk sb into (doing) sth to persuade someone to do something: *Do you think you can talk her into helping us?*
get sb to do sth to persuade or force someone to do something: *I tried to get Jill to come, but she said she was too tired.*
encourage sb to do sth to persuade someone to do something, especially by telling him or her that it is good for him or her: *More high schools are encouraging their students to do community service.*
influence to have an effect on what someone does or thinks: *Sports figures influence kids' ideas about what's cool.*
convince to persuade someone to do something, especially something she or he does not want to do: *Nothing I said could convince him to accompany me.*
coax to persuade someone to do something by talking gently and kindly: *"Come for Christmas," Jody coaxed over the phone.*

P

cajole to persuade someone to do something by praising him or her or making promises to him or her: *I cajoled John into agreeing to let the boys keep the kittens.*
put sb up to sth to persuade or encourage someone to do something wrong or stupid: *One of the other kids must have put him up to it.*
dissuade sb from (doing) sth to persuade someone not to do something: *He didn't make any effort to dissuade me from going.*

P

2 to make someone believe something SYN **convince**: *I am not persuaded by these arguments.* | **persuade sb (that)** *His answer persuaded me that I was wrong.* | **persuade sb of sth** *McFadden must now persuade the jury of her innocence.* [**Origin:** 1500–1600 Latin *persuadere*, from *suadere* **to advise**]

per·sua·sion /pɚˈsweɪʒən/ *n.* **1** the act or skill of persuading someone to do something: *With a little persuasion, he agreed to help.* | *She uses* ***gentle persuasion*** *to get what she wants.* | *We were won over by Kimball's* ***powers of persuasion*** (=skill at persuading people). **2** [C] FORMAL a particular type of belief, especially a political or religious one: *people of all political persuasions* **3 of the female/conservative/vegetarian etc. persuasion** HUMOROUS OR FORMAL belonging to a particular type or group: *a writer of the post-modern persuasion* **4** [U] ENG. LANG. ARTS a type of writing or speech that tries to make people believe that a particular idea or opinion is correct → see also DESCRIPTION, EXPOSITION, NARRATION

per·sua·sive /pɚˈsweɪsɪv, -zɪv/ *adj.* **1** able to influence other people to believe you or to do what you ask them SYN **convincing**: *persuasive arguments.* | *Diane can be very persuasive when she wants to be.* **2** ENG. LANG. ARTS relating to the use of persuasion in speech or writing: *a persuasive essay* —**persuasively** *adv.* —**persuasiveness** *n.* [U]

pert /pɚt/ *adj.* **1** a part of someone's body that is pert looks young and firm **2** a girl or young woman who is pert is fun and amusing, in a way that is a little disrespectful [**Origin:** 1200–1300 Old French *apert* **open, speaking freely**, from Latin *apertus*] —**pertly** *adv.* —**pertness** *n.* [U]

per·tain /pɚˈteɪn/ *v.*
pertain to sth *phr. v.* FORMAL to relate directly to something: *These are important documents* ***pertaining to*** *the case.*

per·ti·na·cious /ˌpɚtˀnˈeɪʃəs/ *adj.* FORMAL continuing to believe something or to do something in a very determined way —**pertinaciously** *adv.* —**pertinacity** /ˌpɚtˀnˈæsət̬i/ *n.* [U]

per·ti·nent /ˈpɚtˀn-ənt/ *adj.* FORMAL directly relating to something that is being considered SYN **relevant**: *pertinent questions* | **+to** *The information is not pertinent to this study.* —**pertinently** *adv.* —**pertinence** *n.* [U] → see also IMPERTINENT

per·tur·ba·tion /ˌpɚtɚˈbeɪʃən/ *n.* [U] PHYSICS a change in the normal path of an object that is moving around a sun or a PLANET, which is caused by the force of GRAVITY from a different object in space

per·turbed /pɚˈtɚbd/ *adj.* worried or annoyed by something: *She seemed a little perturbed by these rumors.* —**perturb** *v.* [T]

per·tus·sis /pɚˈtʌsɪs/ *n.* [U] MEDICINE → see WHOOPING COUGH

Pe·ru /pəˈru/ a country on the west coast of South America, north of Bolivia and south of Ecuador

pe·ruse /pəˈruz/ *v.* [T] FORMAL or HUMOROUS to read something in a careful way: *He spent hours perusing the catalog.* —**perusal** *n.* [C,U]

Pe·ru·vi·an /pəˈruviən/ *adj.* relating to or coming from Peru —**Peruvian** *n.* [C]

per·vade /pɚˈveɪd/ *v.* [T] if a feeling, idea, or smell pervades a place, it spreads through every part of it: *the culture of violence that pervades much of modern society*

per·va·sive /pɚˈveɪsɪv/ *adj.* existing or spreading everywhere: *Alcohol is still a pervasive problem with high school students.* | *the* ***all-pervasive*** (=extremely pervasive) *influence of television* —**pervasiveness** *n.* [U] —**pervasively** *adv.*

per·verse /pɚˈvɚs/ *adj.* **1** behaving in an unreasonable way, especially by doing the opposite of what people want or expect: *She gets a perverse satisfaction from embarrassing people.* | *a perverse policy* **2** PERVERTED —**perversely** *adv.*

per·ver·sion /pɚˈvɚʒən/ *n.* [C,U] **1** a type of sexual behavior that is considered unnatural and unacceptable **2** the process of changing something that is natural or good into something that is unnatural or wrong, or the result of such a change: **a perversion of sth** *Church leaders called their views a perversion of Christ's teachings.*

per·ver·si·ty /pɚˈvɚsət̬i/ *n.* [U] **1** the quality of being perverse: *Max refused the money out of sheer perversity.* **2** PERVERSION

per·vert¹ /pɚˈvɚt/ *v.* [T] **1** to change something in an unnatural and often harmful way: *Negative advertising is perverting the democratic process.* **2** to influence someone so that they begin to think or behave in an immoral way: *People can be perverted and destroyed by power.* [**Origin:** 1300–1400 Old French *pervertir*, from Latin *pervertere*, from *vertere* **to turn**]

per·vert² /ˈpɚvɚt/ *n.* [C] someone whose sexual behavior is considered unnatural and unacceptable

per·vert·ed /pɚˈvɚt̬ɪd/ *adj.* **1** morally unacceptable, especially in a way that changes something good into its opposite: *the perverted logic of Nazi propaganda* | *He takes a perverted pleasure in hurting people.* **2** sexually unacceptable or unnatural: *perverted sexual practices*

pe·se·ta /pəˈseɪt̬ə/ *n.* [C] the former unit of money in Spain until 2002, when it started using the Euro [**Origin:** 1800–1900 Spanish *peso*]

pes·ky /ˈpɛski/ *adj. comparative* **peskier**, *superlative* **peskiest** INFORMAL annoying and causing trouble: *pesky reporters*

pe·so /ˈpeɪsoʊ/ *n. plural* **pesos** [C] the standard unit of money in various countries, including Mexico, Cuba, Colombia, and the Philippines [**Origin:** 1500–1600 Spanish, Latin *pensum* **weight**]

pes·si·mis·m /ˈpɛsəˌmɪzəm/ *n.* [U] a tendency to expect bad things to happen rather than good things OPP **optimism**: **+about** *In his speech, he voiced deep pessimism about the economy.* [**Origin:** 1700–1800 French *pessimisme*, from Latin *pessimus* **worst**]

pes·si·mist /ˈpɛsəmɪst/ *n.* [C] someone who always expects that bad things will happen OPP **optimist**: *Don't be such a pessimist.*

pes·si·mis·tic /ˌpɛsəˈmɪstɪk◂/ *adj.* expecting that bad things will happen in the future or that a situation will have a bad result OPP **optimistic**: *Dad has a* ***pessimistic view*** *of human nature.* | **+about** *I am pessimistic about our chances of success.* —**pessimistically** /-kli/ *adv.*

pest /pɛst/ *n.* [C] **1** a small animal or insect that harms people or destroys things, especially crops or food supplies: *The birds are regarded as pests by farmers* | *methods of* ***pest control*** **2** INFORMAL an annoying person, especially a child: *Stop being such a pest!*

pes·ter /ˈpɛstɚ/ *v.* [T] to annoy someone, especially by asking them many times to do something: **pester sb for sth** *She keeps pestering me for money.* | **pester sb to do sth** *Ryan keeps pestering me to play with him.* [**Origin:** 1500–1600 Old French *empestrer* **to prevent from moving properly**, from Vulgar Latin *pastoria* **something that ties animals' legs together**; influenced by *pest*]

pes·ti·cide /ˈpɛstəˌsaɪd/ *n.* [C] a chemical substance used to kill insects and small animals that destroy crops

pes·ti·lence /ˈpɛstələns/ *n.* [C,U] LITERARY a disease that spreads quickly and kills large numbers of people

pes·ti·len·tial /ˌpɛstəˈlɛnʃəl/ also **pes·ti·lent** /ˈpɛstələnt/ *adj.* **1** MEDICINE causing or relating to pestilence **2** LITERARY or HUMOROUS extremely bad or annoying: *pestilential kids*

pes·tle /ˈpɛsəl, ˈpɛstl/ *n.* [C] a short stick with a heavy round end, used for crushing things in a MORTAR (=a special bowl)

pes·to /ˈpɛstoʊ/ *n.* [U] a SAUCE made of BASIL, GARLIC, PINE NUTS, OLIVE OIL, and cheese

pet¹ /pɛt/ *n.* [C] an animal such as a cat or a dog which you keep and care for at home: *Do you have any pets?* | *a pet shop* | *Some people **keep** rats **as pets**.* → see also TEACHER'S PET

pet² *v.* **petted, petting** [T] to touch and move your hand gently over something, especially an animal: *Do you want to pet the kitty?* ▸see THESAURUS box at **touch¹** → see also HEAVY PETTING, PETTING

pet³ *adj.* **1 a pet project/theory/subject etc.** a plan, idea, or subject that you particularly like or are interested in **2 a pet rabbit/snake/lion etc.** an animal which is usually wild that you keep as a pet → see also **pet peeve** at PEEVE (1), PET NAME

PETA /ˈpit̬ə/ **People for the Ethical Treatment of Animals** a U.S. organization that works to prevent cruelty to animals

pet·al /ˈpɛt̬l/ *n.* [C] BIOLOGY one of the colored leaf-shaped parts of a flower: *rose petals* → see picture at FLOWER¹

-petaled /pɛt̬ld/ [in adjectives] **eight-petaled/blue-petaled etc.** having eight petals, blue petals etc.: *many-petaled flowers*

pe·tard /pəˈtɑrd/ *n.* → see **be hoisted with your own petard** at HOIST¹ (3)

Pete /pit/ *n.* **for Pete's sake** SPOKEN said when you are annoyed, surprised, impatient etc.: *For Pete's sake! Be quiet and listen.*

Pe·ter /ˈpit̬ɚ/ **1 Peter, 2 Peter** two books in the New Testament of the Christian Bible → see also **rob Peter to pay Paul** at ROB (4)

pe·ter¹ /ˈpit̬ɚ/ *v.*

peter out *phr. v.* to gradually become smaller or happen less often and then come to an end: *The hurricane petered out before reaching shore.* | *The discussion gradually petered out.*

peter² *n.* [C] SPOKEN, INFORMAL a PENIS

Peter I /ˌpit̬ɚ ðə ˈfɚst/ also **Peter the Great** (1672–1725) the ruler of Russia from 1682 to 1725

Peter, Saint also **Simon Peter** in the Bible, the leader of the 12 APOSTLES who became the leader of the first Christians

pet·i·ole /ˈpɛt̬iˌoʊl/ *n.* [C] BIOLOGY the thin stem that supports a leaf and attaches it to the stem of a plant

pe·tit bour·geois /ˌpɛti bʊrˈʒwɑ, pəˌti-/ also **petty bourgeois** *adj.* **1** DISAPPROVING paying too much attention to matters such as social position and private possessions, and treating these things as if they are very important: *a petit bourgeois mentality* **2** belonging to the part of the MIDDLE CLASS who are not very wealthy and who own small businesses, stores etc.

petit bour·geoi·sie /ˌpɛti bʊrʒwɑˈzi, pəˌti-/ also **petty bourgeoisie** *n.* DISAPPROVING **the petit bourgeoisie** people belonging to the middle class who are not very wealthy

pe·tite /pəˈtit/ *adj.* **1** a petite woman is short and attractively thin ▸see THESAURUS box at **small¹** **2** small and delicate: *petite hands*

petit four /ˌpɛti ˈfɔr, pəˌti-/ *n.* [C] a type of very small cake served on formal occasions

pe·ti·tion¹ /pəˈtɪʃən/ *n.* [C] **1** a written request signed by a lot of people, asking the government or someone in authority to do something or change something: **+for/against** *Over 200 residents **signed a petition** against the traffic signal.* | *Berisha is part of the opposition group that **drew up the petition**.* **2** LAW an official letter to a court of law, asking for a legal case to be considered: **+for** *The judge rejected Thompson's petition for custody of the children.* **3** FORMAL a formal prayer or request to someone in authority or to God or to a ruler [**Origin:** 1300–1400 Old French, Latin *petitio*, from *petere* **to try to get or find**]

petition² *v.* [I,T] **1** to ask the government or an organization to do something by sending it a petition: **petition (sb) to do sth** *Black leaders have petitioned Congress to change the law.* **2** LAW to make a formal request to someone in authority, to a court of law, or to God: **+for** *Finally, his wife petitioned for divorce.*

pe·ti·tion·er /pəˈtɪʃənɚ/ *n.* [C] **1** someone who writes or signs a petition **2** LAW someone who asks for a legal case to be considered in a court of law

petit mal /ˈpɛti ˌmɑl, -ˌmæl/ *n.* [U] TECHNICAL a form of EPILEPSY which is not very serious → see also GRAND MAL

ˌpet ˈname *n.* [C] a special name you call someone you like

Pe·trarch /ˈpɛtrɑrk, ˈpi-/, also **Fran·ces·co Pe·trar·ca** /frænˌtʃɛskoʊ pəˈtrɑrkə/ (1304–1374) an Italian poet

pet·rel /ˈpɛtrəl/ *n.* [C] BIOLOGY a black and white ocean bird

Pe·tri dish /ˈpitri ˌdɪʃ/ *n.* [C] SCIENCE a small clear dish with a cover which is used by scientists, especially for growing BACTERIA → see picture at LABORATORY

pet·ri·fied /ˈpɛtrəˌfaɪd/ *adj.* **1** extremely frightened, especially when this makes you unable to move or think: **+of** *Aren't you petrified of earthquakes?* ▸see THESAURUS box at **frightened** **2 petrified wood/trees/insects etc.** wood, trees etc. that have changed into stone over a long period of time [**Origin:** 1400–1500 French *pétrifier*, from Greek *petra* **rock**] —**petrify** *v.* [T] —**petrifaction** /ˌpɛtrəˈfækʃən/ *n.* [U]

pet·ro·chem·i·cal /ˌpɛtroʊˈkɛmɪkəl/ *n.* [C] CHEMISTRY a chemical substance obtained from PETROLEUM or natural gas

pet·ro·dol·lars /ˈpɛtroʊˌdɑlɚz/ *n.* [plural] ECONOMICS money earned by the sale of oil

pet·ro·glyph /ˈpɛtrəˌglɪf/ *n.* [C] a picture or set of marks cut into rock, especially one made thousands of years ago

pet·rol /ˈpɛtrəl/ *n.* [U] BRITISH GASOLINE

pe·tro·le·um /pəˈtroʊliəm/ *n.* [U] EARTH SCIENCE oil that is obtained from below the surface of the Earth and is used to make gas, PARAFFIN, and various chemical substances

peˌtroleum ˈjelly *n.* [U] VASELINE

pe·trol·o·gy /pəˈtrɑlədʒi, pɛ-/ *n.* [U] the study of rocks —**petrologist** *n.* [C]

pet·ti·coat /ˈpɛt̬iˌkoʊt/ *n.* [C] a long skirt that was worn under a skirt or dress by women in the past

pet·ti·fog·ger·y /ˈpɛt̬iˌfɑgəri, -ˌfɔg-/ *n.* [U] unnecessary concern with small unimportant details

pet·ti·ness /ˈpɛt̬inɪs/ *n.* [U] behavior or attitudes that are unpleasant or unkind to someone, because you care too much about things that are not really important: *the pettiness of office politics*

pet·ting /ˈpɛt̬ɪŋ/ *n.* [U] **1** the activity of kissing and touching someone as part of a sexual activity → see also HEAVY PETTING **2** the action of touching and moving your hand gently over an animal

ˈpetting zoo *n.* [C] part of a ZOO which has baby animals in it for children to touch

pet·ty /ˈpɛt̬i/ *adj.* *comparative* **pettier**, *superlative* **pettiest** **1** DISAPPROVING small, unimportant, and silly, and not worth worrying or thinking about SYN **trivial**: **petty issue/problem/argument etc.** *a petty dispute* **2** not generous, and caring too much about things that are not really important: *a petty personal attack* | *Sometimes he can be so petty about money* (=he thinks too much about exactly how much people owe him). → see also PETTINESS **3** relating to crimes that are not serious, for example stealing things that are not very valuable: *a rise in the amount of petty crime* | **a petty thief/criminal/offender** (=a criminal who steals things that are not expensive or whose crimes are not very important) **4** DISAPPROVING a petty official etc. is not very important, but uses power in a way that shows they think they are very important: *a petty bureaucrat*

ˌpetty bour'geois *adj.* PETIT BOURGEOIS

ˌpetty bourgeoi'sie *n.* [singular] PETIT BOURGEOISIE

ˌpetty 'cash *n.* [U] money that is kept in an office for making small payments

P

ˌpetty 'larceny *n.* [U] LAW the crime of stealing things that are only worth a small amount of money → see also GRAND LARCENY

ˌpetty 'officer *n.* [C] an officer of low rank in the Navy

pet·u·lant /ˈpɛtʃələnt/ *adj.* behaving in an impatient and angry way for no reason at all, like a child: *his petulant expression* | *You're behaving like a petulant child.* —**petulantly** *adv.* —**petulance** *n.* [U]

pe·tu·nia /pəˈtunyə/ *n.* [C] a garden plant which has pink, purple, or white flowers in the shape of TRUMPETS

pew¹ /pyu/ *n.* [C] a long wooden seat in a church

pew² *interjection* said when something smells very bad: *Pew! What stinks?*

pew·ter /ˈpyut̬ɚ/ *n.* [U] **1** a gray metal made by mixing LEAD and TIN: *a pewter mug* **2** objects made from this metal

pe·yo·te /peɪˈoʊt̬i/ *n.* **1** [U] a drug made from a Mexican CACTUS, which makes people imagine that strange things are happening to them **2** [C] the plant that produces this drug

Pfc., PFC the abbreviation of PRIVATE FIRST CLASS

PG *n.* [C,U] **Parental Guidance** used to show that a movie may include parts that are not appropriate for young children → see also G, PG-13, R³

pg. a written abbreviation of PAGE

PG-13 /ˌpi dʒi θɚˈtin◂/ *n.* [C,U] **Parental Guidance-13** used to show that a movie may include parts that are not appropriate for children under the age of 13 → see also G, PG, R³

pH /piˈeɪtʃ/ also **p'H ˌvalue** *n.* [C usually singular] CHEMISTRY a number on a scale of 0 to 14 which shows how acid or ALKALINE a substance is

phag·o·cyte /ˈfægəˌsaɪt/ *n.* [C] BIOLOGY a blood cell that protects the body by destroying harmful BACTERIA, VIRUSES etc.

phag·o·cy·to·sis /ˌfægəsaɪˈtoʊsɪs/ *n.* [U] BIOLOGY the process in which PHAGOCYTES (=a type of cell) surround and destroy unwanted material such as waste matter and BACTERIA, which helps to protect the body against infection

pha·lanx /ˈfeɪlæŋks/ *n.* [C] FORMAL **1** a large group of people, vehicles etc. that are very close together and difficult to move through: *A phalanx of cameras and reporters awaited the president.* **2** a group of soldiers who stand or move closely together in battle

phal·lic /ˈfælɪk/ *adj.* like a phallus or relating to a phallus: *phallic symbols*

phal·lus /ˈfæləs/ *n.* [C] **1** something that looks like the male sex organ, often used to represent sexual power **2** TECHNICAL the male sex organ SYN **penis**

phan·tasm /ˈfænˌtæzəm/ *n.* [C,U] LITERARY something that exists only in your imagination; an ILLUSION —**phantasmal** /fænˈtæzməl/ *adj.*

phan·tas·ma·go·ri·a /ˌfæntæzməˈgɔriə/ *n.* [C] LITERARY a confused changing strange scene like something from a dream —**phantasmagorical** *adj.*

phan·ta·sy /ˈfæntəsi/ *n. plural* **phantasies** [C,U] an old spelling of FANTASY

phan·tom¹ /ˈfæntəm/ *n.* [C] LITERARY **1** a frightening image of a dead person or strange thing that someone sees or imagines SYN **ghost** ►see THESAURUS box at **ghost¹** **2** something that exists only in your imagination SYN **illusion**

phantom² *adj.* [only before noun] **1** seeming or looking like a phantom: *a phantom ship* **2** seeming real or made to appear real, but not really existing: *a phantom pregnancy*

phar·aoh, Pharaoh /ˈfɛroʊ, ˈfæ-/ *n.* [C] a ruler of ancient Egypt

phar·i·see /ˈfærəˌsi/ *n.* [C] **1** someone who pretends to be religious or morally good, but who is not sincere SYN **hypocrite** **2 Pharisees** a group of Jews who lived at the time of Jesus Christ and who believed in strictly obeying religious laws —**pharisaic** /ˌfærəˈseɪ-ɪk/ *adj.*

phar·ma·ceu·ti·cal /ˌfɑrməˈsut̬ɪkəl/ *adj.* [only before noun] relating to the production of drugs and medicine: *the large pharmaceutical companies*

phar·ma·ceu·ti·cals /ˌfɑrməˈsut̬ɪkəlz/ *n.* [plural] **1** drugs and medicines **2** the large companies that make drugs and medicines

phar·ma·cist /ˈfɑrməsɪst/ *n.* [C] someone who is trained to prepare drugs and medicines and who works in a store or in a hospital

phar·ma·col·o·gy /ˌfɑrməˈkɑlədʒi/ *n.* [U] MEDICINE the scientific study of drugs and medicines —**pharmacologist** *n.* [C] —**pharmacological** /ˌfɑrməkəˈlɑdʒɪkəl/ *adj.*

phar·ma·co·poe·ia /ˌfɑrməkəˈpiə/ *n.* [C] an official book giving information about medicines

phar·ma·cy /ˈfɑrməsi/ *n. plural* **pharmacies** **1** [C] a store or a part of a store where medicines are prepared and sold **2** [U] the study or practice of preparing drugs and medicines [**Origin:** 1300–1400 Late Latin *pharmacia* **giving drugs**, from Greek, from *pharmakeuein* **to give drugs**]

phar·yn·gi·tis /ˌfærɪnˈdʒaɪt̬ɪs/ *n.* [U] MEDICINE a medical condition in which you have a sore swollen pharynx SYN **sore throat**

phar·ynx /ˈfærɪŋks/ *n.* [C] BIOLOGY the tube that goes from the back of the mouth to the place where the separate passages for food and air divide —**pharyngeal** /fəˈrɪndʒəl/ *adj.*

phase¹ /feɪz/ Ac W3 *n.* [C] **1** one of the stages of a process of development or change SYN **stage**: *a new drug that is still in the experimental phase* | **+of** *The first phase of remodeling should be finished by January.* | **+in** *an exciting new phase in your life* | *The work will be done* ***in phases.*** | *It's normal for kids his age to rebel – he's just* ***going through a phase*** (=a phase of childhood development). | *I'm sure his moods are just* ***a passing phase*** (=one that will change). *Teenagers all have them.* ►see THESAURUS box at **stage¹** **2** one of the changes in the appearance of the moon or a PLANET when it is seen from the Earth: **+of** *the phases of the moon* **3** PHYSICS any state in which matter can exist, for example solid, liquid, or gas: *The reaction occurs in the liquid phase of the system.* **4** PHYSICS a part of a repeated pattern in a process or event **5 in phase/out of phase** PHYSICS two or more waves of sound, light, energy etc. are in phase if their highest parts and lowest parts reach the same place at the same time. They are out of phase if these points do not match. [**Origin:** 1800–1900 Modern Latin *phasis*, from Greek, **appearance of a star, phase of the moon**]

phase² Ac *v.* [T]

phase sth ↔ **in** *phr. v.* to introduce something such as a new law or rule gradually: *The new rules will be phased in beginning March 1st.*

phase sth ↔ **out** *phr. v.* to gradually stop using or providing something: *The government began to phase out nuclear power plants.*

phased /feɪzd/ Ac *adj.* happening gradually in a planned way: *a phased withdrawal from the territory*

'phase ˌdiagram *n.* [C] CHEMISTRY a GRAPH showing the conditions at which a substance exists as a solid, liquid, or gas

phat /fæt/ *adj.* SLANG fashionable, attractive, or desirable

Ph.D. /ˌpi eɪtʃ 'di/ *n.* [C] **Doctor of Philosophy** the highest university degree that can be earned, which is given to someone who has done serious RESEARCH, or someone who has this degree → see also DOCTORATE

pheas·ant /'fɛzənt/ *n.* [C,U] BIOLOGY a large colorful bird with a long tail that is hunted for food and sport, or the meat of this bird [**Origin:** 1200–1300 Anglo-French *fesaunt*, from Latin, from Greek *phasianos*, from *Phasis* ancient river in Asia]

phe·no·bar·bi·tal /ˌfinoʊ'bɑrbəˌtɔl/ *n.* [U] a powerful drug that helps you to sleep

phe·nom /fɪ'nɑm/ *n.* [C] INFORMAL someone who is a PHENOMENON: *an 18-year-old tennis phenom*

phe·nom·e·nal /fɪ'nɑmənl/ Ac *adj.* extremely impressive or surprising: *The restaurant is a phenomenal success.* | *a phenomenal performance* —**phenomenally** *adv.*: *phenomenally popular*

phe·nom·e·non /fɪ'nɑmənən, -ˌnɑn/ Ac *n. plural* **phenomena** /-nə/ [C] **1** something that has been seen to happen or exist, and has been studied or described: *Homelessness is not a new phenomenon* | +**of** *the phenomenon of international terrorism* ▸see THESAURUS box at event **2** [usually singular] something or someone that is very unusual, because of a rare quality or ability that they have: *the latest young musical phenomenon* **3** [singular] something or someone that is extremely successful and that everyone is talking about: *Harry Potter is a publishing phenomenon.* [**Origin:** 1500–1600 Late Latin, Greek *phainomenon*, from *phainein* **to show**]

GRAMMAR **phenomenon, phenomena**
Phenomenon is singular and **phenomena** is plural. However, many people use the word **phenomena** when they are speaking about a single thing.

phe·no·type /'finəˌtaɪp/ *n.* [C] BIOLOGY the physical appearance of a living thing, which is the result of both its GENOTYPE (=genes) and its environment → see also GENOTYPE

pher·o·mone /'fɛrəˌmoʊn/ *n.* [C] BIOLOGY a chemical produced by an animal or insect, which can affect the behavior of other animals of the same type, especially by causing sexual attraction

phew /fyu, hwyu/ *interjection* said when you feel tired, hot, or RELIEVED: *Phew! I am so glad it's Friday.*

phi·al /'faɪəl/ *n.* [C] a VIAL

Phi Be·ta Kap·pa /ˌfaɪ ˌbeɪṭə 'kæpə/ *n.* [singular] a society for college students who have done well in their studies

Phil·a·del·phia /ˌfɪlə'dɛlfyə/ a city in the U.S. state of Pennsylvania, which is the fifth largest city in the U.S.

phi·lan·der·er /fɪ'lændərə·/ *n.* [C] DISAPPROVING a man who has sex with many women, without intending to have any serious relationships [**Origin:** 1800–1900 *philander* **lover** (17–19 centuries), from *Philander* name given to a lover in old plays, from Greek *phil-* **loving** + *aner* **man**] —**philandering** *adj.* —**philandering** *n.* [U]

phil·an·throp·ic /ˌfɪlən'θrɑpɪk/ *adj.* a philanthropic person or institution gives money to people who are poor or who need money in order to do something good or useful —**philanthropically** /-kli/ *adv.*

phi·lan·thro·pist /fɪ'lænθrəpɪst/ *n.* [C] a rich person who gives money to help people who are poor or who need money to do useful things

phi·lan·thro·py /fɪ'lænθrəpi/ *n.* [U] the practice of giving money to help people who are poor or who need money to do useful things

phi·lat·e·ly /fə'læṭl-i/ *n.* [U] the activity of collecting stamps for pleasure —**philatelist** *n.* [C] —**philatelic** /ˌfɪlə'tɛlɪk/ *adj.*

-phile /faɪl/ *suffix* [in nouns and adjectives] someone who likes something very much: *a bibliophile* (=someone who likes books) | *Francophile* (=liking France or the French) [**Origin:** French, Greek *-philos* **dear, friendly**]

Phi·le·mon /fɪ'limən/ a book in the New Testament of the Christian Bible

Phil·har·mon·ic /ˌfɪlə·'mɑnɪk◂, ˌfɪlhɑr-/ *adj.* used in the names of ORCHESTRAS: *the Boston Philharmonic*

-philia /fɪliə/ *suffix* [in nouns] **1** TECHNICAL a tendency to feel sexually attracted in a way that is not approved of, that may be part of a mental illness: *necrophilia* (=a sexual attraction to dead bodies) **2** TECHNICAL a diseased or unhealthy tendency to do something: *hemophilia* (=a tendency to bleed) **3** a tendency to like something: *Francophilia* (=liking France)

-philiac /fɪliæk/ *suffix* [in nouns] TECHNICAL **1** someone who feels sexually attracted in a way that is not approved of: *a necrophiliac* **2** someone who has a particular illness: *a hemophiliac*

Phil·ip /'fɪlɪp/**, Chief** (died 1676) a Wampanoag chief who fought against COLONISTS from England who settled on his tribe's land

Philip, Saint in the Bible, one of the 12 APOSTLES

Phi·lip·pi·ans /fɪ'lɪpiənz/ a book in the New Testament of the Christian Bible

Phil·ip·pine /'fɪləˌpin/ *adj.* relating to or coming from the Philippines

Phil·ip·pines, the /'fɪləˌpinz/ a country that consists of over 7,000 islands off the southeast coast of Asia —**Filipino** /ˌfɪlə'pinoʊ/ *n., adj.* → see also FILIPINO

Phil·is·tine /'fɪləˌstin, fɪ'lɪstən/ one of the group of people who lived on the coast of Palestine from the 12th to the 10th century B.C.

phil·is·tine /'fɪləˌstin/ *n.* [C] DISAPPROVING someone who does not like or understand art, literature, music etc. [**Origin:** 1800–1900 *Philistine*; because the Philistines were thought by the Israelites in the Bible to be uncivilized people] —**philistine** *adj.* —**philistinism** *n.* [U]

phil·o·den·dron /ˌfɪlə'dɛndrən/ *n.* [C] a tropical climbing plant with smooth shiny leaves that many people keep in their houses

phi·lol·o·gy /fɪ'lɑlədʒi/ *n.* [U] OLD-FASHIONED ENG. LANG. ARTS the study of the way languages develop and the relationships between languages —**philologist** *n.* [C] —**philological** /ˌfɪlə'lɑdʒɪkəl/ *adj.* → see also LINGUISTICS

phi·los·o·pher /fɪ'lɑsəfə·/ Ac *n.* [C] **1** someone who studies and develops ideas about the nature and meaning of existence and REALITY, good, and evil etc.: *the ancient Greek philosophers* **2** someone who thinks a lot and asks a lot of questions about the world, the meaning of life etc.

phiˌlosopher's 'stone *n.* [singular] an imaginary substance that was thought in the past to have the power to change any other metal into gold

phil·o·soph·i·cal /ˌfɪlə'sɑfɪkəl/ Ac also **phil·o·soph·ic** /ˌfɪlə'sɑfɪk/ *adj.* **1** relating to philosophy: *Rousseau's philosophic writings* **2** accepting difficult or bad situations calmly: +**about** *Jeremy was philosophical about not getting the job.* —**philosophically** /-kli/ *adv.*

phi·los·o·phize /fɪ'lɑsəˌfaɪz/ Ac *v.* [I + about] to think about or talk about things in a serious way, for example about the nature and meaning of life

phi·los·o·phy /fɪ'lɑsəfi/ Ac S2 W3 *n. plural* **philosophies** **1** [U] the study of what it means to exist, what good and evil are, what knowledge is, or how people should live: *She has a degree in philosophy.* | +**of** *the philosophy of science* | **political/moral/social philosophy** *theories of social philosophy* **2** [C] a set of ideas about these subjects: *Eastern religions and philosophies* | +**of** *the philosophy of Nietzsche* **3** [C] the attitude or set of ideas that guides the behavior and actions of a person or organization: *the company's business philosophy* | *My philosophy is: work hard, play hard.* → see also NATURAL PHILOSOPHY

phish·ing /'fɪʃɪŋ/ *n.* [U] COMPUTERS the criminal activity of sending emails or having a WEBSITE that is intended to trick someone into giving away informa-

P

tion such as their bank account number or their computer PASSWORD. This information is then used to get money or goods.

phle·bi·tis /flɪˈbaɪt̬ɪs/ *n.* [U] MEDICINE a medical condition in which your VEINS (=tubes that carry blood through your body) are swollen

phlegm /flɛm/ *n.* [U] the thick yellowish substance produced in your nose and throat, especially when you are sick [**Origin:** 1300–1400 Old French *fleume*, from Latin *phlegma*, from Greek, **flame, phlegm**]

phleg·mat·ic /flɛgˈmæt̬ɪk/ *adj.* calm and not easily excited or worried

P

phlo·em /ˈfloʊɛm/ *n.* [U] BIOLOGY the TISSUE (=matter in the body made of many cells) in plants that carries food substances from the leaves to all parts of the plant

phlox /flɑks/ *n.* [C] a low spreading plant with pink, white, or purple flowers

Phnom Penh /pəˌnɑm ˈpɛn/ the capital and largest city of Cambodia

-phobe /foʊb/ *suffix* [in nouns] someone who has a strong unreasonable dislike or fear of a particular type of person or thing: *technophobes* (=people who are nervous about new TECHNOLOGY, especially computers)

pho·bi·a /ˈfoʊbiə/ *n.* [C] a strong unreasonable fear of something: +**about** *I had a phobia about going to the dentist.* [**Origin:** 1700–1800 Modern Latin, Late Latin *-phobia*, from Greek, from *phobos* **fear**] —**phobic** *adj.*

-phobia /foʊbiə/ *suffix* [in nouns] **1** a strong unreasonable dislike or fear of something, which may be part of a mental illness: *aquaphobia* (=fear of water) **2** a dislike or hatred of a particular type of person or thing: *homophobia* (=dislike of HOMOSEXUALS)

-phobic /foʊbɪk/ *suffix* **1** [in adjectives] suffering from or relating to a particular phobia: *claustrophobic* (=suffering from fear of small spaces) **2** [in nouns] someone suffering from a particular phobia: *an agoraphobic* (=who is afraid of large open spaces) —**-phobically** /-kli/ *suffix* [in adverbs]

Phoe·ni·cian /fɪˈniʃən/ one of the people that lived in Phoenicia on the eastern coast of the Mediterranean from the 12th century to the fourth century B.C.

Phoe·nix /ˈfinɪks/ the capital and largest city of the U.S. state of Arizona

phoe·nix /ˈfinɪks/ *n.* [C] a magic bird in ancient stories, which lives for 500 years, burns itself in a fire, and is then born again from the ASHES

phon- /fən, foʊn/ *prefix* relating to sound, the voice, or the ability to speak: *phonetics* (=science of speech sounds)

phone[1] /foʊn/ S1 W1 *n.* [C] a telephone: *Can I use your phone?* | *What's your **phone number**?* | *I was just leaving when the **phone rang**.* | *Could you **answer the phone*** (=pick it up and talk)*, please?* | *She **picked up the phone*** (=picked up the part that you talk into) *and dialed.* | *My sister is always **on the phone*** (=using the telephone). | *It's time to **get off the phone*** (=stop talking on it) *now.* | **by phone/over the phone** *You can order a new checkbook by phone.* → see also CELL PHONE

THESAURUS

receiver/handset the part of a telephone you speak into and listen to
number/phone number the set of numbers that you press to call someone
busy if a telephone is busy, someone is using it, and you can hear a particular sound that tells you this
busy signal the sound you hear that tells you someone is using the phone you are trying to call
line the wires that connect telephones. If someone is on the line, they are speaking on a telephone connected by that wire.
answering machine a machine that lets you leave a message for someone who is not answering the phone
voice mail a system in which people can leave recorded messages for someone who is not answering the phone
→ CELL PHONE

phone[2] *v.* [I,T] to connect your telephone with someone else's by DIALing numbers, in order to speak to them SYN **call**: *Register with us by phoning this number.*

phone in *phr. v.* **phone sth ↔ in** to telephone a place to report something, give your opinion, ask a question etc. SYN **call in**: *Elliot was arrested for phoning in a bomb threat.* → see also PHONE-IN

THESAURUS

Phone, **call**, and **telephone** all mean "to use the telephone to speak to someone." **Telephone** is only used in fairly formal situations.
You can also say **give somebody a call**.

-phone /foʊn/ *suffix* **1** [in nouns] an instrument or machine related to sound, hearing, or music: *earphones* | *a saxophone* **2** [in nouns] TECHNICAL someone who speaks a particular language: *a Francophone* (=who speaks French) **3** [in adjectives] speaking a particular language: *Francophone* (=where French is spoken)

ˈphone book *n.* [C] a book that contains an alphabetical list of the names, addresses, and telephone numbers of all the people who have a telephone in a particular area

ˈphone booth *n.* [C] a small structure that is partly or completely enclosed, containing a public telephone

ˈphone card *n.* [C] a plastic card with a special number on it that you can use to pay for calls made on a public telephone

ˈphone-in *adj.* **phone-in radio/talk/television show** a radio or television program which ordinary people can call on the telephone to ask questions, give opinions etc.

pho·neme /ˈfoʊnim/ *n.* [C] ENG. LANG. ARTS the smallest unit of speech that can be used to make one word different from another word, such as the "b" and the "p" in "big" and "pig" —**phonemic** /fəˈnimɪk/ *adj.*

pho·ne·mics /fəˈnimɪks/ *n.* [U] ENG. LANG. ARTS the study and description of the phonemes of languages

ˈphone sex *n.* [U] the activity of talking with someone on the telephone about sex in order to become sexually excited

ˈphone tag *n.* [U] INFORMAL a situation in which two people call each other and leave messages on each other's ANSWERING MACHINE but never actually speak to each other: *We've been **playing phone tag** with each other all week.*

ˈphone-ˌtapping *n.* [U] the activity of listening secretly to other people's telephone conversations using special electronic equipment

pho·net·ic /fəˈnɛt̬ɪk/ *adj.* ENG. LANG. ARTS **1** relating to the sounds of human speech **2** using special signs, often different from ordinary letters, to represent the sounds of speech: *a phonetic alphabet*

pho·net·ics /fəˈnɛt̬ɪks/ *n.* [U] ENG. LANG. ARTS the science and study of speech sounds —**phonetician** /ˌfoʊnəˈtɪʃən/ *n.* [C]

ˈphone tree *n.* [C] a list of telephone numbers of the members in an organization, the workers in a company etc., and the order of who should call whom if there is important information that everyone should know

pho·ney /ˈfoʊni/ *adj. comparative* **phonier**, *superlative* **phoniest** another spelling of PHONY

phon·ic /ˈfɑnɪk/ *adj.* TECHNICAL **1** PHYSICS relating to sound **2** ENG. LANG. ARTS relating to speech sounds

phon·ics /ˈfɑnɪks/ *n.* [U] a method of teaching people to read in which they are taught to recognize the sounds that letters represent

phono- /foʊnoʊ, -nə/ *prefix* TECHNICAL relating to sound, the voice, or the ability to speak: *phonology* (=the study of a system of speech sounds)

pho·no·graph /ˈfoʊnəˌɡræf/ *n.* [C] OLD-FASHIONED a RECORD PLAYER

pho·nol·o·gy /fəˈnɑlədʒi/ *n.* [U] ENG. LANG. ARTS the study of the system of speech sounds in a language, or the system of sounds itself —**phonologist** *n.* [C] —**phonological** /ˌfoʊnəˈlɑdʒɪkəl/ *adj.* —**phonologically** /-kli/ *adv.*

pho·ny /ˈfoʊni/ *adj. comparative* **phonier**, *superlative* **phoniest** INFORMAL **1** false or not real, and intended to deceive someone SYN **fake**: *a phony Italian accent* | *a phony driver's license* ►see THESAURUS box at **fake**[2] **2** someone who is phony pretends to be friendly, smart, kind etc., but in fact they are insincere —**phony** *n.* [C] *The photograph is a phony.* —**phoniness** *n.* [U]

phoo·ey /ˈfui/ *interjection* OLD-FASHIONED said to express strong disbelief or disappointment

phos·phate /ˈfɑsfeɪt/ *n.* [C,U] **1** SCIENCE one of the various forms of a salt of PHOSPHORUS, which has various industrial uses **2** [usually plural] a substance containing a phosphate used for making plants grow better

phos·pho·res·cent /ˌfɑsfəˈrɛsənt/ *adj.* SCIENCE a phosphorescent substance shines slightly in the dark because it contains phosphorus, but it produces little or no heat: *a pale green phosphorescent light* —**phosphorescence** *n.* [U]

phos·pho·rus /ˈfɑsfərəs/ *n.* [U] SYMBOL **P** CHEMISTRY a poisonous yellowish ELEMENT that starts to burn when brought out into the air —**phosphoric** /fɑsˈfɔrɪk/ *adj.*: *phosphoric acid*

pho·tic zone /ˈfoʊt̬ɪk ˌzoʊn/ *n.* **the photic zone** BIOLOGY the upper layer in an ocean or a lake which receives enough sunlight for PHOTOSYNTHESIS to take place → see also APHOTIC ZONE

pho·to /ˈfoʊt̬oʊ/ S3 W2 *n. plural* **photos** [C] a photograph, especially one taken for official purposes or to be PUBLISHED SYN **picture**: *The photo appeared in the "New York Times."* | *satellite photos of earth* | *a black-and-white photo* | ***In the photo**, he is punching a TV reporter.*

photo- /foʊt̬oʊ, -t̬ə/ *prefix* TECHNICAL **1** relating to light: *photosensitive* (=that changes when light acts on it) **2** relating to photography: *photojournalism* (=use of photographs in reporting news)

ˈphoto ˌalbum *n.* [C] a special book for putting your personal photos in

ˈphoto booth *n.* [C] a small structure in which you can sit to have photographs taken by a machine

pho·to·cop·i·er /ˈfoʊt̬əˌkɑpiɚ/ *n.* [C] a COPIER

pho·to·cop·y[1] /ˈfoʊt̬əˌkɑpi/ *n. plural* **photocopies** [C] a copy of a document made using a photocopier SYN **copy**

photocopy[2] *v.* [T] to make a copy of a document using a photocopier SYN **copy** ►see THESAURUS box at **copy**[2]

pho·to·e·lec·tric /ˌfoʊt̬oʊ-ɪˈlɛktrɪk◂/ *adj.* PHYSICS using an electric effect that is controlled by light: *photoelectric sensors*

ˌphotoelectric ˈcell *n.* [C] PHYSICS **1** an electronic instrument that uses light to start an electrical effect, often used in BURGLAR ALARMS **2** a PHOTOVOLTAIC CELL

ˌphoto ˈfinish *n.* [C] **1** the end of a race in which the leaders finish so close together that a photograph of the end must be examined to decide who is the winner **2** any competition in which the winner wins by only a very small amount: *Polls show that Sunday's election will be a photo finish.*

pho·to·gen·ic /ˌfoʊt̬əˈdʒɛnɪk/ *adj.* always looking attractive in photographs: *I'm not very photogenic.*

pho·to·graph[1] /ˈfoʊt̬əˌɡræf/ S3 W2 *n.* [C] ESPECIALLY WRITTEN a picture that is made using a camera, especially one that is for official purposes or to be printed or PUBLISHED SYN **photo** SYN **picture**: +**of** *black-and-white photographs of the canyon* | *Broder has been **taking** underwater **photographs** (=making them) since he was 13.* | *You can see the villa **in this photograph**.* [**Origin:** 1800–1900 *photo-* + *-graph* **something written or drawn** (from Greek *graphein* **to write**)]

photograph[2] *v.* **1** [T] ENG. LANG. ARTS to make a picture of someone or something by using a camera and film sensitive to light: *Ruskin refused to be photographed for the article.* **2 photograph well/badly** to look attractive or unattractive in photographs

pho·tog·ra·pher /fəˈtɑɡrəfɚ/ *n.* [C] someone who takes photographs, especially as a professional or as an artist: *a fashion photographer*

pho·to·graph·ic /ˌfoʊt̬əˈɡræfɪk◂/ *adj.* **1** ENG. LANG. ARTS relating to photographs, using photographs, or used in producing photographs: *a photographic image* | *photographic techniques* **2 a photographic memory** the ability to remember exactly every detail of something you have seen

pho·tog·ra·phy /fəˈtɑɡrəfi/ *n.* [U] the art, profession, or method of producing photographs or the scenes in movies: *landscape and wildlife photography*

pho·to·jour·nal·ism /ˌfoʊt̬oʊˈdʒɚnlˌɪzəm/ *n.* [U] the job or activity of showing news stories in newspapers and magazines using mainly photographs instead of words

pho·tom·e·ter /foʊˈtɑmət̬ɚ/ *n.* [C] an instrument that is used for measuring light

pho·to·mon·tage /ˌfoʊt̬oʊmɑnˈtɑʒ/ *n.* [C,U] the process of making a picture by putting many smaller photographs together, or a picture made this way

pho·ton /ˈfoʊtɑn/ *n.* [C] PHYSICS the smallest PARTICLE of light or other form of RADIATION, that has energy but no electric charge or MASS

ˈphoto opporˌtunity also **ˈphoto op** *n.* [C] **1** a chance for someone such as a politician to be photographed for the newspapers or for television in a way that will make them look good **2** INFORMAL a chance to take a picture of someone or something interesting: *You get great photo opportunities from the bridge.*

pho·to·sen·si·tive /ˌfoʊt̬oʊˈsɛnsət̬ɪv◂/ *adj.* SCIENCE sensitive to the action of light, for example by changing color or form: *photosensitive paper*

ˈphoto shoot *n.* [C] an occasion during which a professional photographer takes pictures of a fashion model, an actor etc. for an advertisement, article etc.

Pho·to·stat, **photostat** /ˈfoʊt̬əˌstæt/ *n.* [C] TRADEMARK a type of machine used for making photographic copies, or the copy itself —**photostat** also **photostatic** /ˌfoʊt̬əˈstæt̬ɪk/ *adj.*

pho·to·syn·the·sis /ˌfoʊt̬oʊˈsɪnθəsɪs/ *n.* [U] BIOLOGY the process by which plants that contain CHLOROPHYLL use light to change carbon dioxide and water into CARBOHYDRATE which the plant uses as food → see picture on p 1186

pho·tot·ro·pism /foʊˈtɑtrəˌpɪzəm/ *n.* [U] BIOLOGY the way a plant moves or grows as a reaction to light. For example many plants will grow towards where the light is coming from. → see also GRAVITROPISM, THIGMOTROPISM, TROPISM

pho·to·vol·ta·ic /ˌfoʊt̬oʊvɑlˈteɪ-ɪk◂/ *adj.* able to produce electricity using light: *photovoltaic solar panels*

ˌphotovoltaic ˈcell *n.* [C] PHYSICS an electronic instrument that changes light into electricity

phras·al /ˈfreɪzəl/ *adj.* ENG. LANG. ARTS consisting of or relating to a phrase or phrases

ˌphrasal ˈverb *n.* [C] ENG. LANG. ARTS two or more words including a verb and an adverb or PREPOSITION, which are used together as a verb and have a different meaning from the verb alone. In the sentence "The bomb blew up," "blew up" is a phrasal verb. In this dictionary, phrasal verbs are marked "phr. v."

phrase[1] /freɪz/ S3 W3 *n.* [C] **1** a group of words that are often used together and that have a special meaning: *Darwin's famous phrase: "survival of the fittest"* | *I learned a few French phrases for my trip to Paris.*

THESAURUS

expression a word or phrase that has a particular meaning

idiom a group of words that have a special meaning that is different from the usual meaning of each word
cliché a phrase that has been repeated so often that it is not interesting
saying/proverb a phrase that many people know, that expresses a sensible idea and is used to give advice

2 ENG. LANG. ARTS a group of words without a main verb that together make a subject, an object, or a verb tense. In the sentence "Sarah wore old gray sneakers," "old gray sneakers" is a noun phrase → see also CLAUSE **3** ENG. LANG. ARTS a short group of musical notes that is part of a longer tune or line of music [**Origin:** 1500–1600 Latin *phrasis*, from Greek, from *phrazein* **to point out, explain, tell**] → see also **to coin a phrase** at COIN² (2), **a turn of phrase** at TURN² (10)

phrase² *v.* [T] **1** to express something in a particular way: *How was the question phrased?* **2** ENG. LANG. ARTS to perform music so as to produce the full effect of separate musical phrases

phrase·book /ˈfreɪzbʊk/ *n.* [C] a book that explains useful words and phrases of a foreign language, for people to use when they travel

phra·se·ol·o·gy /ˌfreɪziˈɑlədʒi/ *n.* [U] ENG. LANG. ARTS the way that words and phrases are chosen and used in a particular language or subject: *the standard phraseology of air traffic controllers*

phras·ing /ˈfreɪzɪŋ/ *n.* [U] **1** the way that something is stated, especially when the words that are used are carefully chosen: *the careful phrasing of the report* **2** ENG. LANG. ARTS a way of playing music, reading poetry etc. that separates the notes, words, or lines into phrases: *Sinatra's classic phrasing*

phre·nol·o·gy /frəˈnɑlədʒi/ *n.* [U] the study of the shape of the human head as a way of showing someone's character and abilities, popular especially in the 19th century —**phrenologist** *n.* [C]

phyl·lo dough /ˈfiloʊ ˌdoʊ/ *n.* [U] a type of DOUGH with many very thin layers

phy·log·e·ny /faɪˈlɑdʒəni/ *n. plural* **phylogenies** [C] BIOLOGY the EVOLUTIONARY development of a SPECIES or other group of related living things → see also ONTOGENY

phy·lum /ˈfaɪləm/ *n. plural* **phyla** /-lə/ [C] BIOLOGY one of the main groups into which scientists divide plants and animals. A phylum is larger than a CLASS, but smaller than a KINGDOM.

phys·i·cal¹ /ˈfɪzɪkəl/ Ac S2 W2 *adj.*

1 BODY NOT MIND relating to someone's body rather than their mind or soul: *She was in constant physical pain.* | *physical activity* | *He was obsessed with **physical fitness**.* | *Teachers try to avoid **physical contact** with students.* | *people with severe **physical disabilities***
2 REAL/SOLID relating to real things that can be seen, tasted, felt etc.: *There is no physical evidence to connect him to the crime scene.* | *the physical world around us*
3 VIOLENT involving violent or forceful body movements: *I like physical sports.*
4 SEX relating to sexual attraction or activity: *It was a purely physical relationship.*
5 PERSON INFORMAL someone who is physical likes touching people a lot
6 NATURAL [usually before noun] relating to or following natural laws: *a physical explanation for the phenomenon*
7 SCIENCE [only before noun] a physical science studies energy, natural laws, or things that are not living: *physical chemistry* → see also PHYSICALLY

physical² Ac also **ˌphysical examiˈnation** *n.* [C] a thorough examination of someone's body and general health by a doctor

ˌphysical ˈcapital *n.* [U] all the things made by people, such as machines and buildings, that are used to produce goods or provide a service

ˌphysical ˈchange *n.* [C,U] SCIENCE a change in the physical form of a substance but not in its chemical or ATOMIC qualities

ˌphysical eduˈcation also **phys ed** /ˌfɪz ˈɛd/ ABBREVIATION **P.E.** *n.* [U] sports and physical exercise taught as a school subject

ˌphysical ˈfeature also **ˌphysical characteˈristic** *n.* [C] a natural physical quality or feature of an area of the Earth's surface, such as mountains or valleys or the plants that grow there → see also HUMAN CHARACTERISTIC

ˌphysical geˈography *n.* [U] the study of the Earth's surface and of its rivers, mountains etc. rather than of the countries it is divided into → see also POLITICAL GEOGRAPHY

phys·i·cally /ˈfɪzɪkli/ Ac S3 *adv.* **1** in relation to the body rather than the mind or soul: *As a child, she had been physically and emotionally abused.* | *Do you find him physically attractive?* | *physically demanding work* | *We try to keep **physically fit*** (=having a strong and healthy body). **2 physically impossible/possible** not possible or possible according to the laws of nature or what is known to be true: *It would be physically impossible to open and check all 2.5 million packages.*

ˌphysically ˈchallenged *adj.* having physical prob-

photosynthesis

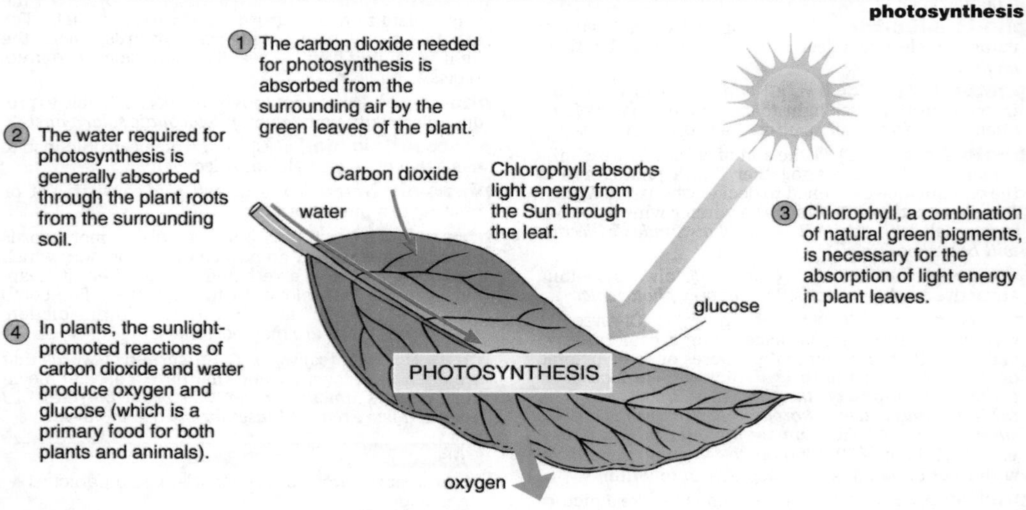
① The carbon dioxide needed for photosynthesis is absorbed from the surrounding air by the green leaves of the plant.
② The water required for photosynthesis is generally absorbed through the plant roots from the surrounding soil.
Carbon dioxide
water
Chlorophyll absorbs light energy from the Sun through the leaf.
③ Chlorophyll, a combination of natural green pigments, is necessary for the absorption of light energy in plant leaves.
glucose
PHOTOSYNTHESIS
④ In plants, the sunlight-promoted reactions of carbon dioxide and water produce oxygen and glucose (which is a primary food for both plants and animals).
oxygen

lems or differences from other people that make it difficult to do physical activities in the usual way: *classes for physically challenged golfers*

ˌphysical ˈmap *n.* [C] a map or drawing that shows the physical features of the Earth, such as mountains, valleys, islands etc.

ˌphysical ˈscience *n.* [U] also **the physical sciences** [plural] SCIENCE the sciences, such as CHEMISTRY, PHYSICS etc., that are concerned with the study of things that are not living

ˌphysical ˈtherapist *n.* [C] someone whose job is to give PHYSICAL THERAPY as a treatment for medical conditions

ˌphysical ˈtherapy *n.* [U] a treatment that uses special exercises, rubbing, heat etc. to treat illnesses and problems with muscles

phy·si·cian /fɪˈzɪʃən/ [W2] *n.* [C] FORMAL a doctor ►see THESAURUS box at doctor[1]

phyˌsician's asˈsistant *n.* [C] someone who is trained to give basic medical treatment, in order to help a doctor

phys·i·cist /ˈfɪzəsɪst/ *n.* [C] PHYSICS a scientist who has special knowledge and training in physics

phys·ics /ˈfɪzɪks/ *n.* [U] PHYSICS the science that studies physical objects and substances, and natural forces such as light, heat, and movement: *a degree in physics* | *a high school physics teacher*

physio- /fɪzioʊ, -ziə/ *prefix* TECHNICAL **1** relating to nature and living things: *physiology* (=study of how the body works) **2** physical: *physiotherapy*

phys·i·og·no·my /ˌfɪziˈɑnəmi, -ˈɑgnə-/ *n.* [C] TECHNICAL the general appearance of a person's face

phys·i·ol·o·gy /ˌfɪziˈɑlədʒi/ *n.* [U] **1** the science that studies how the bodies of living things work **2** BIOLOGY the processes that take place in the bodies and structures of living things: *a study of the physiology of whales* → see also ANATOMY —**physiologist** *n.* [C] —**physiological** /ˌfɪziəˈlɑdʒɪkəl/ *adj.*

phys·i·o·ther·a·py /ˌfɪzioʊˈθɛrəpi/ *n.* [U] MEDICINE PHYSICAL THERAPY —**physiotherapist** *n.* [C]

phy·sique /fɪˈzik/ *n.* [C] the shape and appearance of a human body, especially a man's body: *an athletic physique* → see also FIGURE

phy·to·plank·ton /ˌfaɪtoʊˈplæŋktən/ *n.* [U] BIOLOGY the very small floating plants that are part of PLANKTON → see also ZOOPLANKTON

pi /paɪ/ *n.* [U] TECHNICAL a number, about 3.1416, that is represented by the Greek letter (π) and is equal to the distance around a circle divided by its width. Pi multiplied by the length of the RADIUS (=half the distance across a circle) multiplied by the radius again (=πr^2) gives the area of a circle.

Pia·get /pyɑˈʒeɪ/, **Jean** /ʒɑn/ (1896–1980) a Swiss PSYCHOLOGIST who developed important new ideas about the way that children's minds develop

pi·a·nis·si·mo /piəˈnɪsɪˌmoʊ/ *adj., adv.* ENG. LANG. ARTS played or sung very quietly

pi·an·ist /piˈænɪst, ˈpiənɪst/ *n.* [C] someone who plays the piano very well

pi·an·o[1] /piˈænoʊ/ [S3] *n. plural* **pianos** [C] a large musical instrument that you play by sitting in front of it and pressing the KEYS (=narrow black and white bars): *Do you know how to* ***play the piano?*** | *Jane accompanied me* ***on the piano.*** [**Origin:** 1800–1900 Italian *pianoforte*, from *piano e forte* **quiet and loud**]

piano[2] *adj., adv.* TECHNICAL played or sung quietly

piˈano ˌbar *n.* [C] a bar where someone plays the piano for entertainment

pi·a·no·la /ˌpiəˈnoʊlə/ *n.* [C] a PLAYER PIANO

piˈano stool *n.* [C] a small seat with no back that you sit on while you play the piano

piˈano ˌtuner *n.* [C] someone who makes pianos play at the right PITCH as their job

pi·az·za /piˈɑtsə/ *n.* [C] a public square (=large open area in a city) or market place, especially in Italy

pic /pɪk/ *n.* [C] INFORMAL a picture or movie: *an unusually violent action pic*

pi·cante sauce /pɪˈkɑnt ˌsɔs/ also **picante** *n.* [U] a thick SPICY mixture of crushed TOMATOes, onions, and CHILIs that you put on Mexican food → see also SALSA

pic·a·resque /ˌpɪkəˈrɛsk◂ / *adj.* ENG. LANG. ARTS a picaresque story or NOVEL tells about the adventures and travels of a likable character whose behavior is not always moral

Pi·cas·so /pɪˈkɑsoʊ/, **Pab·lo** /ˈpɑbloʊ/ (1881–1973) a Spanish artist regarded as one of the greatest and most original artists of the 20th century, who helped to develop CUBISM and other styles of ABSTRACT art

P

pic·a·yune /ˌpɪkəˈyun◂ / *adj.* small and unimportant: *a picayune off-Broadway theater*

pic·ca·lil·li /ˌpɪkəˈlɪli/ *n.* [U] a SPICY SAUCE made with small pieces of vegetables

pic·co·lo /ˈpɪkəˌloʊ/ *n. plural* **piccolos** [C] a musical instrument that looks like a small FLUTE

pick up

Larry picked up the can.

Jean picked up her jacket from the dry cleaners.

The truck driver picked up a hitchhiker.

pick[1] /pɪk/ [S1] [W1] *v.* [T]

1 CHOOSE STH to choose someone or something from a group or range of people or things [SYN] **choose**: *Katie picked the blue dress.* | **pick sb as sth** *The magazine's readers picked her as their favorite actor.* | **pick sb/sth for sth** *I didn't get picked for the basketball team.* | **pick sb to do sth** *Two students were picked to represent our school at the debate.* ►see THESAURUS box at choose

2 FLOWERS/FRUIT ETC. to pull off or break off a flower, fruit, nut etc. from a plant or tree: *Laura's in the garden picking tomatoes.* | **pick sb sth** *Here, I picked you an apple.* | **pick a bunch/basketful/couple etc.** *We picked two basketfuls of strawberries.* | *These lilacs are* ***freshly picked*** (=picked very recently). | **go grape/berry etc. picking** (=pick a type of fruit for your own use)

3 SMALL THINGS/PIECES to remove small things from something, or pull off small pieces of something: **pick sth off/from etc.** *She was picking pieces of fluff off her sweater.* | *Stevie, stop* ***picking your nose*** (=putting your finger in your nose to clean it)*!* | *Sam has an annoying habit of* ***picking his teeth*** (=removing pieces of food from your teeth, with your fingers). | *Wolves had* ***picked*** *the sheep's carcass* ***clean*** (=ate all of the meat from the bone).

4 KEEP TOUCHING/PULLING to touch, pull, or SCRATCH

something many times with your fingers: *She kept picking a scab on her arm.*
5 pick and choose INFORMAL to choose only the things you really like or want from a group and ignore the others: *You can't just pick and choose which laws you're going to follow.*
6 pick your way through/across/among etc. to move slowly and carefully, choosing exactly where to put your feet down: *Rescue workers picked their way through the rubble.*
7 pick a fight (with sb) to deliberately start an argument or fight with someone: *Jerry's always trying to pick a fight.*
8 pick sb's brain(s) to ask someone who knows a lot about something for information and advice about it: *I'd like to pick your brains about some legal matters.*
9 pick a lock (with sth) to use something that is not a key to unlock a door, drawer etc.
10 pick sb's pocket to quietly steal something from someone's pocket → see also PICKPOCKET
11 pick holes in sth to criticize a plan, an idea etc.: *I had no trouble picking holes in her theory.*
12 pick a winner INFORMAL an expression meaning "to make a very good choice," sometimes used in a joking way when you think someone has made a very bad choice
13 pick sb/sth to pieces INFORMAL to criticize someone or something very severely and in a very detailed way
14 MUSICAL INSTRUMENT ENG. LANG. ARTS to play a musical instrument by pulling at its strings with your fingers
[**Origin:** 1200–1300 partly from unrecorded Old English *pician*; partly from Old French *piquer* **to prick**] → see also **I have a bone to pick with you** at BONE[1] (5)

pick at sth *phr. v.* **1** to eat something by taking small bites but without much interest, for example because you feel unhappy: *Elaine just sat there picking at her dinner.* **2** to touch something again and again with your fingers, often pulling it slightly: *Don't pick at your scab.*

pick sb/sth ↔ **off** *phr. v.* to shoot people or animals that are some distance away one at a time, by taking careful aim: *One by one, the gunman picked off the soldiers below.*

pick on sb/sth *phr. v.* SPOKEN to treat someone in a way that is not kind: *Stop picking on me!*

pick sb/sth ↔ **out** *phr. v.* **1** to choose someone or something carefully SYN **choose** SYN **select**: *We had fun picking out a present for Susan.* **2** to recognize someone or something in a group of people or things: *It was hard to pick out faces he knew in the crowd.* **3** to play a tune on a musical instrument, slowly or with difficulty: *Connor sat at the piano picking out a simple melody.* **4** if a light picks out something, it shines on it so that it can be seen or seen more clearly

pick over sth *phr. v.* to examine a group of small things very carefully in order to choose the ones you want: *The best fruit had been picked over by the time we got to the store.*

pick through sth *phr. v.* to search through a pile or group of things, and take the one that you want: *Police are still picking through the rubble.*

pick up *phr. v.*
1 LIFT STH UP pick sb/sth ↔ up to lift something up from a surface, usually with your hands: *Mommy can you pick me up?* | *He picked up the letter and read it.* | **pick sth up by sth** *The lioness picked up her cub by its neck.* | *Just as I* ***picked up the phone*** (=lifted it to talk into it), *it stopped ringing.*
2 GO GET SB/STH pick sb/sth ↔ up to go somewhere, usually in a vehicle, in order to get someone or something: *I'll come by tonight to pick up my books.* | *Could you pick me up around eight?* | *For more information, pick up a leaflet at your local post office.*
3 IN A VEHICLE pick sb ↔ up if you pick someone up while you are traveling in a car or other vehicle, you stop so that they can get in and travel with you: *We stopped to pick up a couple of hitchhikers.*
4 BUY STH pick sth ↔ up to buy something, while you are going somewhere or doing something: *Do you want me to pick up some eggs while I'm out?*
5 pick up the bill/tab (for sth) INFORMAL to pay for something that someone else has done, eaten etc.: *The company's picking up the bill for my trip to Hawaii.*
6 WIN STH pick sth ↔ up to win or be given something such as a prize: *She picked up an Oscar for that movie.*
7 CLEAN A PLACE pick sth ↔ up to put things away neatly, or to clean a place this way: *Could you pick all those papers up for me?* | *Pick up the living room before you go to bed.* | *I'm always* ***picking up after*** *him* (=putting things away that he has used).
8 IMPROVE if business, your social life etc. picks up, it improves SYN **improve**: *Sales should pick up again in November.*
9 HABIT/BEHAVIOR pick sth ↔ up if you pick up a habit or a way of behaving, you start to do it because you have spent a lot of time with a particular group of people or in a particular place: *The children had all picked up the local accent.*
10 FEEL BETTER pick sb ↔ up if a medicine, drink etc. picks you up, it makes you feel better → see also PICK-ME-UP
11 pick yourself up to stand up after falling down: *Carol picked herself up and dusted herself off.*
12 sth picks up speed also **sth's speed picks up** if something that is moving picks up speed or its speed picks up, it starts to go faster: *The train was gradually picking up speed.*
13 pick up speed/steam/momentum etc. a) if an idea or system picks up speed, it begins to develop, grow, or become more important: *The economy was picking up steam, and voters were hopeful.* **b)** if a person or group picks up steam, they begin to have more energy or confidence: *The Packers seem to be picking up steam after their win last week.*
14 LEARN pick sth ↔ up to learn a skill, language, or idea without much effort or without being taught in a class: *I've picked up a few words of Russian, since I got here.*
15 NEWS/INFORMATION pick sth ↔ up to learn something such as a useful piece of information, an interesting idea, or a story about someone: *Here's a useful cooking tip I picked up recently.*
16 the wind/beat etc. picks up if the wind, a musical beat etc. picks up, it increases or becomes stronger: *The wind's picking up a little bit.*
17 pick up the slack to work harder when the person who usually does the work cannot or is not doing it: *With Nicole gone, all of our staff will be picking up the slack.*
18 GET AN ILLNESS pick sth ↔ up INFORMAL to get an illness from someone, or to become sick: **pick up sth from sb/sth** *I think I picked up a cold from someone at work.*
19 NOTICE STH pick sth ↔ up to see, hear, or smell something, especially when it is difficult: *Rescue dogs were able to pick up the scent of the child.*
20 RADIO/RECORDING pick sth ↔ up if a machine picks up a sound, signal, or movement, it is able to change it into pictures, record it etc.: *Radar has picked up a new storm front.*
21 START AGAIN pick sth ↔ up if a conversation, meeting etc. picks up or if you pick it up, it starts again from the point where it was interrupted: *Let's pick up again in Chapter 11.* | *Luckily, Maggie was able to* ***pick up where she left off*** *at work, even after being sick for so long.*
22 A CRIMINAL pick sb ↔ up if the police or another official group of people pick someone up, they find them and take them somewhere, to answer questions or to be locked up: *Authorities picked Linden up at a border crossing.*
23 SEX pick sb ↔ up to talk to someone you do not know because you want to have sex with them: *Kathy said some guy tried to pick her up at a bar.*
24 pick up the pieces (of sth) if you pick up the pieces of a business, relationship etc. that has had serious problems, you try to make it work again: *earthquake victims picking up the pieces of their lives*
25 pick up the threads (of sth) if you pick up the threads of a relationship, a way of life, or an idea that

has been interrupted, you try to start it again: *He's trying to pick up the threads of his life again.*
26 pick your feet up used to tell someone to walk properly or more quickly
27 A COLOR pick sth ↔ up if a color or a piece of furniture picks up the color of something else, it has small amounts of that color in it so that it matches: *I like the way the curtains pick up the red and yellow in the rug.*

pick up on sth *phr. v.* **1** to notice something, especially when doing this is difficult SYN **notice** SYN **sense**: *Children easily pick up on tension between their parents.* **2** to notice something and realize that it is important, and take action because of it SYN **spot**: *Genny is good at picking up on trends in the stock market.* **3** to return to a point or an idea that has been mentioned and discuss it more SYN **go back to**: *I'd like to pick up on a point that Steven made earlier.*

pick² S3 *n.* **1 take your pick (of sb/sth)** to choose someone or something from a group of people or things: *The shirt comes in four colors, so take your pick.* **2 the pick of sth** the best thing or things of a group: *It's the pick of this month's new movies.* | **the pick of the crop/bunch/litter** (=the best in the group) **3 have your pick of sth** to be able to choose anyone or anything you want from a group of people or things, because you are very good or very lucky: *Sarah could have her pick of any of the top ten schools in the country.* **4 have/get first pick (of sth)** to be allowed to choose anyone or anything you want from a group of people or things before anyone else is allowed to choose: *She always gets first pick!* **5** [C] INFORMAL someone or something that is chosen from among other people or things SYN **choice**: *Stanhope's horse would be my pick to win the race.* **6** [C] a pickax **7** [C] ENG. LANG. ARTS a small flat object used to pull the strings of an instrument such as a GUITAR when you play it **8** a type of COMB used for very curly hair → see also ICE PICK

pick·a·nin·ny /ˈpɪkəˌnɪni/ *n.* [C] OLD-FASHIONED a word for a small African child, now considered offensive

pick·ax /ˈpɪk-æks/ *n.* [C] a large tool that has a curved iron bar with two sharp points at the end of a long handle

pick·er /ˈpɪkɚ/ *n.* [C] **cotton/fruit/apple etc. picker** a person or machine that picks things, especially crops

pick·et¹ /ˈpɪkɪt/ *n.* [C] **1** also **picket line** a group of people who stand or march in front of a store, factory, government building etc. to protest something or to stop people from going to work during a STRIKE: *A few of the nurses **crossed picket lines** and went back to work.* **2** one person in a picket **3** a soldier or group of soldiers who have the special duty of guarding a military camp → see also PICKET FENCE

picket² *v.* **1** [I,T] to stand or march in front of a store, factory, government building etc. to protest about something or to stop people from going to work during a STRIKE: *Union members picketed the department store when it opened.* **2** [T] to place soldiers around or near a place as guards

ˈpicket ˌfence *n.* [C] a fence made up of a line of strong pointed sticks fastened in the ground

Pick·ett's Charge /ˌpɪkɪts ˈtʃɑrdʒ/ HISTORY an unsuccessful attack by Confederate soldiers during the Battle of Gettysburg in 1863

Pick·ford /ˈpɪkfɚd/, **Mary** (1893–1979) a U.S. movie actress born in Canada

pick·ings /ˈpɪkɪŋz/ *n.* [plural] INFORMAL something or a group of things that you can choose from: **easy/best/rich etc. pickings** *There were rich pickings on the stock market at that time.* | **slim/lean/meager etc. pickings** (=when there are not many good things or opportunities to choose from)

pick·le¹ /ˈpɪkəl/ *n.* **1** [C] a CUCUMBER preserved in VINEGAR or salt water, or a piece of this: *a dill pickle* **2** [U] a strong-tasting liquid made with VINEGAR, used to preserve vegetables **3 be in a (pretty) pickle** OLD-FASHIONED to be in a difficult or confusing situation

pickle² *v.* [T] to preserve food in VINEGAR or salt water: *pickled onions*

pick·led /ˈpɪkəld/ *adj.* OLD-FASHIONED, INFORMAL drunk

ˈpick-me-up *n.* [C] INFORMAL something that makes you feel more cheerful and gives you more energy, especially a drink or medicine

pick·pock·et /ˈpɪkˌpɑkɪt/ *n.* [C] someone who steals things from people's pockets, especially in a crowd

ˈpick-up¹ *n.* **1** [C] also **ˈpickup ˌtruck** a vehicle with a large open part in the back that is used for carrying goods **2** [U] INFORMAL the rate at which a vehicle can increase its speed SYN **acceleration**: *My old car had excellent pick-up.* **3** [C usually singular] INFORMAL an increase or improvement in something SYN **improvement**: *a pick-up in textbook sales* **4** [C] a time or meeting that has been arranged so that someone can take things or people away from a particular place: *Garbage pick-ups are on Tuesdays and Fridays.* | *a shuttle-bus pick-up* **5** [C] an electronic part on an electric GUITAR that makes the sound louder

pick-up² *adj.* [only before noun] a pick-up sports game is not planned and happens because people suddenly decide to play, often with other people they do not know: *a game of pick-up basketball*

ˈpick-up ˌtruck *n.* [C] a PICK-UP

pick·y /ˈpɪki/ *adj.* *comparative* **pickier**, *superlative* **pickiest** INFORMAL someone who is picky is only satisfied with particular things and not others, and so is not easy to please SYN **fussy**: *a picky eater* (=someone who only eats a few foods) | **+about** *Phil's not picky about his clothes.*

pic·nic¹ /ˈpɪknɪk/ S3 *n.* [C] **1** an occasion when people take food and eat it outdoors, especially somewhere such as the beach, a park etc.: *Let's **have a picnic** Sunday afternoon.* ▸see THESAURUS box at **meal** **2 be no picnic** if an activity or situation is no picnic, it is not fun and often very difficult: *A two-hour bus ride to work every day is no picnic.* **3 picnic lunch/supper** the food you take for a picnic [**Origin:** 1700–1800 French *pique-nique*]

picnic² *v.* *past tense and past participle* **picnicked**, **picnicking** [I] to have a picnic: *Several couples were picnicking on the beach.* —**picnicker** *n.* [C]

ˈpicnic ˌarea *n.* [C] an area near a road with outdoor tables, where people in cars can stop and have a picnic

ˈpicnic ˌbasket *n.* [C] a basket used to carry food for a picnic

Pict /pɪkt/ HISTORY one of the people who lived in north and central Scotland from the 3rd to the 9th centuries

pic·to·graph /ˈpɪktəˌgræf/ also **pic·to·gram** /ˈpɪktəˌgræm/ *n.* [C] ENG. LANG. ARTS a picture, SYMBOL, or sign that represents a word or idea, especially one belonging to a set that are used to write a language

pictograph

pic·to·ri·al /pɪkˈtɔriəl/ *adj.* relating to paintings, drawings, or photographs

pic·ture¹ /ˈpɪktʃɚ/ S1 W1 *n.*
1 IMAGE [C] an image that is painted, drawn, printed etc. on a surface: *The picture hung above his desk.* | **+of** *a picture of a sunset* | **draw/paint a picture** *The children drew pictures of their houses.* → see also DRAWING

THESAURUS

sketch a picture that is drawn quickly
painting a picture made using paint
snapshot a photograph that is taken quickly
portrait a painting, drawing, or photograph of a person
cartoon a funny drawing in a newspaper or magazine that tells a story or a joke

caricature a funny drawing of someone that makes a particular feature of his/her face or body look bigger, worse etc. than it really is
illustration a picture in a book
poster a large picture printed on paper, used in order to advertise something or as a decoration on a wall
comic strip a series of pictures drawn inside boxes that tell a story
image a picture seen on a screen, or a formal word for what is in a picture
→ CAMERA, DRAWING

P

2 PHOTOGRAPH [C] a photograph, especially one taken for personal purposes SYN **snapshot**: *Would you like to see our wedding pictures?* | **+of** *Do you have a picture of your family?* | *Excuse me, could you* ***take a picture*** *of us* (=use a camera to take a photograph)*?* | *Leo's picture* (=a photograph of Leo) *is in the paper today.*
3 IDEA IN YOUR MIND [C usually singular] an idea or image in your mind of what something or someone is like: *To get a better picture of how the company is doing, look at sales.* | *I still have a clear picture in my head of my first day in Paris.* | **paint/present/give etc. a picture of sth** *The book paints a vivid picture of life in China.*
4 the situation in a place, an organization, a group etc.: *The picture is the same wherever you go in Africa.* | *It's important not to lose sight of* ***the big picture*** (=the situation as a whole, not just a small part of it).
5 out of the picture also **not in the picture** if someone is in or out of the picture, they are involved or not involved in a situation: *With his main rival out of the picture, he won the election*
6 put/keep sb in the picture to give someone all the information they need to understand a situation, especially one that is changing quickly: *She promised to keep me in the picture as things happened.*
7 be the picture of health/innocence/despair etc. to look very healthy, innocent etc.: *At 82, Mr. Field is the picture of health.*
8 get the picture INFORMAL to understand a situation: *Oh, I get the picture. You're in love with her.*
9 MOVIE [C] ENG. LANG. ARTS a word meaning a movie, used especially by people in the movie industry: *The film won the "Best Picture" award.* | **(the) pictures** OLD-FASHIONED (=movies or movie theaters) → see also MOTION PICTURE
10 TELEVISION/MOVIE SCREEN [C usually singular] the image that appears on a television or movie SCREEN: *The picture's all fuzzy.*
[**Origin:** 1400–1500 Latin *pictura*, from *pictus*, past participle of *pingere* **to paint**] → see also **pretty as a picture** at PRETTY² (4)

picture² S2 *v.* [T] **1** to imagine something, especially by making an image in your mind: *I can still picture her pretty brown eyes.* | **picture sb doing sth** *Doris could picture him standing there in his uniform.* | **picture sb/sth as sth** *I can't picture Jay as a ballet dancer.* ►see THESAURUS box at **imagine** **2** to show someone or something in a photograph, painting, drawing, or movie: **picture sb with sth** *Here, Thuong is pictured with her son Son Hong Vo.* **3** [usually passive] to describe someone or something in a particular way: **picture sb/sth as sth** *Teenagers are usually pictured as lazy.*

'picture book *n.* [C] a children's book that has a lot of pictures and usually a simple story

ˌpicture-'perfect *adj.* exactly right in appearance or quality: *a picture-perfect day*

ˌpicture 'postcard *n.* [C] a POSTCARD with a photograph or picture on the front of it

'picture-postcard *adj.* [only before noun] very pretty: *a picture-postcard view of the Pacific*

'picture show *n.* [C] OLD-FASHIONED a movie, or the occasion when a movie is shown

pic·tur·esque /ˌpɪktʃə'rɛsk/ *adj.* **1** a picturesque place is pretty and interesting, especially in an old-fashioned way: *the picturesque town of Monterey* **2** picturesque language uses unusual, interesting, or sometimes rude words to describe something: *Gordon's picturesque account of the battle* **3** a picturesque person is unusual and interesting, either in the way they look or the way they behave

'picture ˌwindow *n.* [C] a large window made of a single piece of glass

pid·dle /'pɪdl/ *v.* [I] SPOKEN to URINATE
piddle around *phr. v.* SPOKEN to waste time doing things that are not important

pid·dling /'pɪdlɪŋ/ *adj.* small and unimportant: *a piddling amount of money*

pidg·in /'pɪdʒən/ *n.* [C,U] ENG. LANG. ARTS a language that is a mixture of two other languages and is used especially between people who do not speak each other's languages well [**Origin:** 1800–1900 Chinese, English *business*]

pie /paɪ/ S1 *n.* **1** [C,U] a sweet food usually made with fruit baked inside a PASTRY covering: **apple/cherry/pumpkin etc. pie** *my mother's apple pie* | **a piece/slice of pie** *Would you like a piece of pie?* **2** [C,U] a food made of meat or vegetables baked in a PASTRY covering SYN **pot pie**: *steak and kidney pie* **3 slice/share/piece of the pie** a share of something such as money, profits etc.: *The smaller companies want to gain a bigger share of the pie.* **4 pie in the sky** a good plan, promise, or idea that you do not think will happen: *Building a baseball field downtown is just pie in the sky right now.* → see also **easy as pie** at EASY¹ (14), **have a finger in every pie** at FINGER¹ (10), **eat humble pie** at HUMBLE¹ (6), MUD PIE, PIE CHART

pie·bald /'paɪbɔld/ *adj.* a piebald animal has large areas of skin or fur that are two different colors, usually black and white —**piebald** *n.* [C]

piece¹ /pis/ S1 W1 *n.* [C]
1 AMOUNT an amount that has been cut or broken from something, or one of the amounts that something has been cut or broken into: **+of** *a piece of pizza* | *a piece of broken glass* | *The vase has a piece broken off of it.* | **cut/divide/chop etc. sth into pieces** *She cut the cake into eight equal pieces.* | **tear/smash/hack etc. sth to pieces** *The ship was smashed to pieces on the rocks.* | *The lamp lay* ***in pieces*** (=in small parts) *on the floor.*

THESAURUS
scrap a small piece of paper, cloth etc.: *A quilt can be made of scraps of cloth.*
chunk a thick piece of something solid that does not have an even shape: *a stew filled with large chunks of chicken*
lump a small piece of something solid that does not have a definite shape: *a lump of metal*
fragment a small piece that has broken off something, especially glass or metal: *Doctors removed tiny fragments of metal from his leg.*
crumb a very small piece of bread, cake etc.: *She scattered crumbs for the birds.*
slice a thin flat piece of bread, meat etc. cut from a larger piece: *a slice of blueberry pie*
strip a long narrow piece of paper, cloth etc: *She tore a strip off her shirt to make a bandage.*
block a piece of a hard material such as wood or stone with straight sides: *a block of wood*

►see THESAURUS box at **music**, **part¹**
2 SINGLE ITEM a single thing of a particular type: **a piece of sth** *Which piece of luggage is yours?* | *a piece of paper* | *a beautiful piece of furniture* | *a 100-piece tool set* (=with 100 tools in the set)
3 CONNECTED PART one of several parts that something is made of: *Some of the jigsaw pieces are missing.* | *The cars were shipped* ***in pieces*** (=separated into pieces) *and then reassembled.* | *The fireplace was carefully dismantled* ***piece by piece*** (=one part at a time).
4 a piece of sth [usually singular] an amount of something that you do, say, hear, experience etc.: *an excellent piece of work* | **a piece of advice/information/news etc.** *Let me give you a piece of advice.* | **a piece of luck/good fortune** *an unexpected piece of luck*
5 a piece of land/property an area of land: *a fabulous piece of beach-front property*

6 tear/rip/hack etc. sth to pieces to damage something very severely so that it is in many parts: *The lions quickly tore the antelope to pieces.*
7 cut/rip/tear etc. sb to pieces to criticize someone or their ideas very severely: *The President's plan has been ripped to pieces by the press.*
8 (all) in one piece not damaged or injured: *Somehow we made it to Tibet and back in one piece.*
9 give sb a piece of your mind INFORMAL to tell someone that you are very angry with them: *I was so mad that I called back and gave her a piece of my mind.*
10 be a piece of cake INFORMAL to be very easy to do: *Creating graphs is a piece of cake on the computer.*
11 SHARE **a piece of sth** a part or share of something: *They gave the Police Department a piece of the profit.* | **a piece of the action** (=a share of the profits from a business activity, especially an illegal one)
12 go to pieces to be so upset or nervous that you cannot think or behave normally
13 MONEY **a)** a coin of a particular value: **50-cent/100-yen/2-Euro etc. piece** *What can I buy with a 50-cent piece?* **b)** OLD USE a coin: *30 pieces of silver*
14 ART/MUSIC ETC. something that has been produced by an artist, musician, or writer: *When was this piece written?* | **a piece of music/art/writing etc.** *One of the pieces of sculpture is valued at $12,000.*
15 be a piece of crap/junk etc. SPOKEN an impolite way of saying that something is of very low quality: *This printer's a piece of crap!*
16 sb's a (real) piece of work SPOKEN, HUMOROUS used to say that someone behaves in unusual or strange ways, especially when this is annoying or difficult to deal with
17 IN A NEWSPAPER ENG. LANG. ARTS a short written ARTICLE in a newspaper, magazine, or television program: *"The Times"* ***did a*** *nice* ***piece on*** *illegal gambling.*
18 IN GAMES also **game piece** a small object or figure used in playing games such as CHESS
19 GUN SLANG a small gun
20 a piece OLD-FASHIONED a short distance away: *The store is down the road a piece.*
[**Origin:** 1100–1200 Old French, Vulgar Latin *pettia*] → see also **fall to pieces** at FALL[1] (12), MUSEUM PIECE, **pick up the pieces (of sth)** at PICK UP (24), SET PIECE, **the villain (of the piece)** at VILLAIN (2)

piece² S3 *v.*
piece sth ↔ **together** *phr. v.* **1** to think about all the details you have about a situation in order to understand the whole thing: *Investigators are still trying to piece together what caused the fire.* **2** to put all the separate parts of an object into the correct order or position: *A team of five pieced together shards of ancient pottery.*

pi·èce de ré·sis·tance /piˌɛs də rəziˈstɑns/ *n.* [C] the best or most important thing or event in a series, especially when it comes after all the others

piece·meal /ˈpismil/ *adj.* a process that is piecemeal happens slowly in separate unconnected stages and is not well planned: *a piecemeal approach to solving the problem* —**piecemeal** *adv.*: *Hargrave might have to sell the company piecemeal.*

ˈpiece rate *n.* [C] an amount of money that is paid for each thing a worker produces

ˌpieces of ˈeight *n.* [plural] silver coins used in past times in Spain

piece·work /ˈpiswɚk/ *n.* [U] work that is paid according to the number of things you complete or produce rather than the number of hours you work

ˈpie ˌchart *n.* [C] MATH a CHART that consists of a circle divided into parts by lines coming from the center to show how big the different parts of a total amount are → see picture at CHART[1]

ˈpie crust *n.* [C,U] the PASTRY that is under and sometimes covering the fruit or meat in a PIE

pied /paɪd/ *adj.* [only before noun] a pied bird or animal has spots of two or more different colors, usually black and white

pied-à-terre /piˌeɪd ə ˈtɛr/ *n.* [C] a small apartment or house that is not your main home but which you own and stay in sometimes

pied·mont /ˈpidmɑnt/ *n.* [C] EARTH SCIENCE an area of low hills with long gentle slopes, which are near high mountains → see also FOOTHILL

pier

pier /pɪr/ *n.* [C] **1** a structure that is built out into the water, especially so that boats can stop next to it: *The cruise boards at 7 p.m. at Pier 33.* **2** a thick post of stone, wood, or metal used to support something such as a bridge

pierce /pɪrs/ *v.* [T] **1** to make a small hole in or through something using an object with a sharp point: *A bullet pierced his spinal cord.* | ***Pierce a hole in*** *each card to thread the ribbon through.*

THESAURUS
make a hole in sth to cause a hole to appear in something: *Make a hole in the bottom of the can using a hammer and nail.*
prick to make a small hole in the surface of something, using a sharp point: *The nurse pricked my finger and drew a drop of blood.*
punch to make a hole in something using a metal tool or other sharp object: *I had to punch an extra hole in the belt to get it to fit.*
drill to make a hole using a special tool: *They drilled a 180-foot-deep well.*
bore to make a deep round hole in a hard surface: *The tunnel was bored through solid rock.*
▸see THESAURUS box at **hole**[1]

2 have/get sth pierced to have a small hole made in your ears, nose etc. so that you can wear jewelry in it: *Jennie's getting her ears pierced.* **3** if sound, light, pain etc. pierces something you can suddenly hear it, see it, or feel it: *Orange-red flames pierced the dark sky.* **4** to make someone feel an emotion, especially love or sadness, very strongly: *Seeing my father's old letters pierces me with sadness.* [**Origin:** 1200–1300 Old French *percer*]

Pierce /pɪrs/, **Frank·lin** /ˈfræŋklɪn/ (1804–1869) the 14th President of the U.S.

pierced /pɪrst/ *adj.* a part of your body that is pierced has a small hole or holes in it so that you can wear jewelry there: *Are your ears pierced?* | **pierced ears/nose/tongue etc.** *Anne has a pierced nose.*

pierc·ing¹ /ˈpɪrsɪŋ/ *adj.* **1** a piercing sound is high, loud, and usually not nice to listen to: *a piercing scream* ▸see THESAURUS box at **high**[1] **2** piercing wind or cold is very cold and seems to cut into you **3** LITERARY piercing eyes or looks make it seem like someone understands or notices more about you than other people do **4** affecting your emotions very much, especially in a sad way: *a piercing moment of regret* **5** piercing questions, remarks etc. show that someone understands a situation very well and cannot be tricked: *Letterman's piercing humor* **6** LITERARY a piercing light is very strong and bright **7** piercing pain hurts very much —**piercingly** *adv.*

piercing² *n.* [C,U] a BODY PIERCING

Pierre /pɪr/ the capital city of the U.S. state of South Dakota

ˈpie-shaped *adj.* [usually before noun] shaped like a piece that has been cut from a round PIE, with a point at one end and a wide curved edge at the other end

pi·e·ty /ˈpaɪəṭi/ *n.* [U] respect for God and religion, often shown in the way you behave OPP **impiety** → see also PIOUS

pig¹ /pɪg/ S2 *n.* [C] **1** BIOLOGY a farm animal with short legs, a fat body, and a curved tail, that is kept for its meat → see also GUINEA PIG (2) **2** SPOKEN **a)** someone who eats too much or eats more than their share: *You pig! You ate all the cookies!* **b)** someone who behaves in an unpleasant way toward other people: *You're a selfish pig.* → see also **male chauvinist pig** at MALE CHAUVINIST **3 in a pig's eye!** SPOKEN used to show that you do not believe what someone is saying **4 live like a pig** to live in a dirty or messy way or place **5 when pigs fly** used to say that you do not believe something will happen: *"He'll pay us back." "Yeah, when pigs fly."* **6 a pig in a poke** something you bought without seeing it first and that is not as good or valuable as you expected

pig²

pig out *phr. v.* SPOKEN to eat a lot of food: +**on** *We pigged out on pizza.*

pi·geon /ˈpɪdʒən/ *n.* [C] BIOLOGY a gray bird with short legs that is common in cities [**Origin:** 1300–1400 Old French *pijon*, from Late Latin *pipio* **young bird**] → see also CARRIER PIGEON, HOMING PIGEON

ˌpigeon-ˈchested *adj.* someone who is pigeon-chested has a narrow chest that sticks out

pi·geon·hole¹ /ˈpɪdʒənˌhoʊl/ *n.* [C] **1** one of a set of small boxes built into a desk or into a frame on a wall, into which letters or papers can be put **2 put sb/sth into a pigeonhole** to pigeonhole someone or something

pigeonhole² *v.* [T] to decide unfairly that a person, activity etc. belongs to a particular type or group, when the truth is more complicated than that: **pigeonhole sb as sth** *He didn't want to be pigeonholed as an action movie star.*

ˌpigeon-ˈtoed *adj.* someone who is pigeon-toed has feet that point in rather than straight forward

pig·gish /ˈpɪgɪʃ/ *adj.* someone who is piggish eats too much, is dirty, or is unpleasant in their behavior toward other people

pig·gy /ˈpɪgi/ *n. plural* **piggies** [C] SPOKEN a word meaning a "pig," used especially by or to children

pig·gy·back¹ /ˈpɪgiˌbæk/ *adv.* on someone's back or shoulders, or on top of something: *The space shuttle **rode piggyback** on a modified jumbo jet.*

piggyback² *v.* [I] INFORMAL to use something that someone else has done, developed, or made for your own advantage: +**on/onto** *These new firms are piggybacking onto technology that we developed.*

ˈpiggyback ˌride *n.* [C] if you give someone a piggyback ride, you carry them high on your back, holding them with your hands under their legs

ˈpiggy bank *n.* [C] a small container, often in the shape of a pig, in which children can save coins

pig·head·ed /ˈpɪgˌhɛdɪd/ *adj.* DISAPPROVING determined to do things the way you want and refusing to change your mind, even when there are good reasons to do so SYN **stubborn**

ˈpig ˌiron *n.* [U] a form of iron that is not pure, obtained directly from a BLAST FURNACE

pig·let /ˈpɪglɪt/ *n.* [C] a young pig

pig·ment /ˈpɪgmənt/ *n.* [C,U] **1** a natural substance in humans and animals that gives color to skin, blood, hair etc., or all of these substances considered as a group **2** BIOLOGY a substance that produces color in plant or animal TISSUE (=material that makes up the body of the animal or plant), for example MELANIN in skin: *photosynthetic pigments* **3** ENG. LANG. ARTS a dry colored powder that is mixed with oil, water etc. to make paint, or these powders considered as a group

pig·men·ta·tion /ˌpɪgmənˈteɪʃən/ *n.* [U] the coloring of living things: *skin pigmentation*

pig·my /ˈpɪgmi/ *n. plural* **pygmies** [C] another spelling of PYGMY

pig·pen /ˈpɪgpɛn/ *n.* [C] **1** a place where pigs are kept, usually with a building and an outdoor area **2** INFORMAL a very dirty or messy place

pig·skin /ˈpɪgskɪn/ *n.* **1** [singular] INFORMAL the ball used in football **2** [U] leather made from the skin of a pig

pig·sty /ˈpɪgstaɪ/ *n. plural* **pigsties** [C] **1** a very dirty or messy place: *This room's a pigsty.* **2** a pigpen

pig·tail /ˈpɪgteɪl/ *n.* [C] one of two lengths of hair that have been pulled together on either side of the head, and that sometimes are BRAIDED, worn especially by very young girls: *Jenny wore her hair **in pigtails**.* → see picture at HAIRSTYLE

pike /paɪk/ *n.* [C] **1** BIOLOGY a large fish that eats other fish and lives in rivers and lakes **2** SPOKEN a TURNPIKE **3 come down the pike** if an opportunity or something new comes down the pike, it happens or starts to exist: *Jobs like this don't come down the pike that often.* **4** a long-handled weapon used in past times by soldiers

pik·er /ˈpaɪkɚ/ *n.* [C] INFORMAL, DISAPPROVING someone who does not like to spend much money

Pike's Peak /ˌpaɪks ˈpik/ one of the Rocky Mountains in the U.S. state of Colorado

pike·staff /ˈpaɪkstæf/ *n.* [C] the long wooden handle of a PIKE

pi·laf, pilaff /ˈpilɑf/ *n.* [C,U] a dish in which rice and vegetables or meat are cooked together in a pan

pi·las·ter /pɪˈlæstɚ, ˈpɪlæs-/ *n.* [C] a square COLUMN that sticks out partly beyond the wall of a building and is usually only a decoration

Pi·la·tes /pɪˈlɑtiz/ *n.* [U] a type of exercise that strengthens the muscles in the middle part of your body, so that they can better support your whole body

pi·lau /pɪˈlaʊ, -ˈloʊ, ˈpiloʊ/ *n.* [C,U] PILAF

pile¹ /paɪl/ S2 *n.*

1 LARGE AMOUNT/MASS [C] **a)** a large mass of things collected or thrown together: *He swept the leaves into a pile.* | +**of** *piles of cans and bottles* → see also HEAP **b)** a neat collection of several things of the same kind placed on top of each other SYN **stack**: *The folded laundry was separated **into three piles**.* | +**of** *a pile of books* | **put sth on a pile** *Put those letters on the bottom of the pile.*

THESAURUS

heap a large messy pile of things: *All his clothes were in a heap on the floor.*
mound a pile of something with a round shape: *a small mound of rice on the plate*

2 a pile of sth INFORMAL a lot of something SYN **ton**: *a pile of unfinished legislation*

3 at the bottom/top of the pile in a very weak or strong position in society or in an organization: *The mayor has shown little concern for those at the bottom of the pile.*

4 CLOTH/CARPETS [C,U] the soft surface of short threads on a CARPET or some types of cloth, especially VELVET: *a thick red pile carpet* → see also NAP

5 make a pile INFORMAL to make a lot of money

6 POST [C] a heavy big post made of wood, stone, or metal, pushed into the ground and used to support a building, bridge etc.

7 piles [plural] NOT TECHNICAL → see HEMORRHOIDS

[**Origin:** (1) 1400–1500 French, Latin *pila*]

pile² *v.* [T] **1** also **pile up** to make a pile by collecting things together: *Dirty dishes were piled in the sink.* | **pile sth on sth** *The kids piled more pillows on the stack.* **2** to fill something or cover a surface with a lot of something: *Mattie piled her plate with food.* | **be piled (high) with** *Every chair in the room was piled with dirty* *laundry.* | **pile sth into/onto sth** *We piled the bags into the car.*

pile in/into sth *phr. v.* if people pile into a place or vehicle, many of them go into it quickly or in a disorganized way: *Children pile into the gym two afternoons a week.* | *They all piled in and headed for the store*

pile on sth *phr. v.* INFORMAL **1** also **pile it on** to do or talk about something a lot or too much: *Once the press begins to criticize someone, they tend to pile it on.* **2** if people pile on something such as a piece of furniture, many of them sit or lie on it together: *We all piled on the sofa to watch the movie.*

pile out *phr. v.* if a large number of people pile out of a place, they leave it quickly, especially in a disorganized way: +**of** *Commuters piled out of the train.*

pile up *phr. v.* to become much larger in quantity or amount, especially in a way that is difficult to manage, or to make something do this: *Her medical bills began to pile up.* | *Bryant piled up 20 points in the second half of the game.* → see also PILE-UP

'pile ˌdriver *n.* [C] a machine for pushing heavy posts into the ground

'pile-up *n.* [C] INFORMAL an accident in which several vehicles crash into each other: *a six-car pile-up*

pil·fer /ˈpɪlfɚ/ *v.* [I,T] to steal small amounts of things, or things that are not worth much, especially from the place where you work —**pilferer** *n.* [C] —**pilfering** *n.* [U]

pil·grim /ˈpɪlgrəm/ *n.* [C] **1** someone who travels a long way to a holy place for a religious reason **2 the Pilgrims** the group of English people who arrived to settle at Plymouth, Massachusetts, in North America in 1620 [**Origin:** 1100–1200 Old French *peligrin*, from Latin *peregrinus* **foreigner**]

pil·grim·age /ˈpɪlgrəmɪdʒ/ *n.* [C,U] **1** a trip to a holy place for religious reasons: *a pilgrimage to Mecca* ►see THESAURUS box at **trip**[1] **2** a trip to a place related to someone or something famous: *a pilgrimage to Graceland, Elvis' home* **3** a trip to a place that you like very much and where you go often: *the family's annual pilgrimage to the Rockies*

the Pilgrim Fathers

ˌPilgrim 'Fathers *n.* [plural] **the Pilgrim Fathers** the men who were the leaders of the Pilgrims in New England in the 17th century

pil·ing /ˈpaɪlɪŋ/ *n.* [C] a heavy post made of wood, CEMENT, or metal that is used for supporting a building or bridge

pill /pɪl/ S3 *n.* **1** [C] a small solid piece of medicine, that you swallow whole: *vitamin pills* | *I **took** a couple of **pills** for my stuffy nose.* ►see THESAURUS box at **medicine** **2 the pill** a pill taken regularly by some women in order to prevent them having babies: **be/go on the pill** *My doctor advised me to go on the pill.* | *I decided to **go off the pill*** (=stop taking it). **3** INFORMAL someone who annoys you, often a child [**Origin:** 1400–1500 Latin *pilula*, from *pila* **ball**] → see also **a bitter pill (to swallow)** at BITTER (8), MORNING-AFTER PILL

pil·lage /ˈpɪlɪdʒ/ *v.* [I,T] if an army pillages a place, it uses violence to steal from and damage a place that it has taken control of in a war → see also LOOT —**pillage** *n.* [U] —**pillager** *n.* [C]

pil·lar /ˈpɪlɚ/ *n.* [C] **1** a tall upright round post used as a support for a roof SYN **column** **2 pillar of the community/church/society etc.** an active and important member of a group, organization etc. who is respected by many people and is considered to behave in a very moral way **3 a pillar of sth** a very important part of a system of beliefs, especially religious beliefs: *One of the pillars of our society is that everyone has equal access to the legal system.* **4 from pillar to post** moving or changing frequently from one place or situation to another: *The boy has been moved from pillar to post all his life.* **5 a pillar of strength/support (to/for sb)** someone who has a strong character and helps or supports other people **6 pillar of dust/smoke/flame etc.** LITERARY a tall upright mass of dust, smoke, flame etc. SYN **column**

pill·box /ˈpɪlbɑks/ *n.* [C] **1** a small round box for holding PILLS **2** a small strong, usually circular, shelter with a gun inside it, built as a defense **3** also **pillbox hat** a small round hat for a woman

pil·lion /ˈpɪlyən/ *n.* **1** [C] a seat for a second person behind the driver of a MOTORCYCLE or a rider on a horse **2 ride pillion** to sit behind someone who is driving a MOTORCYCLE or riding a horse

pil·lo·ry[1] /ˈpɪləri/ *v.* **pillories, pilloried, pillorying** [T usually passive] if someone is pilloried, they are publicly criticized by a lot of people: **pillory sb for sth** *The Democrats pilloried the President for his military policies.*

pillory[2] *n. plural* **pillories** [C] a wooden frame with holes for the head and hands to be locked into, used in past times as a way of publicly punishing someone → see also THE STOCKS

pil·low[1] /ˈpɪloʊ/ S3 *n.* **1** [C] a cloth bag filled with soft material, that you put your head on when you are sleeping → see also CUSHION **2 a pillow fight** a game in which children hit each other with pillows **3 pillow talk** INFORMAL conversation between lovers in bed [**Origin:** Old English *pyle*, from Latin *pulvinus*]

pillow[2] *v.* [T] **pillow your head on sth** LITERARY to rest your head somewhere, especially so that you can go to sleep

pil·low·case /ˈpɪloʊˌkeɪs/ *n.* [C] a cloth cover for a pillow

pi·lot[1] /ˈpaɪlət/ W2 *n.* [C] **1** someone who operates the controls of an aircraft or SPACECRAFT: *an airline pilot* | +**of** *the pilot of the space shuttle* ►see THESAURUS box at **plane**[1] **2** ENG. LANG. ARTS a television program that is made in order to test whether people like it and would watch it again in the future: *the pilot episode* **3** someone with a special knowledge of a particular area of water, who is employed to guide ships across it: *a harbor pilot* **4 pilot program/test/project etc.** a test that is done to see if an idea, product etc. will be successful: *a pilot project to produce electric cars* [**Origin:** 1500–1600 French *pilote*, from Italian *pedota*, from Greek *pedon* **oar**] → see also AUTOMATIC PILOT

pilot[2] *v.* [T] **1** to test a new idea, product etc. on people to find out whether it will be successful: *The new housing program will be piloted in Chicago and Houston.* **2** to guide an aircraft, SPACECRAFT, or ship as its pilot: *Who was piloting the plane?* **3** [always + adv./prep.] to help someone to go to a place: **pilot sb toward/through etc. sth** *She swiftly piloted me toward the door.* **4 pilot sb through sth** to be responsible for the successful progress of something, especially for making sure that a new law or plan is officially approved: *The Senator piloted the bill through Congress.*

pi·lot·house /ˈpaɪlətˌhaʊs/ *n.* [C] the covered part of a boat, where it is controlled from

'pilot light also **'pilot ˌburner** *n.* [C] **1** a small gas flame that burns all the time and is used for lighting larger gas BURNERS **2** also **pilot lamp** a small electric light on a piece of electrical equipment that shows when it is turned on

Pi·ma /ˈpimə/ a Native American tribe from the southwestern region of the U.S. —**Pima** *adj.*

pi·men·to /pə'mɛntoʊ/ also **pi·mien·to** /pə'myɛntoʊ/ *n.* [C,U] a small red PEPPER often put inside green OLIVES

pimp /pɪmp/ *n.* [C] a man who makes money by controlling PROSTITUTES (=women who have sex with men for money) —**pimp** *v.* [I]

pim·per·nel /'pɪmpɚˌnɛl/ *n.* [C] a small wild plant with flowers in various colors, especially red

pim·ple /'pɪmpəl/ *n.* [C] a small raised red spot on your skin, especially on your face —**pimpled** *adj.* —**pimply** *adj.*

PIN /pɪn/ also **'PIN ˌnumber** *n.* [C] **Personal Identification Number** a secret number that you use when you get money from your bank account using your bank card in a machine

P

pin¹ /pɪn/ S2 *n.* [C]
1 FOR CLOTH a short thin piece of metal with a sharp point at one end, used especially for fastening together pieces of cloth while making clothes
2 WORN ON CLOTHING a) an attractively shaped piece of metal jewelry, sometimes containing jewels, that you fasten to your clothes → see also BROOCH **b)** a round piece of metal that you attach to your clothes that shows that you belong to a particular group or believe in a particular idea: *Her pin said "Peace."*
3 ELECTRICAL one of the pieces of metal that stick out of an electric PLUG
4 FOR SUPPORT a thin piece of metal or wood used as a support for something, or to fasten things together: *Metal pins held the bone together.*
5 you could hear a pin drop SPOKEN used to say that it is very quiet and no one is speaking
6 FOR HAIR a pin made of wire bent into a U-shape to hold long hair in position
7 FOR MARKING POSITION a small thin piece of metal with a sharp point, and a colored top, used for marking the position of someone or something on a map
8 GAMES a) one of the bottle-shaped objects that you try to knock down in a game of BOWLING **b)** an action in the sport of WRESTLING in which you keep your opponent down on their back with both shoulders touching the ground in order to win
9 IN WEAPON a short piece of metal which you pull out of a GRENADE to make it explode a short time later → see also PINS AND NEEDLES, ROLLING PIN, SAFETY PIN

pin² *v.* **pinned, pinning 1** [T always + adv./prep.] to fasten something somewhere, or to join two things together, using a pin: **pin sth to/on/onto** *Some people wore small yellow ribbons pinned to their jackets.* | *She pinned her kids' pictures up on the wall.* **2** [T always + adv./prep.] to make someone unable to move by putting a lot of pressure or weight on them: **pin sb to/under/between etc. sth** *The fourth victim was pinned beneath the car.* **3** [T] to hold someone down on their back on the ground in WRESTLING in order to win

pin sb/sth ↔ **down** *phr. v.* **1** to make someone give clear details or make a definite decision about something: *She refused to be pinned down on details of the investigation.* **2** to understand something clearly or be able to describe it exactly: *It was difficult to pin down exactly what happened that night.* **3** to hold someone firmly on the ground so that they cannot move: *We managed to pin him down until the police came.* **4** to not allow someone to move from a particular place by shooting at them: *Jets were used to pin down rebel units.*

pin sth **on** sb *phr. v.* **1** to blame someone for something, often unfairly: *Don't try to pin the blame on me!* **2 pin your hopes on sb/sth** to hope that something will happen or someone will do something, because all your plans depend on it: *Chris is pinning his hopes on getting into Yale.*

pi·ña co·la·da /ˌpinyə koʊ'lɑdə, -kə-/ *n.* [C] an alcoholic drink made from COCONUT juice, PINEAPPLE juice, and RUM

pin·a·fore /'pɪnəˌfɔr/ *n.* [C] a loose piece of clothing that does not cover your arms, worn by women over their clothes to keep them clean

pi·ña·ta /pi'nyɑtə/ *n.* [C] a decorated paper container filled with candy or small toys, that children try to hit with sticks and break open as a game

Pi·na·tu·bo, Mount /ˌpinə'tuboʊ/ a mountain on the island of Luzon in the Philippines that is an active VOLCANO

pin·ball /'pɪnbɔl/ *n.* [U] an electric game with lights and bells and a sloping board, in which you push buttons to try to keep a ball from rolling off the board

'pinball maˌchine *n.* [C] a machine that you play pinball on

pince-nez /ˌpæns 'neɪ/ *n.* GLASSES worn in past times that were made to fit tightly onto the nose, instead of being held by pieces fitting around the ears

pin·cer /'pɪnsɚ, 'pɪntʃɚ/ *n.* **1** [C usually plural] BIOLOGY one of the pair of CLAWS that some SHELLFISH and insects have, used for holding and cutting food, and for fighting → see picture at CRUSTACEAN **2 pincers** [plural] a tool made of two crossed pieces of metal, used for holding things tightly

'pincers ˌmovement also **'pincer ˌmovement** *n.* [C] a military attack in which two groups of soldiers come from opposite directions in order to catch the enemy between them

pinch¹ /pɪntʃ/ *v.* **1** [T] to press someone's skin very tightly between your finger and thumb, especially so that it hurts: *Stop pinching me!* **2** [I,T] if something you are wearing pinches you, it presses painfully on your skin, because it is too tight: *These shoes pinch my toes.* ▸see THESAURUS box at **hurt¹** **3 pinch yourself** SPOKEN to remind yourself that a situation is real and that you are not imagining it: *I keep pinching myself, and telling myself that I really did win.* → see also PENNY-PINCHING

pinch² *n.* **1 pinch of salt/pepper/cinnamon etc.** a small amount of salt, pepper etc. that you can hold between your finger and thumb: *Stir in a pinch of nutmeg to the mixture.* **2** [C] an act of pressing someone's flesh between your finger and thumb, especially so that it hurts: *Grandma gave us both a pinch on the cheek.* **3 in a pinch** if necessary in a particularly difficult or urgent situation: *My sister can take care of the kids for me in a pinch.* **4 take sth with a pinch of salt** to not completely believe what someone says to you: *You have to take most things Dave says with a pinch of salt.* **5 feel the pinch** to have financial difficulties, especially because you are not making as much money as you used to make: *Local stores and businesses are beginning to feel the pinch.*

pinched /pɪntʃt/ *adj.* **1** not having enough money to do what you want: *the pinched local school system* **2** a pinched face looks thin and unhealthy, for example because the person is sick, cold, or tired

'pinch-hit *v.* [I] **1** to HIT for someone else in baseball **2** to do something for someone else because they are suddenly not able to do it: *I've asked Carl to pinch-hit for me at the meeting tomorrow.* —**pinch-hitter** *n.* [C]

pin·cush·ion /'pɪnˌkʊʃən/ *n.* [C] a soft filled bag for sticking pins in until you need to use them

Pin·dar /'pɪndɚ/ (?522–?443 B.C.) a Greek poet

pine¹ /paɪn/ S3 *n.* **1** [C] also **'pine tree** BIOLOGY a tall tree with long hard sharp leaves that do not fall off in winter: *a grove of pines* **2** [U] the soft pale-colored wood of this tree, used to make furniture, floors etc.: *The doors were made of pine.* | *a pine table*

pine² *v.* [I] to be sad and not continue your life as normal because someone has died or gone away

pine after sb/sth *phr. v.* to miss or want someone or something that you cannot have very much, especially so that you feel sick or unhappy SYN **pine for**

pine away *phr. v.* to gradually become less active, weaker and often sick, especially because you miss someone who has died or gone away: *Don't think I'm pining away because he's left me.*

pine for sb/sth *phr. v.* to miss or want someone or something that you cannot have very much, especially so that you feel sick or unhappy: *Les is still pining for home.*

pin·e·al gland /ˈpɪniəl ˌglænd, ˈpaɪ-/ *n.* [C] a part of the brain that scientists think may be sensitive to light

pine·ap·ple /ˈpaɪnˌæpəl/ *n.* [C,U] BIOLOGY a large yellow-brown tropical fruit or its sweet juicy yellow flesh: *a carton of fresh pineapple juice* → see picture at FRUIT[1]

ˈpine cone *n.* [C] the brown seed container of the PINE tree

ˈpine ˌneedle *n.* [C] a leaf of the pine tree, that is thin and sharp

ˈpine nut *n.* [C] a small seed that grows on some pine trees, that is eaten in salads and other dishes

pine·wood /ˈpaɪnwʊd/ *n.* **1** [C] BIOLOGY a forest of PINE trees **2** [U] the wood from a PINE tree SYN **pine**

pine·y, piny /ˈpaɪni/ *adj.* relating to or containing PINE trees, smelling of PINE

ping[1] /pɪŋ/ *n.* [C] a short high ringing sound: *The dime landed on the floor with a ping.*

ping[2] *v.* [I] to make a short high ringing sound

ping-pong, Ping Pong /ˈpɪŋpɑŋ, -pɔŋ/ *n.* [U] TRADEMARK an indoor game played on a table top by two people with a small light plastic ball and two PADDLES SYN **table tennis**

pin·head /ˈpɪnhɛd/ *n.* [C] **1** the head of a pin **2** [C] INFORMAL an insulting word for someone who is stupid

pin·hole /ˈpɪnhoʊl/ *n.* [C] a very small hole in something, or a small hole made by a pin

ˈpinhole ˌcamera *n.* [C] a very simple camera, in which a pinhole is made at one end of a box, and the film is put inside the box on the side across from the hole

pin·ion[1] /ˈpɪnyən/ *v.* **1** [T always + adv./prep.] to hold or tie up someone's arms or legs very tightly, so that they cannot move freely: *Her arms were pinioned tightly behind her.* **2** [T usually passive] TECHNICAL to cut off the big strong feathers from a bird's wings so that it cannot fly

pinion[2] *n.* [C] TECHNICAL **1** a small wheel, with tooth-like parts on its outer edge, that fits into a larger wheel and turns it or is turned by it → see also RACK-AND-PINION STEERING **2** a bird's wing, especially the outer part, where the strongest flying feathers grow

pink[1] /pɪŋk/ S2 *adj.* red mixed with white: *pink and white stripes* | **bright/hot pink** *bright pink lipstick* | **pale/light pink** *pale pink carnations* → see also **be tickled pink** at TICKLE[1] (3)

pink[2] *n.* **1** [C,U] a pale color made by mixing red and white: *She was dressed **in pink**.* **2** [C] BIOLOGY a garden plant with pink, white, or red flowers **3 in the pink** OLD-FASHIONED in very good health

ˌpink-ˈcollar *adj.* relating to low-paid jobs done mainly by women, for example in offices and restaurants, or relating to the women who do these jobs: *pink-collar jobs* → see also BLUE-COLLAR, WHITE-COLLAR

Pin·ker·ton /ˈpɪŋkɚtən/, **Al·lan** /ˈælən/ (1819–1884) a U.S. DETECTIVE who started the Pinkerton National Detective Agency

pink·eye /ˈpɪŋk-aɪ/ *n.* [U] NOT TECHNICAL a disease that causes the skin around the eyes to swell and become red, and can easily be given to someone else SYN **conjunctivitis**

pink·ie, pinky /ˈpɪŋki/ also **ˈpinkie ˌfinger** *n.* [C] the smallest finger of the human hand

ˈpinking ˌshears also **ˈpinking ˌscissors** *n.* [plural] a special type of scissors that makes points on the edge of the cloth or paper you are cutting

pink·ish /ˈpɪŋkɪʃ/ *adj.* slightly pink

ˌpink ˈslip *n.* [C] INFORMAL **1** a written warning you get when your job is going to end because there is not enough work: *The plant has issued pink slips to over 300 employees.* **2** an official document that proves you own a particular car

pink·y /ˈpɪŋki/ another spelling of PINKIE

ˈpin ˌmoney *n.* [U] OLD-FASHIONED a small amount of money that you can spend on yourself rather than on necessary things

pin·na·cle /ˈpɪnəkəl/ *n.* **1** [singular] the most successful, powerful, exciting etc. part of something: *By 1965, Fellini had **reached the pinnacle of** his commercial success.* **2** [C] a pointed stone decoration, like a small tower, on a building such as a church or castle **3** [C] EARTH SCIENCE a top of a high mountain [**Origin:** 1200–1300 Old French *pinacle*, from Late Latin *pinnaculum*, from Latin *pinna* **wing, wall around the top of a castle**]

pi·noch·le /ˈpiˌnʌkəl/ *n.* [U] a card game for two to four people that uses a special DECK of 48 cards

pin·o·cy·to·sis /ˌpɪnəsaɪˈtoʊsɪs/ *n.* [U] BIOLOGY the process by which some cells take in liquid, by turning a small part of the cell wall inward and then closing this part off with the liquid inside

pin·point[1] /ˈpɪnpɔɪnt/ *v.* [T] **1** to say exactly what the facts about something really are: *Scientists have been unable to pinpoint the cause of the disease.* **2** to find or show the exact position of something or time something happened or will happen: *Satellite pictures helped to pinpoint the location of the weapons.*

pinpoint[2] *n.* [C] **1** a very small point or DOT of something: **+of** *Through a telescope, Jupiter's moons will look like pinpoints of light.* **2 with pinpoint accuracy/precision** very exactly, without even the smallest mistake: *This type of missile can be fired with pinpoint precision.*

pin·prick /ˈpɪnˌprɪk/ *n.* [C] **1** a very small hole in something, similar to one made by a pin **2** [C] a very small area or DOT of something: **+of** *a pinprick of light* **3** a slight feeling that worries or upsets you: **+of** *a pinprick of jealousy*

ˌpins and ˈneedles *n.* **be on pins and needles** to be very nervous and unable to relax, especially because you are waiting for something important: *I was on pins and needles until I found out I'd won.*

pin·stripe /ˈpɪnstraɪp/ *n.* [C] one of the thin light-colored lines that form a pattern on dark cloth

ˈpin-striped also **pinstripe** *adj.* having a pattern of pinstripes: *a pin-striped suit*

pint /paɪnt/ *n.* [C] a unit for measuring liquid, equal to 16 FLUID OUNCES or 0.4732 liters: *a pint of milk* [**Origin:** 1300–1400 Old French *pinte*, from Medieval Latin *pincta*, from Latin, past participle of *pingere* **to paint**]

Pin·ter /ˈpɪntɚ/, **Har·old** /ˈhærəld/ (1930–) a British writer of plays

pin·to /ˈpɪntoʊ/ *n.* [C] a horse with irregular areas of two or more colors on it

ˈpinto bean *n.* [C] a small light brown bean

ˈpint-sized also **ˈpint-size** *adj.* [only before noun] small, and often seeming silly or unimportant: *At age eight Tim was already a pint-sized businessman.*

ˈpin-up *n.* [C] **1** a picture of an attractive person, often a woman without many clothes on, that is put up on a wall to be looked at and admired **2** someone who appears in one of these pictures

pin·wheel /ˈpɪnwil/ *n.* [C] a toy consisting of a stick with curved pieces of plastic at the end that turn around when they are blown

pin·y /ˈpaɪni/ another spelling of PINEY

pi·o·neer[1] /ˌpaɪəˈnɪr/ *n.* [C] **1** one of the first people to do something that other people will later develop or continue to do: **+of/in** *He was a pioneer in the field of biotechnology.* | *a leading pioneer of prison reform* | **a pioneer photographer/geologist etc.** (=one of the first people to develop the skill of photography etc.) **2** one of the first people to travel to a new country or area and begin living there, farming etc.: *Many of the early pioneers left after the first winter.* [**Origin:** 1500–1600 Old French *peonier* **soldier**, from *peon*]

pioneer[2] *v.* [T] to be the first person to do, invent, or use something: *The technique was pioneered at Yale University.*

P

pi•o•neer•ing /ˌpaɪəˈnɪrɪŋ◂/ *adj.* [only before noun] **1** introducing new and better methods or ideas for the first time: *pioneering cancer research* **2** relating to or typical of pioneers, especially the first Europeans who moved west across North America

pio'neer ˌspecies *n.* [C] BIOLOGY a type of plant that is the first plant to grow in an area where nothing has grown before, as a result of which other plants are able to grow there later

pi•ous /ˈpaɪəs/ *adj.* **1** having strong religious beliefs, and showing this in the way you behave ▸see THESAURUS box at **religious** **2** DISAPPROVING pious words, promises, attitudes etc. are intended to sound good or moral, but are probably not sincere: *pious speeches by politicians* → see also PIETY —**piously** *adv.* —**piousness** *n.* [U]

P

pip /pɪp/ *n.* [C] **1** OLD-FASHIONED, INFORMAL an extreme example of a particular type of thing, especially something that is funny or enjoyable **2** one of the spots on DICE or PLAYING CARDS **3** BIOLOGY a small seed from a fruit such as an apple or orange

pipe¹ /paɪp/ [S3] *n.* **1** [C] a tube through which a liquid or gas flows, often under the ground: *The pipes froze and burst during the night.* | *Developers in some hill areas are required to **lay** their own water **pipes**.* | *sewer pipes* **2** [C] a thing used for smoking tobacco, consisting of a small tube with a container shaped like a bowl at one end: *Dad has **smoked a pipe** for years.* | *pipe tobacco* **3** [C] **a)** one of the metal tubes through which air passes when an ORGAN is played **b)** a simple musical instrument shaped like a tube and played by blowing → see also BAGPIPES **4 put/stick that in your pipe and smoke it!** SPOKEN used to tell someone to accept what you have just said, even if they do not like it [**Origin:** Old English *pipa*, from Vulgar Latin, from Latin *pipare* **to make a high sound**]

pipe² *v.* **1** [T usually passive] to send a liquid or gas through a pipe to another place: **be piped in/into/to etc.** *Lots of oil is piped in from Alaska.* **2** [I,T] to make a musical sound using a pipe **3** [I,T] LITERARY to speak or sing in a high voice **4** [T] to decorate food, especially a cake, with thin lines of ICING or cream

pipe down *phr. v.* SPOKEN to stop talking or making a noise, and become calmer and less excited: *Pipe down! I'm trying to study.*

pipe sth ↔ **in**, **pipe** sth **into** sth *phr. v.* to send radio signals or recorded music into a room or building, so that people can hear it while they do other things: *Soft soothing music was piped in over the speaker system.*

pipe up *phr. v.* INFORMAL to begin to say something or start speaking, especially when you have been quiet until then: *Suddenly Dennis piped up, "Mom, can I have a cookie?"*

'pipe ˌcleaner *n.* [C] a length of wire covered with soft material, used to clean the inside of a tobacco pipe

ˌpiped 'music *n.* [U] quiet recorded music played continuously in stores, hotels, restaurants etc.

'pipe dream *n.* [C] a hope, idea, plan etc. that is impossible or will probably never happen

'pipe ˌfitter *n.* [C] someone who puts in and repairs pipes for water, gas etc.

pipe•line /ˈpaɪp-laɪn/ *n.* [C] **1** a line of connecting pipes, often under the ground, used for moving gas, oil etc. over long distances **2 be in the pipeline** if a plan, idea, or event is in the pipeline, it is still being prepared, but it will happen or be completed soon: *Plans for building 1,700 rental units are in the pipeline.*

'pipe ˌorgan *n.* [C] an ORGAN

pip•er /ˈpaɪpɚ/ *n.* [C] a musician who plays a PIPE or the BAGPIPES

'pipe rack *n.* [C] a small frame for holding several tobacco pipes

pi•pette /paɪˈpɛt/ *n.* [C] CHEMISTRY a thin glass tube for sucking up exact amounts of liquid, used especially in chemistry → see picture at LABORATORY

pip•ing¹ /ˈpaɪpɪŋ/ *n.* [U] **1** thin cloth ropes used as decorations on clothes and furniture **2** several pipes, or a system of pipes, used to send liquid or gas in or out of a building

piping² *adv.* INFORMAL **piping hot** very hot: *piping hot soup*

pip•pin /ˈpɪpɪn/ *n.* [C] a small sweet apple

pip•squeak /ˈpɪpskwik/ *n.* [C] INFORMAL someone that you think is not worth respecting or paying attention to, especially because they are young or small or do not have much power

pi•quant /piˈkɑnt, ˈpikənt/ *adj.* **1** having a pleasantly SPICY taste: *a piquant sauce with garlic and red peppers* **2** interesting and exciting [SYN] **intriguing**: *a tale full of piquant characters and vivid descriptions* —**piquantly** *adv.* —**piquancy** /ˈpikənsi/ *n.* [U]

pique¹ /pik/ *v.* **1 pique sb's interest/curiosity** to make someone feel interested in someone or something or want to know more about them: *The tour of the hospital piqued her interest in studying medicine.* **2** [T usually passive] to make someone feel annoyed or upset, especially because they feel insulted: **be/feel piqued** *Privately, he was piqued that his offer was rejected.*

pique² *n.* [U] **1** a feeling of being annoyed or upset, especially because you feel insulted: *He stomped out **in a fit of pique*** (=sudden anger). **2** also **piqué** a type of material made of cotton, silk, or RAYON

pi•ra•cy /ˈpaɪrəsi/ *n.* [U] **1** the illegal copying and sale of books, TAPES, VIDEOS, electronic technology etc.: *software piracy* **2** the crime of attacking and stealing from ships at sea, especially in past times

Pi•ran•del•lo /ˌpɪrənˈdɛloʊ/, **Lu•i•gi** /luˈidʒi/ (1867–1936) an Italian writer of plays and NOVELS

pi•ra•nha /pəˈrɑnə, -ˈræn-/ *n.* [C] BIOLOGY a South American fish with sharp teeth that lives in rivers and eats flesh

pi•rate¹ /ˈpaɪrɪt/ *n.* [C] **1** someone who sailed on the oceans, especially in the past, attacking other boats and stealing things from them **2** someone who dishonestly copies and sells another person's work: *software pirates* —**piratical** /paɪˈrætɪkəl/ *adj.*

pirate² *v.* [T] to illegally copy and sell another person's work, such as a book, design, or invention ▸see THESAURUS box at **copy²** —**pirated** *adj.*: *pirated CDs*

pirate³ *adj.* [only before noun] **1** pirate copies of books, records, films etc. have been made illegally and are sold without the permission of the people who originally produced them: *pirate copies of the movie* ▸see THESAURUS box at **copy²** **2** broadcast or broadcasting illegally: *a pirate radio station* **3** relating to or being a pirate who sailed on the oceans, especially in the past: *a pirate ship*

pir•ou•ette /ˌpɪruˈɛt/ *n.* [C] a very fast turn made on one toe or the front part of one foot, especially by a BALLET dancer —**pirouette** *v.* [I]

pis•ca•to•ri•al /ˌpɪskəˈtɔriəl◂/ *adj.* FORMAL relating to fishing or fishermen (FISHERMAN)

Pis•ces /ˈpaɪsiz/ *n.* **1** [singular] the 12th sign of the ZODIAC, represented by two fish, and believed to affect the character and life of people born between February 21 and March 20 **2** [C] someone who was born between February 21 and March 20

pish /pɪʃ/ *interjection* OLD USE used to show that you are annoyed or impatient

pis•ta•chi•o /pɪˈstæʃiˌoʊ/ *n. plural* **pistachios** [C] a small green nut → see picture at NUT

pis•til /ˈpɪstl/ *n.* [C] BIOLOGY the female part of a flower that produces seeds

pis•tol /ˈpɪstl/ *n.* [C] a small gun you can use with one hand [**Origin:** 1500–1600 French *pistole*, from German, from Czech *pišťal* **pipe**]

'pistol-whip *v.* [T] to hit someone with a pistol

pis•ton /ˈpɪstən/ *n.* [C] a part of an engine consisting of a short solid piece of metal inside a tube, that moves up and down to make the other parts of the engine move

'piston ring *n.* [C] a circular metal spring used to stop gas or liquid from escaping from between a piston and the tube that it moves in

pit¹ /pɪt/ *n.*
1 HOLE [C] **a)** a hole in the ground, especially one made by digging: *He dug a deep pit in the ground.* | *a barbecue pit* **b)** a large hole in the ground from which stones or minerals have been dug SYN **quarry**: *a gravel pit*
2 MARK [C] **a)** a small hollow mark in the surface of something: *tiny scratches and pits in the windshield* **b)** a small hollow mark that is left on your face by ACNE or some diseases → see also PITTED
3 in the pit of your stomach if you feel an emotion in the pit of your stomach, you experience it strongly, often as a bad feeling in your stomach: *a feeling of panic in the pit of his stomach*
4 MESSY PLACE [singular] SPOKEN a house or room that is dirty, messy, or in bad condition: *Eric's house is a total pit.*
5 IN FRUIT [C] BIOLOGY the single large hard seed in some fruits: *a peach pit* → see picture at FRUIT¹
6 be the pits SPOKEN, INFORMAL used to say that something is extremely bad: *This place is the pits.*
7 the pit/pits the place beside the track where cars can come in during a race to be quickly repaired → see also PIT STOP
8 the/a pit of sth LITERARY a situation in which a particular bad quality is too common, or a bad feeling is extremely strong: *the pit of despair*
9 IN A THEATER [C] an ORCHESTRA PIT
10 BUSINESS [C] the area of a STOCK EXCHANGE where people buy and sell STOCKS
11 IN A GARAGE [C] a hole in the floor of a garage that lets you get under a car to repair it
12 BODY PART [C] INFORMAL an ARMPIT
13 the pit (of Hell) also **the fiery pit** BIBLICAL Hell
[**Origin:** (1, 2) Old English *pytt*] → see also **money pit** at MONEY (10), MOSH PIT

pit² *v.* **pitted, pitting** **1** [T] to take out the single hard seed inside some fruits: *Peel and pit two avocados.* **2** [T usually passive] to put small marks or holes in the surface of something, or to consist of these marks or holes: *Potholes pitted the street.* **3** [I] to stop in a car race to get gasoline or to have your car repaired → see also PITTED

pit sb/sth **against** sb/sth *phr. v.* **1** to make someone compete or fight against someone else: *The idea has pitted farmers, developers, and environmentalists against each other.* **2** if you pit yourself or your skills, wits etc. against someone or something, you use your skill, strength, knowledge etc. to deal with or compete against them: *The teams will be pitting their skills against competitors from around the world.*

pit out *phr. v.* SLANG **pit sth ↔ out** to SWEAT so much that your clothes become wet under your arms

pi·ta bread /ˈpitə brɛd/ *n.* [U] a type of flat bread that can be opened so you can put food into it → see picture at BREAD¹

ˈpit bull also **ˌpit bull ˈterrier** *n.* [C] an extremely strong dog with short legs that is sometimes violent

Pit·cairn Is·land /ˌpɪtkɛrn ˈaɪlənd/ an island in the southern Pacific Ocean that is controlled by the U.K.

pitch¹ /pɪtʃ/ *n.*
1 BASEBALL [C] a throw of the ball to the BATTER in baseball: *He **threw a pitch** over the batter's head.* ▶see THESAURUS box at **throw¹**
2 FOR PERSUADING [C] INFORMAL the things someone says to persuade people to buy something, do something, or agree with an idea: *a sales pitch* | *He **made** one last **pitch** for the deal.*
3 MUSIC a) [C,U] a musical note, or how high or low a musical note is: *I've never been able to sing **on pitch**.* **b)** [U] the ability of a musician to play or sing a note at exactly the correct pitch: *Kendrick's pitch was good throughout the first aria.* → see also PERFECT PITCH
4 SOUND/VOICE [C,U] how low or high someone's voice or a sound is: *His voice rose steadily in pitch as he got angrier.*
5 STRONG FEELINGS [singular U] the strength of your feelings or opinions about something: *Racial tensions have risen to **fever pitch*** (=a very excited level) *in recent days.*
6 BLACK SUBSTANCE [U] a black sticky substance that is used on roofs, the bottoms of ships etc. to stop water from coming through → see also PITCH-BLACK, PITCH-DARK
7 SLOPE [singular U] the degree to which something slopes or the angle it is at: *the pitch of the roof*
8 SHIP/AIRCRAFT [C] a movement of a ship or an aircraft in which the front part goes up and the back goes down, and then the front goes down and the back goes up
9 SPORTS FIELD [C] BRITISH an area of ground marked with lines, that some sports are played on: *a cricket pitch*

pitch² *v.*
1 BASEBALL [I,T] to aim and throw a ball to the BATTER in baseball: *He pitched very well Sunday.*
2 THROW [T] to throw something with a lot of force, often aiming carefully: **pitch sth over/into/through etc. sth** *He picked up the paper and pitched it into the fire.*
3 FALL [I always + adv./prep., T always + adv./prep.] to fall suddenly and heavily in a particular direction, or to make someone or something fall in this way: **pitch forward/backward/over etc.** *Greg tripped and pitched forward into the bushes.* | **pitch sb into/over/forward etc.** *A sudden stop pitched her into the windshield.*
4 TRY TO GET BUSINESS [I,T] to try to persuade someone to buy something, make a business deal with you, or let you do some work for them: +**for** *Five companies pitched for the work.* | **pitch sth as sth** *The bonds are pitched as a safe investment.* | **pitch sth at sb/sth** *Her novels are pitched at young single women.*
5 TRY TO GET SUPPORT [T] to try to make people support something by saying how good it is: **pitch sth as sth** *The proposals were pitched as the answer to the company's problems.*
6 SET A LEVEL [T always + adv./prep.] if you pitch a speech, explanation etc. at a particular level of difficulty or to a particular group of people, you make sure that it can be understood by people at that level: **pitch sth at sth** *The puzzles should be pitched at the right level.*
7 pitch a tent also **pitch camp** to set up a tent or a camp for a short time: *We'd better pitch the tent before it gets dark.*
8 SHIP/AIRCRAFT [I] if a ship or an aircraft pitches, it moves up and down in an uncontrolled way with the movement of the water or air → see also ROLL, YAW
9 VOICE/MUSIC [T always + adv./prep.] ENG. LANG. ARTS if you pitch your voice or another sound at a particular level, the sound is produced at that level: **pitch sth high/low** *This song is pitched too high for my voice.* → see also HIGH-PITCHED, LOW-PITCHED
10 SLOPE [I always + adv./prep.] to slope down: **pitch gently/steeply etc.** *The roof pitches sharply to the rear of the house.* → see also PITCHED
11 pitch sb a line INFORMAL to tell someone a story or give them an excuse that is difficult to believe: *She pitched me some line about a bomb scare on the subway.*

pitch sb/sth **against** sb/sth *phr. v.* to make someone fight or compete with someone else

pitch in *phr. v.* INFORMAL **1** to start to work eagerly as a member of a group: *When the harvest comes, the whole family pitches in.* **2** to add your help, support, or money: *The whole team pitched in to buy Kevin a nice present.*

pitch sb/sth **into** sth *phr. v.* to suddenly put someone in a new situation: *The attacks pitched the city into chaos.*

ˌpitch-ˈblack *adj.* completely black or dark: *It was pitch-black outside.*

ˌpitch-ˈdark, pitch dark *adj.* completely dark: *I'm not going in. It's pitch-dark in there!*

pitched /pɪtʃt/ *adj.* a pitched roof is sloping rather than flat

ˌpitched ˈbattle *n.* [C] **1** an angry and usually long argument **2** a battle between armies or groups of people who have already chosen and prepared their

P

positions: *two days of pitched battles between the two armies* → see also SKIRMISH

pitch·er /ˈpɪtʃɚ/ *n.* [C] **1** a container for holding and pouring liquids, that has a handle and a SPOUT (=shaped part for pouring): *a pitcher of iced tea* **2** the player in baseball who throws the ball to the BATTER → see picture at BASEBALL

pitch·fork /ˈpɪtʃfɔrk/ *n.* [C] a farm tool with a long handle and two long curved metal points, used especially for lifting HAY (=dried long grass)

pitch·man /ˈpɪtʃmən/ *n.* [C] someone who tells people why they should buy a particular product

P

pitch·pipe /ˈpɪtʃpaɪp/ *n.* [C] a small pipe that makes particular notes when you blow through it and is used for tuning (TUNE) musical instruments

pit·e·ous /ˈpɪṭiəs/ *adj.* LITERARY expressing suffering and sadness in a way that makes you feel pity: *the piteous cries of hungry children* —**piteously** *adv.*

pit·fall /ˈpɪtfɔl/ *n.* [C] a problem or difficulty that is likely to happen in a particular job, course of action, or activity: *the pitfalls of fame* | *The book helps travelers* ***avoid*** *some of the* ***pitfalls*** *of cross-cultural encounters.*

pith /pɪθ/ *n.* [U] **1** BIOLOGY a white substance just under the outside skin of oranges and similar fruit **2** BIOLOGY a soft white substance that fills the stems of some plants **3 the pith of an argument/issue etc.** the most important and necessary part of an argument etc.

ˌpith ˈhelmet *n.* [C] a large light hard hat worn especially in hot countries, to protect your head from the sun

pith·y /ˈpɪθi/ *adj. comparative* **pithier**, *superlative* **pithiest** a pithy remark, piece of writing etc. is intelligent and strongly stated, without wasting any words: *pithy comments* —**pithily** *adv.* —**pithiness** *n.* [U]

pit·i·a·ble /ˈpɪṭiəbəl/ *adj.* FORMAL making you feel pity: *pitiable victims of war* —**pitiably** *adv.*

pit·i·ful /ˈpɪṭɪfəl/ *adj.* **1** looking or sounding so sad that you feel sympathy: *Margret looked so pitiful, I had to help her.* **2** very bad in quality: *Stu's bass playing is just pitiful.* **3** a pitiful amount is very small and you think it should be more: *a pitiful wage* —**pitifully** *adv.*: *She looked pitifully thin.*

pit·i·less /ˈpɪṭɪlɪs/ *adj.* **1** showing no pity [SYN] **cruel**: *a pitiless dictator* **2** LITERARY pitiless wind, rain, sun etc. is very severe and shows no sign of changing: *the pitiless desert sun* —**pitilessly** *adv.*

pi·ton /ˈpitɑn/ *n.* [C] TECHNICAL a piece of metal used in climbing, that you fasten into the rock to hold the rope

ˈpit stop *n.* [C] **1 make a pit stop** SPOKEN to stop when driving on a long trip to get food, gasoline, or use the toilet **2** a time when you stop in the PIT during a car race to get more gasoline or have repairs done

pit·tance /ˈpɪtˀns/ *n.* [singular] a very small or unfairly small amount of money: *He earned a pittance as an artist.*

pit·ted /ˈpɪṭɪd/ *adj.* **1** having small marks or holes in the surface: *The truck went racing down the pitted side streets.* **2** a pitted fruit has had the single hard seed removed from it: *pitted prunes*

pit·ter-pat·ter /ˈpɪṭɚ ˌpæṭɚ/ also **ˈpitter-pat** *adv.* **go pitter-patter** to make a sound or movement consisting of many quick light beats or sounds: *Anna's heart went pitter-patter as she opened the letter.* —**pitter-patter**, **pitter-pat** *n.* [singular] *the pitter-patter of rain on the roof*

Pitts·burgh /ˈpɪtsbɚg/ an industrial city in the U.S. state of Pennsylvania

pi·tu·i·tar·y /pəˈtuəˌtɛri/ also **piˈtuitary ˌgland** *n. plural* **pituitaries** [C] BIOLOGY the small organ at the base of your brain which produces HORMONES that control the growth and development of your body —**pituitary** *adj.*

ˈpit viper *n.* [C] BIOLOGY a type of poisonous snake, such as a RATTLESNAKE or COPPERHEAD, that has small hollow places below their eyes

pit·y¹ /ˈpɪṭi/ *n.* **1** [U] sympathy for someone who is suffering or unhappy: *a feeling of pity* | **feel/have pity for sb** *I have no pity for people who lie and get caught.* | *Joe hated being an* ***object of pity*** *at school.* **2** [singular] SPOKEN used to show that you are disappointed about something and you wish things could happen differently [SYN] **shame**: **it's a pity (that)** *It's a pity that John couldn't come to the party.* | **it is a pity to do sth** *It would be a pity to spoil the surprise.* | *Students just don't seem interested in math anymore, which is* ***a great pity***. | **That's/What a pity** *"She's not well at all." "Oh that's a pity."* **3 take/have pity on sb** to feel sorry for someone and do something to help them: *Finally, a truck driver took pity on us and gave us a ride.* **4 more's the pity** OLD-FASHIONED used after describing a situation, to show that you wish it was not true: *He's good-looking but married, more's the pity.* [**Origin:** 1200–1300 Old French *pité*, from Latin *pietas* **piety, pity**]

pity² *v.* **pities, pitied, pitying** [T not usually in progressive] to feel sorry for someone because they are in a very bad situation: *I pity anyone who has to live with Rick.*

Pi·us IX, Pope /ˌpaɪəs ðə ˈnaɪnθ/ (1792–1878) the POPE who called together the First Vatican Council, a meeting of Catholic Church leaders from all over the world

Pius XII, Pope /ˌpaɪəs ðə ˈtwɛlfθ/ (1876–1958) the POPE at the time of World War II

piv·ot¹ /ˈpɪvət/ also **ˈpivot point** *n.* [C] **1** PHYSICS a central point or pin on which something balances or turns **2** the one central idea or event that all parts of a plan, process, or idea are based on or arranged around: *Until recently, West Africa was the pivot of the cocoa trade.*

pivot² *v.* **1** [I,T] to turn or balance on a central point, or to make something do this: *The security cameras can pivot to monitor the entire hallway.* **2** [I] to turn quickly on your feet so that you face in the opposite direction

pivot on/around sth *phr. v.* to depend on or be planned around a particular event, or to have a particular idea as the central one: *The entire project pivots on this meeting with the Board of Directors.*

piv·ot·al /ˈpɪvəṭl/ *adj.* having an extremely important effect on the way something develops: +**to** *Foreign trade is pivotal to the nation's economy.* | **a pivotal event/moment/role etc.** *He was a pivotal figure in the campaign.*

pix /pɪks/ *n.* [plural] INFORMAL pictures or photographs

pix·el /ˈpɪksəl/ *n.* [C] COMPUTERS the smallest unit of an image on a television or computer screen

pix·ie, pixy /ˈpɪksi/ *n.* [C] an imaginary creature that looks like a very small human being, has magical powers, and likes to play tricks on people

Pi·zar·ro /pɪˈzɑroʊ/, **Fran·cis·co** /frɑnˈsiskoʊ/ (?1475–1541) a Spanish EXPLORER and soldier who went to South America in 1524, and took control of Peru for Spain

piz·za /ˈpitsə/ [S1] *n.* [C,U] a thin flat round bread, baked with TOMATOes, cheese, and sometimes vegehptables or meat on top [**Origin:** 1800–1900 Italian **pie**]

ˈpizza ˌparlor *n.* [C] a restaurant that serves pizza

piz·zazz /pəˈzæz/ *n.* [U] INFORMAL an exciting strong quality or style: *The show lacks pizzazz.*

piz·ze·ri·a /ˌpitsəˈriə/ *n.* [C] a restaurant that serves pizza

piz·zi·ca·to /ˌpɪtsɪˈkɑṭoʊ/ *n.* [U] musical notes played by pulling on the STRINGS of an instrument

pj's, PJ's /ˈpidʒeɪz/ *n.* [plural] SPOKEN PAJAMAS

Pk. the written abbreviation of PARK

pkg. the written abbreviation of PACKAGE

Pkwy. the written abbreviation of PARKWAY

Pl. the written abbreviation of PLACE

pl. the written abbreviation of PLURAL

plac·ard /ˈplækɚd, -kɑrd/ *n.* [C] a large notice or advertisement put up or carried in a public place: *One placard in the crowd read, "Enough is enough!"*

[**Origin:** 1400–1500 French, Old French *plaquier* **to make flat**]

pla·cate /ˈpleɪkeɪt, ˈplæ-/ *v.* [T] FORMAL to make someone stop feeling angry: *She hoped her apology would placate him.* —**placatory** /ˈpleɪkəˌtɔri/ *adj.*: *placatory words*

place¹ /pleɪs/ S1 W1 *n.* [C]

1 POINT/POSITION any area, point, or position SYN **spot**: *Always keep your passport in a safe place.* | *This is the place where the accident happened.* | ***In places**, there was mold on the walls.* | **a place to do sth** *I couldn't find a place to park.*

THESAURUS

position the exact place where someone or something is, in relation to other things: *The position of the fire tower is marked on the map.*
spot INFORMAL a place, especially a pleasant one where you spend time: *It's a favorite spot for picnics.*
location the place where a hotel, store, office etc. is, or where a movie is made: *The apartment's in an ideal location.*
site a place where something is going to be built, or where something important happened: *the site for the new airport* | *the site of the battle of Gettysburg*
point an exact place, for example on a map: *At this point the trail divides in two.*
somewhere used especially with an adjective or other words to refer in an indefinite way to a place: *She comes from somewhere in Minnesota.*

2 BUILDING/TOWN/COUNTRY ETC. a particular town, country, building, business etc.: *She was born in a place called Black River Falls.* | *I know a good place to get your car serviced.* | *There's a nice Korean place* (=restaurant) *on the corner.* | +**for** *This would be a great place for a party.* | **the right/wrong place** *Are you sure this is the right place?* | **a place to live/eat/stay etc.** *We're looking for a good place to go dancing.* | *Do you need a place to stay?*

3 WHERE SB LIVES INFORMAL the house, apartment, or room where someone lives: *Stuart bought a nice place over on Oak Street.* | **sb's place** *Let's go back to my place for dinner.* ►see THESAURUS box at **home¹**

4 take place to happen, especially after being planned or arranged SYN **happen**: *The next meeting will take place on Thursday.* ►see THESAURUS box at **happen**

5 sb's place of work/employment/business FORMAL a factory, office etc. where you work

6 a place of worship FORMAL a building such as a church, where people have religious ceremonies

7 take the place of sb/sth also **take sb's/sth's place** to exist or be used instead of someone or something else SYN **replace**: *Personal email has virtually taken the place of letters.* | *I don't think anyone could take her place* (=be as important or loved as she is).

8 in place of sb/sth instead of someone or something: *Rolled oats can be used in place of wheat flour in making the bread.*

9 RANK [C] the position that someone gets to in a race or competition: *He's moved up two places to number 4.* | **first/second/third etc. place** *The Canadian team finished in third place.* | **take first/second/third etc. place** *She took second place in the high jump.*

10 in place a) in the correct or usual position: *The decorations are in place for the party.* | **hold/keep sth in place** *Use a piece of twisted wire to hold the material in place.* **b)** if a system, program, or way of doing something is in place, it exists and is being used: *Funding is already in place.*

11 push/press/snap etc. (sth) into/in place to put something into the correct position, or to be put into this position: *They lifted the panel into place.* | *The tubes all snap easily into place.*

12 in sb's place a) if you do something in someone's place, you do it because they were supposed to but could not: *If I can't go, they'll send someone else in my place.* **b)** SPOKEN in someone else's situation: *What would you do in my place?* | **put yourself in sb's place** (=to try to imagine what another person's situation must be like)

13 SPACE/POSITION a space or position in a line of people who are waiting for something: *There are still a few places left on the bus.* | *If you get there first, can you **save** me a **place** in line?*

14 out of place a) not appropriate for a particular situation or occasion: *I felt totally out of place at Cindy's wedding.* **b)** not in the correct or usual position: *Not a thing was out of place in the kitchen.*

15 PURPOSE/POSITION [usually singular] the way that someone or something is considered or used in a situation or in society SYN **role**: +**in** *Work has a very important place in all our lives.* | **sb's place** *They used to say a woman's place was in the home.*

16 a place in the history/record books also **a place in history** a position of being remembered for a long time because of something you have done: *His achievements have earned him a place in history.*

17 STREET Place used in the name of a square, or a short street, or another area in a town that is quite open: *Portland Place*

18 take your place a) to go to a particular position that you need to be in for an activity: *Take your places for the next dance.* **b)** to join, and form an important part of, a group of people or things: *The novel has taken its place among other literary classics.*

19 its place the place where something is usually kept: *Make sure you put everything back in its place.*

20 be no place for sb/sth to be a completely inappropriate place for someone or something: *A library is no place for a party.*

21 all over the place INFORMAL **a)** everywhere: *Dirty clothes were all over the place.* **b)** in a very messy state: *Her hair was all over the place.* **c)** with a lot of confusing, unrelated, or wrong information or ideas: *Her arguments were all over the place.*

22 OPPORTUNITY TO DO STH an opportunity to become a member of a group of people who take part in a particular activity, class etc.: *There are three places left on the cheerleading squad.*

23 POINT IN A BOOK/SPEECH ETC. a point in a book, speech, movie etc.: *I couldn't remember the place where I stopped reading.* | *Sorry, I've **lost** my **place** – what page are we on?*

24 AT A TABLE a knife, fork, spoon, plate etc. arranged on a table for one person to use SYN **place setting**: *Don't forget to **set a place** for Debbie, too.*

25 put sb in their place to show someone that they are not as intelligent or important as they think they are: *I'd like to put her in her place – she thinks she's so smart.*

26 be the place (to do sth) used to say that it is an appropriate place, time, or situation to do or say something: *A board meeting is not the place to discuss your salary.* | *If you want to eat good seafood – **this is the place**.*

27 it is not sb's place (to do sth) if it is not someone's place to do something, it is not appropriate for them to do it, or it is not their responsibility to do it: *It's not your place to tell me what to do!*

28 have no place in sth FORMAL to be completely unacceptable in a particular situation: +**in** *Personal opinion has no place in science.*

29 be going places INFORMAL to start becoming successful in your life: *At only 24, Shelly is already going places.*

[**Origin:** 900–1000 Old French **open space**, from Latin *platea* **broad street**] → see also DECIMAL PLACE, **fall into place** at FALL INTO STH (1), **in the first place** at FIRST¹ (7), **know your place** at KNOW¹ (31), **take second place to sb/sth** at SECOND¹ (11)

place² S2 W1 *v.*

1 OBJECT [T always + adv./prep.] to put something somewhere, especially with care SYN **put**: **place sth in/on/under etc.** *She placed the vase carefully on the table.* | *Place some lemon slices on the fish before serving it.* ►see THESAURUS box at **put**

2 place emphasis/importance/blame etc. (on sb/sth) to decide that someone or something should be empha-

sized, is important, should be blamed etc.: *The school places a lot of emphasis on discipline.* | *He places the blame squarely on the President.*
3 SITUATION [T always + adv./prep.] to force someone or something into a particular situation SYN **put**: *He felt that Jordan's mistakes had placed the family in great danger.*
4 HOW GOOD/IMPORTANT [T always + adv./prep.] to say how good or important you think someone or something is: *I would place health quite high on my list of priorities.* | **place sb/sth above sb/sth** *Companies usually place profit above all else.*
5 POSITION/RANK [T always + adv./prep.] if something places a person at a particular position or rank within a group, it puts them in that position or rank: *The new CD places her among today's top artists.*
6 PRICE/AGE [T] to decide what price something should be or how old something is: **place sth at sth** *The value of the jewels has been placed at one million dollars.*
7 JOB/HOME [T] if an organization or company places someone, it finds an appropriate job or place to live for them: *The temp agency was trying to place me with a law firm.* | *The boy was placed with a foster family.*
8 place an/your order to ask a store or business to provide a product that you need: *Call this number to place your order.*
9 RECOGNIZE SB [T] to remember why you recognize someone, what their name is etc.: *I recognize the name, but I can't place him.*
10 place an ad/advertisement to arrange for an advertisement to be printed in a newspaper or magazine: *He placed an ad in the local newspaper.*
11 place a call FORMAL to make a telephone call: *I'd like to place an overseas call, please.*
12 place sb under arrest if the police place someone under arrest, they take them away because they think the person has done something illegal
13 place sth under (the) control of sth also **place sth under state/government etc. control** to arrange for a country, organization etc. to control something: *Regulation of tobacco has been placed under the agency's control.*
14 place first/second/third etc. to be first, second etc. in a race
15 place sb under surveillance if an organization such as the police places someone under surveillance, they watch them because they think they are doing something illegal
16 place (your) hopes/dreams/faith etc. in sb/sth to hope or believe that someone or something will do something or happen and bring you a good result: *Companies are placing increased reliance on technology.*
17 be well/ideally etc. placed to do sth to be in a good place or situation from which to do something: *The company is well placed to benefit from current trends.*
18 place a/your bet to risk money by guessing the result of a future event, especially a sports event
19 HORSE RACE [I] if a horse places in a race, it comes second

pla·ce·bo /plə'siboʊ/ *n. plural* **placebos, placeboes** [C] **1** MEDICINE a substance given to a patient instead of medicine, without telling them it is not real, either because they are not really sick or because it is part of a test on a drug **2 a/the placebo effect** when a patient becomes well after taking a placebo because they think they are taking real medicine [**Origin:** 1700–1800 Latin **I shall please**, from *placere*]

'place card *n.* [C] a small card with someone's name on it, put on a table to show where they are going to sit

'place kick *n.* [C] a kick at a ball, especially in football, when the ball is placed or held on the ground —**placekicker** *n.* [C]

'place mat *n.* [C] a MAT that you put on a table for each person who is eating there, to protect the table

place·ment /'pleɪsmənt/ *n.* **1** [U] the process of finding a place for someone to live, work, or go to college: *job placement services* | +**of** *the placement of children in foster care* **2** [C,U] the act of placing something in position: +**of** *the placement of fire hydrants on city streets*

'place name *n.* [C] the name of a particular place, such as a town, city, mountain etc.

pla·cen·ta /plə'sɛntə/ *n.* [C] BIOLOGY an ORGAN that forms inside a woman's UTERUS through which blood containing food and oxygen passes to the baby —**placental** *adj.*: *placental tissue*

plac·er min·ing /'plæsɚ ˌmaɪnɪŋ/ *n.* [U] the process of obtaining a valuable mineral such as gold by washing away the sand in which it is contained

'place ˌsetting *n.* [C] the arrangement on a table of knives, forks, spoons, glasses etc. to be used by one person

plac·id /'plæsɪd/ *adj.* calm and peaceful: *the placid water of the lake* [**Origin:** 1600–1700 Latin *placidus*, from *placere* **to please, be decided**] —**placidly** *adv.* —**placidity** /plæ'sɪdət̬i/ *n.* [U]

plack·et /'plækɪt/ *n.* [C] an opening at the top front of a dress, shirt etc. that makes it easier to pull over your head, and that often fastens with buttons

pla·gia·rism /'pleɪdʒəˌrɪzəm/ *n.* **1** [U] the act of using someone else's words, ideas, or work and pretending they are your own: *Plagiarism will not be tolerated in student essays.* **2** [C] an idea, phrase, story etc. that has been copied from someone else's work, without stating that this is where it came from [**Origin:** 1600–1700 *plagiary* **plagiarism** (17–19 centuries), from Latin *plagiarius* **thief**] —**plagiarist** *n.* [C]

pla·gia·rize /'pleɪdʒəˌraɪz/ *v.* [I,T] to take words, ideas etc. from someone else's work and use them in your work, without stating where they came from and as if they were your own ideas etc.: *Kevin was expelled for plagiarizing a term paper.*

plague¹ /pleɪg/ *n.* **1** [U] also **the plague** MEDICINE a very infectious disease that produces high fever and swellings on the body, and often leads to death, especially BUBONIC PLAGUE: *an outbreak of plague* → see also BLACK DEATH **2** [C,U] MEDICINE any disease that causes death and spreads quickly to a large number of people **3 a plague of rats/locusts etc.** an uncontrollable and harmful increase in the numbers of a particular animal or insect **4** [singular] something bad that is very common: +**on** *Domestic violence is a plague on America.* [**Origin:** 1300–1400 Old French *plage*, from Latin *plaga* **hit, wound**] → see also **avoid sb/sth like the plague** at AVOID (2)

plague² *v.* [T] **1** to cause regular discomfort, suffering, or trouble to someone: *Heavy rains continue to plague the state.* **2** to annoy someone, especially by asking them for something again and again: **plague sb with sth** *The kids have been plaguing me with questions.*

plaid /plæd/ *n.* [U] a pattern of squares and crossed colored lines, used mainly on cloth —**plaid** *adj.*: *a plaid dress* → see also TARTAN

plain¹ /pleɪn/ S3 *adj.*
1 CLEAR very clear, and easy to understand or recognize: **it is plain that** *It was plain that Max didn't agree.* | *From the first day I met her, Caroline* ***made it plain that*** (=showed clearly) *she didn't like me.* | *Why don't you just say it* ***in plain English*** (=without using technical or difficult words)? | *This is harassment,* ***plain and simple.*** ►see THESAURUS box at **clear¹**
2 WITH NOTHING SPECIAL/EXTRA without anything added or without decoration SYN **simple**: *a plain blue suit* | *plain vanilla ice cream* | *I just had* ***plain old*** *spaghetti.*
3 as plain as day also **as plain as the nose on your face** very clear to see or understand: *Phil loves her – that's as plain as day.*
4 HONEST showing clearly and honestly what you think about something, without trying to hide anything: *I've never seen her before in my life, and that's* ***the plain truth.***
5 NOT BEAUTIFUL not beautiful or particularly attractive → see also PLAIN JANE
6 (just) plain... SPOKEN **a)** used before a noun to emphasize it: *There's no other word for it. It's just plain mismanagement.* **b)** used before someone's name to

emphasize that it is simple or ordinary or that they do not have a special title: *No, it's not "Doctor Delaney" – it's just plain Mr. Delaney.* → see also PLAIN³
7 in plain sight if something is in plain sight, it is very easy to see or notice, especially when it should be hidden: *They left the drugs lying around in plain sight.*
8 in plain clothes police officers in plain clothes are wearing regular clothes instead of a uniform —**plainness** *n.* [U] → see also PLAINLY, see also PLAIN-CLOTHES

plain² *n.* **1** [C] also **plains** a large area of flat dry land: *the plains of Nebraska* **2** [U] the ordinary stitch in KNITTING

plain³ *adv.* **(just) plain...** INFORMAL used before an adjective in order to emphasize it: *Jason's just plain lucky he wasn't hurt.* → see also PLAINLY

plain·chant /ˈpleɪnˌtʃænt/ *n.* [U] PLAINSONG

ˌplain-ˈclothes *adj.* [only before noun] plain-clothes police are police who wear ordinary clothes so that they can work without being recognized

plain ˈJane *n.* [C] INFORMAL a woman who is not attractive, but is not ugly either

ˈplain-Jane *adj.* [only before noun] INFORMAL a plain-Jane person or thing is not attractive or interesting: *cheap plain-Jane houses*

plain·ly /ˈpleɪnli/ *adv.* **1** in a way that is easy to hear, see, notice etc. SYN **clearly**: *The price is marked plainly on the tag.* | *She was plainly upset.* **2** speaking honestly, and without trying to hide the truth: *She told him plainly that she did not love him.* **3** [sentence adverb] if something is plainly true, necessary, correct etc., it is easy to see that it is true etc. SYN **obviously**: *Plainly, the drug laws are not effective.* **4** simply or without decoration: *a plainly dressed man*

plain·song /ˈpleɪnsɔŋ/ *n.* [U] a type of old Christian church music in which a group of people sing a simple tune together, without musical instruments

plain·spo·ken /ˌpleɪnˈspoʊkən◂/ *adj.* APPROVING saying exactly what you think, especially in a way that people think is honest rather than impolite

plaint /pleɪnt/ *n.* [C] LITERARY a complaint or a sad cry

plain·tiff /ˈpleɪntɪf/ *n.* [C] LAW the person who brings a legal action against another person in a CIVIL COURT (=court of law that deals with the affairs of private citizens rather than crime) → see also DEFENDANT

plain·tive /ˈpleɪntɪv/ *adj.* a plaintive sound is high and sad, like someone crying: *the plaintive cry of wolves* —**plaintively** *adv.*

plait /plæt, pleɪt/ *n.* [C] OLD-FASHIONED a BRAID in a person's hair or a horse's MANE —**plait** *v.* [T]

plan¹ /plæn/ S1 W1 *n.* [C]
1 INTENTION [usually plural] something you have decided to do at a particular time: *His plan is to work abroad for a year.* | *Please don't **change** your **plans** for me.* | *There's been **a change of plan** – I'm not flying to Seattle today.* | *Do you **have plans** Friday night?* | *We still haven't **made plans for*** (=prepared for) *the trip to Tahiti.* | **plans to do sth** *I have no plans to retire.* | *Our **plans fell through*** (=did not happen as you had hoped) *at the last minute.*

> **THESAURUS**
> **plot/conspiracy** a secret plan to do something bad or illegal, especially a plan that involves a lot of people: *a plot to assassinate the President*
> **scheme** a plan, especially to do something bad or illegal: *a scheme to trick people out of their savings*
> **strategy** a careful plan aimed at achieving something difficult: *the government's economic strategy*
> **schedule** a plan of what someone is going to do and when s/he is going to do it: *According to the schedule, there are three meetings about this in October.*
> **timetable** a plan that shows the exact times when something should happen: *Is there a timetable for removing the troops from the country?*

2 METHOD/ARRANGEMENT a set of actions for achieving something in the future, especially one that has been considered carefully and in detail: *the state's highway improvement plan* | +**for** *a plan for a peaceful transfer of power* | **a plan to do sth** *World leaders met to discuss plans to eliminate chemical weapons.* | *Have you decided on **a plan of action**?* | **devise/come up with/work out etc. a plan** *They've devised a plan to ease the flow of traffic downtown.* | *They decided to **go ahead with plans** for the wedding.* → see also INSTALLMENT PLAN
3 go according to plan to happen in the way that was arranged: *If everything goes according to plan, we'll be done in October.*
4 plan A INFORMAL your first plan, which you will use if things happen as you expect: *So, plan A is for Christen to come down on the bus.*
5 plan B INFORMAL your second plan, which you can use if things do not happen as you expect: *If the bus doesn't run on Sunday, then plan B is to drive up and pick her up.*
6 DRAWING a) TECHNICAL a drawing of a building, room, or machine as it would be seen from above, showing the shape, measurements, position of the walls etc.: *an architect's plans* → see also FLOOR PLAN, GROUND PLAN **b)** a drawing that shows exactly how something will be arranged: *a seating plan for the reception*
7 MAP a drawing similar to a map, showing roads, towns, and buildings: *a street-plan of Hartford*
[**Origin:** 1600–1700 French **drawing of a building at ground level**; partly from Latin *planum* **level ground**, partly from French *planter* **to plant**]

plan² S1 W1 *v.* **planned, planning** **1** [I,T] to think carefully about something you want to achieve, and decide exactly how you will do it: *He immediately began planning his escape.* | *It's best to **plan ahead*** (=make plans for a long time in the future) *for international vacations.* | *The graduation ceremony **went** exactly **as planned**.* | **plan what/when/where etc.** *Have you planned what you will say?* | **be planned for tomorrow/next week etc.** *Talks are planned for next Tuesday.* **2** [I,T] to intend to do something: *I'm not planning any career changes right now.* | **plan to do sth** *I was planning to call you tonight.* → see also PLAN ON **3** [T] to decide how you want to make or build something, and exactly what it will be like SYN **design**: *They're still planning the layout of the magazine cover.* → see also PLANNED

plan on sth *phr. v.* **1** to expect something to happen in a particular way SYN **count on**: **plan on sb/sth doing sth** *Don't plan on Todd being on time.* **2** to intend to do something: *How long are you planning on staying?*

plan sth ↔ **out** *phr. v.* to plan something carefully, considering all the possible problems: *I'll get a map so we can plan out our route.*

Planck /plɑŋk/, **Max** /mæks/ (1858–1947) a German scientist who developed the ideas on which QUANTUM THEORY is based

ˌPlanck's ˈconstant *n.* [U] symbol **h** PHYSICS a unit that is used in QUANTUM MECHANICS, equal to 6.626×10^{-34} JOULE-SECONDS. This is the RATIO of the energy of a PHOTON to its FREQUENCY.

plane¹ /pleɪn/ S2 W2 *n.* [C]
1 AIR VEHICLE a vehicle that flies in the air and has wings and at least one engine SYN **airplane**: *It's quicker to go **by plane**.* | *The **plane** will **take off** in 20 minutes.* | *What time does the **plane land**?* | *We were **on the plane*** (=riding inside of a plane) *for more than ten hours.* | **get on/off the plane** *It was raining when I got off the plane.*

> **THESAURUS**
> **airplane** a plane
> **aircraft** a plane or another vehicle that can fly
> **jet** a fast plane with a jet engine
> **Planes that carry people**
> **passenger plane, airliner, jumbo jet**
> **Military planes**
> **bomber, fighter (plane), warplane**

People on a plane
captain, **pilot**, **co-pilot**, **flight crew**, **cabin crew/flight attendants** (=the people whose job is to take care of the passengers), **steward/stewardess** (=a man or woman whose job is to serve food and drinks to passengers)

2 LEVEL/STANDARD a level or standard of thought, development, conversation etc.: *Let's try to keep the discussion on a friendly plane.*
3 MATH a TWO-DIMENSIONAL flat surface in GEOMETRY that contains the straight lines that connect any two of its points
4 FLAT SURFACE a flat or level surface
5 TOOL a tool that has a flat bottom with a sharp blade in it, used for making wooden surfaces smooth
6 TREE also **plane tree** BIOLOGY a large tree with broad leaves that is often planted along streets

plane² *v.* [T] to use a PLANE on a piece of wood to make it smooth

plane³ *adj.* [only before noun] TECHNICAL completely flat and smooth: *a plane surface*

ˈplane geˌometry *n.* [U] MATH the study of lines, shapes etc. that are TWO-DIMENSIONAL (=with measurements in only two directions, not three)

plane·load /ˈpleɪnloʊd/ *n.* [C] the number of people or amount of something that an airplane will hold: *a planeload of refugees*

plan·er /ˈpleɪnɚ/ *n.* [C] a machine or electrical tool for making wooden surfaces smooth

ˈplane ˌsymmetry *n.* [U] BIOLOGY BILATERAL SYMMETRY

plan·et /ˈplænɪt/ S3 W2 *n.* **1** [C] PHYSICS a very large round object in space that moves around the sun or another star; Earth is a planet: *Saturn is the planet with rings around it.* | *the planet Earth* | *Is there life **on** other **planets**?* ▸see THESAURUS box at **space¹** **2 the planet** an expression meaning Earth or the world, used when talking about the environment: *the future of the planet* **3 what planet is sb from/on?** also **sb is (living) on another planet** SPOKEN, HUMOROUS used to say that someone does not seem to understand things that are clear to most people, or that their ideas are not at all practical or sensible [**Origin:** 1100–1200 Old French *planete*, from Late Latin *planeta*, from Greek *planes* **wanderer**] —**planetary** *adj.*

plan·e·tar·i·um /ˌplænəˈtɛriəm/ *n.* [C] a building where lights on a curved ceiling show the movements of planets and stars

plan·gent /ˈplændʒənt/ *adj.* LITERARY a plangent sound is loud and deep and sounds sad

plank /plæŋk/ *n.* [C] **1** a long narrow, usually heavy, piece of wooden board, used especially for making structures to walk on: *a plank of wood* → see also **walk the plank** at WALK¹ (15) **2** one of the main principles that makes up a political PARTY's statement of its aims: *a central plank of the Republican platform* → see also PLATFORM

plank·ing /ˈplæŋkɪŋ/ *n.* [U] many planks that are put together to make a floor

plank·ton /ˈplæŋktən/ *n.* [U] BIOLOGY the very small ORGANISMS that live in the ocean and other areas of water, and are eaten by fish → see picture at FOOD CHAIN

planned /plænd/ *adj.* **1** [only before noun] a planned action or thing is one that you are intending to take or make: *a planned sequel to the book* **2** carefully thought out and decided: *a planned economy* | *The pregnancy wasn't planned.*

ˌplanned obsoˈlescence *n.* [U] the practice of making products that will not be useful or popular for very long, so that people will always have to buy newer, more useful, or popular products to replace them

ˌPlanned ˈParenthood a U.S. organization, with offices all over the country, that provides advice on FAMILY PLANNING

plan·ner /ˈplænɚ/ *n.* [C] **1** someone whose job is to plan things: *a city planner* **2** someone who plans something: *a careful planner* **3** a document, book, or computer program that you can use for planning something

plant¹ /plænt/ S2 W1 *n.* **1** [C] BIOLOGY a living thing that has leaves and roots and grows in earth, especially one that is smaller than a tree: *Don't forget to water the plants.* | *a tomato plant* → see also HOUSEPLANT **2** [C] a factory or building where an industrial process happens: *a textile manufacturing plant* → see also POWER PLANT **3** [C usually singular] something illegal or stolen that is hidden in someone's clothes or possessions to make them seem guilty: *Carlson swore to the police that the drugs were a plant.* **4** [C] someone who is put somewhere or sent somewhere secretly to find out information SYN spy [**Origin:** Old English *plante*, from Latin *planta* **new growth on a plant, part cut off a plant to be grown again**]

plant² S3 W3 *v.* [T]
1 PLANT/SEEDS BIOLOGY to put plants or seeds in the ground to grow: *We planted tomatoes and carrots in the garden.*
2 plant a field/garden/area etc. (with sth) BIOLOGY to plant seeds, plants, or trees in a field, garden etc.: *The field over there is planted with soy beans.*
3 PUT STH SOMEWHERE [always + adv./prep.] INFORMAL to put something firmly in or on something else, or to move somewhere and stay there: **plant sth in/on etc. sth** *She planted her feet wide apart.* | *Grandma **planted** a big wet **kiss** on my cheek.* | **plant yourself** *He planted himself between her and the door.*
4 HIDE ILLEGAL GOODS [T] INFORMAL to hide stolen or illegal goods in someone's clothes, bags, room etc. in order to make them seem guilty: **plant sth on sb** *Someone must have planted the drugs on her.*
5 plant a bomb/device INFORMAL to put a bomb somewhere: *Two men are accused of planting the bomb on the plane.*
6 PERSON [T] to put or send someone somewhere, especially secretly, so that they can find out information: **plant sb in/at etc. sth** *The FBI had planted two agents in the organization.*
7 plant an idea/doubt/suspicion (in sb's mind) to make someone begin to believe an idea, begin to doubt something etc., especially so that they do not realize it was you who gave them the idea: *Their conversation had planted doubts in his mind about the partnership.*

Plan·tae /ˈplænti/ *n.* [singular] BIOLOGY the KINGDOM (=class) of living things that consists of all plants

Plan·tag·e·net /plænˈtædʒənɪt/ the name of the Royal Family of England from 1154 to 1399

plan·tain /ˈplæntˀn/ *n.* [C,U] a type of BANANA that is cooked before it is eaten, or the plant on which it grows [**Origin:** 1500–1600 Spanish *plántano*, from Latin *platanus* type of tree]

plan·tar /ˈplæntɚ, -ˌtɑr/ *adj.* relating to the SOLE (=bottom) of your feet: *plantar warts*

plan·ta·tion /plænˈteɪʃən/ *n.* [C] **1** a large area of land in a hot country, where crops such as tea, cotton, and sugar etc. are grown: *a coffee plantation* **2** a large farm in the U.S. South in the past that used SLAVES to grow cotton, tobacco etc. **3** a large group of trees grown to produce wood

plant·er /ˈplæntɚ/ *n.* [C] **1** an attractive, often decorated, container for growing plants in **2** someone who owns or is in charge of a plantation: *a rice planter* **3** a machine used for planting

plant·ing /ˈplæntɪŋ/ *n.* **1** [C,U] the action of planting a plant or crop: *the planting of new trees* **2** [C usually plural] a plant or crop that has been planted: *Don't forget to water new plantings.*

plaque /plæk/ *n.* **1** [C] a piece of flat metal or stone with writing on it, used as a prize in a competition or to remind people of an event or person: *a commemorative plaque by the entrance to the building* **2** [U] MEDICINE a substance that forms on your teeth, in which BACTERIA that can damage your teeth can live [**Origin:** 1800–1900 French, Dutch *plak*, from *plakken* **to stick**]

plas·ma /ˈplæzmə/ *n.* [U] **1** BIOLOGY the yellowish liquid part of the blood that contains blood cells

2 BIOLOGY the living substance inside a cell SYN **protoplasm** 3 PHYSICS a gas that exists at very high temperatures, for example in stars, which consists of IONS and ELECTRONS

ˌplasma ˈmembrane *n.* [C,U] BIOLOGY a thin layer of material surrounding a cell, through which substances pass in and out SYN **cell membrane**

ˈplasma screen *n.* [C] a type of very thin high-quality television or computer screen made of very small cells that are filled with gas and give off light when electricity passes through them → see also FLAT SCREEN

plas·mid /ˈplæzmɪd/ *n.* [C] TECHNICAL BIOLOGY a small circle of DNA that is separate from the CHROMOSOME and is able to make copies of itself. It is found especially in the cells of BACTERIA. → see picture at BACTERIUM

plas·ter¹ /ˈplæstɚ/ *n.* [U] **1** a substance used to cover walls and ceilings and give a smooth surface, consisting of LIME, water, and sand **2** PLASTER OF PARIS

plaster² *v.* [T usually passive] **1** to spread or stick something all over a surface so that it is thickly covered: **plaster sth with sth** *The wall was plastered with old movie posters.* **2** to cover the pages of a newspaper with a particular story or report: **be plastered across/all over sth** *The boys' names were plastered across the front pages of every newspaper.* **3** to put wet plaster on a wall or ceiling **4** to make your hair lie flat or stick to your head: **be plastered down/to** *His hair was plastered to his forehead with sweat.*

plaster sth ↔ **over** *phr. v.* to cover a hole or an old surface by spreading plaster over it

plas·ter·board /ˈplæstɚˌbɔrd/ *n.* [U] DRYWALL

ˌplaster ˈcast *n.* [C] **1** a hard cover that is used to keep a broken bone in place while it grows together SYN **cast** **2** ENG. LANG. ARTS a copy or model of something made using PLASTER OF PARIS

plas·tered /ˈplæstɚd/ *adj.* [not before noun] INFORMAL very drunk

plas·ter·er /ˈplæstərɚ/ *n.* [C] someone whose job is to cover walls and ceilings with PLASTER

ˌplaster of ˈParis *n.* [U] a mixture of white powder and water that dries quickly, used especially for making models or STATUES

plas·tic¹ /ˈplæstɪk/ S2 W3 *adj.* **1** [only before noun] made of plastic: *a plastic spoon* | *plastic bags* **2** DISAPPROVING, INFORMAL appearing or tasting artificial or not natural SYN **artificial**: *I hate that plastic smile of hers.* **3** TECHNICAL a plastic substance can be formed into many different shapes, and it keeps a shape until it is changed

plastic² S3 *n.* **1** [C,U] CHEMISTRY a light strong material that is chemically produced, that can be made into different shapes when it is soft and is used to make many things: *The doors are made of plastic so they don't dent.* **2** [singular U] INFORMAL a CREDIT CARD, or credit cards considered as a group [**Origin:** 1500–1600 Latin *plasticus* **of shaping**, from Greek *plastikos*, from *plassein* **to shape, form, plaster**]

ˌplastic ˈart *n.* [C,U] TECHNICAL art that shows things in ways in which they can be clearly seen, especially painting or SCULPTURE

ˌplastic ˈbullet *n.* [C] a large bullet made of hard plastic that is intended to injure but not kill, and is used for controlling violent crowds

ˌplastic exˈplosive *n.* [C,U] an explosive substance that can be shaped by hand, or a small bomb made from this

plas·tic·i·ty /plæˈstɪsət̮i/ *n.* [U] TECHNICAL the quality of being easily made into any shape

ˌplastic ˈsurgeon *n.* [C] a doctor who does plastic surgery

ˌplastic ˈsurgery *n.* [U] the medical practice of changing the appearance of people's faces or bodies, either to improve their appearance or to repair injuries

ˌplastic ˈwrap *n.* [U] thin transparent plastic used to cover food in order to keep it fresh

Pla·ta /ˈplɑt̮ə/**, Rí·o de la** /ˈrioʊ dɛ lɑ/ a BAY on the eastern coast of South America, between Argentina and Uruguay, where the Paraná and Uruguay rivers join the Atlantic Ocean

plat du jour /ˌplɑ də ˈʒʊr, ˌplæ-/ *n.* [C] a dish that a restaurant prepares specially on a particular day in addition to its usual food

plate¹ /pleɪt/ S1 W2 *n.*
1 FOOD [C] **a)** a flat and usually round dish that you eat from or serve food from: *a salad plate* | **clean/empty your plate** (=eat everything on your plate) **b)** the amount of food that is on a plate SYN **plateful**: +**of** *a plate of cookies* **c)** a meal served on a large plate in a restaurant SYN **platter**: *a vegetable plate*
2 A SHEET OF METAL [C] a sheet of metal used to protect something: *Steel plates were used to repair the damage to the ship.*
3 **have a lot/too much etc. on your plate** INFORMAL to have a lot to deal with or a lot of things to think about: *I'm sure he has enough on his plate already.*
4 SIGN [C] a flat piece of metal with words or numbers on it, for example on a door or a car: *A brass plate on the door gave his name.* → see also NAMEPLATE
5 **plates** [plural] INFORMAL LICENSE PLATES on a car, truck etc.: *a truck with New Jersey plates*
6 EARTH'S SURFACE [C] EARTH SCIENCE one of the very large areas of rock that form the surface of the Earth → see also PLATE TECTONICS
7 **the plate** the place in baseball where the person hitting the ball stands SYN **home plate** → see also **step up to the plate** at STEP UP (2)
8 IN A CHURCH also **collection plate** a small plate or container, used to collect money in a Christian church
9 GOLD/SILVER ETC. **a)** **gold/silver etc. plate** ordinary metal with a thin covering of gold, silver etc. **b)** [U] articles such as plates, cups, forks, or knives covered with gold or silver
10 **hand/give sb sth on a plate** to make it easy for someone to get or achieve something, so that they do not have to make much effort
11 PICTURES/PHOTOS [C] **a)** a picture in a book, usually in color, that is printed on good-quality paper **b)** a sheet of metal that has been cut or treated so that words or pictures can be printed from its surface **c)** TECHNICAL a thin sheet of glass used especially in past times in photography, with chemicals on it that are sensitive to light
12 PROTECTIVE COVERING [C] TECHNICAL one of the thin sheets of bone, horn etc. that covers and protects the outside of an animal: *The reptile's body is covered with horny plates.*
13 TEETH [C] a thin piece of plastic that fits inside a person's mouth, which false teeth are attached to
[**Origin:** (1, 3, 8) 1400–1500 French *plat* **plate, dish** , from *plat* **flat**, from Vulgar Latin *plattus*] → see also -PLATED

plate² *v.* [T] **be plated with sth** **a)** to have a thin covering of gold, silver etc.: *Even their faucets had been plated with gold.* **b)** to be covered in thin pieces of a hard material such as metal or bone: *The President's limousine is plated with armor.*

pla·teau¹ /plæˈtoʊ/ *n. plural* **plateaus**, **plateaux** /-ˈtoʊz/ [C] **1** EARTH SCIENCE a large area of flat land that is higher than the land around it **2** a period during which the level of cost, achievement etc. does not change much, especially after a period when it was increasing: **reach/hit a plateau** *Attendance at health clubs has reached a plateau.*

plateau² *v.* [I] if costs, achievement etc. plateau, they do not change much, especially after increasing for a period of time: *Interest rates have plateaued at 8%.*

-plated /pleɪt̮ɪd/ [in adjectives] **gold-plated/silver-plated/brass-plated etc.** covered with a thin covering of gold, silver etc.: *a gold-plated necklace* → see also ARMOR-PLATED

plate·ful /ˈpleɪtfʊl/ *n.* [C] all the food that is on a plate: *The pasta was so good, I just had to have a second plateful.*

ˌplate ˈglass *n.* [U] big pieces of glass made in large thick pieces, used especially for store windows

P

plate·let /ˈpleɪtlət/ *n.* [C] BIOLOGY a piece of cell that the body releases into the blood to help stop bleeding after an injury

ˌplate tecˈtonics *n.* [U] EARTH SCIENCE the study of the forming and movement of the large areas of rock that form the surface of the Earth

plat·form /ˈplætfɔrm/ W3 *n.* [C]
1 FOR SPEECHES a raised floor or stage for people to stand on when they are making a speech, performing etc.: *Professor Allen stepped up onto the platform.*
2 STRUCTURE a tall structure built so that people can stand or work above the surrounding area: *a gas drilling platform*
3 POLITICS [usually singular] POLITICS the main ideas and aims of a political party, especially the ones that they state just before an election: *The party's new platform emphasizes rural development.* → see also PLANK
4 CHANCE TO SAY STH a chance for someone to express their opinions, especially their political opinions: *Actors have a good platform to promote their causes.*
5 SUPPORT something that gives you the support, help, power etc. that you need to do something: *The funding will provide a platform for growth.*
6 COMPUTERS a particular type of computer system or SOFTWARE: *a multimedia platform*
7 TRAIN the raised place beside a railroad track where you get on and off a train in a station: *The train to Boston leaves from Platform 9.*
8 platforms [plural] also **platform shoes** shoes with a thick layer of wood, leather etc. beneath the front part and the heel
[**Origin:** 1500–1600 French *plateforme* **diagram, map,** from *plat* **flat** + *forme* **form**]

Plath /plæθ/**, Syl·vi·a** /ˈsɪlviə/ (1932–1963) a U.S. poet

plat·ing /ˈpleɪt̬ɪŋ/ *n.* [U] a thin layer of metal that covers another metal surface: *gold plating*

plat·i·num¹ /ˈplætˀnəm, ˈplætˀn-əm/ *n.* [U] SYMBOL **Pt** CHEMISTRY a silver-gray metal that is an ELEMENT, that does not change color or lose its brightness, and is used in making expensive jewelry and in industry

platinum² *adj.* **1** made of platinum: *a platinum ring* **2** a platinum recording is one of which at least a million copies have been sold: *Eight of his albums **went platinum**.* **3** platinum hair is a silver-white color, especially because it has been colored with chemicals

ˌplatinum ˈblonde *n.* [C] a woman whose hair is a silver-white color, especially one whose hair has been colored with chemicals —**platinum blonde** *adj.*

plat·i·tude /ˈplæt̬əˌtud/ *n.* [C] a statement that has been made many times before and is not interesting or intelligent: *meaningless platitudes* —**platitudinous** /ˌplæt̬əˈtudn-əs/ *adj.*

Pla·to /ˈpleɪt̬oʊ/ (?427–347 B.C.) an ancient Greek PHILOSOPHER, who had a very great influence on European philosophy

pla·ton·ic /pləˈtɑnɪk/ *adj.* **1** a platonic relationship is just friendly, and is not a sexual relationship **2 Platonic** relating to or influenced by the ideas of Plato: *Platonic ideas* —**platonically** /-kli/ *adv.*

pla·toon /pləˈtun/ *n.* [C] a small group of soldiers that is part of a COMPANY and is usually led by a LIEUTENANT [**Origin:** 1600–1700 French *peloton* **ball, small group,** from *pelote* **little ball**]

Platt A·mend·ment, the /ˈplæt əˌmɛndmənt/ HISTORY an addition to the 1901 Cuban CONSTITUTION made by the U.S. government, which gave the U.S. the right to keep ships from their Navy at ports in Cuba and to involve itself in Cuban affairs whenever necessary

plat·ter /ˈplæt̬ɚ/ *n.* [C] **1** a large plate from which food is served: *a serving platter* **2 a chicken/seafood/combo etc. platter** a meal of chicken or other foods arranged on a plate and served in a restaurant **3** OLD-FASHIONED a RECORD

plat·y·pus /ˈplæt̬əpəs/ *n.* [C] a small furry Australian animal that has a beak and feet like a duck, lays eggs, and gives milk to its young

plau·dits /ˈplɔdɪts/ *n.* [plural] FORMAL praise and admiration: **win/draw plaudits** *Her ideas have won plaudits from scientists.*

plau·si·ble /ˈplɔzəbəl/ *adj.* **1** seeming reasonable and likely to be true OPP **implausible**: *Langham's story sounded plausible at the time.* **2** [only before noun] good enough to be considered seriously for a particular job or purpose: *There were no plausible candidates for the job.* [**Origin:** 1500–1600 Latin *plausibilis* **worth applauding,** from *plaudere*] —**plausibly** *adv.* —**plausibility** /ˌplɔzəˈbɪləti/ *n.* [U]

play¹ /pleɪ/ S1 W1 *v.* **plays, played, playing**
1 SPORTS/GAMES a) [I,T] to take part or compete in a game or sport: *Do you want to play, Carl?* | **play basketball/soccer/cards etc.** *The guys are outside playing basketball.* | **play (against) sb** *The Rockets are playing the Bulls this weekend.* | **play sth with sb** *Will you play a game of cards with me?* | **+for** *He played for Denver from 1995 to 1997.* **b)** [T] to use a particular piece, card, person etc. in a game or sport: *She played the ace of clubs.*
2 CHILDREN [I,T] when children play, they do things that they enjoy, often with other people or with toys: *Kendra's in her room playing.* | *Andy loves to play hide-and-go-seek.* | **+with** *He enjoys playing with his grandchildren.* | *Tony has a lot of toys to play with.*
3 MUSIC/INSTRUMENT [I,T] **a)** ENG. LANG. ARTS to perform a piece of music on a musical instrument: *There's a good band playing on Saturday night.* | *She played a piece by Debussy.* | **play in a band/orchestra** *Nancy plays in the school orchestra.* **b)** to have the ability to play a musical instrument: **play (the) piano/guitar/violin etc.** *Matt plays the drums.*
4 RADIO/CD/TAPE ETC. if a radio, STEREO etc. plays or you make it play, it produces sound, especially music: *The bedside radio played softly.* | *Do you have to play your music so loud?* | **play a CD/tape/record** *I usually play my jazz CDs to relax.*
5 play a part/role in sth to have an effect or an influence on something: *Politics played no part in my decision.*
6 IN A PLAY/MOVIE [T] ENG. LANG. ARTS to perform the actions and say the words of a particular character in a theater performance, movie etc.: *Who's playing James Bond in the new movie?* | **play a role/part/character** *Gibson convincingly played the part of the villain.*
7 PLAY/MOVIE [I] ENG. LANG. ARTS if a play or movie is playing at a particular theater, it is being performed or shown there: *The musical is still playing on Broadway.*
8 PERFORM SOMEWHERE [I always + adv./prep., T] ENG. LANG. ARTS to perform in a particular play or place: *They played small local theaters.*
9 POSITION ON A TEAM [T] to have a particular position on a sports team: *I played center in high school.*
10 BEHAVE [T always + adv./prep.] to behave in a particular way in a situation in order to achieve the result or effect that you want: *It's an important meeting so let's think how we're going to play it.* | *Janet wants to **play it safe*** (=avoid taking any risks) *and not put all of our money in stocks.* | **play it carefully/cool etc.** *It's always smarter to play it cool when you first meet a guy.*
11 play it by ear to decide what to do according to the way a situation develops, without making plans before that time: *I'm not sure exactly where I'll go in the summer – I'll play it by ear.*
12 PRETEND [linking verb] to pretend to be a particular kind of person or to have a particular feeling or quality, when this is not typical or true: *If he asks where I was, **play dumb*** (=pretend you do not know the answer). | *Some snakes **play dead** by lying limply on the ground.* | *Don't **play the fool*** (=pretend to be stupid, or behave in a silly way) *with me, young man.* | **play the teacher/the big man etc.** *Susan felt she had to play the good wife.*
13 play ball a) to throw, kick, hit, or catch a ball as a game or activity: *You kids should go outside if you want to play ball.* **b)** INFORMAL to do what someone asks you to do SYN **cooperate**: *If they won't play ball, we'll have to work with another bank.*

14 play a joke/trick on sb to do something to someone as a joke or trick: *The kids in the class decided to play a joke on their teacher.*
15 play by the rules to do what is expected and agreed on: *Some of the salesmen don't play by the rules.*
16 sb's mind/memory etc. plays tricks (on them) if your mind, memory, sight etc. plays tricks on you, you become slightly confused so that you are not sure what is correct: *My mind must be playing tricks on me – I'm sure I left my bag on the chair.*
17 play games to behave in a silly or annoying way by not being direct or serious enough: *Stop playing games and tell me what's going on.*
18 play politics to use a situation or relationships to gain an advantage: *The President is accused of playing politics with disaster relief.*
19 play the ball [always + adv./prep.] to hit a ball in a particular way or to a particular place in a game or sport: *She played the ball low, just over the net.*
20 play God DISAPPROVING to make very important decisions that no person has the right to make, for example whether someone should live or die
21 play your cards right to behave in a smart or skillful way in a situation, so that you gain as much as possible from it: *You'll get a bargain if you play your cards right.*
22 play second fiddle (to sb) to be slightly lower in rank or less important than someone or something else
23 play with fire to do something that is likely to have a very dangerous or harmful result: *Dating the boss's daughter is playing with fire.*
24 play hard to get to pretend that you are not romantically interested in someone so that they will become more interested in you: *You should call her again – I think she's just playing hard to get.*
25 play the race/nationalist/equality etc. card to use a particular subject in a public situation, especially politics, in order to gain an advantage: *She had often played the race card to silence her critics.*
26 play for time to try to delay something so that you have more time to prepare for it or prevent it from happening: *The U.S. strategy has been to play for time.*
27 play (right) into sb's hands to do something that helps someone you are competing with or fighting against, without realizing it: *Foolishly, the enemy had played right into our hands.*
28 play the system to use the rules of a system in a smart way, to gain advantage for yourself: *Accountants know how to play the tax system.*
29 play the market to risk money on the STOCK MARKET as a way of trying to earn more money
30 play the field to have romantic relationships with a lot of different people
31 play the game to do things in the way you are expected to do them or in a way that is usual in a particular situation: *In business, you have to be willing to play the game.*
32 play fast and loose with sb/sth to treat someone in a SELFISH careless way, or to not obey rules or the law carefully: *The mayor liked to play fast and loose with the rules.*
33 play hooky to stay away from school without permission
34 LIGHT [I always + adv./prep.] if light plays on something, it shines on it and moves around on it: *She watched the sunlight playing on the water.*
35 play sb for a sucker/fool to show by the way that you behave toward someone that you think they are stupid
36 SMILE [I always + adv./prep.] LITERARY if a smile plays over someone's lips, they smile quickly and only a little
[**Origin:** Old English *plegan*] → see also **play/keep/hold your cards close to your chest/vest** at CARD¹ (14), see also PLAY WITH

play along *phr. v.* **1** to pretend that you agree with someone's ideas to gain an advantage for yourself or to avoid an argument: *I wasn't sure what he was saying was true, but I decided to play along.* **2** to take part in a game with other people, especially by pretending to play a game you are watching on television

play around *phr. v.* **1** to have a sexual relationship with someone that is not serious or not intended to last very long: +**with** *He wondered if his father had ever played around with other women.* **2** to consider different ideas, try different methods etc. to see what would be best: +**with** *The architect had played around with a few different ideas.* **3** to behave in a silly way or waste time, when you should be doing something more serious SYN **fool around**

play at sth *phr. v.* **1** to do something without being very serious about it or without doing it correctly: *After college, I played at being a writer for a while.* **2** if children play at doing something or being someone, they pretend to do it or be that person

play sth ↔ **back** *phr. v.* to play something that has been recorded on a machine so that you can listen to it or watch it: *I got home and played back my messages.*

play sth ↔ **down** *phr. v.* to try to make something seem less important, serious, or likely than it really is: *The White House is trying to play down the latest scandal.*

play off *phr. v.* **1 play off sth** to deliberately use a feeling, fact, or idea in order to get what you want, often in an unfair way: *She's smart and sly, playing off her sweet image.* **2 play off sb/sth** if one person or thing plays off another, or if they play off each other, they work together in a way that makes the other's good qualities more noticeable

play sb **off against** sb *phr. v.* if you play one person off against another, you encourage them to argue with each other so that you can gain something

play on sth *phr. v.* to use someone's fears, worries, or problems in order to gain an advantage for yourself: *His campaign message plays on people's fear of losing their jobs.*

play out *phr. v.* **1 play sth ↔ out** if a situation or event plays out, is played out, or plays itself out in a particular way, it continues or develops in that way: *It's too soon to say how the situation will play itself out.* **2 play sth ↔ out** to live your life, continue your CAREER etc. in a particular way: *The contestants on the show play out their lives in front of millions.*

play sth ↔ **up** *phr. v.* to emphasize something, especially in a way that makes it seem more important than it really is: *The press has been playing up the racial aspects of the case.*

play up to sb *phr. v.* to behave in a very polite or kind way to someone because you want something from them

play with sth *phr. v.* **1** to keep touching something or moving it around SYN **play around with**: *Stop playing with the remote control!* **2** to consider the possibility of doing something, often not very seriously: *I've been playing with the idea of traveling around the world.* **3 play with words/language** to use words in a smart or amusing way **4 have time/money to play with** to have time or money that is available to be used: *We don't have much time to play with.*

play² S1 W1 *n. plural* **plays**
1 THEATER [C] ENG. LANG. ARTS a story that is written to be performed by actors, especially in a theater: *The play is about two men on trial for murder.* | *one of Shakespeare's most famous plays* | *a play by Chekhov* | *The drama club **puts on a play*** (=performs a play) *every spring.* | *He just got a part **in a play**.* | *She **writes plays** and short stories.* ►see THESAURUS box at **theater**
2 CHILDREN [U] things that people, especially children, do for amusement rather than as work: *Play is important for children.* | *She watched the children **at play**.*
3 GAME/SPORT a) [C] one particular action or set of actions during a sport or game: *On the next play, Johnson ran fifteen yards for a touchdown.* **b)** [U] the action in a sport or game: *Rain stopped play in the third round.* **c)** [U] the style or quality of the playing by a particular player or team in a game or sport: *There was some very good play in the first quarter.*
4 EFFECT/INFLUENCE [U] the state of having an effect or influence or of being used or considered: *the free play of market forces* | **at/in play** *Some strange forces were at*

play. | *During the negotiations, cultural differences will certainly* ***come into play.*** | **bring/put sth into play** *The threat of war was again brought into play.*
5 in play/out of play if a ball is in play or out of play, it is still able or no longer able to be played with according to the rules of the game, especially because it is inside or outside the area allowed by the rules
6 a play for sth an attempt to get something: *Her behavior is obviously a play for attention.*
7 a play on words a use of a word that is interesting or amusing because it can be understood as having two very different meanings SYN **pun**
8 make a play for sb/sth to try to begin a romantic relationship with someone or to try to gain something: *It was obvious that she was making a play for Don.*
9 the play of light/color/shadow etc. the way that light, color, or shadows change and make patterns in a particular situation: *the play of light on the water*
10 in play able to be won or lost in a competition, election etc.: *Some of the Midwestern states are still very much in play.*
11 LOOSENESS [U] if there is some play in something, it is loose and can be moved: **+in** *There's too much play in the rope.*

play·a·ble /ˈpleɪəbəl/ *adj.* **1** able to be played on a particular machine: **+on** *Most DVDs are playable on computers.* **2** a VIDEO GAME that is playable is fun to play, or can be played using a computer, the Internet etc.: *The game is good to look at and incredibly playable.* **3** a field or court that is playable is in good enough condition for a sports game to be played on it **4** a ball that is playable in a sports game is within the playing field, so that a player can try to catch, throw, or hit it **5** able to be played by people of a particular age or ability: *They are looking for music that will be playable for all members of the group.*

ˈplay-ˌacting *n.* [U] behavior in which someone pretends to be serious or sincere, but is not —**play-act** *v.* [I]

ˈplay-ˌaction *n.* **a play-action pass/play** the act of throwing a football after pretending to give it to another player

play·back /ˈpleɪbæk/ *n.* [C,U] the playback of a TAPE that you have recorded is when you play it on a machine in order to watch or listen to it: *You can skip the commercials during playback.*

play·bill /ˈpleɪbɪl/ *n.* [C] a printed paper advertising a play

play·book /ˈpleɪbʊk/ *n.* [C] a book that contains all the PLAYS (=actions in a sports game) that a team uses

play·boy /ˈpleɪbɔɪ/ *n.* [C] a rich man who does not work and who spends his time enjoying himself with beautiful women and fast cars

ˌplay-by-ˈplay *n.* [U] **1** also **play-by-play commentary/description** a description of the action in a sports game or other event as it happens, usually given on television or on the radio: *Hahn does play-by-play for the Kings.* **2 a play-by-play man/announcer/broadcaster** someone who tells what is happening in a sports game as it is happening

ˈplay clothes *n.* [U] clothing that children wear to play in

ˈplay date *n.* [C] a time that parents arrange so that children meet together to play

Play-Doh /ˈpleɪ doʊ/ *n.* [U] TRADEMARK a soft substance like clay made in many different colors, used by children for making shapes

ˌplayed-ˈout *adj.* **1** someone or something who is played-out is not as strong, powerful, attractive etc. as they used to be: *a played-out pony* **2** old-fashioned and not useful anymore: *played-out ideas* → see also **play out** at PLAY[1]

play·er /ˈpleɪɚ/ S1 W1 *n.* [C] **1** someone who takes part in a game or sport: *a tennis player* **2** one of the people, companies, or organizations that is involved in and influences a situation: **+in/on** *Poland has been* ***a major player*** *in the transformation of Eastern Europe.* | *a conference involving the industry's* ***key players*** **3 a CD/record/tape etc. player** a piece of equipment that is used to play CDS, records etc. **4** ENG. LANG. ARTS someone who plays a musical instrument: *a bass player* **5** a man who has sexual relationships with many different women **6** OLD-FASHIONED an actor

ˌplayer piˈano *n.* [C] a piano that is played by machinery inside it. A long roll of paper with holes cut in it gradually turns and tells the machinery which notes to play.

play·ful /ˈpleɪfəl/ *adj.* **1** intended to be fun rather than serious, or showing that you are having fun: *a playful series of ads for milk* | *a playful smile* **2** very active, happy, and wanting to have fun: *a playful kitten* —**playfully** *adv.* —**playfulness** *n.* [U]

play·go·er /ˈpleɪˌgoʊɚ/ *n.* [C] someone who often goes to see plays

play·ground /ˈpleɪgraʊnd/ *n.* [C] **1** an area for children to play, especially at a school or in a park, that often has special equipment for climbing on, riding on etc.: *kids running on the playground* **2** a place where a particular group of people go to enjoy themselves: *a resort that is a playground of the rich and famous*

ˈplay group *n.* [C,U] a group of children, usually between two and four years old, whose parents meet each week so that the children can play together

play·house /ˈpleɪhaʊs/ *n.* [C] **1** ENG. LANG. ARTS a word meaning a "theater," often used as part of a theater's name **2** a small structure like a little house for children to play in

ˈplaying card *n.* [C] FORMAL a CARD

ˈplaying field *n.* [C] a large piece of ground with particular areas marked out for playing football, SOCCER etc. → see also **a level playing field** at LEVEL[2] (3)

play·list, play list /ˈpleɪlɪst/ *n.* [C] the list of songs that a radio station plays

play·mak·er /ˈpleɪˌmeɪkɚ/ *n.* [C] someone in sports such as football or basketball who is skillful at making points or at giving their team an advantage

play·mate /ˈpleɪmeɪt/ *n.* [C] a friend that a child plays with

ˈplay ˌmoney *n.* [U] money used in games that is not real

play·off /ˈpleɪɔf/ *n.* [C usually plural] a game, usually one of a series of games, played by the best teams or players in a sports competition in order to decide the final winner: *The Lakers will meet the Bulls* ***in the playoffs.***

play·pen /ˈpleɪpɛn/ *n.* [C] an enclosed space in which a small child can play safely, that is like an open box with sides made of bars or a net

play·room /ˈpleɪrum/ *n.* [C] a room for children to play in

play·thing /ˈpleɪˌθɪŋ/ *n.* [C] **1** FORMAL a toy **2** someone who you use for your own amusement, without caring about their feelings or needs: *men who treat women as playthings*

play·time /ˈpleɪtaɪm/ *n.* [U] a period of time during which a child can play

play·wright /ˈpleɪraɪt/ *n.* [C] someone who writes plays SYN **dramatist** —**playwriting** *n.*

pla·za /ˈplɑzə, ˈplæzə/ *n.* [C] **1** a group of stores and other business buildings in a town, with outdoor areas between them: *a large shopping plaza* → see also MALL **2** a public area or market place surrounded by buildings, especially in towns in Spanish-speaking countries **3** an area near a HIGHWAY (=large road) where you can stop to buy food or gasoline, use the toilet etc.: *a service plaza* → see also TOLL PLAZA

plea /pli/ *n.* **1** [C] a request that is urgent or full of emotion: *Taylor* ***made an*** *emotional* ***plea*** *for donations.* | **+for** *a mother's plea for help* **2** [C usually singular] LAW a statement by someone in a court of law saying whether they are guilty or not: **make/enter a plea** *Clark entered a plea of "not guilty."* **3** [singular] an excuse for something: *He refused to come* ***on the plea that*** *he had work to do at home.*

ˈplea ˌbargain *n.* [C] an agreement in which you say you are guilty of one crime, in exchange for not going to court for a more serious crime —**plea bargain** *v.* [I,T] —**plea bargaining** *n.* [U]

plead /plid/ W3 *v.* **1** [I,T] to ask for something that you want very much, in a sincere and emotional way SYN **beg**: *"You've got to help me," Mason pleaded.* | **+for** *The President pleaded for tolerance of loyal Arab-Americans.* | **plead with sb (to do sth)** *Leslie pleaded with him to stay.* ▸see THESAURUS box at **ask** **2** [I] *past tense and past participle* **pleaded** or **pled** /plɛd/ LAW to state in a court of law whether or not you are guilty of a crime: *"How do you plead?" "Not guilty, your Honor."* | **plead guilty/innocent/no contest etc.** *Hoskins pled guilty to four charges of theft.* **3** *past tense and past participle* **pleaded** or **pled** /plɛd/ **plead ignorance/poverty/insanity etc.** to give a particular excuse for your actions: *The university pleaded poverty, saying it could not afford to give coaches a raise.* **4** [T] to give reasons why you think something is true or why something should be done: *Residents have a chance to* ***plead*** *their* ***case*** *at tonight's council meeting.* | **plead that** *Taylor pleaded that the proposal would cost the city too much money.*

plead·ing·ly /ˈplidɪŋli/ *adv.* if you say something pleadingly, or look at someone pleadingly, you speak to them or look at them in an emotional way, as though you are asking them to do something

pleas·ant /ˈplɛzənt/ *adj.* **1** enjoyable or attractive and making you feel happy SYN **nice** OPP **unpleasant**: *It's been a very pleasant evening.* | *The restaurant was large and pleasant.* | *What a* ***pleasant surprise!*** | **it is pleasant to do sth** *It was pleasant to think she had won.* ▸see THESAURUS box at **nice** **2** friendly, polite, and easy to talk to OPP **unpleasant**: *Marcia's always pleasant to everybody.* | *a pleasant-looking man* **3** weather that is pleasant is dry and not too hot or cold OPP **unpleasant** —**pleasantly** *adv.*

pleas·ant·ry /ˈplɛzəntri/ *n. plural* **pleasantries** [C usually plural] things that you say to someone in order to be polite, but that are not very important: *She and McDermott* ***exchanged pleasantries.***

please¹ /pliz/ S1 W3 *interjection* **1** used to be polite when asking someone to do something: *Please be quiet!* | *Sit down, please.* | *Would you please hurry up – we're going to be late.* | *Please feel free to ask questions at any time.* **2** used to be polite when asking for something: *Two pancakes for me, please.* | *Could I please go to Becky's house?* **3** said in order to politely accept something that someone offers you: *"Would you like some more wine?" "Yes, please."* **4 Please!** INFORMAL **a)** said when you think what someone has just said or asked is not possible or reasonable: *"Maybe we'll win." "Oh, please! There's no chance."* **b)** used to ask someone to stop behaving badly: *Alison! Please!*

please² W3 *v.* [not in progressive] **1** [I,T] to make someone happy or satisfied: *She did everything she could to please him.* | *a business that wants to please its customers* | *Most young children are* ***eager to please.*** | **be easy/hard etc. to please** *She's hard to please. Everything has to be perfect.* | *Corey is* ***impossible to please*** (=it is impossible to please him). **2** [I not in progressive] used in some phrases to show that someone can do or have what they want: *She does* ***what*** *she* ***pleases.*** | *She lets her kids do* ***whatever*** *they* ***please.*** | *You can spend the money* ***however*** *you* ***please.*** | *You are free to come and go* ***as you please.*** **3 please yourself** SPOKEN said when telling someone to do whatever they like, even though really you think that they are making the wrong choice: *"I don't think I'll go." "Oh, well, please yourself."* **4 please God** used to express a very strong hope or wish: *Everything's going to be fine, please God.* **5 (as) big/nice/bold etc. as you please** SPOKEN very big, nice etc., often in a surprising way: *She walked down the street in her swimming suit, as bold as you please.* **6 if you please** SPOKEN, FORMAL used to politely ask someone to do something: *Spell it for me, if you please.* [**Origin:** 1300–1400 Old French *plaisir*, from Latin *placere* **to please, be decided**]

pleased /plizd/ S3 W3 *adj.* **1** happy or satisfied OPP **displeased**: *Your Dad will be so pleased.* | **+with** *Republican leaders were pleased with the news.* | **+about** *He is genuinely pleased about her success.* | **pleased (that)** *We're all pleased you could come.* | **be pleased to see/hear/learn/announce etc. sth** *I'm pleased to see that his work is improving.* ▸see THESAURUS box at **happy** **2 (I'm) pleased to meet you** SPOKEN used as a polite greeting when you meet someone for the first time **3 pleased with yourself** feeling proud or satisfied because you think you have done something smart, in a way that annoys other people: *Miranda, pleased with herself for getting the answer right, sat down.*

pleas·er /ˈplizɚ/ *n.* **crowd-pleaser/people-pleaser etc.** someone or something that makes other people happy: *A chocolate dessert is a guaranteed crowd-pleaser.*

pleas·ing /ˈplizɪŋ/ *adj.* FORMAL giving pleasure, enjoyment, or satisfaction SYN **agreeable**: *a pleasing nutty flavor* | **+to** *a design that is pleasing to the eye* —**pleasingly** *adv.*

pleas·ur·a·ble /ˈplɛʒərəbəl/ *adj.* FORMAL enjoyable: *a pleasurable experience*

pleas·ure /ˈplɛʒɚ/ S3 W2 *n.* **1** [U] the feeling of happiness, satisfaction, or enjoyment that you get from an experience SYN **enjoyment**: *She sipped her wine* ***with*** *obvious* ***pleasure.*** | *a book to read* ***for pleasure*** | *The music* ***gave*** *her great* ***pleasure.*** | *He seems to* ***take pleasure in*** *proving other people wrong.* **2** [C] an activity or experience that you enjoy very much: *the simple pleasures of life* | *Sleeping on the soft warm sand* ***was a pleasure.*** | **be a pleasure to read/work with/watch etc.** *Carol was a pleasure to work with.* **3** SPOKEN used in some phrases to be polite and show that you are happy to meet someone, do something, ask for something etc.: ***It's a pleasure to*** *finally meet you, Ken.* | *"Give the kids a hug for me."* ***"With pleasure."*** | *"Thanks for coming."* ***"My pleasure."*** | ***It gives*** *me* ***great pleasure*** *to announce the winner.* | *We* ***had the pleasure of*** *being introduced to the President.* **4 at sb's pleasure/at the pleasure of sb** used to say that someone has a particular job because someone in authority has given them that job: *Most commissioners serve at the pleasure of the mayor.* **5 at your pleasure** FORMAL if you can do something at your pleasure, you can do it when you want to and in the way you want to **6 what's your pleasure?** OLD-FASHIONED used to ask someone what they want: *What is your pleasure, Sire?*

ˈpleasure ˌboat also **ˈpleasure ˌcraft** *n.* [C] a boat that someone uses for fun rather than for business

pleat /plit/ *n.* [C] a flat narrow fold in a skirt, a pair of pants, a dress etc. —**pleat** *v.* [T]

pleat·ed /ˈplit̬ɪd/ *adj.* a pleated skirt, pair of pants, dress etc. has a lot of flat narrow folds

plebe /plib/ *n.* [C] INFORMAL a student in his or her first year at the U.S. Military Academy or the U.S. Naval Academy

ple·be·ian¹ /plɪˈbiən/ *adj.* **1** DISAPPROVING relating to ordinary people and what they like, rather than to people with a high social class SYN **lower-class** **2** HISTORY relating to plebeians in ancient Rome

plebeian² *n.* [C] an ordinary person who had no special rank in ancient Rome → see also PATRICIAN

pleb·i·scite /ˈplɛbəˌsaɪt/ *n.* [C,U] POLITICS a system by which everyone in a country, area etc. votes on an important decision that affects the whole area: **+on** *Puerto Rico* ***held a plebiscite*** *on whether to become a state.* → see also REFERENDUM

plec·trum /ˈplɛktrəm/ *n.* [C] a small thin piece of plastic, metal, or wood that you use for playing some musical instruments with strings, such as a GUITAR SYN **pick**

pled /plɛd/ *v.* a past tense and past participle of PLEAD

pledge¹ /plɛdʒ/ *n.* [C] **1** a serious promise or agreement, especially one made publicly or officially SYN **promise**: **+of** *pledges of economic aid* | **a pledge**

to do sth *All six nations have signed a pledge to fight terrorism.* | **make/take/give a pledge** *Parents make a pledge to take their children to rehearsals.* | **keep/fulfill/honor a pledge** *Will he keep his campaign pledges?* **2** a promise to give money to an organization: **+of** *a pledge of $200* | *Donors have* ***made pledges*** *totaling nearly $4 million.* **3 a pledge of love/friendship etc.** a serious promise of love etc. made by two people **4** someone who has promised to become a member of a college FRATERNITY or SORORITY **5** something valuable that you leave with someone else as proof that you will do what you have agreed to do, pay back what you owe etc.

P

pledge² *v.* [T] **1** to make a formal, usually public, promise to do something: **pledge sth to sth/sb** *Moore has pledged $100,000 to the symphony.* | **pledge to do sth** *The mayor pledged to reduce crime.* | **pledge that** *He pledged that he would never lie to her.* | **pledge support/loyalty/solidarity etc.** (=promise to give your support, be loyal etc.) *At school, children* ***pledge allegiance*** *to our country every morning.* **2** to make someone formally promise something: *We were all* ***pledged to secrecy.*** **3** to promise to become a member of a college FRATERNITY or SORORITY **4** to leave something with someone as a PLEDGE

ˌPledge of Alˈlegiance *n.* **the Pledge of Allegiance** an official statement said by American citizens, in which they promise to be loyal to the United States. It is usually said every morning by children in school.

Pleis·to·cene /ˈplaɪstəˌsin/ *adj.* relating to the period in the Earth's history that started about two million years ago and ended about 10,000 years ago, when much of the Earth was covered with ice

ple·na·ry /ˈplinəri, ˈplɛ-/ *adj.* [only before noun] FORMAL **1** involving all the members of a committee, organization etc.: *The party held a plenary session in April.* **2** plenary power or authority is complete and has no limit: *He was given plenary powers to negotiate with the rebels.* —**plenary** *n.* [C]

plen·i·po·ten·ti·ar·y /ˌplɛnəpəˈtɛnʃiˌɛri, -ʃəri/ *n. plural* **plenipotentiaries** [C] FORMAL someone who has full power to take action or make decisions, especially as a representative of their government in a foreign country —**plenipotentiary** *adj.*

plen·i·tude /ˈplɛnəˌtud/ *n.* LITERARY **1 a plenitude of sth** a large amount of something SYN **abundance**: *a plenitude of hope* **2** [U] completeness or fullness

plen·te·ous /ˈplɛntiəs/ *adj.* LITERARY plentiful SYN **abundant**

plen·ti·ful /ˈplɛntɪfəl/ *adj.* more than enough in quantity SYN **abundant**: *a plentiful harvest* —**plentifully** *adv.*

plen·ty¹ /ˈplɛnti/ S2 W3 *pron.* a large quantity that is enough or more than enough: *There's plenty to do and see in New York.* | *"More dessert?" "No thanks, I've had plenty."* | **+of** *Make sure you drink plenty of water.* ▸see THESAURUS box at **enough¹**, **many**

plenty² *adv.* SPOKEN, INFORMAL a lot, or more than enough: **plenty big/fast/warm etc.** *This apartment's plenty big enough for two.* | *There's* ***plenty more*** *chicken if you want it.* | *There are a hundred people in here, and* ***plenty more*** *outside.*

plenty³ *n.* [U] FORMAL **1** a situation in which there is a lot of food and goods available: *It is a disgrace that we still have hunger in this land of plenty.* **2 in plenty** many, or more than enough: *There are errors in plenty in this report.* [**Origin:** 1200–1300 Old French *plenté*, from Latin *plenitas* **fullness**] → see also HORN OF PLENTY

Ples·sy v. Fer·gu·son /ˌplɛsi vɚsəs ˈfɚgəsən/ HISTORY a decision by the Supreme Court in 1896 that stated that SEGREGATION was legal in the U.S. as long as the places or things provided for black people were equal to those provided for white people

pleth·o·ra /ˈplɛθərə/ *n.* **a plethora of sth** FORMAL a very large number of something: *The city faces a plethora of problems.*

pleu·ra /ˈplʊrə/ *n. plural* **pleurae** /-ri/ or **pleuras** [C] BIOLOGY a very thin protective layer of material that covers each lung and the inner walls of the chest —**pleural** *adj.* → see picture at LUNG

pleu·ri·sy /ˈplʊrəsi/ *n.* [U] MEDICINE a serious illness that affects your lungs, causing severe pain in your chest

Plex·i·glas, plexiglass /ˈplɛksiˌglæs/ *n.* [U] TRADEMARK a strong clear type of plastic that can be used instead of glass

plex·us /ˈplɛksəs/ *n.* → see SOLAR PLEXUS

pli·a·ble /ˈplaɪəbəl/ *adj.* **1** able to bend without breaking or cracking SYN **flexible**: *soft pliable leather* ▸see THESAURUS box at **soft** **2** easily influenced and controlled by other people: *He wanted to replace him with a more pliable manager.* —**pliability** /ˌplaɪəˈbɪləṭi/ *n.* [U]

pli·ant /ˈplaɪənt/ *adj.* pliable —**pliancy** *n.* [U]

pli·ers /ˈplaɪɚz/ *n.* [plural] a small tool made of two crossed pieces of metal, used to hold small things, pull things, or to bend and cut wire: *a* ***pair of pliers***

plight /plaɪt/ *n.* [usually singular] a bad, serious, or sad condition or situation: **+of** *the plight of homeless children*

plinth /plɪnθ/ *n.* [C] a square block, usually made of stone, that is used as the base for a PILLAR or STATUE

Plin·y the El·der /ˌplɪni ði ˈɛldɚ/ (A.D. 23–79) an ancient Roman writer known for his NATURAL HISTORY, a very long book full of information about the ideas of his time

Pliny the Young·er /ˌplɪni ðə ˈyʌŋgɚ/ (A.D. ?61–113) an ancient Roman politician and writer known for his letters

Pli·o·cene /ˈplaɪəˌsin/ *adj.* relating to the period in the Earth's history that started about ten million years ago and continued until about four million years ago

PLO, the POLITICS **the Palestinian Liberation Organization** a political organization of Palestinian people, started in 1964. It works to establish a separate state for Palestine that can exist peacefully with Israel.

plod /plɑd/ *v.* **plodded, plodding** [I always + adv./prep.] to walk along slowly because you are tired or bored SYN **trudge**: **+through/along etc.** *Nathan plodded up the stairs to his room.*

plod along/on *phr. v.* to progress at a very slow steady rate, especially in a boring way: **+with** *The movie plods along with predictable twists and turns.* —**plodding** *adj.*: *the plodding pace of negotiations*

plonk /plɑŋk/ *v.* [T] INFORMAL another form of PLUNK

plop¹ /plɑp/ *v.* **plopped, plopping** **1** [I always + adv./prep] to fall somewhere, making a sound like something dropping into water: *The frog plopped back into the river.* **2** [T always + adv./prep.] to drop something, especially into a liquid, or put it down in a careless way so that it makes a sound: **+on/into/onto etc.** *He plopped some mashed potato onto his plate.* **3 plop (yourself) down** to sit down or lie down heavily: *Stan plopped down on the sofa beside me.*

plop² *n.* [C] the sound made by something when it falls or is dropped into liquid

plo·sive /ˈploʊsɪv/ *n.* [C] ENG. LANG. ARTS a CONSONANT sound that is made by completely stopping the flow of air out of your mouth and then suddenly letting it out, as when saying, for example, /b/ or /t/ —**plosive** *adj.*

plot¹ /plɑt/ S3 W3 *n.* [C] **1** ENG. LANG. ARTS the events that form the main story of a book, movie, or play SYN **story line**: *an entertaining plot* | *the opera's* ***convoluted plot*** (=complicated and confusing plot) | *The book's clever* ***plot twists*** (=changes in how the story is progressing) *keep you guessing right to the end.* | *I lost track of the* ***plot line*** (=the basic set of events) *early in the movie.* **2** a secret plan made by a group of people, to do something harmful or illegal: **a plot to do sth** *a plot to bomb U.N. headquarters* | **+against** *a plot against the government* | *She and her lover* ***hatched a plot*** (=started making plans) *to kill her husband.* | *Did the CIA have a role in an* ***assassination plot*** *against*

Castro? ►see THESAURUS box at **plan**[1] **3 the plot thickens** SPOKEN, HUMOROUS used to say that events seem to be becoming more complicated and difficult to understand **4** a small piece of land for building or growing things on: *a vegetable plot* **5** a piece of land in a CEMETERY, in which one person or a group of people are buried when they die: *a family plot* **6** a drawn plan of a building at ground level SYN **ground plan** [**Origin:** Old English **piece of land**]

plot² *v.* **plotted, plotting** **1** [I,T] to make a secret plan to harm a person or organization, especially a political leader or government: *She spent months plotting revenge.* | **plot to do sth** *Nichols had plotted to blow up the building.* | **+against** *The king believed his advisors were plotting against him.* **2** [T] also **plot out** to make lines and marks on a CHART that represent facts, numbers etc.: *The results are plotted in figure 6.1.* **3** [T] also **plot out** MATH to mark, calculate, or follow the position of a moving aircraft, a ship, stars etc.: *They **plotted a course** across the Pacific.* —**plotter** *n.* [C]

plough /plaʊ/ the British and Canadian spelling of PLOW

plov·er /ˈplʌvɚ, ˈploʊ-/ *n.* [C] BIOLOGY a small bird with a round body that lives near the ocean

plow¹ /plaʊ/ *n.* [C] a large piece of equipment used on farms, that cuts and breaks up the surface of the ground so that seeds can be planted, and is pulled by a TRACTOR or animals → see also SNOWPLOW

plow² *v.* **1** [I,T] to use a plow to cut the earth: *In those days the land was ploughed by oxen.* | *He'd finished **plowing the field**.* **2** to push snow off streets using a SNOWPLOW **3** [I always + adv./prep.] to move with a lot of effort or force: **+along/across etc.** *A truck plowed through the mud.*

plow ahead *phr. v.* to continue to do something in spite of opposition or difficulties: **+with** *It was difficult at first, but Harris plowed ahead with her plan.*

plow sth ↔ **back** *phr. v.* to put money that you have earned back into a business in order to make the business bigger and more successful: **+into** *Companies can plow back their profits into new equipment.*

plow into sb/sth *phr. v.* to crash into something or someone, especially while driving, because you are unable to stop quickly enough: *A train derailed and plowed into two houses.*

plow on *phr. v.* to continue trying to achieve something, even though it is difficult, annoying, or boring: *It was not the reaction Margaret had been hoping for, but she plowed on regardless.*

plow through sth *phr. v.* **1** to read or do something completely, even though it is boring, difficult, or takes a long time: *The justices are plowing through 500,000 pages of testimony this week.* | *We plowed through the contents of all the boxes.* **2** to move through something that is blocking your way: *The tornado plowed through Huntsville on Friday.* | *The car plowed through a fence.*

plow sth ↔ **up** *phr. v.* to break up the surface of the ground with a plow

plow·man /ˈplaʊmən/ *n.* [C] OLD USE a man whose job was to guide a plow that was being pulled by a horse

plow·share /ˈplaʊʃɛr/ *n.* [C] the broad curved metal blade of a plow, which cuts and turns over the soil → see also **beat/turn swords into plowshares** at SWORD (2)

ploy /plɔɪ/ *n. plural* **ploys** [C] a way of tricking someone in order to gain an advantage SYN **stratagem**: **political/public relations/marketing etc. ploy** *This is a political ploy, an attempt to scare women into voting against the measure.* | **a ploy to do sth** *a ploy to increase share prices*

pluck¹ /plʌk/ *v.*
1 PULL STH [T] to pull something quickly in order to remove it: **pluck sth from/off etc. sth** *He plucked an apple off the tree.* | *young girls who already **pluck** their **eyebrows*** (=pull out some of the hairs to give their eyebrows the shape they want)
2 TAKE SB/STH AWAY [T always + adv./prep.] to take someone away from a place or situation in a quick and unexpected way: **pluck sb from/off/away etc.** *A large seagull swooped down and plucked a fish out of the water.* | *Rescuers plucked the boy from the water.*
3 CHICKEN/BIRD ETC. [T] to pull the feathers off a dead chicken or other bird before cooking it
4 MUSIC [I,T] ENG. LANG. ARTS to quickly pull at the strings of a musical instrument: **+at** *Someone was plucking at the strings of an old guitar.*
5 pluck up (the) courage to force yourself to be brave and do something you are afraid of doing: *It took me weeks to pluck up the courage to try out for the play.*
6 pluck sth out of the/thin air to say or suggest a number, name etc. that you have just thought of, without thinking about it carefully

pluck at sth *phr. v.* to pull something quickly several times with your fingers, especially because you are nervous or to attract attention: *A little boy plucked at her skirt.*

pluck² *n.* [U] OLD-FASHIONED courage and determination SYN **spunk**: *It **takes** a lot of **pluck** to stand up to a bully.*

pluck·y /ˈplʌki/ *adj.* INFORMAL brave and determined SYN **spunky**: *a plucky heroine*

plug¹ /plʌg/ S3 *n.* [C]
1 ELECTRICITY a) the small object at the end of a wire that is used for connecting a piece of electrical equipment to an OUTLET (=supply of electricity): *the plug on the electric blanket* | *I accidentally **pulled the plug*** (=removed the plug from the electricity supply) *on my computer.* **b)** INFORMAL a place, usually on a wall, where electrical equipment is connected to the electricity supply SYN **outlet**: *Where's the plug in here?*
2 BATHTUB a round flat piece of rubber or plastic used for blocking the hole in a bathtub or SINK
3 USED TO FILL A HOLE an object or substance used to fill or block a hole, tube etc.: *These plugs prevent the water going into your nose.* → see also EARPLUG
4 ADVERTISEMENT INFORMAL a way of advertising a book, movie, idea etc., by talking about it publicly, especially on a television or radio program: *Jennings **put in a plug** for his new movie.*
5 IN AN ENGINE PHYSICS the part of an engine that makes a SPARK, which makes the gas start burning SYN **spark plug**: *Change the plugs every 10,000 miles.*
6 pull the plug INFORMAL **a)** to stop a business or activity from continuing, especially by deciding not to give it any more money: **+on** *NBC has pulled the plug on the comedy series.* **b)** to turn off the machines that are keeping someone who is in a COMA alive: *If I ever get that way, just pull the plug.*
7 PIECE a piece of a substance that has been pressed tightly together: *a plug of tobacco*
[**Origin:** 1600–1700 Dutch, Middle Dutch *plugge*]

plug

plug² S2 *v.* **plugged, plugging** [T] **1** also **plug up** to fill or block a small hole: *Don't pour oil in the sink – it'll plug up the drain.* **2** to advertise a book, movie, idea etc. by talking about it on a television or radio program SYN **promote**: *Whitaker was there to plug his new movie.* ►see THESAURUS box at **advertise** **3** to stop something happening, especially to stop losing or wasting something: *They're scrambling to **plug** the security*

P

holes. **4 plug the gap/hole** to provide something that is needed, because there is not enough: *He is hoping her information will plug the hole in his family history.* **5** OLD-FASHIONED to shoot someone: *They plugged him full of lead.*

plug away *phr. v.* also **plug along** to keep working hard at something: *scientists plugging away in their labs*

plug sth ↔ **in** *phr. v.* **1** to connect a piece of electrical equipment to the main supply of electricity, or to another piece of electrical equipment: *Plug the VCR in and see if it still works.* **2** to add or include numbers or information: *Plug in the website address, and hit "go."*

plug into sth *phr. v.* **1** to connect one piece of electrical equipment to another, or to be connected: **plug sth into sth** *Can you plug the speakers into the stereo for me?* **2** to make use of a service, or get involved in an activity, new area of business etc.: *The agency helps people to plug into social services.*

ˌplug-and-ˈplay *n.* [U] TECHNICAL the ability of a computer and a new piece of equipment to be used together as soon as they are connected

ˈplug-in *adj.* able to be connected to a supply of electricity or to another piece of electrical equipment: *a plug-in microphone*

plum¹ /plʌm/ *n.* **1** [C] BIOLOGY a small round juicy fruit that is purple, red, or yellow and has a single large seed, or the tree that produces this fruit **2** something very good that other people wish they had, such as a good job or part in a movie: *The contract is a plum for Browning and Co.* **3** [U] a dark purple-red color → see also PLUMMY

plum² *adj.* **1 a plum role/job etc.** INFORMAL a good part in a play or movie, a good job etc. that other people wish they had: *He landed a plum role in a TV miniseries.* **2** having a dark purple-red color

plum·age /ˈplumɪdʒ/ *n.* [U] BIOLOGY the feathers covering a bird's body: *the duck's colorful plumage*

plumb¹ /plʌm/ *v.* [T] **1** to make an effort to learn, understand, or explain something completely: *The movie plumbs the psyche of a woman scarred by childhood abuse.* **2 plumb the depths (of despair/misery/bad taste etc.)** to reach the lowest or worst point of something bad: *When his wife left him, Matt plumbed the depths of despair.* **3** to measure the depth of water or to check to see if something is exactly upright using a PLUMB LINE

plumb² *adv.* INFORMAL **1** HUMOROUS completely: *I'm sorry. I plumb forgot.* **2** [always + adv./prep.] INFORMAL exactly: *The bullet hit him plumb between the eyes.*

plumb³ *adj.* TECHNICAL **1** exactly upright or level **2 out of plumb** not exactly upright or level

ˈplumb bob *n.* [C] a small heavy object at the end of a PLUMB LINE

plumb·er /ˈplʌmɚ/ *n.* [C] someone whose job is to repair water pipes, SINKS, toilets etc. [**Origin:** 1300–1400 Old French *plommier* **worker in lead**, from Latin *plumbarius*, from *plumbus* **lead**; because water pipes were originally made of lead]

ˌplumber's ˈhelper *n.* [C] OLD-FASHIONED a PLUNGER

plumb·ing /ˈplʌmɪŋ/ *n.* [U] **1** the pipes that water flows through in a building: *There's something wrong with the plumbing.* | *a shack with no* ***indoor plumbing*** (=water pipes, toilets etc. inside a house) **2** the work of fitting and repairing water pipes, toilets etc.

ˈplumb line *n.* [C] a piece of string with a small heavy object tied to one end, used for measuring the depth of water or for marking a position that is exactly upright, for example when building a wall

plume /plum/ *n.* [C] **1** a small cloud of smoke, dust, etc. that rises up into the air: +**of** *Plumes of hot gas shoot up from Jupiter's surface.* **2** a large feather or group of feathers, especially one that is used as a decoration on a hat **3** EARTH SCIENCE a mass of MAGMA (=very hot melted rock below the surface of the Earth) that is hotter than the magma surrounding it, and which rises up towards the surface of the Earth → see also NOM DE PLUME

plumed /plumd/ *adj.* [only before noun] having or decorated with feathers: *the knights' plumed helmets*

plum·met /ˈplʌmɪt/ *v.* [I] **1** to suddenly and quickly decrease in value or amount: *Sales have plummeted.* | **plummet (from sth) to sth** *Enrollment at the school has plummeted to 25 students.* ►see THESAURUS box at **decrease¹** **2** to fall very suddenly and quickly from a very high place: +**to/toward/down etc.** *The plane plummeted toward the earth.* → see also PLUNGE

plum·my /ˈplʌmi/ *adj.* tasting like a PLUM or containing a lot of PLUMS: *a plummy wine*

plump¹ /plʌmp/ *adj.* **1** a word meaning "slightly fat" but in a fairly pleasant way, used especially about women or children in order to be polite: *a plump woman in her fifties* ►see THESAURUS box at **fat¹** **2** round and full in a way that looks attractive: *plump juicy strawberries* [**Origin:** 1400–1500 Middle Dutch *plomp* **dull, not sharp**] —**plumpness** *n.* [U]

plump² *v.* **1** [T] also **plump up** to make CUSHIONS, PILLOWS etc. softer and rounder by shaking or hitting them **2** [I,T] also **plump up** if dried fruit plumps up, or if you plump it up, it becomes fatter and softer when you put it in liquid: *Soak the raisins in the wine until they plump up.* **3 plump (yourself) down** to sit down suddenly and heavily: *Peggy plumped down in the chair beside Otto.*

ˈplum toˌmato *n.* [C] a type of TOMATO that is egg-shaped and that is often used in cooking

plun·der¹ /ˈplʌndɚ/ *v.* [I,T] **1** to steal money or property from a place, especially while fighting in a war: *Many works of art were plundered by Nazi troops.* **2** [T] to use up all or most of the supplies of something in a careless way: *Are big companies plundering our planet?* —**plunderer** *n.* [C]

plunder² *n.* [U] **1** things that have been stolen during a violent attack, especially during a war SYN **spoils**: *Henry's army returned loaded down with plunder.* **2** the act of plundering: *the plunder of Africa by the European nations*

plunge¹ /plʌndʒ/ *v.*

1 FALL DOWNWARD [I always + adv./prep.] to move, fall, or be thrown suddenly forward or down SYN **plummet**: +**off/into/through etc.** *Her car swerved and plunged through the guardrail.* | *A waterfall plunges off the cliff to the river below.* | *The skydiver* ***plunged to her death*** *from 8,000 feet.* ►see THESAURUS box at **dive¹**

2 DECREASE [I] to suddenly decrease by a large amount SYN **plummet**: *The President's popularity has plunged dramatically in recent weeks.* | *The company's profits plunged by 60 percent.*

3 GO SUDDENLY [I always + adv./prep.] to suddenly go into a place or area: +**into/through/ahead etc.** *Three men left the truck and plunged into the woods.*

4 DO SUDDENLY [I,T] to begin to do something or become involved in something suddenly, especially without thinking about the possible results: **plunge (sb) into sth** *The two women plunged into an animated conversation.* | *She* ***plunged herself into*** *her writing.* | +**ahead** *He put his fears aside and plunged ahead with the plans.*

5 PUSH INTO [I, T always + adv./prep.] to quickly push something firmly and deeply into something else: +**in/into** *She plunged the knife into his neck.* | *Plunge the potatoes into cold water to stop them from cooking.*

6 SHIP [I] if a ship plunges, it moves violently up and down, usually because of high waves

plunge in *phr. v.* also **plunge into sth** to jump or DIVE into water: *Burt plunged into the river fully clothed to save the boy.*

plunge sb/sth **into** sth *phr. v.* to suddenly put someone or something into a bad situation: *Economic changes have plunged many of the elderly into poverty.* | **plunge sb into gloom/despair etc.** (=to suddenly make someone feel very unhappy) *The news* *of her mother's death plunged her into despair.* | *The hall was suddenly* ***plunged into darkness.***

plunge² *n.* **1 take the plunge** to decide to do something risky, especially after delaying it or worrying about it for a long time: *We've decided to take the plunge and get married.* **2** [C usually singular] a sudden quick fall down or forward: *Myers was severely injured in the plunge from the top of the hotel.* **3** [C] a sudden large decrease in the price, value, or amount of something SYN **drop**: +**in** *There has been a 10% plunge in stock prices.* **4** [C usually singular] a jump into water, or a quick swim: +**in** *a plunge in the lake*

plung·er /'plʌndʒɚ/ *n.* [C] **1** a tool used in order to clear waste that is blocking a pipe in a toilet or SINK. It consists of a straight handle with a large rubber cup on its end. **2** TECHNICAL a part of a machine that moves up and down

ˌplunging 'neckline *n.* [C] if a woman's dress or shirt has a plunging neckline, the top part at the front is very low

plunk¹ /plʌŋk/ *v.* [T] INFORMAL **1** to put something down somewhere, especially in a careless noisy way: **plunk sth in/on etc.** *She plunked the bag down on the table.* **2 plunk (yourself) down** to sit down heavily and then relax: *Americans love to plunk themselves down in front of the TV.*

plunk sth ↔ **down** *phr. v.* to spend an amount of money on something: *He plunked down $250 for a necklace for his wife.*

plunk² *n.* [C,U] the sound something makes when it is dropped

plu·per·fect /ˌplu'pɚfɪkt/ *n.* **the pluperfect** ENG. LANG. ARTS the PAST PERFECT tense of a verb

plu·ral¹ /'plʊrəl/ *n.* ENG. LANG. ARTS **1 the plural** the form of a word that represents more than one person or thing. For example, "hands" is the plural of "hand." **2** [C] a plural noun

plural² *adj.* **1 the plural** ENG. LANG. ARTS a plural word or form shows you are talking about more than one thing, person etc.: *a plural pronoun* | *"Have" is the plural form of "has."* **2** FORMAL a plural society, system, or culture is one with people from many different religions, races etc.: *the plural makeup of the United States* [**Origin:** 1300–1400 Old French *plurel*, from Latin *pluralis*, from *plus* **more**]

plu·ral·ism /'plʊrəˌlɪzəm/ *n.* [U] FORMAL the principle that people of different races, religions, and political beliefs can live together peacefully in the same society, or the situation in which this happens —**pluralist** *n.* [C] —**pluralistic** /ˌplʊrə'lɪstɪk/ also **pluralist** *adj.*: *a pluralistic society*

plu·ral·i·ty /plʊ'rælət̬i/ *n. plural* **pluralities** **1** [C,U] POLITICS if one person or party receives a plurality in an election, they receive more votes than any of the other people or parties, but fewer votes than the total number of votes that all the others receive together: *The mayor won with a plurality of 12,000 votes, while the other two candidates had 9,000 and 7,000 votes, respectively* → see also MAJORITY **2** [C] FORMAL a large number of different things: +**of** *In the U.S., there is a plurality of religious beliefs.* **3** [U] ENG. LANG. ARTS the state of being plural

plur·i·bus /'plʊrɪbəs/ → see E PLURIBUS UNUM

plus¹ /plʌs/ Ac S2 W3 *prep.* used to show that one number or amount is added to another OPP **minus**: *Three plus six equals nine. (3 + 6 = 9)* | *The jacket costs $49.95 plus tax.* [**Origin:** 1500–1600 Latin **more** (adjective and adverb)] ►see THESAURUS box at **calculate**

plus² Ac *conjunction* INFORMAL used to add more information: *He's really cute, plus he's got a good job.* | *You need a birth certificate, plus a photo I.D.*

plus³ Ac *adj.* **1 A plus/B plus etc.** a grade used in a system of judging students' work, usually written A+, B+ etc. A B+ is higher than a B, but lower than an A– MINUS OPP **minus** **2** MATH used after a number to mean an amount which is more than that number: *He works ten hours a day plus.* **3** used to say that a number is more than zero, especially in temperatures: *a temperature of plus 12°* **4** [only before noun] used to talk about an advantage or good feature of a thing or situation OPP **minus**: ***On the plus side****, it's a lot cheaper than some of the larger ones.* | **plus factor/point** *The biggest plus factor is that the hotel is right on the beach.*

plus⁴ Ac S2 *n.* [C] **1** INFORMAL something that is an advantage, or a quality you think is good OPP **minus**: **a big/definite/real etc. plus** *Some knowledge of Spanish is a definite plus in the job market.* | *There are* ***pluses and minuses*** (=both good and bad things) *to living in the city.* **2** [usually singular] MATH a PLUS SIGN OPP **minus**

plus-'fours *n.* [plural] pants with loose wide legs that are fastened just below the knee, worn by men in past times when playing GOLF

P

plush¹ /plʌʃ/ also **plush·y** /'plʌʃi/ *adj.* **1** expensive, comfortable, and of good quality SYN **luxurious**: *a plush hotel* **2** made of plush: *plush toys*

plush² *n.* [U] silk or cotton cloth with a surface like short fur

'plus sign *n.* [C] MATH the sign (+), showing that you should add two or more numbers together, or that a number is more than zero

Plu·tarch /'plutɑrk/ (A.D. ?46–?120) an ancient Greek HISTORIAN who wrote about famous Greek and Roman politicians and military leaders

Plu·to /'plut̬oʊ/ **1** in Greek MYTHOLOGY, another name for Hades, the god of the Underworld where the spirits of dead people live **2** an object in space that was considered to be the smallest PLANET until 2006, when it was decided that it was not a planet

plu·toc·ra·cy /plu'tɑkrəsi/ *n. plural* **plutocracies** [C] POLITICS **1** a country ruled by rich people, or a government that is controlled by them **2** a group of rich people who rule a country

plu·to·crat /'plut̬əˌkræt/ *n.* [C] DISAPPROVING someone who has power because they are rich —**plutocratic** /ˌplut̬ə'kræt̬ɪk◂/ *adj.*

plu·to·ni·um /plu'toʊniəm/ *n.* [U] SYMBOL **Pu** CHEMISTRY a RADIOACTIVE metal that is an ELEMENT and is used in the production of NUCLEAR power

ply¹ /plaɪ/ *v.* **plies, plied, plying** **1 ply your trade** FORMAL to work at your business or special skill: *A number of drug dealers ply their trade in the park.* **2** [I always + adv./prep., T] LITERARY if a boat or vehicle plies between two places, it travels to those two places regularly: +**between/across etc.** *Small fishing boats were plying back and forth across the harbor.* | *Graceful sailboats ply the Nile.* **3** [T] OLD USE or LITERARY to use a tool skillfully

ply sb **with** sth *phr. v.* **1** to keep giving someone large quantities of food and drink: *Agents plied him with liquor to get him talking.* **2 ply sb with questions** to keep asking someone questions

ply² *n.* [U] **two-ply/three-ply etc.** a unit for measuring the thickness of plywood, toilet paper, thread, rope etc., based on the number of layers or threads that it has: *double-ply toilet paper*

Plym·outh /'plɪməθ/ **1** the place in the U.S. state of Massachusetts where the Pilgrim Fathers first settled in America **2** a port in southwestern England from which the Pilgrim Fathers sailed to America

ply·wood /'plaɪwʊd/ *n.* [U] a material made of several thin layers of wood stuck together to form a strong board

PM *n.* [C] an abbreviation for PRIME MINISTER

p.m. /ˌpi 'ɛm/ used after numbers to show times from NOON to just before MIDNIGHT: *The party starts at 7 p.m.* (=in the evening) [**Origin:** 1600–1700 Latin *post meridiem* **after noon**] → see also A.M.

PMS *n.* [U] **premenstrual syndrome** the feelings of anger or sadness and the physical pain many women feel just before their PERIOD (=monthly flow of blood)

pneu·mat·ic /nʊ'mæt̬ɪk/ *adj.* **1** able to work using air pressure: *a pneumatic pump* **2** TECHNICAL filled with air: *pneumatic tires*

pneu,matic 'drill *n.* [C] a JACKHAMMER

pneu,matic 'tube *n.* [C] a tube that you can send things through very quickly using air pressure

pneu·mo·coc·cus /ˌnumə'kɑkəs/ *n. plural* **pneumococci** /-'kɑksaɪ, -'kɑkaɪ/ [C] a type of BACTERIA (=very small living things) that causes disease —**pneumococcal** *adj.*

pneu·mo·cys·tis /ˌnumə'sɪstɪs/ *n.* [U] MEDICINE a serious type of pneumonia

pneu·mo·nia /nʊ'moʊnyə/ *n.* [U] MEDICINE a serious illness that affects your lungs and makes it difficult to breathe

P

P.O. **1** the written abbreviation of POST OFFICE **2** the written abbreviation of PETTY OFFICER

Po, the /poʊ/ a river in northern Italy that flows into the Adriatic Sea

P.O. Box /ˌpi 'oʊ ˌbɑks/ *n.* [C] a box in a post office that has a special number, to which you can have your mail sent instead of to your home

p.o.'d /ˌpi 'oʊd◂ / *adj.* SPOKEN, INFORMAL very annoyed

poach /poʊtʃ/ *v.* **1** [T] **a)** to cook an egg without its shell in water that is almost boiling **b)** to cook fish or meat in water or another liquid that is almost boiling: *Poach the chicken in white wine and water.* ▶see THESAURUS box at **cook**[1] **2** [I,T] to persuade someone to leave a team or company and join yours, especially in a secret or dishonest way: *They had poached a major client from a competitor.* **3** [I,T] to illegally catch or shoot animals, birds, or fish, especially on private land without permission **4** [T] to unfairly or illegally use someone else's ideas

poached /poʊtʃt/ *adj.* poached food has been cooked in water that is almost boiling: *poached fruit*

poach·er /'poʊtʃɚ/ *n.* [C] someone who illegally catches or shoots animals, birds, or fish, especially on private land without permission

poach·ing /'poʊtʃɪŋ/ *n.* [U] the activity of illegally catching or shooting animals, birds, or fish, especially on private land without permission: *Kenya wants to prevent the poaching of elephants for their tusks.*

Po·ca·hon·tas /ˌpoʊkə'hɑntəs/ (1595–1617) a Native American woman who helped to develop friendly relations between the English and the Native Americans

pocked /pɑkt/ *adj.* covered with small holes or marks: *the meteor-pocked surface of the moon* —**pock** *v.* [T]

pock·et[1] /'pɑkɪt/ [S2] [W2] *n.* [C]
1 IN CLOTHES a small bag sewn onto or into coats, shirts, pants, or skirts, where you can put things such as money or keys: *Maggie put her **hands in her pockets** to keep them warm.* | *Fred searched his pockets for the ticket.* | **coat/pants/jacket etc. pocket** *He stuffed the phone number in his shirt pocket.* | *A policeman asked him to **empty his pockets*** (=take everything out).
2 MONEY the amount of money available for you to spend: *The ruling means less money in the pockets of investors.* | *He had to pay for the repairs **out of his own pocket*** (=with his own money). | *They're looking for someone with **deep pockets*** (=a lot of money to spend) *to pay for the research.* | *Even children were asked to **dig into** their **pockets** for a contribution.* | **an out-of-pocket expense/charge/cost** (=something you must pay for yourself, rather than your company, your insurance company etc. paying for it) → see also DEEP-POCKETED, POCKETBOOK
3 IN A BAG/DOOR ETC. a small bag, net, or piece of material that is attached to something, so you can put things in it: *You will find the air safety card in the seat pocket in front of you.*
4 SMALL AREA/AMOUNT a small area or amount of something that has a particular quality which is very different from what surrounds it: +**of** *There will be pockets of colder temperatures over the valley today.* | *Government troops crushed the last pockets of resistance in the city.*
5 in sb's pocket if a politician or person in authority is in someone's pocket, they are completely controlled by them and willing to do what they want: *He had several corrupt policemen in his pocket.*
6 GAMES a hole or a small bag on a POOL table that you have to hit the ball into
7 FOOD the hollow area in some kinds of food, which can be filled with other foods: *Stuff the meat into the pocket of the pita bread.*
8 have sth in your pocket to be very sure that you are going to win something such as a competition or election: *It looks like the team has the game firmly in their pocket.*
[**Origin:** 1400–1500 Old North French *pokete*, from *poke* bag] → see also AIR POCKET, **burn a hole in your pocket** at BURN[1] (16), **line your own pockets** at LINE[2] (3), **pick sb's pocket** at PICK[1] (10)

pocket[2] *v.* [T] **1** to steal money, especially money that you are responsible for: *Robbins admitted pocketing $5,300 of the campaign money.* **2** to get a large amount of money, win a prize etc., especially in a way that seems very easy or slightly dishonest: *It's simple – we buy them for $5, sell them for $8, and pocket the difference.* **3** to put something into your pocket: *Tom slipped off his rings and pocketed them.* **4** to hit a ball into a pocket in games such as POOL

pocket[3] *adj.* [only before noun] also **pocket-sized** small enough to be carried in your pocket: *a pocket dictionary*

pock·et·book /'pɑkɪtˌbʊk/ *n.* [C] **1** the amount of money you have, or your ability to pay for things: *Higher prices will **hit** consumers **in the pocketbook*** (=cost them a lot of money). | *Older voters are most concerned about **pocketbook issues*** (=political issues that concern money). **2** OLD-FASHIONED a woman's PURSE (=small bag), especially one without a STRAP **3** a small book with a soft cover that can be carried in a pocket **4** OLD-FASHIONED a WALLET → see also **vote with your pocketbook** at VOTE[1] (7)

'pocket ˌchange *n.* [U] **1** coins that you carry in your pocket **2** a small or unimportant amount of money

pock·et·ful /'pɑkɪtˌfʊl/ *n.* [C] the amount that a pocket will hold: +**of** *a pocketful of quarters*

'pocket knife *n.* [C] a small knife with one or more blades that fold into the handle SYN **jackknife**

'pocket ˌmoney *n.* [U] INFORMAL a small amount of money that you can use to buy things you want: *He earned pocket money by repairing furniture for neighbors.*

'pocket proˌtector *n.* [C] **1** a piece of plastic worn in a shirt pocket to carry pens and prevent ink from ruining your shirt **2 pocket-protector types/guys etc.** someone who likes technical subjects too much, is unfashionable, and is slightly strange

ˌpocket 'veto *n.* [C] POLITICS a method used by the U.S. President to stop a BILL (=suggestion for a new law), in which the President keeps the bill without signing it until Congress is on vacation, so that it cannot become a law

pock·mark /'pɑkmɑrk/ *n.* [C] a small round hollow mark on someone's skin or on the surface of something

pock·marked /'pɑkmɑrkt/ *adj.* covered with small holes or marks: *a pockmarked face* | *The government buildings were pockmarked with bullet holes.* —**pockmark** *v.* [T]

Po·co·nos, the /'poʊkəˌnoʊz/ also **the 'Pocono ˌMountains** a group of mountains in the state of Pennsylvania in the northeastern U.S. that are part of the Appalachians

pod /pɑd/ *n.* [C] **1** BIOLOGY the part of plants such as PEAS and beans that the seeds grow in: *Slice the vanilla pod along one side.* **2** a part of a vehicle or building that is separate from the main part, especially part of a space vehicle: *the space pod's small instrument panel* **3** a long narrow container for gasoline or other substances, especially one carried under an aircraft wing **4** a group of sea animals such as WHALES and DOLPHINS that swim together. **5** a type of natural bag that holds the eggs of some types of insects and fish

pod·cast /ˈpɑdkæst/ *n.* [C] a television or radio show in DIGITAL form that you can DOWNLOAD from a website and watch on your computer or listen to on your MP3 player: *The National Public Radio station website offers a lot of podcasts.* —**podcasting** *n.* [U]

po·di·a·trist /pəˈdaɪətrɪst/ *n.* [C] a doctor who takes care of people's feet and treats foot diseases —**podiatry** *n.* [U]

po·di·um /ˈpoʊdiəm/ *n.* [C] **1** a small raised area for a performer, speaker, or musical CONDUCTOR to stand on **2** a tall thin desk that you stand behind when giving a speech to a lot of people SYN **lectern**: *Mr. Hill rose and went to the podium.*

Po·dunk, **podunk** /ˈpoʊdʌŋk/ *adj.* SPOKEN used to describe a place you think is small, unimportant, and boring: *His car broke down in some podunk little town.*

Poe /poʊ/, **Ed·gar Al·lan** /ˈɛdgɚ ˈælən/ (1809–1849) a U.S. poet and writer of short stories

po·em /ˈpoʊəm/ S2 W3 *n.* [C] ENG. LANG. ARTS a piece of writing that expresses emotions, experiences, and ideas, especially in short lines using words that RHYME (=have a particular pattern of sounds) [**Origin:** 1400–1500 French *poème*, from Latin, from Greek *poiein* **to make, create**]

po·e·sy /ˈpoʊəzi, -əsi/ *n.* [U] OLD USE poetry

po·et /ˈpoʊɪt/ W3 *n.* [C] ENG. LANG. ARTS someone who writes poems

po·et·ess /ˈpoʊət̬ɪs/ *n.* [C] OLD-FASHIONED ENG. LANG. ARTS a female poet

po·et·ic /poʊˈɛt̬ɪk/ also **po·et·i·cal** /poʊˈɛt̬ɪkəl/ *adj.* **1** ENG. LANG. ARTS relating to poetry or typical of poetry: *poetic language* | *poetic imagery* **2** having qualities of deep feeling or graceful expression: *The musician's playing was poetic and sensitive.* —**poetically** /-kli/ *adv.*

po,etic ˈjustice *n.* [U] a situation in which someone is made to suffer for something bad they have done, in a way that you think they deserve: *It did seem to be poetic justice – the bully being bullied.*

po,etic ˈlicense *n.* [U] the freedom that poets and other artists have to change facts, not to obey grammar rules etc., because they are making art or writing poetry

,poet ˈlaureate *n.* [C] a poet who is chosen by a king, queen, or president to write poems on important national occasions

po·et·ry /ˈpoʊətri/ S3 *n.* [U] **1** ENG. LANG. ARTS poems in general, or the art of writing them: *He read me some of his poetry.* | *a poetry class* | **lyric/love/contemporary etc. poetry** *a selection of religious poetry* **2** APPROVING a quality of beauty, gracefulness, and deep feeling: *The way she moves is* ***pure poetry***. | *His golf swing is* ***poetry in motion***.

po·go stick /ˈpoʊgoʊ ˌstɪk/ *n.* [C] a toy used for jumping, that consists of a pole with a spring near the bottom, a bar across the pole that you stand on, and a handle on top

po·grom /ˈpoʊgrəm/ *n.* [C] a planned killing of large numbers of people, especially Jews, usually done for reasons of race or religion SYN **massacre**

poign·ant /ˈpɔɪnyənt/ *adj.* making you feel sad or full of pity: *a poignant story* | *Her death was a* ***poignant reminder*** *that sometimes we are powerless.* [**Origin:** 1300–1400 French, present participle of *poindre* **to prick, sting**, from Latin *pungere*] —**poignancy** *n.* [U] —**poignantly** *adv.*

poin·set·ti·a /pɔɪnˈsɛt̬iə/ *n.* [C] a tropical plant with groups of large red or white leaves that look like flowers

point[1] /pɔɪnt/ S1 W1 *n.*

1 IDEA [C] a single fact, idea, or opinion that is part of an argument or discussion: *That's a* ***good point***. | *My next point is equally important.* | *You* ***have a point*** (=your opinion seems right) – *it is kind of a scary movie.* | *I* ***see your point*** (=understand your opinion), *and in general I agree with you.* | *He* ***made*** *some interesting* ***points*** *during his speech.* | *To* ***prove his point*** (=show that his idea or opinion is right), *Blanchard showed us statistics comparing men and women drivers.* ►see THESAURUS box at **end**[1], **place**[1]

2 GAMES/SPORTS [C] a unit used to show the SCORE in a game or sport: *Reeves* ***scored*** *23* ***points*** *for Arizona.* | *If you forget to draw a card, you* ***lose a point***.

3 the point/sb's point the most important fact or idea: *So what's your point?* | ***The point is****, you've got to get some kind of job.* | *Nobody knows where he went. That's* ***the whole point*** (=the most important fact). | *Those issues are* ***beside the point*** (=they do not relate to the subject). | *Let me* ***come*** *straight* ***to the point***. | *He may not have stolen the money himself, but* ***that's not the point***. | *Would you just* ***get to the point*** (=say the important part of what you want to say)?* | *Whitney* ***missed the point*** (=did not understand the main meaning) *of the whole discussion.* | *The letter was short and* ***to the point*** (=only dealing with the most important subject or idea). | *OK,* ***point taken*** (=said when you accept that what someone says is true). *I won't interfere anymore.* | *She looks like her mother, and, even* ***more to the point*** (=used when mentioning an even more important fact), *acts like her.*

4 IN TIME/DEVELOPMENT [C] a specific moment, time, or stage in something's development: *We're not planning to hire anyone else* ***at this point***. | *The family moved to Oregon* ***at some point*** *in the last century.* | ***At one point****, I really wanted to just give up.* | *Both sides accepted the proposal as* ***a starting point*** (=stage from which something can start) *for negotiations.* | *a* ***turning point*** (=time when things changed) *in the war* | *He was tired* ***to the point of*** *crying.* | **high/low point** (=best/worst moment) *It was the high point of her college career.* | *We've* ***reached a point*** *where we don't have enough money to continue.* ►see THESAURUS box at **stage**[1]

5 PURPOSE [U] the purpose or aim of doing something: +**of** ***The whole point*** *of this legislation is to protect children.* | **point of/in doing sth** ***What's the point*** *of calling a meeting when the chairman can't be there?* | ***There's no point in*** *paying rent if you're not living there.* | *I don't* ***see the point*** *of worrying too much about your diet.*

6 QUALITY/FEATURE [C] a particular quality or feature that someone or something has: *His plan has both good and bad points.* | ***The*** *main* ***selling point*** *of the drug is that it has fewer side effects.* | *Getting along with other people is not Nick's* ***strong point*** (=he is not very good at it). | *She's made a specialty of teaching* ***the finer points*** (=the small details) *of gardening.* | *The church is the* ***focal point*** (=the feature that people pay most attention to) *of this small community.*

7 the point of no return a stage in a process or activity when it becomes impossible to stop it or do something different: *The dam project has* ***reached the point of no return***.

8 on the point of (doing) something going to do something very soon: *The country's economy is on the point of collapse.*

9 MEASURE ON A SCALE [C] a mark or measure on a scale: *Stock prices moved up 27 points today.*

10 the boiling/freezing/melting etc. point (of sth) the temperature at which something boils, freezes, melts etc.

11 IN NUMBERS [C] MATH the sign (.) used to separate a whole number from the DECIMALS that follow it: *one point nine percent* (=1.9%)

12 SHARP END [C] a sharp end of something: *a pencil point*

13 not to put too fine a point on it SPOKEN used when you are saying something in a very direct way that might upset someone: *Everyone there – not to put too fine a point on it – was crazy.*

14 up to a point partly, but not completely: *That's true, up to a point.*

15 make a point of doing sth to do something deliberately: *Bridget made a point of thanking each of us for the gift.*

16 in point of fact used when giving correct information when someone has previously given the wrong

information: *Many people believe surgery is the only answer. In point of fact, a change in diet is often enough.*
17 MATH [C] MATH an exact place on a GEOMETRICAL drawing, which has no width or length or height: *Line A crosses line B at point C.*
18 PLACE [C] a particular place where something happens: *a border crossing point* | *No cars are allowed beyond this point.*
19 PIECE OF LAND [C] a long thin piece of land that stretches out into the ocean
20 PRINT [C,U] a unit for measuring the size of TYPE (=individual letters, numbers etc.) in printing: *I need a 12-point font.*
21 SMALL SPOT [C] a very small spot: *tiny points of light*
22 DIRECTION [C] one of the marks on a COMPASS that shows direction: *the points of the compass*
[**Origin:** 1200–1300 partly from Old French *point* **small hole or spot, point in time or space**, from Latin *punctum*; partly from Old French *pointe* **sharp end**, from Vulgar Latin *puncta*, from Latin *pungere*] → see also **get/earn brownie points** at BROWNIE (4), VANTAGE POINT

point² S1 W1 *v.*
1 SHOW STH WITH YOUR FINGER [I] to show something to someone by holding out your finger or a thin object towards it: *Babies learn to point before they learn to talk.* | **+at** *"Look," she said, pointing at the screen.* | **+to/toward** *Harry pointed excitedly to the waterfall.* | **+up/down/across** *"There they are," she said as she pointed down the mountainside.* | *He* ***pointed his finger*** *at David.* | *The man* ***pointed in the direction of*** *a large yellow house.*

point

2 AIM [I always + adv./prep., T] to aim something in a particular direction, or to be aimed in that direction: **+at/to/toward etc.** *Hundreds of cameras pointed toward the President.* | **point sth at sb/sth** *The man pointed the gun at her head.*
3 MACHINE/CLOCK ETC. [I always + adv./prep.] to show a particular amount, number, time, direction etc. on a machine, clock, COMPASS etc.: *The arrow always points north.* | **+to/toward** *It will be time to go when the big hand points to 12 and the little hand points to 8.*
4 SHOW SB WHERE TO GO [I always + adv./prep., T always + adv./prep.] to show someone which direction to go: *Could you* ***point me in the right direction?*** | *A handmade sign for the party pointed down a dirt road.* ►see THESAURUS box at lead¹
5 SAY WHAT TO DO [T always + adv./prep.] to suggest what someone should do: *My teachers all pointed me toward college.* | *A good financial advisor will be able to* ***point you in the right direction.***
6 SUGGEST STH IS TRUE [I always + adv./prep.] if facts, a situation etc. point to something, they suggest that it is true: *All the evidence seemed to point that way.* | **+to/toward** *His symptoms all point to a stomach ulcer.* | *Everything points to her having died from a drug overdose.*
7 **point the finger at sb** INFORMAL to blame someone or say that they have done something wrong: **+at** *Everyone was pointing the finger at the government, saying they had not done enough to help.*
8 **point the way a)** to show how something could change or develop successfully: **+to/toward** *The development points the way to some new approaches to urban planning.* **b)** to show which direction you need to go to find something: **+to/toward** *No signs point the way to Carson's grave.*
9 **point your toes** to stretch the ends of your feet down, for example when you are dancing

point out *phr. v.* **1** **point sth ↔ out** to tell someone something that they do not already know or have not thought about: *He got very angry when Emily pointed out his mistake.* | *I hadn't noticed the ad until Bill pointed it out.* | **point out that** *Critics point out that there is little evidence to support his theory.* | **point sth out to sb** *Robinson pointed out to them that the changes would actually improve the property.* **2** **point sb/sth ↔ out** to show someone or something to someone by pointing at them: *Luke pointed out two large birds by the water's edge.* | *Several passengers pointed him out to the police.*

point to sth *phr. v.* to mention something because you think it is important and proves something: *Rollings points to improved test scores as evidence that the changes are working.*

point sth ↔ **up** *phr. v.* to make something seem more important or more noticeable SYN **highlight**: *The crash points up the need for new safety regulations.*

ˌpoint-ˈblank *adv.* **1** if you say something point-blank, you do it directly and without trying to explain your reasons: *I* ***asked*** *him* ***point-blank*** *if he had lied.* | *She* ***refused point-blank*** *to answer the question.* **2** a gun fired point-blank is fired very close to the person or thing it is aimed at: *The victim was shot point-blank in the chest.* —**point-blank** *adj.*: *Edwards was shot at* ***point-blank range.***

point·ed /ˈpɔɪntɪd/ *adj.* [usually before noun] **1** having a point at the end: *the dog's pointed brown ears* **2** **a pointed comment/question/look etc.** a direct question, look etc. that deliberately shows that you are annoyed, bored, or that you disapprove of something: *He made a pointed remark about my being late.* —**pointedly** *adv.*

point·er /ˈpɔɪntɚ/ *n.* [C] **1** a useful piece of advice or information that helps you do or understand something SYN **tip**: **+on** *Larry gave me a few pointers on giving a presentation.* **2** COMPUTERS the small picture, usually an ARROW, that you move using a computer's MOUSE to point to the place on the screen where you want to work or start a program: *Move the pointer to the program's icon and double click.* **3** a long stick used to point at things on a map, board etc. **4** the thing, usually a thin piece of metal, that points to a number or direction on a piece of equipment, for example a scale or COMPASS: *The pointer was between 35 and 40 pounds.* **5** **three-pointer/3-pointer** in basketball, an attempt to throw the ball into the basket that will earn three points if it goes in **6** BIOLOGY a hunting dog that stands very still and points with its nose to where birds or animals are hiding → see also THREE-POINTER

poin·til·lism /ˈpwæntlˌɪzəm, ˈpɔɪn-/ *n.* [U] a style of painting popular in the late 19th century, that uses small spots of color all over the painting, rather than BRUSH STROKES —**pointillist** *adj.* —**pointillist** *n.* [C]

point·less /ˈpɔɪntlɪs/ *adj.* **1** without any purpose or meaning SYN **meaningless**: *People stood in groups, making pointless small talk.* | *Life just seemed pointless to me then.* **2** not likely to have any useful result: *Officials say the investigation is pointless.* | **it is pointless to do sth** *I think it would be pointless to discuss this again.* | **it is pointless doing sth** *It's pointless talking to Ken – he won't listen.* —**pointlessly** *adv.* —**pointlessness** *n.* [U]

THESAURUS

futile having no chance of being effective or successful: *a futile attempt to prevent the war*
useless not useful or effective in any way: *The information he provided was useless.*
be a waste of time/money/effort to use time, money, or effort in a way that is not effective, useful, or sensible: *It was a waste of time talking to him – he wouldn't listen.*

ˈpoint man *n.* [C] **1** someone with a very important job or a lot of responsibility for a particular subject in a company or organization: **+on/for** *He was the President's point man on health care.* **2** a soldier who goes ahead of a group to see if there is any danger

ˌpoint of ˈorder *n.* [C] FORMAL a rule used to organize an official meeting: *He raised an objection* ***on a point of order*** (=according to a rule).

ˌpoint of ˈreference *n.* [C] something you already know about that helps you understand a situation

ˌpoint of ˈsale *n.* [C usually singular] the place or store where a product is sold: *Cash registers at the point of sale keep track of the store's stock.*

ˌpoint of ˈview *n.* [C] **1** a particular way of thinking about or judging a situation SYN **perspective**: **from a scientific/technical/business etc. point of view** *The system is seriously flawed from a security point of view.* ►see THESAURUS box at **opinion** **2** ENG. LANG. ARTS if a story is told from the author's or one of the character's point of view, the story is written as though that person is telling the story: *The story is written* ***from*** *a child's* ***point of view.*** | **3** someone's own personal opinion or attitude about something SYN **perspective**: *A trip to the island can be either very relaxing or very boring, depending on your point of view.*

ˈpoint ˌsymmetry *n.* [U] MATH the quality of an object or figure that can be turned 180 degrees around a point and still look the same. In other words, it looks the same UPSIDE DOWN and right side up. → see also REFLECTIONAL SYMMETRY

poin·ty /ˈpɔɪnṭi/ *adj.* INFORMAL POINTED

ˌpointy-ˈheaded *adj.* INFORMAL, DISAPPROVING someone who is pointy-headed is intelligent in a way that is not practical, and behaves in a way that shows they think they know more than anyone else —**ˈpointy head** *n.* [C]

poise /pɔɪz/ *n.* [U] **1** a calm confident way of behaving, and the ability to control your feelings or reactions in difficult situations SYN **composure**: *He was the sort of man who never lost his poise.* **2** a graceful way of moving or standing, so that your body seems balanced and not awkward: *She has the poise of a dancer.* [**Origin:** 1300–1400 Old French *pois* **weight, heaviness**, from Latin *pensum*, from *pendere* **to weigh**]

poised /pɔɪzd/ *adj.* **1** [not before noun] completely ready to do something or for something to happen, when it is likely to happen soon: **poised to do sth** *Hargrove is poised to become the city's first black mayor.* | **+for** *The company seems poised for success.* **2** [not before noun] not moving, but completely ready to move or do something immediately: *The runners stood poised at the start of the race.* | **+for/on/over etc.** *a small animal poised for flight* | **poised to do sth** *A tabby cat was poised to pounce at any second.* | **+over/above** *She stood poised over her son's bed.* **3** behaving in a calm confident way, and able to control your feelings and reactions SYN **composed**: *Heather looked poised and relaxed as she made her way to the stage.* **4 be poised between sth** [not before noun] to be in a position or situation in which two things have an equally strong influence: *The world stood poised between peace and war.*

poi·son¹ /ˈpɔɪzən/ S3 *n.* [C,U] **1** a substance that can kill you or make you very sick if you eat it, breathe it etc.: *The child had swallowed some kind of poison.* | *a box of* ***rat poison*** | *These fruits contain a* ***deadly poison.*** **2** something such as an emotion or idea that makes you behave badly or become very unhappy: *Nationalism is a poison that has caused much suffering.* **3 what's your poison?** SPOKEN a humorous way of asking someone which alcoholic drink they would like [**Origin:** 1200–1300 Old French **drink, poisonous drink, poison**, from Latin *potio*]

poison² *v.* [T] **1** to give someone poison, especially by adding it to food or a drink, in order to harm or kill them: **poison sb** *Hill poisoned her husband for the insurance money.* | **poison sth** *Had someone poisoned his food?* | **poison sb with sth** *Two of the victims had been poisoned with arsenic.* **2** if a substance poisons someone, it makes them very sick or kills them: *A small amount of lead paint can severely poison a child.* | *Seabirds are being poisoned by toxins in the water.* **3** to make land, rivers, air etc. dirty and dangerous, especially by the use of harmful chemicals: *Pesticides are poisoning the rivers.* **4** to have a harmful effect on someone's mind or emotions, or on a situation: *Sex and violence on TV are* ***poisoning*** *our children's* ***minds.*** | *This attitude could poison U.S. relations with Beijing.* **5 poison sb's mind against sb** to make someone dislike another person by saying bad and untrue things —**poisoner** *n.* [C]

ˌpoison ˈgas *n.* [U] gas that causes death or serious injury, used especially against an enemy in a war

poi·son·ing /ˈpɔɪzənɪŋ/ *n.* [C,U] **1** illness that is caused by swallowing, touching, or breathing a poisonous substance: **alcohol/lead/radiation poisoning** (=caused by a particular substance) *a case of carbon monoxide poisoning* **2** the act of giving poison to someone: *There was no evidence of poisoning.* → see also BLOOD POISONING, FOOD POISONING

ˌpoison ˈivy *n.* [U] a plant that has an oily substance on its leaves that makes your skin hurt and ITCH. The leaves have three parts and the plant has white berries.

ˌpoison ˈoak *n.* [U] a plant with leaves similar to an OAK tree's, that makes your skin hurt and ITCH if you touch the leaves

poi·son·ous /ˈpɔɪzənəs/ *adj.* **1** containing poison or producing poison: *The plant's white berries are extremely poisonous.* | *poisonous snakes* ►see THESAURUS box at **harmful** **2** full of bad and unfriendly feelings, and likely to cause harm or anger: *the poisonous atmosphere between the couple* —**poisonously** *adv.*

ˌpoison-ˈpen ˌletter *n.* [C] a letter that is not signed and that says bad things about the person it has been sent to

poison su·mac /ˌpɔɪzən ˈsumæk/ *n.* [U] a plant that has leaves with two parts and green-white berries, and that makes your skin hurt and ITCH if you touch the leaves

poke¹ /pouk/ *v.*

1 WITH A FINGER/STICK ETC. [T] to quickly push your finger or a pointed object into something or someone SYN **jab**: **poke sb in the eye/ribs/arm etc.** *Someone poked me in the eye during basketball practice.* | **poke sb/sth with sth** *Two boys were poking a crab with a stick.* | **+at** *The boys poked at each other and giggled.* ►see THESAURUS box at **push¹**

2 THROUGH A SPACE/HOLE [T always + adv./prep.] to move or push something through a space or out of an opening, so that you can see part of it: **poke sth in/into/through sth** *Sherman poked his camera through the curtains.* | **poke your head around the door/through the window etc.** *Hannah poked her head around the corner to say "Hi."*

3 BE SEEN [I always + adv./prep.] if something is poking through or out of something else, you can see part of it but not all of it: **+out** *Strands of hair poked out from under her hat.* | **+through** *Weeds poked through the cracks.*

4 poke fun at sb/sth to joke about someone or something in a way that is not nice: *Reid was poking fun at his fellow Texans.*

5 poke a hole to make a hole or hollow area in something by pushing something pointed into or through it: **+in/through** *Fire crews poked holes in the roof to lower temperatures inside.*

6 poke holes in sth to find mistakes or problems in a plan or in what someone has said: **+in** *Defense attorneys tried to poke holes in Jimmy's story.*

7 poke your nose in/into sth INFORMAL to try to find out information about or get involved in someone else's private affairs: *My mother-in-law is always poking her nose in our business.*

8 poke the fire to move coal or wood in a fire with a stick to make it burn better

poke along *phr. v.* INFORMAL to move very slowly SYN **dawdle**: *He was poking along at about 40 miles an hour.*

poke around *phr. v.* INFORMAL **1** to look for something by moving a lot of things around SYN **rummage**: **poke around sth** *Fossil collectors come to poke around the mud banks.* | **+in** *Dan was poking around in the cupboard.* **2** to try to find out information about other people's private lives, in a way that annoys them: +**in** *The press keeps poking around in celebrities' private lives.* **3** to spend time somewhere, especially in stores, looking at nothing in particular: **poke around sth** *A few people had stopped to poke around the market.*

poke at sth *phr. v.* **poke at your food/plate** to move food around on your plate but not eat very much

poke² *n.* **1 give sb/sth a poke** to quickly push your fingers, a stick etc. into something or someone: *Vanessa gave me a poke in the ribs.* **2 take a poke at sb** SPOKEN to hit or try to hit someone: *He took a poke at a cop and got arrested.* **3** INFORMAL a criticism of someone or something: +**at** *Keillor is known for his gentle pokes at small-town America.* | *Bennet* ***took a poke at*** *the President's recent refusal to sign the bill.*

P

pok·er /ˈpoʊkɚ/ *n.* **1** [U] a card game that people usually play for money **2** [C] a metal stick used to move wood in a fire to make it burn better

ˌpoker-ˈfaced *adj., adv.* showing no expression on your face: *a poker-faced man* —**poker face** *n.* [singular]

pok·ey¹, poky /ˈpoʊki/ *adj.* INFORMAL doing things very slowly, especially in a way that is annoying: *My old pokey car can only go sixty miles an hour.*

pokey² *n.* [C] OLD-FASHIONED, INFORMAL a JAIL

pol /pɑl/ *n.* [C] INFORMAL a politician

Po·land /ˈpoʊlənd/ a country in central Europe, east of Germany and west of Belarus

po·lar /ˈpoʊlɚ/ *adj.* **1** close to or relating to the North Pole or the South Pole: *one of the best-known polar explorers* **2 polar opposite/opposites** something exactly or completely opposite in character or nature: *O'Brien's dark troubled pictures are the polar opposites of Wheelan's cheerful abstractions.* **3** PHYSICS related to one of the POLES (=ends) of a MAGNET

ˈpolar ˌbear *n.* [C] a large white bear that lives near the North Pole

ˈpolar ˌcap also **ˌpolar ˈice cap** *n.* [C] one of the two large areas of ice on the North and South Poles

po·lar·i·ty /poʊˈlærət̬i, pə-/ *n.* [C,U] **1** FORMAL a state in which people, opinions, or ideas are completely different or opposite to each other: +**between** *There is a growing polarity between the workers and the management.* **2** PHYSICS the state of having either a positive or negative electric charge

po·lar·ize /ˈpoʊləˌraɪz/ *v.* [I,T] FORMAL to divide into clearly separate groups with opposite beliefs, ideas, bx;5or opinions, or to make people do this: *The issue has polarized the country.* —**polarization** /ˌpoʊlərəˈzeɪʃən/ *n.* [U]

ˌpolar ˈmolecule *n.* [C] CHEMISTRY a MOLECULE in which one side has a negative charge and the other side has a positive charge

Po·lar·oid /ˈpoʊləˌrɔɪd/ *n.* TRADEMARK **1** [C] a camera that uses a special film to produce a photograph very quickly **2** [C] a photograph taken with a Polaroid camera **3** [U] a special substance that is put on the glass in SUNGLASSES, car windows etc. to make the sun seem less bright

ˌpolar reˈversal *n.* [C,U] SCIENCE MAGNETIC REVERSAL

ˈpolar ˌzone *n.* [C] EARTH SCIENCE one of the two parts of the Earth that are near the NORTH POLE and the SOUTH POLE, where the weather is always cold → see also TEMPERATE ZONE

pol·der /ˈpoʊldɚ/ *n.* [C] EARTH SCIENCE an area of low land that was formerly under the sea, which is protected from flooding by a specially built wall or bank

Pole /poʊl/ *n.* [C] someone who comes from Poland

pole¹ /poʊl/ [S3] *n.* [C]

1 STICK/POST a long stick or post usually made of wood or metal, often set upright in the ground to support something: *a telephone pole* | *a flag pole* | *a fishing pole*

2 NORTH/SOUTH POLE the most northern or most southern point on a PLANET, especially the Earth: *Amundsen's expedition was the first to reach the Pole.*

3 be poles apart two people or things that are poles apart are as different from each other as it is possible to be: *Tokyo and Washington remain poles apart on the issue.*

4 OPPOSITES one of two situations, ideas, or opinions that are the complete opposite of each other: ***At one pole*** *in the debate is keeping our personal freedoms, and at the other is reducing crime.* | *The two countries remain* ***at opposite poles*** *on this issue.*

5 ELECTRICAL a) PHYSICS one of two points at the ends of a MAGNET where its power is the strongest **b)** one of the two points at which wires can be attached to a BATTERY in order to use its electricity

6 the pole POLE POSITION

[**Origin:** (2–5) 1300–1400 Latin *polus*, from Greek *polos*]

pole² *v.* [I,T] to push a boat along in the water using a pole

pole·cat /ˈpoʊlkæt/ *n.* [C] BIOLOGY **1** a SKUNK **2** a small dark brown wild animal that lives in northern Europe and can defend itself by producing a bad smell

po·lem·ic /pəˈlɛmɪk/ *n.* ENG. LANG. ARTS **1** [C] a written or spoken statement that strongly criticizes or defends a particular idea, opinion, or person: *Essentially, the play is a polemic on the judicial system.* **2** [U] also **polemics** the practice or skill of making such statements

po·lem·i·cal /pəˈlɛmɪkəl/ also **polemic** *adj.* FORMAL or TECHNICAL using strong arguments to criticize or defend a particular idea, opinion, or person: *a polemical article on abortion rights* —**polemically** /-kli/ *adv.*

ˈpole poˌsition *n.* [C,U] the best front position at the beginning of a car or bicycle race

ˈPole Star *n.* **the Pole Star** a star that is almost directly over the North Pole and that can be seen from the northern part of the world

ˈpole vault *n.* **the pole vault** the sport of jumping over a high bar using a long pole —**pole vaulter** *n.* [C] —**pole vaulting** *n.* [U]

po·lice¹ /pəˈlis/ [S2] [W1] *n.* **1 the police** an official organization whose job is to make sure that people obey the law, to catch criminals, and to protect people and property [SYN] **the cops**: *She* ***reported*** *the robbery* ***to the police.*** | *If you don't leave, I'll* ***call the police.*** | *Two men were later* ***arrested by the police.*** | *a police car* **2** [plural] the people who work for this organization: *On Monday, both men finally surrendered to police.* [**Origin:** 1400–1500 French, Late Latin *politia* **government**, from *polites* **citizen**] → see also MILITARY POLICE, SECRET POLICE

THESAURUS

People in the police
police officer/policeman/policewoman
detective a police officer whose job is to discover who is responsible for crimes
plain-clothes police officer a police officer who is wearing ordinary clothes instead of a uniform
cop INFORMAL a police officer

Things the police do
investigate crimes
find/collect evidence
arrest sb
question/interrogate/interview sb
hold/keep sb in custody to keep someone in prison while collecting more information about a crime, or before she or he goes to court
charge sb with a crime to state officially that someone might be guilty of a crime

police² *v.* [T] **1** to control an activity or industry by making sure that people obey the rules [SYN] **regulate**: *The agency was set up to police the nuclear power industry.* | *Most newspapers* ***police themselves*** *and keep to ethical standards.* **2** to keep control over a particular area and protect people and property, using the police, the army etc.: *The five security zones are policed by U.N. forces.* **3** to keep an outside area neat and clean, for example by picking up papers, cans etc. [SYN] **clean up**: *All campers are required to police their* campsite before they leave. **—policing** *n.* [U] *The community is demanding a less aggressive style of policing.*

po,lice bru'tality *n.* [U] violence or threats made by the police against someone who they believe is guilty of a crime

po'lice de,partment *n.* [C] the official police organization in a particular area or city

po'lice dog *n.* [C] a dog trained by the police to find hidden drugs or catch criminals

po'lice force *n.* [C] the police organization in an area: *He resigned from the police force last May.*

po·lice·man /pə'lismən/ *n. plural* **policemen** /-mən/ [C] a male police officer SYN cop

po'lice ,officer *n.* [C] a member of the police SYN cop

po'lice state *n.* [C] POLITICS a country in which the government strictly controls people's freedom to travel, to meet, or to write or speak about politics or other issues

po'lice ,station *n.* [C] the local office of the police in a town, part of a city etc.

po·lice·wom·an /pə'lis,wʊmən/ *n. plural* **policewomen** /-,wɪmɪn/ [C] a female police officer SYN cop

pol·i·cy /'pɑləsi/ Ac S2 W1 *n. plural* **policies** **1** [C,U] a way of doing something that has been officially agreed on and chosen by a political party, business, or other organization: *Do you agree with the administration's policies?* | *the university's admissions policies* | **+on** *the company's policy on maternity leave* | **+of** *The policy of containment* (=preventing the spread of Communism) *led the U.S. into the Vietnam War.* | **defense/housing/foreign etc. policy** *the President's economic policy* | *The Senator urged her colleagues not to* ***adopt a policy*** *that would harm legal immigrants.* **2** [C] a contract with an insurance company, or an official written statement giving all the details of such a contract: *an* ***insurance policy*** | *Have you* ***renewed the*** *car insurance* ***policy?*** | *The* ***policy covers*** *theft and fire.* **3** [C,U] a particular principle that you believe in and that influences the way you behave: *I make it my policy not to gossip.* [**Origin:** (1, 3) 1300–1400 Old French *policie*, from Late Latin *politia* **government**]

pol·i·cy·hold·er /'pɑləsi,hoʊldɚ/ *n.* [C] someone who has bought insurance for something

pol·i·cy·mak·er, policy maker /'pɑləsi,meɪkɚ/ *n.* [C] someone who helps to decide what an organization or government will do and how it will do it

po·li·o /'poʊli,oʊ/ also **po·li·o·my·e·li·tis** /,poʊlioʊmaɪə'laɪtɪs/ *n.* [U] MEDICINE a serious infectious disease of the nerves in the SPINE, which often results in someone being permanently unable to move particular muscles

po·lis /'poʊlɪs/ *n.* [C] HISTORY a CITY-STATE in ancient Greece

pol·i sci /,pɑli 'saɪ/ *n.* [U] SPOKEN a short form of POLITICAL SCIENCE

Po·lish¹ /'poʊlɪʃ/ *adj.* from or relating to Poland, its people, or their language

Polish² *n.* [U] **1** the language of Poland **2 the Polish** [plural] people from Poland

pol·ish¹ /'pɑlɪʃ/ *v.* [T] **1** to make something smooth, bright, and shiny by rubbing it: *Jerry spent all afternoon polishing the car.* ▸see THESAURUS box at **clean²** **2** to improve a piece of writing, a speech etc. by making slight changes before it is completely finished: *Your essay is good, but you need to polish it a little bit.* **—polisher** *n.* [C] **—polishing** *n.* [U]

polish sb/sth ↔ **off** *phr. v.* INFORMAL **1** to finish food, work etc. quickly or easily: *Sam polished off the rest of the pizza.* **2** to kill or defeat someone: *Miami has polished off eleven teams in a row this season.*

polish sth ↔ **up** *phr. v.* **1** also **polish up on sth** to improve a skill or an ability by practicing it: *I'd better polish up my Spanish!* **2** to make something seem better or more attractive to other people: *The company wants to polish up its image.* **3** to polish or make something clean and new looking

polish² *n.* **1** [C,U] a liquid, powder, or other substance that you rub into a surface to make it smooth and shiny: *furniture polish* | *shoe polish* **2** [U] great skill and style in the way someone performs, writes, or behaves: *What this dance troupe lacks in polish, they make up for in enthusiasm.* **3** [singular] a smooth shiny surface produced by polishing, or an act of polishing a surface → see also **spit and polish** at SPIT² (4)

pol·ished /'pɑlɪʃt/ *adj.* **1** shiny because of being rubbed, usually with polish: *dark polished wood* **2** a polished performance, piece of writing, musician, actor etc. is skillful and stylish: *Guillem is a polished ballerina.* **3** polite, confident, and graceful: *a polished lawyer*

pol·it·bu·ro /'pɑlɪt,byʊroʊ/ *n.* [C usually singular] POLITICS the most important decision-making committee of a Communist party or Communist government, especially in the former Soviet Union

po·lite /pə'laɪt/ S3 *adj.* **1** behaving or speaking in a way that is correct for the social situation you are in, and showing that you are careful to consider other people's needs and feelings SYN courteous OPP rude OPP impolite: *The sales clerks were very polite and helpful.* | *polite well-behaved children* | ***Be polite*** *and say thank-you.* | **it is polite to do sth** *It's not polite to talk with your mouth full.* → IMPOLITE

THESAURUS

have good manners to behave in a polite way in social situations: *You teach your children to have good manners by being polite yourself.*
well-behaved behaving in a polite or socially acceptable way: *My kids are generally well-behaved.*
courteous polite and respectful: *He was courteous and helpful.*
civil polite but not very friendly: *I know you don't like him, but try to be civil.*

2 just/only being polite SPOKEN saying something you may not really believe or think, in order to avoid offending someone: *Did she really like the flowers, or was she just being polite?* **3** you make polite conversation, remarks etc. because it is considered socially correct to do this: *We exchanged polite goodbyes before getting on the train.* | *a polite smile* **4 in polite society/circles/company** OFTEN HUMOROUS among people who are considered to have a good education and correct social behavior: *You can't use words like that in polite company.* [**Origin:** 1400–1500 Latin, past participle of *polire*] **—politely** *adv.* **—politeness** *n.* [U]

pol·i·tesse /,pɑli'tɛs/ *n.* [U] FORMAL the ability to behave or speak in a polite way

pol·i·tic /'pɑlə,tɪk/ *adj.* FORMAL sensible and likely to bring advantage SYN prudent: *It would not be politic to ignore the reporters.* → see also BODY POLITIC, POLITICS

po·lit·i·cal /pə'lɪtɪkəl/ S2 W1 *adj.* **1** [no comparative] relating to the government, politics, and public affairs of a country: *an important political issue* | *The U.S. has two main* ***political parties.*** | *Russia's* ***political system*** *has undergone radical changes.* | *political activists* | *political jokes and satire* **2** [no comparative] relating to the ways that different people have power within a group, organization etc.: *Harris was given the job, mainly for political reasons.* **3** POLITICS interested in or active in politics: *Many young people aren't very political.* **4 political football** a difficult problem which opposing politicians argue about or which each side deals with in a way that will bring them advantage: *The issue of teaching evolution in schools has once again become a political football.* → see also POLITICALLY

po,litical 'action com,mittee ABBREVIATION **PAC** *n.* [C] POLITICS an organization formed by a business, UNION, or INTEREST GROUP to help raise money so that people who support their ideas can try to be elected for Congress

po,litical a'sylum *n.* [U] POLITICS the right to remain in another country if you cannot live safely in your own because of the political situation there: *The family was **granted political asylum** in Britain.*

po,litical e'conomy *n.* [U] ECONOMICS the study of the way nations organize the production and use of wealth

po,litical ge'ography *n.* [U] the study of how Earth is divided up into different countries, rather than the way it is marked by rivers, mountains etc. → see also PHYSICAL GEOGRAPHY

P

po·lit·i·cally /pəˈlɪt̬ɪkli/ W3 *adv.* in a political way: *politically active teenagers* | *a politically motivated remark* | [sentence adverb] *Politically, the region is very unstable.*

po,litically cor'rect *adj.* **1** language, behavior, and attitudes that are politically correct are carefully chosen so that they do not offend or insult anyone **2** someone who is politically correct uses politically correct language, behavior etc. —**political correctness** *n.* [U] → see also PC²

po,litical ma'chine *n.* [singular] POLITICS the system of people and organizations that help a politician or party get into power and stay in power

po,litical 'map *n.* [C] a map or drawing that shows the borders between countries, states, capital cities etc.

po,litical 'prisoner *n.* [C] someone who is put in prison because they oppose and criticize the government of their own country

po,litical 'science *n.* [U] POLITICS the study of politics and government —**political scientist** *n.* [C]

po,litical ,sociali'zation *n.* [U] POLITICS the gradual process by which people form and develop political opinions and become interested in politics or involved in political activities: *You should remember that your opinions are biased by your experiences and your political socialization.*

pol·i·ti·cian /ˌpɑləˈtɪʃən/ W2 *n.* [C] **1** someone who works in politics, especially an elected member of the government: *a popular local politician* **2** someone who is skilled at dealing with people or at getting advantages for themselves within an organization: *Jan is the office politician.*

po·lit·i·cize /pəˈlɪt̬əˌsaɪz/ *v.* [T] to make something more political or more involved in politics: *He warned against politicizing the report's conclusions.*

po·lit·i·cized /pəˈlɪt̬əˌsaɪzd/ *adj.* having been made more political or having become involved in politics: *Abortion is a highly politicized issue.* —**politicization** /pəˌlɪt̬əsəˈzeɪʃən/ *n.* [U]

pol·i·tick·ing /ˈpɑləˌtɪkɪŋ/ *n.* [U] political activity, usually done to gain support for yourself or your political group: *election-year politicking*

po·lit·i·co /pəˈlɪt̬əˌkoʊ/ *n. plural* **politicos** [C] a politician or someone who is active in politics; often used in a disapproving way: *Many local politicos were surprised at McKasson's resignation.*

politico- /pəlɪt̬əkoʊ/ *prefix* used in adjectives to say that something involves both politics and something else: *politico-military strategy*

pol·i·tics /ˈpɑləˌtɪks/ S3 W1 *n.* **1** [U] ideas and activities that are concerned with gaining and using power in a country,: *I've been involved in city politics since college.* | *Politics doesn't interest me much.* | **local/state/national politics** *an article on international politics and law* | ***Party politics*** (=activities that are done only to help your political party, rather than to help society in general) *and national security do not mix well.* **2** [U] the profession of being a politician: *Flynn retired from politics in 1986.* | *Helping people is why I **went into politics*** (=became a politician). **3** [plural] the activities of people who are concerned with gaining personal advantage within a group, organization etc.: *the internal politics of the steel industry* | *I'm tired of dealing with **office politics**.* | *an article about **sexual politics*** (=how power is shared between men and women) *at work* **4** [plural] someone's political beliefs and opinions: *His politics are very different from mine.* **5** [U] POLITICAL SCIENCE [**Origin:** 1500–1600 Greek *politika* (plural), from *politikos*]

pol·i·ty /ˈpɑləṭi/ *n.* [C,U] POLITICS a particular form of political or government organization, or a condition of society in which political organization exists

Polk /poʊk/**, James** (1795–1849) the 11th President of the U.S.

pol·ka /ˈpoʊlkə, ˈpoʊkə/ *n.* [C] a very quick simple dance from Eastern Europe for people dancing in pairs, or a piece of music for this dance —**polka** *v.* [I]

'polka dot *n.* [C] one of a number of round spots that form a pattern, especially on cloth: *a green shirt with blue polka dots* —**polka-dot** —**polka-dotted** *adj.*: *a polka-dot dress*

poll¹ /poʊl/ *n.* [C] **1** the process of finding out what people think about something by asking many people the same question, or the result of this: *A recent poll found that 80% of Californians support the governor.* | *The Democratic candidate is ahead **in the polls**.* | **conduct/do/take a poll** *We conducted a poll to find out what parents thought about the bill.* | **+of** *a poll of 1,000 people* | **+on** *a poll on eating habits* | *The **public opinion poll** showed that 25% of us consider ourselves superstitious.*

THESAURUS

survey a set of questions that you ask a large number of people in order to find out about their opinions and behavior: *According to a recent survey, most Americans think there is too much violence on television.*

questionnaire a written set of questions about a particular subject that is given to a large number of people, in order to collect information: *The people who took part in the study filled out a questionnaire about the foods they regularly eat.*

2 the polls [plural] POLITICS the place where you can go to vote in an election: *The polls open at 7 a.m.* | *Ten million voters **went to the polls*** (=voted). | *the party's victory **at the polls*** (=in an election) → see also EXIT POLL, STRAW POLL

poll² *v.* [T] **1** to try to find out what people think about a subject by asking many people the same question SYN **survey**: *Sixty percent of the people polled said they disagreed with the President's economic policies.* ▸see THESAURUS box at **ask** **2** to receive a particular number of votes in an election

'poll book *n.* [C] POLITICS an official record of all the people in a PRECINCT (=area of a town or city with its own local government) who have the legal right to vote

pol·len /ˈpɑlən/ *n.* [U] BIOLOGY a fine powder produced by flowers, which is carried by the wind or by insects to other flowers of the same type, making them produce seeds

'pollen count *n.* [C] a measure of the amount of pollen in the air, usually given to help people who are made sick by it: *The pollen count is high today.*

pol·li·nate /ˈpɑləˌneɪt/ *v.* [T] BIOLOGY to make a flower or plant produce seeds by moving POLLEN from the male plant to the female plant: *Bees help pollinate crops as well as flowers.* —**pollination** /ˌpɑləˈneɪʃən/ *n.* [U]

poll·ing /ˈpoʊlɪŋ/ *n.* [U] **1** POLITICS the activity of voting in a political election: *Polling will take place from 7 a.m. to 10 p.m.* **2** the activity of asking people their opinions

'polling ,station also **'polling ,place** *n.* [C] POLITICS the place where people go to vote in an election

pol·li·wog, **pollywog** /ˈpɑliˌwɑg/ *n.* [C] INFORMAL a TADPOLE

Pol·lock /ˈpɑlək/, **Jack·son** (1912–1956) a U.S. artist known for his very large ABSTRACT paintings which are full of color

Jackson Pollock

poll·ster /ˈpoʊlstɚ/ *n.* [C] POLITICS someone who prepares and asks questions to find out what people think about a particular subject

ˈpoll tax *n.* [C] ECONOMICS a tax of a particular amount that is collected from every citizen of a country, especially in order to be allowed to vote

pol·lut·ant /pəˈlutˀnt/ *n.* [C,U] EARTH SCIENCE a substance in air, water, or soil that is harmful to humans and other ORGANISMS, and is usually the result of human activity: *industrial pollutants in the lake* | *hazardous air pollutants*

pol·lute /pəˈlut/ *v.* [T] **1** EARTH SCIENCE to make air, water, soil etc. dangerously dirty and not good enough for people to use: *beaches polluted by raw sewage* | **pollute sth with sth** *The factory pollutes the air with hydrogen sulfide.* **2** to spoil or ruin something that used to be good SYN **corrupt**: *Money has polluted the democratic spirit of American politics.* **3** to give someone immoral thoughts and make their character bad SYN **corrupt**: *Violent movies and video games are* ***polluting*** *our children's* ***minds***. —**polluted** *adj.*: *polluted rivers* —**polluter** *n.* [C] *a list of the country's worst polluters*

pol·lu·tion /pəˈluʃən/ *n.* [U] **1** the process of making air, water, soil etc. harmful to humans and other ORGANISMS: *The use of electric cars could be a key factor in fighting pollution.* | **+of** *the pollution of our rivers by factories and farms* | **air/water/soil pollution** *air pollution from traffic fumes* ►see THESAURUS box at **environment** **2** EARTH SCIENCE the presence of substances in air, water, soil etc. that are harmful to humans and other ORGANISMS: *rising levels of pollution in rivers* | *Car exhaust emissions are a major* ***source of pollution***.

Pol·ly·an·na /ˌpɑliˈænə/ *n.* [C usually singular] someone who is always cheerful and always thinks something good is going to happen

po·lo /ˈpoʊloʊ/ *n.* [U] a game played between two teams of players riding horses, who use wooden hammers with long handles to hit a small ball → see also WATER POLO

Po·lo /ˈpoʊloʊ/, **Mar·co** /ˈmɑrkoʊ/ (1254–1324) an Italian traveler whose writings gave Europeans their first knowledge of life in the Far East

pol·o·naise /ˌpɑləˈneɪz/ *n.* [C] a slow Polish dance popular in the 19th century, or the music for this dance

ˈpolo shirt *n.* [C] a sport shirt, usually made of cotton, that has a collar, a few buttons near the neck, and that is pulled on over the head

Pol Pot /ˌpoʊl ˈpɑt, ˌpɑl-/ (1926–1998) the leader of the Communist Khmer Rouge group, and Prime Minister of Cambodia from 1975 to 1979, during which time about three million people were killed

pol·ter·geist /ˈpoʊltɚˌgaɪst/ *n.* [C] a GHOST that makes objects move around and makes strange noises

poly- /pɑli/ *prefix* many: *polysyllabic* (=with three or more SYLLABLES) | *polyglot* (=speaking more than one language)

pol·y·an·dry /ˈpɑliˌændri/ *n.* [U] TECHNICAL the custom or practice of having more than one husband at the same time → see also BIGAMY —**polyandrous** /ˌpɑliˈændrəs/ *adj.*

pol·y·es·ter /ˈpɑliˌɛstɚ, ˌpɑliˈɛstɚ/ *n.* [C,U] **1** a type of strong SYNTHETIC cloth: *a blue polyester shirt* **2** TECHNICAL a chemical compound used to make cloth and plastics

pol·y·eth·yl·ene /ˌpɑliˈɛθəˌlin/ *n.* [U] a strong light plastic used to make bags, material for covering food, small containers etc.

po·lyg·a·my /pəˈlɪgəmi/ *n.* [U] TECHNICAL the custom or practice of having more than one husband or wife at the same time → see also BIGAMY —**polygamous** *adj.*

pol·y·gene /ˈpɑliˌdʒin/ *n.* [C] BIOLOGY a GENE whose single effect on physical appearance is too small to see, but which can act together with other GENES to produce an effect that can be seen

pol·y·gen·ic /ˌpɑliˈdʒɛnɪk◂/ *adj.* BIOLOGY relating to or affected by POLYGENES: *a polygenic trait*

pol·y·glot /ˈpɑliˌglɑt/ *adj.* FORMAL speaking or using many languages SYN **multilingual** —**polyglot** *n.* [C]

P

pol·y·gon /ˈpɑliˌgɑn/ *n.* [C] MATH a flat shape with three or more straight sides —**polygonal** /pəˈlɪgənl/ *adj.*

pol·y·graph /ˈpɑliˌgræf/ *n.* [C] TECHNICAL a piece of equipment that is used by the police to find out whether someone is telling the truth SYN **lie detector**

pol·y·he·dron /ˌpɑliˈhidrən/ *n.* [C] MATH a solid shape with many sides, each of which is a polygon

pol·y·math /ˈpɑliˌmæθ/ *n.* [C] FORMAL someone who has a lot of knowledge about many different subjects

pol·y·mer /ˈpɑləmɚ/ *n.* [C] CHEMISTRY **1** a large MOLECULE formed from many smaller molecules **2** a substance made up of these molecules. Polymers can be natural or artificial.

pol·y·mor·phous /ˌpɑliˈmɔrfəs◂/ also **pol·y·mor·phic** /-ˈmɔrfɪk◂/ *adj.* TECHNICAL having many forms, styles etc. during different stages of growth or development: *a polymorphic computer virus*

pol·y·no·mi·al /ˌpɑlɪˈnoʊmiəl/ *n.* [C] MATH an algebraic expression consisting of MONOMIALS (=an expression consisting of a single group of numbers, letters, or indexes) that are added together or SUBTRACTED from each other. For example, expressions such as $7x - 4x + 11$ or $3x^3 + 2x^2 + x - 5$ are polynomials. —**polynomial** *adj.*: *a polynomial equation*

pol·yp /ˈpɑləp/ *n.* [C] **1** MEDICINE a small LUMP that grows inside your body because of an illness, but is not likely to harm you **2** BIOLOGY a sea animal that has a body like a tube and TENTACLES around an opening in its body which it uses both for eating and for getting rid of waste: *a coral polyp*

pol·y·pep·tide /ˌpɑliˈpɛptaɪd/ *n.* [C] CHEMISTRY a PEPTIDE that consists of more than ten AMINO ACIDS

po·lyph·o·ny /pəˈlɪfəni/ *n.* [U] a type of music in which several different tunes or notes are sung or played together at the same time —**polyphonic** /ˌpɑliˈfɑnɪk◂/ *adj.*

pol·y·pro·pyl·ene /ˌpɑliˈproʊpəˌlin/ *n.* [U] a hard light plastic material

pol·y·sac·cha·ride /ˌpɑliˈsækəˌraɪd/ *n.* [C] BIOLOGY any of several CARBOHYDRATES that consist of a number of simple sugars joined together → see also MONOSACCHARIDE

pol·y·se·mous /ˌpɑlɪˈsiməs, pəˈlɪsəməs/ *adj.* ENG. LANG. ARTS a polysemous word has two or more different meanings —**polysemy** /ˈpɑlɪˌsimi, pəˈlɪsəmi/ *n.* [U]

pol·y·sty·rene /ˌpɑliˈstaɪrin◂/ *n.* [U] a soft light plastic material that prevents heat or cold from passing through it, used especially for making containers

pol·y·syl·lab·ic /ˌpɑlisɪˈlæbɪk/ *adj.* ENG. LANG. ARTS a word that is polysyllabic contains more than three SYLLABLES —**polysyllable** /ˈpɑliˌsɪləbəl/ *n.*

pol·y·tech·nic /ˌpɑliˈtɛknɪk/ *n.* [C] a college where you can study technical or scientific subjects

pol·y·the·ism /ˈpɑliθiˌɪzəm/ *n.* [U] the belief that there is more than one god → see also MONOTHEISM —**polytheistic** /ˌpɑliθiˈɪstɪk/ *adj.*

pol·y·un·sat·u·rate /ˌpɑliʌnˈsætʃərɪt/ *n.* [C] a FATTY ACID (=chemical that helps your body produce energy) that is POLYUNSATURATED

pol·y·un·sat·u·rat·ed /ˌpɑliʌnˈsætʃəˌreɪt̬ɪd/ *adj.* polyunsaturated fats or oils come from vegetables and plants, and are considered to be better for your health than animal fats → see also SATURATED FAT

pol·y·ur·e·thane /ˌpɑliˈyʊrəˌθeɪn/ *n.* [U] a plastic used to make paints and VARNISH

pol·y·vi·nyl chlor·ide /ˌpɑlivaɪnl ˈklɔraɪd/ *n.* [U] PVC

po·made /poʊˈmeɪd/ *n.* [U] a sweet-smelling oily substance rubbed on men's hair to make it smooth, used especially in past times

po·man·der /ˈpoʊˌmændɚ/ *n.* [C] a box or ball that contains dried flowers and HERBS and is used to make clothes or a room smell nice

P

pom·e·gran·ate /ˈpɑməˌgrænɪt/ *n.* [C] BIOLOGY a juicy round fruit with a thick red skin and many small seeds inside

pom·mel /ˈpʌməl, ˈpɑ-/ *n.* [C] the high rounded part at the front of a horse's SADDLE

ˈpommel horse *n.* [C] a piece of equipment used in GYMNASTICS that has two handles on top, which you hold onto to swing your body around

pomp /pɑmp/ *n.* [U] FORMAL all the impressive clothes, decorations, music etc. that are traditional for an important official or public ceremony: *The Queen was welcomed with great* ***pomp and circumstance*** (=impressive formal celebrations).

pom·pa·dour /ˈpɑmpəˌdɔr/ *n.* [C] a hair style in which the hair in front is worn brushed up and back over the FOREHEAD (=top part of the face)

Pom·pey /ˈpɑmpi/ (106–48 B.C.) a Roman general and politician who opposed Julius Caesar but was defeated by him in 48 B.C.

pom·pom /ˈpɑmpɑm/ also **pom·pon** /ˈpɑmpɑn/ *n.* [C] **1** a small wool ball used as a decoration on clothing, especially hats **2** a large round ball of loose plastic strings connected to a handle, used by CHEERLEADERS

pomp·ous /ˈpɑmpəs/ *adj.* trying to make people think you are important, especially by using very formal and important sounding words: *a pompous old man | a pompous speech* —**pompously** *adv.* —**pompousness** also **pomposity** /pɑmˈpɑsət̬i/ *n.* [U]

Pon·ce de Le·ón /ˌpɑnsə deɪ leɪˈoʊn/, **Juan** /wɑn/ (1460–1521) a Spanish EXPLORER who took control of Puerto Rico for Spain in 1508 and discovered Florida in 1513

pon·cho /ˈpɑntʃoʊ/ *n. plural* **ponchos** [C] **1** a coat that keeps rain off you and is made of one large piece of material with a cover for your head **2** a coat consisting of one large piece of thick wool cloth like a BLANKET, with a hole in the middle for your head [**Origin:** 1700–1800 American Spanish, Araucanian *pontho* **woolen cloth**]

pond /pɑnd/ *n.* [C] **1** a small area of fresh water that is smaller than a lake: *a goldfish pond* **2 across the pond** also **on the other side of the pond** INFORMAL on the other side of the Atlantic Ocean in the U.K. or the U.S. [**Origin:** 1200–1300 Old English *pund*, from Latin *pondo*]

pon·der /ˈpɑndɚ/ *v.* [I,T] FORMAL to spend time thinking carefully and seriously about a problem, a difficult question, or something that has happened: **+on/over/about** *Scientists still ponder over the origin of man.* | **ponder how/what/whether etc.** *Jay stood still for a moment, pondering whether to go or not.* [**Origin:** 1300–1400 Old French *ponderer* **to weigh**, from Latin *ponderare*, from *pondus* **weight**]

pon·der·ous /ˈpɑndərəs/ *adj.* **1** moving slowly or awkwardly, especially because of being very big and heavy: *Holyfield was slim and quick, giving him an advantage over his ponderous opponent.* **2** boring and too serious: *the professor's ponderous voice* —**ponderously** *adv.* —**ponderousness** *n.* [U]

Pon·ti·ac /ˈpɑnt̬iæk/ (1720?–1769) an Ottawa chief who fought against the British in 1763–1766

pon·tiff /ˈpɑntɪf/ *n.* [C] the POPE [**Origin:** 1500–1600 French *pontif*, from Latin *pontifex* **member of the council of priests in ancient Rome**]

pon·tif·i·cal /pɑnˈtɪfɪkəl/ *adj.* FORMAL **1** relating to the POPE **2** speaking as if you think your judgment or opinion is always right —**pontifically** /-kli/ *adv.*

pon·tif·i·cate¹ /pɑnˈtɪfəˌkeɪt/ *v.* [I] DISAPPROVING to give your opinion about something in a way that shows you think you are always right: **+about/on** *Politicians will happily pontificate on any issue.*

pon·tif·i·cate² /pɑnˈtɪfɪkɪt, -ˌkeɪt/ *n.* [C] TECHNICAL the position or period of being POPE

pon·toon /pɑnˈtun/ *n.* [C] **1** one of several metal containers or boats that are fastened together to support a floating bridge **2** one of two hollow metal containers that are attached to the bottom of an airplane so that it can come down onto water and float

ponˈtoon bridge *n.* [C] a floating bridge that is supported by several pontoons

po·ny¹ /ˈpoʊni/ *n. plural* **ponies** [C] a small horse → see also SHETLAND PONY

pony² *v.*

pony up *phr. v.* **pony up sth** INFORMAL to pay for something: *King wanted $2 million, but neither company would pony up.*

ˈPony Exˌpress *n.* [singular] a mail service in the 1860s that used horses and riders to carry the mail in the U.S.

po·ny·tail /ˈpoʊniˌteɪl/ *n.* [C] hair tied together at the back of your head → see picture at HAIRSTYLE

Pon·zi scheme /ˈpɑnzi ˌskim/ *n.* [C] another name for a PYRAMID SCHEME

pooch /putʃ/ *n.* INFORMAL [C] a dog

poo·dle /ˈpudl/ *n.* [C] a dog with thick curly hair [**Origin:** 1800–1900 German *pudel*, from *pudelhund* **dog that splashes in water**]

poof /puf, pʊf/ *interjection* used when talking about something that happened suddenly: *Then poof! She was gone.*

poof·y /ˈpufi/ *adj.* INFORMAL poofy hair or clothes look big and soft or filled with air: *She wore a poofy blond wig.*

pooh /pu/ *interjection* OLD-FASHIONED **1** used when you are slightly upset about something, especially to avoid saying a swear word **2** used when you think something is stupid or not very good

pooh-bah /ˈpu bɑ/ *n.* [C] INFORMAL a word meaning someone who is important or powerful, used to show that you do not respect them very much

pooh-pooh /ˈpupu, puˈpu/ *v.* [T] INFORMAL to say that you think an idea, suggestion, effort etc. is stupid or not very good: *Energy companies have pooh-poohed the seriousness of global warming.*

pool¹ /pul/ S1 W2 *n.*

1 FOR SWIMMING [C] a hole that has been specially built and filled with water so that people can swim or WADE in it: *I spent the entire afternoon relaxing by the pool.*

2 GAME [U] a game in which you use a stick to knock numbered balls into holes around a cloth-covered table, which is often played in bars: **play/shoot pool** *We went to the bar and played pool.*

3 a pool of water/blood/light etc. a small area of liquid or light on a surface: *There was a pool of oil under the car.*

4 AREA OF WATER [C] a small area of still water in a hollow place: *Kids were looking for crabs in the tide pools.*

5 GROUP OF PEOPLE [C] a group of people who are available to work or to do an activity when they are needed: *a pool of volunteers for community projects | a secretarial pool*

6 SPORTS [C] a game in which people try to win money by guessing the results of football, basketball etc. games, or the money that is collected from these people for this: *the office basketball pool*

7 GROUP OF THINGS [C] a number of things or an amount of money that is shared by a group of people: *He won $50,000 from the pool.*

[**Origin:** (1, 3, 4) Old English *pol*] → see also CARPOOL[1], **dirty pool** at DIRTY[1] (10), GENE POOL

pool² *v.* [T] to combine your money, ideas, skills etc. with those of other people so that you can all use them: *The family **pooled** all of their financial **resources** to start the business.*

'pool hall *n.* [C] a building where people go to play pool

pool·room /'pulrum/ *n.* [C] a room used for playing pool, especially in a bar

pool·side /'pulsaɪd/ *adj.* [only before noun] near or on the side of a swimming pool: *a poolside barbecue* —**poolside** *n.* [U]

'pool ˌtable *n.* [C] a cloth-covered table with pockets in the corners and sides that is used for playing pool

poop¹ /pup/ *n.* **1** [U] INFORMAL solid waste from your BOWELS, used especially when talking to or about children **2** [singular] INFORMAL an act of passing waste from your BOWELS, used especially when talking to or about children **3 the poop** SPOKEN the most recent news about something that has happened, which someone tells you in an informal way: *So, **what's the poop on** the new guy?* **4** [C] TECHNICAL the raised part at the back end of an old sailing ship

poop² *v.* INFORMAL [I,T] to pass solid waste from your BOWELS, used especially when talking to or about children → see also PARTY POOPER

poop out *phr. v.* INFORMAL **1** if something poops out, it stops working: *The laptop's battery pooped out after only two hours.* **2** to stop doing something because you are tired, bored etc.: *Don't **poop out on us*** (=decide not to do something with us) *so soon!*

'poop deck *n.* [C] the floor on the raised part at the back of an old sailing ship

pooped /pupt/ also **ˌpooped 'out** *adj.* [not before noun] INFORMAL very tired SYN **exhausted**: *The dog's all pooped out after her swim.*

poop·er scoop·er /'pupɚ ˌskupɚ/ *n.* [C] INFORMAL a small SHOVEL and a container, used by dog owners for removing their dogs' solid waste from the streets

poo-poo /'pu pu/ *n.* [U] POOP

'poop sheet *n.* [C] INFORMAL written instructions or information

poop·y /'pupi/ *adj.* SPOKEN full of POOP or covered with poop: *a poopy diaper*

poor /pʊr, pɔr/ S1 W1 *adj.*

1 NO MONEY a) having very little money and not many possessions OPP **rich**: *My family was too poor to buy a computer.* | *a poor neighborhood* | *one of the poorest countries in the world* | *My grandparents grew up **dirt poor*** (=very poor). **b) the poor** people who are poor OPP **the rich**: *charities that help the poor*

THESAURUS

needy having very little food or money: *There is financial assistance available for needy students.*
destitute FORMAL having no money, no place to live, no food etc.: *The Depression left many farmers completely destitute.*
impoverished FORMAL very poor: *an impoverished section of New York*
broke not having any money for a period of time: *I'm broke and I need a job.*
disadvantaged having social problems, such as a lack of money, that make it difficult to succeed: *students from disadvantaged backgrounds*
underprivileged poor and not having the advantages of most other people in society: *The arts program gives underprivileged children a chance to experiment with materials they could never afford.*
deprived not having the things that are considered necessary for a comfortable or happy life: *a deprived area in the inner city*
penniless WRITTEN having no money: *She died penniless.*
poverty-stricken extremely poor: *a poverty-stricken community*
→ RICH

2 NOT GOOD not as good as it could be or should be SYN **bad** OPP **good**: *Her chances of recovery are poor.* | *poor living conditions* | *The jacket was **of** very **poor quality*** (=not made well or of good materials). | **poor hearing/eyesight/memory** *Bats have very poor eyesight.* | **do a poor job (of) doing sth** *Public schools have done a poor job educating minorities.* | *My parents are both **in poor health**.* ▸see THESAURUS box at **bad**[1]

3 poor boy/girl/Joe etc. SPOKEN used to show pity for someone because they are so unlucky, unhappy etc.: *Poor Dad, he's had an exhausting week.* | *I feel sorry for the poor animals at the zoo.* | *The **poor thing*** (=used about a person or animal) *looks like she hasn't eaten in days.* | ***Poor old** Phil hasn't been on a date in years.*

4 NOT GOOD AT STH not good at doing something SYN **bad** OPP **good**: *a poor math student* | **+at** *He's poor at reading.*

5 poor in sth lacking things that people need: *The country is poor in natural resources.*

6 finish a poor second/third etc. to finish a race, competition etc. a long way behind the person ahead of you

7 the poor man's sb HUMOROUS used to say that someone is like a very famous performer, writer etc. but is not as good as they are: *He considers himself the poor man's Elvis Presley.*

8 the poor man's sth used to say that something can be used for the same purpose as something else, and is much cheaper: *Herring is the poor man's salmon.*

[**Origin:** 1100–1200 Old French *povre*, from Latin *pauper*] —**poorness** *n.* [U] → see also POORLY, **be (in) good/bad/poor taste** at TASTE[1] (5)

'poor boy also **po' boy** /'poubɔɪ/ *n.* [C] a SUBMARINE SANDWICH

poor·house /'pʊrhaʊs/ *n.* [C] **1** a building in past times where people could live and be fed, which was paid for with public money **2** the state of not having any money: *If Jimmy keeps spending like this, he'll **end up in the poorhouse**.*

poor·ly /'pʊrli/ *adv.* badly OPP **well**: *The article is really poorly written.* | *a poorly lit room*

ˌpoor-'spirited *adj.* LITERARY having no confidence or courage

pop¹ /pɑp/ S2 *v.* **popped, popping**

1 COME OUT OF STH [I always + adv./prep.] to come suddenly or surprisingly out of or away from something: **+out/off/up etc.** *A button popped off my jacket.* | *The lid popped open.*

2 APPEAR [I always + adv./prep.] to suddenly appear somewhere: **pop up/out** *Alison's head popped out from behind the door.* | **up/out popped sth/sb** *The egg cracked and out popped a tiny chick.*

3 PUT STH SOMEWHERE [T always + adv./prep.] INFORMAL to quickly put something somewhere for a short time: **pop sth in/around/over etc.** *I'll just pop these cookies into the oven.*

4 GO QUICKLY [I always + adv./prep.] SPOKEN to go somewhere for a short time: **pop in/out/around/to etc.** *I need to pop into the drug store for a second.* | *I might just **pop in on*** (=quickly visit) *Sarah on the way home.*

5 BREAK [I,T] if something such as a BALLOON or BLISTER pops, or you pop it, it breaks: *The balloon popped with a loud bang.* | *Be careful not to pop that blister.* ▸see THESAURUS box at **break**[1]

6 SHORT SOUND [I,T] to suddenly make a short sound like a small explosion, or to make something do this: *The wood sizzled and popped in the fire.*

7 CORN [I,T] to cook POPCORN (=dried corn) until it swells and bursts open, or to be cooked in this way: *I'll pop some popcorn.*

8 ALCOHOLIC DRINK [I] if a CORK pops or you pop it, it makes a noise as it comes out of a bottle of CHAMPAGNE

9 EARS [I] if your ears pop, you feel the pressure in them suddenly change, for example when you go quickly up or down in an airplane

10 pop the question INFORMAL to ask someone to marry you

11 pop pills INFORMAL to take drugs in the form of PILLS too often
12 HIT [T] SPOKEN to hit someone
13 sb's eyes popped (out of their head) used to say that someone looked extremely surprised or excited
14 pop into your head to think of something suddenly: *The idea just popped into my head.*
15 pop the clutch to take your foot off the CLUTCH in a car when the car is moving slowly, in order to start the engine
[**Origin:** 1300–1400 from the sound]

pop off *phr. v.* INFORMAL **1** to die suddenly **2** to speak quickly without thinking first

pop out *phr. v.* INFORMAL if something you say pops out, you say it suddenly without thinking about it first: *I didn't mean to say it like that – it just popped out.*

pop up *phr. v.* **1** to appear suddenly in a way, or at a time that you did not expect: *New restaurants and stores were popping up everywhere.* | *An error message popped up on screen.* **2 pop sth up** to hit a ball high into the air in a game of baseball so that it is easily caught → see also POP-UP

P

pop² S2 *n.* **1** [C,U] INFORMAL a sweet drink that contains BUBBLES and has no alcohol in it, or a glass or can of this drink SYN **soda**: *a can of pop* ►see THESAURUS box at **soft drink** **2** [U] POP MUSIC: **pop singer/concert/festival etc.** *a pop album* **3** [C] a sudden short sound like a small explosion: *the pop of gunfire* | *The balloon **went pop*** (=made a sudden short sound). **4 $7/$50/25¢ etc. a pop** SPOKEN used when each of something costs a particular amount of money: *Tickets for the show are $150 a pop.* **5** [singular] also **Pops** OLD-FASHIONED a word meaning your "father," used especially when you are talking to him **6 pops** [U] CLASSICAL music that is familiar to many people, especially people who do not usually like CLASSICAL MUSIC: **pops concert/orchestra** *the Boston Pops Orchestra*

pop³ *adj.* [only before noun, no comparative] produced or written for people who do not have special knowledge of a particular field: *pop science*

pop. the written abbreviation of "population"

'pop art *n.* [U] a type of art that was popular in the 1960s, which shows ordinary objects that you see in people's homes, and uses styles and design ideas from advertising and popular drawings

pop·corn /ˈpɑpkɔrn/ S3 *n.* [U] a type of corn that swells and breaks open when heated, and is usually eaten warm with salt and butter

'pop ˌculture *n.* [U] music, movies, products etc. in a particular society that are familiar to and popular with most ordinary people in that society

Pope /poʊp/ *n.* [C] **1** the leader of the Catholic Church: *We went to hear the Pope speak.* | *Pope Benedict XVI* → see also PAPAL **2 Is the Pope Catholic?** HUMOROUS used to say that something is clearly true or certain: *"Do you think he's guilty?" "Is the Pope Catholic?"* [**Origin:** 800–900 Late Latin *papa*, from Greek *papas* **father**, used as a title of bishops]

ˌpop-'eyed *adj.* INFORMAL **1** having your eyes wide open, because you are surprised, excited, or angry **2** having eyes that stick out slightly SYN **bugeyed**

'pop fly *n.* [C] a type of hit in BASEBALL in which the ball is hit high up into the air, making it easy to catch

'pop gun *n.* [C] a toy gun that fires small objects, such as CORKS, with a loud noise

pop·lar /ˈpɑplɚ/ *n.* [C] a fast growing tall tree often grown along roads or used for shade

pop·lin /ˈpɑplɪn/ *n.* [U] a strong shiny cotton cloth

'pop ˌmusic *n.* [U] modern music that is popular with young people and usually consists of simple tunes with a strong beat

pop·o·ver /ˈpɑpˌoʊvɚ/ *n.* [C] a light hollow MUFFIN (=small cake) made with eggs, milk, and flour

pop·pa /ˈpɑpə/ *n.* [singular] INFORMAL another spelling of PAPA

pop·per /ˈpɑpɚ/ *n.* INFORMAL **1** also **'popcorn ˌpopper** [C] a machine that heats POPCORN so that it swells, breaks open, and can be eaten **2 poppers** [plural] a type of illegal drug that makes you feel more active and full of energy

ˌpop psy'chology *n.* [U] ways of dealing with personal problems that are made popular on television or in books, but that are not considered scientific

pop·py /ˈpɑpi/ *n. plural* **poppies** **1** [C] BIOLOGY a plant that has brightly colored, usually red, flowers and small black seeds **2** [U] a red color

pop·py·cock /ˈpɑpiˌkɑk/ *n.* [U] OLD-FASHIONED nonsense

pop·py·seed /ˈpɑpiˌsid/ *n.* [U] the small black seeds of the poppy plant, used in cakes, bread etc.

'pop quiz *n.* [C] a short test that a teacher gives without any warning in order to check whether students have been studying

Pop·si·cle /ˈpɑpsɪkəl/ *n.* [C] TRADEMARK a food made of juice that is frozen onto sticks: *a cherry Popsicle*

'pop star *n.* [C] a famous and successful entertainer who plays or sings POP MUSIC

pop·u·lace /ˈpɑpyələs/ *n.* [singular] FORMAL the ordinary people who live in a country: *the mood of the American populace* → see also POPULATION

pop·u·lar /ˈpɑpyəlɚ/ S2 W1 *adj.* **1** liked by a lot of people OPP **unpopular**: *a popular tourist destination* | *Hilary was very popular at school.* | **+with/among** *Baggy jeans are still popular with teenagers.* | **hugely/immensely/wildly/extremely popular** *a hugely popular sitcom*

THESAURUS

bestseller a book that a lot of people buy
blockbuster a movie that a lot of people watch, especially an exciting movie
hit a movie, song, play etc. that a lot of people pay to see or listen to
craze/fad a fashion, game etc. that is very popular for a short time
cult a movie or a performer that is very popular among a certain group of people
be all the rage to be very popular and fashionable: *Disco was all the rage in the '80s.*
big an informal word for "popular": *He was big a few years ago when he was in a hit TV show.*

2 done or shared by all or most people in the general public: *The idea has a lot of **popular support**.* | **popular belief/opinion** *Popular opinion has turned against the President.* | ***Contrary to popular belief*** (=used to say that a fact that most people believe is not true), *dogs are not colorblind.* **3** [only before noun] intended for or liked by ordinary people, not highly educated people → see also LOWBROW: *He writes popular crime fiction.* | *Is "high art" really better than **popular culture*** (=popular music, movies, TV, art etc.)? → see also POP MUSIC **4** [only before noun] involving the ordinary people in a society, not the political leaders: *a popular movement for democracy* | **popular election/vote** (=one that everyone can take part in) | *The king was exiled following **a popular uprising*** (=when ordinary people try to replace a government). [**Origin:** 1400–1500 Latin *popularis*, from *populus* **people**]

pop·u·lar·i·ty /ˌpɑpyəˈlærət̬i/ *n.* [U] the quality of being liked or supported by a large number of people: *Lee's popularity started to fade.* | **the popularity of sth** *The popularity of camera phones was growing fast.* | **gain/grow/increase in popularity** *Hybrid cars are increasing in popularity.*

pop·u·lar·ize /ˈpɑpyələˌraɪz/ *v.* [T] **1** to make something well known and liked: *He helped to create and popularize rock and roll music.* **2** to make a difficult subject or idea easy to understand for ordinary people who have no special knowledge about it: *books that popularize scientific theories* —**popularization** /ˌpɑpyələrəˈzeɪʃən/ *n.* [U]

pop·u·lar·ly /ˈpɑpyələ·li/ *adv.* **1** by most or many people: *Yeltsin was Russia's first popularly elected president.* | **popularly known/thought/believed etc.** *Musculoligamentous neck sprain is popularly known as "whiplash injury."* **2 popularly priced** if something is popularly priced, it does not cost very much, so that many people buy it: *popularly priced wines*

pop·u·late /ˈpɑpyəˌleɪt/ *v.* [T] if a particular group of people, animals, or plants populate an area, they live there: *The Filipino island of Mindanao is* ***heavily populated*** *by Muslims.*

pop·u·lat·ed /ˈpɑpyəˌleɪt̬ɪd/ *adj.* an area that is populated has people living in it: *The bomb hit a populated area.* | **densely/heavily populated** (=having a lot of people living there) | **thinly/sparsely populated** (=having very few people living there)

pop·u·la·tion /ˌpɑpyəˈleɪʃən/ S3 W1 *n.* **1** [C] the number of people living in a particular area, country etc.: *The population has grown by 10% over the last 15 years.* | **+of** *What is the population of Montana?* | **have a population of sth** *Austria has a population of 7.5 million.* ►see THESAURUS box at **people**[1] **2** [C usually singular] all of the people who live in a particular area: *Most of the population of Canada lives relatively near the U.S. border.* | **the white/urban/American etc. population** (=used to talk about a particular group of people within a larger population) | *the* ***population explosion*** (=rapid increase in a population) *of the 20th century* | *Crime is more prevalent in the major* ***population centers*** (=cities, towns etc. where many people live). **3** BIOLOGY a group of animals, plants, or other living things living in a particular areas especially when they are of the same SPECIES: *Kenya's elephant population*

pop·u·list /ˈpɑpyəlɪst/ *adj.* representing the opinions or interests of ordinary people, not rich, powerful, or very well educated people: *a populist Democrat* —**populist** *n.* [C] —**populism** *n.* [U]

pop·u·lous /ˈpɑpyələs/ *adj.* FORMAL a populous area has a large population in relation to its size: *China is the most populous country in the world.* —**populousness** *n.* [U]

ˈpop-up[1] *adj.* **1** having a hidden part that opens or springs up by itself: *a car with pop-up headlights* | **pop-up card/book** (=one that has pictures that stand up from the page when you open them) **2** COMPUTERS a pop-up advertisement, MENU etc. appears on your computer screen, either because you push a button, or because it is started by a website or piece of SOFTWARE

pop-up[2] *n.* [C] COMPUTERS a window, often containing an advertisement, that suddenly appears on a computer screen

por·ce·lain /ˈpɔrsəlɪn/ *n.* [U] **1** a hard shiny white substance that is used for making expensive plates, cups etc. **2** plates, cups etc. made of this

porch /pɔrtʃ/ S3 *n.* [C] a structure built onto the front or back entrance of a house, with a floor, a roof, and usually RAILINGS, but no walls: **front/back porch** *They were sitting on the front porch drinking beer.* [**Origin:** 1200–1300 Old French *porche*, from Latin *porticus*, from *porta* **gate**]

por·cine /ˈpɔrsaɪn/ *adj.* FORMAL looking like or relating to pigs

por·cu·pine /ˈpɔrkyəˌpaɪn/ *n.* [C] an animal with long sharp needle-like parts growing all over its back and sides

pore[1] /pɔr/ *n.* [C] **1** BIOLOGY one of the small holes in your skin that liquid, especially SWEAT, can pass through → see picture at SKIN[1] **2** BIOLOGY a small hole in the surface of a plant or animal through which the plant or animal can take in or lose liquid **3** BIOLOGY a small hole in rock or soil through which liquid can pass **4 from every pore** in a way that shows a quality or feeling very clearly: *She oozed confidence from every pore* (=she was very confident). [**Origin:** 1300–1400 Old French, Latin *porus*, from Greek *poros* **way through**]

pore[2] *v.*

pore over sth *phr. v.* to read or look at something very carefully for a long time: *We spent all night poring over the contract.*

pork /pɔrk/ S3 *n.* [U] **1** the meat from pigs: *I don't eat pork.* | *pork chops* ►see THESAURUS box at **meat** **2** POLITICS government money spent in a particular area in order to get political advantages [**Origin:** 1200–1300 Old French *porc* **pig**, from Latin *porcus*]

ˈpork ˌbarrel *n.* [singular U] POLITICS a government plan to increase the amount of money spent in a particular area so that a party or politician will become more popular —**pork-barrel** *adj.*: *pork-barrel spending*

pork·er /ˈpɔrkɚ/ *n.* [C] **1** a young pig that is made fat before being killed for food **2** INFORMAL, HUMOROUS a fat person

ˈpork-pie ˌhat also **ˈpork-pie** *n.* [C] a hat made of FELT with a small soft BRIM (=edge)

ˌpork ˈrinds *n.* [plural] small pieces of pig fat that have been cooked in hot oil and are eaten as a SNACK

por·ky /ˈpɔrki/ *adj.* INFORMAL, HUMOROUS fat

por·nog·ra·phy /pɔrˈnɑgrəfi/ also **porn** *n.* [U] **1** also **porno** INFORMAL magazines, movies etc. that show sexual acts and images in a way that is intended to make people feel sexually excited: *a crackdown on pornography on the Internet* | *theaters that show porn* | *a porno magazine* **2** the activity of making these magazines or movies —**pornographer** *n.* [C] —**pornographic** /ˌpɔrnəˈgræfɪk◂/ *adj.*: *pornographic magazines* —**pornographically** /-kli/ *adv.*

po·rous /ˈpɔrəs/ *adj.* allowing liquid, air etc. to pass through slowly: *porous rock* —**porousness** *n.* [U]

por·phy·ry /ˈpɔrfəri/ *n.* [U] a type of hard dark red or purple rock that contains CRYSTALS

por·poise /ˈpɔrpəs/ *n.* [C] a large sea animal that looks similar to a DOLPHIN and breathes air

por·ridge /ˈpɔrɪdʒ, ˈpɑr-/ *n.* [U] soft CEREAL that is cooked with milk or water

port /pɔrt/ *n.* **1** [C,U] a place where ships can be loaded and unloaded: *The submarine was back* ***in port*** *after three months at sea.* | **come into port/leave port** *U.S.S. Kentucky left port at noon.* **2** [C] a town or city with a HARBOR or DOCKS where ships can be loaded and unloaded: *the shipping port of New Bedford* | *Port Angeles, Washington* **3** [C] COMPUTERS a part of a computer where you can connect another piece of equipment: *a printer port* **4** [U] strong sweet Portuguese wine that is usually drunk after a meal: *a glass of port* **5** [U] the left side of a ship or aircraft when you are looking toward the front OPP **starboard**: *the port engine* | ***To port****, we could see the tiny island of Yurishima.* **6 any port in a storm** SPOKEN an expression meaning that you should take whatever help you can when you are in trouble, even if it has some disadvantages [**Origin:** (5) 1500–1600 *port side*; because it was the side from which ships were unloaded.] → see also FREE PORT, PORT OF CALL, PORT OF ENTRY

port·a·ble[1] /ˈpɔrt̬əbəl/ *adj.* **1** able to be carried or moved easily: *a portable phone* | *portable toilets* **2** COMPUTERS a portable computer program can be used on different computer systems: *portable software* **3** if insurance, PENSIONS etc. are portable, workers can take the money from them and move it to a different company or organization when they change jobs —**portability** /ˌpɔrt̬əˈbɪlət̬i/ *n.* [U]

portable[2] *n.* [C] a piece of electronic equipment that can be easily carried or moved

port·age /ˈpɔrt̬ɪdʒ/ *n.* [U] the act of carrying boats over land from one river to another —**portage** *v.* [T]

por·tal /ˈpɔrt̬l/ *n.* [C] **1** COMPUTERS a website on the Internet that helps you find other websites **2** [usually plural] LITERARY a tall and impressive gate or entrance to a building

Por·ta Pot·ti, porta-potty /ˈpɔrt̬ə ˌpɑt̬i/ *n.* [C] TRADEMARK a toilet in a small plastic building that can be moved

P

Port-au-Prince /ˌpɔrt̬ oʊ ˈprɪns/ the capital and largest city of Haiti

por·tend /pɔrˈtɛnd/ *v.* [T] LITERARY to be a sign that something is going to happen, especially something bad: *The rising infection rate portends disaster.*

por·tent /ˈpɔrtɛnt/ *n.* [C] LITERARY a sign or warning that something is going to happen: **+of** *a portent of revolution* → see also OMEN

por·ten·tous /pɔrˈtɛntəs/ *adj.* **1** LITERARY showing that something important is going to happen: *a portentous silence* **2** very serious, in a way that is intended to seem important and impressive: *a portentous voice*

P

por·ter /ˈpɔrt̬ɚ/ *n.* **1** [C] someone whose job is to carry travelers' bags at airports, hotels etc. **2** [C] someone whose job is to take care of the part of a train where people sleep **3** [C] someone whose job is to take care of a building by cleaning it, repairing things etc.

Por·ter /ˈpɔrt̬ɚ/, **Cole** /koul/ (1891–1964) a U.S. musician who wrote many popular songs and MUSICALS

Porter, Kath·erine Anne /ˈkæθrɪn æn/ (1890–1980) a U.S. writer of NOVELS and short stories

Porter, William the real name of the U.S. writer O. Henry

por·ter·house /ˈpɔrt̬ɚhaʊs/ also ˌ**porterhouse ˈsteak** *n.* [C,U] a thick flat piece of high quality BEEF

port·fo·li·o /pɔrtˈfoʊliˌoʊ/ *n. plural* **portfolios** [C] **1** a large flat case used especially for carrying drawings, documents etc. **2** ENG. LANG. ARTS a collection of drawings, paintings, or other pieces of work by an artist, photographer etc. **3** ECONOMICS a collection of STOCK in many different companies, that is owned by one person or by one company, usually in order to reduce the risk involved in buying and selling stock: *an investment portfolio* **4** POLITICS the duties that a particular government official has: *the foreign affairs portfolio*

port·hole /ˈpɔrthoʊl/ *n.* [C] a small round window on the side of a ship or airplane

por·ti·co /ˈpɔrt̬ɪˌkoʊ/ *n.* [C] a covered entrance to a building, consisting of a roof supported by PILLARS

por·tion[1] /ˈpɔrʃən/ Ac S3 W3 *n.* [C] **1** one of the parts that make up something larger: **+of** *Only a small portion of the budget is for training.* | **a large/substantial/significant etc. portion** *A large portion of the book is taken up with pictures.* **2** [usually singular] a share of something, such as responsibility, blame, or a duty, that is divided among a small number of people: **+of** *Both drivers must bear a portion of the blame.* **3** an amount of food for one person, especially when served in a restaurant SYN **serving** SYN **helping** **4 sb's portion** LITERARY something that happens in your life that you cannot avoid SYN **fate**

portion[2] Ac *v.*

portion sth ↔ **out** *phr. v.* to divide something into parts, especially to give them to several people: *Land was portioned out to new settlers.*

Port·land /ˈpɔrtlənd/ **1** the largest city in the U.S. state of Oregon **2** the largest city in the U.S. state of Maine

Port Lou·is /ˌpɔrt ˈluɪs, -ˈlui/ the capital and largest city of Mauritius

port·ly /ˈpɔrtli/ *adj.* someone who is portly, especially an older man, is fat and round —**portliness** *n.* [U]

port·man·teau[1] /pɔrtˈmæntoʊ/ *n.* [C] OLD-FASHIONED a very large SUITCASE that opens into two parts

portmanteau[2] *adj.* [only before noun] FORMAL a portmanteau word is made by combining parts of two other words, for example "infomercial" combines "information" and "commercial"

Port Mores·by /pɔrt ˈmɔrzbi/ the capital and largest city of Papua New Guinea

ˌ**port of ˈcall** *n.* [C usually singular] **1** a port where a ship stops on a trip from one place to another **2** INFORMAL one of a series of places that you visit: *My next port of call was City Hall.*

ˌ**port of ˈentry** *n.* [C] a place, such as a port or airport, where people or goods enter a country

Port of Spain /ˌpɔrt̬ əv ˈspeɪn/ the capital and largest city of Trinidad and Tobago

Por·to No·vo /ˌpɔrt̬ə ˈnoʊvoʊ/ the capital city of Benin

por·trait /ˈpɔrtrɪt/ *n.* ENG. LANG. ARTS **1** [C] a painting, drawing, or photograph of a person: *a family portrait* | **+of** *a portrait of George Washington* ▸see THESAURUS box at **picture**[1] **2** [C] a description or representation of something, for example in a story, play etc.: **+of** *His stories are all harsh portraits of life on the street.* **3** [U] a way of arranging a piece of paper, a photograph etc. that is to be printed so that its longer edges are at the sides and its shorter edges are at the top and bottom → see also LANDSCAPE, SELF-PORTRAIT

por·trait·ist /ˈpɔrtrət̬ɪst/ *n.* [C] someone who paints portraits

por·trai·ture /ˈpɔrtrɪtʃɚ/ *n.* [U] ENG. LANG. ARTS the art of painting or drawing pictures of people

por·tray /pɔrˈtreɪ, pɚ-/ *v.* **portrays, portrayed, portraying** [T] ENG. LANG. ARTS **1** to describe, show, or represent something or someone, especially in a book, movie, article etc. SYN **depict**: *Their music portrays a lifestyle that no longer exists.* | **portray sb as sth** *The President likes to portray himself as a friend of the poor.* ▸see THESAURUS box at **call**[1] **2** to act the part of a character in a play SYN **play**: *In the movie, she portrays an ageing dancer.* [**Origin:** 1200–1300 Old French *portraire*, from Latin *protrahere* **to draw out, show**]

por·tray·al /pɔrˈtreɪəl/ *n.* [C,U] the action of portraying someone or something, or the book, movie, play etc. that results from this: **+of** *He won an Oscar for his portrayal of a dying man.* | *the book's portrayal of Islamic culture*

Por·tu·gal /ˈpɔrtʃəgəl/ a country in southwest Europe, west of Spain

Por·tu·guese /ˌpɔrtʃəˈgiz◂ / *n.* [U] **1** the language of Portugal, Brazil, and some other countries **2 the Portuguese** the people of Portugal —**Portuguese** *adj.*

ˌ**Portuguese man-of-ˈwar** *n.* [C] a large sea creature, like a JELLYFISH, which has long poisonous parts hanging down from its body

Port Vi·la /ˌpɔrt ˈvilə/ the capital and largest city of Vanuatu

pose[1] /poʊz/ Ac *v.* **1 pose a problem/threat/challenge etc.** to exist in a way that may cause a problem, danger, difficulty etc.: *The militia members may pose a terrorist threat.* | *The fish oil apparently poses no danger to humans.* **2** [I,T] to sit or stand in a particular position in order to be photographed or painted, or to make someone do this: **pose for sb/sth** *A group of fans wanted Romano to pose for pictures.* | **pose sb** *The artist posed the model sitting at a table.* **3 pose a question (to sb)** FORMAL to ask a question, especially one that needs to be carefully thought about: *The magazine posed a list of questions to each of the candidates.* **4** [I] to dress or behave as if you have money or social position that you do not really have, in order to seem more impressive to other people [**Origin:** 1300–1400 Old French *poser*, from Late Latin *pausare* **to stop, rest**]

pose as sb *phr. v.* to pretend to be someone else, in order to deceive people: *He posed as a doctor to gain entrance to the day care center.*

pose[2] Ac *n.* [C] **1** the position in which someone stands or sits, especially in a painting, photograph etc.: *Each child is photographed **in a glamorous pose**.* | *Lyn **struck a pose** (=stood or sat in a particular position) with her head to one side.* **2** behavior in which someone pretends to have a quality or social position they do not really have, usually in order to seem impressive to other people: *He likes to sound sophisticated, but it's all a pose.*

Po·sei·don /pəˈsaɪdn/ in Greek MYTHOLOGY, the god of the sea

pos·er /ˈpoʊzɚ/ *n.* [C] a POSEUR

po·seur /poʊˈzɚ/ *n.* [C] someone who pretends to have

a quality or social position they do not really have, usually in order to seem impressive to other people: *They can't sing. They're just a bunch of poseurs with guitars.*

posh /pɑʃ/ *adj.* a posh restaurant, hotel, car etc. is expensive and looks as if it is used by rich people

pos·it /ˈpɑzɪt/ *v.* [T] FORMAL to suggest that a particular idea should be accepted as a fact: *Ptolemy posited that each planet moved in a perfect circle.*

po·si·tion¹ /pəˈzɪʃən/ S1 W1 *n.*

1 **SB IS STANDING/SITTING/LYING ETC.** [C] the way someone stands, sits, or lies: *Are you sitting in a comfortable position?* | **a sitting/kneeling/standing position** *Horton pulled himself slowly to a standing position.* | **change/shift (your) position** *He kept shifting his position in his seat.*

2 **WAY STH IS PLACED/IS POINTING** [C] the way in which an object has been placed or is pointing: *I checked the position of the camera again.* | **in an upright/a vertical/a horizontal position** *Keep the package in an upright position.* | **the on/off/up/down position** *I turned the switch to the "on" position.*

3 **SITUATION** [C usually singular] the situation that someone is in, or the situation relating to a particular subject SYN **situation**: *Next year we'll be in a better* ***financial position*** *to buy a house.* | **in a good/strong etc. position** *The team is in a good position to win the championship.* | **in a difficult/awkward/uncomfortable position** *His request puts us in a difficult position.* | *She's* ***in the enviable position*** (=one that most people would like very much) *of having three job offers.* | *I was* ***in the position of having to*** (=in a difficult situation in which I had to) *teach the people I work for.* | **a position of strength/weakness** *The rebels are negotiating from a position of strength.* | **weaken/undermine sb's position** (=damage someone's chances of success in a particular situation) ►see THESAURUS box at **situation**

4 **PLACE WHERE SB/STH IS** [C] the place where someone or something is, especially in relation to other objects and places: *We were in a good position to see the race.* | +**of** *the position of the village on the map* ►see THESAURUS box at **place¹**

5 **THE CORRECT/USUAL PLACE** [C,U] the place where someone or something is needed or supposed to be, so that they are ready to do something or ready to be used: **in/into position** *Are the men in position?* | *I moved the ladder into position.* | *One of the stage lights was* ***out of position*** (=not in the correct position). | *The guard* ***took up*** *his* ***position*** (=went to the place he should be) *by the door.*

6 **OPINION** [C] an opinion or judgment on a particular subject, especially the official opinion of a government, party, or someone in authority: +**on** *What is the party's position on nuclear power?* | *The airline* ***takes the position that*** (=has the opinion that) *its security is adequate.* | *Flores says she will* ***reconsider her position*** *on the new law.* ►see THESAURUS box at **opinion**

7 **JOB** [C] FORMAL a job: *I have an interview for a position at the college.* | **hold a position/be in a position** *She is the first woman to hold this position.* | **sb's position as sth** *He resigned from his position as chairman.* | **the position of sth** *the position of Chief of Staff to the President* | **a senior/high position** *People in high positions wanted to get rid of him.* | *I decided to* ***apply for the position of*** *assistant manager.* | *I'm sorry,* ***the position has been filled*** (=the company has found someone to do the job). ►see THESAURUS box at **job**

THESAURUS

Describing types of positions

senior used about someone who has an important position in a company or organization: *a senior White House official*

chief used about someone who has the most important or one of the most important positions in a company or organization, used especially in job titles: *the company's chief financial officer*

high-ranking used about someone who has a high position in an organization such as the police, the army, or the government: *high-ranking military officers*

top used about someone who is in a very high position in a large company or organization, or someone in an important profession, for example a lawyer or a doctor, who is very successful in his or her job: *a top administration official* | *one of the country's top chefs*

junior used about someone who does not have an important position or who has less experience than someone doing the same job: *the junior senator from Mississippi*

assistant an assistant manager, director, editor etc. has a position just below a manager etc.: *the store's assistant manager*

8 **SPORTS** [C] the area where someone plays in a sport, or the type of actions they are responsible for doing in the game: *"What position do you play?" "Second base."*

9 **LEVEL/RANK** [C] someone's or something's level or rank in relation to other people in society or in an organization: +**of** *the traditional position of women in society* | *Teachers are in* ***a position of trust*** (=one in which people trust you). | *It is clear that he* ***abused*** *his* ***position*** *as head of the organization* (=used his authority wrongly). | **a position of authority/influence/responsibility** *Is he fit to be in a position of authority over our children?*

10 **RACE/COMPETITION** [C,U] the place of someone or something in a race, competition, list etc. SYN **place**

11 **sb is in no position to do sth** used to say that someone cannot criticize or complain about something because they have done the thing that they are criticizing or complaining about: *I was in no position to argue.*

12 **jockey/maneuver/jostle etc. for position** **a)** to try to get an advantage over other people who are all trying to succeed in doing the same thing: *Republicans are jockeying for position prior to the presidential campaign.* **b)** to try to move into a particular place, especially a place that gives you an advantage, when a lot of other people are trying to move into the same place: *Cameramen jockeyed for position as Jackson arrived at the airport.*

13 **ARMY** [C] a place where an army has put soldiers, guns etc.: *military positions in the hills*

14 **SEX** [C] one of the ways in which two people can sit or lie to have sex

[**Origin:** 1300–1400 French, Latin *positio*, from *positus*, past participle of *ponere* **to put**]

position² *v.* [T] to put someone or something in a particular position: *Nate positioned himself so he could keep an eye on the door.* ►see THESAURUS box at **put**

po'sition ˌpaper *n.* [C] a written statement that shows how a department, organization etc. intends to deal with something

pos·i·tive¹ /ˈpɑzət̬ɪv/ Ac S2 W2 *adj.*

1 **SURE** [not before noun] certain, with no doubt at all SYN **certain** SYN **sure**: *"Are you sure you want to go?" "Positive."* | **positive (that)** *I'm* ***absolutely positive*** *I left it here.* | +**of/about** *I'm not positive of the address, but it's definitely on this street.*

2 **CONFIDENT** considering the good qualities of a situation, person etc., and expecting success SYN **optimistic** OPP **negative**: +**about** *Vernon tried to be positive about the team's 2–6 record.* | **positive attitude/approach/outlook etc.** *You need a positive attitude to find the right job.* | *It's going to be tough, but let's* ***think positive***. → see also **think positively/positive** at THINK (18)

3 **LIKELY TO BE SUCCESSFUL** showing that something is likely to succeed or improve: **a positive sign/indication** *He's breathing on his own again, which is a positive sign.*

4 **APPROVAL/SUPPORT** showing that someone agrees with you, supports what you are doing, and wants you to succeed OPP **negative**: +**about** *Most people have been very positive about the show.* | **a positive response/reaction** *Public response to the ads has been very positive.* | *We've had a lot of* ***positive feedback*** *from the people of this city.*

5 GOOD good, useful, or moral in a way that helps someone or something to improve OPP **negative**: *Reducing stress has a positive effect on health.* | *the song's positive message* | *positive role models for kids*
6 positive proof/evidence/identification etc. proof, EVIDENCE etc. that shows that there is no doubt that something is definitely true SYN **definite**: *The body was flown to Honolulu for positive identification.*
7 MEDICAL/SCIENTIFIC TEST showing signs of what is being looked for OPP **negative**: *If he **tests positive** for steroids, he will be suspended for ten games.* | **come out/up positive** *Phoebe's pregnancy test came out positive.*
8 MATHEMATICS MATH a positive number or quantity is more than zero; (+) is the positive sign OPP **negative**
9 ELECTRICITY [no comparative] PHYSICS having the type of electrical charge that is carried by a PROTON, shown by a (+) sign on a BATTERY OPP **negative**
10 BLOOD MEDICINE having RHESUS FACTOR in your blood OPP **negative**: *type AB positive*
11 GRAMMAR relating to the basic form of an adjective or adverb, such as "small" or "quietly" as opposed to the COMPARATIVE or SUPERLATIVE forms
12 FORCE relating to the end of a MAGNET that turns naturally toward north
13 PHOTOGRAPH [no comparative] TECHNICAL a positive image such as a photograph shows light and colors in the same way as the original image does OPP **negative** —**positiveness** *n.* [U]

positive² Ac *n.* [C] **1** a quality or feature of something that is good or useful OPP **negative**: *You can find positives in any situation.* **2** a number that is higher than zero OPP **negative** **3** TECHNICAL a medical or scientific test result that shows the existence of what is being looked for OPP **negative** **4 the positive** TECHNICAL the basic form of an adjective or adverb, such as "small" or "quietly," as opposed to the COMPARATIVE or the SUPERLATIVE → see also **a false positive/negative** at FALSE (8)

ˌpositive corre'lation *n.* [C] MATH the relationship between two VARIABLES where an increase in one variable always involves an increase in the other OPP **negative correlation**

pos·i·tive·ly /ˈpɑzət̬ɪvli, ˌpɑzəˈtɪvli◂/ Ac *adv.*
1 used to emphasize a strong opinion or surprising statement: *The food in this place is positively disgusting.*
2 SPOKEN used to emphasize that you mean what you are saying SYN **definitely**: *I **absolutely, positively** must remember to send that check.* **3** in a good or useful way OPP **negatively**: *We were affected very positively by the experience.* **4** in a way that shows you agree with something, want it to succeed, or think it is good OPP **negatively**: *Wall Street reacted positively to the announcement.* **5** in a way that shows you are thinking about what is good in a situation rather than what is bad OPP **negatively**: *Try to think more positively about school.* **6** in a way that leaves no possibility of doubt: *They all said positively that they had seen it.* **7 positively charged** TECHNICAL having the type of electrical charge that is carried by PROTONS → see also **think positively/positive** at THINK (18)

ˌpositive rein'forcement *n.* [U] the action of rewarding someone when they do something well, so that they want to continue doing well, rather than punishing them when they do something wrong

pos·i·tiv·ism /ˈpɑzət̬ɪˌvɪzəm/ *n.* [U] a type of PHILOSOPHY based only on real facts that can be proven using science, rather than on ideas —**positivist** *n.* [C]

pos·it·ron /ˈpɑzəˌtrɑn/ *n.* [C] PHYSICS a PARTICLE that has the same mass as an ELECTRON but has a positive electrical CHARGE

pos·se /ˈpɑsi/ *n.* [C] **1** a group of men gathered together by a SHERIFF (=local law officer) in past times to help catch a criminal **2 a posse of sth** a large group of the same kind of people: *Bill plays with a posse of Los Angeles musicians.* **3 sb's posse** SLANG someone's group of friends

pos·sess /pəˈzɛs/ W3 *v.* [T not in progressive] **1** FORMAL to own or have something, especially something valuable, important, or illegal SYN **have** SYN **own**: *Too many nations already possess chemical weapons.* | *Neither of them possesses a credit card.* ►see THESAURUS box at **own²** **2** FORMAL to have an ability, quality etc. SYN **have**: *Every worker possesses valuable skills.* **3 what possessed sb (to do sth)?** SPOKEN said when you cannot understand why someone did something: *I don't know what possessed me to buy such an ugly dress.* **4** LITERARY if a feeling possesses you, you suddenly feel it very strongly and it affects your behavior: *Rage possessed her.* **5** if an evil spirit possesses someone, it takes control of their mind [**Origin:** 1300–1400 Old French *possesser*, from Latin *possidere*]

pos·sessed /pəˈzɛst/ *adj.* [not before noun] **1 like a man/woman possessed** with a lot of energy or violence: *Young played the game like a man possessed.* **2** controlled by an evil spirit **3 be possessed of sth** LITERARY to have a particular quality, ability, belief etc. → see also SELF-POSSESSED

pos·ses·sion /pəˈzɛʃən/ *n.*
1 STH YOU OWN [C usually plural] something that someone owns and keeps or uses themselves: *They lost their home and all their **personal possessions** in the storm.* | **a prized/treasured/cherished possession** *The painting was one of his most prized possessions.* | *We piled **all our worldly possessions*** (=everything you own) *into the truck.*
2 STATE OF HAVING STH [U] FORMAL the state of having or owning something, especially something valuable or important: **sth is in the possession of sb** *The tape is in the possession of prosecutors.* | **sb has possession of sth/sb has sth in their posession** *Anderson says he has possession of the records.* | *We don't **take possession of*** (=be officially able to use something you have bought) *the house till next month.* | **possession is nine-tenths of the law** (=used to say that someone who has something is likely to keep it even if it does not really belong to them)
3 DRUGS/GUN [U] LAW the crime of having something illegally: *Kortz was charged with possession of stolen property.*
4 COUNTRY [C] POLITICS a country controlled or governed by another country: *Britain's former overseas possessions*
5 BALL [U] the state of having control of the ball in some sports: **gain/lose/get etc. possession** *Pittsburgh got possession and scored.*
6 EVIL SPIRITS [U] a situation in which someone's mind is being controlled by an evil spirit
7 in (full) possession of your faculties/senses able to think in a clear and intelligent way, because you are not crazy or affected by old age
8 take possession of sb if a feeling takes possession of you or your mind, it starts to have a strong effect on you that you cannot control

pos·ses·sive¹ /pəˈzɛsɪv/ *adj.* **1** wanting someone to have feelings of love or friendship only for you: *a possessive husband* **2** unwilling to let other people use something you own: **+of/about** *He's pretty possessive about his car.* **3** ENG. LANG. ARTS relating to a word or form of a word such as "my," "theirs," or "Mark's" that shows that one thing or person belongs to or is related to another thing or person —**possessiveness** *n.* [U]

possessive² *n.* ENG. LANG. ARTS **1 the possessive** the form of words such as "your," "its," or "Joshua's" that shows that one thing or person belongs to or is related to another thing or person **2** [C] an adjective, PRONOUN, or noun in the possessive form

posˌsessive 'adjective *n.* [C] ENG. LANG. ARTS an adjective such as "my," "your," or "our" that shows that one thing or person belongs to or is related to another thing or person

posˌsessive 'pronoun *n.* [C] ENG. LANG. ARTS a word that can take the place of a noun such as "mine," "yours," or "ours" which shows that one thing or person belongs to or is related to another thing or person

pos·ses·sor /pəˈzɛsɚ/ *n.* [C] FORMAL someone who has or owns something, especially something valuable or illegal: +**of** *Mike is **the proud possessor** of an antique motorcycle.*

pos·si·bil·i·ty /ˌpɑsəˈbɪləṭi/ S2 W2 *n. plural* **possibilities** **1** [C,U] something that could happen or be true, or the chance that something could happen or be true: *War is still a possibility.* | +**of** *Is there any possibility of that happening?* | *There was no possibility of changing the flight.* | **a possibility (that)** *There's a possibility we won't be here that weekend.* | **a good/definite/distinct etc. possibility** *I don't know if he's leaving, but it's a strong possibility.* | **rule out/exclude a possibility** (=decide that sth is not true, or that it did or will not happen etc.) | **raise/suggest a possibility** (=suggest that something could happen or be true) **2** [C usually plural] an opportunity to do something, or something that can be done or tried: +**for** *Fuel cells are another possibility for powering electric cars.* | *Right now I'm focusing on possibilities for the future.* | *Archer is **exploring the possibilities*** (=thinking about or trying different opportunities) *of opening a club in the city.* | *The U.S. has not yet **exhausted all** diplomatic **possibilities*** (=tried every possible way). | *The house **has** a lot of **possibilities*** (=there are a lot of opportunities for improving it). → see also **within the realm(s) of possibility** at REALM (2)

pos·si·ble[1] /ˈpɑsəbəl/ S1 W1 *adj.* **1** able to be done: *Travel to another planet may soon be possible.* | *There are two possible ways to solve the problem.* | **it is possible (for sb) to do sth** *Is it possible to use the program on a Macintosh?* | *Computer technology has **made it possible** for many people to work at home.* | *I'd like an appointment on Friday afternoon **if possible**.* | **whenever/wherever/where etc. possible** *I walk or use public transportation whenever possible.* | **as long/much/soon etc. as possible** (=as long, much, soon etc. as you can) *Keep your explanation as simple as possible.* | *I want to collect as many of the stickers as possible.* | *The original features of the house have been preserved **as far as possible*** (=to the greatest extent possible). | **do/try everything possible** *Doctors tried everything possible to save her life.* | **in any/every way possible** *Our staff will help you in every way possible.* **2** a possible answer, cause, event etc. might be true, happen, or exist: *There are two possible explanations.* | *Heavy rain is possible later.* | **it is possible (that)** *So you're saying it's possible that Mark did it.* | *"Do you think we can win?" "Well, **anything's possible**."* (=used to say that anything can happen, even if it seems unlikely) **3 would it be possible (for sb) to do sth?** SPOKEN said when asking politely if you can do or have something: *Would it be possible to get together at 6:30 instead of 5?* **4 the best/biggest/fastest etc. possible sth** the best, biggest etc. thing that can exist or be achieved: *the lowest possible price* | *What is the worst possible thing that could happen?* [**Origin:** 1300–1400 French, Latin *possibilis*, from *posse* **to be able**]

possible[2] *n.* [C] someone or something that might be appropriate or acceptable for a particular purpose: *Travolta is another possible for the award.*

pos·si·bly /ˈpɑsəbli/ S2 W2 *adv.* **1** used to say that something may be true or likely, although you are not certain SYN **maybe** SYN **perhaps**: *He's going to stay at least three weeks, possibly longer.* | **quite/very possibly** *He is quite possibly the laziest man I've ever met.* **2** used with MODAL VERBS, especially "can" and "could," to emphasize that something is or is not possible: *I have everything I could possibly need.* | *You can't possibly go to all those stores in one day.* **3** used with modal verbs, especially "can" and "could," to emphasize that someone will do or has done everything they can to help or to achieve something: *We contributed as much as we possibly could to the campaign.* **4 could/can you possibly...?** SPOKEN said when politely asking someone to do something: *Could you possibly wait until later to practice?* **5** SPOKEN used with MODAL VERBS, especially "can" and "could," to emphasize that you are very surprised or shocked by something, or that you cannot understand it: *How could anyone possibly do that to her?*

pos·sum /ˈpɑsəm/ *n.* [C] **1** BIOLOGY an OPOSSUM **2 play possum** INFORMAL to pretend to be asleep or dead so that someone will not annoy or hurt you

post[1] /poʊst/ W3 *n.*
1 PIECE OF WOOD/METAL [C] a strong upright piece of wood, metal etc. that is set into the ground, especially to support something: *a fence post*
2 JOB [C] FORMAL an important job, especially one in the government or military SYN **position**: *the post of deputy environmental secretary* | +**of** *She was offered the post of ambassador.* | *The General **took up** his new **post*** (=started his job) *on Tuesday.* | *Montes has said that he will not **resign** his **post**.* | *We'd like to **fill the post*** (=find someone to do the job) *by next month.* ►see THESAURUS box at **job**
3 SOLDIER/GUARD ETC. [C] the place where someone is expected to be in order to do their job: *Soldiers are not allowed to leave their posts.*
4 INTERNET [C] a message sent to an Internet discussion group so that all members of the group can read it SYN **posting**: *There were hundreds of new posts to read.*
5 SPORTS [C] one of the two upright pieces of wood that players try to kick or hit the ball between in football, HOCKEY etc. SYN **goalpost**
6 MILITARY [C] a military BASE (=place where soldiers live, work etc.)
7 a border/military/customs post a place, especially one on a border, where soldiers or police are guarding, checking etc. something
8 JEWELRY [C] the small metal bar that goes through your ear as part of an EARRING
9 FURNITURE [C] one of the upright parts on the corners of a piece of furniture such as a bed
10 RACE the post the place where a race begins or finishes, especially a horse race: *horses lined up at the post* | **the starting/finishing post** *My horse was first past the finishing post.*
11 BRITISH the MAIL → see also STAGING POST, TRADING POST

post[2] S3 W3 *v.* [T]
1 PUBLIC NOTICE to put up a public notice about something on a wall, BULLETIN BOARD etc.: *Park rangers have posted warnings at the entrance to the trails.*
2 INTERNET MESSAGE COMPUTERS to put a message or computer document on the Internet so that other people can see it: *Could you post this on the website?*
3 keep sb posted SPOKEN to regularly tell someone the most recent news about something: *We don't have any plans yet, but I'll keep you posted.*
4 PROFIT/LOSS ETC. if a company posts its profits, sales, losses etc., it officially reports the money gained or lost in its accounts: *The company posted profits of $14.6 million.*
5 GUARD [usually passive] to send someone somewhere in order to guard a building, check who enters or leaves a place, watch something etc.: **post sb at sth** *Extra guards were posted at the cemetery during the funeral.*
6 JOB [usually passive] to send someone to a different country or place in order to work for a company, or in order to work for a period of time in the army, navy, or government: **post sb to sth** *In 1942, he was posted to India as a fighter pilot.* | *Burton has been **posted overseas** for two years.* ►see THESAURUS box at **job**
7 post bail LAW to pay a specific amount of money in order to be allowed to leave JAIL before your TRIAL: *Mott was released after posting $10,000 bail.*
8 MAIL BRITISH to mail a letter or package

post- /poʊst/ *prefix* later than or after something: *postwar* (=after a particular war) | *postpone* (=do something later) → see also PRE-

post·age /ˈpoʊstɪdʒ/ *n.* [U] the money charged for sending a letter, package etc. by mail: *Please add $3.95 for **postage and handling*** (=charge for packing and sending something you have ordered).

ˈpostage ˌmeter *n.* [C] a machine used by businesses that puts a mark on letters and packages to show that postage has been paid

ˈpostage stamp *n.* [C] FORMAL a stamp

post·al /ˈpoʊstl/ *adj.* [only before noun] **1** relating to the official system that takes letters from one place to another: *postal workers* **2 go postal** SLANG to become very angry and behave in a violent way

P

ˈpostal ˌservice *n.* **the postal service** the organization that provides the service of carrying letters, packages etc. from one part of a country to another

post·card /ˈpoʊstkɑrd/ S3 *n.* [C] a card, often with a picture on it, that can be sent in the mail without an envelope: **+of** *a postcard of the Statue of Liberty*

ˌpost ˈcoital *adj.* happening or done after having sex

post·date /ˌpoʊstˈdeɪt/ *v.* [T] **1** to write a check with a date that is later than the actual date, so that it cannot be used or become effective until that time → see also BACKDATE **2** to happen, live, or be made later in history than something else: *The painting postdates the Renaissance period.* → see also ANTEDATE, PREDATE

P

ˈpost doc *n.* [C] INFORMAL someone who is studying after they have finished their PH.D.

post·doc·tor·al /ˌpoʊstˈdɑktərəl/ *adj.* [only before noun] relating to study done after a PH.D.

post·er /ˈpoʊstɚ/ S3 *n.* [C] a large printed notice, picture etc. used to advertise something or as a decoration: *a poster for the Monterey Jazz festival*

ˈposter child *n.* [C usually singular] **1** also **poster boy/girl** a child with a particular illness or DISABILITY (=physical problem) whose picture appears on a poster advertising the work of an organization that helps children with that problem **2** OFTEN HUMOROUS someone whose behavior represents a particular quality, usually a bad quality: *Washburn is the poster child for wasted talent.*

pos·te·ri·or¹ /pɑˈstɪriɚ, poʊ-/ *n.* [C] HUMOROUS the part of the body you sit on SYN **butt**

posterior² *adj.* [only before noun] TECHNICAL near or at the back of something, especially someone's body OPP **anterior**

pos·ter·i·ty /pɑˈstɛrəṭi/ *n.* [U] people who will live after you are dead: **preserve/record/keep etc. sth for posterity** *The interviews were taped for posterity.*

post·game /ˌpoʊst ˈgeɪm◂ / *adj.* happening after a sports game: *postgame celebrations*

post·grad·u·ate¹ /ˌpoʊstˈgrædʒuɪt/ also **ˌpost-ˈgrad** INFORMAL *adj.* [only before noun] relating to studies done after completing an advanced degree such as an M.A. or Ph.D.: *postgraduate work at the Sorbonne* → see also GRADUATE

postgraduate² also **post-grad** INFORMAL *n.* [C] someone who is studying after completing an advanced degree such as a Ph.D. or an M.A. → see also GRADUATE STUDENT

post·haste /poʊstˈheɪst/ *adv.* LITERARY very quickly

post hoc /ˌpoʊst ˈhɑk◂ / *adj.* FORMAL a post hoc explanation, argument etc. states wrongly that one event caused the event that followed it, and makes this statement based only on the fact that the one event came after another

post·hu·mous /ˈpɑstʃəməs/ *adj.* happening after someone's death, or given to someone or printed after their death: *a posthumous pardon* —**posthumously** *adv.*: *The poems were published posthumously.*

post·hyp·not·ic sug·ges·tion /ˌpoʊsthɪpˌnɑṭɪk səgˈdʒɛstʃən/ *n.* [C] something that someone tells you while you are HYPNOTIZED that is intended to affect your thinking or behavior when you are not hypnotized anymore

post·in·dus·tri·al, **post-industrial** /ˌpoʊstɪnˈdʌstriəl◂ / *adj.* relating to the period in the late 20th century when older types of industries, such as making things in factories, became less important, and computers became more important: *the postindustrial information-based society*

post·ing /ˈpoʊstɪŋ/ *n.* [C] **1** a public notice, especially one advertising a job: *job postings* **2** the act of sending someone to a place to do their job, especially a soldier: *He had a military background with postings overseas.* | **+to** *a posting to Beirut*

Post-it /ˈpoʊst ˌɪt/ *n.* [C] TRADEMARK a small piece of paper that sticks to things, used for leaving notes for people

post·lude /ˈpoʊstlud/ *n.* [C] a piece of music played at the end of a long musical piece or church ceremony → see also PRELUDE

post·man /ˈpoʊstmən/ *n. plural* **postmen** /-mən/ [C] a MAILMAN

post·mark /ˈpoʊstmɑrk/ *n.* [C] an official mark made on a letter, package etc. that shows the place and time it was sent —**postmark** *v.* [T] *All entries must be postmarked by May 1.*

post·mas·ter /ˈpoʊstˌmæstɚ/ *n.* [C] the person who is in charge of a post office

ˌpostmaster ˈgeneral *n.* [C] the person in charge of a national POSTAL SERVICE

post·men·o·paus·al /ˌpoʊstmɛnəˈpɔzəl/ *adj.* TECHNICAL a postmenopausal woman has gone through MENOPAUSE (=stopped having her monthly flow of blood)

post·mod·ern·ism /poʊstˈmɑdɚnˌɪzəm/ *n.* [U] a style of building, painting, writing etc. in the late 20th century that uses an unusual mixture of old and new styles as a reaction against MODERNISM —**postmodern** *adj.*: *postmodern architecture* —**postmodernist** *adj.*: *postmodernist fiction* —**postmodernist** *n.* [C]

post-mor·tem, **postmortem** /ˌpoʊstˈmɔrṭəm/ *n.* [C] **1** also **post-mortem examination** FORMAL an examination of a dead body to discover why the person died SYN **autopsy** **2** an examination of a plan or event that failed, in order to discover why it failed: **+of/on** *a post-mortem of the 2006 campaign*

post·na·sal /ˌpoʊstˈneɪzəl◂ / *adj.* TECHNICAL happening or existing behind your nose inside your head

post·na·tal /ˌpoʊstˈneɪṭl◂ / *adj.* TECHNICAL relating to the time after a baby is born: *postnatal care* → see also POSTPARTUM, PRENATAL

ˈpost ˌoffice S3 *n.* [C] a place where you can buy stamps and send letters, packages etc.

ˈpost office ˌbox *n.* [C] FORMAL a P.O. BOX

post·op·er·a·tive /ˌpoʊstˈɑpərəṭɪv/ also **post-op** /ˌpoʊst ˈɑp◂ / INFORMAL *adj.* TECHNICAL relating to the time after someone has had a medical operation: *postoperative pain* → see also PREOPERATIVE

post·paid /ˌpoʊstˈpeɪd◂ / *adj., adv.* with the POSTAGE already paid

post·par·tum /ˌpoʊstˈpɑrṭəm/ *adj.* TECHNICAL relating to the time just after a woman has a baby: *postpartum hospital stays* | *women suffering from* ***postpartum depression*** (=mental illness in which a woman becomes very unhappy and tired after she has a baby)

post·pone /poʊstˈpoʊn/ *v.* [T] to change an event, action etc. to a later time or date: *The game was postponed because of heavy snow.* | **postpone sth until sth** *The meeting's been postponed until tomorrow.* | **postpone sth for two weeks/a month etc.** *Another delay could postpone the space mission for a year.* | **postpone doing sth** *They've decided to postpone having a family for a while.* | *His trial has been* ***postponed indefinitely*** (=postponed, without saying what the new date will be). [**Origin:** 1400–1500 Latin *postponere*, from *ponere* **to put**] —**postponement** *n.* [C,U]

post·script /ˈpoʊstˌskrɪpt/ *n.* [C] **1** WRITTEN ABBREVIATION **P.S.** a message written at the end of a letter below the place where you sign your name: *The hand-written postscript read, "Thank you Jim!"* **2** something that you add at the end of a story or account that you have been telling someone: *There's an interesting postscript to this tale.*

post·sea·son /ˌpoʊstˈsizən◂ / *adj.* [only before noun] relating to the time after the usual sports SEASON is over: *a postseason game* —**postseason** *n.* [singular] → see also PRESEASON

post·sec·ond·a·ry /ˌpoʊstˈsɛkənˌdɛri/ *adj.* relating to schools or education after you have finished high school: *postsecondary education*

post·test /ˈpoʊsttɛst/ *n.* [C] a test that you take to see how much you have learned after you have studied something or after you have done an activity → see also PRETEST

ˌpost-trauˌmatic ˈstress disˌorder ABBREVIATION **P.T.S.D.** *n.* [U] MEDICINE a mental illness that can develop after a very bad experience such as fighting in a war

pos·tu·late¹ /ˈpɑstʃəˌleɪt/ *v.* [T] FORMAL to suggest that something might have happened or be true: *Darwin postulated the modern theory of evolution.* | +**that** *He postulates that this type of abuse is common.* —**postulation** /ˌpɑstʃəˈleɪʃən/ *n.* [C,U]

pos·tu·late² /ˈpɑstʃəlɪt, -ˌleɪt/ *n.* [C] FORMAL something that is believed to be true, but is not proven, on which an argument or scientific discussion is based: *a mathematical postulate*

pos·ture /ˈpɑstʃɚ/ *n.* **1** [C,U] the position you hold your body in when you sit or stand: *Kerry has really* ***good posture*** (=she holds her body in a way that is straight, natural, and relaxed). | **bad/poor posture** *Poor posture can lead to problems with your back.* **2** [C usually singular] the way you behave or think in a particular situation: *The country then* ***adopted a*** *more hostile military* ***posture.***

pos·tur·ing /ˈpɑstʃərɪŋ/ *n.* [C,U] **1** insincere behavior, attitudes, or statements that are intended to make people believe, notice, admire, or fear you: *political posturing* **2** the action of standing or behaving in a way that you hope will make other people notice and admire you —**posture** *v.* [I]

post·war, post-war /ˌpoʊstˈwɔr◂/ *adj.* [only before noun] happening or existing after a war, especially World War II: *postwar economic growth* | **the postwar period/years/era** *medical advances in the postwar period* —**postwar** *adv.* → see also PREWAR

po·sy /ˈpoʊzi/ *n. plural* **posies** [C] OLD-FASHIONED a flower, or a small group of cut flowers

pot¹ /pɑt/ S2 W3 *n.*

1 COOKING [C] a container used for cooking which is round, deep, and usually made of metal, or the amount of food or liquid that can be contained in this: *an aluminum pot* | *pots and pans* | +**of** *a pot of soup* → see picture at PAN

2 TEA/COFFEE [C] a container with a handle and a small tube for pouring, used to make tea or coffee, or the amount of liquid that can be contained in this: *a coffee pot* | +**of** *a pot of tea*

3 FOR A PLANT [C] a container for a plant, usually made of plastic or baked clay: *Do you think I should put it in a bigger pot?* | +**of** *a pot of lilies*

4 go to pot INFORMAL if something such as a place or an organization goes to pot, it becomes much worse because no one is interested in taking care of it or making it work

5 DRUG [U] INFORMAL an illegal drug smoked like a cigarette, made from the dried leaves of the hemp plant SYN **marijuana**: *She used to* ***smoke pot*** *in highschool.*

6 BOWL [C] a dish, bowl, plate, or other container that is made by shaping clay and then baking it: *broken shards of Roman pots*

7 the pot all the money that people have risked in a game of cards, especially POKER

8 STORING FOOD [C] a glass or clay container used for storing food: *a pot of honey*

9 STOMACH [C] a large round unattractive stomach that sticks out, usually on a man SYN **potbelly**

10 (a case of) the pot calling the kettle black INFORMAL used to say that you should not be criticizing someone for a fault that you also have

[**Origin:** Old English *pott*] → see also CHAMBER POT, MELTING POT

pot² *v.* **potted, potting** [T] to put a plant in a pot filled with soil → see also POTTED

po·ta·ble /ˈpoʊt̬əbəl/ *adj.* FORMAL potable water is safe to drink

pot·ash /ˈpɑtæʃ/ *n.* [U] a type of potassium used especially in farming to make the soil better

po·tas·si·um /pəˈtæsiəm/ SYMBOL **K** *n.* [U] CHEMISTRY a silver-white soft metal that is an ELEMENT and usually exists in compounds formed with other substances

po·ta·to /pəˈteɪtoʊ, -t̬ə/ *n. plural* **potatoes** BIOLOGY **1** [C,U] a round white root with a brown, red, or pale yellow skin, cooked and eaten as a vegetable: *mashed potatoes* | *a baked potato* | *Dad stood at the sink,* ***peeling potatoes*** (=taking the skins off them). **2** [C] a plant that produces potatoes [**Origin:** 1500–1600 Spanish *batata*, from Taino] → see also HOT POTATO, SWEET POTATO

poˈtato chip *n.* [C] one of many thin pieces of potato that have been cooked in oil to make them hard, and that are sold in packages SYN **chip**

poˈtato ˌpeeler *n.* [C] a small tool like a knife, used for removing the skin of a potato

Pot·a·wat·o·mi /ˌpɑt̬əˈwɑt̬əmi/ a Native American tribe from the northeastern central area of the U.S.

pot·bel·lied /ˈpɑtˀˌbɛlid/ *adj.* having a large stomach that sticks out in an unattractive way

ˌpotbellied ˈpig *n.* [C] a type of small pig that people keep as a pet

ˌpotbellied ˈstove *n.* [C] a small round metal STOVE that you burn wood or coal in for heating or cooking, used especially in past times

pot·bel·ly /ˈpɑtˀˌbɛli/ *n.* [C] a large round stomach that sticks out in an unattractive way

pot·boil·er /ˈpɑtˀˌbɔɪlɚ/ *n.* [C] an exciting and romantic book or movie that is produced quickly to make money

po·ten·cy /ˈpoʊtˀnsi/ *n.* [U] **1** the strength of the effect of a drug, medicine, food etc. on your mind or body: *high-potency drugs* | *the potency of the chili* **2** the ability of a man to have sex **3** the power that an idea, argument, action etc. has to influence people: *the political potency of crime issues*

po·tent /ˈpoʊtˀnt/ *adj.* **1** a potent drug, medicine, food etc. has a powerful effect on your body or mind: *unusually potent drugs* **2** powerful and effective: *potent weapons* | *a potent symbol for peace* **3** a man who is potent is able to have sex or able to make a woman PREGNANT —**potently** *adv.* → see also IMPOTENT

po·ten·tate /ˈpoʊtˀnˌteɪt/ *n.* [C] LITERARY a ruler with direct power over his people

po·ten·tial¹ /pəˈtɛnʃəl/ Ac W2 *adj.* [only before noun] a potential customer, problem, effect etc. is not a customer, problem etc. yet, but may become one in the future SYN **possible**: *It is important to identify potential problems early.* | *The 60 potential jurors waited in the courtroom.* | **a potential risk/threat/danger** *the potential health risks associated with the drug* | **a potential customer/buyer/client/investor etc.** (=people who a business wants to attract as customers, buyers etc.) [**Origin:** 1300–1400 Late Latin *potentialis*, from Latin *potentia* **power**]

potential² Ac W3 *n.* [U] **1** the possibility that something will develop in a certain way, or have a particular effect: +**for** *There is some potential for abuse in the system.* | +**of** *We need to explore the potential of this idea further.* | **have the potential to do sth** *The planned bombing had the potential to kill and injure many people.* **2** a natural ability or quality that could develop to make a person or thing very good: *This room* ***has potential.*** | *a young singer* ***with potential*** | **the potential to do sth** *The country shows the potential to be a global economic leader.* | **sb's potential as sth** *In his third year he is finally* ***showing*** *his great* ***potential as a golfer.*** | **achieve/reach/realize your (full) potential** (=succeed in doing as well as you possibly can) **3** PHYSICS the difference in VOLTAGE between two points on an electrical CIRCUIT

poˌtential ˈdifference *n.* [C] PHYSICS the difference in electrical charge between two points in an electric CIRCUIT, measured in VOLTS

poˌtential ˈenergy *n.* [U] PHYSICS the energy that is stored in physical matter when it is not moving → see also KINETIC ENERGY

po·ten·ti·al·i·ty /pəˌtɛnʃiˈæləti/ *n.* [C,U] FORMAL the possibility that something may develop in a particular way

po·ten·tial·ly /pəˈtɛnʃəli/ Ac *adv.* [+ adj./adv.] something that is potentially dangerous, useful, embarrassing etc. does not have that quality now, but it may develop it later: *a potentially dangerous situation* | *a potentially fatal disease*

pot·ful /ˈpɑtˀfʊl/ *n.* [C] the amount that a pot can contain

pot·head /ˈpɑthɛd/ *n.* [C] INFORMAL someone who smokes a lot of MARIJUANA

pot·hold·er /ˈpɑtˌhoʊldɚ/ *n.* [C] a piece of thick material used for holding hot cooking pans

P

pot·hole /ˈpɑthoʊl/ *n.* [C] a large hole in a road caused by traffic and bad weather that makes driving difficult or dangerous —**potholed** *adj.*

po·tion /ˈpoʊʃən/ *n.* [C] **1** LITERARY a drink intended to have a special or magic effect on the person who drinks it: *a love potion* **2** HUMOROUS a medicine, especially one that seems strange, old-fashioned, or unnecessary: *pills and potions*

pot·latch /ˈpɑtlætʃ/ *n.* [C,U] a ceremonial meal among some Native American tribes of the northwest coast, at which one person gives gifts to the other people to show his wealth and high position

pot·luck¹ /ˌpɑtˈlʌk◂/ *n.* **1** [C] a potluck meal **2 take potluck a)** to choose something without knowing very much about it and hope that it will be what you want: *We had to take potluck with hotels.* **b)** to have a meal at someone's home in which you eat whatever they have available

potluck² *adj.* **a potluck meal/dinner/lunch etc.** a meal in which everyone who is invited brings something to eat

Po·to·mac, the /pəˈtoʊmək/ a river in the eastern U.S. that separates the state of Maryland and the city of Washington, D.C. from the states of Virginia and West Virginia

ˌpot ˈpie *n.* [C] meat and vegetables covered with PASTRY and baked in a deep dish

pot·pour·ri /ˌpoʊpʊˈri/ *n.* **1** [U] a mixture of pieces of dried flowers and leaves kept in a bowl to make a room smell nice **2** [C usually singular] a combination or mixture of things, especially things that are not usually put together: *a potpourri of religious ideas*

potpourri

ˈpot roast *n.* [C] a dish that consists of a large piece of BEEF, cooked slowly in a covered pot, often with vegetables

ˈpot shot *n.* **take a pot shot at sb/sth a)** to shoot at someone or something without aiming very carefully **b)** to criticize someone unfairly without thinking carefully about it: *Conservative groups are taking pot shots at the U.N.*

pot·ted /ˈpɑt̬ɪd/ *adj.* [only before noun] a potted plant grows indoors in a pot: *a potted palm*

pot·ter /ˈpɑt̬ɚ/ *n.* [C] someone who makes pots, dishes etc. out of clay

ˌpotter's ˈwheel *n.* [C] a round flat object that spins around very fast, onto which wet clay is placed so that it can be shaped into a pot

pot·ter·y /ˈpɑt̬əri/ *n.* ENG. LANG. ARTS **1** [U] objects made out of baked clay: *American Indian pottery* | *a pottery bowl* **2** [U] the activity of making pots, dishes etc. out of clay: *experts in pottery* | *a pottery class* ►see THESAURUS box at **art¹** **3** [C] a factory where pottery objects are made

ˈpotting soil *n.* [U] special dirt that is used in pots to grow plants in

pot·ty /ˈpɑt̬i/ *n.* [C] **1** a word meaning a potty chair, used by or to children **2 go potty** SPOKEN an expression meaning "to use the toilet," said by or to young children: *Do you have to go potty?* **3 a potty mouth** SPOKEN, INFORMAL a person who has or is a potty mouth uses offensive language

ˈpotty chair *n.* [C] a small chair with a hole in the seat and a bowl under it that is used as a toilet for young children

ˈpotty-train *v.* [T] to teach a child to use a potty chair or toilet —**potty training** *n.* [U] —**potty-trained** *adj.*

pouch /paʊtʃ/ *n.* [C] **1** a small leather, cloth, or plastic bag that you can keep things such as tobacco or money in: *a concealed pouch for your passport* **2** a large bag for holding mail or papers: *a mail pouch* **3** BIOLOGY a pocket of skin on the stomach that MARSUPIALS such as KANGAROOS keep their babies in **4** BIOLOGY a fold of skin like a bag that animals such as SQUIRRELS have inside each cheek to carry and store food **5** an area of loose skin under someone's eyes

Pou·lenc /puˈlæŋk/, **Fran·cis** /frɑnˈsis/ (1899–1963) a French musician who wrote CLASSICAL music

poul·tice /ˈpoʊltɪs/ *n.* [C] something that is put on someone's skin to make it less swollen or painful, often made of a wet cloth with milk, HERBS, or CLAY on it

poul·try /ˈpoʊltri/ *n.* [plural, U] birds such as chickens and ducks that are kept on farms for supplying eggs and meat, or the meat from these birds: *a poultry farmer* | *I eat fish and poultry, but not red meat.*

pounce /paʊns/ *v.* [I] to suddenly jump on an animal, person, or thing after waiting to attack them: *The cat sat still, ready to pounce.* | **+on** *The other woman pounced on her and began fighting.* —**pounce** *n.* [C]

pounce on sb/sth *phr. v.* **1** to notice a mistake, someone's opinion etc. and immediately criticize or disagree with it: *The Colonel pounced on Ryan's reluctance to support the military.* **2** to accept an offer or invitation eagerly SYN **jump at**

pound¹ /paʊnd/ S1 W1 *n.* **1** WRITTEN ABBREVIATION **lb.** [C] a unit for measuring weight, equal to 16 OUNCES or about 0.454 kilograms: *an eight-pound three-ounce baby girl* | **+of** *a pound of apples* | **a/per pound** *Navel oranges are only 39 cents a pound.* | *I've* ***gained*** *ten* ***pounds*** (=become ten pounds heavier) *since last year.* | *I* ***lost*** *20* ***pounds*** (=became 20 pounds lighter) *in the hospital.* **2** [C] **a)** WRITTEN ABBREVIATION **£** the standard unit of money in the U.K. **b)** the standard unit of money in various other countries, such as Egypt and Sudan **3** [C] **the pound a)** a place where dogs and cats that are found on the street are kept until someone comes to get them **b)** a place where cars that have been parked illegally are kept until the owners pay to get them back **4** [U] also **the pound sign/key** the SYMBOL (#), or the button on a telephone with this symbol: *Enter your code, and then press pound.* **5 get/take etc. your pound of flesh** to make someone suffer or pay more money than they can afford, especially because they owe you money [**Origin:** (1–2) Old English *pund*, from Latin *pondo*]

pound² S3 *v.* **1** [I,T] to hit something several times to make a lot of noise, damage it, make it lie flat etc.: *He pounded the desk in frustration.* | **pound against/on sth** *Bill pounded on the front door.* ►see THESAURUS box at **hit¹** **2** [I] if your heart pounds, it beats very hard and quickly: *I stayed calm, but my heart was pounding.* **3** [I always + adv./prep.] to walk or run quickly with heavy loud steps: **pound along/through/down etc. sth** *He came pounding up the narrow trail.* **4** [T] to attack a place continuously for a long time with bombs or SHELLS: *Army cannons continued to pound the city.* → see also **pound/hit the pavement** at PAVEMENT (3)

pound away *phr. v.* **1** to continue to do something difficult without stopping: **+at** *Top scientists are pounding away at the problem.* **2** to continue to hit or attack something: **+at** *Allied warplanes continue to pound away at their targets.*

pound sth **↔ out** *phr. v.* **1** to play music loudly by hitting your piano, drum etc. very hard: *The band pounded out several Beatles' tunes.* **2** to TYPE (=write with a machine) something quickly, especially by hitting the KEYS very hard

Pound /paʊnd/, **Ez·ra** /ˈɛzrə/ (1885–1972) a U.S. poet who lived mostly in Europe, and supported FASCISM and Mussolini during World War II

pound·age /ˈpaʊndɪdʒ/ *n.* [U] **1** an amount charged for every pound in weight **2** INFORMAL body weight or fat that is higher than normal

ˈpound cake *n.* [C] a heavy cake made from flour, sugar, and butter

pound·er /ˈpaʊndɚ/ *n.* **1 a 3-pounder/24-pounder/185-pounder etc. a)** a fish, animal, or person that weighs 3 pounds, 24 pounds etc. **b)** a gun that fires a SHELL that weighs 3 pounds, 24 pounds etc. **2 a quarter/half pounder** a HAMBURGER with a quarter or half pound of meat in it

pound·ing /ˈpaʊndɪŋ/ *n.* **1** [singular U] the action or the sound of something repeatedly hitting a surface very hard, or of your heart beating: *the pounding of hooves* **2 take a pounding a)** if a team or army takes a pounding, it is badly defeated **b)** to be damaged by being hit or hitting something repeatedly: *The ship took a pounding in the storm.* **3** a painful feeling in your head when you can feel your PULSE strongly, often because you are hot, tired, or have a HEADACHE

ˌpound ˈsterling *n.* [singular] TECHNICAL the POUND

pour /pɔr/ S2 W2 *v.*

1 LIQUID [T] to make a liquid or a substance such as salt or sand flow out of or into something: *I'll pour the juice.* | **pour sth into/on/down etc.** *Don't pour that out – I'm going to drink it.* | **pour sb sth** *Could you pour me a glass of water?* ▶see THESAURUS box at **flow**[1]

2 it pours (rain) [I] if it pours, a lot of rain comes out of the sky: *It poured all night.* | *When I got ready to leave it was pouring rain.*

3 LIQUID/SMOKE [I always + adv./prep.] to flow quickly and in large amounts: **+from/down/out** *Smoke poured out of the upstairs windows.* | *Blood was pouring from his nose.*

pour

THESAURUS

flow to move in a steady continuous stream: *This is the place where the river flows into the sea.*
drip to produce small drops of liquid, or to fall in drops: *Rainwater dripped from the trees.*
leak if a liquid leaks, it passes through a hole or crack: *The milk was leaking through a tiny hole in the carton.*
ooze to flow from something very slowly: *Blood oozed through the bandages.*
gush to flow or pour out quickly in large quantities: *Water gushed into the hold of the boat through the hole.*
spurt to flow out suddenly with a lot of force: *Blood spurted from the wound.*
run to flow: *Tears ran down her cheeks.*
come out to pour out of a container, place etc.: *I turned on the faucet, but no water came out.*

4 ARRIVE/LEAVE [I always + adv./prep.] if people or things pour into or out of a place, a lot of them arrive or leave at the same time: **+into/from/through** *Fans poured into the streets to celebrate.* | *Offers of help poured in from all over the country.*

5 LIGHT [I always + adv./prep] if light pours into or out of a place, a lot of light is coming in or out: **pour into/from/through/out of sth** *Light was pouring into the courtyard.*

6 pour on the charm to behave in a very nice and polite way, in order to make someone like you

7 pour cold water over/on sth to spoil someone's plan, idea, or desire to do something by criticizing them: *The mayor is pouring cold water on the report before she's even seen it.*

8 pour scorn on sb/sth to say that something or someone is stupid and not worth considering: *Her boss poured scorn on the suggestion.*

9 pour it on INFORMAL to work very hard and use a lot of energy: *On the court, Rick was pouring it on.* → see also **pour/lay it on thick** at THICK[2] (2)

pour sth **into** sth *phr. v.* to provide a lot of money for something over a period of time: **pour money/aid/dollars etc. into sth** *They continue to pour millions of dollars into research.*

pour sth ↔ **out** *phr. v.* if you pour out your thoughts, feelings etc., you tell someone everything about them, especially because you feel very unhappy: **pour sth ↔ out to sb** *Diane poured all her troubles out to him.* | **pour out your heart/soul** (=tell someone all your feelings, including your most secret ones)

pour·ing /ˈpɔrɪŋ/ *adj.* **(the) pouring rain** very heavy rain: *We waited outside in the pouring rain.*

Pous·sin /puˈsæn/, **Nic·o·las** /ˈnɪkələs/ (1594–1665) a French PAINTER famous for his LANDSCAPES

pout /paʊt/ *v.* [I,T] to push out your lower lip because you are annoyed or unhappy, or in order to look sexually attractive: *Stop pouting and eat your dinner.* —**pout** *n.* [C] —**pouty** *adj.*

pou·tine /puˈtin/ *n.* [U] FRENCH FRIES covered in cheese CURDS and GRAVY, eaten in Canada

pov·er·ty /ˈpɑvɚṭi/ W3 *n.* **1** [U] the situation or experience of being poor: *Too many of our children are being raised* ***in poverty***. | **extreme/dire/abject/grinding poverty** *the region's grinding poverty* **2** [singular, U] FORMAL a lack of a particular quality OPP **wealth**: **+of** *The novel shows a surprising poverty of imagination.* [**Origin:** 1100–1200 Old French *poverté*, from Latin *paupertas*, from *pauper*]

ˈpoverty ˌline also **ˈpoverty ˌlevel**, **ˈpoverty ˌthreshold** *n.* [C] ECONOMICS a level of income below which people are officially considered to be poor

ˈpoverty ˌrate *n.* [C] ECONOMICS the number of people in a country or place who are living on an income below the poverty line, considered in relation to the total number of people living in a place

ˈpoverty-ˌstricken *adj.* extremely poor and having problems because of this: *poverty-stricken neighborhoods*

POW *n.* [C] a PRISONER OF WAR: *All POWs have been released.*

pow /paʊ/ *interjection* used to represent the sound of a gun firing, an explosion, or someone hitting another person hard, especially in COMIC BOOKS

pow·der[1] /ˈpaʊdɚ/ *n.* **1** [C,U] a dry substance in the form of very small grains: *The white powder turned out to be cocaine.* | *She dabbed some* ***face powder*** (=type of makeup) *on her nose.* | *The mustard is sold dry,* ***in powder form.*** **2** [U] EARTH SCIENCE dry light snow consisting of extremely small pieces: *There's a foot of powder on the slopes.* **3** [U] GUNPOWDER **4 take a powder** OLD-FASHIONED to stop doing something or to leave a place quickly, especially to avoid a difficult situation [**Origin:** 1200–1300 Old French *poudre*, from Latin *pulvis* **dust**] → see also BAKING POWDER, CHILI POWDER, CURRY POWDER, TALCUM POWDER

powder[2] *v.* **1** [T] to put powder on something, especially your skin: *The makeup man rushed forward to powder her face.* **2 powder your nose** OLD-FASHIONED or HUMOROUS an expression meaning "to go to the toilet," used by women to avoid saying this directly

ˌpowder ˈblue *n.* [U] a pale blue color —**powder blue** *adj.*

pow·dered /ˈpaʊdɚd/ *adj.* **1** produced or sold in the form of a powder: *powdered milk* **2** covered with powder or with something like powder: *a powdered wig* | **+with** *Their faces were powdered with white dust.*

P

'powder keg *n.* [C] **1** a dangerous situation or place where violence or trouble could suddenly start: *The region has been a powder keg since the killings.* **2** a small container like a BARREL used for holding GUNPOWDER or other substances that explode

'powder puff *n.* [C] a small piece of soft material used by women to spread POWDER on their face or body

'powder room *n.* [C] **1** a polite phrase meaning a "woman's public toilet" **2** a small room with a toilet and SINK in someone's home

pow·der·y /ˈpaʊdəri/ *adj.* **1** like powder or easily broken into powder: *The snow was dry and powdery.* **2** covered with powder

pow·er¹ /ˈpaʊɚ/ S1 W1 *n.*

1 CONTROL [U] the ability or right to control people or events: *We all felt that the chairman had too much power.* | **+over** *People should have more power over the decisions that affect their lives.* | **military/economic/political power** *China's growing economic power* | **exercise/assert power** *The U.S. was clearly prepared to exercise its power.* | *There were some prison guards who **abused** their **power*** (=used it to do bad things). | *There should be more women in **positions of power**.* | *The king had **absolute power*** (=complete power). | **power-crazy/hungry/mad** (=wanting power very much) → see also POWER STRUGGLE, POWER TRIP

2 POLITICAL [U] the position of having political control of a country or government: *He's been **in power** now for eight years.* | **come/rise to power** *When did Napoleon come to power?* | *A new Cambodian government **took power**.* | *The rebels **seized power*** (=get political control using military force) *later that year.* | *The party **lost power** in 1994.* | *Many feared **a return to power** of the old regime.*

3 ENERGY [U] **a)** PHYSICS energy that we get from oil, coal, the sun etc. that can be used for making electricity or for making a machine, car etc. work: *a power source* | **nuclear/wind/solar etc. power** *You can't rely strictly on solar power to move a car very far.* | *The plane **lost power** almost immediately after taking off Thursday.* | *The ship is sailing for Scotland **under its own power*** (=without help from another machine, ship etc.). → see also POWER OUTAGE **b)** the supply of electricity that is used in houses, factories etc.: *Make sure the power is switched off first.* | *Did **the power go out*** (=did the electricity supply stop?) *last night?* | *Four million households **lost power*** (=did not have electricity) *in the storm.* | *The **power came back on** at about 3 a.m.*

4 RIGHT/AUTHORITY [C,U] the legal right or authority to do something: *His presidential powers were limited.* | *The bill would **give** the President new **powers to** declare war.* | **the power to do sth** *The general manager has the power to fire the coach.* | **+over** *Local governments have little power over cable television companies.*

5 STRONG COUNTRY [C] a country that is strong and important, or has a lot of military strength: *Iran is a major power in the Persian Gulf region.* | *the emergence of the U.S. as **a world power*** (=a country that can influence events in any part of the world). | **an economic/a political/a military power** *Japan soon emerged as a leading economic power.* | *Who should be allowed to be **a nuclear power*** (=a country with nuclear weapons)? ►see THESAURUS box at **country¹** → see also SUPERPOWER

6 INFLUENCE [U] the ability to influence people or give them strong feelings: **+of** *Horton was fascinated by the power of dance.* | *the power of sex* | **parent/consumer/student etc. power** (=the influence that a particular group can have on what happens in society)

7 FORCE [U] the physical force or effect produced by something: *the tornado's terrifying power* | **+of** *the power of the explosion* | *the power of the cheetah's long legs* ►see THESAURUS box at **force¹**

8 NATURAL ABILITY [C,U] a natural or special ability to do something: *She claims to have psychic powers.* | **+of** *After the stroke, her father lost the power of speech.* | **the power to do sth** *Science has the power to change our lives.* | **earning/purchasing/bargaining power** (=the ability to earn money, buy things etc.)

9 COMPUTER [U] the ability of a computer or computer system to operate quickly and effectively: *increased computing power*

10 do everything in your power to do everything that you are able or allowed to do: *Doctors are doing everything in their power to save him.*

11 the powers that be INFORMAL the people who have important positions of authority and power, and whose decisions affect your life: *The powers that be do not want this story to be known.*

12 have it in/within your power to do sth also **be in/within your power to do sth** to have the authority or ability to do something: *I wish it was within my power to change the decision.*

13 be in sb's power LITERARY to be in a situation in which someone has complete control over you

14 MATH to the power of 3/4/5 etc. MATH if a number is increased to the power of three, four, five etc., it is multiplied by itself three, four, five etc. times

15 MAKING THINGS LOOK BIGGER [U] the ability of the LENS of BINOCULARS, TELESCOPES etc. to make things look bigger

16 air/sea power the planes or ships that a country has available to use in a war: *The outcome will be decided by air power.*

17 more power to sb SPOKEN used to say that you approve of what someone is trying to do, especially when you would not want to do it: *If Patty's willing to work on the weekend, more power to her.*

18 be beyond/outside sb's power to do sth to not have the authority or ability to do something: *This decision is beyond the power of the lower courts.*

19 the powers of good/evil/light/darkness spirits or magical forces that are believed to influence events in a good or evil way

20 the power behind the throne someone who is able to control and influence decisions made by a leader or someone in authority, often in a secret way

21 a power in the land OLD-FASHIONED someone or something that has a lot of power and influence in a country → see also BALANCE OF POWER, HIGH-POWERED, LOW-POWERED, STAYING POWER

power² *v.* **1** [T usually passive] to supply power to a vehicle or machine: *The motor is powered by gasoline.* **2** [I + adv./prep.] to move quickly and with a lot of strength: **+through/up/down** *Jones powered his way through the San Diego line of defense.* → see also HIGH-POWERED, LOW-POWERED, -POWERED

power sth ↔ **up** *phr. v.* to make a machine start working: *Never move a computer while it is powered up.*

power³ *adj.* **1** controlled by a motor: *Does this car have power windows?* **2 power breakfast/lunch** INFORMAL a business meeting that takes place at breakfast or lunch **3 a power tie/suit etc.** a piece of clothing that makes you look important or confident **4 power dressing** a way of dressing in which you choose the style of your clothes to make others think you are important and confident

'power base *n.* [C] the group of people in a particular area whose support gives a politician or leader their power: *His power base is among working-class Catholics.*

pow·er·boat /ˈpaʊɚˌboʊt/ *n.* [C] a powerful MOTORBOAT that is used for racing

'power ˌbroker *n.* [C] someone who controls or influences which people get political power in a particular area

'power drill *n.* [C] a tool for making holes that works by electricity

-powered /paʊɚd/ *suffix* working or moving by means of a particular type of power: *solar-powered* (=using power from the sun) | *jet-powered* | *battery-powered*

'power ˌfailure *n.* [C] a POWER OUTAGE

pow·er·ful /ˈpaʊɚfəl/ S3 W2 *adj.*

1 IMPORTANT having a lot of influence and strength, and able to control and influence events and other people's actions: *one of the world's most powerful men* | *Africa's most powerful country* | *the hugely powerful gun lobby in the U.S.*

THESAURUS

influential having a lot of power to influence what happens: *an influential Senator on the committee*
strong having a lot of power, influence, or ability: *He is a strong voice in the state assembly.*
dominant more powerful than other people or groups, and able to control what happens: *England was once the dominant power in the world.*

2 MACHINE/WEAPON ETC. a powerful machine, engine, weapon etc. works very effectively and quickly or with great force: *a powerful computer* | *This year's model is even more powerful.*
3 AFFECTING SB'S FEELINGS/IDEAS having a strong effect on someone's feelings or on the way they think: *a powerful story of love* | **powerful reasons/arguments** (=reasons that make you think that something must be true)
4 EFFECT **a powerful effect/influence/impact etc.** a powerful effect or influence is one that is very strong: *Television has a powerful influence on our lives.*
5 TEAM/ARMY ETC. a powerful team, army etc. is very strong and can easily defeat other teams or armies: *the team's powerful offense*
6 MEDICINE a powerful medicine or drug has a very strong effect on your body
7 PHYSICALLY STRONG physically strong: *the eagle's powerful wings*
8 LIGHT/SOUND/TASTE ETC. very strong, bright, loud etc.: *a powerful smell* | *his powerful singing voice*
9 EXPLOSION/KICK/PUNCH ETC. a powerful blow, explosion etc. hits someone with a lot of force or has a lot of force: *The winds were powerful enough to uproot trees.* —**powerfully** *adv.* → see also ALL-POWERFUL

pow·er·house /ˈpaʊɚˌhaʊs/ *n.* [C] INFORMAL **1** an organization or place that produces a lot of ideas and has a lot of influence: *This small company has become a powerhouse in the software market.* **2** someone who is very strong and has a lot of energy: *The band's lead singer is a vocal powerhouse.* **3** someone or something that is very successful, especially in sports: *Sherwin has built the team into a powerhouse.*

pow·er·less /ˈpaʊɚlɪs/ *adj.* unable to stop or control something because you do not have the power, strength, or legal right to do so: **powerless to do sth** *Local police were powerless to stop the violence.* | **+against** *Animals were powerless against the rising flood water.* —**powerlessly** *adv.* —**powerlessness** *n.* [U]

ˈpower line *n.* [C] a large wire carrying electricity above or under the ground

ˌpower of atˈtorney *n.* [C,U] LAW the legal right to do things for another person in their personal or business life, or a document giving this right

ˈpower ˌoutage *n.* [C] a period of time when there is no electricity supply

ˈpower ˌpack *n.* [C] INFORMAL a BATTERY that is used to make electrical objects run

Pow·erPC /ˌpaʊɚ pi ˈsi/ *n.* [C] TRADEMARK a fast CPU that is used in many modern computers

ˈpower plant *n.* [C] **1** a building where electricity is produced to supply a large area **2** PHYSICS the machine or engine that supplies power to a factory, airplane, car etc.

ˈpower ˌpolitics *n.* [U] POLITICS attempts by people or political groups to get control of a particular country's, city's etc. politics

ˈpower-ˌsharing *n.* [U] a situation in which two or more people or groups of people run a government together —**power-sharing** *adj.* [only before noun] *a power-sharing arrangement*

ˈpower ˌstation *n.* [C] a POWER PLANT

ˈpower ˌsteering *n.* [U] a system for STEERing a vehicle that uses power from the vehicle's engine and so needs less effort from the driver

ˈpower ˌstructure *n.* [C] the group of people who have power in a society or country

ˈpower ˌstruggle *n.* [C] a situation in which two or more people, groups, countries etc. are competing to control things: *The government and the military were engaged in a power struggle.*

ˈpower tool *n.* [C] a tool that works by electricity

ˈpower trip *n.* [C usually singular] a situation in which someone in authority gets pleasure from exercising that authority, often in unreasonable ways: *My boss is* ***on** some kind of **power trip** this week.*

Pow·ha·tan¹ /ˌpaʊəˈtæn/ a group of Native American tribes from the eastern U.S.

Powhatan² (1550–1618) an Algonquin chief, father of Pocahontas, who made a peace agreement in 1614 with the English settlers of Jamestown

pow-wow /ˈpaʊ waʊ/ *n.* [C] **1** HUMOROUS a meeting or discussion **2** a meeting or council of Native Americans [**Origin:** 1800–1900 Narragansett *powwaw* **magician**]

pox /pɑks/ *n.* **1** [U] OLD USE the disease SMALLPOX **2 a pox on sb** OLD-FASHIONED used to show that you are angry or annoyed with someone **3 the pox** OLD USE the disease SYPHILIS → see also CHICKENPOX

pp. the written abbreviation of "pages": *See pp. 15–17.*

p.p. written before the name of another person when you are signing a letter for them

ppm *n.* [singular] TECHNICAL **parts per million** a measurement of very small pieces of something, especially something in the air or water: *ozone levels between 0.07 and 0.12 ppm*

PPO *n.* [C] **Preferred Provider Organization** a type of health insurance plan in which members can go to any hospital or doctor, but the insurance company pays more for hospitals and doctors in their system than those outside their system → see also HMO

PPP *n.* [C] COMPUTERS **point-to-point protocol** the information that your computer gives to an ONLINE service PROVIDER over telephone lines, so that you can connect your computer with them and use the Internet, send EMAIL etc.

P.P.S. *n.* [C] a note added after a P.S. in a letter or message

PR *n.* [U] **1** POLITICS **public relations** the work of persuading people to think that a company or organization is a good one: *a PR firm* | **good/bad PR** *The company got some good PR from giving money to the orphanage.* **2** the written abbreviation of Puerto Rico

prac·ti·ca·ble /ˈpræktɪkəbəl/ *adj.* FORMAL able to be used or done successfully in a particular situation: *the most practicable course of action* | **it is practicable (for sb) to do sth** *It's not practicable to publish all the results.* —**practicably** *adv.* —**practicability** /ˌpræktɪkəˈbɪləṱi/ *n.* [U]

prac·ti·cal /ˈpræktɪkəl/ W3 *adj.*
1 REAL SITUATIONS relating to real situations and events rather than ideas OPP **theoretical**: *Voters make their choices based on practical considerations.* | ***a practical approach** to dealing with difficult employees* | *Instructors all have M.B.A.s plus a lot of **practical experience** in business.* | **practical advice/support/help** *The book is full of practical advice for young mothers.*
2 SENSIBLE sensible and basing your decisions on what is possible and likely to succeed, or showing this quality OPP **impractical**: *a practical attitude to marriage* | *She's a very practical person.*
3 LIKELY TO WORK practical plans, methods, advice etc. are likely to succeed or be effective in a situation OPP **impractical**: *Is there a practical alternative to oil-based fuels?* | *It doesn't sound like a very practical solution.*
4 USEFUL/SUITABLE useful or appropriate for a particular purpose, rather than attractive or interesting: *Babysitting coupons are a practical gift any parent will love.* | *Small economy cars are more practical if you live in the city.*

5 **for all practical purposes** used when saying what the real effect of a situation is: *For all practical purposes, the country is bankrupt.*
6 GOOD AT FIXING THINGS good at repairing or making things
[**Origin:** 1500–1600 Late Latin *practicus*, from Greek *prassein* **to do**]

prac·ti·cal·i·ty /ˌpræktɪˈkæləṭi/ *n.* **1 practicalities** [plural] the real facts of a situation rather than ideas about how it might be: *the practicalities of rebuilding the airport* **2** [U] the degree to which a plan, method, or design is appropriate for a situation, and whether or not it is likely to succeed: *We're not sure about the practicality of the new legislation.* **3** [U] the quality of being sensible and basing your plans on what you know is likely to succeed

P

ˌpractical ˈjoke *n.* [C] a trick that is intended to give someone a surprise or shock and make other people laugh —**practical joker** *n.* [C]

prac·ti·cally /ˈpræktɪkli/ S3 *adv.* **1** INFORMAL almost SYN **virtually**: *I practically fainted when I saw him.* | *The theater was practically empty.* | **practically all/every/no etc.** *I have read practically all of his books.* **2** in a sensible way that considers problems: *"But how will we pay for it?" asked John practically.*

ˈpractical ˌnurse *n.* [C] a LICENSED PRACTICAL NURSE

prac·tice¹ /ˈpræktɪs/ S2 W1 *n.*
1 A SKILL **a)** [U] regular activity that you do in order to improve a skill or ability: *You're doing well. You just need a little more practice.* | *Cooking is something that improves **with practice**.* | *Learning to play the guitar isn't easy, **it takes practice**.* **b)** [C,U] a period of time you spend training to improve your skill in doing something: *During the summer, the team has two practices a week.* | **football/hockey/basketball etc. practice** *Sam's at soccer practice.*
2 STH DONE OFTEN [C] something that you do often because of your religion or your society's customs: *the religious beliefs and practices of Hindus* | **the practice of doing sth** *the widespread practice of dumping waste in the sea* | *The use of chemical sprays has **become common practice*** (=become the thing that is normally done). ►see THESAURUS box at **habit**
3 the actual performance of an activity in a real situation, especially in order to see whether it is effective: *the difference between theory and practice* | ***In practice**, the city's transportation system is very inefficient* (=in reality the system is not efficient, even though it was designed to be). | *The office has been slow to **put** the new plans **into practice*** (=use the plans in a real situation).
4 STH DONE OFTEN [C,U] something that people do often, especially a particular way of doing something: *unsafe sexual practices* | **standard/common/general etc. practice** *Lowering prices after the holidays is common practice in the U.S.* | **be good/bad practice** *Changing your computer passwords regularly is considered good practice.* ►see THESAURUS box at **habit**
5 DOCTOR/LAWYER [C,U] the work of a doctor or lawyer, or the place where they work: *Both dentists have **been in practice*** (=worked as dentists) *for twenty years.* | **medical/legal practice** (=a business in which someone works as a doctor or lawyer) → see also GENERAL PRACTICE, PRIVATE PRACTICE
6 be out of practice to have not done something for a long time so that you are unable to do it well: *I love to play tennis, but I'm really out of practice.*
7 practice makes perfect used to say that if you do an activity regularly, you will become very good at it

practice² S1 W2 *v.* **1** [I,T] to do an activity regularly in order to improve your skill or to prepare for a test: *Teresa practices karate two hours a day.* | **practice doing sth** *Gene needs to practice writing essays.* | **practice for sth** *The stunt pilots are practicing for an upcoming air show.* | **practice sth on sb** *Rob has been practicing his comedy routine on me.* | *Coach says I need to **practice hard*** (=practice a lot) *if I want to play next year.*

THESAURUS
rehearse to practice something such as a play or concert before giving a public performance: *The drama group was rehearsing for a performance of "Arsenic and Old Lace."*
work on sth to practice a skill, musical instrument etc. in order to improve: *Jessie has been working on her tennis serve.*
train to prepare for a sports event by exercising and practicing: *Olympic swimmers train for hours every day.*
drill to teach people something by making them repeat the same exercise, lesson etc. many times: *When you're teaching children to read, you don't want to just drill them in the letter sounds, you want them to enjoy a story.*

2 [I,T] to work as a doctor or lawyer: **practice law/medicine/psychiatry etc.** *Harris has practiced law for over thirty years.* | **practice as sth** *He is now practicing as a dentist.* **3** [T] to use a particular method or custom: *The custom of arranging marriages is practiced in some parts of Asia.* | **practice a method/technique** *More and more farmers are practicing organic methods.* **4** [T] if you practice a religion, system of ideas etc., you live your life according to its rules: *Tricia practices Zen Buddhism.* **5 practice what you preach** to do the things that you advise other people to do

prac·ticed /ˈpræktɪst/ *adj.* **1** someone who is practiced in a particular job or skill is good at it because they have done it many times before: *a practiced outdoorsman* | **+in/at** *He was well practiced at giving interviews.* | *Her **practiced eye*** (=ability to deal with something as a result of having seen it many times) *quickly found the problem.* **2** [only before noun] a practiced action has been done so often that it now seems very easy: *With a practiced motion, he grabbed the snake.*

prac·tic·ing /ˈpræktɪsɪŋ/ *adj.* **1 a practicing Catholic/Muslim/Jew etc.** someone who follows the rules and traditions of a particular religion OPP **lapsed** ►see THESAURUS box at **religious** **2 a practicing doctor/lawyer/architect etc.** someone who is working as a doctor, lawyer etc. **3 a practicing homosexual/lesbian/gay etc.** someone who is HOMOSEXUAL and who has sex

prac·ti·cum /ˈpræktɪkəm/ *n.* [C] a school or college course in which students use the knowledge that they have learned in a practical way

prac·tise /ˈpræktɪs/ *v.* the British and Canadian spelling of PRACTICE

prac·ti·tion·er /prækˈtɪʃənɚ/ Ac *n.* [C] **1 a medical/legal/tax etc. practitioner** someone who does a particular job such as a doctor or a lawyer **2** someone who regularly does a particular activity or follows the rules of a particular religion or PHILOSOPHY: *a Christian Science practitioner* | **+of** *a practitioner of Taoist philosophy* → see also FAMILY PRACTITIONER, GENERAL PRACTITIONER, NURSE PRACTITIONER

prae·sid·i·um /prɪˈsɪdiəm, -ˈzɪd-/ *n.* [C] another spelling of PRESIDIUM

prae·to·ri·an guard /priˌtɔriən ˈgɑrd/ *n.* [singular] LITERARY a group of people who are very loyal to someone important or powerful

prag·mat·ic /prægˈmæṭɪk/ *adj.* dealing with problems in a sensible practical way, instead of strictly following a set of ideas: *a pragmatic approach to management problems* | **+about** *He's very pragmatic about his chances of winning.* —**pragmatically** /-kli/ *adv.*

prag·mat·ics /prægˈmæṭɪks/ *n.* [U] ENG. LANG. ARTS the study of how words and phrases are used with special meanings in particular situations

prag·ma·tism /ˈprægməˌtɪzəm/ *n.* [U] a way of dealing with problems in a sensible practical way, instead of following a set of ideas: *a politician known for his pragmatism* —**pragmatist** *n.* [C]

Prague /prɑg/ the capital and largest city of the Czech Republic

ˌPrague ˈSpring, the HISTORY the period from January to August 1968, when the government of Czechoslovakia allowed more political freedom, until the Soviet army entered the country to stop it

Prai·a /ˈpraɪə/ the capital and largest city of Cape Verde

prai·rie /ˈprɛri/ *n.* [C] EARTH SCIENCE a wide open area of mostly flat land that is covered with grass, especially in North America

ˈprairie dog *n.* [C] a small animal with a short tail, which lives in holes on the prairies

praise¹ /preɪz/ W3 *v.* [T] **1** to say that you admire and approve of someone or something, especially publicly OPP **criticize**: *The new freeway plan has been praised by local business leaders.* | **praise sb/sth for sth** *She praised Dorothy for her hard work.* | **highly/much/widely praised** *the university's highly praised work in cancer research* | **praise sb/sth to the skies** OLD-FASHIONED (=to praise someone or something a lot)

THESAURUS

congratulate to tell someone that you are happy that they have achieved something
flatter to say nice things about someone, sometimes when you do not really mean it, often in order to get something you want
compliment sb/pay sb a compliment to say something nice to someone in order to praise them
rave/enthuse about/over sth to talk about something you enjoy or admire in an excited way

2 to give thanks to God and show your respect to him, especially by singing or praying **3 God/Heaven be praised** also **Praise the Lord** used to say that you are pleased something has happened and thank God for it [**Origin:** 1200–1300 Old French *preisier*, from Late Latin *pretiare* **to value highly**]

praise² S3 *n.* [U] **1** words that you say or write in order to praise someone or something OPP **criticism**: **+for** *The teacher deserves praise for the way she handled a difficult situation.* | *Residents were* ***full of praise for*** *the fire department's quick actions* (=they praised it a lot). | *His first novel received* ***high praise*** (=a lot of praise). | **win/earn praise** *The charity has earned widespread praise for its work.* | *a poem* ***in praise of*** *his heroes* | **heap/lavish praise on sb/sth** (=to praise something strongly or many times) **2** an expression of respect and thanks to God: *Let us give praise unto the Lord.* **3 praise be!** OLD-FASHIONED used when you are very pleased about something that has happened → see also **sing sb's praises** at SING (3)

praise·wor·thy /ˈpreɪzˌwɚði/ *adj.* deserving praise: *Honesty is the most praiseworthy quality one can possess.* —**praiseworthiness** *n.* [U]

pra·line /ˈprɑlin, ˈpreɪ-/ *n.* [C,U] a sweet food made of nuts cooked in boiling sugar [**Origin:** 1700–1800 Count Plessis-*Praslin* (1598–1675), French soldier whose cook invented praline]

prance /præns/ *v.* [I] **1** to walk moving your body in a confident way in order to make people notice and admire you, often when this makes you look silly: **+around/in/up** *He started prancing around in front of the cameras.* **2** if a horse prances, it moves with high steps

prank /præŋk/ *n.* [C] a trick, especially one that is intended to make someone look silly SYN **trick**: **pull/play a prank** *Every year, the older kids pull pranks on new students.*

prank·ster /ˈpræŋkstɚ/ *n.* [C] someone who plays tricks on people to make them look silly

prate /preɪt/ *v.* [I + on/about] OLD-FASHIONED to talk in a meaningless boring way about something

prat·fall /ˈprætfɔl/ *n.* [C] an embarrassing accident or mistake, especially one in which you fall down

prat·tle /ˈprætl/ *v.* [I] to talk continuously about silly and unimportant things: *She prattled away, without asking him anything.* ►see THESAURUS box at **talk¹** —**prattle** *n.* [U] —**prattler** *n.* [C]

prawn /prɔn/ *n.* [C] a sea animal like a large SHRIMP, that is used for food

pray¹ /preɪ/ S2 W3 *v.* **prays, prayed, praying 1** [I,T] to speak to God or gods in order to ask for help or give thanks: *You don't have to go to church to pray.* | **pray for sb/sth** *They prayed for peace.* | **pray to sb/sth to do sth** *She prayed to Allah to help her.* **2** [I,T] to wish or hope very strongly that something will happen: **pray that** *Mel prayed that the lawyers could help him.* | **pray for sth** *We're praying for good weather tomorrow.* [**Origin:** 1200–1300 Old French *preier*, from Latin *precari*, from *prex* **request, prayer**]

pray² *adv.* [sentence adverb] OLD-FASHIONED used when politely asking a question or telling someone to do something SYN **please**: *And who,* ***pray tell****, is this?*

prayer /prɛr/ S3 W2 *n.* **1** [C] words that you say when praying to God or gods: *We* ***said a prayer*** *to end the service.* | **+for** *a prayer for the poor* **2** [U] the act of praying, or the regular habit of praying: *the power of prayer* | *a prayer meeting* | *The congregation knelt* ***in prayer*** (=praying). **3** [C] a strong wish or hope for something that you need or want: *The job was* ***the answer to all my prayers*** (=exactly what someone wanted or needed). | *I thought all my* ***prayers were answered*** (=I thought I had gotten everything I wanted) *when I met him.* **4 not have a prayer (of doing sth)** INFORMAL to have no chance of succeeding: *The team didn't have a prayer of winning.* **5 prayers** [plural] a regular religious meeting in a church, school etc., at which people pray together: *morning prayers at the synagogue* → see also LORD'S PRAYER

ˈprayer beads *n.* [plural] a string of BEADS used for counting prayers → see also ROSARY

ˈprayer book *n.* [C] a book containing prayers used in some Christian church services

ˈprayer mat also **ˈprayer rug** *n.* [C] a small MAT which Muslims kneel on when praying

ˈprayer wheel *n.* [C] a piece of wood or metal that is shaped like a drum and turns around on a pole, on which prayers are written, used by Tibet Buddhists

praying man·tis /ˌpreɪ-ɪŋ ˈmæntɪs/ *n.* [C] a long thin green insect that eats other insects

pre- /pri/ *prefix* [in adjectives] **1** before a particular event or period of time OPP **post-**: *prewar* | *pre-breakfast* **2** done before something, or in order to prepare for something OPP **post-**: *prenatal* (=before birth) | *prerecorded* (=recorded before a particular time) **3** before a particular person lived or had power OPP **post-**: *pre-Franco* (=before Franco ruled Spain)

preach /pritʃ/ *v.* **1** [I,T] to give a talk in public about a religious subject, especially about the correct moral way for people to behave: **preach to sb** *He preached to thousands of people.* | **preach (sth) on/about sth** *Pastor Young* ***preached a sermon*** *on forgiveness.* **2** [T] to talk about how good or important something is and try to persuade other people about this: *You're always preaching honesty, and then you lie to me.* **3** [I] to give someone advice in a way that they think is boring or annoying: *Mom, stop preaching – I know what I'm doing.* **4 preach to the choir/converted** to talk about what you think is right or important to people who already have the same opinions as you **5 preach the gospel a)** to tell people about Jesus Christ and try to persuade them to follow Christianity **b)** to try to persuade people to accept something that you believe in very strongly: *As he travels he preaches the gospel of creative healthy cooking.* → see also **practice what you preach** at PRACTICE² (5)

preach·er /ˈpritʃɚ/ *n.* [C] someone who gives talks at religious meetings, especially at a church ►see THESAURUS box at **priest**

preach·y /ˈpritʃi/ *adj.* INFORMAL trying too much to persuade people to accept a particular opinion: *The end of your report gets a little preachy.*

pre·am·ble /ˈpriˌæmbəl/ *n.* [C] FORMAL a statement at

the beginning of a book, document, or talk, explaining what it is about: *the preamble to the Constitution*

pre·ar·ranged /ˌpriəˈreɪndʒd◂/ *adj.* if something is prearranged, it is planned before it happens: *The driver met us at the prearranged time.* —**prearrange** *v.* [T] —**prearrangement** *n.* [U]

Pre·cam·bri·an /priˈkæmbriən/ *n.* **the Precambrian** EARTH SCIENCE the very long period of time in the Earth's history from about 4,600 million years ago, when the hard outer surface of the Earth first formed, until about 570 million years ago, when simple forms of life first appeared on the Earth —**Precambrian** *adj.*: *Precambrian rocks*

pre·car·i·ous /prɪˈkɛriəs, -ˈkær-/ *adj.* **1** a precarious situation or state is likely to become very dangerous: *Levin is in a precarious state of health.* | *a precarious peace* **2** likely to fall, or likely to cause someone to fall: *a precarious rope bridge* [**Origin:** 1600–1700 Latin *precarius* **got by asking, uncertain**] —**precariously** *adv.* —**precariousness** *n.* [U]

pre·cast /ˌpriˈkæst◂/ *adj.* precast CONCRETE is already formed into blocks ready for use to make buildings

pre·cau·tion /prɪˈkɔʃən/ *n.* [C usually plural] **1** something you do in order to prevent something dangerous or bad from happening: *All safety precautions must be followed.* | +**against** *Tourists should always* ***take precautions*** *against theft.* | *Residents of the building were evacuated* ***as a precaution.*** | ***I took the precaution of*** *insuring my camera.* | *All* ***safety precautions*** *must be followed.* **2 take precautions** INFORMAL to use something, especially a CONDOM when you have sex, so that you do not become PREGNANT or get a disease

pre·cau·tion·a·ry /prɪˈkɔʃəˌnɛri/ *adj.* done in order to prevent something dangerous or bad from happening: **a precautionary measure/step** *Troops were sent to the area as a precautionary measure.*

pre·cede /prɪˈsid/ Ac *v.* [T] FORMAL **1** to happen or exist before someone or something or to come before something else in a series OPP **follow**: *The fire was preceded by a loud explosion.* **2** to come before someone or something in order or position: *His name precedes mine on the list.* **3** to go somewhere in front of someone else: *The guard preceded them down the hall.*

prec·e·dence /ˈprɛsədəns/ Ac *n.* [U] **1 take/have precedence** to be more important or urgent than someone or something else, and so need to be done first SYN **priority**: *Should environmental protection take precedence over economic development?* **2** the rank or importance of people or things relative to other people or things SYN **importance**: *Guests were seated* ***in order of precedence.***

prec·e·dent /ˈprɛsədənt/ Ac *n.* **1** [C] an action or official decision that can be used to give legal support to later actions or decisions: +**for** *There is no precedent for this.* | **set/create/establish a precedent** *The case set a precedent for civil rights legislation.* **2** [C,U] something of the same type that has happened or existed before: +**for** *There is no precedent for an empire as vast as that of Russia.* | *An epidemic on this scale is* ***without precedent.*** | *He decided to* ***break with precedent*** (=do something in a different way from before) *and have his lunches with his employees.* **3** [C,U] LAW an official decision by a court on which later decisions are based, or the practice of basing legal decision on these: **set/create/establish a precedent** *The case set a precedent for civil rights legislation.*

pre·ced·ing /prɪˈsidɪŋ, ˈprisidɪŋ/ Ac *adj.* [only before noun] FORMAL happening or coming before the time, place, or part mentioned SYN **previous** OPP **following**: *the statement in the preceding paragraph* | *income tax paid in preceding years*

pre·cept /ˈprisɛpt/ *n.* [C] FORMAL a rule on which a way of thinking or behaving is based: *basic moral precepts* | +**of** *the precepts of Islamic law*

pre·cinct /ˈprisɪŋkt/ *n.* **1** [C] POLITICS an area within a town or city that has its own police force, local government representatives etc.: *the 12th Precinct* **2** [C] POLITICS a voting DISTRICT in the U.S., which is the smallest voting area in U.S. elections: *With 99 percent of precincts reporting, Fordice had 359,884 votes.* **3** [C] the main police station in a particular area of a town or city: *The suspect was taken to the 40th precinct in South Bronx.* **4 precincts** [plural] the area that surrounds an important building: *the precincts of the cathedral* [**Origin:** 1400–1500 Medieval Latin *praecinctum*, from Latin *praecingere* **to put a belt around**]

pre·ci·os·i·ty /ˌprɛʃiˈɑsət̬i/ *n.* [U] LITERARY the attitude of being too concerned about style or detail in your writing or speech, so that it sounds unnatural

pre·cious¹ /ˈprɛʃəs/ *adj.* **1** something that is precious is valuable and important and should not be wasted or used without care SYN **valuable**: *Planes delivered precious supplies of medicine and food.* | +**to** *These schools are too precious to the community to close them.* | **precious seconds/minutes/hours/time** *We cannot afford to waste precious time.* **2** precious memories or possessions are important to you because they remind you of people you like or events in your life: *one of my most precious childhood memories* **3** rare and worth a lot of money: **precious jewels/metal/stones** (=valuable jewels, metal etc.) ▶see THESAURUS box at **valuable** **4** too concerned about style or detail in your writing or speech, so that it seems unnatural: *her precious style of writing*

SPOKEN PHRASES

5 used in order to describe someone or something that is small and pretty: *What a precious little baby girl!* **6** [only before noun] said to show that you are annoyed that someone seems to care too much about something: *Apparently I'd ruined her precious towel.* **7** used to speak to someone you love, especially a baby or small child: *Hello, precious!*

[**Origin:** 1200–1300 Old French *precios*, from Latin *pretiosus*, from *pretium* **price, money**] —**preciously** *adv.* —**preciousness** *n.* [U]

precious² *adv.* INFORMAL **precious little/few** very little or very few: *There are precious few seats inside the court room.*

ˌprecious ˈmetal *n.* [C,U] a rare and valuable metal such as gold or silver

ˌprecious ˈstone also **ˌprecious ˈgem** *n.* [C] a rare and valuable jewel such as a DIAMOND or an EMERALD → see also SEMI-PRECIOUS

prec·i·pice /ˈprɛsəpɪs/ *n.* [C] a very steep side of a high rock, mountain, or cliff

pre·cip·i·tant /prɪˈsɪpət̬ənt/ *n.* [C] TECHNICAL something that causes PRECIPITATION

pre·cip·i·tate¹ /prɪˈsɪpəˌteɪt/ *v.* **1** [T] FORMAL to make something serious happen suddenly or more quickly than was expected: *The President's death precipitated a political crisis.* **2** [I,T] CHEMISTRY to separate a solid from a liquid substance either by chemical action or by gravity, or to be separated in this way **3 precipitate sb somewhere** FORMAL to make someone fall down or forward with great force

pre·cip·i·tate² /prɪˈsɪpət̬ɪt, -ˌteɪt/ *n.* [C,U] CHEMISTRY a solid substance that has been chemically separated from a liquid

pre·cip·i·tate³ /prɪˈsɪpət̬ɪt/ *adj.* FORMAL done too quickly, especially without thinking carefully enough —**precipitately** *adv.*

pre·cip·i·ta·tion /prɪˌsɪpəˈteɪʃən/ *n.* **1** [C,U] EARTH SCIENCE rain, snow etc. that falls on the ground, or the amount of rain, snow etc. that falls: *There is a 30% chance of precipitation.* **2** [C,U] CHEMISTRY a chemical process in which a solid substance forms and falls to the bottom of a solution, either because of gravity or because of a chemical reaction **3** [U] FORMAL the act of doing something too quickly in a way that is not sensible

pre·cip·i·tous /prɪˈsɪpət̬əs/ *adj.* **1** a precipitous change is sudden and bad: *a precipitous drop in property values* **2** a precipitous action or event happens too quickly and is not well planned: *a precipitous decision* **3** dangerously high or steep: *A precipitous path led down the cliff.* —**precipitously** *adv.* —**precipitousness** *n.* [U]

pré·cis /ˈpreɪsi/ *n. plural* **précis** /-siz/ [C] ENG. LANG. ARTS a statement that gives the main idea of a piece of writing, speech etc. —**précis** *v.* [T]

pre·cise /prɪˈsaɪs/ Ac *adj.* **1** precise details, costs, measurements etc. are exact: *There is no precise method of measuring intelligence.* | +**about** *It's difficult to be precise about the number of deaths caused by smoking.* **2** [only before noun] used to emphasize that you are talking about an exact thing SYN **exact**: *At that precise moment, the telephone rang.* **3 to be precise** used to show that you are giving more exact details relating to something you have just said: *He was born in April – on the 4th to be precise.* **4** someone who is precise is very careful about small details or about the way they behave [**Origin:** 1500–1600 French *précis*, from Latin *praecisus*, from *praecidere* **to cut off**] —**preciseness** *n.* [U]

pre·cise·ly /prɪˈsaɪsli/ Ac W3 *adv.* **1** exactly: *We arrived at the hotel at precisely 10:30.* | **precisely what/how/where etc.** *Nick can't remember precisely what he said to her.* **2** used to emphasize that a particular thing is completely true, correct, or important SYN **just**: *She's precisely the kind of person we're looking for.* | *Most of the movie's fans like it* ***precisely because*** *it is so violent.* **3** SPOKEN used to say that you agree completely with someone: *"So it was Clark's mistake." "Precisely."*

pre·ci·sion¹ /prɪˈsɪʒən/ Ac *n.* [U] the quality of being very exact: *The work is done* ***with*** *consistency and* ***precision.***

precision² Ac *adj.* [only before noun] **1** made or done in a very exact way: *Golf is a precision sport.* **2** a precision tool or instrument is used for making or measuring something in a very exact way

pre·clude /prɪˈklud/ *v.* [T] FORMAL to prevent something or make something impossible: **preclude sb from doing sth** *Age does not preclude him from running for office.* —**preclusion** /prɪˈkluʒən/ *n.* [U]

pre·co·cious /prɪˈkoʊʃəs/ *adj.* a precocious child behaves like an adult in some ways, for example by asking difficult and intelligent questions [**Origin:** 1600–1700 Latin *praecox* **becoming ripe early**, from *coquere* **to cook, ripen**] —**precociously** *adv.* —**precociousness** *n.* [U]

pre·cog·ni·tion /ˌprikɑgˈnɪʃən/ *n.* [U] FORMAL the knowledge that something will happen before it does

ˌpre-coˈlonial *adj.* relating to or happening before a place was COLONIZED

pre-Co·lum·bi·an /ˌpri kəˈlʌmbiən/ *adj.* relating to or happening before 1492, when Christopher Columbus came to the Americas: *pre-Columbian Indian cultures*

pre·con·ceived /ˌprikənˈsivd◂/ *adj.* [only before noun] DISAPPROVING preconceived ideas, opinions etc. are formed before you really have enough knowledge or experience, so that they are often wrong: *Karl had a lot of* ***preconceived notions*** *about Americans.*

pre·con·cep·tion /ˌprikənˈsɛpʃən/ *n.* [C] a belief or opinion that you have already formed before you know the actual facts: +**about/of** *Everyone has certain preconceptions of who a drug addict is.*

pre·con·di·tion /ˌprikənˈdɪʃən/ *n.* [C] something that must happen or exist before something else can happen: +**of/for** *The tests are a precondition for high school graduation.*

pre·cooked /ˌpriˈkʊkt◂/ *adj.* precooked food has been partly or completely cooked at an earlier time so that it can be quickly heated up later —**precook** *v.* [T]

pre·cur·sor /ˈpriˌkɚsɚ, prɪˈkɚsɚ/ *n.* [C] FORMAL something that happened or existed before something else and influenced its development: +**of/to** *The instrument is a precursor of the guitar.* | *the precursor to the CIA*

pre·date /priˈdeɪt/ *v.* [T] to have happened or existed earlier in history than something else: *Stone knives predate bows and arrows.* → see also ANTEDATE, BACKDATE, POSTDATE

pre·da·tion /prɪˈdeɪʃən/ *n.* [U] BIOLOGY the general process of one living thing catching and feeding on another: *Predation can have far-reaching effects on biological communities.* → see also PREDATOR, PREY

pred·a·tor /ˈprɛdət̬ɚ/ *n.* [C] **1** BIOLOGY an animal that kills and eats other animals **2** someone who tries to use another person's weakness to get advantages

ˌpredator-ˈprey reˌlationship *n.* [C] BIOLOGY the relationship that exists between two types of living thing, when one type catches and feeds on the other

pred·a·to·ry /ˈprɛdəˌtɔri/ *adj.* **1** BIOLOGY a predatory animal kills and eats other animals for food **2** trying to use someone's weakness to get advantages for yourself: *predatory sales practices*

ˌpredatory ˈpricing *n.* [U] ECONOMICS the practice of selling a product or service for less than the cost of producing it. Companies do this with the intention of getting rid of other similar products in the market before then raising the price of their own product.

pre·dawn /ˌpriˈdɔn◂/ *adj.* relating to or happening before the sun rises: *a predawn police raid*

pre·de·cease /ˌpridɪˈsis/ *v.* [T] FORMAL to die before someone else

pred·e·ces·sor /ˈprɛdəˌsɛsɚ/ *n.* [C] **1** someone who had your job before you started doing it OPP **successor**: **sb's predecessor** *She has been a more aggressive CEO than her predecessor.* **2** a machine, system etc. that existed before another one in a process of development OPP **successor**: **sth's predecessor** *The new model has a more powerful engine than its predecessor.*

pre·des·ti·na·tion /ˌpridɛstəˈneɪʃən/ *n.* [U] **1** the belief that God or FATE has decided everything that will happen and that people cannot change this **2** the belief in some Christian churches that God decided before the beginning of the world who would be saved and go to heaven and who would not

pre·des·tined /priˈdɛstɪnd/ *adj.* something that is predestined is certain to happen because it has been decided by God or FATE: **predestined to do sth** *He's a man who seems predestined to die lonely.* —**predestine** *v.* [I,T]

pre·de·ter·mined /ˌpridɪˈtɚmɪnd/ *adj.* FORMAL decided or arranged before something happens, so that it does not happen by chance: **a predetermined level/limit/amount etc.** *Costs must be kept within predetermined limits.* —**predetermination** /ˌpridɪˌtɚməˈneɪʃən/ *n.* [U]

pre·de·ter·min·er /ˌpridɪˈtɚmənɚ/ *n.* [C] ENG. LANG. ARTS in grammar, a special kind of DETERMINER that is used before other determiners such as "the," "that," or "his." In the phrases "all the boys" and "both his parents," the words "all" and "both" are predeterminers.

pre·dic·a·ment /prɪˈdɪkəmənt/ *n.* [C] a difficult or bad situation in which you do not know what to do, or in which you have to make a difficult choice: *Almost everyone who owns a house is* ***in the same predicament.***

pred·i·cate¹ /ˈprɛdɪkɪt/ *n.* [C] ENG. LANG. ARTS in grammar, the part of a sentence that has the main verb, and that tells what the subject is doing or describes the subject. In the sentence "He ran out of the house," "ran out of the house" is the predicate. → see also SUBJECT

pred·i·cate² /ˈprɛdɪˌkeɪt/ *v.* [T] FORMAL **be predicated on/upon sth** to be based on something as the reason for doing something else: *The company's budget was predicated on selling 10,000 subscriptions.*

pred·i·ca·tive /ˈprɛdɪkət̬ɪv, -ˌkeɪt̬ɪv/ *adj.* ENG. LANG. ARTS a predicative adjective or phrase comes after a verb, for example "happy" in the sentence "She is happy." —**predicatively** *adv.*

pre·dict /prɪˈdɪkt/ Ac W2 *v.* [T] to say that something will happen before it happens: *The newspapers are predicting a close election.* | **predict (that)** *We predict that student numbers will double in the next ten years* | **predict whether/what/how etc.** *It's almost impossible* *to predict when or where a tornado will occur.* | **sth is predicted to do sth** *Unemployment is predicted to decrease by the end of the year.* [**Origin:** 1500–1600 Latin, past participle of *praedicere* **to say beforehand**]

THESAURUS

prophesy/foretell to use religious or magical knowledge to say what will happen in the future: *The priestess at Delphi prophesied that Laius would be killed by his own son.* | *It was foretold the boy would marry the king's daughter.*
forecast to say what is likely to happen in the future, based on information you have: *Sales are forecast to rise.*
foresee to know that something will happen before it happens: *No one could have foreseen what happened next.*
have a premonition to have a feeling that something bad is about to happen: *He had a premonition of impending danger.*

P

pre·dict·a·ble /prɪˈdɪktəbəl/ Ac *adj.* **1** if the result of something is predictable, you know what it will be before it happens OPP **unpredictable**: *The snow had a predictable effect on traffic.* **2** behaving or happening in the way that you expect, especially when this seems boring or annoying OPP **unpredictable**: *Horror movies can be so predictable.* —**predictably** *adv.* [sentence adverb] —**predictability** /prɪˌdɪktəˈbɪləṭi/ *n.* [U]

pre·dic·tion /prɪˈdɪkʃən/ Ac *n.* [C,U] something that you say is going to happen, or the act of saying what you think is going to happen: +**about** *I'd rather not **make a prediction** about how popular the book will be.* | +**that** *His prediction that their marriage wouldn't last was correct.* | +**for** *profit predictions for next year* | +**of** *predictions of climate change* —**predictive** *adj.*

pre·di·gest·ed /ˌpridɪˈdʒɛstɪd◂/ *adj.* predigested information etc. has been put in a simple form and explained so that it is easy to understand

pred·i·lec·tion /ˌprɛdlˈɛkʃən, ˌprid-/ *n.* [C] FORMAL if you have a predilection for something, especially something unusual, you like it very much

pre·dis·posed /ˌpridɪˈspoʊzd/ *adj.* tending to behave in a particular way, or to have a particular health problem: **predispose sb to sth** *Some women are genetically predisposed to breast cancer.* | **predispose sb to do sth** *attitudes and opinions which predispose people to behave in certain ways*

pre·dis·po·si·tion /ˌpridɪspəˈzɪʃən/ *n.* [C] a tendency to behave in a particular way or suffer from a particular illness: +**to/toward** *a predisposition to alcoholism* | **a predisposition to sth** *a predisposition to develop the disease*

pre·dom·i·nance /prɪˈdɑmənəns/ Ac *n.* **1** [singular] if there is a predominance of one type of person or thing in a group, there are more of that type than of any other type: +**of** *the predominance of boys in the class* **2** [U] someone or something that has predominance has the most power or importance in a particular group or area: *Japan's predominance in the world of finance*

pre·dom·i·nant /prɪˈdɑmənənt/ Ac *adj.* more powerful, more common, or more easily noticed than others: *The problem is predominant in men.* | *the predominant views of Victorian society*

pre·dom·i·nant·ly /prɪˈdɑmənəntli/ Ac *adv.* mostly or mainly: *a predominantly middle-class neighborhood* | *The economy is based predominantly on agriculture.*

pre·dom·i·nate /prɪˈdɑməˌneɪt/ Ac *v.* [I] **1** to be more important or powerful than anyone or anything else: *This is a district where Democrats predominate.* **2** to be greater in number or amount than any others: *Before 1860, buffalo predominated in the Great Plains.*

pree·mie /ˈprimi/ *n.* [C] INFORMAL a PREMATURE (=born too early) baby

pre·em·i·nent, **pre-eminent** /priˈɛmənənt/ *adj.* much more important, more powerful, or much better than any others: *preeminent members of the community* —**preeminently** *adv.* —**preeminence** *n.* [U]

pre·empt /priˈɛmpt/ *v.* [T] to make what someone has planned to do or say unnecessary or ineffective by doing or saying something else first: *The deal preempted a strike by city employees.* [**Origin:** 1800–1900 *preemption* (17–21 centuries), from Medieval Latin *praeemere* **to buy before**] —**preemption** /priˈɛmpʃən/ *n.* [U]

pre·emp·tive /priˈɛmptɪv/ *adj.* a preemptive action is done to harm someone else before they can harm you, or to prevent something bad from happening: **a preemptive strike/attack/move etc.** *Planes bombed the area in a preemptive strike.* —**preemptively** *adv.*

preen /prin/ *v.* [I,T] **1** if a bird preens or preens itself, it cleans itself and makes its feathers smooth using its beak **2** also **preen yourself** to look proud because of something you have done **3** also **preen yourself** to spend a lot of time in front of a mirror making yourself look neater and more attractive

pre·ex·ist·ing /ˌpriɪgˈzɪstɪŋ◂/ *adj.* FORMAL existing before something else: *The bill made changes to a preexisting law.* | ***a pre-existing** medical **condition*** (=a medical condition that you have before you take out an insurance policy) —**pre-exist** *v.* [I,T]

pre·fab /ˈprifæb/ *n.* [C] INFORMAL a small prefabricated building —**prefab** *adj.*

pre·fab·ri·cat·ed /priˈfæbrəˌkeɪṭɪd/ *adj.* built from parts made in standard sizes in a factory, so that they can be put together somewhere else: *prefabricated houses* —**prefabricate** *v.* [T] —**prefabrication** /priˌfæbrəˈkeɪʃən/ *n.* [U]

pref·ace¹ /ˈprɛfɪs/ *n.* [C] an introduction at the beginning of a book or speech

preface² *v.* [T] FORMAL to say or do something before the main part of what you are going to say: *Al-Hosni prefaced his speech with a phrase from the Koran.*

pref·a·to·ry /ˈprɛfəˌtɔri/ *adj.* FORMAL forming a preface or introduction: *The chairman made a few prefatory remarks.*

pre·fect /ˈprifɛkt/ *n.* [C] a public official in France, Italy etc. who is responsible for a particular area

pre·fec·ture /ˈprifɛktʃɚ/ *n.* [C] a large area which has its own local government in France, Italy, Japan etc.

pre·fer /prɪˈfɚ/ S2 W2 *v.* **preferred, preferring** [T not in progressive] **1** to like someone or something more than someone or something else, so that you would choose it if you could: *Which color do you prefer – blue or red?* | **prefer sb/sth to sb/sth** *I prefer turkey to chicken.* | **prefer to do sth** *Mom prefers to rent movies and watch them at home.* | **prefer doing sth** *John prefers having morning meetings.* | **sb (would) prefer that** *We would prefer that the details of the crime are not made public yet.* | *Marsha **would prefer** giving birth at home, rather than at the hospital.* **2 I would prefer it if** SPOKEN **a)** used when telling someone politely not to do something: *I'd prefer it if you would not insult my friends.* **b)** used to say that you wish a situation was different: *I would prefer it if we had a bigger house, but we can't afford it.* [**Origin:** 1300–1400 French *préférer*, from Latin *praeferre* **to put in front, prefer**]

pref·er·a·ble /ˈprɛfərəbəl/ *adj.* better or more appropriate: *For this dish, fresh herbs are preferable.* | **preferable to (doing) sth** *Full-time work is definitely preferable to part-time work.*

pref·er·a·bly /ˈprɛfərəbli/ *adv.* used in order to show which person, thing, place, or idea you think would be the best choice: *You should see a doctor, preferably a specialist.*

pref·er·ence /ˈprɛfrəns, -fərəns/ *n.* **1** [C,U] a feeling of liking or wanting someone or something more than another person or thing: +**for** *Many children showed a preference for junk food.* | **have a/any preference** *You choose the one you want. I don't have any preference.* | **have a preference for sb/sth** *Brad has a preference for athletic women.* | **show/express a preference** *Many* *elderly people expressed a strong preference for living in their own homes.* | **a strong/clear preference** *One of the children expressed a strong preference to live with his father.* | **have no strong/particular preference** (=not prefer one thing more than anything else) | *Both methods are effective. It's really a matter of* ***personal preference*** *which you choose.* | *You can list up to five choices,* ***in order of preference*** (=starting with the one you most prefer first, then the next etc.). **2 sb's preference** a person or thing that someone prefers: *My preference would be to start the whole process from the beginning again.* **3 give/show preference to sb** to treat someone more favorably than you treat other people: *In allocating housing, preference was shown to families with young children.* **4 in preference to sth** if you choose one thing in preference to another, you choose it because you think it is better: *I pay with credit cards in preference to cash.*

pref·er·en·tial /ˌprɛfəˈrɛnʃəl◂ / *adj.* [only before noun] preferential treatment, rates etc. are deliberately better for particular people in order to give them an advantage: *Bank officials denied giving the senator any* ***preferential treatment.*** —**preferentially** *adv.*

pre·fer·ment /prɪˈfɚmənt/ *n.* [U] FORMAL the act of getting a more important job

preˌferred ˈstock also **ˈpreference ˌstock** *n.* [C,U] ECONOMICS STOCK on which a company promises to pay a yearly DIVIDEND (=share of the company's profit) even if the company is doing badly and cannot pay a dividend on its other stock → see also COMMON STOCK

pre·fig·ure /ˌpriˈfɪgyɚ/ *v.* [T] FORMAL to be a sign that shows that something will happen later —**prefiguration** /priˌfɪgyəˈreɪʃən/ *n.* [C,U]

pre·fix¹ /ˈpriˌfɪks/ *n.* [C] **1** ENG. LANG. ARTS a group of letters that is added to the beginning of a word to change its meaning and make a new word, such as "un" in "untie" or "mis" in "misunderstand" → see also AFFIX, SUFFIX **2** the first group of numbers in a telephone number **3** a title such as "Ms." or "Dr." used before someone's name [**Origin:** 1600–1700 Modern Latin *praefixum*, from Latin *praefigere* **to fasten before**]

prefix² *v.* [T] **1** ENG. LANG. ARTS to add a prefix to a word, name, or set of numbers **2** FORMAL to say something before the main part of what you have to say SYN **preface**

pre·game /ˈprigeɪm/ *adj.* happening before a game of football, basketball, baseball etc.: *the pregame show* —**pregame** *n.* [C]

preg·nan·cy /ˈprɛgnənsi/ *n. plural* **pregnancies** [C,U] BIOLOGY the condition of being pregnant, or the period of time when a woman is pregnant: *It's harmful to drink alcohol during pregnancy.* | *teenage pregnancies*

preg·nant /ˈprɛgnənt/ S2 W3 *adj.* **1** BIOLOGY if a woman or female animal is pregnant, she has an unborn baby growing inside her: *When did you find out you were pregnant?* | **+with** *My wife was pregnant with our son.* | **six weeks/four months etc. pregnant** *I think she's only three months pregnant.* | **heavily/very pregnant** (=very close to giving birth) | **get/become pregnant** *I got pregnant when I was only 19.* | **get sb pregnant** (=used to say that a man makes a woman pregnant, when this is not wanted or acceptable) **2 a pregnant pause/silence** a pause or silence that is full of meaning or emotion, even though no one says anything **3 pregnant with sth** FORMAL containing a lot of a quality or feeling: *His voice was pregnant with contempt.* [**Origin:** 1400–1500 Latin *praegnans*, from *praegnas*, from *prae-* **before** + *gnatus* **born**]

pre·heat /priˈhit/ *v.* [T] to heat an OVEN to a particular temperature before it is used to cook something: **preheat sth to sth** *Preheat the oven to 375°.*

pre·hen·sile /priˈhɛnsəl/ *adj.* BIOLOGY a prehensile tail, foot etc. can curl around things and hold on to them

pre·his·tor·ic /ˌprihɪˈstɔrɪk◂ / *adj.* relating to the time in history before anything was written down: *prehistoric cave drawings* —**prehistorically** /-kli/ *adv.*

pre·his·to·ry /ˌpriˈhɪstəri/ *n.* [U] the time in history before anything was written down

pre·im·age /ˈprɪˌɪmɪdʒ/ *n.* [C] MATH a GEOMETRIC figure before it is changed in some way, for example by turning it

pre·judge /ˌpriˈdʒʌdʒ/ *v.* [T] to form an opinion about someone or something before you know or have considered all the facts: *I'm not going to prejudge those decisions.* —**prejudgment** *n.* [C,U]

prej·u·dice¹ /ˈprɛdʒədɪs/ *n.* **1** [C,U] an unreasonable dislike of people who are different from you in some way, especially because of their race, sex, religion etc.: **+against** *There is still a lot of prejudice against gays and lesbians.* | **racial/sexual/religious prejudice** (=prejudice against people who belong to a different race, sex, or religion)

THESAURUS

Types of prejudice

racism unfair treatment of people because they belong to a different race: *Some immigrant groups faced racism, for example Jews and Italians, while others, such as Scandinavians, did not.*

discrimination the practice of treating one group of people differently from another in an unfair way: *Discrimination in hiring people for jobs is illegal.*

intolerance the fact of not being willing to accept ways of thinking or behaving that are different from your own: *religious intolerance*

anti-Semitism a strong feeling of hatred toward Jewish people: *Is anti-Semitism on the rise in America and Europe?*

bigotry the behavior and beliefs of someone who has such strong opinions about race, religion, or politics that he or she will not listen to anyone else's opinion: *In the 1930s, bigotry against immigrants increased.*

sexism unfair attitudes and behavior based on the belief that women are weaker, less intelligent, and less important than men: *The armed forces have worked to reduce sexism in their policies.*

People who are prejudiced

racist: *When he expressed his opinion, he was branded a racist.*

bigot someone who has strong unreasonable opinions, especially about race or religion: *his reputation as a bigot*

sexist someone who believes that women are weaker, less intelligent, and less important than men: *Her boss is a sexist.*

2 [U] FORMAL or TECHNICAL harmful effects on something, for example on the results of a legal case: *He was able to refuse the job* ***without prejudice*** (=without it harming his chances of getting the job at another time). [**Origin:** 1200–1300 Old French, Latin *praejudicium*, from *judicium* **judgment**]

prejudice² *v.* [T] **1** to influence someone so that they have an unfair or unreasonable opinion about someone or something: **prejudice sb against sb/sth** *He tried to prejudice the jury against Davis.* **2** LAW to have a bad effect on your opportunities, chances etc. of succeeding in doing something: *A criminal record will prejudice your chances of getting a job.*

prej·u·diced /ˈprɛdʒədɪst/ *adj.* having an unfair feeling of dislike for someone or something, especially someone who is different because they belong to a different race, sex, or religion etc.: **+against** *He denies that he is prejudiced against women.* | *Some of the older employees are prejudiced against using email.*

prej·u·di·cial /ˌprɛdʒəˈdɪʃəl/ *adj.* FORMAL having a bad effect on something, especially by causing people to have an opinion that is not fair or balanced

prel·ate /ˈprɛlət/ *n.* [C] TECHNICAL a BISHOP, CARDINAL, or other important priest in some Christian churches

pre·lim /ˈprilɪm/ *n.* [C usually plural] INFORMAL a PRELIMINARY

pre·lim·i·nar·y¹ /prɪˈlɪməˌnɛri/ Ac *adj.* happening before something that is more important, often in order to prepare for it: *a preliminary report on the causes of the accident* | +**to** *The discussions were preliminary to writing the policy paper.*

preliminary² Ac *n. plural* **preliminaries** [C] **1** something that is done first, to introduce or prepare for something else: *They decided to adopt a child and went through all the preliminaries.* | +**to** *The test is a preliminary to the interview.* **2** [usually plural] the first part of a competition, when it is decided who will go on to the main competition: *the women's 400-meter preliminaries*

P

pre·lit·er·ate /ˌpriˈlɪt̬ərət◂/ *adj.* TECHNICAL a society that is preliterate has not developed a written language → see also ILLITERATE

prel·ude /ˈpreɪlud, ˈprɛlyud/ *n.* [C] **1 be a prelude to sth** to happen just before an important event and make people expect the important event: +**to** *Some analysts see the violence as a prelude to civil war.* **2** ENG. LANG. ARTS a short piece of music at the beginning of a large musical piece **3** ENG. LANG. ARTS a short piece played before a church service → see also POSTLUDE **4** ENG. LANG. ARTS a short piece of music for piano or ORGAN: *Chopin's preludes*

pre·mar·i·tal /priˈmærət̬l/ *adj.* happening or existing before marriage: *premarital sex* —**premaritally** *adv.*

pre·ma·ture /ˌpriməˈtʃʊr◂, -ˈtʊr◂/ *adj.* **1** happening before the natural or appropriate time: *premature deaths caused by smoking* **2** BIOLOGY a premature baby is born before the usual time of birth: *a premature birth* | *The baby was six weeks premature.* **3** done too early or too soon: **it is premature to do sth** *It would be premature to make a decision before all the information comes in.* —**prematurely** *adv.*

pre·med /ˌpriˈmɛd/ *n.* INFORMAL **1** [C] a student who is taking classes that will prepare them for medical school in the U.S. **2** [U] a course of study that prepares students for medical school: *He was in his second year of premed.* | *premed classes*

pre·med·i·cal /priˈmɛdɪkəl/ *adj.* [only before noun] relating to classes that prepare a student for medical school

pre·med·i·tat·ed /priˈmɛdəˌteɪt̬ɪd/ *adj.* a premeditated action, especially a crime, is planned before it happens and done deliberately: *a premeditated murder*

pre·med·i·ta·tion /priˌmɛdəˈteɪʃən/ *n.* [U] the act of thinking about something and planning it before you actually do it

pre·men·strual /priˈmɛnstrəl/ *adj.* BIOLOGY happening just before a woman's PERIOD (=monthly flow of blood)

pre,menstrual 'syndrome *n.* [U] FORMAL → see PMS

pre·mier¹ /prɪˈmɪr, -ˈmyɪr, ˈprimɪr/ *n.* [C] **1** a PRIME MINISTER **2** the chief official and leader of government in a Canadian province **3** the chief official and leader of government in an Australian state

premier² *adj.* FORMAL [only before noun] best or most important: *one of New York's premier hotels*

pre·miere, première /prɪˈmɪr, prəˈmyɛr/ *n.* [C] the first public performance of a movie, play etc.: +**of** *the premiere of Pixar's latest animated film* | *The opera had its* ***world premiere*** (=the first performance in the world) *in March.* —**premiere** *v.* [I,T] → see also SEASON PREMIERE

pre·mier·ship /prɪˈmɪrʃɪp/ *n.* [C,U] POLITICS the period when someone is PRIME MINISTER

prem·ise /ˈprɛmɪs/ *n.* [C] **1** a statement or idea that you accept as true and use as a base for developing other ideas: *a false premise* | **the premise that** *the premise that drug addiction can be cured* | **the premise of sth** *The premise of the novel is that there is life on other planets.* **2 premises** [plural] the buildings and land that a store, restaurant, company etc. uses: *A religious group rents the premises on weekends.* | *Smoking is not allowed* ***on the premises.*** | *The man was escorted* ***off the premises.***

pre·mi·um¹ /ˈprimiəm/ *n.* **1** [C] an amount of money that you pay for something such as insurance: *car insurance premiums* **2** [U] HIGH-OCTANE (=very good quality) gasoline **3 at a premium a)** if something is at a premium, there is little of it available or it is difficult to get: *Hotel rooms are at a premium during the summer.* **b)** if something is sold at a premium, it is sold at a higher price than usual because a lot of people want it **4 put/place a premium on sth** to consider one thing or quality as being much more important than others: *Modern economies place a premium on educated workers.* **5** [C] ECONOMICS an additional amount of money, above a standard rate or amount: *Our customers are willing to* ***pay a premium*** *to get a better Internet connection.*

premium² *adj.* **1** of very high quality: *premium-quality wine* | *The cable company offers both standard and premium services.* **2 a premium price/rate** a price or rate that is much higher than usual

pre·mo·ni·tion /ˌpriməˈnɪʃən, ˌprɛ-/ *n.* [C] a strange feeling that cannot be explained that something, especially something bad, is going to happen: *She* ***had a premonition*** *that something bad would happen.* | +**of** *a premonition of death*

pre·mon·i·to·ry /prɪˈmɑnəˌtɔri/ *adj.* FORMAL giving a warning that something bad is going to happen: *premonitory symptoms of the disease*

pre·na·tal /ˌpriˈneɪt̬l◂/ *adj.* [only before noun] TECHNICAL relating to unborn babies and the care of PREGNANT women: *prenatal care* → see also POSTNATAL

pre·nup·ti·al a·gree·ment /priˌnʌptʃəl əˈgrimənt/ *n.* [C] a legal document that is written before a man and a woman get married, in which they agree to things such as how much money each will get if they DIVORCE

pre·oc·cu·pa·tion /priˌɑkyəˈpeɪʃən/ *n.* **1** [singular, U] the condition of being preoccupied: +**with** *Our society has a preoccupation with getting things done quickly.* **2** [C] something that you give all your attention to: *Their main preoccupation was how to feed their families.*

pre·oc·cu·pied /priˈɑkyəˌpaɪd/ *adj.* thinking or worrying about something a lot, with the result that you do not pay attention to other things: +**with** *The governor has been preoccupied with budget battles.*

pre·oc·cu·py /priˈɑkyəˌpaɪ/ *v.* **preoccupies, preoccupied, preoccupying** [T] if something preoccupies someone, they think or worry about it a lot

pre-op /ˌpriˈɑp◂/ *adj.* INFORMAL preoperative

pre·op·er·a·tive /priˈɑpərət̬ɪv/ *adj.* TECHNICAL relating to the time before a medical operation → see also POSTOPERATIVE

pre·or·dained /ˌpriɔrˈdeɪnd/ *adj.* [not before noun] FORMAL if something is preordained, it is certain to happen in the future because God or FATE has decided it

pre-owned /ˌpriˈoʊnd◂/ *adj.* a word meaning having been previously owned by someone else, used especially as a nice way of saying that something is USED: *pre-owned cars*

prep¹ /prɛp/ *v.* **prepped, prepping** INFORMAL **1** [T] to prepare someone for an operation, examination etc. **2** [I] to prepare for something you will do: *I have to prep for my afternoon class.* **3** [T] to prepare food for cooking in a restaurant

prep² *n.* [C] the written abbreviation of PREPOSITION

pre·pack·aged /ˌpriˈpækɪdʒd◂/ also **pre·packed** /ˌpriˈpækt◂/ *adj.* **1** prepackaged food or other goods are already wrapped and are sold ready to use: *prepackaged salads* **2** DISAPPROVING something which is prepackaged has been designed and planned, and is then used in many different situations without being changed to fit them: *prepackaged ideas about how to fix the economy*

pre·paid /ˌpriˈpeɪd◂/ *adj.* if something is prepaid, it is paid for before it is needed or used: *The shipping charges are prepaid.* | *a prepaid envelope* (=one with a stamp already on it)

prep·a·ra·tion /ˌprɛpəˈreɪʃən/ W3 *n.* **1** [U] the act or process of preparing something: +**for** *I think this game* *was good preparation for the play-offs.* | +**of** *the need for thorough preparation of the sales staff* | *He is practicing every day* ***in preparation for*** (=in order to prepare for) *the race.* | *Plans for the new school are now* ***in preparation.*** **2** [U] the process of getting food ready to eat: *Salads don't need much preparation.* | +**of** *spices used in the preparation of Indian food* **3 preparations** [plural] arrangements for something that is going to happen: +**for** ***Preparations*** *for the upcoming Olympic Games* ***are underway*** (=happening now). | ***Preparations*** *are being* ***made for*** *the President's visit.* **4** [singular, U] something that makes you ready to deal with something else: +**for** *School should be a good preparation for life.* **5** [C] a mixture that has been prepared for a particular purpose, especially a medicine, COSMETIC, or food

pre·par·a·to·ry /prɪˈpærəˌtɔri, -ˈpɛr-, ˈprɛprə-/ *adj.* **1** [only before noun] done in order to get ready for something: *preparatory work on the construction site* **2 preparatory to sth** FORMAL before something else and in order to prepare for it: *The partners held several meetings preparatory to signing the agreement.*

preˈparatory school *n.* [C] a PREP SCHOOL

pre·pare /prɪˈpɛr/ S2 W1 *v.* **1** [I,T] to get ready to do something or deal with something, for example by making plans and arrangements: *I didn't have much time to prepare.* | *The prosecution is still preparing their case.* | **prepare for sth** *The Roman army was preparing for war.* | **prepare to do sth** *Kenny has spent months preparing to take the entrance exam.* | **prepare yourself (for sth)** *I took a few moments to prepare myself before going out on stage.*

THESAURUS

get sth ready: *I've been getting everything ready for the party.*
set sth up to make a piece of equipment ready to be used: *Kim's setting up the computer in the meeting room.*
make preparations to prepare for an important event: *They began to make preparations for the birth of the baby.*

2 [T] to make food: *It took me all day to prepare the dinner.* ►see THESAURUS box at **cook**[1] **3** [T] to decide what information will be in a report, speech, plan etc. and write it down: *Prepare a list of the things that you will need.* | **prepare sth for sb/sth** *I haven't prepared my report for the meeting yet.* **4** [T] to provide someone with the training, skills, experience etc. that they will need to do something or to deal with a bad situation: **prepare sb for sth** *The class prepares students for English exams.* | **prepare sb to do sth** *His training had prepared him to deal with this type of emergency.* **5** [T] to make something ready to be used: **prepare sth for sb/sth** *They are preparing two new satellites for launch.* **6 prepare the way/ground for sth** to make it possible for something to be achieved, or for someone to succeed in doing something: *The Secretary of State's visits prepared the way for peace negotiations.* [**Origin:** 1400–1500 French *préparer*, from Latin *praeparare*, from *parare* **to get, prepare**]

pre·pared /prɪˈpɛrd/ *adj.* **1** [not before noun] ready to do something or to deal with a situation: +**for** *Professor Robbins never seems prepared for class.* | **well/badly/poorly etc. prepared** *The city was poorly prepared to deal with the storm.* | *There was no news and we were* ***prepared for the worst*** (=expecting that something very bad may have happened). **2 be prepared to do sth** to be willing to do something: *How much are they prepared to pay?* | *Nobody was prepared to argue with him.* | *I'm* ***not prepared to*** (=used to say strongly that you are unwilling to do something) *let them take my business without a fight.* **3** [not before noun] arranged and ready to be used: *The dining room is all prepared for our guests.* | *I'll need a few minutes to* ***get*** *everything* ***prepared.*** **4** a prepared speech, statement etc. has already been written or planned at an earlier time: *His lawyer read out a prepared statement.* **5** prepared food is ready to eat, used especially about food that you buy in a store: *a store selling quality prepared foods*

pre·par·ed·ness /prɪˈpɛrɪdnɪs/ *n.* [U] the state of being ready for something: *the country's lack of military preparedness*

pre·pay /priˈpeɪ/ *v.* [I,T] to pay for something before it is needed or used: *If you prepay, the cost of the lunch is only $15.*

pre·pon·der·ance /prɪˈpɑndərəns/ *n.* FORMAL **1 a preponderance of sb/sth** if there is a preponderance of people or things of a particular type in a group, there are more of that type than of any others **2 a preponderance of evidence** LAW a phrase meaning most of the EVIDENCE (=facts and statements) used in a law case shows that one fact is true, but not all of it

pre·pon·der·ant /prɪˈpɑndərənt/ *adj.* FORMAL main or most important —**preponderantly** *adv.*

prep·o·si·tion /ˌprɛpəˈzɪʃən/ *n.* [C] ENG. LANG. ARTS in grammar, a word that is used before a noun, PRONOUN, or GERUND to show place, time, direction etc. In the phrase "a tree in the park," "in" is a preposition. —**prepositional** *adj.* —**prepositionally** *adv.*

ˌprepositional ˈphrase *n.* [C] ENG. LANG. ARTS a phrase consisting of a preposition and the noun, PRONOUN, or GERUND following it, such as "in bed" or "about traveling"

pre·pos·sess·ing /ˌpripəˈzɛsɪŋ◂/ *adj.* FORMAL looking attractive or pleasant

pre·pos·ter·ous /prɪˈpɑstərəs/ *adj.* FORMAL completely unreasonable or silly SYN **absurd**: *a preposterous excuse* [**Origin:** 1500–1600 Latin *praeposterus* **with the back part in front**] —**preposterously** *adv.* —**preposterousness** *n.* [U]

prep·py /ˈprɛpi/ *adj.* INFORMAL preppy clothes or styles are very neat, in a way that is typical of students who go to expensive private schools in the U.S.

ˈprep school *n.* [C] INFORMAL a private school that prepares students for college

pre·pu·bes·cent /ˌpripyuˈbɛsənt◂/ *adj.* FORMAL relating to the time just before a child reaches PUBERTY

pre·quel /ˈprikwəl/ *n.* [C] a book, movie, television program etc. that tells you what happened before the story that has already been told in a popular book or movie

Pre-Raph·a·el·ite /priˈræfeɪəˌlaɪt/ *n.* [C] a member of a group of late 19th-century English painters and artists —**Pre-Raphaelite** *adj.*

pre·re·cord /ˌpririˈkɔrd/ *v.* [T] to record a message, music, a radio program etc. on a machine so that it can be used later —**prerecorded** *adj.*: *a prerecorded message* —**prerecording** *n.* [C,U]

pre·reg·is·ter /priˈrɛdʒɪstɚ/ *v.* [I] to put your name on a list for a particular class, school etc. before the official time to do so —**preregistered** *adj.* —**preregistration** /ˌprirɛdʒɪˈstreɪʃən/ *n.* [U]

pre·req·ui·site /priˈrɛkwəzɪt/ *n.* [C] FORMAL something that is necessary before something else can happen or be done: +**for/to/of** *Good writing skills are a prerequisite for the job.*

pre·rog·a·tive /prɪˈrɑgət̬ɪv/ *n.* [C usually singular] a right that someone has, especially because of their importance or position: **have the prerogative to do sth** *Congress has the prerogative to raise taxes.* | *If you want to leave early,* ***that's your prerogative*** (=used to say that someone has the right to do something, often when you think they should not do it).

pres. **1** the written abbreviation of PRESENT **2 Pres.** the written abbreviation of PRESIDENT

pres·age /ˈprɛsɪdʒ, prɪˈseɪdʒ/ *v.* [T] FORMAL to be a warning or a sign that something is going to happen, especially something bad: *Recent small earthquakes may presage a much larger one.* —**presage** /ˈprɛsɪdʒ/ *n.* [C]

Pres·by·te·ri·an /ˌprɛzbəˈtɪriən, ˌprɛs-/ *n.* [C] a member of the Presbyterian Church —**Presbyterian** *adj.* —**Presbyterianism** *n.* [U]

P

Pres·by·te·ri·ans /ˌprɛzbəˈtɪriənz, ˌprɛs-/ *n.* [plural] a Protestant Christian group that is one of the largest churches in the U.S. and the national church of Scotland

pres·by·ter·y /ˈprɛzbəˌtɛri/ *n.* [C] **1** a local court or council of the Presbyterian church, or the area controlled by that church **2** a house in which a Catholic priest lives **3** the eastern part of a church, behind the area where the CHOIR (=trained singers) sits

pre·school¹ /ˈpriskul/ *n.* [C] a school for young children between three and five years of age, where they learn such things as numbers, colors, and letters SYN nursery school

preschool², pre-school *adj.* relating to the time in a child's life before they are old enough to go to school: *preschool children*

pre·school·er, pre-schooler /ˈpriˌskulɚ/ *n.* [C] a child who does not yet go to school, or one who goes to PRESCHOOL

pre·sci·ent /ˈprɛʃiənt, -ʃənt/ *adj.* FORMAL able to imagine or know what will happen in the future —**prescience** *n.* [U]

pre·scribe /prɪˈskraɪb/ *v.* [T] **1** to officially say what medicine or treatment a sick person should have: **prescribe sth for sb/sth** *Doctors commonly prescribe steroids for children with asthma.* **2** to state officially what someone can and cannot do, or what should be done in a particular situation: *Four years is the minimum jail sentence that federal law prescribes.* [**Origin:** 1400–1500 Latin *praescribere* **to write at the beginning, order**]

pre·scribed /prɪˈskraɪbd/ *adj.* decided by a rule: *the school district's prescribed curriculum*

pre·script /ˈpriˌskrɪpt/ *n.* [C] FORMAL an official order or rule

pre·scrip·tion /prɪˈskrɪpʃən/ *n.* **1** [C] a piece of paper on which a doctor writes what medicine a sick person should have, so that they can get it from a PHARMACIST: *I have to **get this prescription filled*** (=get the medicine that is described in the prescription). **2** [C] a particular medicine or treatment ordered by a doctor for a sick person: *free prescriptions for older people* **3** [C usually singular] an idea or suggestion about how to make a situation, activity etc. successful: **+for** *What's your prescription for a happy marriage?* **4** [U] the act of prescribing a medicine or drug: *the prescription of antibiotics* | *The drug is only available **by prescription*** (=can only be obtained with a written order from a doctor).

pre'scription drug *n.* [C] a type of medicine that you can only get by having a prescription from your doctor

pre·scrip·tive /prɪˈskrɪptɪv/ *adj.* **1** FORMAL stating or ordering how something should be done or what someone should do: *prescriptive teaching methods* **2** TECHNICAL stating how a language should be used, rather than describing how it is used: *prescriptive grammar* —**prescriptively** *adv.*

pre·sea·son /ˌpriˈsizən◂/ *adj.* relating to the time before the beginning of the time of year when a sport is regularly played: *preseason injuries* —**preseason** *n.* [singular] → see also POSTSEASON

pres·ence /ˈprɛzəns/ W2 *n.*
1 IN A PLACE [U] the fact that someone or something is in a place OPP absence: *He didn't seem to be aware of my presence.* | **+of** *The group protested the presence of foreign troops in the country.* | *Tests revealed the presence of poison in her blood.* | *The document was signed **in the presence of** a lawyer* (=while a lawyer is there).
2 APPEARANCE/MANNER [singular, U] the ability to appear impressive to people because of your appearance or the way you behave: *The African dancers have a powerful stage presence.*
3 OFFICIAL GROUP [singular] an official group of people from another country, an army, or the police, who are in a place to watch and influence what is happening: **a military/police presence** *There was a strong police presence at the march.*
4 BUSINESS [singular, U] the fact of a company being noticeable in a particular place, in a way that is good for business: *The sale gives the airline a greater presence in the Northeast.*
5 make your presence felt to have a strong and noticeable effect on the people around you or the situation you are in: *She made her presence felt in her first day on the job.*
6 SPIRIT [C usually singular] a spirit or influence that cannot be seen, but is felt to be near: *an evil presence*

ˌpresence of 'mind *n.* [U] the ability to deal with a dangerous situation calmly and quickly: *Bill **had the presence of mind to** call 911 when the fire got out of control.*

pres·ent¹ /ˈprɛzənt/ S2 W2 *adj.* **1** [not before noun] in a particular place or event, or existing in a particular place OPP absent: *Lead and mercury are present in the drinking water.* | *A feeling of sadness was present in the room.* | *Copies were given to all the members present.* **2** [only before noun] happening or existing now: *the present economic climate* | *Cancer cannot be cured **at the present time**.*

> **THESAURUS**
> **current** happening, existing, or being used now: *What is your current address?*
> **existing** present now and available to be used: *The proposal will strengthen existing immigration laws.*

3 the present day FORMAL the period of history in which we are now living SYN now: *Traditional Indian pottery designs are still used in the present day.* **4 all present and accounted for** used to say that everyone who is supposed to be in a place, at a meeting etc. is now here **5 present company excepted** SPOKEN used when you are saying something bad or impolite about a group of people, in order to tell the people you are with that you do not mean to include them in the statement: *All men are selfish pigs – present company excepted.* → see also PRESENTLY, PRESENT TENSE

pre·sent² /priˈzɛnt/ S2 W2 *v.*
1 GIVE [T] to give something to someone, especially at a formal or official occasion: *The Golden Globe Awards will be presented January 18.* | **present sb with sth** *Captain Dave Schilling presented Patrick with a commendation from the fire department.* | **present sth to sb** *The Princess presented the awards to the winners.* ► see THESAURUS box at give¹
2 INFORMATION/PRODUCT [T] to show something to people or tell them about it for the first time: *The prosecution has now finished presenting its case.* | **present sth to sb** *The report will be presented to the board this week.*
3 INFORMATION [T] to offer or show information about something in a particular way: *All of the following data is presented in metric tons.*
4 THEATER/TELEVISION [T] to give a performance in a theater etc., or broadcast it on television or radio: *The Roxy is presenting a production of "Waiting for Godot" this weekend.*
5 CAUSE STH TO HAPPEN [T] to cause something to happen or exist: **present a problem/difficulty/opportunity etc. (for sb)** *Heavy rains have presented new difficulties for relief workers.* | **present sb with a problem/difficulty/opportunity etc.** *Suddenly I was presented with an opportunity I couldn't ignore.*
6 APPEARANCE [T] to give something or someone a particular appearance or quality: *Restaurants take care to present their food with style.*
7 DESCRIBE STH IN A PARTICULAR WAY [T] to describe or show something in a particular way, especially in order to influence people or make them believe something about it: *How can I present the story so they'll believe me?* | **present sb/sth as sth** *Almost every media story presented these ideas as fact.* | *John **presented himself as** a conservative Republican.*
8 DOCUMENT/TICKET [T] FORMAL to show something such as an official document or ticket to someone in an official position: **present sth to sb** *He presented his passport to the customs official.*

9 **sth presents itself** if a situation, opportunity etc. presents itself, it suddenly happens or exists: *I'm sure a solution will present itself.*
10 **INTRODUCE SB** [T] FORMAL to introduce someone formally, especially to someone important: *May I present my parents, Mr. and Mrs. Benning?*
11 **ARRIVE present yourself** FORMAL if you present yourself at a place, you arrive there and tell someone that you have come: *He presented himself at the Marine base in Virginia.*
12 **present arms** a command to soldiers to hold their weapons upright in front of their bodies as a greeting to someone important
13 **present your apologies/compliments etc.** FORMAL used to express your feelings in a very formal way to someone
14 **ILLNESS** [I] TECHNICAL if an illness presents or a patient presents with particular SYMPTOMS, the patient shows symptoms of the illness

pres•ent[3] /ˈprɛzənt/ S2 W3 *n.* **1** [C] something you give someone on a special occasion SYN **gift**: **+for** *a present for my aunt* | **+from** *The knife was a present from his father.* | **a birthday/Christmas/anniversary present** (=something that you give someone on their birthday, at Christmas etc.) | *He **gave** her lots of **presents** for her birthday.* **2 the present a)** the time that is happening now: *the history of France from the Renaissance to the present* **b)** ENG. LANG. ARTS the form of a verb that shows what exists or is happening now **3 at (the) present** FORMAL at this time SYN **now**: *We have no plans at the present for closing the factory.* **4 for the present** FORMAL now and for a short or unknown time in the future: *For the present, most people are keeping their jobs.* **5 there's no time like the present** used to say that if you are going to do something, you should do it now: *There's no time like the present to change your eating habits.*

pre•sent•a•ble /prɪˈzɛntəbəl/ *adj.* neat and attractive enough to be seen or shown to someone: *At least **make yourself presentable** before you go out.* —**presentably** *adv.*

pres•en•ta•tion /ˌprizənˈteɪʃən, ˌprɛ-/ S2 *n.*
1 GIVE PRIZE [C] the act of giving someone a prize or present at a formal ceremony: **+of** *the presentation of the awards* | *The chairman **made a presentation** to the winner.*
2 SPEECH [C] a formal talk about a particular subject: *Our presentation was followed by a question and answer session.* | *Walters **gave a presentation on** ancient Korean art.* ►see THESAURUS box at **speech**
3 SAYING/SHOWING a) [U] the act of showing something to people or telling them about it officially: **+of** *the presentation of the annual budget* **b)** [C,U] the way in which something is said, offered, shown, explained etc. to others: *When serving a meal, presentation is almost as important as taste.*
4 DOCUMENT/TICKET [C,U] the act of showing someone an official document, ticket etc., so that it can be checked or considered: *The card is issued **upon presentation of** proof of U.S. citizenship.*
5 PERFORMANCE [C] ENG. LANG. ARTS the act of performing something in front of a group of people or on television, radio etc.: **+of** *a new presentation of Shakespeare's "Romeo and Juliet"*
6 BABY [C,U] BIOLOGY the position in which a baby is lying in its mother's body just before it is born —**presentational** *adj.*

presenˈtation ˌcopy *n.* [C] a book that is given to someone by the writer or PUBLISHER

ˈpresent-day *adj.* [only before noun] modern or existing now: *The colonists settled near present-day Charleston.*

pre•sen•tenc•ing /ˌpriˈsɛntˀnsɪŋ/ *adj.* [only before noun] happening before someone receives their SENTENCE (=punishment) in a court of law: *a presentencing hearing*

pre•sent•er /prɪˈzɛntɚ/ *n.* [C] someone who gives a speech or who officially gives a prize or present to someone

pre•sen•ti•ment /prɪˈzɛntəmənt/ *n.* [C] FORMAL a strange and uncomfortable feeling that something is going to happen: **+of** *a presentiment of danger*

pres•ent•ly /ˈprɛzəntli/ *adv.* FORMAL **1** at this time SYN **now** SYN **currently**: *The university presently operates two cancer research centers.* | *Presently, I am unemployed.* ►see THESAURUS box at **now**[1] **2** OLD-FASHIONED in a short time SYN **soon**: *Tea will be served presently.*

ˌpresent ˈparticiple *n.* [C] ENG. LANG. ARTS a PARTICIPLE that is formed in English by adding "ing" to the verb, as in "sleeping." It can be used in COMPOUND forms of the verb to show PROGRESSIVE or CONTINUOUS tenses, as in "She's sleeping," or as an adjective, as in "the sleeping child."

ˌpresent ˈperfect *n.* **the present perfect (tense)** ENG. LANG. ARTS the form of a verb that shows what happened during the period of time up to and including the present, which is formed in English with the present tense of the verb "have" and a PAST PARTICIPLE. In the sentence "Tina has seen the movie twice," "has seen" is in the present perfect.

ˌpresent ˈtense *n.* **the present tense** ENG. LANG. ARTS the form of a verb that shows what is true, what exists, or what happens at the present time. In the sentence "James works for a computer company," "works" is in the present tense.

pres•er•va•tion /ˌprɛzɚˈveɪʃən/ *n.* [U] **1** the act of keeping something unharmed or unchanged: *wildlife preservation* | **+of** *the preservation of native cultures* **2** the degree to which something has remained unchanged or unharmed by weather, age etc.: *Ironically, the older buildings were in a much better **state of preservation**.* → see also SELF-PRESERVATION

pres•er•va•tion•ist /ˌprɛzɚˈveɪʃənɪst/ *n.* [C] someone who works to prevent historical places, buildings etc. from being destroyed

pre•serv•a•tive /prɪˈzɚvət̬ɪv/ *n.* [C,U] a chemical substance that prevents food or wood from decaying

pre•serve[1] /prɪˈzɚv/ W3 *v.* [T] **1** to save something from being harmed or destroyed: *We want to preserve as much open land as possible.* ►see THESAURUS box at **protect** **2** to make something continue without changing: *The island wants to preserve its independence.* **3** to treat food in a special way so that it can be stored for a long time without decaying: *Here's a recipe for preserving fruit in brandy.* **4 preserve sb from sth** to protect someone from something bad or embarrassing: *He was determined to preserve her from harm.* [**Origin:** 1300–1400 French *préserver*, from Latin *servare* **to keep, guard, watch**] → see also WELL-PRESERVED —**preservable** *adj.*

preserve[2] *n.* **1** [C] an area of land or water in which animals, fish, or trees are protected: *a nature preserve* **2** [singular] an activity that only one particular group of people can do, or a place that only those people can use: **+of** *The sport was once the preserve of the wealthy.* **3** [C,U] also **preserves** [plural] a sweet substance such as JAM made from boiling large pieces of fruit with sugar: *a jar of strawberry preserves*

pre•set /ˌpriˈsɛt◂/ *adj.* [usually before noun] decided or set at an earlier time: *The oven will come on at a preset time.* —**preset** *v.* [T]

pre•shrunk /ˌpriˈʃrʌŋk◂/ *adj.* preshrunk clothes are sold after they have been made smaller by being washed: *preshrunk jeans*

pre•side /prɪˈzaɪd/ *v.* [I] to be in charge of an important event, organization, ceremony etc.: *Judge Richter is presiding in the case.* | **+at/over** *Queen Elizabeth II presided at the state dinner held Tuesday.*

preside over sth *phr. v.* **1** to be in a position of authority at a time when important things happen: *It was Prime Minister Yoshida who presided over Japan's post-war economic boom.* **2** to be officially in charge of an organization

pres•i•den•cy /ˈprɛzədənsi/ W3 *n. plural* **presidencies** [C] **1** the job or office of president: *He needs 57*

P

votes to ***win the presidency*** *of the company.* **2** the period of time for which a person is president: *the first year of Bush's presidency*

pres·i·dent /ˈprɛzədənt/ S2 W1 *n.* [C] **1** the official leader of government, in some countries: *Truman became President when Roosevelt died.* | *President Lincoln* | +**of** *the President of Mexico* | *He* ***was elected President*** *in 1996.* **2** someone who is in charge of a business, bank, club, university etc.: +**of** *the president of General Motors* [**Origin:** 1300–1400 French *président*, from Latin, present participle of *praesidere* **to sit in front of, guard, preside over**] → see also VICE PRESIDENT

P

ˌpresident-eˈlect *n.* [singular] someone who has been elected as a new president, but who has not yet started the job

pres·i·den·tial /ˌprɛzəˈdɛnʃəl◂/ W1 *adj.* [usually before noun] **1** relating to a president, or done by a president: *presidential candidates* | *a presidential proclamation* | **a presidential election/campaign** *the 2000 presidential elections* **2** like a president: *He doesn't seem very presidential.*

ˌpresidential ˈprimary *n.* [C] POLITICS in the U.S., an election in which members of a political party in one area vote to decide who will be the party's CANDIDATE for president: **a Republican/Democratic presidential primary** | *the upcoming presidential primaries* (=those happening soon) → see also BLANKET PRIMARY

ˌPresident of the ˈSenate *n.* [C] POLITICS SENATE PRESIDENT

ˌpresident pro ˈtempore also **ˌpresident pro ˈtem** *n. plural* **presidents pro tempore** [C usually singular] POLITICS a member of the U.S. SENATE who is elected by other SENATORS to be in control of the Senate's meetings when the VICE PRESIDENT is not there

ˈPresidents' Day *n.* a U.S. holiday on the third Monday in February to remember the BIRTHDAYS of George Washington and Abraham Lincoln

preˈsiding ˌofficer *n.* [C] POLITICS the person who is officially in charge of controlling the meetings in the U.S. SENATE or the HOUSE OF REPRESENTATIVES. In the Senate, the presiding officer is the SENATE PRESIDENT or the PRESIDENT PRO TEMPORE, and in the House of Representatives, it is SPEAKER OF THE HOUSE.

pre·sid·i·um, praesidium /prɪˈsɪdiəm, -ˈzɪ-/ *n.* [C] POLITICS a committee chosen to represent a large political organization, especially in a COMMUNIST country

Pres·ley /ˈprɛzli/**, El·vis** /ˈɛlvɪs/ (1935–1977) a U.S. singer and GUITAR player, who first became popular as a ROCK 'N' ROLL singer in the mid–1950s, and became one of the most successful and popular singers ever

press¹ /prɛs/ S2 W2 *v.*
1 PUSH AGAINST [I, T always + adv./prep.] to push against a surface, or push someone or something firmly against a surface: +**against/down/on** *People pressed against us from all sides.* | **press sth into/against/to/on sth** *His hands pressed down on both her shoulders.* | *Andy pressed the cool glass to his forehead.* | *Their tiny faces were pressed against the window.*
2 WITH FINGER [T] to push something, especially with your finger, in order to make a machine start, a bell ring etc.: *The pilot pressed a switch on the control panel.* | *Which key do I press to save?*
3 IRON [T] to make clothes smooth using heat SYN **iron**: *I'm not going to press those shirts for you.*
4 TRY TO PERSUADE [I,T] to try hard to persuade someone to do something or tell you something: *I knew that if I pressed him he'd lend me the money.* | +**for** *Employees are pressing for better pay and benefits.* | **press sb on/about sth** *When pressed on the point, the mayor offered no explanation.* | **press sb for sth** *She didn't say much when we pressed her for more details.* | **press sb to do sth** *Both leaders are being pressed to agree quickly on the new treaty.* | **press sb into doing sth** *Alvin had pressed him into teaching at the school.*
5 press charges (against sb) to say officially that someone has done something illegal and must go to court: *Davis refused to press charges against her husband.*
6 HEAVY WEIGHT [T] to put pressure or weight on something to make it flat, crush it etc.: *The crop is then gathered and the grapes are pressed.*

THESAURUS

squash to press something and damage it by making it flat: *The bread got squashed at the bottom of the grocery bag.*
crush to press something very hard so that it is broken or destroyed: *His leg was crushed in the accident.*
mash to press fruit or cooked vegetables until they are soft and smooth: *Mash the potatoes with some milk and butter.*
grind to press something into powder using a special machine: *The flour used to be ground between these two circular stones.*
squeeze to press something from both sides, usually with your fingers, so that a liquid comes out: *Squeeze the toothpaste tube from the bottom.* | *fresh-squeezed orange juice*

7 MOVE [I, T always + adv./prep.] to move in a particular direction by pushing SYN **push**: *Kate* ***pressed forward*** *through the crowd to take her place.* | **press your way through/across etc. sth** *A group of police officers pressed their way through the crowd.*
8 KEEP SAYING/ASKING [T] to continue to say something or ask for something, because you want to make people accept what you are saying: **press a demand/claim/case** *The President was determined to press his case for war.* | *It was not the right time for an argument, so Alex didn't* ***press the point*** (=keep talking about it).
9 press sb's hand/arm to hold someone's hand or arm tightly for a short time, to show friendship, sympathy etc.
10 EXERCISE [T] to push a weight up from your chest without moving your legs or feet SYN **bench press**: *How much can you press?*
11 press sb/sth into service/duty to persuade someone to help you, or to use something to help you do something, because of an unexpected problem or need: *The National Guard was pressed into service to help fight forest fires.*
12 press sth home to repeat or emphasize something, so that people remember it: *The data presses home our point.*
13 press the flesh HUMOROUS if a politician or other famous person presses the flesh, they shake hands with a lot of people
14 RECORD [T] to make a CD, record etc., especially in large numbers in a factory → see also PRESSED

press ahead/on *phr. v.* to continue doing something in a determined way: *We've decided to ignore the setbacks and press on.* | +**with** *The government plans to press ahead with its nuclear program.*

press² W2 *n.*
1 NEWSPAPERS the press [singular] all the organizations, especially newspapers, that provide news and information for the public, or the people who report the stories: *freedom of the press* | *Taylor refuses to speak to the press.* | *The case has been widely reported* ***in the press.*** | **the tabloid/popular/local etc. press** *The tabloid press seized on the scandal.* | *a press photographer* (=who takes photographs for newspapers etc.) | *I don't think the* ***press coverage*** (=the way something is reported by the press) *has been very objective.* | *The editors, citing* ***freedom of the press,*** *refused to pay fines.*
2 PRINTING [C] **a)** a machine that prints books, newspapers, or magazines SYN **printing press b)** a business that prints and sometimes also sells books: *Wesleyan University Press*
3 get good/bad press to be praised or criticized in reports in the newspapers or on television or the radio: *They expected to get some good press for donating the land.*
4 go to press if a newspaper, magazine, or book goes to press, it begins to be printed: *The explosion happened just before the newspaper went to press.*
5 MACHINE [C] a piece of equipment used to put weight

on something in order to make it flat or to force liquid out of it: *a wine press* | *Put the garlic through a press.*
6 PUSH [singular] a light steady push against something small: *The box opens with the press of a button.*
7 CROWD [singular] a crowd of people pushing against each other: *He made his way through the press of people.*
8 RESPONSIBILITY [singular] FORMAL the fact of having a lot of difficult things to do in a short time: **+of** *the press of government business*
9 EXERCISE [C] an exercise in which you push a weight up from your chest without moving your legs or feet, or a piece of equipment you use to do this: *a bench press*
[**Origin:** 1300–1400 Old French *presser*, from Latin *pressare*, from *premere* **to press**] → see also FULL-COURT PRESS, **stop the presses** at STOP[1] (11)

'press ,agency *n.* [C] a NEWS AGENCY

'press ,agent *n.* [C] someone whose job is to supply information or photographs about a particular actor, musician etc. to newspapers, television, or radio

'press box *n.* [C] an enclosed area at a sports ground used by people from newspapers, television, or radio

'press ,clipping *n.* [C usually plural] a short piece of writing or a picture, cut out from a newspaper or magazine

'press ,conference *n.* [C] a NEWS CONFERENCE

'press corps *n.* [C] a group of news reporters working at the same place where something important is happening: *the White House press corps*

pressed /prɛst/ *adj.* **be pressed for time/money etc.** to not have enough time, money etc.: *Frozen dinners are great when you're pressed for time.* → see also HARD-PRESSED

'press ,gallery *n.* [C] an area where news reporters sit, above or at the back of a court of law, Congress, or similar place

press·ing[1] /'prɛsɪŋ/ *adj.* very important and needing to be dealt with immediately SYN **urgent**: *a pressing need for medical supplies* | *Survival is the most pressing concern of any new company.*

pressing[2] *n.* [C] a number of CDs or records made at one time

press·man /'prɛsmən/ *n. plural* **pressmen** /-mən/ [C] INFORMAL someone who writes news reports

'press ,office *n.* [C] the office of an organization or government department which gives information to the newspapers, television, or radio —**press officer** *n.* [C]

'press re,lease *n.* [C] an official statement giving information to the newspapers, television, or radio: *Woodward's attorney said she would* ***issue a press release*** *within a week.*

'press ,secretary *n.* [C] someone who works for an important organization or person and gives information about them to the newspapers, television, or radio

pres·sure[1] /'prɛʃɚ/ S2 W1 *n.*
1 ATTEMPT TO PERSUADE [U] an attempt to persuade someone by using influence, arguments, or threats: **+for** *the pressure for governmental reform* | **+from** *The committee was set up in response to pressure from local people.* | **pressure to do sth** *So far, she has resisted pressure to tell her story to the newspapers.* | *Teachers are* ***under*** *a lot of* ***pressure*** *to improve test scores.* | *His parents have been* ***putting pressure on*** *him to find a job.*
2 ANXIETY [C,U] a way of working or living that causes you a lot of anxiety, especially because you feel you have too many things to do SYN **stress**: *I just can't take the pressure at work anymore.* | **+on** *Students have enough pressure on them as it is.* | **+of** *the pressures of daily deadlines at the newspaper office* | *He performs best* ***under pressure***.
3 INFLUENCE [C,U] events or conditions that cause changes and affect the way a situation develops, especially in economics or politics: *Inflationary pressures will lead to higher prices.* | *The industry is* ***coming under pressure*** *from foreign competition.*
4 WEIGHT [U] the force or weight that is being put on

something: *To stop the bleeding,* ***put pressure*** *directly* ***on*** *the wound* (=push on the wound with your hands or a substance).
5 GAS/LIQUID [U] PHYSICS the force that is produced when gas or liquid is held tightly inside a container: **air/water pressure** *Check the air pressure in your car tires on a regular basis.*
6 WEATHER [C,U] the downward force caused by the weight of the Earth's ATMOSPHERE, which affects the weather: **high/low/rising/falling pressure** | *an area of high pressure* → see also BLOOD PRESSURE, HIGH-PRESSURE

pressure[2] *v.* [T] to try to make someone do something by making them feel it is their duty to do it: **pressure sb to do sth** *They were pressuring me to sell the land.* | **pressure sb into doing sth** *Don't let yourself be pressured into signing anything.* ►see THESAURUS box at **force**[2]

P

'pressure ,cooker *n.* [C] **1** a tightly covered cooking pot in which food is cooked very quickly by the pressure of hot steam **2** a situation or place which causes anxiety or difficulties: *a financial pressure cooker*

pres·sured /'prɛʃɚd/ *adj.* feeling worried because of the number of things you have to do: *I've been feeling pretty pressured at work recently.*

'pressure group *n.* [C] a group or organization that tries to influence the opinions of ordinary people and persuade the government to do something: *environmental pressure groups* → see also INTEREST GROUP

'pressure point *n.* [C] **1** BIOLOGY a point on the body where an ARTERY (=a tube that carries blood) that runs near a bone can be pressed and closed off, to stop blood loss **2** BIOLOGY a place on the body that is MASSAGED or used in treatments such as REFLEXOLOGY or ACUPUNCTURE **3** a place or situation that may involve trouble or problems: *a pressure point for racial tension*

pres·sur·ize /'prɛʃə,raɪz/ *v.* [T usually passive] to keep air or another gas or liquid at a controlled pressure: *The bottles are filled with gas and then pressurized.* —**pressurized** *adj.* —**pressurization** /,prɛʃərə'zeɪʃən/ *n.*

pres·tige /prɛ'stiʒ, -'stidʒ/ *n.* [U] the respect and importance that a person, organization, or profession has, because of their high position in society or the quality of their work: *The job has a certain amount of prestige attached to it.* [**Origin:** 1600–1700 French **deceiving or magic tricks, prestige**, from Latin *praestigiae* **magic tricks**]

pres·tig·ious /prɛ'stɪdʒəs, -'sti-/ *adj.* admired as one of the best and most important: *a prestigious university*

pres·to[1] /'prɛstoʊ/ also **presto-change-o** /,prɛstoʊ 'tʃeɪndʒoʊ/ *interjection* said when something happens so suddenly that it seems hard to believe or seems magical: *You fold it like this and presto! It turns into a hat.*

presto[2] *adj., adv.* ENG. LANG. ARTS played or sung very quickly

pre·sum·a·bly /prɪ'zuməbli/ Ac *adv.* [sentence adverb] used to say that you think something is likely to be true: *It's raining, so presumably the game will be canceled.*

pre·sume /prɪ'zum/ Ac *v.* [T] **1** to think that something is likely to be true, although you are not certain SYN **assume**: *You have your own car, I presume.* | **presume (that)** *I presume you haven't told anyone else about this.* | **be presumed to do sth** *The killers are presumed to have fled to Mexico.* **2** LAW to accept something as true until it is proven to be untrue, especially in law: **be presumed (to be) innocent/dead/guilty** *She is missing and presumed dead.* **3** FORMAL to behave without respect or politeness by doing something that you have no right to do: **presume to do sth** *I would never presume to tell you what you should do.* **4** [usually in present tense] FORMAL to depend on something that is expected to be true SYN **presuppose**: **presume that** *The curriculum presumes that students already have a working knowledge of German.* [**Origin:** 1300–1400

French *présumer*, from Latin *praesumere*, from *sumere* **to take**]

pre·sump·tion /prɪˈzʌmpʃən/ Ac *n.* **1** [C] something that someone thinks is probably true, although they do not know for certain: +**of** *the presumption of a steady rise in home values* | **presumption that** *There is a presumption that parents always want the best for their children.* **2** [C,U] LAW the act of accepting something as true, until it is proven to be untrue: *the presumption of innocence* **3** [U] FORMAL behavior that is not respectful or polite, and that shows you are too confident

P

pre·sump·tive /prɪˈzʌmptɪv/ *adj.* FORMAL or TECHNICAL based on a reasonable belief about what is likely to happen or be true: *a presumptive diagnosis* —**presumptively** *adv.*

pre·sump·tu·ous /prɪˈzʌmptʃuəs/ Ac *adj.* doing something you have no right to do, because of a lack of respect or politeness: +**of** *It would be presumptuous of me to speak on behalf of my colleagues.* —**presumptuousness** *n.* [U]

pre·sup·pose /ˌprisəˈpoʊz/ *v.* [T usually in present tense] FORMAL to depend or be based on a fact that may not be true or a situation that may not exist: **presuppose (that)** *The manual presupposes that the reader is already fairly computer-literate.* —**presupposition** /priˌsʌpəˈzɪʃən/ *n.* [C,U]

pre·tax /ˌpriˈtæks◂ / *adj.* considered before taxes have been calculated or paid: *a pretax profit of $1.4 million* —**pretax** *adv.*

pre·teen /ˌpriˈtin◂ / *adj.* [only before noun] relating to, or made for children who are 11 or 12 years old: *preteen girls* | *preteen fashions* —**preteen** /ˈpritin/ *n.* [C]

pre·tend¹ /prɪˈtɛnd/ S2 W3 *v.* **1** [I,T] to behave as if something is true when you know that it is not: *He's not asleep – he's just pretending.* | **pretend (that)** *We can't just go on pretending that everything is OK.* | **pretend to be** *Rose didn't even pretend to be interested.* | **pretend to do sth** *She picked up a newspaper and pretended to read it.* **2** [T usually in negatives] to claim that something is true when it is not: **pretend to do sth** *I can't pretend to understand all the technical terms* (=I admit I do not understand it). | **pretend (that)** *I won't pretend it was easy to do.* **3** [I,T] to imagine something is true or real, as a game: **pretend (that)** *Let's pretend we live in a cave!* [**Origin:** 1300–1400 Latin *praetendere* **to stretch out in front, make an excuse**]

pretend² *adj.* a word meaning "imaginary," used especially by or with children: *It's not a real gun – it's a pretend one.*

pre·tend·ed /prɪˈtɛndɪd/ *adj.* false or unreal, although seeming to be true or real: *a pretended suicide attempt*

pre·tend·er /prɪˈtɛndɚ/ *n.* [C] **1** someone who claims a right to be king, leader etc., that many people do not accept: +**to** *a pretender to the English throne* **2** someone who pretends to be or do something

pre·tense /ˈpritɛns, prɪˈtɛns/ *n.* [singular U] **1** an attempt to pretend that something is true: **pretense that** *Whiting has abandoned the pretense that* (=has stopped pretending that) *she wrote the book alone.* | *He* ***made no pretense*** *about his motives.* | *Eric moved in with his girlfriend* ***under the pretense of*** *wanting to save money.* **2 have/make no pretense to (doing) sth** FORMAL to not claim that you have a particular quality, skill etc.: *He made no pretense to superiority.* → see also **under false pretenses** at FALSE (6)

pre·ten·sion /prɪˈtɛnʃən/ *n.* [C,U] an attempt to seem more important, more intelligent, of a higher social class etc. than you really are: *Part of his charm lies in his complete lack of pretension.* | +**to** *The musical comedy has few pretensions to high art.* | **literary/social/artistic pretensions** *a publication with literary pretensions*

pre·ten·tious /prɪˈtɛnʃəs/ *adj.* trying to seem more important, more intelligent etc. than you really are OPP **unpretentious**: *a pretentious movie* —**pretentiously** *adv.* —**pretentiousness** *n.* [U]

pret·er·ite, preterit /ˈprɛtərɪt/ *n.* **the preterite** ENG. LANG ARTS the PAST TENSE —**preterite** *adj.*

pre·term /ˌpriˈtɚm◂ / *adj., adv.* happening before the time that a baby is expected to be born: *a preterm delivery*

pre·ter·nat·u·ral /ˌpritɚˈnætʃərəl◂ / *adj.* FORMAL **1** beyond what is usual or normal SYN **extraordinary**: *The story emphasizes the heroine's preternatural beauty.* **2** strange, mysterious, and unnatural: *a preternatural spirit* —**preternaturally** *adv.*

pre·test /ˈpritɛst/ *n.* [C] a test that you take before you have studied something or done an activity to see how much you already know → see also POSTTEST

pre·text /ˈpritɛkst/ *n.* [C] a reason given for an action, used in order to hide your real intentions: +**for** *The incident provided the pretext for war.* | **a pretext to do sth** *They used "poor performance" as a pretext to fire him.* | **on/under the pretext of doing sth** *The thieves enter people's houses under the pretext of making repairs.* | **on/under the pretext that** *His rental car was stopped by police on the pretext that it had a broken tail light.*

Pre·to·ri·a /prɪˈtɔriə/ a city in South Africa which is one of South Africa's three capital cities. The other two are Cape Town and Bloemfontein.

pre·tri·al /ˌpriˈtraɪəl◂ / *adj.* [only before noun] happening before the official TRIAL in a court of law: *a pretrial hearing*

pret·ti·fy /ˈprɪtəˌfaɪ/ *v.* **prettifies, prettified, prettifying** [T] INFORMAL to change something with the intention of making it nicer or more attractive, but often with the effect of spoiling it

pret·ty¹ /ˈprɪti/ S1 W2 *adv.* [+ adj./adv.] INFORMAL **1** fairly, but not completely: *I thought the test was pretty easy.* | *"How are you doing?" "Pretty good."* ►see THESAURUS box at **rather** **2** very SYN **quite**: *Six o'clock? That's pretty early.* **3 pretty much** SPOKEN almost completely: *They're all pretty much the same.* | *"Are you sure you know how to work this?" "Pretty much."* **4 pretty near** SPOKEN almost: *I pretty near froze to death out there.* **5 pretty please** SPOKEN, HUMOROUS said to emphasize that you really want something when you are asking someone for it: *Can I go? Pretty please?* → see also **be sitting pretty** at SIT (9)

pretty² S1 W2 *adj. comparative* **prettier**, *superlative* **prettiest** **1** a pretty woman or girl has a nice attractive face: *a pretty little girl* | *Maria looks much prettier with her hair cut short.* ►see THESAURUS box at **attractive**, **beautiful** **2** pleasant to look at or listen to, without being very beautiful or impressive: *a pretty dress* | *pretty flowers* | *You have a really pretty voice.* **3 not a pretty picture/sight** very bad, upsetting, or worrying: *The plane was completely destroyed – it's not a pretty sight.* **4 pretty as a picture** very pretty **5 not just another/a pretty face** HUMOROUS someone who not only looks attractive, but also has other good qualities or abilities **6** a pretty boy or man looks attractive, but in a way that is more typical of a girl or a woman **7 a pretty boy** a man or boy who is very attractive in a way that is typical of a girl, and who is considered to have succeeded because of his appearance, rather than because of his ability or hard work **8 cost/pay/spend a pretty penny** OLD-FASHIONED to cost, pay etc. a lot of money: *The house cost a pretty penny.* —**prettily** *adv.* —**prettiness** *n.* [U] ► see THESAURUS box at **beautiful**

pretty³ *v.*

pretty sb/sth ↔ **up** *phr. v.* INFORMAL to try to make someone or something look more attractive or acceptable to people: *A bright scarf can pretty up any outfit.*

pret·zel /ˈprɛtsəl/ *n.* [C] a hard salty type of bread baked in the shape of a stick or a loose knot [**Origin:** 1800–1900 German *pretzel, bretzel*, from Latin *brachiatus* **having branches like arms**]

pre·vail /prɪˈveɪl/ *v.* [I] [not in progressive] FORMAL **1** if a person, idea, or principle prevails in a fight or argument, they achieve success in the end: *Justice will* *prevail.* | +**over/against** *The use of force cannot be allowed to prevail over international law.* **2** if a belief, custom, situation etc. prevails, it exists among a group of people or in a certain place: +**in/among etc.** *After the riots, a mood of uncertainty still prevails in the neighborhood.* [**Origin:** 1300–1400 Latin *praevalere*, from *valere* **to be strong**]

prevail on/upon sb *phr. v.* FORMAL to try to persuade someone to do something: **prevail on/upon sb to do sth** *Human rights groups have prevailed upon the governor to intervene.*

pre·vail·ing /prɪˈveɪlɪŋ/ *adj.* [only before noun] **1** existing or accepted in a particular place or at a particular time: *prevailing local customs* **2 a prevailing wind** a wind that blows over a particular area most of the time

prev·a·lent /ˈprɛvələnt/ *adj.* common at a particular time or in a particular place: *Drug abuse is a prevalent problem among the prisoners.* —**prevalence** *n.* [U] *The* ***prevalence of*** *alcoholism among females is estimated to be less than one percent.*

pre·var·i·cate /prɪˈværəˌkeɪt/ *v.* [I] FORMAL to try to hide the truth by not answering questions directly —**prevarication** /prɪˌværəˈkeɪʃən/ *n.* [C,U]

pre·vent /prɪˈvɛnt/ W2 *v.* [T] to do something so that something harmful or bad does not happen: *The rules are intended to prevent accidents.* | **prevent sb/sth from doing sth** *Wrap small ornaments in paper to prevent them from being damaged.* | *We were prevented from entering the site.* [**Origin:** 1400–1500 Latin, past participle of *praevenire* **to come before**] —**preventable** *adj.*: *Smoking is the leading preventable cause of death.*

pre·ven·ta·tive /prɪˈvɛntət̬ɪv/ *adj.* another form of the word PREVENTIVE

pre·ven·tion /prɪˈvɛnʃən/ *n.* [U] the act of preventing something, or the actions that you take in order to prevent something: +**of** *the prevention of cruelty to animals* | **crime/accident/fire prevention** *Effective crime prevention must be our main goal.*

pre·ven·tive /prɪˈvɛntɪv/ also **preventative** *adj.* [only before noun] intended to prevent something that you do not want to happen, such as illness or crime: *preventive health care* (=designed to prevent people from becoming sick) | *Troops were sent to the region as* ***a preventive measure.***

preˌventive deˈtention *n.* [C,U] LAW the act of sending someone to prison when they have been charged with a crime but before their case is judged in a court of law, in order to prevent them becoming involved in more crimes: *Over a thousand so-called "terrorists" remain in preventive detention.*

preˌventive ˈmedicine *n.* [U] MEDICINE medical treatment, advice, and health education that is designed to prevent disease from happening rather than to cure it

pre·view[1] /ˈprivyu/ *n.* [C] **1** an advertisement for a movie or television program that consists of short parts from it to show what it will be like: *There's usually about 15 minutes of previews before the movie.* **2** ENG. LANG. ARTS an occasion when you can see a movie, play etc. before it is shown to the public: +**of** *Previews of the play run this week.* **3** an opportunity to see or experience what something will be like: *Last night's speech provides a preview of the campaign ahead.* → see also SNEAK PREVIEW

preview[2] *v.* [T] **1** to see or watch something before someone else or before the public: *The press will preview the exhibit tomorrow.* **2** to show or perform something before it is shown to or performed for the public

pre·vi·ous /ˈpriviəs/ Ac S3 W2 *adj.* **1** [only before noun] happening or existing before the event, time, or thing that is being mentioned: *They had met briefly on two previous occasions.* | *Andy has two children from a previous marriage.* | *Do you have any* ***previous experience*** *with this type of work?* | **previous offenses/convictions** (=things that a criminal has done, or been judged guilty of, before) ▸see THESAURUS box at **last**[1] **2** coming immediately before another person or thing in a series: *The trees were planted by the previous owner.* | **the previous day/week/year etc.** *I had met them the previous day.* **3 previous to sth** FORMAL before a particular time or event SYN **prior to**: *Previous to 1981 there were no women on the Supreme Court.* [**Origin:** 1600–1700 Latin *praevius* **leading the way**, from *via* **way**]

pre·vi·ous·ly /ˈpriviəsli/ Ac W3 *adv.* before now, or before a particular time: *The robot's work was previously done by three men.* | *a previously unknown drawing by Van Gogh* | **two days/three years etc. previously** *He had returned to Moscow two days previously.*

pre·war, pre-war /ˌpriˈwɔr◂/ *adj., adv.* happening or existing before a war, especially World War II OPP **postwar**: *prewar Poland*

prey[1] /preɪ/ *n.* [U] **1** BIOLOGY an animal that is hunted by another animal or by a person, usually for food: *Snakes track their prey by its scent.* **2 be/fall prey to sth** to be affected by something bad or harmful: *Increasingly, the industry has fallen prey to foreign competition.* **3** someone who can easily be deceived or influenced: *The elderly are* ***easy prey*** *for such con men.* [**Origin:** 1200–1300 Old French *preie*, from Latin *praeda* **something seized**] → see also BIRD OF PREY

prey[2] *v.*

prey on *phr. v.* **1 prey on sb** to try to influence, deceive, or harm weaker people: *Many of the salesmen prey on older people.* **2 prey on sth** if an animal or bird preys on another animal or bird it hunts and eats it: *Cats prey on birds and mice.* **3 prey on sb's mind** to make someone worry continuously: *The accident has been preying on my mind all week.*

prez /prɛz/ *n.* [C] INFORMAL, HUMOROUS a PRESIDENT

price[1] /praɪs/ S1 W1 *n.*

1 MONEY [C,U] the amount of money for which something is sold, bought, or offered: *House prices are beginning to fall again.* | +**of** *the price of gold* | +**for** *We agreed on a price for the bike.* | **raise/increase prices** *The major oil companies raised their prices again last week.* | **cut/reduce prices** *They have cut their prices by almost 30%.* | **a high/low price** *I can't believe how high their prices are!* | **a half/full price** *We got all the furniture for half price.* | *They're selling* ***two*** *bras* ***for the price of one.*** | *There's almost no difference* ***in price*** *between the two rental companies.* | *We're trying to find the right car* ***at the right price.*** | *Recent* ***price cuts*** *have resulted in increased sales.* ▸see THESAURUS box at **cost**[1]

2 SOMETHING BAD [U] something unpleasant that you must accept or experience in order to have or do something that you want: +**of** *He's very busy, but I guess that's the price of success.* | *Travel insurance can be* ***a small price to pay for*** *a vacation without worries.* | *She's gotten the job she wanted, but* ***at what price?*** | *In some countries, reporters* ***pay a high price for*** *doing their job.*

3 at/for a price used to say that you can buy something, but only if you pay a lot of money: *All this modern equipment comes at a price, you know.*

4 put a price (tag) on sth to say how much something costs or is worth: *How can you put a price on a 150-year-old tree?*

5 at any price whatever the cost and difficulties may be: *She's determined to have a child at any price.*

6 not at any price used to say that you would never sell something or do something, even for a lot of money: *Sorry, the car's not for sale at any price.*

7 everyone has their price used to say that you can persuade people to do anything if you give them what they want

8 a price on sb's head a reward for catching or killing someone

9 what price fame/glory etc.? SPOKEN, FORMAL used to suggest that perhaps it was not worth achieving something good, because too many bad things have happened as a result: *As we look at all the pollution, we may ask, what price progress?*

[**Origin:** 1200–1300 Old French *pris*, from Latin *pretium*

price, money] → see also ASKING PRICE, LIST PRICE, MARKET PRICE, **name your price** at NAME² (7), **pay the penalty/price** at PAY¹ (10)

price² [S3] [W3] *v.* [T] **1** [usually in passive] to set the price of something that is for sale: **be reasonably/moderately/competitively priced** *These shoes are pretty reasonably priced.* | **be priced at $10/$50 etc.** *The wine is priced at $15 to $23 per bottle.* **2** to put the price on goods to show how much they cost **3** to compare the prices of things: *I've been pricing new computers.* **4 price yourself out of the market** to demand too much money for the services or goods that you are selling → see also PRICING

'price ,ceiling also **'ceiling price** *n.* [C] ECONOMICS the highest possible price that companies are officially allowed to charge for a product or service [OPP] **price floor**

'price con,trol *n.* [C,U] ECONOMICS a system in which the government sets the prices of things

'price discrimi,nation *n.* [U] ECONOMICS the practice of charging a different price in different areas for the same product or service, usually depending on how much people in each place are willing or able to pay

'price ,fixing *n.* [U] ECONOMICS **1** an illegal agreement between producers and sellers of a product to set its price and make it stay at a high level **2** a system in which the government sets the prices of things

'price floor also **'floor price** *n.* [C] ECONOMICS the lowest possible price that companies are officially allowed to charge for a product or service [OPP] **price ceiling**

'price ,index *n.* [C] ECONOMICS a list of particular goods and services, showing how much their prices change each month, used as a measure of the average increase in the price of goods over a period of time

price·less /'praɪslɪs/ *adj.* **1** so valuable that you cannot calculate a financial value: *priceless works of art* ►see THESAURUS box at **valuable** **2** extremely important or useful: *The ability to motivate people is a priceless asset.* **3** INFORMAL extremely funny or silly: *The look on his face was priceless.*

'price list *n.* [C] a list of prices for things being sold

'price sup,port *n.* [U] ECONOMICS a system in which the government keeps the price of a product at a particular level by giving the producer money or buying the product itself

'price tag *n.* [C] **1** a small ticket showing the price of something **2** the amount that something costs or is worth: *The price tag for the tunnel is $114 million.*

'price war *n.* [C] a situation in which companies that are providing a similar product or service compete against each other very strongly by continuously reducing the price of their products, because each company is trying to get the most customers

pric·ey, pricy /'praɪsi/ *adj.* *comparative* **pricier**, *superlative* **priciest** INFORMAL expensive: *The food's great, but it's a little pricey.*

pric·ing /'praɪsɪŋ/ *n.* [U] the act or result of deciding the price of something you sell: *competitive pricing*

prick¹ /prɪk/ *v.* [T] **1** to make a small hole in the surface of something, using a sharp point: *She had pricked her finger on a rose thorn.* ►see THESAURUS box at **hole¹**, **pierce** **2** to cause a painful stinging feeling on your skin: *Tears pricked my eyes and stung in my throat.* → see also PRICKLE **3 prick sb's conscience** to make someone feel guilty or ashamed: *The campaign has pricked the conscience of the nation.*

prick up *phr. v.* **1 prick sth ↔ up** if someone pricks up their ears, or their ears prick up, they start listening carefully because they have heard something interesting: *Jay pricked up his ears when I mentioned vacation.* **2 prick sth ↔ up** if an animal pricks up its ears, or its ears prick up, it raises them and points them toward a sound

prick² *n.* [C] **1** a slight pain you get when something sharp goes into your skin: *He felt a sudden sting like the prick of a needle.* **2** a small hole made by a sharp point, especially in your skin **3** a sudden slight feeling of unhappiness, worry etc. **4** an act of pricking something → see also PINPRICK

prick·le¹ /'prɪkəl/ *n.* [C] **1** BIOLOGY a long thin sharp point on the skin of some plants and animals **2** a stinging feeling on your skin: *prickles of perspiration*

prickle² *v.* [I,T] to have an uncomfortable stinging feeling on your skin, or to make someone feel this

prickly

prickly plants

prick·ly /'prɪkli/ *adj.* **1** causing problems or disagreements: *a prickly issue* **2** INFORMAL someone who is prickly gets annoyed or offended easily: *a prickly attitude* **3** BIOLOGY covered with prickles: *prickly bushes* **4** something prickly has small points and feels rough and slightly sharp: *His cheeks were prickly with a two-day growth of beard.* **5** if your skin feels prickly, it has a slightly uncomfortable feeling, as if lots of very small points were pricking you —**prickliness** *n.* [U]

,prickly 'pear *n.* [C,U] BIOLOGY a type of CACTUS with yellow flowers, or the fruit of this plant

pric·y /'praɪsi/ *adj.* another spelling of PRICEY

pride¹ /praɪd/ [W3] *n.*

1 SATISFACTION/PLEASURE [U] a feeling of satisfaction and pleasure in what you have achieved, or in what someone connected with you has achieved: *national pride* | *Lance* ***takes*** *obvious* ***pride in*** *his restaurant.* | *She always speaks of her daughter's achievements* ***with*** *great* ***pride****.* | *The team's success is* ***a source of pride*** *for the whole school.* | *I think we all share a* ***sense of pride*** *in what we have accomplished.*

2 take pride in your work/appearance etc. to do something very carefully and well, in a way that gives you a lot of satisfaction: *You should take more pride in your work.*

3 RESPECT [U] a feeling that you like and respect yourself and that you deserve to be respected by other people [SYN] **self-esteem**: *gay pride* | *I felt I had to finish as a matter of pride.* | *I think you may have* ***hurt*** *his* ***pride****.*

4 TOO MUCH PRIDE [U] DISAPPROVING a belief that you are better than other people and do not need their help or support: *He has too much pride to ask for help.*

5 sb's pride and joy someone or something that someone is very proud of, and that is important to them: *The garden is his pride and joy.*

6 the pride of sb/sth a) the thing or person that the people in a particular place are most proud of: *The Olympic champion is the pride of the town.* **b)** the best thing in a group: *The ship was the pride of the U.S. fleet.*

7 LIONS [C] BIOLOGY a group of lions

8 pride of place the most important position: *A statue of Buddha from Thailand holds pride of place in the living room.*

[**Origin:** Old English *pryde*, from *prud* **proud**] → see also **swallow your pride** at SWALLOW¹ (4)

pride² *v.* **pride yourself on (doing) sth** to be especially proud of something that you do well, or of a quality that you have: *Arthur prided himself on his knowledge of Italian art.*

priest /prist/ [S3] [W3] *n.* [C] **1** someone who is specially trained to perform religious duties and ceremonies in some Christian churches: *a Catholic priest* **2** a man with religious duties and responsibilities in some non-Christian religions: *Buddhist priests* [**Origin:** Old English *preost*, from Late Latin *presbyter*, from Greek *presbyteros* **older man, priest**]

THESAURUS

priest someone, usually but not always a man, who is in charge of the prayers, ceremonies, etc. in the Catholic, Episcopal, or Orthodox churches and in some other non-Christian religions
minister/pastor the person who is in charge of the prayers, ceremonies etc. in a Protestant church
rabbi the person who is in charge of the prayers, ceremonies etc. in the Jewish religion
mullah a Muslim teacher of law and religion
preacher someone who gives sermons (=a religious talk as part of a church service) in some Protestant churches
clergyman a religious leader, for example a priest, rabbi, or mullah
chaplain a priest or minister who takes care of the religious needs of an organization such as a college, hospital, prison, or the military
the clergy FORMAL religious leaders as a group

priest·ess /ˈpristɪs/ *n.* [C] a woman with religious duties and responsibilities in some non-Christian religions

priest·hood /ˈpristhʊd/ *n.* **1 the priesthood** the job or position of a priest: *He began his religious training for the priesthood.* **2** [C,U] all the priests of a particular religion or country: *the Babylonian priesthood*

Priest·ley /ˈpristli/**, Joseph** (1733–1804) a British scientist who did important work on the chemistry of gases

priest·ly /ˈpristli/ *adj.* relating to a priest: *priestly robes*

prig /prɪg/ *n.* [C] DISAPPROVING someone who obeys moral rules very carefully, and behaves as if they think they are better than other people —**priggish** *adj.* —**priggishness** *n.* [U]

prim /prɪm/ *adj.* **1** very formal and careful in the way you behave, and easily shocked by anything offensive, sexual etc.: *She's a very* ***prim and proper*** *lady.* **2** [only before noun] prim clothes are neat and formal —**primly** *adv.* —**primness** *n.* [U]

pri·ma bal·le·ri·na /ˌprimə bæləˈrinə/ *n.* [C] the main woman dancer in a BALLET company

pri·ma·cy /ˈpraɪməsi/ Ac *n.* [U] FORMAL the state of being the most powerful or important thing or person: **the primacy of sb/sth (over sb/sth)** *the primacy of national laws over state laws*

pri·ma don·na /ˌprimə ˈdɑnə, ˌprɪmə-/ *n.* [C] **1** DISAPPROVING someone who thinks that they are very good at what they do, and demands a lot of attention, admiration etc. from other people: *Most professional athletes are overpaid prima donnas.* **2** ENG. LANG. ARTS the most important woman singer in an OPERA company → see also DIVA

pri·ma fa·cie /ˌpraɪmə ˈfeɪʃə/ *adj.* [only before noun] LAW seeming to be true, or based on what seems to be true, even though it may later be proved to be untrue: *prima facie evidence* —**prima facie** *adv.*

pri·mal /ˈpraɪməl/ *adj.* [usually before noun] FORMAL **1** BIOLOGY primal feelings or behavior seem to belong to a part of people's character that is ancient and animal-like: *primal fears* **2** basic: *the primal truths of human existence*

pri·mar·i·ly /praɪˈmɛrəli/ Ac W3 *adv.* mainly: *At my last job I worked primarily with immigrants.* | *The advertisement is aimed primarily at children.*

pri·mar·y[1] /ˈpraɪˌmɛri, -məri/ Ac W2 *adj.* [usually before noun] **1** most important or most basic: *Their primary objective is to make money.* | *Low attendance was the primary reason for canceling the shows.* | *Fishing is their* ***primary source of*** *income.* | *Personal safety is* ***of primary importance.*** ►see THESAURUS box at **important** **2** [only before noun] relating to the education of children between five and 11 years old SYN **elementary**: *primary students* | *primary education* **3** TECHNICAL existing or developing before other things: *a primary infection* [**Origin:** 1400–1500 Latin *primarius*, from *primus* **first**] → see also SECONDARY

primary[2] Ac W3 *n. plural* **primaries** [C] **1** POLITICS an election in the U.S. in which people vote to decide who a political party's CANDIDATE will be for a particular position → see also GENERAL ELECTION → see also BLANKET PRIMARY, CLOSED PRIMARY, DIRECT PRIMARY, OPEN PRIMARY, PRESIDENTIAL PRIMARY, RUNOFF PRIMARY **2** a primary color

ˌprimary ˈcare also **ˌprimary ˈhealth care** *n.* [U] basic medical treatment that you receive from a doctor that includes advice as to whether you should see a SPECIALIST (=a doctor who deals only with specific types of medical problems): *a primary care physician* (=a doctor who provides primary care)

ˌprimary ˈcell, volˌtaic ˈcell *n.* [C] CHEMISTRY a piece of equipment that makes electricity from the energy that is produced when two or more chemicals are mixed together. This process can only happen once, and when the electricity is used up, the cell is dead.

primary ˈcolor *n.* [C] in art, one of the three colors – red, yellow, and blue – that can be mixed together to make any other color

ˌprimary ecoˌnomic acˈtivity *n.* [C,U] ECONOMICS an economic activity, such as fishing, farming, or MINING, which makes use of things that exist in nature → see also SECONDARY ECONOMIC ACVTIVITY, TERTIARY ECONOMIC ACVTIVITY

ˌprimary eˈlection *n.* [C] POLITICS a PRIMARY

ˌprimary ˈgrowth *n.* [U] BIOLOGY growth in a plant's stem that happens at the end of its roots and in the top of its stem

ˌprimary ˈmarket also **new ˈissue ˌmarket** *n.* [C] ECONOMICS a market for selling BONDS and STOCK for the first time, not for selling them again later → see also SECONDARY MARKET

ˈprimary ˌschool *n.* [C] an ELEMENTARY SCHOOL

ˌprimary ˈsource *n.* [C] HISTORY a written or spoken description of an event by someone who was actually there when it happened → see also SECONDARY SOURCE

ˌprimary ˈstress *n.* [C,U] ENG. LANG. ARTS the strongest force given, when you are speaking, to a part of a long word, like the force given to "pri" when you say "primary." It is shown in this dictionary by the mark (ˈ). → see also SECONDARY SOURCE

pri·mate /ˈpraɪmeɪt/ *n.* [C] **1** BIOLOGY a member of the group of MAMMALS that includes humans and monkeys **2** also **Primate** the most important BISHOP (=priest with high rank) in a country or an area, especially in the Catholic Church

prime[1] /praɪm/ Ac *adj.* [only before noun] **1** most important: *Our prime concern is for the child's safety.* | *the prime suspect in a murder case* **2** of the very best quality or kind: *prime agricultural land* | *prime cuts of beef* **3 a prime example (of sth)** a very typical example of something: *a prime example of 19th-century architecture* **4 be a prime candidate/target etc. (for sth)** to be the person or thing that is most appropriate or most likely to be chosen for a particular purpose: *He's a prime candidate for the job.*

prime[2] Ac *n.* **1** [singular] the time in your life when you are strongest and most active: **in your prime/in the prime of life** *She died tragically in her prime.* | *Ali was by then a little* ***past his prime*** (=not as strong or good as he used to be). **2** [U] PRIME RATE **3** [C] a PRIME NUMBER

prime[3] Ac *v.* [T] **1** [usually passive] to prepare someone for a situation, so that they know what to do: **prime sb to do sth** *Gonzalez is being primed to take over the leadership position.* | **prime sb for sth** *The riot police have been primed for action.* **2** to put a special layer of paint on a surface, to prepare it for the main layer **3** to prepare a gun or MINE so that it can fire or explode **4** to prepare a water or oil pump by pouring a small amount of water or oil into it **5 prime the pump** to encourage a business, industry, or activity to develop by putting money or effort into it

ˈprime ˌfactor *n.* [C] MATH a number that can be

divided only by itself and the number 1, and is a FACTOR of another number. For example, 7 is a prime factor of 21.

prime fac·tor·i·za·tion /ˌpraɪm ˌfæktərəˈzeɪʃən/ *n.* [C,U] MATH a mathematical expression in which a number is written as the result of multiplying PRIME NUMBERS, for example the prime factorization of 15 is 3 × 5.

ˌprime meˈridian *n.* **the prime meridian** the imaginary line that goes from north to south through Greenwich, England, from which east and west are measured

ˌprime ˈminister, Prime Minister *n.* [C] the chief minister and leader of the government in some countries that have a PARLIAMENTARY system of government: *the prime minister of Turkey*

P

ˌprime ˈmover *n.* [C] **1** someone who has great influence in the development of something important: *prime movers of the nation's economy* **2** TECHNICAL a natural force, such as wind or water, that can be used to produce power

ˌprime ˈnumber *n.* [C] MATH a number that can be divided only by itself and the number 1, for example 3

prim·er¹ /ˈpraɪmɚ/ *n.* **1** [C,U] paint that is spread over the surface of wood, metal etc. before the main covering of paint is put on **2** [C] a tube containing explosive, used to fire a gun, explode a bomb etc.

prim·er² /ˈprɪmɚ/ *n.* [C] **1** a set of basic instructions, explanations etc.: *a primer of good management techniques* **2** OLD-FASHIONED a beginner's book in a school subject

ˈprime ˌrate *n.* [C] ECONOMICS the lowest rate of interest at which money can be borrowed, which banks offer to certain customers

ˌprime ˈrib *n.* [singular U] a piece of good quality BEEF that is cut from the chest of the animal

ˈprime ˌtime *n.* [U] the time in the evening when the greatest number of people are watching television, between about 7:00 and 10:00 or 11:00 **—prime-time** *adj.* [only before noun] *prime-time TV*

pri·me·val /praɪˈmivəl/ *adj.* **1** EARTH SCIENCE belonging to the earliest period in the existence of the universe or the Earth SYN **primordial**: *Primeval clouds of gas formed themselves into stars.* **2** very ancient: *primeval tropical rainforests* **3** primeval emotions or attitudes are very strong, and seem to come from a part of people's character that is ancient and animal-like SYN **primal**

prim·i·tive¹ /ˈprɪməṭɪv/ *adj.*
1 WAY OF LIFE having a simple way of life that existed in the past and does not include modern industries and machines: *a primitive society*
2 EARLY DEVELOPMENT belonging to an early stage in the development of humans or of plants or animals: *primitive man* | *fossils of primitive algae*
3 NOT MODERN very simple or uncomfortable, without modern features: *primitive machinery* | *Conditions at the camp are very primitive.*
4 FEELINGS primitive feelings are not based on reason, and seem to come from a part of people's character that is ancient and animal-like: *primitive urges*
5 ART a) made in a simple style like a child's by an artist with no formal training **b)** made by someone from a primitive society **—primitively** *adv.* **—primitiveness** *n.* [U]

primitive² *n.* [C] **1** OLD-FASHIONED, OFFENSIVE used in the past to mean someone from a simple society who is not used to modern machines or ways of life **2** ENG. LANG. ARTS a painter who paints simple pictures like those of a child **3** ENG. LANG. ARTS a painter or SCULPTOR of the time before the Renaissance

pri·mo·gen·i·ture /ˌpraɪmoʊˈdʒɛnətʃɚ/ *n.* [U] LAW the system by which property owned by a man goes to his oldest son after his death, used especially in the past

pri·mor·di·al /praɪˈmɔrdiəl/ *adj.* FORMAL **1** EARTH SCIENCE existing at the beginning of time or the beginning of the Earth: *the primordial origins of life* **2** in the simplest most basic form: *primordial instincts*

primp /prɪmp/ *v.* [I,T] to make yourself look attractive by arranging your hair, putting on MAKEUP etc.: *She spends hours primping in front of the mirror.*

prim·rose /ˈprɪmroʊz/ *n.* **1** [C] BIOLOGY a small wild plant with colored flowers, or a flower from this plant **2** [U] primrose yellow

ˌprimrose ˈyellow *n.* [U] a light yellow color **—primrose yellow** *adj.*

prince /prɪns/ W3 *n.* [C] **1** also **Prince** the son of a king or queen, or one of their close male relatives: *the royal princes* | *Prince William* **2** also **Prince** a male ruler of a small country or state: *Prince Albert of Monaco* **3** LITERARY OR HUMOROUS a man who is regarded as very special or as the best of a group of men: *He's a prince among men.* [**Origin:** 1100–1200 Old French, Latin *princeps* **leader**, from *primus* **first** + *capere* **to take**]

ˌPrince ˈCharming *n.* [C] INFORMAL OR HUMOROUS a perfect man that a young girl might dream about meeting

Prince Ed·ward Is·land /prɪns ˌɛdwɚd ˈaɪlənd/ a PROVINCE in southeast Canada that is an island in the Gulf of St. Lawrence

prince·ly /ˈprɪnsli/ *adj.* [only before noun] **1 a princely sum/fee/price etc.** an expression meaning a large amount of money, often used in a joking way to mean a very small amount of money: *Harris earned the princely sum of $24 for all her work.* **2** belonging to or relating to a prince: *the princely states* **3** FORMAL very good or generous: *a princely gift*

prin·cess /ˈprɪnsɪs, -sɛs/ *n.* [C] **1** also **Princess** the daughter of a king or queen, or one of their close female relatives: *Princess Anne* **2** also **Princess** the wife of a prince

prin·ci·pal¹ /ˈprɪnsəpəl/ Ac W3 *adj.* [only before noun] most important SYN **main**: *Oil is the country's principal source of income.* | *the principal character in the book* ▸see THESAURUS box at **important** → see also PRINCIPALLY

principal² Ac S3 *n.* **1** [C] someone who is in charge of a school: *The principal called me in to her office.* **2** [singular] an amount of money lent to someone, put into a business etc., on which INTEREST is paid **3** [C often plural] ECONOMICS the main person in a business or organization who can make business decisions **4** [C] ENG. LANG. ARTS the main performer in a play, group of musicians etc. **5** LAW [C] someone who is being represented by someone else in a legal matter

prin·ci·pal·i·ty /ˌprɪnsəˈpæləṭi/ *n. plural* **principalities** [C] a country ruled by a PRINCE

prin·ci·pally /ˈprɪnsəpli/ Ac *adv.* mainly: *The road is used principally for military purposes.*

ˌprincipal ˈparts *n.* [plural] ENG. LANG. ARTS the parts of a verb from which other parts are formed. In English they are the INFINITIVE, past tense, present participle, and past participle.

ˌprincipal ˈroot *n.* [C] MATH the positive ROOT of a number

prin·ci·ple /ˈprɪnsəpəl/ Ac S3 W2 *n.* **1** [C,U] a moral rule or set of ideas about right and wrong, which influences you to behave in a particular way: *He'll do anything for money. The man has no principles.* | *They refused to print the photographs* ***as a matter of principle***. | *Julie doesn't eat meat* ***on principle*** (=because she thinks it is morally wrong, not because she dislikes it). | *I wouldn't work for a tobacco company – it's* ***against*** *my* ***principles***. | **moral/religious principles** *He prided himself on his high moral principles.* | *No, he didn't take much money, but* ***it's the principle of the thing***. | **a man/woman of principle** (=someone who has strong ideas about what is morally right or wrong) **2** [C] a belief or idea on which a set of ideas, a set of laws, a system for doing something etc. is based: *democratic principles* | **+of** *the principle of separation of church and state* | **the principle that** *The method is based on the principle that children learn best through stories.* | *The* ***general principle*** *is that education* *should be freely available.* | **a basic/fundamental/guiding principle** *the basic principles of business management* | *We must go back to* ***first principles*** (=most important and basic beliefs). **3** [C] a basic rule that explains the way something works, such as a machine or a natural force in the universe: *The principles governing the world of physics are unchanging.* | *Archimedes' principle* **4 in principle a)** if you agree in principle, you agree about a general plan or idea but have not thought about the details yet: *The government has agreed in principle to a referendum.* **b)** if you believe in something in principle, you believe in the idea of it but are sometimes willing to take actions that do not support this belief SYN **in theory**: *Many people who support free speech in principle want to restrict it in certain situations.* **c)** if something is possible in principle, there is no good reason why it should not happen, but it has not actually happened yet SYN **in theory**: *It is possible in principle for every candidate to fail.* [**Origin:** 1300–1400 French *principe*, from Latin *principium* **beginning**]

prin·ci·pled /ˈprɪnsəpəld/ Ac *adj.* [usually before noun] **1** having strong clear beliefs about what is morally right and wrong: *principled leadership* **2** based on clear beliefs or ideas: *principled opposition to the idea of lower taxation*

print¹ /prɪnt/ S1 W3 *v.*
1 WORDS BY MACHINE a) [I,T] to produce words, numbers, or pictures on paper or other material, using a machine which puts ink onto the surface: *Why won't this printer print?* | *I need to make a few changes before I print the document.* | **print sth on/across sth** *I called the number that was printed on the form.* | **print sth in sth** *This part should be printed in italics.* | *I'd like to print it in color if I can.* | **print sth with sth** *Stan had the cards printed with his name and address.* **b)** [I] to be printed by a computer: *How long will it take for this file to print?*
2 PRODUCE BOOKS ETC. [T] to produce many copies of a book, newspaper etc.: *His second novel was originally printed in Paris.*
3 IN A NEWSPAPER [T] to include a letter, speech, picture etc. in a newspaper, book, or magazine SYN **publish**: *They printed my letter in the Sunday paper.*
4 WRITE [I,T] to write words by hand without joining the letters: *Please print your name in the blank.*
5 PHOTOGRAPH [T] to produce a photograph on special paper: *How do you want the pictures printed?*
6 print money if a government prints money, it produces paper money, especially in order to pay for something: *The government was printing money to finance a reckless war.* → see also **a license to print money** at LICENSE¹ (7)
7 MARK [T usually passive] to make a mark on a surface by pressing something onto it: *The mark of a child's shoe was clearly printed in the mud.*
print sth ↔ out/off *phr. v.* to produce a printed copy of something you have written using a computer: *I'll print out another copy for you.*

print² S2 W3 *n.*
1 BOOKS/NEWSPAPERS [U] writing that has been printed in books, newspapers etc.: *The information is available in several formats including print and CD-ROM.* | *It's always exciting to see your name* ***in print*** (=printed in a book, newspaper etc.). | *Her work first* ***appeared in print*** *15 years ago.* | *They pay $50 for each story that* ***makes it into print*** (=gets printed).
2 be in print if a book is in print, new copies of it are still being printed: *More than 40 of her books are still in print.*
3 be out of print if a book is out of print, it is not being printed anymore, and you cannot buy new copies
4 the fine/small print the details of a legal document, often in very small writing: *Don't sign anything until you've* ***read the fine print***.
5 LETTERS [U] the letters in which something is printed: *The book is available in large print.*
6 PICTURE [C] ENG. LANG. ARTS **a)** a picture or design that has been printed from a small sheet of metal, block of wood etc.: *The print is a colored woodcut.* **b)** a copy of a painting produced by photography
7 PHOTOGRAPH [C] ENG. LANG. ARTS a photograph in the form of a picture that has been produced from a film: *color prints* | *I ordered two sets of prints.* ▶see THESAURUS box at **camera**
8 MARK [C] **a)** a mark made on a surface or in a soft substance by something that has been pressed onto it: *paw prints* | *I don't want your dirty hand prints all over the walls.* → see also FOOTPRINT **b)** [usually plural] a word for a mark made by the pattern of lines on the ends of your finger, used especially by police SYN **fingerprint**: *We found a set of prints on the door.*
9 MOVIE [C] a copy of a movie: *A new print of "Citizen Kane" has just been released.*
10 CLOTH [C,U] cloth, especially cotton, on which a colored pattern has been printed, or the pattern itself: *a floral print*
[**Origin:** 1200–1300 Old French *preinte*, from *preint*, past participle of *preindre* **to press**, from Latin *premere*]

P

print·a·ble /ˈprɪntəbəl/ *adj.* [usually in negatives] appropriate, polite enough etc. to be printed and read by everyone: *Some of the comments we received were not even printable* (=contained offensive or sexual language). → see also UNPRINTABLE

print·ed /ˈprɪntɪd/ *adj.* **1** put on paper or another surface by a machine using ink: *a printed form* **2** written by hand without joining the letters: *a carefully printed message* **3 the printed word** language in printed form, especially when compared with spoken language **4 the printed page** writing that has been PUBLISHED

ˌprinted ˈcircuit *n.* [C] SCIENCE a set of connections in a piece of electrical equipment consisting of thin lines of metal on a board

ˈprinted ˌmatter *n.* [U] printed material, such as advertisements or books, that can be sent by mail at a cheap rate

print·er /ˈprɪntɚ/ S2 *n.* [C] **1** COMPUTERS a machine connected to a computer that puts documents from the computer onto paper → see also PRINTING PRESS ▶see THESAURUS box at **office** **2** someone employed in the business of printing

print·ing /ˈprɪntɪŋ/ *n.* **1** [U] the action, process, or business of making books, magazines etc. by pressing or copying letters or photographs onto paper: *technical developments in printing* **2** [C] an action of printing copies of a book for sale: *The book is in its fourth printing.* **3** [U] the way someone writes without joining the letters

ˈprinting ink *n.* [U] a type of ink that dries very quickly and is used in printing books, newspapers etc.

ˈprinting press also **ˈprinting maˌchine** *n.* [C] a machine that prints newspapers, books etc., used especially before computers were common

print·mak·ing /ˈprɪntˌmeɪkɪŋ/ *n.* [U] the art of printing pictures using a small sheet of metal, a block of wood etc.

print·out /ˈprɪntaʊt/ *n.* [C,U] a sheet or length of paper with printed information on it, produced from a computer

ˈprint run *n.* [C] all the copies of a book, newspaper etc. that are printed at one time: *an initial print run of one million copies*

ˈprint shop *n.* [C] a small store that prints and copies documents, cards etc. for customers

pri·on /ˈpriɑn/ *n.* [C] BIOLOGY a very small piece of PROTEIN that is thought to cause some infectious brain diseases

pri·or¹ /ˈpraɪɚ/ Ac *adj.* **1 prior to sth** FORMAL before: *Prior to 1492, no human in the Old World had ever eaten corn.* | *They're planning to talk to Joe prior to the meeting.* **2** [only before noun] arranged or happening before the present situation or before something else happens: *Changes may not be made without the prior approval of the City Council.* | **prior knowledge/experience** *Some prior experience with the software is needed.* | *I'm sorry, I have* ***a prior engagement*** (=something you have planned to do) *and won't be able to attend.* | **prior notice/warning** *He was thrown out of the apartment without prior notice.* **3 a prior arrest/conviction** LAW a previous occasion when someone has been ARRESTed for a crime or found guilty of it in a court of law: *Jackson has no history of violence, and no prior convictions.* [**Origin:** 1700–1800 Latin **earlier, older, higher in rank**, from Latin *pri* **before**]

prior² Ac *n.* [C] **1** INFORMAL a previous occasion when someone has been found guilty of a crime: *two priors for homicide* **2** the man in charge of a PRIORY, or the priest next in rank to the person in charge of an ABBEY

P

pri·or·ess /ˈpraɪərɪs/ *n.* [C] the woman in charge of a PRIORY

pri·or·i·tize /praɪˈɔrəˌtaɪz/ Ac *v.* **1** [I,T] to put several jobs, problems etc. in order of importance, so that you can deal with the most important ones first: *Identify all the tasks you have to do, then prioritize.* **2** [T] to deal with one job or problem before everything else, because it is the most important: *We pledge to prioritize the fight against crime.* —**prioritization** /praɪˌɔrət̬əˈzeɪʃən/ *n.* [U]

pri·or·i·ty /praɪˈɔrət̬i/ Ac S3 W3 *n. plural* **priorities** **1** [C] the thing that you think is most important and that needs attention before anything else: *The team's priority is to win.* | *With so little money available, repairs must remain **a low priority**.* | **a top/high/first etc. priority** *Balancing the budget is our number one priority.* **2** [singular, U] the right to be given attention before other people or things: *List your tasks in order of priority.* | **give sb/sth priority** *Restaurant seating is limited and hotel guests are given priority.* | **have/take/get priority (over sth/sb)** *It's normal among teenagers for socializing to take priority over schoolwork.* | **put/place a (high) priority on sth** *We place a high priority on learning at this establishment.* | *Governments should place a higher priority on reducing global warming.* **3 get your priorities straight/right etc.** to form a clear idea of what is most important or urgent: *I need to take a little time off just to get my priorities in order.* —**priority** *adj.* [only before noun]

priˈority ˌmail *n.* [U] a type of mail service that is faster and more expensive than regular mail

pri·o·ry /ˈpraɪəri/ *n.* a place for a group of MONKS or NUNS (=Christian men or women living a religious life separately from other people) which is smaller and less important than an ABBEY

prism /ˈprɪzəm/ *n.* [C] **1** PHYSICS a transparent block of glass that breaks up white light into different colors **2** MATH a geometric SOLID with two matching BASES (=ends) and three or more sides that are all PARALLELOGRAMS or RECTANGLES → see picture at SHAPE¹

pris·mat·ic /prɪzˈmæt̬ɪk/ *adj.* PHYSICS **1** using or containing a PRISM: *prismatic crystal* **2** a prismatic color is very clear and bright

pris·on /ˈprɪzən/ W2 *n.* **1** [C,U] a large building where people are kept as a punishment for a crime, or while waiting to go to court for their TRIAL SYN **jail**: *a maximum security prison* | *He spent 26 years **in prison** for killing his girlfriend.* | *She did not want to **go to prison** again.* | *Nine of the 15 men were **sent to prison** for their role in the conspiracy.* | *Davis was **released from prison** after three months.* | *He is serving **a** 15-year **prison sentence*** (=the length of time someone must stay in prison). **2** [U] the system of sending people to be kept in a prison, or the experience of being sent to a prison: *Prison is an expensive and inefficient way to deal with social problems.* **3** [singular] an unpleasant place or situation which it is difficult to escape from: *Married life had become a prison for her.* [**Origin:** 1100–1200 Old French, Latin *prehensio* **act of seizing**, from *prehendere*] → see also IMPRISON

ˈprison camp *n.* [C] a special prison in which PRISONERS of war are kept

ˈprison cell *n.* [C] a locked room where prisoners are kept

pris·on·er /ˈprɪzənɚ/ W3 *n.* [C] **1** someone who is kept in a prison as a punishment for a crime: *Several of the prisoners are serving life terms.* **2** someone who is taken by force and kept somewhere, for example during a war SYN **captive**: *enemy prisoners* | **keep/hold sb prisoner** *Rebels held him prisoner for four months.* | *Six soldiers were killed and three were **taken prisoner**.*

> **THESAURUS**
> **captive** someone who is kept as a prisoner, especially in a war: *The rebels are holding 54 captives.*
> **hostage** someone who is kept as a prisoner by an enemy, so that the other side will do what the enemy demands: *The terrorists held five Americans hostage.*

3 someone who is completely controlled by a particular situation or feeling: **+of** *He was a prisoner of his own prejudices.* **4 take no prisoners** to show no sympathy to other people when you are trying to achieve something

ˌprisoner of ˈconscience *n.* [C] someone who is put in prison because of their political beliefs

ˌprisoner of ˈwar *n.* [C] a soldier, member of the navy etc. who is caught by the enemy during a war and kept as a prisoner

pris·sy /ˈprɪsi/ *adj.* DISAPPROVING very worried about behaving correctly, and easily shocked by anything offensive or sexual: *a look of prissy disapproval* —**prissily** *adv.* —**prissiness** *n.* [U]

pris·tine /ˈprɪˌstin, prɪˈstin/ *adj.* completely unspoiled by use, or completely clean: *the pristine whiteness of newly fallen snow* | *The old car was **in pristine condition**.*

prith·ee /ˈprɪði/ *interjection* OLD USE please

pri·va·cy /ˈpraɪvəsi/ *n.* [U] **1** the condition of being able to keep your own affairs secret: *I try to protect my family's privacy.* | *Some people think that random drugs tests on employees are **an invasion of privacy**.* | *The **right to privacy** is fundamental.* **2** the condition of being able to be alone, and not seen or heard by other people: *If you want privacy you can close the door.* | **in the privacy of your own home/room etc.** *She preferred to exercise in the privacy of her own home.*

pri·vate¹ /ˈpraɪvɪt/ S2 W1 *adj.*
1 NOT FOR EVERYONE belonging to or for use by only one particular person or group, not for everyone: *private property* | *a private jet* | *Each guest has a private bathroom.*
2 SECRET private feelings, information, or opinions are personal or secret and not for other people to know about: *private documents* | *Don't read that – it's private.*

> **THESAURUS**
> **secret** known or felt only by you, and not talked about or shown to anyone else: *Dreams may reveal our secret desires.*
> **personal** concerning only you: *He asked a lot of personal questions.*
> **innermost** your innermost feelings, desires etc. are the ones you feel most strongly and keep private: *It was like he could read her innermost thoughts.*
> **be none of sb's business** if something is none of your business, it is private and you should not ask about it: *It's none of your business who I go out with.*

3 MEETING/EVENT ETC. a private meeting, conversation etc. involves only a small number of people, and not much information about it is given to other people: *a private discussion* | *a private ceremony*
4 NOT GOVERNMENT [only before noun] not relating to, owned by, or paid for by the government OPP **public**: *a private college* | *private funding*
5 NOT WORK separate from and not relating to your work or your official position: *Susan is trying to bal-*

ance her private life and her work. | *The President made a private visit to the town.*
6 NOT OFFICIAL [only before noun] not representing a government or organization: *a private citizen*
7 QUIET PLACE quiet and without lots of people: *Let's go somewhere more private to talk.*
8 PERSON [only before noun] a private person is one who likes being alone, and does not talk much about their thoughts or feelings: *He doesn't talk much about his family – he's a very private person.*
9 UNDERSTOOD BY FEW [only before noun] only understood by a particular group of people: *a private joke*
10 ARRANGED BETWEEN TWO PEOPLE [only before noun] relating to an agreement between two people that does not involve any official or business organization: *a private sale*
11 LESSON [only before noun] a private lesson is one in which you pay someone to teach you alone rather than with a group of students
[**Origin:** 1300–1400 Latin *privatus*, past participle of *privare* **to deprive**] → see also PRIVATELY

private² *n.* **1 in private** without other people being present OPP **in public**: *I'd rather talk about it with you in private.* **2** [C] also **Private** a soldier of the lowest rank **3 privates** [plural] PRIVATE PARTS

ˌprivate deˈtective *n.* [C] someone who can be employed to look for information or missing people, or to follow people and report on what they do

ˌprivate eduˈcation *n.* [U] education that you must pay for, rather than public education which is provided by the government

ˌprivate ˈenterprise *n.* ECONOMICS **1** [U] the economic system in which private businesses are allowed to compete freely with each other, and the government does not control industry → see also PRIVATE SECTOR ►see THESAURUS box at **business** **2** [C] a business established by a single person or group

pri·va·teer /ˌpraɪvəˈtɪr/ *n.* [C] **1** an armed ship in past times that was not in the navy but attacked and robbed enemy ships carrying goods **2** someone who commanded or sailed on a ship of this type

ˌprivate ˈeye *n.* [C] INFORMAL a PRIVATE DETECTIVE

ˌprivate first ˈclass *n.* [C] a soldier in the U.S. Army or Marines with a rank above PRIVATE

ˌprivate inˈvestigator *n.* [C] a PRIVATE DETECTIVE

pri·vate·ly /ˈpraɪvətli/ *adv.* **1** without other people around: *Could I speak to you privately?* **2** [sentence adverb] not publicly or as part of your official duties: *Privately, officials admit that mistakes were made.* **3** if you feel or think something privately, you do not tell anyone about it: *Many townspeople privately feared the worst.* | [sentence adverb] *Privately, I knew the treatment wasn't working.* **4** without the involvement of the government or without money from the government: *privately owned land* **5** if an arrangement, sale etc. is done privately, it is done directly between two people without any company or organization being involved

ˌprivate ˈparts *n.* [plural] OFTEN HUMOROUS an expression meaning "sex organs," used when you want to avoid naming them directly

ˌprivate ˈpractice *n.* [U] the business of a professional person, especially a doctor or lawyer, who works alone rather than with others

ˌprivate ˈproperty *n.* [U] property owned by a particular person or company, not by the government or by people in general

ˈprivate school *n.* [C] a school not supported by government money, where education must be paid for by the parents of the students

ˌprivate ˈsecretary *n.* [C] a secretary who is employed to help one person, especially with secret business

ˌprivate ˈsector *n.* **the private sector** the industries and services in a country that are owned and run by private companies, and not by the state or government —**private-sector** *adj.* [only before noun] *private-sector jobs* → see also PUBLIC SECTOR

ˌprivate ˈviewing *n.* [C] an occasion when a few people are invited to see a show of paintings, a movie etc. before the public sees it

pri·va·tion /praɪˈveɪʃən/ *n.* [C,U] FORMAL a lack or loss of the things that everyone needs, such as food, warmth, and shelter: *times of privation*

pri·va·ti·za·tion /ˌpraɪvət̬əˈzeɪʃən/ *n.* [C,U] ECONOMICS the action or process of privatizing something

pri·vat·ize /ˈpraɪvəˌtaɪz/ *v.* [T] ECONOMICS to sell an organization, industry, or service that was previously controlled and owned by a government to a private company: *The company was privatized in the 1980s.* → see also NATIONALIZE

P

priv·et /ˈprɪvət/ *n.* [U] a bush with leaves that stay green all year, often grown to form a HEDGE

priv·i·lege /ˈprɪvəlɪdʒ, -vlɪdʒ/ *n.* **1** [C] a special advantage or right that is given only to one person or group: *diplomatic privileges* | *He never asked for special privileges.* | **+of** *Decent health care should not be the privilege of the rich.* **2** [singular] something that you are lucky to have the chance to do, and that you enjoy very much: **the privilege of (doing) sth** *I had the privilege of working with some very talented artists.* | **it is a privilege to do sth** *It's a privilege to finally meet you.* **3** [U] a situation in which people who are rich or of a high social class have many more advantages than other people: *a life of wealth and privilege* **4** [U] the right that lawyers, doctors etc. have to keep information about their discussions with CLIENTS and PATIENTS secret from other people: *attorney-client privilege*

priv·i·leged /ˈprɪvəlɪdʒd/ *adj.* **1** having advantages because of your wealth, high social position etc.: *She comes from a privileged background.* | *Education was available to only* ***the privileged few.*** **2** having a special advantage or a chance to do something that most people cannot do: *Taylor enjoyed privileged access to the presidential files.* | **privileged to do sth** *I feel privileged to serve on the committee.* **3** LAW privileged information is secret and does not have to be given even if a court of law asks for it

priv·y¹ /ˈprɪvi/ *adj.* **1 privy to sth** FORMAL sharing in the knowledge of facts that are secret: *Only a handful of executives were privy to the business plan.* **2** OLD USE secret and private —**privily** *adv.*

privy² *n.* [C] an outside toilet, used in the past ►see THESAURUS box at **toilet**

prix fixe /ˌpri ˈfiks◂, -ˈfɪks/ *adj.* **a prix fixe meal/dinner/menu** a complete meal in a restaurant that is offered for a single price

prize¹ /praɪz/ S3 W3 *n.* [C] **1** something that is given to someone who is successful in a competition, race, game of chance etc.: *First prize is a trip to Orlando.* | **+for** *There was a prize for best costume.* | *Enter now for the chance to* ***win*** *any of these fabulous* ***prizes.*** | **award/give sb an award** *Carter was awarded the Nobel Peace Prize in 2002.* → see also CONSOLATION PRIZE **2** someone or something that is very valuable to you or very important to try to get: *She's going to marry Simon, but I don't think he's much of a prize.* | *The gold watch is the prize of his collection.* [**Origin:** 1500–1600 *prise*, an earlier form of *price*]

prize² *adj.* [only before noun] **1 prize money** money that is given to the person who wins a competition, race etc. **2** good enough to win a prize or to have won a prize: *a herd of prize cattle* → see also PRIZE-WINNING **3** [no comparative] best, most important, or most useful: *one of the team's prize players* → see also PRIZED

prize³ *v.* [T] **1** to regard something as very important or valuable: *He prized his freedom above all else.* **2** to PRY something open or away from something else

prized /praɪzd/ *adj.* extremely important or valuable to someone: *Matsutake mushrooms are* ***highly prized for*** *their fragrance.* | *The transistor radio was the old man's* ***most prized possession.***

prize·fight /ˈpraɪzfaɪt/ *n.* [C] a BOXING match in which the competitors are paid —**prizefighter** *n.* [C] —**prizefighting** *n.* [U]

ˈprize ˌwinner *n.* [C] someone who wins a prize: *a Pulitzer Prize winner*

ˈprize-ˌwinning *adj.* [only before noun] a prize-winning movie, book, person, animal etc. has won a prize: *a prize-winning composer*

pro¹ /proʊ/ W3 *n. plural* **pros** [C] **1** INFORMAL someone who earns money by doing a particular sport or using a particular skill SYN **professional**: *a golf pro* **2** INFORMAL someone who has had a lot of experience with a particular type of situation: *He answered reporters' questions* ***like an old pro***. | *Megan's become* ***a real pro*** *at manipulating people.* **3 the pros and cons (of sth)** the advantages and disadvantages of something: *The brochure explains the pros and cons of each health-care plan.* → see also PRO FORMA, PRO RATA

pro² *adj.* INFORMAL **1** doing a job, sport, or activity for money SYN **professional**: *a pro basketball player* | **turn/go pro** (=become pro) *Both skaters turned pro last year.* **2** done by or relating to people who are paid for what they do SYN **professional**: *pro wrestling*

pro³ *prep.* if you are pro an idea, plan, suggestion etc., you support it or hope that it will succeed: *The party claims to be very pro family.*

pro- /proʊ/ *prefix* favorable toward or supporting something: *a pro-environment governor* | *a pro-democracy demonstration*

pro·ac·tive /proʊˈæktɪv/ *adj.* making changes to improve something before problems happen, rather than reacting to problems and then changing things: *Managers should be proactive in identifying problems.*

pro-am /ˌproʊ ˈæm◂/ *n.* [C] a competition, especially in GOLF, for both PROFESSIONALS (=people who play for money) and AMATEURS (=people who play just for fun)

prob·a·bil·i·ty /ˌprɑbəˈbɪləṭi/ *n. plural* **probabilities** **1** [singular, U] how likely it is that something will happen, exist, or be true: **+of** *The probability of success was pretty low.* | **a strong/high/distinct etc. probability that** *There is a high probablity that other family members will develop the disease.* **2 in all probability** used to say that you think something is very likely to happen: *In all probability, Kelsey will resign by the end of the year.* **3** [C] something that is likely to happen or exist: *War is a real probability.* **4** [C,U] MATH how likely something is to happen, measured in a mathematical calculation: *Genetic tests show a 99.4 percent probability that Hill is the child's father.*

proˈbability distriˌbution *n.* [C] MATH a graph or table that shows all the values that a VARIABLE can have and how likely it is that each value will actually appear

prob·a·ble¹ /ˈprɑbəbəl/ *adj.* likely to exist, happen, or be true OPP **improbable**: *Light rain is probable tomorrow evening.* | *The probable cause of the fire was a cigarette.* | ***It is probable that*** *the jury will find the defendant guilty.* [**Origin:** 1300–1400 French, Latin *probabilis*, from *probare* **to test, prove**]

probable² *n.* [C] someone who is likely to be chosen for a team, to win a race etc.

ˌprobable ˈcause *n.* [U] LAW good reasons to believe that someone has done something illegal: *The police had probable cause to conduct the search.*

prob·a·bly /ˈprɑbəbli/ S1 W1 *adv.* used to say that something is likely to happen, exist, or be true: *I'll probably be late for dinner tonight.* | *"Are you going to the meeting?" "Probably."* | *"Are you going to invite John?" "No,* ***probably not****."*

pro·bate¹ /ˈproʊbeɪt/ *n.* [U] LAW the legal process of deciding that someone's WILL has been correctly made, or the court where this takes place

probate² *v.* [T] LAW to prove that a WILL is legal

pro·ba·tion /proʊˈbeɪʃən/ *n.* [U] **1** LAW a system that allows some criminals to avoid going to prison, if they behave well and see a PROBATION OFFICER regularly for a specific period of time → see also PAROLE: *A judge gave Brown six months'* ***probation***. | **put/place sb on probation** *Preston was put on probation for three years.* **2** a specific period of time in which you must improve your work so that you will not have to leave your job: **put/place sb on probation** *He will be put on probation and fired if the situation does not improve.* **3** a specific period of time during which someone who has just started a job is tested to see whether they are appropriate for that job: *All new employees are* ***on probation*** *for nine months.* —**probationary** *adj.*

pro·ba·tion·er /proʊˈbeɪʃənɚ/ *n.* [C] **1** someone who has broken the law and has been put on probation **2** someone who has recently started a job and who is being tested to see whether they are appropriate for it

proˈbation ˌofficer *n.* [C] LAW someone whose job is to watch, advise, and help people who have broken the law and are on probation

probe¹ /proʊb/ *v.* [I,T] **1** to ask questions in order to find things out, especially things that other people do not want you to know: *He began to probe deeper.* | *Investigators are probing the causes of the train wreck.* | **+into** *What right does he have to probe into my personal life?* **2** to examine something or look for something using your fingers or a long thin instrument: *Anxiously, she probed the wound.* **3** [T] WRITTEN to search or examine a place, especially in order to find something —**probing** *adj.*: *probing questions* —**probingly** *adv.*

probe² *n.* [C] **1** a process by an official organization of trying to find out the truth about something SYN **investigation**: **+into** *a probe into allegations of fraud* **2** a long thin metal instrument that doctors and scientists use to examine parts of the body inside you **3** a SPACE PROBE

pro·bi·ty /ˈproʊbəṭi/ *n.* [U] FORMAL completely moral behavior

prob·lem¹ /ˈprɑbləm/ S1 W1 *n.* [C] **1** a situation that causes difficulties: *Our main problem is lack of funds.* | *The country* ***has*** *huge economic* ***problems***. | **+of** *the problem of homelessness* | **+with** *She has a lot of problems with her family.* | **+for** *The cost of the program is a problem for many people.* | **a big/serious/major problem** *Unemployment is a serious problem in our community.* | *The heavy snow* ***caused problems*** *for commuters.* | *We are working hard to* ***solve the problem***. | *The city is looking for new ways to* ***deal with the problem*** *of street crime.*

> **THESAURUS**
>
> **setback** a problem that stops you from making progress: *The space program suffered a major setback when the space shuttle, Discovery, exploded.*
>
> **snag** INFORMAL a problem, especially one that you had not expected: *There's a snag – I don't have his number.*
>
> **hitch** a small problem that delays or prevents something: *There have been a few last-minute hitches.*
>
> **trouble** when something does not work in the way it should: *The plane developed engine trouble.*
>
> **hassle** SPOKEN a situation that is annoying because it causes problems: *Just trying to store all this stuff is a hassle.*
>
> → DEFECT¹

2 something wrong with your health, your mind, or with part of your body: *I was too embarrassed to discuss the problem with my doctor.* | *long-term* ***health problems*** | **+with** *She has a problem with her eye.* | **a back/heart/kidney etc. problem** *patients with heart problems* | **emotional/psychological problems** *children with severe emotional problems* | **a drug/alcohol/drinking etc. problem** *My father had a serious drinking problem.* | *I'm beginning to think he has a* ***hearing problem***. | *She refuses to admit she has a* ***weight problem*** (=she weighs too much). ►see THESAURUS box at **illness** **3** a question that must be answered, especially one relating to numbers or facts on a test: *The students were given a series of problems to solve.*

SPOKEN PHRASES

4 no problem a) used to say that you are very willing to do something: *"Could you pick some bread up at the store?" "Sure, no problem."* **b)** used after someone has said thank you or said that they are sorry: *"Thanks for letting us stay with you." "No problem."* **5 the problem is...** used before saying what the main problem in a situation really is: *The problem is, we don't have the money for it.* **6 that's sb's problem** used to say that someone else is responsible for dealing with a situation, not you, especially when you think what they are doing is wrong or stupid: *If people don't like the way I look, that's their problem.* **7 What's sb's problem?** used to ask why someone is behaving in an unreasonable way: *What's your problem today?* **8 it's/that's not my problem** used to say you do not care about a problem someone else has: *It's not my problem if she won't listen to reason.* **9 Do you have a problem with that?** also **You got a problem with that?** NONSTANDARD used to ask someone why they oppose you or disagree with you, in a way that shows you think they are wrong: *"You're going to wear that dress?" "Do you have a problem with that?"*

[**Origin:** 1300–1400 French *problème*, from Latin *problema*, from Greek, **something thrown forward**]

problem² *adj.* [only before noun] **a problem child/family/drinker etc.** a child, family, drinker etc. who behaves in a way that is difficult for other people to deal with

prob·lem·at·ic /ˌprɑbləˈmæt̬ɪk/ also **prob·lem·at·ic·al** /ˌprɑbləˈmæt̬ɪkəl/ *adj.* full of problems and difficult to deal with: *Enforcing this law has been problematic.* —**problematically** /-kli/ *adv.*

ˌproblem-soˈlution *adj.* [only before noun] ENG. LANG. ARTS a piece of writing with a problem-solution structure mentions a problem and then a solution to it

ˈproblem-ˌsolving *n.* [U] the process of finding ways of doing things, or finding answers to problems: *Most of the test questions involve problem-solving.* —**problem-solving** *adj.* [only before noun]

pro bo·no /ˌproʊ ˈboʊnoʊ/ *adj.* LAW used to describe work that someone, especially a lawyer, does without getting paid for it: *Turner has agreed to handle the case **on a pro bono basis**.*

pro·bos·cis /prəˈbɑsɪs, -ˈbɑskɪs/ *n. plural* **proboscises** [C] BIOLOGY **1** a long thin tube that forms part of the mouth of some insects and worms **2** the long thin nose of certain animals, such as the ELEPHANT

proˌcedural due ˈprocess *n.* [U] POLITICS the correct legal processes that a government must follow in the way it governs a country: *the Fourteenth Amendment's guarantee of procedural due process*

pro·ce·dure /prəˈsidʒɚ/ Ac S3 W2 *n.* **1** [C,U] the correct or normal method of doing something: **+for** *the procedure for passport applications* | **correct/proper/standard etc. procedure** *The police did not **follow standard procedure** in investigating the murder.* | **security/safety/operating etc. procedure** *The management has tightened security procedures.* **2** [C] a medical treatment or operation that is done in a particular way: **medical/surgical procedure** *The bone marrow is removed in a simple surgical procedure.* —**procedural** *adj.*

pro·ceed /prəˈsid, proʊ-/ Ac W3 *v.* [I] **1** to continue to do something that has already been started: *Negotiations are proceeding smoothly.* | **+with** *Russia decided to proceed with economic reforms.* | **+to** *Let's proceed to the next item on the agenda.* **2 proceed to do sth** an expression meaning to do something next, used especially about something annoying or surprising: *He proceeded to deny the accusations.* **3** [always + adv./prep.] FORMAL to move in a particular direction: **+in/to etc.** *Passengers should proceed to gate 25.* [**Origin:** 1300–1400 Old French *proceder*, from Latin *procedere* **to go forward**] → see also PROCEEDS

proceed against sb *phr. v.* LAW to begin a legal case against someone

proceed from sth *phr. v.* **1** to be caused or produced by something: *Change in an organization usually proceeds from the top and moves down.* **2** to continue a process or way of thinking, starting from a particular point, fact, or belief: *Change the fractions into decimals, and proceed from there.*

proceed to sth *phr. v.* FORMAL if you proceed to the next part of an activity, job etc., you do or take part in the next part of it: *The case is proceeding to trial.*

pro·ceed·ing /prəˈsidɪŋz/ Ac *n.* **1 the proceedings** an event or series of actions: *Brady directs the proceedings at the board meetings.* | *A crowd gathered to **watch the proceedings**.* **2** [C usually plural] LAW actions taken in a law court or in a legal case: **begin/bring/start etc. proceedings** *She has begun divorce proceedings.* | **legal/civil/judicial proceedings** *The county dropped legal proceedings against him.* **3 the proceedings** the official records of meetings

pro·ceeds /ˈproʊsidz/ Ac *n.* [plural] the money that has been gained from doing or selling something: **+of/from** *All the proceeds from the concert will go to charity.*

pro·cess¹ /ˈprɑsɛs, ˈproʊ-/ Ac S1 W1 *n.* [C]
1 DEVELOPMENTS a series of things that happen naturally and result in gradual change: *the human reproductive process* | *the aging process*
2 ACTIONS a series of actions that someone takes in order to achieve a particular result: *groups who oppose the **peace process*** | *the American **political process*** | **process of (doing) sth** *the process of applying to a college* | **slow/long/time-consuming etc. process** *Making the cheese was a slow process.* | **a two-step/five-step etc. process** *The air is cleansed of carbon dioxide in a three-step process.*
3 be in the process of doing sth to have started doing something and not yet be finished: *Our office is in the process of upgrading all the computers.*
4 process of elimination a way of discovering the cause of something, a right answer, or the truth by carefully examining each possibility until only the correct one is left: *A process of elimination may help you find out why your child can't sleep.*
5 in the process while you are doing something or while something is happening: *I spilled the coffee, burning myself in the process.*
6 INDUSTRY a system or a treatment of materials that is used to produce goods: *an advanced industrial process*
7 LAW TECHNICAL a legal case, considered as a series of actions → see also DUE PROCESS

process² Ac S3 W3 *v.* [T] **1** to make food, materials, or goods ready to be used or sold, for example by preserving or improving them in some way: *The fish is processed and canned on the factory ship.* **2** to deal with an official document, request etc. in an official way: *The bank is processing your loan application.* **3** to print a picture from a photographic film **4** to deal with information using a computer → see also DATA PROCESSING

pro·cess³ /prəˈsɛs/ Ac *v.* [I always + adv./prep.] FORMAL to walk or move along in a very slow and serious way, especially as part of a group

pro·cessed /ˈprɑsɛst/ Ac *adj.* processed foods have substances added to them before they are sold that give them color, keep them fresh etc.: ***Highly processed** foods are not as nutritious as fresh foods.* | **processed cheese/meat/food etc.**

pro·ces·sion /prəˈsɛʃən/ *n.* **1** [C,U] a line of people or vehicles moving slowly as part of a ceremony: *a funeral procession* | *They marched **in procession** to the Capitol Building.* **2** [C] several people or things of the same kind, appearing or happening one after the other: **+of** *an **endless procession** of visitors*

pro·ces·sion·al¹ /prəˈsɛʃənl/ *adj.* [only before noun] relating to or used during a procession

processional² *n.* [C] **1** a procession **2** a piece of music that is played during a procession

ˌprocess of incorpoˈration *n.* [U] POLITICS the process by which most of the freedoms and advantages promised in the U.S. BILL OF RIGHTS were included in the FOURTEENTH AMENDMENT, under the part known as the DUE PROCESS CLAUSE

pro·ces·sor /ˈprɑsɛsɚ/ *n.* [C] **1** COMPUTERS the central part of a computer that deals with the commands and information it is given SYN **central processing unit** **2** a machine, person, or industry that processes food or other materials before they are sold or used: *meat processors* → see also FOOD PROCESSOR, WORD PROCESSOR

ˌpro-ˈchoice *adj.* someone who is pro-choice believes that women have a right to ABORTION, and uses this word to describe their own beliefs: *pro-choice activists* → see also PRO-LIFE

P

pro·claim /proʊˈkleɪm, prə-/ *v.* [T] FORMAL **1** to say publicly or officially that something important is true or exists: *Phillips has repeatedly proclaimed his innocence.* | **proclaim sb/sth sth** *The cave was proclaimed a national monument in 1909.* | **proclaim that** *The headlines proclaimed that the war had been won.* **2** to show something clearly or be a sign of something: *They carried signs proclaiming their support.*

proc·la·ma·tion /ˌprɑkləˈmeɪʃən/ *n.* [C, U] an official public statement about something that is important, or the act of making this statement: **proclamation doing sth** *Lincoln **issued a proclamation** freeing the slaves.* | +**of** *the country's proclamation of independence*

Proclamation of 1763, the /prɑkləˌmeɪʃən əv ˌsɛvəntin ˌsɪksti ˈθri/ HISTORY an order by the British king and government in 1763 that COLONISTS in America should not go to live in land west of the Appalachian Mountains without buying the land legally from Native Americans

pro·cliv·i·ty /proʊˈklɪvət̬i/ *n. plural* **proclivities** [C] FORMAL a tendency to behave in a particular way or like a particular thing, especially something bad: +**for/to** *Children have a proclivity to act impulsively.*

pro·con·sul /proʊˈkɑnsəl/ *n.* [C] someone who governed a part of the ancient Roman Empire —**proconsular** *adj.*

pro·con·su·late /proʊˈkɑnsəlɪt/ also **pro·con·sul·ship** /proʊˈkɑnsəlˌʃɪp/ *n.* [C] the rank of a proconsul, or the time during which someone was a proconsul

pro·cras·ti·nate /prəˈkræstəˌneɪt/ *v.* [I] to delay doing something that you ought to do, usually because you do not want to do it SYN **put off**: *Most people procrastinate when it comes to paperwork.* —**procrastinator** *n.* [C] —**procrastination** /prəˌkræstəˈneɪʃən/ *n.* [U]

pro·cre·ate /ˈproʊkriˌeɪt/ *v.* [I,T] FORMAL to produce children or baby animals SYN **reproduce** —**procreation** /ˌproʊkriˈeɪʃən/ *n.* [U]

proc·tor¹ /ˈprɑktɚ/ *n.* [C] someone who watches students during a test to make sure that they do not cheat

proctor² *v.* [T] to watch students during a test to make sure that they do not cheat

proc·u·ra·tor /ˈprɑkyəˌreɪt̬ɚ/ *n.* [C] someone who manages the government of an area, especially in the former Soviet Union, the Roman Catholic Church, or the ancient Roman Empire

pro·cure /proʊˈkyʊr, prə-/ *v.* [T] FORMAL to obtain something, especially something that is difficult to get: **procure sth for sb** *The money will be used to procure medicine and food for local orphanages.* —**procurable** *adj.* —**procurement** *n.* [U] —**procurer** *n.* [C]

prod¹ /prɑd/ *v.* **prodded, prodding** [I,T] **1** to make or persuade someone to do something, especially when they are lazy or unwilling: **prod sb into (doing) sth** *He tried to prod Gordon into responding.* | **prod sb to do sth** *We **push and prod** the kids to finish their projects.* **2** to push or press something with your finger or a pointed object SYN **poke**: *He didn't want doctors **poking and prodding** him.*

prod² *n.* [C usually singular] **1** an instrument used for pushing an animal, in order to make them move in a particular direction: *a **cattle prod*** **2** something that is said or done to encourage or remind someone to do something: *Improving the status of women is a prod to lowering birth rates.* **3** a sudden pressing or pushing movement, using your finger or a pointed object SYN **poke**: *Jerry **gave me a sharp prod** in the back.*

prod·i·gal¹ /ˈprɑdɪgəl/ *adj.* **1** tending to waste what you have, especially money SYN **extravagant**: *a prodigal lifestyle* **2 prodigal son/daughter** a son or daughter who leaves the family and lives in a way they do not approve of, but who is sorry later and returns

prodigal² *n.* [C] HUMOROUS someone who spends money carelessly and wastes their time

pro·di·gious /prəˈdɪdʒəs/ *adj.* very large or great in a surprising or impressive way: *a prodigious feat of engineering* —**prodigiously** *adv.*

prod·i·gy /ˈprɑdədʒi/ *n. plural* **prodigies** [C] **1** a young person who has a great natural ability in a subject or skill: *a tennis prodigy* | *Mozart was a **child prodigy**.* **2** something strange and surprising: *Everest climbers display prodigies of endurance.* [**Origin:** 1400–1500 Latin *prodigium* **sign telling the future, monster**]

pro·duce¹ /prəˈdus/ S2 W1 *v.*
1 GROW/MAKE [T] to grow something or make it naturally: *The region produces most of the state's corn.* | *the body's ability to produce new cells*
2 RESULT IN STH [T] to make something happen or develop, or have a particular result or effect: *The drug produces severe side effects in some people.* | *A second research project has **produced** similar **results**.* | **produce the desired result/effect/behavior etc.** *Will punishment help produce the desired behavior?*
3 SHOW [T] if you produce an object, you bring it out or present it, so that people can see it or consider it: *One of the men suddenly produced a knife.* | *They produced documents proving their claims.*
4 GOODS [I,T] to make things to be sold, using an industrial process: *Nuclear power plants produce 20% of the country's energy.* | *The company produces over 200 sewing machines a month.* → see also MASS-PRODUCED ►see THESAURUS box at **make¹**
5 MAKE WITH SKILL [T] to make something using your skill and imagination: *The artist has produced some very original works.*
6 PLAY/FILM [T] ENG. LANG. ARTS if someone produces a movie, play etc., they provide the money for it and control the way it is made: *Spelling has produced numerous hit TV shows.* → see also PRODUCER
7 BABY [T] FORMAL to have a baby: *A cat may produce kittens three times a year.*
[**Origin:** 1400–1500 Latin *producere*, from *ducere* **to lead**] → see also PRODUCTION → see Word Choice box at PRODUCT

prod·uce² /ˈprɑdus, ˈproʊ-/ *n.* [U] food that has been grown, especially fruits and vegetables: *a farmer's market selling **fresh produce*** | *They sell almost all their **agricultural produce** abroad.*

pro·duc·er /prəˈdusɚ/ W2 *n.* [C] **1** a person, company, or country that makes or grows goods, foods, or materials OPP **consumer**: +**of** *The company is a leading producer of contact lenses.* | **a coffee/wine/car etc. producer** *an international group of steel producers* **2** ENG. LANG. ARTS someone whose job is to control the preparation of a play, movie, broadcast etc., but who does not direct the actors: **TV/movie/record etc. producer** *a successful television producer* → see Word Choice box at PRODUCT ►see THESAURUS box at **movie** → see also DIRECTOR **3** BIOLOGY another word for an AUTOTROPH

proˈducer coˌoperative *n.* [C] ECONOMICS a COOPERATIVE (=business owned equally by all the people working there) that helps small farmers to sell their products

prod·uct /ˈprɑdʌkt/ S2 W1 *n.* **1** [C,U] something useful that is made in a factory, grown, or taken from nature: *None of our products are tested on animals.* | *the advertising of tobacco products* | *I'm allergic to **dairy products*** (=milk, cheese etc.). | *the company's **consumer products*** (=things that people buy) *division*

2 be a/the product of sth a) if someone is the product of a particular background or experience, their character is formed by that background or as a result of that experience: *Sex offenders are often the products of child abuse.* **b)** if something is the product of a particular situation, process etc., it is the result of that situation or process: *Health problems may be a product of poor housing.* **3** [C] MATH the number you get by multiplying two or more numbers in MATHEMATICS: +**of** *The product of 3 times 5 is 15.* **4** [C] CHEMISTRY a substance that is the result of a chemical process: *Hemoglobin is a product of red blood cells.* → see also GROSS DOMESTIC PRODUCT, GROSS NATIONAL PRODUCT

WORD CHOICE **product, produce, production, producer**

• **Production** [U] is the process in which things are made, especially in a factory: *We need to increase production* (NOT *the production*). | *mass production of computers.* A **production** [C] is a play, movie, or program made for the theater, television, or radio: *a new production of Thornton Wilder's play.*

• A **product** [C] is something that is made to be sold: *Dow produces a lot of chemical products.* | *household products such as cleaning liquids and detergents.* Banks and insurance companies also refer to the services they offer as **products**.

• **Produce** [U] (which is pronounced differently from the verb) is a general word for fresh fruit and vegetables: *There are more salad dressings available in the produce section.* If a person, company, or country produces something, they are a **producer** [C]: *Brazil is the world's most important producer of coffee.*

pro·duc·tion /prəˈdʌkʃən/ S2 W1 *n.* **1** [U] the process of making or growing things to be sold as products, or the amount that is produced: *Steel production has decreased by thirty-four percent.* | *Prices have increased to cover* ***production costs****.* | *The booklet, now* ***in production*** (=being made), *will be available in early January.* | *This type of engine never* ***went into production*** (=began to be produced in large numbers). **2** [C] something produced by skill or imagination, especially a play, movie, broadcast etc.: *the Northside Theater Company's production of "A Christmas Carol"* **3** [U] the act or process of making something new, or of bringing something into existence: *the body's production of white blood cells* **4 make a (major) production out of sth** INFORMAL to do something in a way that takes more effort or shows more emotion than is necessary, so that people notice: *Just wash the dishes! You don't have to made a production out of it.* **5** [U] the act of showing something **6** [U] ECONOMICS land, labor, and capital; the three things that are involved in producing all goods and services → see Word Choice box at PRODUCT

proˈduction ˌline *n.* [C] an arrangement of machines and workers in a factory, in which each does one job in the process of making a produce before passing it to the next machine or worker

proˈduction ˌnumber *n.* [C] a scene in a MUSICAL in which a lot of people sing and dance

proˈduction ˌplatform *n.* [C] a large piece of equipment standing on very long legs, used for getting oil out of the ground under the ocean

pro·duc·tive /prəˈdʌktɪv/ *adj.* **1** producing or achieving a lot OPP **unproductive**: *I'm more productive in the morning.* | *a* ***highly productive*** *meeting* | *Despite his health problems, Gilbert lives a* ***productive life*** (=he achieves a lot). **2** relating to the production of goods, crops, or wealth: *Fertilizers make the land more productive.* **3 productive of sth** FORMAL causing or producing something: *The information leak was productive of harmful results.* —**productively** *adv.* —**productiveness** *n.* [U]

proˌductive caˈpacity *n.* [U] ECONOMICS the total amount of goods or services that a country or economic system can produce without causing a large increase in INFLATION (=the continuing increase in prices, or the rate at which prices increase)

proˌductive ˈresources *n.* [plural] ECONOMICS the things, substances, and people that are used when making goods or providing services

pro·duc·tiv·i·ty /ˌproʊdəkˈtɪvəṭi, ˌprɑ-/ *n.* [U] the rate at which goods are produced, and the amount produced, especially in relation to the work, time, and money needed to produce them: **increase/improve/raise productivity** *ways of increasing worker productivity* | *The flu costs industry a lot in* ***lost productivity*** (=days when people cannot work). | *Better equipment led to* ***higher productivity****.*

ˈproduct ˌmarket *n.* [C] ECONOMICS a market in which goods or services are bought by people living on their own or by all the people living together in a house

ˈproduct ˌmix *n.* [C] TECHNICAL the number and type of different products made by a particular company

ˈproduct ˌplacement *n.* [U] a form of advertising in which particular products appear in movies or television shows

prof /prɑf/ *n.* [C] **1** INFORMAL a PROFESSOR **2 Prof.** the written abbreviation of PROFESSOR

pro·fane[1] /proʊˈfeɪn, prə-/ *adj.* **1** showing a lack of respect for God or for holy things: *profane language* | *a loud profane man* **2** FORMAL relating to ordinary life rather than religious or holy things SYN **secular** OPP **sacred**: *sacred and profane art* —**profanely** *adv.*

profane[2] *v.* [T] FORMAL to treat something holy in a way that is not respectful —**profanation** /ˌprɑfəˈneɪʃən, ˌproʊ-/ *n.* [C,U]

pro·fan·i·ty /proʊˈfænəṭi, prə-/ *n. plural* **profanities** **1** [C usually plural, U] offensive words or religious words used in a way that shows you do not respect God or holy things: *The movie is rated "R" for violence and profanity.* **2** [U] an act of showing disrespect for God or for holy things

pro·fess /prəˈfɛs, proʊ-/ *v.* [T] FORMAL **1** to say that you do or are something, especially when it is not really true: *Lewis professed his innocence.* | **profess to be sth** *He professes to be an expert on Islamic art.* | **profess to do sth** *Duke professes to have abandoned his racist views.* **2** to state a personal feeling or belief openly and freely: *He finally professed his love for her.* **3** to have a religion or belief

pro·fessed /prəˈfɛst/ *adj.* [only before noun] FORMAL **1** clearly stating what you believe: *a professed socialist* **2** used to describe a feeling or attitude someone says they have, but which may not be true —**professedly** *adv.*

pro·fes·sion /prəˈfɛʃən/ *n.* **1** [C,U] a job that needs special education and training: *professions such as engineering* | *He's a lawyer* ***by profession****.* | **legal/medical/teaching etc. profession** *She entered the* ***teaching profession*** *in the 1990s.* ▸see THESAURUS box at **job** **2** [singular] all the people in a particular profession: *In the next few years over half the profession will retire.* | **medical/legal/teaching etc. profession** *The medical profession is wary of the changes.* **3** [C] a statement of your belief, opinion, or feeling: *a profession of faith* **4 the world's oldest profession** HUMOROUS the job of being a PROSTITUTE

pro·fes·sion·al[1] /prəˈfɛʃənl/ Ac S3 W2 *adj.* **1** [no comparative] doing a job, sport, or activity for money OPP **amateur**: *a professional singer* | *professional athletes* | **turn/go professional** (=start to do something as a job) **2** [no comparative] done by or relating to people who are paid to do a sport or activity OPP **amateur**: *professional basketball games* **3** [only before noun, no comparative] relating to a job that needs special education and training: *professional development* | *Go to a lawyer for a professional opinion.* | *He needs* ***professional help****.* **4** showing that someone has been well trained and is good at their work, or done by such a person: *These brochures look very professional.* | *a professional approach to his work* **5 professional person/man/woman etc.** someone who works in a profession, or who has an important position in a company or business: *Most professional women find it difficult to balance working with having children.* **6 a profes-**

P

sional liar/complainer etc. HUMOROUS someone who lies or complains too much

professional² Ac W3 *n.* [C] **1** someone who earns money by doing a job, sport, or activity that many other people do just for fun OPP **amateur**: *The competition is open to both amateurs and professionals.* **2** someone who works in a job that needs special education and training: *a group of young professionals* | *Electrical repairs should be left to a* ***trained professional.*** | *nurses and other* ***health professionals*** **3** someone who has a lot of experience and does something very skillfully: *He was a true professional in the field of insurance.* **4 tennis/golf/swimming etc. professional** someone who is very good at a sport and is employed by a private club to teach its members

P

pro·fes·sion·al·ism /prəˈfɛʃnəlˌɪzəm, -ʃənl-/ Ac *n.* [U] the skill and high standards of behavior expected of a professional person: *an employee's competence and professionalism*

proˌfessional ˈlabor *n.* [U] ECONOMICS work that needs a lot of skill, which can only be done by very educated people or by people who have had special training

pro·fes·sion·al·ly /prəˈfɛʃənl-i/ Ac *adv.* **1** as a paid job rather than just for enjoyment: *Schneider has cooked professionally.* **2** as part of your work: *Do you need to use English professionally?* **3** in a way that shows high standards and good training: *a professionally edited video* **4** by someone who has the necessary skills and training: *All plumbing should be professionally installed.*

proˌfessional organiˈzation *n.* [C] ECONOMICS a NONPROFIT organization that does things to improve the conditions and skills of professional people working in jobs that need special training, and which also works to improve the opinion the general public has about the profession

proˌfessional ˈwrestling *n.* [U] a form of entertainment in which people, usually men, fight each other in a way that has been planned before the event —**professional wrestler** *n.* [C]

pro·fes·sor S2 W2, **Professor** /prəˈfɛsɚ/ *n.* [C] a teacher at a college or university, especially one who has a high rank: *Professor Paterson* | **biology/history/Spanish etc. professor** *Who is your economics professor?* | **+of** *a professor of physics* → see also ASSISTANT PROFESSOR, ASSOCIATE PROFESSOR, FULL PROFESSOR

WORD CHOICE **professor, assistant professor, associate professor, full professor, instructor**
In the U.S. most university teachers are called **professor**, which is used for any full-time member of the teaching staff of a university or college. There are three specific ranks: **assistant professor**, **associate professor**, and **full professor. Assistant professor** is the least important position and **full professor** is the most important. An **instructor** is usually a part-time member of a university or college teaching staff. School teachers are never called professors in the U.S.

pro·fes·so·ri·al /ˌprɑfəˈsɔriəl/ *adj.* relating to the job of a professor, or considered typical of a professor: *his professorial appearance* —**professorially** *adv.*

pro·fes·sor·ship /prəˈfɛsɚˌʃɪp/ *n.* [C] the job or position of a college or university professor

prof·fer /ˈprɑfɚ/ *v.* [T] FORMAL **1** to give someone advice, an explanation etc.: *Spencer refused to proffer an apology.* **2** to offer something to someone, especially by holding it out in your hands: *She took a glass proffered by a waiter.* —**proffer** *n.* [C]

pro·fi·cien·cy /prəˈfɪʃənsi/ *n. plural* **proficiencies** [C,U] a high standard of ability and skill: **+in/with/at** *a high level of proficiency in English*

pro·fi·cient /prəˈfɪʃənt/ *adj.* able to do something well or skillfully: **+in/at** *Gwen is proficient in three languages.* | *a proficient typist* —**proficiently** *adv.*

pro·file¹ /ˈproʊfaɪl/ W3 *n.* [C] **1** a side view of someone's head: *He has an attractive profile.* | *a drawing of her* ***in profile*** **2** a short description that gives important details about a person, a group of people, or a place: *a job profile* | **+of** *a short profile of the actor* **3 keep a low profile** to behave quietly and avoid doing things that will make people notice you: *Western visitors to the region are asked to keep a low profile.* **4 raise sb's profile** if a person or organization raises its profile, it gets more attention from the public: *an ad campaign designed to raise the bank's profile* **5** an edge or shape of something seen against a background: *the sharp profile of the mountains against the sky* [**Origin:** 1600–1700 Italian *profilo*, from *profilare* **to draw the edge of something**, from *filare* **to spin**] → see also HIGH-PROFILE

profile² *v.* [T] to write or give a short description of someone or something

pro·fil·ing /ˈproʊfaɪlɪŋ/ *n.* [U] **1** DNA PROFILING **2** the way in which some police organizations stop people from particular races or other groups in order to ask them questions, search them etc., because the police think that these people are more likely to be involved in crimes: *racial profiling* **3** the act of collecting information about people you want to sell something to

prof·it¹ /ˈprɑfɪt/ S3 W1 *n.* **1** [C,U] money that you gain by selling things or doing business, after you have paid your costs: *All the profits will go to cancer research.* | **+of** *a profit of $13.5 million* | **make/turn/earn a profit** *We could sell the CDs for $3 apiece and still make a profit.* | **big/huge/strong/handsome etc. profit** *The project generated huge profits for real estate companies.* | *They fixed up the property and sold it* ***at a profit.*** | **net profit** (=the profit after taxes etc. are paid) | **gross profit** (=the profit before taxes etc. are paid) **2** [U] an advantage that you gain from doing something SYN **benefit**: **+in** *There's no profit to be found in lying.* [**Origin:** 1200–1300 Old French, Latin *profectus*, past participle of *proficere* **to go forward, get something done**] → see also NONPROFIT

profit² *v.* **1** [I,T] FORMAL to be useful or helpful to someone: **profit sb to do sth** *It might profit you to learn about the company before your interview.* | **+from/by** *Many companies profit from hiring minorities.* **2** [I] to gain money from doing something: **+from/by** *Convicted criminals are not permitted to profit from their crimes.*

prof·it·a·bil·i·ty /ˌprɑfɪt̬əˈbɪlət̬i/ *n.* [U] the state of producing a profit, or the degree to which a business or activity produces a profit: *The company is shaving costs to improve profitability.*

prof·it·a·ble /ˈprɑfɪt̬əbəl/ *adj.* **1** producing a profit OPP **unprofitable**: *Many small hospitals are struggling to stay profitable.* | *a* ***highly profitable*** *business* **2** producing a useful result OPP **unprofitable**: *I spent a profitable afternoon at home.* —**profitably** *adv.*

ˌprofit and ˈloss ˌstatement *n.* [C] a financial statement showing a company's income, spending, and profit over a particular period

prof·it·eer /ˌprɑfəˈtɪr/ *n.* [C] someone who makes unfairly large profits, especially by selling things at very high prices when they are difficult to get: *black market profiteers* —**profiteer** *v.* [I] —**profiteering** *n.* [U]

prof·it·less /ˈprɑfətlɪs/ *adj.* not making a profit, or not worth doing —**profitlessly** *adv.*

ˈprofit-ˌmaking *adj.* making a profit: *a profit-making enterprise*

ˈprofit ˌmargin *n.* [C] the difference between the cost of producing something and the price you sell it at

ˈprofit ˌmotive *n.* [U] ECONOMICS the desire to make money, usually given as the reason why a person or business is prepared to do something in order to earn money, especially a lot of money

ˈprofit ˌsharing *n.* [U] a system by which all the people who work for a company receive part of its profits

prof·li·gate /ˈprɑfləgɪt/ *adj.* FORMAL **1** wasting money or other things in a stupid and careless way: *the profligate use of energy resources* **2** behaving in an immoral way and not caring about it at all —**profligacy** *n.* [U] —**profligate** *n.* [C]

pro for·ma /proʊ ˈfɔrmə/ *adj., adv.* FORMAL if something is approved, accepted etc. pro forma, this is part of the usual way of doing things and does not involve any actual choice or decision

pro·found /prəˈfaʊnd/ *adj.* **1** important and having a strong influence or effect: **profound impact/effect/influence etc.** *The study had a profound effect on U.S. health policy.* | *There have been* ***profound changes*** *in climate.* | *a book with profound social implications* **2** showing strong serious feelings SYN **deep**: *a* ***profound sense*** *of sadness* **3** showing great knowledge and understanding SYN **deep**: *a profound remark* | *The essay was very profound.* **4** complete SYN **total**: *profound deafness* | *There was a profound silence after his remark.* **5** LITERARY deep or far below the surface of something SYN **deep** [**Origin:** 1200–1300 Old French *profond* **deep**, from Latin *profundus*, from *fundus* **bottom**] —**profoundly** *adv.*

pro·fun·di·ty /prəˈfʌndət̬i/ *n. plural* **profundities** FORMAL **1** [U] the quality of knowing and understanding a lot, or having strong serious feelings SYN **depth**: *Fairy tales have a surprising profundity.* **2** [C usually plural] something that someone says that shows this quality

pro·fuse /prəˈfyus, proʊ-/ *adj.* **1** given, flowing, or growing freely and in large quantities: *profuse sweating* **2** very eager or generous with your praise, thanks etc.: *profuse apologies* —**profusely** *adv.* —**profuseness** *n.* [U]

pro·fu·sion /prəˈfyuʒən/ *n.* [singular, U] a supply or amount that is almost too large: +**of** *a profusion of photos* | *The vines that grew* ***in wild profusion*** *over the fence.*

pro·gen·i·tor /proʊˈdʒɛnət̬ɚ/ *n.* [C] **1** a person or animal that lived a long time ago, to whom someone or something living now is related SYN **ancestor** **2** FORMAL someone who first thought of an idea a long time ago: +**of** *a progenitor of modern dance*

prog·e·ny /ˈprɑdʒəni/ *n.* [U] **1** TECHNICAL the DESCENDANTS of a person, animal, or plant form SYN **offspring** **2** FORMAL someone's children SYN **offspring** **3** FORMAL something that has developed from something else

pro·ges·ter·one /proʊˈdʒɛstəˌroʊn/ *n.* [U] a female sex HORMONE that is produced by a woman when she is going to have a baby and is also used in CONTRACEPTIVE drugs

prog·na·thous /ˈprɑgnəθəs, prɑgˈneɪθəs/ *adj.* BIOLOGY with a jaw that sticks out more than the rest of the face

prog·no·sis /prɑgˈnoʊsɪs/ *n. plural* **prognoses** /-siz/ [C] **1** a doctor's opinion of how an illness or disease will develop: **prognosis is good/poor/excellent etc.** *Doctors say his prognosis is good.* → see also DIAGNOSIS **2** FORMAL a judgment about the future that is based on information or experience: +**for** *The prognosis for world trade is excellent.*

prog·nos·ti·cation /prɑgˌnɑstəˈkeɪʃən/ *n.* [C,U] a statement about what you think will happen in the future SYN **forecast** —**prognosticate** /prɑgˈnɑstəˌkeɪt/ *v.* [T]

pro·gram¹ /ˈproʊgræm, -grəm/ S1 W1 *n.* [C]
1 PLAN a series of actions which are designed to achieve something important, especially actions that are organized by a government or large organization: *the U.S. space program* | **program to do sth** *a government program to feed the poor* | +**of** *a program of economic aid*
2 TELEVISION/RADIO a show or performance on television or radio, especially one that is played regularly: *a popular* ***television program*** | +**about** *a program about whales* ►see THESAURUS box at **television**
3 COMPUTER a set of instructions given to a computer to make it do a particular job: *a word processing program*
4 EDUCATION a set of classes, activities etc. which have a specific purpose: *The college has a good nursing program.* | *the company's management* ***training program*** | *an* ***educational program*** *for Vietnam veterans*
5 PLAY/PERFORMANCE a printed description of what will happen at a play, concert etc. and which says who the performers are: *a circus program* ►see THESAURUS box at **theater**
6 ACTIVITIES a series of planned activities or events, or a list showing what order they will happen in SYN **schedule**: *the museum's program of exhibitions*
7 get with the program SPOKEN used to tell someone to pay attention to what needs to be done, and to do it
8 MACHINE a series of actions done in a particular order by a machine, for example a washing machine
[**Origin:** 1600–1700 French *programme*, from Greek, from *prographein* **to write before**]

program² S2 W2 *v.* **programmed**, **programming** **1** [T] to set a machine to operate in a particular way: **program sth to do sth** *I've programmed the VCR to record the 9 o'clock movie.* **2** [I,T] COMPUTERS to write a set of instructions for a computer or give a computer instructions, which it uses to perform a particular operation: **program sth to do sth** *They're trying to program computers to produce and understand speech.* | *Hal spends most of his time programming.* **3** [T usually passive] if a person or animal is programmed to do something, they do it without thinking about it, because of their GENES or because of social influences: **program sb to be sth** *The birds are programmed to build their nests in the same way.* **4** to arrange for something to happen as part of a series of planned events: *The orchestra programs very little modern music.* → see also PROGRAMMER

ˈprogram diˌrector *n.* [C] **1** someone who manages an organization or a PROGRAM (=set of planned activities) **2** someone who decides what PROGRAMS to show on a television or radio station

pro·gram·ma·ble /proʊˈgræməbəl, ˈproʊgræm-/ *adj.* COMPUTERS able to be controlled by a computer or electronic program: *a programmable heating system*

pro·gram·mat·ic /ˌproʊgrəˈmæt̬ɪk/ *adj.* FORMAL relating to a program or to how something is organized

pro·gramme /ˈproʊgræm/ the British spelling of PROGRAM, also used in Canada

ˌprogrammed inˈstruction *n.* [U] a method of teaching in which the subject to be learned is divided into small parts, and students have to learn one part correctly before they can go on to the next

pro·gram·mer /ˈproʊˌgræmɚ, -grəmɚ/ *n.* [C] COMPUTERS someone whose job is to write computer PROGRAMS

pro·gram·ming /ˈproʊgræmɪŋ/ *n.* [U] **1** television or radio PROGRAMS, or the activity of producing them: *sports programming* **2** COMPUTERS the activity of writing PROGRAMS for computers **3** COMPUTERS something written by a computer programmer: *Computer viruses are little bits of destructive programming.*

prog·ress¹ /ˈprɑgrəs, -grɛs/ S3 W2 *n.* [U] **1** the process of getting better at doing something, or getting closer to finishing or achieving something: +**on/toward** *the country's progress toward democratic elections* | +**of** *the* ***slow progress*** *of the investigation* | *a* ***lack of progress*** *in the budget talks* | **steady/real/significant etc. progress** *Researchers have* ***made*** *steady* ***progress.*** | **monitor/assess/check sb's progress** *The tests monitor the students' progress.* **2** all the improvements, developments, and achievements that happen in science, society, work etc.: *He dismissed them as simply afraid of progress.* | *technological progress* | *History was seen as a* ***march of progress*** *from savagery to civilization.* | *Are we destroying our planet* ***in the name of progress*** (=because people want progress)*?* **3 in progress** happening now, and not yet finished: *Filming was already in progress.* | *On the easel was a* ***work in progress.*** **4** movement toward a place: *The ship* ***made*** *slow* ***progress*** *through the rough sea.*

pro·gress² /prəˈgrɛs/ *v.* **1** [I] to develop, improve, or achieve things so that you reach a more advanced stage OPP **regress**: *Repair work has progressed quickly.* | +**to**

Will events progress to civil war? | **+beyond** *He was brain damaged, and never progressed beyond the level of a two-year-old child.* | **+toward/towards** *They received rewards as they progressed towards their goals.* **2** [I] ESPECIALLY WRITTEN to move forward slowly: *The men progressed slowly up the stairs.* **3** [I] ESPECIALLY WRITTEN if time or an event progresses, time passes: *She became more relaxed as the day progressed.* **4** [I] ESPECIALLY HUMOROUS to move on from doing one thing to doing another: **+to** *We started with a bottle of wine, and then progressed to whiskey.* **5** [T] to make something such as a plan or idea be developed or start to be used: *I do not know how quickly we can progress the matter.* → see also REGRESS

P

pro·gres·sion /prəˈgrɛʃən/ *n.* **1** [U] a process of change or development: **+of** *the* ***natural progression*** *of the disease* | **progression (from sth) to sth** *She made a rapid progression from young skater to world favorite.* | **+toward/towards** *a progression toward greater equality* **2** [U] movement toward a GOAL or particular place: *the river's progression toward the Gulf of Mexico* **3** [C] a number of things coming one after the other → see also ARITHMETIC PROGRESSION, GEOMETRIC PROGRESSION

pro·gres·sive¹ /prəˈgrɛsɪv/ *adj.* **1** supporting new or modern ideas and methods, especially in politics and education: *progressive policies such as paternity leave* **2** happening or developing gradually over a period of time: *a progressive decline in the country's power* | *a progressive brain disorder* **3** ENG. LANG. ARTS the progressive form of a verb is used to show that an action or activity is continuing to happen, and is shown in English by the verb "be" followed by a PRESENT PARTICIPLE, as in "I was waiting for the bus" —**progressively** *adv.* —**progressiveness** *n.* [U]

progressive² *n.* [C] someone with modern ideas who wants to change things

pro,gressive 'tax *n.* [singular] ECONOMICS a tax that takes a larger PERCENTAGE of money from people with higher incomes than from people with lower incomes → see also REGRESSIVE TAX

'progress re,port *n.* [C] a statement about how something, especially work, is developing

pro·hib·it /proʊˈhɪbɪt, prə-/ Ac W3 *v.* [T] **1** LAW to officially say that an action is illegal or not allowed SYN **forbid** SYN **ban**: *Selling alcohol to people under 21 is prohibited.* | **prohibit sb from doing sth** *Laws prohibited blacks from owning property.* ►see THESAURUS box at **forbid** **2** to make something impossible or prevent it from happening: **prohibit sb/sth from doing sth** *His poor eyesight prohibited him from becoming a pilot.* [**Origin:** 1400–1500 Latin, past participle of *prohibere* **to hold away, prevent**] ►see THESAURUS box at **forbid**

pro·hi·bi·tion /ˌproʊəˈbɪʃən/ Ac *n.* **1** [C,U] LAW the act of officially saying that something is illegal, or the order that says this: **+on/against/of** *a prohibition on cigarette advertising* | *the prohibition of chemical weapons* **2 Prohibition** the period from 1919 to 1933 in the U.S. when the production and sale of alcoholic drinks were forbidden by law

pro·hi·bi·tion·ist /ˌproʊəˈbɪʃənɪst/ *n.* [C] someone who supported Prohibition —**prohibitionism** *n.* [U]

pro·hib·i·tive /proʊˈhɪbət̬ɪv, prə-/ Ac *adj.* **1** prohibitive prices are so high that they prevent people from buying or doing something: *The cost of renovating the old buildings would be prohibitive.* **2** LAW a prohibitive tax or rule prevents people from doing things: *a prohibitive tax on imports* **3 prohibitive favorite** the person, team, or group that is most likely to win a game, election etc.: *The Huskies are prohibitive favorites against Toledo.* —**prohibitively** *adv.*

pro·hib·i·to·ry /proʊˈhɪbəˌtɔri/ *adj.* intended to stop something

proj·ect¹ /ˈprɑdʒɛkt, -dʒɪkt/ Ac S1 W1 *n.* [C] **1** an important and carefully planned piece of work, especially one that is intended to build something, deal with a problem, improve something etc.: *Work on the new freeway project began yesterday.* | *an important* ***research project*** | **major/big project** *a major construction project* **2** a part of a school course that involves careful study of a particular subject over a period of time: **+on** *Our class is* ***doing a project*** *on pollution.* **3 the projects** INFORMAL the buildings that are part of a HOUSING PROJECT [**Origin:** 1300–1400 Latin *projectum*, from the past participle of *proicere* **to throw forward**] → see also HOUSING PROJECT

pro·ject² /prəˈdʒɛkt/ Ac S3 W3 *v.*

1 CALCULATE [T] to calculate the size, amount, or rate of something as it probably will be in the future, using the information you have now: *School officials are projecting a rise in student numbers.* | **project sth to do sth** *Profits are projected to drop by 11%.*

2 MOVIE/PHOTOGRAPH [T] to make the picture of a movie, photograph etc. appear in a larger form on a screen or flat surface: *An image was projected onto a screen on stage.*

3 PLAN be projected to be planned to happen in the future: *the projected closure of the school*

4 HOW SB SEEMS [T] to make other people have a particular idea about you: *You need to* ***project*** *a professional* ***image.*** | *During the campaign, he successfully* ***projected himself as*** *a reliable ordinary guy.*

5 STICK OUT [I] to stick out beyond an edge or surface SYN **protrude**: **+out/from/through etc.** *The garage roof projects two feet over the driveway.*

6 FEELINGS [T] to imagine that other people have the same feelings as you, especially when you do not realize you are doing this: **project sth on/onto sb** *Parents must try not to project their own worries onto their children.*

7 project your voice to speak clearly and loudly so that you can be heard by everyone in a big room

8 IMAGINE to make it seem as though someone is in a different time or place, especially in the future: **project sb/sth into sth** *Reading lets us project ourselves into unfamiliar environments.*

9 THROW [T] TECHNICAL to throw something up or forward with great force

10 PICTURE [T] TECHNICAL **a)** to make a picture of a solid object on a flat surface **b)** to make a map using this method

pro·jec·tile /prəˈdʒɛktl, -ˌtaɪl/ *n.* [C] an object that is thrown or is fired from a weapon, such as a bullet, stone, or SHELL

pro,jectile 'vomiting *n.* [U] the action of VOMITING with a lot of force

pro·jec·tion /prəˈdʒɛkʃən/ Ac *n.* **1** [C] a statement or calculation about what will probably happen, based on information available now: *next year's sales projections* | **earnings/financial/economic/spending etc. projection** *the airline's earnings projections* | **+for** *population projections for the next 25 years* | **+of** *a projection of famine in the area* **2** [C] FORMAL something that sticks out from a surface: *The projections on the tires improve traction on snow and ice.* **3** [U] the act of projecting a movie or picture: *projection equipment* **4** [U] the act of imagining that other people or things are feeling the same emotions as you: **projection of sth onto sb/sth** *the poet's projection of her own moods onto nature* **5** [C] **a)** ENG. LANG. ARTS an image of something that has been projected **b)** the way in which an image of the earth's surface has been projected on a map: *Different projections produce very different-looking maps.*

pro·jec·tion·ist /prəˈdʒɛkʃənɪst/ *n.* [C] someone whose job is to operate the projector in a movie theater

pro·jec·tor /prəˈdʒɛktɚ/ *n.* [C] a piece of equipment that makes a movie or picture appear on a screen or on a flat surface → see also OVERHEAD PROJECTOR

pro·kar·y·ote /proʊˈkæriˌoʊt/ *n.* [C] BIOLOGY a type of ORGANISM whose cells do not have a NUCLEUS. Most prokaryotes have only one cell, for example BACTERIA.

Pro·kof·iev /prəˈkɔfiɛf, -fyəf/, **Ser·gei** /ˈsɚgeɪ/ (1891–1953) a Russian musician who wrote CLASSICAL music

pro·lapse /ˈproʊlæps, proʊˈlæps/ *n.* [C] MEDICINE the

falling down or slipping of an inner part of your body, such as the UTERUS, from its usual position

pro·le·tar·i·at /ˌproʊləˈtɛriət/ *n.* **the proletariat** the class of workers who own no property and work for WAGES, especially in factories, building things etc. —**proletarian** *adj.*

ˌpro-ˈlife *adj.* someone who is pro-life is opposed to ABORTION and uses this word to describe their opinion → see also PRO-CHOICE, RIGHT-TO-LIFE

ˌpro-ˈlifer *n.* [C] a member of a pro-life group

pro·lif·er·ate /prəˈlɪfəˌreɪt/ *v.* [I] if something proliferates, it increases quickly and spreads to many different places: *Fast-food restaurants have proliferated.*

pro·lif·er·a·tion /prəˌlɪfəˈreɪʃən/ *n.* **1** [singular, U] a rapid increase in the amount or number of something: +**of** *the proliferation of nuclear weapons* **2** [U] BIOLOGY the very fast growth of new parts of a living thing, such as cells

pro·lif·ic /prəˈlɪfɪk/ *adj.* **1** someone who is prolific produces a lot of something, especially works of art, books etc.: *hockey's most prolific scorer* **2** an animal or plant that is prolific produces many babies or many other plants **3** LITERARY existing in large numbers: *the prolific bird life* —**prolifically** /-kli/ *adv.*

pro·lix /proʊˈlɪks, ˈproʊlɪks/ *adj.* FORMAL a prolix piece of writing has too many words and is boring

PROLOG /ˈproʊlɑg/ *n.* [U] TRADEMARK a computer language that is similar to human language

pro·logue /ˈproʊlɑg, -lɔg/ *n.* [C usually singular] **1** ENG. LANG. ARTS the introduction to a play, a long poem etc. **2** LITERARY an act or event that leads to a much more important event: +**to** *The failures of the past are a prologue to success.* → see also EPILOGUE

pro·long /prəˈlɔŋ/ *v.* [T] to deliberately make something such as a feeling or activity last longer: *These drugs can prolong lives.*

> **THESAURUS**
>
> **lengthen** to make something continue longer: *The bill would lengthen prison sentences.*
> **extend** to continue for a longer period of time, or to make something continue longer: *Freezing extends the period for which you can store meat.*
> **drag out** to make a situation or event last longer than necessary: *Each side accused the other of dragging out the negotiations.*

pro·lon·ga·tion /ˌproʊlɔŋˈgeɪʃən/ *n.* **1** [U] the act of making something last longer **2** [C] something added to another thing, which makes it longer

pro·longed /prəˈlɔŋd/ *adj.* continuing for a long time: *a prolonged illness*

prom /prɑm/ *n.* [C] a formal dance party for HIGH SCHOOL students, often held at the end of a school year: *the senior prom*

prom·e·nade /ˌprɑməˈneɪd, -ˈnɑd/ *n.* [C] **1** a wide road next to the beach where people can walk for pleasure **2** OLD-FASHIONED a walk for pleasure in a public place

promeˈnade deck *n.* [C] the upper level of a ship where people can walk for pleasure

Pro·me·the·us /prəˈmiθiəs/ in Greek MYTHOLOGY, a TITAN who stole fire from heaven to give to humans

prom·i·nence /ˈprɑmənəns/ *n.* **1** [U] the fact of being important and well known: *The case* ***gained prominence*** (=became well known) *because of the brutal nature of the murders.* | **come/rise to prominence** *The pianist rose to prominence in the 1950s.* **2** [U] the state of being important and easy to notice: *Dance has greater prominence in this year's festival.* | +**of** *the prominence of issues such as abortion during the campaign* **3** [C] FORMAL a part or place that is higher or larger than what is around it

prom·i·nent /ˈprɑmənənt/ W3 *adj.* **1** [C] well known and important: *a prominent business leader* | *a* ***prominent figure*** *in the administration* | *The federal government should* ***play a prominent role*** (=be very involved) *in fighting crime.* **2** important and getting or deserving a lot of attention: *a prominent political issue* **3** something that is prominent is large and sticks out: *a prominent nose* **4** easy to see: **prominent place/position** *The story was given a prominent place on the front page.* | *a prominent display of her new book* [**Origin:** 1400–1500 Latin, present participle of *prominere* **to stick out**]

pro·mis·cu·ous /prəˈmɪskyuəs/ *adj.* **1** having sex with a lot of people: *promiscuous sexual behavior* **2** OLD USE made of many different parts **3** OLD USE not choosing carefully —**promiscuously** *adv.* —**promiscuity** /ˌprɑmɪˈskyuəṭi/ *n.* [U]

prom·ise¹ /ˈprɑmɪs/ S2 W1 *v.* **1** [I,T] to tell someone that you will definitely do something or that something will happen: *The mayor promised a full investigation.* | **promise (that)** *Todd promises that he will write often.* | **promise sb (that)** *You promised me you would be on time.* | **promise to do sth** *Becky promised to help.* | **promise sb sth** *Mom promised us ice-cream if we were good at the store.* | **I/we promise** *"Promise me you won't do anything stupid." "I promise."* | *"I'll help you get it finished."* ***"Promise?"*** (=used to ask if someone promises) | *On Monday, the hostages were released* ***as promised*** (=at the time or place that was promised).

> **THESAURUS**
>
> **swear** to make a very serious promise: *Can teachers be required to swear that they will teach respect for the flag?*
> **take/swear an oath** to make a very serious promise in public: *You must take an oath of loyalty to your country.*
> **vow** to make a serious promise, often to yourself: *She vowed that she would never drink alcohol again.*
> **guarantee** to promise something that you feel very sure about: *The constitution guarantees Americans the right to freedom of speech.*
> **give sb your word** to promise someone very sincerely that you will do something: *He gave us his word and I believe him.*

2 [T] to show signs that make you expect that something will happen: *The game* ***promises to be*** *exciting.* | *The dark clouds promised rain later.* **3 I can't promise anything** SPOKEN used to tell someone that you will try to do what they want, but may not be able to: *I'll try to get us tickets, but I can't promise anything.* **4 I promise you...** SPOKEN used to emphasize that what you are saying is true: *I promise you, it really does work!* **5 promise (sb) the moon/world** if you promise someone the moon, you promise to do things that you cannot really do: *Politicians promise the world and deliver nothing.*

promise² W2 *n.* **1** [C] a statement that you will definitely do something or that something will definitely happen: *You* ***made a promise****, so you have to keep it.* | +**of** *a promise of help* | +**to** *his promise to his father* | **a promise to do sth** *Jim made a promise to quit smoking.* | **promise that** *his promise that I would get a promotion* | +**of** *a promise of cooperation* | **keep/break a promise** (=to do or fail to do something you promised) *Don't make promises you can't keep.* **2** [U] signs that something or someone will be good or successful: *The project seemed* ***full of promise****.* | *John* ***shows*** *a lot of* ***promise*** (=is likely to be good) *as a writer.* | +**of** *More research is needed to* ***fulfill the promise*** *of this powerful technology.* **3** [singular, U] a sign that something, usually something good, will probably happen: +**of** *The air held the promise of spring.* | *Mastering computer skills* ***holds the promise*** *of better jobs.* [**Origin:** 1300–1400 Latin *promissum*, from the past participle of *promittere* **to send out, promise**]

ˈPromised ˌLand *n.* **the Promised Land a)** the land of Canaan, which was promised by God to Abraham and his people in the Bible **b)** a situation or condition that you have wanted for a long time because it will bring you happiness and make you feel safe

prom·is·ing /ˈprɑmɪsɪŋ/ *adj.* showing signs of being successful in the future: *The win is a promising start to the season.* | *a promising young actor* —**promisingly** *adv.*

prom·is·so·ry note /ˈprɑməsɔri ˌnoʊt/ *n.* [C] a document promising to pay money before a particular date

pro·mo /ˈproʊmoʊ/ *n. plural* **promos** [C] **1** INFORMAL a short movie that advertises an event or product **2** a free product, given away in order to advertise something

P

prom·on·to·ry /ˈprɑmənˌtɔri/ *n. plural* **promontories** [C] EARTH SCIENCE a high, long, and narrow piece of land that goes out into the ocean

pro·mote /prəˈmoʊt/ Ac W2 *v.* [T] **1** to help something to develop and be successful: *The council should do more to promote recycling.* | *an exercise that promotes flexibility* **2** [usually passive] to give someone a better and more responsible job in a company OPP **demote**: **promote sb to sth** *Verdon was promoted to senior manager.* **3** to make sure people know about a new product, movie etc., especially by offering it at a reduced price or by advertising it: *a national tour to promote her new book* ▸see THESAURUS box at **advertise** **4** to try to persuade people to believe or support an idea or way of doing things: *Allen goes to schools to promote his anti-drug message.* **5** to be responsible for arranging a large public event such as a concert or a sports game [**Origin:** 1300–1400 Latin, past participle of *promovere* **to move forward**]

pro·mot·er /prəˈmoʊt̬ɚ/ Ac *n.* [C] **1** someone who arranges and advertises concerts or sports events **2** someone who tries to persuade people to believe or support an idea or way of doing things: *a promoter of solar energy*

pro·mo·tion /prəˈmoʊʃən/ Ac *n.* **1** [C,U] a move to a more important job or rank in a company or organization: *He got a promotion and a raise.* | +**to** *the promotion of Moore to vice chairman* **2** [C,U] an activity intended to help sell a product, or the product that is being promoted: *a* ***sales promotion*** *for computers* | +**for** *The network runs promotions for its shows during other programs.* **3** [U] the activity of persuading people to support an idea or way of doing things: +**of** *the promotion of women's rights* **4** [U] the activity of helping something develop and succeed: *the promotion of recycling*

pro·mo·tion·al /prəˈmoʊʃənl/ *adj.* promotional movies, events etc. are made or organized to advertise something: *a promotional brochure*

prompt¹ /prɑmpt/ W3 *v.* **1** [T] to make someone decide to do something, especially something that they had been thinking of doing: *News of the scandal prompted a Senate investigation.* | **prompt sb to do sth** *The decision prompted steel workers to strike.* **2** [T] to make people say or do something as a reaction: *The announcement has prompted criticism from the ACLU.* **3** [I,T] ENG. LANG. ARTS to remind an actor or actress of the next words in a speech **4** [T] COMPUTERS if a computer prompts you to do something, it tells you what to do next or asks you for information: *The program then prompted me to install the ink cartridges.* **5** [T] to encourage someone to speak, or to help a speaker who pauses: *Even when prompted, he won't join the discussion.* [**Origin:** 1300–1400 Medieval Latin *promptare*, from Latin *promptus*, from the past participle of *promere* **to bring out**]

prompt² *adj.* **1** done quickly, immediately, or at the right time: *Complaints receive a prompt response.* **2** [not before noun] someone who is prompt arrives at the right time or does something on time: *Lunch is at two. Try to be prompt.* —**promptness** *n.* [U]

prompt³ *n.* [C] **1** COMPUTERS a sign on a computer screen that shows that the computer has finished one operation and is ready to begin the next: *Turn on your computer and wait until the prompt appears.* **2** ENG. LANG. ARTS a word or words said to an actor in a play, to help them remember what to say

prompt·er /ˈprɑmptɚ/ *n.* [C] someone who tells actors in a play what words to say when they forget

prompt·ing /ˈprɑmptɪŋ/ *n.* **1** [C,U] the act of reminding or encouraging someone to do something: *It took some prompting, but I finally got Jay to clean his room.* **2** [U] the act of telling an actor what to say when they forget

prompt·ly /ˈprɑmptli/ *adv.* **1** immediately: *She promptly went back to sleep.* **2** without delay: *A reply came promptly.* **3** at the right time without being late: *She arrived promptly.* | *The meeting will start promptly at 10 a.m.*

prom·ul·gate /ˈprɑməlˌgeɪt/ *v.* [T] FORMAL **1** to spread an idea or belief to as many people as possible **2** LAW to make a new law come into effect by announcing it officially —**promulgator** *n.* [C] —**promulgation** /ˌprɑməlˈgeɪʃən/ *n.* [U]

pron. *n.* the written abbreviation of PRONOUN

prone /proʊn/ *adj.* **1** likely to do something or suffer from something, especially something bad or harmful: +**to** *Tight muscles are prone to injury.* | **prone to do sth** *The area is prone to flooding.* | **injury-prone/fire-prone/accident-prone etc.** *leak-prone fiberglass boats* **2** FORMAL lying down with the front of your body facing down: *a prone body on the floor* → see also PROSTRATE —**proneness** *n.* [U]

prong /prɔŋ, prɑŋ/ *n.* [C] **1** a thin sharp point of something that has several points, such as a fork **2** one or two or three ways of achieving something which are used at the same time: +**of** *the second prong of the attack* —**pronged** /prɔŋd, prɑŋd/ *adj.*: *a three-pronged approach*

pro·nom·i·nal /proʊˈnɑmənl/ *adj.* ENG. LANG. ARTS relating to or used like a PRONOUN —**pronominally** *adv.*

pro·noun /ˈproʊnaʊn/ *n.* [C] ENG. LANG. ARTS a word that is used instead of a noun or noun phrase, such as "he" instead of "Peter" or "the man," or "it" instead of "the car" → see also DEMONSTRATIVE PRONOUN, PERSONAL PRONOUN

pro·nounce /prəˈnaʊns/ S3 *v.* **1** [T] ENG. LANG. ARTS to make the sound of a letter, word etc., especially in the correct way: *How do you pronounce your last name?* **2** [T] to officially state that something is true: **pronounce sb/sth (to be) sth** *Martins was* ***pronounced dead*** *at 11:07 p.m.* | *I now pronounce you husband and wife.* **3** LAW to give a legal judgment: *The court cannot pronounce judgment in this case.* | *The judge* ***pronounced sentence*** (=said what someone's punishment would be). **4** [I,T] FORMAL to give a judgment or opinion, especially in an official situation: **pronounce (sth) on sth** *Kids will soon be* ***pronouncing judgment*** *on the quality of the games.* | **pronounce yourself** *He pronounced himself surprised by their reaction.* [**Origin:** 1300–1400 Old French *pronuncier*, from Latin *pronuntiare*, from *nuntius* **messenger**]

pro·nounced /prəˈnaʊnst/ *adj.* very easy to notice: *a pronounced limp* | *Her Polish accent is very pronounced.* —**pronouncedly** /prəˈnaʊnsɪdli/ *adv.*

pro·nounce·ment /prəˈnaʊnsmənt/ *n.* [C] FORMAL an official public statement: +**on** *the Pope's latest pronouncement on birth control*

pron·to /ˈprɑntoʊ/ *adv.* SPOKEN quickly or immediately: *The boss wants this report pronto.*

pro·nun·ci·a·tion /prəˌnʌnsiˈeɪʃən/ *n.* **1** [C,U] ENG. LANG. ARTS the way in which a language or a particular word is pronounced: *This word has a different pronunciation in British English.* **2** [singular, U] a particular person's way of pronouncing a word or words: *His pronunciation is very good.*

proof¹ /pruf/ *n.* **1** [C,U] facts, information, documents etc. that prove something is true: +**of** *Drivers should carry proof of insurance.* | **proof that** *There is no proof that the document is authentic.* | **show/provide proof** *Immigrants must be able to show proof of residency.* | **conclusive/absolute/definitive proof** *If we wait for conclusive proof of global warming, it may be impos-*

sible to avoid it. | **proof positive** (=definite proof) **2** [C usually plural] TECHNICAL a printed copy of a piece of writing that is checked carefully for mistakes before the final printing is done **3** [C] a photograph that is used as a test copy before an official copy is made **4** [C] **a)** MATH a test in MATHEMATICS of whether a calculation is correct **b)** a list of reasons that shows a THEOREM (=statement) in GEOMETRY or science to be true **5** [U] a measurement of the strength of some types of alcoholic drinks: **30/40 etc. proof** (=containing 15%, 20% etc. pure alcohol) *40 proof vodka* **6 the proof is in the pudding** also **the proof of the pudding (is in the eating)** used to say that you can only know whether something is good or bad after you have tried it → see also **the burden of proof** at BURDEN[1] (3), **living proof** at LIVING[1] (3)

proof² *adj.* **be proof against sth** FORMAL if something is proof against something else, it is not affected by it: *The varnish makes the wood proof against water.*

-proof /pruf/ *suffix* **1** [in adjectives] designed or made so that something else cannot pass through, or protecting people against that thing → see also -RESISTANT: *a bulletproof vest* (=to protect you from bullets) | *a waterproof jacket* **2** [in adjectives] not easily affected or damaged by someone or something: *a child-proof bottle* (=not able to be opened by a child) | *an ovenproof dish* (=that cannot be harmed by heat) **3** [used in verbs] to treat or make something so that something else cannot pass through it, or so that it gives protection against that thing: *to soundproof a room* **4** [used in verbs] to treat or make something so that it cannot easily be affected or damaged by someone or something: *to burglar-proof your home*

ˌproof of ˈpurchase *n. plural* **proofs of purchase** [C] a special marking on a package of something that proves that you bought it

proof·read /ˈpruf-rid/ *v. past tense and past participle* **proofread** /-rɛd/ [I,T] to read through something that is written or printed in order to correct any mistakes in it —**proofreader** *n.* [C]

Prop. *n.* the abbreviation of PROPOSITION: *Prop. 209*

prop¹ /prɑp/ *v.* **propped, propping** [T always + adv./prep.] to support something by leaning it against something, or by putting something else under, next to, or behind it: **prop sth against/on sth** *He propped his ladder against the house.* | **prop sth open** *Give me something to prop the door open.* ►see THESAURUS box at **lean¹**

prop up

She propped up the books on the shelf with two bookends.

prop sth ↔ **up** *phr. v.* **1** to prevent something from falling by putting something against it or under it: *Steel beams were used to prop up the roof.* **2** to help an ECONOMY, industry, or government so that it can continue to exist, especially by giving money: *The government had propped up the savings and loan industry.* **3 prop yourself up (on/against/with etc. sth)** to hold your body up by leaning against something: *I propped myself up against the wall.*

prop² *n.* [C] **1** ENG. LANG. ARTS a small object such as a book, weapon etc. used by actors in a play or movie: *stage props* **2** INFORMAL a short form of the word PROPELLER **3** something such as money or special laws that help an ECONOMY, industry, or government so that it can continue to exist or be successful: *Low interest rates are the stock market's most important prop.* **4** something or someone that helps you to feel strong or able to deal with a situation: *Many teenagers use alcohol as a prop.* **5** an object placed under or against something to hold it in a position

prop·a·gan·da /ˌprɑpəˈgændə/ *n.* [U] POLITICS information which is false or which emphasizes just one part of a situation, used by a government or political party to make people agree with them: *a propaganda film* | **Nazi/Communist/anti-American etc. propaganda** *Soviet propaganda about the evils of capitalism* | *the spreading of* ***political propaganda*** | **propaganda campaign** (=an organized plan to spread propaganda) —**propagandize** *v.* [I,T] —**propagandist** *n.* [C]

prop·a·gate /ˈprɑpəˌgeɪt/ *v.* FORMAL **1** [T] to spread an idea, belief etc. to many people: *The group launched a website to* ***propagate*** *its* ***ideas***. **2** [I,T] BIOLOGY to grow and produce new plants, or to make a plant do this: *Geraniums are easy to propagate from cuttings.* **3** [T] BIOLOGY if an animal, insect, or CELL etc. propagates itself or is propagated, it increases in number SYN **reproduce** —**propagation** /ˌprɑpəˈgeɪʃən/ *n.* [U]

prop·a·ga·tor /ˈprɑpəˌgeɪt̬ɚ/ *n.* [C] **1** someone who spreads ideas, beliefs etc. **2** a covered box of soil in which seeds are planted to grow

pro·pane /ˈproʊpeɪn/ *n.* [U] a colorless gas used for both cooking and heating

pro·pel /prəˈpɛl/ *v.* **propelled, propelling** [T] **1** to move, drive, or push something forward: *Four engines propel the 8,300-ton ship.* **2** WRITTEN to make someone move in a particular direction, especially by pushing them: *He took her arm and propelled her toward the door.* **3** to move someone into a new situation or make them do something: **propel sb to/into sth** *The movie propelled her to stardom.* → see also PROPULSION

pro·pel·lant, propellent /prəˈpɛlənt/ *n.* [C,U] **1** an explosive for firing a bullet or ROCKET **2** gas pressed into a small space in a container of liquid, which pushes out the liquid when the pressure is taken away —**propellant** *adj.*

pro·pel·ler /prəˈpɛlɚ/ *n.* [C] a piece of equipment consisting of two or more blades that spin around, making an aircraft or ship move

pro·pen·si·ty /prəˈpɛnsət̬i/ *n. plural* **propensities** [C] FORMAL a natural tendency to behave in a particular way or cause something: **a propensity for (doing) sth** *the group's propensity for violence* | **a propensity to do sth** *Some drugs* ***have a propensity*** *to cause birth defects.*

prop·er /ˈprɑpɚ/ S2 W3 *adj.* **1** [only before noun, no comparative] right, appropriate, or correct: *the proper equipment for the job* | *They still think the proper place for a woman is at home with the kids.* **2** socially correct and acceptable OPP **improper**: ***It just wouldn't have been proper to*** *not invite Jeff.* | ***proper behavior*** *at the dinner table* **3** very polite, and careful to do what is socially correct: *a proper young man* **4** [only after noun] relating to the main or most important part of something, and not the parts near it, before it, or after it: *the road that leads to Santa Cruz proper* **5 proper to sth** FORMAL **a)** natural or normal in a particular place or situation: *Please dress in a way proper to the occasion.* **b)** belonging to one particular type of thing: *the reasoning abilities proper to our species* [**Origin:** 1200–1300 Old French *propre*, from Latin *proprius* **own**] → see also PROPERLY

ˌproper ˈfraction *n.* [C] MATH a FRACTION such as ¾, in which the number above the line is smaller than the one below it → see also IMPROPER FRACTION

prop·er·ly /ˈprɑpɚli/ *adv.* **1** correctly, or in a way that is considered right: *Running shoes must fit properly.* | *The company had failed to train their work-*

ers properly. **2** completely and fully SYN **thoroughly**: *Make sure the door is properly closed.*

ˌproper 'noun also **ˌproper 'name** *n.* [C] ENG. LANG. ARTS a noun such as "James," "New York," or "China" that is the name of a particular person, place, or thing and is spelled with a CAPITAL letter → see also COMMON NOUN, NOUN

prop·er·tied /ˈprɑpɚṭid/ *adj.* [only before noun] FORMAL owning a lot of property or land: *the propertied classes*

prop·er·ty /ˈprɑpɚṭi/ S2 W2 *n. plural* **properties** **1** [C,U] a building, a piece of land, or both together: *What's the full market value of the property?* | *Vandals wrecked school property.* | *property taxes* | *There was no criminal violation because the party occurred on **private property**.* **2** [U] the thing or things that someone owns: *At that time, a slave was considered property.* | *Police recovered some of the **stolen property**.* | *The 17-karat diamond ring had once been the **personal property** of Ann-Margret.*

THESAURUS

possessions the things that you own: *The fire destroyed most of their possessions.*
things the things that you own or are carrying: *Kyle won't let anyone touch his things.*
stuff INFORMAL the things that you own or are carrying with you: *All our stuff is still in cardboard boxes.*
belongings things you own, especially things you are carrying with you: *The bell rang, and the students began gathering up their belongings.*
effects FORMAL the things that someone owns: *After Harding's death, the army sent his personal effects to his parents.*
valuables valuable things such as jewelry or cameras which may get stolen: *Please make sure you take any valuables with you.*

3 [C] a quality or power that belongs naturally to something: *People are becoming more aware of garlic's medicinal properties.* | *All sound has three properties: pitch, volume, and duration.* ►see THESAURUS box at **characteristic**[1] → see also REAL PROPERTY

'property deˌveloper *n.* [C] someone who makes money by buying land and building on it

'property ˌtax *n.* [C,U] a tax based on the value of someone's house

pro·phase /ˈproʊˌfeɪz/ *n.* [U] BIOLOGY the first stage of the process that takes place when a cell divides, during which DNA (=genetic material) forms into CHROMOSOMES → see also ANAPHASE, METAPHASE, TELOPHASE

proph·e·cy /ˈprɑfəsi/ *n. plural* **prophecies** **1** [C] a statement that something will happen in the future, especially one made by someone with religious or magic powers: **prophecy (that)** *The **prophecy** that David would become king was **fulfilled**.* **2** [U] the power or act of making a statement about what will happen in the future: *She had the **gift of prophecy*** (=the ability to make prophecies). → see also SELF-FULFILLING PROPHECY

proph·e·sy /ˈprɑfəˌsaɪ/ *v.* **prophesies, prophesied, prophesying** [I,T] **1** to use religious or magical knowledge to say what will happen in the future SYN **foretell**: *The saint prophesied her own death.* ►see THESAURUS box at **predict** **2** to use special knowledge or experience to say that something will happen in the future SYN **predict**: *Economists are prophesying more job cuts.*

proph·et /ˈprɑfɪt/ *n.* [C] **1** a man whom people in the Christian, Jewish, or Muslim religion believe has been sent by God to lead them and teach them their religion: *the prophet Isaiah* **2 the Prophets** the Jewish holy men whose writings form part of the OLD TESTAMENT, or the writings themselves **3 the Prophet** Muhammad, who began the Muslim religion **4** someone who says that they know what will happen in the future: **prophet of doom/disaster** (=someone who says that bad things will happen) **5** someone who introduces and teaches a new idea: **+of** *Gandhi was the prophet of non-violent protests.*

proph·et·ess /ˈprɑfəṭɪs/ *n.* [C] a woman whom people believe has been sent by God to lead them

pro·phet·ic /prəˈfɛṭɪk/ *adj.* correctly saying what will happen in the future: *Lundgren's warnings **proved prophetic**.* —**prophetically** /-kli/ *adv.*

pro·phet·i·cal /prəˈfɛṭɪkəl/ *adj.* like a prophet, or related to the things a prophet says or does

pro·phy·lac·tic[1] /ˌproʊfəˈlæktɪk◂/ *adj.* MEDICINE intended to prevent disease

prophylactic[2] *n.* [C] **1** FORMAL a CONDOM **2** MEDICINE something used to prevent disease

pro·phy·lax·is /ˌproʊfəˈlæksɪs/ *n.* [C,U] MEDICINE a treatment for preventing disease

pro·pin·qui·ty /prəˈpɪŋkwəṭi/ *n.* [U] FORMAL the fact of being near someone or something, or of being related to someone SYN **proximity**

pro·pi·ti·ate /proʊˈpɪʃiˌeɪt/ *v.* [T] FORMAL to do something to please someone, because they have been unfriendly or angry with you and you want them to feel more friendly toward you —**propitiation** /proʊˌpɪʃiˈeɪʃən/ *n.* [U]

pro·pi·ti·a·to·ry /proʊˈpɪʃiəˌtɔri/ *adj.* FORMAL intended to please someone and make them feel less angry toward you and more friendly: *a propitiatory gift of flowers*

pro·pi·tious /prəˈpɪʃəs/ *adj.* FORMAL good and likely to bring good results: **+for** *The most **propitious** time for an attack was lost.* —**propitiously** *adv.*

pro·po·nent /prəˈpoʊnənt/ *n.* [C] someone who supports something or persuades people to do something: **+of** *the proponents of this theory* | **leading/strong/major proponent** *a strong proponent of women's rights* → see also OPPONENT

pro·por·tion[1] /prəˈpɔrʃən/ AC W3 *n.*

1 NUMBER/AMOUNT [C] a part or share of a larger amount or number of something, considered in relation to the whole amount or number: **+of** *A large proportion of their income goes on housing.* | **high/large/small etc. proportion** *Immigrants form a substantial proportion of the city's population.*

2 RELATIONSHIP [C,U] MATH the relationship between two things in size, amount, importance etc.: **proportion of sth to sth** *Girls in the class outnumber the boys by a proportion of three to two.* | *Dad gave approval **in direct proportion to** the difficulty of the task* (=he gave more approval if the task was difficult).

3 APPEARANCE [U] the correct relationship between the size, shape, and position of the different parts of something: *Artists must learn about proportion.* | *Reduce the drawing so that all the elements stay **in proportion**.* | *Her head was large **in proportion to** her thin figure.* | *The porch is **out of proportion with*** (=is too big or too small compared to) *the rest of the house.*

4 SIZE/IMPORTANCE **proportions** the size, importance, seriousness etc. of something: *Try to reduce the task to more manageable proportions.* | **of huge/massive/mammoth etc. proportions** *The region faces a financial crisis of huge proportions.* | **historic/mythic/legendary proportions** *The achievement is almost of mythic proportions* (=it is so important or impressive it seems like things that happen in myths). | **reach crisis/epidemic proportions** (=become so common or frequent that it is a serious problem) *The flu outbreak had reached epidemic proportions.*

5 out of proportion (to sth) a reaction, result, emotion etc. that is out of proportion is too strong or great, compared to the situation in which it happens: *The two men received prison terms that are completely out of proportion to their crime.* | **blow sth (way/totally/all etc.) out of proportion** (=treat something as more serious than it really is) *I think this whole incident has been blown way out of proportion.*

6 keep sth in proportion to react to a situation in a sensible way, and not think that it is worse or more serious than it really is

7 a sense of proportion the ability to judge what is most important in a situation: **have/keep/lose a**

sense of proportion *McCartney seems to have a good sense of proportion about his fame.*
8 MATHEMATICS [U] MATH a mathematical statement showing that the relationship is the same between two pairs of numbers, as in the statement "8 is to 6 as 32 is to 24"
[**Origin:** 1300–1400 Old French, Latin *proportio*, from *portio*] → see also RATIO

proportion² Ac *v.* [T usually passive] FORMAL to put something in a particular relationship with something else, according to size, amount, position etc.: **proportion sth to sth** *Farmers pay to use the pasture, proportioned to the number of animals they graze there.*

pro·por·tion·al /prəˈpɔrʃnəl, -ˈpɔrʃənl/ Ac *adj.* something that is proportional to something else is in the correct or most appropriate relationship to that other thing in size, amount, importance etc.: +**to** *The punishment should be proportional to the crime.* | *The number of representatives each state has is **directly proportional** to its population* (=the number is greater as the population is bigger). | *The cost of the hotel is **inversely proportional** to its distance from the beach* (=the cost becomes lower as the distance becomes greater). —**proportionally** *adv.*

pro,portional represen'tation ABBREVIATION **PR** *n.* [U] POLITICS a system of voting in elections by which all political parties are represented in the government according to the number of votes they receive in the whole country

pro,portional 'tax *n.* [C] ECONOMICS a tax that is charged at a rate that does not change as the amount of income increases, so that the amount of tax in relation to total income remains the same for all levels of income

pro·por·tion·ate /prəˈpɔrʃənɪt/ Ac *adj.* PROPORTIONAL OPP **disproportionate** —**proportionately** *adv.*

pro·por·tioned /prəˈpɔrʃənd/ *adj.* **well/beautifully etc. proportioned** if something is well, beautifully etc. proportioned, its different parts are in a correct relationship to each other, so that it is pleasant to look at OPP **badly/ill proportioned**: *his well-proportioned muscular body* | *a beautifully proportioned dining room*

pro·pos·al /prəˈpoʊzəl/ S3 W1 *n.* **1** [C,U] a plan or suggestion that is given formally to an official person or group, or the act of giving it: *a research proposal* | **proposal to do sth** *The governor has **made a proposal** to raise the tax on gasoline.* | +**for** *a proposal for a high-level meeting* | **accept/reject a proposal** *The Senate rejected a **proposal that** limited the program to two years.* **2** [C] the act of asking someone to marry you: *Did she accept his proposal?*

pro·pose /prəˈpoʊz/ W1 *v.* **1** [T] to formally suggest something such as a plan or course of action, often when the plan etc. is later voted on: *A number of changes have been proposed.* | **propose that** *What do you propose that Michael do?* | **propose doing sth** *They proposed sending troops to the area.* | **propose to do sth** *One council member proposed to close three of the schools.* | **propose a motion/amendment/rule etc.** *She proposed the motion at the next board meeting.* | **propose sth to sb** *No other plan had been proposed to the President.* | **propose sb for sth** *Mr. Nelson proposed him for the award* (=suggested that he receive the award). **2** [T] FORMAL to intend to do something: **propose to do sth** *What do you propose to do about it?* **3 a)** [I] to ask someone to marry you, especially in a formal way: +**to** *Did he propose to her?* **b) propose marriage** FORMAL to ask someone to marry you **4** [T] FORMAL to suggest an idea, method etc. as an answer to a scientific question: **propose that** *It has been proposed that Japanese and Korean are descendants of a common language.* **5 propose a toast (to sb)** to formally ask a group of people at a social event to join you in wishing someone success, happiness etc., while raising a glass and then drinking from it [**Origin:** 1300–1400 Old French *proposer*, from Latin *proponere*, from *ponere* **to put**] —**proposer** *n.* [C]

pro·posed /prəˈpoʊzd/ *adj.* [only before noun] formally suggested to an official person or group: *The proposed regulations would take effect next year.*

prop·o·si·tion¹ /ˌprɑpəˈzɪʃən/ *n.* [C] **1** a statement in which you express an idea, opinion, or belief, which people can examine and judge: *the fundamental propositions of science* | **proposition that** *Our nation is dedicated to the proposition that all men are created equal.* **2** an offer, plan, idea, or suggestion, especially in business or politics: *a good business proposition* | *I'll **make** you **a proposition** – if you pass, I'll buy you that bike.* | **an attractive/interesting/practical etc. proposition** (=an idea that is attractive etc.) | *Farming at that high altitude was usually a **losing proposition*** (=an idea that does not work). **3** also **Proposition** LAW a suggested change or addition to the law of a state of the U.S., which citizens vote on: *Proposition 209 outlawed affirmative action in California.* **4** MATH something that must be proved, or a question to which the answer must be found in GEOMETRY (=type of math dealing with shapes and angles) **5** a statement to someone that you would like to have sex with them —**propositional** *adj.*

proposition² *v.* [T] to suggest to someone that they have sex with you

pro·pound /prəˈpaʊnd/ *v.* [T] FORMAL to suggest an idea, explanation etc. for other people to consider: *Gamow propounded the "Big Bang" theory more than 50 years ago.*

pro·pri·e·tar·y /prəˈpraɪəˌtɛri/ *adj.* [no comparative, usually before noun] FORMAL **1** a proprietary product is one that is only sold under a particular name by a particular company: *proprietary software* **2** relating to who owns something: *He had no **proprietary interest** in the farm* (=he did not own any part of it). **3** proprietary behavior or feelings show that someone or something belongs to you

pro'prietary ,school *n.* [C] a school or college that is owned by a person and that teaches a special skill, such as how to repair a car

pro·pri·e·tor /prəˈpraɪətɚ/ *n.* [C] FORMAL an owner of a business: +**of** *the proprietor of the motel* —**proprietorial** /prəˌpraɪəˈtɔriəl/ *adj.*

pro·pri·e·tress /prəˈpraɪətrɪs/ *n.* [C] OLD-FASHIONED a woman who owns a business

pro·pri·e·ty /prəˈpraɪəṭi/ *n.* FORMAL **1** [U] correct social or moral behavior OPP **impropriety**: *A lot of people seem to have lost their **sense of propriety**.* | +**of** *Critics have questioned the propriety of some of the Senator's loans.* **2 the proprieties** the accepted rules of correct social behavior

pro·pul·sion /prəˈpʌlʃən/ *n.* [U] PHYSICS the force that moves a vehicle forward, or the system used to make this happen: *jet propulsion* —**propulsive** /prəˈpʌlsɪv/ *adj.*: *propulsive force*

pro ra·ta /ˌproʊ ˈreɪṭə, -ˈrɑṭə/ *adj.* TECHNICAL a pro rata payment or share is calculated according to exactly how much of something is used, how much work is done etc. —**pro rata** *adv.*

pro·rate /ˈproʊreɪt, proʊˈreɪt/ *v.* [T] ECONOMICS to calculate a charge, price etc. according to the actual amount of service received rather than by a standard sum

pro·rogue /proʊˈroʊg/ *v.* [T] if a law making institution is prorogued, its meetings officially stop for a period of time → see also ADJOURN, DISSOLVE —**prorogation** /ˌproʊroʊˈgeɪʃən/ *n.* [singular] *the prorogation of Parliament*

pro·sa·ic /proʊˈzeɪ-ɪk/ *adj.* boring, ordinary, or lacking in imagination: *the prosaic details of my life* —**prosaically** /-kli/ *adv.*

pro·sce·ni·um /proʊˈsiniəm, prə-/ *n.* [C] the part of a theater stage that comes forward beyond the curtain

pro·sciut·to /proʊˈʃuṭoʊ/ *n.* [U] uncooked dried Italian HAM (=salted meat) that is cut in very thin pieces

pro·scribe /proʊˈskraɪb/ *v.* [T] LAW to officially say that something is not allowed to exist or be done

SYN **forbid** SYN **prohibit**: *Gambling was proscribed by their religion.* —**proscription** /proʊˈskrɪpʃən/ *n.* [C,U]

prose /proʊz/ *n.* [U] ENG. LANG. ARTS written language in its usual form, as opposed to poetry: *Brown's prose is simple and direct.* [**Origin:** 1200–1300 Old French, Latin *prosa*, from *prorsus*, *prosus* **straight, direct**]

pros·e·cute /ˈprɑsəˌkyut/ *v.* **1** [I,T] LAW to officially say that you think someone is guilty of a crime and try to show they are guilty in a court of law: *Shoplifters will be prosecuted.* | **prosecute sb for (doing) sth** *He is being prosecuted for assault.* | **prosecute sb under a law/Act etc.** *Only five people have been prosecuted under this law.* **2** [I,T] LAW if a lawyer prosecutes someone or a case, it is their job to try to prove that the person is guilty of a crime OPP **defend**: *Who is going to* ***prosecute the case?*** **3** [T] FORMAL to continue doing something, usually until it is finished: *We will continue to prosecute the war.* [**Origin:** 1400–1500 Latin, past participle of *prosequi* **to follow and try to catch**]

ˈprosecuting atˌtorney *n.* [C] a prosecutor who works for a state, COUNTY, or city government in the U.S.

pros·e·cu·tion /ˌprɑsəˈkyuʃən/ *n.* **1 the prosecution** LAW the lawyers acting for the state who try to prove in a court of law that someone is guilty of a crime OPP **defense**: *The prosecution does not have a case against my client.* | *It is expected that Murphy will appear as a* ***witness for the prosection.*** **2** [C,U] LAW the process or act of bringing a legal charge against someone for a crime, or of being judged for a crime in a court of law: *Maxwell could face prosecution for his role in the robbery.* | *Since January, three hate-crime prosecutions have gone to trial.* **3** [U] FORMAL the action of doing something until it is finished: *the prosecution of her duties*

pros·e·cu·tor /ˈprɑsəˌkyut̬ɚ/ W2 *n.* [C] LAW a lawyer who is trying to prove in a court of law that someone is guilty of a crime

pros·e·lyte /ˈprɑsəˌlaɪt/ *n.* [C] FORMAL someone who has recently been persuaded to join a religious group, political party etc. SYN **convert**

pros·e·ly·tize /ˈprɑsələˌtaɪz/ *v.* [I,T] FORMAL to try to persuade someone to join a religious group, political party etc., especially in a way that people find offensive —**proselytizing** *n.* [U] —**proselytizer** *n.* [C]

ˈprose ˌpoem *n.* [C] something that is written in PROSE but that has some of the qualities of poetry —**prose poetry** *n.* [U]

Pro·ser·pi·na /prəˈsɚpɪnə/ the Roman name for the goddess Persephone

pro·sim·i·an /proʊˈsɪmiən/ *n.* [C] BIOLOGY any small PRIMATE that is NOCTURNAL (=sleeps during the day and is awake during the night) and that has large ears and large eyes for seeing in the dark, for example a BUSH BABY

pros·o·dy /ˈprɑsədi, -zə-/ *n.* [U] ENG. LANG. ARTS the patterns of sounds and RHYTHM in poetry, or the rules for arranging these patterns —**prosodic** /prəˈsɑdɪk/ *adj.*

pros·pect¹ /ˈprɑspɛkt/ Ac W2 *n.* **1** [C,U] the possibility that something will happen: **+for** *the prospects for peace* | **prospect of (doing) sth** *There was no prospect of finding work.* | **prospect that** *He had to* ***face the prospect*** *that he might lose.* **2** [singular] something that you expect or know will happen in the future, or the thought of this: *The idea of traveling in Europe was an exciting prospect.* | **the prospect of (doing) sth** *Laura was dreading the prospect of spending Christmas alone.* | *I was thrilled* ***at the prospect of*** *meeting her.* **3** [C] a person, plan, place etc. that has a good chance of success in the future: **+for** *Wilder is considered a* ***good prospect*** *for the next election.* **4** [C usually plural] chances of future success: *You can't marry a man with no job and* ***no prospects!*** | **job/employment prospects** *He went to university to improve his job prospects.* **5** [C] a possible new customer: *A telemarketer calls hundreds of prospects in a day.* **6** [C usually singular] FORMAL a view of a wide area of land, especially from a high place: *a fine prospect of the valley below* **7 in prospect** FORMAL likely to happen in the near future: *A new round of trade talks are in prospect.* [**Origin:** 1400–1500 Latin *prospectus*, from the past participle of *prospicere* **to look forward**]

prospect² Ac *v.* **1** [I,T] to examine an area of land or water, in order to find gold, silver, oil etc.: **+for** *prospecting for gold* **2** [I] to look for something, especially business opportunities: **+for** *The charity is prospecting for new donors.*

pro·spec·tive /prəˈspɛktɪv/ Ac *adj.* [only before noun] **1** likely to do a particular thing or achieve a particular position: *prospective jurors* **2** likely to happen or exist: *the prospective costs of the deal*

pros·pec·tor /ˈprɑspɛktɚ/ *n.* [C] someone who looks for gold, minerals, oil etc.

pro·spec·tus /prəˈspɛktəs/ *n.* [C] a document produced by a company providing details about its business for people who may want to INVEST in it

pros·per /ˈprɑspɚ/ *v.* **1** [I] to be successful and earn a lot of money: *Local businesses are prospering.* **2** [I] to grow and develop in a healthy way SYN **thrive**: *The children prospered under their grandparents' care.* **3** [T] OLD USE to make something succeed [**Origin:** 1300–1400 Old French *prosperer*, from Latin *prosperus* **favorable**]

pros·per·i·ty /prɑˈspɛrət̬i/ *n.* [U] a condition in which people have money and everything that is needed for a good life: *a time of* ***economic prosperity***

pros·per·ous /ˈprɑspərəs/ *adj.* successful and having a lot of money: *a prosperous landowner*

pros·ta·glan·din /ˌprɑstəˈglændɪn/ *n.* [U] BIOLOGY any of a group of substances that are similar to HORMONES and that are found in almost all the TISSUE and organs of the body. They perform a wide variety of important actions such as helping to control smooth muscle activity and BLOOD PRESSURE, and reducing INFLAMMATION.

pros·tate /ˈprɑsteɪt/ also **ˌprostate ˈgland** *n.* [C] BIOLOGY the organ in the body of male MAMMALS that produces a liquid in which SPERM are carried

pros·the·sis /prɑsˈθisɪs/ *n. plural* **prostheses** /-siz/ [C] TECHNICAL an artificial leg, tooth, or other part of the body that takes the place of a missing part —**prosthetic** /prɑsˈθet̬ɪk/ *adj.*

pros·ti·tute¹ /ˈprɑstəˌtut/ *n.* [C] someone, especially a woman, who earns money by having sex with people

prostitute² *v.* [T] **1** FORMAL if someone prostitutes a skill, ability, important principle etc., they use it in a way that does not show its true value, usually to earn money **2 prostitute yourself a)** to have sex in return for money **b)** to do low quality work because you need money, even though you have the ability to do better

pros·ti·tu·tion /ˌprɑstəˈtuʃən/ *n.* [U] **1** the work of prostitutes **2** FORMAL the use of a skill, ability, principle etc., in a way that does not show its true value

pros·trate¹ /ˈprɑstreɪt/ *adj.* **1** lying on your front with your face toward the ground: *They found him* ***lying prostrate*** *on the floor.* → see also PRONE **2** too shocked, upset, damaged etc. to do anything or be effective: **+with** *Judy was prostrate with grief after her father's death.*

prostrate² *v.* [T] **1 prostrate yourself** to lie on your front with your face toward the ground, as an act of religious WORSHIP or a sign of your willingness to obey someone **2** [T usually passive] FORMAL to make someone too shocked, upset, or weak to be able to do anything —**prostration** /prɑˈstreɪʃən/ *n.* [C,U]

prot- /proʊt/ *prefix* another spelling of PROTO-, used before some vowels

pro·tag·o·nist /proʊˈtægənɪst/ *n.* [C] **1** ENG. LANG. ARTS the most important character in a play, movie, or story **2** FORMAL one of the main people or groups involved in a competition, battle, or struggle: *the chief protagonists in the conflict* **3** someone who supports a social or political idea or way of thinking and tries to make it popular: **+of/for** *a protagonist of educational reform* → see also ANTAGONIST

pro·te·an /ˈproʊt̬iən, proʊˈtiən/ *adj.* LITERARY having the ability to change your appearance or behavior again and again: *an actor's protean talents*

pro·tect /prəˈtɛkt/ S2 W1 *v.* [I,T] **1** to keep someone or something safe from harm, damage, or illness: *Are we doing enough to protect the environment?* | *You don't have to lie to protect me anymore, Bill.* | **protect sb/sth from sth** *The laws are designed to protect consumers from unsafe products.* | *The cover protects the machine from dust.* | **protect sb/sth against sth** *We need to protect the country against future terrorist attacks.* | **+against** *The new drug helps protect against the disease.*

THESAURUS

guard to protect someone or something from being attacked or stolen: *Soldiers guarded the gates.*
shield to protect someone or something from being hurt, damaged, or upset: *She brought up her arms to shield her face.*
give/offer/provide protection to protect someone from something harmful: *lotions that provide protection from the sun*
shelter to provide a place where someone is protected from the weather or from danger: *At great risk to themselves, they sheltered Jews from the Nazis.*
preserve to keep someone or something from being harmed, destroyed, or changed too much: *Roosevelt preserved Yellowstone as a national park.*
save to make someone or something safe when they are in danger of being harmed or destroyed: *their fight to save the theater from demolition*

2 [T usually passive] if an insurance company protects your home, car, life etc., it agrees to pay you money if things are stolen or damaged or you are hurt or killed: *Life insurance is vital to protect your family financially.* **3** [T] ECONOMICS to help the industry and trade of your own country by taxing foreign goods: *High customs on foreign goods are meant to protect domestic industries.* **[Origin:** 1400–1500 Latin, past participle of *protegere*, from *tegere* **to cover]** → see also PROTECTIONISM, PROTECTIVE

pro·tect·ed /prəˈtɛktɪd/ **1** a protected animal or plant is kept safe from harm or destruction by special laws: *Spotted owls are* ***a protected species.*** **2** a protected area is one in which it is illegal to hunt the animals that live there or damage the plants **3** a protected building or area is one that is illegal to change without legal permission

pro·tec·tion /prəˈtɛkʃən/ W2 *n.* **1** [U] the act of protecting, or the condition of being protected: *The witnesses were kept under 24-hour police protection.* | **+of** *the protection of endangered species* | **+against** *Wear safety goggles for protection against flying debris.* | **+for** *protection for the city's minorities* | **give/offer/provide protection** *The wall offered some protection against the wind.* | *body armor* ***for extra protection*** **2** [C] something that protects: **+against/from** *Fur is a good protection against the cold.* | **environmental/consumer etc. protections** (=laws that protect the environment, consumers etc.) **3** [U] the promise of payment from an insurance company if something bad happens SYN **coverage** **4** [U] something you use to avoid getting a disease or stop a woman from getting PREGNANT when you have sex, especially a CONDOM **5** [U] protection money

pro·tec·tion·ism /prəˈtɛkʃəˌnɪzəm/ *n.* [U] POLITICS when a government tries to help an industry in its own country by putting a tax on foreign goods or by restricting them from entering the country —**protectionist** *adj.* —**protectionist** *n.* [C]

proˈtection ˌmoney *n.* [U] money paid to criminals to stop them from damaging your property

proˈtection ˌracket *n.* [C] INFORMAL a system in which criminals demand money from you to stop them from damaging your property

pro·tec·tive /prəˈtɛktɪv/ *adj.* **1** [only before noun] used or intended for protection: *protective gloves* **2** wanting to protect someone from harm or danger: **+of** *He's very protective of his younger brother.* **3** ECONOMICS intended to give an advantage to your own country's industry: *a protective tariff on foreign textiles* —**protectively** *adv.* —**protectiveness** *n.* [U]

proˌtective ˈcustody *n.* [U] LAW a situation in which the police make you stay somewhere in order to protect you from people who could harm you: *The children were* ***taken into protective custody.***

proˌtective ˈservices *n.* [U] **child/adult protective services** a government organization that is responsible for making sure that children or old people are being taken care of well by their families

pro·tec·tor /prəˈtɛktɚ/ *n.* [C] someone or something that protects someone or something else: *He sees himself as her protector.* | *a plastic pocket protector*

pro·tec·tor·ate /prəˈtɛktərɪt/ *n.* [C] POLITICS a country with its own government, that is protected and controlled by a more powerful country → see also COLONY

pro·té·gé /ˈproʊt̬əˌʒeɪ, ˌproʊt̬əˈʒeɪ/ *n.* [C] someone, especially a young person, who is taught and helped by someone who has influence, power, or more experience

pro·té·gée /ˈproʊt̬əˌʒeɪ, ˌproʊt̬əˈʒeɪ/ *n.* [C] a girl or woman who is guided and helped by someone who has influence, power, or more experience

pro·tein /ˈproʊtin/ *n.* [C,U] BIOLOGY one of several natural substances that exist in food such as meat, eggs, and beans, which help your body to grow and keep it strong and healthy. Proteins are MACROMOLECULES that are formed by a chain of AMINO ACIDS.

pro tem, Pro Tem /proʊ ˈtɛm/ also **pro tem·po·re** /proʊ ˈtɛmpəri/ *adj.* [only after noun] happening or existing now, but only for a short time: *the President pro tem of the Senate*

pro·test¹ /ˈproʊtɛst/ W3 *n.* **1** [C,U] a strong complaint that shows you disagree with or are angry about something that you think is wrong or unfair: *She ignored his protests and walked away.* | *He accepted his punishment* ***without protest.*** | **+against** *protests against the government's economic policies* | *Six teachers quit* ***in protest*** *of the board's decision.* | *the radical* ***protest movements*** (=group of people who are protesting) *of the 1960s* | **a storm/wave/firestorm of protest** (=a lot of angry protest) **2** [C] an occasion when people come together in public to express disapproval or opposition to something: *Three people died Thursday in violent street protests.* | *a peaceful protest* | **+against** *Thousands of people joined in the protests against the war.* **3 do sth under protest** to do something in a way that shows you do not want to do it because you think it is wrong or unfair: *They finally paid the full bill under protest.*

pro·test² /prəˈtɛst, ˈproʊtɛst/ *v.* **1** [I,T] to say or do something publicly to show that you disagree with or are angry about something that you think is wrong or unfair: **+against/at/about** *Thousands blocked the streets, protesting against the ruling.* | *Students protested the change.* | *"I don't think that's fair!" she protested.*

THESAURUS

march to protest while walking with a group of people from one place to another: *Over a million people marched to protest against the war.*
demonstrate to protest while walking or standing somewhere with a group of people: *Many recent immigrants have demonstrated against the proposed change in the immigration laws.*
riot to protest by behaving in a violent and uncontrolled way: *After the court's verdict, people rioted in the streets of Los Angeles.*
hold/stage a sit-in to protest by refusing to leave a place: *Hundreds of students staged a sit-in.*

P

go on a hunger strike to protest by refusing to eat: *The prisoners went on a hunger strike.*
boycott to protest about the actions of a company or country by refusing to buy something, go somewhere etc.: *The boycott helped bring about political change in South Africa.*
►see THESAURUS box at **complain**

2 [T] to state very firmly that something is true, especially when other people do not believe you: **protest that** *He protested that he hadn't taken the money.* | *He was led away to his jail cell, still* ***protesting his innocence.*** [**Origin:** 1300–1400 French *protester*, from Latin *protestari*, from *testari* **to speak as a witness**]

P

Prot•es•tant /'prɑṭəstənt/ *adj.* relating to a part of the Christian church that separated from the Catholic Church in the 16th century —**Protestant** *n.* [C] —**Protestantism** *n.* [U]

prot•es•ta•tion /ˌprɑṭə'steɪʃən ˌproʊ-/ *n.* [C] FORMAL a strong statement saying that something is true or not true: +**of** *protestations of love*

pro•test•er /'proʊtɛstə-, proʊ'tɛstə-/ *n.* [C] someone who takes part in a public activity to show their opposition to something

pro•tist /'proʊṭɪst/ *n.* [C] BIOLOGY any living thing that is a EUKARYOTE (=a living thing with a cell or cells with an enclosed nucleus) but that is not a plant or an animal, including some BACTERIA, VIRUSES, and ALGAE

pro•tis•ta /proʊ'tɪstə/ *n.* [plural] BIOLOGY the KINGDOM (=biological group) that consists of PROTISTS

proto- /proʊṭoʊ, -ṭə/ *prefix* TECHNICAL existing or coming before other things of the same type SYN **original**: *a proto-fascist group* | *a prototype* (=first form of a new car, machine etc.)

pro•to•col /'proʊṭəˌkɔl, -ˌkɑl/ Ac *n.* **1** [U] the system of rules on the correct and acceptable way to behave in an official situation: *diplomatic protocol* **2** [C] COMPUTERS a set of rules for what form electronic information should be in, so that it can be sent successfully from one computer to another → see also FTP **3** [C] an official statement of the rules that a group of countries have agreed to follow in dealing with a particular problem: *the Kyoto Protocol on greenhouse emissions* **4** [C] the rules that are followed when treating or dealing with a particular illness or medical problem: *an experimental protocol for the study* [**Origin:** 1400–1500 Old French *prothocole*, from Late Greek *protokollon* **first page of a document**]

pro•ton /'proʊtɑn/ *n.* [C] PHYSICS a PARTICLE that exists in the NUCLEUS (=central part) of an atom, and that has a positive electrical charge → see also ELECTRON, NEUTRON → see picture at ATOM

pro•to•plasm /'proʊṭəˌplæzəm/ *n.* [U] BIOLOGY the colorless substance that forms the cells of plants and animals

pro•to•type /'proʊṭəˌtaɪp/ *n.* [C] **1** the first form that a new design of a car, machine etc. has, or a model of it used to test the design before it is produced: +**of/for** *a working prototype of the new aircraft* **2** someone or something that is one of the first and most typical examples of a group or situation: *The law became a prototype for new legislation.*

pro•to•typ•i•cal /ˌproʊṭə'tɪpɪkəl/ *adj.* [no comparative] very typical of a group or a type: *a prototypical spoiled rich kid*

pro•to•zo•an /ˌproʊṭə'zoʊən/ also **pro•to•zo•on** /ˌproʊṭə'zoʊɑn/ *n. plural* **protozoa** /-'zoʊə/ [C usually plural] BIOLOGY a very small living thing that has only one cell —**protozoan** *adj.*

pro•tract•ed /proʊ'træktɪd, prə-/ *adj.* [only before noun] continuing for a long time, especially longer than usual or necessary: *a protracted courtroom battle*

pro•trac•tor /proʊ'træktə-, prə-/ *n.* [C] MATH an instrument, usually in the shape of a half-circle, used for measuring and drawing angles

pro•trude /proʊ'trud/ *v.* [I] to stick out from somewhere: +**from** *A pipe protruded from the wall.* —**protruding** *adj.*: *a protruding stomach*

pro•tru•sion /proʊ'truʒən/ *n.* **1** [C] something that sticks out **2** [U] the condition of sticking out

pro•tu•ber•ance /proʊ'tubərəns/ *n.* [C] FORMAL something that sticks out from the surface of something else —**protuberant** *adj.*

proud /praʊd/ S3 W3 *adj.* **1** feeling pleased with your achievements, family, country etc. because you think they are very good OPP **humble**: *You did it all by yourself? You should be very proud.* | +**of** *Your dad and I are so proud of you.* | **proud to do/be sth** *I'm proud to be an American.* | **proud (that)** *She was proud that she had gotten the job by herself.* | ***the proud owner*** *of a new sports car*

THESAURUS

conceited also **big-headed** INFORMAL very proud of yourself, especially of what you can do, in a way that other people dislike
vain very proud of yourself, especially of your appearance, in a way that other people dislike
arrogant showing that you think you are better than other people
stuck up INFORMAL proud and unfriendly because you think you are better and more important than other people

2 making you feel proud: *Winning an Olympic medal was* ***the proudest moment*** *of her career.* **3** having respect for yourself, so that you are too embarrassed to accept help from other people when you are in a difficult situation: *Many farmers then were too proud to ask for government help.* **4 do sb proud** INFORMAL to make people feel proud of you by doing something well: *The soldiers have done their country proud.* **5** DISAPPROVING thinking that you are more important, skillful etc. than you really are OPP **humble**: *He was a proud man who refused to admit his mistakes.* **6** LITERARY tall and impressive: *the proud cathedral spire* [**Origin:** 1100–1200 Old French *prod, prud, prou* **good, brave**, from Late Latin *prode* **advantage, advantageous**] → see also PRIDE[1] —**proudly** *adv.*

Proust /prust/, **Mar•cel** /mɑr'sɛl/ (1871–1922) a French writer of NOVELS who is considered one of the greatest writers of modern times

prove /pruv/ S2 W1 *v. past tense* **proved**, *past participle* **proved** or **proven** /'pruvən/ **1** [T] to show that something is definitely true, especially by providing facts, information etc. OPP **disprove**: *You're wrong and I can prove it.* | **prove (that)** *Can you prove that you had nothing to do with it?* | **prove sb right/wrong/innocent/guilty etc.** *They say I'm too old, but I'm going to prove them all wrong.* | **prove sb's guilt/innocence** *The trial proved her innocence.* ►see THESAURUS box at **demonstrate** **2** [linking verb] if someone or something proves to be difficult, helpful, a problem etc., you find out that they are difficult, helpful, a problem etc.: **prove (to be) useful/difficult etc.** *The recent revelations may prove to be embarrassing to the President.* | **prove (to be) a disaster/problem/benefit etc.** *The design proved to be a success.* **3 prove yourself** also **prove something** to show how good you are at doing something: *When I started the job, I felt I had to prove myself.* | *He's always acting like he's trying to prove something.* **4 What is sb trying to prove?** SPOKEN said when you are annoyed by someone's behavior, because you think that they are trying too hard to show that they are right or that they know something **5 prove a/your point** if someone does something to prove a point, they do it to show that they are right or that they can do something without having any other good reason: *I'm not going to run the marathon just to prove a point.* **6** [T] LAW to show that a WILL has been made in the correct way —**provable** *adj.* —**provably** *adv.*

prov•en[1] /'pruvən/ *adj.* [usually before noun] tested and shown to be true or good, or shown to exist: ***a proven track record*** *for cutting costs*

proven[2] *v.* a past participle of PROVE

prov·e·nance /'prɑvənəns/ *n.* [U] FORMAL the place where something originally came from

prov·en·der /'prɑvəndɚ/ *n.* [U] OLD-FASHIONED dry food for horses and cattle

prov·erb /'prɑvɚb/ *n.* [C] ENG. LANG. ARTS a short well-known statement that contains advice about life in general. For example, "A penny saved is a penny earned" is a proverb.

pro·ver·bi·al /prə'vɚbiəl/ *adj.* **1 the proverbial sth** used when you describe something using a well-known expression: *He took to the job like the proverbial fish to water.* **2** relating to a proverb **3** well known by a lot of people: *His modesty is proverbial.* —**proverbially** *adv.*

Pro·verbs /'prɑvɚbz/ a book in the OLD TESTAMENT in the Bible

pro·vide /prə'vaɪd/ S2 W1 *v.* [T] **1** to give something to someone or make it available to them, because they need it or want it: *This book provides information on over 1,000 birds.* | *Refreshments will be provided.* | **provide sth for sb** *The university should provide more facilities for disabled students.* | **provide sb with sth** *Someone had provided the reporters with photographs.* | **provide sth to sb** *The water company provides services to eight million people.* **2** to produce something useful as a result: *Liz's story provides a good example of what not to do.* | **provide sb with sth** *The search provided the police with some vital clues.* | **provide sth to/for sb** *Her letter provided hope to women in similar situations.* **3 provide that** FORMAL if a law or rule provides that something must happen, it states that it must happen: *The law provides that employees have the right to join a union.* [**Origin:** 1400–1500 Latin *providere* **to see ahead, provide**, from *videre* **to see**]

provide against sth *phr. v.* FORMAL to make plans in order to deal with a bad situation that might happen

provide for *phr. v.* **1 provide for sb** to give someone the things they need, such as money, food etc.: *He has to provide for his family.* **2 provide for sth** FORMAL if a law, rule, or plan provides for something, it states that something will be done and makes it possible for it to be done: *The new constitution provides for a 650-seat legislature.* **3 provide for sth** FORMAL to make plans in order to deal with something that might happen in the future

pro·vid·ed /prə'vaɪdɪd/ also **pro'vided that** *conjunction* used to say that something will only be possible if something else happens or is done first SYN **as long as**: *He can come with us, provided he pays for his own meals.*

Prov·i·dence /'prɑvədəns/ the capital and largest city of the U.S. state of Rhode Island

prov·i·dence, Providence /'prɑvədəns/ *n.* [U] LITERARY a force that some people believe organizes what happens in our lives, especially what God wants to happen: *divine providence* → see also FATE

prov·i·dent /'prɑvədənt/ *adj.* FORMAL careful and sensible, especially by saving money for the future OPP **improvident**

prov·i·den·tial /ˌprɑvə'dɛnʃəl/ *adj.* FORMAL happening just when you need it or in just the way you need it to happen —**providentially** *adv.*

pro·vid·er /prə'vaɪdɚ/ *n.* [C] **1** a company or person that provides a service: *day-care providers* **2** someone who supports a family

pro·vid·ing /prə'vaɪdɪŋ/ also **pro'viding that** *conjunction* used to say that something will only be possible if something else happens or is done first SYN **provided**: *You can borrow the car, providing I can have it back by 6:00.*

prov·ince /'prɑvɪns/ *n.* **1** [C] also **Province a)** POLITICS one of the large areas into which some countries or EMPIRES are divided, which usually has a government for that area: *Canadian provinces* **b)** [C] HISTORY one of the areas outside Italy that the Roman Empire controlled, but which had its own government **2** FORMAL a subject that someone knows a lot about or something that only they are responsible for SYN **domain**: +**of** *Computers were once the province of scientists and mathematicians.* **3 the provinces** [plural] the parts of a country that are not near to the capital or other large city: *Life in the provinces was difficult.* **4** an area that an ARCHBISHOP (=a Christian priest of the highest rank) is responsible for → see also DIOCESE [**Origin:** 1300–1400 Old French, Latin *provincia* **Roman land**, from *vincere* **to defeat**]

pro·vin·cial¹ /prə'vɪnʃəl/ *adj.* **1** [only before noun] relating to or coming from a province or from the parts of a country that are not near the capital or other large city: *the provincial government of Quebec* **2** DISAPPROVING not interested in anything new or different or in anything that does not relate to your own life and experiences: *provincial attitudes*

provincial² *n.* [C] DISAPPROVING someone who comes from a part of a country that is not near the capital or other large city, especially someone who is not interested in anything new or different

pro·vin·cial·ism /prə'vɪnʃəˌlɪzəm/ *n.* [U] DISAPPROVING the attitude of not being interested in anything new or different or in anything that does not relate to your own life or experience

'proving ground *n.* [C] **1** a place or situation in which something new is tried for the first time or tested **2** an area for scientific testing, especially of vehicles

pro·vi·sion¹ /prə'vɪʒən/ W3 *n.* **1** [C,U] the act of providing something that someone needs: +**of** *the provision of drinking water to rural communities* **2** [C,U] a plan that will provide something that someone may need in the future: +**for** *There is still no provision for a national toxic waste dump.* | *He **made provisions for** his wife and children in his will.* **3 provisions** [plural] food supplies, especially for a long trip: *We had enough provisions for two weeks.* **4** [C] LAW a condition in an agreement or law

provision² *v.* [T] to provide someone or something with a lot of food and supplies, especially for a trip

pro·vi·sion·al /prə'vɪʒənl/ *adj.* **1** intended to exist for only a short time and likely to be changed in the future SYN **temporary**: *a provisional government* **2** provisional offers, arrangements etc. are not yet definite but should become definite in the future —**provisionally** *adv.*

Proˌvisional 'Government, the HISTORY the temporary government that ruled Russia from March 1917 when the CZAR (=Russian king) stopped ruling until the Bolsheviks took control in October 1917

pro·vi·so /prə'vaɪzoʊ/ *n. plural* **provisos** [C] FORMAL a condition that you ask for before you will agree to something: *The money was given to the museum **with the proviso that** it be spent on operating costs.*

pro·voc·a·teur /proʊˌvɑkə'tɚ/ *n.* [C] someone who is employed to encourage people who are working against a government to do something illegal so that the government can catch them

prov·o·ca·tion /ˌprɑvə'keɪʃən/ *n.* [C,U] an action or event that makes someone angry or that is intended to do this: *Carter claims that she attacked him without provocation.*

pro·voc·a·tive /prə'vɑkət̬ɪv/ *adj.* **1** provocative behavior, remarks etc. are intended to make people angry or to cause a lot of discussion: *provocative statements* **2** provocative clothes, movements, pictures etc. are intended to make someone sexually excited: *a provocative bikini* —**provocatively** *adv.*

pro·voke /prə'voʊk/ *v.* [T] **1** to make someone very angry, especially by annoying them: *The dog would not have attacked if it hadn't been provoked.* | **provoke sb into (doing) sth** *Paul tried to provoke Fletch into a fight.* **2** to cause a reaction or feeling, especially a sudden one: *Dole's comments provoked laughter from the press.* | **provoke sb to do sth** *His criticisms only provoked her to work harder.* | **provoke sb into (doing) sth** *She hopes her editorial will provoke readers into thinking seriously about the issue.* [**Origin:** 1300–1400

P

French *provoquer*, from Latin *provocare*, from *vocare* **to call**] → see also THOUGHT-PROVOKING

pro·vost, Provost /ˈproʊvoʊst/ *n.* [C] an important official at a college or university

prow /praʊ/ *n.* [C] ESPECIALLY LITERARY the front part of a ship or boat

prow·ess /ˈpraʊɪs/ *n.* [U] FORMAL great skill at doing something: *athletic prowess*

prowl[1] /praʊl/ *v.* [I,T] **1** if an animal prowls, it moves around an area quietly, especially because it is hunting another animal **2** if someone prowls, they move around an area slowly and quietly, especially because they are looking for something: *Officer Watson prowls the streets at night, looking for drug dealers.*

P

prowl[2] *n.* **1 be on the prowl** to be moving around looking for something or someone in different places: *Lucille is always on the prowl for bargains.* **2** [singular] an act of prowling

ˈprowl car *n.* [C] OLD-FASHIONED a car used by the police to drive around an area

prowl·er /ˈpraʊlɚ/ *n.* [C] someone who moves around secretly or hides in or near someone's house, especially at night, in order to harm them or steal something

prox·i·mate /ˈprɑksəmɪt/ *adj.* FORMAL **1** a proximate cause or result is a direct one, when there are other possible causes as well: *The proximate cause of death was colon cancer.* **2** nearest in time, order, or family relationship —**proximately** *adv.*

prox·im·i·ty /prɑkˈsɪməṭi/ *n.* [U] FORMAL nearness in distance or time: +**to** *We chose the house for its proximity to the school.* | *Here, the rich and poor live* ***in close proximity***.

prox·y /ˈprɑksi/ *n. plural* **proxies** [C] **1** someone that you choose to represent you, especially to vote for you **2 (do sth) by proxy** to do something by arranging for someone else to do it for you

ˈproxy ˌvote *n.* [C] a vote you make by officially sending someone else to vote for you

Pro·zac /ˈproʊzæk/ *n.* [U] TRADEMARK a type of drug that is used to treat DEPRESSION (=a mental illness that makes people very unhappy)

prude /prud/ *n.* [C] DISAPPROVING someone who is very easily shocked by anything relating to sex [**Origin:** 1700–1800 French **good woman, prudish woman**, from *prudefemme* **good woman**] → see also PRUDISH

pru·dence /ˈprudns/ *n.* [U] a sensible and careful attitude that makes you avoid unnecessary risks

pru·dent /ˈprudnt/ *adj.* sensible and careful, especially by trying to avoid unnecessary risks OPP **imprudent**: *prudent investors* | **it is prudent to do sth** *It is prudent to protect your computer from viruses.* —**prudently** *adv.*

pru·den·tial /pruˈdɛnʃəl/ *adj.* OLD-FASHIONED PRUDENT

prud·er·y /ˈprudəri/ *n.* [U] DISAPPROVING prudish behavior

Prud·hoe Bay /ˈprudoʊ ˌbeɪ/ a BAY of the Arctic Ocean on the northern coast of Alaska, where large amounts of oil were discovered in 1968

prud·ish /ˈprudɪʃ/ *adj.* DISAPPROVING very easily shocked by things relating to sex —**prudishly** *adv.* —**prudishness** *n.* [U] → see also PRUDE

prune[1] /prun/ *v.* [T] **1** also **prune sth ↔ back** to cut some of the branches of a tree or bush to make it grow better: *Red dogwoods should be pruned regularly.* **2** to get rid of the unnecessary parts of something: *The state has pruned $275 million from this year's budget.* —**pruning** *n.* [U]

prune[2] *n.* [C] a dried PLUM (=type of fruit)

ˈpruning ˌhook *n.* [C] a knife that is shaped like a hook and is usually on a long pole, used for cutting branches off trees

pru·ri·ent /ˈprʊriənt/ *adj.* FORMAL too strongly interested in sex: *The material would appeal only to* ***prurient interests***. —**prurience** *n.* [U]

prus·sic ac·id /ˌprʌsɪk ˈæsɪd/ *n.* [U] CHEMISTRY a very poisonous acid

pry /praɪ/ *v.* **pries, pried, prying** **1** [T always + adv./prep.] to force something open, or force it away from something else: **pry sth ↔ loose/off/apart etc.** *A raccoon was trying to pry open the lid of the garbage can.* **2** [I] to try to find out details about someone else's private life in an impolite way: *Anna is a private person, and I did not want to pry.* **3 away from prying eyes** in private where people cannot see what you are doing

pry sth **out of** sb *phr. v.* to get money or information from someone with a lot of difficulty: *If you want to know his name, you're going to have to pry it out of her.*

P.S. *n.* [C] **1** also **p.s. postscript** a note added at the end of a letter, giving more information: *Love, Donna P.S. Tell Abby "hello."* **2** the abbreviation of PUBLIC SCHOOL: *P.S. 121* **3** the abbreviation of "Police Sergeant"

psalm /sɑm/ *n.* [C] a song or poem praising God

psalm·ist /ˈsɑmɪst/ *n.* [C] someone who has written a psalm

Psalms /sɑmz/ a book in the Old Testament of the Christian Bible

psal·ter /ˈsɑltɚ/ *n.* [C] a book containing the psalms from the Bible, often with music, for use in a church

psal·ter·y /ˈsɑltəri/ *n.* [C] an ancient musical instrument with strings stretched over a board

pseudo- /sudoʊ/ *prefix* false or not real: *pseudo-intellectuals* (=people who pretend to be intelligent) | *Popular opinion is that astrology is just a pseudoscience* (=not a real science).

pseu·do·nym /ˈsudnˌɪm, ˈsudəˌnɪm/ *n.* [C] an invented name used by someone, especially a writer, instead of their real name: *Charlotte Brontë wrote* ***under the pseudonym*** *of Currer Bell.*

pseu·don·y·mous /suˈdɑnəməs/ *adj.* written or writing under a pseudonym —**pseudonymously** *adv.*

pshaw /pʃɔ/ *interjection* OLD-FASHIONED said to show annoyance, disapproval, or disagreement

psi, p.s.i. *abbreviation* **pounds per square inch** a measure of pressure against a surface

pso·ri·a·sis /səˈraɪəsɪs/ *n.* [U] MEDICINE a disease that makes your skin dry, red, and FLAKY (=coming off in small pieces)

psst /pst/ *interjection* a sound you make very quietly, used to attract someone's attention without other people noticing: *Psst! Come over here.*

PST the abbreviation of PACIFIC STANDARD TIME

psych[1] /saɪk/ *v.*

psych sb **↔ out** *phr. v.* INFORMAL to do or say things that will make your opponent in a game or competition feel nervous or confused, so that it is easier for you to win: *Lawyers try to psych out their opponents.*

psych sb/yourself **up** *phr. v.* INFORMAL to prepare someone mentally before doing something, so that they feel confident: **psych sb/yourself up for sth** *He was trying to psych himself up for the meeting.*

psych[2] *n.* [U] SPOKEN, INFORMAL a short form of PSYCHOLOGY: *a psych major*

psych[3] *adj.* [only before noun] SPOKEN, INFORMAL a short form of PSYCHIATRIC: *the hospital's psych ward*

psych- /saɪk/ *prefix* TECHNICAL relating to the mind, as opposed to the body: *a psychiatrist* | *psychosis* (=serious mental illness) → see also PSYCHO-

psy·che /ˈsaɪki/ *n.* [C usually singular] TECHNICAL or FORMAL someone's mind, or their basic nature, which controls their attitudes and behavior: *The war in Vietnam still lingers in the American psyche.* [**Origin:** 1600–1700 Greek **breath, life, soul, mind**]

psyched /saɪkt/ *adj.* [not before noun] also **psyched up** to be mentally prepared for an event and excited about it: +**about/for** *I'm really psyched about this semester!*

psy·che·del·ic /ˌsaɪkəˈdɛlɪk◂/ *adj.* **1** psychedelic drugs such as LSD make you HALLUCINATE (=see things that do not really exist) **2** psychedelic art, clothing etc. has complicated patterns of strong bright colors, shapes etc.

psy·chi·at·ric /ˌsaɪki'ætrɪk◂/ *adj.* [only before noun] relating to the study and treatment of mental illness: *psychiatric treatment* | *a psychiatric illness*

ˌpsychiatric 'hospital *n.* [C] a hospital where people with mental illnesses are treated

psy·chi·a·trist /saɪ'kaɪətrɪst, sə-/ *n.* [C] a doctor trained in the treatment of mental illnesses: *If you ask me, she needs to* ***see a psychiatrist****.* → see also PSYCHOLOGIST

psy·chi·a·try /saɪ'kaɪətri/ *n.* [U] the study and treatment of mental illnesses

psy·chic[1] /'saɪkɪk/ *adj.* [no comparative] **1** also **psychical** relating to mysterious events involving the power of the human mind: *psychic phenomena* | *psychic healers* **2** having the ability to know what other people are thinking or what will happen in the future, or showing this quality → see also CLAIRVOYANT: *I can't tell what you're thinking – I'm not psychic.* | *a psychic prediction* **3** also **psychical** [only before noun] affecting the mind rather than the body: *psychic disorders* —**psychically** /-kli/ *adv.*

psychic[2] *n.* [C] someone who has mental mysterious powers, such as the ability to receive messages from dead people or to know what will happen in the future

psy·cho /'saɪkoʊ/ *n. plural* **psychos** [C] INFORMAL someone who is likely to suddenly behave in a violent or crazy way —**psycho** *adj.*

psycho- /saɪkoʊ, -kə/ *prefix* TECHNICAL relating to the mind, as opposed to the body: *a psychoanalyst* (=person who helps people with mental illnesses) → see also PSYCH-

psy·cho·ac·tive /ˌsaɪkoʊ'æktɪv◂/ *adj.* TECHNICAL psychoactive drugs, chemicals etc. have an effect on the mind

psy·cho·a·nal·y·sis /ˌsaɪkoʊə'næləsɪs/ *n.* [U] a way of treating someone who is mentally ill by talking to them about their life in the past, their feelings etc., in order to find out the hidden causes of their problems —**psychoanalytic** /ˌsaɪkoʊˌænl'ɪṭɪk/ also **psychoanalytical** *adj.* —**psychoanalytically** /-kli/ *adv.*

psy·cho·an·a·lyst /ˌsaɪkoʊ'ænl-ɪst/ *n.* [C] someone who is trained in psychoanalysis

psy·cho·an·a·lyze /ˌsaɪkoʊ'ænlˌaɪz/ *v.* [I,T] to treat someone or think about a problem using psychoanalysis

psy·cho·bab·ble /'saɪkoʊˌbæbəl/ *n.* [U] INFORMAL, DISAPPROVING language that sounds scientific but is not really, that some people use when talking about their emotional problems

psy·cho·bi·ol·o·gy /ˌsaɪkoʊbaɪ'ɑlədʒi/ *n.* [U] BIOLOGY the study of the body in relation to the mind

psy·cho·dra·ma /'saɪkoʊˌdrɑmə/ *n.* [C] **1** a serious movie, play etc. that examines the complicated minds, feelings and psychological relationships of the characters **2** a way of treating mental illness in which people are asked to act in a situation together to help them understand their emotions

psy·cho·ki·ne·sis /ˌsaɪkoʊkə'nisɪs/ *n.* [U] the action of moving solid objects using only the power of the mind, which some people believe is possible —**psychokinetic** /ˌsaɪkoʊkə'nɛṭɪk/ *adj.*

psy·cho·log·i·cal /ˌsaɪkə'lɑdʒɪkəl/ Ac S3 W3 *adj.* [no comparative] **1** relating to the way that people's minds work and the way that this affects their behavior SYN **mental**: *psychological problems* | *psychological abuse* **2** relating to the study or science of psychology: *Freud's psychological theories* **3** caused by your feelings or thoughts, not by physical things: *Max says he's sick, but I'm sure it's psychological.* **4 psychological warfare** behavior that is intended to make your opponents less confident, especially in a war —**psychologically** /-kli/ *adv.*

psy·chol·o·gist /saɪ'kɑlədʒɪst/ Ac *n.* [C] someone who is trained in psychology: *a child psychologist* → see also PSYCHIATRIST

psy·chol·o·gy /saɪ'kɑlədʒi/ Ac S3 *n.* **1** [U] the study of the mind and how it works: *clinical psychology* | *a psychology class* **2** the mental processes involved in doing a certain activity: +**of** *research into the psychology of racism* **3** [C,U] the usual way in which a particular person or group thinks and reacts: *a terrorist's psychology* | +**of** *the psychology of three-year-olds* **4** [U] INFORMAL knowledge of the way that people think, that makes you able to control what they do: *You have to use psychology to get people to stop smoking.*

psy·cho·met·ric /ˌsaɪkoʊ'mɛtrɪk◂/ *adj.* relating to the measurement of mental abilities and qualities: *psychometric tests*

psy·cho·path /'saɪkəˌpæθ/ *n.* [C] MEDICINE someone who has a serious and permanent mental illness that makes them behave in a violent or criminal way → see also SOCIOPATH —**psychopathic** /ˌsaɪkə'pæθɪk◂/ *adj.*: *a psychopathic killer*

psy·cho·sis /saɪ'koʊsɪs/ *n. plural* **psychoses** /-siz/ [C,U] MEDICINE a serious mental illness that can change your character and make you unable to behave in a normal way → see also PSYCHOTIC

psy·cho·so·cial /ˌsaɪkoʊ'soʊʃəl/ *adj.* TECHNICAL relating to both someone's mind and how they behave with other people: *the psychosocial concerns of cancer patients*

psy·cho·so·mat·ic /ˌsaɪkoʊsə'mæṭɪk/ *adj.* MEDICINE **1** a psychosomatic illness is caused by fear or anxiety rather than by any physical problem **2** relating to the relationship between the mind and physical illness —**psychosomatically** /-kli/ *adv.*

psy·cho·ther·a·py /ˌsaɪkoʊ'θɛrəpi/ *n.* [U] the treatment of mental illness, for example DEPRESSION, by talking to someone and discussing problems, rather than by using drugs or medicine —**psychotherapist** *n.* [C]

psy·chot·ic /saɪ'kɑṭɪk/ *adj.* MEDICINE suffering from PSYCHOSIS, or caused by psychosis: *psychotic delusions* ▸see THESAURUS box at **crazy**[1] —**psychotic** *n.* [C] —**psychotically** /-kli/ *adv.*

psy·cho·tro·pic /ˌsaɪkə'troʊpɪk◂/ *adj.* TECHNICAL psychotropic drugs have an effect on your mind or behavior

PT the written abbreviation of PACIFIC TIME

pt. **1** also **Pt.** the written abbreviation of "part": *Pt. III* **2** the written abbreviation of PINT **3** the written abbreviation of "payment" **4** also **Pt.** the written abbreviation of "point" **5** also **Pt.** the written abbreviation of PORT: *Pt. Moresby*

PTA *n.* [C] **Parent-Teacher Association** an organization of parents and teachers that tries to help and improve a particular school

pter·o·dac·tyl /ˌtɛrə'dæktl/ *n.* [C] a type of large flying REPTILE (=type of animal) that lived many millions of years ago

PTO *n.* [C] **Parent-Teacher Organization** an organization similar to the PTA

Ptol·e·ma·ic sys·tem /ˌtɑlə'meɪ-ɪk ˌsɪstəm/ *n.* [singular] the old system of belief that the Earth was at the center of the universe, with the sun, stars, and PLANETS moving around it

Ptol·e·my[1] /'tɑləmi/ (A.D. ?100–?170) a Greek ASTRONOMER and MATHEMATICIAN who lived and worked in Egypt, and developed the PTOLEMAIC SYSTEM

Ptolemy[2] the name used by the family of kings who ruled Egypt from the 4th century B.C. to the 1st century B.C.

pto·maine /'toʊmeɪn, toʊ'meɪn/ *n.* [C,U] a poisonous substance formed by BACTERIA in decaying food

pub /pʌb/ *n.* [C] a comfortable BAR that often serves food, especially one in the U.K. or Ireland

pu·ber·ty /'pyubəṭi/ *n.* [U] BIOLOGY the stage of physical development during which you change from a child to an adult, for example when a girl begins to MENSTRU-

P

ATE: **reach/enter puberty** *Girls often reach puberty earlier than boys.* | *Boys' voices often crack as they* ***go through puberty***. [**Origin:** 1300–1400 Latin *pubertas*, from *puber* **pubescent**]

pu·bes·cent /pyuˈbɛsənt/ *adj.* BIOLOGY a pubescent boy or girl is going through puberty

pu·bic /ˈpyubɪk/ *adj.* [only before noun] relating to or near to the sexual organs: *pubic hair*

pub·lic¹ /ˈpʌblɪk/ S1 W1 *adj.*
1 ORDINARY PEOPLE [no comparative only before noun] relating to or coming from all the ordinary people in a country or city: *We are responding to a public demand.* | *Public pressure played no part in the decision.* | *Allowing the two banks to merge would not be* ***in the public interest*** (=helpful or useful to ordinary people). | *There was a* ***public outcry*** *about the shooting.* | **public support/opposition** *There has been widespread public support for the new law.*
2 FOR ANYONE [no comparative] available for anyone to use: *a public restroom* | *a public beach* | *Smoking is banned in indoor public places.*
3 GOVERNMENT [no comparative] POLITICS relating to the government and the services it provides for people OPP **private**: *public employees* | **public money/funding/expenditure etc.** *At least $20,000 in public money was spent on the celebration.* | *Jones is not fit for* ***public office*** (=a job that is part of a government).
4 KNOWN ABOUT [no comparative] known about by most people: *The name of the victim has not been* ***made public***. | *Much of the information is already* ***public knowledge***. | *This is not the first time Collins has been* ***in the public eye*** (=on television, radio etc. a lot because you are famous). | *one of the best-known* ***public figures*** (=famous people) *in the country*
5 NOT HIDDEN intended for anyone to know, see, or hear OPP **private**: *a public debate* | *We feel he owes us* ***a public apology***. | *There will be a* ***public inquiry*** *into the sinking of the oil tanker.* | **a public display of emotion/grief/affection etc.** (=an occasion when you show your emotions so that everyone can see)
6 PLACE WITH A LOT OF PEOPLE a public place has a lot of people in it OPP **private**: *It's best to have the first meeting in a public well-lit place.*
7 go public a) to tell everyone about something that was secret: *The chairman didn't want to go public with the information.* **b)** to begin to sell STOCK in your company to become a PUBLIC COMPANY: *Several more biotech companies went public this year.*
8 public life work that you do, especially for the government, that makes you well known to many people: *McGovern retired from public life last year.* | *Ms. Levin has been* ***in public life*** *for 23 years.*
9 sb's/sth's public image the character or attitudes that a famous person, organization etc. is thought by most people to have: *Armstrong is working hard to rebuild his public image.*
10 a public appearance a visit by a famous person in order to make a speech, advertise something etc.: *White will* ***make*** *no more* ***public appearances*** *for the rest of the year.*
11 public enemy number one, public enemy No. 1 the criminal, problem etc. that is considered the most serious threat to people's safety: *Drugs have become public enemy number one.*
[**Origin:** 1400–1500 French *publique*, from Latin *publicus*]

public² W1 *n.* **1 the public** all the ordinary people in a country or city: *The public doesn't really care about electoral reform.* | *The class is free and* ***open to the public***. | *We want the committee to include at least five members of* ***the general public***. | *There have been several complaints from* ***members of the public***. **2 in public** in a place where anyone can know, see, or hear OPP **in private**: *You're not going to wear that in public, are you?* → see also **wash your dirty laundry/linen in public** at DIRTY¹ (9) **3 sb's public** the people who like listening to a particular singer, reading the books of a particular writer etc.: *Musicians have to communicate with their public.*

ˌpublic ˈaccess *n.* [U] **1** the right of ordinary people to go onto particular areas of land or read particular documents: **+to** *Public access to these beaches is guaranteed.* **2** also **public access channel** a television CHANNEL provided by CABLE television, on which anyone can broadcast a program

ˌpublic-adˈdress ˌsystem *n.* [C] a PA

ˌpublic afˈfairs *n.* [plural] events and subjects, especially political ones, that have an effect on people in general: *the university's vice president for public affairs*

ˌpublic asˈsistance *n.* [U] the government programs that help poor people get food, homes, and medical care: *Almost half the community lives* ***on public assistance***.

pub·li·ca·tion /ˌpʌbləˈkeɪʃən/ AC W3 *n.* **1** [U] the process of printing a book, magazine etc. and offering it for sale: **+of** *the publication of her first novel last year* | *The poems were not written* ***for publication***. **2** [C] a book, magazine etc.: *a monthly publication* **3** [U] the act of making something known to people in general: **+of** *the publication of the research findings*

ˌpublic ˈcompany *n.* [C] a company that offers its STOCK for sale to people who are not part of the company

ˌpublic corpoˈration *n.* [C] **1** a PUBLIC COMPANY **2** a business that is run by the government

ˌpublic ˈdebt *n.* [U] ECONOMICS the total amount of money owed by the government of a country SYN **national debt** SYN **federal debt**: *high levels of public debt*

ˌpublic deˈfender *n.* [C] LAW a lawyer who is paid by the government to defend people in court, because they cannot pay for a lawyer themselves → see also DISTRICT ATTORNEY

ˌpublic disˈclosure law *n.* [C usually plural] ECONOMICS a law that makes companies give people all the available information about their products

ˌpublic ˈdocument *n.* [C] ENG. LANG. ARTS a piece of writing that is intended to be read or heard by the public, such as a newspaper, government report, or speech → see also CONSUMER DOCUMENT, FUNCTIONAL DOCUMENT, INFORMATIONAL DOCUMENT, WORKPLACE DOCUMENT

ˌpublic doˈmain *n.* LAW **in the public domain** a play, idea etc. that is in the public domain is available for anyone to perform or use

ˌpublic ˈfunding *n.* [U] money that the government gives to support organizations or events: *public funding for the arts*

ˌpublic ˈgoods *n.* [plural] also **public good** [singular] ECONOMICS goods that are provided by the government and paid for by taxes because they help society as a whole and because they are difficult to produce for profit. Public health, education, and national defense are examples of public goods.

ˌpublic ˈhealth *n.* [U] the health of all the people in an area: *Pollution is a major threat to public health.*

ˌpublic ˈholiday *n.* [C] a special day when people do not go to work and many stores do not open

ˌpublic ˈhousing *n.* [U] houses or apartments built by the government for poor people

ˌpublic inˈquiry *n.* [C] **1** an official attempt to find out the cause of something, especially an accident: *a public inquiry into the bombing* **2** a request for information from an official organization, by people who are not part of that organization

ˌpublic ˈinterest ˌgroup *n.* [C] a group of people who join together in order to try and influence the government of a country to do things that will help most people in the country. For example, there are public interest groups that want to protect the environment or support the interests of people who buy goods in stores.

pub·li·cist /ˈpʌbləsɪst/ *n.* [C] someone whose job is to make sure that people find out about a new product, movie, book etc., or about what a famous person is doing

pub·lic·i·ty /pəˈblɪsəṭi/ *n.* [U] **1** the attention that someone or something gets from newspapers, television etc.: **get/receive/attract publicity** *Wilder received national publicity after the rescue.* | *How can we get some **free publicity** for our company?* | **bad/negative publicity** (=publicity that makes you look bad) | **good/favorable publicity** (=publicity that makes you look good) **2** the business of making sure that people know about a new product, movie etc., or about what a particular famous person is doing: **+for** *Who did the publicity for the show?* | *a publicity campaign for the new book*

pubˈlicity ˌagent *n.* [C] a PRESS AGENT

pubˈlicity ˌstunt *n.* [C] something unusual that someone does to get publicity for a person, organization, product etc.

pub·li·cize /ˈpʌbləˌsaɪz/ *v.* [T] to give information about something to people in general, so that they know about it: *He is giving the interviews to publicize his new movie.* | **well/much/widely/highly publicized** *a highly publicized murder case*

ˌpublic ˈlibrary *n.* [C] a building where people can go to read or borrow books without having to pay

pub·lic·ly /ˈpʌblɪkli/ W3 *adv.* **1** in a way that is intended for anyone to know, see, or hear OPP **privately**: *She never discussed the matter publicly.* | *The company has publicly denied the allegations.* **2** by the government as part of its services OPP **privately**: *a publicly funded housing program* **3** a company that is publicly owned has sold STOCK in it to people who are not part of the company OPP **privately** **4** among the ordinary people in a country or city: *We hope the proposals will be publicly acceptable.*

ˌpublicly ˌheld corpoˈration *n.* [C] ECONOMICS a large company that sells its STOCK on an official STOCK EXCHANGE

ˌpublic-ˈminded *adj.* PUBLIC-SPIRITED

ˌpublic ˈnuisance *n.* [C] **1** LAW an action that is annoying or harmful to many people **2** a person who does things that annoy a lot of people

ˌpublic oˈpinion *n.* [U] the opinions or beliefs that ordinary people have about a particular subject: *Public opinion has now turned against him.*

ˌpublic ˈownership *n.* [U] businesses, property etc. that are under public ownership are owned by the government OPP **private ownership**

ˌpublic ˈpolicy *n.* [C,U] POLITICS the economic and social measures a government publicly says it is going to do: *Full employment became the principal goal of public policy.* | *important public policy issues*

ˌpublic ˈproperty *n.* [U] **1** something, especially an area of land, that is provided for anyone to use, and is usually owned by the government OPP **private property** **2** INFORMAL something that everyone has a right to know about **3** INFORMAL someone who is very famous and cannot have a private life because everything they do is reported in the newspapers, on TV etc.

ˌpublic reˈlations ABBREVIATION **PR** *n.* **1** [plural] the relationship between an organization and the public: *The dispute has been bad for public relations.* **2** [U] the work of explaining to the public what an organization does, so that they will understand it and approve of it: *a public relations firm*

ˌpublic reˈlations ˌexercise *n.* [C] something that an organization does just to make itself popular, rather than because it is the right thing to do

ˌpublic ˈschool *n.* [C] a free local school that any child can go to, which is controlled and paid for by the government → see also PRIVATE SCHOOL

ˈpublic ˌsector *n.* **the public sector** the industries and services in a country that are owned and run by the government: *a job **in the public sector*** —**public-sector** *adj.* [only before noun] → see also PRIVATE SECTOR

ˌpublic ˈservant *n.* [C] someone who works for the government, especially someone who is elected

ˌpublic ˈservice *n.* **1** [C usually plural] ECONOMICS a service or product that a government provides, such as electricity, TRANSPORTATION etc.: *Essential public services are supported by property taxes.* **2** [C] ECONOMICS a service provided to people because it will help them, and not for profit: *Volunteers provide a valuable public service.* **3** [U] POLITICS jobs in the government or its departments: *a long career of public service*

ˌpublic-ˈservice anˌnouncement ABBREVIATION **PSA** *n.* [C] a special message on television or radio, giving information about an important subject

ˌpublic ˈspeaking *n.* [U] the activity of making speeches in public

ˌpublic ˈspending *n.* [U] the money that the government spends on public services: *Public spending for education must be increased.*

ˌpublic-ˈspirited *adj.* thinking about and willing to do what is helpful for everyone in society: *public-spirited citizens*

ˌpublic ˈtelevision *n.* [U] a television program or service that is paid for by the government, large companies, and the public → see also PBS

ˌpublic transporˈtation *n.* [U] bus services, train services etc., that are provided for everyone to use

ˌpublic uˈtility *n.* [C] a private company that is allowed by the government to provide an important service or product, such as electricity or water, to the people in a particular area

ˌpublic ˈworks *n.* [plural] buildings, roads, PORTS etc. that are provided and built by the government for the public to use

pub·lish /ˈpʌblɪʃ/ Ac S2 W1 *v.* **1** [I,T] to arrange for a book, magazine etc. to be written, printed, and sold: *"Moby Dick" was first published in 1851.* | *The company publishes a monthly children's magazine.* **2** [T] if a newspaper, magazine etc. publishes a story, a piece of information etc., it prints it for people to read: **publish an article/letter/story etc.** *The newspaper was criticized for publishing the story.* **3** [T usually passive] to make official information such as a report available for everyone to read: **publish results/findings/information** *Scientists will publish their findings later this year.* **4** [I,T] if a writer or musician publishes their work, they arrange for it to be printed and sold: *How many books has he published?* **5 publish or perish** used to say that people with particular jobs, especially college or university PROFESSORS, must have things that they write published if they want to succeed [**Origin:** 1300–1400 French *publier*, from Latin *publicare* **to make public, publish**] → see also PUBLICATION

pub·lish·er /ˈpʌblɪʃɚ/ Ac W3 *n.* [C] a person or company whose business is to arrange the writing, production, and sale of books, newspapers etc.

pub·lish·ing /ˈpʌblɪʃɪŋ/ Ac *n.* [U] the business of producing books, magazines etc.: *a job in publishing* → see also DESKTOP PUBLISHING, ELECTRONIC PUBLISHING

ˈpublishing house *n.* [C] a company whose business is to arrange the writing, production, and sale of books

Puc·ci·ni /puˈtʃini/, **Gia·co·mo** /ˈdʒɑkəmoʊ/ (1858–1924) an Italian musician who wrote OPERAS

puce /pyus/ *adj.* dark brownish purple [**Origin:** 1700–1800 French *couleur de puce* **flea-color**, from Latin *pulex* **flea**] —**puce** *n.*

puck /pʌk/ *n.* [C] a hard flat circular piece of rubber that you hit with the stick in the game of HOCKEY

puck·er /ˈpʌkɚ/ also **pucker up** *v.* [I,T] **1** INFORMAL if a part of your face puckers or if you pucker it, you pull it tightly together so that lines appear on it: *She puckered her lips and moved to kiss him.* **2** if cloth puckers or something puckers it, it gets lines or folds in it and is not flat anymore —**pucker** *n.* [C] —**puckered** *adj.*

puck·ish /ˈpʌkɪʃ/ *adj.* LITERARY showing that you are amused by other people, and like to make jokes about them: *a puckish grin* —**puckishly** *adv.*

pud·ding /ˈpʊdɪŋ/ *n.* [C,U] **1** a thick sweet creamy food, made with milk, eggs, sugar, and a little flour, and usually served cold: *chocolate pudding* **2** a hot sweet

P

dish, made from cake, rice, bread etc. and milk and eggs, and sometimes with fruit or other sweet things added: *bread pudding* [**Origin:** 1200–1300 Old French *boudin*, from Latin *botellus* **sausage**] → see also **the proof is in the pudding** at PROOF[1] (6)

pud·dle[1] /ˈpʌdl/ *n.* [C] a small pool of water, especially rain water, on a path, street etc.: *a mud puddle*

puddle[2] *v.* [I] if a liquid puddles, it forms a puddle

ˈpuddle ˌjumper *n.* [C] INFORMAL a small airplane that is used to fly short distances

pu·den·dum /pyʊˈdɛndəm/ *n. plural* **pudenda** /-də/ [C] BIOLOGY the sexual organs on the outside of the body, especially a woman's

pudg·y /ˈpʌdʒi/ *adj. comparative* **pudgier**, *superlative* **pudgiest** fatter than usual: *He's short, pudgy, and bald.* —**pudginess** *n.* [U]

Pueb·lo /ˈpwɛbloʊ/ a group of Native American tribes from the southwestern region of the U.S., including the Hopi. They are known for their ADOBE buildings. —**Pueblo** *adj.*

pueb·lo /ˈpwɛbloʊ/ *n.* [C] **1** a small town or group of Native American homes, usually with more than one level, made of stone or ADOBE in the southwest U.S. **2** a small town, especially in the southwest U.S. near Mexico

pu·er·ile /ˈpyʊrəl, -raɪl/ *adj.* FORMAL silly and stupid SYN **childish**: *puerile jokes*

Puer·to Ri·co /ˌpɔrṭə ˈrikoʊ, ˌpwɛrtoʊ-/ an island in the Caribbean Sea, southeast of the U.S. state of Florida. People who live in Puerto Rico are U.S. citizens, but Puerto Rico is not a U.S. state and it governs itself. —**Puerto Rican** *n., adj.*

puff[1] /pʌf/ *v.* **1** [I,T] to breathe in and out while smoking a cigarette, pipe etc.: *He stood by the bar, puffing a cigar.* | +**on/at** *The old man puffed on his pipe.* **2** [I] to breathe quickly and with difficulty after running, carrying something heavy etc.: *He arrived at the door puffing and panting.* → see also **huff and puff** at HUFF[2] (1) **3 a)** [T always + adv./prep.] to blow smoke or steam out of something: *The boiler was puffing thick black smoke.* **b)** [I] if smoke or steam puffs from somewhere, it comes out in little clouds **4** [I always + adv./prep.] if a steam train puffs somewhere, it moves while sending out little clouds of steam: *A train puffed across the bridge.*

puff sth ↔ **out** *phr. v.* **1 puff out your cheeks/chest** to make your cheeks or chest bigger by filling them with air: *He stood up straight and puffed out his chest.* **2** to produce or blow out smoke, steam, or air

puff up *phr. v.* **1 puff sth ↔ up** to become bigger by increasing the amount of air inside, or to make something bigger in this way: *Birds puff up their feathers to keep warm.* | *As the noodles puff up, flip them over in the pan.* **2** if your eye, face etc. puffs up, it swells painfully because of an injury or infection: *He could feel his face puffing up.* **3 puff sb up** to make someone feel very pleased or proud

puff[2] *n.* [C] **1** the action of taking the smoke from a cigarette, pipe etc. into your lungs: +**on** *a nervous puff on a cigarette* | *She* **took a puff** *and began to cough.* **2** a sudden small movement of wind, air, or smoke: +**of** *a puff of smoke* **3** the action of breathing in and blowing air out in short bursts after running, carrying something heavy etc. **4 a cream/cheese/lemon etc. puff** a piece of light PASTRY with a soft mixture of cream or cheese etc. inside

puff·ball /ˈpʌfbɔl/ *n.* [C] a type of round FUNGUS that bursts to let its seeds go

ˌpuffed ˈsleeve *n.* [C] a short SLEEVE that is wider in the middle than at each end

ˌpuffed ˈup *adj.* **1** behaving in a way that shows you are too proud: *He was all puffed up with his own importance.* **2** PUFFY

ˌpuffed ˈwheat *n.* [U] grains of wheat that have been cooked to make them very light, usually eaten with milk for breakfast

puf·fin /ˈpʌfɪn/ *n.* [C] BIOLOGY a North Atlantic sea bird with a black and white body and a large brightly colored beak

ˌpuff ˈpastry *n.* [U] a type of very light PASTRY that PUFFS up when you bake it and has many thin layers

ˈpuff piece *n.* [C] an article in a newspaper, a report on television etc. that is not very serious and makes the person that it is about look very good

puff·y /ˈpʌfi/ *adj. comparative* **puffier**, *superlative* **puffiest** **1** puffy eyes, faces, or cheeks are swollen: *Her eyes were still puffy from crying.* **2** soft and filled with a lot of air: *puffy white clouds* —**puffiness** *n.* [U]

pug /pʌg/ *n.* [C] a small fat short-haired dog with a wide flat face and a short flat nose

Pu·get Sound /ˈpyudʒɪt ˌsaʊnd/ a long narrow BAY of the Pacific Ocean on the northwestern coast of the U.S. in the state of Washington

pu·gi·lism /ˈpyudʒəˌlɪzəm/ *n.* [U] FORMAL the sport of BOXING (=fighting with your hands) —**pugilistic** /ˌpyudʒəˈlɪstɪk/ *adj.*

pu·gi·list /ˈpyudʒəlɪst/ *n.* [C] FORMAL a BOXER

pug·na·cious /pʌgˈneɪʃəs/ *adj.* FORMAL very eager to argue or fight with people —**pugnaciously** *adv.* —**pugnacity** /pʌgˈnæsəṭi/ *n.* [U]

ˈpug nose *n.* [C] a short flat nose that turns up at the end

puke[1] /pyuk/ also **puke up** *v.* [I,T] **1** SPOKEN, INFORMAL to bring food back up from your stomach through your mouth SYN **vomit** SYN **throw up** **2 it makes me (want to) puke!** SPOKEN used to say that something makes you very angry or annoyed

puke[2] *n.* [U] SPOKEN, INFORMAL food brought back up from your stomach through your mouth SYN **vomit**

pukey, puky /ˈpyuki/ *adj.* SLANG very disgusting or unattractive

pul·chri·tude /ˈpʌlkrəˌtud/ *n.* [U] FORMAL beauty, especially of a woman

Pu·lit·zer /ˈpʊlɪtsɚ/, **Joseph** (1847–1911) a U.S. JOURNALIST and newspaper owner, who established the Pulitzer Prizes

ˈPulitzer ˌPrize *n.* one of the eight prizes given every year in the U.S. to people who have produced especially good work in JOURNALISM, literature, or music

pull[1] /pʊl/ S1 W1 *v.*

1 MOVE SB/STH TOWARD YOU [I,T] to use your hands to make someone or something move toward you or in the direction of your hand: *He grabbed the handle and pulled hard.* | *Mom, Ellie's pulling my hair!* | **pull sth into/onto/away etc.** *Help me pull the trunk into the corner.* | *"Come here," he said, pulling her toward him.* | **pull sth open/shut** *Tim got in the car and pulled the door shut.* | **pull sth up/down** *I got in bed and pulled up the covers.*

pull

THESAURUS

tug to pull something suddenly, especially several times with small movements: *Jack tugged on the rope.*
drag to pull something somewhere, usually along the ground: *He dragged his chair closer to the table.*
haul to pull something heavy, often using a rope: *fishermen hauling in their nets*
tow to pull another vehicle or boat: *The plane is towed into position at the landing gate.*
heave to pull or lift something very heavy, especially with one movement: *We managed to heave the piano into position.*
→ PUSH

2 REMOVE WITH FORCE [T] to use force to take something out of the place where it is attached or held: *She's going to have her wisdom teeth pulled.* | **pull sth out/up/off etc.** *Some kid had pulled the doll's head off.*
3 MAKE STH FOLLOW YOU to use a rope, chain, your hands etc. to make something move behind you in the direction that you are moving: *The train was pulling 64 boxcars.* | **pull sth behind/after/along etc.** *He goes by here every day pulling that little wagon behind him.*
4 MOVE YOUR BODY [T always + adv./prep.] **a)** to move your body or a part of your body away from someone or something: **pull sth away/off/out etc.** *Janice pulled her hand out of the cookie jar guiltily.* | **pull yourself/sth free** *He tried to pull his leg free but it was stuck.* **b)** to hold onto something and use your strength to move your body somewhere: **pull yourself up/through etc.** *Bobby had to pull himself up out of the hole.*
5 TAKE STH OUT [T always + adv./prep.] to take something out of a pocket, bag etc. with your hand: **pull sth ↔ out** *She reached in her bag and pulled out her lipstick.* | **pull sth from/out of sth** *Ben pulled a pen from his pocket.*
6 MUSCLE [T] to injure one of your muscles by stretching it too much during physical activity SYN **strain**: *Lift it carefully, or you'll* ***pull a muscle.*** ►see THESAURUS box at **hurt**[1]
7 **pull strings** to secretly use your influence with important people in order to get what you want or to help someone else: *Samuels pulled strings to get her daughter the job.*
8 **pull the/sb's strings** to control something or someone, especially when you are not the person who is supposed to be controlling it: *Who is really pulling the strings at the White House?*
9 **pull your weight** to do your share of the work: *If you don't start pulling your weight around here, you're fired.*
10 CLOTHING [T always + adv./prep.] to put on or take off clothing, usually quickly: **pull sth on/off/up/down** *He ran out the door, pulling on his shirt as he went.* | *She bent over to pull up her socks.*
11 **pull a gun/knife (on sb)** to take out a gun or knife ready to use it
12 TRICK/JOKE/LIE **a)** **pull a stunt/trick/joke/prank etc.** INFORMAL to do something that annoys or harms other people: *boys pulling practical jokes* **b)** [T] SPOKEN to deceive or trick someone: *What are you trying to pull?* | *Are you trying to* ***pull a fast one*** *on me?*
13 CAR [I] if a car pulls to the left or right as you are driving, it moves in that direction because of a problem with its machinery: *The car seems to be pulling to the left.*
14 USE A CONTROL [T] to move a control such as a SWITCH or TRIGGER toward you to make a piece of equipment work: *She raised the gun and pulled the trigger.*
15 MAKE SB/STH NOT TAKE PART [T] to remove someone from an organization, activity etc., so that they do not take part anymore: *The team was pulled at the last minute.* | **pull sb/sth from sth** *She was angry enough to pull her kids from the school.*
16 NATURAL FORCE [T] if a force such as GRAVITY pulls something, it affects it and may make it move toward where the force is coming from
17 ATTRACT/INFLUENCE [T] to make someone want to do something by attracting or influencing them to do it SYN **draw**: **pull sb toward sth** *Recently, I've felt pulled toward a career in medicine.* | **pull sb in different/opposite directions** (=to influence someone to want to do two or more different things)
18 **pull sb's leg** INFORMAL to tell someone something that is not true, as a joke: *I think he was just pulling your leg.*
19 **not pull any punches** INFORMAL to express your disapproval or criticism very clearly, without trying to hide what you feel: *The report doesn't pull any punches in criticizing the administration.*
20 **pull the curtains/blinds** to open or close curtains or BLINDS SYN **draw**
21 **sth is like pulling teeth** used to say that it is very difficult or unpleasant to persuade someone to do something: *Getting the kids to do their homework was like pulling teeth.*
22 **pull to a stop/halt** if a vehicle or the driver pulls to a stop or halt, the vehicle moves more slowly and then stops moving
23 CROWD/VOTES ETC. [T] if an event, performer etc. pulls crowds or a politician pulls a lot of votes, a lot of people come to see them or vote for them SYN **draw**: *Bagert is expected to pull just enough votes to win.*
24 **pull sb's license** INFORMAL to take away someone's LICENSE (=special permission) to do something, especially to drive a car, because they have done something wrong → see also REVOKE
25 **pull a punch** to deliberately hit someone with less force than you could use, so that it hurts less
26 BASEBALL/GOLF [I,T] to hit the ball in baseball, GOLF etc. so that it does not go straight but moves to one side
27 ROW A BOAT [I,T] to make a boat move by using OARS
[**Origin:** Old English *pullian*] → see also **pull yourself up by your bootstraps** at BOOTSTRAPS, **tear/pull your hair out** at HAIR (5), **pull the plug** at PLUG[1] (6), **pull rank (on sb)** at RANK[1] (5), **pull the rug (out) from under sb** at RUG (2), **pull the wool over sb's eyes** at WOOL (4), PUSH

pull ahead *phr. v.* **1** to get in front of another person, vehicle, animal etc. by moving faster than they do, especially in a race **2** to start to make progress faster than someone else or do better than they do: **pull ahead of sb** *One poll showed him pulling ahead of his rivals.*

pull apart *phr. v.* **1** **pull sth ↔ apart** to separate something into two or more pieces or groups: *Pull apart the dough into four equal pieces.* **2** **pull sb/sth apart** to upset someone or make the relationship between people difficult, especially so that a family, group, country etc. becomes divided: *My father's drinking problem pulled the family apart.* **3** **pull sth ↔ apart** to carefully examine or criticize something: *The selection committee pulled each proposal apart.* **4** **pull sb ↔ apart** to separate people or animals when they are fighting **5** if something pulls apart, it breaks into pieces when you pull on it: *Barbecued ribs should pull apart easily with your fingers.*

pull at sth *phr. v.* to take a hold of something and pull it several times SYN **pull on**: *The old man pulled thoughtfully at his beard.*

pull away *phr. v.* **1** to move away from someone quickly when they are trying to touch you or hold you: *I tried to kiss her but she pulled away.* **2** to start to drive away from a place where you had stopped: *He waved as he pulled away.* | **+from** *The bus had already pulled away from the bus stop.* **3** to move ahead of a competitor by going faster or being more successful: *In the final quarter the Bulls pulled away, winning 105–80.*

pull back *phr. v.* **1** **pull sth ↔ back** if an army pulls back or a leader pulls it back, it leaves its present position and moves to a position that is less threatening or dangerous: **pull (sth) back from sth** *The army was pulling back from the east.* → see also PULLBACK **2** to suddenly move your body away from someone or something SYN **draw back** **3** to decide not to do or become involved in something: *Foreign investors have pulled back recently.*

pull down *phr. v.* **1** **pull sth ↔ down** to destroy something or make it stop existing: *Houses were pulled down to make way for a new highway.* **2** **pull down sth** INFORMAL to earn a particular amount of money at your job: *He pulls down at least $65,000 a year.* **3** **pull sb/sth ↔ down** to make someone or something less successful: *There are worries that low sales could pull the economy down.* **4** **pull down a menu** to make a computer PROGRAM show you a list of the things it can do → see also PULL-DOWN

pull for sb/sth *phr. v.* INFORMAL to encourage a person or team to succeed: *Which team are you pulling for?*

pull in *phr. v.* **1** **pull sth ↔ in** INFORMAL if you pull in a lot of money, you earn it: *Smith will pull in about $1.2 million a year.* **2** **pull sth ↔ in** to move a car into a particular space and stop it: *Ken pulled in behind me and parked.* **3** **pull sth ↔ in** to get money, business etc. by doing something to attract people's attention: *Hall pulled in 58% of the vote.* **4 pull sth in** if an event, a show etc. pulls in a lot of people, they go to it or see it: *The movie was still **pulling in crowds** after 18 weeks.* **5** if a train pulls in, it arrives at a station **6 pull sb ↔ in** if a police officer pulls someone in, they take them to a police station because they think they may have done something wrong

pull off *phr. v.* **1 pull sth ↔ off** INFORMAL to succeed in doing something difficult: *The Huskies pulled off a win in Saturday's game.* **2 pull off sth** to drive a car off a road to stop or to turn onto another road: *We pulled off for a bite to eat.* | **pull off the road/highway/freeway etc.** *Pull off the road so we can check the map.*

pull on sth *phr. v.* **1** to take a hold of something and pull it several times SYN **pull at**: *Stop pulling on my skirt.* **2** to take smoke from a pipe or cigarette into your lungs

pull out *phr. v.* **1** to drive onto a road from another road, or from where you have stopped: **+of** *Be careful when you pull out of the driveway.* **2** to stop doing something or being involved in something: **+of** *They're trying to pull out of the deal.* **3 pull sb/sth ↔ out** to remove someone from a situation that they have been involved in: **pull sb out of sth** *After the injury, he had to pull out of the race.* **4 pull sb/sth ↔ out** if a country or its army pulls out of a place or its leaders pull it out, its army leaves that place: *Most of the troops have been pulled out.* | **+of** *U.N. forces have begun to pull out of the region.* → see also PULLOUT **5** if a train pulls out, it leaves a station **6 pull out all the stops** to do everything you can in order to make something succeed: *Fred's pulling out all the stops for his daughter's wedding.*

I,T pull sb/sth **↔ over** *phr. v.* to drive to the side of a road and stop your car, to make someone do this: *I got pulled over for speeding.*

pull through *phr. v.* **1 pull sb through (sth)** to stay alive after you have been very sick or badly injured, or help someone do this: *We're all praying that he'll pull through.* **2 pull through sth** to succeed in dealing with a very difficult situation: *The city managed to pull through its financial crisis.*

pull together *phr. v.* **1** if a group of people pull together, they all work hard to achieve something: *After the hurricane, neighbors pulled together to help each other.* **2 pull yourself together** to force yourself to stop behaving in a nervous, frightened, or disorganized way: *Pull yourself together – you don't want him to see you crying like that.* **3 pull sth ↔ together** to organize something that is not organized and make it work more effectively: *It must have been a lot of work pulling a show like that together.*

pull up *phr. v.* **1** to stop the vehicle that you are driving: *Who is that pulling up out front?* **2 pull up a chair/stool etc.** to get a chair and sit down next to someone who is already sitting **3 pull sth ↔ up** to use force to take plants out of the ground **4 pull sb up short** to make someone suddenly stop doing or thinking a particular thing

pull² *n.*

1 ACT OF PULLING [C] an act of using force to move something toward you or in the same direction that you are moving → see also TUG: *He **gave** the cord **a pull**.*

2 FORCE [C usually singular] PHYSICS a strong force such as GRAVITY, that makes things move in a particular direction: *the moon's pull on the Earth*

3 INFLUENCE [singular, U] INFORMAL special influence that gives you an unfair advantage: *The senator has a lot of pull with the Republicans in Congress.*

4 ATTRACTION [U] the ability to attract people: *the pull of life in the big city*

5 MUSCLE [C] an injury to one of your muscles caused by stretching it too much during exercise: *a groin pull*

6 HANDLE [C] a rope or handle that you use to pull something

7 BASEBALL/GOLF [C] a way of hitting the ball in baseball or GOLF so that it does not go straight, but moves to one side

8 SMOKE [C] an act of taking the smoke from a cigarette, pipe etc. into your lungs

9 DRINK [C] an act of taking a long drink of something: *I took one last **pull** from the water jug.*

pull·back /ˈpʊlbæk/ *n.* [C] **1** an action of moving an army back to a position where it was before: *a pullback of troops from the occupied territories* → see also PULL BACK **2** a situation in which STOCK prices return to a lower level **3** a situation in which a company, organization, or people in general stop doing something or do it less: *a pullback in consumer spending*

ˈpull-ˌdown *adj.* **1 a pull-down menu** a list of things a computer program can do that you can make appear on a computer SCREEN **2** [only before noun] able to be pulled into a lower position: *a pull-down window shade*

pul·let /ˈpʊlɪt/ *n.* [C] a young chicken during its first year of laying eggs

pul·ley /ˈpʊli/ *n. plural* **pulleys** [C] a piece of equipment consisting of a wheel over which a rope or chain is pulled to lift heavy things

ˈpull ˌfactor *n.* [C] a quality or feature of an area that makes people want to move there → see also PUSH FACTOR

Pull·man /ˈpʊlmən/ *n.* [C] **1** also **ˈPullman car** a very comfortable train car, especially one that you can sleep in, or a train made up of these cars **2** also **ˈPullman case** OLD-FASHIONED a very large suitcase

ˈpull-on *adj.* [only before noun] a pull-on shirt, dress etc. does not have any buttons, so you pull it on over your head

pull·out¹ /ˈpʊlaʊt/ *n.* [C] **1** the act of an army, business etc. leaving a particular place or area of activity: *a pullout of troops from the region* → see also PULL OUT **2** part of a magazine, newspaper etc. that can be removed: *a 16-page pullout of office furnishings*

pullout², pull-out *adj.* [only before noun] **1** a pullout part of a magazine or newspaper can be pulled out of the magazine or newspaper and read separately: *a special pullout calendar* **2** pullout parts of a a piece of furniture are able to be slid out and then pushed back in again when they are not needed: *pull-out shelves*

pull·o·ver /ˈpʊlˌoʊvɚ/ *n.* [C] a SWEATER without buttons

ˈpull-up *n.* [C] a CHIN UP

pul·mo·nar·y /ˈpʊlməˌnɛri, ˈpʌl-/ *adj.* BIOLOGY relating to the lungs or having an effect on the lungs

pulp¹ /pʌlp/ *n.* **1** [singular, U] BIOLOGY the soft inside part of a fruit or vegetable: *orange juice with pulp* **2** [U] a very soft substance that is almost liquid, made by crushing or cooking something: *Mash the avocado to a pulp.* **3** [U] a soft substance made of wet wood, cloth etc. that is ground up to make paper: *wood pulp* **4 beat sb to a pulp** INFORMAL to hit someone until they are seriously injured **5** [U] DISAPPROVING books, magazines, movies etc. that are of poor quality or are badly written, and that are often about sex or violence **6** [U] BIOLOGY the soft substance inside a tooth —**pulpy** *adj.* → see picture at TOOTH

pulp² *adj.* [only before noun] pulp magazines, stories etc. are of poor quality or are badly written, and are often about sex and violence: *pulp fiction*

pulp³ *v.* [T] **1** to beat or crush something until it becomes so soft that it is almost liquid **2** to cut up and add water to books, newspapers etc. in order to make paper: *Forms will be shredded, pulped, and recycled.*

pul·pit /ˈpʊlpɪt, ˈpʌl-/ *n.* [C] a structure like a tall box at the front of a church, that a priest or minister stands behind when they speak

pulp·wood /ˈpʌlpwʊd/ *n.* [U] crushed wood that is used to make paper

pul·sar /ˈpʌlsɑr/ *n.* [C] an object like a star that is far away in space and produces a regular radio signal

pul·sate /ˈpʌlseɪt/ *v.* [I] **1** to make repeated sounds or movements that are strong and regular, like a heart beating: *Loud music was pulsating from the speakers.*

2 LITERARY to be strongly affected by a powerful emotion or feeling: +**with** *The whole city seemed to be pulsating with excitement.* —**pulsating** *adj.*

pul·sa·tion /pʌl'seɪʃən/ *n.* **1** [C] BIOLOGY a beat of the heart or any regular beat that can be measured **2** [U] movement that pulsates

pulse¹ /pʌls/ *n.*
1 HEART BEAT [C] **a)** BIOLOGY the regular beat that can be felt, for example at your wrist, as your heart pumps blood around your body: *The man's pulse was weak.* **b)** [usually singular] also **pulse rate** the number of these beats per minute: **take/check sb's pulse** (=count how many time's someone's heart beats in a minute, usually by feeling their wrist)
2 SOUND/LIGHT/ELECTRICITY [C] an amount of sound, light, or electricity that continues for a very short time: *electrical pulses of light*
3 MUSIC/DRUM [C,U] a strong regular beat as in music, or on a drum: *the pulse of steel drums in the parks*
4 HOW A GROUP OF PEOPLE FEEL [U] the ideas, feelings, opinions etc. that are most important or have the most influence in a particular group of people at a particular time: *Stock brokers with a feel for Hong Kong's financial pulse were worried.*
5 sb's pulse quickens/races if someone's pulse quickens etc., it becomes faster because they are excited or nervous
6 set/get sb's pulses racing to make someone feel very excited
7 SEEDS/PLANTS [C usually plural] seeds such as beans, PEAS, and LENTILS that can be eaten, or a plant on which these seeds grow → see also **have/keep your finger on the pulse** at FINGER¹ (8)

pulse² *v.* [I] **1** to move or flow with a steady rapid beat or sound: *He felt the blood pulsing around his body.* **2** if music or sound pulses, it has a loud regular beat **3** LITERARY if a feeling or emotion pulses through someone, they feel it very strongly **4 pulse with excitement/energy/life etc.** if a person or place pulses with excitement, energy etc., they are very exciting, have a lot of energy etc. **5** to push a button on a FOOD PROCESSOR to make the machine go on and off regularly, rather than work continuously

pul·ver·ize /'pʌlvəˌraɪz/ *v.* [T usually passive] **1** to crush something into a powder **2** INFORMAL to completely defeat someone —**pulverization** /ˌpʌlvərə'zeɪʃən/ *n.* [U]

pu·ma /'pumə, 'pyumə/ *n.* [C] a COUGAR

pum·ice /'pʌmɪs/ also **'pumice ˌstone** *n.* **1** [U] EARTH SCIENCE very light silver-gray rock that has come from a VOLCANO, and is crushed and used as a powder for cleaning **2** [C] a piece of this stone used for rubbing your skin to clean it or make it soft

pum·mel /'pʌməl/ *v.* [T]
1 HIT to hit someone or something many times quickly with your FISTS (=closed hands): *She pummeled his bare chest with her fists.*
2 DEFEAT INFORMAL to completely defeat someone in a sport, competition, election etc.
3 STORMS/ATTACKS if storms, winds, or attacks pummel a place, they continue to hit it for a long time and often cause damage
4 CRITICIZE to criticize someone or something strongly again and again, especially in public
5 GIVE TOO MUCH INFORMATION to make someone have to deal with too many ideas, too much information etc. all at the same time

pump¹ /pʌmp/ *n.* **1** [C] a machine for forcing liquid or gas into or out of something: **a water/air/oil etc. pump** (=for moving water, air etc.) | **a hand/foot pump** (=one operated by your hand or foot) → see also BICYCLE¹, STOMACH PUMP **2** [C] a machine at a GAS STATION that is used to put gasoline into cars SYN **gas pump**: *Consumers will be paying more **at the pump*** (=when they buy gas). **3** [C usually plural] a woman's plain shoe that has a short HEEL and does not have BUCKLES or LACES: *a pair of blue leather pumps* → see picture at SHOE¹ **4** [C] an act of pumping [**Origin:** (1, 2) 1400–1500 Middle Low German *pumpe* or Middle Dutch *pompe*] → see also HEAT PUMP, **prime the pump** at PRIME³ (5)

pump² *v.*
1 MOVE LIQUID/GAS [T always + adv./prep.] to make liquid or gas move in a particular direction with a pump: **pump sth into/through/from etc. sth** *A pipe accidentally pumped tons of sewage into Boston Harbor.* | *Blood is pumped around the body by the heart.*
2 FROM UNDER GROUND [T] to bring a supply of water, oil etc. to the surface from under the ground: *We were able to pump clean groundwater from several of the wells.*
3 pump gas to put gasoline into your car at a gas station
4 COME OUT QUICKLY [I always + adv./prep.] when a liquid pumps from somewhere, it comes out in sudden large amounts: +**from/out of etc.** *Oil continued to pump out of the ship's damaged hull.*
5 QUESTIONS [T] INFORMAL to ask someone a lot of questions, in order to find out something: *She wanted to **pump** him **for information** about the deal.*
6 MOVE IN AND OUT/UP AND DOWN [I,T] to move very quickly in and out or up and down, or to make something do this: *She pumped the brake pedal but nothing happened.* | *He kept pumping till water came gushing out.* | *The bikers legs were pumping vigorously.*
7 HEART BEATS [I] if your heart pumps, you can feel it beating quickly because you are excited, frightened etc., or because you have been exercising: *I could feel my heart pumping.*
8 pump sb full of sth to put a lot of drugs into someone's body: *The doctor had him pumped full of pain killers.*
9 pump iron INFORMAL to do exercises by lifting heavy weights
10 have your stomach pumped to have the things inside your stomach removed by a pump, after swallowing something harmful
11 pump sb full of lead/bullets INFORMAL to shoot a lot of bullets into someone

pump away *phr. v.* **1** to move up and down very quickly, or to make something do this **2** if your heart pumps away, you can feel it beating because you are excited, frightened etc., or because you have been exercising

pump sth **into** sb/sth *phr. v.* **1** to spend money on something such as a business, industry, or ECONOMY: *Huge amounts of money are being pumped into research.* **2 pump bullets into sb/sth** INFORMAL to shoot someone several times

pump out *phr. v.* **1 pump sth ↔ out** if something such as music, information, or a supply of products is pumped out or pumps out, a lot of it is produced: *The factory pumps out a million pairs of socks each week.* **2 pump sth ↔ out** to remove liquid from something using a pump: *It took all afternoon to pump out our flooded basement.*

pump up *phr. v.* **1 pump sth ↔ up** to fill a tire, ball etc. with air SYN **inflate** **2 pump sth ↔ up** to increase the value, amount etc. of something: *Exports have pumped up the nation's economy.* **3 pump sb ↔ up** INFORMAL to encourage someone or make them excited about something: *The chanting pumped the team up.* → see also PUMPED **4 pump up the music/volume etc.** SLANG to play music louder

'pump-ˌaction *adj.* **a pump action shotgun/bottle/hairspray etc.** a SHOTGUN, bottle etc. that is operated by pulling or pressing part of it in or out

pumped /pʌmpt/ also **ˌpumped 'up** *adj.* INFORMAL **1** very excited about something: *She often makes big plays that get the whole team pumped up.* **2** with large muscles because you have been exercising: *He came back from the gym all pumped up.*

pum·per·nick·el /'pʌmpɚˌnɪkəl/ *n.* [U] a heavy dark brown bread

pump·kin /'pʌmpkɪn, 'pʌŋkɪn/ S3 *n.* **1** [C,U] BIOLOGY a very large orange fruit that grows on the ground, or the inside of this fruit eaten as food: *pumpkin pie* → see picture on page A35 **2** [singular, not with "the"] a name used for someone you love, especially a child: *What's wrong, pumpkin?* [**Origin:** 1600–1700 *pumpion* **pumpkin**

(16–19 centuries), from French *pompon* **melon, pumpkin**]

ˈpump room *n.* [C] a room at a SPA where you can go to drink the water

pun[1] /pʌn/ *n.* [C] ENG. LANG. ARTS an amusing use of a word or phrase that has two meanings, or of words with the same sound but different meanings. For example, "People are dying to get into that cemetery" can mean that they really want to be buried there, or they are actually dying in order to be buried there: *He was always **making bad puns**.* | *Walters is a large man who carries considerable weight in the Assembly, **no pun intended*** (=used to tell someone that you did not mean to make a pun). | **pardon/excuse/forgive the pun** (=used to say you are making a pun) ►see THESAURUS box at **joke**[1]

pun[2] *v.* **punned, punning** [I] to make a pun

punch[1] /pʌntʃ/ S3 *v.* [T]

1 HIT to hit someone or something hard with your FIST (=closed hand): *The other boys began kicking and punching him.* | **punch sb in/on sth** *Then the guy walked up and punched Jack in the face.* ►see THESAURUS box at **hit**[1]

2 MAKE HOLE to make a hole in something using a metal tool or other sharp object: **punch a ticket/card etc.** *The bus driver will punch your ticket.* | **punch a hole in/through sth** *I got so mad that I punched a hole in the door.* ►see THESAURUS box at **hole**[1], **pierce**

3 PUSH BUTTONS to push a button or key on a machine SYN **push** SYN **press**: *She punched the red button and waited for the doors to open.*

4 HIT STH TO MOVE IT [always + adv./prep.] to hit something in a particular direction using your FIST (=closed hand): **punch sth away/into etc.** *He punched the ball away.*

5 punch holes in an argument/idea/plan etc. to disagree with someone's idea or plan and show what is wrong with it

6 punch the air to make a movement like a punch toward the sky, to show that you are very pleased about something

7 punch the clock INFORMAL to record the time that you start or finish work by putting a card into a special machine

8 punch sb's lights out INFORMAL to hit someone hard in the face so that they become unconscious

9 punch it SPOKEN, INFORMAL to start driving faster immediately

10 CATTLE [T] OLD-FASHIONED to move cattle from one place to another

[**Origin:** 1300–1400 Old French *poinçonner* **to make a hole in**, from *poinçon* **tool for making holes**]

punch in *phr. v.* **1** to record the time that you arrive at work, by putting a card into a special machine: *Mitch made sure he punched in exactly at 8 a.m.* **2 punch sth ↔ in** to put information into a computer by pressing buttons or keys: *I punched in the password.*

punch out *phr. v.* **1** to record the time that you leave work, by putting a card into a special machine: *You should punch out now and take the rest of the day off.* **2 punch sb out** to hit someone so hard that they fall over or become unconscious: *He punched out one of his co-workers.*

punch[2] S3 *n.*

1 HIT [C] a quick strong hit made with your FIST (=closed hand): *a knockout punch* | **+in/on** *a punch on the nose* | *Mike **gave** me **a punch** on the arm.* | **throw a punch** (=try to hit someone)

2 DRINK [C,U] a drink made from fruit juice, sugar, water, and sometimes alcohol: *fruit punch*

3 EFFECTIVE QUALITY [U] a strong, effective, and interesting quality in the way something does something: *The book lacks the punch of his earlier novels.*

4 TOOL [C] also **hole punch** a metal tool for cutting holes or for pushing something into a small hole

5 beat sb/sth to the punch INFORMAL to do or get something before someone else: *The company has managed to beat its rivals to the punch with its new line of computers.*

6 as pleased as punch INFORMAL very happy about something → see also **one-two punch** at ONE-TWO (1), **pack a punch/wallop** at PACK[1] (9), **not pull any punches** at PULL[1] (19), **pull a punch** at PULL[1] (25)

ˈpunch bowl *n.* [C] a large bowl in which punch is served

ˈpunch card *n.* [C] **1** also **ˈpunched card** a card with a pattern of holes in it that was used in past times for putting information into a computer **2** a card that some businesses give you that allows you to get something free or for a reduced price after you have used the business a certain number of times and have had a small hole put in the card each time

ˈpunch-drunk *adj.* **1** INFORMAL PUNCHY **2** a BOXER who is punch-drunk is suffering brain damage from being hit too much

ˈpunching bag *n.* [C] **1** a heavy leather bag hung from a rope, that is PUNCHed for exercise **2** someone who is often blamed and criticized, even though they may not have done anything wrong **3 use sb as a punching bag** INFORMAL to hit or PUNCH someone

ˈpunch line *n.* [C] the last few words of a joke or story that make it funny or surprising

punch·y /ˈpʌntʃi/ *adj. comparative* **punchier**, *superlative* **punchiest** **1** INFORMAL confused, especially because you have had a lot of information to deal with and are very tired SYN **punch-drunk** **2** a punchy piece of writing or speech is very effective because it expresses ideas clearly in only a few words **3** a punchy performance or punchy music is done or played well with a lot of energy —**punchiness** *n.* [U]

punc·til·i·ous /pʌŋkˈtɪliəs/ *adj.* FORMAL very careful to behave correctly and keep exactly to rules —**punctiliously** *adv.* —**punctiliousness** *n.* [U]

punc·tu·al /ˈpʌŋktʃuəl/ *adj.* arriving, happening etc. at exactly the time that has been arranged: *Michael's a very punctual reliable worker.* —**punctually** *adv.* —**punctuality** /ˌpʌŋktʃuˈæləṭi/ *n.* [U]

punc·tu·ate /ˈpʌŋktʃuˌeɪt/ *v.* **1** [T] ENG. LANG. ARTS to divide written work into sentences, phrases etc. using COMMAS, PERIODS etc. **2** [T] to interrupt an activity, situation, period of time etc., especially several times: **be punctuated with/by sth** *Their conversation was punctuated by awkward silences.*

ˌpunctuated equiˈlibrium *n.* [U] BIOLOGY a pattern of EVOLUTION in which a lot of changes happen very quickly, then there is no change for a long time, then a lot of changes happen very quickly, and so on

punc·tu·a·tion /ˌpʌŋktʃuˈeɪʃən/ *n.* [U] ENG. LANG. ARTS the marks used in dividing a piece of writing into sentences, phrases etc.

ˌpunctuˈation mark *n.* [C] ENG. LANG. ARTS a sign, such as a COMMA (,) or QUESTION MARK (?), that is used in dividing a piece of writing into sentences, phrases etc.

THESAURUS

apostrophe the sign ' that is used to show that one or more letters or numbers have been left out, as in "don't." It is also used before "s" to show that something belongs to someone or something, as in "Mark's dog."
parentheses a pair of curved signs ( ) used for enclosing information
brackets a pair of signs [ ] used for enclosing information
comma the sign (,) that is used to show a short pause or to separate things in a list
semicolon the sign (;) that is used to separate different parts of a sentence or list
colon the sign (:) that is used to introduce an explanation, example, quotation etc.
hyphen the sign (-) that is used to join words or syllables
dash the sign (–) that is used to separate two closely related parts of a sentence
ellipsis the sign (...) that is used to show that some words have deliberately been left out of a sentence

period the sign (.) that is used to mark the end of a sentence or the short form of a word
exclamation mark the sign (!) that is used after a sentence or word that expresses surprise, anger, or excitement
question mark the sign (?) that is used at the end of a question
quotation marks a pair of signs (" ") that are put around words, especially to show that you are recording what someone has said
slash a line (/) that is used to separate words, numbers, or letters
backslash a line (\) that is used to separate words, numbers, or letters
asterisk the sign (*) that is used especially to mark something interesting or important
at sign the sign (@) that is used especially in email addresses
ampersand the sign (&) that means "and"

punc·ture¹ /ˈpʌŋktʃɚ/ *n.* [C] a small hole made by a sharp point

puncture² *v.* [T] **1** to make a small hole through the surface of something, so that air or liquid can get out: *You should never puncture old aerosol cans.* **2** to suddenly destroy a feeling or belief, making someone feel unhappy, silly, or confused: *Her happiness was punctured by the news of his death.* **3** LITERARY to interrupt a period of silence by making a noise

pun·dit /ˈpʌndɪt/ *n.* [C] someone who knows a lot about a particular subject, and is often asked for their opinions on it: *political pundits* [**Origin:** 1600–1700 Hindi *pandit*, from Sanskrit *pandita* **wise**]

pun·gent /ˈpʌndʒənt/ *adj.* **1** a pungent taste or smell is strong and sharp: *the pungent smell of onions* **2** pungent remarks or writing criticize something in a very direct and intelligent way —**pungently** *adv.* —**pungency** *n.* [U]

pun·ish /ˈpʌnɪʃ/ W3 *v.* [T] **1** to make someone suffer because they have done something wrong or broken the law: *He knew he would be punished if he was caught.* | **punish sb for (doing) sth** *She deserves to be punished for what she has done.* | **punish sb by doing sth** *Roger punished the children by taking away their toys.* | *Drug traffickers will be* ***severely punished****.* **2** if you punish a crime, you punish anyone who is guilty of it: *Deserting the army during war can be punished by death.* **3 punish yourself (for sth)** to blame yourself for something: *The accident wasn't your fault – stop punishing yourself.* **4** if a system, rule, law etc. punishes a group of people, they are badly affected by it: *The present system punishes the elderly.* [**Origin:** 1300–1400 Old French *punir*, from Latin *punire*, from *poena*, from Greek *poine* **payment, punishment**]

pun·ish·a·ble /ˈpʌnɪʃəbəl/ *adj.* a punishable action may be punished by law, especially in a particular way: *a punishable offense* | +**by** *a crime punishable by death*

pun·ish·ing /ˈpʌnɪʃɪŋ/ *adj.* long, difficult, or extreme, and making you feel tired and weak: *a punishing work schedule* —**punishingly** *adv.*

pun·ish·ment /ˈpʌnɪʃmənt/ W3 *n.* **1** [C] a way in which someone or something is punished: +**for** *The maximum punishment for robbery is 40 years in prison.* | *She was sent to bed early* ***as a punishment****.* | **a harsh/severe punishment** (=one that makes someone suffer a lot)

THESAURUS

sentence a punishment given by a judge in a court: *He was given the maximum ten-year sentence.*
penalty a punishment given to someone who has broken a law, rule, or agreement: *Drug dealers face severe penalties.*
fine an amount of money that you must pay as a punishment for breaking a rule or law: *During the drought, homeowners who used too much water were given a fine.*
community service unpaid work helping other people that someone does as punishment for a crime: *He was ordered to do 60 hours of community service.*
corporal punishment the act of punishing a child by hitting him/her: *Corporal punishment is illegal in schools.*
capital punishment/the death penalty the practice of killing someone as punishment for a crime: *The California legislature re-authorized the use of capital punishment in 1977.*

2 [U] the act of punishing someone or the process of being punished: *The courts are responsible for the punishment of offenders.* | **escape/avoid punishment** *Criminals will not be able to escape punishment.* **3** [U] INFORMAL rough physical treatment SYN **damage**: *Off-road vehicles are designed to withstand a certain amount of punishment.* → see also CAPITAL PUNISHMENT, CORPORAL PUNISHMENT

pu·ni·tive /ˈpyunət̬ɪv/ *adj.* **1 punitive actions/measures/damages etc.** actions etc. that are intended to punish someone: *The airline had to pay $50 million in punitive damages.* **2** so severe that people find it very difficult to pay: *punitive taxes* —**punitively** *adv.*

punk /pʌŋk/ *n.* **1** [U] also **punk ˈrock** a type of loud violent music popular in the late 1970s and the 1980s **2** [C] DISAPPROVING, INFORMAL a young man or a boy who fights and breaks the law: *I'd like to find the punk who broke off my car antenna.* **3** [C] also **punk ˈrocker** someone who dresses like people who like or play punk rock, with brightly colored hair, chains and pins, and torn clothing **4** [U] a substance that burns without a flame and is used to light FIREWORKS etc.

pun·kin /ˈpʌŋkɪn/ *n.* [C] a nonstandard spelling of PUMPKIN

pun·ster /ˈpʌnstɚ/ *n.* [C] someone who makes PUNS

punt¹ /pʌnt/ *n.* **1** [C] a long kick that you make after dropping the ball from your hands, especially in football **2** [C] a long narrow river-boat with a flat bottom and square ends, that is moved by pushing a long pole against the bottom of the river **3** [singular] the act of going out in a punt

punt² *v.* **1** [I,T] to drop the ball from your hands and kick it before it touches the ground, especially in football **2** [I,T] to go or take someone on a river by punt

punt·er /ˈpʌntɚ/ *n.* [C] the player who punts the ball in football

pu·ny /ˈpyuni/ *adj. comparative* **punier**, *superlative* **puniest** **1** small, thin, and weak: *a puny kid* ►see THESAURUS box at **weak¹** **2** unimpressive and ineffective: *puny profits* —**puniness** *n.* [U]

pup¹ /pʌp/ *n.* [C] **1** BIOLOGY a PUPPY **2** BIOLOGY a young SEAL or OTTER: *seal pups* **3** OLD-FASHIONED an insulting word for a young man who is impolite or too confident, and who does not have much experience

pup² *v.* **pupped**, **pupping** [I] TECHNICAL to give birth to pups

pu·pa /ˈpyupə/ *n. plural* **pupas** or **pupae** /-pi/ [C] BIOLOGY a young insect at the stage of its development when it does not feed and is protected inside a special cover, before it becomes an adult —**pupal** *adj.*

pu·pate /ˈpyupeɪt/ *v.* [I] TECHNICAL to become a pupa

pu·pil /ˈpyupəl/ *n.* [C] **1** BIOLOGY the small black round area in the middle of the eye which controls how much light is allowed to enter the eye: *The drops cause the* ***pupils to dilate*** (=get bigger). → see picture at EYE¹ **2** FORMAL someone who is being taught, especially a child SYN **student** [**Origin:** (1) 1300–1400 Old French *pupille*, from Latin *pupa* **girl, doll**; because of the small image of yourself which you can see in someone else's eye]

pup·pet /ˈpʌpɪt/ *n.* [C] **1** a model of a person or animal that you can move by pulling wires or strings, or by putting your hand inside it: *a puppet show* **2** DISAPPROVING a person or organization that is not independent but is controlled by someone else: *a puppet of the ruling party* | **a puppet government/regime/state**

P

etc. (=a government controlled by a more powerful country or organization)

pup·pet·eer /ˌpʌpɪˈtɪr/ *n.* [C] someone who performs with puppets

pup·pet·ry /ˈpʌpɪtri/ *n.* [U] the art of performing with puppets, or the study of this

pup·py /ˈpʌpi/ S2 *n. plural* **puppies** [C] **1** a young dog **2 this/that puppy** SPOKEN, INFORMAL used instead of the name of a thing, especially when you do not know the name: *How do you shut this puppy off?* [**Origin:** 1400–1500 French *poupée* **doll, toy**]

P

ˈpuppy love *n.* [U] a young boy's or girl's love for someone, which people do not regard as serious

ˈpup tent *n.* [C] a small TENT for two people

pur·blind /ˈpɚblaɪnd/ *adj.* FORMAL OR LITERARY stupid or dull

Pur·cell /ˈpɚsəl/, **Henry** (1659–1695) an English musician who wrote CLASSICAL music

pur·chase¹ /ˈpɚtʃəs/ Ac W2 *v.* [T] FORMAL to buy something, especially something big or expensive SYN **buy**: *He purchased the property in 1989.* | **purchase sth from sb/sth** *Tickets may be purchased from the theater box office.* [**Origin:** 1200–1300 Old French *purchacier* **to try to get**, from *chacier* **to run after and try to catch**] ►see THESAURUS box at **buy¹**

purchase² Ac W3 *n.* **1** [C,U] FORMAL the act of buying something: *credit card purchases* | +**of** *the purchase of new computer equipment* | *Many stores will let you* ***make a purchase*** (=buy something) *by telephone.* | **the place/day/date/time of purchase** *Tickets may be returned to the place of purchase for a full refund.* → see also PROOF OF PURCHASE **2** [C] FORMAL something that has been bought: *She paid for her purchases and left.* **3 gain/get a purchase** FORMAL to get a firm hold of something with your hands or feet

ˈpurchase price *n.* [singular] FORMAL the price that you have to pay to buy something or that you paid for something: *The purchase price of the house was $177,500.*

pur·chas·er /ˈpɚtʃəsɚ/ Ac *n.* [C] FORMAL the person who buys something

ˈpurchasing ˌpower *n.* [U] **1** the amount of money that a person or group has available to spend, compared to other people: *the purchasing power of an average American family* **2** the value of a unit of money considered in relation to how much you can buy with it: *The purchasing power of the dollar has declined.*

pur·dah /ˈpɚdə/ *n.* [U] **1** the custom, especially among Muslim people, in which women stay in their home or cover their faces so that they cannot be seen by men **2 in purdah a)** women who are in purdah live according to this custom **b)** staying away from other people

pure /pyʊr/ S3 W3 *adj.*

1 NOT MIXED not mixed with anything else OPP **impure**: *The ring was made of pure gold.* | *pure olive oil* ►see THESAURUS box at **natural¹**

2 COMPLETE [only before noun] complete or total SYN **sheer**: *a smile of pure joy* | **pure luck/chance/coincidence etc.** *It was by pure luck that we found the place.*

3 CLEAN clean, without anything harmful or unhealthy OPP **impure**: *pure drinking water*

4 COLOR [only before noun] clear and not mixed with other colors: *pure white sheets*

5 SOUND very clear and beautiful to hear: *a pure tenor voice*

6 WITHOUT EVIL having the quality of being completely good or moral, especially not having sexual thoughts or experience SYN **innocent** OPP **impure**: *a pure young girl* | *I'm sure he had the purest of motives.*

7 TYPICAL [only before noun] typical of a particular style: *The movie is pure Hollywood.*

8 pure science/math etc. work done in science, math etc. in order to increase our knowledge of it rather than to make practical use of it: *pure research* → see also APPLIED

9 pure and simple INFORMAL used to say that there is only one reason for something: *He wanted revenge, pure and simple.*

10 ART a pure form of art is done exactly according to an accepted standard or pattern

11 as pure as the driven snow OFTEN HUMOROUS morally perfect

[**Origin:** 1200–1300 Old French *pur*, from Latin *purus*] —**pureness** *n.* [U] → see also IMPURE, PURELY, PURIFY, PURITY

pure·blood·ed /ˈpyʊrˌblʌdɪd/ *adj.* with parents, grandparents etc. from only one group or race of people, with no mixture of other groups

pure·bred /ˈpyʊrbrɛd/ *adj.* coming from only one breed of animal, with no mixture of other breeds: *a purebred greyhound* —**purebred** *n.* [C] → see also PEDIGREED, THOROUGHBRED

ˌpure compeˈtition *n.* [U] ECONOMICS PERFECT COMPETITION

pu·ree, purée /pyʊˈreɪ/ *n.* [C,U] food that is boiled or crushed until it is a soft mass that is almost liquid: *tomato puree* —**puree, purée** *v.* [T]

ˌPure Food and ˈDrug Act, the POLITICS a law that controls the production and sale of food, medicine, and alcohol in the U.S. It states that food etc. sold in stores must clearly list all the different things contained in it on the package.

pure·ly /ˈpyʊrli/ *adv.* completely and only, without anything else being involved: *He agreed for purely political reasons.* | *It happened purely by chance.*

pur·ga·tive /ˈpɚgət̬ɪv/ *n.* [C] a medicine or food that makes your BOWELS empty themselves —**purgative** *adj.*

pur·ga·to·ry /ˈpɚgəˌtɔri/ *n.* [U] **1** something that makes you suffer or wait for a long time **2 Purgatory** a place where, according to Catholic beliefs, the souls of dead people must suffer for the bad things they did, until they are pure enough to enter heaven —**purgatorial** /ˌpɚgəˈtɔriəl/ *adj.*

purge¹ /pɚdʒ/ *v.* **1** [T] to force your opponents or people who disagree with you to leave an organization or place, often by using violence: **purge sth of sb/sth** *He has repeatedly purged the armed forces of senior commanders.* | **purge sb/sth (from sth)** *Suspected communists were purged from the government.* **2** [T] FORMAL to remove something or throw something away: *He purged all his files before resigning.* | **purge sth of sth** *They want to purge the French language of English words and phrases.* | **purge sth from sth** *His books were purged from the libraries.* **3** [T] LITERARY to get rid of your bad feelings, such as hatred: **purge sb/sth of sth** *It took her months to purge herself of her feelings of guilt.* **4** [I] to force yourself to VOMIT food, especially because you have an eating disorder **5** [T] TECHNICAL to take a medicine to clear all the waste from your BOWELS

purge² *n.* [C] **1** an action to remove your opponents or people who disagree with you from an organization or place, often using violence: *Stalin's purges in the 1930s* | +**of** *a purge of political extremists* **2** OLD-FASHIONED a medicine that clears all the waste from your BOWELS SYN **purgative**

pu·ri·fi·ca·tion /ˌpyʊrəfəˈkeɪʃən/ *n.* [U] **1** a process that removes the dirty or unwanted parts from something: *water purification* → see picture on p. 1281 **2** acts or ceremonies to remove evil from someone: *ritual purification*

pu·ri·fi·er /ˈpyʊrəˌfaɪɚ/ *n.* [C] a machine that makes water or air clean: *a water purifier*

pu·ri·fy /ˈpyʊrəˌfaɪ/ *v.* **purifies, purified, purifying** [T] **1** to remove the dirty or unwanted parts from something: *Chemicals are used to purify the water.* **2** to get rid of evil from your soul

Pu·rim /ˈpʊrɪm, pʊˈrim/ *n.* [U] a religious holiday on which Jews celebrate their escape from being killed by a king in ancient Persia

pur·ist /ˈpyʊrɪst/ *n.* [C] someone who has very strict ideas about what is right or correct in a particular subject, for example in grammar, art, music etc.: *Baseball purists would be against reducing the number of games.* —**purism** *n.* [U]

Pu·ri·tan /ˈpyʊrətˀn, -tən/ *n.* a member of a Protestant religious group in England in the 16th and 17th centuries, who wanted to make religion simpler and get rid of complicated ceremonies. Many of them went to America to find religious freedom, and their beliefs had a strong influence on the American way of life. —**Puritan** *adj.*

pu·ri·tan /ˈpyʊrətˀn/ *n.* [C] someone who has very strict moral standards and thinks that pleasure is unnecessary or wrong —**puritan** *adj.*: *a puritan upbringing*

pu·ri·tan·i·cal /ˌpyʊrəˈtænɪkəl/ *adj.* DISAPPROVING having extreme attitudes about religion and moral behavior: *a puritanical view toward sex* —**puritanically** /-kli/ *adv.* DISAPPROVING

pu·ri·tan·ism /ˈpyʊrətˀnˌɪzəm/ *n.* [U] **1** a way of living according to very strict rules, especially concerning religion and moral behavior **2 Puritanism** the beliefs and practices of the Puritans

pu·ri·ty /ˈpyʊrət̬i/ *n.* [U] the quality or state of being pure OPP **impurity**: +**of** *the purity of the air* | *White is a symbol of purity.*

purl[1] /pərl/ *v.* [I,T] to use the purl stitch when you KNIT (=make clothes from wool)

purl[2] *n.* [U] one of the types of stitches that you use when you KNIT (=make clothes from wool)

pur·lieus /ˈpərlyuz, -luz/ *n.* [plural] LITERARY the area in and around a place

pur·loin /pəˈlɔɪn, ˈpəlɔɪn/ *v.* [T] FORMAL OR HUMOROUS to steal something, or borrow something without permission

pur·ple /ˈpəpəl/ *adj.* **1** having a dark color that is a mixture of red and blue **2 purple with rage/purple in the face etc.** very red in the face as a result of being angry or embarrassed **3 purple prose** also **a purple passage** DISAPPROVING a piece of writing that uses longer or more LITERARY words than are really necessary, in order to appear impressive to people [**Origin:** 900–1000 Latin *purpura*, from Greek *porphyra* type of shellfish from which purple coloring was obtained] —**purple** *n.* [U]

ˌPurple ˈHeart *n.* [C] a special MEDAL given to U.S. soldiers who have been wounded in battle

pur·plish /ˈpəplɪʃ/ *adj.* slightly purple: *a purplish-blue sweater*

pur·port[1] /pəˈpɔrt/ *v.* [I,T] FORMAL to claim to be someone or something, or to make people believe that something is true, even if it is not: **purport to do/be sth** *The photograph purports to show American pilots missing in Vietnam.* —**purported** *adj.*: *the purported leader of the group* —**purportedly** *adv.*

pur·port[2] /ˈpəpɔrt/ *n.* [U] FORMAL the general meaning of what someone says

pur·pose[1] /ˈpəpəs/ S2 W1 *n.*

1 AIM [C] the aim or result that an event, process, or activity is supposed to achieve: *games with an educational purpose* | +**of** *What is the purpose of his visit?* | **the purpose of sth is to do sth** *The purpose of this exercise is to increase your strength.* | **sb's purpose is to do sth** *The group's main purpose is to help disabled youth.* | **the purpose of doing sth** *The purpose of storing photos in a dark dry place is to prevent fading.* | **sb's purpose in doing sth** *A writer's purpose in telling a story should be to entertain.* | *Troops were sent to the area **for the purpose of** assisting refugees.* | *We delete the data once it has **served its purpose**.* | *It would **serve no useful purpose** to reopen the investigation.* | *Do you use the car **for business purposes**?* → see Grammar box at REASON[1]

THESAURUS

aim something that you want to achieve: *Her aim has always been medical school.*
goal something that you hope to achieve in the future: *Athletes set personal goals for themselves.*
objective something that you are working hard to achieve: *The major objectives have been achieved.*

2 on purpose deliberately SYN **purposely** OPP **by accident**: *Fire investigators believe the fire was set on purpose.*

3 DETERMINATION [U] the feeling of determination that you have when you want to succeed in something: *Starting his own business gave him a new **sense of purpose** in his life.* | *My career was over and I felt I **had no purpose in life**.*

4 for all practical purposes also **for all intents and purposes** used to say that something may not exactly be true, but it is true in general: *For all practical purposes, the project is complete.*

5 for the purpose(s) of sb/sth used to say that someone or something will be considered in a particular way in a discussion, document etc.: *For the purposes of this survey, "white" did not include Hispanics.*

6 to no purpose FORMAL with no results OPP **to good purpose**: *The negotiations lasted for days, apparently to no purpose.*

7 to the purpose OLD-FASHIONED useful or helpful

[**Origin:** 1200–1300 Old French *purpos*, from *purposer* **to intend**, from Latin *proponere*] → see also **accidentally**

water purification

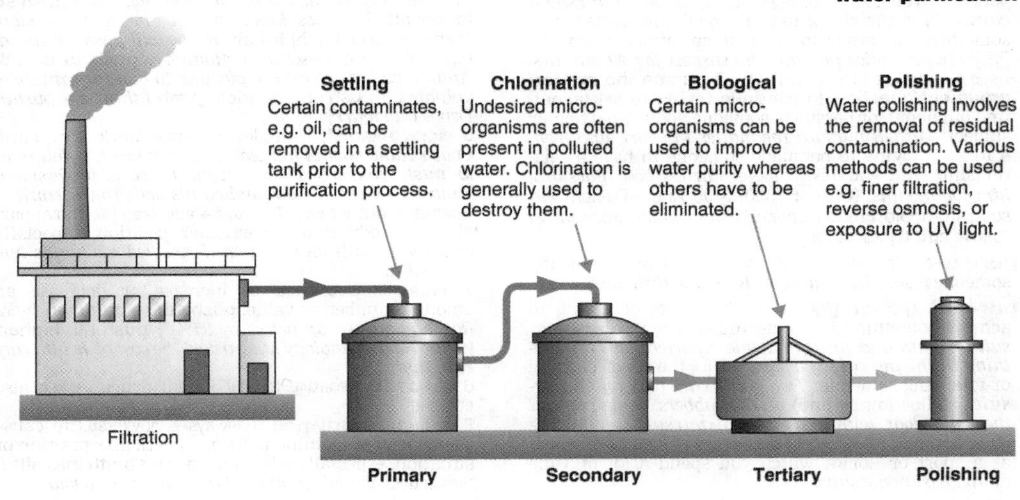
Settling
Certain contaminates, e.g. oil, can be removed in a settling tank prior to the purification process.
Chlorination
Undesired micro-organisms are often present in polluted water. Chlorination is generally used to destroy them.
Biological
Certain micro-organisms can be used to improve water purity whereas others have to be eliminated.
Polishing
Water polishing involves the removal of residual contamination. Various methods can be used e.g. finer filtration, reverse osmosis, or exposure to UV light.
Filtration
Primary
Secondary
Tertiary
Polishing

on purpose at ACCIDENTALLY (2), **defeat the purpose** at DEFEAT[2] (4), PURPOSELY

purpose[2] *v.* [T] OLD USE to intend to do something

pur·pose·ful /ˈpɚpəsfəl/ *adj.* having a clear aim or purpose: *a purposeful and consistent foreign policy* —**purposefully** *adv.* —**purposefulness** *n.* [U]

pur·pose·less /ˈpɚpəslɪs/ *adj.* not having a clear aim or purpose: *The violence is purposeless and impulsive.* —**purposelessly** *adv.* —**purposelessness** *n.* [U]

pur·pose·ly /ˈpɚpəsli/ *adv.* deliberately OPP accidentally: *Tom was purposely not invited to the party.*

P

purr /pɚ/ *v.* **1** [I] if a cat purrs, it makes a soft, low sound in its throat to show that it is pleased **2** [I] if the engine of a vehicle or machine purrs, it works perfectly and makes a quiet smooth sound **3** [I,T] if someone purrs, they speak in a soft, low, and SEXY voice: *"What a good idea," she purred.* —**purr** *n.* [C]

purse[1] /pɚs/ S2 *n.* **1** [C] a bag, often made of leather, in which a woman carries her money and personal things: *I can never find anything in my purse.* → see picture at BAG[1] **2** [singular] FORMAL the amount of money that a person, organization, or country has available to spend: *We must help small businesses without draining **the public purse*** (=money controlled by a government). **3** [C] the amount of money given to someone who wins a sports event, such as a BOXING match or car race: *a $50 million purse for Friday's fight* **4 hold/control the purse strings** to control the money in a family, company etc.: *Maureen definitely holds the purse strings.* **5 tighten/loosen the purse strings** to allow more or less of a family's, company's etc. money to be spent **6** [C] a small container for keeping coins in, made of leather, cloth, plastic etc., used especially by women: *a coin purse* [**Origin:** 1200–1300 Late Latin *bursa* **bag (for money)**]

purse[2] *v.* **purse your lips/mouth** to bring your lips together tightly into a small circle, especially to show disapproval or doubt

purs·er /ˈpɚsɚ/ *n.* [C] an officer who is responsible for the money on a ship and is also in charge of the passengers' rooms, comfort etc.

pur·su·ance /pɚˈsuəns/ *n.* **in pursuance of sth** FORMAL with the aim of doing or achieving something, or during the process of doing this

pur·su·ant /pɚˈsuənt/ *adj.* FORMAL **pursuant to sth** if you do something pursuant to a law, rule, contract etc., you do it according to what the law, rule, contract etc. says

pur·sue /pɚˈsu/ Ac W2 *v.* [T] **1** to continue doing an activity or trying to achieve something over a long period of time: *After college, Jeffrey hopes to **pursue a career in** medicine.* **2** to chase or follow someone or something, in order to catch them, attack them etc. SYN chase: *Police pursued the suspect for 20 minutes.* ►see THESAURUS box at follow **3 pursue the matter/argument/question** to continue trying to ask about, find out about, or persuade someone about a particular subject: *Vardell pursued the matter in court, and won.* **4** to keep trying to persuade someone to have a relationship with you SYN chase: *Carol's been pursuing him for months.* [**Origin:** 1300–1400 Anglo-French *pursuer*, from Old French *poursuir*, from Latin *prosequi* **to follow and try to catch**]

pur·su·er /pɚˈsuɚ/ *n.* [C] someone who is chasing someone else: *They managed to escape their pursuers.*

pur·suit /pɚˈsut/ Ac *n.* **1** [U] the act of trying to achieve something in a determined way: +**of** *the pursuit of truth and justice* | *Some reporters will do anything **in the pursuit of** a story.* **2** [U] the act of chasing or following someone: *Two police cars took off **in pursuit*** (=following behind) *of the robbers.* | *Liz ran out the front door, with Tony **in hot pursuit*** (=following close behind). **3** [C usually plural] FORMAL an activity such as a sport or HOBBY, which you spend a lot of time doing: *leisure pursuits*

pur·ty /ˈpɚt̬i/ *adj.* SPOKEN, NONSTANDARD pretty

pu·ru·lent /ˈpyʊrələnt/ *adj.* MEDICINE containing or producing PUS —**purulence** *n.* [U]

pur·vey /pɚˈveɪ/ *v.* [T] FORMAL to supply goods, services, or information to people

pur·vey·or /pɚˈveɪɚ/ *n.* [C] FORMAL someone who supplies information, goods, or services to people, especially as a business: *a purveyor of office goods*

pur·view /ˈpɚvyu/ *n.* **within/under/outside/beyond the purview of sth** FORMAL within or outside the limits of someone's job, activity, or knowledge: *This matter comes within the purview of the Department of Health.*

pus /pʌs/ *n.* [U] MEDICINE a thick yellowish liquid produced in an infected part of your body: *a blister full of pus*

push[1] /pʊʃ/ S1 W1 *v.*

1 MOVE [I,T] to make someone or something move by pressing with your hands, arms, shoulders etc.: *It's still stuck – you'll have to push harder.* | *Her father was pushing the wheel chair.* | **push sb/sth up/across/away etc.** *Help me push the car into the garage.* | *She pushed him out the door.* | **push sth open/shut** *I slowly pushed the door open.* | +**against** *The horse pushed against the fence.*

THESAURUS

roll to push a round object so that it moves forward: *He rolled the wheel over to the car.*
poke to push someone or something with your finger or something sharp: *Brad poked me in the ribs. "Did you see that," he said.*
shove to push someone or something roughly: *He shoved her against a wall.*
nudge to push someone gently with your elbow to get their attention: *"Move over," she said, nudging my arm.*
elbow to push someone with your elbows, especially in order to move past him or her: *A young man elbowed past him.*
→ PULL

2 BUTTON/SWITCH [I,T] to press a button, SWITCH etc., especially in order to make a piece of equipment start or stop working SYN press: *Push the green button to turn on the machine.*

3 TRY TO GET PAST SB [I, T always + adv./prep.] to use your hands, arms, shoulders etc. to make someone move, especially so that you can get past them: *Stop pushing and wait your turn.* | **push past/through sb** *Furiously, she pushed past him.* | **push your way toward/across/to etc.** *Sandra and I had to push our way to the front of the bus.*

4 ENCOURAGE/PERSUADE [I,T] to encourage or try to persuade someone to accept or do something, especially something that they do not want to do: *The President is pushing his agenda in Congress.* | **push sb to do sth** *My boss keeps pushing me to work more overtime.* | **push (sb) for sth** *Kehoe will push for spending more on after-school activities.* | **push to do sth** *Animal rights groups are pushing to ban the capture of dolphins.* | **push sb into (doing) sth** *I think she pushed Derek into marrying her.*

5 WORK HARD [T] to make someone work very hard: *Coach Kane pushes his players pretty hard.* | *You have to **push yourself** if you want to be a professional dancer.* | *He felt he had **pushed** his body **to the limit**.*

6 MOVE A BODY PART [T always + adv./prep.] to move part of your body into a particular position, especially quickly or with lot of force: *He pushed his hands into his pocket.*

7 INCREASE/DECREASE to increase or decrease an amount, number, or value: **push sth ↔ up/down** *Inflation has pushed up prices by 35%.* | **push sth higher/lower** *New technology has pushed the cost of health care even higher.*

8 DRUGS [T] INFORMAL to sell illegal drugs → see also PUSHER

9 CHANGE A SITUATION [T always + adv./prep.] to cause someone or something to be in a particular position or situation, especially a bad one: **push sb/sth into sth** *It was a decision which pushed the country into war.*

10 ANNOY [T] to annoy someone by doing or saying something, especially again and again: *Had she pushed him too far this time?*
11 ADVERTISE [T] INFORMAL to try to sell more of a product by advertising it a lot SYN **promote**: *We need new ways to push our products.*
12 IDEAS/OPINIONS [T] to try to make people accept your ideas or opinions, especially by talking about them a lot: *I got tired of Robin pushing her environmental agenda at the office.*
13 be pushing 18/30/60 etc. SPOKEN to be nearly 18, 30, 60 etc. years old: *Sheila must be pushing 40 by now.*
14 push sb's buttons to make someone angry by doing or saying something that annoys them: *He really knows how to push Dad's buttons.*
15 push your luck also **push it** INFORMAL to do something or ask for something, when this is likely to annoy someone or be risky: *You'll be pushing it if you ask for more money.*
16 push sth to the back of your mind also **push sth out of your mind** to try to forget about a bad feeling or situation
17 push the envelope to do something that is new and that goes beyond the limits of what has already been done in a particular activity
18 push the point OLD-FASHIONED to keep trying to make someone accept your opinion in a way that they find annoying
19 be pushing up (the) daisies HUMOROUS to be dead
[**Origin:** 1300–1400 Old French *poulser* **to hit, push**, from Latin *pulsare*, from *pellere* **to drive, hit**] → see also PULL

push ahead *phr. v.* to continue with a plan or activity, especially in a determined way: +**with** *The country will push ahead with reforms.*

push sb/sth ↔ **along** *phr. v.* to help someone or something to become successful or make progress

push sb **around** *phr. v.* **1** to tell someone what to do in an impolite or threatening way: *You shouldn't let people push you around like that.* **2** to push someone in a threatening way, often while talking to them in an impolite way: *Some of the bigger boys are pushing the little kids around.*

push aside *phr. v.* **1 push sth ↔ aside** to try not to think about something, especially something bad, so that you can give your attention to something else: *He had to push aside his personal feelings and finish the job.* **2 push sb ↔ aside** to force someone out of their job or position and take the job in their place

push away *phr. v.* **1 push sb ↔ away** to make someone feel that they cannot have a close relationship with you any longer: *I didn't realize I was gradually pushing my friends away.* **2 push sth ↔ away** to stop yourself from thinking about something

push back *phr. v.* **1 push sth ↔ back** to arrange for something to happen at a later time than originally planned: *The deadline has been pushed back.* **2 push sb ↔ back** to force an army or a crowd to move back from their present position

push forward *phr. v.* **1 push sth ↔ forward** to make something continue to happen and be successful: *New ideas are needed to push the peace process forward.* **2** to continue moving toward a place, in spite of difficulties: *As the army pushed forward, the death toll mounted.*

push off *phr. v.* **1** if a boat pushes off from the shore, it moves away from it **2** OLD-FASHIONED to leave a place

push on *phr. v.* **1** to continue doing an activity SYN **push ahead** **2 push sth on sb** to try to make someone accept your ideas or beliefs or buy something that you are selling, especially in a very determined way: *We don't try to push our religion on anybody.* **3** to continue traveling somewhere, especially after you have had a rest: *Hungry and exhausted, the backpackers pushed on.*

push out *phr. v.* **1 push sb ↔ out** to make someone leave a job, position, or organization **2 push sth ↔ out** to cause something to no longer be important, popular, or successful in a particular situation

push sb/sth ↔ **over** *phr. v.* to make someone or something fall to the ground by pushing them: *The dog had pushed over a lamp.*

push sth ↔ **through** *phr. v.* **push sth ↔ through** to get a new law officially accepted: *The party is determined to push through the bill.*

push² S3 *n.*
1 MOVEMENT [C] the act of pushing or pressing something: *If the door's stuck, just **give it a push**.*
2 ATTEMPT [C] to attempt to get or achieve something: *a major diplomatic push* | **a push to do sth** *The club has begun a push to attract new members.* | +**for** *the push for improved productivity*
3 if/when push comes to shove SPOKEN used to say what you can do if a situation becomes very difficult: *If push comes to shove, you can always rent out the house.*
4 ENCOURAGEMENT [singular] something to encourage or persuade someone to do something: *She just **needed** a little **push** to get her started.*
5 MILITARY [C] a planned military attack into the area where the enemy is: *the rebels' final push into the city*
6 with/at the push of a button used to emphasize how easy a machine is to use because it is controlled by pushing a button: *Files can be attached to your email with the push of a button.*

'push-,button *adj.* [only before noun] **1** operated by pressing a button with your finger: *a push-button phone* **2** using computers or electronic equipment rather than traditional methods: *push-button warfare*

push·cart /ˈpʊʃkɑrt/ *n.* [C] a large flat container like a box with wheels, used especially by people who sell goods in the street

push·er /ˈpʊʃɚ/ *n.* [C] INFORMAL someone who sells illegal drugs → see also PENCIL PUSHER

'push ,factor *n.* [C] a quality or feature of an area that makes people want to stop living there and move somewhere else: *The possibility of higher wages elsewhere acted as a push factor out of rural areas.* → see also PULL FACTOR

Push·kin /ˈpʊʃkɪn/, **Al·ek·san·dr** /ˌælɪgˈzændɚ/ (1799–1837) one of Russia's greatest writers who wrote NOVELS, plays, and poetry, and greatly influenced the development of Russian literature

push·o·ver /ˈpʌʃˌoʊvɚ/ *n.* INFORMAL **be a pushover** to be easy to persuade, influence, or defeat: +**for** *Alan's a pushover for beautiful women.*

'push-start *v.* [T] to push a vehicle in order to make the engine start —**push-start** *n.* [C]

'push-up *n.* [C] an exercise in which you lie on the floor on your chest and push yourself up with your arms

push·y /ˈpʊʃi/ *adj. comparative* **pushier**, *superlative* **pushiest** DISAPPROVING so determined to succeed and to get what you want that you behave in an impolite way: *a pushy salesman* —**pushily** *adv.* —**pushiness** *n.* [U]

pu·sil·lan·i·mous /ˌpyusəˈlænəməs/ *adj.* FORMAL weak and frightened of taking even small risks —**pusillanimously** *adv.* —**pusillanimity** /ˌpyusələˈnɪməṭi/ *n.* [U]

puss /pʊs/ *n.* [usually singular] **1** OLD-FASHIONED a word for a cat, used especially when you are calling a cat **2** INFORMAL face → see also SOURPUSS

pus·sy /ˈpʊsi/ *n. plural* **pussies** [C] OLD-FASHIONED, INFORMAL a cat

puss·y·cat /ˈpʊsiˌkæt/ *n.* [C] INFORMAL **1** a cat **2** [usually singular] someone who is very nice and gentle, especially when they may not seem this way: *Jake's a real pussycat once you get to know him.*

puss·y·foot /ˈpʊsiˌfʊt/ also **pussyfoot around** *v.* [I] INFORMAL to be too careful or frightened to make decisions or tell someone exactly what you think: *When she wants something, she doesn't pussyfoot around.*

'pussy ,willow *n.* [C,U] a tree with white flowers that are soft like fur

pus·tule /ˈpʌstʃul/ *n.* [C] MEDICINE a small raised spot on your skin containing PUS (=a thick yellow liquid)

put /pʊt/ S1 W1 *v. past tense and past participle* **put**, **putting**

1 MOVE STH TO PLACE [T always + adv./prep.] to move something to a particular place or position, especially using your hands: *Where did you put the newspaper?* | **put sth in/on/over etc. sth** *I think I put the keys in my coat pocket.* | *We had to put netting over the plants to protect them from birds.* | **put sth ↔ up/down** *He put up his hood when it started to rain.* | *Just* ***put*** *the package* ***over there*** *on the table.*

THESAURUS

place to put something somewhere carefully: *She placed a cool towel on his forehead.*
position to carefully put something in a particular position: *The security cameras are positioned just inside the door.*
slip to put something somewhere quietly or smoothly: *She slipped the necklace over her head.*
stick INFORMAL to put something somewhere without much care: *He stuck a newspaper into his briefcase.*
shove to put something into a space or container carelessly or without thinking much: *Just shove some clothes in a suitcase and let's go!*
thrust to put something somewhere suddenly or forcefully: *She thrust her feet into her sandals and followed him.*
dump to put something down somewhere in a careless way: *You can dump your books over there on the desk.*

2 MOVE A BODY PART [T always + adv./prep.] to move part of your body somewhere: **put sth on/out of/around sth** *Carol put her arms around him.* | *She* ***put up*** *her* ***hand*** *and asked to leave the room.*

3 CHANGE SB'S SITUATION/FEELINGS [T always + adv./prep.] to cause someone or something to be in a particular situation, or cause someone to have a particular feeling: *Davis's goal put his team into the lead.* | **put sb in a good/bad/terrible etc. mood** *Exercising usually helps put me in a better mood.* | *Listening to Larry's stories just about* ***put*** *me* ***to sleep*** (=made me feel sleepy). | **put sb in danger/put sb at risk** *The boys' own actions put them in danger.* | **put sb in a difficult/awkward/embarrassing etc. position** *The offer put me in an awkward position.* | *Higher transportation costs* ***put*** *many companies* ***out of business*** (=make the companies close down). | **put sb out of work/out of a job** *The closure of the factory has put hundreds of people out of work.* | **put sb in charge/control/command (of sth)** *Hall will be put in charge of overseas marketing.* | **put sb/sth out of action** (=damage someone or something with the result that they cannot do their normal activities or be used) | **put sb under pressure/stress** *Tests can put students under a lot of stress.* | *The new rules* ***put*** *private buyers* ***at a disadvantage.***

4 WRITE/PRINT STH [T always + adv./prep.] to write or print something: **put sth in/on/under sth** *Put your name at the top of each answer sheet.* | *I put an ad in the paper last week.*

5 put a stop/an end to sth to stop an activity that is harmful or unacceptable: *The community must work together to put an end to the violence.*

6 put sth behind you to try to forget about a bad experience or mistake so that it does not affect you now: *Counseling helped her put the accident behind her.*

7 EXPRESS [T always + adv./prep.] to say something in a particular way, especially in a way that helps people understand how you feel or what you want: **put sth well/cleverly/succinctly etc.** *She put it very well when she was interviewed on television.* | *Nancy often has trouble* ***putting*** *her thoughts* ***into words*** (=expressing her ideas or feelings). | *You don't have to* ***put it like that*** (=say it in that particular way). | **put simply/simply put** *Simply put, we have no time to waste.*

8 put sth in writing to write something down so that it is official, rather than just being something that is spoken: *Get them to put the job offer in writing.*

SPOKEN PHRASES

9 as sb puts it used to repeat what someone else has said: *As one officer put it, the whole event was "a disaster."*
10 to put it mildly used to say that a situation is actually worse than the way you are describing it: *He was a nuisance, to put it mildly.*
11 to put it bluntly used to tell someone that you are going to say exactly what you think: *To put it bluntly, John, I'm not interested.*
12 how shall/can I put it? used when what you are going to say might sound strange or impolite, or when it is difficult to say exactly what you mean: *He is – how shall I put it? – a little overweight.*
13 I wouldn't put it past sb (to do sth) used to say that you think someone might do something bad or illegal
14 put it/'er there OLD-FASHIONED used to tell someone to shake hands with you, either as a greeting or after making an agreement with them

15 put sth to work/use to use something in an effective way: *Put your skills and knowledge to work for you.*

16 put sb to work to give someone a job to do: *This program will put unemployed people to work.*

17 to put it another way used when trying to explain something in a different way and make it clearer: *To put it another way, raising taxes will mean people have less money to spend.*

18 put sth into action/effect/practice to start using a plan, idea, knowledge etc.: *Forest managers have been slow to put the plan into practice.*

19 put yourself in sb's place/position/shoes to imagine what it is like to be in someone else's situation

20 CONSIDER SB/STH IMPORTANT [T always + adv./prep.] to consider someone or something to have a particular level of importance or quality: **put sth before sth** *The company was accused of putting profit before safety.* | **put sb/sth first/second etc.** *She always puts her family first.*

21 GIVE IMPORTANCE [T always + adv./prep.] to cause someone or something to be in a particular group of good or important people or things: **put sb/sth among/in etc.** *His income puts him among the wealthiest people in the country.*

22 SEND SB SOMEWHERE [T always + adv./prep.] to arrange for or order someone to go to a place for a particular purpose: **put sb in/on etc.** *He ought to be put in prison.* | *Pneumonia put him in the hospital for more than a week.* | *It's time to* ***put*** *the boys* ***to bed*** (=make them go into their beds).

23 put one over on sb INFORMAL to deceive someone into believing something that is not true or that is useless: *They think they've found a way to put one over on the welfare office.*

24 put sb on a plane/train to go with someone to make sure they get on a train, plane etc.: *We went to the airport this morning to put Mom on a plane home.*

25 BUILD [T always + adv./prep.] to build something somewhere: *They're putting a new apartment building on my street.*

26 put sth right to make a situation better, especially after someone has made a mistake or behaved badly: *Larson has promised to put the city's finances right by the end of the year.*

27 THROW [I,T] to throw a SHOT (=a heavy metal ball) in a sports competition

[**Origin:** Old English *putian*] → see also **put/send out feelers** at FEELER, **put your finger on sth** at FINGER[1] (4), **put your foot down** at FOOT[1] (10), **put pressure on** at PRESSURE[1] (1), **put sth to (good) use** at USE[2] (4)

put about *phr. v.* **put sth about** TECHNICAL if a ship puts about or if you put it about, it changes direction

put sth ↔ **across** *phr. v.* to explain your ideas, beliefs etc. in a way that people can understand: *He was trying to put across a serious point.*

put sth ↔ **aside** *phr. v.* **1** to stop thinking about a problem, argument, or disagreement, because you want to achieve something: *They decided to put aside their differences.* **2** to save money regularly, usually for a particular purpose: *Fortunately, they had put aside money for such an emergency.* **3** to stop reading or working with something, in order to start doing something else: *Let's put this question aside for now and continue with the discussion.* **4** to keep a period of time free in order to be able to do something: *Try to put aside an hour each day for exercise.* **5** to keep something so someone can have it or use it later: *I've put aside some of my son's clothes for my sister's baby.*

put sth **at** sth *phr. v.* to calculate and state an amount, someone's age etc., without trying to be very exact: *Official estimates put the damage at over $10 million.*

put away *phr. v.* **1 put sth ↔ away** to put something in the place where it is usually kept: *Could you put the dishes away for me?* **2 put sth ↔ away** to save money: *She was able to put away a few dollars every week.* **3 put sb ↔ away** INFORMAL to put someone in a prison or in a mental hospital: *A maniac like him needs to be put away for a long time.* **4 put sth ↔ away** INFORMAL to eat or drink a lot: *Jack can really put away the food.*

put back *phr. v.* **1 put sth ↔ back** to put something in the place it was before it was moved: *Put the milk back in the fridge.* **2 put sb/sth ↔ back** to cause someone or something to be in the state or situation they were in before: *The program should put 250 people back to work.* **3 put sth ↔ back** to arrange for an event to start at a later time or date SYN **postpone**: *The meeting has been put back until next Thursday.* **4 put sth ↔ back** to delay a process or activity by a number of weeks, months etc.: *This fire could put back the opening date by several weeks.* **5 put sth ↔ back** to make someone or something have something they had before: *This should put a smile back on his face.*

put down *phr. v.*
1 ON A SURFACE **put sth ↔ down** to put something you are holding onto a surface: *He put down his knife and fork.*
2 CRITICIZE **put sb ↔ down** to criticize someone and make them feel silly or stupid: *Meg's mother-in-law is always putting her down.* | *Stop* ***putting yourself down*** (=criticizing yourself)*!*
3 WRITE **put sth ↔ down** to write something, especially a name or number, on a piece of paper or on a list SYN **write down**: *I'm not sure what to put down on the form.*
4 put down a revolution/revolt/rebellion etc. to use force to stop people who are fighting against the government: *Military police were called in to put down the riot.*
5 PAY **put sth ↔ down** to pay part of the total cost of something, so that you can pay the rest later: *We put down a deposit of $100.*
6 BABY **put sb down** to put a baby in its bed
7 put the phone ↔ down to put the part of the telephone that you talk into back onto the telephone when you have finished speaking to someone SYN **hang up**
8 KILL **put sth ↔ down** to kill an animal without causing it pain, usually because it is old or sick: *We had to have the dog put down.*
9 I couldn't put it down SPOKEN used to say that you found a book, toy etc. extremely interesting: *It's such a good book that I couldn't put it down.*
10 AIRCRAFT **put sth ↔ down** FORMAL if an aircraft puts down or if a pilot puts it down, it lands, especially because of an EMERGENCY: *He put the plane down in a field.*
11 put down a motion/an amendment to suggest a subject, plan, change in the law etc. for Congress or a committee to consider

put sb **down as** sth *phr. v.* to guess what someone is like or what they do, without having much information about them: *I didn't think he was unfriendly – I just put him down as shy.*

put down for *phr. v.* **1 put sb down for sth** to put someone's name on a list so that they can take part in an activity, join an organization etc.: *I'll put you down for an appointment on Thursday at 3 p.m.* **2 put sb down for $5/$10 etc.** to write someone's name on a list with an amount of money that they have promised to give: *You can put me down for a $25 donation.*

put sth **down to** sth *phr. v.* to explain the reason for something, especially when you are guessing: *I had a headache but I put it down to the wine.*

put sth ↔ **forth** *phr. v.* FORMAL **1** to suggest a plan, proposal etc. or support it in discussions: *Arguments have been put forth in favor of the construction project.* **2 put forth leaves/shoots/roots etc.** LITERARY if a tree or bush puts forth leaves etc. it begins to grow them

put forward *phr. v.* **1 put sth ↔ forward** to suggest a plan, proposal etc., especially in order to start discussions about something that needs to be decided: *Several proposals have been put forward for discussion.* **2 put sb ↔ forward** to suggest someone who would be good for a particular job, position etc.

put in *phr. v.*
1 INSTALL **put sth ↔ in, put sth in sth** to put a piece of equipment somewhere and connect it so that it is ready to be used SYN **install**: *After we bought the car, we had a better stereo put in.*
2 TIME **put sth ↔ in** to spend time or use energy working or practicing something: *She puts in long hours at the office.*
3 put faith/trust/confidence in sb/sth to trust someone or something or believe that they can do something: *Young says he doesn't put much trust in the polls.*
4 put in an application/a bid/a request etc. to make an official request to have or do something: *Susan put in her application for graduate school last week.*
5 GIVE MONEY **put sth ↔ in** to give money for a particular purpose: *Each of us put in $100 toward the cost.*
6 BANK ACCOUNT **put sth ↔ in, put sth in sth** to add money to a bank account
7 SHIP if a ship puts in, it enters a port

put into *phr. v.*
1 INVEST **put sth into sth** to make money available to be used in a business: *He put his own money into the company.*
2 BANK ACCOUNT **put sth into sth** to add money to a bank account
3 put time/energy/work/enthusiasm etc. into sth to use a lot of time, energy etc. when you are doing an activity: *The kids have put a lot of energy into planning the trip.*
4 ADD QUALITY **put sth into sth** to improve something by adding a particular quality: *Put a little romance into your life.*
5 SHIP **put into sth** if a ship puts into a place, it stops at a port there

put in for sth *phr. v.* to make an official request for something: *Jones put in for a transfer to our Dallas office.*

put off *phr. v.* **1 put sth ↔ off** to arrange to do something at a later time or date, especially because there is a problem, difficulty etc.: *The game has been put off until tomorrow.* | **put off doing sth** *You shouldn't put off going to the dentist.* **2 put sth ↔ off** to delay doing something until later because you do not want to do it now: *You shouldn't put off going to the dentist.* **3 put sb ↔ off, put sb off sth** to make you dislike something or not want to do something: *The car's unusual shape put off many potential customers.* **4 put sb ↔ off** to make someone wait because you do not want to meet them, pay them etc. until later: *You can't keep putting me off – I need the money now.*

put on *phr. v.*
1 CLOTHES **put sth ↔ on** to put a piece of clothing on your body OPP **take off**: *Hurry up and put your shoes on.* ►see THESAURUS box at **dress**[1]

P

2 AFFECT/INFLUENCE put sth on sb/sth to do something that affects or influences someone or something: *The government has put a limit on foreign imports of textiles.* | **put pressure/emphasis/blame etc. on sb/sth** *Tests can put a lot of pressure on students.*
3 ON SKIN put sth ↔ on to put MAKEUP, cream etc. on your skin: *I hardly ever put on lipstick.*
4 START EQUIPMENT put sth ↔ on to make a piece of equipment begin working SYN **turn on**: *It's cold in here. Why don't you put on the heat?*
5 MUSIC put sth ↔ on to put a CD, DVD, TAPE etc. into a machine and start playing it: *Shall I put on another CD?*
6 PRETEND put sth ↔ on to pretend to have a certain feeling, opinion, way of speaking etc. especially in order to get attention: *It annoys me when she puts on her phony British accent.* | *He didn't feel that he had to* ***put on an act*** *to impress her.* → see also **put on a brave face** at BRAVE[1] (2)
7 put on weight/5 pounds etc. to become fatter and heavier: *Dennis has put on a lot of weight recently.*
8 EVENT/CONCERT/PLAY ETC. put sth ↔ on to arrange an event, concert, play etc. or perform in it: *The school puts on a play every year.*
9 COOK put sth ↔ on to start cooking something: *Let me just put the potatoes on first.*
10 you're putting me on! SPOKEN used to tell someone that you think they are joking: *Seth is moving to Alaska? You're putting me on!*
11 RISK MONEY put sth on sth to risk an amount of money on the result of a game, race etc.: *I put $30 on Miami to win the Super Bowl.*
12 put on the brakes a) to make a vehicle stop or slow down by pressing a PEDAL or handle **b)** also **put the brakes on sth** to stop or slow something that is happening
13 ADD put sth on sth to add an amount of money onto the cost of something: *The new tax could put another ten cents on the price of gas.*
14 MEDICAL TREATMENT put sb on sth if a doctor, nurse etc. puts someone on a particular drug, treatment, or DIET, he or she says that person should have it: *The doctor put me on a special diet to lower my cholesterol.*
15 TELEPHONE put sb on, put sb on sth give someone the telephone so that they can talk to someone who has called: *Put Dad on – I want to ask him a question.*
16 GIVE SB A DUTY put sb on sth to give someone a particular duty or responsibility

put out *phr. v.*
1 FIRE/CIGARETTE ETC. put sth ↔ out to make a fire, cigarette etc. stop burning: *It took firefighters several hours to put the blaze out.*
2 MAKE AVAILABLE put sth ↔ out to place things where people can find and use them: *Could you help me put out the sandwiches for lunch?*
3 MAKE EXTRA WORK put sb ↔ out to make additional work or cause problems for someone: *Will it put you out if I bring another guest?*
4 put yourself out to make an effort to do something that will help someone: *Don't put yourself out just for me.*
5 MOVE/TAKE OUTSIDE put sth ↔ out to put something outside the house: *Remember to put the cat out before you go to bed.* | **put the trash/garbage out** (=put dirty or unwanted things outside your house to be taken away) | **put the wash/laundry out** (=put clothes outside to dry)
6 put your hand/foot/arm etc. out also **put out your hand/foot etc.** to move your hand, foot etc. forward and away from your body: *He put his hand out to keep from falling over.*
7 MAKE UNCONSCIOUS put sb out to make someone unconscious before a medical operation
8 INFORMATION put sth ↔ out to officially give information, make statements etc. for people to read or listen to: *The government immediately put out a statement denying the rumor.*
9 PRODUCE A CD/MAGAZINE ETC. put sth ↔ out produce a CD, VIDEO etc. or print a book, magazine etc.: *In the last five years, Williams has put out three new CDs.*
10 put out a light also **put a light out** to make a light stop working by pressing or turning a button
11 BROADCAST put sth ↔ out to broadcast something on radio or television
12 PRODUCE POWER put out sth to produce a particular amount of power → see also OUTPUT
13 put out sb's eye also **put sb's eye out** to remove or severely damage someone's eye
14 SPORTS COMPETITION put sb ↔ out to defeat a sports player or team so that they are no longer in a competition
15 SHIP if a ship puts out, it starts to sail
16 BASEBALL put sb out to prevent a baseball player from winning a point, for example, by catching the ball that they have hit

put through *phr. v.* **1 put sb ↔ through** to connect someone to someone else on the telephone: *"I'd like to speak with Mr. Croft." "I'll put you right through."* **2 put sb through school/college/university** to pay for someone to study at school or college: *I'm grateful to my wife for putting me through law school.* **3 put sb through sth** to make someone experience something very difficult or unpleasant: *I don't think he realizes what he's put me through.* **4 put sb/sth through sth** to test someone or something to make sure that everything is working correctly: *The aircraft was being put through its checks.* → see also **put sb/sth through their/its paces** at PACE[1] (7) **5 put sth ↔ through** to do what is necessary in order to get a plan or suggestion accepted or approved: *The legislation was put through by the Democrats.*

put sth **to** sb *phr. v.* **1 put sth to sb** to suggest something such as a proposal or plan to a group of people and ask them to consider it: *We then put our proposal to the city's board of supervisors.* **2 put sth to a vote** to have people vote on something **3 put sth to sb** to ask someone a question or make a suggestion to them: *I'll* ***put the question to*** *the group for discussion.* | ***I put it to you that*** *in fact you yourself initiated the violence.* **4 put sb to trouble/inconvenience etc.** to make someone do something that will cause them trouble or inconvenience: *I hope I'm not putting you to any trouble by asking for your help.* **5 put your name/signature to sth** to sign a letter, document etc. saying that you agree with what is written in it

put sth **↔ together** *phr. v.* **1** to prepare or produce something by collecting pieces of information, ideas etc.: *You should start by putting together a business plan.* **2** to make a machine, model, piece of furniture etc. by joining all the different parts: *It took days to put the engine together again.* **3** to choose people to be in a team, group etc.: *The state government has put together a team of scientists.* **4 more... than the rest put together** used when comparing two sets of people or things to say that one set contains more than the total of all the other sets: *David earns more than the rest of us put together.*

put sth **toward** sth *phr. v.* to use some money in order to pay part of the cost of something

put sb **under** *phr. v.* if a doctor puts you under, they give you drugs to make you UNCONSCIOUS before SURGERY

put up *phr. v.*
1 BUILD put sth ↔ up to build something such as a wall, fence, building etc.: *They put up a fence to keep intruders out.*
2 TENT/UMBRELLA ETC. put sth ↔ up to spread and raise something that is folded up, so that it is ready to be used: *The tent takes just minutes to put up.*
3 FOR PEOPLE TO SEE put sth ↔ up to attach a picture, notice etc. to a wall or to hang things so that people can see them: *Let's put a few of these posters up in the hallway.* | *Stores are already putting up Christmas decorations.*
4 ATTACH TO A WALL put sth ↔ up to attach a shelf, cupboard etc. to a wall
5 LET SB STAY put sb ↔ up to let someone stay in your house and give them meals: *We could put you up for the night.*

6 PAY FOR SB TO STAY **put sb ↔ up** to pay for someone to stay in a hotel **7 put sth up for sale/auction** to make something available for someone to buy, especially a house or a business: *Thirteen of the bank's branches will be put up for sale.* **8 put sth up for discussion/review etc.** to suggest that an idea, plan, report etc. be discussed or examined **9 put sb up for adoption** to make a child available for another family to ADOPT **10 put up a fight/a struggle/resistance** to argue against or oppose something in a determined way, or to fight against someone who is attacking you: *She put up a brave fight against her attacker.* **11 put up money/$500/$5 million** to give an amount of money for a particular purpose: *Part of that money is being put up by local businessmen.* | *Local residents have* ***put up a reward*** *for information about the crime.* **12 put up or shut up** INFORMAL used to say that someone should either do what needs to be done or stop talking about it **13** ELECTIONS **put sb ↔ up** FORMAL to suggest someone as an appropriate person to be elected to a position

put sb **up to** sth *phr. v.* to encourage someone to do something stupid or dangerous: *Who put you up to this?*

put up with sb/sth *phr. v.* to accept a bad situation or person without complaining SYN **tolerate**: *For many years, residents have put up with the constant noise.* | *I don't know how she puts up with him.*

pu·ta·tive /ˈpyuṭəṭɪv/ *adj.* [only before noun] FORMAL believed or accepted by most people: *the putative father of her child*

ˈput-down *n.* [C] something you say that is intended to make someone feel stupid or unimportant: *The observation was not intended to be a put-down.* → see also **put down** at PUT

ˈput-on *n.* [C] INFORMAL something you say or do to try to make someone believe something that is not true

ˈput ˌoption *n.* [C] ECONOMICS an official contract that gives someone the right to sell STOCKS or BONDS etc. for a specific price until a specific date in the future, usually bought when people think the price of a stock or bond will fall below that price

ˌput ˈout *adj.* INFORMAL **be/feel put out** to feel upset or offended: *She seemed a bit put out when I told her you weren't coming.*

pu·tre·fac·tion /ˌpyutrəˈfækʃən/ *n.* [U] FORMAL the process of decay in a dead animal or plant, during which it smells very bad

pu·tre·fy /ˈpyutrəˌfaɪ/ *v.* **putrefies, putrefied, putrefying** [I] FORMAL if a dead animal or plant putrefies, it decays and smells very bad

pu·tres·cent /pyuˈtrɛsənt/ *adj.* FORMAL beginning to decay and smell very bad —**putrescence** *n.* [U]

pu·trid /ˈpyutrɪd/ *adj.* **1** BIOLOGY putrid dead animals, plants, or parts of the body are decaying and smell very bad **2** INFORMAL very bad or disgusting: *a putrid smell*

putsch /pʊtʃ/ *n.* [C] a secretly planned attempt to remove a government by force → see also COUP

putt /pʌt/ *v.* [I,T] to hit a GOLF BALL lightly a short distance along the ground toward the hole —**putt** *n.* [C]

put·tee /pʌˈti/ *n.* [C usually plural] a long piece of cloth that is wrapped around the leg from the knee down, worn as part of an army uniform in the past

put·ter¹ /ˈpʌṭɚ/ *n.* a type of GOLF CLUB (=stick) to hit the ball a short distance toward or into the hole

putter² *v.* [I always + adv./prep.] **1** to spend time doing things that are not very important, in a relaxed way: **+around/in** *Grandpa spent the morning puttering around the garden.* **2** to walk or move slowly and without hurrying: **+along/down etc.** *The bus was puttering along in the slow lane.*

put·ting /ˈpʌṭɪŋ/ *n.* [U] the action of lightly hitting a GOLF BALL a short distance so that it goes into a hole, or the ability to do this

ˈputting green *n.* [C] one of the smaller smooth areas of grass on a GOLF COURSE where you hit the ball into the hole

put·ty /ˈpʌṭi/ *n.* [U] **1** a soft substance that dries hard and is used to fasten glass into window frames **2 be putty in sb's hands** to be easily controlled or influenced by someone

ˈput-up job *n.* [C] INFORMAL a secret arrangement for something to happen, especially something illegal or something done to trick someone

ˈput-upon *adj.* someone who is put-upon has been treated unfairly by being expected to do too much: *a put-upon wife*

putz¹ /pʌts, pʊts/ *n.* [C] INFORMAL someone, especially a man, who is stupid, annoying, and impolite

putz² *v.*

putz around *phr. v.* to spend time without doing very much, or without doing anything important

puz·zle¹ /ˈpʌzəl/ S3 *n.* [C] **1** a game or toy that has a lot of pieces that you have to fit together: *a child's wooden puzzle* → see also JIGSAW PUZZLE **2** a game in which you have to think hard to solve a difficult question or problem: *a crossword puzzle* **3** [usually singular] something that is difficult to understand or explain: **+to** *Women have always been a puzzle to Brad.* | **+of** *the puzzle of his disappearance* **4 a piece of the puzzle** a piece of information that helps you to understand part of a difficult question, mystery etc.

puzzle² *v.* [T] to confuse someone or make them feel slightly anxious because they do not understand something: *What puzzles me is why her books are so popular.*

puzzle sth ↔ **out** *phr. v.* to solve a confusing or difficult problem after thinking about it carefully

puzzle over sth *phr. v.* to think for a long time about something because you cannot understand it

puz·zled /ˈpʌzəld/ *adj.* confused and unable to understand something: *You look puzzled.* | **+by/at/about** *I was puzzled at her reaction.* | **a puzzled look/expression/stare** *Shew was looking at me with a puzzled stare.*

puz·zle·ment /ˈpʌzəlmənt/ *n.* [U] FORMAL a feeling of being confused and unable to understand something

puz·zler /ˈpʌzlɚ/ *n.* [C] INFORMAL something that is difficult to understand or explain

puz·zling /ˈpʌzlɪŋ/ *adj.* confusing and difficult to understand or explain: *I found his attitude slightly puzzling.*

PVC *n.* [U] a type of plastic, usually used to make pipes, coverings for floors, or other things used in building houses

pvt. the written abbreviation of PRIVATE, the lowest military rank in the army

pwr. the written abbreviation of "power"

PX *n.* [C] a special store for food and other supplies on a U.S. military base

pyg·my /ˈpɪgmi/ *n. plural* **pygmies** [C] **1** also **Pygmy** a person belonging to a race of very small people, especially one of the tribes of central Africa **2** a person, organization, country etc. that is much less powerful, effective etc. than others **3 a pygmy rabbit/hippo/elephant etc.** a very small type of rabbit, HIPPO etc.

py·ja·mas /pəˈdʒɑməz, -ˈdʒæ-/ the British spelling of PAJAMAS

py·lon /ˈpaɪlɑn/ *n.* [C] **1** one of a set of plastic CONES placed on a road to control traffic and protect people who are working there **2** one of the tall metal structures that supports wires carrying electricity **3** a tall structure or post used to support something heavy, especially something that is used to guide aircraft to land

Pyn·chon /ˈpɪntʃən/, **Thomas** (1937–) a U.S. writer of NOVELS

Pyong·yang /ˌpyɑŋˈyɑŋ, ˌpyɔŋ-/ the capital and largest city of North Korea

py·or·rhe·a /ˌpaɪəˈriə/ *n.* [U] a DISEASE of your GUMS that makes your teeth become loose

pyr·a·mid /ˈpɪrəmɪd/ *n.* [C] **1** MATH a solid object that has a four-sided base, and four sides made up of triangles that slope to a point at the top ►see THESAURUS box at **shape**[1] **2** HISTORY a large stone building in the shape of a pyramid, found especially in Egypt and Central America **3** [usually singular] a system or organization in which a small number of people have power or influence over a much larger number of people: *The uneducated poor are at the bottom of the social pyramid.* **4** a pile of objects that have been put into the shape of a pyramid: +**of** *a pyramid of cans* —**pyramidal** /ˌpɪrəˈmɪdl◂ / *adj.*

ˈpyramid ˌscheme *n.* [C] an illegal system of INVESTING money, in which the money of people who invest later is used to pay people in the system who invested earlier

pyre /paɪə/ *n.* [C] a high pile of wood on which a dead body is placed to be burned in a funeral ceremony

Pyr·e·nees, the /ˈpɪrəˌniz/ a range of mountains in southern Europe, that runs between France and Spain, from the Bay of Biscay to the Mediterranean Sea

Py·rex /ˈpaɪrɛks/ *n.* [U] TRADEMARK a special type of strong glass that does not break at high temperatures and is used for making cooking dishes

py·rite /ˈpaɪraɪt/ *n.* [U] a yellow-colored compound of iron and SULFUR [SYN] **fool's gold**

py·ri·tes /pəˈraɪtiz, ˈpaɪraɪts/ *n.* [C] EARTH SCIENCE any of various compounds of SULFUR with a type of metal, usually iron, or iron and COPPER: *iron pyrites*

py·ro /ˈpaɪroʊ/ *n.* [C] SLANG a pyromaniac

py·ro·ma·ni·a /ˌpaɪroʊˈmeɪniə/ *n.* [U] a mental illness that gives you a strong desire to start fires

py·ro·ma·ni·ac /ˌpaɪroʊˈmeɪniˌæk/ *n.* [C] **1** someone who suffers from the mental illness of pyromania **2** INFORMAL, HUMOROUS someone who enjoys making and watching fires

py·ro·tech·nics /ˌpaɪrəˈtɛknɪks/ *n.* **1** [plural] FORMAL OR TECHNICAL a public show of FIREWORKS **2** [U] TECHNICAL the skill or business of making FIREWORKS **3** [plural] an impressive show of someone's skill as a public speaker, musician etc. —**pyrotechnic** *adj.*

Pyr·rhic vic·to·ry /ˌpɪrɪk ˈvɪktəri/ *n.* [C] a victory in which the person who wins suffers so much that the victory was hardly worth winning [**Origin:** 1800–1900 *Pyrrhus* (?312–272 B.C.), Greek king whose army defeated the Romans but had very many killed and wounded]

Py·thag·o·ras /pɪˈθægərəs/ (?582–?507 B.C.) a Greek PHILOSOPHER and MATHEMATICIAN, known for the Pythagorean Theorem, about the relationship between the sides of a TRIANGLE which has one angle of 90°

Py·thag·o·re·an The·o·rem /pɪˌθægəriən ˈθiərəm/ *n.* MATH a rule for calculating the length of one side of a RIGHT TRIANGLE (=one which has one angle of 90°) which states that the SQUARE of the HYPOTENUSE (=longest side) is equal to the sum of the squares of the other two sides. It is written as $a^2 + b^2 = c^2$.

Py·thag·o·re·an trip·le /pɪˌθægəriən ˈtrɪpəl/ *n.* [C] MATH a set of three positive whole numbers, such as 3, 4, and 5, that obey the EQUATION $a^2 + b^2 = c^2$ established by the Pythagorean Theorem

py·thon /ˈpaɪθɑn, -θən/ *n.* [C] BIOLOGY a large tropical snake that kills animals for food by winding itself around them and crushing them

pyx /pɪks/ *n.* [C] a small container in which the holy bread used for the Christian ceremony of COMMUNION is kept

Q,q

Q, q /kyu/ *n. plural* **Q's, q's** [C] **a)** the 17th letter of the English alphabet **b)** a sound represented by this letter

Q., q. the written abbreviation of QUESTION

QA *n.* [U] QUALITY ASSURANCE

Qad·da·fi /gəˈdɑfi, kə-/, **Colonel Mu·am·mar al-** /ˈmuəmɑr æl/ (1942–) the leader of Libya since 1969

Qa·tar /ˈkɑtɑr, kəˈtɑr/ a country in the Middle East, east of Saudi Arabia —**Qatari** /kəˈtɑri/ *n., adj.*

QB the written abbreviation of QUARTERBACK

QED the abbreviation of the Latin phrase "quod erat demonstrandum," used to say that a fact, event etc. proves that what you say is true

Q-rat·ing /ˈkyu ˌreɪt̬ɪŋ/ *n.* [C] a way of describing how well-known by the public someone is

qt. the written abbreviation of QUART

Q-tip /ˈkyu tɪp/ *n.* [C] TRADEMARK a small thin stick with cotton at each end, used for cleaning places that are difficult to reach, such as your ears

Qtr., qtr. the written abbreviation of QUARTER

Quaa·lude /ˈkweɪlud/ *n.* [C] TRADEMARK a drug that makes you feel very relaxed or sleepy, which is often used illegally

quack¹ /kwæk/ *v.* [I] to make the sound that a duck makes

quack² *n.* [C] INFORMAL **1** someone who pretends to be a doctor **2** the sound a duck makes

quack³ *adj.* relating to the activities or medicines of someone who pretends to be a doctor: *a quack remedy for colds*

quack·er·y /ˈkwækəri/ *n.* [U] the activities of someone who pretends to have medical knowledge or skills

quad /kwɑd/ *n.* [C] **1** a square open area with buildings all around it, especially in a school or college **2** a short form of QUADRUPLET **3 quads** [plural] BIOLOGY someone's QUADRICEPS

quadr- /kwɑdr/ *prefix* four: *a quadrangle* (=flat shape with four sides) | *a quadrilateral* (=shape with four straight sides) | *a quadruped* (=animal with four legs)

quad·ran·gle /ˈkwɑdræŋgəl/ *n.* [C] **1** FORMAL a QUAD **2** MATH a flat shape that has four straight sides

quad·rant /ˈkwɑdrənt/ *n.* [C] **1** TECHNICAL a quarter of a circle **2** an area that is one of four equal parts that a larger area is divided into: *the town's southwest quadrant* **3** PHYSICS an instrument for measuring angles, used when sailing or when looking at the stars **4** MATH one of four equal parts into which a PLANE is divided by two straight lines that cross each other at an angle of 90 degrees

quad·ra·phon·ic, quadrophonic /ˌkwɑdrəˈfɑnɪk◂/ *adj.* using a system of sound recording, broadcasting etc. in which the sound comes from four different SPEAKERS at the same time → see also MONO, STEREO²

quad·rat·ic e·qua·tion /kwɑˌdrætɪk ɪˈkweɪʒən/ *n.* [C] MATH an EQUATION such as $ax^2+bx+c=y$, which includes numbers or quantities multiplied by themselves

quad·ri·ceps /ˈkwɑdrəˌsɛps/ *n.* [plural] the large muscle at the front of your THIGH

quad·ri·lat·er·al /ˌkwɑdrəˈlæt̬ərəl/ *n.* [C] MATH a flat shape with four straight sides —**quadrilateral** *adj.*

qua·drille /kwɑˈdrɪl/ *n.* [C] a dance, popular especially in the 19th century, in which the dancers form a square

quad·ril·lion /kwɑˈdrɪlyən/ *number* 1,000,000,000,000,000

quad·ri·ple·gic /ˌkwɑdrəˈplidʒɪk/ *n.* [C] someone who cannot move any part of their body below their neck ►see THESAURUS box at **disabled** —**quadriplegia** *n.* [U] —**quadriplegic** *adj.*

quad·ro·phon·ic /ˌkwɑdrəˈfɑnɪk◂/ *adj.* another spelling of QUADRAPHONIC

quad·ru·ped /ˈkwɑdrəˌpɛd/ *n.* [C] BIOLOGY an animal that has four legs → see also BIPED

quad·ru·ple¹ /kwɑˈdrupəl/ *v.* [I,T] to increase and become four times as big or as high, or to make something do this: *Food prices quadrupled during the war.* | *The company has quadrupled its profits.*

quadruple² *adv.* **1** four times as big or as many **2** having four parts, or involving four of the same type of thing —**quadruple** *adj.*

Q

quad·ru·plet /kwɑˈdruplɪt/ *n.* [C] BIOLOGY one of four babies born at the same time to the same mother

quaff /kwɑf, kwæf/ *v.* [T] LITERARY to drink a lot of something quickly

quag·mire /ˈkwægmaɪə˞, ˈkwɑg-/ *n.* [C usually singular] **1** a difficult or complicated situation: *a legal quagmire* **2** an area of soft wet muddy ground

quail¹ /kweɪl/ *n.* [C,U] BIOLOGY a small fat bird with a short tail that is hunted and shot for food and sport, or the meat from this bird

quail² *v.* [I] LITERARY to be afraid and show it by shaking a little bit

quaint /kweɪnt/ *adj.* unusual and attractive, especially in an old-fashioned way: *a quaint little town* [**Origin:** 1100–1200 Old French *cointe* **clever**, from Latin *cognitus* **known**]

quake¹ /kweɪk/ *v.* [I] **1** to shake slightly in an uncontrolled way, usually because you are afraid: **+with** *Her voice was quaking with fear.* **2** EARTH SCIENCE if the earth, a building etc. quakes, it shakes violently: *The explosion made the whole house quake.* **3 quake in your boots** INFORMAL to feel very afraid or nervous

quake² *n.* [C] INFORMAL an EARTHQUAKE

ˈquake-proof *v.* [T] to build or repair a building so that it is not easily damaged by EARTHQUAKES —**quake-proof** *adj.* —**quake-proofing** *n.* [U]

Quak·ers, the /ˈkweɪkə˞z/ a Christian religious group, also called the Society of Friends, that opposes all violence, has no priests or ceremonies, and holds its religious meetings in silence —**Quaker** *adj.*

qual·i·fi·ca·tion /ˌkwɑləfəˈkeɪʃən/ *n.* **1** [C usually plural] a skill, personal quality, or type of experience that makes you right for a particular job or position: *The only qualification you need is enthusiasm.* | **qualification to do sth** *Does he really have the qualifications to run the agency?* | **+for** *Several senators questioned his qualifications for the Supreme Court.* **2** [U] the action of achieving an official standard in order to do a job, enter a sports competition etc.: *training for qualification as a counselor* | **+for** *Your qualification for a loan depends on your credit history.* | *qualification for the World Cup*

THESAURUS

certificate an official document stating that you have the required knowledge and abilities to do a particular job: *a teaching certificate*
diploma a document showing that someone has successfully completed their high school or college education
degree the qualification that someone gets when they successfully complete a course of study at a college

3 [C,U] something that you add to a statement to limit its effect or meaning: *We welcome the proposal **without qualification**.* **4** [C] *British* something that says you have passed an examination or course to show you have a particular level of skill or knowledge in a subject: *a teaching qualification*

qual•i•fied /ˈkwɑləˌfaɪd/ *adj.* **1** having the right or officially approved knowledge, experience, skills etc., especially for a particular job: *qualified applicants* | **qualified to do sth** *Is she qualified to lead the team?* | **highly/well qualified** *the opinions of highly qualified experts* | **+for** *Karen is well qualified for her new role.* **2** qualified agreement, approval etc. is limited in some way, because you do not completely agree or approve: *The proposal received qualified approval.* **3** having passed a professional examination: *a qualified nurse* **4 a qualified success** a success, but not a complete one because there were still some small problems

qual•i•fi•er /ˈkwɑləˌfaɪɚ/ *n.* [C] **1** someone who has reached the necessary standard for entering a competition **2** a game that you have to win in order to be able to take part in a competition **3** ENG. LANG. ARTS in grammar, a word or phrase that acts as an adjective or adverb, that limits or adds to the meaning of another word or phrase. In the sentence "She rode off happily on her new red bike," the words "happily," "new," and "red" are qualifiers.

qual•i•fy /ˈkwɑləˌfaɪ/ S3 W3 *v.* **qualifies**, **qualified**, **qualifying**
1 HAVE A RIGHT [I,T] to have a right to have or do something, or give someone the right to have or do something: *To qualify, you must be over 18 and single.* | **+for** *You do not qualify for unemployment benefits.* | **qualify to do sth** *You may qualify to vote by mail.* | **qualify sb/sth for sth** *Does this qualify me for citizenship?*
2 MAKE SB SUITABLE [T] if your knowledge, ability etc. qualifies you to do something, it makes you a good person to do it: **qualify sb/sth for sth** *Tomita's fluency in English and Japanese helped qualify her for the job.*
3 BE CONSIDERED STH [I] to have all the necessary qualities to be considered as a particular thing: **+as** *Does photography qualify as an art form?* | *The fees qualify as business expenses.*
4 REACH A STANDARD [I] to pass an examination or reach the standard of knowledge or skill that you need in order to do something: *After qualifying, stock brokers must work for the company for five years.* | **+as** *I finally qualified as a pilot.*
5 COMPETITION [I] to reach the necessary standard to enter or continue in a competition or sports event: **+for** *She qualified for a spot on the Olympic skating team.*
6 ADD SOMETHING [T] to add to something that has already been said, in order to limit its effect or meaning: *He qualified his statement, saying that "the peace process will take some time."*
7 GRAMMAR TECHNICAL [T] if a word or phrase qualifies another word or phrase, it limits or adds to the meaning of it
[**Origin:** 1500–1600 French *qualifier*, from Medieval Latin *qualificare*, from Latin *qualis* **of what kind**]

qual•i•ta•tive /ˈkwɑləˌteɪt̬ɪv/ Ac *adj.* relating to the quality or standard of something, rather than to the amount or number: *qualitative analysis of students' performance* → see also QUANTITATIVE

ˌqualitative ˈdata *n.* [U] MATH data that does not contain numbers or amounts, but ideas, feelings, descriptions etc. → see also QUANTITATIVE DATA

qual•i•ty¹ /ˈkwɑlət̬i/ S2 W1 *n. plural* **qualities** **1** [U] the degree to which something is good or bad: *Supermarket wines vary in quality.* | **of good/high/top quality** *They produce cars of the highest quality.* | **of poor/low quality** *The paints are of poor quality.* | **high/low/top quality sth** *They offer top quality service.* | **air/water etc. quality** *The hot humid weather is affecting air quality.* **2** [C usually plural] a good or bad part of someone's character: *Honesty is an important quality in a friend.* | *Kim has many **good qualities**.* | *Lucas has outstanding **leadership qualities**.* ►see THESAURUS box at characteristic¹ **3** [U] a high standard: *The company guarantees the quality of its service.* | *Tiled bathroom walls are usually a sign **of quality** in new houses.* **4** [C] something that is typical of a substance or object and that makes it different from other things: *the drug's addictive quality* | *The city architecture has its own distinctive quality.* **5 quality of life** how good or bad your life is, shown for example by whether or not you are happy, healthy, able to do the things you want to do etc.: *The drugs promise improved quality of life for cancer patients.*

quality² *adj.* [only before noun, no comparative] having a high standard: *a quality education*

ˈquality asˌsurance *n.* [U] the management of the way goods or services are produced in order to keep the quality good

ˈquality conˌtrol *n.* [U] the practice of checking goods as they are produced, to be sure that their quality is good enough —**quality controller** *n.* [C]

ˈquality ˌtime *n.* [U] the time that you spend giving someone your full attention, especially time spent with your children: *Do you spend enough quality time with your children?*

qualm /kwɑm, kwɔm/ *n.* [C usually plural] a feeling of slight worry because you are not sure that what you are doing is right: *I took the job despite my qualms.* | *The coach **has no qualms about** dropping players who don't perform.*

quan•da•ry /ˈkwɑndəri/ *n. plural* **quandaries** [C] a difficult problem or situation about which you are uncertain what to do: *Kate was **in a quandary over** how to vote.*

quan•ti•fi•er /ˈkwɑntəˌfaɪɚ/ *n.* [C] ENG. LANG. ARTS in grammar, a word or phrase such as "some," "a lot," or "a few" that is used with a noun to show quantity

quan•ti•fy /ˈkwɑntəˌfaɪ/ *v.* **quantifies**, **quantified**, **quantifying** [T] to measure something and express it as a number, especially something that is difficult to measure: *The damage to the tourist industry is difficult to quantify.* —**quantifiable** /ˌkwɑntəˈfaɪəbəl/ *adj.* —**quantification** /ˌkwɑntəfəˈkeɪʃən/ *n.* [U]

quan•ti•ta•tive /ˈkwɑntəˌteɪt̬ɪv/ *adj.* relating to amounts rather than to the quality or standard of something: *a quantitative analysis of stock market trends* —**quantitatively** *adv.* → see also QUALITATIVE

ˌquantitative ˈdata *n.* [U] MATH data that is made up of numbers and amounts → see also QUALITATIVE DATA

quan•ti•ty /ˈkwɑntət̬i/ *n. plural* **quantities** [C,U] **1** an amount of something that can be counted or measured: *The price varies depending on the quantity purchased.* | **+of** *Use equal quantities of flour and butter.* | **a huge/large/vast quantity** *Large quantities of oil were spilled.* | **in large/small quantities** *Sugar is bad for health if consumed in large quantities.* **2** a large amount of something: *I'm still amazed by the sheer quantity of information on the Internet.* | *The cards are cheaper if you buy them **in quantity*** (=a large amount). [**Origin:** 1200–1300 Old French *quantité*, from Latin *quantitas*, from *quantus* **how much**] → see also **be an unknown quantity** at UNKNOWN¹ (3)

ˈquantity ˌtheory *n.* [singular] ECONOMICS an idea about the cause of INFLATION (=a continuing increase in prices, or the rate at which this happens), which says that inflation happens when there is too much money in a country's economic system at a particular time

quan•tum /ˈkwɑntəm/ *n. plural* **quanta** /-tə/ [C] PHYSICS the smallest unit that can be used to measure something such as light or energy. For example, a quantum of light is a PHOTON.

ˌquantum ˈleap also **ˌquantum ˈjump** *n.* [C] a very large and important improvement: *The treatment of breast cancer has taken a quantum leap forward.*

ˌquantum meˈchanics also **ˌquantum ˈphysics** *n.* [U] PHYSICS the scientific study of the way that atoms, PARTICLES, and other very small pieces of MATTER behave and affect each other, based on quantum theory

ˈquantum ˌtheory *n.* [singular] PHYSICS a scientific THEORY that describes the behavior and forces of ELEMENTARY PARTICLES, which is based on the idea that energy, like MATTER exists in very small separate pieces, not in a continuous form

quar·an·tine[1] /ˈkwɔrənˌtin, ˈkwɑr-/ *n.* [U] a period of time when a person or animal is kept apart from others in case they have a disease: *The monkeys were kept* ***in quarantine*** *for 31 days.* | *Doctors have placed the town* ***under quarantine.*** [**Origin:** 1600–1700 Italian *quarantina* **period of forty days**, from Old French, from *quarante* **forty**]

quarantine[2] *v.* [T often passive] to put a person or animal in quarantine

quark /kwɑrk/ *n.* [C] PHYSICS one of six small pieces of MATTER that form the parts of an atom [**Origin:** 1900–2000 invented by Murray Gell-Mann (born 1929), U.S. scientist, based on the phrase "three quarks for Muster Mark" in "Finnegans Wake" (1939) by James Joyce; because originally there were thought to be three quarks]

quar·rel[1] /ˈkwɔrəl, ˈkwɑrəl/ *n.* [C] **1** an angry argument or disagreement: *a bitter family quarrel* | **+with** *She got into a quarrel with her son's coach.* | **+about/over** *They had a quarrel about some girl.* **2** a reason to disagree with something or argue with someone: *I* ***have no quarrel with*** *the court's decision.* [**Origin:** 1300–1400 Old French *querele* **complaint**, from Latin *querela*, from *queri* **to complain**]

quarrel[2] *v.* [I] to have an argument: *I could hear them quarreling next door.* | **+with** *Rivera had quarreled with his tenants once before.* | **+about/over** *We're not going to quarrel about a few dollars.* ►see THESAURUS box at **argue**

quarrel with sth *phr. v.* to disagree with something or complain about something: *Nobody could quarrel with the report's conclusions.*

quar·rel·some /ˈkwɔrəlsəm/ *adj.* LITERARY often arguing, or seeming to enjoy arguing —**quarrelsomeness** *n.* [U]

quar·ry[1] /ˈkwɔri, ˈkwɑri/ *n. plural* **quarries** [C] **1** a place where large amounts of stone, sand etc. are dug out of the ground: *a slate quarry* → see also MINE **2** [singular] an animal or person that someone is hunting or chasing: *The hunter closed in on his quarry.* [**Origin:** (1) 1300–1400 Old French *quarriere*, from an unrecorded *quarre* **square stone**, from Latin *quadrum* **square**]

quarry[2] *v.* [T] to dig out stone, sand etc. from a quarry

quart /kwɔrt/ *n.* WRITTEN ABBREVIATION **qt.** [C] a unit for measuring liquid, equal to 2 PINTS or 0.9463 liters

quar·ter[1] /ˈkwɔrt̬ɚ/ [S1] [W1] *n.* [C]
1 AMOUNT one of four equal or almost equal parts into which something can be divided: *Cut the sandwiches into quarters.* | *a mile and a quarter* | **+of** *A quarter of Canada's population is French speaking.* | ***three quarters of*** *an acre*
2 PART OF AN HOUR one of the four periods of 15 minutes into which each hour can be divided: *I'll meet you in* ***a quarter of an hour.*** | **a quarter to/of three/four/six etc.** (=15 minutes before a particular hour) | **a quarter past/after three/four/six etc.** *It's already a quarter past 7.* | *three-quarters of an hour* (=45 minutes)
3 MONEY a coin that is worth 25 cents (=1/4 of a dollar), used in the U.S. and Canada ►see THESAURUS box at **money**
4 SPORTS one of the four equal periods of time into which games of some sports are divided: *Houston was ahead by 15 points at the end of the first quarter.*
5 BUSINESS ECONOMICS a period of three months, used when discussing business and money: *The company's profits rose in the first quarter of the year.* → see also QUARTERLY[1]
6 in some/various/many etc. quarters, also **from some/all etc. quarters** in or from different groups of people: *We expected criticism from some quarters.*
7 COLLEGE one of the four periods into which a year at school or college is sometimes divided, usually continuing for 10 to 12 weeks → see also SEMESTER: *What classes are you taking this quarter?* ►see THESAURUS box at **university**
8 HOUSE/ROOM quarters [plural] the house or rooms where someone lives, especially someone in the army: *Sleeping quarters are in the barracks.* | **cramped/close/tight quarters** (=a living place where there are too many people and not enough room)
9 PART OF A CITY an area in some cities where a particular type of people typically live or work: *the French Quarter of New Orleans*
10 MOON PHYSICS the period of time twice a month when you can see a quarter of the moon's surface
11 all quarters of the Earth/globe LITERARY everywhere in the world
12 give no quarter OLD USE to show no pity for someone, especially an enemy whom you have defeated
[**Origin:** 1200–1300 Old French *quartier*, from Latin *quartarius*, from *quartus* **fourth**] → see also **in/at close quarters** at CLOSE[2] (1)

quarter[2] *v.* [T] **1** to cut or divide something into four parts: *Quarter two large apples.* **2** to provide someone with a place to sleep and eat, especially a soldier

quarter[3] *quantifier* being a fourth (=1/4) of an amount, size, distance, number etc.: *a quarter-century* | *a quarter-mile* | *It has an area a quarter the size of California's.*

quar·ter·back[1] /ˈkwɔrt̬ɚˌbæk/ *n.* [C] the player in football who directs the OFFENSE and throws the ball → see also MONDAY MORNING QUARTERBACK

quarterback[2] *v.* **1** [I,T] to play in the position of quarterback in football **2** [T] INFORMAL to organize or direct an activity, event etc.: *She quarterbacked the new sales campaign.*

quar·ter·deck /ˈkwɔrt̬ɚˌdɛk/ *n.* [C] the back part of the upper DECK (=floor level) of a ship, used mainly by officers

quar·ter·fi·nal /ˌkwɔrt̬ɚˈfaɪnl/ *n.* [C] one of the set of four games near the end of a competition, whose winners play in the two SEMIFINALS

ˈquarter ˌhorse *n.* [C] a strong horse that is bred to run short races, usually of a quarter of a mile

quar·ter·ly[1] /ˈkwɔrt̬ɚli/ *adj., adv.* produced or happening four times a year: *a quarterly newsletter*

quarterly[2] *n. plural* **quarterlies** [C] a magazine that is produced four times a year

quar·ter·mas·ter /ˈkwɔrt̬ɚˌmæstɚ/ *n.* [C] **1** a military officer in charge of providing food, uniforms etc. **2** a ship's officer in charge of signals and guiding the ship on the right course

ˈquarter note *n.* [C] a musical note that continues for a quarter of the length of a WHOLE NOTE

quar·ter·staff /ˈkwɔrt̬ɚˌstæf/ *n.* [C] HISTORY a long wooden pole used as a weapon, especially in past times

quar·tet /kwɔrˈtɛt/ *n.* [C] **1** ENG. LANG. ARTS four singers or musicians who perform together: *a jazz quartet* | **a woodwind/string/brass quartet** *They hired a string quartet for the wedding.* **2** ENG. LANG. ARTS a piece of music written for four performers **3** four people or things of the same type: **+of** *a quartet of short films* → see also QUINTET, TRIO

quar·tile /ˈkwɔrtaɪl, -t̬l/ *n.* [C] **1** MATH one of four equal parts that a set of data can be divided into → see also PERCENTILE **2** MATH one of the three values in a set of data that divide the set into four equal parts

quar·to /ˈkwɔrt̬oʊ/ *n.* [C] TECHNICAL **1** the size of a piece of paper made by folding a large sheet of paper twice, to produce four sheets, or the paper itself **2** a book with pages of quarto size

quartz /kwɔrts/ *n.* [U] EARTH SCIENCE a hard mineral substance, used in making electronic watches and clocks

qua·sar /ˈkweɪzɑr/ *n.* [C] PHYSICS a very bright, very distant object similar to a star

quash /kwɑʃ/ *v.* [T] FORMAL **1** to stop something, especially talk about something or a feeling that a group of people have: *The company tried to quash the unwanted publicity.* **2** to use force to end protests or to stop people who are not obeying the law: *The police were brought in to quash the strike.* **3** LAW to officially state that a judgment or decision is not legal or correct: *The* *court quashed the convictions after a nine-day hearing.* [**Origin:** (1, 3) 1200–1300 Old French *quasser*, from Latin *cassus* **having no effect, void**]

quasi- /kwɑzi, kweɪzaɪ/ *prefix* like something in some ways SYN **partly**: *quasi-legal* | *a quasi-scientific theory* (=not entirely scientific)

qua·ter·cen·ten·a·ry /ˌkwɑt̬ɚsɛnˈtɛnəri/ *n.* [C] the day or year exactly 400 years after a particular event

quat·rain /ˈkwɑtreɪn/ *n.* [C] ENG. LANG. ARTS a group of four lines in a poem

qua·ver /ˈkweɪvɚ/ *v.* [I,T] if your voice quavers, it shakes as you speak, especially because you are nervous: *Her voice quavered as she described the attack.* —**quaver** *n.* [C] —**quavery** *adj.*

quay /keɪ, ki/ *n. plural* **quays** [C] a place where boats can be tied up or can stop to load and UNLOAD

Q

quay·side /ˈkeɪsaɪd/ *n.* [C] the area next to a quay

quea·sy /ˈkwizi/ *adj.* **1** feeling that you are going to VOMIT SYN **nauseated** SYN **naseous**: *The sway of the boat made passengers queasy.* **2** feeling uncomfortable because an action seems wrong, especially morally wrong: **be/feel queasy about sth** *I felt queasy about giving him money for alcohol.* —**queasiness** *n.* [U]

Que·bec /kwɪˈbɛk/ **1** a PROVINCE in eastern Canada, in which most people speak French as their first language **2** the capital city of Quebec province

Queˈbec ˌAct, the HISTORY the act of British Parliament in 1774 that allowed French people in Quebec to keep their language, Roman Catholic religion, and laws

queen¹ /kwin/ S3 W3 *n.* [C]
1 RULER also **Queen a)** the female ruler of a country: *Queen Victoria* | +**of** *Cleopatra, the queen of Egypt* **b)** the wife of a king ►see THESAURUS box at **king**
2 CARD a playing card with a picture of a queen on it: *the queen of hearts*
3 COMPETITION the woman who wins a beauty competition, or who is chosen to represent a school, area etc.: *Michelle was named **homecoming queen**.* | +**of** *the queen of the Kalispell County Fair*
4 INSECT BIOLOGY a large female BEE, ANT etc., which lays the eggs for a whole group
5 CHESS the most powerful piece in the game of CHESS
6 a woman who is regarded as the best at a particular activity or in a particular field: *Cooper is a former B-movie queen.* | *Tammy Wynette, **the queen of** country music*
[**Origin:** Old English *cwen* **woman, queen**] → see also BEAUTY QUEEN, **homecoming king/queen** at HOMECOMING (3)

queen² *v.* [T] TECHNICAL to change a PAWN into a queen in the game of CHESS

ˈqueen bee *n.* [C] **1** a large female BEE that lays the eggs for a whole group **2** HUMOROUS a woman who behaves as if she is the most important person in a place

queen·ly /ˈkwinli/ *adj.* appropriate for or like a queen

ˌQueen ˈMother *n.* [singular] the mother of the ruling king or queen

Queens /kwinz/ one of the five BOROUGHS of New York City, which is at the western end of Long Island

ˈqueen-size *adj.* **1** a queen-size bed, sheet etc. is larger than the standard size for a bed for two people → see also DOUBLE BED, KING-SIZE, TWIN BED **2** queen-size clothing is for women who are larger than average size

queer /kwɪr/ *adj.* **1** OLD-FASHIONED strange or difficult to explain: *a queer sound* **2 queer in the head** OLD-FASHIONED talking or behaving strangely SYN **crazy** —**queerly** *adv.* —**queerness** *n.* [U]

quell /kwɛl/ *v.* [T] FORMAL **1** to end a violent situation, especially when people are protesting: *Police fired tear gas to quell the rioting.* **2** to reduce or stop feelings of doubt, worry, and anxiety: *The police tried to quell public anxiety about the murders.*

quench /kwɛntʃ/ *v.* [T] **1 quench your thirst** to drink enough to stop you from feeling THIRSTY **2** to satisfy a feeling, especially a feeling of wanting or needing something: **quench sb's thirst/desire etc. for sth** *The magazine quenches the public's thirst for information.* **3 quench a fire/blaze etc.** to make a fire stop burning

quer·u·lous /ˈkwɛrələs, -yələs/ *adj.* FORMAL complaining all the time in an annoying way: *a querulous voice* —**querulously** *adv.* —**querulousness** *n.* [U]

que·ry¹ /ˈkwɪri/ *n. plural* **queries** [C] FORMAL a question you ask to get information, or to check that something is true or correct: *Martin replied to a query from a reporter.* [**Origin:** 1600–1700 *quere* **question** (16–19 centuries), from Latin *quaere!* **ask!**]

query² *v.* **queries, queried, querying** [T] FORMAL **1** to ask a question: *Researchers queried over five thousand voters.* **2** to express doubt that something is true or correct: *Both players queried the umpire's decision.*

que·sa·dil·la /ˌkeɪsəˈdiə/ *n.* [C] a Mexican dish made of TORTILLAS filled with cheese and sometimes meat

quest /kwɛst/ *n.* [C] ESPECIALLY LITERARY a long search for something: *a spiritual quest* | +**for** *the quest for knowledge* —**quest** *v.* [I]

ques·tion¹ /ˈkwɛstʃən, ˈkwɛʃtʃən/ S1 W1 *n.* [C]
1 ASKING FOR INFORMATION [C] a sentence or phrase used to ask for information: *That's an interesting question.* | +**about** *Are there any questions about the homework?* | *Hi Lori, can I **ask** you a quick **question**?* | *You still haven't **answered** my **question**.* | *Reporters **had** a few **questions** for the mayor.* | *Let me **rephrase the question*** (=ask it in a different way). | *Can I ask you **a personal question**?*
2 TEST/COMPETITION [C] a request for information that is intended to test your knowledge, for example in a test or competition: *test questions* | *The first question was really hard.* | *Did you **answer** all the **questions** on the test?* | **get a question right/wrong** (=answer it correctly or incorrectly)
3 SUBJECT/PROBLEM [C] a subject that needs to be discussed or a problem that needs to be solved SYN **issue**: *Several questions had still not been resolved.* | +**of** *the question of animal rights* | ***The question is,** are you going to meet the deadline?*
4 DOUBT [C,U] a quality of being uncertain, or a feeling of doubt about something: +**about** *There was some question about his guilt.* | ***There is no question that** he is a great athlete.* | *Her future is now **in question**.* | **call/bring throw sth into question** (=make people have doubts about something) | *Scientists have **raised questions about*** (=expressed doubt about) *the drug's long-term safety.* | *Whether the promises will be kept is **open to question*** (=not certain).
5 without question a) without any doubt SYN **definitely**: *It is without question the best show on TV.* **b)** without complaining or asking why: *She obeys her husband without question.*
6 the sb/sth in question the person, subject etc. being discussed or talked about: *The man in question is Tom Brown.*
7 out of the question if something is out of the question, you can definitely not have it or not do it, because it is not possible or not allowed: *A new car is out of the question right now.*
8 (that's a) good question! SPOKEN said when you are admitting that you do not know the answer to a question: *"How does he make a living?" "Good question."*
9 be a question of sth used when you are giving the most important fact, part, or feature or something: *If it's a question of money, maybe we can help.*
10 there is no question of (doing) sth used to say that something will definitely not happen: *There is no question of him changing his mind.*
11 beyond question completely certain: *Her honesty is beyond question.*
12 the question on everyone's mind/lips the question that everyone wants to know the answer to, especially because they feel excited about something
13 it's just a question of (doing) sth SPOKEN used to say that something is easy or not complicated: *It's just a question of putting in a couple of screws.*

14 it's only/just a question of time used to say that something is certain to happen at some point in the future: *It was only a question of time before help arrived.*
[**Origin:** 1200–1300 Old French, Latin *quaestio*, from *quaestus*, past participle of *quaerere* **to ask**] → see also **beg the question** at BEG (7), **a leading question** at LEADING¹ (4), **a loaded question** at LOADED (4), **pop the question** at POP¹ (10), **a rhetorical question** at RHETORICAL (3)

question² S1 W2 *v.* [T] **1** to ask someone questions to find out what they know about something, especially about a crime: *We questioned 20,000 voters in our survey.* | **question sb about sth** *Two men are being questioned about the murder.* ▸see THESAURUS box at **ask** **2** to have doubts about something or tell someone about these doubts: *Are you questioning my honesty?* | **question whether/why/how etc.** *Secretly, he questioned whether Jack had ever been married.*

ques·tion·a·ble /ˈkwɛstʃənəbəl/ *adj.* **1** likely to be dishonest or morally wrong: *questionable financial dealings* **2** uncertain or possibly not true or correct: *a questionable assumption* | *The research is of questionable value.* **3** if a sports player is questionable for a game, they may not be able to play

ques·tion·er /ˈkwɛstʃənɚ/ *n.* [C] someone who is asking a question, for example in a public discussion

ques·tion·ing /ˈkwɛstʃənɪŋ/ *adj.* **1** a questioning look or expression shows that you have doubts about something or need some information **2** not accepting things without asking questions —**questioningly** *adv.*

ˈquestion mark *n.* [C] **1** ENG. LANG. ARTS the mark (?) that is used in writing at the end of a question ▸see THESAURUS box at **punctuation mark** **2 there is a question mark over sth** used to say that there is a possibility that it will not be successful or will not continue to exist: *There is a big question mark over the company's future.*

ques·tion·naire /ˌkwɛstʃəˈnɛr/ *n.* [C] a written set of questions about a particular subject given to a large number of people, in order to collect information: *Readers were asked to **fill out a questionnaire** on health issues.*

queue¹ /kyu/ *n.* [C] **1** BRITISH a line of people, vehicles etc., one behind the other, waiting to do or get something SYN **line** **2** a list of jobs that a computer has to do in a particular order: *the print queue* **3** a number of telephone calls that are waiting to be answered in an electronic telephone system: *a phone queue* [**Origin:** 1500–1600 French **tail**, from Latin *cauda*, *coda*]

queue² also **queue up** BRITISH *v.* [I] to form or join a line of people or vehicles waiting to do something or go somewhere SYN **line up**

quib·ble¹ /ˈkwɪbəl/ *v.* [I] to argue about something that is not very important: **+about/over** *I didn't feel like quibbling over the price.*

quibble² *n.* [C] a complaint or criticism about something that is not very important

quiche /kiʃ/ *n.* [C,U] a type of food that consists of PASTRY filled with a mixture of eggs, cheese, vegetables etc.

quiche

quick¹ /kwɪk/ S2 W1 *adj.*
1 FAST done, happening, or existing for only a short time SYN **fast**: *I'll just take a quick shower first.* | *Pasta meals are quick to make.* | *What's the quickest way to the airport?* | *quick movements* | ***That was quick!** I thought you'd be gone for hours.* ▸see THESAURUS box at **short¹**
2 ABLE TO DO STH FAST able to do or produce something fast SYN **fast**: *a quick worker*
3 SMART able to learn and understand things fast: *Carrie's a quick learner.* | *She's **a quick study*** (=someone who learns things quickly) *when it comes to politics.* | *Paul's not very **quick on the uptake*** (=quick to understand what someone is saying). | *Her **quick wits*** (=ability to think quickly) *had gotten her out of many difficult situations.* → see also QUICK-WITTED
4 a quick fix INFORMAL a repair to something or an answer to a problem that happens quickly, but may work for only for a short time: *There's no quick fix for stopping pollution.*
5 NO DELAY happening without any waiting or delay: *Even lowering the price won't guarantee a quick sale.*
6 a quick buck INFORMAL a lot of money that you earn very quickly, especially without much effort: *He's always looking for a way to **make a quick buck**.*
7 be quick to do sth to react quickly to what someone says or does: *She's always quick to criticize.*
8 quick thinking an intelligent decision that is made quickly, or the ability to make decisions like this: *Sue's quick thinking saved the group.*
9 be quick on your feet a) to be able to move quickly and gracefully: *Tom's a big guy, but he's quick on his feet.* **b)** good at reacting quickly and intelligently to difficult questions and in difficult situations: *To be a good learner, you have to be quick on your feet.*
10 be quick (about it) also **make it quick** used to tell someone to hurry: *"Can I just finish this first?" "OK, but be quick about it."*
11 have a quick temper to get angry very easily
12 be quick on the draw a) INFORMAL to be good at reacting quickly and intelligently to difficult questions or in difficult situations **b)** to be able to pull a gun out quickly in order to shoot
13 a quick draw someone who is able to pull a gun out quickly in order to shoot
14 a quick one INFORMAL an alcoholic drink that you have in a hurry
15 quick-and-dirty done fast and using as little money and effort as possible: *a quick-and-dirty solution*
[**Origin:** Old English *cwic* **alive**] → see also QUICKLY —**quickness** *n.* [U]

quick² *interjection* used to tell someone to hurry or come quickly: *Quick! We'll miss the bus!*

quick³ S1 *adv.* SPOKEN, NONSTANDARD **1** quickly: *Come quick! Larry's on TV!* | *It all happened pretty quick.* **2 quick as a flash/wink** very quickly

quick⁴ *n.* [U] **1 the quick** the sensitive flesh under your FINGERNAILS and TOENAILS: *Her nails were **bitten to the quick**.* **2 cut/sting/wound etc. sb to the quick** to make someone very upset **3 the quick and the dead** BIBLICAL [plural] all people, including all those who are alive and all those who are dead

ˈquick bread *n.* [C,U] a bread that you can bake immediately, because it uses BAKING POWDER or BAKING SODA rather than YEAST

ˌquick-ˈchange ˌartist *n.* [C] an entertainer who can change their clothes or appearance very quickly

quick·en /ˈkwɪkən/ *v.* [I,T] **1** to become quicker, or to make something do this: *He quickened his steps as he crossed the street.* | *The **pace** of reform has **quickened** in recent months.* **2** FORMAL if a feeling quickens, or if something quickens it, it becomes stronger or more active SYN **increase**: *Interest in the idea has quickened recently.* **3** OLD USE OR LITERARY to come alive, or to make something come alive

quick·en·ing /ˈkwɪkənɪŋ/ *n.* [U] the first movements of a baby that has not been born yet

quick·ie /ˈkwɪki/ *n.* [C] INFORMAL something done or made quickly and easily —**quickie** *adj.*: *a quickie divorce*

quick·lime /ˈkwɪk-laɪm/ *n.* [U] a white substance obtained by burning LIMESTONE

quick·ly /ˈkwɪkli/ S2 W1 *adv.* **1** fast, or done in a very short amount of time SYN **fast**: *Don't eat too quickly.* | *She walked quickly toward her car.* | *We need to get the work finished **as quickly as possible**.* | *The summer **went by** so **quickly**.* ▸see THESAURUS box at **fast²** **2** after only a very short time SYN **soon**: *I quickly realized that there was something wrong.* **3** for

Q

a short amount of time SYN **briefly**: *Let me just talk to Eve quickly before we go.*

quick·sand /ˈkwɪksænd/ *n.* [C,U] wet sand that is dangerous because it pulls you down into it if you walk on it

quick·sil·ver[1] /ˈkwɪkˌsɪlvɚ/ *n.* [U] **1** OLD USE the metal MERCURY **2 like quicksilver a)** changing in a sudden and unexpected way **b)** moving quickly and often difficult to catch

quicksilver[2] *adj.* [only before noun] LITERARY **1** changing or moving quickly and in a way that you do not expect: *the quicksilver beauty of Khan's singing* **2** able to think and understand things quickly

quick·step /ˈkwɪkstɛp/ *n.* [C] a dance with fast movements of the feet, or the music for this dance

ˌquick-ˈtempered *adj.* easily becoming angry: *My father was quick-tempered and often drunk.*

Q

ˌquick-ˈwitted *adj.* able to understand things quickly and to say things that are funny and smart: *Brady is quick-witted and articulate.* —**quickwittedness** *n.* [U]

quid pro quo /ˌkwɪd proʊ ˈkwoʊ/ *n.* [C] something that you give or do in exchange for something else, especially when this arrangement is not official

qui·es·cent /kwaɪˈɛsənt, kwi-/ *adj.* FORMAL not developing or doing anything, especially when this is only a temporary state —**quiescently** *adv.* —**quiescence** *n.* [U]

qui·et[1] /ˈkwaɪət/ S2 W2 *adj.*

1 NO NOISE making very little or no noise: *The baby's sleeping, so we need to be quiet.* | *The new car is very quiet.* | *I put on some quiet relaxing music.*

THESAURUS

Words used to describe a quiet voice or sound
low a low voice or sound is quiet and deep: *A low humming noise was coming from the refrigerator.*
soft quiet in a way that is pleasant: *She sang a lullaby in a soft voice.*
muffled a muffled sound is very difficult to hear: *the muffled sound of voices in the next room*
hushed if people speak in hushed voices, they speak quietly, especially so that other people cannot hear them: *After a hushed discussion, Jonathan came forward.*
subdued if a person is subdued, she or he is quiet and looks sad: *She looked subdued after her interview.*
inaudible too quiet to be heard: *Her protests were inaudible behind the glass door.*
→ LOUD

Words to describe a quiet place
calm quiet and without activity or trouble: *The streets remained calm again after last week's riots.*
tranquil/peaceful quiet in a way that is pleasant and relaxing: *a tranquil spot for a picnic* | *It was cool and peaceful by the lake.*
sleepy quiet with very little happening: *a sleepy little town*

2 (be/keep) quiet! SPOKEN used to tell someone to stop talking or making noise: *Tanya, be quiet! I'm on the phone.*

3 NOT SPEAKING a) someone who is quiet does not usually talk very much: *He's nice, but kind of quiet.* **b)** not saying much or not saying anything: *Missy's very quiet – is she sick?*

4 NOT MUCH ACTIVITY a quiet place or time is one where there is not much activity: *a quiet neighborhood* | *I'm just going to have a quiet evening at home.* | *The city was quiet after another night of fighting.*

5 BUSINESS if business is quiet, there are not many customers SYN **slow** OPP **busy**: *Business has been pretty quiet recently.*

6 keep sth quiet also **keep quiet about sth** to keep information secret: *We need to keep this quiet – don't tell anyone.*

7 keep sb quiet a) to stop someone from talking, complaining, or causing trouble: *I agreed to help her, just to keep her quiet.* **b)** to stop someone from telling other people about a secret, especially one that may be embarrassing

8 quiet confidence/satisfaction/authority/dignity etc. used to describe feelings in which someone seems very calm not excited: *He spoke with an air of quiet authority.*

9 NOT ROUGH if the ocean or other area of water is quiet, it is calm and not rough

[**Origin:** 1300–1400 Latin *quietus*, from the past participle of *quiescere* **to become quiet, rest**] —**quietness** *n.* [U] → see also QUIETLY

quiet[2] *v.* **1** [I,T] also **quiet down** to become calmer and less noisy, or to make someone do this SYN **calm down**: *The kids finally quieted down and read their books.* | *She gently rocked the baby to quiet him.* **2** [I] also **quiet down** if a situation quiets or quiets down, there is much less activity, or people stop fighting, criticizing, arguing etc. SYN **calm down**: *The fighting seems to have quieted down.* **3** [T] to make someone stop criticizing you or opposing you: *White has quieted the skeptics who said he couldn't do the job.* **4** [T] to make someone feel less frightened or worried: *Her mother quieted her after the nightmare.*

quiet[3] *n.* [U] **1** the state of being quiet, calm, and peaceful: *the quiet of the forest* | *I sat and enjoyed a few minutes of* ***peace and quiet***. **2** silence: *Can I have quiet, please!*

qui·et·ly /ˈkwaɪətli/ W3 *adv.* **1** without making much noise: *Rosa shut the door quietly.* | *"I'm sorry," she said quietly.* **2** in a way that does not attract attention: *When no one was looking, I slipped quietly away.* **3 quietly pleased/amused/confident etc.** having a particular good feeling, without talking about it, or without saying much in general **4** without protesting, complaining, or fighting: *Now are you going to come quietly, or do I have to use force?*

ˌQuiet Revoˈlution *n.* [singular] HISTORY a period of great political, educational, and social change during the 1960s in Quebec, Canada, when the WELFARE STATE was created and French became the official language

qui·e·tude /ˈkwaɪəˌtud/ *n.* [U] FORMAL calmness, peace, and quiet

qui·e·tus /kwaɪˈiṭəs, -ˈeɪṭəs/ *n.* [singular] FORMAL **1** death **2** the end of something

quill /kwɪl/ *n.* [C] **1** BIOLOGY a bird's feather, especially a large one, including the stiff, hard part at the base where the feather joins to the bird's body **2** also **quill pen** a pen made from a large bird's feather, used in past times **3** BIOLOGY one of the sharp needles that grow on the backs of some animals, such as the PORCUPINE

quilt /kwɪlt/ *n.* [C] a warm thick cover for a bed, made by sewing two layers of cloth together with cloth or feathers in between them: *a patchwork quilt* [**Origin:** 1200–1300 Old French *cuilte*, from Latin *culcita* **mattress**]

quilt·ed /ˈkwɪltɪd/ *adj.* quilted cloth has a thick layer of material sewn to it in a pattern of stitches: *a quilted bathrobe*

quilt·ing /ˈkwɪltɪŋ/ *n.* [U] the work of making a quilt, or the material and stitches that you use to make a quilt

quince /kwɪns/ *n.* [C,U] BIOLOGY a hard, yellowish fruit like a large apple, used for making JELLY, or the tree that grows this fruit

qui·nine /ˈkwaɪnaɪn/ *n.* [U] MEDICINE a drug used for treating fevers, especially MALARIA [**Origin:** 1800–1900 Spanish *quina* name of the tree from which quinine is obtained, from Quechua *quinaquina*]

ˈquinine ˌwater *n.* [U] a bitter-tasting drink often mixed in alcoholic drinks such as GIN

quint /kwɪnt/ *n.* [C] INFORMAL a QUINTUPLET

quin·tes·sence /kwɪnˈtɛsəns/ *n.* **the quintessence of sth** FORMAL a perfect type or example of something

quint·es·sen·tial /ˌkwɪntəˈsɛnʃəl/ *adj.* being a perfect example of a particular type of person or thing: *New York is the quintessential big city.* —**quintessentially** *adv.*

quin·tet /kwɪn'tɛt/ *n.* [C] ENG. LANG. ARTS **1** five singers or musicians who perform together **2** a piece of music written for five performers → see also QUARTET, SEXTET, TRIO

quin·tup·let /kwɪn'tʌplɪt, -'tu-/ *n.* [C] BIOLOGY one of five babies born to the same mother at the same time → see also QUADRUPLET, SEXTUPLET

quip /kwɪp/ *v.* [I] to say something short and amusing: *"Giving up smoking is easy," he quipped. "I've done it hundreds of times."* —**quip** *n.* [C]

qui·pu /'kipu/ *n.* [C] HISTORY a group of knotted colored strings, used by the Incas (=ancient people of Peru) as a way of storing information

quire /kwaɪɚ/ *n.* [C] TECHNICAL 24 sheets of paper

quirk /kwɚk/ *n.* [C] **1** a strange habit or feature that someone or something has: *Greg is a nice guy, but he has a few weird personality quirks.* **2 a quirk of fate/nature/history etc.** something strange that happens by chance or for reasons that you do not know or understand: *By a quirk of nature, half the frogs in the pond had more than four legs.*

quirk·y /'kwɚki/ *adj. comparative* **quirkier**, *superlative* **quirkiest** slightly strange or unusual, in an unexpected way: *a quirky sense of humor* —**quirkily** *adv.* —**quirkiness** *n.* [U]

quis·ling /'kwɪzlɪŋ/ *n.* [C] someone who helps an army or enemy country that has taken control of his own country

quit /kwɪt/ S1 *v.* **quit, quitting** **1** [I,T] to leave a job, school etc., especially because you are annoyed or unhappy: *Half of the emplyees have either quit or been fired.* | *She quit school at 16.* | *He had to* ***quit*** *his* ***job*** *to take care of her.*

THESAURUS

give up to stop doing something, or stop trying to do something: *He had given up trying to make her understand.*
resign to officially leave your job or position: *Three board members have resigned.*
give notice to officially tell your employer that you will be leaving your job soon: *You should give three month's notice before leaving your job.*
drop out to stop going to school or stop an activity before you have finished it: *Tucker dropped out of high school when he was 16.*

2 [T] INFORMAL to stop doing something bad or annoying SYN **stop**: ***Quit it****, Robby, or I'll tell Mom!* | **quit doing sth** *I quit smoking two years ago.* | *Quit complaining.* **3** [I,T] INFORMAL to stop doing something: *That kid just never quits moving.* **4** [T] OLD USE to leave a place [**Origin:** 1200–1300 Old French *quiter*, from *quite* **at rest, free of**] → see also QUITS

quite /kwaɪt/ W1 *adv.* **1** [+ adj./adv.] very, but not extremely: *The food here is quite good.* | *She's doing quite well at college.* | *Keegan's quite tall.* ►see THESAURUS box at **rather** **2 not quite** not completely or not exactly: *I'm not quite sure how the system works.* | *"Are you ready?" "Not quite."* | *He didn't say it quite that way, but that's what he meant.* | *Traffic wasn't quite as bad as I expected.* **3** completely: *The situation is quite different today.* | *She seemed quite normal.* **4** used when an amount or number is large, but not extremely large: *There were* ***quite a few*** *people there.* | *We've had* ***quite a bit*** *of snow this year so far.* | *I haven't seen Ed in* ***quite a while****.* **5** used in order to emphasize the fact that something is unusually good, bad etc.: *We got* ***quite a*** *deal on the car.* | *Darby made* ***quite an*** *impression on the kids.* | *I've never met her but I've heard she's* ***quite something*** (=impressive or amazing). | *The annual party has become* ***quite the*** *social event.* **6 quite frankly/honestly** SPOKEN used for emphasizing that you what you are saying is true, often when you know it will surprise or offend someone **7 quite the reverse/opposite/contrary** used to emphasize that a situation is the opposite of what has been mentioned: *She's not lazy – quite the contrary.* **8 quite enough** used to say that any more would be too much: *He's had quite enough to drink.* [**Origin:** 1300–1400 *quit*, *quite* **free of** (13–19 centuries), from Old French *quite*] ►see THESAURUS box at **rather**

Qui·to /'kitoʊ/ the capital city of Ecuador

quits /kwɪts/ *adj.* **call it quits** INFORMAL to stop doing something: *After 8 years of marriage, they're calling it quits.*

quit·tance /'kwɪt˺ns/ *n.* [C] LAW a statement saying that someone does not have to do something anymore, such as paying back money that they owe

quit·ter /'kwɪt̬ɚ/ *n.* [C] INFORMAL DISAPPROVING someone who stops doing a job, activity, or duty because it becomes difficult: *I'm not a quitter, but this job is starting to affect my health.*

quiv·er¹ /'kwɪvɚ/ *v.* [I] **1** to shake slightly, especially because you feel angry, excited, or upset: *Her mouth quivered slightly as she spoke.* | **+with** *His voice quivered with emotion.* **2** to shake slightly: *The ground quivered under my feet.*

quiver² *n.* [C] **1** a slight shake: *I felt a quiver of excitement run through me.* **2** a long case for carrying ARROWS

quix·ot·ic /kwɪk'sɑt̬ɪk/ *adj.* having or showing ideas and plans that are based on hopes, and that are not reasonable or practical: *a quixotic presidential campaign* [**Origin:** 1700–1800 Don *Quixote*, main character of the book "Don Quixote de la Mancha" (1605) by the Spanish writer Cervantes]

quiz¹ /kwɪz/ *n. plural* **quizzes** [C] **1** a short test that a teacher gives to a class: *a biology quiz* **2** a competition in which you have to answer questions **3** a set of questions in a magazine, that ask you questions about yourself, so that you can find out something about your character → see also POP QUIZ

quiz² *v.* **quizzes, quizzed, quizzing** [T] **1** to ask someone a lot of questions: *Journalists quizzed the governor during the half-hour program.* **2** to give a student a short test: *Students are quizzed on their reading.* → see also POP QUIZ

'quiz show *n.* [C] a television show in which people answer questions to test their knowledge in order to try to win prizes or money → see also GAME SHOW

quiz·zi·cal /'kwɪzɪkəl/ *adj.* showing that you are confused or surprised by something, and think it is slightly amusing or strange: *The child gave him a quizzical look.* —**quizzically** /-kli/ *adv.*

quo /kwoʊ/ → see QUID PRO QUO, STATUS QUO

quon·dam /'kwɑndəm/ *adj.* FORMAL relating to an earlier time

Quon·set hut /'kwɑnsət ˌhʌt/ *n.* [C] TRADEMARK a long metal building with a curved metal roof, where soldiers live or where things are stored

quo·rum /'kwɔrəm/ *n.* [C usually singular] the smallest number of people who must be present at a meeting for official decisions to be made: *Do we have a quorum?*

quo·ta /'kwoʊt̬ə/ *n.* [C] **1** an amount or number of something that you are expected to produce, sell, achieve etc., especially in your job: **fill/meet a quota** *Salespeople who fill their quotas earn bonuses.* **2** a limit, especially an official limit, on the number or amount of something you are allowed to have: *Most countries have an immigration quota.* | *a strict quota on imports* | *I think I've had my quota of coffee for the day.* **3** POLITICS an official rule stating that a certain number of jobs or PROMOTIONS (=moves to a more important job or rank) must be given to people from social groups who have been treated unfairly in the past because of their race or sex → see also AFFIRMATIVE ACTION: *He wrote an article about the use of racial preferences and hiring quotas in employment practices.*

quot·a·ble /'kwoʊt̬əbəl/ *adj.* a quotable remark or statement is interesting and noticeable, especially because it is intelligent or amusing

Q

ˈquota ˌsystem *n.* [C] **1** POLITICS a system that puts an official limit on the number of IMMIGRANTS in the United States who are allowed to become U.S. citizens or obtain a GREEN CARD (=official document that shows that a non-citizen can legally live and work in the U.S.) **2** ECONOMICS a system that puts an official limit on particular goods or the amount of a product allowed into a country: *a proposed new U.S. quota system for Mexican-grown tomatoes*

quo·ta·tion /kwoʊˈteɪʃən/ Ac *n.* **1** [C] words from a book, poem etc. that you repeat in your own speech or piece of writing SYN **quote**: **+from** *a quotation from the Bible* **2** [U] the act of quoting something that someone else has written or said **3** [C] a QUOTE of how much money a service will cost

quoˈtation ˌmark *n.* [C usually plural] ENG. LANG. ARTS a mark (" or ") used in writing before and after any words that are being quoted or before and after the exact words someone says

Q

quote¹ /kwoʊt/ Ac S2 W2 *v.* **1** [I,T] to repeat exactly what someone else has said or written: *He's always quoting Shakespeare.* | **quote (sth) from sth** *He quoted a line from a play by Brecht.* | *"We are fighting a war on terror," the president* ***was quoted as saying****.* | *He's a racist, and* ***you can quote me on that****.* | *I think they'll win,* ***but don't quote me*** (=said when what you are saying is not official). **2** [T] to give proof for what you are saying by mentioning a particular example of something SYN **cite**: *Dr. Morse quoted three successful cases in which the drug was used.* **3** [T] to tell a customer the price you will charge them for a service or product → see also ESTIMATE: **quote sb sth** *The other agent quoted us a lower price.* **4 quote ... unquote** SPOKEN used when you are repeating the exact words that someone has said: *They describe themselves as a quote "compassionate conservatives" unquote.* **5 quote** also **and I quote** SPOKEN used when you are going to repeat what someone else has said, to emphasize that it is exactly the way they said it: *Her reaction was, and I quote, "No way."* [**Origin:** 1300–1400 Medieval Latin *quotare*, from Latin *quot* **how many**]

quote² Ac S2 W3 *n.* [C] INFORMAL **1** a QUOTATION from a book, poem etc. **2** a written statement of exactly how much money a service will cost → see also ESTIMATE SYN **quotation** **3 in quotes** words that are in quotes are between a pair of QUOTATION MARKS

quoth /kwoʊθ/ *v.* [T] OLD USE **quoth he/she etc.** a way of saying "he said," "she said" etc.

quo·tid·i·an /kwoʊˈtɪdiən/ *adj.* FORMAL daily or ordinary

quo·tient /ˈkwoʊʃənt/ *n.* [C] **1** MATH the number which is obtained when one number is divided by another **2** the amount of something that something contains or that someone has: *The album contains the band's usual quotient of sentimental love songs.* → see also INTELLIGENCE QUOTIENT

Qur·'an /kəˈræn, -ˈrɑn/ *n.* **the Qur'an** another spelling of KORAN

q.v. *written abbreviation* FORMAL **quod vide** used to tell readers to look in another place in the same book for a piece of information

qwert·y /ˈkwəṭi/ *adj.* a qwerty KEYBOARD on a computer or TYPEWRITER has the keys arranged in the usual way, with Q, W, E, R, T, and Y on the top row

R,r

R[1] /ɑr/ *n. plural* **R's** [C] **1** also **r** *plural* **r's** **a)** the 18th letter of the English alphabet **b)** the sound represented by this letter **2** [C,U] **restricted** used to show that no one under the age of 17 can go to a particular movie unless a parent goes with them → see also NC-17, PG-13 THREE R'S

R[2] the written abbreviation of REPUBLICAN, used to show that someone belongs to that political party: *Senator Charles Grassley, R-Iowa*

R. the written abbreviation of RIVER, used especially on maps

Ra /rɑ/ in Egyptian MYTHOLOGY, the god of the sun

Ra·bat /rəˈbɑt/ the capital city of Morocco

rab·bi /ˈræbaɪ/ *n.* [C] a Jewish priest [**Origin:** 1000–1100 Late Latin, Greek, from Hebrew, **my master**]

rab·bin·ate /ˈræbənɪt, -ˌneɪt/ *n.* **the rabbinate** rabbis considered together as a group

rab·bin·i·cal /rəˈbɪnɪkəl/ *adj.* relating to the writings or teaching of rabbis

rab·bit /ˈræbɪt/ S3 *n.* **1** [C] BIOLOGY a common small animal with long ears and soft fur, that lives in a hole in the ground **2** [U] the fur or meat of a rabbit

ˈrabbit hutch *n.* [C] a wooden CAGE for pet rabbits

ˈrabbit punch *n.* [C] a quick hit on the back of the neck, made with the side of the hand

ˈrabbit ˌwarren *n.* [C] **1** BIOLOGY an area under the ground where wild rabbits live in their holes **2** a building or place with a lot of narrow passages or streets where you can easily get lost

rab·ble /ˈræbəl/ *n.* [singular] **1** a noisy crowd of people who are likely to cause trouble **2 the rabble** DISAPPROVING an insulting word for a group of people that you do not respect, especially people from a lower social class: *They didn't want to mix with the rabble.*

ˈrabble-ˌrouser *n.* [C] someone who tries to make a crowd of people angry and violent, especially in order to achieve political aims —**rabble-rousing** *adj.*: *a rabble-rousing speech* —**rabble-rousing** *n.* [U]

Ra·be·lais /ˌræbəˈleɪ/, **Fran·çois** /frɑnˈswɑ/ (?1494–1553) a French writer who is known for his SATIRE and jokes about sex

rab·id /ˈræbɪd/ *adj.* **1** having very extreme and unreasonable opinions, especially about politics SYN **fanatical**: *rabid liberals* **2** MEDICINE suffering from rabies: *a rabid dog*

ra·bies /ˈreɪbiz/ *n.* [U] MEDICINE a disease that kills animals and people, that you can get if you are bitten by an infected animal

Ra·bin /rɑˈbin,/, **Itz·hak** /ˈɪtʃɑk/ (1922–1995) an Israeli politician who was Prime Minister 1974–1977 and 1992–1995

rac·coon, racoon /ræˈkun/ *n.* **1** [C] BIOLOGY a small North American animal with black fur around its eyes and black and white rings on its tail **2** [U] the thick fur of a raccoon

race[1] /reɪs/ S2 W1 *n.*

1 SPORTS [C] a competition in which each competitor tries to run, drive etc. fastest and finish first: *Over a hundred runners will take part in the race.* | *Lewis* **won** *his final race.* | **a horse/bike/car etc. race** *an exciting motorcycle race* | *It should be an extremely* **close race** (=one in which anyone can win).

2 PEOPLE a) [C] one of the main groups that humans can be divided into according to the color of their skin and other physical features: *human beings of all races* **b)** [U] the fact of belonging to one of these groups: *Mary was discriminated against because of her race.* | *a person of mixed race* **c)** [C] a group of people with the same customs, history, language etc.: *the Nordic races* → see also HUMAN RACE

THESAURUS

nation a country and its social and political structure, or a group of people with the same history and language: *the leaders of several Western nations* | *the Mandan tribe of the Sioux nation*
race one of the groups that people are divided into, based on skin color and other physical features: *Employers may not make decisions about hiring on the basis of race.*
people a race or group of people that live in a particular country. The plural of this meaning of "people" is "peoples": *the native peoples of the United States*
tribe a group of people within a country who are the same race, and who have the same traditions and the same leader: *The Navajo tribe is the second largest in the U.S.*
ethnic group a group of people of the same race, nation, or tribe: *the mix of ethnic groups in this part of Chicago*

3 COMPETITION [C usually singular] a situation in which people, companies etc. are competing with each other to win something or be the first to do something, especially in politics: *The election was a closely fought race.* | **+for** *the race for the presidency* | **the race to do sth** *the race to host the next Olympics* | **be in the race/be out of the race** *Only two candidates are still in the race.* | ***The race was on*** *for domination of the continent.*

4 ATTEMPT TO DO STH QUICKLY [singular] a situation in which you have to do something very quickly because you have very little time available: **a race to do sth** *It's a race to find the killer before he strikes again.*

5 a race against time also **a race against the clock** an attempt to quickly finish doing something very important

6 the races an event at which horses or dogs are raced against each other, especially for money: *a day at the races*

7 ANIMAL/PLANT [C] TECHNICAL a type of animal or plant → see also ARMS RACE, RAT RACE, SPECIES

[**Origin:** (1, 3–6) 1200–1300 Old Norse *ras* **going quickly, running**]

race[2] S3 W3 *v.*

1 SPORTS a) [I,T] to compete against someone or something in a race: *Stevens will not be racing in the final due to an injury.* | **+against** *She will be racing against some of the world's top athletes.* | **race sb to/back/across etc.** *I'll race you to the other side of the pool.* **b)** [T] to use an animal, vehicle, or toy to compete in a race: *He started racing cars when he was 18.*

2 MOVE QUICKLY [I always + adv./prep.,T always + adv./prep.] to move very quickly, or make someone or something do this: **+out/into/by etc.** *I watched the children race across the playground.* | **race sb/sth to sth** *The singer was raced to the hospital.* ►see THESAURUS box at **run**[1], **rush**[1]

3 HURRY TO DO STH [I] to try to do something very quickly because you want to be the first to do it, or because there is very little time available: **race to do sth** *Investors raced to buy shares in the new hi-tech companies.* | **race against time/the clock** *The astronauts are racing against time to repair the spaceship.*

4 HEART/MIND ETC. [I] if your heart, PULSE, or mind races, it works harder and faster than usual, especially because you are sick or anxious: *My heart was racing, and I tried hard not to panic.*

5 sth races through sb's mind if thoughts, ideas etc. race through someone's mind, they think of them very quickly, especially when they are in a very excited or nervous state

6 ENGINE [I] if an engine races, it works faster than it should

ˈrace car also **ˈracing car** *n.* [C] a car that is specially designed for car races

race·course /ˈreɪs-kɔrs/ *n.* [C] a track around which runners, cars etc. race

race·horse /ˈreɪshɔrs/ *n.* [C] a horse specially bred and trained for racing

rac·er /ˈreɪsɚ/ *n.* [C] someone who races a car, bicycle, boat etc.

ˈrace reˌlations *n.* [plural] the relationship that exists between people from different races who are living in the same place

ˈrace ˌriot *n.* [C] violent behavior, such as fighting and attacks on property, caused by hatred between people of different races

race·track /ˈreɪs-træk/ *n.* [C] a track around which runners, horses, cars etc. race

Rach·ma·ni·noff /rɑkˈmɑnɪˌnɔf/, **Ser·gei** /ˈsɚgeɪ/ (1873–1943) a Russian musician who wrote CLASSICAL music

R

ra·cial /ˈreɪʃəl/ W2 *adj.* [only before noun] **1** relating to the relationships between different races of people: *racial equality* | *laws against* ***racial discrimination*** (=unfair treatment because of race) **2** relating to the various races that humans can be divided into: *people from various racial and ethnic groups* | *We welcome all of you, whatever your racial background.* | *programs for* ***racial minorities*** —**racially** *adv.*: *a racially mixed school*

Ra·cine /ræˈsin/**, Jean** /ʒɑn/ (1639–1699) a French writer of plays

rac·ing¹ /ˈreɪsɪŋ/ *n.* [U] the sport of running in races or racing horses, cars etc.: **horse/car/dog etc. racing** *His main interest is car racing.*

racing² *adj.* [only before noun] relating to, designed, or bred for racing: *a racing bicycle*

ˈracing car *n.* [C] a RACE CAR

ˈracing form *n.* [C] a printed sheet that gives information about horse races

rac·ism /ˈreɪsɪzəm/ *n.* [U] **1** unfair treatment of people, or violence against them, because they belong to a different race from your own: *We will not tolerate racism.* ▸see THESAURUS box at **prejudice¹** **2** the belief that different races of people have different characters and abilities, and that the qualities of your own race are the best

rac·ist /ˈreɪsɪst/ *adj.* believing that people of your own race are better than others, and treating people of other races unfairly: *racist comments* —**racist** *n.* [C]

rack¹ /ræk/ S3 *n.* [C] **1** something that you use for storing or hanging things on, usually a small frame with shelves, bars, or hooks: *a spice rack* | *a bicycle rack* | **a book/magazine/newspaper rack** *Celia stood in front of the magazine rack.* → see also LUGGAGE RACK, ROOF-RACK **2** a wire shelf that you put food on while it cooks or while it gets cool **3 a rack of lamb/ribs** a fairly large piece of meat from the side of an animal **4 the rack** a piece of equipment used in the past to make people suffer severe pain by stretching their bodies **5** a three-sided frame used for arranging the balls at the start of a game of POOL **6 go to rack/wrack and ruin** to gradually get into a very bad condition as a result of not being taken care of **7 off the rack** if you buy clothing off the rack, you buy it in a store rather than having it specially made → see also OFF-THE-RACK [**Origin:** (1, 2, 4, 5) 1300–1400 Middle Dutch *rec* **frame**]

rack

spice rack

rack² *v.* **1** another spelling of WRACK → see also NERVE-RACKING **2** [T] also **rack up** to put the balls in the rack at the beginning of a game of POOL

rack sth ↔ **up** *phr. v.* INFORMAL to increase the number or amount of points, experiences, debt etc. that you have over a period of time: *Mullin racked up 41 points in last night's game.*

ˌrack-and-ˈpinion ˌsteering *n.* [U] TECHNICAL a type of system for STEERING a car, truck etc. that uses special bars and COGS

rack·et /ˈrækɪt/ *n.* **1** [singular] INFORMAL a lot of loud noises: *Would you stop that racket, please?* **2** [C] a piece of equipment used for hitting the ball in games such as tennis, consisting of a stick with a net in a round frame: *a tennis racket* **3** [C] a dishonest way of obtaining money, such as by threatening people or selling them illegal goods: *an international smuggling racket* → see also PROTECTION RACKET **4** [C] INFORMAL a job, especially one in which you make a lot of money easily: *the advertising racket* [**Origin:** (2) 1500–1600 French *raquette*, from Italian *racchetta*, from Arabic *rahah* **front of the hand**]

rack·et·eer /ˌrækəˈtɪr/ *n.* [C] someone who is involved in a dishonest method of obtaining money

rack·et·eer·ing /ˌrækəˈtɪrɪŋ/ *n.* [U] the crime of obtaining money dishonestly by means of a carefully planned system

rac·on·teur /ˌrækɑnˈtɚ/ *n.* [C] someone who is good at telling stories in an interesting and amusing way SYN **storyteller**

ra·coon /ræˈkun/ another spelling of RACCOON

rac·quet /ˈrækɪt/ the British and Canadian spelling of RACKET

rac·quet·ball /ˈrækɪtˌbɔl/ *n.* [U] an indoor game in which two players use RACKETS to hit a small rubber ball against the four walls of the court

rac·y /ˈreɪsi/ *adj.* *comparative* **racier**, *superlative* **raciest** racy speech, writing, clothing etc. is exciting and entertaining, usually because it involves sex: *a racy underwear ad* —**racily** *adv.* —**raciness** *n.* [U]

ra·dar /ˈreɪdɑr/ *n.* [C,U] a method of finding the position of things such as airplanes or MISSILES by sending out radio waves: *The planes are invisible to enemy radar.*

ˈradar deˌtector *n.* [C] a piece of electronic equipment that can be used in a car to tell you whether police are using RADAR to check how fast you are driving

ˈradar ˌscreen *n.* **1** [C] a screen that shows where other things such as planes and ships are by using radar **2 the radar screen** a situation in which something is noticed or considered important: *Six years ago, the company wasn't even* ***on the radar screen.***

ˈradar trap *n.* [C] a situation in which police use radar to catch drivers who are going faster than the legal speed

ra·di·al /ˈreɪdiəl/ *adj.* arranged in a circular shape with bars, lines etc. coming from the center: *a spider web's radial framework*

ˌradial ˈsymmetry *n.* [U] BIOLOGY a feature of the shape of some animals, which means that if you cut them through the middle from top to bottom, the two halves of the body will be the same

ˌradial ˈtire also **radial** INFORMAL *n.* [C] a car tire with wires inside the rubber that go completely around the wheel to make it stronger and safer

ra·di·an /ˈreɪdiən/ *n.* [C] MATH a unit for measuring angles. A radian is equal to the angle at the center of a circle with an ARC (=curved part) that is the same length as the RADIUS (=distance from the center to the edge of a circle).

ra·di·ance /ˈreɪdiəns/ *n.* [U] **1** great happiness, health, or energy that shows in the way someone looks: *the radiance of her smile* **2** a soft light that shines from or onto something: *the moon's radiance*

ra·di·ant /ˈreɪdiənt/ *adj.* **1** full of happiness and love, in a way that shows in your face, eyes etc.: *a radiant bride* **2** [only before noun] LITERARY very bright **3** TECHNICAL [only before noun] radiant heat, energy etc. is sent out by radiation —**radiantly** *adv.*: *radiantly beautiful*

ra·di·ate /ˈreɪdiˌeɪt/ *v.* **1** [I always + adv./prep.,T] if someone radiates a feeling or quality, or if it radiates from them, they show it or feel it in a way that is easy to notice: *Syd radiates warmth as he greets his guests.* | **+from** *Tension radiated from his body.* **2** [I always + adv./prep., T] PHYSICS if something radiates light or heat, or if light or heat radiates from something, it is sent out in all directions: *The log fire radiated a cozy glow.* | **+from/out etc.** *We depend on the energy that radiates from the sun.* **3** [I always + adv./prep.] to spread out from a central point SYN **spread**: **+from** *A web of boulevards radiates from the traffic circle.*

ra·di·a·tion /ˌreɪdiˈeɪʃən/ *n.* PHYSICS **1** [U] a form of energy that comes from changes in the NUCLEAR structure of substances such as URANIUM or RADIUM, which is very harmful to living things if present in large amounts: *Sensors detected a dangerous level of radiation.* | *The tumors are treated with radiation.* **2** [U] energy in the form of heat or light sent out as beams that you cannot see: *solar radiation* **3** [U] the process of giving off heat or energy in the form of RAYS or waves, or heat or energy that is given off in this way → see also CONDUCTION **4** [C,U] the action or process of spreading out from a central position: *Clouds prevent the radiation of Earth's warmth into space.*

radiˈation ˌsickness *n.* [U] MEDICINE an illness caused by your body receiving too much radiation

ra·di·a·tor /ˈreɪdiˌeɪt̬ɚ/ *n.* [C] **1** a thing used for heating a room, consisting of a hollow metal container attached to a wall, through which hot water passes **2** the part of a car or aircraft which stops the engine from getting too hot

rad·i·cal¹ /ˈrædɪkəl/ Ac *adj.* **1** a radical change or way of doing something is extremely new and different and often changes something completely: *a radical reform of the tax system* | *a radical decision* **2** POLITICS radical opinions, ideas, leaders etc. support thorough and complete social or political change: *a radical leftist group* | *radical views* **3** important or serious: *Radical differences within the group began to appear.* **4** SLANG very good or enjoyable —**radically** /-kli/ *adv.*

radical² Ac *n.* [C] **1** POLITICS someone who wants thorough and complete social and political change **2** MATH a mathematical ROOT of another number or quantity → see also FREE RADICAL —**radicalism** *n.* [U]

ˌradical eˈquation *n.* [C] MATH an EQUATION containing a radical expression, especially when the radical expression includes a VARIABLE

ˌradical exˈpression *n.* [C] MATH a mathematical expression (=numbers and letters that are being added, subtracted, multiplied, or divided) containing a radical sign

ˌradical ˈfunction *n.* [C] MATH a mathematical FUNCTION (=quantity that changes according to how another mathematical quantity changes) that has a variable under a radical sign, such as $y = \sqrt{x} - 3$

rad·i·cal·ize /ˈrædɪkəˌlaɪz/ *v.* [T] to make a system or idea more extreme, or to make someone want complete social or political change

ˈradical ˌsign *n.* [C] MATH a mathematical sign (√) that shows that you must find the SQUARE ROOT of the quantity after the sign, or if there is an INDEX (=small raised number) before the sign, it shows which ROOT you must find, for example $\sqrt[3]{}$ means that you must find the CUBE ROOT because the index is 3

rad·i·cand /ˈrædɪˌkænd/ *n.* [C] MATH the number or mathematical expression (=numbers and letters representing numbers that are being added, subtracted, multiplied, or divided) that appears after or inside a radical sign, for example $\sqrt{3}$

ra·dic·chi·o /ræˈdikioʊ/ *n.* [U] a type of plant used in SALADS, that is red and has a bitter taste

rad·i·i /ˈreɪdiaɪ/ *n.* the plural of RADIUS

ra·di·o¹ /ˈreɪdiˌoʊ/ S1 W1 *n. plural* **radios** **1** [C] a piece of electronic equipment which you use to listen to programs that are broadcast, such as music and news: *a car radio* | **turn a radio on/off/up/down** *Can you turn your radio down a little bit?* **2 the radio** ENG. LANG. ARTS programs that are broadcast on the radio, considered in general: *How often do you* ***listen to the radio?*** | *I heard the news* ***on the radio.*** **3** [U] ENG. LANG. ARTS the business or activity of making and broadcasting programs which can be heard on a radio: *a career in radio* | **local/national radio** (=programs or companies broadcasting for a local area, or for the whole country) | *a radio personality* | *a radio station* **4** [C,U] a piece of equipment used for sending and receiving spoken messages, or the system that uses this equipment: *a police radio* | *We reached them* ***by radio.*** | *radio contact* [**Origin:** 1900–2000 *radiotelegraphy* (19–21 centuries), from *radio-* + *telegraphy*]

radio² *v.* **radios, radioed, radioing** [I,T] to send a message using a radio: **radio (sb) for sth** *The ship radioed for help.* | **radio (sth) to sb** *I radioed the information back to headquarters.*

radio- /ˈreɪdioʊ/ *prefix* TECHNICAL **1** relating to energy that is sent out as beams: *a radiometer* (=used to measure the amount of energy sent out by something) | *radiography* (=the taking of X-RAYS) **2** relating to something that uses RADIO WAVES: *a radiogram* (=a message sent by radio) **3** relating to energy that comes from NUCLEAR REACTIONS: *radioactive elements*

ra·di·o·ac·tive /ˌreɪdioʊˈæktɪv◂/ *adj.* PHYSICS **1** a radioactive substance contains or produces RADIATION because some of its atoms are changing and decaying: *Plutonium is highly radioactive.* | *radioactive waste* **2** relating to or caused by RADIATION: *radioactive decay*

ˌradioactive ˈdating *n.* [U] SCIENCE a scientific method of calculating the age of a very old object by measuring the amount of a radioactive substance in it SYN **carbon dating**

ˌradioactive ˈwaste *n.* [U] SCIENCE harmful radioactive substances that remain after energy has been produced in a NUCLEAR REACTOR

ra·di·o·ac·tiv·i·ty /ˌreɪdioʊækˈtɪvət̬i/ *n.* [U] PHYSICS **1** the process by which radioactive substances send out RADIATION **2** the energy which is produced in this way: *Workers were exposed to high levels of radioactivity.*

ˈradio ˌbeacon *n.* [C] a station that sends out radio signals to help aircraft stay on the correct course

ra·di·o·car·bon dat·ing /ˌreɪdioʊkɑrbən ˈdeɪt̬ɪŋ/ *n.* [U] FORMAL → CARBON DATING

ˌradio-casˈsette ˌplayer *n.* [C] a piece of electronic equipment that contains both a radio and a CASSETTE DECK

ˌradio-conˈtrolled *adj.* **a radio-controlled airplane/car/vehicle** an airplane, car etc., or a toy copy of this, that is controlled from far away using radio signals

ra·di·o·gram /ˈreɪdioʊˌɡræm/ *n.* [C] a message sent by radio

ra·di·og·ra·pher /ˌreɪdiˈɑɡrəfɚ/ *n.* [C] someone whose job is to take X-RAY photographs of the inside of someone's body, or who treats people for illnesses using an X-ray machine

ra·di·og·ra·phy /ˌreɪdiˈɑɡrəfi/ *n.* [U] MEDICINE the process of taking X-RAY photographs of the inside of someone's body for medical purposes

ra·di·o·i·so·tope /ˌreɪdioʊˈaɪsəˌtoʊp/ *n.* [C] PHYSICS an ISOTOPE (=one of the different possible forms of a RADIOACTIVE atom)

ra·di·ol·o·gist /ˌreɪdiˈɑlədʒɪst/ *n.* [C] a doctor who is trained in the use of RADIATION to treat people

ra·di·ol·o·gy /ˌreɪdiˈɑlədʒi/ *n.* [U] PHYSICS the study and medical use of RADIATION

ˌradio ˈtelephone, radiotelephone *n.* [C] a telephone that works by sending and receiving radio signals

ˌradio ˈtelescope *n.* [C] SCIENCE a very large piece of equipment that receives and records the RADIO WAVES that come from stars and other objects in space

ra·di·o·ther·a·py /ˌreɪdioʊˈθɛrəpi/ *n.* [U] the treatment of illnesses using RADIATION —**radiotherapist** *n.* [C]

R

ˈradio ˌwave *n.* [C usually plural] PHYSICS a form of electric energy that can move through air or space

rad·ish /ˈrædɪʃ/ *n.* [C] a small vegetable whose red or white root is eaten raw and has a strong SPICY taste → see picture on page A35

ra·di·um /ˈreɪdiəm/ *n.* [U] SYMBOL **Ra** CHEMISTRY a rare metal that is an ELEMENT, is RADIOACTIVE, and is used in the treatment of diseases such as CANCER

ra·di·us /ˈreɪdiəs/ *n. plural* **radii** /-diaɪ/ [C] **1** MATH the distance from the center to the edge of a circle or round object: *The moon has a radius of approximately 1,737 kilometers.* **2 within a 10-mile/200-yard etc. radius** within a distance of 10 miles, 200 yards etc. in all directions from a particular place: *The bomb caused damage within a half-mile radius.* **3** TECHNICAL a line drawn straight out from the center of a circle or SPHERE to its edge **4** BIOLOGY the outer bone of the lower part of your arm → see also DIAMETER

ra·don /ˈreɪdɑn/ *n.* [U] SYMBOL **Rn** CHEMISTRY a RADIOACTIVE gas that is an ELEMENT and that can be dangerous in large amounts

R

rad·u·la /ˈrædʒʊlə/ *n.* [C] BIOLOGY a structure like a tongue in the mouth of some MOLLUSKS (=snails, slugs etc), that contains rows of small teeth and is used for getting food off surfaces

raf·fi·a /ˈræfiə/ *n.* [U] a soft substance like string that comes from the leaves of a PALM tree and is used for making baskets, hats, MATS etc.

raff·ish /ˈræfɪʃ/ *adj.* LITERARY behaving or dressing in a confident and cheerful way that shows no concern for what other people think but is still attractive —**raffishness** *n.* [U]

raf·fle¹ /ˈræfəl/ *n.* [C] a type of competition or game in which people buy numbered tickets and can win prizes

raffle² also **raffle off** *v.* [T] to offer something as a prize in a raffle: *They're raffling off a new car at the carnival.*

raft¹ /ræft/ *n.* [C] **1** a flat floating structure, usually made of pieces of wood tied together, used as a boat **2** a small flat rubber boat filled with air **3 a (whole) raft of sth** INFORMAL a large number of things or large amount of something: *The new car has won a raft of awards.* **4** a flat floating structure that you can sit on, jump from etc. when you are swimming

raft² *v.* [I,T] to travel by raft or carry things by raft

raf·ter /ˈræftɚ/ *n.* [C] **1** [usually plural] one of the large sloping pieces of wood that form the structure of a roof **2 be packed/filled to the rafters** to be very full of people or things **3** someone who travels on a raft

raft·ing /ˈræftɪŋ/ *n.* [U] the sport of traveling down a fast-flowing river in a rubber raft

rag¹ /ræg/ *n.*
1 CLOTH [C] a small piece of old cloth, for example one used for cleaning things: *Just get a rag and wipe it up.*
2 in rags wearing old torn clothes: *an old man in rags*
3 go from rags to riches to become very rich after starting your life very poor
4 NEWSPAPER [C] INFORMAL a newspaper that you think is of low quality: *the local rag*
5 MUSIC [C] ENG. LANG. ARTS a piece of RAGTIME music: *Maple Leaf Rag* → see also GLAD RAGS

rag² *v.* **ragged, ragging**
rag on sb *phr. v.* INFORMAL **1** to make jokes and laugh at someone in order to embarrass them **2** to criticize someone in an angry way

ra·ga /ˈrɑgə/ *n.* [C] ENG. LANG. ARTS **1** a piece of Indian music based on an ancient pattern of notes **2** one of the ancient patterns of notes that are used in Indian music

rag·a·muf·fin /ˈrægəˌmʌfɪn/ *n.* [C] LITERARY a dirty young child wearing torn clothes

rag·bag /ˈrægbæg/ *n.* **a ragbag of sth** a confused mixture of things that do not seem to go together or make sense

ˈrag doll *n.* [C] a soft DOLL made of cloth

rage¹ /reɪdʒ/ *n.* [C,U] **1** a strong feeling of anger that is not controlled: *Major Sanderson instantly* ***flew into a rage*** (=suddenly became very angry). | *She threw open the door* ***in a rage.*** | **shaking/trembling/quivering with rage** *I was literally shaking with rage when I heard the news.* **2 road/air etc. rage** a situation in which someone becomes extremely angry and violent while they are driving, sitting on a plane etc. **3 be (all) the rage** INFORMAL to be very popular and fashionable: *Short skirts are all the rage this spring.* **4 the rage for sth** the popularity of or desire for something: *the current rage for makeover shows* [**Origin:** 1200–1300 Old French, Latin *rabies* **anger, wildness**, from *rabere* **to be wild with anger**]

rage² *v.* [I] **1** if something rages, such as a battle, disagreement, or storm, it continues with great violence or strong emotions: *Outside, a storm was raging.* | *The debate* ***rages on.*** **2** LITERARY to feel very angry about something and show this in the way you behave or speak: **+at/about/against** *He raged against the injustice of his situation.*

rag·ged /ˈrægɪd/ *adj.*
1 TORN torn and in bad condition: *ragged clothes*
2 PERSON wearing clothes that are old and torn: *crowds of ragged children*
3 UNEVEN not straight or neat, but with rough uneven edges: *the island's ragged coastline*
4 TIRED tired after using a lot of effort: *The kids have been* ***running me ragged.***
5 NOT DONE WELL not done in a smooth, well-organized and carefully planned way: *a ragged performance*
6 IRREGULAR not happening or done in a regular way: *ragged breathing* —**raggedly** *adv.* —**raggedness** *n.* [U]

rag·ged·y /ˈrægədi/ *adj.* OLD-FASHIONED **1** torn and in bad condition: *raggedy gloves* **2** not straight or neat, but with rough uneven edges: *raggedy hair*

rag·ing /ˈreɪdʒɪŋ/ *adj.* **1** [only before noun] involving or consisting of feelings and emotions that are very strong and difficult to control: *a raging thirst* | *a raging headache* | *a teenager's raging hormones* **2 raging stream/torrent/waters** water that flows fast and with a lot of force

rag·lan /ˈræglən/ *adj.* if a coat, SWEATER etc. has raglan SLEEVES, the sleeves are joined with a sloping line from the arm to the neck

ra·gout /ræˈgu/ *n.* [C,U] a mixture of vegetables and meat boiled together SYN **stew**

rag·tag /ˈrægtæg/ *adj.* **1** disorganized and not working well together: *a ragtag army of rebel soldiers* **2** looking messy, poor, and dirty: *a ragtag refugee camp*

rag·time /ˈrægtaɪm/ *n.* [U] a type of music and dancing with a quick RHYTHM that was popular in the early part of the 20th century

rag·weed /ˈrægwid/ *n.* [U] a North American plant that produces a substance which causes HAY FEVER

rah-rah¹ /ˈrɑrɑ/ *adj.* INFORMAL, DISAPPROVING **1** supporting something without thinking about it enough: *rah-rah patriotism* **2** used to describe someone who tries to encourage people by saying only positive things

rah-rah² *interjection* an expression used in some CHEERS (=shouts of encouragement) at a sports game, or the written expression of what a crowd at a sports game sounds like

raid¹ /reɪd/ *n.* [C] **1** a quick attack on a place by soldiers, airplanes, or ships, intended to cause damage but not take control: *a bombing raid* | **+on/against** *a surprise raid on the naval base* | **carry out/launch a raid** *Allied forces carried out a successful raid on the port.* ►see THESAURUS box at **attack¹** **2** a sudden visit by the police searching for something illegal: **+on** *a police raid on the house of a suspected drug dealer* **3** DISAPPROVING an act of taking and using money that should be used for something else, especially money that belongs to a company or government: *corporate raids of company pension funds* **4** TECHNICAL an attempt by a company to buy enough STOCK in another company to take control of it → see also AIR RAID, PANTY RAID

raid² *v.* [T] **1** if police raid a place, they go there suddenly to search for something illegal: *Armed police raided the house early Wednesday.* **2** to make a sudden attack on a place: *Troops raided rebel villages.* **3** to take or steal a lot of things from a place: *A gang of thieves raided a bank in Rome.* **4** HUMOROUS **raid the refrigerator/closet/pantry etc.** to take a lot of something from a REFRIGERATOR, CLOSET etc.

rail¹ /reɪl/ *n.* **1** [C] a bar that is attached along the side or on top of something such as stairs or a BALCONY: *Hold on to the rail as you walk up the stairs.* → see also RAILING **2** [C usually plural] one of the two long metal tracks attached to the ground that trains move along: *The train came off the rails.* **3** [U] travel by train: *Visitors can enter the city* ***by rail*** *or by boat.* | *rail travel* | *rail service* **4 go/run off the rails** if a system, plan, process etc. goes off the rails, it stops working the way it is supposed to: *The peace process is in danger of going off the rails.* **5 (as) thin/skinny as a rail** extremely thin

rail² *v.* [I] LITERARY to complain angrily about something, especially something that you think is very bad or unfair: **+against/at** *During his sermon, the priest railed against greed.*

rail·ing /ˈreɪlɪŋ/ *n.* [C] a fence consisting of a piece of wood or metal supported by upright posts, especially used on the sides stairs or the edge of a BALCONY → see also RAIL¹ (1)

rail·ler·y /ˈreɪləri/ *n.* [U] FORMAL friendly joking about someone

rail·road¹ /ˈreɪlroʊd/ *n.* [C] **1** a system of traveling or moving things by train: *The railroad is not as extensive as it once was.* | *a railroad track* **2** [C] a track for trains to travel on **3** a company that runs a railroad: *the Southern Pacific railroad* **4 the railroad** all the work, equipment etc. relating to a train system: *Smithers worked* ***on the railroad*** *for more than 50 years.*

railroad² *v.* [T] to force or persuade someone do something without giving them enough time to think about it: **railroad sb into doing sth** *The family says that they were railroaded into selling the land.*

railroad sth **through** (sth) *phr. v.* to make sure that something, especially a law, is decided quickly by an organization such as Congress without giving people time to discuss it thoroughly: *The bill was railroaded through Congress.*

ˈrailroad ˌcrossing *n.* [C] a place where a road and railroad tracks cross each other at the same level

ˈrailroad line *n.* [C] a part of the railroad system that connects two places: *the transcontinental railroad line*

ˈrailroad ˌstation *n.* [C] a TRAIN STATION

ˈrail trail *n.* [C] a path that used to be a railroad track but that has been covered with a hard surface for people to walk, run, or ride bicycles on

rail·way /ˈreɪlweɪ/ *n. plural* **railways** [C] ESPECIALLY CANADIAN, BRITISH a RAILROAD

rai·ment /ˈreɪmənt/ *n.* [U] LITERARY clothes

rain¹ /reɪn/ [S2] [W2] *n.* **1** [C,U] water that falls in small drops from clouds in the sky: *There's been no rain for weeks.* | *Let's wait here until the rain stops.* | *I left my bike out* ***in the rain.*** | ***It looks like rain*** (=it is probably going to rain) *– we'd better go inside.* | **(a) heavy/light rain** (=a large or small amount of rain) | *a rain cloud*

> **THESAURUS**
> **drizzle** light rain with very small drops of water: *a steady drizzle*
> **shower** a short period of rain: *a light shower*
> **downpour** a lot of rain that falls in a short period of time: *a heavy downpour*
> **storm** very bad weather with a lot of wind and rain: *The storm caused flooding.*
> **hail** frozen rain that falls in the form of **hailstones** (=small balls of ice): *a hail storm* | *The hail ruined the corn crop.*
> **sleet** a mixture of snow and rain: *It was cold, and the rain was mixed with sleet.*
> → SNOW, SUNSHINE, WEATHER, WIND

2 the rains [plural] heavy rain that falls during a particular period in the year in tropical countries → see also MONSOON: *The rains have started early this year.* **3 (come) rain or shine** whatever happens or whatever the weather is like: *Burrow runs two miles, rain or shine, everyday.* **4 a rain of arrows/comets/blows etc.** many ARROWS, COMETS etc. falling or coming down from above at the same time [**Origin:** Old English *regn*] → see also ACID RAIN, **(as) right as rain** at RIGHT¹ (13) **—rainless** *adj.*: *a rainless summer*

rain² [S2] *v.* **1** [I] if it rains, drops of water fall from clouds in the sky: *Is it still raining?* | *It rained all day.* | *It was raining hard.*

> **THESAURUS**
> **It's pouring (rain)** it's raining very heavily
> **It's drizzling** a small amount of rain is falling
> **It's sleeting** it's raining and snowing at the same time
> **It's hailing** small balls of ice are falling
> → WEATHER

2 be/get rained out if an event or activity is rained out, it has to stop because there is too much rain: *Yesterday's game was rained out.* **3 when it rains, it pours** SPOKEN used to say that as soon as one thing goes wrong, a lot of other things go wrong as well **4 it's raining cats and dogs** SPOKEN used to say that it is raining very hard **5 rain on sb's parade** if you rain on someone's parade, you say or do something that prevents them from enjoying something good that is happening to them

rain down *phr. v.* **rain sth ↔ down** if something rains down, or is rained down, it falls in large quantities: *The volcano rained down clouds of ash and sparks.* | **rain (sth) down on sb/sth** *Bombs rained down on the town.*

rain·bow /ˈreɪnboʊ/ *n.* [C] a large curve of different colors that can appear in the sky when there is both sun and rain

ˈrain check *n.* [C] **1 take a rain check (on sth)** SPOKEN used to say that you cannot accept an offer or an invitation now but you would like to at a later time: *I'm sorry but I'm busy on Saturday – can I take a rain check?* **2** a piece of paper which allows you to buy a particular product at a special price, given by a store when it does not have any more of the product **3** a ticket for an outdoor event, such as a sports game, that you can use later if rain stopped an event you were at

rain·coat /ˈreɪnkoʊt/ *n.* [C] a coat that you wear to protect yourself from the rain

ˈrain drop *n.* [C] a single drop of rain

rain·fall /ˈreɪnfɔl/ *n.* [C,U] EARTH SCIENCE the amount of rain that falls on an area in a particular period of time: *an annual rainfall of 2.4 inches*

ˈrain ˌforest *n.* [C] EARTH SCIENCE a tropical forest with tall trees that are very close together, growing in an area where it rains a lot: *the Brazilian rain forest*

ˈrain gauge *n.* [C] EARTH SCIENCE an instrument that is used for measuring the amount of rain that falls

Rai·nier, Mount /rəˈnɪr/ a mountain in the U.S. state of Washington which is the highest mountain in the Cascade Range

rain·mak·er /ˈreɪnˌmeɪkɚ/ *n.* [C] **1** someone who makes a lot of money for a company, usually by attracting rich customers **2** someone who claims to be able to make it rain

ˈrain ˌshadow *n.* [C] EARTH SCIENCE an area that is sheltered from the wind and rain by a large hill or mountain, and so gets less rain than the other side of the hill or mountain

rain·storm /ˈreɪnstɔrm/ *n.* [C] a sudden heavy fall of rain

rain·water /ˈreɪnˌwɔt̬ɚ/ *n.* [U] water that has fallen as rain

R

rain·wear /ˈreɪnwɛr/ *n.* [U] WATERPROOF clothes that you wear when it rains

rain·y /ˈreɪni/ *adj. comparative* **rainier**, *superlative* **rainiest** **1** a rainy period of time is one when it rains a lot: *a cold, rainy day* | *The first week was very rainy.* | ***The rainy season** lasts from January to April.* **2 save sth for a rainy day** also **put sth away/aside for a rainy day** to save something, especially money, for a time when you will need it

raise¹ /reɪz/ S1 W1 *v.* [T]
1 TO A HIGHER POSITION to move or lift something to a higher position, place, or level OPP **lower**: *She raised her glass to make a toast.* | *Roy's car raised a cloud of dust as he drove off.* | *I **raised** my **hand** to get her attention.*
2 INCREASE to increase an amount, number, or level SYN **increase** OPP **lower**: *Stores may have to raise prices.* | *Too much coffee can raise your blood pressure.*
3 CHILDREN to take care of your children and help them grow; bring up SYN **bring up** SYN **rear**: *She was raised by her grandparents.* | **raise sb Catholic/ Muslim etc.** *I was raised Catholic.* | *Were you **born and raised** in Alabama?*
4 IMPROVE to improve the quality or standard of something: *Efforts are being made to **raise** employee **morale**.* | *There's a lot of pressure on schools to **raise standards**.*
5 FARMING to grow plants or keep cows, pigs etc. so that they can be sold or used as food: *His sister raises horses in Colorado.* | *These pheasant are **raised on** a corn diet.*
6 raise (sb's) hopes/expectations to make someone hope or expect that something will be success: *I don't want to raise your hopes unnecessarily.*
7 raise consciousness/awareness to make people know and understand more about something: *We hope Stephen's story will raise awareness of mental illness.*
8 raise a subject/question/point/issue etc. **a)** to begin to talk or write about a subject that you want to be considered or a question that you think should be answered SYN **bring up**: *You've raised a number of interesting questions.* **b)** to cause people to start thinking about something: *Johnson's case also raises the issue of free speech.* ▸see THESAURUS box at **mention¹**
9 raise the bar to improve the standard of something so that it is more difficult to achieve a particular level: *The new hybrid has raised the bar for other car makers.*
10 COLLECT MONEY to collect money, support etc. so that you can use it to help people: *We raised nearly $2,000.*
11 raise your voice **a)** to speak loudly or shout because you are angry: *Stop raising your voice, Amanda.* **b)** to make your opinion known, especially when you do not approve of something: *Many voices were raised in dissent.*
12 EYES OR FACE to move your eyes or face so that you are looking up: *He raised his head and looked at her.*
13 raise yourself (up) to lift your body from a sitting position, or the upper part of your body from a lying position: *She raised herself up on her elbows and looked around sleepily.*
14 TO AN UPRIGHT POSITION to move or lift something into an upright position: *If you raise that metal bar, it turns off the ice maker.*
15 raise doubts/fears/suspicions etc. to cause a particular emotion or reaction: *The news raised concern among many in the district.*
16 raise (sb's) spirits to make someone feel less unhappy or worried
17 raise the specter of sth to make people feel afraid that something bad or frightening might soon happen
18 raise (a few) eyebrows to surprise or shock people → see also **raise your eyebrows** at EYEBROW (2)
19 raise Cain OLD-FASHIONED to behave in a wild noisy way that upsets other people
20 raise a smile **a)** to smile when you are not feeling happy **b)** to make someone smile when they are not feeling happy
21 raise your glass (to sb/sth) to celebrate the success or happiness of someone or something by holding up your glass and then drinking from it
22 CARD GAME to make a higher BID than an opponent in a card game
23 raise the alarm LITERARY to warn people about danger
24 BUILD FORMAL to build something such as a MONUMENT: *A statue was raised in memory of the dead.*
25 WAKE SB LITERARY to wake someone who is difficult to wake
26 raise sb from the dead/grave also **raise the dead** BIBLICAL to make someone who has died live again
27 raise the roof INFORMAL **a)** to make a very loud noise when singing, celebrating etc. **b)** to act in a very angry way about something
28 ARMY OLD-FASHIONED to collect together a group of people, especially soldiers: *The rebels quickly **raised an army**.*
29 raise 2/4/10 etc. to the power of 2/3/4 etc. TECHNICAL to multiply a number by itself a particular number of times
[**Origin:** 1100–1200 Old Norse *reisa*]

raise² *n.* [C] an increase in the money you earn: *Why not ask for a raise?* | *Ted got a 10% raise.*

rai·sin /ˈreɪzən/ *n.* [C] a dried GRAPE [**Origin:** 1300–1400 French **grape**, from Latin *racemus* **bunch of grapes**]

rai·son d'ê·tre /ˌreɪzoʊn ˈdɛtrə, -zɑn-/ *n.* [C] the reason something exists, why someone does something etc.

ra·jah, raja /ˈrɑdʒə, -dʒɑ/ *n.* [C] the king or ruler of an Indian state in the past

rake¹ /reɪk/ *n.* **1** [C] a tool with a row of metal teeth at the end of a long handle, used for making soil level, gathering up dead leaves etc. **2** [C] OLD-FASHIONED a man who behaves in an unacceptable way, having many sexual relationships, drinking too much alcohol etc. **3** [C] a stick used by a CROUPIER for gathering in the CHIPS at a table where games are played for money **4** [singular] the angle of a slope: *the rake of the stage*

rake

rake² *v.* **1** also **rake up** [I,T] to move a rake across a surface in order to make the soil level, gather dead leaves etc.: *Her husband was outside raking leaves.* **2** [I always + adv./prep.] to search a place very carefully for something: **+through/around** *I've been raking through my drawers looking for those tickets.* **3** [T] FORMAL **a)** to fire bullets, shells etc. over a wide area by slowly moving a gun so that it points from one side to another: *Guerrillas raked the room with gunfire.* **b)** to affect a wide area by moving a camera, a strong light, your eyes etc. across that area **4 rake sb over the coals** to criticize someone severely for something they have done **5 rake your fingers/nails** to pull your fingers or nails through something or across a surface: *Ken **raked his fingers through** his hair.* **6 rake (the) ashes/coals** to push a stick backward and forward in a fire in order to make the fire go out

rake sth ↔ **in** *phr. v.* INFORMAL to earn a lot of money without trying very hard: *He rakes in about $5,000 a week.* | *The movie is still **raking it in** at the box office.*

rake sth ↔ **up** *phr. v.* INFORMAL to talk about something from the past that people would rather not remember SYN **dredge up**

rak·ish /ˈreɪkɪʃ/ *adj.* **1** making you look relaxed, confident, and stylish, or looking this way: *He wore his hat **at a rakish angle**.* **2** OLD-FASHIONED a rakish man behaves in an unacceptable way, having many sexual relationships, wasting money, drinking too much alcohol etc. —**rakishly** *adv.*

Ra·leigh /ˈrɔli, ˈrɑ-/ the capital city of the U.S. state of North Carolina

Raleigh, Sir Wal·ter /ˈwɔltɚ/ (?1552–1618) an

English EXPLORER who made several trips to North and South America and later wrote books about them

ral·ly¹ /ˈræli/ *v.* **rallies, rallied, rallying** **1** [I,T] to come together or bring people together to support an idea, a political party etc.: *Abrams tried to **rally support** for the plan from Congress.* | **rally to sb's defense/support/aid** *Republicans rallied to the president's defense.* **2** [I] to become stronger again after a period of weakness or defeat: *Stock prices rallied on Monday.* **3** [I,T] if a group of soldiers rally or someone rallies them, they come back together after being scattered

rally around *phr. v.* **rally around sb/sth** if a group of people rally around, they all try to help you in a difficult situation: *Her friends all rallied around when she was sick.*

rally² W3 *n. plural* **rallies** [C] **1** POLITICS a large public meeting, especially one that is held outdoors to support a political idea, protest etc.: *a pro-democracy rally* | *They're **holding a rally** downtown tomorrow.* → see also PEP RALLY **2** a car race on public roads: *the Monte Carlo Rally* **3** an occasion when something becomes stronger again after a period of weakness or defeat: *There was a late rally on the stock exchange.* **4** a series of hits of the ball between players in games like tennis [**Origin:** 1500–1600 French *rallier* **to reunite**, from Old French *alier*]

ˈrallying ˌcry *n. plural* **rallying cries** [C] a word or phrase used to unite people in support of an idea

ˈrallying ˌpoint *n.* [C] an idea, event, person etc. that makes people come together to support something they believe in

RAM /ræm/ *n.* [U] **random access memory** COMPUTERS the part of a computer that keeps information temporarily so that it can be used immediately → see also ROM

ram¹ /ræm/ *v.* **rammed, ramming** **1** [I always + adv./prep., T] to run or drive into something very hard: *Hancock tried to ram the police car.* | **+into** *The truck rammed into her car.* **2** [T always + adv./prep.] to push something into a position using great force: **ram sth into sth** *Ram the posts into the ground.* **3 ram sth down sb's throat** DISAPPROVING to try to make someone accept an idea or opinion by repeating it again and again, especially when they are not interested **4 ram sth home, ram home sth** to make sure someone fully understands something by emphasizing it and by providing a lot of examples, proof etc.: *We've got to ram this message home.*

ram² *n.* [C] **1** BIOLOGY an adult male sheep → see also EWE **2** a BATTERING RAM **3** TECHNICAL a machine that hits something again and again to force it into a position

Ram·a·dan /ˈrɑməˌdɑn/ *n.* [U] the ninth month of the Muslim year, during which Muslims are not allowed to eat or drink during the hours of daylight [**Origin:** 1500–1600 Arabic *ramad* **dryness**]

Ra·ma·ya·na /rəˈmɑyənə/ *n.* [singular] a long poem written in SANSKRIT that is very important in Indian Literature. It tells the story of Prince Rama, and contains the teachings of Hindu wise men.

ram·ble¹ /ˈræmbəl/ *v.* [I] **1** to talk for a long time in a way that does not seem to be clearly organized, with the result that other people find it hard to understand you: *She's getting old and she tends to ramble a little.* **2** [always + adv./prep.] to go on a walk for pleasure, especially without a particular plan **3** if a plant rambles, it grows in all directions

ramble on *phr. v.* to talk or write for a long time in a way that other people find boring: **ramble on about sb/sth** *My father was rambling on about his job.*

ramble² *n.* [C] **1** a long walk for pleasure **2** a speech or piece of writing that is very long and does not seem to be clearly organized

ram·bler /ˈræmblɚ/ *n.* [C] a rose bush that grows in many different directions

ram·bling /ˈræmblɪŋ/ *adj.* **1** a rambling building has an irregular shape and covers a large area: *a rambling old farmhouse* **2** a rambling speech or writing is very long and does not seem to have any clear organization or purpose: *a long rambling letter* **3** a rambling rose grows in all directions, usually up a support of some kind

ram·bunc·tious /ræmˈbʌŋkʃəs/ *adj.* noisy, full of energy, and behaving in a way that cannot be controlled: *two rambunctious boys* —**rambunctiously** *adv.* —**rambunctiousness** *n.* [U]

ram·e·kin /ˈræmɪkən, ˈræmkən/ *n.* [C] a small dish in which food for one person can be baked and served

Ram·e·ses II /ˌræməsiz ðə ˈsɛkənd/ also **ˌRameses the ˈGreat** the king of Egypt from about 1292 to 1225 B.C.

ram·ie /ˈreɪmi, ˈræ-/ *n.* [C,U] a plant from which cloth is made, or the cloth itself

ram·i·fi·ca·tion /ˌræməfəˈkeɪʃən/ *n.* [C usually plural] FORMAL a result or effect of something you do, which may not have expected when you first decided to do it: **legal/political/social etc. ramifications** *the legal ramifications of the case*

ram·i·fy /ˈræməˌfaɪ/ *v.* **ramifies, ramified, ramifying** [I] FORMAL to spread out and form a system or network

ramp¹ /ræmp/ *n.* [C] **1** a slope that has been built to connect two places that are at different levels: *a wheelchair ramp* **2** a road for driving onto or off a large main road: **an off-ramp/on-ramp** *Take the Lake Herman Road on-ramp to Interstate 80.* **3** a moveable STAIRCASE that is used by passengers to get onto or leave an aircraft

ramp² *v.*

ramp down sth *phr. v.* to decrease the amount or quantity of something

ramp up *phr. v.* **ramp sth ↔ up** to start happening more quickly, or to make something do this: *Two new steel mills are ramping up production.*

ram·page¹ /ˈræmpeɪdʒ/ *n.* [C] an occasion when a person or a group rushes around in a wild and violent way, causing damage: *a shooting rampage* | *Rioters **went on a rampage** through the city.*

ram·page² /ræmˈpeɪdʒ, ˈræmpeɪdʒ/ *v.* [I] to rush about in groups wildly or violently, causing damage: **+through** *Anti-government demonstrators rampaged through the capital today.*

ramp·ant /ˈræmpənt/ *adj.* **1** something such as crime or disease that is rampant is bad, happens often in many different places, and is difficult to control: *rampant inflation* | *The drug problem continues to **run rampant**.* **2** BIOLOGY a rampant plant grows and spreads in a way that is not controlled **3** TECHNICAL a rampant figure in HERALDRY is standing on one of its back legs [**Origin:** 1300–1400 French, present participle of *ramper* **to climb, crawl**] —**rampantly** *adv.*

ram·part /ˈræmpɑrt/ *n.* [C usually plural] a wide pile of earth or a stone wall built to protect a castle or city in the past

ram·rod¹ /ˈræmrɑd/ *n.* [C] **1** a stick for pushing GUNPOWDER into an old-fashioned gun, or for cleaning a small gun **2** someone who tries very hard to make someone or a group of people do something or agree with something

ramrod² *adv.* **ramrod straight/stiff** sitting or standing with your back straight and your body stiff —**ramrod** *adj.*: *ramrod posture*

ram·shack·le /ˈræmˌʃækəl/ *adj.* a ramshackle building or vehicle is in bad condition and in need of repair: *a row of ramshackle houses*

ran /ræn/ *v.* the past tense of RUN

ranch /ræntʃ/ *n.* [C] **1** a very large farm in the western U.S. and Canada where sheep, cattle, or horses are raised: *a cattle ranch* **2** a RANCH HOUSE: *a four-bedroom ranch* [**Origin:** 1800–1900 Mexican Spanish *rancho*, from Spanish, **camp, small building, small farm**] → see also **bet the ranch/farm** at BET¹ (6)

ˈranch ˌdressing *n.* [U] a type of SALAD DRESSING, made from YOGURT

R

ranch·er /ˈræntʃɚ/ *n.* [C] someone who owns or is in charge of a ranch: *a cattle rancher*

ˈranch house *n.* [C] **1** a long, narrow house built on one level, usually with a roof that does not slope much **2** a house on a ranch, in which the rancher lives

ranch·ing /ˈræntʃɪŋ/ *n.* [U] the activity or business of operating a ranch

ran·cid /ˈrænsɪd/ *adj.* food that is rancid smells or tastes very bad because the oil or fat in it is not fresh anymore: *rancid butter* —**rancidity** /rænˈsɪdət̬i/ *n.* [U]

ran·cor /ˈræŋkɚ/ *n.* [U] FORMAL a feeling of hatred or anger toward someone, when you cannot forgive them: *He spoke about the war* ***without*** *any* ***rancor****.* —**rancorous** *adj.* —**rancorously** *adv.*

rand /rænd/ *n. plural* **rand** [C] the standard unit of money in South Africa [**Origin:** 1900–2000 The *Rand*, gold-mining area of South Africa]

Rand /rænd/, **Ayn** /aɪn/ (1905–1982) a U.S. writer of NOVELS

R

R & B /ˌɑr ən ˈbi/ *n.* [U] **1** modern popular music which developed from the SOUL and FUNK music of the 1960s and '70s **2 rhythm and blues** a style of popular music in the 1940s and '50s that was a mixture of BLUES and JAZZ and developed into ROCK 'N' ROLL

R & D /ˌɑr ən ˈdi/ *n.* [U] **research and development** the part of a business concerned with studying new ideas and planning new products

R & R /ˌɑr ən ˈɑr/ *n.* [U] **rest and relaxation** a vacation given to people in the army, navy etc. after a long period of hard work or during a war

ran·dom /ˈrændəm/ Ac *adj.* **1** happening, appearing, or chosen without any definite plan, aim, or pattern: *random drug tests* | *The attack appears to have been completely random.* **2 at random** if something is done or happens at random, it does so without any definite plan, aim, or pattern: *We selected the agencies at random from the phone book.* [**Origin:** 1300–1400 Old French *randon* **great speed or force**, from *randir* **to run**] —**randomly** *adv.* —**randomness** *n.* [U]

ˌrandom ˈaccess ˌmemory *n.* [C,U] COMPUTERS RAM

ˌrandom ˈvariable *n.* [C] MATH a VARIABLE (=mathematical quantity that is not fixed and can be any of several amounts) whose value cannot be known certainly, but can be described using PROBABILITY

rang /ræŋ/ *v.* the past tense of RING

range¹ /reɪndʒ/ Ac W2 *n.*

1 GROUP [C, usually singular] a number of things which are all different, but of the same general type: **+of** *Herbs provide a range of aromas and flavors for cooking.* | *We teach the full range of ballroom dances.* | **a wide/broad range of sth** *The party is trying to appeal to a broader range of voters.*

2 NUMBER LIMITS [C] the limits within which amounts, quantities, ages etc. can vary: **age/price etc. range** *Sandwiches come in three sizes and price ranges.* | **in the range of sth** *Starting salaries are in the range of $28,000 to $38,000.* | **beyond/out of sb's range** (=more than someone's limit on price, age etc.)

3 LIMITS TO POWER/ACTIVITY [C] the amount of power or area of responsibility that a person or organization has, or the types of activities they are allowed to do: **+of** *Companies with under 20 employees were outside the range of our survey.*

4 DISTANCE a) [singular, U] the distance within which something can be seen or heard: **+of** *Voice radio has a range of about 100 miles.* | *We just want to get* ***within range*** *to use our binoculars.* | *Make sure towels and shower curtains are* ***out of range*** (=too far away to reach, hear etc.) *of the spray.* | *The walls appear smooth except* ***at close range*** (=very near). **b)** [singular, U] the distance over which a particular weapon can hit things: *What's the gun's range?* | **+of** *missiles with a range of 500 miles* | *Once* ***within range*** (=near enough to hit) *of the target, the plane will drop the bomb.* | *Until the attack began, allied forces stayed* ***out of range*** (=too far away to hit) *of enemy artillery.* | **at close/point-blank/short range** (=from very close) | **long-/short-range missile** *a Pershing short range missile* **c)** [C] the distance which a vehicle such as an airplane can travel before it needs more fuel etc.: **+of** *The Type-2 boat has a range of 4000 miles.*

5 PRODUCTS [C] a set of similar products made by a particular company or available in a particular store: *Sansui planned to broaden its product range to include video equipment.*

6 MUSIC [C usually singular] ENG. LANG. ARTS all the musical notes that a particular singer or musical instrument can make: *Williams is blessed with a 2¼-octave range.*

7 ABILITY [C,U] someone's area of ability, especially as an actor or actress: *an actor of extraordinary range and intensity*

8 MOUNTAINS [C] EARTH SCIENCE a group of mountains or hills, usually in a line: *the Hajar mountain range*

9 PRACTICE WITH WEAPONS [C] an area of land where you can practice using weapons: *a rifle range* → see also DRIVING RANGE

10 LAND [C,U] a large area of land covered with grass, which cattle can eat → see also FREE-RANGE

11 COOKING [C] a STOVE: *a gas range*

12 DATA [C] MATH a measure of the difference between the largest and smallest quantities in a set of data

13 MATH [C] all the different possible values that can be produced by a mathematical FUNCTION (=relation between two mathematical quantities in which one quantity changes according to how the other quantity changes) → see also DOMAIN

[**Origin:** 1200–1300 Old French *renge*, from *rengier*, from *renc*, *reng* **line, place, row**]

range² Ac W3 *v.*

1 INCLUDE [I always + adv./prep.] **a)** if prices, levels, temperatures etc. range from one amount to another, they include both those amounts and anything in between: **range from sth to sth** *The five men are serving prison sentences ranging from 35 to 105 years.* | **range between sth and sth** *Ticket prices range between $12 and $14.* | **range in age/size etc.** (=include many different ages, sizes etc.) **b)** to include a variety of different feelings, actions etc.: **range from sth to sth** *His expression ranges from a painful grimace to a slight smile.*

2 AREA OF LAND [I always + adv./prep.] to move around in or cover an area of land: **+over/through** *Experts say a single mountain lion can range over as much as 64,000 acres.*

3 INCLUDE MANY SUBJECTS [I] to deal with a wide range of subjects or ideas in a book, speech, conversation etc.: **range over sth** *The show ranges over many settings, from 18th-century sailing ships to concert halls.* → see also WIDE-RANGING

4 be ranged FORMAL to be in a particular order or position: *A group of sullen men were ranged along the bar.*

5 be ranged against sth FORMAL to publicly state your opposition to a particular group's beliefs and ideas: *Ranged against the fundamentalists are dozens of political parties.*

range·find·er /ˈreɪndʒˌfaɪndɚ/ *n.* [C] an instrument for finding the distance of an object when firing a weapon or taking photographs

rang·er /ˈreɪndʒɚ/ *n.* [C] **1** someone who is in charge of protecting a forest or area of COUNTRYSIDE: *a park ranger* **2** a police officer in past times, who rode on a horse through country areas **3** a soldier who has been specially trained to make quick attacks

Ran·goon /ræŋˈgun/ the capital and largest city of Myanmar (Burma)

rank¹ /ræŋk/ W3 *n.*

1 POSITION IN ARMY/ORGANIZATION [C,U] the position or level that someone holds in an organization, especially in the police or armed forces: **+of** *officers below the rank of colonel* | **high/senior/low/junior rank** *an officer of fairly high rank* | *He had* ***risen to the rank of*** *major.* | *He steadily* ***rose through the ranks*** (=moved repeatedly to increasingly higher ranks) *of the law firm.* | *He was hauled before a court martial and* ***stripped of his rank*** (=had his rank taken away from him).

THESAURUS

senior used about someone who has an important position in an organization: *a senior White House official*
chief used, especially in job titles, about someone who has the most important or one of the most important positions in an organization: *the company's chief financial officer*
high-ranking used about someone who has a high position in an organization such as the police, the army, or the government: *a high-ranking officer*
top used about someone who is in a very high position in a large company or organization, or someone who is very good, important, or successful in his or her job: *a top administration official* | *one of the country's top chefs*
junior used about someone who has a low or lower position in an organization: *the junior congressman from Mississippi*
assistant an assistant manager, director, editor etc. has a position just below a manager etc.: *the store's assistant manager*

2 the ranks a) the people who belong to an organization or group: **+of** *the ranks of the urban poor* | **in/within the ranks of sb/sth** *The Republicans now face opposition from within their own ranks.* | *A further 450 workers are due to* ***join the ranks*** *of the jobless.* **b)** all the members of the armed forces who are not officers: *He* ***rose from the ranks*** *to become a Field Marshal.*
3 close ranks if the people in a group close ranks, they join together to support each other against other people, especially when there are problems
4 break ranks (with sb) to stop supporting a group that you are a member of: *Two Republicans broke ranks with the party to vote with Democrats.*
5 pull rank (on sb) to use your authority over someone to make them do what you want, especially unfairly: *My boss never pulled rank on me.*
6 LINE [C] a line of people or things: *ranks of empty desks in the classroom* | *The police* ***broke ranks*** (=got out of their lines) *and moved into the crowd.*
7 of the first rank of the highest quality: *an actor of the first rank*
8 SOCIAL CLASS [C,U] someone's position in society: *people of all ranks in society*
[**Origin:** 1300–1400 Old French *renc*, *reng* **line, place, row**] → see also RANK AND FILE

rank² *v.* **1 a)** [I always + adv./prep.] to have a particular position in a list of people or things that are put in order of quality or importance: **rank high/low/first/fourth etc.** *The team has ranked near the bottom of the NFL for two seasons.* | **rank as sth** *It ranks as one of the ten largest drug companies in the world.* | **rank among sb/sth** *We rank among the safest countries in the world.* → see also HIGH-RANKING, TOP-RANKING **b)** [T] to decide the position of someone or something on a list, based on quality or importance: **rank sb/sth fourth/number one etc.** *Mexico's team is ranked 11th in the world.* | **rank sb/sth in order (of sth)** *It was hard to rank the students in order of ability.* **2** [T] to have a higher rank than someone else SYN **outrank**: *A general ranks a captain.*

rank³ *adj.* **1** [only before noun] complete SYN **total**: *There were a few rank beginners in the class.* | *rank hypocrisy* **2** having a very strong and bad smell or taste: *the rank odor of old sweat* —**rankly** *adv.* —**rankness** *n.* [U]

ˌrank and ˈfile *n.* **the rank and file** the ordinary members of an organization rather than the leaders: *The policy will now have to be approved by the rank and file.* —**rank-and-file** *adj.* [only before noun] *rank-and-file members of the union*

Ran·kin /ˈræŋkɪn/, **Jean·nette** /dʒɪˈnɛt/ (1880–1973) a U.S. woman who helped women get the right to vote and was the first woman member of the U.S. House of Representatives

rank·ing¹ /ˈræŋkɪŋ/ *n.* [C] a position on a scale that shows how good someone or something is when compared with others: *She is now fifth in the world rankings.*

ranking² *adj.* [only before noun] a ranking person has the highest position in an organization: *the ship's ranking officer*

ran·kle /ˈræŋkəl/ *v.* [I,T] if something rankles or rankles you, it makes you very annoyed or angry: *His casual style of dress rankled his superiors.*

ran·sack /ˈrænsæk/ *v.* [T] **1** to go through a place stealing things and causing damage: *Roth's home had been ransacked by burglars.* **2** to search a place very thoroughly, often making it messy: *She ransacked the drawers, looking for the ring.*

ran·som¹ /ˈrænsəm/ *n.* [C] an amount of money paid to free someone who is held as a prisoner: *They're demanding $10,000* ***in ransom.*** | *His daughter was kidnapped and* ***held for ransom*** (=kept as a prisoner until money is paid). | *The government refused to* ***pay the ransom.*** | *Police found a* ***ransom note*** (=one demanding money).

ransom² *v.* [T] to set someone free by paying a ransom

rant /rænt/ *v.* [I] to talk or complain in a loud, excited, and rather confused way because you feel strongly about something: **rant about/against sth** *She was still ranting about the unfairness of it all.* | *You don't have to* ***rant and rave*** *to get your point across.*

rap¹ /ræp/ *n.* ENG. LANG. ARTS
1 MUSIC a) [U] a type of popular music in which the words of a song are not sung, but spoken in RHYME to music with a strong beat: *a popular rap singer* **b)** [C] a rap song or the words to a rap song
2 KNOCK [C] a quick light hit or knock: **+on/at** *We heard a sharp rap on the door.*
3 CRIME [C] INFORMAL a statement by the police that someone is responsible for a serious crime SYN **charge**: *a murder rap* → see also RAP SHEET
4 take the rap (for sth) to be blamed or punished for a mistake or crime, especially unfairly
5 beat the rap to avoid being punished for a crime
6 get a bum/bad rap to be unfairly criticized, or to be treated badly
7 a rap on the knuckles a punishment or criticism that is not very severe: *Polluters were getting away with just a rap on the knuckles.*

rap² *v.* **rapped, rapping**
1 HIT [I,T] to hit or knock something quickly: *She rapped the table with her pen.* | **rap at/on sth** *Nina rapped on my door.* ▶see THESAURUS box at **hit¹**
2 MUSIC [I] ENG. LANG. ARTS to say the words of a RAP: **rap about sth** *Kanye West raps about the dark side of the diamond industry.*
3 CRITICIZE [T] to criticize someone angrily: *Nelson is being rapped for his team's loss.*
4 rap sb on the knuckles/rap sb's knuckles to punish or criticize someone for something, but not very severely: *The newspaper rapped the senator's knuckles for the incident.*
5 CONVERSATION [I] OLD-FASHIONED to talk in an informal way to friends
6 SAY [T] to say something loudly, suddenly, and in a way that sounds angry: *The General rapped an order at his men.*

ra·pa·cious /rəˈpeɪʃəs/ *adj.* FORMAL taking everything that you can, especially by using violence: *rapacious real estate developers* —**rapaciously** *adv.* —**rapaciousness** *n.* [U] —**rapacity** /rəˈpæsət̬i/ *n.* [U]

ˈrap ˌartist *n.* [C] someone who writes and sings rap music

rape¹ /reɪp/ *v.* [T] to force someone to have sex when they do not want to: *The girl had been raped and stabbed.* [**Origin:** 1300–1400 Latin *rapere* **to seize**]

rape² *n.* **1** [C,U] the crime of forcing someone to have sex, especially by using violence: *Wilson has been charged with attempted rape.* | *a rape victim* → see also DATE RAPE, RAPIST ▶see THESAURUS box at **attack¹**, **crime**
2 [singular] sudden unnecessary destruction, especially of the environment: *the rape of the American West*
3 [U] BIOLOGY a plant with yellow flowers, grown as animal food and for its oil

R

Raph·a·el¹ /ˈræfiəl/ in the Christian religion, an ARCHANGEL

Raphael² (1483–1520) an Italian painter and ARCHITECT who was one of the most important artists of the RENAISSANCE. His full name in Italian is Raffaello Sanzio.

rap·id /ˈræpɪd/ W3 *adj.* done or happening very quickly and in a very short time SYN **quick**: *The patient made a rapid recovery.* | *rapid economic growth* [**Origin:** 1600–1700 Latin *rapidus* **seizing, sweeping away**, from *rapere*] —**rapidly** *adv.* —**rapidity** /rəˈpɪdəṭi/ *n.* [U]

ˈrapid-fire *adj.* [only before noun] **1** rapid-fire questions, jokes etc. are said quickly one after another **2** a rapid-fire gun can fire shots quickly one after another

rap·ids /ˈræpɪdz/ *n.* [plural] part of a river where the water looks white because it is moving very fast over rocks

ˌrapid ˈtransit ˌsystem also **ˌrapid ˈtransit** *n.* [C] a system for moving people quickly around a city using SUBWAYS or trains above the ground

ra·pi·er¹ /ˈreɪpiɚ/ *n.* [C] a long thin sword with two sharp edges

rapier² *adj.* **a rapier wit** the ability to say things that are very funny, and that often criticize other people

rap·ine /ˈræpən, -paɪn/ *n.* [U] LITERARY the taking away of property by force

rap·ist /ˈreɪpɪst/ *n.* [C] someone who has forced someone else to have sex when they do not want to, especially using violence

rap·pel /ræˈpɛl, rə-/ *v.* **rappelled, rappelling** [I] to go down a cliff or a rock by sliding down a rope and touching the cliff or rock with your feet —**rappel** *n.* [C]

rap·per /ˈræpɚ/ *n.* [C] someone who says, and often writes, the words to RAP songs

rap·port /ræˈpɔr, rə-/ *n.* [singular, U] friendly agreement and understanding between people: **+with** *her rapport with her patients* | **+between** *The rapport between the two men was obvious.* | **establish/build up/develop a rapport (with sb)** *He established a good rapport with his students.* [**Origin:** 1600–1700 French *rapporter* **to carry back, report**]

rap·proche·ment /ˌræproʊʃˈmɑn/ *n.* [singular, U] the establishment of a good relationship between two countries or groups of people, after a period of unfriendly relations: **+with** *the U.S. rapprochement with China*

rap·scal·lion /ræpˈskælyən/ *n.* [C] OLD USE someone who behaves badly, but whom you still like

ˈrap sheet *n.* [C] INFORMAL a list kept by the police of someone's criminal activities

rapt /ræpt/ *adj.* so interested in something that you do not notice anything else: *The congregation listened **in rapt attention**.*

rap·ture /ˈræptʃɚ/ *n.* [U] **1** great excitement and happiness: *He stared **in rapture** at his baby son.* **2 in/into raptures** speaking or behaving in a very excited and happy way because you like something very much: *She **went into raptures about** the food.*

rap·tur·ous /ˈræptʃərəs/ *adj.* FORMAL expressing great happiness or admiration: *rapturous applause* | *a rapturous welcome* —**rapturously** *adv.*

rare /rɛr/ W2 *adj.* **1** not seen or found very often, or not happening very often OPP **common**: *Tim collects rare coins.* | *a rare form of cancer* | **it is rare (for sb) to do sth** *It is rare for him to ask for help.* → see also RARELY, RARITY **2** meat that is rare has only been cooked for a short time and is still red → see also MEDIUM: *I like my steak rare.* **3** TECHNICAL air that is rare has less oxygen than usual because it is in a high place

WORD CHOICE **rare, scarce**

• **Rare** is used to talk about something that is valuable and that there is not much of, or about things that do not happen very often: *a rare first edition of the poems of John Keats* | *A rare tornado struck in Washington state.*

• **Scarce** is used to talk about something that is difficult to get at a particular time or in a particular place, although it may be available at other times: *Consumer goods are scarce and of poor quality.* | *Jobs for college graduates were scarce.*

ˌrare ˈearth also **ˌrare ˈearth ˌelement** *n.* [C] TECHNICAL one of a group of chemical ELEMENTS which are considered metals

rar·e·fac·tion /ˌrɛrəˈfækʃən/ *n.* [C,U] PHYSICS a decrease in the pressure of a gas OPP **compression**

rar·e·fied /ˈrɛrəˌfaɪd/ *adj.* **1** DISAPPROVING rarefied ideas, opinions etc. can only be understood by, or only involve, one small group of people: *He felt uncomfortable in the rarefied New York literary world.* **2** EARTH SCIENCE rarefied air is the air in high places, which has less oxygen than usual

rare·ly /ˈrɛrli/ W3 *adv.* not often: *Alan rarely talked about his work.* | *Brian **rarely, if ever** (=almost never), gets to bed before 3 a.m.*

THESAURUS

not very often: *I go to the movies, but not very often.*

hardly ever almost never: *The kids hardly ever call (=telephone) me.*

seldom MORE FORMAL very rarely: *He seldom slept well.*

→ OFTEN, NEVER, SOMETIMES

rar·ing /ˈrɛrɪŋ/ *adj.* **raring to go** very eager to start an activity: *Carlos was raring to go soon after leaving the hospital.*

rar·i·ty /ˈrɛrəṭi/ *n. plural* **rarities** **1 be a rarity** to not happen or exist very often: *I decided to skip dessert, which is a rarity for me.* **2** [C] something that is valuable or interesting because it is rare: *The CD is packed with live versions and other rarities.* **3** [U] the quality of being rare: *the rarity of the stamps*

ras·cal /ˈræskəl/ *n.* [C] **1** HUMOROUS someone, especially a child, who behaves badly but whom you still like **2** OLD-FASHIONED a dishonest man —**rascally** *adj.*

rash¹ /ræʃ/ *n.* [C] **1** a lot of red spots on someone's skin, caused by an illness or an ALLERGY: *Symptoms include high fever and a rash.* | *My mother **breaks out in a rash** if she eats seafood.* | **heat/diaper rash** (=a rash caused by heat or wearing DIAPERS) **2 a rash of sth** INFORMAL a large number of bad events, changes etc. within a short time: *a rash of car thefts in the neighborhood*

rash² *adj.* doing something too quickly, without thinking carefully about whether it is sensible or not: *a rash decision* | **it is rash (of sb) to do sth** *It would be rash to say the civil war is over.* ►see THESAURUS box at **impulsive** —**rashly** *adv.* —**rashness** *n.* [U]

rasp¹ /ræsp/ *v.* **1** [I,T] to make a rough sound that is not nice to listen to: *Her breath rasped in her throat.* **2** [T] to rub a surface with something rough

rasp² *n.* **1** [singular] a rough noise that is not nice to listen to: *the rasp of a heavy smoker's voice* **2** [C] a metal tool with a rough surface, like a FILE, used for shaping wood or metal

rasp·ber·ry /ˈræzˌbɛri/ S3 *n. plural* **raspberries** [C] **1** BIOLOGY a soft sweet red BERRY (=small fruit) that has many small parts, or the bush that this berry grows on: *raspberry jam* → see picture at FRUIT¹ **2** INFORMAL an impolite sound made by putting your tongue out and blowing SYN **Bronx cheer**

Ras·pu·tin /ræˈspyutˀn/, **Gri·go·ri** /gɪˈgɔri/ (1871–1916) a Russian who claimed to be a holy man, and who had a lot of power in the Russian government because of his influence over Alexandra, the wife of Czar Nicholas II

rasp·y /ˈræspi/ *adj. comparative* **raspier**, *superlative* **raspiest** a raspy voice or sound is rough and not nice to listen to

Ras·ta /ˈræstə, ˈrɑs-/ *n.* [C] INFORMAL a Rastafarian —**Rasta** *adj.*

Ras·ta·far·i·an /ˌræstəˈfɛriən◂, ˌrɑs-/ *n.* [C] someone who believes in a religion that is originally from Jamaica, which has Haile Selassie as its religious leader, and believes that people from the Caribbean will return to Africa —**Rastafarian** *adj.* —**Rastafarianism** *n.* [U]

Ras·ta·man /ˈræstəˌmæn, ˈrɑs-/ *n.* [C] INFORMAL a male Rastafarian, especially one with long hair that has been twisted into DREADLOCKS

rat¹ /ræt/ *n.* [C] **1** BIOLOGY an animal that looks like a large mouse with a long tail **2** SPOKEN someone who has been disloyal to you or deceived you **3 look like a drowned rat** to look very wet and uncomfortable **4 like rats deserting/leaving a sinking ship** used to describe people who leave a company, organization etc. when it is in trouble [**Origin:** Old English *ræt*] → see also PACK RAT, RAT RACE, RATS, RAT TRAP, **smell a rat** at SMELL² (6)

rat² *v.* **ratted**, **ratting** [I] OLD-FASHIONED also **rat on sb** to be disloyal to someone, especially by telling someone in authority about something wrong that person has done

ˌrat-a-ˈtat also **ˌrat-a-tat-ˈtat**, **ˌrat-tat-ˈtat** *n.* [singular] a series of short repeated sounds, for example from a MACHINE GUN

ra·ta·tou·ille /ˌrætæˈtui, ˌrɑ-/ *n.* [U] a dish from France, made of cooked vegetables such as EGGPLANT, ZUCCHINI, TOMATOes, and onions

ratch·et¹ /ˈrætʃɪt/ *n.* [C] a machine part consisting of a wheel or bar with teeth on it, which allows movement in only one direction

ratchet² *v.* [T always + adv./prep.] to increase or decrease by small amounts over a period of time: **ratchet sth ↔ up/down** *Raising the minimum wage would ratchet up real incomes in general.*

rate¹ /reɪt/ S2 W1 *n.* [C]
1 HOW OFTEN the number of times something happens, or the number of examples of something within a certain period: **+of** *The rate of new HIV infections has risen again.* | **at a/the rate of 100 a day/10 a year etc.** *Refugees were crossing the border at the rate of 1000 a day.* | **birth/unemployment/divorce etc. rate** *The unemployment rate rose to 6.5% in February.* | **a high/low rate of sth** *a city with a high rate of street crime* | **success/failure rate** (=the number of times that something succeeds or fails)
2 MONEY a charge or payment that is set according to a standard scale: *hotel rates in the region* | *the bank's lending rates* | **hourly/weekly rate** *In most cases, lawyers charge on an hourly rate.* | **rate of pay/tax/interest etc.** *Nurses are demanding higher rates of pay.* | **a special/reduced/lower etc. rate** *Some hotels offer a special rate for children.* | *We found the **going rate*** (=the usual amount paid for something) *to be about $12 per day.* | ***a fixed rate*** (=one that does not change) *of interest* ►see THESAURUS box at **cost¹**
3 SPEED the change in a quantity measured over a period of time: **at (a)... rate** *Our money was running out **at an alarming rate*** (=so quickly that we were worried). | *the car's slow **rate of speed*** | *I type **at a rate of** 65 words per minute.*
4 at any rate SPOKEN **a)** used when you are stating one definite fact in a situation that is uncertain or unsatisfactory SYN **anyway**: *That's what they said, at any rate.* **b)** used to introduce a statement that is more important than what was said before, especially if it was confusing or unclear SYN **anyway**: *Well, at any rate, the next meeting will be on Wednesday.*
5 at this rate SPOKEN used to say what will happen if things continue to happen in the same way as now: *At this rate, I'll lose $30 million by the end of the season.*
[**Origin:** 1400–1500 French, Medieval Latin *rata*, from Latin *pro rata parte* **according to a fixed part**] → see also CUT-RATE, EXCHANGE RATE, INTEREST RATE, PRIME RATE

rate² S3 W2 *v.* **1 a)** [T usually passive] to think that someone or something has a particular quality, value, or standard: **rate sb (as) sth** *Johnson was rated as the top high-school player in the country.* | *Californian wines are very **highly rated**.* **b)** [I] to be considered as having a particular quality, value, or standard: **sth rates as sth** *That rates as one of the best meals I've ever had.* **2 be rated G/PG/R/X etc.** if a movie is rated G, PG etc. it is officially approved for people of a particular age to see → see also X-RATED **3** [T] to deserve something: *Our restaurant didn't even rate a mention in Beck's guide.*

-rate /reɪt/ [in adjectives] **first-rate/second-rate/third-rate** of good, bad, or very bad quality: *first-rate musicians* | *a third-rate hotel*

ˌrate of ˈchange *n.* [C] MATH a relationship between the changes in a VARIABLE and the length of time over which these changes happen. For example, speed is the rate of change of distance traveled.

ˌrate of exˈchange *n.* [C] ECONOMICS the EXCHANGE RATE

ˌrate of reˈturn *n.* [singular] ECONOMICS a company's profit for a year, expressed as a PERCENTAGE of the money that the company has spent during the year

ˈrat fink *n.* [C] OLD-FASHIONED a RAT

rath·er /ˈræðɚ/ S1 W1 *adv.* **1 rather than** a phrase meaning "instead of," used when you are comparing two things or situations: *Rather than fly directly to LA, why not stop in San Francisco first?* | *He decided to quit rather than accept the new rules.* | *I prefer cooking with olive oil rather than butter.* **2 would rather** used when you would prefer to do or have one thing more than another: *I'd rather not talk about it, okay?* | *We could eat later, if you would rather do that.* | *I could lend him the money, but **I'd rather not**.* | **would rather do sth than (do) sth** *I'd rather die than apologize to him.* | **would rather sb did sth (than sth)** *I'd rather you slept at their house than drive home so late.* **3** [+ adj./adv.] FORMAL to a fairly great degree, often too much: *He was rather irritated that they didn't say anything.* | *a rather blurred photograph*

THESAURUS

fairly used to emphasize an adjective or adverb a little: *The test was fairly easy.* | *The device seemed to give fairly accurate results.*
pretty ESPECIALLY SPOKEN the most usual way of saying "fairly": *The movie was pretty good.* | *It's pretty tough work.*
quite FORMAL used to emphasize something: *The two boys looked quite similar.* | *That's quite an interesting problem.*
kind of INFORMAL used to emphasize something a little: *It was kind of cold out.*

4 or rather used to correct something that you have said, or give more specific information: *There is a problem with parking, or rather with the lack of it.* **5 not...but rather...** used to say that someone does not do something but does something else instead: *The problem is not their lack of funding, but rather their lack of planning.* [**Origin:** Old English *hrathor* **more quickly**]

rat·if·i·ca·tion /ˌrætəfəˈkeɪʃən/ *n.* [U] **1** the act of giving official approval to an agreement: *ratification of the treaty* **2** POLITICS the act of approving an AMENDMENT to the U.S. CONSTITUTION

rat·i·fy /ˈrætəˌfaɪ/ *v.* **ratifies**, **ratified**, **ratifying** [T] POLITICS to make a written agreement official by signing it: **ratify a treaty/agreement etc.** *Both nations ratified the treaty.*

rat·ing /ˈreɪtɪŋ/ W3 *n.* [C] **1** a level on a scale that shows how good, important, popular etc. someone or something is: **sb's approval/popularity/performance etc. rating** *The President's approval rating rose to 78%.* | **a high/low rating** *NBC's new comedy had the highest television rating this season.* | **a favorable/unfavorable rating** *Wall Street analysts gave the shares* *favorable ratings.* **2 the ratings** a list that shows which television programs, movies etc. are the most popular: *CBS will end the series if it continues to drop **in the ratings**.* **3** [usually singular] a letter used to show how much violence, sex, and offensive language a movie contains: *The film was given an X rating in the U.S.* **4** the military class or rank into which an army, navy etc. member is placed, according to their special skills and abilities → see also CREDIT RATING

ra·ti·o /ˈreɪʃiˌoʊ, ˈreɪʃoʊ/ Ac *n. plural* **ratios** [C] **1** a relationship between two amounts, represented by a pair of numbers showing how much bigger one amount is than the other: ***The ratio of** women **to** men on campus is 3:1.* **2** MATH a relationship between two numbers, that is calculated by dividing one number by another. For example, 6 divided by 3 gives a ratio of 2, or 2:1 if it were written out fully. → see also QUOTIENT, PROPORTION

ra·tion¹ /ˈræʃən, ˈreɪ-/ *n.* **1** [C] a specific amount of something such as food or gasoline that you are allowed to have, when there is not much available: **+of** *a daily ration of meat* **2 rations** [plural] the food that is given to a soldier or member of a group each day

ration² *v.* [T] to control the supply of something such as food or gasoline by allowing people to have only a limited amount of it, usually because there is not enough: *Sugar, cooking oil and rice were being rationed.* —**rationing** *n.* [U]

ra·tion·al /ˈræʃənəl/ Ac S3 *adj.* **1** based on clear, practical, or scientific reasons OPP **irrational**: *There is no rational explanation for her disappearance.* **2** sensible and able to make decisions based on intelligent thinking rather than on emotion OPP **irrational**: *We're both rational people. Let's not argue.* | *rational behavior* **3** able to think, understand, and form judgments that are based on facts, in a way that separates humans from animals [**Origin:** 1300–1400 Latin *rationalis*, from *ratio* **calculation, reason**] —**rationally** *adv.* —**rationality** /ˌræʃəˈnæləṭi/ *n.* [U]

ra·tion·ale /ˌræʃəˈnæl/ *n.* [C,U] the reasons and principles on which a decision, plan, belief etc. is based: **+for/behind** *The rationale behind the changes is not clear at all.*

ˌrational eˈquation *n.* [C] MATH an EQUATION that has a rational expression on at least one side of the equal sign

ˌrational exˈpression *n.* [C] MATH a mathematical expression that can be written as a POLYNOMIAL divided by another polynomial

ˌrational ˈfunction *n.* [C] MATH a mathematical FUNCTION (=quantity that changes according to how another mathematical quantity changes) that is written as a RATIO of two POLYNOMIALS

ra·tion·al·ist /ˈræʃənl-ɪst/ *n.* [C] someone who bases their opinions and actions on intelligent thinking, rather than on emotion or religious belief —**rationalism** *n.* [U] —**rationalist** also **rationalistic** /ˌræʃənəˈlɪstɪk◂ / *adj.*

ra·tion·al·ize /ˈræʃnəˌlaɪz, -nlˌaɪz/ Ac *v.* **1** [I,T] to find or invent a reasonable explanation for your behavior or attitudes: *Greg tries to rationalize his cheating by saying everyone else is doing it.* **2** [T] to think about something or improve it in a practical, sensible way: *The Social Security system needs to be rationalized.* **3** [T] MATH to remove the IRRATIONAL NUMBERS in a mathematical EXPRESSION or EQUATION —**rationalization** /ˌræʃnələˈzeɪʃən/ *n.* [C,U]

ˌrational ˈnumber *n.* [C] MATH any REAL NUMBER that can be written as the exact RATIO of two INTEGERS OPP **irrational number**

ˈrat race *n.* [singular] life in business or in big cities in which people are always competing against each other for success in a way that is too difficult and STRESSFUL: *We retired early to **get out of the rat race**.*

rats /ræts/ *interjection* SPOKEN used to express annoyance: *Rats. I forgot to call her.*

rat·tan /ræˈtæn, rə-/ *n.* [U] the plant from which WICKER furniture is made

ˌrat-tat-ˈtat *n.* [singular] RAT-A-TAT

rat·tle¹ /ˈræṭl/ *v.* **1** [I,T] to shake, or make something shake, with quick repeated knocking sounds: *The wind was rattling the windows.* | *Keys rattled in his pocket as he walked.* ►see THESAURUS box at **shake¹** **2** [I always + adv./prep.] if a vehicle or the person in it or on it rattles somewhere, the vehicle moves along making a rattling noise: **+along/past/over etc.** *An old truck rattled past.* **3** [T] INFORMAL to make someone lose confidence or become nervous: *Nothing rattles him.* | *News of the shoot-out **rattled nerves** in the community* (=made people nervous). **4 rattle sb's cage** SPOKEN, HUMOROUS to make someone feel angry or annoyed → see also SABER-RATTLING

rattle around *phr. v.* **1** to move around in an empty space, making a rattling noise: *The ball is filled with tiny stones that rattle around inside.* **2** to live in a house or building that is too big for you or seems empty: *Dad and I rattled around in the house after Mom died.*

rattle sth ↔ **off** *phr. v.* to say something quickly and easily, from memory: *Mark rattled off the list of movies he'd seen.*

rattle on *phr. v.* INFORMAL to talk quickly for a long time, about things that are not interesting: **+about** *Deanna rattled on about her boyfriend.*

rattle² *n.* **1** [singular] the sound that you hear when the parts of something knock against each other: **+of** *the rattle of chains* **2** [C] a baby's toy that makes a noise when it is shaken **3** [C] a wooden or plastic instrument that makes a loud knocking noise, used by people on New Year's Eve and at parties → see also DEATH RATTLE

rat·tled /ˈræṭld/ *adj.* [not before noun] nervous and not confident because of something that has happened: *He's a good player because he doesn't **get rattled** easily.*

rat·tler /ˈrætlɚ, ˈræṭl-ɚ/ *n.* [C] INFORMAL a rattlesnake

rattlesnake

rat·tle·snake /ˈræṭlˌsneɪk/ *n.* [C] BIOLOGY a poisonous American snake that makes a noise like a rattle with its tail

rat·tle·trap /ˈræṭlˌtræp/ *adj.* a rattletrap vehicle is in very bad condition

rat·tling /ˈrætlɪŋ/ *adj., adv.* OLD-FASHIONED **a rattling good story/tale etc.** a very good or interesting story

ˈrat trap *n.* [C] a dirty old building that is in very bad condition

rat·ty /ˈræṭi/ *adj. comparative* **rattier**, *superlative* **rattiest** **1** in bad condition SYN **shabby**: *a ratty bathrobe* **2** like a rat

rau·cous /ˈrɔkəs/ *adj.* **1** impolite, disorganized, noisy, and violent: *Raucous crowds yelled and cheered.* **2** very loud and rough-sounding: *raucous laughter* ►see THESAURUS box at **loud¹** —**raucously** *adv.* —**raucousness** *n.* [U]

raun·chy /ˈrɔntʃi, ˈrɑn-/ *adj. comparative* **raunchier**, *superlative* **raunchiest** INFORMAL **1** sexually exciting or intended to make you think about sex: *raunchy jokes* **2** a raunchy smell is extremely bad —**raunchily** *adv.* —**raunchiness** *n.* [U]

Rausch·en·berg /ˈraʊʃənˌbɚg/, **Rob·ert** /ˈrɑbɚt/ (1925–) a U.S. artist famous for his work in the style of POP ART that sometimes includes photographs or real objects

rav·age /ˈrævɪdʒ/ *v.* [T] to destroy, ruin, or damage something very badly: *The population was ravaged by cholera.*

rav·ag·es /ˈrævɪdʒɪz/ *n.* **the ravages of war/time/disease etc.** the damage or destruction caused by something such as war, disease, storms etc.: *The church escaped most of the ravages of civil war.*

rave¹ /reɪv/ *v.* [I] **1** to talk in a very excited way about something, saying how much you admire or enjoy it:

+**about/over** *Everyone's raving about the new sushi restaurant.* **2** to talk in an angry, uncontrolled way: *Rosen* ***ranted and raved*** *about the team's poor performance.* **3** to talk in a crazy way that is impossible to understand, especially because you are very sick: *He raved for hours, banging his head on the wall.* [**Origin:** 1300–1400 Old French *raver* **to wander, talk wildly**] → see also RAVING

rave² *adj.* **rave reviews/notices** strong praise for a new movie, book, restaurant, product, etc.: **get/receive/win rave reviews** *The band is receiving rave reviews.*

rave³ *n.* [C] **1** an event at which a very large group of young people dance all night to loud music with a strong beat: **rave band/party/culture etc.** *the rave scene of the early 1990s* **2** a piece of writing in a newspaper, magazine etc. that praises a movie, play, or performance very much

rav·el /ˈrævəl/ *v.* [I] **1** if something made from wool or cloth ravels, the threads in it become separated from one another **2** if threads ravel, they become knotted and twisted → see also UNRAVEL

Ra·vel /ræˈvɛl/, **Mau·rice** /mɔˈris/ (1875–1937) a French musician who wrote CLASSICAL music

ra·ven¹ /ˈreɪvən/ *n.* [C] BIOLOGY a large shiny black bird with a large black beak

raven² *adj.* [only before noun] raven hair is black and shiny

ˌraven-ˈhaired *adj.* LITERARY having shiny black hair

rav·en·ing /ˈrævənɪŋ/ *adj.* LITERARY ravening animals are extremely hungry: *a ravening beast*

rav·en·ous /ˈrævənəs/ *adj.* extremely hungry: *The boys ran in, ravenous after their game.* —**ravenously** *adv.*

ra·vine /rəˈvin/ *n.* [C] EARTH SCIENCE a narrow valley with steep sides, formed by running water SYN **gorge**

rav·ing /ˈreɪvɪŋ/ *adj.* INFORMAL **1** talking or behaving in a crazy way: *a raving lunatic* **2 raving success** something that is very successful → see also **stark raving mad** at STARK² (2)

rav·ings /ˈreɪvɪŋz/ *n.* [plural] things someone says that are crazy and have no meaning: +**of** *the ravings of a madman*

ra·vi·o·li /ˌræviˈoʊli/ *n.* [U] small squares of PASTA filled with meat or cheese [**Origin:** 1800–1900 Italian **small turnips**]

rav·ish /ˈrævɪʃ/ *v.* [T] LITERARY **1** to RAPE a woman **2** to make someone feel great pleasure and happiness: *music to ravish the soul*

rav·ish·ing /ˈrævɪʃɪŋ/ *adj.* FORMAL very beautiful: *a ravishing young woman* —**ravishingly** *adv.*

raw¹ /rɔ/ S3 *adj.*

1 FOOD not cooked: *raw vegetables* | *Cabbage can be eaten raw.*

2 INFORMATION information or ideas that have not yet been arranged, checked, or prepared for use: *the* ***raw data*** *sent back by the space probe* | *Dickinson's quiet life provided the* ***raw material*** (=experiences that give an artist, writer etc. ideas) *for her poetry.* | **raw footage** (=film of an event that is not changed before it is shown)

3 MATERIALS raw cotton, sugar, wool etc. are in their natural state and have not been prepared for people to use or deal with: *raw silk* | **raw sewage** (=waste material that has not yet been treated with chemicals) → see also RAW MATERIALS

4 EMOTIONS/QUALITIES raw emotions or qualities are strong and natural, but not completely developed or controlled: *The memories were still raw and painful.* | **raw emotion/passion** *You could see the raw emotion in his eyes.* | *He has enough* ***raw talent*** *to become a star.*

5 PERSON not experienced, not fully trained, or not developed: *We were young and raw.* | **raw recruits** (=people who have just joined the army, navy etc.)

6 get a raw deal to be treated unfairly

7 SKIN a part of your body that is raw is red and sore: *His face was raw and blistered.*

8 LANGUAGE INFORMAL containing a lot of sexual details

9 DESCRIPTIONS giving facts which may not be favorable or nice, without trying to make them seem more acceptable: *a raw account of poverty in the cities*

10 WEATHER very cold and wet: *raw, gusty winds*

[**Origin:** Old English *hreaw*] —**rawness** *n.* [U] → see also **strike/touch/hit a (raw) nerve** at NERVE¹ (5)

raw² *n.* **in the raw a)** in a natural state and not changed or developed: *Her films portray nature in the raw.* **b)** INFORMAL not wearing any clothes

raw·boned /ˈrɔboʊnd/ *adj.* someone who is rawboned, especially a man, is thin and has large bones with the skin stretched over them

raw·hide /ˈrɔhaɪd/ *n.* [U] natural leather that has not been specially treated

ˌraw maˈterials *n.* [plural] materials such as coal, oil etc. in their natural state, before being treated in order to make things

ray /reɪ/ *n. plural* **rays** [C] **1** [often plural] PHYSICS a narrow beam of light from the sun or from something such as a lamp: *the sun's rays* | +**of** *Rays of light filtered through the pine trees.* **2** PHYSICS a beam of heat, electricity, or other form of ENERGY: *a gun that fires invisible rays* → see also COSMIC RAY, GAMMA RAY, X-RAY¹ **3 ray of hope/light/comfort etc.** something that provides a small amount of hope or happiness in a difficult situation: *If only I could see some ray of hope for the future.* **4 ray of sunshine** INFORMAL an expression meaning someone or something that makes a situation seem better: *Little Annie was an unexpected ray of sunshine in her life.* **5** BIOLOGY a large flat ocean fish with a long pointed tail **6** MATH a continuous part of a straight line that starts at a point and goes on without ending

Ray /reɪ/, **Man** /mæn/ (1890–1976) a U.S. artist and photographer, who was one of the leaders of the Dada and SURREALIST movements

ˌray ˈdiagram *n.* [C] PHYSICS a drawing that shows light RAYS, used to find out the size and position of an image formed by a mirror or a LENS

ˈray gun *n.* [C] an imaginary gun in SCIENCE FICTION stories that fires rays that kill people

ray·on /ˈreɪɑn/ *n.* [U] a smooth material like silk used for making clothes

raze /reɪz/ *v.* [T] to completely destroy a town or building

ra·zor /ˈreɪzɚ/ *n.* [C] **1** a sharp instrument used for removing hair, especially from a man's face: *an electric razor* **2 be on a razor edge** to be in a dangerous position where a mistake could be very dangerous: *Politically the country is on a razor edge.*

ˈrazor blade *n.* [C] a small flat blade with a very sharp cutting edge, used in razors

ˌrazor-ˈsharp *adj.* **1** very sharp: *a razor-sharp hunting knife* **2** able to think and understand things very quickly: *her razor-sharp mind*

ˈrazor ˌwire *n.* [U] sharp metal wire in long strings, usually twisted into large circles, that is used to protect buildings or as a fence

razz /ræz/ *v.* [T] INFORMAL to make jokes that insult or embarrass someone SYN **tease**

raz·zle-daz·zle /ˌræzəl ˈdæzəl/ *n.* [U] INFORMAL **1** a lot of activity that is intended to be impressive and excite people: *Behind all the razzle-dazzle is a good movie.* **2** a complicated series of actions intended to confuse your opponent

razz·ma·tazz /ˈræzməˌtæz/ also **raz·za·ma·tazz** /ˈræzəməˌtæz/ *n.* [U] INFORMAL busy or noisy activity that is intended to attract people's attention: *the razzmatazz of old Broadway shows*

RC the written abbreviation of ROMAN CATHOLIC

RCMP *n.* the abbreviation of the ROYAL CANADIAN MOUNTED POLICE → see also MOUNTIE

Rd. the written abbreviation of ROAD, used in addresses

R.D. *n.* [U] **rural delivery** the system of addresses the post office uses to deliver mail in country areas

-rd /rd/ *suffix* used with the number 3 to form ORDINAL numbers: *the 3rd* (=third) *of June* | *his 53rd birthday*

RDA *n.* [singular] MEDICINE **recommended daily allowance** the amount of substances such as VITAMINS, MINERALS or CALORIES that the Food and Nutrition Board of the U.S. National Research Council says you should have each day

re¹ /ri/ *prep.* used especially in business letters to introduce the subject that you are going to write about: *To: John Deacon From: Maria Soames Re: computer system* ►see THESAURUS box at **about¹** → see also IN RE

re² /reɪ/ *n.* [singular] the second note in a musical SCALE according to the SOL-FA system

're /r, ɚ/ *v.* the short form of "are": *We're going to go see them tomorrow.*

re- /ri/ *prefix* **1** again: *rebroadcast* **2** again in a new and better way: *rewrite* **3** back to a former state: *reunited* (=together again as before)

R

reach¹ /ritʃ/ S1 W1 *v.*

1 LEVEL/STANDARD [T] if something reaches a particular rate, amount, degree, etc. it increases or decreases until it gets to that point: *Temperatures are expected to reach the 80s today.* | *Prices have reached record levels.*

2 POINT IN PROCESS/TIME [T] to get to a particular point in a process or in time: *After you reach a certain age, nobody wants to hire you.* | **reach a point/level/stage etc.** *She's reached a point where she's earning a good salary.*

3 WITH YOUR HAND a) [I always + adv./prep., T always + adv./prep.] to move your hand or arm in order to touch, hold, or pick up something: **+for/in/over etc.** *Paula reached up to touch the ceiling.* | *She **reached out her hand** to pet the cat.* **b)** [I,T not in progressive] to manage to touch or pick up something by stretching out your arm: *I can't reach the top shelf.* | *She managed to reach far enough to grab his hand.*

4 SUCCEED [T] to succeed in doing something after discussing it or working on it for a period of time: **reach a decision/agreement/result etc.** *After a long talk, we finally reached a decision.* | **reach a goal/objective/aim** *How will you reach your retirement goals?* | *It only took the jury two hours to **reach a verdict*** (=make a decision in a court case).

5 LENGTH/HEIGHT [I always + adv./prep.,T not in progressive] to be big enough, long enough, or high enough to get to a particular point or level: *The flood waters reached the second floor.* | **reach down/up to sth** *Her skirt reaches down to her ankles.* | **reach as far as sth** *The storm reached as far as the Rocky Mountains.*

THESAURUS

go to reach as far as a particular place: *The road only goes as far as the farmhouse.*
go up/down to sth to reach a particular level: *During the drought, the water in the lake went down below the three foot level.*
come up/down to sth to reach a particular level: *Alex is taller; he comes up to Pat's shoulder now.*

6 SPEAK TO SB [T] to speak to someone or leave a message for them, especially by telephone; SYN **contact**: *You can reach us at (555) 532–7864.*

7 ARRIVE [T] to arrive at a particular place, especially when it has taken a long time or a lot of effort to get there: *We finally reached Chicago at midnight.*

THESAURUS

arrive to reach somewhere after traveling: *The flight should arrive at 6:20.*
get to SPOKEN to reach a place: *By the time I got there, everyone had already left.*
catch to get to a bus, train, plane, etc. on time to get on it: *You'd better hurry if you want to catch the bus.*

►see THESAURUS box at **arrive**

8 BE SEEN/HEARD BY SB [T] if a message, television program etc. reaches a lot of people, they hear it or see it: *Cable TV reaches a huge audience.*

9 RECEIVE INFORMATION [T] if information or a message reaches someone, they receive it: *It took weeks for her letter to reach him.*

10 COMMUNICATE [T] to succeed in making someone understand or accept what you tell them: *I just can't seem to reach him anymore.*

11 reach for the stars to aim for something that is very difficult to achieve

[**Origin:** Old English *ræcan*]

GRAMMAR

You **reach** a place (NOT **reach at** or **reach to** it): *He reached Tokyo at 5 a.m.* You **arrive at** a particular place or building: *When are they arriving at the airport?* You **arrive in** a country or a big city: *to arrive in LA/Tokyo/France.* Sometimes you do not need a preposition at all: *When will they get there/here/home?*

reach out to sb *phr. v.* **1** to show people that you are interested in them and want to listen to them or help them: *Community workers were praised for reaching out to poor families.* **2** to ask someone for help: *He finally reached out to a cousin for help.*

reach² *n.* **1** [singular, U] the distance that you can stretch out your arm to touch something: *a boxer with a long reach* | **out of (sb's) reach/beyond (sb's) reach** *Keep all medicines out of children's reach.* | *The controls were all **within easy reach*** (=easy to touch or use). **2** [singular] the limit of someone's power, authority, or ability to do something: *Large companies are extending their reach.* | **beyond the reach of sb/sth** *Houses are priced beyond the reach of many families.* | **within (sb's) reach** *Set goals that are within your reach.* | *Winning the championship seemed **out of reach**.* **3 within reach (of sth)** within a distance that you can easily travel: *All the main tourist attractions are **within easy reach of** the hotel.* **4** [C usually plural] a straight part of a river between two bends: *the upper reaches of the Nile* **5 the upper/lower reaches of sth** the highest or lowest levels of an organization, group, or system: *the upper reaches of the legal profession*

re·act /ri'ækt/ Ac S3 W3 *v.* [I] **1** to behave in a particular way because of something that has happened or something that has been said to you: *How did Dad react when Vicky said she was pregnant?* | **react to sth** *She reacted angrily to the accusation.* | **react by doing sth** *The audience reacted by shouting and booing.* | **react with sth** *School officials reacted with alarm.* | *She felt insulted, and **reacted accordingly*** (=in a way that could be expected). → see also OVERREACT, RESPOND **2** if a machine or piece of equipment reacts, it performs a particular action because of what is happening in or around it: **react to sth** *The gauge reacts to pressure in the atmosphere.* **3** MEDICINE to become ill when a chemical or drug goes into your body, or because of something you have eaten or touched: **react (badly) to sth** *The patient reacted badly to penicillin.* **4** if prices or financial markets react to something that happens, they increase or decrease in value because of it: **react to sth** *Let's see how the markets reacted to the news.* **5** CHEMISTRY if a chemical substance reacts, it changes when it is in contact with another chemical substance: **react with sth** *An acid reacts with a base to form a salt.*

react against sb/sth *phr. v.* to show that you dislike someone else's rules or way of doing something by deliberately doing the opposite: *He reacted strongly against his religious upbringing.*

re·ac·tant /ri'æktənt/ *n.* [C] CHEMISTRY a chemical substance that is present at the start of a chemical reaction, and which combines with another substance to form a chemical compound

re·ac·tion /ri'ækʃən/ Ac S2 W2 *n.*

1 TO A SITUATION/EVENT [C,U] something that you feel or do because of what has happened to you or been said to you: *Crying is a natural reaction.* | **+to** *her parents' reaction to the news* | **+from** *My suggestion got a positive reaction from the team.* | **sb's first/initial/immediate reaction** *My first reaction was to ignore them.* | *He wrote a letter **in reaction to** the editorial.* | *My **gut***

reaction (=immediate reaction before you have time to think) *was not to trust him.* | **provoke/produce/bring etc. a reaction** *Kids love to provoke a reaction from their parents.* | *There were* ***mixed reactions*** (=both good and bad reactions from people in a group) *to the proposal.*
2 TO FOOD/DRUGS [singular] MEDICINE a bad effect, such as illness, caused by food that you have eaten or a drug that you have taken: *an allergic reaction* | **have/experience/suffer a reaction** *He suffered a severe reaction.* | **+to** *Some people* ***have a*** *mild* ***reaction to*** *the drug.* | **cause/trigger a reaction** *Peanuts can trigger a serious reaction.*
3 CHANGE [singular] a change in people's attitudes, behavior, fashions etc. that happens because they disapprove of what was done in the past: **+against** *a reaction against her father's strictness*
4 reactions [plural] your ability to move quickly when something happens suddenly, especially something dangerous: **quick/slow reactions** *Fighter pilots need to have very quick reactions.*
5 SCIENCE [C,U] **a)** CHEMISTRY a chemical change that happens when two or more chemical substances are mixed together SYN **chemical reaction** **b)** a physical force that is the result of an equally strong physical force in the opposite direction → see also NUCLEAR REACTION
6 AGAINST CHANGE [U] FORMAL strong and unreasonable opposition to all social and political changes → see also CHAIN REACTION

re·ac·tion·ar·y /riˈækʃəˌnɛri/ Ac *adj.* DISAPPROVING strongly opposed to social or political change in a way that is unreasonable: *reactionary politicians* —**reactionary** *n.* [C]

ˌreaction ˈforce *n.* [C] PHYSICS a force that acts in the opposite direction of an ACTION FORCE and with equal strength. For example, where GRAVITY exists, a lack of movement in the direction of the GRAVITATIONAL pull shows that there is a reaction force.

re·ac·ti·vate /riˈæktəˌveɪt/ Ac *v.* [T] to make something start working again, or to start a process again: *California reactivated the death penalty in 1977.*

re·ac·tive /riˈæktɪv/ Ac *adj.* **1** reacting to events or situations rather than starting something new OPP **proactive**: *a reactive foreign policy* **2** CHEMISTRY a reactive chemical substance changes when it is mixed with another chemical substance OPP **non-reactive**

re·ac·tor /riˈæktɚ/ Ac *n.* [C] PHYSICS a NUCLEAR REACTOR

read[1] /rid/ S1 W1 *v. past tense and past participle* **read** /rɛd/
1 WORDS/BOOKS [I,T] **a)** to look at written words and understand what they mean: *I like to read in bed.* | *Always read the directions before you begin.* | *Have you read her new book yet?* | *a* ***widely read*** *newspaper* (=one that is read by many people) **b)** to have the ability to look at words and understand them: *My parents taught me to read.* | *I can read Spanish but I can't speak it very well.*

THESAURUS
flip/flick/thumb through sth to look at parts of a book, magazine, etc. quickly
browse through sth to look at parts of a book, magazine, etc. slowly, but without reading anything thoroughly
skim/scan (through) sth to read something quickly to get the main ideas or to find what you want
pore over sth to read something very carefully for a long time
devour sth to read something quickly and eagerly
plow/wade through sth to read something long and boring
→ WRITE

2 INFORMATION [I,T not in progressive] to find out information from books, newspapers etc.: *Don't believe everything you read in the papers.* | **+that** *I read that garlic is good for your heart.* | **+about/of** *Did you read about the big snow storm in Canada?*
3 READ AND SPEAK [I,T] to say the written words in a book, newspaper etc. so that people can hear them: **read sb sth** *Daddy, will you read me a story?* | **read (sth) to sb** *Mom always read to us at bedtime.* | **read (sth) aloud/out loud** *He opened the letter and began to read it aloud.*
4 MUSIC/MAPS/SIGNS ETC. [T] to look at signs, pictures, maps etc. and understand what they mean: *Can you read music?*
5 COMPUTER [T] COMPUTERS if the DISK DRIVE of a computer reads information from a DISK, it takes the information and puts it into the computer's memory
6 UNDERSTAND STH IN A PARTICULAR WAY [T] to choose to understand a situation, remark, etc. in one of several possible ways: **read sth as sth** *People read his silence as guilt.* | **read sth well/accurately** *He read the situation very well.*
7 SIGN/NEWSPAPER ETC. [T] used to say what the words are on a sign, newspaper HEADLINE etc. SYN **say**: *The headline read: "Firefighters Save Girl From Flames."*
8 STYLE OF WRITING [I always + adv./prep.] used to say that something is written well or badly, or in a particular style: **read well/badly** *The last paragraph reads badly.* | *Toward the end, the book starts to* ***read like*** (=sound similar to) *a list.*
9 UNDERSTAND SB'S THOUGHTS [T] to be able to understand what someone is like or what they are thinking: **read sb's mind/thoughts** *Thanks for the coffee. You read my mind.* | *Don't try to fool me. I* ***can read*** *you* ***like a book*** (=I understand the way you think very well).
10 MEASURING [T] **a)** if a measuring instrument reads a particular number, it shows that number: *The thermometer read 46 degrees.* **b)** to look at the number or amount shown on a measuring instrument such as a gas or electricity meter: *A man came to read the gas meter.*
11 REPLACE WORDS **read sth as sth** also **for sth read sth** used to tell someone to replace a wrong number or word with the correct one: *Please read "5.2% interest" as "5.5% interest."* | *For "November"* (=instead of November) *on line 6, read "September."*
12 read between the lines to guess someone's real feelings or the truth about a situation, from something that is said or written but not expressed directly: *Reading between the lines, I'd say she's not happy.*
13 well-read having read a lot of books and gained a lot of knowledge: *a well-read young man*
14 read sb's lips to understand what someone is saying by watching the way their lips move → see also LIP-READ
15 read my lips SPOKEN used to tell someone that you really mean what you are saying: *Read my lips! I do not want to go out with you!*
16 read sb's palm to look carefully at someone's hand, in order to find out about their future
17 take it as read (that) to feel certain that something is true, even though no one has told you it is true: *I just took it as read that you would get the job.*
18 take sth as read to accept a report, statement etc. as correct and complete without reading or hearing it: *We'll have to take the secretary's report as read.*
19 do you read me? SPOKEN used to ask someone whether they can hear and understand you when you are speaking to them by radio
[**Origin:** Old English *rædan*] → see also READING, **read (sb) the riot act** at RIOT[1] (5)

read for sth *phr. v.* to perform the part of a particular character from a play, as a test of your ability to act in the play SYN **audition**

read sth **back to** sb *phr. v.* to read out loud something that someone has written down for you: *Can you read the last paragraph back to me?*

read sth **into** sth *phr. v.* to think that a situation, action etc. has a meaning or importance that it does not really have: *It was a joke. I think you're reading too much into it.*

read sth ↔ **out** *phr. v.* to say the words that are written in a message, list etc. so that people can hear: *He read out the name of the winners.*

read sth ↔ **through/over** *phr. v.* to read something carefully from beginning to end in order to check

R

details or find mistakes: *Read the contract over carefully before you sign it.*

read up on/about sth *phr. v.* INFORMAL to read a lot about something because you will need to know about it: *I'll have to read up on the tax laws before the meeting tomorrow.*

read² *n.* [singular] **1 a good read** something that you enjoy reading: *It's not great literature, but it's a good read.* **2** someone's judgment about what is happening in a situation: **+on** *He seems to have a good read on his players.*

read·a·ble /ˈridəbəl/ *adj.* **1** interesting or enjoyable to read, and easy to understand OPP **unreadable**: *a long but readable article* **2** writing or print that is readable is clear and easy to read → see also LEGIBLE **3** a computer document or file that is readable by a program can be seen in that program → see also MACHINE READABLE —**readability** /ˌridəˈbɪləṭi/ *n.* [U]

read·er /ˈridɚ/ S2 W2 *n.* [C] **1** someone who reads something: *The book will appeal to young readers.* | *letters from our readers* | **a fast/slow/good/careful etc. reader** *I'm a really slow reader.* | **+of** *readers of the New York Times* | **Times/Post/Newsweek etc. readers** *Post readers may have a very different view of the situation.* | **a great/an avid reader** (=someone who reads often and enjoys it very much) **2** an easy book to help children learn to read, to help people learn a foreign language etc. → see also MIND READER

read·er·ship /ˈridɚˌʃɪp/ *n.* [C,U] the people who read a particular newspaper or magazine: *The magazine has a readership of 60,000.*

read·i·ly /ˈrɛdl-i/ *adv.* **1** quickly and easily: **readily available/accessible** *Fresh cilantro is readily available in most supermarkets.* **2** quickly, willingly, and without arguing: *McGrath readily agreed to go.* | **readily admit/acknowledge** *I readily admit the plan isn't perfect.*

read·i·ness /ˈrɛdinɪs/ *n.* **1** [singular, U] willingness to do something: **readiness to do sth** *Both sides expressed their readiness to begin peace talks.* **2** [U] a state of being prepared and ready for what is going to happen: *They stacked firewood **in readiness for** the long winter ahead.*

read·ing /ˈridɪŋ/ S2 W2 *n.*
1 ACTIVITY/SKILL [U] the activity of looking at and understanding written words: *His hobbies include reading and hiking.* | *The children are separated into groups for reading.* | *reading skills*
2 BOOKS [U] the books, articles etc. that you read: *a child's bedtime reading* | *The book was on a list of **background reading** for the class.* (=reading that is helpful for the class) | **light reading** (=books that are enjoyable and easy to read) | **reading material/matter** (=books, articles etc. that you read, especially for a particular purpose)
3 UNDERSTANDING [C] your opinion of what a particular statement, situation, piece of art etc. means SYN **interpretation**: *What's your reading of the situation?*
4 MEASUREMENT [C] a number or amount shown on a measuring instrument: *Temperature readings were as cold as –2°.*
5 TO A GROUP [C] ENG. LANG. ARTS an occasion when a piece of literature is read to a group of people: *a poetry reading at the bookstore* | **+from** *readings from the classics*
6 FROM HOLY BOOK [C] a piece of writing from a holy book that is read to a group of people as part of a religious service: **+from** *a reading from the Koran*
7 ACT OF READING STH [singular] the act of reading something: *a casual reading of the text*
8 IN CONGRESS [C] POLITICS one of the three occasions in the U.S. Congress when a BILL (=suggested new law) is read and discussed: *the second reading of the Industrial Relations Bill*
9 make (for) good/interesting/boring etc. reading to be enjoyable, interesting etc. to read: *Your report made fascinating reading.*

re·ad·just /ˌriəˈdʒʌst/ Ac *v.* **1** [I] to change the way you do things because of a new situation, job, or way of life: **+to** *It's difficult for prisoners to readjust to life outside prison.* **2** [T] to make a small change to something or to its position: *Remember to readjust the mirrors in the car.* —**readjustment** *n.* [C,U]

ˌread-only ˈmemory *n.* [C,U] COMPUTERS ROM

read·out /ˈridaʊt/ *n.* [C] a record of information that has been produced by a computer, shown on a SCREEN or in print: *an electronic readout of the patient's vital signs* → see also PRINTOUT

read·y¹ /ˈrɛdi/ S1 W1 *adj.*
1 PREPARED [not before noun] prepared for what you are going to do: *Wait a minute. I'm not ready.* | **ready to do sth** *Are you guys ready to go?* | **+for** *I don't feel ready for the test.* | **almost/just about/nearly ready** *We're almost ready to eat.* | **get (sb) ready (for sth)** *She's still getting ready for work.* | *You have to be **ready for anything*** (=prepared to deal with anything that happens) *if you want to win.* | *Ok, are we all **ready to roll*** (=ready to start doing something)*?*
2 FOR IMMEDIATE USE [not before noun] something that is ready has been prepared and can be used, eaten etc. immediately: *Is dinner ready yet?* | *Your dry cleaning will be ready on Thursday.* | **+for** *Is everything ready for the exhibition?* | *Can you **get** breakfast **ready** for the kids?* | *I've got to **have** this report **ready** by Monday morning.* | **ready to use/eat/cook etc.** *The potatoes are ready to cook.* | **ready to be used/eaten/cooked etc.** *These letters are ready to be mailed.* | *The bulldozers are **ready and waiting*** (=used to emphasize that something is ready). | **make sth ready** LITERARY: *The ship was made ready to sail.*
3 be ready for sth SPOKEN to feel that you want something to happen immediately, especially because you cannot deal with a bad situation much longer: *You must be ready for a drink after all that hard work.*
4 be (getting) ready to do sth INFORMAL to be about to do something, or feel strongly as if you could do something: *I was just getting ready to call you.* | *By the end I was ready to scream* (=I felt frustrated enough to scream).
5 WILLING willing and quick to do or give something: **+with** *Jim's father is always ready with advice.* | **ready to do sth** *Management was ready to declare the project a failure.* | *There are hundreds of people who are **ready, willing, and able*** (=used to emphasize that they are very willing) *to work, but there aren't any jobs here.*
6 QUICK [only before noun] quick or without delay: *a ready answer* | *On the Internet, you have **ready access** to huge amounts of information.*
7 ready money/cash money that can be spent at once in coins or paper money: *He was only willing to sell it for ready cash.*
8 (get) ready, (get) set, go! SPOKEN used to tell people to start a race
[**Origin:** 1100–1200 Old English *ræde* **prepared**] → see also READILY, READINESS, **rough and ready** at ROUGH¹ (14)

ready² *n.* FORMAL **at the ready** available to be used immediately: *The crowd stood around, cameras at the ready.*

ready³ *v.* **readies, readied, readying** [T] FORMAL to make something ready

ˌready-ˈmade *adj.* [only before noun] **1** ready-made goods are already made in standard sizes, and are ready for you to use immediately OPP **custom-made**: *ready-made curtains* | *ready-made clothes* **2** ready-made food is already prepared and ready for you to use immediately OPP **homemade**: *ready-made pie crust* **3** ready-made ideas or reasons are provided for you, so that you do not have to think of them yourself: *a ready-made excuse*

ˌready-to-ˈwear *adj.* OLD-FASHIONED ready-to-wear clothes are made in standard sizes, not made specially to fit one person

re·af·firm /ˌriəˈfɚm/ *v.* [T] to formally state an intention, belief etc. again, especially as an answer to a question or doubt: *He reaffirmed his belief that a solution could be found.* | **+that** *The governor has reaffirm-*

ed that education is a top priority. —**reaffirmation** /ˌriæfəˈmeɪʃən/ *n.* [C,U]

Rea·gan /ˈreɪgən/, **Ron·ald** /ˈrɑnld/ (1911–2004) the 40th President of the U.S.

Rea·gan·om·ics /ˌreɪgəˈnɑmɪks/ *n.* [U] HISTORY the economic measures followed by the U.S. government during the 1980s when Ronald Reagan was President, that included reducing taxes, spending less on WELFARE, and increasing military spending

re·a·gent /riˈeɪdʒənt/ *n.* [C] CHEMISTRY a substance that shows that another substance in a compound exists, by causing a chemical REACTION

real[1] /ril/ S1 W1 *adj.*
1 NOT IMAGINARY actually existing and not just imagined: *All of the characters are based on real people.* | *My son still believes that Santa Claus is real.* | *She's much nicer **in real life** than she is in the movie.* | *She'd never seen **a real live** elephant before* (=used to talk about things that are physically present rather than seen on TV, in pictures etc.).
2 IMPORTANT existing as a fact, so that it is important enough to consider, worry about etc.: *It's not a joke. They could be in real danger.* | **no real chance/hope/reason etc.** *There is no real cause for concern.*
3 NOT ARTIFICIAL something that is real is actually what it seems to be and not artificial, false, invented, or a copy SYN **genuine** OPP **fake**: *real leather* | *It was just a practice test, not **the real thing**.* | *This is genuine malt whiskey – **the real McCoy*** (=used to emphasize that something really is what it seems).
4 NOT CLAIMED [only before noun] actual and true, as opposed to being invented or claimed SYN **actual**: *So what's the real reason you were late?* | *Marilyn Monroe's real name was Norma Jean Baker.*
5 used to emphasize what you are saying: *The house is a real mess.* | *The noise is becoming a real problem.*
6 RIGHT QUALITIES [only before noun] having all the right qualities that you expect a particular kind of thing or person to have: *He's never had a real job.* | *Now that's real coffee!*
7 the real world used to talk about the actual experience of living and working with other people, rather than being protected in your parents' home, at school, or at college: *When you're out there **in the real world** you won't have so much help.*
8 MOST IMPORTANT the real questions, problems etc. are the most important ones: *The real issue is how can we help prevent heart disease?*
9 MONEY [only before noun] ECONOMICS a real increase or decrease in an amount of money is one you calculate by including the general decrease in the value of money over a period of time: *a 2% annual growth in real income* | ***In real terms*** (=calculated in this way) *the value of their wages has fallen.*

SPOKEN PHRASES

10 for real seriously, not pretending: *He quit smoking? For real?*
11 get real! used to tell someone that they are being very silly or unreasonable: *"Get real! He'll never make the team."*
12 keep it real to behave in an honest way and not pretend to be different from how they really are
13 is sb for real? used when you are very surprised by or disapprove of what someone has done or said

[**Origin:** 1400–1500 Old French, Medieval Latin *realis* **of things (in law)**, from Latin *res* **thing**]

real[2] S1 *adv.* SPOKEN very: *It was real nice to see you again.*

real[3] *n.* [C] the standard unit of money used in Brazil

ˈreal esˌtate W3 *n.* [U] **1** property in the form of land or houses **2** the business of selling houses or land

ˈreal estate ˌagent *n.* [C] someone whose job is to sell houses or land for other people

ˌreal GDˈP *n.* [singular] ECONOMICS **real gross domestic product** a measure of the total value of all the goods and services produced in a country during a particular period, including an amount for INFLATION (=a continuing increase in prices, or the rate at which this happens). Real GDP is a true measure of a country's ability to produce goods more successfully than it did in the past or to produce them more successfully than other countries.

ˌreal GDˌP per ˈcapita *n.* [singular] ECONOMICS **real gross domestic product per capita** a measure of total goods and services produced by each person living in a country during a particular period, including an amount for INFLATION (=a continuing increase in prices, or the rate at which this happens). The figure is obtained by dividing REAL GDP by the total number of people living in a country.

re·a·lign /ˌriəˈlaɪn/ *v.* **1** [T] to arrange something differently in relation to something else: *We replaced the windows and realigned the door.* **2** to change the way in which a group, company etc. is organized SYN **reorganize**: *Teams are now realigned according to players' ages.* **3 realign yourself with sb** to begin to support and work together with someone again: *They have tried to realign themselves with moderate Democrats.*

re·a·lign·ment /ˌriəˈlaɪnmənt/ *n.* [C,U] **1** the act of changing a group, company etc. so that it is organized in a different way SYN **reorganization**: +**of** *a realignment of the political parties* **2** the process of changing the position of something, especially so that it is in the correct position in relation to something else: *the realignment of broken bones* **3** the act of ending your support for one group and starting to support and work together with a different group: *political realignments*

re·al·ism /ˈriəˌlɪzəm/ *n.* [U] **1** the ability to accept and deal with situations in a practical way, based on what is possible rather than what you would like to happen → see also IDEALISM: *He has hope, but also a scientist's realism.* **2** the quality of being or seeming real: *the realism of video games* **3** also **Realism** ENG. LANG. ARTS a style of art and literature, which started in 19th-century France, in which everything is shown or described as it really is in life → see also CLASSICISM, ROMANTICISM —**realist** *n.* [C]

re·al·is·tic /ˌriəˈlɪstɪk/ *adj.* **1** decisions, plans, or aims that are realistic are based on what is actually possible, rather than on the way you would like things to be OPP **unrealistic**: *Set realistic goals for yourself.* | **it is realistic to do sth** *It's not realistic to expect a promotion so soon.* **2** someone who is realistic thinks in a realistic way OPP **unrealistic**: **be realistic (about sth)** *Be realistic, George. We can't afford this.* **3** ENG. LANG. ARTS pictures, models, plays etc. that are realistic show things as they are in real life: *The game's graphics are amazingly realistic.* | *a realistic television drama*

re·al·is·ti·cally /ˌriəˈlɪstɪkli/ *adv.* **1** in a practical way and according to what is actually possible: *You can realistically expect to pay about $150 a ticket.* | [sentence adverb] *Realistically, there was not much we could do to help.* **2** in a way that shows or describes things as they are in real life: *realistically painted toy soldiers*

re·al·i·ty /riˈæləṭi/ S2 W2 *n.* **1** [C,U] things that actually happen or are true, not things that are imagined or thought about: *the difference between fantasy and reality* | *political realities* | **the reality/realities of sth** *They were unprepared for the reality of city life.* | **the harsh/grim/hard etc. realities** *the harsh realities of prison life* | *They keep saying they'll pay, but **the reality is that** there's no money left.* | *TV is used as **an escape from reality**.* | **in touch/out of touch with reality** (=understanding, or no longer understanding, what is true or real in a situation) **2 in reality** used to say something is different from what people think: *He said he'd retired, but in reality he was fired.* **3** [C] something that actually exists or happens: *Frank's dream of opening a restaurant **became a reality** in 1987.* | *You have the ability to **make** your dream **a reality**.* **4** [U] the fact that something actually exists: *her belief in God's reality*

reˈality ˌcheck *n.* [C usually singular] INFORMAL an occasion when you consider the actual facts of a situation, as opposed to what you would like or what you have imagined: *We made a budget to give ourselves a reality check.*

re,ality T'V *n.* [U] television shows that do not have a SCRIPT and that follow real people, rather than people who are acting, as they take part in actual situations, competitions etc.: *a reality TV show*

re·al·iz·a·ble /ˌriəˈlaɪzəbəl/ *adj.* **1** possible to achieve: *realizable goals* **2** in a form that can be changed into money: *realizable value*

re·al·i·za·tion /ˌriələˈzeɪʃən/ *n.* [singular, U] **1** the act of understanding something that you had not noticed before: **+that** *the realization that I was unhappy in my marriage* | *The city council has* ***come to the realization that*** *the plan is too expensive.* | *There was a* ***growing realization*** *that the war would not end soon.* **2** the act of achieving what you had planned, hoped, or aimed for SYN **achievement**: **+of** *the realization of a childhood dream* **3** FORMAL the act of changing something into money by selling it: **+of** *the realization of assets*

R

re·al·ize /ˈriəˌlaɪz/ S1 W1 *v.* [T not usually in progressive] **1** KNOW STH to know and understand a situation or fact: **realize (that)** *My family realizes that I have to take this job.* | **realize who/what/how etc.** *I wonder if the kids who stole that stuff realize its value.* | **realize sth** *Teenagers don't realize the danger of unprotected sex.*
2 KNOW STH NEW to start to know something that you had not noticed before: **realize (that)** *We didn't realize that it would take so long to get here.* | **realize who/what/how etc.** *I suddenly realized how difficult it was going to be.* | **realize sth** *He'd hurt his arm, but didn't realize it until later.*

THESAURUS

become aware to gradually realize that something is happening or is true: *I became aware that two girls were watching me.*
dawn on sb to realize something for the first time: *It dawned on me that he could be lying.*
sink in to begin to understand something or realize its full meaning: *It took a few minutes for the doctor's words to sink in.*

3 realize an ambition/hope/goal etc. FORMAL to achieve something that you were hoping to achieve: *Two years later she realized her ambition of winning a gold medal.*
4 MONEY FORMAL **a)** to obtain an amount of money, especially by selling something: *We* ***realized a profit on*** *the house.* **b)** to change something that you own into money, especially by selling it: *We were obliged to realize most of our assets.* → see also **sb's worst fears were realized** at WORST[1] (3)

real·ly /ˈrili/ S1 W1 *adv.* **1** a word meaning "very" or "very much," used to emphasize something: *Tom's a really nice guy.* | *His letter really irritated her.* | *It doesn't really matter, does it?* **2** used to talk about what actually happens or is true, rather than what seems to be true or what someone claims is true: *What really happened?* | *That doll might really be valuable.*

SPOKEN PHRASES

3 used to emphasize something you are saying: *I really don't mind.* | *No, really, I'm fine. Don't worry.* **4 really? a)** used to show that you are surprised by what someone has said: *"He'll be ninety-two this year." "Really?"* **b)** used in conversation to show that you are listening to or interested in what the other person is saying: *"It's raining here." "Oh, really? It's nice here."* **5 not really** used to say "no," especially when something is not completely true: *"Are you hungry yet?" "Not really."* **6 (yeah) really** used to express agreement: *"I'm so ready for vacation." "Yeah, really."* **7** used to express disapproval: *Really, Matt, did you have to make such a mess?*

GRAMMAR

Really is often used with an adjective or adverb to mean "very": *I'm really fed up with this job.* | *Mike did really well on his physics test.* **Real** is also used to mean "very," but only in informal speech, and is considered by some people to be grammatically incorrect: *That's a real nice car.*
Really meaning "very" must go immediately before the adjective it strengthens: *He's a really nice man* (=a very nice man). | *Kim's really excited about going to Paris.*
Really in other positions usually emphasizes that what you are saying is true, even though it might not seem to be true: *Really, I'm fine* (=I feel good, even though you might not think so). *Deep down, Shane really is a nice guy.* **Really** is usually used before a verb but not immediately after it (except after the verb **to be**): *It's really cold in here.* | *Dad never really did like traveling.*

USAGE **SPELLING**
Remember there are two l's in **really.**

realm /rɛlm/ *n.* [C] **1** a general area of knowledge, activity, or thought: *the spiritual realm* | **+of** *new discoveries in the realm of science* **2 within the realm(s) of possibility** possible: *I didn't think college was even in the realms of possibility for me.* **3** POLITICS a country ruled over by a king or queen

ˌreal ˈnumber *n.* [C] MATH any number that is not an IMAGINARY NUMBER (=a number that has a part that is the square root of a negative number). Real numbers are either RATIONAL NUMBERS or IRRATIONAL NUMBERS.

re·al·po·li·tik /reɪˈælpɑlɪˌtik/ *n.* [U] POLITICS politics based on practical situations and needs rather than on principles or ideas

ˈreal ˌproperty *n.* [U] ECONOMICS land, buildings etc. that are owned by someone → see also REAL ESTATE

ˈreal-time *adj.* [only before noun] COMPUTERS a real-time computer system deals with information as fast as it receives it —**real time** *n.* [U]: *Airline booking systems need to work in real time.*

Real·tor, realtor /ˈriltɚ/ *n.* [C] TRADEMARK a REAL ESTATE AGENT who belongs to the National Association of Realtors

real·ty /ˈrilti/ *n.* [U] TECHNICAL → see REAL ESTATE

ream[1] /rim/ *n.* **1 reams** [plural] INFORMAL a large amount of writing on paper: **+of** *reams of documents* **2** [C] TECHNICAL a standard amount of paper, consisting of 500 pieces of paper

ream[2] *v.* [T] **1** INFORMAL to cheat someone or treat them badly, especially so that they have to pay too much for something **2** INFORMAL also **ream sb out** to criticize someone severely **3** TECHNICAL to make a hole larger

re·an·i·mate /riˈænəˌmeɪt/ *v.* [T] FORMAL to give someone or something new strength or the energy to start again

reap /rip/ *v.* [I,T] **1** to get something as a result of what you have done: **reap the benefits/profits (of sth)** *Don't let others reap the benefits of your research.* **2** to cut and gather a crop of grain **3 you reap what you sow** SPOKEN used to say that if you do bad things, bad things will happen to you, and if you do good things, good things will happen to you → see also HARVEST

reap·er /ˈripɚ/ *n.* [C] a machine or person that cuts and gathers a crop of grain → see also GRIM REAPER

re·ap·pear /ˌriəˈpɪr/ *v.* [I] to appear again after not being seen for a while: *In March, his cancer reappeared.* | *He reappeared, carrying an umbrella.* —**reappearance** *n.* [C,U]

re·ap·por·tion·ment /ˌriəˈpɔrʃənmənt/ *n.* [U] TECHNICAL the process of changing the numbers of members of the House of Representatives that each state has, based on changes in the states' populations —**reapportion** *v.* [T]

re·ap·praise /ˌriəˈpreɪz/ *v.* [T] to examine something again in order to consider whether you should change your opinion of it: *We have reappraised our economic forecast.* —**reappraisal** *n.* [C,U]

rear[1] /rɪr/ *n.* **1 the rear** the back part of an object, vehicle, or building, or a position at the back of an object or area → see also FRONT: **in/at the rear (of sth)** *The engine is in the rear.* | *There are more seats at the rear of the theater.* **2** [C] also **rear end** INFORMAL the part of your body that you sit on SYN **butt**: *Get up off your rear end and do something.* **3 be bringing up the rear** to be at the back of a line of people or in a race

rear² *adj.* [only before noun] at or near the back of something: *the rear door of the car* | *the plane's right rear tire*

rear³ *v.* **1** [T] to take care of a person or animal until they are fully grown: *She's reared a large family.* | *cattle rearing* **2** [I] also **rear up** if an animal rears, it rises upright on its back legs → see also BUCK **3 be reared on sth** to be given a particular kind of food, books, entertainment etc. regularly while you are a child: *We were reared on junk food and B-movies.* **4 sth rears its ugly head** INFORMAL if a problem or difficult situation rears its ugly head, it appears and is impossible to ignore

ˌrear ˈadmiral, Rear Admiral *n.* [C] a high rank in the navy, or someone who has this rank

rear·guard /ˈrɪrgɑrd/ *n.* **fight a rearguard action a)** to make a determined effort to prevent a change that you think is bad, although it seems too late to stop it: *A rearguard action is being fought against the sale of the land.* **b)** if an army fights a rearguard action, it defends itself at the back against an enemy that is chasing it

re-arm, re-arm /riˈɑrm/ *v.* [I,T] to obtain weapons again or provide someone else with new weapons: *Both armies were rearming heavily for combat.* —**rearmament** *n.* [U]

rear·most /ˈrɪrmoʊst/ *adj.* [only before noun] furthest back SYN **back**: *the rearmost section of the plane*

re·ar·range /ˌriəˈreɪndʒ/ *v.* [T] **1** to change the position or order of things: *We rearranged all the furniture in the living room.* **2** to change the time of a meeting or planned event: *Can we rearrange your appointment for next Thursday?* —**rearrangement** *n.* [C,U]

rear·view mir·ror /ˌrɪrvyu ˈmɪrɚ/ *n.* [C] a mirror in a vehicle that lets the driver see the area behind them → see picture on page A36

rear·ward /ˈrɪrwɚd/ *adj.* in or toward the back of something —**rearward** also **rearwards** *adv.*

rea·son¹ /ˈrizən/ S1 W1 *n.*

1 CAUSE [C] the cause or fact that explains why something has happened or happens, or why someone has done something: **+for** *I told her my reasons for wanting to find a new job.* | **+behind** *He explained the reasons behind the decision.* | **reason (that)** *The reason I called was to ask about the plans for Saturday.* | **reason (why)** *The professor asked the reason why she had been late so often.* | *The real reason we weren't getting along was money.* | **a reason to do sth** *We have to give people a reason to vote for us.* | *McNamara left without* ***giving any reason.*** | **for personal/health etc. reasons** *She resigned for health reasons.* | *The main tower has been closed* ***for reasons of*** *safety.* | *They've decided to change all our job titles,* ***for some reason*** (=for a reason you do not know or cannot understand). | *"Why did you tell him?" "Oh, I* ***had my reasons*** (=had a secret reason for doing it)." | ***For reasons best known to*** *herself,* (=for reasons other people do not understand) *she's sold the house.* | *Geiger was found not guilty* ***by reason of*** *insanity.*

> **THESAURUS**
> **explanation** a reason that you give for why something happened or why you did something: *Is there any explanation for his behavior?*
> **excuse** a reason that you give for why you did something bad: *Mother was disappointed that Jo had not come, and Rosa made excuses for her.*
> **motive** a reason that makes someone do something, especially something bad: *The police have found no motive for the attack.*

2 GOOD OR FAIR REASON [U] a fact that makes it right or fair for someone to do something: **reason to do sth** *Porter* ***has reason to*** *be cautious.* | *There is* ***no reason to*** *panic.* | *Under the circumstances we* ***had every reason to*** (=had very good reasons to) *be suspicious.* | **be no reason to do sth** *There is no reason to believe he will die.* | *Natalie was alarmed by the news, and* ***with good reason.***

3 all the more reason to do sth SPOKEN used to say that what has just been mentioned is an additional reason for doing what you have suggested: *I know there isn't much time, but that's all the more reason to act quickly.*

4 GOOD JUDGMENT [U] sensible judgment and understanding: *In times of war, reason can give way to racism.* | *He says his client wouldn't* ***listen to reason*** (=would not be persuaded by sensible advice). | *They tried to make her* ***see reason*** (=accept advice and make a sensible decision).

5 within reason within sensible limits: *You can go anywhere you want, within reason.*

6 beyond (all) reason a) to an extreme degree: *She spoils the boy beyond all reason.* **b)** in such a state that you are unable to think sensibly: *By this time the child was beyond all reason.*

7 ABILITY TO THINK [U] the ability to think, understand, and form judgments that are based on facts: *the human power of reason* | *Maya feared that she was* ***losing her reason*** (=becoming mentally ill).

8 no reason SPOKEN used when someone asks you why you are doing something and you do not want to tell them: *"Why do ask?" "Oh, no reason."*

[Origin: 1200–1300 Old French *raison*, from Latin *ratio* **calculation, reason]** → see also **rhyme or reason** at RHYME¹ (4), **it stands to reason** at STAND¹ (36)

> **GRAMMAR**
> • **Reason** is often followed by **for, that,** or **why**: *What's the reason for all this noise?* (NOT "the reason **of**" or "**to**") | *the reason that/why he left* (NOT *the reason because/how he left...*). It is also possible to leave out **that**: *the reason he left.* The nature of a **reason** is usually described in a *that* clause: *The reason for the party was that it was Sue's birthday.* In spoken English you may also hear *because* used, although this is considered incorrect by many speakers: *The reason for the party is because it's Sue's birthday.*
> • **Purpose** is often followed by **of** or **in**: *The purpose of the trip/of my coming is to see the President* (NOT *The purpose why I'm coming...*). | *My purpose in coming is to see the President* (NOT *of/for coming...*). People usually say *For this reason/purpose...* (NOT *from/because of this reason..., in/on this purpose* or *for this cause*).

reason² S2 W2 *v.* **1** [T] to form a particular judgment about a situation after carefully considering the facts: **reason (that)** *He reasoned that complaining would do no good.* **2** [I] to think and make judgments: *the ability to reason*

reason sth **out** *phr. v.* to find an explanation or solution to a problem, by thinking of all the possibilities SYN **figure sth out**

reason with sb *phr. v.* to talk to someone in order to try to persuade them to be more sensible: *They tried to reason with him and persuade him to come home.*

rea·son·a·ble /ˈriznəbəl, -zən-/ S3 W3 *adj.* **1** fair and sensible OPP **unreasonable**: *a reasonable request* | *His explanation seemed reasonable to me.* | *Mason is a reasonable man.* | ***It is reasonable to*** *suppose that prices will come down soon.* ►see THESAURUS box at **fair¹** **2** fairly good, but not especially good: *a reasonable standard of living* ►see THESAURUS box at **satisfactory** **3** fairly large or great: *I have a reasonable amount of money saved.* | *Kelly has* ***a reasonable chance of*** *doing well on the exam.* **4** prices that are reasonable seem fair because they are not too high: *good quality furniture at reasonable prices* ►see THESAURUS box at **cheap¹** **5 beyond a reasonable doubt** LAW if something is proved beyond a reasonable doubt, it is shown to be almost certainly true —**reasonableness** *n.* [U]

R

rea·son·a·bly /ˈriznəbli/ *adv.* **1** [+ adj./adv.] to a satisfactory degree, although not completely: *Dad's in reasonably good shape for a 68-year-old.* **2** in a way that is right or fair: *How long before we can reasonably expect to see an improvement?* **3** in a sensible and reasonable way: *Despite her anger, she behaved very reasonably.* **4 reasonably priced** not too expensive: *a reasonably priced restaurant*

rea·soned /ˈrizənd/ *adj.* [only before noun] based on careful thought, and therefore sensible: *a reasoned response*

rea·son·ing /ˈrizənɪŋ/ *n.* [U] the process of thinking carefully about something in order to make a judgment: **+behind** *What is the reasoning behind this proposal?* | **scientific/moral/logical etc. reasoning** *studies of legal reasoning* | *Your* ***line of reasoning*** (=way of thinking or arguing) *is not logical.*

re·as·sur·ance /ˌriəˈʃʊrəns/ *n.* [C,U] something someone says or does that makes you feel less worried or frightened about a problem: **give/offer/provide reassurance** *Parents were giving reassurance to their children.* | **+that** *The mayor gave reassurances that the water was safe to drink.*

re·as·sure /ˌriəˈʃʊr/ *v.* [T] to make someone feel calmer and less worried or frightened about a problem or situation: *Officials reassured callers who were worried about the fires.* | **reassure sb (that)** *He tried to reassure me that my mother would be okay.* → see Word Choice box at INSURE

re·as·sur·ing /ˌriəˈʃʊrɪŋ/ *adj.* making you feel less worried or frightened: *Routines are reassuring to a child.* | **it is reassuring to know/hear etc. sth** *It's reassuring to know that problems like this are rare.* —**reassuringly** *adv.*

re·bate /ˈribeɪt/ *n.* [C] an amount of money that is paid back to you when you have paid too much tax, rent etc.: *a tax rebate* [**Origin:** 1600–1700 *rebate* **to make a rebate** (15–21 centuries), from Old French *rabattre* **to beat down again**]

reb·el¹ /ˈrɛbəl/ *n.* [C] **1** someone who opposes or fights against people in authority: *anti-government rebels* | *rebel soldiers* **2** someone who refuses to do things in the normal way, or in the way that other people want them to: *a teenage rebel* **3** POLITICS someone who opposes the leaders of their organization or political party [**Origin:** 1300–1400 *rebel* **rebellious** (13–21 centuries), from Old French *rebelle*, from Latin, from *bellum* **war**]

re·bel² /rɪˈbɛl/ *v.* **rebelled, rebelling** [I] **1** to oppose or fight against someone in a position of authority: **rebel against sb/sth** *a teenager who rebelled against his father* | *ordinary people rebelling against the government* ►see THESAURUS box at **disobey** **2** WRITTEN if your stomach, legs, mind etc. rebel, you cannot make them work correctly: *He knew he should eat, but his stomach rebelled.*

re·bel·lion /rɪˈbɛlyən/ *n.* [C,U] **1** POLITICS an organized attempt to change the government, or other authority, using violence: *an armed rebellion* | **+against** *a rebellion against the military regime* | **put down/crush a rebellion** (=use violence to stop it) ►see THESAURUS box at **revolution** **2** opposition to someone in authority or to normal or usual ways of doing things: *a rebellion by right-wing members of the party* | **+against** *the artist's rebellion against the styles of other popular painters* → see also REVOLUTION

re·bel·lious /rɪˈbɛlyəs/ *adj.* **1** deliberately disobeying someone in authority: *the rebellious daughter of a military man* | *rebellious behavior* **2** fighting against the government of your country: *rebellious soldiers* —**rebelliously** *adv.* —**rebelliousness** *n.* [U]

re·birth /riˈbɚθ, ˈribɚθ/ *n.* [singular] FORMAL a change by which an important idea, feeling, or organization becomes active again: *a rebirth of nationalism in the region* | *spiritual rebirth*

re·boot /riˈbut/ *v.* [I,T] COMPUTERS if you reboot a computer, or if it reboots, it starts again after it has stopped working

re·born /riˈbɔrn/ *adj.* [not before noun] LITERARY **1 be reborn** to start existing or being active again, often being different and better: *In the past decade, the city has been reborn.* **2 be reborn** to be born again, especially according to some religions, ancient stories etc.

re·bound¹ /ˈribaʊnd, rɪˈbaʊnd/ *v.* **1** [I,T] to catch a basketball after a player has tried but failed to get a point **2** [I] if a ball or other moving object rebounds, it moves quickly back away from something it has just hit: **+off** *The ball rebounded off the rim.* **3** [I] ECONOMICS if prices, values etc. rebound, they increase again after decreasing SYN **recover**: *Share prices rebounded today after last week's losses.* **4** [I] if someone rebounds from something, they become more popular, healthy, happy etc. after a bad experience SYN **bounce back**: **+from** *Can he rebound from the bad publicity?*

rebound on/upon sb *phr. v.* if a harmful action rebounds on someone, it has a bad effect on the person who did it SYN **backfire**

re·bound² /ˈribaʊnd/ *n.* **1 a) on the rebound** someone who is on the rebound is upset or confused because their romantic relationship has just ended: *We met when I was on the rebound from a very messy affair.* **b)** while one or more basketball players are trying to catch a ball that has bounced off the basket after an attempt to make a point has failed: *Johnson was fouled on the rebound.* **c)** a ball that is on the rebound is moving back through the air after hitting something **d)** something that is on the rebound is starting to increase or improve again: *His acting career seems to be on the rebound.* **2** [C] TECHNICAL an act of catching a BASKETBALL after a player has tried but failed to get a point

re·buff /rɪˈbʌf/ *n.* [C] FORMAL an unkind or unfriendly answer to a friendly suggestion or offer of help SYN **snub**: *He ignored her rebuff.* [**Origin:** 1500–1600 Early French *rebuffer*, from Old Italian *ribuffare* **to criticize angrily**] —**rebuff** *v.* [T]

re·build /riˈbɪld/ *v. past tense and past participle* **rebuilt** /-ˈbɪlt/ [T] **1** to build something again, after it has been damaged or destroyed: *Many houses needed to be rebuilt after the earthquake.* ►see THESAURUS box at **repair¹** **2** to make something strong and successful again: *The country is trying to rebuild after years of war.* | *The law will make it hard for people to* ***rebuild their lives*** *after bankruptcy.*

re·buke /rɪˈbyuk/ *v.* [T] FORMAL to speak to someone severely about something they have done wrong SYN **reprimand** SYN **reprove**: **rebuke sb for doing sth** *Jury members were rebuked for speaking with the press.* [**Origin:** 1300–1400 Old North French *rebuker*, from *bukier* **to hit, cut down**] —**rebuke** *n.* [C,U]

re·bus /ˈribəs/ *n.* [C usually singular] a set of pictures in which the names of the objects in the pictures are similar to a word or phrase when they are said out loud. For example, a picture of an eye would represent the word "I."

re·but /rɪˈbʌt/ *v.* **rebutted, rebutting** [T] FORMAL to prove that a statement or a charge made against you is false SYN **refute** —**rebuttal** *n.* [C]

re·cal·ci·trant /rɪˈkælsətrənt/ *adj.* FORMAL refusing to do what you are told to do, even after you have been punished SYN **unruly**: *recalcitrant students* —**recalcitrantly** *adv.* —**recalcitrance** *n.* [U]

re·call¹ /rɪˈkɔl/ S3 W2 *v.* [T]

1 REMEMBER STH [not in progressive] to deliberately remember a particular fact, event, or situation from the past, especially in order to tell someone about it SYN **recollect**: *I couldn't even recall his name.* | **recall that** *Later, he recalled that McGregor had missed the appointment.* | **recall doing sth** *I don't recall ever meeting her.* | **recall what/how/where etc.** *Mrs. Adkins cannot recall what happened the night she was attacked.* | ***As I recall***, *it was particularly hot that summer.*

2 PRODUCT if a company recalls one of its products, it asks you to return it because there may be something wrong with it: *Over 10,000 of the irons had to be recalled.*
3 PERSON to officially tell someone to come back from a place where they have been sent: **recall sb from sth** *The Ambassador was recalled from Washington.*
4 ON A COMPUTER to bring information back onto the screen of a computer
5 BE SIMILAR TO FORMAL if something recalls something else, it makes you think of it because it is very similar: *a style of film-making that recalls Alfred Hitchcock*
6 POLITICS to vote to remove a politician from their political position —**recallable** *adj.*

re•call² /ˈrikɔl, rɪˈkɔl/ *n.* **1** [U] the ability to remember something that you have learned or experienced: *Your recall may improve if you take notes.* | *He has almost* ***total recall*** (=the ability to remember everything) *of everything he reads.* **2** [singular, U] POLITICS a vote to remove someone from their political position, or the act of being removed by a vote: +**of** *the recall of four city council officials* **3** [C] an action in which a company tells people to return a product they bought because there is something wrong with it **4** [singular, U] an official order telling someone to return from a place, especially before they were expected to: *the recall of their ambassador* **5 beyond recall** impossible to bring back or remember

re•cant /rɪˈkænt/ *v.* [I,T] FORMAL to say publicly that you no longer have a belief that you had before, especially a political or religious belief SYN **retract**: *Galileo was forced to recant his belief in the Copernican theory.* —**recantation** /ˌrikænˈteɪʃən/ *n.* [C,U]

re•cap /ˈrikæp, riˈkæp/ *v.* **recapped, recapping** [I,T] to repeat the main points of something that has just been said SYN **recapitulate** —**recap** /ˈrikæp/ *n.* [C]

re•cap•i•tal•ize /riˈkæpɪtḷˌaɪz/ *v.* [T] to INVEST more money into a company or bank, so that it can operate correctly —**recapitalization** /riˌkæpɪtḷ-əˈzeɪʃən/ *n.* [U]

re•ca•pit•u•late /ˌrikəˈpɪtʃəˌleɪt/ *v.* [I,T] FORMAL to repeat the main points of something that has just been said SYN **recap** —**recapitulation** /ˌrikəpɪtʃəˈleɪʃən/ *n.* [C,U]

re•cap•ture /riˈkæptʃɚ/ *v.* [T] **1** to bring back feelings or qualities that were experienced in the past, so that someone can experience them again or see what they were like: *His book recaptures the excitement of life in the Old West.* **2** to catch a prisoner or animal that has escaped **3** to take control of a place again by fighting for it SYN **retake** —**recapture** *n.* [U]

re•cast /riˈkæst/ *v. past tense and past participle* **recast** [T] **1** to give something a new shape or a new form of organization: *The stories have been recast for young readers.* **2** ENG. LANG. ARTS to give parts in a play or movie to different actors —**recasting** *n.* [C,U]

recd. the written abbreviation of "received"

re•cede /rɪˈsid/ *v.* [I] **1** if something you can see or hear recedes, it gets further and further away until it disappears: +**into/from** *The two figures receded into the mist.* **2** if a memory, feeling, or possibility recedes, it gradually goes away: *The threat of attack receded.* | +**into/from** *The postwar division of Europe is receding into the past.* **3** if water recedes, it moves back from an area that it was covering: *The flood waters finally began to recede.* **4** if your hair recedes, you gradually lose the hair at the front of your head: *He was around forty, with a* ***receding hairline***. **5 receding chin** a chin that slopes backward

re•ceipt /rɪˈsit/ S2 *n.* **1** [C] a piece of paper you are given that shows you have paid for something SYN **sales slip**: *credit card receipts* | +**for** *a receipt for a pair of shoes* **2** [U] FORMAL the act or fact of receiving something: +**of** *Payment is due* ***upon receipt*** *of the merchandise.* **3 receipts** [plural] ECONOMICS the money that a business, bank, or government receives: *tax receipts*

re•ceiv•a•ble /rɪˈsivəbəl/ *adj.* needing or waiting to be paid: *the company's* ***accounts receivable*** (=sales that have been made but not yet paid for)

re•ceiv•a•bles /rɪˈsivəbəlz/ *n.* [plural] money that a company owns but that has not yet been paid to it

re•ceive /rɪˈsiv/ S2 W1 *v.* [T]
1 GET STH to get something you are given or sent SYN **get**: *Each child will receive a small gift.* | *Are you still receiving financial aid?* | **receive sth from sb** *In 1962 she received an honorary doctorate from Harvard.* | *Police received calls from residents who heard the gunshots.*
2 EXPERIENCE STH to experience something that happens or something that is done for you SYN **get**: *The writer received a warm welcome.* | *Lee received 324 votes.* | *The study has* ***received*** *considerable* ***attention***. | *Rovner is still in the hospital* ***receiving treatment for*** *a heart problem.* | **receive an injury/blow etc.** *Three firefighters received minor injuries.* | *These officers* ***receive*** *extra* ***training*** *and better equipment.* | *Many new mothers do not* ***receive*** *much* ***support*** *from other family members.*
3 NEWS/INFORMATION if you receive news or information about something, someone tells you it, you read it etc.: *He received the news in silence.* | *Officials have received numerous complaints about airport noise.*
4 REACTION TO STH [usually passive] to react in a particular way to a suggestion, idea, performance etc.: *Hawke's first novel was* ***well received*** *by many critics.*
5 BY RADIO a) if a radio or television receives radio waves or other signals, it makes them become sounds or pictures **b)** to be able to hear a radio message that someone is sending: *Receiving you loud and clear.*
6 PEOPLE FORMAL to accept or welcome someone as a guest or as a member of a group: *She was not well enough to receive visitors.* | **receive sb into sth** *He was later received into the priesthood.*
7 be on the receiving end (of sth) to be the person who is most affected by someone else's actions, usually in a bad way: *I know what it's like to be on the receiving end of criticism.*
[**Origin:** 1300–1400 Old North French *receivre*, from Latin *recipere*, from *capere* **to take**]

re•ceived /rɪˈsivd/ *adj.* [only before noun] FORMAL accepted or considered to be correct by most people: **received wisdom/opinion etc.** *Sontag's articles challenged received notions about photography.*

re•ceiv•er /rɪˈsivɚ/ *n.* [C] **1** the part of a telephone that you hold next to your mouth and ear: **pick up/put down the receiver** *I picked up the receiver and dialed.* | *Cory* ***slammed down the receiver*** (=put it down with force because of anger). ►see THESAURUS box at **phone¹** **2** ECONOMICS someone who is officially in charge of a business or company that is BANKRUPT (=has no money) or that has done something illegal: *Carlson is the court-appointed receiver for the firm.* **3** a player in football who is in a position to catch the ball **4** FORMAL a radio or television, or other equipment that receives signals and changes them into sound **5** someone who buys and sells stolen property **6** someone who is given something SYN **recipient**

re•ceiv•er•ship /rɪˈsivɚˌʃɪp/ *n.* [U] ECONOMICS the state of being controlled by an official receiver: *The resort has* ***gone into receivership***.

re•cent /ˈrisənt/ S3 W1 *adj.* [usually before noun]
1 having happened or started only a short time ago: *recent research into the causes of cancer* | *Irving's* ***most recent*** *novel* | **in recent years/months/times etc.** *The unemployment rate has declined in recent years.* ►see THESAURUS box at **new** **2 in recent memory** during the time that most people are able to remember: *It was one of the worst storms in recent memory.* [**Origin:** 1400–1500 French, Latin *recens* **fresh, recent**] —**recentness** *n.* [U]

re•cent•ly /ˈrisəntli/ S2 W1 *adv.* not long ago: *a recently published book* | *He was* ***until recently*** *the senior manager.* | ***More recently****, he has appeared in several television movies.* → see Grammar box at LATELY

THESAURUS

just only a few minutes, hours, or days ago: *The show just started.* | *I've just been to Roman's house.*
a little/short while ago only a few minutes, hours, or days ago: *She was brought into the emergency room just a little while ago.*
lately in the recent past: *Have you read anything good lately?*
freshly used to say that something was recently made, picked etc.: *freshly baked bread* | *freshly cut flowers*
newly used to say that something happened recently, or that something was made, done etc. recently: *the newly elected governor of New York* | *a newly married couple*

re·cep·ta·cle /rɪˈsɛptəkəl/ *n.* FORMAL a container for putting things in SYN **container**: *a trash receptacle*

re·cep·tion /rɪˈsɛpʃən/ S3 *n.* **1** [C] a large formal party to celebrate an event or to welcome someone: *a* ***wedding reception*** | **+for** *There will be a reception for the visiting professors.* ▸see THESAURUS box at **party**¹, **wedding** **2** [C usually singular] a reaction to a person or idea that shows what you think of them or it: **warm/good/enthusiastic etc. reception** *Winfrey* ***received*** *a warm* ***reception*** (=people welcomed her in a friendly way). | **cool/hostile/chilly etc. reception** *Congress* ***gave*** *the idea a cool* ***reception*** (=they did not like the idea). **3** [U] the quality of television or radio signals that you receive, or the act of receiving them: **get good/bad reception** *We get better reception with the satellite dish.* **4 reception desk/area/room etc.** the desk or area where visitors arriving in a hotel or large organization go first: *Please leave your key at the reception desk.* **5** [C] the act of catching the ball in football: *a 24-yard touchdown reception*

re·cep·tion·ist /rɪˈsɛpʃənɪst/ *n.* [C] someone whose job is to welcome and help people arriving in a hotel or office building, visiting a doctor etc.

re·cep·tive /rɪˈsɛptɪv/ *adj.* willing to consider new ideas or listen to someone else's opinions: *a* ***receptive audience*** | **+to** *a workforce that is receptive to new ideas* —**receptively** *adv.* —**receptiveness** also **receptivity** /ˌrisɛpˈtɪvət̬i/ *n.* [U]

re·cess¹ /ˈrisɛs, rɪˈsɛs/ *n.* **1** [C,U] a time during the day or year when no work is done, in government, a law court etc.: *Congress may pass the bill before the summer recess.* | *One of the lawyers asked the judge for a recess.* **2** [U] a short period of time when children are allowed to go outside to play during the school day SYN **playtime**: **+at/during recess** *We played kickball at recess.* ▸see THESAURUS box at **school**¹ **3** [C] a space in the wall of a room for shelves, cupboards etc. SYN **alcove** **4 the recesses of sth** the hidden parts inside something such as a room: *the dark recesses of the basement*

recess² *v.* [I,T] if a part of the government, a law court etc. recesses, it officially stops work for a period of time: *The judge recessed the trial for two hours.*

re·cessed /ˈrisɛst, rɪˈsɛst/ *adj.* something that is recessed is built into a wall or ceiling in such a way that it does not stick out: *recessed lighting*

re·ces·sion /rɪˈsɛʃən/ *n.* [C] ECONOMICS a period of time during which there is less trade, business activity etc. than usual: *the* ***economic recession*** *of the 1980s* | **deep/severe recession** *a deep recession in Japan* | **go/slip/slide/fall etc. into (a) recession** *Interest rates were lowered to stop the country sliding into a recession.* | **pull/grow/dig out of a recession** *attempts to pull the country out of a recession*

THESAURUS

depression a long period when businesses do not buy, sell, or produce very much and many people do not have jobs: *It took a long time for the economy to recover after the depression.*
slump a period when there is a reduction in business and many people lose their jobs: *a slump in the airline industry*
crash an occasion when the value of stocks on a stock market falls suddenly and by a large amount, causing economic problems: *the effects of the 1987 stock market crash*

re·ces·sive /rɪˈsɛsɪv/ *adj.* BIOLOGY a recessive GENE is only expressed as a physical feature in a child if both parents have the gene and pass it to their child OPP **dominant**: *Blue eyes are recessive.*

re·charge /ˈritʃɑrdʒ, riˈtʃɑrdʒ/ *v.* [T] **1** to put a new supply of electricity into a BATTERY **2** INFORMAL to get your strength and energy back again: *A week in the mountains will* ***recharge my batteries.*** —**rechargeable** *adj.* —**recharge** /ˈritʃɑrdʒ/ *n.* [C]

re·charg·er /riˈtʃɑrdʒɚ/ *n.* [C] a machine that recharges BATTERIES

re·cid·i·vist /rɪˈsɪdəvɪst/ *n.* [C] TECHNICAL a criminal who starts doing illegal things again, even after they have been punished —**recidivism** *n.* [U]

rec·i·pe /ˈrɛsəpi/ S2 W3 *n.* [C] **1** a set of instructions for cooking a particular type of food: **+for** *a recipe for tomato soup* **2 be a recipe for sth** to be likely to cause a particular result, often a bad one: *Critics say the new regulations are a* ***recipe for*** *economic* ***disaster***. [**Origin:** 1300–1400 Latin **take!**, from *recipere*, from *capere* **to take**]

re·cip·i·ent /rɪˈsɪpiənt/ *n.* FORMAL someone who receives something SYN **receiver**: *welfare recipients* | **+of** *the recipient of the Nobel Peace Prize*

re·cip·ro·cal¹ /rɪˈsɪprəkəl/ *adj.* FORMAL a reciprocal arrangement or relationship is one in which two people or groups do or give similar things to each other: *Iran's leaders expected a reciprocal gesture of goodwill.* → see also MUTUAL —**reciprocally** /-kli/ *adv.*

reciprocal² *n.* [C] MATH a MULTIPLICATIVE INVERSE. For example, the reciprocal of 5/3 is 3/5. The product of a number and its reciprocal is 1. [**Origin:** 1500–1600 Latin *reciprocus* **returning the same way**, from *re-* **back** + *pro-* **forward**]

reˌciprocal ˈteaching *n.* [U] a method of teaching that helps students to improve their reading skills. Sometimes the teacher asks a question and the students answer it, and sometimes the students ask a question for the teacher to answer.

re·cip·ro·cate /rɪˈsɪprəˌkeɪt/ *v.* [I,T] **1** to do or give something, because something similar has been done or given to you: *I had been invited to classmates' homes, and I wanted to reciprocate.* **2** to feel the same about someone as they feel about you: *Her love was not reciprocated.* —**reciprocation** /rɪˌsɪprəˈkeɪʃən/ *n.* [U]

rec·i·proc·i·ty /ˌrɛsəˈprɑsət̬i/ *n.* [U] FORMAL a situation in which two people, groups, or countries give each other similar kinds of help or special rights

re·cit·al /rɪˈsaɪt̬l/ *n.* [C] **1** ENG. LANG. ARTS a performance of music or poetry, usually by one performer: *a piano recital* | **+of** *a recital of Italian songs* **2** FORMAL a spoken description of a series of events SYN **recitation**

rec·i·ta·tion /ˌrɛsəˈteɪʃən/ *n.* [C,U] **1** ENG. LANG. ARTS an act of saying a poem, piece of literature etc. that you have learned, for people to listen to SYN **recital**: **+of** *the daily recitation of the Pledge of Allegiance* **2** a spoken description of an event or series of events SYN **recital**: **+of** *a recitation of the company's virtues*

rec·i·ta·tive /ˌrɛsət̬əˈtiv/ *n.* [C,U] TECHNICAL a speech set to music which is sung by one person and continues the story of an OPERA (=musical play) between the songs

re·cite /rɪˈsaɪt/ *v.* **1** [I,T] ENG. LANG. ARTS to say a poem, piece of literature etc. that you have learned, for people to listen to: *Each student had to recite a poem.* **2** [T] to tell someone a series or list of things SYN **relate**: *Clark recited the facts of the case.* —**reciter** *n.* [C]

reck·less /ˈrɛklɪs/ *adj.* not caring or worrying about danger or about the bad results of your behavior

SYN rash: *a reckless, arrogant man* | *a **reckless disregard** for the truth* (=not caring whether something is true) | *The driver was arrested for **reckless driving**.* | *They were playing with a **reckless abandon*** (=without caring about any danger). [**Origin:** Old English *recceleas*] —**recklessly** *adv.* —**recklessness** *n.* [U]

reck•on /ˈrɛkən/ *v.* [T not in progressive] **1** to guess a number or amount, without calculating it exactly SYN **estimate**: *The TV audience in China is reckoned at 800 million.* | **reckon (that)** *Scientists reckon a third of global-warming gases are produced by cars and trucks.* **2** SPOKEN to think or suppose something SYN **guess**: *How long do you reckon it will take?* | **reckon (that)** *I **reckon** she's still mad at you.* **3** to think that someone or something is a particular type of person or thing: **reckon sb/sth as sth** *An earthquake of magnitude 7 is reckoned as a major quake.* **4** FORMAL to calculate an amount [**Origin:** Old English *gerecenian* **to tell, explain**]

reckon on sth *phr. v.* to expect something to happen when you are making plans: *I didn't reckon on how angry he'd be at the idea.*

reckon with sb/sth *phr. v.* **1 a sth to be reckoned with** something or someone that is powerful or has influence, and must be regarded seriously as a possible opponent, competitor, danger etc.: *The Huskies are a team to be reckoned with this season.* | *The rebels are still **a force to be reckoned with**.* **2** to consider a possible problem or have to deal with something difficult when you are making plans for the future: *The government had not then reckoned with the Internet.*

reck•on•ing /ˈrɛkənɪŋ/ *n.* **1** [U] a calculation that is based on a careful guess rather than on exact knowledge: ***By my reckoning**, it weighed about fifty pounds.* **2** [C usually singular, U] a time when you are judged or punished for your actions, or when they have results that affect you: *Global warming is now a certainty, and **the day of reckoning** is near.* → see also DEAD RECKONING

re•claim /rɪˈkleɪm/ *v.* [T] **1** to get back something that once belonged to you: *You may be entitled to reclaim some tax.* **2** to obtain useful products from waste material: *The golf course will use reclaimed wastewater to water the grass.* **3** to make an area of desert, wet land etc. able to be used for farming or building on: *wetlands reclaimed for farming* —**reclamation** /ˌrɛkləˈmeɪʃən/ *n.* [U]

re•cline /rɪˈklaɪn/ *v.* **1** [I] FORMAL to lie or lean back in a relaxed way SYN **lean back**: **+in/on** *Davis was reclining in an easy chair.* **2** [I,T] if you recline a seat or if it reclines, the back of the seat is lowered, so that you can lean back in it

re•clin•er /rɪˈklaɪnɚ/ also **ˌreclining ˈchair** *n.* [C] a large comfortable chair that you can lean back in, with your feet supported by the chair

rec•luse /ˈrɛklus/ *n.* [C] someone who chooses to live alone, and avoids seeing or talking to other people: *Hudson became a recluse after her husband's death.* [**Origin:** 1100–1200 Old French *reclus* **shut up**, from Late Latin *recludere* **to shut up**] —**reclusive** /rɪˈklusɪv/ *adj.*

rec•og•ni•tion /ˌrɛkəgˈnɪʃən/ S3 W3 *n.* **1** [U] the act of recognizing someone or something: *She stared at him without recognition.* | *Many of the bodies were burned **beyond recognition*** (=they had become impossible to recognize). | *Alexander didn't have the **name recognition*** (=people did not know his name or what he had done) *of more experienced politicians.* **2** [singular, U] the act of realizing and accepting that something is true or important: **+of** *a recognition of the needs of these students* | **+that** *the recognition that these drugs do not work for everyone* **3** [singular, U] public respect and thanks for someone's work or achievements: *Women painters got little recognition in those days.* | **+for** *Employees are given recognition for good performance.* | *Ruiz was presented with a gold watch **in recognition of** his 25 years of service.* **4** [U] POLITICS the act of officially accepting that an organization, government, document etc. has legal or official authority: *In 1991, Bush granted **diplomatic recognition** to Russia.* | **+of** *the recognition of treaties and borders* | *Homosexuals want **official recognition** of their permanent relationships.* **5 speech/voice/image etc. recognition** the ability of a computer to recognize voices, shapes etc.

re•cog•ni•zance /rɪˈkɑgnəzəns/ *n.* [U] LAW **1 be released on your own recognizance** if a person who has been CHARGED in a court of law is released on their own recognizance, they are allowed to stay out of prison if they promise to come back to court at a specific time **2** money that someone pays a court etc. in order to promise that they will come back on a particular day or time: *Howe posted a $250 recognizance bond.*

rec•og•nize /ˈrɛkəgˌnaɪz/ S2 W1 *v.* **1** [T not in progressive] to know who someone is or what something is, because you have seen, heard, experienced, or learned about them in the past SYN **identify**: *I recognized her right away.* | *Aaron was humming a tune I didn't recognize.* | *The aim is to help doctors recognize abuse victims.* **2** [T] POLITICS to officially accept that an organization, government, document etc. has legal or official authority: *The U.S. has not recognized the Cuban government since 1961.* **3** [T usually passive] to realize that someone or something is important or very good: *a recognized leader in her profession* | **recognize sb/sth as sth** *Lawrence's novel was eventually recognized as a work of genius.* **4** [T] to admit or accept that something is true SYN **realize**: **recognize (that)** *Hudson recognized that she had to make a change in her lifestyle.* | **recognize what/how/who etc.** *It is important to recognize how little we know about this disease.* ►see THESAURUS box at **admit** **5** [T] to officially and publicly thank someone for something they have done, by giving them a special honor: **be recognized for (doing) sth** *He was recognized for saving many lives.* [**Origin:** 1400–1500 Old French *reconoistre*, from Latin *recognoscere*, from *cognoscere* **to know**] —**recognizable** /ˌrɛkəgˈnaɪzəbəl, ˈrɛkəgˌnaɪ-/ *adj.* —**recognizably** *adv.*

re•coil¹ /rɪˈkɔɪl/ *v.* [I] **1** to feel such a strong dislike of a particular situation that you want to avoid it: **+from/at** *She recoiled at the violence on screen.* | *People **recoiled in horror** from the destruction of the war.* **2** to move back suddenly and quickly from something you do not like or are afraid of SYN **shrink**: **+from/at** *Anna recoiled from his touch.* **3** if a gun recoils, it moves backward very quickly when it is fired [**Origin:** 1100–1200 Old French *reculer*, from *cul* **ass**]

re•coil² /rɪˈkɔɪl, ˈrikɔɪl/ *n.* [singular, U] the backward movement of a gun when it is fired

rec•ol•lect /ˌrɛkəˈlɛkt/ *v.* [T] to be able to remember something, especially by deliberately trying to remember SYN **recall**: *It is painful to recollect these events even now.* | **recollect how/when/what etc.** *Davenport tried to recollect who he had spoken to at the company.* | **recollect that** *She recollected that he had been late that day.*

rec•ol•lec•tion /ˌrɛkəˈlɛkʃən/ *n.* FORMAL **1** [C] something from the past that you remember: *my earliest recollections of childhood* | *The driver **had no recollection of** the crash.* **2** [U] an act of remembering something: ***To the best of my recollection*** (=used when you are not sure that you remember something correctly), *they have never asked us for any money.*

re•com•bi•nant DNA /riˌkɑmbɪnənt ˌdi en ˈeɪ/ *n.* [U] BIOLOGY DNA that has been made artificially using scientific methods that involve combining parts of the DNA from different living things

rec•om•mend /ˌrɛkəˈmɛnd/ S2 W2 *v.* [T] **1** to advise someone to do something, especially because you have special knowledge of a situation or subject SYN **advise**: *The prosecutor recommended a 15-year sentence.* | *The recommended dose is 20 milligrams.* | **recommend that** *Doctors recommend that all children should be immunized.* | **recommend doing sth** *The manufacturers recommend changing the oil every 6,000 miles.* | *We **strongly recommend** buying a bicycle helmet.* ►see THESAURUS box at **advise** **2** to say that

R

something or someone is good, and suggest them for a particular purpose or job: *Can you recommend a good restaurant?* | **recommend sth to sb** *It's a children's book, but I recommend it to everyone.* | **recommend sth for sth** *He recommended some computer equipment for his employers.* | **recommend sb for sth** *His boss recommended him for a promotion.* | *Capra's film is a classic that I **highly recommend**.* **3 sth has much/little/nothing to recommend it** used to say that something has many, few, or no good qualities: *The hotel has little except price to recommend it.*

GRAMMAR

When you use **recommend**, **suggest**, **advise**, **ask**, **insist**, **request**, and **demand** with "that," use only the infinitive form of the verb without "to," even if the subject is singular: *I recommend that this plan be accepted.* | *We ask that the committee review the facts.*

rec·om·men·da·tion /ˌrɛkəmɛnˈdeɪʃən/ W3 *n.* **1** [C] official advice given to someone, especially about what to do: *the government's dietary recommendations* | **+for** *The study has **made recommendations** for improving the program.* | **recommendation that** *a recommendation that the military base be closed* | **recommendation to do sth** *They made a recommendation to limit household water use.* | **+on** *the panel's recommendations on breast cancer screening* ▶see THESAURUS box at **advice** **2** [C,U] a suggestion to someone that they should choose a particular thing or person that you think is very good: *reading recommendations* | *Page was hired **on** Flournoy's **recommendation**.* **3** [C] also **letter of recommendation** a formal letter or statement saying that someone would be an good choice to do a job, study at a particular college etc.: *Schatz's former employer wrote him a recommendation.*

rec·om·pense¹ /ˈrɛkəmˌpɛns/ *v.* [T] FORMAL to give someone a payment for trouble or losses that you have caused them, or a reward for their efforts to help you: **recompense sb for sth** *Nothing can recompense them for their loss.* → see also COMPENSATE

recompense² *n.* [singular, U] FORMAL something that you give to someone for trouble or losses that you have caused them, or as a reward for their help SYN **remuneration**: **+for** *He received no recompense for his work.* → see also COMPENSATION

rec·on·cile /ˈrɛkənˌsaɪl/ *v.* **1** [T] if you reconcile two ideas, situation, or facts, you find a way in which both can be true or acceptable: *How can we reconcile these different goals?* | **reconcile sth with sth** *Newly married couples must reconcile their expectations with the reality of married life.* **2** [I,T] to have a good relationship again with someone after arguing with them: *He and his wife reconciled after two years apart.* | *The couple have apparently **reconciled their differences**.* | **be reconciled with sb** *Ransom hoped to be reconciled with his wife and children.* **3** [T] if you reconcile an account, a CHECKBOOK etc., you make sure that it shows the same amounts going in and out as are shown on a statement from your bank

reconcile sb **to** sth *phr. v.* to make someone able to accept a bad situation: *The food was so good I was almost able to **reconcile myself to** the price.*

rec·on·cil·i·a·tion /ˌrɛkənˌsɪliˈeɪʃən/ *n.* [singular, U] **1** a situation in which two people, countries etc. become friendly with each other again after arguing or fighting: *Her ex-husband hoped for a reconciliation.* | **+between/with** *a reconciliation between the two countries* **2** the process of finding a way that two beliefs, facts etc. that are opposed to each other can both be true or both exist together: **+of/between** *These missionaries sought a reconciliation of native culture and Christianity.*

rec·on·dite /ˈrɛkənˌdaɪt, rɪˈkɑn-/ *adj.* [only before noun] FORMAL recondite information, knowledge etc. is not known about or understood by many people

re·con·di·tion /ˌrikənˈdɪʃən/ *v.* [T] to repair something, especially an old machine, so that it works like a new one —**reconditioned** *adj.*: *a reconditioned engine*

re·con·nais·sance /rɪˈkɑnəsəns, -zəns/ *n.* [C,U] the military activity of sending soldiers and aircraft to find out information about the enemy's forces: *a reconnaissance mission*

re·con·noi·ter /ˌrikəˈnɔɪtə/ [I,T] to try to find out the position and size of your enemy's army, for example by flying airplanes over land where their soldiers are SYN **scout out**

re·con·sid·er /ˌrikənˈsɪdə/ *v.* [I,T] to think again about something in order to decide if you should change your opinion: *I asked him to reconsider.* | *The governor can ask the board to **reconsider** parole **decisions**.* —**reconsideration** /ˌrikənsɪdəˈreɪʃən/ *n.* [U]

re·con·sti·tute /riˈkɑnstəˌtut/ *v.* **1** [T] to make a group, organization etc. exist again in a different form: *The parliament has been reconstituted, but is essentially powerless.* **2** to change dried food back to its original form by added water to it: *reconstituted orange juice* —**reconstitution** /ˌrikɑnstəˈtuʃən/ *n.* [U]

re·con·struct /ˌrikənˈstrʌkt/ Ac *v.* [T] **1** to produce a complete description of an event by collecting pieces of information: *Police are trying to reconstruct the events of last Friday.* **2** to build something again after it has been destroyed or damaged SYN **rebuild**: *She had an operation to reconstruct the bones in her leg.*

re·con·struc·tion /ˌrikənˈstrʌkʃən/ Ac *n.* **1** [U] the work that is done to repair the damage to a city, industry etc., especially after a war: *Gorbachev began the reconstruction and reform of the Soviet system.* **2** [C] a medical operation to replace a bone or a part of the body that has been damaged: *a hip reconstruction* **3** [C usually singular] a description or copy of something that you produce by collecting information about it: **+of** *a reconstruction of a Native American village* | *a reconstruction of the crime* **4 Reconstruction** the period between 1865 and 1877, when the Southern states that had separated from the Union during the Civil War war were reorganized and became part of the Union again

re·cord¹ /ˈrɛkəd/ S1 W1 *n.*
1 INFORMATION [C] information about something that is written down so that it can be looked at in the future: **+of** *Records of births, marriages, and deaths are filed at City Hall.* | **medical/dental/school/financial etc. record** *Medical records are now kept on computers.* | ***written records** from the Middle Ages* | ***Keep a record** of everything you spend.* | ***Records show** he phoned the bank twice that day.* | **worst/hottest/greatest etc. on record** *This month has been the hottest **on record**.*

THESAURUS

diary/journal a book in which you write down the things that have happened to you each day
file a set of written records, or information stored on a computer under a particular name
accounts an exact record of the money that a company has received and spent
books written records of a company's financial accounts
ledger a book in which a company's financial records are kept
roll an official list of names, for example of the people attending a school
log (book) an official record of events, especially on a ship or airplane
register an offical list containing the names of all the people, organizations, or things of a particular type

2 HIGHEST/BEST EVER [C] the fastest speed, longest distance, highest or lowest level etc. that has ever been achieved, especially in a sport: *Dyer scored 36 points, a tournament record.* | *She **broke a** school **record*** (=she did something better than the previous record) *by making all of her free throws.* | *Lewis **holds the record** in the dash.* | *The **world record** for the race is 42 minutes.* | *Walsh **set a** pentathlon **record*** (=achieved a new record) *in 1953.* | *Six million jobs were created in 1978 and 1979 – **an all-time record*** (=the best ever achieved).
3 PAST ACTIVITIES [singular] the facts about how successful, good, honest etc. someone or something has been

in the past: *the team's record of 12 wins and 4 losses.* | +**on** *The Attorney General defended his record on civil rights.* | **have a record** *Mobile homes have a* ***good record*** *for surviving earthquakes.* | **of/for (doing) sth** *a business with a good* ***track record*** *of turning a profit* → see also TRACK RECORD

4 POLICE DOCUMENT [singular] also **criminal record** a document that the police keep that shows a person's criminal activities, time spent in prison etc.: *Hoyle* ***has a record*** *as long as your arm.*

5 MUSIC [C] a round flat piece of plastic with a hole in the middle on which music and sound are stored: *an old Beatles record*

6 off the record if you say something off the record, you do not want people to repeat what you say, for example in newspapers: *Officials, speaking off the record, said they were still worried about the situation.*

7 on (the) record said publicly or officially, so that it may be written down and repeated: *I'm willing to* ***go on record*** *to support the new housing development.* | *Rowe* ***is on record as saying*** *she would consider an advisory position.*

8 for the record used to tell someone that what you are saying should be remembered or written down: *For the record, both men were fined $10,000.*

9 set/put/keep the record straight to tell people the truth about something, because you want to be sure that they understand what the truth really is: *He agreed to the interview in order to set the record straight.*

rec•ord² /rɪ'kɔrd/ S2 W2 *v.* **1** [T] to write information down so that it can be looked at in the future SYN **document**: *The expedition recorded many new species of plants.* | **record that** *The census recorded that the number of Latinos in the area had risen.* **2** [I,T] to store music, sound, television programs etc. on TAPE, CDS etc. so that people can listen to them or watch them again: *Is the machine still recording?* | *The band has just recorded a new album.* | +**on** *The whole incident was recorded on an amateur video tape.* **3** [T] if an instrument records the size, speed, temperature etc. of something, it measures it and keeps that information: *Wind speeds of up to 100 mph have been recorded.* [**Origin:** 1100–1200 Old French *recorder* **to bring to mind**, from Latin *recordari*, from *cor* **heart**]

rec•ord³ /'rɛkɚd/ W3 *adj.* [only before noun] **1** a record event, number, or level is the best, worst, highest, lowest etc. that has ever been achieved or reached: *Record flooding* (=the worst flooding ever) *was reported on the Colorado River.* | *The game was played in front of a record crowd.* | **record high/low** *Temperatures reached a record high yesterday.* **2 in record time** very quickly: *We got home in record time.*

'record-,breaking *adj.* [only before noun] a record-breaking number, level, performance, or person is the highest, lowest, biggest, best etc. of its type that has ever happened or existed: *record-breaking heat* | *a record-breaking swimmer*

re•cord•er /rɪ'kɔrdɚ/ *n.* [C] **1** a piece of electrical equipment that records information, music, movies etc.: *a tape recorder* | *the flight data recorder* **2** ENG. LANG. ARTS a simple wood or plastic musical instrument shaped like a tube, that you play by blowing into it and covering different holes with your fingers to change the notes **3** LAW someone whose job is to officially record things: *the county recorder*

'record-,holder, record holder *n.* [C] the person who has achieved the fastest speed, the longest distance etc. in a sport: *the* ***world record-holder*** *in the 200m backstroke*

re•cord•ing /rɪ'kɔrdɪŋ/ *n.* **1** [C] a piece of music, a speech etc. that has been recorded: *I called her office but just got a recording.* | +**of** *a recording of Vivaldi's "Gloria"* **2** [U] the act of storing music, movies etc. on a TAPE etc.: *automatic recording* | **recording equipment/studio etc.** (=equipment etc. used for recording)

'record ,player *n.* [C] a piece of equipment for playing records → see also STEREO

re•count¹ /rɪ'kaʊnt/ *v.* [T] FORMAL to tell a story or describe a series of events SYN **relate**: *Mama often recounted stories of her childhood.* | **recount how/what** *He recounted how he had met his wife.*

re•count² /'rikaʊnt/ *n.* [C] POLITICS a process of counting votes again, especially because the first result was very close: *Opponents demanded a recount.* —**recount** /ri'kaʊnt/ *v.* [T]

re•coup /rɪ'kup/ *v.* [T] to get back an amount of money you have lost or spent SYN **recover**: *The movie will have to be a huge hit to recoup its cost.* [**Origin:** 1600–1700 French *recouper* **to cut back**, from *couper* **to cut**]

re•course /'rikɔrs, rɪ'kɔrs/ *n.* [singular, U] FORMAL something you do to achieve something or deal with a difficult situation, or the act of doing it: *You* ***have legal recourse*** *if the guarantee is in writing.* | *The family had to survive* ***without recourse to*** (=without being able to use) *government aid.*

re-cov•er /ri'kʌvɚ/ *v.* [T] to put a new cover on a piece of furniture

re•cov•er /rɪ'kʌvɚ/ Ac W3 *v.* **1** [I] to become better after an illness, accident, shock etc. SYN **recuperate**: *Doctors say she will recover quickly.* | *He never* ***fully recovered*** *from the disease.* | +**from** *It will take several months for Boyle to recover from the knee injury.* **2** [I] to return to a normal condition after a period of trouble or difficulty: *The tourist industry is slowly recovering.* | +**from** *The economy has not yet recovered from the recession.* **3** [T] to get back something that was taken from you, lost, or almost destroyed: *Four stolen paintings have recently been recovered.* | **recover sth from sth** *A number of bodies were recovered from the wreckage.* **4** [T] to get back the amount of money that you have spent or that you have lost SYN **recoup**: *The company hopes to recover the cost of developing their new product.* | *The landlord's insurance company may try to* ***recover damages*** *from the renter.* **5** [T] to get back the ability to control your feelings or your body again, after not being able to: *He never recovered the use of his legs.* | *Joyce quickly* ***recovered herself*** (=controlled her emotions) *and blew her nose.* | *She* ***recovered*** *her* ***balance*** *and kept running.* [**Origin:** 1200–1300 Old French *recovrer*, from Latin *recuperare*, from *capere* **to take**] —**recoverable** *adj.*

re•cov•er•y /rɪ'kʌvəri/ Ac W3 *n.* **1** [singular, U] a process of getting better after an illness, injury etc.: +**from** *their recovery from alcoholism* | **a full/complete recovery** *Doctors expect the woman to* ***make a full recovery.*** **2** [singular, U] the process of returning to a normal condition after a period of trouble or difficulty: *Economic recovery is forecast.* | +**from** *The team finally* ***made a recovery from*** *their season-long problems.* **3** [U] the act of getting something that has been taken or lost back: +**of** *the recovery of the stolen jewels*

re'covery ,program *n.* [C] a period of treatment for people who are ADDICTED to drugs or alcohol

re'covery room *n.* [C] a room in a hospital where people first wake up after an operation

re•cre•ate /ˌrikri'eɪt/ Ac *v.* [T] to make something from the past exist again in a new form or be experienced again SYN **recapture**: *Arjelo's novel vividly recreates 15th-century Spain.* —**recreation** /ˌrikri'eɪʃən/ *n.* [C,U]

rec•re•a•tion /ˌrɛkri'eɪʃən/ *n.* [C,U] an activity that you do for pleasure or fun: *Families use the space for recreation.* | **recreation area/room/center etc.** *a recreation center in a poor neighborhood* ▶ see THESAURUS box at **game¹** [**Origin:** 1300–1400 French *récréation*, from Latin, from *recreare* **to make new, refresh**] —**recreational** *adj.*

ˌrecreational 'vehicle *n.* [C] an RV

re•crim•i•na•tion /rɪˌkrɪmə'neɪʃən/ *n.* [C usually plural, U] a situation in which people blame each other, or the things they say when they are blaming each other

rec room /'rɛk rum/ also **recre'ation ,room** *n.* [C] **1** a public room, for example in a hospital, used for social activities or games **2** a room in a private house, where you can relax, play games etc.

re·cru·des·cence /ˌrikruˈdɛsəns/ *n.* [usually singular] FORMAL a time when something, especially something bad, returns or happens again

re·cruit¹ /rɪˈkrut/ S3 W3 *v.* **1** [I,T] to find new people to work in a company, join an organization, do a job etc.: *The district has been trying to recruit more teachers.* **2 a)** [I,T] to get people to join the army or navy → see also CONSCRIPT SYN **enlist** **b)** [T] to form a new army in this way **3** [T] INFORMAL to persuade someone to do something for you SYN **enlist**: **recruit sb to do sth** *We recruited a few of our friends to help us move.* —**recruitment** *n.* [U]

recruit² *n.* [C] **1** someone who has just joined the Army, Navy, or Air Force: *Forty* ***raw recruits*** (=new recruits) *have just started boot camp.* → see also CONSCRIPT **2** someone who has recently joined an organization, team, group of people etc.: *New recruits are sent to the Atlanta office for training.* [**Origin:** 1600–1700 French *recrute* **new growth, new soldiers**, from Old French *recroistre* **to grow up again**]

R

rec·tal /ˈrɛktəl/ *adj.* BIOLOGY relating to the RECTUM

rec·tan·gle /ˈrɛkˌtæŋgəl/ *n.* [C] MATH a shape that has four straight sides, two of which are usually longer than the other two, and a 90° angle inside each of the four corners → see also SQUARE [**Origin:** 1500–1600 Medieval Latin *rectangulus* **having a right angle**, from Latin *rectus* **right** + *angulus* **angle**] → see picture at SHAPE¹

rec·tan·gu·lar /rɛkˈtæŋgyələ/ *adj.* having the shape of a rectangle

rec·ti·fy /ˈrɛktəˌfaɪ/ *v.* **rectified, rectifying, rectifies** [T] FORMAL to correct something that is wrong SYN **correct**: *A number of steps have been taken to rectify the error.* [**Origin:** 1300–1400 French *rectifier*, from Latin *rectus* **right, straight**] —**rectifiable** *adj.* —**rectification** /ˌrɛktəfəˈkeɪʃən/ *n.* [C,U]

rec·ti·lin·e·ar /ˌrɛktəˈlɪniə/ *adj.* MATH formed or moving in a straight line, or consisting of straight lines

rec·ti·tude /ˈrɛktəˌtud/ *n.* [U] FORMAL behavior that is honest and morally correct

rec·to /ˈrɛktoʊ/ *n.* [C] TECHNICAL a page on the RIGHT-HAND side of a book → see also VERSO —**recto** *adj.*

rec·tor /ˈrɛktə/ *n.* [C] **1** a priest in some Christian churches who is responsible for a particular area, group etc. **2** the person in charge of certain colleges and schools [**Origin:** 1300–1400 Latin **governor, ruler**, from *regere* **to rule**]

rec·to·ry /ˈrɛktəri/ *n.* [C] a house where the priest of the local church lives SYN **parsonage**

rec·tum /ˈrɛktəm/ *n.* [C] BIOLOGY the lowest part of your BOWEL → see picture at DIGESTIVE SYSTEM

re·cum·bent /rɪˈkʌmbənt/ *adj.* FORMAL lying down on your back or side

re·cu·per·ate /rɪˈkupəˌreɪt/ *v.* [I] **1** MEDICINE to get better again after an illness or injury SYN **recover**: **+from** *Arkwright is recovering from a knee injury.* **2** ECONOMICS to return to a more normal condition after a difficult time SYN **recover**: *Winston proposed several ways for the industry to recuperate.* —**recuperation** /rɪˌkupəˈreɪʃən/ *n.* [U]

re·cu·per·a·tive /rɪˈkupəˌreɪt̬ɪv, -pərət̬ɪv/ *adj.* recuperative powers or processes help someone or something get better again, especially after an illness: *the recuperative powers of nature*

re·cur /rɪˈkə/ *v.* **recurred, recurring** [I] **1** if something, especially something bad, recurs, it happens again or happens several times: *The cancer may recur.* | *He has a small recurring role in the show.* | *Love is a* ***recurring theme*** *in the book.* **2** MATH if a number or numbers after a DECIMAL POINT recur, they are repeated forever in the same order [**Origin:** 1500–1600 Latin *recurrere* **to run back**, from *currere* **to run**]

re·cur·rence /rɪˈkʌrəns, -ˈkə-/ *n.* [C usually singular, U] FORMAL an occasion when something that has happened before happens again: **+of** *a recurrence of the violence*

re·cur·rent /rɪˈkʌrənt, -ˈkə-/ *adj.* happening or appearing several times: *a recurrent infection* | *The dangers of pride are a* ***recurrent theme*** *in these stories.* —**recurrently** *adv.*

re·cur·sive for·mu·la /rɪˌkəsɪv ˈfɔrmyələ/ *n.* [C] ALGEBRA a mathematical FORMULA that describes each TERM (=number or numbers and letters) in a SEQUENCE (=related list of numbers formed according to a rule) in relation to all the previous terms

re·cuse /rɪˈkyuz/ *v.* [T] FORMAL **recuse yourself** to say that you cannot give advice or take part in something, because you might be too closely involved to be fair —**recusal** *adj.*

re·cy·cla·ble /riˈsaɪkləbəl/ *adj.* EARTH SCIENCE used materials or substances that are recyclable can be recycled: *recyclable bottles* —**recyclable** *n.* [C usually plural]

re·cy·cle /riˈsaɪkəl/ *v.* **1** [I,T] EARTH SCIENCE to put used objects or materials through a special process, so that the material can be used again: *Plastic bottles can be recycled into clothing.* ▸see THESAURUS box at **environment** **2** [T] to use something such as an idea, piece of writing etc. again, instead of developing something new: *The fashion world just keeps recycling old ideas.* —**recycled** *adj.*: *recycled paper*

re·cy·cling /riˈsaɪklɪŋ/ *n.* [U] **1** EARTH SCIENCE the process of treating used things such as paper or steel so that they can be used again: *the city's recycling program* **2** [singular] things such as bottles and plastic containers that are going to be treated and then used again in a recycling process: *Can you take out the recycling?*

red¹ /rɛd/ S1 W1 *adj.* comparative **redder**, *superlative* **reddest** **1** having the color of blood: *a* ***bright red*** *dress* | *He drove straight through a red light.* **2** hair that is red is an orange-brown color ▸see THESAURUS box at **hair** **3** skin that is red is a bright pink color: *Her cheeks were red with excitement.* **4** red wine has a red or purple color **5 be/turn as red (as a beet)** to have a very red face, usually because you are embarrassed **6 not one red cent** INFORMAL used to emphasize that you mean no money at all: *Carter said she wouldn't pay one red cent of her rent until the landlord fixed her roof.* **7** INFORMAL an insulting word meaning COMMUNIST, used especially in past times [**Origin:** Old English *read*] —**redness** *n.* [U] → see also **paint the town (red)** at PAINT² (7), RED FLAG, **be like waving a red flag in front of a bull** at WAVE¹ (7)

red² *n.* **1** [C,U] the color of blood: *The corrections were marked in red* (=in red ink). | *the reds and yellows of the fall trees* **2** [C,U] red wine: *a nice bottle of red* **3 be in the red** INFORMAL to owe more money than you have OPP **be in the black**: *The state is already $3 billion in the red this year.* **4 see red** to become very angry: *I immediately saw red.* **5** [C] INFORMAL an insulting word for someone who has COMMUNIST ideas or opinions, used especially in past times

ˌred aˈlert *n.* [C usually singular] a warning that there is very great danger: *Troops were* ***put on red alert*** *after the bombing.*

ˌred ˈblood cell also **ˌred ˈcorpuscle** *n.* [C] BIOLOGY one of the cells in your blood that carry oxygen to every part of your body → see also WHITE BLOOD CELL

ˌred-ˈblooded *adj.* **red-blooded male/American/patriot etc.** HUMOROUS used in order to emphasize that someone has all of the qualities that a typical man, American etc. is supposed to have

ˌred ˈcarpet *n.* [C usually singular] **1** a long piece of red CARPET that is put on floors for important people to walk on **2** special treatment that you give to someone important who is visiting you: *Williams' hometown* ***rolled out the red carpet*** *to welcome her.*

ˈred chip *n.* [C] a STOCK in a Chinese company that is shown on the Hong Kong STOCK MARKET → see also BLUE CHIP

Red Cloud /ˈrɛd klaʊd/ (1822–1909) a Sioux chief who tried to stop U.S. soldiers from helping people to settle on Sioux land in the northwestern U.S.

red·coat /ˈrɛdkoʊt/ *n.* [C] HISTORY a British soldier during the 18th and 19th centuries

ˌRed ˈCross *n.* **the Red Cross** an international organization that helps people who are suffering as a result of war, floods, disease etc.

red·den /ˈrɛdn/ *v.* [I,T] to become red, or make something red: *Her face reddened in embarrassment.*

red·dish /ˈrɛdɪʃ/ *adj.* slightly red: *reddish-brown lipstick*

re·dec·o·rate /riˈdɛkəˌreɪt/ *v.* [I,T] to change the way a room looks by painting, changing the furniture etc. —**redecoration** /ˌridɛkəˈreɪʃən/ *n.* [U]

re·deem /rɪˈdim/ *v.* [T] FORMAL **1** to make something less bad: *There is little we can do to redeem the situation.* | **redeeming feature/quality/trait etc.** (=the one good thing about someone or something that is generally bad) *The hotel had one redeeming feature – it was cheap.* **2** ECONOMICS to exchange a piece of paper representing an amount of money for that amount of money or for goods equal in cost to that amount of money SYN **exchange**: *Travelers can redeem the coupons for one-way flights.* **3 redeem yourself** to do something that will improve what other people think of you, after you have behaved badly or failed: *The Bears will have a chance to redeem themselves in Saturday's game.* **4** to free someone from the power of evil, especially in the Christian religion: *Christ came to Earth to redeem us from our sins.* → see also REDEEMER **5 redeem a promise/pledge/obligation etc.** FORMAL to do what you promised to do **6** to buy back something that you left with someone you borrowed money from: **redeem sth from sb/sth** *I finally redeemed my watch from the pawnbrokers.* [**Origin:** 1400–1500 French *rédimer*, from Latin *redimere*, from *emere* **to take, buy**] —**redeemable** *adj.*

Re·deem·er /rɪˈdimɚ/ *n.* LITERARY **the Redeemer** Jesus Christ

re·demp·tion /rɪˈdɛmpʃən/ *n.* [U] **1** the state of being freed from the power of evil, believed by Christians to be made possible by Jesus Christ **2** ECONOMICS the act of exchanging a piece of paper worth a particular amount of money for money, goods, or services **3** the state of doing something to improve what people think of you, after you have failed or done something bad: *After his last movie bombed, this script is Brown's shot at redemption.* **4 past/beyond redemption** too bad to be saved, repaired, or improved **5** TECHNICAL the exchange of STOCKS, BONDS etc. for money —**redemptive** /rɪˈdɛmptɪv/ *adj.*

re·de·ploy /ˌridɪˈplɔɪ/ *v.* [T] to move someone or something to a different place or job, especially in the military: *Army tanks were redeployed elsewhere in the region.* —**redeployment** *n.* [U]

re·de·vel·op /ˌridəˈvɛləp/ *v.* [T] to make an area more modern by putting in new buildings or changing or repairing the old ones

re·de·vel·op·ment /ˌridəˈvɛləpmənt/ *n.* [C,U] the act of redeveloping an area, especially in a city: *a redevelopment project downtown*

ˈred-ˌeye *n.* INFORMAL **1** [C] an airplane with PASSENGERS on it that flies at night: *I took the red-eye from Chicago to L.A.* | *a red-eye flight* **2** [U] if someone in a photograph has red-eye, their eyes look red because the photograph was taken using a FLASH (=very bright light on the camera) **3** [U] cheap WHISKEY

ˌred-ˈfaced *adj.* embarrassed or ashamed: *A red-faced Meyer apologized for his choice of words.*

ˌred ˈflag *n.* [C] INFORMAL something that shows or warns you that something might be wrong, illegal etc.: *The transfer of $750,000 from Bowman's account* ***raised the red flag*** *for investigators.*

ˌred ˈgiant *n.* [C] PHYSICS a star that is near the middle of its life, is larger and less solid than the sun, and shines with a reddish light

ˌRed ˈGuards *n.* [plural] groups of students in China in the 1960s who carried out Mao Zedong's POLICIES during the CULTURAL REVOLUTION

red-handed

The security guard caught him red-handed.

ˌred-ˈhanded *adj.* **catch sb red-handed** to catch someone at the moment when they are doing something wrong: *The FBI caught the mayor red-handed using drugs.*

red·head /ˈrɛdhɛd/ *n.* [C] someone who has red hair

ˌred ˈherring *n.* [C] a fact or idea that is not important but that is introduced to take your attention away from the facts that are important, especially in a story

ˌred-ˈhot *adj.* **1** INFORMAL extremely active, exciting, or interesting: *a red-hot news story* | *The Braves have been red-hot in the last few games.* **2** very sexually exciting: *a red-hot love affair* **3** metal or rock that is red-hot is so hot that it shines red: *red-hot lava* **4** a red-hot emotion is very strong: *red-hot anger* **5** INFORMAL very hot: *Be careful with those plates – they're red-hot.*

re·dial /ˈriˌdaɪəl, riˈdaɪəl/ *v.* [I,T] to DIAL a telephone number again

red ˈink *n.* [U] money that a business loses because it spends more than it can earn: *The company faces more red ink in the coming months.*

re·di·rect /ˌridɪˈrɛkt, -daɪ-/ *v.* [T] **1** to send something in a different direction: *The plane was redirected to Cleveland.* **2** to use something for a different purpose: *We must redirect our efforts into preventing environmental damage.*

re·dis·trib·ute /ˌridɪˈstrɪbyut/ Ac *v.* [T] to give something to each member of a group, so that it is divided up in a different way than it was before: **redistribute income/wealth** *Taxes are a way of redistributing income for the welfare of the whole society.* —**redistribution** /ˌridɪstrəˈbyuʃən/ *n.* [U]

ˌred-ˈletter day *n.* [C] INFORMAL a day that you will always remember because something special happens that makes you very happy

ˌred-ˈlight ˌdistrict *n.* [C] the area of a town or city where there are many PROSTITUTES (=people who have sex for money)

ˈred-ˌlining *n.* [U] the act of refusing to give insurance, CREDIT, LOANS etc. to people who live in poor areas of a city, or the act of charging more money for insurance, loans etc. to people in these areas —**red-line** *v.* [T]

ˌred ˈmeat *n.* [U] dark colored meat such as BEEF or LAMB

red·neck /ˈrɛdnɛk/ *n.* [C] INFORMAL DISAPPROVING a man who lives in a country area, is not educated, and has strong unreasonable opinions —**redneck** *adj.*

re·do /riˈdu/ S3 *v.* **redoes** /-ˈdʌz/, *past tense* **redid** /-ˈdɪd/, *past participle* **redone** /-ˈdʌn/ [T] **1** to do something again: *She redid her makeup.* **2** to change the way a room is decorated: *We're redoing the bathroom.*

red·o·lent /ˈrɛdl-ənt/ *adj.* FORMAL **1** making you think of something SYN **reminiscent**: +**of** *The movie's scenery is redolent of mystery.* **2** smelling strongly like something: +**of/with** *a sauce redolent of garlic* —**redolence** *n.* [U]

R

re·dou·ble /riˈdʌbəl/ *v.* [T] **redouble your efforts** to greatly increase your effort as you try to do something

re·doubt·a·ble /rɪˈdaʊt̬əbəl/ *adj.* LITERARY someone who is redoubtable is a person you respect or fear SYN **formidable**

re·dound /rɪˈdaʊnd/ *v.* **redound to sb's fame/credit/honor etc.** FORMAL to make someone more famous, more respected etc.

re·dox re·ac·tion /ˈridɑks riˌækʃən/ *n.* [C] CHEMISTRY a chemical reaction in which one or more ELECTRONS are moved from one atom or MOLECULE to another SYN **oxidation-reduction reaction**

ˌred ˈpepper *n.* **1** [C] a red vegetable that you can eat raw or use in cooking **2** [U] a SPICY red powder used in cooking SYN **cayenne pepper**

re·dress¹ /rɪˈdrɛs/ *v.* [T] FORMAL to correct something that is wrong or unfair SYN **rectify**: *Congress has done little to redress these injustices.* | *Affirmative action was meant to* ***redress the balance*** (=make the situation fair) *for minorities.*

R

re·dress² /ˈridrɛs, rɪˈdrɛs/ *n.* [U] FORMAL money that someone pays you because they have caused you harm, or damaged your property SYN **compensation** SYN **reparation**: *The victims sought redress in the courts.*

ˌRed ˈScare, red scare *n.* [singular] a great fear of COMMUNISM that existed in a country at a particular time

ˌRed ˈSea, the a sea which separates Egypt, Sudan, and Ethiopia from Saudi Arabia and Yemen

ˌred ˈshift *n.* [C] PHYSICS a change in the WAVELENGTH of light and RADIATION from an object in space such as a star, in which the wavelength becomes longer and the light from the object appears more red as the object is moving away from the person looking at it

red·shirt /ˈrɛdʃɚt/ *v.* [I,T] if a college sports player redshirts or the team redshirts him or her, he or she does not play for one year, so that he or she will still be allowed to play during later years of college —**redshirt** *n.* [C]

red·skin /ˈrɛdskɪn/ *n.* [C] OLD-FASHIONED a word meaning a Native American, now considered offensive

ˌred ˈtape *n.* [U] official rules that seem unnecessary and prevent things from being done quickly and easily: *The new rules should help* ***cut the red tape*** *for farmers.*

re·duce /rɪˈdus/ S3 W1 *v.* **1** [T] to make something smaller or less in size, amount, or price SYN **decrease**: *The helmet law reduced injuries in motorcycle accidents.* | **reduce sth by sth** *The city must reduce its spending by 15%.* | **reduce sth (from sth) to sth** *Reduce the oven temperature to 350 degrees.* → see also REDUCTION

THESAURUS

To reduce prices, numbers, or amounts
lower: *The city is trying to lower public transportation costs.*
decrease: *policies to try to decrease unemployment*
cut: *Stores cut prices after Christmas to get rid of excess merchandise.*
slash to reduce an amount or price by a large amount: *School budgets were slashed.*
roll back INFORMAL to reduce prices, costs etc. to a previous level: *a proposal to roll back the gas tax*

To reduce pain
relieve: *Aspirin is effective at relieving headaches.*
ease to reduce pain and make someone feel more comfortable: *Massage can ease the pain from tight muscles.*
lessen: *drugs to lessen pain*
alleviate FORMAL: *Sitting in a warm bath may alleviate the discomfort.*

2 [T] to boil a liquid so that there is less of it **3** [I] to become thinner by losing weight **4 in reduced circumstances** OLD-FASHIONED poorer than you were before **5** [T] MATH to make the form of a mathematical expression simpler without changing its total value SYN **simplify**: *Reduce the fractions you are multiplying by canceling common factors in the numerators and denominators.* **6** [I,T] CHEMISTRY to add ELECTRONS, lose oxygen, or combine with HYDROGEN, or to make an atom or chemical compound do this → see also OXIDIZE [**Origin:** 1300–1400 Latin *reducere* **to lead back**, from *ducere* **to lead**]

reduce sb/sth **to** sth *phr. v.* **1 reduce sb to tears/silence etc.** to make someone cry, be silent etc.: *The music can reduce a listener to tears.* **2 reduce sth to rubble/ashes/ruins etc.** to destroy something, especially a building, completely **3 reduce sb to doing sth** to make someone do something they would rather not do, especially when it involves behaving or living in a way that is not as good as before: *They were reduced to begging on the streets.*

reˈducing ˌagent *n.* [C] CHEMISTRY a chemical substance that REDUCES another substance, especially by giving it ELECTRONS → see also OXIDIZING AGENT

re·duc·tion /rɪˈdʌkʃən/ W3 *n.* **1** [C,U] a decrease in size, price, amount etc.: *The U.S. has agreed to an arms reduction proposal.* | **+in** *Consumers will benefit from the reduction in gasoline prices.* | *The central bank will* ***make*** *no further* ***reductions*** *in interest rates.* **2** [C] a smaller copy of a photograph, map, or picture OPP **enlargement** **3** [C,U] CHEMISTRY a chemical reaction that causes an atom or compound to gain ELECTRONS, lose oxygen, or gain HYDROGEN

re·duc·tion·ism /rɪˈdʌkʃənˌɪzəm/ *n.* [U] FORMAL DISAPPROVING the practice of trying to explain complicated ideas or systems in a very simple way

re·dun·dant /rɪˈdʌndənt/ *adj.* **1** not necessary because something else means or does the same thing: *Phrases such as "female sister" are redundant.* **2** TECHNICAL having additional parts that will make a system work if other parts fail [**Origin:** 1500–1600 Latin, present participle of *redundare*, from *unda* **wave**] —**redundancy** *n.* [U] —**redundantly** *adv.*

re·dux /ˌriˈdʌks/ *adj.* [only after noun] done again, or having come again: *fashions that are the 1960s redux*

red·wood /ˈrɛdwʊd/ *n.* [C,U] a very tall tree that grows in Oregon and California, or the wood from this tree

reed /rid/ *n.* [C] **1** BIOLOGY a type of tall plant like grass that grows in wet places: *Reeds grew all along the river bank.* → see picture on page A31 **2** ENG. LANG. ARTS a thin piece of wood that is attached to a musical instrument such as an OBOE or CLARINET, and that produces a sound when you blow over it

Reed /rid/, **Wal·ter** /ˈwɔltɚ/ (1851–1902) a U.S. doctor who discovered that YELLOW FEVER is caused by MOSQUITO bites

re-ed·u·cate, reeducate /riˈɛdʒəˌkeɪt/ *v.* [T] to teach someone to think or behave in a different way: *Young criminals must be re-educated.*

reed·y /ˈridi/ *adj.* **1** a voice that is reedy is high and not nice to listen to **2** BIOLOGY a place that is reedy has a lot of reeds growing there

reef¹ /rif/ *n.* [C] EARTH SCIENCE a line of sharp rocks, often made of CORAL, or a raised area of sand near the surface of the ocean: *the Great Barrier Reef*

reef² also **reef in** *v.* [T] TECHNICAL to tie up part of a sail in order to make it smaller

ree·fer /ˈrifɚ/ *n.* [C] OLD-FASHIONED a cigarette containing the drug MARIJUANA SYN **joint**

reek /rik/ *v.* [I] **1** to have a strong bad smell SYN **stink**: *This room absolutely reeks.* | **+of** *He reeked of sweat.* **2** to strongly express a particular quality, especially a bad quality: **+of** *His statement reeks of hypocrisy.* —**reek** *n.* [singular]

reel¹ /ril/ *v.* **1** [I always + adv./prep.] to walk in an unsteady way and almost fall over, because you are drunk or as if you are drunk: *A man reeled across the road, talking loudly to nobody.* | **+with** *He was reeling with exhaustion.* **2** [I] to be confused or shocked by a situation: *Bill's letter left us reeling.* | **+with** *The family* *was reeling with shock.* | +**from** *The Democrats are still reeling from their defeat.* **3** [I] if a business, country etc. is reeling, it has had bad things happen to it that are very difficult to deal with: +**from** *The economy was still reeling from the previous year's recession.* **4** [I] also **reel back** to step backward suddenly and almost fall over, especially after being hit or getting a shock: *A punch in his stomach **sent** him **reeling**.* **5** [I] to seem to go around and around: *The room reeled before my eyes, and I fainted.*

reel sb/sth ↔ **in** *phr. v.* **1** to wind the reel on a fishing ROD so that a fish on the line comes toward you: *Sam reeled in a seven-pound fish.* **2** to get or attract a large number of people or things SYN **pull in**: *The show reels in more than 13 million viewers each week.*

reel sth ↔ **off** *phr. v.* INFORMAL **1** to repeat a lot of information quickly and easily: *Jack reeled off a list of names.* **2** to do something repeatedly and quickly: *The UNLV team reeled off 14 straight points to take the lead.*

reel² *n.* [C] **1** a round object onto which things such as film, wire, or a special string for fishing can be wound: *a fishing rod and reel* **2** the amount that one of these objects will hold: *a reel of film* **3** one of the parts of a movie that is contained on a reel: *a scene from the final reel of "High Noon"* **4** ENG. LANG. ARTS a quick FOLK dance, especially one from Scotland or Ireland, or the music for this

re·e·lect, reelect /ˌri ɪˈlɛkt/ *v.* [T] POLITICS to elect someone again —**re-election** /ˌri ɪˈlɛkʃən/ *n.* [C,U]

re·en·act, reenact /ˌri ɪˈnækt/ *v.* [T] to perform the actions of a story, crime etc. that happened in past times: *Children re-enacted the Christmas story.* —**re-enactment** *n.* [C]: *a re-enactment of the crime*

re·en·gi·neer /ˌriɛndʒɪˈnɪr/ *v.* [T] **1** to change the structure of an activity, organization etc. so that it performs better SYN **reorganize**: *They reengineered their banking processes and made it run much more smoothly.* **2** to improve the design of a product

re·en·try, reentry /riˈɛntri/ *n.* [C,U] **1** an act of entering a place again: *The shuttle made a successful re-entry into the Earth's atmosphere.* **2** a situation in which someone starts being involved in something again: +**into** *America's re-entry into the Japanese auto market*

reeve /riv/ *n.* [C] LAW the official who is in charge of the town governments in some Canadian PROVINCES

ref /rɛf/ *n.* [C] INFORMAL a REFEREE

ref. the written abbreviation of REFERENCE

re·fec·to·ry /rɪˈfɛktəri/ *n.* [C] a large room in a MONASTERY, college etc. where meals are served and eaten SYN **cafeteria**

re·fer /rɪˈfɚ/ S3 W1 *v.* **referred, referring**

refer to sb/sth *phr. v.* **1** to mention or speak about someone or something: *One woman used a racist term to refer to African-Americans.* | **refer to sth/sb as sth** *The cafeteria, in the basement, is referred to as "the dungeon."* | **refer to sb/sth by sth** *Celebrities are often referred to by their first names.* **2** to look at a book, map, piece of paper etc. for information: *He spoke without referring to his notes.* **3** if a statement, number, report etc. refers to someone or something, it is about that person or thing: *The blue line on the graph refers to sales.* **4** to send someone or something to another place or person for information, advice, or a decision: **refer sb/sth to sb/sth** *He was referred to a specialist.* [**Origin:** 1300–1400 Latin *referre* **to bring back, report, refer,** from *ferre* **to carry**] → see also CROSS-REFER

ref·er·a·ble /rɪˈfʌrəbəl, -ˈfɚ-/ *adj.* [+ to] FORMAL something that is referable to something else can be related to it

ref·er·ee¹ /ˌrɛfəˈri/ *n.* [C] **1** someone who makes sure that the rules are followed in sports such as football, basketball, or BOXING → see also UMPIRE

THESAURUS

Referee and **umpire** mean the same but are used for different sports.
Use **referee** when you are talking about soccer, ice hockey, basketball, boxing, wrestling, or volleyball.
Use **umpire** when you are talking about baseball.
Tennis and football have both umpires and referees, though the main judge in tennis is usually called the umpire, and the main judge in football is usually called the referee.

2 LAW someone whose job is to be a judge in certain types of law cases: *a juvenile court referee* **3** someone who judges an article or RESEARCH idea before it is PUBLISHed or given money: *Articles submitted to the journal are read by several referees.* **4** someone who is asked to settle a disagreement: *a referee in a neighbor dispute*

referee² *v.* **refereed, refereeing** [I,T] to be the referee for a game

ref·erence /ˈrɛfrəns/ S2 W3 *n.* **1** [C,U] something you say or write that mentions another person or thing: +**to** *There is no **direct reference** to her own childhood in the novel.* | *Oddly, the ad **makes** no **reference to** the product being sold.* | *He made a **passing reference** to cutting the state's debt* (=he mentioned it quickly). **2 reference point** also **point of reference a)** an idea, fact, event, etc. that helps you understand or make a judgment about a situation: *Fitzgerald's case will be the reference point for lawyers in tomorrow's trial.* **b)** something that you can see that helps you to know where you are when you are traveling in an area **3** [U] the act of looking at something for information: *One shelf was filled with reference works* (=reference books). | *Microfilm copies will be kept **for future reference*** (=so that they can be looked at in the future). **4 in/with reference to sth** FORMAL used to say what you are writing or talking about: *I am writing in reference to the job advertised in the paper.* **5** [C] **a)** also **letter of reference** a letter containing information about you that is written by someone who knows you well, usually to a new employer: *For the adoption, the Millers provided references and numerous other documents.* **b)** the person who provides information about your character and abilities: *Ask a teacher to act as one of your references.* **6** [C] a book, article etc. from which information has been obtained: *a list of references* **7** [C] a number that tells you where you can find the information you want in a book, on a map etc.: *a list of streets with map references* → see also CROSS-REFERENCE, **terms of reference** at TERM¹ (18)

ˈreference book *n.* [C] a book such as a dictionary or ENCYCLOPEDIA that you look at to find information

ˈreference ˌlibrary also **ˈreference ˌroom** *n.* [C] a public library or a room in a library, that contains books that you can read but not take away → see also LENDING LIBRARY

ref·er·en·dum /ˌrɛfəˈrɛndəm/ *n. plural* **referenda** /-də/ or **referendums** [C,U] POLITICS an occasion when you vote in order to make a decision about a particular subject, rather than voting for a person: +**on** *Denmark planned to **hold a referendum** on the issue.*

re·fer·ral /rɪˈfʌrəl, -ˈfɚ-/ *n.* [C,U] FORMAL an act of sending someone or something to another person or place for help, information, a decision etc.: +**to** *a referral to a specialist*

re·fill¹ /riˈfɪl/ *v.* [T] to fill something again: *The waiter refilled our wine glasses.* —**refillable** *adj.*: *a refillable lighter*

re·fill² /ˈrifɪl/ *n.* [C] **1** a container filled with a particular substance that you use to fill or replace an empty container, or the substance itself: *refills for an ink pen* | *a prescription refill* **2** SPOKEN another drink to refill your glass: *A large soda is $1.50. Refills are free.*

re·fine /rɪˈfaɪn/ AC *v.* [T] **1** to improve a method, plan, system etc. by gradually making slight changes to it: *Car makers are constantly refining their designs.* **2** to

R

make a substance more pure using an industrial process SYN **purify**: *oil refining*

re·fined /rɪˈfaɪnd/ Ac *adj.* **1** [no comparative] a substance that is refined has been made pure by an industrial process OPP **unrefined** OPP **raw** OPP **crude**: *refined oil* | *refined sugar* **2** someone who is refined is well-educated, polite, and interested in high quality books, music, food etc. SYN **cultivated** OPP **unrefined**: *a refined audience of music-lovers* **3** improved and made more effective OPP **unrefined**: *a refined method of measurement*

re·fine·ment /rɪˈfaɪnmənt/ Ac *n.* **1** [C] an addition or improvement to an existing product, system etc.: *Several rule refinements come into force this season.* **2** [U] the quality of being polite and well-educated, and interested in high quality books, music, food etc.: *His manners showed refinement and good breeding.* **3** [U] the quality of being very good and well-made: *a wine of great delicacy and refinement* **4** [U] the process of improving something: +**of** *the refinement of the measuring device* **5** [U + of] the process of making a substance more pure

R

re·fin·er·y /rɪˈfaɪnəri/ *n. plural* **refineries** [C] a factory where something such as metal, sugar, or oil is made purer: *an oil refinery*

re·fin·ish /riˈfɪnɪʃ/ *v.* [T] to make the surface of something wooden look new again: *Hardwood floors can be sanded and refinished.* —**refinishing** *n.* [U]

re·fit /ˌriˈfɪt/ *v.* **refitted**, **refitting** [I,T] to make a ship, airplane, building etc. ready to be used again, by doing repairs and putting in new machinery: *a refitted shrimp boat* —**refit** /ˈrifɪt/ *n.* [C,U]

re·flect /rɪˈflɛkt/ W2 *v.* **1** [T usually passive] if something such as a mirror or water reflects an image, you can see that image in the mirror etc. SYN **mirror**: **be reflected in sth** *The mountains were reflected in the still water of the lake.* **2** [T not in progressive] to show or be a sign of a particular situation, idea, or feeling: *The poll results reflect widespread anxiety about the economy.* | **be reflected in sth** *His fascination with the circus is reflected in many of his movies.* | **reflect who/what/how etc.** *The department's name was changed to reflect what it does more accurately.* **3** [I,T] PHYSICS if a surface reflects light, heat, or sound, it sends back the light etc. that hits it: *The moon reflects the sun's rays.* | +**off** *Sunlight reflected off the whitewashed houses.* **4** [I,T] to think carefully about something, or to say something that you have been thinking about: +**on** *She reflected on how much had changed.* | **reflect that** *Parker reflected that most people have no idea how hard teachers work.* [**Origin:** 1300–1400 Latin *reflectere* **to bend back**, from *flectere* **to bend**]

reflect on/upon *phr. v.* to influence people's opinion of someone or something, especially in a bad way: *If my kids are rude, that reflects on me as a parent.*

reflection

re·flec·tion /rɪˈflɛkʃən/ *n.* **1** [C] an image reflected in a mirror or similar surface: *I could see my reflection in his sunglasses.* **2** [C,U] careful thought, or an idea or opinion based on this: *Many working women have little time for reflection.* | +**on** *In his latest poems, Paz gives us a series of reflections on death.* | **Upon reflection,** (=after thinking about something) *I came to appreciate my father's wisdom.* **3** [C] something that shows, or is a sign of, a particular situation, fact, or feeling: +**of** *The amount you tip should be a reflection of the kind of service you got.* **4 be a reflection on sb/sth** to show someone's character, abilities, work etc. in an unfavorable way: *Your children's bad behavior is seen as a reflection on you.* | *No matter how hard you clean, the dirt will return. It **is no reflection on** your housekeeping.* **5** [U] PHYSICS the light, heat, sound, or image that is being reflected **6** [C] MATH an exact copy of a GEOMETRIC shape that is a mirror image of the original, so that the right side appears on the left, and the left side appears on the right.

reˌflectional ˈsymmetry also **ˌline ˈsymmetry** *n.* [U] MATH the quality of a flat shape when it has two halves that are exactly the same → see also POINT SYMMETRY

re·flec·tive /rɪˈflɛktɪv/ *adj.* **1** someone who is reflective thinks carefully and deeply about things SYN **contemplative**: *a reflective and soft-spoken man* **2** a reflective surface reflects light: *Bicyclists should wear reflective vests at night.* **3** showing something that is typical or true about a situation: +**of** *The data is reflective of the eating habits of American children.*

re·flec·tor /rɪˈflɛktɚ/ *n.* [C] **1** a small piece of plastic that reflects light and can be fastened to something such as a bicycle, so that it can be seen more easily at night → see picture at BICYCLE[1] **2** PHYSICS a surface that reflects light

re·flex /ˈriflɛks/ *n.* **1** [C] BIOLOGY a sudden movement that the muscles make as a natural reaction to a physical effect: *a baby's sucking reflex* **2 reflexes** [plural] the natural ability to react quickly and well to sudden situations: *Computer games require **quick reflexes**.* **3** [C,U] also **reflex action** something that you do when you react to a situation without thinking: *Hawthorne said she fired the gun as a reflex when her husband shouted.*

ˈreflex ˌarc *n.* [C] BIOLOGY the path followed by nerve signals in the body when they cause a REFLEX action

re·flex·ive /rɪˈflɛksɪv/ *adj.* ENG. LANG. ARTS a reflexive verb or PRONOUN shows that the action in a sentence affects the person or thing that does the action. In the sentences "I enjoyed myself" and "I cut myself," "myself" is reflexive. —**reflexive** *n.* [C]

re·flex·ol·o·gy /ˌriflɛkˈsɑlədʒi/ *n.* [U] a type of ALTERNATIVE MEDICINE in which areas of the feet are touched or rubbed in order to cure or help a medical problem in another part of the body

re·for·es·ta·tion /ˌrifɔrəˈsteɪʃən/ *n.* [U] EARTH SCIENCE the practice of planting trees in an area where they were previously cut down, in order to grow them for industrial use or to improve the environment OPP **deforestation** —**reforest** /riˈfɔrɪst/ *v.* [I,T]

re·form[1] /rɪˈfɔrm/ *v.* **1** [T] to improve a system, law, organization etc. by making a lot of changes to it, so that it operates in a fairer or more effective way: *plans to reform the health care system* ▸see THESAURUS box at **change**[1] **2** [I,T] to change your behavior and become a better person, or to make someone do this: *Dogs that bite can be reformed with good training.* | **reformed criminal/sinner/alcoholic etc.** (=someone who is no longer a criminal, sinner etc.)

reform[2] W2 *n.* [C,U] a change or changes made to a system or organization, in order to improve it: **welfare/immigration/health-care etc. reform** *Tax reforms did not benefit the middle class.* | **economic/democratic/social etc. reform** *a program of economic reform in China* | +**of** *a **sweeping reform** of farm programs*

re-form /ˌri ˈfɔrm/ *v.* [I,T] **1** to start to exist again or to make something start to exist again: *The band isn't re-forming.* **2** to form into lines again, or to make soldiers do this

ref·or·ma·tion /ˌrɛfɚˈmeɪʃən/ *n.* **1** [C,U] an improvement made by changing something a lot: *the reformation of the welfare system* **2 the Reformation** the religious changes in Europe in the 16th century, that resulted in the Protestant churches being established

re·for·ma·to·ry /rɪˈfɔrməˌtɔri/ *n. plural* **reformatories** [C] a REFORM SCHOOL

re·form·er /rɪˈfɔrmɚ/ *n.* [C] someone who tries to improve a system, law, or society: *a great social reformer*

re·form·ist /rɪˈfɔrmɪst/ *adj.* POLITICS wanting to improve systems or situations, especially in politics —**reformist** *n.* [C]

reˈform school *n.* [C] a special school where young people who have broken the law are sent to live

re·fract /rɪˈfrækt/ *v.* [I,T] PHYSICS to change the direction of light or sound, for example when light goes from the air into a liquid or through a transparent substance: *Light is refracted when it hits the surface of the water.*

re·frac·tion /rɪˈfrækʃən/ Ac *n.* [U] PHYSICS a change in the direction of light or sound, for example when it goes from the air into a liquid or through a transparent substance

re·frac·to·ry /rɪˈfræktəri/ *adj.* FORMAL **1** deliberately not obeying someone in authority and being difficult to deal with or control SYN **unruly** **2** TECHNICAL a refractory disease or illness is hard to treat or cure

re·frain¹ /rɪˈfreɪn/ *v.* [I] FORMAL to not do something that you want to do: +**from** *Please refrain from smoking.* [**Origin:** 1300–1400 Old French *refrener*, from Latin *refrenare*, from *frenum* **bridle**]

refrain² *n.* [C] **1** ENG. LANG. ARTS a part of a song that is repeated, especially at the end of each VERSE **2** FORMAL a remark or idea that is repeated often: **common/frequent/constant etc. refrain** *"We'll see," was his frequent refrain.*

re·fresh /rɪˈfrɛʃ/ *v.* **1** [T] to make someone feel less tired or less hot: *A brief nap was enough to refresh him after the flight.* **2 refresh sb's memory/recollection** to make someone remember something: *Leopold looked at the files to refresh his memory.* **3 refresh sb's drink** SPOKEN to add more of an alcoholic drink to someone's glass **4** [I,T] COMPUTERS if you refresh your computer screen while you are connected to the Internet, you make the screen show any new information that has arrived since you first began looking at it —**refreshed** *adj.*

reˈfresher ˌcourse *n.* [C] a course that teaches you about new developments in a particular subject or skill, especially one that you need for your job: *a nursing refresher course*

re·fresh·ing /rɪˈfrɛʃɪŋ/ *adj.* **1** making you feel less tired or less hot: *The ocean breeze was refreshing.* | *a refreshing drink* **2** pleasantly different from what is familiar and boring: *The show is **a refreshing change** from TV's usual programs.* —**refreshingly** *adv.*

re·fresh·ment /rɪˈfrɛʃmənt/ *n.* **1** [C usually plural] food and drinks that are provided at a meeting, party, sports event etc.: *Refreshments will be provided.* | *a refreshment stand* **2** [U] food and drinks in general: *Hosts ought to offer their guests some refreshments.* **3** [U] the experience of being made to feel less tired or hot

ref·ried beans /ˌrifraɪd ˈbinz/ *n.* [plural] a Mexican dish in which beans that have already been cooked are crushed and FRIED with SPICES

re·frig·er·ant /rɪˈfrɪdʒərənt/ *n.* [C] TECHNICAL a substance used in refrigerators, AIR CONDITIONING systems etc.

re·frig·er·ate /rɪˈfrɪdʒəˌreɪt/ *v.* [T] to make something such as food or liquid cold in order to preserve it: *Refrigerate the mixture overnight.* [**Origin:** 1500–1600 Latin, past participle of *refrigerare*, from *frigerare* **to make cold**] —**refrigeration** /rɪˌfrɪdʒəˈreɪʃən/ *n.* [U]

re·frig·er·a·tor /rɪˈfrɪdʒəˌreɪtɚ/ S2 *n.* [C] a large piece of electrical kitchen equipment, shaped like a cupboard, used for keeping food and drinks cold → see also FREEZER SYN **fridge**

re·fuel /riˈfyul/ *v.* **1** [I,T] to fill a vehicle or airplane with FUEL before continuing a trip: *Some military planes can refuel in mid-air.* **2** [T] to make feelings, emotions, or ideas stronger: *The attack refueled fears the war would begin again.*

ref·uge /ˈrɛfyudʒ/ *n.* **1** [C] a place that provides protection from bad weather or danger: *a wildlife refuge* | +**from** *Small huts along the trail provide a refuge from the rain.* | +**for** *a refuge for battered women* **2** [U] safety from harm or danger: *The caves provided refuge in bad weather.* | **take/seek refuge (in sth)** *Several reporters **sought refuge** in the U.S. embassy.* [**Origin:** 1300–1400 Old French, Latin *refugium*, from *refugere* **to run away**]

ref·u·gee /ˌrɛfyʊˈdʒi◂/ *n.* [C] someone who has been forced to leave their country, especially during a war: *Refugees were streaming across the border.* | ***a refugee camp***

re·ful·gent /rɪˈfʊldʒənt/ *adj.* LITERARY very bright —**refulgence** *n.* [U]

re·fund¹ /ˈrifʌnd/ *n.* [C] **1** ECONOMICS an amount of money that is given back to you if you are not satisfied with the goods or services that you have paid for: *You can return it within 30 days for a **full refund**.* | *Two cups were broken, so the store **gave me a refund**.* **2 tax refund** ECONOMICS money that you get back from the government when it has taken too much money in taxes from your wages

re·fund² /rɪˈfʌnd, ˈrifʌnd/ *v.* [T] to give someone their money back, especially when they are not satisfied with the goods or services they have paid for: *Saturday's concert is canceled, and tickets will be refunded.* → see also REIMBURSE

re·fur·bish /rɪˈfɚbɪʃ/ *v.* [T] **1** to thoroughly repair and improve a building by painting it, cleaning it etc. SYN **renovate** **2** to change and improve a plan, idea, or skill [**Origin:** 1600–1700 *furbish* **to clean up** (13–21 centuries), from Old French *forbir*] —**refurbishment** *n.* [C,U]

re·fus·al /rɪˈfyuzəl/ *n.* [C,U] an act of saying firmly that you will not do, give, or accept something: **refusal to do sth** *Samuelson's refusal to take a drug test cost him his job.* | *his **stubborn refusal** to participate* | +**of** *the refusal of the unions to accept pay cuts*

re·fuse¹ /rɪˈfyuz/ S2 W1 *v.* **1** [I] to say or show that you will not do something that someone has asked you to do OPP **agree**: *He tried to persuade her to come with him, but she refused.* | **refuse to do sth** *Steen refused to answer any questions.* | **stubbornly/steadfastly/flatly refuse** *She had stubbornly refused to take my advice.* **2** [I,T] to say that you do not want something that someone tries to give you SYN **turn down** OPP **accept**: *Sutton refused food in protest against conditions in the prison.* | *Their offer is **too good to refuse**.* ►see THESAURUS box at **reject¹** **3** [T] to not give or allow someone to have something that they want: **refuse sb sth** *Immigration authorities refused him a visa.* [**Origin:** 1300–1400 Old French *refuser*, from Latin *refundere* **to pour back**] → see also DECLINE

ref·use² /ˈrɛfyus/ *n.* [U] FORMAL waste material that has been thrown away SYN **garbage** SYN **trash** ►see THESAURUS box at **garbage**

re·fute /rɪˈfyut/ *v.* [T] FORMAL **1** to prove that a statement or idea is not correct SYN **disprove**: **refute a theory/idea etc.** *Several scientists have attempted to refute Moore's theories.* **2** to say that a statement is wrong or not fair: **refute an allegation/charge etc.** *She refuted any allegations of malpractice.* [**Origin:** 1500–1600 Latin *refutare*, from *-futare* **to hit**] —**refutable** *adj.* —**refutation** /ˌrɛfyʊˈteɪʃən/ *n.* [C,U]

reg. a written abbreviation of REGISTRATION

re·gain /rɪˈgeɪn/ *v.* [T] **1** to get something back, especially an ability or quality, that you have lost SYN **recover**: *Iowa State regained the lead in the second half.* | *Will he regain the use of his injured hand?* | *Will the Democrats **regain control** of the House?* | *When she **regained consciousness**, she was lying on the floor.* | *It*

R

took him a moment to **regain** his **composure**. **2** LITERARY to reach a place again

re·gal /ˈrigəl/ *adj.* FORMAL typical of a king or queen, appropriate for a king or queen, or similar to a king or queen in behavior, looks etc. SYN **majestic**: *She gave a regal wave.* —**regally** *adv.*

re·gale /rɪˈgeɪl/ *v.*

regale sb **with** sth *phr. v.* to entertain someone by telling them about something: *Burns regaled his interviewer with tales of his adventures.*

re·ga·lia /rɪˈgeɪlyə/ *n.* [U] traditional clothes and decorations, used at official ceremonies: *Native American dancers in full regalia*

re·gard¹ /rɪˈgɑrd/ *n.*

1 RESPECT [U] feelings of respect for someone or something: **+for** *His statements show* ***little regard*** *for women.* | **have/show regard** *I have a* ***high regard for*** (=have a lot of respect for) *their professionalism.* | *Seventy percent of the voters* ***hold him in low regard*** (=have little respect for him).

2 ATTENTION [U] careful attention that is given to something: **+for** *a proper regard for the law* | **have/show/pay regard** *Leland seems to* ***have little regard for*** *detail in his work.* | *The best people are hired,* ***without regard to*** (=without thinking about) *race.*

3 with/in regard to sth relating to a particular subject: *Important changes are being made in regard to security.*

4 in this/that regard relating to something you have just mentioned: *I had never been in trouble at school, so there were no problems in that regard.*

5 regards [plural] good wishes: ***Send my regards*** *to Mark if you're writing him, okay?* | *I asked Jim to* ***give my regards*** *to his mother.* | *I hope to see you soon.* ***Regards,*** *Tom* (=used to end an informal letter).

6 LOOK [singular] LITERARY a long look without moving your eyes

R

regard² W3 *v.* [T] **1** [not in progressive] to think about someone or something in a particular way SYN **view**: **regard sb/sth as sth** *The book is still regarded as the authority on the subject.* | **regard sb/sth with admiration/fear/concern etc.** *Robert's classmates regarded him with curiosity.* | *The product* ***is highly regarded*** (=people have a very good opinion of it) *worldwide.* | *He was* ***widely regarded*** (=a lot of people have this opinion) *as the best player on the team.* **2** FORMAL to look at someone or something, especially in a particular way: *She regarded him thoughtfully.* ▸see THESAURUS box at **look¹** **3** FORMAL to pay attention to something **4 as regards sth** FORMAL relating to a particular subject: *It is too early to judge the success of these plans, especially as regards the environment.* [**Origin:** 1300–1400 Old French *regarder* **to look back at, regard**, from *garder* **to guard, look at**]

re·gard·ing /rɪˈgɑrdɪŋ/ *prep.* used in letters or speeches to introduce the subject you are writing or talking about SYN **concerning** SYN **with regard to**: *Regarding your recent inquiry, I've enclosed a copy of our new brochure.*

re·gard·less /rɪˈgɑrdlɪs/ *adv.* **1** without being affected by different situations, problems etc.: **+of** *The law requires equal treatment for all, regardless of race, religion, or sex.* **2** if you continue doing something regardless, you do it in spite of difficulties or people telling you not to: *I'm leaving in ten days, regardless.* | **+of** *He does what he wants, regardless of what I say.*

re·gat·ta /rɪˈgɑt̬ə, -ˈgæ-/ *n.* [C] a sports event in which boats race [**Origin:** 1600–1700 Italian *regattare* **to compete**]

re·ge·la·tion /ˌridʒəˈleɪʃən/ *n.* [C,U] PHYSICS the repeated process that happens when ice melts under pressure and then freezes again when the pressure is reduced

re·gen·cy /ˈridʒənsi/ *n.* [C,U] POLITICS a period of government by a regent

re·gen·er·ate /riˈdʒɛnəˌreɪt/ *v.* [T] **1** FORMAL to make something develop and grow strong again, especially something such as an ECONOMY, business etc.: *The Marshall Plan sought to regenerate the shattered Europe of 1947.* **2** to grow again after having been damaged, or to make something grow again: *Given time, the forest will regenerate itself.* | *Brain cells cannot regenerate once they are destroyed.* —**regenerative** /-nəˌreɪt̬ɪv, -nərət̬ɪv/ *adj.* —**regeneration** /rɪˌdʒɛnəˈreɪʃən, ˌridʒɛn-/ *n.* [U]

re·gent /ˈridʒənt/ *n.* [C] POLITICS someone who governs instead of a king or queen, because the king or queen is sick, absent, or still a child —**regent** *adj.* [only after noun]: *the Prince Regent*

reg·gae /ˈrɛgeɪ/ *n.* [U] a type of popular music from the West Indies with a strong regular beat [**Origin:** 1900–2000 Jamaican English *rege* **rags**]

reg·i·cide /ˈrɛdʒəˌsaɪd/ *n.* FORMAL **1** [U] the crime of killing a king or queen **2** [C] someone who does this

re·gime /reɪˈʒim, rɪ-/ Ac W3 *n.* [C] **1** POLITICS a government, especially one that has not been elected fairly or that you disapprove of: **military/totalitarian/Communist etc. regime** *They stood to lose everything they had* ***under a*** *Communist* ***regime.*** | *the country's* ***repressive*** *right-wing* ***regime*** ▸see THESAURUS box at **government** **2** POLITICS a particular system of government or management, especially one that is new or one that was used in the past but is not now: *a new regime of managed health care* **3** a regimen [**Origin:** 1400–1500 French *régime*, from Latin *regimen*]

reˈgime ˌchange *n.* [U] a change in the government of a country that happens because another country forces that government out of power

re·gi·men /ˈrɛdʒəmən/ *n.* [C] FORMAL a special plan of food, exercise etc. that is intended to improve your health: *a fitness regimen*

reg·i·ment /ˈrɛdʒəmənt/ *n.* [C] **1** a large group of soldiers, usually consisting of several BATTALIONS **2** a large number of people, animals, or things: **+of** *a regiment of friends and family*

reg·i·men·tal /ˌrɛdʒəˈmɛntl̩/ *adj.* relating to a regiment: *the regimental commander*

reg·i·ment·ed /ˈrɛdʒəˌmɛntɪd/ *adj.* organized and controlled strictly, often too strictly: *Prison inmates follow a regimented schedule.* —**regimentation** /ˌrɛdʒəmənˈteɪʃən, -mɛn-/ *n.* [U]

re·gion /ˈridʒən/ Ac W1 *n.* [C] **1** a fairly large area of a state, country, or the world, usually without exact limits: *efforts to bring peace to the region* | **polar/border/desert etc. region** *Snow is expected in mountain regions.* ▸see THESAURUS box at **area** **2** a particular part of someone's body: *the regions of the brain that control memory* **3 (somewhere) in the region of sth** used to describe an amount of time, money, etc. without being exact SYN **approximately**: *The cost will be in the region of $40 billion.* [**Origin:** 1300–1400 Old French, Latin *regio*, from *regere* **to rule**]

re·gion·al /ˈridʒənl/ Ac S3 W3 *adj.* relating to a particular region: *the regional sales director* —**regionally** *adv.*

ˌregional ˈcouncil *n.* [C] POLITICS a COUNCIL OF GOVERNMENTS

re·gion·al·ism /ˈridʒənlˌɪzəm/ *n.* [U] loyalty to a particular region of a country and the desire for it to be more politically independent

reg·is·ter¹ /ˈrɛdʒəstɚ/ Ac S2 *n.* **1** [C] an official list containing the names of all the people, organizations, or things of one particular type, or a book that contains this list: *He signed the guest register.* | **+of** *The railroad station is* ***listed on the*** *National* ***Register*** *of Historic Places.* ▸see THESAURUS box at **record¹** **2** [C] a CASH REGISTER **3** [C] a small movable metal plate that controls how much cool or warm air comes into a room: *the hot air registers* **4** [C] ENG. LANG. ARTS the range of musical notes that someone's voice or a musical instrument can reach: **the upper/lower/middle register** *the cello's upper register* **5** [C,U] ENG. LANG. ARTS the words, style, and grammar used by speakers and writers in a particular situation or in a particular type of writing: *Business letters should be written in a formal register.* [**Origin:** 1300–1400 Old French *registre*, from

Medieval Latin *registrum*, from Latin *regerere* **to bring back**]

register² Ac S3 W3 *v.* **1** [I,T] to record a name, details about something etc. on an official list, or to put your name on an official list: *Owners must register their weapons.* | *The tanker is registered in Rotterdam.* | *registered voters* | **register to do sth** *You can register to vote at age 18.* | **+as** *He registered as a bone marrow donor.* | **+with** *You could try registering with an employment agency.* **2** [I,T] to officially arrange to attend a particular school, class, or college SYN **enroll**: **+for** *When do you have to register for classes?* **3** [T] to show or express a feeling: *The faces of the jury registered no emotion.* **4** [I usually in negatives, T] if a fact or something you see registers, or if you register it, you realize or notice it and then remember it: *She told me her name, but it just didn't register at the time.* **5** [T] FORMAL to officially state your opinion about something so that everyone knows what you think: *Call the consumer affairs board to register your complaint.* **6** [I,T] if an instrument registers an amount or if an amount registers on it, the instrument shows or records that amount: *The earthquake registered 7.2 on the Richter scale.*

ˌregistered ˈnurse ABBREVIATION **RN** *n.* [C] someone who has been trained and is officially allowed to work as a nurse

reg·is·trar /ˈrɛdʒəˌstrɑr/ *n.* [C] someone who is in charge of official records, for example in a city or a college

reg·is·tra·tion /ˌrɛdʒəˈstreɪʃən/ Ac S3 *n.* **1** [U] the act of recording names and details on an official list: *voter registration* | **+of** *the registration of births and deaths* | *The registration fee is $75.* | *Registration for new students begins at 9 a.m.* **2** [C] an official piece of paper containing details about a vehicle and the name of its owner: *May I see your license and registration, Ma'am?*

reg·is·try /ˈrɛdʒəstri/ *n.* *plural* **registries** **1** [C] a place where official records are kept: *the Registry of Motor Vehicles* **2** [U] the act of recording information on an official list, or the state of being recorded on such a list: *The registry of the ship is unknown at present.* **3** [C] a list of gifts that people would like to receive when they get married, usually kept at a store: *the* ***bridal registry*** *at Robinson's Department Store*

reg·o·lith /ˈrɛgəlɪθ/ *n.* [C,U] EARTH SCIENCE a layer of loose rock covering the surface of the Earth or another PLANET, which gradually changes shape and color because of the wind, rain, sun etc.: *samples of regolith from the Moon*

re·gress /rɪˈgrɛs/ *v.* [I] to return to an earlier and worse condition, or to a less developed way of behaving OPP **progress**: **+to** *The patient had regressed to an infantile state.* —**regressive** *adj.*

re·gres·sion /rɪˈgrɛʃən/ *n.* [C,U] **1** the act of returning to an earlier condition that is worse or less developed OPP **progression** **2** TECHNICAL the act of thinking or behaving as you did at an earlier time in your life, such as when you were a child

reˈgressive ˌtax *n.* [C] ECONOMICS a tax that has less effect on the rich than on the poor → see also PROGRESSIVE TAX

re·gret¹ /rɪˈgrɛt/ *v.* **regretted, regretting** [T] **1** to feel sorry about something you have done and wish you had not done it: *Do you ever regret taking this job?* | **regret doing sth** *I regretted not having worn a thicker coat.* | **regret (that)** *Most of the men regretted that they hadn't stayed in school.* | **bitterly/deeply regret sth** *It was a stupid thing to do and I deeply regret it* (=regret something very much). | *If we don't deal with the problem now, we'll* ***live to regret*** *it* (=we'll regret it in the future). | ***You'll regret it*** *if you leave your job now.* **2** [not in progressive] FORMAL to be sorry and sad about a situation: *We regret any inconvenience this mistake caused you.* | ***I regret that*** *I have to impose such a short deadline for this project.* **3 I regret to say/inform/tell you that** FORMAL used when you are going to give someone bad news: *I regret to inform you that your contract will not be renewed.* [**Origin:** 1400–1500 Old French *regreter*]

GRAMMAR

Regret is often followed by an *-ing* form of a verb. It can be followed by the *to* form, but this is used mainly in very formal writing. So if you say: *I regret to inform you that your application was not successful,* you mean *I'm sorry, but your application was not successful.* Compare this with: *I regret telling her about my problems.* This means *I'm sorry I told her about my problems, and I wish I hadn't.*

regret² *n.* **1** [C usually plural, U] sadness that you feel about something, because you wish it had not happened or that you had not done it: *Jason detected a note of regret in her voice.* | **+about** *She* ***has no regrets*** (=does not regret) *about not pursuing a TV career.* | **+at** *Dunne* ***expressed regret*** *at having joined the club.* | **with (great/deep) regret** *It is with deep regret that I accept your resignation.* **2 much to sb's regret** FORMAL used to say that someone feels sad or sorry about something: *Much to his regret, he never met his grandfather.* **3 give/send your regrets** FORMAL used when someone is unable to go to a meeting, accept an invitation etc., and they ask someone else to tell people this: *Henry sends his regrets – he has the flu.*

re·gret·ful·ly /rɪˈgrɛtfəli/ *adv.* **1** feeling sad because you do not want to do what you are doing: *"We'd better go," she said regretfully.* **2** [sentence adverb] used to talk about a situation that you wish was different or that you are sorry about SYN **regrettably**: *Regretfully, Elliot was forced to close the business.* —**regretful** *adj.*

re·gret·ta·ble /rɪˈgrɛt̬əbəl/ *adj.* something that is regrettable makes you feel sorry or sad because it has bad results: *Any job losses are regrettable.* | ***It is regrettable that*** *this has been allowed to go on for so long.*

re·gret·ta·bly /rɪˈgrɛt̬əbli/ *adv.* used when you consider a particular situation to be unsatisfactory, and this makes you feel sorry and wish things were different SYN **regretfully**: [sentence adverb] *Regrettably, a lot of the work in the show is of poor quality.* | [+ adj./adv.] *Mr. Hart's comments were regrettably inappropriate.*

re·group /ˌriˈgrup/ *v.* **1** [I] to organize what you are doing in a new or different way, in order to be calmer or more effective: *The party needs time to regroup after its election defeat.* **2** [I,T] to form new groups or form a group again, or to make people do this **3** [I,T] if soldiers regroup or someone regroups them, they form into their correct groups again after a battle, so that they can fight again

reg·u·lar¹ /ˈrɛgyələ˞/ S1 W2 *adj.*
1 REPEATED a regular series of things has the same amount of time or space between each thing and the next: *His breathing was slow and regular.* | *The pillars were spaced* ***at regular intervals.***

THESAURUS

hourly happening or done every hour: *an hourly fee* | *The tour leaves the ticket office hourly.*
daily happening or done every day: *a daily newspaper* | *It rains daily during the rainy season.*
weekly happening or done every week: *a weekly column* | *Our website is updated weekly.*
monthly happening or done every month: *regular monthly meetings* | *The magazine is published monthly.*
yearly happening or done every year: *yearly visits to his mother*
annual happening every year: *the teachers' annual convention*
annually every year: *The Museum of Science attracts 1.7 million visitors annually.*

2 ORDINARY ordinary, without any special features or qualities: *Dr. Garrison is a regular doctor, not a specialist.* | *Do you want decaffeinated or regular coffee?*

3 NORMAL SIZE [only before noun] of a MEDIUM size, neither large nor small: *I'd like a cheeseburger and a regular Coke.*
4 OFTEN [only before noun] happening or doing something very often: *Infants require regular health screening.* | *a regular churchgoer* | *Hemingway was a* ***regular customer*** *here.* | *Get* ***regular exercise****, and eat a healthy diet.* | *Nancy entertains at home* ***on a regular basis****.* | *Fights between the men were a* ***regular occurrence****.*
5 USUAL [only before noun] normal or usual: *What's the regular procedure for filing a complaint?*
6 SHAPE evenly shaped with parts or sides of equal size OPP **irregular**: *a regular hexagon*
7 FACE regular features are SYMMETRICAL, not a strange or unattractive shape, and of normal size OPP **irregular**: *She had dark hair and regular features.*
8 a regular guy/Joe a man who is ordinary, honest, and friendly
9 be/keep/stay regular INFORMAL **a)** to get rid of waste from your BOWELS often enough to be healthy **b)** a woman who is regular has her PERIOD at the same time each month
10 GRAMMAR ENG. LANG. ARTS a regular verb or noun changes its forms in the same way as most verbs or nouns. The verb "dance" is regular, but "be" is not.
11 FOR EMPHASIS OLD-FASHIONED [only before noun] used to emphasize what someone or something is like: *The town's a regular little Venice.*
12 ARMY [only before noun] a regular army has permanent soldiers, whether there is a war or not
[**Origin:** 1300–1400 Old French *reguler*, from Latin *regula* **edge for drawing straight lines, rule**] **—regularity** /ˌrɛgyəˈlærət̬i/ *n.* [U]

regular² *n.* **1** [C] INFORMAL a customer who goes to the same store, bar, restaurant etc., very often: *one of the bar's regulars* **2** [U] the usual type of gasoline that most cars use **3** [C] a soldier whose permanent job is in the army **4** [C] something of regular size, especially food

reg·u·lar·ize /ˈrɛgyələˌraɪz/ *v.* [T] to make a situation that has existed for some time legal or official **—regularization** /ˌrɛgyələrəˈzeɪʃən/ *n.* [U]

reg·u·lar·ly /ˈrɛgyələli, ˈrɛgyəli/ W3 *adv.* **1** at regular times, for example every day, week, or month: *Children are required to attend school regularly.* **2** often: *They go to concerts regularly.* ►see THESAURUS box at **often** **3** evenly arranged or shaped: *regularly shaped crystals*

reg·u·late /ˈrɛgyəˌleɪt/ Ac W3 *v.* [T] **1** to control an activity or process, especially by rules: *Meat and poultry are regulated by the Agriculture Department.* | **be strictly/closely/tightly regulated** *The sale of alcohol is tightly regulated.* **2** to make a temperature, speed, level of activity etc. stay at or near a particular level, and stop it from increasing or decreasing too much SYN **control**: *The drug helps to regulate his heartbeat.*

reg·u·la·tion¹ /ˌrɛgyəˈleɪʃən/ W2 *n.* **1** [C] POLITICS an official rule or order: **building/safety/fire etc. regulations** *The government is working on new food-labeling regulations.* | *There are* ***rules and regulations*** *that we all have to abide by.* ►see THESAURUS box at **rule**¹
2 [U] control over something, especially by rules: *Some reforms have been made in the regulation of childcare.*
3 [C,U] ECONOMICS official rules and orders that a government or CENTRAL BANK uses to control the production and sale of particular goods and services in a country, and to control the process of bringing goods into or sending them out of a country: *Central Bank regulation of the domestic market* | *The total volume of bank credit is restricted by* ***federal government regulations****.*

regulation² *adj.* [only before noun] having or doing all the things asked for in an official rule: *a regulation nine-hole golf course*

reg·u·la·tor /ˈrɛgyəˌleɪt̬ɚ/ Ac *n.* [C] **1** someone who makes sure that a system operates in the right way, or makes it possible for a system to operate correctly or fairly: *federal bank regulators* **2** an instrument for controlling the temperature, speed etc. of something

reg·u·la·to·ry /ˈrɛgyələˌtɔri/ Ac *adj.* FORMAL having the purpose of controlling an activity or process, especially by rules: *the Nuclear Regulatory Commission*

re·gur·gi·tate /rɪˈgɚdʒəˌteɪt/ *v.* FORMAL **1** [I,T] BIOLOGY to bring food that you have already swallowed back out of your mouth SYN **vomit**: *Birds regurgitate food to feed their young.* **2** DISAPPROVING [T] to repeat facts, ideas etc. that you have read or heard without thinking about them yourself: *Students should not just regurgitate facts.* **—regurgitation** /rɪˌgɚdʒəˈteɪʃən/ *n.* [U]

re·hab /ˈrihæb/ *n.* [U] INFORMAL the process of curing someone who has an alcohol or drug problem: *I spent seven months* ***in rehab****.* | *a rehab center*

re·ha·bil·i·tate /ˌriəˈbɪləˌteɪt, ˌrihə-/ *v.* [T] **1** to help someone to live a healthy, useful, or active life again after they have been injured, very sick, or in prison: *The center treats and rehabilitates stroke victims.* **2** to make people think that someone is good again after a period when they thought that person was bad: *He hired a PR company to help rehabilitate his image.* **3** to improve a building or area so that it returns to the good condition it was in before SYN **renovate** [**Origin:** 1500–1600 Medieval Latin, past participle of *rehabilitare*, from Latin *habilitas* **ability**] **—rehabilitation** /ˌriəˌbɪləˈteɪʃən/ *n.* [U]

re·hash /riˈhæʃ/ *v.* [T] DISAPPROVING **1** to use the same ideas again in a new form that is not really different or better: *His new movie just seems to rehash the same old storyline.* **2** to repeat something that was discussed earlier, especially in an annoying way **—rehash** /ˈrihæʃ/ *n.* [C]

re·hears·al /rɪˈhɚsəl/ S3 *n.* **1** [C,U] ENG. LANG. ARTS a period of time or a particular occasion when all the people in a play, concert etc. practice it before a public performance: *I kept forgetting my lines during rehearsal.* | **+for** *a rehearsal for the show* **2** [C] a time when all the people involved in a big event practice it together before it takes place: *a wedding rehearsal* → see also DRESS REHEARSAL

re·hearse /rɪˈhɚs/ *v.* **1** [I,T] ENG. LANG. ARTS to practice or make people practice something such as a play or concert in order to prepare for a public performance: *They rehearsed the scene in her dressing room.* | **+for** *We barely had time to rehearse for the play.* ►see THESAURUS box at **practice**² **2** [T] to practice something that you plan to say to someone: *Norm spent the night before rehearsing what was going to say.* **3** [T] FORMAL to repeat an opinion that has often been expressed before [**Origin:** 1200–1300 Old French *rehercier*, from *herce* **farm tool for breaking up soil**]

re·heat /ˌriˈhit/ *v.* [T] to make a meal or drink hot again: *Reheat the sauce before serving.*

Rehn·quist /ˈrɛnkwɪst/, **William H.** (1924–2005) the Chief Justice of the U.S. Supreme Court from 1986 until his death

Reich /raɪk/ *n.* [singular] HISTORY the German state or EMPIRE during a particular period of history. The First Reich was the Holy Roman Empire (800–1806); the Second Reich existed from 1871 to 1919; and the Third Reich existed from 1933 to 1945.

reign¹ /reɪn/ *n.* [C] **1** the period of time during which someone is king or queen: *the reign of Henry VIII* **2** the period when someone is in charge of an organization, team etc. **3** the period when someone is the CHAMPION of a sport **4** a period during which something important exists or happens somewhere: *the reign of progressive educational ideas* **5 a reign of terror** a period during which a government kills many of its political opponents or puts them in prison [**Origin:** 1200–1300 Old French *regne*, from Latin *regnum*, from *rex* **king**]

reign² *v.* [I] **1** to be the king or queen: *King George VI reigned from 1936 to 1952.* | +**over** *The pharaohs reigned over ancient Egypt.* **2** to exist for a time as the most important or noticeable feature of a place, business, industry etc.: *Confusion reigned after the hurricane.* **3** to be the best, most powerful, or most popular person or thing: *There is no public transportation, so the car **reigns supreme**.*

reign·ing /ˈreɪnɪŋ/ *adj.* [only before noun] **1 the reigning champion** the most recent winner of a competition **2 a reigning monarch/emperor/queen etc.** the person who is reigning over a country at a particular time

re·im·burse /ˌriɪmˈbɚs/ *v.* [T] FORMAL to pay money back to someone when they have had to spend that money for their work or for an organization: **reimburse sb for sth** *The company will reimburse you for travel expenses.* [**Origin:** 1600–1700 *imburse* **to pay** (16–19 centuries), from Old French *borser* **to get money**] → see also REFUND —**reimbursement** *n.* [C,U]

rein¹ /reɪn/ *n.* [C] **1** [usually plural] a long narrow band of leather that is fastened around a horse's head in order to control it **2 give sb (a) free rein** to give someone complete freedom to do something in whatever way they choose **3 keep a (tight) rein on sb/sth** to control someone or something strictly: *We need to keep a tight rein on spending.* **4 the reins** control over an organization or country: *Chef Thuilier will **hand over the reins** of the restaurant to his grandson.* **5 give free/full rein to sth** also **give sth free/full rein** to do something freely, without restricting or controlling yourself at all: *The children can give their imaginations free rein.* [**Origin:** 1200–1300 Old French *rene*, from Latin *retinere*, from *tenere* **to hold**]

rein² *v.*

rein sth ↔ **in** *phr. v.* **1** to start to control a situation more strictly: *Over 3,000 jobs were cut in an attempt to rein in costs.* **2** to make a horse go more slowly by pulling on the reins

re·in·car·nate /ˌriɪnˈkɑrˌneɪt/ *v.* **be reincarnated** to be born again in another body after you have died

re·in·car·na·tion /ˌriɪnkɑrˈneɪʃən/ *n.* **1** [U] the process by which a person or animal is born again in another body after they have died **2** [C] a person or animal that has the soul of a previous person or animal: +**of** *He claimed to be the reincarnation of an ancient warrior.*

rein·deer /ˈreɪndɪr/ *n. plural* **reindeer** [C] a large DEER with long wide horns that lives in very cold places

re·in·force /ˌriɪnˈfɔrs/ Ac *v.* [T] **1** to give support to an opinion, idea, or feeling, and make it stronger: *The study's results reinforce everything we've been saying.* **2** to make a situation or way of behaving less likely to change: *Violent punishments can actually reinforce bad behavior in children.* **3** to make part of a building, structure, piece of clothing etc. stronger: *The dam was reinforced with 20,000 sandbags.* **4** to make a group of people, especially an army, stronger by adding people, equipment etc.

ˌreinforced ˈconcrete *n.* [U] CONCRETE with metal RODS in it, used to make buildings stronger

re·in·force·ment /ˌriɪnˈfɔrsmənt/ Ac *n.* **1 reinforcements** [plural] additional soldiers who are sent to an army to make it stronger: *The police called for reinforcements.* **2** [U] the act of making something stronger: *The bridge is weak and needs reinforcement.* **3** [U] the act of repeating or practicing something so that it will be remembered **4** [U] the process of making a situation or way of behaving less likely to change

re·in·state /ˌriɪnˈsteɪt/ *v.* [T] **1** to put someone back into a job or position of authority that they had before: *She was later reinstated as a director.* **2** to begin to use a law, system etc. again after not using it for a period of time: *The state reinstated capital punishment in 1976.* —**reinstatement** *n.* [C,U]

re·in·sure /ˌriɪnˈʃʊr/ *v.* [T] ECONOMICS to share the insurance of something between two or more companies, so that there is less risk for each —**reinsurance** *n.* [U]

re·in·ter·pret /ˌrinˈtɚprɪt/ Ac *v.* [T] to think about or perform something again or in a different way, especially to understand it in a new way —**reinterpretation** /ˌriɪntɚprəˈteɪʃən/ *n.* [C,U] *a feminist reinterpretation of history*

re·in·vent /ˌriɪnˈvɛnt/ *v.* [T] **1** to change something a lot, so that it is completely different: *The American educational system needs to be reinvented.* **2 reinvent yourself** to change your behavior, style of clothing etc. completely so that people think of you in a different way **3 reinvent the wheel** INFORMAL to waste time trying to find a way of doing something when someone else has already discovered the best way to do it

re·is·sue /riˈɪʃu/ *v.* [T] to produce a CD, book etc. again, after it has not been available for some time —**reissue** *n.* [C]

re·it·e·rate /riˈɪt̬əˌreɪt/ *v.* [T] FORMAL to repeat a statement or opinion in order to make your meaning as clear as possible: *He reiterated his commitment to reform.* —**reiteration** /riˌɪt̬əˈreɪʃən/ *n.* [C,U]

re·ject¹ /rɪˈdʒɛkt/ Ac W2 *v.* [T]

1 OFFER/SUGGESTION to refuse to accept an offer, suggestion, or request OPP **accept**: *Nurses have rejected the latest pay offer.* | *The committee rejected the proposal.*

THESAURUS

refuse to say firmly that you do not want something that you have been offered: *They refused all offers of help.*
turn sth down INFORMAL to say that you do not want something that you have been offered – use this especially when this is surprising: *Sherman turned down several chances to run for president.*
say no SPOKEN to say you do not want something or will not accept a suggestion: *I asked him if he wanted a drink, but he said no.*
decline FORMAL to say politely that you cannot or will not accept an offer: *The Tuckers were invited, but they had to decline.*
→ ACCEPT, AGREE, REFUSE

2 IDEA/BELIEF to decide that you do not believe in or agree with something OPP **accept**: *He has always rejected the idea that a revolution can be peaceful.* | *Opponents have **rejected** her theories **outright*** (=completely).

3 NOT CHOOSE to refuse to accept someone for a job, school etc. OPP **accept**: *Mitchell was rejected by several law schools.*

4 PRODUCT to throw away something that has just been made, because its quality is not good enough OPP **accept**: *Bruised or rotten fruits are rejected.*

5 NOT LOVE to refuse to give someone any love or attention OPP **accept**: *His father rejected him when he was a child.*

6 ORGAN if your body rejects an organ, such as a heart, after a TRANSPLANT operation, it produces substances that attack that organ OPP **accept**

[**Origin:** 1400–1500 Latin, past participle of *reicere* **to throw back**]

re·ject² /ˈridʒɛkt/ Ac *n.* [C] **1** INFORMAL a person who is not liked or accepted by other people **2** a product that has been rejected because it is damaged or imperfect

re·jec·tion /rɪˈdʒɛkʃən/ Ac *n.* **1** [C,U] the act of not accepting or approving an offer, suggestion, request etc.: +**of** *the committee's rejection of his proposal* **2** [C] the act of not accepting someone for a job, school etc.: *He faced rejection after rejection before finding a job.* **3** [C,U] a situation in which someone refuses to give another person any love or attention: *She feared rejection and loneliness.* **4** [U] a situation in which your body rejects an organ, such as a heart, after a TRANSPLANT operation

re·jig·ger /riˈdʒɪɡɚ/ *v.* [T] INFORMAL to arrange or organize something in a different way, especially in order to make it better, more appropriate, more useful etc.: *Is there any way we could rejigger the schedule?*

re·joice /rɪˈdʒɔɪs/ *v.* [I] LITERARY to feel very happy about something and sometimes to show this by celebrating: **+at/over/in** *They were rejoicing over the birth of their first child.* **—rejoicing** *n.* [U] *There was great rejoicing at the victory.*

re·join[1] /ˌriˈdʒɔɪn/ *v.* [T] **1** to go back to a group of people that you were with before: *Sam rejoined the others in the afternoon.* **2** to join an organization again: *Jacobs has rejoined the company.* **3** to join two things together again **4** to go onto a road again after you have been on a different road

re·join[2] /rɪˈdʒɔɪn/ *v.* [T] FORMAL to say something in reply, especially rudely or angrily: *"You're wrong about him," she rejoined.*

R

re·join·der /rɪˈdʒɔɪndɚ/ *n.* [C] FORMAL a clever reply, especially one that criticizes someone or something: *He tried to think of a witty rejoinder.*

re·ju·ve·nate /rɪˈdʒuvəˌneɪt/ *v.* [T] **1** [usually passive] to make someone look or feel young and strong again **2** to make something strong, in good condition, and successful again **—rejuvenation** /rɪˌdʒuvəˈneɪʃən/ *n.* [singular, U]

re·kin·dle /riˈkɪndl/ *v.* [T] **1** to make someone have a particular feeling, thought etc. again: *They met at the reunion and rekindled their romance.* **2** to light a fire or flame again

re·lapse /ˈrilæps/ *n.* [C] **1** a situation in which someone feels sick again after feeling better: **have/suffer a relapse** *He suffered a relapse and had to go back to the hospital.* **2** a situation in which someone starts to behave badly again after they had stopped doing this: *Relapses are common among some recovering alcoholics.* [**Origin:** 1400–1500 Latin, past participle of *relabi* **to slide back**] **—relapse** /rɪˈlæps/ *v.* [I]

re·late /rɪˈleɪt/ S3 W3 *v.* **1** [I] to be connected with someone or something in some way: *I don't understand how the two ideas relate.* | **+to** *How does this job relate to your career goals?* **2** [T] to understand or show two things are connected in some way: **relate sth to sth** *Most writing systems relate letters to sounds fairly closely.* **3** [I] to feel that you understand and have a connection to someone or something: **+to** *Laurie has a hard time relating to children.* | *"I can't do a thing with my hair." "**I can totally relate.**"* **4** [T] FORMAL to tell someone about events that have happened to you or to someone else: *Paige related the story of her legal battles in great detail.* [**Origin:** 1400–1500 Latin, past participle of *referre* **to bring back, report, refer**]

re·lat·ed /rɪˈleɪt̬ɪd/ S2 W2 *adj.* **1** connected in some way: *Police believe that the three murders are related.* | *the problem of drug abuse and other related issues* | **+to** *Art is related to culture.* | **closely/directly related** *The two ideas are closely related.* **2** [not before noun] connected by a family relationship: *Are you and Jim related?* | **+to** *Is Connie related to him?* | **closely/distantly related** *distantly related cousins* **3** related animals, plants, languages etc. belong to the same group **—relatedness** *n.* [U]

-related /rɪleɪt̬ɪd/ *suffix* [in adjectives] **drug-related/stress-related etc.** connected to or caused by drugs, stress etc.: *work-related problems*

reˌlated ˈfunction *n.* [C] MATH a mathematical FUNCTION that includes or is based on a more basic PARENT FUNCTION

reˈlating to *prep.* about or concerning something: *the rules relating to welfare benefits*

re·la·tion /rɪˈleɪʃən/ S3 W1 *n.* **1 in relation to sth** used when comparing two things or showing the relationship between them: *Women's pay is still low in relation to men's.* **2** [C,U] a connection between two or more things: **+between** *There is a direct relation between smoking and lung cancer.* | *His account **bore no relation to*** (=was not connected to) *the truth.* | *The study found **little relation** between IQ and achievement.* **3 relations** [plural] **a)** the way in which people or groups of people behave toward each other: **+between/among** *Relations among the two groups have improved recently.* | **+with** *What are your relations with your ex-husband like?* | *The city has made efforts to improve **race relations**.* **b)** official connections between companies, countries etc.: *Japan established **diplomatic relations** with South Korea in 1965.* | *a politician with experience in **international relations*** **4** [C] a member of your family SYN **relative**: *She invited all her friends and relations.* | *Is Max a relation of yours?* | *His name's Johnson too, but he's **no relation to*** (=he is not a relative) *us.* → see also BLOOD RELATIVE ►see THESAURUS box at **family[1]** **5 have (sexual) relations with sb** OLD-FASHIONED to have sex with someone **6** [C] MATH a set of ORDERED PAIRS of numbers, symbols, words etc., which shows the relationship between the pairs → see also PUBLIC RELATIONS → see Word Choice box at RELATIONSHIP

re·la·tion·al /rɪˈleɪʃənəl/ *adj.* **1** relating to relationships between people: *relational problems* **2** to relationships between things or ideas **3** TECHNICAL a relational computer DATABASE is one which is made to recognize how different types of information are related to each other **4** TECHNICAL a relational word is used as part of a sentence but does not have a meaning of its own, for example the word "have" in "I have gone" → see also NOTIONAL

re·la·tion·ship /rɪˈleɪʃənˌʃɪp/ S1 W1 *n.* **1** [C] the way in which two people or two groups behave toward each other: *Our relationship is purely a professional one.* | **+between** *the special relationship between Britain and the U.S.* | **+with** *What's your relationship with your father like?* | *The two women have an excellent **working relationship**.* | *He had **a love-hate relationship*** (=one in which he liked some things and disliked others) *with his boss.* **2** [C,U] the way in which two or more things are connected and affect each other: **+between** *Do you think there's any relationship between these two events?* | *The tax is unfair and **bears no relationship to** people's ability to pay.* **3** [C] a situation in which two people spend time together or live together, and have romantic or sexual feelings for each other: *She wanted to end their relationship.* | *This was his first serious relationship.* | **+with** *She had a relationship with a married man.* | *No, I'm not married, but I'm **in a relationship** right now.* **4** [U] the way in which you are related to someone in your family: **+to** *"What's your relationship to Sue?" "She's my cousin."*

WORD CHOICE **relationship, relations, relation**

- A **relationship with** someone or something is usually close, and may involve strong feelings: *Jane's stormy relationship with her husband* | *What kind of relationship does she have with her mother?*
- **Relations** is a more official word. **Relations** between people, groups, countries etc. are often about working together or communicating: *Relations between the two countries have improved recently.* |*friendly relations in the workplace.*
- A **relation** or **relationship to** someone or something is usually about a simple fact: *"What's Jane's relationship to Jeff?" "She's his daughter."* | *What relation does temperature have to humidity?*
- A **relationship between** people and other people or things may be either close and full of emotion, or simply a matter of fact: *The relationship between Cynthia and her mother has not always been a loving one.* | *What's the relationship between inflation and interest rates?*

rel·a·tive[1] /ˈrɛlət̬ɪv/ S3 W3 *n.* [C] **1** a member of your family: *She had invited all her friends and relatives to the wedding.* | *Is he a **close relative**?* | *a **distant***

***relative** on my mother's side* ►see THESAURUS box at **family**[1]

THESAURUS

parents
father, dad/daddy INFORMAL
mother, mom/mommy
stepfather/stepmother
brother/sister
grandparents
grandfather/grandpa
grandmother/grandma
great-grandparents
uncle/aunt
nephew/niece
cousin
husband/wife
child/son/daughter
father-in-law/mother-in-law
brother-in-law/sister-in-law

2 an animal or plant that is related to another: *The plant is a relative of the pea.*

relative[2] W3 *adj.* **1** having a particular quality when compared with something else: *a period of relative calm* | *The article compares the **relative merits** of the two cars.* | *She thinks her problems are bad, but **it's all relative**.* **2 relative to sth** relating to or compared with something: *Costs have gone up relative to wages.*

ˌrelative ˈclause *n.* [C] ENG. LANG. ARTS a part of a sentence that has a verb in it, and is joined to the rest of the sentence by "who," "which," "that," "where" etc. For example, in the sentence "The man who lives next door is a doctor," the phrase "who lives next door" is a relative clause.

ˌrelative ˈdating *n.* [U] BIOLOGY a method of deciding how old something is, such as a layer of rock or a FOSSIL, by putting it in an order relative to other layers of rock, fossils etc.

ˌrelative huˈmidity *n.* [U] the amount of water, in the form of VAPOR, that is in the air, usually expressed as a PERCENTAGE

rel·a·tive·ly /ˈrɛlət̬ɪvli/ S3 W2 *adv.* **1** to a particular degree, especially when compared with something similar: *a relatively inexpensive restaurant* | *The system is relatively easy to use.* **2 relatively speaking** used when comparing something with all similar things: *Land prices here are very low, relatively speaking.*

ˌrelative ˈpronoun *n.* [C] ENG. LANG. ARTS a PRONOUN such as "who," "which," or "that" by which a relative clause is connected to the rest of the sentence

rel·a·tiv·ism /ˈrɛlət̬ɪvˌɪzəm/ *n.* [U] the belief that truth and right and wrong are not always the same but change according to the situation or society —**relativist** *adj.* —**relativist** *n.* [C]

rel·a·tiv·i·ty /ˌrɛləˈtɪvət̬i/ *n.* [U] PHYSICS the relationship in PHYSICS between time, space, and MOTION (=movement), according to Einstein's THEORY

re·launch /ˈrilɔntʃ, riˈlɔntʃ, -ˈlɑntʃ/ *v.* [T] **1** to make a new effort to sell a product that is already on sale **2** to start something again in an effort to make it more successful: *The movie helped relaunch his career.* —**relaunch** /ˈrilɔntʃ/ *n.* [C]

re·lax /rɪˈlæks/ Ac S2 W3 *v.*
1 CALM [I,T] to feel calm and comfortable and stop worrying, or to make someone do this: *Hey, relax! There's nothing to worry about!* | *A nice long bath will relax you.*
2 MUSCLE [I,T] if you relax a part of your body or it relaxes, it becomes less stiff or less tight: *Gentle exercise can relax stiff shoulder muscles.*
3 relax rules/controls/regulations etc. to make rules etc. less strict OPP **tighten**: *The laws on the sale of alcohol are being relaxed.*
4 relax your hold/grip a) to hold something less tightly than before OPP **tighten your hold/grip**: +**on** *He relaxed his grip on my arm.* **b)** to become less strict in the way you control something OPP **tighten your hold/grip**: +**on** *The party has no intention of relaxing its hold on the country.*
5 relax your efforts/vigilance/concentration etc. to reduce the amount of effort or attention you give to something
6 HAIR [T] to use strong chemicals such as LYE to make curly hair straight, especially the hair of a black person
[**Origin:** 1300–1400 Latin *relaxare* **to loosen**, from *laxus* **loose**]

re·lax·ant /rɪˈlæksənt/ *n.* [C] something, especially a drug, that makes you relax: *a muscle relaxant*

re·lax·a·tion /ˌrilækˈseɪʃən/ Ac *n.* **1** [C,U] a way of feeling calm and comfortable and enjoying yourself: *I like to cook **for relaxation**.* | *a weekend of **rest and relaxation*** | *relaxation exercises* **2** [C,U] the process of making rules on the control of something less strict: +**of** *a relaxation of export controls* **3** [U] the process of making a muscle softer and less tense

re·laxed /rɪˈlækst/ Ac *adj.* **1** feeling calm and comfortable and not worried: *Everyone looked happy and relaxed, even Bill.* ►see THESAURUS box at **calm**[1] **2** a relaxed situation, activity, or place is comfortable and informal: *a relaxed atmosphere* | *The meeting was very relaxed.* **3** muscles that are relaxed are soft and not tense **4** not strict and not making people obey rules about something: *a relaxed attitude toward discipline*

re·lax·ing /rɪˈlæksɪŋ/ Ac *adj.* making you feel relaxed: *a relaxing bath*

re·lay[1] /ˈrileɪ/ *n.* **1** [C] a RELAY RACE: *the 4 × 100 meter relay* **2** [C,U] a piece of electrical equipment that receives radio or television signals and sends them to a wider area

re·lay[2] /ˈrileɪ, rɪˈleɪ/ *v.* **relays, relayed, relaying** [T] **1** to pass a message from one person or place to another: **relay sth to sb** *Dave relayed the news to the rest of the team.* **2** to send out radio or television signals by relay: *The broadcasts were relayed by satellite.*

re·lay[3] /ˌriˈleɪ/ *v.* **relays, relaid, relaying** [T] to lay something such as a CARPET again

ˈrelay ˌrace *n.* [C] a race in which each member of a team runs or swims part of the total distance

re·lease[1] /rɪˈlis/ Ac S3 W1 *v.* [T]

release

1 SET SB/STH FREE to let a person or animal go after having kept them somewhere: *The bears will be released back into the wild.* | *He was arrested but later released.* | **release sb from sth** *They're going to release me from the hospital tomorrow.*
2 STOP HOLDING to stop holding something that you have been holding tightly or carefully: *Paul released her hand as she sat down.* | **release your hold/grip/grasp on sth** *The dog released its grip on my arm.*
3 MAKE PUBLIC to let news or official information be known and printed: *Police have not released the names of any of the people involved.*
4 FEELINGS to express or get rid of feelings such as anger or worry: *Physical exercise is a good way of releasing tension.*
5 CD/MOVIE to make a CD, movie etc. available for people to buy or see: *The band has just released a new album.*
6 CHEMICAL to let a substance flow out: *Carbon stored in trees is released as carbon dioxide.*
7 FROM A DUTY to allow someone not to do their duty or work: **release sb from sth** *The company is refusing to release him from his contract.*
8 ALLOW TO DROP/FALL/FLY to allow something to drop, fall, or fly away by letting go of it or removing the

R

things that are holding it: *Thousands of bombs were released over the city.*
9 MACHINERY to allow part of a piece of machinery or equipment to move from the position in which it is fastened: *Release the clamp gently.* ▶see THESAURUS box at **drive**[1]
10 MAKE AVAILABLE to make money, land etc. available to be used: *The city has released the land for development.*
[**Origin:** 1200–1300 Old French *relessier*, from Latin *relaxare* **to loosen**]

release[2] Ac S3 W2 *n.*
1 FROM PRISON [singular, U] the act of allowing a person or animal to go free or being allowed to go free: +**from** *Since his release from prison, Logan has not offended again.* | +**of** *the release of all political prisoners*
2 CD/MOVIE [C,U] a new CD, movie etc., or the act of making a CD, movie etc. available to buy or see: *The movie is slated for release in January.* | *the group's latest releases*
3 FEELINGS [U] **a)** a feeling that you are free from the worry or pain that you have been suffering: +**from** *a release from pain* **b)** freedom to show or express your feelings: *Music has always provided me with an emotional release.*
4 OFFICIAL STATEMENT [C,U] an official statement, report etc. that is made available to be printed or broadcast, or the act of making this available: *The figures will be ready for release next month.* | +**of** *the release of classified information* | **a press/news release** *The department has issued a news release announcing the results of its investigation.*
5 CHEMICALS [U] the act of letting a chemical, gas etc. flow out of its usual container: +**of** *the release of toxic gases into the atmosphere*
6 ON A MACHINE [C] a handle, button etc. that can be pressed to allow part of a machine to move

rel·e·gate /ˈrɛləˌgeɪt/ *v.* [T] FORMAL to give someone or something a less important position than before: **relegate sb to sth** *Women were relegated to subordinate roles.* [**Origin:** 1400–1500 Latin, past participle of *relegare* **to send back to do a job**] —**relegation** /ˌrɛləˈgeɪʃən/ *n.* [U]

re·lent /rɪˈlɛnt/ *v.* [I] to change your attitude and become less severe or cruel toward someone or something: *My father finally relented and agreed to drive us to the party.* [**Origin:** 1300–1400 Latin *lentare* **to bend**]

re·lent·less /rɪˈlɛntlɪs/ *adj.* **1** very determined and continuing all the time to try to achieve something: *a relentless search for the truth* | +**in** *Sanders is relentless in his attacks on the government.* **2** something bad that is relentless continues without ever stopping or getting less severe: *The pressure at work was relentless.* | *the relentless heat of the sun* —**relentlessly** *adv.*

rel·e·vant /ˈrɛləvənt/ Ac *adj.* directly relating to the subject or problem being discussed or considered OPP **irrelevant**: *relevant work experience* | +**to** *Kids have to understand how math is relevant to their lives.* | **highly/particularly/directly relevant** *a highly relevant question* | **the relevant authorities/department etc.** (=the people whose job it is to deal with a particular type of thing) [**Origin:** 1500–1600 Latin, present participle of *relevare* **to raise up**] —**relevance** also **relevancy** *n.* [U] —**relevantly** *adv.*

re·li·a·ble /rɪˈlaɪəbəl/ Ac *adj.* able to be trusted or depended on OPP **unreliable**: *I don't know where Jane could be – she's usually very reliable.* | *a reliable form of birth control* | *How reliable is this information?* —**reliably** *adv.* —**reliability** /rɪˌlaɪəˈbɪləṭi/ *n.* [U]

re·li·ance /rɪˈlaɪəns/ Ac *n.* [singular, U] the state of being dependent on something SYN **dependence**: +**on** *We need to reduce our reliance on foreign oil.*

re·li·ant /rɪˈlaɪənt/ Ac *adj.* **be reliant on sb/sth** to depend on someone or something SYN **dependent**: *The local population is heavily reliant on international aid.* → see also SELF-RELIANT

rel·ic /ˈrɛlɪk/ *n.* [C] **1** a very old object that reminds people of the past: *a collection of ancient Roman relics* **2** a custom, organization etc. that began a long time ago and still exists, but which should really have ended long ago: *The custom is a relic of the Middle Ages.* **3** a part of the body or clothing of a holy person which is kept after their death, because it is thought to be holy **4** a type of plant or animal that is very old and has not changed [**Origin:** 1200–1300 Old French *relique*, from Latin *reliquiae* **things left behind**]

re·lief /rɪˈlif/ W3 *n.*
1 COMFORT [singular, U] a feeling of comfort or happiness when something frightening, worrying, or painful has ended or has not happened: *I felt a great* ***sense of relief*** *when the test came back negative.* | ***To our relief****, the deal went though without any problems.* | ***What a relief*** *to finally get away from the office.* | **give/heave/breathe a sigh of relief** *She heaved a sigh of relief when he finally answered the phone.* | *He smiled* ***with relief*** *when he saw us.* | *"Mike says he's too busy to come." "****That's a relief****."* | **it is a relief to do sth** *It was a relief to finally get home.*
2 REDUCTION OF PAIN [U] the reduction of pain or unhappy feelings: +**from** *A spa can provide relief from everyday stresses.* | +**of** *the relief of human suffering* | *The drugs are used for* ***pain relief****.*
3 HELP [U] money, food, clothes etc. given to people who need them: **disaster/earthquake/flood etc. relief** *The group is raising money for famine relief.* | *relief supplies* | *a relief worker*
4 TAX/DEBT [U] a reduction in money owed to someone, such as the government: *tax relief*
5 REPLACEMENT [C] a person or group of people that replaces another one, in order to do their duties: *a relief pitcher*
6 MONEY OLD-FASHIONED money given by the government to help people who are poor, old, unemployed etc.
7 DECORATION [C] a shape or decoration that is raised above the surface it is on → see also BAS-RELIEF
8 **in relief a)** a shape or decoration that is in relief sticks out above the rest of the surface it is on: **in high/low relief** (=sticking out a lot or a little) **b)** if you show a part of the Earth's surface on a map in relief, you show the differences in height between different parts of it
9 **bring/throw sth into (sharp/stark) relief** to make something bad or unpleasant much more noticeable
10 FREEING A TOWN FORMAL the act of freeing a town when it has been surrounded by an enemy → see also **comic relief** at COMIC[1] (2)

re'lief map *n.* [C] a map with the mountains and high parts shown differently from the low parts, especially by being printed in a different color or by being raised

re·lieve /rɪˈliv/ *v.* [T] **1** to make a pain, problem, or bad feeling less severe: *The new road should relieve traffic congestion.* | *The doctor gave me some pills to* ***relieve the pain****.* | **relieve pressure/stress** *Yoga is good for relieving stress.* | **relieve the monotony/boredom (of sth)** *Cross-country skiing relieves the monotony of winter.* ▶see THESAURUS box at **reduce** **2** to replace someone when they have completed their duty or when they need a rest: *After 20 hours, they were relieved by another crew.* **3** **relieve yourself** a polite expression meaning to URINATE **4** FORMAL to free a town that an enemy has surrounded [**Origin:** 1300–1400 Old French *relever* **to raise, relieve**, from Latin *relevare*, from *levare* **to raise**] —**reliever** *n.* [C]: *a pain reliever*

relieve sb **of** sth *phr. v.* **1** FORMAL to take away someone's job because they have done something wrong: **relieve sb of their command/duties/post** *The prison director has been relieved of his post.* **2** FORMAL to help someone by taking something from them, especially something difficult they are doing or something heavy that they are carrying: *Efforts will be made to relieve the country of its massive debt.* **3** HUMOROUS to steal something from someone: *I realized that someone had relieved me of my wallet.*

re·lieved /rɪˈlivd/ *adj.* [not before noun] feeling happy because you are no longer worried about something: **be relieved to see/hear/know etc. sth** *I was so relieved to see that they were not hurt.* | **relieved that** *He* *seemed relieved that he could go home.* | **+at** *We were all greatly relieved at the news.*

re•li•gion /rɪˈlɪdʒən/ S2 W2 *n.* **1** [U] a belief in the life of the spirit and usually in one or more gods: *She's studying philosophy and religion.* | *The Constitution guarantees freedom of religion.* ►see THESAURUS box at **faith** **2** [C] a particular system of this belief and all the ceremonies and duties that are related to it: *the Muslim religion* | *people of all religions* | *Birth control is* ***against her religion*** (=not allowed by her religion). | *Frost has the right to* ***practice his religion****.*

THESAURUS

faith one of the main religions in the world
beliefs ideas that you believe to be true, especially religious ones
creed a set of beliefs, especially religious ones
church the institution of the Christian religion, or one of the separate groups within it: *the issues which face the church today*
denomination a religious group that has slightly different beliefs from other groups who belong to the same religion: *the main Christian denominations*
sect a group of people who have their own set of beliefs or religious habits, especially a group that has separated from a larger group
cult an extreme religious group that is not part of an established religion
faith community a group of people who share a particular set of religious beliefs

Relating to religion
religious relating to religion or to a particular religion, or believing strongly in a religion
holy/sacred considered special and important by believers in a religion: *a holy place* | *sacred texts*
secular not connected with or controlled by a church or other religious authority
believer someone who believes strongly in a religion, especially a Christian religion
atheist someone who does not believe that God exists
agnostic someone who believes that people cannot know whether God exists or not

Religious buildings
church used by Christians
mosque used by Muslims
synagogue used by Jews
temple used by people of other religions such as Buddhists and Hindus

3 find/get religion INFORMAL to suddenly become very religious and change your behavior **4** [singular] an activity or area of interest that is extremely or unreasonably important in someone's life: *Exercise is almost like a religion to Mina.* **5 sth is against sb's religion** INFORMAL, HUMOROUS used to say that someone never does something, and seems to make a point of not doing it: *He never gets up before 10:00 – it's against his religion.* [**Origin:** 1100–1200 Latin *religio*]

re•li•gious /rɪˈlɪdʒəs/ S2 W2 *adj.* **1** [only before noun] relating to religion in general or to a particular religion: *religious groups* | *religious beliefs* ►see THESAURUS box at **religion** **2** believing strongly in your religion and obeying its rules carefully: *She became very religious after the death of her parents.* | *a* ***deeply religious*** *man*

THESAURUS

devout having very strong religious beliefs: *a devout Catholic*
pious believing strongly in a religion, and showing this in how you behave: *a pious woman attending church*
practicing obeying the rules of a particular religion: *a practicing Muslim*
orthodox believing in all the traditional beliefs, laws, and practices of a religion: *orthodox Jews*

—**religiosity** /rɪˌlɪdʒiˈɑsət̬i/ also **religiousness** /rɪˈlɪdʒəsnɪs/ *n.* [U]

re•li•gious•ly /rɪˈlɪdʒəsli/ *adv.* **1** if you do something

religiously, you are always very careful to do it: *She goes to the gym religiously three times a week.* **2** in a way that is related to religion: *religiously oriented education*

re•lin•quish /rɪˈlɪŋkwɪʃ/ *v.* [T] FORMAL to let someone else have your position, power, or rights, especially not willingly: *The president was forced to relinquish power.* | **relinquish sth to sb** *He relinquished control of the company to his son.*

rel•i•quar•y /ˈrɛləˌkwɛri/ *n.* [C] a container for RELICS (=religious objects)

rel•ish[1] /ˈrɛlɪʃ/ *v.* [T] to enjoy an experience or the thought of something that is going to happen: *He relished his moment of glory.* | *Ida relished the thought of spending the summer in Italy.*

relish[2] *n.* **1** [C,U] a cold SAUCE made with foods that are cut up very small, eaten especially with meat to add taste to it: *sweet pickle relish* **2** [U] great enjoyment of something: *She chuckled* ***with relish****.*

re•live /ˌriˈlɪv/ *v.* [T] to remember or imagine something that happened in the past so clearly that you experience the same emotions again: *She began to cry as she relived the experience.*

re•load /ˌriˈloʊd/ *v.* [I,T] to put another bullet into a gun, film into a camera, or PROGRAM into a computer

re•lo•cate /riˈloʊˌkeɪt/ Ac *v.* [I,T] if a group of people or a business relocates or is relocated, they move to a different place: **+to** *I really don't see myself relocating to England.* | **relocate sb/sth to sth** *The head office was relocated to Washington.* —**relocation** /ˌriloʊˈkeɪʃən/ *n.* [U]: *The company will pay $5,000 towards your relocation expenses.*

re•luc•tant /rɪˈlʌktənt/ Ac *adj.* slow and unwilling: *a reluctant smile* | **reluctant to do sth** *At first, Dad was reluctant to lend me the money.* [**Origin:** 1600–1700 Latin, present participle of *reluctari* **to fight against**] —**reluctance** *n.* [singular, U] —**reluctantly** *adv.*

re•ly /rɪˈlaɪ/ Ac *v.*

rely on/upon sb/sth *phr. v.* **1** to trust someone or something to do what you need or expect them to do SYN **count on** SYN **depend on**: *Thanks for your help. I knew I could rely on you.* | **rely on sb/sth to do sth** *You can rely on me to keep this quiet.* | **rely on sb/sth for sth** *Most Americans rely on TV for news.* **2** to depend on something in order to continue to live or exist SYN **depend on**: *Sudan* ***relies heavily on*** *foreign aid.* | **rely on sb/sth for sth** *They rely on the river for their drinking water.* | **rely on sb/sth to do sth** *Most students rely on their parents to support them financially.*

re•main /rɪˈmeɪn/ S3 W1 *v.* **1** [linking verb] to continue to be in the same state or condition SYN **stay**: *He remained silent.* | *Her disappearance remains a mystery.* | *The paintings have remained in perfect condition.* **2** [I] FORMAL to stay in the same place without moving away SYN **stay**: **+at/in/with etc.** *She remained in France for several years.* **3** [I] to continue to exist, after others are gone or have been destroyed: *Very little remains of the original building.* | *Byrd is likely to lose* ***what remains of*** *his fortune.* **4 it remains to be seen** FORMAL used to say that it is still uncertain whether something will happen or is true: *It remains to be seen whether the team can continue its winning streak.* **5 sth remains to be done** something still needs to be done, after other things have been dealt with: *Many questions remain to be answered.* [**Origin:** 1300–1400 Old French *remaindre*, from Latin *remanere*, from *manere* **to stay**] → see also **the fact remains** at FACT (11)

re•main•der /rɪˈmeɪndɚ/ *n.* **1 the remainder** the part of something that is left after everything else is gone or has been dealt with SYN **the rest**: *The remainder must be paid by the end of June.* | **+of** *She quickly ate the remainder of her sandwich.* **2** [C] MATH **a)** in mathematics, a number that is left after you divide one number into another number and it does not divide exactly **b)** in mathematics, a number that is left after

R

you subtract one number from another **3** [C] a book that is sold cheaply because it has not been successful and is no longer being produced

re·main·ing /rɪˈmeɪnɪŋ/ *adj.* [only before noun] the remaining people or things are those that are left when the others are gone, have been used, or have been dealt with: *Add all the remaining ingredients and bring to the boil.*

re·mains /rɪˈmeɪnz/ W3 *n.* [plural] **1** the parts of something that are left after the rest has been destroyed or has disappeared: *ancient remains* | **the remains of sth** *The McDonald family picked through the remains of their house.* **2 sb's remains** FORMAL the body of someone who has died: *A special chapel was built to house Spencer's remains.*

re·make¹ /ˈrimeɪk/ *n.* [C] a CD or movie that has the same music or story as one that was made before: **+of** *a remake of a classic thriller*

remake² /ˌriˈmeɪk/ *v. past tense and past participle* **remade** /-ˈmeɪd/ [T] **1** ENG. LANG. ARTS to film a story or record a song again **2** to build or make something again

R

re·mand /rɪˈmænd/ *v.* [T usually passive] LAW **1** if a court remands someone, it sends them to prison to wait for their TRIAL: *The prosecutor asked the judge to* ***remand*** *Nelson* ***into*** *federal* ***custody***. **2** to send a case to be dealt with in another court

re·mark¹ /rɪˈmɑrk/ W3 *n.* **1** [C] something that you say when you express an opinion or say what you have noticed: *He chose to ignore her last remark.* | *Dan's always* ***making*** *sarcastic* ***remarks***. | *The rumors started because of an* ***offhand remark*** *he made in an interview.* **2 remarks** [plural] the things someone says in a formal speech: *the chairman's* ***opening remarks***

remark² *v.* [T] to say something, especially about something you have just noticed: *"It must be a very old house," John remarked.* | **+that** *Several people remarked that Bill seemed to have changed.* [**Origin:** 1500–1600 French *remarquer*, from *marquer* **to mark**]

remark on/upon sth *phr. v.* to notice that something has happened and say something about it: *People often remark on how beautiful she is.*

re·mark·a·ble /rɪˈmɑrkəbəl/ W3 *adj.* unusual or surprising and therefore deserving attention or praise: *She was a truly remarkable woman.* | *a remarkable achievement* | **+for** *His drawings are remarkable for their accuracy.* | **it is remarkable that** *It's remarkable that no one noticed this fact earlier.* | ***There was nothing remarkable about*** *his life.*

re·mark·a·bly /rɪˈmɑrkəbli/ *adv.* in an amount or to a degree that is unusual or surprising: [+ adj./adv.] *The team played remarkably well.* | [sentence adverb] *Remarkably, everyone had a good time.*

Re·marque, Er·ich Ma·ri·a /rəˈmɑrk, ˈɛrɪk məˈriə/ (1898–1970) a German writer of NOVELS

re·mar·ry /riˈmæri/ *v.* **remarries, remarried, remarrying** [I,T] to marry again after your husband or wife dies, or after the end of a previous marriage —**remarriage** /riˈmærɪdʒ/ *n.* [C]

re·mas·ter /riˈmæstɚ/ *v.* [T] TECHNICAL to make a new copy of an old movie or musical recording using new TECHNOLOGY to improve its quality

re·match /ˈrimætʃ, riˈmætʃ/ *n.* [C] a second game that is played between two teams or people because there was no winner in the first game or there was a disagreement about the result

Rem·brandt /ˈrɛmbrænt/ (1606–1669) a Dutch artist, Rembrandt van Rijn, who is regarded as one of the greatest European painters

re·me·di·al /rɪˈmidiəl/ *adj.* [usually before noun] **1 a remedial class/course/program etc.** a special class, course etc. that helps students who are having difficulty learning something: *remedial math classes* **2** intended to improve something that is wrong or to cure a problem with someone's health: *The company is taking* ***remedial action***.

rem·e·dy¹ /ˈrɛmədi/ *n. plural* **remedies** [C] **1** a way of dealing with a problem or making an unsatisfactory situation better: *The only remedy was to sell part of the company.* | **+for** *There doesn't seem to an effective remedy for the problem.* **2** MEDICINE something such as a medicine that is used to cure an illness or pain that is not very serious: *herbal remedies* | *Inhaling steam is a good* ***home remedy*** *for a sore throat.* → see also **folk medicine/remedy** at FOLK² (2) [**Origin:** 1200–1300 Anglo-French *remedie*, from Latin *remedium*, from *mederi* **to heal**]

remedy² *v.* **remedies, remedied, remedying** [T] to deal with a problem or improve a bad situation: *Her superiors took steps to* ***remedy the situation***.

re·mem·ber /rɪˈmɛmbɚ/ S1 W1 *v.*

1 THE PAST [I,T] to have a picture or idea in your mind of people, events, places etc. from the past: *Do you remember Tony from high school?* | *I still remember that vacation.* | **remember (that)** *I remember the house was very cold.* | **remember sb doing sth** *I remember my grandmother baking us cookies.* | **remember doing sth** *He doesn't even remember coming home.* | ***If I remember correctly****, there was a big bay window at the back.* | **clearly/distinctly/vividly remember sth** *I distinctly remember him saying he would be here at ten.*

2 INFORMATION/FACTS [I,T] to bring information or facts that you know back into your mind: *I can't remember her phone number.* | *Do you remember her name?* | **remember (that)** *I suddenly remembered that I'd left the stove on.* | **remember what/how/why etc.** *Do you remember why she left?*

3 NOT FORGET STH [I,T] to not forget something that you must do, get, or bring: *Did you remember the bread?* | *You were supposed to pick her up, remember?* | **remember to do sth** *It's often hard to remember to take vitamin pills.*

4 KEEP STH IN MIND [T] to keep a particular fact about a situation in your mind: **remember (that)** *Remember that dark colors will make a room look smaller.*

5 HONOR THE DEAD [T] to think about someone who has died with special respect, often in a ceremony: *On Memorial Day, Americans remember their war dead.*

6 be remembered for/as sth to be famous for something that happened or something important that you once did: *Defoe is best remembered for his book "Robinson Crusoe."* | *Graf will be remembered as one of the best women's tennis players.*

7 GIVE SB A PRESENT [T] to give someone a present on a particular occasion: *Aunt Sara always remembers me at Christmas.*

8 remember sb in your will to arrange for someone to have money or property after you die, by writing it in your WILL

9 remember me to sb OLD-FASHIONED, SPOKEN used to ask someone to give a greeting from you to someone else

[**Origin:** 1300–1400 Old French *remembrer*, from Latin *memor* **remembering**]

> WORD CHOICE **remember and remind**
> • **Remember** is used to say that you are the person who is remembering something: *Do you remember Tom and Missy?* | *I can't remember how this thing works.*
> • Use **remind** to say that a person or a thing is making you remember something: *It really reminds me of my hometown.* | *She reminds me of Carla.*

re·mem·brance /rɪˈmɛmbrəns/ *n.* **1** [U] the act of remembering and giving honor to someone who has died: *a day of remembrance* | *He will speak* ***in remembrance of*** *Martin Luther King.* **2** [C,U] FORMAL a memory that you have of a person or event, or the act of remembering it

re·mind /rɪˈmaɪnd/ S1 W2 *v.* [T] **1** to make someone remember something that they must do: *I'd better write this down to remind myself.* | **remind sb to do sth** *Remind me to stop at the bank.* | **remind sb about sth** *Do you think we should remind him about the party?* | **remind sb (that)** *I had to remind her that we still had lots of work to do.* → see Word Choice box at REMEMBER

2 to tell someone about something, especially a fact that they have forgotten, or something important that they need to remember: **remind sb of/about sth** *Remind me of your phone number again.* | **remind sb what/how/when etc.** *Can you remind me what poison oak looks like?* | **remind sb (that)** *He reminded us that his birthday was coming up.*

SPOKEN PHRASES

3 that reminds me used when something has just made you remember something you were going to say or do: *Oh, that reminds me – we're out of milk.* **4 Don't remind me!** used in a joking way when someone has mentioned something that embarrasses or annoys you: *"We have a test tomorrow." "Don't remind me!"* **5 let me remind you** also **may I remind you** FORMAL used to add force to a warning or criticism: *Let me remind you it was your idea to move to the city.*

remind sb **of** sb/sth *phr. v.* **1** to seem similar to someone or something else: *Doesn't she remind you of Nicole?* | *These cookies remind me of my mother's.* **2** to make you think of something that happened or existed in the past: *That song always reminds me of our first date.*

re·mind·er /rɪˈmaɪndɚ/ *n.* [C] **1** that reminds you of something that happened in the past, or of a serious situation that exists now: **+of** *Several ruined buildings are reminders of the earthquake.* | **a reminder that** *The incident is a painful reminder that discrimination occurs in every community.* | *His scars are a* ***constant reminder*** *of the accident.* | *The huge police presence* ***served as a reminder*** *of the terrorist threat.* **2** a letter sent to remind someone to do something, for example to pay a bill **3** you say to remind something to do something that they might forget

Rem·ing·ton /ˈrɛmɪŋtən/, **Fred·eric** /ˈfrɛdrɪk/ (1861–1909) a U.S. PAINTER and SCULPTOR famous for his work showing Native Americans and life in the American West

rem·i·nisce /ˌrɛməˈnɪs/ *v.* [I] to talk or think about pleasant events in your past: **+about** *They were reminiscing about their college days.*

rem·i·nis·cence /ˌrɛməˈnɪsəns/ *n.* [C often plural, U] a spoken or written story about events that you remember: **+of** *reminiscences of the 1960s* → see also MEMOIR

rem·i·nis·cent /ˌrɛməˈnɪsənt/ *adj.* **1 reminiscent of sth** reminding you of something: *a scene reminiscent of an old Hollywood movie* **2** [only before noun] thinking about the past: *a reminiscent smile*

re·miss /rɪˈmɪs/ *adj.* FORMAL [not before noun] careless about doing something that you ought to do: **be remiss in (doing) sth** *We were remiss in not responding to your letter.* | **it would be remiss of sb to do sth** *It would be remiss of the team not to make use of his pitching talent.* [**Origin:** 1400–1500 Latin, past participle of *remittere* **to send back, relax**] —**remissness** *n.* [U]

re·mis·sion /rɪˈmɪʃən/ *n.* [C,U] MEDICINE a period when a serious illness improves for a time: *Juan's cancer is* ***in remission*** *for now.*

re·mit /rɪˈmɪt/ *v.* **remitted, remitting 1** FORMAL to send a payment by mail: *He filed a tax return but failed to remit what he owed.* **2** FORMAL to free someone from a debt or punishment **3** LAW reduce the time someone has to spend in prison

remit sth **to** sb/sth *phr. v.* FORMAL ECONOMICS to send a proposal, plan, or problem back to someone for them to make a decision about → see also UNREMITTING

re·mit·tance /rɪˈmɪtˀns/ *n.* **1** [C] ECONOMICS an amount of money that you send by mail to pay for something **2** [U] the act of sending money by mail

re·mit·tent /rɪˈmɪtˀnt/ *adj.* FORMAL a remittent fever or illness is severe for short periods but improves between those times

rem·nant /ˈrɛmnənt/ *n.* [C] **1** [usually plural] a small part of something that remains after the rest of it has been used, destroyed, or eaten: **+of** *the remnants of the old farmhouse* **2** a small piece of cloth, CARPET etc. left from a larger piece and sold for a cheaper price

re·mod·el /ˌriˈmɑdl/ *v.* [I,T] to change the shape or appearance of something such as a house, room, building etc.: *We're remodeling the basement this winter.*

re·mold /ˌriˈmoʊld/ *v.* [T] FORMAL to change an idea, system, way of thinking etc.

re·mon·strance /rɪˈmɑnstrəns/ *n.* [C,U] FORMAL a complaint or protest

rem·on·strate /ˈrɛmənˌstreɪt, rɪˈmɑnˌstreɪt/ *v.* [I] FORMAL to tell someone that you strongly disapprove of something they have said or done: **+with/against** *She remonstrated with him but he would not listen.*

re·morse /rɪˈmɔrs/ *n.* [U] a strong feeling of being sorry that you have done something very bad: *Watson* ***expressed deep remorse for*** *his crimes.* | *She looked at him* ***without remorse.*** [**Origin:** 1300–1400 Old French *remors*, from Latin *remordere* **to bite again**] —**remorseful** *adj.* —**remorsefully** *adv.*

re·morse·less /rɪˈmɔrslɪs/ *adj.* **1** something bad that is remorseless continues to happen and seems impossible to stop SYN **relentless**: *the remorseless pressure of the job* **2** cruel, and not caring how much other people are hurt: *a remorseless killer* —**remorselessly** *adv.* —**remorselessness** *n.* [U]

re·mort·gage /ˌriˈmɔrgɪdʒ/ *v.* [T] ECONOMICS to borrow money by having a second MORTGAGE on your house, or increasing the one you have → see also REVERSE MORTGAGE, SECOND MORTGAGE

re·mote[1] /rɪˈmoʊt/ S3 W3 *adj.*

1 FAR AWAY far away in space or time: *remote parts of the solar system* | *That part of my life seems very remote now.*

2 NOT NEAR TOWNS far from towns or where people are: *a remote mountain village*

3 CHANCE very unlikely: *The risk of infection is remote.* | **a remote chance/possibility** *There's a remote chance that he's still alive.*

4 VERY DIFFERENT very different from something else, or not closely related to it: **+from** *The book's description of the war seemed very remote from his own experience.*

5 UNFRIENDLY unfriendly, and not interested in people: *a remote, cold man*

6 FROM A DISTANCE [only before noun] **a)** controlled by a piece of equipment that is not directly connected: *remote cameras* **b)** not happening with people in the same place, but involving communication by telephone or computer: *remote education*

7 not the remotest sth not the least or smallest amount of something SYN **not the slightest sth**: *She doesn't have the remotest interest in boys.*

[**Origin:** 1400–1500 Latin, past participle of *removere*, from *movere* **to move**] —**remoteness** *n.* [C]

remote[2] *n.* [C] INFORMAL a remote control

reˌmote ˈaccess *n.* [U] COMPUTERS a system that allows you to use information on a computer that is far away from your computer

reˌmote conˈtrol *n.* **1** [C] a thing you use for controlling a piece of electrical or electronic equipment without having to touch it, for example for turning a television on or off **2** [U] the process of controlling equipment from a distance, using radio or electronic signals: *The bomb is guided by remote control.* **3** [U] COMPUTERS a type of computer SOFTWARE that lets you use a particular computer by connecting it to another one that is far away —**remote-controlled** *adj.*

reˌmote inˌterior ˈangle *n.* [C] MATH either of the two angles inside a TRIANGLE which are not next to the EXTERIOR ANGLE (=angle formed where a side of the triangle meets a line continuing out from another side)

re·mote·ly /rɪˈmoʊtli/ *adv.* **1** [usually in negatives] slightly: *This is* ***not even remotely*** *funny.* **2** from far away: *remotely operated vehicles*

reˌmote ˈsensing *n.* [U] the use of SATELLITES to obtain pictures and information about the Earth

re•mov•a•ble /rɪˈmuvəbəl/ Ac *adj.* easy to remove: *seats with removable covers*

re•mov•al /rɪˈmuvəl/ Ac *n.* [U] **1** the act of taking someone or something away or of getting rid of them: *stain removal* | +**of** *the removal of foreign troops* **2** the act of forcing someone out of an important position or firing them from a job: *the mayor's removal from office* **3** the act of taking off a piece of clothing: *the removal of clothing*

re•move /rɪˈmuv/ Ac S3 W2 *v.* [T] **1** to take someone or something away from, out of, or off the place where they are: *She carefully removed the lid.* | *The old paint will have to be removed first.* | **remove sb/sth from sth** *The children were removed from the home.*

THESAURUS

take off to remove clothing: *She began to take off her clothes.*
tear off to remove part of a piece of paper or cloth by tearing it: *Tear off the coupon below.*
break off to remove a part of something by breaking it: *The high winds broke limbs off trees.*
cut off to remove a part of something by cutting it: *Tree surgeons cut off the dead branches.*
cut out to remove a part of something by cutting round it: *The kids were cutting pictures out of magazines.*
scrape off to remove something using a knife or sharp tool: *It took a wall to scrape the paint off the wood.*
wipe off/up to remove dirt, liquid, etc. with a cloth: *He wiped the sweat off his forehead.* | *Julie wiped up the spilled milk.*
rub off to remove dirt, marks, etc. with a cloth or brush: *He rubbed off some of the rust.*
erase to remove writing from paper, recorded sounds from tape, or information from a computer memory: *If you make a mistake, just erase it.*
cut to remove a part from a movie, book, speech etc.: *The scene was cut from the movie.*

2 to get rid of something so it does not exist anymore: *What's the best way to remove red wine stains?* | *The plan will remove unneeded bureaucracy.* **3** to force someone out of an important position or fire them from a job: **remove sb from power/office etc.** *The mayor will be removed from office.* **4** FORMAL to take off a piece of clothing SYN **take off**: *Irvin paused to remove his sunglasses.* [**Origin:** 1200–1300 Old French *removoir*, from Latin *removere*, from *movere* **to move**]

re•moved /rɪˈmuvd/ *adj.* **1 removed from sth a)** different from something: *The world of TV sitcoms is* ***far removed from*** *reality.* **b)** with little knowledge of a particular subject, issue, situation etc. **2 sb's cousin once/twice etc. removed** the child, GRANDCHILD etc. of your COUSIN, or the cousin of your father, grandfather etc.

re•mov•er /rɪˈmuvɚ/ *n.* [C,U] **paint/stain etc. remover** a substance that takes away paint marks etc.

REM sleep /ˈrɛm slip/ *n.* [U] BIOLOGY a period during sleep when there is rapid movement of the eyes, when you are dreaming

re•mu•ner•ate /rɪˈmyunəˌreɪt/ *v.* [T] FORMAL to pay someone for something they have done for you —**remuneration** /rɪˌmyunəˈreɪʃən/ *n.* [C,U]

re•mu•ner•a•tive /rɪˈmyunərət̬ɪv, -ˌreɪt̬ɪv/ *adj.* FORMAL making a lot of money —**remuneratively** *adv.*

Ren•ais•sance /ˈrɛnəˌzɑns, -ˌsɑns, ˌrɛnəˈsɑns/ *n.* **the Renaissance** the period of time in Europe between the 14th and 17th centuries, when art, literature, PHILOSOPHY, and scientific ideas became very important and a lot of new art etc. was produced: *The city was built during the Renaissance.* | **Renaissance art/architecture etc.** (=art, architecture etc. belonging to the Renaissance period)

ren•ais•sance /ˈrɛnəˌzɑns, -ˌsɑns, ˌrɛnəˈsɑns/ n. [singular] a new interest in something, especially a particular form of art, music etc., that had not been popular for a long period of time: *American classical music is* ***enjoying a renaissance.***

ˌRenaissance ˈman *n.* [C] a man who can do many things well, such as writing, painting etc., and who knows a lot about many different subjects

ˌRenaissance ˈwoman *n.* [C] a woman who can do many things well, such as writing, painting etc., and who knows a lot about many different subjects

re•nal /ˈrinl/ *adj.* [only before a noun] BIOLOGY relating to the KIDNEYS: *acute renal failure*

re•name /riˈneɪm/ *v.* [T usually passive] to give something a new name: *The city was renamed St. Petersburg.*

rend /rɛnd/ *v. past tense and past participle* **rent** /rɛnt/ [T] LITERARY to tear or break something violently into pieces

ren•der /ˈrɛndɚ/ *v.* [T] FORMAL
1 CAUSE TO BECOME to cause someone or something to be in a particular condition: **render sth obsolete/helpless/meaningless etc.** *Pages were missing from the book, rendering it useless.* | **sb unconsious/powerless etc.** *A blow to the head rendered him unconsious.*
2 GIVE SERVICE FORMAL to give help to something or someone or to provide a service: **render assistance/service (to sb)** *Troops are on standby to render assistance.* | *a payment* ***for services rendered***
3 ANNOUNCE STH FORMAL to officially announce a judgment or decision: **render a decision/judgment/opinion etc.** *It is the court's task to render a fair and impartial verdict.*
4 EXPRESS STH FORMAL to express, present, or perform something in a particular way: *Maestas' sculptures were rendered in bronze.* | **render sth into English/Russian/Chinese etc.** (=to translate something into English, Russian etc.)
5 COMPUTER IMAGE TECHNICAL to change GRAPHICS from a computer FILE into an image
6 MELT FAT to melt the fat of an animal as you cook it
7 COVER WALL TECHNICAL to cover an outside wall of a building with PLASTER or CEMENT
render sth ↔ **up** *phr. v.* OLD USE to give something to someone, especially to a ruler or enemy

ren•der•ing /ˈrɛndərɪŋ/ *n.* [C] **1** ENG. LANG. ARTS the particular way a piece of music, poem, movie, play etc. is expressed or performed: *an emotional rendering of the song* **2** a drawing or plan of something such as a building, that shows what it will look like when it is built

ren•dez•vous[1] /ˈrɑndeɪˌvu, -dɪ-/ *n. plural* **rendezvous** /-ˌvuz/ [C] **1** an arrangement to meet at a particular time and place: +**with** *He had arranged a secret rendezvous with a woman named Ruth.* **2** [usually singular] a place where two or more people have arranged to meet **3** [usually singular] a place where a particular group of people often meet: *The bar is a rendezvous for students.* **4** an occasion when two SPACECRAFT or military airplanes or vehicles meet, for example to move supplies from one to the other

rendezvous[2] *v.* [I] **1** to meet someone as you have arranged **2** if two SPACECRAFT or military vehicles or airplanes rendezvous, they meet, for example to move supplies from one to the other

ren•di•tion /rɛnˈdɪʃən/ *n.* **1** [C] ENG. LANG. ARTS the particular way that someone performs a ROLE or plays or sings a piece of music: *a moving rendition of John Lennon's song "Imagine"* **2** [C] ENG. LANG. ARTS a TRANSLATION of a piece of writing **3 extraordinary rendition** the practice of taking people who are thought to be TERRORISTS to a foreign country for INTERROGATION

ren•e•gade /ˈrɛnəˌgeɪd/ *n.* [C] someone who joins the opposing side in a war, political, or religious organization etc., or who does or believes things that are not approved of by society or the organization they belong to [**Origin:** 1400–1500 Spanish *renegado*, from Medieval Latin *renegare* **to say that something is not true**] —**renegade** *adj.* [only before noun]: *renegade cops*

re•nege /riˈnɛg, -ˈnɪg/ *v.* [I] FORMAL to not do something you have promised or agreed to do: **renege on a promise/agreement** *The governor quickly reneged on his election promises.* [**Origin:** 1500–1600 Medieval Latin *renegare* **to say that something is not true**]

re•ne•go•ti•ate /ˌrinɪˈgoʊʃiˌeɪt/ *v.* [I,T] to change a previous agreement between two or more people or groups, especially because one of the groups believes the conditions are unfair: *The company renegotiated contracts with several of its customers.* —**renegotiable** *adj.*

re•new /rɪˈnu/ *v.* [T] **1** to arrange for a contract, membership of a club etc. to continue: **renew a license/contract/lease etc.** *I need to renew my passport this year.* | **renew a membership/subscription** *It's time again to renew your subscription.* **2** to begin to do something again: *Local people have* ***renewed*** *their* ***efforts*** *to save the school.* | **renew a friendship/acquaintance etc.** (=start a relationship again) | **renew an attack/an appeal/a campaign** *The army renewed its attacks on the rebels.* **3** to arrange to continue borrowing a library book or other material for an additional period of time: *Library books can be renewed by telephone.* **4** to replace something that is old or broken with something new: *The state desperately needs to renew its road system.* → see also RENEWED

re•new•a•ble /rɪˈnuəbəl/ *adj.* **1** able to be replaced by natural processes or good management and never used up: *We need to rely less on oil and more on* ***renewable energy*** *sources.* **2** a renewable contract, ticket etc. can be made to continue after the date on which it ends [OPP] **nonrenewable**: *a six-month renewable visa*

reˌnewable ˈresource *n.* [C] a RESOURCE (=something from nature that people use), such plants or animals, that can be replaced after they are used through natural processes → see also FLOW RESOURCE, NONRENEWABLE RESOURCE

re•new•al /rɪˈnuəl/ *n.* [singular, U] **1** a situation when something begins again after a period when it had stopped, or the process of this happening: +**of** *a renewal of fighting* **2** an act of renewing something: *Mark's contract* ***comes up for renewal*** *at the end of the year.* → see also URBAN RENEWAL

re•newed /rɪˈnud/ *adj.* **1** increasing or starting again after not being very strong: **renewed confidence/faith/interest etc.** *a renewed interest in ancient religions* **2** [not before noun] feeling healthy and relaxed again, after feeling sick or tired

ren•net /ˈrɛnət/ *n.* [U] a substance used for making milk thicker in order to make cheese

Re•no /ˈrinoʊ/ a city in the U.S. state of Nevada which is a popular place of people to go to in order to GAMBLE

Reno, Jan•et /ˈdʒænɪt/ (1938–) a U.S. lawyer who, in 1993, became the first woman to have the job of ATTORNEY GENERAL

Ren•oir /rənˈwɑr/, **Pierre Au•guste** /pyɛr ɔˈgust/ (1841–1919) a French PAINTER who was one of the first IMPRESSIONISTS

re•nounce /rɪˈnaʊns/ *v.* [T] **1** to publicly say that you will no longer try to keep something, or will not stay in an important position: *She voluntarily renounced her U.S. citizenship.* | *Wallace* ***renounced all claims to*** *his wife's fortune.* **2** to publicly say that you no longer believe in or support something: *We absolutely renounce all forms of terrorism.* → see also RENUNCIATION

ren•o•vate /ˈrɛnəˌveɪt/ *v.* [T] to repair and paint an old building so that it is in good condition again [**Origin:** 1400–1500 Latin, past participle of *renovare*, from *novare* **to make new**] —**renovation** /ˌrɛnəˈveɪʃən/ *n.* [U]

re•nown /rɪˈnaʊn/ *n.* [U] the quality of being famous and admired because of some special skill or achievement: *an artist* ***of great renown*** | **win/gain/achieve renown as sth** *She won international renown as a popular method.*

re•nowned /rɪˈnaʊnd/ *adj.* known and admired by a lot of people, especially for some special skill, achievement, or quality: *a renowned university* | +**for** *The island was once renowned for its beaches.* | **a renowned statesman/architect etc.** *Daley is a renowned expert in her field.* | +**as** *He's renowned as a brilliant speaker.* ►see THESAURUS box at **famous**[1]

rent[1] /rɛnt/ [S1] *v.* **1** [I,T] to regularly pay money to live in a house or room that belongs to someone else or use something that belongs to someone else: *He finally decided to rent a condo on the lake.* | *We're renting while we look for a house to buy.* ►see THESAURUS box at **borrow**

THESAURUS

lease to pay money to use a building, vehicle, etc. for a specific period of time, usually a long period
tenant someone who is renting a house or room from someone else
landlord/landlady the man or woman who owns the house or room that someone is renting
evict to formally tell your tenant that they must leave the house they are living in

►see THESAURUS box at **cost**[1] **2** [T] to pay money for the use of something for a short period of time: *We rented a couple of movies this weekend.* | *Are you planning to rent a car?* ►see THESAURUS box at **borrow** **3** [I,T] to let someone live in a house, room etc. that you own, in return for money: **rent (sth) to sb** *Some landlords refuse to rent to unmarried couples.* [**Origin:** (1) 1100–1200 Old French *rente* from Vulgar Latin *rendita*]

rent at/for sth *phr. v.* if a house rents at or rents for a particular amount of money, that is how much someone pays in order to use it: *Houses here rent for at least $2,500 a month.*

rent sth ↔ **out** *phr. v.* to make a house, room etc. that you own available to someone in return for money: *They rent out a couple of rooms in their house.*

rent[2] [S3] *n.* **1** [C,U] the amount of money you pay for the use of a house, room, car etc. that belongs to someone else: *The rent is $850 a month.* | *Martin's rent is really low.* | *I always* ***pay the rent*** *on time.* | +**of** *an annual rent of $16,000* | **for rent** (=available to be rented) **2** [C] LITERARY a long narrow cut or hole in something such as cloth

rent•al[1] /ˈrɛntl/ *n.* ECONOMICS **1** [C usually singular] the money that you pay to use a car, television, tools etc. over a period of time: *Ski rental is $20.* **2** [C,U] an arrangement by which you rent something, or the act of renting something: *Card holders get special deals on car rentals and hotels.* **3** [C] something that is rented, especially a car or house

rental[2] *adj.* [only before noun] **1** available to be rented, or being rented: *a rental car* **2** relating to renting something: *a rental fee* | *the rental agreement* **3** a rental company, AGENCY etc. provides cars, houses etc. for people to rent

ˈrent conˌtrol *n.* [U] a situation in which a city or state uses laws to control the cost of renting apartments

ˌrent-ˈfree *adj., adv.* without payment of rent: *Laurie is still living rent-free in our house.* | *rent-free housing*

ˈrent strike *n.* [C] a time when all the people living in a group of houses or apartments refuse to pay their rent, as a protest against something

re•nun•ci•a•tion /rɪˌnʌnsiˈeɪʃən/ *n.* [C,U] FORMAL a decision not to keep a particular set of beliefs, way of life, power, or object: +**of** *the organization's renunciation of violence*

re•o•pen /riˈoʊpən/ *v.* **1** [I,T] if a theater, restaurant etc. reopens or if someone reopens it, it opens again after being closed **2** [I,T] if you reopen a discussion or law case, or if it reopens, you begin it again after it has stopped: *Police reopened the murder investigation in May.* **3** [I,T] if a government reopens the border of their country or if the border reopens, people are allowed to pass through it again after it has been closed

re•or•der /riˈɔrdɚ/ *v.* [I,T] **1** to order a product again: *Supplies are automatically reordered when needed.* **2** to change things or put them in a more appropriate order

R

re·or·ga·nize /ri'ɔrgəˌnaɪz/ *v.* [I,T] to arrange or organize something in a new way: *The company is being completely reorganized.* —**reorganization** /riˌɔrgənə'zeɪʃən/ *n.* [U]

Rep. *n.* [C] **1** the written abbreviation of REPRESENTATIVE: *Rep. Nancy Pelosi* **2** the written abbreviation of REPUBLICAN

rep /rɛp/ *n.* [C] **1** INFORMAL **representative** someone who speaks officially for a company or organization: *a company rep* | *union reps* **2** INFORMAL a SALES REPRESENTATIVE **3** INFORMAL a REPERTORY theater or company **4** SPOKEN a REPUTATION: *Somehow she got a bad rep.* **5** [usually plural] INFORMAL **repetition** one exercise that you do in a series of exercises: *Do 15 reps of each exercise.*

re·pack·age /ˌri'pækɪdʒ/ *v.* [T] **1** to change the way someone or something is shown to the public, so that people will think of them in a new and different way: *The attempt to repackage the gas tax was a complete failure.* **2** to change the way that a product is PACKAGEd, usually in a more attractive way **3** to put something into a different package or container

R

re·paid /ri'peɪd/ *v.* the past tense and past participle of REPAY

re·pair¹ /rɪ'pɛr/ *v.* [T] **1** to fix something that is damaged, broken, or not working correctly SYN **fix**: *The roof needs to be repaired.* | *It will cost millions to* ***repair the damage*** *caused by the fire.* | **get/have sth repaired** *Do you know where I can have my shoes repaired?*

THESAURUS

fix to repair something that is broken or not working correctly: *Someone's coming to fix the washing machine.*
mend to repair a hole in something, especially a piece of clothing: *She was mending a pair of jeans.*
renovate to repair, paint etc. a room, building, or furniture so that it is in good condition again: *They're renovating their kitchen.*
restore to repair something so that it looks new: *They have received government aid to restore the theater.*
service to examine a machine or vehicle and repair it if necessary: *I need to take the car in to get it serviced.*
rebuild to build something again, after it has been damaged or destroyed: *It will take years to rebuild after the earthquake.*

2 FORMAL to do something to improve a bad relationship or situation, especially one that you have caused: *There seemed to be nothing I could do to repair the situation.* [**Origin:** 1300–1400 Old French *reparer*, from Latin *reparare*, from *parare* **to prepare**] → see also IRREPARABLE

repair to sth *phr. v.* OLD-FASHIONED to go to a place that is near: *Shall we repair to the drawing room?*

repair² *n.* **1** [C,U] an act of repairing something: *Many ships dock at the Naval Base* ***for repairs.*** | **+to** *repairs to the city's roads* | *Many of the paintings were damaged* ***beyond repair*** (=so badly that they could not be repaired). | *The building is* ***in serious need of repair.*** | *Two sections of the highway are* ***under repair*** (=being repaired). | **do/carry out/make repairs** *The landlord is responsible for making major repairs.* **2 in good/bad/poor repair** FORMAL in good or bad condition **3** [C] a place on something that has been repaired: *a small repair in the chair's leg* —**repairer** *n.* [C]

re·pair·a·ble /rɪ'pɛrəbəl/ *adj.* able to be repaired

rep·a·ra·ble /'rɛpərəbəl/ *adj.* FORMAL able to be repaired OPP **irreparable**

rep·a·ra·tion /ˌrɛpə'reɪʃən/ *n.* **1 reparations** [plural] money paid by a country for all the deaths, injuries, and damage it has caused, especially after it has been defeated in a war **2** [C,U] FORMAL payment made to or something done for someone for damage, loss, or injury that you have caused them in the past: *He wanted to* ***make*** *some kind of* ***reparation for*** *what he had done.*

rep·ar·tee /ˌrɛpə'ti, -pɑr'ti/ *n.* [U] FORMAL conversation that is very fast and full of intelligent and amusing remarks: *witty repartee*

re·past /rɪ'pæst/ *n.* [C] FORMAL a meal

re·pa·tri·ate /ri'peɪtriˌeɪt/ *v.* [T] **1** POLITICS to send someone back to their own country: *After the war, prisoners were repatriated.* **2** ECONOMICS to send profits or money you have earned back to your own country —**repatriation** /riˌpeɪtri'eɪʃən/ *n.* [U]

re·pay /ri'peɪ/ *v.* **repays**, *past tense and past participle* **repaid, repaying** [T] **1** to pay back money that you have borrowed SYN **pay back**: *She sold her house in order to repay her debts.* | **repay sb sth** *I'll repay you the money you lent me next week.* **2** to reward someone for helping you: **repay sb for sth** *We'll never be able to repay you for all you've done.*

re·pay·a·ble /ri'peɪəbəl/ *adj.* ECONOMICS money that is repayable at a specific time has to be repaid by that time

re·pay·ment /ri'peɪmənt/ *n.* **1** [U] the act of paying back money: *the repayment of a loan* **2** [C] an amount of money that you pay back: *monthly mortgage repayment*

re·peal /rɪ'pil/ *v.* [T] POLITICS if a government repeals a rule or law, it officially ends that rule or law: *Congress voted to repeal the ban.* —**repeal** *n.* [U]

re·peat¹ /rɪ'pit/ S2 W2 *v.*

1 SAY AGAIN [T] to say something again: *I asked him to repeat the question.* | *Sorry, could you repeat that?* | **repeat that** *Martin kept repeating that he was hungry.* | **repeat yourself** *The interviewer asked him to repeat himself* (=say the same thing again). | *Do not,* ***I repeat*** (=used to emphasize what you are saying), *do not leave the area.*

2 DO AGAIN [T] to do something again: *Repeat the exercises twice a day.* | *Todd had to repeat first grade.*

3 TELL STH YOU HEAR [T] to tell someone something that someone else has told you: *Do you promise you won't repeat this to anyone?*

4 IN ORDER TO LEARN [T] to say some words that you have heard or read in order to remember or learn them better: *She read the address and repeated it several times.* | ***Repeat after me:*** *"The customer is always right."*

5 HAPPEN AGAIN [T] if a situation or sequence of events is repeated or repeats itself, it happens again in the same way as something that happened before: *The same situation was repeated in the next race.* | *If* ***history repeats itself,*** *Taylor could win again this year.*

6 BROADCAST [T often passive] to broadcast a television or radio program again: *The awards show will be repeated on Saturday night.*

7 PATTERN [I,T] if a pattern repeats or is repeated, it appears the same way several times or in several places: *The pattern is repeated on the bedspread and drapes.*

8 repeat yourself to say something that you have already said, usually without realizing that you have done it: *Old people tend to repeat themselves.*

9 be worth repeating also **bear repeating** used to say that something is interesting or important enough to say again: *One final warning is worth repeating here.*

[**Origin:** 1300–1400 Old French *repeter*, from Latin *repetere*, from *petere* **to go to, try to find**] —**repeatable** *adj.* → see also REPETITION

repeat² *n.* [C] **1** an event very like something that happened before: **+of** *We simply can't afford a repeat of last year's oil spill.* **2** a television or radio program that is broadcast again SYN **rerun**: *"Is it a repeat?" "No, it's a new episode."* **3** ENG. LANG. ARTS the sign (:) at the end of a line of written music that tells the performer to play the music again, or the act of playing the music again

repeat³ *adj.* [only before noun] doing something or happening more than one time: **a repeat customer/buyer/guest etc.** (=someone who buys goods or services from the same business they bought from before) | **a repeat offender/violator/rapist etc.** (=someone who does the same crime more than once) | *Over half of our profit comes from* ***repeat business.*** | *I will not tolerate a*

repeat performance (=I do not want something bad to happen again).

re·peat·ed /rɪˈpit̬ɪd/ *adj.* [only before noun] done or happening again and again: *There were repeated warnings of snow.* | *Repeated attempts to fix the satellite have failed.*

re·peat·ed·ly /rɪˈpit̬ɪdli/ W3 *adv.* many times: *Davis repeatedly denied that he had ever taken drugs.*

re·peat·er /rɪˈpit̬ɚ/ *n.* [C] **1** TECHNICAL a repeating gun **2** someone who does an activity again, such as a sport, competition, or class

re·peat·ing /rɪˈpit̬ɪŋ/ *adj.* [only before noun] **1** a repeating gun can be fired several times without being loaded again **2** a repeating watch or clock can be made to repeat the last STRIKE (=sound made at an hour or quarter of an hour)

re·pel /rɪˈpɛl/ *v.* **repelled, repelling 1** [T] if something repels you, it is so unpleasant that you do not want to be near it, or it makes you feel sick SYN **repulse** OPP **attract**: *The smell repelled him.* **2** [T] to force an army or group of people who are attacking someone or something to move back and stop attacking them: *The army was able to repel the attack.* **3** [T] to keep something or someone away from you: *The lotion repels biting insects.* **4** [I,T] PHYSICS if two things repel each other they push each other away with an electrical or MAGNETIC force [**Origin:** 1400–1500 Latin *repellere*, from *pellere* **to drive**]

re·pel·lent¹ /rɪˈpɛlənt/ *n.* [C,U] a substance that keeps insects away: *mosquito repellent* → WATER-REPELLENT

repellent² *adj.* disgusting: *Women found him physically repellent.*

re·pent /rɪˈpɛnt/ *v.* [I,T] to feel sorry for something and wish you had not done it, or to say that you feel this way: *Repent your sins and you will be forgiven.* | **+for/of** *Wilson publicly repented for the pain he had caused the family.*

re·pen·tance /rɪˈpɛntˀns/ *n.* [U] the state of being sorry for something you have done

re·pen·tant /rɪˈpɛntˀnt/ *adj.* sorry for something wrong that you have done OPP **unrepentant** —**repentantly** *adv.*

re·per·cus·sion /ˌripɚˈkʌʃən/ *n.* [C] **1** [usually plural] an effect of an event or action, especially a bad effect that happens much later: **+for/on** *The crisis could have severe economic repercussions for the region.* **2** TECHNICAL a sound or force coming back after it hits something

rep·er·toire /ˈrɛpɚˌtwɑr/ *n.* [C usually singular] **1** ENG. LANG. ARTS all of the plays, pieces of music etc. that a performer or group has learned and can perform: *He* ***has a lot of good songs in his repertoire****.* **2** the total number of things that someone or something is able to do: *Kate has a wide repertoire of marketable skills.*

rep·er·to·ry /ˈrɛpɚˌtɔri, -pə-/ *n. plural* **repertories 1** [U] ENG. LANG. ARTS a type of theater work in which a group of actors perform different plays on different days, instead of only doing the same play for a long time: *Her first work was in repertory.* | *a repertory company* **2** [C] a repertoire

rep·e·ti·tion /ˌrɛpəˈtɪʃən/ *n.* **1** [U] doing the same thing many times: *They learn the dance moves through imitation and repetition.* **2** [C] something that is done again: **+of** *We don't want a repetition of last year's disaster.* **3** [U] the act of saying the same thing again: *the repetition of words and phrases* → see also REPEAT

rep·e·ti·tious /ˌrɛpəˈtɪʃəs/ *adj.* saying or doing the same thing several times, especially in such a way that people become bored: *repetitious drills*

re·pet·i·tive /rɪˈpɛt̬ət̬ɪv/ *adj.* done many times in the same way, and often boring: *A lot of the work we have to do is repetitive.* —**repetitively** *adv.*

reˌpetitive ˈstrain ˌinjury *n.* [U] TECHNICAL → see RSI

re·phrase /riˈfreɪz/ *v.* [T] to express something in different words so that its meaning is clearer or more acceptable: *Let me rephrase the question.*

re·place /rɪˈpleɪs/ S2 W2 *v.* [T] **1** to start doing something instead of another person, or start being used instead of another thing: *Have they hired anybody to replace Ken?* | *A new computer has replaced the old one.* **2** to remove someone from their job or something from its place, and put a different person or thing there: *Anderson was replaced in the fifth inning after a wrist injury.* | **replace sth with sth** *The apartments will be torn down and replaced with a shopping plaza.* **3** to get something new to put in the place of something that is broken, stolen, too old etc.: *Two of the tires had to be replaced.* **4** to put something back in its correct place SYN **put back**: **replace sth in/on/beside etc. sth** *She replaced the phone handset on its base.* **5** WRITTEN to happen instead of a previous feeling, thought, atmosphere etc.: *My enthusiasm had been replaced by anxiety.* —**replaceable** *adj.*

re·place·ment /rɪˈpleɪsmənt/ *n.* **1** [C] someone or something that replaces another person or thing: **sb's/sth's replacement** *Who do you think her replacement will be?* | **+for** *They've ordered replacements for the parts that were damaged.* **2** [U] the act of replacing something, often with something newer, better etc.: **+of** *Replacement of the bridge is expected to cost $38 million.* | **hip/knee/joint replacement** (=a medical operation to replace a damaged joint with an artificial one) —**replacement** *adj.*: *a replacement passport* | *replacement costs*

re·play¹ /ˈripleɪ/ *n. plural* **replays** [C] **1** an action in a sport seen on television, that is immediately shown again: *Instant replays showed that Ramirez caught the ball.* **2** something that happens that is very like something that happened before: **+of** *Republicans are hoping for a replay of the 2004 elections.*

re·play² /riˈpleɪ/ *v.* **replays, replayed, replaying** [T] **1** to play again something that has been recorded, such as a VIDEO, television show, or telephone message: *Channel 5 will replay the game's highlights at midnight.* **2** to play a game or sport again: *The game will be replayed on Wednesday.* **3** if you replay something that happened, or it replays in your mind, you think again about it, remembering it in the same order that it originally happened: *Ray's last comment replayed again and again in her head.*

re·plen·ish /rɪˈplɛnɪʃ/ *v.* [T] FORMAL to fill something again or put new supplies into something: *There are not enough new employees to replenish the workforce.* [**Origin:** 1600–1700 Old French *replenir*, from *plein* **full**] —**replenishment** *n.* [U]

re·plete /rɪˈplit/ *adj.* [not before noun] **1** FORMAL containing a lot of something: **+with** *a military ceremony replete with honors* **2** OLD-FASHIONED so full of food or drink that you want no more —**repletion** /rɪˈpliʃən/ *n.* [U]

rep·li·ca /ˈrɛplɪkə/ *n.* [C] a very good copy, especially of a painting or other work of art: *a replica gun* | **+of** *a replica of a wooden Viking boat* [**Origin:** 1800–1900 Italian **something repeated**, from Latin *replicare*]

rep·li·cate¹ /ˈrɛpləˌkeɪt/ *v.* [T] **1** FORMAL to do or make something again in exactly the same way, so that you get the same result SYN **reproduce**: *The western form of democracy cannot always be replicated.* **2** BIOLOGY if a cell, VIRUS etc. replicates, or replicates itself, it divides and produces exact copies of itself SYN **copy**

rep·li·cate² /ˈrɛpləkɪt/ *n.* [C] TECHNICAL an exact copy of something or an exact repeat of a process SYN **copy**: *It is not acceptable to do the experiment once only; you need to produce replicates.* —**replicate** *adj.*

rep·li·ca·tion /ˌrɛpləˈkeɪʃən/ *n.* [U] BIOLOGY the process by which a cell or DNA makes an exact copy of itself: *During replication each strand of DNA generates a new strand.*

re·ply¹ /rɪˈplaɪ/ W3 *v.* **replies, replied, replying 1** [I,T] to answer someone by saying or writing something SYN **answer**: *Sorry it took me so long to reply.* | *"Of course," Natalie replied.* | **+to** *Has anyone replied to your ad in the paper?* | **+that** *He replied that the car belonged to his brother.* | *You must* ***reply in writing*** (=by sending a letter) *within three months.*

R

▸see THESAURUS box at answer[1] **2** [I] to react to an action by doing something else: **reply (to sth) with sth** *Rebel troops replied with increased violence.* | **reply by doing sth** *His parents replied by cutting off his allowance.* [**Origin:** 1300–1400 Old French *replier* **to fold again**, from Latin *replicare*, from *plicare* **to fold**]

reply[2] *n. plural* **replies** [C] **1** something that is said, written, or done as a way of replying SYN **answer**: *I knocked on his door, but there was no reply.* | **+to** *We have still not received any replies to our letters.* | *Aitkins frowned but* ***made no reply*** (=did not say anything). **2 in reply (to sth)** FORMAL **a)** as a way of replying to a question, letter, email etc.: *I am writing in reply to your letter dated May 12.* **b)** as a way of reacting to an action or the behavior of someone else: *The violence came in reply to continued government pressure on the rebels.*

re·po man /ˈripoʊ ˌmæn/ *n.* [C] INFORMAL someone whose job is to REPOSSESS (=take away) cars whose owners have stopped paying for them

R

re·port[1] /rɪˈpɔrt/ S2 W1 *n.* [C] **1** a piece of writing in a newspaper about something that is happening, or part of a television or radio news program: *the weather report* | **+on/about** *There was a report on the situation in Gaza.* | **news/media/press reports** *According to recent news reports, two of the victims are Americans.* ▸see THESAURUS box at newspaper **2** a written or spoken description of a situation or event, giving people the information they need: **+about/of/on** *a police officer's report of the accident* | *Martens* ***gave a report on*** *his sales trip to Korea.* | **file/submit a report** *He filed the report more than three months ago.* ▸see THESAURUS box at account[1] **3** a long formal or official piece of writing that carefully considers a particular subject: **+on** *a report on global warming* | **publish/issue/release a report** *The committee will publish its report in July.* | **the findings/conclusions/recommendations of a report** *The findings of the report suggest that the security situation has not changed.* → see also BOOK REPORT **4** a description of a situation or event, that may or may not be true: **+of** *Police received reports of a bomb threat at the airport at 11:28 p.m.* | **+that** *There are reports that some of the hostages are dead.* **5** FORMAL the noise of an explosion or shot: *a loud report* [**Origin:** 1300–1400 Old French *reporter* **to report**, from Latin *reportare*, from *portare* **to carry**]

report[2] S2 W1 *v.*
1 NEWS [I,T] to give people information about recent events, especially in newspapers and on television and radio: *We aim to report the news as fairly as possible.* | **+on** *Here's Mike Bryer, reporting on the day's stock exchange.* | **+that** *Journalists reported that seven people had been shot.* | ***It was reported that*** *an attack had been made on the police station.*
2 SAY THAT STH IS TRUE/HAS HAPPENED [T] to provide facts and information about something that has happened, has changed, or exists, especially officially: *Doctors reported a 13% increase in the rate of infection.* | **report doing sth** *Witnesses reported seeing three people flee the scene.* | **be reported to be sth/have done sth** *The stolen necklace is reported to be worth $57,000.* | **report (to sb) on sth** *Come back next week and report on your progress.* | **+that** *Inspectors reported that the building was unsafe.*
3 CRIME/ACCIDENT [T] to tell the police or someone in authority that an accident or crime has happened: *I'm here to report a theft.* | **report sth to sb** *We immediately reported the incident to the police.* | **report sb missing/injured/killed etc.** *She reported him missing when he failed to arrive home.*
4 PRODUCE AN OFFICIAL DOCUMENT [I,T] to produce an official and formal statement or report about a particular subject or situation: *The results of the investigation will be reported in October.*
5 COMPLAIN [T] to complain about someone to people in authority: **report sb to sb** *A co-worker reported him to supervisors for drinking on the job.*
6 ARRIVAL [I] to go somewhere and officially state that you have arrived: **+to** *Bradley will report to a federal prison in Petersburg, VA.* | *All soldiers were required to* ***report for duty*** (=say you are ready to work) *on Friday.*

report back *phr. v.* to bring or send back information that you have been asked to find: **+to** *The committee has 60 days to report back to Congress.*

report to sb *phr. v.* to be responsible to someone at work and be managed by them: *In his new job, he will report to the chief executive.*

re·port·age /rɪˈpɔrt̬ɪdʒ, ˌrɛpɔrˈtɑʒ/ *n.* [U] **1** the particular style of reporting used in newspapers, radio, or television **2** the act of reporting news

reˈport card *n.* a written statement by teachers about a child's work at school, sent to their parents

re·port·ed·ly /rɪˈpɔrt̬ɪdli/ *adv.* [sentence adverb] used to say what other people are saying about something, when you cannot be certain if it is true: *He reportedly received $7 million in compensation.* → see also ALLEGEDLY

reˌported ˈspeech *n.* [U] ENG. LANG. ARTS in grammar, the style of speech or writing used to report what someone says without repeating their actual words. The sentence "She said she didn't feel well" is an example of reported speech.

re·port·er /rɪˈpɔrt̬ɚ/ W1 *n.* [C] someone whose job is to write about events for a newspaper or to tell people about events on television or the radio → see also COURT REPORTER, JOURNALIST

re·pose[1] /rɪˈpoʊz/ *n.* [U] FORMAL a state of calm or comfortable rest SYN **rest** —**reposeful** *adj.*

repose[2] *v.* FORMAL **1** [I] if something reposes in a place, it is kept there **2** [I] if someone reposes somewhere they rest there **3 repose your trust/hope etc. in sb** to trust someone to help you

re·pos·i·to·ry /rɪˈpɑzəˌtɔri/ *n. plural* **repositories** [C] **1** a place where things are stored in large quantities: *a furniture repository* | **+of/for** *a repository for nuclear waste* **2** FORMAL a person or book that gives a lot of information: **+of/for** *Parry became a repository for the tribe's history.*

re·pos·sess /ˌripəˈzɛs/ *v.* [T] ECONOMICS to take back cars, furniture, or property from people who stop paying for them as they had arranged —**repossession** /ˌripəˈzɛʃən/ *n.* [C,U]

rep·re·hend /ˌrɛprɪˈhɛnd/ *v.* [T] FORMAL to express disapproval of a person or an action

rep·re·hen·si·ble /ˌrɛprɪˈhɛnsəbəl/ *adj.* FORMAL bad and deserving criticism: *I find their behavior* ***morally reprehensible.***

rep·re·sent /ˌrɛprɪˈzɛnt/ S3 W1 *v.* [T]
1 SPEAK FOR SB a) to speak officially for someone in a court of law and to prepare arguments to support them in court: *Who is representing the defendant?* | *She decided to* ***represent herself*** (=speak for herself, without a lawyer) *during the trial.* **b)** to speak officially for another person or group of people, giving their opinions and taking action for them: *She represents some of Hollywood's biggest stars.* | *The union must* ***represent the interests of*** (=speak for the opinions and needs of) *all its members.*
2 BE STH [linking verb] FORMAL to be or form something SYN **constitute**: **represent a change/advance/increase etc.** *Some pesticides represent a major threat to public health.* | *This treatment represents a significant advance in the field of cancer research.* | **represent ten percent/two-thirds etc.** *European orders represented thirty percent of our sales last year.*
3 GOVERNMENT POLITICS to have been elected to an official government position by the people in a particular area and to do things and make decisions in order to help them: *He represents the 4th Congressional District of Illinois.*
4 EXAMPLE OF STH [T] to be an example of a particular type of thing or quality: *This man represents everything I hate about politicians.*
5 SPORTS if you represent your country, school, town etc. in a sport, you play for the team from that country etc.: *Her ambition is to represent her country at the Olympics.*
6 be represented if a group, organization, area etc. is

represented at an event, people from the group are at the event: *All the local clubs were represented in the parade.* | **be well/poorly represented** *Local parents were well represented at the school board meeting.*
7 represent sb as sth to describe someone or something in a particular way, so that people have a particular opinion of them or it: *Her supporters represent her as a saint.* | *He had* ***represented himself as*** (=pretended to be) *an employee in order to gain access to the files.*
8 SIGN to be a sign or mark that shows something, especially on a map or plan SYN **symbolize**: *The red lines represent the railroad.* | *The direction of the wind is represented by arrows.*
9 ART if a painting, STATUE, piece of music etc. represents something or someone, it shows that thing in a particular way: *paintings representing religious themes* [**Origin:** 1300–1400 Old French *representer*, from Latin *repraesentare*, from *praesentare*]

rep·re·sen·ta·tion /ˌrɛprɪzɛnˈteɪʃən, -zən-/ *n.* **1** [U] the state of having someone to speak, vote, or make decisions for you: *Each state receives equal representation in the U.S. Senate.* → see also PROPORTIONAL REPRESENTATION **2** [C,U] a way of showing or describing something in art, literature, newspapers, television etc., or the fact of doing this SYN **portrayal**: +**of** *a representation of an elephant* | *Islamic art forbids the representation of God.* **3** [U] the work of representing a person or organization, for example in a legal case or official ceremony: *her representation of Garcia in the murder trial* **4 make representations (to sb)** FORMAL to make a formal complaint or statement **5 make false representations** TECHNICAL to describe or explain something in a way that you know is not true

rep·re·sen·ta·tion·al /ˌrɛprɪzɛnˈteɪʃənəl/ *adj.* **1** ENG. LANG. ARTS a representational painting or style of art shows things as they actually appear in real life → see also ABSTRACT **2** relating to a situation in which someone officially speaks or does something for someone else: *Union members receive representational help.*

rep·re·sen·ta·tive¹ /ˌrɛprɪˈzɛntət̬ɪv/ *adj.* [C] **1** typical of a group or thing SYN **typical**: +**of** *The latest incident is representative of a larger trend.* **2** including examples of all the different types of something in a group: **a representative sample/selection** *a representative sample of New York residents* **3** POLITICS a representative system of government allows people to vote for other people to represent them in the government: *a representative democracy*

representative² *n.* [C] **1 Representative** POLITICS a member of the House of Representatives, the Lower House of Congress in the United States **2** a person who has been chosen to speak, vote, or make decisions for someone else: +**of** *an elected representative of the people* → see also SALES REPRESENTATIVE

re·press /rɪˈprɛs/ *v.* [T] **1** to stop yourself from doing something, especially something you want to do: *Brenda repressed the urge to shout at him.* **2** if someone represses feelings, memories etc., their mind has hidden them because they are too upsetting to think about **3** DISAPPROVING to control a group of people by force: *Other nations condemned the ruler for repressing opposition.* → see also SUPPRESS

re·pressed /rɪˈprɛst/ *adj.* **1** having feelings or desires that you do not allow yourself to express or think about: *a repressed young woman* **2** used to describe emotions and memories that someone's mind repressed: *repressed anger*

re·pres·sion /rɪˈprɛʃən/ *n.* [U] **1** cruel and severe control of a large group of people: +**of** *the regime's repression of opposition parties* **2** very strong control of feelings or desires that you are ashamed of, until you feel as if you do not have them anymore: *sexual repression*

re·pres·sive /rɪˈprɛsɪv/ *adj.* **1** a repressive government or law is severe and cruel: *a repressive and brutal dictator* **2** relating to feelings or desires that you do not admit even to yourself, and that you do not allow yourself to express: *an emotionally repressive life*

re·prieve /rɪˈpriv/ *n.* [C] **1** a delay before something bad continues: **be given/granted a reprieve** *Shoppers will be given a temporary reprieve from the new sales tax.* **2** an official order stopping the killing of a prisoner as a punishment: *He was* ***granted a reprieve*** *only hours before his execution.* —**reprieve** *v.* [T usually passive]

rep·ri·mand /ˈrɛprəˌmænd/ *v.* [T] to tell someone officially that something they have done is very wrong: **reprimand sb for (doing) sth** *The officer was officially reprimanded for insulting a local woman.* —**reprimand** *n.* [C]

re·print¹ /ˌriˈprɪnt/ *v.* [T] to print a book, story, newspaper article etc. again

re·print² /ˈriprɪnt/ *n.* [C] **1** a book, story, newspaper article etc. that is printed again **2** an act of printing a book again because all the copies of it have been sold

re·pris·al /rɪˈpraɪzəl/ *n.* [C,U] an act of violence or other strong reaction, to punish your enemies or opponents for something they have done SYN **retaliation**: +**against** *reprisals against unarmed civilians* | *They didn't tell the police* ***for fear of reprisal.*** | *He was shot* ***in reprisal for*** *killing a rival gang member.* [**Origin:** 1400–1500 Old French *reprisaille*, from Old Italian, from *riprendere* **to take back**]

re·prise /rɪˈpriz/ *n.* [C] **1** the act of repeating something such as a piece of writing, a speech, or a performance: *His speech was a reprise of earlier announcements.* **2** ENG. LANG. ARTS a repeat of all or part of a piece of music

re·proach¹ /rɪˈproʊtʃ/ *n.* FORMAL **1** [C,U] criticism or disapproval, or a remark that expresses this: *"You don't need me," she said quietly, without reproach.* **2 above/beyond reproach** impossible to criticize SYN **perfect**: *Vernon's work in the community has been beyond reproach.* **3 a reproach to sb/sth** something that makes a person, society etc. feel bad or ashamed: *These derelict houses are a reproach to the city.*

reproach² *v.* [T] FORMAL to blame or criticize someone in a way that shows you are disappointed, but not angry: **reproach sb for (doing) sth** *Moviemakers have been reproached for showing so much violence.* | *You shouldn't* ***reproach yourself*** *for what has happened.*

re·proach·ful /rɪˈproʊtʃfəl/ *adj.* a reproachful look, remark etc. shows that you are criticizing someone or blaming them —**reproachfully** *adv.*

rep·ro·bate /ˈrɛprəˌbeɪt/ *n.* [C] FORMAL or HUMOROUS someone who behaves in an immoral way: *a nasty old reprobate*

re·proc·ess /riˈprɑsɛs/ *v.* [T] to treat a waste substance so that it can be used again: *a plant that reprocesses nuclear waste*

re·pro·duce /ˌriprəˈdus/ *v.* **1** [I,T] BIOLOGY if a plant or animal reproduces, or reproduces itself, it produces young plants or animals: *The turtles return to the Mexican coast to reproduce.* | *The virus can reproduce itself in under 20 minutes.* **2** [T] to make a photograph or printed copy of something: *The maps have been carefully reproduced.* **3** [T] to make something happen in the same way as it happened before and with the same results SYN **replicate**: *Scientists were unable to reproduce the results of the experiment.* **4** [T] to produce an object or an effect that is as good or effective as something that already exists: *The director manages to reproduce the feeling of a battle at sea.* —**reproducible** *adj.*

re·pro·duc·tion /ˌriprəˈdʌkʃən/ *n.* **1** [U] BIOLOGY the act or process of producing young animals, plants, or any other ORGANISMS: *We are studying the reproduction, diet and health of the dolphins* **2** [U] the act of producing a copy of a book, picture etc.: *the reproduction of works of art* **3** [C] a copy of a work of art, piece of furniture etc.: +**of** *a reproduction of Vincent van Gogh's "Sunflowers"* | **reproduction furniture/chairs etc.** *a reproduction Victorian bed* **4** [U] the act of making a recording of music: *high quality sound reproduction*

re·pro·duc·tive /ˌriprəˈdʌktɪv/ *adj.* [only before noun] BIOLOGY relating to the process of producing young animals or plants: *the human reproductive system*

repro,ductive iso'lation *n.* [U] BIOLOGY conditions that prevent one population of living things from breeding with another, even though the possibility for them to breed together exists, for example a type of behavior, a physical difference, or separation by a land feature

re·proof /rɪ'pruf/ *n.* FORMAL **1** [U] blame or disapproval: *a look of cold reproof* **2** [C] a remark that blames or criticizes someone: *a sharp reproof*

re·prove /rɪ'pruv/ *v.* [T] FORMAL to criticize someone for something that they have done

re·prov·ing /rɪ'pruvɪŋ/ *adj.* FORMAL expressing criticism of something that someone has done: *a reproving stare* —**reprovingly** *adv.*

rep·tile /'rɛptaɪl, 'rɛptl/ *n.* [C] BIOLOGY a type of animal such as a snake or LIZARD whose blood changes temperature according to the temperature around it, and that usually lays eggs [**Origin:** 1300–1400 Old French, Late Latin *reptilis* **creeping**, from Latin *repere* **to creep**]

R

rep·til·i·an¹ /rɛp'tɪliən/ *adj.* like a reptile or relating to reptiles

reptilian² *n.* [C] TECHNICAL a reptile

re·pub·lic /rɪ'pʌblɪk/ *n.* [C] POLITICS a country governed by elected representatives of the people, and led by a president, not a king or queen [**Origin:** 1500–1600 French *république*, from Latin *respublica*, from *res* **thing** + *publica* **public**] → see also MONARCHY

re·pub·li·can¹ /rɪ'pʌblɪkən/ *n.* [C] POLITICS **1 Republican** a member or supporter of the Republican Party in the U.S. → see also DEMOCRAT **2** someone who believes in government by elected representatives only, with no king or queen

republican² *adj.* POLITICS **1 Republican** relating to or supporting the Republican Party in the U.S.: *the Republican candidate for president* **2** relating to or supporting a system of government that is not led by a king or queen and is elected by the people —**republicanism** *n.* [U]

Re,publican 'Party *n.* **the Republican Party** one of the two main political parties of the U.S. → see also DEMOCRATIC PARTY

re·pu·di·ate /rɪ'pyudi,eɪt/ *v.* [T] FORMAL **1** to disagree strongly with someone or something and refuse to have any association with them or it SYN **reject**: *Government officials repudiated the treaty.* **2** to state or show formally that something is not true or not correct SYN **deny**: *He repudiated the allegations of bribery.* **3** OLD-FASHIONED to say formally that you do not have any connection with someone anymore, especially a relative SYN **disown** —**repudiation** /rɪ,pyudi'eɪʃən/ *n.* [U]

re·pug·nance /rɪ'pʌgnəns/ *n.* [U] FORMAL a strong feeling of dislike for something: **+for/of etc.** *a repugnance for pornography*

re·pug·nant /rɪ'pʌgnənt/ *adj.* FORMAL very bad and offensive SYN **disgusting**: *I found his behavior deeply repugnant.* | **+to** *Animal experiments are morally repugnant to many people.* [**Origin:** 1700–1800 French, Latin, present participle of *repugnare* **to fight against**]

re·pulse¹ /rɪ'pʌls/ *v.* [T] FORMAL **1** if something or someone repulses you, you feel they are very bad or DISGUSTING SYN **repel**: *His cold clammy hands repulsed me.* **2** to defeat a military attack SYN **repel**: *Government troops repulsed an attack by rebel forces.* **3** to refuse an offer, proposal, or suggestion in a way that is very direct and often impolite SYN **reject**

repulse² *n.* [singular] **1** FORMAL the act of refusing a proposal or suggestion in an impolite way SYN **rejection** **2** TECHNICAL the defeat of a military attack

re·pul·sion /rɪ'pʌlʃən/ *n.* **1** [singular, U] a very strong feeling of dislike for something, that makes you want to avoid it or feel slightly sick SYN **disgust** SYN **revulsion** OPP **attraction**: *He watched in repulsion as they kissed.* **2** [U] PHYSICS the electric or MAGNETIC force by which one object pushes another one away from it OPP **attraction**

re·pul·sive /rɪ'pʌlsɪv/ *adj.* **1** unpleasant in a way that almost makes you feel sick: *a repulsive smell* | **+to** *The idea of forcing young children to work is repulsive to me.* **2** [only before noun] PHYSICS repulsive forces push objects away from each other —**repulsively** *adv.* —**repulsiveness** *n.* [U]

re·pur·pose /ri'pɚpəs/ *v.* [T] TECHNICAL if something such as equipment, a building, or a document is repurposed, it is used in a new way that is different from its original use, without having to be changed very much

rep·u·ta·ble /'rɛpyətəbəl/ *adj.* respected for being honest or for doing good work: *a reputable newspaper* | *If you buy a used car, go to a reputable dealer.* —**reputably** *adv.*

rep·u·ta·tion /,rɛpyə'teɪʃən/ W3 *n.* [C] the opinion that people have about a particular person or thing based on what has happened in the past: **a good/bad/excellent etc. reputation** *a law firm with a good reputation* | **+for** *The school's reputation for drama is very good.* | **have a reputation for (doing) sth** *Judge Kelso has a reputation for being strict but fair.* | **+as** *She has a reputation as a trouble maker at work.* | **earn/gain/win etc. a reputation as sth** *He gained a national reputation as a campaigner against drugs.* | **ruin/destroy/damage etc. sb/sth's reputation** *The scandal ruined his reputation.* | *The service at Heron Lodge* ***lived up to its reputation*** (=was as bad or good as other people say).

re·pute /rɪ'pyut/ *n.* [U] FORMAL reputation: **of good/low/international etc. repute** *a man of great repute* | *a hotel of international repute*

re·put·ed /rɪ'pyuṭɪd/ *adj.* [only before noun] used to talk about a fact that most people think is true, although it is not possible to be certain: *the reputed leader of a criminal gang* | **be reputed to be/do sth** *She is reputed to be extremely wealthy.*

re·put·ed·ly /rɪ'pyuṭɪdli/ *adv.* [sentence adverb] according to what most people say or think: *The castle was reputedly haunted.*

re·quest¹ /rɪ'kwɛst/ S2 W2 *n.* [C] **1** an act of asking for something politely or formally: **+for** *a request for information* | **+that** *the government's request that troops be withdrawn* | **a request to do sth** *a request to adopt a baby* | *They* ***made an*** *urgent* ***request*** *for more aid.* | **refuse/reject a request** *The bank rejected our request for a loan.* | *He was surprised when his boss* ***agreed to the request.*** | *The study was done* ***at the request of*** *the Chairman* (=because the Chairman asked for it). | *More information is available* ***on request*** (=when you ask for it). | *There were no flowers at the funeral,* ***by request*** (=because they asked specially not to have flowers). | *I'm making drinks. Are there* ***any requests*** (=used to ask people if they want something specific)? **2** a piece of music that is played on the radio because someone has asked for it [**Origin:** 1300–1400 Old French *requeste*, from Vulgar Latin, from *requaerere* **to try to find, need**]

request² S2 W3 *v.* [T] **1** FORMAL to ask for something politely or formally: *To request more information, please call this number.* | **+that** *Students requested that the school provide more computer classes.* | **request sb to do sth** *Guests are requested to wear formal attire.* | **request sth from sb** *You must request permission from a teacher to leave class.*

THESAURUS

ask (for) to say or write something in order to get something: *I asked one of my friends to help me.* | *Tim asked for help.*
demand to ask for something in a strong way because you feel you have a right to it: *The employees are demanding better pay.*

▶see THESAURUS box at **ask** **2** to ask for a particular piece of music to be played on the radio

GRAMMAR

You **request** something (NOT "request for" sth). But you do use **for** with the noun: *requests for money* (NOT *"requests of money"*).

req·ui·em /ˈrɛkwiəm/ also ˌ**requiem ˈmass** *n.* [C] **1** a Christian religious ceremony of prayers for someone who has died **2** ENG. LANG. ARTS a piece of music written for this ceremony

re·quire /rɪˈkwaɪɚ/ Ac S2 W1 *v.* [T not in progressive] **1** if a situation or a problem requires something, it needs that thing SYN **need**: *Higgins' leg will probably require surgery.* | *Most house plants require regular watering.* | *The job requires a lot of time and energy.* ▸see THESAURUS box at **need**[1] **2** [usually passive] to officially demand that people do something, because of a law or rule: **+that** *State law requires that dogs be kept on leashes in public areas.* | **be required to do sth** *You are required by law to wear seat belts.* | **the required number/level/period etc.** *The bill failed to get the required number of votes.* | **sth is required of sb** *Children need to know what is required of them.* | *The book is **required reading** for this class* (=something that people must read for the class). [**Origin:** 1300–1400 Old French *requerre*, from Vulgar Latin *requaerere* **to try to find, need**]

reˌquired reˌserve ˈratio → see RESERVE RATIO

re·quire·ment /rɪˈkwaɪɚmənt/ Ac W2 *n.* [C] **1** something that someone needs or asks for: *Housing requirements change as families grow.* | **+of** *the special requirements of children with learning disabilities* | *She earns enough money to **meet the** family's **requirements*** (=get what the family needs). **2** something that must be done because of a law, rule, contract etc.: **+for** *the city's parking requirements for new buildings* | *The student's grades must **satisfy** the college's admission **requirements*** (=be the same or better as the college's requirements). | *All aircraft must **comply with** the new safety **requirements*** (=be the same or better as the new requirements). | *Most roofs exceed these **minimum requirements*** (=the lowest standard that is allowed).

req·ui·site[1] /ˈrɛkwəzɪt/ *adj.* FORMAL needed for a particular purpose SYN **necessary**: *He lacks the requisite qualifications.*

requisite[2] *n.* [C usually plural] FORMAL something that is needed for a particular purpose: **+of/for** *She believed privacy to be a requisite for a peaceful life.*

req·ui·si·tion[1] /ˌrɛkwəˈzɪʃən/ *v.* [T] to officially demand to have something, especially so that it can be used by an army: *The food was all requisitioned by the army.*

requisition[2] *n.* [C,U] an official demand to have something, usually made by an army or military authority

re·quit·al /rɪˈkwaɪtl/ *n.* [U] FORMAL **1** payment for something done or given **2** something that you do or give to someone because of something they have done or given to you, especially something bad

re·quite /rɪˈkwaɪt/ *v.* [T] FORMAL to give or do something in return for something done or given to you

re-re·lease /ˌri rɪˈlis/ *v.* [T] if a record or movie is re-released, it is produced and sold for a second time, usually with small changes: *Star Wars was re-released in 1997.* —**re-release** /ˈri rɪˌlis/ *n.* [C]

re·route /riˈrut, -ˈraʊt/ *v.* [T] **1** to send vehicles, airplanes, telephone calls etc. to a different place than the one where they were originally going **2** if you reroute a large amount of money, you spend it on something different than had originally been planned

re·run /ˈrirʌn/ *n.* [C] a movie or old television program that is being shown again: *a rerun of "The Jeffersons"* —**rerun** *v.* [T]

re·sched·ule /riˈskɛdʒəl/ Ac *v.* [T] **1** to arrange for something to happen at a different time, because the time you had planned will not work: **reschedule sth for sth** *The press conference had to be rescheduled for March 19.* **2** ECONOMICS to arrange for a debt to be paid back later than was originally agreed

re·scind /rɪˈsɪnd/ *v.* [T] to officially end a law, decision, or agreement that has been made in the past: *The contract was rescinded.*

re·scis·sion /riˈsɪʒən/ *n.* [C,U] FORMAL an official decision or statement that a planned sale, law, agreement etc. will not happen SYN **cancellation**

rescue

res·cue[1] /ˈrɛskyu/ *v.* [T] **1** to save someone or something from a dangerous or unpleasant situation: *Survivors were rescued by helicopter.* | **rescue sb/sth from sth** *She died trying to rescue her children from the blaze.* **2** to prevent a business or plan from failing: *The policy is designed to rescue failing businesses.* [**Origin:** 1300–1400 Old French *rescourre*, from *escourre* **to shake out**, from Latin *excutere*] —**rescuer** *n.* [C]

rescue[2] *n.* [C] **1** an occasion when someone or something is rescued from danger: **+of** *Storms delayed the rescue of the crash victims.* | **rescue team/boat/equipment etc.** *Rescue workers arrived almost immediately.* | **rescue attempt/effort/operation etc.** *a military rescue mission* **2 come to the/sb's rescue a)** to help someone who is having problems or difficulties: *My brother came to the rescue and sent me $1000.* **b)** to save someone who is in a dangerous situation

re·search[1] /ˈrisɚtʃ, rɪˈsɚtʃ/ Ac S1 W1 *n.* [U] **1** serious study of a subject, that is intended to discover new facts or test new ideas: *The book draws on Gardner's own research.* | **+into/on** *research into the causes of cancer* | **research project/team/grant etc.** *AIDS research projects* | **medical/scientific/social/historical etc. research** *new investment in scientific research* | INFORMAL *I'm still **doing research** for my thesis.* | *The scientists have been **conducting** their **research*** (=doing their research) *in the Sudan.* **2** the activity of finding information about something that you are interested in or need to know about: *It's a good idea to **do** some **research** before you buy a house.* [**Origin:** 1500–1600 Old French *recerche*, from *recerchier* **to find out about something thoroughly**] → see also MARKET RESEARCH, R & D

re·search[2] /rɪˈsɚtʃ, ˈrisɚtʃ/ Ac S3 W3 *v.* [T] to study a subject in detail, especially in order to discover new facts or test new ideas: *He spent four years researching material for the play.* | **reasearch into sth** *a project researching into the causes of the disease* —**researcher** *n.* [C]

ˌ**research and deˈvelopment** *n.* [U] → see R & D

re·sell /ˌriˈsɛl/ *v. past tense and past participle* **resold** /-ˈsoʊld/ [T] to sell something that you have bought: *The land was resold for $2 million.* —**resale** *n., adj.*: *the resale of old military vehicles*

re·sem·blance /rɪˈzɛmbləns/ *n.* [C,U] a SIMILARITY between two things, especially in the way they look: **+between** *The resemblance between John and his father was remarkable.* | **bear a (close/striking/strong) resemblance to sb/sth** (=be (very) similar to someone or something) | **bear little/no resemblence**

to sb/sth (=be nothing like someone or something) | **bear a passing resemblance to sb/sth** (=be similar to someone or something)

re·sem·ble /rɪˈzɛmbəl/ W3 *v.* [T not in progressive or passive] to look like, or be similar to, someone or something: *His argument resembles other early philosophers'.* | *an animal that* ***closely resembles*** (=looks very much like) *a monkey* [**Origin:** 1300–1400 Old French *resembler*, from *sembler* **to be like, seem**, from Latin *similare* **to copy**]

re·sent /rɪˈzɛnt/ *v.* [T] to feel angry or upset about a situation or about something that someone has done, especially because you think that it is not fair: **resent (sb) doing sth** *I resented having to work such long hours.* | **deeply/bitterly/strongly resent sth** *The policy was bitterly resented by American voters.* | *Alex* ***resented the fact that*** *she earned more money.* [**Origin:** 1500–1600 French *ressentir* **to feel strongly about**, from *sentir* **to feel**, from Latin *sentire*]

re·sent·ful /rɪˈzɛntfəl/ *adj.* feeling angry and upset about something that you think is unfair SYN **bitter**: +**of/about/at** *She felt resentful at not being promoted.* —**resentfully** *adv.* —**resentfulness** *n.* [U]

re·sent·ment /rɪˈzɛntˀmənt/ *n.* [U] a feeling of anger because something has happened that you think is unfair: *Patrick stared at her with resentment.* | +**at/over/of** *She couldn't let go of her resentment over the divorce.* | +**toward/against** *resentment toward the government*

res·er·va·tion /ˌrɛzɚˈveɪʃən/ S2 W3 *n.* **1** [C] an arrangement made so that a place is kept for you in a hotel, restaurant, airplane etc.: *airline reservations* | *To* ***make reservations*** *call 555-6355.* **2** [C,U] a feeling of doubt because you do not agree completely with a plan, idea, or suggestion: +**about** *He explained his reservations about the plan.* | **have/express reservations (about sth)** *I had strong reservations about the new software.* | *We welcomed her back* ***without reservation*** (=completely). **3** [C] an area of land in the U.S. kept separate for Native Americans to live on: *a Navajo reservation* **4** [C] an area of land where wild animals can live without being hunted SYN **preserve**: *a 50,000 acre private wildlife reservation*

re·serve¹ /rɪˈzɚv/ *v.* [T] **1** to arrange for a place in a hotel, restaurant, airplane etc. to be kept for you: *Do you have to reserve tickets in advance?* | *I'd like to reserve a table for two.* **2** to keep something separate so that it can be used by a particular person or for a particular purpose: **reserve sth for sb/sth** *A separate, smaller room is reserved for smokers.* | *Reserve half of the chicken stock for the sauce.* ►see THESAURUS box at **keep¹** **3** to use or show something only in one particular situation: **reserve sth for sb/sth** *She spoke in a tone of voice she usually reserved for dealing with officials.* **4 reserve the right to do sth** FORMAL an expression meaning that you will do something if you think it is necessary, used especially in notices or official documents: *The management reserves the right to refuse admission.* [**Origin:** 1300–1400 Old French *reserver*, from Latin *reservare* **to keep back**] → see also **suspend/reserve judgment** at JUDGMENT (1)

reserve² *n.* **1** [C] an amount of something kept for future use, especially for difficult or dangerous situations: *$10 million in cash reserves* | +**of** *reserves of food* | *Somehow Debbie maintained an inner reserve of strength.* **2 in reserve** ready to be used if needed in an unexpected situation: *We always keep some money in reserve, just in case.* **3** [U] a quality in someone's character that makes them not like expressing their emotions or talking about their problems: *Later, Darcy drops his reserve and confesses that he loves her.* **4** a RESERVATION **5** [C] a price limit below which something will not be sold, especially in an AUCTION **6 reserves** [plural] a military force that a country has in addition to its usual army: *the army reserves* **7** [C] an area of land that is kept separate in some countries, for example in Canada or Brazil, so that the NATIVE AMERICANS (=original populations of those countries) can live there

re·served /rɪˈzɚvd/ *adj.* **1** unwilling to express your emotions or talk about your problems: *He was particularly reserved around women.* ►see THESAURUS box at **shy¹** **2** a reserved area, seat, place etc. is to be used only by a particular person or for a particular thing: *reserved parking spaces* | +**for** *The front row is reserved for the family of the bride.* —**reservedly** /rɪˈzɚvɪdli/ *adv.* —**reservedness** *n.* [U] → see also **all rights reserved** at RIGHT³ (6), UNRESERVED

Reˌserved ˈPowers *n.* [plural] POLITICS the authority each state in the U.S. has to make decisions, pass laws, etc., whenever the decision, law etc. is not one that the U.S. CONSTITUTION says must be done by CONGRESS → see also ORDINANCE POWERS

Reˌserve ˌOfficer ˈTraining Corps → see ROTC

reˈserve price → see RESERVE

reˌserve ˈratio also **reˌquired reˌserve ˈratio** ABBREVIATION **RRR** *n.* [singular] ECONOMICS the amount of money a bank or financial institution must possess in relation to all the money it has lent. The rate is set by the FEDERAL RESERVE SYSTEM (=the group of U.S. banks that make the rules for all U.S. banks): *The Fed controls the reserve ratio, setting the proportion of deposits that each bank must hold back and not lend.*

re·serv·ist /rɪˈzɚvɪst/ *n.* [C] a soldier in the reserves, who is trained to fight and may join the professional army during a war: *a Marine Corps reservist*

res·er·voir /ˈrɛzəˌvwɑr, -zɚ-, -ˌvwɔr/ *n.* [C] **1** EARTH SCIENCE a lake, often an artificial one, where water is stored before it is supplied to people's houses **2 a reservoir of sth** a large amount of something that has not yet been used: *She found she had reservoirs of unexpected strength.* **3** TECHNICAL a part of a machine or engine where a liquid is kept before it is used **4** TECHNICAL a place where gas or liquid gathers, especially in a rock or in the body

re·set¹ /ˌriˈsɛt/ *v. past tense and past participle* **reset**, **resetting** [T] **1** COMPUTERS to change a clock, control etc. so that it shows a different time or number or is ready to be used again: *Have you reset the alarm clock?* **2** to put a broken bone back into its correct place so that it grows back together correctly **3** to put a jewel into a new piece of jewelry **4** TECHNICAL to make new pages from which to print a book —**reset** /ˈrisɛt/ *n.* [C,U]

re·set² /ˈrisɛt/ *adj.* a reset button or SWITCH is used to make a machine or instrument ready to work again

re·set·tle /riˈsɛtl̩/ *v.* **1** [I,T] to go to live in a new country or area, or help people to do this: *In the 1980s, about 284,000 refugees resettled in California.* | *Families still living on the polluted farmland will be resettled.* **2** [T] to start using an area again as a place to live: *The area was resettled in the latter half of the century.* —**resettlement** *n.* [U]

re·shuf·fle /riˈʃʌfəl/ *v.* [T] to change the jobs of the people who work in an organization, especially in government: *Perez reshuffled his employees' job responsibilities.* —**reshuffle** *n.* [C]

re·side /rɪˈzaɪd/ Ac *v.* [I always + adv./prep.] FORMAL to live in a particular place SYN **live**: *How many people over the age of 18 reside in your household?*

reside in sth/sb *phr. v.* FORMAL **1** to consist of or result from something: *His talent resides in his storytelling abilities.* **2** also **reside with sth/sb** if a power, right etc. resides in something or someone, it belongs to them: *Political power often resides with powerful families.*

res·i·dence /ˈrɛzədəns/ Ac S3 *n.* **1** [U] legal permission to live in a country for a certain amount of time: **permanent/temporary residence** *All those with permanent residence are allowed to vote.* → see also GREEN CARD **2** [C] FORMAL a house, especially a large one: *the ambassador's official residence* ►see THESAURUS box at **home¹** **3** [U] the state of living in a place: *His main* ***place of residence*** *is in Oregon.* | *The college usually has 200 students* ***in residence*** (=living there). | **take up residence** FORMAL (=to start living in a place) **4 artist/poet/scholar etc. in residence** an artist etc. who has been officially chosen by a college or other institution to work there → see also RESIDENCE HALL

'residence ˌhall *n.* [C] a DORMITORY at a college

res·i·den·cy /'rɛzədənsi/ *n.* [U] **1** a period of time when a doctor receives special training in a particular type of medicine, especially at a hospital **2** RESIDENCE

res·i·dent¹ /'rɛzədənt/ Ac W2 *n.* [C] **1** someone who lives or stays in a place such as town or NEIGHBORHOOD, or in an institution: *the elderly residents of a nursing home* | +**of** *residents of Beijing* **2** a doctor working at a hospital where he is being trained

resident² Ac *adj.* **1** [only before noun] working regularly for an particular organization: *the resident conductor at the Oregon Symphony* **2** FORMAL living in a place: +**in** *a German woman, resident in London* **3** [only before noun] living in the place where you work: *resident farm workers* **4 our resident expert/comedian etc.** HUMOROUS used to talk about someone in your group who knows a lot about something, or who is known for doing a particular thing: *He's our resident expert on computer games.*

ˌresident 'alien *n.* TECHNICAL someone from a foreign country who has the legal right to live in the U.S.

res·i·den·tial /ˌrɛzə'dɛnʃəl◂/ Ac *adj.* **1** a residential part of town consists of private houses, with no offices or factories: *a quiet residential neighborhood* **2** relating to homes, rather than offices or businesses: *telephone services for residential customers*

ˌresidential 'care *n.* [U] a system in which people who are old or sick live together in a special house and are taken care of by professionals

ˌresidential 'treatment *n.* [U] treatment in a special home for people who are old, mentally ill, or ADDICTED to drugs or alcohol

ˌresident phy'sician *n.* [C] another name for a RESIDENT

'residents' assoclˌation *n.* [C] an association of people who meet to discuss the problems and needs of the area where they live

re·sid·u·al /rɪ'zɪdʒuəl/ *adj.* [only before noun] remaining after a process, event etc. is finished: *the* ***residual effects*** *of the drug treatment*

res·i·due /'rɛzəˌdu/ *n.* [C] **1** the part of something that is left after the rest has gone or been taken away: *Soap can leave a slight residue on your skin.* | +**of** *a residue of anger and hatred* **2** CHEMISTRY a substance that is left after a chemical process [**Origin:** 1300–1400 Old French *residu*, from Latin *residuum*, from *residere*]

re·sign /rɪ'zaɪn/ W3 *v.* [I,T] **1** to officially and permanently leave your job or position because you want to: **resign from sth** *Shea resigned from the FBI last year.* | **resign as sth** *He resigned as chairman in August.* | **resign your post/position etc.** *She eventually resigned her position as chief executive.* ▸see THESAURUS box at **quit** **2 resign yourself to (doing) sth** to make yourself accept something that you do not like but that cannot be changed: *He seems to have resigned himself to living without her.* [**Origin:** 1300–1400 Old French *resigner*, from Latin *resignare* **to unseal, cancel, give back**] → see also RESIGNED

res·ig·na·tion /ˌrɛzɪg'neɪʃən/ *n.* **1** [C,U] the act of resigning, or a written statement to say you are doing this: *a letter of resignation* | +**of** *the resignation of the chief executive* | +**from** *her resignation from the board of directors* | +**as** *his sudden resignation as Chief of Police* | **hand in your resignation/tender your resignation** (=officially say that you are leaving your job) | *The President refused to* ***accept*** *her* ***resignation.*** **2** [U] the attitude of calmly accepting a bad situation that cannot be changed: *He watched his children argue with resignation.*

re·signed /rɪ'zaɪnd/ *adj.* **1** accepting a situation that you do not like, but cannot change: **resigned to (doing) sth** *She was resigned to spending the day alone.* | *We became* ***resigned to the fact that*** *our team would lose.* **2** a resigned look, sound, action etc. shows that you are making yourself accept something that you do not like: *"Oh well," she said with a resigned smile.* —**resignedly** /rɪ'zaɪnɪdli/ *adv.*

re·sil·ience /rɪ'zɪlyəns/ also **re·sil·ien·cy** /rɪ'zɪlyənsi/ *n.* [U] **1** the ability to quickly become strong, healthy, or happy after a difficult situation, illness etc.: *Their courage and resilience inspired us all.* | *the resilience of the state's economy* **2** PHYSICS the ability of a substance such as rubber to return to its former shape after it has been pressed or bent SYN **flexibility**

re·sil·ient /rɪ'zɪlyənt/ *adj.* **1** able to quickly become strong, healthy, or happy again after an illness, difficult situation, change etc.: *The enemy proved far more resilient than expected.* **2** PHYSICS a resilient substance returns to its former shape after it has been pressed, bent etc. [**Origin:** 1600–1700 Latin, present participle of *resilire* **to jump back**, from *salire* **to jump**] —**resiliently** *adv.*

res·in /'rɛzən/ *n.* **1** [U] BIOLOGY a thick sticky liquid that comes out of some trees **2** [C] CHEMISTRY an artificial plastic substance that is produced chemically and used in industry —**resinous** *adj.*

re·sist /rɪ'zɪst/ W3 *v.* **1** [I,T usually in negatives] to stop yourself from having or doing something that you like or want to do very much: **resist (doing sth)** *I* ***couldn't resist*** *buying these shoes.* | *They made me an offer I* ***can't resist.*** | **resist the temptation/urge etc. to do sth** *She resisted the temptation to laugh at him.* | **hard/impossible to resist** *It's pretty hard to resist Jacob's smile.* **2** [I,T] to oppose or fight someone or something: *Congress continues to resist the anti-weapons bill.* | *He was charged with* ***resisting arrest*** (=fighting against the police who were trying to take him to the police station). **3** [T] to try to prevent change or prevent yourself being forced to do something: *The university resisted pressure to close its art department.* **4** [T] to not be changed or harmed by something: *The virus is able to resist most antibiotics.* [**Origin:** 1300–1400 Latin *resistere*, from *sistere* **to stop**] —**resistable** *adj.*

re·sist·ance /rɪ'zɪstəns/ W3 *n.*
1 AGAINST CHANGE [singular, U] a refusal to accept new ideas or changes: *Attempts to move the prison have* ***met with*** *strong* ***resistance*** *from the community.* | +**to** *It's surprising how little resistance there's been to the new budget plan.*
2 FIGHTING [singular, U] fighting against someone or something that is attacking you: **put up resistance/offer resistance** *Protesters put up some resistance when the police arrived.*
3 AGAINST INFECTION/ILLNESS [singular, U] MEDICINE the natural ability of an animal or plant to stop diseases from harming it: *Vitamins can build up your resistance to colds and the flu.*
4 wind resistance the degree to which a moving object, such as a car or airplane, is made to move more slowly by the air it moves through
5 ELECTRICITY [U] PHYSICS the degree to which a substance can stop an electric current passing through
6 the resistance also **the Resistance** an organization that secretly fights against an enemy that controls their country: *During World War II, he joined the resistance against the Nazis.* | *She was a member of the French Resistance.*
7 the path/line of least resistance the easiest thing to do in a difficult situation
8 EQUIPMENT [C] a RESISTOR → see also PASSIVE RESISTANCE

re·sis·tant /rɪ'zɪstənt/ *adj.* **1** not damaged or affected by something: +**to** *Some insects are resistant to pesticides.* **2** opposed to something and wanting to prevent it happening: +**to** *The company managers were resistant to change.*

-resistant /rɪzɪstənt/ *suffix* [in adjectives] not easily affected or damaged by something: *child-resistant* (=made to be difficult for children to open) | *stain-resistant* (=made so that spills or marks can be easily removed) → see also HEAT-RESISTANT, -PROOF, TAMPER-RESISTANT, WATER-RESISTANT

R

re·sis·tor /rɪˈzɪstɚ/ *n.* [C] PHYSICS a piece of wire or other material used for increasing electrical resistance

res·o·lute /ˈrɛzəˌlut/ *adj.* doing something in a very determined way because you have very strong beliefs, aims etc. SYN **determined** OPP **irresolute**: *a resolute opponent of the new law* —**resolutely** *adv.* —**resoluteness** *n.*

res·o·lu·tion /ˌrɛzəˈluʃən/ Ac W3 *n.* **1** [C] a formal decision or statement agreed on by an official group of people, especially after a vote: *The UN passed a Human Rights resolution by a vote of 130–2.* **2** [singular, U] the final solution to a problem or difficulty: +**of** *a peaceful resolution of the conflict* | +**to** *Drivers may go on strike Monday if there is no resolution to the pay dispute.* **3** [U] APPROVING the quality of having strong beliefs and determination **4** [C] a promise to yourself to do something → see also RESOLVE: *My **New Year's resolution*** (=a resolution made on January 1st) *is to lose weight.* | *Hass **made a resolution** never to return to the South.* **5** [C] POLITICS a formal decision or statement from the U.S. SENATE or the HOUSE OF REPRESENTATIVES that does not have the force of law and does not need to be signed by the American president **6** [singular] ENG. LANG. ARTS the point near the end of a story, book, play etc. when the main CONFLICT between characters or forces is fully dealt with **7** [C,U] SCIENCE the power of a television, camera, MICROSCOPE etc. to give a clear picture of things, or a measure of this: *a high resolution microscope*

R

re·solve¹ /rɪˈzɑlv/ Ac W3 *v.* **1** [T] to find a satisfactory way of dealing with a problem or difficulty SYN **settle**: **resolve a problem/dispute/conflict** *Congressmen called for a third meeting to resolve the conflict.* | *We're hoping they'll **resolve** their **differences*** (=stop arguing and become friendly again) *soon.* | *You can't just wait and hope the problem **resolves itself**!* **2** [I,T] WRITTEN to make a definite decision to do something: **resolve to do sth** *After the divorce she resolved never to marry again.* | +**that** *I resolved that I would stop smoking immediately.* ▸see THESAURUS box at **decide** **3** [I,T] to make a formal decision, especially by voting: +**that** *The city council resolved that the street repairs should be delayed.* **4** [T] TECHNICAL to separate something into its different parts [**Origin:** 1300–1400 Latin *resolvere* **to unloose**, from *solvere*]

resolve into *phr. v.* **1 resolve sth into sth** FORMAL to separate or become separated into parts: *He explained the process by resolving it into a series of simple steps.* **2 resolve (itself) into sth/sb** WRITTEN to gradually change into something else, especially by becoming clearer SYN **become**: *The dark shape resolved into the figure of Mr. Markham.* **3 resolve into sth** TECHNICAL to become separated into parts

resolve² Ac *n.* [U] strong determination to succeed in doing something: *News of the attack **strengthened our resolve** to keep fighting.* | **resolve to do sth** *The party leaders' resolve to pass the law had weakened.*

res·o·nance /ˈrɛzənəns/ *n.* **1** [U] the deep, loud, continuing quality of a sound: *the powerful resonance of Jessie's voice* **2** [C,U] FORMAL the special meaning that something has for you because it relates to your own experiences: *The movie **had** a special emotional **resonance** for me.* **3** [C,U] PHYSICS sound that is produced or increased in an object by sound waves from another object

res·o·nant /ˈrɛzənənt/ *adj.* **1** having a deep, loud, clear sound that continues for a long time: *the baritone's resonant voice* **2 resonant with sth** FORMAL filled with a special meaning, effect, or feeling that continues for a long time **3** TECHNICAL resonant materials increase any sound produced inside them —**resonantly** *adv.*

res·o·nate /ˈrɛzəˌneɪt/ *v.* [I] **1** if something such as an event or message resonates, it continues to have a special meaning or effect: **resonate with sb** *It's an idea that resonates with many voters.* **2** to make a deep, loud, clear sound that continues for a long time: *The music resonated through the streets.* **3** to make a sound that is produced as a reaction to another sound

resonate with sth *phr. v.* **1** to be full of a sound: *a hall resonating with laughter* **2** FORMAL to be full of a particular meaning or feeling: *Stein's speech resonated with bursting hope.*

res·o·na·tor /ˈrɛzəˌneɪt̬ɚ/ *n.* [C] a piece of equipment for making the sound louder in a musical instrument

re·sort¹ /rɪˈzɔrt/ *n.* **1** [C] a place where many people often go for vacation, with hotels, swimming pools etc.: **seaside/beach/mountain etc. resort** *an exclusive island resort in Hawaii* | **resort hotel/beach/town** *The resort town comes alive in the summer months.* | **ski/health/golf etc. resort** *the ski resorts of Aspen, Colorado* **2 last resort** what you will do, use, or try if everything else fails: *I might have to get a second job **as a last resort**.* | *a weapon **of last resort*** (=only used if every other type of weapon fails) [**Origin:** 1300–1400 Old French *resortir* **to come back, resort**, from *sortir* **to go out**]

resort² *v.*

resort to sth *phr. v.* to use something or do something that is bad in order to succeed or deal with a problem: *When polite requests failed, Paul resorted to threats.* | **resort to doing sth** *Homeless teenagers often resort to stealing.*

re·sound /rɪˈzaʊnd/ *v.* [I] **1** if a place resounds with a sound, it is filled with it SYN **echo**: +**with/to** *The auditorium resounded with thunderous applause.* **2** if a sound resounds, it continues loudly and clearly for a long time: +**through/around etc.** *Laughter and cheers resounded throughout the building.* **3** WRITTEN to be talked about a lot: *The war still resounds in the stories people tell.*

re·sound·ing /rɪˈzaʊndɪŋ/ *adj.* **1 resounding success/victory/defeat etc.** a very great or complete success, victory etc., that many people know about: *a resounding defeat for the home team* **2** a resounding answer, especially from a group of people, is very strong and clear: **a resounding yes/no** *The answer appears to be a resounding yes.* **3** [only before noun] a resounding noise is so loud that it seems to continue for a few seconds: *The door slammed with a resounding thud.* ▸see THESAURUS box at **loud¹** —**resoundingly** *adv.*

re·source /ˈrisɔrs, rɪˈsɔrs/ Ac S2 W1 *n.* **1** [C] ECONOMICS something such as land, minerals, or natural energy that exists in a country and can be used to increase its wealth: *Canada's vast mineral resources* | *a country rich in **natural resources*** | *Trees are a **renewable resource**.* **2** [C] ECONOMICS the money, property, people, skills etc. that is available to be used when needed: *The police used every available resource to track down the killer.* | *Several organizations in New Mexico have **pooled** their technical **resources*** (=put together all their separate resources). | *The project has completely **drained** our **resources*** (=used them all). **3** [C] something such as a book, movie, or picture that provides information: *important educational resources* | *a valuable new computer resource* **4 resources** [plural] personal qualities, such as courage and a determination, that you need to deal with a difficult situation: *Jan relied on her **inner resources** to get her through that tough time.* **5** [U] the ability to deal with practical problems: *a man of great resource* [**Origin:** 1600–1700 French *ressource*, from Old French *resourdre* **to rise again, relieve**, from Latin *resurgere*] → see also HUMAN RESOURCES

re·source·ful /rɪˈsɔrsfəl/ Ac *adj.* APPROVING good at finding ways of dealing with practical problems: *a resourceful young man* —**resourcefully** *adv.* —**resourcefulness** *n.* [U]

re·spect¹ /rɪˈspɛkt/ S3 W2 *n.*

1 ADMIRATION [U] admiration for someone, especially because of their personal qualities, knowledge, or skill → see also DISRESPECT: +**for** *I have a lot of respect for Jane's work.* | **win/earn/gain the respect of sb** *She has earned the respect of her fellow athletes.* | *He **commands the respect of*** (=has and deserves the respect of) *many Latino voters in the district.* ▸see THESAURUS box at **admire**

2 CONSIDERATION [U] an attitude of regarding something or someone as important, so that you treat them

in a kind, polite, or careful way: +**for** *I don't think these companies have any respect for the environment.* | *They stayed away* ***out of respect for*** (=because of their respect for) *the wishes of the victim's family.* | *Sales staff should* ***treat*** *all customers* ***with*** *courtesy and* ***respect.*** | *He* ***shows*** *no* ***respect*** *for his teachers.* | **a sign/gesture/mark etc. of respect** *Worshippers cover their heads as a sign of respect.* | *a relationship built on* ***mutual respect*** (=a feeling of respect between two people or groups)
3 in one respect/in some respects/in every respect etc. used to talk about a particular part or parts of a situation that has many parts: *In many respects, our families are very similar.* | *My school was pretty boring, and nothing has changed in that respect.*
4 FOR DANGER [U] a careful attitude toward something or someone that is dangerous: +**for** *The kids have* ***a healthy respect for*** *guns.*
5 with respect to sth FORMAL **a)** concerning or in relation to: *How can parents make better choices with respect to their children's education?* **b)** used to introduce a new subject, or to return to one that has already been mentioned: *With respect to your second question, it's still too early to know.*
6 in respect of sth FORMAL concerning or in relation to: *In respect of civil rights, all citizens are equal under the law.*
7 with (all due) respect SPOKEN, FORMAL used before disagreeing with someone who is in a position of authority, in order to make what you say seem less rude: *With all due respect, sir, I think you're wrong.*
8 respects polite greetings: *John* ***sends his respects.***
9 pay your (last/final) respects (to sb) to go to someone's funeral
[**Origin:** 1300–1400 Latin *respectus* **act of looking back**, from *respicere* **to look back, consider**] → see also SELF-RESPECT

respect[2] S3 W3 *v.* [T] **1** [not in progressive] to admire someone because they have high standards and good personal qualities such as fairness and honesty: *Most of the students liked and respected Mrs. Moline.* | *I disagree, but I respect your opinion.* | **respect sb for (doing) sth** *Dawn never gives up, and I respect her for that.* | **respect sb as sth** *I respect him as a professional.* **2** to be careful not to do anything against someone's wishes, rights, property etc.: *The doctors respected the dying man's wishes.* | *I teach my kids to respect other people's property.* **3** to not break a rule or law: *We ask students to respect school rules.*

re·spect·a·bil·i·ty /rɪˌspɛktəˈbɪləṭi/ *n.* [U] the quality of being considered morally correct and socially acceptable: *The country has recently regained international respectability.*

re·spect·a·ble /rɪˈspɛktəbəl/ *adj.* **1** having standards of behavior, appearance etc. that are socially acceptable and approved of: *a respectable neighborhood* | *hard-working respectable people* **2** good or satisfactory SYN **decent**: *A "B" is a perfectly respectable grade.* —**respectably** *adv.*

re·spect·ed /rɪˈspɛktɪd/ *adj.* admired by many people because of your work, achievements etc.: *a respected member of the community* | *a* ***highly respected*** *surgeon*

re·spect·ful /rɪˈspɛktfəl/ *adj.* feeling or showing respect: *They listened in respectful silence.* | +**of** *He was always respectful of my independence.* —**respectfully** *adv.*

re·spec·tive /rɪˈspɛktɪv/ *adj.* [only before noun] relating or belonging separately to each person who has been mentioned: *The leaders met to discuss the problems facing their respective countries.*

re·spec·tive·ly /rɪˈspɛktɪvli/ *adv.* FORMAL used to say that the things you are mentioning relate separately to each of two or more people or things mentioned before, in the same order as they were mentioned before: *The cups and saucers cost $5 and $3, respectively* (=the cups cost $5 and the saucers $3).

res·pi·ra·tion /ˌrɛspəˈreɪʃən/ *n.* [U] BIOLOGY the process by which ORGANISMS take in oxygen. In humans, this is done by breathing air into the lungs. → see also ARTIFICIAL RESPIRATION

res·pi·ra·tor /ˈrɛspəˌreɪṭɚ/ *n.* [C] **1** MEDICINE a piece of equipment that pumps air into and out of someone's lungs when they cannot breathe without help: *She's been* ***on a respirator*** *since Monday.* **2** something you wear that covers your nose or mouth so you do not breathe dangerous substances

res·pira·to·ry /ˈrɛsprəˌtɔri/ *adj.* TECHNICAL BIOLOGY relating to breathing: *respiratory diseases* | *the respiratory system*

res·pite /ˈrɛspɪt/ *n.* [singular, U] a short time when something bad stops happening, so that the situation is temporarily better: +**from** *a brief respite from the recent hot weather* [**Origin:** 1200–1300 Old French *respit*, from Medieval Latin *respectus* **act of looking back**]

re·splend·ent /rɪˈsplɛndənt/ *adj.* FORMAL very beautiful, bright, and impressive in appearance: *The bride entered the church,* ***resplendent in*** *a white silk gown.* —**resplendently** *adv.*

R

re·spond /rɪˈspɑnd/ Ac S2 W1 *v.* **1** [I] to react to something that has been said or done SYN **react**: +**to** *The fire department responded to the call within minutes.* | **respond (to sth) by doing sth** *Rebels responded by firing missiles into the market square.* | **respond with sth** *The audience responded with wild applause.* **2** [I,T] to say or write something as a reply SYN **reply**: *I asked again, but still he didn't respond.* | **respond to sth** *You didn't respond to any of my emails.* | **respond that** *Officials responded that the policy was likely to be changed.* ►see THESAURUS box at **answer**[1] **3** [I] to improve as a result of a particular kind of treatment: **respond to treatment/medication etc.** *Her cancer responded well to the new medication.* [**Origin:** 1500–1600 Latin *respondere* **to promise in return, answer**, from *spondere*]

re·spon·dent /rɪˈspɑndənt/ Ac *n.* [C] **1** FORMAL someone who answers questions, especially as part of a scientific study **2** LAW someone who has to defend a case in a law court

reˌsponding ˈvariable *n.* [C] BIOLOGY a DEPENDENT VARIABLE

re·sponse /rɪˈspɑns/ Ac S2 W1 *n.* **1** [C,U] something that is done as a reaction to something that has happened or been said: *The decision provoked an angry response from local residents.* | +**to** *The public response to the new model has been very positive.* | *She said she was writing* ***in response to*** (=as a response to) *an ad in the paper.* **2** [C] something that is said or written as a reply: *I wrote to them a month ago but haven't gotten a response yet.* **3** [C] a part of a religious service that is spoken or sung by the people as an answer to a part that is spoken or sung by the priest **4** [C] BIOLOGY a single reaction to a STIMULUS (=something that causes a reaction in living things), for example the way your body reacts to a particular infection

re·spon·si·bil·i·ty /rɪˌspɑnsəˈbɪləṭi/ S2 W1 *n. plural* **responsibilities**
1 IN CHARGE [U] a duty to be in charge of or take care of something or someone, so that you make decisions and can be blamed if something bad happens: *Kelly's promotion means more money and more responsibility.* | +**for** *a manager with responsibility for over 100 employees* | **take/assume responsibility** *Mike agreed to take responsibility for organizing the party.* | *people in* ***positions of responsibility***
2 BLAME [U] blame for something bad that has happened: **accept/take responsibility (for sth)** *Vince refused to accept responsibility for the accident.* | *No one has yet* ***claimed responsibility*** (=said that they were responsible) *for yesterday's bombing.*
3 STH YOU SHOULD DO [C] something you do because it is your duty, or because it is morally correct: *Nick has a lot of responsibilities at home.* | *We all* ***have a responsibility to*** *protect the environment.* | **sb/sth is your responsibility** *The house is my responsibility. I have to pay for repairs.*

4 a sense of responsibility an ability to behave sensibly and make good judgments in a way that shows you can be trusted: *Activities like these help kids develop a sense of responsibility.*
5 a responsibility to sb a duty to help or serve someone because of your work, position in society etc.: *Parents'* ***primary responsibility*** (=most important responsibility) *is to their children.*

re·spon·si·ble /rɪˈspɑnsəbəl/ S2 W2 *adj.*
1 GUILTY [not before noun] if someone is responsible for an accident, mistake, crime etc., it is their fault or they can be blamed: *The people who are responsible will be caught.* | +**for** *Who was responsible for the accident?* | *If anything goes wrong, I will* ***hold*** *you personally* ***responsible.***
2 IN CHARGE OF [not before noun] having a duty to be in charge of or to take care of someone or something: +**for** *Mills is responsible for a budget of over $5 million.* | *Kari will be responsible for the kids while we're away.*
3 CAUSE [not before noun] something that is responsible for a change, problem, event etc., causes the change, problem etc.: +**for** *The floods were responsible for the deaths of over 1,000 people.*
4 be responsible to sb if you are responsible to someone, that person is in charge of your work and you must explain your actions to them: *Cabinet members are directly responsible to the President.*
5 SENSIBLE sensible and able to make good judgments so that you can be trusted, or showing this quality OPP **irresponsible**: *helping children to become responsible adults* | *a responsible attitude*
6 JOB a responsible job or position is one in which the ability to make good judgments and decisions is needed

reˌsponsible deˈvelopment *n.* [U] the process of changing social systems and improving city areas in a responsible way, so that progress is made without damage to the environment

re·spon·si·bly /rɪˈspɑnsəbli/ *adv.* in a sensible way that makes people trust you: *You can trust Jamie to act responsibly.*

re·spon·sive /rɪˈspɑnsɪv/ Ac *adj.* **1** ready to react in a useful or helpful way OPP **unresponsive**: +**to** *We have to be more responsive to the needs of the customer.* **2** easily controlled, and reacting quickly in the way that you want: *a car with responsive brakes* **3** willing to give answers or show your feelings about something OPP **unresponsive**: *She's a very responsive baby.* —**responsively** *adv.* —**responsiveness** *n.* [U]

rest[1] /rɛst/ S1 W1 *n.*
1 the rest what is left after everything else has been used, dealt with etc.: *Two students got A's, but the rest didn't do very well on the test.* | *Who ate the rest of the pizza?* | +**of** *She will have to take medication for the rest of her life.*
2 RELAXING [singular, U] a period of time when you can relax or sleep: *You need to* ***get some rest.*** | *Try and* ***give*** *your ankle* ***a rest*** *so it will heal better.* | *They decided to stop driving and* ***take a*** *short* ***rest.*** | **well-earned/well-deserved rest** (=one that you deserve because you have been working hard)
3 SUPPORT [C] an object used to support something, especially a part of your body or an object while it is not being used: *seats with adjustable head rests*
4 come to rest a) to stop moving: *The plane skidded along the runway and came to rest in a field.* **b)** if your eyes come to rest on something, you stop looking around and look at that one thing
5 put sb's mind to/at rest to make someone feel less anxious or worried
6 at rest TECHNICAL not moving: *The mass was measured while the object was at rest.*
7 lay/put sth to rest to finally prove that an idea is not true and to end discussion or argument about it: *The public's doubts have now been laid to rest.*
8 no rest for the wicked/weary SPOKEN, HUMOROUS said by someone who is tired but who has a lot of things that they must do
9 lay sb to rest an expression meaning "to bury someone who is dead," used when you want to avoid saying this directly: *She was laid to rest next to her husband.*
10 MUSIC [C] **a)** ENG. LANG. ARTS a period of silence of a particular length in a piece of music **b)** a written sign that shows how long the period of silence should be → see picture at MUSICAL[1]
[**Origin:** (2–10) 1400–1500 French *resle*, from *rester* **to remain**, from Latin *restare*]

rest[2] S3 W3 *v.*
1 RELAX **a)** [I] to stop doing working or doing an activity for a time, and usually sit down or lie down: *We stopped and rested for a while at the top of the hill.* **b) rest your feet/legs/eyes etc.** to stop using a part of your body because it is feeling sore or tired
2 GIVE SUPPORT [T always + adv./prep.] to support an object or part of your body by putting it on or against something: **rest sth against/on etc.** *He rested his head on my shoulder.*
3 LIE/LEAN ON [I always + adv./prep.] to lie or lean on something for support: +**against/on etc.** *Their bikes were resting against the fence.* | *He slept peacefully, his head resting on one arm.* ▶see THESAURUS box at **lean**[1]
4 rest assured (that) used to tell someone not to worry, because what you say about a situation is true: *You can rest assured that the car will be ready on time.*
5 rest easy to relax and stop worrying: *I can rest easy, knowing that everything is being taken care of.*
6 sb will not rest until used to say that someone will not be satisfied until something happens: *We will not rest until our demands for justice are met.*
7 COURT OF LAW [I,T] if one side rests or rests its case in a court of law, they stop giving information because they believe they have said enough to prove what they want to prove: *The defense plans to* ***rest its case*** *tomorrow.*
8 I rest my case SPOKEN, HUMOROUS said when something happens or is said that proves that you were right
9 DEAD PERSON [I always + adv./prep.] if a dead person rests somewhere, they are buried there: **final/last resting place** (=the place where someone is buried) → see also RIP
10 rest on your laurels DISAPPROVING to not make any further effort because you are so satisfied with what you have done: *In such a competitive market, a business can't afford to rest on its laurels.*

rest on/upon sth *phr. v.* **1** FORMAL to depend on or be based on something: *Her argument rests on the assumption that the two systems are identical.* **2** if your eyes rest on something, you look at it

rest with sb *phr. v.* if a decision or responsibility rests with someone, they are in charge of it: *Responsibility for training rests with you.*

ˈrest ˌarea *n.* [C] a place near a road where you can stop and rest, use the toilet etc. SYN **rest stop**

re·start /riˈstɑrt/ *v.* [T] to start something such as a machine, a process etc. again after it has stopped: *attempts to restart the peace talks* —**restart** /ˈristɑrt/ *n.* [C usually singular]

re·state /riˈsteɪt/ *v.* [T] to say something again or in a different way, so that it is clearer or more strongly expressed: *The President restated his intention to veto the bill.* —**restatement** *n.* [C,U]

res·tau·rant /ˈrɛsˌtrɑnt, ˈrɛstəˌrɑnt, ˈrɛstərənt/ S1 W2 *n.* [C] a place where you can buy and eat a meal: *a Chinese restaurant* | *We had lunch* ***at a*** *fast-food* ***restaurant.*** [**Origin:** 1800–1900 French *restaurer* **to restore**, from Latin *restaurare* **to renew, rebuild**]

THESAURUS

cafe/coffee shop a place where you can get drinks, cakes, and small meals
fast food restaurant one where you can get meals such as hamburgers, french fries etc.
diner a restaurant where you can eat cheap and simple food
cafeteria a place at work or school where you can get a meal which you take to a table yourself
bistro a small restaurant or bar, especially one serving French-style food

At a restaurant
waiter/waitress/server a man or woman who serves food and drink at the tables in a restaurant
menu a list of all the kinds of food that are available
order to ask for particular food or drink to be brought to you: *Are you ready to order?* | *I ordered a salad.*
check/bill a list showing how much you have to pay for the food you have eaten
leave a tip to leave extra money for the waiter or waitress
service is included used, especially on a bill, to say that you do not have to leave extra money for the waiter or waitress, because it is already included in the cost of your meal

res·tau·ra·teur /ˌrɛstərə'tɚ/ also **res·tau·ran·teur** /ˌrɛstərɑn'tɚ/ *n.* [C] someone who owns and manages a restaurant

rest·ed /'rɛstɪd/ *adj.* [not before noun] feeling healthier, stronger, or calmer because you have had time to relax: *We came back from the trip feeling very rested.*

rest·ful /'rɛstfəl/ *adj.* peaceful and quiet, and making you feel relaxed: *restful music* —**restfully** *adv.*

'rest home *n.* [C] a place where old or sick people can live and be taken care of → see also NURSING HOME

res·ti·tu·tion /ˌrɛstə'tuʃən/ *n.* [U] FORMAL the act of giving back something that was lost or stolen to its owner, or of paying for damage: *The defendant will pay $350,000 in restitution to the victims.*

res·tive /'rɛstɪv/ *adj.* FORMAL impatient because of strict rules or laws, and difficult to control: *The southern region was growing increasingly restive.* —**restively** *adv.* —**restiveness** *n.* [U]

rest·less /'rɛstlɪs/ *adj.* **1** unable or unwilling to keep still, especially because you are nervous or bored: *The kids quickly **grew restless*** (=became restless) *and impatient.* **2** unwilling to stay in one place or do one thing, and always wanting new experiences: *his restless imagination* **3 a restless night** a night during which you cannot sleep or rest —**restlessly** *adj.* —**restlessness** *n.* [U]

re·stock /ˌri'stɑk, 'ristɑk/ *v.* [I,T] to bring in more supplies to replace those that have been used: **restock sth with sth** *Some farmers restocked their farms with imported cattle.*

res·to·ra·tion /ˌrɛstə'reɪʃən/ Ac *n.* [C,U] **1** the act of thoroughly repairing something such as an old building or a piece of furniture so that it looks the same as it did when it was first made: *restoration work* | **+of** *a major restoration of the governor's mansion* **2** the act of bringing back a law, tax, or system of government: **+of** *the restoration of law and order in the region* **3** LAW the act of officially giving something back to its former owner SYN **return**: *Some Native Americans are demanding the restoration of their lands.*

re·stor·a·tive /rɪ'stɔrət̬ɪv/ *adj.* FORMAL making you feel healthier or stronger: *the restorative power of sleep*

re·store /rɪ'stɔr/ Ac W3 *v.* [T]
1 FORMER SITUATION to make a good state, condition, ability, feeling etc. start to exist again: *Utility companies worked for hours to restore power supplies.* | **restore hope/confidence/calm etc.** *The legislature wants to restore the public's confidence in the economy.* | **restore peace/order/discipline etc.** *The National Guard could not immediately restore order.* | **restore sb's sight/hearing etc.** *Can the operation restore his hearing?*
2 REPAIR to repair an old building, piece of furniture, painting etc. so that it is in its original condition: *She's restoring her grandmother's antique dresser.* ►see THESAURUS box at **repair**[1]
3 restore sb/sth to sth to make someone or something be in the condition they were in before, after a period when they have had problems: *The 17th-century house has been **restored to its former glory*** (=made as beautiful as it first was). | **restore sb to power/the throne** (=to make someone president, king, or queen again after a period when they have not been in power)
4 BRING BACK A LAW to bring back a law, tax, right etc.: *a campaign to restore the death penalty*
5 GIVE STH BACK LAW to give back to someone something that was lost or taken from them: **restore sth to sb** *The treaty restored the island of Okinawa to Japan.*
[**Origin:** 1200–1300 Old French *restorer*, from Latin *restaurare* **to renew, rebuild**]

re·stor·er /rɪ'stɔrɚ/ *n.* [C] someone who repairs an old building, piece of furniture, painting etc. so that it is in its original condition: *antique furniture restorers*

re·strain /rɪ'streɪn/ Ac *v.* [T] **1** to control your emotions, especially anger: **restrain yourself (from doing sth)** *She could barely restrain herself from hitting him.* **2** to physically stop someone from doing something or from moving, especially by using force: *It took four officers to restrain Wilson.* **3** to prevent someone from doing something: *an order restraining the union from striking* **4** to control or limit something that tends to increase: *The economy's growth will slow down enough to restrain inflation.* [**Origin:** 1300–1400 Old French *restreindre*, from Latin *restringere*, from *stringere* **to tie tightly, press together**]

re·strained /rɪ'streɪnd/ Ac *adj.* **1** behavior that is restrained is calm and controlled and not too emotional: *She replied in a low, restrained voice.* **2** not too brightly colored or decorated: *restrained earthy shades of yellow*

re'straining ˌorder *n.* [C] an official legal document that prevents someone from doing something

re·straint /rɪ'streɪnt/ Ac *n.* **1** [U] the ability not to do something that you very much want to do, because it would not be sensible: *I admire your restraint.* | **show/exercise/practice restraint** *The police exercised great restraint during the demonstration.* **2** [C usually plural, U] a rule or principle that limits people's activity or behavior: **+on** *restraints on exports* | **impose/lift restraints** (=make or remove rules that control something) **3** [C] something that prevents someone from moving freely, so that they are safe: *a new type of restraint used in children's car seats* **4** [U] FORMAL physical force used to stop someone from moving freely, especially because they are likely to be violent

re·strict /rɪ'strɪkt/ Ac W3 *v.* [T] **1** to limit or control the size, amount, or range of something: *The new law restricts the sale of hand guns.* | **restrict sth to sth** *We will restrict class sizes to 20 students.* | *Imports were **severely restricted**.* **2 restrict yourself to sth** to allow yourself to have only a particular amount of something, or do only a particular type of activity: *He's restricting himself to two cigarettes a day.* **3** to limit or control the movement of someone or something: **restrict sb/sth to sth** *Her disability restricts her to a wheelchair.* **4 restrict sth to sb** to allow only a particular group of people to do or have something: *Should we restrict these violent images to adults?* [**Origin:** 1400–1500 Latin, past participle of *restringere*, from *stringere* **to tie tightly, press together**]

re·strict·ed /rɪ'strɪktɪd/ Ac *adj.* **1** limited or controlled, especially by laws or rules: *a restricted diet* | *restricted parking* | **be restricted to sb/sth** *Visiting hours are restricted to evenings and weekends only.* **2** small or limited in size, area, or amount: *I only have restricted movement in my leg.* | *We work in a very restricted space.* **3 be restricted to sth/sb** to only affect a limited area, group etc.: *The damage was restricted to the west side of town.* **4** a restricted area, document or information can only be seen or used by a particular group of people because it is secret or dangerous: *documents containing restricted data*

re·stric·tion /rɪ'strɪkʃən/ Ac W3 *n.* **1** [C usually plural] a rule or system that limits or controls what you can do or what is allowed to happen: **+on** *restrictions on weapon sales to the region* | *Some states have **imposed restrictions*** (=made restrictions) *on liquor imports.* | ***Restrictions** on trade **were lifted*** (=were removed). | **tough/tight restrictions** *tighter restrictions on the sale of nuclear materials* ►see THESAURUS box at **rule**[1] **2** [U]

R

the act of restricting the size, amount, or range of something

re·stric·tive /rɪˈstrɪktɪv/ Ac *adj.* tending to restrict particular types of activity too much: *The labor laws are too restrictive.* | *a restrictive diet*

reˌstrictive ˈclause also **reˌstrictive ˈrelative ˌclause** *n.* [C] ENG. LANG. ARTS a part of a sentence that says which person or thing is meant. For example, in "the man who came to dinner," the phrase "who came to dinner" is a restrictive clause.

reˌstrictive ˈcovenant *n.* [C] LAW a legal restriction on what the person who owns or uses land can do with it, so that its value and the value of land next to it does not fall

reˌstrictive ˈpractices *n.* [plural] **1** unreasonable limits that one TRADE UNION puts on the kind of work that members of other trade unions are allowed to do **2** an unfair trade agreement between companies that limits the amount of competition there is

ˈrest room, restroom *n.* [C] a room with a toilet, in a public place such as a restaurant, office, or theater

re·struc·ture /ˌriˈstrʌktʃɚ/ Ac *v.* [T] to change the way in which something such as a government, business, or system is organized: *plans to restructure the company*

ˈrest stop *n.* [C] a place near a road where you can stop and rest, use the toilet etc.

re·sult¹ /rɪˈzʌlt/ S2 W1 *n.* **1** [C,U] something that happens or exists because of something that happened before: **+of** *Her cough is the result of years of smoking.* | *Elizabeth suffers memory loss* ***as a result of*** *Alzheimer's disease.* | *More people are using cars,* ***with the result that*** *towns are becoming more polluted.* | **end/final/net result** *The end result of the new regulations will be cleaner air.* | *Global warming is* ***a direct result of*** *human activity.* | *Will the talks* ***produce*** *lasting* ***results?*** | *For* ***best results,*** *use only fresh ingredients.*

THESAURUS

consequences the things that happen as a result of an action, event etc.: *The choice between finishing high school and dropping out has enormous consequences for your future job prospects.*
effect a change that is the result of something: *the harmful effects of pollution*
outcome the final result of a meeting, election, war etc.: *the final outcome of the talks*
upshot the final result of a situation: *The upshot of all this was that the trial had to be delayed.*

2 [C] the final number of points, votes etc. at the end of a competition, game, or election: *the election results* | **+of** *the results of the competition* **3** [C] a piece of information obtained by examining, studying, or calculating something: **+of** *the results of a survey of public opinion* | *My doctor wants to talk to me about my* ***test results.*** | **a positive/negative result** (=one that shows that something is present or happens, or that it is not present or does not happen) **4 results** [plural] **a)** things that happen successfully because of your efforts: *a teacher who knows how to* ***get results*** *from students* **b)** a company's results are the accounts that show how successful it has been over a period of time, usually a year

result² W2 *v.* [I] to happen or exist because of something that happened before: *If you work too long without taking breaks, serious back problems can result.* | **sth results from sth** *injuries resulting from car accidents* [**Origin:** 1400–1500 Latin *resultare* **to jump back, result**, from *saltare* **to jump**]

result in sth *phr. v.* to make something happen SYN **cause**: *Improved farming technology has resulted in larger harvests.*

re·sult·ant /rɪˈzʌltənt, -tˀnt/ *adj.* [only before noun] FORMAL happening or existing as a result of something: *The blast and resultant fire destroyed the building.*

re·sume /rɪˈzum/ W3 *v.* **1** [I,T] FORMAL to start doing something again after stopping or being interrupted: *She hopes to resume work after the baby is born.* **2** [I] if an activity or process resumes, it starts again after a pause: *The trial will resume on Wednesday morning.* **3 resume your seat/place/position** FORMAL to go back to the seat, place, or position where you were before [**Origin:** 1400–1500 Old French *resumer*, from Latin *resumere*, from *sumere* **to take**]

ré·su·mé /ˈrɛzəˌmeɪ, ˌrɛzəˈmeɪ/ *n.* [C] **1** a short written description of your education and your previous jobs, that you send to an employer when you are looking for a new job **2** [+ of] a short description of something such as an article or speech, that gives the main points but no details SYN **summary**

re·sump·tion /rɪˈzʌmpʃən/ *n.* [singular, U] FORMAL the act of starting an activity again after a pause: **+of** *the resumption of classes after Spring Break*

re·sur·face /ˌriˈsɚfɪs/ *v.* **1** [I] to be seen, heard, or noticed again after having disappeared: *One of the missing paintings suddenly resurfaced.* | *Rumors of a merger resurfaced.* **2** [T] to put a new surface on a road **3** [I] to come back up to the surface of the water

re·sur·gence /rɪˈsɚdʒəns/ *n.* [singular, U] the growth of a belief or activity that was common in the past, especially one that is harmful: *the right's political resurgence* | **+of** *There has been a resurgence of interest in his art.* [**Origin:** 1800–1900 *resurgent* (18–21 centuries), from Latin *resurgere* **to rise again**] —**resurgent** *adj.*

res·ur·rect /ˌrɛzəˈrɛkt/ *v.* [T] **1** to make something successful, strong, noticed etc. again: *He has been trying to resurrect his political career.* **2** [T usually passive] to bring someone back to life after they have died

res·ur·rec·tion /ˌrɛzəˈrɛkʃən/ *n.* **1 the resurrection** also **the Resurrection** the return of Jesus Christ to life after his death on the CROSS, which is one of the main beliefs of the Christian religion **2** [U] also **(the) Resurrection (of the Dead)** the return of all dead people to life at the end of the world **3** [U] a situation in which something returns to its previous state or condition: *the city's economic resurrection*

re·sus·ci·tate /rɪˈsʌsəˌteɪt/ *v.* [T] to make someone breathe again or become conscious after they have almost died [**Origin:** 1500–1600 Latin, past participle of *resuscitare*, from *suscitare* **to cause to move around**] —**resuscitation** /rɪˌsʌsəˈteɪʃən/ *n.* [U]

re·tail¹ /ˈriteɪl/ S3 W3 *n.* [U] the sale of goods in stores to customers, for their own use and not for selling to anyone else: *I've worked in retail for two years.* | **retail trade/business etc.** *He owns a chain of retail stores.* → see also WHOLESALE

retail² *v.* **1 retail for/at sth** to be sold at a particular price in stores: *The wine usually retails at $10 a bottle.* **2** [T] TECHNICAL to sell goods in stores **3** /rɪˈteɪl/ [T] FORMAL to tell people about something that happened or is happening [**Origin:** (1–2) 1300–1400 Old French *retaillier* **to divide into pieces**, from *taillier* **to cut**]

retail³ *adv.* if you buy or sell something retail, you buy or sell it in a store: *We bought it retail.*

re·tail·er /ˈriˌteɪlɚ/ W3 *n.* [C] a person or business that sells goods to customers in a store: *a women's clothing retailer*

re·tail·ing /ˈriˌteɪlɪŋ/ *n.* [U] the business of selling goods in stores: *There may be job losses in retailing.*

re·tain /rɪˈteɪn/ Ac W3 *v.* [T] FORMAL **1** to keep or continue to have something, for example a quality, right, or position: *The town has retained much of its charm.* | **retain control/possession of sth** *Russia wants to retain control of the islands.* | **retain your independence/freedom/identity etc.** *The local people are struggling to retain their identity.* → see also RETENTION **2** to prevent heat, liquid etc. from escaping: *The building is designed to retain heat.* **3** to keep or continue to have a document or other object, and not lose it, sell it, or throw it away: *Retain copies of tax documents for at least three years.* **4** to keep facts in your memory: *She has lost the ability to retain most* *short term memories.* **5** if you retain a lawyer or other professional, you pay them to work for you now and in the future **6** if a company retains workers, it continues to employ them, especially over a long period [**Origin:** 1300–1400 Old French *retenir*, from Latin *retinere*, from *tenere* **to hold**]

re·tain·er /rɪ'teɪnɚ/ Ac *n.* [C] **1** ECONOMICS an amount of money paid to someone, especially a lawyer, for work that they are going to do: *He keeps the finest lawyers in the city **on retainer**.* **2** a plastic and wire object that you wear in your mouth to make your teeth stay straight **3** OLD USE a servant, especially one who has always worked for a particular person or family

re'taining ˌwall *n.* [C] a wall that is built to prevent land or water from moving beyond a particular place

re·take¹ /ˌri'teɪk/, *past tense* **retook** /-'tʊk/, *past participle* **retaken** /-'teɪkən/ *v.* [T] **1** to get control of an area again in a war: *Government forces have retaken control of the city.* **2** to film or photograph something again **3** to take a test again because you have previously failed it

re·take² /'riteɪk/ *n.* [C] an act of filming or photographing something again

re·tal·i·ate /rɪ'tæliˌeɪt/ *v.* [I] to do something bad to someone because they have done something bad to you: **retaliate by doing sth** *The demonstrators retaliated by attacking the police station.* | **retaliate against sb** *The terrorists have threatened to retaliate against the government.* [**Origin:** 1600–1700 Late Latin, past participle of *retaliare*, from *talio* **suitable punishment**]

re·tal·i·a·tion /rɪˌtæli'eɪʃən/ *n.* [U] action against someone who has done something bad to you: *O'Connor was shot **in retaliation for** yesterday's attack.* | +**against** *The president ordered immediate military retaliation against the terrorists.*

re·tal·i·a·to·ry /rɪ'tæliəˌtɔri/ *adj.* [usually before noun] FORMAL done against someone because they have harmed you: *retaliatory action*

re·tard /rɪ'tɑrd/ *v.* [T] FORMAL to delay the development of something, or to make something happen more slowly than expected SYN **slow down**: *Cold weather retards the growth of many plants.* —**retardation** /ˌritɑr'deɪʃən/ *n.* [U]

retch /rɛtʃ/ *v.* [I] to try to VOMIT, or feel as if you are going to VOMIT when you do not: *The sight of the body made me retch.*

re·tell /ri'tɛl/ *v. past tense and past participle* **retold** /-'toʊld/ [T] to tell a story again, often in a different way or in a different language

re·ten·tion /rɪ'tɛnʃən/ Ac *n.* [U] **1** PHYSICS the ability or tendency of something to hold liquid, heat etc. within itself: *One of the side effects of the drug is water retention.* **2** FORMAL the act of keeping something: +**of** *The UN voted for the retention of sanctions against the country.* **3** the ability to keep something in your memory: *efforts to improve retention among students*

re·ten·tive /rɪ'tɛntɪv/ Ac *adj.* a retentive memory or mind is able to hold facts and remember them —**retentively** *adv.* —**retentiveness** *n.* [U]

re·think /ˌri'θɪŋk/ *v. past tense and past participle* **rethought** /-'θɔt/ [I,T] to think about a plan or idea again, in order to decide if any changes should be made: *Maybe it's time to rethink our priorities.*

ret·i·cent /'rɛt̬əsənt/ *adj.* unwilling to talk about what you feel or what you know: +**about** *Shaw has always been reticent about discussing his private life.* [**Origin:** 1600–1700 Latin, present participle of *reticere* **to keep silent**, from *tacere*] —**reticence** *n.* [U] —**reticently** *adv.*

re·tic·u·lat·ed /rɪ'tɪkyəˌleɪt̬ɪd/ *adj.* TECHNICAL forming or covered with a pattern of squares and lines that looks like a net —**reticulation** /rɪˌtɪkyə'leɪʃən/ *n.* [C,U]

ret·i·na /'rɛt˺nə/ *n.* [C] BIOLOGY the area at the back of your eye that receives light and sends an image of what you see to your brain [**Origin:** 1300–1400 Medieval Latin] → see picture at EYE¹

ret·i·nue /'rɛt˺nˌu/ *n.* [C] a group of helpers or supporters who are traveling with an important person: *He traveled with a retinue of aides.*

re·tire /rɪ'taɪɚ/ S2 W3 *v.*
1 STOP WORKING [I,T] to stop working, usually because of old age, or to make someone do this: *At 75, Stevens has no plans to retire.* | **retire from sth** *DiMaggio retired from baseball after the '51 season.* | **retire at 60/62/65 etc.** *Most people retire at 65.* | **retire as sth** *Walker retired as chairman of the company in 2006.* | *Jill **retired early*** (=retired before she was old) *to care for her elderly mother.*
2 QUIET PLACE [I] FORMAL to go away to a quiet place: *The jury has retired to consider its verdict.*
3 BED [I] FORMAL to go to bed
4 SPORTS NUMBER [T] if a team retires a player's number or number, they do not use it anymore, in order to show respect to that player
5 BASEBALL [T] in baseball, if a PITCHER retires the BATTER, he makes him STRIKE out
6 ARMY [I] FORMAL to move back from a battle after being defeated
[**Origin:** 1500–1600 Old French *tirer* **to pull**] → see also RETREAT

re·tired /rɪ'taɪɚd/ *adj.* having stopped working, usually because of your age: *a retired teacher* | *My aunt and uncle are both retired.*

re·tir·ee /rɪˌtaɪə'ri/ *n.* [C] someone who has stopped working, usually because of their age

re·tire·ment /rɪ'taɪɚmənt/ S3 W3 *n.* **1** [C,U] the act of retiring from your job, or the time when you do this: *Stitch announced her retirement this year.* | +**from** *his retirement from politics* | *Dr. Franklin **took early retirement*** (=retired at a younger age than is usual) *and moved to Hawaii.* **2** [singular, U] the period after you have retired: *Ask yourself how much income you want to have **in retirement**.* | *He is planning to **come out of retirement** for one last race.*

re'tirement comˌmunity *n.* [C] an area where old people can live independently in separate houses, but close to each other, and where there are various services and activities available to them

re'tirement ˌhome *n.* [C] a place where old people live and are cared for when they are too old to look after themselves → see also NURSING HOME

re'tirement ˌplan *n.* [C] a system for saving money for your retirement, done either through your employer or arranged by yourself → see also PENSION PLAN

re·tir·ing /rɪ'taɪərɪŋ/ *adj.* **1** ESPECIALLY WRITTEN not wanting to be with other people, and tending to avoid social situations, especially with people you do not know SYN **shy** OPP **outgoing** ►see THESAURUS box at **shy¹** **2 the retiring president/manager/director etc.** a president, manager etc. who is soon going to leave their job SYN **outgoing**

re·tool /ri'tul/ *v.* **1** [T] INFORMAL to organize something in a new way: *They've successfully retooled their corporate image.* **2** [I,T] to change or replace the machines or tools in a factory

re·tort¹ /rɪ'tɔrt/ *v.* [T] to reply quickly, in an angry or humorous way: *"That's ridiculous," retorted Simpson.*

retort² *n.* [C] **1** a short and angry or humorous reply: *a nasty retort* **2** CHEMISTRY a bottle with a long narrow bent neck, used for heating chemicals

re·touch /ri'tʌtʃ/ *v.* [T] to make a picture or photograph look more pleasing by painting over unattractive marks or making small changes using a computer

re·trace /ri'treɪs/ *v.* [T] **1 retrace your steps/path/route** to go back exactly the way you have come: *I retraced my steps looking for my keys.* **2** to repeat exactly the same trip that someone else has made: *Riders can retrace the trail taken by the Tour de France.* **3** to do something exactly in the way that you or someone else did it before, in order to get information about what happened in the past: *He hopes to find her by retracing her movements before she disappeared.*

re·tract /rɪˈtrækt/ *v.* **1** [T] to make an official statement saying that something which you said previously is not true SYN **withdraw**: *Later, he retracted his remarks and apologized.* **2** [I,T] BIOLOGY if part of a machine or an animal's body retracts or is retracted, it moves back into the main part SYN **withdraw**: *The cat retracted its claws.* | *One of the plane's wheels wouldn't retract.*

re·tract·a·ble /rɪˈtræktəbəl/ *adj.* **1** a retractable part of something can be pulled back into the main part: *a knife with a retractable blade* **2** having a retractable part: *a retractable razor*

re·trac·tion /rɪˈtrækʃən/ *n.* **1** [C] an official statement saying that something which someone said previously is not true: *The newspaper was forced to publish a retraction.* **2** [U] the act of an animal or machine pulling something back in to its main part

re·train /riˈtreɪn/ *v.* [I,T] to learn or to teach someone the skills that are needed to do a different job: *a federal program to retrain federal workers* | **retrain as sth** *She's hoping to retrain as a teacher.* —**retraining** *n.* [U]

R

re·tread¹ /ˈritrɛd/ *n.* [C] **1** a retreaded tire **2** INFORMAL something that is made or done again, with a few changes added: **+of** *retreads of old TV shows* **3** INFORMAL someone who has been trained to do work which is different from what they did before

re·tread² /riˈtrɛd/ *v.* [T] to put a new rubber surface on an old tire

re·treat¹ /rɪˈtrit/ *v.* [I]

1 CHANGE YOUR DECISION to change your decision about a promise you have publicly made or about a principle you have stated, because the situation has become too difficult: *He was forced to retreat and accept a compromise.* | **reatreat from sth** *The administration was accused of retreating from its promises.*

2 OF AN ARMY to move away from the enemy after being defeated in battle: *The British army retreated into the hills.*

3 MOVE AWAY to move away from or stop being involved in a situation in which you are afraid, embarrassed, or unhappy: *He saw the group of women and retreated.* | **retreat to/from etc. sth** *Ralph retreated upstairs to his room.* | *She chose to retreat into her own imaginary world.*

4 BECOME SMALLER LITERARY if an area of water, snow, or land retreats, it gradually gets smaller: *The flood waters are slowly retreating.*

5 BUSINESS TECHNICAL if the price of STOCKS, INVESTMENTS etc. retreat, they go down

retreat² *n.*

1 CHANGE OF INTENTION [C,U] an act of changing your decision about a promise you publicly made or a principle you stated, because the situation has become too difficult: *the regime's retreat in the face of international criticism* | **+from** *Today's statement is a retreat from their previous position.*

2 OF AN ARMY [C,U] a movement away from the enemy after a defeat in battle OPP **advance**: **+from** *Napoleon's retreat from Moscow* | *The soldiers* ***made a retreat*** *to a nearby town.* | *Rebel soldiers are* ***in full retreat*** (=moving back quickly).

3 MOVEMENT BACK [C,U] a movement away from a situation that is frightening, unpleasant, or embarrassing: *Retreat was the only option when my mom got mad.* | **make/beat a (hasty) retreat** (=move back quickly)

4 PLACE [C] a place you can go to that is quiet or safe: *the family's summer retreat*

5 THOUGHT AND PRAYER [C] a period of time that you spend praying, studying, or thinking about things in a quiet place: *We're* ***going on a retreat*** *with the church.*

6 COVERING SMALLER AREA [singular, U] a gradual movement backward of an area of water, snow, or land so that it gets smaller and covers less of a place: *Ten thousand years ago, the ice began its retreat.*

7 BUSINESS [C] TECHNICAL an occasion when the price of STOCKS, INVESTMENTS etc. goes down

re·trench /rɪˈtrɛntʃ/ *v.* [I] if a government, group, or organization retrenches, it spends less money —**retrenchment** *n.* [C,U]

re·tri·al /ˌriˈtraɪəl, ˈritraɪəl/ *n.* [C] LAW a process of judging a law case in court again, usually because a mistake was made before or because no judgment was reached: *The District Attorney has asked the judge for a retrial.*

ret·ri·bu·tion /ˌrɛtrəˈbyuʃən/ *n.* [singular, U] severe punishment SYN **punishment**: *Employees cannot express their opinions without* ***fear of retribution.*** | **+for** *The family is seeking retribution for his death.* | *The boy's parents believe his illness is* ***divine retribution*** (=punishment from God) *for their sins.* —**retributive** /rɪˈtrɪbyət̬ɪv/ *adj.*

re·triev·al /rɪˈtrivəl/ *n.* [U] **1** COMPUTERS the process of getting back information from a computer system SYN **recovery**: *information retrieval* | **+of** *the storage and retrieval of data* **2** FORMAL [U] the act of getting back something you have lost or left somewhere: *the retrieval of a NASA research satellite*

re·trieve /rɪˈtriv/ *v.* **1** [T] FORMAL to pick up or get back something that has been lost or has been left in the wrong place SYN **recover**: *She bent down to retrieve her earring.* | **retrieve sth from sth** *Divers retrieved a body from the icy river on Wednesday.* **2** [T] COMPUTERS to get back information that has been stored in the memory of a computer **3** [I,T] if a dog retrieves, it finds and brings back birds and small animals its owner has shot [**Origin:** 1400–1500 Old French *retrover* **to find again**, from *trover* **to find**] —**retrievable** *adj.*

re·triev·er /rɪˈtrivɚ/ *n.* [C] a breed of dog can be trained to retrieve birds that its owner has shot → see also GOLDEN RETRIEVER, LABRADOR

ret·ro¹ /ˈrɛtroʊ/ *adj.* deliberately using styles of fashion or design from the recent past: *The room has a retro look.*

retro² *n.* [C] INFORMAL a RETROSPECTIVE

retro- /rɛtroʊ, -trə/ *prefix* back toward the past or an earlier state: *retroactive* (=having an effect on things already done) | *retrograde* (=returning to an earlier and worse state)

ret·ro·ac·tive /ˌrɛtroʊˈæktɪv/ *adj.* FORMAL LAW a law or decision that is retroactive is made now but is effective from a particular date in the past: *a retroactive pay increase* | **+to** *The legislation is retroactive to June 1st.* —**retroactively** *adv.*

ret·ro·fit /ˈrɛtroʊˌfɪt/ *v.* [T] to improve a machine, piece of equipment etc. by putting new and better parts in it after it is made: **retrofit sth with sth** *It is not possible to retrofit an existing car with air bags.* —**retrofit** *n.* [C] —**retrofitting** *n.* [U]

ret·ro·flex /ˈrɛtrəˌflɛks/ *adj.* ENG. LANG. ARTS a retroflex speech sound is made with the end of your tongue pointing backward and up

ret·ro·grade /ˈrɛtrəˌgreɪd/ *adj.* FORMAL **1** involving a return to an earlier and worse situation SYN **backward**: *retrograde racial politics* | *The closure of the factories is seen as* ***a retrograde step.*** **2** TECHNICAL moving backward SYN **backward**: *Venus's rotation is retrograde.* [**Origin:** 1300–1400 Latin *retrogradus*, from *gradi* **to go**]

ret·ro·gress /ˌrɛtrəˈgrɛs/ *v.* [I + to] FORMAL to go back to an earlier and worse state SYN **regress**

ret·ro·gres·sion /ˌrɛtrəˈgrɛʃən/ *n.* [singular, U] FORMAL the action or process of going back to an earlier and worse state SYN **regression**: **+to** *a retrogression to 19th century attitudes toward science*

ret·ro·gres·sive /ˌrɛtrəˈgrɛsɪv◂/ *adj.* FORMAL returning to an earlier and worse situation: *a retrogressive plan* —**retrogressively** *adv.*

ret·ro·spect /ˈrɛtrəˌspɛkt/ *n.* **in retrospect** thinking back to a time in the past, especially with the advantage of knowing more now than you did then: *In retrospect, I would have handled it differently.*

ret·ro·spec·tion /ˌrɛtrəˈspɛkʃən/ *n.* [U] FORMAL thought about the past

ret·ro·spec·tive[1] /ˌrɛtrəˈspɛktɪv/ *adj.* [only before noun] relating to or thinking about the past: *a retrospective look at the 1974 election*

retrospective[2] *n.* [C] something that collects some of the best work an ARTIST, singer, FILMMAKER etc. has done, for example in a single show in a MUSEUM: +**of** *a retrospective of the filmmaker's work*

ret·ro·vi·rus /ˈrɛtroʊˌvaɪrəs/ *n.* [C] BIOLOGY a VIRUS (=very small living thing that causes an infectious illness) that holds its GENETIC information in the chemical substance RNA, rather than in DNA, for example the one that causes AIDS

re·try /riˈtraɪ/ *v.* **retried, retrying** **1** [T] LAW to judge a person or a law case again in court: *The case was later retried.* **2** [I] to do an action on a computer again after it has failed: *Please retry using a different password.* **3** [I] to try to do something again after the first attempt was not successful

ret·si·na /rɛtˈsinə/ *n.* [U] a Greek wine that tastes like the RESIN (=juice) of certain trees

re·turn[1] /rɪˈtɚn/ S2 W1 *v.*

1 GO BACK [I] to go back to a place where you were before, or come back from a place where you have just been: *It was a bright, hot day when she returned.* | +**to** *After receiving her law degree, she returned to Georgia.* | +**from** *Amador had just returned from an appointment.* | *I travel a lot, often* ***returning home*** *late at night.* | *Many of the villagers will leave,* ***never to return.***

2 GIVE BACK [T] **a)** to give something back to its owner, or put something back in its place: *I've got to go by Blockbuster and return those tapes.* | **return sth to sb/sth** *Part of the job was returning borrowed books to the shelves.* **b)** to take something back to the store where you bought it, because you do not like it, it does not fit etc.: *I'm going to return these shoes – they're a little tight.*

3 HAPPEN AGAIN [I] to start to exist again or to have an effect again: *If the pain returns, take two of the tablets every four hours.* | +**to** *Republicans warned against returning to isolationism.*

4 START AGAIN [I] to go back to an activity, job etc. that you were doing before you stopped or were interrupted: +**to** *Santa Anna eventually returned to power in 1853.* | *Yeltsin was anxious to* ***return to work*** *after his bout with pneumonia.*

5 PREVIOUS STATE [I] to be in a previous state or condition again: *Slowly, my breathing* ***returned to normal.***

6 REACT [T] to do something or give something to someone because they have given the same thing to you: *Hitchcock* ***returned the favor*** *by playing on the band's new album.* | *We will* ***return your call*** *as soon as we can.* | *Police took cover in combat positions but did not* ***return fire*** (=shoot back at someone shooting at them).

7 DISCUSS AGAIN [I] to start discussing or dealing with a subject that you have already mentioned, especially in a piece of writing: +**to** *I'll return to your question in a few minutes.*

8 BALL [T] to send the ball back to your opponent in a game such as tennis

9 return a verdict LAW if a JURY returns a VERDICT, they say whether someone is guilty or not

10 PROFIT [T] ECONOMICS if an INVESTMENT returns a particular amount of money, that is how much profit it produces: *Their investment list returned a profit of 34% last year.*

[**Origin:** 1300–1400 Old French *retourner*, from *tourner* **to turn**]

return[2] S3 W1 *n.*

1 GOING BACK [singular] the act of returning from somewhere, or your arrival back in the place where you started from: *We were anxiously awaiting Pedro's return.* | **on/upon sb's return** *On his return from the Holy Land, he stopped at Cotignola.*

2 OF A FEELING/PROBLEM [U] the fact of something such as a problem, feeling, or activity starting to happen or exist again: +**of** *Perhaps her rapid shifts in mood signaled the return of madness.*

3 GIVING BACK [U] the act of giving, putting, or sending something back: *She begged for the return of her kidnapped baby.* | *Both sides are demanding the return of territory lost in the war.*

4 TO AN ACTIVITY [singular] the action of going back to an activity, job, or way of life: +**to** *Cohen says he is not ruling out a return to public life.*

5 in return (for sth) in exchange for something, or as payment for something: *Navy officials reduced the punishment in return for his cooperation.* | *She gave us food and clothing and asked for nothing in return.*

6 PROFIT [U] also **returns** [plural] ECONOMICS the amount of profit that someone gets from money they have used to buy things such as STOCKS, goods, or a business etc.: +**from** *Most people get fairly low returns from their personal investments.* | **return on investment/capital/sales** *U.S. citizens found that they could get a higher return on their capital by investing abroad.* | *These investments bring a high* ***rate of return*** (=level of profit).

7 TAXES [C] a TAX RETURN

8 COMPUTER [U] the key that you press on a computer or TYPEWRITER after you have finished the line you are writing: *Type in your file name and press return.*

9 many happy returns said to someone on their BIRTHDAY, in order to wish them a long life and happiness → see also **the point of no return** at POINT[1] (7)

return[3] *adj.* **by return mail** if you reply to a letter by return mail, you send your reply almost immediately

re·turn·a·ble /rɪˈtɚnəbəl/ *adj.* **1** returnable bottles, containers etc. can be given back to the store, so they can be used again or RECYCLED **2** FORMAL something such as money that is returnable must be given or sent back: *a returnable deposit*

reˌturn adˈdress *n.* [C] the address of the person sending a letter or package, usually shown on the upper left hand corner of an envelope

reˈturn ˌticket *n.* [C] a ticket for your trip back to your home

Reu·ben /ˈrubən/ in the Bible, the head of one of the 12 tribes of Israel

ˈReuben ˌsandwich also **Reuben** *n.* [C] a hot SANDWICH made with CORNED BEEF, Swiss cheese, and SAUERKRAUT on RYE bread

re·u·ni·fy /riˈyunəˌfaɪ/ *v.* **reunified, reunifying** [T] to join the parts of something together again, especially a country that was divided → see also REUNITE —**reunification** /riˌyunəfəˈkeɪʃən/ *n.* [U] *the reunification of Germany*

re·un·ion /riˈyunyən/ S3 *n.* **1** [C] a social meeting of people who have not met for a long time, especially families or people who were at school or college together: **a family/high-school/college etc. reunion** *My twenty-year high school reunion is in August.* **2** [U] a situation in which people meet each other again after a period of being separated: +**with** *his emotional reunion with his wife*

Ré·un·ion /riˈyunyən/ a country consisting of a group of islands in the Indian Ocean, which is controlled by France

re·u·nite /ˌriyuˈnaɪt/ *v.* [I,T usually passive] **1** to bring people together again after a period when they have been separated and have not seen each other, or to come together in this way: *The band will reunite for a U.S. tour.* | **be reunited with sb** *She was recently reunited with the son she gave up for adoption.* **2** to bring together again parts of an organization, country etc. that were fighting or arguing with each other, or to come together in this way: *a desire to reunite the party*

re·use /ˌriˈyuz/ *v.* [T] to use something again: *The plastic bottles can be reused.* —**reusable** *adj.* —**reuse** /riˈyus/ *n.* [U]

rev[1] /rɛv/ *n.* [C] INFORMAL a complete turn of a wheel or engine part, used as a unit for measuring the speed of an engine SYN **revolution**

rev[2] *v.* **revved, revving** [I,T] also **rev up** if you rev an engine, or if an engine revs, you make it work faster: *Joe revved up his motorcycle.*

R

rev up *phr. v.* **rev sth ↔ up** INFORMAL if you rev up a system or organization, or it revs up, it becomes more active: *The phone companies are revving up their marketing campaigns.* → see also REVVED UP

Rev. the written abbreviation of REVEREND: *the Rev. Jesse Jackson*

re·val·ue /riˈvælyu/ *v.* [T] **1** to examine something again in order to calculate its present value: *Once it's sold, the property is revalued at the sale price.* **2** ECONOMICS to increase the value of a country's money in relation to that of other countries OPP **devalue**: *The dollar has just been revalued.* —**revaluation** /riˌvælyuˈeɪʃən/ *n.* [C,U]

re·vamp /riˈvæmp/ *v.* [T] INFORMAL to change something in order to improve it: *ABC plans to revamp the show before next season.* [**Origin:** 1800–1900 *vamp* **to mend** (16–19 centuries)] —**revamping** *n.* [C,U] —**revamp** *n.* [singular]

re·veal /rɪˈvil/ Ac S3 W2 *v.* [T] **1** to make known something that was previously secret or unknown OPP **conceal**: *His letters reveal a different side of his personality.* | *The fact was revealed in the Sunday edition of the paper.* | **reveal (that)** *He revealed that he had spent five years in prison.* | **reveal who/what/why** *She wouldn't reveal how much she had spent on the painting.* **2** to show something that was previously hidden OPP **conceal**: *The curtains opened to reveal a bare stage.* [**Origin:** 1300–1400 Old French *reveler*, from Latin *revelare* **to uncover**]

re·veal·ing /rɪˈvilɪŋ/ Ac *adj.* **1** a remark or event that is revealing shows you something interesting or surprising about a situation or someone else's character: *a revealing insight into her thoughts* **2** revealing clothes allow parts of your body that are usually kept covered to be seen: *revealing swimsuits*

rev·eil·le /ˈrɛvəli/ *n.* [singular, U] a special tune played as a signal to wake soldiers in the morning, or the time at which it is played

rev·el /ˈrɛvəl/ *v.* [I] OLD USE to spend time dancing, eating, drinking etc., especially at a party [**Origin:** 1300–1400 Old French *reveler* **to rebel, revel**, from Latin *rebellare*] —**revel** *n.* [C usually plural]: *drunken revels*

revel in sth *phr. v.* to enjoy something very much, usually because it has a good effect on you: *Leo reveled in his children's success.*

rev·e·la·tion /ˌrɛvəˈleɪʃən/ Ac *n.* **1** [C] a surprising fact about someone or something that was previously secret but that is now being made known: +**about** *He resigned after revelations about his affair.* | +**that** *revelations that two senior police officers had lied in court* **2 sb/sth is a revelation** used to say that someone or something is good, enjoyable, or useful in a surprising way: *His performance was a revelation.* **3** [U] the act of suddenly making known a surprising fact that had previously been secret: *the revelation of previously unknown facts* **4** [C,U] an event, experience etc. that is considered to be a message from God

Rev·e·la·tions /ˌrɛvəˈleɪʃənz/ the last book of the New Testament of the Bible, in which the story of the end of the world is told

rev·el·er /ˈrɛvələ/ *n.* [C usually plural] someone who is having fun singing, dancing etc. in a noisy way, at a party or other celebration

rev·el·ry /ˈrɛvəlri/ *n.* [U] also **revelries** [plural] wild noisy dancing, eating, drinking etc., usually as a celebration of something SYN **celebration**: *the fans' noisy revelries*

re·venge¹ /rɪˈvɛndʒ/ *n.* [U] **1** something you do in order to punish someone who has harmed or offended you: +**for** *The brothers **sought revenge** for their parents' murder.* | *The bombing was carried out **in revenge** for Sunday's massacre.* | **get/take (your) revenge (on sb)** *He vowed that he would get his revenge.* **2** the defeat of someone who has previously defeated you, especially in a sport: *The Yankees will be looking for revenge for last year's embarrassment.* —**revengeful** *adj.*

revenge² *v.* [T] FORMAL **1 revenge yourself on sb** also **be revenged (on sb)** to punish someone who has harmed you or someone you care about **2 be revenged** if an event is revenged someone takes revenge because of it

rev·e·nue /ˈrɛvəˌnu/ Ac W2 *n.* [U] also **revenues** [plural] **1** ECONOMICS money that a business or organization receives over a period of time, especially from selling goods or services: *advertising revenue* | +**from** *revenue from investments* | *an opportunity for the company to **generate revenue*** (=make revenue) | *The plan would cost the government over $150 million in **lost revenue*** (=money that could have been made, but was not). **2** ECONOMICS money that the government receives from tax [**Origin:** 1400–1500 French, past participle of *revenir* **to return**] → see also INTERNAL REVENUE SERVICE

re·ver·ber·ate /rɪˈvɚbəˌreɪt/ *v.* [I] **1** if a loud sound reverberates, it is heard many times as it is sent back from different surfaces, so that the room, building, or area seems to shake SYN **echo**: **reverberate through/across/in etc. sth** *The sound of the bombs reverberated throughout the city.* **2** if a place, room, or building reverberates, it seems to shake because of a loud sound that is sent back from different surfaces SYN **echo**: **reverberate with sth** *The room reverberated with the sound of clapping.* **3** if an event, action, or idea reverberates, it has a strong effect over a wide area: **reverberate through/around etc. sth** *The news reverberated around the globe.*

re·ver·ber·a·tion /rɪˌvɚbəˈreɪʃən/ *n.* **1** [C usually plural] a strong effect that is caused by a particular event SYN **repercussions**: *the political reverberations of the scandal* **2** [C,U] a loud sound that is heard again and again as it is sent back from different surfaces SYN **echo**

re·vere /rɪˈvɪr/ *v.* [T] FORMAL to respect and admire someone or something very much: **revere sb as sth** *She is revered as one of Canada's best writers.* | **be revered (for sth)** *The civil rights leader was revered for his courage and integrity.* [**Origin:** 1600–1700 Latin *revereri*, from *vereri* **to fear, respect**]

Re·vere /rɪˈvɪr/, **Paul** (1735–1818) an American who rode at night on April 18, 1775, to the town of Concord, Massachusetts, in order to warn the people there that the British soldiers were coming

rev·erence¹ /ˈrɛvrəns/ *n.* **1** [U] FORMAL great respect and admiration for someone or something: +**for** *my family's reverence for tradition* **2 your/his reverence** OLD USE used when speaking to or about a priest

reverence² *v.* [T] OLD USE to revere someone or something

Rev·erend /ˈrɛvrənd/ *n.* a title of respect used before the name of a minister of a Christian church: *Reverend Paul Ward*

rev·erend¹ /ˈrɛvrənd/ *n.* [C] a minister of a Christian church

reverend² *adj.* [only before noun] OLD USE deserving respect

ˌReverend ˈMother *n.* [C] OLD USE a title of respect for the woman in charge of a CONVENT SYN **Mother Superior**

rev·erent /ˈrɛvrənt/ *adj.* FORMAL showing a lot of respect and admiration: *The crowd watched her with reverent awe.* —**reverently** *adv.*

rev·er·en·tial /ˌrɛvəˈrɛnʃəl◂/ *adj.* FORMAL having the qualities of great respect and admiration: *He spoke in a reverential voice about his former teacher.* —**reverentially** *adv.*

rev·er·ie /ˈrɛvəri/ *n.* [C,U] a state of imagining or thinking about pleasant things, that is like dreaming: *A knock at the door interrupted my reverie.*

re·ver·sal /rɪˈvɚsəl/ Ac *n.* [C,U] **1** a change to an opposite arrangement, process, or course of action: **a dramatic/sudden/complete reversal** *The decision marks a dramatic reversal in federal policy.* | **a reversal of fortune** (=a change from being successful to unsuccessful or from being unsuccessful to successful) → see also **role reversal** at ROLE (4) **2** [C] a failure or other problem that prevents you from being able to do what you want: *Wilson's campaign has suffered a few embarrassing reversals recently.*

re·verse¹ /rɪˈvɚs/ Ac *v.* **1** [T] to change something, such as a decision, judgment, or process so that it is the opposite of what it was before or so that it goes back to what it originally was: *It will take years to reverse the damage done by pollution.* | **reverse a decision/ruling/verdict etc.** *The judgment was reversed by a higher court.* | **reverse a trend/process/decline etc.** *We need to reverse the trend towards centralized power.* **2** [T] if two people's situations, positions, or ROLES are reversed, each one begins to behave in the way that the other one used to behave: *Our roles as child and parent had now been reversed.* **3** [T] to change the usual order of the parts of something: *Half the new police squad cars have the colors reversed.* **4** [T] to turn something over, so as to show the back of it or so that it faces the opposite way: *The image on the screen was reversed and upside down.* **5 reverse yourself** to change your opinion or position in an argument **6** [I,T] if a car or its driver reverses, they go backward —**reversible** *adj.*: *a reversible jacket* —**reversibility** /rɪˌvɚsəˈbɪləṭi/ *n.* [U]

reverse² Ac *n.* **1 the reverse** the exact opposite of what has just been mentioned SYN **opposite**: *I don't owe you anything. If anything, the reverse is true.* **2 in reverse** in the opposite way to normal or to the previous situation: *We went from the North to the South, but John did the trip in reverse.* **3 into reverse** if a TREND or process goes into reverse or something puts it into reverse, it starts to happen in the opposite way: **put/throw/shift etc. sth into reverse** *The accident threw the airline's plans into reverse.* **4** [U] the control in a vehicle that makes it go backward: **into/in reverse** *Maria put the car into reverse and drove away.* **5** [C] FORMAL a defeat or a problem that delays your plans: *Financial reverses forced Thomas to sell his business.* **6** [singular] the back side of a flat object, for example a coin OPP **obverse**: *the reverse of the coin*

reverse³ Ac *adj.* [only before noun] **1** opposite to what is usual or to what has just been stated: *He was trying to help, but his words had* ***the reverse effect****.* | *The names were listed* ***in reverse order****.* **2 the reverse side (of sth)** the back of something: *the reverse side of the fabric*

reˌverse discrimiˈnation *n.* [U] the practice of giving unfair treatment to a group of people who usually have advantages, in order to be fair to the group of people who have been unfairly treated in the past → see also AFFIRMATIVE ACTION

reˌverse ˈgear *n.* [U] the control in a vehicle that makes it go backward

reˌverse ˈmortgage *n.* [C] TECHNICAL a legal arrangement by which you borrow money from a bank equal to the value of your house, and the LOAN is paid off when the house is sold after your death

re·vers·i·ble /rɪˈvɚsəbəl/ Ac *adj.* **1** if something that has changed is reversible, the thing that was changed can be changed back to the way it was before OPP **irreversible**: *Many chemical reactions are reversible.* **2** a piece of clothing that is reversible can be worn with the part that is normally on the inside showing on the outside: *a reversible jacket*

reˌversible reˈaction *n.* [C] CHEMISTRY a chemical reaction in which the result of the reaction is able to react again and return to its original state

re·ver·sion /rɪˈvɚʒən/ *n.* [singular, U] **1** FORMAL a return to a former, usually bad, condition or habit: **+to** *the country's reversion to a traditional monarchy* **2** LAW the return of property to a former owner: *the reversion of Hong Kong to China*

re·vert /rɪˈvɚt/ *v.*

revert to sth *phr. v.* **1** to go back to a former condition or habit, especially one that was bad: *Brian reverted to his normal happy self as soon as his father returned.* **2** LAW if land or a building reverts to someone, it becomes the property of its former owner again **3** to return to an earlier subject of conversation

re·vet·ment /rɪˈvɛtˀmənt/ *n.* [C] TECHNICAL a surface of stone or other building material that is added to give strength to a wall that holds back loose earth, water etc.

re·view¹ /rɪˈvyu/ S3 W2 *n.* **1** [C,U] an act of carefully examining and considering a situation or process: **+of** *a review of the health care system* | *A new housing plan for the city is now* ***under review*** (=being considered). | *The policy* ***came up for review*** (=the time arrived when it needed to be examined) *in April.* | *The agency has not* ***conducted a review*** (=done a review) *of the budget yet.* | *The jury's verdict is* ***subject to a review*** (=can be reviewed) *by the judge.* **2** [C] ENG. LANG. ARTS an article in a newspaper or magazine that gives an opinion about a new book, play, movie etc.: **+of** *a review of her latest book* | **a restaurant/movie/book etc. review** *She glanced through the book reviews.* | **good/bad reviews** *The movie got good reviews when it first came out.* | *The play has had* ***mixed reviews*** (=some good and some bad ones). **3** [C] a discussion of a particular subject that prepares you for a test: *Monday's class will be a review for the exam.* **4** [U] the activity of writing your opinion about a new book etc. for a newspaper or magazine: *The book was passed to me for review.* **5** [C] an official show of the Army, Navy etc. when a president or officer of high rank is watching: *a naval review* **6** [C] a REVUE [**Origin:** 1400–1500 French *revue*, from *revoir* **to look over**]

review² S3 W3 *v.* **1** [T] to examine, consider, and judge a situation, process, or piece of writing carefully: *The lower court's decision will be reviewed by the Supreme Court.* | *Make sure to review your exam paper before you turn it in.* **2** [I,T] ENG. LANG. ARTS to write an article judging a new book, play, movie etc.: **review sth for sth** *Hayes reviews books for the local paper.* **3** [I,T] to prepare for a test by studying books, notes, reports etc.: **review for sth** *We'll spend this week reviewing for the final.* **4** [T] to officially examine a group of soldiers, ships etc. at a military show

re·view·er /rɪˈvyuɚ/ *n.* [C] someone who writes about new books, plays etc. in a newspaper or magazine

re·vile /rɪˈvaɪl/ *v.* [T] to express hatred of someone or something: *a decision which was reviled by the public* | **reviled as sth** *The president is widely reviled as corrupt.* —**reviler** *n.* [C]

re·vise /rɪˈvaɪz/ Ac *v.* **1** [T] to change your opinions, plans etc. because of new information or ideas: *The college has revised its plans because of local objections.* ►see THESAURUS box at **change¹** **2** [T] ENG. LANG. ARTS to change a piece of writing by adding new information, making improvements, or correcting mistakes: *I'd like you read my story once I've revised it.* | *a* ***revised edition*** *of his earlier book* [**Origin:** 1500–1600 French *réviser*, from Latin *revisere* **to look at again**] —**reviser** *n.* [C]

re·vi·sion /rɪˈvɪʒən/ Ac *n.* ENG. LANG. ARTS **1** [C,U] the process of improving something by correcting it or including new information or ideas: *The hiring plan is undergoing revision.* **2** [C] a change that someone makes to a piece of writing: *I'm making some revisions to the book.* **3** [C] a piece of writing that has been improved and corrected

re·vi·sion·ist /rɪˈvɪʒənɪst/ *adj.* DISAPPROVING not accepting or showing usual beliefs or opinions about a subject, especially in history: *a revisionist history of the war* —**revisionist** *n.* [C] —**revisionism** *n.* [U]

re·vis·it /riˈvɪzɪt/ *v.* [T] **1** to return to a place you once knew well: *Maria wants to revisit her old school.* **2** to discuss something again or think about something again: *The director asked the actors to revisit the text.* **3 sth revisited** an event, fashion etc. revisited reminds you very much of something like it: *The sign above the rack of shirts said, "1965 revisited."*

re·vi·tal·ize /riˈvaɪṭlˌaɪz/ *v.* [T] to make someone or something have strength, energy, or health again: *We*

R

hope to revitalize the neighborhood by providing better housing. | *a revitalizing massage* —**revitalization** /riˌvaɪtl̩-əˈzeɪʃən/ *n.* [U]

re·viv·al /rɪˈvaɪvəl/ *n.* **1** [C,U] the process or fact of something becoming active, popular, or strong again: *an economic revival.* | *The show is enjoying a revival.* | +**of** *a revival of styles from the 1980s* | +**in** *signs of a revival in the auto industry* **2** [C] ENG. LANG. ARTS a new production of a play that has not been performed recently: *a Broadway revival* **3** [C] a public religious meeting that is intended to make people interested in Christianity

re·viv·al·ism /rɪˈvaɪvəˌlɪzəm/ *n.* [U] **1** an organized attempt to make a religion more popular **2** the process of encouraging new interest in something such as a type of art or music —**revivalist** *adj.*

reˈvival ˌmeeting *n.* [C] a REVIVAL

re·vive /rɪˈvaɪv/ *v.* **1** [I,T] to become or make someone become conscious, healthy, or strong again: *Paramedics tried to revive him but could not.* **2** [I,T] to feel or make someone feel better or less tired: *The coffee instantly revived her.* | **revive sb's spirits** (=make someone feel happier) **3** [I,T] to become strong active, or popular again, or to make someone or something do this: *an attempt to revive the steel industry* | *The economy is beginning to revive.* **4** [T] to make someone experience a feeling or memory again: *Seeing Dan revived all my old feelings of jealousy.* **5** [T] to produce a play again after it has not been performed for a long time [**Origin:** 1400–1500 Old French *revivre*, from Latin *revivere* **to live again**]

re·viv·i·fy /riˈvɪvəˌfaɪ/ *v.* **revivifies, revivified, revivifying** [T] FORMAL to give new life and health to someone or something SYN **revitalize**

rev·o·ca·tion /ˌrɛvəˈkeɪʃən/ *n.* [C,U] the act of revoking a law, decision etc.

re·voke /rɪˈvoʊk/ *v.* [T] to officially state that a law, decision, contract etc. is not effective or being used anymore SYN **cancel**: **revoke sth for doing sth** *His driver's license was revoked for driving drunk.* [**Origin:** 1300–1400 Old French *revoquer*, from Latin *revocare* **to call back**]

re·volt¹ /rɪˈvoʊlt/ *n.* **1** [C,U] POLITICS strong and often violent action by a lot of people against their ruler or government: +**against** *a revolt against the central government* | *The 1956 uprising was a* ***popular revolt*** (=one supported by the general population). | *The people rose* ***in revolt.*** | **put down/crush a revolt** (=use military force to stop it) ►see THESAURUS box at **revolution** **2** [C,U] a refusal to accept someone's authority or to obey rules, laws etc.: +**against** *The French Revolution began with a revolt against a new "salt tax."* | *The whole city is* ***in revolt*** *about the new curfew.*

revolt² *v.* **1** [I] POLITICS if a group of people revolt, they take strong and often violent action against the government, usually with the aim of taking power away from them SYN **rebel**: **revolt against sb/sth** *The army revolted against the Communist leadership.* **2** [I] to refuse to accept someone's authority or obey rules, laws etc.: **revolt at/against sth** *The community revolted at the proposal to move the bank downtown.* **3** [T] if something revolts you, it is so bad or upsetting that it makes you feel sick and shocked: *I was revolted by the smell of dead animals.* [**Origin:** 1500–1600 French *révolter*, from Old Italian *rivoltare* **to defeat and remove from power**] → see also REVULSION

re·volt·ing /rɪˈvoʊltɪŋ/ *adj.* very bad or upsetting, often in a way that makes you feel sick SYN **disgusting**: *The food was cold and revolting.* | *a revolting color* —**revoltingly** *adv.*

rev·o·lu·tion /ˌrɛvəˈluʃən/ Ac W2 *n.* **1** [C] a complete change in ways of thinking, methods of working etc.: +**in** *Penicillin began a revolution in the treatment of infectious disease.* | **a social/cultural/technological etc. revolution** *the sexual revolution of the 1960s* | *The printing industry has* ***undergone a revolution*** (=experienced one) *in recent years.* → see also INDUSTRIAL REVOLUTION **2** [C,U] POLITICS a time of great, usually sudden, social and political change, especially the changing of a ruler or political system by force → see also REBELLION: *the Russian Revolution of 1917* | *The country was on the verge of revolution.* → see also COUNTERREVOLUTION

THESAURUS

rebellion an organized attempt to change the government of a country using violence: *an armed rebellion*
revolt a refusal to obey a government, law etc., or an occasion when people try to change the government of a country, often by using violence: *Nasser led the revolt that deposed King Farouk I of Egypt in 1952.*
uprising an occasion when a large group of people use violence to try to change the rules, laws etc. in an institution or country: *Brown tried to get weapons to support a Negro uprising against slavery.*
coup an action in which a group of people, especially soldiers, suddenly take control of their country: *The President was deposed in a violent military coup.*

3 [C,U] one complete circular movement, or continued circular movement, around a certain point: *the planets' revolutions around the sun* **4** [C] a complete turn of a wheel or engine part, used as a unit for measuring the speed of an engine: *a speed of 100 revolutions per minute* [**Origin:** 1300–1400 Old French, Latin *revolutio*, from *revolvere* **to roll back, cause to return**] → see also REVOLVE

rev·o·lu·tion·ar·y¹ /ˌrɛvəˈluʃəˌnɛri◂/ Ac *adj.* **1** completely new and different, especially in a way that leads to great improvements: *revolutionary changes in technology* | *a revolutionary idea* **2** [only before noun] POLITICS relating to a political or social revolution: *revolutionary activity*

revolutionary² Ac *n. plural* **revolutionaries** [C] POLITICS someone who joins in or supports a political or social revolution: *a band of young revolutionaries*

Revoˌlutionary ˈWar, the HISTORY the war in which people in Britain's colonies (COLONY) in North America became independent and established the United States of America. The war began in 1775 and ended in 1781, and a peace agreement was signed in 1783.

rev·o·lu·tion·ize /ˌrɛvəˈluʃəˌnaɪz/ Ac *v.* [T] to completely change the way people think or do things, especially because of a new idea or invention: *Satellites have revolutionized the science of predicting the weather.*

Revolution of 1905, the /rɛvəˌluʃən əv ˌnaɪntin oʊ ˈfaɪv/ *n.* a period of violence in Russia during 1905, when many different groups of people were involved in protest against the unfair treatment of poor people by the CZAR's government

re·volve /rɪˈvɑlv/ *v.* [I,T] to spin around or make something spin around on a central point SYN **rotate**: *The Moon revolves around the Earth.* | *a planet revolving on its axis* [**Origin:** 1300–1400 Latin *revolvere* **to roll back, cause to return**, from *volvere* **to roll**]

revolve around sth *phr. v.* **1** to have something as a main subject or purpose: *Most of the discussion revolved around money.* | *Her life revolves around her children.* **2 sb thinks the world revolves around him/her** INFORMAL used to say that someone thinks they are more important than anyone or anything else

re·volv·er /rɪˈvɑlvɚ/ *n.* [C] a small gun that has a spinning container for bullets, so that several shots can be fired without having to put more bullets in

re·volv·ing /rɪˈvɑlvɪŋ/ *adj.* a revolving object is designed so that it turns with a circular movement: *a revolving stage*

reˌvolving ˈcredit *n.* [U] an arrangement with a store, bank etc. that allows you to borrow money up to a particular amount, and when you pay back some of that money, you can later borrow up to the limit again

re,volving 'door *n.* [C] **1** a type of door in the entrance of a large building, that goes around and around a central point as people go through it **2** used to describe a situation, organization etc. which people leave soon after they have become involved in it: *The job has been a revolving door for seven CEOs.* **3** used to describe a situation, organization etc. that people return to quickly after leaving it, often for a different reason: *Congress is a revolving door, in which former members return as lobbyists.*

revolving door

re•vue /rɪ'vyu/ *n.* [C] a show in a theater, that includes songs, dances, and jokes about recent events

re•vul•sion /rɪ'vʌlʃən/ *n.* [U] a strong feeling of shock and very strong dislike SYN **disgust**: +**at** *Foley expressed revulsion at the killings.*

revved up, **revved-up** /ˌrɛvd 'ʌp/ *adj.* INFORMAL **1** very excited about doing something: *These kids are revved up about going to college.* **2** more active, exciting, or interesting than before: *a revved-up version of an old American folk song* → see also **rev up** at REV²

re•ward¹ /rɪ'wɔrd/ W3 *n.* **1** [C,U] something that you receive because you have done something good or helpful: +**for** *His parents gave him money* ***as a reward for*** *passing exams.* **2** [C,U] something good that you happens to you because of what you do or have done: *the rewards of success* | **financial/monetary rewards** *The work is difficult, but the financial rewards are great.* | *He is finally* ***reaping the rewards*** (=experiencing the rewards) *of all his hard work.* | *For Harper, playing the music has* ***been its own reward*** (=just playing music is enough to make him happy). **3** [C] an amount of money that is offered to someone who finds something that was lost or gives the police information: +**for** *a reward for information on the killer* | *The family has* ***offered a reward*** *of $20,000.*

reward² *v.* [T] **1** to give something to someone because they have done something good or helpful: *How can I reward your kindness?* | **reward sb with sth** *The performers were rewarded with flowers from the audience.* | **reward sb for (doing) sth** *She wanted to reward them for all their efforts.* **2 be rewarded** to achieve something good even when this is difficult: *Finally, Molly's patience was rewarded.* | **be rewarded with/by sth** *The team's efforts have been rewarded with success.* [**Origin:** 1300–1400 Old North French *rewarder* **to regard, reward**, from *warder* **to watch, guard**]

re•ward•ing /rɪ'wɔrdɪŋ/ *adj.* making you feel happy and satisfied because you feel you are doing something useful, important, or interesting, even if you do not earn much money: *Working with kids is a rewarding experience.*

re•wind /ri'waɪnd/ *past tense and past participle* **rewound** /-'waʊnd/ [T] to make a CASSETTE or VIDEOTAPE go backward so you can see or hear it again or from the beginning

re•wire /ri'waɪɚ/ *v.* [T] to put new electric wires in a building, machine, light etc.

re•word /ri'wɚd/ *v.* [T] to say or write something again in different words, in order to make it easier to understand or more appropriate: *Let me reword my question.*

re•work /ri'wɚk/ *v.* [T] to make changes in music or a piece of writing, in order to use it again or to improve it

re•write /ri'raɪt/ *v. past tense* **rewrote** /-'roʊt/, *past participle* **rewritten** /-'rɪt‿n/ [T] **1** to completely change something that has been written, usually in order to improve it: *The professor said I'd have to completely rewrite my paper.* **2 rewrite history** to try to change the way people think about past events, often in a way that is incorrect —**rewrite** /'riraɪt/ *n.* [C]

Rey•kja•vik /'reɪkyəvɪk/ the capital and largest city of Iceland

RFD *n.* [U] the written abbreviation of **rural free delivery** used in the addresses of people who live in the country far from cities and towns

rhap•so•dize /'ræpsəˌdaɪz/ *v.* [I] to talk about something in an eager, excited, and approving way: +**about/over** *Schilling rhapsodized about the beauty of the country.*

rhap•so•dy /'ræpsədi/ *n.* [C] **1** ENG. LANG. ARTS a piece of music that is written to express emotion, and does not have a regular form **2** an expression of eager and excited approval —**rhapsodic** /ræp'sɑdɪk/ *adj.*

Rhe•a /'riə/ in Greek MYTHOLOGY, the wife of the god Cronus and the mother of Zeus

rhe•o•stat /'riəˌstæt/ *n.* [C] PHYSICS a piece of equipment that controls the loudness of a radio or the brightness of an electric light, by limiting the flow of electric current

Rhe•sus fac•tor /'risəs ˌfæktɚ/ *n.* [singular] BIOLOGY a substance that some people have in their red blood cells, which may have a dangerous effect if, for example, a baby that does not have the substance is born to a woman with the substance

rhesus mon•key /'risəs ˌmʌŋki/ *n.* [C] a small monkey from northern India that is often used in medical tests

rhet•o•ric /'rɛt̬ərɪk/ *n.* [U] ENG. LANG. ARTS **1** language that is used, especially by politicians, to influence people, and which may not be sincere or produce any good results: *People want results from politicians, not rhetoric.* **2** the art of speaking or writing to persuade or influence people

rhe•tor•i•cal /rɪ'tɔrɪkəl, -'tɑ-/ *adj.* **1** using speech or writing in special ways in order to persuade people or to produce an impressive effect: *a speech full of* ***rhetorical devices*** (=particular examples of rhetorical language) **2** said or written in a way that is intended to sound impressive, but is not honest and is not based on truth: *a rhetorical commitment to democracy* **3** used to describe a question that is asked without expecting an answer, but is said in order to make a point: *"Why would I choose you?" he said, but the question was rhetorical.* —**rhetorically** /-kli/ *adv.*

rhet•o•ri•cian /ˌrɛt̬ə'rɪʃən/ *n.* [C] FORMAL someone who is trained or skillful in the art of persuading or influencing people through speech or writing

rheum /rum/ *n.* [U] TECHNICAL a thin liquid that comes out of your eyes, when you are asleep —**rheumy** *adj.*

rheu•mat•ic /rʊ'mæt̬ɪk/ *adj.* MEDICINE **1** relating to rheumatism: *rheumatic diseases* **2** suffering from rheumatism

rheu,matic 'fever *n.* [U] MEDICINE a serious infectious disease that causes fever, swelling in your joints, and sometimes damage to your heart

rheu•ma•tism /'rumə ˌtɪzəm/ *n.* [U] MEDICINE a disease that makes your joints or muscles painful and stiff

rheu•ma•toid ar•thri•tis /ˌrumətɔɪd ɑr'θraɪt̬ɪs/ *n.* [U] MEDICINE a disease that continues for many years, and makes your joints painful and stiff, and often makes them lose their correct shape

RH fac•tor /ˌɑr 'eɪtʃ ˌfæktɚ/ *n.* [C] BIOLOGY the RHESUS FACTOR

Rhine, the /raɪn/ an important river in western Europe that flows northward from Switzerland to the Netherlands and into the North Sea

rhine•stone /'raɪnstoʊn/ *n.* [C,U] a jewel made from glass or a transparent rock that is intended to look like a DIAMOND

rhi•no /'raɪnoʊ/ *n. plural* **rhinos** [C] INFORMAL a rhinoceros

rhi·noc·er·os /raɪˈnɑsərəs/ *n.* [C] a large heavy African or Asian animal with thick skin and either one or two horns on its nose [**Origin:** 1200–1300 Latin, Greek, from *rhis* **nose** + *keras* **horn**]

rhi·no·plas·ty /ˈraɪnoʊˌplæsti/ *n.* [U] PLASTIC SURGERY on your nose —**rhinoplastic** /ˌraɪnoʊˈplæstɪk◂ / *adj.*

rhi·zome /ˈraɪzoʊm/ *n.* [C] BIOLOGY the thick stem of some plants, which grows flat along or just under the ground

Rhode Is·land /roʊd ˈaɪlənd/ WRITTEN ABBREVIATION **RI** a state in the northeast of the U.S. which is the smallest U.S. state

Rhodes /roʊdz/ a large Greek island near the coast of Turkey

Rhodes, Cec·il /ˈsɛsəl/ (1853–1902) a South African politician who was born in the U.K.

Rho·de·sia /roʊˈdiʒə/ a former name for Zimbabwe that was used during the period of British rule —**Rhodesian** *n., adj.*

R

rho·do·den·dron /ˌroʊdəˈdɛndrən/ *n.* [C] a bush with bright flowers that keeps its dark green, shiny leaves in winter [**Origin:** 1600–1700 Modern Latin, Greek, from *rhodon* **rose** + *dendron* **tree**]

rhom·boid¹ /ˈrɑmbɔɪd/ *n.* [C] MATH a shape with four sides whose opposite sides are equal SYN **parallelogram**

rhomboid² also **rhom·boid·al** /rɑmˈbɔɪdl/ *adj.* MATH shaped like a rhombus

rhom·bus /ˈrɑmbəs/ *n.* [C] MATH a flat shape with four equal straight sides, especially a shape that is not a square → see picture at SHAPE¹

Rhone, the /roʊn/ a river in southern Europe that flows from southern Switzerland to France and into the Mediterranean Sea

rhu·barb /ˈrubɑrb/ *n.* [U] BIOLOGY a plant with broad leaves and a thick red stem that can be cooked and eaten as a fruit [**Origin:** 1300–1400 Old French *reubarbe*, from Medieval Latin *reubarbarum*, from *rha* **rhubarb** (from Greek) + *barbarus* **foreign**]

rhyme¹ /raɪm/ *n.* ENG. LANG. ARTS **1** [C] a short poem or song, especially for children, using words that rhyme → see also NURSERY RHYME **2** [U] the use of words that rhyme in poetry, especially at the ends of lines **3** [C] a word that rhymes with another word, for example "hop" and "pop": +**for** *I can't find a rhyme for "orange."* **4 rhyme or reason** used in negatives to say that there does not seem to be a sensible reason for something: *There was* ***no rhyme or reason*** *to the decision.* | *The facts are presented one after another* ***without rhyme or reason.***

rhyme² *v.* [not in progressive] **1** [I] ENG. LANG. ARTS if two words or lines of poetry rhyme, they end with the same sound, for example "hop" and "pop": **sth rhymes with sth** *The children were asked if "weight" rhymes with "late".* **2 rhyme sth (with sth)** ENG. LANG. ARTS if you rhyme two words or rhyme one word with another you put them together as rhyme

ˌrhyming ˈcouplet also **ˌrhymed ˈcouplet** *n.* [C usually plural] two lines of poetry that end in words that rhyme

rhythm /ˈrɪðəm/ *n.* **1** [C,U] ENG. LANG. ARTS a regular pattern of beats in music that comes from the arrangement of the notes, the time between them, and how much each note is emphasized: *salsa and other latin rhythms* | +**of** *the rhythm of the music* **2** [U] also **sense of rhythm** the ability to recognize, produce, or follow a rhythm: *She has a great sense of rhythm.* **3** [C,U] a regular repeated pattern of sounds or movements: +**of** *the rhythm of her heartbeat* **4** [C] a regular pattern of events or changes: +**of** *He liked the rhythm of life in the country.* **5** [C] a pattern in an activity that makes it enjoyable to watch or easy to do: *She got into a rhythm early on in the game.* [**Origin:** 1500–1600 Latin *rhythmus*, from Greek, from *rhein* **to flow**]

ˌrhythm and ˈblues *n.* [U] R & B (=a type of music)

rhyth·mic /ˈrɪðmɪk/ also **rhyth·mic·al** /ˈrɪðmɪkəl/ *adj.* having rhythm: *the rhythmic beat of the horses hooves* —**rhythmically** /-kli/ *adv.*

ˈrhythm ˌmethod *n.* **the rhythm method** a method of BIRTH CONTROL that depends on having sex only at a time when the woman is not likely to become PREGNANT

ˈrhythm ˌsection *n.* [C] the part of a band that provides a strong RHYTHM using drums and other similar instruments

RI the written abbreviation of RHODE ISLAND

ri·al /riˈæl, -ˈɑl/ *n.* [C] a RIYAL

rib¹ /rɪb/ *n.* [C] **1** BIOLOGY one of the 12 pairs of curved bones that surround your chest: *a broken rib* | **poke/dig/nudge etc. sb in the ribs** (=to push someone quickly in the ribs with your finger or elbow to get their attention, share a joke with them etc.) → see picture at SKELETON¹ **2** a piece of meat that includes an animal's rib: *barbecued ribs* **3** a curved piece of wood, metal etc. that is used as part of the structure of something such as a boat or building **4** a pattern of raised lines in a KNITted piece of clothing that allow it to stretch [**Origin:** Old English] → see also PRIME RIB, SPARERIBS

rib² *v.* **ribbed, ribbing** [T] to make jokes and laugh at someone in a friendly way: **rib sb about sth** *Jose's teammates ribbed him about the flowers he got.*

rib·ald /ˈraɪbɔld, ˈrɪbəld/ *adj.* ribald songs, remarks, or jokes are humorous and usually about sex

rib·ald·ry /ˈrɪbəldri, ˈraɪ-/ *n.* [U] ribald songs, remarks, or jokes

ribbed /rɪbd/ *adj.* ribbed KNITted material has a pattern of raised lines that allow it to stretch: *a ribbed turtleneck sweater*

rib·bing /ˈrɪbɪŋ/ *n.* [U] **1** friendly jokes and laughter about someone: *What's the matter? Can't you* ***take a little ribbing?*** **2** a pattern of raised lines in KNITted material that allow it to stretch

rib·bon /ˈrɪbən/ S3 *n.*

1 DECORATION [C,U] a long narrow piece of cloth or shiny paper, used to tie things or as a decoration: *She had pink ribbons in her hair.* | *birthday presents tied with ribbon*

2 PRIZE [C] a small arrangement of colored ribbons in the form of a flat flower, that is given as a prize in a competition: *Holly's tomatoes won the* ***blue ribbon*** (=first prize).

3 MILITARY HONOR [C] a piece of ribbon with a special pattern or colors on it, worn to show that you have received a military honor

4 STH LONG AND NARROW [singular] something that is long and narrow: *a 30-mile-long ribbon of beach*

5 SHOWING SUPPORT [C] a narrow piece of colored cloth folded over itself, worn to show support for an organization, principle, or aim

6 cut/tear/slash etc. sb/sth to ribbons to badly damage something by cutting or tearing it in many places

7 TYPEWRITER [C] a long narrow piece of cloth or plastic with ink on it that is used in a TYPEWRITER

[**Origin:** 1500–1600 *riband* **ribbon** (14–21 centuries), from Old French *riban, ruban*]

ˈrib cage *n.* [C] BIOLOGY the structure of RIBS around your lungs, heart, and other organs

ri·bo·fla·vin /ˌraɪbəˈfleɪvən, ˈraɪbəˌfleɪvən/ *n.* [U] CHEMISTRY VITAMIN B2, a substance that exists in meat, milk, and some vegetables, and that is important for your health

ri·bo·so·mal RNA /ˌraɪbəsoʊməl ˌɑr ɛn ˈeɪ/ ABBREVIATION **rRNA** *n.* [U] BIOLOGY RNA that is part of a ribosome → see also TRANSFER RNA

ri·bo·some /ˈraɪbəˌsoʊm/ *n.* [C] BIOLOGY a small part of every living cell, consisting of PROTEIN and the chemical substance ribosomal RNA. Ribosomes react to the GENETIC information contained in TRANSFER RNA by turning AMINO ACIDS into PROTEIN.

rice /raɪs/ S2 W3 *n.* [U] **1** a food that consists of small white or brown grains that you boil in water until they become soft enough to eat: *long-grain rice* **2** BIOLOGY the plant that produces this grain [**Origin:** 1200–1300 Old French *ris*, from Greek *oryza, oryzon*]

rice ˌpaddy *n.* [C] a field in which rice is grown

rice ˌpaper *n.* [U] **1** a type of thin paper made especially in China, used for painting or writing **2** a type of thin paper that can be eaten, which is used in cooking

rice ˈpudding *n.* [U] a sweet food made of rice, milk, and sugar cooked together

rich /rɪtʃ/ S2 W1 *adj.*

1 WEALTHY a) having a lot of money or valuable possessions SYN **wealthy** OPP **poor**: *Her family is very rich.* | *one of the world's richest countries* | *He thought he'd found an easy way to **get rich*** (=become rich). | **filthy/stinking rich** HUMOROUS OR DISAPPROVING (=very rich) **b) the rich** people who have a lot of money and possessions: *The rich send their kids to exclusive private schools.* | *Hollywood homes of **the rich and famous***

THESAURUS

well-off fairly rich, so that you can live very comfortably
wealthy used especially about people whose families have been rich for a long time
prosperous FORMAL rich and successful
well-to-do rich and having a high position in society
affluent FORMAL used about a rich person or society
rolling in it/loaded INFORMAL extremely rich
→ POOR

2 LARGE AMOUNT having or containing a lot of something: **+in** *Oranges are rich in vitamin C.* | *Red meat is **a rich source of** iron.* | **oxygen-rich/oil-rich/calcium-rich etc.** (=containing a lot of oxygen etc.)
3 FULL OF INTEREST full of interesting or important events, ideas etc.: *The area has a rich history.* | **+in** *a story that is rich in detail*
4 FOOD containing foods such as butter, cream, and eggs, which make you feel full very quickly: *a rich chocolate cake*
5 SMELL/FLAVOR having a strong pleasant smell or flavor: *the taste of the rich, dark coffee*
6 COLOR having a beautiful strong color: *a rich dark brown color* ►see THESAURUS box at **color**[1]
7 MUSIC/SOUNDS having a pleasant low sound: *His guitar produces a warm, rich sound.*
8 SOIL/LAND good for growing plants in SYN **fertile**: *Roses require rich soil.* | **+in** *a soil rich in nutrients*
9 CLOTH expensive and beautiful: *the rich velvet of the dress*
[**Origin:** Old English *rice*]

Rich·ard I, King /ˌrɪtʃɚd ðə ˈfɚst/ (1157–1199) a king of England who spent a lot of time fighting in the CRUSADES and in France. He is often called Richard the Lion Heart.

Richard III, King /ˌrɪtʃɚd ðə ˈθɚd/ (1452–1485) a king of England who took the position of king from his brother's son

Ri·che·lieu, Cardinal /ˈriʃəˌlu/ (1585–1642) a French CARDINAL who was the chief minister of France under King Louis XIII

rich·es /ˈrɪtʃɪz/ *n.* [plural] ESPECIALLY LITERARY **1 sb's riches** large amounts of money, property, and expensive possessions belonging to someone SYN **wealth** **2** a large amount of something valuable or interesting: *We explored the riches that the old city had to offer.*

rich·ly /ˈrɪtʃli/ *adv.* **1** heavily or strongly: *The bread was dark and richly flavored.* **2** in a beautiful or expensive way: *richly furnished rooms* **3 richly colored** having beautiful strong colors: *long, richly colored robes* **4 richly deserve** to completely deserve something such as success or punishment **5** in large amounts: *a richly paid position*

Rich·mond /ˈrɪtʃmənd/ the capital city of the U.S. state of Virginia

Rich·ter scale /ˈrɪktɚ ˌskeɪl/ *n.* [singular] a scale that shows how strong an EARTHQUAKE is, with 1 being very weak and 10 being the strongest

Richt·ho·fen /ˈrɪktoʊfən/, **Baron von** (1892–1918) a German pilot known as the Red Baron, who commanded a group of fighter planes in World War I

rick /rɪk/ *n.* [C] a large pile of STRAW or grass that is kept in a field until it is needed

rick·ets /ˈrɪkɪts/ *n.* [U] MEDICINE a disease that children get in which their bones become soft and bent, caused by a lack of VITAMIN D

rick·et·y /ˈrɪkəṭi/ *adj.* a rickety piece of furniture or part of a building is in such bad condition that it looks as if it will break if you use it: *rickety wooden stairs*

Rick·o·ver /ˈrɪkoʊvɚ/, **Hy·man** /ˈhaɪmən/ (1900–1986) a U.S. Navy ADMIRAL and engineer who directed the development of the first SUBMARINE driven by NUCLEAR ENERGY

ˈrick-rack *n.* [U] a type of RIBBON with a shape like small waves, that is used for decoration

rick·shaw /ˈrɪkʃɔ/ *n.* [C] a small vehicle that is pulled by someone walking or riding a bicycle, used in South East Asia for carrying one or two passengers [**Origin:** 1800–1900 Japanese *jinrikisha*, from *jin* **man** + *riki* **strength** + *sha* **vehicle**]

ric·o·chet[1] /ˈrɪkəˌʃeɪ/ *v.* [I] if a moving object, such as a bullet or stone, ricochets, it changes direction when it hits a surface at an angle: **+off** *Bullets were ricocheting off the road next to us.*

ricochet[2] *n.* [C] **1** something such as a bullet or a stone that has ricocheted: *He was hit by a ricochet.* **2** an act of ricocheting

ri·cot·ta /rɪˈkɑṭə/ *n.* [U] a type of soft white Italian cheese [**Origin:** 1800–1900 Italian *ricuocere* **to cook again**]

rid[1] /rɪd/ *adj.* **1 get rid of sb/sth a)** to throw away, sell etc. something you do not want or use anymore: *I got rid of all those old CDs.* **b)** to take action so that you do not have something unpleasant, annoying or unwanted anymore: *I can't get rid of this cough.* | *He opened the windows to get rid of the smell.* **c)** to make someone leave because you do not like them or because they are causing problems: *Andy stayed until 2:00 – we couldn't get rid of him!* **2 be rid of sb/sth** to be no longer affected by someone or something unpleasant, annoying, or unwanted: *I'd give anything to be rid of this headache.*

rid[2] *v. past tense and past participle* **rid, ridding** [**Origin:** 1100–1200 Old Norse *rythja* **to clear land**]

rid sb/sth of sth *v.* **1** to remove something or someone that is bad or harmful from a place, organization etc.: *Ridding the border region of guns will not be easy.* **2 rid yourself of sth** to do something so that you do not have a feeling, thought, or problem that was causing you trouble anymore: *She took classes to rid herself of her Southern accent.*

rid·dance /ˈrɪdns/ *n.* [U] **good riddance** SPOKEN used to say that you are glad that someone or something has gone away

ridden /rɪdn/ the past participle of RIDE

-ridden *suffix* [in adjectives] too full of something, especially something bad: *guilt-ridden* (=feeling very guilty) | *mosquito-ridden*

rid·dle[1] /ˈrɪdl/ *n.* [C] **1** a question that is deliberately confusing and usually has a humorous or clever answer: *See if you can **solve the riddle*** (=find the answer). **2** a mysterious action, event, or situation that you do not understand and cannot explain SYN **mystery**: *the riddle of his death* | *The police have **not solved the riddle** of her disappearance.* **3 talk/speak in riddles** to say things in a mysterious or confusing way that other people cannot understand [**Origin:** Old English *rædelse* **opinion, guess, riddle**]

riddle[2] *v.* [T] to make a lot of small holes in something:

riddle sth with sth *Gunmen riddled the bus with bullets.*

rid·dled /ˈrɪdld/ *adj.* **1** full of something bad: *a drug-riddled neighborhood* | **+with** *a report riddled with errors* **2** damaged or full of holes, especially from bullets: *bullet-riddled bodies* | **+with** *The highway was riddled with potholes.*

ride¹ /raɪd/ S1 W2 *v. past tense* **rode** /roʊd/, *past participle* **ridden** /ˈrɪdn/

1 BICYCLE/MOTORCYCLE [I always + adv./prep., T] to sit on a bicycle or MOTORCYCLE and make it move along: *We used to ride our bikes all summer.* | **+away/down/back etc.** *Nick rode in on his Harley-Davidson.* | **ride (sth) through/down/across etc.** *We rode the trains throughout France.*

2 VEHICLE [I always + adv./prep., T] to travel in a bus, car, or other vehicle: **ride in/on sth** *The kids were riding in the back.* | **ride to/into/back etc.** *I had to ride back to New York on the bus.* | **ride the bus/train/trolley etc.** *Have you ever ridden the tram?*

3 ANIMAL [I,T] to sit on an animal, especially a horse, and make it move along: *Louise taught her kids to ride.* | *Have you ever ridden a horse?* | **+away/across/back etc.** *We watched him ride away.* | **ride on sth** *The bride rode to her wedding on a white horse.* | *She* ***goes riding*** *every weekend.*

R

4 be riding high to feel very happy and confident: *Before Sunday's defeat, the Broncos had been riding high.*

5 IN WATER a) [I always + adv./prep.,T] to move or float on the water: *The kayak rode the waves gently.* **b) ride a wave** to SURF

6 let sth ride INFORMAL **a)** if you let a bad situation ride, you let it continue for a time without doing anything about it, before deciding whether to take any action: *We can't just let this ride – it's too important.* **b)** also **let sth slide** if you let a remark that has annoyed you ride, you do not say anything about it

7 ANNOY SB [T] to annoy someone by repeatedly criticizing them or asking them to do things

8 ride herd on sb/sth to watch and control someone or something carefully: *His assignment was to ride herd on the firm's expenses.*

9 be riding for a fall to be doing something in a way that is too confident, so that you are likely to fail completely

10 ride the rails to travel on a train that carries goods without paying, especially in past times

[**Origin:** Old English *ridan*] → see also **run/ride roughshod over sth** at ROUGHSHOD

ride on sth *phr. v.* if someone's success or the respect that they get is riding on something, it depends on it: *My school career is riding on how well I do this year.*

ride sth ↔ **out** *phr. v.* **1** if a ship rides out a storm, it manages to keep floating until the storm has ended **2** if you ride out a difficult situation, you are not badly harmed by it: *Most large companies may be able to ride out the recession.*

ride up *phr. v.* if a piece of clothing rides up, it moves up so that it is not covering your body in the way it should

ride² S2 W3 *n.* [C]

1 CAR/TRAIN ETC. a trip in a vehicle: *He was asleep for the entire ride.* | **+in/on** *He* ***took us for a ride*** *in his new car.* | **+to/from** *It's a two-hour ride to Montreal.* | *Can we* ***give you a ride*** *home?* | *She usually* ***gets a ride*** *from her sister in the mornings.* | *We could all* ***go for a ride*** *out to Irene's.* | *Maybe I'll be able to* ***hitch a ride*** (=get a ride) *with Steph.* | **a car/train/subway etc. ride** *John took me on my first plane ride.*

2 HORSE/BIKE an occasion when you ride a horse or bicycle somewhere: *The two girls* ***went for a ride*** *in the early morning.* | *a long* ***bike ride***

3 TREATMENT a situation during which you receive a particular type of treatment from someone because of something that you have done: *The president will not have* ***an easy ride*** (=not be treated well) *in today's new's conference.* | **a bumpy/rough ride** *The new bill could be in for a bumpy ride*

4 take sb for a ride INFORMAL to trick, cheat, or lie to someone, especially in order to get money from them

5 come/go along for the ride INFORMAL to join what other people are doing just for pleasure, not because you are seriously interested in it: *I had nothing to do, so I thought I'd go along for the ride.*

6 MACHINE a large machine that people ride on for fun at a FAIR or AMUSEMENT PARK or the time you spend on the ride: *We went on all the rides.* | *I felt dizzy after the ride.*

Ride /raɪd/, **Sal·ly** /ˈsæli/ (1951–) a U.S. scientist and ASTRONAUT who was the first American woman in space

rid·er /ˈraɪdɚ/ *n.* [C] **1** someone who rides a horse, bicycle etc.: *One of the riders had fallen off.* **2** someone who rides a public vehicle, such as a bus or SUBWAY SYN **passenger**: *a survey of subway riders* **3** a statement that is added, especially to an official decision or judgment: *a rider to the bill*

ridge¹ /rɪdʒ/ *n.* [C] **1** EARTH SCIENCE a long area of high land, especially at the top of a mountain: *The sun disappeared behind the ridge.* → see picture on page A31 **2** a long narrow raised area on a surface: *the ridges on the soles of her shoes* | **+of** *a ridge of sand* **3** EARTH SCIENCE a long area of high ATMOSPHERIC pressure that affects the weather **4** the line at the top of a sloping roof, where the two parts of the roof meet

ridge² *v.* [T] to make a ridge or ridges in something

ridged /rɪdʒd/ *adj.* something that is ridged has ridges on its surface: *a ridged cast-iron skillet*

rid·i·cule¹ /ˈrɪdəˌkyul/ *n.* [U] **1** laughter, remarks, or behavior that are unkind and are intended to make someone or something seem or feel stupid: *Her ideas were greeted with ridicule.* | **hold sb/sth up to ridicule** (=to make someone or something look silly in public) **2 an object of ridicule** a person or thing that everyone laughs at and regards as stupid [**Origin:** 1600–1700 French, Latin *ridiculum* **something funny**, from *ridere* **to laugh**]

ridicule² *v.* [T] to laugh at a person, idea, institution etc. because you think it is stupid: *My father ridiculed the idea of me being a football player.* | **ridicule sb for (doing) sth** *He was ridiculed for his old-fashioned clothes.*

ri·dic·u·lous /rɪˈdɪkyələs/ S2 *adj.* silly or unreasonable: *I'd* ***look ridiculous*** *wearing that tiny dress.* | *Oh, for goodness sake,* ***don't be ridiculous.*** | **It's/that's ridiculous** *You can't pay that much for a TV. That's ridiculous!* | **absolutely/totally/utterly ridiculous** *an utterly ridiculous decision* —**ridiculously** *adv.* —**ridiculousness** *n.* [U]

rid·ing /ˈraɪdɪŋ/ *n.* **1** [U] the sport or activity of riding horses **2** [C] an official area in Canada represented by a member of the Canadian PARLIAMENT

RIF *n.* [C] **reduction in force** an expression used by companies to mean an occasion when many people are forced to leave their jobs so the company can save money → see also LAYOFF

rife /raɪf/ *adj.* **1 rife with sth** full of something bad: *a city rife with crime* **2** [not before noun] if something bad is rife, it is very common: *Drug abuse is rife despite the recent crackdown.*

riff /rɪf/ *n.* [C] a series of notes in popular or JAZZ music, especially one that is IMPROVISED and repeated: *a guitar riff*

rif·fle /ˈrɪfəl/ *v.* [T] to quickly turn over the pages of a book, magazine etc.: *Harry riffled through the comics.*

riff·raff /ˈrɪf ræf/ *n.* [U] DISAPPROVING people who are noisy, badly-behaved, or not socially acceptable, who you do not want to have around

ri·fle¹ /ˈraɪfəl/ *n.* [C] a gun with a long BARREL (=tube-shaped part) that you hold up to your shoulder [**Origin:** 1700–1800 *rifle* **to cut grooves on the inside of something, especially a gun barrel** (17–21 centuries), from Old French *rifler* **to cut into a surface, steal**]

rifle² *v.* [T] **1** also **rifle through** to search quickly through a cupboard, drawer etc.: *She rifled through her closet looking for a dress.* **2** to steal things from a place:

The killer had rifled the victim's wallet. **3** SLANG to throw or hit a ball with a lot of force

'rifle range *n.* [C] a place where people practice shooting with rifles

rift /rɪft/ *n.* [C] **1** a situation in which two people or groups have begun to dislike or distrust each other, usually because of a serious disagreement: **+in/within** *Joe's divorce caused a huge rift in the family.* | **+between** *Something caused a rift between the two actors.* | *Collins is trying to* ***heal the rifts*** *in the party.* **2** EARTH SCIENCE a crack or narrow opening in a large mass of rock, cloud etc.

'rift ˌvalley *n.* [C] EARTH SCIENCE a valley with very steep sides, formed by the cracking and moving of the Earth's surface

rig¹ /rɪg/ *v.* **rigged, rigging** [T] **1** to arrange or influence an election, competition etc. in a dishonest way, so that you get the result that you want SYN **fix**: *The game show turned out to be rigged.* **2** if people rig prices or financial markets, they unfairly agree with each other the prices that will be charged so that they can gain an advantage for themselves SYN **fix** **3** also **rig up** to make a piece of equipment, furniture etc. quickly, especially from objects that you find around you: *We rigged up a simple shower in back of the cabin.* **4** to provide something with a piece of equipment for a particular purpose, especially secretly: **rig sth to do sth** *The suitcase was rigged to explode.* | **rig sth with sth** *The car was rigged with explosives.* **5** [usually passive] to provide a ship with ropes, sails etc.: *a fully rigged vessel* [**Origin:** (1–2) 1700–1800 *rig* **trick**]

rig² *n.* [C] **1** also **oil rig** EARTH SCIENCE a large structure used for getting oil from the ground under the ocean **2** a large truck that consists of two parts, one for the engine and the driver and the other for carrying a load SYN **semi** → see also BIG RIG **3** the way in which a ship's sails and MASTS are arranged

Ri·ga /'rigə/ the capital city of Latvia

rig·a·ma·role /'rɪgəməˌroʊl/ *n.* [C] another form of RIGMAROLE

rig·ging /'rɪgɪŋ/ *n.* [U] all the ropes, chains etc. that hold up a ship's sails

right¹ /raɪt/ S1 W1 *adj.*

1 TRUE/CORRECT correct, because of being based on true facts SYN **correct** OPP **wrong**: *The right answer is "spinal cord."* | *The total on the bill isn't right.* | **get sth right** *I got most of the answers right.* | *Their prediction turned out to be* ***half right.***

> **THESAURUS**
> **correct** used about answers, facts, etc. that are right: *Is this information correct?*
> **accurate** used about measurements, descriptions, etc. that are completely right: *The court records must be accurate.*
> **true** based on facts, and not imagined or invented: *a true understanding of the problem*
> → WRONG

2 CORRECT OPINION correct in your opinion or explanation SYN **correct** OPP **wrong**: *You're right, there's another train in five minutes.* | **+about** *You were right about him getting married. The wedding is in May.* | *As time passed, she was* ***proved right*** (=her opinion was proven to be true).

3 CORRECT/NORMAL in the position, order, or state that is correct or where something works best: *Is the patient getting the right medicine?* | **look/feel/sound right** *The engine's not sounding right.*

4 NOT LEFT [only before noun] **a)** relating to or belonging to the side of your body that has the hand that most people write with OPP **left**: *your right foot* **b)** on the same side of something as your right side OPP **left**: *Make a right turn here.* | *the right side of the picture*

5 APPROPRIATE most appropriate for a particular occasion or purpose: *You made the right decision.* | *Ben tried to find the right words to explain.* | **be right for sth** *I have a friend who would be* ***just right*** (=appropriate in every way) *for the job.* | **be right for sb** *She knew that she and Peter were right for each other.*

6 MORALLY CORRECT an action that is right is morally correct OPP **wrong**: *Just because she cheats, doesn't mean it's right for you to do it.* | *Telling her the truth was* ***the right thing to do.*** | **be right to do sth** *Is it right to clone human beings?*

> **SPOKEN PHRASES**
> **7 that's right** **a)** said when something that is said or done is correct: *"You live in Baltimore, don't you?" "That's right."* **b)** said when you remember something or are reminded of it: *Oh, that's right! I had completely forgotten it was today.* **c)** used to show that you think someone is behaving in a silly or unhelpful way: *That's right! You just sit there, and I'll clean up your mess!*
> **8** AS QUESTION used as a question to ask if what you have said is correct or to check that someone understands: *He's the drummer for that band, right?*
> **9** TO AGREE used to agree with what someone says or to show that what they have said is correct: *"We'll have to leave by five." "Right."*
> **10 no one in their right mind would do sth** used to say that you think someone is crazy to do something: *No one in their right mind would ask to hang from a cliff by a little rope.*

11 right side up with the top part at the top, in the correct position OPP **upside down**: *Turn the cake right side up when it's cool.*

12 be in the right place at the right time to be in a place or position that allows you to gain an advantage for yourself, or to do something useful: *I was in the right place at the right time, and I got the job.*

13 (as) right as rain OLD-FASHIONED completely healthy, especially after an illness

14 SOCIALLY the right people, places, schools etc. are considered to be the best or most important: *I wanted to make sure my kids went to the right schools.*

[**Origin:** Old English *riht*] → see also **yeah, right** at YEAH (3)

right² S1 W1 *adv.*

1 exactly in a particular position or place, or at a particular time: *She was standing right in the middle of the road.* | **right here/there** *Your keys are right there where you left them.* | *Good, you're* ***right on time.*** | *I'm sorry I can't talk to you* ***right now*** (=at this moment).

2 IMMEDIATELY immediately and without any delay: **right away/after/before** *We decided to get married right away.* | *It's on right after the 6:30 news.* | *I could see* ***right off the bat*** *that there were going to be problems.* | *We have to deal with the problem* ***right now!***

3 CORRECTLY correctly: *Did they spell your name right?*

4 DIRECTION/SIDE toward the direction or side that is on the right OPP **left**: *Now, turn right onto Main Street.*

5 WELL in a way that is good or satisfactory OPP **badly**: *Everything is* ***going right*** *for us at the moment.* | *Most people don't* ***do it right*** *the first time.* | **come/turn/work out right** (=if a bad situation comes out right, turns out right, or works out right, it eventually gets better or becomes good)

6 right through/into/down etc. all the way, or the whole distance: *The bullet went right through the door.*

7 sb will be right with you also **sb will be right there** SPOKEN used to ask someone to wait because you are coming very soon: *I'm sorry to make you wait. I'll be right there.*

8 be/rank right up there (with sth) INFORMAL to be as good or as important as the very best: *A fireplace is one of the features home buyers want most, right up there with closets and new kitchens.*

9 right and left everywhere or in every way: *Businesses were failing right and left.*

right³ S1 W1 *n.*

1 ALLOWED [C] something, you are morally, legally, or officially allowed to do it: *These people are fighting for basic rights.* | **the right of sb** *the rights and duties of citizens* | **the right of sth** *the right of self-defense* | **a/the right to sth** *All children have a right to free*

R

education. | **the right to do sth** *the right to vote* | **women's/workers'/minorities' etc. rights** *the struggle for women's rights* | **equal rights (for sb)** (=the idea that all people have the same rights that are protected by the legal system) | **be within your rights (to do sth)** (=to be legally allowed to do something, although it may seem unusual) | *The money is yours* ***by right*** (=because you are legally allowed to have it). → see also CIVIL RIGHTS, HUMAN RIGHTS
2 have the right to do sth used to say that someone's action is reasonable: *People have a right to feel safe in their streets.* | *You* ***have no right to*** *tell me how to live my life* (=used to say someone is treating someone in a way that is unreasonable)! | *You* ***have every right to*** *be upset* (=used to emphasize that something is reasonable).
3 the/sb's right the side of your body that has the hand that most people write with, or this side of any place or object OPP **left**: **on/to the right (of sth)** *Owens sat on the right of Smith.* | *Take two steps to the right.*
4 the right/Right political parties or groups such as the REPUBLICANS in the U.S., which strongly support having a CAPITALIST economic system with as little government influence as possible, and which also have socially CONSERVATIVE views OPP **left**: *a bill that is strongly supported by the right* | **the extreme/far right** (=people in this political belief system with the most extreme beliefs)
5 right and wrong used to talk about morally good and bad behavior: *Does the child understand the difference between right and wrong?*
6 LEGAL PERMISSION rights [plural] legal permission to print or use a story, movie etc. in another form: **+to** *They own the rights to a lot of famous Broadway music.* | **all rights reserved** (=used to show that it is illegal to copy written or printed material without special permission)
7 in your own right without depending on anyone or anything else: *Kahlo was Rivera's wife, and an artist in her own right.*
8 be in the right to have the best reasons, arguments etc in a disagreement with someone else: *Both sides are convinced they are in the right.*
9 by rights used to describe what should happen if things are done fairly or correctly: *By rights, the house should be mine now.*
10 do right by sb INFORMAL to do what is morally correct for someone: *We have not yet done right by Native Americans.*
11 the rights and wrongs of sth all the different reasons for and against something: *the rights and wrongs of sex before marriage*
12 HIT [C] a hit using your right hand: *a right to the jaw* —**rightness** *n.* [U] → see also **two wrongs don't make a right** at WRONG[3] (6)

right[4] W3 *v.* [T] **1 right a wrong** to do something to prevent an unfair situation from continuing **2** to put something back into the state or situation that it should be in: *The president promised to right the country's troubled economy.* **3** to put something, especially a vehicle, back into its correct upright position: *A tow truck was called to attempt to right the trailer.*

ˈright ˌangle *n.* [C] **1** MATH an angle of 90°, like the angles inside the corners of a square → see picture at ANGLE[1] **2 at right angles (to sth)** if two things are at right angles, they make a 90° angle where they touch: *The aisles intersect at right angles.* —**right angled** *adj.*: *a right-angled triangle*

ˌright-ˈclick *v.* [I,T] COMPUTERS to press the right button on a computer MOUSE to make the computer do something

right·eous /ˈraɪtʃəs/ *adj.* **1 righteous indignation/anger etc.** strong feelings of anger when you think a situation is not morally right or fair **2** FORMAL morally good and fair **3** SPOKEN, INFORMAL extremely good —**righteously** *adv.* —**righteousness** *n.* [U] → see also SELF-RIGHTEOUS

ˈright field *n.* **1** [singular] the area in baseball in the right side of the OUTFIELD **2** [U] the position of the person who plays in this area → see also LEFT FIELD

right·ful /ˈraɪtfəl/ *adj.* [only before noun] according to what is legally and morally correct: *The city returned the houses to their* ***rightful owners.*** | *Historians are debating Columbus'* ***rightful place*** *in history* (=trying to agree on how important he was). —**rightfully** *adv.* —**rightfulness** *n.* [U]

ˈright-hand, right hand *adj.* [only before noun] on the right side of something OPP **left-hand**: *Washington Avenue will be on your right-hand side.* | *The number is in the top right-hand corner.*

ˌright-ˈhanded *adj.* **1** BIOLOGY a right-handed person uses their right hand for writing, throwing etc. OPP **left-handed** **2** a right-handed tool is designed for right-handed people OPP **left-handed**: *right-handed scissors* —**right-handed** *adv.*

ˌright-ˈhander *n.* [C] someone who uses their right hand for writing, throwing etc. OPP **left-hander**

ˌright-hand ˈman *n.* [singular] the person who supports and helps you the most, especially in your job

right·ist /ˈraɪtɪst/ *adj.* POLITICS supporting RIGHT-WING ideas or groups OPP **leftist**: *a rightist government* —**rightist** *n.* [C] —**rightism** *n.* [U]

right·ly /ˈraɪtli/ *adv.* **1** correctly, or for a good reason SYN **justifiably**: *The novel has been rightly hailed as an American classic.* | *As you rightly pointed out, things are getting worse.* | *Residents are outraged,* ***and rightly so*** (=and they have a good reason to be). **2 rightly or wrongly** used to say that something is true, whether people think it is a good or bad thing: *Rightly or wrongly, many employees feel pushed to work longer hours.* **3 I don't rightly know** also **I can't rightly say** SPOKEN INFORMAL used to say that you are not sure whether something is correct or not

ˌright-ˈminded *adj.* RIGHT-THINKING

ˌright of apˈpeal *n. plural* **rights of appeal** [C] LAW the legal right to ask for a court's decision to be changed

ˌright-of-ˈcenter *adj.* supporting ideas and aims that are between the center and the right in politics OPP **left-of-center**

ˌright of ˈway *n.* **1** [U] the right to drive into or across a road before other vehicles: *You* ***have the right of way*** *at this intersection.* **2** *plural* **rights-of-way** [C,U] the right to go across private land, or the place where you can do this

ˌright ˈon *adj.* INFORMAL **1** someone is right on when they say something that is correct or that you completely agree with: *Parker's column on teenage sexuality is right on.* **2 right on** SPOKEN used to emphasize that you agree with what someone says or does

ˈrights ˌissue *n.* [C] ECONOMICS an offer of STOCK in a company at a cheaper price than usual, to people who own some already

right·size /ˈraɪtsaɪz/ *v.* [I,T] to reduces the number of people a company employs in order to reduce costs —**rightsizing** *n.* [U] → see also DOWNSIZE

ˌright-ˈthinking *adj.* a right-thinking person has opinions, principles, or standards of behavior that you approve of

ˌright-to-ˈdie *adj.* [only before noun] relating to the rights of people who are extremely sick, injured, or unconscious to refuse to use machines or methods that would keep them alive

ˌright-to-ˈlife *adj.* [only before noun] members of a right-to-life organization are opposed to ABORTION, and they use this word to describe their views: *the right-to-life movement* → see also PRO-CHOICE, PRO-LIFE

ˌright-to-ˈwork law *n.* [C] ECONOMICS a law that makes it illegal to force people to join a TRADE UNION

ˌright ˈtriangle *n.* [C] GEOMETRY a TRIANGLE in which the angle opposite the longest side measures 90°

right·ward /ˈraɪt˺wəd/ *adj., adv.* **1** on or toward the right OPP **leftward** **2** on or toward the political RIGHT OPP **leftward**: *a rightward shift in American politics*

ˌright ˈwing *n.* **1 the right wing** political parties or groups such as the REPUBLICANS in the U.S., which strongly support having a CAPITALIST economic system with as little government influence as possible, and which also have socially CONSERVATIVE views OPP **the left wing** **2** [C] the right side of a playing area in sports such as SOCCER or HOCKEY, or a player who plays on this side OPP **left wing** —**right-winger** *n.* [C]

ˌright-ˈwing *adj.* [only before noun] POLITICS belonging to or relating to the right wing OPP **left-wing**: *a right-wing fund raising group*

rig·id /ˈrɪdʒɪd/ Ac *adj.* **1** rigid methods, systems etc. are very strict and difficult to change: *rigid academic standards* | *He keeps a rigid separation between his professional and private life.* **2** someone who is rigid is very unwilling to change their ideas **3** stiff and not moving or bending: *The bike's frame is too rigid.* ►see THESAURUS box at **hard**[1] [**Origin:** 1400–1500 Latin *rigidus*, from *rigere* **to be stiff**] —**rigidly** *adv.* —**rigidity** /rɪˈdʒɪdəti/ *n.* [U]

rig·ma·role /ˈrɪgməˌroʊl/ also **rigamarole** *n.* [singular, U] a long confusing series of actions that seems silly: *I don't want to* ***go through the rigmarole of*** *taking him to court.* [**Origin:** 1700–1800 *ragman roll* document containing a long list, used in a game called "ragman" (15–18 centuries)]

rig·or /ˈrɪgɚ/ *n.* **1** [U] great care and thoroughness in making sure that something is correct: **scientific/academic/intellectual etc. rigor** *The study lacked scientific rigor.* **2 the rigors of sth** the problems and difficulties of a situation: *the rigors of modern life* **3** [U] the quality of being strict or severe

rig·or mor·tis /ˌrɪgɚ ˈmɔrt̬ɪs/ *n.* [U] BIOLOGY the condition in which someone's body becomes stiff after they die

rig·or·ous /ˈrɪgərəs/ *adj.* **1** careful, thorough, and exact: *The car is put through rigorous safety checks.* **2** very severe or strict: *rigorous army training* —**rigorously** *adv.*

rile /raɪl/ *v.* [T] also **rile sb ↔ up** to make someone extremely angry: *He riled the crowd up into an angry frenzy.* —**riled** also **riled up** *adj.*

Ril·ke /ˈrɪlkə/, **Rai·ner Ma·ri·a** /ˈraɪnɚ məˈriə/ (1875–1926) an Austrian poet born in Prague

rim[1] /rɪm/ *n.* [C] **1** the outside edge of something circular: *plates with gold around the rim* | **+of** *The ball hit the rim of the basket.* ►see THESAURUS box at **edge**[1] **2** the edge of an area of land: **+of** *the rim of the canyon* → see also HORN-RIMMED, -RIMMED, WIRE-RIMMED

rim[2] *v.* **rimmed, rimming** [T] to be around the edge of something: *Her eyes were rimmed with black.*

Rim·baud /ræmˈboʊ/, **Ar·thur** /ˈɑrtʊr/ (1854–1891) a French poet

rime /raɪm/ *n.* LITERARY [U] FROST[1]

-rimmed /rɪmd/ [in adjectives] **gold-rimmed/silver-rimmed etc.** having a particular color or type of rim: *a chipped gold-rimmed saucer*

Rim·sky-Kor·sa·kov /ˌrɪmski ˈkɔrsəkɔf/, **Nik·o·lai** /ˈnɪkəlaɪ/ (1844–1908) a Russian musician who wrote CLASSICAL music

rind /raɪnd/ *n.* [C,U] **1** BIOLOGY the thick outer skin of some types of fruit, such as oranges → see also PEEL: *grated lemon rind* **2** the thick outer skin of some foods, such as BACON or cheese

ring[1] /rɪŋ/ S2 W3 *n.*

1 JEWELRY [C] a piece of jewelry that you wear on your finger: **a diamond/gold/silver etc. ring** *her sapphire engagement ring* → see also CLASS RING, ENGAGEMENT RING, WEDDING RING

2 CIRCLE [C] **a)** an object in the shape of a circle: *napkin rings* | *They make great onion rings here.* **b)** a circular line or mark: *My glass left a wet ring on the table.* **c)** a group of people or things arranged in a circle: *A ring of mountains encircles the huge crater.*

3 BELLS [C] the sound made by a bell, or the act of making this sound: *There was a ring at the door.*

4 CRIMINALS [C] a group of people who illegally control a business or criminal activity: **drug/crime/spy etc. ring** *a prostitution ring*

5 have a familiar ring (to it) if something has a familiar ring, you feel that you have heard it before: *His name had a familiar ring to it.*

6 have a ring of truth (to it) to seem likely to be true

7 SPORTS/ENTERTAINMENT a) a small square area surrounded by ropes, where people BOX or WRESTLE **b)** a large circular area surrounded by seats at a CIRCUS **c) the ring** the sport of BOXING: *He retired from the ring at 34.*

[**Origin:** (1–2, 4, 7) Old English *hring*]

ring[2] S2 W3 *v. past tense* **rang** /ræŋ/, *past participle* **rung** /rʌŋ/

1 TELEPHONE [I] if a telephone rings, it makes a sound to show that someone is calling you: *She was about to go out when the phone rang.*

2 BELL a) [I,T] to make a bell make a sound, especially to call someone's attention to you: *We heard them ringing the temple bell.* | **ring for sth** *The sign said "Ring for service."* **b)** [I] if a bell rings, it makes a noise: *I heard the church bells ringing.*

3 EARS [I] if your ears ring, they make a continuous sound that only you can hear, usually because they have been damaged by a loud sound: *My ears were still ringing hours after the concert.*

4 PLACE [I] LITERARY if a place rings with a sound, it is full of that sound: *The cathedral rang with the amazing voices of the choir.*

5 ring a bell (with sb) INFORMAL if something rings a bell, you think you have heard it before: *Does the name Bill Buckner ring a bell?*

6 not ring true if something does not ring true, you do not believe it, even though you are not sure why: *None of her explanations rang true.*

7 ring in your ears if a sound or remark rings in your ears, you remember it clearly and think about it often: *My father's discouraging words still ring in my ears.*

8 ring hollow if words ring hollow, you do not feel that they are true or sincere

9 ring in the New Year to celebrate the beginning of the New Year

ring out *phr. v.* **1** a voice, bell etc. that rings out is making a sound that is loud and clear: *Roars of laughter rang out from the bar.* **2 ring out the old (year)** to celebrate the end of the previous year and the beginning of the new year

ring sth **↔ up** *phr. v.* **1** to press buttons on a CASH REGISTER to record how much money is being put inside when you are selling something: *Can I ring that up for you, sir?* **2** to record or report a particular amount of money that someone, especially a business has made, lost, or spent: *Retailers will probably ring up 5.5% more sales this year than last.*

ring[3] *v.* **ringed** [T] **1** to surround something, especially by forming a circle: *Thousands of protesters ringed the embassy.* | **ring sth with sth** *The area was ringed with barbed wire.* **2** to draw a circular mark around something: *Her eyes were ringed with heavy black liner.* **3** to put a metal ring around a bird's leg

ring·er /ˈrɪŋɚ/ *n.* [C] **1** a piece of equipment that makes a ringing noise: *Turn down the ringer on your phone.* **2** someone who rings church bells or hand bells **3** someone who pretends not to have a skill that they really have, in order to play on a team, enter a competition etc.: *It was discovered that the winning horse was a ringer.* → see also **a dead ringer** at DEAD[1] (23)

ˈring ˌfinger *n.* [C] the finger, which is next to the smallest finger on your left hand, that you traditionally wear a WEDDING RING on

ring·git /ˈrɪŋgɪt/ *n.* [C] the standard unit of money used in Malaysia

ring·ing /ˈrɪŋɪŋ/ *adj.* a ringing sound or voice is loud and clear

ring·lead·er /ˈrɪŋˌlidɚ/ *n.* [C] someone who leads a group that is doing something illegal or wrong

ring·let /ˈrɪŋlɪt/ *n.* [C] a long curl of hair that hangs down

R

ring·mas·ter /ˈrɪŋˌmæstɚ/ *n.* [C] someone who is in charge of the performances in a CIRCUS

ˌRing of ˈFire, the *n.* EARTH SCIENCE the ring of VOLCANIC mountains surrounding the Pacific Ocean

ring·side /ˈrɪŋsaɪd/ *n.* [singular] the area nearest to the performance in a CIRCUS, BOXING match etc.: *ringside seats*

ring·worm /ˈrɪŋwɚm/ *n.* [U] MEDICINE a skin infection that causes red rings, especially on your head

rink /rɪŋk/ *n.* [C] **1** a specially prepared area of ice for skating (SKATE) **2** a special area with a smooth surface where you can go around on ROLLER SKATES

rin·ky-dink /ˈrɪŋki ˌdɪŋk/ *adj.* INFORMAL cheap and of bad quality

rinse¹ /rɪns/ *v.* [T] to use clean water, especially flowing water, to remove dirt, soap etc. from something: *Keith was rinsing the dishes.* | **rinse sth in/with/under sth** *Drain and rinse the noodles under cold water.* | **rinse sth out/away/off etc.** *Irene rinsed the dirt off her hands.* [**Origin:** 1200–1300 Old French *rincer*]

R

rinse sth ↔ **out** *phr. v.* to wash something in clean water without soap: *Don't forget to rinse out your swimsuit.*

rinse² *n.* **1** [C] an act of rinsing something: *Add fabric softener during the final rinse.* **2** [C,U] a product you use to change the color of your hair or to make it more shiny

Ri·o de Ja·nei·ro /ˌrioʊ deɪ ʒəˈnɛroʊ/ also **Rio** a large city and port in east Brazil

Ri·o Grande, the /ˌrioʊ ˈgrænd/ a river in the south of the U.S. that forms part of the border between the U.S. and Mexico. The Mexican name for it is Rio Bravo.

ri·ot¹ /ˈraɪət/ *n.* **1** [C] a situation in which a large crowd of people are behaving in a violent and uncontrolled way, especially when they are protesting about something: *There were riots in several cities.* | *The boy's death touched off* ***race riots*** (=riots caused by a racial problem) *and divided the town.* | *The army was called in to* ***put down the riots*** (=stop them). **2 run riot a)** if people run riot, they behave in a violent, noisy, and uncontrolled way: *Some parents just let their children run riot.* **b)** if your imagination, thoughts etc., run riot, you cannot or do not control them: *Ann let her imagination run riot as she wrote.* **c)** if a plant runs riot, it grows very quickly in an uncontrolled way **3** [singular] SPOKEN someone or something that is very funny or enjoyable: *This guy is a riot.* **4 a riot of color** LITERARY something with many different bright colors: *The garden was a riot of color.* **5 read (sb) the riot act** INFORMAL to give someone a strong warning that they must stop causing trouble: *She read me the riot act for seeing my old girlfriend.* [**Origin:** 1100–1200 Old French **quarrel**]

riot² *v.* [I] if a crowd of people riot, they behave in a violent and uncontrolled way, for example by fighting the police and damaging cars or buildings: *Hundreds of prisoners rioted in the overcrowded prison.* ▸see THESAURUS box at **protest²** —**rioting** *n.* [U] —**rioter** *n.* [C]

ˈriot gear *n.* [U] the special clothing and equipment worn by police officers during a riot

ri·ot·ous /ˈraɪət̬əs/ *adj.* **1** wild, exciting, and uncontrolled in an enjoyable way: *riotous celebrations* **2** uncontrolled, noisy, and violent: *riotous behavior* —**riotously** *adv.* —**riotousness** *n.* [U]

ˈriot poˌlice *n.* [plural] police whose job is to stop riots

RIP the written abbreviation of **Rest in Peace** (=words written on a stone over a grave)

rip¹ /rɪp/ S2 *v.* **ripped, ripping 1** [I,T] to tear something or be torn quickly and violently: *We both fell, and I heard his shirt rip.* | **rip sth ↔ open** *My fingers trembled as I ripped the envelope open.* | **rip sth on sth** *I ripped my skirt on a broken chair.* | **rip sth to shreds/pieces** *Angrily, she ripped the letter to shreds.* **2** [T always + adv./prep.] to remove something quickly and violently, using your hands: **rip sth out/off/down/away** *He ripped off his clothes and dove into the pool.* **3 rip sb/sth to shreds** to strongly criticize someone, or criticize their opinions, remarks, behavior etc.: *I expected him to rip my argument to shreds, but he just smiled.* **4 let rip** INFORMAL **a)** to speak or behave violently or emotionally: *Harriet finally let rip with 20 years of stored resentment.* **b)** to start to do something with a lot of energy: *They really let rip in the second half, scoring 45 points.* **5 let her/it rip** INFORMAL to make a car, boat etc. go as fast as it can **6 rip sb's heart out** to affect someone emotionally so that they feel very sad: *It's a fantastic film – it'll rip your heart out.* **7 rip the heart out of sth** DISAPPROVING to remove the most important part of a plan, law, organization etc.: *The amendment would rip the heart out of the bill.*

rip sb/sth ↔ **apart** *phr. v.* to violently tear or pull someone or something into pieces: *A bomb ripped the plane apart.*

rip into sb *phr. v.* to attack or criticize someone very strongly, especially unfairly: *The defense attorney ripped into Baker.*

rip off *phr. v.* INFORMAL **1 rip sb ↔ off** to charge someone too much money for something: *Insurance companies have been ripping people off for years.* **2 rip sth ↔ off** to steal something: *Burglars ripped off $3,000 worth of stereo and TV equipment.* **3 rip sb/sth ↔ off** to take words, ideas etc. from someone else's work and use them in your work as if they were your own ideas SYN **plagiarize** → see also RIP-OFF

rip on sb/sth *phr. v.* SPOKEN INFORMAL to complain a lot about someone or something: *Gina's always ripping on her boss.*

rip through sth *phr. v.* to move through a place quickly and with violent force: *A tornado ripped through the town.*

rip sth ↔ **up** *phr. v.* to tear something into several pieces: *Tablecloths were ripped up and used for bandages.*

rip² *n.* [C] a long tear or cut: *Anne's jacket has a rip in it.*

rip·cord /ˈrɪpkɔrd/ *n.* [C] **1** the string that you pull to open a PARACHUTE **2** the string that you pull to let gas out of a HOT-AIR BALLOON

ripe /raɪp/ *adj.* *comparative* **riper**, *superlative* **ripest 1** BIOLOGY ripe fruit or crops are fully grown and ready to eat OPP **unripe**: *You'll need a pound of ripe tomatoes.* **2 be ripe for sth** to be ready for something to happen, especially for some kind of change to happen: *The dock area is ripe for development.* **3 the time is ripe (for sth)** used to say it is a good time for something to happen: *The time was ripe for change in the company.* **4 ripe old age a)** a very old age: *Da Ponte lived to* ***the ripe old age of*** *89.* **b)** HUMOROUS a very young age: *Angie was the orchestra's soloist at* ***the ripe old age of*** *22.* **5** ripe cheese has developed a strong taste and is ready to eat **6** HUMOROUS a ripe smell is strong and disgusting [**Origin:** Old English] —**ripeness** *n.* [U]

rip·en /ˈraɪpən/ *v.* [I,T] to become ripe or to make something ripe: *Strawberries do not ripen after picking.*

ˈrip-off *n.* [C] SPOKEN **1** something that is expensive in a way that is unreasonable: *The restaurant was such a rip-off.* **2** music, art, movies etc. that are rip-offs copy something else without admitting this: *This band is just another Coldplay rip-off.* → see also **rip off** at RIP¹

ri·poste¹ /rɪˈpoʊst/ *n.* [C] **1** FORMAL a quick, intelligent, and amusing reply: *his witty ripostes* **2** TECHNICAL a quick return STROKE with a sword in FENCING (=the sport of fighting with swords) [**Origin:** 1700–1800 French, Italian *risposta* **answer**, from *rispondere* **to answer**]

riposte² *v.* **1** [I] FORMAL to reply quickly and in an amusing way **2** [I] TECHNICAL to make a riposte in FENCING

ripped /rɪpt/ *adj.* SLANG having muscles with shapes that are clear and easy to see

rip·ple¹ /ˈrɪpəl/ *v.* **1** [I,T] to move in small waves, or to make something move in this way: *A flag rippled in the breeze.* | *The stone rippled the lake's glassy surface and sank.* **2** [I always + adv./prep.] to pass from one person to another like a wave: +**across/through etc.** *Applause rippled across the audience.*

ripple

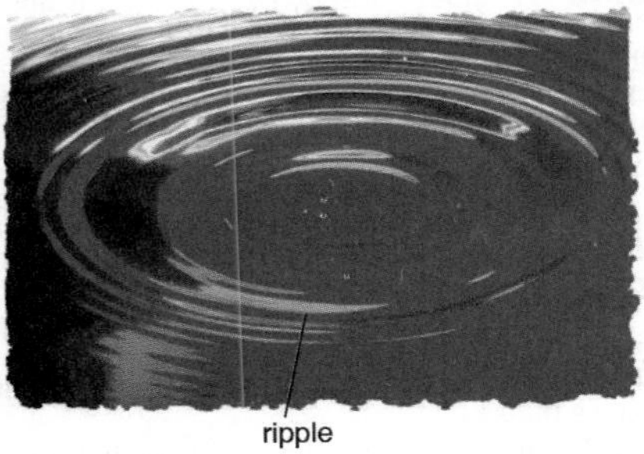

ripple² *n.* [C] **1** a small low wave on the surface of a liquid: *A soft breeze made ripples on the lake.* **2** a sound that gets gradually louder and softer: **a ripple of applause/laughter etc.** *His remark caused a ripple of laughter among the crowd.* **3** a feeling that spreads through a person or a group because of something that has happened: **a ripple of shock/nervousness/fear etc.** *The measures have aroused a ripple of protest abroad.* **4 ripple effect** a situation in which one action causes another, which then causes a third etc. **5** a shape or pattern that looks like a wave: *potato chips with ripples* **6 raspberry/chocolate etc. ripple** a type of ICE CREAM that has different colored bands of fruit, chocolate etc. in it

ˌrip-ˈroaring *adj.* INFORMAL noisy, exciting, and uncontrolled: *The football season got off to a rip-roaring start.*

rise¹ /raɪz/ S3 W1 *v. past tense* **rose** /roʊz/, *past participle* **risen** /ˈrɪzən/ [I]

1 INCREASE to increase in number, amount, or value OPP **fall**: *The level of crime continues to rise.* | **rise by 10%/$5 etc.** *House prices rose by 2.6% in June.* | **rise sharply/rapidly/dramatically** *The costs of bringing up a child have risen rapidly.* | *The divorce rate has* ***risen steadily*** *since the 1950s.* | *As with any investment, earnings* ***rise and fall.*** | *Unemployment was 7.6%* ***and rising.*** ►see THESAURUS box at **increase¹**

2 GO UPWARD also **rise up** to go up OPP **fall**: *Flood waters are still rising in parts of Missouri.* | **rise from sth** *She felt the steam rising up from the cup.* | *The boat* ***rose and fell*** *on the waves.*

3 BECOME SUCCESSFUL to become important, powerful, successful, or rich: **rise (from sth) to sth** *She quickly rose to the position of supervisor.* | *Khrushchev* ***rose to power*** *after Stalin's death in 1953.* | *Lydon* ***rose to fame*** *as Johnny Rotten of the Sex Pistols.* | *Marketing is easy to get into, but* ***rising to the top*** *can be more difficult.* | *She* ***rose through the ranks*** (=progress from a low position to a high position) *to become sales director.* | **rise from the ranks** (=to become an officer in the army after having been an ordinary soldier)

4 VOICE/SOUND also **rise up a)** to be heard: *Their young voices rose up in prayer.* | **rise from sth** *A roar rose from the crowd.* | **rise above sth** *The sound of laughter rose above the wind.* **b)** to become louder or higher: *Her voice rose with an anger that had built up over months.*

5 EMOTION if a feeling or emotion rises, you feel it more and more strongly: *Public anxiety about the economy was rising.* | ***Our spirits rose*** (=we became much happier) *when we saw the lights ahead.*

6 MOUNTAIN/BUILDING/TREE ETC. also **rise up** to be very tall: *The new rollercoaster rises 320 feet into the air.* | **rise to 1,000 feet/2,000 meters etc.** *The tallest peak rises to 2,500 feet above sea level.* | *giant rocks* ***rising from*** (=used to say where the base of something tall is) *the sea*

7 STAND FORMAL to stand up: *She rose to leave.* | **rise from the table/your chair etc.** *"I'm going home," Alice said, rising from the table.* | *The audience* ***rose to its feet,*** *cheering the dancers.* | **all rise** SPOKEN, FORMAL (=used to tell people to stand up at the beginning of a meeting of a court of law)

8 SUN/MOON/STAR to appear in the sky at the normal time OPP **set**: *A crescent moon rose in the sky.*

9 BED OLD-FASHIONED to get out of bed in the morning

10 rise and shine SPOKEN, HUMOROUS used to tell someone to wake up and get out of bed

11 PROTEST/OPPOSITION [I always + adv./prep.] also **rise up** if a large group of people rise, they oppose or fight against people in authority: *The Russian people rose in rebellion in 1917.* | **rise against sb** *Eventually, the steel workers rose up against their bosses.* | **rise in revolt/rebellion** *An entire nation was rising in revolt.*

12 BREAD/CAKES ETC. if bread, cakes etc. rise, they become bigger before they bake or as they bake

13 WIND if the wind rises, it becomes stronger

14 rise from the ashes to become successful again after being almost completely destroyed: *a country that rose from the ashes of civil war*

15 rise from the dead/grave to come alive after having died

16 rise out of sth to be caused by something or begin with something: *The quarrel had risen out of a misunderstanding.*

17 RIVER EARTH SCIENCE if a river rises somewhere, it begins there

[**Origin:** Old English *risan*]

rise above *phr. v.* **1** to work in a determined way so that a problem or difficult situation does not affect or limit you: *I am confident the company will rise above its financial problems.* **2** to keep your moral principles strong and refuse to be affected by words, actions, or feelings that are immoral: *We have to rise above our hatred and protest peacefully.* **3** to be of a higher standard than other things that are similar: *The restaurant needs something to help it rise above the competition.*

rise to sth *phr. v.* **1 rise to the occasion/challenge** to deal successfully with a difficult situation or problem, especially by working harder or performing better than usual: *Can the team rise to the occasion and win for a second time?* **2** if you rise to a remark that is intended to make you angry, you reply to it rather than ignoring it: *She refused to rise to his sexist remarks.*

rise² W2 *n.* **1** [C] an increase in number, amount, or value: +**of** *Profits went up to $24 million, a rise of 16%.* | **rise in costs/prices/taxes etc.** *Officials fear that sudden rises in food prices could cause riots.* | *Violent crime* ***is on the rise*** (=is increasing) *in some European nations.* **2** [singular] the achievement of importance, success, or power OPP **fall**: *the rise of Fascism* | +**of** *"Citizen Kane" details the rise of a ruthless tycoon.* | **rise to power/fame** *the band's sudden rise to fame in the 1960s* | ***the rise and fall of*** (=the achievement of importance, success, power etc. followed by a loss of it) *the Roman Empire* **3** [singular] a movement upward OPP **fall**: *the steady* ***rise and fall of*** *his chest as he slept* **4 give rise to sth** a phrase meaning to be the reason why something happens or begins to exist, used especially in writing: *The success of "Pamela" gave rise to a number of imitations.* | *Daily shaving can give rise to a number of skin problems.* **5 get a rise out of sb** to make someone become annoyed or embarrassed by making a joke about them: *Bill likes to get a rise out of people, to say things just for effect.* **6** [C] a piece of ground that slopes up: *a house built on a steep rise* | +**in** *a slight rise in the road* → see also HIGH-RISE

ris·er /ˈraɪzɚ/ *n.* [C] **1 early/late riser** someone who usually gets out of bed very early or very late **2** the upright part of a step on a set of stairs **3 risers** [plural] a movable set of wooden or metal steps for a group of people to stand on

ris·i·ble /ˈrɪzəbəl/ *adj.* FORMAL something that is risible is so stupid that it deserves to be laughed at [**Origin:** 1500–1600 Late Latin *risibilis*, from Latin *ridere* **to laugh**] —**risibility** /ˌrɪzəˈbɪləti/ *n.* [U]

ris·ing /ˈraɪzɪŋ/ *adj.* **1** increasing in amount or level: *the rising cost of living* **2** [only before noun] becoming more important or famous: *a rising young actor* |

Obama is one of the ***rising stars*** (=a young person who is quickly becoming successful) *in American politics.*

risk¹ /rɪsk/ W1 *n.*

1 CHANCE OF BAD RESULT [C,U] the possibility that something bad or dangerous may happen: *There are a lot of risks involved in starting a small business.* | *How much risk is there with this kind of operation?* | +**of** *the risk of infection* | +**that** *There is a real risk that the wheat crop may be lost.* | +**to** *There is absolutely no risk to the public.* | **reduce/increase the risk of sth** *Healthy eating can help reduce the risk of heart disease.* | **pose a risk (to sb/sth)** *Air bags in cars pose a risk to children.* | **a high/low risk** *The risk of getting malaria here is pretty low.* | *I never walk home alone at night. It's not* ***worth the risk.*** | *There's* ***an element of risk*** (=some risk, but not too much) *in any kind of investment.* ▸see THESAURUS box at **danger**

2 take a risk to do something even though you know there is a fairly strong chance that something bad will happen when you do it: *I knew we were taking a risk when we lent him the money.*

3 at risk be in a situation where you may be harmed: *Millions of lives are at risk because of food shortages.* | **be at risk of sth** *The species is at risk of extinction.* | **be at risk from sth** *Hundreds of people are at risk from radiation poisoning.* | *We would never make a decision that* ***put*** *public health* ***at risk.***

4 CAUSE OF DANGER [C] something or someone that is dangerous or may result in harm: +**to** *Polluted water supplies are a risk to public health.* | *Meat from the infected animals is regarded as* ***a serious health risk.*** | *Untended camp fires pose a tremendous* ***fire risk.*** | *the* ***risk factors*** (=things that influence whether something bad will happen) *for heart disease*

5 run a risk to be in a situation where something bad may happen to you: *If you drink the water here, you run the risk of getting very sick.*

6 at your own risk if you do something at your own risk, you do it even though you understand the possible dangers and have been warned about them: *Danger – enter at your own risk.*

7 at the risk of doing sth used when you think that what you are going to say or do may have a bad result, may offend or annoy people etc.: *At the risk of sounding stupid, can I ask a question?*

8 INSURANCE/BUSINESS [C] ECONOMICS a person or business to whom it is a good or bad idea to give insurance or lend money, because of the amount of money you are likely to make or lose: **a good/bad/poor risk** *Students are not a very good credit risk.*

[**Origin:** 1600–1700 French *risque*, from Italian *risco*] → see also **a calculated risk** at CALCULATED (1), SECURITY RISK

risk² W3 *v.* [T] **1** to put something in a situation in which it could be lost, destroyed, or harmed: **risk sth to do sth** *He had risked his own health to help the sick during the epidemic.* | **risk sth on sth** *You'd be crazy to risk your money on an investment like that!* | *Jim* ***risked his life*** *to help save his partner.* | *I'm getting too old to* ***risk life and limb*** (=risk being killed or hurt) *for a cheap thrill.* **2** to get into a situation where something bad may happen to you: *They had risked death in order to get their families to America.* | **risk doing sth** *These families risk losing their homes.* **3** to do something that you know may have dangerous or bad results: **risk doing sth** *I decided to risk having the operation right away.* | *You could leave a little later for the airport, but you may not want to* ***risk it.***

'risk ˌmanagement *n.* [U] the prevention or reduction of dangerous accidents or mistakes in a business or organization

'risk-ˌtaking *n.* [U] the practice of doing things that involve risks in order to achieve something —**risktaker** *n.* [C]

risk·y /ˈrɪski/ *adj. comparative* **riskier**, *superlative* **riskiest** involving a risk that something bad will happen: *Travel in the region is still considered risky.* | *a risky financial investment* | **it is risky to do sth** *Doctors say it's too risky to try and operate.* | +**for** *Large projects can be very risky for an individual company.* | *Buying a used car is a* ***risky business.*** —**riskily** *adv.* —**riskiness** *n.* [U]

ri·sot·to /rɪˈzɑt̬oʊ, -ˈsɑtoʊ, -ˈzoʊ-/ *n.* [U] a hot food made by adding hot liquid to rice a little at a time, often with cheese and pieces of meat, fish, or vegetables

ris·qué /rɪsˈkeɪ/ *adj.* a joke, remark etc. that is risqué is slightly shocking, especially because it is about sex: *risqué humor*

rite /raɪt/ *n.* [C] a ceremony that is always performed in the same way, usually for religious purposes: *funeral rites* | *The women of the village* ***perform*** *these traditional* ***rites.*** → see also LAST RITES

ˌrite of 'passage *n. plural* **rites of passage** [C] a special ceremony or action that is a sign of a new stage in someone's life, especially when a boy starts to become a man

rit·u·al¹ /ˈrɪtʃuəl/ *n.* [C,U] **1** a ceremony that is always performed in the same way, in order to mark an important religious or social occasion: *ancient dances and rituals* | *The Chinese surround silk with myth and ritual.* **2** something that you do regularly and in the same way each time: *Set up a regular time for homework; make it a ritual.* | **a daily/a nightly/a weekly/an annual etc. ritual** *the daily ritual of mealtimes*

ritual² *adj.* [only before noun] **1** done as part of a rite or ritual: *ritual prayers* **2** done in a specific and expected way, but without real meaning or sincerity: *ritual campaign promises* [**Origin:** 1500–1600 Latin *ritualis*, from *ritus*] —**ritually** *adv.*

rit·u·al·is·tic /ˌrɪtʃuəˈlɪstɪk◂/ *adj.* ritualistic words, types of behavior etc. always follow the same pattern, especially because they form part of a ritual: *ritualistic ceremonies* | *ritualistic violence* —**ritualistically** /-kli/ *adv.*

ritz·y /ˈrɪtsi/ *adj. comparative* **ritzier**, *superlative* **ritziest** INFORMAL fashionable and expensive: *We had dinner at a ritzy hotel.* [**Origin:** 1900–2000 *Ritz* hotels, international group of fashionable and expensive hotels founded by César Ritz]

ri·val¹ /ˈraɪvəl/ W3 *n.* [C] **1** a person, group, or organization that you compete with in sports, business, a fight etc. SYN **competitor**: *He took control of the party by eliminating rivals.* | **sb's rival** *This gives the company a competitive advantage over its rivals.* | +**for** *one of his rivals for the job* | **rival company/nation/team etc.** *two rival Arab tribes* | **sb's nearest/closest rival** *She was two minutes faster than her nearest rival.* | *The two boxers were* ***old rivals*** (=had been rivals for a long time). | *The Red Sox play tonight against their* ***arch rivals*** (=the team with whom they feel the strongest competition), *the Yankees.* **2** one of a number of things that people can choose between: *The newest model has several advantages over its rivals.* | *He* ***has few rivals*** (=is better than most) *as a writer of detective stories.* [**Origin:** 1500–1600 Latin *rivalis* **someone who uses the same stream as another, rival in love**, from *rivus* **stream**]

rival² *v.* [T] to be as good or important as someone or something else: *The college's facilities rival those of Harvard and Yale.* | **rival sth in sth** *The storm rivaled hurricane Katrina in intensity.* → see also UNRIVALED

ri·val·ry /ˈraɪvəlri/ *n. plural* **rivalries** [C,U] continuous competition: *Most of the killings result from gang rivalry.* | *ethnic rivalries* → see also at SIBLING RIVALRY

riv·en /ˈrɪvən/ *adj.* FORMAL split violently apart: *Somalia's south remains riven by tribal feuds.*

riv·er /ˈrɪvɚ/ S2 W2 *n.* [C] **1** EARTH SCIENCE a natural and continuous flow of water in a long line across a country into an ocean, lake etc.: *the Mississippi River* | **up/down (the) river** (=in the same direction as the river flows, or in the opposite direction) *We went down river in a canoe.* → see picture on page A31 **2** a large amount of moving liquid: +**of** *A river of mud flowed down the hill.* [**Origin:** 1200–1300 Old French *rivere*, from Latin *riparius* **of a river bank**] → see also **sell sb down the river** at SELL¹ (11)

Ri·ve·ra /rɪˈvɛrə/, **Di·e·go** /diˈeɪgoʊ/ (1886–1957) a Mexican PAINTER famous for his wall paintings showing the life and history of the Mexican people

ˈriver ˌbasin *n.* [C] EARTH SCIENCE an area from which all the water flows into the same river

ˈriver bed *n.* [C] EARTH SCIENCE the ground over which a river flows

riv·er·side /ˈrɪvɚˌsaɪd/ *n.* [singular] the land on the banks of a river: **riverside city/home etc.** *a beautiful riverside park*

riv·et¹ /ˈrɪvɪt/ *v.* [T] **1** to attract and hold someone's attention: *We stopped the car, riveted by the bizarre scene ahead of us.* | **be riveted on/to sth** *All eyes were riveted to the tiny television set.* **2** to fasten something with rivets

rivet² *n.* [C] a metal pin used to fasten pieces of metal together

riv·et·ing /ˈrɪvəṭɪŋ/ *adj.* something that is riveting is so interesting or exciting that you cannot stop watching it or listening to it: *his riveting performance as a drug addict*

riv·i·er·a /ˌrɪviˈɛrə/ *n.* **the Riviera** a warm coast that is popular with people who are on vacation, especially the Mediterranean coast of France [**Origin:** 1700–1800 Italian **coast, shore**]

riv·u·let /ˈrɪvyəlɪt/ *n.* [C] a very small stream of liquid, especially water: *Rivulets of rain ran down the window.*

Riy·adh /ˈriyɑd/ the capital and largest city of Saudi Arabia

ri·yal, **rial** /riˈɑl, -ˈæl/ *n.* [C] the standard unit of money in Saudi Arabia and other Arab countries

RN *n.* [C] the abbreviation of REGISTERED NURSE

RNA *n.* [U] BIOLOGY **ribonucleic acid** an important chemical that exists in all living cells. It is involved in making PROTEINS and also in the process of INHERITANCE.

roach /roʊtʃ/ *n.* **1** BIOLOGY a COCKROACH **2** SLANG the end part of a MARIJUANA cigarette **3** BIOLOGY a European fish similar to a CARP

road /roʊd/ S1 W1 *n.* **1** [C,U] a specially prepared hard surface for cars, buses, bicycles etc. to travel on: *They live on a very busy road.* | *a narrow road* | **up/down/along the road** (=further along the road) *I ran down the road to see what was happening.* | **by/at the side of the road** *Two police cars were parked by the side of the road.* | *Alaska's ferry system connects cities that can't be reached* ***by road***. | *Turn left on the next* ***main road***. | *They turned off the highway onto a* ***side road*** (=smaller road). | *A twisting* ***dirt road*** (=without a hard surface) *led to her house.* → see also ROADWORK → see Word Choice box at STREET

THESAURUS

Types of road
street a road in a town, with houses or stores on each side
main street a road in the middle of a town where many stores, offices etc. are
avenue a road in a town, often with trees on each side
boulevard a wide road in a town or city
lane a narrow road in the country, or one of the two or three parallel areas on a road which are divided by painted lines to keep traffic apart
main road a large and important road
the main drag INFORMAL the main road through a town
back/side road a small road that is not used much
highway a very wide road for traveling fast over long distances
freeway/expressway a very wide road in a city or between cities, on which cars can travel very fast without stopping
toll road a road that you pay to use
turnpike a large road for fast traffic that you pay to use
interstate a road for fast traffic that goes between states

2 on the road a) traveling in a car, especially for long distances: *We were back on the road before dawn.* **b)** if a group of actors or musicians is on the road, they are traveling from place to place giving performances **c)** if your car is on the road, you have paid for the repairs, tax etc. necessary for you to legally drive it: *It costs a lot of money to keep these old cars on the road.* **3 on the road to peace/recovery/democracy etc.** developing in a way that will result in peace etc.: *We are already on the road to economic recovery.* **4 the road to sth** a process or series of events that will achieve something or have a particular result: *the first steps on the road to success* **5 down the road** INFORMAL in the future: *We might get married, but that's much further down the road.* **6 down a road** INFORMAL following a particular course of action: *We've been down that road before, and we know it doesn't work.* **7 one for the road** SPOKEN a last alcoholic drink before you leave a party, bar etc. **8 the road to hell is paved with good intentions** used to say that it is not enough to intend to do something good, because people are judged by their actions, not by their intentions [**Origin:** Old English *rad* **ride, journey**] → see also **the end of the road** at END¹ (12), **hit the road** at HIT¹ (22)

road·block /ˈroʊdblɑk/ *n.* [C] **1** a place where the police are stopping traffic: *Police* ***set up*** *ten* ***roadblocks*** *around Las Cruces.* **2** something that stops the progress of a plan: *a major roadblock in the peace talks*

ˈroad hog *n.* [C] INFORMAL someone who drives with their car taking up most of a road and does not let others drive by

road·house /ˈroʊdhaʊs/ *n.* [C] a restaurant or bar on a main road outside a city

road·ie /ˈroʊdi/ *n.* [C] INFORMAL someone whose job is moving equipment for a group of musicians when they are traveling to different places to perform

road·kill /ˈroʊdkɪl/ *n.* [U] INFORMAL animals that are killed by cars and other vehicles

ˈroad ˌmanager *n.* [C] someone who makes arrangements for entertainers when they are traveling

ˈroad map *n.* [C] **1** a map of all the roads in an area **2** a plan for achieving something: *The U.S. must come up with a road map for achieving peace in Iraq.*

ˈroad rage *n.* [U] violence and angry behavior by car drivers toward other car drivers

road·run·ner /ˈroʊdˌrʌnɚ/ *n.* [C] BIOLOGY a small American bird that runs very fast and that usually lives in deserts

road·show /ˈroʊdʃoʊ/ *n.* [C] a set of performances, meetings, or events in which each one is held in a different city or town: *a roadshow to promote the company to investors*

road·side /ˈroʊdsaɪd/ *n.* [singular] the land at the edges of a road: **a roadside cafe/restaurant etc.** *a roadside hamburger place*

ˈroad sign *n.* [C] a sign next to a road, that gives information to drivers

ˈroad test *n.* [C] **1** a test to check that a vehicle is in good condition and safe to drive **2** the part of a driving test which involves driving on roads, rather than answering questions —**roadtest** *v.* [T]

ˈroad trip *n.* [C] a long trip you take in a car, usually with friends

road·way /ˈroʊdweɪ/ *n. plural* **roadways** [C,U] the part of the road used by vehicles

road·work, **road work** /ˈroʊdwɚk/ *n.* [U] repairs that are being done to a road: *Roadwork has slowed traffic to a crawl.*

road·wor·thy /ˈroʊdˌwɚði/ *adj.* a vehicle that is roadworthy is in good condition and safe enough to drive —**roadworthiness** *n.* [U]

roam /roʊm/ *v.* **1** [I,T] to walk, travel, or move around an area, usually for a long time, with no clear purpose or direction: *At one point, buffalo freely roamed North America.* | *The kids roamed the neighborhood on their*

R

bikes. | +**around/through/over etc.** *He's been roaming around Italy for the last two or three months.* **2** [I] if your eyes roam over something, you look slowly at all parts of it: +**over** *Harry's eyes roamed over her body.*

roam·ing /ˈroʊmɪŋ/ *n.* [U] **1** the process that a cell phone uses when it is in a different area from usual, and has to connect to a different network **2** the act of walking or traveling, usually for a long time, with no clear purpose or direction: *After 18 years of roaming, she settled down in Missouri.*

roan /roʊn/ *n.* [C] a horse that is a light reddish brown color —**roan** *adj.*

roar[1] /rɔr/ *v.* **1** [I] if a lion roars, it makes a very loud, frightening sound with its mouth wide open: *The lions roared in their cages.* **2** [T] to say or shout something in a deep, powerful voice, showing anger another emotion: *"Get out!" he roared.* ►see THESAURUS box at **shout**[1] **3** [I always + adv./prep.] to move very quickly and noisily: +**past/down etc.** *Cars full of young kids roared by with streamers flying.* **4** [I] to make a deep, very loud noise: *There was a huge fire roaring in the fireplace.* **5** [I] to suddenly laugh very loudly: *When she told him about the call, he* ***roared with laughter***. **6** [I,T] WRITTEN if a crowd roars, the people in the crowd all shout together because they are angry or excited, making a very loud noise: *The crowd roared in delight.* **7** [I always + adv./prep] to suddenly start performing much better in a sports game, especially so that you move ahead of your opponent: **roar past/back/ahead etc.** *The Dolphins roared past the Houston Oilers in the second half.* [**Origin:** Old English *rarian*]

R

roar[2] *n.* [C] **1** a continuous loud noise, especially one made by wind, water, a machine, or a crowd of people: *the roar of the surf* | *the roar of the airplane's engines* | *The crowd noise had risen to a roar.* **2** a deep, loud noise made by an animal such as a LION, or by someone's voice: *Nadia let out a roar of laughter.*

roar·ing /ˈrɔrɪŋ/ *adj.* **1** [only before noun] making a deep, very loud, continuous noise: *a roaring waterfall* **2 roaring fire** a roaring fire in a FIREPLACE is large and gives off a pleasant warmth **3 roaring drunk** very drunk and noisy **4 a roaring success** a person, business, performance etc. that is a roaring success is extremely successful

roast[1] /roʊst/ *v.* **1** [I,T] to cook something, such as meat, in an OVEN or over a fire ►see THESAURUS box at **cook**[1] **2** [I,T] to heat nuts, coffee, beans etc. quickly in order to dry them and give them a pleasant taste: *dry-roasted peanuts* **3** [T] INFORMAL to strongly criticize or make insulting remarks about someone or something: *Many fans roasted the players after the game.*

roast[2] *n.* [C] **1** a large piece of roasted meat → see also POT ROAST **2** an occasion at which people celebrate a special event in someone's life by telling funny stories or giving speeches about them: *We're going to have a roast for Jack when he retires.* **3** an outdoor party at which food is cooked on an open fire SYN **cookout**: *an oyster roast*

roast[3] *adj.* [only before noun] roasted: *roast beef*

roast·ing /ˈroʊstɪŋ/ also **ˌroasting ˈhot** *adj.* INFORMAL very hot, especially so that you feel uncomfortable: *a roasting hot day*

rob /rɑb/ *v.* **robbed, robbing** [T] **1** to steal money or property from a person, bank etc.: *The man is wanted for robbing several gas stations.* | *We* ***got robbed*** *last summer.* | **rob sb of sth** *Her first husband had robbed her of her fortune.* ►see THESAURUS box at **steal**[1] **2** to cause someone to no longer have something or someone good, for example a good quality, or a person you love: **rob sb/sth of sth** *A hamstring injury had robbed him of his speed.* | *The accident robbed the children of their mother.* **3 rob the cradle** INFORMAL to have a sexual relationship with someone who is a lot younger than you **4 rob Peter to pay Paul** INFORMAL to use money that you needed for something to pay for something else

rob·ber /ˈrɑbɚ/ *n.* [C] someone who steals money or property: *a bank robber*

ˌrobber ˈbaron *n.* [C] a powerful person who uses money and influence to get more money, businesses, land etc., in a way that is slightly dishonest

rob·ber·y /ˈrɑbəri/ *n. plural* **robberies** [C,U] the crime of stealing things from a bank, store etc., especially using violence: *The weapon was used in this morning's robbery.* | *He got a 20-year sentence for* ***armed robbery*** (=robbery using a gun). → see also **highway robbery** at HIGHWAY, MUGGING

robe[1] /roʊb/ *n.* [C] **1** also **robes** a long loose piece of clothing, especially one worn for official ceremonies: *the judge's black robes* **2** a long loose piece of clothing that you wear over your night clothes or after a bath SYN **bathrobe** [**Origin:** 1200–1300 Old French **stolen things, (stolen) clothes**]

robe[2] *v.* FORMAL **be robed in sth** to be dressed in a particular way: *The hostess looked very glamorous, robed in emerald velvet.*

Rob·erts /ˈrɑbɚts/, **John** (1955–) a U.S. judge who became the Chief Justice of the U.S. Supreme Court in 2005

Robes·pierre /ˌroʊbzˈpyɛr/, **Max·i·mil·i·en** /ˌmæksɪˈmɪliən/ (1758–1794) one of the leaders of the French Revolution

rob·in /ˈrɑbɪn/ *n.* [C] **1** BIOLOGY a common North American bird with a red breast and brown back **2** BIOLOGY a European bird like an American robin, but smaller [**Origin:** 1500–1600 *robin redbreast* **robin**, from *Robin*, form of the male name *Robert*]

Robin Hood /ˈrɑbɪn ˌhʊd/ in old English stories, a man who is remembered especially for robbing the rich and giving to the poor

Rob·in·son /ˈrɑbənsən/, **Jack·ie** /ˈdʒæki/ (1919–1972) a baseball player who was the first African-American person to be allowed to play in the MAJOR LEAGUES

Robinson, Sug·ar Ray /ˈʃʊgɚ reɪ/ (1920–1989) a BOXER who was the world CHAMPION in the 1940s and 1950s

ro·bot /ˈroʊbɑt, -bʌt/ *n.* [C] **1** a machine that can move and do some of the work of a person, and is usually controlled by a computer: *assembly line robots* **2** a machine that looks like a person, and can talk and walk and do some things that humans can do, especially in stories: *a planet inhabited by robots* **3** DISAPPROVING someone who works or behaves like a machine, without showing their thoughts or feelings [**Origin:** 1900–2000 Czech *robota* **work**] —**robotic** /roʊˈbɑtɪk/ *adj.*

ro·bot·ics /roʊˈbɑtɪks/ *n.* [U] SCIENCE the study of how robots are made and used

ro·bust /roʊˈbʌst, ˈroʊbʌst/ *adj.* **1** a robust person is strong and healthy: *a robust mother of four boys* **2** a robust system, organization etc. is strong and not likely to have problems: *Retail sales have been robust this year.* **3** a robust object is strong and not likely to break: *The chair was more robust than it looked.* ►see THESAURUS box at **strong** **4** robust food or FLAVORS have a good, strong taste: *a robust cheese* **5** behaving or speaking in a strong and determined way: *The Governor gave a robust defense of his policies.* [**Origin:** 1500–1600 Latin *robustus* **strong (like an oak tree)**, from *robur* **oak, strength**] —**robustly** *adv.* —**robustness** *n.* [U]

rock[1] /rɑk/ S2 W2 *n.*
1 STONE a) [U] EARTH SCIENCE stone, or a type of stone that forms part of the Earth's surface: *Geologists study the exposed sections of rock.* | *The road was flanked by boulders and tall* ***rock formations*** (=shapes made naturally from rock). **b)** [C] a piece of stone, especially a large one: *Eugene stood on a rock and called for help.* | *A ship was driven onto the rocks during the storm.*
2 MUSIC [U] also **rock music** ENG. LANG. ARTS a type of popular modern music with a strong loud beat, played using GUITARS and drums: *a rock concert* | *The station plays rock, blues, and jazz.*
3 be on the rocks INFORMAL a relationship or business

that is on the rocks is having a lot of problems and is likely to fail soon: *His third marriage was on the rocks.* **4 scotch/vodka etc. on the rocks** INFORMAL an alcoholic drink that is served with ice but with no water added
5 be (stuck) between a rock and a hard place INFORMAL to have a choice between two things, both of which are bad or dangerous
6 JEWEL [C usually plural] INFORMAL a DIAMOND or other jewel
7 as solid/steady as a rock a) very strongly built or well supported and not likely to break or fall: *The walls were still solid as a rock after 50 years.* **b)** someone who is as solid or steady as a rock is very strong and calm in difficult situations and you can depend on them → see also ROCK-SOLID
[**Origin:** (1, 3–7) 1300–1400 Old North French *roque* from Vulgar Latin *rocca*]

rock² S3 *v.* **1** [I,T] to move gently, leaning backward and forward or from one side to the other, or to make something do this: *The chair squeaked as I rocked back and forth* | *Waves from a passing freighter rocked the boat.* **2** [T] to make the people in a place or organization feel very shocked or surprised, especially because they have to deal with problems or changes: *The company was rocked by massive changes in the computer business.* **3 rock the boat** INFORMAL to cause problems for other members of a group by criticizing something or trying to change the way something is done: *As long as you don't rock the boat, nobody cares what you do.* **4 sb/sth rocks** SLANG said to show that you strongly approve of someone or something or are grateful to them: *Thanks, man. You rock!* **5** [T] EARTH SCIENCE if an explosion or EARTHQUAKE (=violent movement of the earth) rocks an area, it makes it shake

rock•a•bil•ly /ˈrɑkəˌbɪli/ *n.* [U] a type of music that combines rock music and traditional country music

ˌrock and ˈroll *n.* [U] ROCK 'N' ROLL

ˈrock ˈbottom *n.* **hit/reach rock bottom** INFORMAL to become as unhappy or unsuccessful as it is possible to be: *Our marriage had finally hit rock bottom.*

ˈrock-ˌbottom *adj.* a rock-bottom price is as low as it can possibly be: *rock-bottom real estate prices*

ˈrock ˌclimbing *n.* [U] the sport of climbing up very steep rock surfaces such as the sides of mountains —**rock climber** *n.* [C]

ˈrock-ˌcrystal *n.* [U] pure natural QUARTZ (=a very hard mineral) that is transparent

Rock•e•fel•ler /ˈrɑkəˌfɛlɚ/, **John D.** (1839–1937) a U.S. businessman and PHILANTHROPIST who started the Standard Oil Company in 1870

Rockefeller, John D., II (1874–1960) the son of John D. Rockefeller who gave the U.N. the land for its HEADQUARTERS, and built the Rockefeller Center in New York City

ˈRockefeller Founˌdation, the an organization that supports scientific RESEARCH, especially to improve the environment and social conditions

rock•er /ˈrɑkɚ/ *n.* [C] **1** a ROCKING CHAIR **2** one of the curved pieces of wood at the bottom of a ROCKING CHAIR **3** a musician who plays ROCK 'N' ROLL music, or someone who likes this kind of music: *rocker Carl Perkins* **4 be off your rocker** SPOKEN to be crazy

rock•et¹ /ˈrɑkɪt/ W3 *n.* [C] **1** a vehicle used for traveling or carrying things into space, which is shaped like a big tube ▶see THESAURUS box at space¹ **2** a similar object used as a weapon, especially one that carries a bomb: *The rocket attacks are coming from a nearby neighborhood.* **3** a small tube fastened to a stick, that contains explosive powder and is used as a FIREWORKS **4 sth isn't rocket science** HUMOROUS used to say that something is very easy to do, and only stupid people would be unable to do it: *Making a sandwich isn't rocket*

R

rock cycle

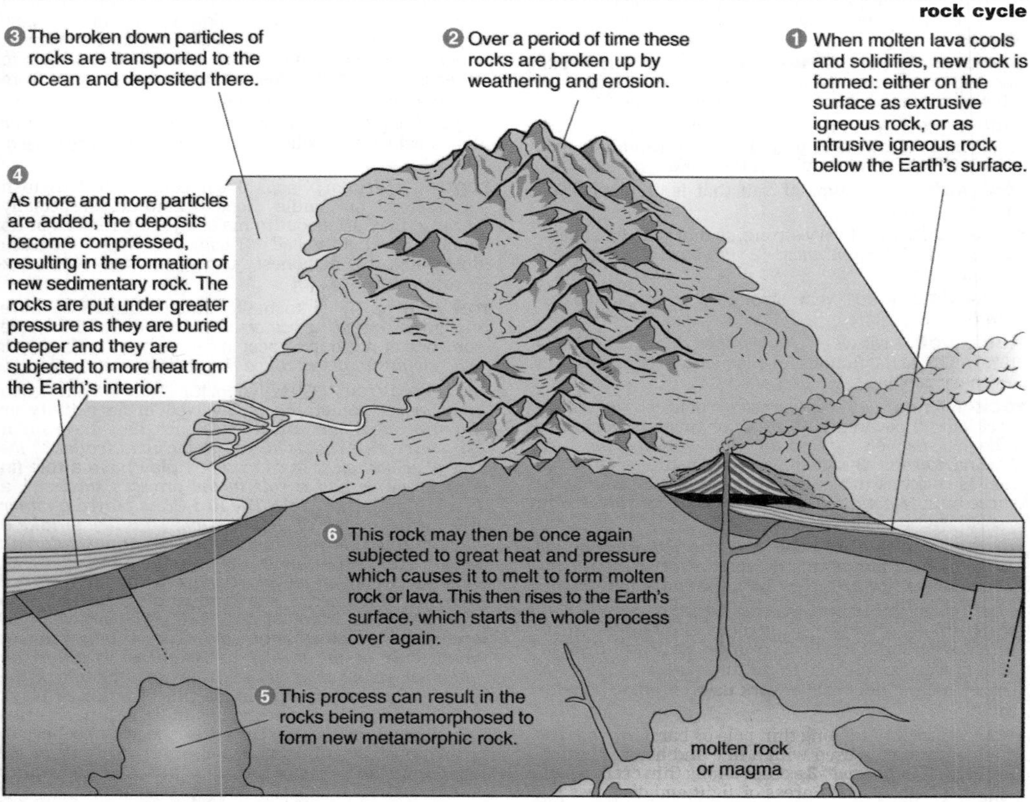
③ The broken down particles of rocks are transported to the ocean and deposited there.
② Over a period of time these rocks are broken up by weathering and erosion.
① When molten lava cools and solidifies, new rock is formed: either on the surface as extrusive igneous rock, or as intrusive igneous rock below the Earth's surface.
④ As more and more particles are added, the deposits become compressed, resulting in the formation of new sedimentary rock. The rocks are put under greater pressure as they are buried deeper and they are subjected to more heat from the Earth's interior.
⑥ This rock may then be once again subjected to great heat and pressure which causes it to melt to form molten rock or lava. This then rises to the Earth's surface, which starts the whole process over again.
⑤ This process can result in the rocks being metamorphosed to form new metamorphic rock.
molten rock or magma

science, you know. → see also ROCKET SCIENTIST [**Origin:** 1600–1700 Italian *rocchetta* **small stick used in spinning thread**, from *rocca* **stick used in spinning**]

rocket² *v.* [I] **1** also **rocket up** if a price or amount rockets, it increases quickly and suddenly: *Prices rocketed up overnight.* | **rocket (from sth) to sth** *Profits rocketed to $10 million.* **2** [always + adv./prep.] to move somewhere very fast SYN **shoot**: **+through/along etc.** *They rocketed by in their sleek limousines.* **3** [always + adv./prep.] to achieve a successful position very quickly: **rocket (sb) to sth** *The album rocketed to number one in the charts.* | *The movie rocketed Newman to stardom.*

'rocket ˌlauncher *n.* [C] a weapon like a tube used for firing military rockets into the air

'rocket ˌscientist *n.* [C] **1** a scientist whose work is related to rockets **2 it doesn't take a rocket scientist (to do sth)** also **you don't have to be a rocket scientist (to do sth)** HUMOROUS used to say that something is very easy to do, and only stupid people would be unable to do it: *It doesn't take a rocket scientist to understand that this was no accident.* **3 sb is no rocket scientist** HUMOROUS used to say that someone is very stupid

R

rock·fall /ˈrɑkˌfɔl/ *n.* [C] a pile of rocks that are falling or have fallen

'rock ˌgarden *n.* [C] a type of garden where there are rocks with small plants growing between them

ˌrock-'hard *adj.* extremely hard

'rocking chair *n.* [C] a chair that has two curved pieces of wood under its legs, so that you can make it lean backward and forward in a repeated, gentle movement, as you sit in it → see picture at CHAIR¹

'rocking horse *n.* [C] a wooden horse for children that leans backward and forward in a repeated gentle movement when you sit on it

'rock ˌmusic *n.* [U] a type of popular modern music with a strong loud beat, played using GUITARS and drums

Rock·ne /ˈrɑkni/, **Knute** /nut/ (1888–1931) a U.S. football COACH famous for developing new methods of playing that made his team extremely successful

rock 'n' roll /ˌrɑk ən ˈroʊl/ *n.* [U] a type of music with a strong loud beat and played on GUITARS and drums, which first became popular in the 1950s

'rock salt *n.* [U] a type of salt that is obtained from under the ground

ˌrock-'solid *adj.* **1** very strong, so that you can depend on it: *rock-solid commitment* **2** very hard and not likely to break

ˌrock-'steady *adj.* very strong or very calm: *rock-steady nerves*

Rock·well /ˈrɑkwɛl/, **Nor·man** /ˈnɔrmən/ (1894–1978) a U.S. artist famous for his pictures of the lives of ordinary people

rock·y /ˈrɑki/ *adj.* *comparative* **rockier**, *superlative* **rockiest** **1** covered with rocks or made of rock: *The village sits on a rocky hill overlooking the Mediterranean.* **2** INFORMAL a relationship or situation that is rocky is difficult and may not continue or be successful: *Negotiations **got off to a rocky start** today.* —**rockiness** *n.* [U]

ˌRocky 'Mountains, the also **the Rockies** a long range of high mountains in North America that runs from Alsaka down to New Mexico, and separates the Midwest of the U.S. from the West Coast

ro·co·co /rəˈkoʊkoʊ/ *adj.* rococo buildings and furniture have a lot of curly decoration and were fashionable in Europe in the 18th century [**Origin:** 1800–1900 French *rocaille* **decorative work using stones**, from *roc* **rock**]

rod /rɑd/ *n.* [C] **1** a long thin pole or bar: *a curtain rod* **2** a long thin pole used with a line and hook for catching fish: *a fishing rod* **3** BIOLOGY a long thin CELL in your eye, that helps you see areas of light and darkness but not color → see also CONE [**Origin:** Old English *rodd*] → see also HOT ROD, LIGHTNING ROD

rode /roʊd/ *v.* the past tense of RIDE

ro·dent /ˈroʊdnt/ *n.* [C] BIOLOGY one of a group of small animals with long sharp front teeth, such as rats or rabbits [**Origin:** 1800–1900 Latin, present participle of *rodere* **to chew with the front teeth**]

ro·de·o /ˈroʊdiˌoʊ, roʊˈdeɪoʊ/ *n.* *plural* **rodeos** [C] a type of entertainment in which COWBOYS ride wild horses, catch cattle with ropes, and ride in races [**Origin:** 1800–1900 Spanish *rodear* **to surround**]

Rod·gers /ˈrɑdʒɚz/, **Richard** (1902–1979) a U.S. COMPOSER famous for writing MUSICALS with Lorenz Hart and Oscar Hammerstein

Ro·din /roʊˈdæn/, **Au·guste** /oʊˈgust/ (1840–1917) a French SCULPTOR who is considered the greatest sculptor of his time

roe /roʊ/ *n.* [C,U] fish eggs eaten as a food

roent·gen, röntgen /ˈrɛntˀgən, ˈrʌnt-/ *n.* [C] TECHNICAL the international measure for X-RAYS

Roent·gen, Röntgen /ˈrɛntˀgən, ˈrʌntˀ-/, **Wil·helm** /ˈvɪlhɛlm/ (1845–1923) a German scientist who discovered X-rays

Roeth·ke /ˈrɛtki/, **The·o·dore** /ˈθiədɔr/ (1908–1963) a U.S. poet

Roe v. Wade /ˌroʊ vɚsəs ˈweɪd/ LAW a decision by the Supreme Court in 1973 that made ABORTION in the first three months of PREGNANCY legal in the U.S.

rog·er /ˈrɑdʒɚ/ *interjection* used in radio conversations to say that a message has been understood

Rog·ers /ˈrɑdʒɚz/, **Will** (1879–1935) a U.S. humorous writer and performer, famous for his jokes that criticized politicians

Ro·get /roʊˈʒeɪ/, **Peter Mark** (1779–1869) a British doctor who wrote the first English THESAURUS

rogue¹ /roʊg/ *adj.* [only before noun] **1** not behaving in the usual or correct way and often causing trouble: *a rogue gene* | **rogue state/regime** (=a country or government that does not conform to the laws that most other governments do, and is considered a danger to other nations) **2** a rogue wild animal lives apart from the main group and is often dangerous

rogue² *n.* [C] a man who behaves in a slightly bad or dishonest way, but whom people still like —**roguery** *n.* [U]

rogu·ish /ˈroʊgɪʃ/ *adj.* **1** someone with a roguish expression or smile looks amused, especially because they are about to make a joking remark or do something slightly bad **2** someone who is roguish does slightly dishonest things —**roguishly** *adv.* —**roguishness** *n.* [U]

roil /rɔɪl/ *v.* [T] **1** to make water, clouds etc. move violently: *Joy-riding boaters roiled the water.* **2** to make someone or a group or people feel nervous or annoyed: *Wild swings in prices roiled the stock market.*

role, rôle /roʊl/ Ac S2 W1 *n.* [C] **1** the way in which someone or something is involved in an activity or situation, and how much influence they have on it SYN **part**: **+in** *What is his role in the investigation?* | *the role of government in education* | **play/have a role (in sth)** *Everyone had a role in the project's success.* | **a leading/major/key role** *The Red Cross played a major role in the country's rehabilitation.* | *I'd like to **take a more active role** (=be more involved) at my children's school.* **2** ENG. LANG. ARTS the character played by an actor in a play or movie SYN **part**: *Brendan **played the role of** Romeo.* | **the lead/leading/starring role** *Alexander had sung leading roles in more than 50 operas.* | **a major/minor role** *Costner only plays a minor role in the movie.* | *"Peter Pan" features an unknown young actor in **the title role*** (=the role of the character whose name is in the title of a film or play). **3** the position that someone has in society, in an organization etc., or the way they are expected to behave in a relationship with someone else: *her new role in the company* | *I enjoy my role as a husband and father.* **4 role reversal** a situation in which two people, usually a man and a woman or a child and a parent, take each other's traditional roles: *At 19, I had to take my dad to the hospital, which was a scary role reversal.* [**Origin:** 1600–1700 French *rôle* **roll, role**, from Old French *rolle* **rolled up document**]

ˈrole ˌmodel *n.* [C] someone whose behavior, attitudes etc. people try to copy because they admire them: **+for/to** *She is a role model for many women in business.*

ˈrole-play *n.* [C,U] an exercise in which you behave in the way that someone else would behave in a particular situation, especially to help you learn something: *ideas for classroom role-play* —**role-play** *v.* [I,T]

roll[1] /roʊl/ S1 W2 *v.*

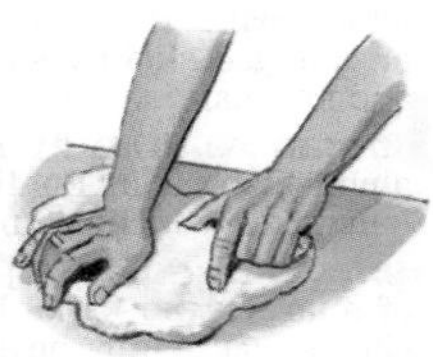

1 ROUND OBJECT [I always + adv./prep.,T always + adv./prep.] if something that is round rolls or if you roll it, it moves along a surface by turning over and over: *One of the eggs rolled off the counter.* | *The kids were rolling a tire down the hill.* | **roll sth in sth** *Roll the scallops in the Cajun spice mix.* ►see THESAURUS box at **push**[1]
2 PERSON/ANIMAL [I always + adv./prep.] also **roll over** to turn your body over one or more times while lying down: *Ralph rolled onto his stomach.* | *I'm trying to teach my dog to roll over.*
3 STH WITH WHEELS [I always + adv./prep., T always + adv./prep.] to move on wheels, or make something that has wheels move: **+into/forward/past etc.** *The truck rolled to a stop.* | **roll sth to/around/by etc.** *The waitress rolled the dessert cart over to our table.*
4 PAPER/STRING ETC. [T] also **roll up** to bend or wind something such as paper, string etc. into the shape of a tube or ball: *She rolled up the poster and put it in a cardboard tube.* | **roll sth into sth** *Roll the dough into small balls.*
5 DROP OF LIQUID [I always + adv./prep.] to move over a surface smoothly without stopping: **+down/onto etc.** *Sweat rolled off his forehead.*
6 WAVES/CLOUDS [I always + adv./prep.] to move in a particular direction: **+into/toward etc.** *Huge waves rolled onto the beach.*
7 roll your eyes to move your eyes around and up, especially in order to show that you are annoyed: *My friends roll their eyes when I mention her name.*
8 GAME [I,T] if you roll DICE, you throw them as part of a game
9 SHIP/PLANE [I] if a ship or airplane rolls, it leans one way and then another with the movement of the water or air
10 MAKE STH FLAT [T] to make something flat by moving something heavy over it: *Roll the dough into a 12-inch square.*
11 SOUND [I] if drums or THUNDER roll, they make a long low series of sounds
12 MACHINE/CAMERA [I] if a machine such as a movie camera or a PRINTING PRESS rolls, it operates
13 (all) rolled into one if something is several different things rolled into one, it includes qualities of all those things: *The band's sound was metal and punk and rap all rolled into one.*
14 get rolling if a plan, business etc. gets rolling, it starts operating: *The project finally got rolling a year ago.*
15 be rolling in money/dough/cash/it to have or earn a lot of money
16 roll out of bed INFORMAL to get out of bed: *In college, I rarely rolled out of bed before noon.*
17 be rolling in the aisles if people in a theater, AUDIENCE etc. are rolling in the aisles, they are laughing a lot
18 be ready to roll INFORMAL used to say you are ready to do something or go somewhere: *After months of planning, we were finally ready to roll.*
19 roll with the punches to deal with problems or difficulties by doing whatever you need to do, rather than by trying only one method: *A business needs to roll with the punches in order to survive.*
20 ATTACK [T] INFORMAL to rob someone, especially when they are drunk and asleep: *Punks on the streets would roll drunks for small change.*
21 roll your r's to pronounce the sound /r/ using your tongue in a way that makes the sound very long
22 a rolling stone gathers no moss used to say that someone who often changes jobs, moves to different places etc. is not able to have any real relationships or responsibilities
23 roll a cigarette to make your own cigarette, using loose tobacco and special paper
[**Origin:** 1300–1400 Old French *roller*, from Vulgar Latin *rotulare*, from Latin *rotula*] → see also **set/start the ball rolling** at BALL[1] (5), **heads will roll** at HEAD[1] (25)

roll around *phr. v.* if something such as a time or event that happens regularly rolls around, it happens again: *By the time dinner time rolls around, the boys are very tired.*

roll sth ↔ **back** *phr. v.* **1** to reduce the price of something: *Ticket prices will be rolled back to 1968 levels for one week.* **2** to reduce the influence or power of a system, government etc., especially because it has too much power: *The bill would roll back the tax cuts of 2004.* **3** to force your opponents in a war to move back from their position

roll sth ↔ **down** *phr. v.* **1 roll a window down** also **roll down a window** to open a car window **2 roll your sleeves/pants down** to unfold the ends of your SLEEVES or the legs of your pants so that they are their usual length

roll in *phr. v.* **1** to happen or arrive in large numbers or quantities: *The money rolled in, and the business grew.* **2** if clouds, mist etc. roll in, they begin to cover an area of the sky or land: *It looks like the fog is already rolling in.* **3** INFORMAL if someone rolls in, they arrive much later than usual or expected, and you are annoyed because they are so late: *Rebecca sometimes rolls in around noon.*

roll sth ↔ **out** *phr. v.* **1** to make something flat and thin by pushing a special wooden roller over it: *Roll the pastry out flat.* **2** to make something flat and straight after it has been curled into a tube shape or a ball: *We rolled out our sleeping bags under the stars.* **3** to make a new product available for people to buy or use: *The network will be rolling out ten new TV shows in September.* **4 roll out the red carpet** to make special preparations for an important visitor

roll over *phr. v.* **1** to turn your body around once so that you are lying in a different position SYN **turn over**: *I rolled over and went back to sleep.* **2 roll sb/sth over** to turn someone's body over on the ground SYN **turn over**: *We have to roll him over onto his back.* **3** to make no effort to stop someone from doing something bad to you: *We can't just roll over and let them take our house away!* **4 roll sth ↔ over** to officially arrange to pay a debt at a later date than the date that was first agreed

roll up *phr. v.* **1** to curl something such as cloth or paper into a tube shape: *We rolled the carpet up.* **2 roll your sleeves/pants up** to turn the ends of your SLEEVES, pants etc. over several times so that they are shorter **3 roll your sleeves up** to start doing a job, even though it is difficult or you do not want to do it: *She just rolls up her sleeves and gets the job done.* **4 roll a window up** also **roll up a window** to close the window of a car **5 roll up into sth** if an animal rolls up into a ball, it forms its body into a ball shape

roll[2] S2 W3 *n.*
1 PAPER/FILM/MONEY ETC. [C] a piece of paper, film, money etc. that has been rolled into the shape of a tube: *The wallpaper costs $20 a roll.* | **+of** *a roll of film*
2 BREAD [C] a small round LOAF of bread for one person: *hot, fresh rolls* | *a cinnamon roll* → see picture at BREAD[1]
3 LIST OF NAMES an official list of names, especially of people at a meeting, in a class etc.: *The first thing we do in class is* ***call the roll*** (=say the list of names to check who is there). | *Half a million people have left* ***the welfare rolls*** (=a list of people without jobs who claim money from the state). | **the (voter) rolls** (=a list of the

people who are allowed to vote) ►see THESAURUS box at record[1]
4 roll of drums/thunder a long, low, fairly loud sound made by drums etc.
5 be on a roll INFORMAL to be having a lot of success with what you are trying to do: *Don't stop now. You're on a roll!*
6 GAME [C] the action of throwing DICE as part of a game SYN **throw**: *a roll of the dice*
7 SHIP/PLANE [C] the movement of a ship or airplane when it leans from side to side with the movement of the water or air
8 SKIN/FAT [C] a thick layer of skin or fat, usually just below your waist or around your neck: +**of** *rolls of loose skin*
9 a roll in the hay INFORMAL, HUMOROUS an act of having sex with someone

'roll bar *n.* [C] a strong metal bar over the top of a car, intended to protect the people inside if the car turns over

'roll call *n.* [C,U] the act of reading out an official list of names to check who is there

R

ˌrolled 'oats *n.* [plural] a type of OATS, used for making OATMEAL

roll·er /ˈroʊlɚ/ *n.* [C] **1** a tube-shaped piece of wood, metal etc. that can be rolled over and over, used for painting, crushing, making things smoother etc.: *a paint roller* **2** a small plastic or metal tube used for making hair curl SYN **curler** **3** a long, powerful wave: *Booming rollers crashed on the beach.* **4** a tube-shaped piece of metal or wood, used for moving heavy things that have no wheels → see also HIGH ROLLER

Roll·er·blade /ˈroʊlɚˌbleɪd/ *n.* [C] TRADEMARK ROLLER SKATE, IN-LINE SKATE —**rollerblade** *v.* [I] —**rollerblading** *n.* [U] → see picture at SKATE[1]

'roller ˌcoaster *n.* [C] **1** a track with sudden steep slopes and curves, which people ride on in special cars at FAIRS and AMUSEMENT PARKS **2** a situation that is impossible to control, because it keeps changing very quickly: *The last six months have been* ***an emotional roller coaster*** (=a situation that causes your emotions to change in extreme ways) *for our family.*

'roller skate *n.* [C] a special boot with four wheels attached under it —**roller-skate** *v.* [I] —**roller skating** *n.* [U] → see also IN-LINE SKATE

'roller ˌtowel *n.* [C] a cloth you use for drying your hands in a public place, which is joined together at the ends and wound around a bar of wood or metal

rol·lick·ing /ˈrɑlɪkɪŋ/ *adj.* [only before noun] noisy and cheerful: *a rollicking song*

roll·ing /ˈroʊlɪŋ/ *adj.* [only before noun] **1** rolling hills have many long gentle slopes **2** done or happening in stages over a period of time, not all at once: *The college has a rolling admissions policy.* **3** if you have a rolling walk, you move from side to side as you walk

'rolling mill *n.* [C] a factory or machine in which metal is rolled into large, flat, thin pieces

'rolling pin *n.* [C] a long tube-shaped piece of wood used for making PASTRY flat and thin before you cook it

'rolling stock *n.* [U] all the trains, BOXCARS, passenger cars etc. that are used on a railroad

'roll-on *adj.* a roll-on DEODORANT or other liquid is contained in a bottle with a ball in the neck which you move across your skin —**roll-on** *n.* [C]

roll·o·ver /ˈroʊlˌoʊvɚ/ *n.* **1** [C] a process in which money is moved from one bank account or INVESTMENT to another without any tax or other money having to be paid, or an account that is arranged in this way: *Many CD rollovers happen in October.* **2** [C] an accident in which a car turns over onto its roof

'roll-top ˌdesk *n.* [C] a desk that has a cover that you roll back when you open it

Ro·lo·dex /ˈroʊloʊˌdɛks/ *n.* [C] TRADEMARK a small container that sits on a desk and holds cards with people's names, addresses, and telephone numbers on them

ro·ly-po·ly /ˌroʊli ˈpoʊli◂/ *adj.* a roly-poly person is round and fat

ROM /rɑm/ *n.* [U] **Read-Only Memory** COMPUTERS the part of a computer where permanent information and instructions are stored → see also RAM

ro·maine /roʊˈmeɪn, ˈroʊmeɪn/ *n.* [U] a type of LETTUCE with long leaves

Ro·man /ˈroʊmən/ *adj.* **1** HISTORY relating to ancient Rome or the Roman Empire **2** relating to the city of Rome —**Roman** *n.* [C]

ro·man /ˈroʊmən/ *n.* [U] TECHNICAL the ordinary style of printing that uses small upright letters, like the style used for printing these words → see also ITALICS

ro·man à clef /roʊˌmɑn ɑ ˈkleɪ/ *n.* [C] a NOVEL in which real events and people are given different names or changed slightly, so that they seem to be invented and not real

ˌRoman 'alphabet *n.* **the Roman Alphabet** the alphabet used in English and many other European languages, which begins with the letters A, B, C

ˌRoman 'candle *n.* [C] a type of FIREWORKS in the shape of a large CANDLE that burns quickly and brightly and shoots SPARKS into the air

ˌRoman 'Catholic *adj.* belonging or related to the part of the Christian religion whose leader is the Pope —**Roman Catholic** *n.* [C] —**ˌRoman Ca'tholicism** *n.* [U]

ˌRoman ˌCatholic 'Church, the the largest church of the Christian religion, that has the Pope as its leader

ro·mance[1] /ˈroʊmæns, roʊˈmæns/ W3 *n.* **1** [C] an exciting and often short relationship between two people who love each other: *Their romance began in high school.* | *It was just a* ***summer romance*** (=one that happens during a vacation). *Paris is where her* ***whirlwind romance*** (=one that happens very suddenly and quickly) *started.* **2** [U] love, or a feeling of being in love: *The romance had gone out of their relationship.* **3** [U] the feeling of excitement and adventure that is related to a particular place, activity etc.: *the romance of life in the Wild West* **4** [C] ENG. LANG. ARTS a story, book, or movie about two people who fall in love with each other: *a historical romance* **5** [C] ENG. LANG. ARTS a story that has brave characters and exciting events: *a Medieval romance* [**Origin:** 1200–1300 Old French *romans* **French, something written in French**, from Latin *romanicus* **Roman**]

romance[2] *v.* [T] OLD-FASHIONED to try to persuade someone to love you

Ro'mance ˌlanguage *n.* [C] ENG. LANG. ARTS a language that comes from Latin, for example French or Spanish

Ro·man·esque /ˌroʊməˈnɛsk◂/ *adj.* in the style of building that was popular in Western Europe in the 11th and 12th centuries, which had many round ARCHES and thick PILLARS

Ro·ma·ni·a /roʊˈmeɪniə, rʊ-/ a country in southeast Europe, east of Hungary and west of the Black Sea —**Romanian** *n., adj.*

ˌRoman 'law *n.* [U] LAW → see CIVIL LAW

ˌRoman 'nose *n.* [C] a nose that curves out near the top

ˌroman 'numeral *n.* [C] MATH a number in a system first used in ancient Rome, that uses the combinations of the letters I, V, X, L, C, D, and M to represent numbers → see also ARABIC NUMERAL

Romano- /roʊmɑnoʊ, rə-/ *prefix* ancient Roman and something else: *Romano-British art*

Ro·ma·nov /ˈroʊmənɔf/ the name of a family of Russian CZARS who ruled from 1613 to 1917

Ro·mans /ˈroʊmənz/ a book in the New Testament of the Christian Bible

ro·man·tic[1] /roʊˈmæntɪk/ W3 *adj.*
1 SHOWING LOVE if you are romantic, or if you do romantic things, you treat the person that you love in a special way that makes them feel loved and special: *I wish my boyfriend was more romantic.*

2 PRODUCING LOVE making you have feelings of love for someone: *a romantic, candle-lit restaurant* | *She sent him a romantic note.*
3 RELATING TO LOVE [only before noun] relating to feelings of love or a loving relationship: *I'm not ready for a romantic relationship.* | *a marriage based on* ***romantic love*** (=love where people fall in love, rather than for example, love for friends or family)
4 UNREALISTIC romantic ideas are not based the way things really are, but on how someone would like them to be OPP **realistic**: **a romantic idea/view/notion** *I had a very romantic idea of what life on a farm was like.*
5 STORY/MOVIE about love: *a romantic comedy*
6 BEAUTIFUL beautiful in a way that strongly affects your emotions: *the wild and romantic west coast of Ireland*
7 LITERATURE/ART also **Romantic** relating to Romanticism: *the Romantic poets* —**romantically** /roʊˈmæntɪk/ *adv.*

romantic² *n.* [C] **1** someone who shows strong feelings of love and likes doing things that are related to love, such as buying flowers, presents etc.: *I'm a romantic who likes picnics and candlelight dinners.* **2** someone who is not practical, and bases their ideas too much on an imagined idea of the world **3** also **Romantic** ENG. LANG. ARTS a writer, painter etc., whose work is based on Romanticism

ro·man·ti·cism, **Romanticism** /roʊˈmæntəˌsɪzəm/ *n.* [U] a way of writing or painting that was popular in the late 18th and early 19th century, in which feelings and wild natural beauty were considered more important than anything else → see also CLASSICISM, REALISM

ro·man·ti·cize /roʊˈmæntəˌsaɪz/ *v.* [T] DISAPPROVING to talk or think about things in a way that makes them seem more romantic or attractive than they really are: *The movie romanticizes life on the streets.* —**romanticized** *adj.*: *romanticized memories of childhood*

Ro·ma·ny /ˈroʊməni/ *n.* **1 the Romany** the GYPSY people **2** [U] the language of the GYPSY people

Rome /roʊm/ the capital and largest city of Italy

Ro·me·o /ˈroʊmioʊ/ *n.* [C] OFTEN HUMOROUS a man who tries to attract all the women he meets in a ROMANTIC or sexual way: *He's the office Romeo.*

romp¹ /rɑmp/ *v.* [I] **1** to play in a noisy way, especially by running, jumping etc.: **+around/through etc.** *Children romped around happily in the puddles.* **2** [always + adv./prep.] to defeat another team or player in a sports competition very easily: **romp to a win/victory** *The women's team romped to a 132–81 win over Texas.* [**Origin:** 1700–1800 *ramp* **to behave threateningly** (14–19 centuries), from French *ramper*]

romp² *n.* [C] **1** an occasion when one sports team defeats another one very easily: **+over** *Nebraska's 59–28 romp over Utah State* **2** an occasion when people play noisily and roughly **3** INFORMAL a movie, play, book etc. that is funny, and full of exciting scenes: *"Tom Jones" is a bawdy romp through 18th-century England.*

romp·ers /ˈrɑmpɚz/ *n.* [plural] a piece of clothing for babies, made like a top and pants joined together

ron·do /ˈrɑndoʊ/ *n. plural* **rondos** [C] a piece of music in which the main tune is repeated so that one tune starts before the previous one finishes

rönt·gen /ˈrɛntˀgən, ˈrʌnt-/ *n.* [C] another spelling of ROENTGEN

roof¹ /ruf, rʊf/ S2 W3 *n.* [C]
1 OF A BUILDING the outside surface or structure on top of a building, vehicle, tent etc.: *We'll need a ladder to get up on the roof.* | *I left my coffee cup on the roof of the car.*
2 a roof over your head somewhere to live: *We always had food on the table and a roof over our heads.*
3 go through the roof INFORMAL **a)** if a price, cost etc. goes through the roof, it increases to a very high level **b)** also **hit the roof** to suddenly become very angry: *If Dad sees you he'll hit the roof!*
4 MOUTH the roof of your mouth the hard upper part of the inside of your mouth
5 UNDER GROUND the highest part of a passage under the ground, a CAVE etc.: *the roof of the cave*
6 under the same roof also **under one roof** in the same building or home: *You can buy groceries, hardware, and other services all under one roof.*
7 under sb's roof SPOKEN in someone's home: *While you're living under my roof, you'll follow my rules.*
[**Origin:** Old English *hrof*] → see also **raise the roof** at RAISE¹ (27), SUNROOF

roof² *v.* [T usually passive] **1** to put a roof on a building **2 metal-roofed/tile-roofed etc.** having a roof that is covered with a particular material

roof·ies /ˈrufiz/ *n.* [plural] SLANG an illegal drug that is sometimes used to make someone unconscious so they can be RAPED

roof·ing /ˈrufɪŋ/ *n.* [U] material such as SHINGLES or TILES etc., used for making or covering roofs

ˈroof-rack *n.* [C] a LUGGAGE RACK

roof·top /ˈruftɑp/ *n.* [C] the upper surface of a roof: *A cat was up on the rooftop.* → see also **shout sth from the rooftops** at SHOUT¹ (2)

rook¹ /rʊk/ *n.* [C] **1** one of the pieces in a game of CHESS SYN **castle** **2** BIOLOGY a large black European bird like a CROW

rook² *v.* [T] OLD-FASHIONED to cheat someone, especially to get their money SYN **cheat**

rook·er·y /ˈrʊkəri/ *n.* [C] a group of NESTS made by rooks or other birds that live together, such as PENGUINS

rook·ie /ˈrʊki/ *n.* [C] **1** someone who is in their first year of playing a professional sport: *He is likely to win the "Rookie of the Year" award.* **2** someone who has just started doing a job and has little experience: *The police at the crime scene were all rookies.* | **a rookie cop/soldier etc.** *a rookie radio reporter*

room¹ /rum, rʊm/ S1 W1 *n.*
1 IN A BUILDING [C] an area of the inside of a building that has its own walls, floor, and ceiling: *I looked at all the people in the room.* | *We're staying in room 804.* | *He's upstairs in his room* (=his bedroom). | **bathroom/dining room/meeting room etc.** *I think I'll put the lamp in the guest room.* | **a meeting/lecture/guest etc. room** *I think I'll put the lamp in the guest room.* | **one-room/two-room** *Carl lives in a one-room apartment downtown.* | **single/double room** (=a room in a hotel for one person or for two)
2 SPACE [U] enough space for a particular person, thing, or activity SYN **space**: **there is room (for sb/sth)** *There isn't any more room in the closet.* | **there is room (in sth)** *There's plenty of room in the trunk for your bags.* | **have room (for sth)** *We have plenty of room here for a party.* | **make room (for sb/sth)** *Move over and make some room for me.* | **room to do sth** *The kids don't have much room to play in the yard.* | **leave room (for sb/sth)** *Please leave room for people to get past.* | *That old TV* ***takes up too much room.*** | **leg-room/head-room** (=space for your legs or head in a vehicle) → see also **elbow room** at ELBOW¹ (5)
3 OPPORTUNITY/POSSIBILITY [U] the chance to do something, or the possibility that something exists or can happen: **+for** *Does the job offer room for advancement?* | *There was no* ***room for error*** *on his final long-jump attempt.* | *Teachers feel they have no* ***room for maneuver*** (=possibility of changing what you do). | *You did well on the last project, but there's* ***room for improvement*** (=you can and should improve). | **room for debate/discussion/doubt etc.** *The evidence is clear. There is little room for doubt.* | **room to do sth** *Dad always gave us room to make our own mistakes.*
4 there's not enough room to swing a cat INFORMAL used to say that an area or room is not very big
[**Origin:** Old English *rum*] → see also LIVING ROOM, SITTING ROOM

room² S3 *v.* [I] OLD-FASHIONED **1 room with sb** to share a room or a house with someone, especially when you are in college: *Dan roomed with Steve at Harvard.* **2** to rent and live in a room somewhere: **+in** *Didn't you used to room in their house?*

R

ˌroom and ˈboard *n.* [U] a room to sleep in and food: *Room and board at school costs $450 a month.*

room·er /ˈrumɚ/ *n.* [C] someone who pays rent to live in a house with its owner

room·ful /ˈrumfʊl/ *n.* [C] a large number of things or people that are all together in one room: +**of** *a roomful of reporters*

room·ie /ˈrumi/ *n.* [C] SPOKEN A ROOMMATE

ˈrooming house *n.* [C] a house where you can rent a room to live in

room·mate /ˈrum-meɪt/ S2 *n.* [C] **1** someone who you share a room with, especially when you are in college: *I ran into my old college roommate today.* **2** someone you share a room, apartment, or house with: *We were roommates back in Chicago.*

ˈroom ˌservice *n.* [U] a service provided by a hotel, by which food, drink etc. can be sent to a guest's room

ˈroom ˌtemperature *n.* [U] the normal temperature inside a house, used to talk about the temperature at which a food or drink should be served: *Red wine tastes best* ***at room temperature.***

R

room·y /ˈrumi, ˈrʊmi/ *adj. comparative* **roomier**, *superlative* **roomiest** a house, car etc. that is roomy is large and has a lot of space inside it —**roominess** *n.* [U]

Roo·se·velt /ˈroʊzəˌvɛlt/, **El·ea·nor** /ˈɛlɪnɚ/ (1884–1962) the wife of President Franklin D. Roosevelt, known for her work on human rights

Roosevelt, Frank·lin D. /ˈfræŋklɪn di/ (1882–1945) the 32nd President of the U.S., who helped to end the Depression of the 1930s by starting a program of social and economic changes called the New Deal

F.D. Roosevelt

Roosevelt, The·o·dore /ˈθiədɔr/ (1858–1919) the 26th President of the U.S.

ˌRoosevelt ˈCorollary, the HISTORY a statement by President Theodore Roosevelt in 1904 saying that the U.S. had the right to take action in Latin American countries to protect its own economic interests. This was an addition to the Monroe Doctrine of 1823 which said that European countries did not have the right to take action in Latin American countries.

roost¹ /rust/ *n.* [C] a place where birds rest and sleep → see also **rule the roost** at RULE² (6)

roost² *v.* [I] **1** BIOLOGY if a bird roosts, it rests or sleeps somewhere **2 sb's chickens come home to roost** also **sth comes home to roost** used to say that someone's past mistakes are causing problems for them now: *Their extravagant overspending has come home to roost.*

roost·er /ˈrustɚ/ *n.* [C] a male chicken

root¹ /rut, rʊt/ S2 W2 *n.* [C]
1 PLANT BIOLOGY the part of a plant or tree that grows under the ground and gets water and MINERALS from the soil: *Cover the roots with plenty of soil.* | *tree roots*
2 CAUSE OF A PROBLEM the main cause of a problem: +**of** *The roots of the problem are very complex* | **be/lie at the root of** *Allergies are at the root of a lot of health problems.* | *A good mechanic should be able to* ***get to the root of the problem.*** | *What do you see as the* ***root cause*** (=main reason) *of the Civil War?*
3 OF AN IDEA/BELIEF the main part of an idea or belief which all the other parts come from: *Jazz* ***has its roots in*** *the folk songs of African-American culture.* | **be/lie at the root of sth** *Biblical writings lie at the root of Western culture.*
4 sb's roots a place that you are connected to because you or your family come from it: *He decided to* ***return to*** *his East Coast* ***roots*** *after his marriage failed.*
5 put down roots if you put down roots somewhere, you start to feel that this place is your home and to have relationships with the people there: *Just as I was putting down roots, our family had to move up north.*
6 TOOTH/HAIR ETC. the part of a tooth, hair etc. that connects it to the rest of your body → see picture at TOOTH
7 take root a) if an idea, method, activity etc. takes root, people begin to accept or believe it: *The theory is slowly taking root in our schools.* **b)** if a plant takes root, it starts to grow where you have planted it
8 LANGUAGE ENG. LANG. ARTS the basic part of a word that shows its main meaning, to which other parts can be added. For example, the word "coldness" is formed from the root "cold" and the suffix "ness." → see also STEM
9 MATHEMATICS a number that when it is multiplied by itself a particular number of times, equals the number that you have: *2 is the fourth root of 16 (2 × 2 × 2 × 2 = 16).*
[**Origin:** 1100–1200 Old Norse *rot*] → see also CUBE ROOT, GRASS ROOTS, SQUARE ROOT

root² *v.* **1** [I always + adv./prep.] INFORMAL to search for something by moving things around SYN **rummage**: +**through/in/around** *I rooted through my purse for a pen and a notebook.* **2** [I always + adv./prep.] if an animal roots somewhere, it looks for food under the ground with its nose **3 a)** [I] BIOLOGY to grow roots: *New shrubs will root easily in summer.* **b) root itself** if a plant roots itself, it makes itself fixed in the ground or between rocks, bricks etc. by growing roots: *Weeds had rooted themselves between the rocks.*

root for sb *phr. v.* INFORMAL **1** to give support and encouragement to someone in a competition, test, or difficult situation, because you want them to succeed: *We're all rooting for you, Bill.* **2** to support a sports team or player by shouting and cheering: *Most of the crowd was rooting for Foreman.*

root sth ↔ **out** *phr. v.* **1** to find out where a particular kind of problem exists and get rid of it: *Drastic measures have been taken to root out corruption.* **2** to find something by searching for it: *I'll have to root his address out.*

root sth ↔ **up** *phr. v.* to dig or pull a plant up with its roots

ˈroot beer *n.* [C,U] a sweet brown non-alcoholic drink made from the roots of some plants

ˈroot caˌnal *n.* [C] a treatment in which a DENTIST removes a decaying area in the root of a tooth

ˈroot ˌcellar *n.* [C] a room under the ground in which vegetables such as potatoes are kept, especially in past times

ˈroot crop *n.* [C] a vegetable or plant that is grown so that its root parts can be used

root·ed /ˈrut̬ɪd/ *adj.* **1 be rooted in sth** to have developed from something or be the result of something: *This feeling of rejection is often rooted in childhood.* **2 be rooted to the spot/chair/floor etc.** to be so shocked, surprised, or frightened that you cannot move **3** [not before noun] if a plant is rooted somewhere, it is held in the ground firmly by its roots: *The bush was too firmly rooted to dig up easily.*

ˈroot hair *n.* [C] BIOLOGY one of very many small hairs that stick out from the surface of a plant's root

root·less /ˈrutlɪs/ *adj.* having nowhere that you feel is really your home: *His life in California felt rootless.* —**rootlessness** *n.* [U]

ˈroot ˌvegetable *n.* [C] a vegetable such as a potato or CARROT that grows under the ground

ˈroot word *n.* [C] ENG. LANG. ARTS a word that is used as a base to make other longer words by adding a PREFIX or a SUFFIX to it. For example, "undrinkable" includes the root word "drink."

rope¹ /roʊp/ S3 *n.* **1** [C,U] very strong, thick string, made by twisting together many threads of HEMP, NYLON, or other material: *a piece of rope* | *She lowered the basket on a rope.* **2 the ropes a)** all the things someone needs to know to do a job or deal with a system: *Nathan* ***knows the ropes*** *– he's been in the company for 15 years.* | *I spent the first few months just* ***learning the ropes.*** | **show/teach sb the ropes** *Jon will show you the ropes and answer any questions.* **b)** the rope fence that surrounds an area used for BOXING or WRESTLING **3 give sb enough rope (to hang themselves)** INFORMAL to give someone freedom to do what they want to do, because you think they will cause problems for themselves **4 be on the ropes** INFORMAL to be in a very bad situation, in which you are likely to be defeated: *The army says the rebels are on the ropes.* [**Origin:** Old English *rap*] → see also **be at the end of your rope** at END[1] (15), JUMP ROPE

rope[2] *v.* **1** [T always + adv./prep.] to tie things together using rope: **rope sth to sth** *We roped the suitcases to the top of the car.* | **rope sb/sth together** *Mountaineers rope themselves together for safety.* **2** [T] to catch an animal using a circle of rope

rope sb ↔ **in** *phr. v.* INFORMAL to persuade someone to help you in a job, or to join in an activity, especially when they do not want to: *Did you get roped in too?*

rope sb **into** sth *phr. v.* INFORMAL to persuade someone to help you in a job, or to join in an activity, especially when they do not want to: **rope sb into doing sth** *Denise roped us into helping set up for the party.*

rope sth ↔ **off** *phr. v.* to surround an area with ropes, especially in order to separate it from another area: *Sidestreets had been roped off for the parade.*

'rope ˌladder *n.* [C] a LADDER made of two long ropes connected by wooden pieces that you stand on

Roque·fort /ˈroʊkfɚt/ *n.* [U] a type of cheese that is white with STRIPES of blue MOLD

Ror·schach test /ˈrɔrʃɑk ˌtɛst/ *n.* [C] a method of testing someone's character, by making them say what spots of ink with various shapes look like

ro·sa·ry /ˈroʊzəri/ *n. plural* **rosaries** **1** [C] a string of BEADS used by Catholics for counting prayers **2 the Rosary** the set of prayers that are said by Catholics while counting rosary BEADS

rose[1] /roʊz/ S3 *n.* **1** [C] BIOLOGY a flower that has a pleasant smell, and is usually red, pink, white, or yellow, or the bush that this grows on: *a dozen red roses* **2** [U] a pink color **3 be coming up roses** INFORMAL be happening or developing in the best possible way **4 come out (of sth) smelling like a rose** also **come out smelling like roses** INFORMAL to get an advantage from a situation, when you ought to have been blamed, criticized, or harmed by it [**Origin:** Old English, Latin *rosa*] → see also **a bed of roses** at BED[1] (11)

rose[2] *adj.* having a pink color

rose[3] *v.* the past tense of RISE

ro·sé /roʊˈzeɪ/ *n.* [C,U] pink wine

ro·se·ate /ˈroʊziɪt/ *adj.* POETIC pink

Ro·seau /roʊˈzoʊ/ the capital and largest city of Dominica

rose·bud /ˈroʊzbʌd/ *n.* [C] BIOLOGY the flower of a rose before it opens

'rose bush *n.* [C] the plant that roses grow on

'rose-ˌcolored *adj.* **1** having a pink color **2 see/view etc. sth through rose-colored glasses** to think that something is better than it really is, because you do not notice anything bad: *She sees the world through rose-colored glasses.*

'rose hip *n.* [C,U] the small red fruit from some kinds of rose bushes, used in medicines and juices

rose·mar·y /ˈroʊzˌmɛri/ *n.* [U] leaves that have a strong, pleasant smell and are used in cooking, or the bush that these come from

Ro·sen·berg /ˈroʊzənˌbɚg/, **Ju·li·us** /ˈdʒuliəs/ (1918–1953) a U.S. citizen who was a SPY for the Soviet Union with his wife Ethel Rosenberg (1915–1953)

'rose-ˌtinted *adj.* ROSE-COLORED

Ro·set·ta Stone, the /roʊˈzɛt̬ə ˌstoʊn/ a large, ancient stone that was found in Egypt in 1799, which had the same piece of writing on it in three different writing systems: Greek letters, Egyptian letters, and ancient Egyptian HIEROGLYPHICS. This important discovery made it possible for people to translate hieroglyphics for the first time.

ro·sette /roʊˈzɛt/ *n.* [C] a shape like a round flat flower that has been made from stone, wood, cloth etc. and is used for decoration

rose·wa·ter /ˈroʊzˌwɔt̬ɚ/ *n.* [U] a liquid made from roses which has a pleasant smell

rose·wood /ˈroʊzwʊd/ *n.* [U] a hard dark red wood, used for making expensive furniture

Rosh Ha·sha·nah, Rosh Hashana /ˌrɑʃ həˈʃɑnə/ *n.* [C,U] the Jewish New Year, in late September or early October

Ro·sie the Riv·et·er /ˌroʊzi ðə ˈrɪvət̬ɚ/ HISTORY a woman factory worker who appeared as a character in U.S. government movies and POSTERS that praised women for doing hard but important work during World War II, such as making weapons and aircraft

ros·in /ˈrɑzən/ *n.* [U] a solid, slightly sticky, substance that you rub on the BOW of a VIOLIN etc., to help it move smoothly on the strings —**rosin** *v.* [T]

Ross /rɔs/, **Bet·sy** /ˈbɛtsi/ (1752–1836) the woman who is believed to have made the first U.S. flag

Ros·tand /roʊˈstɑnd/, **Ed·mond** /ˈɛdmənd/ (1868–1918) a French writer of plays

ros·ter /ˈrɑstɚ/ *n.* [C] **1** a list of the names of people on a sports team, in an organization etc.: *the best players on the team roster* **2** a list of people's names that shows the jobs they must do and the times when they must do them: *duty rosters* [**Origin:** 1700–1800 Dutch *rooster* **frame for cooking things on, list**, from *roosten* **to roast**]

ros·trum /ˈrɑstrəm/ *n.* [C] a small PLATFORM (=raised area) that you stand on when you are making a speech or CONDUCTING musicians [**Origin:** 1500–1600 Latin **beak, front part of a ship**, from *rodere* **to chew with the front teeth**]

ros·y /ˈroʊzi/ *adj. comparative* **rosier**, *superlative* **rosiest** **1** pink: *rosy cheeks* **2** seeming to offer hope of success or happiness: *a rosy financial report* —**rosiness** *n.* [U]

rot[1] /rɑt/ *v.* **1** [I,T] BIOLOGY to decay by a gradual natural process, or to make something do this: *The trees were left to rot.* | *Moisture can rot your house's foundation.* ▶see THESAURUS box at **decay[1]** **2 rot in jail/prison etc.** to have to say and suffer for a long time in an unpleasant place [**Origin:** Old English *rotian*]

rot away *phr. v.* **rot sth ↔ away** to decay completely and disappear or break into small pieces, or to make something do this: *The top of the coffin had rotted away.*

rot[2] *n.* [U] **1** BIOLOGY the natural process of decaying, or the part of something that has decayed: *Overwatering causes root rot.* **2** LITERARY a state in which something becomes bad or does not work as well as it should: *moral rot* **3** OLD-FASHIONED nonsense → see also DRY ROT

ro·ta·ry /ˈroʊt̬əri/ *adj.* [usually before noun] **1** turning in a circle around a central point, like a wheel: *the rotary movement of the helicopter's blades* **2** having a main part that does this: *a rotary dial phone*

Ro·ta·ry Club /ˈroʊt̬əri ˌklʌb/ *n.* an organization of business people in a town who work together to raise money for people who are poor or sick

ro·tate /ˈroʊteɪt/ *v.* **1** [I,T] to turn with a circular movement around a central point, or to make something do this: *The Earth rotates on its axis once every 24 hours.* | *Rotate the pan halfway through baking.* ▶see THESAURUS box at **turn[1]** **2** [I,T] to change the places of things or people, or to make people or things do this, especially in a circular direction: *Rotating the tires every few months helps them last longer.* | *The players rotate before each serve.* **3** [I,T] if a job rotates, or if people rotate jobs, they each do a job for a particular period of time and then change to another: *The chair-*

R

manship of the committee rotates annually. **4** [T] TECHNICAL to regularly change the crops grown on a piece of land, in order to preserve the quality of the soil [**Origin:** 1600–1700 Latin, past participle of *rotare*, from *rota* wheel]

ro·ta·tion /roʊˈteɪʃən/ *n.* **1** [U] GEOMETRY the action of a solid object turning with a circular movement around a central point inside it: *the rotation of the Earth* **2** [C] one complete turn around a central point SYN **revolution**: *The wheel takes a second to make one rotation.* **3** [U] the practice of changing regularly from one thing to another, or regularly changing the person who does a particular job: *job rotation* | *The three plays will be shown **in rotation*** (=one after the other in a repeating order) *throughout the summer.* **4** [C] a period of time spent doing a particular job, when you will soon change to a different job for the same employer: *a new doctor's rotation in the emergency room* **5** [U] TECHNICAL the practice of regularly changing the crops that are grown on a piece of land, in order to preserve the quality of the soil SYN **crop rotation** **6** [C] GEOMETRY a change in the position of a flat GEOMETRIC shape when the shape turns around a fixed point —**rotational** *adj.*

R

roˌtational ˈsymmetry *n.* [U] MATH the quality that a shape or object has if it looks exactly the same in more than one position when it is turning around a central point → see also POINT SYMMETRY

ROTC /ˈrɑtsi, ˌɑr oʊ ti ˈsi/ *n.* **Reserve Officers Training Corps**; an organization that trains students to be U.S. Army or Navy officers

rote¹ /roʊt/ *adj.* a rote action, process etc. involves repeating something many times, without thinking about it carefully or without understanding: *rote memorization*

rote² *n.* [U] **by rote** if you do something by rote, you do it the same way every time, without thinking about it: *Each morning, we recited the Pledge of Allegiance **by rote.***

ROTFL also **rotfl** **rolling on the floor laughing** used by people communicating on the Internet, through TEXT MESSAGES etc. to say that they are laughing very hard at something that someone else has written

rot·gut /ˈrɑtgʌt/ *n.* [U] SLANG strong cheap low-quality alcohol

Roth·ko /ˈrɑθkoʊ/, **Mark** (1903–1970) a U.S. artist, born in Russia, famous for his large paintings of squares and RECTANGLES in different colors

ro·tis·ser·ie /roʊˈtɪsəri/ *n.* [C] a piece of equipment for cooking meat by turning it around and around on a metal ROD over heat

ro·to·gra·vure /ˌroʊt̬əgrəˈvyʊr/ *n.* **1** [U] TECHNICAL a method of printing words and pictures from a COPPER CYLINDER **2** [C] OLD-FASHIONED the color magazine of a newspaper, especially a Sunday newspaper, that has been printed in this way

ro·tor /ˈroʊt̬ɚ/ *n.* [C] TECHNICAL **1** a part of a machine that turns around on a central point **2** also **rotor blade** the long flat part on top of a HELICOPTER that turns around and around

ro·to·till·er /ˈroʊt̬əˌtɪlɚ/ *n.* [C] a machine with a motor and sharp blades that is used to cut up land to prepare it for growing plants —**rototill** *v.* [I,T]

rot·ten¹ /ˈrɑtˀn/ *adj.* **1** badly decayed: *rotten eggs* | *The floor in the bathroom is all rotten.* ►see THESAURUS box at **old** **2** INFORMAL very unpleasant or disgusting: *I had a rotten day.* **3** INFORMAL of a very low quality, standard, or ability: *The service was rotten.* | *a rotten driver* | **+at** *You're rotten at lying.* **4** INFORMAL behaving in an unpleasant way: *You rotten little brat!* **5 feel rotten a)** to feel sick: *I've felt rotten all day.* **b)** to feel unhappy and guilty about something: **+about** *I feel rotten about having to fire him.* **6 a rotten apple** one bad person who has a bad effect on all the others in a group [**Origin:** 1200–1300 Old Norse *rotinn*] —**rottenly** *adv.* —**rottenness** *n.* [U]

rotten² *adv.* INFORMAL **spoil sb rotten** to treat someone too well or too kindly, especially a child: *Brittany's grandparents spoil her rotten.*

ˌrotten ˈborough *n.* [C] HISTORY a CONSTITUENCY in England before 1832 in which very few people had the right to vote

Rott·wei·ler, rottweiler /ˈrɑtˀˌwaɪlɚ/ *n.* [C] a type of strong and sometimes dangerous dog, often used as a guard dog

ro·tund /roʊˈtʌnd/ *adj.* HUMOROUS having a fat round body —**rotundity** *n.* [U]

ro·tun·da /roʊˈtʌndə/ *n.* [C] a round building or hall, especially one with a DOME (=a round bowl-shaped roof)

rou·ble /ˈrubəl/ another spelling of RUBLE

rou·é /ruˈeɪ/ *n.* [C] LITERARY, DISAPPROVING a man who believes that pleasure is the most important thing in life

rouge /ruʒ/ *n.* [U] pink or red powder or cream that women put on their cheeks —**rouge** *v.* [T]

rough¹ /rʌf/ S3 *adj.*
1 NOT SMOOTH having an uneven surface OPP **smooth**: *His hands were big and rough.* | *rough tree bark*
2 NOT EXACT not exact, not containing many details, or not in a final form SYN **approximate**: *Prices shown are only a rough guideline.* | *the **rough draft*** (=first writing) *of his first novel* | *Can you give me a **rough idea** of when the job will be finished?* | *This figure is only a **rough estimate**.*
3 NOT GENTLE using force or violence: *Football's a rough sport.* | *The prisoners complained of rough treatment.*
4 HAVING A LOT OF PROBLEMS/DIFFICULTIES [usually before noun] a rough period of time is one in which you have a lot of problems or difficulties: *I've had a rough day.* | *This year has been **a rough ride*** (=difficult time) *for the bank.* | *Melody admitted that there have been **rough patches*** (=difficult times) *in her marriage.* | *You look like you had a **rough night*** (=you slept badly).
5 CITY/AREA ETC. a rough area is a place where there is a lot of violence or crime: *She grew up in a rough part of town.*
6 UNPLEASANT unpleasant, often in a way that seems unfair: **+on** *The changes have been rough on the staff.* | *"She said she never loved me." "That's rough."*
7 be rough on sb to treat someone in an kind way, for example by criticizing them in an angry way SYN **be hard on sb**: *Don't be too rough on her – it was a mistake.*
8 have rough edges also **be rough around the edges** to have small parts that are not completely correct, finished etc. but are not a serious problem: *The play still has a few rough edges.*
9 WEATHER/SEA with strong wind or storms: *The ship went down in rough seas.*
10 NOT COMFORTABLE uncomfortable, with difficult conditions: *The trip was long and rough.*
11 VOICE/SOUND not sounding soft or gentle, and often sounding fairly angry: *a deep, rough voice*
12 rough stuff SPOKEN violent behavior
13 SIMPLE/NOT WELL MADE simple and often not very well made SYN **crude**: *a rough wooden table*
14 rough and ready not perfect for a particular situation or purpose, but good enough
15 rough justice punishment that is not decided in a court in the usual legal way, and that is often severe or unfair: *the rough justice of the Old West*
[**Origin:** Old English *ruh*] —**roughness** *n.* [U] → see also ROUGHLY

rough² *n.* **1 the rough** uneven ground with long grass on a GOLF course **2 take the rough with the smooth** to accept the bad things in life as well as the good ones **3** [C] a picture drawn very quickly, that does not show all the details → see also **a diamond in the rough** at DIAMOND (5)

rough³ *v.* **rough it** INFORMAL to live for a short time in conditions that are not very comfortable, especially when CAMPING: *I don't mind roughing it for a while.*

rough sb **up** *phr. v.* INFORMAL to attack someone and hurt them by hitting them SYN **beat up**

rough[4] *adv.* **play rough** to play in a violent way in which someone could get hurt

rough·age /ˈrʌfɪdʒ/ *n.* [U] BIOLOGY a substance contained in some vegetables and fruits that is not easily DIGESTed, and so helps your BOWELs to work SYN **fiber**

ˌrough and ˈtumble *n.* [U] a situation in which people fight or compete with one another, often in a cruel way: +**of** *the rough and tumble of politics* —**rough-and-tumble** *adj.*: *the rough-and-tumble world of Wall Street*

ˌrough ˈdiamond *n.* [C] a DIAMOND that has not yet been cut and polished to use as jewelry → see also **a diamond in the rough** at DIAMOND (5)

rough·en /ˈrʌfən/ *v.* [I,T] to become rough, or to make something rough: *Sand the surface to roughen it before repainting.*

ˌrough-ˈhewn *adj.* rough-hewn wood or stone has been roughly cut and its surface is not yet smooth

rough·house /ˈrʌfhaʊs/ *v.* [I] to play roughly or fight: *No more roughhousing, you two!*

rough·ly /ˈrʌfli/ W3 *adv.* **1** not exactly SYN **approximately**: *Martin makes roughly $150,000 a year.* | **roughly equal/comparable/similar etc.** *two rocks of roughly equal size* | *The word is **roughly translated** as "spiritedness."* ►see THESAURUS box at **about**[2] **2** not gently or carefully: *She roughly pushed me toward the door.* **3** not neatly or exactly: *The wood was roughly cut.*

rough·neck /ˈrʌfnɛk/ *n.* [C] **1** a member of a team of people who make or operate an OIL WELL **2** INFORMAL someone who usually behaves in a rough, rude, or angry way

rough·shod /ˈrʌfʃɑd/ *adj.* **run/ride roughshod over sth** to behave in a way that ignores other people's feelings or opinions: *The court cannot be allowed to ride roughshod over the rights of the accused.*

rou·lette /ruˈlɛt/ *n.* [U] a game in which a small ball is spun around on a moving wheel, and people try to win money by guessing which hole it will fall into → see also RUSSIAN ROULETTE

round[1] /raʊnd/ S3 W3 *adj.* **1** shaped like a circle: *The table was round.* | *a woman with a round face* ►see THESAURUS box at **shape**[1] **2** shaped like a ball: *small round berries* **3** curved: *the cathedral's round arches* **4** fat and curved SYN **plump**: *a short round man* **5** a round number is a whole number, often ending in 0, that is usually not exact: *Just give me $50. That's a nice round number.* | ***In round numbers**, you'll need to make about $1,000 to break even.* —**roundness** *n.* [U] → see also ROUNDLY, **a square peg in a round hole** at SQUARE[1] (11)

round[2] S3 W2 *n.* [C]
1 SERIES a number or set of events that are related: +**of** *the final round of voting* | *A third round of talks will begin next month.* ►see THESAURUS box at **stage**[1]
2 COMPETITION one of the parts of a competition that you have to finish or win before you can go to the next part: *The winners will play each other in the next round.* | **the opening/final round** *the opening round of the championship* | *Davis won his last **qualifying round**.* ►see THESAURUS box at **competition**
3 GUN SHOT a single shot from a gun, or a bullet for one shot: *a round of ammunition* | *Gunmen **fired** more than 100 **rounds** into the car.*
4 ALCOHOL a drink for each of the people in a group, or your turn to buy a drink for each of them: *Joe bought the first **round of drinks**.*
5 a round of applause a period when people CLAP to show that they enjoyed a performance: *The audience **gave her a big round of applause**.*
6 rounds [plural] the usual visits that someone, especially a doctor, regularly makes as part of their job: *The theft was discovered by a security guard **making** his **rounds**.*
7 make the rounds a) to go around from one place to another, often looking for work: +**of** *Ryan is making the rounds of talk shows to promote her new movie.* **b)** if a story, joke, illness etc. makes the rounds, it is passed from one person to another: *The story has been making the rounds for some time.*
8 GOLF a complete game of GOLF
9 BOXING one of the periods of fighting in a BOXING or WRESTLING match that are separated by short rests: *Hamed won the fight in the seventh round.*
10 CIRCLE something that has a circular shape: *Slice the potatoes into rounds.*
11 SONG ENG. LANG. ARTS a song for three or four singers, in which each one sings the same tune, starting at different times
12 a series of activities that you have to do regularly, especially activities that are not very interesting: *He dreaded the **daily round of** phone calls from unhappy customers.* | *She was weary of the **endless round of** parties.*
13 in the round a play that is performed in the round is performed on a central stage surrounded by the people watching it
[**Origin:** 1200–1300 Old French *roont*, from Latin *rotundus*]

round[3] S3 *v.* [T] **1** to go around something such as a bend or the corner of a building: *As I rounded the corner, I could see that the house was on fire.* **2** to make something into a round shape: *The edges of the counter have been rounded to make them safer.*

round sth ↔ **down** *phr. v.* to reduce an exact figure to the nearest whole number → see also ROUND UP

round off *phr. v.* **1** to change an exact figure to the nearest whole number: *Prices are **rounded off to the nearest** dollar.* **2 round sth ↔ off** to do something as a way of ending an event, performance etc. in an appropriate or satisfactory way: **round sth off with sth** *We rounded off our dinner with homemade apple pie.* **3 round sth ↔ off** to take the sharp edges off something: *Round off the corners with a pair of scissors.*

round sth ↔ **out** *phr. v.* to make an experience more thorough or complete: *Next week's performance of Strauss' "Elektra" rounds out the opera season.*

round up *phr. v.* **1 round sb/sth ↔ up** to find and gather together a group of people or things: *Neighbors helped round up the cattle.* → see also ROUNDUP **2 round sb ↔ up** to search for and find a particular group of people and keep them prisoner: *Police rounded up dozens of suspects.* **3 round sth ↔ up** to increase an exact figure to the next highest whole number → see also ROUND DOWN

round[4] S2 *adv.* [only after verb] **1** AROUND **2 round about** SPOKEN about a particular time or amount: *We'll probably get there round about 9:00.*

round[5] S3 *prep.* AROUND: *People used to believe that the sun went round the Earth.* → see also ROUND-THE-CLOCK

round·a·bout /ˈraʊndəˌbaʊt/ *adj.* not done in the shortest, most direct way possible SYN **indirect**: *a roundabout route* | ***In a roundabout way**, she admitted she was wrong.*

ˌround ˈcharacter *n.* [C] ENG. LANG. ARTS a round character in a book, movie etc. seems like a real person because he or she has many different qualities

round·ed /ˈraʊndɪd/ *adj.* having a round shape SYN **curved** → see also WELL-ROUNDED

round·house /ˈraʊndhaʊs/ *n.* [C usually singular] a hit or kick in which you swing your FIST (=closed hand) or foot with a wide circular movement at someone —**roundhouse** *adj.*

round·ly /ˈraʊndli/ *adv.* **roundly condemn/criticize etc.** to condemn or criticize etc. someone strongly and severely: *All the major parties roundly condemned the attack.*

ˌround ˈrobin *n.* [C] a competition in which every player or team plays against each of the other players or teams

ˌround-ˈshouldered *adj.* having shoulders that are bent forward or that slope down

ˈround steak *n.* [U] a piece of meat from the top part of the leg of a cow

ˈround-ˌtable *adj.* [only before noun] a round-table discussion or meeting is one in which everyone can talk about things in an equal way

ˈround-the-clock *adj.* [only before noun] all the time, both day and night: *round-the-clock weather reports* → see also **around the clock** at CLOCK[1] (4)

ˈround trip *n.* [C] a trip to a place and back again

ˈround-trip *adj.* [only before noun] a round-trip ticket is for a trip to a place and back again → see also ONE-WAY

round·up /ˈraʊndʌp/ *n.* [C] **1** an occasion when people or animals of a particular type are all brought together, often using force: *a cattle roundup* **2** a short description of the main parts of the news, on the radio or on television: *a news roundup* → see also **round up** at ROUND[3]

R

rouse /raʊz/ *v.* **1** [I,T] to wake up, or to wake someone up: **rouse sb from sleep/dreams etc.** *The heavy rain roused me from sleep.* **2** [T] to make someone start doing something, especially when they have been too tired or unwilling to do it: **rouse sb to sth** *The campaign is designed to rouse young people to action.* **3** [T] to make someone feel a particular emotion, such as anger or fear → see also AROUSE

rous·ing /ˈraʊzɪŋ/ *adj.* a rousing song, speech etc. makes people feel excited and eager to do something

Rous·seau /ruˈsoʊ/, **Hen·ri** /ɑnˈri/ (1844–1910) a French PAINTER famous for his paintings in bright colors and a simple flat-looking style

Rousseau, Jean-Jacques /ʒɑn ʒɑk/ (1712–1778) a French writer and PHILOSOPHER whose work had a great influence on the French Revolution

roust /raʊst/ *v.* [T] to make someone move from a place, especially using force or for a reason that is not nice: *Thousands of people were rousted from their homes by the fire.*

roust·a·bout /ˈraʊstəˌbaʊt/ *n.* [C] a man who does work for which he needs to be strong but not skilled, especially in a port, an OILFIELD, or a CIRCUS

rout[1] /raʊt/ *v.* [T] to defeat someone completely in a battle, competition, or election: *The army was routed in a fierce battle.*

rout[2] *n.* [singular] a complete defeat in a battle, competition, or election: *A 3–0 rout of Canada qualified the U.S. for the World Cup.*

route[1] /rut, raʊt/ Ac S2 W3 *n.* [C] **1** the way from one place to another, especially a way that is regularly used and can be shown on a map: *a scenic route* | **+to/from** *What's the best route from here to the station?* | **take/follow a route** *We weren't sure which route we should take.* **2** a road, railroad, or imaginary line along which vehicles often travel: *The airline was fourced to sell some of its European routes.* | *a bus route* **3** a way of doing something or achieving a particular result: *I arrived at the same conclusion by a different route.* | **+to** *Money is not always the route to happiness.* **4 Route** used with a number as the name of some main roads in the U.S.: *I took Route 20 east from Chicago.* [**Origin:** 1100–1200 Old French, Vulgar Latin *rupta (via)* **broken way**, from Latin *ruptus* **broken**] → see also EN ROUTE, PAPER ROUTE, RURAL ROUTE, SNOW ROUTE, TRADE ROUTE

route[2] Ac *v.* [T] to send someone or something using a particular route: **route sth through/by/via sth** *All calls were routed through a switchboard to my office.* → see also REROUTE

rou·tine[1] /ruˈtin/ *n.* **1** [C,U] the usual or normal way in which you do things, or the usual series of things that you do: *Her daily routine consisted of work, dinner, then TV and bed.* | *Russ is the type of person who likes routine.* | *It's best to try to* **get into a routine.** | *I got a phone call in the middle of my morning* **exercise routine.** **2** [C] ENG. LANG. ARTS a set of movements, jokes, songs etc. that form part of a performance: *a dance routine* | *a comedy routine* **3** [C] DISAPPROVING, INFORMAL a false way of behaving that is intended to achieve a particular result: *I won't fall for that routine again.* **4** [C] COMPUTERS a set of instructions given to a computer so that it will do a particular operation —**routinize** /ruˈtinaɪz, ˈrutˀnˌaɪz/ *v.* [T]

rou·tine[2] /ˌruˈtin◂/ *adj.* **1** happening as a normal part of a job or process and not because of any special problem: *a routine blood test* | *Systems need to be updated* **on a routine basis.** ►see THESAURUS box at normal[1] **2** ordinary and boring: *My job at the newspaper had become routine.*

rou·tine·ly /ruˈtinli/ *adv.* if something is routinely done, it is usually done as part of the normal process of working, doing a job etc.: *We routinely test patients for high blood pressure.*

roux /ru/ *n. plural* **roux** /ruz, ru/ [C,U] a mixture of flour and butter that is used for making SAUCES

rove /roʊv/ *v.* [I always + adv./prep.] **1** to travel from one place to another SYN **roam**: *Bands of armed men rove the countryside.* **2** if someone's eyes rove, they look continuously from one part of something to another

rov·er /ˈroʊvɚ/ *n.* [C] **1** LITERARY someone who travels or moves around from place to place and does not stay long in one place **2** a ROBOT that can move over rough ground

rov·ing /ˈroʊvɪŋ/ *adj.* **1 a roving reporter/photographer** someone who works for a newspaper or television company and travels from place to place to do their job **2 a roving eye** OLD-FASHIONED someone who has a roving eye is always looking for a chance to have sexual relationships

row[1] /roʊ/ S2 W2 *n.* [C] **1** a line of things or people next to each other: **+of** *A row of palm trees lined the street.* | *The girls stood in a row* **in a row.** | *The desks were all arranged* **in rows.** | *The hills are planted with* **row upon row** *of grape vines.* **2** a line of seats in a theater, large room etc.: **the front/back row** *We sat in the front row.* **3** TECHNICAL a line of numbers, information etc. that goes across the page in a TABLE (=type of list) → see also COLUMN **4 in a row** used to say that the same thing happens or is done a number of times, one after the other: *They won six times in a row.* **5 a hard/tough row to hoe** INFORMAL a situation or problem that is difficult for someone to deal with

row[2] /roʊ/ *v.* **1** [I,T] to make a boat move across water using OARS (=long poles that are flat at one end): *We rowed the boat across the lake.* **2** [T] to take someone somewhere in a boat that you are rowing: *He rowed us down the river.* **3** [I] to row in a boat as a sport

row[3] /raʊ/ *n.* [C] BRITISH a short angry argument

row·boat /ˈroʊboʊt/ *n.* [C] a small boat that you move through the water with OARS (=long poles that are flat at the end)

row·dy[1] /ˈraʊdi/ *adj. comparative* **rowdier**, *superlative* **rowdiest** behaving in a noisy, rough, uncontrolled way that is likely to cause arguments and fighting: *The boys at the party got a little rowdy.* ►see THESAURUS box at loud[1] —**rowdily** *adv.* —**rowdiness** *n.* [U]

rowdy[2] *n.* [C usually plural] OLD-FASHIONED someone who behaves in a rough noisy way

row house /ˈroʊ haʊs/ *n.* [C] a house that is part of a line of houses that are joined to each other

row·ing /ˈroʊɪŋ/ *n.* [U] the sport or activity of making a boat move through water with OARS

ˈrowing maˌchine *n.* [C] a piece of exercise equipment on which you perform the action of rowing a boat

ˌrow opeˈrations *n.* [plural] MATH methods that you use to change a MATRIX in order to solve a set of mathematical EQUATIONS

roy·al[1] /ˈrɔɪəl/ W3 *adj.* [only before noun] **1** relating to, belonging to, or involving a king or queen or their family → see also REGAL: *the royal palace* | *a royal wedding* **2** very impressive, as if done for a king or queen: *Williams got the* ***royal treatment*** *on her visit to Washington.* **3** INFORMAL used to emphasize how bad or annoying someone or something is: *They've made a royal mess of things.* **4 the royal "we"** OFTEN HUMOROUS the use of the word "we" instead of "I" by the British Queen or King [**Origin:** 1200–1300 Old French *roial*, from Latin *regalis*] —**royally** *adv.*

royal[2] *n.* [C] INFORMAL a member of a royal family

ˌroyal ˈblue *n.* [U] a deep, bright blue color —**royal blue** *adj.*

ˌroyal ˈflush *n.* [C usually singular] a set of cards that someone has in a card game, which are the five most important cards in a SUIT (=one of the four different types of card): the ACE, KING, QUEEN, JACK, and ten

ˌRoyal ˈHighness *n.* [C] **your/his/her Royal Highness** used when speaking to or about a royal person, especially a PRINCE or PRINCESS

roy·al·ist /ˈrɔɪəlɪst/ *n.* [C] someone who supports a king or queen, or believes that a country should be ruled by kings or queens —**royalist** *adj.*

roy·al·ty /ˈrɔɪəlti/ *n. plural* **royalties** **1** [C usually plural] ECONOMICS a payment made to the writer of a book or piece of music, or to someone whose idea, invention etc. is used by someone else to make money. The amount paid depends on how many copies of the book, song, or product are sold: *The Baltimore company will also receive royalties from sales of the drug in Europe.* | *He was paid $1.2 million in royalties for his best-selling book.* | *royalty payments* **2** [U] members of a royal family

rpm /ˌɑr pi ˈɛm/ **revolutions per minute** a measurement of the speed at which an engine or RECORD PLAYER turns

RR, R.R. **1 rural route** used in addresses in country areas of the U.S., to show which area a letter should go to **2** a written abbreviation of RAILROAD

rRna *n.* [U] BIOLOGY the abbreviation of RIBOSOMAL RNA

RSI *n.* [U] MEDICINE **repetitive strain injury** pain in your hands, arms etc. caused by doing the same movements very many times, especially when typing (TYPE)

RSVP[1] an abbreviation that is used on invitations to ask someone to tell you if they can come or not [**Origin:** 1800–1900 French *répondez, s'il vous plaît* **please reply**]

RSVP[2] *v.* **RSVP's, RSVP'd** **1** [I,T] to tell someone who gave you an invitation whether you can go or not: *Eighteen people hadn't RSVP'd for the wedding.* **2** [I] to arrange for a place to be kept for you at an event —**RSVP** *n.* [C]

rte. a written abbreviation of ROUTE

rub[1] /rʌb/ S2 *v.* **rubbed, rubbing**
1 MOVE STH OVER A SURFACE [I,T] to move your hand, a cloth etc. backward and forward over a surface while pressing against it: *Would you rub my back?* | *I had to rub hard to get the marks off.* | *Ann woke up and* ***rubbed her eyes.*** | **rub sth with sth** *He rubbed his face with a wet washcloth.* ►see THESAURUS box at **touch**[1]
2 PRESS STH AGAINST STH [T] to press something against something else and move it around: **rub sth against/on sth** *He rubbed the toe of his shoe against his calf.* | **rub sth together** *We tried to make a fire by rubbing two sticks together.*
3 PUT SUBSTANCE ON STH [T always + adv./prep.] to put a substance into or onto the surface of something by pressing it and moving it around with your hand, a cloth etc.: **rub sth on/into/over etc. sth** *She rubbed lotion on her arms.* | **rub sth with sth** *Rub the fish with salt.*
4 rub shoulders/elbows with sb INFORMAL to spend time with rich or famous people: *As a reporter he gets to rub shoulders with the rich and famous.*
5 rub sb the wrong way INFORMAL to annoy someone by the way you behave toward them: *Jeff sometimes rubs people the wrong way.*
6 rub salt into a wound INFORMAL to make a bad situation even worse for someone
7 rub sb's nose in it INFORMAL to keep reminding someone about something they did wrong or failed to do, especially in order to punish them
8 be rubbing your hands INFORMAL to be pleased because something has happened which gives you an advantage, especially because something bad has happened to someone else
9 not have two pennies/nickels/dimes to rub together OLD-FASHIONED to have no money

rub (up) against sth *phr. v.* to press against someone or something else and move around: *The cat rubbed against her legs.*

rub down *phr. v.* **1 rub sth ↔ down** to make a surface dry or smooth by rubbing it with a cloth or SANDPAPER **2 rub sb ↔ down** to MASSAGE someone (=rub their muscles), especially after hard exercise **3 rub sb/sth ↔ down** to dry a person or animal by rubbing them with a cloth, TOWEL etc. → see also RUBDOWN

rub sth **↔ in** *phr. v.* **1** INFORMAL to remind someone about something they want to forget, especially because they are embarrassed about it: *I know I was wrong – you don't have to* ***rub it in.*** **2** to put a cream or oil onto someone's skin or hair and press and move it around to make it go in

rub off *phr. v.* **1 rub sth ↔ off, rub sth off sth** to remove something from a surface by rubbing it: *She rubbed off her lipstick.* **2** to remove something from a surface by rubbing it, or to come off a surface because of being rubbed: **+on/onto** *Newspaper ink had rubbed off on my hand.*

rub off on sb *phr. v.* if a feeling, quality, or habit rubs off on someone, they start to have it because they are with another person who has it: *Her enthusiasm rubs off on everybody.*

rub sb **out** *phr. v.* INFORMAL to murder someone SYN **bump off**

rub[2] *n.* **1** the action of rubbing something or massaging (MASSAGE) someone for a short time: *Can I have a* ***back rub?*** **2 the rub** LITERARY a particular problem or difficult situation: *The rub is that disposable diapers will last 500 years in a landfill.* **3** a mixture of SPICES, oil etc. that you put on meat before cooking it to give it more FLAVOR: *lemon and ginger rub*

rub·ber /ˈrʌbɚ/ *n.*
1 SUBSTANCE [U] a substance used to make tires, GLOVES, boots etc., which is made from the juice of a tropical tree or artificially: *a rubber ball*
2 FOR SEX [C] INFORMAL a CONDOM
3 BASEBALL [C] the piece of white rubber where the PITCHER (=person who throws the ball) stands in a baseball game
4 rubbers [plural] OLD-FASHIONED a rubber shoe or boot that you wear over an ordinary shoe when it rains or snows SYN **galoshes**
5 CARD GAME [C] a series of games of BRIDGE (=a card game)
6 where the rubber hits/meets the road INFORMAL a situation in which you use an idea rather than just thinking or talking about it, especially one in which you find out whether the idea is practical or not

ˈrubber band *n.* [C] a thin circular piece of rubber used for holding things together

ˈrubber boot *n.* [C] a tall boot made of rubber that keeps your foot and the lower part of your leg dry → see picture at BOOT[1]

ˌrubber ˈbullet *n.* [C] a bullet made of rubber that is not intended to seriously hurt or kill people, but is used to control violent crowds

ˌrubber ceˈment *n.* [U] a type of glue that dries slowly, allowing you to change the position of something

R

ˈrubber check *n.* [C] INFORMAL a check that the bank refuses to accept because the person who wrote it does not have enough money in the bank to pay it

rub·ber·neck /ˈrʌbɚˌnɛk/ *v.* [I] INFORMAL to twist your neck around trying to look at something surprising, especially while you are driving a car —**rubbernecker** *n.* [C]

ˈrubber plant *n.* [C] a plant with large shiny dark green leaves that is often grown indoors

ˌrubber ˈstamp *n.* [C] a small piece of rubber with a handle, used for printing dates or names on paper

ˌrubber-ˈstamp *v.* [T] to give official approval to something without really thinking about it: *The board rubber-stamped the plan at its meeting Friday.*

rub·ber·y /ˈrʌbəri/ *adj.* **1** looking or feeling like rubber: *The steak was a little rubbery.* **2** if your legs or knees are rubbery, they feel weak or unsteady

rub·bing /ˈrʌbɪŋ/ *n.* [C] a copy of a shape or pattern made by rubbing a pencil, WAX, CHALK etc. onto a piece of paper laid over it: *a brass rubbing*

R

ˈrubbing ˌalcohol *n.* [U] MEDICINE a type of alcohol used for cleaning wounds or skin

rub·bish /ˈrʌbɪʃ/ *n.* [U] **1** INFORMAL an idea, statement etc. that is rubbish is silly or wrong and does not deserve serious attention SYN **nonsense** **2** GARBAGE

rub·ble /ˈrʌbəl/ *n.* [U] broken stones or bricks from a building or wall that has been destroyed: *The town was reduced to rubble in the war.*

rub·down /ˈrʌbdaʊn/ *n.* [C] **1** the action of rubbing someone's body to make them relaxed, especially after exercise SYN **massage** **2** the action of rubbing a surface to make it smooth or clean → see also **rub down** at RUB[1]

rube /rub/ *n.* [C] DISAPPROVING, INFORMAL someone, usually from the country, who has no experience of other places and thinks in a simple way

Rube Gold·berg /ˌrub ˈgoʊldbɚg/ *adj.* [only before noun] a Rube Goldberg machine, system etc. is very complicated and not practical, in an amusing way

ru·bel·la /ruˈbɛlə/ *n.* [U] MEDICINE an infectious disease that causes red spots on your body, and can damage an unborn child SYN **German measles**

Ru·bens /ˈrubənz/, **Peter Paul** (1577–1640) a Flemish PAINTER, famous for his paintings in which the women have fairly large fat bodies

Ru·bi·con /ˈrubɪˌkɑn/ *n.* **cross the Rubicon** to do something that you cannot later change, that will have extremely important effects in the future

ru·bi·cund /ˈrubɪkənd/ *adj.* LITERARY someone who is rubicund is fat and has a red face

ru·bid·i·um /ruˈbɪdiəm/ *n.* [U] SYMBOL **Rb** CHEMISTRY a soft silver-white metal that is an ELEMENT

ru·ble, rouble /ˈrubəl/ *n.* [C] the standard unit of money in Russia and Belarus

ru·bric /ˈrubrɪk/ *n.* [C] FORMAL **1** a title for a group of things that all have the same particular qualities: *I think the general rubric for the conference will be business-climate issues.* **2** the title written at the top of a piece of writing: *The names were listed under the rubric "Contributors."* **3** a set of rules that are used to judge something: *This type of student's report card replaces letter grades with an elaborate rubric of skills and goals.* [**Origin:** 1200–1300 Old French *rubrique* **words written in red**, from Latin *rubrica*]

ru·by /ˈrubi/ *n. plural* **rubies** **1** [C] a red jewel **2** [U] also **ruby red** the color of this jewel [**Origin:** 1300–1400 Old French *rubis*, *rubi*, from Latin *rubeus* **reddish**]

ruched /ruʃt/ *adj.* a ruched curtain or piece of clothing has parts of it gathered together so that it has soft folds in it

ruck·sack /ˈrʌksæk/ *n.* [C] a BACKPACK [**Origin:** 1800–1900 German **back sack**]

ruck·us /ˈrʌkəs/ *n.* [singular] INFORMAL a noisy argument or confused situation: *What's all the ruckus about?*

rud·der /ˈrʌdɚ/ *n.* [C] a flat part at the back of a ship or aircraft that can be turned in order to control the direction in which the ship or aircraft moves

rud·der·less /ˈrʌdɚlɪs/ *adj.* without any clear direction or purpose, especially because a leader has gone away

rud·dy /ˈrʌdi/ *adj. comparative* **ruddier**, *superlative* **ruddiest** **1** a ruddy face looks pink and healthy: *ruddy cheeks* **2** LITERARY red: *a ruddy glow* —**ruddiness** *n.* [U] —**ruddy** *adv.*

rude /rud/ S2 *adj.* **1** speaking or behaving in a way that is not polite and is likely to offend or annoy people OPP **polite**: *He's one of the rudest people I've ever met.* | *I don't mean to be rude, but I have to get going.* | +**to** *Why were you so rude to him?* | **be rude of sb** *"She didn't even say thank you." "Well, that was rude of her."* | **it's rude (of sb) to do sth** *It's rude to stare.*

THESAURUS

impolite FORMAL not polite: *Chewing with your mouth open is impolite.*
insulting saying or doing something that insults someone: *He said some very insulting things.*
tactless carelessly saying or doing things that are likely to upset someone: *It was tactless to ask her if she'd gained weight.*
offensive likely to upset or offend people: *His remarks are offensive to African Americans.*
insolent FORMAL deliberately rude: *He was insolent toward the teacher.*
disrespectful not showing the proper respect for someone or something: *The players should not be disrespectful to the coach.*
impertinent not showing the proper respect for someone: *an impertinent answer*

2 a rude awakening/shock a situation in which you suddenly realize something upsetting or bad: *If they expect to win easily, they are in for a rude awakening.* **3** LITERARY made in a simple, basic way SYN **crude**: *rude wooden shacks* [**Origin:** 1200–1300 Old French, Latin *rudis* **raw, rough**] —**rudely** *adv.* —**rudeness** *n.* [U]

ru·di·men·ta·ry /ˌrudəˈmɛntri, -ˈmɛntəri/ *adj.* **1** a rudimentary knowledge or understanding of a subject is very simple and basic SYN **basic** OPP **sophisticated**: *a rudimentary knowledge of music* **2** rudimentary equipment, methods, systems etc. are very basic and not advanced SYN **basic**: *rudimentary tools* **3 a rudimentary tail/wing/eye** a part of an animal that has only developed into a very simple form

ru·di·ments /ˈrudəmənts/ *n.* [plural] FORMAL **the rudiments of sth** the most basic parts of a subject, which you learn first SYN **basics**: *the rudiments of baseball*

rue /ru/ *v.* [T] LITERARY to wish that you had not done something SYN **regret**: *She **rued the day** she met him.*

rue·ful /ˈrufəl/ *adj.* feeling or showing that you wish you had not done something: *a rueful smile* —**ruefully** *adv.*

ruff /rʌf/ *n.* [C] **1** a stiff circular white collar, worn in the 16th century **2** BIOLOGY a circle of feathers or fur around the neck of an animal or bird

ruf·fi·an /ˈrʌfiən/ *n.* [C] OLD-FASHIONED a violent man who is involved in crime

ruf·fle[1] /ˈrʌfəl/ *v.* **1** [T] to make a smooth surface uneven: *The wind ruffled Jill's hair.* **2** [T] to offend or upset someone slightly: *Yancy's aggressive style has **ruffled some feathers*** (=annoyed some people). **3** [I,T] if a bird ruffles its feathers or the feathers ruffle, they stand out from the bird's body

ruffle[2] *n.* [C] a band of thin cloth sewn in folds, used as a decoration around the edge of something such as a dress

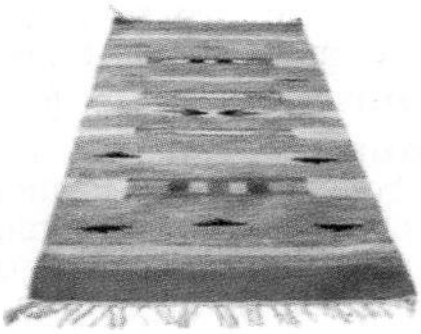

rug

rug /rʌg/ S3 *n.* [C] **1** a piece of thick cloth or wool that covers part of a floor, used for warmth or as a decoration → see also CARPET: *a large circular rug* **2 pull the rug (out) from under sb** also **pull the rug (out) from under sb's feet** INFORMAL to suddenly take away something that someone was depending on to achieve what they wanted: *He promised support, then pulled the rug out from under us.* **3** HUMOROUS a TOUPEE [**Origin:** 1500–1600 From a Scandinavian language] → see also **sweep sth under the rug/carpet** at SWEEP¹ (14)

rug·by /ˈrʌgbi/ *n.* [U] an outdoor game played by two teams with an OVAL (=egg-shaped) ball that you kick or carry [**Origin:** 1800–1900 *Rugby* School in England, where the game is said to have been invented]

rug·ged /ˈrʌgɪd/ *adj.* **1** land that is rugged is rough and uneven: *the rugged landscape of the West* **2** a man who is rugged is good-looking and has strong features which are often not perfect: *Ann admired Joe's rugged good looks.* **3** a rugged car or piece of equipment etc. is strongly built and not likely to break easily SYN **sturdy**: *a rugged mountain bike* **4** rugged behavior is confident and determined but not always polite: *a rugged individualist* —**ruggedly** *adv.* —**ruggedness** *n.* [U]

rug·rat /ˈrʌgræt/ *n.* [C] SPOKEN, HUMOROUS a small child

ru·in¹ /ˈruɪn/ S3 *v.* [T] **1** to spoil or destroy something completely: *All their furniture was ruined in the flood.* | *The scandal nearly ruined his career.* ▸see THESAURUS box at **destroy** **2** ECONOMICS to make someone lose all their money: *A long strike would ruin the company.* —**ruined** *adj.* [only before noun]: *ruined houses* ▸see THESAURUS box at **destroy**

ruin² *n.* **1** [U] a situation in which you have lost all your money, your social position, or the good opinion that people had about you: *financial ruin* | *Unwise investments put him **on the road to ruin**.* **2** [C] the part of a building that is left after the rest has been destroyed: *ancient ruins* | *an 800-year-old Mayan ruin* | ***the ruins of** the old abbey* **3 be/lie in ruins a)** if a building is in ruins, it has fallen down or been badly damaged: *Whole blocks of the city were in ruins after the war.* **b)** if someone's life, hopes, plans, or an organization is in ruins, they are having great problems and cannot continue: *Our economy lies in ruins.* **4 the ruins of sth** the parts of something such as an organization, system, or set of ideas that remain after the rest has been destroyed: *He contemplated the ruins of his marriage.* **5 fall into ruin** also **go to ruin** to become damaged or destroyed because of lack of care: *The 18th century mansion has fallen into ruin.* **6 be the ruin of sb/sth** OLD-FASHIONED to be the thing that spoils or destroys something, especially someone's life or CAREER: *Manning's love for alcohol was the ruin of him.* [**Origin:** 1300–1400 Old French *ruine*, from Latin *ruina*] → see also **go to rack and ruin** at RACK¹ (6)

ru·in·a·tion /ˌruəˈneɪʃən/ *n.* [singular, U] FORMAL a situation in which someone or something is ruined, or the cause of this

ru·in·ous /ˈruɪnəs/ *adj.* **1** causing a lot of damage: *Alcohol is as ruinous as illegal drugs.* **2** costing much more than you can afford: *ruinous taxes* —**ruinously** *adv.*: *ruinously expensive*

rule¹ /rul/ S1 W1 *n.*
1 OFFICIAL INSTRUCTION [C] an official instruction that says how things must be done or what is allowed, especially in a game, organization, or job: +**of** *What are the rules of the game?* | **follow/observe/obey rules** *Employees are expected to obey certain rules.* | *You can't come in if you're not a member – it's **against the rules**.* | *Elizabeth was expelled for **breaking the** school's **rules**.* | **bend/stretch the rules** (=allow someone to not obey a particular rule on a particular occasion) | *Each club has its own **rules and regulations**.* | *We have **unwritten rules** (=unofficial rules) about what kind of behavior is considered appropriate.* | *I'm sorry, but **rules are rules** (=used when you are saying a rule cannot be broken) and you can't go in there.*

THESAURUS
law a rule that people in a particular country, city, or state must obey: *The law requires motorcyclists to wear helmets.*
regulation an official rule or order: *the airlines' safety regulations*
restriction a rule or set of laws that limits what you can do or what is allowed to happen: *new restrictions on immigration*
guidelines rules or instructions about the best way to do something: *Judges have been given new guidelines on the sentencing of criminals.*
statute FORMAL a law or rule: *a federal statute prohibiting sex discrimination*

2 GOVERNMENT [U] the government of a country by a particular group of people or using a particular system: *For 150 years, the country was **under** Turkish **rule**.* | *calls for **majority rule*** (=the situation in which the largest group of people control the government) | **military/colonial/direct etc. rule** *the end of colonial rule*
3 the rule of law a situation in which the people and government of a country obey the laws: *An efficient state is based on the rule of law.*
4 as a (general) rule used to say that something usually happens or is usually true: *As a rule, men tend to be taller than women.*
5 be the rule used to say that something is the usual situation: *Early marriage used to be the rule in many parts of the world.*
6 ADVICE [C] something that you should do in a particular situation, or a statement about what you should do: *the rules of etiquette* | ***There are really no hard and fast rules*** (=there are no definite rules) *for decorating.* | *Problems can be avoided by **following** a few simple **rules**.* | ***The rule is**, if you feel any pain, stop exercising.*
7 a rule of thumb a rough method of calculation, based on practical experience: *You should tip bellmen $1 to $2 per bag, as a rule of thumb.*
8 make it a rule (to do sth) to try to make sure that you always do something: *I make it a rule not to take friends on as clients.*
9 SCIENCE/GRAMMAR [C] ENG. LANG. ARTS a statement about what usually happens in the grammar of a language or in a scientific process: +**of** *the rules of punctuation*
10 FOR MEASURING [C] OLD-FASHIONED a RULER
[**Origin:** 1200–1300 Old French *reule*, from Latin *regula* **edge for drawing straight lines, rule**] → see also **sb/sth is the exception that proves the rule** at EXCEPTION (4), GOLDEN RULE, GROUND RULES, HOME RULE, **play by the rules** at PLAY¹ (15), SLIDE RULE

rule² S3 W1 *v.*
1 GOVERNMENT [I,T] to have the official power to control a country and the people who live there: *The country was ruled by Spain until 1821.* | *Queen Victoria ruled for 64 years.* | **rule (over) sth/sb** *He ruled over an empire that stretched from Persia across to China.*
2 COURT/LAW [I always + adv./prep.,T] LAW to make an official decision about something, especially a legal problem: *The Medical Examiner's office ruled the death a murder.* | **rule that** *The court ruled that he was being held illegally.* | +**on** *The Supreme Court has yet to rule on the case.* | +**against** *A state appeals court ruled against her last month.* | *In the end, the court **ruled in her favor**.* → see also RULING¹
3 CONTROL/INFLUENCE [T] if a feeling or desire rules someone, it has a powerful and controlling influence on their actions: *We can't let ourselves be ruled by fear.*

R

4 BE MOST IMPORTANT [I] to be more important or have more influence than other things: *In this community, tradition rules.*
5 rule sb/sth with an iron fist/hand to control a group of people in a very severe way
6 rule the roost INFORMAL to be the most powerful person in a group
7 let your heart rule your head to make decisions based on what you feel, not what you think
8 sb/sth rules SPOKEN used to say that the team, school, place etc. mentioned is better than anyone else: *Jefferson High School rules!* → see also OVERRULE

rule out *phr. v.* **1 rule sb/sth ↔ out** to decide that someone or something is not possible or appropriate: *Police have ruled her out as a suspect.* | *Doctors have* ***ruled out the possibility of*** *surgery.* **2 rule sth ↔ out** to make it impossible for something to happen: *High prices rule out a vacation for many people.*

rule•book /ˈrulbʊk/ *n.* [C] a book of rules, especially one that is given to workers in a job or that contains the rules of a sport

R

ruled /ruld/ *adj.* ruled paper has parallel lines printed across it

rul•er /ˈrulɚ/ *n.* [C] **1** MATH a flat narrow piece of plastic, metal etc. with straight edges, that you use for measuring things or drawing straight lines: *a 12-inch ruler* **2** someone such as a king or queen who has official power over a country or area ▶see THESAURUS box at **king**

rul•ing¹ /ˈrulɪŋ/ *n.* [C] an official decision, especially one made by a court: **+on** *the court's rulings on civil rights issues*

ruling² *adj.* [only before noun] the ruling group in a country or organization is the group that controls it: *the ruling party*

rum /rʌm/ *n.* [C,U] a strong alcoholic drink made from sugar, or a glass of this drink

rum•ba /ˈrʌmbə/ *n.* [C,U] a popular dance from Cuba, or the music for this dance

rum•ble¹ /ˈrʌmbəl/ *v.* [I] **1** to make a series of long low sounds: *Thunder rumbled over the mountains.* **2** if a car, truck, airplane rumbles somewhere, it moves slowly while making a series of long low sounds: **+along/past etc.** *A truck rumbled past.* **3** if your stomach rumbles, it makes a noise, especially because you are hungry **4** OLD-FASHIONED to fight with someone

rumble² *n.* **1** [singular] a series of long low sounds: *the rumble of a freight train* **2** [C] OLD-FASHIONED a fight

ˈrumble strip *n.* [C] an area of road, usually at the side, that has a rough surface which makes a noise when you drive on it. It is used to warn drivers that they are too close to the edge of the road, or sometimes on the main part of a road to warn drivers that they are coming up to traffic lights or stop signs.

rum•bling /ˈrʌmblɪŋ/ *n.* **1** [C usually plural] remarks that show that people are starting to become annoyed, or that a difficult situation is developing: *rumblings of discontent* **2** [C usually singular] a rumbling noise: *the rumbling of thunder*

ru•men /ˈrumən/ *n. plural* **rumens** or **rumina** /-mənə/ [C] BIOLOGY a separate enclosed part in the stomach of an animal, such as cow, which stores and partly changes food the animal has just eaten before passing it into the other part of the stomach

ru•mi•nant /ˈrumənənt/ *n.* [C] BIOLOGY an animal such as a cow that has several stomachs and eats grass

ru•mi•nate /ˈruməˌneɪt/ *v.* [I] **1** FORMAL to think for a long time about something: **+about/on etc.** *He was ruminating on the injustices of the world.* **2** BIOLOGY if animals such as cows ruminate, they bring food back into their mouths from their stomachs and CHEW it again [**Origin:** 1500–1600 Latin, past participle of *ruminare*, from *rumen* **throat**] —**rumination** /ˌruməˈneɪʃən/ *n.* [C,U]

rum•mage¹ /ˈrʌmɪdʒ/ *v.* [I always + adv./prep.] also **rummage around** to search for something by moving things around in a careless way: **+in/through etc.** *Andrea rummaged through her purse for a tissue.*

rummage² *n.* [U] old clothes, toys etc. that you do not want anymore

ˈrummage sale *n.* [C] an event at which old clothes, toys etc. are sold as a way of getting money, for example to help a school or church

rum•my /ˈrʌmi/ *n.* [U] a simple card game

ru•mor /ˈrumɚ/ *n.* [U] **1** information that is passed from one person to another and which may or may not be true, especially information about someone's personal life or about an official decision: **a rumor that** *I heard a rumor that he was getting married.* | **+of** *The government denied rumors of corruption.* | **+about** *rumors about the mayor's personal life* | ***Rumor has it that*** *she was fired.* | *He accused us of* ***spreading rumors*** *about him.* | **a rumor spreads/goes around/circulates** *A rumor began to circulate that the company was closing.* **2 the rumor mill** the people, considered as a group, that discuss something and pass rumors to each other [**Origin:** 1300–1400 Old French *rumour*, from Latin *rumor*]

ru•mored /ˈrumɚd/ *adj.* used to describe something that people are saying secretly or in an unofficial way, and which may or may not be true: *rumored plans of a merger* | ***It's rumored that*** *he spent time in prison.* | **be rumored to be (doing) sth** *Allen is rumored to be moving to Montana.*

ru•mor•mon•ger /ˈrumɚˌmʌŋgɚ, -ˌmɑŋ-/ *n.* [C] DISAPPROVING someone who tells other people rumors

ru•mour /ˈrumɚ/ the British and Canadian spelling of RUMOR

rump /rʌmp/ *n.* **1** [C] BIOLOGY the part of an animal's back that is just above its back legs **2** [C] BIOLOGY the part of your body that you sit on SYN **bottom** **3 the rump of sth** [singular] the part of a country, organization etc. that remains after most of the other parts have left or been taken away

rum•ple /ˈrʌmpəl/ *v.* [T] to make hair, clothes etc. less neat —**rumpled** *adj.*: *rumpled sheets*

ˈrump steak *n.* [C,U] meat that comes from the part of a cow that is just above its back legs

rum•pus /ˈrʌmpəs/ *n.* [singular] INFORMAL a lot of noise, especially made by people arguing or playing

ˈrumpus room *n.* [C] OLD-FASHIONED a room in a house that is used by the family for games, parties etc.

run¹ /rʌn/ S1 W1 *v. past tense* **ran** /ræn/, *past participle* **run**, **running**
1 MOVE a) [I] to move very quickly, by moving your legs more quickly than when you walk: *If we run, we can still catch the bus.* | **+down/over/through etc.** *I ran down the stairs as fast as I could.* | *She ran screaming through the house.* | **+to** *She ran to him and hugged him.* | **+away/off** *They turned and ran away.* | *He* ***ran for his life*** (=to avoid being killed) *as bullets flew around him.* **b)** [I,T not in passive] to move in this way as a sport or for exercise: *I run every morning.* | **run 2 miles/10 kilometers/400 meters etc.** *He ran 4 miles on Saturday.*

THESAURUS
sprint to run as fast as you can for a short distance: *I sprinted toward the end zone.*
dash/tear to run very fast in a hurried way: *Lorraine dashed to her room to get her books.*
jog/go jogging to run quite slowly for exercise over a long distance: *I jog three times a week.*
race to go somewhere very quickly: *I raced home from school.*
bolt to suddenly run somewhere very fast, especially in order to escape or because you are frightened: *At the sound of the bell, the kids bolted for the door.*
→ WALK

2 BE IN CHARGE OF [T] to control or be in charge of a company, an organization, or a system: *Christina runs a restaurant in Houston.* | *No one really knows who's running the country.* | **well-run/badly run** *a well-run*

business | a large **state-run** factory ▶see THESAURUS box at control[1]
3 IN A RACE [I,T] to take part in a running race: *I've never run a marathon before.* | **+in** *Owens is running in the 200 meters.*
4 GO SOMEWHERE [I] SPOKEN to go somewhere quickly, either by foot or in a car: **+to** *I need to run to the store for some milk.* | **+over/out/back etc.** *Let me just run out to the car and get it.* | **run and do sth** *Run and get me a towel.* | *Sorry, **I have to run*** (=I need to leave quickly).
5 MACHINES a) [I] if a machine runs, it operates: *How has your car been running lately?* | *We had the computer **up and running*** (=working) *in less than an hour.* | **run on electricity/gas/fuel etc.** *The car runs on solar energy.* | **run off a battery/generator etc.** (=use something as a power source) **b)** [T] to make a machine operate: *They don't run the furnace in the summertime.*
6 COMPUTER PROGRAM [I,T] COMPUTERS if a computer program runs or you run it, it operates: *You'd better run the spell checker before you print it.* | *You have too many programs running.*
7 ELECTION [I] POLITICS to try to be elected in an election: *Seven candidates ran in the last election.* | **run for sth** *She ran for Congress in 2004.* | **run against sb** *Adams has not said if he will run against Dornan.*
8 TEST/PROCESS [T] to do something such as a test, check, or EXPERIMENT, in which you do things in a particular order: **run a check/test/experiment (on sb/sth)** *The doctors need to run a few tests first.*
9 run late/early/on time to arrive, go somewhere, or do something late, early, or at the right time: *Don called – he's running late, so we'll start without him.*
10 NEWS/STORIES/ADVERTISEMENTS [I,T] if something runs in a newspaper or magazine or on television or someone runs it, it is printed or broadcast: *Her story ran in the local papers.* | *They ran the ad for several weeks.*
11 FLOW [I] to flow, especially in or from a particular direction or place: *Do you hear water running?* | **+down/along etc.** *Tears started to run down her cheeks.* | *A stream ran through the garden.* ▶see THESAURUS box at flow[1], pour
12 FAST/OUT OF CONTROL [I always + adv./prep.] to move too fast or in an uncontrolled way: **+into/down/through etc.** *Her car ran off the road and into a tree.*
13 PLAY/MOVIE ETC. [I] to continue being performed or shown regularly in one place: *The exhibit runs through May at the Museum of Art.*
14 AMOUNT/PRICE [I,T] to be at a particular level, amount, price etc.: **run sb $20/$50 etc.** *New headlights are going to run you about 40 bucks.* | **be running at sth** *Inflation was running at 5%.* | *Weekly rates **run to** $3,750 during June, July, and August.*
15 HAPPEN [I] to happen or take place, especially in the way that was intended: *The course will run from September to June.* | *Things didn't **run** as **smoothly** as we'd hoped.* | *The president claims that the military campaign is **running according to plan**.*
16 BUSES/TRAINS ETC. a) [I] if a bus, train etc. service runs, it takes people from one place to another at specific times of the day: *The buses don't run on holidays.* | **+to/between etc.** *A ferry runs between the island and the mainland.* **b)** [T] if someone runs a bus, train etc. service, they make it operate: *Caltrain runs commuter trains to San Jose.*
17 NOSE/EYES [I] if someone's nose or eyes are running, liquid is flowing out of them
18 OFFICIAL PAPERS [I] to officially be able to be used for a particular period of time: *The contract runs for a year.*
19 ROADS/PIPES/FENCES/LINES [I always + adv./prep., T always + adv./prep.] if something long and thin such as a river, road, or wire runs in a particular direction or someone runs it there, that is where it is or where someone puts it: **+along/through etc.** *A small path runs between the dunes.* | *A narrow twisting road **runs the length of** the valley.* | **run sth along/through etc. sth** *Run the cables under the carpet.*
20 MOVE SMOOTHLY [I] to move smoothly along something such as a track: *The drapes run along these special tracks.*
21 be running low/short if a supply of something is running low or running short, there is very little of it left: *Our food supply was running low.* | *Time was running short.*
22 be running low on sth also **be running short of sth** to have very little left of something that you normally keep a supply of: *The plane was running low on fuel.*
23 MOVE STH OVER A SURFACE [T always + adv./prep.] to move or rub something lightly along a surface: **run sth down/through/along sth** *He ran his fingers through her hair.* | *Run the scanner over the barcodes.*
24 run your eyes over/along/down etc. sth to look quickly at something: *I ran my eyes down the list of names.*
25 PAIN/FEELING [I always + adv./prep.] if pain or another feeling runs through you or a part of your body, you feel it very strongly: **+through/down/up etc.** *Alvin felt a sharp pain run down his left arm.* | *Sophie felt a chill of fear run through her.*
26 run drugs/guns/whiskey etc. to bring drugs or guns into a country illegally in order to sell them SYN smuggle → see also DRUG RUNNER, GUN-RUNNING
27 STORY/DISCUSSION ETC. [I] to develop in a particular way or include particular things SYN go: *Their argument runs like this.*
28 run in the family if something such as a quality, disease, or skill runs in the family, many people in that family have it: *Good looks must run in the family.*
29 run a temperature/fever to have a body temperature that is higher than normal, because you are sick
30 run a (red) light to drive quickly through TRAFFIC LIGHTS instead of stopping: *The ambulance ran a red light.*
31 run an errand to go to a store, office etc. to buy or get something that you need: *I have to stop off near here to run an errand.*
32 COLORS [I] if color runs, it spreads from one area of cloth to another, when the cloth is wet: *I hope these jeans don't run when I wash them.*
33 PAINT/INK ETC. [I] if paint, ink, or MAKEUP runs, it moves onto an area where you did not intend it to go: *Your mascara's running.*
34 run for cover a) to run toward a place where you will be safe from being attacked, especially by bullets **b)** to try to protect yourself from criticism, a bad situation etc.: *Signs of trouble on Wall Street sent investors running for cover.*
35 run for it to run as quickly as possible in order to escape: *Someone's coming – run for it!*
36 run (sth) aground/ashore if a ship runs aground, or someone runs it aground, it hits rocks or the ground and cannot move because the water is not deep enough
37 run its course to continue in the expected way until finished: *Once the disease has run its course, it's not likely to return.*
38 run (sb) a bath to fill a bathtub with water (for someone)
39 be running high if feelings are running high, people are becoming angry or upset about something: *Emotions were running high during the trial.*
40 run dry a) if a river or WELL (=hole in the ground for getting water) runs dry, there is no water left **b)** if a supply of something such as ideas, money etc. runs dry, it ends or is used up: *The show's creativity had run dry after the second season.*
41 HOLE IN CLOTHES [I] if a hole in PANTYHOSE runs, it gets longer in a straight line
42 come running a) INFORMAL to react in a very eager way when someone asks or tells you to do something: *He only has to ask and I come running.* **b)** SPOKEN to ask someone for help, advice, or sympathy when you have a problem: **+to** *Don't come running to me when everything goes wrong!*
43 run sb's life INFORMAL to keep telling someone what they should do all the time, in a way that they find annoying: *Stop trying to run my life!*
44 be running scared to have become worried about the power of an enemy or opponent: *Their new software has the competition running scared.*
45 run rings/circles around sb INFORMAL to be able to do

R

something much better than someone else can: *Sophie can run circles around anyone who disagrees with her.* **46 run wild** to behave in an uncontrolled way: *Football fans ran wild through the city.*

[**Origin:** Old English *rinnan*] → see also **run amok** at AMOK, **make your blood run cold** at BLOOD (11), **run counter to** at COUNTER[3] (1), **cut and run** at CUT[1] (25), **run/go deep** at DEEP[2] (4), **run the gauntlet** at GAUNTLET (3), **run riot** at RIOT[1] (2), RUNNING[1], RUNAROUND

run across sb/sth *phr. v.* to meet or find someone or something by chance: *I ran across some old love letters in a drawer.*

run after sb/sth *phr. v.* to chase someone or something: *She ran after him, calling his name.*

run along *phr. v.* SPOKEN OLD-FASHIONED used to tell someone, especially children, that they must leave, or that you must leave now: *Now you kids run along to bed.*

run around *phr. v.* **1** to run in an area, without a definite direction or purpose: *Put your puppy on the floor and let him run around.* **2** INFORMAL to be very busy doing many small jobs: *She's been running around all day getting things ready.*

run around with sb *phr. v.* to spend a lot of time with someone, especially in a way that other people disapprove of SYN **run with**

run away *phr. v.* **1** to leave a place, especially secretly, in order to escape from someone or something: *He wanted to run away and join the circus when he was a kid.* | +**from** *Sandy had run away from home several times in her teens.* → see also RUNAWAY[2] **2** to try to avoid a problem or situation because it is difficult or embarrassing: +**from** *Baker is not one to run away from a fight.*

run away with *phr. v.* **1 run away with sb** DISAPPROVING to leave a place secretly or illegally with someone else SYN **run off with**: *His wife has run away with another man.* **2 let your imagination/emotions/feelings run away with you** to allow your ideas, feelings etc. start to control how you behave and stop you from thinking in a sensible way anymore: *I can't let my emotions run away with me.* **3 run away with sth** INFORMAL to win a competition or sports game very easily: *The Warriors ran away with the championship.* **4 run away with sth** to steal something SYN **run off with**

run sth **by** sb *phr. v.* **1** to ask someone about something in order to get their opinion or permission: *You'd better run that contract by a lawyer.* **2 run that by me again** SPOKEN used to ask someone to explain something again, because you did not completely understand

run down *phr. v.* **1 run sb/sth ↔ down** to drive into a person or animal and kill or injure them: *He was run down by a drunk driver.* **2 run sth ↔ down** if a clock, machine, BATTERY etc. runs down or something runs it down, it has no more power and stops working: *If you leave the radio on, it will run down the battery.* **3 run sb/sth ↔ down** INFORMAL to say things that are impolite, bad, or unfair about someone or something: *Never run down your previous employer to a new one.* **4 run down sth** to quickly read a list of people or things: *Let me run down the guestlist again.* **5** if time, a clock etc. is running down, the available time is coming to an end: *With the clock running down, Dole scored another basket.* → see also RUNDOWN, RUN-DOWN

run into *phr. v.* **1 run into sb** INFORMAL to meet someone by chance: *We ran into Ruth this morning.* **2 run into sb/sth** to hit someone or something with a car or other vehicle: *I nearly ran into a tree.* **3 run into sth** to accidentally hit a part of your body on something: *He's always running into things.* **4 run into difficulties/problems/debt etc.** to start to experience difficulties: *The business has run into serious financial problems.* **5 run into (the) hundreds/thousands/millions etc.** to reach a total of several hundreds, thousands etc.: *Insurance claims are expected to run into the millions.* **6 run into sth** if one thing runs into another, for example another word, color, or quality, it joins it and mixes with it so that it is difficult to notice where one ends and the other begins **7 run sth into the ground a)** to use something a lot without taking care of it or repairing it, so that you destroy it: *She ran that old car into the ground.* **b)** to manage a business so badly that it fails completely: *Within a couple of years, he had run the family business into the ground.*

run off *phr. v.* **1** DISAPPROVING to leave a place or person in a way that people disapprove of: *His wife ran off and left him.* | +**to** *They ran off to New York together.* **2 run sth ↔ off** to quickly print several copies of something: *We need to run off a hundred and fifty copies of this.* **3 run sb off, run sb off sth** to force someone to leave a particular place, especially a road: *He ran the intruders off with a gun.* | *Someone tried to **run** me **off the road**.* **4 run off at the mouth** INFORMAL to talk too much: *Boyd seems to enjoy running off at the mouth to the press.*

run off with *phr. v.* **1 run off with sb** DISAPPROVING to leave a place with someone, because you are having a sexual relationship that people do not approve of SYN **run away with**: *Maria left her husband and ran off with Henry.* **2 run off with sth** to take something without permission: *Someone ran off with Robert's scuba gear.*

run on *phr. v.* **1** to continue happening for longer than expected or planned: *Our meetings usually run on for hours.* **2** to continue speaking for a long time about something that is boring: +**about** *My dad will run on for hours about golf.*

run out *phr. v.* **1** if you run out of something, you use all of it and do not have any left: *I've got some money you can borrow if you run out.* | +**of** *I hope we don't run out of paint.* | *We're starting to run out of ideas.* **2** if something runs out, it is all used and there is none: *My patience was running out.* | *Time is starting to run out.* **3** if an agreement, contract, official document etc. runs out, it reaches the end of the period when it is officially allowed to continue SYN **expire**: *My contract runs out in September.* **4 run out of steam/gas etc.** INFORMAL to have no energy or eagerness left for something that you are trying to do: *I'm running out of steam – why don't we quit for the day?* **5 run sb out of town** OLD-FASHIONED to force someone to leave a place, because they have done something wrong

run out on sb *phr. v.* DISAPPROVING to leave someone, especially your family, when you should not because you are responsible for them: *My dad ran out on me and my mom when I was ten.*

run over *phr. v.* **1 run sb/sth ↔ over** to hit someone or something with a car or other vehicle, and drive over them: *The dog had been run over by a car.* **2 run over sth** to look at or read something again so that you understand it better, or so that you are prepared for something: *Sean ran over his notes one last time.* **3 run over sth** to explain something so that someone else understands it, especially a series of points or instructions: *I'll just run over the main points again.* **4 run over sth in your head/mind** to think about something: *He ran over all the possibilities in his mind.* **5** also **run over time** to continue past the arranged time: *The meetings usually run over by a few minutes.* **6** if a container runs over, there is so much liquid inside that some flows out SYN **overflow**

run through *phr. v.* **1 run through sth** to repeat something in order to practice it or make sure it is correct SYN **go through** SYN **run over**: *I want to run through the speech one more time.* **2 run through sb's mind/head** if something runs through your mind, you cannot help thinking about it or remembering: *The same thought kept running through his mind.* **3 run through sth** to quickly read or look at something, especially in order to check or find something: *Joe ran through a list of the jobs to be done.* **4 run through sth** to think about, talk about, or explain something quickly, especially a series of events, reasons, or instructions: *The woman quickly ran through* *the instructions with me.* **5 run through sth** to be present in many parts of something or continue through it, for example in an artist's work or in a society: *This theme runs through the whole book.* **6 run sth through sth** to put something through a machine, a computer program etc. so that it can be dealt with: *Police ran the information through their databases.* **7 run through sth** to use all of a supply of something, especially money: *He ran through several thousand dollars before police caught him.* **8 run sb through** LITERARY to push a sword completely through someone → see also RUN-THROUGH

run to *phr. v.* **1 run to sb** to ask someone to help or protect you, especially when you should not need their help: *You can't keep running to your parents every time you have a problem.* **2 run to sth** to be or reach a particular number or amount, especially a large number or amount **3** FORMAL **sb's taste runs to sth** used to say that someone likes a particular type of thing

run up *phr. v.* **1 run up a bill/expenses/debts** to use a lot of something or borrow a lot of money, so that you will have to pay a lot of money: *He's been running up huge phone bills.* **2 run sth ↔ up** to achieve a particular number of points in a game or competition **3 run sth ↔ up** to raise a flag on a pole

run up against sth/sb *phr. v.* to have to deal with unexpected problems or a difficult opponent: *They finally ran up against a team they couldn't beat.*

run with *phr. v.* **1 run with sth** to develop an idea or plan by adding your own ideas and efforts: *Mike picked up the idea and ran with it.* **2 run with sb** spend a lot of time with someone, especially in a way that other people disapprove of SYN **run around with**: *She started running with the wrong crowd.*

run² S1 W1 *n.*

1 ON FOOT a) [C] a period of time spent running, or a distance that you run as a sport or for exercise: *a 5-mile run* | *I'm about to* ***go for a run.*** **b)** [singular] the act of running: *I* ***broke into a run*** (=started running) *when I spotted her across the field.* | *It was still raining hard, but we* ***made a run for*** (=suddenly started raining) *the car.* | *The kids set off* ***at a run*** (=running) *for the swing sets.*

2 BASEBALL [C] a point won in baseball: *He* ***scored*** *936* ***runs*** *in 12 seasons.*

3 PLAY/MOVIE [C] ENG. LANG. ARTS a continuous series of performances of a play, movie etc. in the same place: *The play had a three-month run on Broadway.*

4 SERIES [C usually singualr] a series of successes or failures: **+of** *a run of six consecutive defeats* | **a run of good/bad luck** (=several lucky or unlucky things happening quickly after each other)

5 do sth on the run while you are on your way somewhere, or doing something else: *I always seem to eat on the run these days.*

6 a run on sth a situation in which a lot of people suddenly buy a particular product: *There's always a run on roses before Valentine's Day.* | **a run on the dollar/pound/yen etc.** (=a situation in which a lot of people sell dollars etc. and the value goes down)

7 a run on a bank also **a bank run** an occasion when a lot of people all take their money out of a bank at the same time

8 ELECTION [C, usually singular] an attempt to be elected: *Turner is* ***making*** *his first* ***run for*** *public office.*

9 NUMBER PRODUCED [C] the number of units of a product that are produced at one time: *a limited run of 200 copies*

10 make a run for it to suddenly start running in order to escape: *When the guard turned, we made a run for it.*

11 on the run a) be trying to escape or hide, especially from the police: *Mel had been on the run since he escaped from jail.* **b)** if an army or an opponent is on the run, they may soon be defeated: *Government forces have the rebels on the run.* **c)** very busy and continuously rushing to get from one place to another: *She's constantly on the run.*

12 TRIP [C usually singular] a trip by train, ship, truck etc., made regularly between two places: *It's a 45-minute run between the two cities.*

13 SLOPE [C] **a)** a sloping area of land that you can SKI down: *Both resorts offer beginner to expert runs.* **b)** a special area or track for people to slide down on a SLED or BOBSLED **c)** a trip down a slope in a sport such as SKIING

14 IN CLOTHES [C] a long hole in a pair of PANTYHOSE

15 give sb a (good) run for their money to do well in an election, competition etc. so that your opponent has to use all their skill and effort to defeat you: *He didn't win, but he gave Rogers a run for his money.*

16 have the run of sth to be allowed to use a place when and how you want: *We had the run of the house all week.*

17 have a good/long run used to say that someone does something successfully for a long time, especially when this period of success has come to an end: *We've had a good run, but we knew it couldn't last forever.*

18 the runs [plural] INFORMAL DIARRHEA (=an illness that makes you need to go to the toilet often)

19 MUSIC [C] ENG. LANG. ARTS a set of notes played or sung quickly up or down a SCALE in a piece of music

20 CARD GAMES [C] a set of cards with numbers in a series, held by one player

21 FOR ANIMALS [C] an enclosed area where animals such as chickens or rabbits are kept → see also DRY RUN, FUN RUN, **in the long run** at LONG¹ (8), **in the short term/run** at SHORT¹ (11), TRIAL RUN

run·a·bout /ˈrʌnəˌbaʊt/ *n.* [C] OLD-FASHIONED a small car used for short trips

run·a·round /ˈrʌnəˌraʊnd/ *n.* **give sb the runaround** INFORMAL to deliberately avoid giving someone a definite answer, especially when they are asking you to do something: *The insurance company keeps giving me the runaround.* → see also **run around** at RUN¹

run·a·way¹ /ˈrʌnəˌweɪ/ *adj.* [only before noun] **1** a runaway vehicle or animal is out of control and moving fast: *a runaway freight train* **2** happening very easily or quickly, and not able to be controlled: *"Scarlett" became a runaway bestseller.* **3** a runaway person has left the place where they are supposed to be: *runaway teens*

runaway² *n. plural* **runaways** [C] someone, especially a child, who has left home without telling anyone and does not intend to go back → see also **run away** at RUN¹

ˌrun-ˈdown, rundown *adj.* **1** a building or area that is run-down is in very bad condition SYN **dilapidated**: *run-down houses* **2** [not before noun] someone who is run-down is tired or not healthy ▶see THESAURUS box at **tired**

run·down /ˈrʌndaʊn/ *n.* [C usually singular] a quick report or explanation of an idea, situation, event etc. SYN **summary**: **+of/on** *Here's a rundown of what you can expect at most resorts.*

rune /run/ *n.* [C] **1** ENG. LANG. ARTS one of the letters of the alphabet used in ancient times by people in Northern Europe **2** a magic song or written sign —**runic** *adj.*

rung¹ /rʌŋ/ *v.* the past participle of RING

rung² *n.* [C] **1** one of the bars that form the steps of a LADDER **2** INFORMAL a particular level or position in an organization or system: **+of/on** *Community colleges are the bottom rung of the state's higher education ladder.* **3** a bar between two legs of a chair

ˈrun-in *n.* [C] **1** an argument or disagreement, especially with someone in an official position: **+with** *He* ***had a run-in*** *with his boss.* **2 a run-in with the police/authorities/law** if you have a run-in with the police etc., you have trouble with them because you have broken a law

run·ner /ˈrʌnɚ/ *n.* [C] **1** someone who runs as a sport or for pleasure: *a long-distance runner* | **a good/fast/slow etc. runner** *I'm not a very fast runner.* **2** in baseball, a player who waits on one of the bases so they can run to the next base when the ball is hit: *Mays was up, with two runners on base.* → see picture at BASEBALL **3** someone who walks or runs from place to place carrying messages, especially in past times SYN **messenger** **4** one of the two thin pieces of metal

R

under a SLED, or the single piece of metal under a SKATE, that allows it to go over snow and ice smoothly **5** a long narrow piece of cloth or CARPET: *a red table runner for Christmas* **6** the bar of wood or metal that a drawer or curtain slides along **7** BIOLOGY a stem with which a plant such as a STRAWBERRY spreads itself along the ground and then puts down roots to form a new plant → see also DRUG RUNNER, FRONTRUNNER

ˌrunner-ˈup *n. plural* **runners-up** [C] the person or team that comes second in a race or competition

run·neth /ˈrʌnəθ/ *v.* → see **my cup runneth over** at CUP[1] (13)

run·ning[1] /ˈrʌnɪŋ/ *n.* **1** [U] the act or sport of running: *He **goes running** every morning.* | **running shoes/shorts etc.** *an expensive pair of running shoes* **2 the running of sth** the process of managing or organizing a business, home, organization etc.: *Maria helped her mother with the running of the household.* **3 be in the running/out of the running** to have some hope or no hope of winning a race or competition: *They remain in the running for a spot in the tournament.* | *She's out of the running for a medal.*

R

running[2] *adj.* [only before noun] **1 running water a)** a building that has running water has pipes which provide water to its BATHROOM, kitchen etc.: *a cabin with no running water* **b)** water that is flowing or moving: *the sound of running water* | *Scrub the potatoes thoroughly **under running water**.* **2 running commentary** a spoken description of an event, especially a race or game, made while the event is happening: ***Keep up a running commentary** as you demonstrate the experiment.* **3 running battle/argument/joke etc.** an argument or joke that continues or is repeated over a long period of time: *They've had a running battle about the fence for over five years.* **4 running total** a total that continues to increase as new costs, amounts etc. are added: *Keep a running total of your expenses.* **5 running time** the length of time from the beginning to the end of a movie or television program: *a running time of 194 minutes* **6 running sore** a sore area on your skin, that has liquid coming out of it **7 in running order** a machine that is in running order is working correctly **8 the running order** the order in which the different parts of an event have been arranged to take place: *There are a few changes in the running order for the teachers' conference.*

running[3] *adv.* **two years/five times etc. running** for three years etc. without a change or interruption SYN **in a row**: *The business has had increased sales for three years running.*

ˈrunning ˌback *n.* [C,U] a player whose main job is to run with the ball in football

ˈrunning ˌcosts *n.* [plural] the amount of money that is needed to operate an organization, system etc.

ˌrunning ˈjump *n.* [C] a jump made by running up to the point at which you leave the ground

ˈrunning mate *n.* [C usually singular] POLITICS when someone who is trying to become president, GOVERNOR etc. chooses a running mate, they choose the person who will become the VICE PRESIDENT, LIEUTENANT GOVERNOR etc. if they are elected: *Kennedy chose Johnson as his running mate in the 1960 presidential election.*

run·ny /ˈrʌni/ *adj.* INFORMAL **1** a runny nose, runny eyes etc. have liquid coming out of them, usually because you have a cold **2** something, especially a food, that is runny is not as solid or thick as normal or as you want: *The scrambled eggs were a little bit runny.*

ˈrun-off *n.* **1** [C] POLITICS a second competition or election that is arranged when there is no clear winner of the first one: *a run-off election* → see also PLAY-OFF, **run off** at RUN[1] **2** [U] rain or other liquid that flows off the land into rivers, oceans etc.: *the run-off from melting snow*

run·off pri·ma·ry /ˌrʌnɔf ˈpraɪmɛri/ *n.* [C] POLITICS an election in the U.S. in which the two people who won the most votes in a political party's DIRECT PRIMARY are the only CANDIDATES, and the winner of those two becomes the official party candidate → see also BLANKET PRIMARY

ˌrun-of-the-ˈmill *adj.* not special or interesting in any way SYN **ordinary**: *a run-of-the-mill performance*

ˈrun-on ˌsentence *n.* [C] ENG. LANG. ARTS a sentence that has two main CLAUSES without connecting words or correct PUNCTUATION

runt /rʌnt/ *n.* [C] **1** BIOLOGY the smallest and least developed baby animal of a group born at the same time: *the runt of the litter* **2** INFORMAL a small, unimportant person who you do not like

ˈrun-through *n.* [C] a short practice before a performance, test etc.: *a brief run-through before the concert*

ˈrun-up *n.* **1 the run-up to sth** the period of time just before an important event: *the run-up to the elections* **2** [C] the act of running, or the distance that you run, before you kick a ball, jump over a pole etc.

run·way /ˈrʌnweɪ/ *n. plural* **runways** [C] **1** a long specially prepared hard surface like a road that aircraft leave from or come down on ▸see THESAURUS box at **airport** **2** ENG. LANG. ARTS a long narrow part of a stage that goes out into the area where the AUDIENCE sits

ru·pee /ˈrupi, ruˈpi/ *n.* [C] the standard unit of money in some countries such as India and Pakistan [**Origin:** 1600–1700 Hindi *rupaiya*, from Sanskrit *rupya* **silver made into coins**]

ru·pi·ah /ruˈpiə/ *n.* [C] the standard unit of money in Indonesia

rup·ture[1] /ˈrʌptʃɚ/ *n.* **1** [C,U] an occasion when something suddenly breaks apart or bursts: *A pipeline rupture halted supplies of natural gas.* **2** [C] a situation in which two countries or groups of people suddenly disagree and often end their relationship with each other SYN **breach**: +**between** *the rupture of relations between the two countries* | +**with** *a rupture with his family* **3** [C] a sudden harmful change in a situation: *a major rupture in the social system* | *Children experience a parent's death as a rupture in their lives.*

rupture[2] *v.* [I,T] **1** to break or burst, or make something break or burst: *A blood vessel in his brain had ruptured.* **2** [T] to damage good relations between people or a peaceful situation: *The noise of a motorcycle ruptured the peace of the afternoon.*

ru·ral /ˈrʊrəl/ S2 W3 *adj.* **1** happening in or relating to the country, not the city SYN **country** OPP **urban**: *a magazine about rural life* | *Crime is a concern in both rural and urban areas.* **2** like the country or reminding you of the country OPP **urban**: *Compared to Los Angeles, Santa Barbara is rural.* [**Origin:** 1400–1500 Old French, Latin *ruralis*, from *rus* **open land**]

ˌrural deˈlivery *n.* the full form of R.D.

ˌrural free deˈlivery WRITTEN ABBREVIATION **RFD** *n.* [U] free delivery of mail provided by the U.S. Post Office to people living in country areas

ˈrural ˌroute *n.* → see RR

ruse /ruz/ *n.* [C] something you do in order to deceive someone SYN **trick**

rush[1] /rʌʃ/ S3 W3 *v.*

1 MOVE QUICKLY [I always + adv./prep.] to move very quickly, especially because you need to be somewhere very soon SYN **hurry**: *There's plenty of time – we don't need to rush.* | +**out/past/through/along etc.** *I rushed into the hall to get a ticket.* | *People were rushing past her down the steps.*

THESAURUS

race to go somewhere as fast as you can: *Carter raced downstairs.*

dash to run somewhere very fast, especially only a short distance: *Bob dashed across the road to his friend's house.*

hurry to do something or go somewhere more quickly than usual, especially because there is not much time: *People hurried into stores to escape the rain.*

charge to move quickly forward: *The boys charged up the trail, laughing and yelling.*

speed to move very fast, used about cars, trains etc., or the people traveling in them: *Several cars sped by.*
→ RUN[1]

2 DO STH QUICKLY [I,T] to do or decide something very quickly, especially so that you do not have time to do it carefully or well: *He doesn't intend to rush his decision.* | **rush it/things** *He's recovering well, but shouldn't rush things.* | **+to** *The press is guilty of* ***rushing to judgment*** (=deciding someone is guilty of something) *in these cases.* → see also RUSH INTO
3 rush to do sth to do something eagerly and without delay: *Investors rushed to buy the newly issued stocks.*
4 TAKE/SEND URGENTLY [T always + adv./prep.] to take or send something or someone to a place very quickly, especially because of an unexpected problem: **rush sb to somewhere** *She was* ***rushed to the hospital*** *with severe chest pain.* | *The army rushed reinforcements to the front.*
5 MAKE SB HURRY [T] to try to make someone do something more quickly than they want to: *I don't mean to rush you but I really need to get going.* | **rush sb into doing sth** *Don't let them rush you into signing the contract.*
6 LIQUID [I always + adv./prep.] if water or another liquid rushes somewhere, it moves quickly through or into a place: *Water rushed through the gutters.*
7 BLOOD [I] if blood rushes to your face or your head, your face becomes red because you feel embarrassed, shy, angry, or excited about something: **+to** *He smiled, and the blood rushed to her face.*
8 FOOTBALL [I,T] to carry the ball forward: *Lawrence rushed for 68 yards and one touchdown.*
9 ATTACK [T] to attack someone suddenly and in a group: *Police in riot gear rushed the demonstrators.*
10 UNIVERSITIES a) [T] to give parties for students, have meetings with them etc., in order to decide whether to let them join your FRATERNITY or SORORITY (=type of club) **b)** [I,T] to go through the process of trying to be accepted into these clubs: *She decided to rush the Tri-Delta sorority.*
[**Origin:** 1300–1400 Old French *ruser* **to drive back, deceive**, from Latin *recusare*]

rush around *phr. v.* to try to do a lot of things in a short period of time: *Dean rushed around trying to get everything ready.*

rush into sth *phr. v.* to get involved in something without taking enough time to think carefully about it: *She refuses to be rushed into any decision.* | *He's asked me to marry him, but I don't want to* ***rush into anything.***

rush sth ↔ **out** *phr. v.* to make a new product, book etc. available for sale very quickly

rush sth ↔ **through** *phr. v.* to deal with official or government business more quickly than usual: *The environmental bill was rushed through the House in one month.*

rush² *n.*
1 HURRY [singular, U] a situation in which you need to hurry SYN **hurry**: *Slow down! What's the* ***big rush?*** | *a* ***frantic rush*** *for the ferry* | **be in a rush to do sth** *Eric* ***was in no rush to*** *make a decision.* | *Take your time.* ***There's no rush.*** | *If you* ***are in a rush*** *and can't stop to eat, grab some fruit.*
2 BUSY PERIOD the rush the time in the day, month, year etc. when a place or group of people are particularly busy: *The accident happened during the evening rush.* | *the Christmas rush* → see also RUSH HOUR
3 PEOPLE WANTING STH [singular] a situation in which a lot of people suddenly try to do or get something: **+on** *A scheduled increase in passport fees has caused a rush on the passport office.* | **the rush to do sth** *Libraries are being sacrificed in the* ***mad rush*** *to put computers in schools.* → see also GOLD RUSH
4 FAST MOVEMENT [singular] a sudden fast movement of things or people: *From the darkness behind her there came a rush of wings.* | **rush of air/wind/water** *the rush of water down the mountainside*
5 PLANT [C] BIOLOGY a type of tall grass that grows in water, often used for making baskets, MATS etc.
6 FEELING a) [C] INFORMAL a strong, usually pleasant feeling that you get from taking a drug or from doing something exciting: *Skateboarding is a real rush once you know how to do it.* **b) rush of excitement/panic etc.** a sudden very strong feeling of excitement etc.: *I felt a rush of passion I had never known before.*
7 STUDENTS [C usually singular] the time when university students who want to join a FRATERNITY or SORORITY (=type of club) go to a lot of parties in order to see which one they would like to join: *rush week* | *a rush party*
8 FOOTBALL [C] an act of moving the ball forward
9 rushes [plural] ENG. LANG. ARTS the first prints of a movie before it has been EDITED SYN **dailies**

rushed /rʌʃt/ *adj.* done very quickly or too quickly, because there was not enough time: *The restaurant's service was rushed and impersonal.*

'rush hour *n.* [C,U] the time of day when the roads, buses, trains etc. are most full, because people are traveling to or from work: *heavy rush hour traffic*

Mount Rushmore

Rush•more, Mount /ˈrʌʃmɔr/ also **Mount ˌRushmore ˌNational Meˈmorial** a mountain in the U.S. state of South Dakota, where the rock has been cut into the shape of the faces of four U.S. presidents: Washington, Jefferson, Lincoln, and Theodore Roosevelt

Rus•sell, Ber•trand /ˈbɚtrənd/ (1872–1970) a British PHILOSOPHER and mathematician

Russell, Bill /bɪl/ (1934–) a U.S. basketball player

Russell, Charles (1852–1916) a U.S. religious leader who started the Jehovah's Witnesses

rus•set /ˈrʌsɪt/ *n.* [U] LITERARY a reddish-brown color —**russet** *adj.*

Rus•sia /ˈrʌʃə/ a very large country in Eastern Europe and northern Asia, officially called the Russian Federation, that reaches from the Arctic Ocean in the north and Ukraine in the west to the Pacific Ocean in the east —**Russian** *n., adj.*

ˌRussian ˌOrthodox ˈChurch, the the main Christian church in Russia, that was formed in the 11th century by separating from the Catholic Church, and is closely related to the Greek Orthodox Church

ˌRussian Revoˈlution, the HISTORY the events in Russia in 1917 which ended the rule of the CZARS and led to the governing of Russia by the Bolsheviks under Lenin

ˌRussian rouˈlette *n.* [U] a game in which you risk killing yourself by shooting at your head with a gun that has six spaces for bullets but only one bullet in it

rust¹ /rʌst/ *n.* [U] **1** the reddish-brown substance that forms on iron and steel when they get wet: *Clean and oil gardening tools to prevent rust.* **2** a plant disease that causes reddish-brown spots [**Origin:** Old English] → see also RUSTPROOF, RUSTY

rust² *v.* [I,T] to become covered with rust, or to make something become covered in rust: *a pile of rusting farm machinery*

rust away *phr. v.* to be gradually destroyed by rust

ˈRust Belt, the an area in the northern U.S., including parts of the states of Illinois, Michigan, Indiana, Ohio, and Wisconsin, where many large industries, especially the steel and car industries, used to employ many people but have become less successful

rus·tic¹ /ˈrʌstɪk/ *adj.* **1** simple, old-fashioned, and not spoiled by modern developments, in a way that is typical of the country: *rustic cabins in the mountains* **2** [only before noun] roughly made from wood: *a rustic bench* —**rusticity** /rʌˈstɪsəṭi/ *n.* [U]

rustic² *n.* [C] LITERARY someone from the country, especially a farm worker

rus·tle¹ /ˈrʌsəl/ *v.* **1** [I,T] if leaves, papers, clothes etc. rustle, or if you rustle them, they make a soft noise as they rub against each other: *A light breeze rustled the treetops.* | *Her taffeta dress rustled as she moves past.* **2** [T] to steal farm animals such as cattle, horses, or sheep

rustle sth ↔ **up** *phr. v.* INFORMAL to find or make something quickly, especially a meal: *She rustled up some dinner from leftovers.*

R

rustle² *n.* [singular] the noise made when something rustles: +**of** *a rustle of leaves*

rus·tler /ˈrʌslɚ/ *n.* [C] someone who steals farm animals such as cattle, horses, or sheep

rust·proof /ˈrʌstpruf/ *adj.* metal that is rustproof will not RUST

rust·y /ˈrʌsti/ *adj.* **1** metal that is rusty is covered in RUST: *an old rusty bicycle* **2** if you are rusty, you are not as good at something as you used to be, because you have not practiced it for a long time [SYN] **out of practice**: *I was a little rusty, and my timing was off.* —**rustiness** *n.* [U]

rut¹ /rʌt/ *n.* **1** [C] a deep narrow track left in soft ground by a wheel **2 in a rut** living or working in a situation that never changes, so that you feel bored: *I sometimes feel that my relationship with Jeff is* ***stuck in a rut.*** **3** [U] also **the rut** BIOLOGY the period of the year when some male animals, especially DEER, are sexually active

rut² *v.* [I] TECHNICAL if animals, especially DEER, are rutting, they are having sex or are ready to have sex because of the time of year

ru·ta·ba·ga /ˈruṭəˌbeɪgə/ *n.* [C] a large round yellow vegetable that grows under the ground [**Origin:** 1700–1800 Swedish *rotabagge*, from *rot* **root** + *bagge* **bag**]

Ruth /ruθ/ a book in the Old Testament of the Christian Bible

Ruth, Babe /beɪb/ (1895–1948) a baseball player who is famous for getting more HOME RUNS than anyone before him

Ruth·er·ford /ˈrʌðɚfɚd/, **Er·nest** /ˈɚnɪst/ (1871–1937) a British scientist, born in New Zealand, who discovered the structure of the atom and was the first person to split the NUCLEUS of an atom

ruth·less /ˈruθlɪs/ *adj.* **1** so determined to get what you want that you do not care if you have to hurt other people in order to get it: *the cold, ruthless look in her eyes* | *a ruthless criminal* **2** determined and firm when making difficult decisions: *He ran the company with ruthless efficiency.* [**Origin:** 1300–1400 *ruth* **pity** (12–19 centuries), from *rue*] —**ruthlessly** *adv.* —**ruthlessness** *n.* [U]

Rut·ledge /ˈrʌtlɪdʒ/, **John** (1739–1800) a CHIEF JUSTICE on the U.S. Supreme Court

rut·ted /ˈrʌṭɪd/ *adj.* a surface that is rutted has deep narrow tracks in it left by the wheels of vehicles

RV *n.* [C] **recreational vehicle** a large vehicle, usually with cooking equipment and beds in it, that a family can use for traveling or camping [SYN] **camper**

Rw·an·da /ruˈɑndə/ a country in east central Africa between Tanzania and the Democratic Republic of Congo —**Rwandan** *n., adj.*

Rx. *n.* the written abbreviation of PRESCRIPTION

rye /raɪ/ *n.* [U] **1** a type of grain that is used for making bread and WHISKEY: *a pastrami sandwich on rye* **2** also **rye whis·key** a type of WHISKEY made from rye: *a bottle of rye* [**Origin:** Old English *ryge*]

rye·grass /ˈraɪgræs/ *n.* [U] a type of grass that is grown as food for animals

S,s

S[1], **s** /ɛs/ *n. plural* **S's, s's** [C] **a)** the 19th letter of the English alphabet **b)** a sound represented by this letter

S[2] **1** the written abbreviation of "small," used on clothes to show the size **2** used to show that a television show has scenes involving sex

S. also **S** the written abbreviation of "south" or "southern"

-'s /z, s/ INFORMAL **1** the short form of "is": *Alan's on vacation.* | *What's in here?* | *Pam's leaving today.* **2** the short form of "has": *Paul's already left.* **3** a short form of "us," used only in "let's": *Let's go.* **4** a short form of "does," used in questions after "who," "what" etc.: *How's that look?*

S & L /ˌɛs ənd ˈɛl/ *n.* [C] INFORMAL the short form of SAVINGS AND LOAN association

S & P 500 /ˌɛs ən ˌpi faɪv ˈhʌndrɪd/ also **Standard & Poor's 500 stock index, Standard & Poor's Index** *n.* [singular] **the S & P 500** ECONOMICS a list that shows the daily changes in the price of STOCKS in 500 large U.S. companies, used as a measure of the changes in the U.S. STOCK MARKET: *The S & P 500 is down 1.17 points to 396.47.*

sab·ba·tar·i·an /ˌsæbəˈtɛriən/ *n.* [C] FORMAL someone who strongly believes that the Sabbath should be a holy day on which people do not work —**sabbatarian** *adj.*

Sab·bath /ˈsæbəθ/ *n.* **1 the Sabbath a)** Sunday, considered as a day of rest and prayer by most Christian churches **b)** Saturday, considered as a day of rest and prayer in the Jewish religion and some Christian churches **2 keep/break the Sabbath** to obey or not obey the religious rules of this day [**Origin:** 900–1000 Latin *sabbatum*, from Hebrew *shabbath* **rest**]

sab·bat·i·cal /səˈbæt̬ɪkəl/ *n.* [C,U] a period when someone, especially someone in a college or university job, stops doing their usual work in order to study or travel: *He's going* ***on sabbatical*** *next fall.* | *She* ***took a sabbatical*** *in order to finish the book.* —**sabbatical** *adj.*

sa·ber /ˈseɪbɚ/ *n.* [C] **1** a light pointed sword with one sharp edge, used in FENCING **2** a heavy sword with a curved blade, used in past times

saber-ˌrattling *n.* [U] a phrase meaning the action of threatening to use military force, used when you do not think this is very frightening or serious

Sa·bin /ˈseɪbɪn/, **Al·bert** /ˈælbɚt/ (1906–1993) a U.S. doctor who developed a new VACCINE against POLIO

sa·ble[1] /ˈseɪbəl/ *n.* [C,U] an expensive fur used to make coats, or the small animal that this fur comes from

sable[2] *adj.* POETIC black or very dark in color

sab·o·tage[1] /ˈsæbəˌtɑʒ/ *v.* [T] **1** to secretly damage or destroy equipment, vehicles etc. that belong to an enemy or opponent, so that they cannot be used: *Every single plane had been sabotaged.* **2** to deliberately spoil someone's plans because you do not want them to succeed [SYN] **undermine**: *He used his influence to sabotage her career.*

sabotage[2] *n.* [U] the act of deliberately damaging or destroying equipment, vehicles etc. in order to prevent an enemy or opponent from using them: ***acts of sabotage*** *by the terrorists* [**Origin:** 1800–1900 French *saboter* **to walk along noisily, do work badly, sabotage**, from *sabot* **wooden shoe**]

sab·o·teur /ˌsæbəˈtɚ/ *n.* [C] someone who deliberately damages, destroys, or spoils someone else's property or activities, in order to prevent them from doing something

sac /sæk/ *n.* [C] BIOLOGY a part inside a plant or animal that is shaped like a bag and contains liquid or air

Sac·a·ja·we·a /ˌsækədʒəˈwiə/ (1786–1812) a Native American woman who acted as a guide to Meriwether Lewis and William Clark on their travels from St. Louis to the Pacific Ocean

sac·cha·rin /ˈsækərɪn/ *n.* [U] a chemical substance that tastes sweet and can be used instead of sugar in food and drinks

sac·cha·rine /ˈsækərin/ *adj.* too romantic in a way that seems silly and insincere [SYN] **sentimental**: *the movie's saccharine ending*

sac·er·do·tal /ˌsæsɚˈdoʊt̬l, ˌsækɚ-/ *adj.* LITERARY relating or belonging to a priest

sa·chem /ˈseɪtʃəm/ *n.* [C] the name for a leader of some Native American tribes

sa·chet /sæˈʃeɪ/ *n.* [C] a small bag that contains dried HERBS or flowers that have a nice smell: *a lavender sachet* [**Origin:** 1400–1500 French *sac* **bag**]

sack[1] /sæk/ *n.* [C] **1** a large bag, usually made of paper, that you use for carrying food or other things that you have bought [SYN] **bag**: *a sack of groceries* | *a brown paper sack* **2** a large bag made of strong rough cloth, that you use for storing or carrying flour, coal, vegetables etc. [SYN] **bag**: *a sack of potatoes* **3 hit the sack** SPOKEN to go to bed **4 in the sack** INFORMAL a phrase meaning in bed, used especially when you are talking about sexual activity that takes place in bed **5** an occasion in a football game when someone makes the QUARTERBACK fall down **6 the sack of sth** FORMAL a situation in which an army goes through a place, destroying or stealing things and attacking people: *the sack of Rome* [**Origin:** Old English *sacc*, from Latin *saccus*, from Greek *sakkos* **bag, sackcloth**]

S

sack[2] *v.* [T] **1** to make the QUARTERBACK fall down in a football game **2** if an army sacks a place, they go through it destroying or stealing things and attacking people: *The invaders sacked Delphi.* **3** to force someone to leave their job [SYN] **fire**

sack out *phr. v.* SPOKEN to go to sleep: *He sacked out on the sofa.*

sack·cloth /ˈsæk-klɔθ/ also **sack·ing** /ˈsækɪŋ/ *n.* [U] rough cloth used for making sacks

ˈsack race *n.* [C] a race in which the competitors have to jump forward with both legs inside a large cloth bag

sac·ra·ment /ˈsækrəmənt/ *n.* [C] **1 the Sacrament** the bread and wine that are eaten at COMMUNION (1) (=an important Christian ceremony) **2** one of the important Christian ceremonies, such as marriage or communion —**sacramental** /ˌsækrəˈmɛntl◂ / *adj.*

Sac·ra·men·to /ˌsækrəˈmɛntoʊ/ the capital city of the U.S. state of California

sa·cred /ˈseɪkrɪd/ *adj.* **1** relating to a god or religion, and so treated with great respect [OPP] **profane**: *sacred writings* | *In India, cows are considered sacred.* | **+to** *The Black Hills are sacred to the Sioux and Cheyenne.* ▸see THESAURUS box at **religion** **2** extremely important and greatly respected [SYN] **sacrosanct**: *Human life is sacred.* | *Our time with our kids is sacred.* | **+to** *Good food is sacred to the French.* **3 is nothing sacred?** SPOKEN used to express shock when something that you think is very important is being changed or harmed: *Look at how those girls are dressed! Is nothing sacred anymore?* [**Origin:** 1300–1400 Past participle of *sacre* **to make holy** (13–17 centuries), from Old French *sacrer*] —**sacredly** *adv.* —**sacredness** *n.* [U]

ˌsacred ˈcow *n.* [C] DISAPPROVING a belief that is so important to some people that they will not let anyone criticize it

sac·ri·fice[1] /ˈsækrəˌfaɪs/ *n.* **1** [C,U] the act of deciding not to have or do something valuable or important to you, in order to get something that is more important, especially for someone else: *Parenthood often calls for sacrifice.* | *Gandhi worked for the independence of India, at great* ***personal sacrifice****.* | *David's mother* ***made*** *many* ***sacrifices*** *to send him to college.* **2 a)** [C,U] the act of offering something to a god, especially in past times, by killing an animal or a person in a religious ceremony: *They **made sacrifices to** their gods to keep them happy.* **b)** [C] an object or animal that is killed for a god in a religious ceremony: *The ceremony included a **human sacrifice*** (=a person killed as a sacrifice). **3** LITERARY **the ultimate/supreme/final sacrifice** the act of dying while you are fighting for something that you strongly believe in: *These soldiers were prepared to **make the ultimate sacrifice** in defense of freedom.* **4** a hit in baseball that you make so that a runner can go ahead to the next BASE, even though you are OUT (=not allowed to play anymore at that time)

sacrifice² *v.* [T] **1** to give up something valuable or important, in order to get something that you feel is more important, or in order to help someone else: **sacrifice sth for sth** *Don't sacrifice your health for your job.* | *Rugiero was willing to **sacrifice his life*** (=die) *for his country.* | **sacrifice sth to do sth** *Jim sacrificed a promising career to stay home with his kids.* **2** to offer something or someone to a god as a sacrifice

sac·ri·fi·cial /ˌsækrəˈfɪʃəl◂/ *adj.* **1** relating to or offered as a sacrifice: *a sacrificial ceremony* **2 a sacrificial lamb** someone or something that suffers, especially unfairly, so that someone or something more important can succeed: *Flood waters were allowed to cover agricultural land, which served as a sacrificial lamb in order to protect towns downstream.* —**sacrificially** *adv.*

S

sac·ri·lege /ˈsækrəlɪdʒ/ *n.* [C,U] **1** the act of treating something holy in a way that does not show respect **2** the act of treating something badly when someone else thinks it is very important: **sacrilege to do sth** *It would **be sacrilege** to destroy the scenic effect of these waterfalls.* —**sacrilegious** /ˌsækrəˈlɪdʒəs/ *adj.* —**sacrilegiously** *adv.*

sac·ris·tan /ˈsækrəstən/ *n.* [C] TECHNICAL someone whose job is to take care of the holy objects in a church

sac·ris·ty /ˈsækrəsti/ *n. plural* **sacristies** [C] TECHNICAL a small room in a church where holy cups and plates are kept, and where priests put on their ceremonial clothes SYN **vestry**

sac·ro·sanct /ˈsækroʊˌsæŋkt/ *adj.* something that is sacrosanct is considered to be so important that no one is allowed to criticize or change it SYN **sacred**: *Marriage is no longer sacrosanct.*

SAD /sæd/ *n.* [U] the abbreviation of SEASONAL AFFECTIVE DISORDER

sad /sæd/ S2 W3 *adj. comparative* **sadder**, *superlative* **saddest** **1** unhappy, especially because something bad has happened to you or someone else OPP **happy**: **feel/look/sound sad** *I felt so sad for them.* | *Dad looked sad and worried.* | **be sad to hear/see/read etc. sth** *We're sad to see him go.* | *The children talk about what **makes them sad**.* | **+about** *Tim was excited about the new job, but sad about leaving.* | **sad that** *She felt deeply sad that she had not been able to hold her baby.* | **a sad smile/face/expression etc.** *There was such a sad look in her eyes.*

THESAURUS

unhappy not happy, because you are in a situation, job, or relationship that you do not enjoy, and it seems likely to continue: *an unhappy marriage* | *Many parents were unhappy with the education the school was providing.*
miserable very sad, especially because you are lonely or sick: *I couldn't help feeling miserable.*
upset sad because something bad or disappointing has happened: *She's still very upset about her father's death.*
depressed sad for a long time because things are wrong in your life: *He got very depressed after he lost his job.*
down/low INFORMAL a little sad about things in your life: *Whenever I felt down, I'd read his letter.*
homesick sad because you are away from your home, family, and friends: *Many students get homesick in their first year.*
distressed very upset: *the distressed mother of the missing boy*
distraught so upset that you cannot think clearly or behave calmly: *Her husband was distraught when she left him.*
heartbroken extremely sad because of something that has happened: *He died of pneumonia, and his parents were heartbroken.*
gloomy sad because you think a situation will not improve: *a gloomy mood*
glum used especially to say that someone looks sad: *The place was full of glum men with no jobs.*

2 making you feel unhappy: *My brother told us the sad news.* | **a sad book/song/movie etc.** *a sad song about love* | **it is sad to see/hear etc.** *It was sad to see all that food going to waste.* | **a sad time/day/moment etc.** *This is a sad day for us all.* **3** very bad or unacceptable: *It's pretty sad that in an Italian restaurant they can't cook pasta well.* | *America's public schools are in a **sad state**.* | ***Sad to say**, he hadn't saved much.* | ***The sad thing is**, children don't get a chance just to play.* | **it's sad that/when/if** *It's sad that more people don't get involved.* **4** SPOKEN a sad person is someone who you think is boring, stupid, or very bad at doing something: *You stayed home waiting for him to call? You are so sad.* **5 sad sack** INFORMAL someone who is very boring or not skillful at doing things **6 sadder but wiser** having learned something from a bad experience: *He came out of the relationship sadder but wiser.* [**Origin:** Old English *sæd* **having had enough**] —**sadness** *n.* [singular, U] → see also SADLY

Sa·dat /səˈdɑt/, **An·war al-** /ˈɑnwɑr æl/ (1918–1981) the President of Egypt from 1970 to 1981, who tried to bring peace between the Arabs and Israelis

Sad·dam Hus·sein /səˌdɑm huˈseɪn, ˌsɑdəm-/ (1937–) the President of Iraq from 1979 until 2003, when the U.S. removed him from power

sad·den /ˈsædn/ *v.* [T] FORMAL to make someone feel sad or disappointed: ***It saddens** me **that** the children have been dragged into this mess.*

sad·dle¹ /ˈsædl/ *n.* **1** [C] a seat made of leather that is put on a horse's back so that someone can ride it **2** [C] a seat on a bicycle or MOTORCYCLE **3 be in the saddle** INFORMAL **a)** to be in a position in which you have power or authority: *Madison is **back in the saddle** at company headquarters.* **b)** to be riding a horse

saddle² *v.* [T] to put a saddle on a horse

saddle up *phr. v.* to put a saddle on a horse

saddle sb **with** sth *phr. v.* to give someone a job, problem etc. that is difficult or boring and that they do not want: *College kids are saddled with lots of debt before they even graduate.*

sad·dle·bag /ˈsædlˌbæg/ *n.* [C] a bag used for carrying things, that is attached to the saddle on a horse or bicycle

sad·dler /ˈsædlɚ/ *n.* [C] someone who makes saddles and other leather products

sad·dler·y /ˈsædləri, ˈsædl-ri/ *n. plural* **saddleries** **1** [C,U] saddles and leather goods made by a saddler, or the store where these are sold **2** [U] the art of making saddles and other leather goods

ˈsaddle shoe *n.* [C] a shoe that has a toe and heel of one color, with a different color in the middle

ˈsaddle soap *n.* [U] a type of soap used for cleaning and preserving leather

ˈsaddle sore¹ *n.* [C usually plural] a sore spot on your skin that you can get after riding a horse for a long period of time

saddle sore² *adj.* [not before noun] feeling stiff and sore after riding a horse or bicycle

sa·dism /ˈseɪdɪzəm/ *n.* [U] **1** behavior in which someone gets pleasure from being cruel to someone else: *the sadism of the prison guards* **2** behavior in which someone gets sexual pleasure from hurting someone else [**Origin:** 1800–1900 French *sadisme*, from the Marquis de *Sade* (1740–1814), French writer who described cruel sexual practices] → see also MASOCHISM

sa·dist /ˈseɪdɪst/ *n.* [C] someone who enjoys being cruel to other people → see also MASOCHIST

sa·dis·tic /səˈdɪstɪk/ *adj.* cruel and enjoying making other people suffer: *the sadistic guards* —**sadistically** /-kli/ *adv.* → see also MASOCHISTIC

sad·ly /ˈsædli/ *adv.* **1** in a way that shows that you are sad SYN **unhappily**: *Sam looked sadly out the window.* **2** [sentence adverb] in a way that shows a situation is bad or unlucky, and you wish it were different SYN **unfortunately**: *Sadly, the business failed.* **3** very or very much: *He was a popular man who will be sadly missed.* | *They're* ***sadly mistaken*** *if they think they're going to win.* | *An understanding of their problems was* ***sadly lacking.***

sa·do·mas·o·chism /ˌseɪdoʊˈmæsəˌkɪzəm/ *n.* [U] FORMAL the practice of getting sexual pleasure from hurting someone or being hurt —**sadomasochist** *n.* [C] —**sadomasochistic** /ˌseɪdoʊˌmæsəˈkɪstɪk/ *adj.*

sa·fa·ri /səˈfɑri/ *n.* [C] **1** a trip to see or hunt wild animals, especially in Africa: **go/be on safari** *Amy and John went on safari for their honeymoon.* **2 safari suit/jacket** a suit or JACKET that is made of light-colored material, and usually has a belt and two pockets on the chest [**Origin:** 1800–1900 Arabic *safariy* **of a trip**]

safe[1] /seɪf/ S2 W2 *adj.*

1 NOT CAUSING HARM not likely to cause any physical injury or harm OPP **dangerous**: *Flying is one of the safest forms of travel.* | **be safe to do sth** ***Is it safe*** *to drink the water?* | +**for** ***Make*** *your home* ***safer*** *for your children.* | *People stood at a* ***safe distance*** *to watch.*

2 NOT IN DANGER [not before noun] not in danger of being lost, harmed, or stolen SYN **secure** OPP **unsafe**: *She doesn't* ***feel safe*** *at home on her own.* | +**from** *The birds build their nests high up, safe from predators.* | ***Keeping*** *art* ***safe*** *from thieves is a worry for museums everywhere.* | *The missing children were found* ***safe and sound*** (=unharmed after a dangerous experience).

3 PLACE a safe place is one where something is not likely to be stolen or lost, or where someone is not likely to be hurt or harmed: *It's a fairly safe neighborhood.* | *Keep your passport* ***in a safe place.*** | *Make sure you put your ticket* ***somewhere safe.***

4 NO RISK not involving any risk and very likely to succeed: *a safe investment* | *Tom's plan seemed simple and safe.*

5 safe trip/arrival/return etc. a trip etc. in which no one is harmed or lost: *They prayed for their father's safe return.*

6 SUBJECT a safe subject in a conversation, movie, book etc. is not likely to upset anyone or make people argue: *She tends to choose safe topics for her films.*

7 it's safe to say SPOKEN used when you are certain that something is true or correct: *It's safe to say that he's one of our best players.*

8 better (to be) safe than sorry SPOKEN used to say that it is better to be careful now, even if this takes time, effort etc., so that nothing bad will happen later: *I think I'll take my umbrella along – better safe than sorry.*

9 be on the safe side to do something in order to be certain to avoid a bad situation: *Just to be on the safe side, drink bottled water.*

10 be in safe hands to be with someone who will take good care of you: *Parents want to make sure they're leaving their children in safe hands.*

[**Origin:** 1200–1300 Old French *sauf*, from Latin *salvus* **safe, healthy**] —**safely** *adv.*: *Drive safely!* → see also **it's a safe/sure bet (that)** at BET[2] (5), **play it safe** at PLAY[1] (10)

safe[2] *n.* [C] a strong metal box or cupboard with special locks where you keep money and valuable things SYN **strongbox**

ˌsafe ˈconduct *n.* [singular, U] official protection for someone when they are passing through a dangerous area: *Rafael was* ***granted safe conduct*** *out of the country.*

safe·crack·er /ˈseɪfˌkrækə/ *n.* [C] someone who opens SAFES illegally, in order to steal things from them

ˈsafe-deposit ˌbox *n.* [C] a small box used for storing valuable objects, usually kept in a special room in a bank

safe·guard[1] /ˈseɪfgɑrd/ *v.* [I,T] to protect something from harm or damage SYN **guard**: *Be sure to safeguard your passport at all times.* | *Slave owners wanted to* ***safeguard*** *their* ***interests.*** | **safeguard (sth) against sth** *Vaccinations safeguard against disease.*

safeguard[2] *n.* [C] something such as a rule, action etc. that is intended to protect someone or something from possible dangers or problems SYN **protection**: *environmental safeguards* | +**against** *a safeguard against loss*

ˌsafe ˈhaven *n.* [C,U] a place where someone can go to in order to escape from possible danger or attack

ˌsafe ˈhouse *n.* [C] a house where someone can hide and be protected

safe·keep·ing /ˌseɪfˈkipɪŋ/ *n.* [U] the state of being kept safe, or the action of keeping something safe: *The artworks are stored in a bank vault* ***for safekeeping.***

ˌsafe ˈsex *n.* [U] ways of having sex that reduce the risk of the spread of AIDS and other sexual diseases, especially the use of a CONDOM

safe·ty /ˈseɪfti/ S2 W2 *n.*

1 NOT IN DANGER [U] the state of being safe from danger or harm: *Our job is to maintain safety on the streets.* | +**of** *concerns about the* ***health and safety*** *of employees* | *We must be able to send our children to school* ***in safety.*** | **for sb's safety** *Several women said they* ***feared for*** *their* ***safety*** (=they are afraid they are not safe anymore). | ***For your own safety,*** *please remain seated until the plane comes to a complete stop.* | ***For safety's sake,*** *keep kids away when barbecuing food.*

2 HARMFUL/NOT HARMFUL [U] the state of not being dangerous or likely to cause harm or injury: +**of** *There is concern over the safety of the new drug.* | **safety measures/precautions/checks** (=things that are done in order to make sure that something is safe)

3 SAFE PLACE [U] a place where you are safe from danger: +**of** *She finally reached the safety of the shelter.* | **lead/take etc. sb to safety** *Firefighters led the kids to safety.* | *He swam at least three miles before he* ***reached safety.***

4 there's safety in numbers SPOKEN used to say that a dangerous or bad situation is better if there are a lot of people with you

5 SPORTS [C] TECHNICAL a way of getting two points in football by making the other team put the ball down in its own GOAL

6 GUN a small lock on a gun that stops it from being fired by accident

7 safety harness/helmet/glasses etc. equipment that keeps you safe when you do something dangerous

ˈsafety belt *n.* [C] a SEAT BELT

ˈsafety ˌcurtain *n.* [C] a thick curtain that can be lowered at the front of a theater stage to prevent fire from spreading

ˈsafety deˌposit ˌbox *n.* [C] a SAFE-DEPOSIT BOX

ˈsafety glass *n.* [U] **1** strong glass that has been specially treated so that it breaks into very small pieces that are not sharp, used for example in car windows **2** glass that is made by putting a thin plastic sheet between two pieces of glass, so that if the glass is broken the pieces stay on the plastic

ˈsafety lamp *n.* [C] a special lamp used by MINERS, that has a flame which will not make gases explode

ˈsafety match *n.* [C] a match that can only be lit by rubbing it along a special surface on the side of its box

ˈsafety net *n.* [C] **1** a large net that is used to catch someone who is performing high above the ground if they fall **2** a system or arrangement that exists to help you if you have serious problems or get into a

S

difficult situation: +**for** *Welfare provides a safety net for people who are unable to work.* **3** ECONOMICS actions taken by a government to help or protect companies or financial institutions that have serious financial problems: *the federal safety net that protects the banking industry*

ˈsafety pin *n.* [C] a curved metal pin for fastening things together. The point of the pin fits into a cover.

ˈsafety ˌrazor *n.* [C] a RAZOR that has a cover over part of the blade to protect your skin

ˈsafety valve *n.* [C] **1** a part of a machine that allows gas, steam etc. to be let out when the pressure becomes too great **2** something you do that allows you to express strong feelings such as anger without doing any harm: *Humor can be a safety valve in high pressure situations.*

saf·flow·er /ˈsæflaʊɚ/ *n.* [C,U] a plant with orange flowers, grown for its oil which is used in cooking

saf·fron /ˈsæfrən/ *n.* [U] **1** bright yellow SPICE that is used in cooking to give food a special taste and color. It comes from a flower. **2** a bright orange-yellow color

sag /sæg/ *v.* **sagged, sagging** [I] **1** to hang down or bend in the middle, especially because of the weight of something. SYN **sink down**: *The shelves sagged under the weight of hundreds of books.* | *His whole body seemed to sag with relief.* **2** to become weaker or less valuable: *Stock prices sagged again today.* —**sag** *n.* [singular, U]

sa·ga /ˈsɑgə/ *n.* [C] **1** ENG. LANG. ARTS a long story about events that happen over many years: +**of** *"Roots" is the saga of an African-American family, from slavery to the present day.* **2** INFORMAL a long and complicated series of events, or a description of this: +**of** *She launched into the saga of her on-again off-again engagement.* **3** ENG. LANG. ARTS one of the stories written about the Vikings of Norway and Iceland

sa·ga·cious /səˈgeɪʃəs/ *adj.* FORMAL able to understand and judge things very well SYN **wise** SYN **astute** —**sagaciously** *adv.*

sa·gac·i·ty /səˈgæsət̬i/ *n.* [U] FORMAL good judgment and understanding SYN **wisdom**

sage¹ /seɪdʒ/ *n.* **1** [U] a plant with gray-green leaves that are used in cooking **2** [C] LITERARY someone, especially an old man, who is very wise

sage² *adj.* LITERARY very wise, especially as a result of a lot of experience: *sage advice* —**sagely** *adv.*

sage·brush /ˈseɪdʒbrʌʃ/ *n.* [U] a small plant that is very common in dry areas in the western U.S.

sag·gy /ˈsægi/ *adj.* INFORMAL something that is saggy hangs down or bends more than it should: *saggy blue socks*

Sag·it·tar·i·us /ˌsædʒəˈtɛriəs/ *n.* **1** [U] the ninth sign of the ZODIAC, represented by an animal that is half-horse and half-human, and believed to affect the character and life of people born between November 22 and December 21 **2** [C] someone who was born between November 22 and December 21

sa·gua·ro /səˈgwɑroʊ/ *n. plural* **saguaros** [C] a type of large CACTUS with branches that curve up, that grows in the southwestern U.S.

Sa·har·a, the /səˈhærə/ also **the Saˌhara ˈDesert** the world's largest desert which covers a very large area of North Africa

Sa·hel /səˈheɪl, -ˈhil/ *n.* EARTH SCIENCE a very dry area in north Africa, near the Sahara desert

said¹ /sɛd/ *v.* the past tense and past participle of SAY

said² *adj.* [only before noun] LAW mentioned before: *The said person has committed similar offenses in the past.*

sail¹ /seɪl/ *v.* **1** [I always + adv./prep.,T] to travel across an area of water in a boat or ship: +**away/to/across etc.** *We'll sail from Miami to Nassau.* | *She watched the fishing boats sail away.* | *My dream is to sail the South Pacific.* ►see THESAURUS box at **travel¹** **2** [I,T] to direct or control the movement of a boat or ship: *There was a picture of Dick sailing his boat in the Caribbean.* | *My father taught me to sail.* **3** [I] to start a trip by boat or ship: *The ship sailed at dusk.* | +**for** *What year did Columbus sail for the New World?* **4** [I always + adv./prep.] to move quickly and smoothly through the air: +**over/past/through etc.** *A ball came sailing over the fence.* **5** [I always + adv./prep.] to move forward gracefully and confidently: +**by/past/over etc.** *She sailed by without looking at him.*

sail through *phr. v.* to succeed very easily on a test or in a competition or get through a difficult process easily: *The bill sailed through Congress.*

sail² *n.* [C] **1** a large piece of strong cloth attached to the MAST (=tall pole) of a boat, so that the wind will push the boat along: **raise/lower the sails** (=put the sails up or down) **2 set sail** to begin a trip by boat or ship: +**for/from** *We set sail for Savannah in the morning.* **3 under sail** LITERARY moving along on a ship or boat that has sails

sail·board /ˈseɪlbɔrd/ *n.* [C] a flat board with a sail, that you stand on in the sport of WINDSURFING SYN **windsurfer**

sail·board·ing /ˈseɪlˌbɔrdɪŋ/ *n.* [U] WINDSURFING —**sailboarder** *n.* [C]

sail·boat /ˈseɪlboʊt/ *n.* [C] a small boat with one or more sails

sail·ing /ˈseɪlɪŋ/ *n.* **1** [U] the sport or activity of traveling in or controlling a small boat with sails: *We* ***went sailing*** *in the clear waters off the island.* **2 sth is smooth/clear sailing** used to say that a situation is not causing problems and is easy to deal with: *The next few months are not going to be smooth sailing for the company.* **3** [C] a time when a passenger ship leaves a port: *Luckily, there was another sailing at two o'clock.*

ˈsailing ship also **ˈsailing ˌvessel** *n.* [C] a large ship with sails

sail·or /ˈseɪlɚ/ *n.* [C] **1** someone who works on a ship, especially a member of a navy **2 a good/bad sailor** someone who does or does not feel sick when they are in a boat

ˈsailor suit *n.* [C] a blue and white suit that looks like an old-fashioned sailor's uniform, worn by small boys

saint /seɪnt/ S2 *n.* [C] **1 a)** someone who is given a special honor by the Christian church after they have died, because they were very good or holy: *paintings of saints and martyrs* **b)** WRITTEN ABBREVIATION **St.** the title given to someone who has been given this honor: *Saint Patrick* **2** INFORMAL someone who is extremely good, kind, or patient: *Thanks so much for doing that. You're a saint.* **3 sb is no saint** used to say that someone has some faults: *He's a nice guy, but he's no saint.* [**Origin:** 1100–1200 Old French, Late Latin *sanctus*, from Latin, **holy**] → see also **the patience of a saint** at PATIENCE (3)

Saint Ber·nard /ˌseɪnt˺ bɚˈnɑrd/ *n.* [C] a very large strong dog with long brown and white hair

saint·ed /ˈseɪntɪd/ *adj.* **1** [only before noun] LITERARY having been made a saint by the Christian church **2** OFTEN HUMOROUS someone who is sainted is extremely good, kind, or patient

saint·hood /ˈseɪnthʊd/ *n.* [U] the state of being a saint

saint·ly /ˈseɪntli/ *adj.* completely good and honest, with no faults: *She was a simple, loving and saintly woman.* —**saintliness** *n.* [U]

Saint Pat·rick's Day /seɪnt ˈpætrɪks ˌdeɪ/ *n.* [C,U] a holiday on March 17 when people, especially people whose families originally came from Ireland, wear green clothes and honor Saint Patrick

Saint-Saëns /sænˈsɑns/**, Ca·mille** /kæˈmil/ (1835–1921) a French musician who wrote CLASSICAL music

ˈsaint's day *n.* [C] the day of the year when the Christian church remembers a particular SAINT

saith /ˈseɪəθ, sɛθ/ OLD USE says

sake¹ /seɪk/ S3 *n.* [U] **1 for the sake of sb/sth** also **for sb's/sth's sake** in order to help, improve, or please someone or something: *They stayed together for the sake of the children.* | *She agreed to go for James's sake.*

2 for God's/Christ's/goodness'/Heaven's etc. sake SPOKEN **a)** said when you are annoyed, surprised, impatient etc.: *For God's sake, be patient!* **b)** used when you are telling someone how important it is to do something or not to do something: *For heaven's sake, don't be late!* **3 for its own sake** also **sth for sth's sake** if something is done for its own sake, it is done for the value of the experience itself, not for any advantage it will bring: *art for art's sake* **4 for the sake of it** if you do something for the sake of it, you do it because you want to and not for any particular reason: *He was just talking for the sake of it.* **5 for the sake of argument** SPOKEN if you say something for the sake of argument, what you say may not be true, but it will help you to have a discussion: *Let's say, just for the sake of argument, that you have $5,000 to invest.*

sake² /'sɑki, -keɪ/ *n.* [U] a Japanese alcoholic drink made from rice

Sa·kha·rov /'sɑkərɔf/, **An·drei** /'ɑndreɪ/ (1921–1989) a Russian scientist who helped to develop the Soviet HYDROGEN BOMB and was also known for his criticism of the Soviet government

sal·a·ble, saleable /'seɪləbəl/ *adj.* something that is salable can be sold, or is easy to sell SYN **marketable**: *a salable crop* —**salability** /ˌseɪlə'bɪləṭi/ *n.* [U]

sa·la·cious /sə'leɪʃəs/ *adj.* showing too much interest in sex: *The tabloid newspapers love salacious gossip.* [**Origin:** 1600–1700 Latin *salax* **liking to jump, full of sexual desire**, from *salire* **to jump**] —**salaciously** *adv.* —**salaciousness** *n.* [U]

sal·ad /'sæləd/ S1 *n.* [C,U] **1** a mixture of raw vegetables, usually including LETTUCE: *a tomato and cucumber salad* | *Would you* ***toss the salad*** (=mix it all together)? | *a salad bowl* **2** raw or cooked food that is cut into small pieces and served cold: *potato salad* [**Origin:** 1300–1400 Old French *salade*, from Old Provençal *salada*, from *salar* **to add salt to**]

'salad bar *n.* [C] a place in a restaurant where you can choose what to put into your own salad

'salad days *n.* [plural] OLD-FASHIONED the time of your life when you are young and not very experienced

'salad ˌdressing *n.* [C,U] a SAUCE that you put on SALADS to give them a special taste

sal·a·man·der /'sæləˌmændɚ/ *n.* [C] a small animal similar to a LIZARD, which lives in water and on land

sa·la·mi /sə'lɑmi/ *n.* [C,U] a large SAUSAGE with a strong taste, that is eaten cold in thin SLICES [**Origin:** 1800–1900 Italian *salare* **to add salt to**, from *sale* **salt**]

sal·a·ried /'sælərid/ *adj.* receiving money each month for the work you do, rather than money for each hour you work: *salaried workers*

sal·a·ry /'sæləri/ S2 W2 *n. plural* **salaries** [C,U] money that you receive as payment from the organization or business you work for, usually paid to you every month: *How can they afford that car* ***on*** *Todd's* ***salary***? | **annual/yearly salary** *an annual salary of $35,000* | *His* ***base salary*** *is $46,000 a year, but bonuses and overtime can add another $10,000.* | *a* ***starting salary*** (=the salary you get when you begin a job) *of $22,000 a year* | *a TV news anchor who* ***earns*** *a huge* ***salary*** [**Origin:** 1200–1300 Latin *salarium* **money to pay for salt**, from *sal* **salt**] → see also WAGE ►see THESAURUS box at pay²

sal·a·ry·man /'sælərimæn/ *n. plural* **salarymen** /-mɛn/ [C] a man who works in an office in Japan, often for many hours every day

sale /seɪl/ S1 W1 *n.*

1 ACT OF SELLING [C,U] the act of giving property or other goods to someone in exchange for money: **+of** *laws regarding the sale of alcohol* | *Every time Harvey* ***makes a sale***, *he gets $50 commission.* | *increased sales to the Middle East*

2 for sale available to be bought: *Sorry, it's not for sale.* | *a for sale sign* | *They* ***put*** *their house* ***up for sale*** (=made it available to be bought).

3 LOWER PRICES [C] a period of time when stores sell their goods at lower prices than usual: *All the Christmas sales start right after Thanksgiving.* | *I got these shoes* ***in the*** *Macy's* ***sale***. | *Nordstrom's is* ***having a sale***.

4 on sale a) available to be bought at a lower price than usual: *I got my shoes on sale for half price.* **b)** available to be bought: **be/go on sale** *Tickets for the concert will go on sale in June.*

5 sales a) [plural] the total number of products that are sold during a particular period of time: *We're expecting sales to top $5 million this year.* | *the company's* ***sales figures*** | *a drop in* ***retail sales*** (=things sold in stores) | **+of** *Sales of automobiles are up this year.* | **home/car/computer etc. sales** *Computer sales are slowing down.* | *The company had close to $700 million* ***in sales*** *this year.* **b)** [U] the part of a company that deals with selling products: *She works as* ***sales manager*** *at a magazine.* | *Are you interested in a career in sales?*

6 AVAILABLE TO BUY [C] an occasion when people bring particular things to a place in order to sell them: *a craft sale* | *a bake sale to raise money for the school* | **garage/yard sale** (=when people sell things they do not want anymore from their yard or garage) *I bought some golf clubs at a yard sale.*

7 AUCTION [C] an event at which things are sold to the person who offers the highest price SYN **auction**: *an exhibit and sale of Chinese art*

8 sales campaign an effort made by a company to try to increase the number of products it sells

9 sales pitch/talk the things that someone says when they are trying to persuade you to buy something SYN **spiel**

[**Origin:** 1000–1100 Old Norse *sala*] → see also BILL OF SALE, POINT OF SALE

sale·a·ble /'seɪləbəl/ *adj.* another spelling of SALABLE

Sa·lem /'seɪləm/ **1** the capital city of the U.S. state of Oregon **2** a town in the U.S. state of Massachusetts, famous for the Salem Witch Trials in 1692, when many women were taken to a court of law and then officially killed for using magic

sales·clerk /'seɪlzklɚk/ *n.* [C] someone who sells things in a store

sales·girl /'seɪlzgɚl/ *n.* [C] OLD-FASHIONED a young woman who sells things in a store

sales·man /'seɪlzmən/ *n. plural* **salesmen** /-mən/ [C] a man whose job is to persuade people to buy his company's products: **computer/car/insurance etc. salesman** *the leading bond salesman at Salomon*

sales·man·ship /'seɪlzmənˌʃɪp/ *n.* [U] the skill or ability to persuade people to buy things as part of your job

sales·per·son /'seɪlzˌpɚsən/ *n. plural* **salespeople** /-ˌpipəl/ [C] someone whose job is selling things, especially by persuading people to buy their company's products

'sales repreˌsentative also **'sales rep** *n.* [C] someone who travels around, usually within a particular area, selling their company's products

'sales slip *n.* [C] a RECEIPT

'sales tax *n.* [C,U] ECONOMICS a tax that you have to pay in addition to the cost of something you are buying

sales·wom·an /'seɪlzˌwʊmən/ *n. plural* **saleswomen** /-ˌwɪmɪn/ [C] a woman whose job is selling things, especially by persuading people to buy her company's products

sa·li·ent /'seɪliənt/ *adj.* FORMAL the salient points or features of something are the most important or most noticeable parts of it: **salient point/feature/fact etc.** *Four salient points emerged from our study.* [**Origin:** 1600–1700 Latin, present participle of *salire* **to jump**] —**salience** *n.* [U]

sa·line¹ /'seɪlin, -laɪn/ *adj.* containing or consisting of salt: *saline solution* —**salinity** /sə'lɪnəṭi/ *n.* [U]

saline² *n.* [U] a special mixture of water and salt, used in medical treatment

S

Sal·in·ger /ˈsælɪndʒɚ/, **J. D.** (1919–) a U.S. writer best known for his book "The Catcher in the Rye"

J.D. Salinger

Salis·bur·y steak /ˌsɔlzbɛri ˈsteɪk, ˌsɑlz-, -bəri/ *n.* [C] a food made of GROUND BEEF that is mixed with SPICES, formed into a flat shape, and cooked

Sa·lish /ˈseɪlɪʃ/ a group of Native American tribes from the northwestern U.S. and western Canada that speak the same language

sa·li·va /səˈlaɪvə/ *n.* [U] BIOLOGY the liquid that is produced naturally in your mouth SYN **spit**

sal·i·var·y gland /ˈsæləˌvɛri ˌglænd/ *n.* [C] BIOLOGY a part of your mouth that produces saliva → see picture at DIGESTIVE SYSTEM

sal·i·vate /ˈsæləˌveɪt/ *v.* [I] **1** BIOLOGY to produce more saliva in your mouth than usual, especially because you see or smell food **2** HUMOROUS to be very interested or eager to do something or try something: +**at/over** *Drug companies are salivating over the profit opportunities of the new technology.* —**salivation** /ˌsæləˈveɪʃən/ *n.* [U]

Salk /sɔk, sɔlk/, **Jo·nas** /ˈdʒoʊnəs/ (1914–1995) a U.S. scientist famous for producing the first successful VACCINE against POLIO

sal·low /ˈsæloʊ/ *adj.* sallow skin looks slightly yellow and unhealthy —**sallowness** *n.* [U]

sal·ly¹ /ˈsæli/ *n. plural* **sallies** [C] **1** an amusing intelligent remark SYN **wisecrack** **2** a sudden quick attack and return to a position of defense

sally² *v.* **sallies**, **sallied**, **sallying**

sally forth *phr. v.* to leave somewhere that is safe in order to do something that you expect to be difficult or dangerous: *Each morning they sallied forth in search of jobs.*

salm·on /ˈsæmən/ *n.* **1 a)** [C] *plural* **salmon** BIOLOGY a large fish with silver skin and pink flesh that lives in the ocean but swims up rivers to lay its eggs, or the meat of this fish **b)** [U] this fish eaten as food **2** [U] a pink-orange color [**Origin:** 1200–1300 Anglo-French *salmun*, from Latin *salmo*]

sal·mo·nel·la /ˌsælməˈnɛlə/ *n.* [U] MEDICINE a type of BACTERIA in food, especially chicken or eggs, that makes you sick: *a case of* ***salmonella poisoning*** [**Origin:** 1900–2000 Modern Latin, from Daniel E. *Salmon* (1850–1914), U.S. scientist]

sa·lon /səˈlɑn/ S3 *n.* [C] **1** a place where you can get your hair cut, have beauty treatments etc.: **hair/beauty/tanning etc. salon** *an expensive hair salon* **2** a store where fashionable and expensive clothes are sold: *a bridal salon* **3** OLD-FASHIONED a room in a very large house where people can meet and talk **4** ENG. LANG. ARTS a regular meeting of famous people at which they talk about art, literature, or music [**Origin:** 1600–1700 French, from Italian *salone* **large hall**]

sa·loon /səˈlun/ *n.* [C] **1** a public place where alcoholic drinks were sold and drunk in the western U.S. in the 19th century SYN **bar** **2** a large comfortable room where passengers on a ship can sit and relax

sal·sa /ˈsælsə, ˈsɔl-/ S3 *n.* **1** [U] a SAUCE usually made from onions, TOMATOES, and CHILIES, that you put on Mexican food → see also PICANTE SAUCE **2** [C,U] ENG. LANG. ARTS a type of Latin American music, or the dance done to this music [**Origin:** 1900–2000 Spanish **sauce**]

SALT /sɔlt/ *n.* POLITICS **Strategic Arms Limitation Talks** talks held between the U.S. and the former Soviet Union in 1972 and 1979, which led to two official written agreements limiting the number of NUCLEAR WEAPONS each country kept → SALT TREATY

salt¹ /sɔlt/ S2 W2 *n.* **1** [U] a natural white mineral, usually in the form of very small grains, that is added to food to make it taste better or to preserve it: *Season the sauce with salt and pepper.* | *a* ***pinch of salt*** (=a small amount) → see also ROCK SALT, SEA SALT, TABLE SALT **2 the salt of the earth** someone who is ordinary, but good and honest **3** [C] CHEMISTRY a type of chemical substance that is formed when an acid is combined with a BASE **4 old salt** a SAILOR who has had a lot of experience sailing on the ocean [**Origin:** Old English *sealt*] → see also BATH SALTS, EPSOM SALTS, **take sth with a grain of salt** at GRAIN (6), **rub salt into a wound** at RUB¹ (6), SMELLING SALTS, **worth his/her salt** at WORTH¹ (7)

salt² *v.* [T] **1** to add salt to food to make it taste better: *Lightly salt the water and add the pasta.* | *salted peanuts* **2** to add salt to food to preserve it: *salted fish* **3** to put salt on the roads to prevent them from becoming icy

salt sth ↔ **away** *phr. v.* to save money for the future, sometimes money you have earned dishonestly: *They had salted away over $45 million in overseas bank accounts.*

salt³ *adj.* [only before noun] **1** preserved by salt: *salt pork* **2** consisting of SALTWATER: *a salt lake*

ˌsalt-and-ˈpepper *adj.* hair that is salt-and-pepper has dark hairs mixed with white hairs

salt·box /ˈsɔltˌbɑks/ *n.* [C] a house that has two levels in front and one level in back

ˈsalt ˌcellar *n.* [C] a SALT SHAKER

sal·tine /sɔlˈtin/ *n.* [C] a type of CRACKER (=thin hard dry bread) with salt on top of it

ˌSalt Lake ˈCity the capital and largest city of the U.S. state of Utah

ˈsalt marsh *n.* [C] an area of flat wet ground near the sea with many different varieties of grass growing on it, that is regularly flooded by salt water

salt·pe·ter /ˌsɔltˀˈpit̬ɚ/ *n.* [U] a substance used in making GUNPOWDER (=powder that causes explosions) and matches

ˈsalt ˌshaker *n.* [C] a small container for salt, with holes in the top

SALT Trea·ty /ˈsɔlt ˌtrit̬i/ also **ˈSALT Aˌgreement** *n.* [C] POLITICS written agreements between the U.S. and the former Soviet Union (SALT I signed in 1972 and SALT II signed in 1979) limiting the number of NUCLEAR WEAPONS each country kept

ˈsalt truck *n.* [C] a large vehicle that puts salt or sand on the roads in the winter to make them less icy

salt·wa·ter¹, **salt water** /ˈsɔltˀˌwɔt̬ɚ, -ˌwɑ-/ *n.* [U] water that contains salt, especially naturally in the ocean

saltwater² *adj.* [only before noun] **1** BIOLOGY living in salty water or in the ocean OPP **freshwater**: *saltwater fish* **2** EARTH SCIENCE containing saltwater OPP **freshwater**: *a saltwater tank*

salt·y /ˈsɔlti/ *adj. comparative* **saltier**, *superlative* **saltiest** **1** tasting like or containing salt: *The soup is a little too salty.* ▶see THESAURUS box at **taste¹** **2** OLD-FASHIONED slightly impolite or talking about sex, but in a way that is amusing: *She's a surprisingly salty lady.* | *salty language*

sa·lu·bri·ous /səˈlubriəs/ *adj.* FORMAL pleasant and good for your health SYN **healthful**: *the salubrious climate of northern Italy*

sal·u·ta·ry /ˈsælyəˌtɛri/ *adj.* FORMAL a salutary experience is usually unpleasant, but it has a positive result or teaches you something: *The war could have a* ***salutary effect*** *on other countries in the region.*

sal·u·ta·tion /ˌsælyəˈteɪʃən/ *n.* **1** [C] a word or phrase used at the beginning of a letter or speech, such as "Dear Mr. Smith" SYN **greeting** **2** [C,U] FORMAL something you say or do when greeting someone SYN **greeting**

sa·lu·ta·to·ri·an /səˌlutəˈtɔriən/ *n.* [C] a student who has received the second-best grades in their class all through high school or college, and who usually gives a speech at the GRADUATION ceremony → see also VALEDICTORIAN

sa·lute[1] /sə'lut/ *v.* **1** [I,T] to move your right hand to your head, especially in order to show respect to an officer in the Army, Navy etc.: *He saluted the captain.* | *Students do not have to* ***salute the flag*** *if they have religious reasons for not doing so.* **2** [T] to praise someone for the things they have achieved, especially publicly SYN **honor**: **salute sb as sth** *Bush saluted Madison as "the father of our Constitution."* | **salute sb for sth** *Today we salute these citizens for their commitment to our community.* **3** OLD-FASHIONED to greet someone in a polite way, especially by moving your hand or body [**Origin:** 1300–1400 Latin *salutare*, from *salus* **health, safety, greeting**]

salute[2] *n.* [C] **1** an act of raising your right hand to your head as a sign of respect, usually done by a soldier to an officer: *As they left, he* ***gave them a salute.*** | *He raised his hand* ***in salute.*** **2** something that expresses praise to someone for something they have achieved, or that expresses honor or respect to something: **a salute to sb/sth** *a musical salute to Hollywood movies of the 1940s* | *They raised their glasses* ***in salute.*** **3** an occasion when guns are fired into the air in order to show respect for someone important: *a 21-gun salute*

sal·vage[1] /'sælvɪdʒ/ *v.* [T] **1** to save something from a situation in which other things have already been damaged, destroyed, or lost: **salvage sth from sth** *They stood clutching the possessions they had salvaged from their homes.* **2** to make sure that something is not lost completely or does not completely fail, when it is in a bad situation: *Can the peace process be salvaged?* | *He fought to* ***salvage his reputation*** (=do something so that he would not lose people's respect).

salvage[2] *n.* [U] **1** the act of saving things from a situation in which other things have already been damaged, destroyed, or lost: *a salvage operation* **2** things that have been saved in this way: *We found the statue in a local salvage yard.*

sal·va·tion /sæl'veɪʃən/ *n.* [U] **1** in the Christian religion, the state of being saved from evil SYN **redemption** **2** something that prevents or saves someone from danger, loss, or failure: +**of** *Construction of the factory proved to be the salvation of the local economy.* | **be sb's/sth's salvation** *The AA has been Ron's salvation.*

Sal,vation 'Army *n.* **the Salvation Army** a Christian organization that tries to help poor people

salve[1] /sæv/ *n.* [C,U] **1** a substance that you put on sore skin to make it less painful SYN **ointment** **2** something you do to reduce bad feelings in a situation: *Our goal is to provide a salve for consumers' fears.*

salve[2] *v.* [T] **salve your conscience/feelings/ego** to do something to make yourself or someone else feel less guilty or less emotionally hurt SYN **assuage**: *Buying his wife flowers helped to salve his conscience.*

sal·ver /'sælvɚ/ *n.* [C] a large metal plate used for serving food or drinks at a formal meal: *a silver salver* [**Origin:** 1600–1700 French *salve*, from Spanish *salva* **testing of food to check for poison, large metal plate on which tested food was given to the king**]

sal·vo /'sælvoʊ/ *n. plural* **salvos** or **salvoes** [C] **1** the firing of several guns during a battle or as part of a ceremony: +**of** *a salvo of automatic gunfire* **2** one of a series of questions, statements etc. that you use to try to win an argument or competition: **opening/last/first etc. salvo** *Sanders* ***fired the first salvo*** *against the development plan.*

Sa·mar·i·tan /sə'mærət̚n/ also **good Samaritan** *n.* [C] someone, especially a stranger, who helps you when you have problems or are in a difficult situation [**Origin:** 1600–1700 from the Bible story of a person from Samaria (an area of ancient Palestine), who stopped and helped a man who had been attacked and robbed]

sam·ba /'sɑmbə, 'sæm-/ *n.* [C,U] a fast dance from Brazil, or the type of music played for this dance

same[1] /seɪm/ S1 W1 *adj.* [only before noun]
1 NOT DIFFERENT a) the same person, place, thing etc. is one particular person etc. and not a different one: *Harry and I went to the same school.* | +**as** *Recycling will be picked up on the same day as your garbage.* | **the same... (that)** *Put the book back in the same place you took it from.* **b)** used to say two or more people, things etc. are exactly like each other: *I know how you feel – I have the same problem.* | *The same thing could happen again.* | +**as** *He gets the same grades as I do, but he never studies.* | **the same... (that)** *Brenda came in wearing the same dress that Jean had on.* | **the very/exact same sth** *The exact same thing happened to Linda yesterday.* | *She received less pay for* ***exactly the same*** *duties.* | *John reacted in* ***much the same*** *way as my mother had.*
2 NOT CHANGING used to say that a particular person or thing does not change: *Her perfume has always had the same effect on me.* | *He's the* ***same old*** *Peter, grouchy as ever.* | *It's the* ***same old*** (=used when you have heard something many times before) *excuse – not enough time.*
3 at the same time a) if two things happen at the same time, they both happen together: *We both started talking at the same time.* **b)** used to introduce a fact which must also be considered: *We don't want to lose him. But at the same time, he has to realize that company regulations must be obeyed.*
4 same difference SPOKEN used to say that different actions, behavior etc. have the same result or effect: *"We'll have to use lemons instead of limes." "Same difference."*
5 by the same token a phrase meaning in the same way, or for the same reasons, used when you want to say that something else is also true even though it is very different or surprising: *I want to win, but by the same token, I don't want to hurt Sam's confidence.*
6 be on the same page SPOKEN used to say that two or more people understand each other and are thinking about something in the same way: *I just want to make sure we're all on the same page before we start.*
7 same old, same old SPOKEN used to say that a situation has not changed at all: *"How are you doing, Dave?" "Same old, same old."*
8 be in the same boat to be in the same difficult situation that someone else is in
[**Origin:** 1100–1200 Old Norse *samr*] → see also **amount to the same thing** at AMOUNT[2] (2)

> **GRAMMAR**
> Remember that the adjective **same** always has "the" or "this," "that" etc. before it: *We all ordered the same thing.* | *He drove back to Fairview that same night.*

same[2] S1 *pron.* **1 the same a)** used to say that two or more people or things are exactly like another: *Oranges are an excellent source of vitamin C. The same is true for strawberries and spinach.* | *The coins look the same, but one's a fake.* | +**as** *Our results were* ***exactly the same*** *as his.* | *Fred looks* ***much the same****, despite the passing years.* | *Temperatures were in the mid-80s today; expect* ***more of the same*** (=another thing like the one just mentioned) *for the weekend.* **b)** someone or something that does not change: *Things just won't* ***be the same*** *without you around.* | *Life would never* ***be the same again.*** **2 just/all the same** in spite of a particular situation or opinion, or in spite of something you have just mentioned etc. SYN **nevertheless**: *The potatoes were a little overcooked, but delicious all the same.* | *I'm not likely to run out of money, but all the same, I'm careful.* **3 (and the) same to you!** SPOKEN **a)** used as a friendly reply to a greeting: *"Have a happy New Year!" "Thanks – same to you."* **b)** used as an angry reply to an impolite remark: *"You idiot! I hope you get run over!" "Same to you!"* **4 same here** SPOKEN used to say that you feel the same way as someone else: *"I'm exhausted!" "Same here."* → see also **it's all the same to sb** at ALL[2] (14), **one and the same** at ONE[2] (23)

S

same[3] S1 W1 *adv.* **1 the same (as sth)** in the same way: *"Pain" and "pane" are pronounced* ***exactly the same.*** | *I used your recipe, but my cookies don't taste the same as yours.* **2 same as sb** SPOKEN just like someone else: *He works hard, same as you.* | **same as usual/ever/always** *"How's school?" "Oh, same as always."*

same·ness /ˈseɪmnɪs/ *n.* [U] a boring lack of variety, or the quality of being very similar to something else

ˌsame-ˈsex *adj.* **same-sex marriage/relationship etc.** a marriage, relationship etc. between two men or two women SYN **homosexual**

Sa·miz·dat /ˈsɑmɪzˌdɑt/ *n.* [singular] a system in former SOVIET countries by which people secretly copied and passed around literature and newspapers that were not allowed by the government

Sa·mo·a /səˈmoʊə/ → see AMERICAN SAMOA, WESTERN SAMOA —**Samoan** *n., adj.*

sam·o·var /ˈsæməvɑr/ *n.* [C] a large metal container used in Russia to boil water for making tea

sam·pan /ˈsæmpæn/ *n.* [C] a small boat used in China and Southeast Asia [**Origin:** 1600–1700 Chinese *sanban*, from *san* **three** + *ban* **board, plank**]

S

sam·ple[1] /ˈsæmpəl/ S3 W3 *n.* [C] **1** a small part or amount of something that is examined in order to find out something about the whole thing SYN **specimen**: **+of** *I'll need to look at a sample of his handwriting.* | **blood/urine/water etc. sample** *The study is based on air samples taken in seven locations.* **2** a small amount of a product that people can try in order to find out what it is like: **+of** *free samples of ice cream* **3** a group of people who have been chosen from a larger group to give information or answers to questions: *The sample consisted of 344 elementary school teachers.* | *The survey was based on telephone interviews with a* ***random sample*** (=one in which you choose people without knowing anything about them) *of Americans.* | *We selected a* ***representative sample*** (=one that is planned to include several different types of people) *of 650 elderly people.* **4** a small part of a song from a CD or record that is used in a new song [**Origin:** 1200–1300 Old French *essample*, from Latin *exemplum*]

sample[2] *v.* [T] **1** to taste a food, go to a place, try an activity etc. in order to see what it is like SYN **try**: *I decided to sample the chocolate cheesecake.* | *You should sample the local nightlife while you're here.* ▶see THESAURUS box at **taste**[2] **2** [often passive] to choose some people from a larger group in order to ask them questions or get information from them: *The results are based on a poll of 1,000* ***randomly sampled*** *adults.* **3** to use a small part of a song from a CD or record in a new song

ˈsample proˌportion *n.* [C] MATH a PERCENTAGE of a larger sample of data, that can be examined and used to make judgments about the whole sample

sam·pler /ˈsæmplɚ/ *n.* [C] **1** a piece of cloth with different stitches on it, made to show how good someone is at sewing **2** a machine that can record sounds or music so that you can change them and use them for a new piece of music **3** a machine or tool that takes a small amount of something such as water or blood so that you can examine it **4** a set of small amounts of something, for example food or a produce, for someone to try: *a sampler platter of desserts*

ˈsample space *n.* [singular] MATH a list of all the possible results of an EXPERIMENT to find out how likely something is to happen. For example, in an experiment on rolling a dice, the sample space is 1, 2, 3, 4, 5, 6. This is used in STATISTICS.

ˈsampling ˌmethod *n.* [C] MATH one of a number of methods that can be used to collect data about people. The methods are different from each other in the way that the people who are studied are chosen.

Sam·u·el /ˈsæmyuəl/ **1 Samuel, 2 Samuel** two books in the Old Testament of the Christian Bible

sam·u·rai /ˈsæmʊˌraɪ/ *n. plural* **samurai** [C] a member of a powerful military class in Japan in past times —**samurai** *adj.*: *a samurai sword*

Sa·na'a /sæˈnɑ/ the capital city of Yemen

san·a·to·ri·um /ˌsænəˈtɔriəm/ *n. plural* **sanatoriums** or **sanatoria** /-riə/ [C] a type of hospital for sick people who are getting better but still need rest and a lot of care, especially in past times when many people suffered from TUBERCULOSIS (=a serious disease of the lungs)

sanc·ti·fy /ˈsæŋktəˌfaɪ/ *v.* **sanctifies, sanctified, sanctifying** [T] **1** to make something holy SYN **consecrate** **2** to make something socially or religiously acceptable, or to give something official approval: *The idea of progress has been sanctified in our culture.* —**sanctification** /ˌsæŋktəfəˈkeɪʃən/ *n.* [U]

sanc·ti·mo·ni·ous /ˌsæŋktəˈmoʊniəs/ *adj.* DISAPPROVING behaving as if you are morally better than other people, in a way that is annoying SYN **self-righteous**: *a sanctimonious speech about family values* —**sanctimoniously** *adv.* —**sanctimoniousness** *n.* [U]

sanc·tion[1] /ˈsæŋkʃən/ *n.* **1 sanctions** [plural] POLITICS official orders or laws stopping trade, communication etc. with another country, as a way of forcing its leaders to make political changes: **+against** *international sanctions against Iraq* | **+on** *The U.S.* ***imposed sanctions*** (=started using sanctions against) *on China for breaking trade agreements.* | *The government is not yet ready to* ***lift*** *these* ***sanctions*** (=stop using them). | **economic/trade sanctions** *The U.N. may impose economic sanctions.* **2** [U] FORMAL official permission, approval, or acceptance: *He acted without religious or government sanction.* **3** [C] a form of punishment that can be used if someone disobeys a rule or law: *The court* ***imposed*** *the harshest possible* ***sanction.*** [**Origin:** 1400–1500 Old French, Latin *sanctio*, from *sancire*]

sanction[2] *v.* [T] FORMAL **1** to officially accept or allow something SYN **approve** SYN **authorize**: *Gambling will be not be sanctioned in any form.* **2 be sanctioned by sth** to be made acceptable by something: *Young men's bad behavior was sanctioned by tradition.* **3** to punish someone for disobeying a rule or law: *The number of doctors sanctioned by state medical boards has risen.*

sanc·ti·ty /ˈsæŋktət̬i/ *n.* [U] **1 the sanctity of life/marriage etc.** the quality that makes life, marriage etc. so important that it must be respected and preserved: *the sanctity of the Constitution* **2** FORMAL the holy or religious character of a person or place

sanc·tu·ar·y /ˈsæŋktʃuˌɛri/ *n. plural* **sanctuaries** **1** [U] safety and protection from danger, or protection from police, soldiers etc.: *He is suspected of* ***giving sanctuary to*** *terrorists.* | **find/seek sanctuary** *Hundreds of civilians have sought sanctuary at churches and embassies.* **2** [C] a place that is safe and provides protection, especially for people who are in danger SYN **refuge**: **+for** *The center is a sanctuary for battered women.* **3** [C] an area for birds or animals where they are protected and cannot be hunted: **bird/wildlife etc. sanctuary** *Pollution is threatening the marine sanctuary.* **4** [C] the part of a church where Christian religious services take place **5** [C] the part of a religious building that is considered to be the most holy

sanc·tum /ˈsæŋktəm/ *n.* [C] **1 inner sanctum** HUMOROUS a place or room that only a few important people are allowed to enter: *the inner sanctums of city government* **2** also **sanctum sanctorum** /ˌsæŋktəm sæŋkˈtɔrəm/ a holy place inside a TEMPLE

sand[1] /sænd/ S2 W3 *n.* **1** [U] a substance consisting of very small grains of rocks and minerals, that forms beaches and deserts: *The children played happily in the sand.* | *a mixture of sand and cement* **2** [C usually plural, U] an area of beach: *miles of golden sands* | *We walked along the sand.* **3 the sands of time** LITERARY moments of time that pass quickly **4** a light yellowish or grayish brown color [**Origin:** Old English]

sand[2] S3 *v.* **1** [I,T] also **sand down** to make a surface smooth by rubbing it with SANDPAPER or using a special piece of equipment **2** [T] to put sand onto an icy road to make it safer

san·dal /ˈsændl/ *n.* [C] a light open shoe that is fastened onto your foot by bands of leather, cloth etc., and that is worn in warm weather: *a pair of sandals* [**Origin:** 1300–1400 Latin *sandalium*, from Greek, from *sandalon*] → see picture at SHOE[1]

san·dal·wood /ˈsændlˌwʊd/ *n.* [U] nice-smelling wood from a southern Asian tree, or the oil from this wood, which is often used in PERFUMES

sand·bag¹ /ˈsændbæg/ *n.* [C] a bag filled with sand, which is used for protection against floods, explosions etc.

sandbag² *v.* **sandbagged**, **sandbagging** **1** [I,T] to put sandbags around a building in order to protect it from a flood, explosion etc. **2** [T] to try to prevent someone from doing something or being successful, especially in an unfair way: *The agency tried to sandbag Kahn's book, worried it would reveal secrets.*

sand·bank /ˈsændbæŋk/ *n.* [C] EARTH SCIENCE a raised area of sand in or by a river, ocean etc.

sand·bar /ˈsændbɑr/ *n.* [C] a long pile of sand in a river or the ocean formed by the movement of the water

sand·blast /ˈsændblæst/ *v.* [T] to clean or polish metal, stone, glass etc. with a machine that sends out a powerful stream of sand

sand·box /ˈsændbɑks/ *n.* [C] a special box or area with sand for children to play in

Sand·burg, Carl /ˈsændbɚg, kɑrl/ (1878–1967) a U.S. writer and poet

sand·cas·tle /ˈsændˌkæsəl/ *n.* [C] a small model of a castle made out of wet sand by children playing on a beach

sand dune *n.* [C] a hill of sand formed by the wind in a desert or near the ocean → see picture on page A31

sand·er /ˈsændɚ/ also **ˈsanding maˌchine** *n.* [C] an electric tool with a rough surface that moves very quickly, used for making surfaces smooth, especially wooden surfaces

sand fly *n.* [C] a small fly that bites people and lives on beaches

San·di·nis·ta /ˌsændɪˈnistə/ *n.* [C usually plural] HISTORY a member of a group in Nicaragua that removed President Somoza from power in 1979 and formed a SOCIALIST government —**Sandinista** *adj.*

sand·lot /ˈsændlɑt/ *n.* [C] an area of empty land in a town or city, where children often play sports or games: *a sandlot ball game* → see also PARK

sand·man /ˈsændmæn/ *n.* [singular] an imaginary man who is supposed to make children go to sleep by putting sand in their eyes

sand·pa·per¹ /ˈsændˌpeɪpɚ/ *n.* [U] strong paper covered on one side with sand or a similar substance, that you rub on wood in order to make the surface smooth

sandpaper² *v.* [T] to rub something with sandpaper

sand·pip·er /ˈsændˌpaɪpɚ/ *n.* [C] BIOLOGY a small bird with long legs and a long beak that lives around muddy or sandy shores

sand·stone /ˈsændstoʊn/ *n.* [U] EARTH SCIENCE a type of soft yellow or red rock, often used in buildings

sand·storm /ˈsændstɔrm/ *n.* [C] EARTH SCIENCE a storm in the desert in which sand is blown around by strong winds

sand trap, **sandtrap** *n.* [C] a hollow place on a GOLF COURSE, filled with sand, from which it is difficult to hit the ball

sand·wich¹ /ˈsændwɪtʃ/ *n.* [C] two pieces of bread with cheese, meat etc. between them: *a peanut butter and jelly sandwich* [**Origin:** 1700–1800 Earl of *Sandwich* (1718–92), who ate sandwiches so that he could continue gambling without leaving the table] → see also CLUB SANDWICH, **give sb a knuckle sandwich** at KNUCKLE[1] (3), OPEN-FACED SANDWICH

sandwich² *v.* [T usually passive] to be in a very small space between two other things: **sandwich sth (in) between sth** *I sat there, sandwiched between two huge women.*

ˈsandwich board *n.* [C] two boards with advertisements or messages on them, which someone wears so that the boards hang in front and behind them as they walk around in public

sand·y /ˈsændi/ *adj.* **1** covered with sand or containing a lot of sand: *a sandy beach* **2** hair that is sandy is a yellowish-brown color —**sandiness** *n.* [U]

sane /seɪn/ *adj.* **1** mentally healthy and able to think in a normal and reasonable way OPP **insane** OPP **mentally ill**: *He was judged to be sane by several psychiatrists.* **2** reasonable and using or showing sensible thinking SYN **sensible**: *Mass transit is the only sane way to get around New York.* **3 keep sb sane** also **stay/remain sane** to stop someone from thinking about their problems and becoming upset: *I work out to keep myself sane.* [**Origin:** 1600–1700 Latin *sanus* **healthy, sane**] —**sanely** *adv.* → see also SANITY

San Fran·cis·co /ˌsæn frənˈsɪskoʊ/ a city in the U.S. state of California which is built on hills next to the Pacific Ocean

ˌSan Franˌcisco ˈBay an INLET of the Pacific Ocean on the western coast of the U.S. in the state of California

sang /sæŋ/ *v.* the past tense of SING

Sang·er, Mar·garet /ˈsæŋɚ, ˈmɑrgrɪt/ (1883–1966) a U.S. woman who started the attempt to make BIRTH CONTROL available to everyone in the U.S.

sang-froid /ˌsæŋˈfwɑ/ *n.* [U] FORMAL courage and the ability to keep calm in dangerous or difficult situations [**Origin:** 1700–1800 French **cold blood**]

San·gre de Cris·to Mountains, the /ˌsɑŋgreɪ də ˌkrɪstoʊ ˈmaʊntˀnz/ a RANGE of mountains in the southwestern U.S. that is part of the Rocky Mountains and runs from Colorado to New Mexico

san·gri·a /sæŋˈgriə, sæn-/ *n.* [U] a drink made from red wine, fruit, and fruit juice [**Origin:** 1900–2000 Spanish *sangría* **bleeding, sangria**, from *sangre* **blood**]

san·gui·na·ry /ˈsæŋgwəˌnɛri/ *adj.* LITERARY involving violence and killing SYN **bloody**

san·guine /ˈsæŋgwɪn/ *adj.* FORMAL **1** cheerful and hopeful about the future SYN **optimistic**: +**about** *Collins was not sanguine about the team's prospects.* **2** red and healthy looking SYN **ruddy**: *a sanguine complexion* [**Origin:** 1300–1400 French *sanguin*, from Latin *sanguineus*, from *sanguis* **blood**] —**sanguinely** *adv.*

san·i·tar·y /ˈsænəˌtɛri/ *adj.* **1** clean and not involving any danger to your health OPP **unsanitary**: *All food must be stored in sanitary containers.* **2** [only before noun] relating to removal of dirt and waste, so that places are kept clean and healthy for people to live in: *a lack of **sanitary facilities** (=toilets) in the field* | *poor **sanitary conditions** in the refugee camps*

ˌsanitary ˈlandfill *n.* [C] a place where waste is buried under the ground SYN **dump**

ˌsanitary ˈnapkin also **ˌsanitary ˈpad** *n.* [C] a piece of soft material that a woman wears in her underwear for the blood when she has her PERIOD

san·i·ta·tion /ˌsænəˈteɪʃən/ *n.* [U] the protection of public health by removing and treating waste, dirty water etc.

ˌsaniˈtation ˌworker *n.* [C] FORMAL someone who removes the waste material that people put outside their houses SYN **garbage man**

san·i·tize /ˈsænəˌtaɪz/ *v.* [T] **1** DISAPPROVING to remove particular details from a report, story etc., in order to make it less offensive or unpleasant, often so that it is not complete or interesting: *a sanitized biography of a complex man* **2** to clean something thoroughly, removing dirt and BACTERIA

san·i·ty /ˈsænəṭi/ *n.* [U] **1** the condition of being mentally healthy OPP **insanity**: *I began to doubt his sanity.* | *Could she be **losing her sanity**?* **2** the ability to think in a normal and sensible way: *Let's hope sanity prevails on Capitol Hill and they vote against this bill.*

S

San Jo·sé /ˌsæn hoʊˈzeɪ/ the capital and largest city of Costa Rica

San Juan /sæn ˈwɑn/ the capital city of the U.S. TERRITORY of Puerto Rico

sank /sæŋk/ *v.* a past tense of SINK

San Ma·ri·no /ˌsæn məˈrinoʊ/ a very small country in northeast Italy

San Mar·tín /sæn mɑrˈtin/**, Jo·sé de** /hoʊˈseɪ də/ (1778–1850) a military leader who helped the countries of Argentina, Chile, and Peru to gain INDEPENDENCE from the Spanish

sans /sænz, sɑn/ *prep.* HUMOROUS without: *He was wearing running shoes, sans socks.*

San Sal·va·dor /sæn ˈsælvəˌdɔr/ the capital and largest city of El Salvador

San·skrit /ˈsænskrɪt/ *n.* [U] an ancient language of India

sans ser·if /ˌsæn ˈserəf, ˌsænz-/ *n.* [U] TECHNICAL a style of printing in which letters have no SERIFS (=wider parts at the ends of lines)

San·ta Claus /ˈsæntə ˌklɔz/ also **Santa** *n.* an imaginary old man with red clothes and a long white BEARD who, children believe, brings them presents during the night before Christmas [**Origin:** 1700–1800 Dutch *Sinterklaas*, from *Sint Nikolaas* **Saint Nicholas**, patron saint of children]

S

San·ta Fe /ˌsæntə ˈfeɪ/ the capital city of the U.S. state of New Mexico

ˌSanta Fe ˈTrail, the an important road in the western area of the U.S. starting in Missouri and ending in Santa Fe, which was used in the 19th century by American SETTLERS

San·tee /sænˈti/ also **ˌSantee ˈSioux** the eastern part of the Sioux tribe of Native Americans

San·te·ri·a /ˌsæntəˈriə/ a religion based on traditional African beliefs and Catholic Christian beliefs

San·ti·a·go /ˌsæntiˈɑgoʊ/ the capital and largest city of Chile

San·to Do·min·go /ˌsæntoʊ dəˈmɪŋgoʊ/ the capital and largest city of the Dominican Republic

São Pau·lo /saʊm ˈpaʊloʊ/ the largest city in southeast Brazil

São To·mé /ˌsaʊn təˌmeɪ/ the capital city of São Tomé and Príncipe

São Tomé and Prín·ci·pe /ˌsaʊn təˌmeɪ ən ˈprɪnsɪpə/ a small country that consists of a group of islands off West Africa in the Gulf of Guinea

sap[1] /sæp/ *n.* **1** [U] BIOLOGY the watery substance that carries food through a plant **2** [C] INFORMAL a stupid person who is easy to deceive or treat badly SYN **fool**

sap[2] *v.* **sapped, sapping** [T] to gradually take away something such as strength or energy SYN **weaken**: **sap sb's courage/energy/strength** *The illness had sapped Diane's strength.*

sa·pi·ent /ˈseɪpiənt/ *adj.* LITERARY very wise —**sapiently** *adv.* —**sapience** *n.* [U]

sap·ling /ˈsæplɪŋ/ *n.* [C] a young tree

sa·pon·i·fi·ca·tion /səˌpɑnəfəˈkeɪʃən/ *n.* [U] CHEMISTRY a chemical process in which an ALKALI reacts with fats and oils to form soap

sap·phic /ˈsæfɪk/ *adj.* LITERARY LESBIAN

sap·phire /ˈsæfaɪɚ/ *n.* **1** [C,U] EARTH SCIENCE a transparent bright blue jewel **2** [U] a bright blue color [**Origin:** 1200–1300 Old French *safir*, from Latin, from Greek, from Hebrew *sappir*, from Sanskrit *sanipriya* **dear to the planet Saturn**]

sap·py /ˈsæpi/ *adj. comparative* **sappier**, *superlative* **sappiest** **1** expressing love and emotions in a way that seems silly: *a sappy love song* **2** BIOLOGY full of SAP (=liquid in a plant)

sap·robe /ˈsæproʊb/ *n.* [C] BIOLOGY a living thing that obtains its food from substances that are decaying

sap·wood /ˈsæpwʊd/ *n.* [U] BIOLOGY the younger outer wood in a tree, that is not as dark or hard as the wood in the middle, through which water, SAP, and other liquids are moved around the plant

sar·a·band, **sarabande** /ˈsærəˌbænd/ *n.* [C] a slow piece of music based on a type of 17th century dance

Sar·a·cen /ˈsærəsən/ *n.* [C] OLD USE a word for a Muslim, used in the Middle Ages

Sar·a·je·vo /ˌsærəˈyeɪvoʊ/ the capital and largest city of Bosnia-Herzegovina

Sa·ran Wrap /səˈræn ˌræp/ *n.* [U] TRADEMARK thin transparent plastic that you use to wrap or cover food, in order to keep it fresh SYN **plastic wrap**

sar·casm /ˈsɑrˌkæzəm/ *n.* [U] a way of speaking or writing that involves saying the opposite of what you really mean in order to make a joke that is not nice, or to show that you are annoyed: *a hint of sarcasm in his voice* [**Origin:** 1500–1600 French *sarcasme*, from Late Latin, from Greek *sarkazein* **to tear flesh, bite your lip angrily, sneer**]

sar·cas·tic /sɑrˈkæstɪk/ *adj.* saying things that are the opposite of what you mean in order to make a joke that is not nice, or to show that you are annoyed: *Nick can be very sarcastic.* —**sarcastically** /-kli/ *adv.*: *"Oh good," she said sarcastically.*

sar·coph·a·gus /sɑrˈkɑfəgəs/ *n. plural* **sarcophagi** [C] a decorated stone box for a dead body, used in ancient times

sar·dine /sɑrˈdin/ *n.* **1** [C] BIOLOGY a small fish that can be eaten, that is often packed in flat metal boxes **2 be packed/crammed in/pushed together etc. like sardines** to be pushed tightly together in a small space: *We were packed like sardines on the train.*

sar·don·ic /sɑrˈdɑnɪk/ *adj.* speaking or smiling in a way that is not nice and shows you do not have a good opinion of someone or something: *a sardonic laugh* [**Origin:** 1600–1700 French *sardonique*, from Greek *sardonios*, from *sardanios*; influenced by *Sardonios* **Sardinian**, because of a plant from Sardinia (an Italian island), which causes the face to twist into a smile] —**sardonically** /-kli/ *adv.*

sarge /sɑrdʒ/ *n.* [singular] SPOKEN, INFORMAL used as a way to talk to or about a SERGEANT

Sar·gent /ˈsɑrdʒənt/**, John Sing·er** /dʒɑn ˈsɪŋɚ/ (1856–1925) a U.S. painter who worked mainly in London, known for his paintings of rich and important people

sa·ri /ˈsɑri/ *n.* [C] a long piece of cloth that you wrap around your body like a dress, worn especially by women from India

sa·rong /səˈrɑŋ, -ˈrɔŋ/ *n.* [C] a loose skirt consisting of a long piece of cloth wrapped around your waist, worn especially by men and women in Malaysia and some islands in the Pacific Ocean

sarsa·pa·ril·la /ˌsæspəˈrɪlə, ˌsɑrs-/ *n.* [U] a sweet drink made from the root of the SASSAFRAS plant [**Origin:** 1500–1600 Spanish *zarzaparrilla*, from *zarza* **bush** + *parrilla* **small vine**]

sar·to·ri·al /sɑrˈtɔriəl/ *adj.* [only before noun] FORMAL relating to good-quality clothes or how they are made: *sartorial elegance* [**Origin:** 1800–1900 Latin *sartorius*, from *sartor* **someone who makes clothes**] —**sartorially** *adv.*

Sar·tre /ˈsɑrtrə/**, Jean-Paul** /ʒɑn pɔl/ (1905–1980) a French PHILOSOPHER and writer, famous for his influence on the development of EXISTENTIALISM

SASE *n.* [C] **self-addressed stamped envelope** an envelope that you put your name, address, and a stamp on, so that someone else can send you something

sash /sæʃ/ *n.* [C] **1** a long piece of cloth that you wear around your waist like a belt **2** a long piece of cloth that you wear over one shoulder and across your chest as a sign of a special honor **3** a wooden frame that has a sheet of glass inside it to form part of a window [**Origin:** (1, 2) 1500–1600 Arabic *shash* **fine cloth**]

sa·shay /sæˈʃeɪ/ *v.* **sashays, sashayed, sashaying** [I always + adv./prep.] to walk in a confident FEMININE way while moving your body from side to side, especially so that people look at you

sa·shi·mi /sɑˈʃimi/ *n.* [U] a type of Japanese food consisting of small pieces of fresh fish that have not been cooked

Sas·katch·e·wan /səˈskætʃəwən, -ˌwɑn/ a PROVINCE in central Canada

Sas·quatch /ˈsæskwɑtʃ/ *n.* another name for BIGFOOT

sass[1] /sæs/ *v.* [T] DISAPPROVING INFORMAL to talk in an impolite way to someone you should respect

sass[2] *n.* [U] INFORMAL **1** DISAPPROVING impolite remarks made to someone who should be respected **2** APPROVING a confident attitude that shows you do not care what other people think

sas·sa·fras /ˈsæsəˌfræs/ *n.* [C,U] a small Asian or North American tree, or the pleasant-smelling roots of this tree used in food and drinks

sas·sy /ˈsæsi/ *adj. comparative* **sassier**, *superlative* **sassiest** **1** DISAPPROVING a sassy child is not polite to someone they should respect **2** APPROVING confident and showing that you do not care what other people think

SAT /sæt/ *n.* [C] TRADEMARK **Scholastic Aptitude Test** an examination that high school students take before they go to college

sat /sæt/ *v.* the past tense and past participle of SIT

Sat. a written abbreviation of Saturday

Sa·tan /ˈseɪtˀn/ *n.* the Devil, considered to be the main evil power and God's opponent

sa·tan·ic /səˈtænɪk, seɪ-/ *adj.* **1** relating to the Devil or practices that treat the Devil like a god: *a satanic cult* **2** extremely cruel or evil: *a satanic grin* —**satanically** /-kli/ *adv.*

sa·tan·ism /ˈseɪtˀnˌɪzəm/ *n.* [U] the practice of respecting or WORSHIPing the Devil as a god —**satanist** *n.* [C] —**satanist** *adj.*

sa·tay /ˈsɑteɪ/ *n.* [U] a dish originally from southeast Asia, made of pieces of meat which are cooked on small sticks and eaten with a PEANUT SAUCE

satch·el /ˈsætʃəl/ *n.* [C] a leather bag that you carry over your shoulder, used especially in past times by children for carrying books to school

sat·ed /ˈseɪṱɪd/ *adj.* [T] LITERARY feeling that you have had enough, or more than enough, of something to satisfy you —**sate** *v.* [T]

sat·el·lite /ˈsæṱlˌaɪt/ S3 W2 *n.* [C] **1** PHYSICS a machine that has been sent into space and goes around the Earth, moon etc., used for radio, television, and other electronic communication: *the launch of a communications satellite* | *This broadcast comes live* ***by satellite*** *from New York.* ►see THESAURUS box at **space**[1] **2** PHYSICS a moon that moves around a PLANET ►see THESAURUS box at **space**[1] **3** a country, organization, store etc. that is controlled by or is dependent on another larger one: *a satellite store* **4** a town that has developed next to a large city [**Origin:** 1500–1600 French, Latin *satelles* **personal servant or guard**]

satellite ˌdish *n.* [C] a large circular piece of metal that receives special television signals so that you can watch satellite television

satellite ˈtelevision also **ˌsatellite TˈV** *n.* [U] television programs that are broadcast using satellites in space, and that can only be received by people who have a satellite dish

sa·ti /sʌˈti, ˈsʌti/ *n.* another spelling of SUTTEE

sa·ti·ate /ˈseɪʃiˌeɪt/ *v.* [T usually passive] LITERARY to completely satisfy a desire or need for something such as food or sex, sometimes so that you feel you have had too much —**satiated** *adj.* —**satiety** /səˈtaɪəṱi/ *n.* [U]

sat·in /ˈsætˀn/ *n.* [U] a type of cloth that is very smooth and shiny [**Origin:** 1300–1400 Old French] —**satin** *adj.*

sat·in·wood /ˈsætˀnˌwʊd/ *n.* [C,U] a tree that grows in India and Sri Lanka, or the hard smooth wood that comes from this tree

sat·in·y /ˈsætˀn-i/ *adj.* smooth, shiny, and soft

sat·ire /ˈsætaɪɚ/ *n.* ENG. LANG. ARTS **1** [U] a way of talking or writing about something, for example politics and politicians, in which you deliberately make them seem funny so that people will see their faults: *Gelbart is a writer of comedy and social satire.* **2** [C] a play, book, story etc. written in this way: *a political satire* [**Origin:** 1500–1600 French, Latin *satura, satira*, from *(lanx) satura* **full plate, mixture**] —**satirical** /səˈtɪrɪkəl/ *adj.* —**satiric** *adj.* —**satirically** /-kli/ *adv.*

sat·i·rist /ˈsæṱərɪst/ *n.* [C] ENG. LANG. ARTS someone who writes satire

sat·i·rize /ˈsæṱəˌraɪz/ *v.* [T] to use satire to make people see someone or something's faults: *The book satirizes small-town politics.*

sat·is·fac·tion /ˌsæṱɪsˈfækʃən/ *n.* **1** [C,U] a feeling of happiness or pleasure because you have achieved something or gotten what you wanted OPP **dissatisfaction**: *Our goal is 100% customer satisfaction.* | +**with** *general satisfaction with local schools* | *He looked at his work* ***with satisfaction.*** | *She* ***got*** *a deep* ***satisfaction from*** *her volunteer work.* | *I'm looking for greater* ***job satisfaction*** (=enjoyment of your job). **2** [U] FULFILLMENT of a need, demand, claim, desire etc.: *sexual satisfaction* | +**of** *the satisfaction of physical needs* **3 have/get the satisfaction of doing sth** to get a small amount of pleasure from a situation that is unsatisfactory in other ways: *It's unfair, but at least you have the satisfaction of knowing you were right.* **4 to sb's satisfaction** if something is done to someone's satisfaction, it is done as well or as completely as they want, so they are pleased

sat·is·fac·to·ry /ˌsæṱɪsˈfæktəri, -tri/ *adj.* acceptable, or good enough for a particular situation or purpose: *His progress this year has been satisfactory.* | **a satisfactory explanation/response/answer etc.** *There seems to be no satisfactory explanation.* | **a satisfactory result/outcome/resolution etc.** *a satisfactory outcome for everyone* | +**to** *The arrangement is satisfactory to both sides.* ►see THESAURUS box at **adequate** —**satisfactorily** *adv.*

THESAURUS

good enough having a standard that is satisfactory for a particular purpose or situation: *Is he good enough to play in the major leagues?*
acceptable good enough for a particular purpose: *The essay was acceptable, but not brilliant.*
adequate enough in quantity or of a good enough quality for a particular purpose: *Many children do not receive adequate nutrition.*
all right/okay acceptable, but not excellent: *The food was okay.* | *Was the movie all right?*
reasonable fairly good, large, or high: *a reasonable level of performance*

sat·is·fied /ˈsæṱɪsˌfaɪd/ *adj.* **1** pleased because something has happened in the way that you want, or because you have achieved something OPP **dissatisfied**: *No matter what I do, she's never satisfied.* | *a satisfied smile* | *satisfied customers* | +**with** *I'm not satisfied with the haircut.* | *It's always so hard to* ***keep*** *everyone* ***satisfied.*** | **completely/entirely satisfied** *I'm not entirely satisfied with my job.* **2** feeling sure that something is right or true: +**that** *The jury was satisfied that he had done nothing wrong.* **3 (are you) satisfied?** SPOKEN used to show that someone has annoyed you by asking too many questions or making too many demands: *I'm here now – are you satisfied?* → see also SELF-SATISFIED

sat·is·fy /ˈsæṱɪsˌfaɪ/ S3 W3 *v.* **satisfies, satisfied, satisfying** [T] **1** to make someone happy by providing what they want or expect: *Nothing I did ever seemed to satisfy my father.* **2** if something satisfies someone's needs or wants, it gives them what they need or want: *We aim to satisfy consumer demand.* | **satisfy a request/desire/need etc.** *The program is designed to satisfy the needs of adult learners.* | *Magazines like this* ***satisfy*** *people's* ***curiosity*** *about celebrities' lives.* | **sat-**

S

isfy sb's hunger/thirst/appetite *A salad won't be enough to satisfy your appetite.* **3** FORMAL to make someone feel sure that something is right or true SYN convince: **satisfy sb/yourself of sth** *Jackson tried to satisfy us of his innocence.* | **satisfy sb/yourself that** *Phil satisfied himself that no one was there and closed the door.* **4 satisfy a requirement/condition/criterion etc.** FORMAL to be good enough for a particular purpose, standard etc.: *The cheapest products satisfy only minimum safety requirements.* **5 satisfy a debt/obligation** FORMAL to pay a debt that you owe **6 satisfy an equation** TECHNICAL to be a correct answer to an EQUATION in mathematics etc. [**Origin:** 1400–1500 Old French *satisfier*, from Latin *satisfacere*, from *satis* **enough** + *facere* **to make**]

sat·is·fy·ing /ˈsætɪsˌfaɪ-ɪŋ/ *adj.* **1** making you feel pleased and happy, especially because you have gotten what you wanted: *I find my work very satisfying.* | **it is satisfying to do sth** *It's satisfying to know that people enjoyed your performance.* **2** food that is satisfying is good and makes you feel that you have eaten enough: *a satisfying meal* —**satisfyingly** *adv.*

Sa·trap /ˈseɪtræp, ˈsæt-/ *n.* [C] the person in charge of governing a PROVINCE in ancient Persia

S

sat·u·rate /ˈsætʃəˌreɪt/ *v.* [T] **1** FORMAL to make something very wet SYN soak: *Heavy rains had saturated the ground.* **2** to fill something completely with a large number of things, or with a large amount of something: **saturate sth with sth** *The campaign saturated prime time television with ads.* **3 saturate the market** to offer so much of a product for sale that there is more of it than people want to buy **4** CHEMISTRY to DISSOLVE (=mix until something becomes part of a liquid) as much of a solid into a chemical mixture as possible

sat·u·rat·ed /ˈsætʃəˌreɪtɪd/ *adj.* [no comparative] **1** extremely wet: +**with** *The pillow was saturated with blood.* ▸see THESAURUS box at wet[1] **2** completely filled with something or a large number of things: +**with** *The system is saturated with fraud and corruption.* **3** CHEMISTRY if a chemical mixture is saturated, it has had as much of a solid DISSOLVED (=mixed until it has become part of the liquid) into it as possible: *a saturated salt solution* **4 the market (for sth) is saturated** used to say that so much of a product has been offered for sale that people do not want to buy any more things of that kind

ˌsaturated ˈfat *n.* [C,U] a type of fat from meat and milk products that is less healthy than other kinds of fat from vegetables or fish

sat·u·ra·tion /ˌsætʃəˈreɪʃən/ *n.* [U] **1** the act or result of making something completely wet **2** a situation in which something is very full of a particular type of thing, so that no more can be added **3 saturation bombing** a military attack in which all of a particular area has a lot of bombs dropped on it **4 saturation coverage/advertising** a situation in which there is so much information, advertising etc. about something that everyone has heard about it **5** CHEMISTRY the state of a chemical mixture that has reached its SATURATION POINT

satuˈration ˌpoint *n.* [C usually singular] **1** a situation in which no more people or things can be added because there are already too many: *The coffee bar market has almost **reached** its **saturation point**.* **2** CHEMISTRY the state that a chemical mixture reaches when it has had as much of a solid substance DISSOLVED (=mixed until it becomes part of the liquid) into it as possible

Sat·ur·day /ˈsætədi, -ˌdeɪ/ *n.* [C,U] the seventh day of the week, between Friday and Sunday: *Carrie's plane leaves Saturday.* | *Jim's going to Tucson **on Saturday**.* | *We were in Hawaii **last Saturday**.* | *Would **next Saturday** be a good time for me to visit?* | *Let's get together **this Saturday*** (=the next Saturday that is coming). | *Jack always washes his car **on Saturdays*** (=each Saturday). | *Steve's birthday is **on a Saturday** this year.* | **Saturday morning/afternoon/night etc.** *Don't forget that we have a soccer game Saturday morning.* → see Grammar box at SUNDAY [**Origin:** 800–900 Translation of Latin *Saturni dies* **day of Saturn**]

ˌSaturday night ˈspecial *n.* [C] a small cheap gun that is easy to buy and easy to hide in your clothing

Sat·urn /ˈsætən/ *n.* **1** PHYSICS the PLANET that is sixth in order from the Sun and is surrounded by large rings → see picture at SOLAR SYSTEM **2** in Roman MYTHOLOGY, the father of Zeus and god of farming

sat·ur·na·li·a /ˌsætəˈneɪliə/ *n.* [C] LITERARY an occasion when people enjoy themselves in a very wild and uncontrolled way

sat·ur·nine /ˈsætənaɪn/ *adj.* [no comparative] LITERARY looking sad and serious, especially in a threatening way

sa·tyr /ˈseɪtə/ *n.* [C] **1** a creature in ancient Greek literature who was half human and half goat and represented pleasure and enjoyment **2** FORMAL or HUMOROUS a man who is always thinking about sex or trying to get sexual pleasure

sauce /sɔs/ S2 W3 *n.* **1** [C,U] a thick liquid that is served with food to add a particular taste: *chicken in a rich creamy sauce* | **tomato/chocolate etc. sauce** *scallops with garlic sauce* | **barbecue/teriyaki/white sauce** (=a particular type of sauce) **2 the sauce** OLD-FASHIONED alcoholic drinks: *Alice seems to be **hitting the sauce** (=drinking a lot) a lot lately.* [**Origin:** 1300–1400 Old French, Latin *salsa*, from *sallere* **to add salt to**]

sauce·pan /ˈsɔs-pæn/ *n.* [C] a deep round metal container with a handle that is used for cooking on top of the STOVE

sau·cer /ˈsɔsə/ *n.* [C] a small round plate that curves up at the edges, that you put a cup on → see also FLYING SAUCER

sau·cy /ˈsɔsi/ *adj.* *comparative* **saucier**, *superlative* **sauciest** **1** slightly shocking, but amusing or sexually attractive: *saucy swimwear* **2** OLD-FASHIONED impolite and not showing enough respect, but often in a way that is amusing: *a saucy spirited girl* —**saucily** *adv.* —**sauciness** *n.* [U]

Saudi A·ra·bi·a /ˌsɔdi əˈreɪbiə, ˌsaʊ-/ a country in the Middle East, east of the Red Sea —**Saudi Arabian** also **Saudi** *n., adj.*

sau·er·kraut /ˈsaʊəˌkraʊt/ *n.* [U] a German food made from CABBAGE that has been left in salt so that it tastes sour

Sauk, Sac /sɔk/ a Native American tribe from the northeastern central area of the U.S.

Sault Sainte Ma·rie Ca·nals /ˌsu seɪnt məˌri kəˈnælz/ a system of three CANALS connecting two of the Great Lakes in North America, Lake Superior and Lake Huron

sau·na /ˈsɔnə/ *n.* [C] **1** a room that is heated to a very high temperature by hot air, where people sit because it is considered healthy **2** a period of time when you sit or lie in a room like this: *Gordon **took a sauna** after his swim.*

saun·ter /ˈsɔntə, ˈsɑn-/ *v.* [I always + adv./prep.] to walk in a slow way, that makes you look confident or proud: +**along/around/in etc.** *A young man sauntered into the bar.* —**saunter** *n.* [singular]

sau·sage /ˈsɔsɪdʒ/ S2 *n.* [C,U] a mixture of meat, especially PORK (=meat from a pig), that has been cut up very small, and SPICES, usually made into a tube shape: *Do you want bacon or sausage with your eggs?* [**Origin:** 1400–1500 Old North French *saussiche*, from Late Latin *salsicia*, from Latin *salsus* **salted**]

Saus·sure /soʊˈsʊr/, **Fer·di·nand de** /ˈfədɪnɑn də/ (1857–1913) a Swiss LINGUIST whose ideas are considered the beginning of modern LINGUISTICS

sau·té /sɔˈteɪ/ *v.* **sautéed, sautéing** [T] to cook something quickly in a little hot oil: *Sauté the onions until soft.* [**Origin:** 1800–1900 French, past participle of *sauter* **to jump**]

sav·age[1] /ˈsævɪdʒ/ *adj.* **1** very cruel and violent: *a savage dog* | *Police described the attack as unusually savage.* | **a savage attack/murder/beating etc.** *Jake was the victim of a savage beating.* **2** criticizing someone or something very severely: **savage attack/criticism etc.** *a savage attack on the president's policies* **3** very severe and harmful: *savage cuts in government spending* **4** [only before noun] OLD-FASHIONED a word to describe a person or group from a country where the way of living seems very simple and undeveloped, now considered offensive SYN **primitive** **5** [only before noun] LITERARY sharp and dangerous-looking [**Origin:** 1200–1300 Old French *sauvage*, from Latin *silvaticus* **of the woods, wild**] —**savagely** *adv.* —**savageness** *n.* [U]

savage² *n.* [C] OLD-FASHIONED a word for someone from a country where the way of living seems very simple and undeveloped, now considered offensive → see also **noble savage** at NOBLE¹ (4)

savage³ *v.* [T] **1** to criticize someone or something very severely: *His performance was savaged by critics.* **2** to attack someone violently, causing serious injuries

sav·age·ry /ˈsævɪdʒri/ *n. plural* **savageries** [C,U] **1** extremely cruel and violent behavior **2** very strong angry feelings that are shown in the way someone speaks or behaves

sa·van·na, savannah /səˈvænə/ *n.* [C,U] EARTH SCIENCE a large flat area of grassy land in a warm part of the world [**Origin:** 1500–1600 Spanish *zavana*, from Taino *zabana*]

Sa·van·nah /səˈvænə/ the oldest city in the U.S. state of Georgia

sa·vant /sæˈvɑnt, sə-/ *n.* [C] LITERARY someone who knows a lot about a particular subject

save¹ /seɪv/ S1 W1 *v.*
1 FROM HARM/DANGER [T] to make someone or something safe from danger, harm, or destruction: *Doctors were unable to save his damaged leg.* | **save sb/sth from sth** *Neighbors managed to save the school from closure.* | *Her quick action* ***saved my life*** (=prevented me from dying). | *Doug was determined to* ***save*** *his* ***marriage*** (=prevent a divorce). ▶see THESAURUS box at protect
2 MONEY IN A BANK [I,T] also **save up** to keep money, and often to gradually add more money over a period of time, so that you can use it later: *We'll have to save more money if we want a new car.* | **+for** *I'm saving up for a trip to Europe.* | **save (up) to do sth** *We're trying to save money to buy a house.* → see also SAVER
3 NOT WASTE [T] to use less money, time, energy etc. so that you do not waste any: *We can save 15 minutes by taking the expressway.* | **save sb sth** *These changes could save the company up to $500,000 a year.* | **save money/time/energy etc.** *I did it myself to save time.*
4 TO USE LATER [T] to keep something so that you can use or enjoy it in the future: *We'll eat half of it and save the rest for later.* | **save sth for sth** *I'm saving the champagne for a special occasion.* | **save sth to do sth** *Save the bones to make soup with.* ▶see THESAURUS box at keep¹
5 COLLECT [T] also **save up** to keep all the objects of a particular kind that you can find, so that they can be used for a special purpose: *My grandmother saved up all her old magazines.*
6 HELP TO AVOID [T] to help someone by making it unnecessary for them to do something that is inconvenient or that they do not want to do: **save doing sth** *Speak to her now to save calling her later.* | **save sb (doing) sth** *If you lend me the money, it will save me a trip to the bank.* | **save sb the trouble/bother etc. (of doing sth)** *Just use the canned soup and save yourself the trouble.*
7 KEEP FOR SB [T] to stop people from using something, so that it is available for someone else: *Will you save my place in line?* | **save sth for sb** *Kate asked us to save some dinner for her.* | **save sb sth** *We'll save you a seat.*
8 COMPUTER [I,T] COMPUTERS to make a computer keep the work that you have done on it: *Have you saved your document?*
9 you saved my life SPOKEN used to thank someone who has gotten you out of a difficult situation or solved a problem for you: *Thanks for the ride – you really saved my life.*
10 save sb's skin/bacon/neck/butt INFORMAL to make it possible for someone to escape from an extremely difficult or dangerous situation: *The money arrived just in time to save my neck.*
11 can't do sth to save your life SPOKEN to be completely unable to do something: *I can't read a map to save my life.*
12 sb's/sth's saving grace the one good thing that makes someone or something acceptable: *The movie's only saving grace was its dazzling special effects.*
13 save the day to make a situation end successfully when it seemed likely to end badly: *Andy saved the day by lending me the money.*
14 SPORTS [T] to stop the other team from getting a GOAL in a sport such as SOCCER or HOCKEY
15 save sb from himself/herself to prevent someone from doing something that is likely to harm them in the end
16 RELIGION [I,T] in the Christian church, to free someone from the power of evil and SIN
[**Origin:** 1200–1300 Old French *salver*, from Late Latin *salvare*, from Latin *salvus*] → see also **save your breath** at BREATH (4), **save face** at FACE¹ (7)
save on sth *phr. v.* to avoid wasting something by using as little as possible of it: *To save on expenses, Tracy moved in with her mother.*

save² *n.* [C] an action by the GOALKEEPER in SOCCER or HOCKEY that prevents the other team from getting a GOAL

save³ also **ˈsave for** *prep.* FORMAL except for: *She answered all the questions save one.*

save⁴ also **ˈsave that** *conjunction* FORMAL used for mentioning the only person or thing about which a statement is not true SYN **except that**

saver /ˈseɪvɚ/ *n.* [C] someone who saves money in a bank → see also FACE SAVER, SCREEN SAVER

-sav·er /seɪvɚ/ *suffix* [in nouns] **a time-saver/money-saver/energy-saver etc.** something that prevents loss or waste: *Shopping online is a great time-saver.*

sav·ing /ˈseɪvɪŋ/ S3 *n.* **1 savings** [plural] all the money that you have saved, especially in a bank: *She lost their* ***life savings*** *in a Vegas casino.* **2** also **savings** [C] an amount of something that you have not used or do not have to spend: **+of** *The sales price represents a savings of $100.* | **+in** *The new engines will lead to savings in fuel.* **3** [U] ECONOMICS the act of keeping money and adding to it so that you can use it later

ˈsavings acˌcount *n.* [C] ECONOMICS a bank account that pays INTEREST on the money you have in it, and which allows you to take money out of your account without having to tell your bank several days or weeks before you do this → see also CHECKING ACCOUNT, DEPOSIT ACCOUNT, NOW ACCOUNT

ˌsavings and ˈloan *n.* [C] ECONOMICS a business that lends money, usually so that you can buy a house, and into which you can pay money to be saved

ˈsavings bank *n.* [C] ECONOMICS a bank whose business is mainly from savings accounts and from LOANS on houses

ˈsavings bond *n.* [C] ECONOMICS a BOND sold by the U.S. government that cannot be sold from one person to another

ˈsavings rate *n.* [C] ECONOMICS **1** the part of your income which you have left after you have paid your taxes, bills etc., that you save rather than spend: *the decline in personal savings rates in the U.S.* **2** the rate of INTEREST paid on a SAVINGS ACCOUNT

sav·ior /ˈseɪvyɚ/ *n.* **1** [C usually singular] someone or something that saves you from a difficult or dangerous situation: *A wealthy investor turned out to be the company's savior.* **2 the/our Savior** in the Christian religion, a name for Jesus Christ, because he is believed to save people from SIN and death

sav·oir-faire /ˌsævwɑr ˈfɛr/ *n.* [U] the ability to do or say the right things, especially in social situations: *people with money and savoir-faire*

sa·vor¹ /ˈseɪvɚ/ *v.* [T] **1** to enjoy the taste or smell of something very much: *Marty took time to savor each*

S

bite of his steak. **2** to make an activity or experience last as long as you can, because you are enjoying every moment of it: *We savored the early morning quiet.*

savor² *n.* [singular, U] FORMAL **1** a taste or smell, especially one that is pleasant: *a delicate savor* **2** interest and enjoyment: *Life seems to have lost its savor.*

sa·vor·y¹ /ˈseɪvəri/ *adj.* **1** having a pleasant and attractive smell or taste: *savory grilled vegetables* **2** [used with negative] something that is not savory seems morally unacceptable, or not nice OPP **unsavory**: *It's not the most savory topic for discussion.* **3** having a taste that is not sweet, especially a salty or SPICY taste OPP **sweet**: *savory snacks* [**Origin:** 1200–1300 Old French *savouré*, past participle of *savourer*, from *savour*]

savory² *n.* [U] a plant whose leaves are used in cooking to add taste to meat, vegetables etc.

sav·vy¹ /ˈsævi/ *adj. comparative* **savvier**, *superlative* **savviest** having the practical knowledge and ability to deal with a situation successfully: *savvy consumers* | **computer-savvy/media-savvy etc.** (=having knowledge about a particular subject)

savvy² *n.* [U] practical knowledge and ability: *political savvy*

saw¹ /sɔ/ *v.* the past tense of SEE

saw² *n.* [C] **1** a tool that has a flat metal blade with an edge that has been cut into a series of "V" shapes, used for cutting wood **2** a well-known wise statement SYN **proverb**: *that* ***old saw*** *about being careful what you wish for* [**Origin:** Old English *sagu*]

saw

saw³ *v. past tense* **sawed**, *past participle* **sawed** or **sawn** /sɔn/ [I,T] to cut something using a saw: **+through** *The prisoners sawed through the bars in their cell.* ►see THESAURUS box at **cut¹**

saw at sth *phr. v.* to try to cut something with a repeated backward and forward movement: *Dad sawed at the steak.*

saw sth ↔ **off** *phr. v.* to remove something by cutting it off with a saw: *We sawed off the dead branches.*

saw·bones /ˈsɔbounz/ *n.* [C] OLD-FASHIONED HUMOROUS a medical doctor, especially a SURGEON

saw·buck /ˈsɔbʌk/ *n.* [C] OLD-FASHIONED a $10 BILL

saw·dust /ˈsɔdʌst/ *n.* [U] very small pieces of wood that fall when you cut wood with a SAW

ˈsawed-off *adj.* **a sawed-off shotgun/rifle** a SHOTGUN that has had its BARREL (=long thin part) cut short, so that it is easier to hide

saw·horse /ˈsɔhɔrs/ *n.* [C] a small wooden structure shaped like an "A," usually used in pairs, on which you put a piece of wood that you are sawing

saw·mill /ˈsɔmɪl/ *n.* [C] a factory where trees are cut into boards using machines

sawn /sɔn/ *v.* a past participle of SAW

saw·yer /ˈsɔyɚ/ *n.* [C] OLD USE someone whose job is sawing wood

sax /sæks/ *n.* [C] INFORMAL a saxophone

Sax·on /ˈsæksən/ *n.* [C] a member of the German race that went to live in England in the fifth century —**Saxon** *adj.*

sax·o·phone /ˈsæksəˌfoun/ *n.* [C] a metal musical instrument with a single REED, used mostly in JAZZ and dance music [**Origin:** 1800–1900 French, from Adolphe *Sax* (1814–94), Belgian musician who invented the instrument]

sax·o·pho·nist /ˈsæksəˌfounɪst/ *n.* [C] someone who plays the saxophone

say¹ /seɪ/ S1 W1 *v.* **says** /sɛz/, *past tense and past participle* **said** /sɛd/, **saying**

1 THOUGHT/OPINION [I only in questions and negatives, T] to express a thought, opinion, explanation etc. in words: *What did you say?* | *"I don't care," he said.* | *"Is Joyce coming?" "I don't know – she didn't say."* | **say (that)** *Carol said you were looking for me.* | **say sth to sb** *What did Don say to you?* | **say how/why/who etc.** *Did she say how long she's going to be gone?* | **say something/anything/nothing** *He said something in Japanese.* | **something/anything/nothing to say** *I couldn't think of anything to say to her.* | **a nice/stupid/weird etc. thing to say** *That's a terrible thing to say, Wayne.* | **say yes/no (to sth)** *Every time I ask to go, Mom says no.* | **say hello/goodbye/please/thank you etc.** (=greet someone, speak to them when you are leaving, ask for something politely etc.) | *I think he's a little scared, even if he won't* ***say so.*** | *He* ***said something about*** *being glad he was home.* | *Look, I've* ***said I'm sorry*** (=apologized) *– what more do you want?* | *I'd just like to* ***say a few words*** (=make a short speech) *about the schedule.*

THESAURUS

mention to say something but without giving many details: *He mentioned that he'd seen you yesterday.*
add to say something more about something: *Is there anything you'd like to add?*
express to say how you feel about something: *Her mother expressed concern about how Lisa was doing in school.*
point out to say something that other people had not noticed or thought of: *"It's upside down," Liz pointed out.*
imply to say something in a way that is not direct, especially something bad: *He seemed to be implying that I'd stolen it!*
whisper to say something very quietly: *"Is the baby asleep?" she whispered.*
mumble/mutter to say something quietly so that your words are not clear, for example when you are annoyed or embarrassed: *He mumbled something about working late.* | *"It's not fair," she muttered.*
murmur to say something in a soft, slow, gentle voice: *He murmured words of love.*
stammer/stutter to speak with a lot of pauses and repeated sounds, because you have a speech problem, or because you are nervous or excited: *Eric stammered his thanks, and blushed.*
growl to say something in a low angry voice: *"Shut up," he growled.*
snarl to say something in a nasty angry way: *"Get the hell out of here!" he snarled.*

2 GIVE INFORMATION [T not in passive] to give information in written words, numbers, or pictures: *What does the letter say?* | *The hall clock said 9:00.* | **say (that)** *The report says that safety standards need to be improved.* | **say to do sth** *The label says to take one pill before meals.* | **say who/what/how etc.** *The card doesn't even say who sent the flowers.* | ***It says here*** *the restaurant has live music.*

3 WANT TO EXPRESS [T] used to explain what you mean, or to find out what someone else means: *What are you trying to say?* | **say (that)** *Are you saying I'm fat?*

4 TELL SB TO DO STH [I,T not in progressive] to tell someone to do something or tell them what they are allowed to do: **say to do sth** *She said to give her a call when we get to the hotel.* | **say (that)** *Did Mom say you could come?*

5 say sth to yourself to think something: *I said to myself, "That can't be right."*

6 SPEAK WORDS OF STH [T] to speak the words of play, poem, prayer etc.: *I'll* ***say a prayer*** *for you.* | *She* ***said her lines*** *without much emotion.*

7 say sth to sb's face to make a remark that is negative or not nice directly to the person that the remark is about: *He wants me to leave, but he's too nice to say it to my face.*

8 COMMON OPINION [T] to express an opinion that a lot of people have: *Experts say that the painting is by a German artist.* | **they/people say (that)** *They say you only ever use a small portion of your brain.* | ***You know what they say*** *– you can't teach an old dog new tricks.*

9 be said to do/be sth to be considered by many to do something or to have certain qualities: *She's said to be the richest woman in the world.*
10 SHOW CHARACTER/QUALITIES [T] to show what someone or something's real character or qualities are: *What you wear* ***says a lot about*** *who you are.* | *The test scores* ***don't say much for*** *the quality of the teaching.*
11 HAVE MEANING [T] to have or show a meaning that someone can understand: *Most modern art doesn't say much to me.* | *Julie's whole attitude just said "New York"* (=it was typical of what you would find there). | *The expression on his face* ***said it all*** (=showed what he was feeling).
12 PRONOUNCE [T] to pronounce a word or sound: ***How do you say*** *your last name?*
13 this/that is not to say used to make it clear that something is not true, when you think someone might think that it is: *I was angry at him, but that's not to say I stopped loving him.*
14 to say nothing of sth used to say that you have described only some of the bad points about something: *He gave her clothes and a car, to say nothing of the jewelry.*
15 it's not for sb to say used to say that someone is not the person who should give an opinion or make a decision
16 say your piece to give your opinion about something, especially when you are annoyed about something

SPOKEN PHRASES

17 be saying used to emphasize that you are trying to explain what you mean in a way that someone will understand better, especially in a situation in which you are arguing with someone and do not want them to be angry: ***I'm just saying*** *it would be easier if we made a copy.* | ***I'm not saying*** *it's a bad idea, just that we need to think about it.* | ***All I'm saying is*** *that it would be better to do this first.* | *No one really wants to help out,* ***you know what I'm saying?***
18 (let's) say a) used when you are imagining a situation and talking about what you would do or what would happen SYN **suppose**: *Let's say you won $3 million. How would you spend it?* **b)** used to suggest something as an example: *Can you come to dinner? Say, 7:00?*
19 let's just say used when you do not want to give any details about something, usually because it is an important secret or the details are very bad or boring: *Let's just say he wasn't very happy.*
20 who says (that)...? used to say that you do not agree with a statement, opinion etc.: *Who says Tommy and I are still going out?*
21 says who? said when you do not believe what someone has said, and you want to know who has suggested that this is true: *"You can't go in there." "Says who?"*
22 anything/whatever you say used to tell someone that you agree to do what they want, accept their opinion etc., especially because you do not want an argument: *"Let's paint the room orange." "Anything you say, dear."*
23 you can say that again used to say that you completely agree with someone: *"We're too old for this." "You can say that again."*
24 that said also **having said that** used to say that something is true in spite of what you have just said: *They played very badly. That said, they're still a very good team.*
25 I can't say (that) used to say that you definitely do not think or feel something: *I can't really say that I enjoyed the experience.*
26 I have to say used to emphasize what you are saying: *I have to say I wasn't very impressed.*
27 who can say? also **who's to say?** used to say that no one can know something for certain: *It's unlikely that he'll be successful, but who can say?*
28 what do you say? a) used to ask someone if they agree with a suggestion: *Let's go for a ride? What do you say?* | ***What do you say we*** *split the two sandwiches?* **b)** used to remind a young child to say "please" or "thank you"

SPOKEN PHRASES

29 say when said when you want someone to tell you when to stop doing something or when you have given them enough of something, especially a drink
30 say what? SLANG used when you have not heard something that someone said, or when you cannot believe that something is true
31 (just) say the word used to tell someone they have only to ask and you will do what they want: *Just say the word and I'll get rid of her.*
32 I'll say this/that (much) for sb used when you want to mention something good about someone, especially when you have been criticizing them: *I'll say this much for Barry – he's very confident.*
33 that's not saying much used to emphasize that even though one thing is better or different from another, the difference is not very large: *I'm better with computers than my sister, but that's not saying much.*
34 when all is said and done used to remind someone about an important point that they should remember: *When all is said and done, she's still part of our family.*
35 to say the least used to say that you could have described something, criticized someone etc. a lot more severely than you have: *These maps are difficult to understand, to say the least.*
36 sth goes without saying used to say that something is so clear that it does not really need to be stated: ***It goes without saying that*** *a well-rested person is a better worker.*
37 something/a lot/not much etc. to be said for sth used to say that there are some, a lot of, not many etc. advantages to something: *There's something to be said for the new energy policy.*
38 that/which is to say used before describing what you mean in more detail: *Laura uses a special, which is to say expensive, shampoo and conditioner.*
39 you said it! a) used to say that you agree with someone: *"That was hard!" "You said it!"* **b)** also **you said it, not me** used when someone says something that you agree with, although you would not have actually said it yourself because it is not nice or not polite: *"I'm no good at this." "Hey, you said it!"*
40 I'll say! used to agree or say yes strongly
41 what do you have to say for yourself? used to ask someone for an explanation when they have done something wrong
42 say no more also **enough said** used to say that there is no need to say any more because you already understand everything even though it was not said directly
43 I'd rather not say used when you do not want to tell someone something: *"Where were you last night?" "I'd rather not say."*
44 have something to say about sth to be angry about something: *Your Dad will have something to say about this when he gets home.*
45 I wouldn't say no (to sth) used to say that you would like something, and would accept it if you were offered it: *I wouldn't say no to a cup of coffee.*
46 you could say that used to answer "yes" to someone's question when you do not want to give any more details: *"Is he a friend of yours?" "You could say that."*
47 what/whatever sb says, goes used to emphasize who is in control in a situation: *Around here, what the boss says, goes.*
48 wouldn't you say? used to ask someone if they agree with something you have just said: *It's a little ridiculous, wouldn't you say?*
49 if I (do) say so myself used when you say something good about yourself or your achievements, but do not want to seem too proud: *This cake is really good, if I do say so myself.*
50 you don't say! a) HUMOROUS used to show that you are not surprised at all by what someone has just told you **b)** OLD-FASHIONED used to say that you are surprised by what someone has just told you

S

[**Origin:** Old English *secgan*] → see also **say cheese** at CHEESE (2), **easier said than done** at EASY² (5), **say a mouthful** at MOUTHFUL (4), **no sooner said than done** at SOON (13)

say² S2 W3 *n.* [singular, U] **1** the right to take part in deciding something: **have a/some say in sth** *Local people want to have a say in decisions that affect them.* | *The chairman* ***has the final say.*** **2 have/get your say** to have the opportunity to give your opinion about something: *You've had your say – now it's my turn.*

say³ S2 *interjection* used to express surprise, or to get someone's attention so that you can tell them something: *Say, isn't that Mr. Hammel over there?*

say·ing /ˈseɪ-ɪŋ/ *n.* [C] **1** a well-known short statement that expresses an idea most people believe is true and wise → see also PROVERB ►see THESAURUS box at **phrase¹** **2 as the saying goes** used to introduce a particular phrase that people often say: *Blondes, as the saying goes, have more fun.* → see also **sth goes without saying** at SAY¹ (36)

ˈsay-so *n.* [singular] INFORMAL **1 sb's say-so** someone's permission: *Nobody here leaves* ***without*** *my* ***say-so.*** **2 on sb's say-so** based on someone's personal statement without any proof

S

SC the written abbreviation of South Carolina

scab¹ /skæb/ *n.* [C] **1** MEDICINE a hard layer of dried blood that forms over a cut or wound while it is getting better **2** an insulting word for someone who works while the other people in the same factory, office etc. are on STRIKE

scab² also **scab over** *v.* **scabbed, scabbing** [I] if a cut or wound scabs or scabs over, a scab forms over it

scab·bard /ˈskæbəd/ *n.* [C] LITERARY a metal or leather cover for the blade of a knife or sword

scab·by /ˈskæbi/ *adj. comparative* **scabbier**, *superlative* **scabbiest** scabby skin is covered with scabs

sca·bies /ˈskæbiz/ *n.* [U] MEDICINE a skin disease caused by very small insects

scab·rous /ˈskæbrəs/ *adj.* LITERARY impolite or shocking, especially in a sexual way: *scabrous rumors*

scads /skædz/ *n.* [plural] OLD-FASHIONED INFORMAL **scads of sth** large numbers or quantities of something

scaf·fold /ˈskæfəld, -foʊld/ *n.* [C] **1** a structure built next to a building or high wall, for workers to stand on while they build, repair, or paint the building **2** a structure that can be moved up and down to help people work on high buildings **3** a structure with a raised PLATFORM on which criminals are killed, especially in past times, by hanging or cutting off their heads [**Origin:** 1200–1300 Old North French *escafaut*, from Vulgar Latin *catafalicum* **stage, platform, scaffold**]

scaf·fold·ing /ˈskæfəldɪŋ/ *n.* [U] poles and boards that are built into a structure for workers to stand on when they are working on the outside of a building or next to a high wall

scal·ar /ˈskeɪlə/ *n.* [C] TECHNICAL **1** also **ˌscalar ˈquantity** MATH a quantity that has size but no direction and is represented by a number, for example quantities of time, energy, and MASS **2** MATH a number or value that is multiplied by all the numbers in a MATRIX in scalar multiplication

ˌscalar multipliˈcation *n.* [U] MATH the process of multiplying all the numbers in a MATRIX by a particular number

ˌscalar ˈproduct *n.* [C] MATH a number that is the result of multiplying the lengths of two VECTORS together with the COSINE of the angle between them SYN **dot product**

scal·a·wag /ˈskæliwæg/ *n.* [C] OLD-FASHIONED **1** a dishonest person who causes trouble **2** HISTORY a white southern Republican after the Civil War

scald¹ /skɔld/ *v.* [T] **1** to burn your skin with hot liquid or steam: *I scalded myself on the hot water pipe.* **2** if you scald vegetables, you put them in boiling water for a short time **3** to heat a liquid to a temperature just below the BOILING POINT [**Origin:** 1100–1200 Old North French *escalder*, from Late Latin *excaldare* **to wash in warm water**]

scald² *n.* [C] a burn caused by hot liquid or steam

scald·ing /ˈskɔldɪŋ/ *adj.* **1** extremely hot: *a cup of scalding coffee* ►see THESAURUS box at **hot** **2** scalding criticism is very severe

scale¹ /skeɪl/ S3 W3 *n.*

1 SIZE/LEVEL [singular, U] the size, level, or amount of something, especially in relation to something else or to what is normal: *The photograph doesn't give you an idea of the building's scale.* | **+of** *The scale of the disaster soon became evident.* | **on a large/small/broad etc. scale** *Emergency aid is needed on a massive scale.* | **large-scale/small-scale** *a small-scale research project*

2 MEASURING SYSTEM [C] a system for measuring the force, speed, amount etc. of something, or for comparing it with something else: *The salary scale goes from $60,000 to $175,000.* | *Hurricanes are graded* ***on a scale*** *from 1 to 5.*

3 on a scale of 1 to 10 SPOKEN used when you are telling someone how good you think something is: *On a scale of 1 to 10, this book rates a nine and a half* (=it is very good).

4 WEIGHT a) a machine that you use to weigh people or objects: *a bathroom scale* **b)** also **scales** a piece of equipment with two dishes, used especially in the past for weighing things by comparing them to a known weight: *a pair of scales* → see also **tip the balance/scales** at TIP² (3), **tip the scales at 150/180/200 etc. pounds** at TIP² (5)

5 RANGE [C usually singular] the whole range of different types of people, things, ideas etc., from the lowest level to the highest: **at the top/upper/bottom/lower end of the scale** *Jaguar makes cars at the top end of the price scale.*

6 MAP/MODEL [C usually singular, U] the relationship between the size of a map, drawing, or model and the actual size of the place or thing that it represents: *maps with a scale of 1:25,000* | *The building plans must be exactly* ***to scale*** (=with all parts shown in the right size in relation to each other).

7 MEASURING MARKS [C] a set of marks with regular spaces between them that are on a tool or instrument used for measuring: *the scale on a thermometer*

8 FISH [C usually plural] BIOLOGY one of the small flat pieces of skin that cover the bodies of fish, snakes etc.

9 MUSIC [C] ENG. LANG. ARTS a series of musical notes moving up or down in PITCH with particular distances between each note: *the F major scale*

10 MINIMUM PAY [U] an amount of money that must be paid to someone who belongs to a UNION: *Many of the actors worked* ***for scale.***

11 WATER PIPES [U] a white substance that forms around the inside of hot water pipes or containers in which water is boiled

12 the scales fall from sb's eyes LITERARY used to say that someone suddenly realizes what has been clear to other people → see also FULL-SCALE

scale² *v.* [T] **1** FORMAL to climb to the top of something that is high and difficult to climb: *The climbers will attempt to scale Mount Everest.* **2** to make something the right size for use by a particular person or group: **+to** *Salaries are scaled according to the level of responsibility.* **3** to remove the SCALES (=skin) from a fish

scale sth ↔ **back/down** *phr. v.* to reduce the size of an organization, plan etc. so that it operates at a lower level: *The company has scaled back its workforce.*

scale sth ↔ **up** *phr. v.* to increase the amount or size of something

ˈscale ˌdrawing *n.* [C] a drawing of an object, building, or area etc. that is larger or smaller than the actual object, building etc. Maps and BLUEPRINTS are examples of a scale drawing.

sca·lene /ˈskeɪlin/ *adj.* MATH a scalene TRIANGLE is a three-sided shape in which the sides are all different lengths → see also EQUILATERAL → see picture at TRIANGLE

scal·lion /ˈskælyən/ *n.* [C] a young onion with a small round end and a long green stem SYN **green onion**

scal·lop /ˈskæləp, ˈskɑləp/ *n.* [C] **1** BIOLOGY a small sea creature that has a hard flat shell made of two parts that fit together, or the flesh from this animal eaten as food **2** one of a row of small curves decorating the edge of clothes, curtains etc.

scal·loped /ˈskæləpt, ˈskɑ-/ *adj.* **1** having a series of small curves around the edges for decoration: *a dress with a scalloped neckline* **2 scalloped potatoes/corn etc.** potatoes, corn etc. that have been baked in a cream or cheese SAUCE

scalp¹ /skælp/ *n.* [C] **1** BIOLOGY the skin on the top of your head **2** the skin and hair that was cut off an enemy's head in the past as a sign of victory **3 be out for/be after/want etc. sb's scalp** INFORMAL to want to defeat or punish someone severely [**Origin:** 1300–1400 From a Scandinavian language]

scalp² *v.* [T] **1** INFORMAL to buy tickets for an event and sell them again at a much higher price **2** to cut off a dead enemy's scalp as a sign of victory

scal·pel /ˈskælpəl/ *n.* [C] a small very sharp knife used by doctors in operations

scal·per /ˈskælpɚ/ *n.* [C] a person who makes money by buying tickets for an event and selling them again at a very high price

scal·y /ˈskeɪli/ *adj. comparative* **scalier**, *superlative* **scaliest** **1** an animal, such as a fish, that is scaly is covered with small flat pieces of hard skin **2** scaly skin is dry and rough —**scaliness** *n.* [U]

scam¹ /skæm/ *n.* [C] INFORMAL a dishonest way of getting money by tricking people, especially one that is carefully planned: *an insurance scam*

scam² *v.* **scammed**, **scamming** [T] INFORMAL to trick someone into giving you money

ˈscam ˌartist *n.* [C] INFORMAL someone who tries to get money by tricking people

scamp /skæmp/ *n.* [C] OLD-FASHIONED a child who has fun by tricking people, especially in an amusing way

scam·per /ˈskæmpɚ/ *v.* [I always + adv./prep.] to run with quick short steps, like a child or small animal: +**across/out/off etc.** *A mouse scampered across the floor.*

scam·pi /ˈskæmpi/ also **ˌshrimp ˈscampi** *n.* [U] a dish of large SHRIMP cooked with butter and GARLIC

scan¹ /skæn/ *v.* **scanned**, **scanning** **1** also **scan through** [I,T] to read something quickly in order to understand its main meaning or to find some particular information: *Stern started every day by scanning the want ads.* **2** [I,T] COMPUTERS to use a SCANNER (=piece of computer equipment) to copy a document or a picture into DIGITAL form: *You can* ***scan in*** *pictures and then manipulate them on screen.* **3** [T] if a machine scans an object or a part of your body, it passes a BEAM of ELECTRONS over it to produce a picture of its surface or of what is inside: *All luggage is scanned before the flight.* | **scan sb/sth for sth** *Women are now regularly scanned for breast cancer.* **4** [I,T] if a machine, instrument, or computer program scans something, it searches it carefully to find something: **scan (sth) for sth** *The program scans for computer viruses.* **5** [T] to examine an area carefully but quickly, because you are looking for a particular person or thing: *Surveillance cameras constantly scan the sidewalks.* | **scan sth for sth** *I scanned the room for familiar faces.* **6** TECHNICAL **a)** [I] poetry that scans has a regular pattern of beats **b)** [T] to find or show a regular pattern of beats in a poem or line of poetry [**Origin:** 1300–1400 Late Latin *scandere*, from Latin, **to climb**] → see also SCANSION

scan² *n.* **1** [C] a test done by a SCANNER (=special machine that produces a picture of the inside of something): *a bone scan* **2** [singular] the act of looking at or reading something quickly: *a quick scan of the headlines*

scan·dal /ˈskændl/ W3 *n.* **1** [C,U] behavior or events, often involving famous people, that are considered to be shocking or not moral: *a financial scandal* | *Jameson's wife left him after the* ***scandal broke*** (=became known to everyone). **2** [singular] a very bad situation that exists and that you think should be changed by someone in authority: *the scandal of poverty in our richest cities* [**Origin:** 1100–1200 Late Latin *scandalum* **offense**, from Greek *skandalon*]

scan·dal·ize /ˈskændlˌaɪz/ *v.* [T] to do something that shocks people very much: *His announcement scandalized the nation.*

scan·dal·mon·ger /ˈskændlˌmʌŋgɚ, -ˌmɑŋ-/ *n.* [C] DISAPPROVING someone who tells people shocking things about someone else, often things that are not true —**scandalmongering** *n.* [U]

scan·dal·ous /ˈskændl-əs/ *adj.* completely immoral and shocking: *scandalous behavior* —**scandalously** *adv.*

Scan·di·na·vi·a /ˌskændɪˈneɪviə/ an area of northern Europe consisting of Norway, Sweden, Denmark, Finland, and Iceland

Scan·di·na·vi·an /ˌskændəˈneɪviən◂/ *n.* [C] someone from the area of northern Europe that includes Norway, Sweden, Denmark, Finland, and Iceland —**Scandinavian** *adj.*: *Scandinavian languages*

scan·ner /ˈskænɚ/ *n.* [C] **1** COMPUTERS a piece of computer equipment that copies an image from paper into a computer → see picture at COMPUTER **2** PHYSICS a machine that moves a BEAM of ELECTRONS over something in order to produce a picture of what is inside: *scanners for medical use*

scan·sion /ˈskænʃən/ *n.* [U] TECHNICAL the pattern of regular beats in poetry, or the marks you write to represent this

scant /skænt/ *adj.* [only before noun] **1** not enough: *We had scant time to rehearse.* **2 a scant cup/teaspoon etc.** a little less than a full amount of a particular measurement

scant·y /ˈskænti/ *adj. comparative* **scantier**, *superlative* **scantiest** **1** not much or not as much as is needed: *scanty evidence* **2** scanty clothes do not cover very much of your body: *a scanty bikini* —**scantily** *adv.*: *scantily clad models*

-scape /skeɪp/ *suffix* [in nouns] a wide view of a particular area, especially in a picture: *the cityscape of New York* | *seascapes* (=pictures of the ocean)

scape·goat /ˈskeɪpgoʊt/ *n.* [C] someone who is blamed for something bad that happens, even if it is not their fault [**Origin:** 1500–1600 *scape* (from *scape* **to get away** (13–20 centuries), from *escape*) + *goat*] —**scapegoat** *v.* [T]

scap·u·la /ˈskæpyələ/ *n. plural* **scapulae** /-li/ or **scapulas** [C] BIOLOGY one of the two flat bones on each side of your upper back SYN **shoulder blade** → see picture at SKELETON¹

scar¹ /skɑr/ *n.* [C] **1** a permanent mark that is left after you have had a cut or wound: +**on** *He has a scar on his left cheek.* | *Will the surgery* ***leave a scar?*** ►see THESAURUS box at **mark²** **2** a permanent emotional or mental effect caused by a bad experience: **mental/emotional scars** *The emotional scars remained after the relationship ended.* | *The mental* ***scars*** *could take a long time to* ***heal.*** **3** an ugly permanent mark on something: *The buildings* ***bear the scars of*** *the last month's fighting.* [**Origin:** 1300–1400 Old French *escare*, from Late Latin *eschara*, from Greek]

scar² *v.* **scarred**, **scarring** **1** [T] to have or be given a permanent mark on your skin because of a cut or wound: *Her arm was scarred with cigarette burns.* | *David survived the crash but will* ***be scarred for life.*** **2** [T] if a bad, difficult, or upsetting experience scars you, it has a permanent effect on your character or feelings: *She was deeply scarred by her father's suicide.* | *battle-scarred young men* **3** [T] to spoil the appearance of something, especially by damaging it: *Huge quarries scar the landscape.* **4** [I] also **scar over** MEDICINE if a wound scars, it becomes healthy but leaves a permanent mark on your skin

scar·ab /ˈskærəb/ also **ˈscarab ˌbeetle** *n.* [C] a large

S

black BEETLE (=insect with a hard shell), or an object in the shape of this insect

scarce[1] /skɛrs/ *adj.* **1** if food, clothing, water etc. is scarce, there is not enough of it available: *Water is always scarce in these parts.* | *scarce oil resources* | *Natural gas is **in scarce supply**.* → see Word Choice box at RARE **2 make yourself scarce** INFORMAL to leave a place, especially in order to avoid a bad situation [**Origin:** 1200–1300 Old North French *escars*, from Vulgar Latin *excarpsus* **pulled out**]

scarce[2] *adv.* LITERARY scarcely

scarce·ly /ˈskɛrsli/ *adv.* **1** almost not, or almost none at all SYN **hardly**: *The city had scarcely changed.* | *They had **scarcely any** money.* | *Ted **scarcely ever** left the house.* | **can/could scarcely do sth** *She could scarcely believe her eyes.* **2** just barely, or only a very short time ago SYN **barely**: **have scarcely done sth when** *He had scarcely gone to sleep when the phone rang.* **3** definitely not, or almost certainly not: *She can scarcely be blamed for what happened.* → see Word Choice box at ALMOST

scar·ci·ty /ˈskɛrsət̬i/ *n.* [singular, U] a situation in which there is not enough of something SYN **shortage**: **+of** *The scarcity of medical supplies was becoming critical.*

S

scare[1] /skɛr/ S2 *v.* **1** [T] to make someone feel frightened SYN **frighten**: *I'm sorry – I didn't mean to scare you!* | ***It scares me** how angry he gets.* | *A siren went off and **scared the living daylights out of** me.* **2 scare easily** to become frightened easily: *I don't scare easily, you know.* [**Origin:** 1100–1200 Old Norse *skirra*, from *skjarr* **shy, fearful**] → see also SCARED, SCARY

scare sb ↔ **into** sth *phr. v.* to make someone do something by frightening them or threatening them: **scare sb into doing sth** *The story scared me into quitting smoking.*

scare sb/sth ↔ **off/away** *phr. v.* **1** to make someone or something go away by frightening them: *An alarm system can scare burglars away.* **2** to make someone uncertain or worried, so that they do not do something they were going to do: *Violence on the island has scared off tourists.*

scare sth ↔ **up** *phr. v.* INFORMAL **1** to get or find something, even though this is difficult: *I might be able to scare up two tickets to the game.* **2** to make something, although you have very few things to make it from: *Susie scared up some lunch while we unpacked.*

scare[2] *n.* **1** [singular] a sudden feeling of fear SYN **fright**: *Lisa **gave** her parents **a scare** when she didn't come home after school.* **2** [C] a situation in which a lot of people become frightened about something: *a bomb scare*

scare·crow /ˈskɛrkroʊ/ *n.* [C] an object made to look like a person, that a farmer puts in a field to frighten birds away

scared /skɛrd/ S2 *adj.* frightened of something, or nervous about something SYN **frightened** SYN **afraid**: *At first, I was really scared.* | **+of** *He's really scared of snakes.* | **+(that)** *She was scared that she might slip and fall on the ice.* | **scared of doing sth** *He's scared of being caught.* | **scared to do sth** *Mary was scared to tell the truth.* | **scared stiff/scared to death** (=extremely frightened)

scare·dy-cat /ˈskɛrdiˌkæt/ *n.* [C] INFORMAL an insulting word for someone who is easily frightened, used especially by children

ˈscare quotes *n.* [plural] QUOTATION MARKS (" ") that are put around a word or phrase to show that it has a special meaning, rather than quotation marks that are put around what someone says

ˈscare ˌstory *n.* [C] a report, especially in a newspaper, that makes a situation seem more serious or worrying than it really is

ˈscare ˌtactics *n.* [plural] methods of persuading people to do something by frightening them: *The company used scare tactics to sell medical alert systems to the elderly.*

scarf[1] /skɑrf/ *n. plural* **scarfs** or **scarves** /skɑrvz/ [C] **1** a long narrow piece of material that you wear around your neck to keep it warm **2** a square piece of material that a woman wears over her head or around her neck, usually as a decoration [**Origin:** 1500–1600 Old North French *escarpe*, from Old French *escherpe* **bag hung around the neck**]

scarf[2] also **scarf down/up** *v.* [T] INFORMAL to eat something very quickly: *I scarfed down a candy bar between classes.*

scar·i·fy /ˈskɛrəfaɪ, ˈskær-/ *v.* **scarifies, scarified, scarifying** [T] **1** to break and make the surface of a road or field loose, using a pointed tool **2** TECHNICAL to make small cuts on an area of skin using a sharp knife **3** LITERARY to criticize someone very severely

scar·let /ˈskɑrlɪt/ *n.* [U] a bright red color [**Origin:** 1200–1300 Old French *escarlate*, from Medieval Latin *scarlata*, from Persian *saqalat* type of cloth] —**scarlet** *adj.*

ˌscarlet ˈfever *n.* [U] MEDICINE a serious infectious illness that mainly affects children, causing a sore throat and red spots on your skin

ˌscarlet ˈwoman *n.* [C] OLD-FASHIONED a woman who has sexual relationships with many different people

scarp /skɑrp/ *n.* [C] EARTH SCIENCE a line of natural cliffs

scarves /skɑrvz/ *n.* a plural of SCARF

scar·y /ˈskɛri/ S1 *adj. comparative* **scarier**, *superlative* **scariest** INFORMAL **1** frightening: *a scary movie* | *It's scary to think about what could happen.* **2** worth getting worried about: *We're so deep in debt it's scary.* → see also SCARE[1]

scat[1] /skæt/ *n.* [U] **1** ENG. LANG. ARTS a style of JAZZ singing, in which a singer sings sounds rather than words **2** solid waste from the body of a wild animal SYN **droppings**

scat[2] *interjection* OLD-FASHIONED used to tell an animal, especially a cat, or a small child to go away

scath·ing /ˈskeɪðɪŋ/ *adj.* scathing remarks, COMMENTS etc. criticize someone or something very severely [**Origin:** 1700–1800 *scathe* **to harm** (12–20 centuries), from Old Norse *skatha*] —**scathingly** *adv.*

scat·o·log·ic·al /ˌskæt̬lˈɑdʒɪkəl/ *adj.* FORMAL too interested in or relating to human waste, in a way that people find offensive: *scatological humor* —**scatology** /skæˈtɑlədʒi/ *n.* [U]

scat·ter /ˈskæt̬ɚ/ *v.* [I,T] **1** if a lot of things scatter, or if someone scatters them, they are thrown or dropped over a wide area in an irregular way: **+over/on etc.** *The marbles scattered and rolled across the room.* | *Scatter a few flower petals over the table for a decorative effect.* | **scatter sth with sth** *The work table was scattered with pencils and crayons.* **2** if a group of people scatter, or if something scatters them, everyone suddenly moves in different directions, especially to escape danger: *Soldiers used tear gas to scatter the crowd.* **3 be scattered to the four winds** LITERARY to be broken apart or separated and lost **4** PHYSICS if waves or PARTICLES scatter, or if something scatters them, they are made to go in different directions in an irregular way → see also SCATTERED, SCATTERING

scat·ter·brained /ˈskæt̬ɚˌbreɪnd/ *adj.* not thinking in a practical way, so that you forget or lose things —**scatterbrain** *n.* [C]

ˈscatter ˌdiagram also **ˈscatter plot** *n.* [C] MATH a GRAPH that shows the relationship between two sets of data by showing values from one set along the X-AXIS and values from the other set along the Y-AXIS

scat·tered /ˈskæt̬ɚd/ *adj.* **1** spread over a wide area in an irregular way: **+over/across/around etc.** *Toys were scattered all over the floor.* **2** happening or coming at irregular times over a period of time: *scattered gunfire* | **scattered showers/thunderstorms/rain** *Expect scattered showers this evening.* **3** not able to pay attention to things, for example because you have too many things to think about or are very upset **4 be**

scattered with sth if an area is scattered with something, it has a number of things over it, with large, irregular spaces between them

scat·ter·ing /ˈskæt̬ərɪŋ/ *n.* [C usually singular] a small number of things or people spread out over a large area: **+of** *a scattering of villages*

scav·enge /ˈskævɪndʒ/ *v.* [I,T] **1** BIOLOGY if an animal scavenges, it eats anything that it can find: **scavenge (sth) for sth** *Rats were scavenging for food.* **2** if someone scavenges, they search through things that other people do not want for food or useful objects: **scavenge (sth) for sth** *Children in the garbage dumps scavenge for glass and plastic bottles.* [**Origin:** 1600–1700 *scavenger* (16–21 centuries), from *scavager* **tax collector, someone who cleans streets**] —**scavenger** *n.* [C]

ˈscavenger hunt *n.* [C] a game in which people are given a list of unusual things that they must find and bring back

sce·nar·i·o /sɪˈnɛriˌoʊ, -ˈnær-/ Ac *n. plural* **scenarios** [C] **1** a situation that could possibly happen but has not happened yet: **a likely/possible/plausible scenario** *The most likely scenario is that 90 jobs will be lost.* | **the worst-case/nightmare scenario** (=the worst possible situation) **2** ENG. LANG. ARTS a written description of the characters, place, and things that will happen in a movie, play etc.

scene /sin/ S2 W1 *n.* [C]

1 PLAY/MOVIE ENG. LANG. ARTS **a)** a single piece of action that happens in one place in a movie, book etc.: *a love scene* | *That's my favorite scene in the movie.* **b)** part of a play during which there is no change in time or place: *Act V, Scene 2 of "Hamlet"* | *the opening scene of the play* ►see THESAURUS box at **part**[1]

2 ACCIDENT/CRIME [usually singular] the place where an accident, crime etc. happened: *Emergency workers rushed to the scene.* | *Police were called to **the scene of the crime**.* | **on/at the scene** *Reporters were soon on the scene.* | **the crime/murder scene** *His fingerprints were found at the murder scene.*

3 [singular] a particular set of activities and the people who are involved in them: *I was tired of the same old scene.* | **the music/fashion/political etc. scene** *She's a newcomer to the political scene.* | *the New Orleans jazz scene*

4 WHAT YOU SEE a view of a place or the things happening there that someone sees: *a lively street scene* | **+of** *There was a scene of utter confusion outside the courthouse.*

5 PICTURE ENG. LANG. ARTS a picture showing a view of a place: *framed desert scenes*

6 behind the scenes a) secretly, while other things are happening publicly: *Brown worked behind the scenes on the deal.* **b)** where work on a movie, play, TV program etc. that is not seen by the public is done, as opposed to the acting

7 set the scene a) to provide the conditions in which an event can happen: *His experiments set the scene for later discoveries.* **b)** to describe the situation before you begin to tell a story: *Let me just take a minute to set the scene.*

8 ARGUMENT a loud angry argument, especially in a public place: *Be quiet. You're **making a scene**.*

9 not your scene SPOKEN not the type of thing you like: *Dance clubs aren't really my scene.*

10 be/come/appear on the scene to be or become involved in a situation, activity etc.: *By then, there was a new boyfriend on the scene.*

11 a bad scene INFORMAL a difficult or bad situation

[**Origin:** 1500–1600 French *scène*, from Latin *scena*, *scaena* **stage, scene**]

scen·er·y /ˈsinəri/ *n.* [U] **1** the natural features of a particular part of a country, such as mountains, forests, deserts etc.: *spectacular mountain scenery* ►see THESAURUS box at **country**[1] **2** ENG. LANG. ARTS the painted background, furniture etc. used on a theater stage → see also **a change of scenery** at CHANGE[2] (4)

sce·nic /ˈsinɪk/ *adj.* surrounded by views of beautiful nature: *a scenic ocean drive* | *Let's **take the scenic route** (=go a longer, more beautiful way) home.* —**scenically** /-kli/ *adv.*

scent[1] /sɛnt/ *n.* [C,U] **1** a pleasant smell that something has: **+of** *The scent of incense filled the air.* ►see THESAURUS box at **smell**[1] **2** the smell of a particular animal or person that some other animals, for example dogs, can follow: *The dogs followed the animal's scent.* **3 throw sb off the scent** to give someone false information to prevent them from catching you or discovering something **4 the scent of scandal/panic/victory etc.** a particular quality that people can notice in a situation **5** OLD-FASHIONED a liquid that you put on your skin to make it smell nice SYN **perfume**

scent[2] *v.* [T] **1** to give a particular smell to something: *The fragrance of lilacs scented the evening air.* **2 scent fear/danger/victory etc.** LITERARY to feel sure that something is going to happen **3** if an animal scents another animal or a person, it knows that they are near because it can smell them [**Origin:** 1300–1400 Old French *sentir* **to feel, smell**, from Latin *sentire* **to feel**]

scent·ed /ˈsɛntɪd/ *adj.* having a particular smell, especially a nice one: *scented candles* | **pine-scented/lemon-scented etc.** *pine-scented cleaners*

scent·less /ˈsɛntlɪs/ *adj.* without a smell SYN **odorless**

scep·ter /ˈsɛptɚ/ *n.* [C] a short decorated stick carried by kings or queens at ceremonies

sceptic /ˈskɛptɪk/ the British and Canadian spelling of SKEPTIC

scep·ti·cal /ˈskɛptɪkəl/ the British and Canadian spelling of SKEPTICAL

scep·ti·cism /ˈskɛptəˌsɪzəm/ the British and Canadian spelling of SKEPTICISM

scha·den·freu·de /ˈʃɑdnˌfrɔɪdə/ *n.* [U] FORMAL a feeling of pleasure that you get when something bad happens to someone else [**Origin:** 1800–1900 German *schaden* **harm** + *freude* **pleasure**]

sched·ule[1] /ˈskɛdʒəl, -dʒul/ Ac S1 W2 *n.* [C]

1 PLAN FOR DOING STH a plan of what is going to happen or be done and when it will happen or be done: *a schedule of events* | *We've got a very **tight schedule** for this project.* | **ahead of/on/behind schedule** (=before, at, or after the planned time) ►see THESAURUS box at **plan**[1]

2 WHAT SB MUST DO a list of everything that someone has to do and when they plan to do it: *Let me just check my schedule.* | **a busy/full schedule** *How can he fit everything into his busy schedule?*

3 CLASS LIST a list of all the classes that a student is taking at one time and the times they take place: *What's your schedule like this fall?*

4 BUS/TRAIN ETC. a list that shows the times that buses, trains etc. leave or arrive at a particular place: **a bus/train/airline etc. schedule** *Do you have a current bus schedule?*

5 FORMAL LIST a formal list of something, for example prices: *a schedule of fees*

[**Origin:** 1300–1400 Old French *cedule* **piece of paper, note**, from Late Latin *schedula*, from Latin *scheda* **sheet of papyrus**]

schedule[2] Ac S2 W2 *v.* [T usually passive] to plan that something will happen at a particular time: **be scheduled for June/Monday/4:00 etc.** *Rehearsal is scheduled for 2:00.* | **be scheduled for completion/release/publication etc.** *The bridge is scheduled for completion next year.* | **be scheduled to do sth** *I'm scheduled to see Dr. Good next week.*

sched·uled /ˈskɛdʒəld/ *adj.* **1** happening or planned according to a schedule: *There are seven scheduled stops on the Senator's campaign trip.* | *scheduled maintenance* | *We now return to our **regularly scheduled** programming.* **2 a scheduled flight** an airplane service that flies at the same time every day or every week

Schel·ling /ˈʃɛlɪŋ/**, Frie·drich von** /ˈfridrɪk vɑn/ (1775–1854) a German PHILOSOPHER

sche·ma /ˈskimə/ *n. plural* **schemas** or **schemata** /skiˈmɑt̬ə/ [C] **1** a simple drawing that shows the main parts of something SYN **diagram** **2** a THEORY or way of looking at something

sche·mat·ic¹ /skiˈmæṭɪk/ Ac *adj.* showing the main parts of something in a simple way: *a schematic diagram* —**schematically** *adv.*

schematic² Ac *n.* [C] a simple drawing of a structure, especially of an electrical or MECHANICAL system that shows its main parts

sche·ma·tize /ˈskiməˌtaɪz/ *v.* [T] FORMAL to arrange something in a system

scheme¹ /skim/ Ac W3 *n.* [C] **1** an intelligent plan, especially to do something dishonest or illegal: *a get-rich-quick scheme* | **a scheme to do sth** *He came up with a scheme to steal his uncle's fortune.* ▸see THESAURUS box at **plan¹** **2** a system that you use to organize information, ideas etc.: *a classification scheme* → see also COLOR SCHEME **3 in the scheme of things** in the way things generally happen, or are organized: *What I'm doing doesn't matter in the larger scheme of things.* [**Origin:** 1500–1600 Latin *schema* **arrangement, figure**, from Greek, from *echein* **to have, hold, be in a condition**]

scheme² Ac *v.* [I] to secretly make intelligent and dishonest plans to get or achieve something: **+against** *He knew that people were scheming against him.* | **scheme to do sth** *They were charged with scheming to defraud the government.* —**schemer** *n.* [C] —**scheming** *adj.*: *a scheming woman*

scher·zo /ˈskɛrtsoʊ/ *n.* [C] a cheerful piece of music played quickly —**scherzo** *adj., adv.*

Schil·ler /ˈʃɪlɚ/, **Frie·drich von** /ˈfridrɪk vɑn/ (1759–1805) a German writer of plays, poetry, and history

schism /ˈsɪzəm, ˈskɪzəm/ *n.* [C,U] the separation of a group into two groups, caused by a disagreement about its aims and beliefs, especially a separation in the Christian church —**schismatic** /sɪzˈmæṭɪk, skɪz-/ *adj.*

schist /ʃɪst/ *n.* [U] EARTH SCIENCE a type of rock that naturally breaks apart into thin flat pieces

schiz·o /ˈskɪtsoʊ/ *n.* [C] SLANG a SCHIZOPHRENIC —**schizo** *adj.*

schiz·oid /ˈskɪtsɔɪd/ *adj.* **1** TECHNICAL typical of schizophrenia: *a schizoid personality disorder* **2** INFORMAL quickly changing between opposite opinions or attitudes

schiz·o·phre·ni·a /ˌskɪtsəˈfriniə/ *n.* [U] MEDICINE a serious mental illness in which someone's thoughts and feelings are not based on what is really happening around them [**Origin:** 1900–2000 German *schizophrenie*, from Greek *schizo-* **split** + *phren* **mind**]

schiz·o·phren·ic¹ /ˌskɪtsəˈfrɛnɪk/ *adj.* **1** TECHNICAL relating to schizophrenia, or typical of schizophrenia **2** INFORMAL quickly changing from one opinion, attitude etc. to another: *a schizophrenic trade policy*

schizophrenic² *n.* [C] someone who has schizophrenia

schle·miel /ʃləˈmil/ *n.* [C] a stupid person, especially one who is easily tricked

schlep /ʃlɛp/ *v.* **schlepped, schlepping** INFORMAL **1** [T] to carry or pull something heavy SYN **lug**: **schlep sth down/out/along etc. sth** *We had to schlep the luggage up three flights of stairs.* ▸see THESAURUS box at **carry¹** **2** [I always + adv./prep.] to go somewhere when it will be slow, boring, or a lot of effort to do so [**Origin:** 1900–2000 Yiddish *shleppen*, from Middle High German *sleppen*] —**schlep** *n.* [C]

schlep around *phr. v.* to spend your time doing nothing useful

Schlie·mann /ˈʃlimɑn/, **Hein·rich** /ˈheɪnrɪk/ (1822–1890) a German ARCHAEOLOGIST who discovered the ancient city of Troy

schlock /ʃlɑk/ *n.* [U] INFORMAL things that are cheap, bad, or useless [**Origin:** 1900–2000 Yiddish *shlak*, from Middle High German *slag* **hit**] —**schlocky** *adj.*

schmaltz·y /ˈʃmɔltsi, ˈʃmɑl-/ *adj.* comparative **schmaltzier**, superlative **schmaltziest** INFORMAL a schmaltzy piece of music, book etc. deals with strong emotions such as love and sadness in a way that seems silly and not serious enough: *a schmaltzy love song* [**Origin:** 1900–2000 *schmaltz* **schmaltzy quality** (20–21 centuries), from Yiddish *shmalts* **melted fat**] —**schmaltz** *n.* [U]

schmo /ʃmoʊ/ *n.* plural **schmoes** [C] INFORMAL a stupid person → see also **Joe Blow/Schmo** at JOE (1)

schmooze /ʃmuz/ *v.* [I] INFORMAL to talk about unimportant things at a social event in a friendly way that is not always sincere: **+with** *He spent time schmoozing with local TV executives.* [**Origin:** 1800–1900 Yiddish *shmuesn* **to talk**] —**schmoozer** *n.* [C]

schmuck /ʃmʌk/ *n.* [C] SPOKEN a stupid person [**Origin:** 1800–1900 Yiddish *shmok* **penis, stupid person**, from German *schmuck* **decoration, jewelry**]

schnapps /ʃnæps/ *n.* [U] a strong alcoholic drink [**Origin:** 1800–1900 German *schnaps*, from Low German *snappen* **to snap**]

schnau·zer /ˈʃnaʊzɚ, ˈʃnaʊtsɚ/ *n.* [C] a type of small gray or black dog with fairly short wavy hair

schnit·zel /ˈʃnɪtsəl/ *n.* [C,U] a flat piece of meat, especially VEAL, covered with small pieces of bread and cooked in oil

schnook /ʃnʊk/ *n.* [C] SPOKEN a stupid or unimportant person

schnoz, **schnozz** /ʃnɑz/ *n.* [C] HUMOROUS a nose

Schoen·berg /ˈʃɚnbɚg/, **Ar·nold** /ˈɑrnəld/ (1874–1951) an Austrian musician who wrote modern CLASSICAL music

schol·ar /ˈskɑlɚ/ W3 *n.* [C] **1** someone who knows a lot about a particular subject, especially one that is not a science subject: *Biblical scholars* **2** someone who has been given a SCHOLARSHIP (=money) to study at a college or university: *a Rhodes scholar*

schol·ar·ly /ˈskɑlɚli/ *adj.* **1** relating to the serious study of a particular subject: *scholarly research* **2** someone who is scholarly spends a lot of time studying, and knows a lot about a particular subject

schol·ar·ship /ˈskɑlɚˌʃɪp/ S3 *n.* **1** [C] an amount of money that is given to someone by an organization to help pay for their education, especially because they are very smart or for another particular reason → see also FINANCIAL AID: **+to** *a $1,000 scholarship to ISU* | *He attended Yale* ***on a scholarship.*** | **a football/academic/drama etc. scholarship** (=a scholarship given for someone who plays on a sports team or has a particular skill) | **a full/full-ride scholarship** (=a scholarship that pays all of a student's costs) → GRANT¹ **2** [U] the knowledge, work, or methods involved in serious studying: *a work of great scholarship*

scho·las·tic /skəˈlæstɪk/ *adj.* [only before noun] FORMAL **1** relating to schools, learning, or teaching: *outstanding scholastic achievement* **2** relating to scholasticism

scho·las·ti·cism /skəˈlæstəˌsɪzəm/ *n.* [U] a way of studying thought, especially religious thought, based on things written in ancient times

school¹ /skul/ S1 W1 *n.*

1 WHERE CHILDREN LEARN [C,U] a place where children are taught: *Do you walk to school?* | *What* ***school*** *does your son* ***go to?*** | *Lisa always buys her lunch* ***at school.*** | *The kids are* ***in school*** *most of the day.* | **a school bus/building etc.** *school books* → see also CHARTER SCHOOL, PAROCHIAL SCHOOL, PRIVATE SCHOOL, PUBLIC SCHOOL

THESAURUS

At school

class a period of time during which children are taught a particular subject

period one of the equal parts that a school day is divided into: *his fifth period class*

classwork school work done by children while they are in a class rather than at home
homework work that students are asked to do at home
assignment a piece of work that a student is asked to do
essay a short piece of writing about a particular subject by a student
recess a time when children are allowed to go outside to play during the school day
study to spend time reading, going to classes etc. to learn about a subject, especially to do this in order to prepare for a test
extracurricular relating to activities that students do at school that are not part of their regular classes
→ STUDENT

2 TIME AT SCHOOL [U] **a)** the time when students have classes in a school during the day: *Hurry or you'll be late for school.* | *School starts at 8:30.* | **before/after school** *I have football practice after school.* **b)** the time during your life when you go to a school: *She started school when she was four.* | *Ann's one of my old friends from school.* | *We have three kids* ***in school*** *now.*
3 UNIVERSITY a) [C,U] a college or university, or the time when you study there: *Both their kids are away at school now.* | *You should apply to Duke – it's a good school.* | *I took five years to get through school.* **b)** [C] a department or group of departments that teaches a particular subject at a university: +**of** *the Harvard School of Business* | **law/medical/graduate etc. school** *I worked my way through graduate school.*
4 TEACHERS/STUDENTS [singular, U] the students and teachers at a school: *The whole school was sorry when she left.*
5 SPECIAL SUBJECT [C] a place where a particular subject or skill is taught: *a language school* | +**of** *the Eastman School of Music*
6 ART/LITERATURE [C] a number of artists, writers etc. who are considered as a group because their styles of work are very similar: *the Impressionist school*
7 a school of thought an opinion or way of thinking about something that is shared by a group of people: *There are two main schools of thought on the subject.*
8 FISH [C] BIOLOGY a large group of fish, WHALES, DOLPHINS etc. that swim together: +**of** *a school of tuna* ►see THESAURUS box at **group**[1]
9 of/from the old school having old-fashioned traditional values or qualities, and not willing to change them: *a family doctor of the old school*
10 the school of hard knocks OLD-FASHIONED the difficult or bad experiences you have in life
[**Origin:** Old English *scol*, from Latin *schola*, from Greek *schole* **discussion, school**]

school[2] *v.* [T often passive] to train or teach someone: **school sb in sth** *They school you in the practical aspects of golf.*

school·bag /ˈskulbæg/ *n.* [C] a bag that a child carries his or her books and other things for school in

ˌschool ˈboard *n.* [C] a group of people who are elected to govern a school or group of schools in the U.S.

school·book /ˈskulbʊk/ *n.* [C] a book that is used in school classes SYN **textbook**

school·boy /ˈskulbɔɪ/ *n.* [C] OLD-FASHIONED a boy attending school

school·child /ˈskul-tʃaɪld/ *n. plural* **schoolchildren** /-ˌtʃɪldrən/ [C] OLD-FASHIONED a child attending school

ˈschool day *n.* [C] **1** a day of the week when children are usually at school **2 sb's school days** the time in someone's life when they attend school

ˈschool ˌdistrict *n.* [C] an area in a U.S. state that includes a number of schools which are governed together

school·girl /ˈskulgɚl/ *n.* [C] OLD-FASHIONED a girl attending school

school·house /ˈskulhaʊs/ *n.* [C] a building for a small school, especially in a small town or the country in past times: *a one-room schoolhouse*

school·ing /ˈskulɪŋ/ *n.* [U] school education: *Walter only had seven years of schooling.*

school·kid /ˈskul-kɪd/ *n.* [C] INFORMAL a child attending school

school·marm /ˈskulmɑrm/ *n.* [C] **1** a female school teacher in the past **2** a woman teacher who is considered to be old-fashioned, strict, and easily shocked by immoral things —**schoolmarmish** *adj.*

school·mas·ter /ˈskulˌmæstɚ/ *n.* [C] OLD-FASHIONED a male teacher, especially in a British private school

school·mate /ˈskulmeɪt/ *n.* [C] someone who goes or went to the same school as you

ˈschool ˌmistress *n.* [C] OLD-FASHIONED a female teacher, especially in a British private school

ˈschool night *n.* [C] a night before you have to go to school the next morning: *You guys should be in bed – it's a school night.*

school·room /ˈskulrum/ *n.* [C] a room where classes are taught

school·teach·er /ˈskulˌtitʃɚ/ *n.* [C] a teacher

school·work /ˈskulwɚk/ *n.* [U] work done for or during school classes

school·yard /ˈskulyɑrd/ *n.* [C] the area next to a school building where the children can go or play when they are not having lessons

schoo·ner /ˈskunɚ/ *n.* [C] **1** a fast sailing ship with two sails **2** a large tall glass for beer

Scho·pen·hau·er /ˈʃoʊpənˌhaʊɚ/, **Ar·tur** /ˈɑrtʊr/ (1788–1860) a German PHILOSOPHER

Schrö·ding·er /ˈʃroʊdɪŋɚ/, **Er·win** /ˈɚvɪn/ (1887–1961) an Austrian scientist whose ideas were an important part of the development of QUANTUM MECHANICS

Schu·bert /ˈʃubɚt/, **Franz** /frɑnz/ (1797–1828) an Austrian musician who wrote CLASSICAL music

Schu·mann /ˈʃumɑn/, **Rob·ert** /ˈrɑbɚt/ (1810–1856) a German musician who wrote CLASSICAL music

schuss /ʃʊs/ *v.* [I] to SKI quickly down a mountain in a straight line

schwa /ʃwɑ/ *n.* [C] ENG. LANG. ARTS **1** a vowel typically heard in parts of a word that are spoken without STRESS, such as the "a" in "about" **2** the sign (/ə/), used to represent this sound

Schwar·zen·eg·ger /ˈʃwɔrtsənˌɛgɚ/, **Ar·nold** /ˈɑrnəld/ (1947–) an Austrian who became a U.S. citizen, and who was formerly a BODY BUILDER and actor before being elected as the GOVERNOR of California in 2003

Schweit·zer /ˈʃwaɪtsɚ/, **Al·bert** /ˈælbɚt/ (1875–1965) a German doctor, famous for starting a hospital in Gabon and treating people who were suffering from LEPROSY

sci·at·ic /saɪˈæṭɪk/ *adj.* BIOLOGY relating to the HIPS: *the sciatic nerve*

sci·at·i·ca /saɪˈæṭɪkə/ *n.* [U] pain in the lower back, HIPS, and legs

sci·ence /ˈsaɪəns/ S2 W1 *n.* **1** [U] knowledge about the physical world, especially based on examining, testing, and proving facts: *developments in science and technology* **2** [U] the study of science: *a course in science* | *Mr. Paulson is a science teacher.* **3** [C] a particular part of science, for example BIOLOGY, CHEMISTRY, or PHYSICS: *the physical sciences* **4** [C] the study of a subject based on examining, testing, and proving facts: *library science* **5 sth is not an exact science** used to say that something involves a lot of guessing, and that there is not just one right way to do it: *Opinion polling is hardly an exact science.* **6 have sth down to a science** to have so much experience doing something that you can do it very well without making any mistakes, wasting anything etc. [**Origin:** 1300–1400 Old French, Latin *scientia* **knowledge**, from *scire* **to know**] → see also COMPUTER SCIENCE, NATURAL SCIENCE, **sth isn't rocket science** at ROCKET[1] (4), SOCIAL SCIENCE

ˈscience ˌfair *n.* [C] a competition, often at a school,

S

where students must make or do something that is related to science and then show it to the judges: *a project on volcanoes for the science fair*

ˌscience ˈfiction *n.* [U] ENG. LANG. ARTS a type of writing that describes imaginary future developments in science and their effect on life, for example traveling in time or to other PLANETS with life on them

ˈscience park *n.* [C] an area in a city where there are a lot of companies or organizations that do scientific work

sci·en·tif·ic /ˌsaɪənˈtɪfɪk/ S3 W2 *adj.* **1** [no comparative] relating to science, or using its methods: *scientific research* | *the international scientific community* **2** done very carefully, using an organized system OPP **unscientific**: *The selection process wasn't very scientific.* —**scientifically** /-kli/ *adv.*

ˌscientific ˈlaw *n.* [C] SCIENCE a statement about the way something works in nature, that is considered to be true at all times, and is the result of using scientific method

ˌscientific ˈmethod *n.* [U] SCIENCE a thorough method for doing scientific study, in which scientists test their ideas about how things work by doing EXPERIMENTS

ˌscientific noˈtation *n.* [U] MATH a way of writing very small and very large numbers. For example, 1×10^9 means one billion or 1,000,000,000; 1×10^{-9} means one billionth or 0.000000001.

ˌscientific ˈtheory *n.* [C,U] SCIENCE a set of ideas or scientific principles that many scientists accept as a reasonable and suitable explanation for why something exists or happens: *If current scientific theory is correct, the Earth is around 4.6 billion years old.* | *competing scientific theories*

sci·en·tist /ˈsaɪəntɪst/ W2 *n.* [C] someone who works or is trained in science → see also ROCKET SCIENTIST

Sci·en·tol·o·gy /ˌsaɪənˈtɑlədʒi/ *n.* [U] a religion that was started in the 1950s by the U.S. SCIENCE FICTION writer L. Ron Hubbard, officially called the Church of Scientology —**Scientologist** *n.* [C]

sci-fi /ˌsaɪ ˈfaɪ/ *n.* [U] INFORMAL SCIENCE FICTION

scim·i·tar /ˈsɪmɪtɚ, -ˌtɑr/ *n.* [C] a sword with a curved blade

scin·til·la /sɪnˈtɪlə/ *n.* [singular] FORMAL a very small amount of something: *There was **not a scintilla of** evidence to prove it.*

scin·til·late /ˈsɪntlˌeɪt/ *v.* [I] LITERARY to shine with small quick flashes of light SYN **sparkle** —**scintillation** /ˌsɪntlˈeɪʃən/ *n.* [U]

scin·til·lat·ing /ˈsɪntlˌeɪṭɪŋ/ *adj.* FORMAL interesting, intelligent, and amusing: *scintillating conversation*

sci·on /ˈsaɪən/ *n.* [C] **1** LITERARY a young member of a famous or important family **2** BIOLOGY a living part of a plant that is cut off, especially to be fastened to another plant

scissors

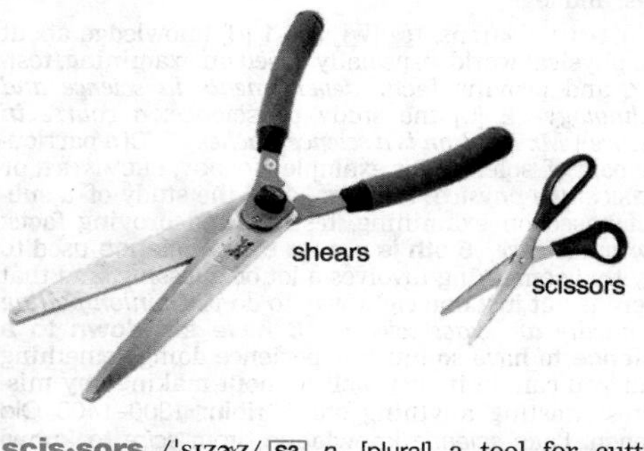

scis·sors /ˈsɪzɚz/ S3 *n.* [plural] a tool for cutting paper, fabric, card etc. made of two sharp blades that are fastened in the middle and have two holes for your fingers at one end: *a pair of scissors* [**Origin:** 1300–1400 Old French *cisoires*, from Late Latin *cisorium* **cutting tool**]

scl·era /ˈsklɪərə, ˈsklɪrə/ *n* [C] MEDICAL BIOLOGY the white outer layer of your eye → see picture at EYE[1]

scle·ro·sis /skləˈroʊsɪs/ *n.* [C,U] MEDICINE a disease that causes an organ or soft part of your body to become hard → see also MULTIPLE SCLEROSIS —**sclerotic** /skləˈrɑṭɪk/ *adj.*

scoff /skɔf, skɑf/ *v.* [I] FORMAL to laugh at a person or idea, and talk about them in a way that shows you think they are stupid: +**at** *Parker scoffed at the movie's critics.*

scoff·law /ˈskɔflɔ, ˈskɑf-/ *n.* [C] someone who often breaks the law, but in a way that is not very serious

scold[1] /skoʊld/ *v.* [T] to angrily criticize someone, especially a child, about something they have done: **scold sb for doing sth** *June scolded the boys for taking the candy without permission.* —**scolding** *n.* [C,U]

scold[2] *n.* [C] OLD-FASHIONED someone who often complains or criticizes

sco·li·o·sis /ˌskoʊliˈoʊsɪs/ *n.* [U] TECHNICAL a medical condition in which someone's SPINE is curved in a way that is not normal

sconce /skɑns/ *n.* [C] an object that is attached to a wall and holds CANDLES or electric lights

scone /skoʊn, skɑn/ *n.* [C] a small round type of bread, sometimes containing dried fruit

scoop

scoop[1] /skup/ *n.* [C] **1** a round deep spoon used for holding or serving food such as flour, sugar, or ICE CREAM: *an ice cream scoop* **2** also **scoopful** an amount of food served with this kind of spoon: +**of** *a big scoop of mashed potatoes* **3** an important or exciting news story that is printed in one newspaper or shown on one television station before any of the others know about it: *All the reporters were looking for a scoop.* **4 the scoop** INFORMAL news or new information about something: +**on** *the scoop on the best sales* | *Jones got **the inside scoop** on the band.* | **what's the scoop?** (=used to ask someone for information or news about something) [**Origin:** 1300–1400 Middle Dutch *schope*]

scoop[2] *v.* [T] **1** to pick something up with a scoop, a spoon, or with your curved hand: **scoop sth up/out/off etc.** *Cut the melon in half and scoop out the seeds.* **2** to be the first newspaper to print an important news report: *Charlie loved to scoop the competition.*

scoop sth ↔ **up** *phr. v.* if a lot of people scoop something up, they buy it quickly so that soon there is none left

ˈscoop ˌneck *n.* [C] a round fairly low neck on a woman's TOP or dress

scoot /skut/ *v.* INFORMAL **1** [I] to move to one side, especially to make room for someone or something else: +**over** *Can you scoot over?* **2** [I] to move quickly and suddenly: +**off/away/past etc.** *Matt scooted over the bridge on his skateboard.* **3** [T] to make someone or something move a short distance by pushing or pulling: *I scooted my chair over to their table.* **4 scoot!** SPOKEN used to tell someone to move or to leave a place quickly

scoot·er /ˈskuṭɚ/ *n.* [C] **1** also **ˈmotor ˌscooter** a type of small less powerful MOTORCYCLE **2** a child's vehicle with two small wheels, an upright handle, and a narrow board that you stand on with one foot, while the other foot pushes against the ground

scope[1] /skoʊp/ Ac *n.* [U] **1** the range of things that a subject, activity, book etc. deals with: *We need to define the scope of the program.* | *His efforts were too limited **in scope** to have an effect.* | **beyond/within the scope of sth** *A discussion of all the possible treatments is beyond the scope of this book.* | **broaden/expand the scope of sth** *The network is trying to expand the scope* *of children's TV.* | **narrow/limit the scope of sth** *Democrats want to limit the scope of the investigation.* **2** the opportunity to do or develop something: +**for** *Is there much scope for initiative in this job?* **3** an instrument or part of a piece of equipment used for looking at things through: *a rifle scope* [**Origin:** 1500–1600 Italian *scopo* **purpose**, from Greek *skopos*]

scope² Ac *v.* [T]

scope sb/sth ↔ **out** *phr. v.* INFORMAL to look at someone or something to see what they are like: *A couple of guys were scoping out the girls.*

Scopes trial, the /ˈskoʊps ˌtraɪəl/ HISTORY a TRIAL in Tennessee in 1925 at which John T. Scopes had to go to a court of law because he had taught about EVOLUTION in school. He was found guilty of breaking the law, but was later ACQUITted.

scorch¹ /skɔrtʃ/ *v.* **1** [I,T] if you scorch something, or if it scorches, its surface burns slightly and changes color: *The iron was too hot, and I scorched my shirt.* **2** [T] if strong heat scorches you, it burns you: *The hot sand scorched our feet.* **3** [T] if strong heat scorches plants, it dries them and kills them

scorch² *n.* **1** [C] a mark made on something where its surface has been burned **2** [U] brown coloring on plants caused by some plant diseases

ˌscorched-ˈearth ˌpolicy *n.* [C] the destruction by an army of everything useful in an area, especially crops and buildings, so that the land cannot be used by an enemy

scorch·er /ˈskɔrtʃɚ/ *n.* [C usually singular] INFORMAL an extremely hot day: *Today's going to be a scorcher.*

scorch·ing /ˈskɔrtʃɪŋ/ *adj.* **1** extremely hot SYN **searing**: *scorching temperatures* **2** criticizing someone or something in an extreme way SYN **scathing**: *a scorching appraisal of his work*

score¹ /skɔr/ S2 W3 *n.* [C]

1 IN A GAME the number of points that each team or player has won in a game or competition: *What's the score?* | *The score is tied at 82.* | *Barbara, can you* ***keep score*** (=keep a record of the points won)? | *The* ***final score*** *was 76–72.* | +**of** *She won with a score of 37.5.*

2 ON A TEST the number of points a student has earned for correct answers on a test: *Average* ***test scores*** *have fallen in recent years.*

3 RESULT OF SCIENTIFIC TEST/SURVEY a number of points or a rank that shows the result of a scientific test or of a SURVEY: *a high* ***IQ score*** (=measure of intelligence) | *A score between 70 and 90 shows you like to take risks.*

4 MUSIC ENG. LANG. ARTS a written or printed copy of a piece of music, especially for a large group of performers, or the music itself: *a* ***musical score*** | *Williams* ***wrote the score*** *for the movie.*

5 on that score SPOKEN concerning the particular thing you have just mentioned: *You won't get any complaints from me on that score.*

6 scores of sth a lot of: *Scores of reporters gathered outside the courthouse.*

7 settle a score to do something to harm or hurt someone who has harmed or hurt you in the past SYN **retaliate**: *Stanford settled an old score Friday by defeating Siena 94–72.*

8 know the score INFORMAL to know the real facts of a situation, including any bad ones: *If the salespeople knew the score, surely the managers did too.*

9 MARK a mark that has been cut onto a surface with a sharp tool: *deep scores in the wood*

10 NUMBER OLD USE twenty

[**Origin:** 1000–1100 Old Norse *skor* **mark cut into a surface, count, twenty**] → see also **know the score** at KNOW¹ (24)

score² S3 W2 *v.*

1 WIN POINTS [I,T] to win a point in a game, competition, or on a test: *Oregon scored twice in the last three minutes of the game.* | **score a point/run/touchdown etc.** *Mays scored the winning goal.*

2 IN A TEST/EXPERIMENT [I,T] to get points in a test, experiment, or SURVEY: *Most of the students scored above the national average.* | **score high/low** *Girls scored higher than boys in spelling.* | *Kentucky scored lowest on voter turnout.*

3 GIVE POINTS [T] to give a particular number of points in a game, competition, or test: *Participants will be scored on their performance in each event.*

4 score points (with sb) INFORMAL to do or say something to please someone or to make them feel respect for you: *Score points with your girlfriend by sending her flowers.*

5 SUCCEED [I,T] INFORMAL to be very successful in something you do: *He has scored again with this enjoyable movie.*

6 MUSIC ENG. LANG. ARTS **a)** to write the music for a movie, BALLET etc. **b)** to arrange a piece of music for a group of instruments or voices

7 GET DRUGS [I,T] SLANG to succeed in buying or getting illegal drugs

8 SEX [I] INFORMAL to have sex with someone

9 PAPER [T] to mark a line on a piece of paper, using a sharp instrument: *Scoring the paper first makes it easier to fold.*

score·board /ˈskɔrbɔrd/ *n.* [C] a board on which the points won in a game are shown

score·card /ˈskɔrkɑrd/ *n.* [C] **1** a printed card used by someone watching a game or race to record what happens **2** a system that is used for checking or testing something

score·keep·er /ˈskɔrˌkipɚ/ *n.* [C] someone who keeps an official record of the points won in a game

scor·er /ˈskɔrɚ/ *n.* [C] **1** a player who wins a point or GOAL **2** a scorekeeper

scorn¹ /skɔrn/ *n.* [U] the feeling that someone or something is stupid or does not deserve respect SYN **contempt**: +**for** *He could barely disguise his scorn for her.* | *They had treated the American flag* ***with scorn.*** | **heap/pour scorn on** (=strongly criticize something you think is stupid) *Republican leaders are heaping scorn on the plan.*

scorn² *v.* [T] to show that you think that a person, idea, or suggestion is stupid, unacceptable, or does not deserve respect SYN **disdain**: *Skinner's ideas were scorned by many psychologists.*

scorn·ful /ˈskɔrnfəl/ *adj.* feeling or showing scorn SYN **disdainful**: *a scornful look* | +**of** *He was scornful of religion.* —**scornfully** *adv.*

Scor·pi·o /ˈskɔrpiˌoʊ/ *n.* **1** [singular] the eighth sign of the ZODIAC, represented by a scorpion, and believed to affect the character and life of people born between October 23 and November 21 **2** [C] someone who was born between October 23 and November 21

scor·pi·on /ˈskɔrpiən/ *n.* [C] a tropical creature like an insect with a curving tail and a poisonous sting

Scot /skɑt/ *n.* [C] someone from Scotland

Scotch¹ /skɑtʃ/ *n.* [C,U] a type of WHISKEY (=strong alcoholic drink) made in Scotland, or a glass of this: *a Scotch and soda*

Scotch² *adj.* SCOTTISH

scotch /skɑtʃ/ *v.* [T] to stop something happening by firmly doing something to prevent it: *The mayor* ***scotched rumors*** *that he would be running for the Senate.*

ˌScotch ˈtape *n.* [U] TRADEMARK thin clear plastic in a narrow band that is sticky on one side, used for sticking light things such as paper together

ˈscotch-tape *v.* [T] to stick things together with Scotch tape

scot-free /ˌskɑt ˈfri/ *adv.* **get off scot-free** INFORMAL to avoid being punished, although you deserve to be [**Origin:** 1200–1300 *scot* **tax** (13–19 centuries), from Old Norse *skot* **shot, payment**]

Scot·land /ˈskɑtlənd/ a country in the United Kingdom, north of England

Scots·man /ˈskɑtsmən/ *n. plural* **Scotsmen** /-mən/ [C] a man who comes from Scotland

Scots·woman /ˈskɑts,wʊmən/ *n. plural* **Scotswomen** /-,wɪmɪn/ [C] a woman who comes from Scotland

Scott /skɑt/, **Dred** /drɛd/ (?1795–1858) an African-American who was born a slave, famous for a legal case in which he claimed that he should be a free man

Scott, Sir Wal·ter /ˈwɔltɚ/ (1771–1832) a Scottish writer and poet

Scot·tish /ˈskɑṭɪʃ/ *adj.* from or relating to Scotland

scoun·drel /ˈskaʊndrəl/ *n.* [C] OLD-FASHIONED a bad or dishonest man SYN **rogue**

scour /skaʊɚ/ *v.* [T] **1** to search an area, document etc. very carefully and thoroughly: *Rescue teams scoured the ruins for signs of more victims.* **2** also **scour out** to clean something very thoroughly by rubbing it with a rough material SYN **scrub**: *pots that had been scoured* ▸see THESAURUS box at **clean**[2] **3** also **scour out** to form a hole by continuous movement over a long period: *Over the years, the stream had scoured out a round pool in the rock.* —**scour** *n.* [singular]

scourge[1] /skɚdʒ, skɔrdʒ/ *n.* [C] **1** something that causes a lot of harm or suffering: +**of** *Gun violence is the scourge of our society.* **2** a WHIP used to punish people in past times [**Origin:** 1100–1200 Anglo-French *escorge*, from Old French *escorgier* **to whip**]

S

scourge[2] *v.* [T] LITERARY **1** to cause a lot of harm or suffering to a place or group of people **2** to hit someone with a whip as punishment in past times SYN **whip**

ˈscouring pad *n.* [C] a small ball of wire or rough plastic used in order to clean cooking pots and pans

scout[1] /skaʊt/ *n.* [C] **1** a soldier, plane etc. that is sent to search an area in front of an army and get information about the enemy: *Scouts reported on the position of the tanks.* **2** someone whose job is to look for good sports players, musicians etc. in order to employ them: *Davis caught the attention of NBA scouts a few years ago.* | *a* ***talent scout*** *for Maverick Records* → see also TALENT SCOUT **3 a) the Scouts** the organization of the BOY SCOUTS or the GIRL SCOUTS **b)** a member of the BOY SCOUTS or the GIRL SCOUTS

scout[2] *v.* **1** [I] also **scout around** to look for something in a particular area SYN **search**: +**for** *They're scouting for a site on which to build new offices.* **2** [T] also **scout out** to examine a place or area in order to get information about it, especially in a military situation SYN **reconnoiter**: *He set out to scout the surrounding countryside.* | *companies scouting out business opportunities* **3** [T] also **scout for** to find out about the abilities of sports players, musicians etc., in order to employ the best ones [**Origin:** 1300–1400 Old French *escouter* **to listen**, from Latin *auscultare*]

scout·ing /ˈskaʊṭɪŋ/ *n.* [U] the activities that BOY SCOUTS and GIRL SCOUTS take part in

scout·mas·ter /ˈskaʊtˀ,mæstɚ/ *n.* [C] a man who is the leader of a group of BOY SCOUTS

scow /skaʊ/ *n.* [C] a large boat with a flat bottom, used mainly for carrying heavy goods

scowl[1] /skaʊl/ *v.* [I] to look at someone in an angry way SYN **glower**: +**at** *Nancy scowled at me from across the room.*

scowl[2] *n.* [C] an angry or disapproving expression on someone's face

Scrab·ble /ˈskræbəl/ *n.* [U] TRADEMARK a game in which players try to make words from the separate letters they have

scrab·ble /ˈskræbəl/ *v.* [I always + adv./prep.] to try to find something quickly by feeling with your fingers, especially among a lot of other things: **scrabble for sth** *She scrabbled under the bed for her slippers.* [**Origin:** 1500–1600 Dutch *schrabbelen* **to scratch**]

scrag·gly /ˈskrægli/ *adj.* INFORMAL growing in a way that looks uneven and not well taken care of: *a scraggly beard*

scram /skræm/ *v.* **scrammed, scramming** [I usually in imperative] SPOKEN to leave a place very quickly, especially so that you do not get caught: *Scram, kid!*

scram·ble[1] /ˈskræmbəl/ *v.*

1 CLIMB [I always + adv./prep.] to climb up, down, or over something quickly and with difficulty, especially using your hands to help you: +**up/down/over etc.** *The suspect scrambled over a fence.* | *Fans scrambled onto the stage.*

2 MOVE QUICKLY [I always + adv./prep.] to move somewhere quickly, especially in an awkward way: +**to/out/from etc.** *Campers scrambled to safety when a flash flood came down the canyon.* | *I scrambled out of bed, late as usual.*

3 DO STH QUICKLY [T] to try to do something difficult very quickly: **scramble to do sth** *Everyone had to scramble to finish the project on time.*

4 STRUGGLE/COMPETE [I,T] to struggle to get or reach something, or compete with other people to do this: +**for** *People were scrambling for the seats in the front row.* | **scramble to do sth** *working parents who are scrambling to make a living*

5 INFORMATION/MESSAGE [T] to use special equipment to mix messages, radio signals etc. into a different form, so that they cannot be understood by other people without the correct equipment: *Cable TV companies scramble their signals, so you can't watch without paying.*

6 scramble an egg to cook an egg by mixing the white and yellow parts together and heating it

7 FOOTBALL if a football player, especially the QUARTERBACK, scrambles, he runs around with the football in order to avoid being TACKLED (=stopped by the defense)

8 MIX [T] to mix words, ideas, sentences etc., so that they are not in the right order and do not make sense: *In this game, the letters of the words are scrambled.*

9 scramble to your feet to stand up quickly and awkwardly: *He scrambled to his feet as the ambassador entered the room.*

10 scramble sb's brains INFORMAL to make someone unable to think clearly or reasonably: *This amount of LSD is enough to scramble anyone's brains.*

11 AIRCRAFT [I,T] TECHNICAL if military airplanes scramble or if someone scrambles them, they are sent up into the air very quickly in order to escape or to attack an enemy

scramble[2] *n.* [singular] **1** a situation in which people compete with and push each other in order to get what they want: +**for** *There was a scramble for the best seats.* | **a scramble to do sth** *a scramble to reach the exits* **2** a situation in which something has to be done very quickly, with a lot of rushing around: *It was a* ***mad scramble*** *trying to get things ready in time.*

ˌscrambled ˈeggs *n.* [plural] eggs that have been cooked after mixing the white and yellow parts together

scram·bler /ˈskræmblɚ/ *n.* [C] a machine that mixes up a radio or telephone message so that it cannot be understood without special equipment → see also DESCRAMBLER

scrap[1] /skræp/ *n.* **1** [C] a small piece of paper, cloth etc.: +**of** *a message on a scrap of paper* | *Save those fabric scraps to make a quilt.* ▸see THESAURUS box at **piece**[1] **2** [U] materials or objects that are not used anymore for the purpose they were made for, but can be used again in another way: *The Kempers sold their old car to a scrap dealer.* | **scrap metal** (=metal from old cars, machines etc. that is melted and used again) **3** [C] a small piece of information, truth etc.: +**of** *There isn't a scrap of evidence.* **4 scraps** [plural] pieces of food that are left after you have finished eating: **table/kitchen scraps** *They fed the dog on table scraps.* **5** [C] INFORMAL a short fight or argument: *He got into a scrap with a neighbor boy.* ▸see THESAURUS box at **fight**[2] [**Origin:** (1–4) 1300–1400 Old Norse *skrap* **scraps**]

scrap[2] *v.* **scrapped, scrapping 1** [T] to decide not to use a plan or system: *The program was finally scrapped.* **2** [T] to get rid of an old machine, vehicle etc., and use its parts in some other way: *Thousands of older planes will be scrapped.* **3** [I] INFORMAL to have a short fight or argument

scrap·book /ˈskræpbʊk/ *n.* [C] a book with empty pages where you can stick pictures, newspaper articles, or other things you want to keep

scrape¹ /skreɪp/ *v.* **1** [T] to remove something from a surface or clean a surface, using the edge of a knife, stick etc.: *You'll need to scrape the windshield – it's covered in ice.* | **scrape sth away/off etc.** *Barbara used a stick to scrape the mud off her boots.* | **scrape sth clean** *Scrape your plate clean and put it in the sink.* **2** [I always + adv./prep., T] to rub against a rough surface in a way that causes slight damage or injury, or to make something do this SYN **graze**: **+on/against etc.** *The side of the car scraped against the wall.* | **scrape sth on/against etc. sth** *Tim fell down and scraped his knee on the sidewalk.* **3** [I,T] to make a noise by rubbing roughly against a surface SYN **grate**: *Metal scraped loudly as the snowplow drove past.* | **scrape (sth) along/down/against etc.** *Branches scraped against the house in the wind.* **4 scrape the bottom of the barrel** INFORMAL to have to use something even though it is not very good, because there is nothing better available: *We'll really be scraping the bottom of the barrel if we hire him.*

scrape by *phr. v.* **1** to have just enough money to live SYN **get by**: **+on** *We had to scrape by on welfare for two years.* **2** to just manage to succeed in passing a test or dealing with a difficult situation

scrape in/into *phr. v.* to just manage to succeed in getting a job, getting into college, etc.: **scrape into sth** *Dave just scraped into the local college.*

scrape through *phr. v.* to just manage to succeed in passing a test or dealing with a difficult situation: **scrape through sth** *Dani just scraped through her driving test.*

scrape sth ↔ **together/up** *phr. v.* to get enough money for a particular purpose, when this is difficult: *She scraped together enough money to start a small florist business.*

scrape² *n.* **1** [C] a mark or slight injury caused by rubbing against a rough surface SYN **abrasion**: *a few* ***cuts and scrapes*** *on her back* ▸see THESAURUS box at **injury** **2** [C] a situation in which you get into trouble or have difficulties: **+with** *He had a few scrapes with the law as a kid* **3** [C usually singular] the noise made when one surface rubs roughly against another: *She got up with a scrape of her chair.*

scrap·er /ˈskreɪpɚ/ *n.* [C] a tool whose edge is used to remove something from a surface: *a paint scraper*

ˈscrap heap *n.* **1 the scrap heap** INFORMAL the situation of not being wanted or used any longer, especially in a way that seems unfair: *Older employees may just end up* ***on the scrap heap***. **2** [C] a pile of unwanted things, especially pieces of metal

scra·pie /ˈskreɪpi/ *n.* [U] a serious disease that sheep get

scrap·ings /ˈskreɪpɪŋz/ *n.* [plural] small pieces that have been SCRAPEd from a surface

scrap·py /ˈskræpi/ *adj.* INFORMAL APPROVING having a strong determined character and being willing to fight or argue with people: *a scrappy team that plays hard*

ˈscrap yard, scrapyard *n.* [C] a business that buys old materials and goods and sells the parts that can be used again

scratch¹ /skrætʃ/ S2 *v.*

1 RUB YOUR SKIN [I,T] to rub your skin with your nails, especially because it ITCHes: *Try not to scratch.* | *Tom scratched his nose.* | **+at** *She scratched at the bites on her arm.* ▸see THESAURUS box at **touch¹**

2 MAKE A MARK [T] to make a small cut or mark on something by pulling something sharp or rough across it: *Don't use that cleaner – it'll scratch the sink.*

3 CUT YOUR SKIN [I,T] to cut someone's skin slightly with your nails or with something sharp: *I scratched my hand on a rusty nail.* | *Careful – that cat scratches.*

4 ANIMAL [I always + adv./prep.] if an animal scratches, it rubs its feet against something, often making a noise: *A few chickens were scratching around in the yard.* | **+at** *The dog kept scratching at the door to be let in.*

5 scratch the surface to deal with only a very small part of a subject: *So far, we have only scratched the surface of the information available on this topic.*

6 scratch your head INFORMAL to not know the answer or solution to something, and to have to think hard about it: *The last question really left us scratching our heads.* | *Budget directors are scratching their heads about how to deal with the shortfall.*

7 NOISE [I always + adv./prep.] to make a noise by rubbing something with a sharp or pointed object: *His pen scratched along the paper.*

8 REMOVE STH [T always + adv./prep.] to remove something from a surface by rubbing it with something sharp: **scratch sth off/away etc.** *I scratched off some of the paint.*

9 NOT DO STH [T] if you scratch an idea, a plan etc., you decide that you will not do it: *Well, I guess we can scratch that idea.*

10 NOT INCLUDE SB/STH [T] if you scratch someone off a list, you take their name off the list: **scratch sb/sth from/off sth** *Jones was scratched from the lineup due to an injury.*

11 you scratch my back, I'll scratch yours SPOKEN used to say that you will help someone if they agree to help you

12 REMOVE FROM RACE [T usually passive] to remove someone from a race or competition before it begins

scratch sth ↔ **out** *phr. v.* to draw a line through a word, in order to remove it: *Phil's name had been scratched out with a black pen.*

scratch² S3 *n.* **1** [C] a thin mark or cut on the surface of something or on someone's skin: **+on** *a scratch on the car door* | *Several people were treated for minor* ***cuts and scratches***. | *Miraculously, Liz survived the fall* ***without a scratch*** (=not injured at all). **2 from scratch** if you do or start something from scratch, you begin it without using anything that existed or was prepared before: *The company was* ***started from scratch*** *in 1995, but has grown quickly.* | *Doug baked the cake from scratch* (=not using a cake mix from a box). **3** [C] a sound made by something sharp or rough being rubbed on a hard surface: *the scratch of a match being lit*

scratch³ *adj.* [no comparative] a scratch player in a sport, especially GOLF, does not have a HANDICAP

ˌscratch-and-ˈsniff *adj.* [only before noun] a scratch-and-sniff book, printed advertisement etc. has a special dry substance on its surface that produces a smell when you scratch it

ˈscratch pad *n.* [C] several sheets of cheap paper fastened together at the top or side, used for writing notes or lists

ˈscratch ˌpaper *n.* [U] cheap paper, or paper that has already been used on one side, that you use for making notes, lists etc.

scratch·y /ˈskrætʃi/ *adj.* *comparative* **scratchier**, *superlative* **scratchiest** **1** scratchy clothes or materials feel rough and uncomfortable **2** a scratchy voice sounds deep and rough **3** a scratchy throat feels sore **4** a scratchy record makes a lot of noise because it is old or damaged —**scratchiness** *n.* [U]

scrawl¹ /skrɔl/ *v.* [T] to write in a careless and messy way, so that your words are not easy to read, though they are often large SYN **scribble**: *Jim scrawled his signature across the bottom of the page.*

scrawl² *n.* [C, singular] something written in a messy careless way, or a messy careless way of writing: *The note was written in Gwen's childish scrawl.*

scraw·ny /ˈskrɔni/ *adj.* *comparative* **scrawnier**, *superlative* **scrawniest** a scrawny person or animal looks thin, unattractive, and weak [**Origin:** 1800–1900 *scranny* **thin**]

scream¹ /skrim/ S2 W3 *v.* **1** [I] to make a loud high noise with your voice because you are hurt, frightened, excited etc. SYN **shriek**: *There was a loud bang, and people started screaming.* | *a screaming baby* | **+with/in** *She was screaming with pain.* | *He threw himself onto*

S

*the floor, **kicking and screaming**.* ►see THESAURUS box at shout[1] **2** [I,T] also **scream out** to shout something in a very loud high voice because you are angry or frightened SYN yell: *"Get out!" she screamed.* | *They were screaming insults at each other.* | +**for** *I screamed for help.* | +**at** *She's been screaming at her kids all morning.* **3** [I] to make a very loud high noise: *The police car sped by with its siren screaming.* → see also **scream/yell bloody murder** at BLOODY[1] (3)

scream[2] *n.* [C] **1** a loud high sound made with your voice because you are very frightened, angry, hurt, or excited SYN shriek SYN yell: *There were screams coming from the alley.* | *We heard a **piercing scream** followed by two gunshots.* | **scream of joy/pain etc.** *the children's screams of excitement* | *He **let out a scream** of terror.* **2** a very loud high sound: *the scream of a jet taking off* **3 be a scream** INFORMAL used to describe someone or something that is very funny: *Did you see that show last night? What a scream!*

scree /skri/ *n.* [U] EARTH SCIENCE an area of loose broken rocks on the side of a mountain

screech /skritʃ/ *v.* **1** [I] if a vehicle or its wheels screech, they make a loud high noise as it is stopping: *The plane's tires screeched as it touched down.* | *screeching brakes* | **screech to a halt/stop/standstill** (=stop very suddenly with a loud noise) **2** [I,T] to make a loud high noise with your voice, especially because you are angry SYN shriek: *"Where is it?" Callie screeched.* [**Origin:** 1500–1600 *scritch* **to screech** (13–20 centuries), from the sound] —**screech** *n.* [singular] *a screech of tires*

S

screen[1] /skrin/ S2 W2 *n.*

1 TV/COMPUTER [C] the flat glass part of a television or computer, on which you see words, pictures etc.: *a huge TV screen* | *It's easier to correct your work **on screen** than on paper.*

2 MOVIES a) [C] the large white surface that pictures are shown on in a movie theater **b)** [singular, U] movies in general: *Her play was adapted for **the big screen**.* | *She was a star of **stage and screen**.* | *He first appeared on the **silver screen** (=in movies) in the 1930s.*

3 DOOR/WINDOW [C] a wire net fastened inside a frame in front of a window or door that allows air into the house but keeps insects out

4 MOVABLE WALL [C] a piece of furniture like a thin wall that can be moved around, used to divide one part of a room from another SYN partition: *a screen around the patient's bed*

5 STH THAT HIDES a) [C] something tall and wide that hides a place or thing: *a screen of high bushes* **b)** [singular] something that hides what someone is doing: +**for** *The business was a screen for drug dealing.*

6 SPORTS [C] a player or group of players in a game such as BASKETBALL who protect the player who has the ball

7 TEST FOR ILLNESS a SCREENING

[**Origin:** 1300–1400 Old French *escren*, from Middle Dutch *scherm*] → see also SMOKESCREEN, SUNSCREEN

screen[2] S3 *v.* [T] **1** to do tests on people, blood etc. to find out whether they have a particular illness: *Blood banks now screen all blood supplies.* | **screen sb for sth** *Women over 50 should be screened for breast cancer.* **2** to hide or protect something by putting something in front of it: **screen sth (off) from sth** *The hedge screens the yard from the street.* **3** to find out information about people in order to decide whether you can trust them or whether they are the right people to work for you: *Applicants are screened for security reasons.* **4** to show a movie or television program: *The movie will be screened on television for the first time on Saturday night.* **5** to check things to see whether they are acceptable or appropriate: *You can use an answering machine to **screen** your **calls**.*

screen sth ↔ **out** *phr. v.* **1** to remove people or things that are not acceptable or not appropriate SYN filter out: *The software screens out sites that are not appropriate for children.* **2** to prevent something from entering or passing through: *The low clouds screened out all but a hint of sunshine.*

'screen ˌdoor *n.* [C] a door that will let air in but keep insects out, that consists of a wire net inside a frame and is put outside the main door

'screen dump *n.* [C] COMPUTERS a picture of everything that appears on a computer screen at a particular time, that you can print or save in your computer

ˌscreened 'porch also **'screen porch** *n.* [C] an area with a roof but no walls, built onto the outside of the ground floor of a house and with SCREENS to let air in but keep insects out

screen·ing /'skrinɪŋ/ *n.* **1** [C,U] MEDICINE medical tests that are done to make sure that someone does not have a disease or is generally healthy: +**for** *screenings for breast cancer* **2** [C,U] the showing of a movie or television program: *the 7:30 screening of the movie* **3** [U] tests or checks done to make sure that someone or something is appropriate or acceptable for a particular purpose: *security screening* | *the screening of potential jurors*

screen·play /'skrinpleɪ/ *n.* [C] the words that are written down for actors to say in a movie or television program SYN script: *He wrote the screenplay for "Psycho."*

'screen ˌprinting *n.* [U] SILK-SCREENING

'screen ˌsaver *n.* [C] COMPUTERS a computer program that makes a moving image appear on a computer screen when the image on it has not changed for a period of time, so that the screen does not become damaged

'screen ˌtest *n.* [C] an occasion when someone is filmed while performing, in order to see if they are good enough to act in a movie

screen·writ·er /'skrinˌraɪt̬ɚ/ *n.* [C] someone who writes plays for movies or television programs —**screenwriting** *n.* [U]

screw[1] /skru/ S3 *n.* **1** [C] a thin pointed piece of metal that you push and turn in order to fasten pieces of metal or wood together: *You just need to **tighten** these two **screws** here.* **2 have a screw loose** also **have a few screws loose** INFORMAL HUMOROUS to be slightly crazy **3 tighten/put the screws (on sb)** INFORMAL to force someone to do something by threatening them: *The law tightens the screws on industries that pollute.* [**Origin:** 1400–1500 Old French *escroe* **inner screw, nut**, from Latin *scrofa* **female pig**]

screw[2] *v.*

1 ATTACH [I,T always + adv./prep.] to attach one object to another using a screw: **screw (sth) into/onto/to sth** *The kitchen cabinets are screwed to the walls.* | *The table legs just screw into the top like this.*

2 CLOSE BY TURNING [T always + adv./prep.] to fasten or close something by turning it until it cannot be turned anymore SYN twist: **screw sth on/together etc.** *The kids always forget to screw the cap back on the bottle.*

3 screw up your eyes/face/mouth etc. to move the muscles around your eyes, mouth etc. in a way that makes them seem narrow: *Lynn screwed up her face in disgust.* | *I screwed my eyes tight and concentrated.*

4 PAPER/CLOTH [T always + adv./prep.] also **screw up** to twist paper or cloth into a small round shape: **screw sth (up) into sth** *She screwed her handkerchief into a ball.*

5 screw sb also **screw sb over** SLANG to cheat someone or treat them in a dishonest or unfair way SYN cheat: *The dealer really screwed us over when we bought this car.* | **screw sb out of sth** *Sue's sister screwed her out of her share of the money.*

6 be screwed SLANG to be in a lot of trouble or in a very difficult situation: *If Dad finds out about this, we're screwed!* → see also **have your head screwed on (right/straight)** at HEAD[1] (22)

screw around *phr. v.* INFORMAL **1** to spend time doing silly things: *Some kids were screwing around outside.* **2** to cause trouble or problems for someone, especially by changing something that they think should not be changed: +**with** *Someone's been screwing around with my computer.*

screw up *phr. v.* **1** INFORMAL to make a bad mistake or do something very stupid SYN mess up: *If you screw* *up again, you're fired!* **2 screw sth ↔ up** INFORMAL to spoil something by doing something stupid, especially by making something not organized SYN **mess sth up**: *Dave screwed up my files, so now I can't find anything.* | *She realized that she had screwed up her life.* **3 screw sb ↔ up** INFORMAL to make someone feel very unhappy, confused, or anxious, especially for a long time SYN **mess sb up**: *Living with my parents is enough to screw anybody up.* → see also SCREWED UP **4 screw up your courage** also **screw up the/enough courage to do sth** to try to be brave enough to do something you are very nervous about: *Mike screwed up his courage and started dialing her number.*

screw·ball /ˈskrubɔl/ *n.* [C] INFORMAL **1** someone or something who seems very strange or crazy **2 screwball comedy** a movie or television program that is funny because crazy things happen

screw·driv·er /ˈskruˌdraɪvɚ/ *n.* [C] **1** a tool with a narrow blade at one end that you use for turning screws **2** an alcoholic drink made from VODKA and orange juice

ˌscrewed ˈup *adj.* INFORMAL **1** someone who is screwed up has a lot of emotional problems because of bad or unhappy experiences in the past **2** not arranged in the correct order, or not in the correct place: *the state's screwed-up finances*

ˈscrew top *n.* [C] a cover that you twist onto the top of a bottle or other container

screw·y /ˈskrui/ *adj.* INFORMAL an idea, plan etc. that is screwy seems strange or crazy SYN **crazy**

scrib·ble[1] /ˈskrɪbəl/ *v.* **1** [T] to write something quickly and in a messy way: *She scribbled her phone number on a slip of paper.* **2** [I] to draw marks that have no meaning: *Ashley scribbled all over her bedroom walls in crayon.* ▶see THESAURUS box at **draw**[1]

scribble[2] *n.* **1 scribbles** [plural] meaningless marks or pictures, especially done by children **2** [singular, U] messy writing that is difficult to read

scrib·bler /ˈskrɪblɚ/ *n.* [C] INFORMAL a writer, especially an unimportant one

scribe /skraɪb/ *n.* [C] **1** someone whose job was to make written copies of books or documents, especially before printing was invented **2** HUMOROUS a writer, especially a JOURNALIST

scrim·mage /ˈskrɪmɪdʒ/ *n.* [C] a practice game of football, basketball etc. → see also LINE OF SCRIMMAGE —**scrimmage** *v.* [I]

scrimp /skrɪmp/ *v.* [I] to try to save as much money as you can, even though you have very little, especially by buying cheaper things SYN **economize**: *My parents **scrimped and saved** to pay for my education.*

scrimp on sth *phr. v.* to pay too little money for something or buy something that is cheap and of bad quality: *Airlines can't scrimp on security measures.*

scrip /skrɪp/ *n.* **1** [U] an official piece of paper that someone can use like money in a particular situation **2** [C] SPOKEN a PRESCRIPTION

script[1] /skrɪpt/ S2 *n.* **1** [C] ENG. LANG. ARTS the written form of a speech, play, movie etc.: *Mamet wrote the script himself.* | *a movie script* **2** [C,U] ENG. LANG. ARTS the set of letters used in writing a language SYN **alphabet**: *Arabic script* **3** [singular, U] FORMAL writing done by hand, especially with the letters of the words joined SYN **handwriting**: *a beautiful 18th-century script* [**Origin:** 1300–1400 Latin *scriptum* **something written**, from *scribere*]

script[2] *v.* [T] **1** to write a speech, play, movie etc.: *The film was scripted by author Armistead Maupin.* **2** to plan all the details of an event, with the result that it does not seem natural: *The day's events were **carefully scripted** to avoid reporters' questions.* —**scripted** *adj.*

scrip·tur·al /ˈskrɪptʃərəl/ *adj.* relating to or based on holy books

scrip·ture /ˈskrɪptʃɚ/ *n.* **1** [U] also **the (Holy) Scriptures** [plural] the Christian Bible **2** [C,U] the holy books of a particular religion: *Buddhist scriptures*

script·writ·er /ˈskrɪptˌraɪtɚ/ *n.* [C] someone who writes SCRIPTS for movies, television etc.

scrod /skrɑd/ *n.* [U] the white meat of a young fish, especially COD or HADDOCK

scroll[1] /skroʊl/ *n.* [C] **1** ENG. LANG. ARTS a long piece of paper that can be rolled up, and is used as an official document, especially in past times **2** a decoration shaped like a roll of paper [**Origin:** 1400–1500 *scrow* **scroll** (13–17 centuries), from Old French *escroue* **piece of paper, scroll**; influenced by *roll*]

scroll[2] *v.* [I,T] COMPUTERS to move information on a computer screen up or down so that you can read it: **+up/down** *Scroll down a little – look.* | **+through** *He scrolled through the text.*

scroll·work /ˈskroʊlwɚk/ *n.* [U] TECHNICAL decoration in the shape of scrolls

Scrooge, **scrooge** /skrudʒ/ *n.* [C] INFORMAL someone who hates spending money SYN **miser** [**Origin:** 1800–1900 Ebenezer *Scrooge*, character in "A Christmas Carol" (1843) by Charles Dickens]

scro·tum /ˈskroʊṭəm/ *n.* *plural* **scrota** /-ṭə/ or **scrotums** [C] BIOLOGY the bag of skin attached to the outside of the body that contains the TESTICLES of men and male animals

scrounge /skraʊndʒ/ *v.* [I,T] to get money or something you want by asking other people for it or searching through other things for it, rather than by paying for it: **+up** *She uses whatever she can scrounge up in her sculptures.* | **scrounge (around) for sth** *Children were scrounging around in garbage cans for food.* [**Origin:** 1900–2000 *scrunge* **to steal**] —**scrounger** *n.* [C]

scrub[1] /skrʌb/ *v.* **scrubbed, scrubbing 1** [I,T] to rub something hard, especially with something rough, in order to clean it: *The kitchen floor needs to be scrubbed.* | *the children's **freshly scrubbed** faces* ▶see THESAURUS box at **clean**[2] **2** [T usually passive] INFORMAL to decide not to do something that you had planned, especially because there is a problem SYN **cancel**: *The shuttle launch was scrubbed just ten minutes before liftoff.* [**Origin:** 1200–1300 Low German or a Scandinavian language]

scrub sth ↔ **down** *phr. v.* to clean the surface of something thoroughly

scrub sth ↔ **out** *phr. v.* to clean the inside of something thoroughly: *She scrubbed out the toilet.*

scrub up *phr. v.* to wash your hands and arms before doing a medical operation

scrub[2] *n.* **1** [U] BIOLOGY low bushes and trees that grow in very dry soil SYN **brush** **2 scrubs** [plural] INFORMAL a loose green shirt and pants worn by doctors during medical operations

scrub·ber /ˈskrʌbɚ/ *n.* [C] a plastic or metal object or a brush that you use to clean pans or floors

ˈscrub brush *n.* [C] a stiff brush that you use for cleaning things → see picture at BRUSH[1]

scrub·by /ˈskrʌbi/ *adj.* covered by low bushes: *scrubby terrain*

scrub·land /ˈskrʌblænd/ *n.* [U] EARTH SCIENCE land that is covered with low bushes

scruff /skrʌf/ *n.* **by the scruff of the neck** if you hold a person or animal by the scruff of their neck, you hold the flesh, fur, or clothes at the back of the neck

scruff·y /ˈskrʌfi/ *adj.* *comparative* **scruffier**, *superlative* **scruffiest** dirty and messy and not taken care of very well: *a scruffy sweatshirt* [**Origin:** 1800–1900 *scruff* **messy person** (19–21 centuries), from *scurf*]

scrum /skrʌm/ *n.* [C] a part of a game of RUGBY, in which the players all push close together in a circle with their heads down and try to get the ball with their feet

scrump·tious /ˈskrʌmpʃəs/ *adj.* INFORMAL food that is scrumptious tastes very good SYN **delicious**

scrunch /skrʌntʃ/ also **scrunch up** *v.* [T always + adv./prep.] INFORMAL to crush and twist something into a

S

smaller shape: *She scrunched the letter into a ball.* | *He scrunched his eyes up, trying to see.*

scrunch·ie /ˈskrʌntʃi/ *n.* [C] a circular rubber band that is covered with cloth, used for holding hair in a PONYTAIL

scru·ple¹ /ˈskrupəl/ *n.* [C usually plural] a belief about right and wrong that prevents you from doing something bad: *He* ***has*** *absolutely* ***no scruples about*** *claiming other people's work as his own.* [**Origin:** 1400–1500 Old French *scrupule*, from Latin *scrupulus* **small sharp stone, cause of mental discomfort**]

scruple² *v.* **not scruple to do sth** FORMAL to be willing to do something, even though it may have harmful or bad effects: *They did not scruple to bomb innocent civilians.*

scru·pu·lous /ˈskrupyələs/ *adj.* **1** careful to be completely honest and fair SYN **principled** OPP **unscrupulous**: *a scrupulous lawyer* | +**about** *They were scrupulous about repaying their loans.* **2** very careful and thorough so that everything is done and nothing is missed: *a* ***scrupulous attention to detail*** —**scrupulously** *adv.*: *scrupulously clean* —**scrupulousness** *n.* [U]

scru·ti·nize /ˈskrutˀnˌaɪz/ *v.* [T] to examine someone or something very thoroughly and carefully SYN **examine**: *He* ***scrutinized*** *the photo* ***closely***.

scru·ti·ny /ˈskrutˀn-i/ *n.* [U] careful and thorough examination of someone or something SYN **examination**: **careful/close/intense scrutiny** *There will be a closer scrutiny of tax returns.* | *Their fund-raising methods have* ***come under scrutiny*** *from the Justice Department.* [**Origin:** 1400–1500 Latin *scrutinium*, from *scrutari* **to search, examine**, from *scruta* **unwanted things, trash**]

SCSI /ˈskʌzi/ *n.* [U] COMPUTERS **Small Computer Systems Interface** something that helps a small computer work with another piece of electronic equipment, such as a PRINTER, especially when they are connected by wires

scu·ba div·ing /ˈskubə ˌdaɪvɪŋ/ *n.* [U] the sport of swimming under water while breathing through a tube that is connected to a container of air on your back [**Origin:** 1900–2000 *self-contained underwater breathing apparatus*] —**scuba diver** *n.* [C]

scuba diving

scud /skʌd/ *v.* **scudded, scudding** [I always + adv./prep.] LITERARY if clouds scud across the sky, they move quickly

scuff /skʌf/ *v.* [T often passive] to make a mark on a smooth surface by rubbing it against something rough —**scuff** *n.* [C]

scuffed /skʌft/ *adj.* marked because of being rubbed against something rough: *scuffed brown shoes*

scuf·fle /ˈskʌfəl/ *n.* [C] a short fight that is not very violent or serious SYN **fight** SYN **tussle**: +**with/between** *A brief* ***scuffle broke out*** *between fans after the game.* ▸see THESAURUS box at **fight²** —**scuffle** *v.* [I]

scuf·fling /ˈskʌflɪŋ/ *n.* [U] soft noises made by someone or something that is moving around where you cannot see it: *scuffling noises behind the wall*

ˈscuff mark *n.* [C] a mark made on something when something rough has been rubbed against it

scull¹ /skʌl/ *n.* [C] **1** a small light boat for only one person, used in races **2** one of the OARS that you use to move this boat along

scull² *v.* [I,T] to ROW a small light boat

scul·le·ry /ˈskʌləri/ *n. plural* **sculleries** [C] a room next to the kitchen, especially in a large old house, where cleaning jobs were done in past times

sculpt /skʌlpt/ *v.* [T often passive] **1** ENG. LANG. ARTS to shape stone, wood, clay etc. in order to make a solid object that represents someone or something: *The statue is sculpted in solid marble.* **2** to make something into a particular shape as a result of a natural process, for example the movement of a river

sculpt·ed /ˈskʌlptɪd/ *adj.* [only before noun] having a clear smooth shape that looks as though an artist has made it: *high sculpted cheekbones*

sculp·tor /ˈskʌlptɚ/ *n.* [C] someone who makes sculptures

sculp·tur·al /ˈskʌlptʃərəl/ *adj.* [only before noun] having a clear shape that looks as though an artist has made it

sculp·ture /ˈskʌlptʃɚ/ *n.* **1** [U] ENG. LANG. ARTS the art of making objects out of stone, wood, clay etc.: *modern painting and sculpture* ▸see THESAURUS box at **art¹** **2** [C] an object made out of stone, metal, clay etc. by an artist: *a life-size bronze sculpture* [**Origin:** 1300–1400 Latin *sculptura*, from *sculpere* **to carve**]

sculp·tured /ˈskʌlptʃɚd/ *adj.* **1** [only before noun] decorated with sculptures, or formed into a particular shape by an artist: *sculptured plaques and statues* **2** having a smooth attractive shape: *his sculptured muscles*

scum /skʌm/ *n.* **1** [singular, U] a dirty substance that forms on the surface of a liquid: *soap scum on the bathtub* **2** [C] *plural* **scum** SPOKEN a bad and nasty person: *They treated me like scum.* | **scum of the earth** (=the worst people you can imagine) —**scummy** *adj.*

scum·bag /ˈskʌmbæg/ *n.* [C] SPOKEN a bad and nasty person

scup·per /ˈskʌpɚ/ *n.* [C] TECHNICAL a hole in the side of a ship that allows water to flow back into the ocean

scur·ri·lous /ˈskɚələs, ˈskʌr-/ *adj.* FORMAL scurrilous remarks, articles etc. contain damaging and untrue statements about someone [**Origin:** 1500–1600 Latin *scurrilis*, from *scurra* **stupid person**]

scur·ry /ˈskɚi, ˈskʌri/ *v.* **scurries, scurried, scurrying** [I always + adv./prep.] to move quickly with short steps SYN **hurry**: +**along/past/across** *A mouse scurried across the floor.*

S-curve /ˈɛs kɚv/ *n.* [C] a curve in a road in the shape of an "S," that can be dangerous to drivers

scur·vy /ˈskɚvi/ *n.* [U] MEDICINE a disease caused by not eating foods such as fruit and vegetables that contain VITAMIN C

scut·tle¹ /ˈskʌtl̩/ *v.* **1** [T] to ruin or end someone's plans or chance of being successful: *The senator did his best to scuttle the tax increase.* **2** [I always + adv./prep.] to move quickly with short steps, especially because you are afraid and do not want to be noticed SYN **scurry**: +**along/past/down** *Crabs scuttled out of their holes.* **3** [T] to sink a ship by making holes in the bottom, especially in order to prevent it from being used by an enemy SYN **sink**

scuttle² *n.* [C] a container for carrying coal

scut·tle·butt /ˈskʌtl̩ˌbʌt/ *n.* [U] INFORMAL stories about other people's personal lives, especially stories that are unkind and untrue SYN **gossip** SYN **rumor**

scuz·zy /ˈskʌzi/ *adj. comparative* **scuzzier**, *superlative* **scuzziest** INFORMAL disgusting and dirty: *a scuzzy part of the city*

scythe /saɪð/ *n.* [C] a farming tool that has a long curved blade attached to a long wooden handle, and is used to cut grain or long grass

SD the written abbreviation of SOUTH DAKOTA

SDI *n.* the abbreviation for STRATEGIC DEFENSE INITIATIVE

S.E., SE the written abbreviation of SOUTHEAST

sea /si/ W1 *n.* **1** [C] EARTH SCIENCE a large area of salty water that is mostly enclosed by land: *the Mediterranean Sea* **2** [singular, U] a word meaning "ocean," used especially when talking about traveling in a ship or boat: *the creatures of **land and sea** | Waste is dumped **in the sea**.* | *ships **at sea*** (=on the ocean) | *Five sailors were **lost at sea*** (=drowned). | *Some troops arrived **by sea*** (=traveling in a ship). | *The bottle gradually drifted **out to sea*** (=away from land). | *The bay was calmer than **the open sea*** (=part of the sea far from land). **3 a sea of sth** a large number or quantity of something: *She looked out over a vast sea of cars.* **4 the seas** LITERARY the ocean, used especially when you are not talking about a particular ocean **5 be/feel at sea** to be confused or not sure what to do SYN **bewildered**: *It was her first day, and she felt completely at sea.* **6** [C] PHYSICS one of the broad plains on the moon and Mars [**Origin:** Old English *sæ*] → see also HIGH SEAS, **the seven seas** at SEVEN (4)

ˈsea aˌnemone *n.* [C] a small brightly-colored animal that sticks onto rocks under the surface of the ocean and looks like a flower

sea•bed, sea bed /ˈsibɛd/ *n.* [singular] the land at the bottom of the ocean SYN **seafloor**

sea•bird /ˈsibɚd/ *n.* [C] a bird that lives near the ocean and finds food in it

sea•board /ˈsibɔrd/ *n.* [C] **the eastern/Atlantic seaboard** the part of the eastern U.S. that is near the Atlantic Ocean

sea•borne /ˈsibɔrn/ *adj.* carried on or arriving in ships: *a seaborne attack*

ˈsea breeze *n.* [C] a cool light wind that blows from the ocean onto the land

ˈsea ˌcaptain *n.* [C] the CAPTAIN of a ship

ˈsea change *n.* [singular] a very big change in something: *a **sea change in** society's values*

ˈsea dog *n.* [C] LITERARY or HUMOROUS someone with a lot of experience of ships and sailing

sea•far•ing /ˈsiˌfɛrɪŋ/ *adj.* [only before noun] **1** relating to the life and activities of a sailor: *seafaring tales* **2** working or traveling on ships: **seafaring nation/people** *The Portuguese are a seafaring nation.* —**seafaring** *n.* [U] —**seafarer** *n.* [C]

sea•floor /ˈsiflɔr/ *n.* [singular] the land at the bottom of a sea or ocean

seafood

sea•food /ˈsifud/ *n.* [U] animals from the ocean that you can eat, for example fish and SHELLFISH

sea•front /ˈsifrʌnt/ *adj.* [only before noun] OCEANFRONT

sea•go•ing /ˈsiˌgoʊɪŋ/ *adj.* [only before noun] built to travel on the ocean SYN **oceangoing**: *a seagoing vessel*

sea•gull /ˈsigʌl/ also **gull** *n.* [C] BIOLOGY a common gray and white bird that lives near the ocean

sea•horse /ˈsihɔrs/ *n.* [C] BIOLOGY a small sea fish with a head and neck that look like those of a horse

seal¹ /sil/ *n.* [C]

1 ANIMAL BIOLOGY a large sea animal that has smooth fur, eats fish, and lives around coasts, especially in cold areas → see picture at FOOD CHAIN

2 STOP WATER/DIRT ENTERING a piece of rubber or plastic used on a pipe, machine, container etc. to prevent air, water, dirt etc. from going into or out of it: *an airtight seal*

3 NEW CONTAINER a piece of WAX, paper etc. that you have to break in order to open a new container: *Check that the seal on the medicine has not been broken.*

4 seal of approval if you give something your seal of approval, you say that you approve of it, especially officially: *The project has received the city council's seal of approval.*

5 a) SPECIAL MARK a mark that has a special design and shows the legal or official authority of a person or organization: *stationery decorated with the Texas state seal* **b)** an object used to make this mark

6 STAMP a special type of stamp with a picture on it, that you cannot use to mail a letter but that is bought to help a CHARITY

7 under seal information or documents that are under seal are kept secret, especially by a court of law: *Court papers regarding pretrial information are under seal.*

[**Origin:** (1) Old English *seolh*]

seal² *v.* [T]

1 ENTRANCE/CONTAINER also **seal up** to close an entrance or a container with something that stops air, water etc. from coming into or out of it: *The doorway had been sealed up with bricks.*

2 ENVELOPE/PACKAGE to close an envelope, package etc. by using something sticky to hold its edges in place: *She sealed the box with clear tape.*

3 BUILDING/COUNTRY if a building, area, or country is sealed, no one can enter or leave it: *The country has sealed its borders.*

4 seal a deal/agreement/promise etc. to do something that makes a deal, agreement etc. more formal or definite

5 seal sb's fate to make something, especially something bad, sure to happen: *Rogerson's fate was sealed when he got behind the wheel of his car, completely drunk.*

6 seal a victory/win to make a victory certain: *His three-point shot sealed the victory.*

7 KEEP SECRET if a court of law or a business seals information, documents, offers etc., they keep them secret → see also UNSEAL

8 WOOD to cover the surface of something with something that will protect it: *The stain both colors and seals the wood.* → see also **my lips are sealed** at LIP (5)

seal sth ↔ **in** *phr. v.* to stop what something contains from getting out: *Cook the meat over a high heat to seal in the juices.*

seal sth ↔ **off** *phr. v.* to stop people from entering an area or building, because it is dangerous: *Police have sealed off the area.*

ˈsea lane *n.* [C] a SHIPPING LANE

seal•ant /ˈsilənt/ *n.* [C,U] a substance that is put on the surface of something to protect it from air, water etc.

sealed /sild/ *adj.* **1** closed in a way that prevents something from getting in or out: *The list of winners' names was delivered in a sealed envelope.* | *a sealed container* **2** sealed information, documents, offers etc. are kept secret by a court of law or business → see also UNSEALED

ˈsea legs *n.* [plural] **find/get your sea legs** to begin to be able to walk normally, not feel sick etc. when you are traveling on a ship

seal•er /ˈsilɚ/ *n.* **1** [C,U] a layer of paint, polish etc. put on the surface of something to protect it from air, water etc. **2** [C] a person or ship that hunts SEALS

ˈsea ˌlevel *n.* [U] the average height of the ocean, used as a standard for measuring other heights and depths, such as the height of a mountain: **above/below sea level** *The city is 2,500 feet above sea level.*

sea•lift /ˈsilɪft/ *n.* [C] an act of moving people or things by boat, when it is difficult or dangerous to use roads or aircraft

seal•ing /ˈsilɪŋ/ *n.* [U] the hunting or catching of SEALS

ˈsealing wax *n.* [U] a red substance that melts and becomes hard again quickly, used for closing letters, documents etc., especially in past times

ˈsea ˌlion *n.* [C] a large type of SEAL that lives near the coast in the Pacific Ocean

seal·skin /ˈsilskɪn/ *n.* [C,U] the skin or fur of some types of SEALS, used for making leather or clothes

seam /sim/ *n.* [C] **1** a line where two pieces of cloth, leather etc. have been stitched together: *Neil's shirt was torn at the shoulder seam.* **2** EARTH SCIENCE a layer of a mineral, especially coal, under the ground **3 be coming/falling apart at the seams a)** if a plan, organization etc. is coming or falling apart at the seams, so many things are going wrong with it that it will probably fail: *The country's whole economy is coming apart at the seams.* **b)** if a piece of clothing is coming or falling apart at the seams, the stitches on it are coming unfastened **4 be bursting/bulging at the seams** if a room, building etc. is bursting or bulging at the seams, it is so full of people that hardly anyone else can fit into it **5** a line where two pieces of metal, wood etc. have been fastened together

sea·man /ˈsimən/ *n. plural* **seamen** /-mən/ [C] **1** a sailor on a ship or in the navy who is not an officer SYN **sailor** **2** someone who has a lot of experience of ships and the ocean

sea·man·ship /ˈsimənˌʃɪp/ *n.* [U] the skills and knowledge that an experienced sailor has

ˈsea mile *n.* [C] a NAUTICAL MILE

S

seam·less /ˈsimlɪs/ *adj.* **1** done or happening so smoothly that you cannot tell where one thing stops and another begins: *a seamless mix of musical styles* **2** not having any SEAMS: *seamless stockings*

seam·less·ly /ˈsimlɪsli/ *adv.* happening or done so smoothly that you cannot tell where one thing stops and another begins: *The novel shifts seamlessly from the present to the past.*

seam·stress /ˈsimstrɪs/ *n.* [C] OLD-FASHIONED a woman whose job is SEWING and making clothes SYN **dressmaker** → see also TAILOR

seam·y /ˈsimi/ *adj. comparative* **seamier**, *superlative* **seamiest** involving bad things such as crime, violence, or immoral behavior SYN **sordid**: ***the seamy side of*** *Hollywood* [**Origin:** 1800–1900 *seamy* **having the rough side of the seam showing** (17–19 centuries), from *seam*]

sé·ance /ˈseɪɑns/ *n.* [C] a meeting where people try to talk to or receive messages from the spirits of dead people

sea·plane /ˈsipleɪn/ *n.* [C] an airplane that can take off from and land on the surface of water

sea·port /ˈsipɔrt/ *n.* [C] a town or city on or near a coast with a HARBOR that large ships can use

ˈsea ˌpower *n.* **1** [U] the size and strength of a country's navy **2** [C] a country with a powerful navy

sear /sɪr/ *v.* **1** [I always + adv./prep.,T] to burn something with a sudden powerful heat SYN **scorch**: *Brush fires seared the hillsides.* **2** [T] to cook the outside of a piece of meat quickly at a high temperature, in order to keep its juices in **3** [I,T always + adv./prep.] to have a very strong sudden and bad effect on you: **+into/in** *The image of the crash was seared into her memory.*

search[1] /sɚtʃ/ W2 *n.* **1** [C usually singular] an attempt to find someone or something that is difficult to find: **+for** *the search for the wreck of the Titanic* | *Police have* ***called off the search for*** (=officially stopped looking for) *the missing children.* | *The company* ***launched a*** *nationwide* ***search*** *for a new CEO.* | *Officers* ***conducted a search*** *of the property.* | *a* ***thorough search*** *of the area* **2** [C] if a computer does a search or if someone does a search on a computer, they command the computer to find certain information: *A search found several good websites.* | *a* ***computer search*** *of major newspapers* | **perform/run/do a search** *Police ran a database search of the license numbers of stolen cars.* **3 in search of sb/sth** looking for someone or something: *They traveled widely in search of work.* **4** [singular, U] an attempt to find a solution to a problem or an explanation for something: **+for** *the search for the meaning of life* **5 search and rescue** the process of searching for someone who is lost and who may need medical help, for example in the mountains or in the ocean → see also STRIP SEARCH

search[2] S3 W2 *v.*
1 LOOK FOR [I,T] to look carefully for someone or something that is difficult to find: *Police searched the house.* | **+for** *Lynn searched for a parking place.* | **+through** *I searched through the papers on my desk, looking for the receipt.* | **search sth for sth** *Investigators searched the records for evidence of fraud.* ►see THESAURUS box at **look**[1]
2 COMPUTER [T] to tell a computer to find certain information: *some useful tips for searching the web* | **search sth for sth** *Try searching the Internet for information on hotels.*
3 PERSON [T] if someone in authority searches you or the things you are carrying, they look for things that you might be hiding: *All visitors will be searched before entering the prison.*
4 SOLUTION/EXPLANATION ETC. [I] to try to find a solution to a problem or an explanation for something: **+for** *Scientists are still searching for a cure.*
5 Search me! SPOKEN used to tell someone that you do not know the answer to a question: *"How much longer is it going to take?" "Search me!"*
6 EXAMINE [T] to examine something very carefully in order to find something out, decide something etc.: *Our leaders will have to search their consciences before agreeing to this deal.*
7 search-and-destroy mission/operation an attempt to find and destroy something such as an enemy's property during a military battle
[**Origin:** 1300–1400 Old French *cerchier* **to go around, examine, search**, from Late Latin *circare* **to go around**]

search sth ↔ **out** *phr. v.* to find or discover something by looking carefully for it: *The gallery's owners search out works by talented young artists.*

ˈsearch ˌengine *n.* [C] COMPUTERS a computer program that helps you find information on the Internet

search·ing /ˈsɚtʃɪŋ/ *adj.* [only before noun] **1** intended to find out all the facts about something: **searching examination/questions/investigation etc.** *Immigration officers asked some searching questions.* **2 searching look** a look from someone who is trying to find out as much as possible about someone else's thoughts and feelings: *She gave Mike a long searching look.* —**searchingly** *adv.*

search·light /ˈsɚtʃlaɪt/ *n.* [C] a powerful light that can be turned in any direction, used for finding people, guarding places etc.

ˈsearch ˌparty *n.* [C] a group of people organized to look for someone who is missing or lost: *Anxious parents* ***sent out a search party*** *to look for the two boys.*

ˈsearch ˌwarrant *n.* [C] a legal document that gives the police official permission to search a building

sear·ing /ˈsɪrɪŋ/ *adj.* [only before noun] **1** extremely hot: *the* ***searing heat*** *of the desert* **2** searing pain is severe and feels like a burn **3** searing writing or remarks criticize someone or something in a severe way: *a searing portrait of our society*

Sears /sɪrz/, **Richard** (1863–1914) a U.S. businessman who started the MAIL ORDER company Sears Roebuck

ˈsea salt *n.* [U] a type of salt made from ocean water, used in cooking

sea·scape *n.* [C] a picture or painting of the ocean

ˈsea ˌserpent *n.* [C] an imaginary large snake-like animal that people used to think lived in the ocean

sea·shell /ˈsiʃɛl/ *n.* [C] the empty shell of a small ocean creature: *seashells on the beach*

sea·shore /ˈsiʃɔr/ *n.* **the seashore** the land along the edge of the ocean, usually consisting of sand and rocks → see also BEACH ►see THESAURUS box at **shore**[1]

sea·sick /ˈsiˌsɪk/ *adj.* feeling very sick because of the movement of a boat or ship —**seasickness** *n.* [U]

sea·side /ˈsisaɪd/ *adj.* [only before noun] relating to the land next to a sea or ocean: *a seaside resort*

sea·son¹ /ˈsizən/ S2 W1 *n.*
1 IN A YEAR [C] one of the four main periods that a year is divided into, which are spring, summer, fall, and winter
2 TIME FOR ACTIVITY [C usually singular, U] the period of time in a year during which a particular activity takes place: *The Lakers need to work on their defense this season.* | *new dramas for the fall season* (=the time in the fall when new television programs are shown) | *The orchestra's* ***season finale*** (=last concert during the season) *will include works by Bach and Mozart.* | **football/basketball/hockey etc. season** (=when football, basketball etc. are officially played) | **hunting/fishing season** (=the time when it is legal to hunt or fish) *When does fishing season open this year?* | **deer/duck etc. season** (=when it is legal to hunt deer, ducks etc.) | *He was caught hunting* ***out of season*** (=when it is not legally allowed).
3 USUAL TIME STH HAPPENS [C usually singular, U] a period of time in a year during which something usually happens: *This region has a fairly short* ***growing season*** (=when flowers and plants grow). | *Peaches are* ***in season*** (=ripe and ready to eat) *now.* | *Fruit is more expensive* ***out of season*** (=when it is not the time of year in your area when they are ready to eat). | +**for** *the season for strawberries* | **the rainy/dry/wet etc. season** (=when there is a lot of rain, dry weather etc.)
4 VACATION/HOLIDAY PERIOD [singular, U] the time of year when most people take their vacation, or when there are special holidays: **high/peak season** (=the busiest part of this time) *You can expect to pay $150 for a cabin* ***in the high season.*** | **off/low season** (=the time when most people are not taking vacations) *Our trip to Italy in the off season was a bargain.* | *There are free tours during the* ***tourist season.*** | **the holiday season** (=Thanksgiving to New Year's Day, including Christmas, Hanukkah etc.) *The game was a top seller during the holiday season.* | **season's greetings** (=used especially on card to say you hope someone has a nice Christmas, Hanukkah etc.)
[**Origin:** 1300–1400 Old French *saison*, from Latin *satio* **act of planting seeds**] → see also OPEN SEASON

season² *v.* [T] **1** to add salt, pepper, SPICES etc. to something you are cooking to make it taste better: **season sth with sth** *a creamy sauce lightly seasoned with herbs* | *Add the milk and* ***season to taste*** (=add salt or pepper in the amount you think tastes right). ►see THESAURUS box at **cooking¹** **2** to make wood hard and ready to use by gradually drying it

sea·son·a·ble /ˈsiznəbəl/ *adj.* FORMAL seasonable weather conditions are typical for the time of year OPP **unseasonable**: *seasonable temperatures* —**seasonably** *adv.* → see also UNSEASONABLY

sea·son·al /ˈsizənəl/ *adj.* [usually before noun] **1** happening, available, or needed during a particular season: *fresh seasonal fruits* | **seasonal workers/labor/employment etc.** *seasonal farm workers* **2** relating to or affected by the seasons of the year: *seasonal variation in rainfall levels*

ˌseasonal afˌfective disˈorder ABBREVIATION **SAD** *n.* [U] an illness that makes people feel sad and tired in the winter, because there is not enough light from the sun

sea·son·al·ly /ˈsisənəli/ *adv.* according to what is usual for a particular season: **seasonally adjusted figures/rates/data etc.** (=numbers about sales, unemployment etc. that are changed according to what usually happens at a particular time of year)

sea·soned /ˈsizənd/ *adj.* **1 seasoned traveler/campaigner/veteran etc.** someone who has a lot of experience in a particular activity SYN **experienced** **2** seasoned food has salt, pepper, SPICES etc. added to it

ˌseasoned ˈsalt *n.* [U] a mixture of salt and other SPICES, especially PAPRIKA, used in cooking and to give food a special taste

sea·son·ing /ˈsizənɪŋ/ *n.* [C,U] salt, pepper, SPICES etc. that give food a more interesting taste

ˈseason preˌmiere *n.* [C] the first show of the year for a continuing television series, usually shown in the fall

ˈseason ˌticket *n.* [C] a ticket that allows you to go to all the sports games played by a particular team in a year, all the concerts in a series etc., and that costs less than buying a separate ticket for each game, concert etc.: *a season ticket to the Pasadena Playhouse*

ˈsea stack *n.* [C] EARTH SCIENCE a tall thin upright rock structure in the ocean near an island or large area of land, formed by the gradual effect of the wind and waves moving against the land

seat¹ /sit/ S2 W1 *n.*
1 PLACE TO SIT [C] a place where you can sit, for example a chair, especially in a restaurant, airplane, theater etc.: *There are two seats left in the back row.* | *a 65,000-seat stadium* | *Please* ***take a seat*** (=sit down). | *Mr. Benson came in and* ***took his seat*** (=sat down in his seat). | *Would you like a* ***window*** *or* ***aisle seat*** (=in an airplane)? | *Anne, in the* ***passenger seat*** (=the seat next to the driver in a car), *was not hurt.* | *Who was in the* ***driver's seat?*** | **the back/front seat** (=the seats in the back or front of a car) | ***Reserved seats*** (=specific seats that you say you want when you buy a ticket) *for the game are $15.*
2 OFFICIAL POSITION [C] POLITICS a position as a member of a government or a group that makes official decisions: +**on** *a seat on the board of directors* | +**in** *Republicans hold 235 of the 435 seats in the House.* | **Senate/House seat** *Several incumbents are in danger of* ***losing*** *their House* ***seats.***
3 PART OF A CHAIR [C usually singular] the flat part of a chair etc. that you sit on: *a chair with a broken seat* | *Who left the toilet seat up?*
4 baby/child/car seat a special chair that you put in a car for a baby or small child
5 BICYCLE ETC. [C] the part of a bicycle, MOTORCYCLE etc. that you sit on SYN **saddle** → see picture at BICYCLE¹
6 seat of government/power FORMAL a place, usually a city, where a government is based
7 take a back seat (to sb/sth) to have less influence or importance: *Foreign policy will take a back seat to domestic problems for a while.*
8 on the edge of your seat waiting with great excitement to see what will happen next: *The movie's last scenes* ***kept us on the edge of our seats.***
9 be in/on the hot seat INFORMAL to be in a difficult position in which you have to make important decisions or answer a lot of questions: *The Eagles' coach found himself in the hot seat after Sunday's huge loss.*
10 be in the driver's seat to control what happens in an organization, relationship, or situation
11 do sth by the seat of your pants to do something by using only your own skill and experience, without any help from anyone or anything else
12 CLOTHES [singular] the part of your pants that you sit on: *The seat of his jeans was dirty.*
13 BODY PART [singular] the part of your body that you sit on SYN **bottom** SYN **rear end**
[**Origin:** 1100–1200 Old Norse *sæti*] → see also **a back seat driver** at BACK SEAT (2), COUNTY SEAT, LOVESEAT, WINDOW SEAT

seat² *v.* [T] **1 seat yourself beside/in/on etc.** FORMAL to sit down somewhere: *Archer seated himself in the armchair.* **2** [always + adv./prep.] to arrange for someone to sit somewhere: **seat sb beside/on/near etc.** *The hostess seated us next to the kitchen door.* **3** [not in progressive] if a room, vehicle, table etc. seats a certain number of people, it has enough seats for that number: *The arena seats 30,000.*

ˈseat belt also **ˈsafety belt** *n.* [C] a strong belt attached to the seat of a car or an airplane, that you fasten around yourself for protection in an accident → see picture on page A36

seat·ed /ˈsitɪd/ *adj.* **1** if someone is seated, they are sitting down: +**at/near/beside etc.** *Jan was seated near the door.* | *Please* ***remain seated*** *until the plane has come to a complete stop.* **2 be seated** SPOKEN used to ask people politely to sit down: *Ladies and gentlemen, please be seated.*

S

-seater /siṭɚ/ *suffix* **two-seater/four-seater etc.** a vehicle, piece of furniture etc. with two seats, four seats etc.

seat·ing /ˈsiṭɪŋ/ *n.* [U] **1** ENG. LANG. ARTS all the seats in a theater, STADIUM etc.: *a **seating capacity** of only 30* **2** the places where people will sit, according to an arrangement: **seating plan/arrangements etc.** *the seating plan for the banquet*

seat·mate /ˈsit˺meɪt/ *n.* [C] someone who sits next to you on an airplane

ˌseat-of-the-ˈpants *adj.* INFORMAL relating to a way of doing something in which you do not plan ahead, but instead do things using your skill and knowledge of the current situation: *a seat-of-the-pants approach to work*

Se·at·tle /siˈæṭl/ a city and port in the U.S. state of Washington in the northwest of the U.S.

ˈsea ˌurchin *n.* [C] a small round animal that lives in the ocean and has a hard shell covered in sharp points

sea·wall /ˈsiwɔl/ *n.* [C] a wall built along the edge of the ocean to stop the water from flowing over an area of land

sea·ward /ˈsiwɚd/ *adj.* facing or directed toward the ocean —**seaward** also **seawards** *adv.*

sea·wat·er /ˈsiˌwɔṭɚ/ *n.* [U] salty water from the ocean

S

sea·way /ˈsiweɪ/ *n. plural* **seaways** [C] **1** a river or CANAL used by ships to go from the ocean to places that are not on the coast **2** a line of travel regularly used by ships on the ocean

sea·weed /ˈsiwid/ *n.* [U] one of several different types of common plants that grow in the ocean

sea·wor·thy /ˈsiˌwɚði/ *adj.* a ship that is seaworthy is safe and in good condition —**seaworthiness** *n.* [U]

se·ba·ceous /sɪˈbeɪʃəs/ *adj.* BIOLOGY related to a part of the body that produces special oils

se·bum /ˈsibəm/ *n.* [U] BIOLOGY a special oil that is produced by the skin

SEC → see SECURITIES AND EXCHANGE COMMISSION, THE

sec /sɛk/ *n.* **1 a sec** SPOKEN a very short time: *"Are you coming?" "**Just a sec** (=wait a short time) – I'm almost ready." | I'll be there **in a sec**.* **2 sec.** the abbreviation of SECOND: *10 min. and 15 sec.*

se·cant /ˈsikænt, -kənt/ *n.* [singular] MATH **1** a straight line that cuts through a circle or curve at two or more places **2** the RATIO of the HYPOTENUSE of a RIGHT TRIANGLE to the side next to a particular angle

se·cede /sɪˈsid/ *v.* [I] FORMAL to formally stop being part of a country or organization: +**from** *Quebec voted on seceding from Canada.* —**secession** /sɪˈsɛʃən/ *n.* [U]

se·ces·sion·ist /sɪˈsɛʃənɪst/ *n.* [C] someone who wants an area to formally stop being part of a country, especially someone who wanted the South to stop being part of the U.S. around the time of the Civil War

se·clude /sɪˈklud/ *v.* [T] FORMAL to keep yourself or someone else away from other people SYN **isolate**

se·clud·ed /sɪˈkludɪd/ *adj.* **1** a secluded place is private and quiet because it is a long way from other places and people: *a secluded beach* **2 a secluded life/existence** a way of living that is quiet and private because you do not see many people

se·clu·sion /sɪˈkluʒən/ *n.* [U] the state of being private and away from other people: *The victim's family has remained **in seclusion** since the shooting.*

sec·ond[1] /ˈsɛkənd/ S1 W1 *adj.* **1** 2nd; the person, thing, event etc. that comes after the first one: *her second year of school | the second act of the play | King's second novel became a bestseller. | Dave's second wife* **2** the position in a competition or scale that comes after the one that is the best, most successful, biggest etc.: *She won second prize. | They're in second place in the league.* | **second biggest/most successful/most important etc.** *the second-largest city in the state | The teacher's influence is **second only to** (=is most important, common, best etc. except for one other thing) that of the parent.* **3** another example of the same thing, or another in addition to the one you have: *They're thinking of buying a second home in Florida. | There is a second reason why this important. | The program for teen mothers **gives them a second chance** to finish high school. | Most insurance companies ask you to **get a second opinion*** (=ask a different doctor to examine you) *before having major medical treatment.* **4 have second thoughts (about sth)** to have doubts about a decision you have made: *Stan was having second thoughts about marrying Julie.* **5 on second thought** SPOKEN used to say that you have changed your opinion or decision about something: *On second thought, I don't think I'll wear this jacket.* **6 not give sth a second thought** to not think or worry about something at all: *Most people just drive around and don't give the environment a second thought.* **7 without a second thought** if you do something without a second thought, you do it without worrying about it at all: *Those people would have killed him without a second thought.* **8 be second to none** to be the best: *His musical technique is second to none.* **9 second best** something that is not as good as the best: *We shouldn't have to **settle for second best*** (=accept something that is not as good as the best). **10 a second look/glance** an occasion when you look at or consider something again, especially because it is interesting or surprising: *A second look at these stories shows that they are more important than they first seem. | No one **gave him a second glance**.* **11 take second place to sb/sth** to be thought of or treated as less important than someone or something else: *Her wants take second place to Joe's.* **12 second wind** if you get your second wind, you begin to feel less tired than before, especially when playing a sport, doing physical work etc. **13 every second year/day/thing etc.** the second, then the fourth, then the sixth year etc.: *The committee meets every second Monday.*

second[2] S1 W1 *n.* **1** [C] a unit for measuring time. There are 60 seconds in a minute: *Heat the sauce in the microwave **for 45 seconds**. | It should only **take** four or five **seconds** to transfer the data.* **2** [C] a very short period of time: *I'll be ready in **a few seconds**. | Hold still, this will only **take a second**. | He should be here **any second*** (=in a very short time). *| The whole thing was over **in seconds*** (=after a few seconds). *| At least 30 shots were fired **in a matter of seconds*** (=in a very short time). *| "Are you coming?" "**Just a second*** (=wait a short time) *– I have to put my shoes on."* → see also SPLIT SECOND → see Word Choice box at MOMENT **3 seconds** [plural] **a)** another serving of the same food after you have eaten your first serving: *Are you going back for seconds?* **b)** clothes or other goods that are sold cheaply in stores because they are not perfect **4** [U] INFORMAL SECOND BASE **5** [C] TECHNICAL one of the 60 parts into which a MINUTE of an angle is divided. It can be shown as a symbol after a number. **6** [C] someone who helps someone else in a fight, especially in BOXING or, in the past, a DUEL [**Origin:** (1, 2, 5) 1300–1400 Medieval Latin *secunda*, from *secunda pars minuta* **second small part, one sixtieth of a minute**, from Latin *secundus*]

second[3] [adverb] **1** next after the first one: **finish second/come in second** *Alice finished second in the 100-meter dash.* **2** [sentence adverb] used to add another piece of information to what you have already said or written SYN **secondly**: *Well, first of all, it's too expensive and second, we don't have anywhere to put it.*

second[4] *pron.* **1 the second** the next thing on a list etc. after the first one: *A third reason for rejecting the plan, closely related to the second, is the effect on the environment. | Maria's birthday is on the second* (=the 2nd day of the month). **2 the Second** ABBREVIATION **II** used after the name of a king, queen, pope etc. who has the same name as someone who held that position in the past: *Pope John Paul the Second* (=written as "Pope John Paul II")

second[5] *v.* [T] **1** to formally support a suggestion or plan made by another person in a meeting: **second a motion/proposal etc.** *The motion to purchase a new copier was seconded by Ms. Green.* **2 I'll second that**

SPOKEN used to say that you completely agree with what someone has just said: *"I could use a cold drink right now." "I'll second that!"*

Second A'mendment *n.* HISTORY a written change to the U.S. CONSTITUTION, which gives all citizens the right to BEAR ARMS (=carry weapons). The Second Amendment was made in 1791.

sec·ond·ar·y /ˈsɛkənˌdɛri/ *adj.* **1** not as important or urgent as something else: *the novel's secondary characters* | **be secondary to sth** *In their movies, plot is secondary to flashy special effects.* | **be of secondary importance/be a secondary consideration** *Teenagers want their clothes to look good – comfort is of secondary importance to them.* ►see THESAURUS box at **unimportant** **2 secondary education/schooling etc.** the education, teaching etc. of children between the ages of 11 and 18 —**secondarily** *adv.*

secondary ˌeconomic acˈtivity *n.* [C,U] ECONOMICS an economic activity that involves making a product from materials that exist in nature → see also PRIMARY ECONOMIC ACTIVITY, TERTIARY ECONOMIC ACTIVITY

secondary ˈgrowth *n.* [U] BIOLOGY an additional increase in the width of the roots and stems of large plants such as bushes and trees, which supports the growing plant and helps it develop → see also PRIMARY GROWTH

secondary inˈfection *n.* [C] an infection that develops from another illness that someone has

secondary ˈmarket *n.* [C] ECONOMICS a market for selling BONDS and STOCKS again, after they have already been sold for the first time

secondary ˌschool *n.* [C] a school for children between the ages of 11 and 18 → see also ELEMENTARY SCHOOL

secondary ˈsource *n.* [C] **1** a book, article etc. that ANALYZES something such as a piece of literature or a historical event and that can be used to support your ideas in an ESSAY **2** HISTORY a description of an event by someone who was not there when it happened → see also PRIMARY SOURCE

secondary ˈstress *n.* [C,U] ENG. LANG. ARTS the second strongest STRESS that is put on part of a word or sentence when you speak it, and shown in this dictionary by the mark (/ˌ/)

second baˈnana *n.* [C usually singular] HUMOROUS someone who has a less important job than someone else, especially on a television show or in an organization

second ˈbase *n.* [singular] the second of the four places you have to run to in games such as baseball before gaining a point

second ˈchildhood *n.* [singular] **1** a time when an old person starts to behave and think like a small child, because their mental abilities are not as good as they used to be **2** a time when someone, especially a man who is between 40 and 60 years old, decides that they want to behave like a young person again and have an exciting life

second ˈclass *n.* [U] **1** the system in the U.S. for delivering newspapers, magazines, advertisements etc. through the mail → see also FIRST CLASS **2** the part of a train or ship in some countries outside the U.S., that is cheaper but not as comfortable as FIRST CLASS

second-ˈclass *adj.* **1** [only before noun] considered to be less important or good than other people or things: *Women were treated as **second-class citizens**.* **2** of a lower standard or quality than the best: *a second-class education* **3 second-class ticket/fare/compartment/cabin etc.** relating to cheaper and less comfortable travel on a train or ship in some countries outside the U.S. → see also FIRST-CLASS

second ˈcoming *n.* **the Second Coming** the time when Christians believe that Jesus Christ will return to Earth

Second ˌContinental ˈCongress, the HISTORY a group of representatives from the American colonies COLONY that met several times from 1775 to 1789 to make decisions about how the new country should be run and make laws

ˌsecond ˈcousin *n.* [C] a child of a COUSIN of one of your parents

ˌsecond-deˈgree *adj.* **1 second-degree murder/manslaughter/burglary etc.** a crime that is less serious than the most serious type, especially because it was not planned **2 second-degree burns** TECHNICAL the second most serious form of burns

ˌsecond-ˈguess *v.* [T] **1** to criticize something after it has already happened, especially by saying what should have been done: *He refused to second-guess his coach's decision.* **2** to try to say what will happen or what someone will do before they do it: *I won't try to second-guess the president's decision.*

ˈsecond ˌhand *n.* [C] the long thin piece of metal that points to the seconds on a clock or watch

second·hand /ˌsɛkəndˈhænd◂ / *adj.* **1** not new, and used by someone else before you SYN **used**: *secondhand clothing* ►see THESAURUS box at **old** **2 secondhand store/bookstore/shop etc.** a store that sells things that have been used by other people, at cheap prices **3** secondhand information, reports, opinions etc. are told to you by someone who is not the person who originally said it OPP **first hand** —**secondhand** *adv.*

ˌsecondhand ˈsmoke *n.* [U] smoke from someone else's cigarette, pipe etc. that you breathe in

ˌsecond-in-comˈmand *n.* [C] the person who has the next highest rank to the leader of a group, especially in a military organization

ˌsecond ˈlanguage *n.* [C usually singular] a language that you speak in addition to the language you learned as a child

ˌsecond ˌlaw of ˌthermodyˈnamics *n.* [singular] PHYSICS a principle of PHYSICS that says that in a system with no outside influences, the amount of ENTROPY (=disorder) will tend to increase over time. This explains why heat moves to cooler areas until the temperature everywhere in a system is equal, and therefore there is less structure in the system.

ˌsecond lieuˈtenant *n.* [C] a middle rank in several of the U.S. military forces, or someone who has this rank

sec·ond·ly /ˈsɛkəndli/ *adv.* [sentence adverb] used when you want to give a second point or fact, or give a second reason for something: *Firstly, we don't need it, and secondly, it's really expensive.*

ˌsecond ˈmortgage *n.* [C] a legal arrangement in which you borrow additional money from a bank when you already have one MORTGAGE that you are still paying back

ˌsecond ˈnature *n.* [U] **be/become second nature (to sb)** something that is second nature to you is something you have done so often that you do it almost without thinking: *Driving becomes second nature after a while.*

ˌsecond ˈperson *n.* **the second person** ENG. LANG. ARTS a form of a verb or PRONOUN that is used to show the person you are speaking to. For example, "you" is a pronoun in the second person, and "you are" is the second person singular and plural of the verb "to be" —**ˈsecond-person** *adj.* [only before noun] → see also FIRST PERSON

ˌsecond-ˈrate *adj.* [usually before noun] not very good, or not as good as the best of its type SYN **mediocre**: *a second-rate author*

ˌsecond ˈsight *n.* [U] the ability to know what will happen in the future, or to know about things that are happening somewhere else, that some people claim to have

ˌsecond-ˈstring *adj.* [only before noun] not regularly part of a team, group etc., but sometimes taking someone else's place in it: *the Vikings' second-string quarterback* → see also FIRST-STRING

ˌSecond World ˈWar *n.* **the Second World War** HISTORY WORLD WAR II

S

se·cre·cy /ˈsikrəsi/ *n.* [U] **1** the process of keeping something secret, or the state of being kept a secret: *The atom bomb project was* ***shrouded in secrecy*** (=kept completely secret). | **absolute/complete secrecy** *They stressed the need for complete secrecy.* **2 swear sb to secrecy** to make someone promise that they will not repeat what you have told them

se·cret¹ /ˈsikrɪt/ W2 *adj.* **1** known about by only a few people and kept hidden from others: *secret information* | *secret meetings with the rebels* | *They* ***kept*** *their relationship* ***secret from*** *their parents* (=they did not tell them). | **secret compartment/passage/hiding place etc.** *Agents found the drugs in a secret compartment in Campbell's suitcase.* | **secret ingredient/recipe/formula** *The cookies are made to a secret recipe.* → see also TOP-SECRET

THESAURUS

confidential used about information, especially in business or government, that is secret and not intended to be shown or told to other people
classified used about information that the government has ordered to be kept secret from most people
sensitive used about information that is kept secret because there would be problems if the wrong people knew it
covert used about things that are done secretly, especially by a government or official organization: *CIA covert activities*
undercover used about things that are done secretly by the police in order to catch criminals or find out information: *an undercover operation*
→ PRIVATE¹

2 secret weapon something that will help you gain a big advantage over your competitors, that they do not know about **3** [only before a noun] secret feelings, worries, or actions are ones that you do not want other people to know about: *Her secret fear was that Jim would leave her.* | *his* ***secret life*** *with his mistress* ▶see THESAURUS box at **private¹** **4 secret admirer** someone who is in love with another person, without that person's knowledge [**Origin:** 1300–1400 Old French, Latin *secretus*, past participle of *secernere* **to separate**]

secret² S3 W2 *n.* [C] **1** something that is kept hidden or that is known about by only a few people: *I can't tell you that –* ***it's a secret.*** | *Can you* ***keep a secret*** (=not tell a secret to anyone)? | *I'll* ***tell you a secret, if you*** *promise not to tell anybody else.* | ***It is*** *certainly* ***no secret that*** (=many people know that) *the store is losing a lot of money.* | *Here's a* ***dirty little secret*** *about college: many people never finish.* | *This is just* ***our little secret.*** | ***The secret*** *would come* ***out*** (=not be a secret anymore) *sooner or later.* | *Pam's lasagna recipe is a* ***closely-guarded secret*** (=one that is carefully kept). | *This beach is one of the area's* ***best-kept secrets*** (=no one knows about it). | **deep/dark secret** *The family's happy exterior hid some dark secrets.* **2 in secret** in a private way or place that other people do not know about: *The negotiations were conducted in secret.* **3** [singular] a particular way of achieving a good result, that is the best or only way: **the secret to (doing) sth** *The secret to making good pie crust is to use very cold water.* | *Your hair always looks so great –* ***what's your secret*** (=how do you do it)? | *What do you think is* ***the secret of*** *her* ***success?*** **4 make no secret of sth** to make your opinions about something clear: *Marge made no secret of her dislike for Terry.* **5 the secrets of nature/the universe etc.** the things no one yet knows about nature, the universe etc. → see also TRADE SECRET

ˌsecret ˈagent *n.* [C] someone whose job is to find out and report on the military and political secrets of other countries SYN **spy**

sec·re·tar·i·al /ˌsɛkrəˈtɛriəl/ *adj.* relating to the work of a secretary

Sec·re·tar·i·at /ˌsɛkrəˈtɛriət/ a horse famous for winning many horse races in the U.S.

sec·re·tar·i·at /ˌsɛkreˈtɛriət/ *n.* [C] POLITICS a government office or the office of an international organization with a secretary or SECRETARY GENERAL who is in charge: *the United Nations Secretariat in New York*

sec·re·tar·y /ˈsɛkrəˌtɛri/ S3 W2 *n. plural* **secretaries** [C] **1** someone who works in an office typing (TYPE) letters, keeping records, answering telephone calls, arranging meetings etc.: *My secretary will fax you all the details.* → see also PRESS SECRETARY **2** an official who is chosen by the U.S. President to be in charge of a large government department and a member of the CABINET: *the Secretary of Defense* → see also SECRETARY OF STATE **3** a member of an organization who is chosen to write down notes from meetings, write letters etc.: *the secretary of the chess club*

ˌsecretary ˈgeneral, secretary-general *n.* [C] POLITICS the most important official in charge of a large organization, especially an international organization: *the U.N. Secretary-General*

ˌSecretary of ˈState *n. plural* **Secretaries of State** [C] the head of the U.S. government department that deals with the U.S.'s relations with other countries

ˌsecret ˈballot *n.* [C,U] a way of voting in which people write their choices on a piece of paper in secret, or an act of voting in this way: *The chairman was elected* ***by secret ballot.***

se·crete /sɪˈkrit/ *v.* [T] **1** BIOLOGY if a part of an animal or plant secretes a substance, it produces that substance: *The toad's skin secretes a deadly poison.* → see also EXCRETE **2** FORMAL to hide something SYN **hide**: *The money had been secreted in a Swiss bank account.*

se·cre·tion /sɪˈkriʃən/ *n.* BIOLOGY **1** [C] a substance, usually liquid, produced by part of a plant or animal **2** [U] the production of this substance: *the secretion of hormones*

se·cre·tive /ˈsikrət̬ɪv/ *adj.* a secretive person or organization likes to keep their thoughts, intentions, or actions hidden from others: *a secretive nation* | **be secretive about sth** *Officials have been secretive about sales projections.* —**secretively** *adv.* —**secretiveness** *n.* [U]

se·cret·ly /ˈsikrɪtli/ *adv.* in a way that is kept hidden from other people SYN **covertly**: *Harris secretly recorded his conversation with the senator.*

ˌsecret poˈlice *n.* **the secret police** a police force controlled by a government, that secretly tries to defeat the political enemies of that government

ˌsecret ˈservice *n.* **the Secret Service** a U.S. government department that deals with special kinds of police work, especially protecting the President

ˌsecret soˈciety *n.* [C] a social, political etc. organization that meets in secret and whose members must keep its activities and rules secret from other people

sect /sɛkt/ *n.* [C] a group of people with their own particular set of beliefs and practices, especially one that has separated from a larger religious group [**Origin:** 1300–1400 Old French *secte* **group, sect**, from Latin *secta* **way of life, type of people**]

sec·tar·i·an /sɛkˈtɛriən/ *adj.* **1 sectarian violence/conflict/fighting etc.** violence, CONFLICT etc. that is related to the strong feelings between people of different religious groups **2** supporting a particular religious group and its beliefs: *a sectarian school* —**sectarianism** *n.* [U]

sec·tion¹ /ˈsɛkʃən/ Ac S1 W2 *n.*
1 PLACE/OBJECT [C] one of the parts that something such as an object or place is divided into: *The plane's tail section was found in a cornfield.* | **+of** *This is one of the older sections of town.* | *the reference section of the library* | *seats in the* ***smoking section*** | *The bookcase can be taken apart and stored* ***in sections.*** ▶see THESAURUS box at **part¹**
2 GROUP OF PEOPLE [C] a separate group within a larger group of people SYN **segment**: **+of** *a large section of the American public*
3 brass/rhythm/woodwind/string etc. section ENG.

LANG. ARTS the part of a band or ORCHESTRA that plays the BRASS, RHYTHM etc. instruments
4 BOOK/NEWSPAPER/REPORT [C] one of the separate parts of something written, such as a newspaper or book: *Who has the sports section?* | *the final section of this chapter*
5 LAW one of the parts of a law or legal document: *Article I, Section 8 of the U.S. Constitution*
6 MEDICAL/SCIENTIFIC TECHNICAL **a)** [C,U] a medical operation that involves cutting → see also **cesarean section** at CESAREAN (1) **b)** [C] a very thin flat piece that is cut from skin, a plant etc. to be looked at under a MICROSCOPE
7 SIDE/TOP VIEW [C,U] a picture that shows what a building, part of the body etc. would look like if it were cut from top to bottom or side to side → see also CROSS SECTION
8 AREA OF LAND [C] a square area of land in the central and western U.S. that is one mile long on each side
9 MATHEMATICS [C] MATH the shape that is made when a solid figure is cut by a flat surface in mathematics: *conic sections*
[**Origin:** 1300–1400 Latin *sectio*, from *secare* **to cut**]

section² Ac *v.* [T] **1** to separate something into parts: *Peel and section the oranges.* **2** TECHNICAL to cut a section from skin, a plant etc. **3** TECHNICAL to use a flat surface to cut a solid figure in mathematics **4** TECHNICAL to cut a part of the body in a medical operation

section sth ↔ **off** *phr. v.* to divide an area into parts, especially by putting something between the parts: *Part of the yard had been sectioned off for growing vegetables.*

sec·tion·al /ˈsɛkʃənl/ *adj.* **1** relating to one group of people within a larger group or society: *community groups and their sectional interests* **2** made up of sections that can be put together or taken apart: *a sectional sofa* **3** a sectional drawing or view of something shows what it would look like if it were cut from top to bottom, or from side to side

sec·tion·al·ism /ˈsɛkʃənlˌɪzəm/ *n.* [U] POLITICS when someone, especially a politician, shows that he or she is concerned only with what is best for one part of a country, not what is best for the whole country

sec·tor /ˈsɛktɚ/ Ac W2 *n.* [C] **1** a part of an area of activity, especially of business, trade etc.: **+of** *the manufacturing sector of the economy* | **the public/private sector** (=business controlled by the government or by private companies) **2** one of the parts into which an area is divided, especially for military reasons: *recent disturbances in the city's Christian sector* **3** GEOMETRY an area in a circle enclosed by two straight lines drawn from the center to the edge

sec·u·lar /ˈsɛkyəlɚ/ *adj.* **1** not relating to or controlled by a church or other religious authority → see also SACRED: *The government is secular.* | *secular music* ▸see THESAURUS box at **religion** **2** TECHNICAL a secular priest lives among ordinary people, rather than with other priests in a MONASTERY [**Origin:** 1300–1400 Old French *seculer*, from Latin *saecularis* **coming once in an age**]

sec·u·lar·ism /ˈsɛkyələˌrɪzəm/ *n.* [U] **1** a system of social organization that does not allow religion to influence the government, or the belief that religion should not influence a government: *Turkey's secularism* **2** the quality of behaving in a way that shows religion does not influence you: *the secularism of popular culture* —**secularist** *n.* [C]

sec·u·lar·ize /ˈsɛkyələˌraɪz/ *v.* [T] to remove the control or influence of religious groups from a society or an institution —**secularization** /ˌsɛkyələrəˈzeɪʃən/ *n.* [U]

se·cure¹ /sɪˈkyʊr/ Ac *adj.*
1 NOT LIKELY TO CHANGE a secure situation is one that you can depend on because it is not likely to change: *a secure income* | *I wish my job were more secure.*
2 PROTECTED a) locked or guarded so that people cannot get in or out, or steal anything SYN **safe**: *Keep your passport in a secure place.* | *secure government buildings* **b)** safe from and protected against damage or attack: *a secure online transaction* | **+from** *The new computer system is secure from hackers.*
3 FEELING SAFE feeling safe and protected from danger SYN **safe**: *People should feel secure when they walk the streets of this city.*
4 CONFIDENT a) feeling confident and certain about a situation and not worried that it might change OPP **insecure**: *a happy and secure child* | *By 30, he was successful and* ***financially secure*** (=having enough money to live on). | *She smiled,* ***secure in the knowledge that*** *her children were safe.* **b)** feeling confident about yourself and your abilities OPP **insecure**: *Marie's not as secure as she wants us to believe.*
5 FIRMLY ATTACHED firmly attached, tied, or fastened: *Are you sure that shelf is secure?*
[**Origin:** 1500–1600 Latin *securus*, from *se* **without** + *cura* **care**]

secure² Ac *v.* [T] **1** to get or achieve something that will be permanent, especially after a lot of effort: *The last-minute goal secured their position in the final.* | *Negotiators are working to* ***secure*** *the hostages'* ***release***. **2** to make something safe from being attacked, harmed, or lost: *Troops were brought in to secure the area.* **3** to attach or tie something firmly in a particular position: **secure sth to sth** *He secured the boat to the dock.* **4** ECONOMICS to legally promise that if you cannot pay back money you have borrowed from someone, you will give them goods or property of the same value instead: *Fox used company money to secure a personal loan.* —**secured** *adj.*: *a secured loan*

se·cure·ly /sɪˈkyʊrli/ Ac *adv.* **1** tied, attached etc. tightly or firmly, especially in order to make something safe: **securely locked/fastened/tied etc.** *Make sure the latch is securely fastened.* **2** in a way that keeps something safe from being stolen or lost: *The system allows you to transfer the money securely online.*

Se̦curities and Exˈchange Comˌmission, the a U.S. government organization which makes sure that people and companies obey laws about the sale of company STOCKS and BONDS

se·cu·ri·ty /sɪˈkyʊrət̬i/ Ac *n.*
1 KEEPING SB/STH SAFE [U] things that are done in order to keep a place, person, or thing safe: ***Security*** *was* ***tight*** *at yesterday's ceremony.* | *I was surprised at the* ***lax security*** *during the president's visit.* | *They have* ***tightened security*** *at the jail.* | **security measures/checks/procedures etc.** *security checks at the airport* | *He was transferred to a* ***high security*** *federal prison.* | *They maintain very* ***tight security*** (=careful protection using a lot of soldiers, police etc.) *along the border.*
2 SAFETY [U] the safety of a country or person: *a threat to our security* | *The trip has been canceled for reasons of* ***national security***.
3 SAFE SITUATION/FEELING [U] a feeling of confidence that you are safe and things will continue in the same way and not change: *Parenting is about giving a child security and love.* | *Unions are working for greater* ***job security*** (=not being in danger of losing your job) *for low-paid workers.* | *This insurance plan offers your family* ***financial security*** (=enough money to live on) *in the event of your death.* | *Carrying a lot of equipment can give climbers* ***a false sense of security***.
4 securities [plural] ECONOMICS official documents such as STOCKS or BONDS that people buy in order to earn money from INTEREST
5 PROTECTION FROM LOSS ETC. [U] protection in something like a computer or banking system that prevents things from being lost, and prevents people from finding information, stealing things etc.: *increased Internet security*
6 GUARDS [U] people who deal with the protection of buildings and equipment, especially people who do this for a company or store: *If you see anything suspicious, call security.* | *security personnel* → see also SECURITY GUARD
7 BORROWING MONEY [U] ECONOMICS something such as property that you promise to give someone if you cannot pay back money you have borrowed from them: **+for** *They used their home as security for the loan.*

S

se'curity ˌblanket *n.* [C] **1** a BLANKET that children like to hold and touch to comfort themselves **2** something that makes someone feel less nervous or anxious in bad or worrying situations

se'curity ˌclearance *n.* [C,U] official permission for someone to see secret documents, enter a building etc. that someone is given after a strict checking process

se'curity deˌposit *n.* [C] an amount of money that you give to a LANDLORD before you rent a house or apartment, and that is returned to you after you leave if you have not damaged the property

se'curity force *n.* [C usually plural] a group of people whose job is to protect a country, an official building etc.

se'curity ˌguard *n.* [C] someone whose job is to guard a building, a vehicle carrying money etc.

se'curity ˌlight *n.* [C] a light that turns on when someone tries to enter a dark building or area

se'curity ˌrisk *n.* [C] someone or something that you cannot trust, and that could cause serious problems for the safety of a government or organization: *Large windows pose a security risk.*

se'curity ˌservice *n.* [C] POLITICS a government organization that protects a country's secrets against enemy countries or protects the government against attempts to take away its power

secy. a written abbreviation of "secretary"

se·dan /sɪ'dæn/ *n.* [C] a large car that has four doors, seats for at least four people, and a TRUNK

se'dan chair *n.* [C] a seat on two poles with a cover around it, on which an important person was carried in the past

se·date¹ /sɪ'deɪt/ *adj.* **1** calm, serious, and formal, without excitement or strong feelings **2** walking or moving slowly: *a sedate pace* —**sedately** *adv.* —**sedateness** *n.* [U]

sedate² *v.* [T usually passive] to give someone drugs to make them sleepy or calm, especially so that they do not feel pain: *She was **heavily sedated** for the pain.*

se·da·tion /sɪ'deɪʃən/ *n.* [U] MEDICINE the use of drugs to make someone sleepy or calm, often so that they do not feel pain: *The patient was still **under sedation**.*

sed·a·tive /'sɛdət̬ɪv/ *n.* [C] MEDICINE a drug used to make someone sleepy or calm

sed·en·tar·y /'sɛdnˌtɛri/ *adj.* FORMAL **1** a sedentary job etc. is one in which you sit down a lot and do not move or exercise very much: *a sedentary lifestyle* **2** a sedentary person is someone who sits a lot and does not exercise **3** TECHNICAL a sedentary group of people tend always to live in the same place [**Origin:** 1500–1600 French *sédentaire*, from Latin *sedentarius*, from *sedere* **to sit**]

Se·der /'seɪdɚ/ *n.* [C] a special dinner which takes place on the first two nights of Passover and is held to remember the occasion when the Jewish people left Egypt

sedge /sɛdʒ/ *n.* [U] a plant similar to grass that grows in groups on low wet ground

sed·i·ment /'sɛdəmənt/ *n.* [C,U] **1** solid substances that settle at the bottom of a liquid: *sediment in the wine* **2** EARTH SCIENCE material that is left on the surface of the Earth as the result of the movement of water, wind, or GLACIERS

sed·i·ment·a·ry /ˌsɛdə'mɛntri, -'mɛntəri/ *adj.* EARTH SCIENCE made of the solid substances that settle at the bottom of oceans, rivers, lakes etc.: *sedimentary rock*

sed·i·men·ta·tion /ˌsɛdəmən'teɪʃən/ *n.* [U] EARTH SCIENCE the natural process by which small pieces of rock, earth etc. settle at the bottom of the ocean etc. and form a solid layer

se·di·tion /sɪ'dɪʃən/ *n.* [U] FORMAL speech, writing, or actions intended to encourage people to disobey a government, in places where this is considered a crime

se·di·tious /sɪ'dɪʃəs/ *adj.* FORMAL intended to encourage people to disobey the government, in places where this is considered a crime: *a seditious conspiracy* —**seditiously** *adv.*

se·duce /sɪ'dus/ *v.* [T] **1** to persuade someone to have sex with you, especially in a way that is attractive and not too direct **2** [usually passive] to make someone want to do something by making it seem very attractive or interesting to them: *Graduates are often seduced by the huge salaries offered by large firms.* [**Origin:** 1400–1500 Latin *seducere* **to lead away**, from *ducere* **to lead**] —**seducer** *n.* [C]

se·duc·tion /sɪ'dʌkʃən/ *n.* **1** [C,U] an act of persuading someone to have sex with you for the first time **2** [C usually plural] something that strongly attracts people, but often has a bad effect on their lives: *the seductions of city life*

se·duc·tive /sɪ'dʌktɪv/ *adj.* **1** sexually attractive: *a charming and seductive man* **2** very interesting or attractive to you, in a way that persuades you to do something you would not usually do: *L.A. is a dangerous yet seductive city.* | *a seductive offer* —**seductively** *adv.* —**seductiveness** *n.* [U]

se·duc·tress /sɪ'dʌktrɪs/ *n.* [C] a woman who uses her sexual attractiveness to persuade someone to have sex with her

sed·u·lous /'sɛdʒələs/ *adj.* LITERARY hard working and determined: *a sedulous worker* —**sedulously** *adv.*

see

Lisa was blindfolded so she couldn't see anything.

They looked at the paintings.

Richard is watching TV.

see off

His family came to the airport to see him off.

see¹ /si/ S1 W1 *v. past tense* **saw** /sɔ/, *past participle* **seen** /sin/

1 ABILITY TO SEE [I,T not in progressive] to be able to use your eyes to look at things and know what they are:

Dad doesn't see as well as he used to. | **can/can't see** *I can't see anything without my glasses.*
2 NOTICE/EXAMINE [T not in progressive] to notice, examine, or recognize someone or something by looking: *She turned and saw him.* | *May I see your ticket, please?* | **can/can't see** *You can see the Empire State Building from here.* | **see where/what/who etc.** *Did you see who it was?* | **see (that)** *Oh, I see you got a new TV.* | **see sb/sth doing sth** *I saw her dancing with John.* | **see sb/sth do sth** *He saw the two women leave about 7:00.* | **see if/whether** *Can you see if Robert's there?* | ***Have you seen** my keys?* | ***As you can see**, we haven't finished yet.*

THESAURUS

You **see** something either without planning to or when you try to. You can say that you **saw** a particular movie, program, play etc., but you cannot say "see television."
You deliberately **look at** a picture or something else that is not moving, or **look at** someone or something for a short period of time.
You **watch** TV, a movie, something that happens for a period of time, or a place where something might happen.
notice to see something interesting or unusual: *I noticed a police car outside their house.*
spot to suddenly see something, especially something you are looking for: *I finally spotted her near the gates of the stadium.*
catch sight of sb/sth to suddenly see someone or something: *Lila's smile faded as she caught sight of me.*
catch/get a glimpse of sth also **glimpse** to see something, but only for a very short time: *I caught a glimpse of him getting onto a subway car.*
make out to see something, but only with difficulty: *Ahead, I could just make out the figure of a woman.*
witness to see something happen, especially a crime or an accident: *Two cab drivers witnessed the mugging.*
Unable to see
partially-sighted also **visually handicapped/impaired** unable to see well because of a physical problem with your eyes
blind unable to see anything

3 UNDERSTAND STH [I,T not in progressive] to understand or realize something: **see why/what/who etc.** *I can see why she was upset.* | ***I see what you mean** – her voice is really irritating.* | *I **could never see the point of*** (=could not understand the reason for or importance of something) *making us write in pencil.* ►see THESAURUS box at **understand**
4 NOTICE STH IS TRUE [T not in progressive] to notice that something is happening or that something is true: *After a month of practice, you will see a difference in your playing.* | **see (that)** *I can see there might be problems.*
5 FIND OUT [T] to find out information or a fact: **see what/when/who/how etc.** *Let's go see what Mom is doing.* | **see if/whether** *I'll call Tina and see if she's going.*
6 IN THE FUTURE [I,T] to find out about something in the future: **see if/whether** *I'll be interested to see whether he replies to my letter.* | **see how/what/when etc.** *I might come – I'll see how I feel tomorrow.* | *We just have to **wait and see** what happens.* | *Everything will be fine – **you'll see**.* | **see how it goes/see how things go** (=used when you are going to do something and will deal with problems as they appear)
7 TELEVISION/MOVIE [T not in progressive] to watch a television program, movie, play etc.: *We saw a great show on PBS last night.*
8 VISIT/MEET SB [T] **a)** to visit or meet someone: *Hi, I'm here to see Mary Jorgensen.* | *I'll see you at 2:30 at the mall.* **b)** to be visited by someone: *Danielle's still too sick to see anyone today.*
9 MEET BY CHANCE [T not in progressive] to meet someone by chance: *We saw Kathy and her mom at the airport.*
10 HAVE A MEETING [T] to have an arranged meeting with someone: *Ally has been seeing an analyst for years.* | **see sb about sth** *Why don't you see Bryan about the job?*
11 SPEND TIME WITH SB [T] to spend time with someone: *I've **been seeing a lot of** Joanne lately.* | **see more/less etc. of sb** *Do you see much of Rick these days?*
12 be seeing sb to be having a romantic relationship with someone: *Is Marge still seeing Tom?*
13 WHERE INFORMATION IS [T only in imperative] used to tell you where you can find information: *See p. 58.* | *See local listings for movie times.* | **see above/below** *The results are shown in Table 7a (see below).*
14 CONSIDER STH IN A PARTICULAR WAY [T always + adv./prep.] to regard or consider someone or something in a particular way: *Having a child makes you see things differently.* | **see sb/sth as sth** *I see the job as a challenge.* | *The decision is seen as a setback for the White House.* | **the way sb sees it/as sb sees it** *The way I see it, we have two choices.* | **be seen to be sth** *The country was seen to be an economic threat.*
15 see sth through sb's eyes to see something or think about it in the way that someone else does

SPOKEN PHRASES

16 see you! used to say goodbye when you know you will see someone again: ***See you later**, Colleen.* | **see you tomorrow/at 3:00/Sunday etc.** *I'll see you all in two weeks.* | **see you in a while/a bit/an hour etc.** *We'll see you folks in a little while.* | *Okay then, **I'll be seeing you*** (=see you soon)*!*
17 I see used to show that you are listening to what someone is telling you and that you understand it: *"First you need to switch the machine on like this." "Oh, I see."*
18 we'll see said when you do not want to make a decision about something immediately, especially when you are talking to a child: *"Can I come with you, Mommy?" "We'll see, sweetheart."*
19 let's see also **let me see** used to show that you are trying to remember or find something: *Okay, let's see, what were we talking about?*
20 you see used when you are explaining something to someone: *You see, he spends most of his time over at Bart's house.*
21 ...see used to check that someone is listening and understands what you are explaining to them: *You mix the flour and the eggs like this, see.*
22 I'll see what I can do used to say that you will try to help someone without promising to do it: *"I really need it by tomorrow." "I'll see what I can do."*
23 see what sb/sth can do to find out how good someone or something is at what they are supposed to be able to do: *Let's take this car out to the track and see what it can do.*
24 I don't see why not used to say yes in answer to a question or request: *"Can we go to the park?" "I don't see why not."*
25 now I've seen everything also **now I've seen it all** used to say that you think something is very silly or shocking
26 seen one, seen 'em all also **once you've seen one, you've seen them all** used to say that things of a particular type become boring because they are very similar to each other: *Once you've seen one of his movies, you've seen them all.*
27 see your way (clear) to do sth FORMAL to be able and willing to help someone: *If you could see your way to help us, it would be greatly appreciated.*
28 CHECK STH [T not in progressive] to make sure or check that something is done correctly: **+that** *It's your job to see that it's done correctly.* | *Don't worry – I'll **see to it**.*
29 WARNING [T only in imperative] used as a warning that something is important and must be done: **see (that)** *Just see that you behave while you're there.*

30 see (sth) for yourself also **see sth with your own eyes** to look at something so that you can find out if it is true, rather than believing what someone else tells

S

you: *Ed came outside to see for himself what was going on.*
31 EXPERIENCE [T not in progressive] to experience something: *Dr. McNeil had never seen an injury like this before.* | *I never thought I'd* ***live to see the day*** *you'd be buying me dinner.* | *He's an experienced politician, who* ***has seen it all before****.*
32 IMAGINE [T not in progressive] to form a picture or idea of something or someone in your mind SYN **imagine**: *He could see a great future for her in music.* | *I just* ***can't see*** *Marla* ***as*** *a teacher.* | **see yourself doing sth** *I don't see myself doing this job forever.*
33 see sth coming to realize that there is going to be a problem before it actually happens: *Everyone had seen the layoffs coming.*
34 see eye to eye [usually in negatives] if two people see eye to eye, they agree with each other: **+with** *I don't always see eye to eye with my father on politics.*
35 be seeing things to imagine that you see something which is not really there
36 see fit (to do sth) FORMAL to consider an action to be appropriate and sensible: *Management has not seen fit to replace the system yet.* | *The committee is free to use the funds* ***as it sees fit****.*
37 TIME/PLACE [T] if a time or place has seen a particular event or situation, it happened or existed in that time or place: *The U.S. saw a huge wave of immigration in the early 1900s.*
38 have seen better days INFORMAL to be in a bad condition: *The car has definitely seen better days.*
39 see sth for what it is also **see sb for what they are** to realize that someone or something is not as good or nice as they seem
40 you have to see sth to believe it also **sth has to be seen to be believed** used to say that something is so bad, big, unusual etc. that you would not believe it could exist or happen if you did not see it yourself
41 not see the forest for the trees to be unable to understand something because you are looking too much at small details rather than the whole thing
42 see the last of sb/sth to not see someone or something again because they have gone or are finished: *I hope we've seen the last of him.*
43 (see and) be seen (to look at and) to be noticed by people who are important in society: *The restaurant is still the place to be seen in L.A.*
44 see the world to travel to many different countries so that you can get a lot of different experiences
45 see the light **a)** to realize that something is true or must be done **b)** to have a special experience that makes you believe in a religion
46 GO WITH SB [T always + adv./prep.] to go somewhere with someone to make sure that they get there: *He insisted on* ***seeing*** *me* ***home****.* | *Let me* ***see you to the door****.*
47 see the light of day to start to exist, be seen, be used etc., especially after being planned, hidden, unused etc. for a long time: *Supporters doubt the law will ever see the light of day.*
48 see reason/sense to realize that you are being stupid or unreasonable
49 GAME OF CARDS [T not in progressive] to risk the same amount of money as your opponent in a card game
50 not see beyond the end of your nose to be so concerned with yourself and what you are doing that you do not realize what is happening to other people around you
[**Origin:** Old English *seon*] → see also **see the color of sb's money** at COLOR[1] (11), **see red** at RED[2] (4), **it remains to be seen** at REMAIN (4), SEEING

see about sth *phr. v.* **1** to make arrangements or preparations for something to happen, or to deal with something: *She had gone to a lawyer to see about a divorce.* | **see about doing sth** *Kenji will have to see about getting a visa.* **2 we'll see about that** SPOKEN **a)** used to say that you intend to stop someone from doing something they are planning to do: *Kim thinks she's coming too, huh? Well, we'll see about that!* **b)** also **we'll have to see about that** used to say that you do not know if something will be possible

see sth **against** sth *phr. v.* to consider something together with something else: *This sales growth must be seen against the backdrop of the city's overall economic expansion.*

see sb **around** *phr. v.* INFORMAL **1** to notice someone regularly in places where you go, without speaking to them: *I never actually met her, but I've seen her around.* **2 see you around** SPOKEN used to say goodbye to someone when you have not made a definite arrangement to meet again

see in *phr. v.* **1 see sth in sb/sth** to notice a particular quality in someone or something that makes you like them: *Janna had the same sense of fun that I saw in her father.* **2 not know what sb sees in sb** also **what does sb see in sb?** used to say that you do not understand why someone likes someone else: *What does Ron see in her?* **3 see in the new year** to celebrate the beginning of a new year

see off *phr. v.* **1 see sb ↔ off** to go to an airport, train station etc. to say goodbye to someone: *We went to the station to see him off.* **2 see sb/sth ↔ off** to defend yourself successfully in a fight or battle, or beat an opponent in a game: *The company has successfully seen the competition off.*

see out *phr. v.* **1 see sb out** to go to the door with someone to say goodbye to them when they leave: *Don't get up –* ***I'll see myself out*** (=used to tell someone they do not have to come to the door with you). **2 see sth ↔ out** to continue doing something or being somewhere until a particular period of time has finished

see through *phr. v.* **1 see through sth** to recognize the truth about something that is intended to deceive you: *I can see through your little plan.* **2 see through sb** to know what someone is really like, especially what their bad qualities are: *He was no good at bluffing, and I* ***saw right through*** *him.* **3 see sth through** to continue doing something, especially something difficult or not nice, until it is finished: *Martin made it clear that he intends to see the project through.* **4 see sb through** also **see sb through sth** to give help and support to someone during a difficult time: *The money should see me through a few months of unemployment.*

see to sb/sth *phr. v.* to deal with something or do something for someone: *She's upstairs seeing to the baby.* | *Would you* ***see to it that*** *Michelle gets that report?*

see² *n.* [C] TECHNICAL an area governed by a BISHOP

seed¹ /sid/ S3 W3 *n.*
1 PLANTS **a)** [C] BIOLOGY a small hard object produced by plants, containing an EMBRYO, from which a new plant grows: *sunflower seeds* | *an apple seed* | **plant/sow seeds** *Sow the seeds one inch deep in the soil.* | *I grew the plant* ***from seed****.* **b)** [U] a quantity of seeds: *grass seed*
2 seeds of sth something that makes a new situation start and develop: **+of** *the seeds of revolution* | *The letter planted seeds of doubt in Sally's mind.*
3 SPORTS [C] a player or team which is given a particular position according to how likely they are to win a competition: ***The top seed*** *has made it to the quarter finals.* | **the number one/two/three etc. seed** (=the person or team who is in the first, second etc. position)
4 go to seed **a)** if someone or something goes to seed, they become ugly, fat, or unhealthy, especially because they are getting old or are not taken care of well: *The old central bus station is going to seed.* **b)** if a plant or vegetable goes to seed, it starts producing flowers and seeds as well as leaves
5 FAMILY [U] BIBLICAL the group of people who have a particular person as their father, grandfather etc., especially when they form a particular race
[**Origin:** Old English *sæd*]

seed² *v.*
1 REMOVE SEEDS [T usually passive] to remove seeds from fruit or vegetables: *Seed and slice the peppers.*
2 RANK [T usually passive] to give a player or team in a

competition a particular position, according to how likely they are to win: **be seeded second/third etc.** *She was seeded fifth in the competition.* | *a top-seeded player*
3 PLANT [T usually passive] BIOLOGY to plant an area of ground with seeds
4 CLOUDS [T] to put a chemical substance into clouds from an airplane, in order to produce rain
5 PRODUCE SEEDS [I] BIOLOGY to produce seeds

seed·bed /ˈsidbɛd/ *n.* [C] **1** a place or condition that encourages something to develop: +**of** *The city's slums were a seedbed of rebellion.* → see also HOTBED **2** an area of ground where young plants are grown from seeds before they are planted somewhere else

seed ˌcapital *n.* [U] seed money

seed coat *n.* [C] BIOLOGY a protective cover surrounding the seeds of a plant, that prevents it from becoming too dry

seed cone *n.* [C] BIOLOGY in a tree that produces both male and female cells, a container for holding the female cells during the time when male cells are developing → see also PINE CONE

seed·ling /ˈsidlɪŋ/ *n.* [C] a young plant grown from seed

seed ˌmoney *n.* [U] the money you have available to start a new business

seed pearl *n.* [C] a very small and often imperfect PEARL

seed·y /ˈsidi/ *adj. comparative* **seedier**, *superlative* **seediest** INFORMAL a seedy person or place looks dirty or poor, and is often involved in or connected with illegal, immoral, or dishonest activities: *a seedy nightclub* —**seediness** *n.* [U]

see·ing /ˈsiɪŋ/ *conjunction* SPOKEN also **ˈseeing as (how)**, **ˈseeing that** because a particular fact or situation is true SYN **since**: *Seeing as it's your birthday, why don't we go out for a meal?*

Seeing ˈEye ˌdog *n.* [C] TRADEMARK a dog trained to guide blind people

seek /sik/ Ac S3 W1 *v. past tense and past participle* **sought** /sɔt/ [T]
1 TRY TO DO STH FORMAL to try to achieve or get something: *Do you think the president will seek re-election?* | **seek to do sth** *Local schools are seeking to reduce the dropout rate.* | **seek refuge/asylum/shelter** *Thousands of people crossed the border, seeking refuge from the war.* | *Justice is not about* ***seeking revenge****.* | **seek damages/compensation** *Workers are entitled to seek compensation for their injuries.* | **attention-seeking/publicity-seeking** (=trying to get people's attention)
2 seek (sb's) advice/help/assistance etc. FORMAL to ask someone for advice or help: *You may need to seek professional help.*
3 LOOK FOR FORMAL to look for something you need: *A man is being sought by police following the attack.* ▸see THESAURUS box at **look**[1]
4 seek your fortune LITERARY to go to another place hoping to gain success and wealth
5 MOVE to move naturally toward something or into a particular position: *Water seeks its own level.*
[**Origin:** Old English *secan*] → see also HEAT-SEEKING, SELF-SEEKING, SOUGHT-AFTER

seek sb/sth ↔ **out** *phr. v.* to look very hard for someone or something: *We're always seeking out new talent.*

seek·er /ˈsikɚ/ *n.* [C] someone who is trying to find or get something: **job/asylum/treasure etc. seeker** *Autograph seekers should arrive early at the game.*

seem /sim/ S1 W1 *v.* [linking verb, not in progressive]
1 to appear to be true, to be a particular thing, or to have a particular quality, feeling, or attitude SYN **appear**: *You seem kind of nervous.* | *He seems an odd choice.* | **seem strange/important/funny etc. to sb** *Does that seem right to you?* | +**like** *Terri seems like a nice girl.* | *We waited for what seemed like a long time.* | **seem to be sth** *Lack of money seems to be the main problem.* | **seem to do sth** *The kids seem to like each other.* | *Jill's voice seemed to be coming from very far away.* | **it seems to sb (that)** *It seems to me that you don't have much choice.* | **it seems like/as if/as though** *It seems like Jerry is always working.* | **it seems likely/unlikely/clear (that)** *It seems likely he will miss the next game.* | **it seems (that)/it would seem (that)** *It seems that one of your students cheated on the test.* | *"So Bill is leaving her?" "****So it seems*** (=it appears to be true)*."*

THESAURUS

appear FORMAL to seem to have particular qualities: *Light colors make a room appear bigger than it is.*
look to seem to be something, especially by having a particular appearance: *Mrs. Fraser looked very worried.* | *Things look very difficult for the company.*
sound to seem to have a particular quality when you hear or read about someone or something: *It sounds like a wonderful trip.* | *He made it all sound very complicated.*
come across as sth to seem to have certain qualities: *She comes across as a really happy person.*

2 used to make what you are saying less strong or certain, or more polite: *There seems to be some misunderstanding.* | **seem to have done sth** *I seem to have lost my keys.* **3 can't/couldn't seem to do sth** used to say that you have tried to do something, but cannot do it: *I just can't seem to relax.* [**Origin:** 1100–1200 Old Norse *sœma* **to be appropriate to**, from *sœmr* **appropriate**]

S

seem·ing /ˈsimɪŋ/ *adj.* [only before noun] FORMAL appearing to be something, especially when this is not actually true SYN **apparent**: *Don't be fooled by her seeming lack of concern.*

seem·ing·ly /ˈsimɪŋli/ *adv.* **1** [+ adj.] appearing to have a particular quality when this is not actually true SYN **apparently**: *seemingly impossible task* **2** [sentence adverb] FORMAL according to the facts as you know them: *There is seemingly nothing we can do to stop the project.*

seeml·y /ˈsimli/ *adj. comparative* **seemlier**, *superlative* **seemliest** OLD-FASHIONED appropriate for a particular situation or social occasion, according to accepted standards of behavior OPP **unseemly**

seen /sin/ *v.* the past participle of SEE

seep /sip/ *v.* [I always + adv./prep.] **1** to flow slowly through small holes or spaces: +**in/into/through etc.** *Water was seeping through the walls.* **2** LITERARY to gradually go, come, or spread

seep·age /ˈsipɪdʒ/ *n.* [singular, U] a gradual flow of liquid through small spaces or holes: *oil seepage*

seer /ˈsiɚ/ *n.* [C] ESPECIALLY LITERARY someone who can see into the future and say what will happen

seer·suck·er /ˈsɪrˌsʌkɚ/ *n.* [U] a light cotton cloth with an uneven surface and a pattern of lines on it

see·saw[1] /ˈsisɔ/ *n.* [C] **1** a piece of equipment that children play on, made of a board that is balanced in the middle, so that when the child sitting on one end goes up the other goes down SYN **teeter-totter** **2** a situation in which someone or something keeps changing from one state or condition to another and back again

seesaw[2] *v.* [I] to move from one condition to another and back again

seethe /sið/ *v.* [I] **1** to feel a bad emotion, especially anger, so strongly that you are almost shaking: *He went to bed seething.* | +**with** *Daniel was seething with jealousy.* **2 be seething with sth** if a place is seething with people, insects etc., there are a lot of them all moving quickly in different directions: *The area was seething with tourists.* **3** LITERARY if a liquid seethes, it moves violently, for example because it is boiling

ˈsee-through *adj.* a see-through material or surface allows you to see through it: *a see-through blouse* → see also TRANSPARENT

seg·ment /ˈsɛgmənt/ S3 *n.* [C] **1** a part of something that is in some way different from or affected differently than the whole: *The program included a short segment about pet owners.* | +**of** *A large segment of the population does not exercise at all.* | *products for a variety of* ***market segments*** **2** BIOLOGY a part of a fruit, flower, or insect that naturally divides into parts: *orange segments* → see picture at FRUIT[1] **3** MATH the part of a line between two points **4** MATH a part of a circle that is separated from the rest of the circle by a straight line across it [**Origin:** 1500–1600 Latin *segmentum*, from *secare* **to cut**] —**segment** /ˈsɛgmənt, sɛgˈmɛnt/ *v.* [T]

seg·men·ta·tion /ˌsɛgmənˈteɪʃən/ *n.* [U] the act of dividing something into smaller parts, or the state of being divided in this way

seg·ment·ed /ˈsɛgmɛntɪd/ *adj.* made up of separate parts that are connected to each other: *an insect's segmented body*

seg·re·gate /ˈsɛgrəˌgeɪt/ *v.* [T often passive] to separate one group of people from others, or to separate people into several groups because they are different from each other in some way, for example because they are of a different race, sex, or religion OPP **desegregate**: *In two of these tests, the people were segregated by gender.* | *Not long ago, schools in the South were racially segregated.* | *segregated residential areas* | **segregate sb from sb** *Juvenile offenders should be segregated from adults.* [**Origin:** 1500–1600 Latin, past participle of *segregare*, from *se-* **apart** + *grex* **herd**] → see also INTEGRATE

seg·re·gat·ed /ˈsɛgrəˌgeɪtɪd/ *adj.* a segregated school, institution, or other place can only be used by members of one race, religion, sex etc. → see also INTEGRATED

seg·re·ga·tion /ˌsɛgrəˈgeɪʃən/ *n.* [U] **1** POLITICS the practice of keeping people of different races or religions apart and making them live, work, or study separately → see also INTEGRATION: *racial segregation* **2** BIOLOGY the process by which a CHROMOSOME divides into its two parts so that each half appears in a separate GAMETE (=cell involved in sexual reproduction)

se·gue /ˈsɛgweɪ/ *v.* **segued, segueing** [I] to move or change smoothly from one song, idea, activity, condition etc. to another: +**into** *The band segued smoothly into the next song.* —**segue** *n.* [C]

Seine, the /seɪn, sɛn/ a river in northern France that flows through Paris and Rouen and northward into the English Channel

seis·mic /ˈsaɪzmɪk/ *adj.* [only before noun] **1** EARTH SCIENCE relating to or caused by EARTHQUAKES or powerful explosions: *seismic activity* **2** very great, serious, or important: *seismic changes in international relations*

ˌseismic acˈtivity *n.* [U] EARTH SCIENCE EARTHQUAKES or other shaking movements in the surface of the Earth

ˌseismic ˈwave *n.* [C] EARTH SCIENCE a shaking movement in the Earth's surface that continues for a length of time and moves over a large area, caused when the very large sheets of rock that form the surface of the Earth move against each other

seis·mo·graph /ˈsaɪzməˌgræf/ *n.* [C] EARTH SCIENCE an instrument that measures and records the movement of the earth during an EARTHQUAKE —**seismographic** /ˌsaɪzməˈgræfɪk◂/ *adj.*

seis·mol·o·gy /saɪzˈmɑlədʒi/ *n.* [U] EARTH SCIENCE the scientific study of EARTHQUAKES —**seismologist** *n.* [C]

seize /siz/ W3 *v.* [T]

1 GRAB to take firm hold of someone or something suddenly and with a lot of force SYN **grab**: *"Come with me," said Nat, seizing him by the arm.* | **seize sth from sb** *He seized the scissors from her.* ►see THESAURUS box at **hold**[1]

2 TAKE CONTROL to take control of a place suddenly and quickly, using military force: **seize power/control** *His party seized power in a military coup.*

3 TAKE PRISONER to suddenly catch someone and make sure they cannot get away: *Three hostages were seized at gunpoint.*

4 TAKE STH AWAY if the police or government officers seize something, they take away illegal goods such as drugs or guns: *Authorities have seized over 200 pounds of marijuana this year.*

5 AFFECT SB [usually passive] if a feeling seizes someone, it suddenly affects them strongly: *A wave of panic seized her.* | **be seized with/by sth** *He was suddenly seized with guilt.*

6 seize a chance/opportunity etc. to quickly and eagerly do something when you have the chance to do it: *As usual, I seized the opportunity to voice my own opinion.*

7 seize the day/moment used to say that you should do something now, when you have the chance to do it, rather than waiting until a later time

8 seize the initiative to gain an advantage by quickly doing something before someone else does it

[**Origin:** 1200–1300 Old French *saisir* **to take possession of**, from Medieval Latin *sacire*]

seize on/upon sth *phr. v.* to suddenly become very interested in an idea, excuse, what someone says etc.: *White House staffers seized upon the senator's comments.*

seize up *phr. v.* **1** if an engine or part of a machine seizes up, its moving parts stop working and cannot move anymore, for example because of lack of oil **2** if a part of your body such as your back seizes up, you suddenly cannot move it and it is very painful

sei·zure /ˈsiʒɚ/ *n.* **1** [C,U] the act of taking away illegal goods such as drugs or guns by the police or government officers: *drug seizures* | +**of** *the seizure of guns and other weapons* **2** [C,U] the act of suddenly taking control of something, especially by force **3** [C] MEDICINE a sudden condition in which someone becomes unconscious and cannot control the movements of their body, which continues for a short time: **have/suffer a seizure** *One of the restaurant customers suffered an epileptic seizure.*

sel·dom /ˈsɛldəm/ *adv.* almost never SYN **rarely**: *She seldom eats at home.* | *Council meetings are seldom longer than an hour.* | *Seldom have I read such a powerful book.* [**Origin:** Old English *seldan*]

se·lect[1] /sɪˈlɛkt/ Ac S3 W2 *v.* [T] **1** to choose someone or something by carefully thinking about which is the best, most appropriate etc. SYN **choose** SYN **pick**: *I selected four postcards.* | **select sb/sth to do sth** *We selected Sarah to be our representative.* | **select sb/sth from sth** *They selected the winner from six finalists.* ►see THESAURUS box at **choose** **2** COMPUTERS to use the MOUSE to choose a word or picture on a computer screen, usually by CLICKING on it: *Go to the File menu and select "Save."*

select[2] Ac *adj.* FORMAL **1** [only before noun] a select group of people or things is a small special group that has been carefully chosen: *a select group of students* | *Funds should not just be available to* ***a select few.*** **2** only lived in, visited, or used by a small number of rich people SYN **exclusive**: *a very select residential area* [**Origin:** 1500–1600 Latin, past participle of *seligere* **to select**, from *legere* **to gather, choose**]

seˌlect comˈmittee *n.* [C] a small group of politicians and advisers from various parties, chosen to examine a particular subject SYN **special committee**: *the Senate Select Committee on Ethics*

se·lect·ed /sɪˈlɛktɪd/ Ac *adj.* [only before noun] carefully chosen from among a group of similar people or things: *a book of selected poems by T. S. Eliot*

se·lec·tion /sɪˈlɛkʃən/ Ac S3 W3 *n.*

1 ACT OF CHOOSING [U] the careful choice of a particular person or thing from among a group of similar people or things: +**of** *the selection of a Supreme Court justice* | *The judges will* ***make*** *their final* ***selection*** *this afternoon.* | +**as** *Ross's selection as the Republican Party's candidate*

2 RANGE [C usually singular] a number of different things of the same kind that are available for you to buy, choose, or use SYN **range**: +**of** *We offer a selection of*

hot and cold dishes. | **a wide/good selection of sth** *a wide selection of digital cameras*
3 GROUP [C usually singular] a number of things that have been chosen from among a group of things: **+of** *She showed me a selection of her drawings.* | **+from** *a selection of songs from Broadway musicals*
4 CHOICE [C] someone or something that has been chosen from among a group of people or things SYN **choice**: *Is it too late to change my selection?*
5 SONG [C] a song that someone performs or records: *He produced six of the selections on the new album.* → see also NATURAL SELECTION

se·lec·tive /sɪˈlɛktɪv/ Ac *adj.* **1** careful about what you choose to do, buy, allow etc.: *selective colleges* | **+about** *We've always been selective about our clients.* **2** affecting or relating to the best or most appropriate people or things from a larger group: *selective breeding* **3 a selective memory** a memory that seems to choose what to remember and what to forget —**selectively** *adv.* —**selectivity** /sɪˌlɛkˈtɪvəṭi/ *n.* [U]

seˌlective ˈbreeding *n.* [U] BIOLOGY the deliberate mating (MATE) of two animals in order to produce animals that are considered better than existing animals

Seˌlective ˈService *n.* [U] the U.S. government system in which young men must put their names on an official list and choose which part of the armed forces they would join if there were a war

Seˌlective ˌTraining and ˈService Act, the HISTORY a U.S. law passed in 1940 that said that all young men had to put their names on an official list for military service

se·lec·tor /sɪˈlɛktɚ/ Ac *n.* [C] TECHNICAL a piece of equipment that helps you find the right position for something, for example the correct station on a radio

se·le·ni·um /sɪˈliniəm/ *n.* [U] SYMBOL **Se** CHEMISTRY a poisonous ELEMENT that is not a metal and is used in some electrical instruments to make them sensitive to light

self /sɛlf/ W2 *n. plural* **selves** /sɛlvz/ **1** [usually singular] the person you are, including your character, your typical behavior, your abilities etc.: **sb's usual/normal self** *Marcus wasn't his usual smiling self today.* | **be/look/feel (like) your old self** *Jim was beginning to feel like his old self again.* | *Many people deny their* ***true selves*** (=what they are really like). **2** [U] TECHNICAL someone's conscious understanding of being a separate person, different from other people: *a child's developing* ***sense of self*** **3 be a shadow/ghost of your former self** to not be as healthy, strong, cheerful etc. as you used to be **4** [U] a word written in business letters, official documents etc. meaning the same person that has just been mentioned **5 your good self** HUMOROUS used to mean "you" [**Origin:** Old English]

self- /sɛlf/ *prefix* **1** by yourself or by itself: *He's self-taught* (=he taught himself). | *self-adhesive labels* (=that stick by themselves) **2** done by or to yourself or itself: *a self-portrait* (=a picture of yourself, that you have drawn or painted yourself) | *self-restraint* (=the ability to stop yourself from doing something that is not sensible)

self-abneˈgation *n.* [U] FORMAL a lack of interest in your own needs and desires SYN **abnegation**

self-abˈsorbed *adj.* concerned only with yourself and the things that affect you: *I was too self-absorbed to notice how unhappy she was.* —**self-absorption** *n.* [U]

self-ˌactualiˈzation *n.* [U] FORMAL the process of developing and improving your own abilities so that you become happier and more satisfied with your life

self-adˈdressed *adj.* a self-addressed envelope has your name and address on it, so that someone can use it to send you something in the mail → see also SASE

self-adˈhesive *adj.* a self-adhesive stamp, BANDAGE etc. has a sticky surface and does not need liquid or glue to make it stay attached to something else

self-agˈgrandizement *n.* [U] the act of making yourself seem bigger, more important, or more powerful than you are —**self-aggrandizing** *adj.*

ˌself-apˈpointed *adj.* [only before noun] having given yourself a job, position etc., especially without the approval of other people: *self-appointed guardians of public morals*

ˌself-asˈsurance *n.* [U] confidence and the belief that you are able to deal with people and problems easily

ˌself-asˈsured *adj.* calm and confident about what you are doing

ˌself-aˈwareness *n.* [U] knowledge and understanding of yourself —**self-aware** *adj.*

ˌself-ˈcentered *adj.* interested only in yourself and not really caring what is happening to other people SYN **selfish** —**self-centeredness** *n.* [U]

ˌself-conˈfessed *adj.* [only before noun] admitting that you have a particular quality, especially one that is bad: *a self-confessed television addict*

ˌself-ˈconfident *adj.* sure that you can do things well, that people have a good opinion of you, that you are attractive etc., and not shy or nervous in social situations —**self-confidently** *adv.* —**self-confidence** *n.* [U]

ˌself-conˈgratulatory *adj.* DISAPPROVING behaving in an annoying way that shows you think you have done very well at something: *a self-congratulatory smile* —**ˌself-congratuˈlation** *n.* [U] DISAPPROVING

S

ˌself-ˈconscious *adj.* **1** worried and embarrassed about what you look like or what other people think of you: *I felt really self-conscious when they started filming.* | **+about** *Leo's still self-conscious about his accent.* ▶see THESAURUS box at **shy**[1] **2** self-conscious art, writing etc. shows that the artist or writer is paying too much attention to how the public will react to them —**self-consciously** *adv.* —**self-consciousness** *n.* [U]

ˌself-conˈtained *adj.* **1** something that is self-contained is complete in itself, and does not need other things or help from somewhere else to make it work: *a self-contained heating unit* **2** someone who is self-contained tends not to be friendly or show their feelings

ˌself-contraˈdictory *adj.* containing two opposite statements or ideas that cannot both be true —**self-contradiction** *n.* [C,U]

ˌself-conˈtrol *n.* [U] the ability to behave calmly and sensibly even when you feel very excited, angry etc.: *Matt's lack of self-control has gotten him into a lot of trouble.* —**self-controlled** *adj.*

ˌself-deˈception *n.* [U] the act of making yourself believe something is true, when it is not really true: *In difficult situations, most of us practice some degree of self-deception.* —**self-deceptive** *adj.*

ˌself-deˈfeating *adj.* causing more problems and difficulties in a situation, instead of preventing or dealing with the ones that already exist: *the self-defeating cycle of overeating and dieting*

ˌself-deˈfense *n.* [U] **1** something that you do to protect yourself or your property: *Keller insists he shot the man* ***in self-defense*** (=to protect himself). **2** skills that you learn to protect yourself if you are physically attacked: *a self-defense class*

ˌself-deˈnial *n.* [U] the practice of not doing or having the things you enjoy, either because you cannot afford it, or for moral or religious reasons —**self-denying** *adj.*

ˌself-ˈdeprecating *adj.* trying to make your own abilities or achievements seem unimportant: *self-deprecating humor*

ˌself-deˈscribed *adj.* [only before noun] using a particular word or words to describe yourself, even if other people would not describe you in this way: *Tom is a self-described ladies' man.*

self-de·struct /ˌsɛlf dɪˈstrʌkt/ *v.* [I] **1** if something self-destructs, it destroys itself by exploding **2** if a group, organization etc. self-destructs, it stops working effectively and becomes disorganized, especially because of disagreements **3** if someone self-destructs, they do something that will cause them to fail, especially deliberately

ˌself-desˈtruction *n.* [U] **1** the practice of deliberately doing things that are likely to seriously harm or kill you: *Her poems reveal that she was bent on self-destruction* (=determined to harm or kill herself). **2** the act of something destroying itself by exploding

ˌself-deˈstructive *adj.* likely to seriously harm yourself or prevent yourself from succeeding: *a self-destructive lifestyle of drugs and alcohol*

ˌself-determiˈnation *n.* [U] the right of the people of a particular country to govern themselves and to choose the type of government they will have

ˌself-ˈdiscipline *n.* [U] the ability to make yourself do the things you know you ought to do, without someone making you do them: *Working at home takes a lot of self-discipline.* —**self-disciplined** *adj.*

ˌself-ˈdoubt *n.* [U] the feeling that you and your abilities are not good enough

ˌself-ˈeducated *adj.* having taught yourself by reading books etc., rather than learning things in school

ˌself-efˈfacing *adj.* FORMAL not wanting to attract attention to yourself or your achievements, especially because you are not socially confident SYN **modest**: *self-effacing modesty* —**self-effacement** *n.* [U]

ˌself-emˈployed *adj.* working for yourself, and not directly employed by a company: *Kerry is a self-employed graphic designer.* —**self-employment** *n.* [U] → see also FREELANCE

ˌself-esˈteem *n.* [U] the feeling that you are someone who deserves to be liked, respected, and admired: *Losing the job was a real blow to his self-esteem.* | **low/poor/high self-esteem** (=not much self-esteem or a lot of it) | **boost/bolster/build (sb's) self-esteem** *Looking good can boost your self-esteem.*

ˌself-ˈevident *adj.* FORMAL clearly true and needing no more proof SYN **obvious**: *self-evident truths*

ˌself-examiˈnation *n.* **1** [C,U] MEDICINE the practice of checking parts of your body for early signs of some diseases **2** [U] careful thought about whether your actions and your reasons for them are right or wrong

ˌself-exˈplanatory *adj.* clear and easy to understand without needing further explanation: *The form is pretty self-explanatory.*

ˌself-exˈpression *n.* [U] the expression of your feelings, thoughts, ideas etc., especially through activities such as painting, writing, or acting etc.: *She viewed dance as a form of self-expression.* —**self-expressive** *adj.*

ˌself-fulˌfilling ˈprophecy *n.* [C usually singular] a statement about what is likely to happen in the future that becomes true, because you expected it to happen and therefore changed your behavior so that it did happen

ˌself-ˈgoverning *adj.* POLITICS a self-governing area, country, or organization is controlled by its own members rather than by someone from another country or organization

ˌself-ˈgovernment *n.* [U] the government of a country or part of a country by its own citizens, rather than by another country or group SYN **self-rule**

ˌself-ˈhelp *n.* [U] the use of your own efforts to deal with your problems instead of depending on other people: *self-help books* | *a self-help group* (=a group of people with a particular illness or problem who help each other)

self•hood /ˈsɛlfhʊd/ *n.* [U] TECHNICAL the knowledge of yourself as an independent person separate from others

ˌself-ˈimage *n.* [C] the idea you have of your own abilities, physical appearance, and character: *people with a poor self-image*

ˌself-imˈportant *adj.* behaving in a way that shows you think you are more important than other people: *a self-important pompous little man* —**self-importantly** *adv.*

ˌself-imˈposed *adj.* a self-imposed rule, condition, responsibility etc. is one that you have made yourself accept, and which no one has asked you to accept: *self-imposed exile*

ˌself-imˈprovement *n.* [U] the activity of trying to learn more skills or to deal with problems better

ˌself-inˈdulgent *adj.* **1** allowing yourself to have or do things you enjoy but do not need, especially if you do this too much **2** DISAPPROVING a self-indulgent movie, book etc. only expresses the director's or writer's feelings and interests, which are not interesting to other people —**self-indulgence** *n.* [U] —**self-indulgently** *adv.*

ˌself-inˈflicted *adj.* self-inflicted pain, problems, illnesses etc. are those you have caused yourself: *a self-inflicted wound*

ˌself-ˈinterest *n.* [U] the act of caring about only what is best for you rather than other people OPP **altruism**: *He acted purely out of self-interest.* —**self-interested** *adj.*

self•ish /ˈsɛlfɪʃ/ *adj.* caring only about yourself and not about other people: *He's completely selfish.* | *She agreed to go along for purely selfish reasons.* —**selfishly** *adv.* —**selfishness** *n.* [U]

ˌself-ˈknowledge *n.* [U] FORMAL an understanding of your own character, your reasons for doing things etc.

self•less /ˈsɛlflɪs/ *adj.* APPROVING caring about other people more than about yourself: *selfless devotion to others* —**selflessly** *adv.* APPROVING —**selflessness** *n.* [U] APPROVING

ˌself-ˈmade *adj.* a self-made man or woman has become successful and rich by their own efforts, and did not have advantages such as money or a high social position when they started: *a self-made millionaire*

ˌself-oˈpinionated *adj.* DISAPPROVING believing that your own opinions and ideas are always right and that everyone else should always agree with you

ˌself-perˈpetuating *adj.* a self-perpetuating situation, activity, belief etc. is able to continue by itself without the help of anyone or anything else

ˌself-ˈpity *n.* [U] the feeling of being sorry for yourself because you have been unlucky or you think people have treated you badly: *He sat around **wallowing in self-pity*** (=seeming to enjoy feeling sorry for himself). —**self-pitying** *adj.*

ˌself-ˈportrait *n.* [C] a drawing, painting, or description that you do of yourself

ˌself-posˈsessed *adj.* calm, confident, and in control of your feelings, even in difficult or unexpected situations —**self-possession** *n.* [U]

ˌself-preserˈvation *n.* [U] protection of yourself in a threatening or dangerous situation: *What seems to motivate Congress is self-preservation – a desire to get re-elected.*

ˌself-proˈclaimed *adj.* [only before noun] DISAPPROVING having given yourself a position or title without the approval of other people: *self-proclaimed experts*

ˌself-ˈregulatory also **ˌself-ˈregulating** *adj.* a self-regulatory system, industry, or organization is one that controls itself, rather than having an independent organization or laws to make sure that rules are obeyed —**ˌself-reguˈlation** *n.* [U]

ˌself-reˈliant *adj.* able to decide what to do by yourself, without depending on the help or advice of other people: *David learned to be self-reliant at a young age.* —**self-reliance** *n.* [C]

ˌself-reˈspect *n.* [U] a feeling of being confident about yourself and your abilities and that you deserve to be treated well by other people: *The program gives kids a sense of pride and self-respect.*

ˌself-reˈspecting *adj.* [only before noun] having respect for yourself and your abilities and beliefs: ***No self-respecting** wine drinker **would** enjoy wine that came from a box.*

ˌself-reˈstraint *n.* [U] the ability not to do or say

something you really want to, because you know it is more sensible not to do or say it

ˌself-ˈrighteous *adj.* DISAPPROVING proudly sure that your beliefs and attitudes are good and right, in a way that annoys other people: *self-righteous indignation* —**self-righteously** *adv.* DISAPPROVING —**self-righteousness** *n.* [U] DISAPPROVING

ˌself-rising ˈflour *n.* [U] a type of flour that contains BAKING POWDER

ˌself-ˈrule *n.* [U] POLITICS the government of a country or part of a country by its own citizens, rather than by another country or group SYN **self-government**

ˌself-ˈsacrifice *n.* [U] the act of doing without things you want, need, or care about in order to help someone else —**self-sacrificing** *adj.*

self·same /ˈsɛlfseɪm/ *adj.* [only before noun] LITERARY exactly the same: *They met and were married on **the selfsame** day.*

ˌself-ˈsatisfied *adj.* DISAPPROVING too pleased with yourself and what you have done: *a self-satisfied grin* —**ˌself-satisˈfaction** *n.* [U] DISAPPROVING

ˌself-ˈseeking *adj.* DISAPPROVING doing things only because they will give you an advantage that other people do not have: *self-seeking politicians*

ˌself-ˈservice also **ˌself ˈserve** *adj.* a self-service restaurant, store etc. is one in which you get things for yourself and then pay for them: *a self-service gas station* —**self-service** *n.* [U]

ˌself-ˈserving *adj.* DISAPPROVING showing that you will only do something if it will gain you an advantage: *a self-serving political maneuver*

ˌself-ˈstarter *n.* [C] someone who is able to work successfully on their own without needing other people's help or a lot of instructions

ˈself-styled *adj.* [only before noun] having given yourself a title or position without having a right to it: *a self-styled religious leader*

ˌself-sufˈficient *adj.* providing all the things you need without help from outside: *a self-sufficient farm* —**self-sufficiency** *n.* [U]

ˌself-supˈporting *adj.* **1** able to earn enough money to support yourself **2** able to stay upright without support

ˌself-susˈtaining *adj.* continuing or able to continue existing, working, developing etc. without needing help from anyone else: *a self-sustaining economic recovery*

ˌself-ˈtaught *adj.* having learned a skill or subject by yourself, rather than in a school: *a self-taught artist*

ˌself-ˈtitled *adj.* [only before noun] a self-titled CD, record etc. has as its title the name of the group or singer who performs on it

ˌself-ˈwilled *adj.* very determined to do what you want, even when this is unreasonable —**self-will** *n.* [U]

self-wind·ing /ˌsɛlf ˈwaɪndɪŋ/ *adj.* a self-winding watch is one that you do not have to WIND to make it work

ˌself-ˈworth *n.* [U] the feeling that you deserve to be liked and respected: *Work gave me a sense of self-worth and purpose.*

sell[1] /sɛl/ S1 W1 *v. past tense and past participle* **sold** /soʊld/

1 GIVE STH FOR MONEY [I,T] to give something to someone in exchange for money OPP **buy**: *More than a million copies of the book have been sold.* | **sell sth to sb** *I sold the piano to a friend.* | **sell sb sth** *He offered to sell me his car.* | **sell sth for $100/$50 etc.** *She sold the painting for $150.* | **sell sth at a profit/loss** (=to sell something for more or less money than you originally paid for it)

THESAURUS

put sth up for sale to give money to be used for a particular purpose: *The farm was put up for sale.*
auction/auction off to sell things at a special event to the person who offers the most money: *The artist's drawings and posters were auctioned off.*
peddle to go from place to place trying to sell something, especially something illegal or cheap: *vendors peddling ice cream in the park*
export to sell goods to another country: *farms in the area export two-thirds of the world's wheat*
deal in sth to buy and sell a particular type of product: *He deals in antiques.*

2 FOR SALE [T] to offer something for people to buy: *Do you sell stamps?*
3 BE BOUGHT [I] to be bought by someone in exchange for money: *We're hoping the house will sell quickly.* | *Their first album sold millions.* | **sell well/badly** *The car is selling well in Japan.* | **sell for $100/$50/$3 etc.** *Nierman's paintings sell for thousands of dollars.*
4 MAKE SB WANT STH [T] to make people want to buy something: *Scandals sell newspapers.* | **sell sth to sb** *The car's eco-friendly design should help sell it to consumers.*
5 IDEA/PLAN a) [T] to try to make someone accept a new idea or plan: **sell sth to sb** *He needed to sell the idea to his colleagues.* **b)** [I] to become accepted: *There are doubts about whether the policy will sell in small-town America.*
6 sell yourself a) to be able to make yourself seem impressive to other people: *If you want a promotion, you've got to sell yourself better.* **b)** also **sell your body** to have sex with someone for money
7 sell sb/sth short to not give someone or something the praise, attention, or reward that they deserve: *Don't sell yourself short – you're very capable!*
8 sell your soul (to the devil) to agree to do something bad in exchange for money, power etc.
9 sell your vote to take money from someone who wants you to vote for a particular person or plan
10 sell sb a bill of goods to trick someone into accepting or believing something that is not good or true by making it seem better than it is
11 sell sb down the river INFORMAL to do something that harms a group of people who trusted you to help them, in order to gain money or power for yourself
[**Origin:** Old English *sellan*] → see also **be selling/going like hotcakes** at HOTCAKE

sell sth ↔ **off** *phr. v.* **1** to sell something, especially for a low price, because you need the money, or because you want to get rid of it: *They sold off their surplus cattle.* **2** to sell all or part of a business

sell sb **on** sth *phr. v.* to persuade someone that an idea or plan is good: *We're still trying to sell Dad on a family trip to Hawaii.* | **be sold on (doing) sth** *He could see she was sold on the idea.*

sell out *phr. v.* **1** if a product, tickets, places at a concert etc. sell out, they are all sold and there are none left: *Tickets for the concert sold out in an hour.* → see also SOLD OUT **2** if a store sells out of something, it has no more of that particular thing left to sell → see also SOLD OUT **3 sell sth ↔ out** if an event, performance etc. sells out a place, it is so popular that all the tickets for it are sold → see also SELLOUT **4** DISAPPROVING to change your beliefs or principles, especially in order to get more money or some other advantage: *His friends accused him of selling out.* → see also SELLOUT **5 sell sb ↔ out** INFORMAL, DISAPPROVING to disappoint someone by not doing what they expected you to do, or by helping and supporting someone else instead: *The government has sold out middle class Americans.* → see also SELLOUT **6** to sell your business, your share in a business, or a piece of property: *He was forced to sell out to pay off his debts.*

sell[2] *n.* **a hard/tough sell** something that is difficult to persuade people to buy or accept: *This tax hike is going to be a hard sell to voters.* → see also SOFT SELL

sell·er /ˈsɛlɚ/ *n.* [C] **1** someone who sells something OPP **buyer** **2 a big/top/poor etc. seller** a product that sells well, badly etc. → see also BESTSELLER

ˌseller's ˈmarket *n.* [singular] a situation in which there is not much of a particular thing, such as houses or property, available for sale, so prices tend to be high OPP **buyer's market**

ˈselling point *n.* [C] something about a product that will make people want to buy it: *The school's strongest selling point is its excellent sports facilities.*

ˈselling price *n.* [C] the price at which something is actually sold → see also ASKING PRICE

sell·out, sell-out /ˈsɛlaʊt/ *n.* [C usually singular] **1** a performance, sports game etc. for which all the tickets have been sold: *The concert is expected to be a sellout.* | *The team played before* ***a sellout crowd*** *of 65,000.* **2** INFORMAL someone who other people think has not done what they promised to do or who is not loyal to their old friends or supporters anymore, especially because they are trying to become more popular, richer etc.: *If I took the job, I'd feel like a sellout.* **3** INFORMAL a situation in which someone has not done what they promised to do or were expected to do by the people who trusted them: *Waters' new film may be considered a sellout by his older fans.* → see also **sell out** at SELL[1]

selt·zer /ˈsɛltsɚ/ also **ˈseltzer ˌwater** *n.* [U] water that contains BUBBLES of gas

sel·vage /ˈsɛlvɪdʒ/ *n.* [C] the edge of a piece of cloth, made strong in such a way that the threads will not come apart

selves /sɛlvz/ *n.* the plural of SELF

Selz·nick /ˈsɛlznɪk/, **Da·vid O.** /ˈdeɪvɪd oʊ/ (1902–1965) a U.S. movie PRODUCER

se·man·tic /səˈmæntɪk/ *adj.* ENG. LANG. ARTS relating to the meanings of words [**Origin:** 1600–1700 Greek *semantikos* **having meaning**, from *semainein* **to mean**, from *sema* **sign**] —**semantically** /-kli/ *adv.*

se·man·tics /səˈmæntɪks/ *n.* ENG. LANG. ARTS **1** [plural,U] the meaning of words and phrases: *The difference in the versions is just a matter of semantics.* **2** [U] TECHNICAL the study of the meaning of words and other parts of language

sem·a·phore /ˈsɛməˌfɔr/ *n.* **1** [U] a system of sending messages using two flags, that you hold in different positions to represent letters and numbers **2** [C] a light that is used to send signals, for example on a railroad

sem·blance /ˈsɛmbləns/ *n.* **a/some semblance of sth** a condition or quality that is similar to another one: *The countries now have some semblance of a free press.*

se·men /ˈsimən/ *n.* [U] BIOLOGY the liquid containing SPERM that is produced by the male sex organs in humans and animals

se·mes·ter /səˈmɛstɚ/ [S2] *n.* [C] one of the two periods of time, usually about 15 to 18 weeks long, into which a year at high schools, colleges, and universities is divided [**Origin:** 1800–1900 German, Latin *semestris* **half-yearly**, from *sex* **six** + *mensis* **month**] → see also QUARTER

sem·i /ˈsɛmaɪ/ *n. plural* **semis** [C] **1** a very large heavy truck consisting of two connected parts, that carries goods over long distances → see also SEMITRAILER **2** [usually plural] INFORMAL a SEMIFINAL

semi- /sɛmi, sɛmaɪ/ *prefix* **1** exactly half: *a semicircle* **2** partly but not completely: *a semi-invalid* (=someone who is not well enough to go out very much) | *semi-literate people* (=who can only read a little) **3** happening, appearing etc. twice in a particular period → see also BI-: *a semiweekly visit*

sem·i·an·nu·al /ˌsɛmiˈænyuəl, -maɪ-/ *adj.* happening, appearing etc. twice a year: *a semiannual report* —**semiannually** *adv.*

ˌsemi-ˈarid, semiarid *adj.* having only a little rain and producing only some small plants: *a semi-arid climate*

ˌsemi-autobioˈgraphical *adj.* a semi-autobiographical book contains some true information about the writer's own life and some descriptions of events that did not really happen

sem·i·au·to·mat·ic /ˌsɛmiˌɔtəˈmæt̬ɪk, -maɪ-/ *adj.* a semiautomatic weapon moves each new bullet into position ready for you to fire, so that you can fire the next shot very quickly —**semiautomatic** *n.* [C] → see also AUTOMATIC

sem·i·cir·cle /ˈsɛmiˌsɚkəl/ *n.* [C] **1** MATH half a circle ►see THESAURUS box at **shape**[1] **2** a group arranged in a curved line, as if on the edge of half a circle: *A semicircle of chairs faced his desk.* —**semicircular** /ˌsɛmiˈsɚkyəlɚ/ *adj.*

semiˌcircular caˈnal *n.* [C] BIOLOGY one of three tubes inside your INNER EAR that gives your brain information about the position and direction of your body and helps to keep you balanced

sem·i·co·lon /ˈsɛmiˌkoʊlən/ *n.* [C] ENG. LANG. ARTS a PUNCTUATION MARK (;) used to separate independent parts of a sentence or list

sem·i·con·duct·or /ˈsɛmikənˌdʌktɚ, -maɪ-/ *n.* [C] PHYSICS a substance, such as SILICON, that allows some electric currents to pass through it and that is used in electronic equipment for this purpose —**semiconducting** *adj.* [only before noun] → see also CONDUCTOR

sem·i·con·scious /ˌsɛmiˈkɑnʃəs, -maɪ-/ *adj.* only partly conscious and not able to understand everything that is happening around you

sem·i·dark·ness /ˌsɛmiˈdɑrknɪs, -maɪ-/ *n.* [U] a place or situation in which there is not much light

sem·i·fi·nal /ˈsɛmiˌfaɪnl, ˈsɛmaɪ-, ˌsɛmiˈfaɪnl/ *n.* [C] one of two sports games, whose winners then compete against each other to decide who wins the whole competition

sem·i·fi·nal·ist /ˌsɛmiˈfaɪnl-ɪst, ˌsɛmaɪ-/ *n.* [C] a person or team that competes in a semifinal

sem·i·gloss /ˈsɛmiglɔs, -maɪ-/ *n.* [U] semigloss paint has a smooth and slightly shiny surface when it is dry

sem·i·lu·nar valve /ˌsɛmilunɚ ˈvælv, -maɪ-/ *n.* [C] MEDICAL BIOLOGY one of two small parts on your heart that open and close to prevent blood flowing back into the left and right VENTRICLES → see picture at HEART

sem·i·nal /ˈsɛmənl/ *adj.* **1** FORMAL a seminal book, piece of music etc. is important and contains new ideas or facts, so that it influences the way in which ideas in science, art, history etc. develop in the future **2** [only before noun] BIOLOGY producing or containing SEMEN

sem·i·nar /ˈsɛməˌnɑr/ [S3] *n.* [C] **1** a class at a university or college for a small group of students and a teacher to study and discuss a particular subject: *Teaching takes place in lectures and seminars.* ►see THESAURUS box at **university** **2** a meeting at which people give talks, reports etc. on a particular subject, sometimes as a form of training: *a sales seminar*

sem·i·nar·i·an /ˌsɛməˈnɛriən/ *n.* [C] a student at a seminary

sem·i·nar·y /ˈsɛməˌnɛri/ *n. plural* **seminaries** [C] a college for training priests or ministers

Sem·i·nole /ˈsɛmɪˌnoʊl/ *n.* a group of Native Americans of the Creek tribe, from the southwestern area of the U.S.

sem·i·no·mad·ic /ˌsɛminoʊˈmædɪk, ˌsɛmaɪ-/ *adj.* seminomadic people move from place to place to live according to the seasons, but they also have a fixed place where they grow some crops → see also NOMADIC

se·mi·ot·ics /ˌsɛmiˈɑt̬ɪks/ also **sem·i·ol·o·gy** /ˌsɛmiˈɑlədʒi/ *n.* [U] ENG. LANG. ARTS the way in which people communicate through signs and images, or the study of this —**semiotician** /ˌsɛmiəˈtɪʃən/ *n.* [C] —**semiologist** /ˌsɛmiˈɑlədʒɪst/ *n.* [C] —**semiotic** /ˌsɛmiˈɑt̬ɪk/ *adj.*

sem·i·per·me·a·ble /ˌsɛmiˈpɚmiəbəl, -maɪ-/ *adj.* TECHNICAL a semipermeable surface allows some substances to pass through it, but not others: *a semipermeable membrane*

ˌsemi-ˈprecious, semiprecious *adj.* a semiprecious jewel or stone is valuable, but not as valuable as a DIAMOND, RUBY etc.

sem·i·pri·vate /ˌsɛmiˈpraɪvɪt, -maɪ-/ *adj.* **1** a semiprivate room, area etc. is one that you share with one or two other people **2** partly, but not completely, privately owned or run

ˌsemi-proˈfessional also **sem·i·pro** /ˌsɛmiˈproʊ, -maɪ-/ INFORMAL *adj.* [usually before noun] relating to being paid for doing a sport, playing music etc., but not doing it as a main job: *a semipro boxer* | *the semi-professional baseball leagues* —**semiprofessional** also **semipro** INFORMAL *n.* [C]

sem·i·re·tired /ˌsɛmirɪˈtaɪəd, -maɪ-/ *adj.* a semi-retired person only works part of the time they used to work, especially because they are getting older and want time to do other things

ˌsemi-ˈskilled *adj.* **a)** a semi-skilled worker is not highly SKILLED or professional, but needs some skills for the job they are doing **b)** a semi-skilled job is one that you need some skills to do, but you do not have to be highly SKILLED

sem·i·sweet /ˌsɛmiˈswit◂ / *adj.* semisweet chocolate is only slightly sweet and has a darker color than MILK CHOCOLATE

Sem·ite /ˈsɛmaɪt/ *n.* [C] someone who belongs to the race of people that includes Jews, Arabs, and, in ancient times, Babylonians, Assyrians etc. → see also ANTI-SEMITISM

Se·mit·ic /səˈmɪṭɪk/ *adj.* **1 a)** belonging to the group of people that includes Arabs, some Jews, and, in ancient times, Babylonians, Assyrians etc. **b)** belonging or relating to any of the languages of these people **2** OLD USE another word for JEWISH → see also ANTI-SEMITIC

sem·i·trail·er /ˈsɛmaɪˌtreɪlə/ *n.* [C] a part of a large truck like a long box, that is pulled by the main part of the truck and has its front end supported by the main part → see also SEMI (1)

sem·i·trop·i·cal /ˌsɛmiˈtrɑpɪkəl◂ / *adj.* EARTH SCIENCE SUBTROPICAL

ˈsemi-ˌvowel *n.* [C] ENG. LANG. ARTS a sound made in speech that sounds like a vowel, but is in fact a CONSONANT, such as /w/ or /y/

sem·i·week·ly /ˌsɛmiˈwikli, -maɪ-/ *adj., adv.* appearing or happening twice a week: *a semiweekly newspaper column*

sem·o·li·na /ˌsɛməˈlinə/ *n.* [U] small grains of crushed wheat, used especially in making PASTA

Sen. *n.* [C] the written abbreviation of SENATOR: *Sen. Biden*

sen·ate /ˈsɛnɪt/ *n.* **1 a) the Senate** the smaller and higher-ranking of the two parts of the government with the power to make laws, in countries such as the U.S., Canada, and Australia → see also HOUSE OF REPRESENTATIVES: *The Senate approved the bill.* | *He was elected to the Senate in 1996.* **b)** [C] a similar part of the government in many U.S. states: *the Kansas state senate* **2** [C] the governing council at some universities **3 the Senate** [singular] the highest level of government in ancient Rome [**Origin:** 1100–1200 Old French *senat*, from Latin *senatus*, from *senex* **old man**]

ˌSenate ˈPresident also **ˌPresident of the ˈSenate** *n.* [C] POLITICS the person who is officially in charge of controlling the meetings in a SENATE. In the U.S. SENATE, the Senate President is the VICE PRESIDENT.

sen·a·tor, Senator /ˈsɛnəṭə/ W2 *n.* [C] a member of a senate: *Senator Frist* | *a Michigan state senator* —**senatorial** /ˌsɛnəˈtɔriəl/ *adj.*: *senatorial duties*

send /sɛnd/ S1 W1 *v.* [T] *past tense and past participle* **sent** /sɛnt/

1 HAVE STH TAKEN BY MAIL ETC. to arrange for something to go or be taken to another place, especially by mail: *Kristen sent some pictures from the party.* | **send sb sth** *You should send Pat some flowers to say thank you.* | **send sth to sb/sth** *How much is it to send a letter to Australia?* | *Many countries have sent emergency aid supplies to the area.* | **send sth by mail/ship/air etc.** *I'll send you the documents by courier.* | **send sth up/over/to etc.** *He ordered coffee and rolls to be sent up to his room.*

2 ELECTRONIC/COMPUTER ETC. to make a message, electronic signal etc. go somewhere using radio equipment, computers etc.: *Please send a fax to confirm the reservation.* | *The ship sent a distress call.* | **send sb sth** *I'll send you an email tomorrow.*

3 MAKE SB GO SOMEWHERE to tell someone to go somewhere or arrange for them to go there, usually so that they can do something for you there: *Who sent you?* | *The U.N. is sending troops.* | **send sb to sth** *They sent him to prison for five years.* | **send sb to do sth** *A reporter was sent to cover the story.* | **send sb over/home/to etc.** *The children were sent home from school early.*

4 send sth out/up/forth etc. to produce small pieces or parts, or to make them come out: *In the fireplace, a log broke in two and sent up a shower of sparks.*

5 send (sb) your love/regards/best wishes etc. SPOKEN to ask someone to give your greetings, good wishes etc. to someone else: *Dad sends his love.*

6 CAUSE SB/STH TO MOVE [always + adv./prep.] to make someone or something move somewhere, especially through the air, by pushing them, throwing them etc.: **send sth through/over etc. sth** *He kicked the ball and sent it straight through the window.* | **send sb/sth flying/sprawling/reeling etc.** *The force of the blow sent me reeling to the floor.*

7 send sb/sth doing sth to cause someone or something to do something: *The sound of gunfire sent people running for cover.* | *Poor harvests had sent prices soaring.*

8 send word (to sb) to tell someone something by sending them a letter or message: *Ruth* ***sent word that*** *she would be in town for a few days.*

9 send (sb) a message to tell people something or make them think that something is true: *It would send all the wrong messages if we changed the policy now.*

10 send shivers/chills up (and down) your spine to make you feel very frightened or excited

11 send sb packing INFORMAL to tell someone who is not wanted that they must leave immediately

[**Origin:** Old English *sendan*]

send sb ↔ **away** *phr. v.* to send someone to another place, especially to live there: *Greg was sent away to school at the age of seven.*

send away for sth *phr. v.* to write and ask a company or organization to mail something to you SYN **send off for** SYN **send in for**: *I sent away for one of their catalogs.*

send sth ↔ **back** *phr. v.* to return something to where it came from: **send sth back to sb** *Please fill the form out and send it back to us.*

send sth ↔ **down** *phr. v.* to make something decrease in value or price

send for sb/sth *phr. v.* **1** to ask or order that something be brought or sent to you: *Send for your free sample today!* **2** FORMAL to ask or order someone to come to you by sending them a message: *I think we should send for the doctor.*

send in *phr. v.* **1 send sth ↔ in** to take something, usually by mail, to a place where it can be dealt with: *I've sent in applications for a couple of jobs.* **2 send sth ↔ in** to make soldiers, police etc. go somewhere to deal with a very difficult or dangerous situation: *It's time to send in the ground troops.* **3 send sb ↔ in** to tell someone to go into a room where someone else is: *Mr. Jones is here – should I send him in?*

send in for sth *phr. v.* to write and ask a company or organization to mail something to you SYN **send away for** SYN **send off for**

send sb **into** sth *phr. v.* to make someone feel a particular way or experience a particular condition: *Planning a big dinner party sends me into a panic.*

send off *phr. v.* **1 send sth ↔ off** to take something somewhere by mail: *I sent off the letter this morning.* **2 send sb ↔ off** to make someone go to another place, or to arrange for them to go there: **send sb off to sth** *At 16, Eleanor was sent off to boarding school.*

send off for sth *phr. v.* to write and ask a company or organization to mail something to you SYN **send away for** SYN **send in for**

send sth ↔ **on** *phr. v.* to send something that has been received to another place so that it can be dealt with: *We send any complaints on to the Head Office.*

S

send out *phr. v.* **1 send sth ↔ out** to mail something from one place to a lot of people or places: *Information packets have been sent out to the students.* **2 send sb ↔ out** to make a person or group of people go somewhere in order to do a particular job: *Search parties were sent out to look for survivors.* **3 send sth ↔ out** to broadcast or produce a signal, light, sound etc.: *The plane sent out a distress call.*

send out for sth *phr. v.* to ask a restaurant or store to deliver food to you at home or at work

send up *phr. v.* **1 send sth ↔ up** to make something increase in value or price: *The shortage is bound to send prices up.* **2 send up sb/sth** to make something look silly or stupid by copying it in a very funny way SYN **spoof** → see also SEND-UP **3 send sb ↔ up** INFORMAL to send someone to prison

send·er /ˈsɛndɚ/ *n.* [C] the person who sent a particular letter, package, message etc.

send·off /ˈsɛndɔf/ *n.* [C] a party or other occasion when people gather together to say goodbye to someone who is leaving: **give sb a good/big/warm etc. sendoff** *Craig's teammates gave him a big sendoff.*

ˈsend-up *n.* [C] the act of copying someone or something in a way that makes them look funny or stupid SYN **spoof**: **+of** *a very funny send-up of the mayor's speech* → see also **send up** at SEND

S

Sen·e·ca¹ /ˈsɛnɪkə/ (?4 B.C.–A.D. ?65) a Roman PHILOSOPHER, politician, and writer of plays

Seneca² [plural] a Native American tribe from the northeast region of the U.S.

ˌSeneca Falls Conˈvention, the HISTORY the first large meeting in the U.S. about women's rights, held at Seneca Falls, New York, in 1848

Sen·e·gal /ˈsɛnɪˌgɔl/ a country in West Africa on the Atlantic coast —**Senegalese** /ˌsɛnɪgəˈliz/ *n., adj.*

se·nes·cent /sɪˈnɛsənt/ *adj.* FORMAL becoming old and showing the effects of getting older: *a senescent industry* —**senescence** *n.* [U]

se·nile /ˈsinaɪl/ *adj.* NOT TECHNICAL MEDICINE mentally confused or behaving strangely, because of old age: *a senile old man* —**senility** /sɪˈnɪləṭi/ *n.* [U]

senile de·men·tia /ˌsinaɪl dɪˈmɛnʃə/ *n.* [U] MEDICINE a medical condition that can affect the minds of old people, making them confused and not able to think well → see also ALZHEIMER'S DISEASE

Se·nior /ˈsinyɚ/ *adj.* [only after noun] WRITTEN ABBREVIATION **Sr.** used after the name of a father whose son has the same name → see also JUNIOR: *Ken Griffey, Sr.*

se·nior¹ /ˈsinyɚ/ S2 W2 *adj.* **1** having a higher position or rank OPP **junior**: *the firm's senior managers* | **+to** *She's senior to me in our department.* ▸see THESAURUS box at **position¹**, **rank¹** **2** being about 60 or older, or relating to people like this: *reduced fares for senior travelers* [**Origin:** 1300–1400 Latin **older**, from *senex* **old**]

senior² S2 *n.* [C] **1** a student in the last year of HIGH SCHOOL or college: *Jen will be a senior this year.* | *my senior year of college* → see also FRESHMAN, JUNIOR² (1), SOPHOMORE **2** a senior citizen: *a housing development for active seniors* | *Seniors can get a 10% discount.* **3 be two/five/ten etc. years sb's senior** to be two, five, ten etc. years older than someone OPP **junior**: *Her husband was nine years her senior.*

ˌsenior ˈcitizen *n.* [C] someone who is about 60 or older ▸see THESAURUS box at **old**

ˌsenior ˈhigh school also **ˌsenior ˈhigh** *n.* [C] a school for students in 9th or 10th grade through 12th grade, between the ages of about 14 and 18 SYN **high school** → see also JUNIOR HIGH SCHOOL

se·nior·i·ty /ˌsinˈyɔrəṭi, -ˈyɑr-/ *n.* [U] **1** the length of time you have worked for a company or organization: *Salary is based mainly on seniority.* **2** the situation of being higher in rank or older than someone else: *He achieved a position of seniority.*

ˌsenior ˈmoment *n.* [C] HUMOROUS a time when you suddenly cannot remember something that you usually know because you are getting older

ˌsenior ˈprom *n.* [C] a formal dance party for students in their last year of HIGH SCHOOL

sen·na /ˈsɛnə/ *n.* [U] BIOLOGY a tropical plant with a fruit that is often used to make a medicine to help your BOWELS work

sen·sa·tion /sɛnˈseɪʃən/ *n.* **1** [C,U] a physical feeling that you get from one of your five SENSES, especially the sense of touch SYN **feeling**: *A cold sensation suddenly ran down my spine.* | **+of** *She felt the ticklish sensation of wanting to sneeze.* **2** [U] the ability to feel things, especially through your sense of touch SYN **feeling**: **+in** *Jerry realized that he had no sensation in his legs.* **3** [C] an emotional feeling or an idea in your mind, caused by a particular event, experience, or memory SYN **feeling**: *I **had the strange sensation that** I had been here before.* **4** [C usually singular] someone or something that the public suddenly becomes very interested in and excited about: *The band became an overnight pop sensation.* **5** [singular] extreme excitement or interest, or someone or something that causes this: **cause/create a sensation** *The opera caused a sensation in Moscow.*

sen·sa·tion·al /sɛnˈseɪʃənl/ *adj.* **1** very interesting and exciting: *sensational findings* **2** DISAPPROVING intended to interest, excite, or shock people rather than inform them: *sensational journalism* **3** INFORMAL very good or impressive: *She still looks sensational at 56.* —**sensationally** *adv.*

sen·sa·tion·al·ism /sɛnˈseɪʃənlˌɪzəm/ *n.* [U] DISAPPROVING a way of reporting events or stories that makes them seem as strange, exciting, or shocking as possible —**sensationalist** *adj.*

sen·sa·tion·al·ize /sɛnˈseɪʃənlˌaɪz/ *v.* [T] DISAPPROVING to deliberately make something seem as strange, exciting, or shocking as possible: *The media tend to sensationalize crimes like these.*

sense¹ /sɛns/ S1 W1 *n.*

1 FEELING [C] a feeling about something SYN **feeling**: **+of** *I felt a great sense of relief.* | *The neighborhood has a real sense of community.* | **get/have the sense that** *I got the sense that things weren't exactly right.*

2 JUDGMENT [U] good understanding and judgment, especially about practical things: *At 15, she seemed to have no sense at all.* | **have the sense to do sth** *I hope he had the sense to take an umbrella.* → see also COMMON SENSE

3 make sense a) to have a clear meaning and be easy to understand: *Read this and tell me if it makes sense.* **b)** to have a good reason or explanation: *His behavior just didn't seem to make sense.* **c)** to be a sensible thing to do: **it makes sense (for sb) to do sth** *It doesn't make sense to drive if you can walk.*

4 SEE/SMELL/TOUCH ETC. [C] BIOLOGY one of the five natural powers of sight, hearing, feeling, taste, and smell, that give us information about the things around us: *We perceive the world around us through our senses.* | *Good art should appeal to **the senses**.* | **sense of smell/taste/touch etc.** *Dogs have an incredibly keen sense of smell.* → see also SIXTH SENSE

5 ABILITY [singular] a natural ability that makes it easy for you to understand or know something: **a sense of rhythm/timing/form etc.** *Steiner's drawings show a strong sense of color.* | *Kay doesn't have much **fashion sense**.* | *I respect Don's **business sense**.* | **a sense of justice/fairness** *Kids have a natural sense of justice.*

6 come to your senses to realize that what you are doing is not sensible: *One day he'll come to his senses and see what a fool he's been.*

7 bring sb to their senses to make someone think or behave in a reasonable and sensible way: *It's too bad it took a lawsuit to bring them to their senses.*

8 make (some/any) sense of sth to understand something, especially something difficult or complicated: *Can you make any sense of this article?*

9 talk/knock some sense into sb to make someone behave in a more sensible way by talking to them or treating them in a firm way

10 there's no sense in (doing) sth SPOKEN used to say

that it is not sensible to do something: *There's no sense in spending a fortune on kids' clothes.*
11 a sense of direction a) the ability to know which way you should be going in a place you do not know well **b)** an idea about what your aims in life are: *Rehabilitation programs have created a sense of direction for the inmates.*
12 a sense of humor the ability to understand or enjoy things that are funny, or to make people laugh: *Jessica managed to keep her sense of humor throughout the ordeal.*
13 THE MEANING OF STH [C] the meaning of a word, phrase, sentence etc.: *The word "record" has several different senses.* | *He's a gentleman* ***in every sense of the word*** (=using all possible meanings of this word). | *It's not really a hotel* ***in the*** *conventional* ***sense.***
14 in a/one sense in one particular way, but without considering all the other facts or possibilities: *What he says is right in a sense.*
15 in no sense used to emphasize that something is definitely not true: *He is in no sense an unkind person.*
16 in a (very) real sense used to emphasize the fact that something is definitely true: *The country had, in a very real sense, been misled.*
17 take leave of your senses to start to behave in an unreasonable or stupid way: *You challenged him to a fight? Have you taken leave of your senses?*
18 a sense of occasion a feeling or understanding that an event or occasion is very serious or important
19 regain your senses OLD-FASHIONED to stop feeling FAINT or slightly sick
[**Origin:** 1300–1400 Old French *sens*, from Latin *sensus*, from *sentire* **to feel**] → see also **see reason/sense** at SEE[1] (48)

sense² S3 W3 *v.* [T] **1** to feel that something exists or is true, without being told or having proof: *Max sensed her distrust of him.* | **sense (that)** *Fran sensed that something was wrong.* | **sense what/how/who etc.** *We could sense how unhappy she was.* **2** if a machine senses something, it discovers and records it: *The gauge senses the temperature and adjusts the heating accordingly.*

sense·less /ˈsɛnslɪs/ *adj.* **1** happening or done for no good reason or with no purpose: *a senseless killing* **2** unconscious: *He fell and knocked himself senseless.* —**senselessly** *adv.* —**senselessness** *n.* [U]

ˈsense ˌorgan *n.* [C] BIOLOGY a part of your body through which you see, smell, hear, taste, or feel something

sen·si·bil·i·ty /ˌsɛnsəˈbɪləṭi/ *n. plural* **sensibilities** **1** [C,U] the way that someone feels about something or reacts to particular subjects or types of behavior: *The posters in his office* ***offended the sensibilities of*** *some of his coworkers.* **2** [singular, U] the ability to understand feelings, especially those expressed in literature or art: *a deep artistic sensibility*

sen·si·ble /ˈsɛnsəbəl/ *adj.* **1** showing good judgment SYN **reasonable**: *She seems very sensible.* | *We aim to help clients make financially sensible choices.* | **it is sensible to do sth** *It isn't sensible to climb these mountains alone.* **2** sensible shoes or clothes are practical and comfortable rather than fashionable SYN **practical**: *sensible walking shoes* **3** healthy and containing a balanced variety of food: *Always eat a sensible diet.* **4 be sensible of sth** LITERARY to know or recognize something **5** FORMAL noticeable: *a sensible increase in temperature* —**sensibly** *adv.*

sen·si·tive /ˈsɛnsəṭɪv/ S2 W3 *adj.*
1 UNDERSTANDING PEOPLE APPROVING able to understand other people's feelings and problems, and careful not to upset people OPP **insensitive**: *Underneath all that macho stuff, he's really a sensitive guy.* | **+to** *Nurses have to be sensitive to patients' needs.*
2 EASILY OFFENDED easily hurt, upset, or offended by things that people say: *Joel is such a sensitive boy.* | **+about** *Laura's very sensitive about her weight.* | **+to** *She remained very sensitive to criticism.* → see also HYPERSENSITIVE (2)
3 EASILY DAMAGED easily damaged or hurt: *a baby's sensitive skin* | **+to** *Some people are more sensitive to the sun than others.* | *Wetlands are* ***environmentally sensitive*** *areas.*
4 COLD/PAIN ETC. able to feel physical sensations, especially pain, more than usual: *Tell me if any of these spots are sensitive.* | **+to** *My teeth are really sensitive to hot and cold.*
5 REACTING TO SMALL CHANGES able to notice, measure, or react to very small changes or differences: *This is a very sensitive recorder – it picks up every word you say.* | *Dogs have very sensitive noses.*
6 LIKELY TO CAUSE PROBLEMS a sensitive subject needs to be dealt with carefully, for example because it may offend people or make people angry: *a sensitive issue*
7 SECRET sensitive information or documents need to be kept secret, because harm would result if the wrong people knew about them: ***highly sensitive*** *information* ▸see THESAURUS box at **secret**[1]
8 ART/MUSIC ETC. able to understand or express yourself through art, music, literature etc.: *a sensitive musician* —**sensitively** *adv.* —**sensitiveness** *n.* [U]

-sensitive /sɛnsəṭɪv/ *suffix* [in adjectives] **light-sensitive/heat-sensitive etc.** used in adjectives to say what causes a change or reaction in something: *light-sensitive photographic paper*

sen·si·tiv·i·ty /ˌsɛnsəˈtɪvəṭi/ *n.*
1 UNDERSTANDING [singular, U] the ability to understand other people's feelings and problems: *Victims of crime must be treated with sensitivity.* | *His comments showed* ***a lack of sensitivity.*** | **+to** *a sensitivity to women's issues*
2 ABILITY TO BE DAMAGED [C,U] the fact that someone or something can be damaged, hurt, or made sick, especially by reacting to chemicals, animal fur, or other substances: *chemical sensitivity* | **+of** *the sensitivity of the environment* | **+to** *sensitivity to sunlight*
3 sensitivities [plural] someone's feelings and the fact that they could be upset or offended: *the religious sensitivities of the Muslim community*
4 ABILITY TO BE OFFENDED [U] the fact of being easily hurt, offended, or upset by the things that people say: *He misjudged the sensitivity of his audience.*
5 REACTION TO CHANGES [U] the ability to notice, measure, or react to small changes or differences: *the sensitivity of the instruments* | *the market's price sensitivity*
6 IN ART/MUSIC ETC. [C,U] the quality of being able to express emotions through art, music, literature etc.: *He played the part with extraordinary sensitivity.*
7 ABILITY TO CAUSE PROBLEMS [U] the fact that a subject is likely to offend people or make them angry: *the sensitivity of the issue*
8 QUALITY OF BEING SECRET [U] the fact that information or documents need to be kept secret

sensiˈtivity ˌtraining *n.* [U] a type of training that teaches people to have more respect for people of different races, people who are DISABLED etc.

sen·si·tize /ˈsɛnsəˌtaɪz/ *v.* [T usually passive] **1** to make someone able to notice a particular problem or situation and give it attention OPP **desensitize**: **be sensitized to sth** *Volunteers need to be sensitized to the cultural differences they will encounter.* **2** SCIENCE to treat a material or a piece of equipment so that it will react to physical or chemical changes OPP **desensitize** **3** if someone is sensitized to a particular substance, their body begins to have a bad reaction whenever they touch it, breathe it etc. —**sensitization** /ˌsɛnsəṭəˈzeɪʃən/ *n.* [U]

sens·or /ˈsɛnsɚ, -sɔr/ *n.* [C] TECHNICAL a piece of equipment used for discovering the presence of light, heat, sound, movement etc., especially in small amounts

sen·so·ry /ˈsɛnsəri/ *adj.* [only before noun] BIOLOGY relating to or using your SENSES of sight, hearing, smell, taste, or touch: *sensory deprivation* → see also ESP (1)

ˌsensory reˈceptor *n.* [C] BIOLOGY a living cell that reacts to light, sound, smell, taste, or touch and then sends information to the body's NERVOUS SYSTEM

sen·su·al /ˈsɛnʃuəl/ *adj.* **1** making you think of physical pleasure, especially sexual pleasure: *sensual lips* **2** a sensual person enjoys physical pleasures, especially sex **3** relating to the feelings of your body rather than your mind: *sensual pleasures* —**sensuality** /ˌsɛnʃuˈæləṭi/ *n.* [U] —**sensually** /ˈsɛnʃuəli/ *adv.*

sen·su·al·ist /ˈsɛnʃuəlɪst/ *n.* [C] someone who is only interested in physical pleasure

sen·su·ous /ˈsɛnʃuəs/ *adj.* **1** pleasing to your senses: *a rich sensuous smell* **2** attractive in a sexual way: *full sensuous lips* —**sensuously** *adv.* —**sensuousness** *n.* [U]

sent /sɛnt/ *v.* the past tense and past participle of SEND

sen·tence¹ /ˈsɛntˀns, -təns/ S2 W2 *n.* [C] **1** ENG. LANG. ARTS a group of words that usually contains a subject and a verb, expresses a complete idea, or asks a question, and that, when written in English, begins with a capital letter and ends with a PERIOD, QUESTION MARK, or EXCLAMATION POINT: *a short sentence* | *Write your answers in **full sentences**.* **2** LAW a punishment that a judge gives to someone who has been found guilty of a crime: *a six-year prison sentence* | *He faces a possible **life sentence*** (=staying in prison until he dies). | *The murder charge could result in a **death sentence*** (=punishment by death). | *He had **served a short sentence*** (=spent time in prison) *for robbery.* | *The judge gave her **a suspended sentence*** (=punishment that will happen only if she breaks the law again during a particular time). | **a heavy/light sentence** (=long or short time in prison) | **pass/pronounce sentence** (=to officially state what a punishment will be) ►see THESAURUS box at **punishment** [**Origin:** 1200–1300 Old French, Latin *sententia* **feeling, opinion, sentence**, from *sentire* **to feel**]

sentence² *v.* [T often passive] LAW if a judge sentences someone found guilty of a crime, they officially and legally give them a punishment: **sentence sb to sth** *She was sentenced to three years in prison.* | *He was convicted and **sentenced to death**.*

ˈsentence ˌadverb *n.* [C] ENG. LANG. ARTS an adverb that expresses an opinion about the whole sentence that contains it

sen·ten·tious /sɛnˈtɛnʃəs/ *adj.* FORMAL, DISAPPROVING telling people how they should behave —**sententiously** *adv.*

sen·tient /ˈsɛnʃənt/ *adj.* FORMAL or TECHNICAL having feelings and knowing that you exist: *Humans are sentient beings.*

sen·ti·ment /ˈsɛntəmənt/ *n.* **1** [C,U] FORMAL an opinion or feeling you have about something: *His sentiments were echoed all over the city.* | *"I hate all this junk mail we get." "**My sentiments exactly*** (=I agree)." | **public/popular sentiment** *The governor misjudged public sentiment.* | **anti-war/anti-Washington etc. sentiment** *growing anti-war sentiment* **2** [U] feelings of pity, love, sadness etc. that are often considered to be too strong or not appropriate for a particular situation: *There's no place for sentiment in business.*

sen·ti·men·tal /ˌsɛntəˈmɛntl◂/ *adj.* **1** relating to or easily affected by emotions such as love, sympathy, sadness etc., often in a way that seems silly or inappropriate for a particular situation: *I suppose we get more sentimental as we grow older.* | *a sentimental farewell* ►see THESAURUS box at **emotional** **2** based on or relating to your feelings rather than on practical reasons: *He kept the car **for sentimental reasons**.* **3** ENG. LANG. ARTS a story, movie, book etc. that is sentimental deals with emotions such as love and sadness in a way that seems silly and insincere: *sentimental lyrics* **4 sentimental value** if something has sentimental value, it is not worth much money, but it is important to you because it reminds you of someone you love or a happy time in the past: *The photos were of great sentimental value.* —**sentimentally** *adv.*

sen·ti·men·tal·ist /ˌsɛntəˈmɛntl-ɪst/ *n.* [C] someone who behaves or writes in a sentimental way —**sentimentalism** *n.* [U]

sen·ti·men·tal·i·ty /ˌsɛntəmɛnˈtæləṭi, -mən-/ *n.* [U] the quality of being sentimental

sen·ti·men·tal·ize /ˌsɛntəˈmɛntlˌaɪz/ *v.* [I,T] to speak, write or think about something in a way that mentions only the good or happy things about something, but not the bad things: *These historical novels tended to sentimentalize the past.*

sen·ti·nel /ˈsɛntˀnl, -tɪnəl/ *n.* [C] OLD-FASHIONED a sentry

sen·try /ˈsɛntri/ *n. plural* **sentries** [C] a soldier standing outside a building as a guard

ˈsentry box *n.* [C] a tall narrow shelter with an open front where a soldier can stand while guarding a building

Seoul /soʊl/ the capital and largest city of South Korea

se·pal /ˈsipəl, ˈsɛ-/ *n.* [C] BIOLOGY one of the small leaves that contains a young flower before the flower opens, and which stays directly under the flower → see picture at FLOWER¹

sep·a·ra·ble /ˈsɛpərəbəl/ *adj.* two things that are separable can be separated or considered separately OPP **inseparable**: **+from** *Is physical health really separable from mental health?* —**separably** *adv.* —**separability** /ˌsɛpərəˈbɪləṭi/ *n.* [U]

sep·a·rate¹ /ˈsɛprɪt/ S2 W2 *adj.* [no comparative] **1** not joining or touching: *The music rooms are in a separate building.* | **+from** *The offices are separate from the factory.* | **keep sth separate (from sth)** *Keep the raw meat separate from the cooked meat.* | **keep sth and sth separate (from each other)** *Keep the blue and green cards separate from each other.* **2** ideas, information, activities etc. that are separate are not related or do not affect each other in any way: *That's a separate issue.* | *The two things are entirely separate.* | **+from** *My social life is completely separate from my work.* | **keep sth separate (from sth)** *Keep your love life separate from your studies.* **3** [only before noun] not the same one SYN **different**: *Write each list on a separate sheet of paper.* | *He asked her out on two separate occasions.* | **its/sb's own separate sth** *Each province has its own separate army.* **4 go your separate ways a)** if people who have been in a relationship, especially a romantic relationship, go their separate ways, they end their relationship: *After six years of marriage, they decided to go their separate ways.* **b)** if people who have been traveling together go their separate ways, they start traveling in different directions —**separately** *adv.*

sep·a·rate² /ˈsɛpəˌreɪt/ S2 W2 *v.*

1 BE BETWEEN [T often passive] if something separates two places or two things, it is between them so that they are not touching each other or connected with each other: *A picket fence separates her lawn from the neighbor's.* | **separate sth from sth** *The island is separated from the land by a wide canal.*

2 DIVIDE [I,T] to divide or split into different parts, or layers, or to make something do this: *The paint had separated.* | **separate (sth) into sth** *He asked us to separate into groups.* | *Separate the hair into sections.* | *First **separate the eggs*** (=divide the white part from the yellow part) *and beat the whites.*

THESAURUS

divide to separate something into a number of smaller parts: *The teacher divided the class into groups.*
split to separate something into two or more groups, parts etc.: *We'd both worked on it, so we split the prize money.*
break up to separate something into smaller parts: *The phone company was broken up to encourage competition.*
segregate to separate one group of people from others because of race, sex, religion etc.: *Schools were racially segregated.*

3 STOP LIVING TOGETHER [I] to stop living with your husband or wife, because both of you do not want to be together anymore → see also DIVORCE: *My parents separated when I was two.* | **separate from sb** *Ginny separated from her husband last year.* ►see THESAURUS box at **divorce²**

4 RECOGNIZE DIFFERENCE [T] to recognize that one idea is different from another, and to deal with each idea alone: **separate sth from sth** *The patient finds it difficult to separate fact from fantasy.*
5 MOVE APART [I,T] to move apart, or make people move apart: *When we reached the airport we separated.* | **get/be separated from sb** *They got lost after being separated from their tour group in the mountains.*
6 MAKE SB/STH DIFFERENT **separate sb/sth from sb/sth** to be the thing that makes someone or something different from other similar people or things: *What separates her from the rest of the applicants?*
7 BE THE DIFFERENCE BETWEEN SB/STH [T] used to say how much older, better, etc. someone or something is than another person or thing: *Only one game separates the teams in the race for the top of the league.*
8 BE THE DISTANCE BETWEEN SB/STH [T] used to say how much distance there is between people or things: *Less than a mile separated the two towns.*
9 PSYCHOLOGY **separate from sb** TECHNICAL to stop having a very close connection with someone else, usually your mother: *the baby's need to separate from the mother*
10 separate the men from the boys INFORMAL to make it clear which people are brave or strong and which are not
11 separate the sheep from the goats also **separate the wheat from the chaff** to choose the good and useful things or people and get rid of the others
[**Origin:** 1400–1500 Latin, past participle of *separare*, from *se-* **apart** + *parare* **to prepare, get**]

separate sth ↔ **out** *phr. v.* to make a person or thing separate from the rest of a group or whole: *We separated out the students who will benefit from extra help.*

sep·a·rat·ed /ˈsɛpəˌreɪt̬ɪd/ *adj.* not living with your husband or wife anymore → see also DIVORCED: *My parents are separated.* | +**from** *I've been separated from my husband for six months.*

sep·arates /ˈsɛprɪts/ *n.* [plural] women's clothing, such as skirts, shirts, and pants, that can be worn in different combinations

sep·a·ra·tion /ˌsɛpəˈreɪʃən/ *n.* **1** [U] the act of separating or the state of being separate: *the separation of church and state* | *the separation of the country into two states* **2** [C,U] the state of being apart from other people or things, or the period of time when this happens: *The family had to endure a two-year separation.* | +**from** *The worst part of the divorce was the separation from his three children.* **3** [C] a situation in which a husband and wife agree to live apart even though they are still married → see also DIVORCE

sepaˈration anxˌiety *n.* [U] TECHNICAL a feeling of being very nervous and upset when someone important to you leaves you, especially that a child has when its parents go away

sepaˌration of ˈpowers *n.* [singular, U] the situation that exists when each of the three parts of government, the EXECUTIVE, LEGISLATIVE, and JUDICIAL branches, are independent of each other and do different things

sep·a·ra·tist /ˈsɛprət̬ɪst/ *n.* [C] POLITICS a member of a group in a country that wants to establish a new separate country with its own government —**separatism** *n.* [U]

sep·a·ra·tor /ˈsɛpəˌreɪt̬ɚ/ *n.* [C] a machine for separating liquids from solids, or cream from milk

se·pi·a /ˈsipiə/ *n.* [U] **1** a dark reddish brown color **2 a sepia photograph/print** a photograph, picture etc., especially an old one, that is this color **3** an ink used for drawing which has this color [**Origin:** 1300–1400 Latin **cuttlefish**, from Greek; because the color is obtained from a liquid in cuttlefishes' bodies]

se·poy /ˈsipɔɪ/ *n.* [C] HISTORY an Indian soldier under the command of the British in India

sep·sis /ˈsɛpsɪs/ *n.* [U] MEDICINE an infection in part of the body, in which PUS is produced

Sep·tem·ber /sɛpˈtɛmbɚ/ ABBREVIATION **Sept.** *n.* [C,U] the ninth month of the year, between August and October: *Students go back to school **in September**.* | *Classes start **on September 5**.* | *Noah started first grade **last September**.* | ***Next September** I'll be a senior in high school.* | *Quinn will arrive **September 24**.* → see Grammar box at JANUARY [**Origin:** 1000–1100 Old French *Septembre*, from Latin *September*, from *septem* **seven**; because it was the seventh month of the ancient Roman year]

sep·tet /sɛpˈtɛt/ *n.* [C] ENG. LANG. ARTS **1** a group of seven singers or musicians who perform together **2** a piece of music written for seven performers

sep·tic /ˈsɛptɪk/ *adj.* MEDICINE INFECTED: *a septic wound*

sep·ti·ce·mi·a /ˌsɛptəˈsimiə/ *n.* [U] MEDICINE a serious condition in which infection spreads from a small area of your body through your blood SYN **blood poisoning**

ˌseptic ˈtank *n.* [C] a large container kept under ground used for putting human body waste into

sep·tu·a·ge·nar·i·an /ˌsɛptuədʒəˈnɛriən/ *n.* [C] someone who is between 70 and 79 years old

sep·tum /ˈsɛptəm/ *n.* [C] TECHNICAL a thin MEMBRANE that separates two hollow areas in a body organ, for example the nose

sep·ul·cher /ˈsɛpəlkɚ/ *n.* [C] a small room or building in which the bodies of dead people were put in the past

se·pul·chral /səˈpʌlkrəl/ *adj.* **1** LITERARY sad, serious, and slightly frightening: *a sepulchral voice* **2** TECHNICAL relating to burying dead people

se·quel /ˈsikwəl/ *n.* **1** [C] ENG. LANG. ARTS a book, movie, play etc. that continues the story of an earlier one, usually written or made by the same person: +**to** *She's writing a sequel to her very successful first novel.* **2** [C usually singular] an event that happens as a result of something that happened before

se·quence /ˈsikwəns/ Ac *n.* [C,U] **1** a series of related events, actions etc. which have a particular order and usually lead to a particular result: +**of** *a sequence of keystrokes* | *Owen closed his eyes and thought about the **sequence of events** that had led up to this.* **2** [C,U] the order in which things happen, or are supposed to happen: *The system follows a logical sequence.* | *Each edition is numbered separately **in sequence*** (=in order). | *The chapters may be studied **out of sequence*** (=not in the order in which they are arranged). **3** [C] ENG. LANG. ARTS one part of a story, movie etc. that deals with a single subject or action: *the action sequence at the beginning of the movie* **4** [C] MATH a list of numbers that are formed according to a rule in which a particular operation is performed on each previous number to make the next number → see also ARITHMETIC SEQUENCE, GEOMETRIC SEQUENCE [**Origin:** 1300–1400 Late Latin *sequentia*, from Latin *sequi* **to follow**]

se·quenc·ing /ˈsikwənsɪŋ/ *n.* [U] FORMAL the arrangement of things into an order, especially the arrangement of events or actions

se·quen·tial /sɪˈkwɛnʃəl/ Ac *adj.* FORMAL relating to or happening in a sequence: *a sequential arrangement* —**sequentially** *adv.*

se·ques·ter /sɪˈkwɛstɚ/ *v.* [T] FORMAL to force a group of people, such as a JURY, to stay away from other people

se·ques·tered /sɪˈkwɛstɚd/ *adj.* LITERARY a sequestered place is quiet and far away from people

se·quin /ˈsikwɪn/ *n.* [C] a small shiny round flat piece of plastic that you SEW onto clothing for decoration [**Origin:** 1500–1600 French, Italian *zecchino*, from *zecca* **place where coins are made**, from Arabic *sikka* **coin**] —**sequined** also **sequinned** *adj.*

se·quoi·a /sɪˈkwɔɪə/ *n.* [C] an EVERGREEN tree from the western U.S. that can grow very tall and wide and can live for thousands of years → see picture on page A31

Se·quoy·ah /sɪˈkwɔɪə/ (?1760–1843) a Native American of the Cherokee tribe, famous for inventing a way of writing the Cherokee language

S

se·ra·glio /sə'rælyoʊ, -'rɑl-/ *n.* [C] LITERARY a HAREM

ser·aph /'sɛrəf/ *n. plural* **seraphs** or **seraphim** /-rəfɪm/ [C] one of the ANGELS that protect the seat of God, according to the Bible

se·raph·ic /sə'ræfɪk/ *adj.* LITERARY extremely beautiful or pure, like an ANGEL

Ser·bi·a /'sɚbiə/ a country in Eastern Europe which was once part of Yugoslavia

sere /sɪr/ *adj.* LITERARY very dry

ser·e·nade[1] /ˌsɛrə'neɪd/ *n.* [C] ENG. LANG. ARTS **1** a song that a man performs for the woman he loves, especially standing below her window at night **2** a piece of gentle music [**Origin:** 1600–1700 French *sérénade*, from Italian *serenata*, from *sereno* **clear, calm**]

serenade[2] *v.* [T] if you serenade someone, you sing or play music to them to show them that you love them

ser·en·dip·i·ty /ˌsɛrən'dɪpət̬i/ *n.* [U] LITERARY the process of accidentally discovering something that is interesting or valuable: *The discovery was pure serendipity.* [**Origin:** 1700–1800 *Serendip* ancient name of Sri Lanka; because it was an ability possessed by the main characters in the old Persian story, "The Three Princes of Serendip"]

S

se·rene /sə'rin/ *adj.* **1** someone who is serene is very calm and relaxed: *her serene smile* **2** a place or situation that is serene is very peaceful: *a serene landscape of gentle hills* [**Origin:** 1400–1500 Latin *serenus* **clear, calm**] —**serenely** *adv.* —**serenity** /sə'rɛnət̬i/ *n.* [U]

serf /sɚf/ *n.* [C] someone who lived and worked on land that they did not own and who had to obey the owner of this land during the Middle Ages in Europe → see also SLAVE

serf·dom /'sɚfdəm/ *n.* [U] the state of being a serf

serge /sɚdʒ/ *n.* [U] strong cloth, usually made of wool

ser·geant /'sɑrdʒənt/ *n.* [C] a low rank in the army, air force, police etc., or someone who has this rank

ˌsergeant-at-'arms *n.* [C] an officer in an organization such as Congress whose job is to make sure that members obey the rules and that meetings stay organized

ˌsergeant 'major *n.* [C] a military rank in the U.S. Army or Marine Corps, or someone who has this rank

se·ri·al[1] /'sɪriəl/ *adj.* [only before noun] **1 a serial killer/rapist/arsonist etc.** someone who does the same crime several times, often in the same way **2 serial killings/murders/rapes etc.** crimes of the same kind that are done by the same person over a period of time **3** TECHNICAL acting on instructions or information in the order that it comes, one piece of information after the other → see also PARALLEL: *serial computer processing* **4** printed or broadcast in several separate parts —**serially** *adv.*

serial[2] *n.* [C] a long story or NOVEL that is broadcast or printed in several separate parts on television, in a newspaper etc.

se·ri·al·ize /'sɪriəˌlaɪz/ *v.* [T usually passive] to print or broadcast a story in several separate parts: *His book was first serialized in "The New Yorker."* —**serialization** /ˌsɪriələ'zeɪʃən/ *n.* [U]

ˌserial mo'nogamy *n.* [U] HUMOROUS the practice of having a series of MONOGAMOUS relationships that continue for only a short time —**serial monogamist** *n.* [C]

'serial ˌnumber *n.* [C] a number put on things that are produced in large quantities so that each one is slightly different: *The stolen weapon was identified by its serial number.*

se·ries /'sɪriz/ Ac S2 W1 *n. plural* **series** [C]
1 SIMILAR ACTIONS [usually singular] several events or actions of the same kind that happen one after the other: +**of** *There has been a series of attacks on tourists in the city this summer.*
2 EVENTS WITH A RESULT a group of events that are related and have a particular result: +**of** *An ongoing series of problems made the sale of the company necessary.*
3 TV/RADIO [usually singular] a set of television or radio programs in which each one tells the next part of a story or deals with the same kind of subject: *The new movie is based on the classic TV series from the '60s.* ►see THESAURUS box at **television**
4 BOOKS/MAGAZINES ETC. a set of books, magazines etc. that deal with the same subject, tell stories about the same characters etc.: *Jance has written a series of books that take place in Seattle.*
5 SIMILAR THINGS a group of similar things: *a series of numbers at the bottom of the computer screen* | *As she smiled, her mouth pushed her cheeks into a series of tiny wrinkles.*
6 PLANNED EVENTS a group of events or actions of the same kind that are planned to happen one after another in order to achieve something: *a lecture series* | *Beethoven's Ninth Symphony will be the first in a series of concerts at the new concert hall.* → see also WORLD SERIES
7 in series TECHNICAL being connected so that electricity passes though the parts of something electrical continuously in the correct order
8 MATH the sum of SEQUENCE (=set of numbers that are formed by a rule)
[**Origin:** 1600–1700 Latin *serere* **to join**]

ser·if /'sɛrəf/ *n.* [C] a short flat line at the top or bottom of some printed letters → see also SANS SERIF

se·ri·ous /'sɪriəs/ S1 W1 *adj.*
1 SITUATION/PROBLEM a serious situation, problem, accident etc. is extremely bad or dangerous: *Drugs are a serious problem here.* | *Luckily the damage was not serious.* | **a serious illness/injury/accident** *a serious car accident*
2 someone who is serious is not joking or pretending, but really means what they say: *Is that a serious offer?* | *"I'd like you to come with us." "Are you serious?"* | **serious about (doing) sth** *Is she serious about quitting her job?* | *Stop pushing me! **I'm serious*** (=used to emphasize that something is important)! | *My mother was **dead serious*** (=extremely serious), *and I knew it.* | ***Be serious** now* (=used to tell someone to stop joking). | *Marry Jason? **You can't be serious*** (=used to tell someone that what they have just said sounds impossible to believe)!
3 CAREFUL careful and thorough: *a serious article* | **serious consideration/thought/attention** *We'll give your request serious consideration.*
4 ROMANTIC RELATIONSHIP a serious romantic relationship is intended to continue for a long time: *It was my first serious relationship.* | +**about** *Are you serious about her?* | **a serious boyfriend/girlfriend** *his first serious girlfriend*
5 PERSON **a)** someone who is serious is always very sensible and quiet and does not laugh: *a serious young man* **b)** not laughing or not seeming happy, because you are worried, unhappy, or think something is very important: *The lawyer listened with a serious face.*
6 IMPORTANT important: *Work was a serious business to Tom.*
7 SPORTS/ACTIVITIES ETC. very interested in something, and spending a lot of time involved with it: *My brother is a serious golfer.* | +**about** *People in France are very serious about their food.*
8 LARGE IN AMOUNT SPOKEN INFORMAL used to emphasize that something is large in amount: *She's been earning serious money.*
9 VERY GOOD INFORMAL [only before noun] very good and often expensive: *That's a serious computer setup!*
[**Origin:** 1400–1500 French *sérieux*, from Late Latin *seriosus*, from Latin *serius*] —**seriousness** *n.* [U]

se·ri·ous·ly /'sɪriəsli/ S2 W2 *adv.*
1 NOT JOKING in a way that shows you are not joking and you mean what you say: *Allow me to speak seriously for a moment.* | *Seriously, though, are you going to see her again?*
2 VERY MUCH/BADLY very badly or to a great degree: *There was something seriously wrong.*
3 take sb/sth seriously to believe that someone or something is worth paying attention to or should be

respected: *As a teacher, it's important that the kids take you seriously.* | *Don't take anything he says too seriously.*
4 CAREFULLY very carefully and thoroughly: *You need to think seriously about your future.*
5 ROMANTIC RELATIONSHIP in a way that shows that you intend to continue a romantic relationship for a long time: *They started dating seriously about eight months ago.*
6 seriously? SPOKEN used to ask someone if they really mean what they have just said: *"You've got the job." "Seriously?"*

ser·mon /ˈsɝmən/ *n.* [C] **1** a religious talk given as part of a Christian church service, usually based on a part of the Bible: **give/preach/deliver a sermon** *A young priest gave the sermon.* **2** DISAPPROVING a talk in which someone tries to give you unwanted moral advice SYN lecture: *I don't need any sermons from you about my family life.*

ser·mon·ize /ˈsɝməˌnaɪz/ *v.* [I] DISAPPROVING to give a lot of unwanted moral advice in a serious way SYN preach

ser·o·to·nin /ˌserəˈtoʊnɪn/ *n.* [U] a chemical in the body that helps carry messages from the brain

ser·pent /ˈsɝpənt/ *n.* [C] **1** BIOLOGY a snake, especially a large one **2 the Serpent** the evil snake in the Garden of Eden according to the Bible [**Origin:** 1200–1300 Old French, Latin, present participle of *serpere* **to creep**]

ser·pen·tine /ˈsɝpənˌtin, -ˌtaɪn/ *adj.* **1** twisting or winding like a snake: *a serpentine river* **2** complicated and difficult to understand: *the movie's serpentine plot*

ser·rat·ed /səˈreɪt̬ɪd, ˈsɛˌreɪt̬ɪd/ *adj.* having a sharp edge made of a row of connected V shapes like teeth: *Use **a serrated knife** to slice the bread.* —**serration** /səˈreɪʃən/ *n.* [C,U]

ser·ried /ˈserid/ *adj.* LITERARY pressed closely together SYN crowded

se·rum /ˈsɪrəm/ *n.* [C,U] **1** MEDICINE a liquid containing substances that fight infection, that is put into a sick person's blood → see also VACCINE **2** BIOLOGY the watery part of blood or the liquid from a plant —**serous** *adj.*

serv·ant /ˈsɝvənt/ *n.* [C] **1** someone who is paid to clean someone's house, cook for them, answer the door etc. **2 servant of sb/sth** someone who is controlled by someone or something, or does useful things for them: *I remain a faithful servant of the state.* → see also CIVIL SERVANT

serve[1] /sɝv/ S1 W1 *v.*
1 FOOD/DRINK [I,T] to give someone food or drink, especially as part of a meal: *Light refreshments will be served.* | **serve sb** *A team of waiters served us.* | **serve sth with sth** *I'm planning to serve the chicken with a light cream sauce.* | **serve sth to sb** *Your meals can be served to you in your room.* | **serve sth hot/cold etc.** *Serve the pie warm or at room temperature.* | **breakfast/lunch/dinner is served** (=used in hotels and similar places to say when breakfast, lunch etc. is provided) ▶see THESAURUS box at cooking[1]
2 serve two/three/four etc. (people) if food serves two, three etc. people, there is enough for that number of people: *This recipe serves six.*
3 BE USEFUL/HELPFUL [I,T] to be useful or helpful for a particular purpose or reason: **serve as sth** *The sofa also serves as a bed.* | *Do the raised lines **serve a purpose*** (=have a particular use), *or are they just for decoration?* | *McKenna's background in publishing **serves her well*** (=is very useful) *in her new position.* | *We wanted to build a community that **served the needs of*** (=was useful for) *all its members.*
4 DO A HELPFUL JOB [I,T] to spend a period of time doing a job, especially one that helps the organization, country etc.: *School board members serve a two-year term.* | **serve in the army/military etc.** *She served in the Peace Corps in the 1960s.* | **serve on a board/committee etc.** *Ann serves on various local committees.* | **serve as sth** *Powell served as Secretary of State for President Bush's first term.* | *Christine was proud to **serve her country*** (=in the military or doing government work).
5 STORE/RESTAURANT [T] FORMAL to help the customers in a store, restaurant etc., especially by bringing them the things that they want: *Please fill out this questionnaire so that we may better serve you.*
6 HAVE AN EFFECT [I,T] FORMAL to have a particular effect or result: **serve to do sth** *The incident served to emphasize the need for security.*
7 PRISON [T] to spend a particular period of time in prison: *He's **serving a life sentence** for murder.* | *McAllen is still **serving time*** (=spending time in prison) *for manslaughter.*
8 (it) serves sb right (for doing sth) SPOKEN used to say that you think someone deserves something bad that happens to them, because they have been stupid or unkind: *Serves him right – he shouldn't have cheated in the first place.*
9 PROVIDE STH [T] to provide a group of people with something that is necessary or useful: *The airline now serves 37 cities.*
10 SPORTS [I,T] to start playing in a game such as tennis or VOLLEYBALL by throwing the ball up in the air and hitting it to your opponent
11 serve a summons/writ etc. to officially send or give someone a written order to appear in a court of law
12 serve an apprenticeship to learn a job or skill by working for a particular period of time for someone who has a lot of experience
13 CHURCH [I] to help a priest during the EUCHARIST
[**Origin:** 1100–1200 Old French *servir*, from Latin *servire* **to be a slave, serve**] → see also **justice has been done/served** at JUSTICE (3), **if memory serves** at MEMORY (8)

serve sth ↔ **out** *phr. v.* to continue doing something until the end of a particular period of time: *The Senator's failing health means he may not be able to serve out his term.*

serve sth ↔ **up** *phr. v.* to put food onto plates so that people can eat it

serve[2] *n.* [C] the action in a game such as tennis or VOLLEYBALL in which you throw the ball in the air and hit it to your opponent: *It's your serve.*

serv·er /ˈsɝvɚ/ *n.* [C] **1** someone who brings you your food in a restaurant: *Our server told us about the day's specials.* ▶see THESAURUS box at **restaurant**
2 COMPUTERS **a)** the main computer on a NETWORK, that controls all the others **b)** one of the computers on a network that provides a special service: **a file/print/mail server** *All important data is stored on a central file server.* **3** a special spoon or tool for putting a particular kind of food onto a plate: *a silver cake server* **4** a player who hits a ball to begin a game in tennis, VOLLEYBALL etc. **5** someone who helps a priest during the EUCHARIST

serv·ice[1] /ˈsɝvɪs/ S1 W1 *n.*
1 STORE/HOTEL ETC. [U] the help that people who work in a store, restaurant, bar etc. give you: **good/quick/excellent service** *The service was really good at that French restaurant.* | **poor/slow/terrible service** *The service was terrible.* | *high standards of **customer service*** (=service that a shop, restaurant, company etc. gives to its customers)
2 WORK DONE FOR SB [U] also **services** [plural] FORMAL work that someone does for a company, organization, person etc.: **+to** *Horne was given an award in recognition of services to the city.* | **20/30 years etc. of service** *He was thanked for his ten years of service to the company.* | *He **offered his services** as a tennis coach.* | *We **employed the services of** a lawyer.* | *Jordan had a long and distinguished career in **public service*** (=work done for the public or the government). | *Please accept this as payment for **services rendered*** (=used on a bill you give to someone for work you have done for them).
3 BUSINESS [C,U] advice or work that a company provides for people to buy: *The company provides phone and Internet service to 30 million people.* | **a babysitting/cleaning/delivery etc. service** *We offer a gift-buying service for busy businesspeople.* | *The bank offers a range of financial services.* → see also SERVICE INDUSTRY

4 OFFICIAL SYSTEM [C,U] a government system or private organization that provides help, or the help provided by these systems or organizations: *the amount spent by the government on public services* | *I'm looking for information on family planning services.* | **police/medical/fire etc. service** *emergency ambulance service* | *interruptions to postal service in the area* | ***The Postal Service*** (=the government organization that delivers mail) *will print 45 million stamps this year.*
5 RELIGION [C] a formal religious ceremony, for example in church: *A special church **service** was **held** in the city for victims of the fire.* | **a marriage/funeral etc. service** *A larger memorial service will be held for Burns later this month.*
6 HELP [singular, U] help that you give to someone: *Don't thank me – I'm glad to **be of service*** (=be able to help someone). | *Unions may charge for **services rendered*** (=help that has been given to non-members). | **at sb's service** FORMAL (=if someone or something is at your service, they are available to help you)
7 jury/military/community etc. service something that ordinary people can be asked to do for the public as a public duty or as a punishment: *All young men must do one year of military service.*
8 GOVERNMENT [C usually singular] used in the names of organizations that work directly for a government: *the foreign service* | *the U.S. customs service*
9 the service a country's military forces, especially considered as a job: *My first duty station in the service was in North Carolina.*
10 SPORTS [C] an act of hitting a ball through the air in order to start a game, for example in tennis
11 CAR/MACHINE [C] an examination and repair of a machine or car to keep it working correctly
12 dinner/tea service a set of matching plates, bowls, cups etc. → see also **on active duty/service** at ACTIVE[1] (7), **pay lip service to sth** at PAY[1] (15), **press sb/sth into service/duty** at PRESS[1] (11)

service² W2 *v.* [T] **1** to examine a machine or vehicle and repair it if necessary: *I'm having the car serviced next week.* ►see THESAURUS box at **repair¹** **2** to provide people with something they need or want: *The parking lot was built to service both campuses.* **3** TECHNICAL to pay the INTEREST on a debt —**servicing** *n.* [U]

service³ *adj.* **service door/elevator etc.** a door, ELEVATOR etc. that is only for the use of people working in a place, rather than the public

serv·ice·a·ble /ˈsɚvɪsəbəl/ *adj.* **1** good enough to be used for a particular purpose: *These boots are still perfectly serviceable.* **2** fairly good, but not excellent: *The food was serviceable, but not stunning.* —**serviceability** /ˌsɚvɪsəˈbɪləṭi/ *n.* [U]

ˈservice ˌcharge *n.* [C] an amount of money that is added to the price of something in order to pay for services that you use when buying it: *There is a $1 service charge for each ticket purchased online.*

ˈservice ˌclub *n.* [C] a usually national organization made of smaller local groups in which members do things to help their COMMUNITY

ˌservice coˈoperative *n.* [C] ECONOMICS a COOPERATIVE (=a company, shop etc. in which all of the people who work there own an equal share of it) that provides a service rather than produces goods

ˈservice eˌconomy *n.* [C] a country or an economic system in which most people work for businesses that provide services, rather than businesses involved in MANUFACTURING (=producing goods)

ˈservice ˌindustry *n.* [C,U] an industry that provides a service rather than a product, for example the insurance industry, advertising, TOURISM etc.

serv·ice·man /ˈsɚvɪsˌmæn, -mən/ *n. plural* **servicemen** /-ˌmɛn, -mən/ [C] a man who is a member of the military

ˈservice road *n.* [C] a FRONTAGE ROAD

ˈservice ˌstation *n.* [C] a place that sells gas, food etc.

serv·ice·wom·an /ˈsɚvɪsˌwʊmən/ *n. plural* **servicewomen** /-ˌwɪmɪn/ [C] a woman who is a member of the military

ser·vi·ette /ˌsɚviˈɛt/ *n.* [C] CANADIAN, BRITISH a paper NAPKIN

ser·vile /ˈsɚvəl, -vaɪl/ *adj.* **1** DISAPPROVING very eager to obey someone without questioning them **2** relating to SLAVES or to being a slave —**servilely** *adv.* —**servility** /sɚˈvɪləṭi/ *n.* [U]

serv·ing¹ /ˈsɚvɪŋ/ *n.* [C] an amount of food that is enough for one person SYN **helping**: *The recipe makes four servings.* | **servings of fruits/vegetables/grains etc.** *Eat five servings of fruits and vegetables per day.*

serving² *adj.* **a serving spoon/dish/platter etc.** a spoon, dish etc. that is used to serve food

ser·vi·tor /ˈsɚvəṭɚ/ *n.* [C] OLD USE a male servant

ser·vi·tude /ˈsɚvəˌtud/ *n.* [U] the condition of being a SLAVE or being completely under the control of someone

ses·a·me /ˈsɛsəmi/ *n.* [U] a tropical plant grown for its seeds and oil, used in cooking → see also OPEN SESAME

ses·sion /ˈsɛʃən/ S2 W2 *n.* [C] **1** a period of time used for a particular activity, especially by a group of people: *He made changes to the song during a recording session.* | *a practice session* **2** POLITICS a formal meeting or group of meetings, especially of a law court or government organization: *Court will remain **in session**.* | *We'll resume the debate in the next **session of Congress**.* **3** a part of the year when classes are given at a college or university: *This course will only be offered during the fall session.* [**Origin:** 1300–1400 Old French, Latin *sessio* **act of sitting, session**, from *sedere* **to sit**]

set¹ /sɛt/ S1 W1 *v. past tense and past participle* **set**, **setting**
1 PUT [T always + adv./prep.] to carefully put something down somewhere, especially something that is difficult to carry SYN **put**: **set sth (down) on sth** *She set her cup of coffee on the table.* | **set sth down** *Dan set the tray down.* | **set sth aside** *Set the sauce aside to cool.*
2 ESTABLISH STH [T] to establish a way of doing something which then continues or is copied: *Managers should **set an example*** (=behave in a good or sensible way that other people can copy) *to their staff.* | **set a pattern/tone/trend etc.** *The speech set the tone for the whole conference.* | *He **set a** new world **record*** (=do something better than anyone else has ever done) *with that jump.* | **set a precedent** (=if an event or action sets a precedent, it shows people a way of doing something which they can use or copy)
3 DECIDE STH [T] to decide on a time, date, amount etc., or decide what the rules or limits for something should be: **set a time/date (for sth)** *Have you set a date for the wedding?* | **set a price/budget etc. at sth** *The price of oil has been set at $46 a barrel.* | **set guidelines/standards/conditions/limits etc.** *The city has set strict guidelines for new buildings.* | *The company has just **set** new **targets** for the next three years.* | **set (yourself) a goal** *I set myself the goal of becoming sports editor of the college paper.*
4 set fire to sth also **set sth on fire/ablaze/alight** to make something start burning: *Protesters set fire to a truck and two buses.*
5 MOVIE/PLAY/STORY [T usually passive] if a movie, play, story etc. is set in a place or period, it happens there or at that time: *The play is set in Madrid in the year 1840.*
6 BUILDING/TOWN/CITY be set [always + adv./prep.] if a building, town etc. is set in a particular position, it is in that position: *The house was set back from the road.* | *a medieval village set high on a hill*
7 MACHINE/CLOCK ETC. [T] to move part of a machine, clock etc. so that it is in a particular position and is ready to be used: *Did you set the alarm?* | **set sth on/to sth** *I set the oven on "broil."*
8 set sth in motion to make something start happening, especially by means of an official order: *The plan was set in motion on January 1.*
9 set the table to arrange plates, knives, cups etc. on a table so that it is ready for a meal
10 set your mind/sights/heart on sth also **have your mind/sights/heart set on sth** to be determined to

achieve something or decide that you definitely want to have it: *She had her heart set on a big wedding.*
11 **set a trap** **a)** to make a trap ready to catch an animal **b)** to invent a plan to catch a criminal or show that someone is doing something wrong
12 **set to work** to start doing something in a determined way, especially something that is difficult and needs a lot of effort: +**on** *He sat down and set to work on the illustrations.*
13 **set sail** to start sailing somewhere: *We set sail at sunrise.*
14 **set sb to work** to make someone start doing a particular kind of work for you: *They set her to work in the hot fields.*
15 **SUN** [I] when the sun sets, it seems to move close to the horizon and then goes below it SYN **go down**: *We went outside to watch the sun set.*
16 **LIQUID/GLUE/CEMENT ETC.** [I] to become hard and solid: *How long does it take for the glue to set?*
17 **set sb straight/right** to tell someone the right way to do something or the true facts about something: *He thought we had to pay for everything, but I set him straight.* → see also **set/put/keep the record straight** at RECORD[1] (9)
18 **set the world on fire** INFORMAL to be very successful and have a great effect on someone or something: *She went to New York expecting to set the world on fire.*
19 **set sth to music** to write music for a story or a poem, so that it can be sung
20 **set sb free/loose** to allow someone or an animal to be free: *After six years in prison, Louis was set free.*
21 **set store by sth** to consider something to be very important: *Mama always set great store by honesty.*
22 **FACE** WRITTEN if your face or mouth sets into an unpleasant or unhappy expression, or you set your face or mouth in that way, you start to have that expression: *His mouth was set in a thin angry line.*
23 **PRINTING** to arrange the words and letters of a book, newspaper etc. so it is ready to be printed: *In those days books had to be set by hand.*
24 **set sth right** also **set sth to rights** to deal with any problems, mistakes etc. and make a situation the way it should be: *This company needs a dramatic shake-up to set things right.*
25 **BONE** MEDICINE **a)** [T] if you set a broken bone, you move the broken ends so that they are in the right place to grow together again **b)** [I] if a broken bone sets, it joins together again
26 **HAIR** [T] to arrange someone's hair while it is wet so that it has a particular style when it dries
27 **be set into sth** to be attached to the surface of something: *Sculpted panels were set into the walls.*
[**Origin:** Old English *settan*]

set about *phr. v.* **1 set about sth** WRITTEN to start doing something, especially something that needs a lot of time and effort: *He set about his task with determination.* | **set about doing sth** *Lou set about decorating their new house.* **2 set about sb** OLD USE to attack someone by hitting and kicking them

set against *phr. v.* **1 set sb against sb** to make someone start to fight or argue with another person, especially a person who they had friendly relations with before: *He set her against her own family.* **2 be set against sth** if a movie, play, story etc. is set against a place or period, it happens there or at that time: *It's a novel of passion and love set against the glitter of the international jet set.* **3 set sb against sth** to make someone not want to do something: *Her early experiences had set her against living in the city.*

set apart *phr. v.* **set sb/sth apart** to make someone or something different and often better than other people or things: *Our ability to reason sets us apart from other animals.*

set sth ↔ **aside** *phr. v.* **1** to keep something, especially money or time, for a special purpose and only use it for that purpose: +**for** *The shelter set aside 32 spaces for homeless kids.* | *Try to set aside some time each day for exercise.* **2** to decide that you will not be influenced by a particular feeling, belief, or principle, because something else is more important: *They agreed to set their differences aside.* **3** to decide that a previous legal decision or agreement does not have any effect anymore: *The judge set aside the verdict of the lower court.*

set back *phr. v.* **1 set sb/sth ↔ back** to delay the progress or development of something, or delay someone from finishing something: *The fire set back construction of the building by three months.* **2 set sb back** to delay someone in finishing something: *My illness set me back a couple of weeks.* **3 set sb back** INFORMAL to cost someone a particular amount of money: *Most of these wines will set you back $15 to $20.*

set down *phr. v.* **1 set down sth** to establish how something should be done in an official set of rules or an official document: *The government has set down clearer guidelines for teachers.* **2 set sth ↔ down** to write about something so that you have a record of it: *I wanted to set my feelings down on paper.*

set forth *phr. v.* **1 set sth ↔ forth** FORMAL to write or talk about an idea, argument, or a set of figures: *The review committee has set forth its conclusions in a report.* **2** LITERARY to begin a journey: *They set forth into the unknown.*

set in *phr. v.* if something sets in, especially something bad, it begins and seems likely to continue for a long time: *We wanted to leave before winter set in.* | *Fear set in as the tornado approached.*

set off *phr. v.* **1 set sth ↔ off** to make something start happening, especially when you do not intend to do so: *The news set off widespread panic.* **2 set sth ↔ off** to make something such as an ALARM system start operating, especially when you do not intend to do so: *Something burning in the oven set off the smoke alarm.* **3 set sth ↔ off** to make a bomb explode, or cause an explosion: *Any movement could have set off the bomb.* **4** to start to go somewhere SYN **leave**: *Jeri and I set off on foot for the beach.* **5 set sth ↔ off** if a piece of clothing, color, decoration etc. sets something off, it makes it look noticeable and attractive: *The blue in your shirt really sets off your eyes* **6 set sb off** to make someone laugh, cry, get angry etc. about something: *He knows just what to say to set me off.*

set out *phr. v.* **1** ESPECIALLY WRITTEN to start a trip, especially a long one: +**on** *On May 17 1673, they set out on their dangerous journey.* | +**for** *We set out for St. Petersburg the next day.* **2** to start doing something or making plans to do something in order to achieve a particular result: **set out to do sth** *When she was 18, Amy set out to find her biological parents.* | **set out on sth** *My nephew is just setting out on a career in journalism.* **3 set sth ↔ out** to write or talk about something such as a group of facts, ideas, or reasons, especially in a clearly organized way: *It's important to set your ideas out logically.* **4 set sth ↔ out** to put a group of things down and arrange them: *Lois set out the sugar bowl and the napkins on the table.*

set up *phr. v.*
1 **COMPANY/ORGANIZATION ETC.** **set sth ↔ up** to start a company, organization, committee etc. SYN **establish**: *They want to set up their own import-export business.* | *Jack got his law degree, then **set up shop** (=set up a business) as a real estate lawyer.*
2 **ARRANGE/ORGANIZE** **set sth ↔ up** to make the necessary arrangements so that something, such as a meeting or event, can happen: *I can set up an appointment for you to have a massage.*
3 **EQUIPMENT** to prepare the equipment that will be needed for an activity so that it is ready to be used: *The next band was already setting up on the other stage.* | **set sth ↔ up** *My brother set up the modem on my computer.*
4 **BUILD/PUT UP** **set sth ↔ up** to place or build something somewhere, usually a temporary structure: *A press headquarters was set up outside the stadium.* | *We **set up camp** (=put up a tent or group of tents) before dinner.*
5 **MAKE SB SEEM GUILTY** **set sb ↔ up** to deliberately make other people think that someone has done something wrong or illegal: *He said that the FBI had set him up.*
6 **SPORTS** **set sth ↔ up** to hit or kick a ball into a

particular position so that another player can kick or hit it to get a point: *He scored two goals himself, and set up a third.*

7 PROVIDE MONEY **set sb ↔ up** to provide someone with the money that they need, especially so that they can start a business: *My parents set me up in business after I got my degree.*

8 set up housekeeping/house to start living in your own home, especially with someone else, instead of living with your parents

9 RELATIONSHIP **set sb ↔ up** to arrange for two people to meet, especially because you think they might start a romantic relationship: *Two of our friends set us up.*

set² S1 W1 *n.*

1 GROUP OF THINGS [C] a group of things that form a whole: *a train set* | +**of** *a set of golf clubs* | *A strange set of events led me to this job.* | *The older generation have a different set of values.*

2 a TV/television set a television: *a color television set*

3 MOVIE [C] ENG. LANG. ARTS a place where a movie or television program is acted and filmed: **on (the) set** *She was on the set early to read over her lines.*

4 STAGE [C] ENG. LANG. ARTS the painted background, furniture, and other structures used on a stage for a play: *The set is still being built.*

5 SPORTS [C] one part of a game such as tennis or VOLLEYBALL: *In the second set, Sampras led 5–4.*

6 MUSIC [C] ENG. LANG. ARTS a series of songs performed by one band or singer as part of a concert: *They played a 90-minute set.*

7 PEOPLE [C usually singular] a group of people with similar interests: *the skateboarding set* → see also JET SET

8 the set of sb's face/jaw/shoulders etc. the expression on your face or the way you hold your body, which tells people how you are feeling: *His determination to win was obvious from the set of his jaw.*

9 HAIR [singular] OLD-FASHIONED an act of arranging your hair in a particular style when it is wet

10 FIRMNESS [singular] the state of becoming firm or solid: *You'll get a better set if you use gelatin.*

11 MATH [C] a collection of numbers, shapes etc. in MATHEMATICS: *The set (x, y) has two members.*

12 RADIO [C] a piece of equipment for receiving radio signals: *a ham radio operator's set*

13 ONION [C] BIOLOGY a small brown root planted in order to grow onions: *onion sets*

set³ *adj.* [no comparative]

1 AMOUNT/TIME a set time, amount etc. has been decided by someone and cannot be changed SYN **fixed**: *Workers earn a set amount for each piece they sew.* | *The evening meal is served at a set time.*

2 READY [not before noun] INFORMAL prepared for something: +**for** *Get set for a full evening of hot entertainment.* | *Okay, I'm* ***all set****, let's get going.* | **be (all) set to do sth** *He was set to go, but Mel stopped him.* | **get set for sth/get set to do sth** *OK everyone, get set for some fun.* | *"On your marks –* ***get set*** (=used to say "get ready" before a race) *– go!"*

3 be (dead) set on (doing) sth to be very determined to do something: *Mark is absolutely set on owning his own business.*

4 be (dead) set against (doing) sth to be very opposed to something: *Her parents were dead set against the marriage.*

5 set to do sth likely to do something: *The hot weather looks set to continue.*

6 EXPRESSION if your face is set, it has a fixed expression on it, especially an angry or worried one, and does not move: *Her face was pale and set.*

7 set ideas/views/opinions/beliefs set opinions or beliefs are ones you are not likely to change: *My mother has very set ideas about how to bring up children.*

8 be set in your ways DISAPPROVING to be used to doing things in a particular way and not willing to change: *He's so set in his ways. He'll never try it.*

9 set into sth built into the surface of something: *There was a door set into the stone wall.*

10 set with gems/jewels etc. decorated with jewels: *a ring set with four precious stones*

set·back /ˈsɛt˺bæk/ *n.* [C] something that delays or prevents progress, or makes things worse than they were: *The ruling is a major setback for civil rights activists.* → see also **set back** at SET¹

Se·ton /ˈsit˺n/, **Saint Elizabeth** (1774–1821) the first woman in the U.S. to be made a SAINT by the Catholic Church

ˌset ˈpiece *n.* [C] a speech, piece of music, painting etc. that follows a well-known formal pattern or style, and is often very impressive: *The trial scene at the end of the movie is a classic set piece.*

set·tee /sɛˈti/ *n.* [C] a long seat with a back and usually with arms, for more than one person to sit on

set·ter /ˈsɛṭɚ/ *n.* [C] **1** BIOLOGY a long-haired dog, often trained to find animals or birds so they can be shot **2 a policy-setter/record-setter/price-setter etc.** someone who decides something as part of their job: *corporate budget-setters* **3 a style-setter/standard-setter/example-setter etc.** someone who does things that other people admire and try to copy: *Be the example-setter for your kids.* → see also PACESETTER, TRENDSETTER

set·ting /ˈsɛṭɪŋ/ *n.* **1** [C usually singular] the place where something is or where something happens, and the general environment surrounding the thing or event: *Imagine working in a beautiful setting overlooking the bay.* | *Most patients were initially treated in a hospital setting.* **2** [C usually singular] ENG. LANG. ARTS the place or time that the action of a book, movie etc. happens: +**for** *Ireland is the setting for his latest movie.* **3** [C] the position in which you put the controls on a machine or instrument: *the iron's temperature settings* | *The heater was* ***on*** *the highest* ***setting****.* **4** [C] the metal that holds a stone in a piece of jewelry, or the way the stone is fastened: *a diamond ring in a gold setting* **5** [C] ENG. LANG. ARTS music that is written to go with a poem, prayer etc. **6 the setting of the sun** LITERARY the time when the sun goes down → see also PLACE SETTING

set·tle¹ /ˈsɛṭl/ S2 W2 *v.*

1 ARGUMENT [T] to end an argument by agreeing on something: **settle a dispute/argument/issue etc.** *Attempts to settle the trade dispute have failed.* | *Mom, we need your opinion to settle a bet.* | *I hope your brothers can* ***settle their differences*** (=agree to stop arguing or fighting).

2 COURTCASE [I,T] to make an agreement that ends a court case or stops it before it goes to the courts at all: *Her company paid $5.8 million to settle the lawsuit.* | **settle with sb (for sth)** *He finally settled with his former employers for an undisclosed sum.* | *Maybe they'll be willing to* ***settle out of court*** (=come to an agreement before going to a court of law).

3 GO AND LIVE SOMEWHERE **a)** [I always + adv./prep., T always + adv./prep.] to go to live in a new place, and stay there for a long time, or to send someone to do this: *Many Jewish immigrants settled in the Lower East Side.* | *In 1990 about 200 Somali refugees were settled in the city.* **b)** [T usually passive] to go to a place where no people have lived permanently before and start to live there: *Historians are unsure when the territory was first settled.*

4 COMFORTABLE [I,T always + adv./prep.] to put yourself, a part of your body, or someone else in a comfortable position: **settle (sb/sth) back/into/down etc.** *Stan settled back to read his paper.* | *The nurse settled grandpa into a chair.* | **settle yourself in/on etc. sth** *She settled herself by an oak tree on a hill overlooking the town.*

5 MOVE DOWN [I] **a)** if dust, snow etc. settles, it comes down and stays in one place: +**on/in** *A layer of fine white dust was settling on the wet pavement.* → see also **the dust settles** at DUST¹ (4) **b)** if something such as a building or the ground settles, it sinks slowly to a lower level: *The chimney's foundation has settled and needs to be replaced.*

6 settle a bill/an account/a claim to pay money that is owed: *Officials sold the house to settle a tax bill.*

7 ORGANIZE BUSINESS/MONEY [T] to deal with all the details of a business or of someone's money or property, so that nothing further needs to be done: *Kevin returned to the States to* ***settle his affairs****.* | *It'll take*

months to ***settle the estate*** (=deal with someone's money and property after they die, for example by giving it to the person's relatives).
8 DECIDE [T] to decide on something, especially so that you can make definite arrangements: *Nothing is settled yet.* | *There's not much time to* ***settle the details*** *of our trip.* | *"It's raining."* ***"That settles it*** (=used to say that you have finally made a decision). *I'm staying home."*
9 FEELING/QUALITY [I always + adv./prep.] if a quality or feeling settles over a place or on someone, it has a strong effect: +**over/on** *A sense of peace settled on the town.*
10 WEATHER/NIGHT [I] if something such as darkness or FOG settles over an area, it comes into the sky: +**on/over** *Dusk began to settle over the island.*
11 BIRD/INSECT if a bird, insect etc. settles, it flies down and rests on something: +**on** *A butterfly settled on a branch near our window.*
12 QUIET/CALM [I,T] to become quiet or calm, or to make someone or something quiet or calm: **settle your nerves/stomach** (=stop your nerves or stomach from being upset)
13 settle a score also **settle an account** to do something to hurt or cause trouble for someone because they have harmed or offended you: *She's got a few old scores to settle with her former friend.*
14 FACE [I] if a particular expression settles on your face, it stays there

settle down *phr. v.* **1** to stop talking or behaving in an excited way, or to make someone do this: *Would you kids just settle down for a minute?* | **settle sb ↔ down** *Sometimes we take the baby for a ride in the car to settle him down.* **2** to start living in a place with the intention of staying there and behaving in a responsible way, getting married, having a good job etc.: *I'm not ready to settle down yet.* **3** to make yourself comfortable somewhere, especially because you will be there a long time: **settle down to do sth** *She settled down on the couch to read.* **4 settle down to sth** to start giving all of your attention to a job, activity etc.: *I read my mail, then settled down to some serious work.*

settle for sth *phr. v.* to accept something even though it is not the best, or not what you really want: *There wasn't any real coffee, so we had to settle for the instant kind.*

settle in *phr. v.* also **settle into sth** to begin to feel happy and relaxed in a new situation, home, job, or school: **settle (sb) into sth** *They'll need time to settle into their new house.* | **settle (sb) in** *People were settling in for an afternoon of music in the park.* | *Church members helped settle the young family in.*

settle on/upon sth/sb *phr. v.* **1** to decide or agree on something: *Doug finally settled on the broiled salmon for $14.95.* | *The committee has finally settled on a new leader.* **2 sb's eyes/gaze settle on sb/sth** WRITTEN used to say that someone notices someone or something and looks at them for a while: *Her eyes settled on the boy in the corner.*

settle up *phr. v.* to pay what you owe on an account or bill: **settle up with sb** *I'll settle up with the waiter.*

settle² *n.* [C] a long wooden seat with a high back that usually has a hollow place for storing things under the seat

set·tled /ˈsɛt̬ld/ *adj.* **1** remaining the same, and not likely to change SYN **fixed**: *We can accept that as settled, then.* | *a well-to-do settled community* **2 feel/be settled** to feel comfortable about living or working in a particular place: *I still don't feel settled in my new job.* → see also UNSETTLED

set·tle·ment /ˈsɛt̬lmənt/ W3 *n.*
1 OFFICIAL AGREEMENT [C,U] an official agreement or decision that ends an argument between two sides: **reach/achieve a settlement** *We hope to reach a settlement by February.* | *an* ***out-of-court settlement*** (=an agreement made without the two sides having to go to court) | **divorce/peace/financial etc. settlement** (=the agreement about what the two sides will do after a divorce, after fighting stops etc.)
2 GROUP OF HOUSES [C] a group of houses and buildings where people live, in an area where no group lived before: *New settlements sprang up along the railroad.*
3 NEW AREA/PLACES [U] the movement of a new population into a place to live there: +**of** *the settlement of the American West*
4 PAYMENT [U] ECONOMICS the act of paying all the money that you owe: +**of** *the settlement of all his debts* | *The defendant paid over $200,000* ***in settlement*** *of the matter.*
5 SINKING [U] EARTH SCIENCE the slow sinking of a building, the ground under it etc.

ˈsettlement ˌhouse *n.* [C] a building in a poor area of a city where services are provided for the local people

set·tler /ˈsɛtlɚ, ˈsɛt̬l-ɚ/ *n.* [C] someone who goes to live in a new place where there are few people: *Eddie's great-grandfather was one of the town's first settlers.*

set·up /ˈsɛt̬ʌp/ *n.* **1** [C usually singular] the way something is organized or arranged: *We have a new setup in the classroom.* **2** [C,U] the act of organizing something new, such as a business or a computer system: *Trained technicians can help with installation and setup.* **3** [C] several pieces of equipment that work together in a system: *If you're serious about photography, you'll need your own darkroom setup.* **4** [C usually singular] INFORMAL a dishonest plan that is intended to trick you: *How do I know this isn't a setup?* **5** [C usually singular] the first part of a story, movie, or joke that describes the general situation and introduces the characters in it → see also **set up** at SET¹

ˈsetup ˌcost *n.* [C] ECONOMICS another word for START-UP COST

Seu·rat /səˈrɑ/, **Georges** /ʒɔrʒ/ (1859–1891) a French painter famous for developing the method of painting known as POINTILLISM

Seuss /sus/, **Dr.** (1904–1991) a U.S. children's writer whose funny stories, poems, and pictures are very popular with young children

sev·en /ˈsɛvən/ *number* **1** 7 **2** seven o'clock: *Come over* ***at around seven.*** **3 the seven-year itch** HUMOROUS the idea that after seven years of being married, people feel less satisfied with their relationship and may want to have sex with other people **4 the seven seas** LITERARY all the oceans of the world: *They traveled the seven seas, hoping to find new lands.* [**Origin:** Old English *seofon*] → see also SEVENTH¹

sev·en·teen /ˌsɛvənˈtin◂/ *number* 17 —**seventeenth** *adj., pron., n.*

sev·enth¹ /ˈsɛvənθ/ *adj.* **1** 7th; next after the sixth: *The store is on Seventh Avenue.* **2 be in seventh heaven** INFORMAL to be extremely happy: *She got a puppy for Christmas, and she was in seventh heaven.*

seventh² *pron.* **the seventh** the 7th thing in a series: *I'll call you when I get back on the seventh* (=the 7th day of the month).

seventh³ *n.* [C] 1/7; one of seven equal parts

Seventh-Day Ad·vent·ist /ˌsɛvənθ deɪ ˈædvəntɪst/ *n.* [C] a member of a Christian group that goes to church on Saturdays and believes that Jesus Christ will soon come again to Earth

ˌseventh-inning ˈstretch *n.* [singular] a period of time in the middle of the seventh INNING of a baseball game, when the teams stop playing and the people watching the game can stand up and walk around

seventieth¹ /ˈsɛvəntiɪθ/ *adj.* 70th; next after the sixty-ninth: *my father's seventieth birthday*

seventieth² *pron.* **the seventieth** the 70th thing in a series

sev·en·ty /ˈsɛvənt̬i/ *number* **1** 70 **2 the seventies** also **the '70s** the years from 1970 through 1979 **3 sb's seventies** the time when someone is 70 to 79 years old: **in your early/mid/late seventies** *I'd guess she's in her late seventies.* **4 in the seventies** if the temperature is in the seventies, it is between 70° and 79° FAHRENHEIT: **in the high/low seventies** *The temperature was in the high seventies and sunny.*

S

ˌseventy-ˈeight *n.* [C] an old-fashioned record that turns 78 times a minute while it is being played

sev·er /ˈsɛvɚ/ *v.* [T] FORMAL **1** to cut through something completely, separating it into two parts, or separating a smaller part from the whole: *Martin's hand was severed in the accident.* | *The bullet severed a main artery.* **2** to end a relationship with someone, or a connection with something: *She wanted to* ***sever all ties with*** (=have no more contact with) *her family.*

sev·eral¹ /ˈsɛvrəl/ S1 W1 *quantifier, pron.* a number of people or things that is more than a few, but not a lot: *I've been to Florida several times.* | *Several people volunteered to help.* | *We waited several more seconds before knocking.* | **+of** *Several of the students received awards for their work.* | **several hundred/thousand etc.** *The suit cost several hundred dollars.*

several² *adj.* [only before noun, no comparative] FORMAL or LAW different and separate SYN **respective**: *They deal with their several responsibilities* [**Origin:** 1400–1500 Anglo-French, Medieval Latin *separalis*, from Latin *separare*] —**severally** *adv.*

sev·erance /ˈsɛvrəns/ *n.* [U] **1** a situation in which someone has to leave a company because their employer does not have a job for them anymore: *The company has a voluntary severance program.* **2** severance pay **3** the act of ending a relationship with someone or a connection with something: *the severance of trade with Germany*

S

ˈseverance pay *n.* [U] money that you get when you leave a company because your employer does not have a job for you anymore

se·vere /səˈvɪr/ W3 *adj.* **1** very bad, or serious enough for you to worry about: *severe pain* | *The victims suffered severe head injuries.* | *severe economic problems* **2** severe weather conditions are extremely hot, cold, dry etc. and are bad or dangerous: *severe thunderstorms* | *a severe frost* **3** severe punishment is extreme, and intended to prevent more crimes or wrong behavior SYN **harsh**: *Severe penalties will be imposed for late payment.* **4** severe criticism is very extreme and shows that you think someone has done something very badly or done something very wrong SYN **harsh** OPP **mild**: *her severe and public criticism of the president* **5** someone who is severe is very strict and demands that rules of behavior be obeyed or standards be followed SYN **stern**: *Her severe smile softened.* **6** simple and formal in style with little or no decoration or beauty SYN **plain**: *She wore a severe black dress and no make-up.* **7** very difficult and needing a lot of effort or skill: *a* ***severe test*** *of my skill* [**Origin:** 1500–1600 French *sévère*, from Latin *severus*] —**severity** /səˈvɛrəṭi/ *n.* [C,U] *We didn't realize the severity of her illness.*

se·vere·ly /səˈvɪrli/ *adv.* **1** very badly or to a great degree: *a severely damaged building* | *severely disabled children* | *Medical facilities are severely limited in the area.* **2** in an unfriendly or disapproving way: *"Don't be unkind," said Wendy severely.* **3** in a way that is strict and intended to prevent more crimes or wrong behavior: *We knew we would be severely punished* **4** in a plain simple style with little or no decoration or beauty: *Her hair was pulled back severely from her face.*

sew /soʊ/ S2 *v. past tense* **sewed**, *past participle* **sewn** /soʊn/ or **sewed** [I,T] to use a needle and thread to fasten pieces of cloth together, or to attach something such as a button to clothes: *Where did you learn to sew so well?* | **sew sth on/onto sth** *Can you sew a patch on my jeans?* | **sew sth together** *Sew the two sides of the fabric together.* [**Origin:** Old English *siwian*]

sew up *phr. v.* **1 sew sth ↔ up** to finish a business agreement or plan and get the result you want: *The deal should be sewn up in a week.* **2 have sth (all) sewn up** to gain control over a situation so that you are sure to win or gain something: *It looks like the Republicans have the election sewn up.* **3** INFORMAL to close a wound on someone's body using stitches: *The doctor sewed up Jared's arm in minutes.* **4** to close or repair something by sewing it: *You should sew up that rip in your pants.*

sew·age /ˈsuɪdʒ/ *n.* [U] the mixture of waste from the human body and used water that is carried away from houses by sewers: *a sewage treatment plant* | ***Raw sewage*** (=sewage that has not been treated) *was being pumped into the bay.*

Sew·ard /ˈsuɚd/**, William Henry** (1801–1872) a U.S. politician who helped to arrange the deal in which the U.S. bought Alaska from Russia in 1867

sew·er /ˈsuɚ/ *n.* [C] a pipe or passage under the ground that carries away waste material and used water from houses, factories etc.: *the city's sewer system* [**Origin:** 1400–1500 Old French *esseweur*, from *essewer* **to carry away water**, from Vulgar Latin *exaquare*]

sew·er·age /ˈsuərɪdʒ/ *n.* [U] the system by which waste material and water are carried away in sewers and then treated to stop them from being harmful

sew·ing /ˈsoʊɪŋ/ *n.* [U] **1** the activity or skill of making or repairing clothes or other things made of cloth, or decorating cloth with a needle and thread **2** something you have sewn or are going to sew: *My grandmother picked up her sewing.*

ˈsewing maˌchine *n.* [C] a machine used for stitching cloth or clothes together

sewn /soʊn/ *v.* a past participle of SEW

sex¹ /sɛks/ AC S2 W1 *n.* **1** [U] BIOLOGY physical activity between two people that involves the joining of their sexual organs, done either to produce babies, or for pleasure SYN **sexual intercourse**: *There is too much sex and violence on TV.* | *At what age should kids learn about sex?* | *They believe it's wrong to* ***have sex*** (=do this activity) *outside marriage.* | *He had* ***had sex with*** *several partners.* | *We always explain how to practice* ***safe sex*** (=ways of having sex without spreading disease). | *the dangers of* ***unprotected sex*** (=sex without a condom) **2** [C,U] BIOLOGY the male or female nature of a person, animal, or plant: *Are the twins the same sex?* **3** [C] all men considered as a group, or all women considered as a group: *differences between the sexes* | *He's very nervous around members of* ***the opposite sex*** (=people that are not his own sex). [**Origin:** 1300–1400 Latin *sexus*] → see also SAME-SEX, SINGLE-SEX

sex² AC *v.* [T] BIOLOGY to find out whether an animal is male or female

ˈsex act *n.* [C] a particular way in which people have sex

ˈsex apˌpeal *n.* [U] the quality of being sexually attractive: *a star with real glamour and sex appeal*

ˈsex change *n.* [C usually singular] a medical operation or treatment that changes someone's body so that they look like someone of the other sex

ˈsex ˌchromosome *n.* [C] BIOLOGY either of the two CHROMOSOMES in humans and some animals that directly influence whether someone is male or female. People have one pair of sex chromosomes. Females have two X CHROMOSOMES, and males have one X CHROMOSOME and one Y CHROMOSOME.

ˈsex discrimiˌnation also **ˌsexual discrimiˈnation** *n.* [U] unfair treatment because of which sex you are

ˈsex drive *n.* [U] someone's ability or physical need to have sex

ˈsex edˌucation also **sex ed** /ˈsɛks ɛd/ INFORMAL *n.* [U] education in schools about the physical processes and emotions involved in sex

ˈsex ˌgoddess *n.* [C] INFORMAL a woman, especially someone famous, who many people think is sexually attractive

ˈsex ˌindustry *n.* [singular] the businesses and activities related to PROSTITUTION and PORNOGRAPHY (=movies, magazines etc. that show sex)

sex·ism /ˈsɛkˌsɪzəm/ AC *n.* [U] unfair attitudes and behavior based on the belief that women are weaker, less intelligent, and less important than men: *racism and sexism in the military*

sex·ist /ˈsɛksɪst/ *adj.* DISAPPROVING **1** relating to the belief that women are weaker, less intelligent, and less important than men: *sexist comments* **2** believing in sexism: *He's such a sexist pig.* —**sexist** *n.* [C]

ˈsex ˌkitten *n.* [C] OLD-FASHIONED a woman who is considered to be very sexually attractive and who behaves like a young girl

sex·less /ˈsɛkslɪs/ *adj.* **1** not sexually attractive **2** not involving sexual activity, in a way that does not seem normal or usual: *a sexless relationship* **3** BIOLOGY neither male nor female: *a sexless being*

ˈsex life *n.* [C] someone's sexual activities: *He has a very active sex life.*

ˈsex ˌmaniac *n.* [C] INFORMAL someone who always wants to have sex, thinks about it all the time, and is unable to control these feelings

ˈsex ˌobject *n.* [C] someone you consider only as a way to satisfy your sexual desire, rather than as a person with feelings and desires of their own

ˈsex ofˌfender *n.* [C] someone who is guilty of a crime related to sex —**sex offense** *n.* [C]

ˈsex ˌorgan *n.* [C] a part of the body that is involved with the production of children, such as the PENIS or VAGINA

sex·pot /ˈsɛkspɑt/ *n.* [C] INFORMAL a word meaning a "sexually attractive woman," that many women think is offensive

ˈsex ˌsymbol *n.* [C] someone famous who represents society's idea of what is sexually attractive

sex·tant /ˈsɛkstənt/ *n.* [C] a tool for measuring angles between stars in order to calculate the position of your ship or aircraft

sex·tet /sɛksˈtɛt/ *n.* [C] ENG. LANG. ARTS **1** a group of six singers or musicians performing together **2** a piece of music for six performers

ˈsex ˌtherapy *n.* [U] the treatment of someone's sexual problems by talking to them over a long period of time about their feelings —**sex therapist** *n.* [C]

sex·ton /ˈsɛkstən/ *n.* [C] someone whose job is to take care of a church building, and sometimes ring the church bells and dig graves

Sex·ton /ˈsɛkstən/, **Ann** /æn/ (1928–1974) a U.S. poet

ˈsex ˌtourism *n.* [U] the activity of traveling to other countries in order to have sex, especially in order to do sexual activities that are illegal in your own country —**sex tourist** *n.* [C]

sex·tup·let /sɛkˈstʌplɪt/ *n.* [C] BIOLOGY one of six people who are born at the same time and have the same mother

sex·u·al /ˈsɛkʃuəl/ Ac S3 W1 *adj.* [no comparative] **1** relating to sex: *a disease passed on by sexual contact* | *sexual relationships* **2** relating to the social relationships between men and women: *sexual stereotypes* **3** relating to the way people or animals have babies: *sexual reproduction* —**sexually** *adv.*: *young people who are sexually active*

ˌsexual asˈsault *n.* [C,U] LAW the crime of forcing someone to have sex or touching someone sexually while threatening them

ˌsexual ˈcongress *n.* [U] LITERARY sexual intercourse

ˌsexual haˈrassment *n.* [U] sexual remarks, looks, or touching done to someone who does not want it, especially from someone that they work with

ˌsexual ˈintercourse *n.* [U] FORMAL the act of two people having sex with each other

sex·u·al·i·ty /ˌsɛkʃuˈæləti/ Ac *n.* [U] **1** the things people do and feel that are related to their desire or ability to have sex: *a study of human sexuality* **2** SEXUAL ORIENTATION

ˌsexually transˌmitted disˈease ABBREVIATION **STD** *n.* [C,U] MEDICINE a disease such as AIDS, HERPES etc., that is passed on through having sex

ˌsexual orienˈtation *n.* [U] the fact that someone is sexually attracted to people of the same sex or the opposite sex

ˌsexual ˈpolitics *n.* [U] ideas and activities that are concerned with how power is shared between men and women, and how this affects their relationships

ˌsexual ˈpreference *n.* [U] SEXUAL ORIENTATION

ˌsexual reˈlations *n.* [plural] FORMAL sexual activity between two people

ˌsexual reproˈduction *n.* [U] BIOLOGY the process in which two cells from different parents join to produce the first cell of a new living person, animal, plant etc.

ˈsex ˌworker *n.* [C] a polite expression for a PROSTITUTE

sex·y /ˈsɛksi/ *adj.* *comparative* **sexier**, *superlative* **sexiest** **1** sexually exciting or attractive: *a sexy woman* | *a sexy black dress* ▸see THESAURUS box at beautiful **2** INFORMAL sexy ideas or products are ones that many people think are very interesting and exciting —**sexily** *adv.* —**sexiness** *n.* [U]

Sey·chelles, the /seɪˈʃɛlz/ a country that consists of about 85 small islands in the Indian Ocean, to the east of Kenya —**Seychellois** /ˌseɪʃɛlˈwɑ/ *adj.*

SF *adj.*, *n.* the abbreviation of SCIENCE FICTION

SGML *n.* [U] COMPUTERS **Standard Generalized Markup Language** a special computer language used to send computer information from one piece of computer SOFTWARE to another

Sgt. the written abbreviation of SERGEANT

Shab·bat /ʃəˈbɑt, ˈʃɑbəs/ *n.* [C,U] Saturday, considered as a day of rest and prayer in the Jewish religion

shab·by /ˈʃæbi/ *adj.* *comparative* **shabbier**, *superlative* **shabbiest** **1** old and in bad condition from being used for a long time: *a shabby suit* | *shabby hotel rooms* **2 shabby treatment** behavior toward someone that is unfair and not nice: *I don't know what we did to deserve such shabby treatment.* **3 sth is not (too) shabby** INFORMAL used to show that you think something is very good: *Our profits were up by 35% last year. That's not too shabby.* **4** wearing clothes that are old and in bad condition: *a shabby old man* [**Origin:** 1600–1700 *shab* **scab, worthless man** (11–19 centuries), from Old English *sceabb* **scab**] —**shabbily** *adv.* —**shabbiness** *n.* [U]

shack¹ /ʃæk/ *n.* [C] a small building made of cheap materials: *They lived in a one-room shack.*

shack² *v.*

shack up *phr. v.* INFORMAL to live with someone who you have sex with but are not married to: +**with** *He shacked up with some woman in Newark.*

shack·le /ˈʃækəl/ *v.* [T usually passive] **1** to restrict what someone can do: *The company is shackled by a lack of capital.* **2** to put shackles on someone

shack·les /ˈʃækəlz/ *n.* [plural] **1 the shackles of slavery/communism etc.** LITERARY the limits put on your freedom and happiness by SLAVERY, COMMUNISM etc. **2** a pair of metal rings joined by a chain that are used for fastening together a prisoner's hands or feet: *He was led into the courthouse **in shackles**.*

shad /ʃæd/ *n.* [C,U] BIOLOGY a north Atlantic fish used for food

shade¹ /ʃeɪd/ S3 *n.*

1 AREA OF DARKNESS [U] an area that is cooler and darker because the light of the sun cannot reach it: *a plant that likes shade* | *Let's find a table **in the shade**.* | *They were sitting **in the shade of** an old oak tree.* → see also SHADOW

2 COLOR [C] a particular degree of a color: *The room was decorated in pastel shades.* | **a shade of pink/green etc.** *a beautiful deep shade of blue* ▸see THESAURUS box at color¹

3 FOR WINDOW [C] a piece of cloth or other material that can be rolled down to cover a window inside a building: *I don't think they're home – all the **shades are drawn*** (=pulled down to cover the windows). | *a cardboard sun shade for the car window*

4 FOR BLOCKING LIGHT [C] something that reduces or blocks light: *lamps with beautiful silk shades*

5 IN A PICTURE [U] the dark places in a picture: *the artist's skillful use of **light and shade***

6 a shade very slightly, or a little bit: *She was a shade*

S

under five feet tall. | *The results were a shade better than expected.*
7 shades of meaning/opinion/feeling etc. meanings, opinions etc. that are slightly different from each other SYN **nuance**: *One phrase can have many shades of meaning, depending on the context.*
8 shades [plural] INFORMAL SUNGLASSES
9 shades of sb/sth used to say that something reminds you of someone or something else: *The food was terrible. Shades of lunch in the school cafeteria.*
10 shades of gray slightly different opinions or ways of looking at a situation that are not completely right or wrong, or completely good or bad: *Tom's view of the world doesn't allow for many shades of gray.*
11 put sth in the shade to be so good or impressive that other similar things or people seem much less important or interesting: *They're planning a festival that will put all the others in the shade.*
12 have it made in the shade HUMOROUS to have everything you need in order to be happy
[**Origin:** Old English *sceadu*]

shade² *v.* [T] **1** to protect something from direct light: *a narrow road shaded by rows of trees* | **shade your eyes/face etc.** *She shaded her eyes and watched the plane fly overhead.* | **shade sb from sth** *There was only one umbrella to shade us from the sun.* **2** also **shade in** ENG. LANG. ARTS to make part of a picture or drawing darker: *The park areas have been shaded on the map.*
shade into sth *phr. v.* FORMAL if one thing shades into another, it gradually changes into the other thing: *Bedford felt his impatience shading into anger.*

'shade tree *n.* [C] a tree that is planted in order to give SHADE

shad·ing /ˈʃeɪdɪŋ/ *n.* **1** [U] ENG. LANG. ARTS the areas of a drawing or painting that have been made to look darker **2** [C,U] a slight difference between things, situations, or ideas: *the subtle shadings of legal language*

shad·ow¹ /ˈʃædoʊ/ W3 *n.*
1 DARK SHAPE [C] a dark shape that someone or something makes on a surface when they are between that surface and the light: *I saw his shadow on the wall.* | **+of** *the shadow of a bird flying overhead* | *The apple tree* ***cast a shadow*** (=made a shadow) *across the front lawn.*
2 PERSON [C] a dark shape, especially of a person, that you cannot see well because it is in a dark place: *Just then, a dark shadow emerged from the mist.*
3 DARKNESS [U] also **shadows** [plural] darkness caused by something that prevents light from entering a place: *A tall man came out of the shadows.* | *The room was half* ***in shadow.*** | ***In the shadows****, something moved.*
4 BAD EFFECT/INFLUENCE [singular] the bad effect or influence that something has, which makes other things seem less enjoyable, attractive, or impressive: **in/under the shadow of sth** *life in the shadow of dictatorship* | **cast a shadow over/on sth** *The scandal cast a shadow over the rest of his career.*
5 beyond/without a shadow of a doubt leaving no doubt at all: *His guilt has been proved beyond a shadow of a doubt.*
6 be a shadow of your former self to be much weaker or less powerful than before: *Following years of heavy losses, the company is only a shadow of its former self.*
7 in the shadow of sb also **in sb's shadow** less happy and successful than you could be, because someone else gets noticed much more: *Kate grew up in the shadow of her movie-star sister.*
8 shadows under sb's eyes small dark areas under someone's eyes that show they are tired
9 sb's shadow someone who follows someone else everywhere they go → see also **afraid of your own shadow** at AFRAID (7), EYE SHADOW, FIVE O'CLOCK SHADOW

shadow² *v.* [T] **1** to follow someone closely in order to watch what they are doing: *Detectives shadowed the two men for weeks.* **2** to spend time with someone at work in order to learn about their job: *The students spent a week shadowing attorneys and office staff.* **3** [usually passive] to cover something with a shadow, or make it dark: *His rugged face was shadowed by darkness.*

'shadow ˌboxing *n.* [U] fighting with an imaginary opponent, especially as training for BOXING —**shadow-box** *v.* [I]

'shadow ˌpuppet *n.* [C] a flat PUPPET on thin sticks that makes special shapes on a wall when you shine a light behind it

shad·ow·y /ˈʃædoʊi/ *adj.* **1** mysterious and difficult to know anything about: *a shadowy network of terrorist groups* **2** full of shadows, or difficult to see because of shadows: *a shadowy room* | *a shadowy figure at the back of the crowd*

shad·y /ˈʃeɪdi/ *adj. comparative* **shadier**, *superlative* **shadiest** **1** protected from the sun or producing shade: *It was shady under the trees.* | *shady streets* **2** probably dishonest or illegal: *Managers had been involved in some* ***shady deals.***

shaft¹ /ʃæft/ *n.* **1** [C] a passage that goes up through a building or down into the ground, so that someone or something can get in or out: **mine/elevator/ventilation shaft** *a 300-foot elevator shaft* **2 shaft of light/sunlight** a narrow beam of light **3** [C] a long handle on a tool, SPEAR etc. **4 get the shaft** INFORMAL to be treated unfairly, especially by being dismissed from your job **5** [C] a thin long piece of metal in an engine or machine that turns and passes on power or movement to another part of the machine → see also DRIVE SHAFT **6** [C] LITERARY an ARROW **7** [usually plural] one of a pair of poles between which a horse is tied to pull a vehicle

shaft² *v.* [T usually passive] SLANG to treat someone unfairly, especially by dishonestly getting money from them: *It's the poor who will* ***get shafted*** *when the law is changed.*

shag¹ /ʃæg/ *n.* **1** [U] a type of covering for a floor, made with long pieces of YARN: **shag carpeting/rug** (=with a surface like this) **2** [C] a type of hair style in which the hair is cut to different lengths all over the head, so that it is not smooth **3** [U] strong-tasting TOBACCO with thick leaves cut into small thin pieces

shag² *v.* **shagged**, **shagging** [I,T] to practice catching a baseball that has been hit rather than thrown: *The fielders were* ***shagging balls*** *hit by the coach.*

shag·gy /ˈʃægi/ *adj. comparative* **shaggier**, *superlative* **shaggiest** **1** shaggy hair or fur is long and messy: *a shaggy black beard* **2** having shaggy hair or fur: *a shaggy dog* —**shagginess** *n.* [U]

ˌshaggy-'dog ˌstory *n.* [C] a long joke that often ends in a silly or disappointing way

Shah /ʃɑ/ *n.* [C] the title of the kings of Iran, used in past times

shake¹ /ʃeɪk/ S2 W2 *v. past tense* **shook** /ʃʊk/, *past participle* **shaken** /ˈʃeɪkən/
1 MOVEMENT [I,T] to move up and down or from side to side with quick repeated movements, or to make someone or something do this: *Shake the bottle well.* | *His wife shook him awake.* | *Never shake a baby.* | *The whole house started to shake.* | **shake sth out of/off/from sth** *She shook the sand out of her shoes* (=removed it by shaking them).

shake

shaking hands

THESAURUS

tremble to shake because you are frightened or upset: *The dog was trembling with fear.*
shiver to shake because you are very cold: *She stood there, shivering in her thin jacket.*
wobble to shake from side to side: *The pile of books wobbled and fell.*
vibrate to shake continuously with small fast movements: *The steering wheel vibrated under my hands.*
rattle to shake and make a noise: *The windows rattled in the wind.*

2 BODY [I] if someone shakes, or if a part of their body shakes, they make small sudden movements from side

to side or up and down, especially because they are frightened, cold, or sick SYN **tremble**: *His hand shook as he signed the paper.* | *What's the matter? You're* ***shaking like a leaf*** (=shaking a lot because you are very nervous or frightened). | **shake with anger/fear/laughter etc.** *Her body was shaking with laughter.*
3 shake your head to turn your head from side to side as a way of saying no or to show disapproval, surprise, or sadness: *"Do you know why?" He shook his head.* | **shake your head in disgust/despair etc.** *She shook her head in dismay.*
4 shake hands (with sb) also **shake sb's hand** to hold someone's hand in your hand and move it up and down, as a greeting or as a sign you have agreed on something: *"It's nice to meet you," Hal said, shaking Mark's hand.*
5 SHOCK [T] to shock and upset someone or a group of people very much: *News of the accident shook the tiny farming community.* | *She was* ***badly shaken*** *by the experience.*
6 shake sb's confidence/faith/belief to make someone feel less confident, less sure about their beliefs etc.: *The trial had shaken his belief in the legal system.*
7 shake your fist (at sb) to show that you are angry by holding up and shaking your tightly closed hand
8 VOICE [I] if your voice shakes, it sounds nervous or uncertain: +**with** *Tim's voice shook with emotion.*
9 ESCAPE [T] also **shake off** to escape from someone who is chasing you: *They managed to shake the police car that was following them.*
10 GET RID OF [T] also **shake off** to get rid of an illness, a problem, something annoying etc.: *I can't seem to shake off this cold.* | *Parker hopes to shake his image as a dull unimaginative politician.*
11 be shaking in your boots INFORMAL to be very nervous or worried: *Employees were shaking in their boots at the thought of more layoffs.*
12 more sth than you can shake a stick at HUMOROUS a lot or very many: *There are more fast-food places in this town than you can shake a stick at.*
13 shake a leg SPOKEN to hurry and start doing something now: *Come on, shake a leg!*
14 shake your booty HUMOROUS to dance to popular music
[**Origin:** Old English *sceacan*] → see also **shake/rock sth to its foundations** at FOUNDATION (8)

shake sb ↔ **down** *phr. v.* **1** INFORMAL to get money from someone by using threats: *Corrupt officials were shaking down local business owners.* **2** to search a person or place thoroughly → see also SHAKEDOWN

shake on sth *phr. v.* SPOKEN to agree on a decision or business agreement by shaking hands: *Let's* ***shake on it.***

shake out *phr. v.* **1 shake sb out of sth** to make someone change an attitude, emotion, or opinion, especially one that you do not approve of: *She tried to* ***shake herself out of it,*** *but soon began crying again.* **2 shake sth ↔ out** to shake a cloth, bag, sheet etc. so that it is not folded any more, or so that small pieces of dirt or dust come off: *He shook out his napkin and put it in his lap.* **3** to change naturally over a period of time until the final result is clear, especially when some things are removed from the situation: *The project was put on hold to see how things were going to shake out.* **4 shake sth ↔ out** to change a situation by removing things from it that are not useful or that do not make a profit: *It will take time to shake out all the bugs in the new system.*

shake sb/sth ↔ **up** *phr. v.* **1** to make changes to an organization in order to make it more effective: *A new manager is coming in to* ***shake things up.*** → see also SHAKEUP **2** to give someone a very bad shock, so that they feel very upset and frightened: *The accident shook her up a lot.* → see also SHAKEN, SHOOK UP

shake² *n.* [C] **1** a cold drink made of milk, ICE CREAM, and fruit or chocolate SYN **milkshake**: *a strawberry shake* **2** an act of shaking: *She* ***gave*** *him* ***a little shake,*** *to wake him up.* **3 the shakes** NOT TECHNICAL nervous shaking of your body caused by illness, fear, too much alcohol etc.: *She would* ***get the shakes*** *before going on stage.* **4 no great shakes** INFORMAL if you say that someone or something is no great shakes, you think they are not very good: *He's no great shakes as a singer.* **5** [C] a small flat square piece of wood, used with many other pieces to cover a roof: *a shake roof* → see also **give/get a fair shake** at FAIR¹ (9)

shake·down /ˈʃeɪkdaʊn/ *n.* **1** [C] INFORMAL an act of getting money from someone by using threats SYN **extortion** **2** [C] a thorough search of a place or a person: *No guns were found during the shakedown.* **3** a final test of something such as a boat or airplane before it is put into general use, to find any remaining problems: *a shakedown flight* **4** [C usually singular] a period of time during which something changes, especially when things are removed from it: *The market is in the process of a shakedown.*

shak·en /ˈʃeɪkən/ also **ˌshaken ˈup** *adj.* [usually not before noun] upset, shocked, or frightened by something bad that has happened to you: *He had been* ***badly shaken*** *by the attack.*

shake·out /ˈʃeɪkaʊt/ *n.* [C] **1** [usually singular] ECONOMICS a situation in which several companies fail because they cannot compete with stronger companies in difficult economic conditions **2** a SHAKEUP

Shak·er /ˈʃeɪkɚ/ *adj.* Shaker furniture is made in a plain, simple, and attractive style: *a Shaker chair*

shak·er /ˈʃeɪkɚ/ *n.* [C] **1** a container with holes in the lid, used to shake salt, sugar etc. onto food: *a salt shaker* **2** also **cocktail shaker** a container in which drinks are mixed → see also **mover and shaker** at MOVER (2)

Shak·ers /ˈʃeɪkɚz/ a Christian religious group that started in England in 1747 and was established in the U.S. in 1774. Members live and work together in their own small towns, and do not have sex. No new members were accepted after the 1970s.

Shakes·peare /ˈʃeɪkspɪr/, **William** (1564–1616) an English writer of plays and poems, who is generally regarded as the greatest of all English writers

Shake·spear·e·an /ʃeɪkˈspɪriən/ *adj.* [only before noun] ENG. LANG. ARTS **1** relating to the work of Shakespeare: *Shakespearean scholars* **2** in the style of Shakespeare: *a drama of Shakespearean length*

shake·up /ˈʃeɪk-ʌp/ *n.* [C] a process in which an organization makes a lot of big changes in a short time to improve its effectiveness: *a management shakeup across the company*

shak·y /ˈʃeɪki/ *adj. comparative* **shakier**, *superlative* **shakiest** **1** weak and unsteady because of old age, illness, or shock: *My legs felt shaky.* | *a shaky voice* **2** not completely certain or correct: *The evidence is shaky, at best.* | *She refused to admit she was wrong, even though she was on very* ***shaky ground*** (=her reasons were not good). **3** not good and likely to fail: *a shaky relationship* | *The team's morale has been shaky.* | *Their work together got off to a* ***shaky start*** (=things went badly when they first started working together). **4** not firm or steady SYN **wobbly**: *a shaky ladder* —**shakily** *adv.* —**shakiness** *n.* [U]

shale /ʃeɪl/ *n.* [U] EARTH SCIENCE a smooth soft rock that breaks easily into thin flat pieces

shall /ʃəl; *strong* ʃæl/ S2 W2 *modal verb* **1** FORMAL used in official documents to show a law, command, promise etc.: *No such authorization shall be given without the manager's written consent.* **2 shall I/we?** SPOKEN FORMAL used to make a suggestion, or ask a question that you want the other person to decide about: *Shall I turn on the light?* | *Shall we meet around six o'clock?* **3** FORMAL or OLD-FASHIONED used to emphasize that something will definitely happen, or that you are determined that something will happen: *The truth shall make you free.* | *As we shall see in the next chapter, many of these practices are still in use.* **4 we shall see** FORMAL used when you do not know what will happen in the future, or when you do not want to give someone a definite answer [**Origin:** Old English *sceal*]

shal·lot /ˈʃælət, ʃəˈlɑt/ *n.* [C] a vegetable like a small onion

S

shal·low /ˈʃæloʊ/ *adj.* **1** not deep, and measuring only a short distance from the top to the bottom OPP **deep**: *a shallow pan* | *The water's shallow here.* | *the shallow end of the pool* → see picture at DEEP[1] **2** not interested in or not showing any understanding of important or serious matters: *a shallow argument* | *If he's only interested in your looks, that just shows how shallow he is.* **3 shallow breathing** breathing that only takes in small amounts of air —**shallowly** *adv.* —**shallowness** *n.* [U]

shal·lows /ˈʃæloʊz/ *n.* **the shallows** an area of shallow water: *Small fish live in the shallows.*

sha·lom /ʃɑˈloʊm, ʃə-/ *interjection* a Hebrew word used to say hello or goodbye

shalt /ʃəlt; *strong* ʃælt/ *v.* **thou shalt** BIBLICAL a phrase meaning "you shall," used when talking to one person

sham[1] /ʃæm/ *n.* [C] **1** [usually singular] something or someone that deceives people by seeming good, real, or true when it is not: *The election was a sham.* | *Do we want our justice system to just be a sham?* **2** a cover for a PILLOW, that has decorated edges SYN **pillowcase**

sham[2] *adj.* [only before noun] made to appear real in order to deceive people: *a sham marriage*

S

sha·man /ˈʃɑmən, ˈʃeɪ-/ *n.* [C] someone with religious authority in some tribes, who is believed to be able to talk to spirits, cure illnesses etc. —**shamanism** *n.* [U] —**shamanistic** /ˌʃɑməˈnɪstɪk/ *adj.*

sham·ble /ˈʃæmbəl/ *v.* [I always + adv./prep.] to walk slowly and awkwardly, without lifting your feet off the ground very much SYN **shuffle**: **+along/in/over etc.** *He then shambled over toward me.*

sham·bles /ˈʃæmbəlz/ *n.* **1** [singular, U] if something is in shambles, it is failing because it is not at all organized and there is a lot of confusion: *The whole meeting was a shambles from start to finish.* | *The economy was* ***in a*** *complete* ***shambles****.* | *My life was* ***in shambles****.* **2** [singular] if a place is in shambles, it is very messy: *This kitchen is a shambles!* [**Origin:** 1900–2000 *shambles* place where animals are killed for meat, scene of great killing or destruction]

shame[1] /ʃeɪm/ S3 *n.*

1 it's a shame (that) also **what a shame** SPOKEN used when you wish a situation was different, and you feel sad, disappointed, or angry: *It's a shame you have to leave so soon.* | *What a shame we missed the beginning of the concert!* | *"Jeff says he can't come tonight." "Oh, that's such a shame!"* | *It's a* ***crying shame*** *that our schools don't have enough money for textbooks.*

2 GUILTY FEELING [U] the guilty and embarrassed feeling you have when you know you have done something wrong: *He felt a deep sense of shame.* | *How could you do this?* ***Have you no shame*** (=do you not feel guilty)*?* | *Her face was flushed* ***with shame****.* | **hang/bow your head in shame** (=look downward and avoid looking at other people because you feel ashamed) ▸see THESAURUS box at **guilt**[1]

3 Shame on you! SPOKEN used to tell someone that they should feel shame because of something they have done

4 NO RESPECT [U] loss of honor and respect SYN **disgrace**: ***There's no shame in*** *finishing second* (=it should not make you feel ashamed). | *You've* ***brought shame on*** *this family.*

5 put sb/sth to shame INFORMAL to be so much better than someone or something else that it makes the other thing seem very bad or ordinary: *Matt's cooking puts mine to shame.*

[**Origin:** Old English *scamu*] → see also ASHAMED

shame[2] *v.* **1 shame sb into doing sth** to force someone to do something by making them feel ashamed: *His wife shamed him into handing the money back.* **2** [T] to make someone feel ashamed, or feel they have lost honor and respect: *It shamed him to have to ask Jan for help.* **3** [T] to be so much better than someone or something else that you make them seem bad or feel embarrassed: *His playing that day shamed experienced musicians.*

shame·faced /ˈʃeɪmfeɪst/ *adj.* looking ashamed or embarrassed about having behaved badly or having done something wrong: *A shamefaced spokesperson admitted that mistakes had been made.* —**shamefacedly** /ˈʃeɪmˌfeɪsɪdli/ *adv.*

shame·ful /ˈʃeɪmfəl/ *adj.* shameful behavior is so bad that people think you should be ashamed of it SYN **disgraceful**: *a shameful waste of resources* —**shamefully** *adv.*

shame·less /ˈʃeɪmlɪs/ *adj.* not seeming to be ashamed of your bad behavior, although other people think you should be ashamed: *He's a shameless flirt.* —**shamelessly** *adv.* —**shamelessness** *n.* [U]

sham·poo[1] /ʃæmˈpu/ *n. plural* **shampoos** **1** [C,U] a liquid soap for washing your hair **2** [C,U] a liquid soap used for cleaning CARPETS **3** [C] an act of washing your hair or having it washed: *$45 for a shampoo, cut, and blow-dry* [**Origin:** 1700–1800 Hindi *cāpo*, from *cāpna* **to press, shampoo**]

shampoo[2] *v.* [T] to wash something with shampoo

sham·rock /ˈʃæmrɑk/ *n.* [C] a small plant with three green leaves on each stem, that is the national sign of Ireland

Shang·hai /ʃæŋˈhaɪ/ the largest city in China

shang·hai /ʃæŋˈhaɪ/ *v.* [T usually passive] OLD-FASHIONED to trick or force someone into doing something they do not want to do

Shan·gri-La /ˌʃæŋgrɪˈlɑ/ *n.* [singular] a perfect place that is very beautiful and where everyone is happy SYN **paradise**

shank /ʃæŋk/ *n.* **1** [C,U] a piece of meat cut from the leg of an animal: *lamb shanks* **2** [C] a straight narrow part of a tool or other object: *the shank of a button* **3** [C usually plural] BIOLOGY the part of a person's or animal's leg between the knee and ANKLE

shan't /ʃænt/ *modal verb* OLD USE the short form of "shall not"

shan·ty /ˈʃænti/ *n. plural* **shanties** [C] **1** a small, roughly built house made from thin sheets of wood, TIN, plastic etc. that very poor people live in **2** also **shantey** another spelling of CHANTEY

shan·ty·town /ˈʃæntiˌtaʊn/ *n.* [C] an area in or near a city where poor people live in shanties

shape[1] /ʃeɪp/ S2 W2 *n.*

1 ROUND/SQUARE ETC. FORM a) [C,U] the form that something has, that you see or feel SYN **form**: *What shape is your table?* | *You can recognize a tree by the shape of its leaves.* | *a cake* ***in the shape of*** (=having the same shape as) *a football* | *People* ***come in all shapes and sizes****.* | **round/square etc. in shape** *The lamp was triangular in shape.* **b)** [C] a particular shape, or a thing that is that shape: *The kids cut out shapes from pieces of cardboard.* | *a toddler's book about shapes and colors*

THESAURUS

Types of shapes

square a shape with four straight sides that are equal in length and four angles of 90 degrees
circle a round shape that is like an O
semicircle half a circle
triangle a shape with three straight sides and three angles
rectangle a shape with four straight sides and four angles of 90 degrees
oval a shape like a circle, but which is longer than it is wide
cylinder an object in the shape of a tube
cube a solid object with six equal square sides
pyramid a shape with a square base and four triangular sides that meet in a point at the top
sphere a shape like a ball

Describing types of shapes

square shaped like a square: *a square box*
circular/round shaped like a circle: *a circular table*
semicircular shaped like a semicircle: *a semicircular arch above the door*
triangular shaped like a triangle: *sails divided into triangular sections*

rectangular shaped like a rectangle: *a simple rectangular building*
oval shaped like an oval: *an oval swimming pool*
cylindrical shaped like a cylinder: *The statue is on top of a tall cylindrical column.*
spherical shaped like a ball: *The planet Saturn is not completely spherical.*

2 in good/bad/poor etc. shape in good, bad etc. condition, or in good, bad etc. health: *My old bike is still in pretty good shape.* | *The economy is in worse shape now than it was last year.* | *Kaplan seemed to be in better shape than either of us.*
3 in shape/out of shape in a good or bad state of physical FITNESS: *I am so out of shape.* | *I really need to* ***get in shape*** *before summer.* | **keep/stay in shape** *He plays basketball to* ***keep in shape.*** | **in good/awful/great etc. shape** *Eddie is in better shape than anyone else on the team.*
4 take shape to develop into a clear and definite form: *An idea was* ***beginning to take shape*** *in his mind.*
5 CHARACTER OF STH [singular] the way something looks, works, or is organized: *Computers have completely* ***changed the shape of*** *our industry.* | *We will* ***not*** *tolerate racism* ***in any way, shape or form*** (=not of any type). | *This new technique is* ***the shape of things to come*** (=an example of the way things will develop in the future).
6 be in no shape to do sth to be sick, weak, drunk etc., and so not able to do something well: *Mel was in no shape to drive home after the party.*
7 in the shape of sth used to explain what something consists of: *Help* ***came in the shape of*** *a loan from his parents.*
8 THING NOT SEEN CLEARLY [C] a thing or person that you cannot see clearly enough to recognize: *a dark shape behind the trees* → see also **bent out of shape** at BENT[2] (3), **whip sb/sth into shape** at WHIP[1] (6)

shape² S3 W3 *v.* [T] **1** to influence something such as a belief, opinion etc. and make it develop in a particular way: *Children's desires are shaped by what they see on TV commercials.* **2** to make something have a particular shape, especially by pressing it: ***Shape*** *the dough* ***into*** *small balls.* [**Origin:** Old English *scieppan*]

shape up *phr. v.* INFORMAL **1** to improve your behavior or work: *If you don't shape up, I'll have to contact your parents.* **2 be shaping up** to make progress and develop in a particular way: *Ken's plans for the business are shaping up well.* | **be shaping up as sth** *Immigration is shaping up as a major issue in the campaign.* | **be shaping up to be sth** *February is shaping up to be one of the wettest months on record.* **3 shape up or ship out** SPOKEN used to tell someone that if they do not improve, they will be made to leave a place or their job

shaped /ʃeɪpt/ *adj.* having a particular shape: *The building* ***was shaped like*** *a giant pyramid.* | **egg-shaped/V-shaped etc.** *an L-shaped living room*

shape·less /ˈʃeɪplɪs/ *adj.* **1** not having a clear or definite shape, especially in a way that looks unattractive: *The prisoners wear shapeless orange uniforms.* **2** something such as a book or plan that is shapeless does not have a clear structure SYN **formless**: *a shapeless tedious movie*

shape·ly /ˈʃeɪpli/ *adj.* having a body that has an attractive shape: *her long shapely legs* —**shapeliness** *n.* [U]

shard /ʃɑrd/ *n.* [C] a sharp piece of broken glass, metal etc.: **+of** *shards of ancient pottery*

share¹ /ʃɛr/ S1 W1 *v.*
1 USE EQUALLY [I,T] to have or use something that other people also have or use, often at the same time: *We don't have enough books for everyone, so you'll have to share.* | **share sth with sb** *Do you mind sharing a room with Jenny?*
2 LET SB USE STH [I,T] to let someone have or use something that belongs to you: *Learning to share is hard for toddlers.* | **share sth with sb** *You'll have to share your toys with your little brother.*
3 SAME INTEREST/OPINION ETC. [T] to have the same opinion, experience, feeling etc. as someone else: *Mike finally found a girl who shares his interest in football.* | *They come from different cities, but they* ***share a common*** *culture.* | **share sth with sth** *Stubbornness was a characteristic he shared with his mother.*
4 DIVIDE [I,T] to divide something between two or more people: *We can share the cost of gas.* | **share (sth) with sb** *Everybody brings a dish to share with everyone else.* ▶see THESAURUS box at give[1]
5 RESPONSIBILITY [T] to be equally responsible for doing something, paying for something etc.: *We all share some of the blame for the accident.* | *They* ***share the responsibility*** *for their kids.*
6 TELL SB STH [I,T] to tell other people about an idea, secret, problem etc.: *Time is set aside for the kids to share their experiences.* | **share sth with sb** *Sonia shared a very touching story with the group.*
7 share and share alike SPOKEN used to say that you should share things fairly and equally with everyone
8 share your life (with sb) if you share your life with someone, you spend your life together with them as their husband, wife etc.

share in sth *phr. v.* to take part in something, or to have a part of something that other people also have: *His daughters did not share in his happiness.* | *Owning stock allows you to share in a corporation's profits.*

share² S3 W1 *n.* **1** [singular] the part of something that you own or are responsible for: **+of** *I wrote a check*

S

shapes

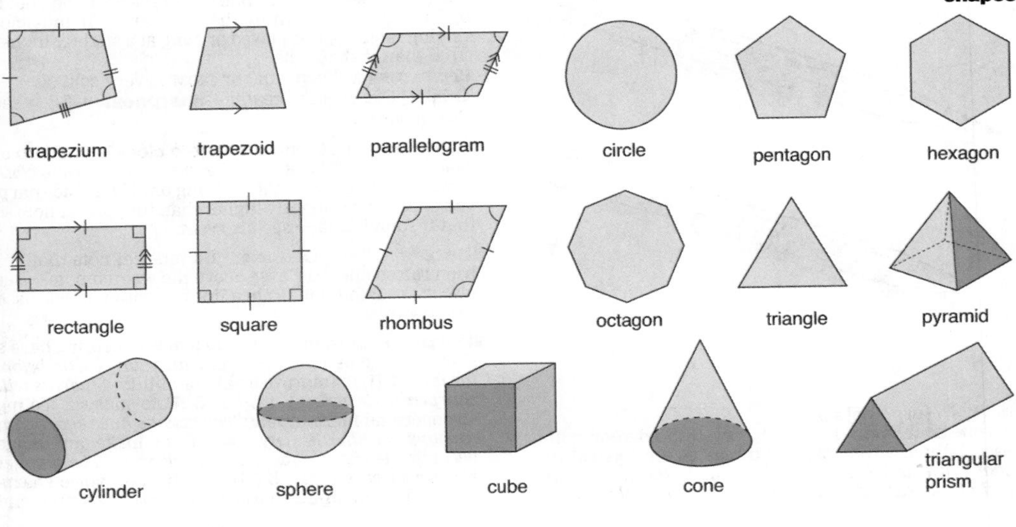

for my share of the phone bill. | **+in** *Bonuses are a way of giving employees a share in the profits.* | *I* ***do*** *my* ***share*** *of the housework.* **2 your (fair) share a)** as much as or more of something than you could reasonably expect to have: *She's had* ***more than*** *her* ***fair share of*** *problems recently.* | *You've sure had your share of bad luck, haven't you?* **b)** as much as everyone else, or as much as you deserve to have: *We'll make sure everyone gets their fair share.* | *I've made my share of mistakes.* **3** [singular] your part in an activity, event etc.: **+in** *Employees are always given a share in the decision-making process.* **4** [C] a part of an amount: **+of** ***A large share of*** *their income goes toward rent.* **5** [C] ECONOMICS one of the equal parts into which the ownership of a company is divided, used especially when you are talking about the number of parts or the price of each one → see also STOCK: *The price has gone up to $4.50 a share.* | **+in/of** *Sandy owns 200 shares of Microsoft stock.* **6** [C] OLD-FASHIONED a PLOWSHARE [**Origin:** Old English *scearu* **cutting, division**] → see also **the lion's share (of sth)** at LION (2), TIMESHARE —**sharing** *n.* [U]

share·crop·per /ˈʃɛrˌkrɑpɚ/ *n.* [C] a poor farmer who uses someone else's land, and gives the owner part of the crop in return —**sharecropping** *n.* [U]

ˌshared ˈreading *n.* [U] TECHNICAL a learning activity in which the teacher and the students read the same story together

share·hold·er /ˈʃɛrˌhoʊldɚ/ also **share·own·er** /ˈʃɛrˌoʊnɚ/ W3 *n.* [C] ECONOMICS someone who owns STOCK in a business SYN **stockholder**

share·ware /ˈʃɛrwɛr/ *n.* [U] COMPUTERS free or cheap computer SOFTWARE, usually produced by small companies, that you can use for a short time before you decide whether to buy it → see also FREEWARE

sha·ri·a /ʃɑˈriə/ *n.* [U] a system of religious laws followed by Muslims

shark /ʃɑrk/ *n.* [C] **1** *plural* **shark** or **sharks** BIOLOGY a large fish with several rows of very sharp teeth, that lives in the ocean and is often considered to be dangerous to humans → see picture at FOOD CHAIN **2** INFORMAL someone who cheats other people out of money SYN **swindler**: **card/pool shark** (=someone who cheats when playing cards or POOL in order to win money) → see also LOAN SHARK

shark·skin /ˈʃɑrkskɪn/ *n.* [U] a type of material with a smooth shiny surface

sharp

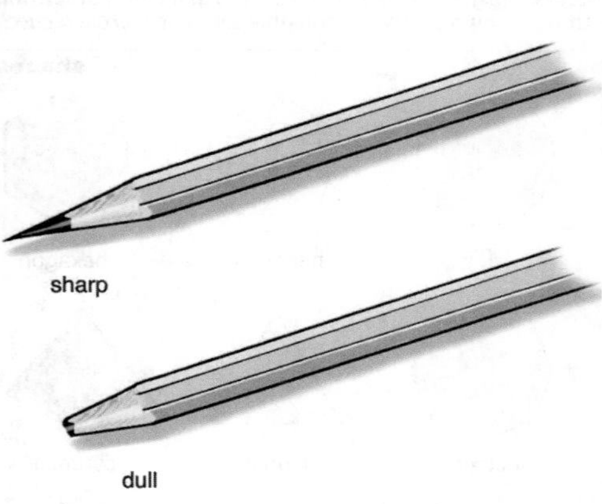

sharp¹ /ʃɑrp/ W3 *adj.*
1 THIN EDGE/POINT having a very thin edge or point, especially one that can cut things easily OPP **blunt**: *sharp pencils* | *Make sure the knife is sharp.* | *Cut the end of the stick into a sharp point.* | *The blade has a* ***razor-sharp*** (=very sharp) *edge.* ►see THESAURUS box at taste¹
2 INCREASE/DECREASE a sharp increase, fall etc. is very sudden and very big SYN **steep**: *a sharp rise in prices* | *a sharp decline in unemployment* | *sharp cuts in welfare benefits*
3 DIRECTION a sharp turn or bend changes direction suddenly: *We came to a* ***sharp turn*** *in the road.* | *a sharp angle*
4 INTELLIGENT able to think and understand things very quickly, and not easily deceived OPP **dull** OPP **stupid**: *a sharp young attorney* | *My great-aunt Nellie is 87, but she's still* ***as sharp as a tack*** (=able to think very quickly and clearly).
5 CRITICISM speaking in a way that shows you disapprove of something or are angry about it: *the sharp tone of her comments* | *The proposed tax increase drew* ***sharp criticism*** *from Republican senators.* | *His mother* ***has a*** *very* ***sharp tongue*** (=she speaks in a very disapproving way).
6 CLEAR/DEFINITE clear and definite, so that there is no doubt and something is very easy to notice: *There are no sharp differences between the two political parties.* | *The accident brought problems at the factory into* ***sharp focus.*** | *His happy mood was* ***in sharp contrast*** *to the rest of the family's gloom.*
7 PAIN sudden and severe, but not continuing for a long time OPP **dull**: *I felt a sharp pain in my back.*
8 FEELINGS [only before noun] a sharp feeling is a sudden unhappy or bad feeling, such as sadness: *He felt a sharp stab of guilt.* | *a sharp sense of disappointment*
9 SOUNDS loud, short, and sudden: *a sharp cry of pain*
10 NOTICE able to see, hear, or notice things that are hard to see, hear, or notice: *My son, with his sharp eyes, noticed the animal first.* | *The job requires someone with* ***a sharp eye for detail*** (=the ability to notice and deal with details).
11 keep a sharp eye out for sth to watch carefully so that you do not miss something: *We ought to keep a sharp eye out for animal tracks.*
12 keep a sharp eye on sb to watch someone very carefully, especially because you do not trust them: *Security guards kept a sharp eye on Mattson as he walked through the store.*
13 CLOTHES attractive and stylish: *lawyers in sharp suits*
14 SHAPE not rounded or curved SYN **angular**: *her sharp features*
15 TASTE having a strong slightly bitter taste: *sharp Cheddar cheese*
16 PICTURE if an image or picture is sharp, you can see all the details very clearly OPP **fuzzy**: *This TV set gives you a very sharp picture.*
17 MOVEMENT quick and sudden: *The wind blew across the lake in sharp gusts.* | *a sharp intake of breath*
18 MUSIC a) F/D/C etc. sharp a musical note that is sharp has been raised by one HALF STEP from the note F, D, C etc. and is shown by the sign (#) **b)** if music or singing is sharp, it is played or sung at a slightly higher PITCH than it should be
19 WEATHER a sharp wind or FROST is very cold
[**Origin:** Old English *scearp*] —**sharpness** *n.* [U] → see also SHARPLY

sharp² *adv.* **1 at ten-thirty/two o'clock etc. sharp** at exactly 10:30, 2:00 etc.: *We're meeting at ten o'clock sharp.* **2** ENG. LANG. ARTS if you sing or play music sharp, you sing or play slightly higher than the correct note so that it sounds bad → see also FLAT

sharp³ *n.* [C] ENG. LANG. ARTS **1** a musical note that has been raised one HALF STEP above the written note → see also FLAT **2** the sign (#) in a line of written music used to show this

sharp·en /ˈʃɑrpən/ *v.* **1** [T] to make something have a sharper edge or point: *Sharpen all your pencils before the test.* **2** [T] to improve a skill or ability: *Students will sharpen their writing skills.* **3** [T] to make a feeling stronger and more urgent: *The actions have sharpened tensions within the city.* **4** [I,T] to make an image become clearer, or to become clearer: *The images sharpened on screen.* **5** [I,T] if someone's voice sharpens, or if something sharpens it, it becomes high and loud, in an unpleasant way: *"Why?" he said, his voice sharpening.* **6** to make something clearer or more noticeable: *He rewrote the speech to sharpen the message.*

sharp·en·er /ˈʃɑrpənɚ/ *n.* [C] a tool or machine for sharpening pencils, knives etc.

ˌsharp-ˈeyed *adj.* able to see very well and notice small details: *Two sharp-eyed readers spotted the mistake.*

sharp·ly /ˈʃɑrpli/ *adv.* **1** if something rises, falls, increases etc. sharply, it rises, falls, increases etc. quickly and suddenly: *Sales declined sharply in the last quarter.* | *sharply rising prices* **2** in a severe and disapproving way: *The White House reacted sharply to the accusations.* | *a **sharply critical** report* **3** clearly and definitely, in a very noticeable way: *Opinion is sharply divided.* | *Schools in rich areas **contrast sharply with*** (=are very different from) *those in poorer parts of the city.* **4** quickly and suddenly: *The plane **turned sharply** to the left before diving out of control.*

sharp·shoot·er /ˈʃɑrpˌʃuṭɚ/ *n.* [C] someone who is very skillful at hitting what they aim at when shooting a gun

ˌsharp-ˈtongued *adj.* [usually before noun] often saying things in a cruel or criticizing way

ˌsharp-ˈwitted *adj.* able to think and react very quickly SYN **quick-witted**

Shas·ta, Mount /ˈʃæstə/ a mountain in the Cascade Range that is in the U.S. state of California and is an inactive VOLCANO

shat·ter /ˈʃæṭɚ/ *v.* **1** [I,T] to break suddenly into very small pieces, or to make something break in this way: *The force of the crash shattered the windshield.* | *The storm was so bad that windows shattered.* | **+into** *The plane shattered into pieces upon impact.* ►see THESAURUS box at **break**[1] **2** [T] to completely destroy someone's hopes or beliefs: *Their lives were completely shattered by the accident.* **3 shatter a record** to do better in a race or competition than anyone else has: *She shattered the world record by more than five seconds.*

shat·ter·ing /ˈʃæṭərɪŋ/ *adj.* very shocking and upsetting: *Her death was a shattering blow.* → see also EARTH-SHATTERING

shat·ter·proof /ˈʃæṭɚˌpruf/ *adj.* glass that is shatterproof is specially made so that it will not form sharp dangerous pieces if it is broken

shave[1] /ʃeɪv/ S3 *v.* **1** [I,T] to cut off hair very close to the skin, especially from the face, using a RAZOR: *He hadn't shaved in over a week.* | **shave your head/legs/armpits etc.** *I washed my hair and shaved my legs.* **2** [T] to remove very thin pieces from the surface of something using a sharp tool: *Shave some fresh Parmesan cheese over the salad before serving.* [**Origin:** Old English *scafan*]

shave

shave sth ↔ **off** *phr. v.* **1** to remove hair by shaving: *Dave shaved off his mustache!* **2** to reduce an amount or number very slightly: *She shaved two seconds off her previous time in the 10,000 meters.* **3** to remove very thin pieces from the surface of something, using a knife or other cutting tool: *Fill the crack with putty and shave off any excess after it dries.*

shave[2] *n.* [C usually singular] **1** an act of shaving your face: *He needed a shave.* **2 a close shave a)** a situation in which you just avoid an accident or something bad: *The icy weather caused a few close shaves on the road.* **b)** a shave that cuts a man's hair very close to his face

shav·en /ˈʃeɪvən/ *adj.* with all the hair shaved off → see also CLEAN-SHAVEN, UNSHAVEN

shav·er /ˈʃeɪvɚ/ *n.* [C] **1** a small piece of electrical equipment used for shaving → see also RAZOR **2** INFORMAL OLD-FASHIONED a small boy

ˈshaving brush *n.* [C] a brush used for spreading soap or shaving cream over a man's face when he shaves

ˈshaving cream *n.* [U] a mixture made of soap that a man puts on his face when he SHAVES

shav·ings /ˈʃeɪvɪŋz/ *n.* [plural] very thin pieces of a hard material, especially wood, that are cut from a surface with a sharp blade

Shaw /ʃɔ/, **George Ber·nard** /dʒɔrdʒ bɚˈnɑrd/ (1856–1950) an Irish writer famous especially for his funny plays which criticized society and the moral values of the time

shawl /ʃɔl/ *n.* [C] a piece of soft cloth, usually in a square or TRIANGULAR shape, that is worn around the shoulders or head, especially by women

Shaw·nee /ʃɔˈni/ *n.* a Native American tribe from the central northern region of the U.S. —**Shawnee** *adj.*

she[1] /ʃi/ S1 W1 *pron.* [used as the subject of a verb] **1 a)** a woman or girl who has been mentioned already, or who the person you are talking to already knows about: *What did she tell you to do?* | *You'd better ask Amy – she knows how to use the copier.* | *I saw you talking to that girl. Who is she?* **b)** a female animal that has been mentioned already **2** used to talk about a car, ship, or other vehicle that has been mentioned already: *She's a good reliable little car.*

she[2] *n.* [singular] INFORMAL a female: *What a cute puppy! Is it a he or a she?*

s/he /ˌʃi ɚ ˈhi/ *pron.* used in writing when the subject of the sentence can be either male or female: *If any student witnesses a crime, s/he should contact campus police immediately.*

she- /ʃi/ *prefix* female: *a she-goat*

sheaf /ʃif/ *n. plural* **sheaves** /ʃivz/ [C] **1** several pieces of paper held or tied together: **+of** *a sheaf of papers* **2** a bunch of wheat, corn etc. tied together after it has been cut

shear[1] /ʃɪr/ *v. past tense* **sheared**, *past participle* **sheared** or **shorn** /ʃɔrn/ **1** [T] to cut the wool off a sheep **2 be shorn of sth a)** to have something valuable or important taken away from you: *Party leaders were shorn of their power.* **b)** LITERARY to have something removed: *a room shorn of any decoration* **3** [T usually passive] LITERARY to cut off someone's hair

shear off *phr. v.* if something shears off a part of something, or the part shears off, it is separated from the rest, especially after being pulled or hit with a lot of force: **shear off sth** *The tornado sheared off part of the Swensons' roof.*

shear·er /ˈʃɪrɚ/ also **ˈsheep ˌshearer** *n.* [C] someone who cuts the wool off sheep

shears /ʃɪrz/ *n.* [plural] a heavy tool for cutting things, that looks like a big pair of scissors: *a **pair of** garden **shears*** → see also PINKING SHEARS, WIND SHEAR → see picture at SCISSORS

sheath /ʃiθ/ *n. plural* **sheaths** /ʃiðz, ʃiθs/ [C] **1** a simple close-fitting dress **2** a cover for the blade of a knife or other sharp object **3** BIOLOGY a close-fitting part of a plant or animal that acts as a protective covering

sheathe /ʃið/ *v.* **1 be sheathed in sth** to be completely covered by something, especially something protective: *Their sofa was sheathed in clear plastic.* **2** [T] LITERARY to put a knife or sword into a sheath

sheath·ing /ˈʃiðɪŋ/ *n.* [C usually singular] a protective outer cover, for example for a building or a ship

sheaves /ʃivz/ *n.* the plural of SHEAF

she·bang /ʃɪˈbæŋ/ *n.* **the whole shebang** INFORMAL the whole thing SYN **everything**: *She's in charge of the whole shebang.*

shed[1] /ʃɛd/ *v. past tense and past participle* **shed**, **shedding**
1 GET RID OF [T] to get rid of something that you do not

S

need or want anymore: *The magazine hopes to **shed** its old-fashioned **image**.* | *I'd like to **shed** a few **pounds*** (=lose weight and become thinner).
2 ANIMAL/PLANT [I,T] BIOLOGY to have hair, skin, or leaves fall off as part of a natural process: *Short-haired dogs don't shed as much as long-haired ones.* | *As it grows, a snake will regularly shed its skin.*
3 DROP/TAKE OFF [T] to drop something, allow it to fall, or to take it off quickly: *Inside, the two men shed their coats and sat down.*
4 shed tears to cry: *She shed no tears when he left.*
5 shed blood to kill or injure people, especially during a war or a fight: *Too much blood has already been shed in this conflict.* → see also BLOODSHED
6 WATER [T] if something sheds water, the water flows off its surface, instead of sinking into it
7 LAMP ETC. [T] if a lamp or other SOURCE of light sheds a particular type of light, it lights the area around it: *The candle shed a dim glow over her face.* → see also **throw/shed/cast light on sth** at LIGHT[1] (9)

shed² *n.* [C] **1** a small building, often made of wood or metal, used especially for storing things: *The ladder is in the tool shed.* | *a storage shed* **2** a large industrial building where work is done, large vehicles are kept, or machinery is stored

S

she'd /ʃid/ **1** the short form of "she had": *She'd taken everything with her.* **2** the short form of "she would": *She'd like to come with us.*

'she-ˌdevil *n.* [C usually singular] HUMOROUS a very cruel woman

sheen /ʃin/ *n.* [singular, U] a soft smooth shiny appearance SYN luster: *the sheen of the polished table*

sheep /ʃip/ S2 *n. plural* **sheep** [C] **1** BIOLOGY a farm animal that eats grass and is kept for its wool and its meat: *a sheep ranch* | **a flock/herd of sheep** (=a group of sheep) **2 like sheep** if people behave like sheep, they do not think about what to do for themselves, but follow what everyone else does or thinks: *Tour guides led them around like sheep.* [**Origin:** Old English *sceap*] → see also BLACK SHEEP, **count sheep** at COUNT[1] (13), LAMB, MUTTON, **a wolf in sheep's clothing** at WOLF[1] (2)

'sheep dip *n.* [C,U] a chemical used to kill insects that live in sheep's wool, or a special bath in which this chemical is used

'sheep dog, sheepdog *n.* [C] **1** a dog that is trained to control sheep **2** a type of dog that is often trained to control sheep → see also OLD ENGLISH SHEEPDOG

sheep·ish /ˈʃipɪʃ/ *adj.* uncomfortable or embarrassed because you know that you have done something silly or wrong SYN embarrassed: *She **looked** relieved at first, then a little **sheepish**.* —**sheepishly** *adv.* —**sheepishness** *n.* [U]

sheep·skin /ˈʃipˌskɪn/ *n.* **1** [C,U] the skin of a sheep with the wool still on it: *a sheepskin coat* **2** [C] INFORMAL a DIPLOMA (=official document that shows you have completed your studies at a college or university)

sheer /ʃɪr/ *adj.* [no comparative] **1 the sheer amount/weight/size etc.** used to emphasize how much of something there is or how heavy, big etc. something is: *The building's sheer size makes it expensive to heat.* | +**of** *We were overwhelmed by the sheer number of applications.* **2 sheer luck/happiness/stupidity etc.** luck, happiness etc. with no other feeling or quality mixed with it SYN pure: *the look of sheer joy on her face* | *It was sheer luck that the last shot went into the basket.* **3** a sheer drop, cliff, slope etc. is very steep and almost VERTICAL SYN steep **4** NYLON, silk etc. that is sheer is very thin and fine, so that it is almost transparent: *sheer curtains*

sheet /ʃit/ S1 W2 *n.* [C] **1** a large piece of thin cloth that you put on a bed to lie on or lie under SYN bedlinen: *clean sheets* | *Hotel housekeepers **change the sheets** (=put clean sheets on a bed) every day.* **2** a thin flat piece of something such as paper, glass, or metal, that usually has four sides: *Write each answer on a separate sheet.* | +**of** *Cover the dish with a sheet of plastic wrap.* | *a blank **sheet of paper*** → see also SHEET METAL **3** a large flat area of something such as ice or water that is spread over a surface: +**of** *Freezing weather turned puddles into sheets of ice.* **4** a sheet of rain or fire is a very large moving mass of it: *The rain was coming down in sheets.* | +**of** *Sheets of flame shot into the air.* **5** TECHNICAL a rope or chain attached to a sail on a ship, that controls the angle between a sail and the wind [**Origin:** Old English *scyte*] → see also BAKING SHEET, BALANCE SHEET, COOKIE SHEET, RAP SHEET, TIME SHEET, **as white as a sheet** at WHITE[1] (3)

sheet·ing /ˈʃit̬ɪŋ/ *n.* [U] material such as plastic or metal that is made into thin flat sheets and used to cover something and protect it: *The roof was covered in plastic sheeting.*

'sheet ˌmetal *n.* [U] metal in the form of thin sheets

'sheet ˌmusic *n.* [U] music that is printed on single sheets and not fastened together inside a cover

Sheet·rock /ˈʃitˀrɑk/ *n.* [U] TRADEMARK a type of board made of two large sheets of CARDBOARD with PLASTER between them, used to cover walls and ceilings

sheik, sheikh /ʃik, ʃeɪk/ *n.* [C] **1** an Arab ruler or prince **2** a Muslim religious leader or teacher

sheik·dom, sheikhdom /ˈʃikdəm/ *n.* [C] a place that is governed by an Arab ruler or prince

shek·el /ˈʃɛkəl/ *n.* [C] **1** the standard unit of money in Israel **2** HUMOROUS money: *Cahn made a few shekels on the deal.*

shelf /ʃɛlf/ S2 *n. plural* **shelves** /ʃɛlvz/ **1** [C] a long flat narrow board fastened to a wall or in a frame or cupboard, that you can put things on: *shelves of books* | *supermarket shelves* | **top/bottom shelf** *Put it back on the top shelf.* | *boxes that take up a lot of **shelf space*** **2 off the shelf** available to be bought immediately, without having to be specially designed or ordered: *off-the-shelf computer software packages* **3 on the shelf** if a plan, idea etc. is on the shelf, it is not used or considered: *The proposal will have to be **put on the shelf** until we can get more funding.* **4** [C] EARTH SCIENCE a narrow surface of rock or ice shaped like a shelf **5 fly off the shelves** to be sold in large numbers: *We can't keep the toy in stock – it's just been flying off the shelves.* [**Origin:** 1300–1400 Middle Low German *schelf*] → see also SHELVE

'shelf life *n.* [C usually singular] the length of time that food, chemicals etc. can be stored before they become too old to eat or use: *Chocolate has a shelf life of nine months.*

shell¹ /ʃɛl/ S3 W3 *n.* [C] **1 a)** BIOLOGY a hard outer part that covers or protects a nut, egg, or seed: *Throw away any eggs with cracked shells.* | *a peanut shell* **b)** the hard protective covering of some animals, for example a SNAIL, CRAB, or CLAM: *The turtle poked its head out of its shell.* | *shells on the beach* **2** a metal tube containing a bullet and an explosive substance, used in a gun: *shotgun shells* **3** a metal container, like a large bullet, which is full of an explosive substance and is fired from a large gun: *Rebels fired **mortar shells** directly into the town square.* **4** a covering made of PASTRY that surrounds a food: *a prepared pie shell* | *taco shells* **5** the outside structure of something: *The buildings were just burned-out shells.* | *a parka with a waterproof nylon shell* **6 sb's shell** if someone goes into their shell, they are shy and do not want to talk to people; if they come out of their shell, they become more confident and less shy: *She's really **come out of her shell** since she went to college.* | *The more his father shouted, the more he **retreated into his shell**.* [**Origin:** Old English *sciell*]

shell² *v.* [T] **1** to fire shells from large guns at something: *Rebels shelled the town.* **2** to remove something such as beans, nuts, or SHELLFISH from a shell or a POD

shell out *phr. v.* INFORMAL **shell out sth** to pay a lot of money for something, especially when it is more than you want to spend: +**for** *She ended up shelling out for two rooms.* | **shell out sth** *Dave had to shell out over $2,000 to get his car fixed.*

she'll /ʃɪl, ʃil/ the short form of "she will": *She'll be back in a minute.*

shel·lac[1] /ʃə'læk/ *n.* [U] a type of transparent paint used to protect surfaces or to make them hard

shellac[2] *v.* **shellacks**, **shellacked**, **shellacking** [T] **1** to paint something with shellac **2** to completely defeat someone

shel·lack·ing /ʃə'lækɪŋ/ *n.* [U] INFORMAL a complete defeat: *their shellacking of Florida State*

Shel·ley, Ma·ry Woll·stone·craft /'ʃɛli, 'mɛri 'wʊlstənˌkræft/ (1797–1851) an English writer, whose best-known NOVEL is "Frankenstein"

Shelley, Per·cy Bysshe /'pɚsi bɪʃ/ (1792–1822) an English poet

shell·fire /'ʃɛlˌfaɪɚ/ *n.* [U] another word for SHELLING

shell·fish /'ʃɛlˌfɪʃ/ *n. plural* **shellfish** [C,U] an animal that lives in water, that has a shell but no BACKBONE, and that may be eaten as food

ˈshell game *n.* [C] **1** a dishonest method of doing something, in which you appear to be doing one thing when you are really doing another: *Critics called the proposal a shell game.* **2** a game in which a player guesses which cup a small object is hidden under, after the cups have been moved around several times

shell·ing /'ʃɛlɪŋ/ also **shellfire** *n.* [U] the firing of large guns at a place: *The shelling of the town continued well into the night.*

ˈshell shock *n.* [U] OLD-FASHIONED a type of mental illness caused by the terrible experiences of fighting in a war or battle

ˈshell-shocked *adj.* **1** INFORMAL feeling tired, confused, or anxious because of a recent difficult experience: *Cindy looked a little shell-shocked after her driving test.* **2** OLD-FASHIONED mentally ill because of the terrible experiences of war

shel·ter[1] /'ʃɛltɚ/ *n.* **1** [U] a place to live, considered as one of the basic needs of life: *They are in desperate need of food and shelter.* **2** [U] protection from danger or from wind, rain, hot sun etc.: **+of** *We reached the shelter of the caves.* | **in/into/under the shelter of sth** *They stood in the shelter of the railroad station.* | *Several people* ***took shelter*** *indoors when the rain started.* | *They had to* ***run for shelter*** *when gunshots rang out.* **3** [C] a safe place where people or animals who have no homes or are in danger can go to live and receive help SYN **refuge**: **+for** *a shelter for battered women* | *a* ***homeless shelter*** (=for people who do not have a place to live) | *We got our dog from the* ***animal shelter***. **4** [C] a building or an area with a roof over it that protects you from the weather or other dangerous conditions outside: *a bus shelter* (=a small structure with a roof, where you wait for a bus) | **a bomb/an air-raid/a fallout shelter** (=a place that protects people from bombs dropped by airplanes) → see also BOMB SHELTER, TAX SHELTER

shelter[2] *v.* **1** [T] to provide a place where someone or something is protected, especially from the weather or from danger: *They risked their lives to shelter Jews during World War II.* | **shelter sth from sth** *A row of trees shelters the house from the wind.* ►see THESAURUS box at **protect** **2** [I] to stay in or under a place where you are protected from the weather or from danger: **+from** *People stood in doorways, sheltering from the rain.*

shel·tered /'ʃɛltɚd/ *adj.* **1 a sheltered life/childhood/existence etc.** a life etc. in which someone has been very protected from difficult or bad experiences: *Paula had a very sheltered upbringing.* **2** a place that is sheltered is protected from weather conditions: *a sheltered spot for a picnic*

shelve /ʃɛlv/ *v.* [T] **1** to decide not to continue with a plan, idea etc., although you might continue with it at a later time: *Plans for the new stadium have been shelved.* **2** to put something on a shelf, especially books **3** [I always + adv./prep.] land that shelves slopes slightly

shelves /ʃɛlvz/ *n.* the plural of SHELF

shelv·ing /'ʃɛlvɪŋ/ *n.* [U] **1** a set of shelves attached to a wall **2** wood, metal etc. used for shelves

Shen·an·do·ah /ˌʃɛnən'doʊə/ a river in northwest Virginia in the eastern U.S.

ˌShenan'doah ˌValley, the a valley in northwest Virginia in the eastern U.S., between the Blue Ridge Mountains and the Allegheny Mountains

she·nan·i·gans /ʃə'nænɪgənz/ *n.* [plural] INFORMAL **1** bad behavior that is not very serious SYN **mischief** **2** slightly dishonest activities

Shep·ard, Al·an /'ʃɛpɚd, 'ælən/ (1923–1998) a U.S. ASTRONAUT who was the first American in space

shep·herd[1] /'ʃɛpɚd/ *n.* [C] someone whose job is to take care of sheep

shepherd[2] *v.* [T always + adv./prep.] to lead or guide a group of people somewhere, making sure that they go where you want them to go: **shepherd sb into/out/toward etc.** *The tour guides shepherded the rest of the group onto the bus.*

shep·herd·ess /'ʃɛpɚdɪs/ *n.* [C] OLD-FASHIONED a woman or girl whose job is to take care of sheep

sher·bert /'ʃɚbɚt/ *n.* [U] NONSTANDARD SHERBET

sher·bet /'ʃɚbɪt/ *n.* [U] a sweet frozen food, similar to ICE CREAM, made with water, fruit, sugar, and milk

Sher·i·dan, Rich·ard Brins·ley /'ʃɛrədən, 'rɪtʃɚd 'brɪnzli/ (1751–1816) an Irish writer of plays

sher·iff /'ʃɛrɪf/ *n.* [C] LAW a law officer of a COUNTY in the U.S., who is elected and has the highest rank of the officers in that county [**Origin:** Old English *scirgerefa*, from *scir* **area with its own government** + *gerefa* **person in charge of an area**]

S

Sher·lock /'ʃɚlɑk/ *n.* SPOKEN used when you think someone is being stupid, because they should have understood something more easily or sooner: *"It's Saturday tomorrow, right?" "Yeah, Sherlock."*

Sher·man, William /'ʃɚmən/ (1820–1891) a Union general in the U.S. Civil War

ˌSherman Anti'trust Act, the HISTORY a law passed by Congress in 1890 that made it illegal for companies to work together to limit competition and control prices

Sher·pa /'ʃɚpə/ *n.* [C] a Himalayan person who is often employed to guide people through mountains

sher·ry /'ʃɛri/ *n.* [C,U] a pale or dark brown strong wine, originally from Spain [**Origin:** 1500–1600 *sherris* **sherry** (16–18 centuries), from *Xeres* (now *Jerez*), city in southwestern Spain]

she's /ʃiz/ **1** the short form of "she is": *She's coming now.* **2** the short form of "she has": *She's changed the guidelines.*

Shet·land po·ny /ˌʃɛtlənd 'poʊni/ *n.* [C] a small strong horse with long rough hair

shh /ʃʃ/ *interjection* used to tell people to be quiet: *Shh! I can't hear what he's saying.*

Shi·a /'ʃiə/ *adj.* relating to the Shiite branch of the Muslim religion —**Shia** *n.* [C]

shi·at·su /ʃi'ɑtsu/ *n.* [U] a Japanese form of MASSAGE (=pressing and rubbing someone's body) [**Origin:** 1900–2000 Japanese *shiatsuryoho*, from *shi* **finger** + *atsu-* **pressure** + *ryoho* **treatment**]

shib·bo·leth /'ʃɪbələθ, -lɛθ/ *n.* [C] FORMAL an old idea, custom, or principle that you think is not important or appropriate for modern times [**Origin:** 1600–1700 a Hebrew word meaning **stream**, used (according to the Bible) by the Gileadite people as a way of recognizing their enemies, who could not pronounce the sh properly]

shield[1] /ʃild/ *n.* [C] **1 a)** a large piece of metal, wood, or leather that soldiers in past times used to protect themselves when fighting **b)** also **riot shield** a piece of equipment made of strong plastic, used by police or soldiers to protect themselves against angry crowds → see also HUMAN SHIELD **2** something that protects a person or thing from harm or damage: *the heat shields on the space shuttle* | **+against** *The immune system is our body's shield against infection.* **3** the small piece of metal that a police officer wears to show that he or she is a police officer SYN **badge** **4** a shape that is wide at the top and curves to a point at the bottom, or a drawing or model of this: *the shields on his tie*

shield² *v.* [T] to protect someone or something from being harmed or damaged SYN **protect**: *Beneath him, shielded by his body, lay a baby.* | **shield sb/sth from sb/sth** *Her manager had shielded her from a lot of the bad publicity.* ►see THESAURUS box at **protect**

shift¹ /ʃɪft/ Ac S3 W2 *v.*
1 MOVE [I,T] to move from one place or position to another, or make something do this: *Joe shifted uncomfortably from one foot to another.* | *She shifted her gaze from me to Bobby.*
2 NEW SUBJECT [T always + adv./prep.] to change a situation, discussion etc. by giving special attention to one idea or subject instead of to a previous one: **shift attention/emphasis/focus etc.** *The White House hopes to shift the media's attention away from foreign policy issues.* | **attention/emphasis/focus etc. shifts** *The focus shifted to whether the team would make the playoffs.* | *Students are expected to* ***shift gears*** *frequently, to go from Shakespeare to geometry to Spanish verbs.*
3 OPINIONS [I] if someone's opinions, beliefs etc. shift, they change: *Public opinion was beginning to shift to the right.*
4 COSTS/SPENDING [T always + adv./prep.] to change the way that money is paid or spent: *Investors were shifting funds from U.S. to Asian stocks.* | *We must shift more resources toward health care.*
5 shift the blame/responsibility to make someone else responsible for something, especially for something bad that has happened: *Defense lawyers tried to shift the responsibility for the crime on to the victim.*
6 IN A CAR [I,T] to change the GEARS when you are driving: *I shifted into second gear.*
[**Origin:** Old English *sciftan* **to divide, arrange**]

shift for yourself *phr. v.* if you have to shift for yourself, you have to take care of yourself, when usually other people help you do this: *These children were left alone to shift for themselves.*

shift² Ac S3 W2 *n.* [C] **1** a change in the way people think about something, in the way something is done etc. SYN **change**: **+from/to** *a* ***major shift*** *from manufacturing to service industries* | **+in** *a* ***fundamental shift*** *in the state's education policy* **2 a)** one of the periods during each day and night when a particular group of workers in a factory, hospital etc. are at work: *Dave had to* ***work a*** *12-hour* ***shift*** *yesterday.* | *They worked* ***double shifts*** (=two shifts, one immediately after the other) *over the weekend.* | *Thirty employees worked* ***in shifts*** *to get the job done.* | **the day/night/early/late shift** *Earl's on the night shift this week.* | *a nurse working the* ***swing shift*** (=a period that is usually from 3:00 to 11:00 p.m.) **b)** the workers who work during one of these periods: **night/day/early/late shift** *What time does the early shift come on duty?* **3** COMPUTERS the KEY on a computer KEYBOARD or TYPEWRITER that you press to print a capital letter: *To run the spellchecker, press SHIFT and F7.* **4** a simple straight loose-fitting woman's dress

ˌshifting ˈagriculture *n.* [U] the practice of farming an area of land until the soil cannot produce any more crops, then moving to farm an area of land in another place

ˈshift key *n.* [C] the KEY on a computer KEYBOARD or TYPEWRITER that you press to print a capital letter

shift·less /ˈʃɪftlɪs/ *adj.* OLD-FASHIONED lazy and seeming to have no interest in working hard or trying to succeed SYN **idle**

shift·y /ˈʃɪfti/ *adj.* looking dishonest: *a shifty fast-talking lawyer* —**shiftiness** *n.* [U]

shi·i·ta·ke /ʃiˈtɑki/ *n. plural* **shiitake** [C] a type of MUSHROOM that is often used in Chinese and Japanese cooking

Shi·ite /ˈʃi-aɪt/ *n.* [C] a member of one of the two main groups in the Muslim religion → see also SUNNI —**Shiite** *adj.*

shik·sa /ˈʃɪksə/ *n.* [C] a word used by Jewish people to talk about a woman who is not Jewish

shill /ʃɪl/ *n.* [C] DISAPPROVING **1** someone who is paid to say that they like and use a product in an advertisement, in order to encourage other people to buy that product: *weight-loss products advertised by celebrity shills* **2** someone who pretends to be a customer in order to make other people interested in doing something such as GAMBLING —**shill** *v.* [I]

shil·ling /ˈʃɪlɪŋ/ *n.* [C] **1** a unit of money used in past times in Great Britain. There were 20 shillings in a pound. **2** a unit of money used in Kenya, Uganda, Tanzania, and Somalia

shil·ly-shal·ly /ˈʃɪli ˌʃæli/ *v.* **shilly-shallies, shilly-shallied, shilly-shallying** [I] INFORMAL to waste time or take too long to make a decision SYN **vacillate**

Shi·loh /ˈʃaɪloʊ/ a place in the U.S. state of Tennessee where many soldiers on both sides were killed in a battle in 1862 during the Civil War

shim /ʃɪm/ *n.* [C] a piece of wood, metal etc. that is wider at one end than the other, used to fill a space between two things that do not fit together well

shim·mer /ˈʃɪmɚ/ *v.* [I] to shine with a soft light that seems to shake slightly SYN **glimmer**: *The lake shimmered in the moonlight.* ►see THESAURUS box at **shine¹** —**shimmer** *n.* [singular, U]

shim·my /ˈʃɪmi/ *v.* **shimmies, shimmied, shimmying** [I] to move forward or back while also quickly moving slightly from side to side

shin /ʃɪn/ *n.* [C] BIOLOGY the front part of your leg between your knee and your foot [**Origin:** Old English *scinu*] → see also SHIN SPLINTS

shin·bone /ˈʃɪnboʊn/ *n.* [C] BIOLOGY the front bone in your leg below your knee

shin·dig /ˈʃɪndɪg/ *n.* [C] OLD-FASHIONED a noisy party

shine¹ /ʃaɪn/ W3 *v. past tense and past participle* **shone** /ʃoʊn/ **1** [I] to produce bright light: *It wasn't very warm, but at least the* ***sun*** *was* ***shining***. | *The moon shone brightly in the sky.* | **+in/on** *That lamp's shining in my eyes.*

THESAURUS

flash to shine brightly for a very short time: *Lightning flashed across the sky.*
flicker to shine with an unsteady light: *The candle flickered and went out.*
twinkle to shine in the dark but not very brightly or continuously: *stars twinkling in the sky*
glow to shine with a warm soft light: *A fire was still glowing in the fireplace.*
sparkle/glitter to shine with many small bright points of light: *The lake sparkled in the sunshine.*
shimmer to shine with a soft light that seems to shake slightly: *The lake shimmered in the moonlight.*
gleam if something smooth and clean gleams, it shines: *The silverware had been polished until it gleamed.*
glint to reflect back light strongly when light falls on it: *The sun glinted off the windows.*
glisten to shine and look wet or oily: *Tears glistened on her cheeks.*

2 [I] to look bright and shiny: *She polished the table until it shone.* **3** *past tense and past participle* **shined** to make something bright by rubbing it SYN **polish**: *You'd better shine your shoes first.* **4** [T] to hold or point a lamp, light etc. so that the light from it goes in a particular direction: **shine sth into/across/onto etc.** *She shone the flashlight around the room.* **5** [I] if your eyes shine, or your face shines, you have an expression of happiness: *The kids' eyes shone with excitement.* **6** [I not in progressive] to be very good at something and be noticed doing it: *The concert will give young musicians their chance to shine.* [**Origin:** Old English *scinan*]

shine through *phr. v.* if a quality that someone or something has shines through, you can easily see that it is there: *Her intelligence shines through in all her work.*

shine² *n.* **1** [singular, U] the brightness that something has when light shines on it: *a product that adds shine to your hair* **2 take a shine to sb/sth** INFORMAL to like someone or something very much when you have just met them or seen them for the first time SYN **take a liking to sb/sth** **3** [singular] an act of making something bright by polishing it: *Your shoes need a shine.* → see also **(come) rain or shine** at RAIN¹ (3)

shin·er /ˈʃaɪnɚ/ *n.* [C] INFORMAL a black or purple area of skin around your eye, because you have been hit there

shin·gle¹ /ˈʃɪŋgəl/ *n.* **1** [C] one of many thin flat pieces of building material, fastened in rows to cover a roof or wall **2 hang out your shingle** to start your own business, especially as a doctor or lawyer **3 shingles** [U] a disease caused by an infection of the nerve endings, which produces painful red spots, usually on one side of the body only **4** [U] EARTH SCIENCE small round pieces of stone on a beach

shingle² *v.* [T] to put shingles on a roof —**shingled** *adj.*

shin·ing /ˈʃaɪnɪŋ/ *adj.* [only before noun] **1** excellent in a way that is easy to see: **a shining achievement/moment** *This was his shining moment.* **2 a shining example of sth** someone or something that should be admired because it clearly shows a particular quality: *The house is a shining example of Art Deco architecture.*

shin·ny /ˈʃɪni/ *v.* **shinnies, shinnied, shinnying** [I] **shinny up/down (sth)** to climb up or down a tree, pole etc. by using your hands and legs

ˈshin splints *n.* [plural] a condition in which you have pain and swelling in your shins, usually caused by running on hard surfaces

Shin·to /ˈʃɪntoʊ/ also **Shin·to·ism** /ˈʃɪntoʊˌɪzəm/ *n.* [U] the ancient religion of Japan that has gods who represent various parts of nature, and gives great importance to people who died in the past [**Origin:** 1700–1800 Japanese, Chinese *shin tao* **way of the gods**]

shin·y /ˈʃaɪni/ *adj. comparative* **shinier**, *superlative* **shiniest** smooth and bright: *a shiny black limousine* | *Her hair was thick and shiny.* —**shininess** *n.* [U]

ship¹ /ʃɪp/ S3 W2 *n.* [C] **1** a large boat used for carrying people or things on the ocean: *a cruise ship* | *a cargo ship* | *Supplies are brought in* ***by ship***.

THESAURUS

Ships that carry people
cruise ship, **liner**, **ferry**
Ships that carry goods
freighter, **tanker**, **barge**, **cargo ship**
Military ships
aircraft carrier, **battleship**, **cruiser**, **destroyer**, **gunboat**, **frigate**, **minesweeper**, **submarine**, **warship**

2 a large vehicle used for traveling in space [**Origin:** Old English *scip*] → see also **jump ship** at JUMP¹ (24), **run a tight ship** at TIGHT¹ (9)

ship² S3 W3 *v.* **shipped**, **shipping** **1** [I,T] to deliver goods to someone, or to deliver them to a store so that they are available for people to buy: *We can ship a replacement to you within 24 hours.* | *The updated version is scheduled to ship on July 1.* **2** [T] to send or carry something by ship: **ship sth out/to etc.** *Supplies were shipped to Britain from the U.S.* **3** [T usually passive] to order someone to go somewhere: **ship sb off/out etc.** *He was shipped off to boarding school at age 11.* → see also **shape up or ship out** at SHAPE UP (3)

ship out *phr. v.* if a soldier ships out, he is sent to the place where he will be fighting: *In the fall of 1943, Stewart's unit shipped out for Italy.*

-ship /ʃɪp/ *suffix* [in nouns] **1** a particular position or job, or the time during which you have it: *American citizenship* | *He was offered a professorship.* **2** the state of having something: *car ownership* | *a long friendship* | *A year's membership costs $35.* **3** a particular art or skill: *her fine musicianship* | *a work of great scholarship* → see also -MANSHIP **4** all the people in a particular group: *a magazine with a readership of 9,000* (=with 9,000 readers) **5** used to form particular titles for people: *your Ladyship*

ship·board¹ /ˈʃɪpbɔrd/ *n.* [U] **on shipboard** on a ship

shipboard² *adj.* [only before noun] on a ship: *shipboard navigation systems*

ship·build·ing /ˈʃɪpˌbɪldɪŋ/ *n.* [U] the industry of making ships —**shipbuilder** *n.* [C]

ship·load /ˈʃɪploʊd/ *n.* [C] the amount of goods or the number of people a ship can carry: +**of** *Several shiploads of grain arrived in the harbor that day.*

ship·mate /ˈʃɪpmeɪt/ *n.* [C] a SAILOR's shipmate is another sailor who is working on the same ship

ship·ment /ˈʃɪpmənt/ *n.* [C,U] a load of goods being delivered, or the act of sending them: *The order is ready for shipment.* | **arms/oil/drug/food etc. shipment** *an illegal arms shipment* | +**of** *a large shipment of auto parts*

ship·per /ˈʃɪpɚ/ *n.* [C] a company that sends goods to places

ship·ping /ˈʃɪpɪŋ/ *n.* [U] **1** the price charged for delivering goods: *Add $2.00 for* ***shipping and handling***. **2** ships considered as a group: *The port is closed to all shipping.* **3** the action of delivering goods, especially by ship: *a shipping company*

ˈshipping adˌdress *n.* [C] the address where you want something to be sent when you buy it on the Internet

ˈshipping clerk *n.* [C] someone whose job is to send and receive goods at a company

ˈshipping ˌlane also **ˈsea lane** *n.* [C] an officially approved path of travel that ships must follow

ship·shape /ˌʃɪpˈʃeɪp◂/ *adj.* [not before noun] neat and clean: *Hotels are warned when rooms aren't shipshape.*

ˌship-to-ˈshore *adj.* [only before noun] providing communication between a ship and people on land: *ship-to-shore radio*

ship·wreck¹ /ˈʃɪp-rɛk/ *n.* [C] **1** the destruction of a ship in an accident: *survivors of the shipwreck* **2** a ship that has been destroyed in an accident: *a 450-year-old shipwreck*

shipwreck² *v.* **be shipwrecked** if someone or a boat or ship is shipwrecked, they are in an accident in which a ship is destroyed

ship·wright /ˈʃɪp-raɪt/ *n.* [C] someone who builds or repairs ships

ship·yard /ˈʃɪp-yɑrd/ *n.* [C] a place where ships are built or repaired

shirk /ʃɚk/ *v.* [T] to deliberately avoid doing something you should do, because you are lazy: **shirk your responsibilities/duties/obligations** *Federal agents will not shirk their duty.* —**shirker** *n.* [C] —**shirking** *n.* [U]

shirk from sth *phr. v.* to deliberately avoid something or refuse to do something, especially because you are afraid: *The president won't shirk from a fight over the tax.*

shirred /ʃɚd/ *adj.* shirred material is decorated with several lines of stitches sewn in a way that makes many small folds between the stitches

shirt /ʃɚt/ S1 W2 *n.* [C] **1** a piece of clothing that covers the upper part of your body and your arms, and usually has a collar and buttons down the front → see also BLOUSE: *I have to wear a shirt and tie to work.* **2 sb would give you the shirt off their back** INFORMAL used to say that someone is very generous: *Dan's the kind of guy who would give you the shirt off his back.* **3 keep your shirt on** SPOKEN used to tell someone who is becoming angry that they should stay calm **4 no shirt, no shoes, no service** used on signs in restaurants and stores to say that if you are not wearing a shirt or shoes, you cannot come in [**Origin:** Old English *scyrte*] → see also STUFFED SHIRT

shirt·dress /ˈʃɚt˺drɛs/ *n.* [C] a woman's dress in the style of a long shirt SYN **shirtwaist**

shirt·front /ˈʃɚtfrʌnt/ *n.* [C] the part of a shirt that covers your chest

shirt·sleeve /ˈʃɚtsliv/ *n.* **1 in (your) shirtsleeves** wearing a shirt but no JACKET: *Most of the men were working in their shirtsleeves.* **2** [C] the part of a shirt that covers your arm

shirt·tail /ˈʃɚtˀteɪl/ *n.* [C] the part of a shirt that is below your waist and is usually put inside your pants: *Tuck in your shirttail.*

shirt·waist /ˈʃɚtweɪst/ also **ˈshirtwaist ˌdress** *n.* [C] a SHIRTDRESS

shish ke·bab /ˈʃɪʃ kəˌbɑb/ *n.* [C] small pieces of meat and vegetables that are put on a long thin metal stick and cooked

shiv·er¹ /ˈʃɪvɚ/ *v.* [I] to shake slightly because you are cold or frightened: *The water was cold, and Robbie shivered.* | +**with** *Juanita was shivering with fear.* ▸see THESAURUS box at **shake¹** [**Origin:** 1400–1500 *chiver* **to shiver**]

shiver

shiver² *n.* [C] **1** a slight shaking movement of your body caused by cold or fear SYN **tremble** SYN **quiver**: +**of** *A shiver of anxiety* ***ran through*** *her.* **2 give you the shivers** INFORMAL to make you feel afraid: *Just thinking about flying gives me the shivers.* → see also **send shivers/chills up (and down) your spine** at SEND (10)

shiv·er·y /ˈʃɪvəri/ *adj.* shaking slightly because of cold, fear, or illness

shoal /ʃoʊl/ *n.* [C] **1** BIOLOGY a large group of fish swimming together ▸see THESAURUS box at **group¹** **2** EARTH SCIENCE a small hill of sand just below the surface of water that makes it dangerous for boats

shock¹ /ʃɑk/ S3 *n.*
1 EVENT/SITUATION [C usually singular] if something that happens is a shock, you did not expect it, and it makes you feel very surprised and usually upset: +**to** *Their divorce was a big shock to everyone.* | *Chuck's death* ***came as a*** *complete* ***shock*** *to all of us.* | **be a shock to see/hear/find etc.** *It was a shock to discover just how bad conditions were.*
2 BAD FEELING [singular, U] the feeling of surprise you have when something that you do not expect happens, especially something bad or frightening: *The team was* ***in shock*** *after the defeat.* | **the shock of (doing) sth** *Mom never really got over the shock of Dad's death.* | *The whole town was* ***in a state of shock*** *at the news.* | *If you think it's easy, you're* ***in for a shock.***
3 ELECTRICITY [C] also **electric shock, electrical shock** PHYSICS a sharp painful feeling caused by a dangerous flow of electricity passing through your body: *Ouch! The light switch just* ***gave me a shock.***
4 MEDICAL [U] MEDICINE a medical condition in which someone looks pale and their heart and lungs are not working correctly, usually after a sudden very bad experience: *Several passengers were treated for shock.* | *A small boy was brought in, in a* ***state of shock.***
5 SHAKING [C,U] violent shaking caused for example by an explosion or an EARTHQUAKE: *The shock of the explosion could be felt miles away.* → see also SHOCK WAVE
6 CAR [C usually plural] a SHOCK ABSORBER
7 SUDDEN CHANGE [C] a sudden unexpected change that threatens the economic situation, way of life, or traditions of a group of people: *the oil shocks of the 1970s*
8 a shock of hair a very thick mass of hair
[**Origin:** (1–7) French *choc*, from *choquer* **to strike against**] → see also CULTURE SHOCK, SHELL SHOCK, SHOCKED, TOXIC SHOCK SYNDROME

WORD CHOICE **shock, surprise, shocking, surprising**
• **Shock** and **shocking** are both fairly strong words. If something **is, comes as**, or **gives you** a **shock**, it is unexpected and often very bad: *It came as a real shock to hear she was in the hospital.* | *It will take a long time to get over the shock of his wife's death.*
• You can use **surprise** and **surprising** to talk about something that is unexpected, but is not necessarily bad: *It was a nice surprise when Brenda dropped in.* | *There are a number of surprising differences between life in America and in my country.*
• Something that is **shocking** is extremely bad, often in an offensive or immoral way: *shocking cruelty* | *The shocking news of her murder came late Friday night.*

shock² *v.* [T] **1** to make someone feel very surprised and upset, and unable to believe what has happened: *The hatred in her voice shocked him.* | *Obviously, her suicide shocked the whole school.* **2** to make someone feel very offended, by talking or behaving in an immoral or socially unacceptable way: *Many readers were shocked by the obscenities in the article.* **3** to give an electric shock to someone

ˈshock abˌsorber *n.* [C] a piece of equipment connected to each wheel of a vehicle to make traveling more comfortable and less BUMPY

shocked /ʃɑkt/ S3 *adj.* feeling surprised and very upset by something unexpected, bad, or immoral: +**at** *We were shocked at their terrible working conditions.* | **shocked to see/hear/learn etc.** *I was very shocked to hear of Brian's death.* | *There was a moment of* ***shocked silence.***

THESAURUS
aghast WRITTEN shocked: *We were aghast at the devastation caused by the storm.*
shaken shocked by something that has happened to you: *He was very shaken by the accident.*
appalled/horrified very shocked: *I was appalled by his decision.*
traumatized so badly shocked that you are affected for a very long time: *traumatized ex-soldiers*
outraged very shocked and angry: *Women were outraged at the treatment she received in Congress.*
devastated very shocked and sad: *He was devastated when she left him.*

shock·er /ˈʃɑkɚ/ *n.* [C] a movie, news story etc. that shocks you

shock·ing /ˈʃɑkɪŋ/ *adj.* very offensive or upsetting: *shocking photographs of mass graves* | ***It's shocking that*** *so little has been done to help.* —**shockingly** *adv.* → see Word Choice box at SHOCK¹

ˌshocking ˈpink *n.* [U] a very bright pink color —**shocking pink** *adj.*

ˈshock jock *n.* [C] someone on a radio show who plays music and talks about subjects that offend many people

shock·proof /ˈʃɑkpruf/ *adj.* a watch, machine etc. that is shockproof is made or designed so that it is not easily damaged if it is dropped or hit

ˈshock ˌtactics *n.* [plural] methods of achieving what you want by deliberately shocking someone

ˈshock ˌtherapy also **shock treatment** *n.* [U] **1** treatment of mental illness using powerful electric shocks **2** the use of extreme methods to change a system or solve a problem as quickly as possible: *programs of economic shock therapy*

ˈshock troops *n.* [plural] soldiers who are specially trained to make sudden quick attacks on the enemy

ˈshock wave *n.* **1 shock waves** [plural] strong feelings of shock that people feel when something bad happens suddenly: *The plane crash* ***sent shock waves through*** *the aviation industry.* **2** [C,U] EARTH SCIENCE a very strong wave of air pressure or heat from an explosion, an EARTHQUAKE etc.

shod¹ /ʃɑd/ *v.* the past tense and past participle of SHOE

shod[2] *adj.* FORMAL wearing a particular type of shoes: **be shod in sth** *His feet were shod in thick-soled sandals.*

shod·dy /'ʃɑdi/ *adj. comparative* **shoddier**, *superlative* **shoddiest** **1** made or done cheaply or carelessly: *shoddy workmanship* **2** unfair and dishonest: *shoddy journalism* [**Origin:** 1800–1900 *shoddy* **cloth made from reused wool** (19–20 centuries)] —**shoddily** *adv.*: *shoddily built housing* —**shoddiness** *n.* [U]

shoes

shoe[1] /ʃu/ S1 W2 *n.* [C] **1** something that you wear to cover your feet, made of leather or some other strong material: *new leather shoes* | *She was* ***wearing*** *jeans and tennis* ***shoes***. | *a new* ***pair of shoes*** | *He* ***took off*** *his* ***shoes*** *and socks.* | *I* ***put on*** *my* ***shoes*** *and coat.* | *expensive* ***running shoes*** | *I can't walk in* ***high-heeled shoes***. → see also BOOT, TENNIS SHOE **2 be in sb's shoes** to be in someone else's situation, especially a bad one: *I wouldn't want to be in Frank's shoes right now.* **3 step into sb's shoes** also **fill sb's shoes** to do a job that someone else used to do, and do it as well as they did: *It'll be hard to find someone to fill Pam's shoes.* **4 if the shoe fits (, wear it)** SPOKEN used to say that if a remark that has been made about you is true, then you should accept it: *"Are you saying I'm a liar?" "Well, if the shoe fits..."* **5** a U-shaped piece of iron that is nailed onto a horse's foot SYN **horseshoe** **6** the part of a BRAKE that presses on a wheel to make a vehicle stop [**Origin:** Old English *scoh*]

shoe[2] *v. past tense and past participle* **shod** /ʃɑd/, **shoeing** [T] to put a shoe on a horse

shoe·box /'ʃubɑks/ *n.* [C] a CARDBOARD box that shoes are sold in, and that people often keep other things in

shoe·horn[1] /'ʃuhɔrn/ *n.* [C] a curved piece of metal or plastic that you can put inside the back of a shoe when you put it on, to help your heel go in easily

shoehorn[2] *v.* [T] to put someone or something into a space that is too small: **+into** *Twelve players are shoehorned into a tiny dressing room.*

shoe·lace /'ʃuleɪs/ *n.* [C] a thin piece of material, like string, that goes through holes in the front of your shoes and is used to tie them SYN **lace**

shoe·mak·er /'ʃuˌmeɪkɚ/ *n.* [C] someone who makes shoes and boots SYN **cobbler**

Shoe·mak·er /'ʃuˌmeɪkɚ/, **Wil·lie** /'wɪli/ (1931–2003) a U.S. JOCKEY who won thousands of horse races and is considered one of the best jockeys ever

shoe·shine /'ʃuʃaɪn/ *n.* [C usually singular] an act of polishing your shoes or having them polished by someone else

shoe·string /'ʃuˌstrɪŋ/ *n.* **1 on a shoestring** INFORMAL if you do something on a shoestring, you do it without spending much money: *The program was run on a shoestring.* **2 a shoestring business/operation/budget etc.** a business, organization etc. that does not have much money available to spend: *a shoestring campaign for governor* **3** a shoelace

'shoestring po,tatoes *n.* [plural] potatoes that have been cut into very thin pieces, thinner than FRENCH FRIES, and then cooked in hot oil

shoe·tree /'ʃuˌtri/ *n.* [C] an object shaped like a shoe that you put inside a shoe so that it keeps its shape

sho·gun /'ʃoʊgən/ *n.* [C] a military leader in Japan until the middle of the 19th century

shone /ʃoʊn/ *v.* the past tense and past participle of SHINE

shoo[1] /ʃu/ *interjection* used to tell a child or an animal to go away

shoo[2] *v.* [T always + adv./prep.] to make a child, animal, or insect go away by waving your arms, especially because they are annoying you: **shoo sb out/away etc.** *He shooed the kids out of the kitchen.*

'shoo-in *n.* [C usually singular] INFORMAL someone who is expected to win a race, election etc. easily: *He looked like* ***a shoo-in to win*** *the Democratic nomination.*

shook /ʃʊk/ *v.* the past tense of SHAKE

,shook 'up *adj.* [not before noun] SPOKEN NONSTANDARD very frightened, shocked, or upset because of something that has happened SYN **shaken**

shoot[1] /ʃut/ S1 W1 *v. past tense and past participle* **shot**/ʃɑt/

1 KILL/INJURE [T] to injure or kill someone or an animal using a gun: *I thought he was going to shoot me.* | *She shot herself with one of her husband's hunting rifles.* | **shoot sb in the leg/head etc.** *He was shot in the leg while trying to escape.* | **shoot sb to death/shoot sb dead** *One woman was shot dead in an attempted robbery.* | *The guards have orders to* ***shoot*** *intruders* ***on sight*** (=shoot as soon as you see someone). | *The men were* ***shot at point-blank range*** (=from very close).

2 FIRE A GUN [I,T] **a)** to fire a weapon and make bullets come out of it: *Stop or I'll shoot!* | **+at** *He took aim and shot at the target.* | *The soldiers had orders to* ***shoot to kill*** (=shoot at someone with the intention of killing them). | **shoot a gun/rifle etc.** *Todd's grandfather taught him how to shoot a rifle.* **b)** if a gun shoots or shoots a particular type of bullet, it sends out a bullet: *It's just a toy – it doesn't shoot real bullets.*

3 ARROW [T] to make an ARROW come from a BOW: *They shot arrows from behind the bushes.*

4 MOVE QUICKLY [I,T always + adv./prep.] to move quickly in a particular direction, or to make something move in this way: *Flames were shooting skyward.* | **+past/along etc.** *Two kids shot past us on in-line skates.* | **shoot sth up/in/along etc.** *The fountain shoots water 20 feet into the air.*

5 TRY TO MAKE A POINT [I,T] to throw or hit a ball or PUCK

in a sport such as basketball or HOCKEY toward the place where you can gain points: *O'Neal shot from behind the three-point line.*
6 BECOME FAMOUS/SUCCESSFUL [I always + adv./prep.] to move up in rank or become famous or very successful very quickly: *Her new album shot straight to the top of the charts.* | **shoot to fame/stardom/prominence** *Julia Roberts shot to fame in "Pretty Woman."*
7 PAIN [I always + adv./prep.] if pain shoots through your body, you feel it going quickly through it: +**through/along/down** *A sharp pain suddenly shot down her right arm.* | **shooting pain/pains** *She had shooting pains in her arms and legs.*
8 PHOTO/MOVIE [I,T] to take photographs or make a movie of something: *The movie was shot in New Zealand.*
9 shoot hoops/baskets INFORMAL to play basketball or practice playing it
10 shoot pool INFORMAL to play a game of POOL
11 shoot a 68/71 etc. to get a particular number of points in a game of GOLF
12 START SPEAKING [used in the imperative] SPOKEN, INFORMAL used to tell someone to start speaking: *"I have a couple of questions for you." "Okay, shoot."*
13 shoot yourself in the foot to say or do something stupid that will cause you a lot of trouble: *If he keeps talking, pretty soon he'll shoot himself in the foot.*
14 shoot the breeze/bull INFORMAL to have an informal conversation about unimportant things
15 shoot a look/glance (at sb) to look at someone quickly, especially so that other people do not see, to show them how you feel: *Linda shot an angry glance in Doug's direction.*
16 shoot your mouth off INFORMAL to talk about something that you should not talk about or that you know nothing about
17 shoot it out (with sb) INFORMAL to fight using guns, especially until one person or group is defeated or killed
18 shoot from the hip to say what you think in a direct way, without thinking about it first
19 shoot questions at sb to ask someone a lot of questions very quickly: *The prosecutor shot a series of rapid questions at Hendrickson.*
20 shoot the rapids to ride in a small boat over rough water in a river, especially as a sport
21 shoot straight a) to shoot a gun so that the bullet goes where you want it to go **b)** INFORMAL to speak honestly and directly with someone
22 DRUGS [I,T] SLANG to take illegal drugs by using a needle SYN **shoot up**
23 shoot your wad INFORMAL to have used all of your money, power, energy etc.
[**Origin:** Old English *sceotan*] → see also **blame/shoot the messenger** at MESSENGER (2)

shoot down *phr. v.* **1 shoot sth ↔ down** to destroy an airplane while it is flying: *His plane was shot down behind enemy lines.* **2 shoot sb ↔ down** to kill someone with a gun, especially someone who cannot defend themselves: *The army were accused of shooting down unarmed demonstrators.* **3 shoot sb/sth ↔ down** to say that what someone is suggesting is wrong or stupid: *I tried to help, but all my suggestions were **shot down in flames**.*

shoot for sth *phr. v.* INFORMAL to try to achieve a particular aim, especially one that is very difficult SYN **aim for**: *We are shooting for a 50% increase in sales this year.*

shoot up *phr. v.* **1** to increase quickly in number or amount: *Insurance premiums shot up following the earthquake.* **2** to grow taller or higher very quickly: *Suddenly, a huge orange flame shot up.* | *Peter really shot up over the summer.* **3 shoot sb/sth ↔ up** to injure or damage someone or something by shooting them with bullets: *Then two men came in and shot up the entire lobby.* **4** SLANG to take illegal drugs by using a needle

shoot² *n.* [C] **1** BIOLOGY the part of a plant that comes up above the ground when it is just beginning to grow **2** an occasion when someone takes photographs or makes a movie: *a fashion shoot* | *a photo shoot* → see also **sth is a crap shoot** at CRAP (6), TURKEY SHOOT

shoot³ *interjection* INFORMAL used to show that you are annoyed or disappointed about something: *Oh, shoot! I forgot to go to the bank.*

'shoot-'em-up *n.* [C] **1** a movie, TV program, or book in which there is a lot of action, shooting, and killing **2** a simple computer game in which you try to kill as many enemies as possible —**shoot-'em-up** *adj.* [only before noun]

shoot·er /'ʃuṭə/ *n.* [C] **1** a basketball player who is good at throwing the ball through the basket in order to gain points **2** someone who shoots a gun **3** INFORMAL a gun → see also SIX-SHOOTER, TROUBLESHOOTER

shoot·ing /'ʃuṭɪŋ/ *n.* **1** [C] a situation in which someone is injured or killed by a gun: *Ambulances rushed to the scene of the shooting.* | +**of** *the accidental shooting of a policeman* **2** [U] the process of taking photographs or making a movie: *We had two weeks of rehearsals before shooting began.* **3** [U] the sport of shooting a gun

'shooting ˌgallery *n.* [C] **1** a place where people shoot guns at objects to win prizes **2** SLANG an empty building in a city, where people buy illegal drugs and put them into their bodies with needles

ˌshooting 'star *n.* [C] a small piece of rock or metal from space, that burns brightly as it falls toward the Earth SYN **meteor**

shoot·out /'ʃutaʊt/ *n.* [C] **1** a fight using guns: *Brown was killed **in a shootout with police**.* **2** a sports competition, especially in basketball or GOLF, in which people take turns throwing or hitting a ball to see who can gain the most points

ˌshoot-to-'kill *adj.* [only before noun] **a shoot-to-kill order/rule/authorization etc.** orders or rules for police or soldiers that they should try to shoot and kill anyone doing something wrong

shop¹ /ʃɑp/ S2 *v.* **shopped, shopping** [I] to go to one or more stores to buy things: *Mom's out shopping with Grandma.* | +**for** *I was shopping for a new dress but couldn't find anything I liked.* | +**at** *I usually shop at Lucky's.* [**Origin:** Old English *sceoppa* **stall**] → see also SHOPPING, WINDOW SHOPPING

shop around *phr. v.* to compare the price and quality of different things before you decide which to buy: *If you shop around, you can probably find a lower price.* | +**for** *We shopped around for the best deal on a new car.*

shop² S1 W2 *n.*
1 SMALL STORE [C] a small store that sells one particular type of goods: *a gift shop* → see also COFFEE SHOP
2 MAKING/REPAIRING THINGS [C] a place where things are made or repaired: *a welding shop* | *Our car's still in the shop* (=being repaired). → see also BODY SHOP, SHOP STEWARD
3 SCHOOL SUBJECT [U] also **shop class** a subject taught in schools that shows students how to use tools and machinery to make or repair things: *Doug made this table **in shop**.* | **wood/metal/print etc. shop** *I'm taking metal shop this semester.*
4 set up shop INFORMAL to start a business: *Dr. Rosen has set up shop downtown.*
5 close up shop INFORMAL to close a business, usually permanently: *Finnegan's Bar is closing up shop after 35 years.* → see also **talk shop** at TALK¹ (3)

shop·a·ho·lic /ˌʃɑpə'hɔlɪk, -'hɑlɪk/ *n.* [C] HUMOROUS someone who goes shopping very often and buys more things than they should

ˌshop 'floor *n.* **the shop floor** the area in a factory where the ordinary workers do their work

shop·keep·er /'ʃɑpˌkipə/ *n.* [C] someone who owns or is in charge of a small store SYN **storekeeper**

shop·lift /'ʃɑpˌlɪft/ *v.* [I] to take something from a store without paying for it —**shoplifter** *n.* [C] *Shoplifters will be prosecuted.* ▸see THESAURUS box at **steal¹**

shop·lift·ing /'ʃɑpˌlɪftɪŋ/ *n.* [U] the crime of stealing things from stores, for example by hiding them in your bag or under your clothes

shoppe /ʃɑp/ *n.* [C usually singular] a way of spelling "shop," used especially in the names of stores to make them seem old-fashioned and attractive: *Ye Olde Candy Shoppe*

shop·per /ˈʃɑpɚ/ *n.* [C] **1** someone who buys things in stores, or who is looking for something to buy: *The streets were crowded with holiday shoppers.* ►see THESAURUS box at **customer** **2** a type of newspaper, filled mainly with advertisements, that is delivered free to every house in a particular area

shop·ping /ˈʃɑpɪŋ/ S2 *n.* [U] **1 go shopping** to go to one or more stores to buy things, often for enjoyment: +**for** *Kari and I went shopping for swimsuits.* | **go grocery/clothes/shoe etc. shopping** (=to go to one or more stores in order to buy food, clothes etc.) **2** the activity of going to stores to buy things: *Shopping is one of my favorite pastimes.* | *She was tired after* ***doing all the shopping*** *and laundry.* | **Christmas/holiday shopping** (=buying presents for Christmas, Hanukkah etc.)

shopping ˌbag *n.* [C] a large bag made of heavy paper with a flat bottom and two handles, that you get when you buy something in a store

shopping ˌcart *n.* [C] a large metal basket on wheels that you push around in a store when you are shopping

shopping ˌcenter *n.* [C] a group of stores built together in one area, often in one large building

shopping ˌlist *n.* [C] a list of things, especially food, that you need to buy

shopping ˌmall *n.* [C] a large building containing many stores SYN **mall**

shopping ˌplaza *n.* [C] a row of stores built together with an area for parking cars in the front SYN **strip mall**

shopping ˌspree *n.* [C] an occasion when you buy a lot of things from a lot of stores and spend a lot of money: *She* ***went on a shopping spree*** *and spent over $1,500 on clothes.*

shop ˈsteward *n.* [C] a worker who is elected by members of a UNION in a factory or other business to represent them in dealing with managers

ˈshop talk *n.* [U] INFORMAL conversation about your work, which other people may find boring

shop·worn /ˈʃɑpwɔrn/ *adj.* **1** something that is shopworn is slightly damaged or dirty because it has been in a store for a long time **2** an idea that is shopworn is not interesting anymore because it has been discussed many times before

shore¹ /ʃɔr/ W3 *n.* **1** [C,U] the land along the edge of a large area of water, such as an ocean or lake: *Only a few survivors reached the shore.* | **from/to shore** *We could see a boat about a mile from shore.* | *a resort* ***on the shores of*** *Lake Michigan* | *We only had a couple of hours* ***on shore*** (=away from a ship). → see picture on page A31

THESAURUS

coast the land next to the ocean: *The island is 15 miles off the coast of Newfoundland.*
beach an area of sand or small stones at the edge of an ocean or lake: *a clean beach with golden sand*
seashore the area of land next to the ocean: *seashore resort towns*
bank the edge of a river: *the banks of the Mississippi river*

2 these/American/foreign etc. shores ESPECIALLY LITERARY a particular country that has a border on the ocean: *It was the first college founded on these shores.* [**Origin:** 1300–1400 Middle Dutch, Middle Low German *schore*] → see also ASHORE, OFFSHORE, ONSHORE

shore² *v.*

shore sth ↔ **up** *phr. v.* **1** to help or support something that is likely to fail or is not working well: *The government has made attempts to shore up the struggling economy.* **2** to support a wall with large pieces of wood, metal etc. to stop it from falling down

ˈshore leave *n.* [U] a period of time that a SAILOR is allowed to spend on land, away from their work: *The crew members were* ***on shore leave*** *in New York.*

shore·line /ˈʃɔrlaɪn/ *n.* [C,U] the land at the edge of a lake, river, ocean etc. SYN **coastline**: *the bay's 6,000 miles of shoreline*

shorn /ʃɔrn/ *v.* a past participle of SHEAR

short¹ /ʃɔrt/ S1 W1 *adj.*

1 LENGTH/DISTANCE measuring a small amount in length or distance OPP **long**: *a short skirt* | *Anita had her hair cut short.* | *a short stick* | **a short walk/flight/drive** *The hotel is only a short walk from the beach.* | *There was a loud explosion* ***a short distance*** *away.* ►see THESAURUS box at **hair**

2 TIME a) happening or continuing for only a little time OPP **long**: *a short speech* | *I've just been living here* ***a short time.*** | *Both her parents died within* ***a short space of time.*** | ***A short while*** *later, the doorbell rang.* **b)** happening or seeming to happen for less time than usual: *Today's meeting should be fairly short.* | *Winter is coming, and the days are getting shorter.* | **a few short hours/days/weeks etc.** *He'd known her for only a few short days.*

THESAURUS

brief used about short events and periods of time: *a brief interview*
quick used about short events: *a quick discussion*
short-lived existing or happening for only a short time: *The ensuing peace was short-lived.*
momentary continuing for a very short time: *a momentary silence*
passing short and not very serious: *a passing phase*
ephemeral FORMAL existing or popular for only a short time: *an ephemeral summertime romance*

3 PERSON of less than average height OPP **tall**: *She's short with brown hair.* | *He's much shorter than I am.*

4 BOOK/NAME/LIST ETC. a short piece of writing or name etc. does not have many words or details in it OPP **long**: *a short poem* → see also SHORT STORY

5 be short (of sth) to not have enough of something that you need, especially when you need a particular amount more: *Can you lend me a couple of dollars? I'm still a little short.* | *Supporters are still three votes short of passing the bill.* | *Our libraries are short of funds.*

6 just short of sth also **a little short of sth** a little less than something: *The total cost will be just short of $17 million.*

7 be short on sth to have less of something than you should have: *He's a nice guy, but a little short on common sense.* | *The president's speech was* ***long on*** *promises* ***and short on*** *details.*

8 time is short used to say that there is probably not enough time to do what you need to do: *Let's get to work – time's getting short.*

9 have a short memory to quickly forget something that you should remember, especially something bad or important: *The American public has a very short memory.*

10 short notice if something is short notice, you are told about it only a short time before it happens: *Yolanda had to fly to New York* ***on very short notice.***

11 in the short term/run during the period of time that is not very far into the future: *The problems will be difficult to resolve in the short term.* → see also SHORT-TERM

12 be in short supply if something is in short supply, there is not enough of it available: *Fresh water was in very short supply.*

13 short and sweet not taking a long time, and better or less boring than you expect: *They won't listen to a long lecture, so just keep it short and sweet.*

14 short of breath unable to breathe easily, especially because you are unhealthy and have been exercising

15 in short order in a short time and without delay: *The bombers destroyed the enemy's camp in short order.*

16 make short work of sth to finish something

S

quickly and easily, especially a meal or a job: *The kids made short work of the sandwiches.*
17 be short for sth to be a shorter way of saying a name: *Her name is Alex, short for Alexandra.*
18 nothing/little short of sth used to emphasize that something is very good, very surprising etc.: *Dana's recovery seemed nothing short of a miracle.*
19 have a short temper/fuse to get angry very easily
20 draw/get the short straw also **get the short end of the stick** to be given something difficult or bad to do, especially when other people have been given something better
21 VOWEL ENG. LANG. ARTS short vowels in English are the sounds of a in "bat," e in "bet," i in "bit," o in "box," and u in "but"
22 be short with sb to speak to someone using very few words, in a way that seems impolite or unfriendly [**Origin:** Old English *scort*] → see also **life is too short (to do sth)** at LIFE (26), **get/be given short shrift** at SHRIFT —**shortness** *n.* [U]

short² S3 *adv.* **1 short of (doing) sth** [sentence adverb] without actually doing something: *Short of locking her in, he couldn't stop her from leaving.* **2 short of sth a)** a little nearer than the place you were trying to reach: *The path ends just short of the summit.* | **three feet/five miles etc. short of sth** *The plane touched down 200 yards short of the runway.* **b)** a little less than a particular number or amount: *He was just short of six feet tall.* **c)** a short period of time before something: **two weeks/a month etc. short of sth** *Art died two weeks short of his 70th birthday.* **3 come up short** to be in a situation in which you do not have enough of something that you need, or in which you are not successful: *We've been to the state tournament four times, but we've come up short every time.* → see also **cut sb short** at CUT¹ (18), **cut sth short** at CUT¹ (17), **fall short (of sth)** at FALL¹ (10), **be running short** at RUN¹ (21), **be running short on sth** at RUN¹ (22), **stop short** at STOP¹ (12), **stop short of (doing) sth** at STOP¹ (9)

short³ S2 *n.* **1 shorts** [plural] **a)** short pants ending at or above the knees: *a pair of shorts* **b)** men's underwear: *He came to the door in his shorts.* → see also BOXER SHORTS **2 in short** used when you want to say, in just a few words, what is the most important point about a situation: *In short, the project is just too expensive.* **3 for short** as a shorter way of saying a name: *My name's Jennifer – Jen for short.* **4** [C] INFORMAL a short movie shown before the main movie in a theater **5** [C] PHYSICS a SHORT CIRCUIT: *There must be a short in the system.* → see also **the long and the short of it** at LONG³ (3)

short⁴ *v.* **1** [I,T] also **short out** PHYSICS to SHORT-CIRCUIT, or make something do this: *The fire was caused by a toaster that shorted out.* **2** [T] INFORMAL to give someone less of something than they should receive **3** [T] to sell STOCKS, currencies (CURRENCY) etc. that you do not yet own, and then buy them later, when the price has become lower, in order to make a profit → see also SHORT SELLING

short·age /ˈʃɔrt̬ɪdʒ/ *n.* [C,U] **1** a situation in which there is not enough of something that people need: **+of** *a severe shortage of skilled labor* | **a water/food/housing etc. shortage** *water shortages in the summer* **2 there is no shortage of sth** used to say that there is a lot or too much of something: *There was no shortage of volunteers.*

short·bread /ˈʃɔrtˀbrɛd/ *n.* [U] a hard, sweet cookie made with a lot of butter

short·cake /ˈʃɔrtˀkeɪk/ *n.* [U] cake over which a sweet fruit mixture is poured: *strawberry shortcake*

ˌshort-ˈchange *v.* [T often passive] **1** to treat someone unfairly by not giving them what they deserve: *Fans felt they had been short-changed by the short performance.* **2** to give back too little money to someone who has paid for something with more money than was needed

ˌshort ˈcircuit *n.* [C] the failure of an electrical system caused by bad wires or a fault in a connection in the wires

ˌshort-ˈcircuit *v.* **1** [I,T] PHYSICS to have a short circuit or cause a short circuit in something **2** [T] to prevent something from being successful **3** [T] to get something done without going through the usual long methods

short·com·ing /ˈʃɔrtˀˌkʌmɪŋ/ *n.* [C usually plural] a fault in someone's character or abilities, or in a product, system etc., that makes something less successful or effective than it should be: *The situation made me aware of my own shortcomings.* | **+in/of** *serious shortcomings in our safety procedures*

short·cut, short cut /ˈʃɔrtˀkʌt/ *n.* [C] **1** a quicker more direct way of going somewhere than the usual one: *Carlos decided to **take a shortcut** home across the field.* **2** a quicker way of doing something: **+to** *There aren't really any shortcuts to learning English.* **3** COMPUTERS an ICON or a combination of keys that lets you do something on a computer more quickly and easily

ˌshort-day ˈplant *n.* [C] BIOLOGY a plant that only produces flowers during times when there is less daylight, for example in autumn → see also LONG-DAY PLANT

short·en /ˈʃɔrtˀn/ *v.* [I,T] to make something shorter in time or length, or to become shorter OPP **lengthen**: *How much does it cost to get pants shortened?* | *The days are shortening now.*

short·en·ing /ˈʃɔrtˀn-ɪŋ, -nɪŋ/ *n.* [U] butter, LARD, or solid fat made from vegetable oil that you mix with flour when making cookies, PASTRY etc.

short·fall /ˈʃɔrtfɔl/ *n.* [C] the difference between the amount you have and the amount you need or expect: *a $4 billion budget shortfall* | **+in** *a shortfall in world food supplies* | **+of** *an estimated shortfall of $2 million*

short·hand¹ /ˈʃɔrthænd/ *n.* [U] **1** a fast method of writing that uses special signs or shorter forms to represent letters, words, and phrases → see also LONGHAND: *The notes were written **in shorthand**.* **2** a shorter but sometimes less clear way of saying something: **be shorthand for sth** *SFX is Hollywood shorthand for "special effects."*

shorthand² *adj.* [only before noun] using a shorter but sometimes less clear way of saying something: *Over the years, the phrase became **a shorthand way of** saying that someone wasn't qualified for the job.*

short·hand·ed /ˌʃɔrtˈhændɪd◂/ *adj.* having fewer helpers or workers than you need: *We're a little shorthanded this week.*

ˈshort-haul *adj.* a short-haul aircraft or flight travels a fairly short distance → see also LONG-HAUL

short·ie /ˈʃɔrt̬i/ *adj.* [only before noun] INFORMAL a shortie coat, JACKET, skirt etc. is one that is shorter than the usual length

short·ies /ˈʃɔt̬iz/ *n.* [plural] INFORMAL also **shortie pajamas** a set of clothes consisting of a shirt and a pair of short pants, for a woman to wear in bed → see also SHORTY

ˈshort list *n.* [C] a list of the most appropriate people for a job, prize etc., chosen from all the people who were considered: *Weber's name was **on the short list** of candidates for the superintendent's job.*

short-lived /ˌʃɔrtˈlɪvd◂/ *adj.* continuing for only a short time: *Our happiness was short-lived.*

short·ly /ˈʃɔrtli/ W3 *adv.* **1** soon: *Ms. Jones will be back shortly.* | **shortly before/after** *The accident happened shortly before noon.* ►see THESAURUS box at **soon** **2** speaking in an impatient unfriendly way: *"I've already told them that," Jim said shortly.*

ˌshort-order ˈcook *n.* [C] someone in a restaurant kitchen who makes the food that can be prepared easily or quickly

ˌshort-ˈrange *adj.* [only before noun] **1** designed to travel or operate only within a short distance: *a short-range nuclear missile* **2 a short-range plan/goal/forecast etc.** plans, goals etc. that relate only to the period that is not very far into the future: *short-range weather forecasts*

short 'ribs *n.* [plural] a piece of meat from a cow that includes part of the bones that go around its chest

short 'selling *n.* [U] the practice of selling STOCKS, currencies (CURRENCY) etc. that you do not yet own, and then buying them later, when the price has become lower, in order to make a profit —**short sale** *n.* [C]

short-sheet *v.* [T] to fold the top sheet on a bed so that no one can get into it, as a trick

short·sight·ed, short-sighted /ˌʃɔrtˈsaɪt̬ɪd◂/ *adj.* **1** DISAPPROVING not considering the possible effects in the future of something that seems to save time, money, or effort now OPP **farsighted**: *a shortsighted energy policy* **2** NEARSIGHTED —**shortsightedly** *adv.* —**shortsightedness** *n.* [U]

short-'staffed *adj.* [not before noun] having fewer than the usual or necessary number of workers

short·stop /ˈʃɔrtstɑp/ *n.* [C] the player on a baseball team who tries to stop any balls that are hit between second and third BASE

short 'story *n.* [C] ENG. LANG. ARTS a short written story about imaginary situations, usually containing only a few characters

short-'tempered *adj.* easily becoming angry or impatient

short-'term *adj.* [usually before noun] continuing for only a short time, or relating only to the period that is not very far into the future OPP **long-term**: *The treatment may bring short-term benefits.* | *short-term economic forecasts* | *a short-term loan* → see also **short-term memory** at MEMORY (1), **in the short term** at SHORT[1] (11)

short·wave, short wave /ˈʃɔrtˀweɪv/ *n.* [U] radio broadcasting on waves of less than 60 meters in length, which can be sent around the world → see also LONG WAVE, MEDIUM WAVE

short·y /ˈʃɔrt̬i/ *n.* [C usually singular] **1** INFORMAL someone who is not very tall **2** SLANG a girl or woman, especially someone's GIRLFRIEND → see also SHORTIES

Sho·sho·ne /ʃoʊˈʃoʊni/ *n.* a group of Native American tribes from the southeastern region of the U.S. —**Shoshone** *adj.*

Shos·ta·ko·vich /ˌʃɑstəˈkoʊvɪtʃ/, **Dmi·tri** /dəˈmitri/ (1906–1975) a Russian musician who wrote CLASSICAL music

shot[1] /ʃɑt/ S2 W2 *n.*
1 GUN an act of firing a gun: *The first shot missed Randy's head by just a few inches.* | *He quickly* ***fired*** *three* ***shots****.* | *Someone* ***took a shot at*** *her as she was getting out of her car.* | *One of the police officers fired* ***a warning shot****.*
2 SOUND [C] the sound of a gun being fired: *Where were you when you heard the shot?* | *A second* ***shot rang out****.*
3 SPORTS [C] an attempt to throw, kick, or hit the ball toward the place where you can gain points, especially in basketball, tennis, HOCKEY, or SOCCER: *I was open, so I* ***took the shot****.* | *He only* ***made*** *one* ***shot*** *in six attempts.*
4 PHOTOGRAPH [C] a photograph of a particular thing, view, person etc.: **get/take a shot (of sth)** *Al got some good shots of the parade as it went past.*
5 MOVIE/TV [C] a continuous view of something in a movie or television program, that is produced by having the camera in a particular position: *In the opening shot, we see a train come into the station.*
6 ATTEMPT [C] an attempt to do something or achieve something: **+at** *This will be his second shot at the championship.* | *Rhonda was willing to* ***take a shot at*** *singing on stage.* | *I've never tried before, but I'll* ***give it a shot****.* | *I'm not promising I'll succeed, but I'll* ***give it my best shot****.*
7 MEDICINE [C] an amount of a medicine that is put into your body with a needle, or the act of doing this: *You should* ***have a*** *tetanus* ***shot*** *every ten years or so.*
8 DRINK [C] a small amount of a strong alcoholic drink: **+of** *a shot of whiskey*
9 BULLETS [U] **a)** small metal balls that are shot, many at a time, from a SHOTGUN **b)** OLD USE large metal balls that are shot from a CANNON
10 REMARK [C] an angry remark: *She couldn't resist a* ***parting shot*** *at Brian: "I never loved you anyway!"* | *That joke about his height was a* ***cheap shot*** (=a rude remark that is not necessary). | **the first/opening shot** (=an attack at the beginning of a political argument or campaign)
11 a good/bad etc. shot someone who can shoot a gun well, badly etc.: *Sgt. Cooper is an excellent shot.*
12 HEAVY BALL [C] a heavy metal ball that competitors try to throw as far as possible in the sport of the SHOT PUT
13 a shot in the dark an attempt to guess something without having any facts or definite ideas: *My answer to the last question was a complete shot in the dark.*
14 a shot in the arm something that makes you more confident or more successful: *The new factory will give the local economy a real shot in the arm.*
15 a 10-to-1/50-to-1 etc. shot a horse, dog etc. in a race, whose chances of winning are expressed as numbers that show the ODDS
16 like a shot if you do something like a shot, you do it very quickly and eagerly: *She was out of the room like a shot.*
17 a warning shot also **a shot across sb's bow** something you say or do to warn someone that you are going to oppose them → see also BIG SHOT, **call the shots** at CALL[1] (11), **not by a long shot** at LONG SHOT (2), MUG SHOT

shot[2] *adj.* [not before noun] **1 be shot** SPOKEN to be in a bad condition after being used too much or treated badly: *My back tires are shot.* | *His confidence was* ***shot to pieces****.* **2 be shot through with sth** FORMAL **a)** to have a lot of a particular quality or feeling: *All the stories were shot through with gentle humor.* **b)** if a piece of cloth is shot through with a color, it has very small threads of that color woven into it

shot[3] *v.* the past tense and participle of SHOOT

shot·gun /ˈʃɑtˀgʌn/ *n.* [C] **1** a long gun that fires a lot of small round bullets and that is held to your shoulder to fire, used especially for killing birds or animals **2 ride/call shotgun** SLANG to ride in the front seat of a car next to the driver, or to say you want to do this: *My kids always argue over who gets to ride shotgun.*

ˌshotgun 'wedding also **ˌshotgun 'marriage** *n.* [C] **1** a wedding that has to take place immediately because the woman is going to have a baby **2** a situation in which two organizations, groups, people etc. are forced to join together, when this is not what one or both parties would really want

'shot put *n.* **the shot put** a sports competition in which you throw a heavy metal ball as far as you can —**shot putter** *n.* [C]

should /ʃəd; *strong* ʃʊd/ S1 W1 *modal verb* negative short form **shouldn't** **1** used to say what is the right or sensible thing to do, or a good thing to do SYN **ought to**: *You really should see a doctor.* | *Children shouldn't play in the street.* | *What should I do?* | **should have done sth** *You should have called me right away.* **2** used to talk about what is correct, for example what the correct amount is, or what is the correct way of doing something SYN **ought to**: *Every sentence should start with a capital letter.* | *There should be ten tickets, but there are only nine.* **3** used to say that you expect something to happen or be true SYN **ought to**: *She should pass the test easily.* | *They should be here by 8:00.* | *There should be some milk in the refrigerator.* **4** FORMAL used in instructions and orders: *All passengers should have their passports ready.* **5** FORMAL used to talk about something that may happen or may be true: *What if one of us should get lost?* | **should sb/sth do sth** *Should you need help* (=if you need help), *call me.* **6 you shouldn't have** SPOKEN used as a friendly way of thanking someone who has given you something, and for saying that you were not expecting it **7 you should have seen/heard sth** SPOKEN used to emphasize how funny, strange, beautiful etc. something was that you saw or heard: *You should have seen the look on her face when I told her.* **8 I should think/hope/imagine** SPOKEN used to show a strong reaction to something, based on

S

what you think is correct or morally right: *"My new car is really nice." "Well, **I should hope so**, considering how much you paid for it!"* | *"I wasn't going to give her any extra help." "**I should think not**, after the way she treated you last time."* **9 who/what should... but... etc.** OLD-FASHIONED or HUMOROUS used to show that you were surprised when something happened, a particular person appeared etc.: *Who should I meet but my old pal, Frank!* **10 I should think (that)** FORMAL, SPOKEN used to say what you believe or expect to be true or correct: *I should think he'd be grateful for some time off.* [**Origin:** Old English *sceolde* **owed, had to**] → see also **how should/would I know?** at KNOW[1] (57)

should·a /ˈʃʊdə/ *v.* SPOKEN a way of saying "should have"

shoul·der[1] /ˈʃoʊldɚ/ S2 W2 *n.*

1 BODY PART [C] BIOLOGY one of the two parts of the body at each side of the neck where the arm is connected: *Ben put his arm around Kari's shoulders.* | *I rested my head on his shoulder.* | *Tom is tall and strong with **broad shoulders**.* | *When we asked Mike about it, he just **shrugged his shoulders*** (=raised his shoulders to show that he did not know or care). | **look/glance over your shoulder** *I looked over my shoulder to see if anyone was following me.*

2 watch/look/read over sb's shoulder to stand behind someone and look at, read etc. something in front of them, sometimes so that you can criticize it: *I can't work with you watching over my shoulder.*

3 CLOTHES [C] the part of a piece of clothing that covers your shoulder: *a jacket with padded shoulders*

4 ROAD [C usually singular] an area of ground beside a road where drivers can stop their cars if they are having trouble: *I pulled onto the shoulder to check my brakes.*

5 a shoulder to cry on someone who will listen to your problems and give you sympathy: *If you ever need a shoulder to cry on, just call me.*

6 MEAT [C,U] BIOLOGY the upper part of the front leg of an animal that is used for meat: *pork shoulder*

7 stand/walk etc. shoulder to shoulder to stand, walk etc. very close together in a row

8 shoulder to shoulder (with sb) together, in order to achieve the same thing: *They were working shoulder to shoulder with local residents.*

9 on sb's shoulders if a difficult or unpleasant responsibility is on someone's shoulders, they are the person that has that responsibility: *The blame rests squarely on Jim's shoulders.*

[**Origin:** Old English *sculdor*] → see also **have a chip on your shoulder** at CHIP[1] (5), **give sb/sth the cold shoulder** at COLD[1] (8), **head and shoulders above the rest/others** at HEAD[1] (44), **look over your shoulder** at LOOK[1] (4), **rub shoulders with sb** at RUB[1] (4), -SHOULDERED

shoulder[2] *v.* **1** [T] **shoulder a responsibility/duty/cost etc.** to accept a difficult or unpleasant responsibility, duty etc.: *Most of the cost was shouldered by private corporations.* **2** [T] to lift something onto your shoulder to carry it **3 shoulder your way through/into etc. sth** to move through a large crowd of people by pushing with your shoulder: *She shouldered her way through the onlookers.*

ˈshoulder bag *n.* [C] a bag or PURSE that you use for carrying things, that hangs from a long STRAP over your shoulder

ˈshoulder blade *n.* [C] BIOLOGY one of the two flat bones on each side of your back SYN **scapula** → see picture at SKELETON[1]

-shouldered /ʃoʊldɚd/ [in adjectives] **broad-shouldered / square-shouldered / round-shouldered etc.** having shoulders that have a particular size or shape

ˈshoulder-high *adj.* as high as your shoulder: *a shoulder-high hedge*

ˈshoulder-length *adj.* shoulder-length hair hangs down to your shoulders

ˈshoulder pad *n.* [C usually plural] a thick flat piece of material that is attached under the shoulder of a piece of clothing to make your shoulders look bigger

ˈshoulder strap *n.* [C] a long narrow piece of material that goes over the shoulder on a piece of women's clothing or on a bag etc.

should·n't /ˈʃʊdnt/ *v.* the short form of "should not": *You shouldn't have told her.*

shouldst /ʃʊdst/ *v.* OLD USE or BIBLICAL **thou shouldst** you should

should've /ˈʃʊdəv/ *v.* the short form of "should have": *Dana should've come with us.*

shout[1] /ʃaʊt/ W3 *v.* **1** [I,T] to say something very loudly: *You don't need to shout. I'm standing right here.* | *"Get out of the way!" she shouted.* | +**for** *We could hear them shouting for help.* | +**at** *I wish he'd stop shouting at the children.* | **shout sth at sb** *He was shouting insults at the other driver.* | **shout at sb to do sth** *Neil shouted at us to be quiet.*

THESAURUS

call (out) to shout in order to get someone's attention
scream/shriek to shout in a very loud high voice because you are angry, excited etc.
yell to shout, for example because you are angry or excited, or because you want to get someone's attention
cry out to make a sudden loud noise, for example when you are suddenly hurt or afraid
raise your voice to say something more loudly than usual, often because you are angry about something
cheer to shout to show that you like a team, performance etc.
bellow/roar to shout loudly in a deep voice
holler INFORMAL to shout loudly

2 shout sth from the rooftops to tell everyone about something, because you want them to know about it —**shouting** *n.* [U]

shout sb ↔ **down** *phr. v.* to shout in order to prevent someone from being heard: *Some of the speakers were shouted down by the crowd.*

shout sth ↔ out *phr. v.* to say something suddenly in a loud voice: *Several students shouted out the answer.*

shout[2] *n.* **1** [C] a loud call expressing anger, pain, excitement etc.: *Lisa's voice rose to a shout.* | *Mindy **gave a** little **shout** when her name was called.* | **a shout of joy/delight/pain etc.** *The news was greeted with shouts of excitement.* **2 give sb a shout** SPOKEN to go and find someone and tell them something: *Give me a shout when you're ready to go.* **3 send a shout out to sb** SLANG to say hello to someone you know when you are on the radio or TV

shove[1] /ʃʌv/ *v.* **1** [I,T] to push someone, in a rough or careless way, using your hands or shoulders: **shove sb toward/into etc. sth** *He shoved her toward the car.* | *People were **pushing and shoving** at the barriers to get a better view.* | *Several of the girls **shoved their way** to the front.* ►see THESAURUS box at **push[1]** **2** [T always + adv./prep.] to put something somewhere carelessly or without thinking about it much: **shove sth into/under etc. sth** *Amy just shoved everything under the bed.* | *He shoved a handful of popcorn into his mouth.*

THESAURUS

stick to put something somewhere in a careless way: *Just stick the books on the table for now.*
thrust to push something somewhere suddenly or forcefully: *David thrust his hands into his pockets.*
dump to drop or put something somewhere in a careless way: *I dumped the groceries on the floor and ran to answer the phone.*
cram to force something into a small space: *He crammed his books and coat into his locker.*

►see THESAURUS box at **put** **3 shove it/sth** SPOKEN used to tell someone in a very rude way that you do not want something and that you are very angry: *Tell him he can* *shove his stupid job.* [**Origin:** Old English *scufan* **to push away**]

shove sb **around** *phr. v.* INFORMAL to treat someone in a rude way, especially by giving them orders: *Pretty soon, they won't be able to shove me around anymore.*

shove off *phr. v.* **1** INFORMAL to go away **2 shove off!** SPOKEN used to rudely tell someone to go away or to stop annoying you **3** to push a boat away from the land, usually with a pole

shove² *n.* [C] a strong push: ***Give the door a good shove*** *— it might open.* → see also **if/when push comes to shove** at PUSH² (3)

shov·el¹ /ˈʃʌvəl/ *n.* [C] **1** a tool used for digging or moving soil, snow etc., that has a large square, rounded, or pointed blade and a long handle → see also SPADE **2** a part of a large vehicle or machine used for moving or digging soil

shovel² *v.* **shoveled, shoveling** also **shovelled, shovelling 1 a)** [I,T] to lift and move soil, snow etc. with a shovel: *They shoveled dirt back into the grave.* **b)** [T] to make a surface clean by using a shovel: **shovel the driveway/sidewalk etc.** *Chris, I asked you two days ago to shovel the front walk.* **2 shovel sth into/onto etc. sth** to put something into a place quickly: *He was shoveling spaghetti into his mouth.*

shov·el·ful /ˈʃʌvəlˌfʊl/ *n.* [C] the amount of soil, snow etc. that you can carry on a shovel

show¹ /ʃoʊ/ S1 W1 *v. past tense* **showed**, *past participle* **shown** /ʃoʊn/

1 LET SB SEE [T] to let someone see something, for example by holding it out so that they can look at it: **show sb sth** *Billy showed us the scar from his operation.* | **show sth to sb** *You have to show your ticket to the woman at the gate.*

2 PROVE STH [T] to provide facts or information that make it clear that something is true, that something exists, or that something has happened SYN **demonstrate**: *The latest figures show a rise in unemployment.* | **show (that)** *The polls show voters are dissatisfied with the administration.* | **show sb (that)** *We have shown our critics that we can succeed.* | **show (sb) how/what etc.** *She just wants a chance to show what she can do.* | **be shown to be/do sth** *Red wine has been shown to reduce the risk of heart disease.* ►see THESAURUS box at **demonstrate**

3 EXPLAIN STH [T] to tell someone how to do something, by explaining it to them, often by doing it yourself so that they can see you SYN **demonstrate**: **show sb sth** *Can you show me the right way to hold a racket?* | **show sb how (to do sth)** *He showed me how to download the pictures onto my computer.* ►see THESAURUS box at **explain**

4 IMAGES/INFORMATION ETC. [T] **a)** if a picture, map etc. shows something, you can see it in the picture, on the map etc.: *Fig. 3 shows the average monthly rainfall in Miami.* | **show sb/sth as sth** *The picture shows him as a stocky man.* | **be shown as/by/with etc. sth** *In the chart, the various departments are shown in different colors.* **b)** if a clock or other measuring instrument shows a time, a number etc., you can see that time etc. on it

5 FEELINGS/QUALITIES a) [T] to let your feelings, attitudes, or personal qualities be clearly seen in the way you behave, the way you look etc.: *Mark isn't afraid to show his feelings.* | *Mary showed great interest in the children.* | **show how/what etc.** *All right. Show us how tough you are.* | **show your appreciation/gratitude** *How can I ever show my appreciation?* **b)** [I] if your feelings, attitudes, or personal qualities show, they can be clearly seen: *Her irritation clearly showed on her face.*

6 show signs of sth used to say that something is starting to become noticeable: *The economy is beginning to show some signs of improvement.* | *At 65, Nelson* ***shows no signs of*** *slowing down.*

7 GUIDE SB [T] to go with someone and guide them to a place: **show sb to/into sth** *The maid showed him into the living room.* | **show sb in/out** *I can show myself out.* | *Come on, I'll* ***show*** *you* ***the way.*** ►see THESAURUS box at **lead¹**

8 POINT AT STH [T] to help someone see where a place or thing is, especially by pointing to it: *Show me which tooth hurts.* | **show sb where** *Can you show me exactly where he fell?*

9 CAN BE SEEN a) [I] if something shows, it is easy to see: *Is my slip showing?* | *The scar doesn't show.* **b)** [T] if material shows dirt or a mark, it is easy to see the dirt or mark on it: *Light-colored carpeting really shows the dirt.*

10 have something/nothing etc. to show for sth if you have something to show for your efforts, hard work etc., you have achieved something as a result of them: *At the end of the year, I had nothing to show for all my work.*

11 MOVIE/TV a) [I] if a movie or television program is showing, it is available on a screen for people to see: *The movie is showing at theaters across the country.* **b)** [T] to make a movie or television program available on a screen for people to see: *The game will be* ***shown live*** *on Channel 5 tonight.* → see also SHOWING

12 ART [T] to put a group of paintings or other works of art in one place so that people can come and see them: *Her recent sculptures are being shown at the Hayward Gallery.* → see also SHOWING

13 EXPERIENCE [T] to change or experience something, especially an increase or decrease: *All categories of sales had shown an increase.* | **show a profit/loss** (=to make a financial profit or loss)

14 it just shows also **it (just) goes to show** SPOKEN said when an event or experience you have been talking about proves something: *It just goes to show how little I know about football.*

15 show sb the door to make it clear that someone is not welcome and should leave a building

16 show sb a good time HUMOROUS to take someone to a lot of social events and other types of entertainment so that they enjoy themselves

17 show your true colors to behave in a way that shows what your real character is, especially if you are dishonest or not nice

18 ANIMAL [T] to put an animal into a competition with other animals

19 show your face to go somewhere, especially when there is a good reason for you not to be there or you are embarrassed about being there: *I don't think he'll show his face around here again.*

20 ARRIVE [I] INFORMAL to arrive at the place where someone is waiting for you SYN **show up**: *I came to meet Hank, but he never showed.*

21 ... and it shows used to say that something, especially something bad, is very clear to see: *This is the director's first feature film,* ***and it shows*** (=it is obviously not very good).

22 show your hand to make your true power or intentions clear, especially after you have been keeping them secret

23 I'll show him/them etc. SPOKEN used to say that you will prove to someone that you are better, more effective etc. than they think you are: *Is that so? Well, I'll show them!*

24 show sb who's boss INFORMAL to prove to someone who is threatening your authority that you are more powerful than they are

25 show the way if you show the way for other people, you do something new that others then try to copy

26 HORSE RACE [I] if a horse shows in a race, it finishes third → see also WIN

[**Origin:** Old English *sceawian* **to look, look at, see**]

show sb ↔ **around** (sth) *phr. v.* to go around a place with someone when they first arrive there, to show them what is interesting, useful etc.: *She'd never been to the city before, so I offered to show her around.* | *Let me show you around the house.*

show off *phr. v.* **1** DISAPPROVING to try to make people notice and admire your abilities, achievements, or possessions: *He was showing off on the tennis court.* → see also SHOW-OFF **2 show sth ↔ off** to show something to a lot of people because you are very proud of it: *Gary was looking for an opportunity to show off his boxing skills.* **3 show sth ↔ off** if one thing shows off something else, it makes the other

S

thing look especially attractive: *The white dress showed off her tan.*

show up *phr. v.* **1** to arrive, especially at the place where someone is waiting for you: *Sue showed up 20 minutes late for class.* **2** to be easy to see or notice: *The white marks really show up against the dark fabric.* | *Her tumor didn't show up on the scan.* **3 show sb ↔ up** to make someone feel stupid or embarrassed in public, especially by doing something better than they can do it: *Robin's not talking to me because I showed her up at racquetball.*

show² S1 W1 *n.*
1 TV/RADIO [C] a program on television or on the radio: *a TV show* | *It's one of the best shows on TV.* → see also GAME SHOW, TALK SHOW ▸see THESAURUS box at **television**
2 PERFORMANCE [C] an entertaining performance, especially one that includes music, dancing, or jokes: *a Broadway show* | *The show starts at 7:30.* | *We're going to* ***see a show*** *this Friday.* | *The kids* ***put on a*** *puppet* ***show*** *in the back yard.* → see also FLOOR SHOW
3 COLLECTION OF THINGS [C] an occasion when a lot of similar things are brought together in one place so that people can come and look at them or they can compete to see which is best: **a flower/dog/cat etc. show** *Dad took us to the boat show at the civic center.* | **hold/stage a show** *The gallery is holding a show of her work next month.* → see also FASHION SHOW
4 a show of sth something that someone does in order to make a particular feeling or quality clear to someone else: **+of** *a show of gratitude* | *Armed police drove through the city in* ***a show of force.*** | *Demonstrators flooded the streets as* ***a show of support*** *for the king.*
5 make a show of (doing) sth also **put on a show of (doing) sth** to do something in a very clear way because you want other people to notice that you are doing it: *The government made a show of moving troops near the border.*
6 for show if something is for show, or is done for show, its main purpose is to look attractive to people: *We don't eat off those plates. They're just for show.*
7 a show of hands a vote taken by counting the raised hands of the people at a meeting, in a class etc.: *Let's see a show of hands. Who wants to go outside?*
8 run the show INFORMAL to be in charge of a situation: *Who's running the show?*
9 let's get this show on the road SPOKEN used to tell people it is time to start working or start a trip
10 on show if something is on show, it is in a place where it can be seen by the public SYN **on display** → see also **steal the show/scene/limelight** at STEAL¹ (4)

ˌshow and ˈtell *n.* [U] an activity for children in which they bring an object to school and tell the other children about it

show·biz /ˈʃoʊbɪz/ *n.* [U] INFORMAL SHOW BUSINESS

show·boat¹ /ˈʃoʊboʊt/ *v.* [I] INFORMAL to do things to try to make people notice and admire you

showboat² *n.* [C] a large river boat, usually with an engine that is run by steam, with a theater on it

ˈshow ˌbusiness *n.* [U] the entertainment industry, for example television, movies, theater etc.

show·case¹ /ˈʃoʊkeɪs/ *n.* [C] **1** an event or situation that is designed to show the good qualities of a person, organization, product etc.: **+for** *The convention is a showcase for new software products.* **2** a glass box containing objects for people to look at in a store, at an art show etc.

showcase² *v.* [T] to show someone or something to the public in a favorable way: *The gallery showcases talented young artists.*

show·down /ˈʃoʊdaʊn/ *n.* [C usually singular] a meeting, argument, fight etc. that will settle a disagreement or competition that has continued for a long time: **+between/with** *a showdown between the top two teams in the league* | **+with** *a showdown with the president over the budget*

show·er¹ /ˈʃaʊə/ S2 *n.* [C]
1 PLACE FOR WASHING a place where you can stand to wash your whole body with water that comes from above you, or the pipe that the water comes through: *She turned off the shower.* | *If anybody calls, tell them I'm* ***in the shower.*** | *a shower curtain*
2 ACT OF WASHING an act of washing your body while standing under a shower: *You'll feel better after a nice hot shower.* | *Steve didn't even have time to* ***take a shower*** *this morning.*
3 RAIN/SNOW a short period of rain or snow: *Tomorrow's forecast calls for a few scattered showers.* | *a snow shower* ▸see THESAURUS box at **rain¹**
4 THINGS IN THE AIR a lot of small light things falling or appearing together: **+of** *a shower of sparks*
5 PARTY a party at which presents are given to a woman who is going to get married or have a baby: *a baby shower* | *Donna's having a* ***bridal shower*** *for Julie next week.*
[**Origin:** Old English *scur*]

shower² *v.* **1** [I] to wash your whole body while standing in a shower **2** to generously give someone a lot of things, or a large amount of something: *Medals were showered on the soldiers returning from battle.* | **shower sb with praise/admiration/honors etc.** *Luke showered her with gifts.* **3** [I always + adv./prep.,T] to scatter a lot of small light things onto a person or place, or to be scattered in this way: **+down/over/upon** *Confetti showered down as the crowd cheered wildly.* | **shower sb/sth with sth** *The volcano erupted, showering the city with ash.*

ˈshower cap *n.* [C] a plastic hat that keeps your hair dry in a shower

ˈshower gel *n.* [U] a type of liquid soap that you use to wash yourself in a shower

ˈshower head *n.* [C] the part of a SHOWER that has many small holes in it for water to come out

show·er·y /ˈʃaʊəri/ *adj.* raining frequently for short periods

show·girl /ˈʃoʊgəl/ *n.* [C] one of a group of women who sing or dance in a musical show, usually wearing clothing decorated in bright colors, feathers etc.

ˈshow house *n.* [C] a house that has been built and filled with furniture to show buyers what similar new houses look like

show·ing /ˈʃoʊɪŋ/ *n.* **1** [C] an occasion when a movie, collection of art works etc. is shown to the public: **+of** *the 7:30 showing of the movie* | *We had* ***a private showing*** *at the museum.* **2** [C usually singular] the level of success or failure someone is achieving in a competition, process etc.: **a good/strong/poor etc. showing** *The party made a poor showing in the last election.*

ˈshow ˌjumping *n.* [U] a sport in which horses with riders have to jump a series of fences as quickly and skillfully as possible

show·man /ˈʃoʊmən/ *n. plural* **showmen** /-mən/ [C] someone who is good at entertaining people and getting a lot of public attention

show·man·ship /ˈʃoʊmənˌʃɪp/ *n.* [U] skill at entertaining people and getting public attention

shown /ʃoʊn/ *v.* the past participle of SHOW

show-off /ˈʃoʊɔf/ *n.* [C] INFORMAL, DISAPPROVING someone who always tries to show how smart or skillful they are so that other people will admire them

show·piece /ˈʃoʊpis/ *n.* [C usually singular] something that is intended to show the public how good, successful etc. someone or something is: *He built the casino as the showpiece of his business empire.*

show·place /ˈʃoʊpleɪs/ *n.* [C] a place that someone wants people to see, because of its beauty, historical interest etc.

show·room /ˈʃoʊrum/ *n.* [C] a large room where you can look at things that are for sale such as cars or electrical goods: *a car showroom*

ˈshow-ˌstopping *adj.* a show-stopping performance or song is extremely good or impressive: *a show-stopping dance number* —**showstopper** *n.* [C]

show·time /ˈʃoʊtaɪm/ *n.* **1** [C,U] the time when a movie or other type of entertainment is supposed to begin **2** [U] INFORMAL the time when an activity is supposed to begin: *Okay, everybody. **It's showtime!***

ˈshow ˌtrial *n.* [C] LAW an unfair legal TRIAL that is organized by a government, especially a Communist one, for political reasons, not in order to find out whether someone is guilty

ˈshow tune *n.* [C] a song that is used in a MUSICAL (=play in a theater with music)

show·y /ˈʃoʊi/ *adj. comparative* **showier**, *superlative* **showiest** very colorful, big, expensive etc., especially in a way that is meant to attract people's attention: *cheap, showy jewelry* —**showily** *adv.* —**showiness** *n.* [U]

shrank /ʃræŋk/ *v.* the past tense of SHRINK

shrap·nel /ˈʃræpnəl/ *n.* [U] small pieces of metal from a bomb, bullet etc. that are scattered when it explodes: *shrapnel wounds* [**Origin:** 1800–1900 Henry *Shrapnel* (1761–1842), British army officer who invented such bombs]

shred¹ /ʃrɛd/ *n.* **1** [C] a small thin piece that is torn or cut roughly from something: +**of** *a shred of paper* | **tear/rip/cut sth to shreds** *The puppy had ripped my shoes to shreds.* | *His shirt was **in shreds**.* **2 a shred of sth** a very small amount of something: *He took away her last shred of dignity.* | **not a shred of proof/evidence/doubt etc.** | *The police didn't have a shred of evidence* (=none at all) *against her.* **3 in shreds** completely ruined: *Our wonderful plans were in shreds.* **4 tear/rip sb/sth to shreds** to criticize someone or something very severely and very thoroughly: *Other researchers tore the theory to shreds.*

shred² *v.* **shredded, shredding** [T] **1** to cut or tear something into small thin pieces: *Shred the cabbage as finely as possible.* ►see THESAURUS box at **cut¹** **2** to put a document into a shredder

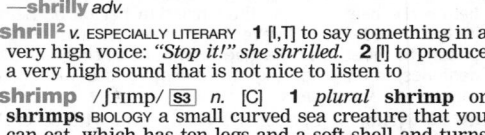

shred

shred·der /ˈʃrɛdɚ/ *n.* [C] a machine that cuts documents into long, narrow pieces so that no one can read them

shrew /ʃru/ *n.* [C] **1** BIOLOGY a very small animal like a mouse with a long pointed nose **2** OLD-FASHIONED a woman who is not nice and always argues and disagrees with people

shrewd /ʃrud/ *adj.* **1** good at judging what people or situations are really like, especially in a way that makes you successful in business, politics etc.: *a shrewd businesswoman* **2** well judged and likely to be right or successful: *shrewd investments* [**Origin:** 1200–1300 *shrew* in the old meaning **very bad man**] —**shrewdly** *adv.*: *He shrewdly decided not to get involved.* —**shrewdness** *n.* [U]

shrew·ish /ˈʃruɪʃ/ *adj.* DISAPPROVING a shrewish woman is one who always argues and disagrees with people

shriek¹ /ʃrik/ *v.* **1** [I] to make a very high loud sound, especially because you are excited, afraid, or angry: *Terrified, the girl shrieked and ran.* | **shriek with joy/pain/fright etc.** *Several people in the audience shrieked with laughter.* ►see THESAURUS box at **shout¹** **2** [I,T] to say something in a high loud voice because you are excited, afraid, or angry: *"No!" she shrieked.* | **shriek (sth) at sb** *The girls shrieked insults at each other.*

shriek² *n.* [C] **1** a loud high sound that you make with your voice because you are frightened, excited, angry etc.: +**of** *a shriek of terror* | *Then he **let out** a piercing **shriek**.* **2** a loud high sound made by an animal or a machine: *the shriek of the police siren*

shrift /ʃrɪft/ *n.* **get/be given short shrift** to not get much attention or sympathy from someone: *Her suggestions were given short shrift by the chairman.*

shrill¹ /ʃrɪl/ *adj.* **1** a shrill sound is very high and not nice to listen to [SYN] **piercing**: *his aunt's shrill voice* | *the shrill whistle of the train* ►see THESAURUS box at **high¹**, **loud¹** **2** shrill words express repeated, often unreasonable complaints or criticism: *the media's shrill criticism of the policy* —**shrillness** *n.* [U] —**shrilly** *adv.*

shrill² *v.* ESPECIALLY LITERARY **1** [I,T] to say something in a very high voice: *"Stop it!" she shrilled.* **2** [I] to produce a very high sound that is not nice to listen to

shrimp /ʃrɪmp/ [S3] *n.* [C] **1** *plural* **shrimp** or **shrimps** BIOLOGY a small curved sea creature that you can eat, which has ten legs and a soft shell and turns pink when it is cooked → see picture at CRUSTACEAN **2** INFORMAL an insulting word for someone who is very small

ˌshrimp ˈcocktail *n.* [C,U] shrimp served with a red SAUCE, eaten before the main part of a meal

shrimp·ing /ˈʃrɪmpɪŋ/ *n.* [U] the activity of fishing for shrimp —**shrimper** *n.* [C]

shrine /ʃraɪn/ *n.* [C] **1** a place that is connected with a religion, a holy event, or holy person, and that people visit to pray: *a Shinto shrine* **2** a place that people visit or respect because it is connected with a famous person or event, or with someone dead who they do not want to forget: *the Lenin shrine in Moscow* **3 a shrine to sb/sth** an area that has been specially decorated to honor a particular person: *Linda transformed a corner of her bedroom into a shrine to Elvis.* [**Origin:** Old English *scrin*, from Latin *scrinium* **case, box**]

Shrin·er /ˈʃraɪnɚ/ *n.* [C] someone who belongs to a secret society, in which members help each other become successful, do good things for others etc.

shrink¹ /ʃrɪŋk/ *v. past tense* **shrank** /ʃræŋk/ or **shrunk** /ʃrʌŋk/, *past participle* **shrunk** **1** [I,T] to become smaller or to make something smaller through the effects of heat or water: *My sweater shrank in the dryer.* → see also PRESHRUNK, SHRUNKEN **2** [I,T] to become smaller in amount, size, or value, or to make something become smaller in this way: *Profits have been shrinking over the last year.* | *This drug can shrink some tumors.* **3** [I always + adv./prep.] to move back and away from something, especially because you are frightened: +**back/away/from** *The children shrank back as she spoke.* [**Origin:** Old English *scrincan*]

shrink from sth *phr. v.* to avoid doing something that is difficult or that you do not want to do: *We do not intend to shrink from our basic responsibilities.* | *Many people tend to shrink from discussing their personal lives.*

shrink² *n.* [C] INFORMAL, HUMOROUS a PSYCHIATRIST

shrink·age /ˈʃrɪŋkɪdʒ/ *n.* [U] the process of shrinking, or the amount that something shrinks: *There's bound to be some shrinkage as the wood dries out.*

ˌshrinking ˈviolet *n.* [C] HUMOROUS someone who is very shy: *Maggie is definitely **no shrinking violet**.*

ˈshrink-wrap *n.* [U] a type of clear plastic that is used for wrapping goods for sale —**shrink-wrapped** *adj.*

shriv·el /ˈʃrɪvəl/ also **shrivel up** *v.* [I,T] **1** if something shrivels or something such as heat or sun shrivels it, it becomes smaller and its surface is covered in lines because it is very dry or old: *My plants have all shriveled up and died.* **2** to gradually become less and less or smaller and smaller, or to make something do this: *Profits have shriveled since the beginning of the year.* —**shriveled** *adj.*: *the old man's shriveled face*

ˈshroom /ʃrum/ *n.* [usually plural] SLANG **1** a MUSHROOM **2** a type of MUSHROOM taken as an illegal drug

shroud¹ /ʃraʊd/ *n.* [C] **1** a cloth that is wrapped around a dead person's body before it is buried **2** something that hides or covers something: **a shroud of mist/smoke/darkness etc.** *The castle stood in a shroud of mist.* **3 a shroud of secrecy/mystery/silence etc.** LITERARY a feeling or quality that surrounds a situation and hides its true nature

shroud² *v.* **1** [T usually passive] to cover or hide something: **be shrouded in mist/smoke etc.** *The ship was shrouded in clouds of steam and gray smoke.* **2 be**

S

shrouded in mystery/secrecy etc. to be mysterious, secret etc.: *The work is shrouded in secrecy.*

Shrove Tues·day /ˌʃroʊv ˈtuzdi/ *n.* [C,U] the day before the beginning of the Christian period of Lent [**Origin:** 1400–1500 Shrove from *shrive* (of a Christian priest) **to hear and forgive someone's sins** (11–21 centuries), from Old English *scrifan*] → see also ASH WEDNESDAY, MARDI GRAS

shrub /ʃrʌb/ *n.* [C] BIOLOGY a small bush with several woody stems [**Origin:** Old English *scrybb*]

shrub·ber·y /ˈʃrʌbəri/ *n. plural* **shubberies** [C,U] a group of shrubs planted close together

shrug[1] /ʃrʌg/ *v.* **shrugged**, **shrugging** [I,T] to raise and then lower your shoulders in order to show that you do not know something or do not care about something: *He* ***shrugged*** *his* ***shoulders*** *and went back to his work.*

shrug sth ↔ **off** *phr. v.* **1** to treat something as unimportant and not worry about it: *She tried to shrug off his remarks.* **2** to succeed in getting rid of something such as a cold, a sore throat, or a problem that is having a bad effect on you or your work

shrug[2] *n.* [C usually singular] **1** a movement of your shoulders up and then down again **2** a short JACKET or SWEATER worn by women that covers the shoulders, arms, and chest

S

shrunk /ʃrʌŋk/ *v.* the past tense and past participle of SHRINK

shrunk·en /ˈʃrʌŋkən/ *adj.* having become smaller or been made smaller: *an old shrunken woman*

shtetl /ˈʃtɛtl̩, ˈʃteɪtl̩/ *n.* [C] a small Jewish town or area of a city in Eastern Europe in the past

shtick, **schtick** /ʃtɪk/ *n.* [U] a typical quality or feature that someone, especially a COMEDIAN or other entertainer, is known for

shuck /ʃʌk/ *v.* [T] **1** also **shuck off** to take off a piece of clothing: *He shucked off his wet coat and hat in the hallway.* **2** to remove the outer cover of a vegetable such as corn, or the shell of OYSTERS **3** also **shuck off** to get rid of something that you do not want anymore

shucks /ʃʌks/ *interjection* INFORMAL used to show you are a little disappointed about something → see also AW SHUCKS[2]

shud·der[1] /ˈʃʌdɚ/ *v.* [I] **1** to shake for a short time because you are afraid or cold, or because you think something is disgusting: *Dave tried to kiss Julia but she shuddered and turned away.* **2** if a vehicle or machine shudders, it shakes violently: *The car shuddered briefly as its engine died.* **3 I shudder to think** used to say that you do not want to think about something because it is too bad or disgusting: *I shudder to think what will happen to him now.*

shudder at sth *phr. v.* to think that something is very bad or disgusting: *He shuddered at the thought of meeting them again.*

shudder[2] *n.* [C usually singular] **1** a quick shaking movement: *"Do you think he'll come back?" she asked with a shudder.* | *The building* ***gave*** *a sudden* ***shudder****.* **2 send a shudder through sb/sth** to cause someone or an organization to be afraid: *The news sent a shudder through the business community.*

shuf·fle[1] /ˈʃʌfəl/ *v.* **1** [I always + adv./prep.] to walk without lifting your feet off the ground, often in a slow and awkward way: +**along/toward/down etc.** *She shuffled across the floor to answer the telephone.* **2** [I,T] to move something such as papers into a different order or into different positions: *She shuffled the papers on her desk.* | +**through** *Mr. Murphy shuffled through some files in the drawer.* **3** [T] to move people around into different positions or jobs, usually within the same organization or department: **shuffle sb around** *Bryant has shuffled the team's starting players around several times.* **4** [I,T] to mix PLAYING CARDS around into a different order before playing a game with them: *Is it my turn to shuffle?* **5 shuffle your feet** to move your feet slightly, especially because you are bored or embarrassed: *Monica shuffled her feet nervously and stared at the floor.* —**shuffler** *n.* [C] → see also RESHUFFLE[1]

shuffle[2] *n.* **1** [singular] a slow walk in which you do not lift your feet off the ground **2** [C usually singular] an act of moving things or people around to different positions: *a shuffle of top management* **3** [C] the act of mixing cards into a different order before playing a game **4 be/get lost in the shuffle** to not be noticed or considered because there are so many other things to deal with

shuf·fle·board /ˈʃʌfəlˌbɔrd/ *n.* [U] a game played especially by passengers on ships, in which you use a long stick to push a flat round object toward an area with numbers on it

shui /ʃweɪ/ → see FENG SHUI

shun /ʃʌn/ *v.* **shunned**, **shunning** [T] to avoid someone or something deliberately: *Wilson is a quiet man who shuns publicity.* | *Victims of the disease were shunned by society.*

shunt[1] /ʃʌnt/ *v.* [T] **1** [usually + adv./prep.] to move someone or something to another place, especially in a way that seems unfair: **shunt sb aside/off/around etc.** *Employees were shunted from one department to another.* **2** TECHNICAL to make something such as blood flow between two parts of the body, especially by making a special passage in a medical operation **3** TECHNICAL to make electricity flow through a different path **4** TECHNICAL to move a train or railroad car onto a different track

shunt[2] *n.* [C] TECHNICAL **1** a small passage that a doctor puts between two parts of someone's body to let something such as blood flow between them SYN **bypass** **2** a connection that allows electricity to flow through a different path **3** an action of moving a train or railroad car to a different track

shush[1] /ʃʌʃ, ʃʊʃ/ *v.* [T] to tell someone to be very quiet, especially by putting your fingers against your lips or by saying "shush": *He stood up and shushed the class.*

shush[2] *interjection* used to tell someone, especially a child, to be quiet

shut[1] /ʃʌt/ S1 W2 *v.* **shut**, **shutting**

1 CLOSE [I,T] to close something, or to become closed SYN **close** OPP **open**: *Can you shut the window?* | *The door shut behind him as he left.* | *She lay down on the bed and shut her eyes.*

2 BOOK/MAGAZINE ETC. [T] to put together the covers of a book, magazine etc. so that it is closed SYN **close** OPP **open**: *He shut his book and leaned back in the chair.*

3 shut your mouth/trap/face! SPOKEN used to tell someone in a rude and angry way to stop talking

4 shut your eyes/ears to sth FORMAL to deliberately refuse to notice or pay attention to something: *You can't just shut your eyes to the situation.*

5 shut your ears (to sth) to deliberately not listen to something

[**Origin:** Old English *scyttan*]

shut sb/sth ↔ **away** *phr. v.* **a)** to put someone or something in a place away from other people where they cannot be seen: *In the past, disabled people were often shut away.* **b) shut yourself away** to stay home or go somewhere quiet, so that you can be alone: *She shut herself away in her room to work on her novel.*

shut down *phr. v.* **1 shut sth ↔ down** if a company, factory etc. shuts down or is shut down, it stops operating either permanently or temporarily: *Protesters hope to shut the nuclear plant down.* → see also SHUTDOWN **2 shut sth ↔ down** if a large machine, computer, or other piece of equipment shuts down, or if someone shuts it down, it stops working or is turned off: *The machine automatically shuts down if it is not used for 20 minutes.* → see also SHUTDOWN **3 shut sb ↔ down** to prevent an opposing sports team or player from playing well or getting points

shut sth **in** sth *phr. v.* **1** to shut a door, drawer etc. against something so that it gets trapped there: *Ouch! I shut my finger in the door.* **2 shut the door in sb's face** to close a door when someone is standing on the other side because you do not want to see them or talk to them

shut off *phr. v.* **1 shut sth ↔ off** if a machine, tool etc. shuts off, or if you shut it off, it stops operating: *The iron shuts off automatically if it gets too hot.* | *Do you know how to shut the alarm off?* **2 shut sth ↔ off** to stop goods or supplies from being available or being delivered: *Crews had to shut off gas service for four hours.* → see also SHUTOFF **3 shut yourself off** to avoid meeting and talking to other people: **+from** *After his wife's death, Pete shut himself off from the rest of his family.* **4 be shut off from sth** to be separated from other people or things, especially so that you are not influenced by them: *The valley is completely shut off from the modern world.*

shut out *phr. v.* **1 shut sb ↔ out** to deliberately not let someone join in an activity or share your thoughts and feelings: *Don't just shut me out. I want to help.* | *Many of the working poor are* ***being shut out of*** *the healthcare system.* **2 shut sb/sth ↔ out** to prevent someone or something from entering a place: *Heavy curtains shut out the sunlight.* **3 shut sth ↔ out** to stop yourself from thinking about or noticing something, so that you are not affected by it: *She could not shut out the noise of the lawnmower.* **4 shut sb ↔ out** to defeat an opposing sports team and prevent them from getting any points: *Colorado shut out Kansas City 3–0.* → see also SHUTOUT

shut up *phr. v.* **1 shut up!** SPOKEN **a)** used to tell someone rudely to stop talking: *Just shut up and listen!* **b)** used to show that you are surprised, shocked, or excited by what someone has just said **2** INFORMAL **shut sb up** to stop talking or be quiet, or to make someone do this: **+about** *I wish Ted would shut up about that stupid bike.* | *Maybe this will shut her up.* **3 shut sb ↔ up** to keep someone in a place away from other people, and prevent them from leaving: **be shut up in sth** *All the stores were closed and citizens were shut up in their houses.*

shut² *adj.* [not before noun; no comparative] not open SYN **closed** OPP **open**: *One of his eyes was swollen shut.* | *Make sure you* ***keep*** *the doors and windows* ***shut***. | **slam/bang/swing etc. shut** *She heard the cell door clang shut.* | **pull/kick/slide/slam etc. sth shut** *Dave got in the car and pulled the door shut.* → see also **keep your mouth shut** at MOUTH¹ (2)

shut·down /ˈʃʌtˀdaʊn/ *n.* [C] **1** the act of stopping a factory, business etc. from operating SYN **closure**: *a shutdown of the factory* **2** an occasion when a large machine, computer, or other piece of equipment stops operating → see also **shut down** at SHUT¹

ˈshut-eye *n.* [U] INFORMAL sleep: **get/catch some shut-eye** *Let's try and get some shut-eye tonight.*

ˈshut-in *n.* [C] someone who is sick or DISABLED and cannot leave their house very easily

shut·off /ˈʃʌt̬ɔf/ *n.* **1** [C,U] the act of stopping the supply of something such as gas or water **2** [C] something that can stop the supply of something such as gas or water: *an automatic safety shutoff* → see also **shut off** at SHUT¹

shut·out /ˈʃʌt̬aʊt/ *n.* [C] a sports game in which one team prevents the other from getting any points → see also **shut out** at SHUT¹

shut·ter¹ /ˈʃʌt̬ɚ/ *n.* [C] **1** [usually plural] one of a pair of wooden or metal covers fastened to the sides of a window on the outside of a house, used either to protect the window or for decoration **2** ENG. LANG. ARTS a part of a camera that opens for a very short time to let light onto the film

shutters

shutter² *v.* [T usually passive] to close a business, office etc. permanently or temporarily

shut·ter·bug /ˈʃʌt̬ɚˌbʌg/ *n.* [C] INFORMAL someone who likes to take a lot of photographs

shut·tered /ˈʃʌt̬ɚd/ *adj.* **1** with closed shutters **2** a shuttered business or store is closed, either permanently or temporarily

shut·tle¹ /ˈʃʌt̬l/ *n.* [C] **1** a SPACE SHUTTLE **2** an airplane, bus, or train that makes regular short trips between two places: *If I take the 6:30 shuttle, I'll be there in time for the meeting.* **3** a pointed tool used in weaving, to pass a thread over and under the threads that form the cloth

shuttle² *v.* **1** [I always + adv./prep.] to travel frequently between two places: **+between** *Susan shuttles between New York and Washington for her job.* **2** [T] to move people from one place to another place that is fairly near: *Passengers were shuttled to downtown hotels by bus.*

shut·tle·cock /ˈʃʌt̬lˌkɑk/ *n.* [C] a BIRDIE

ˈshuttle diˌplomacy *n.* [U] international talks in which someone travels between countries and talks to members of the governments, for example to make a peace agreement

shy¹ /ʃaɪ/ *adj. comparative* **shier** or **shyer**, *superlative* **shiest** or **shyest** **1** nervous and embarrassed about talking to other people, especially people you do not know: *Carl is a very quiet shy boy.* | *a shy smile* | *She was too shy to talk to anyone.* | *He was* ***painfully shy*** (=extremely shy) *as a teenager.*

S

THESAURUS

timid not brave or confident: *She's a good player, but timid on the court.*
bashful shy and not willing to say very much: *Rachel blushed and gave me a bashful smile.*
reserved not liking to express your emotions or talk about your problems: *a quiet reserved man*
introverted thinking a lot about your own interests, problems etc., and not liking to be with other people: *an introverted teenager*
withdrawn quiet, and not wanting to talk to other people: *After the accident, he became anxious and withdrawn.*
antisocial not liking to meet people and talk to them: *My family was fairly antisocial and we seldom had visitors.*
retiring FORMAL not wanting to be with other people: *a shy and retiring woman*
self-conscious worried and embarrassed about what you look like or what other people think of you: *A group of self-conscious teenage boys watched the girls.*
→ INSECURE, SOCIABLE

2 shy about (doing) sth [usually in negatives] unwilling to do something or get involved in something: *Don't be shy about asking questions.* | *John has strong opinions, and he's* ***not shy about*** (=he's very willing to do it) *sharing them.* **3 be shy (of sth)** to have or be slightly less than a particular amount of something: *The Democrats are three votes shy of a majority.* | *The singer was just shy of 24.* [**Origin:** Old English *sceoh*] —**shyly** *adv.*: *She smiled shyly and started to blush.* —**shyness** *n.* [U] → see also **once bitten twice shy** at BITE¹ (16), CAMERA-SHY, GUN-SHY

shy² *v.* **shies, shied, shying**

shy at sth *phr. v.* if a horse shies at something, it makes a sudden movement away from it because it is frightened

shy (away) from sb/sth *phr. v.* also **shy away** **1** to avoid doing or dealing with something because you are not confident enough or you are worried or nervous about it: *The board members tend to shy away from controversial topics.* **2** to move away from someone or avoid them because you are nervous or frightened

shy·ster /ˈʃaɪstɚ/ *n.* [C] INFORMAL a dishonest person, especially a lawyer or BUSINESSMAN

Si·a·mese cat /ˌsaɪəmiz ˈkæt/ *n.* [C] a type of cat

that has blue eyes, short gray or brown fur, and a dark face and feet

Siamese twin /ˌsaɪəmiz ˈtwɪn/ *n.* [C usually plural] one of two people who are born joined to each other SYN **conjoined twin** [**Origin:** 1800–1900 From such a pair (Chang and Eng) who were born in Siam (now Thailand)]

Si·be·ri·a /saɪˈbɪriə/ a very large area in Russia, between the Ural Mountains and the Pacific Ocean

sib·i·lant¹ /ˈsɪbələnt/ *adj.* FORMAL ENG. LANG. ARTS making or being a sound such as "s" or "sh"

sibilant² *n.* [C] ENG. LANG. ARTS a sibilant sound such as "s" or "sh" in English

sib·ling /ˈsɪblɪŋ/ *n.* [C] FORMAL a brother or sister [**Origin:** Old English *sibb* **related**]

ˌsibling ˈrivalry *n.* [U] competition between brothers and sisters for their parents' attention or love

sib·yl /ˈsɪbəl/ *n.* [C] one of a group of women in ancient Greece and Rome who were thought to know the future

sic¹ /sɪk/ *adv.* FORMAL ENG. LANG. ARTS used in PARENTHESES or BRACKETS after a word in writing that you have copied from another document in order to show that you know the word was not spelled or used correctly: *Jenna's letter began "Dear Santa Clouse [sic],..."*

S

sic² *v.* **sicced, siccing** [T] **sic 'em!** SPOKEN used to tell a dog to attack someone

sic on *phr. v.* **1 sic sth on sb** to tell a dog to attack someone **2 sic sb on sb** to tell someone in authority that someone has done something wrong, so that they are punished

Si·ci·ly /ˈsɪsəli/ an island in the Mediterranean Sea, which is part of Italy and is close to Italy's most southern point —**Sicilian** /səˈsɪliən/ *n., adj.*

sick¹ /sɪk/ S1 W2 *adj.*

1 NOT HEALTHY suffering from a disease or illness → see also ILL: *a sick child* | *His mother's very sick.* | **+with** *She's been sick with the flu.* | *Dan **got** really **sick** when we were on vacation.* | *Three employees were **out sick*** (=not at work because they were sick) *yesterday.* | *Leslie **called in sick*** (=telephoned to say she would not come to work because she was sick) *today.* | *Ron was **sick as a dog*** (=very sick) *all week.*

THESAURUS

feel sick to feel sick in your stomach and as if you might vomit
not feel good/well to feel sick: *Mommy, I don't feel good.*
ill sick: *She became ill on the first day at sea.*
not very well: *You don't look very well* (=you look sick).
under the weather SPOKEN slightly sick: *I've been a little under the weather lately.*

2 NOT FEELING WELL having an unpleasant feeling in your stomach, especially as if you might VOMIT: *I **felt sick** after I ate all that candy.* | *She got **sick to** her **stomach** and went to lie down.* | *The smell of rotting garbage **made him sick**.*
3 be sick to bring food up from your stomach through your mouth SYN **vomit**: *I think I'm going to be sick.* → see also THROW UP
4 be sick (and tired) of sth also **be sick to death of sth** to be angry and bored with something that has been happening for a long time: *I am sick and tired of her excuses.* | *They must be sick of living in that little apartment.*
5 make me/you sick SPOKEN **a)** to make you feel very angry: *It's enough to make you sick, the way they treat old people.* **b)** SPOKEN, HUMOROUS used humorously to say that you are JEALOUS of someone: *He's so cute it makes me sick.*
6 be worried sick also **be sick with worry** to be extremely worried: *Why didn't you call? We've been worried sick!*
7 STRANGE/CRUEL a) someone who is sick does things that are strange and cruel, and seems mentally ill: *One of his neighbors described him as "a very sick man."* | *This letter must be the product of **a sick mind**.* | *Whoever did this must be **sick in the head**.* **b)** sick stories, jokes etc. deal with death and suffering in a cruel or disgusting way: *Is this somebody's idea of a sick joke?*
8 sick at heart very unhappy, upset, or disappointed about something: *All the cruelty and injustice made her sick at heart.*
9 SLANG very good
[**Origin:** Old English *seoc*] → see also CARSICK, HOMESICK, SEASICK, **take ill/sick** at TAKE¹ (46)

sick² *n.* **the sick** [plural] people who are sick: *She devoted herself to the care of the sick and poor.*

sick·bay /ˈsɪkbeɪ/ *n.* [C] a room on a ship, at a military BASE etc. where there are beds for people who are sick

sick·bed /ˈsɪkbɛd/ *n.* [C usually singular] the bed where a sick person is lying: *He responded in a message **from his sickbed**.*

ˌsick ˈbuilding ˌsyndrome *n.* [U] a condition in which chemicals and GERMS stay in the air in an office building and make the people who work there sick

ˈsick day *n.* [C] a day that you are allowed to spend away from work because you are sick: *I haven't **taken** any **sick days** this year.*

sick·en /ˈsɪkən/ *v.* **1** [T] to make you feel shocked and angry, especially because you strongly disapprove of something: *The thought of such cruelty sickened her.* **2** [I,T] to become very sick, or to make someone sick: *A gas attack in the main train station sickened hundreds of people.* | *The buffalo **sickened and died** in captivity.*

sicken of sth *phr. v.* FORMAL to lose your desire for something or your interest in it: *She soon sickened of City Hall politics and moved on.*

sick·en·ing /ˈsɪkənɪŋ/ *adj.* **1** very shocking, annoying, or upsetting SYN **disgusting**: *the sickening attitude of those in power* | ***It's sickening** the way they treat their animals.* **2** disgusting, and making you feel as if you want to VOMIT SYN **nauseating**: *the sickening smell of rotting meat* **3 a sickening thud/crash etc.** a sound that is not nice to listen to, and that makes you think someone has been injured or something has been broken **4** SPOKEN making you feel JEALOUS or annoyed: *She's so beautiful **it's sickening**.* —**sickeningly** *adv.*

sick·ie /ˈsɪki/ *n.* [C] INFORMAL, HUMOROUS A SICKO

sick·le /ˈsɪkəl/ *n.* [C] a tool with a blade in the shape of a hook, used for cutting wheat or long grass

ˈsick leave *n.* [U] time that you are allowed to spend away from work because you are sick

ˌsickle cell aˈnemia *n.* [U] MEDICINE a serious illness that mainly affects people whose families originally came from Africa, in which the blood cells change shape, causing weakness and fever

sick·ly /ˈsɪkli/ *adj.* **1** weak, unhealthy, and often sick: *a pale sickly child* **2** a sickly smell, taste etc. is disgusting and makes you feel sick —**sickly** *adv.*: *the sickly sweet smell of cheap perfume*

sick·ness /ˈsɪknɪs/ *n.* **1** [U] the state of being sick: *absence from work due to sickness* ►see THESAURUS box at **illness** **2 motion/car/air sickness** a feeling that some people get while traveling, that they are about to VOMIT → see also ALTITUDE SICKNESS, MORNING SICKNESS, SLEEPING SICKNESS **3** [C] a particular illness SYN **illness** SYN **disease**: *Alcoholism is a sickness.* **4** [C,U] the serious problems and weaknesses of a social, political, or economic system: *the sickness in our Western culture*

sick·o /ˈsɪkoʊ/ *n.* [C] INFORMAL someone who gets pleasure from things that most people find disgusting or upsetting: *What kind of sicko would write something like that?*

sick·out /ˈsɪkaʊt/ *n.* [C] an organized protest by workers at a company who say they are sick and stay home on the same day

ˈsick pay *n.* [U] money paid by an employer to a worker who cannot work because of illness

sick·room /ˈsɪk-rum/ *n.* [C] a room where someone who is very sick lies in bed

Sid·dhar·tha /sɪˈdɑrθə, -tə/ the original name of the Buddha

side[1] /saɪd/ S1 W1 *n.* [C]
1 PART OF AN AREA one of the two areas that are on the left or the right of an imaginary line, or on the left or the right of a border, wall, river etc.: *This side of town is pretty run down.* | **+of** *my side of the bed* | *The hat had a flower* ***on one side***. | *Cars pulled over* ***to one side*** *to let the ambulance past.* | **either side/both sides** *The mountains rose on either side of the valley.* | **the far/other/opposite side** (=the area farthest from you or across from you) *He pointed to a girl* ***on the*** *other* ***side*** *of the room.* | **north/west/south etc. side** *the south side of the river* | **left/right side** *The stroke affected the right side of her body.* | **the right-hand/left-hand side** *Assets are listed* ***on the*** *left-hand* ***side*** *of the chart.*
2 NEXT TO [usually singular] the place or area directly next to someone or something, on the right or the left: **left/right side** *a chair* ***to the*** *left* ***side*** *of the desk* | **+of** *Stand* ***on this side*** *of me so Dad can take a picture.* | *Her husband stood* ***at her side***. | *Two large screens stood* ***on either side*** (=one on the left side and one on the right side) *of the stage.*
3 side by side a) next to each other: *They lay side by side on the couch.* **b)** if people live, work etc. side by side, they do it together, have a good relationship, and help each other: *Doctors and scientists are working side by side to find a cure.* **c)** if two things exist side by side, they exist at the same time, even though this may seem difficult or impossible: *In Egypt, fundamentalism and feminism have long existed side by side.*
4 OUTER SURFACE a) an outer surface of something that is not its front, back, top, or bottom: **+of** *the door at the side of the building* | *Toni ran her finger down the side of her glass.* | *a dent in the side of the car* **b)** one of the flat surfaces or edges of a shape: *A cube has six sides.*
5 EDGE the part of an object or area that is farthest from the middle, at or near the edge SYN **edge**: *Jack sat down on the side of the bed.* | *She stopped at the side of the road.*
6 INNER SURFACE one of the usually flat surfaces on the inside of a hollow object or area: **+of** *Scrape the batter from the sides of the bowl.*
7 OF A THIN OBJECT one of the two surfaces of a thin flat object: **+of** *You can write on both sides of the paper.* | *The record has a scratch on one side.*
8 from side to side moving continuously, first in one direction then in the other: *The boat swayed from side to side as waves hit it.*
9 SUBJECT/SITUATION one part or feature of a subject, problem, or situation, especially when compared with another part: ***Look on the bright side*** (=think about the positive parts), *Tim. At least you learned something.* | **technical/financial/social etc. side** *Who's in charge of the creative side of the project?* | **serious/funny etc. side** *She wrote about the lighter side of family life.* | **on the plus/minus/positive/negative side** *On the positive side, the program has helped farmers.* | *It's a children's book about fairies, but it does have a* ***dark side*** (=serious or frightening feature).
10 OPINION/ATTITUDE one person's opinion or attitude in an argument or disagreement SYN **point of view**: *Well, I can* ***see*** *both* ***sides***. *They both have a point.* | *Tell me your* ***side of the story***.
11 ARGUMENT/WAR ETC. one of the people, groups, or countries opposing each other in an argument, war etc.: *a peace deal that is acceptable to both sides* | *the Union side during the Civil War* | *At least we're* ***on*** *the winning* ***side***. | *You're on my side, aren't you, Pat?* | *Hey,* ***whose side are you on, anyway*** (=why are you supporting the other side)*?*
12 take sides to choose to support a particular person or opinion: *Parents should try to avoid taking sides in sibling arguments.*
13 MOUNTAIN/VALLEY one of the sloping areas of a hill, mountain etc.: **+of** *A trail wound up the side of the mountain.* | **hillside/mountainside** *sheep grazing on the hillside*
14 on/from all sides also **on/from every side a)** in or from every direction: *The farm is surrounded on all sides by wheat fields.* | *Troops opened fire from all sides.* **b)** by or from a lot of people with different opinions: *Panel members expect criticism from all sides.*
15 PART OF SB'S CHARACTER [usually singular] one part of someone's character, especially when compared with another part: *It was a side of Shari I hadn't seen before.* | **sb's emotional/romantic/funny etc. side** *Todd seldom lets people see his softer side.*
16 PART OF YOUR BODY BIOLOGY the left or right part of your body from under your arm to the top of your leg: *We need to roll her onto her left side.* | *She was lying on her side on the bed.*
17 FAMILY the parents, grandparents etc. of your mother or your father: *Ken is Scottish* ***on*** *his mother's* ***side***. | *My mother's* ***side of the family*** *is from Canada.*
18 sb's side of a deal/bargain what someone agrees to do as part of an agreement: *Will he* ***keep*** *his* ***side of*** *the deal?*
19 on the high/heavy/small etc. side a little too high, too heavy etc.: *Alice is a little on the quiet side, but she's a good worker.*
20 on the side a) in addition to your regular job: *They run a catering business on the side.* → see also SIDELINE[1] **b)** food that is served on the side in a restaurant is served next to the main food on a plate, and you usually have a choice about what it will be: *steak with a baked potato on the side*
21 FOOD a small amount of food that you order in a restaurant in addition to your main meal: **+of** *a hamburger with a side of fries*
22 have sth on your side also **sth is on your side** to have an advantage that increases your chances of success: *Time is on our side – sooner or later, they'll do something stupid.*
23 be at sb's side/stay by sb's side/not leave sb's side to be with someone, and take care of them or support them: *She stayed by his side all through the trial.*
24 get on sb's good/bad side also **get on the right/wrong side of sb** SPOKEN to make someone very pleased with you or very angry with you: *I don't know what I did to get on her bad side.*
25 take/draw sb to one side to take someone away from other people for a short time for a private talk: *"Can I talk to you for a minute?" Rachel said as she took me to one side.*
26 a side of beef/pork one half of an animal's body, cut along the BACKBONE, to be used for food
27 put/set sth to one side to save something to be dealt with or used later: *He set the letter to one side for Kate to read.*
28 on the right/wrong side of 30, 40 etc. SPOKEN HUMOROUS younger or older than 30, 40 etc.
29 on the wrong/right side of the law INFORMAL breaking or not breaking the law: *De Niro plays a lawyer, on the right side of the law.*
30 the best/biggest etc. sth this side of sth/sb HUMOROUS used to say that something is very good, big etc.: *They serve the best baked beans this side of Boston.*
31 criticize/nag/hassle etc. sb up one side and down the other to criticize someone, treat them in an unkind way etc. a lot, without worrying about how they feel
32 the other side of the coin a different or opposite way of thinking about something: *The food wasn't exceptional, but the other side of the coin is that lunches are reasonably priced.*
33 two sides of the same coin two problems or situations that are so closely connected that they are really just two parts of the same thing: *Kohl later said that German unity and European integration were "two sides of the same coin."*
[**Origin:** Old English] → see also **get up on the wrong side of the bed** at BED[1] (8), **err on the side of caution/mercy etc.** at ERR (1), FLIP SIDE, **right side up** at RIGHT[1] (11), **be on the safe side** at SAFE[1] (9), -SIDED, **split your sides** at SPLIT[1] (11)

side[2] S3 *adj.* [only before noun] **1** in or on the side of something: *Josie slipped out through a side exit.* **2 a**

side view a view of something as it looks from the side: *The next slide shows a side view of the building.*

side³ *v.*

side against sb *phr. v.* to argue against a person or group in an argument, fight etc.

side with sb *phr. v.* to support a person or group in an argument, fight etc.: *Liz tends to side with her Dad in difficult family decisions.*

side·arm¹ /ˈsaɪdɑrm/ *n.* [C often plural] a weapon carried or worn at someone's side, for example a gun or sword

sidearm² *adj., adv.* a sidearm throw in a sport is one in which you throw the ball with a sideways movement of your arm

side·bar /ˈsaɪdbɑr/ *n.* [C] **1** a separate part of something such as a newspaper article, where additional information is given **2** LAW an occasion when the lawyers and the judge in a TRIAL discuss something without letting the JURY hear

ˈside ˌbenefit *n.* [C] an additional advantage or good result that comes from something, besides its main purpose: *A side benefit to lowering speed limits was a reduction in pollution caused by cars.*

S

side·board /ˈsaɪdbɔrd/ *n.* [C] a long low piece of furniture usually in a DINING ROOM, used for storing plates, glasses etc.

side·burns /ˈsaɪdbɚnz/ *n.* [plural] hair that grows down the sides of a man's face in front of his ears [**Origin:** 1800–1900 *burnsides* type of beard in which the chin is shaved, from Ambrose *Burnside* (1824-81), U.S. general who wore such a beard]

side·car /ˈsaɪdkɑr/ *n.* [C] a small seat on wheels that can be attached to the side of a MOTORCYCLE for an additional passenger

-sided /saɪdɪd/ [in adjectives] **six-sided/hard-sided etc.** having the number or type of sides mentioned: *a one-sided view of the issue* | *soft-sided luggage*

ˈside dish *n.* [C] a small amount of food such as a vegetable that you eat with a main meal

ˈside efˌfect *n.* [C] **1** MEDICINE an effect that a drug has on your body, in addition to curing pain or illness: *Drowsiness is one possible side effect.* | **serious/harmful/adverse etc. side effect** *The most serious side effect is an increase in the risk of blood clots.* **2** an unexpected result of a situation or event: *A side effect of tuna fishing is the death of dolphins.*

ˈside ˌissue *n.* [C] a subject or problem that is not as important as the main one, and may take people's attention away from the main subject: *The environment should not be a side issue in this election.*

side·kick /ˈsaɪdˌkɪk/ *n.* [C] someone who spends time with or helps another more important person, especially on a television show or in a movie

side·line¹ /ˈsaɪdlaɪn/ *n.* **1 the sidelines** [plural] **a)** the area just outside the lines that form the edge of a sports field: *Tom stood **on the sidelines**, cheering his teammates.* **b)** the state of not taking part in an activity even though you want to or should do it: *Trading was light yesterday as small investors remained **on the sidelines**.* **2** [C] a line at the side of a sports field, which shows where the players are allowed to play **3** [C] an activity that you do in addition to your main job or business in order to earn more money: *He raised chickens **as a sideline**.*

sideline² *v.* [T usually passive] if someone is sidelined, they are unable to play in a sports game because they are injured, or unable to take part in an activity because they are not as good as someone else: *Horn will be sidelined for three weeks by a sprained ankle.*

side·long /ˈsaɪdlɔŋ/ *adj.* **a sidelong glance/look** a way of looking at someone by moving your eyes to the side, especially so that it seems secret, dishonest, or disapproving: *Fred kept sneaking sidelong glances at Lynn.* —**sidelong** *adv.*

ˈside ˌorder *n.* [C] a small amount of food ordered in a restaurant to be eaten with a main meal, but served on a separate dish: *a side order of onion rings*

si·de·re·al /saɪˈdɪriəl/ *adj.* TECHNICAL relating to or calculated using the stars: *the sidereal day*

ˈside road *n.* [C] SIDE STREET

side·sad·dle /ˈsaɪdˌsædl/ *adv.* **ride/sit sidesaddle** to ride or sit on a horse with both of your legs on the same side of the horse

side·show /ˈsaɪdʃoʊ/ *n.* [C] **1** a separate small part of a CARNIVAL or CIRCUS, where you pay to see something, such as people with strange physical appearances **2** an event that is much less important or serious than another one: *Advertising at the Olympics should be a sideshow, not the main event.*

side·split·ting /ˈsaɪdˌsplɪtɪŋ/ *adj.* extremely funny: *a sidesplitting imitation of the president*

side·step /ˈsaɪdstɛp/ *v.* **sidestepped, sidestepping** **1 sidestep a problem/question/rule etc.** to avoid doing or talking about something that is difficult SYN **avoid**: *The board sidestepped the issue of discrimination.* **2** [I] to step quickly sideways to avoid being hit or walking into someone —**sidestep** *n.* [C]

ˈside street also **ˈside road** *n.* [C] a street, road etc. that is smaller than a main street but is often connected to it

side·swipe /ˈsaɪdswaɪp/ *v.* [T] to hit the side of a car while passing in another car so that the two sides touch quickly: *The bus sideswiped several parked cars.*

side·track /ˈsaɪdtræk/ *v.* [T] **1** to make someone stop doing what they should be doing, or stop talking about what they started talking about, by making them interested in something else: *Don't let yourself **get sidetracked** by the audience's questions.* **2** to delay or stop the progress of something: *An effort to improve security was sidetracked by budget problems.*

ˌside-view ˈmirror *n.* [C] a mirror attached to the side of a car → see picture on page A36

side·walk /ˈsaɪdwɔk/ S3 *n.* [C] a raised hard surface along the side of a street for people to walk on

ˈsidewalk caˌfé *n.* [C] a type of restaurant with tables and chairs outdoors on the sidewalk

side·wall /ˈsaɪdwɔl/ *n.* [C] **1** the surface on the side of a car tire, that does not touch the road **2** a wall that forms the side of a room or building

side·ways /ˈsaɪdweɪz/ *adv.* **1** to or toward one side: *The car slid sideways into the barrier.* **2** with the side, rather than the front or back, facing forward: *I had to turn sideways to get in.* —**sideways** *adj.*: *Mike gave him a sideways glance.*

side-wheel·er /ˈsaɪdˌwilɚ/ *n.* [C] an old-fashioned type of ship which is pushed forward by a pair of large wheels at the sides

side·wind·er /ˈsaɪdˌwaɪndɚ/ *n.* [C] BIOLOGY a type of snake that lives in dry areas of Mexico and the southwestern U.S., and that moves along the ground in a sideways movement

sid·ing /ˈsaɪdɪŋ/ *n.* **1** [U] long narrow pieces of wood, metal, or plastic, used for covering the outside walls of houses **2** [C] a short railroad track connected to a main track, where trains are kept when they are not being used

si·dle /ˈsaɪdl/ *v.* [I always + adv./prep.] to walk toward something or someone slowly and quietly, as if you do not want to be noticed: **+up/toward/along** *Mr. Tang sidled into the room.*

SIDS /sɪdz/ *n.* [U] SUDDEN INFANT DEATH SYNDROME

siè·cle /siˈɛklə/ → see FIN DE SIÈCLE

siege /sidʒ/ *n.* [C,U] **1** a situation in which an army or the police surround a place and try to gain control of it by stopping supplies of food, weapons etc. from reaching it: **+of** *the 900-day-long Nazi siege of Leningrad* | *Security forces have **laid siege to*** (=started a siege in) *two areas of the city.* **2** a situation in which someone or a group of people enters a place and holds the people inside as prisoners **3 be under siege a)** to be surrounded by an army or the police in a siege: *The fort was under siege.* **b)** to be criticized or attacked by a lot of questions, problems, threats etc. over a period of time: *The President was under siege from war protesters.* **4 siege mentality** the feeling among a group of people that they are surrounded by enemies and must do everything they can to protect themselves [**Origin:** 1100–1200 Old French *sege* **seat, siege**, from Latin *sedere* **to sit**] → see also BESIEGE

si·en·na /si'ɛnə/ *n.* [U] a yellowish-brown color

si·er·ra /si'ɛrə/ *n.* [C,U] a row or area of sharply pointed mountains [**Origin:** 1500–1600 Spanish, Latin *serra* **saw**]

Si'erra Club a U.S. organization that tries to protect the environment, especially natural areas such as forests, mountains, and rivers

Sierra Le·one /si,ɛrə li'oʊn/ a country in West Africa between Liberia and Guinea —**Sierra Leonean** *n., adj.*

Sierra Ma·dre, the /si,ɛrə 'mɑdreɪ/ a system of mountain ranges in central Mexico

Sierra Ne·va·da, the /si,ɛrə nə'vædə, -'vɑ-/ also **the Sierras** a mountain range in the U.S. state of California, which separates the coast of California from the rest of the U.S.

si·es·ta /si'ɛstə/ *n.* [C] a short sleep in the afternoon, especially in warm countries: *We finished lunch and went inside to* ***take a siesta***. [**Origin:** 1600–1700 Spanish, Latin *sexta (hora)* **sixth hour, noon**]

sieve¹ /sɪv/ *n.* [C] **1** a round wire kitchen tool with a lot of small holes, used for separating solid food from liquid or small pieces of food from large pieces **2** a round wire tool for separating small objects from large objects

sieve² *v.* [T] to put something through a sieve → see picture on page A32

sift /sɪft/ *v.* [T] **1** to put flour, sugar etc. through a sifter or similar container in order to remove large pieces ►see THESAURUS box at **cooking¹** → see picture on page A32 **2** also **sift through** to examine information, documents etc. carefully in order to find something out or decide what is important and what is not: *She was sifting through some of her mother's old letters.*

sift sth ↔ **out** *phr. v.* to separate something from other things: **+from** *It's hard to sift out the truth from the lies in this case.*

sift·er /'sɪftɚ/ *n.* [C] a container with a handle and a lot of small holes in the bottom, used for removing large pieces from flour or for mixing flour and other dry things together in cooking

sigh¹ /saɪ/ *v.* **1** [I,T] to breathe out making a long sound, especially because you are bored, disappointed, tired etc.: *"I know," she sighed.* | **sigh deeply/heavily** *Ted sighed deeply and turned around.* | *When it was over, Penny* ***sighed with relief***. **2** [I] LITERARY if the wind sighs, it makes a long sound like someone sighing: *The wind sighed in the trees.* **3 sigh for sth** LITERARY to be sad because you are thinking about a pleasant time in the past: *Emilia sighed for her lost youth.* [**Origin:** Old English *sican*]

sigh² *n.* [C] an act or sound of sighing: **+of** *With a sigh of exhaustion, she watched them leave.* | **let out/give/heave etc. a sigh** *She let out a deep sigh.* | *"I'm glad that's over," she said,* ***breathing a sigh of relief***.

sight¹ /saɪt/ S3 W2 *n.*

1 ABILITY TO SEE [U] the physical ability to see SYN **vision**: *She had an operation to restore her sight.* | *Mrs. Rosen is* ***losing*** *her* ***sight***.

2 ACT OF SEEING [singular, U] the act of seeing something: **+of** *Martha couldn't bear the sight of children begging in the streets.* | *Ray always faints* ***at the sight of*** *blood.* | *We* ***caught sight of*** (=suddenly saw) *the mayor on her way into City Hall.*

3 THING YOU SEE [C] something you can see, especially something unusual, beautiful etc.: **common/familiar sight** *Limousines are a common sight in Los Angeles.* | **awesome/strange/beautiful etc. sight** *The balloons rose into the air – it was a wonderful sight.* | *Some children are easily distracted by all the* ***sights and sounds*** *of the classroom.* | *Are you sure you want to come in? It's* ***not a pretty sight*** (=very ugly or frightening). | *Thousands of people were marching – it was* ***a sight to behold*** (=it was an unusual, impressive etc. thing to see).

4 PLACES TO SEE the sights famous or interesting places that tourists visit: *My brother* ***showed*** *us all* ***the sights*** *of New York.* | *In the afternoon, you'll have time to relax or* ***see the sights***. → see also SIGHTSEEING

5 in/within sight a) inside the area that you can see: *She walked fast, but it was easy to keep her in sight.* | *It was a beautiful day, with* ***not*** *a cloud* ***in sight***. | *There were* ***no*** *adults* ***within sight***. | *I looked around, but Dad was* ***nowhere in sight***. | *The boys get home and eat* ***everything in sight***. | *At last the ship* ***came into sight*** (=came inside the area that you can see). **b)** likely to happen soon: *Peace is now in sight.* | *Today is the 15th day of the heat wave, with* ***no end in sight***.

6 within/in sight of sth a) in the area where you can see something: *The boat was stopped by the Coast Guard within sight of land.* | *At last they* ***came in sight of*** *the city.* **b)** in a position where you will soon be able to get something or achieve something: *Just when he was within sight of his goal, the funding was cut.*

7 on sight as soon as you see someone: *Lisa disliked him on sight.* | *Troops were given orders to* ***shoot on sight***.

8 out of sight outside the area that you can see: *Keep valuables out of sight.* → see also OUT-OF-SIGHT

9 disappear/vanish from sight to disappear: *Then the plane vanished from sight on the radar screen.*

10 not let sb out of your sight to make sure that someone stays near you: *Stay here, and don't let the baby out of your sight.*

11 sight unseen if you buy or choose something sight unseen, you do it without looking at the thing first: *How could you rent a house sight unseen?*

12 can't stand the sight of sb/sth also **hate the sight of sb/sth** to dislike someone or something very much: *Alan and Sam can't stand the sight of each other.*

13 a sight for sore eyes SPOKEN someone or something that you feel very happy to see

14 out of sight, out of mind used to say that if you cannot see someone or something, you stop thinking about them/it and forget about them/it

15 GUN [C usually plural] the part of a gun or other weapon that guides your eye when you are aiming at something

16 be/look a sight to look very funny, stupid, or messy: *She must have been quite a sight with her hair in curlers.*

17 in your sights if you have something or someone in your sights, you intend to achieve it or get it for yourself, or to attack them: *Rogers* ***had*** *victory firmly* ***in*** *his* ***sights***.

[**Origin:** Old English *gesiht*] → see also **at first sight/glance** at FIRST¹ (5), **know sb by sight** at KNOW¹ (5), **lose sight of sb/sth** at LOSE (18), **set your mind/sights/heart on sth** at SET¹ (10)

sight² *v.* [T] to see something from a long distance away or for a short time: *A mountain lion was sighted in the local area last night.*

sight·ed /'saɪt̬ɪd/ *adj.* someone who is sighted can see, and is not blind → see also CLEAR-SIGHTED, FARSIGHTED, NEARSIGHTED

'sight gag *n.* [C] something that an actor or COMEDIAN does that makes people laugh because it looks funny

sight·ing /'saɪt̬ɪŋ/ *n.* [C] an occasion on which something is seen, especially something rare or something that people are hoping to see: *reports of UFO sightings*

sight·less /'saɪtlɪs/ *adj.* LITERARY blind

sight-read /'saɪt˺rid/ *v. past tense and past participle* **sight-read** /-rɛd/ [I,T] to play or sing written music when you look at it for the first time, without practicing it first —**sight-reader** *n.* [C] —**sight-reading** *n.* [U]

sight·see·ing /'saɪt,siɪŋ/ *n.* [U] the activity of visiting famous or interesting places, especially as a tourist: *We can* ***go sightseeing*** *tomorrow.*

S

sight·se·er /ˈsaɪtˌsiɚ/ *n.* [C] someone, especially a tourist, who is visiting a famous or interesting place

ˈsight word *n.* [C] ENG. LANG. ARTS a word which a reader recognizes immediately as a whole without needing to examine its different parts

sign¹ /saɪn/ S1 W1 *n.*

1 GIVES INFORMATION [C] a piece of paper, metal etc. in a public place, with words or drawings on it that give people information, warn them about something, tell them what to do etc.: *a stop sign* | *What did that sign say?* | *a **warning sign** on the pier*

2 STH THAT PROVES STH [C] an event, fact etc. that shows that something is happening or will happen, or that something is true or exists SYN **indication**: **+of** *Do you see any signs of improvement in her condition?* | *The three wise men read the signs in the sky that said a king was born in Bethlehem.* | **sign (that)** *The drop in unemployment is one sign that the economy is getting better.* | **a good/bad sign** *He agreed to come, which was a good sign.* | *Raised blood pressure is a **warning sign**.* | *the **telltale signs** of drug abuse* | *Some runners were starting to **show signs of** fatigue.* | *Police found **no sign of** forced entry.* | *Holiday decorations in the stores are **a sure sign that** summer is over.* | ***There were signs of** a struggle – several chairs were knocked over.*

S

THESAURUS

indication a sign: *He gave no indication that he saw me.*
indicator a sign that people look for and can recognize which tells them what is happening or is true: *a key indicator of economic well-being*
evidence facts or signs that show clearly that something exists or is true: *evidence that spring is on its way*
signal a sign that shows something, which may cause someone to take action: *She called me by my full name, always a signal that she was angry.*
mark a sign, especially that you respect or honor someone: *People stood in silence as a mark of respect.*
symptom a sign that an illness or problem exists: *Seizures are a common symptom of these tumors.*

3 MOVEMENT OR SOUND [C] a movement, sound etc. that you make in order to tell someone to do something or give them information SYN **gesture** SYN **signal**: **sign that** *I made a sign that I understood Anna.* | **give/make a sign** *The President gave reporters the **thumbs-up sign**.* | **sign for sb to do sth** *Three short blasts of the whistle was the sign to begin.*

4 PICTURE/SYMBOL [C] a picture, shape etc. that has a particular meaning SYN **symbol**: *Write your answer after the equals sign.* | *a dollar sign*

5 there is no sign of sb/sth used to say that someone or something is not in a place or cannot be found: *I waited for an hour but there was no sign of her.*

6 a sign of life a) a movement that shows that someone is alive, or something that shows that there are people in a particular place: *Apart from a few lights, there was no sign of life on the block.* **b)** something that shows that a situation is becoming more active: *The nation's economy is starting to **show** a few faint **signs of life**.*

7 a sign of the times something that shows how the world or society has changed recently: *Marriages that last only a few weeks are a sign of the times.*

8 the sign of the cross the hand movement that some Christians make in the shape of a cross, to show respect for God or to protect themselves from evil

9 STARS [C] also **star sign** a group of stars, representing one of 12 parts of the year, that some people believe influences your behavior and your life: *What's your sign?*

10 LANGUAGE SIGN LANGUAGE

[**Origin:** 1200–1300 Old French *signe*, from Latin *signum* **mark, sign, image, seal**]

sign² S1 W1 *v.* **1** [I,T] to write your SIGNATURE on a letter or document to show that you wrote it, agree with it etc.: *Just sign here by the X.* | *Would you like to sign our guest book?* | *She **signed her name** at the bottom of the page.* **2** [T] to make a document, agreement etc. official and legal by writing your SIGNATURE on it: *Each tenant will have to sign the lease.* | *The President **signed** the bill **into law** yesterday.* **3** [T] if an organization such as a football team or music company signs someone, that person signs a contract agreeing to work for it: *Simmons was signed as a free agent in 1994.* | **+for/to/with** *Eventually the group signed with Motown records.* **4 sign on the dotted line** INFORMAL to officially agree to something, especially by signing a contract **5** [I,T] to use SIGN LANGUAGE **6 signed, sealed, and delivered** also **signed and sealed** with everything finished and taken care of as needed, especially with all the necessary legal documents signed: *Until it's all written down, signed and sealed, there really is no agreement.* —**signer** *n.* [C]

sign sth ↔ **away** *phr. v.* to sign a document that takes away your legal right to do something, or that gives your property or legal right to someone else: *Several people had been tricked into signing away their right to sue.* | *The contract was so complicated, I felt like I was **signing my life away**.*

sign for sth *phr. v.* to sign a document to prove that you have received something: *Who signed for the package?*

sign in *phr. v.* **1** to write your name on a form, in a book etc. when you enter a place such as a hotel, an office, or a club: *All visitors must sign in at the front desk.* **2 sign sb in** to write someone else's name in a book so that they are allowed to enter a club, an office etc.

sign off *phr. v.* to say goodbye at the end of a television or radio broadcast, or at the end of a letter

sign off on sth *phr. v.* to officially say or show that you approve of a document, plan, or idea: *Congress has not yet signed off on the deal.*

sign on *phr. v.* to sign a document agreeing to help or work for someone, or to persuade someone to do this: *All the show's stars have signed on for another season.* | **sign sb on** *Ferguson signed King on as host of the program.*

sign out *phr. v.* **1** to write your name in a book when you leave a place such as a hotel, an office, or a club **2 sign sth ↔ out** to write your name on a form or in a book to show that you have taken or borrowed something: *Somebody had already signed out the last VCR.* **3 sign sb ↔ out** to write in a book that someone is allowed to leave somewhere such as a school, an office etc.: *Parents must sign students out when picking them up for doctor's appointments.*

sign sth ↔ **over** *phr. v.* to sign an official document that gives your property or rights to someone else: **+to** *Richard signed over his shares to his son.*

sign up *phr. v.* **1** to put your name on a list because you want to take part in an activity: **+for** *Over 25 people have signed up for the self-defense class.* | **sign up to do sth** *All four of their sons signed up to join the army.* **2 sign sb ↔ up** to officially allow someone to work for a company or join an organization: *Unions have been having trouble signing up enough new members.*

sign·age /ˈsaɪnɪdʒ/ *n.* [U] all the signs used in a building, along a road etc.

sig·nal¹ /ˈsɪgnəl/ S3 W3 *n.* [C] **1** a sound or action that you make in order to give information to someone or tell them to do something: ***At the signal** he turned off the lights.* | **signal (for sb) to do sth** *The general **gave the signal** for his troops to advance.* → see also BUSY SIGNAL, SMOKE SIGNAL **2** an event or action that shows what someone feels, what exists, or what is likely to happen: **signal (that)** *The figures are a signal that the economy is improving.* | *A red **warning signal** flashed.* | *The move was **a clear signal** of support for his policies.* | *Our society sure gives kids **mixed signals** about sexuality.* | *It was a **strong signal** that he should look for another job.* | **send/give a signal** *This will send the wrong signal to potential investors.* ►see THESAURUS box at sign¹ **3** a series of light waves, sound waves etc. that carry an image, sound, or message, for example in radio or television: *The telephone changes sound waves into electrical signals.* | **send (out)/transmit/emit a signal** *the equipment needed to transmit digital signals* | **receive/pick up a signal** *The Coast Guard picked up a distress signal from a freighter.* **4** a piece of equipment with colored lights, used on a road or railroad to tell drivers when they can continue or when they must stop: *We waited for the signal to turn green.*

signal[2] *v.* **1** [I,T] to make a sound or action in order to give information or tell someone to do something: *The whistle signaled the end of the game.* | **+for** *Koln signaled for silence.* | **+to** *Mike signaled to the waiter.* | **signal (to) sb to do sth** *The policeman signaled him to come along.* **2** [T] to make something clear by what you say or do: *Both sides have signaled their willingness to talk.* | **signal (that)** *Mexico has signaled that it may reject the request.* **3** [T] to be a sign or proof that something is going to happen: *The melting of the ice signals the start of spring.* **4** [I] to show the direction you intend to turn in a vehicle, by using lights SYN **indicate**: *The driver in front of us was signaling left.*

signal[3] *adj.* FORMAL **a signal achievement/success/failure etc.** a very important achievement, success etc.

sig·nal·ize /ˈsɪgnəˌlaɪz/ *v.* [T] FORMAL to be a clear sign of something

sig·nal·ly /ˈsɪgnəli/ *adv.* FORMAL in a way that is very noticeable: *The school has failed signally to deal with this problem.*

sig·nal·man /ˈsɪgnəlmən/ *n. plural* **signalmen** /-mən/ [C] **1** a member of the army or navy who is trained to send and receive signals **2** someone whose job is to control railroad signals

sig·na·to·ry /ˈsɪgnəˌtɔri/ *n. plural* **signatories** [C] one of the people or countries that sign an official agreement, especially an international one: **+to/of** *a meeting of the 35 signatories of the Helsinki Pact*

sig·na·ture[1] /ˈsɪgnətʃɚ/ *n.* [C] **1** your name written in the way you usually write it, for example at the end of a letter, on a contract, or on a check: *I couldn't read his signature.* | *a petition with 4,000 signatures* | **+on** *You need a parent's signature on your report card.* **2** something that is closely connected in people's minds with a particular event, person, company etc. because they use it a lot: **+of** *Negative TV ads became the signature of the campaign.* **3** [U] FORMAL the act of signing something SYN **signing**: *The bill came to the president's desk **for signature**.* → see also AUTOGRAPH, KEY SIGNATURE, TIME SIGNATURE

signature[2] *adj.* [only before noun] closely connected in people's minds with a particular person, company etc. because it is used a lot by that person or company: *Smith's signature singing style*

sign·board /ˈsaɪnbɔrd/ *n.* [C] a flat piece of wood, CARDBOARD etc. in a public place, with writing on it that gives people information

sig·net /ˈsɪgnɪt/ *n.* [C] a metal object used for printing a small pattern in WAX as an official SEAL

ˈsignet ring *n.* [C] a ring that has a signet on it

sig·nif·i·cance /sɪgˈnɪfɪkəns/ Ac *n.* [U] **1** the importance of an event, action etc., especially because of the effects or influence it will have in the future: **+of** *the significance of climate change* | **+for** *The research will **have** enormous **significance** for arthritis sufferers.* | **historical/political/social etc. significance** *the town's historical significance in the American Revolution* | **+to** *the area's significance to the film industry* | **great/little significance** *The changes **were of** very little **significance**.* **2** the meaning of a word, sign, action etc., especially when this is not immediately clear: **+of** *a discussion about the significance of the poem*

sig·nif·i·cant /sɪgˈnɪfɪkənt/ Ac S3 W2 *adj.* **1** having an important effect or influence, especially on what will happen in the future OPP **insignificant**: *a significant change in the policy* | **historically/politically/economically etc. significant** *a historically significant site in Greece* | *It was a **highly significant** event.* ▸see THESAURUS box at **important** **2** large enough to be noticeable or have noticeable effects OPP **insignificant**: *A significant number of drivers still do not wear seat belts.* | *There was no **statistically significant** difference between the two groups.* **3** [only before noun] a significant look, smile etc. has a special meaning that is not known to everyone SYN **meaningful**: *They exchanged significant glances.*

sigˌnificant ˈfigure also **sigˌnificant ˈdigit** *n.* [C] MATH a DIGIT (=sign that represents a number) in a number that is known to be exact. Significant figures start with the first digit on the left that is not a zero, and end with the last digit on the right which is not zero (unless the zero is known to be an exact value). So the number 0.302 has three significant figures, and the number 0. 0302 also has only three significant figures.

sig·nif·i·cant·ly /sɪgˈnɪfɪkəntli/ Ac W3 *adv.* **1** in an important way or to a large degree: *The scores of the two groups were not significantly different.* | **significantly better/greater/worse etc.** *People living near the reactor have significantly higher rates of cancer.* | **increase/reduce/go up/drop etc. significantly** *The population has increased significantly.* **2** [sentence adverb] used to say that something is very important: *Significantly, these mothers enjoyed their work, whereas the other group did not.* **3** in a way that seems to have a special meaning SYN **meaningfully**: *Barb glanced significantly in my direction.*

sigˌnificant ˈother *n.* [C] your GIRLFRIEND, BOYFRIEND, wife, or husband

sig·ni·fi·ca·tion /ˌsɪgnəfəˈkeɪʃən/ *n.* [C] FORMAL the intended meaning of a word

sig·ni·fy /ˈsɪgnəˌfaɪ/ Ac *v.* **signifies, signified, signifying** [T not in progressive] **1** to represent, mean, or be a sign of something: *The image of a lion signifies power and strength.* | **signify (that)** *"N/A" signifies that the information was not available.* **2** FORMAL to make a wish, feeling, or opinion known by doing something SYN **convey**: *Many people wore red ribbons to signify their support.* **3** [I] to be important enough to have an effect on something: *The amount doesn't really signify in the overall results.*

sign·ing /ˈsaɪnɪŋ/ *n.* **1** [U] the act of writing your name on something such as an agreement or contract: *Both leaders were present for the signing of the peace treaty.* **2** [C] a ceremony or event at which someone writes their name on something: *book signings* **3** [U] the use of sign language to communicate

ˈsign ˌlanguage *n.* [C,U] ENG. LANG. ARTS a language that uses hand movements instead of spoken words, used by people who cannot hear

sign·post /ˈsaɪnpoʊst/ *n.* [C] **1** a pole that supports a sign near a road, or a sign that is supported by a pole **2** something that helps you to understand how something is organized, or to notice something: *These events were the signposts of change.*

Sikh /sik/ *n.* [C] a member of an Indian religious group that developed from Hinduism in the 16th century [**Origin:** 1700–1800 a Hindi word meaning **disciple, follower**] —**Sikhism** *n.* [U] —**Sikh** *adj.*

Si·kor·sky /sɪˈkɔrski/, **I·gor** /ˈigɔr/ (1889–1972) a U.S. engineer, born in the Ukraine, who designed the first HELICOPTER

si·lage /ˈsaɪlɪdʒ/ *n.* [U] grass or other plants cut and stored so that they can be used as winter food for farm animals

si·lence[1] /ˈsaɪləns/ W2 *n.*
1 NO NOISE [U] complete absence of sound or noise SYN **quiet**: **+of** *the silence of the night* | ***Silence fell*** (=it began to be quiet) *over the desert.* | **break/shatter the silence** *The silence was suddenly broken by a loud scream.* | **absolute/complete/dead silence** *the complete silence of the forest at night*
2 NO TALKING [C,U] complete quiet because no one is talking, or a period of complete quiet: *There was a long silence before anyone answered.* | *We walked along **in silence** for a few blocks.* | **embarrassed/awkward/stunned etc. silence** *Peter's comments were met with*

S

an awkward silence. | **complete/total/dead silence** *They ate in total silence.*
3 NO DISCUSSION/ANSWER [U] failure or refusal to discuss something or answer questions about something: +**on** *The government's silence on such an important issue seems very strange.* | *The answer was a* ***deafening silence*** (=very noticeable refusal to discuss something).
4 NO COMMUNICATION [C,U] failure to write a letter to someone, call them on the telephone etc.: *After years of silence, she wrote to me.*
5 a minute of silence also **one-minute/two-minute etc. silence** a period of time when everyone stops talking as a sign of respect and honor toward someone who has died

silence² *v.* [T] **1** to make someone stop expressing opposition or criticism: *The government silenced political opponents.* **2** to make someone stop talking, or stop something from making a noise → see also SHUSH: *Danny silenced him with a gesture.*

si·lenc·er /ˈsaɪlənsɚ/ *n.* [C] a thing that is put on the end of a gun so that it makes less noise when it is fired

si·lent /ˈsaɪlənt/ [W3] *adj.* **1** not saying anything: *Phil was silent for a moment.* | *The audience* ***fell silent*** (=became completely quiet) *as Jackson began to speak.* | **remain/keep/stay silent** *I shake my head and remain silent.* → see also **sb is the strong silent type** at STRONG (28) **2** failing or refusing to talk about something or express an opinion: +**on/about** *The report was silent on the subject.* | *You have the right to* ***remain silent.*** **3** without any sound, or not making any sound [SYN] **soundless**: *The house was strangely silent.* | *a silent alarm at the bank* **4 give sb the silent treatment** to not speak to someone because you are angry or upset about something they did **5** ENG. LANG. ARTS a silent letter in a word is not pronounced: *The "b" at the end of "thumb" is silent.* [**Origin:** 1400–1500 Latin, present participle of *silere* **to be silent**] —**silently** *adv.*

ˌsilent maˈjority *n.* **the silent majority** the ordinary people in a country, who are not active politically and who do not make their opinions known

ˌsilent ˈmovie also **ˌsilent ˈfilm** *n.* [C] an old-fashioned movie with no sound, mainly made before about 1928

ˌsilent ˈpartner *n.* [C] someone who owns part of a business, but who is not actively involved in the way it operates

sil·hou·ette¹ /ˌsɪluˈɛt, ˈsɪluˌɛt/ *n.* **1** [C] a dark image, shadow, or shape, that you see against a light background: *We could see her silhouette through the curtains.* | +**against** *the silhouette of the tree against the moon* **2** [C,U] a drawing of someone or something that shows their outer shape, usually from the side, filled in with black against a light background: *a collection of portraits and silhouettes* | *The stamp shows a woman* ***in silhouette.*** **3** [C] a particular shape that clothes have: *wool suits with a new narrower silhouette* [**Origin:** 1700–1800 French, from Étienne de *Silhouette* (1709–1767), French politician famous for not liking to spend money, and therefore appropriately giving his name to a cheap simple picture]

silhouette² *v.* **be silhouetted (against sth)** to appear as a dark shape in front of a light background: *the mountains silhouetted against the sky*

sil·i·ca /ˈsɪlɪkə/ *n.* [U] EARTH SCIENCE a chemical compound that exists naturally as sand, QUARTZ, and FLINT, used in making glass

sil·i·cate /ˈsɪləˌkeɪt, -kət/ *n.* [C,U] EARTH SCIENCE one of a group of common solid mineral substances that exist naturally in the Earth's surface

sil·i·con /ˈsɪlɪkən, -ˌkɑn/ *n.* [U] SYMBOL **Si** CHEMISTRY an ELEMENT that exists as a solid or as a powder and is often used for making glass, bricks, and parts for computers

ˌsilicon ˈchip *n.* [C] COMPUTERS a computer CHIP

sil·i·cone /ˈsɪləˌkoʊn/ *n.* [U] SCIENCE one of a group of chemicals that are not changed by heat or cold, do not let water pass through them, and are used in making artificial rubber, body parts, and many other products

ˌSilicon ˈValley a part of California in the area between San Francisco and San José, which is known as a center of the computer industry

sil·i·co·sis /ˌsɪləˈkoʊsɪs/ *n.* [U] an illness of the lungs caused by breathing SILICA, common among people who work in mines

silk /sɪlk/ *n.* **1** [U] a thin smooth soft cloth made from very thin thread which is produced by a silkworm: *a silk blouse* **2 silks** [plural] TECHNICAL the colored shirts worn by JOCKEYS (=people who ride horses in races) **3 you can't make a silk purse out of a sow's ear** SPOKEN used to say that you cannot make something good out of something that is of bad quality [**Origin:** Old English *seolc*]

silk·en /ˈsɪlkən/ *adj.* LITERARY **1** soft, smooth, and shiny like silk [SYN] **silky**: *her silken skin* **2** made of silk: *red silken robes*

ˈSilk Road, the HISTORY the road that led from China to the Mediterranean, used for trade in ancient times and in the Middle Ages

ˈsilk-screening also **ˈscreen ˌprinting** *n.* [U] a way of printing by forcing paint or ink onto a surface through a stretched piece of cloth —**silk-screen** *v.* [T]

silk·worm /ˈsɪlk-wɚm/ *n.* [C] a type of CATERPILLAR which produces silk thread

silk·y /ˈsɪlki/ *adj.* *comparative* **silkier**, *superlative* **silkiest** **1** soft, smooth, and shiny, like silk [SYN] **silken**: *silky long hair* **2** a silky voice is gentle and pleasant to listen to, and is used especially when trying to persuade someone to do something —**silkiness** *n.* [U]

sill /sɪl/ *n.* [C] the narrow shelf at the base of a window frame

sil·ly¹ /ˈsɪli/ [S2] *adj.* *comparative* **sillier**, *superlative* **silliest** **1** stupid in a CHILDISH or embarrassing way: *I feel so silly in this outfit.* | *a silly hat* | *She's just* ***being silly.*** **2** not sensible, or showing bad judgment [SYN] **foolish**: *They asked a lot of* ***silly questions.*** | *It's silly to build another room onto the house now.* | *"Can I go by myself?"* ***"Don't be silly;*** *you're too little."* **3** SPOKEN not serious or practical: *They served coffee in these silly little cups.* **4 bore/scare/beat etc. sb silly** to make someone extremely bored, SCARED etc. **5 drink/laugh/scare yourself silly** to drink, laugh etc. so much that you stop behaving in a sensible way [**Origin:** Old English *sælig* **happy**] —**silliness** *n.* [U]

silly² *n.* [singular] SPOKEN a name used to tell someone that you think they are being stupid: *No, silly, put it over there!*

si·lo /ˈsaɪloʊ/ *n.* *plural* **silos** [C] **1** a tall structure like a tower that is used for storing grain, winter food for farm animals etc. **2** a large structure under the ground from which a large MISSILE can be fired

silt¹ /sɪlt/ *n.* [U] EARTH SCIENCE sand, mud, soil etc. that is carried in water and then settles at a curve in a river or at the point where a river flows into the ocean

silt² *v.*
silt up *phr. v.* to fill or become filled with silt: *The reservoirs had silted up.*

sil·ver¹ /ˈsɪlvɚ/ *n.* **1** [U] SYMBOL **Ag** CHEMISTRY a valuable shiny light-gray metal that is an ELEMENT and is used to make jewelry, knives, coins etc.: *a cup made of solid silver* **2** [U] spoons, forks, dishes etc. that are made of silver: *Use a soft cloth to polish the silver.* **3** [U] the color of silver **4** [C] a SILVER MEDAL [**Origin:** Old English *seolfor*]

silver² [W3] *adj.* **1** made of silver: *a silver necklace* **2** having the color of silver: *a silver Mercedes* **3 give/hand sth to sb on a silver platter** to make it very easy for someone to get something or succeed at something **4 silver bullet** a quick painless cure for an illness, or something that solves a difficult problem in an easy way: *More investment isn't a silver bullet for poor neighborhoods.* → see also **be born with a silver spoon in**

your mouth at BORN (7), **every cloud has a silver lining** at CLOUD[1] (6)

silver[3] *v.* [T] **1** to cover a surface with a thin shiny layer of silver or another metal, for example in order to make a mirror **2** LITERARY to make something shine and look the color of silver → see also GILD

ˌsilver anniˈversary *n.* [C] the date that is exactly 25 years after the beginning of something, especially a marriage → see also DIAMOND ANNIVERSARY, GOLDEN ANNIVERSARY

ˌsilver ˈdollar *n.* [C] a one-dollar coin used in the U.S. in past times

sil•ver•fish /ˈsɪlvɚfɪʃ/ *n. plural* **silverfish** or **silverfishes** [C] a small silver-colored insect that is found in houses and sometimes damages paper or cloth

ˌsilver ˈmedal *n.* [C] a MEDAL made of silver that is given to the person who finishes second in a race or competition → see also GOLD MEDAL

ˌsilver ˈmedalist *n.* [C] someone who has won a silver medal

ˌsilver ˈplate *n.* [U] metal that is covered with a thin layer of silver —**silver-plated** *adj.*: *a silver-plated candlestick*

ˌsilver ˈscreen *n.* **the silver screen** the movie industry in Hollywood, in past times: *stars of the silver screen*

sil•ver•smith /ˈsɪlvɚˌsmɪθ/ *n.* [C] someone who makes things out of silver

ˌsilver-ˈtongued *adj.* good at talking to people and persuading them

sil•ver•ware /ˈsɪlvɚˌwɛr/ *n.* [U] knives, spoons, and forks made of silver or another metal

sil•ver•y /ˈsɪlvəri/ *adj.* **1** shiny and silver in color: *the silvery light of the moon* **2** ESPECIALLY LITERARY having a pleasant light musical sound: *a silvery laugh*

Sim•e•on /ˈsɪmiən/ in the Bible, the head of one of the 12 tribes of Israel

sim•i•an /ˈsɪmiən/ *adj.* BIOLOGY relating to monkeys or similar to a monkey or APE —**simian** *n.* [C]

sim•i•lar /ˈsɪmələ/ Ac S2 W1 *adj.* **1** almost the same, but not exactly the same OPP **different**: *We have similar tastes in music.* | **+to** *Tom's voice is very similar to his brother's.* | **+in** *The two cars are similar in size.* | **remarkably/strikingly similar** *The two women told strikingly similar stories.* | *Their writing styles are* ***quite similar.***

THESAURUS

like similar in some way to something else: *It tastes a little like chicken.*
alike very similar: *She and her sister look alike.*
akin to sth similar to something: *For me, the work was so enjoyable it was akin to play.*
identical exactly the same: *The two pictures were identical.*
matching having the same color, style, or pattern as something else: *a matching handbag and shoes*

2 [no comparative] MATH similar GEOMETRIC FIGURES have the same shape and equal angles, but do not have to be the same size [**Origin:** 1500–1600 French *similaire*, from Latin *similis* **like, similar**]

sim•i•lar•i•ty /ˌsɪməˈlærət̬i/ Ac *n. plural* **similarities** **1** [singular, U] the fact of being like someone or something else, but not being exactly the same SYN **resemblance**: **+between** *a* ***striking similarity*** *between the two designs* | **+to** *the drug's similarity to natural hormones* | *The attack* ***bore*** *a remarkable* ***similarity*** *to several crimes last year.* **2** [C] a way in which things or people are similar: **+in** *the* ***similarities and differences*** *in their political systems* | **+between/with** ***There are similarities*** *with German, but Yiddish is a separate language.* | *They are both blonde, but the* ***similarity ends there.***

sim•i•lar•ly /ˈsɪmələli/ Ac W3 *adv.* in a similar way: *Liz's mother reacted similarly when I told her about it later.* | [sentence adverb] *Sales of existing homes went up 2% last month. Similarly, construction of new homes rose as well.*

sim•i•le /ˈsɪməli/ *n.* ENG. LANG. ARTS **1** [C] an expression that describes something by comparing it with something else, using the words "as" or "like." For example, "as white as snow" is a simile. **2** [U] the use of expressions like this → see also METAPHOR

SIMM /sɪm/ *n.* [C] TECHNICAL **Single In-line Memory Module** a piece of electronic equipment that gives a computer more RAM

sim•mer[1] /ˈsɪmɚ/ *v.* **1** [I,T] to cook something slowly in a liquid that is gently boiling: *Simmer the soup for 20 minutes.* **2** [I] if something such as an argument is simmering, it develops slowly over a long period of time before people express their feelings: *the ethnic conflicts that have been simmering in the country*

simmer down *phr. v.* **1** to become calm again after you have been angry: *After they'd simmered down, it was never mentioned again.* **2 simmer down!** SPOKEN used to tell someone to be less excited, angry etc.: *Simmer down, you two! Supper's almost ready.*

simmer[2] *n.* [singular] the condition of boiling gently: *Bring the vegetables to a simmer.*

si•mo•ny /ˈsaɪməni, ˈsɪm-/ *n.* [U] TECHNICAL the action by a Christian of buying or selling holy or spiritual things, usually regarded as wrong

Simon Ze•lo•tes /ˌsaɪmən zɪˈloʊtiz/ also **Simon the Ca•naan•ite** /-ðə ˈkeɪnəˌnaɪt/ in the Bible, one of the 12 APOSTLES

sim•pa•ti•co /sɪmˈpɑt̬ɪkoʊ, -ˈpæ-/ *adj.* INFORMAL **1** someone who is simpatico is easy to like **2** in agreement: *Not all couples are simpatico during long car trips.*

sim•per /ˈsɪmpɚ/ *v.* [I] to smile in a silly annoying way —**simper** *n.* [C]

sim•ple /ˈsɪmpəl/ S2 W1 *adj.*

1 EASY not difficult or complicated to do or understand: *I'm sure there's a perfectly simple explanation.* | *He couldn't even answer very simple questions.* | *The system is* ***relatively simple.*** | **simple to do/make etc.** *The projects are all simple to make.* | *Make a chart of jobs to do, but* ***keep it simple.*** | *Just call her up –* ***it's as simple as that.***

THESAURUS

easy not difficult: *It was an easy class.*
straightforward simple and easy to understand: *a straightforward explanation*

2 PLAIN without a lot of decoration or unnecessary things added SYN **plain**: *a simple black dress* | *The chicken was served with a simple cream sauce.* | *the building's simple clean lines*
3 ONLY [only before noun] used to emphasize that only one thing is involved: *Players practice hard for one simple reason: if they don't, they don't play.* | **the simple truth/fact is...** *The simple truth is that we don't have enough money.* | **pure/plain and simple** *It was racism, pure and simple.*
4 NOT HAVING MANY PARTS consisting of only a few necessary parts, and not having a complicated structure: *simple organisms such as bacteria* | *a few simple tools*
5 NOT SPECIAL honest and ordinary, and not special in any way: *Joe was just a simple farmer.*
6 the simple life life without too many possessions or modern machines, especially in the COUNTRYSIDE
7 GRAMMAR TECHNICAL simple tenses are not formed with an AUXILIARY such as "have" or "be"
8 STUPID OLD-FASHIONED not intelligent
[**Origin:** 1200–1300 Old French **plain, uncomplicated**, from Latin *simplus*, from *sim-* **one** + *-plus* **multiplied by**]
→ see also **pure and simple** at PURE (9)

ˌsimple ˈfracture *n.* [C] MEDICINE a broken or cracked bone that does not cut through the flesh that surrounds it → see also COMPOUND FRACTURE

ˌsimple ˈinterest *n.* [U] ECONOMICS INTEREST that is calculated on the sum of money that you first INVESTED and not on any interest it has earned → see also COMPOUND INTEREST

ˌsimple-'minded *adj.* not very intelligent, and not able to understand complicated things

'simple ˌsugar *n.* [C] BIOLOGY a sugar such as GLUCOSE, that does not break down into other sugars during HYDROLYSIS (=a common chemical reaction involving water and another substance) SYN **monosaccharide**

sim·ple·ton /'sɪmpəltən/ *n.* [C] OLD-FASHIONED someone who has a very low level of intelligence

sim·plic·i·ty /sɪm'plɪsəṭi/ *n.* [U] APPROVING the quality of being simple and not complicated, especially when this is attractive or useful: *The design was beautiful in its simplicity.* | ***For the sake of simplicity,*** *the task is divided into three parts.* | *The solution* ***was simplicity itself*** (=was very simple).

sim·pli·fy /'sɪmpləˌfaɪ/ *v.* **simplifies, simplified, simplifying** [T] **1** to make something easier or less complicated: *The laws have been simplified to shorten the process of divorce.* **2** ALGEBRA to change an EQUATION, FRACTION, or other mathematical expression into its simplest form, using ARITHMETIC and ALGEBRA → see also OVERSIMPLIFY —**simplified** *adj.*: *a simplified version of Chinese script* —**simplification** /ˌsɪmpləfə'keɪʃən/ *n.* [C,U]

S

sim·plis·tic /sɪm'plɪstɪk/ *adj.* DISAPPROVING treating difficult subjects in a way that is too simple: *a simplistic view of the world* —**simplistically** /-kli/ *adv.*

sim·ply /'sɪmpli/ S2 W1 *adv.* **1** only SYN **just**: *It's not* ***simply a matter of*** *money.* | *Many students do not finish the test* ***simply because*** *they run out of time.* **2** used to emphasize what you are saying: *The strain on the rope was simply too much, and it broke.* | *We simply don't have the resources to compete with large corporations.* | *It was* ***quite simply*** *the best meal I'd ever eaten.* **3** used to emphasize how easy it is to do something: *Simply fill out the coupon and take it to your local store.* **4** in a way that is easy to understand: *She writes very simply and clearly.* | **put simply/simply put/to put it simply** (=expressing something in a clear way) *Simply put, I am very disappointed.* **5** in a plain and ordinary way, without spending much money: *They live very simply in the country.*

sim·u·la·crum /ˌsɪmyə'lækrəm, -'leɪ-/ *n. plural* **simulacra** /-krə/ [C + of] FORMAL something that is made to look like another thing

sim·u·late /'sɪmyəˌleɪt/ Ac *v.* [T] **1** to make or produce something that is not real but has the appearance or feeling of being real: *This machine can simulate conditions in space.* **2** LITERARY to pretend to have a feeling SYN **feign**: *He found it impossible to simulate grief.*

sim·u·lat·ed /'sɪmyəˌleɪṭɪd/ Ac *adj.* not real, but made to look, feel etc. like a real thing, situation, or feeling: *simulated leather* | *a simulated space flight*

sim·u·la·tion /ˌsɪmyə'leɪʃən/ Ac *n.* [C,U] the activity of producing conditions that are similar to real ones, especially in order to test something, or the conditions that are produced: *a* ***computer simulation*** *used to train pilots* | +**of** *Rescue crews are participating in a simulation of a major traffic accident.*

sim·u·la·tor /'sɪmyəˌleɪṭə/ *n.* [C] a machine that is used for training people by letting them feel what real conditions are like, for example in a plane: *a flight simulator*

sim·ul·cast /'saɪməlˌkæst/ *v. past tense and past participle* **simulcast** [T usually passive] to broadcast a program on television and radio, or on more than one television or radio station, at the same time —**simulcast** *n.* [C]

si·mul·ta·ne·ous /ˌsaɪməl'teɪniəs/ *adj.* happening or done at exactly the same time: *In simultaneous raids on five homes, police seized over $5 million worth of cocaine.* [**Origin:** 1600–1700 Medieval Latin *simultaneus*, from Latin *simul* **at the same time**] —**simultaneously** *adv.*: *The two cameras are operated simultaneously.* —**simultaneity** /ˌsaɪməltə'neɪəṭi/ *n.* [U]

sin¹ /sɪn/ *n.* **1** [C,U] an action that is against religious rules and is considered to be offensive to God SYN **transgression**: *The Bible says adultery is a sin.* | *No one is completely without sin.* | +**of** *the sin of greed* | *He* ***confessed*** *his* ***sins*** *to one of the priests.* **2** [C usually singular] something that you think is wrong and strongly disapprove of: ***It's a sin to*** *waste all this food.* | ***It's no sin to*** (=it is acceptable to) *look at other men once in a while.* **3 as miserable/ugly/guilty etc. as sin** SPOKEN very unhappy, ugly etc. —**sinless** *adj.* → see also **live in sin** at LIVE¹ (16), **cover/hide a multitude of sins** at MULTITUDE (3), ORIGINAL SIN, SINFUL

sin² *v.* **sinned, sinning** [I] **1** to break God's laws SYN **transgress**: +**against** *He has sinned against God.* **2 be more sinned against than sinning** OLD-FASHIONED used to say that someone should not be blamed for what they have done wrong, because they have been badly treated by other people

sin³ TECHNICAL the written abbreviation of SINE

Si·nai /'saɪnaɪ/ the northeastern part of Egypt, which is a piece of land between the two narrow upper parts of the Red Sea, the Gulf of Suez and the Gulf of Aqaba

since¹ /sɪns/ S1 W1 *conjunction* **1** at or from a time after a particular time or event in the past: *A lot has happened since we graduated from college.* | *I haven't seen Michelle since I moved away from Los Angeles.* **2** continuously during the period of time after a particular time or event in the past: *Darla's been really happy since she started work.* | *We've been friends* ***ever since*** *we met in first grade.* **3** used to give the reason for something: *I'll be 40 next month, since you ask.* | *Since nobody's replied yet, I guess they're not interested.* [**Origin:** Old English *siththan*, from *sith tham* **since that**]

since² S2 W1 *prep.* **1** at or from a time after a particular time or event in the past → see also FOR: *Unemployment is now at its lowest point since World War II.* | *Sarah's been sick since Friday.* | ***Ever since*** *the accident, I haven't been able to use my right hand.* **2 since when?** SPOKEN used in questions to show surprise, anger etc.: *Oh, yeah? Since when are you in charge around here?*

WORD CHOICE since, for, ago

- **Since** is mainly used when you want to talk about a situation or activity that started at some time in the past and has continued to the time when you are speaking. It is used with verbs in the present perfect tense: *We've been here since Tuesday morning.* | *Doug hasn't been the same since his father died six months ago* (NOT *He hasn't been the same since six months/six months before.*).
- **For** is used where you want to give the length of a period of time, but do not need to say exactly when it started or finished. It goes with all tenses of verbs: *We lived there for a long time.* | *Tony will be staying with us for three days.* When you use **for** with the present perfect tense, it gives a period of time that ends at the time of speaking: *I've been waiting for two hours* (NOT *since two hours*).
- **Ago** is used mainly with the simple past tense to show the point in time when something happened: *Marlene called ten minutes ago* (NOT *since ten minutes*).

since³ S2 W2 *adv.* [used with the present perfect and the past perfect tenses] **1** at a time in the past after a particular time or event: *Her husband died over ten years ago, but she has since remarried.* | *Many of our friends have since moved away.* | *Greg left work Tuesday afternoon and hasn't been seen since.* **2** for the whole of a long period of time after a particular time or event in the past: *We bought this house in 1986 and have lived here* ***ever since.*** → see also **long since** at LONG² (9)

sin·cere /sɪn'sɪr/ *adj.* **1** a sincere feeling, belief, statement etc. is honest and true, and based on what you really feel and believe SYN **genuine**: *I would like to express my sincere appreciation for your hard work.* | *a sincere effort to reach an agreement* **2** APPROVING someone who is sincere is honest and says what they really feel or believe, usually in a kind way OPP insincere: *She's a really sincere person.* | +**in** *They were completely sincere in their beliefs.* [**Origin:** 1500–1600 Latin *sincerus* **clean, pure**]

sin·cere·ly /sɪn'sɪrli/ *adv.* **1** if you feel or believe something sincerely, you really feel or believe it and are not just pretending SYN truly: *Steve sincerely believed he was doing the right thing.* | *We sincerely regret any trouble this has caused.* **2 Sincerely (yours),...** also **Yours sincerely,...** an expression that you write at the end of a formal letter before you sign your name

sin·cer·i·ty /sɪn'sɛrəṭi/ *n.* [U] **1** the quality of honestly believing something or really meaning what you say: *Diplomats expressed doubts about his sincerity.* | +**of** *the sincerity of their commitment to the project* **2 in all sincerity** very sincerely and honestly SYN in all candor: *I think in all sincerity it would be better to give up now.*

Sin·clair /sɪŋ'klɛr/, **Up·ton** /'ʌptən/ (1878–1968) a U.S. writer best known for his NOVEL about the MEAT-PACKING industry in Chicago

sine /saɪn/ *n.* [C] MATH the FRACTION that you calculate for an angle in a RIGHT TRIANGLE, by dividing the length of the side opposite the angle by the length of the HYPOTENUSE (=longest side) → see also COSINE, TANGENT (3)

si·ne·cure /'saɪnɪˌkyʊr, 'sɪn-/ *n.* [C] a job which you get paid for, even though you do not have to do very much work

si·ne qua non /ˌsɪni kwɑ 'nɑn/ *n.* [singular] FORMAL something that you must have, or which must exist, for something else to be possible: +**for/of** *Strength of character is the sine qua non of leadership.*

sin·ew /'sɪnyu/ *n.* **1** [C,U] BIOLOGY a long strong piece of TISSUE in your body that connects a muscle to a bone SYN tendon **2** [C usually plural] LITERARY something that gives strength or support to a government, country, or system: *Rope is the sinew of any sailing vessel.*

sin·ew·y /'sɪnyui/ *adj.* **1** a sinewy person has strong muscles that you can see under their skin: *a big man with long sinewy arms* **2** sinewy meat has a lot of sinews in it, and is not easy to cut or eat

sin·ful /'sɪnfəl/ *adj.* **1** morally wrong, or guilty of doing something morally wrong SYN wicked: *sinful behavior* | *They believe that humans are sinful by nature.* **2** very wrong or bad: *a sinful waste of taxpayers' money* —**sinfully** *adv.*

sing /sɪŋ/ S1 W2 *v.* *past tense* **sang** /sæŋ/, *past participle* **sung** /sʌŋ/ **1** [I,T] to produce musical sounds, songs etc. with your voice: *Daryl sang in his high school choir.* | *Everyone sang "Happy Birthday."* | +**to** *She sang softly to herself as she worked.* | **sing sb sth** *Sing me a little of it, and I'll see if I know it.* | *They drove along,* ***singing*** *old Beatles* ***songs***. | *She started to* ***sing*** *him* ***to sleep*** (=sing until a baby or child falls asleep). **2** [I] BIOLOGY if birds sing, they produce high musical sounds **3 sing sb's praises** to praise someone very much: *Diane really admires you – she's always singing your praises.* **4 sing a different/new tune** to say something that is different from what you said before: *If he'd known this earlier, he might have sung a different tune.* **5 sing from the same hymn sheet/hymnbook/sheet of music etc.** used to say that a group of people are all expressing the same opinion or have the same aim **6** [I always + adv./prep.] LITERARY to make a high continuous sound: *A kettle was singing on the stove.* **7** [I] OLD-FASHIONED to tell someone or the police everything you know about a crime, especially a crime you were involved in yourself SYN inform: *Pretty soon, Vinnie was singing like a canary.* **8** [I + of,T] LITERARY to praise someone in poetry [**Origin:** Old English *singan*]

sing along *phr. v.* to sing with someone else who is already singing: +**to** *Jackie was singing along to the radio.* | +**with** *Kern invited the audience to sing along with him.*

sing out *phr. v.* to sing or shout out clearly and loudly: *"Good morning, Mrs. James!" Eddie sang out.*

sing. the written abbreviation of SINGULAR

sing·a·long /'sɪŋəˌlɔŋ/ *n.* [C] an informal occasion when people sing songs together

Sing·a·pore /'sɪŋgəˌpɔr/ **1** a small country on an island in Southeast Asia, between Malaysia and Indonesia **2** the capital city of Singapore —**Singaporean** /ˌsɪŋə'pɔriən/ *n., adj.*

singe /sɪndʒ/ *v.* **singed, singeing** [I,T] to burn the surface or edge of something slightly, or to be burned slightly: *The match burned down, singeing her fingers.*

sing·er /'sɪŋɚ/ S3 *n.* [C] someone who sings, especially as a profession: *an opera singer* | *the band's* ***lead singer*** (=main singer) → see also VOCALIST

Sing·er /'sɪŋɚ/, **I·saac** /'aɪzək/ (1811–1875) a U.S. inventor who was the first person to make and sell SEWING MACHINES

Singer, I·saac Ba·shev·is /'aɪzək bə'ʃɛvɪs/ (1904–1991) a Jewish-American writer, born in Poland, who is best known for his short stories written in Yiddish

ˌsinger-'songwriter *n.* [C] someone who writes songs and sings them

sin·gle¹ /'sɪŋgəl/ S1 W1 *adj.*
1 ONE [only before noun] only one: *The Cubs won the game by a single point.* | *These trees can grow over a foot in a single summer.* | *There was* ***not a single*** (=not even one) *person in sight.*
2 NOT MARRIED not married, or not involved in a romantic relationship with anyone SYN unmarried: *Is Jeff still single?* → see also SINGLE PARENT ▶see THESAURUS box at married
3 every single thing/person/one etc. used to emphasize that something is true for every thing, person etc. in a group: *Mike's mom calls him every single day.* | *Every single time I go on a plane, I get sick.*
4 the single biggest/greatest/worst etc. used to emphasize that something or someone is the biggest, greatest etc. of their kind: *Education is the single most important issue today.* | *Housing is our single biggest monthly expense.*
5 a single bed/room etc. a bed, room etc. that is meant for or used by only one person → see also DOUBLE: *You have to pay extra for a single room.*
6 ONE PART having only one part, quality etc., rather than having two or more: *a single strand of pearls* | *a single-lane bridge*
[**Origin:** 1200–1300 Old French, Latin *singulus*]

single² *n.* [C] **1** a musical recording of only one song, or a CD of that song that you can buy: *her latest single* | *The band has had several* ***hit singles***. **2** an action of hitting a ball with a bat that allows the person who hits the ball to reach first BASE in baseball **3 singles** [U] a game, especially in tennis, played by one person against another: *the women's singles championship* → see also DOUBLES **4** a piece of paper money worth one dollar: *Does anybody have five singles?* **5 singles** [plural] people who are not married or involved in a romantic relationship: *The show is especially popular among young singles.* | *a singles bar* (=where single people can go to drink and meet new people)

single³ *v.* [I] to hit the ball far enough to be able to run to first BASE in baseball: *Rodriguez singled to left field.*

single sb/sth ↔ **out** *phr. v.* to choose one person or thing from among a group, especially in order to praise them or criticize them: *I don't know why I was singled out.* | +**for** *Why single out one group for special treatment?*

ˌsingle-'breasted *adj.* a single-breasted JACKET or suit has only one set of buttons at the front → see also DOUBLE-BREASTED

ˌsingle 'digits *n.* **in (the) single digits** a number, rate etc. that is in single digits is less than ten: *Temperatures dipped into the single digits overnight.* —**single-digit** *adj.* [only before noun] *single-digit inflation*

ˌsingle-'family *adj.* [only before noun] **a single-family house/home etc.** a house that is built for one family to live in

S

ˌsingle ˈfile *n.* **in single file** moving in a line, with one behind another: *The class walked in single file down the hall.* —**single file** *adv.*: *They passed single file through the gap in the hedge.*

ˌsingle-ˈhandedly also **ˌsingle-ˈhanded** *adv.* done by one person without help from anyone else: *She raised her child single-handedly.* —**single-handed** *adj.* [only before noun] *a single-handed yacht race*

ˌsingle ˈissue ˌparty *n.* [C] POLITICS a political party that is active in only one area of politics, and that does not have any interest in the other activities involved in governing a country: *Single issue parties are rarely successful in becoming elected, but they do influence voters.*

ˌsingle ˈmarket *n.* [C] a group of countries in which there is freedom of movement of goods, services, money, and workers, and with an agreement on rules for production and trade. The European Union is a single market.

ˌsingle-ˈminded *adj.* having one clear aim and working very hard to achieve it: *a single-minded pursuit of success* —**single-mindedly** *adv.* —**single-mindedness** *n.* [U]

sin·gle·ness /ˈsɪŋɡəlnɪs/ *n.* FORMAL **1 singleness of purpose** great determination when you are working to achieve something **2** [U] the state of being unmarried

ˌsingle ˈparent *n.* [C] a mother or father who takes care of their children on their own, without a partner

ˌsingle-reˈplacement reˌaction also **disˈplacement reˌaction** *n.* [C] CHEMISTRY a chemical reaction in which a single ELEMENT replaces another element in a COMPOUND

ˈsingle-sex *adj.* **single-sex school/college/education etc.** a school, college etc. for either males or females, but not for both together OPP **coed**

ˈsingle-spaced *adj.* [usually before noun] single-spaced lines of words on a printed page are close together, rather than having a space between them: *a three-page single-spaced letter* —**single-space** *v.* [T] —**single-spacing** *n.* [U] → see also DOUBLE-SPACED

sin·gle·ton /ˈsɪŋɡəltən/ *n.* [C] someone who does something or goes somewhere alone

sin·gly /ˈsɪŋɡli/ *adv.* alone, or one at a time SYN **separately**: *Are the rolls sold singly or by the dozen?*

sing·song /ˈsɪŋsɔŋ/ *n.* [singular] a way of speaking in which your voice repeatedly rises and falls —**singsong** *adj.*: *a singsong voice*

sin·gu·lar¹ /ˈsɪŋɡyələ˞/ *adj.* **1** ENG. LANG. ARTS a singular noun, verb, form etc. is used when writing or speaking about one person or thing: *If the subject is singular, use a singular verb.* **2** [only before noun] FORMAL very great or very noticeable SYN **exceptional** SYN **extraordinary**: *a singular achievement* | *Congress showed a singular lack of understanding of the issue.* **3** [only before noun] used to emphasize the fact that there is only one of something SYN **single**: *The singular objective is to improve the company's performance.* **4** [only before noun] LITERARY very unusual or strange: *such singular behavior*

singular² *n.* **the singular** the form of a word used when writing or speaking about one person or thing

sin·gu·lar·i·ty /ˌsɪŋɡyəˈlærət̮i/ *n. plural* **singularities** **1** [C] TECHNICAL an extremely small point in space that contains an extremely large amount of material, which does not obey the usual laws of nature, especially inside a BLACK HOLE or at the beginning of the universe **2** [U] OLD-FASHIONED strangeness **3** [U] FORMAL the fact of being the only one of its kind: *a work that shows his singularity as a writer*

sin·gu·lar·ly /ˈsɪŋɡyələ˞li/ *adv.* **1** in a way that is very noticeable: *a singularly beautiful woman* **2** OLD-FASHIONED in an unusual way SYN **strangely**

Sin·ha·lese /ˌsɪnhəˈliz/ *n.* [C] **1** someone from one of the groups of people who live in Sri Lanka **2** one of the languages of Sri Lanka —**Sinhalese** *adj.*

sin·is·ter /ˈsɪnɪstə˞/ *adj.* making you feel that something evil, wrong, or illegal is happening or will happen: *a sinister laugh* | *A sinister figure lurked in the shadows.* | **there is something/nothing sinister...** *There was something sinister about the way things happened.* [**Origin:** 1400–1500 Old French *sinistre*, from Latin *sinister* **left-handed, unlucky**] → see also OMINOUS

sink¹ /sɪŋk/ W3 *v.* *past tense* **sank** /sæŋk/ or **sunk** /sʌŋk/ *past participle* **sunk**

1 IN WATER [I] to go down below the surface of water, mud etc. OPP **float**: *He threw in a coin, and it sank to the bottom of the pool.* | *The boat sank after hitting a rock.* | *The guns were sinking deeper and deeper in the mud.* ►see THESAURUS box at **dive¹** → see picture at FLOAT¹

2 DAMAGE SHIP [T] to damage a ship so badly that it goes down below the surface of water: *Three ships were sunk that night by enemy torpedoes.*

3 MOVE LOWER [I] to move down to a lower level: *The building's foundations have sunk several inches in recent years.* | *Gradually, the sun sank below the horizon.*

4 FALL/SIT DOWN [I] to fall down or sit down heavily, especially because you are very tired and weak: **+into/on/down etc.** *Tom sank down on the sofa, completely exhausted.*

5 GET WORSE [I always + adv./prep.] to gradually get into a worse condition: **sink into crisis/despair/decay etc.** *The country was sinking into political crisis.* | *Two days after the accident, Joyce sank into a coma.*

6 LOWER AMOUNT/VALUE [I] to go down in amount or value SYN **drop**: *The price of crude oil could sink even further.*

7 SPORTS [T] to put a ball into a hole or basket in games such as GOLF or basketball: *Pierce sank a three-point basket two minutes into the game.*

8 DIG INTO GROUND [T] if you sink something such as a well or part of a building, you dig a hole to put it into the ground: *The first exploratory oil well was sunk in late 1987.*

9 sb's heart sinks also **sb's spirits sink** used to say that someone loses hope or confidence: *My heart just sank when I read Patty's letter.*

10 be sunk SPOKEN to be in a situation when you are certain to fail or have a lot of problems: *If that check doesn't come today, we're really sunk.*

11 sink like a stone/rock also **sink without a trace** **a)** if something in water sinks like a stone, it sinks to the bottom very quickly **b)** if someone or something sinks like a stone, it is not popular and people forget about it very quickly: *The movie sank like a stone.*

12 SOUND [I] if a sound sinks, it becomes very quiet: **+into** *Sarah's voice sank into a whisper.*

13 have/get a sinking feeling to have or get a bad feeling when you suddenly realize that something bad is going to happen: *I had a sinking feeling in the pit of my stomach.*

14 sink so low also **sink to doing sth** to be dishonest enough or SELFISH enough to do something very bad or unfair SYN **stoop**: *How could he have sunk so low?*

15 sink or swim to succeed or fail without help from anyone else: *Law school is tough – it really is sink or swim.*

[**Origin:** Old English *sincan*]

sink in *phr. v.* if information, facts etc. sink in, you gradually understand them or realize their full meaning: *It took a moment for what he had said to sink in.*

sink sth **into** sth *phr. v.* **1** to spend a lot of money on something SYN **invest**: *They had sunk their entire savings into their house.* **2** to put something sharp into someone's flesh, into food etc.: *Walters sank his harpoon into the whale.* **3 sink your teeth into sth** **a)** to bite into something or start to eat it: *We couldn't wait to sink our teeth into one of those burgers.* **b)** to become actively involved in something that you think is very interesting: *a movie role he can really sink his teeth into*

sink² S3 *n.* [C] an open container in a kitchen or BATHROOM that you can fill with water and use for washing your hands or face, or for washing dishes etc.

SYN washbasin → see also **everything but the kitchen sink** at KITCHEN (2)

sink·er /ˈsɪŋkɚ/ *n.* [C] **1** a small heavy object that is attached to a string or net to keep it in the water when you are fishing → see also **hook, line, and sinker** at HOOK[1] (12) **2** a type of throw in baseball in which the ball drops very low as it crosses HOME PLATE

sink·hole /ˈsɪŋkhoʊl/ *n.* [C] **1** a large hole that forms in the ground **2** something that costs a lot of money over a long period of time, or uses a lot of time and other things: *The fighter plane program was a budget sinkhole.*

ˈsinking ˌfund *n.* [C] ECONOMICS money saved regularly by a business to pay for something in the future

sin·ner /ˈsɪnɚ/ *n.* [C] someone who has SINNED by not obeying God's laws

Sino- /saɪnoʊ/ *prefix* relating to China: *Sino-Japanese trade*

ˈsin tax *n.* [C] an additional tax that is put on the price of certain things that are unhealthy, such as cigarettes and alcohol

sin·u·ous /ˈsɪnyuəs/ *adj.* curving and twisting smoothly, like the movements of a snake: *a tree with sinuous branches* | *the sinuous movements of her head and arms*

si·nus /ˈsaɪnəs/ *n. plural* **sinuses** [C] BIOLOGY one of the hollow spaces in the bones of your face that are filled with air and are connected to the inside of your nose

si·nus·i·tis /ˌsaɪnəˈsaɪtɪs/ *n.* [U] a condition in which your sinuses swell up and become painful

Sioux /su/ a Native American tribe from the central northern region of the U.S. —**Sioux** *adj.*

sip[1] /sɪp/ *v.* **sipped, sipping** [I,T] to drink something slowly, taking very small mouthfuls: *Tom sipped his coffee thoughtfully.* | **+on/at** *He ate his sandwich and sipped on a soda.*

sip[2] *n.* [C] a very small amount of a drink: **+of** *a sip of coffee* | *Fraker poured some wine and **took a sip**.*

si·phon[1] /ˈsaɪfən/ *n.* [C] **1** a bent tube used for getting liquid out of a container, used by holding one end of the tube at a lower level than the end in the container **2** a type of bottle for holding SODA WATER, which is forced out of the bottle using gas pressure

siphon[2] *v.* [T] **1** to remove liquid from a container by using a siphon: **siphon sth off/out/into etc.** *Crews began siphoning oil from the leaking boat.* **2** ECONOMICS to take money from a business, account etc. dishonestly, in order to use it for a purpose for which it was not intended: **siphon sth off/from etc.** *Over $30 billion in relief aid had been siphoned off into foreign bank accounts.*

Si·quei·ros /sɪˈkeɪroʊs/, **Da·vid** /ˈdeɪvɪd/ (?1896–1974) a Mexican PAINTER famous for his wall paintings of political subjects

sir /sɚ/ S2 W3 *n.* **1** FORMAL used when speaking to a man in order to be polite or to show respect → see also MA'AM: *Excuse me, sir. Is this your jacket?* | *"Are you on duty tonight, Corporal?" "Yes, sir."* | *Dear Sir or Madam...* (=used at the beginning of a formal letter to someone you do not know) **2 Sir** a title used before the first name of a man who is a KNIGHT or a BARONET in Great Britain: *Sir James Wilson* **3 no/yes sir!** SPOKEN, INFORMAL used to emphasize a statement or an answer to a question: *I'm never going to do any more work for them. No sir!* [**Origin:** 1200–1300 Old French, Latin *senior* **older**]

sire[1] /saɪɚ/ *n.* **1 Sire** OLD USE used when speaking to a king **2** [C usually singular] BIOLOGY the father of a four-legged animal, especially a horse → see also DAM

sire[2] *v.* [T] **1** to be the father of an animal, especially a horse: *The stallion has sired several race winners.* **2** OLD-FASHIONED to be the father of a child

sir·ee, sirree /səˈri/ *n.* **no/yes siree (Bob)!** SPOKEN, INFORMAL used to emphasize a statement or an answer to a question: *But locking my keys in the truck's not the worst of it, no siree!*

si·ren /ˈsaɪrən/ *n.* [C] **1** a piece of equipment that makes very loud warning sounds, used on police cars, FIRE TRUCKS etc.: *the wail of police sirens* **2 a siren call/song** encouragement to do something that sounds very attractive, especially when this could have bad results: *Investors were lured by the siren call of Internet stocks.* **3** a word used especially in newspapers meaning a woman who is very attractive, but also dangerous to men **4 the Sirens** a group of women in ancient Greek stories, whose beautiful singing made SAILORS sail toward them into dangerous water

sir·loin /ˈsɚlɔɪn/ also **ˈsirloin ˌsteak** *n.* [C,U] expensive meat, cut from a cow's lower back

si·roc·co /sɪˈrɑkoʊ/ *n.* [C] EARTH SCIENCE a hot wind that blows from the desert of North Africa across to southern Europe

sir·ree /səˈri/ *n.* another spelling of SIREE

sis /sɪs/ *n.* SPOKEN a name used when speaking to your sister

si·sal /ˈsaɪsəl/ *n.* [C,U] a Central American plant whose leaves produce strong FIBERS which are used in making rope

sis·ter /ˈsɪstɚ/ S1 W1 *n.* [C] **1** a girl or woman who has the same parents as you: *He has two sisters and a brother.* | **big/older sister** *My older sister is a teacher.* | **little/younger sister** *Where's your little sister?* ►see THESAURUS box at **relative[1]** **2** also **Sister** a NUN: *Sister Mary Margaret* **3 a sister company/organization/ship etc.** a company etc. that belongs to the same group or organization: *one of the bank's sister companies* **4** SPOKEN a way of talking to or about an African American woman, used by African Americans **5** SPOKEN a word used by women to talk about other women and to show that they have feelings of friendship and support toward them: *We have to support our sisters in southern Africa.* [**Origin:** Old English *sweostor*]

ˈsister ˌcity *n.* [C] a city or town that has formed a relationship with a similar city in another country in order to encourage visits between them

sis·ter·hood /ˈsɪstɚˌhʊd/ *n.* **1** [U] a strong loyalty among women who share the same ideas and aims, especially relating to the improvement of women's rights and opportunities **2** [C] an organization of women, especially a religious one

ˈsister-in-ˌlaw *n. plural* **sisters-in-law** [C] **1** the sister of your husband or wife **2** your brother's wife **3** the wife of the brother of your husband or wife

sis·ter·ly /ˈsɪstɚli/ *adj.* typical of a loving sister: *sisterly affection*

sit /sɪt/ S1 W1 *v. past tense and past participle* **sat** /sæt/, **sitting**

1 IN A CHAIR ETC. a) [I] to be on a chair, in a seat, or on the ground, with the top half of your body upright and your weight resting on your BUTTOCKS: **+on/in etc.** *We sat on the floor, sorting through the pictures.* | *She was sitting in her rocking chair by the window.* | **+by/next to/beside etc.** *Who usually sits next to you in class?* | **sit doing sth** *Todd just sat staring into space for a while.* | **sit at a desk/table etc.** *I walked in and saw Steve sitting at the kitchen table.* | *He was restless, unable to **sit still**.* | *Several children **sat cross-legged** on the floor in front of her.* **b)** [I always + adv./prep.] also **sit down** to get into a sitting position after you have been standing up: *Jim walked over and sat beside her.* **c) sit upright** to sit in a position in which your back is straight, or to get into this position after lying down or bending: *An older woman was sitting upright at the desk.* | *She suddenly **sat bolt upright** (=very straight), staring at him.* **d)** [T always + adv./prep.] also **sit sb down** to make someone sit somewhere or help them to sit somewhere: **sit sb on/in etc.** *Just sit the children over here and give them something to drink.*

2 OBJECTS/BUILDINGS ETC. [I] to be in a particular position or condition: **+on/in etc.** *Your book is sitting on the shelf, right where you left it.* | **sit empty/unused/vacant etc.** *Most of the stores had sat vacant for years.*

3 DO NOTHING [I always + adv./prep.] to stay in one place

for a long time, especially sitting down, doing nothing useful or helpful: *I spent two hours just sitting on the freeway.* | *Are you just going to* ***sit there*** *all afternoon?* | *I'm not going to* ***sit here*** *and listen to you two argue.*
4 ANIMAL/BIRD a) [I always + adv./prep.] to be in, or get into, a resting position, with the tail end of the body resting on a surface: *Jeff's dog sat next to his chair as we talked.* **b) Sit!** used to tell a dog to sit with the tail end of its body on the ground or floor **c)** [I always + adv./prep.] if a bird sits on its eggs, it covers them with its body to make the eggs HATCH (=open)
5 sit tight a) SPOKEN to stay where you are and not move: *Just sit tight – I'll be there in ten minutes.* **b)** to stay in the same situation, and not change your mind or do anything new: *You might want to sit tight a few months and see what happens to the stock market.*
6 not sit well with sb if a situation, plan etc. does not sit well with someone, they do not like it: *The policy did not sit well with voters.*
7 COMMITTEE/COURT ETC. [I] **a)** to be a member of a committee, court, or other official group: **+on** *Critics have claimed that he is not qualified to sit on the court.* **b)** to have a meeting in order to carry out official business SYN **meet**: *The Court of Appeals sits in San Francisco.*
8 BABY/CHILD [I] SPOKEN to take care of a baby or child while its parents are out SYN **babysit**: **+for** *Kelly sits for them once a week.*
9 be sitting pretty to be in a very good or favorable position: *At that stage in the campaign, she was sitting pretty in the polls.*
10 sit on the fence to avoid saying which side of an argument you support or what your opinion is about a particular subject: *You can't sit on the fence any longer – what's it going to be?* → see also FENCE-SITTER
11 sit on your hands to delay taking action when you should do something: *The council has just been sitting on its hands on this issue.*
12 sit in judgment (on/over sb) to give your opinion about whether someone has done something wrong, especially when you have no right to do this
13 PICTURE/PHOTO [I + for] to sit somewhere so that you can be painted or photographed

sit around *phr. v.* to spend a lot of time sitting and doing nothing very useful: *Mostly we sat around and talked.*

sit back *phr. v.* **1** to get into a comfortable position and relax: *You* ***sit back and relax*** *– I'll fix dinner.* **2** to make no effort to get involved in something or influence what happens: *Don't just sit back and wait for new business to come to you.*

sit by *phr. v.* to take no action that would stop something bad from happening: *You're not going to just sit by and let this happen, are you?*

sit down *phr. v.* **1** to get into a sitting position or be in a sitting position: *Come on in and sit down.* | *We all sat down for dinner.* **2 sit sb down** to make someone sit down somewhere, or help them to sit down: *I helped her into the room and sat her down in the armchair.* **3 sit sb down** to make someone sit down and listen to something, especially when you are angry or need to tell them something important: *Your need to sit Bobby down and explain why we can't afford to go.* **4 sit down and do sth** to try to solve a problem or deal with something that needs to be done, by giving it all your attention: *Sit down and work out what you spend each month.*

sit in *phr. v.* **1** to be present at a meeting, but not take an active part in it: **+on** *We sat in on a couple of French classes.* **2 sit in for sb** to do a job, go to a meeting etc. instead of the person who usually does it: *Sawyer sat in for Jennings on the evening news for a week.*

sit on sth *phr. v.* INFORMAL to delay dealing with something: *If you have a genuine complaint, don't just sit on it.*

sit sth ↔ **out** *phr. v.* **1** to not take part in something such as a game or dance, especially when you usually take part: *Johnson sat out the game with a shoulder injury.* **2** to stay where you are until something finishes, especially something boring or bad SYN **wait out**: *When the war started, her family decided to stay in the country and* ***sit it out.***

sit through sth *phr. v.* to attend a meeting, performance etc., and stay until the end, even if it is very long and boring: *We had to sit through three hours of speeches.*

sit up *phr. v.* **1** to be in a sitting position or get into a sitting position after you have been lying down: *By Monday, Tina was well enough to sit up in bed.* **2 sit sb up** to help someone to sit after they have been lying down **3** to sit in a chair with your back up straight: ***Sit up straight*** *and finish your dinner.* **4** to stay up very late: *Rick sat up all night studying for his physics final.* **5 sit up and take notice** to suddenly start paying attention to someone or something: *The speech made voters sit up and take notice.*
[**Origin:** Old English *sittan*]

WORD CHOICE sit, sit at/in front of/on/in, sit down, seat, be seated
• You **sit at** a table, piano, or desk (unless you choose to **sit on** them!), and also **at** a computer or the controls of a car or airplane. However, you **sit in front of** the television or the fire (though you can also **sit by** or **around** a fire).
• You **sit on** something that has a flat level surface such as the floor, the grass, a simple hard chair, a bench, a sofa, or a bed.
• You **sit in** a tree, long grass, a car, a room, an armchair, or the driver's seat of a car.
• When you are talking about the action of moving from standing to sitting, it is more common to use **sit down** rather than **sit** on its own: *Afterward, everyone sat down again* (NOT *sat again*). *Please sit down.*
• Note that **seat** as a verb is only transitive. It is fairly formal, and is used in these ways: *The theater seats 500 people* (=has seats for 500 people). | *The hostess will seat you* (=show you where you can sit).
• **Be seated** is a formal expression for **sit down**. At a formal dinner or in church, for example, you might hear: *Please be seated* (=please sit down).

sit·ar /ˈsɪtɑr/ *n.* [C] a musical instrument from India that looks like a GUITAR and has two sets of strings, a long wooden neck, and a round body

sit·com /ˈsɪt˺kɑm/ *n.* [C,U] **situation comedy** a funny television program in which the same characters appear in different situations each week

ˈsit-down *adj.* **1** a sit-down meal or restaurant is one in which you sit at a table and eat a formal meal: *a sit-down dinner party* **2 a sit-down strike/protest** an occasion when a large group of people protests something by sitting down in a public place and not leaving until their demands are listened to

site¹ /saɪt/ Ac S3 W1 *n.* [C] **1** a place where something important or interesting happened: *a historical site* | **+of** *the site of a Civil War battle* ►see THESAURUS box at **place¹** **2** an area of ground where something is being built or will be built: *a construction site* | **+of/for** *The school board has approved the site for the high school.* **3** a place that is used for a particular purpose: *a camp site* | **+of/for** *a nesting site for birds* **4 on site** at the place where something happens: *An engineer will be on site to supervise the construction.* **5** a WEBSITE
[**Origin:** 1300–1400 Old French, Latin *situs*, from *sinere* **to leave, put**]

site² Ac *v.* **be sited** be placed or built in a particular place: **+in/near etc.** *The zoo is sited in the middle of the city.*

ˌsite-speˈcific *adj.* designed and made to be used in a particular place, or relating to a particular place: *site-specific artworks*

ˈsit-in *n.* [C] POLITICS a type of protest in which people refuse to leave the place where they work or study until their demands are dealt with SYN **protest**: **hold/stage a sit-in** *Students staged a sit-in to protest the firing of a popular professor.*

sit·ter /ˈsɪt̬ɚ/ *n.* [C] **1** SPOKEN A BABYSITTER **2** someone who sits or stands somewhere so that someone else can paint them or take photographs of them

sit·ting /ˈsɪtɪŋ/ *n.* [C] **1 at/in one sitting** during one continuous period when you are sitting in a chair: *I read the whole book in one sitting.* **2** one of the times when a meal is served in a place where there is not enough space for everyone to eat at the same time: *Dinner is served in three sittings.* **3** an occasion when you have yourself painted or photographed

Sitting ˈBull (?1834–1890) a Sioux chief famous for fighting against General George Custer

Sitting Bull

sitting ˈduck *n.* [C] someone who is easy to attack or easy to cheat: *We were like sitting ducks for pickpockets.*

sitting room *n.* [C] OLD-FASHIONED the room in a house where you sit, relax, watch television etc. SYN **living room**

sit·u /ˈsɪtu, ˈsaɪtu/ → see IN SITU

sit·u·ate /ˈsɪtʃuˌeɪt/ *v.* **1** [T] to describe or consider something as being part of something else or relating to something else: **situate sth in sth** *Students will be expected to situate the novel in its historical context.* **2** [T always + adv./prep.] to put something in a particular place or position: *Tax preparation services generally situate themselves in storefront offices.*

sit·u·at·ed /ˈsɪtʃuˌeɪtɪd/ *adj.* **be situated** to be in a particular place or position SYN **be located**: *The house is situated on a small hill.* | **beautifully/conveniently/ideally etc. situated** *Troops occupied a town strategically situated near the Chinese border.*

sit·u·a·tion /ˌsɪtʃuˈeɪʃən/ S1 W1 *n.* [C] a combination of all the things that are happening and all the conditions that exist at a particular time in a particular place: *Everyone knew how serious the situation was.* | **deal with/handle a situation** *She handled a difficult situation very well.* | *What would you do if you were **in my situation**?* | **economic/political/financial situation** *Discuss your financial situation with an accountant.*

THESAURUS

state of affairs FORMAL a situation: *Teenagers must rebel against their parents to some degree; this is a healthy state of affairs.*
circumstances the conditions that affect a situation, action, event etc: *When the circumstances are more dangerous, more supervision is needed.*
things life in general and the way it is affecting people: *Things have improved since then.*
position the situation that someone is in, especially when this affects what they can and cannot do: *They were in a strong position to negotiate higher rates.*
case a situation that exists, especially as it affects a particular person or group: *Sometimes small events have enormous consequences, which is the case here.*

ˌsituation ˈcomedy *n.* [C,U] FORMAL a SITCOM

ˈsit-up *n.* [C] an exercise to make your stomach muscles strong, in which you sit up from a lying position, while keeping your feet on the floor SYN **crunch**: *He **does** a hundred **sit-ups** every day.*

SI U·nit /ˌɛs ˈaɪ ˌyunɪt/ *n.* [C] SCIENCE a standard unit of measurement in the INTERNATIONAL SYSTEM OF UNITS, used for measuring distance, weight, time, temperature, electric current, amounts of a substance, and strength of light. There are seven SI Units: the meter, kilogram, second, AMPERE, KELVIN, MOLE, and CANDELA.

six /sɪks/ *number* **1** 6 **2** six o'clock: *I'll be home **at six**.* **3 it's six of one and half a dozen of the other** SPOKEN used to say there is not much difference between two possible choices, situations etc. **4 six figures** a number that is between 100,000 and one million dollars: *a salary in the low six figures* **5 six feet under** HUMOROUS dead and buried [**Origin:** Old English]

ˌSix Day ˈWar, the HISTORY a war between Israel on one side and Egypt, Jordan, and Syria on the other, that was fought in June 1967. As a result of the war, Israel gained control of several areas of land.

ˈsix-figure *adj.* [only before noun] used to describe a number between 100,000 and one million, especially an amount of money

six·fold /ˌsɪksˈfould◂/ *adv.* by six times as much or as many —**sixfold** *adj.* [only before noun] *a sixfold increase*

ˌsix-ˈfooter *n.* [C] INFORMAL someone who is at least six feet (1.83 meters) tall

ˈsix-pack *n.* [C] **1** six cans of a drink, especially beer, sold together as a set: +**of** *a six-pack of beer* **2** INFORMAL well-developed muscles that you can see on a man's stomach → see also **Joe Six-Pack** at JOE (3)

ˈsix-ˌshooter *n.* [C] INFORMAL a type of short gun that can hold six bullets, especially one that was used in the western U.S. in the past

six·teen /ˌsɪkˈstin◂/ *number* 16

six·teenth¹ /ˌsɪkˈstinθ◂/ *adj.* 16th; next after the fifteenth: *the sixteenth century*

sixteenth² *pron.* **the sixteenth** the 16th thing in a series: *Let's have dinner on the sixteenth* (=the 16th day of the month).

sixteenth³ *n.* [C] 1/16; one of sixteen equal parts

ˈsixteenth ˌnote *n.* [C] a musical note which continues for a sixteenth of the length of a WHOLE NOTE

sixth¹ /sɪksθ/ *adj.* 6th; next after the fifth: *June is the sixth month.*

sixth² *pron.* **the sixth** the 6th thing in a series: *I'll call you on the sixth* (=the 6th day of the month).

sixth³ *n.* [C] 1/6; one of six equal parts: *The money represents about **a sixth of** my income.* | **one-sixth/five-sixths etc.** *Only one-sixth of the electorate voted.*

ˌsixth ˈsense *n.* [singular] a special feeling or ability to know things, without using any of your five ordinary senses such as your hearing or sight: *Rob has a sixth sense for making the right investment.*

six·ti·eth¹ /ˈsɪkstiɪθ/ *adj.* 60th; next after the fifty-ninth: *It's my father's sixtieth birthday tomorrow.*

sixtieth² *pron.* **the sixtieth** the 60th thing in a series

six·ty /ˈsɪksti/ *number* **1** 60 **2 the sixties** also **the '60s** the years from 1960 through 1969 **3 sb's sixties** the time when someone is 60 to 69 years old: **in your early/mid/late sixties** *I'd guess she's in her late sixties.* **4 in the sixties** if the temperature is in the sixties, it is between 60° and 69° FAHRENHEIT: **in the high/low sixties** *It was in the high sixties and sunny.*

siz·a·ble, sizeable /ˈsaɪzəbəl/ *adj.* fairly large: *a sizable crowd*

size¹ /saɪz/ S1 W1 *n.*
1 HOW BIG [C,U] how big or small something is: *reductions in class sizes in schools* | *There are restrictions on **the size** and weight **of** packages we can ship.* | *Jensen's house **is the same size as** ours.* | *The human heart **is** about **the size of** a fist.* | *It can take many years for the salmon to reach its **full size**.* | *Leave the dough in a warm place until it has doubled **in size**.* | **small/large size** *Despite its small size, the car has a lot of room inside.* | **be half/twice/three times etc. the size of sb/sth** *The city is twice the size of Chicago.* | **(of) this/that size** *Nobody thought a town this size could support an orchestra.* | **in all/different/various shapes and sizes** *Pasta comes in all different shapes and sizes.*
2 VERY BIG [U] the fact of being very big: *I couldn't believe **the size of** their house!* | *The most impressive thing about the diamond is its **sheer size**.*
3 CLOTHES/PRODUCTS [C] one of a set of standard measures according to which clothes and other goods are produced and sold: *The shirts are available in three*

S

sizes. | **a size 6/8/12 etc.** *Do you have these pants in a size 12?* | **take/wear a size** *What size shoes does Kelly wear?* | **shoe/shirt/dress etc. size** *I'm not sure what his shirt size is.* | *"I'm looking for a jacket." **"What size are you?"***
4 cut/chop/trim etc. sth to size to cut something so that it is the right size for a particular use: *Trim the paper to size.*
5 size matters HUMOROUS used to say that larger things are better than smaller things
6 that's about the size of it SPOKEN used to agree that what someone has said about a situation is a good or correct way of describing it
7 GLUE [U] SIZING
[**Origin:** 1100–1200 Old French *assise* **sitting to make a legal judgment or a judgment on standard amounts**, from *asseoir* **to seat**] → see also **cut sb down to size** at CUT[1], -SIZE, -SIZED, **try sth on for size** at TRY ON (2)

size[2] *v.* [T] **1** [usually passive] to make something into a particular size or sizes: *Most costume patterns are sized for children.* **2** [usually passive] to sort things according to their size **3** to cover or treat something with SIZING

size sb/sth ↔ **up** *phr. v.* to look at or consider a person or situation and make a judgment about them: *They stood at opposite sides of the room, sizing each other up.*

S

-size /saɪz/ [in adjectives] **1** of a particular size, or about the same size and shape as something SYN **-sized**: *an average-size room* | *poster-size color photos* **2** used to say that something is big enough or small enough for a particular purpose: *a pocket-size microscope* | *family-size cartons of juice* → see also BITE-SIZE, KING-SIZE, QUEEN-SIZE

size·a·ble /ˈsaɪzəbəl/ another spelling of SIZABLE

-sized /saɪzd/ *adj.* of a particular size, or about the same size and shape as something SYN **-size**: *a medium-sized dog* | *pea-sized hailstones* | **good-sized/fair-sized/decent-sized** (=big enough for a particular purpose)

siz·ing /ˈsaɪzɪŋ/ *n.* [U] **1** a thick sticky liquid used for giving stiffness and a shiny surface to cloth, paper etc. **2** the way things are grouped according to size

siz·zle /ˈsɪzəl/ *v.* [I] **1** to make a sound like water falling on hot metal, while cooking: *Bacon was sizzling in the pan downstairs.* **2** to be very exciting: *The city sizzles during the annual jazz festival.* —**sizzle** *n.* [singular, U]

siz·zler /ˈsɪzlɚ/ *n.* [C] something that is very exciting

siz·zling /ˈsɪzlɪŋ/ *adj.* **1** very hot: *a sizzling summer day* **2** very exciting, especially in a sexual way: *sizzling sex scenes*

SJ a written abbreviation used after a priest's name, to show that he is a JESUIT

ska /skɑ/ *n.* [U] a kind of popular music originally from Jamaica with a fast regular beat, similar to REGGAE

skates

skate[1] /skeɪt/ *n.* **1** [C] one of a pair of boots with metal blades on the bottom, for moving quickly on ice SYN **ice skate** **2** [C] one of a pair of boots or frames with small wheels on the bottom, for moving quickly on flat smooth surfaces SYN **roller skate** SYN **in-line skate** **3** [C,U] *plural* **skate** or **skates** BIOLOGY a large flat ocean fish that can be eaten [**Origin:** (1, 2) 1600–1700 Dutch *schaats* **stilt**, **skate**, from Old North French *escache* **stilt**]

skate[2] S3 *v.* [I] **1** to move on skates: *The children skated on the frozen pond.* → ICE-SKATE, ROLLER-SKATE ▸see THESAURUS box at **slide**[1] **2** to ride on a skateboard SYN **skateboard** **3 be skating on thin ice** INFORMAL to be doing something that may get you into trouble if you are not careful —**skater** *n.* [C]

skate over/around sth *phr. v.* to avoid mentioning a problem or subject, or not give it enough attention: *I could tell he was skating around the issue of pay.*

skate·board /ˈskeɪt˺bɔrd/ *n.* [C] a short board with two small wheels at each end, which you can stand on and ride for fun or as a sport —**skateboard** *v.* [I] —**skateboarder** *n.* [C] → see picture at SKATE[1]

skate·board·ing /ˈskeɪt˺bɔrdɪŋ/ *n.* [U] the activity of riding a skateboard for fun or as a sport

ˈskate park also **ˈskating park** *n.* [C] a special area outside where you can SKATEBOARD, IN-LINE SKATE, or ROLLER-SKATE

skat·ing /ˈskeɪṭɪŋ/ *n.* [U] **1** the activity of moving around on SKATES for fun or as a sport **2** the activity of riding on a SKATEBOARD SYN **skateboarding**

ˈskating ˌrink *n.* [C] a place or building where you can SKATE

ske·dad·dle /skɪˈdædl/ *v.* [I] HUMOROUS to leave a place quickly, especially because you do not want to be caught

skee·ter /ˈskiṭɚ/ *n.* [C] SPOKEN, INFORMAL a word meaning MOSQUITO, used mainly in the southern U.S.

skeet shoot·ing /ˈskit ˌʃuṭɪŋ/ *n.* [U] the sport of shooting at clay objects that have been thrown into the air —**skeet shooter** *n.* [C]

skein /skeɪn/ *n.* [C] **1** a long loosely wound piece of YARN **2** a complicated series of things that are related to each other: +**of** *a complex skein of stories*

skel·e·tal /ˈskɛlətl/ *adj.* **1** BIOLOGY like a skeleton, or relating to a skeleton: *Police found only skeletal remains.* **2** extremely thin and bony: *skeletal fingers* ▸see THESAURUS box at **thin**[1] **3** containing only the most basic parts: *a skeletal analysis*

skel·e·ton[1] /ˈskɛlət˺n/ *n.* [C]
1 BONES a) BIOLOGY the structure consisting of all the bones in a human or animal body: *the human skeleton* | +**of** *the skeleton of a dinosaur* **b)** a set of these bones or a model of them, fastened in their usual positions, used for example by medical students
2 STRUCTURE the supporting structure of a building, bridge etc.: *The office building's steel skeleton rose above the skyline.*
3 THIN an extremely thin person or animal: *After three years in prison, he had been reduced to a skeleton.*
4 BASIC PART the most important parts of something, to which more detail can be added later: *We have agreed the skeleton of the plan.*
5 a skeleton in the closet an embarrassing or bad secret about something that happened to you in the past: *Everyone **has a few skeletons in the closet.***
[**Origin:** 1500–1600 Modern Latin, Greek, from *skeletos* **dried up**]

skeleton[2] *adj.* **a skeleton staff/crew/service etc.** only enough workers or services to keep an operation or organization running

ˈskeleton key *n.* [C] a key made to open a number of different locks

skep·tic /ˈskɛptɪk/ *n.* [C] someone who has doubts about whether something is true, right, or good: *religious skeptics* [**Origin:** 1500–1600 Greek *skeptikos* **thoughtful**, from *skeptesthai* **to look, consider**]

skep·ti·cal /ˈskɛptɪkəl/ *adj.* **1** having doubts about whether something is true, right, or good: +**about/of** *Initially, he was skeptical about whether the stories were*

skeleton

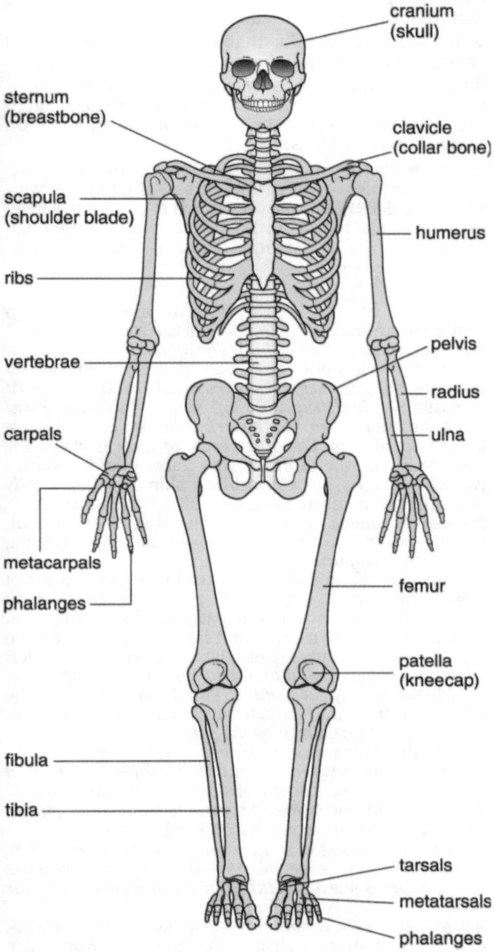

true. | **highly/deeply skeptical** *Some scientists remain highly skeptical of the theory.* **2** tending to doubt or not believe what other people tell you: *an increasingly skeptical American public* —**skeptically** /-kli/ *adv.*

skep·ti·cism /ˈskɛptəˌsɪzəm/ *n.* [U] an attitude of doubt about whether something is true, right, or good

sketch¹ /skɛtʃ/ *n.* [C] ENG. LANG. ARTS **1** a simple quickly made drawing that does not show much detail: +**of** *a sketch of a child* | *a* ***rough sketch*** *of the building* | **do/make/draw a sketch** *I usually do a couple of pencil sketches before I start a painting.* ►see THESAURUS box at **drawing**, **picture¹** **2** a short humorous scene on television, in the theater etc., that is part of a larger show: *a comedy sketch* **3** a short written or spoken description: *a brief sketch of the artist's life* [**Origin:** 1600–1700 Dutch *schets*, from Italian *schizzo*, from *schizzare* **to splash**]

sketch² *v.* [I,T] ENG. LANG. ARTS **1** to draw a sketch of something ►see THESAURUS box at **draw¹** **2** also **sketch out** to describe something in a general way, giving the basic ideas: *We've sketched out what needs to be covered this semester.*

sketch sth ↔ **in** *phr. v.* to add more information about something: *I'd like to sketch in a few details for you.*

sketch·pad /ˈskɛtʃpæd/ also **sketch·book** /ˈskɛtʃbʊk/ *n.* [C] a number of sheets of paper fastened together and used for drawing

sketch·y /ˈskɛtʃi/ *adj. comparative* **sketchier**, *superlative* **sketchiest** **1** not thorough or complete, and not having enough details to be useful: *Details of the accident are still sketchy.* **2** INFORMAL not completely safe or able to be trusted: *The neighborhood is a little sketchy at night.* —**sketchily** *adv.*

skew /skyu/ *v.* [T] **1** to affect a test or an attempt to get information in a particular way, which makes the results incorrect: *The error could skew the findings of the research.* **2** to influence someone's opinion or judgment in a way that makes it not fair or reasonable [**Origin:** 1300–1400 Old North French *escuer* **to avoid**]

skewed /skyud/ *adj.* **1** a skewed opinion, piece of information, result etc. is incorrect, especially because it has been affected by a particular thing or because you do not know all the facts: *The media's coverage of the election was skewed in favor of the ruling party.* **2** something that is skewed is not straight and is higher on one side than the other → see also ASKEW

skew·er¹ /ˈskyuɚ/ *n.* [C] a long metal or wooden stick that is put through pieces of meat and vegetables before they are cooked

skewer² *v.* [T] **1** to make a hole through a piece of food with a skewer → see picture on page A32 **2** to press a long sharp object into a thing or person **3** to criticize someone very strongly, often in a way that other people find humorous: *He skewered the popular press for its simplistic approach to social problems.*

ˈskew lines *n.* [plural] MATH straight lines that are not in the same PLANE are not parallel, and do not touch each other or cross

ski¹ /ski/ *n. plural* **skis** [C] **1** one of a pair of long thin narrow pieces of wood or plastic that you fasten to your boots and use for moving on snow: *a pair of skis* | *ski equipment* **2** a long thin narrow piece of strong material, fastened under a small vehicle so that it can travel on snow [**Origin:** 1700–1800 Norwegian, Old Norse *skith* **stick of wood, ski**]

ski² *v.* **skied**, **skiing** [I] to move on skis as a sport, or in order to travel on snow: *I'm learning to ski.* ►see THESAURUS box at **slide¹** → see also SKIER

ˈski boot *n.* [C] a specially made stiff boot that fastens onto a ski → see picture at BOOT¹

skid

skid¹ /skɪd/ *v.* **skidded**, **skidding** [I] if a vehicle or wheel skids, it suddenly slides sideways and you cannot control it: +**off/across etc.** *The car skidded off the icy road.* ►see THESAURUS box at **slide¹**

skid² *n.*

1 SLIDING MOVEMENT [C] a sudden sliding movement of a vehicle, that you cannot control: *Tony slammed on the brakes and the car* ***went into a skid*** (=started to skid). | *Long* ***skid marks*** *on the pavement showed that the driver had tried to brake.*

2 on the skids INFORMAL in a situation that is bad and getting worse: *Truck sales have been on the skids.*

3 hit the skids to suddenly become much worse or less successful

4 put the skids on sth INFORMAL to make it likely or certain that something will fail

5 grease the skids to prepare a situation so that something can happen more easily

6 **HELICOPTER** [C usually plural] a flat narrow part that is under some aircraft such as HELICOPTERS, used in addition to wheels for landing
7 **USED TO LIFT/MOVE** [C usually plural] a piece of wood that is put under a heavy object to lift or move it
8 **NOT SUCCESSFUL** [C usually singular] a period of time during which someone or something is not successful: *a six-game losing skid*

ˌskid ˈrow, Skid Row *n.* **1 be on skid row** if someone is on skid row, they drink too much alcohol and have no job, nowhere to live etc. **2** [U] a part of a city with a lot of old buildings in bad condition, where poor people who drink too much alcohol spend their time

ski·er /ˈskiɚ/ *n.* [C] someone who SKIS

skies /skaɪz/ *n.* the plural of SKY

skiff /skɪf/ *n.* [C] a small light boat for one person

ski·ing /ˈski-ɪŋ/ S3 *n.* [U] the sport of moving down hills or across land in the snow, wearing SKIS: *We're **going skiing** in Colorado this winter.*

ˈski jump *n.* [C] a long steep sloping PLATFORM, which people go down on SKIS and jump off in sports competitions

ˈski ˌjumping *n.* [U] a sport in which people wearing SKIS slide down a ski jump and jump off the end as far as possible

skil·ful /ˈskɪlfəl/ *adj.* the British and Canadian spelling of SKILLFUL

ˈski lift *n.* [C] a piece of equipment that carries SKIERS up to the top of a SKI SLOPE

skill /skɪl/ S2 W1 *n.* **1** [U] the ability to do something well, especially because you have learned and practiced it: *The game takes a lot of skill.* | **+at/in** *Gibson's skill at hitting the ball is outstanding.* | *The whole team played **with great skill** and determination.* | **a level/degree of skill** *The job requires a high degree of skill.* **2** [C] a particular ability that someone has because they have learned and practiced it: **develop/learn/acquire a skill** *You're never too old to learn new skills.* | **computer/management/communication etc. skills** *I need to improve my computer skills.* | *Many of the employees have limited English **language skills**.* | *Reading and writing are **basic skills** that everyone should have.* ►see THESAURUS box at **ability** [**Origin:** 1100–1200 Old Norse *skil* **good judgment, knowledge**]

skilled /skɪld/ *adj.* **1** someone who is skilled has the training and experience that is needed to do something well OPP **unskilled**: *a skilled technician* | **+at/in** *He was not skilled at debating.* | *She is a **highly skilled** (=very skilled) dancer.* | *There is a shortage of **skilled labor** in the area.* **2** skilled work needs people with special abilities or training to do it OPP **unskilled**

skil·let /ˈskɪlɪt/ *n.* [C] a flat heavy cooking pan with a long handle SYN **frying pan**

skill·ful /ˈskɪlfəl/ *adj.* **1** good at doing something, especially something that needs special ability or training: *a skillful surgeon* | **+at** *She's very skillful at drawing.* **2** made or done very well, showing a lot of ability: *I was impressed by her skillful handling of the situation.* —**skillfully** *adv.*

skim /skɪm/ *v.* **skimmed**, **skimming** **1** [T] to remove something from the surface of a liquid, especially floating oil or solids: **skim sth off/from sth** *Skim any oil off the surface of the sauce.* **2** [I,T] to read something quickly to find the main facts or ideas in it: *Jack opened the paper and skimmed the headlines.* | **+through** *I skimmed through the article.* **3** [I,T] to move along quickly, nearly touching a surface: *Seagulls were skimming the waves.*

skim sth ↔ **off** *phr. v.* **1** to take money illegally or dishonestly: *For years his business partner had been skimming off the profits.* **2** to take part of something that other people want, especially the best part of it: *Top universities skim off the best students.*

ˈski mask *n.* [C] a warm KNIT hat that covers most of your head and face

skim·mer /ˈskɪmɚ/ *n.* [C] **1** a ship that is used for cleaning up oil from the surface of the ocean **2** a bird that flies low over the ocean

ˌskim ˈmilk *n.* [U] milk that has had all the fat and cream removed from it → see also ONE PERCENT MILK

skimp /skɪmp/ *v.* [I] to not spend enough money or time on something, or not use enough of something, so that what you do is unsuccessful or of bad quality: **+on** *Don't skimp on the cream.*

skimp·y /ˈskɪmpi/ *adj.* *comparative* **skimpier**, *superlative* **skimpiest** **1** a skimpy dress, skirt etc. is very short and does not cover very much of a woman's body ►see THESAURUS box at **clothes** **2** not providing enough of something: *a skimpy meal* —**skimpily** *adv.* —**skimpiness** *n.* [U]

skin¹ /skɪn/ S2 W2 *n.*
1 BODY [U] **a)** BIOLOGY the natural outer layer of a human or animal body: *Her skin was red from the sun.* | *Soap can irritate your skin.* | *The toad's skin produces a poisonous substance.* | *a skin disease* | **sensitive/delicate skin** *Babies have very sensitive skin.* | **soft/smooth** *She had beautiful soft skin.* | **fair/pale/dark/olive etc. skin** *a man with dark skin and dark eyes* | **a layer/fold of skin** *The outer layer of skin is called the epidermis.* **b)** the skin on your face: **oily/dry skin** *a cleanser for oily skin* | **good/bad skin** *Todd has really bad skin* (=unhealthy looking skin). → -SKINNED
2 FROM AN ANIMAL [C,U] BIOLOGY the skin of an animal, sometimes including its fur, used to make leather, clothes etc.: *leopard skins*
3 FOOD [C,U] **a)** BIOLOGY the natural thin outer cover of some fruits and vegetables: *potato skins* | *onion skin* **b)** the outer cover of a SAUSAGE SYN **casing**
4 ON A LIQUID [C,U] a thin solid layer that forms on the top of some liquids when they get cold or are left without a cover: *a skin on the top of the pudding*
5 by the skin of your teeth if you do something by the skin of your teeth, you just barely succeed in doing it: *Jeff just got into college by the skin of his teeth.*
6 have thin/thick skin to be easily upset or not easily upset by criticism: *You need to have thick skin to be a salesperson.* → see also THICK-SKINNED, THIN-SKINNED
7 be (all) skin and bones INFORMAL to be extremely thin in a way that is unattractive and unhealthy
8 get under sb's skin if someone gets under your skin, they annoy you, especially by the way they behave: *Kids will say some mean things to try and get under your skin.*
9 make sb's skin crawl to make someone feel nervous, disgusted, or slightly afraid: *The thought of him touching me just makes my skin crawl.*
10 it's no skin off sb's nose SPOKEN used to say that someone does not care what another person thinks or does, because it does not affect them: *It's no skin off our nose if they don't want to come along.*
11 OUTER LAYER [C] the outer layer of a vehicle, building, or object
12 COMPUTERS [C] the way in which information appears on a computer screen, especially when this can be changed easily
[**Origin:** 1100–1200 Old Norse *skinn*] → see also **jump out of your skin** at JUMP¹ (6), **save sb's skin/bacon/neck/butt** at SAVE¹ (10)

skin² *v.* **skinned**, **skinning** **1** [T] to remove the skin from an animal, fruit, or vegetable: *Skin and slice the tomatoes.* **2** [T] to hurt a part of your body by rubbing off some skin: *She fell and skinned her knee.* **3 skin sb alive** INFORMAL to punish someone very severely: *Richard would skin me alive if he ever found out.* **4 there is more than one way to skin a cat** used to say that there is more than one way to achieve something **5** [T] INFORMAL to completely defeat someone

skin·care /ˈskɪnkɛr/ *adj.* skincare products are intended to improve the condition of your skin, especially the skin on your face —**skin care** *n.* [U]

ˌskin ˈdeep *adj.* something that is skin deep seems to be important or effective, but in fact it is not, because it only affects the way things appear: *Beauty is only skin deep.*

ˈskin ˌdiving *n.* [U] the sport of swimming under water with light breathing equipment, but without a protective suit —**skin diver** *n.* [C]

skin flick *n.* [C] SLANG a PORNOGRAPHIC movie (=one with a lot of sex in it)

skin·flint /ˈskɪnˌflɪnt/ *n.* [C] DISAPPROVING someone who hates spending money or giving it away SYN **miser**

skin graft /ˈskɪngræft/ *n.* [C] a medical operation in which healthy skin is removed from one part of your body and used on another to replace burned or damaged skin

skin·head /ˈskɪnhɛd/ *n.* [C] a young white person who has hair that is cut very short, especially one who behaves violently toward people of other races

skin·less /ˈskɪnlɪs/ *adj.* [only before noun] skinless meat, especially chicken, has had the skin removed from it

-skinned /skɪnd/ [in adjectives] **dark-skinned/smooth-skinned/brown-skinned etc.** having a particular type or color of skin

Skin·ner /ˈskɪnɚ/, **B.F.** (1904–1990) a U.S. PSYCHOLOGIST famous for developing the ideas of BEHAVIORISM

skin·ny¹ /ˈskɪni/ *adj. comparative* **skinnier**, *superlative* **skinniest** very thin, especially in a way that is unattractive: *skinny little kids* ►see THESAURUS box at **thin¹**

skinny² *n.* **the skinny** SPOKEN information, especially secret information, about someone or something: *What's the skinny on the new guy?*

skinny-ˌdipping *n.* [U] swimming with no clothes on: *Some of us* ***went skinny-dipping*** *in the lake.*

skin-ˈtight *adj.* [only before noun] skin-tight clothes fit extremely tightly against your body

skip¹ /skɪp/ S3 *v.* **skipped, skipping**

1 NOT DO STH [T] to not do something that you usually do, or that you should do: *Skipping meals is not a good way to lose weight.* | **skip class/school** *He skipped school three days in a row.*

2 NOT DEAL WITH STH [I,T] to not read, mention, or deal with something that would normally come or happen next: *I decided to skip the first two chapters.* | **+to** *Well, let's skip to question eight for now.* | **+over** *Can we skip over the details?*

3 CHANGE SUBJECTS [I always + adv./prep.] to go from one subject or activity to another in no particular order: **+around** *I wish you wouldn't keep skipping around.* | **skip from sth to sth** *She keeps skipping from one topic to another.*

4 MOVE ON FOOT [I] to move forward with little jumps between big jumping steps: *Shelly skipped down the sidewalk.* ►see THESAURUS box at **jump¹**

5 skip it! SPOKEN INFORMAL used to say angrily and rudely that you do not want to talk about something

6 skip town/the country to leave a place suddenly and secretly, especially to avoid being punished or paying debts

7 skip a year/grade to start a new school year in a class that is one year ahead of the class you would normally enter

8 skip a rock/stone to throw a smooth flat stone into a lake, river etc. in a way that makes it jump across the surface

9 BALL [I always + adv./prep.] if a ball or something similar skips off a surface, it quickly moves away from that surface after hitting it: **+off/along/across etc.** *The ball skipped off his glove and bounced toward the fence.*

10 skip rope to jump over a rope as you swing it over your head and under your feet, as a game or for exercise SYN **jump rope**

skip out *phr. v.* to leave suddenly and secretly, especially in order to avoid being punished or paying money: *They skipped out without paying.* | **+on** *Joel skipped out on his wife when she was eight months pregnant.*

skip² *n.* [C] a quick light stepping and jumping movement

ˈski pants *n.* [plural] thick pants with long thin pieces of cloth that fasten over your shoulders, worn while SKIing

ˈski plane *n.* [C] an airplane that has long thin narrow parts on the bottom instead of wheels, for landing on snow

ˈski pole *n.* [C] one of two pointed short poles used for balancing and for pushing against the snow when SKIing

skip·per¹ /ˈskɪpɚ/ *n.* [C] **1** the person in charge of a boat or ship **2** INFORMAL the person in charge of a sports team SYN **coach**

skipper² *v.* [T] **1** to be in charge of a boat or ship **2** to be in charge of a sports team, business etc.

skirl /skɚl/ *v.* [I] to make a high sharp sound, like the sound of BAGPIPES —**skirl** *n.* [singular]

skir·mish¹ /ˈskɚmɪʃ/ *n.* [C] **1** a fight between small groups of soldiers, ships etc., especially one that happens away from the main part of a battle ►see THESAURUS box at **war** **2** a short argument, especially between political opponents [**Origin:** 1300–1400 Old French *escaramouche*, from Old Italian *scaramuccia*]

skirmish² *v.* [I] to be involved in a short fight or argument

skirt¹ /skɚt/ S2 *n.* [C] **1** a piece of outer clothing worn by women and girls, which hangs down from the

S

skin

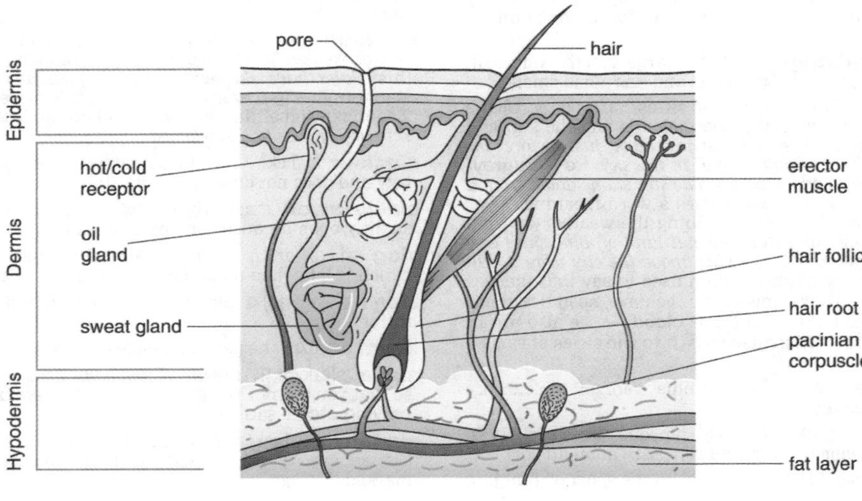

waist like the bottom part of a dress → see also DRESS: *She was wearing a short skirt.* **2** something that covers or protects something: *a skirt around the base of the Christmas tree* **3** also **skirts** OLD-FASHIONED the part of a dress or coat that hangs down from the waist [**Origin:** 1200–1300 Old Norse *skyrta* **shirt**]

skirt² also **skirt around** *v.* [T] **1** to go around the outside edge of a place or area: *The hurricane skirted the coast of Florida.* **2** to avoid talking about an important subject, especially because it is difficult or embarrassing: *The report skirted around the important issues.*

'ski run *n.* [C] a marked track on a slope for SKIing

'ski slope *n.* [C] a snow-covered part of a mountain which has been prepared for people to SKI down

skit /skɪt/ *n.* [C] a short humorous performance

skit·ter /'skɪt̬ɚ/ *v.* [I] to run very quickly and lightly, like a small animal

skit·tish /'skɪt̬ɪʃ/ *adj.* **1** a skittish horse or other animal gets excited or frightened very easily **2** a skittish person is nervous and afraid to do anything because of something bad that could happen: *skittish investors* —**skittishly** *adv.* —**skittishness** *n.* [U]

skiv·vies /'skɪviz/ *n.* [plural] OLD-FASHIONED INFORMAL a man's underwear

S

Skop·je /'skoʊpyeɪ, 'skɔ-/ the capital and largest city in Macedonia

skul·dug·ger·y /ˌskʌl'dʌgəri/ *n.* [U] OFTEN HUMOROUS secretly dishonest or illegal activity

skulk /skʌlk/ *v.* [I always + adv./prep.] to hide or move around secretly, trying not to be noticed, especially when you are intending to do something bad SYN **lurk**: +**around/in/behind etc.** *Someone was skulking in the shadows.*

skull /skʌl/ *n.* [C] BIOLOGY the bones of a person's or animal's head [**Origin:** 1200–1300 From a Scandinavian language] → see picture at SKELETON¹

ˌskull and 'crossbones *n.* [singular] **1** a picture of a human skull with two bones crossed below it, used in the past on the flags of PIRATE ships → see also JOLLY ROGER **2** a picture of a human skull with two bones crossed below it, used on containers to show that what is inside is poison or very dangerous

skull·cap /'skʌlkæp/ *n.* [C] a small round close-fitting hat for the top of the head, worn sometimes by Christian priests or Jewish men → see also YARMULKE

skunk¹ /skʌŋk/ *n.* **1** [C] BIOLOGY a small black and white North American animal that produces a very strong bad smell if it is attacked or afraid **2** INFORMAL [C] a person who does bad things **3** [U] SLANG the drug MARIJUANA

skunk² *v.* [T] INFORMAL to defeat a player or team very easily, especially so that they do not gain any points at all

'skunk ˌcabbage *n.* [C,U] a large North American plant that grows in wet areas and has a bad smell

sky /skaɪ/ S3 W2 *n. plural* **skies** **1** [singular, U] the space above the earth, where clouds and the sun and stars appear: *The sky turned dark just before the storm.* | *There wasn't a cloud **in the sky**.* | **a blue/gray/cloudy/cloudless etc. sky** *The sun shone down from a clear blue sky.* **2 skies** WRITTEN a word meaning "sky," used especially when describing the weather or what the sky looks like in a place: *a land of blue skies and warm sunshine* | ***The skies** above the city were a dull brown.* **3 the sky's the limit** used to say that there is no limit to what someone can achieve, spend, win etc. [**Origin:** 1200–1300 Old Norse **cloud**] → see also **pie in the sky** at PIE (4), **praise sb/sth to the skies** at PRAISE¹ (1)

ˌsky 'blue *n.* [U] the bright blue color of a clear sky —**sky-blue** *adj.*

sky·cap /'skaɪkæp/ *n.* [C] someone whose job is to carry passengers' bags and SUITCASES at an airport

sky·div·ing /'skaɪˌdaɪvɪŋ/ *n.* [U] the sport of jumping from an airplane and falling through the sky before opening a PARACHUTE —**skydive** *v.* [I] —**skydiver** *n.* [C]

ˌsky-'high *adj., adv.* **1** extremely high: *sky-high real estate prices* **2 blow sth sky-high a)** to destroy something completely with an explosion **b)** to completely spoil a situation and cause a lot of problems

sky·jack /'skaɪdʒæk/ *v.* [T] to use violence or threats to take control of an airplane —**skyjacker** *n.* [C] —**skyjacking** *n.* [C]

sky·lark /'skaɪlɑrk/ *n.* [C] BIOLOGY a small bird that sings while flying high in the sky

sky·light /'skaɪlaɪt/ *n.* [C] a window in the roof of a building

sky·line /'skaɪlaɪn/ *n.* [C] the shape made by tall buildings or hills against the sky

'sky ˌmarshal also **'air ˌmarshal** *n.* [C] a specially trained person who carries a gun and whose job is to travel on a passenger plane and protect it from attacks by TERRORISTS

sky·rock·et /'skaɪˌrɑkɪt/ *v.* [I] to increase suddenly and greatly: *Inflation has skyrocketed.*

sky·scrap·er /'skaɪˌskreɪpɚ/ *n.* [C] a very tall modern city building

sky·ward /'skaɪwɚd/ also **skywards** *adv.* LITERARY up into the sky, or toward the sky: *The bird soared skyward.* —**skyward** *adj.*

sky·writ·ing /'skaɪˌraɪt̬ɪŋ/ *n.* [U] words that are written high in the air by an airplane that leaves lines of white smoke behind it

slab /slæb/ *n.* [C] **1** a thick flat four-sided piece of a hard material such as stone: *a concrete slab* **2 a slab of cake/beef/butter etc.** a large flat piece of cake, meat etc.

slack¹ /slæk/ *adj.* **1** with less business activity than usual: *Business was slack.* **2** hanging loosely, or not pulled tight: *a slack rope* **3** DISAPPROVING not taking enough care or making enough effort to do things right SYN **lax**: *slack security* ▸see THESAURUS box at **lazy** —**slackly** *adv.* —**slackness** *n.* [U]

slack² *n.* **1 pick/take up the slack** to do something that needs to be done because someone else is not doing it anymore: *You shouldn't expect your colleagues to take up the slack.* **2 slacks** [plural] pants, especially ones made out of good material but that are not part of a suit: *slacks and a sweater* **3 cut/give sb some slack** SPOKEN to not be strict with someone or criticize them: *Cut her some slack – she's in a difficult position.* **4** [U] looseness in the way that something such as a rope hangs or is fastened: *Leave a little slack in the line.* **5** [U] money, space, time etc. that an organization or person has, but does not need

slack³ also **slack off** *v.* [I] to make less of an effort than usual, or be lazy in your work: *This is no time to be slacking off!*

slack·en /'slækən/ *v.* [I,T] **1** to gradually become slower, weaker, less active etc., or to make something do this: *Sales have slackened over the past five years.* | **slacken your pace/speed** (=go or walk more slowly) **2** to make something looser, or to become looser: *The skin of her face had slackened.*

slack·er /'slækɚ/ *n.* [C] DISAPPROVING someone who is lazy and does not do all the work they should

slack-jawed /'slæk dʒɔd/ *adj.* having your mouth slightly open because you are shocked or stupid

slag /slæg/ *n.* [U] a waste material similar to glass, which is left when metal is obtained from rock

'slag heap *n.* [C] a pile of waste material at a mine or factory

slain /sleɪn/ *v.* the past participle of SLAY

slake /sleɪk/ *v.* [T] LITERARY **1 slake your thirst** to drink so that you are not THIRSTY anymore **2 slake a desire/craving etc.** to satisfy a desire etc.

sla·lom /'slɑləm/ *n.* [U] a race for people on SKIS or in KAYAKS (=a type of boat) down a curving course marked by flags

slam¹ /slæm/ *v.* **slammed, slamming**
1 DOOR ETC. [I,T] if a door, window etc. slams, or if someone slams it, it closes with a loud noise: *We heard a car door slam outside.* | *Don't slam the door!* | *Greg came in and* ***slammed*** *the door* ***shut*** *behind him.*
2 PUT STH SOMEWHERE [T always + adv./prep.] to put something on or against a surface with a fast violent movement: **slam sth down** *Henry slammed the phone down angrily.* | **slam sth on/against/into etc. sth** *She slammed her fork on the table and started shouting.*
3 CRITICIZE SB/STH [T] INFORMAL to criticize someone or something strongly: **slam sb/sth for sth** *The committee was slammed for its unfair selection procedure.*
4 HIT WITH FORCE [I always + adv./prep.,T] to hit or attack someone or something with a lot of force: *Huge storms continue to slam the region.* | **+into/against etc.** *He slammed into the back of a parked car.*
5 slam (on) the brakes a) to make a car stop very suddenly by pressing on the BRAKES very hard **b)** to make a process, program etc. stop studdenly
6 slam the door in sb's face a) to close a door hard when someone is trying to come in **b)** to rudely refuse to meet someone or talk to them
7 slam a car into gear/reverse etc. to change GEAR very quickly and roughly when driving a car

slam² *n.* [C usually singular] the noise or action of a door, window etc. slamming → see also GRAND SLAM

'slam ˌdancing *n.* [U] a way of dancing to PUNK music in which people jump around violently and hit each other with their bodies —**slam-dance** *v.* [I]

'slam dunk *n.* [C] **1** an act of putting the ball through the net in basketball, by throwing it down very hard from above the net **2** a very forceful impressive act: *a huge legal slam dunk*

'slam-dunk *v.* [I,T] to put a ball through the net in basketball, by jumping very high and throwing the ball down through the net using a lot of force

slam·mer /'slæmɚ/ *n.* **the slammer** INFORMAL prison

slan·der¹ /'slændɚ/ *n.* [U] **1** false spoken statements about someone that are intended to damage the good opinion that people have of that person ►see THESAURUS box at **lie³** **2** the crime of making false spoken statements of this kind → see also LIBEL —**slanderer** *n.* [C]

slander² *v.* [T] to say untrue things about someone in order to damage other people's good opinion of them → see also LIBEL

slan·der·ous /'slændərəs/ *adj.* a slanderous statement about someone is not true, and is intended to damage other people's good opinion of them: *slanderous remarks*

slang /slæŋ/ *n.* [U] ENG. LANG. ARTS very informal language that includes new and sometimes offensive words, and that is used especially by people who belong to a particular group, such as young people or criminals: **+for** *"Grunt" is army slang for an infantry soldier.* | **a slang word/expression/term** *There were a lot of slang expressions in the movie.* —**slangy** *adj.*

slant¹ /slænt/ *v.* **1** [I,T] to slope, or move in a sloping line, or to make something do this: *The sun's rays slanted through the trees.* **2** [T] to give information or ideas in a way that gives more support to a particular opinion, group of people, or set of ideas, especially in a way that is unfair: *The researchers were accused of slanting their findings to support their theories.*

slant² *n.* [singular] **1** a way of writing about or thinking about a subject that shows strong support for a particular opinion or set of ideas SYN **bias**: *The article had an anti-American slant.* **2** a particular way of thinking about something that is different from the previous way of thinking about it, or different from the way other people think about it: **a new/fresh/different slant on sth** *Recent events have put a new slant on the president's earlier comments.* **3** a sloping position or angle: **at/on a slant** *The house seems to be built on a steep slant.*

slant·ed /'slænṭɪd/ *adj.* **1** sloping to one side: *a slanted roof* **2** providing facts or information in a way that unfairly supports one opinion, one side of an argument etc. SYN **biased**: **+toward/against** *The book is heavily slanted toward American business methods.*

slap¹ /slæp/ S3 *v.* **slapped, slapping** **1** [T] to hit someone quickly with the flat part of your hand: *Mrs. Williams slapped the children's hands away from the candy.* | *Sarah* ***slapped*** *Zack* ***across the face.*** ►see THESAURUS box at **hit¹** **2** [T always + adv./prep.] to put something down on a surface with force, especially when you are angry: **slap sth down** *"Here," she said, slapping the drinks down.* | **slap sth (down) on sth** *Ed slapped his hand down on the table.* **3 slap sb on the back** to hit someone on the back in a friendly way, often as a way of praising them

slap against sb/sth *phr. v.* to hit a surface with a lot of force, making a loud sharp sound: *Gray sheets of rain slapped against the windowpanes.*

slap sb **around** *phr. v.* to violently hit someone more than once with your hand

slap sb **down** *phr. v.* to criticize someone's ideas, questions etc. in an unfair and cruel way, so that they lose confidence

slap on *phr. v.* **1 slap sth ↔ on, slap sth on sth** to put or spread something quickly or carelessly onto a surface: *We just slapped a coat of paint on the wall.* **2 slap sth on sth** to suddenly announce a new charge, tax etc., especially unfairly or without warning: *The government slapped a 20% tax on all luxury goods.*

slap² *n.* [C] **1** a quick hit with the flat part of your hand: *She* ***gave*** *him a* ***slap*** *across the face.* **2 a slap in the face** an action that seems to be deliberately intended to offend or upset someone, especially someone who has tried very hard to do something: *Gwynn considered the salary they were offering a slap in the face.* **3 a slap on the wrist** a punishment that you think is not severe enough **4 a slap on the back** an action of hitting someone on the back in a friendly way, especially as a way of praising them [**Origin:** 1600–1700 Low German *slapp*, from the sound]

slap·dash /'slæpdæʃ/ *adj.* careless and done too quickly: *a slapdash piece of work*

slap·hap·py /'slæpˌhæpi/ *adj.* silly, careless, and likely to make mistakes

'slap shot *n.* [C] a way or act of hitting the PUCK in HOCKEY by moving your stick a long way back and then hitting the puck with a lot of force

slap·stick /'slæpˌstɪk/ *n.* [U] humorous acting in which the performers fall down, throw things at each other etc.: *slapstick comedy*

slash¹ /slæʃ/ *v.* **1** [I always + adv./prep.,T] to cut something violently with a knife, sword etc.: *Someone had slashed the car's tires.* | **+through** *The leopard's claws slashed through soft flesh.* **2** [T] to reduce an amount, price etc. by a large amount: *Car manufacturers have slashed prices on some of the latest models.* ►see THESAURUS box at **reduce** **3** [I always + adv./prep.] to try to cut or hit something, by making several swinging movements with a knife, sword, stick etc.: **+at** *She slashed wildly at the bushes with a knife.* **4 slash your wrists** to cut the VEINS in your wrists with the intention of killing yourself **5** [I always + adv./prep.] LITERARY to move somewhere in a violent way: *Tornadoes slashed through the region.*

slash² S3 *n.* [C] **1** a quick movement made with a knife, sword etc. in order to cut someone or something **2** also **slash mark** ENG. LANG. ARTS a line (/) used in writing to separate words, numbers, or letters ►see THESAURUS box at **punctuation mark** **3** a long narrow wound on someone's body, or a long narrow cut in something **4** LITERARY a short line of bright color, especially red

ˌslash-and-'burn *adj.* [only before noun] **1** slash-and-burn farming is a way of clearing land in tropical areas by cutting down and burning plants so that crops can be grown there for a few years **2** DISAPPROVING used to describe an action that is too extreme and has a harmful effect

slat /slæt/ *n.* [C] a thin flat piece of wood, plastic etc.,

S

used especially in furniture —**slatted** *adj.*: *a slatted bench*

slate¹ /sleɪt/ *n.* **1** [U] EARTH SCIENCE a dark gray rock that can easily be split into flat thin pieces **2 slate blue/gray** a dark blue or gray color **3** [C] POLITICS a list of people that voters can choose in an election, or who are being considered for an important job: *the party's slate of candidates* **4** [C] a small black board or a flat piece of slate in a wooden frame that can be written on with CHALK or a special stick made of rock, used in schools in the past [**Origin:** 1300–1400 Old French *esclat* **thin piece split off**, from *esclater* **to burst, splinter**] → see also **a clean slate** at CLEAN¹ (9), **wipe the slate clean** at WIPE¹ (3)

slate² *v.* [T usually passive] to expect or plan something: **be slated to do/be sth** *He is slated to appear at the Jazz Festival next year.* | **be slated for sth** *Every house on this block is slated for demolition.*

slath·er /ˈslæðɚ/ *v.* [T] to cover something with a thick layer of a soft substance: **slather sb/sth with sth** *She slathered herself with lotion.*

slat·tern /ˈslætɚn/ *n.* [C] OLD-FASHIONED a dirty messy woman

S

slaugh·ter¹ /ˈslɔtɚ/ *v.* [T] **1** to kill an animal for food **2** to kill a lot of people in a cruel or violent way: *Hundreds of civilians had been slaughtered by government troops.* ►see THESAURUS box at **kill¹** **3** to defeat an opponent in a sports game by a large number of points

slaughter² *n.* [U] **1** the act of killing large numbers of people in a cruel or violent way **2** the act of killing animals for food → see also **like a lamb to the slaughter** at LAMB¹ (5)

slaugh·ter·house /ˈslɔtɚˌhaʊs/ *n.* [C] a building where animals are killed

Slav /slɑv/ *n.* [C] someone who comes from one of the countries of Eastern or Central Europe who speak Slavic languages such as Russian, Bulgarian, Polish etc.

slave¹ /sleɪv/ S2 W3 *n.* [C] **1** someone who is owned by another person and works for them for no money → see also MASTER: *They treated her like a slave.* | *freed slaves* **2 be a slave to/of sth** to be completely influenced by something, so that you cannot make your own decisions: *Don't be a slave to fashion.* [**Origin:** 1200–1300 Old French *esclave*, from Medieval Latin *sclavus*, from *Sclavus* **Slavic person**; because in the early Middle Ages many Slavic people in central Europe were slaves]

slave² *v.* [I always + adv./prep.] to work very hard with little time to rest: **+away/over/for** *I slaved all day over a hot stove to cook this meal.*

ˈslave ˌdriver *n.* [C] **1** someone who forces SLAVES to work **2** HUMOROUS an employer who makes people work extremely hard

ˈslave ˌlabor *n.* [U] **1** work done by SLAVES, or the people who do this work: *The death camps were built by slave labor.* **2** work for which you are paid an unfairly small amount of money —**slave laborer** *n.* [C]

slav·er¹ /ˈsleɪvɚ/ *n.* [C] **1** someone who sells slaves **2** OLD USE a ship for slaves

slav·er² /ˈslævɚ, ˈslɑ-/ *v.* [I] LITERARY to let SALIVA (=liquid produced inside your mouth) come out of your mouth, especially because you are hungry SYN **drool** SYN **slobber**

slaver over sth *phr. v.* to be very excited about something, especially in an impolite or stupid way SYN **drool over**

slav·er·y /ˈsleɪvəri/ *n.* [U] **1** the system of having slaves: *Slavery was abolished after the Civil War.* **2** the condition of being a slave: *Her ancestors had been captured and **sold into slavery**.*

ˈslave state *n.* [C] one of the southern U.S. states in which it was legal to own slaves before the Civil War

ˈslave trade *n.* **the slave trade** the business of buying and selling slaves, especially Africans who were taken to America in the 18th and 19th centuries

Slav·ic /ˈslɑvɪk/ *adj.* from or relating to Russia or countries of Eastern or Central Europe, such as Poland or Bulgaria: *Slavic languages* → see also SLAV

slav·ish /ˈsleɪvɪʃ/ *adj.* DISAPPROVING **slavish devotion/imitation etc.** behavior or actions that show that you cannot make your own decisions about what you should do: *the slavish adherence to old ideas* —**slavishly** *adv.* DISAPPROVING —**slavishness** *n.* [U] DISAPPROVING

slaw /slɔ/ *n.* [U] INFORMAL COLE SLAW

slay /sleɪ/ *v. past tense* **slew** /slu/, *past participle* **slain** /sleɪn/ [T] **1** a word meaning "to kill someone violently," used especially in newspapers or old stories SYN **murder**: *St. George slew the dragon.* | *slain civil rights leader Martin Luther King Jr.* **2** also **slayed** SPOKEN to amuse someone a lot: *That guy really slays me!* —**slayer** *n.* [C]

slay·ing /ˈsleɪ-ɪŋ/ *n.* [C] a word meaning an act of killing someone, used especially in newspapers SYN **murder**

sleaze /sliz/ *n.* DISAPPROVING **1** [U] immoral behavior, especially involving sex or lies: *sleaze and corruption in politics* **2** [C] also **sleazebag**, **sleazeball**, **sleazebucket** INFORMAL someone who behaves in an immoral or dishonest way

slea·zy /ˈslizi/ *adj. comparative* **sleazier**, *superlative* **sleaziest** DISAPPROVING **1** low in quality and relating to immoral behavior: *sleazy tabloids* **2** a sleazy place is dirty, cheap, or in bad condition, and immoral or dishonest people usually go there: *a sleazy motel* **3** someone who is sleazy is immoral or dishonest, and makes you feel uncomfortable [**Origin:** 1900–2000 *sleazy* (of cloth) **too thin or light** (17–20 centuries)] —**sleaziness** *n.* [U]

sled¹ /slɛd/ *n.* [C] a small vehicle used for riding or traveling over snow, made from a board with two long narrow pieces of metal fastened under it, often used by children or in some sports → BOBSLED, DOGSLED, SLEIGH, TOBOGGAN

sled² *v.* **sledded**, **sledding** [I] to travel or ride on a sled

ˈsled dog *n.* [C] a dog that is used in a team to pull a sled over snow

sledge·ham·mer /ˈslɛdʒˌhæmɚ/ *n.* [C] a large heavy hammer

sleek¹ /slik/ *adj.* **1** APPROVING smooth, attractive, sometimes shiny, and often narrow or thin: *a sleek black car* | *sleek new office buildings* **2** APPROVING sleek hair or fur is straight, shiny, and healthy-looking: *The cat purred as Ben stroked its sleek fur.* **3** looking or sounding good or done very well, often in a way that is not sincere —**sleekly** *adv.* —**sleekness** *n.* [U]

sleek² *v.* [T] LITERARY to make hair or fur smooth and shiny by putting water or oil on it

sleep¹ /slip/ S1 W1 *v. past tense and past participle* **slept** /slɛpt/

1 REST [I] to rest your mind and body, usually at night when you are lying in bed with your eyes closed: *I normally sleep on my back.* | *How many hours do you sleep a night?* | *Don't set the alarm – I want to **sleep late** (=sleep until late in the morning) tomorrow.* | **sleep well/soundly** *Did you sleep well?*

THESAURUS

Use **sleep** when you are giving more information, for example how long or how deeply someone sleeps, or where they sleep: *Most people sleep for about eight hours.* | *He slept downstairs.* In other cases, it is usual to say that someone **is asleep**. Do not use **sleep** to talk about starting to sleep. Use **fall asleep** or **go to sleep**. Use **get to sleep** to talk about having difficulty falling asleep: *It took me hours to get to sleep.*
doze/snooze to sleep lightly for a short time, especially when you did not intend to: *He was dozing in front of the TV.*
doze off to fall asleep, especially when you did not intend to: *I dozed off while reading.*

take a nap to sleep for a short time during the day: *The baby takes two hour-long naps every day.*
oversleep to sleep for longer than you intended: *I overslept and was late for work.*
toss and turn to keep changing your position in bed because you cannot sleep: *I lay awake, tossing and turning.*
not sleep a wink to not be able to sleep at all: *Peter didn't sleep a wink that night.*

2 sleep like a log/baby to sleep very well, without waking up for a long time **3 not sleep a wink** to not sleep at all **4 sleep tight (don't let the bedbugs bite)** SPOKEN used especially to children before they go to bed, to say that you hope they sleep well: *Good night, kids. Sleep tight!* **5** NO ACTIVITY [I] if a city or building sleeps, it is quiet during the night because most of the people are asleep: *New York is the city that never sleeps.* **6** NUMBER OF PEOPLE [T] to have enough beds for a particular number of people: **sleep two/four/six etc.** *The cabin can sleep four comfortably.* **7 let sleeping dogs lie** to deliberately avoid mentioning a problem or argument that you had in the past, so that you do not cause any problems → see also OVERSLEEP

sleep around *phr. v.* DISAPPROVING to have sex with a lot of different people

sleep in *phr. v.* to deliberately sleep later than usual in the morning: *I'm going to sleep in tomorrow.*

sleep sth ↔ **off** *phr. v.* to sleep until you do not feel sick anymore, especially after drinking too much alcohol: *It's better to let him* ***sleep it off***.

sleep on sth *phr. v.* if you sleep on a decision or problem, you wait to deal with it until the next day: *I'll* ***sleep on it***, *and let you know in the morning.*

sleep over *phr. v.* a word meaning "to sleep at someone else's house for a night," used especially by children: *Is it okay if I sleep over at Kristi's tonight?*

sleep through sth *phr. v.* **1** to sleep while something is happening and not be woken by it: *I can't believe I slept through the storm!* **2 sleep through the night** to sleep continuously during the whole night: *At least the baby's sleeping through the night now.*

sleep together *phr. v.* to have sex: *I'm sure those two are sleeping together.*

sleep with sb *phr. v.* to have sex with someone, especially someone you are not married to: *She slept with her friend's husband.*

sleep[2] S2 W2 *n.* **1** BEING ASLEEP [U] the natural state of resting your mind and body, usually at night: *Most adults need seven or eight hours sleep a night.* | *I didn't* ***get*** *much* ***sleep*** *last night.* | *I just couldn't* ***get to sleep*** (=start to sleep) *last night.* | *Ed often talks* ***in*** *his* ***sleep*** (=while he is sleeping). **2 go to sleep a)** to start sleeping: *I went to sleep at 9:00, and woke up at 6:00.* | *Nick turned his alarm off, and* ***went back to sleep***. **b)** if a part of your body goes to sleep, you cannot feel it for a short time because it has not been getting enough blood **3** PERIOD OF SLEEPING [singular] a period of sleeping: *She* ***fell into a deep sleep***. | *What you need is* ***a good night's sleep*** (=a night when you sleep well). **4 lose sleep over sth** to worry about something: *It's just a practice game – I wouldn't lose any sleep over it.* **5 put sb to sleep a)** to make someone fall asleep, especially by being very boring: *His lectures always put me to sleep.* **b)** to make someone unconscious before a medical operation by giving them drugs **6 put sth to sleep** to give drugs to a sick animal so that it dies without too much pain **7 sb can do sth in their sleep** used to say that someone is able to do something very easily, especially because they have done it many times before **8 sing/rock/lull etc. sb to sleep** to sing to someone, move them gently etc. until they start sleeping **9** IN YOUR EYES [U] NOT TECHNICAL a substance that forms in the corners of your eyes while you are sleeping [**Origin:** Old English *slæp*]

sleep·er /ˈslipɚ/ *n.* [C] **1** someone who is asleep: **a light/heavy sleeper** (=someone who wakes easily, or does not wake easily) **2** a movie, book etc. which is successful, even though people did not expect it to be **3 a)** also **ˈsleeper car** a part of a train with beds for passengers to sleep in **b)** a bed on a train for a passenger to sleep in **4** a piece of clothing for a baby, that covers its whole body including its feet, and that is usually worn to sleep in

ˈsleeping bag *n.* [C] a large warm bag that you sleep in, especially when camping

ˈsleeping car *n.* [C] a part of a train with beds for passengers

ˈsleeping pill *n.* [C] a PILL that helps you to sleep

ˈsleeping ˌsickness *n.* [U] MEDICINE a serious disease that is carried by the TSETSE FLY (=a type of African insect) and that causes extreme tiredness and fever, and makes you lose weight

sleep·less /ˈsliplɪs/ *adj.* **1 a sleepless night** a night when you are unable to sleep **2** unable to sleep: *the sleepless parents of newborn babies* —**sleeplessly** *adv.* —**sleeplessness** *n.* [U]

sleep·o·ver /ˈslipˌoʊvɚ/ *n.* [C] a party for children in which they spend the night at someone's house

sleep·walk·er /ˈslipˌwɔkɚ/ *n.* [C] someone who walks while they are sleeping —**sleepwalk** *v.* [I] —**sleepwalking** *n.* [U]

S

sleep·wear /ˈslipwɛr/ *n.* [U] clothes such as PAJAMAS, that you wear in bed

sleep·y /ˈslipi/ S3 *adj.* *comparative* **sleepier**, *superlative* **sleepiest** **1** tired and ready to sleep: *I'm so sleepy I can't keep my eyes open.* **2** a sleepy town or area is very quiet, and not much happens there ►see THESAURUS box at **quiet**[1] —**sleepily** *adv.* —**sleepiness** *n.* [U]

sleep·y·head /ˈslipiˌhɛd/ *n.* [C] SPOKEN someone, especially a child, who looks as if they want to go to sleep

sleet /slit/ *n.* [U] ice mixed with rain that falls when it is very cold ►see THESAURUS box at **rain**[1], **snow**[1] —**sleet** *v.* [I]

sleeve /sliv/ *n.* [C] **1** the part of a piece of clothing that covers your arm, or that covers part of your arm: **long/short sleeves** *a dress with long sleeves* → see also -SLEEVED **2 have something up your sleeve** to have a secret plan or idea that you are going to use later: *He still has a few tricks up his sleeve.* → see also **have an ace up your sleeve** at ACE[1] (5) **3** a stiff paper cover that protects a book or a record SYN **jacket** **4** a tube that surrounds a machine part [**Origin:** Old English *sliefe*] → see also **laugh up your sleeve** at LAUGH[1] (10), **roll your sleeves up** at ROLL UP (ROLL)[1]

-sleeved /slivd/ also **-sleeve** /sliv/ [in adjectives] **long-sleeved/short-sleeved** also **long-sleeve/short-sleeve** having sleeves that are long or short: *a short-sleeved shirt*

sleeve·less /ˈslivlɪs/ *adj.* a sleeveless JACKET, dress etc. has no sleeves

sleigh /sleɪ/ *n.* [C] a large vehicle pulled by animals, in which you sit to travel over snow → see also SLED

sleigh

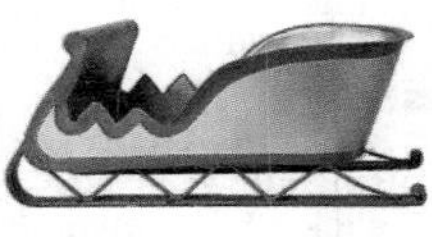

sleight of hand /ˌslaɪt̬ əv ˈhænd/ *n.* [U] **1** quick skillful movements with your hands, especially when performing magic tricks **2** the use of skillful tricks and lies to achieve something

slen·der /ˈslɛndɚ/ *adj.* **1** APPROVING thin and tall or long, graceful, and attractive: *She is slender and stylish.* | *slender birch trees* ►see THESAURUS box at **thin**[1] **2** small and not enough to be useful, helpful, or effective: *a slender majority* —**slenderness** *n.* [U]

slept /slɛpt/ *v.* the past tense and past participle of SLEEP

sleuth /sluθ/ *n.* [C] OLD-FASHIONED someone who tries to find out information about a crime SYN detective [Origin: 1800–1900 *sleuthhound* **dog used for tracking people** (14–20 centuries), from *sleuth* **track** (12–15 centuries) (from Old Norse *sloth*) + *hound*]

sleuth·ing /ˈsluθɪŋ/ *n.* [U] the activity of finding information about someone or something, especially information about a crime: *DNA testing is a form of genetic sleuthing.*

slew¹ /slu/ *n.* **a slew of sth** a large number of things: *We've received a slew of complaints.*

slew² *v.* the past tense of SLAY

slice¹ /slaɪs/ *n.* **1** [C] a flat piece of bread, meat etc. cut from a larger piece: *Cut the cheese into thin slices.* | **+of** *a slice of bread* ►see THESAURUS box at **piece¹** **2** [C] a part or share of something good: **+of** *Everyone wants their slice of the profits.* **3** [C] a way of hitting the ball in sports such as tennis and GOLF that makes the ball go to one side with a spinning movement, rather than straight ahead **4 a slice of life** a description or scene in a movie, play, or book that shows life as it really is **5** [C] a tool or machine used for slicing food SYN slicer [Origin: 1400–1500 Old French *esclice* **thin piece broken off**, from *esclicier* **to splinter**]

S

slice² *v.* **1** [T] also **slice up** to cut meat, bread etc. into thin flat pieces: *Could you slice the bread?* | *Slice up the onions thinly.* ►see THESAURUS box at **cut¹** → see picture on page A32 **2** [I always + adv./prep.,T] to cut something easily with one long movement of a sharp knife or edge: **+into/through** *The blade is so sharp it can slice through a tin can.* | **slice sth in two/half** (=slice something into two equal pieces) **3** [I always + adv./prep.,T] to move quickly and easily through something such as water or air, or to make something do this: **+through/into** *The speedboat sliced through the water.* **4** [T] to hit the ball in sports such as tennis or GOLF so that it spins sideways instead of moving straight forward **5 any way you slice it** SPOKEN in any way you choose to consider the situation: *It's the truth, any way you slice it.* —**slicer** *n.* [C]

slice sth ↔ **off** *phr. v.* to separate something by cutting it with one long movement of a sharp knife or edge: *He accidentally sliced off the end of his finger.*

ˌsliced ˈbread *n.* [U] **1** bread that is sold already cut into slices **2 be the best/greatest thing since sliced bread** HUMOROUS to be very good, helpful, useful etc.

slick¹ /slɪk/ *adj.* **1** done or made in a way that seems very impressive or attractive: *a slick advertising campaign* **2** good at persuading people, often in a way that does not seem honest: *a slick used-car salesman* **3** smooth and slippery: *slick paper* | **+with** *The roads were slick with snow.* **4** very good or attractive: *The new software is pretty slick.* **5** working or moving very smoothly, skillfully, and effectively —**slickly** *adv.* —**slickness** *n.* [U]

slick² *n.* [C] **1** an area of oil on the surface of water or on a road SYN oil slick **2** a smooth car tire used for racing **3 a slick of oil/blood/sweat etc.** a small amount of something wet or sticky **4** a magazine printed on good quality paper with a shiny surface, usually with a lot of color pictures

slick³ *v.*

slick sth ↔ **back** *phr. v.* to smooth hair backward by using oil, water etc.

slick sth ↔ **down** *phr. v.* to make hair lie down and be smooth and shiny by using oil, water etc.

slick·er /ˈslɪkɚ/ *n.* [C] a coat made of smooth shiny material to keep out the rain → see also CITY SLICKER

slide¹ /slaɪd/ S3 W3 *v.* *past tense and past participle* **slid** /slɪd/

1 MOVE SMOOTHLY [I,T] to move smoothly over a surface while continuing to touch it, or to make something move in this way: **+along/across/down etc.** *Francesca slid across the ice.* | **slide sth across/along etc. sth** *She slid my drink along the bar.*

THESAURUS

slip to slide a short distance accidentally, and fall or lose your balance slightly: *I slipped in the mud.*
skid used to say that a vehicle suddenly slides sideways or forwards in an uncontrollable way: *The driver lost control and skidded into the wall.*
glide to move smoothly and quietly on water, ice, or a smooth surface: *Skaters glided across the ice.*
slither to move along like a snake, or to slide in an awkward way, for example on a muddy surface: *The passage was so narrow we had to slither through it on our bellies.*
skate to move smoothly on ice when wearing skates (=boots with metal blades underneath)
ski to move smoothly on snow when wearing skis (=boots with long pieces of wood or plastic underneath)

2 MOVE QUIETLY [I,T always + adv./prep.] to move somewhere quietly without being noticed, or to move something in this way: **+into/out etc.** *He slid out of the room when no one was looking.* | **slide sth into/out etc.** *She slid a gun into her pocket.*
3 BECOME LOWER [I] if prices, amounts, rates etc. slide they become lower: *Stock prices continued to slide.*
4 GET INTO A BAD SITUATION [I] to begin to have a problem or gradually get into a worse situation than before: **+into** *It's easy to slide into debt.* | **+toward** *The country was sliding toward war.*
5 let sth slide a) SPOKEN to deliberately ignore a mistake, problem, remark etc. without becoming angry or trying to punish it: *Well, I guess we can* ***let it slide*** *this time.* **b)** to let a situation get gradually worse, without trying to stop it: *Management has let safety standards slide at the plant.*
[Origin: Old English *slidan*]

slide² S3 *n.* [C]
1 FOR CHILDREN a large structure with steps leading to the top of a long sloping surface for children to slide down: *Don't go down the slide head first.*
2 PICTURE a small piece of film in a frame that shows a picture on a screen or wall, when you shine light through it: *a series of color slides*
3 PRICE/AMOUNT [usually singular] a fall in prices, amounts etc.: **+in** *a slide in gold prices*
4 INTO A WORSE SITUATION [usually singular] a situation in which something gradually gets worse, or someone develops a problem: **+into** *his slide into depression*
5 SCIENCE a small piece of thin glass used for holding something when you look at it under a MICROSCOPE
6 MUSIC/MACHINE ENG. LANG. ARTS a movable part of a machine or musical instrument, such as the U-shaped tube of a TROMBONE
7 EARTH/SNOW a sudden fall of earth, stones, snow etc. down a slope: *a rock slide* → see also LANDSLIDE, MUDSLIDE
8 MOVEMENT [usually singular] a sliding movement across a surface: *The car went into a slide.*

ˈslide proˌjector *n.* [C] a piece of equipment that shines a light through SLIDES so that pictures appear on a screen or wall

slid·er /ˈslaɪdɚ/ *n.* [C] a fast throw of a baseball in which the ball suddenly changes direction when it gets close to the BATTER

ˈslide rule *n.* [C] MATH an old-fashioned instrument that looks like a ruler with a middle part that slides, used for calculating

ˌsliding ˈdoor *n.* [C] a door that slides open from side to side, rather than swinging from one side on HINGES

ˌsliding ˈscale *n.* [C usually singular] a system for calculating how much you pay for taxes, medical treatment etc., in which the amount that you pay changes when there are different conditions: *Therapists' fees are figured* ***on a sliding scale.***

slight¹ /slaɪt/ W3 *adj.* **1** [usually before noun] very small or not important: *a slight headache* | *a slight improvement* **2 not the slightest chance/doubt/difference etc.** no chance, doubt etc. at all: *I didn't have the slightest idea who that man was.* **3 not in the slightest** not at all: *"Are you worried about the test?"*

"Not in the slightest." **4** thin and delicate: *a slight young woman* ►see THESAURUS box at **thin**[1]

slight[2] *v.* [T] FORMAL to offend someone by treating them rudely or without respect —**slighted** *adj.*

slight[3] *n.* [C] a remark or action that offends someone: **+to/against** *His comment wasn't meant to be a slight against your abilities.*

slight·ly /ˈslaɪtli/ S3 W2 *adv.* **1** to a small degree SYN **a little**: *a slightly different color* | *Women make up slightly more than half the population.* | *She moved the picture* ***ever so slightly*** (=by a very small amount) *to the right.* **2 slightly built** having a thin and delicate body

slim[1] /slɪm/ *adj. comparative* **slimmer**, *superlative* **slimmest** **1** attractively thin: *a slim waist* ►see THESAURUS box at **thin**[1] **2 a slim chance/possibility etc.** very little chance etc. of getting what you want: *They have only a slim chance of winning.* **3** very small in amount or number: *The team has a slim lead.* **4** not wide or thick: *a slim volume* **5 slim pickings** INFORMAL used to say that there is not enough of something [**Origin:** 1600–1700 Dutch **bad, of low quality**]

slim[2] *v.* **slimmed**, **slimming**

slim down *phr. v.* also **slim** **1 slim sth ↔ down** to become smaller in size or amount, or to reduce the size or amount of something: *They want to slim down the company.* **2 slim sb/sth ↔ down** to become thinner by losing weight, or to make a person or a body part thinner in this way: *I'm trying to slim down.*

slime /slaɪm/ *n.* [U] **1** a thick slippery substance that looks or smells bad **2** a slippery substance that comes from the bodies of SNAILS and SLUGS [**Origin:** Old English *slim*]

slime·ball /ˈslaɪmbɔl/ *n.* [C] SLANG someone who is immoral, disgusting, and cannot be trusted

slim·ming /ˈslɪmɪŋ/ *adj.* making you look thinner: *Black is a slimming color.*

slim·y /ˈslaɪmi/ *adj. comparative* **slimier**, *superlative* **slimiest** **1** covered with slime, or wet and slippery like slime: *slimy mud* **2** INFORMAL friendly in a way that makes you feel uncomfortable, because it seems insincere or dishonest: *a slimy politician* —**sliminess** *n.* [U]

sling[1] /slɪŋ/ *v. past tense and past participle* **slung** /slʌŋ/ [T always + adv./prep.] **1** to throw or put something somewhere with a wide careless movement: **sling sth around/over etc. sth** *Pat picked up his bag and slung it over his shoulder.* **2** [usually passive] to hang something loosely: **(be) slung around/over/on etc. sth** *Dave wore a tool belt slung around his waist.* **3 sling hash** OLD-FASHIONED SLANG to work as a WAITRESS or WAITER in a cheap restaurant → see also GUNSLINGER, LOW-SLUNG, MUDSLINGING

sling[2] *n.* [C] **1** a piece of cloth tied around your neck to support your injured arm or hand: *She had her arm* ***in a sling*** *for months.* **2** a set of ropes or strong pieces of cloth that hold heavy objects to be lifted or carried **3 slings and arrows** criticism and remarks that are intended to hurt someone's feelings **4** a special type of bag that fastens over your shoulders, in which you can carry a baby next to your body **5** a narrow piece of leather or cloth on a gun, used for carrying it over your shoulder **6** a simple weapon consisting of a long thin piece of rope with a piece of leather in the middle, used in the past for throwing stones

sling·back /ˈslɪŋbæk/ *n.* [C] a type of woman's shoe that is open at the back and has a narrow band going around the heel → see picture at SHOE[1]

sling·shot /ˈslɪŋʃɑt/ *n.* [C] a small stick in the shape of a Y with a thin band of rubber at the top, used by children to shoot stones

slink /slɪŋk/ *v. past tense and past participle* **slunk** /slʌŋk/ [I always + adv./prep.] to move somewhere quietly and secretly, especially because you are afraid or ashamed: **+away/off/around etc.** *He slunk back into his office.*

slink·y /ˈslɪŋki/ *adj. comparative* **slinkier**, *superlative* **slinkiest** a slinky dress, skirt etc. is smooth and tight and shows the shape of a woman's body

slip[1] /slɪp/ S2 W2 *v.* **slipped**, **slipping**

1 SLIDE/FALL [I] to slide a short distance accidentally, and fall or lose your balance slightly: *He slipped and fell.* | **+on** *Brenda slipped on the icy sidewalk.* ►see THESAURUS box at **fall**[1], **slide**[1]

2 MOVE SECRETLY [I always + adv./prep.] to move quickly, smoothly, or secretly: **+out/through/by etc.** *She slipped out without saying goodbye.* | *They slipped past the sleeping guard.*

3 PUT STH SOMEWHERE [T] to put something somewhere or give someone something quietly, secretly, or smoothly, especially by sliding it: **slip sth around/into/through etc.** *Someone slipped a note under my door.* | *Ann slipped the book into her bag.* | **slip sb sth** *Dave slipped me $20 when Jerry wasn't looking.* ►see THESAURUS box at **put**

4 FALL/DROP [I] to become loose and fall off or from something in a sliding movement: **+off/down/from etc.** *Her bag slipped off her shoulder.*

5 NOT HOLD [I] if something slips, it fails to stay firmly on a surface or on the thing it is holding, and slides across the surface or thing: *The knife slipped and cut my finger.* → see also SLIPPAGE

6 GET WORSE [I] to become worse or lower than before: *Standards have slipped in many parts of the industry.* | **+from/to** *The team slipped from second place to fourth.* | *Pre-tax profits slipped 13% to $247 million.* → see also SLIPPAGE

7 slip through the cracks if someone or something slips through the cracks, they are not caught or helped by the system that is supposed to catch or help them: *Some kids slip through the cracks of the educational system.*

8 slip your mind if something slips your mind, you forget it or forget to do something, especially because you are too busy: *I meant to call you, but it completely slipped my mind.*

9 be slipping if a person is slipping, they are starting to make mistakes, or to become less efficient than they were before

10 slip through your fingers/hands if something such as an opportunity, offer etc. slips through your fingers, you just fail to get or keep it: *Don't let a chance like that slip through your fingers!*

11 BECOME LATE if a SCHEDULE (=plan of times when things are supposed to happen) slips, things begin to happen or be done later than they are supposed to: *Schedules slipped and costs rose.* → see also SLIPPAGE

12 slip one over on sb INFORMAL to deceive someone or play a trick on them SYN **put one over on sb**

13 let sth slip to accidentally mention a piece of information that you had wanted to keep a secret: *He* ***let it slip that*** *they were planning to get married.*

14 slip a disk to suffer an injury when one of the connecting parts between the bones in your back moves out of place → see also SLIPPED DISK

15 SLIDE [I always + adv./prep.] LITERARY to move smoothly and often quietly, especially by sliding across a surface SYN **slide**: **+down/into** *The sun slipped slowly down behind the mountains.*

16 GET FREE [T] to get free from something that is holding you: *The dog slipped his collar and ran away.*

slip away *phr. v.* **1** if something such as an opportunity or someone's power slips away, it gradually disappears or is lost: *Somehow victory had slipped away.* **2** to die peacefully **3** if time slips away, it passes without your realizing how quickly it is passing

slip by *phr. v.* **1** if an opportunity slips by, someone does not take advantage of it: *He had somehow* ***let the opportunity slip by.*** **2** if time slips by, it passes without your realizing how quickly it is passing: *The years just seem to slip by.*

slip sth **↔ in** *phr. v.* to use a word or say something without attracting too much attention: *He slipped in a few jokes to liven the speech up.*

slip into sth *phr. v.* **1** to put clothes on quickly: *I'll just slip into something more comfortable.* **2** to start being in a particular condition without intending to do this or often realizing what is happening: *He had begun to slip into debt.* | *Myrtle slipped into a coma.*

S

slip sth ↔ **off** *phr. v.* to take clothes off quickly: *Greg sat down and slipped his shoes off.*

slip sth ↔ **on** *phr. v.* to put clothes on quickly: *Amanda slipped on her robe.*

slip out *phr. v.* if something slips out, you say it without really intending to: *Occasionally, a sarcastic comment slipped out.*

slip out of sth *phr. v.* to take clothes off quickly: *Keith slipped out of his jacket.*

slip up *phr. v.* to make a mistake: *He does occasionally slip up and forget his medication.* | **+on** *He slipped up on just one detail.*

[**Origin:** 1200–1300 Middle Dutch, Middle Low German *slippen*] → see also SLIP-UP

slip² S3 *n.*

1 PAPER [C] a small or narrow piece of paper: *a credit-card slip* | **+of** *She wrote the address on a slip of paper.* → see also PINK SLIP

2 MISTAKE [C] a small mistake: *She didn't **make** a single **slip**.*

3 a slip of the tongue/pen something that you say or write by accident, when you meant to say or write something else: *His comment was clearly a slip of the tongue.* → see also FREUDIAN SLIP

4 UNDERWEAR [C] a piece of underwear similar to a thin dress or skirt, that a woman wears under a dress or skirt

5 give sb the slip to successfully escape from someone who is chasing you: *Eddie gave her the slip in the hotel lobby.*

6 GETTING WORSE [C usually singular] an occasion when something becomes worse or lower than before: **+in** *a slip in stock prices*

7 SLIDE/FALL [C] an act of sliding a short distance, or of falling by sliding

8 a slip of a girl/boy/thing OLD-FASHIONED, HUMOROUS a small thin young person

9 BOAT [C] a space in the water in which you can keep a boat when it is not being used

10 CLAY [U] a thin mixture of clay and water, used in making pots

11 PLANT a small part of a plant that has been cut off and put into soil or water to grow into a new plant, or that has been attached to another plant

slip·case /ˈslɪpkeɪs/ *n.* [C] a hard cover like a box that a book is kept in

ˈslip ˌcover *n.* [C] a loose plastic or cloth cover for furniture

slip·knot /ˈslɪpnɑt/ *n.* [C] a knot that you can make tighter or looser by pulling one of its ends

ˈslip-on *n.* [C] a type of shoe without a fastening, that you can slide onto your foot —**slip-on** *adj.*: *slip-on shoes*

slip·page /ˈslɪpɪdʒ/ *n.* **1** [U] the act of sliding slightly, especially accidentally **2** [C,U] the act of becoming worse or lower than before, or of gradually changing, especially to a worse state: *a slippage in profits* **3** [C,U] failure to do something at the planned time or at the planned cost

ˌslipped ˈdisk *n.* [C usually singular] a painful injury caused when one of the connecting parts between the bones in your back moves out of place

slip·per /ˈslɪpɚ/ *n.* [C] a light soft shoe that you wear indoors, especially to keep your feet warm → see picture at SHOE¹

slip·per·y /ˈslɪpəri/ *adj.* *comparative* **slipperier**, *superlative* **slipperiest** **1** something that is slippery is difficult to hold, walk on etc. because it is wet or GREASY: *a slippery floor* **2 a/the slippery slope** the beginning of a process or habit that is hard to stop and that will develop into something extremely bad: *a slippery slope toward more serious drug abuse* **3** DISAPPROVING someone who is slippery cannot be trusted and usually manages to avoid being punished: *a slippery salesman* **4** a problem, job etc. that is slippery is difficult to deal with: *a slippery economic problem* —**slipperiness** *n.* [U]

slip·shod /ˈslɪpʃɑd/ *adj.* done too quickly and carelessly: *slipshod management*

slip·stream /ˈslɪpstrim/ *n.* [C usually singular] the area of low air pressure just behind a fast-moving vehicle

ˈslip-up *n.* [C] a careless mistake → see also **slip up** at SLIP¹

slip·way /ˈslɪpweɪ/ *n.* [C] a sloping track that is used for moving boats into or out of the water

slit¹ /slɪt/ *v.* *past tense and past participle* **slit**, *present participle* **slitting** [T] **1** to make a straight narrow cut in cloth, paper, skin etc.: *Deb **slit** the envelope **open** with a knife.* **2 slit sb's throat** to kill someone by cutting their throat with a knife **3 slit your wrists** to cut the VEINS in your wrists with the intention of killing yourself

slit² *n.* [C] a long straight narrow cut or hole: *a skirt with a slit up the side*

slith·er /ˈslɪðɚ/ *v.* [I always + adv./prep.] to slide smoothly across a surface, twisting or moving from side to side: **+through/across etc.** *A snake slithered through the weeds.*

slith·er·y /ˈslɪðəri/ *adj.* slippery in an unpleasant way

sliv·er /ˈslɪvɚ/ *n.* [C] **1** a very small thin sharp piece of something that has broken off a larger piece: *slivers of broken glass* **2** a narrow piece or part of something: *a sliver of cake* → see also SPLINTER

sliv·o·vitz /ˈslɪvəvɪts, ˈsli-/ *n.* [U] a strong alcoholic drink made in southeastern Europe from PLUMS

slob /slɑb/ *n.* [C] INFORMAL DISAPPROVING someone who is lazy, dirty, messy, and impolite [**Origin:** 1700–1800 Irish Gaelic *slab* **mud**]

slob·ber /ˈslɑbɚ/ *v.* [I] INFORMAL to let SALIVA (=the liquid produced by your mouth) come out of your mouth and run down SYN **drool**: *The dog slobbered all over my hand.*

slobber over sb/sth *phr. v.* to show how much you like or want something in an extreme way that embarrasses or annoys other people SYN **drool over**

sloe /sloʊ/ *n.* [C] BIOLOGY a small bitter fruit like a PLUM

ˈsloe gin *n.* [U] an alcoholic drink made with sloes, GIN, and sugar

slog¹ /slɑg/ *v.* **slogged**, **slogging** [I always + adv./prep.] **1** to walk or travel with difficulty, especially through mud, over wet ground etc.: **+down/up/through etc.** *We had to slog through mud to get to the farm.* **2** to work hard at something without stopping, especially when the work is boring and difficult: **+through** *Detectives slogged through hours of interviews.*

slog² *n.* [singular] **1** something you do that takes a lot of effort and time: *The campaign will be a long hard slog.* **2** a long and tiring walk

slo·gan /ˈsloʊgən/ *n.* [C] a short easily remembered phrase used in advertising, politics etc.: *a campaign slogan* [**Origin:** 1500–1600 Scottish Gaelic *sluagh-ghairm* **army cry**]

sloop /slup/ *n.* [C] a type of boat with one central MAST (=pole for sails)

slop¹ /slɑp/ *v.* **slopped**, **slopping** **1** [I always + adv./prep.,T always + adv./prep.] if liquid in a container slops or someone slops it, it moves around in an uncontrolled way or over the edge: **+around/about/over** *The water slopped around in the bucket.* | **slop sth over/into etc. sth** *Don't slop your soup on the tablecloth.* **2 slop sth onto/on/into/in sth** to put something wet such as liquid or food somewhere in a careless way, so that it does not stay neatly in one place **3** [T] to feed slop to pigs

slop² *n.* [U] **1** also **slops** [plural] food waste that is used to feed animals **2** DISAPPROVING food that is too soft and tastes bad **3** OLD-FASHIONED waste from the human body: *a slop bucket* **4** DISAPPROVING writing or speech that is too emotional or romantic

slope¹ /sloʊp/ *n.* [C] **1** a piece of ground or a surface that is higher at one end than the other: *The car rolled down the slope into the lake.* | **a gentle/steep slope** *They climbed up the steep slope.* **2** [usually plural] an area in the mountains where people go SKIING: *the beginner* slopes | David can't wait to get **on the slopes**. → see also SKI SLOPE **3** the side of a hill or mountain: *the lower slopes of the mountains* **4** [usually singular] the angle at which something slopes in relation to a HORIZONTAL (=flat) surface: *a 30° slope* **5** [usually singular] GEOMETRY the rate at which the VERTICAL positions of points on a line or PLANE change in relation to the change in their HORIZONTAL positions → see also **a/the slippery slope** at SLIPPERY (2)

slope² *v.* [I] if the ground or a surface slopes, it is higher at one end than the other: **+up/down/away etc.** *The front yard slopes down to the street.*

slop·py /ˈslɑpi/ *adj. comparative* **sloppier**, *superlative* **sloppiest** **1** DISAPPROVING not done carefully or thoroughly: *sloppy handwriting* | *sloppy work* **2** sloppy clothes are loose-fitting and do not look neat SYN **messy**: *a sloppy old sweater* **3** wet and messy or unpleasant: *a sloppy kiss* **4** DISAPPROVING expressing feelings of love too strongly and in a silly way: *The movie is a sloppy romance.* —**sloppily** *adv.* —**sloppiness** *n.* [U]

sloppy joe, sloppy Joe /ˌslɑpi ˈdʒoʊ/ *n.* [C] a type of SANDWICH made with GROUND BEEF that has been cooked in TOMATO SAUCE

slosh /slɑʃ/ *v.* **1** [I always + adv./prep.,T always + adv./prep] if a liquid sloshes in a container or someone or something sloshes it, it moves quickly against the sides of its container and makes a noise: **slosh (sth) around** *Water sloshed around in the bottom of the boat.* **2** [T always + adv./prep.] to put a liquid in a container or on a surface in a careless way **3** [I always + adv./prep.] to walk through water or mud in an active loud way

sloshed /slɑʃt/ *adj.* [not before noun] INFORMAL very drunk

slot¹ /slɑt/ S3 *n.* [C] **1** a long narrow hole in a surface, especially one that you can put things through: *The disk goes into this slot here.* | *a mail slot* **2** a time, position, or opportunity for something: *A new comedy is scheduled for the 9 p.m. time slot.* **3** a job in a company or organization: *He was asked to take over the CEO slot.* **4 the top/bottom/second etc. slot** a particular position in a group of similar people or things that are competing with each other [**Origin:** 1300–1400 Old French *esclot* **hollow place in the bone in the middle of the chest**]

slot² *v.* **slotted**, **slotting** [I,T always + adv./prep.] to go into a slot, or to put something in a slot

sloth /slɔθ, sloʊθ/ *n.* **1** [C] BIOLOGY a furry animal of Central and South America that moves very slowly and hangs from tree branches **2** [U] LITERARY laziness

sloth·ful /ˈslɔθfəl/ *adj.* LITERARY lazy or not active —**slothfully** *adv.* —**slothfulness** *n.* [U]

ˈslot maˌchine *n.* [C] a machine used for playing a game, that starts when you put money into it and from which you can win money

ˌslotted ˈspoon *n.* [C] a large spoon with holes in it

slouch¹ /slaʊtʃ/ *v.* [I] to stand, sit, or walk with your shoulders bent forward in a way that makes you look tired or lazy: *Ralph sat slouching at his desk.*

slouch² *n.* **1 be no slouch** to be very good or skillful at something: *He's no slouch when it comes to innovative projects.* **2** [singular] a way of standing, sitting, or walking with your shoulders bent forward that makes you look tired or lazy

slough¹ /slʌf/ *v.* [T] to get rid of a dead outer layer of skin SYN **slough off** SYN **shed**: *A snake sloughs its old skin.*

slough off *phr. v.* **1 slough sth ↔ off** to get rid of a dead outer layer of skin, or to come off in this way **2 slough sth ↔ off** to get rid of a feeling, belief etc. SYN **shed**: *We need to slough off the company's bad image.*

slough² /slaʊ, slu/ *n.* **1** [C] EARTH SCIENCE an area of land covered in deep dirty water or mud **2 a slough of despair/neglect etc.** LITERARY a bad situation or condition that you cannot get out of easily

Slo·vak Re·pub·lic, the /ˌsloʊvɑk rɪˈpʌblɪk/ also **Slo·va·ki·a** /sloʊˈvɑkiə/ a country in eastern Europe between the Ukraine and the Czech Republic, that was formed in 1993 when Czechoslovakia was divided —**Slovakian, Slovak** *n., adj.*

Slo·ve·ni·a /sloʊˈvinyə/ a country in southeast Europe, between Austria and Croatia, that was formerly part of Yugoslavia —**Slovenian** *n., adj.*

slov·en·ly /ˈslʌvənli, ˈslɑ-/ *adj.* dirty, messy, and careless: *a fat slovenly woman* [**Origin:** 1500–1600 *sloven* **dirty messy person**] —**slovenliness** *n.* [U]

slow¹ /sloʊ/ S2 W2 *adj.*

1 MOVE not moving quickly or able to move quickly OPP **fast** OPP **quick**: *a slow stroll around the park* | *a slow walker* | *The car was traveling at a very slow speed.*

2 DO/HAPPEN taking a long time, or a longer time than usual OPP **quick** OPP **fast**: *a slow process* | *slow workers* | *Economic growth remains slow.* | **slow to do sth** *The wound was slow to heal.* | **slow in doing sth** *New ideas have been slow in coming.* | *The project got off to* ***a slow start.*** | *The legal system can be* ***painfully slow.***

3 BUSINESS if business or trade is slow, there are not many customers, or not much is sold: *It's been a pretty slow day.*

4 MUSIC slow music is not played quickly: *a slow song*

5 CLOCK [not before noun] if a clock is slow, it is showing a time earlier than the correct time OPP **fast**: **ten minutes/five minutes etc. slow** *My watch is about five minutes slow.*

6 the slow lane a) the slow lane on a large road is the one farthest to the right, where the slowest vehicles are supposed to drive **b)** if someone is in the slow lane, they are not making progress as quickly as other people, organizations etc.: *Vanguard Healthcare prefers to stay in the slow lane.*

7 STUPID not good or quick at understanding things OPP **quick**: *Danny is a little bit slow.* | *a slow learner*

8 slow on the uptake not good at understanding things quickly

9 be slow going if a job, trip etc. is slow going, it is difficult to make progress quickly

10 slow off the mark not reacting to a situation quickly

11 BUS/TRAIN ETC. [only before noun] a slow train, boat etc. stops at many stations, places etc. instead of going directly from one main place to another OPP **fast**

12 a slow news day a day on which nothing important happens and there is nothing interesting in the newspapers or on the television news

13 do a slow burn also **go into a slow burn** to slowly become angry: *Coach Bowen stood on the sidelines, doing a slow burn.*

14 PHOTOGRAPHY slow film does not react to light very easily OPP **fast**

15 a slow oven an OVEN that is set at a fairly low temperature

[**Origin:** Old English *slaw*] → see also SLOWLY

slow² S3 W2 *v.* [I,T] to become slower, or to make something slower: *Economic growth has slowed.* | **slow (sth) to a crawl/trickle/halt etc.** *The scandal has slowed business to a trickle.*

slow down also **slow up** *phr. v.* **1 slow sb/sth ↔ down** to become slower, or to make someone or something slower OPP **speed up**: *Slow down – you're driving too fast!* | *The ice on the road slowed us down.* | *All this paperwork has really slowed up our application process.* **2 slow sb ↔ down** to become less active or busy than you usually are, or to make someone less active or busy: *Marge's arthritis is starting to slow her down.*

slow³ *adv.* SPOKEN slowly: *You'd better go slow around this corner.*

slow·down /ˈsloʊdaʊn/ *n.* **1** [C usually singular] a reduction in activity or speed: *a slowdown in consumer spending* **2** [C] a period when people deliberately work slowly in order to protest about something

slow·ly /ˈsloʊli/ S3 W2 *adv.* **1** at a slow speed or rate: *Ann drove away slowly.* | *Can you speak more slowly?* |

S

Her condition is slowly improving. **2 slowly but surely** if you do something slowly but surely, you do it more slowly than expected, but it is clear that you are making progress

ˌslow ˈmotion *n.* [U] movement on television or in a movie that is shown at a slower speed than it really happened: *They replayed the goal* ***in slow motion***. —**slow-motion** *adj.* [only before noun]

ˈslow-pitch *n.* [U] a game like SOFTBALL, played by mixed teams of men and women

slow·poke /ˈsloʊpoʊk/ *n.* [C] SPOKEN someone who moves or does things too slowly

ˌslow-ˈwitted *adj.* not good at understanding things SYN **stupid**

sludge /slʌdʒ/ *n.* [U] **1** the thick nearly solid substance that is left when SEWAGE (=the liquid waste from houses, factories etc.) has been cleaned **2** a soft thick substance like mud, especially at the bottom of a liquid —**sludgy** *adj.*

slug¹ /slʌg/ *n.* [C] **1** BIOLOGY a small slow-moving creature with a soft body like a SNAIL, but without a shell **2** a bullet **3** INFORMAL a small amount of a strong alcoholic drink: *a slug of whiskey* **4** a piece of metal shaped like a coin, used to get a drink, ticket etc. from a machine illegally

S

slug² *v.* **slugged, slugging** [T] **1** to hit someone hard with your closed hand: *Jimmy slugged Paul in the stomach.* **2** to hit a baseball hard **3 slug it out** if two people slug it out, they fight in a fierce way: *The candidates will slug it out in next week's debate.*

slug sth ↔ **back** *phr. v.* to drink an alcoholic drink, especially by swallowing large amounts at the same time

slug·fest /ˈslʌgfɛst/ *n.* [C] INFORMAL **1** a situation in which people are arguing or fighting with each other in a very angry and rude way: *a political slugfest* **2** a very rude and loud competition between two or more people, sports teams or musical groups

slug·ger /ˈslʌgɚ/ *n.* [C] a baseball player who hits the ball very hard

slug·gish /ˈslʌgɪʃ/ *adj.* moving. happening, or reacting more slowly than normal: *I've felt sluggish all day.* | *sluggish sales* —**sluggishly** *adv.* —**sluggishness** *n.* [U]

sluice¹ /slus/ *n.* [C] a passage for water to flow through, with a special gate that can be opened or closed to control the flow

sluice² *v.* **1** [T] to wash something with a lot of water **2** [I always + adv./prep.] if water sluices somewhere, a large amount of it suddenly flows there

slum¹ /slʌm/ *n.* [C] an area of a city that is in very bad condition, where very poor people live: +**of** *the slums of Rio* | *She grew up* ***in the slums***. ►see THESAURUS box at **area**

slum² *v.* **slummed, slumming** [I] also **slum it** OFTEN HUMOROUS to spend time in conditions that are much worse than you are used to: *I don't want to spend a lot, but I don't want to slum it either.*

slum·ber¹ /ˈslʌmbɚ/ *v.* [I] LITERARY to sleep

slumber² *n.* [singular, U] also **slumbers** [plural] LITERARY sleep

ˈslumber ˌparty *n.* [C] a children's party at which a group of children spend the night at one child's house

slum·lord /ˈslʌmlɔrd/ *n.* [C] DISAPPROVING someone who owns houses in a poor area and charges high rents for buildings that are in bad condition

slum·my /ˈslʌmi/ *adj.* INFORMAL a slummy area is one where very poor people live and the buildings are in bad condition

slump¹ /slʌmp/ *v.* [I] **1** to suddenly go down in price, value, or number: *Sales slumped by 20% last year.* | +**to** *The currency slumped to a record low.* **2** [always + adv./prep.] to fall or lean against something because you are not strong enough to stand: +**back/over/on/to etc.** *He slumped against the wall.* **3** if your shoulders or head slump, they bend forward because you are unhappy, tired, unconscious etc.

slump² *n.* [C] **1** ECONOMICS a sudden decrease in prices, sales, business activity etc.: *an economic slump* | +**in** *a slump in exports* ►see THESAURUS box at **recession** **2** a period of time when a company, sports team etc. is not successful

slumped /slʌmpt/ *adj.* sitting with your body leaning backward or forward because you are tired or unconscious: *Brad was slumped in front of the TV.*

slung /slʌŋ/ *v.* the past tense and past participle of SLING

slunk /slʌŋk/ *v.* the past tense and past participle of SLINK

slur¹ /slɚ/ *v.* **slurred, slurring** **1** [I,T] to speak in an unclear way, without separating your words or sounds correctly: **slur your speech/words** *After a few drinks, Bev started slurring her words.* **2** [T] to criticize someone or something unfairly **3** [T] ENG. LANG. ARTS to play a group of musical notes smoothly together [**Origin:** (2) 1600–1700 *slur* **thin mud** (15–19 centuries)] —**slurred** *adj.*: *slurred speech*

slur² *n.* **1** [C] an unfair criticism, or an offensive remark: +**on** *a slur on my reputation* | **racial/ethnic/anti-Semitic etc. slur** (=an offensive remark, based on someone's race, religion etc.) **2** [singular] an unclear way of speaking, in which the words are not separated **3** [C] ENG. LANG. ARTS a curved line written over or under musical notes to show they must be played together smoothly

slurp /slɚp/ *v.* [I,T] to make a noisy sucking sound while drinking a liquid ►see THESAURUS box at **drink¹** —**slurp** *n.* [C]

Slur·pee /ˈslɚpi/ *n.* [C,U] TRADEMARK a SLUSH

slur·ry /ˈslɚi, ˈslʌri/ *n.* [U] a thin mixture of water and another substance such as mud, CEMENT, or animal waste

slush /slʌʃ/ *n.* **1** [U] partly melted snow: *slush and snow* ►see THESAURUS box at **snow¹** **2** [C,U] a drink made with crushed ice and a sweet liquid: *a cherry slush* —**slushy** *adj.*

ˈslush fund *n.* [C] a sum of money kept for dishonest purposes, especially by a politician

sly¹ /slaɪ/ *adj. comparative* **slier** or **slyer**, *superlative* **sliest** or **slyest** **1 a sly smile/glance/wink etc.** a smile, look etc. that shows that you are hiding something you know from other people **2** very skillful in the way that you use tricks and lies to get what you want: *Be careful, she can be pretty sly.* —**slyly** *adv.* —**slyness** *n.* [U]

sly² *n.* **on the sly** secretly, especially when you are doing something that you should not do: *Dick had started drinking again on the sly.*

smack¹ /smæk/ *v.* **1** [I,T] to hit or crash into something, or to hit something against something else so that it makes a short loud noise: +**into** *The plane smacked into the side of the mountain.* | **smack sth against/into etc. sth** *Canseco smacked the last pitch into the left-field seats.* **2 smack your lips** to make a short loud noise with your lips because you are hungry **3** [T] to hit someone hard with your hand: *He turned and smacked me in the chest.* ►see THESAURUS box at **hit¹**

smack of sth *phr. v.* FORMAL to seem to have a particular quality: *Their failure to publish the article smacks of censorship.*

smack² *n.* **1** [C] a hard hit with your hand: *She gave Danny's hand a smack.* **2** [C] a short loud noise, caused especially when something hits something else **3 give sb a smack on the lips/cheek** INFORMAL to kiss someone loudly **4** [U] SLANG the illegal drug HEROIN

smack³ *adv.* INFORMAL **1 smack (dab) in the middle** exactly or directly in the middle of something: *We found ourselves smack in the middle of a huge fight.* **2** if something moves smack into or against something, it hits it with a lot of force, making a loud noise: *I drove smack into the side of the garage.*

smack·er /ˈsmækɚ/ also **smack·er·oo** /ˌsmækəˈru/ *n.* [C] INFORMAL **1** a dollar: *It cost me 50 smackers.* **2** a loud kiss

small[1] /smɔl/ S1 W1 *adj.*
1 SIZE not large in size or amount OPP **large**: *a small car* | *This T-shirt is too small for me.* | *a small increase in food prices* | ***a small amount of** money* → see Word Choice box at LITTLE[1]

THESAURUS
little small in size: *a little dog*
tiny very small: *a tiny baby*
minute extremely small: *A minute amount of this poison can kill.*
cramped used about a space that is too small: *a cramped apartment*
petite used about a woman who is short and thin in an attractive way
→ BIG

2 GROUP/NUMBER consisting of only a few people or things SYN **large**: *The classes are small and the people are friendly.* | *a small group of friends* | *Only **a small number of** cases were affected.*
3 UNIMPORTANT a small problem, job, mistake etc. is not important or severe: *a small mistake* | *We made only a few small changes.* | *There's a small problem.*
4 NOT WORTH MUCH MONEY not costing a large amount of money: *a small gift*
5 CHILD a small child is young: *She has three small children.* ▸see THESAURUS box at **young**[1]
6 a small business/firm/company etc. a business that does not have many EMPLOYEES, and usually deals with a limited number of products or activities
7 small farmer/investor someone whose activities do not involve large amounts of land or money
8 a small fortune a lot of money: *It's going to cost us a small fortune to fix the roof.*
9 in a/some small way if something helps, affects, influences etc. something else in a small way, it has an effect, but not an important one: *It was good to feel we helped in some small way.*
10 ALPHABET small letters are the smaller of the two forms that we use, for example "b" rather than "B" SYN **lower case**
11 feel/look small to feel or look stupid, unimportant, or ashamed: *She loved to make me look small.*
12 in no small measure/part/degree to a great degree: *The success of the project is due in no small measure to you.*
13 no small achievement/task/feat etc. a large achievement: *Getting the two sides to talk to each other is no small achievement.*
14 VOICE a small voice is quiet and soft: *"It still hurts," he said in a small voice.*
15 small potatoes something that is not very important, especially when compared with something else: *Four thousand dollars is small potatoes for a big company.*
16 (it's a) small world SPOKEN said when you are surprised to learn that someone knows a person who you know, goes to a place where you go etc.: *"Did you know David works with my wife?" "Really? Small world."*
17 a socialist with a small "s"/a libertarian with a small "l" etc. someone who believes in the principles you have mentioned, but is not a member of a political party or group with that name
[**Origin:** Old English *smæl*] → see also **(it's) no/small/little wonder** at WONDER[2] (2) —**small** *adv.*: *He writes so small I can't read it.* —**smallness** *n.* [U]

small[2] *n.* **the small of sb's back** the lower part of someone's back where it curves in, just above their BUTTOCKS

small arms *n.* [plural] guns that are held in one or both hands for firing

small-boned *adj.* a small-boned person is short and thin

small-ˈcaliber *adj.* [only before noun] a small-caliber gun fires small bullets

small ˈchange *n.* [U] **1** money in coins of low value **2** an amount of money that seems small, when it is compared with another amount: *Twenty million dollars is small change in Washington.*

ˌsmall ˈclaims court *n.* [C] LAW a court where people can try to get small amounts of money from other people or from companies, when they have been treated unfairly

ˈsmall fry *n.* [plural,U] **1** children **2** unimportant people or things

ˈsmall hours *n.* [plural] **the small hours** the early morning hours, between about one and four o'clock SYN **the wee hours**

ˌsmall inˈtestine *n.* [singular] BIOLOGY the long tube that food goes through after the stomach and before the LARGE INTESTINE, where it is broken down into its chemical parts and taken into the blood → see also LARGE INTESTINE → see picture at DIGESTIVE SYSTEM

small·ish /ˈsmɔlɪʃ/ *adj.* fairly small OPP **largish**: *a smallish woman*

ˌsmall-ˈminded *adj.* DISAPPROVING only interested in things that affect you, and too willing to judge people according to your own opinions: *The tone of the book is small-minded and intolerant.* → see also NARROW-MINDED —**small-mindedness** *n.* [U] DISAPPROVING

small·pox /ˈsmɔlpɑks/ *n.* [U] MEDICINE a serious infectious disease in the past that caused spots that left marks on the skin and often killed people → see also CHICKENPOX

ˈsmall ˌprint *n.* [U] **the small print** FINE PRINT

ˌsmall-ˈscale *adj.* [only before noun] **1** not involving a lot of people, money etc. OPP **large-scale**: *small-scale research projects* **2** a small-scale map, model etc. is drawn or made smaller than usual and does not show many details OPP **large-scale**

ˈsmall ˌscreen *n.* **the small screen** television → see also BIG SCREEN

ˈsmall talk *n.* [U] polite friendly conversation about unimportant subjects: *Guests stood with their drinks, **making small talk** about the weather.*

ˈsmall-time *adj.* [only before noun] not important or successful: *a small-time drug dealer* → see also BIG-TIME —**small-timer** *n.* [C]

ˈsmall-town *adj.* [only before noun] **1** relating to a small town: *a small-town newspaper* **2** relating to the qualities, ideas, and opinions that people who live in small towns are supposed to have, such as honesty and politeness, but sometimes also a lack of interest in anything new or different: *small-town values*

smarm·y /ˈsmɑrmi/ *adj.* *comparative* **smarmier**, *superlative* **smarmiest** DISAPPROVING polite in an insincere way that you do not like or trust

smart[1] /smɑrt/ S1 W3 *adj.*
1 INTELLIGENT intelligent OPP **dumb** OPP **stupid**: *He's a smart guy.* | *You're way too smart to be doing this job.* ▸see THESAURUS box at **intelligent**
2 GOOD DECISION a) making good judgments or decisions: *Here are a few tips every smart traveler should know.* | *a smart businesswoman* **b)** a smart decision, plan etc. shows good judgment or thinking OPP **dumb** OPP **stupid**: *Buying the house was **a smart move*** (=a good decision).
3 IMPOLITE saying funny things in a way that does not show respect: *That's enough of your smart remarks for now.* | *Don't **get smart with** me.* | *That girl **has a smart mouth*** (=says rude things that do not show respect). → see also SMART-MOUTHED
4 the smart money opinions and judgments made by intelligent people who know a lot about a particular situation, especially relating to INVESTMENTS: *The smart money says that biotech is the next big thing.*
5 TECHNOLOGY [only before noun] COMPUTERS smart machines, weapons, materials etc. have a computer system that makes them able to make decisions and react to different situations appropriately: *smart weapons* → see also SMART BOMB

S

6 **FASHIONABLE** OLD-FASHIONED neat and fashionable, or used by fashionable people SYN **sharp**: *a smart suit*
7 **WELL-DRESSED** OLD-FASHIONED wearing neat attractive clothes and having a generally neat and clean appearance
8 **QUICK** a smart movement is done quickly and with force: *Marvin gave me a smart kick under the table.*
[**Origin:** Old English *smeart*] —**smartness** *n.* [U] → see also SMARTS

smart² *adv.* INFORMAL in a way that shows intelligence and good judgment: *We've got to work smarter, not harder.*

smart³ *v.* [I] **1** to be upset because someone has hurt your feelings or offended you: +**from** *The Eagles were still smarting from their loss to Arizona.* **2** if a part of your body smarts, it hurts with a stinging pain: *The smoke made my eyes smart.* ►see THESAURUS box at **hurt¹**

smart off *phr. v.* INFORMAL to make funny impolite remarks

smart al·eck /ˈsmɑrt̬ ˌælɪk/ *n.* [C] INFORMAL DISAPPROVING someone who always says funny impolite things, or who always has the right answer in a way that is annoying

ˈsmart bomb *n.* [C] a bomb that is fired from an aircraft and guided by a computer

S

ˈsmart card *n.* [C] a small plastic card with an electronic part that records information

smart·en /ˈsmɑrtˀn/ *v.*

smarten up *phr. v.* **1 smarten sth ↔ up** to improve your behavior and the way you do things and behave more intelligently **2 smarten sth ↔ up** to make something look better, for example by cleaning or painting it

smart·ly /ˈsmɑrtli/ *adv.* **1** in a neat fashionable way: *a smartly dressed man* **2** quickly: *Stocks rose smartly in active trading.* **3** using force: *He hit the ball smartly toward left field.*

ˈsmart-ˌmouthed *adj.* INFORMAL making a lot of funny impolite remarks

smarts /smɑrts/ *n.* [plural] INFORMAL the ability to think quickly and make good judgments SYN **intelligence**: *political smarts* → see also STREET SMARTS

smart·y /ˈsmɑrt̬i/ *n. plural* **smarties** [C] a SMART ALECK

smart·y·pants /ˈsmɑrt̬iˌpænts/ *n.* [C] HUMOROUS someone who always says funny impolite things or always has the right answer, in an annoying way

smash¹ /smæʃ/ *v.* **1** [I,T] to break into many small pieces violently or loudly, or to make something do this by dropping, throwing, or hitting it: *The burglars smashed a window to get in.* | **smash (sth) to bits/pieces** *The bottle rolled off the table and smashed to pieces.* ►see THESAURUS box at **break¹** **2** [I always + adv./prep.,T always + adv./prep.] to hit an object or surface violently, or to make something do this: +**against/down/into etc.** *She was killed when her car smashed into a tree.* | **smash sth against/down/into etc. sth** *He smashed his fist down on the table.* **3** [T] to defeat or destroy something such as an enemy or an organization: *Police say they have smashed a major crime ring.* **4** [T] to ruin something such as someone's hopes or happiness: *His confidence had been smashed to pieces.* **5 smash a record** to do much better than someone or something has done before in a race, competition etc. **6** [T] to hit a high ball with a strong DOWNWARD action, in tennis or similar sports

smash sth ↔ **in** *phr. v.* **1** to hit something so violently that you break it and make a hole in it: *The door had been smashed in.* **2 smash sb's head/face in** INFORMAL to hit someone very hard in the head or face

smash sth ↔ **up** *phr. v.* to deliberately damage or destroy something: *Forty inmates smashed up their prison cells.* → see also SMASH-UP

smash² *n.* **1** [C] a very successful new play, book, movie etc. SYN **smash hit**: *the latest Broadway smash* **2** [singular] the loud sound of something breaking **3** [C] a hard DOWNWARD hit of the ball in tennis or similar sports

smashed /smæʃt/ *adj.* [only before noun] INFORMAL very drunk or affected by a drug

ˈsmash hit *n.* [C] a very successful new play, book, movie etc. SYN **smash**

smash·ing /ˈsmæʃɪŋ/ *adj.* OLD-FASHIONED very good: *The show was a **smashing success**.*

ˈsmash-up *n.* [C] a serious car or train accident

smat·ter·ing /ˈsmæt̬ərɪŋ/ *n.* **a smattering of sth** a small number or amount of something: *He received only a smattering of applause.* [**Origin:** 1500–1600 *smatter* **to splash, talk with little knowledge** (15–19 centuries)]

smear¹ /smɪr/ *v.* **1** [T] to spread a liquid or soft substance over a surface, especially in a careless or messy way: **smear sth on/over etc.** *She smeared suntan lotion on her shoulders.* **2** [I,T] to make something such as ink, paint, MAKEUP etc. messy by rubbing it, getting it wet etc., or to become messy in this way SYN **smudge**: *She had been crying and her makeup had smeared.* | *His sweaty hand was smearing the ink as he wrote.* **3** [T] to make dirty or oily marks on something SYN **smudge**: *Don't smear my glasses.* | **smear sth with sth** *Halle's face was smeared with butter.* **4** [T] to spread an untrue story about someone in order to harm them: *The story was an attempt to smear his campaign opponent.* [**Origin:** Old English *smeoru* **fatty material**]

smear² *n.* [C] **1** a dirty or oily mark on something: +**of** *smears of blood* ►see THESAURUS box at **mark²** **2** an attempt to harm someone by spreading untrue stories about them **3** a soft food made of cheese or other things that can be spread on something, especially a BAGEL SYN **spread** **4** an area of human cells that are put on a SLIDE to be examined under a MICROSCOPE → see also PAP SMEAR —**smeary** *adj.*

ˈsmear camˌpaign *n.* [C] a deliberate plan to tell untrue stories about someone, especially a politician, in order to harm them

smell¹ /smɛl/ S1 W3 *n.* **1** [C] the quality that people and animals recognize by using their nose: *What's that smell?* | *A delicious smell was coming from the kitchen.* | +**of** *The air was filled with the smell of flowers.*

THESAURUS

You can use **smell** in a general way to talk about something that you notice or recognize using your nose. It can be used to mean a good smell or a bad smell: *There was a strong smell of fish in the house.* | *The smell of bread baking always reminds me of my grandma.*

A good smell
aroma a strong pleasant smell, used especially about food: *the aroma of fresh coffee*
scent/fragrance/perfume a pleasant smell: *the sweet fragrance of roses*

A bad smell
stink a very bad smell: *the stink of rotting fish*
stench/reek a very strong bad smell: *the stench of urine*
odor FORMAL a bad smell: *the odor of alcohol on his breath*

2 [C] a bad smell → see also ODOR: *I think the smell is getting worse.* **3** [U] the ability to notice or recognize smells: *A mole finds its food by smell alone.* | *Dogs have a very good **sense of smell**.*

smell² W3 *v.*
1 HAVE A PARTICULAR SMELL [linking verb] to have a particular smell: *I love the way the house smells at Christmas.* | **smell nice/good/bad etc.** *You smell nice!* | *Something smells terrible!* | +**like** *Your perfume smells like roses.* | +**of** *The apartment smelled of paint.*
2 HAVE A BAD SMELL [I not in progressive] to have a bad smell SYN **stink**: *Your feet smell.*
3 RECOGNIZE A SMELL [T not in progressive] to notice or recognize a particular smell: *Do you smell smoke?* | *I **can smell** something burning.*
4 USE YOUR NOSE [T] to put your nose near something to

discover what type of smell it has SYN sniff: *Smell these roses!*
5 smell trouble/danger etc. to feel that something bad is going to happen: *Actually, I should have smelled trouble earlier.*
6 smell a rat to guess that something wrong or dishonest is happening
7 smell fishy (to sb) to seem likely to be dishonest, illegal etc.: *The deal smelled fishy to many people on Wall Street.*
8 smell something fishy to think something is likely to be dishonest or untrue
9 sth doesn't smell right (to sb) used to say that a situation does not seem right
10 come up/out smelling like a rose to get an advantage from a situation, when you ought to have been blamed, criticized, or harmed by it
11 ABLE TO SMELL [I] to have the ability to notice and recognize smells

smell sb/sth ↔ **out** *phr. v.* **1** to find something because you have a natural ability to do this: *He has an instinct for smelling out weakness in others.* **2** to find something by smelling: *Dogs are able to smell out their prey.*

smell sth ↔ **up** *phr. v.* to fill a place with an unpleasant smell: *He smelled up the place with his cigars.*

-smelling /smɛlɪŋ/ *suffix* [in adjectives] having a particular smell: *sweet-smelling flowers*

smelling salts *n.* [plural] a strong-smelling chemical that you hold under someone's nose to make them conscious again

smell·y /ˈsmɛli/ *adj. comparative* **smellier**, *superlative* **smelliest** having a strong bad smell: *smelly socks* —**smelliness** *n.* [U]

smelt[1] /smɛlt/ *v.* [T] to melt a rock that contains metal in order to remove the metal

smelt[2] *v.* an old-fashioned form of the past tense and past participle of SMELL

smelt[3] *n.* [C] BIOLOGY a small fish that lives in cold lakes and oceans

smidg·en, smidgeon /ˈsmɪdʒən/ also **smidge** /smɪdʒ/ *n.* INFORMAL **1 a smidgen/smidge (of sth)** a very small amount of something: *Add a smidgeon of salt.* **2 a smidgen/smidge** a little: *Open the window a smidge.*

smile[1] /smaɪl/ S2 W2 *v.* **1** [I] to have or make a happy expression on your face in which your mouth curves up → see also FROWN: *She smiled and said "Good morning."* | **+at** *Susan smiled at him and waved.* | **+about** *What are you smiling about?* → GRIN[1] (1)

THESAURUS

grin to smile continuously with a very big smile: *He grinned happily as she came toward him.*
beam to smile because you are very pleased about something: *Jenny ran across the room, beaming with pleasure.*
smirk to smile in an unpleasant way, for example because you are pleased about someone else's bad luck: *I stood there, unable to remember anything, and then saw my brother smirking.*

2 smile to yourself to be amused by something, often without showing it: *Mark read the message and smiled to himself.* **3** [T] to say or express something with a smile: *"I knew you'd come," she smiled.* **4 God/luck/fortune smiles on sb** if God, luck etc. smiles on you, you have very good luck —**smiling** *adj.* [only before noun] *smiling children* —**smilingly** *adv.*: *Melissa smilingly reached for a cigarette.*

smile[2] S3 W2 *n.* [C] **1** an expression on your face in which your mouth curves up to show that you are happy, amused, friendly etc. → see also FROWN: *Juan had a big smile on his face.* | *"How's it going?" Maya asked **with a smile**.* | *She **gave** the children **a** little **smile**.* → GRIN[2] **2 be all smiles** to look very happy, especially because of something good that has happened

smil·ey /ˈsmaɪli/ *n.* [C] a sign that looks like a face when you look at it sideways, for example :-) used in EMAIL messages to show that you are happy or pleased about something

ˈsmiley face *n.* [C] a simple picture of a smiling face, drawn as a circle with two eyes and a mouth inside it

smirk /smɚk/ *v.* [I] to smile in a way that is not nice, and that shows that you are pleased by someone else's bad luck: **+at** *What are you smirking at?* ▸see THESAURUS box at smile[1] [**Origin:** Old English *smearcian* **to smile**] —**smirk** *n.* [C]

smite /smaɪt/ *v. past tense* **smote** /smoʊt/, *past participle* **smitten** /ˈsmɪtˀn/ [T] **1** OLD USE to hit something or someone hard **2** BIBLICAL to destroy, attack, or punish someone → see also SMITTEN[1]

smith /smɪθ/ *n.* [C] someone who makes and repairs things made of iron SYN **blacksmith**

-smith /smɪθ/ *suffix* [in nouns] someone who makes something: *a gunsmith* (=someone who makes guns) | *a silversmith* (=someone who makes things out of silver) | *a wordsmith* (=someone who writes, for example a reporter)

Smith /smɪθ/, **Ad·am** /ˈædəm/ (1723–1790) a Scottish ECONOMIST famous for his belief in FREE ENTERPRISE, which has had an important influence on modern economic and political ideas

Smith, John (1580–1631) an English EXPLORER who started Jamestown, Virginia, the first permanent COLONY in America

Smith, Joseph (1805–1844) a U.S. religious leader who started the MORMON religion

Smith, Mar·garet Chase /ˈmɑrgrɪt tʃeɪs/ (1897–1995) a U.S. politician who was the first woman to be elected to both the Senate and the House of Representatives

smith·er·eens /ˌsmɪðəˈrinz/ *n.* **smash/blow/blast etc. sth to smithereens** INFORMAL to destroy something completely by breaking it violently into very small pieces

Smith·son /ˈsmɪθsən/, **James** (1765–1829) a British scientist who left the money to start the Smithsonian Institution after his death

Smith·so·ni·an In·sti·tu·tion, the /smɪθˌsoʊniən ɪnstɪˈtuʃən/ also **the Smithsonian** a large group of MUSEUMS and scientific institutions in Washington, D.C., which was established in 1846 using money left by James Smithson

smith·y /ˈsmɪθi/ *n. plural* **smithies** [C] a place where iron objects such as HORSESHOES were made and repaired in past times

smit·ten[1] /ˈsmɪtˀn/ *adj.* feeling that you love someone or like something very much, especially suddenly: **+with** *Eric's completely smitten with Jenny.*

smitten[2] *v.* the past participle of SMITE

smock /smɑk/ *n.* [C] a loose piece of clothing like a long shirt, worn over your clothes to prevent them from getting dirty: *an artist's smock*

smock·ing /ˈsmɑkɪŋ/ *n.* [U] a type of decoration made on cloth by pulling the cloth into small regular folds which are held tightly with stitches —**smock** *v.* [T] —**smocked** *adj.*

smog /smɑg, smɔg/ *n.* [U] unhealthy air, often brown in color, caused by gases from cars and smoke from factories etc. —**smoggy** *adj.*

smoke[1] /smoʊk/ S3 W3 *n.* **1** [U] white, gray, or black gas that is produced by something burning: *a cloud of smoke* | *cigarette smoke* | *We could still smell the smoke from the fire.* **2** [C usually singular] INFORMAL an act of smoking a cigarette etc.: *He went outside for a smoke.* | *I haven't **had a smoke** in nine days.* **3** [C] INFORMAL a cigarette: *a pack of smokes* **4 go up in smoke a)** to be destroyed by fire **b)** if your plans go up in smoke, you cannot do what you intended to do **5 smoke and mirrors** actions that are intended to deceive people, or to make them believe something that is not true: *The business proposal was all smoke and mirrors.* **6 where**

there's smoke, there's fire used to say that if something bad is being said about someone or something, it is probably partly true [**Origin:** Old English *smoca*] —**smokeless** *adj.*

smoke² S1 W2 *v.* **1 a)** [I,T] if someone smokes, they regularly use cigarettes, a pipe etc.: *Do you smoke?* | *Dana started smoking again.* | **smoke cigarettes/cigars/a pipe** *My grandfather smoked a pipe.* | **smoke like a chimney** (=to smoke a lot) **b)** [I,T] to suck or breathe in smoke from a cigarette, pipe etc.: *Do you mind if I smoke?* | **smoke a cigarette/cigar/pipe** *Greg sat alone, smoking a cigarette.* **2** [I] if something smokes, it has smoke coming out of it: *The house was still smoking when we arrived.* **3** [T] to give fish or meat a special taste by hanging it in smoke to preserve it —**smoking** *n.* [U]

smoke out *phr. v.* **1 smoke sb/sth ↔ out** to fill a place with smoke in order to force a person or animal to come out **2 smoke sb ↔ out** to force someone who is causing a particular problem to make themselves known

'smoke a,larm *n.* [C] a piece of electronic equipment that warns you when there is smoke or fire in a building

S

'smoke bomb *n.* [C] something that you throw that produces clouds of smoke, used to prevent people from seeing clearly

smoked /smoʊkt/ *adj.* **smoked salmon/bacon/sausage etc.** fish, meat etc. that has been left in smoke to preserve it and give it a special taste

'smoke de,tector *n.* [C] a SMOKE ALARM

,smoked 'glass *n.* [U] glass that is a dark gray color

,smoke-filled 'room *n.* [C] a place where a group of powerful people meet in secret to make decisions, especially about politics

,smoke-'free *adj.* **a smoke-free area/zone etc.** a place where you are not allowed to smoke

smoke•house /'smoʊkhaʊs/ *n.* [C] a building where meat, fish etc. is hung in smoke to preserve it and give it a special taste

,smokeless to'bacco *n.* [U] a type of tobacco that is held in the mouth for a long time and sometimes CHEWed, but not swallowed or smoked

smok•er /'smoʊkɚ/ *n.* [C] **1** someone who smokes cigarettes, CIGARS etc. OPP **nonsmoker**: *Mike is a very* ***heavy smoker*** (=he smokes a lot). | **a cigarette/cigar/pipe smoker** *Most cigarette smokers would like to quit.* **2** a piece of equipment that produces smoke, used to give meat, fish etc. a special taste

smoke•screen /'smoʊkskrin/ *n.* [C] **1** something that you do or say to hide your real plans or actions **2** a cloud of smoke produced so that it hides soldiers, ships etc. during a battle

'smoke ,signal *n.* [C] a signal that is sent out to people who are far away, using the smoke from a fire

smoke•stack /'smoʊkstæk/ *n.* [C] a tall CHIMNEY at a factory or on a ship

'smokestack ,industry *n.* [C usually plural] a big traditional industry, such as making cars

smok•ing¹ /'smoʊkɪŋ/ *n.* [U] the activity of breathing in tobacco smoke from a cigarette, pipe etc.: *the dangers of cigarette smoking* | **stop/give up/quit smoking** *I quit smoking 12 years ago.*

smoking² *adj.* [only before noun, no comparative] **a smoking area/section/room etc.** a place where people are allowed to smoke

,smoking 'gun *n.* [C usually singular] definite proof of who is responsible for something or how something really happened

'smoking jacket *n.* [C] a type of man's formal JACKET made of expensive material, usually worn at home in the evening

smok•y /'smoʊki/ *adj. comparative* **smokier**, *superlative* **smokiest** **1** filled with smoke: *a smoky room* **2** producing too much smoke: *a smoky old diesel engine* **3** having the taste, smell, or appearance of smoke: *smoky bacon* —**smokiness** *n.* [U]

smol•der /'smoʊldɚ/ *v.* [I] **1** if something smolders, it burns slowly without a flame ►see THESAURUS box at **burn¹** **2** if someone smolders or if their strong feelings smolder, the feelings are not fully expressed

smol•der•ing /'smoʊldərɪŋ/ *adj.* [only before noun] **1** burning slowly without a flame: *smoldering plane wreckage* **2** a smoldering feeling is strong but not fully expressed: *smoldering resentment* **3** very sexually attractive or sexually exciting

smooch /smutʃ/ *v.* [I,T] INFORMAL if two people smooch, they kiss each other in a romantic way —**smooch** *n.* [C]

smooth¹ /smuð/ *adj.*
1 SURFACE a smooth surface is completely even, without any BUMPS OPP **rough**: *a smooth pebble* | *the smooth surface of the glass* | *The stone steps had been* ***worn smooth.*** ►see THESAURUS box at **flat¹**
2 SOFT smooth skin, hair, or fur is soft and pleasant to touch, and your hand moves easily over it OPP **rough**: *The conditioner leaves your hair* ***silky smooth.***
3 LIQUID a smooth liquid mixture has no big pieces in it OPP **lumpy**: *a smooth sauce*
4 WITHOUT PROBLEMS a system, operation, or process that is smooth operates well and without problems: *a smooth transition* | *The negotiations have hardly been smooth.* → see also **go smoothly** at SMOOTHLY (2)
5 smooth sailing if something is smooth sailing, it is easy and happens without any problems
6 a smooth ride a situation in which you do not experience any problems or no one opposes you when you are trying to do something
7 MOVEMENT a smooth movement, style, way of doing something etc. is graceful and has no sudden awkward changes OPP **jerky**: *Swing the tennis racket in one smooth motion.*
8 RIDE/TRIP a smooth ride or trip is comfortable because the vehicle you are in does not shake much while you are traveling OPP **bumpy**: *a smooth flight*
9 PERSON someone who is smooth is polite, confident, and relaxed, but also makes you feel that you cannot trust them: *a smooth lawyer* → see also SMOOTH-TALKING
10 TASTE a smooth drink such as WHISKEY or coffee is not bitter, but tastes good and is easy to swallow
11 SOUND soft and pleasant to listen to: *a smooth reassuring voice*
[**Origin:** Old English *smoth*] —**smoothness** *n.* [U] → see also SMOOTHLY

smooth² *v.* [T] **1** to take away the roughness from the surface of something: *Use a file to smooth sharp edges.* | **smooth sth down/off/out etc.** *Smooth down all surfaces before you start painting.* **2** to make something flat by moving your hands across it: **smooth sth out/open etc.** *They smoothed out the map on the table.* | **smooth sth down/back etc.** *She smoothed back her hair.* **3** [always + adv./prep.] to rub a liquid, cream etc. gently over a surface or into a surface: **smooth sth into/over sth** *She smoothed suntan lotion over her legs.* **4 smooth the way (for sth)** to make it easier for something to happen, by dealing with any problems first **5 smooth sb's ruffled feathers** to calm someone down when they are angry or offended

smooth sth ↔ **out** *phr. v.* **1** to get rid of problems or difficulties: *She spends most of her time smoothing out quarrels between participants.* **2** to make something happen in an even regular way by getting rid of the irregular parts

smooth sth ↔ **over** *phr. v.* to make problems or difficulties seem less important: *Later I tried to* ***smooth things over****, but he wasn't interested.*

smooth•ie /'smuði/ *n.* [C] **1** a thick drink made of fruit and fruit juices that have been mixed together until they are smooth **2** INFORMAL someone who is good at persuading people, but does not seem to be sincere

smooth•ly /'smuðli/ *adv.* **1** in a steady way, without stopping and starting again: *A small panel slid smoothly back.* **2** without problems, as planned or intended: **go/work/run etc. smoothly** *Nancy keeps the* *office running smoothly.* **3** if you say something smoothly, you say it in a calm and confident way **4** in a way that produces a smooth surface

ˈsmooth-ˌtalking *adj.* a smooth-talking person is good at persuading people and saying nice things, but you do not trust them: *a smooth-talking salesman* —**smooth talker** *n.* [C]

smor·gas·bord /ˈsmɔrgəsˌbɔrd/ *n.* [C] **1** a large variety of foods which are put on a long table so that people can serve themselves **2 a smorgasbord of sth** a large variety of different things

smote /smoʊt/ *v.* the past tense of SMITE

smoth·er /ˈsmʌðɚ/ *v.* [T] **1** to cover the whole surface of something with something else: **smother sth with/in sth** *My steak was smothered in onions and gravy.* **2** to kill someone by putting something over their nose and mouth to stop them from breathing: *She smothered her baby with a pillow.* **3** to express your feelings for someone too strongly, so that your relationship with them cannot develop normally: *I had to leave – I felt like I was being smothered.* **4 smother sb with kisses** to kiss someone a lot **5** to stop yourself from showing a feeling SYN **stifle**: *Nancy smothered a laugh.* **6** to make a fire stop burning by preventing air from reaching it **7** to completely defeat someone who opposes you [**Origin:** 1100–1200 *smother* **thick smoke** (12–19 centuries), from Old English *smorian* **to suffocate**]

smudge¹ /smʌdʒ/ *n.* [C] a dirty mark: *a lipstick smudge on the rim of the cup* ▸see THESAURUS box at **mark²** —**smudgy** *adj.*

smudge² *v.* **1** [I,T] to make writing, painting etc. become unclear by touching or rubbing it, or to become unclear in this way: *Renee wiped at her eyes, smudging her makeup.* **2** [T] to make a dirty mark on a surface: *Someone had smudged the paper with their greasy hands.*

smug /smʌg/ *adj.* DISAPPROVING showing too much satisfaction with your own skill or success: *What are you looking so smug about?* | *a smug grin* —**smugly** *adv.* —**smugness** *n.* [U]

smug·gle /ˈsmʌgəl/ *v.* [T] **1** to take something or someone illegally from one country to another: **smuggle sth into/out of/across etc. sth** *Thousands of antiques are smuggled out of the country every year.* **2** to take someone or something secretly to a place where they are not allowed to be: **smuggle sb/sth in/out** *I'll smuggle you in through the back door.* | **smuggle sth into/to/from etc. sth** *He somehow smuggled his notes into the exam.*

smug·gler /ˈsmʌglɚ/ *n.* [C] someone who takes something illegally from one country to another: *a drug smuggler*

smug·gling /ˈsmʌglɪŋ/ *n.* [U] the crime of taking things illegally from one country to another

smut /smʌt/ *n.* [U] **1** DISAPPROVING books, stories, pictures etc. that offend some people because they are about sex **2** a type of plant disease that attacks crops and causes a black substance to form on the plants: *corn smut*

smut·ty /ˈsmʌṭi/ *adj. comparative* **smuttier**, *superlative* **smuttiest** DISAPPROVING smutty books, stories, pictures etc. offend some people because they are about sex —**smuttiness** *n.* [U]

snack¹ /snæk/ S3 *n.* [C] **1** a small amount of food that is eaten between main meals or instead of a meal: *The café serves drinks and snacks.* | **have/grab a snack** *I only had time to grab a quick snack.* **2** also **snack food** a food, such as POTATO CHIPS or PEANUTS, that is sold to be eaten as a snack

snack² *v.* [I] to eat small amounts of food between main meals or instead of a meal: +**on** *He's always snacking on junk.*

ˈsnack bar *n.* [C] a place where you can buy snacks, such as SANDWICHES and CANDY BARS

sna·fu /ˈsnæfu, snæˈfu/ *n.* [C] a situation in which a plan does not happen in the way it should

snag¹ /snæg/ *n.* [C] **1** a disadvantage or problem, especially one that is not very serious: *The grand opening* ***hit a snag*** *when no one could find the key.* ▸see THESAURUS box at **problem¹** **2** a thread that has been pulled out of a piece of cloth by accident because it has gotten stuck on something sharp or pointed **3** a part of a dead tree that sticks out, especially one that is under water and can be dangerous

snag² *v.* **snagged, snagging** **1** [T] INFORMAL to succeed in getting someone or something: *They managed to snag Hanks for the leading role.* **2** [I,T] to damage something by getting it stuck on something, or to become damaged in this way: *I snagged my sweater again.*

snail /sneɪl/ *n.* [C] **1** BIOLOGY a small soft creature that moves very slowly and has a hard shell on its back **2 at a snail's pace** if something happens or is done at a snail's pace, it happens extremely slowly

ˈsnail mail *n.* [U] HUMOROUS an expression meaning letters that are sent through the mail and not by EMAIL

snake¹ /sneɪk/ *n.* [C] **1** BIOLOGY an animal with a long thin body and no legs, that often has a poisonous bite: **a poisonous/venomous snake** *Paul was bitten by a poisonous snake.* **2** also **snake in the grass** someone who cannot be trusted [**Origin:** Old English *snaca*]

snake² *v.* **1** [I always + adv./prep.,T always + adv./prep.] if a river, road, train, or line snakes somewhere, it moves in long twisting curves: +**along/past/down etc.** *The line for tickets snaked around the block.* | *The train was* ***snaking its way*** *through the mountains.* **2** [T always + adv./prep.] if you snake something somewhere, you move it in long twisting curves

S

snake·bite /ˈsneɪkbaɪt/ *n.* **1** [C,U] the bite of a poisonous snake **2** [C] an alcoholic drink that contains TEQUILA, which is drunk quickly from a small glass before you suck a piece of LEMON with salt on it in your hand

ˈsnake ˌcharmer *n.* [C] someone who entertains people by controlling snakes as they play music to them

ˈsnake eyes *n.* [plural] a situation in a game in which a pair of DICE both show the number one

ˈsnake oil *n.* [U] something that is claimed to be a solution to a problem, but is not effective

ˈsnake oil ˌsalesman also **ˈsnake oil ˌpeddler** *n.* [C] someone who deceives people by persuading them to accept false information, solutions that are not effective etc.

ˈsnake pit *n.* [C] a place or situation that is not organized and where people are quick to criticize one another

snake·skin /ˈsneɪkˌskɪn/ *n.* [U] the skin of a snake used to make shoes, bags etc.

snak·y /ˈsneɪki/ *adj.* moving or lying in twisting curves: *a snaky road*

snap¹ /snæp/ S3 *v.* **snapped, snapping**

1 BREAK [I,T] if something snaps or if you snap it, it breaks with a sudden sharp noise: *A twig snapped under my feet.* | *The wind snapped branches and power lines.* | **snap (sth) in two/half etc.** (=to break something into two pieces, or to break into two pieces) ▸see THESAURUS box at **break¹**

2 MOVE INTO POSITION [I always + adv./prep.,T always + adv./prep.] to move into a particular position suddenly, making a short sharp noise, or to make something move like this: *The cops snapped the handcuffs back onto the prisoner.* | **snap open/shut/together/on/off** *The pieces just snap together like this.* | **snap sth open/shut/together/on/off** *She snapped her briefcase shut.* → see also SNAP-ON

3 FASTEN [I always + adv./prep.,T always + adv./prep.] to fasten or attach something using a snap, or to become fastened in this way SYN **unsnap**: *The dress snaps up the back.* | *Zip up the tent and then snap the flap over it.* | *We snapped on our fanny packs and went out for the day.*

4 MOVE SUDDENLY [I always + adv./prep.,T always + adv./prep.] to move into a particular position suddenly and

with a lot of force or energy and often with a short sharp noise, or to make something do this: **snap back/down/around etc.** *Pete stopped with a jolt, his head snapping back.* | **snap (sth) back/down/around etc.** *The boys snapped their towels at each other.*
5 SAY STH ANGRILY [I,T] to say something quickly in an angry or annoyed way: *"Can't you see I'm eating?" Mattie snapped.* | **+at** *Walter snapped at me for no reason.*
6 snap your fingers to make a short sharp noise by moving one of your fingers quickly against your thumb, for example in order to get someone's attention
7 BECOME ANGRY/ANXIOUS ETC. [I] **a)** to suddenly stop being able to control your anger, anxiety, or other feelings in a difficult situation: *When he hit me, I just snapped.* **b)** if someone or someone's mind snaps, they suddenly become mentally ill
8 PHOTOGRAPH [T] to take a photograph: *Mel snapped a picture of me and Sonia.* → see also SNAPSHOT
9 NOISE [I] LITERARY to make a short sharp noise: *The fire snapped and crackled.*
10 GUM [T] to cause GUM in your mouth to make a short sharp noise
11 ANIMAL [I] if an animal such as a dog snaps, it tries to bite you: **+at** *Ginger was snapping at their heels.*
12 FOOTBALL [T] to pass the ball to the QUARTERBACK to start a play
13 snap to it SPOKEN used to tell someone to hurry and do something immediately
14 snap to attention if soldiers snap to attention, they suddenly stand very straight
15 STOP [T] to end a series of events: *The victory snapped a series of setbacks for the team.*
[**Origin:** 1400–1500 Dutch, Low German *snappen*]

snap off *phr. v.* **1 snap sth ↔ off, snap sth off sth** if something snaps off or is snapped off, it breaks with a short sharp noise so that it is no longer attached to the thing it was attached to before: *The tip of the tree snapped off when it fell.* | *Snap off the ends of the beans.* **2 snap sth ↔ off** if you snap off a light or a piece of electrical equipment or it snaps off, it stops working suddenly, often making a short sharp noise

snap on *phr. v.* **snap sth ↔ on** if you snap on a light or a piece of electrical equipment or it snaps on, it starts working suddenly, often making a short sharp noise

snap out of sth *phr. v.* **1 snap out of it** to stop being sad or upset and make yourself feel better **2** to suddenly start paying attention or behaving normally again: *When I snapped out of my daydream, it was already 10:00.*

snap up *phr. v.* **1 snap sth ↔ up** to buy something immediately, especially because it is very cheap: *People from out of state are coming in and snapping up real estate.* **2 snap sb/sth ↔ up** to eagerly take an opportunity to have someone as part of your company, team etc.: *He was snapped up by a major law firm before he even graduated.*

snap² *n.* **1** [singular] a sudden loud sound, especially made by something breaking or closing: *Nick closed the lid **with a snap**.* **2** [C] a small metal fastener on clothes that works when you press its two parts together → see picture at FASTENER **3 be a snap** INFORMAL to be very easy to do: *Pasta dough is a snap to make.* **4** [C] the act of starting play in a game of football by passing the ball to the QUARTERBACK **5** [C] a thin hard cookie: *ginger snaps* **6 a snap of your fingers** a sudden sound made by quickly moving one of your fingers against your thumb → see also COLD SNAP

snap³ *adj.* **a snap judgment/decision** a judgment or decision made quickly and without enough thought or preparation

ˈsnap bean *n.* [C] a long thin green bean that is very CRISP

snap·drag·on /ˈsnæpˌdrægən/ *n.* [C] a garden plant with white, red, or yellow flowers [**Origin:** 1500–1600 Because the flowers are thought to look like a dragon's mouth]

ˈsnap-on *adj.* [only before noun] a snap-on part of a toy or tool can be attached and removed easily

snap·per /ˈsnæpɚ/ *n.* [C,U] BIOLOGY a type of fish that lives in warm parts of the ocean, or the meat from this fish

ˈsnapping ˌturtle *n.* [C] a type of TURTLE with a powerful mouth that makes a short sharp noise when it closes quickly

snap·pish /ˈsnæpɪʃ/ *adj.* easily annoyed and often speaking in an angry way

snap·py /ˈsnæpi/ *adj. comparative* **snappier**, *superlative* **snappiest** **1** spoken or written in a short, clear, and often funny way: *Keep your slogan **short and snappy**.* **2 make it snappy** SPOKEN used to tell someone to hurry: *Get me a drink, and make it snappy.* **3** snappy clothes, objects etc. are attractive and fashionable —**snappily** *adv.* —**snappiness** *n.* [U]

snap·shot /ˈsnæpʃɑt/ *n.* [C] **1** an informal photograph: **+of** *I sent some snapshots of the kids.* ►see THESAURUS box at **picture¹** **2** a piece of information or a description that quickly gives you an idea of what the situation is like at a particular time: **+of** *The book gives us a snapshot of life in the Middle Ages.*

snare¹ /snɛr/ *n.* [C] **1** something that is intended to trick someone and get them into a difficult situation **2** a snare drum **3** a trap for catching an animal, especially one that uses a wire or rope to catch the animal by its foot

snare² *v.* [T] **1** to catch an animal by using a snare SYN **trap** **2** to catch someone, especially by tricking them

ˈsnare drum *n.* [C] a small flat drum that makes a hard sharp sound when you hit it

snarf /snɑrf/ also **snarf down** *v.* [T] INFORMAL to eat something quickly, often in a messy or noisy way

snarl /snɑrl/ *v.* **1** [I] if an animal snarls, it makes a low angry sound and shows its teeth: **+at** *The dog snarled at me.* **2** [I,T] to curl your lips and say something in a nasty angry way: *"What do they want?" snarled Will.* ►see THESAURUS box at **say¹** **3** [I,T usually passive] also **snarl up** if traffic snarls or is snarled, it is blocked and cannot move **4** [T usually passive] also **snarl up** to make something become caught or twisted in a mass of string, hair etc.: *Dolphins sometimes get snarled up in the nets.* **5** [I] also **snarl up** if hairs, threads, wires etc. snarl, they become twisted and messy and are difficult to separate **6** [I,T usually passive] also **snarl up** to make it hard for something to progress or continue successfully: *The process keeps getting snarled up in paperwork.* [**Origin:** (1, 2) 1500–1600 *snar* **to snarl** from the sound] —**snarl** *n.* [C] *traffic snarls*

ˈsnarl-up *n.* [C] **1** a confused situation that prevents work from continuing **2** a situation in which traffic cannot move SYN **snarl**

snatch¹ /snætʃ/ *v.* [T] **1** to take something away from someone with a quick violent movement SYN **grab**: *Lewis rudely snatched the letter.* | **snatch sth away/up/back etc.** *Kari tried to snatch the phone away.* **2** to take someone or something away from a place by force: *The child was snatched as he played outside the house.* **3** to steal something quickly, when you have an opportunity, especially by taking it in your hands suddenly: *Someone snatched her purse.* **4** to quickly take the opportunity to do something when you do not have much time: *He tried to snatch a few hours' sleep.*

snatch at sth *phr. v.* to quickly put out your hand to try to take or hold something SYN **grab at**

snatch sth **↔ up** *phr. v.* to eagerly buy or take something because it is cheap or because you want it very much SYN **snap up**

snatch² *n.* [C] **1 a snatch of conversation/music/song etc.** a short and incomplete part of a conversation, song etc. that you hear **2 in snatches** for short periods: *His words came to her in snatches.*

snaz·zy /ˈsnæzi/ *adj. comparative* **snazzier**, *superlative* **snazziest** INFORMAL bright, fashionable, and attractive: *a snazzy new car* —**snazzily** *adv.*

S

Snead /snid/, **Sam** /sæm/ (1912–2002) a U.S. GOLF player

sneak¹ /snik/ S3 *v. past tense and past participle* **snuck** /snʌk/ or **sneaked** **1** [I always + adv./prep.] to go somewhere secretly and quietly in order to avoid being seen or heard: +**in/past/around etc.** *She snuck out of the house once her parents were asleep.* ▸see THESAURUS box at walk¹ **2** [T always + adv./prep.] to take someone or something somewhere secretly: **sneak sth through/by/past etc.** *He had sneaked his camera into the show.* | **sneak sb sth** *I snuck her a note asking her to meet me.* **3 sneak a look/glance/peek** to look at something quickly and secretly, especially something that you are not supposed to see **4** [T] INFORMAL to quickly and secretly steal something that is not important or that does not have much value: *I used to sneak cigarettes from my dad.*

sneak up *phr. v.* to come close to someone very quietly, so that they do not see you until you reach them: +**on/behind etc.** *Don't sneak up on me like that!*

sneak up on sb *phr. v.* if something sneaks up on you, it happens sooner than you expected it to

sneak² *n.* [C] INFORMAL someone who is not liked because they do things secretly and cannot be trusted

sneak³ *adj.* [only before noun] **1** doing things or done very secretly and quickly, so that people do not notice you or cannot stop you: *a sneak attack* **2 a sneak peek (at sth)** an opportunity to see an example of a product, TV show etc. before it is available to people in general → see also SNEAK PREVIEW

sneak·er /ˈsnikɚ/ *n.* [C usually plural] a type of light soft shoe, used for sports SYN tennis shoe → see picture at SHOE¹

sneak·ing /ˈsnikɪŋ/ *adj.* **1 have a sneaking suspicion/feeling (that)** to have a slight feeling that something is wrong, without being sure **2 have a sneaking admiration/respect/admiration for sb/sth** to have a secret feeling of admiration for someone or something

sneak ˈpreview *n.* [C] an occasion when you can see a movie, play etc. before it is shown to people in general

sneak·y /ˈsniki/ *adj. comparative* **sneakier**, *superlative* **sneakiest** doing things in a secret and dishonest or unfair way —**sneakily** *adv.*

sneer¹ /snɪr/ *v.* [I,T] to smile or speak in an unkind way that shows you have no respect for someone or something: *"Is that your best suit?" she sneered.* | +**at** *The critics sneered at his paintings.* —**sneering** *adj.*: *a sneering letter* —**sneeringly** *adv.*

sneer² *n.* [C] an unkind smile or remark that shows you have no respect for someone or something

sneeze¹ /sniz/ *v.* [I] **1** BIOLOGY to have a sudden uncontrolled burst of air come out of your nose and mouth, for example when you have a cold **2 be nothing to sneeze at** to be good or impressive enough to be considered carefully [**Origin:** Old English *fneosan*]

sneeze² *n.* [C] an act or sound of sneezing

sneeze guard *n.* [C] a piece of plastic that is hung over food at a restaurant where people serve themselves, to keep them from sneezing on the food

snick·er /ˈsnɪkɚ/ *v.* [I] to laugh quietly in a way that is not nice at something which is not supposed to be funny: +**at** *She snickered at his poetry.* ▸see THESAURUS box at laugh¹ —**snicker** *n.* [C]

snide /snaɪd/ *adj.* unkind, but often in a smart indirect way: **a snide remark/comment** *a snide remark about her clothes* —**snidely** *adv.*

sniff¹ /snɪf/ S3 *v.* **1** [I,T] to breathe air in through your nose in order to smell something: *He opened the milk and sniffed it.* **2** [I] to breathe air into your nose in short breaths, loudly enough so that it can be heard: *She sniffed a few times and stopped crying.* **3** [T] to say something in a way that shows you think something is not good or impressive enough for you: *"Is that all?" she sniffed.* **4** [T] to take an illegal drug such as COCAINE through your nose [**Origin:** 1300–1400 From the sound] → see also GLUE SNIFFING

sniff at sth *phr. v.* **1** to think or show you think that someone or something is not very good or not good enough for you **2 be nothing to sniff at** to be good or impressive enough to be considered carefully SYN be nothing to sneeze at

sniff sth ↔ **out** *phr. v.* **1** to discover or find something by its smell: *Officers used dogs to sniff out bodies in the rubble.* **2** to find out or discover something: *He could always sniff out talent in others.*

sniff² *n.* [C] an act or sound of sniffing

snif·fle¹ /ˈsnɪfəl/ *v.* [I] to sniff repeatedly to stop liquid from running out of your nose, especially when you are crying or when you are sick

sniffle² *n.* **1** an act or sound of sniffling **2 have the sniffles** to have a slight cold

snif·ter /ˈsnɪftɚ/ *n.* [C] a special large round glass for drinking BRANDY

snig·ger /ˈsnɪgɚ/ *v.* [I] SNICKER

snip¹ /snɪp/ *v.* **snipped**, **snipping** [I,T] to cut something using scissors with a quick small cut: **snip sth ↔ off/open etc.** *She snipped off a loose thread.* ▸see THESAURUS box at cut¹

snip² *n.* [C] a quick small cut with scissors

snipe¹ /snaɪp/ *v.* [I] **1** to criticize someone in an angry way: +**at** *Critics are sniping at him in the press.* **2** to shoot from a hidden position at people who are not protected —**sniping** *n.* [U]

snipe² *n.* [C] BIOLOGY a bird with a very long thin beak that lives in wet areas, and is often shot as a sport

snip·er /ˈsnaɪpɚ/ *n.* [C] someone who shoots from a hidden position at people who are not protected

snip·pet /ˈsnɪpɪt/ *n.* [C] a small piece of information, music etc.: +**of** *a few snippets of conversation*

snip·py /ˈsnɪpi/ *adj.* INFORMAL criticizing in a slightly angry way

snit /snɪt/ *n.* **be in a snit** to be annoyed about something, in a way that seems unreasonable

snitch¹ /snɪtʃ/ *v.* INFORMAL **1** [I] to tell someone in authority about something that another person has done wrong, because you want to cause trouble for that person: +**on** *Someone must have snitched on me.* **2** [T] to quickly steal something that is not important or that does not have much value

snitch² *n.* [C] someone who is not liked because they tell someone in authority when other people do things that are wrong or against the rules

sniv·el /ˈsnɪvəl/ *v.* [I] to behave or speak in a weak complaining way, especially when you are crying

snob /snɑb/ *n.* [C] DISAPPROVING **1** someone who thinks they are better than people from a lower social class **2 a movie/wine/fashion etc. snob** someone who knows a lot about movies, wine etc. and thinks their opinions are better than other people's **3 snob appeal** something, especially an expensive product, that has snob appeal is liked by people who think they are better than other people [**Origin:** 1800–1900 *snob* **shoemaker, person of low social rank** (18–19 centuries)]

snob·ber·y /ˈsnɑbəri/ *n.* [U] the attitudes and behavior of snobs

snob·bish /ˈsnɑbɪʃ/ also **snob·by** /ˈsnɑbi/ *adj.* having attitudes, behavior etc. that are typical of a snob —**snobbishly** *adv.* —**snobbishness** *n.* [U]

snoop /snup/ *v.* [I] to try to find out private information about someone or something by secretly looking at their things: +**around/through etc.** *I caught him snooping around in my office.* [**Origin:** 1800–1900 Dutch *snoepen* **to buy or eat secretly**] —**snoop** *n.* [C] —**snooper** *n.* [C]

snoop·y /ˈsnupi/ *adj. comparative* **snoopier**, *superlative* **snoopiest** INFORMAL always trying to find out private information about someone or something SYN nosy

S

snoot /snut/ *n.* [C] INFORMAL your nose

snoot·y /ˈsnuṭi/ *adj. comparative* **snootier**, *superlative* **snootiest** INFORMAL, DISAPPROVING impolite and unfriendly, because you think you are better than other people

snooze¹ /snuz/ *v.* [I] **1** to sleep for a short time ▸see THESAURUS box at **sleep¹** **2 you snooze, you lose** used to tell someone that they will miss something if they do not pay attention and act quickly

snooze² *n.* INFORMAL **1** [C usually singular] a short period of sleep **2** [C] something that is very boring

ˈsnooze aˌlarm also **ˈsnooze ˌbutton** *n.* [C usually singular] part of an ALARM CLOCK you push to turn off the ALARM for a short period of time, allowing you to sleep a little longer

snore /snɔr/ *v.* [I] to breathe in a loud way through your mouth and nose while you are sleeping ▸see THESAURUS box at **breathe** [**Origin:** 1300–1400 From the sound] —**snore** *n.* [C] —**snorer** *n.* [C]

snor·kel /ˈsnɔrkəl/ *n.* [C] **1** a tube that allows a swimmer to breathe air under water **2** a piece of equipment that allows a SUBMARINE to take in air when it is under water

S

snor·kel·ing /ˈsnɔrkəlɪŋ/ *n.* [U] the activity of swimming under water using a snorkel: *We **went snorkeling** in the Caribbean last winter.* —**snorkel** *v.* [I]

snort¹ /snɔrt/ *v.* **1** [I] to make a loud noise by forcing air out through your nose, in order to express anger or annoyance, or while laughing: **+at** *Foster snorted at the idea.* **2** [T] to say something in a way that shows you are angry or annoyed, or that you think something is stupid: *"You must be nuts," Carla snorted.* **3** [T] to take illegal drugs such as COCAINE by breathing them in through your nose

snort² *n.* [C] **1** a loud sound made by breathing through your nose, especially to show anger, annoyance, or amusement **2** a small amount of a drug that is breathed in through the nose **3** INFORMAL a small amount of a strong alcoholic drink: **+of** *a snort of whiskey*

snot /snɑt/ *n.* INFORMAL, IMPOLITE **1** [U] the thick MUCUS (=liquid) produced in your nose **2** [C] someone who is SNOTTY

ˈsnot-nosed *adj.* **a snot-nosed kid/brat etc.** INFORMAL, IMPOLITE an expression used to describe a child by someone who does not like the child

snot·ty /ˈsnɑṭi/ *adj. comparative* **snottier**, *superlative* **snottiest** INFORMAL **1** DISAPPROVING thinking that you are better than other people, and criticizing people in an unkind way because of this: *Don't get all snotty with me.* **2** wet and dirty with MUCUS from your nose

snout /snaʊt/ *n.* [C] the long nose of some kinds of animals, such as pigs

snow¹ /snoʊ/ S2 W2 *n.* **1** [U] water frozen into soft white pieces that fall from the sky in cold weather and cover the ground: *The trees were covered with snow.* | *Over six inches of **snow fell** last night.*

THESAURUS

snowflakes pieces of falling snow
sleet a mixture of snow and rain
slush snow on the road that has partly melted and is very wet
blizzard a storm with a lot of snow and a strong wind
frost white powder that covers the ground when it is cold
hail drops of rain that fall as ice, which are called **hailstones**
→ RAIN, WEATHER, WIND

2 [C] a period of time in which snow falls: *The storm was one of the **heaviest snows** this winter.* | *a snow flurry* **3 snows** a large amount of snow that has fallen at different times during a season: *winter snows* **4** [U] NOT TECHNICAL small white spots on a television picture that are caused by bad weather conditions, weak television signals etc. **5** [U] SLANG the illegal drug COCAINE [**Origin:** Old English *snaw*]

snow² S2 *v.* **1 it snows** if it snows, snow falls from the sky: *It snowed all night.* | *Is it snowing?* **2** [T] to persuade someone to believe or support something, especially by lying to them: *Millions of readers were snowed into believing it was a true story.* **3 be snowed in** to be unable to travel from a place because so much snow has fallen there: *We were snowed in for three days.* **4 be snowed under a)** if an area is snowed under, a lot of snow has fallen there so that people are unable to travel **b)** to have more work than you can deal with

snow·ball¹ /ˈsnoʊbɔl/ *n.* [C] **1** a ball made of snow that someone has pressed together: *a snowball fight* **2 a snowball effect** if something has a snowball effect on other things, it starts a series of events or changes that grow bigger and bigger, faster and faster etc.

snowball² *v.* [I] if a plan, problem, business etc. snowballs, it grows bigger at a faster and faster rate: *The penalties and late fees began to snowball.*

ˈsnow belt *n.* **the Snow Belt** the north-central and northeastern parts of the U.S., where the weather is very cold and there is a lot of snow in the winter

snow·bird, Snowbird /ˈsnoʊbɚd/ *n.* [C] someone, especially a RETIRED person, who leaves their home in a cold part of the U.S. or Canada to live in a warm part of the U.S. for the winter

ˈsnow ˌblindness *n.* [U] eye pain and difficulty in seeing things, caused by looking at snow in bright light

ˈsnow-ˌblower *n.* [C] a machine that clears snow from SIDEWALKS, roads etc. by picking it up and blowing it away with a lot of force

snow·board /ˈsnoʊbɔrd/ *n.* [C] a long wide board made of plastic, which people stand on and ride down snow-covered hills for fun

snowboarding

snow·board·ing /ˈsnoʊˌbɔrdɪŋ/ *n.* [U] the sport or activity of going down snow-covered hills while standing on a snowboard —**snowboard** *v.* [I] —**snowboarder** *n.* [C]

snow·bound /ˈsnoʊbaʊnd/ *adj.* blocked or prevented from leaving a place by large amounts of snow: *snowbound travelers*

ˈsnow ˌbunny *n.* [C] INFORMAL a word meaning a very attractive young woman at a SKI RESORT, considered offensive by most women

ˈsnow-capped *adj.* LITERARY snow-capped mountains are covered in snow at the top

ˈsnow cone *n.* [C] a type of food made from crushed ice with a colored fruit-FLAVORED liquid poured over it, served in a CONE-shaped paper cup

ˈsnow day *n.* [C] a day when schools, businesses etc. are closed because there is too much snow for people to travel

snow·drift /ˈsnoʊˌdrɪft/ *n.* [C] a deep mass of snow piled up by the wind

snow·drop /ˈsnoʊdrɑp/ *n.* [C] a European plant with a small white flower which appears in early spring

snow·fall /ˈsnoʊfɔl/ *n.* [C,U] an occasion when snow falls from the sky, or the amount that falls in a particular period of time: *the first snowfall of the season*

snow·field /ˈsnoʊfild/ *n.* [C] EARTH SCIENCE a wide area of land that is always covered in snow

snow·flake /ˈsnoʊfleɪk/ *n.* [C] a small soft flat piece of frozen water that falls as snow

ˈsnow job *n.* [C usually singular] INFORMAL an act of making someone believe something that is not true

ˈsnow line *n.* **the snow line** the level above which snow on a mountain never melts

snow·man /ˈsnoʊmæn/ *n. plural* **snowmen** /-mɛn/ [C] a figure of a person made of big balls of snow, made especially by children

ˈsnow melt *n.* [singular, U] the water that flows out of an area as snow melts, or the time when this happens SYN **melt**

snow·mo·bile /ˈsnoʊmoʊˌbil/ *n.* [C] a small vehicle with a motor, that moves over snow or ice easily

ˈsnow pea *n.* [C] a type of PEA whose outer part is eaten as well as its seeds

snow·plow /ˈsnoʊplaʊ/ *n.* [C] a vehicle or piece of equipment on the front of a vehicle that is used to push snow off roads or railroad tracks

ˈsnow route *n.* [C] an important road in a city that cars must be removed from when it snows, so that the snow can be cleared away from it

snow·shoe /ˈsnoʊʃu/ *n.* [C] one of a pair of wide flat frames with many thin pieces of leather or plastic across, that you attach to your shoes so that you can walk on snow without sinking

snow·storm /ˈsnoʊstɔrm/ *n.* [C] a storm with strong winds and a lot of snow

snow·suit /ˈsnoʊsut/ *n.* [C] a warm piece of clothing that covers a child's whole body

ˈsnow tire *n.* [C] a special car tire with a pattern of deep lines, used when driving on snow or ice

ˌsnow-ˈwhite *adj.* pure white

snow·y /ˈsnoʊi/ *adj. comparative* **snowier**, *superlative* **snowiest** **1** full of snow or snowing: *snowy weather* **2** LITERARY pure white: *snowy hair* —**snowiness** *n.* [U]

snub[1] /snʌb/ *v.* **snubbed, snubbing** [T] **1** to treat someone rudely, especially by ignoring them when you meet **2 snub your nose (at sb/sth)** to show that you do not respect someone or something, or do not care what they think of you —**snub** *n.* [C]

snub[2] *adj.* **snub nose** a nose that is short and flat and points slightly up

ˌsnub-ˈnosed also **ˌsnub-ˈnose** *adj.* [only before noun] **1 a snub-nosed pistol/revolver etc.** a small gun with a very short BARREL (=tube where the bullets come out) **2** having a short nose that points slightly up

snuck /snʌk/ *v.* a past tense and past participle of SNEAK

snuff[1] /snʌf/ *v.* **1** [T] also **snuff out** to stop a CANDLE from burning by pressing the burning part with your fingers or by covering it with a snuffer **2** [T] also **snuff out** to stop or end something in a sudden forceful way: *Any hopes of a comeback have now been snuffed out.* **3** [T] also **snuff out** INFORMAL to kill someone **4** [I,T] to breathe air into your nose in a noisy way SYN **sniff** [**Origin:** (1–3) 1300–1400 *snuff* burned part of a used candle (14–19 centuries)]

snuff[2] *n.* [U] **1 a)** a type of tobacco in powder form, which people breathe in through their noses **b)** a type of tobacco in small pieces, which people put in their mouth and chew, but do not swallow **2 up to snuff** good enough for a particular purpose

snuff·er /ˈsnʌfɚ/ *n.* [C] a tool with a small cup-shaped end on a handle, used for stopping CANDLES from burning

ˈsnuff film also **ˈsnuff ˌmovie** *n.* [C] a movie that shows someone really being killed, often while they are having sex

snuf·fle /ˈsnʌfəl/ *v.* [I] to breathe through your nose in a noisy way, making low sounds —**snuffle** *n.* [C]

snug /snʌg/ *adj.* **1** someone who is snug feels comfortable, happy, and warm: *The children were safe and snug in their beds.* **2** a snug room or space is small, warm, and comfortable and makes you feel protected **3** snug clothes fit closely —**snugly** *adv.* —**snugness** *n.* [U]

snug·gle /ˈsnʌgəl/ *v.* [I always + adv./prep.] **1** to settle into a warm comfortable position: +**up/down/into etc.** *I snuggled down under the covers.* **2 (be) snuggled in/along/between etc. sth** to be fit into a small space, in a way that seems comfortable: *We found the cottage snuggled into a hollow of the hill.*

so[1] /soʊ/ S1 W1 *adv.* **1** [+ adj./adv.] used to emphasize a quality or describe a particular degree of a quality: *I felt so sick yesterday.* | *I never knew Rob could sing so well.* | *Why are you so mad at me?* | *Do we have to leave so early?* | *Thank you **so much**!* | *There were **so many** people there.* | *Why was **so little** time spent on this?* | ***So few** people really understand what we're doing.* | *Inside, the house is **not so** impressive.* **2 so tall/fat/tired etc. (that)** used to say that because someone or something is very tall, fat etc., something happens or someone does something: *He was so weak that he could hardly stand up.* | *It's so simple even a child could use it.* **3** a word meaning "also," used before a MODAL VERB, an AUXILIARY VERB, or a form of "be" to add a positive statement to another positive statement that has just been mentioned: *Ashley's a great swimmer, and **so is** her brother.* | *"I have a lot to do today." "**So do I.**"* | *Average incomes have risen recently, but **so have** prices.* | **so will/can/should etc. sb/sth** *If you're having dessert, then so will I.* **4** used to talk about an idea, suggestion, situation etc. that has been mentioned before: *"He's a better player than I am." "Maybe so."* | *If you haven't chosen, please **do so** now.* | *I didn't understand his instructions and **said so**.* | **think/hope/suppose etc. so** *"Is it supposed to rain tomorrow?" "No, I don't think so."* | **so I hear/so it seems etc.** *"We're moving next month." "So I hear."* **5 and so forth (and so on)** also **and so on (and so forth)** used after a list to show that there are other similar things that could also be mentioned, without actually naming them: *The study included women of different ages, races, and so forth.* **6 ...or so** used when you cannot be exact about a number, amount, or period of time: *We're leaving in five minutes or so.* **7 so to speak** SPOKEN used when you are saying something in words that do not have their usual meaning: *We have to pull down the barriers, so to speak, of poverty.* **8 not so much... as...** used to say that one description of someone or something is less appropriate or correct than another: *I'm not so much angry as disappointed.* **9 without so much as a sth** also **not so much as a sth** used when you are surprised or annoyed that someone did not do something: *The car survived the accident without so much as a dent.* | *I never received so much as a reply.* **10 so... as to be sth** FORMAL used with two adjectives or adverbs with similar meanings, to emphasize how extreme a particular quality is: *The insect is so small as to be almost invisible.* **11 so... a sth** FORMAL used to emphasize an adjective, especially when what is being mentioned is surprising or unusual: *He had never spoken to so large a crowd before.* **12 so much the better** used to say that if something happens, it will make the situation even better than it already is: *You can use dried parsley, but if you have fresh, so much the better.* **13 so as (not) to do sth** FORMAL in order to do something, or not to do something: *Work carefully so as not to tear the delicate material.* **14 only so much/many** used to say that there is only a limited quantity of something: *There's only so much rudeness that I'm willing to tolerate.* **15 not so... as sb/sth** FORMAL used in comparisons to say that someone or something has less of a particular quality than another person or thing SYN **not as... as sb/sth** **16** FORMAL used to emphasize

S

the degree to which someone experiences a particular feeling: *I so enjoy her company.*

SPOKEN PHRASES

17 used to introduce the next part of a story you are telling someone: *So anyway, we decided to go to a movie.* **18** used to get someone's attention, especially in order to ask them a question: *So, Lisa, how's the new job going?* **19** used with a movement of your hand to show how big, high etc. something or someone is SYN **this**: *Oh, he must be about so tall.* **20** used to check that you understand something: *So this one's the original, and this one's the copy, right?* **21** used when asking a question about what has just been said: *"He's gone to Atlanta on business." "So when will he be back?"* **22 like so** used when you are showing someone how to do something: *Then turn the paper over and fold it, like so.* **23 so much for sth** used to say that something you tried to do did not work as it was supposed to, or that something that was promised did not happen: *The gate was unlocked. So much for security.* **24 so long!** INFORMAL a friendly way of saying goodbye **25 so be it** used to show that you do not like or agree with something, but you will accept it anyway: *If we have to break the rules, then so be it.* **26 I do so/it is so etc.** used especially by children to say that something is true, can be done etc. when someone else says that it is not, cannot etc. SYN **too**: *"You don't know how to ride a bike." "I do so!"* **27 not so good/well/bad etc.** used to mean the opposite of a particular quality, without saying this directly, especially when you were expecting something else: *The results are not so good* (=they are fairly bad). | *The food here is not so bad* (=it is fairly good). **28** INFORMAL used like "definitely" before phrases to emphasize what you are saying: *Orange is just so not the right color for Kari.* | *I am so going to punish you for that.* **29 sb/sth is so Bob/L.A./'80s etc.** SLANG used to say that someone or something is typical of or appropriate for a particular person, place, style etc.: *Jenna's attitude is so L.A.* | *That dress is so you!* **30 so help me (God)** used to emphasize how determined you are: *So help me, I'm going to make sure it doesn't happen again.*

[**Origin:** Old English *swa*] → see also **even so** at EVEN[1] (5), **so far** at FAR[1] (7), **just so** at JUST[1] (29), **as/so long as** at LONG[2] (5) → see Grammar box at SUCH[1]

so² S1 W1 *conjunction* **1** used to give the reason why something happens, why someone does something etc. SYN **therefore**: *I got hungry, so I made a sandwich.* | *There were no buses, so we walked.* **2 so (that) a)** in order to make something happen, make something possible etc.: *I lowered my voice so she wouldn't hear.* | *Can I borrow your map so that I don't get lost?* **b)** used to say that something happens as a result of something else SYN **with the result that**: *Nobody spoke to me, so that I felt unwelcome.*

SPOKEN PHRASES

3 So (what)? also **so what if...?** INFORMAL used to say in a slightly rude way that you do not think that something is important: *"He's taller than you." "So what?"* | *So what if we're a little late?* **4** INFORMAL used for saying that you accept a fact but do not think it is important: *So I made a mistake – I'm only human.*

►see THESAURUS box at **thus**

so³ *adj.* [not before noun] **1** true or correct: *Please, say it isn't so!* | *"Kaye said she fixed the car herself." "**Is that so?**"* | *Did you do it, and **if so**, why?* **2** used instead of repeating an adjective that you have mentioned before: *She's upset and understandably so.* | **more so/less so/too much so etc.** *She feels relaxed here, even more so than at home.* | *"You're serious, aren't you?" "Very much so."* **3 be just/exactly so** to be arranged neatly, with everything in the right place: *Everything on Maxine's desk has to be just so.* → see also SO-SO

so⁴ *interjection* used, often in a joking way, to show surprise or that you have found something out about someone: *So! This is where you've been hiding.*

so⁵ *n.* [singular] the fifth note in a musical SCALE according to the SOL-FA system SYN **sol**

soak¹ /soʊk/ S3 *v.* **1** [I,T] to cover something with a liquid for a period of time, especially in order to make it softer or easier to clean, or to be covered by liquid in this way: *Soak the beans overnight.* | *Let the pan soak a while before you scrub it.* | **soak sth in sth** *She soaked the fish in lemon juice.* **2** [T] if a liquid soaks someone or something, it makes them completely wet: *The heavy rain soaked his clothes.* **3** [T] to make someone or something completely wet by putting liquid on them or putting them in liquid: *Police turned on hoses, soaking protesters.* | **soak sth with/in sth** *He took a rag and soaked it with gasoline.* **4** [I] to spend a long time taking a bath **5** [T] INFORMAL to make someone pay too much money in prices or taxes: *The tax is designed to soak the rich.* [**Origin:** Old English *socian*]

soak sth ↔ **in** *phr. v.* to notice or think about what you are learning, seeing, or experiencing: *Just give me a couple of minutes to **soak it all in**.*

soak into sth *phr. v.* if a liquid soaks into cloth, soil, food etc., it goes into it

soak off *phr. v.* **soak sth ↔ off, soak sth off sth** to remove something by leaving it covered with a liquid for a period of time: *Soak the label off the jar.*

soak through *phr. v.* **soak through sth** if a liquid soaks through cloth, soil etc., it goes through it: *Blood had soaked through the sock.*

soak sth ↔ **up** *phr. v.* **1** if something soaks up a liquid, it takes the liquid into itself: *This material soaks up water like a sponge.* **2** if you soak up a liquid, you use paper, a soft cloth etc. to remove the liquid from something **3** to enjoy something by watching it closely or becoming involved in it: *A walking tour is a great way to soak up the city's history.* **4** to learn something quickly and easily: *Small children soak up language at an amazing rate.* **5** to use a lot of something that is available, especially money

soak² *n.* [C] **1** a long and enjoyable time spent taking a bath **2 an old soak** HUMOROUS someone who is often drunk

soaked /soʊkt/ *adj.* **1** very wet or wearing very wet clothes SYN **drenched**: **be soaked in/with sth** *His shirt was soaked in sweat.* | *The boys were **soaked to the skin** but still smiling.* ►see THESAURUS box at **wet**[1] **2 be soaked in sth** to have a lot of a particular quality: *The city is soaked in history.*

-soaked /soʊkt/ *suffix* [in adjectives] **1 rain-soaked/sweat-soaked/blood-soaked etc.** used when saying what has made something very wet **2** having a lot of a particular quality or affected a lot by something: *a sun-soaked vacation*

soak·ing¹ /ˈsoʊkɪŋ/ also **ˌsoaking ˈwet** *adj.* very wet: *Tom's shoes were soaking wet.* ►see THESAURUS box at **wet**[1]

soaking² *n.* [C usually singular] an act of making something completely wet

ˈso-and-so *n. plural* **so-and-so's** **1** [U] an expression meaning some person or thing, used when you do not give a specific name → see also SUCH AND SUCH: *I'd find myself thinking, "I wonder what so-and-so is doing?"* **2** [C] OLD-FASHIONED a very unpleasant or unreasonable person

soap¹ /soʊp/ S3 *n.* **1** [U] the substance that you use to wash your body or other things → see also DETERGENT: *a bar of soap* | *Wash thoroughly with **soap and water**.* **2** [C] INFORMAL a SOAP OPERA [**Origin:** Old English *sape*]

soap² also **soap up** *v.* [T] to rub soap on or over someone or something

soap·box /ˈsoʊpbɑks/ *n.* a means by which someone can express their opinions in a strong and forceful way: **be/get/climb on your soapbox** *She's always getting on her soapbox about some political cause.*

ˈsoap ˌopera *n.* [C] a television story about the daily lives of the same group of people, which is broadcast regularly. In the past, soap operas were on the radio.

soap·stone /ˈsoupstoun/ *n.* [U] EARTH SCIENCE a soft stone that feels like soap

soap·suds /ˈsoupsʌdz/ *n.* [plural] the mass of small BUBBLES that form on top of soapy water

soap·y /ˈsoupi/ *adj. comparative* **soapier**, *superlative* **soapiest** containing soap, or like soap: *warm soapy water* —**soapiness** *n.* [U]

soar /sɔr/ *v.* [I] **1** to increase quickly to a high level: *The temperature soared to 90°.* | *soaring real estate prices* **2 a)** to fly, especially very high up in the sky, floating on air currents: *An eagle soared above us.* **b)** to go quickly upward to a great height: *The ball soared through the air.* **3** if your spirits or hopes soar, you begin to feel very happy or hopeful: *Adam's smile sent her spirits soaring.* **4** [not in progressive] if buildings, trees, towers etc. soar, they look very tall and impressive: *The cliffs soar a hundred feet above the ocean.* [**Origin:** 1300–1400 Old French *essorer*, from Vulgar Latin *exaurare*, from Latin *aura* **air**]

sob /sɑb/ *v.* **sobbed**, **sobbing** [I] to cry loudly while breathing in short sudden bursts: *Louise was sobbing uncontrollably.* ►see THESAURUS box at **cry**[1] —**sob** *n.* [C]

so·ber[1] /ˈsoubɚ/ *adj.* **1** not drunk: *Are you sober enough to drive?* **2** having a serious attitude to life: *a sober hard-working young man* **3** plain and not brightly colored: *a sober gray suit* **4** serious and making you think carefully about things: *sober reality* [**Origin:** 1300–1400 Old French *sobre*, from Latin *sobrius*] —**soberly** *adv.*

sober[2] *v.* [I,T]

sober up *phr. v.* **sober sb ↔ up** to gradually become less drunk, or make someone become less drunk: *They tried to sober her up by giving her some coffee and food.*

so·ber·ing /ˈsoubərɪŋ/ *adj.* making you feel very serious: *a sobering thought*

so·bri·e·ty /səˈbraɪəṭi/ *n.* [U] **1** the condition of not being drunk or not drinking alcohol: *Terry's father had periods of sobriety but always went back to drinking.* **2** FORMAL behavior that shows a serious attitude toward life

so·bri·quet /ˈsoubrɪˌkeɪ/ *n.* [C] LITERARY an unofficial title or name SYN **nickname**

ˈ**sob ˌstory** *n.* [C] INFORMAL a story, especially one that is not true, that someone tells you in order to make you feel sorry for them

ˈ**so-called** Ac W3 *adj.* [only before noun] **1** used to describe someone or something that has been given a name which you think is wrong: *The so-called experts couldn't tell us what was wrong.* **2** used to show that someone or something is usually called a particular name: *the use of so-called "smart bombs"*

soc·cer /ˈsɑkɚ/ S2 *n.* [U] a sport played by two teams of 11 players, who try to kick a round black and white ball into their opponents' GOAL [**Origin:** 1800–1900 *association (football)*; because it was originally played under the rules of the English Football Association] → see also FOOTBALL

ˈ**soccer mom** *n.* [C] a mother who spends a lot of time driving her children to sports practice, music lessons etc., considered as a typical example of women from the middle to upper classes in U.S. society

so·cia·ble /ˈsouʃəbəl/ *adj.* friendly and liking to be with other people OPP **unsociable**: *a sociable likeable woman* —**sociably** *adv.* —**sociability** /ˌsouʃəˈbɪləṭi/ *n.* [U]

THESAURUS

outgoing liking to meet and talk to new people: *an outgoing popular girl*
extroverted confident, and enjoying being with other people: *an extroverted salesman*
gregarious friendly and enjoying being and talking with other people: *a gregarious man who loves telling stories*
→ SHY

so·cial[1] /ˈsouʃəl/ S1 W1 *adj.* **1** relating to human society and its organization, or the quality of people's lives: *the country's serious social problems* | *the existing* ***social order*** | *the struggle for* ***social justice*** | *a period of rapid* ***social change*** **2** relating to the position in society that you have, according to your job, family, wealth etc.: *improvements in women's social and economic status* | *Students come from a wide variety of* ***social classes*** (=groups of people who have the same social position). **3** relating to the way you meet people and form relationships: *social interaction* | *Group play helps children develop* ***social skills*** (=the ability to meet people easily and deal well with them). | *He lacked all the usual* ***social graces*** (=good and polite behavior toward other people). **4** relating to the time you spend with your friends for enjoyment: *The church organizes a number of* ***social events*** *during the summer.* | *Brenda had a very active* ***social life*** (=activities done with friends for fun) *in college.* | *Even* ***social drinking*** (=drinking alcohol with friends, at parties etc.) *is dangerous for an alcoholic.* | *I'm afraid this isn't a* ***social call*** (=a visit to someone for pleasure rather than business). **5** a social person enjoys meeting and talking to other people SYN **sociable** OPP **antisocial** **6** BIOLOGY social animals live together in groups in their natural state: *Elephants are social animals.* [**Origin:** 1600–1700 Latin *socialis*, from *socius* **someone you spend time with**] —**socially** *adv.*: *socially acceptable behavior* | *Jan only drinks socially.*

social[2] *n.* [C] OLD-FASHIONED a party for the members of a group, club, or church

ˌ**social ˈclimber** *n.* [C] DISAPPROVING someone who tries to get accepted into a higher social class by becoming friendly with people who belong to that class

ˌ**social ˈcontract** *n.* [singular] an arrangement by which people in a society accept that they all have rights and duties, and give up some freedoms so that they are protected by the state

ˌ**social ˈDarwinism** *n.* [U] the belief that there are people in society who are naturally more intelligent and skillful than others and who will be most successful, and that the state should not try to affect people's success

ˌ**social deˈmocracy** *n.* POLITICS **1** [U] a political and economic system, especially in many European countries, based on some ideas of SOCIALISM combined with DEMOCRATIC principles, such as personal freedom and government by elected representatives **2** [C] a country, especially in Europe, with a government based on this system —**social democrat** *n.* [C]

ˈ**social disˌease** *n.* [C] OLD-FASHIONED a SEXUALLY TRANSMITTED DISEASE SYN **STD**

ˌ**social engiˈneering** *n.* [U] POLITICS the practice of making changes in laws in order to change society according to a political idea

ˌ**Social ˈGospel, the** also **the ˌSocial ˈGospel ˌMovement** *n.* HISTORY a U.S. political movement formed in the late 19th and early 20th century by PROTESTANT Christians who believed that the moral rules of the Bible could be used as an answer to many of the country's social problems

ˌ**social instiˈtution** *n.* [C] one of five important institutions considered by many people to form the basic structure of western society. They are: family, religion, education, the ECONOMY, and government.

so·cial·ism /ˈsouʃəˌlɪzəm/ *n.* [U] POLITICS an economic and political system in which large industries are owned by the government, and taxes are used to take some wealth away from richer citizens and give it to poorer citizens → see also CAPITALISM

so·cial·ist[1] /ˈsouʃəlɪst/ *adj.* POLITICS **1** based on socialism, or relating to a political party that supports socialism: *socialist principles* **2** a socialist country or government has a political and economic system based on socialism

socialist[2] *n.* [C] POLITICS someone who believes in

socialism, or who is a member of a political party that supports socialism → see also CAPITALIST

ˌsocialist 'realism *n.* [U] a set of beliefs about art, literature, and music which says that their main purpose is to educate people about Marxism and socialism

so·cial·ite /'soʊʃəˌlaɪt/ *n.* [C] someone who is well known for going to many fashionable parties

so·cial·i·za·tion /ˌsoʊʃələ'zeɪʃən/ *n.* [U] **1** the process by which people are made to behave in a way that is acceptable in their society: *Schools are an important tool in the socialization of American citizens.* **2** the process of making something work according to SOCIALIST ideas: *the socialization of medicine*

so·cial·ize /'soʊʃəˌlaɪz/ *v.* **1** [I] to spend time with other people in a friendly way: +**with** *He doesn't socialize with his co-workers.* **2** [T] to train someone to behave in a way that is acceptable in the society they are living in: *Punishing children is not the best way to socialize them.*

ˌsocialized 'medicine *n.* [U] medical care provided by a government and paid for through taxes

ˌsocial mo'bility *n.* [U] the ability to move easily from one social class to another

ˌsocial 'science *n.* **1** [U] the study of people in society, which includes history, politics, ECONOMICS, SOCIOLOGY, and ANTHROPOLOGY **2** [C] one of these subjects → see also NATURAL SCIENCE —**social scientist** *n.* [C]

S

ˌSocial Se'curity *n.* [U] a U.S. government program into which workers must make regular payments, and which pays money regularly to old people and people who are unable to work: *people living* ***on Social Security*** → see also PENSION

ˌSocial Se'curity ˌnumber *n.* [C] a number that is given to each person in the U.S. by the government and is used to IDENTIFY people on official forms, in computer records etc.

ˌsocial 'service *n.* [C usually plural] POLITICS a service that is provided by the government to help people who are poor or have problems such as mental illness, difficulty finding a job, family problems etc.

'social ˌstudies *n.* [U] a subject of study in school that includes history, government, GEOGRAPHY etc.

ˌsocial 'welfare *n.* [U] programs to help people who are poor, do not have jobs etc.

'social work *n.* [U] work done by government or private organizations to improve bad social conditions and help people who are poor or who have family problems etc.

'social ˌworker *n.* [C] someone who is trained to help people with particular social problems, such as family problems, being unable to work etc.

so·ci·e·tal /sə'saɪətl/ *adj.* [only before noun] relating to a particular society, or the way society is organized: *societal changes*

so·ci·e·ty /sə'saɪəti/ S2 W1 *n. plural* **societies**
1 PEOPLE IN GENERAL [C,U] all the people who live together in a country or area, and the structures such as laws, customs etc. that affect their lives and make it possible for them to live together: *We live in a society that values hard work.* | *Prisons are meant to protect society from criminals.* | *recent changes in American society* | *Children are the most vulnerable* ***members of society***. | *the role of religion* ***in society*** | **a segment/sector/level of society** *Drug abuse occurs in all segments of society.* ►see THESAURUS box at **people**[1]
2 ORGANIZATION [C] used in the names of some organizations that have members who share similar interests, aims etc.: *the local historical society* | +**of/for** *the Society for the Prevention of Cruelty to Animals* ►see THESAURUS box at **organization**
3 UPPER CLASS [U] the fashionable group of people who are rich and go to many social events: *members of New York's* ***high society*** | *a society wedding*
4 CLASS [U] a particular group of people within a society: *a study of American working class society* | *His comments outraged* ***polite society*** (=people who are considered to have good education and correct social behavior).
5 WITH OTHER PEOPLE [U] FORMAL the act of being together with other people, or the people you are together with: *Holidays are times to enjoy the society of your family.*
6 ANIMALS [C,U] BIOLOGY a group of closely related animals of the same SPECIES who work together and help each other

Soˌciety of 'Friends, the → see QUAKERS, THE

Soˌciety of 'Jesus, the → see JESUIT

socio- /soʊsioʊ, soʊʃioʊ/ *prefix* TECHNICAL **1** relating to society: *sociology* (=study of society) **2** social and something else: *socioeconomic factors*

so·ci·o·cul·tur·al /ˌsoʊsioʊ'kʌltʃərəl/ *adj.* based on a combination of social and CULTURAL conditions: *sociocultural values* —**socioculturally** *adv.*

so·ci·o·ec·o·nom·ic /ˌsoʊsioʊˌɛkə'nɑmɪk, -ˌikə-/ *adj.* [only before noun] ECONOMICS based on a combination of social and economic conditions —**socioeconomically** /-kli/ *adv.*

so·ci·ol·o·gy /ˌsoʊsi'ɑlədʒi/ *n.* [U] the scientific study of societies and the behavior of people in groups → see also ANTHROPOLOGY —**sociologist** *n.* [C] —**sociological** /ˌsoʊsiə'lɑdʒɪkəl/ *adj.*: *a sociological study of the working class* —**sociologically** /-kli/ *adv.*

so·ci·o·path /'soʊsiəˌpæθ, -ʃiə-/ *n.* [C] TECHNICAL someone whose behavior toward other people is considered unacceptable, strange, and possibly dangerous SYN **psychopath** —**sociopathic** /ˌsoʊsiə'pæθɪk/ *adj.*

so·ci·o·po·lit·i·cal /ˌsoʊsioʊpə'lɪtɪkəl, ˌsoʊʃi-/ *adj.* [only before noun] based on a combination of social and political conditions: *changes in the sociopolitical system* —**sociopolitically** /-kli/ *adv.*

sock[1] /sɑk/ S2 *n.* **1** [C] a piece of clothing made of soft material that you wear on your foot inside your shoe: *a pair of socks* | *Put your* ***shoes and socks*** *on.* **2** [C usually singular] INFORMAL a hard hit, especially with your hand closed: *Larry gave him a sock in the arm.* **3 put a sock in it** SPOKEN used to tell someone in a joking way to stop talking [**Origin:** (1, 3) Old English *socc*, from Latin *soccus* **light shoe**] → see also **knock sb's socks off** at KNOCK[1] (7)

sock[2] *v.* [T] **1** to hit someone very hard: *Bill socked her so hard that the bruise lasted a week.* **2 be/get socked with sth** to be suddenly affected by something bad: *I got socked with a big tax bill.* **3 sock it to sb** [usually in imperative] to do something or tell someone something in a direct and forceful way **4 be socked in** if an airport or area is socked in, it is very difficult to see far and no one can travel because of bad FOG, snow, or rain
sock sth **away** *phr. v.* to keep money in a safe place, to use later: *He's been socking money away for years.*

sock·et /'sɑkɪt/ *n.* [C] **1** a hollow part of something that another part fits into: *eye sockets* **2** a place in a wall where you can connect electrical equipment to the supply of electricity SYN **outlet**

sock·eye /'sɑk-aɪ/ *n. plural* **sockeye** [C,U] a type of SALMON (=fish) that is commonly used for food

Soc·ra·tes /'sɑkrəˌtiz/ (?469–399 B.C.) a Greek PHILOSOPHER from Athens, who was the teacher of Plato and is known for developing a method of examining ideas according to a system of questions and answers —**Socratic** /sə'krætɪk/ *adj.*

Soˌcratic 'method *n.* [singular] a method of teaching first used by Socrates in ancient Greece. The teacher does not give information directly, but instead asks the student a series of questions, as a way of directing the student to improve their thinking and knowledge.

sod /sɑd/ *n.* [U] a piece of dirt with grass growing on top of it

so·da /'soʊdə/ S3 *n.* **1** [C,U] a sweet drink that contains BUBBLES and has no alcohol in it SYN **pop**: *a can of soda* ►see THESAURUS box at **soft drink** **2** [U] also **soda water** water containing BUBBLES of gas, often added to alcoholic drinks **3** [C] an ICE CREAM SODA **4** [U] one of several types of chemical compound containing SODIUM in powder form, that is used for cleaning or in making other products in industry → see also CAUSTIC SODA [**Origin:** 1400–1500 Italian, name of a plant from which soda is obtained] → see also BAKING SODA

'soda ˌcracker *n.* [C] a type of thin hard dry bread with salt on it SYN **saltine**

'soda ˌfountain *n.* [C] a place, often inside a DRUGSTORE, with a long COUNTER (=type of high table) at which SOFT DRINKS, drinks made with ICE CREAM etc. were served, especially in the 1940s and 1950s

'soda jerk *n.* [C] someone who worked at a soda fountain, making drinks

'soda pop *n.* [U] OLD-FASHIONED SODA

'soda ˌwater *n.* [U] SODA

sod·den /ˈsɑdn/ *adj.* very wet and completely full of water: *sodden fields*

so·di·um /ˈsoʊdiəm/ *n.* [U] CHEMISTRY **1** SYMBOL **Na** a silver-white metal that is an ELEMENT and usually exists in combination with other substances **2** SODIUM CHLORIDE (=salt): *a low-sodium diet*

ˌsodium bi'carbonate *n.* [U] TECHNICAL → BAKING SODA

ˌsodium 'chloride *n.* [U] CHEMISTRY the type of salt that is used in cooking and on foods

sod·om·ite /ˈsɑdəˌmaɪt/ *n.* [C] OLD USE someone who is involved in sodomy

sod·om·y /ˈsɑdəmi/ *n.* [U] LAW or OLD USE a sexual act in which a man puts his sexual organ into someone's ANUS, especially that of another man

so·fa /ˈsoʊfə/ *n.* [C] a comfortable piece of furniture with raised arms and a back, that is wide enough for three or more people to sit on [**Origin:** 1600–1700 Arabic *suffah* **long seat**] → see also COUCH

'sofa bed *n.* [C] a sofa that has a bed inside that can be folded out

So·fi·a /ˈsoʊfiə/ the capital and largest city of Bulgaria

soft /sɔft/ S2 W2 *adj.*

1 NOT HARD a) not hard, firm, or stiff, but easy to press OPP **hard**: *a soft pillow* | *The ground was still soft after the rain.* **b)** less hard than average: *a soft lead pencil* | *a soft cheese*

THESAURUS

pliable used about a material or substance that can be bent or pressed without breaking or cracking: *The leather was soft and pliable.*
squishy INFORMAL soft and able to be squeezed: *a squishy red foam ball*
spongy soft and full of holes that contain air or liquid like a sponge: *The soil seemed spongy.*
springy used about something that is soft and comes back to its normal shape after being pressed or walked on: *springy grass*
tender used about food that is easy to cut and eat, especially because it has been well cooked: *a tender steak*
mushy used about food that is soft, wet, and unpleasant: *mushy overcooked broccoli*

2 NOT ROUGH having a surface that is smooth and pleasant to touch OPP **rough**: *a soft cloth* | *The cream will leave your skin softer and smoother.*
3 NOT LOUD a soft sound, voice, or music is quiet and often pleasant to listen to OPP **loud** OPP **harsh**: *soft music* | *He calmed down and his voice became softer.* ▸see THESAURUS box at **quiet**[1]
4 COLOR/LIGHT [only before noun] soft colors or lights are pleasant and relaxing because they are not too bright OPP **harsh** OPP **bright**: *Soft lighting creates a romantic atmosphere.* | *soft blues and grays* ▸see THESAURUS box at **color**[1]
5 NO HARD EDGES not having any hard edges or pointed shapes: *soft curves*
6 GENTLE gentle and not strong or forceful SYN **gentle**: *a soft breeze* | *a soft kiss*
7 NOT STRICT DISAPPROVING not strict and seeming weak OPP **tough**: *If you appear to be soft, people take advantage of you.* | +**on** *No politician wants to seem soft on crime.* | *Courts have been **taking a soft line** with young offenders.*
8 SENSITIVE APPROVING kind, gentle, and sympathetic to other people: *Very few people ever saw his softer side.* | *He has **a soft heart** beneath that cold exterior.*
9 SALES/MARKETS decreasing in price, value, or in the amount sold: *Analysts expressed fears of a softer U.S. market for large cars.* | *soft real estate prices*
10 WATER CHEMISTRY soft water does not contain many minerals, so that it forms BUBBLES from soap easily
11 have a soft spot for sb/sth to like someone or something, even though other people might not: *Garner has always had a soft spot for stray animals.*
12 a soft touch a) someone from whom you can easily get money, because they are nice or easy to deceive: *Brad knew I was a soft touch.* **b)** a gentle way of dealing with something: *Negotiators will need a soft touch.*
13 WEAK BODY having a body that is not in a strong physical condition, because you do not do enough exercise: *He'd gotten soft after all those years in a desk job.*
14 SPEECH SOUND TECHNICAL a soft CONSONANT is made without stopping the flow of air from your mouth completely OPP **hard**: *the soft "g" in "gem"*
15 TOO EASY a soft job, life etc. is too easy and does not involve much work or much hard physical work
16 soft in the head HUMOROUS crazy or very stupid
17 be soft on sb OLD-FASHIONED to be romantically attracted to someone
[**Origin:** Old English *softe*] → see also **soft underbelly** at UNDERBELLY (1) —**softly** *adv.*: *She stroked his head softly.* | *Music played softly in the background.* —**softness** *n.* [U]

soft·ball /ˈsɔftbɔl/ *n.* **1** [U] a game similar to baseball that is played on a smaller field with a larger softer ball **2** [C] a ball that is slightly larger and less hard than a baseball, used to play this game

ˌsoft-'boiled *adj.* a soft-boiled egg has been boiled in its shell long enough for the white part to become solid, but the yellow part in the center is still soft → see also HARD-BOILED

'soft-ˌcore *adj.* [usually before noun] showing or describing sexual behavior and situations in a way that is intended to be sexually exciting, but without fully showing sexual acts or organs: *soft-core pornography* → see also HARDCORE, SOFT PORN

soft·cov·er /ˈsɔftˌkʌvɚ/ *n.* [C] a book with a cover made of thick paper that can bend SYN **paperback** → see also HARDCOVER

'soft drink *n.* [C] a cold drink that does not contain alcohol, especially one that is sweet and has BUBBLES

THESAURUS

Soft drink, **soda**, **pop**, and **soda pop** all mean the same thing. **Soft drink** is a general word that is used everywhere in the U.S. **Soda** is mainly used in the Northeast and Southwest. **Pop** is used mainly in the Midwest and West. **Soda pop** is fairly old-fashioned, but it is still used in some parts of the U.S., especially in the Midwest.

soft·en /ˈsɔfən/ *v.* **1** [I,T] to become less hard or firm, or to make something less hard or firm SYN **soften up** OPP **harden**: *Leave the butter at room temperature to soften.* | *He squeezed the clay in his hands to soften it.* **2** [T] to make something smoother and more pleasant to touch: *Moisturizer softens and protects your skin.* **3** [T] to make the bad effect of something less severe: *Congress has decided to soften the projected welfare cuts.* | **soften the blow/impact etc.** *If you have bad news to tell someone, try to find a way to soften the blow.* **4** [I,T] if your attitude, image etc. softens, or if something softens it, it becomes less severe, less critical etc., and more sympathetic OPP **harden**: *Lawmakers have softened their stance on immigration in recent months.* **5** [I,T] if your expression or voice softens, or if something softens it, you look or sound nicer and more gentle OPP **harden**: *His voice softened when he spoke to her.*

soften up *phr. v.* **1 soften sth ↔ up** to become less hard or firm, or to make something less hard or firm SYN **soften** **2 soften sb ↔ up** to be nice to someone before you ask them to do something, so that they will agree to help you: *I could tell he was trying to soften me up.* **3 soften sb ↔ up** to make an enemy's defenses weaker so that they will be easier to attack, especially by bombing them

soft·en·er /ˈsɔfənɚ/ *n.* [C] a substance that you add to water to make clothes feel soft after washing: *a fabric softener* → see also WATER SOFTENER

ˌsoft ˈfocus *n.* [U] a way of photographing or filming things so that the edges of the objects in the photograph do not appear clear or sharp

soft·heart·ed /ˌsɔftˈhɑrt̬ɪd◂ / *adj.* easily affected by feelings of pity or sympathy for other people

soft·ie, **softy** /ˈsɔfti/ *n. plural* **softies** [C] someone who is too easily affected by feelings of pity or sympathy, or who is too easily persuaded

ˌsoft ˈlanding *n.* [C] a situation in which a SPACECRAFT comes down onto the ground gently and without any damage

ˈsoft ˌmoney *n.* [U] money that is given to a political group rather than to a specific politician, so that the amount that can be given is not limited by law

ˌsoft ˈpalate *n.* [C] BIOLOGY the soft part of the back of the top of your mouth

ˌsoft-ˈpedal *v.* [T] to make something seem less important or less urgent than it really is: *The President soft-pedaled criticism of the regime on his recent visit.*

ˌsoft ˈporn *n.* [U] magazines, pictures etc. that show people wearing no clothes in a way that is intended to be sexually exciting, but that does not fully and clearly show sexual acts → see also HARDCORE, SOFT-CORE

ˈsoft rock *n.* [U] a type of ROCK MUSIC that does not have a strong beat and that includes many songs about love → see also HARD ROCK

ˌsoft ˈsell *n.* [singular] a way of advertising or selling things that involves gently persuading people to buy something in a friendly and indirect way → see also HARD SELL

ˈsoft-ˌshoe *n.* [U] a way of dancing in which you make soft noises with your shoes on the floor

ˌsoft ˈshoulder *n.* [C] the edge of a road, when this edge is made of dirt rather than a hard material

ˌsoft-ˈspoken *adj.* having a pleasant gentle voice, and not talking very much

soft·ware /ˈsɔft-wɛr/ S3 W1 *n.* [U] COMPUTERS the sets of programs that tell a computer what to do: *word-processing software* | *a software developer* → see also HARDWARE

soft·wood /ˈsɔft-wʊd/ *n.* [C,U] wood from trees such as PINE and FIR that is cheap and easy to cut, or a tree with this type of wood → see also HARDWOOD

soft·y /ˈsɔfti/ *n.* [C] another spelling of SOFTIE

sog·gy /ˈsɑgi/ *adj. comparative* **soggier**, *superlative* **soggiest** too wet and soft, in a way that is unpleasant: *a soggy sandwich* —**soggily** *adv.* —**sogginess** *n.* [U]

soi·gné, **soignée** /swɑnˈyeɪ/ *adj.* FORMAL dressed or arranged in an attractive fashionable way

soil¹ /sɔɪl/ W3 *n.* **1** [C,U] BIOLOGY the top layer of the earth in which plants grow SYN **dirt**: *Most herbs grow well in dry soil.* | **good/rich/fertile soil** *a rich loamy soil* ▸see THESAURUS box at **ground¹** **2 on U.S./French/foreign etc. soil** in the U.S., in France, in a foreign country etc.: *We were glad to be back on American soil.* **3 sb's native soil** your own country **4 fertile soil for sth** a situation where new ideas, political groups etc. can easily develop and succeed: *Poverty provides the most fertile soil for revolution.* **5 the soil** LITERARY farming as a job or way of life: *Medieval peasants were bound to the soil.* [**Origin:** 1200–1300 Anglo-French **piece of ground**, from Latin *solium* **seat**]

soil² *v.* [T] **1** FORMAL to make something dirty, especially with waste from your body: *He didn't want the guards to see he had soiled himself.* **2 soil your hands** [usually in negatives] to do something or become involved with something that is dirty, immoral, or dishonest —**soiled** *adj.*: *soiled diapers*

soi·ree, **soirée** /swɑˈreɪ/ *n.* [C] LITERARY or HUMOROUS a fashionable evening party

so·journ /ˈsoʊdʒɚn/ *n.* [C] LITERARY a short period of time that you stay in a place that is not your home: *a brief sojourn in Europe* —**sojourn** *v.* [I]

sol /sɑl, sɔl/ *n.* [U] SO

sol·ace /ˈsɑlɪs/ *n.* [U] a feeling of emotional comfort at a time of great sadness or disappointment: **seek/find solace in sth** *After his wife's death, Rob sought solace in religion.*

so·lar /ˈsoʊlɚ/ *adj.* [only before noun] PHYSICS **1** relating to the sun → see also LUNAR: *a solar observatory* **2** using the power of the sun's light and heat: *solar energy* [**Origin:** 1400–1500 Latin *solaris*, from *sol* **sun**]

ˌsolar ˈcell *n.* [C] PHYSICS a piece of equipment that can produce electric power from SUNLIGHT

ˌsolar eˈclipse *n.* [C] an occasion when the moon moves between the sun and the Earth, so that the sun cannot be seen for a short time from the Earth

so·lar·i·um /səˈlɛriəm, soʊ-/ *n.* [C] a room, usually enclosed by glass, where you can sit in bright SUNLIGHT

ˌsolar ˈpanel *n.* [C] a piece of equipment, usually on the roof of a building, that uses the sun's energy to heat water or to make electricity

solar plex·us /ˈsoʊlɚ ˌplɛksəs/ *n.* [singular] BIOLOGY the front part of your body below your chest, which hurts very much if you are hit there

solar system

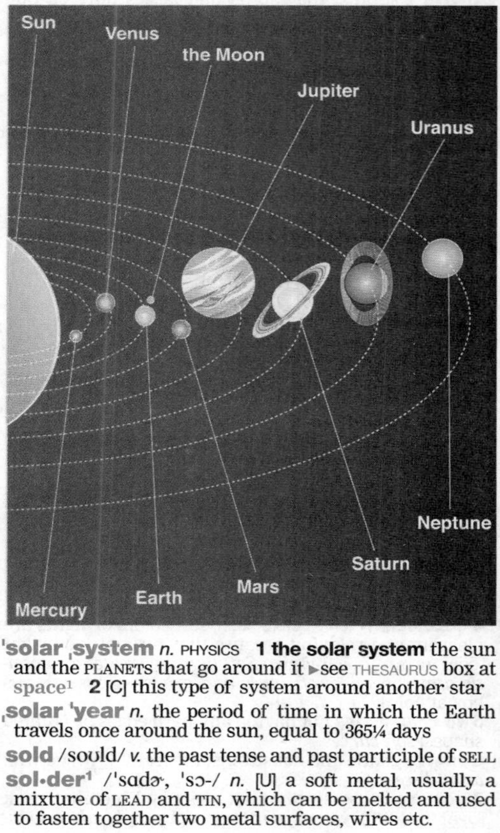

ˈsolar ˌsystem *n.* PHYSICS **1 the solar system** the sun and the PLANETS that go around it ▸see THESAURUS box at **space¹** **2** [C] this type of system around another star

ˌsolar ˈyear *n.* the period of time in which the Earth travels once around the sun, equal to 365¼ days

sold /soʊld/ *v.* the past tense and past participle of SELL

sol·der¹ /ˈsɑdɚ, ˈsɔ-/ *n.* [U] a soft metal, usually a mixture of LEAD and TIN, which can be melted and used to fasten together two metal surfaces, wires etc.

solder² *v.* [T] to fasten or repair metal surfaces with solder

ˈsoldering ˌiron *n.* [C] a tool that is heated, usually by electricity, and used for melting solder and putting it on surfaces

sol·dier¹ /ˈsoʊldʒɚ/ W2 *n.* [C] a member of a country's army, especially someone who is not an officer [**Origin:** 1200–1300 Old French *soudier*, from *soulde* **pay**, from Late Latin *solidus* **gold coin**]

soldier² *v.*

soldier on *phr. v.* to continue working in spite of difficulties

sol·dier·ing /ˈsoʊldʒərɪŋ/ *n.* [U] the life or job of a soldier

sol·dier·ly /ˈsoʊldʒɚli/ *adj.* FORMAL typical of a good soldier

ˌsoldier of ˈfortune *n. plural* **soldiers of fortune** [C] someone who works as a soldier for anyone who will pay him SYN **mercenary**

sol·dier·y /ˈsoʊldʒəri/ *n.* [singular, U] LITERARY a group of soldiers

ˌsold ˈout *adj.* **1** a concert, performance etc. that is sold out has no more tickets left **2** [not before noun] if a store is sold out of something, it has no more of that particular thing left to sell → see also **sell out** at SELL¹

sole¹ /soʊl/ Ac *adj.* [only before noun] **1** the sole person, thing etc. is the only one SYN **only**: *Our sole concern is the safety of our workers.* | *She was the sole woman at the conference.* | *the **sole survivor** of the crash* | *He came here **with the sole purpose of** causing trouble.* **2** a sole duty, right, responsibility etc. is one that is not shared with anyone else: *Maureen was given sole custody of the children.* [**Origin:** 1200–1300 Old French *soul*, from Latin *solus* **alone**]

sole² Ac *n.* **1** [C] the bottom surface of your foot, especially the part you walk or stand on: *Don't go barefoot, or you'll burn **the soles of your feet**.* **2** [C] the flat outer part on the bottom of a shoe, not including the heel: *shoes with rubber soles* | *There's something **on the sole of my shoe**.* → see picture at SHOE¹ **3** [C,U] *plural* **sole** or **soles** BIOLOGY a flat ocean fish, or the meat from this fish → see also -SOLED

sole³ Ac *v.* [T usually passive] to put a new sole on a shoe

sol·e·cism /ˈsɑləˌsɪzəm, ˈsoʊ-/ *n.* [C] FORMAL **1** ENG. LANG. ARTS a mistake in grammar **2** a mistake that breaks the rules of polite behavior

-soled /soʊld/ [in adjectives] **thick-soled/leather-soled etc.** having soles that are thick, made of leather etc.

sole·ly /ˈsoʊli/ Ac *adv.* not involving anything or anyone else SYN **only**: *I will hold you **solely responsible** for anything that goes wrong.*

sol·emn /ˈsɑləm/ *adj.* **1** very serious in behavior or style: *a solemn expression* | *solemn music* **2 a solemn promise/pledge/word etc.** a promise that is made very seriously and with no intention of breaking it: *Jurors swear a solemn oath.* **3** performed in a very serious way: *a solemn ceremony* [**Origin:** 1300–1400 Old French *solemne*, from Latin *solemnis* **ceremonial, formal, solemn**] —**solemnly** *adv.* —**solemnity** /səˈlɛmnət̬i/ *n.* [U]

sol·em·nize /ˈsɑləmˌnaɪz/ *v.* **1 solemnize a marriage** FORMAL to perform a wedding ceremony in a church **2** [T] to make a ceremony more formal and serious, especially by having a prayer or other religious part in it

ˌsole proˈprietorship *n.* [C] ECONOMICS a company or business that is owned by only one person

sol-fa /soʊl ˈfɑ/ *n.* [U] the system in which the notes of the musical SCALE are represented by seven short words (DO, RE, MI, FA, SO, LA, TI), used especially in singing

so·lic·it /səˈlɪsɪt/ *v.* [I,T] **1** to ask someone for money, help, or information: *Certain federal employees are forbidden from soliciting campaign funds.* | **solicit sth from sb** *School officials have been soliciting ideas from parents.* **2** to sell something by taking orders for a product or service, usually by going to people's houses or businesses: *No soliciting on company premises is allowed.* **3** LAW to offer to have sex with someone in exchange for money [**Origin:** 1400–1500 Old French *solliciter* **to disturb, take charge of**, from Latin *sollicitare*] —**solicitation** /səˌlɪsəˈteɪʃən/ *n.* [C,U]

so·lic·i·tor /səˈlɪsət̬ɚ/ *n.* [C] **1** FORMAL someone who tries to sell things to people, usually by going to people's houses or calling them on the telephone **2** LAW the main lawyer for a city, town, or government department **3** LAW a type of lawyer in the U.K. who gives advice, does the necessary work when property is bought and sold, and defends people, especially in the lower courts of law → see also BARRISTER

soˌlicitor ˈgeneral *n.* [C] LAW a government lawyer next in rank below the ATTORNEY GENERAL

so·lic·it·ous /səˈlɪsət̬əs/ *adj.* FORMAL caring very much about someone's safety, health, or comfort: +**of** *He was always very solicitous of other people's opinions.* —**solicitously** *adv.* —**solicitousness** *n.* [U]

so·lic·i·tude /səˈlɪsəˌtud/ *n.* [U] FORMAL eager care about someone's health, safety etc. SYN **solicitousness**

S

sol·id¹ /ˈsɑlɪd/ W3 *adj.*

1 FIRM/HARD PHYSICS hard or firm with a fixed shape and VOLUME, and not liquid or a gas: *Coconut oil is solid at room temperature.* | *a solid object* | *Is the baby eating solid food yet?* | *I was glad to be back on solid ground.* | *The lake was **frozen solid**.* ►see THESAURUS box at **hard¹**

2 STRONGLY MADE strong and well made: *a solid piece of furniture* | *The frame is **as solid as a rock**.*

3 NOT HOLLOW having no holes or spaces inside: *a solid chocolate bunny* | *a solid block of wood*

4 solid gold/silver/oak etc. consisting completely of gold, silver, oak etc.: *solid gold bracelets*

5 GOOD WORK/PREPARATION having a lot of practical value because of good preparation, strong principles etc.: *five years of solid achievement* | *Kids need a **good solid** education in high school.* | *Good communication provides a **solid foundation** for marriage.*

6 DEPENDABLE someone or something that is solid can be trusted and depended on: *He's a very solid player.* | *a company with a **solid reputation*** | **solid evidence/facts** *They could not support their claims with solid evidence.* | *Romer gave every impression of being a **solid citizen**.*

7 COLOR consisting of one color only, with no pattern: *a solid green background* | *Solid colors are more flattering than stripes.*

8 WITHOUT SPACES continuous, without any spaces or breaks: *a solid line on the graph*

9 TIME without any pauses: **five solid hours/two solid weeks etc.** *Josh stayed in bed for three solid days.*

10 on solid ground confident because you are dealing with a subject you are sure about, or because you are in a safe situation: *He checked with other scientists to make sure he was on solid ground.*

11 LOYAL [usually before noun] always loyal to a person or political party: *solid supporters of the president*

12 GEOMETRY MATH having length, width, and height SYN **three-dimensional**: *A sphere is a solid figure.*

13 GOOD SLANG very good or impressive

[**Origin:** 1300–1400 Old French *solide*, from Latin *solidus*] —**solidly** *adv.*: *solidly built* —**solidness** *n.* [U] → see also SOLIDITY

solid² *adv.* **1 be booked/jammed/packed solid** to have no more seats, places etc. available at all: *Most state park campgrounds are already booked solid for the summer.* **2 five hours solid/two weeks solid etc.** used to emphasize that something happened or someone did something for a continuous period of time: *We drove for four hours solid to get here on time.*

solid³ *n.*

1 OBJECT [C] PHYSICS a firm object or substance that has a shape that does not change; not a gas or a liquid: *Water changes from a liquid to a solid when it freezes.*

2 solids [plural] foods that are not in liquid form: *She hasn't been able to eat solids for a week.*
3 SHAPE MATH a shape that has length, width, and height
4 COLOR [C usually plural] a solid color
5 PART OF LIQUID [C usually plural] CHEMISTRY the part of a SOLUTION that has the qualities of a solid when it is separated from the liquid: *milk solids*
6 HELPFUL ACTION [C] SLANG something you do to help someone else SYN **favor**

sol·i·dar·i·ty /ˌsɑləˈdærəṭi/ *n.* [U] **1** loyalty and general agreement between all the people in a group, or between different groups, because they all have the same aim: *A lot of people joined with us as an act of solidarity.* | **+with** *He said the attack was carried out to show his solidarity with the Chechen people.* **2 Solidarity** a Polish LABOR UNION that became very powerful in the 1980s and forced Poland's COMMUNIST government to make important political and economic changes. This was part of the process which led to the ending of COMMUNIST power in Eastern Europe.

so·lid·i·fy /səˈlɪdəˌfaɪ/ *v.* **solidifies, solidified, solidifying** [I,T] **1** to become solid, or make something solid: *Remove any solidified fat from the top of the soup.* **2** to make an agreement, plan, attitude etc. firmer and less likely to change, or to become firmer and less likely to change: *This is the play that solidified William's reputation as a leading playwright.* —**solidification** /səˌlɪdəfəˈkeɪʃən/ *n.* [U]

S

so·lid·i·ty /səˈlɪdəṭi/ *n.* [U] **1** the strength or hardness of something: *the massive solidity of his muscles* **2** the quality of something that is permanent and can be depended on: *These data confirm the underlying solidity of the labor market.*

ˌsolid-ˈstate *adj.* **1** solid-state electrical equipment contains electronic parts, such as SILICON CHIPS, rather than MECHANICAL parts **2** PHYSICS solid-state PHYSICS is concerned with the qualities of solid substances, especially the way in which they CONDUCT electricity

so·lil·o·quy /səˈlɪləkwi/ *n. plural* **soliloquies** [C,U] ENG. LANG. ARTS a speech in a play in which a character talks to himself or herself, so that the AUDIENCE knows the character's thoughts → see also COLLOQUY —**soliloquize** *v.* [I]

sol·ip·sism /ˈsɑləpˌsɪzəm, ˈsɔ-/ *n.* [U] TECHNICAL the idea in PHILOSOPHY that the only thing you can be certain about is your own existence and your own thoughts and ideas

sol·ip·sis·tic /ˌsɑləpˈsɪstɪk/ *adj.* **1** FORMAL DISAPPROVING concerned only with yourself and the things that affect you SYN **self-centered** **2** TECHNICAL relating to solipsism in PHILOSOPHY

sol·i·taire /ˈsɑləˌtɛr/ *n.* **1** [U] a game of cards for one person **2** [C] a single jewel, or a piece of jewelry with a single jewel in it, especially a large DIAMOND: *a diamond solitaire*

sol·i·tar·y¹ /ˈsɑləˌtɛri/ *adj.* **1** [only before noun] a solitary person or thing is the only one you can see in a place: *A solitary figure stood at the end of the bar.* → see Word Choice box at ALONE **2** [only before noun] done or experienced without anyone else around: *a long solitary walk* **3** spending a lot of time alone, usually because you like being alone: *Hamilton was described as a solitary man.* | *a solitary life* **4 not a/one solitary sth** used to emphasize that there is not even one word, thing etc.: *We don't have a solitary bed available.* —**solitariness** *n.* [U]

solitary² *n.* [U] INFORMAL solitary confinement

ˌsolitary conˈfinement *n.* [U] an additional punishment for a prisoner in which they are kept alone and are not allowed to see anyone else

sol·i·tude /ˈsɑləˌtud/ *n.* [U] the state of being alone, especially when this is what you enjoy: *Carl spent the morning **in solitude**.*

so·lo¹ /ˈsoʊloʊ/ *n. plural* **solos** [C] **1** ENG. LANG. ARTS **a)** a piece of music written for or performed by one performer → see also DUET: *She was nervous about singing a solo.* **b)** a part of a piece of music in which one performer plays the most important part, with or without the other performers playing along: *a drum solo* **2** a job or performance that is done alone, especially an aircraft flight

solo² *adj., adv.* **1** relating to a singer or musician who plays alone, rather than as part of a band: *a solo album* **2** related to or played as a musical solo: *a solo passage for violin* **3** done alone, without anyone else helping you: *Ron's first solo flight* | *When did you first fly solo?* ►see THESAURUS box at **alone**

solo³ *v.* [I] **1** to perform a solo in a piece of music **2** to fly an aircraft alone

so·lo·ist /ˈsoʊloʊɪst/ *n.* [C] a musician who performs a solo

Sol·o·mon /ˈsɑləmən/ (10th century B.C.) a king of Israel, the son of King David, who built the TEMPLE in Jerusalem and is known for being extremely wise

ˈSolomon ˌIslands, the a country that consists of several islands in the southwest Pacific, to the east of Papua New Guinea

sols·tice /ˈsɑlstɪs, ˈsɔl-/ *n.* [C] the time when the sun is farthest north or south of the EQUATOR: **the summer/winter solstice** (=the longest or shortest day of the year) → see also EQUINOX

sol·u·ble /ˈsɑlyəbəl/ *adj.* **1** CHEMISTRY a soluble substance can be DISSOLVED in a liquid OPP **insoluble** → see also WATER-SOLUBLE **2** FORMAL a soluble problem can be solved OPP **insoluble** —**solubility** /ˌsɑlyəˈbɪləṭi/ *n.* [U]

sol·ute /ˈsɑlyut/ *n.* [C] CHEMISTRY the substance that has DISSOLVED in a chemical SOLUTION

so·lu·tion /səˈluʃən/ S3 W2 *n.* **1** [C] a way of solving a problem or dealing with a difficult situation: *The easiest solution is not always the best one.* | **+to/for** *There is no simple solution to the problem of unemployment.* | *We're trying to **find a solution** that both sides can support.* **2** [C] the correct answer to a question or problem, for example on a test or in a piece of schoolwork: **+to** *The solution to last week's puzzle is on page 12.* **3** [C] MATH any number or value that makes an EQUATION true **4** [C,U] CHEMISTRY a mixture of two or more substances, especially a solid and a liquid, in which the MOLECULES of both substances have completely combined together SYN **homogenous mixture**: *saline solution* | **a strong/weak solution** *a weak solution of fertilizer* ►see THESAURUS box at **mixture**

soˌlution of an eˈquation *n.* [C] MATH the values which when given to the different parts in an EQUATION make the equation true

solve /sɑlv/ S2 W2 *v.* [T] **1** to find or provide a way of dealing with a problem: *Simply making drugs legal will not solve our nation's drug problem.* **2** to find the correct answer to a question or problem, or the explanation for something that is difficult to understand: *Casey is very good at solving crossword puzzles.* | **solve a crime/mystery/case** *Rice's murder has never been solved.* [**Origin:** 1400–1500 Latin *solvere* **to loosen, solve, dissolve, pay**] —**solvable** *adj.*

sol·vent¹ /ˈsɑlvənt/ *n.* [C,U] **1** a liquid that is able to turn a solid substance into a liquid, or that can remove a substance from a surface **2** CHEMISTRY a liquid in which a substance is DISSOLVED to form a SOLUTION

solvent² *adj.* having enough money to pay your debts OPP **insolvent**: *Will Social Security be solvent in 50 years?* —**solvency** *n.* [U]

Sol·zhe·ni·tsyn /ˌsoʊlʒəˈnɪtsən/, **Alexander** (1918–) a Russian writer of NOVELS

So·ma·li·a /səˈmɑliə/ a country in east Africa that is east of Ethiopia and Kenya, and next to the Indian Ocean —**Somali** *n., adj.*

som·ber /ˈsɑmbɚ/ *adj.* **1** sad and serious SYN **grave**: *She was in a somber mood.* **2** dark and without any bright colors: *a somber gray dress* [**Origin:** 1700–1800 French *sombre*] —**somberly** *adv.* —**somberness** *n.* [U]

som·bre·ro /səmˈbrɛroʊ, sɑm-/ *n. plural* **sombreros** [C] a Mexican hat for men that is tall with a wide, round edge [**Origin:** 1500–1600 Spanish *sombra* **shade**] → see picture at HAT

some[1] /səm; *strong* sʌm/ S1 W1 *quantifier* **1** a number of people or things or an amount of something, when the actual number or amount is not stated → see also ANY: *There's some bread in the kitchen.* | *It's a good idea to take some cash with you.* | *I know some people who work there.* **2** a number of people or things or an amount of something, but not all: *Some people believe in life after death.* | *In some cases, the damage could not even be repaired.* **3** FORMAL a fairly large amount of something: *The talks have been continuing for some time.* [**Origin:** Old English *sum*]

GRAMMAR

• **Some of** cannot be followed directly by a noun. Use "the," "this," "those" etc., or a possessive: *Some of the students went home early* (NOT *Some of students...*). | *I talked to some of my friends after the concert* (NOT *some of friends...*). However, **some of** can be followed directly by a pronoun: *Some of us thought the food was overcooked.*

• **Some** is followed directly by a noun when you are talking about part of something in general: *Some people have trouble staying within a budget.* | *Some foods need to be refrigerated.* Use **some of** when you are talking about part of a particular thing, group etc.: *Some of us left before the end of the movie.* | *Some of the strawberries we bought were bad.*

some[2] /sʌm/ S1 W1 *pron.* **1** a number of people or things or an amount of something, when the exact number or amount is not stated → see also ANY: *We need more wine. Could you get some?* | *"Do you have any tape?" "Yeah, there's some in my desk drawer."* | *Don't buy stamps because I have some here.* **2** a number of people or things or an amount of something, but not all: *Many businesses are having problems and some have already closed.* | *Most of the corn is fed to livestock, but some is sold.* | *Some have suggested that the president was lying.* | +**of** *Some of us had to leave the meeting early.* | *Can I have some of your cake?* **3 and then some** INFORMAL and more: *"They say he earns $2.5 million a season." "And then some."*

some[3] /sʌm/ S1 W1 *determiner* **1** used to talk about a person or thing, when you do not know or say exactly which: *Can you give me some idea of the cost?* | **some kind/type/form/sort of sth** *Tina must be suffering from some kind of depression.* | ***For some reason*** *he won't return my phone calls.* | *Isn't there* ***some other*** (=another) *method we can use?* **2** SPOKEN INFORMAL used when you are talking about a person or thing that you do not know, remember, or understand, or when you think it does not matter: *Some guy called for you today.* **3 some...or other/another** used when you do not want to mention a specific person or thing, or when you think it does not matter: *Everyone will need to see a doctor at some time or another.* **4** SPOKEN INFORMAL very good, bad, impressive, or extreme: *That was some party last night!* **5 some friend/help! etc.** SPOKEN used, especially when you are annoyed, to mean someone or something has disappointed you by not behaving in the way you think they should: *Some friend you are!*

some[4] /səm; *strong* sʌm/ *adv.* **1 some more** an additional number, amount, or degree of something: *Would you like some more pie?* | *I think we still need to practice some more.* **2 some ten people/50%/$100 etc.** FORMAL an expression meaning about ten people, 50%, $100 etc.: *Dr. Brown began his career some 30 years ago.* **3** SPOKEN INFORMAL a little: *We could work some and then rest a while.* | *The service has improved some.*

-some /səm/ *suffix* **1** [in adjectives] tending to behave in a particular way, or having a particular quality: *a troublesome boy* (=who causes trouble) | *a bothersome back injury* (=that BOTHERS you very much) **2** [in nouns] a group of a particular number: *a golf foursome* (=four people playing GOLF together)

some·bod·y[1] /ˈsʌmˌbɑdi, -ˌbʌdi/ S1 W2 *pron.* **1** used to mean a person, when you do not know, or do not say, who the person is SYN **someone**: *There's somebody waiting to see you.* | *Somebody's car alarm kept me awake all night.* | **somebody new/different etc.** *I think they're getting somebody famous to sing at the festival.* | *They offered the job to* ***somebody else*** (=a different person). | *We could ask John* ***or somebody*** (=or a similar person). | ***Somebody or other*** *decided it was my fault.* **2 be somebody** to be an important, successful, or famous person: *He wants to be somebody.*

somebody[2] *n. plural* **somebodies** [C] a person who is important, successful, or famous OPP **nobody**

some·day /ˈsʌmdeɪ/ *adv.* at an unknown time in the future, especially a long time in the future SYN **one day**: *Maybe someday I'll tell him.*

some·how /ˈsʌmhaʊ/ S2 W2 *adv.* **1** in some way, or by some means, although you do not know how: *We'll get the money back somehow.* | *They fixed it* ***somehow or other.*** **2** in some way that you do not say or that you cannot describe or explain: *His comments were slightly offensive somehow.* **3** for some reason that you cannot explain: *Somehow I knew she would say that.*

some·one /ˈsʌmwʌn/ S1 W1 *pron.* **1** used to mean a person, when you do not know, or do not say, who the person is SYN **somebody**: *Someone was pounding on the door.* | *Could someone please turn on the lights?* | **someone new/different etc.** *That limo must be for someone important.* | *We'll have to find* ***someone else*** (=a different person) *to finish the job.* | *You should have told Dad* ***or someone*** (=or a similar person). **2 be someone** to be an important, famous, or successful person

S

some·place[1] /ˈsʌmpleɪs/ S2 *adv.* [not usually in questions or negatives] in or to a place, but you do not say or know exactly where SYN **somewhere**: *I left my keys someplace.* | **someplace safe/different etc.** *Put the money someplace safe.* | *If the café is full, we can just go* ***someplace else*** (=to a different place).

someplace[2] *pron.* a place, although you do not say or know exactly where SYN **somewhere**: *She just got back from someplace.* | **someplace to do sth** *We're looking for someplace to live.* | *They're planning a trip to Germany* ***or someplace*** (=or a similar place).

som·er·sault /ˈsʌmɚˌsɔlt/ *n.* [C] a movement in which someone rolls or jumps forward or backward, so that their feet go over their head before they stand up again: **do/turn a somersault** *Janice did a backward somersault on the mat.* [**Origin:** 1500–1600 Old French *sombresaut*, from Latin *super* **over** + *saltus* **jump**] —**somersault** *v.* [I]

some·thing[1] /ˈsʌmθɪŋ/ S1 W1 *pron.* [not usually in questions or negatives] **1** used to mean a particular thing when you do not know its name, do not know exactly what it is etc.: *There's something in my eye.* | *Come here – I want to show you something.* | *Sarah said something about coming over later.* | **something new/old/big/better etc.** *They're working on something important.* | *I like this car, but I need something bigger.* | *Don't buy her flowers – get her* ***something else*** (=a different thing). | *There's* ***something wrong with*** (=a problem with) *the printer.* | *They were arguing about* ***something or other.*** ▸see THESAURUS box at **thing** **2 something to eat/drink/read/do etc.** some food, a drink, a book, an activity etc.: *Do you want something to eat?* | *There is always something to do here.* | *I need to find something to wear to Amy's wedding.* **3 do something** to take action, usually in order to improve a bad situation: *Don't just stand there – do something.* | +**about** *I wish they'd do something about the noise.* **4 have something to do with sth** to be connected with or related to a particular person or thing, but in a way that you are not sure about: *I know Steve's job has something to do with investments.* **5 something like 100/2,000 etc.** APPROXIMATELY 100, 2,000 etc.: *Something like 400 people attended the meeting.* **6 thirty-something/forty-something etc.** used to say that someone's age is between 30 and 39, between 40 and 49 etc., when you do not know exactly **7 something about sb/sth** a quality or feature of someone or something that you recognize, but cannot say exactly what it is: *Something about Frank's attitude worried her.* | *There's something strange about* the woman's eyes in the painting. **8 make something of yourself** to become successful or famous **9 something of a sth** FORMAL used to say that someone or something is a particular thing to some degree: *The news came as something of a surprise.* **10 something like sb/sth** similar in some way to someone or something: *The bird is something like a crow.* **11 there is something to sth** used to admit that something must be good, helpful etc., when you did not believe this earlier: *Well, if the treatment worked for Jean, there must be something to it.* **12 something for nothing** something good, useful, or desirable that you get without working or paying for it, or without making any effort: *Don't expect to get something for nothing.*

SPOKEN PHRASES

13 ...or something used when you cannot remember, or do not want to give, another example of something you are mentioning: *Here's some money. Get yourself a sandwich or something.* **14 be something** to be impressive and deserve admiration: *Her performance was really something.* **15 be something else a)** to be impressive **b)** to be annoying: *Your attitude is something else, you know.* **16 sixty something/John something etc.** used when you cannot remember the rest of a number or name: *The last bus leaves at eleven something* (=sometime between 11:00 and 12:00). **17 that's saying something** INFORMAL used to emphasize that something is particularly good, bad etc.: *His poetry is worse than mine, and that's saying something.* **18 that's something** used to say that there is at least one thing that you should be glad about in a situation that is mostly bad: *We still have a little money left. That's something.* **19 something fierce** INFORMAL very much, or in a very severe way

S

something² *n.* **a little something** SPOKEN INFORMAL **a)** a small or inexpensive gift **b)** a small meal or SNACK

some·time¹ /ˈsʌmtaɪm/ S2 *adv.* at a time in the future or in the past, although you do not know exactly when: *Our house was built sometime around 1900.* | *It's a long story. I'll tell you about it sometime.* | *Let's meet again **sometime soon**.*

sometime² *adj.* [only before noun] **1** FORMAL used to say that someone used to be something, but is not anymore SYN **former**: *his rival and sometime friend* **2** used to say that someone does or is something part of the time, but not always: *a sometime actor*

some·times /ˈsʌmtaɪmz/ S1 W1 *adv.* on some occasions, but not all: *I sometimes have to work late.* | *Sometimes, she stayed in bed until the afternoon.* | *"Do you ever wish you were back in Japan?" "Sometimes."*

THESAURUS

occasionally sometimes but not often: *We see each other occasionally.*
(every) once in a while/every so often sometimes but not regularly: *I call her every once in a while.*
from time to time sometimes but not often or regularly: *A situation like this arises from time to time.*
→ OFTEN, NEVER, RARELY

some·what /ˈsʌmwʌt/ Ac S3 W2 *adv.* more than a little, but not very: *The new model is somewhat different from the previous one.* | *The town has changed somewhat since I was a child.* | *The cause of the accident is still **somewhat of a** mystery.*

some·where¹ /ˈsʌmwɛr/ S1 W2 *adv.* [not usually in questions or negatives] **1** in or to a place, but you do not say or know exactly where: *Let's go for a walk somewhere.* | **somewhere warm/different etc.** *It would be nice to go somewhere warm.* | **+in/near/behind etc.** *There must be a restaurant somewhere near here.* | *You might be able to find a cheaper one **somewhere else*** (=in a different place). **2** used to show that an amount or number is not exact and may be a little more or less: *The price of the painting nowadays would be **somewhere around** $8,000.* | *The old man was **somewhere between** 90 **and** 100.* | *The project will cost **somewhere in the region of** $50,000.* **3 get somewhere** to make progress: *Now we're really getting somewhere!*

somewhere² *pron.* a place, although you do not say or know exactly where: *We could move to somewhere like Bermuda.* | **somewhere to do sth** *Tonya needs somewhere to keep her skis.* | *Can we get some money from **somewhere else**?* | *We could go to the park **or somewhere*** (=or a similar place). ►see THESAURUS box at **place¹**

some·wheres /ˈsʌmwɛrz/ *adv.* SPOKEN NONSTANDARD somewhere

som·me·lier /ˌsʌməlˈyeɪ/ *n.* [C] someone who works in a restaurant and whose job is to advise people on the right wines to drink

som·nam·bu·list /sɑmˈnæmbyəlɪst/ *n.* [C] FORMAL someone who walks while they are asleep SYN **sleepwalker** —**somnambulism** *n.* [U] —**somnambulistic** /sɑmˌnæmbyəˈlɪstɪk/ *adj.*

som·no·lent /ˈsɑmnələnt/ *adj.* LITERARY **1** making you want to sleep: *a slow somnolent folk song* **2** almost starting to sleep —**somnolence** *n.* [U]

Som·nus /ˈsɑmnəs/ the Roman name for the god Hypnos

son /sʌn/ S1 W1 *n.*
1 CHILD [C] someone's male child → see also DAUGHTER: *Our son Jamie is five years old.* | *They have three sons and a daughter.* → see also **like father like son** at FATHER¹ (5) ►see THESAURUS box at **relative¹**
2 YOUNG MAN used by an older person as a friendly way to address a boy or young man: *What's your name, son?*
3 the Son Jesus Christ; the second member of the Trinity, the three parts of God in the Christian religion that include God the Father and the HOLY SPIRIT
4 FROM A PLACE [C] WRITTEN a man, especially a famous man, from a particular place or country: *Mozart, Salzburg's most famous son* → see also **favorite son** at FAVORITE¹ (2)
5 DESCENDANT [C usually plural] LITERARY a man who has a particular ANCESTOR, or whose ancestors come from a particular place or were involved in a particular thing: **+of** *the sons of Abraham* | *the sons of the Revolution*
6 my son used by a priest to address a man or boy
[**Origin:** Old English *sunu*]

so·nar /ˈsoʊnɑr/ *n.* [U] SCIENCE equipment on a ship or SUBMARINE that uses sound waves to find out the position of objects under the water [**Origin:** 1900–2000 *sound navigation ranging*]

so·na·ta /səˈnɑt̬ə/ *n.* [C] a piece of music with three or four parts that is written for a piano, or for a piano and another instrument

Sond·heim /ˈsɑndhaɪm/, **Ste·phen** /ˈstivən/ (1930–) a U.S. SONGWRITER and COMPOSER famous for writing many successful MUSICALS

Song, Sung /sʊŋ/ HISTORY the DYNASTY that ruled China from 960 to 1279. During this time there were many developments in TECHNOLOGY, PHILOSOPHY, and art.

song /sɔŋ/ S1 W1 *n.*
1 MUSIC a) [C] ENG. LANG. ARTS a short piece of music with words that you sing: *We played guitars and **sang songs**.* | *Who **wrote this song**?* | **a pop/folk/love etc. song** *a Russian folk song* **b)** [U] songs or singing in general: *an evening of Irish song and dance* ►see THESAURUS box at **music**
2 burst/break into song to suddenly start singing
3 BIRD/ANIMAL [C,U] BIOLOGY the musical sounds made by birds or some other animals, such as WHALES: *the song of a lark*
4 for a song very cheaply: *He was able to buy the house for a song.*
5 a song and dance (about sth) INFORMAL an explanation or excuse that is too long and complicated
6 sb's song a song that reminds two people in a romantic relationship of when they first met: *Listen, they're **playing our song**.*
[**Origin:** Old English *sang*]

song·bird /ˈsɔŋbɚd/ *n.* [C] a bird that can make musical sounds

song·book /ˈsɔŋbʊk/ *n.* [C] a book with the words and music of many songs

ˈsong ˌcycle *n.* [C] a group of songs that are all about a particular important event

ˌSong of ˈSolomon also **ˌSong of ˈSongs** a book in the Old Testament of the Christian Bible

song·ster /ˈsɔŋstɚ/ *n.* [C] **1** ENG. LANG. ARTS a singer, especially someone who sings well **2** BIOLOGY a songbird

song·stress /ˈsɔŋstrɪs/ *n.* [C] WRITTEN a female singer

song·writ·er /ˈsɔŋˌraɪṭɚ/ *n.* [C] someone who writes the words and usually the music of a song —**songwriting** *n.* [U]

son·ic /ˈsɑnɪk/ *adj.* [only before noun] PHYSICS relating to sound, SOUND WAVES, or the speed of sound

ˌsonic ˈboom *n.* [C] PHYSICS a loud sound like an explosion, that an airplane makes when it starts to travel faster than the speed of sound

ˈson-in-ˌlaw *n. plural* **sons-in-law** [C] the husband of your daughter → see also DAUGHTER-IN-LAW

son·net /ˈsɑnɪt/ *n.* [C] ENG. LANG. ARTS a poem with 14 lines that RHYME with each other in a special pattern [**Origin:** 1500–1600 Italian *sonetto*, from Old Provençal *sonet* **little song**]

son·ny /ˈsʌni/ *n.* OLD-FASHIONED, SPOKEN used when speaking to a boy or young man who is much younger than you: *Now, you just listen to me, sonny.*

ˌson of a ˈgun *n. plural* **sons of guns** [C] SPOKEN **1** HUMOROUS a man you like or admire: *Billy's a tough old son of a gun.* **2** a man that you are annoyed with **3** an object that is difficult to deal with **4 son of a gun!** used to express surprise

ˌSon of ˈGod *n.* **the Son of God** also **the Son of Man** used by Christians to mean Jesus Christ

son·o·gram /ˈsɑnəˌgræm/ *n.* [C] TECHNICAL an image, for example of an unborn baby inside its mother's body or of a body organ, that is produced by a machine that passes ELECTRONS through the body SYN **ultrasound**

son·o·rous /ˈsɑnərəs, səˈnɔrəs/ *adj.* having a pleasantly deep loud sound: *a sonorous voice*

soon /sun/ S1 W1 *adv.* **1** in a short time from now, or a short time after something else happens: *It will be getting dark soon.* | *I finished my business sooner than I expected.* | *We soon realized how difficult the job was going to be.* | *They should be back* ***pretty soon.*** | ***Soon after*** *his return, Robert received a letter.* | ***How soon*** (=How quickly) *can you get here?*

THESAURUS

in a minute SPOKEN used when talking about something that will happen within a few minutes: *I'll be ready in a minute.*
any minute now SPOKEN used when something will happen in a very short time from now, but you do not know exactly when: *Margo should be here any minute now.*
before long soon or in a short time: *She had the poem memorized before long.*
shortly FORMAL soon: *He left Germany shortly before the war started.*
in the near future in the next few weeks or months: *They promised to contact us again in the near future.*

2 as soon as immediately after something has happened: *I came as soon as I heard the news.* | *I'll come over to your place* ***as soon as I can.*** **3 as soon as possible** ABBREVIATION **ASAP** as quickly as possible: *Please send us your reply as soon as possible.* **4 sooner or later** used to say that something is certain to happen at some time in the future, though you cannot be sure exactly when: *She's bound to find out sooner or later.* **5 the sooner (...) the better** used to say that it is important for something to happen very soon: *The sooner we get these bills paid off, the better.* | *They knew they had to leave town, and the sooner the better.* **6 the sooner..., the sooner...** used to say that if something happens soon, then something else that you want will happen soon after that: *The sooner I get this work done, the sooner I can go home.* **7 too soon** too early: ***It's still too soon to say*** *whether the operation was successful.* | ***All too soon,*** *it was time to leave.* **8 not a moment too soon** also **none too soon** almost too late, and when you thought that something was not going to happen in time: *The doctor finally arrived and not a moment too soon.* **9 soon enough** very soon, or earlier than you expect: *Soon enough, it started to rain.* **10 sb would (just) as soon do sth** used to say that someone would prefer to do something, or would prefer that something happen: *I'd just as soon stay home and watch a DVD.* **11 sb would sooner do sth (than sth)** if you would sooner do something, you would really prefer to do it, especially instead of something that seems bad, used to say that someone would prefer to do something, especially something very unpleasant, than something else: *She would sooner kill herself than sell the store.* **12 no sooner had/has/is/does... than...** used to say that something happened almost immediately after something else: *No sooner had he sat down than the phone rang.* **13 no sooner said than done** used to say that you will do something immediately [**Origin:** Old English *sona* **immediately**]

S

soot /sʊt/ *n.* [U] black powder that is produced when something is burned —**sooty** *adj.*

soothe /suð/ *v.* [T] **1** to make someone feel calmer and less anxious, upset, or angry: *She soothed the baby with a lullaby.* **2** to make a pain or a bad feeling less severe: *A massage would soothe his aching muscles.* [**Origin:** Old English *sothian* **to prove the truth**, from *soth* **true**] —**soothing** *adj.*: *gentle soothing music* —**soothingly** *adv.*

sooth·say·er /ˈsuθˌseɪɚ/ *n.* [C] OLD USE someone who people believe has the ability to say what will happen in the future

sop¹ /sɑp/ *v.* **sopped, sopping**
sop sth ↔ **up** *phr. v.* to remove liquid from a surface by using something that ABSORBS (=takes the liquid into itself) the liquid: *He used bread to sop up the tomato juice on his plate.* → see also SOPPING

sop² *n.* [C usually singular] DISAPPROVING **1** something that you offer to someone in order to prevent them from complaining or getting angry about something: +**to** *Repealing the bill is a sop to the wealthy.* **2** a piece of food used for DIPping in a liquid

so·phis·ti·cate /səˈfɪstəkɪt, -ˌkeɪt/ *n.* [C] someone who is sophisticated

so·phis·ti·cat·ed /səˈfɪstəˌkeɪṭɪd/ *adj.* **1** confident and having a lot of life experience and good judgment about socially important things such as art, fashion etc. OPP **unsophisticated**: *a sophisticated and charming man* **2** a sophisticated machine, system, method etc. is very well designed, very advanced, and often works in a complicated way OPP **unsophisticated**: *sophisticated equipment* | *a* ***highly*** (=very) ***sophisticated*** *computer system* ▸see THESAURUS box at **advanced**, **modern** **3** having a lot of knowledge and experience with difficult or complicated subjects, and therefore able to understand them well OPP **unsophisticated**: *Teens are a lot more sophisticated today than they were in the past.* **4** intended for people who know a lot about things such as art, fashion etc. OPP **unsophisticated**: *sophisticated designer clothes* **5** involving a lot of complicated ideas or processes OPP **unsophisticated**: *sophisticated research* [**Origin:** 1300–1400 Medieval Latin, past participle of *sophisticare* **to deceive with words, hide the true nature of something**, from Latin *sophisticus*] —**sophistication** /səˌfɪstəˈkeɪʃən/ *n.* [U] *the sophistication of modern weapons systems*

soph·ist·ry /ˈsɑfɪstri/ *n. plural* **sophistries** FORMAL **1** [U] the skillful use of reasons or explanations that seem correct but are really false, in order to deceive people **2** [C] a reason or explanation that seems correct but is really false, used in order to deceive people

Soph·o·cles /ˈsɑfəˌkliz/ (?496–406 B.C.) a Greek writer of plays, who developed Greek TRAGEDY as a style of theater

soph·o·more /ˈsɑfəmɔr/ S3 *n.* [C] a student in the second year of high school or college → see also FRESHMAN

soph·o·mor·ic /ˌsɑfəˈmɔrɪk◂ / *adj.* FORMAL DISAPPROVING childish and not very sensible: *a sophomoric sense of humor*

sop·o·rif·ic¹ /ˌsɑpəˈrɪfɪk◂ / *adj.* FORMAL **1** making you feel ready to sleep: *His voice had an almost soporific effect.* **2** tired and ready to sleep SYN **sleepy**

soporific² *n.* [C] FORMAL something that makes you feel ready to sleep

sop·ping /ˈsɑpɪŋ/ also **ˌsopping ˈwet** *adj.* very wet: *My shoes were sopping.*

so·pra·no /səˈprænoʊ/ *n. plural* **sopranos** [C] a woman, girl, or young boy whose singing voice is very high —**soprano** *adj.* [only before noun]

sor·bet /sɔrˈbeɪ, ˈsɔrbət/ *n.* [C,U] a frozen sweet food made of fruit juice, sugar, and water → see also ICE CREAM, SHERBET [**Origin:** 1500–1600 Old French **fruit drink**, from Old Italian *sorbetto*]

sor·cer·er /ˈsɔrsərə/ *n.* [C] a man in stories who uses magic and receives help from evil spirits

sor·cer·ess /ˈsɔrsərɪs/ *n.* [C] a woman in stories who uses magic and receives help from evil spirits

sor·cer·y /ˈsɔrsəri/ *n.* [U] magic that uses the power of evil spirits

sor·did /ˈsɔrdɪd/ *adj.* **1** involving immoral or dishonest behavior: *a sordid affair* **2** very dirty and disgusting: *the sordid slums of modern cities* [**Origin:** 1500–1600 Latin *sordidus*, from *sordes* **dirt**]

sore¹ /sɔr/ S3 *adj.* **1** a part of your body that is sore is painful and often red because of a wound or infection, or because you have used a muscle too much: *My legs are still sore today.* | *Val woke up with **a sore throat** and a temperature of 102°.* ▸see THESAURUS box at **painful** **2 a sore point/spot/subject** something that is likely to make someone upset or angry when you talk about it: *Money is still a sore point with many employees.* **3 a sore loser** someone who always gets very angry and upset when they lose a game, competition etc. **4 stick/stand out like a sore thumb** INFORMAL if someone or something sticks out like a sore thumb, they are very noticeable because they are different from everyone or everything else **5** WRITTEN great: *We are in sore need of help.* **6** [not before noun] OLD-FASHIONED upset, angry, and annoyed, especially because you have not been treated fairly: +**at/about** *Is he still sore at us?* [**Origin:** Old English *sar*] → see also **a sight for sore eyes** at SIGHT¹ (13)

sore² *n.* [C] a painful, often red, place on your body caused by a wound or infection → see also BEDSORE, COLD SORE

sore·head /ˈsɔrhɛd/ *n.* [C] INFORMAL someone who is angry in an unreasonable way

sore·ly /ˈsɔrli/ *adv.* very much or very seriously: *Medical supplies are sorely needed.* | *He will be sorely missed.*

sor·ghum /ˈsɔrgəm/ *n.* [U] a type of grain that is grown in tropical areas

so·ror·i·ty /səˈrɔrət̮i, -ˈrɑr-/ *n. plural* **sororities** [C] a club for women students at some colleges and universities → see also FRATERNITY

sor·rel /ˈsɔrəl, ˈsɑ-/ *n.* BIOLOGY **1** [U] a plant with sour-tasting leaves that are used in cooking **2** [C] a light brown or reddish-brown horse

sor·row¹ /ˈsɑroʊ, ˈsɔ-/ *n.* **1** [U] a feeling of great sadness, usually because someone has died or because something terrible has happened to you: **great/deep sorrow** *a time of great sorrow* **2** [C] an event or situation that makes you feel great sadness: *the joys and sorrows of life* → see also **drown your sorrows** at DROWN (3)

sorrow² *v.* [I] LITERARY to feel or express sorrow

sor·row·ful /ˈsɑroʊfəl, -rəfəl/ *adj.* FORMAL very sad: *a sorrowful poem* —**sorrowfully** /-fli/ *adv.*

sor·ry /ˈsɑri, ˈsɔri/ S1 W2 *adj. comparative* **sorrier**, *superlative* **sorriest**

1 ASHAMED [not before noun] feeling ashamed or unhappy about something bad you have done: *I told him I was sorry.* | +**(that)** *She was sorry that she'd upset him.* | +**for** *I think he's sorry for what he's done.* | +**about** *We're sorry about all the mess, Mom.* | *I wish he would just call and **say** he's **sorry**.*

2 a) be/feel sorry for sb to feel pity or sympathy for someone because something bad has happened to them or because they are in a bad situation: *For a minute, she felt sorry for the girl.* **b) feel sorry for yourself** to feel unhappy because you are in a bad situation, especially when other people think you should not be unhappy: *Stop feeling so sorry for yourself!*

3 DISAPPOINTED [not before noun, no comparative] feeling sad about a situation, and wishing it were different: +**(that)** *I'm sorry you didn't enjoy the meal.* | +**about** *I'm so sorry about your accident.* | **sorry to do sth** *I won't be sorry to leave this place.* | **sorry to hear/see/learn** *I was sorry to hear that your mother had died.*

4 VERY BAD [only before noun] very bad, especially in a way that makes you feel pity or disapproval: *He wanted to forget the whole sorry episode.* | *the **sorry state** of the environment* | *The old building was **a sorry sight**.*

5 a sorry excuse for sth something that is of very poor quality, someone who is bad at their job etc.: *a sorry excuse for a movie*

SPOKEN PHRASES

6 (I'm) sorry a) used to excuse yourself and tell someone that you wish you had not done something that has affected them badly, hurt them, embarrassed them etc.: *"Hey, you stepped on my foot." "Sorry."* | *Oh, sorry, am I sitting in your chair?* | +**about** *Sorry about that. I'll buy you a new one.* | +**(that)** *Sorry I'm late.* | +**for** *I'm so sorry for the rude things I said.* | **sorry to do sth** *I'm sorry to keep you waiting.* **b)** used as a polite way of introducing disappointing information or a piece of bad news: *I'm sorry, we don't have any tickets left.* | ***I'm sorry but** you'll have to leave.* **c)** used as a polite way of interrupting someone: **sorry to bother/interrupt/disturb etc. you** *Sorry to bother you, but I need to get a book from the shelf.* **d)** used when you have said something that is not correct, and want to say what is correct: *Turn left, sorry, right at the traffic lights.* **e)** used to politely disagree with someone: ***I'm sorry, but** that just isn't true.* **f)** used to refuse an offer or to say "no": *"Are you coming to lunch?" "No, sorry, I have some work to finish."* **g)** used to show sympathy to someone who has just told you that something bad has happened to them: *"My husband died last year." "I'm sorry."*

7 (I'm) sorry? used to ask someone to repeat something that you have not heard correctly SYN **pardon**: *Sorry? What did you say?*

8 you'll be sorry used to tell someone they will wish they had not done something: *Let me go or you'll be sorry!*

9 I'm sorry to say used to say that you are disappointed that something has happened: *We lost, I'm sorry to say.*

[**Origin:** Old English *sarig*, from *sar*; influenced by *sorrow*] → see also **better (to be) safe than sorry** at SAFE¹ (8) → see Word Choice box at EXCUSE¹

sort¹ /sɔrt/ S1 W1 *n.*

1 TYPE/KIND [C] a group or class of people, things etc. that have similar qualities or features SYN **kind** SYN **type**: +**of** *What sort of music do you like?* | **the/that/this sort of thing** *It's just the sort of thing your mother would say.* | *They had **all sorts of** (=many different kinds of) seafood on the menu.* | *Several members of the team suffered injuries **of one sort or another** (=of various different types).* | **of this/that sort** *Accidents of this sort are relatively common.* ▸see THESAURUS box at **type¹**

2 some sort of sth also **sth of some sort** used when something is of a particular type, but you do not know the exact details about it: *He's some sort of scientist.* | *There was a game of some sort going on inside.*
3 sort of INFORMAL **a)** to some degree but not in a way that you can easily describe [SYN] **kind of**: *"Do you know what I mean?" "Sort of." | I sort of felt I should help them. | It's sort of a condensed one-day version of the course.* **b)** used when you are not sure you are using the best word to describe something [SYN] **kind of**: *He was sort of running and jumping at the same time. | The dress was a sort of bluish color.* **c)** used to make what you are saying sound less strong or direct [SYN] **kind of**: *Well, I sort of thought we could maybe go out sometime.*
4 of sorts also **of a sort** used when something is of a particular type, but is not a very good example of it, or is similar to something in some way: *We were given a meal of sorts.*
5 out of sorts feeling a little upset, annoyed, or sick: *Mandy's been out of sorts all week.*
6 PERSON [C usually singular] someone with a particular type of character [SYN] **kind** [SYN] **type**: *Uncle Ralph was always a good-natured sort.* | *He's **the sort of person who** is always late.*
7 COMPUTER [C] if a computer does a sort, it puts things in a particular order
[**Origin:** 1300–1400 Old French *sorte*, from Latin *sors* **chance, what you get by luck, share, condition**] → see Usage note at KIND[1]

sort² [S1] *v.* [T] to put things in a particular order, or arrange them in groups according to size, rank, type etc.: *The eggs are sorted according to size.* | **sort sth into sth** *She sorted the clothes into neat piles.*
sort out ↔ sb/sth *phr. v.* **1** to organize something that is mixed up or messy: *It took us all day to sort out all the paperwork.* **2** to separate one type of thing from another: *I've sorted out the papers that can be thrown away.* **3** to successfully deal with a problem or difficult situation: *Mike's still trying to sort out his personal life.*
sort through sth *phr. v.* to look for something among a lot of similar things, especially while you are arranging these things into an order: *Maria began sorting through the documents.*

sort·a /ˈsɔrt̬ə/ INFORMAL used in writing to represent the way some people say "sort of" when they are talking: *I was sorta worried about them.*

sor·tie¹ /ˈsɔrti, sɔrˈti/ *n.* [C] **1** a short flight made by an airplane over enemy land, in order to bomb a city, military defenses etc.: *air sorties* **2** a short trip

sortie² *v.* [I] TECHNICAL to make a short flight over enemy land or an attack on an enemy's position

SOS *n.* [singular] **1** a signal that a ship or aircraft sends to say that it is in danger and needs help quickly **2** an urgent request for help [**Origin:** 1900–2000 *S* and *O*, letters chosen because they were easy to send by Morse code, but often understood as short for *"save our souls"*]

ˈso-so *adj., adv.* neither very good nor very bad [SYN] **average**: *"How are you feeling?" "Oh, so-so."* | *a so-so movie*

sot /sɑt/ *n.* [C] OLD-FASHIONED someone who is drunk all the time

sot·to vo·ce /ˌsɑtoʊ ˈvoʊtʃi/ *adv.* FORMAL in a very quiet voice, so that other people cannot easily hear

souf·flé /suˈfleɪ/ *n.* [C,U] a baked food that contains a lot of air and is made with eggs, flour, milk, and often cheese

sough /saʊ, sʌf/ *v.* [I] LITERARY if the wind soughs, it makes a soft sound when passing through trees —**sough** *n.* [U]

sought /sɔt/ [Ac] *v.* the past tense and past participle of SEEK

ˈsought-ˌafter *adj.* [usually before noun] wanted by a lot of people, but rare or difficult to get: **most/highly sought-after** *one of the most sought-after speakers in the country*

souk /suk/ *n.* [C] a market in an Arab city

soul /soʊl/ [S3] [W2] *n.*
1 SPIRIT [C] the part of a person that is not physical and contains their thoughts, feelings, character etc., that many people believe continues to exist after they die: *the souls of the dead* → see also SPIRIT
2 INNER CHARACTER [U] the part of a person that contains their true character, where their deepest thoughts and feelings come from: *He felt a restlessness deep **in his soul**.* | *Meditation **is good for the soul*** (=makes you feel better inside). | *Ed thinks that anyone who doesn't like poetry **has no soul**.*
3 PERSON [C] LITERARY a person: **a sensitive/brave/simple etc. soul** *Only a few brave souls ventured out in the storm.* | *Tina swore she would **not tell a soul*** (=no one).
4 MUSIC [U] SOUL MUSIC
5 STRONG EMOTIONS [U] a special quality of a painting, piece of music, performance etc. that makes people feel strong emotions: *Her performance was technically perfect, but it lacked soul.*
6 SPECIAL QUALITY [U] the special quality or part that gives something its true character: *A lot of local residents say the downtown area is losing its soul.*
7 be the soul of discretion/politeness/honesty HUMOROUS to have and show a lot of a particular positive quality
[**Origin:** Old English *sawol*] → see also **bare your soul** at BARE² (2), **bless my soul!** at BLESS (8), **keep body and soul together** at BODY (11), **God rest his/her soul** at GOD (4), **the heart and soul of sth** at HEART (29), **sell your soul (to the devil)** at SELL¹ (8), SOUL MUSIC

ˈsoul ˌbrother *n.* [C] INFORMAL an expression meaning an "African-American man," used especially by young African-Americans in the 1960s and 1970s

ˈsoul-desˌtroying *adj.* extremely boring or making you feel extremely unhappy: *soul-destroying work*

ˈsoul food *n.* [U] traditional foods that are cooked and eaten by African-Americans in the southern U.S.

soul·ful /ˈsoʊlfəl/ *adj.* expressing deep, usually sad emotions: *a soulful voice* —**soulfully** *adv.* —**soulfulness** *n.* [U]

soul·less /ˈsoʊl-lɪs/ *adj.* **1** lacking emotions or sympathy: *soulless multinational corporations* **2** lacking the attractive qualities that make people happy: *a soulless suburb* —**soullessly** *adv.* —**soullessness** *n.* [U]

ˈsoul mate *n.* [C] someone you have a very close relationship with because you share the same emotions and interests

ˈsoul ˌmusic *n.* [U] a type of popular music that often expresses deep emotions, usually performed by African-American singers and musicians

ˈsoul patch *n.* [C] a small square area of hair that a man grows just below his bottom lip

ˈsoul-ˌsearching *n.* [U] careful examination of your thoughts and feelings, because you are very worried about whether or not it is right to do something: *After **doing** some serious **soul-searching**, I decided to resign.*

ˈsoul ˌsister *n.* [C] INFORMAL an expression meaning an "African-American woman," used especially by young African-Americans in the 1960s and 1970s

sound¹ /saʊnd/ [S1] [W1] *n.*
1 NOISE [C] something that you hear: *a vowel sound* | *There were strange sounds coming from the next room.* | **+of** *Just then, we heard the sound of voices outside.* | **a clicking/tearing/hissing etc. sound** *Rattling sounds came from his throat.* | *We tried **not to make a sound*** (=to be completely quiet) *as we went upstairs.* | *the **sights and sounds of** the big city* → see Word Choice box at NOISE
2 ENERGY [U] VIBRATIONS that travel through air, water etc. and that humans can hear: *Light travels faster than sound.* | *The planes can travel faster than **the speed of sound**.*
3 TV/RADIO ETC. [U] what you hear coming from a television, a radio, in a movie theater etc.: *He was watching a football game with the sound off.* | **turn the sound up/down/on/off** *Turn the sound up a little.*

S

4 MUSICAL STYLE [C usually singular] the particular quality that a singer's or group's music has: *Every successful band has its own unique sound.*
5 WATER [C] a narrow area of water that connects two larger areas of water: *Puget Sound*
6 not like the sound of sth to feel worried by something that you have heard or read: *"There's been a slight change in our plans." "I don't like the sound of that."*
7 from the sound of it/sth judging from what you have heard or read: *From the sound of it, things are worse than we thought.*
[**Origin:** 1200–1300 Old French *son*, from Latin *sonus*]

sound² S1 W1 *v.*
1 SEEM [linking verb + adj./prep.] if someone or something sounds a particular way, they seem to have a particular quality when you hear or read about them: *The trip sounds really exciting.* | *Fifty dollars sounds about right.* | **sound good/fun/difficult etc. to sb** *That sounds pretty good to me.* | +**like** *Nick sounds like a nice guy.* | **it sounds like/as if/as though** *It sounds as if Nancy will need another operation.* | *I'll come over and take you out for dinner. **How does that sound?*** ►see THESAURUS box at **seem**
2 NOISE [linking verb] if a noise sounds a particular way, that is how it seems to you when you hear it: *Their songs all sound the same.* | *The voice sounded familiar.* | +**like** *I heard what sounded like fireworks.* | **it sounds like/as if/as though** *The banging sounded as if it was coming from next door.*
3 VOICE [linking verb] to seem to show a particular quality with your voice: *Jen sounded kind of tired on the phone.* | +**like** *You sound just like my mother.* | **sound like/as if/as though** *He sounded like he had a cold or something.*
4 WARNING [T] to publicly give a warning or tell people to be careful: *Several earlier studies had **sounded** similar **warnings**.* | **sound a note of caution/optimism/despair etc.** *I would, however, sound a note of caution here.* | *Health officials have **sounded the alarm*** (=warning about danger) *about a possible flu outbreak.* → see also **sound the death knell** at DEATH KNELL (1)
5 MAKE A NOISE [I,T] if something sounds or if you sound it, it makes a noise: *If gas levels get too high, a warning bell will sound.* | *Sound your horn to warn other drivers.*
6 MEASURE DEPTH [T] EARTH SCIENCE to measure the depth of the ocean, a lake etc. → see also SOUNDINGS

sound off *phr. v.* **1** to express strong opinions about something, especially when you are complaining angrily: +**on/about** *Madden regularly sounds off on a variety of topics.* **2** if soldiers sound off, they shout out numbers or their names to show that they are there

sound out *phr. v.* **1 sound sb/sth ↔ out** to talk to someone in order to find out what they think about a plan or idea: **sound sb ↔ out about/on sth** *They may want to sound you out on the subject first.* **2 sound sth ↔ out** ENG. LANG. ARTS to pronounce a new or difficult word by slowly saying the sounds of each letter in it: *Children start by learning to print and sound out words.*

sound³ *adj.*
1 SENSIBLE sensible, correct, and likely to produce the right results OPP **unsound**: *sound advice* | *sound investments* | **environmentally/financially/ideologically etc. sound** *environmentally sound farming methods*
2 DEPENDABLE dependable and good for basing something else on: *a sound basis for a good marriage* | *His conclusions are based on sound evidence.*
3 HEALTHY ESPECIALLY LAW physically or mentally healthy: *Was he **of sound mind*** (=not mentally ill) *when he wrote the will?*
4 GOOD CONDITION in good condition and not damaged OPP **unsound**: *On the surface, the house appeared to be **structurally sound**.*
5 SLEEP/SLEEPER [only before noun] sound sleep is deep and peaceful: *He's a very sound sleeper.*
6 a sound thrashing a) the experience of being hit very violently, especially as a punishment **b)** a very bad defeat → see also **safe and sound** at SAFE¹ (2) —**soundness** *n.* [U]

sound⁴ *adv.* **sound asleep** deeply asleep

'sound ˌbarrier *n.* **1 the sound barrier** the sudden increase in the pressure of air against a vehicle, especially an aircraft, when it reaches the speed of sound: *The world's fastest car **broke the sound barrier*** (=went faster than the speed of sound) *during a test in Nevada yesterday.* **2** [C] a high wall that is built along the side of a road to block the noise of the traffic on the road

'sound bite *n.* [C] a very short part of a speech or statement, especially one made by a politician, that is broadcast on television or the radio

sound·board /'saʊndbɔrd/ also **'sounding board** *n.* [C] **1** a piece of electronic equipment that is used to control sound levels at a concert, in a recording STUDIO etc. **2** a thin board over which the strings of a piano, VIOLIN etc. are put in order to increase the sound of the instrument SYN **sounding board** **3** a SOUNDING BOARD²

'sound card *n.* [C] a piece of electronic equipment that allows a computer to produce sounds

'sound check *n.* [C] the process of checking that all the equipment needed for broadcasting or recording is working correctly

'sound efˌfects *n.* [plural] sounds produced artificially for a television or radio program, a movie etc.

'sounding board *n.* [C] **1** someone you discuss your ideas with in order to find out if they are good: +**for** *John always used her as a sounding board for new ideas.* **2** a board that is placed behind someone who is speaking to a large group of people so that the speaker can be heard more easily SYN **soundboard**

sound·ings /'saʊndɪŋz/ *n.* [plural] **1** careful or secret questions that you ask someone in order to find out what they think about something: *recent soundings of voters on various issues* **2** measurements you make to find out how deep water is

sound·less /'saʊndlɪs/ *adj.* without any sound: *a soundless light rain* —**soundlessly** *adv.*: *Hawks flew soundlessly above us.*

sound·ly /'saʊndli/ *adv.* **1** if you sleep soundly, you sleep deeply and peacefully **2** completely or severely: *Our proposal was soundly rejected by the board.*

sound·proof¹ /'saʊndpruf/ *adj.* a soundproof wall, room etc. is one that sound cannot pass through or into

soundproof² *v.* [T] to make something soundproof

sound·stage /'saʊndsteɪdʒ/ *n.* [C] a large room that has been specially made so that no sounds from outside the room can be heard, used for filming movies and television programs

'sound ˌsystem *n.* [C] a very large STEREO system, especially one that includes the equipment a band needs to control its sound at a performance

sound·track /'saʊndtræk/ *n.* [C] ENG. LANG. ARTS **1** the recorded music from a movie **2** the part of a piece of film where the sound is recorded

'sound wave *n.* [C] PHYSICS a movement of pressure caused by a release of energy, traveling through something such as air or water and heard as sound

soup¹ /sup/ S2 *n.* **1** liquid cooked food often containing small pieces of meat, fish, or vegetables: *tomato soup* **2 be in the soup** OLD-FASHIONED INFORMAL to be in trouble [**Origin:** 1600–1700 French *soupe* **piece of bread dipped in liquid, soup**]

soup² *v.*

soup sth ↔ up *phr. v.* INFORMAL to improve something by making it bigger, more attractive, or more exciting: *We spent half a year souping up my old Volkswagen Beetle.* → see also SOUPED-UP

soup·çon /sup'soʊn/ *n.* [singular] FORMAL or HUMOROUS a small amount of something: *a soupçon of irony* [**Origin:** 1700–1800 French **suspicion**]

ˌsouped-'up *adj.* a souped-up car or other machine has

been made more powerful, especially by adding special parts to it: *a souped-up old Chevy*

ˈsoup ˌkitchen *n.* [C] a place where people with no money and no homes can get free food

ˈsoup spoon *n.* [C] a wide spoon that is used for eating soup

soup·y /ˈsupi/ *adj.* INFORMAL having a thick liquid quality like soup: *soupy mud*

sour[1] /saʊɚ/ S3 *adj.*
1 TASTE having a sharp acid taste, like the taste of a LEMON: *a sour apple* → see also BITTER, SWEET[1] ▸see THESAURUS box at taste[1]
2 NOT FRESH milk or other food that is sour is not fresh and has a bad taste: *The milk smells a little sour.* | **turn/go sour** (=become sour)
3 UNFRIENDLY looking unfriendly or unhappy: *She always had the same sour expression.* → see also SOUR-FACED
4 SMELL a sour smell is unpleasant and not fresh: *sour breath*
5 sour grapes DISAPPROVING a situation in which someone is pretending that they dislike something because they want it but cannot have it: *This may sound like sour grapes, but I don't think I would have taken the job anyway.*
6 a sour note a situation, experience, event, or action that is not enjoyable, pleasant, or satisfactory: *The meeting* ***ended on a sour note.***
7 turn/go sour INFORMAL if a relationship or plan turns or goes sour, it becomes less enjoyable, pleasant, or satisfactory: *We dated two years and then things went sour.*
[**Origin:** Old English *sur*] —**sourly** *adv.* —**sourness** *n.* [U]

sour[2] *v.* [I,T] **1** if a relationship or someone's attitude sours, or if something sours it, it becomes unfriendly or unfavorable: *The incident soured relations between the two countries.* | **+on** *Investors seem to have soured on the company.* **2** if milk sours or something sours it, it begins to have a bad taste because it is not fresh anymore

source[1] /sɔrs/ Ac S3 W1 *n.* [C] **1** a thing, place, activity etc. that you get something from: *They get their money from various sources.* | **a food/energy/light source** *relatively clean energy sources* | **+of** *Milk is a very good source of calcium.* | *the region's main source of income* **2** the cause of something, especially a problem, or the place where it starts: **+of** *Money is often a major source of tension for married couples.* **3** a person, book, or document that supplies you with information: *All of your sources have to be listed at the end of the paper.* | *My sources tell me you're about to resign.* | ***A reliable source*** *in the Justice Department confirmed the story.* | **a primary/secondary source** (=information that comes directly from a particular event, or information that has passed through someone or something else) **4** EARTH SCIENCE the place where a stream or river starts: *the source of the Mississippi* [**Origin:** 1300–1400 Old French *sourse*, from *sourdre* **to rise, spring out**, from Latin *surgere*]

source[2] Ac *v.* [T] to find out where something can be obtained from

ˈsource code *n.* [U] COMPUTERS the original form a computer program is written in before it is changed into a form that a particular type of computer can read → see also MACHINE CODE

ˈsource ˌlanguage *n.* [C usually singular] TECHNICAL the original language of something such as a document, from which it is to be translated → see also TARGET LANGUAGE

ˌsour ˈcream *n.* [U] cream that has been made sour by adding a type of BACTERIA

sour·dough /ˈsaʊɚdoʊ/ *n.* [U] uncooked DOUGH (=bread mixture) that is left to FERMENT before being used to make bread: *sourdough bread*

ˈsour-faced *adj.* someone who is sour-faced looks unfriendly or unhappy

sour·puss /ˈsaʊɚpʊs/ *n.* [C] HUMOROUS someone who is always in a bad mood, complains a lot, and is never satisfied

sou·sa·phone /ˈsuzəˌfoʊn/ *n.* [C] a very large musical instrument made of metal, which you blow into, used especially in marching bands

souse /saʊs/ *v.* [T] to put something in water or pour water over something, making it completely wet

soused /saʊst/ *adj.* INFORMAL drunk

south[1] /saʊθ/ S1 W1 *n.* [singular, U] **1** WRITTEN ABBREVIATION **S.** the direction toward the bottom of the world, that is on the right of someone facing the rising sun: *Which way is south?* | *The airport is a few miles* ***to the south of*** *the city.* | *They planned to attack the city* ***from the south.*** **2 the south** the southern part of a country, state etc.: **+of** *the south of France* | *They lived in a small town* ***in the south.*** **3 the South** the southeastern part of the U.S.: *Don spent most of his childhood in the South.* → see Word Choice box at NORTH[1]

south[2] *adj.* **1** WRITTEN ABBREVIATION **S.** in, to, or facing the south: *Our office is located on the south side of the street.* **2** a south wind comes from the south SYN **southerly**
[**Origin:** Old English *suth*]

south[3] S3 W3 *adv.* **1** toward the south: *The window faces south.* | *Go south on Highway 1.* | **+of** *The city is about 120 miles south of Bangkok.* **2 go south** INFORMAL if a situation, organization, or standard of quality goes south, it becomes very bad although it was once very good: *After four years, their relationship began to go south.* **3 down South** in or to the southeastern part of the U.S.: *His sister still lives down South.* → see also UP NORTH

South, the the southeastern states of the U.S. which were part of the Confederacy during the Civil War

South ˈAfrica a country at the southern end of Africa —**South African** *n., adj.*

ˌSouth Aˈmerica *n.* one of the CONTINENTS which includes land south of the Caribbean Sea and north of Antarctica —**South American** *n., adj.*

south·bound /ˈsaʊθbaʊnd/ *adj., adv.* traveling or leading toward the south: *southbound traffic* | *The car was driving southbound on Route 43.*

South Car·o·li·na /ˌsaʊθ kærəˈlaɪnə/ ABBREVIATION **S.C.** a state in the southeast U.S.

South Da·ko·ta /ˌsaʊθ dəˈkoʊt̬ə/ ABBREVIATION **S.D.** a state in the northern central U.S.

south·east[1] /ˌsaʊθˈist◂/ *n.* [U] **1** WRITTEN ABBREVIATION **S.E.** the direction that is exactly between south and east **2 the southeast** the part of a country, state etc. that is in the southeast **3 the Southeast** the area of the U.S. that includes the states of Alabama, Florida, Georgia, and South Carolina

southeast[2] *adj.* [only before noun] **1** WRITTEN ABBREVIATION **S.E.** in or from the southeast SYN **southeastern**: *the southeast corner of the state* **2** a southeast wind comes from the southeast SYN **southeasterly**

southeast[3] *adv.* [only before noun] toward the southeast

south·east·er /saʊθˈistɚ/ *n.* [C] a strong wind or storm coming from the southeast

south·east·er·ly /saʊθˈistɚli/ *adj.* **1** toward or in the southeast: *The rain front is moving in a southeasterly direction.* **2** a southeasterly wind comes from the southeast

south·east·ern /ˌsaʊθˈistɚn/ *adj.* in or from the southeast part of a country SYN **southeast**

south·east·ward /ˌsaʊθˈistwɚd/ also **southeastwards** *adv.* toward the southeast —**southeastward** *adj.*

south·er·ly /ˈsʌðɚli/ *adj.* **1** in or toward the south **2** a southerly wind comes from the south

south·ern /ˈsʌðɚn/ S3 W2 *adj.* **1** in or from the south part of a country, state etc.: *southern Mexico* **2 Southern** relating to the southeastern part of the U.S.: *Southern hospitality*

ˌSouthern ˈColonies, the HISTORY five of the

S

English colonies (COLONY) in America: Virginia, Maryland, North Carolina, South Carolina, and Georgia

South·ern·er, southerner /ˈsʌðənɚ/ *n.* [C] someone who lives in or comes from the southern part of a country, especially from the southeastern part of the U.S.

ˌsouthern ˈhemisphere *n.* **the southern hemisphere** the half of the world that is south of the EQUATOR

ˌSouthern ˈLights *n.* **the Southern Lights** bands of colored light in the night sky, seen in the most southern parts of the world such as Australia → see also NORTHERN LIGHTS

south·ern·most /ˈsʌðənˌmoust/ *adj.* furthest south: *the southernmost tip of Florida*

ˌSouth Koˈrea a country in East Asia, west of Japan and east of China. It is officially called the Republic of Korea. —**South Korean** *n., adj.*

ˌSouth Paˈcific *n.* **the South Pacific** the southern part of the Pacific Ocean where there are groups of islands, such as New Zealand and Polynesia

south·paw /ˈsauθpɔ/ *n.* [C] someone who uses their left hand more than their right hand, especially said about baseball PITCHERS and BOXERS

S

ˌSouth ˈPole *n.* **the South Pole** the most southern point on the Earth's surface, and the land around it → see also MAGNETIC POLE, NORTH POLE

south·ward /ˈsauθwɚd/ also **southwards** *adv.* toward the south: *The fleet sailed southward.* —**southward** *adj.*

south·west¹ /ˌsauθˈwɛst◂ / *n.* [U] **1** WRITTEN ABBREVIATION **S.W.** the direction that is exactly between south and west **2 the southwest** the part of a country, state etc. that is in the southwest **3 the Southwest** the area of the U.S. that includes the states of New Mexico, Arizona, Texas, California, Nevada, and sometimes Colorado and Utah

southwest² *adj.* **1** WRITTEN ABBREVIATION **S.W.** in or from the southwest SYN **southwestern**: *the southwest part of the county* **2** a southwest wind comes from the southwest SYN **southwesterly**

southwest³ *adv.* toward the southwest

south·west·er /sauθˈwɛstɚ/ *n.* [C] a strong wind or storm coming from the southwest

south·west·er·ly /sauθˈwɛstɚli/ *adj.* **1** in or toward the southwest **2** EARTH SCIENCE a southwesterly wind comes from the southwest

south·west·ern /ˌsauθˈwɛstɚn/ *adj.* in or from the southwest part of a country, state etc. SYN **southwest**: *southwestern Indiana*

south·west·ward /ˌsauθˈwɛstwɚd/ also **southwestwards** *adv.* toward the southwest —**southwestward** *adj.*

sou·ve·nir /ˌsuvəˈnɪr, ˈsuvəˌnɪr/ *n.* [C] an object that you keep to remind yourself of a special occasion or a place you have visited: *We bought T-shirts as souvenirs.* | *a souvenir shop* | +**of** *I got a model of the Eiffel Tower as a souvenir of Paris.* | +**from** *a souvenir from our trip to Las Vegas* [**Origin:** 1700–1800 French *souvenir* **to remember**] —**souvenir** *adj.* [only before noun] *souvenir plates*

sou'west·er /sauˈwɛstɚ/ *n.* [C] **1** a hat made of shiny material that keeps the rain off, with a wide piece at the back that covers your neck **2** INFORMAL a SOUTHWESTER

sov·er·eign¹ /ˈsɑvərɪn/ *n.* [C] **1** FORMAL a king or queen ►see THESAURUS box at **king** **2** ECONOMICS a gold coin used in the past

sovereign² *adj.* POLITICS **1** a sovereign country or state is independent and governs itself **2** having or relating to the highest power in a country: *sovereign authority*

sove·reign·ty /ˈsɑvrənti/ *n.* [U] POLITICS **1** the power and right to govern: +**of** *the sovereignty of Congress* | +**over** *Spain's claim of sovereignty over the territory* **2** the power that an independent country has to govern itself: *the defense of our national sovereignty*

So·vi·et /ˈsouviɪt, -viˌɛt/ *adj.* from or relating to the former U.S.S.R. (Soviet Union) or its people

so·vi·et /ˈsouviɪt, -viˌɛt/ *n.* [C] HISTORY **1** one of the groups of elected workers who made laws at different levels of government in the Soviet Union **2** also **Soviet** a citizen of the Soviet Union

ˌSoviet ˈUnion, the a country in Europe and Asia that existed from 1917 to 1991 and was the largest country in the world. It was officially called the Union of Soviet Socialist Republics, or U.S.S.R.

sow¹ /sou/ *v. past tense* **sowed**, *past participle* **sown** /soun/ or **sowed** [I,T] **1** to plant or scatter seeds on a piece of ground: **sow sth with sth** *They sowed the field with barley.* **2 sow the seeds of sth** to do something that will cause a bad situation in the future: *Through their arrogance, they sowed the seeds of their own destruction.* **3 sow your wild oats** if a man sows his wild oats, he has sex with many different women, especially when he is young —**sower** *n.* [C] → see also **you reap what you sow** at REAP (3)

sow² /sau/ *n.* [C] a fully grown female pig OPP **boar** → see also **you can't make a silk purse out of a sow's ear** at SILK (3)

sown /soun/ *v.* a past participle of sow

sox /sɑks/ *n.* [plural] NONSTANDARD another spelling of "socks"

soy /sɔɪ/ also **soy·a** /ˈsɔɪə/ *n.* [U] soy beans [**Origin:** 1600–1700 Japanese *shoyu*, from Chinese *shi-yau*]

ˈsoy bean also **ˈsoya bean** *n.* [C] the bean of an Asian plant from which oil and food containing a lot of PROTEIN is produced

ˈsoy sauce *n.* [U] a dark brown salty liquid that is used especially in Japanese and Chinese cooking

spa /spɑ/ *n.* [C] **1** a place where people go in order to improve their health or beauty, especially through swimming, exercise, beauty treatments etc. SYN **health spa** **2** a town where the water has special minerals in it, and where people go to improve their health by drinking the water or swimming in it **3** a bath or pool that sends currents of hot water around you SYN **Jacuzzi** [**Origin:** 1600–1700 *Spa* Belgian town with a spa]

space¹ /speɪs/ S1 W1 *n.*

1 EMPTINESS [U] the amount of an area, room, container etc. that is empty or available to be used SYN **room**: +**for** *There's space for a table and two chairs.* | **more/less/enough etc. space** *I wish I had more space in my apartment.* | **space to do sth** *He had plenty of space to work.* | *Let's* ***make space*** *on the shelf for my books.* | *Leave enough* ***space*** *for the suitcases.* | *A piano would* ***take up*** *too much* ***space***. | **closet/storage/office etc. space** *They have a lot of storage space.* | *The mirrors create* ***a sense of space*** (=a feeling that a room has lots of space).

2 EMPTY AREA [C] an empty area, especially one that can be used for a particular purpose: *a parking space* | *Please write any comments in the space provided.* | *She* ***cleared a space*** *on her desk.*

3 BEYOND EARTH [U] PHYSICS the area beyond the Earth where the stars and PLANETS are: *the first man in space* | *space exploration* | *the icy blackness of* ***outer space*** (=the farthest areas of space)

THESAURUS

Things in space

star a large ball of burning gas in space

planet a very large round natural object that orbits (=moves around) a star

sun a star around which planets move

solar system a sun and the planets moving around it

moon/satellite a natural object that moves around a planet

meteor a piece of rock or metal that moves through space and falls toward the Earth

asteroid a piece of rock that moves around the Sun, especially between Mars and Jupiter
comet an object in space like a bright ball with a long tail, that moves around the Sun
constellation a group of stars that form a particular pattern when seen from the Earth
galaxy one of the large groups of stars that make up the universe
black hole an area in outer space into which everything near it, including light, is pulled
pulsar a small star that produces radiation and radio waves in regular amounts
quasar a very bright object in space that is similar to a star and produces radio waves

Vehicles used in space
spacecraft a vehicle that is able to travel in space. Some types of spacecraft may carry people.
rocket a spacecraft shaped like a tube, that does not carry people
(space) shuttle a spacecraft that is designed to go into space and return to Earth several times, on which people travel
(space) probe a spacecraft without people in it that sends information about space back to Earth
space station a large spacecraft that stays above the Earth and is a base for astronauts
satellite a machine that travels in space around the Earth, moon etc., used for radio, television, and other electronic communication

Someone who travels in space
astronaut, **cosmonaut** (=a Russian astronaut)

4 BETWEEN THINGS [C] an empty area between two things, or between two parts of something SYN **gap**: **+between** *the space between the house and the garage* ▶see THESAURUS box at **hole**[1]
5 WHERE THINGS EXIST [U] all of the area in which everything exists, and in which everything has a position or direction: *cultural views of time and space* | *Calculate the exact* ***point in space*** *where two lines meet.*
6 in/within the space of sth within a particular period of time: *Two managers have resigned within the space of seven months.*
7 a short space of time a short period of time: *They achieved a lot in a short space of time.*
8 EMPTY LAND [C,U] land, or an area of land that has not been built on: *Much of the land will be preserved as* ***open space****.* | *the* ***wide-open spaces*** *of Australia*
9 FREEDOM [U] the freedom to do what you want or to be alone when you need to: *I really need my space sometimes.* | *Do you want me to go home and* ***give you some space****?*
10 IN WRITING/TYPING [C] **a)** an empty space between written, typed, or printed words, lines etc.: *Insert a space here.* **b)** the width of a TYPED letter of the alphabet
11 IN A NEWSPAPER [U] the amount of a newspaper, magazine, or book that is used for a particular subject: *The story* ***got*** *very little* ***space in*** *the major newspapers.*
12 stare/look/gaze into space to look straight in front of you without looking at anything in particular, usually because you are thinking
[**Origin:** 1200–1300 Old French *espace*, from Latin *spatium* **area, room, length of space or time**] → see also **breathing space** at BREATHING ROOM

space[2] S3 *v.* **1** [T always + adv./prep.] also **space out** to arrange objects or events so that they have a particular amount of space or time between them: *Space the cookies out on a pan.* | **space sth two years/three feet etc. apart** *The injections are spaced four months apart.* | **be evenly/equally spaced** *The lights have been evenly spaced on the tunnel's walls.* → see also SPACED, SPACING **2** [I] also **space out** INFORMAL to stop paying attention and just look in front of you without thinking, especially because you are bored or because you have taken drugs: *I completely spaced out during the lecture.* → see also SPACED-OUT **3** [T] also **space off** INFORMAL to forget to do something: *I totally spaced off the meeting.*

'space-age *adj.* very modern: *space-age design*

'space bar *n.* [C] the part at the bottom of a TYPEWRITER or KEYBOARD that you press to make a space

'space ˌcadet *n.* [C] INFORMAL someone who forgets things, does not pay attention, and often behaves strangely

'space ˌcapsule *n.* [C] the part of a spacecraft that is designed to carry and protect people in space

space·craft /'speɪs-kræft/ *n.* [C] a vehicle that is able to travel in space

spaced /speɪst/ *adj.* **1** arranged or happening with a particular amount of space or time between each: **closely/widely/evenly/neatly etc. spaced** *closely spaced teeth* **2** INFORMAL spaced-out → see also DOUBLE-SPACED, SINGLE-SPACED

ˌspaced-'out also **spaced** *adj.* INFORMAL not fully conscious of what is happening around you, especially because you are extremely tired or because you have taken drugs → see also **space out** at SPACE[2] (2)

'space ˌheater *n.* [C] a small machine for heating a room

space·man /'speɪsmæn, -mən/ *n. plural* **spacemen** /-mɛn, -mən/ [C] **1** INFORMAL a man who travels into space SYN **astronaut** **2** a creature from another world, especially in children's stories

'space probe *n.* [C] a SPACECRAFT without people in it, that is sent into space to collect information about the conditions there and send it back to Earth

space·ship /'speɪsˌʃɪp/ *n.* [C] a vehicle for carrying people through space, especially in stories

'space ˌshuttle *n.* [C] a space vehicle that can land like an airplane, so that it can be used more than once

'space ˌstation *n.* [C] a place or vehicle in space that is used as a base for people traveling in space or for scientific tests

space·suit /'speɪs-sut/ *n.* [C] a special suit for wearing in space, that covers and protects your whole body and provides an air supply

ˌspace-time con'tinuum *n.* [U] TECHNICAL the universe considered as having four measurements: length, width, depth, and time

space·walk /'speɪswɔk/ *n.* [C] the act of moving around outside a SPACECRAFT while in space, or the time spent outside it

space·y /'speɪsi/ *adj.* INFORMAL behaving as though you are not fully conscious of what is happening around you

spac·ing /'speɪsɪŋ/ *n.* [U] **1** the amount of space between each printed letter, word, or line on a page: **single spacing/double spacing etc.** (=the arrangement of lines of words on a page with no spaces, one space etc. between them) → see also SPACE[1] (10) **2** the amount of space or time between objects or events: *the proper spacing of garden plants* → see also SPACE[1] (4)

spa·cious /'speɪʃəs/ *adj.* a spacious house, room etc. is large and has lots of space to move around in —**spaciousness** *n.* [U]

spack·le /'spækəl/ *n.* [U] a substance used to fill holes in walls, that becomes very hard when it dries —**spackle** *v.* [I,T]

spade /speɪd/ *n.* [C] **1** a SHOVEL for digging in the ground **2 a)** a PLAYING CARD belonging to the SUIT of spades **b) spades** [plural] the SUIT (=group of cards) that have one or more black shapes that look like pointed leaves printed on them: *the queen of spades* **3 call a spade a spade** to say exactly what you think is true, without trying to be polite **4 in spades** INFORMAL to a great degree, or in large amounts: *He's got talent in spades.* [**Origin:** (2—4) 1500–1600 Italian *spada* Spanish *espada* **broad sword** (used as a mark on cards)]

spade·work /'speɪdwɚk/ *n.* [U] hard work that has to be done in preparation before something can happen → see also LEGWORK

spa·ghet·ti /spə'gɛt̬i/ S3 *n.* [U] a type of PASTA in very

S

long thin pieces, that is cooked in boiling water [**Origin:** 1800–1900 Italian *spago* **string**]

spa,ghetti 'western *n.* [C] a movie about American COWBOYS, especially one made in Europe by an Italian director during the 1960s and 1970s

Spain /speɪn/ a country in southwest Europe, between France and Portugal —**Spanish** /'spænɪʃ/ *adj.*

spake /speɪk/ BIBLICAL or POETIC a past tense of SPEAK

Spam /spæm/ *n.* [U] TRADEMARK a type of inexpensive CANNED meat made mainly of PORK

spam /spæm/ *v.* **spammed**, **spamming** [I,T] DISAPPROVING to send the same email message to many different people who have not asked for it and do not want to read it, usually as a way of advertising something —**spam** *n.* [U] —**spamming** *n.* [U]

'spam ,blocking *n.* [U] ways of stopping unwanted emails from being sent to you, for example by having a list of addresses from which you will not accept emails

span¹ /spæn/ *n.* [C] **1** a period of time: *There were at least 86 attacks within a three-month span.* | +**of** *the span of recorded history* → see also ATTENTION SPAN, LIFESPAN **2** the part of a bridge, ARCH etc. that goes across from one support to another, or the bridge itself **3** the distance from one side of something to the other: *The central arch has a span of 90 feet.* → see also WINGSPAN

span² *v.* **spanned**, **spanning** [T] **1** to include all of a period of time: *Her teaching career has spanned 33 years.* **2** to include all of a particular space or area: *Their search spanned three continents.* **3** if a bridge spans an area of water, it goes from one side to the other **4** to include a number of different things: *Our membership spans all ages.*

Span·dex, **spandex** /'spændɛks/ *n.* [U] TRADEMARK a type of stretchy material that fits tightly on your body, especially used to make sports clothes

span·gle /'spæŋgəl/ *n.* [C] a small piece of shiny metal or plastic sewn on to clothes to give them a shining effect → see also SEQUIN

span·gled /'spæŋgəld/ *adj.* **1** covered with lights or bright shapes: +**with** *As night fell, the city became spangled with lights.* | **star-spangled/gold-spangled/sun-spangled etc.** (=covered in bright stars, gold, sunlight etc.) **2** covered in spangles: *a spangled evening gown*

Spang·lish /'spæŋglɪʃ/ *n.* [U] HUMOROUS a mixture of the Spanish and English languages

Span·iard /'spænyəd/ *n.* [C] a Spanish person

span·iel /'spænyəl/ *n.* [C] a type of dog with long ears that hang down [**Origin:** 1300–1400 Old French *espaignol* **Spaniard, spaniel**, from Latin *Hispania* **Spain**] → see also COCKER SPANIEL

Span·ish¹ /'spænɪʃ/ *adj.* from or relating to Spain

Spanish² *n.* **1** [U] the language of Spain and parts of North, Central, and South America **2 the Spanish** [plural] the people who live in Spain or are from Spain

,Spanish-A,merican 'War, the HISTORY a war between the U.S. and Spain in 1898, which resulted in Spain giving up its claim on Cuba and giving Puerto Rico, the Philippines, and Guam to the U.S.

spank /spæŋk/ *v.* [T] **1** to hit someone on their BUTTOCKS with your open hand, especially a child as a punishment: *I often **got spanked** by my parents.* ►see THESAURUS box at hit¹ **2** INFORMAL to defeat someone badly in a sport [**Origin:** 1700–1800 From the sound]

spank·ing¹ /'spæŋkɪŋ/ *n.* [C] the act of hitting someone on their BUTTOCKS with your open hand, especially a child as a punishment: *If you do that again, you're going to **get a spanking**!*

spanking² *adv.* INFORMAL **spanking new/clean etc.** very new, clean etc.: *a spanking new community center*

spar /spɑr/ *v.* **sparred**, **sparring** [I] **1** to practice BOXING with someone **2** to argue with someone, especially in a pleasant friendly way: +**with/over** *Republicans are still sparring with Democrats over the health bill.* → see also SPARRING MATCH, SPARRING PARTNER

spare¹ /spɛr/ *adj.*
1 a spare key/battery/bulb etc. a key, BATTERY etc. that you have in addition to the ones you normally use, so that it is available if another is needed
2 AVAILABLE [only before noun] not being used and available to be used: *I have two spare tickets for tonight's game.* | *There are beggars on every corner asking for **spare change*** (=coins of small value that you do not need).
3 TIME [only before noun] a spare moment, minute, hour etc. is one in which you are not working or do not have to be doing something: *In his **spare time**, he volunteers at a homeless shelter.*
4 PLAIN a spare style of writing, painting etc. is plain or basic and uses nothing unnecessary: *the artist's spare use of color*
5 THIN tall and thin
[**Origin:** Old English *spær*] → see also SPARE ROOM, SPARE TIRE

spare² *v.* [T]
1 GIVE to let someone have or use someone or something because you do not need them or are not using them: **spare sb sth** *Could you spare me a dollar or two?* | **spare sb/sth to do sth** *We're too busy to spare anyone to help you today.*
2 TIME to use some of your time to do something for someone, especially when you have a lot of other things to do: *I'm sorry, I can't spare the time right now.* | **spare sth to do sth** *Can you spare a couple of minutes to talk about next week's program?*
3 money/time to spare if you have time, money etc. to spare, there is some left in addition to what you have used or need: *If any of you have time to spare, we could always use the help.*
4 NOT DAMAGE OR HARM [T usually passive] to not damage or harm someone or something even though other people or things are being damaged, killed, or destroyed: *The hostages' lives were spared.*
5 spare sb the trouble/difficulty/pain etc. of (doing) sth to prevent someone from having to do something difficult or upsetting: *I wanted to spare you the trouble of picking me up.*
6 spare sb (the details) to not tell someone all the details about something, because it is boring, it makes them angry etc.: *"They own three houses: one in the country, one in..." **"Spare me!"***
7 with seconds/minutes/time etc. to spare seconds, minutes etc. before something had to happen: *They got to the airport with seconds to spare.*
8 spare no expense/effort to spend as much money as necessary or to do everything you can to make something really good, even if it is expensive or difficult: *They spared no expense in building the library.*
9 spare sb's feelings to avoid doing something that would upset someone: *He lied to spare her feelings.*
10 without a moment to spare also **with not a moment to spare** happening at the very last possible moment
11 spare a thought for sb to think about another person who is in a worse situation than you are
12 spare the rod, spoil the child OLD-FASHIONED used to say that if you do not SPANK your child when he or she is bad, he or she will not learn how to behave well

spare³ *n.* [C] **1** an additional thing of a particular kind that you keep so that it is available: *I brought two batteries just in case I needed a spare.* **2** a SPARE TIRE **3** a situation in BOWLING in which you knock down all the PINS (=bottle shaped objects) with a ball in two attempts → see also STRIKE

,spare 'part *n.* [C] a new part for a vehicle or machine, that is used to replace a part that is damaged or broken

spare·ribs /'spɛr,rɪbz/ *n.* [plural] the meat from the RIBS (=chest bones) of a pig, served on the bones as a meal

,spare 'room *n.* [C] a BEDROOM in your house, that is kept for guests to use when they come to stay

spare 'tire *n.* [C] **1** an additional wheel with a tire on it, that you keep in a car for use if another tire gets damaged → see picture on page A36 **2** HUMOROUS a large area of fat around someone's waist

spar·ing·ly /ˈspɛrɪŋli/ *adv.* using or doing only a little of something: *Salt should be used sparingly in cooking.* —**sparing** *adj.*

spark¹ /spɑrk/ *n.*
1 FIRE [C] a very small piece of brightly burning material produced by a fire or by hitting or rubbing two hard objects together: *sparks from the fire*
2 ELECTRICITY [C] PHYSICS a flash of light caused by electricity passing across a space: *electric sparks from a broken wire*
3 CAUSE [C] a small action or event that quickly causes trouble or violence: +**for** *The judge's verdict provided the spark for the riots.*
4 INTELLIGENCE/ENERGY [U] a quality of intelligence or energy that makes someone successful or fun to be with: *She was tired, and lacked her usual spark.*
5 a spark of interest/excitement/anger etc. a small amount of a feeling or quality, or the beginning of a feeling or quality that could grow: *There was a spark of interest in his eyes when I mentioned her name.*
6 SEXUAL ATTRACTION [singular] a feeling of sexual attraction: *Jim is a really nice guy, but there's just no spark.*
7 (the) sparks fly if sparks fly, people argue angrily: *Sparks flew when Julia accused other members of the team of cheating.*
[**Origin:** Old English *spearca*]

spark² *v.*
1 CAUSE TROUBLE also **spark off** [T] to be the cause of trouble or violence: *The shootings have sparked a national debate over gun control.*
2 spark (sb's) interest/hope/curiosity etc. to make someone become interested in something, make someone feel hopeful, curious etc.: *Field trips could spark students' interest in science careers.*
3 CAUSE FIRE [T] to start a fire or explosion: *A discarded cigarette sparked the brush fire.*
4 PRODUCE SPARKS [I] PHYSICS to produce sparks of fire or electricity: *The loose wire was sparking.*
5 ENCOURAGE WRITTEN to encourage someone to try harder to do something well, by doing it well yourself SYN **inspire**: **spark sb to sth** *Jackson's playing sparked his team to a 97–89 victory.*

spar·kle¹ /ˈspɑrkəl/ *v.* [I] **1** to shine in small bright flashes: *The crystal chandelier sparkled.* ►see THESAURUS box at shine¹ **2** if someone's eyes sparkle, they shine brightly, especially because the person is happy or excited: +**with** *The children's eyes sparkled with happiness.* **3** to be very lively and interesting → see also SPARKLING

sparkle² *n.* **1** [C,U] a bright shiny appearance, with small points of flashing light **2** [singular, U] a sparkle in someone's eyes is a bright shining quality their eyes have, especially because they are happy or excited **3** [U] a quality that makes something seem interesting and full of life

spark·ler /ˈspɑrklɚ/ *n.* [C] a FIREWORK in the shape of a thin stick, that gives off SPARKS of fire as you hold it in your hand

spark·ling /ˈspɑrklɪŋ/ *adj.* **1** shining brightly with points of flashing light: *a sparkling lake* **2** a sparkling drink has BUBBLES of gas in it: *a glass of sparkling apple juice* **3** full of life and intelligence: *a sparkling personality*

ˌsparkling ˈwine *n.* [C,U] a white wine with a lot of BUBBLES, such as CHAMPAGNE

ˈspark plug *n.* [C] a part in a car engine that produces an electric SPARK to make the mixture of gas and air start burning

ˈsparring match *n.* [C] a friendly argument that is not serious

ˈsparring ˌpartner *n.* [C] **1** someone you practice BOXING with **2** someone you regularly have friendly arguments with

spar·row /ˈspæroʊ/ *n.* [C] BIOLOGY a small brown bird, very common in many parts of the world [**Origin:** Old English *spearwa*]

sparse /spɑrs/ *adj.* existing only in small amounts: *He combed his sparse hair.* | *Information on the disease is sparse.* [**Origin:** 1700–1800 Latin *sparsus* **spread out**, from the past participle of *spargere* **to scatter**] —**sparsely** *adv.*: *a sparsely populated area* —**sparseness** *n.* [U]

Spar·ta /ˈspɑrt̬ə/ HISTORY an important CITY-STATE in the southern part of ancient Greece, which was known for the military organization of its society

spar·tan /ˈspɑrtˀn/ *adj.* spartan conditions or ways of living are simple and without any comfort: *a spartan apartment* [**Origin:** 1600–1700 *Spartan* **of Sparta** (16–21 centuries), from *Sparta* city in ancient Greece whose people lived simply]

spasm /ˈspæzəm/ *n.* [C] **1** BIOLOGY a sudden uncontrolled TIGHTENing of your muscles: *back spasms* **2 a spasm of grief/laughter/coughing etc.** a sudden strong feeling or reaction that continues for a short period [**Origin:** 1300–1400 Old French *spasme*, from Latin, from Greek *spasmos*, from *span* **to pull**]

spas·mod·ic /spæzˈmɑdɪk/ *adj.* **1** BIOLOGY of or relating to a muscle spasm **2** happening for short irregular periods, not continuously SYN **intermittent** —**spasmodically** /-kli/ *adv.*

spas·tic /ˈspæstɪk/ *adj.* MEDICINE having CEREBRAL PALSY, a disease that prevents control of the muscles —**spastic** *n.* [C]

spat¹ /spæt/ *v.* the past tense and past participle of SPIT

spat² *n.* [C] **1** INFORMAL a short unimportant argument: *a lovers' spat* **2** [usually plural] one of a set of special pieces of cloth worn in past times over men's shoes and fastened with buttons

spate /speɪt/ *n.* **a spate of sth** a large number of similar things that happen in a short period of time, especially bad things: *a spate of burglaries*

spa·tial /ˈspeɪʃəl/ *adj.* FORMAL **1** relating to the position, size, shape etc. of things **2** relating to people's ability to understand the position, size, shape etc. of things: *spatial skills* —**spatially** *adv.*

spat·ter /ˈspæt̬ɚ/ *v.* [I always + prep.,T] if liquid spatters somewhere or something spatters it, drops of it fall or are thrown on the surface: **spatter on/over/across etc. sth** *Blood spattered across the floor.* | **spatter sth on/over/across etc. sb/sth** *Try not to spatter grease on the stove.* | **spatter sb/sth with sth** *A passing truck spattered us with mud.* —**spatter** *n.* [C,U]

spat·u·la /ˈspætʃələ/ *n.* [C] **1** a kitchen tool with a wide flat part at the end of a long handle for lifting food out of a cooking pan **2** a tool with a wide flat part used for spreading and mixing things

spawn¹ /spɔn/ *v.* **1** [I,T] BIOLOGY if a fish or FROG spawns it produces eggs in large quantities at the same time **2** [T] to make something happen or start to exist, especially a large number of things: *The book has spawned several movies.*

spawn² *n.* [U] BIOLOGY the eggs of a fish, FROG etc. laid together in a soft mass

spay /speɪ/ *v.* **spays, spayed, spaying** [T] BIOLOGY to remove part of the sex organs of a female animal so that it is not able to have babies → see also NEUTER

speak /spik/ S1 W1 *v. past tense* **spoke** /spoʊk/, *past participle* **spoken** /ˈspoʊkən/
1 IN CONVERSATION [I always + adv./prep.] to talk to someone about something or have a conversation: +**to** *I haven't spoken to him since last Monday.* | +**with** *The director would like to speak with you this afternoon.* | +**of/about** *Dad never spoke about his family at all.* | **speak to/with sb about sth** *Have you spoken to Harriet about the party?*
2 SAY WORDS [I] to use your voice to produce words: *She was too nervous to speak.* | *He spoke very softly.* | +**to** *John, speak to me! Are you OK?* | *I was so emotional I* ***couldn't speak.***
3 A LANGUAGE [T not in progressive] to be able to speak a particular language: *Elaine speaks Spanish and*

S

Russian. | *He* ***doesn't speak a word of*** *French* (=he doesn't speak French at all). | **can/can't speak English/Japanese etc.** *Several children in the class cannot speak English.* → see also -SPEAKING
4 FORMAL SPEECH [I] to make a formal speech: *I get nervous if I have to speak in public.* | **+at** *I've been invited to speak at the annual convention.* | **+about/on** *She will be speaking on education reform.* | *Kendrick* ***spoke in favor of*** (=said things that showed he supports) *cutting taxes.* | *Only one member* ***spoke against*** (=said things to oppose) *the new rules.* → see also SPEAKER, SPEECH
5 generally/strictly/technically etc. speaking used when you are saying what is true in a general, strict etc. way: *Strictly speaking, it's my money, not yours.*
6 EXPRESS IDEAS/OPINIONS [I always + adv./prep.] to say something that expresses your ideas or opinions: **speak well/highly of sb/sth** *Dan speaks very highly of* (=says good things about) *you.* | **speak as a parent/teacher/Democrat etc.** *Speaking as a lawyer, I think you're making a mistake.* | *Personally speaking, I don't like the way she dresses.* | **speak badly/ill of sb/sth** (=say bad things about someone or something)
7 ON TELEPHONE [I] to talk to someone using the telephone: *"Who's speaking, please?" "This is Mike Palmer."* | **+to/with** *"May I speak to Laura Davis?" "Speaking."*

S

8 speak your mind to say exactly what you think about something, even when this might offend people: *Sam has never been shy about speaking his mind.*
9 sth speaks volumes (about/for sb/sth) used to say that something expresses a feeling or idea very clearly, without using words: *The look on his face spoke volumes about his opinion.*
10 be on speaking terms (with sb) also **be speaking (to sb)** [usually in negatives and questions] if two people are not on speaking terms, they do not talk to each other, especially because they have argued: *Claire and Andy aren't speaking.*
11 speak out of turn to say something when you do not have the right or authority to say it
12 speak in tongues to talk using strange words as part of a Christian religious experience
13 speak with one voice if a group of people speak with one voice, they all express the same opinion
[**Origin:** Old English *sprecan, specan*] → see also **actions speak louder than words** at ACTION (14), **in a manner of speaking** at MANNER (4), **so to speak** at SO[1] (7), **be spoken for** at SPOKEN[2] (2)

speak for *phr. v.* **1 speak for sb/sth** to represent a person or group of people by expressing their feelings, thoughts, or beliefs: *I speak for the families of this city in saying that we want better schools.* **2 speak for yourself** SPOKEN used to tell someone that you do not have the same opinion as they do: *"We're not interested in going." "Hey, speak for yourself."* **3 speak for itself/themselves** to show something so clearly that no explanation is necessary: *The results speak for themselves.*

speak of sth *phr. v.* **1** LITERARY to show clearly that something happened or that it exists: *The lines on her face spoke of her frustration.* **2 speaking of sb/sth** SPOKEN used when you want to say more about someone or something that has just been mentioned: *Speaking of birthdays, don't you have one coming up?* **3 speak of the devil** SPOKEN said when the person you have just been talking about arrives at the place where you are **4 no... to speak of** also **nothing/none to speak of** used to say that there is very little of something or not enough to be important or easily noticed: *Grace had no personality to speak of.* | *"Have you had any rain?" "None to speak of."*

speak out *phr. v.* to publicly speak in protest about something, especially when protesting could be dangerous: **+about/in favor of/against** *Smith was not afraid to speak out against the war.*

speak to sb *phr. v.* **1** to talk to someone who has done something wrong, to tell them not to do it again: **speak to sb about sth** *Someone needs to speak to him about being on time.* **2** if something such as a poem, painting, or piece of music speaks to you, you like it because it expresses a particular meaning, quality, or feeling to you

speak up *phr. v.* **1** used to ask someone to speak louder: *Speak up, please – I can't hear you.* **2** to express your opinion freely and clearly: *If anyone is against the plan, now is the time to speak up.*

speak up for sb/sth *phr. v.* to speak in support of someone or something: *You'll have to learn to speak up for yourself.*

-speak /spik/ *suffix* [in nouns] the special language or difficult words that are used in a particular business or activity: *computerspeak*

speak·eas·y /ˈspikˌizi/ *n.* [C] a place in the U.S. in the 1920s and 1930s where you could buy alcohol illegally

speak·er /ˈspikɚ/ S1 W2 *n.* [C]
1 IN PUBLIC someone who makes a formal speech to a group of people: *Is he a good speaker?* | **+at** *Dole will be the main speaker at graduation.* | *a brilliant* ***public speaker*** | *We have a special* ***guest speaker*** *today.*
2 OF A LANGUAGE someone who speaks a particular language: **+of** *speakers of Cantonese* | **a French speaker/English speaker etc.** *The agency desperately needs Arabic speakers.*
3 SOUND EQUIPMENT the part of a radio, record player, or sound system where the sound comes out → see picture at COMPUTER
4 SAYING STH FORMAL someone who is saying something: *the relationship between speaker and listener*
5 POLITICIAN [usually singular] also **the Speaker of the House** the politician who controls discussions in the House of Representatives in the U.S. Congress

-speaking /ˈspikɪŋ/ *suffix* [in adjectives] **French-speaking/Italian-speaking etc. a)** able to speak a particular language: *a German-speaking secretary* **b)** containing mainly people who speak a particular language as their first language: *a Turkish-speaking region*

spear¹ /spɪr/ *n.* [C] **1** a pole with a sharp pointed blade at one end, used as a weapon **2** a thin pointed stem of a plant, shaped like a spear: *asparagus spears*

spear² *v.* [T] **1** to push a pointed object, usually a fork, into something, so that you can pick it up **2** to push or throw a spear into someone or something, especially in order to kill them **3** to block an opponent illegally in American football by hitting them with your HELMET **4** to hit an opponent illegally in ice HOCKEY with the blade of your ice hockey stick

spear·head¹ /ˈspɪrhɛd/ *v.* [T] to lead an attack or organized action: *The anti-smoking campaign is spearheaded by the government.*

spearhead² *n.* [C usually singular] a person or group of people who lead an attack or organized action

spear·mint /ˈspɪrmɪnt/ *n.* [U] **1** a fresh MINT taste, often used in candy: *spearmint chewing gum* **2** BIOLOGY the MINT plant that this taste comes from

spec /spɛk/ *n.* INFORMAL **1** [C usually plural] one of the details in the plan for how fast, large etc. something such as a building, car, or piece of electrical equipment should be SYN **specification**: *software specs* | **build/make sth to (sb's) spec(s)** (=build something exactly according to the details of the plan) **2 specs** [plural] OLD-FASHIONED GLASSES to help you see **3 on spec** if you do something on spec, you do it without being sure that you will get what you are hoping for

spe·cial¹ /ˈspɛʃəl/ S1 W1 *adj.* **1** not ordinary or usual, but different in some way and often better or more important: *He's been on a special diet since his heart attack.* | *No special equipment is needed.* | *No one gets special treatment here.* | **+about** *What's so special about her?* | **anything/something/nothing special** *Are you doing anything special for Christmas?* | *The good china was used only* ***on special occasions*** (=for important social events). | *Changes are allowed only in* ***special circumstances.*** | *a* ***special edition*** (=a special type of something produced only for a short time) *of Faulkner's first novel* | *Each village has its* ***own special*** *charm.* **2** particularly important to someone: *a special* friend | +**to** *You know you're very special to me.* | *She was a teacher who* ***made*** *every child* ***feel special.*** | *Her younger son* ***had a special place in*** *her* ***heart.*** **3** [only before noun] greater or more than usual: *I made a special effort to be nice to him.* **4** [only before noun] having a particular job to do: *a special envoy in the peace talks* [**Origin:** 1100–1200 Old French *especial*, from Latin *specialis* **particular**]

special² *n.* [C] **1** something that is not usual or ordinary, and is made or done for a special purpose: *a TV special on the election* **2** a particular product that is sold for a lower price at a particular time: *What are your lunch specials?* **3 on special** being sold at a special low price SYN **on sale**: *Breyer's ice cream is on special this week.*

ˌspecial 'agent *n.* [C] someone who works for the FBI

ˌspecial com'mittee *n.* [C] POLITICS a small group of politicians and advisers from various parties, chosen to examine a particular subject SYN **select committee**: *the U.S. Senate Special Committee on Aging*

ˌspecial de'livery *n.* [C,U] a service that delivers a letter or package very quickly

ˌspecial ˌeconomic 'zone also **ˌspecial 'enterprise ˌzone** *n.* [C] ECONOMICS an area in China where the government is helping economic development by allowing foreign companies and banks to buy property, operate companies etc., and by allowing local companies to make their own business decisions

ˌspecial edu'cation *n.* [U] the education of children who have particular physical problems or learning problems

ˌspecial ef'fect *n.* [C usually plural] an unusual image or sound in a movie or television program that has been produced artificially: *The movie has great special effects.*

ˌspecial 'forces *n.* [plural] soldiers who have been specially trained to fight against GUERRILLA or TERRORIST groups

ˌspecial 'interest ˌgroup *n.* [C] POLITICS a group of people who all share the same political, social, or business aims, especially groups who try to influence the government

ˌspecial 'interests *n.* [plural] special interest groups in general

spe·cial·ist /ˈspɛʃəlɪst/ W3 *n.* [C] **1** someone who knows a lot about a particular subject, or is very skilled at it SYN **expert**: *a telecommunications specialist* | +**in** *a specialist in African politics* ►see THESAURUS box at **expert¹** **2** a doctor who knows more about one particular type of illness or treatment than other doctors: *You'll have to see a specialist.* | *a cancer specialist* ►see THESAURUS box at **doctor¹** —**specialist** *adj.* [only before noun]

spe·cial·i·za·tion /ˌspɛʃələˈzɪʃən/ *n.* **1** [U] ECONOMICS the business practice of limiting what your company produces or does to one particular product or activity, or to a small number of related products or activities: *industry specialization* **2** [C,U] an activity or subject that you know a lot about: *In my area of specialization – corporate law – you have to keep up-to-date with new rulings.* | *a mathematics major with a specialization in computing*

spe·cial·ize /ˈspɛʃəˌlaɪz/ W3 *v.* [I] to limit all or most of your study, business, work etc. to a particular thing: +**in** *The store specializes in interior design books.*

spe·cial·ized /ˈspɛʃəˌlaɪzd/ *adj.* relating to one particular purpose, type of work, type of product etc. OPP **general**: *specialized training in computer programming* | *The agency helps businesses fill* ***highly specialized*** (=very specialized) *positions.*

spe·cial·ly /ˈspɛʃəli/ *adv.* **1** for one particular purpose, and only for that purpose: *The kayaks are specially designed for use in the ocean.* **2** SPOKEN for a particular person SYN **especially**: *We ordered pizza specially for you.*

ˌspecial 'needs *n.* [plural] needs that someone has because they have mental or physical problems: *children with special needs* | *special needs education*

ˌspecial 'offer *n.* [C] a low price charged for a product for a short time: +**on** *a special offer on dishwashers*

ˌSpecial Oˌlympics Inter'national an organization that gives sports training to children and adults who have disabilities (DISABILITY) and organizes sports competitions for them

ˌspecial 'prosecutor *n.* [C] LAW in the U.S., an independent lawyer who is chosen to examine the actions of a government official and find out if they have done anything wrong or illegal

'special ˌschool *n.* [C] a school for children with physical problems or problems with learning

ˌspecial ˌtheory of rela'tivity *n.* [singular] PHYSICS the first of Einstein's two scientific descriptions of the relationship between matter, time, and space, which shows that mass and energy are related and that time, DIMENSION, and MASS are affected by speed. The theory is based on the ideas that the speed of light in a VACUUM does not change and that the rules of PHYSICS are the same everywhere in the universe. → see also GENERAL THEORY OF RELATIVITY

spe·cial·ty¹ /ˈspɛʃəlti/ *n. plural* **specialties** [C] **1** a type of food that is always very good in a particular area or restaurant: *Their specialty is prime rib.* **2** a subject or job that you know a lot about or have a lot of experience of: *Sports medicine is her specialty.*

S

specialty² *adj.* [only before noun] **1** specialty products are special or unusual in some way, and are therefore usually expensive **2 a specialty store/restaurant/shop** a store or restaurant that sells products or foods that are special or unusual in some way

spe·ci·a·tion /ˌspiʃiˈeɪʃən/ *n.* [U] BIOLOGY the process by which one existing species of animal, plant etc. gradually changes over a long period of time and forms into two or more different species that are GENETICally different

spe·cie /ˈspiʃi, -si/ *n.* [U] ECONOMICS money in the form of gold or silver coins

spe·cies /ˈspiʃiz, -siz/ W2 *n. plural* **species** [C] BIOLOGY a group of animals or plants that are all similar and can breed together to produce young animals or plants: *a rare plant species* | *All dogs are members of the same species.* | +**of** *There are over 40 species of birds living on the island.* [**Origin:** 1300–1400 Latin **appearance, kind**, from *specere* **to look (at)**] → see also ENDANGERED SPECIES

'species diˌversity *n.* [U] BIOLOGY the number of different species of animals, plants, and other living things that exist on the Earth or in a particular place, as well as how they are spread across a particular area: *Another result of cutting down the forests will be the loss of species diversity.*

spe·cif·ic¹ /spɪˈsɪfɪk/ Ac S2 W2 *adj.* **1** [only before noun] a specific thing, person, or group is one particular thing, person, or group: *a specific example* | *The game is intended for specific age groups.* **2** detailed and exact SYN **precise**: *He gave us specific instructions.* | *Can you* ***be more specific about*** *what you're looking for?* **3 specific to sth** FORMAL limited to, or affecting, only one particular thing: *issues specific to senior citizens* —**specificity** /ˌspɛsəˈfɪsəṭi/ *n.* [U]

specific² Ac *n.* **1 specifics** [plural] particular details that must be decided exactly: +**of** *She would not comment on the specifics of the lawsuit.* | *I don't want to* ***go into specifics.*** **2** [C] MEDICINE a drug that has an effect only on one particular DISEASE

spe·cif·i·cally /spɪˈsɪfɪkli/ Ac S3 W3 *adv.* **1** concerning or intended for one particular type of person or thing only: *Their campaign is specifically aimed at young mothers.* **2** in a detailed or exact way: *I specifically asked you not to hit your sister!* **3** [sentence adverb] used when you are adding more exact information: *Casual dress is not acceptable. Specifically, men must wear a shirt and tie.*

spec·i·fi·ca·tion /ˌspɛsəfəˈkeɪʃən/ Ac *n.* [C usually plural] **1** a detailed instruction about how something should be designed or made SYN spec: **build/manufacture/make sth to (sb's) specifications** *The furniture is made to your own specifications.* **2** a clear statement of what is needed or wanted: *job specifications*

spe͵cific 'gravity *n.* [U] PHYSICS the weight of a substance divided by the weight of the amount of water that would fill the same space

spe͵cific 'heat *n.* [U] CHEMISTRY the amount of heat that is needed to raise the temperature of one gram of a substance by one degree Celsius

spe·ci·fy /'spɛsə͵faɪ/ Ac *v.* **specifies, specified, specifying** [T] to state something in an exact and detailed way: *The President did not specify a date for his visit to Peru.* | **specify who/what/how etc.** *He did not specify what surgery was required.* | **specify that** *The rules clearly specify that competitors are not allowed to accept payment.* —**specified** *adj.*: *Application forms must be submitted before the specified deadline.*

spec·i·men /'spɛsəmən/ *n.* [C] **1** BIOLOGY a small amount or piece of something that is taken from a plant or animal, so that it can be tested or examined: *a blood specimen* **2** a single example of something: *a very fine specimen of 12th-century glass* **3** HUMOROUS someone who has a very attractive or strong body, especially an ATHLETE [**Origin:** 1600–1700 Latin *specere* **to look (at)**]

S

spe·cious /'spiʃəs/ *adj.* FORMAL seeming to be true or correct, but actually false: *specious logic* —**speciously** *adv.* —**speciousness** *n.* [U]

speck /spɛk/ *n.* [C] a very small mark, spot, or piece of something: +**of** *specks of paint on the floor*

speck·le /'spɛkəl/ *n.* [C] small marks or spots covering a background of a different color

speck·led /'spɛkəld/ *adj.* covered with many small marks or spots: *speckled eggs*

spec·ta·cle /'spɛktəkəl/ *n.* **1 make a spectacle of yourself** to behave in an embarrassing way that is likely to make other people notice you and laugh at you: *Jody made a complete spectacle of herself by getting drunk at the wedding.* **2** [C usually singular] something that you see that is very impressive, surprising, shocking etc.: *It was an odd spectacle.* | +**of** *the magnificent spectacle of a herd of elephants* **3** [C,U] an impressive or exciting public show or event **4 spectacles** [plural] OLD-FASHIONED a pair of GLASSES for your eyes

spec·tac·u·lar[1] /spɛk'tækyələ˞/ *adj.* **1** very impressive and exciting: *a spectacular view of the Grand Canyon* **2** very extreme or sudden, and therefore attracting a lot of attention: *the city's spectacular growth* —**spectacularly** *adv.*

spectacular[2] *n.* [C] an event or performance that is very large and impressive

spec·tate /'spɛkteɪt/ *v.* [I] to watch a sports event

spec·ta·tor /'spɛkteɪt̬ə˞/ *n.* [C] someone who is watching an event or game: *There were over 40,000 spectators at the game.*

'spectator ͵sport *n.* [C] a sport that people go and watch

spec·ter /'spɛktə˞/ *n.* [C] **1 the specter of sth** something that people are afraid of because it may affect them soon: *The country now faces the specter of civil war.* **2** [C] LITERARY a GHOST ▶see THESAURUS box at **ghost**[1]

spec·tra /'spɛktrə/ *n.* the plural of SPECTRUM

spec·tral /'spɛktrəl/ *adj.* **1** PHYSICS relating to or made by a SPECTRUM **2** LITERARY relating to or like a specter

spec·tro·scope /'spɛktrə͵skoʊp/ *n.* [C] PHYSICS an instrument used for forming and looking at spectra (SPECTRUM) —**spectroscopy** /spɛk'trɑskəpi/ *n.* [U] —**spectroscopic** /͵spɛktrə'skɑpɪk/ *adj.*

spec·trum /'spɛktrəm/ *n. plural* **spectra** /-trə/ [C] **1** a complete range of opinions, ideas, situations etc., going from one extreme to its opposite: +**of** *a wide spectrum of opinions* | *The bill drew support* ***from across the*** *political* ***spectrum.*** | **the whole/entire/full spectrum (of sth)** *news stories covering the full spectrum of events* | **one end/the other end/the opposite end etc. of the spectrum** *The two articles here represent opposite ends of the spectrum.* **2** PHYSICS the set of bands of colored light into which a beam of light can be separated by passing it through a PRISM **3** PHYSICS a complete range of radio, sound etc. waves **4** ELECTROMAGNETIC SPECTRUM

spec·u·late /'spɛkyə͵leɪt/ *v.* **1** [I,T] to think or talk about the possible causes or effects of something without knowing all the facts or details: +**on/about** *Police would not speculate on a motive.* | **speculate that** *Some economists speculate that inflation will increase next year.* **2** [I] ECONOMICS to buy goods, property, or STOCK in a company etc. hoping that you will make a large profit when you sell them: +**in** *He made his fortune by speculating in real estate.* [**Origin:** 1500–1600 Latin, past participle of *speculari* **to watch (secretly)**, from *specere* **to look (at)**] —**speculator** *n.* [C]

spec·u·la·tion /͵spɛkyə'leɪʃən/ *n.* [C,U] **1** the act of guessing without knowing all the facts about something, or the guesses that you make: +**about** *speculation about a potential run for President* | **speculation that** *There is speculation that he may have left the country.* | *Stock prices fell* ***amid speculation that*** *oil prices would rise.* | **pure/wild/idle speculation** (=speculation that is unlikely to be true) **2** ECONOMICS the act of trying to make a profit by speculating: *currency speculation*

spec·u·la·tive /'spɛkyələt̬ɪv, -͵leɪt̬ɪv/ *adj.* **1** based on guessing, not on information or facts: *The theories are* ***highly speculative.*** **2** ECONOMICS bought or done in the hope of making a profit later: *speculative stocks* **3** done while trying to guess something: *a speculative look* —**speculatively** *adv.*

sped /spɛd/ *v.* the past tense and past participle of SPEED

speech /spitʃ/ S1 W1 *n.* **1** [C] a talk, especially a formal one about a particular subject, given to a group of people: *a campaign speech* | *I have to write my speech for tomorrow.* | +**on** *a speech on the environment* | **give/make/deliver a speech** *Her father made a long speech at the wedding.* | +**to** *a speech to the troops before the battle* | +**by** *a speech by the chairman of the company*

> **THESAURUS**
>
> **address** a formal speech that someone makes to a group of people: *the commencement address*
> **talk** an occasion on which someone speaks to a group of people about a particular subject or about their experiences: *a talk on his travels in Africa*
> **lecture** a talk, especially one given to students in a university: *a psychology lecture*
> **presentation** a talk about a particular subject, especially one at which you describe or explain something: *The students were asked to give a brief presentation on what they had done over the summer.*

2 [U] the ability to speak: *Only humans are capable of speech.* **3** [U] ENG. LANG. ARTS spoken language rather than written language: *In speech we use a smaller vocabulary than in writing.* **4** [U] the particular way in which someone speaks: *His speech was slurred, and he sounded drunk.* **5** [C] a set of lines that an actor must say in a play [**Origin:** Old English *spræc*, *spæc*] → see also DIRECT SPEECH, FIGURE OF SPEECH, **freedom of speech/religion etc.** at FREEDOM (1), INDIRECT SPEECH, PART OF SPEECH, REPORTED SPEECH

speech·i·fy /'spitʃə͵faɪ/ *v.* **speechifies, speechified, speechifying** [I] INFORMAL to make speeches in order to seem important

'speech im͵pediment *n.* [C] a permanent physical or nervous problem that makes it difficult for you to pronounce particular sounds

speech·less /'spitʃlɪs/ *adj.* **1** unable to speak because you are so angry, upset, surprised etc.: +**with** *Allen was nearly speechless with fear.* | *His remarks* ***left her speechless*** (=made her speechless). **2 I'm speechless** SPOKEN used to say that you are so angry, upset, surprised etc. that you do not know what to say —**speechlessly** *adv.* —**speechlessness** *n.* [U]

speech ˌsynthesizer *n.* [C] a computer system that produces sounds like human speech

speech ˌtherapy *n.* [U] MEDICINE treatment that helps people who have difficulty speaking correctly —**speech therapist** *n.* [C]

speech·writ·er /ˈspitʃˌraɪtɚ/ *n.* [C] someone who writes speeches for other people as their job

speed¹ /spid/ S2 W2 *n.*
1 RATE OF TRAVEL [C,U] how fast something moves or travels: *average wind speed* | +**of** *the speed of light* | *The train can travel* ***at a speed of*** *110 mph.* | *The ferry* ***has a top speed of*** (=the fastest it can possibly go is) *25 mph.* | **at full/top speed** *He came running toward me at full speed.* | **at high/low speed** *The car drove off at high speed.* | *We raced down the mountain* ***at breakneck speed*** (=dangerously fast). | *The rocks began to* ***gather speed*** (=gradually start to travel faster) *as they tumbled down the hillside.*
2 RATE OF ACTION [U] how fast something happens or is done: *the computer's data transmission speed* | +**of** *the speed of change in the region* | *They're putting up new houses* ***at lightning speed.***
3 up to speed (on/with sth) having the information you need to understand what has been happening in a particular situation: *We need to* ***bring*** *everyone* ***up to speed on*** *the project.*
4 FAST [U] the quality of moving or doing something fast: *A good player needs strength and speed.* | *They acted* ***with speed*** *and efficiency.*
5 DRUG [U] SLANG an illegal drug that makes you very active SYN **amphetamine**
6 PHOTOGRAPHY [C] **a)** the degree to which photographic film is sensitive to light **b)** the time it takes for a camera SHUTTER to open and close: *a shutter speed of 1/250 second*
[**Origin:** Old English *sped* **success, quickness**] → see also -SPEED

speed² S3 *v. past tense and past participle* **sped** /spɛd/ or **speeded** **1** [I always + adv./prep.] to go quickly: +**along/down/past/away etc.** *The car sped along the dusty highway.* ►see THESAURUS box at **rush¹**
2 [T always + adv./prep.] to take someone or something somewhere very quickly: **speed sb to/away/back etc.** *Security guards sped her to a waiting helicopter.*
3 [I usually progressive] to be driving faster than the legal limit: *I'm sure I wasn't speeding, officer.* | *Mort* ***got caught speeding*** *again.* **4** [T] to make something happen faster SYN **speed up**: *The good news should speed his recovery.* → see also SPEEDING

speed by *phr. v.* if time speeds by, it seems to pass very quickly

speed up *phr. v.* **speed sth ↔ up** to move or happen faster, or to make something move or happen faster: *Speed up – we're going to be late.* | *The new system will speed up the registration process.*

-speed /spid/ [in adjectives] **five-speed/ten-speed etc.** having five, ten etc. GEARS: *a five-speed transmission* → see also TEN-SPEED

speed·boat /ˈspidbout/ *n.* [C] a small boat with a powerful engine, designed to go fast

speed bump *n.* [C] a narrow raised part across a road that forces traffic to go slowly

speed ˌdemon *n.* [C] HUMOROUS someone who drives a car, MOTORCYCLE etc. very fast

speed ˌdial also **ˈspeed ˌdialing** *n.* [U] a special feature on a telephone that lets you DIAL someone's telephone number very quickly by pressing one button —**speed-dial** *v.* [I,T]

speed·ing /ˈspidɪŋ/ *n.* [U] the offense of driving faster than the law allows: *a ticket for speeding*

speed ˌlimit *n.* [C] the fastest speed allowed by law on a particular piece of road, water, railroad etc.: *The speed limit is 45 mph.*

speed·om·e·ter /spɪˈdɑmətɚ/ *n.* [C] an instrument in a vehicle that shows how fast it is going → see picture on page A36

ˈspeed ˌreading *n.* [U] a method of reading very quickly —**speed-read** *v.* [I,T]

ˈspeed ˌskating *n.* [U] the sport of racing on ice wearing ICE SKATES

speed·ster /ˈspidstɚ/ *n.* [C] **1** a car that is designed to go very fast **2** INFORMAL someone who drives or runs very fast

ˈspeed trap *n.* [C] a place on a road where police wait to catch drivers who are going too fast

speed·up /ˈspidʌp/ *n.* [C usually singular] an increase in the speed of something or the rate at which a process happens: +**in** *a speedup in the economy*

speed·way /ˈspidweɪ/ *n.* [C] a special track that is used for racing MOTORCYCLES or cars as a sport

speed·y /ˈspidi/ *adj. comparative* **speedier**, *superlative* **speediest** **1** happening or done quickly or without delay SYN **quick**: *We hope you make a speedy recovery.* **2** able to move or do things very quickly SYN **fast** —**speedily** *adv.* —**speediness** *n.* [U]

spell¹ /spɛl/ S1 W3 *v.* **1** [I,T] ENG. LANG. ARTS to form a word by writing or naming the letters in order: *"How do you spell your name?" "R-E-I-D."* | *Excuse me, but my name is* ***spelled wrong*** *on the list.* | *I don't think you* ***spelled*** *that word* ***right.*** | *Does Kathy* ***spell*** *her name* ***with a*** *C or a K?* **2** [T not in passive] ENG. LANG. ARTS if letters spell a word, they form it: *"B-O-O-K" spells "book."* **3** to be going to lead to something bad happening: **spell trouble/disaster/danger etc.** *The bad weather could spell disaster for farmers.* **4** [T] INFORMAL to do someone else's work for them for a short period so that they can rest [**Origin:** 1200–1300 Old French *espeller*]

spell sth ↔ **out** *phr. v.* **1** to explain something clearly and in detail: *Do I have to spell everything out for you?* | **spell out how/what etc.** *Morgan spelled out how he would make the company profitable again.* **2** ENG. LANG. ARTS to show how a word is spelled by writing or saying the letters separately and in order: *Could you spell your last name out for me?* **3** ENG. LANG. ARTS to write a word in its complete form instead of using an ABBREVIATION

spell² S2 *n.* [C] **1** a piece of magic that someone does or the special words or ceremonies used in doing it: *The witch* ***cast a spell on*** (=did a piece of magic to change something about) *the young prince.* | *Only a kiss could* ***break the spell*** (=stop the spell from working). | *The whole town seemed to be* ***under a spell.*** ►see THESAURUS box at **magic¹** **2** a period of a particular type of activity, weather etc., usually a short period: *After a brief spell in the army, I returned to teaching.* | +**of** *a spell of bad luck* | **a cold/wet/dry spell** *We had another cold spell last month.* **3** a very short period of feeling sick: *a dizzy spell* **4** a power that attracts and influences you so strongly that it completely controls your feelings: **be/fall/come under sb's spell** *She fell under the spell of the cult's leader.* **5 break the spell** to make a time stop feeling special

spell·bind·ing /ˈspɛlˌbaɪndɪŋ/ *adj.* extremely interesting and holding your attention completely —**spellbinder** *n.* [C]

spell·bound /ˈspɛlbaʊnd/ *adj.* extremely interested in something you are listening to: *Stories of his trips to Asia* ***held us spellbound*** *for hours.*

ˈspell-ˌchecker *n.* [C] COMPUTERS a computer PROGRAM that checks what you have written and makes your spelling correct —**spell-check** *v.* [I,T]

spell·er /ˈspɛlɚ/ *n.* [C] **1 a good/bad/poor speller** someone who is good or bad at spelling words correctly **2** a book for teaching spelling

spell·ing /ˈspɛlɪŋ/ *n.* ENG. LANG. ARTS **1** [U] the act of spelling words correctly or the ability to do this: *Ben has always been good at spelling.* | *a spelling mistake* **2** [C] the way in which a word is spelled: +**of** *"Tyre" is the British spelling of "tire."*

ˈspelling bee *n.* [C] a competition for students in a

S

school in which the winner is the one who spells the most words correctly

spe·lunk·ing /spɪˈlʌŋkɪŋ, ˈspilʌŋk-/ *n.* [U] the sport of walking and climbing in CAVES —**spelunker** *n.* [C]

spend /spɛnd/ S1 W1 *v. past tense and past participle* **spent** /spɛnt/
1 MONEY [I,T] to use your money to buy goods or services: *Everyone spends too much at Christmas.* | *I've already* ***spent*** *all my* ***money***. | **spend sth on sth** *We spend about $150 a week on food.* | **spend sth on sb** *Mom never spends any money on herself.* | **spend $5/$10/$20 etc.** *I only want to spend about $20.* | *The $100 for my new shoes was* ***money well spent*** (=a sensible way of spending money).
2 TIME [T] to use time doing a particular thing or pass time in a particular place: *We spent a week in Honolulu.* | *She spends hours on the phone.* | **spend sth doing sth** *I spent most of the weekend cleaning the house.* | *I'm trying to* ***spend*** *more* ***time with*** *my family.*
3 spend the night (at sth) to sleep in a different place from usual through the night: *She spent the night at a friend's.*
4 spend the night with sb to stay for the night and have sex with someone
5 EFFORT [T] to use effort or energy to do something SYN **expend**: *We spent a lot of energy looking for a nice apartment.*
6 spend money like there's no tomorrow/like water/like it's going out of style etc. to spend a lot of money very quickly and carelessly
[**Origin:** 1100–1200 Partly from Latin *expendere* and partly, later, from Old French *despendre*, from Latin *dispendere* **to weigh out**]

spen·der /ˈspɛndɚ/ *n.* [C] someone who spends money: *The casino hopes to attract* ***big spenders*** (=people who like to spend large amounts of money).

spend·ing /ˈspɛndɪŋ/ *n.* [U] the amount of money spent, especially by a government or organization, or the activity of spending money: +**on** *spending on education* | *spending cuts* | **government/public/defense etc. spending** *massive government spending* | **increase/raise/reduce/cut spending** *We've actually increased welfare spending.*

ˈspending ˌmoney *n.* [U] money that you have available to spend on your own personal pleasure

spend·thrift /ˈspɛndˌθrɪft/ *n.* [C] someone who spends money carelessly, even when they do not have a lot of it

spent¹ /spɛnt/ *v.* the past tense and past participle of SPEND

spent² *adj.* **1** already used, and now empty or useless: *spent bullet shells* **2** LITERARY extremely tired **3 be a spent force** to be a political idea or organization that does not have any power or influence anymore

sperm /spɚm/ *n. plural* **sperm** or **sperms** **1** [C] also **sperm cell** BIOLOGY a cell produced by the sex organs of a male animal, which is able to join with the female egg to produce a new life **2** [U] the liquid from the male sex organs that these cells swim in SYN **semen**

sper·ma·ce·ti /ˌspɚməˈsiṭi, -ˈsɛ-/ *n.* [U] a solid oily substance found in the head of the SPERM WHALE and used in making skin creams, CANDLES etc.

sper·mat·o·zo·on /spɚˌmæṭəˈzouɑn, -ˈzouən/ *n. plural* **spermatozoa** /-ˈzouə/ [C] TECHNICAL a SPERM

ˈsperm bank *n.* [C] a place where SEMEN is kept to be used in medical operations that help women to become PREGNANT

ˈsperm count *n.* [C usually singular] a medical measurement of the number of sperm a man has, which shows if he is able to make a woman PREGNANT

sper·mi·cide /ˈspɚməˌsaɪd/ *n.* [C,U] a cream or liquid that kills SPERM, used while having sex to prevent the woman from becoming PREGNANT —**spermicidal** /ˌspɚməˈsaɪdl◂/ *adj.*: *spermicidal jelly*

ˈsperm whale *n.* [C] BIOLOGY a large WHALE, hunted for its oil, fat, and SPERMACETI

spew /spyu/ *v.* **1** also **spew out/forth** [I always + adv./prep.,T] to flow out of something in quantities that are too large, or to make something, especially something unwanted, flow out in this way: +**from/into/over etc.** *Black smoke spewed out from the car's exhaust pipe.* | **spew sth into/over etc. sth** *The factory spews huge amounts of carbon dioxide into the air.* **2** also **spew out/forth** [I always + adv./prep.,T] if you spew a lot of bad or negative things or they spew out of you, you say them very quickly: *The group uses the Internet to spew religious hatred.* **3** [I,T] SPOKEN to VOMIT

SPF **sun protection factor** a number on a bottle of SUNSCREEN that tells you how much protection it gives you from the sun: *SPF 25*

sphere /sfɪr/ Ac *n.* [C] **1** something that has the shape of a ball: *The Earth is not a* ***perfect sphere*** (=it is not perfectly round). **2** a particular area of activity, work, knowledge etc.: *Small business is the fastest-growing sphere of the economy.* | **in the political/economic/public etc. sphere** *reforms in the political sphere* **3** MATH a solid object in the shape of a ball, in which every point on the surface is exactly the same distance from the center. ►see THESAURUS box at **shape¹** → see picture at SHAPE¹ **4 sb's sphere of influence** the area where a person, country, organization etc. has power to control and change things: *America's sphere of influence* [**Origin:** 1200–1300 Old French *espere*, from Latin *sphaera*, from Greek *sphaira* **ball, sphere**]

-sphere /sfɪr/ *suffix* [in nouns] TECHNICAL relating to the air or gases surrounding the Earth: *the atmosphere*

spher·i·cal /ˈsfɪrɪkəl, ˈsfɛr-/ Ac *adj.* having the shape of a sphere

ˌspherical geˈometry *n.* [U] MATH the part of GEOMETRY (=study of shapes) that deals with SPHERES

sphe·roid /ˈsfɪrɔɪd/ *n.* [C] TECHNICAL a shape that is similar to a ball, but not perfectly round

sphinc·ter /ˈsfɪŋktɚ/ *n.* [C] BIOLOGY a muscle that surrounds an opening or passage in your body, and can become tight in order to close it: *the anal sphincter*

sphinx /sfɪŋks/ *n.* [C] an ancient Egyptian image of a lion with a human head, lying down

spic-and-span /ˌspɪk ən ˈspæn/ another spelling of SPICK-AND-SPAN

spice¹ /spaɪs/ *n.* **1** [C,U] one of the various types of powders or seeds that you put into food you are cooking to give it a special taste: *herbs and spices* → see picture at RACK **2** [singular, U] interest or excitement that is added to something: *The secrecy added spice to their affair.* [**Origin:** 1200–1300 Old French *espice*, from Late Latin *species* **spices**] → see also **variety is the spice of life** at VARIETY (5)

spice² *v.* [T] to add spice to food —**spiced** *adj.*: *spiced wine*

spice sth ↔ **up** *phr. v.* **1** to make food taste better by adding spices to it: **spice sth up with sth** *Spice the sauce up with chili powder.* **2** to add interest or excitement to something: *We need some advice on how to spice up our love life.*

spick-and-span, **spic-and-span** /ˌspɪk ən ˈspæn/ *adj.* completely clean and neat

spic·y /ˈspaɪsi/ *adj. comparative* **spicier**, *superlative* **spiciest** **1** spicy food has a pleasantly strong taste, and gives you a pleasant burning feeling in your mouth: *spicy Italian sausage* ►see THESAURUS box at **taste¹** **2** relating to sex and therefore exciting and slightly shocking: *spicy gossip* —**spiciness** *n.* [U]

spi·der /ˈspaɪdɚ/ *n.* [C] a small creature with eight legs, which catches insects using a spiderweb [**Origin:** Old English *spithra*, from *spinnan* **to spin**]

spider

spi·der·web /ˈspaɪdɚˌwɛb/ *n.* [C] a very fine network of sticky threads made by a spider to catch insects SYN **web** → see also COBWEB

spi·der·y /ˈspaɪdəri/ *adj.* covered with or made of lots of long thin uneven lines: *spidery handwriting*

spiel /ʃpil, spil/ *n.* [C] INFORMAL a short speech that someone has used many times before, especially one that is intended to persuade people to buy something

Spiel·berg /ˈspilbɚg/, **Ste·ven** /ˈstivən/ (1947–) a U.S. movie DIRECTOR

spif·fy /ˈspɪfi/ *adj.* INFORMAL looking new, neat, and attractive

spig·ot /ˈspɪgət/ *n.* [C] **1** an outdoor TAP **2** a TAP on a large container that controls the flow of liquid from it

spike¹ /spaɪk/ *n.* [C]
1 POINTED THING something long and thin with a sharp point, especially a pointed piece of metal: *a row of spikes on top of the wall*
2 INCREASE a sudden large increase in the number or rate of something: **+in** *a spike in unemployment*
3 LINE TECHNICAL a sharp point on a GRAPH that shows that the number or rate of something has increased quickly
4 SHOES a) a sharp metal point on the bottom of a sports shoe **b) spikes** [plural] special sports shoes with metal points on the bottom that are worn by people who run races, play GOLF, or play baseball
5 VOLLEYBALL in the game of VOLLEYBALL, a strong hit of the ball that makes it move down to the floor very fast

spike² *v.* **1** [I] if the number or rate of something spikes, it increases quickly and by a large amount: *Energy use has spiked this month.* **2** [T] to add alcohol or a drug to what someone is drinking: **spike sth with sth** *He claimed his drinks had been spiked with drugs.* **3** [T] to push a sharp tool or object into something **4 spike the ball a)** to powerfully throw a football down on the ground to celebrate a TOUCHDOWN **b)** to powerfully hit a VOLLEYBALL down over the net

spik·y /ˈspaɪki/ *adj.* **1** spiky hair is stiff and stands up on top of your head **2** having long sharp points: *a spiky cactus*

spill¹ /spɪl/ S2 *v. past tense and past participle* **spilled** or **spilt** /spɪlt/
1 LIQUID [I,T] if you spill a liquid or if it spills, it accidentally flows over the edge of a container: *I almost spilled my coffee.* | **+on/over etc.** *Oil had spilled onto the concrete.* | **spill sth down/on/over sth** *He spilled paint all over the carpet.*
2 PEOPLE [I always + adv./prep.] if people spill out of somewhere, they move out in large groups: **spill (out) into/onto etc. sth** *People spilled out into the street.*
3 LIGHT [I always + adv./prep.] if light spills somewhere, it shines through a window, door, hole etc. into a place or onto something: **+into/onto/through etc.** *Sunlight spilled into the room.*
4 spill the beans INFORMAL to tell something that someone else wanted you to keep a secret
5 spill your guts INFORMAL to tell someone everything about your private life or about a personal secret
6 spill (sb's) blood LITERARY to kill or wound people
[**Origin:** Old English *spillan* **to kill, destroy, waste**] → see also **cry over spilled milk** at CRY¹ (6)

spill over *phr. v.* **1** if a problem or bad situation spills over, it spreads and begins to affect other places, people etc.: **+into** *The violence has spilled over into neighboring countries.* **2** to develop into a worse situation, feeling etc.: **+into** *The situation could spill over into chaos.*

spill² *n.* [C] **1** an act of spilling something, or an amount of something that is spilled: *an oil spill* **2** a fall from a horse, bicycle etc.: *He* ***took a spill*** *on his motorcycle.* **3** a piece of wood or twisted paper for lighting lamps, fires etc.

spill·age /ˈspɪlɪdʒ/ *n.* [C,U] the act of spilling something, or the amount of something that is spilled SYN **spill**

spill·o·ver /ˈspɪlˌoʊvɚ/ *n.* [C,U] the effect that one situation or problem has on another situation: **a spillover effect/benefit/cost** *The crisis will have a spillover effect on other small banks.*

ˈspillover ˌcost *n.* [C] ECONOMICS a cost involved in the production of goods in large numbers using machinery, that affects people who do not have any control over the number being produced

spill·way /ˈspɪlweɪ/ *n.* [C] a passage that lets water flow over or around a DAM (=wall for holding back water)

spilt /spɪlt/ *v.* a past tense and past participle of SPILL

spin¹ /spɪn/ S3 W3 *v. past tense and past participle* **spun** /spʌn/, **spinning**
1 TURN AROUND [I,T] to turn around and around very quickly, or to make someone or something do this: *The Earth spins as it moves around the sun.* | *The children were spinning a top.* | **spin (sb/sth) around** *The dancers spun around on the stage.* ►see THESAURUS box at **turn¹**
2 OPPOSITE DIRECTION [I,T] to turn your body or a vehicle you are driving quickly so that you are facing in the opposite direction, or to make someone or something do this: *She spun to face him.* | **spin (sb/sth) around** *He spun the car around and took off down the street.*
3 SEEM TO MOVE [I] if something spins, it seems to move and you feel DIZZY, for example because you are shocked, excited, or drunk: *I lay down and the room started to spin.* | *My* ***head was spinning****.*
4 DESCRIBE [T] to present information to the public in a particular way so that they will have a particular opinion of it: *He could spin any story to make the president look good.*
5 spin a yarn/story/tale to tell a story, especially using a lot of imagination
6 INSECT [T] if a SPIDER or insect spins a WEB or COCOON, it produces thread to make it
7 WOOL/COTTON [I,T] to make cotton, wool etc. into thread by twisting it
8 spin your wheels to try to do something without having any success: *I felt like I was just spinning my wheels trying to make him understand.*
9 DRIVE [I always + adv./prep.] to drive or travel quickly: **+past/along etc.** *A Mercedes spun past at about 100 miles per hour.*

spin sth ↔ **off** *phr. v.* **1** to form a separate and partly independent company from parts of an existing company **2** to produce a new television program using characters from another program
[**Origin:** Old English *spinnan*] → see also SPIN-OFF

spin out *phr. v.* if a car spins out, the driver loses control of it and the car spins around

spin² *n.*
1 TURNING [C] an act of turning around quickly, or making something do this: *a series of complicated flips and spins* | *He* ***gave*** *the roulette wheel* ***a spin****.* | *The plane nosedived and* ***went into a spin****.*
2 CAR [C] INFORMAL a short trip in a car for pleasure: *Let's* ***take*** *your new car* ***for a spin****.*
3 BALL [U] if you put spin on a ball in a game such as tennis or SOCCER, you deliberately make the ball turn very quickly so that it is difficult for your opponent to hit
4 POLITICS/BUSINESS [singular, U] the things someone, especially a politician or business person, tells people about a situation in order to influence the way people think: *Company representatives tried to* ***put a*** *positive* ***spin on*** *the lay-offs.* → see also SPIN CONTROL, SPIN DOCTOR

S

5 SB'S ATTITUDE [singular, U] the way someone thinks about a particular subject or the attitude they have toward it SYN angle: +**on** *What's your spin on what's been happening?*
6 **in/into a spin** confused and anxious about what to do, or starting to feel this way: *The latest allegations have Republicans in a spin.*
7 SCIENCE [singular] TECHNICAL a quality of an ELEMENTARY PARTICLE that influences its behavior with other particles

spi·na bif·i·da /ˌspaɪnə ˈbɪfədə/ *n.* [U] MEDICINE a serious condition in which a person's SPINE does not develop correctly before they are born, so that their SPINAL CORD is not protected

spin·ach /ˈspɪnɪtʃ/ *n.* [U] a vegetable with large dark green leaves [**Origin:** 1300–1400 Old French *espinache*, from Arabic *isfanakh*, from Persian] → see picture on page A35

spi·nal /ˈspaɪnl/ *adj.* BIOLOGY relating to or affecting your SPINE: *spinal injuries*

ˈspinal ˌcolumn *n.* [C] BIOLOGY your SPINE

ˈspinal cord *n.* [C] BIOLOGY the thick string of nerves enclosed in your SPINE by which messages are sent to and from your brain → see picture at BRAIN[1]

S

ˈspin conˌtrol *n.* [U] the act of describing a situation in politics or business so that the public has a particular opinion of it

spin·dle /ˈspɪndl/ *n.* [C] **1** a part of a machine shaped like a stick, around which something turns **2** a round pointed stick used for twisting the thread when you are spinning wool **3** BIOLOGY a small structure within a living cell that helps to separate the CHROMOSOMES when the cell is dividing

spin·dly /ˈspɪndli/ *adj.* long and thin in a way that looks weak: *spindly legs*

ˈspin ˌdoctor *n.* [C] POLITICS someone whose job is to give information to the public in a way that gives the best possible advantage to a politician or organization

spine /spaɪn/ *n.* [C] **1** BIOLOGY the row of bones down the center of your back that supports your body and protects your SPINAL CORD SYN **backbone**: *an injury to the spine* → see picture at BRAIN[1] **2** the part of a book that the pages are fastened onto: *a book with a leather spine* **3** BIOLOGY a stiff sharp point on an animal or plant: *a hedgehog's spines* [**Origin:** 1300–1400 Latin *spina*]

ˈspine-ˌchilling *adj.* a spine-chilling story or film is very frightening in a way that people enjoy —**spine-chiller** *n.* [C]

spine·less /ˈspaɪnlɪs/ *adj.* **1** lacking courage and determination: *a spineless coward* **2** BIOLOGY without a spine: *spineless creatures such as jellyfish* —**spinelessly** *adv.* —**spinelessness** *n.* [U]

spin·et /ˈspɪnət/ *n.* [C] **1** a small UPRIGHT PIANO **2** a musical instrument of the 16th and 17th centuries, which is played like a piano

ˈspine-ˌtingling *adj.* making you feel very excited or frightened in an enjoyable way

spin·na·ker /ˈspɪnɪkɚ/ *n.* [C] a sail with three points that is at the front of a boat, used when the wind is directly behind

spin·ner /ˈspɪnɚ/ *n.* [C] **1** someone whose job is to make thread by twisting cotton, wool etc. **2** a thing used for catching fish that moves around and around when pulled through the water

spin·ner·et /ˌspɪnəˈrɛt/ *n.* [C] BIOLOGY a small organ on the body of a SPIDER, from which the SILK comes out of the spider's body when it is making a WEB

spin·ning /ˈspɪnɪŋ/ *n.* [U] a type of exercise in which a group of people ride EXERCISE BIKES together while they listen to music or a teacher

spinning jen·ny /ˈspɪnɪŋ ˌdʒɛni/ *n. plural* **spinning jennies** [C] an industrial machine used in past times for making cotton, wool etc. into thread

ˈspinning wheel *n.* [C] a simple machine consisting of a wheel on a frame, that people used in their homes in the past for making cotton, wool etc. into thread

ˈspin-off *n.* [C] **1** a television program involving characters that were previously in another program or movie **2** something good or useful that happens as an unexpected result of something else **3** a separate and partly independent company that is formed from parts of an existing company, or the action of forming a company in this way **4** a product such as a CD, book, or toy that is related to a movie, television show etc. SYN **tie-in**

Spi·no·za /spɪˈnoʊzə/, **Ba·ruch** /bəˈruk/ (1632-1677) a Dutch PHILOSOPHER

spin·ster /ˈspɪnstɚ/ *n.* [C] OLD-FASHIONED an unmarried woman, usually one who is not young anymore and who seems unlikely to marry —**spinsterhood** *n.* [U]

ˌspin the ˈbottle *n.* [U] a game in which people sitting in a circle spin a bottle in the middle and when the bottle stops spinning and points to someone, that person must do something, such as kiss another person

spin·y /ˈspaɪni/ *adj. comparative* **spinier**, *superlative* **spiniest** having a lot of SPINES: *a spiny cactus*

spi·ral¹ /ˈspaɪrəl/ *n.* [C] **1** a line in the form of a curve that winds around a central point, moving farther away from the center all the time **2** a process, usually a harmful one, in which something gradually but continuously rises, falls, gets worse etc.: +**of** *a spiral of violence* | *The news sent stocks into* ***a downward spiral.*** | **an inflationary spiral** (=a continuing rise in wages and prices because an increase in one causes an increase in the other) [**Origin:** 1500–1600 Medieval Latin *spiralis* (adjective), from Latin *spira* **coil**] —**spiral** *adj.*

spiral² *v.* **spiraled** also **spiralled**, **spiraling** also **spiralling** [I] **1** [always + adv./prep.] to move in the shape of a spiral: +**to/around/up/down etc.** *Yellow smoke spiraled upward.* **2** if a situation spirals, it gets worse, more violent etc. in a way that cannot be controlled: *The controversy has* ***spiraled out of control.*** **3** if debt or the cost of something spirals, it increases quickly in a way that cannot be controlled —**spiraling** *adj.*: *the spiraling cost of health care*

ˌspiral ˈnotebook *n.* [C] a book made of plain pieces of paper that are attached to a metal spiral, which you can write notes in

ˌspiral ˈstaircase *n.* [C] a set of stairs arranged in a circular pattern so that they go around a central point as they get higher

spire /spaɪɚ/ *n.* [C] a roof that rises steeply to a point on top of a tower, especially on a church

spi·ril·lum /spaɪˈrɪləm/ *n. plural* **spirilla** /-lə/ [C] BIOLOGY BACTERIA (=small living things which can cause illness or disease) with a SPIRAL or curved shape that must have oxygen to live

spir·it¹ /ˈspɪrɪt/ S2 W2 *n.*
1 CHARACTER [singular, U] the qualities that make someone live or behave the way they do, and make them different from other people: *I'm 85, but I still feel young* ***in spirit.*** | **a wild/independent/proud etc. spirit** *She was impressed by his independent spirit.* | *Such challenges cannot defeat* ***the human spirit.*** → see also FREE SPIRIT, **a kindred spirit/soul** at KINDRED[1], -SPIRITED
2 spirits [plural] the way someone feels at a particular time, for example if they are cheerful or sad: **in good/high spirits** *He is in good spirits despite his illness.* | **lift/raise sb's spirits** *The warm morning sun lifted our spirits.* | *They didn't let the loss* ***dampen their spirits*** (=make them less cheerful). | *She listens to music to* ***keep her spirits up*** (=avoid becoming less cheerful). | **sb's spirits lift/rise/sink** (=someone becomes more or less cheerful)
3 DETERMINATION [U] APPROVING courage, energy, and determination: *She played* ***with great spirit.*** | *I admire the team's* ***fighting spirit.*** | *Years in prison did not* ***break*** *Mandela's* ***spirit*** (=make him lose courage and determination).
4 NO BODY [C] a creature without a physical body that some people believe exists, such as an ANGEL or a dead person who has returned to this world and has strange

or magical powers: *evil spirits* ▸see THESAURUS box at ghost[1]
5 SOUL [C] the part of someone that you cannot see, that consists of the qualities that make up their character, which many people believe continues to live after the person has died: *She felt sure his spirit was in heaven.* → see also SOUL
6 ATTITUDE/FEELING [singular, U] the attitude that you have toward something or while you are doing something: +**of** *a new spirit of cooperation* | **team/community/public etc. spirit** (=a strong feeling of belonging to a particular group and wanting to help them)
7 TYPICAL QUALITIES [singular] the set of ideas, beliefs, feelings etc. that are typical of a particular period in history, a place, or a group of people: +**of** *Tourism has not destroyed the spirit of Bali.* | **the spirit of the age/times** *His beliefs conflicted with the spirit of the age.*
8 INTENTION [U] the way a law or rule was intended to be used when it was written: *His actions may not be illegal, but they violate* ***the spirit of the law****.* → see also THE LETTER OF THE LAW
9 DRINK [C usually plural] OLD-FASHIONED a strong alcoholic drink such as WHISKEY or BRANDY
10 get/enter into the spirit (of sth) to start to feel as happy, excited etc. as the people around you: *Judith just couldn't get into the spirit of the holiday.*
11 the Spirit the HOLY SPIRIT
12 in spirit if you say you will be somewhere in spirit or with someone in spirit, you cannot be with them but you will be thinking about them: *If I can't make it to the wedding, I'll be there in spirit.*
13 that's the spirit SPOKEN used to express approval of someone's behavior or attitude
14 the spirit is willing but the flesh is weak HUMOROUS used to say that you would like to do something, but are not strong enough, either physically or mentally, to do it
15 when/as the spirit moves you when you feel that you want to do something
[**Origin:** 1200–1300 Anglo-French, Latin *spiritus* **breath, spirit**]

spirit² *v.*
spirit sb/sth ↔ **away/off** *phr. v.* to take someone or something away quickly and secretly

spir·it·ed /ˈspɪrɪṭɪd/ *adj.* APPROVING having or showing a lot of energy and determination: *a spirited and independent girl* | **a spirited defense/debate etc.** *a spirited discussion of the issue*

-spirited /spɪrɪṭɪd/ [in adjectives] **sweet-spirited/tough-spirited/rebellious-spirited etc.** having a particular type of character → see also HIGH-SPIRITED, LOW-SPIRITED, MEAN-SPIRITED, PUBLIC-SPIRITED

spir·it·less /ˈspɪrɪtlɪs/ *adj.* **1** having no energy or determination **2** not cheerful: *spiritless celebrations* —**spiritlessness** *n.* [U]

spir·i·tu·al¹ /ˈspɪrɪtʃuəl, -tʃəl/ W3 *adj.* [only before noun] **1** relating to your spirit rather than to your body or mind: *Yoga has spiritual as well as physical benefits.* **2** relating to religion SYN **religious**: *a spiritual leader* **3** very interested in your soul, God, or religion, but not necessarily in a particular religion: *She's deeply spiritual.* **4 a spiritual home** a place where you feel you belong because you share the ideas and attitudes of that society —**spiritually** *adv.*

spiritual² *n.* [C] a religious song of the type sung originally by African-Americans

spir·i·tu·al·ism /ˈspɪrɪtʃʊˌlɪzəm/ *n.* [U] the belief that dead people may send messages to living people, usually through a MEDIUM (=someone with special powers) —**spiritualist** *n.* [C] —**spiritualistic** /ˌspɪrɪtʃʊˈlɪstɪk/ *adj.*

spir·i·tu·al·i·ty /ˌspɪrɪtʃuˈæləṭi/ *n.* [U] the quality of being interested in or related to religion or religious matters

spir·i·tu·ous /ˈspɪrɪtʃuəs/ *adj.* [only before noun] TECHNICAL containing alcohol

spit¹ /spɪt/ *v. past tense and past participle* **spit** *or* **spat** /spæt/, **spitting**
1 LIQUID FROM YOUR MOUTH [I] BIOLOGY to force a small amount of SALIVA (=the liquid in your mouth) out of your mouth: +**at/on/into** *Somebody spit at me.* | *Eli, stop spitting on the floor.*
2 FOOD/DRINK ETC. [T always + adv./prep.] to force something out of your mouth SYN **spit out**: **spit sth into/on/onto sth** *Don't spit your gum on the ground.*
3 SAY STH [T] to say something quickly in a very angry way SYN **spit out**: *"You're worthless!" Greg spat out.*
4 SMALL PIECES [I,T] to send out small pieces of something, for example fire or hot oil, into the air: *The volcano began rumbling and spitting ash on July 3.*
5 CAT [I] if a cat spits, it makes short angry sounds
6 be within spitting distance (of sb/sth) SPOKEN INFORMAL to be very close to someone or something
7 I could (just) spit SPOKEN INFORMAL used to say that you are very angry or annoyed
[**Origin:** Old English *spittan*]
spit sth ↔ **out** *phr. v.* **1** to force something out of your mouth: *If you don't like it, spit it out.* **2** to say something quickly in a very angry way: *She spat out his name with contempt.* **3 spit it out** SPOKEN INFORMAL used to ask someone to tell you something that they seem too frightened or embarrassed to say: *Come on Jean, spit it out!*
spit sth ↔ **up** *phr. v.* **1** to bring food or drink up from your stomach and out through your mouth SYN **vomit**: *The baby is always crying and spitting up.* **2 spit up blood** to cough so that blood comes out through your mouth, especially because you are injured or sick

spit² *n.* **1** [U] BIOLOGY the watery liquid that is produced in your mouth SYN **saliva** **2** [C] a long thin stick that you put through meat so that you can turn it when cooking it over a fire **3** [C] EARTH SCIENCE a long narrow piece of land that sticks out into the ocean, a river etc. **4 spit and polish** INFORMAL the act of cleaning something thoroughly

spit·ball /ˈspɪt˺bɔl/ *n.* [C] a small piece of paper that children put in their mouths and then spit or throw at each other

spite¹ /spaɪt/ *n.* **1 in spite of sth** without being affected or prevented by something SYN **despite**: *In spite of her success, Sue is depressed.* | *She loves him* ***in spite of the fact that*** *he drinks too much.* → see Word Choice box at DESPITE **2** [U] a feeling of wanting to hurt or upset people, for example because you are JEALOUS or think you have been unfairly treated: *He hid her purse* ***out of spite*** (=because of spite). | **pure/sheer spite** **3 in spite of yourself** if you do something in spite of yourself, you do it although you did not expect or intend to do it: *She laughed in spite of herself.*

spite² *v.* [T only in infinitive] **do sth (just) to spite sb** to do something deliberately in order to annoy or upset someone: *The neighbors make noise just to spite us.* → see also **cut off your nose to spite your face** at CUT OFF (10)

spite·ful /ˈspaɪtfəl/ *adj.* deliberately nasty to someone in order to hurt or upset them: *a spiteful remark* —**spitefully** *adv.* —**spitefulness** *n.* [U]

spit·fire /ˈspɪtfaɪɚ/ *n.* [C] someone, especially a woman, who becomes angry very easily

ˌspitting ˈimage *n.* **be the spitting image of sb** to look exactly like someone else

spit·tle /ˈspɪṭl/ *n.* [U] SALIVA (=liquid from your mouth) that is outside your mouth

spit·toon /spɪˈtun/ *n.* [C] a container used in the past to SPIT into

Spitz /spɪts/, **Mark** (1950–) a U.S. swimmer famous for winning seven GOLD MEDALS at the Olympic Games in Munich in 1972

splash¹ /splæʃ/ *v.*
1 LIQUID FALLS/HITS STH [I] if a liquid splashes, it hits or falls on something, usually making a noise: +**against/on/over** *The waves splashed against the rocks.*

S

2 MAKE SB/STH WET [T] to make someone or something wet by making water or another liquid hit them: *The kids were splashing each other.* | **splash sth on/over etc. sth** *He splashed cold water on his face.* | **splash sb/sth with sth** *A car drove past, splashing all of us with mud.*
3 MAKE LIQUID FLY [I] to make liquid fly up in the air with a loud noise by hitting it or by moving around in it or through it: +**around** *The boys were splashing around in the ocean.* | +**through** *The truck splashed through a stream.*
4 splash sth across/on/over sth [usually passive] if a newspaper splashes a story or picture across its pages, it prints it very large so that it is easy to notice: *The story was splashed across the front page.*
5 POUR [T always + adv./prep.] to put liquid somewhere in a careless way
splash down *phr. v.* if a SPACECRAFT splashes down, it lands in the ocean
[**Origin:** 1700–1800 *plash* **to splash** (16–19 centuries)] → see also SPLASHDOWN

splash² *n.* [C]
1 SOUND the sound of a liquid hitting something or being moved around quickly: *She fell into the river with a loud splash.*
2 LIQUID an amount of liquid that splashes, or the act of splashing: +**of** *a splash of cold water*
3 make a splash INFORMAL to do something that gets a lot of public attention: *His performance made quite a splash on Broadway.*
4 COLOR a small area of a bright color: +**of** *a splash of color*
5 SMALL AMOUNT [usually singular] a small amount of liquid added to a drink or food: +**of** *a splash of lemon*
6 MARK a mark made by a liquid splashing onto something else

S

splash·down /ˈsplæʃdaʊn/ *n.* [C,U] a landing by a SPACECRAFT in the ocean

splash·y /ˈsplæʃi/ *adj. comparative* **splashier**, *superlative* **splashiest** big, bright, or very easy to notice SYN **flashy**

splat¹ /splæt/ *n.* [singular] INFORMAL a noise like something wet hitting a surface hard

splat² *v.* **splatted**, **splatting** [I,T] to put or drop something soft or wet onto a surface with enough force to make a noise, or to hit a surface and make this noise

splat·ter /ˈsplæt̬ɚ/ *v.* [I,T] to cover something with small drops of liquid: *Grease splattered everywhere.* | **splatter sb/sth with sth** *A passing car splattered us with mud.* | **be splattered with sth** *The sheets were splattered with blood.* —**splatter** *n.* [C,U]

splay /spleɪ/ also **splay out** *v.* [I,T usually passive] if fingers or legs splay or are splayed, they spread farther apart, often in a way that looks strange

ˌsplay-ˈfooted *adj., adv.* with your feet wide apart and flat

spleen /splin/ *n.* **1** [C] BIOLOGY an organ near your stomach that controls the quality of your blood **2** [U] FORMAL anger: *The meeting gave him a chance to **vent** his **spleen*** (=express his anger).

splen·did /ˈsplɛndɪd/ *adj.* FORMAL **1** excellent or very fine: *You're all doing a splendid job.* **2** beautiful and impressive: *a splendid view* [**Origin:** 1600–1700 Latin *splendidus*, from *splendere* **to shine**] —**splendidly** *adv.*: *The plan worked splendidly.*

splen·dif·er·ous /splɛnˈdɪfərəs/ *adj.* INFORMAL HUMOROUS splendid

splen·dor /ˈsplɛndɚ/ *n.* [plural, U] impressive beauty and richness, or features that show this quality, especially in a large building or large place: *the splendors of imperial Rome*

sple·net·ic /splɪˈnɛt̬ɪk/ *adj.* LITERARY often in a bad mood and angry

splice¹ /splaɪs/ *v.* [T] **1** to join the ends of two pieces of rope, film etc. so that they form one continuous piece **2** to combine parts of different GENES to try to give specific features or qualities to an animal or plant

splice² *n.* [C] **1** the place where the ends of two things such as rope or film have been joined together so that they form one continuous piece **2** the place where parts of GENES have been joined together → see also COMMA SPLICE

splic·er /ˈsplaɪsɚ/ *n.* [C] a machine for joining pieces of film or recording TAPE neatly together

splint /splɪnt/ *n.* [C] a flat piece of wood, metal etc., used for keeping a broken bone in position while it HEALS

splin·ter¹ /ˈsplɪntɚ/ *n.* [C] a small sharp piece of wood, glass, or metal, that has broken off a larger piece: *I've got a splinter in my finger.* | +**of** *splinters of glass* —**splintery** *adj.* → see also SLIVER

splinter² *v.* [I,T] **1** to separate into smaller groups or parts, or to make a large group or organization do this, especially because of a disagreement: *The civil rights movement began to splinter.* **2** if a hard substance such as wood, glass, stone etc. splinters, or someone or something splinters it, it breaks into thin sharp pieces

ˈsplinter group also **ˈsplinter organiˌzation** *n.* [C] a group of people that has separated from a political or religious organization because they have different ideas

split¹ /splɪt/ S2 *v. past tense and past participle* **split**, *present participle* **splitting**
1 DISAGREE [I,T] if a group of people splits or is split, it divides into two or more groups, because one group strongly disagrees with the other: *The issue has split legal scholars.* | +**over/on** *Lawmakers split along party lines over the budget.* | +**from/with** *The left wing split from the main organization.* | **split sth in two/split sth down the middle** *The war has split the nation in two.*

split

2 INTO PARTS [I,T] to divide or separate into different parts or groups, or to make something do this: *The trail splits when you reach the lake.* | +**into** *The corporation will split into three smaller companies.* | **split sth into sth** *I'm going to split the class into three groups.* | **split in two/half** *After independence, the country split in two.* ►see THESAURUS box at **separate²**
3 BREAK OR TEAR [I,T] if something splits or if you split it, it tears or breaks, usually along a straight line: *He's outside splitting logs.* | *The branch split under our weight.* | **split open/apart** *One of the bags had split open.* | **split (sth) in two/half** *Split the rolls in half.* ►see THESAURUS box at **break¹**
4 SHARE [T] to divide something into separate parts, so that two or more people each get a part SYN **divide**: *They sold the house and split the proceeds.* | **split sth with/between/among sb** *I'll split this sandwich with you.* | **split the bill/cost/check** *They agreed to split the cost of repairs.* | **split sth down the middle/split sth fifty-fifty** (=divide something equally) | **split sth three/four etc. ways** (=into three, four, or more equal parts)
5 split the difference to agree on an amount that is exactly between two amounts that have been mentioned
6 INJURE [T] if you or something else splits your head or your lip, it gets badly cut, especially because you fall against something or get hit by something: *She fell and **split** her **head open**.*
7 STOCK [I,T usually passive] ECONOMICS if STOCK in a company splits or is split, it is divided into more shares that are each less valuable, but together are worth the same amount as the original shares
8 COMPETITION [T] if two teams split a competition, they both have equal SCORES in it
9 split hairs to argue that there is a difference between

two things, when the difference is really too small to be important
10 LEAVE [I] SLANG to leave quickly
11 split your sides (laughing) to laugh very hard

split off *phr. v.* **1 split sth ↔ off** to completely separate from a group, or to make part of a group do this: *They plan to split off part of the business.* | **+from** *Norway split off from Sweden in 1905.* **2 split sth ↔ off** to break something away from something so that it is completely separate, or to break off in this way: *A piece of the cliff split off and fell to the valley floor.*

split up *phr. v.* **1 split sb ↔ up** if people split up or someone or something splits them up, they end their marriage or relationship: *My parents split up when I was three.* | *Why would she try to split them up?* | **+with** *Taylor's splitting up with his wife.* **2 split sb ↔ up** if people who work or perform together split up or someone or something splits them up, they stop working or performing together: *The band split up in 2003.* **3 split sb/sth ↔ up** to divide into separate groups, or to make a pair or group of people or things do this: *Let's split up and meet back here in a half an hour.* | **split (sb/sth) up into sth** *The teacher split up the class into three groups.* **4 split sth ↔ up** to divide or separate something into different parts: **split sth up into sth** *You should really split the article up into sections.*

split[2] S3 *n.* [C]
1 DISAGREEMENT a serious disagreement that divides an organization or group of people into smaller groups: **+in/within** *a deep split within the church* | **+between/among** *a split between party moderates and conservatives* | **+over** *a split over economic policy*
2 TEAR a tear or crack in something made of cloth, wood etc.: **+in** *a split in the seam of his pants*
3 SHARE the way in which something, especially money, is shared between several people: **a three-way/four-way etc. split** (=a share of something that is divided equally between three, four etc. people) | **a 50-50/60-40/70-30 etc. split** (=a split in which each person or group gets 50%; one person gets 60% and the other 40% etc.)
4 DIFFERENCE a clear separation or difference between two things, ideas, opinions etc.: *a startling split between men's and women's views of sexual harassment*
5 BAND/TEAM ETC. the act of ending a relationship in which you work or perform together with other people: **+with** *the band's split with their manager*
6 RELATIONSHIP the act of ending a marriage or a similar relationship: **+with** *her split with her husband*
7 STOCK an occasion when the STOCK in a company is divided into more shares that are each less valuable, but together are worth the same amount as the original shares SYN **stock split**
8 do the splits also **do a split** to spread your legs wide apart so that your legs touch the floor along their whole length → see also BANANA SPLIT

split[3] *adj.* [not usually before noun] **1** in a state of disagreement, with two groups of people having directly opposing opinions: **+on/over** *The party is split over immigration laws.* | *Voters are* ***evenly split*** *on the war.* **2** if a society or other group is split into two or more groups, it contains two very separate groups: *Society remains split along racial lines.* **3** having a tear or a crack

ˌsplit ˈend *n.* **1 split ends** [plural] a condition of someone's hair in which the ends have split into several parts **2** [C] in football, a RECEIVER who lines up several yards away from the rest of the team

ˌsplit inˈfinitive *n.* [C] ENG. LANG. ARTS a phrase in which you put an adverb or other word between "to" and an INFINITIVE, as in "to easily win." Some people think this is incorrect English.

ˌsplit-ˈlevel *adj.* a split-level house, room, or building has floors at different heights in different parts —**split-level** *n.* [C]

ˌsplit ˈpea *n.* [C] a dried PEA split into its two halves

ˌsplit personˈality *n.* [C] NOT TECHNICAL a condition in which someone has two very different ways of behaving

ˌsplit ˈscreen *n.* [C] a method of showing two different scenes or pieces of information at the same time on a movie, television, or computer screen

ˌsplit ˈsecond *n.* **a split second** an extremely short period of time: *For a split second I thought we were going to crash.* —**split-second** *adj.*: *a split-second decision*

ˌsplit ˈshift *n.* [C] a period of work that is divided into two or more parts on the same day

ˌsplit ˈticket *n.* [C] POLITICS a vote in U.S. elections in which the voter has voted for some CANDIDATES of one party and some of the other party —**split-ticket** *adj.*

split·ting /ˈsplɪt̬ɪŋ/ *adj.* a splitting HEADACHE is very bad

splotch /splɑtʃ/ *n.* [C] INFORMAL a large mark with an irregular shape, for example of mud, paint etc.: *big greasy splotches* —**splotchy** *adj.*

splurge /splɚdʒ/ *v.* [I] INFORMAL to spend more money than you can usually afford: **+on** *We splurged on an expensive hotel.* —**splurge** *n.* [C]

splut·ter /ˈsplʌt̬ɚ/ *v.* [I] to SPUTTER

Spock /spɑk/, **Dr. Benjamin** (1903–1998) a U.S. doctor whose books giving advice on how parents should take care of their children had a great influence on parents

spoil /spɔɪl/ S3 *v.*
1 RUIN STH [T] to have a bad effect on something, so that it is not attractive, enjoyable, useful etc.: *We didn't let the rain spoil our day.* | *I don't want to spoil the surprise.* | *Mom got home early, which* ***spoiled everything*** (=completely ruined our plan).
2 FOOD [I] to start to decay: *Most of the food in the refrigerator had spoiled.*
3 CHILD [T] to give a child whatever they want or let them do what they want, often with the result that they behave badly: *His grandparents* ***spoil him rotten.***
4 TREAT KINDLY [T] to take care of or treat someone in a way that is too kind or generous: *Roses? You're spoiling me, Bill.* | ***Spoil yourself*** *and select the deluxe package.*
5 ALWAYS EXPECT QUALITY to make someone get used to something good, so that they do not like experiencing or getting anything less good: *We've been spoiled by all the good restaurants around here.*
6 VOTING [T] POLITICS to mark a BALLOT wrongly so that your vote is not included
7 spoil your appetite to eat something before a meal, with the result that you do not feel hungry and don't want or enjoy your meal
8 be spoiling for a fight/argument to be very eager to fight or argue with someone
[**Origin:** 1200–1300 Old French *espoillier*, from Latin *spoliare* **to strip, rob**] → see also SPOILER, SPOILS

spoil·age /ˈspɔɪlɪdʒ/ *n.* [U] TECHNICAL the process of food spoiling, or the condition of being spoiled

spoiled /spɔɪld/ *adj.* **1** someone, especially a child, who is spoiled is impolite and behaves badly because they are always given what they want or allowed to do what they want: *Mary, you're just* ***a spoiled brat*** (=a spoiled annoying child). | *That kid is* ***spoiled rotten*** (=very spoiled). **2** used to having a pleasant life or good experiences: *We're really spoiled with the good weather here.* **3** spoiled food has started to decay

spoil·er /ˈspɔɪlɚ/ *n.* [C] **1** a raised part on a car that stops the car from lifting off the road at high speeds **2** a piece of an aircraft wing that can be lifted up to slow the airplane down **3** information about how a book, movie, TV show etc. ends that spoils the surprise of finding out what happens **4** a person or team that spoils another's winning record **5** a book, article etc. that is produced to take attention away from another similar book and spoil its success

spoils /spɔɪlz/ *n.* [plural] **the spoils** FORMAL or LITERARY **a)** things taken by an army from a defeated enemy, or things taken by thieves: *the spoils of war* **b)** profits or advantages gained through political power or through competition → see also **to the victor go/belong the spoils** at VICTOR (2)

spoil·sport /ˈspɔɪlspɔrt/ *n.* [C] INFORMAL someone who spoils other people's fun

ˈspoils ˌsystem *n.* [C] the practice of giving jobs or advantages to your supporters when you have been elected to a government position. In the U.S., President Jackson was an early supporter of this practice.

spoke¹ /spoʊk/ *v.* the past tense of SPEAK

spoke² *n.* [C] one of the thin metal bars that connect the outer ring of a wheel to the center, especially on a bicycle → see picture at BICYCLE¹

spok·en¹ /ˈspoʊkən/ *v.* the past participle of SPEAK

spoken² *adj.* **1** [usually before noun] used to describe the form of language that you speak rather than write → see also WRITTEN: **spoken English/Chinese/German etc.** *Her spoken English was poor.* | *Slang is a feature of spoken language.* | **the spoken word** (=spoken language) **2 be spoken for a)** if something is spoken for, you cannot buy it or use it because it is being kept for someone else who has already claimed or paid for it **b)** if someone is spoken for, they are married or already have a serious relationship with someone → see also SOFT-SPOKEN, WELL-SPOKEN

S

-spoken /spoʊkən/ *suffix* [in adjectives] speaking in a particular way: *a soft-spoken man* (=who speaks quietly)

ˌspoken-ˈword *adj.* relating to language that is spoken rather than written or sung

spokes·man /ˈspoʊksmən/ W2 *n. plural* **spokesmen** /-mən/ [C] someone, especially a man, who has been chosen to speak officially for a group, organization, or government: **+for** *a spokesman for NASA*

spokes·per·son /ˈspoʊksˌpɚsən/ *n. plural* **spokespeople** /-ˌpipəl/ [C] a spokesman or spokeswoman

spokes·wom·an /ˈspoʊksˌwʊmən/ *n. plural* **spokeswomen** /-ˌwɪmɪn/ [C] a woman who has been chosen to speak officially for a group, organization, or government: *a hospital spokeswoman*

spo·li·a·tion /ˌspoʊliˈeɪʃən/ *n.* [U] FORMAL the violent or deliberate destruction or spoiling of something

sponge¹ /spʌndʒ/ *n.* **1** [C,U] a piece of a soft natural or artificial substance that is full of small holes and is used for washing or cleaning something **2** [C] BIOLOGY a simple sea creature from which natural sponge is produced **3 like a sponge** used to say that someone can learn and remember things easily: *She absorbed information like a sponge.* [**Origin:** 1000–1100 Latin *spongia*, from Greek]

sponge² *v.* **1** [T always + adv./prep.] to remove liquid or a mark with a wet cloth or sponge: **sponge sth off/out/up** *Sponge up the wine right away.* **2** [I] to get money, free meals etc. from other people, without doing anything for them: **+off** *He's been sponging off his friends for years.* **3** [T] to wash something with a wet cloth or sponge **4** [T always + adv./prep.] to put paint, a liquid etc. on a surface using a sponge

ˈsponge bath *n.* [C] an act of washing your whole body with a wet cloth, usually when you cannot use a BATHTUB or SHOWER

ˈsponge cake *n.* [C,U] a light cake made from eggs, sugar, and flour but usually no butter or oil

spong·er /ˈspʌndʒɚ/ *n.* [C] someone who gets money, free meals etc. from other people and does nothing for them in return

spong·y /ˈspʌndʒi/ *adj.* *comparative* **spongier**, *superlative* **spongiest** soft and full of holes that contain air or liquid like a SPONGE: *The earth was spongy underfoot.* —**sponginess** *n.* [U]

spon·sor¹ /ˈspɑnsɚ/ W3 *n.* [C] **1** a person or company that pays for a show, broadcast, sports event etc. in exchange for the right to advertise at that event: *one of the sponsors of the Olympic Games* **2** a person, organization, or country that supports an activity and helps it to succeed: *The U.S. is one of the main sponsors of the agreement.* **3** POLITICS someone who officially introduces or supports a proposal for a new law: *the bill's sponsors* **4** a person or company who officially agrees to help someone else, or to be responsible for what they do: *You cannot get a work visa without an American sponsor.* **5** someone who agrees to give someone else money for a CHARITY if they walk, run, swim etc. a particular distance **6** someone who officially supports someone who is being BAPTIZED or CONFIRMED → see also GODPARENT [**Origin:** 1600–1700 Latin *spondere* **to promise**]

sponsor² *v.* [T] **1** to give money to or pay for a sports event, show, broadcast etc., especially so that you can advertise your products at the event: *The race is being sponsored by the Traveler's Club.* **2** POLITICS to officially support a proposal for a new law: *The two senators sponsored the bill together.* **3** to officially agree to help someone or be responsible for what they do: *To get a visa, you need someone to sponsor you.* **4** to agree to give someone money for CHARITY if they walk, run etc. a particular distance **5** to officially agree to support someone who is being BAPTISED or CONFIRMED in a Christian church

spon·sor·ship /ˈspɑnsɚˌʃɪp/ *n.* [U] **1** support, usually financial support for an activity or event, often so that you can advertise at that event: *the tobacco industry's sponsorship of sporting events* **2** an agreement to help someone or be responsible for what they do: *the sponsorship of new immigrants* **3** the condition of having officially introduced or supported a proposal for a new law: *the Congressman's sponsorship of the bill*

spon·ta·ne·i·ty /ˌspɑntəˈneɪət̬i, ˌspɑntˀnˈeɪ-/ *n.* [U] the quality of being spontaneous: *He loved her spontaneity and directness.*

spon·ta·ne·ous /spɑnˈteɪniəs/ *adj.* **1** happening or done without being planned or organized: *spontaneous applause* **2** APPROVING doing things when you want to, without planning or organizing them first: *I'm trying to be more spontaneous.* **3** TECHNICAL happening suddenly in a natural way [**Origin:** 1600–1700 Late Latin *spontaneus*, from Latin *sponte* **of your own free will**] —**spontaneously** *adv.* —**spontaneousness** *n.* [U]

sponˌtaneous comˈbustion *n.* [U] burning caused by chemical changes inside something rather than by heat from outside

spoof¹ /spuf/ *n.* [C] a funny book, play, movie etc. that copies a serious or important one and makes it seem silly: **+of/on** *a spoof on spy films of the '60s* [**Origin:** 1800–1900 invented name for a game involving deception] —**spoof** *v.* [T]

spoof² *adj.* [only before noun] **1** designed as a spoof **2** used to describe emails, WEBSITES etc. that are designed to look as if they belong to real companies and trick people into giving out personal information, CREDIT CARD numbers etc.: *spoof emails*

spook¹ /spuk/ *v.* [T] INFORMAL to frighten a person or an animal: *Something must have spooked the horses.*

spook² *n.* [C] INFORMAL **1** a GHOST **2** SLANG a SPY

spook·y /ˈspuki/ *adj.* *comparative* **spookier**, *superlative* **spookiest** INFORMAL strange or frightening, especially in a way that makes you think of GHOSTS: *a spooky old house*

spool /spul/ *n.* [C] a small CYLINDER or object shaped like a small wheel that you wind thread, wire, TAPE, camera film etc. around

spoon¹ /spun/ S2 *n.* [C] **1** a tool used for eating, cooking, or serving food, consisting of a small bowl-shaped part and a long handle: *knives, forks, and spoons* **2** a SPOONFUL [**Origin:** Old English *spon* **piece of wood split off**] → see also **be born with a silver spoon in your mouth** at BORN (7), GREASY SPOON, SOUP SPOON, SPOONFUL, WOODEN SPOON

spoon² *v.* **1** [T always + adv./prep.] to put food somewhere with a spoon **2** [I,T] to lie on your side next to someone so that your front is against their back → see also SPOONING

spoon·bill /ˈspunbɪl/ *n.* [C] BIOLOGY a type of large water bird with long legs and a long flat BILL

spoo·ner·ism /ˈspunəˌrɪzəm/ *n.* [C] ENG. LANG. ARTS a phrase in which the speaker makes the mistake of exchanging the first sounds of two words, with a funny result, for example "sew you to a sheet" for "show you to a seat" [**Origin:** 1900–2000 William *Spooner* (1844–1930), British university teacher who supposedly often made such mistakes]

ˈspoon-feed *v. past tense and past participle* **spoon-fed** [T] **1** to give too much information and help to someone: *Teachers should avoid spoon-feeding facts to students.* **2** to feed someone, especially a baby, with a spoon

spoon·ful /ˈspunfʊl/ *n.* [C] the amount that a SPOON will hold: +**of** *a spoonful of sugar*

spoon·ing /ˈspunɪŋ/ *n.* [U] OLD-FASHIONED romantic behavior, especially kissing

spoor /spʊr, spɔr/ *n.* [C] BIOLOGY the track of foot marks or FECES (=solid waste) left by a wild animal

spo·rad·ic /spəˈrædɪk/ *adj.* happening often but not regularly or continuously SYN **intermittent**: *sporadic gunfire* [**Origin:** 1600–1700 Medieval Latin *sporadicus*, from Greek, from *sporaden* **scattered in different places**] —**sporadically** /-kli/ *adv.*

spore /spɔr/ *n.* [C] BIOLOGY a cell that is like a seed and is produced by living things which have only a single set of GENES, such as MUSHROOMS or BACTERIA. Spores can develop into new mushrooms, bacteria etc.: ***Fungus spores** are often spread by the wind.* [**Origin:** 1800–1900 Modern Latin *spora*, from Greek, **act of planting seeds, seed**]

spork /spɔrk/ *n.* [C] a plastic object shaped like a spoon but with points on the end like a fork, usually given to customers in FAST FOOD restaurants

sport¹ /spɔrt/ S2 W1 *n.*
1 GAMES [C] a physical activity in which people compete against each other: *Soccer is Mark's favorite sport.* | *I've been **playing sports** all my life.* | *I'm not very good at **team sports**.* → see also SPECTATOR SPORT, SPORTS

THESAURUS

Places where people play sports
field a large area of ground, usually covered with grass, where team sports are played: *a soccer field*
stadium a large sports field with seats all around it for people to watch team sports or track and field competitions: *a football stadium*
ballpark/park a stadium where baseball is played
court an area with lines painted on the ground, for tennis, basketball etc.: *a volleyball court*
diamond the area in a baseball field that is within the shape formed by the four bases, also used to refer to the whole field
track a special area for running on
gym a large room with machines which you can use to do exercises
(swimming) pool a place where you can swim
health club a building where you can do various different sports

▸see THESAURUS box at **game¹**

2 OUTDOOR ACTIVITY [C] an outdoor activity such as hunting, fishing, HIKING etc.: *Fishing is a solitary sport.* → see also BLOOD SPORT
3 CHEERFUL PERSON also **good sport** a cheerful person who is willing to help or let you do what you want and does not complain about things: *We teased her a lot but she was always **a good sport about** it.* | ***Be a sport** and lend me your car.*
4 a good/bad/poor sport someone who can deal with defeat without becoming angry or upset, or someone who cannot do that: *I don't like playing with him – he's not a very good sport.*
5 FUN [U] FORMAL fun or amusement: *Lions are usually hunted **for sport**, not for food.*
6 BOY SPOKEN OLD-FASHIONED a friendly way of talking to a boy
7 make sport of sb FORMAL to make someone seem stupid by joking about them or copying them
8 the sport of kings OLD-FASHIONED horse racing
[**Origin:** 1300–1400 *disport*] → see also WATER SPORTS, WINTER SPORTS

sport² *v.* **1** to wear or show something publicly, especially in a proud way: *Will was sporting a gold chain around his neck.* **2** [I] LITERARY to play together happily

ˈsport coat *n.* [C] a SPORTS JACKET

sport·fish·ing /ˈspɔrtˌfɪʃɪŋ/ *n.* [U] the activity of fishing as a HOBBY, rather than a job

sport·ing /ˈspɔrt̬ɪŋ/ *adj.* **1 a)** [only before noun] relating to sports: *a sporting event* | *The store sells clothes and **sporting goods*** (=sports equipment). **b)** relating to or joining in outdoor sports such as hunting or horse racing: *the sporting life* **2 a sporting chance (of doing sth)** a fairly good chance of succeeding or winning

spor·tive /ˈspɔrt̬ɪv/ *adj.* LITERARY **1** enjoying fun and making jokes in a friendly way SYN **playful** **2** interested in sports

ˈsport jacket *n.* [C] a SPORTS JACKET

sports /spɔrts/ S3 *adj.* [only before noun] **1** relating to sports or used for sports: *a sports tournament* | *sports equipment* **2** on the subject of sports: *the sports section* (=part of a newspaper)

ˈsports bra *n.* [C] a special type of BRA that is designed for women to wear while playing sports

ˈsports car *n.* [C] a low fast car, often with a roof that can be folded back

sports·cast /ˈspɔrts-kæst/ *n.* [C] a television broadcast of a sports game —**sportscaster** *n.* [C]

ˈsports ˌcenter *n.* [C] a building where many different types of indoor sport are played

ˈsports coat *n.* [C] a SPORTS JACKET

ˈsports day *n.* [C] a FIELD DAY

ˈsport shirt *n.* [C] a SPORTS SHIRT

ˈsports jacket *n.* [C] a man's comfortable JACKET, worn on informal occasions

sports·man /ˈspɔrtsmən/ *n. plural* **sportsmen** /-mən/ [C] a man who plays several different sports, especially outdoor sports → see also SPORTSWOMAN

sports·man·like /ˈspɔrtsmənˌlaɪk/ *adj.* behaving in a fair, honest, and polite way when competing in sports, or showing this quality

sports·man·ship /ˈspɔrtsmənˌʃɪp/ *n.* [U] behavior that is fair, honest, and polite in a game or sports competition: **good/bad sportsmanship** *We try to teach the kids good sportsmanship.*

ˈsports ˌscholarship *n.* [C] money given to some college students to pay for all or part of their education, because they are good enough to play for one of the college's sports teams

ˈsports shirt *n.* [C] a shirt for men that is worn on informal occasions

sports·wear /ˈspɔrtswɛr/ *n.* [U] **1** clothes that are appropriate for informal occasions **2** clothes that are worn to play sports or when you are relaxing

sports·wom·an /ˈspɔrtsˌwʊmən/ *n. plural* **sportswomen** /-ˌwɪmɪn/ [C] a woman who plays many different sports, especially outdoor sports

sports·writ·er /ˈspɔrtsˌraɪt̬ɚ/ *n.* [C] someone whose job is to write about sports for a newspaper or magazine

ˈsport top *n.* [C] a special top that can be moved up and down to open or close a bottle, used especially on plastic bottles of drinking water

ˌsport-uˈtility ˌvehicle *n.* [C] a type of vehicle that is bigger than a car and is made for traveling over rough ground

sport·y /ˈspɔrt̬i/ *adj. comparative* **sportier**, *superlative* **sportiest** INFORMAL designed to look attractive in a bright informal way: *a sporty little car* —**sportiness** *n.* [U]

S

spot[1] /spɑt/ S1 W2 *n.* [C]
1 **PLACE** a particular place or area, especially a pleasant place where you spend time: *a quiet spot on the beach* | *It took 20 minutes to find a parking spot.* | **on this/that spot** *There was once a church on this spot.* | **the exact/very/same spot** *This is said to be the exact spot where the king was executed.* | **a camping/swimming/vacation spot** (=a place that is suitable for a particular activity) ▸see THESAURUS box at **place**[1]
2 **AREA OF COLOR** a small round area of color that is a different color from the rest of the surface around it: *a white dog with brown spots*
3 **MARK** a small mark on something, especially one that is made by a liquid: **+on** *grease spots on her blouse* | **+of** *A few spots of blood were found in the car.* ▸see THESAURUS box at **mark**[2]
4 **DIFFERENT AREA** a small area on a surface that is rougher, smoother, softer etc. than the rest: *a bald spot on the top of his head*
5 **PLACE ON BODY** a particular place on your body, especially one that is uncomfortable: *Is this spot painful?*
6 **on the spot a)** immediately, without careful planning: *They offered me a job on the spot.* **b)** at the place where something is happening: *Fortunately, there was a doctor on the spot.*
7 **POSITION** a position in a competition or event: *a spot on the Olympic team*
8 **ADVERTISEMENT** a short radio or television advertisement, especially one for a politician: *a 30-second spot on the local radio station*
9 **APPEARANCE** a short appearance on television, radio etc.: *a* **guest spot** *on "The Tonight Show"*
10 **PART** a particular part of a performance, a piece of writing etc.: *The essay is good, but a few spots still need some work.*
11 **put sb on the spot** to make someone feel embarrassed by asking them to do something or answer a question they do not want to, especially in front of other people: *You shouldn't put friends on the spot by asking them to hire your family members.*
12 **SITUATION** INFORMAL a difficult situation: *They* ***put*** *us* ***in a*** *very difficult* ***spot*** *by canceling at the last minute.* | **a tough/rough/difficult etc. spot** *They're in a really tough spot right now.*
13 **MARK ON SKIN** a small round red area on someone's skin that shows that they are sick: *a chickenpox spot*
14 **LIGHT** a SPOTLIGHT
15 **a five-spot/ten-spot etc.** SPOKEN OLD-FASHIONED a piece of paper money worth five dollars, ten dollars etc. → see also BLIND SPOT, **a bright spot** at BRIGHT (9), **a high point/spot** at HIGH[1] (12), **hit the spot** at HIT[1] (16), **hot spot** at HOT (31), **be rooted to the spot/chair/floor etc.** at ROOTED (2), **have a soft spot for sb/sth** at SOFT (11), TROUBLE SPOT, **a weak point/spot** at WEAK[1] (12)

spot[2] S3 W3 *v.* **spotted, spotting** [T]
1 **SEE** to notice someone or something, especially when you are looking for them or when they are difficult to see: *I finally spotted Greg in the crowd.* | **spot sb/sth doing sth** *He was spotted leaving the building at 4:30 a.m.* | **be easy/hard/difficult to spot** *Drug addicts are often easy to spot.* ▸see THESAURUS box at **see**[1]
2 **NOTICE QUALITY** to notice that someone or something has a special ability or quality that can be used and developed: *At the audition he was spotted by a talent scout.*
3 **GAME** to give the other player in a game an advantage: **spot sb sth** *He spotted me six points and he still won.*
4 **HELP** to make sure that someone does not get hurt while they do an activity such as GYMNASTICS or WEIGHTLIFTING, by being there to help them move in the correct way if needed
5 **LIQUID** if liquid spots a surface, small drops of it fall on the surface → see also SPOTTED

spot[3] *adj.* [only before noun] TECHNICAL involving paying for or delivering something immediately, not at some future time: *spot prices for crude oil*

ˌspot ˈcheck *n.* [C] a quick examination of a few things or people from a group, to check whether everything is correct or satisfactory: *Customs officers make random spot checks.* —**spot-check** *v.* [I,T + for]

spot·less /ˈspɑtlɪs/ *adj.* **1** completely clean: *The kitchen was spotless.* ▸see THESAURUS box at **clean**[1] **2** a spotless reputation, record, character etc. shows that someone is completely honest, has a good character, and good past behavior: *a spotless military record* —**spotlessly** *adv.* —**spotlessness** *n.* [U]

spot·light[1] /ˈspɑtlaɪt/ *n.* **1 a)** [C] a very powerful light whose beam can be directed at someone or something **b)** [C usually singular] the round area of light made by this beam on the ground, stage etc.: *She stepped into the spotlight to make her speech.* **2 the spotlight** attention that someone receives in the newspapers, on television etc.: *The announcement put Rogers* ***in the spotlight*** (=receiving a lot of attention) *again.* **3 shine/put/turn etc. a spotlight on sth** to direct attention to something: *The disaster has thrown a spotlight on the nation's poor.*

spotlight[2] *v. past tense and past participle* **spotlighted** or **spotlit** [T] **1** to direct attention to someone or something: *The article spotlights the growth of Islam in the U.S.* **2** to shine a strong beam of light on something

spot·ted /ˈspɑt̬ɪd/ *adj.* [usually before noun] having small round marks on the surface: *a spotted dog* | **+with** *The patio was spotted with bird droppings.*

spot·ter /ˈspɑt̬ɚ/ *n.* [C] **1** someone whose job is to look for a particular thing or person: **a weather/traffic/celebrity etc. spotter** *a weather spotter for the National Weather Service* **2** someone who prevents someone else from getting hurt while they do an activity like GYMNASTICS or WEIGHTLIFTING, by being there to help them move correctly if needed → see also TREND-SPOTTER

spot·ty /ˈspɑt̬i/ *adj. comparative* **spottier**, *superlative* **spottiest 1** good only in some parts, but not in others SYN **patchy**: *a spotty performance* **2** happening or done sometimes, but not regularly, as you expect: *spotty bus service* **3** covered with spots

spouse /spaʊs/ *n.* [C] FORMAL a husband or wife: *Spouses and children are welcome.* [**Origin:** 1100–1200 Old French *espous(e)*, from Latin *sponsus* **promised (in marriage)**] —**spousal** /ˈspaʊzəl/ *adj.*

spout[1] /spaʊt/ *n.* [C] **1** a small tube or pipe on a container that you pour liquid out through: *the spout of a teapot* **2** a sudden strong stream of liquid that comes out of somewhere very fast → see also WATERSPOUT

spout[2] *v.* **1** [I always + adv./prep.,T] if liquid or fire spouts from somewhere or something spouts it, it comes out very quickly in a powerful stream: *A statue in the fountain was spouting water.* | **+from** *Oil continues to spout from the damaged well.* **2** [I,T] also **spout off** INFORMAL to talk a lot about something in a boring way, especially without thinking about what you are saying: *He's just spouting nonsense again.* | **+about** *We all had to listen to him spouting off about politics.* **3** [I] if a WHALE spouts, it sends out a stream of water from a hole in its head

sprain /spreɪn/ *v.* [T] MEDICINE to damage a joint in your body by suddenly twisting it: *Amy fell and sprained her ankle.* ▸see THESAURUS box at **hurt**[1] —**sprain** *n.* [C]

sprang /spræŋ/ *v.* the past tense of SPRING

sprat /spræt/ *n.* [C] a small European HERRING

sprawl[1] /sprɔl/ *v.* [I always + adv./prep.] **1** also **sprawl out** to lie or sit with your arms or legs stretched out in a lazy or careless way: **+in/on etc.** *She sprawled out lazily on the bed.* **2** if buildings or a town sprawl, they spread out over a wide area in a messy and unattractive way: *The suburbs sprawl outward from the city center.* **3 send sb sprawling** to hit or push someone so that they fall over in an uncontrolled way

sprawl[2] *n.* [U] **1** a large area of buildings that are spread out in a messy and unattractive way: *More freeways will just mean more* ***urban sprawl.*** **2** [singular] a position in which you have your arms or legs stretched out in a lazy or careless way

sprawled /sprɔld/ *adj.* [not before noun] **sprawled (out) in/on etc. sth** lying or sitting with your arms or legs stretched out in a lazy or careless way: *He was sprawled in an armchair.*

sprawl·ing /ˈsprɔlɪŋ/ *adj.* spreading over a wide area in a messy or unattractive way: *a sprawling city*

spray[1] /spreɪ/ S3 *v.* **sprays, sprayed, spraying** **1** [T] to force liquid out of a container, HOSE etc. in a stream of small drops into the air or onto someone or something: **spray sb/sth with sth** *She sprayed herself with perfume.* | **spray sth on/onto/over sb/sth** *Someone had sprayed blue paint on his car.* | **spray crops/plants etc.** (=cover them with liquid chemicals to protect them from insects or disease) **2** [I always + adv./prep.] if liquids or small pieces spray somewhere, they are quickly scattered through the air: +**over/around/from etc.** *Grass cuttings sprayed from the mower.* **3 spray (sb/sth with) bullets/gunfire** to shoot many bullets from a gun quickly: *Gunmen sprayed the crowd with bullets.* **4** [I,T] if a cat sprays, it sprays URINE around an area to show other cats where it lives

spray[2] S3 *n. plural* **sprays**
1 SPECIAL LIQUID [C,U] liquid that is forced out of a special container in a stream of very small drops: *hair spray* | *bug spray* (=for killing insects)
2 OCEAN [U] water in very small drops blown from the ocean or a wet surface: *I felt the spray from the waves on my face.*
3 CONTAINER [C] a can or other container with a special tube that forces liquid out in a stream of small drops: *an aerosol spray*
4 FLOWERS [C] an attractive arrangement of flowers, jewels, or small branches used for decoration: +**of** *a spray of irises*
5 a spray of bullets/dust etc. a lot of very small objects or pieces moving quickly through the air
6 LIQUID [C] an amount of liquid that goes through the air in very small drops: +**of** *a spray of saliva*
7 ANIMAL [C] liquid that an animal such as a SKUNK forces out of its body in very small drops, that usually has a strong smell → see also PEPPER SPRAY

ˈspray ˌbottle *n.* [C] a bottle with a pump inside it and a special top that you press in order to make liquid come out of it

ˈspray can *n.* [C] a can that keeps what is inside it under pressure so it can be sprayed out, used for substances such as paint, HAIR SPRAY, and cooking oil

spray·er /ˈspreɪɚ/ *n.* [C] a piece of equipment used for SPRAYing liquid, especially to protect crops from insects or disease

ˈspray gun *n.* [C] a piece of equipment held like a gun, which SPRAYS liquid in very small drops

ˈspray paint *n.* [U] paint that is SPRAYed from a can —**spray-paint** *v.* [I,T]

spread[1] /sprɛd/ S2 W2 *v. past tense and past participle* **spread**
1 AFFECT MORE PEOPLE [I,T] if an activity, problem, feeling etc. spreads or someone or something spreads it, it starts involving or affecting more and more people: *As violence spreads, more people are leaving their homes.* | +**throughout/to/across etc.** *The practice has spread from cities to villages.* | **spread sth throughout/to across etc. sth** *The attacks spread terror throughout the region.*
2 LIQUID/FIRE ETC. [I,T] if liquid, fire, smoke etc. spreads or someone or something spreads it, it moves so that it covers a larger area: *The forest fire is spreading out of control.* | +**through/across/over etc.** *A pool of liquid started to spread across the floor.* | **spread sth through/across/over etc. sth** *High winds have spread the flames to neighboring houses.*
3 DISEASE a) [I,T] if disease spreads or someone or something spreads it, it is passed from one person or animal to another, so that it affects more and more people or animals: *The disease spread rapidly among the poor.* | *Malaria is spread by mosquitoes.* **b)** [I] to affect more and more of someone's body: +**to** *The cancer has spread to her liver.*
4 INFORMATION a) [I] to become known about by more and more people: +**to/through/over etc.** *Rumors about Amy spread through the school.* | ***Word spread that*** *Mitchell had resigned.* | *News of her arrival* ***spread like wildfire*** (=became known very quickly). **b)** [T] to tell a lot of people about something: *Johnson is working to* ***spread the word*** *about the benefits of prenatal care.* | **spread lies/rumors/gossip** *After they broke up, he spread nasty rumors about her.*
5 OPEN/ARRANGE [T] to open something so that it covers a bigger area, or arrange a group of things so that they cover a flat surface SYN **spread out**: **spread sth on/over/across etc. sth** *He spread a towel on the sand.* | *She spread her papers across the table.*
6 SOFT SUBSTANCE a) [T] to put a soft substance onto a surface in order to cover it: **spread sth on/over sth** *She spread the frosting evenly over the cake.* | **spread sth with sth** *Spread the bread lightly with butter.* **b)** [I] to be soft enough to be put onto a surface in order to cover it: *If you warm up the butter it'll spread more easily.* → see picture on page A32
7 spread across/over/throughout etc. sth also **be spread across/over etc. sth** to cover, stretch, or exist over a large area SYN **spread out**: *Water lilies spread across the surface of the pond.* | *The 250 stores are spread throughout the country.*
8 PEOPLE/PLANTS/ANIMALS [I always + adv./prep.] to begin to live or grow in other areas or countries: +**throughout/over/to etc.** *The hemp plant spread to India sometime before 800 B.C.*
9 spread (out/apart) your legs/arms/fingers etc. to move your legs, arms etc. as far apart as possible: *She spread her arms wide.*
10 OVER TIME [T] to do something or make something happen gradually over a period of time, rather than all at once SYN **spread out**: **spread sth over sth** *The musical performances will be spread over three days.*
11 SHARE [T] to share work, responsibility, money etc. among several people or things: *Spreading the work will help us meet the project deadline.* | *We can spread the risk by investing in several areas.* | *The city plans to* ***spread the burden*** *of new taxes as evenly as possible.*
12 spread yourself thin to try to do too many things at the same time so that you do not do any of them effectively
13 EXPRESSION [I always + adv./prep.] to gradually become noticeable on someone's face or mouth: +**across/over** *A big smile spread across her face.*
14 spread 'em SPOKEN used by police to tell someone to stand with their arms and legs wide apart so their bodies can be searched
15 spread seeds/manure/fertilizer to scatter seeds, MANURE etc. on the ground
16 spread its wings if a bird or insect spreads its wings, it opens them wide
17 spread your wings to start to have an independent life and experience new things: *Living on my own gave me a chance to spread my wings.*
[**Origin:** Old English *sprædan*]

spread out *phr. v.* **1** if a group of people spread out, they move apart from each other so that they cover a wider area: *We spread out and began to search the field.* **2 spread sth ↔ out** to open something so that it covers a bigger area, or arrange a group of things so that they cover a flat surface: *He spread the map out on the desk.* **3 spread sth ↔ out** to do something or make something happen gradually over a period of time, rather than all at once: *You can spread out the payments over a year.* **4** also **be spread out** to cover, stretch, or exist over a large area: *The old town spreads out below the cliff.*

spread[2] *n.*
1 the spread of sth the increase in the area or number of people affected by something, or in the number of people who do something; the development of something so that it affects or is known about by more people or involves a larger area: *the spread of disease*
2 SOFT FOOD [C,U] a soft food that you spread on bread: **cheese/chocolate etc. spread** (=cheese, chocolate etc. in a soft form)
3 ARTICLE/ADVERTISEMENT [C] a special article or adver-

S

tisement in a newspaper or magazine: *a two-page spread in Sunday's paper*
4 LARGE MEAL [C] INFORMAL a large meal for several guests on a special occasion: *They had quite a spread at the wedding reception.*
5 CLOTH [C] a BEDSPREAD
6 HAND/WINGS [U] the area covered when the fingers of a hand, or a bird's wings, are fully stretched
7 GAME [singular] the number of points between the SCORES of two opposing teams: *a four-point spread*
8 MONEY [singular] ECONOMICS the difference between the prices at which something is bought and sold, or the interest rates for lending and borrowing money
9 FARM [C] a large area of land owned by one person, especially a farm or RANCH
10 RANGE [C usually singular] a range of people, things, or numbers: *a broad spread of investments*
11 AREA [singular] the total area in which a group of things exists: *the spread of the bullet holes*
12 a spread of land/water an area of land or water → see also **middle-aged spread** at MIDDLE-AGED (2)

spread-ea·gled /ˌsprɛd ˈigəld◂/ also **spread-eagle** *adj.* lying with arms and legs stretched out

spread·sheet /ˈsprɛdʃit/ *n.* [C] **1** an arrangement of information about sales, taxes, profits etc. in COLUMNS and rows **2** also **spreadsheet program** [C], **spreadsheet software** [U] COMPUTERS a type of computer program that produces spreadsheets

spree /spri/ *n.* [C] a short period of time in which you do a lot of something that you enjoy, especially spending money or drinking alcohol: *Mom **went on a** shopping **spree** and bought three new outfits.* | **a buying/drinking/shooting etc. spree** *Tyson began his crime spree by robbing a liquor store.*

sprig /sprɪg/ *n.* [C] a small stem or part of a branch with leaves or flowers on it: +**of** *a sprig of parsley*

spright·ly /ˈspraɪtli/ *adj. comparative* **sprightlier**, *superlative* **sprightliest** **1** a sprightly old person is still active and full of energy **2** done with a lot of energy —**sprightliness** *n.* [U]

spring¹ /sprɪŋ/ S2 W2 *n.*
1 SEASON [C,U] the season between winter and summer, when leaves and flowers appear: *It stays cold until early spring.* | *The white blossoms appear **in the spring**.* | *They were married **in the spring of** 1997.* | *The store just opened **this spring**.* | **last/next spring** (=the spring before or after this spring) | *spring flowers*
2 WATER [C] a place where water comes up naturally from the ground: *There are several hot springs in the area.*
3 PIECE OF METAL [C] something, usually a twisted piece of metal, that will return to its previous shape after it has been pressed down or pulled → see also BOX SPRING
4 BED/CHAIR ETC. [U] the ability of a chair, bed etc. to return to its normal shape after being pressed down: *There's not much spring left in this mattress.*
5 a spring in sb's step a way of walking that shows someone is happy and full of energy
6 SUDDEN JUMP [singular] a sudden quick movement or jump in a particular direction

spring² *v. past tense* **sprang** /spræŋ/ or **sprung** /sprʌŋ/, *past participle* **sprung**
1 JUMP [I always + adv./prep.] to move suddenly and quickly in a particular direction, especially by jumping: +**out of/from/towards etc.** *Tom sprang out of bed and ran downstairs.* | *The puppy sprang up and caught the ball.* | *Ward **sprang to** his **feet** (=stood up suddenly) when she entered the room.*

spring out

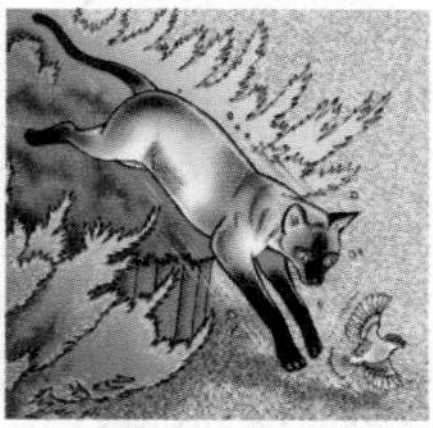

2 MOVE SUDDENLY [I always + adv./prep.] if something springs back, open etc., it moves quickly, suddenly, and with force: +**back/up** *The branch sprang back (=after being pushed away) and hit him in the face.* | **spring open/shut** *As she turned the key, the door sprang open.*
3 spring to (sb's) mind if someone or something springs to mind, you immediately think of them: *Two questions spring to mind.*
4 spring into action to suddenly start taking action: *Church members have sprung into action to save the building.*
5 spring to/into life to suddenly start moving or start working: *Finally, the engine sprang to life.*
6 EXPRESSION/TEARS [I always + adv./prep.] to appear suddenly on someone's face or in their eyes: +**into/to** *Tears sprang to his eyes.*
7 spring a leak if a boat or a container springs a leak, it begins to let liquid in or out through a crack or hole
8 spring into existence/being to suddenly begin to exist
9 spring to sb's defense to quickly defend someone who is being criticized
10 spring a trap **a)** if an animal springs a trap, it makes the trap move and catch it **b)** to trick someone into saying or doing something
11 spring a surprise to make something unexpected or unusual happen
12 spring to attention if soldiers spring to attention, they stand suddenly upright
13 PRISON [T] INFORMAL to help someone leave prison or escape from there → see also **hope springs eternal** at HOPE² (7)

spring for sth *phr. v.* INFORMAL to pay for something: *I'll spring for dinner tonight.*

spring from sth *phr. v.* to be caused by something: *Most of my inner strength springs from my religious beliefs.*

spring sth **on** sb *phr. v.* to tell someone some news that surprises or shocks them: *It's not fair to spring this on her without any warning.*

spring up *phr. v.* to suddenly appear or start to exist: *New universities sprang up all over the country.*

spring·board /ˈsprɪŋbɔrd/ *n.* [C] **1** something that helps you to start doing something or be successful, especially in your CAREER: +**for/to** *The movie was his springboard to fame.* **2** a strong board for jumping on or off, used when DIVING or doing GYMNASTICS

spring·bok /ˈsprɪŋbɑk/ *n.* [C] a small South African DEER that can run fast

ˌspring ˈbreak *n.* [C] a vacation from school in the spring that is usually one or two weeks long

ˌspring ˈchicken *n.* [C] **sb is no spring chicken** HUMOROUS used to say that someone is not young anymore

ˌspring-ˈcleaning *n.* [U] the process of cleaning a house thoroughly, usually once a year —**spring-clean** *v.* [I,T]

spring·er span·iel /ˌsprɪŋɚ ˈspænyəl/ *n.* [C] a type of SPANIEL (=type of dog)

ˌspring ˈfever *n.* [U] a sudden feeling of energy and a desire to do something new and exciting that you have in the spring

Spring·field /ˈsprɪŋfild/ the capital city of the U.S. state of Illinois

ˌspring ˈonion *n.* [C] a GREEN ONION

ˈspring roll *n.* [C] an EGG ROLL

ˌspring ˈtide *n.* [C] EARTH SCIENCE a large rise and fall in the level of the ocean at the time of the NEW MOON and the FULL MOON. The sun, moon, and Earth are all in a line at this time, which causes a stronger GRAVITATIONAL pull on the ocean than usual. → see also NEAP TIDE

spring·time /ˈsprɪŋtaɪm/ *n.* [U] the time of the year when it is spring

ˌspring ˈtraining *n.* [U] the period during which a baseball team gets ready for competition

spring·y /ˈsprɪŋi/ *adj. comparative* **springier**, *superlative* **springiest** something that is springy comes back to its former shape after being pressed, pulled, or walked on

sprin·kle¹ /ˈsprɪŋkəl/ *v.* **1** [T] to scatter small drops of liquid or small pieces of something: **sprinkle sth on/over sth** *He had sprinkled rose petals on the bed.* | **sprinkle sb/sth with sth** *Sprinkle the clay with water.* → see picture on page A32 **2** [I] if it is sprinkling, it is raining lightly

sprinkle sth **with** sth *phr. v.* to put some jokes, phrases, objects etc. in every part of something, especially something such as a speech or piece of writing: *He sprinkles his stories with the names of famous people.*

sprinkle² *n.* [C] **1** small pieces of food, or a light layer of these: *chocolate sprinkles* | +**of** *a sprinkle of coconut* **2** a light rain

sprin·kler /ˈsprɪŋklɚ/ *n.* [C] **1** a piece of equipment with holes that is on the ground, used for scattering water on grass or soil **2** a piece of equipment with holes that is on a ceiling and scatters water if there is a fire

sprin·kling /ˈsprɪŋklɪŋ/ *n.* **a sprinkling of sth** a small quantity or amount of something: *a sprinkling of snow*

sprint¹ /sprɪnt/ *v.* [I] to run very fast for a short distance: +**along/across/up etc.** *Lewis sprinted across the finish line.* ►see THESAURUS box at **run¹** [**Origin:** 1500–1600 from a Scandinavian language]

sprint² *n.* **1** [singular] a short period of running very fast **2** [C] a short race in which runners run very fast, swimmers swim very fast etc. over a short distance: *a 200-meter sprint*

sprint·er /ˈsprɪntɚ/ *n.* [C] someone who runs in fast races over short distances

sprite /spraɪt/ *n.* [C] a FAIRY, especially one who is graceful or who likes playing tricks on people

spritz /sprɪts/ *v.* [T] to SPRAY a liquid in short bursts —**spritz** *n.* [C] *a spritz of perfume*

spritz·er /ˈsprɪtsɚ/ *n.* [C,U] a drink made with SODA WATER and white wine

sprock·et /ˈsprɑkɪt/ *n.* [C] **1** also **sprocket wheel** a wheel with a row of teeth (TOOTH) that fit into and turn something such as a bicycle chain or a photographic film with holes **2** one of the teeth on a wheel of this kind

sprout¹ /spraʊt/ *v.* **1** [I] BIOLOGY if leaves or BUDS sprout, they appear and begin to grow **2** [I,T] BIOLOGY if vegetables, seeds, or plants sprout, they start to grow, producing SHOOTS, or BUDS: *Trees were sprouting new leaves.* | *The seeds had begun to sprout.* **3** [I + adv./prep.] also **sprout up** to appear suddenly in large numbers: *Office buildings are sprouting up everywhere.* **4** [I,T] to grow suddenly, or grow something suddenly, especially hair, horns, or wings: *Jim seemed to have sprouted a beard overnight.* [**Origin:** Old English *sprutan*]

sprout² *n.* [C] **1** [usually plural] BIOLOGY an ALFALFA seed that has grown a short stem and is eaten **2** a BEAN SPROUT **3** BIOLOGY a new growth on a plant SYN **shoot** **4** a BRUSSELS SPROUT

spruce¹ /sprus/ *n.* [C,U] a tree that grows in northern countries and has short leaves shaped like needles

spruce² *v.*

spruce up *phr. v.* **1 spruce sth ↔ up** INFORMAL to make yourself or something look neater and cleaner: *We wanted to spruce the house up before selling it.* **2 spruce yourself up** INFORMAL to make yourself look neater and cleaner: *Meg went upstairs to spruce up before dinner.*

sprung /sprʌŋ/ *v.* a past tense and the past participle of SPRING

spry /spraɪ/ *adj. comparative* **sprier** or **spryer**, *superlative* **spriest** or **spryest** a spry old person is active and cheerful —**spryly** *adv.*

spud /spʌd/ *n.* [C] INFORMAL a POTATO

spume /spyum/ *n.* [U] LITERARY a type of FOAM that forms on top of waves when the ocean is rough

spun /spʌn/ *v.* the past tense and past participle of SPIN

spunk /spʌŋk/ *n.* [U] INFORMAL APPROVING the quality of being brave and determined and having a lot of energy —**spunky** *adj.*

spur¹ /spɚ/ *n.* [C]
1 ON A BOOT a sharp pointed object on the heel of a rider's boot which is used to encourage a horse to go faster
2 on the spur of the moment without planning ahead of time: *I bought the ticket on the spur of the moment.* → see also SPUR-OF-THE-MOMENT
3 INFLUENCE a fact or event that makes you try harder to do something: +**to** *The speech was a spur to action for many people.*
4 BONE a short piece of bone that grows out inside a part of your foot or body where it should not
5 RAILROAD a railroad track or road that goes away from a main line or road
6 LAND EARTH SCIENCE a piece of high ground that sticks out from the side of a hill or mountain
7 CHICKEN the stiff sharp part that sticks out from the back of a male chicken's leg
8 BRANCH a small short branch that grows off a larger branch, especially on a fruit tree

spur² *v.* **spurred, spurring** **1** [T] to make an improvement or change happen faster: *Lower taxes would spur investment.* **2** [T] also **spur on** to encourage someone to try harder in order to succeed: *The teammates spurred each other on.* | **spur sb (on) to (do) sth** *Her misfortunes spurred her to write.* | *The thought of losing our house* ***spurred*** *me* ***into action*** (=made me start doing something). **3** [I,T] to encourage a horse to go faster, especially by kicking it with the spurs on your boots

spu·ri·ous /ˈspyʊriəs/ *adj.* **1** not based on facts or good reasoning and not GENUINE or true SYN **false**: *a spurious claim* **2** insincere: *spurious sympathy* [**Origin:** 1500–1600 Late Latin *spurius*, from Latin (noun), **child of unmarried parents**] —**spuriously** *adv.* —**spuriousness** *n.* [U]

spurn /spɚn/ *v.* [T] LITERARY to refuse to accept someone or something, especially because you think you are better than they are [**Origin:** Old English *spurnan*]

ˌspur-of-the-ˈmoment *adj.* [only before noun] a spur-of-the-moment decision or action is made or done suddenly without planning

spurt¹ /spɚt/ *v.* **1** [I,T] if liquid, flames etc. spurt from something or something spurts them out, they pour out of it quickly and suddenly and with force: *The wound was spurting blood.* | +**from/out of** *Flames spurted from the engine.* ►see THESAURUS box at **flow¹**, **pour** **2** [I always + adv./prep.] to suddenly start moving more quickly, especially for a short time

spurt² *n.* [C] **1** a stream of liquid, flames etc. that comes out of something suddenly and with force: +**of** *spurts of flame* **2** a short sudden increase of activity, effort, or speed: *a growth spurt* | *the recent spurt in sales* **3 in spurts** if something happens or is done in spurts, it happens suddenly and for short periods of time

Sput·nik, sputnik /ˈspʊtnɪk, ˈspʌt-/ *n.* [C,U] HISTORY an early Soviet SATELLITE. Sputnik 1 was the first artificial satellite that went around the Earth, in 1957.

sput·ter /ˈspʌt̬ɚ/ *v.* **1** [I] if something such as an engine or a fire sputters, it makes short soft uneven noises like very small explosions: *The engine sputtered and died.* **2** [I,T] to talk quickly in short confused phrases, especially because you are angry or shocked: *"What do you mean?" Annabelle sputtered.* **3** [I] also **sputter along** if a system, team, machine etc. sputters, it does not work very effectively: *The country's move toward democracy is sputtering along.*

spu·tum /ˈspyut̬əm/ *n.* [U] BIOLOGY liquid in your mouth which you have coughed up from your lungs

spy¹ /spaɪ/ *n. plural* **spies** [C] someone whose job it is to find out secret information about another country, organization, or group: *an enemy spy*

spy² *v.* **spies, spied, spying** **1** [I] to secretly collect information about an enemy country or an organization you are competing against: +**for** *He was accused of spying for North Korea.* **2** [T] LITERARY to suddenly see

S

someone or something, especially after searching for them SYN spot —**spying** *n.* [U]

spy on sb *phr. v.* to watch someone secretly: *We sneaked upstairs to spy on my sister.*

spy·glass /ˈspaɪglæs/ *n.* [C] a small TELESCOPE used by SAILORS in the past

ˈspy ˌmaster, spymaster *n.* [C] a spy who is responsible for a group of spies

spy·ware /ˈspaɪwɛr/ *n.* [U] COMPUTERS computer programs that secretly record information about which WEBSITES you use and send the information to other people or companies

sq. the written abbreviation of "square"

squab /skwɑb/ *n.* [C,U] BIOLOGY a young PIGEON, or the meat of this bird

squab·ble /ˈskwɑbəl/ *v.* [I] to argue continuously about something unimportant: +**about/over** *They're always squabbling over money.* ►see THESAURUS box at argue —**squabble** *n.* [C]

squad /skwɑd/ *n.* [C] **1** the group of police officers responsible for dealing with a particular type of crime: **the drug/riot/vice etc. squad** *The bomb squad was called in.* **2** an organized group of players that make up a sports team: *a football squad* **3** a small group of soldiers working together for a single purpose: *a drill squad* **4** a group of CHEERLEADERS [**Origin:** 1600–1700 French *escouade*, from *escadre*, from Italian *squadra* **square**] → see also DEATH SQUAD, FIRING SQUAD, PEP SQUAD

S

ˈsquad car *n.* [C] a car used by police when they are on duty SYN **patrol car**

squad·ron /ˈskwɑdrən/ *n.* [C] a military force consisting of a group of aircraft or ships

squal·id /ˈskwɑlɪd/ *adj.* **1** dirty and disgusting, because of a lack of care or money: *squalid living conditions* **2** involving DISHONESTY or low moral standards: *a squalid affair* → see also SQUALOR

squall¹ /skwɔl/ *n.* [C] a sudden strong wind, especially one that brings rain or snow

squall² *v.* [I] if a baby or child squalls, it cries loudly

squal·or /ˈskwɑlɚ/ *n.* [U] the condition of being SQUALID: *The refugees are forced to **live in squalor**.*

squan·der /ˈskwɑndɚ/ *v.* [T] to carelessly waste money, opportunities, time etc. on things that are not useful: **squander sth on sth** *He squandered his money on drinking and gambling.* —**squanderer** *n.* [C]

Squan·to /ˈskwɑntoʊ/ (?1585–1622) a Native American who helped the first English people to come to live in America, by showing them where to hunt and fish and how to plant corn

square¹ /skwɛr/ S3 *adj.*

1 SHAPE MATH having four straight equal sides and 90° angles inside each corner: *a square table* ►see THESAURUS box at **shape¹** → see picture at SHAPE¹

2 a square mile/meter etc. an area of measurement equal to a square with sides a mile long, a meter long etc.: *an area of 22 square miles* | +**of** *4,000 square kilometers of forest*

3 ANGLE forming a 90° angle, or seeming to do this: *square corners* | *a square jaw*

4 five feet/two meters etc. square having the shape of a square with sides that are five feet, two meters etc. long: *The room is two yards square.*

5 a square meal a good satisfying meal

6 STRAIGHT/LEVEL parallel to a straight line: +**with** *The windows should be square with the sill.*

7 be there or be square INFORMAL HUMOROUS used to say that someone should go to a party, event etc. because all the popular people will be there

8 HONEST OLD-FASHIONED honest and fair, especially in business: *It's important to be square with clients.* | *We just want **a square deal**.*

9 BORING INFORMAL OLD-FASHIONED someone who is square is boring and unfashionable

10 be (all) square INFORMAL OLD-FASHIONED if two people are square, they do not owe each other any money

11 a square peg in a round hole INFORMAL someone who is in a job or situation that is not appropriate for them —**squareness** *n.* [U]

square² S3 W3 *n.* [C]

1 SHAPE a) a shape with four straight equal sides with 90° angles at the corners **b)** a piece of something in this shape: +**of** *a square of green cloth* ►see THESAURUS box at **shape¹**

2 IN A TOWN a broad open area in the middle of a town, that is usually in the shape of a square, or the buildings surrounding it: *Our hotel was **on the main square**.*

3 square one the situation from which you started to do something: ***Let's go back to square one** and try again.* | *Police **are back at square one** in their investigation.*

4 NUMBER MATH the result of multiplying a number by itself: *The square of 4 is 16.* → see also SQUARE ROOT

5 IN A GAME a space on a board used for playing a game such as CHESS

6 BORING PERSON OLD-FASHIONED INFORMAL someone who is boring and unfashionable

7 TOOL a flat tool with a straight edge, often shaped like an L, used for drawing or measuring 90° angles

[**Origin:** 1200–1300 Old French *esquarre*, from Vulgar Latin *exquadra*, from *exquadrare* **to make square**]

square³ *v.*

1 MULTIPLY [T] MATH to multiply a number by itself

2 square your shoulders to push back your shoulders with your back straight, usually to show your determination

3 square an account also **square the books** to give someone money or do something for them so that you do not owe them anything anymore

4 MAKE STH STRAIGHT [T] to make something straight or parallel

5 SPORTS [T] to win the same number of points or games as your opponent

6 square the circle to attempt something impossible

square sth ↔ **away** *phr. v.* INFORMAL to finish something, especially by putting the last details in order: *I have a few things to **get squared away** before I leave.*

square off *phr. v.* **1** to get ready to fight or argue with someone: +**with** *Local ranchers are squaring off with the government over the regulations.* **2 square sth ↔ off** to make something square with straight edges or corners

square up *phr. v.* to pay money that you owe

square with *phr. v.* **square sth with sth** if you square two ideas, statements etc. with each other or if they square with each other, they can be accepted together even though they seem different: *His story simply does not square with the facts.* | *How do you square that with your political beliefs?*

square⁴ *adv.* [only after verb] **1** directly and firmly SYN **squarely**: ***Look him square in the eye** and tell him you won't do it.* **2** MATH at 90° to a line SYN **squarely** → see also **fair and square** at FAIR³ (1)

squared /skwɛrd/ *adj.* **1 3/9/10 etc. squared** MATH the number 3, 9, 10 etc. multiplied by itself: *3 squared equals 9.* **2** having a square shape: *squared corners*

ˈsquare dance *n.* [C] a type of dance in which four pairs of dancers face each other in a square, and someone calls out the movements they should do —**square dancing** *n.* [U]

ˈsquare knot *n.* [C] a type of knot that will not come undone easily

square·ly /ˈskwɛrli/ *adv.* [only after verb] **1** directly or in the middle, not at an angle or to one side: *She hit him squarely on the nose.* **2** completely and with no doubt: *He put the blame squarely on the U.S.* **3** directly and honestly, without trying to avoid something **4** MATH at 90° to a line

ˌsquare ˈmatrix *n.* [C] MATH a MATRIX that has the same number of ROWS (=lines of information going across) and COLUMNS (=lines of information going down)

ˌsquare-ˈrigged *adj.* a square-rigged ship has its sails set across it and not along its length

ˌsquare ˈroot *n.* [C] MATH the square root of a number

is the number which, when multiplied by itself, equals that number: *The square root of 9 is 3.*

squar·ish /ˈskwɛrɪʃ/ *adj.* shaped almost like a square

squash¹ /skwɑʃ, skwɔʃ/ *v.* **1** [T] to press against someone or something, making them flatter and often breaking or damaging them: *Move over – you're squashing me!* | *The cake* ***got*** *a little* ***squashed*** *on the way here.* ▸see THESAURUS box at **press¹** **2** INFORMAL [I always + adv./prep.,T always + adv./prep.] to push yourself or something else into a space that is too small **3** INFORMAL [T] to defeat an opponent completely **4** [T] to use your power or authority to stop something, especially something that is causing trouble SYN **quash** **5** [T] to control or ignore an emotion [**Origin:** 1500–1600 Old French *esquasser*, from Latin *quassare* **to shake**]

squash² *n.* **1** [C,U] BIOLOGY one of a group of large heavy hard fruits, such as PUMPKINS and ZUCCHINI, that are eaten as vegetables **2** [U] a game played by two people who use RACKETS to hit a small rubber ball against the four walls of a square court

squashed /skwɑʃt/ *adj.* broken or made flat by being pressed hard: *a squashed spider*

squat¹ /skwɑt/ *v.* **squatted, squatting** [I] **1** also **squat down** to get into a position where you are balancing on your feet, with your knees bent and your bottom off the ground: *Howard squatted down to check the tire.* **2** to be in a position where you are balancing on your feet, with your knees bent and your bottom off the ground: *A group of young men were squatting by the roadside.* **3** to live in a building or on a piece of land without permission and without paying rent: *Families are still squatting in war-damaged buildings.* [**Origin:** 1300–1400 Old French *esquatir*, from *quatir* **to press**, from Vulgar Latin *coactire* **to press together**]

squat² *adj.* short and thick or low and wide in an unattractive way: *a squat old man*

squat³ *n.* **1** [C] a squatting position **2 not pay/do/know etc. squat** SLANG not pay, do, know etc. anything → see also DIDDLY

squat·ter /ˈskwɑṭɚ/ *n.* [C] someone who lives in an empty building or on a piece of land without permission and without paying rent

squaw /skwɔ/ *n.* [C] OLD-FASHIONED a word for a Native American woman, now usually considered offensive

squawk /skwɔk/ *v.* [I] **1** if a bird squawks, it makes a loud sharp angry sound **2** INFORMAL to complain loudly and angrily —**squawk** *n.* [C]

squeak¹ /skwik/ *v.* **1** [I] to make a very short high noise or cry that is not loud: *This chair keeps squeaking.* | *I could hear a mouse squeaking.* **2** [I,T] to say something in a very high voice, especially because you are nervous, afraid, or excited **3 squeak by/through/past (sth)** INFORMAL to succeed, win, or pass a test, class, or competition by a very small amount, so that you just barely avoid failure: *I just squeaked by in algebra.* **4 squeak out a victory/win/pass etc.** to just barely win, pass etc. a test or competition [**Origin:** 1300–1400 from the sound]

squeak² *n.* [C] a very short high noise or cry: *the squeak of the wooden floorboards*

squeak·y /ˈskwiki/ *adj. comparative* **squeakier**, *superlative* **squeakiest** making very high noises that are not loud: *a squeaky door* | *Her voice is kind of high and squeaky.* —**squeakily** *adv.* —**squeakiness** *n.* [U]

ˌsqueaky ˈclean *adj.* INFORMAL **1** completely clean **2** never having done anything morally wrong: *a squeaky clean reputation*

squeal¹ /skwil/ *v.* **1** [I] to make a long loud high sound or cry: *The truck squealed to a stop.* | **+with/in** *The children squealed with delight.* **2** [T] to say something in a loud high-pitched voice: *"Let me go!" she squealed.* **3 squeal (on sb)** INFORMAL to tell the police or someone in authority about someone you know who has done something wrong —**squealer** *n.* [C]

squeal² *n.* [C] a long loud high sound or cry: **+of** *squeals of laughter*

squeam·ish /ˈskwimɪʃ/ *adj.* easily shocked or upset, or easily made to feel sick by seeing unpleasant things: **+about** *Some people are squeamish about blood.* —**squeamishly** *adv.* —**squeamishness** *n.* [U]

squee·gee /ˈskwidʒi/ *n.* [C] a tool with a thin rubber blade and a short handle, used for removing or spreading a liquid on a surface

squeeze¹ /skwiz/ S3 *v.*

1 PRESS WITH HAND [I,T] to press something firmly in, especially with your hand: *Cathy gently squeezed my hand.*

2 GET LIQUID OUT [T] to press or twist something in order to get liquid out of it: *First, squeeze the oranges.* | **squeeze sth out of sth** *She squeezed the water out of her hair.* | **squeeze sth on/onto sth** *Emily squeezed lemon into her tea.* ▸see THESAURUS box at **press¹** → see picture on page A32

3 FIT INTO SMALL SPACE [I always + adv./prep.,T always + adv./prep.] to make something fit into a space or pass through an opening that is too small, or to get into such a space or pass through such an opening: **+into/through/past/between** *Five of us squeezed into the back seat of the car.* | *Could I just squeeze past?* | **squeeze sb/sth into sth** *Somehow I squeezed the car into the tiny parking space.* | **squeeze (sb/sth) in** *We could probably squeeze one more person in.*

4 squeeze out/into/through sth to succeed, win, or pass a test, class, or competition by a very small amount, so that you just barely avoid failure: *Atlanta managed to squeeze out a one-point victory.*

5 squeeze your eyes shut/closed to close your eyes very tightly

6 LIMIT MONEY [T] ECONOMICS to strictly limit the amount of money that is available to a company or organization, so that it is difficult for them to do things: *Cuts in federal funding are squeezing poor families.*

[**Origin:** 1500–1600 *quease* **to press, squeeze** (15–17 centuries), from Old English *cwysan*]

squeeze in *phr. v.* **squeeze sb/sth ↔ in** to manage to meet someone or do something although you are very busy: *We'll see if we can squeeze in a round of golf.* | *I could squeeze you in at 4:00.*

squeeze out *phr. v.* **1 squeeze sb/sth ↔ out** to force someone or something to stop taking part in something by making it very difficult for them to continue: *Local bookstores are being squeezed out by national chains.* **2 squeeze sth ↔ out** to squeeze something wet in order to remove the liquid from it: *Squeeze the cloth out first.*

squeeze sth **out of** sb *phr. v.* to force someone to tell you something: *See if you can squeeze more information out of them.*

squeeze² *n.* **1** [C] an act of pressing something firmly, usually with your hands: *Henry reached over and* ***gave*** *her arm* ***a squeeze.*** **2 a (tight) squeeze** a situation in which there is just barely enough room for things or people to fit somewhere: *It'll be a tight squeeze, but you can ride in the back seat.* **3** [singular] ECONOMICS a situation in which salaries, prices, borrowing money etc. are strictly controlled, so that it becomes difficult for someone to do something: *Small businesses are beginning to* ***feel the*** *financial* ***squeeze.*** **4 a squeeze of lemon/lime etc.** a small amount of juice obtained by squeezing a piece of fruit **5 put the squeeze on sb** INFORMAL to try to persuade someone to do something, especially by using threats **6** a SQUEEZE PLAY **7 your/her/his (main) squeeze** INFORMAL HUMOROUS someone's BOYFRIEND or GIRLFRIEND

squeeze·box /ˈskwizbɑks/ *n.* [C] INFORMAL an ACCORDION

ˈsqueeze play *n.* [C] **1** a play in baseball in which a BATTER tries to BUNT the ball in order to give a RUNNER on third base a chance to gain a point **2** pressure put on someone in order to get what you want

squeez·er /ˈskwizɚ/ *n.* [C] a small tool for squeezing (SQUEEZE) juice from fruit such as LEMONS

squelch /skwɛltʃ/ *v.* [I,T] to stop something such as an idea or action from developing or spreading: *Barrett* has tried to squelch the rumors. [**Origin:** 1600–1700 from the sound] —**squelch** *n.* [C]

squib /skwɪb/ *n.* [C] **1** LITERARY a short amusing piece of writing **2** a small exploding FIREWORK

squid /skwɪd/ *n. plural* **squid** or **squids** [C] a sea creature with a long body and ten arms around its mouth → see picture at FOOD CHAIN

squig·gle /ˈskwɪgəl/ *n.* [C] a short line that curls and twists, especially in writing or drawing —**squiggly** *adj.*: *squiggly lines*

squint /skwɪnt/ *v.* [I] to look at something with your eyes partly closed in order to see better, especially because the light is very bright: *She smiled and squinted against the sun.* | +**at** *He was squinting at the screen.* —**squint** *n.* [singular] —**squinty** also **squinty-eyed** *adj.*: *a squinty-eyed tough guy*

squire¹ /skwaɪɚ/ *n.* [C] a young man in the Middle Ages who learned how to be a KNIGHT by serving one

squire² *v.*

squire around *phr. v.* **squire sb ↔ around, squire sb around sth** to take someone to different places and treat them well

squirm /skwɚm/ *v.* [I] **1** to twist your body from side to side, especially because you are uncomfortable or nervous: *The baby squirmed in her arms.* **2** to feel very embarrassed or ashamed: *Pornography is a subject that* ***makes*** *most Americans* ***squirm****.* —**squirm** *n.* [singular] —**squirmy** *adj.*

squirm out of sth *phr. v.* INFORMAL to avoid doing something you do not want to do, or to avoid a bad situation

squir·rel¹ /ˈskwɚəl/ *n.* [C] a small animal that climbs trees and eats nuts and that has a long furry tail [**Origin:** 1300–1400 Anglo-French *esquirel*, from Latin *sciurus*, from Greek *skiouros*, from *skia* **shadow** + *oura* **tail**]

squirrel² *v.*

squirrel sth ↔ **away** *phr. v.* to keep something, especially money, in a safe place to use later

squir·rel·ly, squirrely /ˈskwɚəli/ *adj.* INFORMAL DISAPPROVING unable to sit still or be quiet, and often a little strange

squirt¹ /skwɚt/ *v.* **1** [I,T] if you squirt liquid or it squirts, it is forced out of a narrow hole in a thin fast stream: +**from** *Blood squirted from the wound.* | **squirt sth (on sb/sth)** *David squirted ketchup on his fries.* **2** [T] to hit or cover someone or something with a thin fast stream of liquid: **squirt sb/sth with sth** *Some kids squirted her with a water pistol.*

squirt² *n.* [C] **1** a fast thin stream of liquid **2** SPOKEN a word used when speaking to a small child **3 a little squirt** SPOKEN a person who you do not like or respect, especially a small person

ˈsquirt ˌbottle *n.* [C] a plastic bottle that you SQUEEZE to make a substance come out of it, used especially for food such as KETCHUP and MUSTARD

ˈsquirt gun *n.* [C] a WATER PISTOL

squish /skwɪʃ/ *v.* **1** [I,T] INFORMAL to press against someone or something, making them flatter and often breaking or damaging them SYN **squash** **2** [I always + adv./prep.,T always + adv./prep.] INFORMAL to push yourself or something else into a space that is too small SYN **squash** **3** [I always + adv./prep.] to make a soft sucking sound by moving in or through something soft and wet like mud —**squished** *adj.*

squish·y /ˈskwɪʃi/ *adj. comparative* **squishier**, *superlative* **squishiest** soft, able to be squeezed, and usually wet or full of liquid: *a squishy jellyfish* —**squishiness** *n.* [U]

Sr. **1** [only after noun] the written abbreviation of SENIOR: *Douglas Fairbanks, Sr.* **2** the written abbreviation of Sister, used in front of the name of a NUN: *Sr. Bernadette*

Sri Lan·ka /sri ˈlɑŋkə, ʃri-/ a country in south Asia which is an island in the Indian Ocean, southeast of India —**Sri Lankan** *n., adj.*

SRO, S.R.O. *n.* **1** [U] **standing room only** used when all the seats in a theater, sports STADIUM etc. are full and there is only room left for people to stand **2** [C] **single-room occupancy** a small cheap apartment consisting of one room, a toilet, and a small kitchen area

S.S. **1** the abbreviation of SOCIAL SECURITY **2** the abbreviation of STEAMSHIP

SSA **Social Security Administration** the U.S. government department that manages SOCIAL SECURITY programs

ssh /ʃʃ/ *interjection* used to ask for silence or less noise: *Ssh! Be quiet.*

St. **1** the written abbreviation of "street" used in addresses: *Wall St.* **2** the written abbreviation of SAINT: *St. Andrew*

-st /st/ *suffix* used with the number 1 to form ORDINAL numbers: *1st* (=first) *prize* | *my 21st birthday*

stab¹ /stæb/ *v.* **stabbed, stabbing** **1** [T] to push a knife or other sharp object into someone in order to hurt or kill them: **stab sb with sth** *She stabbed him with a knife.* | **stab sb in the heart/arm etc.** *A man tried to stab her in the arm.* | *Two men were* ***stabbed to death*** *during the riot.* **2** [T] to push a sharp object quickly into something: *She stabbed the egg yolk with her fork.* **3** [I,T] to make quick pushing movements with your finger or something pointed: +**at** *She stabbed at his chest with her finger.* | **stab sth with sth** *He spoke angrily, stabbing the air with his pen.* **4 stab sb in the back** to do something that harms someone who likes and trusts you SYN **betray** → see also STABBING¹, STABBING²

stab² *n.* [C] **1** an act of stabbing or trying to stab someone: *a stab wound* **2** [C] INFORMAL an attempt at doing something: **take/make a stab at (doing) sth** *I wasn't sure of the answer, but I took a stab at it.* **3 a stab of pain/fear/envy etc.** a sudden sharp feeling of pain, fear etc. **4 a stab in the back** something bad that someone does to you, especially someone whom you like and trust **5** [C] a quick pushing movement with your hand or something pointed

stab·bing¹ /ˈstæbɪŋ/ *n.* [C] a crime in which someone is stabbed

stabbing² *adj.* a stabbing pain is sharp and sudden, as if it had been made by a knife

sta·bil·i·ty /stəˈbɪləṭi/ Ac *n.* [U] **1** the quality of not changing frequently or suddenly OPP **instability**: *a long period of political stability* | +**of** *the financial stability of the community* **2** the condition of being steady and not likely to fall or move in an unsafe way OPP **instability**: +**of** *the structural stability of the building* **3** the quality of having a healthy mental and emotional state OPP **instability**: *emotional stability* **4** CHEMISTRY the ability of a substance to stay in the same state OPP **instability**

sta·bi·lize /ˈsteɪbəˌlaɪz/ Ac *v.* **1** [I,T] to reach a state where there are no more frequent or sudden changes, or to make something do this: *The patient's condition has now stabilized.* **2** [T] to make something steady and not likely to fall or move in an unsafe way —**stabilization** /ˌsteɪbələˈzeɪʃən/ *n.* [U]

sta·bi·liz·er /ˈsteɪbəˌlaɪzɚ/ *n.* [C] **1** CHEMISTRY a chemical that helps something such as a food to stay in the same state **2** a piece of equipment that helps make something such as an aircraft or ship steady

ˈstabilizing seˌlection *n.* [U] BIOLOGY when particular animals, plants etc. prove to be most suitable for life in their environment because their GENES lie in the middle range of those present across the whole SPECIES

sta·ble¹ /ˈsteɪbəl/ Ac *adj.* **1** steady and not likely to fall or move in an unsafe way OPP **unstable**: *That chair doesn't look very stable.* **2** not changing frequently and not likely to suddenly become worse OPP **unstable**: *a stable relationship* | *stable government* | *She is* ***in*** *a critical but* ***stable condition*** (=not likely to suddenly become sicker). **3** with a healthy mental and emotional state OPP **unstable**:

He's not a very stable person. **4** CHEMISTRY a stable substance tends to stay in the same chemical or ATOMIC state OPP **unstable** [**Origin:** 1200–1300 Old French *estable*, from Latin *stabilis*, from *stare* **to stand**] → see also STABILITY —**stably** *adv.*

stable² Ac *n.* [C] **1** a building where horses, cattle etc. are kept **2 stables** [plural] **a)** a stable or a group of stables **b)** a business that keeps or trains horses for competition or for people to ride for fun **3** a group of racing horses that has one owner or trainer **4 a)** a group of people who work for the same company, play on the same team etc. **b)** a group of products or companies that belong to the same company or person: *the company's stable of hotels and casinos*

stable³ Ac *v.* [T] to put or keep a horse in a stable

sta·ble·man /ˈsteɪbəlmæn/ *n. plural* **stablemen** /-mən/ [C] a man who works in a stable and takes care of horses

sta·ble·mate /ˈsteɪbəlˌmeɪt/ *n.* [C] **1** something that is made by the same company or someone who works for the same company as something or someone else **2** a horse from the same STABLE as another horse

sta·bling /ˈsteɪblɪŋ/ *n.* [U] space for horses to be stabled

stac·ca·to /stəˈkɑt̬oʊ/ *adv.* with the notes cut short and played separately in a way that does not flow smoothly → see also LEGATO —**staccato** *adj.*

stack¹ /stæk/ S3 *n.* [C] **1** a neat pile of things, one on top of the other SYN **pile**: +**of** *a stack of books* | *stacks of unopened boxes* **2 the stacks** [plural] the rows of shelves in the part of a library where most of the books are kept **3 a stack of sth** also **stacks of sth** INFORMAL a large amount: *We get stacks of junk mail every day.* **4** COMPUTERS a temporary store of information on a computer **5** a tall CHIMNEY **6** a large pile of grain, grass etc. that is stored outside [**Origin:** 1200–1300 Old Norse *stakkr*] → see also **blow your top/stack** at BLOW¹ (9), HAYSTACK

stack² *v.* **1** [I,T] also **stack up** to form a neat pile or make things into a neat pile: *These chairs stack easily.* | *Stack the plates up here.* **2** [T usually passive] to put piles of things on a place or in a place: +**with** *The coffee table was stacked with magazines.* **3 stack the shelves** to put goods for sale onto the shelves in a store, especially a food store **4 stack the deck/cards a)** INFORMAL to make a situation difficult so that someone cannot succeed: +**against** *In business, the deck is often stacked against women.* **b)** INFORMAL to arrange cards dishonestly in a game **5** [I,T] also **stack up** if aircraft stack or are stacked around an airport, they are made to fly around it until they can land → see also **the odds are (stacked) against sb/sth** at ODDS (1)

stack up *phr. v.* INFORMAL **1** used to talk about how good something is when compared to something else SYN **compare**: +**against** *How does my kids' school stack up against others?* **2** if a number of things stack up, they gradually collect or get stuck in one place: *My phone messages had started to stack up.*

sta·di·um /ˈsteɪdiəm/ W3 *n. plural* **stadiums** or **stadia** /-diə/ [C] a building for sports, consisting of a field surrounded by rows of seats: *a baseball stadium* [**Origin:** 1300–1400 Latin, Greek *stadion* **unit of length, racetrack**]

staff¹ /stæf/ S1 W1 *n.* **1** [C,U] *plural* **staffs** the people who work for an organization: *The entire staff has done a great job.* | +**of** *Our department has a staff of seven.* | *The New York Yankees have a strong pitching staff.* | ***Staff members*** *were encouraged to make suggestions.* | *Joan is the only lawyer we have* ***on staff.*** ▸see THESAURUS box at **colleague** **2** [C] *plural* **staffs** a pole for flying a flag on SYN **flagpole** **3** [C] *plural* **staves** /steɪvz/ **a)** OLD-FASHIONED a long thick stick to help you walk **b)** a long thick stick that an official holds in some ceremonies **4** [C] *plural* **staves** or **staffs** ENG. LANG. ARTS the set of five lines that music is written on **5 the staff of life** LITERARY a basic food, especially bread [**Origin:** Old English *stæf* **stick**] → see also GENERAL STAFF, GROUND STAFF

staff² *v.* [T usually passive] to be the workers in an organization, or to provide the workers: *The clinic is staffed by retired doctors.* —**staffing** *n.* [U] *staffing levels* → see also OVERSTAFFED, UNDERSTAFFED

staff·er /ˈstæfɚ/ *n.* [C] someone who is paid to work for an organization: *a staffer in the White House*

ˈstaff ˌofficer *n.* [C] a military officer whose job is to help an officer of a higher rank

ˈstaff ˌsergeant *n.* [C,U] a lower rank in the U.S. Army, Air Force, or Marines, or someone who has this rank

stag /stæg/ *n.* [C] **1** BIOLOGY a fully grown male DEER SYN **buck** **2 go stag** INFORMAL if a man goes stag, he goes to a party without a woman → see also STAG PARTY

stage¹ /steɪdʒ/ S2 W1 *n.*

1 TIME/STATE/PART [C] a particular time or state that something reaches as it grows or develops, or a part of a process, competition etc. → see also PHASE: *The negotiations were reaching a critical stage.* | *the* ***early stages*** *of the disease* | *the* ***final stages*** *of the war* | ***At this stage****, it is not clear what will happen.* | *the* ***first stage*** *of the project* | *The goods are loaded onto trucks for* ***the next stage*** *of the trip.* | *Construction of the bridge is in its* ***final stage.*** | *All kids* ***go through a stage*** *when they're embarrassed by their parents.* | *Don't worry; it's* ***just a stage*** (=used to say that a child is only behaving in a particular way because of the stage he or she is at in development).

THESAURUS

part one of the pieces or features of something, such as an event or period of time: *The early part of his life was spent in New York.*
phase a separate part in a process of development or change: *Schools will receive extra funding in both phases of the plan.*
point a specific moment, time, or stage in something's development: *At this point in the season the team is finally starting to work together.*
round one of a number of events that are related: *the first round of the competition*

2 THEATER **a)** [C,U] ENG. LANG. ARTS the raised floor in a theater on which plays are performed: *the stage in the school auditorium* | *I get nervous every time I go* ***on stage.*** | **stage left/right** (=from the left or right side of the stage, from the view of an actor facing the people watching) **b) the stage** plays as a form of entertainment: *The show was directed for the stage by James Lapine.* | *a gala featuring stars of* ***stage and screen*** (=theater and movies) ▸see THESAURUS box at **theater**
3 ACTING **the stage** ENG. LANG. ARTS acting as a profession, especially in plays: *In Shakespeare's time, women were not allowed* ***on the stage*** (=to act in plays).
4 center stage if someone or something is center stage, it has everyone's attention, or is very important: *Immigration has* ***taken center stage*** *in the election.*
5 PLACE [singular] a place or area of activity where something important happens: *Geneva has been the stage for many such conferences.* | *China is one of the few countries strong enough to challenge the U.S.* ***on the world stage.***
6 set the stage for sb/sth to prepare for something or make something possible: *The beatings by police set the stage for the riots.*
[**Origin:** 1200–1300 Old French *estage*, from Latin *stare* **to stand**]

stage² *v.* [T] **1** to organize an event, especially a public event: **stage a strike/demonstration/concert etc.** *Environmental activists staged a protest in front of City Hall.* | *The police have staged raids on drug dealers.* **2** to organize how a play will be done: *Leverich also staged "The Glass Menagerie."* **3 stage a comeback** to start doing something again after you have stopped for a while: *He tried to stage a comeback during the last few months of the campaign.*

stage·coach /ˈsteɪdʒkoʊtʃ/ *n.* [C] a closed vehicle

S

pulled by horses, that in past times carried passengers and letters

stage·craft /ˈsteɪdʒkræft/ *n.* [U] the skill of making a performance of a play or show interesting

ˈstage diˌrection *n.* [C] a written instruction to an actor to do something in a play

ˌstage ˈdoor *n.* [C] the side or back door in a theater, used by actors and theater workers

ˈstage fright *n.* [U] nervousness felt by someone who is going to perform in front of a lot of people

stage·hand /ˈsteɪdʒhænd/ *n.* [C] someone who works on a theater stage, getting it ready for a play or for the next part of a play

ˌstage-ˈmanage *v.* [T] INFORMAL to organize a public event, such as a meeting, in a way that will give you the result that you want: *The press conference was carefully stage-managed.*

ˈstage ˌmanager *n.* [C] someone in charge of the parts of a play's performance that do not involve acting, such as the lights, SCENERY etc.

ˈstage ˌmother *n.* [C] DISAPPROVING a mother who tries too hard to make her child succeed in SHOW BUSINESS

S

ˈstage ˌname *n.* [C] a name used by an actor instead of his or her real name

stage·struck /ˈsteɪdʒˌstrʌk/ *adj.* loving to see plays, or wanting very much to become an actor

ˌstage ˈwhisper *n.* [C] **1** ENG. LANG. ARTS an actor's loud WHISPER that other actors on the stage pretend not to hear **2** a loud WHISPER that is intended to be heard by everyone

stage·y /ˈsteɪdʒi/ *adj.* another spelling of STAGY

stag·fla·tion /stægˈfleɪʃən/ *n.* [U] ECONOMICS an economic condition in which there is INFLATION (=a continuing rise in prices) but many people do not have jobs and businesses are not doing well

stag·ger[1] /ˈstægɚ/ *v.* **1** [I always + adv./prep.] to walk or move in an unsteady way, almost falling over SYN **reel**: *He staggered and fell.* | +**away/into/down etc.** *The ship lurched, and he staggered backward.* | ***Staggering under the weight,*** *she carried the suitcases into the station.* ▸see THESAURUS box at **walk[1]** **2** [I] to be struggling to deal with a difficult situation SYN **reel**: *The country is* ***staggering under the weight*** *of its debt.* **3** [T] to arrange people's working hours, VACATIONS etc. so that they do not all begin and end at the same time **4** [T usually passive] to make someone feel very surprised or shocked: *We were all staggered by the news of her death.* **5** [T] to start a race with each runner at a different place on a curved track

stagger[2] *n.* [C usually singular] an unsteady movement of someone who is having difficulty walking

stag·ger·ing /ˈstægərɪŋ/ *adj.* very surprising, shocking, and hard to believe SYN **amazing**: *The population grew at a staggering rate.* —**staggeringly** *adv.*

stag·ing /ˈsteɪdʒɪŋ/ *n.* **1** [C,U] ENG. LANG. ARTS the activity or art of performing a play, including the acting, clothes etc.: *a modern staging of "Macbeth"* **2** [U] a flat raised surface that is put up for a short time for people to stand and work on

ˈstaging ˌarea *n.* [C] **1** a place where soldiers meet and where military equipment is gathered before it is moved to another place **2** a place where an event is organized from: *the staging area for the parade*

ˈstaging post *n.* [C] **1** a place where people, planes, ships etc. stop on a long trip, for example to rest or get supplies → see also STOPOVER **2** a staging area

stag·nant /ˈstægnənt/ *adj.* [no comparative] **1** stagnant water or air does not move or flow and often smells bad: *stagnant pools of water* **2** not changing, developing, or making progress SYN **inactive**: *Ticket sales have been stagnant.* —**stagnancy** *n.* [U] —**stagnantly** *adv.*

stag·nate /ˈstægneɪt/ *v.* [I] to stop developing or making progress: *a stagnating economy* —**stagnation** /stægˈneɪʃən/ *n.* [U]

ˈstag ˌparty *n.* [C] a party for men only, especially on the night before a man's wedding SYN **bachelor party**

stag·y, stagey /ˈsteɪdʒi/ *adj.* behavior that is stagy is not natural, so that people move in a way that is slightly too deliberate, speak slightly too loudly or softly etc.: *The performance was dramatic without being stagy.* —**stagily** *adv.*

staid /steɪd/ *adj.* serious, old-fashioned, and boring: *staid scientific journals* —**staidly** *adv.* —**staidness** *n.* [U]

stain[1] /steɪn/ S3 *v.* **1** [I,T] to accidentally make a mark on something, especially one that cannot be removed, or to be marked in this way: *Sweat stained his cowboy hat.* | +**with** *a carpet stained with red wine* **2** [T] to change the color of something, especially something made of wood, by using a special chemical or DYE **3 stain sb's name/honor/reputation etc.** LITERARY to damage the good opinion that people have about someone [**Origin:** 1400–1500 partly from Old French *desteindre* **to discolor**; partly from Old Norse *steina* **to paint**]

stain[2] *n.* **1** [C] a mark that is difficult to remove, especially one made by a liquid such as blood, coffee, or ink: +**on** *The tablecloth had a large stain on it.* | **a blood/ink/wine etc. stain** *blood stains on the floor* ▸see THESAURUS box at **mark[2]** **2** [C,U] a special liquid used to make something such as wood dark **3 a stain on sb's character/reputation etc.** LITERARY something that someone has done that is wrong or illegal, that other people know about

ˌstained ˈglass *n.* [U] glass of different colors used for making pictures and patterns in windows, especially in a church: *stained glass windows*

stain·less /ˈsteɪnlɪs/ *adj.* made of stainless steel

ˌstainless ˈsteel *n.* [U] a type of steel that does not RUST: *stainless steel sinks*

stair /stɛr/ S2 W2 *n.* **1 stairs** [plural] a set of steps built for going from one level of a building to another → see also STEP: *The children sat* ***on the stairs,*** *listening.* | **up/down the stairs** *Jerry ran up the stairs.* | *We carried the groceries up four* ***flights of stairs*** (=sets of stairs). | **the bottom/foot of the stairs** *There was a letter at* ***the foot of the stairs.*** | **the top/head of the stairs** *I left my briefcase at the top of the stairs.* → see also DOWNSTAIRS, UPSTAIRS[1] **2** [C] one of the steps in a set of stairs: *The second stair creaks when you step on it.* **3** [C] LITERARY a set of stairs: *I heard footsteps coming up the stair.* [**Origin:** Old English *stæger*]

staircase

stair·case /ˈstɛrkeɪs/ *n.* [C] a set of stairs inside a building, including its supports and the side parts that you hold on to

stair·way /ˈstɛrweɪ/ *n. plural* **stairways** [C] a staircase, especially a large or impressive one

stair·well /ˈstɛrwɛl/ *n.* [C] the space that goes through all the floors of a building, where the stairs are

stake[1] /steɪk/ W3 *n.*

1 be at stake if something that you value very much is at stake, you will lose it if a plan or action is not successful: *Thousands of lives are at stake.* | *At stake is the company's survival.*

2 (have) a stake in sth a) if you have a stake in something, you will get advantages if it is successful, and you feel that you have an important connection with it: *The system gives workers a stake in the company.* | *Jobs give young people a stake in society.* **b)** if you have a stake in a business, you have INVESTED money in it: *Hudson had an 80% stake in the airline.*

3 the stake a post to which a person was tied in past

times to be killed by being burned: *Witches were* ***burned at the stake.***
4 MONEY RISKED [C usually plural] money that people risk on the result of a game, race etc., all of which is taken by the winner: *a game of high-stakes poker*
5 high stakes a) if you play for high stakes, you risk a lot of money in a game **b)** if the stakes are high when you are trying to do something, you risk losing a lot or it will be dangerous if you fail: *For Tanya, it is a struggle to stay in school, but the stakes are high.*
6 SHARP POST [C] a pointed piece of wood, metal etc. that is pushed into the ground to hold a rope, mark a particular place etc.: *tent stakes*
7 pull up stakes INFORMAL to move from one place to another
[**Origin:** Old English *staca* **sharp post**]

stake² *v.* [T] **1** to risk losing something that is valuable or important to you, if a plan or action is not successful: **stake sth on sb/sth** *He staked his reputation on the success of the project.* **2 stake (out) a claim a)** to say publicly that you think you have a right to have or own something: *Both countries have staked a claim to the islands.* **b)** to prove that you deserve to have something: *Griffey had already staked a claim to the Most Valuable Player award.* **3** to risk money or possessions on a race or competition SYN **wager** SYN **bet**: *One time he staked his house on a roll of the dice.* **4** also **stake off** to mark or enclose an area of ground with stakes: *The grassy area was staked off.* **5** also **stake up** to support something with stakes: *Stake up the tomato plants.* **6 I'd stake my life on it** SPOKEN used when saying that you are completely sure that something is true, or that something will happen: *I know it's real; I'd stake my life on it.*

stake sth ↔ **out** *phr. v.* INFORMAL **1** to watch a place secretly and continuously: *Officers staked out the apartment all evening.* **2** to mark or control a particular area so that you can have it or use it: *Flower sellers arrive early to stake out a good spot.* **3** to be successful in a particular area of business: *In three years, they have staked out over 30% of the shoe market.* **4** to state your opinions about something clearly, so that people know what you will do and how your opinions are different from other people's: *The president used the speech to stake out his position on the budget.* → see also STAKEOUT

stake·hold·er /ˈsteɪkˌhoʊldɚ/ *n.* [C] **1** someone who has INVESTED money into something, or who has some important connection with it, and who therefore will be affected by its success or failure: *employees and stakeholders* **2** LAW someone, usually a lawyer, who takes charge of a property or amount of money during a legal disagreement or during a sale **3** someone chosen to hold the money that is risked by people on a race, competition etc. and to give all of it to the winner

stake·out /ˈsteɪkaʊt/ *n.* [C] during a stakeout, the police watch a place secretly and continuously in order to catch people doing something illegal

sta·lac·tite /stəˈlæktaɪt/ *n.* [C] EARTH SCIENCE a sharp pointed object hanging down from the roof of a CAVE, which is formed gradually by water that contains minerals as it drops slowly from the roof

sta·lag·mite /stəˈlægmaɪt/ *n.* [C] EARTH SCIENCE a sharp pointed object coming up from the floor of a CAVE, formed by drops from a stalactite

stale /steɪl/ *adj.* **1** bread or cake that is stale is not fresh or good to eat because it is slightly old OPP **fresh**: *stale cookies* | *French bread* ***goes stale*** *quickly.* ►see THESAURUS box at **old** **2** not interesting or exciting anymore: *stale old gossip* | *After two years, their marriage began to* ***go stale.*** **3** air, breath, or liquid that is stale is not fresh or pleasant OPP **fresh**: *the smell of stale smoke* | *stale coffee* **4** if a person gets stale, they have no new ideas, interest, or energy, especially because they have been doing the same thing for too long: *I like him; he's young, he's not stale.* —**staleness** *n.* [U]

stale·mate /ˈsteɪlmeɪt/ *n.* [C,U] **1** a situation in which it seems impossible to settle an argument or disagreement, and neither side can get an advantage SYN **deadlock**: *Can they* ***break the stalemate*** *in the peace negotiations?* **2** a position in CHESS in which neither player can win —**stalemate** *v.* [T]

Sta·lin /ˈstɑlɪn/**, Joseph** (1879–1953) a Russian politician, born in Georgia, who was leader of the former Soviet Union from the death of Lenin (1924) until his own death

stalk¹ /stɔk/ *n.* [C] BIOLOGY a long narrow stem of a plant, that supports the leaves, fruits, or flowers: *Two flowers usually develop on each stalk.* → see picture at FLOWER¹

stalk² *v.* **1** [T] to follow an animal or person quietly in order to catch or kill it: *a tiger stalking its prey* | *the rapist who is stalking women* ►see THESAURUS box at **follow** **2** [T] to follow and watch someone over a long period of time, in a way that is annoying or threatening, and that is considered a crime: *She was stalked by an obsessed fan.* **3** [I always + adv./prep.] to walk in a proud or angry way, with long steps: **+out/off/away** *Yvonne stalked out of the room in disgust.* **4** [T] if something bad stalks people or a place, it threatens them: *It is a disease that stalks the young.*

stalk·er /ˈstɔkɚ/ *n.* [C] someone who follows and watches another person over a long period of time, in a way that is annoying or threatening

stalk·ing /ˈstɔkɪŋ/ *n.* [U] the crime of following and watching someone over a long period of time, in a way that is annoying or threatening

ˈstalking ˌhorse *n.* [C] POLITICS someone or something that people pay attention to, in a way that hides the actions of another person or hides the real purpose of an action

stall¹ /stɔl/ *n.* **1** [C] a table or a small store with an open front, especially outdoors, where goods are sold SYN **booth** SYN **stand**: *a stall at a flea market* **2** [C] also **shower/toilet/bathroom stall** a small enclosed private area for washing or using the toilet **3** [C] an enclosed area in a building for an animal, especially a horse or cow **4** [C usually singular] an occasion when an engine stops working: *The plane* ***went into a stall*** (=the engine stopped working). **5** [C] an occasion when something stops improving or developing: *The economy has* ***gone into a stall.*** **6** [C usually plural] a seat in a row of long seats for priests and singers in some larger churches: *choir stalls* [**Origin:** (1–3, 6) Old English *steall*]

stall² *v.* **1** [I,T] if an engine stalls or you stall it, it stops because there is not enough power or speed to keep it going: *The car kept stalling.* | *An inexperienced pilot can easily stall a plane.* **2** [I] to stop making progress or developing: *Negotiations have stalled.* **3** [I] to deliberately delay because you are not ready to do something, answer questions etc.: *Management seems to be* ***stalling for time*** *on the new contracts.* **4** [T] INFORMAL to make someone wait or stop something from happening until you are ready SYN **delay**: *Dad's coming! See if you can stall him for a minute.*

stal·lion /ˈstælyən/ *n.* [C] a male horse that is fully grown, kept for breeding → see also MARE

stal·wart¹ /ˈstɔlwɚt/ *n.* [C] someone who works hard and is loyal to a particular organization or set of ideas: *a stalwart of the Democratic Party*

stalwart² *adj.* **1 stalwart supporter/ally etc.** a very loyal and strong supporter **2** FORMAL strong in appearance [**Origin:** Old English *stælwierthe* **useful, strong**] —**stalwartly** *adv.*

sta·men /ˈsteɪmən/ *n.* [C] BIOLOGY the male part of a flower, that produces POLLEN → see also ANTHER → see picture at FLOWER¹

stam·i·na /ˈstæmənə/ *n.* [U] physical or mental strength that lets you continue doing something for a long time without getting tired SYN **endurance**: *Brooks just doesn't have the stamina to play the whole game.* [**Origin:** 1700–1800 Latin, plural of *stamen* **thread, thread of life**]

stam·mer¹ /ˈstæmɚ/ *v.* [I,T] to speak or say something with a lot of pauses and repeated sounds, either

S

because you have a speech problem, or because you are nervous, excited etc. SYN **stutter**: *He blushed and stammered his thanks.* ▶see THESAURUS box at **say**[1] —**stammerer** *n.* [C] —**stammeringly** *adv.*

stammer[2] *n.* [C usually singular] a speech problem which makes someone speak with a lot of pauses and repeated sounds SYN **stutter**: *"G-g-get up," she said with a slight stammer.*

stamp[1] /stæmp/ S2 *n.* [C]
1 MAIL also **postage stamp** FORMAL a small piece of paper that you buy and stick onto an envelope or package before sending it, that shows you have paid to use the mail system: *a 32-cent stamp* | **a sheet/book of stamps** (=set of stamps that you buy)
2 TOOL a tool for pressing or printing a mark or pattern onto a surface, or the mark made by this tool: *a date stamp* | *a stamp in your passport*
3 sb's stamp of approval someone's statement that they accept something or give permission for something: *The mayor **gave** his **stamp of approval** to the plan.*
4 put your stamp on sth to affect something so that it changes in a particular way, especially in a way that makes people notice you: *It will take time for him to put his own stamp on the organization.*
5 FOOT an act of stamping, especially with your foot: *an angry stamp of her foot*
6 QUALITY a particular quality or type of character: *a man **of a** literary **stamp*** | **have/bear the stamp of sth** *The speech bore the stamp of authority.*
7 EXCHANGE FOR GOODS a TRADING STAMP: *Do you save stamps?* → see also FOOD STAMP, RUBBER STAMP

stamp[2] *v.*
1 MAKE A MARK [T] to put a pattern, sign, or letters on something using a special tool: *The folder was stamped "Secret."* | *The woman stamped my passport.* | **stamp sth on sth** *the expiration date stamped on the bottle* | **stamp sth with sth** *Each engine is stamped with a serial number.*
2 FOOT [I,T] to lift your foot off the ground and put it down hard SYN **stomp**: *The audience stamped and shouted.* | *"Be quiet!" she said, **stamping** her **foot*** (=because she was angry). | *He **stamped** his **feet** to keep warm.* | **stamp on sth** *She screamed and stamped on a cockroach.*
3 WALK NOISILY [I always + adv./prep.] to walk somewhere in a noisy way by putting your feet down hard on the ground, especially because you are angry or cold SYN **stomp**: *She stamped down the stairs.*
4 AFFECT SB/STH [T] to have an important or permanent effect on someone or something: *The experience was **stamped on** her **memory**.* | **stamp sth on sth** *He soon stamped his authority on the college.*
5 MAIL [T] to stick a stamp onto a letter, package etc.
stamp sb **as** sth *phr. v.* to show that someone has a particular type of character: *Some Republicans are trying to stamp him as unpatriotic.*
stamp sth ↔ **out** *phr. v.* **1** to prevent something bad from continuing: *The law is an attempt to stamp out political corruption.* **2** to put out a small fire by stepping hard on the flames **3** to make a shape or object by pressing hard on something using a machine or tool

ˈ**Stamp Act, the** HISTORY a British law passed in 1765 that began a tax on newspapers and other documents in the American colonies (COLONY)

stam·pede[1] /stæmˈpid/ *n.* [C] **1** a sudden rush of frightened animals all running in the same direction **2** a sudden rush by a lot of people, all wanting to do the same thing or go to the same place SYN **rush**: *a stampede toward the doors* [**Origin:** 1800–1900 American Spanish *estampida*, from Spanish, **crush**]

stampede[2] *v.* [I,T] **1** if animals stampede, they suddenly start running together in the same direction, because they are frightened: *stampeding buffalo* **2** if people stampede, they run together in the same direction, because they are frightened or excited SYN **rush**: *Children stampeded out of the school doors.* **3 be/get stampeded** to feel forced to do something you do not really want to do, because a lot of other people are doing it and want you to do it too: **be stampeded into doing sth** *Kennedy refused to be stampeded into starting new nuclear tests.*

ˈ**stamping ground** *n.* [C] STOMPING GROUND

stance /stæns/ *n.* [C usually singular] **1** an opinion that is stated publicly: +**on/against** *the senator's stance on tax cuts* | **take/adopt a stance** *The company has taken a **tough stance** on contract negotiations.* **2** a position in which you stand, especially when doing a particular activity: *You need to improve your stance and swing.* → see also POSTURE

stanch /stæntʃ/ *v.* [T] to STAUNCH

stan·chion /ˈstæntʃən/ *n.* [C] a strong upright bar used to support something

stand[1] /stænd/ S1 W1 *v. past tense and past participle* **stood** /stʊd/
1 BE ON YOUR FEET [I] to support yourself on your feet in an upright position: *She was so weak that she could barely stand.* | *I was standing a few feet away from him.* | +**in/behind/beside etc.** *He stood on the corner, waiting for a bus.* | *Don't **just stand there*** (=stand and not do anything) *– help me!* | **stand (somewhere) doing sth** *I stood there waiting.* | *Could you **stand still*** (=not move) *for just a minute?* | **stand on your toes/stand on tiptoe** (=support yourself on your toes) → see also STANDSTILL
2 RISE [I,T] also **stand up** to rise to an upright position on your feet, or to make someone do this SYN **rise**: *We all stood and clapped.* | *Stand up, Joey.* | **stand sb (up) on sth** *Dad stood me up on a chair so I could see.*
3 STEP [I always + adv./prep.] to step a short distance: **stand back/aside** (=step backwards or sideways) *Helen stood back to admire the painting.* | *The doctors told everyone to **stand clear*** (=move away from something).
4 UPRIGHT POSITION [I,T always + adv./prep.] to be upright in a particular position, or to put something somewhere in an upright position: *Few houses were left standing after the tornado.* | *There's a parking lot where the theater once stood.* | **stand sth on/in/over etc.** *Stand the bookcase against the wall over there.* ▶see THESAURUS box at **lean**[1]
5 IN A STATE/SITUATION [I always + adv./prep., linking verb] to be in, stay in, or get into a particular state or situation: *The kitchen door **stood open**.* | *The house has **stood empty** since Mrs. Green died.* | *Warships are standing on alert in case there is an attack.* | **the way things stand/as things stand** *As things stand, we'll be lucky to finish the job by Monday.* | **where/how do things stand?** *Where do things stand in terms of the budget?* | **stand united/divided** (=agree or disagree completely) *He urged the nation to stand united against terrorism.* | **stand prepared/ready to do sth** (=be prepared to do something whenever it is necessary) | *We teachers need to **stand together*** (=stay united) *if we want better pay.* → see also **be/stand in awe of sb** at AWE[1] (2)
6 ACCEPT A SITUATION [I,T] to be able to accept or deal well with a difficult situation SYN **tolerate**: *I **can't stand it**! You're being such a fool!* | **can/could stand** *I could barely stand the pain.* | **stand letting/allowing etc. sb doing sth** *How can you stand letting her talk to you like that?*
7 BE GOOD ENOUGH [T] to be done or made well enough to be successful, strong, or useful for a long time: *The paint is designed to stand all kinds of weather.* | *His poetry will **stand the test of time*** (=stay popular). → see also **stand up**
8 stand to do sth to be likely to do or have something: *He stands to make a good deal of money.* | *Who **stands to gain** from this situation?* | **stand to win/lose** *Kirkland stands to lose his business if he misses a payment.*
9 NOT MOVE [I] to stay in a particular place without moving: *Leave the mixture to stand for an hour.*
10 AT A LEVEL/AMOUNT [I always + adv./prep.] to be at a particular level or amount: +**at** *Unemployment stands at 6%.*
11 A RANK/POSITION [I always + adv./prep.] to have a particular rank or position when compared to similar things or people: *He stands high on the list of suitable*

candidates. | How does our country's level of debt **stand in relation to** other countries?
12 HEIGHT [I always + adv./prep., linking verb] FORMAL to be a particular height: *The radio antenna* ***stands*** *867 feet* ***high.*** | *John* ***stands*** *six feet* ***tall.***

SPOKEN PHRASES

13 NOT LIKE can't/couldn't stand to not like someone or something at all, or think that something is extremely bad or disgusting SYN **can't bear**: *Her father can't stand liver.* | *Doug couldn't stand her.* | **can't stand sb/sth doing sth** *Bert can't stand anyone touching him.* | **can't stand the sight/smell/taste etc. of sth** *Alison can't stand the sight of blood.* | **can't stand to see/hear/do etc.** *I couldn't stand to see good food going to waste.* | **can't stand seeing/hearing/doing etc.** *I can't stand listening to her complain.* → see also **stand for sth**
14 SUGGEST STH TO SB could stand used to say very directly that it would be a good idea for someone to do something or for something to happen: *It looks like the kitchen could stand a good cleaning.* | **could stand to do sth** *You could stand to lose a few pounds.*
15 if you can't stand the heat, get out of the kitchen used to say that you should leave a job or situation if you cannot deal with its difficulties
16 do sth standing on your head to do something easily: *I've done it so many times I could do it standing on my head.*
17 I stand corrected FORMAL used to admit that your opinion or something that you just said was wrong

18 stand trial to be brought to a court of law to have your case examined and judged: **+on/for** *Jenkins will stand trial on corruption charges.*
19 stand alone a) to continue to do something alone, without help from anyone else: *She does not stand alone in her fight against this law.* **b)** to be much better than anyone or anything else: *Piaget's sheer volume of research stands alone.*
20 stand fast/firm also **stand your ground a)** to refuse to change your opinions, intentions, or decisions: *The city council stood firm, rejecting the plan.* | **+on/against** *Priests were urged to stand firm against divorce.* **b)** to not allow someone to force you to move backward: *The Eagles' defense stood firm, not letting Washington score.*
21 stand in line to stand in a line of people, in order to wait for your turn to do something: *At 6 a.m. people were already standing in line to buy bread.*
22 STILL EXIST [I not in progressive] to continue to exist, be correct, or be VALID: *My offer still stands.* | *The court of appeal has ruled that the conviction should stand.*
23 stand still to not change or progress at all, although time has passed: *Space technology has not stood still.* | ***Time*** *seems to* ***stand still*** *in this historic hotel.*
24 stand a chance/hope (of doing sth) to be likely to be able to do something or to succeed: *You'll stand a better chance of getting a job with a degree.* | *The Eagles* ***don't stand a chance against*** *New York.*
25 LIQUID [I] a liquid that stands does not flow or is not made to move: *Mosquitos usually lay their eggs in standing water.*
26 stand tall a) to be proud and feel ready to deal with anything: *He encouraged his students to stand tall.* **b)** to stand with your back straight and your head raised: *She stood tall and faced him.*
27 know how/where you stand (with sb) to know how someone feels about you, or what you are allowed to do in a particular situation: *I never know where I stand with him.* | *It helps to know where you stand legally.*
28 stand pat INFORMAL to refuse to change a decision, plan etc.: **+on** *For now, the German Central Bank is standing pat on interest rates.*
29 stand at attention if soldiers stand at attention, they stand very straight and stiff to show respect: *The guards stood at attention as the general walked past.*
30 stand on your head/hands to support yourself on your head or hands, with your feet in the air
31 where sb stands someone's opinion about something, or the official rule about something: **+on** *I'm not sure where I stand on the issue of gun control.*
32 from where I stand also **from where I'm standing** according to what you know or feel: *Well, from where I stand, it looks like you've found a good job.*
33 stand guard (over sb/sth) to watch someone or something so that they do not do anything wrong or so that nothing bad happens to them: *Soldiers stand guard on the street corners.*
34 stand accused a) to be the person in a court of law who is being judged for a crime: *Irvin stands accused of murder.* **b)** if you stand accused of doing something bad or wrong, other people say that you have done it: *The radio station stands accused of racism.*
35 stand on your own two feet INFORMAL to be able to do what you need to do, earn your own money etc., without help from others: *She needs to learn to stand on her own two feet.*
36 it stands to reason used to say that something should be completely clear to anyone who is sensible: *If the thefts are all in the same area, it stands to reason it's the same kids doing it.*
37 stand in sb's way also **stand in the way** to prevent someone from doing something: *You can't stand in the way of progress!* | *If he was so determined to do it, who was I to stand in his way?*
38 stand sb in good stead FORMAL to be very useful to someone when needed: *Saving the company millions should stand me in good stead for a promotion.*
39 stand sth on its head to show that a belief, idea etc. is completely untrue: *Galileo's discovery stood medieval thought on its head.*
40 stand or fall by/on to depend on something for success: *The whole nation stands or falls on the Constitution.*
41 not stand on ceremony FORMAL to not worry about the formal rules of polite behavior
[**Origin:** Old English *standan*] → see also **make sb's hair stand on end** at HAIR (11), **not have a leg to stand on** at LEG (9), BYSTANDER, STANDBY[1]

stand against sb/sth *phr. v.* to oppose a person, organization, plan, decision etc.: *As a nation, we stand against terrorism.*

stand around *phr. v.* to stand somewhere and not do anything: *There were plenty of people just standing around.* | **stand around doing sth** *Some kids were just standing around talking.*

stand by *phr. v.* **1 stand by sth** to keep a promise or agreement, or to say that something is still true: *I stand by what I said earlier.* **2 stand by sb** to stay loyal to someone and support them, especially in a difficult situation: *He's really stood by her during her illness.* **3** to be ready to do something if necessary: *A rescue helicopter is standing by.* | **+for** *Stand by for the countdown.* **4** to not do anything to help someone or prevent something from happening: *They will not stand by and let you take away their homes.*

stand down *phr. v.* **1 stand sb down** if a soldier stands down or is stood down, he stops working for the day or stops what he is doing to obey someone: *We stood down at six.* **2** FORMAL to agree to leave your position or to stop trying to be elected, so that someone else can have a chance: *He is standing down from his post in January.* → see also **step down** at STEP[2]

stand for sth *phr. v.* **1** if a letter, number, picture, or sign stands for something, it represents a word, name, or idea, especially in a short form SYN **represent**: *V.A. stands for Veterans Administration.* **2** to support a particular set of ideas, values, or principles: *Samuels hasn't made it clear to voters exactly what he stands for.* **3** to allow or accept something: *Maggie won't stand for any alcohol in her house.*

stand in for sb *phr. v.* to do someone else's job or take their place for a short time: *Hall will stand in for Troy as quarterback.* → see also STAND-IN

stand out *phr. v.* **1** to be very easy to see or notice: *We want the picture on the cover to stand out.* | *At six foot seven, Rich really* ***stands out in a crowd.*** | **stand out a mile/stand out like a sore thumb** *His bright*

S

green jacket stood out a mile. **2** to be clearly better than other similar people or things: **stand out as sth** *Owen stands out as the best young player in the game.* | **+from/among/above** *Three of the cars we tested stood out from the rest.* **3** to rise up from a surface SYN **project**: *The veins stood out on his arms.* → see also STANDOUT

stand over sb *phr. v.* to stand very close behind or above someone and watch as they work, especially to make sure they do nothing wrong: *I can't concentrate with him standing over me like that.*

stand up *phr. v.* **1** to be on your feet, or to rise to your feet: *I've been standing up all day.* | *Jim stood up stiffly.* **2 stand up straight** to stand in a very upright way, so that your shoulders are not forward: *Stand up straight and pay attention.* **3** to stay healthy in a difficult environment or in good condition after a lot of hard use: **+to** *My old truck can stand up to just about anything.* **4** to be proved to be true, correct, useful etc. when tested: **stand up under/to sth** *The data may not stand up to further testing.* | *Without a witness, these charges will never **stand up in court*** (=be successfully proved in a court of law). **5 stand sb up** INFORMAL to not meet someone who you have arranged to meet: *I can't believe she stood me up.* **6 stand up and be counted** to make it very clear what you think about something, when this is dangerous or might cause trouble for you → see also STAND-UP[1]

S

stand up for sb/sth *phr. v.* to support or defend a person or idea when they are being attacked: *Thanks for standing up for me.* | *Don't be afraid to stand up for what you believe in.*

stand up to sb/sth *phr. v.* to refuse to accept unfair treatment from a person or organization: *He's a hero to Arabs because he stood up to the United States.*

stand[2] S2 W2 *n.*

1 FOR SUPPORT [C] a piece of furniture or equipment used to support something: *a music stand* | *an umbrella stand*

2 FOR SELLING [C] a table or small structure, usually outside or in a large building, used for selling or showing things SYN **stall**: *They have the largest stand at the conference.* | *an ice cream stand* → see also NEWSSTAND

3 the stands a) the place where people sit to watch a sports game SYN **grandstand** SYN **bleachers**: *There were over 40,000 people in the stands.* **b)** the places where magazines and newspapers can be bought: *The new edition of "Time" will **hit the stands*** (=become available to be bought) *Tuesday.*

4 OPINION/ATTITUDE [C usually singular] a position or opinion that you state firmly and publicly SYN **position**: **+on/against** *What is their stand on environmental issues?* | *The organization has not **taken a stand** on abortion.*

5 the stand the place in a court of law where someone sits when lawyers ask them questions: *On Monday, Richards will **take the stand*** (=begin answering questions). | *Wilcox looked nervous **on the stand*** (=when he was answering questions).

6 OPPOSE/DEFEND [C] a strong effort to defend yourself or to oppose someone or something: **take/make/mount a stand (against sth)** *Neighborhood residents are taking a stand against drug dealers.*

7 a group of trees of one type growing close together SYN **copse**: *a stand of pines*

8 taxi/cab stand a place where taxis stop and wait for passengers → see also GRANDSTAND, ONE-NIGHT STAND

stand·a·lone /ˈstændəˌloʊn/ *adj.* **1** COMPUTERS a standalone computer works on its own without being part of a NETWORK **2** TECHNICAL a standalone company is one that is not part of a larger company

stan·dard[1] /ˈstændɚd/ S2 W2 *n.*

1 LEVEL OF QUALITY [C,U] a level of quality, skill, ability, or achievement that is considered to be necessary or acceptable in a particular situation, and by which someone or something is judged: *Air quality standards vary from state to state.* | **+of** *the school's standards of behavior* | **strict/rigorous/tough standards** *The airline has rigorous **safety standards**.* | *The hotel must **maintain** its high **standards** of service.* | *Unless your scuba diving equipment is **up to standard*** (=good enough), *do not use it.* | **a high/low standard** *These students **set** high **standards** for themselves.* | **meet/reach/attain a standard** *They have to reach a certain standard or they won't pass.* | **raise/lower a standard** *Asher launched a campaign to raise standards of health care.*

2 USED WHEN COMPARING [C usually plural] the ideas of what is good or normal that someone uses to compare one thing with another: *Shakespeare is the standard against which other playwrights are measured.* | *It was a luxurious house **by local standards**.* | *Ella was 41 years old, hardly a girl **by any standard*** (=according to anyone's opinion or values).

3 MORAL PRINCIPLES standards [plural] moral principles about what kind of behavior or attitudes are acceptable: *There is a concern about the **moral standards** of today's youth.* | **high/low standards** *Our leaders need high **ethical standards**.*

4 MEASUREMENT [C] SCIENCE an agreed system, method, or unit for measuring weight, PURITY, value etc.: *the official government standard for the purity of silver*

5 a standard a car that uses a STICK SHIFT system to control its GEARS → see also AUTOMATIC

6 SONG [C] ENG. LANG. ARTS a popular song that has been sung by many different singers, or a piece of music that has been played by many different musicians, especially over many years: *She sang all the **old standards**.* | *popular jazz standards*

7 FLAG [C] a flag used in ceremonies: *the royal standard*

8 MILITARY POLE [C] a pole with a picture or shape at the top carried in past times at the front of an army

[**Origin:** 1100–1200 Old French *estandard* **battle-flag**]

→ see also DOUBLE STANDARD, LIVING STANDARD

standard[2] S3 W2 *adj.* **1** accepted as normal or usual: *A work week of 40 hours is standard in the U.S.* | *What's the standard rate of pay for a babysitter?* | *Modems are **standard equipment** on PCs sold for home use.* | **standard practice/procedure** (=the usual way of doing things) *Searching luggage at airports is now standard practice.* ►see THESAURUS box at **normal**[1] **2** regular and usual in shape, size, quality etc. OPP **nonstandard**: *standard size paper* **3** the form of a language that most people use and consider correct: *the word's standard spelling* → see also NONSTANDARD, SUBSTANDARD

ˌstandard ˈatmosphere *n.* [C] PHYSICS an ATMOSPHERE

ˈstandard-ˌbearer *n.* [C] **1** an important leader in a moral argument or political group **2** the soldier who carries the STANDARD (=flag) at the front of an army

ˌstandard deˈduction *n.* [C usually singular] a specific amount of the money you earn that you do not have to pay tax on

ˌstandard deviˈation *n.* [C] MATH in STATISTICS, a calculation which shows how much each value in a set is different from the MEAN of the values in the set

ˌstandard ˈentropy *n.* [U] PHYSICS the ENTROPY of a substance in its standard state at 25° Celsius

ˌstandard-ˈissue *adj.* **1** included in ordinary military equipment **2** a standard-issue thing is the ordinary type of that thing: *The movie is a standard-issue romance.*

stan·dard·ize /ˈstændɚˌdaɪz/ *v.* [T] to make all the things of one particular type the same as each other: *Should the U.S. standardize the school curriculum?* —**standardization** /ˌstændɚdəˈzeɪʃən/ *n.* [U]

ˌstandardized ˈtest *n.* [C] a test that is taken by a large number of people and is designed to measure their knowledge or ability: *standardized tests of reading ability*

ˌstandard of ˈliving *n.* [C usually singular] ECONOMICS the amount of wealth, comfort, and goods that a particular person, group, country etc. has: *Many cross the border seeking a better standard of living.*

ˌstandard ˈtime *n.* [singular] **1** the time to which all clocks in a particular area of the world are set **2** the time of the year from late October to early April when clocks are set one hour back from DAYLIGHT SAVING TIME

stand·by[1], **stand-by** /ˈstændbaɪ/ *plural* **standbys** *n.* **1** [C] something that is kept to be used when needed: *Oatmeal was Mom's standby for breakfast.* | *a generator for standby power in emergencies* **2 on standby a)** ready to help immediately if you are needed: *City firefighters have been **kept on standby** for the past three days.* **b)** if you are on standby to travel on a plane or train or to attend something such as a play, you may be allowed to get a ticket if places become available: *There are no tickets left, but we can **put** you **on standby**.* **c)** if a piece of electrical equipment is on standby, the power is on, but it is not being used: *The phone's battery will last up to 200 hours on standby.* **3** [C] someone or something that you can always depend on or that will always be appropriate: *Duck à l'orange is an **old standby** on French menus.* —**standby** *adv.*: *I was able to fly standby to Miami.* → see also **stand by** at STAND[1]

standby[2] *adj.* [only before noun] a standby ticket is one that you can get only if places become available, for example if other people cannot use their tickets

ˈstand-in *n.* [C] **1** ENG. LANG. ARTS someone who takes the place of an actor for some parts of a movie **2** someone who does the job or takes the place of someone else for a short time SYN **substitute**: *The vice-president acted as a stand-in for the president during the debate.* → see also STAND IN FOR SB

stand·ing[1] /ˈstændɪŋ/ *adj.* [only before noun] **1** permanently agreed or arranged: **a standing invitation/offer** *You have a standing invitation to our cabin.* **2 standing order a)** a permanent rule that a group of people such as a committee, council etc. follow: *U.N. troops have standing orders to attack if they are fired upon.* **b)** an agreement to buy something regularly: *Two of the firm's key customers canceled their standing orders.* **3** done from or in a standing position: *He pulled himself up to a standing position.* | *Seifert's speech received **a standing ovation*** (=when people stand up to CLAP). **4 a standing joke** something that happens often and that people make jokes about: *My spelling mistakes became a standing joke in the office.*

standing[2] *n.* **1** [U] someone's rank or position in a system, organization, society etc., based on what other people think of them or compared to others of the same type: **+in/among/with etc.** *The policy has damaged his standing among environmentalists.* | *China has improved its international standing.* | **low/high standing** *the party's low standing in the polls* **2 standings** [plural] the list that shows what rank a team, person etc. has in a competition: *The Rockets are second in the NBA standings.* **3 of five/many etc. years' standing** used to show the time during which something such as an agreement has existed: *It was a social policy of 60 years' standing.*

ˌstanding ˈarmy *n.* [C] a professional permanent army, rather than one that has been formed for a war

ˈstanding comˌmittee *n.* [C] a group of members of Congress chosen to consider possible new laws

ˈstanding room *n.* [U] space for standing in a theater, STADIUM etc.: *There was **standing room only** (=no seats were left) in the court room.*

ˌstanding ˈwave also **ˌstationary ˈwave** *n.* [C] PHYSICS a type of wave that has regular repeating patterns of fixed points with no change or VIBRATION and changing points of the greatest possible change or vibration, caused when two waves of the same size moving in the opposite direction meet

Stan·dish /ˈstændɪʃ/, **Miles** /maɪlz/ (?1584–1656) an English soldier who came to America with the Pilgrim Fathers on the Mayflower ship

stand·off /ˈstændɔf/ *n.* [C] a situation in which neither side in a fight or battle can gain an advantage

stand-off·ish /stænˈdɔfɪʃ/ *adj.* INFORMAL fairly unfriendly and formal SYN **aloof**: *She was cold and stand-offish.* —**stand-offishly** *adv.* —**stand-offishness** *n.* [U]

stand·out /ˈstændaʊt/ *n.* [C] a person or thing in a group that is much better than all the rest: *Marple was a basketball standout in high school.* —**standout** *adj.*: *a standout performance*

stand·pipe /ˈstændpaɪp/ *n.* [C] a pipe that provides water in a public place in the street

stand·point /ˈstændpɔɪnt/ *n.* [C usually singular] a way of thinking about people, situations, ideas etc. SYN **point of view**: ***From a** financial **standpoint**, the plan made very good sense.*

stand·still /ˈstændˌstɪl/ *n.* **a standstill** a situation in which there is no movement or activity at all: *The sudden snow storm **brought** the entire city **to a standstill**.* | **come/grind to a standstill** *The country came to a standstill during the games.* | *Traffic was **at a standstill** on the freeway.*

ˈstand-up[1], **standup** *adj.* [only before noun] **1** stand-up COMEDY involves one person telling jokes as a performance: *a stand-up comedian* **2** able to stay upright: *a stand-up mirror* **3 a stand-up guy** APPROVING a man who other people like because he is honest and admits when he is wrong: *Fred's a stand-up guy.* **4** a stand-up meeting, meal etc. is one in which people stand up during it: *a stand-up wedding reception* → see also **stand up** at STAND[1]

stand-up[2], **standup** *n.* [U] stand-up COMEDY: *Mark used to **do stand-up** at Roxy's bar.*

Stan·i·slav·sky /ˌstænɪˈslɑfski/, **Con·stan·tin** /ˈkɑnstəntin/ (1863–1938) a Russian actor and theater DIRECTOR who developed a new way of acting, called method acting, which involves actors using their own emotions and experiences

S

stank /stæŋk/ *v.* the past tense of STINK

Stan·ley /ˈstænli/, **Hen·ry Mor·ton** /ˈhɛnri ˈmɔrt̚n/ (1841–1904) a British EXPLORER who was sent by a U.S. newspaper to find David Livingstone in Africa in 1871

Stan·ton /ˈstænt̚n/, **E·liz·a·beth Ca·dy** /ɪˈlɪzəbəθ ˈkeɪdi/ (1815–1902) a U.S. woman who helped women get the right to vote

stan·za /ˈstænzə/ *n.* [C] ENG. LANG. ARTS a group of lines in a repeated pattern that form part of a poem SYN **verse**

staph /stæf/ *n.* [C] **staphylococcus** a type of BACTERIA that causes serious infections: *a staph infection*

sta·ple[1] /ˈsteɪpəl/ *n.* [C] **1** a small piece of thin wire that is used to hold pieces of paper together, by using a special tool to push the ends through the paper and bend them over **2** a small U-shaped piece of metal with pointed ends, used to hold something in place **3** a food that is needed and used all the time: *Tortillas are a staple of Mexican cooking.* **4** someone or something that is often seen or often happens in a particular place: *The song is a staple of the band's live shows.* **5** ECONOMICS the main product that a country or company produces, or its main source of income: *Military contracts are still a staple of the business.* [**Origin:** (1, 2) Old English *stapol* **post**]

staple[2] *v.* [T] to fasten two or more things together with a staple: **staple sth to sth** *A credit card slip was stapled to the receipt.* | **staple sth together** *I stapled the poems together into a little book.* ▸see THESAURUS box at **fasten**

staple[3] *adj.* [only before noun] **1** forming the greatest or most important part of something: *Oil is Nigeria's staple export.* **2 staple diet/food** the food that you normally eat: *Potatoes are part of the staple diet in Russia.* **3** used often or all of the time: *Market research is a staple tool of business.*

ˈstaple gun *n.* [C] a tool used for putting strong staples into walls or pieces of wood

sta·pler /ˈsteɪplɚ/ *n.* [C] a tool used for putting STAPLES into paper

star[1] /stɑr/ S2 W1 *n.* [C]
1 IN THE SKY PHYSICS a large ball of burning gases in space that can be seen at night as a point of light in the sky: *The stars are beautiful tonight.* | *Already the first **stars were out**.* | *We slept **under the stars*** (=outdoors, without a shelter). | ***Bright stars** filled the sky.* | *A few **stars twinkled** in between the clouds.* → see also FALLING STAR, SHOOTING STAR ▸see THESAURUS box at **space**[1]

2 FAMOUS PERFORMER/PLAYER a famous and successful performer in entertainment or a famous player in sports: *His first movie made him a star.* | **basketball/football/soccer etc. star** *Former tennis star Björn Borg also attended the party.* | **movie/Hollywood star** *All the Hollywood stars came to the premiere.* | **rock/pop star** *his dream of becoming a rock star* | *By the age of 20, she was already* ***a big star*** (=very famous performer). | *She's a* ***rising star*** (=someone who is becoming famous) *in the world of opera.* → see also MOVIE STAR, POP STAR, STAR² ▸see THESAURUS box at **famous, movie**

3 MAIN ACTOR IN MOVIE/TV the person who has the main part, or one of the main parts, in a movie, television show, play etc.: +**of** *Clooney was then one of the stars of "ER."*

4 SHAPE a) a shape with four or more points, which represents the way a star looks in the sky: *The flag's 50 stars represent the 50 states.* **b)** a mark in this shape, used to draw attention to something written SYN **asterisk**: *I put stars next to the items we still need to buy.* **c)** a piece of cloth or metal in this shape, worn to show someone's rank or position

5 HOTELS/RESTAURANTS a mark used in a system for judging the quality of hotels and restaurants: **three-star/four-star/five-star** *a five-star restaurant*

6 BEST PERFORMER the person who gives the best performance in a movie, play, television show etc.: *The real star of this movie is the baby polar bear.* | *In Italy, Mehta was* ***the star of the show.*** | *Rivera's first* ***star turn*** (=great performance) *was in "West Side Story."* | *Keiko, a killer whale, had been the show's* ***star attraction*** (=the performer people most wanted to see).

7 SUCCESSFUL PERSON INFORMAL someone who is particularly successful at a job, course of study etc.: *After college, Weiss became a star in sports journalism.* | **a star player/performer/salesman etc.** *He's one of our star players.* | *He is known as* ***a rising star*** (=someone who is becoming successful and famous) *in Japanese politics.*

8 see stars to see flashes of light, especially because you have been hit on the head: *I bumped my head so hard that I saw stars.*

9 have stars in your eyes to imagine that something you want to do, especially something that might make you famous, is much more exciting or attractive than it really is → see also STARRY-EYED

10 sth is written in the stars INFORMAL used to say that what happens is controlled by FATE (=a power that some people believe controls the future)

[**Origin:** Old English *steorra*] → see also **be born under a lucky/unlucky star** at BORN (8), EVENING STAR, FIVE STAR GENERAL, FOUR-STAR GENERAL, MORNING STAR, **reach for the stars** at REACH¹ (11), **thank your lucky stars** at THANK (4)

star² W3 *v.* **starred, starring 1** [I] ENG. LANG. ARTS if someone stars in a movie, television show, or play, that person acts as one of the main characters in it: +**in** *He has starred in several successful TV series.* | +**as** *Fiennes stars as the evil wizard Voldemort.* | *his* ***starring role*** (=the most important character) *in "The Godfather"* **2** [T] ENG. LANG. ARTS if a movie, television show, or play stars someone, that person acts the part of the main character SYN **feature**: *a movie starring John Travolta* | **star sb as...** *"Mary Poppins" starred Julie Andrews as the singing nanny .* **3** [T] to put an ASTERISK (=a star-shaped mark) next to something written: *The most important points have been starred.*

star·board /ˈstɑrbɚd/ *n.* [U] the side of a ship or aircraft that is on your right when you are facing forward —**starboard** *adj.* → see also PORT

starch¹ /stɑrtʃ/ *n.* **1** [U] BIOLOGY a white substance that provides your body with energy but has no taste, and is found in foods such as grain, rice, and potatoes **2** [C] a food that contains this substance: *Starches such as potatoes are a part of most good diets.* **3** [U] a substance that is mixed with water and is used to make cloth stiff **4 take the starch out of sb** to make someone feel less confident

starch² *v.* [T] to make cloth stiff, using starch —**starched** *adj.*: *a starched white uniform*

starch·y /ˈstɑrtʃi/ *adj.* **1** BIOLOGY containing a lot of starch: *starchy foods* **2** DISAPPROVING very formal and correct in your behavior: *the starchy department head* —**starchily** *adv.* —**starchiness** *n.* [U]

ˈstar-crossed *adj.* LITERARY being in a situation that prevents something happy or good from happening: *star-crossed lovers* (=people who love each other but cannot be together)

star·dom /ˈstɑrdəm/ *n.* [U] the state of being a famous performer or sports player: *Denver* ***rose to stardom*** *in the 1970s.*

star·dust /ˈstɑrdʌst/ *n.* [U] LITERARY an imaginary magic substance like shiny powder

stare¹ /stɛr/ W2 *v.* [I] **1** to look at something or someone for a long time without moving your eyes: +**at** *What are you staring at?* | **stare (at sb/sth) in disbelief/amazement/horror etc.** *Zach stared at him in disbelief.* | *She sat* ***staring into space*** (=looking for a long time at nothing). | *I stood and* ***stared out the window*** (=looked for a long time at something through a window). ▸see THESAURUS box at **eye², look¹** **2 be staring sb in the face a)** INFORMAL to be very clear and easy to see: *The solution is staring you in the face.* **b)** to seem impossible to avoid: *Defeat was staring us in the face.*

stare sb down *phr. v.* to look at someone for so long that they start to feel uncomfortable and look away [**Origin:** Old English *starian*] —**staredown** *n.*

stare² *n.* [C] a long steady look: *Their argument attracted the stares of passing shoppers.* | *The question simply got a* ***blank stare*** (=a stare with no understanding or expression). | **a hard/cold/hostile etc. stare** (=a stare that shows a particular emotion, such as anger, dislike etc.) *She* ***gives*** *the team* ***a*** *hard* ***stare****, then says, "Go play like you mean it."*

star·fish /ˈstɑrˌfɪʃ/ *n.* [C] a flat sea animal that has five arms forming the shape of a star

star·fruit /ˈstɑrfrut/ *n.* [C] BIOLOGY a pale green tropical fruit that has a shape similar to a star

star·gaz·er /ˈstɑrˌgeɪzɚ/ *n.* [C] **1** someone who likes to look at stars **2** INFORMAL someone who studies ASTRONOMY or ASTROLOGY **3** someone with ideas or plans that are impossible or not practical

star·gaz·ing /ˈstɑrˌgeɪzɪŋ/ *n.* [U] the activity of looking at stars —**stargaze** *v.* [I]

stark¹ /stɑrk/ *adj.* **1** very simple and plain in appearance, with little color or decoration SYN **austere**: *stark white walls* | *the stark beauty of the desert* **2** used about unpleasant things that are very clear and obvious SYN **harsh**: *Ethnic divisions in the region remain stark.* | *the* ***stark realities*** *of life in the slums* **3** [only before noun] complete or total, used especially when you are talking about something unpleasant: *This year's dryness is* ***in stark contrast to*** (=completely opposite to) *the record rains of last spring.* [**Origin:** Old English *stearc* **stiff, strong**] —**starkly** *adv.* —**starkness** *n.* [U]

stark² *adv.* INFORMAL **1 stark naked** not wearing any clothes at all **2 stark raving mad** completely crazy

star·less /ˈstɑrlɪs/ *adj.* with no stars showing in the sky

star·let /ˈstɑrlɪt/ *n.* [C] a young actress who plays small parts in movies and hopes to become famous

star·light /ˈstɑrlaɪt/ *n.* [U] the light that comes from the stars, often considered to be romantic

star·ling /ˈstɑrlɪŋ/ *n.* [C] BIOLOGY a greenish-black bird that is very common in Europe and North America

star·lit /ˈstɑrˌlɪt/ *adj.* LITERARY made brighter by light from the stars: *a starlit night*

Star of Da·vid /ˌstɑr əv ˈdeɪvɪd/ *n.* [C usually singular] a star with six points that represents the Jewish religion or the state of Israel

star·ry /ˈstɑri/ *adj.* having many stars: *a starry winter sky*

starry-ˈeyed *adj.* INFORMAL happy and hopeful about things in a way that is silly or UNREALISTIC: *starry-eyed young actresses*

Stars and ˈStripes *n.* **the Stars and Stripes** the flag of the U.S.

star·ship /ˈstɑrʃɪp/ *n.* [C] a word for a SPACECRAFT that can take people between stars and PLANETS, used in SCIENCE FICTION stories

star sign *n.* [C] a ZODIAC sign

star-sixty-ˈnine also **ˌstar-six-ˈnine** *v.* [T] SPOKEN to call back the last person who called you by pressing the buttons *, 6, and 9 on the telephone

Star-Spangled ˈBanner *n.* **the Star-Spangled Banner a)** the NATIONAL ANTHEM (=national song) of the U.S. **b)** LITERARY the flag of the U.S.

star-ˌstudded *adj.* including many famous performers: *a star-studded cast*

START /stɑrt/ **Strategic Arms Reduction Talks/Treaty** HISTORY an agreement in 1991 between the U.S. and the Soviet Union to reduce the numbers of a type of NUCLEAR weapon that can travel a long distance

start¹ /stɑrt/ S1 W1 *v.*

1 BEGIN DOING STH [I,T] to do something you were not doing before, and continue doing it SYN **begin**: *There's so much to do, I don't know where to start.* | *They're starting construction next spring.* | **start doing sth** *I'm going to start washing the dishes.* | **start to do sth** *It had just started to rain.* | *She* ***started*** *crying* ***again*** (=began crying after she had stopped). | *We'd better* ***get started*** (=start doing something) *if we want to finish this job today.*

2 BEGIN HAPPENING [I,T] to begin happening, or to make something begin happening: *What time does the movie start?* | *Lightning started a fire that burned 500 acres.* | **start sb doing sth** *Some dust in the closet started him sneezing.* | *The party was just* ***getting started*** *when we arrived.* | **starting now/today/tomorrow etc.** *The series will be shown on CBS starting next fall.*

3 A PARTICULAR BEGINNING [I always + adv./prep.,T] also **start off** to begin something in a particular way, or to begin in a particular way: *A healthy breakfast is a good way to start the day.* | **+with/in/on etc.** *The festivities started with a huge fireworks display.* | **+as** *The whole thing started as a joke.* | **start (sth) by doing sth** *Chao starts by explaining some basic legal concepts.* | **start sth with/on etc. sth** *I like to start my workout with some sit-ups.* | **start well/badly/slowly etc.** *The season has started badly for the Giants.*

4 JOB/SCHOOL [I,T] to begin a new job, or to begin going to school, college etc.: *It sounds like an exciting job. When do you start?* | **start school/college/work** *When she started school, Mari couldn't speak English at all.*

5 CAR/ENGINE ETC. [I,T] also **start up** if you start a car or engine or if it starts, it begins to work: *The car wouldn't start this morning.* | **get the car/engine etc. started** *Can you help me get the lawn mower started?*

6 LIFE/PROFESSION [I always + adv./prep.,T] also **start out** to begin your life or profession in a particular way or place: **+as** *She started as a dancer in the 1950s.* | **start sth doing sth** *Collins started his adult life driving a taxi.* | *Can you give me any tips on how to* ***get started in*** *business?*

7 TRIP [I] also **start off/out** to begin traveling or moving in a particular direction: *We'll have to start early to get to Grandma's by lunchtime.* | **+from/across/up etc.** *I started up the mountain at noon and reached the top by four.*

8 BUSINESS/ORGANIZATION ETC. [T] also **start up** to make something begin to exist SYN **establish**: *A group of women in the neighborhood have started an investment club.* | **start a business/company/firm** *Brad left his father's company to start a business of his own.*

9 start from scratch/zero to begin doing a job or activity completely from the beginning: *Peter the Great had to start from scratch when he built St. Petersburg.*

10 ROAD/RIVER [I always + adv./prep.] if a river, road etc. starts somewhere, it begins in that place: **+in/at** *The trail starts at the west end of the campground.*

11 PRICES [I always + adv./prep.] if prices start at or from a particular number, that is the lowest number at which you can get or buy something: **+at/from** *Summer rates at the hotel start at $199.*

12 SPORTS [I,T] if a player starts in a game, or if someone starts them, they begin playing when the game begins, especially because they are one of the best players on a team: **+for** *Astacio started for the Dodgers on Tuesday night.*

13 to start with SPOKEN **a)** said to emphasize the first of a list of facts or opinions you are stating: *I'm not going to Vegas. To start with, I don't like gambling, and anyway I can't get time off work.* **b)** said when talking about the beginning of a situation, especially when it changes later: *I was nervous to start with, but after a while I was fine.*

14 MOVE SUDDENLY [I] to move your body suddenly, especially because you are surprised or afraid: *A loud knock at the door made her start.* | **+from** *Emma started from her chair and rushed to the window.*

15 start afresh/anew to stop doing what you are doing and begin doing it again better or differently: *She moved to Texas to start anew after the divorce.*

16 start a family to have your first baby: *His mom hopes he'll settle down and start a family.*

17 START A FIGHT/ARGUMENT ETC. to deliberately cause trouble, especially by beginning a fight, argument etc.: *Don't go trying to start a fight.* | *"Tim, don't hit your sister." "She* ***started it!****"* | **start something/anything** *If you start something in there, don't expect me to back you up.*

18 start a rumor to tell other people something, usually something bad or untrue: *Someone started a rumor that I was pregnant.*

19 start young to begin doing something when you are young: *Great musicians start young.*

20 be back where you started to try to do something and fail, so that you finish in the same situation that you were in before: *He'd worked hard for ten years, but now he was right back where he'd started.*

21 Don't (you) start with me! SPOKEN used to tell someone not to complain, argue, or annoy you

start back *phr. v.* to begin returning to the place you came from: **+to/down/up etc.** *I started back down the mountain.*

start in *phr. v.* to begin criticizing someone or complaining to them about something: *Mother, don't you start in again, or I'll leave.* | **+on** *Before I knew it, she'd started in on my wife.*

start in on sth *phr. v.* INFORMAL to begin eating something: *Finally he started in on his burger.*

start off *phr. v.* **1** to begin an activity in a particular way, or to help someone do this: **start off (by) doing sth** *Let's start off by introducing ourselves.* | **start sb/sth off with sth** *Our coach started us off slowly with some simple exercises.* **2** to be a particular thing or have a particular quality at the beginning of something, especially when this changes later: *The week started off slowly, but by Wednesday I was busy again.* | **+as** *I started off as a drummer.* **3** to move in a particular direction, or begin a trip: *I sat in the car for a minute before starting off.* | **+to/toward/back etc.** *Tim started off in the opposite direction.*

start on *phr. v.* **1 start on sth** to begin doing something or using or eating something: *You'd better start on your homework.* | *Mona started on a second piece of chicken.* **2 start sb on sth** to make someone start doing something regularly, especially because it will be good for them: *Try starting your baby on solid foods at four months old.* **3 get (sb) started on sth** if you get started on something or someone gets you started on it, you start talking about it for a long time without stopping: *Don't get him started on one of his stories!*

start out *phr. v.* **1** to begin happening or existing in a particular way, especially when this changes later: *"The Star" started out as a small weekly newspaper.* **2** to begin your life, profession, or an important period of time: *When we were just starting out, no one came to our concerts.* | **+as** *Blake started out as a salesman, but afterward got into advertising.* | **start**

sth out *Kate started her career out as a model.* **3** to begin a trip, or begin moving in a particular direction: *They had just started out when she tripped and hurt her ankle.*

start over *phr. v.* to start doing something again from the beginning, especially because you want to do it better: *If you make a mistake, just erase it and start over.*

start up *phr. v.* **1 start sth ↔ up** if you start up a business, company etc., or it starts up, it begins to exist: *New software companies are starting up in the area.* → see also START-UP[2] **2 start sth ↔ up** if an engine, car etc. starts up, or you start it up, it begins to work: *The whistle blew and the train started up.* **3** if a sound, activity, or event starts up, it begins to exist or happen: *After a few minutes the music* ***started up again.***
[**Origin:** Old English *styrtan* **to jump**] → see Word Choice box at COMMENCE

> WORD CHOICE **start, begin**
> These words usually mean the same thing. However, **start** has some special meanings for which **begin** cannot be used. Use **start** to talk about making a machine work: *I couldn't start the car this morning.* We also use **start** to talk about making something begin to exist: *Matt's thinking about starting his own business.*

S

start[2] S2 W2 *n.*
1 BEGINNING [C usually singular] the first part of something, for example a book, activity, or period of time, or the point at which it begins to develop SYN **beginning** OPP **end**: **+of** *We were late and missed the start of the movie.* | *The assassination marked the start of the war.* | ***From the start*** (=from the moment it began and all the time after that), *their marriage seemed headed for disaster.* | *The case was handled badly* ***from start to finish.*** | **get off to a good/bad start** *The day had gotten off to a bad start.* | **a good/bad start to sth** *The team had a good start to the season.* | *Despite a* ***slow start****, the business is now doing well.* | ***At the start of*** *the book, the boy is living with his aunt and uncle.* | **the start of the year/day/season etc.** *We moved to New York at the start of the year.*
2 it's a start SPOKEN used to say that something you have achieved may not be impressive, but it will help with a bigger achievement: *One exercise class a week isn't enough, but it's a start.*
3 for a start INFORMAL used to emphasize the first of a list of facts or opinions you are stating: *I don't think she'll get the job. She's too young, for a start.* → see also FOR STARTERS
4 make a start to begin doing something: **+on** *I'll make a start on the dishes.*
5 SUDDEN MOVEMENT [singular] a sudden movement of the body, usually caused by fear or surprise: *I awoke* ***with a start*** *and reached for the phone.* | *The sound of scratching on the window* ***gave me a start*** (=frightened or surprised me).
6 CHANCE IN LIFE [singular] the beginning of your life, job etc. and the things that happen to you then, which affect your chances of being happy and successful later: *He* ***got his start*** *in politics as a campaign volunteer.* | *The family is hoping to make a* ***fresh start*** *in the U.S.A.* | *Good health care for the mother* ***gives*** *babies a healthy* ***start.*** | *We all want our kids to have the best possible* ***start in life.*** | *She was the one who* ***gave*** *me my* ***start*** *in show business.*
7 BE AHEAD/HAVE AN ADVANTAGE [C usually singular] if you have a start on other people, you begin doing something before them, which gives you a better chance of being successful SYN **lead**: **+on** *The prisoners had a three-hour start on their pursuers.* | *Germany's military buildup in the 1930s* ***gave it a*** *huge* ***start*** *on Britain and France.* → see also HEAD START
8 the start the place where a race begins: *The horses were all lined up at the start.* → see also FALSE START, **in/by fits and starts** at FIT[2] (6)

start·er /ˈstɑrt̬ɚ/ *n.* **1** [C] a member of a sports team who plays when the game begins, especially because they are one of the best players: *No one on the bench is as good as any of the starters.* **2 for starters** INFORMAL used to emphasize the first of a list of facts, opinions, questions etc.: *"What do you want to know about him?" "What's his name, for starters?"* **3** [C,U] a substance containing BACTERIA that is used to start the process of making cheese, YOGURT etc. **4** [C] a piece of equipment for starting a machine, especially an electric motor for starting an engine **5** [C] someone who gives the signal for a race to begin **6** [C] a person, horse, car etc. that is in a race when it starts **7** [C] an APPETIZER → see also NONSTARTER, SELF-STARTER

ˈstarter home *n.* [C] a small house or apartment bought by people who are buying their first home

ˈstarter kit *n.* [C] the basic equipment and instructions that you need to start doing something

ˈstarter ˌmotor *n.* [C] a STARTER

ˈstarting ˌblock *n.* [C] **1 starting blocks** a pair of blocks attached to the ground, that a runner pushes his or her feet against at the start of a race **2** the block that a swimmer pushes his or her feet against at the start of a race

ˈstarting gate *n.* [C] a gate or pair of gates that open to allow a horse or dog through at the start of a race

ˈstarting line *n.* **the starting line** the line at which a race begins → see also FINISH LINE

ˈstarting ˌline-up *n.* [C] the best players on a sports team, who play when the game begins

ˈstarting point *n.* [C] **1** an idea or situation from which a discussion, process, or PROJECT can develop: *The article was a starting point for discussion.* **2** a place from which you start a trip, race etc.

ˈstarting price *n.* [C] the lowest possible price for something such as a car or house without any special features, or the lowest price you are willing to accept for something you are selling

start·le /ˈstɑrt̬l/ *v.* [T] to make someone feel suddenly surprised or slightly shocked, often so that they make a sudden movement SYN **make sb jump**: *You startled me! I didn't hear you come in.*

start·led /ˈstɑrt̬ld/ *adj.* feeling suddenly surprised or slightly shocked: **be startled to see/hear/learn etc.** *I was startled to see her there.* | *his startled look*

star·tling /ˈstɑrt̬lɪŋ/ *adj.* very unusual or surprising: *a startling change in attitudes* | ***It was startling to*** *see it like that, with no warning.* **—startlingly** *adv.*: *startlingly beautiful*

ˈstart-up[1] *adj.* relating to beginning and developing a new business: *start-up costs*

start-up[2] *n.* [C] COMPUTERS a new small company or business: *Internet start-ups*

ˈstart-up ˌcost also **ˈsetup ˌcost** *n.* [C usually plural] ECONOMICS the amount of money that needs to be spent before a new business or product starts to produce any income

star·va·tion /stɑrˈveɪʃən/ *n.* **1** [U] suffering or death caused by lack of food: *People were dying of starvation.* **2 a starvation diet** INFORMAL a situation in which you eat very little food, especially to become thinner **3 starvation wages** extremely low WAGES

starve /stɑrv/ S3 *v.* **1** [I] to suffer or die because you do not have enough to eat: *The world cannot stand by while these people starve.* | *Thousands of refugees* ***starved to death.*** **2** [T] to prevent someone from having enough food to live: *The poor dogs had been starved.* **3** [I,T] to not give or not be given something very important such as love or money, with harmful results: **starve (sb) for sth** *The children were starved for affection.* | **be starved of sth** *schools that are starved of resources* **4 be starving** also **be starved** SPOKEN to be very hungry: *I'm starving! When do we eat?* **5 starve yourself** to not eat enough food, especially in order to become thin **6 starve sb into (doing) sth** to force someone to do something by preventing them from getting food or money: *The Navy thought they could* ***starve*** *the enemy* ***into submission*** *through a blockade.*
[**Origin:** Old English *steorfan* **to die**]

starve sb out *phr. v.* to force someone to leave a place by preventing them from getting food: *The government tried to starve out the rebels.*

Star Wars *n.* an informal name for the STRATEGIC DEFENSE INITIATIVE

stash¹ /stæʃ/ *v.* [T always + adv./prep.] INFORMAL to store something in a safe, often secret, place: **stash sth away** *She found the gin that Bill had stashed away.* | **stash sth in/under sth** *He has stashed millions in foreign banks.*

stash² *n.* [C] INFORMAL an amount of something that is kept in a secret place, especially money, weapons, or drugs

sta·sis /ˈsteɪsɪs, ˈstæ-/ *n.* [U] FORMAL a state or period in which there is no change or development → see also STATIC¹

stat /stæt/ *n.* [C] INFORMAL a STATISTIC

state¹ /steɪt/ S1 W1 *n.*
1 CONDITION [C] the mental, emotional, or physical condition that someone or something is in at a particular time: *When the gas cools, it condenses back to its liquid state.* | **+of** *We were in a state of shock afterward.* | *Exercise can improve your* ***state of mind*** (=the way you think and feel). | **sb's mental/emotional/physical state** *The poem is a reflection of her mental state.* | *Our schools are* ***in a*** *terrible* ***state*** (=their condition is bad). | **a state of war/siege** *The two countries are still officially in a state of war.* → see also STATE OF EMERGENCY
2 PART OF A COUNTRY [C] POLITICS one of the areas with limited law-making powers that together make up a country controlled by a central government, such as the U.S.: **+of** *the state of Iowa* | *the state government* | **state employees/property/regulations etc.** *Most state employees will have the day off.* | **state-owned/state-funded/state-subsidized etc.** *the state-run pension plan*
3 A COUNTRY [C] POLITICS a country considered as a political organization: *Not all* ***member states*** *of the EU joined the currency union.* | **a democratic/totalitarian etc. state** (=with that type of government) *China is still a Communist state.* → see also POLICE STATE ▸see THESAURUS box at **country¹**
4 GOVERNMENT [singular, U] also **the State** POLITICS the government or political organization of a country: *It is the duty of the state to pass laws for the common good.* | **matters/affairs of state** (=the business of the government) → see also HEAD OF STATE, WELFARE STATE
5 CEREMONY [U] POLITICS the official ceremonies and events relating to governments and rulers: *The Queen will visit Texas as part of her official* ***state visit***. → see also **lie in state** at LIE¹ (13)
6 a state of affairs a situation: **sad/strange/worrisome etc. state of affairs** *How is he dealing with this confusing state of affairs?*
7 in/into a state SPOKEN being or becoming very nervous, anxious, or excited: *I knew I was* ***working myself into a state****, but I couldn't stop worrying.*
8 the state of play the position reached in an activity or process that has not finished yet: *I can't comment on the state of play in the negotiations.*
[**Origin:** 1100–1200 Old French *estat*, from Latin *status*, from the past participle of *stare* **to stand**]

state² S3 W2 *v.* [T] **1** to formally say or write a piece of information or your opinion: *Please state your full name for the record.* | **state (that)** *He stated that his department was not responsible for the mistake.* | *To say the city has serious problems is* ***stating the obvious*** (=saying something that is already clear). **2** if a document, newspaper, ticket etc. states information, it contains the information written clearly: *The receipt clearly states that refunds are not allowed.*

state atˈtorney *n.* [C] LAW a lawyer who represents the state in court cases

state ˌcollege *n.* [C] a college that receives money from the U.S. state it is in to help pay its costs

state court *n.* [C] LAW a court in the U.S. which deals with legal cases that are related to state laws or a state's CONSTITUTION

state·craft /ˈsteɪtkræft/ *n.* [U] the skill or activity of working in government or DIPLOMACY

ˈState Deˌpartment → see DEPARTMENT OF STATE, THE

state·hood /ˈsteɪthʊd/ *n.* [U] **1** POLITICS the condition of being an independent nation **2** the condition of being one of the states making up a nation, such as the U.S.

State·house, statehouse /ˈsteɪthaʊs/ *n.* **the Statehouse** POLITICS the building where the people who make laws in a U.S. state do their work

state·less /ˈsteɪtlɪs/ *adj.* POLITICS not officially being a citizen of any country: *Millions of refugees remain stateless.* —**statelessness** *n.* [U]

ˌstate ˈline *n.* [C] POLITICS the border between two states in the U.S.

state·ly /ˈsteɪtli/ *adj.* **1** done slowly and with a lot of ceremony: *She walked back in the same stately manner as before.* **2** impressive in style and size: *a stately old house*

state·ment /ˈsteɪt˺mənt/ S2 W1 *n.* [C] **1** something you say or write publicly or officially to let people know your intentions or opinions, or to record facts: **+that** *The statement that boys are good at math and girls are not is plainly wrong.* | **+about/on** *He made several negative statements about her performance.* | **make/issue/give a statement** (=say something in a very official way) *Vernon issued a statement today, confirming his resignation.* | *In* ***a sworn statement*** (=one that you officially say is true), *Thomas denied any improper behavior.* | **get/take a statement** (=officially write down what someone says) *Brady took statements from both witnesses.* | **public/official statement** *School administrators have made a number of public statements about this issue.* | **false/inaccurate/misleading statement** (=one that is wrong) *He was accused of making false statements in court.* → see also MISSION STATEMENT **2** a list showing amounts of money paid, received, owing etc. and their total: *a bank statement* | *the company's annual financial statement* **3** something you do, make, wear etc. that causes people to have a particular opinion about you: *The type of car you drive* ***makes a statement*** *about who you are.* → see also FASHION STATEMENT

S

Stat·en Is·land /ˌstæt˺n ˈaɪlənd/ an island which is the smallest of the five BOROUGHS of New York City

ˌstate of eˈmergency *n.* [C] a situation that a government officially says is very dangerous, and in which it uses special laws to control the situation: *The governor* ***declared a state of emergency*** *during the blizzard.*

ˌstate-of-the-ˈart *adj.* using the most modern and recently developed methods, materials, or knowledge: *state-of-the-art electronics*

ˌstate ˈpark *n.* [C] a large park owned and managed by a U.S. state, often in an area of natural beauty

state·room /ˈsteɪtrum/ *n.* [C] a private room or place for sleeping on a ship, train etc.

States /steɪts/ *n.* INFORMAL **the States** a word meaning the U.S., used especially by someone when they are outside the U.S.

ˌstate's atˈtorney *n.* a STATE ATTORNEY

ˈstate ˌschool *n.* INFORMAL a STATE COLLEGE or STATE UNIVERSITY

ˌstate's ˈevidence *n.* **turn state's evidence** if a criminal turns state's evidence, they give information in a court of law about other criminals

state·side, Stateside /ˈsteɪtsaɪd/ *adj., adv.* INFORMAL a word meaning "in the U.S." or "relating to the U.S.," used by people when they are not in the U.S.: *He was assigned for duty stateside.*

states·man /ˈsteɪtsmən/ *n.* *plural* **statesmen** /-mən/ [C] a political or government leader, especially one who is respected as being wise, honorable, and fair —**statesmanlike** *adj.* —**statesmanship** *n.* [U]

ˈstates' ˌrights *n.* [plural] the rights or powers that U.S.

states have because the Constitution has not given those rights to the Federal government: *Jefferson was a strong advocate of states' rights.*

states·wo·man /ˈsteɪtsˌwʊmən/ *n. plural* **stateswomen** /-ˌwɪmɪn/ [C] a political or government leader, especially one who is respected as being wise, honorable, and fair

ˌstate ˈtrooper *n.* [C] a member of a police force that is controlled by one of the U.S. state governments, who works anywhere in that state

ˈstate uniˌversity *n. plural* **state universities** [C] a university which receives money from the U.S. state it is in to help pay its costs

state·wide /ˈsteɪtˀwaɪd/ *adj.* affecting or involving all people or parts of a U.S. state: *statewide elections*

stat·ic¹ /ˈstæt̬ɪk/ *adj.* not moving, changing, or developing, especially when movement or change would be good OPP **dynamic**: *Unfortunately, the high divorce rate* ***remains static***. [**Origin:** 1800–1900 Modern Latin *staticus*, from Greek *statikos* **causing to stand**] → see also STASIS, DYNAMIC

static² *n.* [U] **1** PHYSICS noise caused by electricity in the air that blocks or spoils the sound from radio or TV **2** PHYSICS static electricity **3** INFORMAL complaints or opposition to a plan, situation, or action: *That's my final decision, so don't give me any static.*

ˌstatic ˈcharacter *n.* [C] ENG. LANG. ARTS a character in a book, movie etc. who is not well developed and who does not change during the story

ˌstatic ˈcling *n.* [U] a force caused by static electricity, that causes things such as clothes to stick together

ˌstatic elecˈtricity *n.* [U] PHYSICS electricity that is not flowing in a current, but collects on the surface of an object and gives you a small electric shock

stat·ics /ˈstæt̬ɪks/ *n.* [U] PHYSICS the science dealing with the forces that produce balance in objects that are not moving → see also DYNAMIC

sta·tion¹ /ˈsteɪʃən/ S1 W1 *n.*

1 TRAVEL [C] a place where public vehicles regularly stop so that passengers can get on and off, goods can be loaded etc., or the building or buildings at such a place: **a bus/train/subway station** *I'll meet you at the train station.* | *Grand Central Station*

2 ACTIVITY OR SERVICE [C] a building or place that is a center for a particular type of service or activity: *a police station* | *I need to stop at the gas station on the way home.* | *a radar station*

3 TV/RADIO [C] **a)** one of the many different signals you can receive on your television or radio, that a company broadcasts on → see also CHANNEL: **a TV/television/radio station** *a popular local radio station* | **a jazz/rock/country etc. station** *See if you can find a country music station.* | *I can only* ***get*** *a couple of* ***stations*** *on this radio.* **b)** an organization which makes television or radio broadcasts, or the building where this is done: *She works for a television station in Utah.*

4 POSITION [C] a place where someone stands or sits in order to be ready to do something quickly if needed: *the clerk's station behind the counter*

5 SOCIAL RANK [C] OLD-FASHIONED your position in society: **above/below sb's station** *She married a man far below her station.*

6 MILITARY [C] a small military establishment

7 SHIPS [U] TECHNICAL a ship's position in relation to others in a group, especially a military ship

8 FARM [C] a large RANCH (=farm) for sheep or cattle in Australia or New Zealand

[**Origin:** 1500–1600 French, Latin *statio* **place for standing or stopping**, from *stare* **to stand**]

station² *v.* [T usually passive] to put someone in a particular place in order to do a particular job or military duty: **be stationed in/at sth** *Dad was stationed in Europe during the war.* | *There were police officers stationed at every exit.*

sta·tion·a·ry /ˈsteɪʃəˌnɛri/ *adj.* not moving: *The truck hit a stationary vehicle.*

ˌstationary ˈbike also **ˌstationary ˈbicycle** *n.* [C] an EXERCISE BIKE

ˌstationary ˈwave *n.* [C] PHYSICS a STANDING WAVE

ˈstation break *n.* [C] a pause during a radio or television program, so that local stations can give their names or broadcast advertisements

sta·tion·er /ˈsteɪʃənɚ/ *n.* [C] FORMAL someone in charge of a store that sells stationery

sta·tion·er·y /ˈsteɪʃəˌnɛri/ *n.* [U] **1** special paper for writing letters on, usually with matching envelopes **2** materials that you use for writing, such as paper, pens, pencils etc.

ˈstation ˌhouse *n.* [C] the local office of the police or fire department in a town, part of a city etc.

ˈstation ˌmaster *n.* [C] someone who is in charge of a train station

ˈstation ˌwagon *n.* [C] a large car with a door and a lot of space at the back for boxes, suitcases etc.

sta·tis·tic /stəˈtɪstɪk/ Ac W2 *n.* **1 statistics a)** [plural] MATH a collection of numbers which represents facts or measurements: *official crime statistics* | **+for** *statistics for injuries at work* **b)** [U] the science of dealing with and explaining such numbers → see also VITAL STATISTICS **2** [singular] MATH a single number which represents a fact or measurement: *a depressing statistic* | **a statistic that** *I read a statistic that over 10,000 Americans a day turn 50.* **3 become/be a statistic** INFORMAL to die of a disease, in an accident etc. and be considered only as an example of the way you died, not as a person [**Origin:** 1700–1800 German *statistik* **study of political facts and figures**, from Modern Latin *statisticus* **of politics**] —**statistical** *adj.*: *statistical analysis* —**statistically** /-kli/ *adv.*: *The variation is not statistically significant.*

stat·is·ti·cian /ˌstæt̬əsˈtɪʃən/ Ac *n.* [C] MATH someone who works with statistics

sta·tive /ˈsteɪt̬ɪv/ *adj.* TECHNICAL ENG. LANG. ARTS a stative verb describes a state rather than an action or event, and is not usually used in PROGRESSIVE forms. For example, in the sentence "This book belongs to me," "belong" is stative.

stats /stæts/ *n.* [plural,U] INFORMAL STATISTICS

stat·u·ar·y /ˈstætʃuˌɛri/ *n.* [U] FORMAL statues

stat·ue /ˈstætʃu/ *n.* [C] an image of a person or animal that is made in solid material such as stone or metal and is usually large: *a bronze statue* | **+of** *a statue of George Washington* → see also SCULPTURE

ˌStatue of ˈLiberty, the *n.* a large STATUE of a woman on Liberty Island in New York Harbor, given to the U.S. by France in 1884. The TORCH she holds in her right hand represents freedom.

Statue of Liberty

stat·u·esque /ˌstætʃuˈɛsk◂/ *adj.* large and beautiful in an impressive way, like a statue: *a tall statuesque woman*

stat·u·ette /ˌstætʃuˈɛt/ *n.* [C] a small statue for putting on a table or shelf → see also BUST

stat·ure /ˈstætʃɚ/ *n.* [C,U] FORMAL **1** the degree to which someone is admired or regarded as important: *There is no one of equal stature to replace him.* **2** someone's height or size: **small/short/tall in stature** *Cecilia is short in stature.*

sta·tus /ˈsteɪt̬əs, ˈstæ-/ Ac S2 W2 *n. plural* **statuses** **1** [C,U] the official or legal position or condition of a person, group, country etc.: *They have asked for refugee status.* | *the country's favorable trade status* | **+as** *her status as an amateur athlete* | *What is your* ***marital status*** (=whether you are married or not)? **2** [U] your social or professional rank or position, considered in relation to other people: **+of** *the status of women in* *traditional cultures* | **high/low status** *He worked a number of jobs with low status.* | *The* ***social status*** *of doctors has always been high.* **3** [U] respect and importance that someone or something is given or considered to have SYN **prestige**: *the actress's celebrity status* | *He has* ***achieved*** *legendary* ***status*** *for his designs.* | *The band has a* ***cult status*** (=is liked very much by a small group of people) *in the U.S.* **4 the status of sth** what is happening at a particular time in a situation: *Could you check on the status of my order?* **5 sb's (HIV) status** whether or not someone is infected with HIV [**Origin:** 1700–1800 Latin, from the past participle of *stare* **to stand**]

ˈstatus bar *n.* [C] a BAR on a computer screen that gives you information about the program or programs you are using

ˈstatus ofˌfender *n.* [C] LAW a young person who the government or courts are responsible for because they have done things such as running away from home or not going to school many times, and their parents cannot control them → see also DELINQUENT

status quo /ˌsteɪt̬əs ˈkwoʊ, ˌstæ-/ *n.* **the status quo** the condition of a situation as it is: *She's not afraid to challenge the status quo.* | **maintain/preserve etc. the status quo** (=keep things as they are)

ˈstatus ˌsymbol *n.* [C] something that you have or own that is thought to show high social STATUS or power: *expensive cars and other status symbols*

stat·ute /ˈstætʃut/ *n.* [C] **1** LAW a law that has been passed by a LEGISLATURE and formally written down: *The procedure is determined* ***by statute.*** ►see THESAURUS box at **rule**[1] **2** a formal rule of an institution or organization: *university statutes*

ˌstatute of limiˈtations *n.* [C] LAW a law which gives the period of time within which action may be taken on a legal question or crime: *Police did not investigate because* ***the*** *three-year* ***statute of limitations*** *had* ***run out.***

stat·u·to·ry /ˈstætʃəˌtɔri/ *adj.* FORMAL LAW decided or controlled by law: *statutory requirements for clinical laboratories* —**statutorily** *adv.*

ˌstatutory ofˈfense *n.* [C] TECHNICAL a crime that is described by a law and can be punished by a court

ˌstatutory ˈrape *n.* [C] LAW the act of having sex with someone who is below a particular age

staunch[1] /stɔntʃ, stɑntʃ/ *adj.* giving strong loyal support to another person, organization, belief etc.: *a staunch conservative* | *staunch allies* ►see THESAURUS box at **faithful**[1] [**Origin:** 1400–1500 Old French *estanche*, from *estancher*] —**staunchly** *adv.* —**staunchness** *n.* [U]

staunch[2] also **stanch** *v.* [T] to stop the flow of liquid, especially of blood from a wound: *He used the cloth to try to staunch the flow of blood.*

stave[1] /steɪv/ *v. past tense and past participle* **staved** or **stove**

stave sth ↔ **off** *phr. v.* to keep someone or something from reaching you or affecting you for a period of time: *She brought along some fruit to stave off hunger.*

stave[2] *n.* [C] **1** one of the thin curved pieces of wood fitted close together to form the sides of a BARREL **2** ENG. LANG. ARTS a musical STAFF

staves /steɪvz/ *n.* a plural of STAFF

stay[1] /steɪ/ S1 W1 *v.* **stays, stayed, staying**

1 NOT LEAVE [I] to continue to be in the same place and not leave: *Can you stay a little longer?* | *We should stay and help.* | **+in** *She stayed in bed all day.* | **stay here/there** *Stay here in case anybody calls.* | **stay (for) a minute/day/week etc.** *I can only stay a few minutes.* | *We just* ***stayed at home*** *and worked on the house.* | **stay home from school/work** *He had the flu, so he stayed home from school.* | *They* ***stayed late*** *to finish the report.* | **stay for lunch/a drink/dinner etc.** *Would you like to stay for dinner?*

2 NOT CHANGE [linking verb] to continue to be in a particular position, condition, or state, without changing SYN **remain**: *Try to stay calm.* | *It was hard to stay awake.* | *I hope we can stay friends.* | **+in/out of/on etc.** *Get out of this house and stay out!* | *Why do some people stay in abusive relationships?* | *Hotel rates will* ***stay the same*** *next year.*

3 VISIT/LIVE SOMEWHERE [I] to live in a place temporarily, especially as a visitor or guest: *How long are they going to stay?* | **+at/in** *We'll stay at a hotel.* | **+with** *You're welcome to stay with us.* | **stay for a week/month etc.** *Why don't you come and stay for a few days?* | *She needs* ***a place to stay*** *for a while.*

4 stay the night also **stay overnight** to remain somewhere, especially at someone else's house, from one evening to the next day SYN **stay over**: *She stayed overnight at her cousin's.*

5 stay put SPOKEN to remain in one place and not move: *Stay put until I get back.*

6 stay the course to finish something in spite of difficulties: *The president is vowing to stay the course.*

7 stay tuned **a)** SPOKEN said on TV or radio stations to tell people not to change to a different station: *Stay tuned for more on this late-breaking story.* **b)** INFORMAL used to tell someone to continue paying attention to see how a situation develops

8 stay an order/ruling/execution etc. LAW if a judge stays an order, ruling etc., they stop a particular decision from being used or a particular action from happening

9 stay! SPOKEN used to tell a dog not to move

10 stay sb's hand LITERARY to stop someone from doing something

[**Origin:** 1400–1500 Old French *ester* **to stand, stay**, from Latin *stare*] → see also **here to stay** at HERE[1] (6)

stay after *phr. v.* **stay after sth** to remain somewhere for a particular purpose after an event there has finished: *She had to stay after school.*

stay around *phr. v.* to not leave a person or a place: *Fans stayed around to celebrate with the team.*

stay away *phr. v.* to not go near someone or something: *Tourists have stayed away because of the bad weather.* | **+from** *I told you to stay away from my sister.*

stay behind *phr. v.* to remain somewhere after others have left: *I'll stay behind and wait for her.*

stay in *phr. v.* to spend the evening at home rather than go out: *Let's stay in and watch TV.*

stay on *phr. v.* to continue to do a job or to study after the usual or expected time for leaving: *He was set to retire, but stayed on as a favor to his boss.*

stay out *phr. v.* to remain away from home during the evening or night: *She stayed out late last night.*

stay out of sth *phr. v.* to not become involved in something that other people are involved in, such as an argument, a fight etc.: *Stay out of this, Ben. It's none of your business.* | *Try to* ***stay out of trouble*** *this once, OK?*

stay over *phr. v.* to remain somewhere, especially at someone else's house, from one evening to the next day: *A couple of her friends stayed over last night.*

stay together *phr. v.* if two people or a family stay together, they continue to live together and remain in their relationship

stay up *phr. v.* to not go to bed when you would normally go to bed: *We stayed up all night talking.*

stay with sb *phr. v.* **1** to remain in a relationship with someone **2** to remain in someone's memory: *The memory of that night stayed with him for years.*

stay[2] S2 *n.* **1** [C usually singular] a limited time of living in a place: *a short stay in the hospital* **2** [C,U] LAW the act of stopping an action because a judge has ordered it: **a stay of execution/deportation etc.** (=a sometimes temporary stop of the punishment) **3** [C] a strong wire or rope used for supporting a ship's MAST **4** [C] a short piece of plastic, bone, or wire used to keep a shirt COLLAR or a CORSET stiff

ˈstay-at-ˌhome *adj.* [only before noun] **1** INFORMAL always staying at home and never doing exciting things **2** staying at home, rather than working somewhere else, usually to take care of children: *a stay-at-home mom* —**stay-at-home** *n.* [C]

S

ˈstaying ˌpower *n.* [U] the ability or energy to keep doing something difficult until it is finished: *No one should doubt our staying power or determination in this mission.*

St. Chris·to·pher and Ne·vis /seɪnt ˌkrɪstəfɚ ən ˈnivɪs/ → see ST. KITTS AND NEVIS

STD *n.* [U] **sexually transmitted disease** MEDICINE a disease such as HERPES, GONORRHEA etc. that is passed from person to person through sex

std. a written abbreviation of "standard"

stead /stɛd/ *n.* **1 do sth in sb's stead** FORMAL to do something that someone else usually does or was going to do: *She went to the meeting in the mayor's stead.* **2 stand/put/hold sb in good stead** to be very useful to someone when needed: *His five years of training stood him in good stead.*

stead·fast /ˈstɛdfæst/ *adj.* LITERARY **1** very loyal and never changing: *steadfast devotion* ►see THESAURUS box at faithful[1] **2** certain that you are right about something and refusing to change your position or opinion in any way: **+in** *They are steadfast in their refusal to sell the land.* [**Origin:** Old English *stedefæst* **fixed in place**] —**steadfastly** *adv.* —**steadfastness** *n.* [U]

S

stead·y[1] /ˈstɛdi/ *adj. comparative* **steadier**, *superlative* **steadiest**
1 NOT MOVING firmly held in a particular position and not moving or shaking: *Hold the ladder steady.* | *Gluing toothpicks takes* ***a steady hand*** *and a lot of patience.*
2 CONTINUOUS moving, happening, or developing in a continuous or gradual way: *steady rain* | *She's been making steady progress.* | *Her breathing was slow and steady.* | **a steady stream/flow/trickle etc.** *a steady stream of traffic*
3 steady work/income/employment etc. work or pay that will definitely continue over a long period of time: *a steady job*
4 NOT CHANGING a steady level, speed etc. stays about the same: *Chen maintained a steady pace throughout the race.* | **hold/remain steady** *Inflation held steady at 3%.*
5 VOICE calm and smooth: *She spoke in a low steady voice.*
6 LOOK without moving your eyes: *a steady gaze*
7 PERSON sensible and able to be depended on: *a steady worker*
8 a steady boyfriend/girlfriend someone that you have been having a regular romantic relationship with
9 a steady relationship a serious and strong relationship that continues for a long time
10 steady as she goes SPOKEN used to tell someone to keep the same speed and direction when STEERING a boat —**steadily** *adv.* —**steadiness** *n.* [U]

steady[2] *v.* **steadies, steadied, steadying** **1** [I,T] to hold someone or something so they become more balanced or controlled, or to become more balanced or controlled: *He grabbed the desk to steady himself.* **2** [I,T] to become calmer, or to make someone calmer: *He took a deep breath to* ***steady his nerves.*** **3** [I] to stop increasing or decreasing and remain about the same SYN **stabilize**

steady[3] *adv.* **go steady (with sb)** to have a long regular romantic relationship with someone

steady[4] *n.* [C] OLD-FASHIONED, INFORMAL a BOYFRIEND or GIRLFRIEND that someone has been having a romantic relationship with

steady[5] *interjection* used when you want to tell someone to be careful or not to cause an accident: *Steady! Watch what you're doing.*

ˌsteady-ˈstate ˌtheory *n.* TECHNICAL the idea that the degree to which space is filled with things has always been the same and that these things move away from each other as new atoms begin to exist → see also BIG BANG THEORY

steak /steɪk/ S2 *n.* **1** [C,U] good quality BEEF (=meat from a cow), or a large thick piece of any good quality red meat: *a grilled steak* **2 a cod/salmon/tuna etc. steak** [C] a large thick piece of fish [**Origin:** 1400–1500 Old Norse *steik*]

steak·house /ˈsteɪkhaʊs/ *n.* [C] a restaurant that serves steak

ˈsteak knife *n.* [C] a sharp knife used for cutting meat during a meal

steak tar·tare /ˌsteɪk tɑrˈtɑr/ *n.* [U] steak that is cut into very small pieces and eaten raw, usually with a raw egg

steal[1] /stil/ S1 W2 *v. past tense* **stole** /stoʊl/, *past participle* **stolen** /ˈstoʊlən/
1 TAKE STH [I,T] to take something that belongs to someone else: *Somebody stole my bike.* | *It's wrong to steal.* | **+from** *She got caught stealing from the store.* | **steal sth from sb** *He stole money from the company.*

THESAURUS

burglarize to go into a building, car etc. and steal things from it: *When they got back to their hotel, they found their rooms had been burglarized.*
rob to steal money or other things from a bank, store, or person: *He robbed several gas stations in the area.*
mug to attack someone in the street and steal something from him or her: *He had been mugged at gunpoint.*
shoplift to steal something from a store by leaving without paying for it: *One in ten teenagers have shoplifted.*
rip off sth INFORMAL to steal something: *Someone had ripped off $3,000 worth of stereo equipment.*
→ CRIME, CRIMINAL

2 USE IDEAS to use someone else's ideas without getting permission or admitting they are their ideas: *She accused her coworker of stealing her ideas for the project.*
3 MOVE SOMEWHERE LITERARY [I always + adv./prep.] to move quietly without anyone noticing you: **+into/across etc.** *Garrick stole out of the house early.*
4 steal the show/scene/limelight to do something, especially when you are acting in a play, that makes people pay more attention to you than to other people: *The children's performance stole the show.*
5 steal a look/glance etc. to look at someone or something quickly and secretly
6 BASEBALL [I,T] to run to the next BASE in the game of baseball before someone hits the ball
7 BASKETBALL/HOCKEY ETC. [T] to suddenly take control of the ball, PUCK etc. from your opponent in sports such as basketball or HOCKEY
8 steal a kiss to kiss someone quickly when they are not expecting it
9 steal sb's thunder to get the success and praise someone else should have gotten, by doing what they had intended to do
10 steal a march on sb to gain an advantage over someone by doing something that they had planned to do before they have a chance to do it
[**Origin:** Old English *stelan*] → see also **win/capture/steal sb's heart** at HEART (15)

steal[2] *n.* [C] INFORMAL **1 be a steal** to be very inexpensive: *The wine is a steal at $9.* **2** the act of suddenly taking control of the ball, PUCK etc. from your opponent in sports such as basketball or HOCKEY **3** the act of running to the next BASE in the game of baseball before someone hits the ball

stealth /stɛlθ/ *n.* [U] **1** the action of doing something very quietly, slowly, or secretly so that no one notices you **2** also **Stealth** a system of making military aircraft that cannot be discovered by RADAR instruments: **a stealth bomber/fighter/aircraft etc.** (=an airplane made using this system) [**Origin:** 1200–1300 from an unrecorded Old English *stælth* **stealing**]

stealth·y /ˈstɛlθi/ *adj.* moving or doing something quietly and secretly: *the stealthy movements of a hunter* —**stealthily** *adv.*

steam[1] /stim/ *n.* [U]
1 GAS CHEMISTRY the hot mist that water produces when it is boiled: *Steam rose from the hot tub.*

2 MIST ON SURFACE the mist that forms on windows, mirrors etc. when warm wet air suddenly becomes cold: *steam on the bathroom mirror*
3 POWER power that is produced by boiling water to make steam, in order to make things work or move: **a steam engine/locomotive etc.** (=an engine, train etc. that works by the power produced by steam)
4 let/blow off steam to get rid of your anger or excitement in a way that does not harm anyone, by doing something active: *Recess is a good chance for kids to blow off steam.*
5 pick/build/get up steam also **gather/gain steam a)** if an engine picks up steam, it gradually starts to go faster **b)** if plans, beliefs, actions etc. pick up steam, they gradually become more important and more people become interested in them: *The rebuilding plan is picking up steam.*
6 run out of steam also **lose steam** to no longer have or start having less of the energy or the desire to continue doing something, especially because you are tired: *The team just ran out of steam before the game was over.*
7 under your own steam if you go somewhere under your own steam, you get there without help from anyone else
[**Origin:** Old English] → see also **full speed/steam ahead** at FULL[1] (11)

steam[2] *v.* **1** [I] if something steams, steam rises from it, especially because it is hot: *The hot engine was steaming.* **2** [T] to cook something in steam: *Do you want me to steam the broccoli?* ►see THESAURUS box at cook[1] **3** [I always + adv./prep.] to travel somewhere in a boat or train that uses steam to produce power: **+into/from/up etc.** *A ship steamed up the river.* → see also STEAMED, STEAMING

steam ahead *phr. v.* to continue growing or developing at a fast rate

steam sth ↔ **off** *phr. v.* to use steam to remove something

steam sth ↔ **open** *phr. v.* to use steam to open something: *He steamed open the letter.*

steam up *phr. v.* **steam sth ↔ up** to cover something with steam, or become covered with steam: *When I walked inside, my glasses steamed up.* | *Our breath was steaming up the car windows.*

'steam bath *n.* [C] a STEAM ROOM, or the period of time spent in this room

steam·boat /'stimboʊt/ *n.* [C] a boat that uses steam to produce power and is used for sailing along rivers and coasts

'steam clean *v.* [T] to clean something by using a machine that produces steam

steamed /stimd/ *adj.* **1** cooked with steam: *steamed vegetables* **2** SPOKEN angry or annoyed

steam·er /'stimɚ/ *n.* [C] **1** a STEAMSHIP **2** a container used to cook food in steam

'steamer trunk *n.* [C] a large box, used especially in the past for carrying clothes and other objects when you travel

steam·ing /'stimɪŋ/ *adv.* **1** also **steaming hot** very hot with steam rising up: *a bowl of steaming hot soup* **2** SPOKEN also **steaming mad** extremely angry

'steam iron *n.* [C] an electric IRON that produces steam in order to make clothes easier to IRON

steam·roll /'stimroʊl/ *v.* [I,T] INFORMAL to make sure something happens by using all your power and influence

steam·roll·er[1] /'stim,roʊlɚ/ *n.* [C] **1** a heavy vehicle with a large wide ROLLER at the front that you drive over road surfaces to make them flat **2** someone or something that defeats or destroys its opponents completely

steamroller[2] *v.* [I,T] INFORMAL to steamroll

'steam room *n.* [C] a room that is filled with steam that people sit in to relax → see also SAUNA

steam·ship /'stim,ʃɪp/ *n.* [C] a large ship that uses steam to produce power

'steam ,shovel *n.* [C] a large machine that digs and moves earth

steam·y /'stimi/ *adj.* *comparative* **steamier**, *superlative* **steamiest** **1** full of steam or covered in steam: *a steamy locker room* **2** sexually exciting and slightly shocking: *steamy love scenes*

steed /stid/ *n.* [C] POETIC a strong fast horse

steel[1] /stil/ *n.* **1** [U] strong metal that can be shaped easily, consisting of iron and CARBON: *The bridge is made of steel.* **2** [U] the industry that makes steel: *The main industries in the area are coal and steel.* **3** [C] a thin bar of steel used to make knives sharp [**Origin:** Old English *style, stele*] → see also **nerves of steel** at NERVE[1] (8), STAINLESS STEEL

steel[2] *adj.* [only before noun] **1** made of steel: *a steel gate* **2** relating to steel or the industry that makes steel: *the steel towns of Pennsylvania* **3** very strong: *a steel grip*

steel[3] *v.* [T] **steel yourself** to prepare yourself for something that will be uncomfortable or upsetting

,steel 'band *n.* [C] a group of people who play music on steel drums together

,steel 'drum *n.* [C] a type of drum from the West Indies made from oil BARRELS, which you hit in different areas to produce different musical sounds

,steel-'gray *adj.* having a dark gray color —**steel gray** *n.* [U]

,steel gui'tar *n.* [C] a musical instrument with ten strings that is played using a steel bar and a PEDAL (=a bar you press with your foot)

steel·mak·er /'stil,meɪkɚ/ *n.* [C] a company that makes steel —**steelmaking** *n.* [U]

'steel mill *n.* [C] a factory where steel is made

,steel 'wool *n.* [U] a rough material made of fine steel threads, that is used to make surfaces smooth, remove paint etc.

steel·work·er /'stil,wɚkɚ/ *n.* [C] someone who works in a factory that makes steel

steel·works /'stilwɚks/ *n.* a steel mill

steel·y /'stili/ *adj.* **1 steely determination/pride/stare etc.** an extremely strong and determined attitude, expression etc. **2** LITERARY having a gray color like steel

,steely-'eyed *adj.* having an expression in your eyes that shows you are strong and determined

steep[1] /stip/ *adj.* **1** a road, hill etc. that is steep slopes at a high angle: *The road's too steep to ride up on a bike.* | *They live on a steep hill.* **2** steep prices, charges etc. are unusually expensive: *The prices are a little steep.* **3** a steep increase or rise in something is a very big increase: *a steep increase in the cigarette tax* [**Origin:** Old English *steap* **high, steep, deep**] —**steeply** *adv.* —**steepness** *n.* [U]

steep[2] *v.* **1 be steeped in history/tradition/politics etc.** to have a lot of a particular quality: *The town is steeped in history.* **2** [I,T] if something steeps or you steep it in a liquid, it remains in the liquid for a while so that it becomes soft or has the same taste as the liquid: **steep sth in sth** *Steep the herbs in hot water.*

steep·en /'stipən/ *v.* [I,T] if a slope, road etc. steepens or something steepens it, it becomes steeper

stee·ple /'stipəl/ *n.* [C] a tall pointed tower on the roof of a church

stee·ple·chase /'stipəl,tʃeɪs/ *n.* [C] **1** a long race in which horses jump over gates, water etc. **2** a long race in which people run and jump over fences, water etc.

stee·ple·jack /'stipəl,dʒæk/ *n.* [C] someone whose work is repairing towers, tall CHIMNEYS etc.

steer[1] /stɪr/ *v.*
1 CAR/BOAT ETC. [I,T] to control the direction a vehicle is going, for example by turning a wheel: *His hands were full, so he was steering with his knees.* | **steer sth into/around/toward etc. sth** *He steered the boat toward the island.*
2 INFLUENCE SB/STH [T] to guide someone's behavior or

S

the way a situation develops: **steer sb/sth away from sth** *The program aims to steer teenagers away from drugs.* | **steer sb/sth toward sth** *Kyle kept steering the conversation back toward politics.*
3 GUIDE SB TO A PLACE to guide someone to a place, especially while touching them: **steer sb toward/to/into etc. sth** *She took my arm and steered me into the room.*
4 steer clear (of sb/sth) INFORMAL to try to avoid someone or something bad or difficult: *I steered clear of the subject of her divorce.*
5 BE IN CHARGE OF [T always + adv./prep.] to be in charge of an organization, team etc. and make decisions that help it be successful, especially during a difficult time: **steer sth through/to etc. sth** *Corbin successfully steered the company through recession.*
6 steer a course to choose a particular way of doing something: **steer a middle course** (=choose a course of action that is not extreme)
[**Origin:** Old English *stieran*]

steer² *n.* [C] a young male cow that has had its sex organs removed → BULLOCK, HEIFER

steer·age /ˈstɪrɪdʒ/ *n.* [U] the part of a passenger ship where people who had the cheapest tickets used to travel in the past

steer·ing /ˈstɪrɪŋ/ *n.* [U] the parts of a car, truck, boat etc. that allow you to control its direction: *power steering*

ˈsteering ˌcolumn *n.* [C] a long piece of metal in a car or other vehicle that connects the steering wheel to the equipment that moves the wheels

ˈsteering comˌmittee *n.* a committee that guides or directs a particular activity

ˈsteering wheel *n.* [C] a wheel that you turn to control the direction of a car, boat etc. → see picture on page A36

steers·man /ˈstɪrzmən/ *n. plural* **steersmen** /-mən/ [C] someone who STEERS a ship

stein /staɪn/ *n.* [C] a tall cup for drinking beer, often decorated and with a lid

Stein /staɪn/, **Ger·trude** /ˈgɚtrud/ (1874–1946) a U.S. writer famous for the new and unusual style of her NOVELS, poems, and other work

Stein·beck /ˈstaɪnbɛk/, **John** (1902–1968) a U.S. writer of NOVELS

John Steinbeck

Stein·em /ˈstaɪnəm/, **Glo·ri·a** /ˈglɔriə/ (1934–) a U.S. writer and FEMINIST who was a leading member of the WOMEN'S MOVEMENT in the 1960s

Stel·la /ˈstɛlə/, **Frank** (1936–) a U.S. PAINTER famous for his ABSTRACT paintings using GEOMETRIC shapes

stel·lar /ˈstɛlɚ/ *adj.* [usually before noun] **1** extremely good: *He gave **a stellar performance**.* **2** PHYSICS relating to the stars → see also INTERSTELLAR **3** relating to famous actors, performers etc.

stem¹ /stɛm/ *n.* [C] **1** BIOLOGY a long thin part of a plant, from which leaves, flowers, or fruit grow: *roses with long stems* **2** the long thin part of a wine glass, VASE etc., between the base and the wide top **3** the narrow tube of a pipe used to smoke tobacco **4** ENG. LANG. ARTS the part of a word that stays the same when different endings are added to it, for example "driv-" in "driving" and "driven" **5 from stem to stern** all the way from the front to the back, especially of a ship [**Origin:** Old English *stefn, stemn*] → see also BRAIN STEM

stem² *v.* **stemmed, stemming** [T] **1 stem the tide/flow/growth etc. of sth** to stop something from spreading or developing: *The government is trying to stem the flow of drugs into the country.* **2** FORMAL to stop the flow of a liquid: *He used a rag to stem the bleeding.*
stem from sth *phr. v.* to develop as a result of something else: *A lot of her emotional problems stem from her childhood.*

ˌstem-and-ˈleaf plot *n.* [C] MATH a way of showing QUANTITATIVE DATA (=data in number form) that involves writing the different parts of each number in separate COLUMNS (=lists going down). The first DIGIT or digits of a number (= the stem) is written in the first column, and the remaining digits (= leaves) of all the data that begin with that stem are written next to it in the second column.

-stemmed /stɛmd/ *suffix* [in adjectives] **long-stemmed/short-stemmed etc.** having a long stem, a short stem etc.: *long-stemmed roses*

stench /stɛntʃ/ *n.* [C usually singular] **1** a very strong bad smell: *the stench of rotting fish* ▸see THESAURUS box at **smell¹** **2 the stench of injustice/corruption/treachery etc.** something that makes you believe that something very bad and dishonest is happening

sten·cil¹ /ˈstɛnsəl/ *n.* [C] **1** a piece of plastic, wood, paper etc. in which patterns or letters have been cut, used to make a pattern on a surface by drawing or painting through the holes **2** a pattern made using a stencil

stencil² *v.* [T] **1** to make a pattern, letters etc. using a stencil **2** to decorate something using a stencil

Sten·dhal /stænˈdɑl, stɑn-/ (1783–1842) a French writer of NOVELS

Sten·gel /ˈstɛŋgəl/, **Ca·sey** /ˈkeɪsi/ (1891–1975) a U.S. baseball player and manager, famous for making the New York Yankees very successful

sten·o /ˈstɛnoʊ/ *n.* OLD-FASHIONED INFORMAL **1** [C] a stenographer **2** [U] stenography

ste·nog·ra·pher /stəˈnɑgrəfɚ/ *n.* [C] OLD-FASHIONED someone whose job is to write down what someone else is saying, using stenography, and then type a copy of it

ste·nog·ra·phy /stəˈnɑgrəfi/ *n.* [U] OLD-FASHIONED a system of writing quickly by using signs or shorter forms for letters, words, and phrases SYN **shorthand**

sten·to·ri·an /stɛnˈtɔriən/ *adj.* LITERARY a stentorian voice is very loud and powerful [**Origin:** 1600–1700 *Stentor* man with a very loud voice in an ancient Greek story]

step¹ /stɛp/ S1 W1 *n.*
1 MOVEMENT [C] the movement you make when you put one foot in front of the other when walking: *a baby's first steps* | *Jane hesitated, then **took a step** forward.* | *I **retraced** my **steps*** (=went back the way I had come) *for two blocks looking for the money.*
2 ACTION [C] one of a series of things that you do in order to deal with a problem or produce a particular result: *Baker said his next step will be to demand a new trial.* | **+toward** *an important step toward peace* | *The treaty is **a first step** toward arms control.* | *We have **taken steps** to ensure that such an accident cannot happen again.* | **a major/big/important etc. step** *The discovery of penicillin was a major step forward in medicine.* | *Environmentalists call the change **a step in the right direction**.* | *Critics call the government decision **a step backward*** (=an action that makes a situation worse) *for human rights.* | **a step on/along the path/road/way** *The deal is an important step on the path to economic recovery.* → see also STEP-BY-STEP ▸see THESAURUS box at **action**
3 STAIR [C] a flat narrow piece of wood or stone, especially one in a series, that you put your foot on when you are going up or down, especially outside a building SYN **stair**: *Ellen ran up the steps.* → see also DOORSTEP (1)
4 IN A PROCESS [C] a stage in a process → see also STAGE: *Record your result, and go on to step three.* | *The argument now goes **a step further**.* | *Pam supported him **every step of the way*** (=during every stage of the process). | *Changes must be made **one step at a time**.*
5 POSITION [C] a position or rank on a scale: *the lowest step of the salary scale* | **a step up/down** *I think Mike's a step up from Rosa's last boyfriend.*

6 DANCING [C] a movement of your feet in dancing: *dance steps* | *I can't remember all the steps.*
7 **in step** a) having ideas that agree with what other people think or with what is usual, acceptable etc.: +**with** *It's important to keep in step with the people you represent.* b) moving your feet in the same way as people you are walking or marching with
8 **out of step** a) having ideas that are different from what other people think or from what is usual, acceptable etc.: +**with** *The President is out of step with the majority of Americans.* b) moving your feet in a different way from people you are walking or marching with
9 SOUND [C] the sound you make when you set your foot down while walking SYN **footstep**: *Marge could hear a man's steps in the hall.*
10 DISTANCE [C] the distance you move when you take a step while walking: *The theater is just a few steps from Times Square.*
11 **be/keep/stay one step ahead (of sb)** to be better prepared for something or know more about something than someone else: *We have to keep one step ahead of the competition.*
12 **stay one step ahead of police/investigators etc.** to manage not to be caught by someone who is trying to find or catch you
13 EXERCISE a) also **step aerobics** [U] a type of exercise you do by walking onto and off a flat piece of equipment several inches high: *a beginners' step class* b) [C] a piece of equipment used for doing step
14 MUSIC [C] ENG. LANG. ARTS the difference in PITCH between two musical notes that are separated by one KEY on the piano
[**Origin:** Old English *stæpe*] → see also **fall into step with sb/sth** at FALL INTO (9), **a spring in sb's step** at SPRING[1] (5), **watch your step** at WATCH[1] (14)

step[2] S2 W2 *v.* **stepped, stepping** [I always + adv./prep.]
1 MOVE to raise one foot and put it down in front of the other one to move along: +**forward/back/down etc.** *Step aside and let the doctor through.* | +**inside/outside/in/out etc.** *Could you step into the hall for a minute?* | *Please **step this way*** (=come the way I am showing you).
2 STAND ON STH to bring your foot down on something: +**in/on etc.** *Yuck! What did you step in?*
3 **step on sb's toes** to offend or upset someone, especially by trying to do their work: *I'm new here, so I don't want to step on anyone's toes.*
4 **step out of line** to behave badly by breaking rules or disobeying orders
5 **step on it** also **step on the gas** to drive faster: *If you don't step on it we'll miss the plane.*

step aside *phr. v.* to leave your job or official position, especially in order to let someone else have it

step back *phr. v.* to stop thinking too much about small details and consider something in a more general way

step down *phr. v.* to leave your job or official position SYN **resign**: +**as** *Arnez is stepping down as chairman.* | +**from** *She's stepping down from the committee.*

step forward *phr. v.* to come and offer help, information etc.: *No witnesses to the robbery have yet stepped forward.*

step in *phr. v.* to become involved in a discussion, disagreement etc., especially in order to stop the trouble SYN **intervene**: *The police stepped in to break up the fight.*

step into sth *phr. v.* to become involved in a situation, or start doing something: *Because of her previous experience, she easily stepped into the role of producer.* → see also **step into the breach** at BREACH[1] (5)

step on sb *phr. v.* to treat someone badly, especially as you try to gain more power or influence than them

step out *phr. v.* to leave your home or office for a short time: *Rhonda just stepped out – may I take a message?*

step up *phr. v.* 1 **step sth ↔ up** to increase the amount of an activity or the speed of a process in order to improve a situation: *They have stepped up security at the airport.* → see also STEPPED-UP 2 also **step up to the plate** to agree to help someone or to be responsible for doing something: *Residents will have to step up if they want to rid this area of crime.*

step- /stɛp/ *prefix* related, not by birth, but because a parent has remarried: *my stepfather* (=the man who has married my mother) | *her stepchildren* (=her husband's children from an earlier relationship)

step·broth·er /ˈstɛpˌbrʌðɚ/ *n.* [C] a boy or man whose father or mother has married your mother or father

ˌstep-by-ˈstep *adj.* [only before noun] a step-by-step plan, method etc. does things carefully and in a particular order —**step by step** *adv.*: *Rich went through the instructions step by step.*

step·child /ˈstɛp-tʃaɪld/ *n. plural* **stepchildren** /-ˌtʃɪldrən/ [C] a STEPDAUGHTER or STEPSON

step·daugh·ter /ˈstɛpˌdɔt̬ɚ/ *n.* [C] a daughter that your husband or wife has from a relationship before your marriage

step·fa·ther /ˈstɛpˌfɑðɚ/ *n.* [C] the man who is married to your mother but who is not your father

Ste·phen /ˈstivən/**, Saint** in the Bible, a follower of Jesus who was the first Christian MARTYR

step·lad·der /ˈstɛpˌlædɚ/ *n.* [C] a LADDER with two sloping parts that are joined at the top so that it can stand without support, and which can be folded flat

step·moth·er /ˈstɛpˌmʌðɚ/ *n.* [C] a woman who is married to your father but who is not your mother

step·par·ent /ˈstɛpˌpɛrənt/ *n.* [C] a STEPFATHER or STEPMOTHER

steppe /stɛp/ *n.* [C,U] also **the steppes** a large area of land without trees, especially an area in Russia, parts of Asia, and southeast Europe

ˈstepped-up *adj.* done more quickly or with more effort than before: *stepped-up factory production* → see also **step up** at STEP[2]

ˈstepping stone, stepping-stone *n.* [C] 1 something that helps you to progress toward achieving something, especially in your work: +**to/toward** *a stepping stone toward political unification* 2 one of a row of large flat stones that you walk on to get across a stream

step·sis·ter /ˈstɛpˌsɪstɚ/ *n.* [C] a girl or woman whose father or mother has married your mother or father

step·son /ˈstɛpsʌn/ *n.* [C] a son that your husband or wife has from a relationship before your marriage

-ster /stɚ/ *suffix* [in nouns] 1 someone who is connected with, deals with, or uses a particular thing: *a gangster* (=member of a group of criminals) | *a trickster* (=someone who deceives people with tricks) | *a pollster* (=someone who asks people for their opinions) 2 someone who has a particular quality: *a youngster* (=a young person) 3 SPOKEN INFORMAL added to someone's name and used with "the" to make a NICKNAME: *the Bradster* (=nickname for "Brad")

ster·e·o[1] /ˈstɛriˌoʊ, ˈstɪr-/ *n. plural* **stereos** 1 [C] a machine for playing CDS, records etc. that produces sound from two or more SPEAKERS: *a car stereo* | *It sounds better **on your stereo** than mine.* 2 **in stereo** if music, a radio program etc. is in stereo, it is being played or broadcast using a system in which sound is directed through two speakers

stereo[2] also **ster·e·o·phon·ic** /ˌstɛriəˈfɑnɪk◂, ˌstɪr-/ *adj.* using a system of sound recording or broadcasting in which the sound is directed through two SPEAKERS to make it seem more real: *stereo equipment* → see also MONO, QUADRAPHONIC

ster·e·o·scop·ic /ˌstɛriəˈskɑpɪk◂, ˌstɪr-/ *adj.* a stereoscopic photograph, picture etc. is made so that when you look at it through a special machine it looks THREE-DIMENSIONAL

ˈstereo ˌsystem *n.* [C] a set of equipment for playing music on, usually including a CD PLAYER, radio, and speakers

S

ster·e·o·type[1] /ˈstɛriəˌtaɪp, ˈstɪr-/ *n.* [C] an idea of what a particular group of people is like that many people have, especially one that is wrong or unfair: *racial stereotypes* | +**about** *stereotypes about the homeless* | *Lee does not **fit the stereotype of** a lawyer.* —**stereotypical** /ˌstɛriəˈtɪpɪkəl/ *adj.*

stereotype[2] *v.* [T usually passive] to decide, usually unfairly, that some people have particular qualities or abilities because they belong to a particular race, sex, or social class: **stereotype sb as sth** *Too many children's books stereotype girls as helpless and weak.* —**stereotyped** *adj.* —**stereotyping** *n.* [U]

ster·ile /ˈstɛrəl/ *adj.* **1** BIOLOGY completely clean and not containing any BACTERIA: *a sterile laboratory* **2** BIOLOGY not able to produce babies SYN **infertile** OPP **fertile**: *The operation left her sterile.* **3** a sterile building, room, place etc. is not interesting, exciting, or attractive and does not make you feel comfortable **4** lacking new ideas or imagination: *a sterile debate* **5** BIOLOGY sterile land cannot be used for growing crops OPP **fertile** —**sterility** /stəˈrɪləṭi/ *n.* [U]

ster·il·ize /ˈstɛrəˌlaɪz/ *v.* [T] BIOLOGY **1** to make something completely clean and kill any BACTERIA in it: *Sterilize the needle in boiling water.* **2** to perform an operation that makes a person or animal unable to have babies —**sterilizer** *n.* [C] —**sterilization** /ˌstɛrələˈzeɪʃən/ *n.* [C,U]

S

ster·ling[1] /ˈstɚlɪŋ/ *adj.* **sterling qualities/character/record etc.** excellent qualities, character etc.

sterling[2] *n.* [U] **1** sterling silver **2** the standard unit of money in the United Kingdom, based on the POUND

ˌsterling ˈsilver *n.* [U] metal that is over 92% pure silver

stern[1] /stɚn/ *adj.* **1** very serious and strict, often in a way that does not seem friendly: *a stern judge* **2** done in a very strict and severe way: *a stern warning* **3** [only before noun] very difficult and testing someone's ability and skill: *a stern challenge* **4 be made of sterner stuff** to have a strong character and be more determined than other people to succeed in a difficult situation —**sternly** *adv.* —**sternness** *n.* [U]

stern[2] *n.* [C usually singular] the back part of a ship → see also BOW

ster·num /ˈstɚnəm/ *n. plural* **sternums** or **sterna** /-nə/ [C] BIOLOGY your BREASTBONE → see picture at SKELETON[1]

ste·roid /ˈstɛrɔɪd, ˈstɪrɔɪd/ *n.* [C] MEDICINE a chemical compound produced in the body, but also given as a drug by doctors for injuries and used illegally by people doing sports to improve their performance

steth·o·scope /ˈstɛθəˌskoʊp/ *n.* [C] an instrument used by doctors to listen to someone's heart or breathing

Stet·son, stetson /ˈstɛtsən/ *n.* [C] TRADEMARK a tall hat with a wide BRIM (=edge), worn especially in the American West [**Origin:** 1900–2000 John B. *Stetson* (1830–1906), U.S. hatmaker]

ste·ve·dore /ˈstivəˌdɔr/ *n.* [C] someone who loads and unloads ships as their job [**Origin:** 1700–1800 Spanish *estibador*, from *estibar* **to pack**, from Latin *stipare*]

Ste·vens /ˈstivənz/**, Wal·lace** /ˈwɑləs/ (1879–1955) a U.S. poet

Ste·ven·son /ˈstivənsən/**, Ad·lai** /ˈædleɪ/ (1900–1965) a U.S. politician who competed twice in the election for President, and helped to establish the U.N. in 1946

Stevenson, Rob·ert Lou·is /ˈrɑbɚt ˈlui/ (1850–1894) a Scottish writer of NOVELS

stew[1] /stu/ *n.* **1** [C] a cooked dish, made of meat and vegetables that are cooked slowly together in liquid: *beef stew* **2 in a stew** INFORMAL confused or anxious, especially because you are in a difficult situation

stew[2] *v.* **1** [T] to cook something slowly in liquid **2 stew (in your own juices)** INFORMAL to worry or become angry because of something bad that has happened or a mistake you have made

stew·ard /ˈstuɚd/ *n.* [C]
1 SHIP someone whose job is to manage the food and drinks on a ship, or to serve them to passengers
2 PROTECTOR someone who takes care of something and protects it, such as nature or public property or money: *Not all ranchers are good stewards of the land.*
3 AIRPLANE OLD-FASHIONED a male FLIGHT ATTENDANT ►see THESAURUS box at **plane**[1]
4 UNION a SHOP STEWARD
5 HOUSE AND LAND someone whose job is to take care of a house and its land, such as a large farm
6 FOOD a man who arranges the supply and serving of food in a club, college etc.
7 RACE someone who is in charge of a horse race, meeting, or other public event
[**Origin:** Old English *stiweard* **hall-guard**]

stew·ard·ess /ˈstuɚdɪs/ *n.* [C] OLD-FASHIONED a female FLIGHT ATTENDANT

stew·ard·ship /ˈstuɚdˌʃɪp/ *n.* [U] the way in which someone controls and takes care of an event, an organization, or someone else's property

stewed /stud/ *adj.* **1** cooked slowly in liquid: *stewed tomatoes* **2** [not before noun] INFORMAL drunk

St. George's /seɪnt ˈdʒɔrdʒɪz/ the capital city of Dominica

stick[1] /stɪk/ S1 W2 *v. past tense and past participle* **stuck** /stʌk/
1 ATTACH [I,T] to attach something to something else with a substance such as glue, or to become attached to a surface: *This stamp won't stick.* | +**to** *The sand sticks to your skin and gets in your eyes.* | **stick (sth) together** *The oil keeps the pasta from sticking together.* | **stick sth to/in/on etc. sth** *She stuck her gum on the bottom of the desk.*
2 PUT [T always + adv./prep.] INFORMAL to put something somewhere, especially quickly and without thinking carefully: **stick sth in/on/under etc.** *You can stick your things under the bed.* ►see THESAURUS box at **put, shove**[1]
3 PUSH IN [I always + adv./prep.,T always + adv./prep.] if a pointed object sticks into or through something or you stick it there, it is pushed into it: +**into/through etc.** *The sharp pins stuck into her arms.* | **stick sth in/into/through etc. sth** *The boy stuck his finger up his nose.*
4 MOVE BODY PART [T always + adv./prep.] if you stick a part of your body somewhere, you move it into that position: **stick sth in/inside/under etc.** *She stuck her head in the window and looked around.*
5 DIFFICULT TO MOVE [I] if something sticks, it becomes firmly attached in one position so that it is difficult to move: *This drawer keeps sticking.* | *The wheels **stuck fast*** (=could not be moved at all) *in the mud.*
6 make sth stick INFORMAL **a)** to make people accept that someone is guilty of something: *Is there enough evidence to make the charges stick?* **b)** to make a change become permanent or effective: *The administration has succeeded in making this policy stick.*
7 stick in sb's throat if words stick in someone's throat, they are unable to say what they want, especially because they are upset
8 stick in sb's craw if a situation or someone's behavior sticks in someone's craw, it is so annoying that they cannot accept it
9 NAME [I] if a name that someone has invented sticks, people continue to use it: *The other kids called him "Speedy," and the name stuck.*
10 stick to sb's ribs food that sticks to your ribs makes you feel satisfied and become heavier
11 sb can stick sth SPOKEN INFORMAL used to rudely and angrily say that you do not want what someone is offering you
12 CARD GAME [I] to decide not to take any more cards in some card games
[**Origin:** Old English *stician*] → see also **stay/stick in sb's mind** at MIND[1] (41), **stick/poke your nose into sth** at NOSE[1] (3), STUCK[2] → see also **stick out like a sore thumb** at SORE[1] (4)

stick around *phr. v.* INFORMAL to stay in the same

place for a little longer, especially in order to wait for something that you expect to happen: *Stick around – there'll be dancing later.*

stick by *phr. v.* **1 stick by sb** to continue to give your support to a friend who has problems: *My wife has **stuck by me through thick and thin**.* **2 stick by sth** to do what you said you would do or what you think you should do: *Richards is sticking by her decision not to approve the spending bill.*

stick out *phr. v.*
1 COME UP OR FORWARD if a part of something sticks out, it comes out further than the rest of a surface or comes out through a hole: *It's kind of cute the way his ears stick out.* | **+of/from/through** *Paul's legs were sticking out from under the car.*
2 MOVE BODY PART OUT **stick sth ↔ out** to deliberately make part of your body come forward or away from the rest of your body: *"Nice to meet you," Pat said, sticking out her hand.*
3 stick your tongue out (at sb) to quickly put your tongue outside your mouth and back in again, to be rude
4 stick out (in sb's mind) to seem more important to someone than other people or things: *One concern that sticks out in everyone's mind is the cost of the new stadium.*
5 stick it out to continue to the end of an activity that is difficult, painful, or boring: *I'm going to stick it out just to prove to him that I can do it.*
6 stick your neck out INFORMAL to take the risk of saying or doing something that may be wrong or that other people may disagree with

stick to sth *phr. v.*
1 DO WHAT YOU SAY to do or keep doing what you said you would do or what you believe in: *Have you been sticking to your diet?* | **stick to your decision/principles etc.** *I told you I'd be there, and I stuck to my word.*
2 CONTINUE WITH SAME THING to keep using or doing one particular thing and not change to anything else: *He should stick to writing fiction.* | *If you're driving, stick to soft drinks.*
3 stick to it to continue to work or study in a very determined way in order to achieve something: *When I set a goal, I stick to it.* → see also STICK-TO-IT-IVENESS
4 stick to the point/subject/facts to talk only about what you are supposed to be talking about or what is certain: *"Please stick to the facts," said the judge.*
5 stick to the rules INFORMAL to do something exactly according to the rules
6 stick to your guns INFORMAL to refuse to change your mind about something even though other people are trying to persuade you that you are wrong
7 stick it to sb to make someone suffer, pay a high price etc.: *Politicians like to stick it to the tourists because the tourists don't vote.*
8 stick to your story SPOKEN to continue to say that what you have told someone is true, even though they do not believe you
9 stick to your knitting HUMOROUS to continue to pay attention to your own work, and not get involved in or ask questions about things that other people are doing

stick together *phr. v.* INFORMAL if people stick together, they continue to support one another even when they have problems: *We're a family and we stick together no matter what.*

stick up *phr. v.* **1** if a part of something sticks up, it is raised up or points up above a surface: *My hair is sticking up, isn't it?* | **+from/through etc.** *Part of the plane was sticking up out of the water.* **2 stick 'em up** SPOKEN INFORMAL used to tell someone to raise their hands when threatening them with a gun

stick up for sb *phr. v.* INFORMAL to defend someone who is being criticized, especially when no one else will defend them: *You're her husband – you should stick up for her.* | **stick up for yourself** *She's always known how to stick up for herself.*

stick with *phr. v.* INFORMAL **1 stick with sb** to stay close to someone: *Just stick with me. I'll explain everything as we go along.* **2 stick with sth** to continue doing or using something the way you did or planned to do before: *Let's stick with the original plan.* **3 stick with sth** to continue doing something, especially something difficult: *We're going to **stick with it** till we get the job done.* **4 stick with sb** to remain in someone's memory: *Those words will stick with me for the rest of my life.* **5 stick sb with sb/sth** to make someone accept something, do something, spend time with someone etc. when they do not want to: *They stuck me with the most difficult project again.* → see also **be stuck with sth** at STUCK² (5) **6 stick with sb** to stay loyal to someone and support them, especially in a difficult situation SYN **stick by**

stick² S2 W3 *n.*
1 FROM A TREE [C] a long thin piece of wood that has fallen or been cut from a tree: *a bundle of sticks*
2 a long thin or round piece of something: **+of** *a stick of gum* | *a stick of butter* | **a carrot/bread/cinnamon etc. stick** *She was chewing a celery stick.* → see also FISH STICK
3 SPORTS [C] a long specially shaped piece of wood that you use for hitting the ball or PUCK in sports such as HOCKEY
4 CAR [C] INFORMAL a STICK SHIFT
5 FOR A PARTICULAR PURPOSE [C] a long thin piece of wood used for a particular purpose: *a walking stick* | *a measuring stick* → see also DRUMSTICK, NIGHTSTICK, YARDSTICK
6 get on the stick SPOKEN to start doing something you should be doing
7 the sticks INFORMAL a place that is very far from a town or city: *They live somewhere out in the sticks.*
8 sticks and stones can/may break my bones (but words can never hurt/harm me) SPOKEN used especially by children to say that it does not worry you if someone says things to you that are not nice
9 a stick of furniture a piece of furniture → see also **a carrot-and-stick approach** at CARROT (3), **more sth than you can shake a stick at** at SHAKE¹ (12)

stick·ball /ˈstɪkbɔl/ *n.* [U] a game like BASEBALL that is played in the street by children, using a small ball and a stick

stick·er /ˈstɪkɚ/ S3 *n.* [C] a small piece of paper or plastic with a picture or writing on it that you can stick on to something → see also LABEL

ˈsticker price *n.* [C usually singular] the price of something, especially a car, that is written on it or given in advertisements, but that may be reduced by the person selling it

ˈsticker shock *n.* [U] HUMOROUS the surprise you feel when you find out how expensive something is, especially a car

ˈstick ˌfigure *n.* [C] a very simple drawing of a person that uses straight lines for the arms, body, and legs

ˈsticking point *n.* [C] the thing that prevents an agreement from being made in a discussion: *a major sticking point in the negotiations*

ˈstick-in-the-ˌmud *n.* [C] DISAPPROVING someone who is not willing to try anything new or have fun

stick·ler /ˈstɪklɚ/ *n.* **be a stickler for rules/detail/punctuality etc.** to think that rules, details etc. are very important and that other people should also think they are very important

ˈstick man *n.* [C] a STICK FIGURE

ˈstick-on *adj.* [only before noun] stick-on material has a sticky substance on its back so that you can stick it on to something: *stick-on name tags* —**stick-on** *n.* [C]

stick·pin /ˈstɪkˌpɪn/ *n.* [C] a decorated pin worn as jewelry

ˈstick shift *n.* [C] **1** a movable metal bar in a car that you use to control its GEARS **2** a car that uses a stick shift system to control its gears → see also AUTOMATIC

stick-to-it-ive·ness /ˌstɪk ˈtu ɪṭ əvnɪs/ *n.* [U] INFORMAL the ability to continue doing something that is difficult or tiring to do

ˈstick-up *n.* [C] INFORMAL a situation in which someone steals money from people in a bank, store etc. by threatening them with a gun

stick·y /ˈstɪki/ S3 *adj.* *comparative* **stickier**, *superlative* **stickiest** **1** made of or covered with a substance that sticks to surfaces: *There's something sticky on the floor.* **2** sticky weather makes you feel uncomfortable and very hot, wet, and dirty: *a hot sticky day in August* **3** a sticky situation, question, or problem is difficult or dangerous to deal with: *a sticky political issue* **4 have sticky fingers** INFORMAL to be likely to steal something —**stickiness** *n.* [U]

ˈsticky note also **sticky** *n.* [C] a small piece of paper that sticks to things, used for leaving notes for people SYN **Post-it®**

stiff¹ /stɪf/ *adj.*

1 BODY if a part of your body is stiff or you are stiff, your muscles hurt and it is difficult to move: *My legs are stiff from going running last night.* | **a stiff neck/back/joint etc.** *Sleeping on the plane gave me a stiff neck.* | *I **felt** really **stiff** after playing basketball last week.* ►see THESAURUS box at **painful**

2 PAPER/MATERIAL ETC. hard and difficult to bend: *a shirt with a stiff collar* ►see THESAURUS box at **hard¹**

3 MIXTURE a stiff mixture is thick and almost solid, so that it is not easy to mix: *Beat the egg whites until stiff.*

4 STRICT/SEVERE more difficult, strict, or severe than usual: **a stiff sentence/penalty/fine** *new stiffer penalties for drug dealers* | **stiff competition/opposition/resistance** *The company is facing stiff competition from Canadian manufacturers.*

5 UNFRIENDLY unfriendly or very formal, so that other people feel uncomfortable: *Their goodbyes were stiff and formal.*

6 a stiff drink/whiskey etc. a very strong alcoholic drink

7 a stiff wind/breeze a fairly strong wind

8 stiff as a board SPOKEN extremely hard and difficult to bend

9 keep a stiff upper lip to try to keep calm and not show your feelings in a situation when most people would become upset

[**Origin:** Old English *stif*] —**stiffly** *adv.* —**stiffness** *n.* [U]

stiff² *adv.* **1 bored/scared stiff** INFORMAL extremely bored or SCARED **2 frozen stiff** extremely cold, or frozen and hard

stiff³ *n.* [C] SLANG the body of a dead person → see also WORKING STIFF

stiff⁴ *v.* [T] INFORMAL to not pay someone money that you owe them or that they expect to be given, especially by not leaving a TIP in a restaurant

ˈstiff-arm *v.* [T] **1** to prevent someone from getting close to you by pushing them with your arm stretched out **2** to refuse to talk to someone or give them information, especially when you are being attacked or criticized —**stiff-arm** *n.* [C]

stiff·en /ˈstɪfən/ *v.* **1** [I] to suddenly become unfriendly, angry, or anxious: *Nora stiffened when she heard her ex-boyfriend's name.* **2** [I,T] to become stronger, more severe, or more determined, or to make something do this: *Opposition to the building of a new runway has stiffened.* | *Their opposition only **stiffened** my **resolve**.* **3** [I] also **stiffen up** to become painful and difficult to move: *My back had stiffened up overnight.* **4** [I,T] to make material, hair etc. stiff so that it will not bend easily, or to become stiff: *Starch is used to stiffen the fabric.*

ˌstiff-ˈnecked *adj.* LITERARY DISAPPROVING proud and refusing to change or obey SYN **stubborn**

sti·fle /ˈstaɪfəl/ *v.* [T] **1** to stop something from happening or developing: *Martial law continues to stifle political debate in the country.* **2** to stop yourself from doing something you want to do or expressing a feeling: *She stifled the urge to scream.* | **stifle a yawn/smile etc.** *I was unable to stifle my laughter.* **3** [usually passive] if you are stifled by something, it stops you breathing comfortably: *He was almost stifled by the fumes.*

sti·fling /ˈstaɪflɪŋ/ *adj.* **1** very hot and difficult to breathe in: *stifling heat* **2** a stifling situation stops you from developing your own ideas and character

stig·ma /ˈstɪgmə/ *n.* **1** [singular, U] a strong feeling in society that a type of behavior or a particular condition is shameful: **the stigma of (doing) sth** *the social stigma of mental illness* | *There is **a stigma attached to** single parenthood.* | *Being fat **carries a stigma** that starts early.* **2** [C] BIOLOGY the top sticky part of the female structure of a flower, which receives the POLLEN that allows it to form new seeds [**Origin:** 1500–1600 Latin **mark, mark burned on the skin**, from Greek, from *stizein* **to tattoo**]

stig·ma·ta /stɪgˈmɑt̬ə, ˈstɪgmət̬ə/ *n.* [plural] the marks on the hands and feet of Jesus Christ caused by nails, or similar marks that appear on the bodies of some holy people

stig·ma·tize /ˈstɪgməˌtaɪz/ *v.* [T usually passive] to make someone feel they should be ashamed of their situation: *Single mothers often feel that they are stigmatized by society.* —**stigmatization** /ˌstɪgmət̬əˈzeɪʃən/ *n.* [U]

stile /staɪl/ *n.* [C] a set of steps placed on either side of a fence so that people can climb over it

sti·let·to /stɪˈlɛt̬oʊ/ *n.* *plural* **stilettoes** or **stilettos** [C] **1** also **stiletto heel a)** a high thin heel of a woman's shoe **b)** a shoe that has this kind of heel **2** a small knife with a thin BLADE [**Origin:** 1600–1700 Italian *stilo* **knife**, from Latin *stilus* **pointed stick, stylus, style of writing**]

still¹ /stɪl/ S1 W1 *adv.* **1** used to emphasize that a situation has continued up to now or another particular point in time and is continuing at that moment: *It's still raining.* | *Do you still have her phone number?* | *There's still some food left.* | *They still haven't arrived.* | *Did she still live in Tokyo when you met her?* | **still to do/go/come** *There were more surprises still to come.* **2** in spite of what has just been said or done SYN **nonetheless** SYN **nevertheless**: *She worked hard but she still failed the test.* | [sentence adverb] *She's probably out. Still, you could try calling her.* **3** [sentence adverb] used when mentioning a good feature of a situation or a good thing that happened, after mentioning a bad one SYN **nonetheless** SYN **nevertheless** SYN **however**: *The hotel was terrible. Still, the weather was good.* **4 still more/another/other/further etc.** even more in amount or degree SYN **even**: *Kevin grew still more depressed.* | *Still others have begun to complain.* **5 better/harder/worse etc. still** also **still better/harder/worse etc.** even better, harder etc. than something else SYN **even**: *Dan found biology difficult, and physics harder still.* | *The situation is making me unhappy. Worse still, it's affecting the kids.* **6 be still going strong** to continue to be active or successful, even after a long time: *They've been married for 42 years, and they're still going strong.*

WORD CHOICE **still, already, yet**

- **Still** can mean that you are surprised that something has continued for longer than you might expect: *You mean Jenny still hasn't found a job?*
- **Already** is usually used in positive sentences to mean that you are surprised that something has happened earlier than you thought it would: *Are they here already?*
- **Yet** is used in negatives and questions to talk about things that you expect to happen, but have not happened: *I haven't had breakfast yet.* | *Has Bill arrived yet?*
- Using **yet** instead of **still** in a positive sentence is rare and a little formal: *We have yet to hear the truth.* | *The city council may yet surprise us.* In conversation, you are more likely to say something like: *We still don't know the truth.*

GRAMMAR

Still usually comes immediately before any negative word: *She still isn't ready.* | *You still don't understand.* | *A solution has still not been found* (or *...still hasn't,* NOT *...has not still*). **Still** usually comes immediately after a positive modal verb: *I can still remember* (NOT *still can remember*). | *He may still be there* (NOT *be still there*).

Otherwise **still** comes after the verb **to be** and immediately before any main verb: *She's still eating* (NOT *still is eating*). | *It's still raining.* | *We still have time* (NOT *have still time*). | *I still love her.* **Yet** often comes either immediately after a negative word or at the end of a clause, but there is a difference of style. In formal written English, you might read: *We do not yet know the answer.* In informal conversation you might say: *I don't know the answer yet* (NOT *I don't know yet the answer*).

still² S3 *adj.* [no comparative] **1** not moving: *a still pond* | **keep/stand/lie etc. still** *The kids find it hard to sit still.* **2** quiet and calm: *For once, the house was completely still.* **3** not windy: *a hot still airless day* **4 still waters run deep** used to say that someone who is quiet may have very strong feelings or a lot of knowledge **5** without BUBBLES or gas: *still mineral water* [**Origin:** Old English *stille*] —**stillness** *n.* [U]

still³ *n.* [C] **1** ENG. LANG. ARTS a photograph of a scene from a movie **2** a piece of equipment for making alcoholic drinks out of grain or potatoes **3 the still of the night/evening etc.** LITERARY the calm and quiet of the night, evening etc.

still⁴ *v.* [I,T] LITERARY **1** to become quiet or still, or to make someone or something do this **2** if an unpleasant feeling, such as doubt or fear, stills or is stilled, it becomes weaker or goes away

still·birth /ˈstɪlbɚθ, ˌstɪlˈbɚθ/ *n.* [C,U] a birth in which the baby is born dead → see also ABORTION

still·born /ˌstɪlˈbɔrn◂ / *adj.* **1** BIOLOGY born dead: *a stillborn baby* **2** ending before having had a chance to start: *a stillborn romance*

ˌstill ˈlife *n. plural* **still lifes** [C,U] a painting or photograph of an arrangement of objects, especially flowers and fruit

stilt /stɪlt/ *n.* [C usually plural] **1** one of two poles on which you can stand and walk high above the ground: *Circus performers were walking* ***on stilts.*** **2** one of a set of poles that support a building, so that it is raised above ground or water level

stilt·ed /ˈstɪltɪd/ *adj.* a stilted style of writing or speaking is formal and unnatural: *the movie's stilted dialogue* —**stiltedly** *adv.*

Stil·ton /ˈstɪltˀn/ *n.* [U] a type of English cheese that has a strong taste [**Origin:** 1700–1800 *Stilton* village in Cambridgeshire, England where the cheese was originally sold]

stim·u·lant /ˈstɪmyələnt/ *n.* [C] **1** MEDICINE a drug or substance that makes you feel more active and full of energy: *Nicotine is a stimulant.* **2** something that encourages more of a particular activity SYN **stimulus**: +**to** *a stimulant to the economy*

stim·u·late /ˈstɪmyəˌleɪt/ *v.* [T] **1** to encourage or help an activity to begin or develop further: *Will the tax cuts stimulate the economy?* **2** to encourage someone by making them excited about and interested in something: *We try to stimulate the children's imaginations.* **3** BIOLOGY to make a plant or part of the body become active or stronger: *The drug stimulates the immune system.* —**stimulative** *adj.* —**stimulation** /ˌstɪmyəˈleɪʃən/ *n.* [U]

stim·u·lat·ing /ˈstɪmyəˌleɪtɪŋ/ *adj.* **1** exciting or full of new ideas: *a stimulating discussion of world politics* **2** making you feel more active: *the stimulating effects of coffee*

stim·u·lus /ˈstɪmyələs/ *n. plural* **stimuli** /-laɪ/ **1** [C usually singular, U] BIOLOGY something that helps a process to develop more quickly or more strongly: +**to/for** *Tourism provided an important stimulus to the local economy.* **2** [C] something that makes someone or something move or react: *visual stimuli*

sting¹ /stɪŋ/ *v. past tense and past participle* **stung** /stʌŋ/ **1** [I,T] BIOLOGY if an insect or a plant stings you, it causes a sharp pain and that part of your body swells: *Henry was stung by a bee.* **2** [I,T] to make something hurt with a sudden sharp pain for a short time, or to hurt in this way: *The paper cut on my finger really stings.* | *Cigarette smoke stings my eyes.* ▶see THESAURUS box at **hurt¹** **3** [I,T usually passive] if a remark or criticism stings, it makes you feel upset and embarrassed: *She had been stung by this criticism.* | **sting sb into (doing) sth** *Her harsh words stung him into action.* [**Origin:** Old English *stingan*]

sting² *n.* **1** [C] BIOLOGY a wound or mark made when an insect or plant stings you: *a bee sting* **2** [singular] a sharp pain in your eyes or skin, caused by being hit, by smoke etc.: +**of** *She felt the sting of tears in her eyes.* **3** [singular] the upsetting or bad effects of a situation: *the sting of discrimination* | *A few hundred dollars won't* ***take the sting out of*** (=makes it easier to deal with the bad effects of) *losing my job.* **4** [C] a situation in which the police catch criminals by pretending to be involved in criminal activity themselves

sting·er /ˈstɪŋɚ/ *n.* [C] the sharp needle-like part of an animal or insect's body that can be pushed through the skin of a person or animal, often leaving poison

sting·ing /ˈstɪŋɪŋ/ *adj.* **a stinging report/letter/rebuke etc.** a report, letter etc. that severely and strongly expresses criticism

ˈstinging ˌnettle *n.* [C] a wild plant with leaves that sting and leave red marks on the skin

sting·ray /ˈstɪŋreɪ/ *n.* [C] BIOLOGY a large fish with a flat body and several sharp points on its back near its tail

stin·gy /ˈstɪndʒi/ *adj. comparative* **stingier**, *superlative* **stingiest** **1** not generous, especially with money, when you can easily afford to be OPP **generous**: *He's too stingy to give money to charity.* **2** a stingy amount of something, especially food, is too small to be enough —**stingily** *adv.* —**stinginess** *n.* [U]

stink¹ /stɪŋk/ S3 *v. past tense* **stank** or **stunk** /stʌŋk/, *past participle* **stunk** [I] **1** to have a strong and very bad smell SYN **reek**: *Your shoes stink.* | *It stinks in here.* | +**of** *He came home stinking of beer.* | *The school's bathrooms* ***stink to high heaven*** (=stink very much). **2 sth stinks** SPOKEN INFORMAL **a)** used to say that something is bad or that you do not like it: *Don't eat there – the food stinks!* **b)** used to say that you think something is not fair or reasonable: *"My mom won't let me go." "That stinks."* [**Origin:** Old English *stincan*]

stink of sth *phr. v.* to seem to be bad or seem to be related to something bad: *The whole administration stinks of corruption.*

stink sth ↔ **up** INFORMAL *phr. v.* **1** to fill a place with a very bad smell: *His cigar stunk up the whole car.* **2 stink up the place** to perform badly in a play, game etc.

stink² *n.* **1** [C] a very bad smell: +**of** *the stink of burning rubber* ▶see THESAURUS box at **smell¹** **2 make/raise/cause etc. a stink** to complain very strongly because you are annoyed about something: *I made a stink about it, and they gave me my money back.*

ˈstink bomb *n.* [C] a small container that produces an extremely bad smell when it is broken

stink·er /ˈstɪŋkɚ/ *n.* [C] INFORMAL **1** someone who behaves badly, especially a child **2** a movie, book, sports team etc. that is very bad

stink·ing /ˈstɪŋkɪŋ/ *adj.* **1** having a very strong bad smell: *a can of stinking garbage* **2** [only before noun] SPOKEN used to emphasize what you are saying when you are angry or do not like something: *I don't want to watch that stinking TV show.* **3 stinking rich** INFORMAL an expression meaning "extremely rich," used especially when you think this is unfair **4 stinking drunk** very drunk

stink·y /ˈstɪŋki/ *adj. comparative* **stinkier**, *superlative* **stinkiest** INFORMAL smelling very bad SYN **smelly**: *stinky socks*

stint¹ /stɪnt/ *n.* [C usually singular] a period of time spent doing a particular job or activity: +**as/in/at/with** *He did a four-year stint in the Marines.*

stint² *v.* [I usually in negatives] to give or use too little of something: +**on** *They didn't stint on alcohol at the party.*

sti·pend /ˈstaɪpɛnd, -pənd/ *n.* [C] a particular amount

S

of money paid regularly to someone such as a priest or student, as a salary or money to live on

stip·ple /ˈstɪpəl/ *v.* [T] to draw or paint a picture or pattern using very short STROKES or spots instead of longer lines —**stippled** *adj.* —**stippling** *n.* [U]

stip·u·late /ˈstɪpyəˌleɪt/ *v.* [T] to say that something must be done, when you are making an agreement or offer: **stipulate that** *His will stipulated that his fortune be given to his two daughters.*

stip·u·la·tion /ˌstɪpyəˈleɪʃən/ *n.* [C,U] something that must be done which is stated as part of an agreement: **stipulation that** *The agreement included a stipulation that half the money be spent on low-income housing.*

stir[1] /stɚ/ W3 *v.* **stirred**, **stirring** **1** [T] to move a liquid or substance around with a spoon or stick in order to mix it together: *Stir the paint to make sure it is smooth.* | **stir sth with sth** *She stirred her coffee with a plastic spoon.* | **stir sth in/into sth** *Stir the flour into the mixture.* ►see THESAURUS box at **cooking**[1], **mix**[1] **2** [I] WRITTEN to move slightly or change your position, especially because you are uncomfortable, anxious, or you are about to wake up: *The sleeping child stirred.* **3 a)** [T] to make someone have a strong feeling or reaction: **stir memories/emotions etc.** *The music stirred childhood memories.* | *The Arizona landscape* ***stirs the imagination.*** **b)** [I] if a feeling stirs in you, you begin to feel it: +**in/inside/within** *Excitement stirred inside her.* **4** [T] to make someone feel they must do something: **stir sb to do sth** *The incident has stirred students to protest.* **5** [I,T] to make something move slightly, or to move slightly: *A gentle breeze stirred the curtains.* [**Origin:** Old English *styrian*]

stir up *phr. v.* **1 stir sth ↔ up** to deliberately try to cause arguments or problems between people: *John was always* ***stirring up trouble*** *in class.* | *Dave's just trying to* ***stir things up*** *because he's jealous.* **2 stir sb ↔ up** to make someone feel excited or that they must do something: *His speech really stirred up the crowd.* **3 stir sth ↔ up** to make something move around in the air or in water: *The wind stirred up the powdery sand.*

stir[2] *n.* **1** [C usually singular] a feeling of excitement or annoyance: **create/cause a stir** *His comments created quite a stir.* **2** [C usually singular] an act of stirring something **3** [C,U] OLD-FASHIONED SLANG a prison

ˌstir-ˈcrazy *adj.* INFORMAL extremely nervous and upset, especially because you feel trapped in a place: *I'll* ***go stir-crazy*** *if I don't get out of this house.*

ˈstir-fry *v.* **stir-fries**, **stir-fried**, **stir-frying** [T] to cook something by cutting it into small pieces and cooking it in a small amount of hot oil for a short time —**stir-fry** *n.* [C] —**stir-fried** *adj.*

stir·ring[1] /ˈstɚɪŋ/ *adj.* producing strong feelings or excitement in someone: *a stirring speech* —**stirringly** *adv.*

stirring[2] *n.* [C often plural] an early sign that something is starting to happen, or that you are beginning to feel a particular emotion: **a stirring of love/doubt/rebellion etc.** *the first faint stirrings of doubt*

stir·rup /ˈstɚəp, ˈstɪrəp/ *n.* [C] **1** a ring of metal that hangs from each side of a horse's SADDLE for someone to put their foot in as they ride the horse **2** a U-shaped object that is used for supporting or holding something such as your feet **3** a band of cloth that goes under your foot on some pants

ˈstirrup ˌpants *n.* [plural] women's pants made of a material that stretches, that have bands at the bottom of the legs that fit under your feet

stitch[1] /stɪtʃ/ *n.*
1 SEWING [C] the result of sewing by taking a thread into and out of a piece of cloth: *She sewed with small neat stitches.*
2 FOR WOUND [C usually plural] a piece of special thread that fastens the edges of a wound together: *She needed five stitches in her forehead.*
3 in stitches INFORMAL unable to stop laughing: **keep/have sb in stitches** *Tony kept us in stitches all evening.*
4 PAIN [C usually singular] a sharp pain in the side of your body, that you can get by running or laughing very hard: *After jogging about a mile, I suddenly got a stitch in my side.*
5 FUNNY [C usually singular] INFORMAL someone or something that is very funny
6 KNITTING [C] one of the small circles that are formed when you are KNITting, that join together to make a SWEATER etc. → see also **drop a stitch** at DROP[1] (32)
7 STYLE [C,U] a particular way of sewing or KNITting that makes a particular pattern: *Purl and plain are the two main stitches in knitting.*
8 not have a stitch on INFORMAL to be wearing no clothes
9 not have a stitch to wear to not have any clothing that is appropriate for a particular occasion
10 a stitch in time (saves nine) SPOKEN used to say that it is better to deal with problems early than to wait until they get worse
[**Origin:** Old English *stice* **prick**]

stitch[2] *v.* [T] to sew two pieces of cloth together, or to sew a decoration onto a piece of cloth: **stitch sth onto/across/to etc. sth** *She stitched the lace onto the cloth.*

stitch sth ↔ **together** *phr. v.* to put different things or parts of something together to make one larger thing: *They have managed to stitch together a national network of banks.*

stitch sth ↔ **up** *phr. v.* **1** to put stitches in cloth or a wound in order to fasten parts of it together: *She stitched up the cut and left it to heal.* **2** to get a deal or agreement completed satisfactorily so that it cannot be changed: *The deal was stitched up in minutes.*

stitch·er·y /ˈstɪtʃəri/ *n.* [U] NEEDLEWORK

stitch·ing /ˈstɪtʃɪŋ/ *n.* [U] a line of stitches in a piece of material

St. John's /seɪnt ˈdʒɑnz/ the capital city of Antigua and Barbuda

St. Kitts and Ne·vis /seɪnt ˌkɪts ən ˈnivɪs/ also **St. Christopher and Nevis** a country consisting of two islands in the Caribbean Sea

St. Law·rence Riv·er, the /seɪnt ˌlɔrəns ˈrɪvɚ/ a river in North America that flows from Lake Ontario to the Gulf of St. Lawrence and forms part of the border between the U.S. and Canada

St. ˌLawrence ˈSeaway, the a system of CANALS in North America connecting the St. Lawrence River and all the Great Lakes. It was built by the U.S. and Canada and was opened in 1959.

St. Lou·is /seɪnt ˈluɪs/ a city in the U.S. state of Missouri which is a port on the Mississippi River

St. Lu·cia /seɪnt ˈluʃə/ a country that is an island in the Caribbean Sea

stoat /stoʊt/ *n.* [C] a small thin animal with brown fur that is similar to a WEASEL, and kills other animals

stock[1] /stɑk/ S3 W1 *n.*
1 IN A STORE [C,U] a supply of a particular type of thing that a store has to sell: *Buy now while stocks last!* | +**of** *We have a huge stock of quality carpets.* | *Let me check if our other store has that CD* ***in stock*** (=available at a particular store). | *I'm sorry, that swimsuit is completely* ***out of stock*** (=unavailable at a particular store) *in your size.*
2 FINANCE a) [U] shares of OWNERSHIP in a company that are sold to the public: +**in** *How much stock do you own in the company?* | **sell/issue stock** *The company plans to issue more stock to raise capital.* **b)** [C usually plural] the stock of a particular company, especially when considering how valuable it is: *The company's stock rose 8% this year.* | *the buying of stocks and bonds* | **technology/tobacco/financial etc. stocks** *Technology stocks are still a risky investment.*
3 COOKING [C,U] a liquid made by boiling meat or bones and vegetables, which is used to make soups or to add FLAVOR to other dishes: *chicken stock*
4 AMOUNT AVAILABLE [C] the total amount of something in a particular area that is available to be used: *Some fish stocks in the North Atlantic have dropped radically.*
5 SUPPLIES [C] a supply of something that you keep and

can use when you need to: +**of** *large stocks of chemical weapons*
6 a stock of jokes/knowledge/words etc. the jokes, knowledge, words etc. that someone knows or has
7 take stock (of sth) to think carefully about the things that have happened in a situation in order to decide what to do next: *While in the hospital, Jeremy took stock of his life.*
8 ANIMALS [U] farm animals, especially cattle SYN **livestock**
9 GUN [C] the part of a gun that you hold or put against your shoulder, usually made of wood
10 RESPECT [U] the amount of respect that someone gets from other people SYN **standing**: **sb's stock is high/low** *Simon's stock is high in the network news business.*
11 FAMILY [U] the type or group of people that your family belonged to in the past and may still belong to: **of Scottish/Protestant/good etc. stock** *His parents were of hard-working peasant stock.*
12 the stocks a) a wooden structure in a public place to which criminals were fastened by their feet or hands in the past as a punishment **b)** a wooden structure in which a ship is held while it is being built
13 PLANT a) a plant that you can cut stems off to make new plants grow **b)** a thick part of a stem onto which another plant can be added so that the two plants grow together
14 THEATER [C,U] ENG. LANG. ARTS a STOCK COMPANY → see also SUMMER STOCK
15 FLOWER [C] BIOLOGY a plant with pink, white, or light purple flowers and a sweet smell
16 CLOTHING [C] a wide band of cloth that goes around the neck so that the ends hang in front of your chest, worn especially by some priests
[**Origin:** Old English *stocc* **tree-trunk, block of wood**]
→ see also LAUGHING STOCK, **lock, stock, and barrel** at LOCK² (3), ROLLING STOCK

stock² *v.* [T] **1** if a store stocks a particular product, it keeps a supply of it to be sold: *The store stocks a wide range of kitchen equipment.* **2** to provide a supply of something so that it is ready to use: **stock sth with sth** *They stocked the cabin with plenty of food.* → see also WELL-STOCKED **3** to put fish in a lake or river: **stock sth with sth** *They plan to stock the lake with trout.*
stock up *phr. v.* to buy a lot of something to use when you need to: +**on** *I have to stock up on snacks for the party.*

stock³ *adj.* **a stock excuse/question/remark etc.** an excuse, question etc. that people often say or use, especially when they cannot think of anything more interesting or original

stock·ade¹ /stɑˈkeɪd/ *n.* [C usually singular] a wall or fence made of large upright pieces of wood, built to defend a place

stockade² *v.* [T] to put a stockade around a place in order to defend it

stock·breed·er /ˈstɑkˌbridɚ/ *n.* [C] a farmer who breeds cattle

stock·brok·er /ˈstɑkˌbroʊkɚ/ *n.* [C] ECONOMICS someone whose job is to buy and sell STOCKS, BONDS etc. for other people —**stockbroking** *n.* [U]

ˈstock car *n.* [C] **1** a car that has been made stronger so that it can compete in a race where cars often crash into each other **2** a railroad car used for cattle

ˈstock cerˌtificate *n.* [C] ECONOMICS an official document that shows that you own STOCK in a company

ˈstock ˌcompany *n.* [C] **1** ECONOMICS a company whose money is divided into STOCK so that many people own a small part of it **2** ENG. LANG. ARTS a group of actors who work together doing several different plays

ˈstock exˌchange *n.* ECONOMICS **1** [C usually singular] a place where STOCKS are bought and sold SYN **stock market**: *the New York Stock Exchange* **2 the stock exchange** [singular] the business of buying and selling STOCK SYN **the stock market**

stock·hold·er /ˈstɑkˌhoʊldɚ/ *n.* [C] ECONOMICS someone who owns STOCK in a business

Stock·holm /ˈstɑkhoʊlm/ the capital and largest city of Sweden

ˈstock ˌindex *n.* [C] an official and public list of STOCK PRICES

stock·ing /ˈstɑkɪŋ/ *n.* [C usually plural] **1** a thin close-fitting piece of clothing that covers a woman's leg and foot → see also PANTYHOSE, TIGHTS **2** OLD-FASHIONED a man's sock **3 in your stockinged/stocking feet** wearing socks but no shoes → see also BODY STOCKING, CHRISTMAS STOCKING

ˈstocking ˌcap *n.* [C] a type of soft hat that fits close around your head, used to keep you warm

ˈstocking ˌmask *n.* [C] a stocking or NYLONS that someone wears over their face, especially when doing something illegal

ˌstock-in-ˈtrade *n.* [U] **1** something that is typical of a particular person or thing, especially what they say or do: *Charm was his stock-in-trade.* **2** the things that a person, company, or organization uses in their work or deals in **3** TECHNICAL the goods kept by a business so that it can operate by selling them

stock·man /ˈstɑkmən/ *n. plural* **stockmen** /-mən/ [C] a man whose job it is to take care of farm animals

ˈstock ˌmarket W3 *n.* ECONOMICS **1 the stock market** [singular] **a)** the business of buying and selling STOCK SYN **the stock exchange**: *She made a lot of money on the stock market.* **b)** the average value of STOCKS sold in a STOCK EXCHANGE: *The stock market keeps going up.* **2** [C usually singular] a place where STOCKS are bought and sold SYN **stock exchange**

ˈstock ˌoption *n.* [C usually plural] an opportunity for an EMPLOYEE to buy STOCK in his or her company at a lower price than the usual price

stock·pile¹ /ˈstɑkpaɪl/ *n.* [C] a large supply of goods, weapons etc. that are kept ready to be used in the future, especially when they may become difficult to obtain: +**of** *stockpiles of nuclear missiles*

stockpile² *v.* [T] to keep adding to a supply of goods, weapons etc. that you are keeping ready to use if you need them in the future: *Rebel groups continue to stockpile weapons.*

stock·pot /ˈstɑkpɑt/ *n.* [C] a pot in which you make cooking STOCK

ˈstock price *n.* [C] the price of one share of a company's STOCK

stock·room /ˈstɑkrum/ *n.* [C] a room for storing things in a store or office

ˈstock split *n.* [C] a situation in which the STOCK in a company is divided into more shares that are less valuable, but which together are worth the same amount as the original shares: *a two-for-one stock split*

ˌstock-ˈstill *adv.* not moving at all

stock·y /ˈstɑki/ *adj. comparative* **stockier**, *superlative* **stockiest** a stocky person is short and heavy and looks strong —**stockily** *adv.* —**stockiness** *n.* [U]

stock·yard /ˈstɑkyɑrd/ *n.* [C] a place where cattle, sheep etc. are kept before being taken to a market and sold

stodg·y /ˈstɑdʒi/ *adj. comparative* **stodgier**, *superlative* **stodgiest** **1** a stodgy person is boring and behaves rather formally **2** stodgy writing or organizations are boring, formal, and old-fashioned: *the stodgy banking industry* —**stodginess** *n.* [U]

sto·gie /ˈstoʊgi/ *n.* [C] INFORMAL a CIGAR, especially a thick cheap one

sto·ic¹ /ˈstoʊɪk/ also **sto·ic·al** /ˈstoʊɪkəl/ *adj.* not complaining or feeling unhappy when bad things happen to you [**Origin:** 1500–1600 *Stoic* **follower of the ancient Greek thinker Zeno, who said that happiness results from accepting what happens in life**] —**stoically** /-kli/ *adv.*

stoic² *n.* [C] someone who does not show their emotions and does not complain when something bad happens to them

stoi·chi·om·e·try /ˌstɔɪkiˈɑmətri/ *n.* [U] CHEMISTRY the study and calculation of the quantities of sub-

S

stances in a chemical reaction, and the relation between these quantities

sto·i·cism /ˈstoʊɪˌsɪzəm/ *n.* [U] patience and calmness when bad things happen to you

stoke /stoʊk/ also **stoke up** *v.* [T] **1** to move the coal or wood around in a fire used for cooking or heating, or to add more coal or wood to the fire **2** to cause something to increase: *Rising oil prices stoked inflation.* | **stoke fear/anger/resentment etc.** *The recent budget cuts have stoked public outrage.*

stoked /stoʊkt/ *adj.* [not before noun] SPOKEN very excited about something good that is going to happen: *I'm stoked about the trip.*

stok·er /ˈstoʊkɚ/ *n.* [C] someone whose job is to put coal or other FUEL into a FURNACE

stole¹ /stoʊl/ *v.* the past tense of STEAL

stole² *n.* [C] a long straight piece of cloth or fur that a woman wears across her shoulders

sto·len¹ /ˈstoʊlən/ *v.* the past participle of STEAL

stolen² *adj.* having been taken illegally: *stolen cars*

stol·id /ˈstɑlɪd/ *adj.* someone who is stolid does not react to situations or seem excited by them when most people would react —**stolidly** *adv.*

S

sto·lon /ˈstoʊlɑn/ *n.* [C] BIOLOGY **1** a long stem that grows out from a plant and produces roots where it touches the ground. New plants grow from those roots. **2** part of the body wall of some very simple animals that grow together in one place on which new members of the COLONY grow

sto·ma /ˈstoʊmə/ *n. plural* **stomas** or **stomata** /-mət̬ə/ [C] BIOLOGY one of the many very small holes on the surface of a leaf, that controls the amount of water and gases that enter and leave the plant

stom·ach¹ /ˈstʌmək/ S2 W3 *n.* [C] **1** BIOLOGY the organ inside your body where food is DIGESTED: *I had a pain in my stomach.* → see picture at DIGESTIVE SYSTEM **2** the front part of your body, below your chest: *He punched me in the stomach.* **3 do sth on an empty/a full stomach** to do something when you have not eaten or have just eaten: *Don't take the pills on an empty stomach.* **4 turn sb's stomach** to make someone feel sick or upset: *The smell was enough to turn my stomach.* **5 have the stomach for sth** also **have the stomach to do sth** [usually in negatives and questions] to have enough determination or courage to do something unpleasant, difficult, or dangerous: *The soldiers had no stomach for a fight.* [**Origin:** 1300–1400 Old French *estomac*, from Latin *stomachus* **throat, stomach**] → see also **have/get butterflies in your stomach** at BUTTERFLY (2), **in the pit of your stomach** at PIT¹ (3), **sick to your stomach** at SICK¹ (2), **have a strong stomach** at STRONG (29)

stomach² *v.* [T usually in questions and negatives] **1** to be able to do, accept, or deal with something, especially something unpleasant or bad SYN **endure**: **can/could stomach** *He couldn't stomach the sight of blood.* | **hard/difficult to stomach** *He found her attitude hard to stomach.* **2** to be able to eat something without becoming sick

stom·ach·ache, stomach ache /ˈstʌməkˌeɪk/ *n.* [C] pain in your stomach or near your stomach

ˈstomach pump *n.* [C] a machine with a tube that doctors use to suck out the food or liquid inside someone's stomach, especially after they have swallowed poison

sto·ma·ta /ˈstoʊmətə/ *n.* BIOLOGY a plural of STOMA

stomp /stɑmp, stɔmp/ *v.* **1** [I always + adv./prep.] to walk somewhere in a noisy way by putting your feet down hard onto the ground, usually because you are angry SYN **stamp**: +**off/out/into etc.** *She stomped off in a huff.* **2** [I,T] to put your foot down onto someone or something with a lot of force SYN **stamp**: +**on** *Several rioters stomped on an American flag.*

ˈstomping ˌground *n.* **sb's stomping ground** a favorite place where someone often goes

stone¹ /stoʊn/ S2 W2 *n.*
1 ROCK [U] EARTH SCIENCE a hard solid mineral substance SYN **rock**: *a huge block of stone* | *The temple is made of stone.*
2 PIECE OF ROCK [C] a small rock of any shape, found on the ground: *Kids were throwing stones into the water.*
3 JEWELRY [C] a jewel SYN **gemstone**: *sapphires, diamonds, and other* ***precious stones***
4 MEDICAL [C] MEDICINE a ball of hard material that can form in organs such as your BLADDER or KIDNEYS: *gall stones*
5 a stone's throw from sth also **a stone's throw away** INFORMAL very close to something: *The hotel is only a stone's throw from the beach.*
6 be made of stone also **have a heart of stone** to have no emotions or pity for someone
7 not be carved/etched/written etc. in stone used to say an idea or plan could change: *None of the plans are set in stone.*
8 FRUIT [C] BRITISH the large hard part at the center of some fruits, such as a PEACH, that contains the seed SYN **pit**
9 WEIGHT [C] BRITISH unit for measuring weight, equal to 14 pounds or 6.35 kilograms
[**Origin:** Old English *stan*] → see also FOUNDATION STONE, **kill two birds with one stone** at KILL¹ (12), **leave no stone unturned** at LEAVE¹ (35), PAVING STONE, STEPPING STONE, **sticks and stones can/may break my bones** at STICK² (8)

stone² *adj.* made of stone: *a stone wall* | *stone tools*

stone³ *v.* [T] **1** to throw stones at someone or something: *Rioters blocked roads and stoned vehicles.* **2 stone sb (to death)** to kill someone by throwing stones at them, usually as a punishment

Stone /stoʊn/**, Har·lan** /ˈhɑrlən/ (1872–1946) a CHIEF JUSTICE on the U.S. Supreme Court

ˈStone Age *n.* **the Stone Age** HISTORY a very early time in human history, when only stone was used for making tools, weapons etc. → see also BRONZE AGE, IRON AGE

ˌstone-ˈcold¹ *adj.* **1** completely cold, in a way that is bad **2** definite, with no possibility that things are or will be different: *a stone-cold certainty* **3** if a player or a sports team is stone-cold, they are not able to get any points

ˈstone-cold² *adv.* **stone-cold sober** having drunk no alcohol at all

stoned /stoʊnd/ *adj.* [not before noun] **1** INFORMAL feeling very excited or extremely relaxed because you have taken an illegal drug **2** OLD-FASHIONED very drunk

ˌstone ˈdead *adj.* used to emphasize that a person or animal is dead

ˌstone ˈdeaf *adj.* completely unable to hear

ˈstone-faced also **ˈstony-faced** *adj.* showing no emotion or friendliness

ˈstone-ground *adj.* stone-ground flour is made by crushing grain between two MILLSTONES

stone·ma·son /ˈstoʊnˌmeɪsən/ *n.* [C] someone whose job is cutting stone into pieces to be used in buildings → see also MASON

ston·er /ˈstoʊnɚ/ *n.* [C] SLANG someone who smokes MARIJUANA very often

stone·wall /ˈstoʊnwɔl/ *v.* [I] to delay a discussion, decision etc. by talking a lot and refusing to answer questions

stone·ware /ˈstoʊnwɛr/ *n.* [U] pots, bowls etc. that are made from a special hard clay

stone·washed /ˈstoʊnwɑʃt/ *adj.* stonewashed JEANS etc. have been made softer by a washing process in which they are beaten with stones

stone·work /ˈstoʊnwɚk/ *n.* [U] the parts of a building that are made of stone, especially when they are used for decoration

ston·y /ˈstoʊni/ *adj. comparative* **stonier**, *superlative* **stoniest** **1** covered by stones or containing stones: *the stony hillside* **2** without friendliness or pity: *They drove home in stony silence.* → see also **stony-faced** at STONE-FACED (1) **3 fall on stony ground** if a request, suggestion, joke etc. falls on stony ground, it is ignored or people do not like it —**stonily** *adv.*

stood /stʊd/ *v.* the past tense and past participle of STAND

stooge /studʒ/ *n.* [C] **1** DISAPPROVING INFORMAL someone who is used by someone else to do something unpleasant, dishonest, or illegal **2** a performer in a COMEDY show who another performer makes jokes about and makes look stupid

stool /stul/ S3 *n.* [C] **1** a seat without any supporting part for your back or arms: *a bar stool* → see picture at CHAIR[1] **2** BIOLOGY a piece of solid waste from your body [**Origin:** Old English *stol*]

stool·pi·geon /ˈstul,pɪdʒən/ *n.* [C] INFORMAL someone, especially a criminal, who helps the police to catch another criminal, usually by giving them information SYN **informer**

stoop[1] /stup/ *v.* [I] **1** also **stoop down** to bend your body forward and down: *David stooped down to tie his shoes.* **2** DISAPPROVING to do something bad or morally wrong, which you do not normally do: *I didn't think even you could **stoop so low**!* | **+to** *She would never stoop to blackmail.* | **stoop to sb's/that/this level** *You don't have to stoop to his level to be successful.* **3** to stand with your back and shoulders bent forward

stoop[2] *n.* **1** [C] a raised area at the door of a house, usually big enough to sit on **2** [singular] if you have a stoop, your shoulders slope forward or seem too round

stooped /stupt/ *adj.* having a stoop: *a stooped old man*

stoop·ing /ˈstupɪŋ/ *adj.* stooping shoulders are bent forward or have become too round

stop[1] /stɑp/ S1 W1 *v.* **stopped, stopping**
1 NOT CONTINUE [I,T] to not continue to do something or happen anymore, or to make someone or something not continue to do something or happen: *Can we stop now? I'm tired.* | *By noon the rain had stopped.* | *The referee stopped the fight.* | *Apply pressure to stop the bleeding.* | **stop doing sth** *We couldn't stop laughing.* | *The phone stopped ringing.*

THESAURUS
have/take a break to stop doing something for a short time in order to rest: *Okay, everyone, take a ten-minute break.*
break to stop for a short time in order to rest or eat something: *We broke for lunch at one o'clock.*
pause to stop speaking or doing something for a short time before starting again: *He paused for a moment to consider the question.*

2 **stop that/it** SPOKEN said when you want someone to stop annoying, upsetting, or hurting you or someone else: *Stop it! You're hurting me.*
3 NOT MOVE FARTHER [I,T] to not walk, move, or travel any farther, or to make someone or something not walk, move etc. farther: *Stop! There's a car coming.* | *He stopped the car and got out.* | *Someone stopped me and asked for directions.* | **at/outside/behind etc.** *You didn't stop at that stop sign.* | **stop sb/sth at outside/behind etc.** *They were stopped at the border.* | *His new truck can **stop on a dime*** (=stop very quickly).
4 PAUSE [I] to pause in an activity, trip etc. in order to do something before continuing: *Let's stop a minute.* | **stop for sth** *This looks like a good place to stop for lunch.* | **+at** *I need to stop at the gas station first.* | *Does this bus stop at Pine Street?* | **stop to do sth** *They stopped to admire the view.* | **stop and do sth** *She had to stop and rest.* | **stop to think/consider** *When you stop to think about it, it doesn't make sense.*
5 PREVENT [T] to prevent someone from doing something or something from happening SYN **prevent**: *I'm leaving now, and you can't stop me.* | **stop sb/sth from doing sth** *How can we stop the virus from spreading?* | *They're trying to stop kids from smoking before they start.* | **stop yourself from doing sth** *He couldn't stop himself from worrying.* | ***There's nothing to stop** you **from** applying for the job yourself.*
6 END [I] to not go or stretch beyond a particular point SYN **end**: *The road stops at the farm.*
7 TURN OFF [I,T] if a machine or piece of equipment stops or someone stops it, it does not continue working: *How do you stop the tape recorder?* | *The clock stopped.*
8 **stop at nothing (to do sth)** to do anything, even if it is cruel, dishonest, or illegal, to get what you want: *Johnson **would stop at nothing** to win an election.*
9 **stop short of (doing) sth** to not do something that is extreme, although you almost do it: *He stopped short of calling him a liar.*
10 **stop a check** also **stop payment (on a check)** to tell your bank to not pay money for a check that you have written to someone
11 **stop the presses a)** to make a PRINTING PRESS stop working, especially because something very important has happened and you need to add it to the newspaper before it finishes printing **b)** to close a company that prints newspapers, magazines, or books **c)** SPOKEN HUMOROUS said before telling someone surprising news: *Stop the presses! Lewis is coming back.*
12 **stop (dead) in your tracks** also **stop short** to suddenly stop moving, especially because something has frightened or surprised you
[**Origin:** Old English *stoppian* **to block up**]

stop back *phr. v.* to go back to a place you have been to earlier: *Can you stop back later? I'm really busy right now.*

stop by *phr. v.* **stop by sth** to make a short visit to a place or person, especially while you are going somewhere else: *I'll stop by this evening.*

stop in *phr. v.* INFORMAL to make a short visit to a place or person, especially while you are going somewhere else: *I just stopped in to say hello.* | **+at** *I need to stop in at the office for a minute.*

stop off *phr. v.* to make a short visit to a place while you are going somewhere else: **+in/at etc.** *I'm going to stop off at the mall after work.*

stop over *phr. v.* to stop somewhere and stay a short time before continuing a long trip, especially when traveling by airplane: **+in** *The plane stops over in Dubai on the way to India.* → see also STOPOVER

stop sth ↔ **up** *phr. v.* **1** to block something such as a pipe so that water, smoke etc. cannot go through it **2** **be stopped up** if your nose or head is stopped up, it is full of thick liquid because you have a cold

stop[2] S2 W3 *n.* [C]
1 **put a stop to sth** to prevent something from continuing or happening: *She decided to put a stop to their relationship.*
2 DURING TRIP a time when you stop during a trip for a short time, or the place where you stop: *an overnight stop in London* | *Charleston was the first stop on the tour.* | *The ship **makes stops** in five ports.*
3 **come/roll/skid etc. to a stop** to stop moving: *The bus came to a stop outside the school.*
4 **come to a stop** to stop happening: *The music came to a stop.*
5 **bring sth to a stop a)** to stop something from moving **b)** to stop something from continuing: *His comment brought the discussion to a complete stop.*
6 BUS/TRAIN a place where a bus or train regularly stops for people to get on and off: *I'm getting off at the next stop.*
7 CHECK the action or fact of telling your bank not to pay money for a check that you have written to someone: *I'll have to **put a stop on** that check.*
8 MUSIC ENG. LANG. ARTS **a)** one of a set of handles that you push in or out in an ORGAN to control the amount of sound it produces **b)** a set of pipes on an ORGAN that produce sound
9 CONSONANT ENG. LANG. ARTS a CONSONANT sound, like /p/, /b/, or /k/, made by stopping the flow of air completely and then suddenly letting it out of your mouth → see also **pull out all the stops** at PULL OUT (6)

ˌstop-and-ˈgo *adj.* stop-and-go driving or traffic stops and starts frequently instead of flowing smoothly

stop·cock /ˈstɑpkɑk/ *n.* [C] a VALVE that can be opened or closed with a TAP (=object you turn) to control the flow of a liquid in a pipe

S

stop·gap /ˈstɑpgæp/ *n.* [C] something or someone that you use for a short time until you can replace it with something better —**stopgap** *adj.* [only before noun] *stopgap measures*

stop·light /ˈstɑplaɪt/ *n.* [C] also **stoplights** [plural] a set of colored lights used to control and direct traffic

stop·o·ver /ˈstɑpˌoʊvɚ/ *n.* [C] a short stay somewhere between parts of a trip, especially on a long airplane trip: *a two-day stopover in Hong Kong* → see also **stop over** at STOP[1]

stop·page /ˈstɑpɪdʒ/ *n.* **1** [C] a situation in which workers stop working for a short time as a protest: *a work stoppage* **2** [C,U] the act of stopping something from moving or happening: *a stoppage of payments* **3** [C] something that blocks a tube or container

stop·per /ˈstɑpɚ/ *n.* [C] a thing that fits tightly in the top part of a bottle to close it —**stopper** *v.* [T]

ˈstopping ˌdistance *n.* [C,U] the distance that a driver is supposed to leave between their car and the one in front in order to be able to stop safely

stop·watch /ˈstɑpwɑtʃ/ *n.* [C] a watch used for measuring the exact time it takes to do something, especially to finish a race

S

stor·age /ˈstɔrɪdʒ/ S3 *n.* [U] **1** the act of keeping or putting something in a special place while it is not being used: *The attic was used for storage.* | +**of** *the storage of radioactive material* | **storage space/capacity** (=the amount of space or room that can be used for storing things) **2 in storage** things in storage are being kept in a special place, usually for a charge, until you need to use them: *Most of my furniture's in storage.* **3** the act of keeping information on a computer, or the amount of memory available on a computer for this purpose **4** the price you pay for having goods or furniture stored

ˈstorage ˌroom *n.* [C] a room that is used to store things

store[1] /stɔr/ S1 W1 *n.* [C] **1** a place where goods are sold → see also SHOP: *a retail store* | **a shoe/clothing/grocery etc. store** (=one that sells one type of goods) | *I need to* **go to the store** (=go to a store that sells food) *for some milk.* → see also CONVENIENCE STORE, DEPARTMENT STORE, DRUGSTORE

THESAURUS

Stores that sell particular types of goods
bookstore/clothes store/record store etc. a store that sells one type of goods
grocery store a store that sells food and other things used in the home
supermarket a large store that sells many different kinds of food and things people need for the house
bakery a place or area within a grocery store where bread, cakes, cookies etc. are made or sold
delicatessen/deli a small store or an area within a grocery store that sells cheese, cooked meat, bread etc.
liquor store a small store where alcohol is sold
drugstore a store where you can buy medicines, beauty products etc.
hardware store a store that sells equipment and tools that you use in your home and yard
nursery/garden center a place where plants and trees are grown and sold
newsstand a place on a street where newspapers and magazines are sold
boutique a small store that sells fashionable clothes or decorations
Stores that sell different types of goods
convenience store a store where you can buy food, newspapers etc., that is often open 24 hours each day
department store a large store that sells many different products, such as clothes, kitchen equipment etc.
chain store one of a group of stores owned by the same company
superstore a very big store, especially one that has many different types of products, or one that has a lot of one type of product
Stores that sell goods more cheaply
outlet store a store that sells things for less than the usual price
warehouse store a store that sells things in large amounts at lower prices
People who use or work in stores
customer someone who buys the things sold in a store
sales assistant/clerk someone whose job is to help customers to buy things
cashier someone whose job is to receive and pay out money in a store

2 in store (for sb) if something unexpected such as a surprise or problem is in store, it is going to happen: *He had a surprise in store for her.* **3** a supply or large amount of something, especially that you keep to use later: +**of** *The book is a store of knowledge about Dickens.* | *the body's stores of fat* **4** a large building in which supplies or goods are kept → see also **set store by sth** at SET[1] (21), STOREHOUSE

store[2] W3 *v.* [T] **1** to keep something somewhere until you need it: *Here's a tip for storing wine.* | +**in/at** *All of my old books are stored in boxes in the attic.* ▸see THESAURUS box at **keep**[1] **2** to keep a substance or form of energy so that it is available for use later: +**in** *The body stores energy in the muscles.* **3** to keep facts or information in your brain or a computer: +**on** *How many files can you store on a CD-ROM?* [**Origin:** 1200–1300 Old French *estorer* **to build, supply, store**, from Latin *instaurare* **to make new, restore**]

store sth ↔ **away** *phr. v.* to put something away and keep it until you need it

store sth ↔ **up** *phr. v.* **1** to collect and keep a supply of something so that you can use it in the future SYN **stockpile**: *The group was storing up ammunition.* **2** to remember things so that you can use them or tell someone about them later: *Writers store up experiences to use in their novels.* **3** to deliberately not allow yourself to show your strong feelings but to keep thinking about them, especially for a long time: *She had stored up a lot of resentment over the years.*

ˈstore brand *n.* [C] a type of goods that is produced for a particular store and has the store's name on them → see also NAME BRAND

ˈstore deˌtective *n.* [C] someone who is employed in a large store to watch the customers and to stop them from stealing

store·front /ˈstɔrfrʌnt/ *n.* [C] **1** the part of a store that faces the street **2 a storefront office/church/school etc.** a small office, church etc. in a shopping area

store·house /ˈstɔrhaʊs/ *n.* [C] **1 a storehouse of information/memories etc.** something that contains a lot of information etc. **2** OLD-FASHIONED a building where things are stored SYN **warehouse**

store·keep·er /ˈstɔrˌkipɚ/ *n.* [C] someone who owns or manages a store

store·room /ˈstɔr-rum/ *n.* [C] a room where goods are stored

storied /ˈstɔrid/ *adj.* [only before noun] LITERARY being the subject of many stories SYN **famous**

-storied /stɔrid/ *suffix* [in adjectives] **two-storied/five-storied etc.** having two, five etc. floors: *a six-storied building*

stork /stɔrk/ *n.* [C] BIOLOGY a tall white bird with long legs and a long beak

storm[1] /stɔrm/ S3 W3 *n.* **1** [C] EARTH SCIENCE a period of very bad weather when there are strong winds, a lot of rain, snow, and dust, and sometimes LIGHTNING: *The tree blew down in the storm.* | **a violent/severe storm** *Expect severe storms overnight.* | **a storm hits/strikes** *A terrible storm hit the island.* ▸see THESAURUS box at **rain**[1], **wind**[1] **2** [C usually singular] a situation in which people suddenly express very strong feelings about

something that someone has said or done: **a storm of protest/controversy/criticism etc.** *The proposal provoked a storm of criticism.* | **stir/whip/blow up a storm** *His latest comments have whipped up a storm.* | *He was unaware of the ethical **storm brewing** around him.*
3 take sth by storm a) to be very successful in a particular place: *She took the literary world by storm.* **b)** to succeed in getting possession of a place by attacking it using large numbers of soldiers
4 dance/sing/cook etc. up a storm INFORMAL to do something with all your energy [**Origin:** Old English]

storm² *v.* **1** [T] to suddenly attack and enter a place using a lot of force: *An angry crowd stormed the embassy.* **2** [I always + adv./prep.] to go somewhere in a noisy fast way that shows you are extremely angry: +**out of/into/off etc.** *Sally stormed into his office for an explanation.* **3** [I,T] LITERARY to shout something because you feel extremely angry **4** [I always + adv./prep.] to be successful very quickly: *The team stormed into the lead.*

storm ˌcellar *n.* [C] a place under a house or under the ground where you can go to be safe during violent storms

storm cloud *n.* [C] **1** EARTH SCIENCE a dark cloud that you see before a storm **2** [usually plural] a sign that something very bad is going to happen: ***Storm clouds are gathering** over the trade negotiations.*

storm door *n.* [C] a second door that is fitted outside a door to a house to give protection against rain, snow, wind etc.

storm surge *n.* [C] a sudden rise in the level of the sea caused by a tropical storm, which results in large amounts of water flooding the land

storm·troop·er /ˈstɔrmˌtrupɚ/ *n.* [C] a member of a special group of German soldiers in World War II who were trained to be very violent

storm ˌwindow *n.* [C] a special window that gives protection against rain, snow, wind etc.

storm·y /ˈstɔrmi/ *adj. comparative* **stormier**, *superlative* **stormiest** **1** stormy weather, a stormy sky etc. is full of strong winds, heavy rain or snow, and dark clouds: *a stormy winter night* **2** a stormy relationship, meeting etc. is full of strong and often angry feelings: *a stormy meeting* | *Their relationship has often been stormy.*

sto·ry /ˈstɔri/ S1 W1 *n. plural* **stories** [C]
1 TRUE/IMAGINARY EVENTS a description of imaginary or true events, especially one that is said or written in order to entertain people: *The movie is based on a true story.* | *Don't be frightened, Connie – it's only a story* (=it is imaginary). | +**about/of** *a story about friendship and courage* | *the story of "Snow White"* | **tell/read sb a story** *Mommy, will you read me a story?* | **the full/whole story** *I don't think she's telling us the whole story.* | **a ghost/love/detective etc. story** (=a story about ghosts, love etc.) | ***Bedtime stories** are an important part of our evening ritual.*

THESAURUS

tale a story about things that happened long ago, or things that may not have really happened: *tales of adventure* | *fairy tales*
myth a very old story about gods, magical creatures etc.: *the Greek myths about Zeus*
legend an old story about brave people or magical events: *the legend of Robin Hood*
fable a traditional story that teaches a moral lesson: *the fable of the race between the tortoise and the hare*
yarn a long story that is not completely true: *We listened to Grandpa's yarns about the early days on the farm.*

2 NEWS a report in a newspaper or news broadcast about a recent event: *a front-page story* | *What makes a good story?* | *The paper **ran a** three-page **story*** (=published it) *on the flood.* | **a/the cover story** (=the main story in a magazine that is about the picture on the cover) | *The **story** of their affair first **broke** in July.* → see also **success story** at SUCCESS (4) ►see THESAURUS box at **newspaper**
3 HISTORY a description of the most important events in someone's life or in the development of something: *the Tina Turner story* | *the story of Western culture* | +**behind** *What's the story behind the painting?* → see also LIFE STORY
4 BUILDING a floor or level of a building: *an apartment on the fifth story* → -STORIED
5 MOVIE/PLAY ETC. what happens in a movie, play, or book SYN **plot**
6 EXCUSE an excuse or explanation, especially one that you have invented: *She **gave me some story** about having to work late.* | *Jim kept **changing** his **story**.*
7 sb's side of the story the way that a particular person describes what happened: *I still haven't heard Linda's side of the story.*
8 WHAT PEOPLE SAY information that people tell each other, but that may not be true SYN **rumor**: *There are a lot of wild stories going around.* | *Polly's mother's mother, **so the story goes*** (=people are saying this), *ran away when she was 15.* ►see THESAURUS box at **account¹**

SPOKEN PHRASES

9 it's the same old story used to say that the present bad situation has often happened before: *It's the same old story – too much work and not enough time.*
10 that's the story of my life used after a disappointing experience to mean that similar disappointing things always seem to happen to you
11 but that's another story used when you have mentioned something that you are not going to talk about on this occasion
12 be a different story to be very different in some way or be in a different situation: *It looks like a nice house, but inside it's a different story.*
13 that's not the whole story used to say that there are more details that people need to know in order to understand the situation
14 it's the same story here/there etc. used to say the same thing is happening in another place: *Unemployment is rising here, and it's the same story across the country.*
15 end of story used to mean that there is nothing more to say about a particular subject: *I'm not going to lend you any more money, end of story.*
16 A LIE a word meaning a "lie," used by or to children: *Have you been telling stories again?*

[**Origin:** 1200–1300 Old French *estorie*, from Latin *historia*] → see also **cock and bull story** at COCK¹ (2), **hard luck story** at HARD¹ (20), **it's a long story** at LONG¹ (12), **(to make a) long story short** at LONG¹ (11), SHORT STORY, SOB STORY

-story /stɔri/ *suffix* [in adjectives] **two-story/three-story etc.** used to say how many floors a building has: *a 12-story hotel*

sto·ry·book¹ /ˈstɔriˌbʊk/ *n.* [C] a book of stories for children

storybook² *adj.* **a storybook ending/marriage/romance etc.** an ending, marriage, romance etc. that is so happy or perfect that it is like one in a children's story

ˈstory line *n.* [C] the main set of related events in a book, play, movie, TV show etc. SYN **plot**

sto·ry·tell·er /ˈstɔriˌtɛlɚ/ *n.* [C] someone who tells stories, especially to children

stoup /stup/ *n.* [C] **1** a container for holy water near the entrance to a church **2** a glass or MUG used for drinking in past times

stout¹ /staʊt/ *adj.* **1** fairly fat and heavy or having a thick body: *a short stout woman* ►see THESAURUS box at **fat¹** **2** LITERARY strong and thick: *a stout wooden beam* **3** strong and determined: *a stout defense in court* —**stoutness** *n.* [U] —**stoutly** *adv.*

stout² *n.* [U] a strong dark beer

stout·heart·ed /ˈstaʊtˌhɑrt̬ɪd/ *adj.* LITERARY brave and determined

stove¹ /stoʊv/ S2 *n.* [C] **1** a piece of kitchen equipment on which you cook food in pots and pans, and that contains an OVEN **2** a thing used for heating a room or for cooking, which works by burning wood, coal, oil, or gas: *a wood-burning stove* [**Origin:** 1400–1500 Middle Dutch, Middle Low German, **heated room**, from Vulgar Latin *extufa*, from Greek *typhein* **to smoke**]

stove² *v.* a past tense and past participle of STAVE

stove·pipe hat /ˌstoʊvpaɪp 'hæt/ *n.* [C] a tall black silk hat worn by men in the past

'stove top *n.* [C] the top of a stove where the BURNERS (=the parts where the heat comes from) are

'stove-top *adj.* [only before noun] **1** made to be used on top of a STOVE: *a stove-top grill* **2** able to be cooked using only the stove top

stow /stoʊ/ *v.* [T always + adv./prep.] to put or pack something neatly away in a space until you need it again: *I stowed my bag under my seat.*

stow away *phr. v.* to hide on a ship or airplane in order to travel secretly or without paying → see also STOWAWAY

stow·age /'stoʊɪdʒ/ *n.* [C] space available on a boat for storing things

stow·a·way /'stoʊəˌweɪ/ *n.* [C] someone who hides on a ship or airplane in order to avoid paying or to travel secretly

S

Stowe /stoʊ/, **Har·ri·et Bee·cher** /'hæriɪt 'bitʃɚ/ (1811–1896) a U.S. writer famous for her NOVEL "Uncle Tom's Cabin," which influenced many people to oppose SLAVERY

St. Pat·rick's Day /seɪnt 'pætrɪks ˌdeɪ/ *n.* [C,U] SAINT PATRICK'S DAY

St. Paul /seɪnt 'pɔl/ the capital city of the U.S. state of Minnesota

St. Pe·ters·burg /seɪnt 'piṭɚzˌbɚg/ a city in Russia, on the Baltic Sea, that was the capital of Russia from 1712 to 1918. It was called Leningrad from 1924 until 1991.

strad·dle /'strædl/ *v.* [T] **1** to sit or stand with your legs on either side of someone or something: *He straddled his bike.* **2** if something straddles a line, road, or river, part of it is on one side and part on the other side: *The forest straddles the border.* **3** to include different areas of activity

strafe /streɪf/ *v.* [T] to attack a place by flying an airplane low over the ground and firing many bullets

strag·gle /'strægəl/ *v.* [I usually + adv./prep.] **1** if members of a group straggle somewhere, they move at different speeds, so that there are large spaces between them: +**in/into/toward etc.** *Students were beginning to straggle in from lunch.* **2** to move, grow, or spread out in a messy way in different directions

strag·gler /'stræglɚ/ *n.* [C] someone who is behind the others in a group, especially because they walk more slowly

strag·gly /'strægli/ *adj.* *comparative* **stragglier**, *superlative* **straggliest** growing in a messy way and spreading out in different directions: *straggly hair*

straight¹ /streɪt/ S1 W2 *adv.*

1 IN A LINE in a line or direction that is not curved or bent: *Terry was so tired he couldn't walk straight.* | +**ahead/at/down etc.** *She walked straight past me.* | *He combs his hair straight back.* | *He **looked** me **straight in the eye** and lied!*

2 IMMEDIATELY [+ adj./adv.] immediately or without delay: +**to/down/back etc.** *Let's get straight down to business.* | *You should have gone straight to the police.* | *Be sure to come **straight home**.*

3 ONE AFTER THE OTHER happening one after the other in a series, especially an unusually long series: *It's rained for eight days straight.*

4 LEVEL/UPRIGHT in an upright or level position or in a position that is correct in relation to something else: *I can't get the picture to hang straight.* | **sit/stand up straight** *Sit up straight and pay attention.*

5 SEE/THINK if you cannot think or see straight, you cannot think or see clearly

6 tell/ask sb straight (out) SPOKEN to tell someone something clearly without trying to hide your meaning: *I asked her straight out if she was lying.*

7 come straight out and say/admit/tell etc. sth also **come straight out with sth** SPOKEN to tell someone something without waiting

8 say sth straight to sb's face also **tell sb sth straight to their face** SPOKEN to say something to someone in a very clear and direct way, especially something that will offend or upset them: *I told him straight to his face what I thought of him.*

9 straight out of sth very much like something in a particular kind of movie, book etc.: *a main street straight out of a 1950s movie*

10 NOT FUNNY performed in a serious way rather than a funny way

11 go straight INFORMAL to stop being a criminal and live an honest life

12 straight up SLANG used to emphasize that what you are saying is true

13 straight up? SLANG used to ask someone if they are telling the truth → see also, **(straight/right) from the horse's mouth** at HORSE¹ (2)

straight² S3 *adj.*

1 NOT BENDING/CURVING something that is straight goes in one direction and does not bend or curve: *a straight road* | *Keep your legs straight.* | *She has **straight** black **hair*** (=hair without curls). | *Light always travels **in a straight line**.* ►see THESAURUS box at **hair**

2 LEVEL/UPRIGHT level or upright, or in the correct position in relation to something else: *Is my tie straight?*

3 ONE AFTER ANOTHER immediately one after another in a series, especially in an unusually long series: *an amazing record of 43 straight wins* | *She won the game **in straight sets**.*

4 TRUTHFUL honest and truthful: *Just give me a straight yes or no.* | +**with** *Are you going to be straight with me or not?* | *Jack never gives me **a straight answer**.* | *Voters need more **straight talk**.*

5 a straight face a serious expression on someone's face that does not show that they are joking or saying something untrue: *How can you say that **with a straight face?*** | *I couldn't **keep a straight face**.* → see also STRAIGHTFACED

6 get straight A's/B's etc. to earn the grade "A," "B" etc. in all of your school subjects

7 ALCOHOLIC DRINKS a straight alcoholic drink has no water or any other drink added

8 SEX attracted to people of the opposite sex → see also GAY SYN **heterosexual** → LESBIAN

9 NOT FUNNY not involving or involved in COMEDY: *a straight role* → see also STRAIGHT MAN

10 ONLY ONE TYPE completely one particular type of something: *It's not a straight historical novel.*

11 BORING OLD-FASHIONED DISAPPROVING behaving in a way that is accepted as normal by many people but which you think is boring

12 CHOICE/EXCHANGE a straight choice, exchange etc. involves only two possible choices, exchanges etc.

SPOKEN PHRASES

13 get sth straight to understand the facts about a situation and be able to tell them correctly: *I wanted to get the facts straight.* | ***Let me get this straight** – you just want lettuce for dinner.*

14 set sb straight (on sth) to make someone understand the facts about a situation

15 set things straight to do something or say something to solve a problem or fix a mistake

16 DRUGS SLANG not using illegal drugs

17 NOT OWING SB MONEY [not before noun] OLD-FASHIONED not owing money to someone or being owed money by someone anymore SYN **even**

[**Origin:** 1300–1400 from an old past participle of *stretch*] → see also **set/put/keep the record straight** at RECORD¹ (9)

straight³ S2 *n.* [C] **1** [usually plural] someone who is sexually attracted to people of the opposite sex → see also GAY, LESBIAN SYN heterosexual **2 the straight and narrow** an honest and moral way of living: *The program **keeps** the kids **on the straight and narrow**.* **3** if you have a straight in a card game, you have been given several cards whose numbers are CONSECUTIVE, for example 2, 3, 4, 5, 6 **4 the straight** the straight part of a RACETRACK SYN straightaway

ˌstraight ˌangle *n.* [C] MATH an angle that measures exactly 180°

ˈstraight-arm *v.* [T] to STIFF-ARM someone —**straight-arm** *n.* [C]

ˌstraight ˈarrow *n.* [C] INFORMAL someone who never does anything illegal or unusual and exciting

straight·a·way¹ /ˈstreɪt̬əˌweɪ/ *n.* [singular] the straight part of a RACETRACK

straight·a·way² /ˌstreɪt̬əˈweɪ/ *adv.* at once SYN immediately

straight·edge /ˈstreɪt̬ɛdʒ/ *n.* [C] a long flat piece of wood, plastic, or metal used for drawing straight lines or checking to see if something is straight

straight·en /ˈstreɪtˀn/ S3 *v.* **1** [I,T] to make something straight so that it does not bend or curve, or to become straight SYN straighten out: *Try straightening your arm.* | *After a few miles the river straightens.* **2** [T] to move something so that it is upright, level, or in the correct position in relation to something else: *He paused to straighten his tie.* **3** [I,T] to make your back straight, or to stand up straight after bending down SYN straighten up: *Alan straightened in his chair.* **4** [T] to make something neat and clean SYN straighten up: *Mom told me to straighten my room.*

straighten out *phr. v.* **1 straighten sth ↔ out** to deal with the things that are causing problems or confusion in a situation: *There are a few things that we need to straighten out between us.* **2 straighten sb ↔ out** to deal with someone's bad behavior or personal problems: *Five years in the Navy helped straighten him out.* **3 straighten sth ↔ out** to make something straight so that it does not bend or curve, or to become straight: *She slowly straightened out her legs.*

straighten up *phr. v.* **1** to begin to behave well after behaving badly: *You'd better straighten up, young lady!* **2 straighten sth ↔ up** to make something neat and clean: *I straightened up the house.* **3** to make your back straight, or to stand up straight after bending down

straight·faced /ˌstreɪtˈfeɪst◂/ *adj.* serious and not showing by the expression on your face that you are really joking or saying something that is not true → see also **a straight face** at STRAIGHT² (5)

straight·for·ward /ˌstreɪtˈfɔrwəd◂/ Ac *adj.* **1** simple and easy to understand OPP complicated: *The directions are fairly straightforward.* ►see THESAURUS box at simple **2** honest about your feelings or opinions and not hiding anything: *Wes is a straightforward person.* ►see THESAURUS box at honest —**straightforwardly** *adv.* —**straightforwardness** *n.* [U]

straight·jack·et /ˈstreɪtˌdʒækɪt/ *n.* [C] another spelling of STRAITJACKET

straight-ˈlaced *adj.* another spelling of STRAIT-LACED

ˈstraight man *n.* [C] a male entertainer who works with a COMEDIAN, providing him or her with opportunities to make jokes

ˈstraight ˌrazor *n.* [C] a cutting tool with a straight blade that a man uses to SHAVE, used especially in the past

ˈstraight ˌshooter *n.* [C] INFORMAL an honest person who you can trust

straight ˈticket *n.* [C] POLITICS in an election in the U.S., a vote in which someone chooses the CANDIDATES of only one particular political party: *This time I voted a straight ticket.*

strain¹ /streɪn/ *n.*

1 WORRY [C,U] worry caused by having to deal with a problem or having to work too hard over a long period of time SYN stress: +**of** *the strain of raising eight kids* | *At the time, we were both **under a lot of strain**.* | *The long working hours **put a severe strain on** employees.*

2 DIFFICULTY [C] a problem or difficulty that is caused when a system, organization etc. is used too much or has too much to deal with: +**on** *the strain on water resources* | *His loan payments were **putting a strain on** his finances.* | **break/crack/collapse etc. under the strain** *The legal system almost cracked under the strain.*

3 IN A RELATIONSHIP [C,U] problems and bad feelings that develop in a relationship between two people or groups SYN tension: *The strain in their friendship was beginning to show.*

4 FORCE [U] PHYSICS a force that pulls, stretches, or pushes something SYN stress: +**on** *The strain on the cables supporting the bridge is enormous.* | **break/snap/collapse etc. under the strain** *The beams collapsed under the strain.*

5 INJURY [C,U] an injury to a muscle or part of your body caused by using it too much: *eye strain* | *a knee strain*

6 PLANT/DISEASE/ANIMAL [C] BIOLOGY a breed or type of plant, disease, or animal: +**of** *a deadly strain of influenza*

7 the strains of sth LITERARY the sound of music being played: +**of** *the strains of a Beethoven sonata*

8 QUALITY [singular] a particular quality that people have: +**of** *a strong strain of nationalism in the country*

[**Origin:** (1–5) 1300–1400 Old French *estraindre*, from Latin *stringere*]

strain² *v.*

1 PART OF BODY [T] to injure a muscle or part of your body by making it work too hard → see also SPRAIN: *You'll strain your eyes trying to read in this light.* ►see THESAURUS box at hurt¹

2 EFFORT [I,T] to try very hard to do something, using all your physical or mental strength: **strain to do sth** *I strained to remember where I had met him before.* | **strain your ears/eyes** (=try very hard to hear or see) | *Don't **strain yourself** (=try too hard) – we can finish the report tomorrow.*

3 LIQUID [T] to separate solid things from a liquid by pouring the mixture through something with very small holes in it: *Strain the sauce through a sieve.* → see picture on page A32

4 BEYOND A LIMIT [T] to cause problems by forcing a system, organization etc. to be used too much or deal with more than is normal or acceptable: *Repairs to the roof have severely strained the school's budget.*

5 RELATIONSHIPS [T] to cause problems between people, countries etc.: *The bombing has **strained relations** between the two communities.* | **strain sb's friendship/relationship/marriage etc.** *The loan ended up straining their friendship.*

6 PULL/PUSH [I] to pull hard at something or push hard against something: +**against** *Spectators strained against the barriers to get a closer look.* | +**at** *The dog barked, straining at his chain.*

7 be straining at the leash INFORMAL to be eager to be allowed to do what you want

strained /streɪnd/ *adj.* **1** a strained situation makes people feel nervous and uncomfortable, and unable to behave naturally SYN tense: *Relations between the two countries are still strained.* **2** showing the effects of worry or too much work: *a strained expression* **3** a strained muscle or other part of your body has been injured because you have made it work too hard **4** strained fruit and vegetables have been put through something with very small holes to make it easy for babies to eat

strain·er /ˈstreɪnɚ/ *n.* [C] a kitchen tool for separating solids from liquids: *a tea strainer*

strait /streɪt/ *n.* [C] also **straits** [plural] EARTH SCIENCE a narrow passage of water between two areas of land, usually connecting two large areas of water, for example two oceans: *the Strait of Magellan* → see also **be in dire straits** at DIRE (1)

strait·ened /ˈstreɪtˀnd/ *adj.* FORMAL **straitened circumstances** a situation that is difficult because of a lack of money

S

strait·jack·et, **straightjacket** /ˈstreɪtˌdʒækɪt/ *n.* [C] **1** a special piece of clothing that is used to control the movements of someone who is mentally ill and violent **2** something such as a law or set of ideas that puts very strict or unfair limits on someone: *the straitjacket of tradition*

ˌstrait-ˈlaced, **straight-laced** *adj.* having strict old-fashioned ideas about moral behavior

Strait of Ma·gel·lan, the /ˌstreɪt̬ əv məˈdʒɛlən/ a narrow area of sea between Tierra del Fuego and the mainland of South America that connects the Atlantic Ocean with the Pacific Ocean

strand¹ /strænd/ *n.* [C] **1** a single thin piece of thread, wire, hair etc.: +**of** *a strand of silk* **2 a strand of pearls/beads** a single row of PEARLS or BEADS on a string, worn as jewelry **3** one of the parts of a story, problem etc.: *Plato draws all the strands of the argument together at the end.* **4** LITERARY a beach

strand² *v.* [T usually passive] to put someone in a place or situation from which they need help to leave

strand·ed /ˈstrændɪd/ *adj.* a stranded person, animal, or vehicle has been left in a situation from which they need help to leave: *stranded motorists* | +**in/on/at etc.** *We were now stranded in the desert, without water.* | *Icy weather* ***left*** *thousands of airline passengers* ***stranded***.

S

strange¹ /streɪndʒ/ S1 W2 *adj.* **1** unusual or surprising, especially in a way that is difficult to explain or understand SYN **weird** SYN **odd**: *a strange noise* | *Gabby is a strange girl.* | ***That's strange.*** *Ben was just here.* | **it is strange that** *It's strange that Linda hasn't even called.* | **it is/feels strange to do sth** *It was strange to see someone else wearing my clothes.* | ***There's something really strange about*** *their relationship.* | ***For some strange reason*** *she's decided she doesn't want to go.* | ***Strange as it may seem***, *I actually prefer the cold weather.*

THESAURUS

funny a little strange or unusual: *I heard a funny noise downstairs.*
peculiar strange, unfamiliar, or a little surprising: *a peculiar taste*
mysterious strange in a way that is hard to explain or understand: *At that time, the sudden epidemics of polio were mysterious and frightening.*
odd strange, especially in a way that you disapprove of or cannot understand: *It seemed like an odd thing to say.*
weird strange and different from what you are used to: *a weird experience* | *weird clothes*
bizarre very unusual and strange in a way that is hard to explain or understand: *Her bizarre behavior was caused by a mental illness.*
eccentric an eccentric person is strange and different in a way that people think is slightly amusing: *an eccentric old man*

2 a strange person or thing is not familiar because you have not seen or met them before: *Meryl was all alone in a strange city.* **3 truth/fact etc. is stranger than fiction** used to say that what happens in the real world is often more unusual than what happens in stories **4 feel strange** to have an unusual and slightly unpleasant feeling, physically or emotionally: *I was tired, and felt a little strange.* [**Origin:** 1200–1300 Old French *estrange* **foreign**, from Latin *extraneus*] —**strangeness** *n.* [U]

strange² *adv.* [only after verb] NONSTANDARD in a way that is different from what is normal: *They were all looking at me kind of strange.*

strange·ly /ˈstreɪndʒli/ *adv.* **1** in a way that is different from what is normal SYN **oddly**: *She began behaving strangely.* | *The whole city was strangely peaceful.* **2** [sentence adverb] used to say that something is unusual or surprising SYN **oddly**: *Strangely, I wasn't afraid anymore.* → see also **strangely/oddly/funnily enough** at ENOUGH¹ (3)

strang·er /ˈstreɪndʒɚ/ W3 *n.* [C] **1** someone you do not know: *Don't take candy from strangers.* | **a complete/perfect/total stranger** *I can't just go up and talk to a total stranger.* **2 be no stranger to sth** to have had a lot of a particular type of experience: *Derek is no stranger to controversy.* **3** someone in a new and unfamiliar place **4 Don't be a stranger!** SPOKEN said when someone is leaving to invite them back to visit you often **5 Hello, stranger!** SPOKEN, HUMOROUS said to greet someone you have not seen for a long time

stran·gle /ˈstræŋgəl/ *v.* [T] **1** to kill someone by pressing on their throat with your hands, a rope etc. → see also CHOKE: *Freitas was strangled with a nylon cord.* **2** to limit or prevent the growth or development of something: *The economy is being strangled by inefficiency.* [**Origin:** 1200–1300 Old French *estrangler*, from Latin *strangulare* **to strangle**] —**strangler** *n.* [C]

stran·gled /ˈstræŋgəld/ *adj.* **a strangled cry/sound/gasp etc.** a cry, sound, gasp etc. that is suddenly stopped before it is finished

stran·gle·hold /ˈstræŋgəlˌhoʊld/ *n.* [C] **1** [usually singular] complete control over a situation, organization etc.: +**on** *a four-decade stranglehold on power* **2** a strong hold around someone's neck that is meant to stop them from breathing

stran·gu·la·tion /ˌstræŋgyəˈleɪʃən/ *n.* [U] the act of killing someone by strangling them, or the fact of being killed in this way —**strangulate** /ˈstræŋgyəˌleɪt/ *v.* [T]

strap¹ /stræp/ *n.* [C] **1** a narrow band of strong material that is used to carry, fasten, or hang something: *The purse has a wide leather strap.* | *a bra strap* **2** a narrow piece of strong material, usually in a LOOP, that hangs from the ceiling of a bus or train for passengers to hold onto **3** a narrow piece of leather used for beating someone in the past → see also CHINSTRAP, SHOULDER STRAP

strap² *v.* **strapped**, **strapping** [T always + adv./prep.] to fasten someone or something in place with one or more straps: **strap sth into/on/down etc.** *Chuck strapped the suitcase to the roof of the car.*

strap sb ↔ **in** *phr. v.* to fasten a belt around someone in a car or other vehicle

strap·less /ˈstræplɪs/ *adj.* **a strapless dress/gown/top etc.** a dress or shirt that has no straps or other cloth over your shoulders

strapped /stræpt/ *adj.* **strapped (for cash)** INFORMAL having little or no money at the moment

strap·ping /ˈstræpɪŋ/ *adj.* [only before noun, no comparative] a strapping young man or woman is strong, tall, and looks healthy and active

Stras·berg /ˈstræsbɚg/**, Lee** /li/ (1901–1982) a U.S. teacher of acting and theater DIRECTOR, famous for using and developing the ideas of method acting

stra·ta /ˈstræt̬ə, ˈstreɪt̬ə/ *n.* EARTH SCIENCE the plural of STRATUM

strat·a·gem /ˈstræt̬ədʒəm/ *n.* [C] FORMAL a trick or plan to deceive an enemy or gain an advantage

stra·te·gic /strəˈtidʒɪk/ also **stra·te·gi·cal** /strəˈtidʒɪkəl/ Ac W3 *adj.* **1** done or useful as part of a plan to achieve or win something, especially in a military, business, or political situation: *strategic planning* | *a strategic alliance* | *a strategic location* | *strategic decisions* **2 strategic arms/weapons/bombing etc.** weapons or attacks designed to reach an enemy area from your own and destroy the enemy's ability to fight → see also TACTICAL **3** TECHNICAL used in fighting wars: *strategic materials such as iron or steel* —**strategically** /-kli/ *adv.*

Straˌtegic Deˈfense Iˌnitiative ABBREVIATION **SDI** *n.* [C] a military plan for destroying an enemy's MISSILES before they could reach the U.S., using LASERS attached to SATELLITES in space. The plan was put forward by President Reagan in the 1980s and strongly supported by him during his time as President. Many scientists believed that the plan was impossible to achieve, and people commonly called it Star Wars.

stra,tegic 'value *n.* [U] the importance or usefulness of things or places for providing a country or an army with a military advantage: *The fort has little strategic value but it symbolizes the authority of the government.*

strat·e·gist /'strætədʒɪst/ Ac *n.* [C] someone who is good at planning, especially military movements: *military strategists*

strat·e·gy /'strætədʒi/ Ac S2 W1 *n. plural* **strategies** **1** [C] a well-planned action or series of actions for achieving an aim, especially in a military, business, or political situation: *learning strategies* | *military strategies* | **a strategy for doing sth** *We need a new strategy for dealing with drug abuse.* | **a strategy to do sth** *What's the current strategy to attract younger viewers?* | **a marketing/a business/an economic strategy** *the government's long-term economic strategy* ▶see THESAURUS box at **plan**[1] **2** [U] the skill of planning military movements **3** [U] skillful planning in general: *The company needs to focus on strategy.* [**Origin:** 1800–1900 Greek *strategia* **art of leading an army**, from *strategos*]

strat·i·fi·ca·tion /,strætəfə'keɪʃən/ *n.* [C,U] **1** the way that a society develops into different social classes **2** the way that different layers of earth, rock etc. develop over time **3** the position that different layers of something have in relation to each other —**stratify** /'strætə,faɪ/ *v.* [I,T]

strat·i·fied /'strætə,faɪd/ *adj.* **1** having different social classes: *a highly stratified society* **2** EARTH SCIENCE having several layers of earth, rock etc.: *stratified rock*

strat·o·sphere /'strætə,sfɪr/ *n.* **1 the stratosphere** the part of the air surrounding the Earth above the TROPOSPHERE, starting at about six miles above the Earth **2** a very high position, level, or amount: *Oil prices soared* ***into the stratosphere.***

stra·tum /'strætəm, 'streɪ-/ *n. plural* **strata** /'strætə, 'streɪtə/ [C] **1** EARTH SCIENCE a layer of rock of a particular kind, especially one with different layers above and below it **2** a social class in a society **3** a layer of earth, such as one where tools, bones etc. from an ancient CIVILIZATION are found by digging

Strauss /straʊs/, **Jo·hann** /'yoʊhɑn/ **1 Johann Strauss the Elder** (1804–1849) an Austrian musician who wrote CLASSICAL music **2 Johann Strauss the Younger** (1825–1899) an Austrian musician who wrote more than 400 WALTZES

Strauss, Le·vi /'livaɪ/ (1829–1902) a U.S. clothing MANUFACTURER who was the first person to make JEANS and started the clothing company Levi Strauss

Strauss, Rich·ard /'rɪkɑrt/ (1864–1949) a German musician who wrote CLASSICAL music

Stra·vin·sky /strə'vɪnski/, **I·gor** /'igɔr/ (1882–1971) a Russian musician who wrote modern CLASSICAL music

straw[1] /strɔ/ *n.* **1 a)** [U] the dried stems of wheat or similar plants that are used for animals to sleep on, and for making things such as baskets, MATS etc. → see also HAY: *a bale of straw* **b)** [C] a single dried stem of wheat or a similar plant **2** [C] a thin tube of paper or plastic for sucking a drink from a bottle or cup **3 the last straw** also **the straw that breaks the camel's back** the last problem in a series of problems that finally makes you give up, get angry etc.: *Having to work late on a Friday was the last straw!* **4 be grasping/clutching at straws** to be trying everything you can to succeed, even though the things you are trying are not likely to help or work [**Origin:** Old English *streaw*] → see also **you can't make bricks without straw** at BRICK[1] (3), **draw straws** at DRAW[1] (24), **draw the short straw** at DRAW[1] (25)

straw[2] *adj.* [only before noun] **1** made of straw: *a straw hat* **2 a straw man** a weak opponent or imaginary argument that can easily be defeated

straw·ber·ry /'strɔ,bɛri/ S3 *n. plural* **strawberries** [C] BIOLOGY a soft red juicy fruit with small pale seeds on its surface, or the plant that grows this fruit [**Origin:** Old English *streawberige*, from *streaw* + *berige* **berry**]

'strawberry blond *adj.* strawberry blond hair is light reddish yellow —**strawberry blond** *n.* [C]

'straw-,colored *adj.* light yellow

,straw 'poll also **,straw 'vote** *n.* [C] POLITICS an unofficial test of people's opinions before an election, to see what the result is likely to be

stray[1] /streɪ/ *v.* **strays, strayed, straying** [I] **1** to move away from the place where you should be, without intending to: **+into/onto/from** *Three of the soldiers strayed into enemy territory.* **2** to begin to deal with or talk about a different subject than the main one, without intending to: *For an instant his tired mind strayed.* | **+into/onto/from** *Let's not stray too far from the topic.* **3** if your eyes stray, you begin to look at something else, usually without intending to **4** if your hands or fingers stray somewhere, you touch something you should not, or touch something without really intending to **5** to start doing something that is wrong or immoral, when usually you do not behave in this way **6 stray from the fold/path etc.** to do or believe something differently from other people in a group you belong to

stray[2] *adj.* [only before noun] **1** a stray animal, such as a dog or cat, is lost or has no home **2** accidentally separated from other things of the same kind: *He was killed by a stray bullet.*

stray[3] *n.* [C] **1** an animal that is lost or has no home **2** INFORMAL someone or something that has become separated from others of the same kind

streak[1] /strik/ *n.* [C]
1 COLORED LINE a colored or dirty line, especially one that has an irregular shape or has been made accidentally: *Her mascara ran in streaks down her face.* ▶see THESAURUS box at **line**[1]
2 CHARACTER a part of someone's character that is different from the rest of their character: *She has a stubborn streak.* | **+of** *a streak of independence*
3 PERIOD a period of time during which you continue to be successful or to fail: *a streak of bad luck* | **be on a winning/losing streak** (=have a period of time when you continue to win or lose)
4 HAIR a line of lighter color in your hair SYN **highlight**: *gray streaks*
5 a streak of lightning/fire/light etc. a long straight burst of LIGHTNING, fire etc.

streak[2] *v.* **1** [T usually passive] to cover something with streaks: *The evening sky was streaked red and orange.* | **be streaked with sth** *Her face was streaked with sweat.* **2** [I always + adv./prep.] to run or fly somewhere so fast you can hardly be seen: **+across/along/down etc.** *Two jets streaked across the sky.* **3** [I] to run across a public place with no clothes on to shock people **4** [T] to have someone put lines of lighter color in your hair, or to put these lines in someone else's hair

streak·er /'strikɚ/ *n.* [C] someone who runs across a public place with no clothes on to shock people

streak·y /'striki/ *adj.* **1** marked with streaks, or in the form of streaks **2** a streaky sports player or team plays very well for a period of time, and then plays badly for a period of time

stream[1] /strim/ W3 *n.* [C] **1** EARTH SCIENCE a natural flow of water that moves across the land and is narrower than a river: *a mountain stream* → see also DOWNSTREAM, UPSTREAM **2 a stream of sth** a long and almost continuous series of events, people, objects etc.: *a stream of insults* | **a steady/a constant/an endless etc. stream of sth** *A steady stream of visitors came to the house.* **3** a flow of water, air, smoke etc., or the direction in which it is flowing: *A stream of air swirled the dust into clouds.* → see also GULF STREAM, JET STREAM **4** TECHNICAL a sound or VIDEO that you play on your computer directly from the Internet, without saving it onto your computer [**Origin:** Old English] → see also BLOODSTREAM, MAINSTREAM[1], ON-STREAM, STREAM OF CONSCIOUSNESS

stream[2] *v.*
1 FLOW [I always + adv./prep.] to flow quickly and in great

S

amounts: +**out/in/onto etc.** *Tears streamed down her cheeks.*
2 MOVE CONTINUOUSLY [I always + adv./prep.] to move in a continuous flow in the same direction: +**out/across/past etc.** *People streamed past us.*
3 LIGHT [I always + adv./prep.] if light streams somewhere, it shines through an opening into a place or onto a surface: +**in/through/from etc.** *Sunlight was streaming through the open windows.*
4 PRODUCE LIQUID [I] to produce a continuous flow of liquid: +**with** *His eyes were streaming with tears.*
5 FLOAT [I always + adv./prep., usually in progressive] to move freely in a current of wind or water: +**in/out/behind etc.** *Elise ran, her hair streaming out behind her.*
6 FROM INTERNET [I,T] COMPUTERS if you stream sound or VIDEO or if it streams, you play it on your computer directly from the Internet, rather than saving it onto your computer

stream·er /ˈstrimɚ/ *n.* [C] **1** a long narrow piece of colored paper, used for decoration on special occasions **2** a long narrow flag

stream·ing /ˈstrimɪŋ/ *adj.* TECHNICAL streaming AUDIO, VIDEO etc. are sounds or moving images that you play directly from the Internet without saving them onto your computer

stream·line /ˈstrimlaɪn/ *v.* [T] **1** to make something such as a business, organization etc. work more simply and effectively **2** to form something into a smooth shape so that it moves easily through the air or water —**streamlined** *adj.*: *streamlined cars*

ˌstream of ˈconsciousness *n.* [U] ENG. LANG. ARTS the expression of thoughts and feelings in writing exactly as they pass through your mind, without the usual ordered structure they have in formal writing

street /strit/ S1 W1 *n.* [C] **1** a public road in a city or town that has houses, stores etc. on one or both sides: *a busy city street* | *They live on Clay Street.* | *street signs* | *a street corner* | **down/along/up the street** *We walked slowly down the street.* | *Someone just moved in **across the street**.* | *Look both ways before you **cross the street**.* ▶see THESAURUS box at road **2 the street/streets** the busy public parts of a city where there is a lot of activity, excitement, and crime, or where people without homes live: *I try to stay off the street at night.* | *She spent a year homeless, living **on the streets**.* **3 the man/woman on the street** the average person, who represents the general opinion about things **4 a one-way/two-way street** a process that fully involves the opinions and feelings of only one person or group, or of both people or groups: *Marriage is a two-way street.* **5 back on the street/streets** if a criminal is back on the streets, he or she has been allowed to leave prison
[**Origin:** Old English *stræt*] → see also BACKSTREET, **be on easy street** at EASY[1] (17), **take to the streets/highways etc.** at TAKE TO (2), **walk the streets** at WALK[1] (13)

> WORD CHOICE **street, road**
> • A **street** is in a town or city, and usually has stores and other buildings beside it: *a street corner* (NOT *"road corner"*).
> • A **road** is usually in the country, but sometimes very wide **streets** are also called **roads**: *the road to Rochester* (NOT *street*).

street·car /ˈstritˀkɑr/ *n.* [C] a type of bus that runs on electricity along metal tracks in the street

ˌstreet ˈcleaner *n.* [C] **1** a vehicle that uses water and large brushes to clean streets **2** someone whose job is to clean streets —**street cleaning** *n.* [U]

ˈstreet clothes *n.* [plural] ordinary clothes that people wear, rather than uniforms or other special clothes

streetlight /ˈstritlaɪt/ also **street·lamp** /ˈstritlæmp/ *n.* [C] a light at the top of a tall post in the street

ˈstreet map *n.* [C] a map showing the position and names of all the streets in a town or city

ˈstreet muˌsician *n.* [C] a musician who performs outdoors in towns and cities to earn money

ˈstreet ˌpeople *n.* [plural] people who have no home and live on the streets

street·scape /ˈstritskeɪp/ *n.* [C] a view or plan of a street or a group of streets in a city

ˈstreet smarts *n.* [U] the ability to deal with difficult situations on the streets of a big city —**street-smart** *adj.*

ˈstreet ˌvalue *n.* [C,U] the price for which a drug can be sold illegally to people

street·walk·er /ˈstritˀwɔkɚ/ *n.* [C] a PROSTITUTE who stands on the street to attract customers

street·wise /ˈstritˀwaɪz/ *adj.* smart and experienced enough to deal with difficult situations on the streets of a big city: *a streetwise detective*

strength /strɛŋkθ, strɛnθ/ S3 W2 *n.*
1 PHYSICAL [U] the physical power and energy that makes someone strong OPP weakness: *a man of great physical strength* | *He barely **had the strength to** lift the fork.* | *Kim's been exercising to **build up** her **strength**.* | *Sarah hit him **with all** her **strength**.* ▶see THESAURUS box at force[1]
2 DETERMINATION [U] the quality of being brave or determined in dealing with difficult or bad situations OPP weakness: *moral strength* | **the strength to do sth** *Your support has given me the strength to carry on.* | *She couldn't **find the strength** to leave him.* | *Rosa Parks had enormous **strength of character*** (=strong ability to deal with difficult situations). | *Schuller found **an inner strength** that helped him through his recovery.* → see also **pillar of strength** at PILLAR
3 FEELING/BELIEF ETC. [U] how strong a feeling, belief, or relationship is SYN depth: +**of** *the strength of a mother's love* | *I admire **the strength of** her **convictions**.*
4 ORGANIZATION/COUNTRY ETC. [U] the political, military, or economic power of an organization, country, or system OPP weakness: +**of** *the strength of the U.S. economy* | **military/air/naval strength** *Britain's military strength* | *The unions organized **a show of strength*** (=something that shows how powerful it is).
5 USEFUL QUALITY OR ABILITY [C] a particular quality or ability that gives someone or something an advantage OPP weakness: *His charm is one of his greatest strengths* | +**of** *the strengths of the plan* | *Managers need to know their employees' **strengths and weaknesses**.*
6 OBJECT [U] how strong an object or structure is, especially its ability to last for a long time without breaking OPP weakness: +**of** *the strength of the concrete structures*
7 SUBSTANCE/MIXTURE [C,U] how strong a substance or mixture such as an alcoholic drink, medicine, or cleaning liquid is → see also -STRENGTH
8 MONEY [U] the value of a country's money when compared to other countries' money OPP weakness: +**of** *the strength of the euro*
9 on the strength of sth because of something that persuaded you: *He was hired immediately on the strength of her recommendation.*
10 NATURAL FORCE [U] how strong a natural force such as a wind or current of water is: +**of** *the awesome strength of the river*
11 NUMBER OF PEOPLE [U] the number of people in a team, army etc.: +**of** *the strength of Hispanic voters in Texas* | *Security forces were out **in strength*** (=in large numbers).
12 COLOR/TASTE/LIGHT ETC. [U] how strong a color, taste, light etc. is
13 give me strength! SPOKEN used when you are annoyed or angry about something
14 go from strength to strength to become more and more successful
[**Origin:** Old English *strengthu*] → see also **not know your own strength** at KNOW[1] (32), **a position of strength** at POSITION[1] (3)

-strength /strɛŋkθ, strɛnθ/ *suffix* [in adjectives] **full-strength/half-strength/industrial-strength etc.** used to describe how strong a medicine, cleaning solution, chemical mixture etc. is: *a maximum-strength pain reliever*

strength·en /ˈstrɛŋkθən, ˈstrɛnθən/ *v.*
1 FEELING/BELIEF/RELATIONSHIP [I,T] to become stronger, or make something such as a feeling, belief, position, or relationship stronger SYN deepen OPP weaken: *Our friendship has strengthened over the years.* | **strengthen sb's resolve/determination/conviction** *Steve's opposition only strengthened her resolve to go ahead.* | **strengthen ties/bonds/links** *The university hopes to strengthen its ties with the local community.*
2 FINANCIAL SITUATION [I,T] if the financial situation of a country or company strengthens or is strengthened, it improves or is made to improve OPP weaken: *Our first priority is to strengthen the economy.*
3 BODY/STRUCTURE [T] to make something such as your body or a building stronger OPP weaken: *Swimming will strengthen your upper body.* | *Supports were added to strengthen the outer walls.*
4 MONEY [I,T] to increase in value, or to make money do this OPP weaken: **+against** *The dollar has strengthened against other currencies.*
5 TEAM/ARMY ETC. [T] to make an organization, army etc. more powerful, especially by increasing the number or quality of the people in it OPP weaken: *We're looking for ways to strengthen our sales team.*
6 PROOF/REASON [T] to give support to a reason or an attempt to prove something OPP weaken: *Fresh evidence has strengthened the case against him.*
7 strengthen sb's hand to make someone more powerful or give them an advantage over an opponent
8 WIND/CURRENT [I] to increase in force OPP weaken: *The wind strengthened during the night.*

stren·u·ous /ˈstrɛnyuəs/ *adj.* **1** needing great effort or strength: *strenuous exercise* **2** active and determined: *strenuous objections* —**strenuously** *adv.*

strep /strɛp/ *n.* [U] **1** also **strep throat** an illness caused by streptococcus in which your throat is very painful **2** streptococcus

strep·to·coc·cus /ˌstrɛptəˈkɑkəs/ *n. plural* **streptococci** /-ˈkɑksaɪ, -ˈkɑkaɪ/ [C] a type of BACTERIA that causes infections, especially in your throat —**streptococcal** *adj.*

strep·to·my·cin /ˌstrɛptoʊˈmaɪsən, -tə-/ *n.* [U] a strong drug used in medicines to kill BACTERIA

stress¹ /strɛs/ Ac S3 W3 *n.*
1 WORRY [U] continuous feelings of worry about your work or personal life, that prevent you from relaxing: *The headaches were caused by stress.* | *the emotional stress of divorce* | *Single mothers are always **under** a lot **of stress**.*
2 DIFFICULTY [C usually plural] a situation that causes continuous feelings of worry: *everyday stresses* | *the **stresses and strains** of being a manager*
3 EMPHASIS [U] the special attention or importance given to a particular idea, fact, or activity SYN emphasis: **put/lay stress on sth** *The school puts a great deal of stress on good manners.*
4 FORCE [C,U] PHYSICS the physical force or pressure on an object: **put/place stress on sth** *Exercise puts stress on bones as well as muscles.*
5 LOUDNESS [C,U] ENG. LANG. ARTS the degree of force or loudness with which a part of a word is pronounced or a note in music is played, which makes it sound stronger than other parts or notes → see also ACCENT: **the stress is/falls on sth** *The stress is on the first syllable.*
[**Origin:** 1300–1400 *distress*]

stress² Ac W3 *v.* [T] **1** ENG. LANG. ARTS to emphasize a statement, fact, or idea SYN emphasize: **stress that** *The report stressed that student math skills need to improve.* | *Crawford continues to **stress the need for** more housing downtown.* | *Experts **stress the importance of** a balanced diet.* ►see THESAURUS box at emphasize **2** to emphasize a word or part of a word so that it sounds louder or more forceful: *The word "basket" is stressed on the first syllable.*

stress sb ↔ **out** *phr. v.* INFORMAL to make someone so worried or nervous that they cannot relax: *Studying for finals always stresses me out.*

stressed /strɛst/ Ac *adj.* **1** also **stressed-out** INFORMAL so worried and tired that you cannot relax: *I always eat when I'm stressed.* | *stressed-out nurses* **2** [only before noun] TECHNICAL a stressed object, especially a metal object, has had a lot of pressure or force put on it **3** ENG. LANG. ARTS a stressed word or SYLLABLE is emphasized so that it sounds louder or more forceful OPP unstressed

ˈstress ˌfracture *n.* [C] a small crack in a bone, caused by repeated pressure on that part of your body

stress·ful /ˈstrɛsfəl/ Ac *adj.* a stressful job, experience, or situation makes you worry a lot: *Moving to a new house is very stressful.*

ˈstress mark *n.* [C] ENG. LANG. ARTS a mark that shows which part of a word is emphasized the most

ˈstress-reˌlated *adj.* caused by STRESS: *stress-related illness*

stretch¹ /strɛtʃ/ S2 W3 *v.*
1 MAKE STH BIGGER/LOOSER [I,T] to make something bigger or looser by pulling it, or to become bigger or looser in this way: *The rope stretched and then broke.* | *What's the best way to stretch shoes?*
2 BODY [I,T] to bring your arms, legs, or body to full length: *Carl sat up in bed and stretched.* | *She stretched her arms and yawned.* | **+across/over etc.** *Ann stretched across and grabbed the phone.* ►see THESAURUS box at exercise²

stretch

3 CHANGE SHAPE [I not in progressive] if material stretches, it can become bigger or longer when you pull it and then return to its original shape when you stop
4 IN SPACE [I always + adv./prep.] to spread out or cover a large area SYN stretch out: **+to/into/away etc.** *A line of people stretched around the block.*
5 TIME/SERIES [I always + adv./prep.,T] to continue over a period of time or in a series, or make something do this: **+into/on/over etc.** *The research program stretched over several years.* | **stretch sth to sth** *They have stretched their winning streak to 11 games.*
6 MAKE STH TIGHT [T] to pull something so that it is tight: *The canvas is stretched over a wooden frame.*
7 MAKE STH LAST [I,T] if you stretch an amount of money, food etc. or you make it stretch, you make it last for a longer time than it usually would by using it carefully: *I'm going to have to stretch this $60 until payday.*
8 BE ENOUGH [I always + adv./prep.] to be enough to buy something: *I knew Grandma's money would only stretch so far.*
9 stretch sb/sth to the limit also **stretch sb/sth to the breaking point** to push someone or something beyond a point that is reasonable by asking for too much, using too much etc.: *Working families are already stretched to the limit.*
10 be stretching it INFORMAL to say something that makes something seem more important, bigger etc. than it really is: *Calling him a "world class" athlete is stretching it.*
11 stretch the truth/facts to say or write something that is not completely true: *Reporters sometimes stretch the facts to catch a reader's eye.*
12 stretch your legs INFORMAL to go for a walk, especially after sitting for a long time
13 stretch (sb's) credulity/patience etc. to be almost beyond the limits of what someone can believe, accept etc.: *Her theories about reincarnation stretch credulity.*
14 ABILITIES [T] to make someone use all of their skill, abilities, or intelligence: *I want a job that stretches me.*
15 stretch a/the point to say something that makes something seem more important, bigger, worse etc. than it really is
[**Origin:** Old English *streccan*] —**stretchable** *adj.*

stretch out *phr. v.*
1 be stretched out to be lying with your body and legs straight in order to relax: *The dog was stretched out in front of the fire.*
2 LIE DOWN INFORMAL to lie down, usually in order to sleep or rest: *I just want to stretch out for a few minutes.*
3 HAND/FOOT **stretch sth ↔ out** to put out your hand, foot etc. in order to reach something: *Jimmy stretched out his hand to take the candy.*
4 CLOTHING **stretch sth ↔ out** if you stretch out a piece of clothing, or it stretches out, it becomes bigger or looser by being worn or pulled: *No, you can't wear my sweater – you'd stretch it out.*
5 IN SPACE to spread out or cover a large area
6 IN TIME **stretch sth ↔ out** to make something last for longer than is usual or expected

stretch² *n.*
1 LENGTH OF LAND/WATER [C] an area of land or water, especially one that is long and narrow: +**of** *an empty stretch of highway*
2 TIME [C] a continuous period of time: +**of** *a stretch of three weeks without sunshine* | *New doctors are forced to work 36 hours* ***at a stretch****.*
3 not by any stretch (of the imagination) also **by no stretch (of the imagination)** SPOKEN used to emphasize that a negative statement is true: *Raising children isn't easy by any stretch of the imagination.*
4 STH DIFFICULT something that is difficult to do or believe: *Playing a teenager is* ***a bit of a stretch*** *for the 35-year-old actress.*
5 BODY [C] the action of stretching a part of your body out to its full length, or a particular way of doing this: *Do some stretches before you exercise.*
6 the home/final stretch a) the last part of a track before the end of a race **b)** the last part of an activity, trip, or process
7 MATERIAL [U] the ability a material has to increase in length or width without tearing: *The fabric has lost its stretch.* → see also STRETCHY
8 do a stretch (for sth) INFORMAL to spend a period of time in prison for a crime

stretch·er /ˈstrɛtʃɚ/ *n.* [C] a covered frame for carrying someone who is too injured or sick to walk

stretch lim·o /ˌstrɛtʃ ˈlɪmoʊ/ also **ˌstretch ˈlimousine** *n.* [C] a very large comfortable car that has been made longer than usual

ˈstretch mark *n.* [C usually plural] a mark left on your skin as a result of it stretching too much, especially during PREGNANCY

stretch·y /ˈstrɛtʃi/ *adj. comparative* **stretchier**, *superlative* **stretchiest** stretchy material, clothes etc. can stretch when you pull them and then return to their original shape

strew /stru/ *v. past tense* **strewed**, *past participle* **strewn** /strun/ or **strewed** [T usually passive] FORMAL **1** to scatter things around a large area: **be strewn around/about/across etc. sth** *There were clothes strewn across the floor.* **2 be strewn with sth** to be covered with things that are scattered around in a messy way: *The street was strewn with broken glass.* **3 be strewn with sth** to contain a lot of something

stri·at·ed /ˈstraɪˌeɪt̮ɪd/ *adj.* TECHNICAL having narrow lines or bands of color SYN **striped**

stri·a·tion /straɪˈeɪʃən/ *n.* [C,U] **1** EARTH SCIENCE one of many deep straight lines that have been made in the surface of a rock when a GLACIER moves over it, or the process in which this happens: *types of glacial striation* **2** one of a number of narrow lines or bands of color SYN **stripe**

strick·en¹ /ˈstrɪkən/ *adj.* FORMAL very badly affected by trouble, illness etc.: **drought-stricken/cancer-stricken/tragedy-stricken etc.** *Fires are common in this drought-stricken region.* → see also GRIEF-STRICKEN, PANIC-STRICKEN, POVERTY-STRICKEN

stricken² *v.* a past participle of STRIKE¹ (10,22)

strict /strɪkt/ *adj.* **1** demanding that rules be obeyed: *a strict teacher* | +**about** *The hospital is very strict about visiting hours.* | +**with** *Mom and Dad were always very strict with us kids.* **2** a strict order or rule is one that must be obeyed: *strict laws against drugs* | *I'm telling you this* ***in the strictest confidence*** (=it must be kept completely secret). **3** [usually before noun] exact and correct, often in a way that seems unreasonable: *The book is not actually "autobiographical"* ***in the strict sense.*** **4 a strict Muslim/vegetarian etc.** someone who obeys all the rules of a particular religion, belief etc. [**Origin:** 1400–1500 Latin *strictus*, past participle of *stringere* **to tie tightly, press together**] —**strictness** *n.* [U]

strict·ly /ˈstrɪktli/ *adv.* **1** exactly and completely: *The report is strictly confidential.* **2 strictly speaking** used when you are using words or explaining rules in an exact and correct way: *Strictly speaking, spiders are not insects.* **3** only for a particular person, thing, or purpose and nothing else: *I play the piano strictly for fun.* **4** in a way that must be obeyed: *Local driving regulations are strictly enforced.*

stric·ture /ˈstrɪktʃɚ/ *n.* [C often plural] FORMAL **1** a rule that strictly limits what you can do: +**against/on** *the Church's strictures on birth control* **2** a severe criticism

stride¹ *n.*
1 STEP [C] a long step: *Len was out of the room in two strides.*
2 IMPROVEMENT [C] an improvement in a situation or in the development of something: **make great/major/giant etc. strides** *We've made tremendous strides in reducing crime.*
3 take sth in stride to not allow something to annoy, embarrass, or upset you: *Neil took the criticism in stride.*
4 WAY OF WALKING [singular] the pattern of your steps, or the way you walk or run: *a quick decisive stride*
5 hit your stride to become comfortable with a job so you can do it continuously and well
6 break (your) stride a) to begin moving more slowly or to stop when you are running or walking **b)** if you break your stride, you allow someone or something to interrupt or annoy you, rather than continuing smoothly
7 knock/throw/keep sb off stride to make someone unable to do something effectively by not allowing them to give all their attention to it
8 (match sb) stride for stride also **go stride for stride with sb** to manage to be just as fast, strong, skilled etc. as someone else even if they keep making it harder for you

stride² /straɪd/ *v. past tense* **strode** /stroʊd/, *past participle* **stridden** /ˈstrɪdn/ [I always + adv./prep.] to walk quickly with long steps ►see THESAURUS box at **walk¹** [**Origin:** Old English *stridan*]

stri·dent /ˈstraɪdnt/ *adj.* **1** forceful and determined: *strident critics* **2** a strident sound or voice is not nice to listen to because it is loud and often high [**Origin:** 1600–1700 Latin, present participle of *stridere* **to make a rough unpleasant noise**] —**stridently** *adv.* —**stridency** *n.* [U]

strife /straɪf/ *n.* [U] FORMAL trouble between two or more people or groups SYN **conflict**: *ethnic strife*

strike¹ /straɪk/ S3 W1 *v. past tense and past participle* **struck** /strʌk/
1 HIT [I always + adv./prep.,T] FORMAL to hit or knock something hard SYN **hit**: *The girl was struck and killed by a speeding car.* | +**on/against** *The rain struck hard against the window.* | **strikes sb on/in sth** *The ball struck him in the face.* ►see THESAURUS box at **hit¹**
2 THOUGHT/IDEA [T not in progressive] if a thought, idea, fact etc. strikes you, you think of it, notice it, or realize that it is important, interesting, surprising, bad etc.: *We were struck by her patience with all the children.* | **it strikes sb that** *It suddenly struck me that I hadn't spoken to Debbie in months.*
3 strike sb as (being) sth to seem to have a particular quality or feature: *Mr. West struck me as a very good businessman.* | *His arguments struck us as completely ridiculous.* | ***How does*** *breakfast in bed* ***strike you*** (=do

you like the idea)? | **it strikes sb as strange/odd/funny etc. that** *Didn't it strike you as odd that they chose Martin?*
4 STOP WORK [I] if a group of workers strike, they stop working for a time as a protest against their pay, working conditions etc.: *The flight attendants are threatening to strike.* | **+for/against** *Over 100,000 factory workers are striking for higher wages.* | **+over** *Public employees are striking over pay.*
5 WITH YOUR HAND [T] FORMAL to deliberately hit someone or something hard, especially with your hand SYN **hit**: *She struck him hard across the face.* | **strike sth with sth** *Jumping up, he struck the table with his fist.* | *She* ***struck*** *the dog* ***a blow*** *with her umbrella.*
6 ATTACK [I] to attack suddenly: *Police fear that the killer will strike again.* | *The snake releases the mouse after striking.* | **+at** *Fighter bombers struck at the presidential palace.*
7 strike a balance (between sth) to give the correct amount of importance or attention to two opposing things: *She's trying to strike a balance between family and work.*
8 STH BAD HAPPENS [I] if something bad strikes, it suddenly happens: *Tragedy struck two days later.*
9 strike a deal/bargain (with sb) to agree to do something if someone else does something for you: *Republicans have struck a deal with Democrats on tax cuts.*
10 DISEASE [T usually passive] FORMAL *past participle* **stricken** to make someone become sick: **be stricken by/with sth** *He was stricken with polio when he was just two.*
11 strike a cheerful/conciliatory/cautious etc. note also **strike a... tone** to express a particular feeling or attitude: *Davis tried to strike a hopeful note in his speech.*
12 strike a chord to be or say something that other people agree with or have sympathy with: *The book* ***struck a deep chord with*** *the American Jewish community.*
13 strike a match to make a match burn by hitting it against a hard surface
14 strike gold/oil etc. to suddenly find gold, oil etc., especially after you have been looking for it
15 strike gold to become very successful at something and earn a lot of money
16 CLOCK [I,T] when a clock strikes, or it strikes one, three, six etc., its bell sounds one, three, six etc. times to show the time: *The tower bell was beginning to* ***strike the hour*** (=strike when it is exactly one o'clock, two o'clock etc.).
17 LIGHTNING [I,T] when LIGHTNING strikes something, it hits and damages it
18 strike sb dead if something, especially LIGHTNING or God, strikes you dead, they hit you and kill you very suddenly
19 strike a blow for sth to do something to help achieve or protect a principle, aim, or group: *We feel we have struck a blow for freedom of speech.*
20 strike a blow to/at/against sth to have a harmful effect on people's beliefs, an organization etc.: *The court has struck another blow to the state's civil rights commission.*
21 within striking distance (of sth) a) close enough to reach or attack a place easily **b)** close enough to be reached, attacked, or achieved easily: *The city was now within striking distance.* **c)** very close to achieving something: *Ryan is within striking distance of the world record.*
22 strike sb/sth from sth FORMAL *past participle* **stricken** to remove a name or a thing from something written: *His testimony was* ***stricken from the record*** (=removed from the official court record).
23 GAIN ADVANTAGE [I] to do something that gives you an advantage or harms your opponent in a fight, competition etc.: *The home team struck first with two touchdowns in the first quarter.*
24 strike it rich to suddenly make a lot of money: *They're hoping to strike it rich in Las Vegas.*
25 LIGHT [T] to fall on a surface: *Watch what happens when light strikes the prism.*
26 strike terror/fear into sb's heart to make someone feel afraid
27 strike a pose to stand or sit with your body in a particular position
28 strike while the iron is hot to do something immediately rather than waiting until a later time when you are less likely to succeed
29 be struck dumb to be unable to speak, usually because you are very surprised → see also DUMBSTRUCK
30 TENT/SAIL/SET [T] to take down a tent, sail, or SET (=structures built for a play): *We* ***struck camp*** *at daybreak.*
31 be struck with horror/terror/awe etc. to suddenly feel very shocked, afraid etc. → see also AWESTRUCK
32 COINS [T usually passive] to make a coin
[**Origin:** Old English *strican* **to touch lightly, go**] → see also **hit/strike home** at HOME[2] (5), STRICKEN[1], STRIKING

strike at sb/sth *phr. v.* **1** to deliberately try to hit someone or something with your hand or a weapon: *She struck at him with her fists.* **2** to have a harmful effect on someone or something: *The bombing* ***struck at the heart of*** (=affected the most important part of) *the local community.*

strike back *phr. v.* to attack or criticize someone who has attacked or criticized you first: **+at** *White struck back at critics of his educational policies.*

strike down *phr. v.* **1 strike sth ↔ down** if a court strikes down a law, it decides not to allow it **2 strike sb ↔ down** to make someone die or become very sick: *Thousands of people were struck down by the disease.* **3 strike sb ↔ down** LITERARY to hit someone so hard that they fall down

strike on/upon sth *phr. v.* to discover something or have a good idea about something, especially when this is sudden, unexpected, or happens by accident SYN **hit on**: *Richard eventually struck on a plan for solving his financial difficulties.*

strike out *phr. v.*
1 BASEBALL strike sb ↔ out to fail to hit the ball in baseball three times so that you are not allowed to continue trying, or to make someone do this → see also STRIKEOUT
2 strike out on your own to start doing something new or living by yourself, without other people's help
3 ATTACK to criticize or attack someone suddenly or violently: **+at** *Depressed men often strike out at their wives and children.*
4 IN A DIRECTION to start moving in a particular direction, especially in a determined way: **+across/toward/through etc.** *The men struck out toward the mountains.*
5 NOT SUCCEED SPOKEN to be unsuccessful at something: *"Did you kiss her?" "No, I struck out."*
6 WORD strike sth ↔ out OLD-FASHIONED to draw a line through something written on a piece of paper SYN **cross out**

strike through sth *phr. v.* to draw a line through something written on a piece of paper SYN **cross out**

strike up *phr. v.* **1 strike up a friendship/conversation/correspondence etc. (with sb)** to start to become friendly with someone, start talking to them etc.: *I struck up a conversation with the taxi driver on the way to the airport.* **2 strike sth ↔ up** to begin playing a piece of music **3 strike up the band** to tell a band to begin playing a piece of music

strike upon sth *phr. v.* to STRIKE ON something

strike[2] W2 *n.*
1 WORKERS [C,U] a period of time when a group of workers stop working as a protest against their pay, working conditions etc.: **+over** *The strike over pay cuts lasted three weeks.* | **+against** *a strike against a major airline* | *About 300 workers* ***went on strike*** *Tuesday over wages.* | *Workers are* ***on strike*** *for a second day today.* | *The leadership* ***called the strike*** (=asked people to stop working) *to protest dangerous working conditions.* | *Union leaders are calling for* ***a general strike*** (=one involving most of the workers in the country). | *The* ***strike was called off*** (=ended) *late last night.* | **a machinists'/players' etc. strike** *During the teachers' strike, all schools were closed.*
2 MILITARY [C] a military attack, especially by aircraft

dropping bombs: +**against/on** *preemptive military strikes on specific targets* | **an air/a nuclear etc. strike** *The air strikes took the enemy by surprise.* | *The country is threatening to* ***launch*** *air* ***strikes*** *against its neighbors.*
3 two/three etc. strikes against sb/sth two, three etc. things that make it extremely difficult for someone or something to be successful
4 BASEBALL [C] an attempt to hit the ball in baseball that fails, or a ball that is thrown to the BATTER in the correct area, but is not hit → see also FOUL
5 BOWLING [C] a situation in BOWLING in which you knock down all the PINS (=bottle shaped objects) with a ball on your first attempt → see also SPARE
6 GOLD/OIL [C] the discovery of something valuable such as gold or oil by digging in the ground: *an oil strike* → see also HUNGER STRIKE, LIGHTNING STRIKE, OIL STRIKE, RENT STRIKE, THREE-STRIKES

strike·bound /ˈstraɪkbaʊnd/ *adj.* unable to move, happen, or work because of a strike

strike·break·er /ˈstraɪkˌbreɪkɚ/ *n.* [C] someone who takes the job of someone who is on strike → see also SCAB —**strikebreaking** *n.* [U]

strike·out /ˈstraɪk-aʊt/ *n.* [C] in baseball, the action of throwing three STRIKES so that the BATTER is not allowed to try to hit the ball anymore → see also **strike out** at STRIKE[1]

S

ˈstrike pay *n.* [U] money paid by a union to workers who are not working because they are on STRIKE

strik·er /ˈstraɪkɚ/ *n.* [C] someone who is not working because they are on STRIKE

ˈstrike zone *n.* [C] in baseball, the area over HOME PLATE between the BATTER's knees and the top of the arms, where the ball must be thrown to be considered a STRIKE

strik·ing /ˈstraɪkɪŋ/ *adj.* **1** unusual or interesting enough to be noticed: **a striking contrast/example/parallel etc.** *striking similarities between the two cultures* ►see THESAURUS box at **noticeable** **2** very attractive, often in an unusual way: *a man with striking features* —**strikingly** *adv.* → see also **within striking distance** at STRIKE[1] (21)

Strind·berg /ˈstrɪndbɚg/, **August** (1849–1912) a Swedish writer of plays

string[1] /strɪŋ/ S2 W3 *n.*
1 THREAD [C,U] a strong thread made of several threads twisted together, used for tying or fastening things: *a piece of string* | *The pen was hanging from a string on the wall.*
2 GROUP/SERIES [C] **a)** a number of similar things or events coming one after another: +**of** *a string of questions about my past* **b)** a line of similar things: +**of** *a string of tiny islands off the coast* **c)** a group of similar things: +**of** *She owns a string of health clubs.*
3 no strings (attached) having no special conditions or limits on an agreement, relationship etc.: *Howard's lent me the money with no strings attached.*
4 a string of pearls/beads/lights etc. several objects of the same kind connected with a thread, chain etc. SYN **strand**
5 the strings [plural] also **the string section** the part of an ORCHESTRA that consists of stringed instruments, such as VIOLINS
6 ON AN INSTRUMENT [C] one of the long thin pieces of wire, NYLON etc. that is stretched across a musical instrument and produces sound: *a guitar string*
7 ON A RACKET [C] one of the pieces of NYLON that is stretched across the frame of a tennis RACKET or a similar type of racket, to form the surface that you hit the ball with
8 COMPUTERS [C] a group of letters, words, or numbers, one after the other, especially in a computer program
9 first/second/third string a team or group with the highest, second highest etc. level of skill
10 have sb on a string INFORMAL to be able to make someone do whatever you want
[**Origin:** Old English *streng*] → see also G-STRING, **pull strings** at PULL[1] (7), **pull the/sb's strings** at PULL[1] (8), **hold/control the purse strings** at PURSE[1] (4), -STRING

string[2] *v. past tense and past participle* **strung** /strʌŋ/ [T] **1** to put things together onto a thread, chain etc.: *She strung the beads on a cord.* **2** [always + adv./prep.] to hang things in a line, high up, especially for decoration: **string sth up/along/across etc.** *Paper lanterns were strung up across the courtyard.* **3 be strung (out) along/across etc. sth** WRITTEN to be spread out in a long line SYN **string out**: *The 200 houses are strung along a narrow five-mile road.* **4** to put a string or a set of strings onto a musical instrument → see also HIGH-STRUNG, STRUNG OUT

string sb along *phr. v.* INFORMAL to deceive someone for a long time by making them believe that you will help them, that you love them etc.: *He's never going to marry you – he's just stringing you along.*

string sth ↔ out *phr. v.* INFORMAL to make something last longer: *The process could string out the dispute for months.*

string sth ↔ together *phr. v.* **1** to combine two or more things together to make something that is complete, good, useful etc., especially when you have trouble doing it: *He managed to string together enough financial aid to go to college.* **2 string words/phrases/sentences together** to say or write something that makes sense to other people, especially when you have trouble doing it: *He was so drunk he could hardly string two words together.*

string up *phr. v.* INFORMAL **1 string sb ↔ up** to kill someone by hanging them **2 string sth ↔ up** to hang something in a high position

-string /strɪŋ/ [in adjectives] **first-string/second-string/third-string** relating to or being a member of a sports team with the highest, second highest etc. level of skill: *a first-string quarterback*

ˈstring bean *n.* [C] **1** BIOLOGY a GREEN BEAN **2** SPOKEN INFORMAL a very tall thin person

stringed instruments

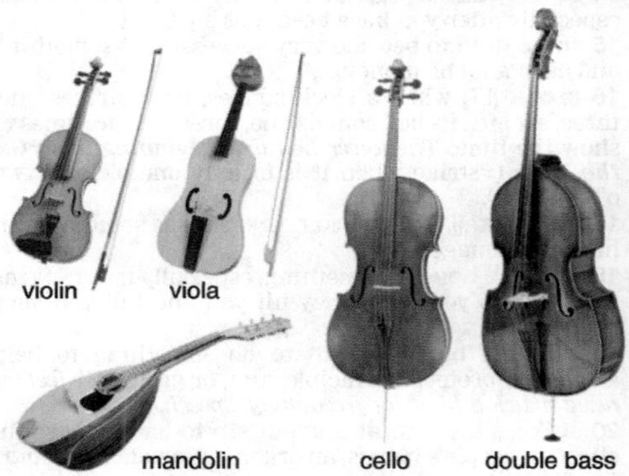

ˌstringed ˈinstrument *n.* [C] a musical instrument, such as a VIOLIN, that produces sound from a set of STRINGS

strin·gent /ˈstrɪndʒənt/ *adj.* **1** a stringent law, rule, standard etc. is very strict and must be obeyed **2** stringent economic conditions exist when there is a severe lack of money and strict controls on the supply of money —**stringently** *adv.* —**stringency** *n.* [U]

string·er /ˈstrɪŋɚ/ *n.* [C] **1** someone who regularly sends in news stories to a newspaper, but who is not employed by that newspaper **2 a first-stringer/second-stringer/third-stringer** one of the players on a sports team who has the highest, second highest etc. level of skill

ˈstring tie *n.* [C] a narrow piece of cloth worn around your neck and tied in a bow

string·y /ˈstrɪŋi/ *adj. comparative* **stringier**, *superlative* **stringiest** **1** stringy meat, fruit, or vegetables are full of thin pieces that are difficult to eat **2** stringy hair is very thin and looks like string, especially because it is dirty **3** a stringy person or part of their body is very thin so that their muscles show through their skin

strip[1] /strɪp/ S3 *v.* **stripped, stripping**
1 TAKE OFF YOUR CLOTHES [I] **a)** to take off your clothes: *Jack stripped and jumped into the shower.* | *The boys* ***stripped naked*** (=removed all their clothes) *and jumped in the pond.* | *The doctor had me* ***strip to the waist*** (=take off the clothes on the top half of my body) *to examine my chest.* | **strip (down) to sth** *She stripped down to her bra and panties.* → see also **strip off** **b)** to take off your clothes in a sexually exciting way as entertainment for someone else ▸see THESAURUS box at **piece**[1]
2 TAKE OFF SB'S CLOTHES [T] to take off someone else's clothes: *The prisoner was stripped and beaten.* | **strip sb to sth** *They stripped us to our underwear and took our clothes.*
3 REMOVE A LAYER [T] to remove something that is covering the surface of something else SYN **strip away** SYN **strip off**: *Strip the wax with solvent.* | **strip sth from sth** *We used paint thinner to strip the paint from the doors.* → see also **strip off**
4 BUILDING/CAR ETC. [T] to remove everything that is inside a building, all the equipment from a car etc. so that it is completely empty: *The apartment had been* ***stripped bare***.
5 DAMAGE [T] to damage or break the GEARS in a machine or the THREADS (=lines) on a screw so that they do not work correctly anymore
6 BED [T] to take all the sheets off a bed
7 ENGINE/MACHINE [T] to separate an engine, machine, or piece of equipment into pieces in order to clean or repair it
[**Origin:** Old English *-strypan*] → see also ASSET STRIPPING

strip sth ↔ **away** *phr. v.* **1** to remove the surface of something, or remove a layer that is covering the surface of something: *Strip away the old paint.* **2** to remove something that prevents you from seeing what someone or something is really like: *I wanted to strip away all the lies and find out the truth.*

strip sth ↔ **down** *phr. v.* **1** to make something much simpler or more basic → see also STRIPPED-DOWN **2** to separate an engine, machine, or piece of equipment into pieces in order to clean or repair it

strip of *phr. v.* **1 strip sb of sth** to take away something important from someone, for example their title, property, or power, especially as a punishment: *He was stripped of his medal after failing a drug test.* **2 strip sth of sth** to remove a lot of something from something else, especially in a way that causes damage: *Some shampoos strip your hair of its natural oils.*

strip off *phr. v.* **1 strip sth ↔ off** to quickly take off a piece of clothing: *She stripped off her wet clothes.* **2 strip sth ↔ off, strip sth off sth** to remove the surface of something, or remove a layer of something that is covering the surface: *We need to strip off the wallpaper first.*

strip[2] S3 *n.* [C] **1** a long narrow piece of paper, cloth etc.: *a strip of bacon* | *She tore the paper into strips.* **2** a long narrow area of land: *a strip of sand between the cliffs and the ocean* **3** a road with a lot of stores, restaurants etc. along it: *the Las Vegas strip* **4** a COMIC STRIP → see also LANDING STRIP

strip club *n.* [C] a place where people go to see performers who take off their clothes in a sexually exciting way

stripe /straɪp/ *n.* [C] **1** a line of color, especially one of several lines of color all close together: *a shirt with black and white stripes* ▸see THESAURUS box at **line**[1]
2 politicians/musicians/scientists etc. of all stripes INFORMAL all different types of politicians, musicians etc.: *Politicians of all stripes are praising the deal.* **3** a narrow piece of material worn on the arm of a uniform as a sign of rank → see also **earn your stripes** at EARN (5), STARS AND STRIPES

striped /straɪpt, ˈstraɪpɪd/ *adj.* having lines or bands of color: *a blue and white striped T-shirt*

strip joint *n.* [C] INFORMAL a STRIP CLUB

strip·ling /ˈstrɪplɪŋ/ *n.* [C] LITERARY a boy who is almost a young man

ˈstrip mall *n.* [C] a row of stores built together, with a large area for parking cars in front of it

ˈstrip mine *n.* [C] EARTH SCIENCE a very large hole that is made in the ground to remove metal, coal etc. from the earth —**strip-mine** *v.* [I,T] —**strip mining** *n.* [U]

ˌstripped-ˈdown *adj.* [only before noun] having only the basic features, with everything special and additional removed → see also STRIP DOWN

strip·per /ˈstrɪpɚ/ *n.* [C] **1** someone whose job is to take off their clothes in a sexually exciting way in order to entertain people **2** a tool or liquid used to remove something from a surface: *paint stripper*

ˈstrip ˌpoker *n.* [C] a game of POKER (=card game) in which players that lose take off pieces of their clothing

ˈstrip search *n.* [C] a process in which you have to remove your clothes so that your body can be checked, usually for hidden drugs —**strip-search** *v.* [T]

ˈstrip show *n.* [C] a form of entertainment where people take off their clothes in a sexually exciting way

strip·tease /ˈstrɪptiz/ *n.* [C,U] a performance in which someone, especially a woman, takes off their clothes in a sexually exciting way

strive /straɪv/ *v. past tense* **strove** /stroʊv/, *past participle* **striven** /ˈstrɪvən/ *n.* [I] FORMAL to make a great effort to achieve something: +**for** *We are striving for social justice and peace.* | **strive to do sth** *We strive to be 100% accurate.*

strobe light /ˈstroʊb laɪt/ also **strobe** *n.* [C] a light that flashes on and off very quickly, often used in places where you can dance

strode /stroʊd/ *v.* the past tense of STRIDE

stroke[1] /stroʊk/ *n.* [C]
1 ILLNESS MEDICINE an occasion when an ARTERY (=tube carrying blood) in your brain suddenly bursts or becomes blocked: *She died of a massive stroke.* | **have/suffer a stroke** *My father suffered a stroke that left him unable to speak.*
2 SWIMMING/ROWING **a)** one of a set of movements in swimming or rowing in which you move your arms or the OAR forward and then back: *She swam with strong steady strokes.* **b)** a style of swimming or rowing: *the back stroke*
3 SPORTS a movement of the upper part of your body that you use to hit the ball in games such as tennis and GOLF: *a backhand stroke*
4 a stroke of (good) luck/fortune something lucky that you did not expect to happen: *Finding the key was a real stroke of luck.*
5 PEN/BRUSH **a)** a single movement of a pen or brush when you are writing or painting: *He paints with a series of quick strokes.* **b)** a line made by doing this: *Some Chinese characters contain over 60 strokes.* → see also BRUSH STROKE
6 a stroke of genius/inspiration etc. a very good idea about what to do to solve a problem: *It was a stroke of genius to film the movie in Toronto.*
7 with/at a stroke of the pen if you do something with a stroke of the pen, you do it by signing a piece of paper
8 at the stroke of seven/ten etc. at exactly seven o'clock, ten o'clock etc.
9 a bold/master stroke something very brave or effective that someone does to achieve something
10 at a/one stroke also **with a/one stroke** with a single sudden action
11 HIT an action of hitting someone with something such as a whip or a thin stick
12 CLOCK/BELL [C] a single sound made by a clock giving the hours, or by a bell, GONG etc.
13 a stroke of lightning a bright flash of LIGHTNING, especially one that hits something → see also **different strokes (for different folks)** at DIFFERENT (4)

stroke[2] *v.* [T] **1** to move your hand gently over something: *She was sitting on the sofa, stroking her cat.* ▸see THESAURUS box at **touch**[1] **2** [always + adv./prep.] to move

S

something somewhere with gentle movements of your hand: *He gently stroked the hair from her eyes.* **3** [always + adv./prep.] to hit a ball in tennis, baseball, GOLF etc. **4** to say nice things to someone to make them feel good, especially because you want something from them SYN **flatter**: *He expects his girlfriend to* ***stroke his ego***.

stroll /stroul/ *v.* [I,T] to walk somewhere in a slow relaxed way: **+along/across/around etc.** *We strolled through the gardens, admiring the flowers.* | *After dinner I strolled the deserted beach.* ►see THESAURUS box at **walk**[1] —**stroll** *n.* [C]

stroll·er /ˈstroulə/ *n.* [C] a small chair on wheels in which a small child sits and is pushed along → see also BABY CARRIAGE

stroll·ing /ˈstroulɪŋ/ *adj.* [only before noun] a strolling musician plays music while walking among listeners

strong /strɔŋ/ S1 W1 *adj.*

1 PHYSICAL having a lot of physical power so that you can lift or move heavy things, do hard physical work etc. OPP **weak**: *strong arms* | *My brother is stronger than I am.* | *He's 65 and still* ***strong as an ox*** (=very strong).

2 NOT EASILY DAMAGED not easily damaged, broken, or destroyed OPP **weak**: *a strong rope* | *Is that branch strong enough to hold you?*

S

THESAURUS

tough used about a material that is not easily cut, damaged, or made weaker: *The toys are made of tough plastic.*
heavy-duty used about a particular type of thing that is stronger or less easily damaged than other types: *a heavy-duty garbage sack*
sturdy/robust used about a strong object, vehicle etc.: *a sturdy table*
durable used about materials and products that will remain in good condition for a long time even when they are used a lot: *A rope made of these synthetic materials is more durable than a cotton rope.*
unbreakable too strong to be broken: *an unbreakable bond between the two brothers*
indestructible too strong to be destroyed: *The wood of the yellow locust tree is virtually indestructible.*

►see THESAURUS box at **bright**

3 POWERFUL having a lot of power or influence and therefore likely to be successful OPP **weak**: *a strong president* | *a strong national defense* | *We believe we are* ***in a strong*** *negotiating* ***position***. ►see THESAURUS box at **powerful**

4 DONE WITH POWER produced with or using a lot of power or force OPP **weak**: *She gave the door a strong kick, and it flew open.*

5 BELIEFS/OPINIONS a strong feeling, opinion, belief etc. is one that you feel very sure or serious about: *There has been strong support for the strike.* | **strong views/opinions/feelings etc.** *Many people have strong feelings on the matter.* | *He has* ***a strong sense of*** *right and wrong.*

6 SURE/DETERMINED having opinions, beliefs etc. that you are very sure about, and willing to take action because of them: *I'm a strong believer in regular exercise.* | *a strong supporter of the Libertarian Party*

7 EMOTIONS a strong emotion, desire etc. has a great effect on you: *a strong temptation* | *I didn't know your* ***feelings for*** *her* ***were*** *so* ***strong*** (=you liked her so much).

8 ARGUMENT/REASON ETC. likely to persuade other people that something is true or the correct thing to do OPP **weak**: *The conclusions are supported by* ***strong evidence***. | *The argument against closing the school is very strong.*

9 ABLE TO DEAL WITH DIFFICULTY determined and able to deal with a difficult or upsetting situation OPP **weak**: *I don't think she's strong enough to handle the news.*

10 RELATIONSHIP a strong relationship, friendship etc. is one in which people are very loyal to each other and the relationship is likely to last a long time: *a strong emotional bond with the boy* | *strong trade ties between the two nations*

11 TASTE/SMELL having a taste or smell that you notice easily: *a strong garlic taste* | *The smell of onions was pretty strong.*

12 INFLUENCE/EFFECT a strong influence or effect has the power to change a situation or person in an important way: **have a strong influence/effect on sb/sth** *These events could have a strong influence on the outcome of the election.*

13 LIKELY likely to succeed or happen: *a strong candidate for best supporting actor* | **a strong possibility/probability/chance** *There is a strong possibility that he wouldn't survive.*

14 50/600/10,000 etc. strong used to give the number of people in a crowd or organization: *The crowd was over 100,000 strong.*

15 SKILLFUL/SUCCESSFUL very good or successful at doing something: *Dallas is a stronger team than Pittsburgh.* | *a strong economy*

16 ALCOHOL/DRUGS ETC. having a lot of a substance such as alcohol that gives something its effect: *strong pain killers* | *This margarita is really strong.*

17 DONE WELL done very well or skillfully OPP **weak**: *The stock gave another strong performance last year.*

18 sb's strong point/suit the thing someone does best: *Tact was never your strong suit.*

19 WIND/WATER ETC. strong wind, water etc. moves with great force

20 MONEY ECONOMICS a strong CURRENCY (=the type of money used in a country) does not easily lose its value compared with other currencies OPP **weak**

21 LIGHT/COLOR bright and easy to see OPP **weak**: *The light was not very strong.*

22 be (still) going strong to continue to be active or successful, even after a long time: *After 20 years, the band is still going strong.*

23 HEALTHY healthy, especially after you have been sick OPP **weak**: *I don't think her heart is very strong.*

24 ACCENT a strong ACCENT is a way of pronouncing words that shows clearly that someone comes from a particular area or country: *a strong Russian accent*

25 strong language speech or writing that contains a lot of swearing: *The film contains strong language and violence.*

26 WORDS/LANGUAGE ETC. openly criticizing someone or something: *strong words about the organization's mistakes*

27 NOSE/CHIN ETC. large and noticeable, especially in an attractive way OPP **weak**: *Imelda's strong features reflect her Indian heritage.*

28 sb is the strong silent type used to say that someone, usually a man, does not say very much but seems confident, physically strong, and interesting

29 a strong stomach a) the ability to watch something that shows people bleeding, being hurt etc. without feeling sick or upset: *It's a very violent film. You'll need a strong stomach to sit through it.* **b)** the ability to do something risky without becoming frightened

30 strong medicine a way of dealing with a problem that is very severe, but is expected to be effective

31 TECHNICAL a strong verb or form does not add a regular ending in the past tense, but may change a vowel OPP **weak**

[**Origin:** Old English *strang*] → see also **come on strong/fast** at COME ON (8), STRONGLY

ˌstrong ˈacid *n.* [C] CHEMISTRY an acid that completely separates into IONS (=atoms with an electric charge) when it is mixed with water → see also WEAK ACID

ˈstrong-ˌarm *adj.* [only before noun] INFORMAL **strong-arm methods/tactics etc.** methods that use force or violence, especially when this is not necessary —**strong-arm** *v.* [T]

ˌstrong ˈbase *n.* [C] CHEMISTRY a BASE (=chemical substance that combines with an acid to form a salt) that separates completely into HYDROXIDE IONS and metal ions when it is mixed with water → see also WEAK BASE

strong·box /ˈstrɔŋbɑks/ *n.* [C] a box, usually made of metal, that can be locked and that valuable things are kept in

strong e'lectrolyte *n.* [C] CHEMISTRY a liquid that allows electricity to travel through it effectively because it contains a lot of IONS (=atoms with an electric charge) → see also WEAK ELECTROLYTE

strong·hold /'strɒŋhoʊld/ *n.* [C] **1** an area where there is a lot of support for a particular attitude, way of life, political party etc.: *a traditional Democratic stronghold* **2** an area that is strongly defended by a military group: *a rebel stronghold*

strong inter'action also **ˌstrong 'force** *n.* [singular] PHYSICS the force that keeps PROTONS and NEUTRONS together in the NUCLEUS of an atom → see also WEAK INTERACTION

strong·ly /'strɒŋli/ W3 *adv.*
1 BELIEVING if you feel or believe something strongly, you are very sure and serious about it: *We strongly believe that she is innocent.*
2 VERY MUCH very much or to a high level or degree: *He was strongly attracted to one of his co-workers.*
3 EXPRESSING OPINION in a way that shows you really want to persuade someone to do something: **strongly urge/advise/encourage** *Her doctor strongly advised her to stop smoking.*
4 SMELL/TASTE in a way that is easy to smell or taste: *Harold's suit smelled strongly of mothballs.*
5 WITH FORCE with a lot of power or physical force: *The wind blew strongly.*
6 NOT EASILY DAMAGED in a way that is not easily damaged, broken, or destroyed: *a strongly built house*
7 LIKELY TO SUCCEED in a way that shows a lot of activity or energy and seems likely to be successful: *The album is selling strongly.*

strong·man /'strɒŋmæn/ *n. plural* **strongmen** /-mɛn/ [C] **1** a man with a lot of political power who uses force to keep that power **2** a very strong man who performs at a CIRCUS

strong-'minded *adj.* not easily influenced by other people to change what you believe or want SYN determined OPP weak-minded —**strong-mindedly** *adv.* —**strong-mindedness** *n.* [U]

strong room *n.* [C] a special room in a bank, shop etc. where valuable objects can be kept safely

strong-'willed *adj.* knowing exactly what you want to do and being determined to achieve it, even if other people advise you against it OPP weak-willed

stron·ti·um /'strɑnṭiəm/ *n.* [U] SYMBOL **Sr** CHEMISTRY a soft metal that is one of the chemical ELEMENTS

strop /strɑp/ *n.* [C] a narrow piece of leather used to make RAZORS sharp

strove /stroʊv/ *v.* the past tense of STRIVE

struck /strʌk/ *v.* the past tense and past participle of STRIKE

struc·tur·al /'strʌktʃərəl/ Ac *adj.* relating to the structure of something: *structural damage* | *structural changes in the economy* —**structurally** *adv.*

structural engi'neer *n.* [C] an engineer skilled in planning the building of large structures such as bridges —**structural engineering** *n.* [U]

struc·tur·al·ism /'strʌktʃərəˌlɪzəm/ *n.* [U] ENG. LANG. ARTS a method of studying language, literature, society etc. in which you examine the different parts or ideas in a subject to find a common pattern —**structuralist** *adj., n.*

struc·ture¹ /'strʌktʃɚ/ Ac S2 W2 *n.*
1 HOW THINGS ARE CONNECTED [C,U] the way in which the parts of something are connected with each other and form a whole: *good sentence structure* | *The cells have a similar structure.*
2 BUILDING [C] something that has been built, especially something large such as a building or bridge: *a large glass and concrete structure*
3 RELATIONSHIPS [C,U] the way in which relationships between people or groups are organized in a society or in an organization: *the structure of society* | *a new management structure* | **social/political/economic structure** *changes in the traditional political structure* | *challenges to the existing* ***power structure*** (=the way society gives power to particular people)
4 ORGANIZED SITUATION [C,U] the condition of having ideas, activities etc. that are carefully organized and planned: *Children need structure and stability.*
5 STH THAT FORMS [C] BIOLOGY something that forms or grows naturally, especially a part of a person, animal, or plant: *bony structures in the arm*
[**Origin:** 1400–1500 Latin *structura* **act of building**, from *struere* **to make into a pile, build**]

structure² Ac *v.* [T] to arrange the different parts of something into a pattern or system in which each part is connected to the others: *He still has not decided how to structure the business.*

struc·tured /'strʌktʃɚd/ Ac *adj.* carefully organized, planned, or arranged: *The school day is* ***highly structured.*** | *a* ***loosely structured*** (=planned, but without involving too many details) *program of events*

stru·del /'strudl/ *n.* [C,U] a type of Austrian or German cake, made of PASTRY with fruit inside

strug·gle¹ /'strʌgəl/ W2 *v.* [I] **1** to try extremely hard to achieve something, or deal with something, even though it is very difficult and you may not be completely successful: *Johnny is struggling in school.* | **struggle to do sth** *I struggled to keep from crying.* | **+with** *The airline is struggling with high fuel costs.* | **+for** *Millions of people are struggling for survival.* **2** to use all your power to fight against someone who is attacking you or holding you: **+with/against** *Liz struggled fiercely with her attacker.* | **+for** *The two men struggled for the gun.* **3** to move somewhere with great difficulty: **+toward/into etc.** *Fern struggled up the stairs to her bedroom.* **4** to use a lot of energy to try to do or move something that is very difficult to do or move: **+with** *I struggled with the window but couldn't get it open.*
struggle on *phr. v.* to continue doing something that you find difficult, tiring etc.

struggle² W2 *n.* **1** [C,U] a long hard fight to get freedom, political rights etc.: **+for** *the nation's struggle for independence* | *a* ***power struggle*** *for control of the party* | **+against** *a struggle against the government* ►see THESAURUS box at **fight²** **2** [C,U] a long period of time in which you try to deal with a difficult problem, disease etc.: **+with/against** *Kelly's struggle with cancer* **3** [C] a fight between two people for something, or an attempt by one person to escape from the other: *Police said there were no signs of a struggle.* **4 be a struggle (for sb)** to be an activity, job etc. that is very difficult for someone to do: *Reading is a struggle for Tim.*

strum /strʌm/ *v.* **strummed, strumming** [I,T] to play an instrument such as a GUITAR by moving your fingers up and down across its strings

strum·pet /'strʌmpɪt/ *n.* [C] OLD USE an insulting word meaning a woman who has sex for money

strung /strʌŋ/ *v.* the past tense and past participle of STRING

ˌstrung 'out, strung-out *adj.* INFORMAL **1** strongly affected by drugs and unable to react normally: *strung-out junkies* | **+on** *The kids were all strung out on drugs.* **2** extremely tired and worried

strut¹ /strʌt/ *v.* **strutted, strutting** [I] **1** to walk proudly with your head high and your chest pushed forward, showing that you think you are important: *Jackson strutted around on stage between songs.* **2 strut your stuff** INFORMAL to show your skill at doing something [**Origin:** Old English *strutian* **to make an effort**]

strut² *n.* **1** [C] a long thin piece of metal or wood used to support a part of a building, the wing of an aircraft etc. **2** [singular] a proud way of walking, with your head high and your chest pushed forward

strych·nine /'strɪknaɪn, -nən, -nin/ *n.* [U] a very poisonous substance sometimes used in small amounts as a medicine

Stu·art /'stuɚt/ the name of the royal family that ruled Scotland from 1371 to 1603, and ruled Britain from 1603 to 1649 and from 1660 to 1714

stub¹ /stʌb/ *n.* [C] **1** the short part that is left when the rest of something long and thin, such as a cigarette or pencil, has been used: *a cigar stub* **2** the part of a ticket that is returned to you after it has been torn, as proof that you have paid **3** a piece of a check that is left after the main part has been torn off **4** something that is short, because the rest of it has been cut off, or because it has not developed

stub² *v.* **stubbed**, **stubbing** [T] **stub your toe** to hurt your toe by hitting it against something ►see THESAURUS box at **hit¹**

stub sth ↔ **out** *phr. v.* to stop a cigarette from burning by pressing the end of it against something

stub·ble /ˈstʌbəl/ *n.* [U] **1** short stiff hairs that grow on a man's face, a woman's legs etc. when they have not SHAVED for a period of time **2** short stiff pieces left in the fields after wheat, corn etc. has been cut —**stubbly** *adj.*

stub·born /ˈstʌbɚn/ *adj.* **1** DISAPPROVING determined not to change your mind, even when people think you are being unreasonable: *Why are you so stubborn?* | *Amos has* ***a stubborn streak*** (=stubborn part of his character) *that makes him very difficult to work with.* | *She's* ***as stubborn as a mule*** (=very stubborn). **2 stubborn opposition/determination/resistance etc.** very strong and determined opposition, desire to do something etc. **3** difficult to remove, deal with, or use: *stubborn stains* —**stubbornly** *adv.* —**stubbornness** *n.* [U]

stub·by /ˈstʌbi/ *adj.* *comparative* **stubbier**, *superlative* **stubbiest** short and thick or fat: *stubby little fingers*

stuc·co /ˈstʌkoʊ/ *n.* [U] a type of PLASTER or CEMENT mixture that is used especially to cover the outside walls of houses

stuck¹ /stʌk/ *v.* the past tense and past participle of STICK

stuck² *adj.* [not before noun] **1** firmly fastened or attached in a particular position and unable to move or be moved: *This drawer is stuck.* | **+in** *The boat was stuck in the mud.* | *The candy* ***got stuck*** *in my teeth.* | *Somehow he* ***got*** *his toe* ***stuck*** *in the drain.* **2** unable to move forward quickly or at all because there are vehicles or people in front of you: *We would have been here sooner, but we were* ***stuck in traffic***. **3** unable to do any more of something that you are working on because it is too difficult: *Can you help me with my homework, Dad? I'm stuck.* **4** unable to escape from a boring or difficult situation: **+in/at** *Bob was stuck in meetings all afternoon.* **5 be stuck with sb/sth** to be unable to get rid of someone or something you do not want to keep or deal with: *We're only renting the house, so we're stuck with this wallpaper.* **6 be stuck for sth** to be unable to think of something or to find something that you need to have: *For once Anthony was stuck for words.* **7 be stuck on sb** INFORMAL to be attracted to someone

ˌstuck-ˈup *adj.* INFORMAL DISAPPROVING proud and unfriendly because you think you are better and more important than other people

stud /stʌd/ *n.* **1** [C] a small round piece of metal or stone on a stick that goes through your ear, nose, tongue etc. as jewelry **2** [C] INFORMAL a man who is very sexually attractive **3** [C] an upright board in a wall that is used to form the frame of a house **4** [C] a small round piece of metal that is stuck into a surface for decoration **5 a)** [U] the use of animals, such as horses, for breeding: *a stud farm* **b)** [C] a male animal with good qualities, especially a horse or dog, used for breeding **6** [C] a small piece of metal on a TIRE, that prevents slipping on snow and ice

stud·book /ˈstʌdbʊk/ *n.* [C] a list of names of race horses from which other race horses have been bred

stud·ded /ˈstʌdɪd/ *adj.* **1** decorated with a lot of studs or small jewels etc.: *a studded belt* | **jewel-studded/silver-studded/nail-studded etc.** *a diamond-studded watch* **2 studded with sth** WRITTEN covered or filled with a lot of something → see also STAR-STUDDED

stu·dent /ˈstudnt/ S1 W1 *n.* [C] **1** someone who is studying at a school, college etc.: *high school students* | **a law/a medical/an engineering etc. student** *a first-year medical student at UCSF* | **an undergraduate/a graduate student** (=a student who is taking courses for his or her first university degree, or after completing this degree) | **a student teacher/nurse** (=someone who is learning to be a teacher or nurse) | **a (straight) A/B/C etc. student** (=someone who always earns A's, B's etc. for their school work) **2 a student of sth** someone who is very interested in a particular subject: *a student of human nature*

ˌstudent ˈbody *n.* [C] all of the students in a high school, college, or university, considered as a group

ˌstudent ˈcouncil *n.* [C,U] the group of students at a school who are elected to represent the students in meetings and who organize school activities

ˌstudent ˈgovernment *n.* [C,U] the group of students in a school or college who are elected to represent the students in meetings and who organize school activities

ˌstudent ˈloan *n.* [C] a method of paying for your education in which college students borrow money from a bank or the government and repay it when they start working

ˌstudent ˈteaching *n.* [U] the period of time during which students who are learning to be teachers practice teaching in a school

ˌstudent ˈunion *n.* [C] **1** a building at a college where students go to meet socially, buy books, relax etc. **2** an organization of students at a college or university who are concerned with students' rights

stud·ied /ˈstʌdid/ *adj.* a studied way of behaving is deliberate and often not sincere, because it has been planned carefully

stu·di·o /ˈstudiˌoʊ/ S3 W2 *n.* *plural* **studios** [C]
1 FOR RECORDING ENG. LANG. ARTS a room where television and radio programs are made and broadcast, or where music is recorded: *a recording studio*
2 MOVIE COMPANY also **studios** [singular] ENG. LANG. ARTS a movie company or the buildings it owns and uses to make its movies: *Universal Studios*
3 ARTIST'S ROOM ENG. LANG. ARTS a room where a painter or photographer regularly works
4 ART COMPANY ENG. LANG. ARTS a company that produces pictures or photographs
5 APARTMENT also **studio apartment** a small apartment with one main room
6 DANCE/MUSIC ROOM ENG. LANG. ARTS a room where dancing or music lessons are given, or that dancers use to practice in

ˌstudio ˈaudience *n.* [C] a group of people who watch and are sometimes involved in a television or radio program while it is being made

stu·di·ous /ˈstudiəs/ *adj.* **1** spending a lot of time studying and reading **2** careful in your work: *studious attention to detail* —**studiously** *adv.* —**studiousness** *n.* [U]

ˌstud ˈpoker *n.* [U] a type of POKER (=card game) in which each player has one or more cards face up, so that the other players can see them

stud·y¹ /ˈstʌdi/ S1 W1 *n.* *plural* **studies**
1 PIECE OF WORK [C] a piece of work that is done to find out more about a particular subject or problem, and usually includes a written report: *a scientific study* | **+of/into** *a study of children with polio* | *studies into the causes of climate change* | **make/conduct/carry out etc. a study** *The study was carried out between January and May 2001.*
2 SUBJECT [U] a particular type of subject that people learn about and study, especially a science: *Linguistics* ***is the study of*** *language.*
3 studies [plural] used in the names of subjects that people study: *a class in Chinese studies*
4 sb's studies [plural] the work that someone does in order to learn about a particular subject, especially the

classes they take at a college or university: *Karen gave up her studies when she had a baby.*
5 ROOM [C] a room in a house that is used for work or studying
6 CAREFUL THOUGHT [U] the act of examining something very carefully and in a lot of detail: *The report merits careful study.*
7 be a study in sth to be a perfect example of something: *Franklin and Eleanor Roosevelt were a study in contrasts.*
8 SCHOOL WORK [U] the activity of studying for school, college etc.: *His full-time job leaves little time for study.*
9 ART [C] a small detailed drawing, especially one that is done to prepare for a large painting: *Renoir's studies of flowers*
10 MUSIC [C] ENG. LANG. ARTS a piece of music, usually for piano, that is often intended for practice
[**Origin:** 1100–1200 Old French *estudie*, from Latin *studium* **mental effort, eagerness, study**]

study² S1 W1 *v.* **studies, studied, studying**
1 FOR A CLASS/TEST [I] to do work such as reading to prepare for a class, test etc.: *She's always studying.* | **+for** *I have to stay home and study for a quiz.*
2 LEARN ABOUT A SUBJECT [I,T] to learn about a subject by spending time reading, going to classes etc.: *He's studying biology at college.* | **study to be a doctor/lawyer etc.** *Alex is studying to be an engineer.* | **+for** *Several of the young men were studying for the priesthood.* | *He* ***studied*** *violin* ***under*** (=was trained by) *Andor Toth.* ►see THESAURUS box at **learn**, **school¹**
3 EXAMINE A PROCESS [T] to watch and examine something carefully over a period of time in order to find out more about it: *He studied the behavior of gorillas.* | **study how/why/when etc.** *They're studying how stress affects health.*
4 CONSIDER STH [T] to spend a lot of time carefully examining a plan, document, problem etc.: *We are studying the possibility of moving our offices.* | **study how/why/when etc.** *University officials are studying how to increase enrollment.*
5 LOOK AT STH [T] to look at something very carefully: *They studied the map for a few moments.*

ˈstudy group *n.* [C,U] a group of students that meets in order to help each other study for a class at a college, or the time when they do this

ˈstudy hall *n.* [U] a period of time during a school day when a student must go to a particular place to study instead of to a regular class

stuff¹ /stʌf/ S1 W2 *n.* [U]
1 SUBSTANCE INFORMAL a substance or material of any kind: *What's that sticky stuff on the table?*
2 THINGS INFORMAL a number of different things: *They sent me a bunch of stuff about the university.* | *Where's all the camping stuff?* | **sb's stuff** *You can put your stuff over here for now.* ►see THESAURUS box at **property**
3 IDEAS INFORMAL the things that people say, think, write etc.: **+about** *She said some mean stuff about my brother.* | *You don't believe* ***all that stuff****, do you?* | *I try not to think about* ***stuff like that****.*
4 ACTIVITIES INFORMAL the activities that someone does: *I've got so much stuff to do this weekend.*
5 WORK/ART INFORMAL something someone has made, written, painted etc.: *I've read some of her stuff.*
6 ...and stuff SPOKEN INFORMAL used for saying that there are other things, ideas, actions etc. similar to what you have just mentioned, without saying exactly what they are: *He used to yell at me and stuff.*
7 do/show your stuff SPOKEN to do what you are good at or what you have trained or prepared to do
8 the stuff of dreams/fantasy/novels etc. exactly the kind of thing that dreams, FANTASY, NOVELS etc. consist of: *What Johnson did at the Olympics is the stuff of legend.*
9 CHARACTER [U] INFORMAL the qualities of someone's character: *Becky's got* ***the right stuff*** (=qualities that make her able to deal with difficulties) *to become a good doctor.* | *I thought you were* ***made of sterner stuff*** (=more determined).
[**Origin:** 1300–1400 Old French *estoffe*, from *estoffer* **to provide with things needed**] → see also **the hard stuff** at HARD¹ (15), **hot stuff** at HOT (13), **kid stuff** at KID¹ (4), **know your stuff** at KNOW¹ (63), **strut your stuff** at STRUT¹ (2)

stuff² W3 *v.*
1 PUSH [T always + adv./prep.] to push or put something into a small space, especially in a careless hurried way: **stuff sth into/in/up etc. sth** *I stuffed some clothes into a bag.*
2 FILL [T] to fill something until it is full: **stuff sth with sth** *He stuffed his pockets with candy.*
3 FILL WITH STH SOFT [T] to fill something with soft material: **stuff sth with sth** *She stuffed the rag doll with old socks.*
4 FOOD [T] to fill a chicken, TOMATO etc. with a mixture of bread or rice, onion etc.
5 DEAD ANIMAL [T] to fill the skin of a dead animal in order to make the animal look alive
6 stuff yourself (with sth) also **stuff your face (with sth)** INFORMAL to eat so much food that you cannot eat anything else
7 sb can stuff sth INFORMAL IMPOLITE used to say very angrily or rudely that you do not want what someone is offering

stuffed /stʌft/ S3 *adj.*
1 FULL [not before noun] completely full, so that nothing more will fit in: *The trunk was* ***stuffed full of*** *old books.*
2 UNABLE TO EAT MORE [not before noun] completely full, so that you cannot eat any more
3 FOOD filled with a mixture of something such as bread or rice, onion etc.: *stuffed peppers*
4 TOY [only before noun] a stuffed toy is a cloth figure that has been filled with a soft substance: *There were* ***stuffed animals*** *all over her bed.*
5 DEAD ANIMAL a stuffed dead animal has been filled with a substance so it looks like it did when it was alive

ˌstuffed ˈshirt *n.* [C] DISAPPROVING someone who behaves in a very formal way and thinks that they are important

ˌstuffed-ˈup *adj.* if you or your nose is stuffed-up, you are unable to breathe easily through your nose because you have a cold

stuff·ing /ˈstʌfɪŋ/ *n.* [U] **1** a mixture of bread, onion, HERBS, and other foods, that you put inside a chicken, TURKEY etc. before cooking it SYN **dressing** **2** soft material that is used to fill something such as a CUSHION → see also

stuff·y /ˈstʌfi/ *adj. comparative* **stuffier**, *superlative* **stuffiest** **1** a stuffy room or building does not have enough fresh air in it: *It's very stuffy in here.* **2** DISAPPROVING a stuffy person is too formal and has old-fashioned ideas —**stuffily** *adv.* —**stuffiness** *n.* [U]

stul·ti·fy·ing /ˈstʌltəˌfaɪ-ɪŋ/ *adj.* extremely boring and making you lose the ability to think of new ideas: *a stultifying job* [**Origin:** 1700–1800 Late Latin *stultificare* **to make stupid**, from Latin *stultus* **stupid**] —**stultify** *v.* [T] —**stultification** /ˌstʌltəfəˈkeɪʃən/ *n.* [U]

stum·ble /ˈstʌmbəl/ *v.* **1** [I] to hit your foot against something or put your foot down awkwardly while you are walking or running, so that you almost fall: *One runner stumbled and almost fell.* | **+over/on** *I stumbled over the step.* ►see THESAURUS box at **fall¹** **2** [I always + adv./prep.] to walk in an unsteady way and often almost fall: **+in/out/across etc.** *He was stumbling around in the dark.* **3** [I always + adv./prep.] to stop or make a mistake when you are reading to people or speaking: **+over/at/through** *Harrison stumbled through his speech.* —**stumble** *n.* [C]
stumble across sb/sth *phr. v.* to discover something or meet someone when you do not expect to SYN **stumble on**: *I stumbled across one of my old diaries.*
stumble into sth *phr. v.* to become involved in something by chance: *I really just stumbled into acting.*
stumble on/upon sb/sth *phr. v.* to discover something or meet someone when you do not expect to SYN **stumble across**

S

ˈstumbling ˌblock *n.* [C] a problem or difficulty that prevents you from achieving something: +**to** *the main stumbling blocks to progress*

stump¹ /stʌmp/ *n.* [C] **1** BIOLOGY the bottom part of a tree that is left in the ground after the rest of it has been cut down **2** the short part of someone's leg, arm etc. that remains after the rest of it has been cut off **3** the small useless part of something that remains after most of it has broken off or worn away **4 on the stump** if a politician is on the stump, he or she is on a trip, making public speeches, meeting voters, and trying to get their support

stump² *v.* **1** [T] to ask someone such a difficult question that they are completely unable to think of an answer: *The case has stumped the police for months.* **2** [I,T] POLITICS to travel around an area, meeting people and making speeches in order to gain political support **3** [I + up/along/across] to walk with heavy steps [SYN] **stomp** —**stumped** *adj.* [not before noun]

ˈstump speech *n.* [C] a speech made by a politician while traveling around to get political support

stump·y /ˈstʌmpi/ *adj. comparative* **stumpier**, *superlative* **stumpiest** INFORMAL short and thick in an unattractive way

S

stun /stʌn/ *v.* **stunned**, **stunning** [T not in progressive] **1** to surprise or upset someone so much that they do not react immediately: *The decision stunned many people.* **2** to make someone unconscious for a short time: *The impact of the ball had stunned her.* → see also STUNNED, STUNNING

stung /stʌŋ/ *v.* the past tense and past participle of STING

ˈstun gun *n.* [C] a weapon that produces a very strong electric current and can be used to make animals or people unconscious

stunk /stʌŋk/ *v.* a past tense and the past participle of STINK

stunned /stʌnd/ *adj.* **1** too surprised or shocked to speak: *He looked completely stunned.* | *The audience sat in **stunned silence**.* ►see THESAURUS box at **surprised** **2** almost unconscious and unable to move normally, especially because you have been hit on the head

stun·ner /ˈstʌnɚ/ *n.* [C] INFORMAL **1** someone or something that is very attractive or impressive, especially a woman **2** something that surprises you, especially a situation or event

stun·ning /ˈstʌnɪŋ/ *adj.* **1** extremely attractive or beautiful: *You look stunning.* ►see THESAURUS box at **attractive**, **beautiful** **2** very surprising or shocking: *a stunning victory* ►see THESAURUS box at **surprising** —**stunningly** *adv.*

stunt¹ /stʌnt/ *n.* **1** [C] a dangerous action that is done to entertain people, especially in a movie **2** [C] DISAPPROVING something that is done to attract people's attention, especially in advertising or politics → see also PUBLICITY STUNT **3 pull a stunt** DISAPPROVING to do something that is silly or embarrassing, or that is slightly dangerous: *The next time you pull a stunt like that, you're fired.*

stunt² *v.* [T] to stop someone or something from growing to their full size or developing correctly: *Does coffee really **stunt** your **growth**?*

ˈstunt man *n.* [C] a man whose job is to take the place of an actor when something dangerous has to be done in a movie

ˈstunt ˌwoman *n.* [C] a woman whose job is to take the place of an actress when something dangerous has to be done in a movie

stu·pa /ˈstupə/ *n.* [C] a holy Buddhist structure with a round roof

stu·pe·fied /ˈstupəˌfaɪd/ *adj.* **1** extremely surprised or shocked **2** unable to act or think clearly —**stupefy** *v.* [T] —**stupefaction** /ˌstupəˈfækʃən/ *n.* [U]

stu·pe·fy·ing /ˈstupəˌfaɪ-ɪŋ/ *adj.* **1** making you feel extremely surprised or shocked: *a stupefying amount of money* **2** making you unable to act or think clearly —**stupefy** *v.* [T]

stu·pen·dous /stuˈpɛndəs/ *adj.* [no comparative] extremely large or impressive: *a stupendous achievement* —**stupendously** *adv.*

stu·pid /ˈstupɪd/ [S1] [W3] *adj.* **1** showing a lack of good sense or good judgment [SYN] **dumb**: *We did a lot of stupid things in high school.* | *a stupid question* | **it is stupid (of sb) to do sth** *It was stupid of me to give her money.* | *That was a really **stupid thing to do**.* **2** OFFENSIVE having a low level of intelligence, so that you have difficulty learning or understanding things [SYN] **dumb**: *She understands – she's not stupid.* | **feel/look stupid** *Her college friends make me feel stupid.* **3** SPOKEN making you annoyed or impatient [SYN] **dumb**: *I can't get this stupid radio to work.* | *That shirt **looks stupid** with those pants.* **4 stupid with shock/exhaustion/fear etc.** LITERARY unable to think clearly because you are extremely shocked, tired, frightened etc. [**Origin:** 1500–1600 French *stupide*, from Latin *stupidus*, from *stupere* **to surprise extremely, stun**] —**stupidly** *adv.*: *Stupidly, she took their advice.*

stu·pid·i·ty /stuˈpɪdət̬i/ *n. plural* **stupidities** **1** [C,U] behavior that shows a lack of thought or good judgment: *He was injured because of his own stupidity.* **2** [U] the quality of having a low level of intelligence so that you have difficulty learning or understanding things

stu·por /ˈstupɚ/ *n.* [C,U] a state in which you cannot think, speak, see, or hear clearly, usually because you have drunk too much alcohol or taken drugs: *He spent his wedding night **in a drunken stupor**.*

stur·dy /ˈstɚdi/ *adj. comparative* **sturdier**, *superlative* **sturdiest** **1** a sturdy object is strong, well-made, and not easily broken: *The table was old but sturdy.* | *sturdy walking boots* ►see THESAURUS box at **strong** **2** strong and healthy-looking but not thin: *sturdy legs* **3** [only before noun] determined and not easily persuaded to change your opinions [**Origin:** 1200–1300 Old French *estourdi* **stupidly brave, stunned**, from Vulgar Latin *exturdire* **to behave like a thrush that has got drunk from eating grapes**] —**sturdily** *adv.* —**sturdiness** *n.* [U]

stur·geon /ˈstɚdʒən/ *n.* [C,U] BIOLOGY a large fish, from which CAVIAR is obtained, or the meat of this fish

stut·ter¹ /ˈstʌt̬ɚ/ *v.* **1** [I,T] to speak with difficulty because you cannot stop yourself from repeating the first CONSONANT of some words → see also STAMMER ►see THESAURUS box at **say¹** **2** [I] if something such as a machine stutters, it makes quick exploding noises and does not work smoothly

stutter² *n.* [C usually singular] an inability to speak normally because you stutter

St. Vin·cent and the Gren·a·dines /seɪnt ˌvɪnsənt ən ðə ˈgrɛnədinz/ a country that consists of a group of islands in the Caribbean Sea

sty /staɪ/ *n. plural* **sties** [C] **1** also **stye** MEDICINE an infected place on the edge of your EYELID, which becomes red and swollen **2** a place where pigs are kept [SYN] **pigsty** **3** a very messy or dirty room [SYN] **pigsty**

Styg·i·an /ˈstɪdʒiən/ *adj.* LITERARY dark and making you feel nervous or afraid [**Origin:** 1500–1600 Latin *stygius*, from Greek, from *Styx* river in ancient Greek stories which people cross over when they die]

style¹ /staɪl/ [AC] [S2] [W1] *n.*
1 WAY OF MAKING/PERFORMING [C,U] a particular way of performing, designing, or producing something, especially one that is typical of a particular person, group, period of time, place etc.: +**of** *the Italian style of cooking* | **a writing/playing/singing etc. style** *Hemingway's direct writing style* | **an architectural/a musical etc. style** *I like a wide variety of musical styles.* | **in (a/the) classical/Gothic/1920s etc. style** *The paintings are done in an expressionistic style.* | **in the style of sb/sth** *a painting in the style of Van Gogh*
2 WAY OF BEHAVING/DOING [C] the particular way that someone deals with something or behaves, especially

one that expresses a particular attitude: +**of** *Voters seem to like his style of leadership.* | **a management/teaching/directing etc. style** *She has a very informal teaching style.* | *Confrontation* ***is not*** *his* ***style.*** | *I like your* ***style*** (=approve of the way you do things), *Simpson.* | *I think a job at the bank would be* ***more*** *her* ***style*** (=more typical of what she does or likes).
3 FASHION/DESIGN [C,U] a particular design or fashion for something such as clothes, hair, furniture etc.: *the latest styles for this season* | +**of** *a new style of sunglasses* | *Are tight jeans* ***in style*** (=fashionable) *this year?*
4 FASHIONABLE QUALITY [U] the quality of being fashionable and stylish: *The room was decorated* ***with style.*** | *Teenagers like to develop their own* ***sense of style.*** → see also STYLISH
5 ATTRACTIVE QUALITY [U] a confident and attractive quality that makes people admire you, and that is shown in your appearance or the way you do things: *Sue may be hard to work with, but she definitely* ***has style.*** | *The spokesman handled all the questions* ***with style.***
6 USE OF LANGUAGE [C,U] a particular set of rules for using words, FORMATting documents, spelling etc.: *It's not considered good style to use abbreviations in essays.* → see also STYLISTIC
7 in style a) fashionable at the present time: *Short hair is back in style.* **b)** in a very impressive, expensive, or comfortable way: **in great/grand/fine etc. style** *Leonora arrived at the ball in grand style.*
8 out of style not fashionable at the present time: *Some clothes never go out of style.*
9 FLOWER [C] BIOLOGY the long thin part of the female structure in a flower, that is between the OVARY and the STIGMA → see picture at FLOWER[1]
[**Origin:** 1200–1300 Latin *stilus* **pointed stick, stylus, style of writing**] → see also **cramp sb's style** at CRAMP[2] (3)

style[2] Ac *v.* [T] **1** to cut someone's hair in a particular way: *I only let Betty style my hair.* **2** [usually passive] ENG. LANG. ARTS to design something such as clothing, furniture, or cars **3 style yourself (as) sth** FORMAL to give yourself a particular title or name, or to behave as if you are a particular type of person: *He styles himself as a tough guy.* → see also SELF-STYLED

style sth **on/after** sth *phr. v.* to copy the style or appearance of something

-style /staɪl/ *suffix* **1** [in adjectives] like something that is typical of a particular place, period of history, person etc.: *Victorian-style buildings* **2** [in adverbs] in a way that is typical of a particular type of person or thing: *He likes to cook Japanese-style.*

sty·ling[1] /ˈstaɪlɪŋ/ *n.* [U] **1** the process of cutting or arranging someone's hair: *styling products* **2 stylings** [plural] the way in which someone performs music, jokes etc.: *breathy vocal stylings* **3** the design and appearance of an object, especially a car or furniture

styling[2] also **stylin'** /ˈstaɪlɪn/ Ac *adj.* SLANG attractive and fashionable SYN **cool**

ˈstyling ˌbrush *n.* [C] a heated brush used, especially by women, to make their hair a particular shape

styl·ish /ˈstaɪlɪʃ/ Ac *adj.* attractive in a fashionable way: *a stylish black suit* —**stylishly** *adv.* —**stylishness** *n.* [U]

styl·ist /ˈstaɪlɪst/ *n.* [C] **1** someone who cuts or arranges people's hair as their job **2** ENG. LANG. ARTS someone who has carefully developed a good style of writing

sty·lis·tic /staɪˈlɪstɪk/ *adj.* ENG. LANG. ARTS related to the style of a piece of writing or art —**stylistically** /-kli/ *adv.*

sty·lis·tics /staɪˈlɪstɪks/ *n.* [U] ENG. LANG. ARTS the study of style in written or spoken language

styl·ized /ˈstaɪəˌlaɪzd/ Ac *adj.* ENG. LANG. ARTS drawn, written, or done in a style or way that is not normal, natural, or REALISTIC —**stylize** *v.* [T]

sty·lus /ˈstaɪləs/ *n. plural* **styluses** or **styli** /-laɪ/ [C] **1** COMPUTERS a pointed instrument like a pen used to write on a computer screen in order to put information into the computer **2** a pointed instrument used in the past for writing on WAX **3** the small pointed part of a RECORD PLAYER that touches the record

sty·mie /ˈstaɪmi/ *v.* [T] INFORMAL to prevent someone from doing what they have planned or want to do SYN **thwart**

sty·ptic pen·cil /ˈstɪptɪk ˌpɛnsəl/ *n.* [C] a type of medicine in the shape of a pencil that is used to stop the bleeding of small cuts, especially cuts from shaving (SHAVE)

Sty·ro·foam /ˈstaɪrəˌfoʊm/ *n.* [U] TRADEMARK a soft light plastic material that prevents heat or cold from passing through it, used especially to make containers: *a Styrofoam cup*

sua·sion /ˈsweɪʒən/ *n.* [U] FORMAL → PERSUASION

suave /swɑv/ *adj.* a suave man is polite, confident, and relaxed, sometimes in an insincere way [**Origin:** 1500–1600 French **pleasant, sweet**, from Latin *suavis*] —**suavely** *adv.* —**suavity, suaveness** *n.* [U]

sub[1] /sʌb/ *n.* [C] INFORMAL **1** a SUBMARINE **2** a long bread roll split open and filled with meat, cheese etc. SYN **submarine sandwich** **3** a SUBSTITUTE TEACHER **4** a SUBSTITUTE in sports such as football

sub[2] *v.* **subbed, subbing** [I] INFORMAL to act as a SUBSTITUTE for someone: +**for** *Roy's subbing for Chris in tonight's game.*

sub- /sʌb/ *prefix* **1** under or below a particular level or thing: *sub-zero temperatures* (=below zero) | *subtitles* **2** part of a bigger whole: *a subdivision of a large city* **3** less important or powerful than the main person or thing: *an electrical substation* **4** almost or nearly: *subtropical heat* **5** further south than another place: *sub-Saharan Africa*

sub·arc·tic /ˌsʌbˈɑrktɪk, -ˈɑrt̬ɪk/ *adj.* near the Arctic Circle, or typical of this area

subˌarctic ˈclimate *n.* [C usually singular] a type of weather with extremely cold winters and short warm summers, found for example in Alaska and Scandinavia → see also CONTINENTAL CLIMATE

sub·a·re·a /ˈsʌbˌɛriə/ *n.* [C] an area that is part of a larger area

sub·a·tom·ic /ˌsʌbəˈtɑmɪk◂/ *adj.* PHYSICS smaller than an atom or existing within an atom

ˌsubatomic ˈparticle *n.* [C] PHYSICS a piece of matter smaller than an atom

sub·com·mit·tee /ˈsʌbkəˌmɪt̬i/ *n.* [C] a small group formed from a committee to deal with a particular subject in more detail

sub·com·pact /ˌsʌbˈkɑmpækt/ *n.* [C] a type of very small and inexpensive car

sub·con·scious[1] /ˌsʌbˈkɑnʃəs/ *adj.* [no comparative] subconscious feelings, desires etc. are hidden in your mind and you do not know that you have them: *a subconscious fear of success* —**subconsciously** *adv.*

subconscious[2] also **subˌconscious ˈmind** *n.* [singular] the part of your mind that has thoughts and feelings that you do not always realize you have: *The anger was buried deep in her subconscious.*

sub·con·ti·nent /ˌsʌbˈkɑntˀn-ənt, -tənənt/ *n.* [C] **1** EARTH SCIENCE a very large area of land that is part of a CONTINENT **2 the (Indian) subcontinent** EARTH SCIENCE the area of land that includes India, Pakistan, and Bangladesh —**subcontinental** *adj.*

sub·con·tract /ˌsʌbˈkɑntrækt/ *v.* [T] also **subcontract sth ↔ out** if a company subcontracts work, they pay other people to do part of their work for them —**subcontract** *n.* [C]

sub·con·trac·tor /ˌsʌbˈkɑntræktɚ/ *n.* [C] someone who does part of the work of another person or firm

sub·cul·ture /ˈsʌbˌkʌltʃɚ/ *n.* [C] a particular group of people within a society and their behavior, beliefs, and activities, often a group that many people disapprove of: *the drug subculture of the inner city*

S

sub·cu·ta·ne·ous /ˌsʌbkyuˈteɪniəs◂ / *adj.* BIOLOGY beneath your skin: *subcutaneous fat* —**subcutaneously** *adv.*

sub·di·vide /ˌsʌbdəˈvaɪd, ˈsʌbdəˌvaɪd/ *v.* [T] to divide something that is already divided, into smaller parts or groups

sub·di·vi·sion /ˈsʌbdəˌvɪʒən/ *n.* **1** [C] an area of land that has been subdivided for building houses on **2** [C,U] the act of dividing something that has already been divided, or the parts that result from doing this

sub·due /səbˈdu/ *v.* [T] **1** to stop a person or group from behaving violently, especially by using force: *Police used pepper spray to subdue the man.* **2** FORMAL to take control of a place by defeating the people who live there **3** FORMAL to prevent your emotions from being so strong SYN **repress** [**Origin:** 1300–1400 Old French *soduire* **to lead into bad actions**, from Latin *subducere* **to remove**; influenced by Latin *subdere* **to force to obey**]

sub·dued /səbˈdud/ *adj.* **1** unusually quiet and possibly unhappy: *Richard seems very subdued tonight.* ▸see THESAURUS box at **quiet**[1] **2** with less excitement or activity than you would expect, or less busy than usual: *Inflation remained subdued in September.* **3** subdued lighting, colors etc. are not bright SYN **soft** **4** not loud SYN **quiet**: *subdued voices*

sub·freez·ing /ˌsʌbˈfrizɪŋ◂ / *adj.* subfreezing temperatures are below 32°F (0°C)

sub·group /ˈsʌbgrup/ *n.* [C] a separate, smaller, and sometimes less important part of a group

sub·head·ing /ˈsʌbˌhɛdɪŋ/ *n.* [C] a short phrase used as a title for a small part within a longer piece of writing

sub·hu·man /ˌsʌbˈhyumən◂ / *adj.* **1** not considered to have all the qualities of a normal human being, and therefore less valuable **2** subhuman conditions are very bad or cruel SYN **inhuman**

subj. a written abbreviation for SUBJECT

sub·ject[1] /ˈsʌbdʒɪkt/ S2 W1 *n.* [C]
1 THING TALKED ABOUT the thing you are talking about or considering in a conversation, discussion, book, movie etc. SYN **topic**: +**of** *The subject of childhood obesity is getting a lot of attention.* | *Stop* ***changing the subject*** (=starting to talk about something different)*!* | *Several good books have been written* ***on the subject of*** *personality disorders.* | *Can we just* ***drop the subject*** (=stop talking about it) *now, please?* | **be a subject of debate/discussion/gossip etc.** *Kennedy's death continues to be a subject of debate.* | **a delicate/sensitive/touchy subject** *You know money is a touchy subject with her.* | **get/be/stay off the subject** *Somehow we got off the subject and started talking about TV.*
2 SCHOOL an area of knowledge that you study at a school or college: *History was my favorite subject in school.*
3 TEST SCIENCE a person or animal that is used in a test or EXPERIMENT, especially a medical or PSYCHOLOGICAL one: *Half of the subjects were given caffeine.*
4 ART ENG. LANG. ARTS the thing you are dealing with when you paint a picture, take a photograph etc.: *Monet loved to use gardens as his subjects.*
5 GRAMMAR ENG. LANG. ARTS a noun, noun phrase, or PRONOUN that usually comes before a main verb and represents the person or thing that performs the action of the verb, or about which something is stated. For example, in the sentence "She hit John" the subject is "she," and in "Elephants are big" the subject is "elephants." → see also OBJECT: +**of** *the subject of the sentence*
6 COUNTRY someone who was born in a country that has a king or queen, or someone who has a right to live there → see also CITIZEN: *a British subject*
[**Origin:** 1300–1400 Old French, Latin *subjectus*, from *subicere* **to put under your control**]

subject[2] *adj.* **1 subject to sth a)** possibly or likely to be affected by something, especially something bad: *Several highways are subject to closing due to snow.* | *Prices are* ***subject to change*** *at any time.* **b)** dependent on something else: *The agreement is subject to approval by teachers.* **c)** if you are subject to a set of rules or laws, you must obey them: *When you are in a foreign country, you are subject to its laws.* **d)** if something is subject to a tax, charge etc., then that amount of money must be paid in connection to it **2** [only before noun] POLITICS a subject country, state, people etc. are strictly governed by another country or group of people

sub·ject[3] /səbˈdʒɛkt/ *v.*
subject to *phr. v.* **1 subject sb to sth** to force someone to experience something very bad, upsetting, or difficult, especially over a long time: *Police subjected him to hours of questioning.* **2 subject sth to sth** to make something be treated in a particular way or experience something: *The vaccine has been subjected to extensive laboratory tests.*

sub·jec·tion /səbˈdʒɛkʃən/ *n.* [U] FORMAL **1** the state of being ruled or controlled by someone SYN **subjugation** **2** the act or process of forcing a country or group of people to be ruled by you SYN **subjugation**

sub·jec·tive /səbˈdʒɛktɪv/ *adj.* **1** a subjective statement, report, attitude etc. is influenced by personal opinion and can therefore be unfair: *Hiring decisions can be very subjective.* **2** [no comparative] existing only in your mind or imagination: *Our perception of colors is subjective.* **3** ENG. LANG. ARTS related to the subject in grammar → see also OBJECTIVE —**subjectively** *adv.* —**subjectivity** /ˌsʌbdʒɛkˈtɪvəti/ *n.* [U]

ˈsubject ˌmatter *n.* [U] what is being talked about in speech or writing, or represented in art

sub·ju·gate /ˈsʌbdʒəˌgeɪt/ *v.* [T] to defeat a person or group and make them obey you —**subjugation** /ˌsʌbdʒəˈgeɪʃən/ *n.* [U]

sub·junc·tive /səbˈdʒʌŋktɪv/ *n.* [C,U] ENG. LANG. ARTS a verb form or a set of verb forms in grammar, used in some languages to express doubt, wishes, or possibility. For example, in "if I were you," "were" is the subjunctive of the verb "to be." → see also IMPERATIVE, INDICATIVE[2] —**subjunctive** *adj.*

sub·lease /ˈsʌblis/ *n.* [C] an agreement in which someone who rents property from its owner then rents that property to someone else —**sublease** *v.* [I,T]

sub·let /sʌbˈlɛt, ˈsʌblɛt/ *v. past tense and past participle* **sublet**, **subletting** [I,T] to rent to someone else a property that you rent from its owner —**sublet** /ˈsʌblɛt/ *n.* [C]

sub·li·mate /ˈsʌbləˌmeɪt/ *v.* [I,T] FORMAL to use the energy that comes from particular feelings and desires, especially sexual feelings, to do something that is more acceptable to society

sub·li·ma·tion /ˌsʌbləˈmeɪʃən/ *n.* [U] **1** FORMAL the process of sublimating **2** CHEMISTRY the process in which a solid substance changes into a gas, without ever becoming a liquid

sub·lime[1] /səˈblaɪm/ *adj.* [no comparative] **1** excellent in a way that makes you feel extremely happy **2** very great or extreme, especially in a way that shows that someone does not notice or care about what is happening around them: *sublime insensitivity* —**sublimely** *adv.* —**sublimeness** *n.* [U] —**sublimity** /səˈblɪməti/ *n.* [U]

sublime[2] *n.* **1 the sublime** something that has excellent qualities and that makes you feel extremely happy **2 from the sublime to the ridiculous** used to say that a serious and important thing or event is being followed by something silly, unimportant, or bad

sub·lim·i·nal /ˌsʌbˈlɪmənl/ *adj.* affecting your mind in a way and at a level that you are not conscious of: *They deny that their songs contain* ***subliminal messages.***

sub·lin·gual /ˌsʌbˈlɪŋgwəl/ *adj.* under your tongue

sub·ma·chine gun /ˌsʌbməˈʃin ˌgʌn/ *n.* [C] a type of MACHINE GUN that is light and easily carried

sub·ma·rine[1] /ˈsʌbməˌrin, ˌsʌbməˈrin/ *n.* [C] a ship, especially a military one, that can stay under water ▸see THESAURUS box at **ship**[1]

submarine² *adj.* [only before noun] TECHNICAL growing, used, or existing under the ocean: *submarine mountain ranges*

sub·ma·rin·er /ˌsʌbməˈrinɚ, ˌsʌbˈmærɪnɚ/ *n.* [C] a sailor who lives and works in a submarine

submarine 'sandwich *n.* [C] a SUB

sub·merge /səbˈmɚdʒ/ *v.* **1** [I,T] to go under the surface of water, or to put something under water or another liquid ▸see THESAURUS box at **dive¹** **2** [T] to hide something such as information or feelings SYN **suppress** **3 submerge yourself in sth** to make yourself very busy doing something SYN **immerse** —**submergence** *n.* [U]

sub·merged /səbˈmɚdʒd/ *adj.* just under the surface of water or another liquid: *submerged icebergs*

sub·mersed /səbˈmɚst/ *adj.* submersed plants live under the water

sub·mers·i·ble /səbˈmɚsəbəl/ *n.* [C] a vehicle that can travel under water

sub·mer·sion /səbˈmɚʒən/ *n.* [U] the activity of going under water, or the state of being completely covered in liquid

sub·mis·sion /səbˈmɪʃən/ Ac *n.* **1** [U] the state of accepting that someone has power over you and you have to obey them: **+to** *submission to the will of God* | **force/frighten/beat etc. sb into submission** *They often beat the wild horses into submission.* | *His head was bowed* ***in submission***. **2** [C,U] the act of giving a plan, piece of writing etc. to someone in authority for them to consider or approve, or the plan, piece of writing etc. itself: *Submissions must be received by May 1.* | **+of** *the deadline for the submission of proposals* | **+to** *Plans were drawn up for submission to the council.* **3** [C] LAW a request or suggestion that is given to a judge for them to consider

sub·mis·sive /səbˈmɪsɪv/ *adj.* always willing to obey someone, even if they are unkind to you —**submissively** *adv.* —**submissiveness** *n.* [U]

sub·mit /səbˈmɪt/ Ac S3 W3 *v.* **submitted, submitting** **1** [T] to give a plan, piece of writing etc. to someone in authority for them to consider or approve: **submit sth to sb/sth** *The agency must submit its budget to the board each July.* **2** [I,T] FORMAL to agree to obey a person, group, set of rules etc., or to agree to do something, especially because you have no choice: **+to** *Workers have refused to submit to drug tests.* | *He demanded that she submit to him.* **3** [T] FORMAL to suggest or say something: **submit that** *I submit that the judge was biased.* [**Origin:** 1300–1400 Latin *submittere* **to lower, submit**, from *mittere* **to send**]

sub·nor·mal /ˌsʌbˈnɔrməl◂/ *adj.* less or lower than normal: *subnormal temperatures*

sub·or·bit·al /ˌsʌbˈɔrbɪtl/ *adj.* TECHNICAL making less than one complete ORBIT (=trip around the Earth)

sub·or·di·nate¹ /səˈbɔrdənɪt/ Ac *n.* [C] someone who has a lower position and less authority than someone else in an organization

subordinate² Ac *adj.* [no comparative] **1** in a lower position with less authority than someone else: **+to** *The CIA Director is subordinate to the Secretary of Defense.* | **a subordinate role/status/position** *the subordinate role of women in many societies* **2** less important than something else: **+to** *The aims are subordinate to the mission's primary goal.* → see also SUBSERVIENT

sub·or·di·nate³ /səˈbɔrdnˌeɪt/ Ac *v.* [T] to put someone or something in a less important position: **subordinate sth to sb/sth** *Product research is often subordinated to sales tactics.* —**subordination** /səˌbɔrdnˈeɪʃən/ *n.* [U]

suˌbordinate 'clause *n.* [C] ENG. LANG. ARTS a DEPENDENT CLAUSE

sub·orn /səˈbɔrn/ *v.* [T] LAW to persuade someone to tell lies in a court of law or to do something else that is illegal, especially for money —**subornation** /ˌsʌbɔrˈneɪʃən/ *n.* [U]

sub·par /sʌbˈpɑr/ *adj.* below an expected level of quality: *a subpar performance*

sub·plot /ˈsʌbplɑt/ *n.* [C] ENG. LANG. ARTS a PLOT (=set of events) that is less important than and separate from the main plot in a story, play etc.

sub·poe·na¹ /səˈpinə/ *n.* [C] LAW a written order stating that you must come to a court of law and be a WITNESS or that a document must be produced in court

subpoena² *v.* **subpoenaed** [T] LAW to order someone to come to a court of law and be a WITNESS or say that a document must be produced in court

sub ro·sa /ˌsʌb ˈroʊzə/ *adv.* secretly —**sub-rosa** *adj.*

sub·rou·tine /ˈsʌbruˌtin/ *n.* [C] a part of a computer PROGRAM containing a set of instructions for doing a small job that is part of a larger job

sub·scribe /səbˈskraɪb/ *v.* **1** [I] to pay money to regularly have copies of a newspaper or magazine delivered to you, or to ask to receive something such as a NEWSLETTER by email OPP **unsubscribe**: **+to** *We subscribe to the "New York Times."* **2** ECONOMICS to give money regularly for a service: **+to** *Which Internet service provider do you subscribe to?* **3** to pay money regularly to be a member of an organization or to help its work **4** [T] FORMAL to sign your name [**Origin:** 1400–1500 Latin *subscribere*, from *scribere* **to write**]

subscribe to sth *phr. v.* if you subscribe to an idea, view etc., you agree with it or support it: *I have never subscribed to the belief that people are basically good.*

sub·scrib·er /səbˈskraɪbɚ/ *n.* [C] **1** someone who pays money to regularly receive copies of a newspaper or magazine, or who asks to receive something such as a NEWSLETTER by email: **+to** *subscribers to the magazine* **2** someone who gives money regularly for a service: *cable subscribers* **3** someone who pays money to be part of an organization or to help its work **4** someone who agrees with or supports a particular idea: **+to** *I'm not a big subscriber to that view.* **5** FORMAL someone who signs their name on a document

sub·script /ˈsʌbskrɪpt/ *adj.* [only before noun] written or printed next to and below a number, letter etc. → see also SUPERSCRIPT —**subscript** *n.* [C]

sub·scrip·tion /səbˈskrɪpʃən/ *n.* [C] **1** an amount of money you pay regularly to receive copies of a newspaper or magazine: *a newspaper subscription* | **+to** *A subscription to the magazine costs $29 a year.* | *You can* ***cancel your subscription*** *at any time.* **2** an amount of money you pay regularly for a service **3** an amount of money you pay regularly to be a member of an organization or to help its work

sub·sec·tion /ˈsʌbˌsɛkʃən/ *n.* [C] a part of a SECTION

sub·se·quent /ˈsʌbsəkwənt/ Ac *adj.* FORMAL **1** [only before noun] coming after or following something else: *Subsequent events proved me wrong.* ▸see THESAURUS box at **later²**, **next¹** **2 subsequent to sth** after something: *New evidence emerged subsequent to their conviction.* [**Origin:** 1400–1500 Latin, present participle of *subsequi* **to follow closely**, from *sequi* **to follow**] → see also CONSEQUENT

sub·se·quent·ly /ˈsʌbsəˌkwɛntli, -kwəntli/ Ac *adv.* FORMAL after an event in the past: *New safety guidelines were subsequently adopted.* ▸see THESAURUS box at **after³**

sub·ser·vi·ent /səbˈsɚviənt/ *adj.* **1** DISAPPROVING too willing to do what other people want you to do: **+to** *Women were expected to be subservient to men.* **2 subservient to sth** FORMAL less important than something else SYN **subordinate** —**subserviently** *adv.* —**subservience** *n.* [U]

sub·set /ˈsʌbsɛt/ *n.* [C] a set that is part of a larger set

sub·side /səbˈsaɪd/ *v.* [I] **1** if a feeling, noise, bad weather condition etc. subsides, it gradually becomes less strong or severe: *The pain began to subside.* **2** FORMAL if something such as water, land, or a building subsides, it gradually sinks to a lower level **3** EARTH SCIENCE if water, especially flood water, subsides, it gradually goes under the ground or back to a normal level

sub·si·dence /səbˈsaɪdns, ˈsʌbsədəns/ *n.* [C,U] TECH-

S

NICAL the process by which land sinks to a lower level, or the state of land or buildings that have sunk

sub·sid·i·ar·y¹ /səbˈsɪdiˌɛri/ Ac *n. plural* **subsidiaries** [C] a company that is owned or controlled by another company: +**of** *the European subsidiary of a U.S. company* ►see THESAURUS box at **company**

subsidiary² Ac *adj.* FORMAL less important than a similar or related thing

sub·si·dize /ˈsʌbsəˌdaɪz/ Ac *v.* [T] ECONOMICS if a government or organization subsidizes a company, activity etc., it pays part of its costs: *Many day care facilities are subsidized by the city.* —**subsidized** *adj.*: *subsidized housing* —**subsidization** /ˌsʌbsədəˈzeɪʃən/ *n.* [U]

ˌsubsidized ˈloan *n.* [C] ECONOMICS a special LOAN (=money you borrow) given to students in the U.S., on which the interest payments are paid by the government while the student is attending school, college, or university

sub·si·dy /ˈsʌbsədi/ Ac *n. plural* **subsidies** [C] ECONOMICS money that is paid by a government or organization to make prices lower, support someone who is producing goods etc.: *Congress may cut some subsidies to farmers.* [**Origin:** 1300–1400 Latin *subsidium* **soldiers kept in reserve, support, help**, from *sub-* **near** + *sedere* **to sit**]

S

sub·sist /səbˈsɪst/ *v.* [I] **1** to stay alive when you have only small amounts of food or money SYN **survive**: +**on** *I subsisted on canned soup.* **2** LAW to continue to exist

sub·sis·tence /səbˈsɪstəns/ *n.* [U] **1** the condition of having enough food or money to live, but no more: *Settlers to the area threatened the bears' subsistence.* **2** a small amount of money or food that is just enough to provide you with the basic things people need to have: *Factory workers were paid a* ***subsistence wage.*** | ***subsistence farming*** (=growing just enough food to live on).

subˌsistence ˈagriculture also **subˌsistence ˈfarming** *n.* [U] ECONOMICS farming in which someone only produces enough food to feed his or her own family, often because the land is too poor to produce a lot of crops

subˌsistence eˈconomy *n.* [C] ECONOMICS a TRADITIONAL ECONOMY

subˈsistence ˌlevel *n.* [singular, U] a very poor standard of living, in which people only have the things that are completely necessary for life and nothing more

sub·soil /ˈsʌbsɔɪl/ *n.* [U] EARTH SCIENCE the layer of soil between the surface and the lower layer of hard rock

sub·son·ic /ˌsʌbˈsɑnɪk◂ / *adj.* slower than the speed of sound: *subsonic aircraft*

sub·spe·cies /ˈsʌbˌspiʃiz, -ˌspisiz/ *n.* [C] BIOLOGY a group of similar plants or animals, which is smaller than a SPECIES

sub·stance /ˈsʌbstəns/ W3 *n.*

1 MATERIAL [C] a type of solid, liquid, or gas that has particular qualities: *The leaves are covered with a sticky substance.* | **illegal/controlled/banned substance** *Marijuana is still an illegal substance.* | **toxic/hazardous/dangerous substance** *The product contains harmful substances.*

2 IMPORTANCE [U] FORMAL the quality of being important, or of dealing with important subjects in a serious way SYN **significance**: **matters/issues of substance** *Some progress has been made on matters of substance.* | *It was an entertaining speech, but without much substance.*

3 MAIN IDEAS [singular, U] FORMAL the most important ideas of what someone says or in a piece of writing SYN **essence**: +**of** *No one knows what the substance of their conversation was.* | ***In substance,*** *he means that we must work harder.* | *My disagreements with him have more to do with* ***style*** *than* ***substance*** (=I disagree with the way he does things, not with his ideas).

4 TRUTH [U usually in questions and negatives] FORMAL basic facts that are true: +**of** *Brown did not deny the substance of the reports.* | +**to** ***There was no substance to*** *the rumors* (=they were not true).

5 a man/woman of substance LITERARY a man or woman who has a lot of money and power

[**Origin:** 1200–1300 Old French, Latin *substantia*, from *substare* **to stand under**]

ˈsubstance aˌbuse *n.* [U] the habit of taking too many illegal drugs, in a way that harms your health SYN **drug abuse**

sub·stand·ard /ˌsʌbˈstændəd◂ / *adj.* not as good as the average, and not acceptable: *substandard medical care* → see also NONSTANDARD, STANDARD²

sub·stan·tial /səbˈstænʃəl/ W3 *adj.* **1** large in amount, number, or degree SYN **considerable**: *A substantial number of houses were damaged.* | *The breakfast they provide is substantial.* ►see THESAURUS box at **big** **2** large and strongly made: *a substantial mahogany desk* **3** FORMAL having a lot of influence or power, usually because of wealth: *a very substantial family in the wool trade*

sub·stan·tial·ly /səbˈstænʃəli/ *adv.* **1** very much or a lot SYN **considerably**: *Attendance at the conference was substantially lower this year.* | *The first chapter had been changed substantially.* **2** in the most important or basic way SYN **essentially**: *The two articles were substantially the same.*

sub·stan·ti·ate /səbˈstænʃiˌeɪt/ *v.* [T] FORMAL to prove the truth of something that someone has said, claimed etc.: *No evidence has been found to substantiate the story.* —**substantiation** /səbˌstænʃiˈeɪʃən/ *n.* [U]

sub·stan·tive¹ /ˈsʌbstəntɪv/ *adj.* FORMAL, APPROVING important or serious, or dealing with important or serious issues: *Most substantive work in Congress takes place in committees.* | *substantive political issues* —**substantively** *adv.*

substantive² *n.* [C] ENG. LANG. ARTS a noun —**substantival** /ˌsʌbstənˈtaɪvəl/ *adj.*

sub·sta·tion /ˈsʌbˌsteɪʃən/ *n.* [C] a place where electricity is passed on from the place that produces it into the main system

sub·sti·tute¹ /ˈsʌbstəˌtut/ Ac *n.* [C] **1** something new or different that you use instead of something else that you used previously: *a sugar substitute* | +**for** *Chewing tobacco is not a safe substitute for cigarettes.* **2** someone who does someone else's job for a limited period of time, especially on a sports team or in a school: *We had a substitute today for history.* **3 be no substitute for sth** to not have the same good or desirable qualities as something or someone else: *Vitamin pills are no substitute for a healthy diet.*

substitute² Ac *v.* **1** [T] to use something new or different instead of something else: **substitute sth for/with sth** *You can substitute yogurt for cream in the recipe.* **2** [I,T] to do someone's job until the person who usually does it is able to do it again: +**for** *He substituted for the lead singer, who was sick.*

ˌsubstitute ˈteacher *n.* [C] a teacher who teaches a class when the usual teacher is sick

sub·sti·tu·tion /ˌsʌbstəˈtuʃən/ Ac *n.* [C,U] someone or something that you use instead of the person or thing you would normally use, or the act of using them: *The coach* ***made*** *two* ***substitutions*** *in the second half.* | **substitution of sth for sth** *the substitution of English for French as the world's common language*

substiˈtution efˌfect *n.* [C] ECONOMICS a way in which some customers react to an increase in the cost of a product, by buying less of the product and more of another product

sub·stra·tum /ˈsʌbˌstreɪt̬əm, -ˌstræ-/ *n. plural* **substrata** /-t̬ə/ [C] **1** EARTH SCIENCE a layer that lies beneath another layer, especially in the earth: *a substratum of rock* **2** FORMAL a quality that is hidden

sub·struc·ture /ˈsʌbˌstrʌktʃə/ *n.* [C] **1** one of the STRUCTURES within a society or organization that combines with others to form a whole **2** a solid base under the ground that supports a building above the ground

sub·sume /səbˈsum/ *v.* [T] FORMAL to include someone or something as part of a larger group, rather than considering them as separate: **subsume sb/sth under sth** *The women's athletic department will be subsumed under the men's.*

sub·ten·ant /ˌsʌb'tɛnənt/ *n.* [C] someone who pays rent for an office, apartment etc. to the person who is renting it from the owner —**subtenancy** *n.* [C,U] → see also SUBLET

sub·tend /səb'tɛnd/ *v.* [T] TECHNICAL to be opposite to a particular angle or ARC, and form the limits of it in GEOMETRY

sub·ter·fuge /'sʌbtəˌfyudʒ/ *n.* [C,U] FORMAL a secret trick or slightly dishonest way of doing something, or the use of this: *The reporter had used subterfuge to gain admission.*

sub·ter·ra·ne·an /ˌsʌbtə'reɪniən◂ / *adj.* EARTH SCIENCE beneath the surface of the Earth: *subterranean passages*

sub·text /'sʌbtɛkst/ *n.* [C] a hidden or second meaning in something that someone says or writes: *The subtext of many baby care books is that good mothers stay home with their kids.*

sub·ti·tle¹ /'sʌbˌtaɪtl/ *n.* [C] ENG. LANG. ARTS **1 subtitles** [plural] the words printed at the bottom of a movie to translate what is being said by the actors, when the movie is in a foreign language: *a French film with English subtitles* **2** a less important title below the main title in a book

subtitle² *v.* [T usually passive] **1** to print subtitles at the bottom of a movie **2** to give a subtitle to a book —**subtitled** *adj.*

sub·tle /'sʌtl/ *adj.* **1** not easy to notice or understand unless you pay careful attention OPP **obvious**: *the subtle changes in color in the leaves* | *a **subtle form** of racism* | **subtle differences/variations/distinctions** *Babies can hear subtle differences in pronunciation that adults cannot.* **2** a subtle taste or smell is pleasant and delicate OPP **strong**: *a subtle hint of almond* **3** a subtle person, plan, method etc. skillfully hides what they really want or intend to do or does it in a very indirect way: *She wasn't ever subtle in giving her opinion.* | *He put a lot of subtle pressure on his employees.* **4** very smart about noticing and understanding things SYN **sensitive**: *a subtle mind* [**Origin:** 1300–1400 Old French *soutil*, from Latin *subtilis* **finely woven, subtle**] —**subtly** *adv.*

sub·tle·ty /'sʌtlti/ *n. plural* **subtleties** **1** [U] the quality that something has when it has been done in an intelligent, skillful, and indirect way: *the subtlety of his performance* | *"How long are you staying?" I asked, with no subtlety at all.* **2** [C usually plural] a thought, idea, or detail that is important but difficult to notice or understand: +**of** *Some of the subtleties of the language are lost in translation.*

sub·to·tal /'sʌbˌtoʊtl/ *n.* [C] the total of a set of numbers, especially on a bill, before other numbers are also added to form a complete total: *the subtotal before sales tax is added*

sub·tract /səb'trækt/ *v.* [T] MATH to take a number or an amount from a larger number or amount: **subtract sth from sth** *If you subtract 10 from 30, you get 20.* [**Origin:** 1500–1600 Latin, past participle of *subtrahere* **to pull from beneath, remove**] → see also ADD, DEDUCT, MINUS¹ (1)

sub·trac·tion /səb'trækʃən/ *n.* [C] MATH the act of subtracting → see also ADDITION

sub·trop·i·cal /ˌsʌb'trɑpɪkəl/ *adj.* EARTH SCIENCE relating to or typical of an area that is near a tropical area: *subtropical climates*

sub·urb /'sʌbəb/ *n.* [C] an area away from the center of a town or city, where a lot of people live: *a Chicago suburb* | +**of** *Lakewood is a suburb of Denver.* | *My family moved to **the suburbs** when I was ten.* [**Origin:** 1300–1400 Latin *suburbium*, from *urbs* **city**]

sub·ur·ban /sə'bəbən/ *adj.* **1** relating to a suburb, or in a suburb: *suburban life* | *a suburban shopping center* **2** boring and having very traditional beliefs and interests: *suburban attitudes*

sub·ur·ban·ite /sə'bəbəˌnaɪt/ *n.* [C] a word meaning someone who lives in a suburb, often used to show disapproval

sub·ur·bi·a /sə'bəbiə/ *n.* [U] **1** suburban areas in general: *a home in suburbia* **2** the behavior, opinions, and ways of living that are typical of people who live in a suburb: *middle-class suburbia*

sub·ven·tion /səb'vɛnʃən/ *n.* [C] FORMAL a gift of money, usually from a government, for a special use

sub·ver·sion /səb'vəʒən/ *n.* [U] POLITICS secret activities that are intended to encourage people to oppose the government

sub·ver·sive¹ /səb'vəsɪv/ *adj.* subversive ideas, activities etc. are secret and intended to encourage people to oppose a government, religion etc.: *subversive organizations* —**subversively** *adv.* —**subversiveness** *n.* [U]

subversive² *n.* [C] someone who is subversive

sub·vert /səb'vət/ *v.* [T] FORMAL **1** POLITICS to try to destroy the power and influence of a government or established system etc.: *an attempt to subvert the democratic process* **2** to destroy someone's beliefs or loyalty

sub·way /'sʌbweɪ/ *n. plural* **subways** [C] a railroad that runs under the ground, used in a city as a form of PUBLIC TRANSPORTATION SYN **metro**: *the New York subway system*

S

ˌsub-'zero, **subzero** *adj.* sub-zero temperatures are lower than zero or the temperature at which water freezes

suc·ceed /sək'sid/ W2 *v.*
1 NOT FAIL [I] if you succeed, you do what you have tried or wanted to do OPP **fail**: *Work hard, and you'll succeed.* | **succeed in (doing) sth** *Very few people succeed in losing weight and keeping it off.*
2 HAVE A GOOD RESULT [I] if something succeeds, it has the result or effect it was intended to have OPP **fail**: *Teachers and parents will have to work together for the program to succeed.* | **succeed in (doing) sth** *Our advertising campaign has succeeded in attracting more customers.*
3 JOB [I] to do well in your job, especially because you have worked hard at it for a long time: +**as** *Nobody thought he would ever succeed as an artist.* | +**in** *Determination will help you succeed in business.*
4 FOLLOW SB IN A POSITION [I,T] to be the next person to take a position or rank after someone else: **succeed sb as sth** *Wolcott will succeed Dr. Johansen as director of the museum.*
5 REPLACE [T] FORMAL to come after and replace something else: *By the early '90s, CDs had succeeded records in popularity.*
6 nothing succeeds like success used to say that success often leads to even greater success
7 only succeed in doing sth used when someone does the opposite of what they intended to do: *You've only succeeded in upsetting your mother.*
[**Origin:** 1300–1400 Latin *succedere* **to go up, follow after, succeed**, from *sub-* **near** + *cedere* **to go**]

suc·ceed·ing /sək'sidɪŋ/ *adj.* coming after something else: *She became more well-known with each succeeding novel.*

suc·cess /sək'sɛs/ W1 *n.* **1** [U] the achievement of something that you have tried to do or wanted to do OPP **failure**: *The experiment was a success.* | *The plan had no **chance of success**.* | *I tried phoning him, **without success**.* | **success in (doing) sth** *The program helps people **have** long-term **success** in losing weight.* | *What is the **key to** your **success**?* **2** [C] if something is a success, it earns a lot of money, is popular etc. OPP **failure**: +**of** *the success of the business he started* | **a great/huge/resounding etc. success** *The show was a big success.* | *The lunch buffet has **proved a** resounding **success*** (=has become successful). | *If anyone can **make a success out of** it, he can.* | *The book has **enjoyed** great **success*** (=it has been very successful). **3** [C] someone who does very well in their job, sport, in society etc. OPP **failure**: +**in**

his success in Hollywood | +**as** *Hal was not a great success as a rock singer.* **4 success story** someone or something that becomes successful, especially when this happens in spite of difficulties: *The program is only one of the school's success stories.*

suc·cess·ful /sək'sɛsfəl/ S3 W2 *adj.* **1** having the effect or result you intended: *The surgery was successful.* | *a **highly successful** campaign* | **successful in (doing) sth** *They have been very successful in marketing their jeans to teenagers.* **2** a successful person earns a lot of money or is very well known and respected: *a successful entrepreneur* | *a **highly successful** lawyer* | **successful in (doing) sth** *She has been successful in the music business.* | +**as** *She had become increasingly successful as a poet.* **3** a successful business, movie etc. makes a lot of money: *a successful law firm* | *a **highly successful** product* —**successfully** *adv.*

suc·ces·sion /sək'sɛʃən/ Ac *n.* **1 a succession of sb/sth** a number of people or things of the same type that happen or follow one after another: *I heard a succession of loud bangs outside.* **2 in succession** happening one after the other without anything different happening in between: *They've won the championship four times **in succession**.* | **in close/quick succession** (=quickly one after the other) *He fired two shots in quick succession.* **3** [U] the act of taking over an office or position, or the right to be the next to take it: +**to** *Ferdinand was first in line of succession to the throne.* → see also ACCESSION

suc·ces·sive /sək'sɛsɪv/ Ac *adj.* [only before noun] coming or following one after the other: *How will this affect successive generations* (=our children, our grandchildren etc.)*?* | *seven successive years of drought* —**successively** *adv.*

suc·ces·sor /sək'sɛsɚ/ Ac *n.* [C] **1** someone who takes a job or position previously held by someone else: +**as** *Ms. Barrick will be Sloan's successor as treasurer.* | +**to** *He is seen as a possible successor to the outgoing Secretary of State.* **2** FORMAL a machine, system etc. that exists after another one in a process of development OPP **predecessor**: *The refrigerator was the successor to the ice box.*

suc·cinct /sək'sɪŋkt, sə'sɪŋkt/ *adj.* APPROVING clearly expressed in a few words: *a succinct explanation* [**Origin:** 1400–1500 Latin, past participle of *succingere* **to tuck up**, from *sub-* **under, close to** + *cingere* **to put a belt around**] —**succinctly** *adv.* —**succinctness** *n.* [U]

suc·cor /'sʌkɚ/ *n.* [U] LITERARY help that is given to someone who is having problems —**succor** *v.* [T]

suc·co·tash /'sʌkətæʃ/ *n.* [U] a dish made from corn, beans, and TOMATOes cooked together

suc·cu·bus /'sʌkyəbəs/ *n. plural* **succubi** /-baɪ, -bi/ [C] LITERARY a female DEVIL that has sex with a sleeping man → see also INCUBUS

suc·cu·lent[1] /'sʌkyələnt/ *adj.* juicy and good to eat: *succulent tropical fruit* —**succulence** *n.* [U]

succulent[2] *n.* [C] BIOLOGY a plant such as a CACTUS that has thick soft leaves or stems that can hold a lot of liquid

suc·cumb /sə'kʌm/ *v.* [I] FORMAL **1** to stop opposing someone or something that is stronger than you, and allow them to take control SYN **give in**: +**to** *The country has not yet succumbed to pressure to stop nuclear testing.* | *I **succumbed to temptation** and ordered the pie.* **2** if you succumb to an illness, you become very sick or die of it: +**to** *Lewis succumbed to cancer in 2003.* [**Origin:** 1400–1500 French *succomber*, from Latin *succumbere*, from *sub-* **under, close to** + *cumbere* **to lie down**]

such[1] /sʌtʃ/ S1 W1 *determiner* **1** used to talk about a person, thing etc. that is like the one that has already been mentioned: *Such behavior is not acceptable.* | *He was an expert on such matters.* | **some/many/few/any/no such sth** (=some person or thing of that kind) *California has no such law.* **2 such sth as sth** used for giving an example: *The problem exists in such places as Korea.* | *such writers as Hemingway and Twain* **3** used to emphasize a quality that someone or something has: *I've never seen **such a** clean garage.* | *It's **such a** long way to go.* | *They're such nice people.* **4** used to talk about the results that are caused by a quality that something or someone has: **such a sth that...** *It's such a tiny kitchen that only one of us cooks at a time.* | *The drink is being marketed **in such a way** as to appeal to children.* | **to such an extent/degree that** *It disrupted things to such an extent that it took weeks to recover.* **5 there's no such person/thing etc. as** used to say that a particular person or thing does not exist: *There is no such thing as magic.* **6 such...as** FORMAL OR LITERARY used to emphasize that there is a small amount of something or that it is of poor quality: *Such food as they gave us was warm and nutritious.* [**Origin:** Old English *swilc*]

> **GRAMMAR** **such, so**
> Use **such** and **so** to emphasize a particular quality that a person has. Use **so** before an adjective or adverb: *Janet's so nice!* | *Why does Rick always have to talk so loudly?* If the adjective is before a noun, however, use **such** or **such a**: *Janet and Ted are such nice people.* | *He's such a stupid jerk!*

such[2] S2 W2 *pron.* **1** used to talk about a person, thing etc. that is like the one that has already been mentioned: *Such was the punishment for students who talked in class.* | *Birth is a natural process and should be treated **as such*** (=as a natural process). **2 such as** used when giving an example of something: *supplies such as food and medicine* | *Characters such as Mickey Mouse and Snoopy are still popular with youngsters.* **3 such as sth is** used to show that you think something is not good enough or that there is not enough of it: *We examined the evidence, such as it was.* **4 be such that** also **be such as to do sth** FORMAL OR LITERARY used to give a reason or explanation for something: *Brown's influence was such that he was never investigated.* | *The force of the explosion was such as to break windows several streets away.* **5 and such** SPOKEN and people or things like that: *a store that sells computers and such* **6 not...as such a)** SPOKEN used to say that the word you are using to describe something is not exactly correct: *The committee doesn't have a plan of action as such.* **b)** used to say that something does not include or is not related to all things or people of a particular type: *We have nothing against men as such.* **7 such of sb/sth as** FORMAL those people or things of a particular group or type: *Such of you as wish to leave may do so now.*

'such and ˌsuch, such-and-such *pron.*, *determiner* SPOKEN used instead of a particular name, time, amount etc., so that you can talk about it without saying exactly what it is: *He's always asking me why I did such and such.*

such·like /'sʌtʃlaɪk/ *pron.* things of that kind: *money for food, clothes, and suchlike* —**suchlike** *adj.* [only before noun]

suck[1] /sʌk/ S2 *v.* [I,T]
1 PUT IN MOUTH to hold something in your mouth and pull on it with your tongue and lips, often to drink or eat something: *He's eight years old and he still sucks his thumb.* | *The baby was very premature and couldn't suck.* | +**on** *Molly was sucking on a candy cane.* | +**at** *The baby sucked at his mother's breast.*
2 DRINK/BREATHE to take liquid or air into your mouth by making your lips tight and using the muscles of your mouth to pull the liquid or air in: *The insects feed by sucking the animal's blood.* | **suck sth in** *Miguel put the cigarette to his mouth and sucked in some smoke.* | **suck sth up** *Jenny sucked up the milkshake with her straw.*
3 PULL to pull someone or something with great power and force to a particular place: +**down/into** *A bird got sucked into the jet's engines.* | **suck sb/sth under** *The strong waves threatened to suck us under.*
4 BE BAD [I] SPOKEN INFORMAL to be very bad: *The food there sucks.* | +**at** *She really sucks at tennis.*
5 TAKE FROM [T] to take something such as energy,

money etc. from something else, when this is a bad thing to happen: *He felt as if all the warmth had been sucked from his body.* | **suck sth out of sb/sth** *Poverty seemed to* ***suck the life*** *out of us.* | *These people are* ***sucking*** *the country* ***dry*** (=taking everything from someone or something, especially money).
6 suck sb into sth to make someone become involved in a particular situation, event etc., especially a bad one: *I refuse to let them suck me into their argument.*
7 suck in your stomach to pull your stomach in using your stomach muscles, so that it looks smaller: *He caught sight of himself in the mirror and sucked in his stomach.*
[**Origin:** Old English *sucan*]

suck up *phr. v.* **1** INFORMAL DISAPPROVING to say or do a lot of nice things in order to make someone like you or to get what you want: **suck up to sb** *Brad's always sucking up to the teacher.* **2 suck it up** SPOKEN used to tell someone to do something and stop worrying or complaining about how bad or difficult it is: *The other team is playing really well, but we just have to suck it up and do better.*

suck² *n.* [C] an act of sucking

suck·er¹ /ˈsʌkɚ/ *n.* [C] **1** INFORMAL someone who is easily deceived, tricked, or persuaded to do something, especially something that does not give them any advantage: *You sent them money? Sucker!* | *There really is* ***a sucker born every minute*** (=used to say that many people do stupid things). **2 be a sucker for sb/sth** to like someone or something very much, so that you cannot refuse them: *I'm a sucker for babies.* **3** SPOKEN a thing: *How much did that sucker cost you?* **4** a LOLLIPOP **5** BIOLOGY a part of an insect or of an animal's body that it uses to hold on to or stick to a surface: *Tree frogs have suckers on their feet.* **6** BIOLOGY a part of a plant that grows from the root or lower stem of a plant to become a new plant

sucker² *v.*

sucker sb **into** sth *phr. v.* to persuade someone to do something they do not want to do, especially by tricking them or lying to them

sucker punch *v.* [T] INFORMAL to hit someone very quickly when they do not expect to be hit —**sucker punch** *n.* [singular]

suck·le /ˈsʌkəl/ *v.* BIOLOGY **1** [T] to feed a baby or young animal with milk from the breast **2** [I] if a baby or young animal suckles, it sucks milk from a breast → see also BREAST-FEED, NURSE² (3)

suck·ling /ˈsʌklɪŋ/ *n.* [C] LITERARY a young human or animal still taking milk from its mother's breast

suckling pig *n.* [C] a young pig that was still taking milk from its mother, which is sometimes cooked whole and eaten on special occasions

suck·y /ˈsʌki/ *adj.* SLANG very bad or not fun: *a sucky job*

su·crose /ˈsukroʊz, ˈsyu-/ *n.* [U] CHEMISTRY the most common form of sugar → see also FRUCTOSE, LACTOSE

suc·tion /ˈsʌkʃən/ *n.* [U] SCIENCE **1** the process of removing air or liquid from a container or enclosed space so that another substance can be pulled in, or so that two surfaces stick together: *the suction of the vacuum cleaner* **2** the force that causes a substance to be pulled into a closed space when the air or liquid already present is removed

suction cup *n.* [C] a small round piece of rubber or plastic that sticks to a surface by suction

suction pump *n.* [C] a pump that works by removing air from an enclosed space, so that the substance to be pumped is pulled in

Su·dan /suˈdæn/ also **the Sudan** a country in northeast Africa, south of Egypt and west of Ethiopia

Su·da·nese /ˌsudnˈiz/ *adj.* coming from or relating to Sudan —**Sudanese** *n.* [C]

sud·den /ˈsʌdn/ S1 W3 *adj.* **1** happening, coming, or done quickly or when you do not expect it: *A sudden storm drenched us.* | *a* ***sudden change*** *of plans* **2 (all) of a sudden** suddenly: *All of a sudden the lights went out.* [**Origin:** 1200–1300 Old French *sodain*, from Latin *subitaneus*, from *subitus* **sudden**] —**suddenness** *n.* [U]

ˌsudden ˈdeath *n.* [U] if a game goes into sudden death, both teams have equal points at the end, so the game continues until one player or team gains the lead and wins

ˌSudden ˌInfant ˈDeath ˌSyndrome *n.* [U] MEDICINE a situation in which a baby stops breathing and dies while it is sleeping, for no known reason SYN **crib death**

sud·den·ly /ˈsʌdnli/ S2 W1 *adv.* quickly and without warning, when you do not expect it: *Suddenly there was a knock on the door.* | *Jane suddenly realized that everyone else had left.*

Su·do·ku /suˈdoʊku/ *n.* [U] TRADEMARK a puzzle in which you put numbers between 1 and 9 into empty squares that are arranged into rows, COLUMNS (=upright rows), and boxes. When you have finished, each row, column, and box must contain the numbers from 1 to 9 once only.

suds /sʌdz/ *n.* [plural] **1** the BUBBLES formed on the top of water with soap in it **2** INFORMAL beer —**sudsy** *adj.*

sue /su/ S3 W3 *v.* [I,T] **1** LAW to make a legal claim against someone, especially for money, because they have harmed you in some way: *If the builders don't fulfill their side of the contract, we'll sue.* | *The girl's parents sued the school.* | **sue sb for libel/negligence/malpractice etc.** *Aaron is being sued for fraud.* | **sue sb for $100,000/damages/compensation etc.** *Tonelli was sued for $40,000 by a former employee.* | *At the time, she didn't want to* ***sue for divorce*** (=in order to end a marriage). **2 sue for peace** FORMAL if a country or army sues for peace, they ask for peace, especially because there is no other good choice: *They had hoped to force the North to sue for peace.* [**Origin:** 1100–1200 Anglo-French *suer* **to follow, make a legal claim to,** from Vulgar Latin *sequere*]

suede /sweɪd/ *n.* [U] soft leather with a slightly rough surface: *a suede jacket* [**Origin:** 1600–1700 French *(gants de) Suède* **Swedish (gloves)**]

su·et /ˈsuɪt/ *n.* [U] hard fat from around an animal's KIDNEYS, used in cooking

Su·ez /ˈsuɛz/**, the Gulf of** an INLET of the Red Sea at its northern end, that is between the main part of northern Egypt and Sinai

ˌSuez Caˈnal, the a CANAL in northeast Egypt that connects the Mediterranean Sea to the Gulf of Suez and the Red Sea

suf·fer /ˈsʌfɚ/ S3 W1 *v.*
1 PAIN/ILLNESS [I,T] to experience physical or mental pain or illness: *Hardesty suffered severe burns to his face.* | *I hate to see animals suffer.* | **+from** *She suffers from asthma.*
2 BAD SITUATION [I,T] to be in a very bad situation that makes things very difficult for you: *Small businesses have suffered financially during the recession.* | **+for** *People all over the world are suffering for their religious beliefs.* | *If workers cannot learn to adapt, they will* ***suffer the consequences*** (=have something bad happen to them). | **+from** *a country suffering from record unemployment*
3 BAD EXPERIENCE [T] if someone suffers a bad or difficult experience, it happens to them: *Many immigrants suffer discrimination.* | *The Democrats have just* ***suffered*** *a huge* ***defeat*** *in the polls.* | **suffer damage/injury/loss** *Many houses suffered damage from the flood.*
4 BECOME WORSE [I] to become worse in quality because a bad situation is affecting something or because no one is taking care of it: *My grades suffered as a result of having to work more hours.*
5 not suffer fools gladly to not be patient with people you think are stupid
6 suffer sb to do sth OLD USE to allow someone to do something

[**Origin:** 1100–1200 Old French *souffrir*, from Vulgar Latin *sufferire*]

suf·fer·ance /ˈsʌfərəns/ *n.* **on/at/by (sb's) sufferance** FORMAL if you live or work somewhere on sufferance, you are allowed to do it by someone who would prefer you did not do it

suf·fer·er /ˈsʌfərə/ *n.* [C] someone who suffers, especially from a particular illness: *cancer sufferers*

suf·fer·ing /ˈsʌfərɪŋ/ *n.* [C,U] physical or mental pain and difficulty: *the sufferings of the poor* | *the* ***pain and suffering*** *they went through*

suf·fice /səˈfaɪs/ *v.* [not in progressive] **1** [I] FORMAL to be enough: *A one-page letter should suffice.* | **suffice to do sth** *A single example will suffice to make the point.* **2 suffice (it) to say (that)** used to say that the statement that follows is enough to explain what you mean, even though you could say more: *Suffice it to say that it didn't go well.*

suf·fi·cien·cy /səˈfɪʃənsi/ Ac *n.* FORMAL **1** [U] the state of being or having enough: *The war has affected the country's economic sufficiency.* **2 a sufficiency of sth** a supply that is enough: *a sufficiency of raw materials*

suf·fi·cient /səˈfɪʃənt/ Ac W3 *adj.* [no comparative] FORMAL as much as is needed for a particular purpose SYN **enough** OPP **insufficient**: *There was not sufficient evidence to prosecute.* | *Was the time set aside for discussion sufficient?* | **sufficient sth to do sth** *There is sufficient reason to believe that he is lying.* | **+for** *The apartment was barely sufficient for a family of four.* [**Origin:** 1300–1400 Latin, present participle of *sufficere* **to put under, suffice**] —**sufficiently** *adv.* → see also SELF-SUFFICIENT ▸see THESAURUS box at **adequate**

suf·fix /ˈsʌfɪks/ *n.* [C] ENG. LANG. ARTS a letter or letters added to the end of a word to form a new word. For example, you can add the suffix "ness" to the word "kind" to form "kindness." [**Origin:** 1600–1700 Modern Latin *suffixum*, from Latin *suffigere* **to fasten beneath**] → see also AFFIX², PREFIX

suf·fo·cate /ˈsʌfəˌkeɪt/ *v.* **1** [I,T] to die or make someone die by preventing them from breathing: *It's important to leave the car window open a little, so that your pet doesn't suffocate.* **2 be suffocating** to feel uncomfortable because there is not enough fresh air: *Can you open a window? I'm suffocating.* **3** [T] to prevent a relationship, plan, business etc. from developing well or being successful: *Jealousy can suffocate a relationship.* [**Origin:** 1400–1500 Latin, past participle of *suffocare*, from *sub-* **under, close to** + *fauces* **throat**] —**suffocation** *n.* [U]

suf·fo·cat·ed /ˈsʌfəˌkeɪtɪd/ *adj.* **feel suffocated** to feel like you are not free or do not have enough space: *I felt suffocated living in the city.*

suf·fra·gan /ˈsʌfrəgən/ *adj.* [only before noun] a suffragan BISHOP helps another bishop of higher rank in their work —**suffragan** *n.* [C]

suf·frage /ˈsʌfrɪdʒ/ *n.* [U] POLITICS the right to vote in national elections

suf·fra·gette /ˌsʌfrəˈdʒɛt/ *n.* [C] POLITICS a woman who tried to gain the right to vote for women, especially in the early 20th century

suf·fra·gist /ˈsʌfrədʒɪst/ *n.* [C] POLITICS someone who tries to obtain the right to vote for particular groups of people, especially women or people above a certain age

suf·fuse /səˈfyuz/ *v.* [I,T] LITERARY **1** if warmth, color, liquid etc. suffuses something or someone, it covers or spreads through them: *The landscape was suffused in golden light.* **2** to spread through all of a situation, group of people, country etc.: *Religion suffuses the country's approach to all issues.* **3 be suffused with sth** if a person or situation is suffused with a feeling, they are full of that feeling —**suffusion** /səˈfyuʒən/ *n.* [U]

Su·fi /ˈsufi/ *n.* [C] a believer in Islam who practices a form of MYSTICISM, trying to come close to God through prayer and MEDITATION —**Sufism** *n.* [U]

sug·ar¹ /ˈʃʊgə/ S2 W2 *n.* **1** [U] a sweet white or brown substance that is obtained from plants and used to make food and drinks sweet: *Do you take sugar in your coffee?* | *a cup of sugar* **2** BIOLOGY one of several sweet substances formed in plants → see also GLUCOSE **3** OLD-FASHIONED SPOKEN used to address someone you like very much [**Origin:** 1200–1300 Old French *çucre*, from Medieval Latin *zuccarum*, from Arabic *sukkar*]

sugar² *v.* [T] to add sugar or cover something with sugar

ˈsugar beet *n.* [U] a vegetable that grows under the ground, from which sugar is obtained → see also BEET

sug·ar·cane /ˈʃʊgəkeɪn/ *n.* [U] a tall tropical plant from whose stems sugar is obtained

ˌsugar-ˈcoated *adj.* **1** made to seem better than something really is: *a sugar-coated view of life* **2** covered with sugar —**sugar-coat** *v.* [T]

ˈsugar cube *n.* [C] a square piece of solid sugar

ˈsugar ˌdaddy *n.* [C] INFORMAL an older man who gives a young woman presents and money in return for having a relationship with her and possibly for sex

sug·ared /ˈʃʊgəd/ *adj.* covered in sugar: *sugared cereals*

sug·ar·less /ˈʃʊgəlɪs/ *adj.* containing no sugar: *sugarless gum*

ˈsugar ˌmaple *n.* [C] a type of MAPLE tree that grows in North America, whose SAP (=liquid from the tree) is used to make MAPLE SYRUP

sug·ar·y /ˈʃʊgəri/ *adj.* **1** containing sugar or tasting like sugar: *sugary snacks* **2** language, emotions etc. that are sugary are too nice and seem insincere: *the song's sugary lyrics*

sug·gest /səgˈdʒɛst, səˈdʒɛst/ S2 W1 *v.* **1** [T] to tell someone your ideas about what they should do, where they should go etc.: *Who suggested this restaurant?* | **suggest doing sth** *I suggest talking to a lawyer first.* | **suggest (that)** *Mark's sister suggested that we go to Mexico this summer.* | **suggest how/where/what etc.** *The students can suggest how their work should be displayed.* **2** [T] to make someone think that a particular thing is true SYN **indicate**: *Current data suggests that there could be life on Mars.* | **suggest (that)** *The article suggested that Rivas may resign.* | **evidence/research/studies etc. suggest (that)** *The data suggests that fathers want to be more involved with their kids' lives.* ▸see THESAURUS box at **demonstrate** **3** [T] to tell someone about someone or something that is appropriate for a particular job or activity SYN **recommend**: **suggest sth for sth** *This accounting technique is suggested for use in health care programs.* → see Grammar box at RECOMMEND **4 I'm not suggesting** SPOKEN used to say that what you have said is not exactly what you intended to say: *I'm not suggesting that she's stupid or anything.* **5** [T] to make someone think of something that is similar to something else, or help them to imagine it: *He spread his hands to suggest the size of the fish.* [**Origin:** 1500–1600 Latin, past participle of *suggerere* **to put under, provide, suggest**, from *sub-* **under, close to** + *gerere* **to carry**]

sug·gest·i·ble /səgˈdʒɛstəbəl/ *adj.* easily influenced by other people or by things you see and hear: **highly/very suggestible** *At that age, kids are highly suggestible.*

sug·ges·tion /səgˈdʒɛstʃən/ S3 W3 *n.* **1** [C,U] an idea, plan, or possibility that someone mentions, or the act of mentioning it: *a list of holiday gift suggestions* | **suggestion that** *The suggestion that the children work together on the stories had interesting results.* | *Can I* ***make a suggestion?*** | *Let me know if you* ***have any suggestions.*** | *My boss is always* ***open to suggestions*** (=willing to listen to ideas). | ***At the suggestion of*** *his attorneys* (=because they suggested it), *he stopped talking to the press.* **2 suggestion of/that** a sign or possibility of something: *There was a suggestion of illegal drug use.* | *Chilton denied any suggestion of wrongdoing.* **3** [U] an indirect way of making people accept an idea: *Don't underestimate* ***the power of suggestion.*** **4 a suggestion of sth** a slight amount or sign of something: *She looked at him with just a suggestion of a smile.*

sug·ges·tive /səg'dʒɛstɪv/ *adj.* **1** a remark, behavior etc. that is suggestive makes you think of sex: *suggestive lyrics* **2** reminding you of something: **+of** *The sounds were suggestive of whales calling to each other.* **—suggestively** *adv.* **—suggestiveness** *n.* [U]

su·i·ci·dal /ˌsuə'saɪdl/ *adj.* **1** wanting to kill yourself: *He felt depressed and suicidal.* **2** likely to lead to a lot of damage or trouble: *It would be suicidal for the senator to oppose this policy.* **3** likely to lead to death: *The mission was suicidal.*

su·i·cide /'suəˌsaɪd/ W3 *n.* [C,U] **1** the act of killing yourself: *I learned later that she had* ***committed suicide.*** | *He suffered from depression and* ***attempted suicide.*** | *There was a* ***suicide note*** *on the table.* ▸see THESAURUS box at **kill**[1] **2 suicide attack/bombing/mission etc.** an attack etc. in which the person who carries out the attack deliberately kills himself or herself in the process of killing other people: *the suicide bombings that cause chaos and grief* **3 political/social/economic etc. suicide** something you do that ruins your good position in politics, your social life, the economy etc. [**Origin:** 1600–1700 Latin *sui* **of oneself** + English *-cide*]

'suicide ˌbomber *n.* [C] someone who hides a bomb on their body and explodes it in a public place, killing himself or herself and other people, usually for political reasons

'suicide pact *n.* [C] an arrangement between two or more people to kill themselves at the same time

'suicide watch *n.* [C] a period of time during which a prisoner is guarded carefully to prevent them from killing themselves

suit[1] /sut/ S2 W2 *n.* [C] **1** a set of clothes made of the same material, usually including a JACKET (=short coat) with pants or a skirt: *a blue wool suit* | *a man* ***wearing a suit*** *and tie* | *a dark* ***business suit*** → see also MORNING SUIT **2 jogging/swimming/bathing etc. suit** a piece of clothing or a set of clothes used for running, swimming etc. → see also SWIMSUIT, WET SUIT **3** LAW a problem or complaint that a person or company brings to a court of law to be settled SYN **lawsuit**: *Larkin has* ***filed suit*** (=officially brought the problem to a court of law) *against the corporation.* | *the testimony in a* ***civil suit*** **4** one of the four types of cards in a set of playing cards **5 sb's strong suit** something that you are good at: *Politeness is not his strong suit.* **6 plead/press your suit** OLD USE to ask a woman to marry you [**Origin:** 1200–1300 Old French *siute* **act of following, group of helpers**, from Vulgar Latin *sequita*] → see also **in your birthday suit** at BIRTHDAY (2), **follow suit** at FOLLOW (8)

suit[2] *v.* **1** [T] to be acceptable, appropriate, or CONVENIENT for a particular person or in a particular situation: *There are activities to suit everyone.* | *It takes time to find a college that will* ***suit*** *your child's* ***needs.*** | *"Eight o'clock?" "That* ***suits me fine*** (=is completely acceptable for me)." | **suit sth to sb/sth** *She had the ability to suit her performances to the audience.* **2 well/best/ideally etc. suited** to have the right qualities to do something: **+for** *Megan is well suited for library work.* | **+to** *Soups are perfectly suited to winter suppers.* **3** [T not in passive] clothes or colors that suit someone make them look attractive: *That coat really suits Paul.* | *Red suits you.* **4 suit yourself** SPOKEN used to tell someone they can do whatever they want to, even though it annoys you or you think they are not doing the right thing: *"I think I'll just stay home tonight." "Suit yourself."*

suit·a·bil·i·ty /ˌsuṭə'bɪləṭi/ *n.* [U] the degree to which something or someone has the right qualities for a particular purpose: **+as** *Critics doubt his suitability as a leader.*

suit·a·ble /'suṭəbəl/ *adj.* having the right qualities for a particular person, purpose, or situation SYN **appropriate** OPP **unsuitable**: *a suitable place to live* | **+for** *The show is not suitable for young children.* | **+to** *a school that is suitable to your child's needs* **—suitableness** *n.* [U]

suit·a·bly /'suṭəbli/ *adv.* **1 suitably dressed/prepared/equipped etc.** wearing the right clothes, having the right information, equipment etc. for a particular situation: *He was not suitably dressed for a wedding.* **2 suitably impressed/amazed/outraged etc.** showing or having the amount of feeling or quality that you would expect in a particular situation: *Bruck is suitably cautious about his future.*

suit·case /'sut˥keɪs/ *n.* [C] a large bag or box with a handle, used for carrying clothes and possessions when you travel → see picture at CASE[1]

suite /swit/ *n.* [C] **1** a set of expensive rooms in a hotel: *the honeymoon suite* **2** a set of rooms or offices in an office building **3** ENG. LANG. ARTS a piece of music made up of several short parts: *the Nutcracker Suite* **4** COMPUTERS a group of related computer PROGRAMS that make a set **5** a set of matching furniture for a room: *a new dining room suite*

suit·ing /'suṭɪŋ/ *n.* [U] TECHNICAL material used for making suits, especially woven wool

suit·or /'suṭɚ/ *n.* [C] **1** OLD-FASHIONED a man who wants to marry a particular woman **2** someone or a company that is trying to buy or gain control of another company

Suk·koth, Sukkot /'sʊkəs, sʊ'koʊs/ *n.* [singular] a Jewish holiday in the fall when people remember the time when Jews traveled from Egypt to Israel in ancient times

sul·fate /'sʌlfeɪt/ *n.* [C,U] a chemical compound formed from SULFURIC ACID: *copper sulfate*

sul·fide /'sʌlfaɪd/ *n.* [C,U] a mixture of sulfur with another substance

sul·fur /'sʌlfɚ/ *n.* [U] SYMBOL **S** CHEMISTRY an ELEMENT that is usually in the form of a light yellow powder with a strong unpleasant smell, and is used in drugs, explosives, and industry

ˌsulfur di'oxide *n.* [U] a poisonous gas that is a cause of air POLLUTION in industrial areas

sul·fu·ric a·cid /sʌlˌfyʊrɪk 'æsɪd/ *n.* [U] a powerful acid

sul·fur·ous /'sʌlfərəs, sʌl'fyʊrəs/ *adj.* related to, full of, or used with sulfur

sulk /sʌlk/ *v.* [I] to show that you are annoyed about something by being silent and having an unhappy expression on your face: *You can't sit around sulking all day.* **—sulk** *n.* [C]

sulk·y /'sʌlki/ *adj.* **1** showing that you are sulking: *a sulky frown* **2** sulking, or tending to sulk: *a sulky child* **—sulkily** *adv.* **—sulkiness** *n.* [U]

sul·len /'sʌlən/ *adj.* **1** angry and silent, especially because you feel you have been treated unfairly: *The girl was sullen and uncooperative.* **2** LITERARY a sullen sky or ocean is dark and looks as if bad weather is coming SYN **gloomy**: *a sullen gray sky* **—sullenly** *adv.* **—sullenness** *n.* [U]

sul·ly /'sʌli/ *v.* **sullies, sullied, sullying** [T] FORMAL OR LITERARY to spoil or reduce the value of something that was perfect: *a scandal that* ***sullied his reputation***

sul·phate /'sʌlfeɪt/ *n.* [C,U] another spelling of SULFATE

sul·phide /'sʌlfaɪd/ *n.* [C,U] another spelling of SULFIDE

sul·phur /'sʌlfɚ/ *n.* [U] another spelling of SULFUR

sul·phu·ric ac·id /sʌlˌfyʊrɪk 'æsɪd/ *n.* [U] another spelling of SULFURIC ACID

sul·tan /'sʌlt˥n/ *n.* [C] a ruler in some Muslim countries

sul·tan·a /sʌl'tænə/ *n.* [C] the wife, mother, or daughter of a sultan

sul·tan·ate /'sʌltəˌneɪt/ *n.* [C] POLITICS **1** a country ruled by a sultan: *the sultanate of Oman* **2** the position of a sultan, or the period of time during which he rules

S

sul·try /ˈsʌltri/ *adj.* **1** weather that is sultry is very hot with no wind and air that feels wet SYN **humid** **2** a woman who is sultry makes other people feel strong sexual attraction for her: *a sultry voice* —**sultriness** *n.* [U]

sum¹ /sʌm/ Ac W3 *n.*
1 MONEY [C] an amount of money: **+of** *The house was sold for the sum of $1.1 million.* | *He had invested a large* ***sum of money****.* | **a large/small/substantial etc. sum** *One hundred dollars was a considerable sum in those times.* → see also LUMP SUM, **princely sum/fee/price etc.** at PRINCELY (1)
2 [C] MATH the total produced when you add two or more numbers or things together: **+of** *The sum of the three angles of a triangle is 180°.*
3 greater/more than the sum of its parts having a quality or effectiveness as a group that you would not expect from the quality of each member separately
4 [C] a simple calculation done by adding, SUBTRACTING, multiplying, or dividing
5 in sum used before a statement that gives the main information about something in a few simple words: *In sum, we need to cut costs.*
[**Origin:** 1200–1300 Old French *summe*, from Latin *summa*, from *summus* **highest**] → see also SUM TOTAL

S

sum² Ac *v.* **summed, summing**
sum up *phr. v.* **1** to give the main information contained in a report, speech, discussion etc. in a short statement at the end SYN **summarize**: ***To sum up****, exercise and diet are equally important.* | **sum sth up** *In your final paragraph, sum up your argument.* **2 sum sth ↔ up** to describe something or show its typical qualities using only a few words, pictures etc.: *The city's problem can be summed up in three words: too many people.* | *That image sums up the whole movie.* **3 sum sth ↔ up** if a lawyer or judge sums up at the end of a TRIAL, he or she explains the main facts of the case **4 sum sth ↔ up** to form a judgment or opinion about someone or something: *Pat summed up the situation at a glance.* **5 that (about) sums it up** SPOKEN used to say that you have said everything that is important about a subject → see also SUMMATION

Su·me·ri·an /suˈmɛriən/ one of the people who lived in the part of Mesopotamia that is now Iraq from about 3500 B.C. until about 2000 B.C. —**Sumerian** *adj.*

sum·ma cum lau·de /ˌsʊmə kʊm ˈlaʊdə, -deɪ/ *adv.* with highest honor; if you GRADUATE summa cum laude, you have achieved the highest level in your college or university degree → see also CUM LAUDE, MAGNA CUM LAUDE

sum·mar·i·ly /səˈmɛrəli/ *adv.* FORMAL immediately, without paying attention to the usual processes, rules etc.: *He had been* ***summarily dismissed****.*

sum·ma·rize /ˈsʌməˌraɪz/ Ac *v.* [I,T] to make a short statement giving only the main information and not the details of a plan, event, report etc.: *The memo summarized the discussion.*

sum·ma·ry¹ /ˈsʌməri/ Ac *n. plural* **summaries** [C] a short statement that gives the main information about something, without giving all the details: **+of** *a summary of his research findings* | ***In summary****, this type of treatment will not help everyone.*

summary² Ac *adj.* [only before noun, no comparative] **1** FORMAL done immediately, without paying attention to the usual processes, rules etc.: *a summary execution* **2** a summary report, statement etc. gives only the main information about something, but not the details OPP **full**

sum·ma·tion /səˈmeɪʃən/ Ac *n.* [C] FORMAL **1** a statement giving the main facts, but not the details of something, especially one made by lawyers at the end of a TRIAL **2** the total amount or number you get when two or more things are added together

sum·mer¹ /ˈsʌmɚ/ S1 W1 *n.* **1** [C,U] the season of the year when the sun is hottest and the days are longest, between spring and fall: *the summer of 1972* | *We were away for most of the summer.* | *It never rains here* ***in the summer****.* | *Do you have any vacation plans* ***this summer****?* | **last/next summer** *We went to the county fair last summer.* | **early/late summer** *a Saturday afternoon in late summer* | **summer clothes/jobs/sports etc.** (=clothes, jobs, sports etc. that are used or done in the summer) **2 20/50 etc. summers** LITERARY 20, 50 etc. years of age: *He looked younger than his 70 summers.* [**Origin:** Old English *sumor*] → see also INDIAN SUMMER, SUMMERY

summer² *v.* [I always + adv./prep.] to spend the summer in a particular place

ˈsummer ˌcamp *n.* [C,U] a place where children can stay during the summer, and take part in various activities

ˈsummer home *n.* [C] a house that you live in only in the summer

ˈsummer house *n.* [C] **1** also **summerhouse** a building in a yard or park, where you can sit in warm weather **2** a summer home

ˈsummer school *n.* [C,U] courses you can take in the summer at a school or college

ˌsummer ˈsolstice *n.* [singular] the longest day of the year, which in the northern HEMISPHERE (=top half of the Earth) is around June 21

ˈsummer stock *n.* [U] a group of actors who work together on several plays during the summer, or the plays performed by these actors

sum·mer·time /ˈsʌmɚˌtaɪm/ *n.* [U] the time of the year when it is summer: *It's very hot here* ***in the summertime****.*

sum·mer·y /ˈsʌməri/ *adj.* appropriate for summer, or reminding you of the summer: *a light summery dress*

sum·mit /ˈsʌmɪt/ W3 *n.* [C] **1** POLITICS an important meeting or set of meetings between the leaders of something, especially the leaders of governments: *a U.S.–Russian summit* | *a national education summit* | **a summit meeting/conference** *A summit meeting with China is likely by the end of the year.* **2** EARTH SCIENCE the top of a mountain: *the first woman to* ***reach the summit*** *of Pike's Peak* → see picture on page A31 **3 the summit of sth** FORMAL the greatest amount or highest level of something SYN **peak**: *the summit of his career*

sum·mit·ry /ˈsʌmɪtri/ *n.* [U] FORMAL a situation in which important summit meetings are held

sum·mon /ˈsʌmən/ *v.* [T] FORMAL **1** to formally order or ask someone to come to a particular place: *Russo saw the fight and summoned the police.* | **summon sb to sth** *Republican leaders were summoned to the White House.* **2** to officially order someone to come to a court of law: **summon sb to do sth** *She was summoned to testify.* **3** also **summon up** to make a great effort to use your strength, courage, energy etc.: *I couldn't summon up the energy to argue with her.* **4** also **summon up** if something summons a memory, thought etc., it makes you remember it or think of it: *Christmas always summons up childhood memories.* [**Origin:** 1200–1300 Old French *somondre*, from Latin *summonere* **to remind secretly**]

sum·mons /ˈsʌmənz/ *n. plural* **summonses** [C] LAW an official order to appear somewhere, especially in a court of law: *Pasqua was* ***issued a summons****.*

su·mo /ˈsumoʊ/ also **ˌsumo ˈwrestling** *n.* [U] a Japanese form of WRESTLING, done by men who are very fat —**sumo wrestler** *n.* [C]

sump /sʌmp/ *n.* [C] the lowest part of a DRAINAGE system where liquids or wastes remain

sump·tu·ous /ˈsʌmptʃuəs/ *adj.* very impressive and expensive SYN **luxurious**: *a sumptuous banquet* —**sumptuously** *adv.* —**sumptuousness** *n.* [U]

ˌsum ˈtotal *n.* **the sum total** the whole amount of something, especially when this is less than expected or needed: **+of** *And that's the sum total of my knowledge about it.*

Sun. the written abbreviation of Sunday

sun¹ /sʌn/ S1 W2 *n.* **1 the sun** the large bright yellow circular object that shines in the sky during the day, that gives us light and heat, and around which the

Earth moves: *The sky was blue and the* ***sun*** *was* ***shining***. | **the sun rises/comes up/sets/goes down** *The sun rises in the east and sets in the west.* | *The rain stopped and the* ***sun came out*** (=you could see the sun). → see picture at SOLAR SYSTEM **2** [U] the heat and light that come from the sun: *That side of the house gets the most sun.* | *I can't sit* ***in the sun*** *anymore – it's too hot.* **3** [C] PHYSICS any star around which PLANETS move: *a distant sun* ▸see THESAURUS box at **space**[1] **4 (everything/anything) under the sun** used to emphasize that you are talking about a very large range of things: *We talked about everything under the sun.* **5 get/catch some sun** INFORMAL to spend time outside in the sun, especially long enough that your skin becomes slightly red or brown: *It looks like you got a little sun today.* [**Origin:** Old English *sunne*] → see also **make hay while the sun shines** at HAY (2), **there's nothing new under the sun** at NEW (17)

sun[2] *v.* **sunned, sunning** [I,T] also **sun yourself** to sit or lie outside while the sun is shining: *people sunning themselves by the pool*

ˈsun-baked *adj.* made very hard and dry by the sun

sun·bathe /ˈsʌnbeɪð/ *v.* [I] to sit or lie outside in the sun, especially in order to become brown

sun·beam /ˈsʌnbim/ *n.* [C] a beam of light from the sun

sun·bed /ˈsʌnbɛd/ *n.* [C] a metal structure the size of a bed, that you lie on to make your skin brown using light from special lamps → see also SUNLAMP

ˈSun Belt, Sunbelt *n.* **the Sun Belt** the southern or southwestern parts of the U.S., where the sun shines a lot

ˈsun block, sunblock *n.* [C,U] cream or oil that you rub into your skin, in order to stop the sun's light from burning you

sun·bon·net /ˈsʌnˌbɑnɪt/ *n.* [C] a hat worn in past times by women as protection from the sun

sun·burn /ˈsʌnbɚn/ *n.* [C,U] red and painful skin that you can get from spending too much time in the sun —**sunburned** also **sunburnt** *adj.* → see also SUNTAN

sun·burst /ˈsʌnbɚst/ *n.* [C] a pattern or drawing that looks like the sun with lines coming out from the center

sun·dae /ˈsʌndi, -deɪ/ *n.* [C] ice cream with sweet sauce poured over it, with nuts, whipped cream etc. on top: *a hot fudge sundae*

Sun·day /ˈsʌndi, -deɪ/ WRITTEN ABBREVIATION **Sun.** *n.* *plural* **Sundays** [C,U] the first day of the week, between Saturday and Monday: *Football season starts Sunday.* | *It snowed* ***on Sunday***. | *We had friends over* ***last Sunday***. | *We're going to go on a picnic* ***next Sunday***. | *What are you going to do* ***this Sunday*** (=the next Sunday that is coming)? | *I always read the paper* ***on Sundays*** (=each Sunday). | *Christmas falls* ***on a Sunday*** *this year.* | **Sunday morning/afternoon/night etc.** *We're going out to breakfast Sunday morning.* [**Origin:** Old English *sunnandæg*]

GRAMMAR

On Sunday/Monday/Tuesday etc. is used with the past tense to talk about a particular day in the week that has just passed, or with the present tense to talk about a particular day in the week that is coming: *It rained on Sunday.* | *We are leaving on Sunday.* Only use "the" in front of the name of a day if you are talking about a particular day of a particular week: *Let's meet on the Sunday before Easter.*

ˈSunday school *n.* [C,U] a class in a church where children go on Sundays to be taught about the Christian religion

sun deck *n.* [C] an area next to a house or on a ship, where people can sit in order to be in the sun

sun·der /ˈsʌndɚ/ *v.* [T] LITERARY to break something into parts, especially violently SYN **split** → see also ASUNDER

sun·dial /ˈsʌndaɪl/ *n.* [C] an object used for telling the time, by looking at the position of a shadow made on a stone circle by a pointed piece of metal

sun·down /ˈsʌndaʊn/ *n.* [U] SUNSET

ˈsun-drenched *adj.* a sun-drenched place is one where the sun shines most of the time: *the sun-drenched Mediterranean*

sun·dress /ˈsʌndrɛs/ *n.* [C] a dress that women wear in hot weather, that does not cover the arms or shoulders

ˈsun-dried *adj.* [only before noun] sun-dried food has been left in the sun to dry in order to give it a particular taste: *sun-dried tomatoes*

sun·dries /ˈsʌndriz/ *n.* [plural] FORMAL small objects that are not important enough to be named separately → see also SUNDRY

sun·dry /ˈsʌndri/ *adj.* [only before noun, no comparative] FORMAL **1** not similar enough to form a group SYN **miscellaneous**: *They manufacture clothing and sundry other products.* **2 all and sundry** everyone, not just a few carefully chosen people → see also SUNDRIES, **various and sundry sth** at VARIOUS (2)

sun·fish /ˈsʌnfɪʃ/ *n. plural* **sunfish** or **sunfishes** [C] BIOLOGY an ocean fish that has a large flat circular body

sun·flow·er /ˈsʌnˌflaʊɚ/ *n.* [C] a very tall plant with a large yellow flower and seeds that can be eaten

sunflower

sung /sʌŋ/ *v.* the past participle of SING

sun·glass·es /ˈsʌnˌglæsɪz/ *n.* [plural] dark glasses that you wear to protect your eyes when the sun is very bright SYN **shades**

ˈsun god *n.* [C] a god in some ancient religions who represents the sun or has power over it

ˈsun hat *n.* [C] a hat that you wear to protect your head from the sun → see picture at HAT

sunk /sʌŋk/ *v.* a past tense and the past participle of SINK

sunk·en /ˈsʌŋkən/ *adj.* **1** [only before noun] having fallen to the bottom of the ocean or a lake: *sunken ships* **2** [only before noun] built or placed at a lower level than the surrounding floor, ground etc.: *a sunken living room* **3 sunken cheeks/eyes** if someone has sunken cheeks or eyes, they look thin, old, or unhealthy

sun·lamp /ˈsʌnlæmp/ *n.* [C] a lamp that produces a special light used for making your skin brown

sun·less /ˈsʌnlɪs/ *adj.* LITERARY having no light from the sun SYN **dark**: *a sunless prison cell*

sun·light /ˈsʌnlaɪt/ *n.* [U] natural light that comes from the sun: *The water sparkled in the sunlight.* | **bright/direct sunlight** *This plant needs direct sunlight.* | **sunlight pours/streams** *Sunlight poured through the windows.*

sun·lit /ˈsʌnˌlɪt/ *adj.* made brighter by light from the sun: *a sunlit valley*

Sun·na, Sunnah /ˈsʊnə/ *n.* **the Sunna** a set of Muslim customs and rules based on the words and acts of Muhammad

Sun·ni /ˈsʊni/ *n.* [C] a Muslim who follows one of the two main branches of the Muslim religion → see also SHIITE

sun·ny /ˈsʌni/ *adj. comparative* **sunnier**, *superlative* **sunniest** **1** full of light from the sun: *a sunny kitchen* | ***It's sunny*** *today.* ▸see THESAURUS box at **sunshine** **2** INFORMAL cheerful and happy: *a sunny smile*

ˌsunny-side ˈup *adj., adv.* [not before noun] an egg that is cooked sunny-side up is cooked on one side only, and not turned over in the pan

ˈsun porch *n.* [C] a room with large windows and often a glass roof, designed to let in a lot of light

sun·rise /ˈsʌnraɪz/ *n.* **1** [U] the time when the sun first appears in the morning: *Sunrise is at 6:10 tomorrow.* | *A farmer's work begins* ***at sunrise.*** **2** [C,U] the colored part of the sky where the sun first appears in the morning: *a beautiful sunrise*

ˈsunrise ˌindustry *n.* [C] an industry, such as ELECTRONICS or making computers, that uses modern processes and takes the place of older industries → SUNSET INDUSTRY

sun·roof /ˈsʌnruf/ *n.* [C] **1** a part of the roof of a car that you can open to let in air and light → see picture on page A36 **2** a flat roof of a building where you can sit when the sun is shining

sun·screen /ˈsʌnskrin/ *n.* [C,U] a cream or oil that you rub into your skin to stop the sun from burning you

sun·set /ˈsʌnsɛt/ *n.* **1** [U] the time of day when the sun disappears and night begins: *The park is open from 8 a.m. to sunset.* | *The flag is taken down* ***at sunset.*** **2** [C,U] the colored part of the sky where the sun gradually disappears at the end of the day: *a purple and orange sunset* **3 ride/head/sail etc. off into the sunset** HUMOROUS to leave a place or a job without plans of ever coming back because you believe you have finished everything you wanted to do

ˈsunset ˌindustry *n.* [C] an industry that uses old equipment and methods, usually in an area that once had many industries like it, and that is becoming less successful: *sunset industries such as steel* → SUNRISE INDUSTRY

sun·shade /ˈsʌnʃeɪd/ *n.* [C] something that you put in your car window to stop the sun from shining in

sun·shine /ˈsʌnʃaɪn/ *n.* [U] **1** the light and heat that come from the sun when there are no clouds: *the warm spring sunshine* | ***Bright sunshine*** *came in the window.*

THESAURUS

When the sun is shining
sunny/fine: *a warm sunny day*
bright/fair used especially in weather reports
It's a nice/beautiful/glorious day
There isn't a cloud in the sky

When the sun cannot be seen
cloudy/gray
It's overcast it's very dark and likely to rain
→ RAIN, SNOW, WEATHER, WIND

2 INFORMAL happiness: *Petey was the only* ***ray of sunshine*** *in her life.* **3** SPOKEN used to address someone you love, or someone who is making you annoyed: *Good morning, sunshine.* | *Look, sunshine, get to work!*

sun·spot /ˈsʌnspɑt/ *n.* [C] PHYSICS a small dark area on the sun's surface

sun·stroke /ˈsʌnstroʊk/ *n.* [U] MEDICINE fever, weakness etc. caused by being outside in the sun for too long

sun·tan /ˈsʌntæn/ *n.* [C] attractively brown skin that someone with pale skin gets when they spend a lot of time in the sun SYN **tan** —**suntanned** *adj.* → see also SUNBURN

ˈsuntan ˌlotion also **ˈsuntan ˌoil** *n.* [C,U] a cream or oil that you rub into your skin to stop the sun from burning you

sun·up /ˈsʌnʌp/ *n.* [U] INFORMAL SUNRISE

ˈsun ˌworshiper *n.* [C] INFORMAL someone who likes to lie in the sun to get a suntan

Sun Yat-Sen /ˌsʊn yɑt ˈsɛn/ (1866–1925) a Chinese political leader who established the National Party in China, and helped to remove the last Manchu emperor from power. He became the first President of the new Republic of China in 1911.

sup /sʌp/ *v.* **supped, supping** [I] OLD USE to eat supper

supe /sup/ *n.* [C] SPOKEN **1** a SUPERVISOR **2** a SUPERINTENDENT

su·per¹ /ˈsupɚ/ S2 W2 *adj.* INFORMAL extremely good SYN **wonderful**: *You guys did a super job.* | *"I'll see you at 8." "Super!"* [**Origin:** 1800–1900 *superfine* **of the highest quality** (17–21 centuries), from *super-* + *fine*]

super² *adv.* SPOKEN extremely: *He's super nice.*

super³ *n.* [C] SPOKEN a SUPERINTENDENT

super- /supɚ/ *prefix* **1** larger, greater, stronger etc. than other things or people of the same type: *a supermarket* | *a supertanker* **2** above others, or in a more powerful position than others: *a supervisor*

su·per·a·bun·dance /ˌsupərəˈbʌndəns/ *n.* **a superabundance of sth** FORMAL more than enough of something —**superabundant** *adj.*

su·per·an·nu·at·ed /ˌsupɚˈænyuˌeɪtɪd/ *adj.* FORMAL old, and not useful or not working anymore: *superannuated computer equipment*

su·perb /sʊˈpɚb/ *adj.* [no comparative] extremely good SYN **excellent**: *The meal was superb.* | *a superb performance* [**Origin:** 1500–1600 Latin *superbus* **proud, grand,** from *super*] —**superbly** *adv.*

ˈSuper Bowl *n.* [C usually singular] a football game played once a year to decide which professional team is the best in the U.S.

su·per·bug /ˈsupɚˌbʌg/ *n.* [C] MEDICINE a type of BACTERIA that cannot be killed using the drugs that have usually been used to kill bacteria

su·per·charged /ˈsupɚˌtʃɑrdʒd/ *adj.* **1** a supercharged engine is very powerful because air or FUEL is supplied to it at a higher pressure than normal **2** extremely powerful, strong etc.: *the company's supercharged performance*

su·per·cil·i·ous /ˌsupɚˈsɪliəs/ *adj.* FORMAL DISAPPROVING behaving as if you think that other people are less important than you: *a supercilious laugh*

su·per·com·put·er /ˈsupɚkəmˌpyut̬ɚ/ *n.* [C] COMPUTERS a computer that is more powerful than almost all other computers

su·per·con·duc·tiv·i·ty /ˌsupɚˌkɑndʌkˈtɪvət̬i/ *n.* [U] PHYSICS the ability of some substances to allow electricity to flow through them very easily, especially at very low temperatures —**superconductive** /ˌsupɚkənˈdʌktɪv/ *adj.*

su·per·con·duc·tor /ˈsupɚkənˌdʌktɚ/ *n.* [C] PHYSICS a substance that allows electricity to flow through it very easily, especially at very low temperatures —**superconducting** *adj.*

su·per·cool /ˌsupɚˈkul/ *v.* [T usually passive] TECHNICAL to cool a liquid below the temperature at which it would normally freeze, without the liquid becoming solid

super-du·per /ˌsupɚ ˈdupɚ◂/ *adj.* SPOKEN, INFORMAL extremely good SYN **super**

su·per·e·go /ˌsupɚˈigoʊ/ *n.* [C usually singular] TECHNICAL a word meaning your "conscience," used in Freudian PSYCHOLOGY → see also EGO, ID

su·per·fi·cial /ˌsupɚˈfɪʃəl/ *adj.*
1 **NOT COMPLETE/THOROUGH** not examining or understanding something in a complete or thorough way: *a superficial understanding of physics* | *a superficial examination of the scene*
2 **APPEARANCE** seeming to have a particular quality, especially when you do not examine something closely, although this is not true or real: *Despite their superficial similarities, the two novels are very different.*
3 **SURFACE** affecting only the surface of your skin or the outside part of something, and therefore not serious: *a superficial wound*
4 **PERSON** DISAPPROVING someone who is superficial does not think about things that are serious or important SYN **shallow**: *All the other girls seemed silly and superficial.*
5 **NOT IMPORTANT** not important or not having a big effect SYN **minor**: *superficial changes in government policies*

6 TOP LAYER EARTH SCIENCE existing in or relating to the top layer of something, especially soil, rock etc. —**superficially** *adv.* —**superficiality** /ˌsupɚfɪʃiˈæləṭi/ *n.* [U]

su·per·flu·ous /sʊˈpɚfluəs/ *adj.* FORMAL more than is needed or wanted SYN unnecessary [**Origin:** 1300–1400 Latin *superfluus*, from *superfluere* **to overflow**] —**superfluously** *adv.* —**superfluousness** *n.* [U]

Su·per·fund /ˈsupɚˌfʌnd/ *n.* [singular] a law that provides money from the U.S. government to clean up areas that have been POLLUTED with dangerous substances, but that also allows the government to demand money in a court of law from the companies that made the area dirty

Su·per·glue /ˈsupɚglu/ *n.* [U] TRADEMARK a very strong glue that sticks very quickly and is difficult to remove —**superglue** *v.* [T]

su·per·he·ro /ˈsupɚˌhɪroʊ/ *n. plural* **superheroes** [C] a character in stories who uses special powers, such as great strength or the ability to fly, to help people

su·per·high·way /ˌsupɚˈhaɪweɪ/ *n. plural* **superhighways** [C] FORMAL a very large road on which you can drive fast for long distances → see also INFORMATION SUPERHIGHWAY

su·per·hu·man /ˌsupɚˈhyumən◂ / *adj.* much greater than ordinary human powers or abilities: **superhuman strength/power etc.** *a superhuman effort to finish*

su·per·im·pose /ˌsupɚɪmˈpoʊz/ *v.* [T] **1** to put one picture, image, or photograph on top of another so that both can be partly seen: **superimpose sth on/onto sth** *A photo of dancers was superimposed onto the beach scene.* **2** to combine two systems, ideas, opinions etc. so that one influences the other: **superimpose sth on/onto sth** *Superimposing capitalism on another economic system is apt to cause problems.* —**superimposition** /ˌsupɚɪmpəˈzɪʃən/ *n.* [U]

su·per·in·tend /ˌsupɚɪnˈtɛnd/ *v.* [T] FORMAL to be in charge of something, and control how it is done SYN supervise —**superintendence** *n.* [U]

su·per·in·tend·ent /ˌsupɚɪnˈtɛndənt/ *n.* [C] **1** also **superintendent of schools** someone who is in charge of all the schools in a particular area in the U.S. **2** someone who is in charge of an apartment building and is responsible for making repairs in the building **3** someone who is officially in charge of a place, job, activity etc.: *the superintendent of Yellowstone National Park*

su·pe·ri·or[1] /səˈpɪriɚ, sʊ-/ *adj.* [no comparative] **1** better, more powerful, more effective etc. than a similar person or thing, especially one that you are competing against OPP inferior: +**to** *He genuinely believed that men were superior to women.* | **far/vastly/clearly superior** *a vastly superior navy* **2** [only before noun] FORMAL of very good quality OPP inferior: *superior craftsmanship* | *a superior academic record* **3** DISAPPROVING thinking that you are better than other people OPP inferior: *a superior attitude* | +**to** *She always acts so superior to everyone else.* **4** having a higher position or rank than someone else OPP inferior: *Are you questioning the orders of a superior officer?* **5** TECHNICAL higher in position SYN upper [**Origin:** 1300–1400 Old French *superieur*, from Latin *superior* **further above**] → see also MOTHER SUPERIOR, INFERIOR

superior[2] *n.* [C] someone who has a higher rank or position than you, especially in a job: *Do you have a good working relationship with your* ***immediate superior*** (=the person in the position directly above yours)? → see also INFERIOR

Su·pe·ri·or, Lake /səˈpɪriɚ, sʊ-/ the largest of the five Great Lakes on the border between the U.S. and Canada

Suˌperior ˈCourt, superior court *n.* [C,U] a court of law that has more authority than other courts in a particular area

su·pe·ri·or·i·ty /səˌpɪriˈɔrəṭi, -ˈɑr-/ *n.* [U] **1** the quality of being better, more skillful, more powerful etc. than other people or things: +**of** *the superiority of this product* | +**over** *The organization has a technical superiority over its rivals.* | +**in** *U.S. superiority in air power* **2** an attitude that shows you think you are better than other people: *She spoke with an* ***air of superiority***.

su·per·la·tive[1] /səˈpɚləṭɪv, sʊ-/ *adj.* [no comparative] **1** excellent: *superlative special effects* **2** ENG. LANG. ARTS a superlative adjective or adverb expresses the highest degree of a particular quality. For example, the superlative form of "tall" is "tallest." → see also COMPARATIVE

superlative[2] *n.* **1 the superlative** ENG. LANG. ARTS the superlative form of an adjective or adverb. For example, "biggest" is the superlative of "big." → COMPARATIVE **2** [C] a word that shows you think someone or something is very good: *a movie that has earned superlatives from critics*

su·per·la·tive·ly /səˈpɚləṭɪvli/ *adv.* extremely

su·per·man /ˈsupɚˌmæn/ *n. plural* **supermen** /-ˌmɛn/ [C] a man of unusually great ability or strength

su·per·mar·ket /ˈsupɚˌmɑrkɪt/ *n.* [C] a large store where customers can buy many different kinds of food and things for the house

su·per·mod·el /ˈsupɚˌmɑdl/ *n.* [C] an extremely famous fashion MODEL

su·per·mom /ˈsupɚmɑm/ *n.* [C usually singular] INFORMAL a mother who takes care of her children, cooks, cleans the house etc., in addition to having a job outside the house, and who is admired because of this

su·per·nat·u·ral[1] /ˌsupɚˈnætʃərəl◂ , -tʃrəl◂ / *adj.* impossible to explain by natural causes, and therefore seeming to involve the powers of gods or magic: *supernatural powers* —**supernaturally** *adv.*

supernatural[2] *n.* **the supernatural** events, powers, and creatures that cannot be explained, and seem to involve gods or magic: *belief in the supernatural*

su·per·no·va /ˌsupɚˈnoʊvə/ *n. plural* **supernovas** or **supernovae** /-vi/ [C] PHYSICS a very large, very bright exploding star → see also NOVA

su·per·nu·mer·ar·y /ˌsupɚˈnuməˌrɛri/ *n. plural* **supernumeraries** [C] **1** FORMAL someone or something that is additional to the number of people or things that are needed **2** TECHNICAL someone who is in a play, OPERA etc. without speaking, usually as part of a large group of people —**supernumerary** *adj.*

sup·er·pow·er /ˈsupɚˌpaʊɚ/ *n.* [C] POLITICS a nation that has very great military and political power

su·per·script /ˈsupɚˌskrɪpt/ *adj.* [only before noun] written or printed above a number, letter etc. —**superscript** *n.* [C,U] → see also SUBSCRIPT

su·per·sede /ˌsupɚˈsid/ *v.* [T] if a new idea, product, or method supersedes another one, it becomes used instead because it is more modern or effective or has more authority SYN replace: *The new deal supersedes the old agreement.*

su·per·size[1] /ˈsupɚˌsaɪz/ *adj.* [only before noun] a supersize drink or meal in a FAST FOOD restaurant is the largest size that the restaurant serves

supersize[2] *v.* [T] to buy or sell the largest meal or drink sold in a FAST FOOD restaurant: *I always supersize my French fries.*

su·per·son·ic /ˌsupɚˈsɑnɪk◂ / *adj.* faster than the speed of sound: *a supersonic jet* → see also SUBSONIC

su·per·star /ˈsupɚˌstɑr/ *n.* [C] an extremely famous performer, especially a musician, movie actor, or sports player

su·per·sti·tion /ˌsupɚˈstɪʃən/ *n.* [C,U] DISAPPROVING a belief that some objects or actions are lucky or unlucky, or that they cause events to happen, based on old ideas of magic: *the old superstition that black cats are unlucky*

su·per·sti·tious /ˌsupɚˈstɪʃəs/ *adj.* DISAPPROVING influenced by superstitions: *a superstitious woman* —**superstitiously** *adv.*

su·per·store /ˈsupɚˌstɔr/ *n.* [C] a very large store that sells many different types of product

su·per·struc·ture /ˈsupɚˌstrʌktʃɚ/ *n.* [singular, U]

S

1 a structure that is built on top of the main part of something such as a ship or building **2** FORMAL a political or social system that has developed from a simpler system: *the superstructure of capitalism*

su·per·tank·er /ˈsupɚˌtæŋkɚ/ *n.* [C] an extremely large ship that can carry large quantities of oil or other liquids

ˌSuper ˈTuesday *n.* [U] a Tuesday in March during a year in which there is an election for U.S. President, when important PRIMARY ELECTIONS take place in many states

su·per·vise /ˈsupɚˌvaɪz/ *v.* [I,T] to be in charge of an activity or person, and make sure that things are done in the correct way: *Ruff supervises a staff of more than 200 lawyers.*

su·per·vi·sion /ˌsupɚˈvɪʒən/ *n.* [U] the act of supervising someone or something: *The children were left without adult supervision.* | *The medicine should only be taken **under** a doctor's **supervision**.*

su·per·vis·or /ˈsupɚˌvaɪzɚ/ S3 *n.* [C] **1** someone who supervises a person or activity **2** someone who is a member of the city, COUNTY etc. government in some parts of the U.S. —**supervisory** /ˌsupɚˈvaɪzəri/ *adj.*: *supervisory responsibilities*

S

su·per·wom·an /ˈsupɚˌwʊmən/ *n. plural* **superwomen** /-ˌwɪmɪn/ [C] a woman who is very successful in her job and also takes care of her children and home

su·pine /suˈpaɪn, ˈsupaɪn/ *adj.* FORMAL **1** lying on your back → see also PRONE: *a supine position* **2** allowing other people to make decisions instead of you, in a way that seems very weak: *a supine press* —**supinely** *adv.*

sup·per /ˈsʌpɚ/ S3 *n.* [C,U] an informal meal that is eaten in the evening SYN **dinner**: *Let's go for a walk after supper.* | *What's **for supper**?* | *The Nelsons are coming **for supper**.* | *He went home to **have supper** with his wife and kids.* | *Come on, Callie, **eat** your **supper**.* [**Origin:** 1200–1300 Old French *souper*]

ˈsupper club *n.* [C] a small NIGHTCLUB, where you can eat, drink, dance etc.

sup·per·time /ˈsʌpɚtaɪm/ *n.* [U] the time of the evening when people eat supper

sup·plant /səˈplænt/ *v.* [T] FORMAL to take the place of a person or thing so that they are not used anymore, not in a position of power anymore etc.: *Money has supplanted class as a determiner of status in America.*

sup·ple /ˈsʌpəl/ *adj.* **1** leather, skin, wood etc. that is supple is soft and bends easily **2** someone who is supple bends and moves easily and gracefully: *Exercise will help keep you supple.* [**Origin:** 1200–1300 Old French *souple*, from Latin *supplex* **bending under, willing to obey**] —**suppleness** *n.* [U]

sup·ple·ment¹ /ˈsʌpləmənt/ Ac *n.* [C] **1** something that you add to something else to improve it or make it complete: *vitamin supplements* | +**to** *It was an important supplement to their regular income.* ►see THESAURUS box at **addition** **2** an additional part at the end of a book, or a separate part of a newspaper, magazine etc.: *a Sunday supplement* **3** an amount of money that is added to the price of a service, hotel room etc.: *You will have to pay a **single supplement** if you join the tour alone.*

sup·ple·ment² /ˈsʌpləˌmɛnt/ Ac *v.* [T always + adv./prep.] to add something, especially to what you earn or eat, in order to increase it to an acceptable level: **supplement sth with sth** *You may need to supplement your diet with calcium.* | **supplement sth by (doing) sth** *He supplemented his income by writing freelance articles.* —**supplementation** /ˌsʌpləmɛnˈteɪʃən/ *n.* [U]

sup·ple·men·ta·ry /ˌsʌpləˈmɛntəri/ Ac *adj.* **1** also **supplemental** provided in addition to what already exists SYN **additional**: *supplementary insurance coverage* **2** TECHNICAL two supplementary angles can combine to form an angle of 180° → see also COMPLEMENTARY

sup·pli·ant /ˈsʌpliənt/ *n.* [C] LITERARY a supplicant —**suppliant** *adj.*

sup·pli·cant /ˈsʌplɪkənt/ *n.* [C] LITERARY someone who asks for something, especially from someone in a position of power or from God

sup·pli·ca·tion /ˌsʌpləˈkeɪʃən/ *n.* [C,U] LITERARY the action of asking or praying for help from someone in power or from God —**supplicate** /ˈsʌpləˌkeɪt/ *v.* [I,T]

sup·pli·er /səˈplaɪɚ/ *n.* [C] **1** a company that provides a particular product: +**of** *Libya is Italy's largest supplier of oil.* **2** someone who provides someone with something, especially illegal drugs

sup·ply¹ /səˈplaɪ/ S2 W2 *n. plural* **supplies** **1** [C] an amount of something that is available to be sold, bought, or used: *The nation's fuel supplies will not last forever.* | +**of** *a plentiful supply of cheap labor* | **money/water/food etc. supply** *The Federal Reserve Bank controls the money supply.* **2 supplies** [plural] food, clothes, and things necessary for daily life or for a particular activity: *Supplies were brought in by air.* | **emergency/relief supplies** *Emergency supplies are being sent to the flooded region.* | **medical/school/cleaning etc. supplies** *agencies taking food and medical supplies to the area* | *paper and office supplies* **3 gas/electricity/water etc. supply** a system that is used to supply gas, electricity, water etc.: *Los Angeles needed a reliable water supply.* **4** [C,U] the act or process of providing something: +**of** *Blood clots can stop the supply of blood to the brain, causing a stroke.* **5 a supply ship/convoy/route etc.** a ship, a group of trucks, a ROUTE etc. used for bringing or storing supplies → see also MONEY SUPPLY, **be in short supply** at SHORT¹ (12)

supply² W3 *v.* **supplies, supplied, supplying** [T] **1** to provide people with something that they need or want, especially regularly over a long period of time: *Paint for the project was supplied by the city.* | **supply sb with sth** *In the 1850s, Stanford's business supplied miners with shovels.* | **supply sth to sb** *They were arrested for supplying drugs to street dealers.* **2 be well/poorly/generously supplied with sth** to have a lot of something, a little of something etc.: *The lounge was well supplied with ashtrays.*

supˌply and deˈmand *n.* [U] ECONOMICS the relationship between the amount of goods or services that are for sale and the amount that people want to buy, in a way that influences prices: *the laws of supply and demand* (=an economic rule that says the price of a product or service will usually drop if the supply is greater than the number of people who want to buy it, and that the price will usually increase if there is only a limited supply and a lot of people want to buy it)

supˈply curve also **ˌmarket supˈply curve** *n.* [C] ECONOMICS a GRAPH (=drawing with lines showing how sets of measurements are related to each other) showing the different prices of a product depending on the quantity supplied → see also DEMAND CURVE, SUPPLY SCHEDULE

supˈply line *n.* [C usually plural] the different ways, places etc. that an army uses to send food and equipment to its soldiers during a war: *The bombing **cut off** enemy **supply lines**.*

supˈply ˌschedule also **ˌmarket supˈply ˌschedule** *n.* [C] ECONOMICS a list showing the price of goods, with different prices depending on the amount being bought or when they are bought → see also DEMAND SCHEDULE, SUPPLY CURVE

supˌply-side ecoˈnomics *n.* [U] the idea that if the government reduces taxes, producers will be able to make more goods and this will improve a country's economic situation

sup·port¹ /səˈpɔrt/ S2 W1 *v.* [T]

1 AGREE WITH SB/STH to say that you agree with an idea, group, person etc. and usually help them because you want them to succeed: *The changes are supported by the Democratic party.* | **support sb in sth** *We must support teachers in their efforts to keep schools drug-free.* | *The U.S. **strongly supports** the trade agreement.*

2 PROVIDE MONEY TO LIVE to provide enough money for someone to pay for all the things they need: *He wasn't*

earning enough to support his family. | **support yourself** *If she can't support herself, how's she going to support a child?* | **support sb by doing sth** *She supports herself by giving piano lessons.*
3 HELP SB to help someone by being nice to them during a difficult time in their life: *My friends and family have all supported me through the divorce.*
4 HOLD STH UP to hold the weight of something, keep it in place, or prevent it from falling: *The pillars support the ceiling.*
5 GIVE MONEY TO STH to give money to a group, organization, or event etc. to encourage it or pay for its costs: *Support the Girl Scouts – buy a box of cookies.*
6 **support a habit** to get and use money to pay for a bad habit, such as taking drugs: *Paul started dealing drugs to support his own cocaine habit.*
7 PROVE STH to show or prove that something is true or correct: **be supported by sth** *Wang's theory is supported by archeological evidence.*
8 COMPUTERS to provide information and material to improve a computer program or system to make it continue working: *I don't think they support that version of the program anymore.*
9 LAND/AIR/WATER if land, water, or air can support people, animals, or plants, it is of good enough quality, clean enough, has enough food etc. to provide a place where they can live successfully: *This land is dry and can't support many cattle.* | *The lake is too polluted to support fish.*
10 MONEY/PRICES to do something to prevent prices, the value of a country's money etc. from decreasing
[**Origin:** 1300–1400 Old French *supporter*, from Latin *supportare* **to carry**] —**supportable** *adj.* → see also INSUPPORTABLE

support[2] S2 W1 *n.*
1 APPROVAL [U] approval, encouragement, and often help for a person, idea, plan etc.: +**for** *There is a lot of support for the plan.* | *The idea has the* ***strong support*** *of the president.* | *Congress has* ***given*** *its* ***support to*** *the military action.* | *A number of people spoke* ***in support of*** *the new rule.* | *Thompson has* ***won the support of*** *half the party.* | *The mayor is trying to* ***drum up support for*** (=get many people's approval for) *the new subway line.*
2 SYMPATHY/HELP [U] sympathetic encouragement and help that you give to someone: *Thanks for all your support – it's been a hard year.* | +**of** *the loving support of my family* → see also **moral support** at MORAL[1] (3)
3 HOLD STH UP [C,U] something that presses on something else to hold it up or in position, or the result of doing this: *the wooden supports of the bridge* | *This sofa has good back support.* | *She leaned against the wall* ***for support.***
4 MONEY [C,U] money that you give a person, group, organization etc. to help pay for their costs: *The GI bill provided* ***financial support*** *for soldiers who wanted a college education.* | ***With your support,*** *we can help these youngsters.* → see also CHILD SUPPORT, PRICE SUPPORT
5 SOLDIERS [U] help or protection that is given by one group of soldiers to another group who are fighting in a battle: *logistical support* | **air/ground support** (=help or protection that comes from people in aircraft or people on the ground)
6 **support staff/services/systems etc.** people or equipment that help other people to achieve something: *the school's teachers and support staff*
7 FOR PART OF BODY [C] something that you wear to hold a weak or damaged part of your body in the right place: **back/neck/knee etc. support** *She untied her ankle supports.*
8 COMPUTERS TECHNICAL SUPPORT

sup·port·er /səˈpɔrt̬ɚ/ W2 *n.* [C] **1** someone who supports a particular person, group, or plan: +**of** *a supporter of abortion rights* | **a strong/firm/staunch etc. supporter** *Cox is one of Carter's biggest supporters.*
2 a JOCKSTRAP

sup'port group *n.* [C] a group of people who meet to help each other with a particular problem, for example ALCOHOLISM

sup'port hose *n.* [U] special PANTYHOSE that hold your legs very firmly and help blood move through your legs

sup·port·ing /səˈpɔrt̬ɪŋ/ *adj.* **1 a supporting part/role/actor etc.** a small part in a play or movie, or the actor who plays such a part **2 supporting wall/beam etc.** a wall, piece of wood etc. that supports the weight of something

sup·port·ive /səˈpɔrt̬ɪv/ *adj.* APPROVING giving help or encouragement, especially to someone who is in a difficult situation: *My family is very supportive.* | +**of** *All the team members are very supportive of each other.*

sup·pose /səˈpoʊz/ S1 W1 *v.* **1 be supposed to do/be sth a)** used to say what someone should or should not do, especially because of rules or what someone in authority has said: *You're not supposed to smoke in the building.* | *What time are you supposed to be there?* **b)** used to say what was or is expected or intended to happen, especially when it did not happen: *No one was supposed to know about it.* | *Was that supposed to be a joke?* | *The band is supposed to perform at the club on Friday.* **c)** used to say that something is believed to be true by many people, although it might not be true or you might disagree: *I didn't really like the book, but the movie is supposed to be very funny.* | *The house is supposed to be haunted.* **2** [T not in progressive] to think that something is probably true, based on what you know SYN presume: *There were many more deaths than was first supposed.* | **suppose (that)** *After all his attention, Mattie supposed he would ask her to marry him.* | ***There is no reason to suppose that*** (=it is unlikely that) *he is lying.* **3** [T not in progressive] FORMAL to expect something will happen or be true, and then base your plans on it SYN presuppose: *The company's plan supposes a steady increase in orders.*

SPOKEN PHRASES

4 I suppose a) used to say you think something is true, although you are uncertain about it SYN I guess: *I suppose you're right.* | *"The kids will love it, don't you think?" "****I suppose so.****"* | **I suppose (that)** *I suppose things worked out for the best.* **b)** used when agreeing to let someone do something, especially when you do not really want them to do it SYN I guess: *"Can we come with you?" "Oh,* ***I suppose so.****"* **c)** used when saying in an angry way that you expect something is true SYN I guess: **I suppose (that)** *I suppose you want mine too!* **d)** used to say that you think that something is probably true, although you wish it were not and hope someone will tell you it is not SYN I guess: **I suppose (that)** *I suppose I'll have to take this over to Gene's house.* **e)** used when guessing that something is true SYN I guess: *She looked about 50, I suppose.* **5 suppose** also **supposing** used to ask someone to imagine what would happen if a particular situation existed: *Suppose Bobby really is telling the truth. What then?* **6 what's that supposed to mean?** said when you are annoyed by what someone has just said: *"It sounds like things aren't going too well for you lately." "What's that supposed to mean?"* **7 I don't suppose (that) a)** used to ask a question in an indirect way, especially if you think the answer will be "no": *I don't suppose you have any idea where my address book is, do you?* **b)** used to ask for something in a very polite way: *I don't suppose you'd be willing to go get the napkins?* **c)** used to say that you think it is unlikely that something will happen: *I don't suppose I'll ever see her again.* **8 do you suppose (that)...?** used to ask someone's opinion about something, when you know that they do not have any more information about the situation than you do: *Do you suppose people will ever live on Mars?* | **what/who/why etc. do you suppose...?** *How do you suppose he got here?*

[**Origin:** 1300–1400 Old French *supposer*, from Latin *supponere* **to put under, substitute**]

sup·posed /səˈpoʊzd/ *adj.* [only before noun] claimed by other people to be true or real, although you do not think they are right: *Even the supposed experts are unable to explain what's happening.*

S

sup·pos·ed·ly /səˈpoʊzɪdli/ S3 *adv.* used when saying what many people say or believe is true, especially when you disagree with them: [sentence adverb] *Anne is coming for a visit in March, supposedly.* | [adj./adv.] *How could a supposedly intelligent person make so many stupid mistakes?*

sup·po·si·tion /ˌsʌpəˈzɪʃən/ *n.* [C,U] something that you think is true, even though you are not certain and cannot prove it: *The report will be based on fact, not supposition.* | **supposition (that)** *The police are acting on the supposition that she took the money.*

sup·pos·i·to·ry /səˈpɑzəˌtɔri/ *n. plural* **suppositories** [C] MEDICINE a small piece of solid medicine that is placed in someone's RECTUM or VAGINA

sup·press /səˈprɛs/ *v.* [T] **1** POLITICS to stop people from opposing the government, especially by using force: *The Communist government suppressed all dissent.* **2** to prevent people from knowing about important information or opinions, especially when they have a right to know: *The police were accused of suppressing evidence.* **3** to prevent something from growing or developing, or from working effectively: *The virus suppresses the body's immune system.* **4** to stop yourself from showing your feelings or from doing an action: **suppress a grin/laugh/burp etc.** *Harry could hardly suppress a smile.* —**suppressed** *adj.*: *suppressed rage* —**suppressible** *adj.* —**suppression** /səˈprɛʃən/ *n.* [U] → see also REPRESS

S

sup·pres·sant /səˈprɛsənt/ *n.* **a cough/appetite/pain etc. suppressant** a drug or medicine that makes you cough less, makes you less hungry etc.

sup·press·or /səˈprɛsɚ/ *n.* [C] something that prevents something from developing, working effectively, or being noticeable: *a noise suppressor* —**suppressor** *adj.* [only before noun] TECHNICAL

su·pra·na·tion·al /ˌsuprəˈnæʃənl/ *adj.* FORMAL POLITICS involving more than one country, and often having more authority than these countries: *a supranational organization*

su·prem·a·cist /sʊˈprɛməsɪst/ *n.* [C] someone who believes that their own particular group or race is better than any other → see also WHITE SUPREMACIST

su·prem·a·cy /səˈprɛməsi, sʊ-/ *n.* [U] the position in which you are more powerful or advanced than anyone else: **+in** *his supremacy in the 400 meter race*

su·preme /səˈprim, sʊ-/ *adj.* **1** having the highest position of power, importance, or influence: *the supreme commander of the fleet* | *In the U.S., the automobile* ***reigns supreme*** (=has a position of great importance). **2** [only before noun] the greatest possible: *a supreme act of courage* | *They've made* ***a supreme effort*** *to repair the damage.* **3 make the supreme sacrifice** to die for your country, for a principle etc.

Suˌpreme ˈBeing *n.* [singular] LITERARY God

Suˌpreme ˈCourt *n.* **1** LAW **the Supreme Court** the court of law with the most authority in the U.S. **2** [C] a court of law in most U.S. states with more authority than all other courts in that state

su·preme·ly /səˈprimli/ *adv.* [+ adj./adv.] extremely, or to the greatest possible degree: *a supremely talented musician*

Supt. the written abbreviation of SUPERINTENDENT

sur·cease /ˈsɚsis/ *n.* [U + of] LITERARY an end to something, especially to pain, sadness, suffering etc. —**surcease** *v.* [I,T]

sur·charge /ˈsɚtʃɑrdʒ/ *n.* [C] money that you have to pay in addition to the basic price of something: **+on** *a 10% surcharge on all imports* —**surcharge** *v.* [T]

sure[1] /ʃʊr, ʃɚ/ S1 W1 *adj.*

1 CERTAIN YOU KNOW STH [not before noun] confident that you know something or that something is true or correct SYN **certain**: *I think Leah lives here, but I'm not sure.* | **sure (that)** *Are you sure you know how to get there?* | **+about** *"That's the man I saw last night." "Are you quite sure about that?"* | **+of** *There's something wrong – I'm sure of it.* | **not sure how/where/when etc.** *He was not sure how she would respond.* | **not sure if/whether** *I'm not sure if I'm pronouncing this name correctly.* | *I'm* ***pretty sure*** *it was John.*

2 CERTAIN ABOUT YOUR FEELINGS [not before noun] certain about what you feel, want, like etc.: **sure (that)** *Are you sure you really want a divorce?* | **not sure what** *I'm not sure what I want to study in college.* | **+of** *Don't commit yourself unless you're sure of your feelings.*

3 make sure a) to check that something is true or has been done: *I know I asked you before, but I just wanted to make sure.* | **make sure (that)** *First, make sure that the printer has paper in it.* **b)** to do something so that you can be certain of the result: **make sure (that)** *I'll walk you home to make sure no one bothers you.* | **+of** *Thomas would be sorry – she would make sure of that.* → see Word Choice at INSURE

4 CERTAIN TO SUCCEED certain to happen, succeed, or have a particular result: **sure to do sth** *He's sure to get nervous and say something stupid.* | *Not having sex is the only* ***sure way*** *to avoid getting pregnant.* | **a sure bet/thing** (=something that is certain to happen, win, or succeed)

5 DEFINITELY TRUE definitely true: ***One thing is sure****: we don't have enough money to pay for this.*

6 DEPENDABLE [only before noun] showing that something will definitely happen or is definitely true SYN **reliable**: **a sure sign/indication** *Those black clouds are a sure sign of rain.*

7 for sure a) INFORMAL certainly or definitely: *No one knows for sure what happened.* **b)** SPOKEN used to emphasize that something is true: *He wasn't using drugs,* ***that's for sure.*** | ***One thing's for sure*** (=this is true and certain)*: he's not going to make the same mistake again.* **c)** SLANG used to agree with someone

8 sure of yourself confident in your own abilities and opinions, sometimes in a way that annoys other people

9 be sure to do sth used to tell someone to remember to do something: *Be sure to read all the directions carefully.*

10 sure of sth confident that you have, will get, will achieve, or will keep something: *They can be sure of a warm welcome.* | *For the first time in my life, I wasn't sure of my ability.*

11 sure thing SPOKEN used to agree to something: *"Could you help lift this?" "Sure thing."*

12 to be sure used to admit that something is true, before saying something that is the opposite: *It was difficult, to be sure, but somehow we managed to finish the job.*

13 a sure footing a) a situation in which your feet are placed firmly so they cannot slide → see also SURE-FOOTED **b)** a situation that is calm, and in which there is little danger of failure: *The government is trying to get the economy back* ***on a sure footing****.*

14 HOLD a sure hold is strong and firm

[**Origin:** 1300–1400 Old French *sur*, from Latin *securus*, from *se* **without** + *cura* **care**] —**sureness** *n.* [U]

sure[2] S1 W2 *adv.*

1 sure enough INFORMAL used to say that something did actually happen in the way that you said it would: *Sure enough, Mike managed to get lost.*

SPOKEN PHRASES

2 YES used to say "yes" to someone: *"Can you give me a ride to work tomorrow?" "Sure."*

3 ACCEPTING THANKS used as a way of replying to someone when they thank you: *"Thanks a lot." "Sure, no problem."*

4 USED TO EMPHASIZE STH used to emphasize a statement: *It sure is hot out here.* | *"The turkey looks great." "It sure does."*

5 USED BEFORE STATEMENT used at the beginning of a statement admitting that something is true, especially before adding something very different: *Sure, he's cute, but I'm still not interested.* ▸see THESAURUS box at **certainly**

6 sure you do/can/will etc. used to remind, encourage, or persuade someone when they doubt something: *"I don't remember him." "Sure you do."*

ˌsure-ˈfire, surefire *adj.* [only before noun] INFORMAL certain to succeed: *a sure-fire winner* | *a sure-fire way to make a million dollars*

ˌsure-ˈfooted, surefooted *adj.* able to walk without sliding or falling in a place where it is not easy to do this

sure·ly /ˈʃʊrli, ˈʃɚli/ W3 *adv.* **1** [sentence adverb] used to show that you think something must be true, especially when people seem to be disagreeing with you: *Surely he knew the money was stolen.* ▶see THESAURUS box at **certainly** **2** OLD-FASHIONED certainly: *Such sinners will surely be punished.* **3** OLD-FASHIONED used to say "yes" to someone or to express agreement with them → see also **slowly but surely** at SLOWLY (2)

sur·e·ty /ˈʃʊrət̬i/ *n. plural* **sureties** **1** [C,U] LAW money someone gives to make sure that someone will appear in court **2** [C,U] WRITTEN the condition of being sure about something, or something you are sure about SYN **certainty** **3** [C] ECONOMICS someone who will pay a debt, appear in court etc. if someone else fails to do so

surf¹ /sɚf/ *v.* **1** [I,T] to ride on ocean waves standing on a special board **2 surf the Internet/Net/Web** to use a computer to look through information on the Internet for anything that interests you —**surfer** *n.* [C] → see also SURFING

surf² *n.* [U] **1** the white substance that forms on top of ocean waves as they move toward the shore **2 surf's up** SPOKEN used to say that there are plenty of waves for SURFING **3 surf 'n' turf** also **surf and turf** an expression used in some restaurants for a meal of SHELLFISH, usually LOBSTER, and STEAK

sur·face¹ /ˈsɚfəs/ W2 *n.* [C]
1 OUTSIDE LAYER the outside or top layer of something: *the moon's surface* | *an uneven road surface* | +**of** *the surface of the glass* | *Dead leaves floated* **on the surface** *of the water.* | **below/beneath the surface** *They dig tunnels several feet below the surface.*
2 the surface the qualities someone or something seems to have until you learn more about them: ***On the surface****, Ed seemed calm.* | **below/beneath/under the surface** *There is a lot of bad feeling just below the surface.* | **come/rise to the surface** *Tensions eventually come to the surface.*
3 WORK AREA an area on a desk, table etc. used for working: *Work on a clean flat surface.*
4 SIDE OF AN OBJECT TECHNICAL one of the sides of an object: *A cube has six surfaces.*
5 PLAYING AREA the area on which a sport is played, or the substance on which it is played
[**Origin:** 1600–1700 French *sur-* **above** + *face* **face**] → see also **scratch the surface** at SCRATCH¹ (5)

surface² *v.* **1** [I] if information or feelings surface, they become known about or easy to notice: *Rumors about the killings have begun to surface in the press.* **2** if someone or something surfaces, they suddenly appear somewhere, especially after being gone or hidden for a period of time: *Three years later, Toole surfaced in Cuba.* **3** [I] to rise to the surface of water: *Suddenly one whale surfaced right beside our boat.* **4** [T] to put a surface on a road

surface³ *adj.* [only before noun] **1** appearing to be true or real, but not representing what someone really feels or what something is really like SYN **superficial**: *a surface resemblance* **2** on or relating to the surface of something, especially the ground, water etc.: *the surface layer of soil* **3** relating to the part of the Army, Navy etc. that travels by land or on the ocean, rather than by air or UNDERWATER: *the Navy's surface ships*

ˈsurface ˌarea *n.* [C] MATH the total measurement of the area of all the surfaces of an object

ˈsurface ˌmail *n.* [U] the system of sending letters or packages to other countries by trucks, ships etc., rather than by airplanes

ˌsurface ˈtension *n.* [U] PHYSICS the way the MOLECULES in the surface of a liquid stick together so that the surface is held together

surface-to-air ˈmissile *adj.* a MISSILE that is fired at airplanes from the land or from a ship

Surface Transporˈtation ˌBoard, the ABBREVIATION **STB** POLITICS the U.S. government organization that makes rules that control railroads, the business of moving goods by truck etc.

surf·board /ˈsɚfbɔrd/ *n.* [C] a long piece of plastic, wood etc. that you stand on to ride over ocean waves for fun

sur·feit /ˈsɚfɪt/ *n.* FORMAL **a surfeit of sth** an amount of something that is too large or more than you need SYN **excess**

surfing

surf·ing /ˈsɚfɪŋ/ *n.* [U] **1** the activity or sport of riding over the waves on a special board: *In Hawaii we went surfing every day.* **2 Internet/Web/Net surfing** the activity of using a computer to look through the Internet for something that interests you → see also CHANNEL SURFING, WINDSURFING

S

surge¹ /sɚdʒ/ *v.* [I] **1** [always + adv./prep.] to suddenly move forward very quickly: +**forward/through/into etc.** *The crowd surged forward.* **2** to increase suddenly by a large amount: *Auto sales surged more than 60% last year.* **3** also **surge up** if a feeling surges or surges up, you begin to feel it very strongly: *Rage surged up inside him.* **4** [always + adv./prep.] if a large amount of water, electricity etc. surges somewhere, it moves there very suddenly and powerfully: *Waves surged over the seawalls.*

surge² *n.* [C usually singular] **1** a sudden increase in something such as demand, profit, interest etc.: +**in** *a surge in sales of the book* | +**of** *a tremendous surge of interest in Chinese medicine* **2** a sudden strong feeling: +**of** *a surge of excitement* **3** a sudden powerful movement of a lot of water, electricity etc.: *a power surge* | +**of** *a sudden surge of flood water* **4** a sudden movement of a lot of people: +**of** *The city is preparing for a surge of visitors this summer.*

sur·geon /ˈsɚdʒən/ *n.* [C] a doctor who does operations in a hospital [**Origin:** 1300–1400 Anglo-French *surgien*, from Old French *cirurgie*, from Latin, from Greek *cheirourgos* **working with the hand**] → see also DENTAL SURGEON ▶see THESAURUS box at **doctor**

ˌSurgeon ˈGeneral *n.* **the Surgeon General** the medical officer with the highest rank in the U.S. Public Health Service or a similar state organization

ˈsurge proˌtector also **ˈsurge supˌpressor** *n.* [C] a piece of electrical equipment that prevents a sudden large increase in electricity from affecting other equipment, especially computers, connected to it

sur·ger·y /ˈsɚdʒəri/ S2 W3 *n. plural* **surgeries**
1 [C,U] medical treatment in which a surgeon cuts open your body to repair or remove something inside → see also OPERATION: *heart surgery* | +**on** *She required surgery on her right knee.* | **have/undergo surgery on sth** *He underwent surgery to remove a blood clot.* | **major/minor surgery** *The condition can be treated with minor surgery.* → see also COSMETIC SURGERY, PLASTIC SURGERY
2 [U] the part of medical science concerned with this type of treatment **3** [C,U] the process of performing surgery, or the place where this is done in a hospital: *Dr. Bremner is* ***in surgery*** *right now.*

sur·gi·cal /ˈsɚdʒɪkəl/ *adj.* [only before noun] **1** MEDICINE relating to or used for medical operations: *surgical instruments* | *a surgical procedure* **2 with surgical precision** extremely carefully in order to affect only a particular area or part of something, without affecting anything else —**surgically** /-kli/ *adv.*: *The tumor was surgically removed.*

ˌsurgical ˈstrike *n.* [C] a carefully planned quick military attack intended to destroy something in a particular place without damaging the surrounding area

Su·ri·nam, **Suriname** /ˌsʊrɪˈnɑm/ a country on the northern coast of South America between Guyana and French Guiana —**Surinamese** /ˌsʊrənɑˈmiz/ *adj.*

sur·ly /ˈsɚli/ *adj. comparative* **surlier**, *superlative* **surliest** in a bad mood, unfriendly, and often rude: *surly teenagers* [**Origin:** 1500–1600 *sirly* **like a lord, proud and grand** (14–17 centuries), from *sir*] —**surliness** *n.* [U]

sur·mise /sɚˈmaɪz/ *v.* [T] FORMAL to guess that something is true using the information you know already: **surmise (that)** *I could only surmise from their behavior that they had met before.* [**Origin:** 1500–1600 Old French, past participle of *surmetre* **to accuse**, from Latin *supermettere* **to throw on**] —**surmise** *n.* [C,U]

sur·mount /sɚˈmaʊnt/ *v.* [T] FORMAL **1** to succeed in dealing with a problem or difficulty SYN **overcome** **2** [usually passive] to be above or on top of something —**surmountable** *adj.*

S

sur·name /ˈsɚneɪm/ *n.* [C] FORMAL a LAST NAME [**Origin:** 1300–1400 *sur-* **above, beyond** (from Old French) + *name*]

sur·pass /sɚˈpæs/ *v.* [T] **1** to be even better or greater than someone or something else: *China will likely surpass the U.S. as the world's largest market.* | **surpass expectations/hopes/dreams** (=be better than you had expected, hoped etc.) **2 surpass yourself** FORMAL to do something even better than you have ever done before

sur·pass·ing /sɚˈpæsɪŋ/ *adj.* [only before noun] LITERARY much better than that of other people or things: *a young woman of surpassing beauty*

sur·plice /ˈsɚplɪs/ *n.* [C] a piece of clothing made of white material worn over other clothes by priests or singers in church

sur·plus¹ /ˈsɚplʌs/ *n.* [C,U] **1** an amount of something that is more than is wanted, needed, or used: **+of** *There is a slight surplus of oil worldwide.* **2** ECONOMICS the amount of money that a country or company has left after it has paid for all the things it needs: *a budget surplus* **3** ECONOMICS a TRADE SURPLUS

surplus² *adj.* **1** [only before noun] more than is wanted, needed, or used: *surplus grain* | *Anne bought a surplus Army Jeep.* **2 be surplus to needs/requirements etc.** FORMAL to not be necessary anymore

ˌsurplus ˈbudget *n.* [C] ECONOMICS BUDGET SURPLUS

sur·prise¹ /sɚˈpraɪz, səˈpraɪz/ W2 *n.*

1 EVENT [C] an unexpected or unusual event: *What a surprise! I didn't expect to see you.* | **+to** *This will be a surprise to most people in the office.* | *Her answer* ***came as a surprise.*** | *It should* ***come as no surprise*** (=be expected) *that Stuart is being promoted.* | **a big/complete/total/great surprise** *Their engagement announcement was a big surprise.* → see Word Choice box at SHOCK¹

2 FEELING [C,U] the feeling you have when something unexpected or unusual happens: *Then –* ***much to my surprise*** (=in a way that surprised me) *– they offered me the job.* | **in/with surprise** *Gretchen looked up in surprise as Dale walked in.* | **get/have a surprise** *She got a surprise when she saw who had written the letter.* | *The new managers were* ***in for a few surprises*** (=likely to experience surprise). | **a nasty/rude surprise** *We had a rude surprise when the bill arrived.*

3 catch/take sb by surprise a) to surprise or shock someone by happening in a way that is not expected: *Ernie's kiss took her by surprise.* **b)** to suddenly attack a place or an opponent when they are not ready: *The sudden attack took the government by surprise.*

4 GIFT/PARTY ETC. [C] an unexpected present, trip etc. which you give to someone or organize for them, often on a special occasion: **+for** *I have a little surprise for you.*

5 surprise! SPOKEN said when you show someone something that you know will surprise them, or when they arrive at a surprise party for them

6 surprise, surprise HUMOROUS used when saying in a joking way that you expected something to happen or be true: *The study showed – surprise, surprise – that coffee makes you more alert.*

7 METHOD [U] the use of methods which are intended to cause surprise: ***The element of surprise*** *is a useful tool in making an arrest.*

[**Origin:** 1400–1500 Old French, past participle of *surprendre* **to take over, surprise**]

surprise² W3 *v.* [T] **1** to make someone feel surprised: *It was the tone of his voice that surprised me.* | *The report's conclusions have surprised many analysts.* | **sth does not surprise sb** *Russ's success doesn't surprise me at all.* | **it surprises sb (that)** *Looking back, does it surprise you that she left?* | **it surprises sb to see/find/know etc.** *It surprised me to hear how difficult she is to work with.* | **it wouldn't surprise me if** *It wouldn't surprise me if they got a divorce.* | **surprise sb with sth** *They may surprise you with their ingenuity.* **2** to find, catch, or attack someone when they are not expecting it, especially when they are doing something they should not be doing: *A security guard surprised the burglars in the storeroom.*

surprise³ *adj.* [only before noun] not expected: *a surprise visitor* | *a suprise announcement*

sur·prised /sɚˈpraɪzd/ S1 *adj.* **1** having the feeling you get when something unusual or unexpected happens: *I was so surprised when I saw you walk in!* | **+at/by** *He was surprised at how angry Sabina sounded.* | **surprised (that)** *No one is really surprised that the negotiations failed.* | **surprised to see/hear/learn etc.** *I bet she'll be really surprised to see me.* | *I* ***wouldn't be surprised if*** *Jacobs won the tournament* (=I think it is likely this will happen). | ***Don't be surprised if*** *no one shows up* (=this is likely to happen). | *I was* ***pleasantly surprised*** *by what I saw.*

THESAURUS

amazed very surprised: *I was amazed that someone so big could be so quick.*
shocked feeling surprised, and often upset or offended: *We were all shocked by the news.*
astonished very surprised: *Her lawyer was astonished at the verdict.*
astounded very surprised: *Ed was astounded at how much the town had changed.*
flabbergasted very surprised and shocked: *People were flabbergasted; something like this couldn't happen.*
stunned too surprised and shocked to speak: *We watched in stunned disbelief.*
dumbfounded too surprised and confused to speak: *"Frank's here," said my father. I stood there dumbfounded. I hadn't seen Frank in ten years.*
nonplussed so surprised that you do not know what to say or do: *Henry seemed nonplussed by what Doreen had said.*
taken aback surprised by what someone says or does: *At first she was taken aback, but then she laughed.*

2 [only before noun] showing that someone is surprised: *She gave him a surprised look.*

surˈprise ˌparty *n.* [C] a party that is given for someone who does not expect it, at which the guests shout "Surprise!" when that person arrives

sur·pris·ing /sɚˈpraɪzɪŋ/ *adj.* unusual or unexpected: *surprising news* | *Our findings were somewhat surprising.* | **it is surprising (that)** *It's surprising that Heidi chose not to take the job.* | **it is surprising how/what etc.** *It's surprising how quickly you get used to things.* | **hardly/scarcely surprising** *Her confession is hardly surprising, given the evidence against her.* | ***A surprising number of*** *people said yes.* → see Word Choice box at SHOCK²

THESAURUS

extraordinary unusual and surprising: *It's an extraordinary book.*
amazing very surprising or unexpected, and sometimes difficult to believe: *It's amazing how fast some animals can run.*
shocking surprising and upsetting: *That so many children live in poverty in our rich country is shocking.*
astonishing very surprising, and often difficult to believe: *The population of the world is growing at an astonishing rate.*
astounding very surprising, and almost impossible to believe: *the astounding success of her second novel*
staggering very surprising and shocking, especially because something is so large: *a staggering sum of money*
stunning very surprising and shocking: *In a stunning announcement, the senator said he was retiring.*
unbelievable so surprising that you can hardly believe it: *The change in her was unbelievable.*

sur·pris·ing·ly /sɚˈpraɪzɪŋli/ *adv.* at a time or in a way that is surprising or unexpected: [+ adj./adv.] *The test was surprisingly easy.* | [sentence adverb] *Surprisingly, John agreed to come.* | ***Not surprisingly**, Barbara left him when she found out about the affair.*

sur·real /səˈril/ *adj.* a surreal situation or experience is very strange, like something from a dream

sur·re·al·ism /səˈriəˌlɪzəm/ *n.* [U] ENG. LANG. ARTS a style of 20th-century art or literature in which the artist or writer connects unrelated images and objects in a strange way —**surrealist** *adj.* —**surrealist** *n.* [C]

sur·re·al·is·tic /səˌriəˈlɪstɪk/ *adj.* **1** seeming very strange because of a combination of many unusual unrelated events, images etc. **2** ENG. LANG. ARTS relating to surrealism SYN surrealist —**surrealistically** /-kli/ *adv.*

sur·ren·der[1] /səˈrɛndɚ/ *v.*
1 STOP FIGHTING [I] also **surrender yourself** to say officially that you want to stop fighting because you realize that you cannot win: *All three gunmen had surrendered by the end of the day.* | +**to** *After 74 days of battle, the army surrendered to the British.*

THESAURUS

give in to accept that you have lost a fight, game etc.: *Eventually she gave in.*
concede to admit that you are not going to win a game, argument, battle etc.: *Davis conceded defeat in the election.*
admit/accept defeat to accept that you have not won something: *In July 1905, Russia admitted defeat in its war with Japan.*

2 LAND/WEAPONS [T] to give your soldiers or land to an enemy after they have beaten you in a battle: **surrender sb/sth to sb** *They were given two hours to surrender their weapons to authorities.*
3 GIVE UP STH IMPORTANT [T] to give up something that is important or necessary, often because you feel forced to: *Ventura surrendered custody of all six of her children.*
4 **surrender (yourself) to sth** to allow yourself to do, feel, or be influenced by something that you have been fighting against: *Colette surrendered to temptation and took out a cigarette.*
5 IMPORTANT DOCUMENT [T] FORMAL to give something such as a LICENSE or a PASSPORT to someone in authority so that it cannot be used anymore: **surrender sth to sb** *The court ordered Bond to surrender his passport to the authorities.*

surrender[2] *n.* [singular, U] **1** the act of saying officially that you want to stop fighting because you realize that you cannot win: *terms of surrender* | +**of** *the surrender of Germany* | *The allies demanded **unconditional surrender*** (=the act of accepting total defeat). **2** the act of giving up weapons, land, people etc to someone who has defeated you or to the police: +**of** *the surrender of weapons* **3** the act of giving up something, usually because you are forced to: +**of** *a surrender of power* **4** LITERARY the act of allowing yourself to do, feel, or be influenced by something that you have been fighting against: +**to** *his total surrender to drug addiction*

sur·rep·ti·tious·ly /ˌsɚəpˈtɪʃəsli, ˌsʌrəp-/ *adv.* FORMAL secretly, quickly, or quietly, so that other people do not notice: *Helen eyed him surreptitiously.* —**surreptitious** *adj.* —**surreptitiousness** *n.* [U]

sur·rey /ˈsɚi, ˈsʌri/ *n. plural* **surreys** [C] a light CARRIAGE with two seats, which was pulled by a horse and was used in the past

sur·ro·gate[1] /ˈsɚəgɪt, ˈsʌrə-/ *adj.* [only before noun] a surrogate person or thing is one that takes the place of someone or something else

surrogate[2] *n.* [C] **1** someone or something that takes the place of someone or something else **2** a surrogate mother —**surrogacy** *n.* [U]

ˌsurrogate ˈmother *n.* [C] a woman who has a baby for another woman who is unable to give birth, and then gives her the baby after it is born —**surrogate motherhood** *n.* [U]

sur·round[1] /səˈraʊnd/ W2 *v.* [T]
1 BE ALL AROUND to be all around someone or something: *A high fence surrounds the building.* | *The lake is surrounded by trees.*
2 **surround sth with sth** to put things all around something: *They surrounded the site with barbed wire.*
3 POLICE if police or soldiers surround a place, they arrange themselves in positions all the way around it: *FBI agents surrounded the house.* | *Police **have** the building **surrounded**.*
4 GROUP OF PEOPLE if a lot of a particular type of people surround you, they are near you or are important in your life: *At work, I'm surrounded by idiots.*
5 BE RELATED to be closely related to a situation or event: *A great deal of controversy has surrounded the new drug.*
6 **surround yourself with sb/sth** to choose to have certain people or things near you all the time: *He surrounds himself with women.*
[**Origin:** 1400–1500 Old French *suronder* **to overflow, flood**, from Late Latin *superundare*, from Latin *unda* **wave**]

surround[2] *n.* [C] an area around the edge of something, especially one that is decorated or made of a different material

sur·round·ing /səˈraʊndɪŋ/ *adj.* [only before noun] near or around a particular place: *the surrounding villages*

sur·round·ings /səˈraʊndɪŋz/ *n.* [plural] the objects, buildings, natural things etc. that are around a person or thing at a particular time: *It took a while to get used to my new surroundings.*

surˈround ˌsound *n.* [U] a system of four or more SPEAKERS (=pieces of equipment that sound comes out of) used with movies and television so that the sounds from the movie come from all directions —**surround-sound** *adj.* [only before noun]

sur·tax /ˈsɚtæks/ *n.* [U] ECONOMICS an additional tax, especially on money you earn if it is higher than a particular amount

sur·veil /sɚˈveɪl/ *v.* **surveilled**, **surveilling** [T] INFORMAL to watch a person or place carefully because they may be connected with criminal activities

sur·veil·lance /sɚˈveɪləns/ *n.* [U] **1** the act of carefully watching a person or place because they may be connected with criminal activities: *The suspects are still **under surveillance**.* | **a surveillance camera/tape etc.** (=equipment used for surveillance) **2** the act of carefully watching the military activities of another country to see what they are planning to do: **a surveillance plane/mission/satellite etc.** *surveillance flights over enemy territory*

S

sur·vey[1] /ˈsɚveɪ/ Ac W2 *n.* [C] **1** a set of questions that you ask a large number of people in order to find out about their opinions or behavior: **conduct/carry out/take a survey** *The university is conducting a survey of students' views.* | **a survey shows/reveals/says/finds sth** *The survey showed that children's eating habits are changing.* ▸see THESAURUS box at **poll**[1] **2** an examination of an area of land in order to make a map of it: *a geological survey* **3** a general description or report about a particular subject or situation: +**of** *a survey of modern English literature*

sur·vey[2] /sɚˈveɪ, ˈsɚveɪ/ Ac *v.* **surveys, surveyed, surveying** [T] **1** to ask a large number of people questions in order to find out their attitudes or opinions: *Over 1,000 people were surveyed for this report.* **2** to look at or consider someone or something carefully, especially in order to form an opinion about them: *They got out of the car to survey the damage.* **3** to examine and measure an area of land and record the details on a map [**Origin:** 1400–1500 Old French *surveeir* **to look over**]

ˈ**survey** ˌ**course** *n.* [C] a college course that gives an introduction to a subject for people who have not studied it before

S

sur·vey·or /sɚˈveɪɚ/ *n.* [C] someone whose job is to measure and record the details of an area of land

sur·viv·al /sɚˈvaɪvəl/ Ac W3 *n.* [U] **1** the state of continuing to exist, when there is a risk you might die: +**of** *the survival of endangered species* | *Doctors say his* ***chances of survival*** *are not good.* | *the survival rate for people with the disease* | **a fight/struggle for survival** (=a struggle to continue to exist) **2** the state of continuing to exist in spite of difficulties or dangers: *Many small firms are now fighting for survival.* | +**of** *the survival of the domestic steel industry* **3 survival of the fittest** a situation in which only the strongest and most successful people or things continue to exist

sur·vi·val·ist /sɚˈvaɪvəlɪst/ *n.* [C] someone who carefully prepares so that they will survive something bad that they think is going to happen, such as a war, especially by storing food and weapons —**survivalist** *adj.* —**survivalism** *n.* [U]

surˈvival kit *n.* [C] a set of things in a special container that you need to help you stay alive if you get hurt or lost

sur·vive /sɚˈvaɪv/ Ac S2 W2 *v.*
1 STAY ALIVE [I,T] to continue to live after an accident, war, illness etc.: *Only 12 of the passengers survived.* | *She survived the attack.*
2 CONTINUE TO EXIST [I,T] to continue to exist in spite of many difficulties or dangers: *A few pages of the original manuscript still survive.* | *The company survived the recession.*
3 AFFORD WHAT YOU NEED [I] to manage to live, buy food etc. when you have very little money: +**on** *We can't survive on just one salary.*
4 CONTINUE TO LIVE NORMALLY [I,T] to continue to live normally and not be too upset by your problems: *I'm sure she will survive this crisis.*
5 LIVE LONGER [T usually passive] to live longer than someone else, usually someone closely related to you: *He is survived by his wife and two children.*
[**Origin:** 1400–1500 Old French *survivre* **to live longer than,** from Latin *supervivere*] —**survivable** *adj.* —**survivability** /sɚˌvaɪvəˈbɪləti/ *n.* [U]

sur·vi·vor /sɚˈvaɪvɚ/ Ac *n.* [C] **1** someone or something that still exists in spite of having been almost destroyed or killed: *Unfortunately, there were no survivors.* | *breast cancer survivors* | +**of** *the survivors of the plane crash* | **the sole/lone survivor** (=the only person who survives) **2** someone who is still alive when a close relative has died: *Miss Arthur never married and* ***left no survivors.*** **3** someone who manages to live their life without being too upset by problems: *Don't worry about Kurt – he's a survivor.* **4** a company, business etc. that continues to exist in spite of many difficulties

sus·cep·ti·bil·i·ty /səˌsɛptəˈbɪləti/ *n. plural* **susceptibilities** [C,U] **1** how likely someone is to suffer from a particular illness, or the condition of being likely to suffer from it: +**to** *He has a genetic susceptibility to colon cancer.* **2** how likely someone or something is to be damaged, hurt, or badly affected by something: +**to** *the economy's susceptibility to inflation* **3 sb's susceptibilities** [plural] someone's feelings about something SYN **sensibilities**

sus·cep·ti·ble /səˈsɛptəbəl/ *adj.* **1** likely to suffer from a particular illness: +**to** *He's very susceptible to chest infections.* **2** likely to be damaged, hurt, or badly affected by something: +**to** *Soil on the slopes is susceptible to erosion.* **3** easily influenced or persuaded by other people SYN **impressionable** **4 susceptible of change/interpretation/analysis etc.** FORMAL able to be changed, considered in a different way etc. [**Origin:** 1600–1700 Late Latin *susceptibilis*, from Latin *suscipere* **to take up, admit**]

su·shi /ˈsuʃi/ *n.* [U] a type of Japanese food consisting of small cakes of cooked rice with raw fish, vegetables etc. inside or on top

ˈ**sushi bar** *n.* [C] a small restaurant where sushi is served

sus·pect[1] /səˈspɛkt/ W3 *v.* **1** [T not in progressive] to think that something bad or secret is probably happening, true, or likely: *Through it all, he never suspected anything.* | **suspect (that)** *I suspected that she was not telling the truth.* | *Police say they do not* ***suspect foul play*** (=think that murder was likely) *in the man's death.* ▸see THESAURUS box at **think** **2** [T not in progressive] to think that someone is probably guilty of a crime: *Despite the evidence, no one suspected them.* | **suspect sb of (doing) sth** *Burton was suspected of poisoning her husband.* **3** [T not in progressive] to doubt that something is true: *We eventually began to suspect his loyalty.* [**Origin:** 1400–1500 Latin *suspectare*, from the past participle of *suspicere* **to look up at, admire, distrust**]

sus·pect[2] /ˈsʌspɛkt/ *n.* [C] **1** someone who is thought to be guilty of a crime: *a murder suspect* | **the prime/chief suspect** *He is the police's prime suspect in the case.* **2** something that is thought to be the cause of a problem, illness etc.

suspect[3] *adj.* **1** likely not to be good, believable, honest, dependable etc.: *The food looked a little suspect to me.* | *a suspect business deal* | *Some of the data they used was* ***highly suspect.*** **2** [only before noun] suspect packages, goods etc. look as if they contain something illegal or dangerous

sus·pect·ed /səˈspɛktɪd/ *adj.* **1** likely or believed to be illegal or dangerous: *Employees are asked to report any suspected fraud.* | **a suspected criminal/terrorist/spy etc.** *The police tried to arrest the suspected burglar.* **2** a suspected illness or medical condition is one which doctors think a person may have, although they are not sure

sus·pend /səˈspɛnd/ Ac *v.* [T]
1 STOP STH to officially stop something from continuing, especially for a short time: *Sales of the drug have now been suspended.*
2 LEGAL PERMISSION to officially state that a document cannot be used legally for a period of time: *His driver's license has been suspended.*
3 FROM SCHOOL/JOB ETC. to make someone leave school, a job, or an organization temporarily, especially because they have broken the rules: **suspend sb (from sth)** *Knight was suspended from her job without pay.*
4 HANG STH to hang someone or something, especially something heavy, from something else SYN **hang**: **suspend sb/sth from sth** *Two large stainless steel frames were suspended from the ceiling.* | **suspend sb/sth by sth** *The bridge was suspended by wire cables.*
5 be suspended in water/air/space etc. TECHNICAL if something is suspended in a liquid or in air, it floats in it without moving much
6 be suspended in time to seem as if no change or progress has happened after a long period of time: *The town seemed suspended in time.*
7 suspend (your) disbelief to forget or allow yourself

to forget that something such as a performance, movie etc. is not real or true → see also **suspend/reserve judgment** at JUDGMENT (1)

sus,pended ani'mation *n.* [U] **1** a state in which someone's body processes are slowed down to a state almost like death **2** a feeling that you cannot do anything because you have to wait for what happens next

sus,pended 'sentence *n.* [C] LAW a punishment given by a court in which the criminal will only go to prison if they do something else illegal within a particular period of time

sus·pend·ers /sə'spɛndɚz/ *n.* [plural] two bands of cloth that go over your shoulders and fasten to your pants to hold them up

sus·pense /sə'spɛns/ *n.* [U] **1** a feeling of excitement or nervousness when you do not know what will happen next: **keep/hold sb in suspense** *Don't keep me in suspense – tell me what happened!* | ***The suspense is killing me*** (=the suspense is making me too nervous)! **2** a type of movie, book etc. that makes you feel excited or nervous because you do not know what will happen next: *Do you prefer action or suspense?* | *a suspense novel* —**suspenseful** *adj.*: *a suspenseful story*

sus·pen·sion /sə'spɛnʃən/ Ac *n.*
1 STOPPING [U] the act of officially stopping something from continuing for a period of time: **+of** *a suspension of military activities*
2 LEGAL PERMISSION [U] the act of stating officially that a document cannot be used legally for a period of time: **+of** *the suspension of his medical license*
3 REMOVAL [C] the removal of someone from a team, job, school etc. for a period of time, especially to punish them: **+from** *a ten-day suspension from school*
4 CAR EQUIPMENT [U] equipment attached to the wheels of a vehicle which makes riding in the vehicle feel smoother, especially on bad roads
5 suspension of disbelief the condition of forgetting or allowing yourself to forget that something such as a performance, movie etc. is not real or true
6 MIXTURE [C] CHEMISTRY a liquid mixture containing very small pieces of solid material that have not DISSOLVED in the liquid → see also COLLOID

sus'pension ,bridge *n.* [C] a bridge that is hung from strong steel ropes attached to towers

sus,pensory 'ligament *n* [C] BIOLOGY a band of strong TISSUE, similar to muscle, that holds an organ or part of the body in place, especially the LENS of your eye → see picture at EYE[1]

sus·pi·cion /sə'spɪʃən/ *n.* **1** [C,U] a feeling that someone is probably guilty of a crime or that something is wrong in a situation: **+of** *suspicions of child abuse* | **+about** *I told him my suspicions about Henry.* | *We can't prove anything yet, but we **have** our **suspicions**.* | *His unusual spending habits **aroused** the FBI's **suspicions*** (=made them think he was doing something wrong). | *The things he told me **confirmed** my **suspicions** about Jean.* | *Wheeler was arrested **on suspicion of** drunk driving* (=because police thought he was drunk). | *Hudson **came under suspicion of** committing the murders* (=police think he murdered someone). | **above/beyond suspicion** (=definitely not guilty of a crime) **2** [U] a feeling that you do not like or trust someone: *New people in the town were regarded **with suspicion**.* **3 I have a (sneaking) suspicion** also **I have my suspicions** to think you know something that is supposed to be secret: *I have a suspicion that everything will change when the boss gets back.* **4 a suspicion of sth** LITERARY a very small amount of something seen, heard, tasted etc.

sus·pi·cious /sə'spɪʃəs/ *adj.* **1** thinking that someone might be guilty of a crime or of doing something wrong, without being sure: **+of/about** *Police became suspicious of them after a tip-off.* | *His strange behavior **made me suspicious**.* **2** likely to be illegal or morally wrong SYN **suspect**: *a suspicious package* | **under/in suspicious circumstances** *His wife disappeared under suspicious circumstances.* | **anything/something suspicious** *Residents are asked to report anything suspicious to police.* | **a suspicious character** (=a person you do not know, who is behaving in a way that makes

you suspicious) **3** feeling that you do not like or trust someone or something: **+of** *Many people are suspicious of new technology.*

sus·pi·cious·ly /sə'spɪʃəsli/ *adv.* **1** in a way that shows you think someone has done something wrong or dishonest: *The soldiers watched us suspiciously.* **2** a way that makes people think that something bad or illegal is happening: *The two men were behaving suspiciously.* **3 suspiciously quiet/nice/good/friendly etc.** too quiet, nice, good, friendly etc. so that you think something might be wrong or illegal: *The price seemed suspiciously low.* **4 sth looks/sounds etc. suspiciously like sth** used to say that something looks, sounds etc. very much like something else, especially something bad: *His compliments often sound suspiciously like insults.*

Sus·que·han·nock /ˌsʌskwə'hænək/ a Native American tribe that formerly lived in the northeastern area of the U.S.

sus·tain /sə'steɪn/ Ac W3 *v.*
1 MAKE STH CONTINUE FORMAL [T] to make something continue over a period of time SYN **maintain**: *Increased construction could help sustain job growth.*
2 sustain damage/injury/defeat etc. FORMAL to be damaged, hurt, defeated etc.: *The driver sustained a severe head injury.*
3 FOOD/WATER [T] to provide enough food, water etc. for people to stay alive: *The land can barely sustain its population.*
4 GIVE STRENGTH [T] to make it possible for someone to stay strong or hopeful: *The thought of getting home was the only thing that sustained me in the hospital.*
5 WEIGHT [T] FORMAL to hold up the weight of something SYN **support**: *The floor cannot sustain the weight of a piano.*
6 (objection) sustained LAW used by a judge in a court of law to say that someone was right to object to another person's statement → see also **(objection) overruled** at OVERRULE (2)
7 IDEA [T] FORMAL to support or prove an idea, argument etc.
[**Origin:** 1200–1300 Old French *sustenir*, from Latin *sustinere* **to hold up, sustain**]

sus·tain·a·ble /sə'steɪnəbəl/ Ac *adj.* an action or process that is sustainable can continue or last for a long time: *sustainable economic growth*

sus,tainable de'velopment *n.* [U] the practice of limiting how much coal, oil, and other natural materials a country or industry uses, so that they continue to last for a long time

sus·te·nance /'sʌstənəns/ Ac *n.* [U] **1** BIOLOGY food that people, animals, or plants need to stay alive and healthy SYN **nourishment** **2** LITERARY something that gives you strength or hope **3** FORMAL the act of making something continue

sut·tee, sati /sʌ'ti, 'sʌti/ *n.* [U] the ancient custom in the Hindu religion of burning a wife with her husband when he dies

su·ture /'sutʃɚ/ *n.* [C,U] the act of sewing a wound together, or a stitch used to do this —**suture** *v.* [T]

SUV *n.* [C] a SPORT-UTILITY VEHICLE

Su·va /'suvə/ the capital city of Fiji

su·ze·rain·ty /'suzərənti, -reɪn-/ *n.* [U] POLITICS the right of a country or leader to rule over another country —**suzerain** *n.* [singular]

svelte /svɛlt/ *adj.* thin and graceful: *a svelte young man* [**Origin:** 1800–1900 French, Italian *svelto* **stretched**, from *svellere* **to pull out**]

Sven·ga·li /svɛn'gɑli/ *n.* [C] DISAPPROVING a man who has great influence or power over someone's mind and makes them do bad or immoral things [**Origin:** 1900–2000 *Svengali*, character who uses hypnotism to get control over people in the book Trilby (1894) by George du Maurier]

S.W., SW the written abbreviation of SOUTHWEST

S

swab[1] /swɑb/ *n.* [C] **1** a short stick with cotton on the end, used to clean a wound, clean your ears, or put medicine on your body → see also Q-TIP: *a cotton swab* **2** a small piece of soft material used to clean a wound or put medicine on someone's body **3** a small amount of something that is taken from someone's body using a swab, in order to do a medical test

swab[2] *v.* **swabbed, swabbing** [T] **1** also **swab down** to clean something, especially the floors of a ship **2** to clean a wound with a piece of material

swad·dle /ˈswɑdl/ *v.* [T] to wrap a young baby tightly to keep its arms and legs from moving

ˈswaddling ˌclothes *n.* [plural] OLD USE pieces of cloth wrapped around young babies to keep their arms and legs from moving

swag /swæg/ *n.* **1** [C] a deep fold of material, especially in or above a curtain **2** [U] SLANG the goods stolen when someone is robbed → see also LOOT

swag·ger[1] /ˈswægɚ/ *v.* [I always + adv./prep.] to walk in a relaxed way, taking large steps, in a way that shows that you are extremely confident: +**down/in/out etc.** *J.D. swaggered over to the bar to get a drink.*

swagger[2] *n.* [singular, U] **1** a relaxed way of walking that shows you are very confident **2** a way of talking or behaving that shows you are very confident

S

Swa·hi·li /swɑˈhili/ *n.* [U] a language that is spoken in several countries in East Africa, for example in Kenya and Tanzania

swain /sweɪn/ *n.* [C] LITERARY **1** a young man who is in love with a girl **2** a young man from the country

swal·low[1] /ˈswɑloʊ/ S3 *v.*
1 FOOD [I,T] to make food or drink go down your throat and to your stomach: *Chew your food well before you swallow.*
2 NERVOUSLY [I] to make a movement with your throat as if you are swallowing food, especially because you are nervous: *She swallowed twice, preparing to tell him the truth.* | *I **swallowed hard** and opened the door.*
3 BELIEVE/ACCEPT [T] INFORMAL to immediately believe a story, explanation etc. that is not actually true: *I found the story a little **hard to swallow*** (=difficult to believe). ►see THESAURUS box at **believe**
4 swallow your pride to do something even though it embarrasses you or you feel that you should not have to do it: *I swallowed my pride and did as I was told.*
5 FEELING [T] to stop yourself from showing your feelings, especially bad feelings: *Mary tried hard to swallow her anger.*
[**Origin:** Old English *swelgan*] → see also **a bitter pill (to swallow)** at BITTER (8)

swallow up *phr. v.* **1 swallow sth ↔ up** if a company, organization, or country swallows up a smaller one, the smaller one becomes part of it and does not exist on its own anymore **2** LITERARY **swallow sb/sth ↔ up** if someone or something is swallowed up by something, they become hidden or covered by it and disappear: *He was swallowed up by the fog.* **3 swallow sth ↔ up** if something swallows up an amount of money, time etc., it uses a large amount or all of it: *Housing costs swallowed up most of their income.* **4 swallow sth ↔ up** if land is swallowed up, it is used for building houses, roads etc.

swallow[2] *n.* [C] **1** BIOLOGY a small bird with a tail in the shape of an UPSIDE DOWN V and long pointed wings that flies quickly and gracefully **2** an act of making food, drink etc. go down your throat

swal·low·tail /ˈswɑloʊˌteɪl/ *n.* [C] a black and yellow BUTTERFLY with two long thin parts at the bottom of its wings

swam /swæm/ *v.* the past tense of SWIM

swa·mi /ˈswɑmi/ *n.* [C] a Hindu religious teacher

swamp[1] /swɑmp, swɔmp/ *n.* [C,U] EARTH SCIENCE a large area of low wet land near a river, where wild plants and trees grow → see also BOG —**swampy** *adj.*: *swampy ground* → see picture on page A31

swamp[2] *v.* [T] **1** [usually passive] to suddenly give someone a lot of work, problems etc. to deal with: **be swamped with sth** *We've been swamped with new orders all week.* **2** [usually passive] if people swamp a place, they fill it in large numbers **3** if a lot of water swamps a place, it suddenly covers it, especially in a way that causes damage **4** LITERARY if a feeling swamps someone, they feel it very strongly and it prevents them from thinking about anything else

swan /swɑn/ *n.* [C] BIOLOGY a large white, or sometimes black, bird with a long graceful neck, that lives on rivers and lakes

ˈswan dive *n.* [C] a DIVE into water, that starts with your arms stretched out from the sides of your body

swank·y /ˈswæŋki/ *adj. comparative* **swankier**, *superlative* **swankiest** INFORMAL very fashionable, expensive, and designed to make people notice: *a swanky hotel*

ˈswan song *n.* [C] the last piece of work or last performance of a poet, painter etc.

swap[1] /swɑp/ *v.* **swapped, swapping** INFORMAL **1** [I,T] to exchange something with someone, especially so that each of you gets what you want SYN **trade**: **swap sth for sth** *He swapped his watch for a box of cigars.* | **swap sth with sb** *I swapped hats with Mandy.* | **swap sb sth for sth** *I'll swap you my earrings for yours.* ►see THESAURUS box at **exchange**[2] **2** [T] to tell information to someone and be given information in return: *Harvey and I spent the evening **swapping** travel **stories**.* **3** [I,T] to do the things that someone else has been doing, and let them do the things that you have been doing: *Why don't we swap jobs?* **4** [T] to get rid of one thing, or stop using it, and buy or get a different one, or start using a different one: **swap sth for sth** *I think we should swap this car for a smaller one.* **5 swap places/seats (with sb)** to let someone sit or stand in your place, so that you can have their place **6 swap places (with sb)** to do someone else's job, live their life etc., and let them have your job, live your life etc. [**Origin:** 1500–1600 *swap* **to hit** (14–19 centuries), from the sound; from the practice of striking the hands together when agreeing a business deal]

swap[2] *n.* [C] INFORMAL **1** [usually singular] an exchange of one thing for another: *a swap of arms for hostages* **2** a swap meet

ˈswap ˌmeet *n.* [C] an occasion when people meet to buy and sell used goods, or to exchange them

swarm[1] /swɔrm/ *n.* [C] **1** BIOLOGY a large group of insects or other animals which move together, especially BEES: +**of** *a swarm of locusts* **2** a crowd or large number of people: +**of** *Swarms of tourists visit the resort every summer.*.

swarm[2] *v.* [I always + adv./prep.,T] **1** if people swarm somewhere, they go there quickly as a very large crowd: *Reporters swarmed the area outside the courtroom.* **2** BIOLOGY if insects or other animals swarm, they fly together in a very large group: *Flies swarmed around him.*

swarm with sb/sth *phr. v.* to be full of a moving crowd of people or animals: *The downtown was swarming with police.*

swar·thy /ˈswɔrði, -θi/ *adj. comparative* **swarthier**, *superlative* **swarthiest** a swarthy man has dark skin and often looks slightly dangerous

swash·buck·ling /ˈswɑʃˌbʌklɪŋ, ˈswɔʃ-/ *adj.* WRITTEN enjoying adventures and fighting, or involving people like this: *a swashbuckling hero* —**swashbuckler** *n.* [C]

swas·ti·ka /ˈswɑstɪkə/ *n.* [C] **1** a sign of a cross with each end bent at 90° used as a SYMBOL of the Nazi party **2** a similar sign with the ends of the cross bent in the opposite way used as an ancient religious SYMBOL [**Origin:** 1800–1900 Sanskrit *svastika*, from *svasti* **being well, good luck**]

SWAT /swɑt/ *adj.* [only before noun] **special weapons and tactics** relating to a specially trained group of police who handle the most dangerous and violent situations: *a SWAT team*

swat /swɑt/ *v.* **swatted, swatting** [T] **1** to hit an insect to try to kill it **2** to hit someone on their bottom with your open hand or an object, especially as a punishment SYN spank **3** to hit something with your open hand, especially in a way that makes it move or change direction SYN slap: *She swatted his hand away.* [**Origin:** 1600–1700 *squat* in its original meaning **to crush** (13–19 centuries)] —**swat** *n.* [C]

swat at sb/sth *phr. v.* to move your hand to try to hit someone or something, especially an insect

swat sth ↔ **away/down** *phr. v.* to prevent an idea, action etc. from being considered or done because you think it is annoying or not good enough

Swatch /swɑtʃ/ *n.* [C] TRADEMARK a type of watch made by a Swiss company, often made of brightly colored plastic

swatch /swɑtʃ/ *n.* [C] a piece of cloth that is used as an example of a type of material or its quality

swath /swɑθ/ also **swathe** /swɑθ, sweɪð/ *n.* [C] FORMAL **1** a long band of cloth, color, light etc.: *a swath of beige cloth* **2** a long narrow area of land that is different from the land on either side of it: *The fire had destroyed huge swaths of land.* **3 cut a swath through sth** to destroy a large amount or part of something, or cause a lot of damage to it: *The current economic crisis has cut a swath through the car industry.*

swathe /swɑθ, sweɪð/ *v.* LITERARY **be swathed in sth** to be dressed, wrapped, or covered in a large piece of cloth

swat·ter /ˈswɑt̬ɚ/ *n.* [C] a FLYSWATTER

sway¹ /sweɪ/ *v.* **sways, swayed, swaying** **1** [I,T] to move slowly from one side to another, or make something do this: *The trees swayed in the breeze.* | *Connie swayed her hips in time with the music.* **2** [T] to influence someone who has not yet decided about something so that they change their opinion: *Will these arguments sway voters?*

sway² *n.* [U] **1** power to rule or influence people SYN control: **+over** *His sway over the committee is impressive.* | **+with/among** *sway among young voters* | **+in** *limits to the U.S.'s sway in South Asia* | **have/hold/gain sway** *No one has more sway with her than her mother.* | *The region is* ***under the sway of*** (=controlled by) *militia groups.* **2** a gentle swinging movement from side to side

sway·backed /ˈsweɪbækt/ *adj.* **1** having a back that curves in too much **2** a swaybacked bridge, building etc. has a top surface that curves down in the middle

Swa·zi·land /ˈswɑziˌlænd/ a country in southeast Africa between South Africa and Mozambique —**Swazi** *n., adj.*

swear /swɛr/ S2 *v.* *past tense* **swore** /swɔr/, *past participle* **sworn** /swɔrn/

1 OFFENSIVE LANGUAGE [I] to use offensive language, especially because you are angry: *I've never heard her swear.* | **swear at sb/sth** *I'm sorry I swore at you.* | **swear like a sailor/trooper** (=use very offensive language)

2 STATE THE TRUTH [T not in progressive] SPOKEN to emphasize that what you have said is the truth: **swear (that)** *He swore that he didn't tell Tim.* | ***I swear to God*** *I didn't take anything out of your room.* | *She* ***swears up and down*** (=used to emphasize something) *that it wasn't her.* | **swear on the Bible/your life etc.** *I swear on my life I don't know where the money is.*

3 I could have sworn that... also **I could swear that...** SPOKEN used to say that you were sure about something, but now you are not sure: *I could've sworn that I'd met her before.*

4 SERIOUS/OFFICIAL PROMISE [T] to make a very serious promise: **swear (that)** *Sam swore that he would always support them.* | **swear to do sth** *Do you swear to tell the whole truth?* | *All of us* ***swear an oath*** *to protect our country as military officers.* | *Bouchard refused to* ***swear allegiance to*** (=promise to be loyal to) *the queen.* ►see THESAURUS box at **promise¹**

5 swear sb to secrecy/silence to make someone promise not to tell anyone what you have told them

swear by sth *phr. v.* INFORMAL to believe strongly that something is good or effective: *She swears by vitamin C as a cure for colds.*

swear sb ↔ **in** *phr. v.* **1** to make someone promise publicly to be loyal to a country, official job etc.: **swear sb in as sth** *McCrory was sworn in as city manager last March.* **2** LAW to make someone give an official promise in a court of law: *The jury had to be sworn in first.*

[**Origin:** Old English *swerian*] → see also SWEARING-IN

swear sth ↔ **off** *phr. v.* to promise to stop doing something that is bad for you: *I'm swearing off alcohol after last night!*

swear to sth *phr. v.* **1** LAW to say that something is true, especially in a court of law: *The maid saw her leave at 1:30, and she's willing to swear to it.* **2 I couldn't/wouldn't swear to (doing) sth** used to say that you think something is true, but you are not certain: *I think I parked across the street, but I wouldn't swear to it.*

ˌswearing-ˈin also **ˌswearing-ˈin ˌceremony** *n.* [U] an official ceremony when someone promises publicly to be loyal to a country, do an official job well and honestly etc.

ˈswear word *n.* [C] a word that is considered to be offensive or shocking by most people

sweat¹ /swɛt/ *v.*

1 LIQUID FROM SKIN [I] BIOLOGY to have liquid coming out through your skin, especially because you are hot, frightened, or exercising: *It's so hot, I can't stop sweating.* | *All the stress was* ***making*** *her* ***sweat.*** | *You're* ***sweating like a pig*** (=sweating a lot).

2 WORK [I] INFORMAL to work hard: *They sweated and saved for ten years to buy a house.* | **+over** *He'd sweated over the plans for six months.* | *Many people have* ***sweated blood*** (=worked very hard) *to build up the company.*

3 WORRY [I] INFORMAL to be anxious, nervous, or worried about something: *Let them sweat – I'll make my decision tomorrow.* | *We were* ***sweating bullets*** (=worrying) *until we found out we wouldn't lose our jobs.*

4 don't sweat it SPOKEN used to tell someone not to worry about something

5 don't sweat the small stuff SPOKEN used to tell someone not to worry about unimportant things

6 PRODUCE LIQUID [I] if something such as a container with a liquid in it or cheese sweats, liquid from the air or from inside it appears on its surface

sweat sth ↔ **off** *phr. v.* to lose weight by sweating: *I sweated off a few pounds in the steam room.*

sweat sth ↔ **out** *phr. v.* **1** to get rid of an illness or something bad in your body by making yourself sweat a lot: *I was in bed for two days sweating out a fever.* **2** to worry while you wait for something to happen: *We had to* ***sweat it out*** *for a few hours until the test results came back.* **3** to continue something until it is finished, even though it is difficult **4 sweat it out** to do hard physical exercise

sweat sth **out of** sb *phr. v.* INFORMAL to find out information from someone by asking lots of questions and threatening them

sweat² *n.*

1 LIQUID ON SKIN [singular, U] BIOLOGY liquid that comes out through your skin when you are hot, frightened, or exercising SYN perspiration: *Sweat was pouring down his face.* | *The men were* ***dripping with sweat*** *after an hour's work.* | **break (into) a sweat/break out in a sweat** (=to start sweating) | *It was cold, but I was* ***working up a sweat.***

2 a (cold) sweat the action of sweating because you are nervous or frightened: *I woke up from the nightmare* ***in a cold sweat.***

3 sweats [plural] INFORMAL a SWEAT SUIT or SWEAT PANTS

4 no sweat SPOKEN used to say that you can do something easily: *I'll finish this by tomorrow, no sweat.*

5 WORK [singular] hard work, especially when it is boring or difficult: *It'll take a lot of sweat to make this work.*

6 the sweat of sb's brow LITERARY the hard effort that someone has made in their work

7 in/into a sweat feeling or beginning to feel very nervous or worried about something: **get/break into a sweat** *It's not worth getting into a sweat about.*

S

8 (the) sweats [plural] the action of sweating because you are sick: *Do you suffer from* ***night sweats*** (=sweating while you sleep)?

sweat·band /ˈswɛtbænd/ *n.* [C] **1** a narrow band of cloth that you wear around your head or wrist to stop sweat from running down when you are running, playing a sport etc. **2** a narrow piece of cloth that you wear sewn or stuck in the inside of a hat

ˈsweat ˌequity *n.* [U] a share in the OWNERSHIP of something that someone gets because of work they have put into it, or the work itself

sweat·er /ˈswɛt̬ɚ/ S2 *n.* [C] a piece of warm wool, cotton etc. clothing for the top half of your body, that has long SLEEVES [**Origin:** 1800–1900 *sweat*; because it was originally worn when doing exercise, to make you sweat]

ˈsweat gland *n.* [C] BIOLOGY a small organ under your skin that produces sweat

ˈsweat pants *n.* [plural] soft thick pants, worn especially for sports

sweat·shirt /ˈswɛt-ʃɚt/ S3 *n.* [C] a piece of thick cotton clothing with long SLEEVES, worn on the top half of your body, especially for playing sports

sweat·shop /ˈswɛt-ʃɑp/ *n.* [C] a small business or factory, especially an illegal one, where people work hard in bad conditions for very little money

ˈsweat sock *n.* [C] a type of sock that you wear when you play sports

ˈsweat suit *n.* [C] a set of clothes made of thick soft material, worn especially for sports

sweat·y /ˈswɛt̬i/ *adj. comparative* **sweatier**, *superlative* **sweatiest** **1** covered with SWEAT: *sweaty palms* **2** smelling like sweat: *sweaty clothes* **3** a sweaty can, glass, or food has drops of liquid on its surface **4** very hot or difficult, and making you SWEAT: *a sweaty job*

Swe·den /ˈswidn/ a country on the PENINSULA of Scandinavia in northern Europe —**Swede** *n.* [C] —**Swedish** *adj., n.* [U]

sweep¹ /swip/ W2 *v. past tense and past participle* **swept** /swɛpt/

1 CLEAN STH [T] to clean the floor or ground using a BROOM, or remove dirt, dust etc. by doing this: *I just finished sweeping the kitchen floor.* | **sweep sth off/out/up etc.** *Could you sweep the snow off the patio for me?*

2 PUSH STH SOMEWHERE [T always + adv./prep.] to move something to a particular place or in a particular direction with a brushing or swinging movement: *I swept the papers quickly into the drawer.*

3 WIND/WAVES ETC. a) [I always + adv./prep.] to move somewhere quickly with a lot of force: +**across/through etc.** *A series of tornadoes swept through Kansas.* **b)** [T always + adv./prep.] to push someone or something somewhere with a lot of force: *Strong waves swept the boy out into the surf.* | *Half of the town was* ***swept away*** *by the hurricane.*

4 BECOME POPULAR/COMMON [I always + adv./prep.,T] if an idea, feeling, or activity sweeps a group of people or sweeps across, over etc. a group, it quickly becomes very popular or commonly used: +**across/through etc.** *The fashion trends are sweeping through the teenage population.* | **sweep the nation/country/state etc.** *Rumors of the scandal are sweeping the capital.*

5 GROUP a) [I always + adv./prep.] if a group of people or animals sweep somewhere, they quickly move there together: +**through/along etc.** *Soldiers swept through the city looking for rebels.* **b)** [T always + adv./prep.] if a crowd sweeps someone somewhere, it forces them to move in the same direction it is moving in: **sweep sb along/away etc.** *I got swept along by the crowds of commuters.*

6 POLITICS a) [I] if a political party sweeps an election, its members win most of the separate elections: *The party is expected to sweep the fall elections.* **b) sweep to power/victory** also **sweep into office** to be elected to an important position very easily and by a large number of votes: *Reformers swept to power by promising change.* **c) sweep sb to power/victory** also **sweep sb into office** to make it possible for someone to be elected to an important position very easily and by a large number of votes

7 SPORTS/GAMES [T] to win all of the games in a series of games: *The Dodgers swept the series.*

8 PERSON [I always + adv./prep.] if someone sweeps somewhere, they move quickly and confidently, especially because they are impatient or like to look important: +**into/through etc.** *She swept into the room.*

9 VEHICLE [I always + adv./prep.] if a vehicle sweeps somewhere, it moves quickly and smoothly without stopping or changing directly: +**by/past** *A large van swept past.*

10 sweep sb off their feet to make someone feel suddenly and strongly attracted to you in a romantic way

11 LIGHTS/EYES [I always + adv./prep.,T] if lights or someone's eyes sweep an area, they move or look quickly around it: *The helicopter's searchlights swept the streets below.* | +**over/across/around etc.** *His eyes swept over the audience.*

12 TOUCH A SURFACE [T] if something such as a dress sweeps the floor, ground etc., it touches it lightly as you move

13 FORM A CURVE [I always + adv./prep.,T] LITERARY to form a long curved shape: +**down/around etc.** *The hills swept down to the sea.*

14 sweep sth under the rug/carpet to try to keep something a secret, especially something you have done wrong

15 CHIMNEY [T] to clean something such as a CHIMNEY with a long brush

sweep sb ↔ **along** *phr. v.* to make someone so interested or involved in something that they forget about other things

sweep sth ↔ **aside** *phr. v.* to refuse to pay attention to something someone says: *Doubts about the drug's safety were swept aside.*

sweep away *phr. v.* **1 sweep sth ↔ away** to completely destroy something or make something disappear: *Poverty will be swept away.* **2 sweep sb ↔ away** to make someone so interested or involved in something that they forget about other things: *We were swept away by her enthusiasm.*

sweep sth ↔ **back** *phr. v.* if you sweep your hair back, you pull it back from your face, especially so that it stays in that style: *Kerry swept her hair back into a bun.*

sweep over sb *phr. v.* if a feeling sweeps over you, you feel it immediately: *The joy of winning swept over him.*

sweep up *phr. v.* **1 sweep sth ↔ up** to clean a place using a BROOM, or to pick up dirt, dust etc. in this way: *Could you sweep up the glass?* | *I'll just sweep up before I go.* **2 sweep sb ↔ up** to pick someone up in one quick movement: *Joe swept her up in his arms and kissed her.* **3 sweep your hair up** to pull your hair back away from your face so that it is on top of your head, especially so that it stays in that style

sweep² *n.* [C] **1** a long swinging movement of your arm, a weapon etc.: *She dismissed the idea with a sweep of her hand.* **2** [usually singular] a search or attack that moves over a large area: *Police made a sweep of the area.* **3** a series of several games that one team wins against another team; a series of several games or competitions in which one person or team wins all the games or competitions **4 the sweep of sth a)** a long curved line or area of land: *the sweep of the hills in the distance* **b)** the quality that an idea, plan, piece of writing etc. has of considering or affecting many different and important things: *the broad sweep of history* **5** a CHIMNEY SWEEP → see also **clean sweep** at CLEAN¹ (10)

sweep·er /ˈswipɚ/ *n.* [C] **1** someone or something that sweeps **2** a SOCCER player who plays in a position behind all of the other defending players on a team

sweep·ing /ˈswipɪŋ/ *adj.* **1** affecting many things, or making an important difference to things: **sweeping changes/cuts/laws etc.** *The computer industry has undergone sweeping changes.* | **a sweeping gesture** (=an action that affects many people or things) **2** DISAP-

PROVING **sweeping** statements or ideas are very general, do not consider details, and are usually unfair or untrue: *You're always making* ***sweeping generalizations*** *about women drivers.* **3** [only before noun] including a lot of information about a particular subject, especially about events that happened at different times and places: *a sweeping novel* **4 a sweeping victory** a very great victory in which someone wins by a large amount **5** gently curving: *a sweeping staircase* **6** very wide and open: *a sweeping view of the valley*

sweep·ings /ˈswipɪŋz/ *n.* [plural] dirt, dust etc. that is left to be swept up

sweeps /swips/ *n.* also **sweeps month/period etc.** a period of time during the year when TV stations try to find out which shows are the most popular

sweep·stakes /ˈswipsteɪks/ *n.* [C usually singular] **1** a type of competition in which you have a chance to win a prize if your name is chosen **2** a type of BETting in which the winner gets all of the money risked by everyone who BETS **3** a competition, election, argument etc. in which you cannot guess who will win or get the most advantages: *the presidential sweepstakes*

sweet¹ /swit/ S1 W2 *adj.*
1 TASTE having a taste like sugar → see also BITTER OPP **sour**: *The pie is a little too sweet for me.* | *sweet juicy peaches* ▸see THESAURUS box at **taste¹**
2 CHARACTER kind, gentle, and friendly: *Fran is such a sweet person.* | **it is sweet of sb to do sth** *It was sweet of you to help.*
3 FEELINGS making you feel happy and satisfied: *Revenge is sweet.* | *It was now her turn to enjoy* ***the sweet smell of success*** (=the pleasant feeling of being successful).
4 SMELL having a pleasant smell SYN **fragrant**: *a rose with a very sweet smell*
5 SOUND pleasant to listen to: *a sweet singing voice*
6 CHILDREN/SMALL THINGS looking pretty and attractive SYN **cute**: *Jessica looks so sweet in that hat.*
7 Sweet! SPOKEN used to say that you think that something is very good: *"I got four tickets to the concert." "Sweet!"*
8 a sweet deal a business or financial deal in which you get an advantage, pay a low price etc.: **give/get a sweet deal** *I got a sweet deal on the car.*
9 take your own sweet time also **do sth in your own sweet time** to take as long as you want to do something, without caring whether other people approve, especially in a way that annoys other people: *He just takes his own sweet time, doesn't he?*
10 have a sweet tooth to like things that taste like sugar
11 sweet nothings things that you say to someone that you have a romantic relationship with: *He* ***whispered sweet nothings in her ear***.
12 sweet sixteen INFORMAL used to describe a girl when she is 16 years old, or a party that is given for her when she turns 16
13 be sweet on sb OLD-FASHIONED to be very attracted to or in love with someone
14 WATER/AIR LITERARY fresh and clean with a pleasant taste or smell
[**Origin:** Old English *swete*] → see also **home sweet home** at HOME¹ (14), **short and sweet** at SHORT¹ (13), SWEETNESS —**sweetly** *adv.*

sweet² S3 *n.* **1 sweets** [plural] sweet food or candy **2 my sweet** OLD-FASHIONED used when speaking to someone you love

ˌsweet-and-ˈsour *adj.* [only before noun] sweet-and-sour food in Chinese cooking has both sweet and sour tastes together

sweet·bread /ˈswitbrɛd/ *n.* [C] OLD-FASHIONED a small organ from a sheep or young cow, used as food

sweet·corn /ˈswitˀkɔrn/ *n.* [U] a type of corn that people eat

sweet·en /ˈswitˀn/ also **sweeten up** *v.* **1** [I,T] to make something sweeter, or become sweeter: *Sweeten the sauce with honey.* **2** [T] INFORMAL to make an offer or deal better by giving something more: *They offered a cash bonus to sweeten the deal.* | **sweeten the pot** (=to make a business offer more attractive) **3** [T] LITERARY to make someone kinder, gentler etc.

ˌsweetened conˈdensed milk *n.* [U] CONDENSED MILK

sweet·en·er /ˈswitˀn-ɚ, -nɚ/ *n.* **1** [C,U] a substance used to make something taste sweeter: *artificial sweeteners* **2** [C] INFORMAL something that you give to someone to persuade them to do something

ˌsweet ˈgum *n.* [C] a tree with hard wood and groups of seeds like PRICKLY balls, common in North America

sweet·heart¹ /ˈswithɑrt/ S3 *n.* [C] **1** a way of addressing someone you love **2** INFORMAL a kind person **3 sb's sweetheart** OLD-FASHIONED the person that someone loves **4** OLD-FASHIONED an informal way of talking to a woman you do not know, which most women find offensive

sweetheart² *adj.* **a sweetheart deal/arrangement/contract** an unfair agreement that gives special advantages to a particular person or business because they are powerful or because they are friends of someone involved in the deal

sweet·ie /ˈswit̬i/ S3 *n.* [C] **1** INFORMAL a way of addressing someone you love **2** someone or something that is small, pretty, and easy to love

ˈsweetie pie *n.* [C] SPOKEN a way of addressing someone you love

sweet·ness /ˈswitnɪs/ *n.* [U]
1 TASTE the sweet taste that something has: *the fruit's natural sweetness*
2 KINDNESS kindness in the way someone speaks or behaves: *the sweetness of the girl's smile*
3 SMELL the pleasant smell that something has: *the sweetness of her perfume*
4 FEELING the pleasant feeling that you have when you have achieved something: *the sweetness of victory*
5 SOUND the pleasant musical sound that something has
6 be all sweetness and light to be very pleasant and friendly → see also SWEET¹

ˈsweet pea *n.* **1** [C] BIOLOGY a climbing plant with sweet-smelling flowers in various colors **2** [singular] a way of addressing someone you love, used especially when speaking to children

ˌsweet poˈtato *n.* [C] a sweet-tasting vegetable that looks like a red potato and is yellow inside → see also YAM

ˈsweet roll *n.* [C] a small sweet PASTRY

ˈsweet spot *n.* [C] **1** the area on a RACKET, BAT, or CLUB that is most effective in hitting a ball **2** INFORMAL a situation or position in which you can be successful

ˈsweet-talk *v.* [T] INFORMAL to try to persuade someone to do something by talking to them in a nice way —**sweet talk** *n.* [U]

ˌsweet-ˈtempered *adj.* having a character that is kind and gentle

sweet wil·liam /ˌswit ˈwɪlyəm/ *n.* [C,U] a plant with sweet-smelling flowers

swell¹ /swɛl/ *v. past tense* **swelled**, *past participle* **swollen** /ˈswoʊlən/ or **swelled**
1 SIZE [I] also **swell up** to gradually increase in size: *His ankle was beginning to swell up.* | *Wood swells if it becomes wet.*
2 AMOUNT/NUMBER [I,T] to gradually increase in amount or number, or to make something increase in this way: *The river was swelling rapidly with the constant rain.* | *Large numbers of refugees have* ***swollen the ranks of*** (=increased the number of) *the unemployed.*
3 swell with pride/anger/confidence etc. to feel very proud, angry, confident etc.
4 SOUND [I] LITERARY to become louder: *Music swelled around us.*
5 SHAPE [I,T] also **swell (sth) out** to become round in shape rather than flat, or to make something do this: *The wind swelled the sails.*
6 OCEAN [I] to move suddenly and powerfully up

S

[**Origin:** Old English *swellan*] → see also GROUNDSWELL, SWOLLEN[2]

swell[2] *n.* **1 a)** [C] a single long wave in the ocean away from the shore **b)** [singular] the way in which the ocean moves up and down **2** [C usually singular] ENG. LANG. ARTS an increase in sound level, especially in music SYN **crescendo** **3** [C] LITERARY a situation in which something increases in number or amount: **+of** *a growing swell of support* → see also GROUNDSWELL **4 a swell of sth** a sudden strong feeling: *a swell of pride* **5 the swell of sth** the roundness and fullness of something **6** [C] OLD-FASHIONED a fashionable or important person

swell[3] *adj.* OLD-FASHIONED very good

swell·ing /ˈswɛlɪŋ/ *n.* **1** [U] the condition of having swollen **2** [C] an area of your body that has become larger than normal, because of illness or injury

swel·ter /ˈswɛltɚ/ *v.* [I] to feel too hot and uncomfortable [**Origin:** 1400–1500 *swelt* **to die, become unconscious because of heat** (11–20 centuries), from Old English *sweltan* **to die**]

swel·ter·ing /ˈswɛltərɪŋ/ *adj.* too hot, and making you feel uncomfortable: *sweltering heat*

swept /swɛpt/ *v.* the past tense and past participle of SWEEP

S

ˌswept-ˈback *adj.* **1** swept-back hair is brushed backward from your face **2** swept-back wings on an aircraft form the shape of the letter "V"

swerve

swerve /swɚv/ *v.* [I] to make a sudden sideways movement while moving forward, especially in order to avoid hitting something: *She swerved to avoid the biker.* | **+across/off etc.** *The bus swerved off the road.* [**Origin:** Old English *sweorfan* **to wipe, put away**] —**swerve** *n.* [C]

swerve from sth *phr. v.* to change from an idea or course of action

swift[1] /swɪft/ *adj.* **1** happening quickly and immediately: *My letter received a swift reply.* **2** [only before noun] moving, or able to move, very fast: *a swift runner* **3 be swift to do sth** to do something as soon as you can, without any delay **4 not too swift** INFORMAL not very intelligent **5 swift of foot** LITERARY able to run fast —**swiftly** *adv.* —**swiftness** *n.* [U]

swift[2] *n.* [C] BIOLOGY a small brown bird that has pointed wings, flies very fast, and is similar to a SWALLOW

Swift /swɪft/, **Jon·a·than** /ˈdʒɑnəθən/ (1667–1745) an Irish writer famous for his book "Gulliver's Travels" who wrote many other SATIRICAL stories and articles

swig /swɪg/ *v.* **swigged, swigging** [T] INFORMAL to drink something by taking large amounts into your mouth at one time ►see THESAURUS box at **drink[1]** —**swig** *n.* [C]

swill[1] /swɪl/ also **swill down** *v.* [T] INFORMAL to drink something, especially alcohol, in large amounts

swill[2] *n.* [U] **1** food for pigs, mostly made of unwanted pieces of human food **2** INFORMAL food that you think is very bad

swim[1] /swɪm/ S3 *v. past tense* **swam** /swæm/, *past participle* **swum** /swʌm/, **swimming** **1** [I,T] to move yourself through water using your arms, legs etc., or to cross an area of water by doing this: *Can you swim?* | *Dad swims 50 laps in the pool every morning.* | **swim the breaststroke/backstroke etc.** (=to swim using a particular movement) **2** [I] if your head swims, you start to feel confused or DIZZY: *The heavy incense was **making my head swim**.* **3** [I] if something you are looking at swims, it seems to move because you feel DIZZY: *The numbers swam before my eyes.* **4 be swimming in sth** to be covered by a lot of liquid: *The eggs were swimming in oil.* **5 swim with/against the tide/current/stream** to do or say the same things as, or different things from, what most people do [**Origin:** Old English *swimman*]

swim[2] *n.* **1** [C] a period of time that you spend swimming: *Let's **go for a swim**.* **2 in the swim (of things)** INFORMAL involved in a situation and knowing what is happening

ˈswim ˌbladder *n.* [C] BIOLOGY an AIR BLADDER

ˈswim club *n.* [C] **1** a place where people can go to swim and take swimming lessons, and where swim teams compete against other clubs **2** a team from this type of place

swim·mer /ˈswɪmɚ/ *n.* [C] **1** someone who swims, especially in competitions: **a good/strong swimmer** (=someone who swims well) **2** someone who is swimming

swim·ming /ˈswɪmɪŋ/ S2 *n.* [U] the sport or activity of swimming: *Swimming is great exercise.* | *swimming lessons* | *Let's **go swimming** this afternoon.*

ˈswimming cap *n.* [C] a type of tight-fitting hat that you wear when you swim to keep your hair dry

ˈswimming hole *n.* [C] INFORMAL a POND (=area of water like a small lake) where you can go swimming

swim·ming·ly /ˈswɪmɪŋli/ *adv.* OLD-FASHIONED **go swimmingly** to happen as planned without problems

ˈswimming pool *n.* [C] a structure that has been built and filled with water for people to swim in SYN **pool**

ˈswimming suit *n.* [C] a SWIMSUIT

ˈswimming trunks *n.* [plural] a piece of clothing like SHORTS, worn by men for swimming

swim·suit /ˈswɪmsut/ *n.* [C] a piece of clothing worn for swimming

ˈswim team *n.* [C] a team that competes in swimming competitions

swim·wear /ˈswɪmwɛr/ *n.* [U] clothing worn for swimming

swin·dle /ˈswɪndl/ *v.* [T] to get money from someone by deceiving them: **swindle sb out of sth** *He swindled his business partner out of $3 million.* ►see THESAURUS box at **cheat[1]** [**Origin:** 1700–1800 *swindler* **person who swindles** (18–21 centuries), from German *schwindler* **someone confused or unbalanced**] —**swindle** *n.* [C]

swine /swaɪn/ *n. plural* **swine** [C] **1** BIOLOGY a pig **2** INFORMAL someone whose behavior is extremely rude or DISGUSTING → see also **cast pearls before swine** at CAST[1] (19)

swine·herd /ˈswaɪnhɚd/ *n.* [C] OLD USE someone who takes care of pigs

swing[1] /swɪŋ/ S3 W3 *v. past tense and past participle* **swung** /swʌŋ/

1 MOVE BACKWARD/FORWARD [I,T] to move backward and forward or side to side from a particular point, or to make something do this: *The sign was swinging in the wind.* | *Two boys sat on the table, swinging their legs.* | *The gate swung gently **back and forth**.*

2 MOVE IN A CURVE [I always + adv./prep.,T always + adv./prep.] to move quickly in a smooth curve, or to make something move like this: **swing open/shut** *The heavy door swung shut.* | **swing sth through/into/around etc. sth** *Pat swung the bag over his shoulder and left.*

3 TRY TO HIT [I,T] to move your arm or something you are holding to try to hit someone or something: *Rickey swung his fist and hit Tom on the chin.* | **+at** *I swung at the ball and missed.* | **swing sth at sb/sth** *She swung her bag at him.*

4 CHANGE QUICKLY [I,T] if emotions, opinions, or situations swing or something swings them, they change quickly to the opposite of what they were: **swing from sth to sth** *Her mood would swing from joy to despair.* | **swing to the left/right** (=to become more politically liberal or conservative)
5 VEHICLE [I always + adv./prep.,T always + adv./prep.] if a vehicle swings or its driver swings it in a particular direction, it turns or moves in a curve in that direction: *A black car swung into the driveway.*
6 swing into action to suddenly begin work that needs to be done, using a lot of energy and effort: *The medical team arrived and swung into action.*
7 ARRANGE STH [T] SPOKEN to make arrangements for something to happen, although it takes a lot of effort to do this: *I'll come over Friday if I can **swing it**.*
8 PLAY [I] to sit on a SWING and make it move backward and forward by bending your legs: *Let's see who can swing the highest.*
9 MUSIC [I] INFORMAL if music swings, it has a strong, enjoyable RHYTHM
10 be swinging OLD-FASHIONED INFORMAL to be fun, exciting, and enjoyable
11 sb swings both ways INFORMAL used to say that someone is BISEXUAL
[**Origin:** Old English *swingan* **to beat, go quickly**] → see also **there's not enough room to swing a cat** at ROOM[1] (4), **the swinging sixties** at SWINGING (2)

swing around *phr. v.* **1 swing sth ↔ around** to turn around quickly or make something turn around quickly, to face in the opposite direction: *She swung around to face him.* | *He swung the boat around and headed for shore.* **2** if a wind swings around, it changes direction suddenly and quickly

swing by *phr. v.* **swing by sth** INFORMAL to visit a place or person for a short time, usually for a particular purpose: *I told Tom I might swing by later.*

swing for sth *phr. v.* OLD-FASHIONED to be killed by HANGING as a punishment for a crime

swing through *phr. v.* **swing through sth** INFORMAL to visit a place very quickly, especially as part of a larger trip: *He swung through Seattle last week as part of a promotional tour.*

swing² *n.*
1 SEAT WITH ROPES [C] **a)** a seat hanging from ropes or chains, that children sit on and make move forward and backward through the air: *Hannah loves to **play on the swings**.* **b)** a seat big enough for two or more people that hangs from ropes or chains: *a porch swing*
2 ATTEMPT TO HIT [C] a swinging movement made with your arm, a weapon etc., especially in order to hit something: +**of** *He split the log with one swing of the ax.* | *Jackson **took a swing at*** (=tried to hit) *the other man.*
3 CHANGE [C] a large change, especially in opinions, ideas, or feelings: +**to/toward/away from** *a political swing to the left* | +**in** *a dramatic swing in public opinion* → see also **a mood swing** at MOOD SWING
4 BASEBALL/GOLF [singular] the swinging movement of your arms and body when you hit the ball in baseball or GOLF
5 be in the swing of sth also **get into the swing of sth** INFORMAL to be or become fully involved in an activity or situation: *I'll need your help until I **get into the swing of things**.*
6 the swing of sth a regular continuous movement from side to side: *the swing of a pendulum*
7 MUSIC [U] ENG. LANG. ARTS JAZZ music of the 1930s and 1940s, usually played by a big band, or a dance done to this music
8 a swing through sth a trip in which you visit several places within an area in a short time: *a three-day swing through southern California* → see also **in full swing** at FULL[1] (8)

swing·er /ˈswɪŋɚ/ *n.* [C] OLD-FASHIONED INFORMAL **1** someone who has sexual relationships with many people **2** someone who is very active and fashionable, and goes to many parties, NIGHTCLUBS etc.

swing·ing /ˈswɪŋɪŋ/ *adj.* OLD-FASHIONED **1** exciting, fun, and enjoyable: *a swinging party* **2 the swinging sixties** the years 1960 to 1969, thought of as a time when there was an increase in social and sexual freedom

ˈswinging door *n.* [C] a door that can be pushed open from either side, and swings shut by itself

ˈswing set *n.* [C] a tall metal frame with SWINGS hanging from it, for children to play on

ˈswing shift *n.* [singular] workers who work from three or four o'clock in the afternoon until eleven or twelve o'clock at night, or this period of work

swipe¹ /swaɪp/ *v.* **1** [T] to pull a special plastic card through a machine to record information on a computer: *Please swipe your credit card.* **2** [T] INFORMAL to steal something: *Someone swiped my cell phone.* **3** [I,T] to hit someone or something by swinging your arm

swipe at sb/sth *phr. v.* to try to hit, reach, or touch something by swinging your arm, hand, or an object

swipe² *n.* [C] **1** a public criticism of someone or something in a speech or in writing: *In her latest article, she **takes a swipe at** her critics.* **2** the action of hitting or trying to hit someone or something by swinging your arm very quickly: *He just **took a swipe at*** (=tried to hit) *me.*

swirl¹ /swɚl/ *v.* **1** [I,T] to turn around quickly in a twisting circular movement, or make something do this: *Her skirt swirled as she danced.* | **swirl sth around** *He swirled the brandy around in his glass.* **2** [I] if stories, RUMORS, ideas etc. swirl, a lot of people start to talk about them

swirl² *n.* [C] **1** a swirling movement **2** an amount of something that is swirling around: +**of** *a swirl of dust* **3** ENG. LANG. ARTS a twisting circular pattern: +**of** *bright swirls of color*

swish /swɪʃ/ *v.* **1** [I,T] to move or make something move quickly through the air with a smooth quiet sound: *The horse swished its tail.* **2** [T] to move liquid around in your mouth **3** [T] to win points in a basketball game by throwing the ball through the basket in a way that makes a smooth quiet sound [**Origin:** 1700–1800 from the sound] —**swish** *n.* [singular]

Swiss¹ /swɪs/ *adj.* coming from or relating to Switzerland

Swiss² *n.* [plural] **the Swiss** the people of Switzerland

ˌSwiss ˈchard *n.* [U] CHARD

ˌSwiss ˈcheese *n.* [U] a type of cheese with holes in it

ˌSwiss ˈsteak *n.* [C,U] a thick flat piece of BEEF covered in flour and cooked in a SAUCE

switch¹ /swɪtʃ/ S2 *v.*
1 CHANGE [I,T] to change from doing or using one thing to doing or using another: +**from/to** *She worked as a teacher before switching to journalism.* | *The department has switched from film to digital photographs.* | +**between** *Students here often switch between English and Spanish.*
2 EXCHANGE [T] if you switch two things, you replace or exchange one with the other: *We must have switched umbrellas by mistake.* | **switch seats/places etc. (with sb)** *Do you mind if we switch seats so that I can sit next to my husband?*
3 MOVE SB/STH [T always + adv./prep.] to move someone or something to another place, position, organization etc.: **switch sb/sth (from sth) to sth** *He switched the knife to his right hand.*
4 TIME/EVENT [T always + adv./prep.] to change the time when a planned event will take place: **switch sth (from sth) to sth** *The meeting time has been switched to 3:00.*
5 MACHINE [T] to change the way a machine operates by using a switch or button: **switch sth to sth** *Switch the freezer to "defrost."*
6 WORK [I,T] if you switch with someone who does the same job as you or switch shifts with them, you exchange your working times with theirs for a short time SYN **trade**

switch off *phr. v.* **1 switch sth ↔ off** if you switch off a machine, electric light, radio etc. or if a machine does this, it stops working SYN **turn off**: *Switch off the lights before you leave.* **2** if two people switch off, they take turns doing a job **3** INFORMAL to stop listening or paying attention: *I found myself switching off during the meeting.*

switch on *phr. v.* **switch sth ↔ on** if you switch on a machine, electric light, radio etc. or if a machine does this, it starts working SYN **turn on**: *Is it okay if I switch the TV on?* | *The tape recorder switches on when you begin talking.*

switch over *phr. v.* to change completely from one method, product etc. to another: **+from/to** *More and more people are switching over to online banking.*

switch² S3 W3 *n.* [C] **1** the part on a light, radio, machine etc. that starts or stops the flow of electricity when you push it up or down: *a light switch* | *Where's the on switch?* | **flip/flick/throw a switch** (=turn on something with a switch) **2** a complete change from one thing to another: *The switch to a free market economy will not be easy.* | *Some of the farms have* ***made a switch*** *from agricultural to dairy production.* **3 make the switch** [usually passive] to exchange one object for another similar object, especially secretly or accidentally **4** a thin stick of wood that bends easily, used in past times for hitting children as a punishment or for making animals move

S

switch·back /ˈswɪtʃbæk/ *n.* [C] a road that goes up a steep hill in a series of sharp turns, or one of these turns

switch·blade /ˈswɪtʃbleɪd/ *n.* [C] a knife with a blade inside the handle which springs out when you press a button

switch·board /ˈswɪtʃbɔrd/ *n.* [C] a central system used to connect telephone calls in an office building, hotel etc.: *switchboard operators* → see also **jam the switchboard** at JAM¹ (6)

switch·er·oo /ˌswɪtʃəˈru/ *n.* [singular] INFORMAL a situation in which someone secretly SWITCHes one object for a similar object

ˈswitch-ˌhitter *n.* [C] a baseball player who can hit the ball well from either side of HOME PLATE —**switch-hit** *v.* [I]

Swit·zer·land /ˈswɪtsələnd/ a country in western Europe, surrounded by France, Germany, Austria, and Italy → see also SWISS

swiv·el¹ /ˈswɪvəl/ *v.* **1** also **swivel around** [I,T] to turn around a central point, or make something do this: *The lamp swivels to focus light exactly where you want it.* **2** also **swivel around** [I] if someone swivels, they turn around quickly

swivel² *n.* [C] an object that joins two parts of something in such a way that one or both parts can turn around freely

ˈswivel chair *n.* [C] a chair that can turn around to face a different direction without the legs moving → see picture at CHAIR¹

swiz·zle stick /ˈswɪzəl ˌstɪk/ *n.* [C] a small stick for mixing drinks

swol·len¹ /ˈswoʊlən/ *v.* a past participle of SWELL

swollen² *adj.* **1** a swollen part of your body is bigger than usual because of illness or injury: *My knee's still really swollen from the accident.* **2** a swollen river has more water in it than usual

swoon /swun/ *v.* [I] **1** to feel so much excitement, happiness, or admiration that you feel physically weak: **+over** *I was not the only one swooning over Antonio.* **2** OLD-FASHIONED to become unconscious and fall down SYN **faint** —**swoon** *n.* [singular]

swoop /swup/ *v.* [I usually + adv./prep.] **1** if a bird or aircraft swoops, it moves suddenly and steeply down through the air, especially to attack something: **+in/down/from etc.** *A huge owl swooped down from the tree.* **2** to make a sudden attack or ARREST: **+in/on etc.** *Soldiers swooped in and rescued the hostages.* —**swoop** *n.* [C] → see also **at/in one fell swoop** at FELL³ (1)

swoosh /swʊʃ, swuʃ/ *v.* [I] to make a sound by moving quickly through the air —**swoosh** *n.* [C]

sword /sɔrd/ *n.* [C] **1** a weapon with a long pointed blade and a handle, used in the past: **draw your sword** (=to pull out your sword so you can use it) **2 beat/turn swords into plowshares** to stop fighting or thinking about war and start living peacefully **3 a/the sword of Damocles** LITERARY the possibility of something bad or dangerous happening at any time **4 put sb to the sword** LITERARY to kill someone with a sword → see also **cross swords (with sb)** at CROSS¹ (12)

sword·fish /ˈsɔrdˌfɪʃ/ *n.* [C] BIOLOGY a large fish with a very long pointed upper jaw

sword·play /ˈsɔrdpleɪ/ *n.* [U] the activity of fighting with swords

swords·man /ˈsɔrdzmən/ *n. plural* **swordsmen** /-mən/ [C] someone who fights with a sword, or someone who is skilled in this

swords·man·ship /ˈsɔrdzmənˌʃɪp/ *n.* [U] skill in fighting with a sword

swore /swɔr/ *v.* the past tense of SWEAR

sworn¹ /swɔrn/ *v.* the past participle of SWEAR

sworn² *adj.* **1 a sworn statement/testimony/deposition etc.** a statement, TESTIMONY etc. that someone makes after officially promising to tell the truth **2 a sworn enemy** one of two people or groups of people who hate each other very much **3 sb's sworn duty** something that someone has to do because they have promised to do it

swum /swʌm/ *v.* the past participle of SWIM

swung /swʌŋ/ *v.* the past tense and past participle of SWING

syb·a·rit·ic /ˌsɪbəˈrɪt̬ɪk◂/ *adj.* FORMAL wanting or enjoying expensive pleasures and comforts [**Origin:** 1600–1700 Latin *Sybariticus*, from *Sybaris* ancient Italian city whose people lived in great wealth and comfort] —**sybarite** /ˈsɪbəˌraɪt/ *n.* [C]

syc·a·more /ˈsɪkəˌmɔr/ *n.* [C] an eastern North American tree with broad leaves, or the wood of this tree

syc·o·phant /ˈsɪkəfənt/ *n.* [C] DISAPPROVING someone who praises important or powerful people in order to get something from them [**Origin:** 1500–1600 Latin *sycophanta* **someone who tells about the bad actions of another, flatterer**, from Greek *sykophantes*] —**sycophantic** /ˌsɪkəˈfæntɪk/ *adj.*

Syd·ney /ˈsɪdni/ the largest city in Australia, which is the capital city of the state of New South Wales

syl·la·bar·y /ˈsɪləˌbɛri/ *n. plural* **syllabaries** [C] TECHNICAL a writing system in which each character represents a syllable

syl·lab·ic /sɪˈlæbɪk/ *adj.* ENG. LANG. ARTS **1** based on or relating to syllables: *syllabic stress* **2** TECHNICAL a syllabic CONSONANT forms a whole syllable

syl·la·ble /ˈsɪləbəl/ *n.* [C] ENG. LANG. ARTS a word or part of a word which contains a single vowel sound [**Origin:** 1300–1400 Old French *sillabe*, from Latin, from Greek *syllabe*, from *syllambanein* **to gather together**]

syl·la·bus /ˈsɪləbəs/ *n. plural* **syllabuses** or **syllabi** /-baɪ/ [C] a plan that states what students at a school or college should learn in a particular class [**Origin:** 1600–1700 Modern Latin, from a mistaken reading of Latin *sittyba* **label**] → see also CURRICULUM

syl·lo·gism /ˈsɪləˌdʒɪzəm/ *n.* [C] TECHNICAL a statement with three parts, the first two of which prove that the third part is true, for example "all men will die; Socrates is a man; therefore Socrates will die" —**syllogistic** /ˌsɪləˈdʒɪstɪk/ *adj.*

sylph /sɪlf/ *n.* [C] LITERARY **1** an attractively thin and graceful girl or woman **2** an imaginary female spirit that, according to ancient stories, lived in the air

sylph·like /ˈsɪlfˌlaɪk/ *adj.* LITERARY attractively thin and graceful

syl·van /ˈsɪlvən/ *adj.* LITERARY in the forest or belonging to the forest

sym- /sɪm/ *prefix* together or with; used instead of SYN- before the letters "b," "m," or "p"

sym·bi·o·sis /ˌsɪmbiˈoʊsɪs, -baɪ-/ *n.* [U] **1** a relationship between people or organizations that depend on each other equally **2** BIOLOGY the relationship between two different living things that exist very closely together and depend on each other for particular advantages —**symbiotic** /ˌsɪmbiˈɑṭɪk◂ / *adj.*: *a symbiotic relationship*

sym·bol /ˈsɪmbəl/ Ac *n.* [C] **1** ENG. LANG. ARTS a picture, shape, color etc. that has a particular meaning or represents an idea: *The cross is the most important symbol in Christianity.* | +**of** *The dove is a symbol of peace.* **2** a letter, number, or sign that represents a sound, an amount, a chemical substance etc.: *mathematical symbols* | +**for** *"H" is the scientific symbol for hydrogen.* **3** someone or something that represents a quality or idea: +**of** *Cadillacs were seen as symbols of wealth and prestige.* [**Origin:** 1400–1500 Latin *symbolum*, from Greek *symbolon* **proof of who someone is, checked by comparing its other half**] → see also SEX SYMBOL, STATUS SYMBOL

sym·bol·ic /sɪmˈbɑlɪk/ Ac also **sym·bol·i·cal** /sɪmˈbɑlɪkəl/ *adj.* **1** a symbolic event, speech, action etc. represents something important, but does not really change anything: *The president's trip to Russia was mostly symbolic.* | *a symbolic gesture* **2** representing an idea or quality: +**of** *Each candle is symbolic of one life.* **3** using pictures, shapes, colors etc. to represent ideas or qualities: *a symbolic painting* —**symbolically** /-kli/ *adv.*

sym·bol·ism /ˈsɪmbəˌlɪzəm/ Ac *n.* [U] **1** the use of pictures, shapes, colors etc. to represent an idea: *religious symbolism* **2** an idea or quality that something represents: +**of** *The symbolism of the characters is obvious.*

sym·bol·ize /ˈsɪmbəˌlaɪz/ Ac *v.* [T] if one thing, event etc. symbolizes an idea or quality, it represents the idea or quality: *Wedding rings symbolize a couple's commitment to each other.* —**symbolization** /ˌsɪmbələˈzeɪʃən/ *n.* [U]

symmetrical /səˈmɛtrɪkəl/ also **sym·met·ric** /səˈmɛtrɪk/ *adj.* MATH having two halves that are exactly the same in shape, size, and arrangement OPP **asymmetrical**: *symmetrical shapes* —**symmetrically** /-kli/ *adv.*

sym·me·try /ˈsɪmətri/ *n.* [U] **1** MATH the quality of being symmetrical: *We were impressed by the symmetry and the elegance of the city.* **2** the quality that a situation has when two events or actions seem to be balanced or equal in some way: *There was a certain symmetry to coming back to New York, where I started my artistic life all those years ago.*

sym·pa·thet·ic /ˌsɪmpəˈθɛṭɪk/ *adj.* **1** caring about someone who has a problem and able to understand how they feel: *She was very sympathetic when I told her.* | +**to/toward** *Most people feel sympathetic to the victims of crime, not the criminals.* | *Mom was always there with* ***a sympathetic ear*** (=willingness to listen to someone else's problems). **2** [not before noun] supporting an idea, plan, request etc., or willing to consider it: +**to/toward** *The senator is very sympathetic to environmental issues.* **3 a sympathetic figure/character** LITERARY someone in a book, play etc. who most people like **4** [only before noun] showing a good understanding of what is needed in a situation, event etc. SYN **sensitive** —**sympathetically** /-kli/ *adv.*

sym·pa·thize /ˈsɪmpəˌθaɪz/ *v.* [I] **1** to feel sorry for someone because you understand their problems: *I sympathize, but I don't know how to help.* | +**with** *I can sympathize with those who have lost loved ones.* **2** to support someone's ideas or actions: +**with** *Many people sympathized with the strikers.*

sym·pa·thiz·er /ˈsɪmpəˌθaɪzɚ/ *n.* [C] someone who supports the aims of an organization or political party but does not belong to it SYN **supporter**: *Communist sympathizers*

sym·pa·thy /ˈsɪmpəθi/ *n. plural* **sympathies** **1** [U] the feeling of being sorry for someone who is in a bad situation and understanding how they feel: *I think he just wants a little sympathy.* | **have/feel sympathy for sb** *I have a lot of sympathy for single mothers.* | *I* ***have*** *absolutely* ***no sympathy for*** *students who cheat on tests.* | *He's just trying to* ***play on your sympathy*** (=make you feel sorry for him in order to gain an advantage). **2** [plural,U] feelings of sadness for someone whose relative or friend has died, or who has suffered something else very bad → see also CONDOLENCES: *messages of sympathy* | *a sympathy card* | **our/my sympathies are with sb** *Our sympathies are with the families of the victims.* | **our/my sympathies go out to sb** *My sympathies go out to the boy's mother.* | **send/extend etc. sympathies (to sb)** (=to send a message of sympathy to someone) **3** [plural,U] belief in or support for a plan, idea, or action, especially a political one: *Willard is* ***in sympathy with*** *many Green Party issues.* | **have/express sympathy for sth** *Sullivan expressed sympathy for the striking federal workers.* | *The local population's* ***sympathies lie with*** *the rebels.* | **communist/Republican/left-wing etc. sympathies** *He is known for his pro-socialist sympathies.* **4** [U] a feeling that you understand someone because you are similar to them **5 in sympathy** FORMAL if two things happen in sympathy, one happens and then the second one happens in the same way as a result of the first

sym·pho·ny /ˈsɪmfəni/ *n. plural* **symphonies** [C] ENG. LANG. ARTS **1** a long piece of music usually in four parts, written for an ORCHESTRA: *Tchaikovsky's Symphony No. 6* **2** also **symphony orchestra** a large group of CLASSICAL musicians led by a CONDUCTOR **3** a performance by a symphony —**symphonic** /sɪmˈfɑnɪk/ *adj.*

S

sym·po·si·um /sɪmˈpoʊziəm/ *n. plural* **symposiums** or **symposia** /-ziə/ [C] **1** a formal meeting in which people who know a lot about a particular subject have discussions about it: +**on** *a symposium on women's health* **2** a group of articles on a particular subject collected together in a book

symp·tom /ˈsɪmptəm/ W3 *n.* [C] **1** a physical condition which shows that you have a particular illness: *cold symptoms* | +**of** *Common symptoms of diabetes are weight loss and fatigue.* **2** a sign that a serious problem exists: +**of** *The high crime rate is a symptom of a wider social problem.* [**Origin:** 1500–1600 Latin *symptoma*, from Greek, **something that happens, symptom**]

symp·to·mat·ic /ˌsɪmptəˈmæṭɪk/ *adj.* **1 be symptomatic of sth** if a situation or type of behavior is symptomatic of something, it shows that a serious problem exists: *Poor grades could be symptomatic of a learning disorder.* **2** MEDICINE related to medical symptoms —**symptomatically** /-kli/ *adv.*

syn- /sɪn/ *prefix* together or with: *a synthesis* (=combining of separate things)

syn·a·gogue /ˈsɪnəˌgɑg/ *n.* [C] a building where Jewish people meet for religious services SYN **temple** [**Origin:** 1100–1200 Old French *synagoge*, from Late Latin, from Greek **gathering of people, synagogue**]

syn·apse /ˈsɪnæps, sɪˈnæps/ *n.* [C] TECHNICAL BIOLOGY the space between two nerve cells in your body, across which information travels to make muscles, GLANDS etc. work

sync, synch /sɪŋk/ *n.* **in sync a)** two or more parts of a machine, process etc. that are moving or happening at the same time and same speed OPP **out of sync**: +**with** *The soundtrack wasn't in sync with the movie.* **b)** matching something or in agreement with someone OPP **out of sync**: +**with** *The Congressman's position is in sync with the will of the people he represents.*

syn·chro·nic·i·ty /ˌsɪŋkrəˈnɪsəṭi/ *n.* [U] the fact of two or more events happening at the same time or place, when these events are believed to be connected in some way

syn·chro·nize /ˈsɪŋkrəˌnaɪz/ *v.* **1** [T] to arrange for two or more actions to happen at exactly the same time **2 synchronize your watches** to make two or more watches or clocks show exactly the same time **3** [I,T] if the sound and action of a movie synchronize or if you synchronize them, they go at exactly the same speed —**synchronization** /ˌsɪŋkrənəˈzeɪʃən/ *n.* [U]

ˌsynchronized ˈswimming *n.* [U] a sport in which swimmers move together in patterns in the water to music

syn·chro·nous /ˈsɪŋkrənəs/ *adj.* two or more things that are synchronous are working or moving together at the same speed

syn·co·pa·tion /ˌsɪŋkəˈpeɪʃən/ *n.* [U] a RHYTHM in a line of music in which the BEATS that are usually weak are emphasized —**syncopated** /ˈsɪŋkəˌpeɪṭɪd/ *adj.*: *syncopated rhythms*

syn·co·pe /ˈsɪŋkəpi/ *n.* [U] TECHNICAL **1** a way of making a word shorter by leaving out sounds or letters in the middle of it, for example changing "cannot" to "can't" **2** the loss of consciousness when someone faints

syn·di·cate¹ /ˈsɪndəkɪt/ *n.* [C] a group of people or companies who join together in order to achieve a particular aim: +**of** *a syndicate of banks* [**Origin:** 1600–1700 French *syndicat*, from *syndic* **someone who does business for another**, from Late Latin *syndicus*]

syn·di·cate² /ˈsɪndɪˌkeɪt/ *v.* **1** [T usually passive] to sell written work, photographs, television shows etc. to a number of different organizations so that they can appear in many different places: *His column is syndicated throughout America.* **2** [I,T] to form into a syndicate —**syndicated** *adj.*

syn·di·ca·tion /ˌsɪndɪˈkeɪʃən/ *n.* [U] **be in syndication** if a TV show is in syndication, different local TV stations pay to show it

syn·drome /ˈsɪndroʊm/ *n.* [C] **1** MEDICINE a set of physical or mental problems considered together as a disease → see also DOWN'S SYNDROME, PREMENSTRUAL SYNDROME, SUDDEN INFANT DEATH SYNDROME **2** a set of qualities, events, or behaviors that is typical of a particular type of problem

syn·er·gy /ˈsɪnɚdʒi/ *n.* [U] TECHNICAL the additional energy or greater effect that is produced by two or more people combining their energy and ideas

syn·od /ˈsɪnəd/ *n.* [C] an important meeting of church leaders to make decisions concerning the church

syn·o·nym /ˈsɪnəˌnɪm/ *n.* [C] ENG. LANG. ARTS a word with the same meaning or almost the same meaning as another word in the same language, such as "sad" and "unhappy" [**Origin:** 1400–1500 Latin *synonymum*, from Greek, from *synonymos* **synonymous**] → see also ANTONYM

syn·on·y·mous /sɪˈnɑnəməs/ *adj.* **1** an idea, thing, or person etc. that is synonymous with something else has an extremely close connection to it, so that if you think of one, you also think of the other.: +**with** *At one point IBM was practically synonymous with personal computers.* **2** ENG. LANG. ARTS synonymous words have the same or nearly the same meaning —**synonymously** *adv.*

syn·op·sis /sɪˈnɑpsɪs/ *n. plural* **synopses** /-siz/ [C] ENG. LANG. ARTS a short description giving the general idea and the most important facts from something longer, for example a book SYN **summary**

syn·tac·tic /sɪnˈtæktɪk/ *adj.* ENG. LANG. ARTS relating to syntax: *the sentence's syntactic structure* —**syntactically** /-kli/ *adv.*

syn·tax /ˈsɪntæks/ *n.* [U] **1** ENG. LANG. ARTS the way words are arranged in order to form sentences or phrases, or the rules of grammar which control this → see also MORPHOLOGY, SEMANTICS **2** COMPUTERS the rules that describe how words and phrases are used in a computer language [**Origin:** 1500–1600 French *syntaxe*, from Late Latin *syntaxis*, from Greek, from *syntassein* **to arrange together**]

syn·the·sis /ˈsɪnθəsɪs/ *n. plural* **syntheses** /-siz/ **1** [C] something in which different ideas, styles, pieces of information etc. are combined: +**of** *The show is a synthesis of dance forms.* **2** [U] the act of combining different ideas, styles, pieces of information etc.: +**of** *the synthesis of existing research* **3** [U] the act of producing a substance by combining other substances through chemical or BIOLOGICAL means: +**of** *the synthesis of thyroid hormone in the body* **4** [C] the production of sounds, speech, or music electronically

syn·the·size /ˈsɪnθəˌsaɪz/ *v.* [T] **1** CHEMISTRY to produce a substance by combining other substances through chemical or BIOLOGICAL means: *The body needs vitamin D to synthesize calcium.* **2** to combine different ideas, experiences, or pieces of information together to make something new: *A good reader synthesizes information from various sources.* **3** ENG. LANG. ARTS to produce sounds, speech, or music electronically

syn·the·sized /ˈsɪnθəˌsaɪzd/ *adj.* **1** produced by combining different things, especially making something similar to a natural product by combining chemicals: *synthesized hormones* **2** synthesized sounds are produced using a machine such as a synthesizer

syn·the·siz·er /ˈsɪnθəˌsaɪzɚ/ *n.* [C] an electronic instrument that produces the sounds of various musical instruments → see also SPEECH SYNTHESIZER

ˈsynthesizing ˌquestion *n.* [C] TECHNICAL a question in a test which asks a student to combine different ideas in an answer

syn·thet·ic /sɪnˈθeṭɪk/ *adj.* produced by combining different artificial substances, rather than being naturally produced: *synthetic fibers* —**synthetically** /-kli/ *adv.*

syn·thet·ics /sɪnˈθeṭɪks/ *n.* [plural] chemical substances that are made to be like natural substances, especially cloth

syph·i·lis /ˈsɪfəlɪs/ *n.* [U] MEDICINE a very serious disease that is passed from one person to another during sexual activity

Syr·i·a /ˈsɪriə/ a country in west Asia, south of Turkey and west of Iraq —**Syrian** *n., adj.*

sy·ringe¹ /səˈrɪndʒ/ *n.* [C] an instrument for taking blood from someone's body or putting liquid, drugs etc. into it, consisting of a hollow plastic tube and a needle [**Origin:** 1400–1500 Medieval Latin *syringa*, from Greek *syrinx* **tube**]

syringe² *v.* [T] to clean something with a syringe

syr·up /ˈsɚəp, ˈsɪrəp/ *n.* **1** [U] a sweet sticky liquid eaten especially on PANCAKES, made from the SAP of a maple tree SYN **maple syrup** **2** [U] thick sticky liquid made from sugar, eaten on top of or mixed with other foods: *chocolate syrup* **3** [singular, U] a sweet liquid made from sugar and water, that is slightly thick: *Drain the syrup from the can of peaches.* **4** [C,U] medicine in the form of a thick sweet liquid: *cough syrup* [**Origin:** 1300–1400 Old French *sirop*, from Medieval Latin, from Arabic *sharab* **drink, wine, syrup**]

syr·up·y /ˈsɚəpi, ˈsɪrəpi/ *adj.* **1** thick and sticky like syrup or containing syrup **2** DISAPPROVING too kind or SENTIMENTAL in a way that seems silly or insincere

sys·tem /ˈsɪstəm/ S1 W1 *n.* [C]

1 METHOD an organized set of ideas, methods, or ways of working: *the U.S. legal system* | +**of** *our system of government* | +**for** *Ben has a unique system for filing documents.* | ***Under the** new **system** you can access your account directly.* | *Is there **a system in place** to deal with complaints?*

2 RELATED PARTS a group of related parts that work together as a whole for a purpose or with a particular result: *a car alarm system* | *nuclear weapons systems* | *our solar system and its planets* | *There is a huge weather system moving through the area over the next few days.*

3 BIOLOGY BIOLOGY the parts in a human or animal body that work together to do a particular job: *the digestive system* | *the immune system* (=the parts of the body that protect against disease) | *the nervous system*

4 COMPUTERS COMPUTERS a group of computers that are connected to each other: *The software kept crashing **the system**.* → see also OPERATING SYSTEM

5 sb's system a phrase meaning someone's body, used when you are talking about its medical or physical condition: *Too much alcohol is bad for your system.*

6 get sth out of your system INFORMAL to get rid of strong, bad, or upsetting feelings
7 the system INFORMAL all of the official rules and powerful groups or organizations that seem to control your life and limit your freedom: *Harris has spent his entire career fighting the system.* | *He was always looking for ways to **beat the system*** (=avoid or break the rules).
8 all systems (are) go ESPECIALLY HUMOROUS used to say that you are ready to do something or that something is ready to happen
[**Origin:** 1600–1700 Late Latin *systema*, from Greek, from *synistanai* **to combine**] → see also SOLAR SYSTEM

sys·tem·at·ic /ˌsɪstəˈmæt̬ɪk◂/ *adj.* organized carefully and done thoroughly: *Let's do this in a systematic way.* | **systematic destruction/discrimination/corruption etc.** *the systematic slaughter of innocent people* —**systematically** /-kli/ *adv.*

sys·tem·a·tize /ˈsɪstəməˌtaɪz/ *v.* [T] to put facts, numbers, ideas etc. into a particular order —**systematization** /ˌsɪstəmət̬əˈzeɪʃən/ *n.* [U]

sys·tem·ic /sɪˈstɛmɪk/ *adj.* **1** affecting all of a system: *systemic police corruption* **2** BIOLOGY affecting your whole body: *a systemic infection* —**systemically** /-kli/ *adv.*

ˈsystems ˌanalyst *n.* [C] COMPUTERS someone whose job is to study a company's computer needs and provide them with the appropriate SOFTWARE and equipment —**systems analysis** *n.* [U]

ˈsystem ˌsoftware *n.* [U] COMPUTERS computer PROGRAMS that make up the OPERATING SYSTEM (=a system that controls the way a computer works) → see also APPLICATION

S

T,t

T, t /ti/ *n. plural* **T's, t's** [C] **1 a)** the 20th letter of the English alphabet **b)** the sound represented by this letter **2 to a T** INFORMAL perfectly or exactly: *He matched the description to a T.*

T.A. *n.* [C] a TEACHING ASSISTANT

tab[1] /tæb/ *n.* [C]
1 MONEY YOU OWE a) a bill that is added up at the end of a period of time, showing how much you owe for drinks, food etc.: *He ordered dinner and* ***put it on his tab.*** | *In two days, she* ***ran up a bar tab*** *of $175.* **b)** the amount of money that you owe for a meal in a restaurant, drinks in a bar etc. SYN **bill** SYN **check** ►see THESAURUS box at **bill**[1]
2 pick up the tab to pay for something, especially when it is not your responsibility to pay: *Taxpayers will have to pick up the tab for the new stadium.*
3 keep (close) tabs on sb/sth INFORMAL to watch someone or something carefully to check what they are doing: *He keeps tabs on everyone in the building.*
4 ON A CAN/BOX ETC. a small piece of metal, plastic, or paper that you pull to open a container
5 SMALL PIECE OF PAPER/PLASTIC a small piece of paper or plastic you attach to a page, FILE etc. in order to find it easily
6 IN TYPING a) a setting that you make on a computer or TYPEWRITER so that when you press a special button, you move forward to a particular place on a line of TEXT **b)** a TAB KEY
7 DRUGS SLANG a solid form of the illegal drug LSD

tab[2] *v.* **tabbed, tabbing 1** [I] to press the TAB KEY on a computer or TYPEWRITER to move forward to a particular place on a line of TEXT **2** [T usually passive] to choose someone or something for an activity or AWARD

Ta·bas·co /təˈbæskoʊ/ also **taˈbasco ˌsauce** *n.* [U] TRADEMARK a very SPICY red liquid made from CHILIS, used in cooking

tab·by /ˈtæbi/ *n. plural* **tabbies** [C] a cat with orange, gray, or brown marks on its fur **—tabby** *adj.*

tab·er·na·cle /ˈtæbɚˌnækəl/ *n.* [C] **1** a church or other building used by some Christian groups **2 the tabernacle** the small tent in which the ancient Jews kept their most holy objects **3** a box in which holy bread and wine are kept in Catholic churches

ˈtab key *n.* [C] a button on a computer or TYPEWRITER that you push, in order to move forward to a particular place on a line of TEXT

ta·ble[1] /ˈteɪbəl/ S1 W1 *n.*
1 FURNITURE a piece of furniture with a flat top supported by legs: *the dining room table* | *He put the box* ***on the table.*** | *She sat down* ***at the table.*** | *Could you help me* ***set the table*** (=put knives, forks etc. on a table before a meal)? | *The waiter* ***cleared the table*** (=took the empty plates, glasses etc. off a table). | **reserve/book a table** (=ask a restaurant to keep a table available for you) → see also CARD TABLE, COFFEE TABLE, HEAD TABLE
2 SPORT/GAME a special table for playing a particular indoor sport or game on: *a ping-pong table*
3 LIST a list of numbers, facts, or information arranged in rows across and down a page: *The figures are shown in the table below.* | *See Table 3 for cost comparisons.* → see also MULTIPLICATION TABLE, TABLE OF CONTENTS, TIMES TABLE
4 at the table when sitting at a table eating a meal: *It's not polite to blow your nose at the table.*
5 a place/seat/voice etc. at the table an opportunity to take part in important or official discussions or decisions
6 on the table officially suggested and being considered: *The offer on the table is a 10% wage increase.*
7 under the table INFORMAL money that is paid under the table is paid secretly and illegally → see also **turn the tables (on sb)** at TURN[1] (13)
[**Origin:** 1100–1200 Old French, Latin *tabula* **board, list**]

table[2] S3 *v.* [T] **table a bill/measure/proposal etc.** to delay considering a proposal until a later time

tab·leau /tæbloʊ/ *n. plural* **tableaux** /-blouz/ [C] **1** a place, situation, or description that is like a beautiful or exciting picture or a scene from a book, movie etc. **2** a large painting or photograph **3** also **tableau vivant** a group of people who do not speak or move arranged on stage to look like a painting

ta·ble·cloth /ˈteɪbəlˌklɔθ/ *n.* [C] a cloth used for covering a table

ˈtable ˌlamp *n.* [C] a small lamp that is made to be used on a table → see picture at LAMP

ta·ble·land /ˈteɪbəl-lænd/ also **tablelands** *n.* [C] EARTH SCIENCE a large area of high flat land SYN **plateau**

ˈtable ˌlinen *n.* [U] all the cloths used during a meal, such as NAPKINS and tablecloths

ˈtable ˌmanners *n.* [plural] the way in which someone eats their food, considered according to the usual rules of social behavior about eating

ˌtable of ˈcontents *n.* [C] a list at the beginning of a book that tells you the order and the page numbers of the CHAPTERS

ˈtable salt *n.* [U] salt in the form of extremely small white grains, commonly used for adding taste to food

ta·ble·spoon /ˈteɪbəlˌspun/ W3 *n.* [C] **1 a)** a special spoon used for measuring small amounts in cooking, equal to three TEASPOONS or 15 ml **b)** also **ta·ble·spoon·ful** /ˈteɪbəlˌspunfʊl/ the amount a tablespoon can hold **2** a large spoon commonly used for eating or serving food

tab·let /ˈtæblɪt/ *n.* [C] **1** a small flat hard piece of medicine with rounded corners → see also PILL: *vitamin C tablets* ►see THESAURUS box at **medicine** **2** a set of pieces of paper for writing on that are glued together at the top **3** a flat piece of stone or metal with words cut into it

ˈtable ˌtennis *n.* [U] an indoor game played on a table by two or four players who hit a small plastic ball to each other across a net SYN **ping-pong**

ta·ble·top[1], table top /ˈteɪbəlˌtɑp/ *n.* [C] the flat top surface of a table

tabletop[2], table-top *adj.* [only before noun] done, existing, or kept on a table

ta·ble·ware /ˈteɪbəlwɛr/ *n.* [U] the plates, glasses, knives etc. used when eating a meal

ˈtable ˌwine *n.* [C,U] a fairly cheap wine intended for drinking with meals

tab·loid /ˈtæblɔɪd/ *n.* [C] a newspaper that has small pages, a lot of photographs, stories about sex, famous people etc., and not much serious news ►see THESAURUS box at **newspaper** [**Origin:** 1900–2000 *Tabloid* a trademark for a medicinal tablet (19–20 centuries); because of the small size of the tablet] **—tabloid** *adj.* [only before noun]

ta·boo[1] /təˈbu, tæ-/ *adj.* **1** a taboo subject, word, activity etc. is one that people avoid because they think it is extremely offensive or embarrassing **2** TECHNICAL too holy or evil to be touched, or used

taboo[2] *n. plural* **taboos** [C] a religious or social custom which means a particular activity or subject must be avoided: **+about/on/against** *a taboo against marrying outside the group* | **break a taboo** (=to do something that is forbidden by a taboo)

tab·u·lar /ˈtæbyələ/ *adj.* arranged in the form of a TABLE (=set of numbers arranged in rows across and down a page)

tab·u·la ra·sa /ˌtæbyələ ˈrɑzə, -sə/ *n. plural* **tabulae rasae** [C usually singular] LITERARY your mind in its original state, before you have learned anything

tab·u·late /ˈtæbyəˌleɪt/ *v.* [T] to arrange figures or

information together in a set or a list so that they can be easily compared —**tabulation** /ˌtæbyəˈleɪʃən/ *n.* [U]

ta·chom·e·ter /tæˈkɑmət̬ɚ/ *n.* [C] a piece of equipment used to measure the speed at which the engine of a vehicle turns

tac·it /ˈtæsɪt/ *adj.* tacit agreement, approval, support etc. is given without actually being spoken or officially agreed to —**tacitly** *adv.* —**tacitness** *n.* [U]

tac·i·turn /ˈtæsəˌtɚn/ *adj.* FORMAL speaking very little, so that you seem unfriendly —**taciturnly** *adv.* —**taciturnity** /ˌtæsəˈtɚnət̬i/ *n.* [U]

tack¹ /tæk/ *n.*
1 PIN [C] a short pin with a large round flat top, for attaching notices to boards, walls etc. SYN **thumbtack**
2 WAY OF DOING STH [C,U] a method that you use to achieve something: *If that doesn't work, we'll **try a different tack**.*
3 NAIL [C] a small nail with a sharp point and flat top
4 SHIP a) [C,U] the direction of a sailing ship, based on the direction of the wind and the position of its sails **b)** [C] the action of changing the direction of a sailing boat, or the distance it travels between these changes: *a long tack into the bay*
5 SEWING [C] a long loose stitch used for fastening pieces of cloth together before SEWING them
6 HORSES [U] all the equipment you need for horse riding

tack² *v.* **1** also **tack up** [T always + adv./prep.] to attach something to a wall, board etc. using a TACK: **tack sth to sth** *A note was tacked to the door.* **2** [I] to change the course of a sailing ship so that the wind blows against its sails from the opposite direction **3** [T] to fasten pieces of cloth together with long loose stitches, before SEWING them

tack sth ↔ **on** also **tack** sth **on/onto** sth *phr. v.* INFORMAL to add something to something that already exists or is complete, especially in a way that seems badly planned: *They had tacked a clause onto the end of the contract.*

tack·le¹ /ˈtækəl/ *v.* **1** [T] to make a determined effort to deal with a difficult problem: *The committee decided to tackle the budget problems in a new way.* **2** [I,T] to force someone to the ground so that they stop running, especially in a game such as football or RUGBY: *He was tackled on the 40-yard line.* **3** [I,T] to try to take the ball away from an opponent in a game such as SOCCER

tackle² *n.* [C] **1 a)** the act of stopping an opponent by forcing them to the ground, especially in football or RUGBY **b)** the act of trying to take the ball from an opponent in a game such as SOCCER **2** [C] a player in football who stops other players by tackling them or preventing them from moving forward **3** [U] the equipment used in some sports, especially fishing **4** [C,U] ropes and PULLEYS (=wheels) used for lifting heavy things, moving a ship's sails etc.

tack·y /ˈtæki/ *adj. comparative* **tackier**, *superlative* **tackiest** **1** DISAPPROVING showing that you do not have good judgment about what is fashionable, socially acceptable etc.: *It's really tacky to request gifts on an invitation.* **2** DISAPPROVING cheap looking and of very bad quality: *tacky souvenirs* **3** slightly sticky [**Origin:** (1–2) 1800–1900 *tacky* **horse in poor condition** (1800–1900).] —**tackily** *adv.* —**tackiness** *n.* [U]

ta·co /ˈtɑkoʊ, ˈtæ-/ *n. plural* **tacos** [C] a type of Mexican food consisting of a corn TORTILLA that is folded in half and filled with meat, beans etc. [**Origin:** 1900–2000 Mexican Spanish, Spanish, **wad, snack**]

tact /tækt/ *n.* [U] the ability to be polite and careful about what you say or do so that you do not upset or embarrass other people [**Origin:** 1600–1700 French **sense of touch**, from Latin *tactus*, from *tangere* **to touch**]

tact·ful /ˈtæktfəl/ *adj.* careful not to say or do anything that will upset or embarrass other people OPP **tactless**: *There was no tactful way of telling him the truth.* —**tactfully** *adv.*

tac·tic /ˈtæktɪk/ *n.* **1** [C] a method that you use to achieve something: *negotiating tactics* | *None of our tactics worked.* **2 tactics** [plural] the way in which military forces are arranged in order to win a battle, or the science of arranging them → see also SCARE TACTICS

tac·ti·cal /ˈtæktɪkəl/ *adj.* **1** relating to what you do to achieve what you want at a later time, especially in a game or large plan: *tactical decisions* | *a tactical advantage* | **a tactical error/mistake/blunder** (=a mistake that will harm your plans later) **2 a tactical weapon/missile/aircraft etc.** a weapon, airplane etc. that is only used over short distances to support military forces → see also STRATEGIC **3** relating to the way military forces are organized in order to win battles: *the military's tactical options* —**tactically** /-kli/ *adv.*

tac·ti·cian /tækˈtɪʃən/ *n.* [C] someone who is very good at TACTICS

tac·tile /ˈtæktl/ *adj.* **1** relating to your sense of touch: *a tactile sensation* **2** wanting to touch things or be touched often

tact·less /ˈtæktlɪs/ *adj.* likely to upset or embarrass someone without intending to OPP **tactful**: *a tactless comment* —**tactlessly** *adv.* —**tactlessness** *n.* [U]

tad /tæd/ *n.* SPOKEN, OLD-FASHIONED **a tad** a small amount, or to a small degree: *It's a tad expensive.*

tad·pole /ˈtædpoʊl/ *n.* [C] a small creature that has a long tail, lives in water, and grows into a FROG or TOAD

Tae-Bo /ˌtaɪˈboʊ/ *n.* [U] a type of exercise that combines dancing, kicking, and quick hand movements

taek·won do /taɪ ˈkwɑn doʊ/ *n.* [U] a style of fighting from Korea in which you kick, hit with your hands etc.

taf·fe·ta /ˈtæfət̬ə/ *n.* [U] a shiny stiff cloth made from silk or NYLON

taf·fy /ˈtæfi/ *n. plural* **taffies** [C,U] a type of soft CHEWY candy

Taft /tæft/, **William** (1857–1930) the 27th President of the U.S.

Taft-Hart·ley Act, the /ˌtæft ˈhɑrtli ˌækt/ HISTORY a law passed by Congress in 1947 that said certain things that LABOR UNIONS did were not allowed, and allowed the President to stop a STRIKE for 80 days if it would be dangerous to the country

tag¹ /tæg/ S3 *n.*
1 PIECE OF PAPER/PLASTIC [C] a small piece of paper, plastic etc. attached to something to show what it is, who owns it, what it costs etc.: *a name tag* | *Where's the price tag?* → see also DOG TAG
2 GAME [U] a children's game in which one player chases and tries to touch the others: **Tag! (You're it!)** (=said when a player manages to touch someone they are chasing)
3 tags [plural] INFORMAL the LICENSE PLATE on a car
4 DESCRIPTION [C] INFORMAL a word or phrase which is used to describe a person, group, or thing, but which is often unfair or not correct SYN **label**
5 COMPUTERS [C] COMPUTERS a computer CODE attached to a word or phrase in a computer document in order to arrange the information in a particular way
6 NAME/SYMBOL [C] INFORMAL someone's name or symbol that they paint illegally on a wall, vehicle etc.
7 GRAMMAR [C] ENG. LANG. ARTS a phrase such as "can't we?" or "is it?" that is added to a sentence to make it into a question → see also TAG QUESTION
8 ON A STRING [C] a metal or plastic point at the end of a piece of string or SHOELACE that prevents it from splitting → see also PHONE TAG

tag² *v.* **tagged, tagging** [T] **1** to fasten a tag onto something: *Each bird was tagged and released into the wild.* **2** to give someone or something a name or title, or think of them in a particular way that is difficult to change: **be tagged (as) sth** *He had been tagged "a slow learner" in the second grade.* **3** to touch someone you are chasing in a game of tag, or to touch someone with the ball in baseball **4** INFORMAL to illegally paint your name on a wall, vehicle etc. **5** COMPUTERS to attach a LABEL or CODE to a piece of information in a computer

tag along *phr. v.* INFORMAL to go somewhere with

someone, although you are not wanted or needed: *I hated it when my sister tagged along.*

tag sth ↔ **on** *phr. v.* to add something to something that already exists or is complete

tag·a·long /ˌtægəˈlɔŋ/ *n.* [C] INFORMAL someone who goes somewhere with someone else, especially when they are not wanted —**tag-along** /ˈtægəˌlɔŋ/ *adj.* [only before noun]

tag·ging /ˈtægɪŋ/ *n.* [U] INFORMAL the illegal activity of painting your name or sign on a wall, a vehicle etc.

ta·glia·tel·le /ˌtælyəˈtɛli, ˌtɑ-/ *n.* [U] a type of PASTA that is cut in very long thin flat pieces

ˈtag line *n.* [C] a sentence or phrase in an advertisement or advertising song that is the most important or easiest to remember

ˈtag ˌquestion *n.* [C] TECHNICAL a question that is formed by adding a phrase such as "can't we?," "wouldn't he?," or "is it?" to a sentence

ˈtag sale *n.* [C] a sale of used things that someone does not want anymore, or a sale at which the normal prices for things have been reduced

Ta·hi·ti /təˈhiṭi/ an island in French Polynesia, in the Pacific Ocean, which is governed by France —**Tahitian** /təˈhiʃən/ *n., adj.*

Ta·hoe /ˈtɑhoʊ/**, Lake** a large lake in the southwestern U.S. on the border between the states of Nevada and California

T

tai chi /ˌtaɪ ˈtʃi/ *n.* [U] a Chinese form of physical exercise that trains your mind and body in balance and control

tai·ga /ˈtaɪgə/ *n.* **the taiga** EARTH SCIENCE a forest of PINE trees (=trees with needle-shaped leaves that stay on the tree in winter) between the TUNDRA and the STEPPES of northern Russia and Asia

tail[1] /teɪl/ [S2] *n.* [C]

1 ANIMAL BIOLOGY the movable part at the back of an animal's body: *The dog was **wagging** its **tail**.* → see also -TAILED

2 BACK PART [usually singular] the back part of something, especially something that is moving away from you: *I took my place at the tail of the line.*

3 AIRCRAFT the back part of an aircraft

4 SHIRT the bottom part of your shirt at the back, that you put inside your pants [SYN] **shirttail**

5 tails [plural] INFORMAL a man's suit coat with two long parts that hang down the back, worn to formal events [SYN] **tailcoat**

6 tails [U] SPOKEN the side of a coin that does not have a person's head on it: *Which do you want, heads or tails?*

7 the tail end of a sth the last part of an event, situation, or period of time: *I only saw the tail end of the movie.*

8 be on sb's tail also **ride sb's tail** to follow another car too closely

9 FOLLOW [C] INFORMAL someone who is employed to watch and follow someone, especially a criminal: *He **put a tail on** his wife.*

10 with your tail between your legs embarrassed or unhappy because you have failed or been defeated

11 work/play/laugh etc. your tail off to work, play etc. very hard

12 it's (a case of) the tail wagging the dog INFORMAL used to say that an unimportant thing is wrongly controlling a situation

[**Origin:** Old English *tægel*] → see also **turn tail (and run)** at TURN[1] (23)

tail[2] *v.* [T] INFORMAL to follow someone and watch what they do, where they go etc.: *The police have been tailing him for several months.* ▸see THESAURUS box at **follow**

tail off *phr. v.* to become gradually smaller or weaker, sometimes stopping completely: *Profits tailed off toward the end of the year.*

tail·back /ˈteɪlbæk/ *n.* [C] the player who is the farthest back from the front line in football, and who often runs with the ball

tail·bone /ˈteɪlboʊn/ *n.* [C] NOT TECHNICAL the bone at the very bottom of your back [SYN] **coccyx**

tail·coat /ˈteɪlkoʊt/ *n.* [C] a man's suit coat with two long parts that hang down the back, worn to formal events

-tailed /teɪld/ *suffix* [in nouns] **white-tailed/long-tailed/ring-tailed etc.** having a tail that is white, long etc.

tail·gate[1] /ˈteɪlgeɪt/ *n.* [C] **1** a door at the back of a truck or car that opens out and down **2** a TAILGATE PARTY

tailgate

tailgate[2] *v.* [I,T] to drive too closely behind another vehicle —**tailgater** *n.* [C]

ˈtailgate ˌparty *n.* [C] a party before a football game where people eat and drink in the PARKING LOT of the place where the game is played

tail·light /ˈteɪl-laɪt/ *n.* [C] one of the two red lights at the back of a vehicle → see picture on page A36

tai·lor[1] /ˈteɪlɚ/ *n.* [C] someone whose job is to make clothes, especially men's clothes, that are measured to fit each customer perfectly

tailor[2] *v.* [T] to make something so that it is exactly right for someone's particular needs: **tailor sth for/to sb/sth** *We tailored the part specifically for her.*

tai·lored /ˈteɪlɚd/ *adj.* **1** a tailored piece of clothing is made to fit very well **2** made to fit a particular need or situation: *carefully tailored legislation*

tai·lor·ing /ˈteɪlərɪŋ/ *n.* [U] the work of making clothes or the style in which they are made

ˌtailor-ˈmade *adj.* exactly right or appropriate for someone or something: **+for** *The job's tailor-made for you.*

tail·pipe /ˈteɪlpaɪp/ *n.* [C] the pipe on the back of a car, truck etc. that gases from the engine come out of → see also EXHAUST PIPE

tail·spin /ˈteɪlspɪn/ *n.* [C] **1 in/into a tailspin** in or into a situation with many big problems that you cannot control, so that the situation becomes worse and worse: *Raising interest rates could send the economy into a tailspin.* **2** an uncontrolled fall of an airplane through the air, in which the back of the airplane spins in a wider circle than the front

tail wind, tailwind /ˈteɪl wɪnd/ *n.* [C] a wind blowing in the same direction that a vehicle is traveling

taint[1] /teɪnt/ *v.* [T usually passive] **1** if something bad taints a situation or person that it is connected with, it makes the person or situation seem bad or less desirable: *His reputation has been tainted by scandal.* **2** to ruin something by adding an unwanted substance to it: *The water supply had been tainted with dangerous chemicals.*

taint[2] *n.* [singular] the appearance of being related to something shameful or terrible: **+of** *the taint of corruption*

taint·ed /ˈteɪntɪd/ *adj.* **1** a tainted substance, especially food or drink, is not safe because it is spoiled or contains poison: *a tainted blood supply* **2** affected by or related to something illegal, dishonest, or morally wrong: *tainted money*

Tai·pei /ˌtaɪˈpeɪ/ the capital and largest city of Taiwan

Tai·wan /ˌtaɪˈwɑn/ an island near the southeast coast of China, which was formerly called Formosa —**Taiwanese** /ˌtaɪwɑˈniz◂/ *n., adj.*

Ta·ji·ki·stan /tɑˈdʒikɪˌstɑn, -ˌstæn/ a country in central Asia, between Uzbekistan and China, formerly part of the Soviet Union —**Tajik** *n., adj.*

Taj Ma·hal, the /ˌtɑdʒ məˈhɑl/ a beautiful white building in Agra, India, built in the middle of the 17th century by the ruler Shah Jahan as a MAUSOLEUM for his wife, Mumtaz Mahal

take

He took off his coat.

The plane took off.

take¹ /teɪk/ S1 W1 *v. past tense* **took** /tʊk/, *past participle* **taken** /ˈteɪkən/

1 MOVE SB/STH [T] to move someone or something with you when you go from one place to another: *Take an umbrella in case it rains.* | *Her mother's already taken her home.* | **take sb/sth to sth** *Take this note to the principal's office, please.* | *He needs someone to take him to the hospital.* | **take sb sth** *We should take your grandma some of these flowers.* | **take sb/sth into sth** *They took me into another room.* | **take sb/sth with you** *Don't forget to take your passport with you.* | *The kids begged Susan to **take** them **along**.* | *Someone came and **took** the dishes **away**.* ►see THESAURUS box at **bring** → see also BRING

2 DO STH [T] used with some nouns to say that you do the actions relating to the noun: *Take a look at this.* | *Hurry up. I need to take a shower too.* | *Let's take a walk around the block.*

3 TIME [T] if something takes a particular amount of time, that is the amount of time necessary to do it or for it to happen: *How long is this going to take?* | *What took you so long?* | **take (sb) ten minutes/three hours etc.** *The whole process takes two hours.* | **it takes (sb) ten minutes/three hours etc. to do sth** *It takes me about 20 minutes to get to work.*

4 ACCEPT/CHOOSE to accept or choose to have something, especially something that is offered to you: *He should have taken that job.* | *Did she take your advice?* | **take sth from sb** *Never take candy from strangers.* | *She refuses to take help from anyone.* | **take (the) credit/blame/responsibility (for sth)** (=to say that you deserve the credit, blame, or responsibility for something)

5 STUDY [T] to study a particular subject: *What classes are you taking next semester?* | *Steve took piano for years.*

6 TEST [T] to do a test or examination: *I'm going to see if I can take the test early.*

7 REMOVE STH [T always + adv./prep.] to remove something from a particular place: **take sth off/out of/from sth** *Take your feet off the seats.* | *Can you take the turkey out of the oven for me?*

8 NEED [T] to need a particular quality, amount of money, amount of effort etc. in order for you to achieve something or make something happen SYN **require**: *Raising children takes a lot of hard work.* | **it takes sth to do sth** *It will take nearly $650,000 to restore the house.* | **take courage/guts** *It takes courage to admit you're wrong.* | *They can still win, but it'll **take some doing**.*

9 PHOTOGRAPH to use a camera or similar piece of equipment to make a picture: +**of** *Could you take a picture of us?* | *I think we'd better take an X-ray.*

10 STEAL/BORROW [T] to steal something or borrow something without someone's permission: *The burglars took just about everything.* | *Did you take my pen again?*

11 HOLD/PUT [T] to reach for something and then hold it or put it somewhere: *Let me take your coats.* | *He took her hand and smiled.* | **take sb by the hand/arm** *She took me by the hand and led me into the living room.*

12 GET CONTROL [T] to get possession or control of someone or something: *Rebel forces have taken the capital.* | **take sb prisoner/hostage** *Six soldiers were taken prisoner.*

13 take control/charge/power/office to begin being in control of something or having a position of power: *The Communists took power in 1948.* | **take control/charge of sth** *Young people need to learn to take charge of their own lives.*

14 ACCEPT STH BAD/ANNOYING [T] INFORMAL to accept a bad situation or someone's bad or annoying behavior without becoming upset: *I can't take much more of this stress.* | *He's not very good at taking criticism.* | *The death of a loved one is always **hard to take**.* | **take it like a man** (=to accept a bad situation or physical beating without complaining or showing emotion)

15 take credit cards/checks/cash etc. to accept CREDIT CARDS, checks etc. as a form of payment SYN **accept**: *Do you take checks?*

16 MEDICINE/DRUG [T] to take a drug into your body: *Take two tablets before bed.* | **take sth for sth** *You really need to take something for that cough.* | *They say he used to **take drugs*** (=take illegal drugs).

17 MACHINE/VEHICLE [T] if a machine, vehicle etc. takes a particular type of gasoline, BATTERY etc., you have to use that in it: *What kind of gas does your car take?*

18 TAXI/BUS/TRAIN/ROAD ETC. [T] to use a taxi, bus, train etc. to go somewhere, or to travel using a particular road: *Let's take a cab.*

19 CONSIDER [T] to consider or react to someone or something in a particular way: *I can't **take** his suggestions very **seriously**.* | **take sth well/badly/hard** *She didn't take the news very well.* | **take sth lightly/personally etc.** *Try not to take his criticism personally.* | **take sth as sth** *I guess I'll take that as a compliment.* | **take sth as evidence/proof/a sign (of sth)** *I don't think we can take this as proof of her guilt.*

20 WRITE [T] to write down information that you have just been given: *Did you take notes during the lecture?* | *He's not here right now. Can I **take a message**?*

21 CAUSE SB TO GO [T always + adv./prep.] to lead someone somewhere or cause them to go there: *My job takes me all over the world.* | **take sb to/across/through etc. sth** *The highway takes you through some beautiful country.*

22 MEASURE [T] to test or measure something: *Hold still while I take your temperature.*

23 AS A GUEST [T] to bring someone with you to a restaurant, movie etc. and pay for them or be responsible for them: **take sb to sth** *Who are you taking to the dance?*

24 ROAD [T] to use a particular street or road to travel on: *Take the freeway – it'll be quicker.* | **take a right/left** *When you get to State Street, take a right.* | *I think maybe we **took a wrong turn**.*

25 EMOTION/ATTITUDE [T] used with some nouns that represent emotions or attitudes, to say that someone has or feels that emotion or attitude: *Dad **takes an interest in** everything we do.* | **take pleasure/joy/pride etc. in (doing) sth** *I took great pleasure in telling him he was wrong.* | *Howard **took pity on** the man and gave* *him some food.* | *I* ***take offense at*** (=feel offended by) *what he said.* | *She* ***took comfort from*** *the fact that he was just a phone call away.*

SPOKEN PHRASES

26 I take it (that) used to say that based on something you have noticed, you think something else is likely to be true: *I take it you two have already met.*
27 take sb/sth (for example) said when you want to give an example of something you have just been talking about: *Not everyone's happy about the changes. Take me, for example.*
28 take it or leave it used to say that what you have offered will not change: *I'll give you $50 for the bike – take it or leave it.*
29 take it from me used to persuade someone that what you are saying is true: *Take it from me – she's trouble.*
30 what do you take me for? used to say that you would never do something that someone has suggested you might do: *I'm not going to do it alone. What do you take me for – a fool?*
31 it takes all kinds (to make a world) said when you think what someone is doing, likes etc. is very strange
32 take it outside to go outside to continue an argument or fight

33 SUFFER STH [T] to experience something bad because you cannot avoid it: *Employees are being forced to take a 5% pay cut.* | *The company has* ***taken a loss*** *of over $45 million.* | **take a hammering/beating** (=to be defeated or go through a difficult period)
34 LEVEL [T always + adv./prep.] to make someone or something go to a higher level or position: **take sth to/into sth** *Does he have the talent to take him to the top?* | *I want to* ***take*** *the matter* ***further*** *and make a formal complaint.*
35 take it upon/on yourself to do sth to decide to do something without permission or approval: *Judy just took it upon herself to make the arrangements.*
36 sb can take sth or leave it used to say that someone does not care whether they have, see, or do something: *Pizza? I can take it or leave it.*
37 FOOD/DRINKS [T not in progressive] to use something such as salt, sugar, milk etc. in your food or drinks: **take sth in sth** *Do you take lemon in your tea?* | *I* ***take*** *my* ***coffee black***.
38 EAT/DRINK [T] to eat or drink something, especially in small amounts: *He took a mouthful of water from the bottle.*
39 SIZE [T] to wear a particular size of clothes or shoes: *What size shoe do you take?*
40 HAVE SPACE/STRENGTH FOR [T not in progressive or passive] to have only enough space or strength to contain or support a particular amount of something, or a particular number of things: *The shelf won't take any more books.*
41 NEWSPAPER [T] to have a particular newspaper delivered regularly to your house
42 USE [T usually in imperatives] a word meaning to use something, used when giving instructions: *Take one tortilla and top with cheese, tomatoes, and beans.*
43 NUMBERS [T] to subtract one number from another number SYN **take away**: **take sth from sth** *Take 4 from 9 and what do you get?*
44 IN GAMES/SPORTS [T] to get possession of something from an opponent in a game or sport
45 take a bend/fence/corner etc. [T] to try to get over or around something in a particular way: *You're driving too fast to take that curve.*
46 take ill/sick also **be taken ill** OLD-FASHIONED to suddenly become very sick
47 STH WORKS [I] if something that is supposed to change something else takes, it is successful and continues to work: *The dye didn't take and I had to redo it.*
48 SEX [T] LITERARY if a man takes a woman, he has sex with her
[**Origin:** 1000–1100 Old Norse *taka*] → see also **take care** at CARE[1] (5), **take a hike** at HIKE[1] (4), **take sth lying down** at LIE DOWN, **take part** at PART[1] (4), **take place** at PLACE[1] (4), **point taken** at POINT[1] (3), TAKEN[2], TAKEOFF, **have what it takes** at WHAT[1] (15) ►see THESAURUS box at **bring**

take sb **aback** *phr. v.* to surprise or shock someone: *He was a little taken aback by my response.*

take after sb *phr. v.* to look or behave like an older relative: *Everyone says I take after my mother.*

take apart *phr. v.* **1 take sth ↔ apart** to separate something into pieces SYN **dismantle** OPP **put together**: *Tom was always taking things apart in the garage.* **2 take sb ↔ apart** INFORMAL to beat someone very easily in a game or sport **3 take sth ↔ apart** to search a place very thoroughly and make a big mess

take away *phr. v.* **1 take sth ↔ away** to remove something or make it stop existing: *This should take some of the pain away.* **2 take sth ↔ away** to remove a possession from someone and not allow them to have it anymore: *If you can't play nice, I'll take the toys away.* **3 take sb ↔ away** if the police, government etc. take someone away, they remove them from their home and put them somewhere by force: *Soldiers came in the night and took him away.* **4 take sth ↔ away** MATH to subtract one number from another number

take away from sth *phr. v.* to spoil the good effect or success of something SYN **detract**: *The sad news took away from our enjoyment of the evening.*

take back *phr. v.* **1 take sth ↔ back** to admit that you were wrong to say something: *I take back everything I said.* **2 take sth ↔ back** to take something you have bought back to a store because it does not fit, is not what you wanted etc.: *If the shirt doesn't fit, take it back.* **3 take sb ↔ back** to be willing to start a romantic relationship again with someone after ending it: *After all the things I said, I don't think she'd ever take me back.* **4 take sb back** to make someone remember a time in the past: *Boy, that song really takes me back.*

take sth **↔ down** *phr. v.* **1** to remove something from its place, usually so that it is lower down or in several pieces: *When are you going to take down your Christmas decorations?* | *Help me take down the tent.* **2** to write something on a piece of paper in order to remember it or have a record of it: *Let me take down your name and number.*

take sth **from** sth *phr. v.* to get something from something such as a book, collection etc.: *The book's title is taken from an old folk song.*

take in *phr. v.*
1 UNDERSTAND/REMEMBER take sth ↔ in to understand and remember new facts and information: *I need a minute to take in what he told me.*
2 DECEIVE take sb ↔ in to deceive someone completely: *You have to be pretty dumb to be taken in by an offer like that.*
3 MONEY take sth ↔ in to collect or earn an amount of money: *How much did you take in at the sale?*
4 CAR/EQUIPMENT ETC. take sth ↔ in to bring something to a place in order to have it repaired: *I'm going to take the car in tomorrow for a tune-up.*
5 PROVIDE HOME take sb/sth ↔ in to let a person or an animal stay in your house or a shelter, especially because they have nowhere else to stay: *Brett's always taking in stray animals.*
6 CLOTHES take sth ↔ in to make a piece of clothing narrower so that it fits you OPP **let out**
7 POLICE take sb ↔ in if the police take someone in, they take them to a police station to ask them questions about a crime
8 VISIT/SEE take in sth to visit a place while you are in the area
9 MOVIE/PLAY ETC. take in sth OLD-FASHIONED to go to see something such as a movie, play etc.
10 WORK take in sth to do work for someone else in your home

take off *phr. v.*
1 REMOVE STH take sth ↔ off, take sth off sth to remove something, especially a piece of clothing OPP **put on**: *Could you take off your shoes before you come in?*
2 AIRCRAFT/SPACE VEHICLE to rise into the air at the beginning of a flight: *What time did the plane finally take off?*

3 LEAVE A PLACE INFORMAL to leave somewhere suddenly, especially without telling anyone
4 WORK take sth ↔ off, take sth off sth to not go to work for a period of time: *I'm taking Friday off to go to the dentist.* | *I need to take some time off work.*
5 WEIGHT take sth ↔ off to become thinner and lighter, especially by losing a particular amount of weight: *He's taken a lot of weight off recently.*
6 SUCCESS to suddenly start being successful: *His singing career has really taken off.*

take on *phr. v.*
1 COMPETE/FIGHT take sb/sth ↔ on to compete or fight against someone or something: *Tonight the 49ers take on the Raiders in Oakland.*
2 CHANGE QUALITY take on sth to begin to have a different quality or appearance: *Her face took on a fierce expression.*
3 DO WORK take sth ↔ on to start doing some difficult work or to start being responsible for something important: *I've taken on far too much work lately.*
4 HIRE take sb ↔ on to start to employ someone SYN **hire**: *We've taken on three new employees this month.*
5 PLANE/BUS ETC. take sb/sth ↔ on if a plane, ship, bus etc. takes on people or things, they come onto it or are put onto it

take out *phr. v.*
1 REMOVE take sth ↔ out to remove something from inside a container or place: *She opened her briefcase and took a letter out.*
2 AS GUEST/DATE take sb ↔ out to take someone to a restaurant, theater, club etc. and pay for their meal or entertainment: *I'm taking Melinda out for dinner tonight.*
3 FROM BANK take sth ↔ out to arrange to get something officially, especially from a bank, insurance company, or a court of law: *The couple took out a $200,000 loan.*
4 ADVERTISEMENT take sth ↔ out to arrange for an advertisement to be printed in a newspaper or magazine: *She took out ads in all the local papers.*
5 FROM BANK ACCOUNT take sth ↔ out to get money from your bank account
6 FROM LIBRARY take sth ↔ out to borrow a book from a library SYN **check out**
7 take a lot out of sb also **take it out of sb** to make someone feel very tired: *My job takes a lot out of me.*
8 KILL/DESTROY take sb/sth ↔ out INFORMAL to kill someone, or destroy something: *The bombing took out the entire village.* → see also TAKEOUT

take sth **out on** sb *phr. v.* to treat someone badly because you are feeling angry, tired etc.: *Don't* ***take it out on*** *me! It's not my fault.*

take over *phr. v.* **1 take sth over** to begin to do what someone else was doing, especially being in charge of something: *She wants me to take over when she retires.* | *His brother took over the running of the business.* **2 take sth ↔ over** to take control of something: *The company was taken over by Sony in 1989.* → see also TAKEOVER

take to *phr. v.* **1 take to sb/sth** to start to like someone or something: *We took to each other right away.* **2 take to the streets/highways etc.** to go out into the streets for a particular purpose, usually to protest something: *Thousands of people took to the streets in protest.* **3 take to sth** to start doing something regularly or as a habit: **take to doing sth** *Lately he's taken to staying up till the middle of the night.* | *After his business failed, he* ***took to drink*** (=started drinking alcohol regularly). **4 take to sth like a duck to water** to learn how to do something very easily or to quickly change your behavior and attitudes to match a new situation **5 take to your bed** OLD-FASHIONED to go to your bed and stay there, especially because you are sick

take up *phr. v.*
1 SPACE/TIME take up sth if something takes up a particular amount of time or space, it fills or uses it: *I don't want to take up too much of your time.* | *Our new car takes up the whole garage.* | **be taken up with sth** *Most of my time is taken up with work.*
2 ACTIVITY/SUBJECT take sth ↔ up to become interested in a particular activity or subject and spend time doing it: *She recently took up golf.*
3 take up residence FORMAL to start living somewhere
4 take up arms LITERARY to fight a battle using weapons
5 FLOOR/CARPET ETC. take sth ↔ up to remove something that is attached to the floor
6 IDEA/SUGGESTION/SUBJECT take sth ↔ up to begin discussing or considering something: *Now the papers have taken up the story.*
7 OFFER take sth ↔ up to accept an offer or CHALLENGE that someone has made: *I took up the invitation to visit.*
8 JOB/RESPONSIBILITY take up sth to start a new job or have a new responsibility
9 POSITION take up sth to put yourself in a particular position ready for something to happen, or so that you can see better
10 CLOTHES take sth ↔ up to reduce the length of a skirt or pair of pants
11 CONTINUE AN ACTIVITY take sth ↔ up to continue a story or activity that someone else started, or that you started but had to stop

take sb **up on** sth *phr. v.* to accept an invitation that someone has made: *Thanks for the offer. I might take you up on it.*

take up with *phr. v.* **1 take sth ↔ up with sb** to discuss something with someone, especially a complaint or problem: *If you're unhappy, you should take it up with your supervisor.* **2 take up with sb** OLD-FASHIONED to begin a friendship or a romantic relationship, especially with someone you should not have a relationship with

take[2] S3 W3 *n.* [C] **1** an attempt to record a movie scene, song, action etc. without stopping: *They were able to film the scene in one take.* **2** INFORMAL an opinion about a person, situation, or idea: **+on** *Let's hear your take on what just happened.* **3** INFORMAL [usually singular] the amount of money earned by a store or business in a particular period of time **4 be on the take** INFORMAL if someone in an official position is on the take, they are receiving money for doing things that are wrong or illegal **5** [usually singular] the number of fish or animals caught at one particular time

take·down /ˈteɪkdaʊn/ *n.* [C] a movement in WRESTLING in which you put your opponent on his or her back on the ground

ˈtake-home ˌpay *n.* [U] the amount of money that you receive from your job after taxes etc. have been taken out

tak·en[1] /ˈteɪkən/ *v.* the past participle of TAKE

taken[2] *adj.* [not before noun] **1 taken (with sb/sth)** attracted by a particular person, idea, plan etc.: *She seems quite taken with him.* **2** a seat or place that is taken is not available because it is being saved for someone else OPP **free**

take·off /ˈteɪk-ɔf/ *n.* **1** [C,U] the time when an airplane or ROCKET rises into the air → see also LIFT-OFF: *The plane crashed shortly after takeoff.* **2** [C] an amusing performance that copies a show, movie, or the way someone behaves: *a takeoff of a morning talk show* **3** [C] the act of leaving the ground as you make a jump → see also **take off** at TAKE[1]

take·out, take-out /ˈteɪk-aʊt/ *n.* [C,U] a meal that you buy at a restaurant to eat at home or somewhere else —**takeout** *adj.*

take·o·ver /ˈteɪkˌoʊvɚ/ *n.* [C] **1** an act of getting control of a country or political organization, especially by using force: **+of** *the military takeover of the government* **2** the act of getting control of a company by buying most of the STOCK in it → see also **hostile takeover/bid/buyout** at HOSTILE (4)

tak·er /ˈteɪkɚ/ *n.* **1** [C] someone who accepts or buys something that is offered: *There have been* ***no takers*** *for the multimillion-dollar property.* **2 a risk-taker/test-taker/hostage-taker etc.** someone who takes risks, tests etc. **3** [C] someone who accepts support and help from other people, but who is not willing to give them support or help

talc /tælk/ *n.* [U] **1** talcum powder **2** a soft smooth mineral that feels like soap and is used for making paints, plastics etc.

tal·cum pow·der /ˈtælkəm ˌpaʊdɚ/ *n.* [U] a fine powder which you put on your skin after washing to make it dry or smell nice

tale /teɪl/ W2 *n.* [C] **1** a story about imaginary, usually exciting, events: +**of** *tales of adventure* | *a folk tale* (=traditonal story) ►see THESAURUS box at **story** **2** a description of an event or situation, often one containing strong emotions or one that is not completely true: *The guys sat around* ***telling tales*** *of adventure.* | *Bankers are used to hearing* ***tales of woe*** *from would-be borrowers.* **3 live/survive to tell the tale** to still be alive after a dangerous or frightening event [**Origin:** Old English *talu*] → see also FAIRY TALE, **old wives' tale** at OLD (20), **tall tale** at TALL (4), TATTLETALE

tal·ent /ˈtælənt/ W3 *n.* **1** [C,U] a special natural ability or skill: *You need talent and hard work to be a tennis player.* | +**for** *Gary has a talent for making people laugh.* | **a man/woman of many talents** (=someone who has the ability to do several things very well) | **a talent contest/show/competition** (=a competition in which people show how well they can sing, dance, tell jokes etc.) ►see THESAURUS box at **ability** **2** [C,U] a person or people with a special natural ability or skill: *As a singer, she's a great talent.* [**Origin:** 1400–1500 *talent* unit of weight or money in the ancient world (9–21 centuries), from Latin *talentum*, from Greek *talanton*; from a story in the Bible in which a man gives talents to his three servants, and two of them use them well]

T

tal·ent·ed /ˈtæləntɪd/ *adj.* having a very good natural ability or skill in a particular activity: *a talented journalist*

ˈtalent scout *n.* [C] someone whose job is to find young people who are good at a sport or activity

tal·is·man /ˈtælɪsmən, -lɪz-/ *n.* [C] an object that is believed to have magic powers of protection

talk¹ /tɔk/ S1 W1 *v.*

1 CONVERSATION [I] to say things to someone, especially in a conversation: *I could hear people talking in the next room.* | +**to/with** *It's been nice talking to you.* | +**about** *Let's not talk about the accident.* | *Sandy talks about herself all the time.* | *Once Lou* ***gets talking*** (=starts having a conversation), *you know you're going to be there a while.*

THESAURUS

have a conversation to talk informally to another person or people in order to ask questions, exchange ideas etc.: *The two men were having a long conversation.*
chat (with/to sb)/have a chat to talk to someone in a friendly way about things that are not very important: *She's chatting with Chris.* | *We ended up having a chat about sailing.*
converse FORMAL to have a conversation with someone: *Students like her because she can converse with them in their own language.*
visit (with sb) INFORMAL to have a conversation with someone, especially about your personal lives: *My aunt and uncle used to stop by to visit with my parents every week.*
discuss to talk seriously about ideas or plans: *We'll discuss the matter at the meeting.*
gossip to talk about other people's private lives when they are not there: *People have started to gossip about his wife.*
whisper to talk quietly, usually because you do not want other people to hear what you are saying: *He turned to his mother and whispered something in her ear.*
go on to talk too much or for too long about something: *She went on and on about how good she was at basketball.*
ramble (on) to talk for a long time in a way that does not seem organized, and that other people think is boring: *He rambled on for an hour about fishing.*
prattle to talk continuously about silly and unimportant things: *We had to sit and listen to her prattling on about her children.*

2 DISCUSS [I,T] to discuss something with someone, especially an important or serious subject: *We need to talk right now.* | +**about/of** *We've been talking about getting married.* | +**to/with** *I'd like to talk with you in private.* | **talk sports/business/politics etc.** *I don't feel like talking business right now.*

3 talk shop INFORMAL to talk about things that are connected with your work, especially at a social event, in a way that other people find boring

4 SPEECH [I] to give a speech SYN **speak**: +**on/about** *Prof. Simmons will talk on the benefits of genetic research.*

5 SAY WORDS [I] to produce words in a language: *He's only one year old and he's already starting to talk.* | *Is this one of those birds that can talk?*

6 talk about sth to discuss something in writing in a book, newspaper, magazine etc.: *The next two chapters talk about further developments in this field.*

7 SECRET INFORMATION [I] to give someone important secret information because they force you to: *Even after three days of interrogation, Maskell* ***refused to talk.***

8 PRIVATE LIVES [I] to discuss other people's private lives and behavior, usually in a disapproving way: *If we're seen together, people might talk.*

9 talk to yourself to say things out loud, which are not directed at another person: *"What did you say?" "Nothing, I was just talking to myself."*

10 COMPUTERS [I] if a machine such as a computer talks to another machine, it sends information to it

SPOKEN PHRASES

11 what are you talking about? a) said when the person you are talking to has just said something that you think is clearly stupid or wrong, or based on a wrong idea: *What are you talking about? I gave you the money weeks ago.* **b)** used to ask someone what their conversation is about

12 I don't know what sb is talking about used to say that you did not do something bad that someone says you did and that you do not know anything about the situation: *"Tell me who you sold the drugs to." "I don't know what you're talking about."*

13 know what you are talking about to know a lot about a particular subject: *I know what I'm talking about because I was there when it happened.*

14 talk about rich/funny/stupid etc. used to emphasize that the person or thing you are talking about is very rich, funny, stupid etc.: *Talk about lucky. That's the second time he's won this week!*

15 look who's talking also **sb can talk, sb's a fine one to talk** used to say that someone should not criticize someone else because they are just as bad: *"You need to get more exercise." "Look who's talking!"*

16 now you're talking said when you think someone's suggestion is a very good idea

17 we're/you're talking (about) sth a) used to tell someone what will be necessary in order to do or get what they are asking you about: *For a new set of tires, you're talking $250.* **b)** used in conversation to emphasize or remind someone that a particular kind of thing is involved in a situation: *We're talking about matters of national security.*

18 I'm talking to you! used when you are angry because the person you are talking to is not paying attention to you

19 talk sb's ear off to talk too much to someone

20 sth is like talking to a brick wall used to say that it is difficult and annoying to try to speak with someone because they do not seem to listen to or understand you

21 that's what I'm talking about used to say that you strongly agree with what someone has said or like something you have just heard or seen

22 be talking [usually in negatives and questions] INFORMAL if two people are not talking they refuse to talk to each

other because they have argued: *Pat and Alan are still not talking.*
23 **do (all) the talking** INFORMAL to explain or speak for a group of people in a difficult situation: *Just let me do the talking.*
24 **talk your way out of sth** INFORMAL to escape from a bad or embarrassing situation by giving explanations, excuses etc.
25 **talk tough (on sth)** INFORMAL to tell people very strongly what you want from them or what you will do: *The President is talking tough on crime.*
26 **talk dirty** INFORMAL to talk in a sexual way to someone in order to make them feel sexually excited
27 **talk trash** INFORMAL to say impolite or offensive things to or about someone, especially to opponents in a sports competition
28 **talk (some) sense into sb** INFORMAL to persuade someone to behave in a sensible way: *Someone needs to talk sense into Rob before he gets hurt.*
29 **talk sense/nonsense** INFORMAL to say sensible or stupid things
30 **be the booze/drugs/alcohol etc. talking** INFORMAL used to say that someone is saying something only because they have had too much to drink, taken drugs etc.
31 **talk out of both sides of your mouth** DISAPPROVING to say opposite things to different people in order to try to please everyone
32 **talk the talk (of sb/sth)** to say the things that people expect or think are necessary in a particular situation → see also WALK THE WALK
33 **talk turkey** INFORMAL to talk seriously about important things, especially in order to agree on something
34 **be talking through your hat** DISAPPROVING to talk as if you know about something, when in fact you do not
35 **talk smack** INFORMAL to criticize someone or something in an unpleasant way
36 **talk a blue streak** OLD-FASHIONED, INFORMAL to talk very quickly, without stopping

talk around sth *phr. v.* to discuss a problem without really dealing with the important parts of it

talk back *phr. v.* to answer someone rudely after they have criticized you or told you to do something: **+to** *Don't talk back to your father!*

talk down *phr. v.* **1 talk sb/sth ↔ down** to give instructions on a radio to a PILOT so that they can bring an aircraft to the ground safely **2 talk sb ↔ down** to persuade someone to come down from a high place when they are threatening to jump and kill themselves **3 talk sb/sth ↔ down** to talk about someone or something in a way that makes them seem unsuccessful, boring, bad etc. OPP **talk up**

talk down to sb *phr. v.* to talk to someone as if they were stupid when in fact they are not SYN **patronize**: *Kids hate it when you talk down to them.*

talk sb **into** sth *phr. v.* to persuade someone to do something: *Why did I let you talk me into this?* | **talk sb into doing sth** *Linda finally talked me into buying a new car.*

talk sth ↔ **out** *phr. v.* INFORMAL to talk about a problem in order to solve it: *There are still a lot of details that we need to talk out.*

talk sb **out of** sth *phr. v.* to persuade someone not to do something: **talk sb out of doing sth** *Can't you talk them out of selling the house?*

talk sth ↔ **over** *phr. v.* to discuss a problem or situation with someone before you decide what to do: *Don't worry – we have plenty of time to talk it over.* | **talk sth over with sb** *I'm going to have to talk it over with Dale first.* | *Let's* ***talk things over*** *next week.*

talk through *phr. v.* **1 talk sth ↔ through** to discuss all of something so that you are sure you understand it: *They need to meet again to talk through their plans.* **2 talk sb through sth** to give someone instructions on how to do something by giving them a little information at a time: *Tech support talked me through the software installation.*

talk sb/sth ↔ **up** *phr. v.* to talk about someone or something in a way that makes them seem successful, interesting, good etc. OPP **talk down**: *The administration has been eager to talk up the deal.*

talk[2] S1 W1 *n.*
1 CONVERSATION [C] a conversation: *After a long talk, we decided to break up.* | *Rob and I* ***had*** *a really good* ***talk*** *last night.* | **+about** *I think it's time we had a talk about your future here in the company.* | **+with** *Her talk with Eddie had convinced her he was telling the truth.*
2 talks [plural] formally organized discussions between governments, organizations etc.: *The talks have reached an important stage.* | **+with** *Talks with the rebels have failed.* | **+about** *talks about the future of the Middle East* | *The President* ***held talks*** *with Chinese officials.* | **peace/trade/budget etc. talks** *The peace talks look promising.* | *Talks* ***broke down over*** *money issues.*
3 SPEECH [C] a speech or LECTURE: *an entertaining talk* | **+on/about** *a talk on local history* | **+by** *a series of talks by well-known writers* | **+to** *a talk to the entire student body* | **give/do/deliver a talk** *Last week, she gave a talk at the University of Minnesota.* ►see THESAURUS box at **speech**
4 DISCUSSION [U] the activity of talking about something, especially something that may not happen or be true, or what is said about it: *In those days there was talk if two people lived together without being married.* | ***There's talk of*** *more factory closures in the area.* | ***There's talk that*** *she might resign.*
5 talk is cheap INFORMAL used to say that you do not believe someone will do what they say
6 TYPE OF CONVERSATION [U] a particular type of conversation or thing that is talked about: *That's enough of that kind of talk.* | **girl/guy/football etc. talk** *It's girl talk – nothing you'd be interested in.*
7 be all talk (and/but no action) SPOKEN to always be talking about what you have done or what you are going to do without ever actually doing anything
8 be the talk of the town/company etc. to be the person or thing that everyone is talking about because they are very interested, excited, shocked etc.: *The trial has been the talk of the campus.*
9 sth is only/just talk used to say that something has been talked about, but it is possibly or probably not going to happen: *It's just talk. He'll never do it.* → see also BABY TALK, PEP TALK, **pillow talk** at PILLOW[1] (3), SMALL TALK, SWEET-TALK

talk·a·tive /ˈtɔkətɪv/ *adj.* someone who is talkative likes to talk a lot SYN **loquacious** —**talkativeness** *n.* [U]

talk·er /ˈtɔkɚ/ *n.* [C] INFORMAL someone who talks a lot or talks in a particular way: *Will's a talker, all right.* | **smooth/slick talker** (=someone who says nice things but who you do not trust) *He's a smooth talker who'll tell you exactly what you want to hear.*

talk·ie /ˈtɔki/ *n.* [C] OLD-FASHIONED a movie with sounds and words

ˌtalking ˈbook *n.* [C] a book that has been recorded for blind people to listen to

ˌtalking ˈhead *n.* [C] INFORMAL someone on television who is not performing, but instead is reading the news, giving opinions, or discussing something. Usually they are filmed so that you only see their shoulders and heads.

ˈtalking-to *n.* **give sb a talking-to** INFORMAL to talk to someone angrily because you are annoyed about something they have done

ˌtalk ˈradio *n.* [U] a type of radio program in which listeners call the radio station to give their opinions or to discuss a subject

ˈtalk show *n.* [C] a television or radio show on which people talk about their lives and are asked questions

talk·y /ˈtɔki/ *adj.* INFORMAL containing a lot of talking, especially about things that are not very interesting: *The play is terribly talky and slow.*

tall /tɔl/ S1 W2 *adj.* **1** a person, building, tree etc. that is tall has a greater than average height: *He was tall* *and thin.* | *a house surrounded by tall trees* → see picture at HIGH¹

WORD CHOICE

Use **tall** to describe people, trees, and upright narrow objects.
Use **high** to describe mountains, walls, fences etc.
You can use both **tall** and **high** to describe buildings, but **tall** is more commonly used.
Use **high** to talk about how far something such as a shelf is from the ground.

2 used when you say or ask what the height of something or someone is: *Lorna is a little taller than her husband.* | ***How tall** is the Eiffel Tower?* | **three feet/two meters etc. tall** *Tammy is only five feet tall.* **3 be a tall order** INFORMAL if a request or piece of work is a tall order, it will be almost impossible for you to do: *Finding time to read to their kids is a tall order for busy parents.* **4 tall tale/story** a story that is difficult to believe, because the events in it are very exciting, dangerous etc. **5** a tall drink contains a small amount of alcohol mixed with a large amount of juice, SODA etc. **6 a tall drink of water** OLD-FASHIONED, HUMOROUS someone, especially a woman, who is very tall [**Origin:** Old English *getæl* **quick, ready**] —**tallness** *n.* [U] → see also **stand tall** at STAND¹ (26), **walk tall** at WALK¹ (10)

Tal·la·has·see /ˌtæləˈhæsi/ the capital city of the U.S. state of Florida

tall·boy /ˈtɔlbɔɪ/ *n.* [C] a can of beer that holds 16 OUNCES

Tal·linn /ˈtɑlɪn/ the capital and largest city of Estonia

tal·low /ˈtæloʊ/ *n.* [U] hard animal fat used for making CANDLES

tal·ly¹ /ˈtæli/ *n. plural* **tallies** [C] a record of how much you have spent, won, obtained etc. so far SYN **count**: *The final tally showed Sanchez having 984 more votes than her opponent.* | *a **running tally*** (=a record that adds something up as it happens) *of your expenses* | ***Keep a tally** of how many cars pass.*

tally² *v.* **tallies, tallied, tallying** **1** also **tally up** [T] to calculate the total number of something: *Absentee ballots were tallied three days after the election.* **2** [I] if numbers or statements tally, they match each other exactly SYN **agree**: +**with** *Lilly says things that don't always tally with the truth.*

Tal·mud /ˈtɑlmʊd, ˈtælməd/ *n.* **the Talmud** the collection of writings that make up Jewish law about religious and non-religious life —**Talmudic** /tɑlˈmudɪk/ *adj.*

tal·on /ˈtælən/ *n.* [C] a sharp powerful curved nail on the feet of some birds that catch animals for food

ta·ma·le /təˈmɑli/ *n.* [C] a SPICY Mexican dish made of meat and other foods that are then wrapped in DOUGH made from corn, then in corn HUSKS, and then cooked in steam

tam·a·rind /ˈtæmərɪnd/ *n.* [C] BIOLOGY a tropical tree, or the fruit of this tree [**Origin:** 1500–1600 Spanish and Portuguese *tamarindo*, from Arabic *tamr hindi* **Indian date**]

tam·bou·rine /ˌtæmbəˈrin/ *n.* [C] a circular musical instrument, usually covered with skin or plastic, that has small pieces of metal around the edge. You hit it with your hand or shake it to make a noise.

tame¹ /teɪm/ *adj.* **1** an animal that is tame is not wild anymore, because it has been trained to live with people SYN **domesticated** OPP **wild** **2** boring or unexciting SYN **dull**: *a pretty tame rollercoaster* —**tamely** *adv.* —**tameness** *n.* [U]

tame² *v.* [T] **1** to train a wild animal to obey you and not to attack people → see also DOMESTICATE **2** to reduce the power or strength of something and prevent it from causing trouble: *attempts to tame inflation*

ta·mox·i·fen /təˈmɑksəfən/ *n.* [U] a drug that is used to treat breast CANCER

tamp /tæmp/ *v.* [T always + adv./prep.] also **tamp down** to press or push something down by lightly hitting it several times

Tam·pa /ˈtæmpə/ a city, port, and holiday RESORT in the U.S. state of Florida

Tam·pax /ˈtæmpæks/ *n.* [U] TRADEMARK the name of a common type of TAMPON

tam·per /ˈtæmpɚ/ *v.*

tamper with sth *phr. v.* to touch something or make changes to it without permission, especially in order to deliberately damage it: *The telephone line had been tampered with.*

ˈtamper-proof *adj.* a package or container that is tamper-proof is made in a way that prevents someone from opening it before it is sold

ˈtamper-reˌsistant also **ˈtamper-ˌevident** *adj.* a package or container that is tamper-resistant is made so that you can see if someone has opened it before it is sold in stores

tam·pon /ˈtæmpɑn/ *n.* [C] a tube-shaped mass of cotton or similar material that a woman puts inside her VAGINA during her PERIOD (=monthly flow of blood)

tan¹ /tæn/ *adj.* **1** having a pale yellowish brown color: *a tan suit* **2** having darker skin after spending time in the sun SYN **tanned**: *She came home tan and glowing.*

tan² *n.* **1** [U] a light yellowish brown color **2** [C] the brown color that someone with pale skin gets after they have been in the sun SYN **suntan**: *Monica got a nice tan.* **3** [C] an abbreviation of TANGENT

tan³ *v.* **tanned, tanning** **1** [I,T] if you tan, or the sun tans you, your skin becomes darker because you spend time in the sun: *I don't tan – I just get red.* **2** [T] to make animal skin into leather by treating it with a type of acid → see also **have/tan sb's hide** at HIDE² (2), TANNING BED, TANNING SALON

tan·dem /ˈtændəm/ *n.* [C] **1 in tandem** doing something together or at the same time as someone or something else: *The two skaters glided by in tandem.* | +**with** *The company is **working in tandem** with a software developer on the product.* **2** two people who work well together: *The tandem of Mitchell and Bookman combined for three touchdowns.* **3** also **ˈtandem ˌbicycle** a bicycle built for two riders sitting one behind the other

tan·door·i /tænˈdʊri/ *adj.* tandoori chicken, lamb etc. is an Indian dish that has been cooked in a large closed clay pot

Ta·ney /ˈtɔni/, **Rog·er** /ˈrɑdʒɚ/ (1777–1864) a CHIEF JUSTICE on the U.S. Supreme Court

Tang /tɑŋ/ HISTORY the DYNASTY that ruled China from 618 to 907. It is considered to be a very good period in China's history, with progress made in literature, art, science, and TECHNOLOGY.

tang /tæŋ/ *n.* [singular] a strong, slightly sour, but pleasant taste or smell: *The lemon added a nice tang to the sauce.* —**tangy** *adj.*: *tangy barbecue sauce*

Tan·gan·yi·ka /ˌtæŋgənˈyikə/**, Lake** a large lake in central Africa between the Democratic Republic of Congo and Tanzania

tan·ge·lo /ˈtændʒəloʊ/ *n.* [C] BIOLOGY a fruit that is a CROSS (=mixture) between a TANGERINE and a GRAPEFRUIT

tan·gent /ˈtændʒənt/ *n.* [C] **1 go off on a tangent** to suddenly start thinking or talking about a completely new and different subject: *Let's stay with the topic and not go off on a tangent.* **2** MATH a straight line that touches the outside of a curve but does not cut across it **3** MATH a number relating to an angle in a RIGHT TRIANGLE that is calculated by dividing the length of the side across from the angle by the length of the side next to it → see also COTANGENT

tan·gen·tial /tænˈdʒɛnʃəl/ *adj.* FORMAL tangential information, remarks etc. are only related to a particular subject in a slight or indirect way: *Some of the questions had only tangential relevance to the subject.* —**tangentially** *adv.*

tan·ger·ine /ˌtændʒəˈrin/ *n.* [C] BIOLOGY a small sweet fruit like an orange with a skin that comes off easily

[**Origin:** 1600–1700 French *Tanger* **Tangier**, city in Morocco]

tan·gi·ble /ˈtændʒəbəl/ *adj.* **1** easy to see or notice, so that there is no doubt OPP **intangible**: *the tangible benefits of the new system* | *tangible rewards for good behavior* | **tangible proof/evidence** *The wins are tangible proof of her skill as a coach.* **2** FORMAL able to be seen and touched: *tangible personal property* **3 tangible assets/property etc.** property such as buildings, equipment etc. —**tangibly** *adv.* —**tangibility** /ˌtændʒəˈbɪləṱi/ *n.* [U]

tan·gle¹ /ˈtæŋgəl/ *n.* [C] **1** a twisted mass of something such as hair or thread SYN **snarl**: *It takes forever to comb the tangles out of my hair.* | +**of** *a tangle of electrical cords* **2** a confused situation: +**of** *a tangle of immigration laws* | *a confused tangle of emotions* **3** an argument or fight: +**with** *I did not want to get in a tangle with the press.*

tangle² *v.* **1** [I] to fight or argue with someone: +**with** *He's the last person you want to tangle with.* **2** [I,T] also **tangle up** to become twisted together or make something become twisted together in a messy way SYN **snarl**: *My hair tangles easily.*

tan·gled /ˈtæŋgəld/ also **ˌtangled ˈup** *adj.* **1** twisted together in a messy way SYN **snarled**: *The phone cord is* ***all tangled up.*** **2** complicated or consisting of many confusing parts: *her tangled emotions* | *his* ***tangled web of*** *illegal business deals*

tan·go¹ /ˈtæŋgoʊ/ *n. plural* **tangos** [C] a fast dance from South America, or a piece of music for this dance

tango² *v.* [I] **1** ENG. LANG. ARTS to dance the tango **2 it takes two to tango** SPOKEN used to say that if a problem involves two people, then both people are equally responsible

tank¹ /tæŋk/ S2 W3 *n.* [C] **1** a large container for storing liquid or gas: *The hot water tank is leaking.* | *a large* ***fish tank*** (=a tank that fish are kept in) | *Some water must have gotten into the* ***gas tank.*** | *the boat's* ***fuel tank*** | *an underground* ***storage tank*** **2** also **tankful** the amount of liquid or gas held in a tank: +**of** *a half tank of gas* **3** a heavy military vehicle that has a large gun and runs on two metal belts that go around its wheels **4** a large artificial pool for storing water [**Origin:** 1600–1700 Portuguese *tanque* **pool**] → see also SEPTIC TANK, THINK TANK

tank² *v.* [I] **1** SLANG to decrease quickly or be very unsuccessful: *The movie tanked at the box office.* **2** SLANG [T] to deliberately lose a sports game that you could have won

tank up *phr. v.* **1** INFORMAL to put gasoline in your car so that the tank is full **2** SLANG to drink a lot of alcohol, especially beer

tan·kard /ˈtæŋkɚd/ *n.* [C] a large metal cup, usually with a handle and lid, used for drinking beer

tanked /tæŋkt/ also **ˌtanked ˈup** *adj.* [not before noun] SLANG drunk or affected by drugs

tank·er /ˈtæŋkɚ/ *n.* [C] a vehicle or ship specially built to carry large quantities of gas or liquid, especially oil → see also OIL TANKER

ˈtank top *n.* [C] a shirt with a wide round opening for your neck and no SLEEVES

tanned /tænd/ *adj.* having a darker skin color because you have been in the sun

tan·ner /ˈtænɚ/ *n.* [C] someone whose job is to make animal skin into leather by TANNING

tan·ner·y /ˈtænəri/ *n. plural* **tanneries** [C] a place where animal skin is made into leather by TANNING

tan·nin /ˈtænɪn/ also **tan·nic ac·id** /ˌtænɪk ˈæsɪd/ *n.* [U] an acid used in preparing leather, making ink etc.

ˈtanning bed *n.* [C] a piece of equipment shaped like a box with special lights inside, that you lie in to get a TAN

ˈtanning saˌlon *n.* [C] a place where you pay to use a tanning bed

tan·ta·lize /ˈtæntlˌaɪz/ *v.* [T] to make someone feel a strong desire to have or do something, especially when they cannot have it or do it or when they must wait

[**Origin:** 1500–1600 *Tantalus* king in an ancient Greek story who had to stand up to his chin in water under a fruit tree, but was unable to reach either the water to drink or the fruit to eat]

tan·ta·liz·ing /ˈtæntlˌaɪzɪŋ/ *adj.* making you feel a strong desire to have or do something, especially when you must wait or when you cannot have or do it: *a tantalizing hint as to how the book might end* —**tantalizingly** *adv.*

tan·ta·mount /ˈtæntəˌmaʊnt/ *adj.* **be tantamount to sth** if an action, suggestion, plan etc. is tantamount to something bad, it has the same effect or is almost as bad SYN **equivalent to**: *Journalists argued that the law was tantamount to censorship.*

tan·trum /ˈtæntrəm/ *n.* [C] a sudden short period when someone, especially a child, behaves very angrily and unreasonably: **throw/have a tantrum** *Rachel threw a tantrum when we didn't get her an ice cream cone.* | *a child's* ***temper tantrum***

Tan·za·ni·a /ˌtænzəˈniə/ a country in east Africa between Kenya and Mozambique —**Tanzanian** *n., adj.*

Tao /taʊ, daʊ/ *n.* [U] the natural force that unites all things in the universe, according to Taoism

Tao Chi /ˌdaʊ ˈtʃi, ˌtaʊ-/ (1630–1714) a Chinese PAINTER who was one of the greatest artists of the Qing dynasty

Tao·ism /ˈtaʊɪzəm, ˈdaʊ-/ *n.* [U] a way of thought developed in ancient China, based on the writings of Lao Tzu, emphasizing a natural and simple way of life

tap¹ /tæp/ *n.*

1 WATER/GAS [C] a piece of equipment for controlling the flow of water, gas etc. from a pipe or container → see also FAUCET: *a drink of water from the tap* | **turn on/off the tap** *She turned off the tap.*

2 on tap a) beer that is on tap comes from a BARREL, rather than from a bottle or can **b)** INFORMAL something that is on tap is ready to use when you need it: *Plenty of good food will be on tap at the fair.*

3 HIT [C] an act of hitting something lightly, especially to get someone's attention SYN **pat**: +**at/on** *Rita felt a tap on her shoulder.*

4 SOUND [C] a sound of something hitting something else lightly: *There was a tap at the door.*

5 TELEPHONE [C] an act of secretly listening to someone's telephone, using electronic equipment: *The FBI had put a tap on his phone line.*

6 BARREL [C] a specially shaped object used for letting liquid out of a BARREL, especially beer

7 DANCING [U] also **tap dancing** dancing in which you wear special shoes with pieces of metal on the bottom, which make a loud sound on the floor as you move: *tap shoes* | *ballet, tap, and modern classes*

8 taps [U] a song or tune played on the BUGLE at night in an army camp, and at military funerals

tap² S3 W3 *v.* **tapped, tapping**

1 HIT LIGHTLY [I,T] to hit your fingers, foot, or something you can hold lightly on something, for example to get someone's attention, because you are nervous etc. → see also KNOCK SYN **rap**: +**on** *I tapped on the window.* | **tap sth on/against etc.** *Ted nervously tapped his fingers on the desk.* | *She kept tapping her pencil on the desk.* | *They tapped their glasses together and drank.* | **tap sb on the arm/shoulder etc.** *One of the students tapped Mia on the shoulder.* | *John was* ***tapping his feet to the music.*** ►see THESAURUS box at **hit¹**

2 ENERGY/MONEY [T] also **tap into** to use or take what is needed from something such as an energy supply or amount of money: *The company tapped pension funds to pay its debts.*

3 IDEAS [T] also **tap into** to make as much use as possible of the ideas, experience, knowledge etc. that a group of people has: *He has tapped into people's anxieties about the future.*

4 TELEPHONE [T] to listen secretly to someone's telephone by using a special piece of electronic equipment: *Investigators had tapped the phone line.*

5 CHOOSE SB [T] to choose someone to do something, especially to have an important job: *Williams is expected to be tapped as the new director of operations.*
6 TREE [T] to get liquid from the TRUNK of a tree by making a hole in it
[**Origin:** (1) 1100–1200 Old French *taper* **to hit with the flat part of the hand**]

tap sth ↔ **in** *phr. v.* to hit or kick a ball into a hole or GOAL from a short distance away, in sports such as GOLF or SOCCER

tap sb/sth ↔ **out** *phr. v.* **1** to hit something lightly, especially with your fingers or foot, to make a sound: *He tapped out the rhythm.* **2** to write something with a TYPEWRITER or computer: *She tapped out a memo.* **3** INFORMAL to use all of the money or energy that someone or something has: *Our ski trip to Colorado tapped me out.* → see also TAPPED OUT

tap·as /ˈtæpəs, -pæs/ *n.* [U] small dishes of food eaten as part of the first course of a Spanish meal [**Origin:** 1900–2000 Spanish, plural of *tapa* **cover, lid**]

ˈtap ˌdancing *n.* [U] dancing in which you wear special shoes with pieces of metal on the bottom, which make a loud sound on the floor as you move —**tap-dance** *v.* [I] —**tap dancer** *n.* [C]

tape¹ /teɪp/ Ac S1 W2 *n.*
1 RECORDING a) [U] narrow plastic material covered with a special MAGNETIC substance, on which sounds, pictures, or computer information can be recorded and played: *I don't like the sound of my voice* ***on tape*** (=recorded on tape). **b)** [C] a special plastic box containing a length of tape that sound can be recorded on SYN **cassette**: *He lent me some of his old tapes.* | **+of** *I'd like a tape of the concert.* **c)** [C] a special plastic box containing a length of tape that sound and pictures can be recorded on SYN **videotape**: *Bring me* ***a blank tape*** (=with nothing recorded on it) *and I'll record the movie for you.*
2 STICKY MATERIAL [U] a narrow length of sticky material used to stick things together: *a photo stuck to the wall with tape* → see also DUCT TAPE, MASKING TAPE, SCOTCH TAPE
3 the tape a string stretched out across the finishing line in a race and broken by the winner
4 FOR MEASURING a TAPE MEASURE
5 THIN PIECE OF MATERIAL [C,U] a long thin piece of material used in sewing, tying things together, marking an area etc.
[**Origin:** Old English *tæppe*] → see also RED TAPE

tape² Ac S2 *v.* **1** [I,T] also **tape-record** to record sound or pictures onto a TAPE SYN **record**: *Do you mind if I tape this interview?* **2** [T] to stick something onto something else using TAPE SYN **stick**: **tape sth to sth** *Why is this envelope taped to the refrigerator?* ▶see THESAURUS box at **fasten** **3** [T] also **tape up** to fasten a package, box etc. with TAPE: *This is taped up so well I can't get it open.* **4** [T usually passive] also **tape up** to tie a BANDAGE firmly around an injured part of someone's body: *Wilkins had his knee taped up.*

ˈtape deck *n.* [C] the part of a TAPE RECORDER that winds the tape, and records and plays back sound, used as part of a system

ˈtape drive *n.* [C] a small machine attached to a computer that passes information from a computer to a tape or from a tape to a computer

ˈtape ˌmeasure *n.* [C] a long narrow band of cloth or steel, marked with INCHES, centimeters etc., which is used for measuring things

ˈtape ˌplayer *n.* [C] a piece of electrical equipment that can play back sound on TAPE

ta·per¹ /ˈteɪpɚ/ *v.* [I,T] to become gradually narrower toward one end, or to make something narrower at one end: *The jeans taper toward the ankle.*

taper off *phr. v.* to decrease gradually SYN **diminish**: *The rain tapered off at sunset.* —**tapering** *adj.*: *long tapering fingers* → see also TAPERED

taper² *n.* [C] **1** a very thin CANDLE **2** a piece of string covered in WAX, used for lighting lamps and CANDLES **3** [usually singular] a gradual decrease in the width of a long object

ˈtape-reˌcord *v.* [T] to record sound using a tape recorder

ˈtape reˌcorder *n.* [C] a piece of electrical equipment that can record sound on TAPE and play it back

ˈtape reˌcording *n.* [C] something that has been recorded with a tape recorder: *a tape recording of the phone call*

ta·pered /ˈteɪpɚd/ *adj.* having a shape that gets narrower toward one end: *long tapered fingers*

tap·es·try /ˈtæpɪstri/ *n. plural* **tapestries** [C,U] **1** heavy cloth or a large piece of cloth on which colored threads are woven to produce a picture, pattern etc. **2** something that is made up of many different people and things: *the tapestry of life*

tape·worm /ˈteɪpwɚm/ *n.* [C] BIOLOGY a long flat PARASITE that lives in the BOWELS of humans and other animals

tap·i·o·ca /ˌtæpiˈoʊkə/ *n.* [U] small hard white grains made from the crushed dried roots of CASSAVA, or a DESSERT made of this

ta·pir /ˈteɪpɚ/ *n.* [C] an animal like a pig with thick legs, a short tail, and long nose, that lives in tropical America and Southeast Asia

ˌtapped ˈout *adj.* INFORMAL not having any more of something, especially money: *The city is almost tapped out.*

tap·root /ˈtæprut/ *n.* [C] BIOLOGY the main root of some plants, that grows straight down and produces smaller side roots

ˈtap ˌwater *n.* [U] water that comes out of a FAUCET, rather than a bottle

taq·ue·ri·a /ˌtækəˈriə/ *n.* [C] an informal Mexican restaurant, especially in the southwest U.S.

tar¹ /tɑr/ *n.* [U] **1** a black substance, thick and sticky when hot but hard when cold, used especially for making road surfaces → see also COAL TAR **2** a sticky substance that is formed by burning tobacco, and that gets into the lungs of people who smoke: **high/low/medium tar** *high tar cigarettes*

tar² *v.* **tarred, tarring** [T] **1** to cover a surface with tar **2** to spoil the good opinion that people have about someone: *Kleider has been tarred by recent business scandals.* **3 be/get tarred with the same brush** to be blamed along with someone else for their faults or crimes **4 tar and feather sb a)** to cover someone in tar and feathers, done as a cruel punishment in past times **b)** to criticize or punish someone very severely and publicly

Ta·ra·hu·ma·ra /ˌtærəhuˈmɑrə/ a Native American tribe from northern Mexico

tar·an·tel·la /ˌtærənˈtɛlə/ *n.* [C] a fast Italian dance, or the music for this dance

ta·ran·tu·la /təˈræntʃələ/ *n.* [C] a large poisonous SPIDER from southern Europe and tropical America [**Origin:** 1500–1600 Medieval Latin, Old Italian *tarantola*, from *Taranto* city in southern Italy, where such spiders are found]

Ta·ra·wa /təˈrɑwə, ˈtærəˌwɑ/ the capital city of Kiribati

tar·dy /ˈtɑrdi/ *adj.* FORMAL **1** done or doing something later than it should have been done: *a tardy response to my letter* **2** arriving late, especially for a class at school SYN **late**: *He was tardy three times this semester.* —**tardily** *adv.* —**tardiness** *n.* [U]

tar·get¹ /ˈtɑrgɪt/ Ac W2 *n.* [C]
1 OBJECT OF ATTACK an object, person, or place that is deliberately chosen to be attacked: **+for/of** *Fort Sumter was the target of the first shot fired in the Civil War.* | *The camps were* ***prime targets*** *for enemy attack.* | *As the youngest and smallest, Scott was an* ***easy target****.*
2 AN AIM something that you are trying to achieve, such as a total, an amount, or a time SYN **goal**: *The company will* ***reach*** *its* ***target*** *of 12% growth this year.* | *Our year-end results were right* ***on target*** (=where we

hoped they would be). | **sales/growth etc. target** *Dealers are under pressure to **meet** (=achieve) sales **targets**.*
3 OBJECT OF AN ACTION the person or place that is most directly affected by an action, especially a negative one: **+of/for** *The cable TV company has been a target of criticism.* | *The area is a **prime target*** (=very likely target) *for redevelopment.* | *Voters' worries about jobs make them **easy targets** for this kind of campaign message.*
4 SHOOTING something that you practice shooting at, especially a round board with circles on it: *The area is used by the army for **target practice**.*
5 target group/area/audience etc. a limited group, area etc. that something such as a plan or idea is aimed at: *The target market is 14- to 25-year-old men.* → see also TARGET LANGUAGE
[**Origin:** 1200–1300 Old French *targette*, from *targe* **small shield**]

target² Ac *v.* [T] **1** to make something have an effect on a limited group or area: **target sth at/on sb/sth** *The ad campaign has been targeted at adults who smoke.* **2** to aim something at someone or something: **target sth at/on sb/sth** *The missiles are targeted at several key military sites.* **3** to choose a particular person or place to do something to, especially to attack or criticize them: **target sb/sth for sth** *Guerrilla groups targeted him for assassination.*

target ˌcell *n.* [C] BIOLOGY a living cell that can recognize and take in a particular HORMONE (=a substance produced by the body of an animal, plant etc. that influences its growth and development)

target ˌlanguage *n.* [C usually singular] ENG. LANG. ARTS the language that something such as a document is going to be translated into → see also SOURCE LANGUAGE

target popuˌlation *n.* [C] MATH the whole group of people or things who are being studied in someone's RESEARCH. For example, "men aged between 35 and 45" might be a target population. A representative number of people are chosen from the whole group.

Tar Heel *n.* [C] an informal name for someone who comes from North Carolina

tar·iff /ˈtærɪf/ *n.* [C] ECONOMICS a tax on goods coming into a country or going out of a country: **+on** *high tariffs on imported goods* [**Origin:** 1500–1600 Italian *tariffa*, from Arabic *ta'rif* **list of money to be paid**]

tar·mac /ˈtɑrmæk/ *n.* **1** [U] a mixture of TAR and very small stones, used for making the surface of roads SYN **asphalt** **2 the tarmac** an area covered with tarmac, especially where airplanes take off or land: *Reporters waited **on the tarmac** for the President.* [**Origin:** 1900–2000 *Tarmac*, a trademark, from *tarmacadam* **tarmac** (19–20 centuries) (from John L. *McAdam* (1756–1836), Scottish engineer who invented the process)]

tar·nish¹ /ˈtɑrnɪʃ/ *v.* **1** [T] if an event or fact tarnishes someone's REPUTATION, record, image etc., it makes it worse: *The scandal tarnished Wilson's political image.* **2** [I,T] if metals such as silver, COPPER, or BRASS tarnish, or if something tarnishes them, they become dull and lose their color —**tarnished** *adj.*: *tarnished silverware*

tarnish² *n.* [singular, U] **1** loss of color or brightness on metal **2** the fact of someone's REPUTATION, record, image etc. becoming worse

ta·ro /ˈtɑroʊ/ *n.* [U] a tropical plant grown for its thick root which is boiled and eaten

tar·ot /ˈtæroʊ/ *n.* [singular, U] a set of 78 cards with pictures on them, which some people believe you can use for telling what might happen to someone in the future

tarp /tɑrp/ also **tar·pau·lin** /tɑrˈpɔlɪn/ *n.* [C,U] a large heavy cloth or piece of plastic that water cannot go through, used for protecting things from the rain

tar·pa·per /ˈtɑrˌpeɪpɚ/ *n.* [U] thick paper that has been covered in TAR, used in covering houses or roofs

tar·ra·gon /ˈtærəgɑn, -gən/ *n.* [U] the leaves of a small plant, used in cooking to give food a special taste

tar·ry¹ /ˈtæri/ *v.* **tarries, tarried, tarrying** [I] LITERARY **1** to stay in a place, especially when you should leave SYN **linger** **2** to delay or be slow in going somewhere

tar·ry² /ˈtɑri/ *adj.* covered with TAR (=a thick black liquid)

tar·sals /ˈtɑrsəlz/ *n.* [plural] BIOLOGY any of the bones that form the ANKLE joint → see picture at SKELETON¹

tar·sus /ˈtɑrsəs/ *n. plural* **tarsi** /-saɪ, -si/ [C] BIOLOGY your ANKLE or one of the seven small bones in your ankle —**tarsal** *adj.*

tart¹ /tɑrt/ *adj.* **1** food that is tart has a slightly sour taste: *a tart green apple* **2 tart reply/remark etc.** a reply, remark etc. that is sharp and not nice —**tartly** *adv.*: *"Isn't that interesting," Clarke said tartly.* —**tartness** *n.* [U]

tart² *n.* **1** [C,U] a small PIE, usually containing fruit **2** [C] INFORMAL an insulting word for a woman whose appearance or behavior makes you think that she is too willing to have sex SYN **hussy** **3** [C] OLD-FASHIONED, INFORMAL a PROSTITUTE

tart³ *v.*
tart up *phr. v.* INFORMAL **1 tart yourself up** OFTEN HUMOROUS if a woman tarts herself up, she tries to make herself look attractive, by putting on jewelry, MAKEUP etc. **2 tart sth ↔ up** to try to make something more attractive by decorating it, often in a way that other people think looks cheap or ugly

tar·tan /ˈtɑrt̚n/ *n.* [C,U] a traditional Scottish pattern of colored squares and crossed lines, or cloth with this pattern, especially wool cloth —**tartan** *adj.*

Tar·tar /ˈtɑrt̬ɚ/ *n.* [C] **1** a member of the groups of people from Central Asia that attacked Western Asia and Eastern Europe in the Middle Ages **2** a TATAR —**Tartar** *adj.*

tar·tar /ˈtɑrt̬ɚ/ *n.* **1** [U] BIOLOGY a hard yellowish substance that forms on your teeth and can damage them **2** [U] TECHNICAL a reddish-brown substance that forms on the inside of wine BARRELS → see also CREAM OF TARTAR

ˌtartar ˈsauce *n.* [U] a cold white SAUCE often eaten with fish, made from eggs, oil, PICKLES, CAPERS etc.

Tash·kent /tæʃˈkɛnt, tɑʃ-/ the capital city of Uzbekistan

task /tæsk/ Ac W2 *n.* [C] **1** a piece of work that must be done, especially one that is difficult or that must be done regularly: *Patients need help with tasks such as dressing and eating.* | **difficult/daunting task** *We now face the difficult task of getting the bill through Congress.* | **simple/easy task** *a simple task such as making breakfast* | *Mothers often have the **thankless task** of organizing family, house, and work.* | **task of doing sth** *After the floods, we were faced with the task of repairing the damage.* | *New workers will be shown how to **perform** routine **tasks** first.* | **main/primary task** *Our main task is to improve the economy.* **2 take someone to task** to tell someone that you strongly disapprove of something they have done [**Origin:** 1200–1300 Old North French *tasque*, from Medieval Latin *tasca* **tax or service to be done for a ruler**]

ˈtask force *n.* [C] **1** a group formed for a short time to deal with a particular problem: *a government task force on urban education* **2** a military force sent to a place for a special purpose

task·mas·ter /ˈtæskˌmæstɚ/ *n.* someone who makes people work very hard: **a hard/stern/tough taskmaster** *Our high school coach was a tough taskmaster.*

Tas·ma·ni·a /tæzˈmeɪniə/ a large island near the southeast coast of Australia, which is one of the states of Australia —**Tasmanian** *n., adj.*

tas·sel /ˈtæsəl/ *n.* [C] a large number of threads tied together into a round ball at one end and hung as a decoration on clothes, curtains etc. —**tasseled** *adj.*

taste¹ /teɪst/ S2 W3 *n.*
1 FOOD/MOUTH a) [singular, U] the feeling that is produced by a particular food or drink when you put it in your mouth SYN **flavor**: **sweet/salty/sour etc. taste** *The medicine **has a** slightly bitter **taste**.* | **+of** *I didn't*

like the taste of the coffee. **b)** [C usually singular] a small amount of food or drink that you put in your mouth to try it: *Can I **have a taste** of your pie?* **c)** [U] the sense by which you know one food from another: *Smoking can damage your sense of taste.*

THESAURUS

delicious very good
disgusting/horrible/awful very bad
sweet like sugar
tasty having a pleasant taste, but not sweet
sour like a lemon
salty containing a lot of salt
bitter having a sharp strong taste like black coffee without sugar
hot/spicy containing spices that give you the feeling that your mouth is burning
sharp having a strong slightly sour taste
mild not having a strong or hot taste
bland not having an interesting taste

2 JUDGMENT [U] someone's judgment about what is good or appropriate when they choose clothes, music, art etc.: *No one with any taste would buy a painting like that.* | **good/bad taste (in sth)** *Kate has such good taste.*

3 STH YOU LIKE [C,U] the type of thing that you tend to like or like to do: *The resort caters to people with expensive tastes.* | **+for** *A rafting trip will **satisfy your taste** for adventure.* | **+in** *We have similar tastes in music.* | *She had the whole house redecorated **to her taste**.* | *The room was **too** dark **for my taste**.* | *Olives are an **acquired taste*** (=something that you start to like only when you have tried it several times).

4 EXPERIENCE [C usually singular] a small example or short experience of something that shows you what it is like: **+of** *The program **gives** city kids **a taste** of the wilderness.* | *Going away to college was his **first taste** of freedom.*

5 be (in) good/bad/poor taste to be appropriate or inappropriate for a particular occasion: *I thought Craig's joke was in pretty poor taste.*

6 FEELING [singular] the feeling you have after an experience, especially a bad experience: *Being laid off with so little notice **left a bad taste in** my **mouth**.* | **+of** *the sweet taste of victory*

7 to taste if you add salt, SPICES etc. to taste, you add as much as you think makes the food taste right. The phrase is used in instructions for cooking. → see also **there's no accounting for taste** at ACCOUNT FOR (5), **an acquired taste** at ACQUIRE (4)

taste² S1 W3 *v.* **1** [linking verb] to have a particular type of taste: **taste good/awful etc.** *This cake tastes delicious.* | **taste sweet/bitter/salty etc.** *I don't like cranberries – they taste kind of sour.* | **taste like sth** *I've never had rabbit, but they say it tastes like chicken.* | *The coffee **tasted like dishwater*** (=used to say that coffee or tea is too weak). | **sweet-tasting/strong-tasting etc.** (=having a sweet, strong etc. taste) *a bitter-tasting medicine* **2** [T] to eat or drink a small amount of something to see what it is like: *Taste your eggs before you put salt on them.* | *Did you taste the salsa?*

THESAURUS

try to eat or drink something to see if you like it: *Try the chicken burritos there – they're really good.*
sample to eat just a little bit of a food or drink, to see what it is like: *You'll have a chance to sample various types of wine.*

3 [T not in progressive] to experience the taste of food or drink: *I can't taste anything with this cold.* | ***Can you taste the difference?*** **4 taste fame/freedom etc.** to have a short experience of something that you want more of: *There was a lot of hard work before we first tasted success.* [**Origin:** 1200–1300 Old French *taster* **to touch, test, taste**, from Vulgar Latin *taxitare*]

ˈtaste bud *n.* [C usually plural] BIOLOGY one of the small parts on the surface of your tongue with which you can taste things

taste·ful /ˈteɪstfəl/ *adj.* made, decorated, or chosen using good judgment about what is appropriate or good: *the lawyer's tasteful dark suit* —**tastefully** *adv.*: *a tastefully furnished apartment* —**tastefulness** *n.* [U] → see also TASTY

taste·less /ˈteɪstlɪs/ *adj.* **1** offensive or not appropriate for a particular situation: *a tasteless TV talk show* | *tasteless jokes* **2** food or drink that is tasteless is not good, because it has no particular taste: *The salad was tasteless.* **3** made, decorated, or chosen with bad judgment about what is good or appropriate: *gaudy and tasteless designs* —**tastelessly** *adv.* —**tastelessness** *n.* [U]

tast·er /ˈteɪstɚ/ *n.* [C] someone whose job is to test the quality of foods, wines etc. by tasting them: *a wine taster*

tast·ing /ˈteɪstɪŋ/ *n.* [C,U] an event that is organized so that you can try different foods or drinks to see if you like them, or the activity of doing this: *a wine and cheese tasting*

tast·y /ˈteɪsti/ *adj. comparative* **tastier**, *superlative* **tastiest** **1** tasty food has a good taste → see also TASTEFUL: *a tasty soup* ►see THESAURUS box at **taste¹** **2** INFORMAL tasty news, GOSSIP etc. is especially interesting and is often related to sex or surprising behavior —**tastiness** *n.* [U]

tat /tæt/ *n.* [C] INFORMAL a short form of TATTOO → see also TIT FOR TAT

ta·ta·mi /təˈtɑmi, tə-/ *n.* [U] woven pieces of straw used as a covering for a floor in a house, especially in Japan: *tatami mats*

Ta·tar /ˈtɑt̬ɚ/ *n.* **1** [C] a member of a group of people who live in parts of Russia, Ukraine, and Central Asia **2** [U] one of the languages of these people —**Tatar** *adj.*

ta·ter /ˈteɪt̬ɚ/ *n.* [C] SPOKEN a potato

Ta·ter Tots, tater tots /ˈteɪt̬ɚ tɑts/ *n.* [plural] TRADEMARK potatoes that are cut into small pieces, made into balls, frozen, and then FRIED or baked

tat·tered /ˈtæt̬ɚd/ *adj.* clothes, books etc. that are tattered are old and torn: *a tattered blue sofa*

tat·ters /ˈtæt̬ɚz/ *n.* [plural] **1 in tatters a)** ruined or badly damaged: *After the war, the country's economy was in tatters.* **b)** clothes that are in tatters are old and torn **2** clothing or pieces of cloth that are old and torn

tat·ting /ˈtæt̬ɪŋ/ *n.* [U] a type of LACE that you make by hand, or the process of making it

tat·tle /ˈtæt̬l/ *v.* [I] **1** if a child tattles, they tell a parent or teacher that another child has done something bad SYN **tell**: **+on** *Robert is always tattling on me for things I didn't do.* **2** OLD-FASHIONED to talk about small unimportant things, or about other people's private affairs SYN **gossip** —**tattling** *n.* [U] —**tattler** *n.* [C]

tat·tle·tale /ˈtæt̬lˌteɪl/ *n.* [C] a word meaning someone who tattles, used by or to children

tat·too¹ /tæˈtu/ *n. plural* **tattoos** **1** [C] a picture or message that is permanently marked on your skin with a needle and ink: *a tattoo of a lion* **2** [singular] a rapid continuous beating of drums, especially played as a military signal, or a sound like this **3** [C] a signal played on a drum or BUGLE (=type of horn) to tell soldiers to go to bed at night [**Origin:** (1) 1700–1800 Tahitian *tatau*]

tattoo² *v.* [T] **1** to make a permanent picture or message on someone's skin with a needle and ink **2** to mark someone in this way —**tattooed** *adj.*: *heavily tattooed arms*

tatˈtoo ˌartist also **tat·too·ist** /tæˈtuɪst/ *n.* [C] someone whose job is tattooing

tatˈtoo ˌparlor *n.* [C] a place where you go to get a tattoo

tat·ty /ˈtæt̬i/ *adj.* INFORMAL looking old and dirty, or in a bad condition SYN **shabby**

taught /tɔt/ *v.* the past tense and past participle of TEACH

taunt¹ /tɔnt, tɑnt/ *v.* [T] to try to make someone angry or upset by saying things that are not nice: *The older boys taunted Chris and called him a girl.* —**taunting** *adj.* —**tauntingly** *adv.*

taunt² *n.* [C often plural] a remark or joke intended to make someone angry or upset

taupe /toʊp/ *n.* [U] a brownish gray color —**taupe** *adj.*

Tau·rus /ˈtɔrəs/ *n.* **1** [U] the second sign of the ZODIAC, represented by a BULL, and believed to affect the character and life of people born between April 20 and May 20 **2** [C] someone who was born between April 20 and May 20: *Lisa's a Taurus.*

taut /tɔt/ *adj.* **1** stretched tight: *The rope was taut.* **2** showing signs of worry or anxiety: *Catherine looked upset, her face taut.* **3** having firm muscles: *taut stomach muscles* **4** not using more words or time than necessary to tell a story: *a taut suspenseful thriller*

tau·tol·o·gy /tɔˈtɑlədʒi/ *n. plural* **tautologies** [C,U] TECHNICAL a statement in which you say the same thing twice using different words in a way that is not necessary, for example "He sat alone by himself." —**tautological** /ˌtɔt̬əˈlɑdʒɪkəl/ *adj.* —**tautologically** /-kli/ *adv.* → see also REDUNDANT

tav·ern /ˈtævən/ *n.* [C] a place where alcoholic drinks can be bought and drunk SYN **bar** [**Origin:** 1200–1300 Old French *taverne*, from Latin *taberna* **small simple building, shop**]

taw·dry /ˈtɔdri/ *adj.* **1** showing low moral standards: *a tawdry scandal* **2** cheaply and badly made: *tawdry jewelry* [**Origin:** 1600–1700 *tawdry lace* **necklace** (16–18 centuries), from *St. Audrey's lace*, from *St. Audrey* 7th-century queen of Northumbria, England; because it was originally sold at fairs in honor of St. Audrey] —**tawdriness** *n.* [U]

taw·ny /ˈtɔni/ *adj.* brownish yellow in color: *a lion's tawny fur*

tax¹ /tæks/ S1 W1 *n.* **1** [C,U] an amount of money that you must pay to the government according to your income, property, goods etc., and that is used to pay for public services: *The city will have to* ***raise taxes*** *to pay for the roads.* | +**on** *a tax on gasoline* | *All workers* ***pay taxes.*** | ***The tax burden*** (=amount of taxes all people must pay) *is not shared equally in this state.* | **before-tax/after-tax** *The company reported an after-tax profit of $1.2 million.* **2** [singular] FORMAL something that uses a lot of your strength, PATIENCE etc. → see also CAPITAL GAINS TAX, INCOME TAX, PROPERTY TAX, SALES TAX

tax² *v.* [T] **1** to charge a tax on a product, income, property etc., or make someone pay a tax: **tax sth at 10%/a high rate etc.** *Company profits are currently taxed at 34%.* | *The rich are taxed at a higher rate than the poor.* | **tax sb on sth** *You are not taxed on pension money you have saved in the plan until you receive it.* | *Gasoline is* ***heavily taxed*** *in Europe.* **2** to make someone have to work hard or make a strong effort: **tax sb's strength/patience/mind etc.** *The kids are taxing my patience today.* [**Origin:** 1200–1300 Old French *taxer* **to make a judgment about, tax**, from Latin *taxare* **to feel, make a judgment about, blame**] —**taxable** *adj.*: *taxable income* → see also TAXING

taxable ˈincome *n.* [C,U] ECONOMICS the income on which a person or company must pay tax. It is their total income less any money they are allowed to earn or take away before paying tax: *Taxpayers can reduce their taxable income by as much as $2,000 a year if they manage their investments properly.*

tax asˌsessor *n.* [C] ECONOMICS someone whose job is to officially decide the value of someone's house or property, in order to calculate how much tax they must pay

tax·a·tion /tækˈseɪʃən/ *n.* [U] ECONOMICS the system or process of charging taxes, or the money paid for taxes: *high levels of taxation* | *The colonists objected to* ***taxation without representation*** (=being taxed without having anyone speaking for you in government).

tax aˌvoidance *n.* [U] ECONOMICS the practice of finding legal ways to pay less tax → see also TAX EVASION

tax base *n.* [C usually singular] ECONOMICS **1** all the people and companies who pay tax, and the total amount they pay **2** income, goods, and property on which people or companies must pay tax

ˈtax ˌbracket *n.* [C] ECONOMICS a particular range of income levels on which the same rate of tax is paid

ˈtax break *n.* [C] ECONOMICS a special reduction in taxes that the government allows for a particular purpose or group of people: *a tax break for small business owners*

ˈtax colˌlector *n.* [C] someone who works for the government and makes sure that people pay their taxes

ˈtax cut *n.* [C] an official decision by the government to charge people less tax on what they earn

ˌtax-deˈductible, tax deductible *adj.* ECONOMICS tax-deductible costs can be SUBTRACTED from your total income before you calculate how much tax you owe: *Contributions to charities are tax deductible.*

ˌtax-deˈferred *adj.* ECONOMICS not taxed until a later time: *tax-deferred savings*

ˈtax eˌvasion *n.* [U] ECONOMICS the crime of paying too little tax, or paying no tax at all

ˌtax-exˈempt *adj.* not taxed, or not having to pay tax: *tax-exempt savings* | *a tax-exempt charity*

ˈtax ˌexile *n.* [C] ECONOMICS someone who moves to another country in order to avoid paying high taxes in their own country

ˌtax-ˈfree *adj.* not taxed: *tax-free winnings*

ˈtax ˌhaven *n.* [C] ECONOMICS a place where people go to live in order to avoid paying high taxes in their own countries

tax·i¹ /ˈtæksi/ *n. plural* **taxis** [C] a car with a driver that you pay to take you somewhere SYN **cab**: ***I took a taxi*** *to the airport.* | *He left the restaurant and* ***hailed a taxi*** (=waved or shouted at a taxi to make it stop). [**Origin:** 1900–2000 *taxicab*]

taxi² *v.* **taxis** or **taxies**, **taxied**, **taxiing** [I] if an airplane taxis, it moves slowly along the ground before taking off or after landing

tax·i·cab /ˈtæksiˌkæb/ *n.* [C] a taxi

tax·i·der·mist /ˈtæksəˌdəmɪst/ *n.* [C] someone whose job is taxidermy

tax·i·der·my /ˈtæksəˌdəmi/ *n.* [U] the art of specially preparing the skins of dead animals, birds, or fish, and then filling them with a special material so that they look as though they are alive

ˈtax inˌcentive *n.* [C] ECONOMICS a reduction in the amount of tax people or companies are charged, used as a way of encouraging people to do something, such as work harder, start a new business etc.: *The government announced a number of measures, including tax incentives to encourage the redevelopment of brownfield sites* (=areas where factories used to be).

tax·ing /ˈtæksɪŋ/ *adj.* needing a lot of effort SYN **demanding**: *a taxing job*

ˈtaxi stand *n.* [C] a place where taxis wait for customers

tax·i·way /ˈtæksiˌweɪ/ *n.* [C] the hard surface like a road that an airplane drives on to get from the airport to the RUNWAY

tax·man /ˈtæksmæn/ *n. plural* **taxmen** /-mɛn/ [C] **1** a TAX COLLECTOR **2 the taxman** ECONOMICS the government department that collects taxes

tax·on /ˈtæksɑn/ *n.* [C] BIOLOGY any of the groups into which plants or animals are placed in a system that organizes plants and animals by their natural relationship with each other → see also TAXONOMY

tax·on·o·my /tækˈsɑnəmi/ *n. plural* **taxonomies** [C,U] BIOLOGY the science of organizing things such as plants or animals into a system of different groups according to the features that they share, and of giving them names —**taxonomic** /ˌtæksəˈnɑmɪk◂/ *adj.*

tax·pay·er /ˈtæksˌpeɪə/ *n.* [C] ECONOMICS a person or organization that pays tax: *How much will this cost* ***the taxpayers?*** | *The stadium is being built with* ***taxpayer money.***

T

ˈtax reˌlief *n.* [U] ECONOMICS a reduction in the amount of tax you have to pay, especially as a result of a change in a law

ˈtax reˌturn *n.* [C] ECONOMICS the form on which you calculate your taxes and which you must send to the government

ˈtax ˌshelter *n.* [C] ECONOMICS a plan or method that allows you to legally avoid paying taxes

ˈtax year *n.* [C] ECONOMICS the period of 12 months in which your income is calculated for paying taxes

Tay·lor /ˈteɪlɚ/, **Zach·a·ry** /ˈzækəri/ (1784–1850) the 12th President of the U.S.

TB *n.* **1** [U] **tuberculosis** MEDICINE a serious infectious disease that affects your lungs and other parts of your body **2** [C] the written abbreviation of TAILBACK

TBA **to be announced** used to say that a piece of information will be decided or given at a later time: *game time TBA*

T-ball /ˈti bɔl/ *n.* [U] TRADEMARK an easy form of baseball for young children in which you hit the ball off a special stick

Tbi·li·si /təbəˈlisi/ the capital and largest city of Georgia

T-bill /ˈti bɪl/ *n.* [C] ECONOMICS a TREASURY BILL

T-bond /ˈti bɑnd/ *n.* [C] ECONOMICS a TREASURY BOND

T-bone steak /ˌti boʊn ˈsteɪk/ also **ˈT-bone** *n.* [C] a thinly cut piece of BEEF that has a T-shaped bone in it

T

tbs., tbsp. *n.* [C] the written abbreviation of TABLESPOON: *1 tbs. sugar*

T cell, T-cell /ˈti sɛl/ *n.* [C] BIOLOGY a type of WHITE BLOOD CELL that helps the body fight disease

Tchai·kov·sky /tʃaɪˈkɔfski/, **Pe·ter Il·yich** /ˈpitɚ ˈɪlɪtʃ/ (1840–1893) a Russian musician who wrote CLASSICAL music

TDD *n.* [C,U] **telecommunications device for the deaf** a piece of equipment that allows people who cannot hear to send and receive messages using a telephone, by TYPING them or reading them on a small screen

TE *n.* [C] the written abbreviation of TIGHT END

tea /ti/ S1 W3 *n.* **1 a)** [U] a hot brown drink made by pouring boiling water onto the dried leaves from a particular bush: *How about a cup of tea?* → see also ICED TEA **b)** [C,U] the dried leaves of a particular Asian bush, used for making tea, or a particular type of these leaves **c)** [U] bushes whose leaves are used to make tea **2 mint/chamomile/herbal etc. tea** a hot drink made by pouring boiling water onto the leaves or flowers of a particular plant, sometimes used as a medicine **3** [C] an informal party, usually in the afternoon, and usually with things such as SANDWICHES and cake to eat: *an afternoon tea* **4 (not) for all the tea in China** OLD-FASHIONED, INFORMAL used to say that you would refuse to do something, whatever happened: *I wouldn't marry her for all the tea in China.* [**Origin:** 1600–1700 Chinese *te*] → see also **not be your cup of tea** at CUP[1] (11)

tea·bag /ˈtibæg/ *n.* [C] a small paper bag with tea leaves inside, used for making tea

teach /titʃ/ S1 W1 *v. past tense and past participle* **taught** /tɔt/

1 SCHOOL/COLLEGE ETC. [I,T] to give lessons at a school, college, or university, or to help someone learn about something by giving them information SYN **instruct**: *Russell has been teaching in Japan for almost ten years.* | *I teach 18- to 21-year-olds.* | **teach sth to sb** *Volunteers were sent to teach reading to inner-city children.* | **teach sb about sth** *We need to do more to teach teenagers about sexual health.* | **teach English/mathematics/history etc.** *Do you know who's teaching biology this semester?* | **teach school/college etc.** *She teaches third grade in Little Rock.*

THESAURUS

instruct FORMAL to teach someone, especially in a practical way and about a practical skill: *A nurse instructs the patients in how to perform the tests at home.*
tutor to teach one student or a small group, especially when that student or group needs help in a particular subject: *I found work tutoring Mexican students in English.*
train to teach a person or group of people in the particular skills or knowledge they need to do a job, or to teach an animal to do something: *It will take at least a month to train the new assistant.* | *The dogs are trained to sniff suitcases for drugs.*
educate to teach people over a long period of time, in many different types of knowledge: *It is difficult to educate children in buildings that are not in good condition.* | *The agency tries to educate people about the dangers of drugs.*

2 SHOW SB HOW [T] to show someone how to do something: *It's not hard. I'll teach you.* | **teach sb (how) to do sth** *My mother taught me how to drive.* | *Eli's teaching me to play chess.* | **teach sb sth** *Can you teach me one of your card tricks?*
3 BEHAVIOR/IDEAS [T] to show or tell someone how they should behave or what they should think: **teach sb to do sth** *Parents need to teach their children to treat other people with respect.* | **teach sb sth** *No one ever taught him the difference between right and wrong.* | **teach sb that** *Family histories can teach children that families stick together through tough times.*
4 EXPERIENCE SHOWS STH [T] if an experience or situation teaches you something, it helps you to understand something about life: **teach sb sth** *What has this taught you?* | **teach sb to do sth** *Playing sports has taught me never to give up.* | **teach sb about sth** *The whole episode taught me a lot about my husband.* | **teach sb that** *Experience has taught me that witnesses' memories fade quickly.*
5 that'll teach you (to do sth) SPOKEN used when something bad has just happened to someone, especially because they ignored your warning: *That'll teach you to park in a loading zone.*
6 teach sb a lesson INFORMAL **a)** to make someone want to avoid doing something bad or unwise again: *I hope your night in the cells has taught you a lesson.* **b)** to deliberately hit someone many times, because of something they have done that you do not like SYN **beat sb up**: *What happened to you? Somebody try to teach you a lesson?*
7 you can't teach an old dog new tricks used to say that older people often do not want to change or cannot change the way they do things
[**Origin:** Old English *tæcan* **to show, teach**]

Teach /titʃ/, **Ed·ward** /ˈɛdwɚd/ also **Blackbeard** (died 1718) a British PIRATE

teach·er /ˈtitʃɚ/ S1 W1 *n.* [C] someone whose job is to teach, especially in a school: *Mrs. Sherwood was my first-grade teacher.* | **history/English/chemistry etc. teacher** *He became a high school music teacher.*

THESAURUS

A **teacher** is usually someone who works in a school: *Marie is a high school teacher.*
A **teacher** can also be someone who helps a person learn something: *a guitar teacher*
A **professor**, **lecturer**, or an **instructor** teaches in a university or college. A **professor** has a higher rank than a **lecturer** or an **instructor**.
An **instructor** is also someone who teaches a sport or a practical skill such as swimming or driving: *a driving instructor* | *a scuba-diving instructor*
A **tutor** gives private lessons to one student or a small group of students, usually to help them when they are studying a difficult subject: *a math tutor*
A **coach** trains a person or team in a sport: *a football coach*
→ SCHOOL, UNIVERSITY

ˌteacher's ˈpet *n.* [C] INFORMAL a child who other children think is the teacher's favorite student, so that they dislike him or her

ˈteach-in *n.* [C] a situation in which people protest a political or social problem by meeting to give information about it and discuss it: *Students held a teach-in to protest the war.*

teach·ing /ˈtitʃɪŋ/ *n.* [U] **1** the work or profession of a teacher: *Ann's planning to go into teaching* (=become a teacher). | *I did my* ***student teaching*** (=period of teaching done while training to be a teacher) *in an inner-city school.* **2** also **teachings** [plural] the moral, religious, or political ideas spread by a particular person or group: **+of** *the teachings of Confucius* | **Christian/biblical/Islamic/religious etc. teachings** *church teachings on sexual issues*

teaching asˌsistant *n.* [C] a GRADUATE student at a university who teaches classes

teaching ˌhospital *n.* [C] a hospital where medical students receive practical training from experienced doctors

tea·cup /ˈtikʌp/ *n.* [C] a cup that you serve tea in

tea ˌgarden *n.* [C] a public garden where people can buy and drink tea

tea·house /ˈtihaʊs/ *n.* [C] a special building in China or Japan where tea is served, often as part of a ceremony

teak /tik/ *n.* **1** [U] a very hard yellowish-brown wood that is used for making ships and good-quality furniture **2** [C] the South Asian tree that this wood comes from

tea ˌkettle, **teakettle** *n.* [C] a metal container with a handle and a SPOUT that is used for boiling water

teal /til/ *n.* **1** [U] a greenish blue color **2** [C] BIOLOGY a small wild duck —**teal** *adj.*

tea leaves *n.* **1** [plural] the small finely cut pieces of leaves used for making tea **2 read the tea leaves** to look at tea leaves in the bottom of a cup to try to find out what will happen in the future

team¹ /tim/ Ac S1 W1 *n.* [C] **1** a group of people who play a game or sport together against another group: **baseball/football/basketball etc. team** *the school volleyball team* | *It's great to* ***play*** *on a winning* ***team.*** | *How long have you been* ***on the team?*** | *Scott didn't* ***make the*** *soccer* ***team*** (=was not chosen for the team) *this year.* **2** a group of people who have been chosen to work together to do a particular job: **+of** *a team of lawyers* | *the sales team* | *They* ***work*** *effectively* ***as a team.*** ▸see THESAURUS box at **group¹** **3** two or more animals that are used to pull a vehicle [**Origin:** Old English **young of an animal, group of animals pulling something**]

team² Ac *v.* [I,T] also **team up** to join with someone so you can work together on something, or to make someone work with someone else on something: **+with** *He teamed with Annie Lennox for a top 10 hit.* | **+team up to do sth** *Archeologists and volunteers are teaming up to uncover the mysteries of the site.*

team·mate /ˈtim-meɪt/ *n.* [C] someone who plays on the same team as you

team ˌplayer *n.* [C] INFORMAL someone who works well with other people in order to achieve something, especially in business

team ˈspirit *n.* [U] willingness to work with other people as part of a team

team·ster /ˈtimstɚ/ *n.* [C] someone who controlled pairs or groups of animals that pulled vehicles in past times

Team·sters, the /ˈtimstɚz/ a large U.S. UNION, mainly for people who drive trucks

team·work /ˈtimwɚk/ *n.* [U] the actions of a group of people that help them to work together effectively

tea ˌparty *n.* [C] **1** a small party in the afternoon at which tea, cake etc. is served **2 be no tea party** INFORMAL to be very difficult or not nice to do

tea·pot /ˈtipɑt/ *n.* [C] a container for making and serving tea, which has a handle and a SPOUT → see also **a tempest in a teapot** at TEMPEST (2)

tear¹ /tɪr/ W3 *n.* [C usually plural] BIOLOGY a drop of salty liquid that comes out of your eye when you are crying: *a tear on your face* | *tear-stained cheeks* | *She came home* ***in tears*** (=crying). | *Danny* ***burst into tears*** (=suddenly started crying) *and ran out.* | *In court Burg* ***broke down in tears*** (=started crying). | ***Fighting back tears*** (=trying very hard not to cry), *she kissed her son goodbye.* | *I could tell you stories that would* ***bring tears to your eyes*** (=make you almost cry). | **tears stream/run/roll down sb's face/cheeks** *She just sat there, the tears rolling down her cheeks.* | *His mother* ***wiped away his tears.*** | *He's a tough director who can* ***reduce*** *actors* ***to tears*** (=make someone cry). | *We're not* ***shedding any tears*** (=crying because we are sad) *over his resignation.* | **tears of joy/anger/sadness etc.** *Tears of gratitude shone in his eyes.* | *I could see that Sam was* ***close to tears*** (=almost crying). → see also **crocodile tears** at CROCODILE (3)

tear² /tɛr/ S2 W3 *v. past tense* **tore** /tɔr/, *past participle* **torn** /tɔrn/

1 PAPER/CLOTH a) [T] to damage something such as paper or cloth by pulling it too hard or letting it touch something sharp SYN **rip**: *How did you tear your pocket?* | **tear sth out of sth** *Don't tear pages out of the book.* | **tear off sth** *She tore off a sheet of paper.* | *I* ***tore a hole*** *in my new blouse.* | *Celia grabbed the envelope and* ***tore it open.*** **b)** [I] if paper or cloth tears, a hole appears in it, or it splits, because it has been pulled too hard or has touched something sharp: *The paper is old and tears easily.* ▸see THESAURUS box at **break¹**

2 REMOVE STH [T always + adv./prep.] to pull something violently from a person or place: **tear sth from/away/off etc.** *He tore the letter from my hand.* | *The hurricane tore the roofs off houses.*

3 MOVE QUICKLY [I always + adv./prep.] to move somewhere very quickly, especially in a dangerous or careless way: **+away/up/past etc.** *Would you kids stop tearing around the house?* | *The cat tore through the hallway.* ▸see THESAURUS box at **run¹**

4 tear sb/sth to shreds/pieces a) to tear something into very small pieces: *She tore the letter to pieces.* **b)** to criticize someone or something very severely: *He tore Russell's argument to shreds.*

5 MUSCLE [T] to damage a muscle or LIGAMENT (=a strong band connected to your muscles)

6 tear sb limb from limb to attack someone in a very violent way: *Garcia's opponents are angry enough to tear him limb from limb.*

[**Origin:** Old English *teran*] → see also **tear/pull your hair out** at HAIR (5), **tear/rip sb's heart out** at HEART (16), TORN²

tear sb/sth ↔ **apart** *phr. v.* **1** to break something into many small pieces, especially in a violent way: *A tornado tore apart airplanes at the small airport.* **2** to make the members of an organization or group start having severe disagreements with each other: *Disagreement over the minister is tearing our church apart.* **3** to make someone feel extremely unhappy or upset: *Seeing him in that hospital bed tore me apart.* **4** to make a close relationship between two or more people end in a sad way, especially by making one person move away: *War tore the family apart.* **5** to criticize someone very strongly: *My dad didn't like him and just tore him apart.*

tear at sb/sth *phr. v.* to pull violently at someone or something: *The children were screaming and tearing at each other's hair.*

tear sb **away** *phr. v.* to make yourself or someone else leave a place or stop doing something when you or they do not really want to: **+from** *We're going to a movie if she ever* ***tears herself away*** *from that computer.*

tear sth ↔ **down** *phr. v.* to knock down a building or structure: *The fence was later torn down.*

tear into sb/sth *phr. v.* **1** to attack someone, especially by hitting them very hard: *The two boys tore into each other.* **2** to start doing something with a lot of energy: *"This looks great!" Jen said, tearing into her dinner.* **3** to criticize someone very strongly, especially unfairly: *Then Bob started tearing into her for spending money.*

tear sth ↔ **off** *phr. v.* to remove your clothes as

quickly as you can: *Kelly tore off his shirt and jumped in the pool.*

tear sb/sth ↔ **up** *phr. v.* **1** to destroy a piece of paper or cloth by tearing it into small pieces SYN **rip up**: *Tear up the check before you throw it away.* **2** to remove or damage something such as a floor, road etc.: *The streets were torn up for repairs.* **3** to make someone feel extremely unhappy or upset: *When I hear people criticize the food we serve, it just tears me up.* **4** to damage or ruin a place, especially by behaving violently: *Kari tore up the apartment looking for her keys.* **5 tear up an agreement/contract etc.** to say that you no longer accept an agreement or contract

tear³ /tɛr/ *n.* [C] a hole in a piece of cloth, paper etc. where it has been torn → see also **wear and tear** at WEAR² (1)

tear⁴ /tɪr/ *v.* [I] if your eyes tear, they produce tears because it is cold, you are sick etc.

tear up *phr. v.* to almost start crying: *Ed teared up when he talked about his father.*

tear·drop /ˈtɪrdrɑp/ *n.* [C] **1** BIOLOGY a single drop of salty liquid that comes from your eye when you cry **2** a shape that is pointed at one end and wide and round at the other end

tear·ful /ˈtɪrfəl/ *adj.* crying a little, or almost crying: *a tearful goodbye* —**tearfully** *adv.*

tear gas /ˈtɪr gæs/ *n.* [U] a gas that stings your eyes, used by the police to control crowds —**teargas** *v.* [T]

tear·jerk·er /ˈtɪrˌdʒɚkɚ/ *n.* [C] INFORMAL a movie, book, story etc. that is very sad and makes you cry

tea·room /ˈtirum/ *n.* [C] a restaurant where tea and small meals are served

tease¹ /tiz/ S2 *v.* **1** [I,T] to make jokes and laugh at someone in order to have fun by embarrassing them, either in a friendly way or in a way that is not nice SYN **rib** SYN **needle** SYN **josh**: **only/just teasing** *I'm sorry; I was just teasing.* | *The other girls teased me a lot.* | **tease sb about sth** *His friends were teasing him about his girlfriend.* **2** [T] to deliberately annoy an animal: *He'll bite you if you don't stop teasing him.* **3** [I,T] to deliberately make someone sexually excited without intending to have sex with them **4** [T] to comb your hair in the opposite direction to that in which it grows, so that it looks thicker [**Origin:** Old English *tæsan*]

tease sth ↔ **out** *phr. v.* **1** to succeed in finding information, the meaning of something etc., even though this is difficult and may take a long time: *Students are taught to tease out the meaning from difficult texts.* **2** to gently loosen or straighten hairs or threads that are stuck together, so they become loose or straight again: *She teased out the knots in her hair.* **3 tease sth out of sb** to persuade someone to tell you something that they do not want to tell you

tease² *n.* [C] INFORMAL **1** someone who enjoys embarrassing or annoying people slightly by making jokes about them, often in a friendly way **2** someone who deliberately makes you sexually excited, but has no intention of having sex with you **3** something that is intended to make people interested in an event, movie, or program that is going to happen later or that is going to become available later: *The tease aims to keep you watching, prevent you from changing the channel.* → see also STRIPTEASE

teas·er /ˈtizɚ/ *n.* [C] INFORMAL an advertisement, event, piece of writing etc. that makes you interested in something that is going to happen or be shown later: *a teaser for a soap opera* → see also BRAIN TEASER

ˈtea ˌservice *n.* [C] a matching set of cups, plates, pot etc., used for serving tea

tea·spoon /ˈtispun/ W3 *n.* [C] **1** a small spoon that you use for eating and for mixing sugar into tea, coffee etc. **2 a)** a special spoon used for measuring small amounts in cooking, equal to ⅓ of a TABLESPOON or 5 ml **b)** also **tea·spoon·ful** /ˈtispunfʊl/ the amount a teaspoon can hold

teat /tɪt, tit/ *n.* [C] one of the small parts on a female animal's body that her babies suck milk from

tech /tɛk/ *n.* [C] **1 technical** used in the names of colleges or universities where students study science subjects or subjects that involve making, building, or repairing things, such as engineering or computer science: *a freshman at Texas Tech* **2** a TECHIE **3 tech company/stock/industry etc.** a company, STOCK etc. that is involved in computers, SOFTWARE, the Internet etc.

tech·ie /ˈtɛki/ *n.* [C] INFORMAL someone who knows a lot about computers and electronic equipment —**techie** *adj.* [only before noun] *techie toys*

tech·ni·cal /ˈtɛknɪkəl/ Ac S3 W2 *adj.*

1 INDUSTRY/SCIENCE relating to practical knowledge, skills, or methods, especially in industrial or scientific work: *a job requiring technical knowledge* | *The company provides good customer service and technical expertise.* | *The workers needed more technical training.* → see Word Choice box at TECHNIQUE

2 DETAILS involving small details and needing a lot of attention and special knowledge or skill: *Jurors must deal with many technical legal questions.* | *Many books on furniture making are too technical or require artistic skills.*

3 LANGUAGE a technical word or language is difficult for most people to understand because it is connected with one particular subject or used in one particular job: *The* ***technical term*** *for a heart attack is an "infarction."*

4 technical problem/difficulty a problem involving the way a machine or system works: *The space probe's launch was delayed due to a technical problem.*

5 ACCORDING TO RULES according to the exact details in a set of rules: *a technical foul* | *This is a technical violation of the treaty.*

6 SKILLS technical skills or ability are the skills needed to do something difficult, especially in music, art, sports etc.: *a dancer with excellent technical skills*

[**Origin:** 1600–1700 Greek *technikos* **of art, skillful**, from *techne* **art, skill**]

ˈtechnical ˌcollege *n.* [C] a college where students study practical subjects that prepare them for particular types of jobs, especially jobs involving machines or science → see also JUNIOR COLLEGE

tech·ni·cal·i·ty /ˌtɛknɪˈkæləṭi/ *n. plural* **technicalities** [C] **1** LAW a small detail in a law or a set of rules, especially one that forces you to make a decision that seems unfair: *The murderer was acquitted* ***on a technicality*** (=because of a technicality). **2** [usually plural] the small details of how to do something or how a system or process works, which you need training to understand: *the technicalities of laser printing*

tech·ni·cally /ˈtɛknɪkli/ Ac S3 *adv.* **1** according to the exact details of rules, laws etc.: [sentence adverb] *Technically, you are responsible if someone gets injured on your property.* | [+ adj./adv.] *The union was then technically illegal.* **2** relating to the special skills needed for a particular activity, especially in sports, music etc.: [+ adj./adv.] *The dance is technically very difficult.* **3** relating to scientific work, or the use or design of machines or equipment: *This machine is technically simpler than later models.* **4 technically possible/impossible/difficult etc.** possible, impossible etc. using the scientific knowledge that is available now: *In the future, it will be technically possible to live on the moon.*

ˈtechnical ˌschool *n.* [C] a TECHNICAL COLLEGE

ˌtechnical supˈport also **ˌtech supˈport** *n.* [U] COMPUTERS **1** help or information that you receive to improve a computer program or system, make it continue working, or use it correctly **2** the department of a company that provides help with using computers

tech·ni·cian /tɛkˈnɪʃən/ *n.* [C] **1** a skilled scientific or industrial worker: *a dental technician* | *an automotive technician* **2** someone who is very good at the skills of a particular sport, art etc.: *Whether he was a great artist or not, Dali was a superb technician.*

Tech·ni·col·or /ˈtɛknəˌkʌlɚ/ *n.* [U] TRADEMARK a method of making color movies that produces very clear bright colors

tech·ni·col·or /ˈtɛknəˌkʌlɚ/ *adj.* [only before noun] having many very bright colors, usually too bright: *Sam's technicolor jacket*

tech·nique /tɛkˈnik/ Ac S3 W2 *n.* **1** [C] a special skill or way of doing something, especially one that has to be learned: *The surgery is done using a new technique.* | **technique for (doing) sth** *some basic techniques for creating documents* | **+of** *the techniques of drawing and painting* **2** [U] the level of skill or the set of skills that someone uses to do something, especially in art, music, sports etc.: *the artist's impressive style and technique*

WORD CHOICE **technique, technology, technical, high-tech**

- The noun **technique** [C] is a specific way of doing something, usually involving some skill: *We want our teachers to learn the latest teaching techniques.*
- **Technology** is a noun that means the scientific knowledge which is used for practical purposes such as making machines, electronic equipment etc.: *The technology* (NOT *the technique*) *to make photographs did not exist in the 16th century.* | *Space research has produced major advances in computer technology* (NOT *computer technique*).
- **Technical** is an adjective and means detailed practical knowledge of something involving science, technology, or machines: *Her job requires a lot of technical training* (NOT *technique training*).
- **High-tech** is also an adjective. It is short for *high technology* (NOT *high technique* or *high technical*) and is used about things that use the most modern technology.

tech·no /ˈtɛknoʊ/ *n.* [U] a type of popular electronic dance music with a fast strong beat

techno- /tɛknə/ *prefix* relating to machines and electronic equipment: *technophobia* (=dislike and fear of computers, machines etc.) | *techno-literacy* (=skill in using computers)

tech·noc·racy /tɛkˈnɑkrəsi/ *n. plural* **technocracies** [C,U] POLITICS a social system in which people with a lot of scientific or technical knowledge have a lot of power

tech·no·crat /ˈtɛknəˌkræt/ *n.* [C] a skilled scientist who has a lot of power in industry or government

tech·no·log·i·cal /ˌtɛknəˈlɑdʒɪkəl◂/ Ac *adj.* SCIENCE relating to technology: **technological advances/improvements/innovations etc.** *Technological progress in the computer industry has been rapid.*

tech·no·log·i·cally /ˌtɛknəˈlɑdʒɪkli/ Ac *adv.* in a way that is related to technology: *a technologically advanced factory*

tech·nol·o·gist /tɛkˈnɑlədʒɪst/ *n.* [C] SCIENCE someone who works in a job using equipment that needs special knowledge of technology: *an X-ray technologist*

tech·nol·o·gy /tɛkˈnɑlədʒi/ Ac S3 W1 *n. plural* **technologies** [C,U] machines, equipment, and ways of doing things that are based on modern knowledge about science and computers: *new satellite technology* | *environmentally safe technologies for pest control* | *We use* ***cutting-edge technology*** *to ensure product quality.* → see Word Choice box at TECHNIQUE

tech·no·phobe /ˈtɛknəfoʊb/ *n.* [C] INFORMAL someone who does not like modern machines, such as computers —**technophobia** /ˌtɛknəˈfoʊbiə/ *n.* [U]

ˈtech supˌport *n.* [U] INFORMAL → see TECHNICAL SUPPORT

tec·ton·ic /tɛkˈtɑnɪk/ *adj.* relating to PLATE TECTONICS

tecˌtonic ˈplate *n.* [C] one of the very large areas of rock that form the surface of the Earth, and that move around in relation to each other in a way that can cause EARTHQUAKES etc. → see also PLATE TECTONICS

tec·ton·ics /tɛkˈtɑnɪks/ *n.* [U] PLATE TECTONICS

Te·cum·seh /təˈkʌmsə/ (?1768–1813) a Shawnee chief, famous for trying to unite the Native American tribes in North America so that together they could fight against white people to keep their land

ted·dy /ˈtɛdi/ *n. plural* **teddies** [C] **1** a teddy bear **2** a piece of clothing for women, intended to be worn in bed or under other clothes, consisting of PANTIES and a top with thin STRAPS over the shoulders, all in one piece

ˈteddy bear *n.* [C] a soft toy in the shape of a bear [**Origin:** 1900–2000 Theodore (*"Teddy"*) Roosevelt (1858–1919), U.S. President, who liked hunting bears]

te·di·ous /ˈtidiəs/ *adj.* something that is tedious continues for a long time and is not interesting SYN **boring** SYN **dull**: *a tedious lecture* —**tediously** *adv.* —**tediousness** *n.* [U]

te·di·um /ˈtidiəm/ *n.* [U] the quality of being boring and seeming to continue for a long time: *the tedium of the long drive*

tee¹ /ti/ *n.* [C] **1** a small object that you use in GOLF to hold the ball above the ground before you hit it **2** a flat raised area of ground where you first hit the ball toward each hole in a game of GOLF

tee²

tee off *phr. v.* **1** to hit the ball off the tee in a game of GOLF **2 tee sb off** INFORMAL to make someone angry: *His attitude really tees me off.*

ˈtee-ball *n.* [U] another spelling of T-BALL

ˌteed ˈoff *adj.* [not before noun] INFORMAL annoyed or angry

teem /tim/ *v.* [I]

teem with sth *phr. v.* to be full of people, animals etc. SYN **swarm with**: *Local lakes* ***are teeming with*** *fish.*

teem·ing /ˈtimɪŋ/ *adj.* full of people, animals etc. that are all moving around: *the teeming city streets*

teen¹ /tin/ *adj.* [only before noun] INFORMAL relating to teenagers, or used or done by teenagers: *teen actresses* | *teen smoking* | *a teen magazine*

teen² *n.* **1** [C usually plural] a teenager: *charity work done by teens* **2 sb's teens** the period of your life when you are between 13 and 19 years old: *Lisa was* ***in her teens*** *when she met him.* | **early/late teens** *By his early teens he was an accomplished pianist.*

teen·age /ˈtineɪdʒ/ also **teen·aged** /ˈtineɪdʒd/ *adj.* [only before noun] aged between 13 and 19, or relating to someone of that age: *my teenage daughter* | *the problem of teenage pregnancy*

teen·ag·er /ˈtiˌneɪdʒɚ/ S3 *n.* [C] someone who is between 13 and 19 years old ▸see THESAURUS box at **child**

tee·ny /ˈtini/ also **teen·sy** /ˈtinzi/ *adj.* INFORMAL very small SYN **tiny**

teen·y·bop·per /ˈtiniˌbɑpɚ/ *n.* [C] OLD-FASHIONED a girl between the ages of about nine and 14, who is very interested in popular music, teenage fashions etc.

teeny wee·ny /ˌtini ˈwini◂/ also **teen·sy ween·sy** /ˌtinzi ˈwinzi/ *adj.* INFORMAL a word meaning "very small," used especially by or to children

tee·pee /ˈtipi/ *n.* [C] another spelling of TEPEE

ˈtee ˌshirt *n.* [C] another spelling of T-SHIRT

tee·ter /ˈtit̬ɚ/ *v.* [I] **1** to stand or move in an unsteady way as if you are going to fall: **+on/along/across etc.** *Stacks of books teetered on his desk.* **2 be teetering on the brink/edge of sth** to be very close to an extreme and dangerous situation: *The country is teetering on the brink of a financial crisis.*

ˈteeter-ˌtotter *n.* [C] a piece of equipment that children play on, made of a board that is balanced in the middle, so that when one end goes up the other goes down SYN **seesaw**

teeth /tiθ/ *n.* the plural of TOOTH

teethe /tið/ *v.* [I] **be teething** if a baby is teething, its first teeth are growing —**teething** /ˈtiðɪŋ/ *n.* [U]

T

ˈteething ˌpains also **ˈteething ˌproblems** *n.* [plural] small problems that a company, product, system etc. has when it is first starting or first being used

tee·to·tal·er /ˈtiˌtoʊtl̩ɚ/ *n.* [C] someone who never drinks alcohol

TEFL /ˈtɛfəl/ *n.* [U] the teaching of English as a foreign language → see also TESOL

Tef·lon /ˈtɛflɑn/ *n.* [U] TRADEMARK a type of plastic that things will not stick to, often used on the inside surfaces of cooking pans

Te·gu·ci·gal·pa /təˌgusɪˈgælpə/ the capital and largest city of Honduras

Teh·ran, Teheran /tɛˈrɑn, -ˈræn/ the capital and largest city of Iran

tel. the written abbreviation of "telephone number"

Tel A·viv /ˌtɛl əˈviv/ the second largest city of Israel, which is on the coast of the Mediterranean Sea

tele- /tɛlə/ *prefix* **1** at or over a long distance SYN far: *a telescope* | *telecommunications* **2** by or for television: *a teleplay* **3** using a telephone: *telesales*

tel·e·cast /ˈtɛləkæst/ *n.* [C] a broadcast on television —**telecast** *v.* [T]

tel·e·com /ˈtɛləkɑm/ *n.* [U] the abbreviation of TELECOMMUNICATIONS: *the telecom industry*

tel·e·com·mu·ni·ca·tions /ˌtɛləkəˌmyunəˈkeɪʃənz/ W3 also **telecommunication** *n.* [U] the process or business of sending and receiving messages by telephone, radio, television etc.: *public telecommunications networks*

tel·e·com·mut·er /ˈtɛləkəˌmyut̬ɚ/ *n.* [C] an EMPLOYEE who works at home using computers, telephones etc. to communicate with people at work —**telecommute** *v.* [I] —**telecommuting** *n.* [U]

tel·e·con·ference¹ /ˈtɛləˌkɑnfrəns/ *n.* [C] a business meeting in which people in different places talk to each other using telephones or VIDEO equipment —**teleconferencing** *n.* [U]

teleconference² *v.* [I] to have a meeting in which people in different places talk to each other using telephones and VIDEO equipment

tel·e·gen·ic /ˌtɛləˈdʒɛnɪk/ *adj.* someone who is telegenic looks attractive on television: *a telegenic actress*

tel·e·gram /ˈtɛləˌgræm/ *n.* [C] a message sent by telegraph

tel·e·graph¹ /ˈtɛləˌgræf/ *n.* **1** [U] an old-fashioned method of sending messages using radio or electrical signals, in which short and long signals are used to represent letters of the alphabet **2** [C] a piece of equipment that receives or sends messages in this way —**telegraphic** /ˌtɛləˈgræfɪk◂/ *adj.* —**telegraphically** /-kli/ *adv.*

telegraph² *v.* **1** [I,T] to send a message by telegraph **2** [T] to let people clearly see what you intend to do, without saying anything: *A boxer shouldn't telegraph his punches.*

te·leg·ra·pher /təˈlɛgrəfɚ/ *n.* [C] someone whose job is to send and receive messages by telegraph

te·leg·ra·phy /təˈlɛgrəfi/ *n.* [U] TECHNICAL the process of sending messages by TELEGRAPH

tel·e·ki·ne·sis /ˌtɛləkɪˈnisɪs, -kaɪ-/ *n.* [U] the ability to move physical objects using only the power of your mind —**telekinetic** /ˌtɛləkɪˈnɛt̬ɪk◂/ *adj.*: *telekinetic powers*

Te·le·mann /ˈtɛləˌmɑn/, **Ge·org** /ˈgeɪɔrg/ (1681–1767) a German musician who wrote CLASSICAL music

tel·e·mar·ket·ing /ˌtɛləˈmɑrkət̬ɪŋ/ *n.* [U] a method of selling products in which you call people on the telephone and try to persuade them to buy something —**telemarketer** *n.* [C]

te·lem·e·try /təˈlɛmətri/ *n.* [U] TECHNICAL the use of special scientific equipment to measure something and send the results somewhere by radio

te·le·ol·o·gy /ˌtiliˈɑlədʒi, ˌtɛ-/ *n.* [U] the belief that all natural things and events were specially planned for a particular purpose —**teleological** /ˌtiliəˈlɑdʒɪkəl◂, ˌtɛ-/ *adj.*

tel·e·path·ic /ˌtɛləˈpæθɪk◂/ *adj.* **1** someone who is telepathic has a mysterious ability to know what other people are thinking **2** a telepathic message is sent from one person to another by using thoughts

te·lep·a·thy /təˈlɛpəθi/ *n.* [U] a way of communicating in which thoughts are sent from one person's mind to someone else's, without speaking, writing, or signs

tel·e·phone¹ /ˈtɛləˌfoʊn/ S2 W2 *n.* **1** [C,U] a piece of equipment that you use to speak to someone in another place, or the system of communication that makes it possible for you to do this SYN **phone**: *Is that my **telephone ringing?*** | *a cordless telephone* | *a telephone conversation* | *Reservations can be made **by telephone**.* | *I was **on the telephone*** (=using the telephone) *when Dave came in.* | *What's your **telephone number?*** | *You got a **telephone call** from Sue yesterday.* | *It was just someone trying to sell me something **over the telephone*** (=using the telephone). | *It was her job to **answer the telephone**.*

THESAURUS

lift/pick up the receiver to move the part of a telephone you speak into close to your face
dial a number to press the buttons or turn the dial (=wheel with numbered holes) on a telephone
answer the telephone/phone to pick up and speak into a telephone when it rings
hang up also **put down the telephone/phone** to put the part you speak into onto the main part again
there is no answer nobody answers the telephone when you call a number
a number/line is busy someone else is speaking on that line when you call, so you cannot speak to the person you want
dial/have the wrong number to dial or have dialed a number which is not the number of the person you want to speak to
get through to succeed in speaking to someone on the telephone
voice mail a system which lets people leave recorded messages for you on your telephone when you are unable to answer it
answering machine a machine on which people can leave recorded messages for you when you are unable to answer the telephone
→ PHONE

2 [C] the part of a telephone that you hold close to your ear and mouth SYN **receiver**: *Fran said goodbye and **hung up the telephone**.* | *Ripley **picked up the telephone** and dialed.* **[Origin:** 1800–1900 *tele-* + Greek *phone* **sound, voice]** —**telephonic** /ˌtɛləˈfɑnɪk◂/ *adj.*

telephone² *v.* [I,T] FORMAL to speak to someone by telephone SYN **call**: *Their neighbors telephoned the police.* ▸see THESAURUS box at **phone²**

ˈtelephone ˌbook *n.* [C] a PHONE BOOK

ˈtelephone ˌbooth *n.* [C] a PHONE BOOTH

ˈtelephone diˌrectory *n.* [C] a PHONE BOOK

ˈtelephone exˌchange *n.* [C] a central building or office where telephone calls are connected to other telephones

ˈtelephone ˌpole *n.* [C] a tall wooden pole that supports telephone wires

ˈtelephone tag *n.* [U] PHONE TAG

te·leph·o·ny /təˈlɛfəni/ *n.* [U] COMPUTERS computer HARDWARE and SOFTWARE that allow a computer to make and receive telephone calls

tel·e·pho·to lens /ˌtɛləfoʊt̬oʊ ˈlɛnz/ *n.* [C] a special camera LENS used for taking clear photographs of things that are far away

tel·e·play /ˈtɛləˌpleɪ/ *n.* [C] a story written for a television program or movie

tel·e·print·er /ˈtɛlə,prɪntə/ *n.* [C] a TELETYPE

Tel·e·Promp·Ter, teleprompter /ˈtɛlə,prɑmptə/ *n.* [C] TRADEMARK a machine from which someone speaking on television reads the words of their speech

tel·e·scope¹ /ˈtɛlə,skoʊp/ *n.* [C] SCIENCE a piece of scientific equipment shaped like a tube with special LENSes inside, used for making distant objects such as stars and PLANETS look larger and closer → see also RADIO TELESCOPE → see picture at OPTICAL

telescope² *v.* **1** [T usually passive] to make a process or set of events happen in a shorter time: **be telescoped into sth** *The play's three acts are telescoped into a two-hour program.* **2** [I,T] if something telescopes or you telescope it, it becomes longer or shorter by sliding parts over each other: *The legs telescope to make the tripod higher or lower.*

tel·e·scop·ic /,tɛlə'skɑpɪk◂/ *adj.* **1** also **tel·e·scop·ing** /ˈtɛlə,skoʊpɪŋ/ made of parts that slide over each other so that the whole thing can be made longer or shorter: *a tripod with telescopic legs* **2** made or done using a telescope: *a telescopic picture of Mars* **3** making distant things look bigger: *a telescopic lens*

tel·e·thon /ˈtɛlə,θɑn/ *n.* [C] a special television program in which famous people provide entertainment and ask people to give money to help other people

Tel·e·type /ˈtɛlətaɪp/ *n.* [C] **1** TRADEMARK a machine that prints or sends messages that are sent along telephone lines SYN **teleprinter** **2** a message that is sent or received by this machine

tel·e·type·writ·er /,tɛlə'taɪpraɪtə/ *n.* [C] a Teletype

tel·e·van·gel·ist /,tɛlə'vændʒəlɪst/ *n.* [C] a Christian minister who regularly talks about Christianity on television, often asking people to give money to his or her church —**televangelism** *n.* [U]

tel·e·vise /ˈtɛlə,vaɪz/ *v.* [T] to broadcast something on television: *The debate will be **televised live**.*

tel·e·vi·sion /ˈtɛlə,vɪʒən/ S2 W1 *n.* **1** [C] also **'tele-vision ,set** FORMAL a piece of electronic equipment shaped like a box with a screen, on which you can watch programs SYN **TV**: *a 36-inch television* | **turn/switch a television on/off** *Turn that television off!* **2** [U] the programs broadcast in this way SYN **TV**: *Frank **watches television** all the time.* | **television program/show/commercial etc.** *a television program for kids*

THESAURUS

Types of television programs
show/program: *This is my favorite show.*
movie/film: *There's a good movie on Channel 7 at nine o'clock.*
soap (opera) a program that is on TV regularly, often every day, about the same group of people
sitcom a funny TV program which has the same people in it every week in a different story
game show a program in which people play games in order to try and win prizes
talk show a program in which people answer questions about themselves
cartoon a movie or program that uses characters that are drawn and not real
series a set of TV programs about the same group of people or about a particular subject, shown regularly: *a new drama series about cops and lawyers*
documentary a program that gives information about a subject
the news: *the six o'clock news*
episode one of the programs in a series
reality (TV) show a program that shows all the details of what people do in their daily lives or in a special situation

3 on television broadcast or being broadcast on television: *What's on television tonight?* **4** [U] the business or activity of making and broadcasting programs on television: *Blair has spent his entire career **in television**.* | **television producer/reporter/cameraman etc.** *Jenner works as a television sports commentator.* | **network/cable/public television** (=the companies that produce shows on the main free stations, on cable stations, or on the public broadcasting system) *It has been a difficult year for network television.*

tel·ex /ˈtɛlɛks/ *n.* **1** [U] the system of sending messages from one business to another on the telephone network, using a TELETYPE machine **2** [C] a message sent in this way —**telex** *v.* [I,T]

tell /tɛl/ S1 W1 *v. past tense and past participle* **told** /toʊld/

1 SAY/INFORMATION [T] to give someone facts or information about something: **tell sb (that)** *Tell Teresa I said hi.* | *I wish someone had told me that the meeting was canceled.* | **tell sb sth** *Tell me your phone number again.* | **tell sb who/why/what etc.** *She wouldn't tell me why she was angry.* | **tell sb about sth** *Did you tell Jennifer about the party?* | **tell a story/joke/secret etc.** *My father always cried when he told this story.* | *Patrick tells lies all the time.* | *For once, I think he's **telling the truth**.*

THESAURUS

order to tell someone that they must do something, especially using your official power or authority: *He ordered his men to fire.*
instruct to officially tell someone what to do: *The doctor instructed him to get more exercise.*
command used to say that a military leader, ruler etc. tells someone officially to do something: *The soldiers commanded him to stop.*
issue orders/instructions used to say that someone with authority tells people exactly what they should do: *Paredes issued orders for a renewed defense of the city.*
demand to firmly or angrily ask an organization or a person to do something: *The government demanded the immediate release of the journalist.*
insist to say that someone must do something: *My mother insisted that I take my sister with me.*

►see THESAURUS box at **explain**

2 KNOW [I, T not in progressive] to know something or be able to recognize something because of certain signs that show this: **can/could tell** *She might have been lying. Ben couldn't tell.* | **tell (that)** *I could tell Darren was really nervous.* | **tell when/how etc.** *It was **hard to tell** what she was thinking.* | **tell by/from sth** *I can tell by the way he talks that he's from the South.*

3 WHAT SB SHOULD DO [T] to say that someone must do something: **tell sb to do sth** *Mom told me to take out the trash before I leave.* | **tell sb (that)** *Denise was told she had to work overtime tonight.* | **tell sb what/how etc.** *Stop trying to tell me what to do all the time.* | ***Do as you're told*** (=obey me) *and don't ask questions.*

4 RECOGNIZE DIFFERENCE [T not in progressive] to be able to see how one person or thing is different from another: **tell sth from sth** *Most experts can tell an expensive diamond from a cheap one.* | *It's fairly easy to **tell the difference** between good coffee and bad coffee.*

5 WARN [T usually in past tense] to warn someone that something bad might happen: **tell sb (that)** *Alan told Marge she shouldn't walk alone at night.* | **tell sb to do sth** *Helen told me not to trust Robert.*

6 BE A SIGN OF STH [T not in progressive or passive] to give information in ways other than talking: **tell sb (that)** *The red light tells you it's recording.* | **tell sb what/why etc.** *The bear's sense of smell tells it where its prey is hiding.* | **tell sb about sth** *Studying meteorites can tell us about the origins of the universe.*

7 tell yourself to try to persuade yourself about something, because it is difficult to accept or because it worries you: *I kept telling myself that it wasn't my fault.*

8 BAD BEHAVIOR [I] INFORMAL to tell someone in authority about something wrong that someone has done SYN **tattle**: *If you don't give back my pencil, I'm going to tell.* | **+on** *I was afraid my little sister would tell on us.*

T

9 AFFECT [I not in progressive] to have an effect on someone, especially a harmful one: *His years in the army certainly tell in his attitude to his work.* | +**on** *The strain was beginning to tell on her.* → see also TELLING

10 tell time to be able to know what time it is by looking at a clock

SPOKEN PHRASES

11 (I/I'll) tell you what a) used when you are suggesting or offering something: *I'll tell you what, I'll pay for the movie if you drive.* **b)** used to emphasize what you are saying: *I tell you what, he's so cool.*

12 I tell you also **I'm telling you**, **let me tell you** used to emphasize that what you are saying is true, even though it may be difficult to believe: *I tell you, I've never seen anything like it before.*

13 (I) told you (so) used when you have warned someone about a possible danger that has now happened and they have ignored your warning

14 to tell (you) the truth used to emphasize that you are being very honest: *To tell you the truth, I can't stand Sandy's cooking.*

15 tell me used before asking a question: *Tell me, does this look okay?* | *So tell me – what're you doing in Argentina?*

16 I'll tell you something/one thing/another thing also **let me tell you something/one thing/another thing** used to make someone pay attention to what you are going to say: *Let me tell you something – if I catch you kids smoking, you'll be grounded for a year at least.*

17 I couldn't tell you used to tell someone that you do not know the answer to their question: *"Is it supposed to rain tomorrow?" "I couldn't tell you."*

18 I can't tell you a) used to say that something is a secret, so you cannot answer their question: *"Where are we going?" "I can't tell you – it's a surprise."* **b)** used to say that you cannot express your feelings or describe something well: *I can't tell you how grateful I am for your help.*

19 I'm not telling (you) used to say that you refuse to tell someone something

20 tell it like it is to say exactly what you think or what is true, without hiding anything that might upset or offend people: *Don always tells it like it is.*

21 don't tell me used to interrupt someone because you know what they are going to say or because you want to guess, especially when you are annoyed: *Don't tell me we're out of milk!*

22 sb tells me (that) used to say what someone has told you: *Debbie tells me you're looking for a new job.*

23 there's no telling what/how etc. used to say that it is impossible to know what has happened or what will happen next: *There's no telling how he'll react to the news.*

24 to hear sb tell it used to say that someone gave their opinion of an event, which may not be completely true or correct: *To hear Betsy tell it, you'd think we burned the house down.*

25 you're telling me used to emphasize that you already know and agree with something that someone has just said: *"Wow, this is really hard work." "You're telling me!"*

26 tell me about it used to say that you already know how bad something is, especially because you have experienced it yourself: *"I'm totally sick of my boss." "Yeah, tell me about it."*

27 you never can tell also **you can never tell** used to say that you cannot be certain about what will happen in the future: *"Maybe they'll get married." "You never can tell."*

28 tell sb where to get off SLANG to tell someone angrily that they have done or said something insulting or unfair: *"Did you give him the money?" "No, I told him where to get off."*

29 tell me another one used when you do not believe what someone has told you

[**Origin:** Old English *tellan*] → see also **all told** at ALL[2] (17)

tell sb/sth **apart** *phr. v.* if you can tell two people or things apart, you can see the difference between them, so that you do not confuse them SYN **distinguish between**: *I've never been able to tell the twins apart.*

tell of sb/sth *phr. v.* LITERARY to describe an event or person: *Chavez often told of his mother's kindness to strangers.*

tell sb ↔ **off** *phr. v.* to talk angrily to someone because they have done something wrong: *My mother told him off.*

Tell /tɛl/, **William** a Swiss FOLK HERO of the 14th century, who opposed the Austrians who ruled Switzerland

tell·er /ˈtɛlɚ/ *n.* [C] **1** ECONOMICS someone whose job is to receive and pay out money in a bank **2** POLITICS someone who counts votes → see also ATM, STORYTELLER

Tel·ler /ˈtɛlɚ/, **Ed·ward** /ˈɛdwɚd/ (1908–2003) a U.S. scientist, born in Hungary, who worked on the development of the ATOMIC BOMB and HYDROGEN BOMB

tell·ing /ˈtɛlɪŋ/ *adj.* **1** having a great or important effect SYN **significant**: *a telling impact on the industry* **2** showing the true character or nature of someone or something, often without being intended: **telling detail/remark/sign etc.** *The problem was a telling sign of disaster to come.* —**tellingly** *adv.*

tell·tale /ˈtɛlteɪl/ *adj.* **telltale signs/marks etc.** signs etc. that clearly show something has happened or exists, especially something bad that is a secret: *There was a telltale smell of alcohol on the captain's breath.*

tel·o·phase /ˈtɛləˌfeɪz, ˈti-/ *n.* [C] BIOLOGY the fourth and final stage in the process by which a cell divides, during which the CHROMOSOMES move to the opposite end of the cell and two new NUCLEI (=central part of the cells of living things) are formed → see also ANAPHASE, METAPHASE, MITOSIS, PROPHASE

tem·blor /ˈtɛmblɚ, -blɔr/ *n.* [C] FORMAL an EARTHQUAKE

te·mer·i·ty /təˈmɛrət̬i/ *n.* [U] **have the temerity to do sth** FORMAL to risk doing or saying something even though you know it may offend or annoy someone or get you in trouble

temp[1] /tɛmp/ *n.* [C] an office worker who is only employed for a short period of time

temp[2] *v.* [I] to work as a temp

tem·per[1] /ˈtɛmpɚ/ *n.*

1 TENDENCY TO BE ANGRY [C,U] a tendency to become angry suddenly: *Robin* ***has quite a temper***. | *Jill needs to learn to* ***control*** *her* ***temper***. | **a bad/quick/violent etc. temper** *I wouldn't argue with him too much – he's got a short temper.* | ***Tempers flared*** (=people became angry) *during the protest.*

2 lose your temper (with sb/sth) to suddenly become so angry that you cannot control yourself: *I've never seen him lose his temper with anyone.*

3 [singular, U] an uncontrolled feeling of anger that continues for a short time: *In* ***a fit of temper*** (=a quick expression of anger), *she smashed the vase against the wall.*

4 ATTITUDE [singular] FORMAL the general attitude that people have in a particular place at one time SYN **mood**: +**of** *Gandhi knew the temper of the country.*

5 EMOTIONAL STATE [singular, U] a particular emotional state SYN **mood**: **in a good/bad/foul etc. temper** *She's been in a bad temper all day.*

6 temper, temper SPOKEN, HUMOROUS said to tell someone that they should stop showing their anger in a silly or unreasonable way → see also BAD-TEMPERED, EVEN-TEMPERED, ILL-TEMPERED, -TEMPERED

temper[2] *v.* [T] **1** FORMAL to make something less severe or extreme, especially by adding something that has the opposite effect: **temper sth with sth** *They have tempered their enthusiasm with common sense.* **2** to make metal as hard as is needed by heating it and then putting it in cold water → see also TEMPERED

tem·per·a /ˈtɛmpərə/ *n.* ENG. LANG. ARTS **1** [U] a type of paint used for painting pictures and signs, which contains a thick liquid such as egg **2** [C] a picture painted with tempera paint

tem·per·a·ment /ˈtɛmprəmənt/ *n.* [C,U] the emotional part of someone's character, especially how likely they are to be happy, angry etc.: *My father and I have very similar temperaments.*

tem·per·a·men·tal /ˌtɛmprəˈmɛntl/ *adj.* **1** likely to suddenly become upset, excited, or angry: *a temperamental horse* **2** a temperamental machine, system etc. does not always work correctly **3** relating to the emotional part of someone's character —**temperamentally** *adv.*

tem·perance /ˈtɛmprəns/ *n.* [U] **1** OLD-FASHIONED the practice of never drinking alcohol for moral or religious reasons **2** FORMAL sensible control of the things you say and do, especially the amount of alcohol you drink

ˈtemperance ˌmovement *n.* [C usually singular] HISTORY a group of people whose aim was to prevent or strictly limit the drinking of alcohol, especially in the late 1800s and early 1900s

tem·perate /ˈtɛmprɪt/ *adj.* **1 a temperate climate/region/area etc.** a type of weather or a part of the world that is never very hot or very cold **2** FORMAL temperate behavior is calm and sensible → see also INTEMPERATE

ˈtemperate ˌzone *n.* [C] EARTH SCIENCE one of the two parts of the Earth that are between the POLAR ZONES and the TROPICS, where the weather is not usually very hot nor very cold → see also POLAR ZONE

tem·pera·ture /ˈtɛmprətʃɚ/ S3 W2 *n.* **1** [C,U] a measure of how hot or cold a place or thing is: *It was sunny, but the temperature was well below zero.* | ***A rapid change in temperature** could kill a fish.* | *The exhibit room has to be kept at **a constant temperature**.* | **air/water/surface etc. temperature** *The water temperature should be at least 180 degrees.* | **temperatures in the 40s/50s/60s etc.** *We expect clear skies and temperatures in the 70s.* | **high/low temperature** *Steel is produced at very high temperatures.* | **a rise/fall etc. in temperature** *Next week we should expect a fall in temperatures.* | **the temperature rises/goes up** (=it gets warmer) | **the temperature falls/drops/goes down** (=it gets colder) → see also ROOM TEMPERATURE **2** [C,U] the temperature of your body, especially used as a measure of whether you are sick or not: *The nurse **took*** (=measured) *my **temperature**.* | *Exercise raises your **body temperature**.* **3 have a temperature** also **be running a temperature** to have a body temperature that is higher than normal, especially because you are sick **4** [C usually singular] the way people are reacting to a particular situation, for example whether they are behaving angrily or calmly: *The political temperature rose after the jobs crisis became even worse.* [**Origin:** 1400–1500 Latin *temperatura* **mixture**, from *temperare* **to divide up properly, mix, keep within proper limits, temper**]

tem·pered /ˈtɛmpɚd/ *adj.* tempered metal has been made hard by heating it and then putting it in cold water: *tempered steel* → see also TEMPER[2]

-tempered /tɛmpɚd/ *suffix* [in adjectives] **good-tempered/foul-tempered/quiet-tempered etc.** usually in a good, bad etc. mood: *a sweet-tempered woman*

ˈtemper ˌtantrum *n.* [C] a TANTRUM

tem·pest /ˈtɛmpɪst/ *n.* **1** [C] EARTH SCIENCE a violent storm **2 a tempest in a teapot** an unimportant matter that a lot of people become upset about

tem·pes·tu·ous /tɛmˈpɛstʃuəs/ *adj.* **1** FORMAL a tempestuous relationship or period of time involves a lot of difficulty and strong emotions **2** LITERARY a tempestuous ocean or wind is very rough and violent SYN **stormy** —**tempestuously** *adv.* —**tempestuousness** *n.* [U]

tem·plate /ˈtɛmpleɪt/ *n.* [C] **1** a thin sheet of plastic or metal in a special shape or pattern used to help cut other materials in a similar shape **2** a computer document containing some basic information that you use as a model for writing other documents, such as business letters, envelopes etc. **3** something that is used as a model for another thing [**Origin:** 1600–1700 French *templet*, from *temple* **instrument in a loom for keeping the cloth stretched**]

tem·ple /ˈtɛmpəl/ *n.* [C] **1** a building where people go to WORSHIP in some religions, such as the Jewish, Hindu, Buddhist, Sikh, and Mormon religions: *an ancient Greek temple* ►see THESAURUS box at **religion** **2** [usually plural] BIOLOGY one of the two fairly flat areas on each side of your FOREHEAD **3** one of the two narrow pieces on the sides of a pair of glasses that fit over your ears [**Origin:** (1) 800–900 Latin *templum*]

tem·po /ˈtɛmpoʊ/ *n. plural* **tempos** [C] **1** ENG. LANG. ARTS the speed at which music is played or should be played **2** the speed at which something happens SYN **pace**: *the slow tempo of island life*

tem·po·ral /ˈtɛmpərəl/ *adj.* FORMAL **1** relating to or limited by time **2** relating to practical instead of religious affairs

ˌtemporal ˈlobe *n.* [C] BIOLOGY one of the two lower parts of the brain at either side

tem·po·rar·y /ˈtɛmpəˌrɛri/ Ac S3 W3 *adj.* **1** continuing for only a limited period of time OPP **permanent**: *a temporary ceasefire* | *temporary jobs* | *She was employed **on a temporary basis**.* **2** intended to be used for only a limited period of time OPP **permanent**: *temporary housing* **3** employed for only a limited period of time OPP **permanent**: *temporary workers* **4** temporary FILES on a computer hold information that is needed only for a short time. [**Origin:** 1500–1600 Latin *temporarius*, from *tempus* **time**] —**temporariness** *n.* [U] —**temporarily** /ˌtɛmpəˈrɛrəli/ *adv.*: *The elevator is temporarily out of order.*

tem·po·rize /ˈtɛmpəˌraɪz/ *v.* [I] FORMAL to delay or avoid making a decision in order to gain time

tempt /tɛmpt/ *v.* [T] **1** to try to persuade someone to do something by making it seem attractive: **tempt sb to do sth** *They're offering free gifts to tempt people to join.* | **tempt sb into doing sth** *We hope to tempt young people into studying science.* **2** to make someone want to have or do something, even though they know they really should not: *Leaving valuables in your car will tempt thieves.* | *"Would you like some more cake?" "**Don't tempt me**."* | **be tempted to do sth** *I was tempted to tell him what I really thought.* **3 tempt fate a)** to do something that involves unnecessary risk and may cause serious problems: *People are tempting fate by building homes in the canyons where fires are common.* **b)** to say too confidently that something will have a good result, that there will be no problems etc., when it is likely that there will be problems

temp·ta·tion /tɛmpˈteɪʃən/ *n.* **1** [C,U] a strong desire to have or do something even though you know you should not: **temptation to do sth** *There's always a temptation to blame others for your situation.* | *Try to **resist the temptation** to snack between meals.* | *Rick **gave in to the temptation*** (=did something although he knew he should not) *to steal the watch.* **2** [C,U] something that makes you want to have or do something, even though you know you should not: *Chocolate in the house is a great temptation!*

tempt·ing /ˈtɛmptɪŋ/ *adj.* something that is tempting seems very good and you would like to have it or do it: *a tempting job offer* | *That pie looks tempting.* | **it is tempting to do sth** *It's tempting to believe her story, but there's no proof.* —**temptingly** *adv.*

tempt·ress /ˈtɛmptrɪs/ *n.* [C] OLD-FASHIONED a woman who makes a man want to have sex with her

tem·pur·a /ˈtɛmpərə, tɛmˈpʊrə/ *n.* [U] a Japanese dish of vegetables and SEAFOOD covered in BATTER and cooked in hot oil

tem·pus fu·git /ˌtɛmpəs ˈfyudʒɪt/ LITERARY a phrase meaning "time flies"; used to say that time passes very quickly

ten[1] /tɛn/ *number* **1** 10 **2** ten o'clock: *My appointment's **at ten**.* **3 ten to one** INFORMAL used to say that

T

something is very likely: *Ten to one Marsha will be late.* [**Origin:** Old English *tien*] → see also TENTH[1]

ten² *n.* [C] **1** a piece of paper money worth $10: *Do you have two tens for a twenty?* **2 a (perfect) ten** INFORMAL used to give a perfect SCORE in sports, or humorously to praise someone or something: *I'd give the service at the deli a ten.*

ten·a·ble /ˈtɛnəbəl/ *adj.* FORMAL **1** a tenable belief, argument etc. is reasonable and can be defended successfully OPP **untenable** **2** a tenable situation can continue because any problems can be dealt with OPP **untenable**

te·na·cious /təˈneɪʃəs/ *adj.* determined to do something and unwilling to stop trying even when the situation becomes difficult —**tenaciously** *adv.* —**tenaciousness** also **tenacity** /təˈnæsət̬i/ *n.* [U]

ten·an·cy /ˈtɛnənsi/ *n. plural* **tenancies** FORMAL **1** [C] the period of time that someone rents a house, land etc. **2** [C,U] the right to use a house, land etc.: *joint tenancy*

ten·ant /ˈtɛnənt/ *n.* [C] someone who lives in a house, room etc. and pays rent to the person who owns it

ˌtenant ˈfarmer *n.* [C] someone who farms land that is rented from someone else

ˌTen Comˈmandments *n.* [plural] the ten laws that God gave to Moses, according to the Bible. They are an important part of the Jewish and Christian religions.

T

tend /tɛnd/ S2 W1 *v.* **1 tend to do sth** to often do a particular thing, especially something that is bad or annoying, and to be likely to do it again: *Bill tends to talk too much when he's nervous.* | *Jobs in restaurants tend not to pay very well.* **2** [T] to take care of something by doing what is necessary to keep it in a good condition or to improve its condition: *He's outside tending the garden.* **3 tend bar** to work as a BARTENDER

tend to sb/sth *phr. v.* to take care of someone or something and deal with their problems and needs: *She was in the bedroom tending to her son.*

tend toward sth *phr. v.* to have a particular quality or feature more than others: *Her approach tends toward the traditional.*

tend·en·cy /ˈtɛndənsi/ S3 W3 *n. plural* **tendencies** [C] **1** a PROBABILITY that you will develop, think, or behave in a certain way: **a tendency to do sth** *His tendency to be critical made him unpopular.* | *The copier **has a tendency** to jam.* | **+toward/to** *a tendency toward alcoholism* | **+for** *teenagers' tendencies for acne problems* | *There is **a growing tendency** for people to change jobs more often.* **2 artistic/alcoholic/aggressive etc. tendencies** particular skills, weaknesses, or desires that make someone behave in a particular way: *For years, Kurt kept his suicidal tendencies a secret.* [**Origin:** 1600–1700 Medieval Latin *tendentia*, from Latin *tendere* **to stretch**]

ten·den·tious /tɛnˈdɛnʃəs/ *adj.* FORMAL a tendentious speech, remark, book etc. expresses a strong opinion that is intended to influence people —**tendentiousness** *n.* [U]

ten·der¹ /ˈtɛndɚ/ *adj.* **1** easy to cut and eat, especially because of being well cooked OPP **tough**: *a tender steak* ►see THESAURUS box at **soft** **2** gentle and careful in a way that shows love: *a tender kiss* **3** a tender part of your body is painful if someone touches it: *My arm is still a little tender.* ►see THESAURUS box at **painful** **4** easily damaged: *tender young plants* **5 tender loving care** sympathetic treatment and a lot of attention SYN **TLC** **6 a tender age** HUMOROUS or LITERARY the time when you are young or do not have much experience: *Wayne began working in the family store **at the tender age of** five.* —**tenderly** *adv.* —**tenderness** *n.* [U]

tender² *v.* [T] **1** [T] FORMAL to formally offer something to someone, especially in business: **tender sth to sb** *About 66% of the corporation's shares have been tendered to the phone company.* | *They **tendered** him a $3.5 million offer to play next season.* | *She **tendered** her **resignation*** (=officially said that she was going to leave her job) *on Friday.* **2** [T] OLD-FASHIONED to give money as a payment

tender³ *n.* [C] **1** a small boat that takes people or supplies between the shore and a larger boat **2** OLD-FASHIONED part of a steam train used for carrying coal and water for the engine → see also BARTENDER, LEGAL TENDER, TENDER OFFER

ten·der·foot /ˈtɛndɚfʊt/ *n.* [C] INFORMAL someone who does not have much experience doing something

ˌtender-ˈhearted *adj.* very kind and gentle —**tender-heartedly** *adv.* —**tender-heartedness** *n.* [U]

ten·der·ize /ˈtɛndəˌraɪz/ *v.* [T] to make meat softer and easier to eat by preparing it in a special way

ten·der·iz·er /ˈtɛndəˌraɪzɚ/ *n.* [C,U] a substance that is put onto raw meat to make it softer and easier to eat after it is cooked

ten·der·loin /ˈtɛndɚlɔɪn/ *n.* [U] meat that is soft and easy to eat, cut from each side of the BACKBONE of cows or pigs

ˈtender ˌoffer *n.* [C] TECHNICAL a formal statement of the price you would charge for doing a job or providing goods or services

ten·di·ni·tis /ˌtɛndəˈnaɪt̬ɪs/ *n.* [U] continuous pain in a tendon because of an injury

ten·don /ˈtɛndən/ *n.* [C] BIOLOGY a band of strong white TISSUE that connects a muscle to a bone

ten·dril /ˈtɛndrəl/ *n.* [C] **1** BIOLOGY a thin curling stem without leaves by which a climbing plant fastens itself to a support **2** LITERARY a thin curling piece of something thin, such as hair or smoke

ten·e·ment /ˈtɛnəmənt/ also **ˈtenement ˌbuilding**, **tenement house** *n.* [C] a large building divided into apartments, especially in the poorer areas of a city

ten·et /ˈtɛnɪt/ *n.* [C] a principle or belief, especially one that is part of a larger system of beliefs: *Individualism is **a basic tenet of** Western culture.*

ten·fold /ˈtɛnfoʊld/ *adj., adv.* FORMAL ten times as much or as many of something

ˌten-gallon ˈhat *n.* [C] a tall hat made of soft material with a wide BRIM, worn especially by COWBOYS

Ten·nes·see /ˌtɛnəˈsi/ WRITTEN ABBREVIATION **TN** a state in the southeastern U.S.

ten·nies /ˈtɛniz/ *n.* [plural] INFORMAL TENNIS SHOES

ten·nis /ˈtɛnɪs/ S3 *n.* [U] a game for two people or two pairs of people who use RACKETS to hit a small soft ball backward and forward over a net: *a game of tennis* | *We **played tennis** all afternoon.* | *a tennis racket*

ˈtennis ˌbracelet *n.* [C] a type of BRACELET (=band worn around the wrist) which is made of many small valuable stones, such as DIAMONDS, which are connected together in a row

ˈtennis court *n.* [C] the four-sided area that you play tennis on

ˌtennis ˈelbow *n.* [U] a medical problem in which your elbow becomes very painful after you have bent it too often

ˈtennis shoe *n.* [C] a light shoe used for sports, with a rubber surface on the bottom → see picture at SHOE[1]

Ten·ny·son /ˈtɛnɪsən/, **Al·fred** /ˈælfrɪd/, **Alfred, Lord Tennyson** (1809–1892) an English poet

Te·noch·ti·tlán /teˌnoʊtʃtiˈtlɑn/ HISTORY the capital city of the Aztecs, which was where Mexico City now stands

ten·on /ˈtɛnən/ *n.* [C] an end of a piece of wood, that has been cut to fit exactly into a MORTISE in order to form a strong joint

ten·or /ˈtɛnɚ/ *n.* ENG. LANG. ARTS **1 a)** [C] a man with a singing voice that can reach the range of notes just below the lowest woman's voice, or this man's voice **b)** [U] the part of a piece of music a tenor sings **c)** [C] a musical instrument with the same range of notes as a tenor **2 the tenor of sth** FORMAL the general character, attitude, or meaning of something SYN **tone** —**tenor** *adj.*: *a tenor saxophone*

tense[1] /tɛns/ Ac S3 *adj.* **1** feeling very nervous and worried because of something bad that might happen: *Williams looked a little tense before the game.* ▸see THESAURUS box at **worried** **2** a tense situation, moment etc. is one in which you feel very anxious and worried because of something bad that might happen: *nine months of tense negotiations* | *The atmosphere was extremely tense.* **3** unable to relax your body or part of your body because your muscles feel tight: *I can feel you're really tense in your lower back.* | *tense muscles* [**Origin:** 1600–1700 Latin **stretched**, from the past participle of *tendere* **to stretch**] —**tensely** *adv.* —**tenseness** *n.* [U] → see also TENSION

tense[2] Ac *v.* [I,T] also **tense up** to make your muscles tight and stiff, or to become tight and stiff: *He put his arm around me, and I tensed up.* | *He tensed his body in anticipation of the impact.*

tense[3] Ac *n.* [C,U] ENG. LANG. ARTS any of the forms of a verb that show an action or state in the past, present, or future time. "I study" is in the present tense, "I studied" is in the past tense, and "I will study" is in the future tense.

tensed 'up *adj.* [not before noun] INFORMAL feeling so nervous or worried that you cannot relax

ten•sile /'tɛnsəl/ *adj.* able to be stretched: *tensile rubber*

tensile 'strength *n.* [U] TECHNICAL the ability of materials such as steel, CONCRETE, and cloth to bear pressure or weight

ten•sion /'tɛnʃən/ Ac W3 *n.*
1 NO TRUST [C,U] the feeling that exists when people or countries do not trust each other and may suddenly attack each other or start arguing: *racial tension* | **+between** *The obvious tension between them made everyone else uncomfortable.* | **racial/ethnic/political etc. tension** *Widespread unemployment has fueled social tensions.* | **tension grows/mounts/builds etc.** *Tension in the region has grown recently.* | **break/defuse/ease/relieve etc. tension** *Everyone laughed, breaking the tension.*
2 NERVOUS FEELING [U] a nervous, worried, or excited feeling that makes it impossible for you to relax: *The tension as we waited for the news was unbearable.* | **reduce/relieve/ease etc. tension** *Exercise is the ideal way to relieve tension after a hard day.*
3 DIFFERENT INFLUENCES [C,U] a situation in which different needs, forces, or influences work in different directions and make the situation difficult: **+between** *the tension between work and family life*
4 TIGHTNESS [U] tightness or stiffness in a wire, rope, muscle etc.: *Often a hot bath will help relieve **muscle tension**.*
5 FORCE [U] PHYSICS the amount of force that stretches something: *The rope can take up to 300 pounds of tension.*

ten-speed *n.* [C] a bicycle with ten GEARS

tent /tɛnt/ S3 *n.* [C] **1** a shelter consisting of a sheet of cloth supported by poles and ropes, used for camping or at an outdoor party or FESTIVAL: *We can **pitch our tent** (=put our tent up) over there.* → see also OXYGEN TENT **2** OFTEN HUMOROUS a very loose-fitting dress or BLOUSE [**Origin:** 1200–1300 Old French *tente*, from Latin *tenta*, from the past participle of *tendere* **to stretch**]

ten•ta•cle /'tɛntəkəl/ *n.* [C] **1** BIOLOGY one of the long thin parts of a sea creature such as an OCTOPUS which it uses for holding things **2 tentacles** [plural] DISAPPROVING the bad or harmful influence or effects that something has on someone or something else: *a terrorist network with worldwide tentacles*

ten•ta•tive /'tɛntət̬ɪv/ *adj.* **1** not definite or certain, because you may want to change your mind: *a tentative agreement* **2** having or showing a lack of confidence SYN **hesitant**: *a tentative smile* —**tentatively** *adv.*: *Our meeting is tentatively scheduled for 2 p.m. Monday.* —**tentativeness** *n.* [U]

tent 'city *n.* [C] a place where a lot of people live in tents because they have no other homes

ten•ter•hooks /'tɛntɚhʊks/ *n.* **on tenterhooks** nervous or excited because you are waiting to find something out or waiting for something to happen

tenth[1] /tɛnθ/ *adj.* 10th; next after the ninth: *October is the tenth month.*

tenth[2] *pron.* **the tenth** the 10th thing in a series: *Let's have dinner on the tenth* (=the 10th day of the month).

tenth[3] *n.* [C] 1/10; one of ten equal parts: ***a tenth of a** mile* | **one-tenth/two-tenths/three-tenths etc. (of sth)** *one-tenth of the nation's workforce*

ten•u•ous /'tɛnyuəs/ *adj.* **1** a tenuous situation or relationship is weak or uncertain and likely to change or end: *The connection between the two theories is tenuous.* **2** LITERARY very thin and easily broken —**tenuously** *adv.* —**tenuousness** *n.* [C]

ten•ure /'tɛnyɚ/ *n.* [U] **1** the right to stay permanently in a teaching job: *It's become much more difficult to get tenure at the university.* **2** FORMAL the period of time when someone has an important job: *The company has doubled in value during her tenure.* **3** LAW the legal right to live in a house or use a piece of land for a period of time

ten•ured /'tɛnyɚd/ *adj.* **1** a tenured teacher, PROFESSOR etc. has gained the right to stay permanently in a teaching job **2** a tenured position at a school, college, or university is one from which a teacher or PROFESSOR cannot be dismissed in most situations

'tenure-track *adj.* [only before noun] a tenure-track teaching position at a college or university is one which can lead to the person in that position getting tenure in the future

Ten•zing Nor•gay /ˌtɛnzɪŋ 'nɔrgeɪ/ (1914–1986) a Nepalese mountain climber and guide. He and Sir Edmund Hillary were the first people to reach the top of Mount Everest.

te•pee, teepee, tipi /'tipi/ *n.* [C] a round tent with a pointed top, used by some Native Americans [**Origin:** 1700–1800 Dakota Sioux *tipi*, from *ti* **to live in a place** + *pi* **to use for**]

tep•id /'tɛpɪd/ *adj.* **1** a tepid feeling, reaction etc. shows a lack of excitement or interest: *tepid praise* **2** tepid liquid is slightly warm, especially in an unpleasant way: *tepid coffee* → see also LUKEWARM —**tepidly** *adv.* —**tepidness** *n.* [U]

te•qui•la /tə'kilə/ *n.* [C,U] a strong alcoholic drink made in Mexico from the AGAVE plant [**Origin:** 1800–1900 Spanish *Tequila* area of Mexico]

ter•a•byte /'tɛrəˌbaɪt/ *n.* [C] COMPUTERS a unit for measuring the amount of information a computer can store or use, equal to about a TRILLION BYTES

ter•cen•ten•a•ry /ˌtɚsɛn'tɛnəri, tɚ'sɛnt̚nˌɛri/ *n.* *plural* **tercentenaries** [C] the day or year exactly 300 years after a particular event

Te•re•sa /tə'risə/**, Mother** → MOTHER TERESA

Te•resh•ko•va /ˌtɛrɪʃ'koʊvə/**, Val•en•ti•na** /ˌvælən'tinə/ (1937–) a Russian ASTRONAUT who was the first woman in space

ter•i•ya•ki /ˌtɛri'yɑki/ *n.* [U] a Japanese dish containing meat which has been kept in a liquid mixture before cooking, to give it a special taste —**teriyaki** *adj.* [only before noun] *teriyaki sauce*

term[1] /tɚm/ S1 W1 *n.* [C]
1 WORD/EXPRESSION [C] a word or expression that has a particular meaning, especially one that concerns a particular subject: *There are a lot of specialized terms in medicine.* | **+for** *"Multimedia" is the term for any technique combining sounds and images.* | **a medical/legal/scientific etc. term** *"Sub rosa" is the legal term for a secret agreement.* | **in general/broad/simple etc. terms** *We explain in simple terms what the treatment involves.* | **a term of endearment/respect/abuse etc.** (=a word or expression used to say you love someone, to show respect for someone etc.)
2 in terms of sth as far as something is concerned or only in relation to something: *In terms of quality ingredients, this is the best ice cream you can buy.* | **explain/**

T

describe/measure etc. sth in terms of sth *The program's results can be measured in terms of improved performance.* | **in terms of what/how/who etc.** *There are great differences among the children in terms of what they can do.*

3 in financial/artistic/psychological etc. terms if you describe or consider something in financial, artistic etc. terms, you are mainly interested in the financial, artistic etc. side of it: *Failure to solve the problem will be expensive in both financial and human terms.* | *Most people in the capital are wealthy,* ***in relative terms.*** | ***In real terms*** (=when the effects of other things such as inflation are considered), *average household income has dropped.*

4 come to terms with sth to accept a bad situation or event and not feel upset or angry about it anymore: *It took years for Rob to come to terms with his mother's death.*

5 come to terms (with sb) to reach an agreement or end an argument with someone: *Do you still think you can come to terms with them?*

6 think/talk in terms of doing sth to consider or discuss doing something, especially in a particular way: *We've got to think in terms of expanding the agency's services.*

7 in the long/short/near etc. term also **over the long/short/near etc. term** considered over a period from now until a long, short etc. time in the future: *Cutting staff may reduce costs in the short term.* → see also LONG-TERM, SHORT-TERM

T

8 on equal terms (with sb/sth) also **on the same terms (as sb/sth)** having the same advantages, rights, or abilities as anyone else: *Women are demanding to compete for jobs on equal terms with men.*

9 be on good/bad/friendly etc. terms (with sb) to have a good, bad, friendly etc. relationship with someone: +**with** *Tim's still on good terms with his ex-wife.*

10 INSTITUTION a period of time during which a government, court, or other official organization regularly meets: *The court's term runs from September to May.*

11 PRISON a period of time that someone must spend in prison: +**of** *a lengthy term of imprisonment* | **a prison/jail term** *Reynolds could get a prison term of up to 85 years.*

12 TIME DOING A JOB [C] a period of time for which someone is elected to an important government job: **a term of/in office** *Mayor Johnson announced that he would not seek another term of office.*

13 SCHOOL/COLLEGE [C] one of the periods that the school or college year is divided into: **summer/fall/winter/spring term** *He's been accepted at the college for the fall term.* → see also MIDTERM² (1), SEMESTER

14 CONDITIONS terms [plural] the conditions of an agreement, contract, legal document etc.: *These terms are completely unacceptable.* | +**of** *The terms of the agreement are still being negotiated.* | **according to/under the terms of sth** *Under the terms of the agreement, the debt would be repaid over 20 years.* | *Sign here to accept the various* ***terms and conditions.*** | *They were to borrow the money under very* ***favorable terms.***

15 PERIOD OF AGREEMENT [C] ECONOMICS the period of time that a contract, LOAN etc. continues for: *Officials now are trying to extend the term of the loan by two years.* | *My contract was for a* ***fixed term*** *of five years.*

16 in sb's terms according to one person's set of opinions: *In his terms, the play is not about black experience, but about human experience.*

17 on your (own) terms according to the conditions that you want or ask for: *Owens lived life on his own terms.*

18 terms of reference the agreed limits of what an official committee or report has been asked to study

19 HAVING A BABY [U] TECHNICAL the end of the period of time that a woman is PREGNANT: *Carrie's medical condition will make it hard to* ***carry*** *the baby* ***to term*** (=keep the baby until the normal time for it to be born).

20 NUMBER/SIGN [C] MATH one of the numbers or signs used in a mathematical calculation

[**Origin:** 1200–1300 Old French *terme* **edge, limit, end,** from Latin *terminus*] → see also **a contradiction in terms** at CONTRADICTION (3), **in glowing terms** at GLOWING (2), **be on speaking terms (with sb)** at SPEAK (10), **in no uncertain terms** at UNCERTAIN (3)

term² *v.* [T usually passive] **1** to use a particular word or expression to name or describe something: **term sb/sth (as) sth** *She apologized for what she termed "a dumb mistake."* | *The meeting could hardly be termed a success.* **2 be termed out of office** to have to leave a political position because the law says someone can be in that position for only a particular number of years

ter·mi·nal¹ /ˈtɚmənl/ Ac *adj.* **1** a terminal illness cannot be cured, and causes death: *terminal cancer* ►see THESAURUS box at **airport** **2 a terminal decline/decay** the state of becoming worse and worse, and never getting better **3 terminal boredom** HUMOROUS the feeling of being extremely bored **4** [only before noun] TECHNICAL existing at the end of something: *terminal buds* —**terminally** *adv.*: *terminally ill patients*

terminal² Ac *n.* [C] **1** a large building where people wait to get onto airplanes, buses, or ships, or where goods are loaded: *Baggage claim is in* ***the main terminal.*** | *They're building a new* ***passenger terminal.*** | **an air/a bus/a ferry/a rail terminal** *I'll take you to the bus terminal.* **2** COMPUTERS a piece of computer equipment consisting of at least a KEYBOARD and a screen, that you use for putting in or taking out information from a large computer: *a computer terminal* **3** PHYSICS one of the points at which you can connect wires in an electrical CIRCUIT

ˈterminal aˌdapter *n.* [C] COMPUTERS a piece of electronic equipment that allows information from one computer to be sent along special ISDN telephone lines to another computer

ˈterminal ˌside also **ˌterminal ˌside of an ˈangle** *n.* [C] MATH the side or line at which the measurement of an angle stops → see also INITIAL SIDE

ˌterminal veˈlocity *n.* [U] PHYSICS the highest speed that can be reached by an object falling down through the air. At this speed, air RESISTANCE stops any ACCELERATION.

ter·mi·nate /ˈtɚməˌneɪt/ Ac *v.* **1** [I,T] FORMAL if something terminates, or if you terminate it, it ends: *The contract terminates at the end of the year.* | *Doctors may* ***terminate a pregnancy*** *when the life of the mother is at risk.* **2** [T] FORMAL to remove someone from a job SYN **fire**: *Two of his co-workers were terminated.* **3** [T] INFORMAL to kill someone

ter·mi·na·tion /ˌtɚməˈneɪʃən/ Ac *n.* [C,U] **1** FORMAL the act of ending something, or the end of something: +**of** *the termination of his employment* **2** BIOLOGY a medical operation to end the life of a developing child before it is born SYN **abortion** **3** FORMAL the act of removing someone from a job SYN **dismissal**

ter·mi·nol·o·gy /ˌtɚməˈnɑlədʒi/ *n. plural* **terminologies** [C,U] ENG. LANG. ARTS the technical words or expressions that are used in a particular subject: *medical terminology* —**terminological** /ˌtɚmənəˈlɑdʒɪkəl◂/ *adj.*

ter·mi·nus /ˈtɚmənəs/ *n. plural* **termini** /-naɪ/ or **terminuses** [C] the station or stop at the end of a train line or bus service

ter·mite /ˈtɚmaɪt/ *n.* [C] an insect that eats and destroys wood from trees and buildings

ˈterm ˌlimit also **ˈterm limiˌtation** *n.* [C] a particular number of years that the law allows someone to stay in a particular political position

ˈterm ˌpaper *n.* [C] a long piece of written work by a school or college student, as the most important piece of work in a course

tern /tɚn/ *n.* [C] BIOLOGY a black and white sea bird that has long wings and a tail with two points

ter·na·ry /ˈtɚnəri/ *adj.* TECHNICAL consisting of three parts → see also BINARY

Ter·ra /ˈtɛrə/ the Roman name for the goddess Gaea

ter·race /ˈtɛrɪs/ *n.* [C] **1** a flat outdoor area next to a building or on a roof, where you can sit outside to eat, relax etc. **2** a flat area cut out of a slope, usually one in a series that rises up the slope, that is often used to grow crops [**Origin:** 1500–1600 Old French **pile of earth, terrace**, from Latin *terra* **earth, land**]

ter·raced /ˈtɛrɪst/ *adj.* [only before noun] a terraced field, slope, garden etc. has been cut into a series of flat areas along the side of the slope: *terraced rice fields*

ter·ra cot·ta, terracotta /ˌtɛrəˈkɑt̬ə◂/ *n.* [U] **1** hard reddish-brown baked CLAY **2** a reddish-brown color —**terra cotta** *adj.*

terra fir·ma /ˌtɛrə ˈfɚmə/ *n.* [U] USUALLY HUMOROUS land, rather than water or air: *We were glad to be back on terra firma again.*

ter·rain /təˈreɪn/ *n.* [C,U] EARTH SCIENCE a particular type of land: *rocky terrain*

ter·ra·pin /ˈtɛrəpɪn/ *n.* [C] a small TURTLE (=animal with four legs and a hard shell) that lives in water in warm areas

ter·rar·i·um /təˈrɛriəm/ *n. plural* **terraria** /-riə/ or **terrariums** [C] a large glass container that you grow plants in as a decoration

ter·res·tri·al /təˈrɛstriəl/ *adj.* **1** relating to the Earth, rather than the moon or other PLANETS → see also EXTRATERRESTRIAL[2] **2** EARTH SCIENCE living on or relating to land rather than water —**terrestrially** *adv.*

ter·ri·ble /ˈtɛrəbəl/ S1 W3 *adj.* **1** extremely severe in a way that causes harm or damage SYN **horrible**: *a terrible accident* ►see THESAURUS box at **horrible** **2** extremely bad SYN **awful**: *The movie was terrible.* | *I have a terrible memory.* ►see THESAURUS box at **bad**[1] **3** [not before noun] feeling sick SYN **awful**: *"How are you today?" "Terrible."* **4** [not before noun] feeling guilty or unhappy about something SYN **awful**: **feel terrible about (doing) sth** *I feel terrible about what happened.* **5** making you feel afraid, upset, or shocked: *a terrible noise* **6 the terrible twos** INFORMAL the period of time when a child is two years old and difficult to deal with [**Origin:** 1300–1400 Old French, Latin *terribilis*, from *terrere* **to frighten**]

ter·ri·bly /ˈtɛrəbli/ *adv.* **1** [+ adj./adv.] very SYN **extremely**: *I'm terribly sorry to have kept you waiting.* | *John's **not terribly** interested in school.* **2** very badly: *The team played terribly.*

ter·ri·er /ˈtɛriɚ/ *n.* [C] a small active type of dog that was originally used for hunting

ter·rif·ic /təˈrɪfɪk/ S3 *adj.* **1** very good, especially in a way that makes you feel happy and excited SYN **fantastic**: *That's a terrific idea.* | *Your dress looks terrific!* **2** very large in size or degree SYN **tremendous**: *a terrific bang*

ter·rif·i·cally /təˈrɪfɪkli/ *adv.* **1** [+ adj./adv.] very SYN **extremely** **2** very well

ter·ri·fied /ˈtɛrəˌfaɪd/ *adj.* very frightened: *a terrified old woman* | **+of** *The children were terrified of the dog.* | **+at** *They were terrified at the thought of getting caught.* | **terrified (that)** *We were terrified that the bridge would collapse.*

ter·ri·fy /ˈtɛrəˌfaɪ/ *v.* **terrifies, terrified, terrifying** [T] to make someone extremely afraid: *Speaking in public terrifies me.*

ter·ri·fy·ing /ˈtɛrəˌfaɪ-ɪŋ/ *adj.* extremely frightening: *a terrifying experience* —**terrifyingly** *adv.*

ter·rine /təˈrin, tɛ-/ *n.* [C,U] food made of cooked meat, fish, or fruit formed into a LOAF shape and served cold, or the dish this is served in

ter·ri·to·ri·al /ˌtɛrəˈtɔriəl◂/ *adj.* **1** [no comparative] relating to land that is owned or controlled by a particular country: *a territorial dispute* **2** BIOLOGY territorial animals closely guard the area of land that they consider to be their own —**territoriality** /ˌtɛrətɔriˈæləṭi/ *n.* [U]

territorial ˈwaters *n.* [plural] POLITICS the ocean near a country's coast, which that country has legal control over

ter·ri·to·ry /ˈtɛrəˌtɔri/ W3 *n. plural* **territories**
1 GOVERNMENT LAND [C,U] POLITICS land that is owned or controlled by a particular government, ruler, or military force: **U.S./British/Chinese etc. territory** *Hong Kong became Chinese territory again in 1997.* | **occupied/enemy/disputed/hostile etc. territory** *The plane was flying over enemy territory.* | *There is a narrow strip of **neutral territory** between the two countries.*
2 TYPE OF LAND [U] land of a particular type: *mountainous territory* | **uncharted/unexplored territory** *Chile is a country filled with unexplored territory.*
3 NOT A STATE [C] POLITICS land that belongs to a country, but is not a state, PROVINCE etc.: *The island of Guam is a U.S. territory.*
4 EXPERIENCE [U] a particular area of experience or knowledge: **familiar/unfamiliar/new/uncharted etc. territory** *We are moving into unfamiliar territory with this new software.*
5 ANIMAL/GROUP [C,U] BIOLOGY the area that an animal considers to be its own and will defend against others
6 come/go with the territory to be a natural and accepted part of a particular job, situation, place etc.: *Criticism comes with the territory when you're a public figure.*
7 BUSINESS [C,U] an area of business, especially in selling, for which someone is responsible: *a sales territory*
8 SPORT [U] the area of a field that a player or team is defending
[**Origin:** 1300–1400 Latin *territorium* **land around a town**, from *terra* **earth, land**]

ter·ror /ˈtɛrɚ/ *n.* **1** [U] a feeling of extreme fear: *She could see the terror in his eyes.* | *She screamed **in terror**.* | *We **lived in terror of** waking Dad when he was napping.* | *a moment of **sheer terror*** (=complete terror) ►see THESAURUS box at **fear**[1] **2** [U] violent action against ordinary people for political purposes SYN **terrorism**: *a campaign of terror* | *the war on terror* **3** [C] an event or situation that makes people feel extremely frightened, especially because they think they may die: **+of** *the terrors of war* **4** [C] INFORMAL a very annoying person, especially a child: *That Johnson kid's a real terror!* **5 hold no terrors for sb** FORMAL to not frighten or worry someone → see also **a holy terror** at HOLY (4), **reign of terror** at REIGN[1] (5), **strike terror/fear into sb's heart** at STRIKE[1] (26)

ter·ror·ism /ˈtɛrəˌrɪzəm/ *n.* [U] the use of violence such as bombing, shooting, or KIDNAPPING against ordinary people to obtain political demands SYN **terror**: *the continuing threat of international terrorism* | *a horrible **act of terrorism***

ter·ror·ist /ˈtɛrərɪst/ *n.* [C] someone who uses violence such as bombing, shooting etc. against ordinary people to obtain political demands → see also GUERRILLA —**terrorist** *adj.* [only before noun] *a terrorist attack* —**terroristic** /ˌtɛrəˈrɪstɪk◂/ *adj.*

ter·ror·ize /ˈtɛrəˌraɪz/ *v.* [T] to deliberately frighten people by threatening to harm them, especially so they will do what you want: *Drug dealers have been terrorizing the neighborhood.*

ter·ry·cloth /ˈtɛriˌklɔθ/ also **ter·ry** /ˈtɛri/ *n.* [U] a type of thick cotton cloth with uncut threads on both sides, used to make TOWELS etc.

terse /tɚs/ *adj.* a terse reply, message etc. uses very few words and often shows that you are annoyed —**tersely** *adv.* —**terseness** *n.* [U]

ter·ti·ar·y /ˈtɚʃiˌɛri, -ʃəri/ *adj.* TECHNICAL third in place, degree, or order

ˌtertiary ˌeconomic acˈtivity *n.* [C,U] ECONOMICS an economic activity in which a service is provided, for example operating a hotel or providing insurance, rather than producing goods or obtaining materials such as oil or coal from the ground → see also PRIMARY ECONOMIC ACTIVITY, SECONDARY ECONOMIC ACTIVITY

TESL /ˈtɛsəl/ *n.* [U] **teaching English as a second language** the activity of teaching English to people who live in a country where English is spoken, but who do not speak English as their first language

Tes·la /ˈtɛslə/**, Nik·o·la** /ˈnɪkələ/ (1856–1943) a U.S. scientist, born in Croatia, who discovered how to produce ALTERNATING CURRENT and made other important developments in electricity and radio

TESOL /ˈtisɔl/ *n.* [U] the teaching of English to speakers of other languages

tes·sel·la·tion /ˌtɛsəˈleɪʃən/ *n.* [C] MATH a pattern made of repeating shapes that fit exactly together

test¹ /tɛst/ S1 W1 *n.* [C]

1 KNOWLEDGE/ABILITY a set of questions, exercises, or practical activities to measure someone's skill, ability, or knowledge: *I have a test tomorrow.* | **+on** *You'll have a test on irregular verbs tomorrow.* | *Why didn't you have to* ***take the test?*** | **a math/French/biology etc. test** *How'd you do on your algebra test?* | **pass/fail a test** *Foreign students have to pass a language test.* | **a driving/swimming/reading etc. test** *I failed my driving test the first time.* | **an intelligence/memory/personality/aptitude test** *He scored high on intelligence tests.* | *Teachers are under pressure to improve* ***test scores.***

2 SUBSTANCE/OBJECT a) a scientific examination of a substance or object done in order to find out something: *a series of blood tests* | *an HIV test* | **+on** *tests on the hair from the scene of the crime* | **+for** *a test for chemicals in the water* | **run/carry out/do a test** *They ran tests on the manuscript in an attempt to date it.* | *Employees are required to* ***take a*** *drug* ***test.*** | *I'm still waiting for my* ***test results*** *from the hospital.* **b)** equipment used for carrying out a scientific or medical test: *a home pregnancy test*

3 BODY PART a medical examination of your body or a part of it to check if it is working well or not: *a hearing test*

4 DIFFICULT SITUATION [usually singular] a difficult situation in which the qualities of someone or something are clearly shown: *Dealing with adolescents can be a real test.* | **a test of character/strength/skill etc.** *It looks as though the meeting will be a test of wills.* | *The training sessions turned out to be an* ***endurance test.***

5 put sb/sth to the test to put someone or something into a situation that shows how good or effective they are: *It's time we put the theory to the test.*

6 MACHINE/PRODUCT a process used to find out whether equipment or a product works correctly or is safe: *nuclear weapons tests* | **+on** *tests on cosmetics* | *All the cars undergo rigorous* ***safety tests.*** | **test site/equipment/procedure** *NASA has improved its test procedures.*

7 STANDARD something that is used as a standard to judge or examine something else: **+of** *Profits are the ultimate test of a company's success.*

[**Origin:** 1300–1400 Old French **pot for testing metals**, from Latin *testum* **clay pot**] → see also BREATH TEST, MEANS TEST, **stand the test of time** at STAND¹ (7), TEST CASE

test² S1 W2 *v.*

1 SUBSTANCE/OBJECT [I,T] to scientifically examine a substance or object in order to find out something: **+for** *The kit is designed to test for HIV infection.* | **test sb/sth for sth** *The water should be tested for lead.* | *They tested her for diabetes.* ►see THESAURUS box at **check**¹

2 test positive/negative (for sth) to get a particular result when a medical test is done on you: *Half the team tested positive for steroids.*

3 BODY PART [T] MEDICINE to medically examine someone's body or a part of it to check if it is working well or not: *I need to get my eyes tested.*

4 KNOWLEDGE/ABILITY a) [T] to measure someone's skill, ability, or knowledge, using a test: *This section tests your mathematical skills.* | **test sb on sth** *Which chapters are you going to test us on?* **b) test well/badly/poorly** to perform well or badly on a test: *I don't test very well.*

5 MACHINE/PRODUCT [T] also **test out** to try using something to see if it works in the correct way: *The store began testing the machines last May.* | **test sth on sb/sth** *These cosmetics have not been tested on animals.*

6 SHOW HOW GOOD/STRONG [T] **a)** to show how good or strong someone's or something's qualities are, especially by putting them in a difficult situation: *The next six months will test your powers of leadership.* **b)** if something tests your patience, nerves, faith etc., it almost destroys your patience, sense of calm etc. because it is so hard to deal with: *Her son's death severely tested her religious faith.*

7 IDEA/PLAN [T] also **test out** to try an idea, plan, explanation etc. in order to find out if it is correct: *There was a comprehensive study to test the theory.*

8 test the waters to check people's reaction to a plan before you decide to do anything → see also **just testing** at JUST¹ (26), **tried and tested** at TRIED²

tes·ta·ment /ˈtɛstəmənt/ *n.* [C] FORMAL **1 a testament to sth** something that shows or proves something else very clearly: *The aircraft's safety record is a testament to its design.* **2** LAW a WILL → see also NEW TESTAMENT, OLD TESTAMENT

ˈtest ban *n.* [C] an agreement between countries to stop testing NUCLEAR WEAPONS

ˈtest case *n.* [C] LAW a legal case that establishes a particular principle and is then used as a standard which other similar cases can be judged against

ˈtest drive *n.* [C] an occasion when you drive a car to see if it works well or if you like it so that you can decide if you want to buy it —**test-drive** *v.* [T]

test·er /ˈtɛstɚ/ *n.* [C] **1** a person or piece of equipment that tests something **2** a small bottle of PERFUME, a tube of LIPSTICK etc., in a store, for customers to try

ˈtest-fly *v.* [T] to fly an aircraft to see if it operates in the correct way

tes·ti·cle /ˈtɛstɪkəl/ *n.* [C] BIOLOGY one of the two round organs that produce SPERM in a male, that are enclosed in a bag of skin below the PENIS —**testicular** /tɛˈstɪkyəlɚ/ *adj.*

tes·ti·fy /ˈtɛstəˌfaɪ/ W3 *v.* **testifies, testified, testifying 1** [I,T] LAW to make a formal statement of what is true, especially in a court of law: *Mr. Molto has agreed to testify at the trial.* | **+for/against** *Several witnesses testified against the officer.* | **+about** *You will be called to testify about what you saw.* | **testify that** *She testified that he had attacked her.* **2** [I,T] FORMAL to be a clear sign that something is true: **+to** *The empty stores testify to the depth of the recession.* **3** [I] to stand up and tell people about how God has helped you in your life

tes·ti·mo·ni·al /ˌtɛstəˈmoʊniəl/ *n.* [C] **1** something that is said or given to someone to show thanks, praise, or admiration, especially in front of other people: *Ed stood and* ***gave a testimonial to*** (=said nice things about) *his mother.* **2** a formal written statement describing someone's character and abilities **3** a favorable statement someone makes about a product, used especially in advertising to encourage other people to buy and use that product

tes·ti·mo·ny /ˈtɛstəˌmoʊni/ W3 *n. plural* **testimonies** [C,U] **1** LAW a formal statement that something is true, such as the one a WITNESS makes in a court of law: *His testimony was crucial to the prosecution's case.* ►see THESAURUS box at **court**¹ **2** a fact or situation that shows or proves something very clearly: **+to/of** *The results are a testimony to the coach's skill and hard work.*

ˈtesting ground *n.* [C] **1** a place where machines, cars etc. are tried to see if they work **2** a situation, place, or problem in which you can try new ideas and methods to see if they work

tes·tis /ˈtɛstɪs/ *n. plural* **testes** /-tiz/ [C] BIOLOGY a TESTICLE

ˈtest ˌmarket *n.* [C] a small area where a new product is sold to find out how people like it before it is sold everywhere else —**test-market** *v.* [T] *The new beer will be test-marketed in San Diego.*

tes·tos·ter·one /tɛˈstɑstəˌroʊn/ *n.* [U] BIOLOGY the HORMONE (=type of chemical substance) in males that gives them their male qualities

ˈtest ˌpattern *n.* [C] a pattern or picture that is shown on television when there are no programs

ˈtest ˌpilot *n.* [C] a pilot who flies new aircraft in order to test them

ˈtest run *n.* [C] an occasion when you try doing something or using something to make sure everything works before you really need to do or use it

test tube *n.* [C] SCIENCE a small glass container with a long narrow shape and a round bottom, used in science → see picture at LABORATORY

test-tube ˌbaby *n.* [C] NOT TECHNICAL a baby that started to develop from an egg removed from a woman's body, that was then put back inside the woman to continue developing

tes·ty /ˈtɛsti/ *adj. comparative* **testier**, *superlative* **testiest** impatient and easily annoyed —**testily** *adv.* —**testiness** *n.* [U]

tet·a·nus /ˈtɛtˀn-əs, -nəs/ *n.* [U] MEDICINE a serious illness caused by BACTERIA that enter your body through cuts and wounds and make your muscles, especially your jaw, become stiff

tête-à-tête¹ /ˌteɪt̬ ə ˈteɪt, ˌtɛt̬ ə ˈtɛt/ *n.* [C] a private conversation between two people

tête-à-tête² *adv.* [only after verb] if two people meet, speak, or eat tête-à-tête, they are together in private

teth·er¹ /ˈtɛðɚ/ *n.* [C] **1** a rope or chain that something, especially an animal, is tied to so that it can only move around within a limited area **2 be at the end of your tether** to be so worried, tired etc., that you feel you cannot deal with a difficult or upsetting situation

tether² *v.* [T + to] to tie something, especially an animal, to a post so that it can only move around within a limited area

teth·er·ball /ˈtɛðɚˌbɔl/ *n.* [U] a game in which two people hit a ball hanging by a rope from the top of a pole in opposite directions to see who can make the rope wrap all the way around the pole first

Te·ton Range, the /ˈtitɑn ˌreɪndʒ/ also **the Tetons** a RANGE of mountains in the northwestern U.S. that is part of the Rocky Mountains and is in the states of Idaho and Wyoming

tetra- /tɛtrə/ *prefix* having four of something: *a tetrahedron*

tet·ra·cy·cline /ˌtɛtrəˈsaɪklin/ *n.* [U] a type of ANTIBIOTIC (=medicine)

tet·ra·he·dron /ˌtɛtrəˈhidrən/ *n.* [C] MATH a solid shape with four sides that are shaped like TRIANGLES

Teu·ton /ˈtutˀn/ HISTORY a member of one of the ancient German tribes of northwestern Europe

Teu·ton·ic /tuˈtɑnɪk/ *adj.* **1** HISTORY relating to the ancient Germanic peoples of northwestern Europe: *Teutonic mythology* **2** HUMOROUS having qualities that are thought to be typical of German people: *Teutonic efficiency*

Tex·as /ˈtɛksəs/ a large state in the southern U.S., on the border of Mexico —**Texan** *n., adj.*

Texas toast *n.* [U] a type of TOAST (=heated bread) that is very large and thick

Texas ˌWar for Indeˈpendence, the also **ˌTexas Revoˈlution, the** HISTORY the successful attempt by people in Texas to gain INDEPENDENCE from Mexico in 1835–1836

Tex-Mex /ˌtɛks ˈmɛks◂/ *adj.* INFORMAL relating to the music, cooking etc. of Mexican-American people in Texas, or the Southwest in general: *a Tex-Mex restaurant* —**Tex-Mex** *n.* [U]

text¹ /tɛkst/ Ac S2 W2 *n.* **1** [U] the writing in a book, magazine etc. rather than the pictures or notes, or any written material: *a single column of text* | *I only edit the text, not the artwork.* **2** [C] ENG. LANG. ARTS a book or other piece of writing that is related to learning or intended for study: *religious texts* **3** a textbook: *a chemistry text* **4 the text of sth** the exact words of a speech, article etc.: *Newspapers printed **the full text of** the speech.* **5** [C] a written message sent using a CELL PHONE SYN **text message** ►see THESAURUS box at **cell phone** **6** [C] a short piece from the Bible that someone reads and talks about during a religious service [**Origin:** 1300–1400 Old French *texte*, from Latin *textus* **woven material**]

text² *v.* [I,T] to send someone a written message using a CELL PHONE SYN **text message**: *I'll text you later.* —**texting** *n.* [U]

text·book¹ /ˈtɛkstbʊk/ *n.* [C] a book that contains information about a subject that people study: *a biology textbook* ►see THESAURUS box at **book¹**

textbook² *adj.* [only before noun] done or happening exactly as something should be done or as it should happen: **a textbook case/example** *The project was a textbook case of the value of basic research.*

tex·tile /ˈtɛkstaɪl/ *n.* **1** [C] a word used mainly in business for woven material that is made in large quantities: *textiles such as silk and cotton* | **textile industry/market etc.** *a textile manufacturer* **2 textiles** [plural] the industry that makes cloth

ˈtext ˌmessage¹ *n.* [C] a written message sent using a CELL PHONE SYN **text** ►see THESAURUS box at **cell phone**

text message² *v.* [I,T] to send someone a written message using a CELL PHONE SYN **text** —**text messaging** *n.* [U]

ˈtext ˌstructure *n.* [C,U] ENG. LANG. ARTS the way in which a writer organizes a piece of writing

tex·tu·al /ˈtɛkstʃuəl, -tʃəl/ Ac *adj.* ENG. LANG. ARTS relating to the way that a book, magazine etc. is written: *a detailed textual analysis of the stories*

tex·ture /ˈtɛkstʃɚ/ *n.* [C,U] **1** the way a surface, substance, or material feels when you touch it, and how smooth or rough it looks: *a rough texture* | *the grainy texture of the film* | +**of** *the smooth texture of silk* **2** the degree of solidness, wetness etc. that a substance, particularly food, has: *a soft cheese with a creamy texture* | *The pudding is very light **in texture**.* **3** ENG. LANG. ARTS the way the different parts are combined in a piece of writing, music, art etc. in order to affect you in a particular way: *the rich texture of Shakespeare's English* —**textural** *adj.* —**texturally** *adv.* → see also -TEXTURED

tex·tured /ˈtɛkstʃɚd/ *adj.* **1** having a surface that is not smooth: *textured stockings* **2** having many different parts that are combined to produce a particular effect: *richly textured storytelling*

-textured /tɛkstʃɚd/ *suffix* [in adjectives] **coarse-textured/smooth-textured/fine-textured etc.** having a particular type of texture

ˌtextured ˌvegetable ˈprotein *n.* [U] a substance made from beans, that can be used in cooking instead of meat

TGIF *interjection* **thank God it's Friday** used to say that you are glad the WORKWEEK is almost finished

-th /θ/ *suffix* **1** forms ORDINAL numbers, except with those that end with 1, 2, or 3: *the 17th of June* | *a fifth of the total* → see also -ND, -RD, -ST **2** OLD USE or BIBLICAL another form of the SUFFIX -ETH: *he doth* (=does)

Thack·er·ay /ˈθækəri/, **Wil·liam Make·peace** /ˈwɪlyəm ˈmeɪkpis/ (1811–1863) a British writer of NOVELS

Thad·de·us /ˈθædiəs/ in the Bible, one of the 12 APOSTLES, also called Jude

Thai·land /ˈtaɪlænd/ a country in Southeast Asia, north of Malaysia and east of Myanmar. Before 1949, Thailand was called Siam. —**Thai** *n., adj.*

thal·a·mus /ˈθæləməs/ *n.* [C] BIOLOGY the area of the brain that is used to organize the information from your eyes, ears etc.

tha·lid·o·mide, Thalidomide /θəˈlɪdəˌmaɪd/ *n.* [U] a drug given to people to make them calm, used in the past until it was discovered that it harmed the development of the arms and legs of unborn babies

thal·li·um /ˈθæliəm/ *n.* [U] SYMBOL **Tl** CHEMISTRY a soft metal ELEMENT (=basic substance) that is very poisonous

Thames, the /tɛmz/ a river in England that flows from the west through London

than¹ /ðən; *strong* ðæn/ S1 W1 *conjunction* **1** used to introduce the phrase that represents the second person

T

or thing in a comparison: *He's stronger than I am.* | *It's a nice car, but it costs* ***more than*** *we want to pay.* | *We earned* ***less*** *this year* ***than*** *in previous years.* **2 would rather/sooner... than...** used to say that you prefer one thing to another: *I'd rather drive than take the subway.* **3 no sooner had/was etc. ... than...** also **hardly had/was etc. ... than...** used to say that something had just happened when something else happened: *No sooner had I gotten into the house than the phone rang.* [**Origin:** Old English *thanne, thænne*] → see also **other than** at OTHER[1] (8), **rather than** at RATHER (1)

WORD CHOICE as, than
In spoken and informal English, many people use object pronouns such as "me," "him" etc. after **than**: *Doris is older than me*. Many teachers think this is incorrect. They say that the form of the pronoun that follows **than** should depend on whether it is the subject or object of a verb (even when the verb is not there): *Doris is older than I* (=than I am). | *The news upset my wife more than me* (=than it upset me). In informal speech, we often use object pronouns such as "me," "her," "him" etc. before words like **as**, **than**, and **be** when making comparisons: *He's a lot older than her.* | *You got the same grade as me.* In written or formal English, it is better to use subject pronouns such as "I," "she," "he" etc.: *The other players are as good as he.* | *My daughter is more beautiful than I.*

T

than² S1 W1 *prep.* **1** used to introduce the second person or thing in a comparison: *My brother is easier to get along with than my sister.* | *She says she feels a little better than yesterday.* | *Repairing the machine is cheaper than buying a new one.* | *Your job is* ***more*** *exciting* ***than*** *mine.* | *Women were often paid* ***less than*** *men.* **2 more/less/fewer etc. than** used to say that a number or amount is over or under a particular figure: *If it costs more than $60, I won't buy it.* | *She's leaving in less than a week.* **3 more/less...than** used to say that one description is more correct than another: *She was more upset than angry.* | *The words were less a request than an order.* **4** used with some words such as "else" or "other" to mean "except" or "besides": *Do you speak any language other than English?*

thang /θæŋ/ *n.* [C usually singular] SLANG a humorous way of saying "thing"

thank /θæŋk/ S1 W3 *v.* [T] **1** to tell someone that you are pleased and grateful for something they have done, or to be polite about it: *I haven't had a chance to thank him yet.* | **thank sb for (doing) sth** *Did you thank Aunt Edith for the present?* | *He thanked us all for coming.* **2 have sb to thank (for sth) a)** used when saying who is responsible for something good that has happened **b)** used when saying who you blame for something bad that has happened: *It looks like we have Sheila to thank for this little mix-up.*

SPOKEN PHRASES
3 thank goodness/heavens/God said to show that you are very glad about something: *Thank goodness final exams are over.* | **+for** *Thank heavens for email!* **4 thank your lucky stars (that)** used to tell someone that they are very lucky, especially because they have avoided a bad or dangerous situation: *Thank your lucky stars the boy wasn't seriously hurt.* **5 you'll thank me (for sth)** used to tell someone not to be annoyed with you for doing or saying something, because it will be helpful to them later **6 I'll thank you (not) to do sth** FORMAL used to tell someone in an angry way not to do something

[**Origin:** Old English *thancian*] → see also THANK YOU

thank·ful /ˈθæŋkfəl/ *adj.* [not before noun] grateful and glad about something that has happened, especially because without it the situation would be much worse: **+for** *We really have a lot to be thankful for.* | **thankful (that)** *I was just thankful that it didn't rain.* | **thankful to do/be sth** *He felt thankful to be alive.* —**thankfulness** *n.* [U]

thank·ful·ly /ˈθæŋkfəli/ *adv.* **1** [sentence adverb] used to say that you are glad that something has happened, especially because a difficult situation has ended or been avoided: *Thankfully, there were no injuries.* **2** feeling grateful and glad about something, especially because a difficult situation has ended or been avoided

thank·less /ˈθæŋklɪs/ *adj.* **1** a thankless job is difficult and you do not get any praise for doing it: **a thankless role/task/work** *Being a parent can seem like a thankless task.* **2** LITERARY a thankless person is not grateful SYN **ungrateful**

thanks¹ /θæŋks/ *interjection* INFORMAL
1 GRATEFUL used to tell someone that you are grateful for something they have given to you or done for you SYN **thank you**: *Could you hold the door for me? Thanks.* | **+for** *Thanks for dinner – it was delicious.* | **thanks for doing sth** *It was good to talk to you. Thanks for calling.*
2 thanks a lot also **thanks a bunch** INFORMAL **a)** used to tell someone that you are very grateful for something they have given you or done for you: *Thanks a lot for the ride.* **b)** used when you are annoyed about something and do not really mean thank you at all: *"I forgot to bring your money." "Well, thanks a lot!"*
3 OFFER used as a polite way of accepting something that someone has offered you: *"More coffee?" "Oh, thanks."*
4 COMPLIMENT used as a polite way of reacting when someone has said something nice to you: *"I like your haircut." "Thanks."*
5 no, thanks used to say politely that you do not want something: *"Do you want to dance?" "No, thanks. I'm kind of tired."*
6 QUESTION used when politely answering someone's question about how you or your family are doing: *"Hi, Bill, how are you?"* ***"Fine, thanks."***
7 thanks for nothing used to tell someone in an angry or humorous way that they have not helped you

thanks² *n.* [plural] **1** the things you say or do to show that you are grateful to someone: *a letter of thanks* | *He left without* ***a word of thanks***. | *Let us* ***give thanks to*** *God.* **2 thanks to sb a)** used to say that something good has happened because of someone or something: *We've raised $50,000, thanks to everyone's generosity.* **b)** used to thank a person or organization for doing something very helpful or useful: **many/special thanks to sb** *Many thanks to Ron for such an interesting evening.* **c)** used to say angrily or humorously that someone or something has caused a problem: *Thanks to Ted, I've got to work late again.* **3 no thanks to sb/sth** SPOKEN in spite of what someone or something did or did not do: *We managed to win, no thanks to you.*

Thanks·giv·ing /ˌθæŋksˈgɪvɪŋ/ *n.* **1** [C,U] also **Thanksˈgiving ˌDay** a holiday in the U.S. and Canada when families have a large meal together to be thankful for food, health, families etc., and to celebrate the time when the people who first came to North America from England were saved from dying by Native Americans who gave them food and showed them how to grow crops. In the U.S., the holiday is in November and in Canada, it is in October. **2** [U] the period of time just before and after this day: *Where are you going for Thanksgiving?*

thanks·giv·ing /ˌθæŋksˈgɪvɪŋ/ *n.* [C,U] an expression of thanks to God

ˈthank you S1 *interjection*
1 GRATEFUL used to tell someone that you are grateful for something they have given to you or done for you SYN **thanks**: *"Mommy, this is for you!" "Thank you, Jenny."* | **+for** *Thank you for the letter.* | **thank you for doing sth** *Thank you for helping me last week.*
2 COMPLIMENT used as a polite way of reacting when someone has said something nice to you: *"That's a beautiful outfit." "Thank you."*
3 OFFER used as a polite way of saying that you would like something that someone has offered: *"Can I give you a ride home?" "Oh, thank you."*
4 no, thank you used to say politely that you do not want something: *"Can I help?" "No, thank you, I'm almost finished."*
5 QUESTION used when politely answering someone's

question about how you or your family are: *"How are you feeling today?" "Much better, thank you."* **6** ANNOYED used at the end of a sentence when telling someone firmly that you do not want their help or advice and are slightly annoyed by it: *I can do it myself, thank you.*

thank-you *n.* [C] something you say or do in order to thank someone: *She baked them some cookies as a thank-you.* —**thank-you** *adj.* [only before noun] *a thank-you note*

Tharp /θɑrp/, **Twy·la** /ˈtwaɪlə/ (1941–) a U.S. dancer and CHOREOGRAPHER of modern dance and BALLET

that¹ /ðæt/ S1 W1 *pron.* **1** *plural* **those** /ðoʊz/ used to talk about a person, thing, idea etc. that has already been mentioned or is already known about: *Don't worry about that.* | *She's really funny – that's why I like her so much.* | *I'm not sure why she'd want to marry a man like that.* | *Those were her exact words.* | *"I have to go," she said, and* ***with that*** (=after doing that) *she hung up the phone.* **2** *plural* **those** /ðoʊz/ used to talk about someone or something that is farther from you than someone or something else or that is nearer to the person you are talking to than to you, especially when you are looking or pointing at them: *Is that my pen?* | *Our tomatoes never get as big as those.* | *Who was that you were talking to?* | *That's a cute dress you're wearing.* **3** /ðət/ used after a noun as a RELATIVE PRONOUN like "who," "whom," or "which" to introduce a CLAUSE: *Here's a list of the things that we still need to do.* | *What's the name of the girl that works with Ron?* | *Josh is the one that she used to live with.* | **the year/time etc. that** *I'll never forget the day that she was born.* | *Do you know the* ***reason that*** *Paul canceled the meeting?* → see Word Choice box at WHICH, WHO **4** used to introduce a CLAUSE after a noun phrase that contains a SUPERLATIVE or a word such as "first" or "only": *Trina's the nicest person that I've ever met.* | *The only thing that matters to him is money.* **5** *plural* **those** /ðoʊz/ FORMAL used when talking about a particular thing of a particular type or kind: +**of** *His own experience is different from that of his friends.* **6 those** [plural] used to talk about a particular type of people: *There are those who still insist the world is flat.* **7 that is (to say)** used to correct a statement or give more exact information about something: *I loved him – that is, I thought I did.*

SPOKEN PHRASES

8 that's it a) said when something is complete, completely finished, or unable to be changed: *That's it, then. There's nothing more we can do.* **b)** also **that does it** said when you are angry about a situation and you do not want it to continue: *That does it – I'm leaving.* **c)** said in order to tell someone that they are doing something correctly **9 that's that** said when something is completely finished or when a decision will not be changed: *We're offering $2,700, and that's that.* **10 that's life/men/politics etc.** used to say that something is typical of a particular situation, group of people etc.: *I guess I made a mistake, but hey, that's life.* **11 that's all there is to it a)** used to emphasize that something is true and cannot be changed: *She's smarter than me and that's all there is to it.* **b)** said to emphasize that something is easy to do **12 at that** said to give more information about something mentioned before: *She's pregnant and having twins at that!*

[**Origin:** Old English *thæt*] → see also THIS

GRAMMAR

In informal speech or writing, **that** is often not used at the beginning of clauses that follow a verb, noun, or adjective, especially when the subject of the main clause and the **that** clause are the same: *He says he's going to come next week* (instead of: *He says that he...*). | *I was sick – that's the reason I didn't come* (instead of: *...the reason that I...*). | *I'm sorry I can't help you* (instead of: *I'm sorry that I...*). In more formal speech and writing, **that** is used more often: *Authorities suspect that one man died in the fire.* | *New research shows that reading to children from birth improves intellectual development.*

that² /ðæt/ S1 W1 *determiner plural* **those** /ðoʊz/ **1** used to talk about someone or something that is farther from you than someone or something else or that is nearer to the person you are talking to than to you, especially when you are looking or pointing at them: *No, I wanted that one over there.* | *Who's that man in the car?* | *Those shoes are prettier than these.* **2** used to talk about a person, thing, idea etc. that has already been mentioned or is already known about: *I saw that woman again today.* | *That last test was a lot easier than this one.* | *They met again later that year.* | *What did you do with those sandwiches?* → see also THIS

that³ /ðət; *strong* ðæt/ S1 W1 *conjunction* **1** used after verbs, nouns, and adjectives to introduce a CLAUSE that tells what someone says or thinks, or which states a fact, gives a reason etc.: *She says that she'll come.* | *Are you sure that they live on Park Lane?* | *I can't believe that she told you.* | **it is surprising/interesting/lucky etc. that** *It's disappointing that we lost.* **2 a) so big/tall etc. that...** very big, very tall etc. with the result that something happens or someone does something: *I was so scared that I almost wet my pants.* **b) such a big man/such a tall house etc. that...** a very big man, a very tall house etc. with the result that something happens or someone does something: *It was such a bad snowstorm that they shut the airport down.* **3** FORMAL in order that, or so that something may happen or someone may do something: *We pray that he may recover soon.* **4** FORMAL used at the beginning of a CLAUSE to make it a noun that can be used, for example, as the subject of a sentence: *That he talked about it to reporters surprises me.* **5** LITERARY used when you wish that something would happen, that you could do something etc.: *Oh, that Mother were alive to see this.* → see also **so (that)** at SO² (2)

that⁴ /ðæt/ S2 *adv.* [+ adj./adv.] SPOKEN **1 that long/many/big etc. a)** used to say how long, how many etc., especially because you are showing the size, number etc. with your hands: *The fish was about that long.* **b)** [usually in negatives and questions] as much as long, many etc. as something really is or as someone has said, when the degree or the amount is great: *I didn't know the situation was that bad.* | *Is it really going to cost that much?* **2 not (all) that much/long/big etc.** not very much, long etc.: *The show isn't all that funny.*

thatch /θætʃ/ *n.* **1** [C,U] STRAW, leaves, or REEDS used to make a roof, or a roof made of this **2** [singular] HUMOROUS a thick messy pile of hair on someone's head

thatched /θætʃt/ *adj.* made with dried STRAW, REEDS, leaves etc.: *a thatched roof* —**thatch** *v.* [I,T]

Thatch·er /ˈθætʃɚ/, **Mar·garet** /ˈmɑrgrɪt/ (1925–) a British politician who was the U.K.'s first woman Prime Minister, from 1979 until 1990

thaw¹ /θɔ/ *v.* **1** also **thaw out** [I,T] if ice or snow thaws or if warm weather thaws it, it becomes warmer and turns into water **2** also **thaw out** [I,T] if frozen food thaws or you thaw it, it unfreezes until it is ready to cook **3** also **thaw out** [I,T] if your body or a part of it thaws or you thaw it, it gets warmer again after having been extremely cold **4** [I] to become friendlier and less formal or serious

thaw² *n.* **1** [C] an improvement in relations between two countries after a period of opposition: *the thaw in East-West tensions* **2** [singular] a period of warm weather during which snow and ice melt

the¹ /ðə; *before a vowel* ði; *strong* ði/ S1 W1 *determiner* **1** used to talk about a particular person or thing that has already been mentioned, is already known about, or is the only one anywhere or in a particular situation: *Here's one shoe, but where's the other one?* | *Be sure to ask the doctor about that spot.* | *Where is the lowest point on Earth?* | *The Earth moves around the sun.* → see also A **2** used when you are saying which person or thing you mean: *That's the guy I was telling you about.* | *the house with a red door* | *I prefer the blue one.* **3** used before nouns that describe actions and changes when they are followed by "of": *the death of his*

T

mother | *the arrival of guests* | *the cleaning of hotel rooms* **4** used to talk about a person or a thing that is part of our natural environment or part of daily life: *We'll have to finish this in the morning.* | *What's the weather like in Singapore?* | *I heard it on the radio.* **5** used to talk about a part of someone's body: *She kissed him right on the lips* (=his lips). | *How's the arm* (=your arm)*?* | *diseases of the liver* **6** used as part of the names of some countries and areas, and in the names of oceans, mountain ranges, rivers, groups of islands, and some deserts: *the United States* | *the Pacific Ocean* **7** used before an adjective to make it into a noun when you are talking about or showing all the people who that adjective describes: *a school for the deaf* | *She devoted her life to helping the poor.* | *wars between the English and the French* **8** used before a plural noun to talk about or show a particular kind of thing: *How late are the stores open tonight?* | *The winters in California are very mild.* **9** used before a singular noun to talk about a particular type of person or thing in a general way: *The tiger is a beautiful animal.* | *The computer has changed people's lives.* **10** used before talking about or showing a particular date: *the third of October* | *Could we meet again on the 12th?* **11** used to talk about or show a period of time, especially one that continues for ten or a hundred years: *the war years* | *fashions of the '70s* (=the 1970s) | *political change in the early 1900s* **12** used to form a phrase that tells when something happened: *The day I left Uganda my troubles started.* | *He had been hired the previous year.* **13** used before a noun, especially in negative sentences to show an amount or degree needed for a particular purpose: **the sth (to do sth)** *I don't have the time to answer all these questions.* | *We wanted to ask but we didn't have the courage.* | **the sth for sth** *Does he have the experience for this job?* **14** used before the names of musical instruments when talking about the activity of playing them: *He plays the violin.* **15** a particular type of sport or a sports event: *Who won the long jump?* **16** used to talk about some types of entertainment: *They often go to the opera.* **17 the flu/the measles/the mumps etc.** used before the names of certain common illnesses: *I got the chickenpox from my brother.* **18** used before an adjective to make it into a noun when you are talking about or showing a situation that that adjective describes: *I'm afraid you're asking for the impossible.* **19** used to talk about measurements and amounts when describing how something is calculated, sold etc.: *They sell fabric by the yard.* | *We get paid by the hour.* | *My car gets over 30 miles to the gallon.* **20** INFORMAL used before the name of a thing that represents a particular activity: *He's let **the bottle*** (=drinking alcohol) *ruin his life.* | *Ever since the accident she's been afraid to **get behind the wheel*** (=drive a car). **21** used before the name of a family in the plural to talk about all the members of that family: *our neighbors the Dunbars* **22** used in titles after names that tell how someone is different from other people with the same name: *Peter the Great* | *Pliny the Younger* **23** SPOKEN said with strong pronunciation before a noun to show that it is the best, most famous etc. person or thing of its kind: *"Her friend is Julia Roberts." "Not the Julia Roberts?"* | *Paris is the city for romance.* **24** SPOKEN said before a word that describes someone or something when you are angry, JEALOUS, surprised etc.: *He lost his keys, the idiot!* **25** SPOKEN used after "what," "why" etc. in many expressions showing surprise or anger: *What the heck was that?*
[**Origin:** Old English]

GRAMMAR

- Do not use **the** with uncountable or plural nouns when you are using the general sense of the noun: *My favorite food is ice cream.* | *Glen really likes dogs.*
- Use **the** with uncountable or plural nouns when you mean a particular thing or a particular group of things: *The ice cream we bought yesterday tastes funny.* | *Did you see the dogs in that window?*
- Use **the** if you are mentioning specific things that are already known to the reader or listener: *I'm sorry. I gave the dress to Maggie.*
- Also use **the** before a noun that is followed by a phrase that says more specifically what type of thing you mean: *The life of an artist is not always easy.* | *This is the best steak I've ever eaten.*
- DO NOT use **the** in the following situations (unless there is extra information that tells specifically which thing you are talking about):

1. With many times of day and night and names of days, months etc., especially after "at," "by," and "on": *at noon* | *We'll be there by dawn.* | *on Tuesday* (but: *during the night* | *Let's have dinner on the Tuesday after next.*)
2. When you are talking about meals, especially after "at," "before," "during," "after," "for," and the verb "have": *We'll do it after dinner.* | *What's for lunch?* | *We had breakfast in bed.* (but: *The dinner we had at Marcia's house was delicious.*)
3. In many fixed expressions such as: *by car/bus etc.* | *at school/college etc.* | *to bed/jail/church etc.* | *arm in arm* | *from beginning to end*
4. With names of languages and most diseases: *She speaks Norwegian.* | *My father has cancer.*
5. With most names of streets, places, countries, mountains, people, businesses etc.: *Pine Street* | *I'm flying into O'Hare airport.* | *South Korea* | *Florida* | *Mount Fuji* | *Let's eat at Burger King.* However, some such names always contain **the**, especially the names of countries that are plural: *the United States* | *Russ is staying at the Hilton.*

- Use **the** before the names of rivers, oceans, and groups of mountains: *the Mississippi* | *the Indian Ocean* | *the Himalayas.*

the² S3 *adv.* **1 the more/the faster etc. ..., the more/less/faster etc.** used to show that two things increase or change together, in a connected way: *The more I thought about the idea, the more I liked it.* | *"When do you want this done?" "The sooner the better."* **2** used before the SUPERLATIVE form of adjectives and adverbs to emphasize that something is as big, good etc. as it is possible to be: *Frieda likes you the best.* | *Which is the least expensive?* **3** used before the COMPARATIVE form of adjectives and adverbs to show that someone or something has more or less of a particular quality than before: **the better/the worse** *America will be the better for these changes.* | *They replaced the painting with a copy and the public was **none the wiser*** (=not realizing what has happened).

the- /θi/ *prefix* another form of the PREFIX THEO-

the·a·ter S2 W2, **theatre** /ˈθiət̬ɚ/ *n.*
1 PLACE FOR PLAYS [C] a building or place with a stage where plays are performed: *an open-air theater* | *the Orpheum Theatre*

THESAURUS

Types of performance
play a story that is performed by actors
musical a play that uses singing and dancing to help tell the story, as well as talking
opera a musical play in which all the words are sung rather than spoken
ballet/dance a performance given by dancers
concert a performance given by musicians or singers

At the theater
box office the place where tickets are sold
balcony the higher level of seats, upstairs
program a small book that describes what will happen at a performance and includes information about the performers
intermission a time when the performance stops for a short time and people can talk or have a drink
stage the raised part at the front of the theater where the performance takes place
orchestra pit the place below the stage where the musicians sit

2 PLACE FOR MOVIES [C] a building where movies are shown SYN **movie theater**
3 PLAYS [U] **a)** plays as a form of entertainment: *the history of American theater* | *People want **good theater***

(=plays of high quality) *at reasonable prices.* **b)** the work of acting in, writing, or organizing plays: *Reed began his career* ***in the theater*** *in 1957.*
4 WAR [C] a large area where a war is being fought: **a theater of war/operations etc.** *the Pacific theater of war during World War II*
5 HOSPITAL [C] a special room in a hospital where people can watch a medical operation being done
[**Origin:** 1300–1400 Old French *theatre*, from Latin, from Greek *theatron*, from *theasthai* **to watch**]

the·a·ter·go·er /'θiətɚˌgoʊɚ/ *n.* [C] someone who regularly watches plays at the theater

theater-in-the-'round *n.* [U] the performance of a play on a central stage with the people watching sitting in a circle around it

the·a·tre /'θiətɚ/ *n.* [C] another spelling of THEATER

the·at·ri·cal /θi'ætrɪkəl/ *adj.* **1** ENG. LANG. ARTS relating to the performing of plays: *a theatrical troupe* **2** ENG. LANG. ARTS relating to movies that are shown in theaters rather than on television: *the movie's* ***theatrical release*** (=to be shown in theaters) **3** behaving in a loud or very noticeable way that is intended to get people's attention SYN **dramatic** —**theatrically** /-kli/ *adv.*

the·at·ri·cals /θi'ætrɪkəlz/ *n.* [plural] performances of plays

the·at·rics /θi'ætrɪks/ *n.* [plural] behavior that is very loud or noticeable and intended to get people's attention

thee /ði/ *pron.* OLD USE the OBJECT form of THOU SYN **you**

theft /θɛft/ *n.* **1** [U] the crime of stealing: *He was charged with auto theft.* ►see THESAURUS box at **crime** **2** [C] an act of stealing something: *Most of the thefts occurred at night.* | **+of** *the theft of $200 from the office* → see also THIEF

their /ðɚ; *strong* ðɛr/ S1 W1 *possessive adj.* [possessive form of "they"] **1** belonging or relating to the people, animals, or things that have been mentioned or are known about: *Bill and Sue and their two boys* | *I love koala bears – their faces are so cute.* | *The buildings had all their windows smashed.* **2** used to avoid saying "his" or "her" in relation to words like "anyone," "no one," "everyone" etc.: *Everyone has their own room.*
[**Origin:** 1100–1200 Old Norse *theirra* **theirs**]

GRAMMAR **they, them, themselves, their, theirs**

In spoken and informal English, it is very common for people to use **they, them, themselves, their**, or **theirs** to talk about a singular noun or a singular pronoun such as "anyone" or "everyone." This is especially common when it is not clear whether they are speaking about men or women or both: *If a student needs help, I am always happy to talk to them.* | *Someone left their umbrella in the closet.* Many teachers do not approve of using these pronouns in this way. They suggest using "he or she," "him or her," "his or her" etc.: *Someone left his or her umbrella in the closet.*

theirs /ðɛrz/ S3 *possessive pron.* [possessive form of "they"] **1** the thing or things belonging to or relating to the people or things that have been mentioned or are known about: *Our report was better than theirs.* | *These are our books. Theirs are over there.* **2** used to avoid saying "his" or "hers" in relation to words like "anyone," "no one," "everyone" etc.: *Everyone wants what is theirs.* → see also HIS

the·ism /'θiɪzəm/ *n.* [U] TECHNICAL **1** belief in the existence of one God **2** belief in the existence of a god or gods —**theistic** /θi'ɪstɪk/ *adj.* —**theistically** /-kli/ *adv.*

them¹ /ðəm, əm; *strong* ðɛm/ S1 W1 *pron.* **1** the object form of "they": *I looked for my keys but couldn't find them.* | *We lent them our car.* | *The puppies were so cute I wanted to buy them all.* **2** used to avoid saying "him" or "her" in relation to words like "anyone," "no one," "everyone" etc.: *If anyone calls, tell them I'll be back later.* [**Origin:** 1100–1200 Old Norse *theim*] → see Grammar box at THEIR

them² /ðɛm/ *determiner* SPOKEN, NONSTANDARD those: *I couldn't understand all them big words.*

the·mat·ic /θɪ'mætɪk/ Ac *adj.* relating to a particular theme, or organized according to themes: *the thematic structure of the novel*

the,matic 'map *n.* [C] TECHNICAL a map that is used to show GEOGRAPHICAL information such as the use of the land, CLIMATE, or population levels in different areas

theme /θim/ Ac S3 W2 *n.* [C] **1** a main subject or idea in a piece of writing, speech, movie etc.: **+of** *The theme of her speech was freedom and choice.* | *There have been dozens of movies* ***on the same theme.*** **2** a particular style: *The bar is decorated in a sports theme.* **3** also **theme music/song** ENG. LANG. ARTS music or a song that is often played during a movie or musical play or at the beginning and end of a television or radio program: **+from/to** *the theme from "Star Wars"* **4** ENG. LANG. ARTS a short simple tune that is repeated and developed in a piece of music: *Freia's theme in Wagner's opera* **5** ENG. LANG. ARTS a short piece of writing on a particular subject that you do for school SYN **essay**
[**Origin:** 1200–1300 Latin *thema*, from Greek, **something laid down, theme**]

-themed /θimd/ [in adjectives] **holiday-themed/gay-themed/Civil War-themed etc.** having a particular style or relating to a particular group of people: *a rock 'n' roll-themed club*

'theme park *n.* [C] a type of park where you can have fun riding on big machines such as a ROLLER COASTER or a FERRIS WHEEL, but where the whole park is based on one subject such as space travel or water

'theme ,party *n.* [C] a party where everyone has to dress in a particular way relating to a particular subject

them·selves /ðəm'sɛlvz, ðɛm-/ S1 W1 *pron.* **1** [reflexive form of "they"] used to show that the people who do something are affected by their own action: *Those guys only talk about themselves.* | *Do you think they killed themselves?* **2** used to emphasize a plural subject or object: *The teachers themselves had made the same mistake.* | *Guests were greeted by the band members themselves.* **3** used to say that a group of people does something without anyone or anything else helping or being involved: *Why don't they just do it themselves?* **4** also **themself** SPOKEN, NONSTANDARD used to avoid saying "himself" or "herself" in relation to words like "everyone," "anyone," "no one" etc.: *Everyone who used the tool hurt themselves with it.* **5 in themselves** also **in and of themselves** considered without other related ideas or situations: *These are major problems in themselves.* **6 (all) by themselves a)** alone: *They're old enough to go to the pool by themselves.* **b)** without help from anyone or anything else: *The spots on your skin will disappear by themselves.* **7 (all) to themselves** if people have something to themselves, they do not have to share it with anyone: *They had the whole beach to themselves.* **8 not be/feel/seem etc. (like) themselves** if people or animals are not themselves, they do not feel or behave in the way they usually do, for example because they are upset or sick → see Grammar box at THEIR

then /ðɛn/ S1 W1 *adv.* **1** at a particular time in the past or future: *What was the town like then?* | *It was then that I heard a noise.* | *We get the results next week, so we won't know anything* ***until then.*** | *We moved to Phoenix in '88, and* ***from then on*** (=starting at that time) *we've lived in this house.* | *A hundred dollars was a lot of money* ***back then*** (=a long time ago when things were different). | ***Only then*** *did I realize she was lying.* | *Olga turned out the lights.* ***Just then*** *the door opened.* | *If we washed the dishes,* ***then and only then*** *would Mom let us watch TV.* **2** after something has happened SYN **next**: *First she was a singer. Then she became a dancer.* | *I walked the dog, then cooked dinner.* **3** SPOKEN said to show that what you are saying is related in some way to what has been said before SYN **in that case**: *"He said he'd call if he got lost." "Then you don't need to worry about it."* | *"Friday's no* good." "Then how about Saturday?" **4** used when saying what the result of a situation or action is: *Don't make eye contact – then they won't ask for money.* | *If you won't tell him, **then** I will.* **5** used when what you think is true or correct based on something else: *You haven't heard the news then?* | *If they're not here by now, **then** they probably aren't coming.* **6 but then (again)** ESPECIALLY SPOKEN used to say that although something is true, something else is also true, which makes the first thing seem less important: *William didn't succeed the first time, but then very few people do.* **7** SPOKEN used to add something to what you have just said: *She works long hours. Then there's the family to take care of.* **8 then and there** also **there and then** immediately: *If I come across a mistake, I fix it right then and there.* **9** SPOKEN said at the beginning of a sentence, after something such as "right," "OK," or "now," in order to get people's attention: *OK then, let's get started.* **10** SPOKEN used at the end of a conversation, especially to show that something has been agreed on: *Good, that's settled then.* **11** ESPECIALLY WRITTEN used to mention what you have been talking about or give a SUMMARY of it: *This, then, was the situation we were in.* → see also **(every) now and then** at NOW[1] (23)

then- /ðen/ *prefix* **the then-president/then-director/then-21-year-old etc.** the president, director etc. at a particular time in the past: *his then-wife* —**then** *adj.* [only before noun]

T

thence /ðens/ *adv.* LITERARY **1** from there **2** for that reason

thence·forth /ˈðensˌfɔrθ, ˌðensˈfɔrθ/ *adv.* LITERARY starting from that time

theo- /θiə/ *prefix* relating to God or gods: *theology* (=study of religion)

the·oc·ra·cy /θiˈɑkrəsi/ *n. plural* **theocracies** [C] a social system or state controlled by religious leaders —**theocratic** /ˌθiəˈkræṭɪk◂ / *adj.*

the·o·crat /ˈθiəˌkræt/ *n.* [C] a religious leader who is one of the people who rule a theocracy

the·o·lo·gian /ˌθiəˈloʊdʒən/ *n.* [C] someone who has studied theology

ˌ**theological ˈseminary** *n.* [C] a college for training people to become church ministers, priests, or RABBIS

the·ol·o·gy /θiˈɑlədʒi/ *n. plural* **theologies** **1** [U] the study of religion and religious ideas and beliefs **2** [C,U] a particular system of religious beliefs and ideas: *a comparison of Eastern and Western theologies* —**theological** /ˌθiəˈlɑdʒɪkəl◂ / *adj.* —**theologically** /-kli/ *adv.*

the·oph·yl·line /θiˈɑfələn/ *n.* [U] a drug like CAFFEINE that is used to treat heart and breathing problems

the·o·rem /ˈθiərəm, ˈθɪrəm/ *n.* [C] MATH a statement, especially in mathematics, that you can prove by reasoning

the·o·ret·i·cal /ˌθiəˈreṭɪkəl/ Ac *adj.* **1** also **the·o·ret·ic** /ˌθiəˈreṭɪk◂ / relating to or based on ideas, especially scientific ideas, rather than practical work or experience OPP **practical**: *theoretical research* **2** also **theoretic** relating to a set of ideas, especially scientific ideas that explain something: *the theoretical framework for his work* **3** a theoretical situation or condition could exist but does not really exist: *a theoretical but unlikely risk of infection* **4 theoretical physics/chemistry etc.** a part of science or mathematics that deals with ideas and CALCULATIONS rather than with EXPERIMENTS

the·o·ret·i·cal·ly /ˌθiəˈreṭɪkli/ Ac *adv.* **1** used to say that something could happen, but it is extremely unlikely: *It's theoretically possible for everyone in the class to get 100%.* **2** [sentence adverb] used to say what is supposed to be true in a particular situation, especially when the opposite is true: *Theoretically, she's the boss, but she's hardly ever here.*

the·o·rist /ˈθiərɪst/ Ac also **the·o·re·ti·cian** /ˌθiərəˈtɪʃən/ *n.* [C] someone who develops ideas within a particular subject that explain why particular things happen or are true: *a leading feminist theorist*

the·o·rize /ˈθiəˌraɪz/ *v.* [I,T] to think of a possible explanation for an event or fact: **+about/on** *Physicists can still only theorize about how the universe began.* | **theorize (that)** *Police theorize that the two men were working together.*

the·o·ry /ˈθiəri, ˈθɪri/ Ac S2 W2 *n. plural* **theories** **1** [C] an idea or set of ideas that is intended to explain something about life or the world, especially one that has not yet been proven to be true: *new scientific theories* | **+about/on** *theories on the spread of crime* | **+of** *Einstein's theory of relativity* | **a/the theory that** *the theory that the dinosaurs were wiped out by an asteroid* | *There's plenty of evidence to **support the theory**.* **2** [C] an idea that someone thinks is true: **+on/about** *It seems that everyone has a theory about the case.* | **a/the theory that** *Police are working on the theory that he may have been kidnapped.* **3** [U] the general principles or ideas that a subject is based on: *music theory* **4 in theory** used to say that something seems to be true, but may not be true because other things may influence a situation: *In theory, more competition is good for consumers.* → see also IN PRACTICE [**Origin:** 1500–1600 Late Latin *theoria*, from Greek, from *theorein* **to look at**]

ther·a·peu·tic /ˌθerəˈpyuṭɪk/ *adj.* **1** MEDICINE relating to the treatment or cure of disease: *the plant's therapeutic properties* **2** making you feel calm and relaxed: *I find swimming very therapeutic.* —**therapeutically** /-kli/ *adv.*

ther·a·peu·tics /ˌθerəˈpyuṭɪks/ *n.* [U] MEDICINE the part of medical science concerned with the treatment and cure of illness

ther·a·pist /ˈθerəpɪst/ *n.* [C] **1** a trained person whose job is to help people with their emotional problems, especially by talking to them and asking them to talk about their feelings: *Have you thought about **seeing a therapist**?* **2** someone who has been trained to give a particular form of treatment for a physical or medical condition: *a speech therapist*

ther·a·py /ˈθerəpi/ S2 W3 *n. plural* **therapies** **1** [C,U] MEDICINE the treatment of an illness or injury over a fairly long period of time, especially without using drugs or operations: *years of physical therapy* | **+for** *radiation therapy for cancer* **2** [U] the treatment or examination of someone's mental problems by talking to them for a long time about their feelings: *Julie's been **in therapy** for two years.* **3** [C usually singular] an activity that makes you feel happier and more relaxed [**Origin:** 1800–1900 Modern Latin *therapia*, from Greek *therapeia*, from *therapeuein* **to attend, treat**] → see also OCCUPATIONAL THERAPY, PHYSICAL THERAPY, SPEECH THERAPY

Ther·a·va·da Bud·dhism /θerəˌvɑdə ˈbudɪzəm/ *n.* [U] one of the two main forms of Buddhism, and the main religion in Sri Lanka, Thailand, and Cambodia. It emphasizes that the best way to reach the perfect state of holiness is through study and MEDITATION. → see also MAHAYNA BUDDHISM

there[1] /ðer/ S1 W1 *pron.* **there is/are/exists/remain etc.** used to say that something exists or happens: *Is there any milk left?* | *There were some sheep in the field.* | *There must be a reason she's acting like this.* | *Suddenly there was a loud crash.* | *There's a document missing, isn't there?* | *There remained the problem of money.* | ***There seem to be** so many squirrels this year.*

GRAMMAR

When **there** is the subject of the sentence, the form of the verb depends on whether the noun that follows it is singular or plural. If the noun is singular, the verb is singular; if the noun is plural, the verb is plural: *There are two Vietnamese students in my class.* | *There's a letter for you in the kitchen.* In informal spoken English, many people use **there's** before a plural noun: *There's two cookies left in the package.* This should not be used in formal writing.

there[2] S1 W1 *adv.* **1** in or to a particular place that is not where you are or near you: *Australia? No, I've never been there.* | *We could go to my apartment and have lunch there.* | *When I looked up, she was standing **right there**.* | **out/in/under etc. there** *Don't go in there right now.* | *We flew to Athens, and sailed **from there** to Crete.* | *Don't worry. We'll **get there*** (=arrive) *before the stores close.* | *How long has Kim lived **over there** in Thailand?* | *It's too far to drive **there and back** in one day.* **2** at a particular point in a story, situation, process etc.: *Don't stop there! Tell me the rest!* | *We've still got work to do, but we're **getting there**.* **3** if something is there, it exists or is available: *The stain was still there.* | *The offer's there if you want it.* **4 be there (for sb)** to be ready to help someone or be kind to them when they have problems: *My parents were always there for me.* **5 sb/sth is there to do sth** used to say what someone or something's duty or purpose is: *Police are there to make sure everyone obeys the laws.*

SPOKEN PHRASES

6 used when you are talking about or pointing to someone or something that is not near you: *Sign the document there and there.* | *Who's that man **over there**?* | *"Where's my pen?" "It's **right there** in front of you!"* **7** used to say which statement, idea, or reason you agree with, want to say more about etc.: *I'm not sure I agree with you there.* **8 there is sb/sth** also **there he/she/it etc. is a)** said to make someone look or pay attention to something: *There's the statue I was telling you about.* **b)** said when you have found someone or something you were looking for, or someone you have been waiting for arrives: *There you are – I've been looking all over for you.* **9 there you go a)** also **there you are** said when giving something to someone or when you have done something for someone: *"There you go." "Thanks."* **b)** used in order to tell someone that they have done something correctly or understood something: *Can you turn just a little to the left? There you go.* **c)** also **there you are, there you have it** said when something has been proved or explained: *"I can't do everything I used to, but I am almost 70." "Well, there you go."* **d)** also **there you are, there it is** used to show that you accept that an unsatisfactory situation cannot be changed: *I'd have liked more children, but there it is.* **10 is sb there?** used when you want to speak to someone on the telephone and someone else answers: *Hello, is Sandy there?* **11 sit/stand/lie etc. there** used to emphasize that someone is lazy or useless: *She just sits there while I do all the work.* **12 there he/she etc. goes again** said when someone starts saying or doing something again that you do not approve of: *There she goes again complaining about money.* **13 there goes sth a)** used for showing your disappointment when you lose something, for example an opportunity, or when something that happens prevents you from doing something: *There go our chances of winning the championship.* | *Look at all that food – there goes my diet!* **b)** also **there it goes** used for saying that you can hear something such as a bell ringing: *There goes the dryer – can you check on the clothes?* **14 there goes sb/sth** also **there he/she/it etc. goes** said when you see someone or something moving past you or away from you: *Look, there goes a fire engine.* **15 hi/hello/hey there** said when greeting someone, especially when you have just noticed them: *Hi there. You must be Liane.* **16 sb's not all there** used to say that someone is not very intelligent and seems slightly crazy **17 been there, done that (got/bought the T-shirt)** used to say that something is not interesting or impressive because you have already done it, perhaps several times **18 that book there/those shoes there etc.** said when showing or pointing to where something is: *Can you hand me that towel there?*

[Origin: Old English *thær*] → see also HERE[1], **then and there** at THEN (8)

there[3] *interjection* **1** said when you give something to someone: *There. I hope that's enough.* **2** said to express success or satisfaction, especially when you have finished something: *There! It's done.* **3 so there!** said to someone to show that you do not care what they think and you are not going to change your behavior: *I'm going to do what I like, so there!* **4 there, there** said to comfort someone who is upset: *There, there. It's not the end of the world.*

there·a·bouts /ˌðɛrəˈbaʊts, ˈðɛrəˌbaʊts/ *adv.* near a particular time, place, number etc., but not exactly: *The women were all 50 **or thereabouts**.*

there·af·ter /ðɛrˈæftɚ/ *adv.* FORMAL after a particular event or time SYN **afterward**: *He moved to France and died **shortly thereafter**.*

there·by /ðɛrˈbaɪ, ˈðɛrbaɪ/ Ac *adv.* FORMAL with the result that something else happens: *He redesigned the process, thereby saving the company thousands of dollars.*

there·fore /ˈðɛrfɔr/ S3 W2 *adv.* FORMAL as a result of something that has just been mentioned SYN **so** SYN **for that reason**: *Their car was bigger and therefore more comfortable.* ▸see THESAURUS box at **thus**

there·in /ðɛrˈɪn/ *adv.* **1 therein lies sth** FORMAL used to say that something is caused by or comes from a particular situation: *270 votes are necessary to win, and therein lies the problem.* **2** FORMAL or LAW in that place, or in that piece of writing → see also HEREIN

there·of /ðɛrˈʌv/ *adv.* FORMAL or LAW concerning something that has just been mentioned: *The company's success, or its **lack thereof**, depends on the quality of its product.*

there·on /ðɛrˈɔn/ *adv.* FORMAL or LAW **1** on the thing that has just been mentioned **2** THEREUPON

there·to /ðɛrˈtu/ *adv.* FORMAL or LAW **1** to something that has just been mentioned **2** concerning an agreement or piece of writing that has just been mentioned

there·to·fore /ˈðɛrt̬əˌfɔr/ *adv.* LAW before or until a particular time

there·un·der /ðɛrˈʌndɚ/ *adv.* FORMAL or LAW **1** under something that has just been mentioned **2** according to a document, law, or part of an agreement that has just been mentioned

there·up·on /ˈðɛrəˌpɑn, ˌðɛrəˈpɑn/ *adv.* FORMAL **1** immediately after something else has happened, and usually as a result of it SYN **then** **2** concerning a subject that has just been mentioned

therm /θɚm/ *n.* [C] a measurement of heat equal to 100,000 BTUs

therm- /θɚm/ *prefix* another form of THERMO-, used before some vowels

ther·mal[1] /ˈθɚməl/ *adj.* [only before noun] **1** relating to or caused by heat: *thermal energy* **2** thermal clothing is made from special material to keep you warm in very cold weather: *thermal underwear* **3** EARTH SCIENCE thermal water is heated naturally under the earth: *thermal springs*

thermal[2] *n.* [C] **1** EARTH SCIENCE a rising current of warm air **2 thermals** INFORMAL special warm clothing, especially underwear

ˌthermal caˈpacity *n.* [U] CHEMISTRY HEAT CAPACITY

ther·mi·on·ics /ˌθɚmiˈɑnɪks/ *n.* [U] TECHNICAL the part of science that deals with the flow of ELECTRONS from heated metal

thermo- /θɚmoʊ, -mə/ *prefix* TECHNICAL relating to heat SYN **therm-**: *a thermostat* (=for controlling temperature)

ther·mo·dy·nam·ics /ˌθɚmoʊdaɪˈnæmɪks/ *n.* [U] PHYSICS the science that deals with the relationship between heat and other forms of energy —**thermodynamic** *adj.*

ther·mom·e·ter /θɚˈmɑmət̬ɚ/ *n.* [C] SCIENCE a piece of equipment that measures the temperature of the air, of your body etc.

ther·mo·nu·cle·ar /ˌθɚmoʊˈnukliɚ/ *adj.* thermonuclear weapons use a NUCLEAR reaction, involving the splitting of atoms, to produce very high temperatures and a very powerful explosion

ˌthermoˌnuclear ˈfusion *n.* [U] PHYSICS NUCLEAR

FUSION that takes place when the NUCLEI of light atoms, for example those of HYDROGEN, crash into each other at very high speeds and temperatures

ther·mo·plas·tic /ˌθɚməˈplæstɪk◂/ *n.* [C,U] CHEMISTRY a plastic that is soft and bendable when heated but hard when cold

Ther·mos, **thermos** /ˈθɚməs/ *n.* [C] TRADEMARK a special container that is designed to keep drinks hot or cold

ther·mo·stat /ˈθɚməˌstæt/ *n.* [C] an instrument used for keeping a room or a machine at a particular temperature

the·sau·rus /θɪˈsɔrəs/ *n. plural* **thesauruses** or **thesauri** /-raɪ/ [C] ENG. LANG. ARTS a book in which words are put into groups with other words that have similar meanings

these /ðiz/ *determiner, pron.* the plural of THIS

the·sis /ˈθisɪs/ Ac *n. plural* **theses** /-siz/ [C] **1** a long piece of writing about a particular subject that you do as part of an advanced university degree, such as a MASTER'S DEGREE: +**on** *Keller wrote his master's thesis on Swedish choral music.* **2** FORMAL an idea or statement that tries to explain why something happens: *The book seems to have no central thesis.*

ˈthesis ˌstatement *n.* [C] the statement in a piece of writing that gives the main idea or the writer's opinion

thes·pi·an /ˈθɛspiən/ *n.* [C] FORMAL or HUMOROUS an actor [**Origin:** 1800–1900 *Thespis* 6th-century B.C. Greek writer of plays] —**thespian** *adj.*

T

Thes·sa·lo·ni·ans /ˌθɛsəˈloʊniənz/ **1 Thessalonians, 2 Thessalonians** two books in the New Testament of the Christian Bible

they /ðeɪ/ S1 W1 *pron.* [used as the subject of a verb] **1** used to talk about two or more people or things that have already been mentioned or are known about: *Sara and Michael said they won't be able to come.* | *Look at these flowers. Aren't they beautiful?* | *Your parents are coming too, aren't they?* **2** used instead of "he" or "she" after words like "anyone," "no one," "everyone" etc.: *If anyone else arrives, they'll have to wait.* **3** used to talk about the people in a particular place, the people involved in a particular activity, the people in government etc., when you do not know them or name them: *What do they call oranges in Spain?* | *Where are they going to build the new highway?* **4 they say/think etc.** SPOKEN used to say what people in general think, believe, are saying etc.: *They say it's safer to fly than to drive.* [**Origin:** 1100–1200 Old Norse *their*] → see Grammar box at THEIR

they'd /ðeɪd/ **1** the short form of "they had": *They said they'd already seen it.* **2** the short form of "they would": *They'd all like to meet you.*

they'll /ðeɪl, ðɛl/ the short form of "they will": *They'll be here around noon.*

they're /ðɚ; *strong* ðɛr/ the short form of "they are": *They're spending Christmas in Florida.*

they've /ðeɪv/ the short form of "they have," when "have" is an AUXILIARY VERB: *They've lived there about three years.*

thi·a·min, **thi·a·mine** /ˈθaɪəmən/ *n.* [U] BIOLOGY a natural chemical in some foods, that you need in order to prevent particular illnesses

thick[1] /θɪk/ S3 W3 *adj.*

1 NOT THIN measuring a large distance or a larger distance than usual, between two opposite surfaces or sides OPP **thin**: *a thick slice of bread* | *The walls were thick and solid.*

2 [not before noun] measuring a particular distance between two opposite sides or surfaces: *The price of the glass will depend on how thick it is.* | **two feet thick/12 inches thick etc.** *The brick wall is about 16 inches thick.*

3 LIQUID not containing much water and moving or flowing slowly OPP **thin**: *a thick tasty sauce*

4 SMOKE/CLOUD ETC. filling the air, and difficult to see through or breathe in SYN **dense** OPP **thin**: *thick clouds of black smoke* | *We drove through thick fog.*

5 HAIR/FUR ETC. consisting of many hairs growing closely together OPP **thin**: *thick black hair* ►see THESAURUS box at **hair**

6 be thick with sth a) to be covered with a thick layer of something: *The furniture was thick with dust.* **b)** to be filled with a lot of something such as smoke: *The room was thick with cigarette smoke.* **c)** to be filled with a lot of things: *The roads were thick with holiday travelers.*

7 TREES/BUSHES ETC. growing very close together, or having a lot of leaves, so there is not much space in between SYN **dense** OPP **thin**: *a thick forest*

8 WAY OF SPEAKING clearly belonging to a particular place or part of the country: **a thick Irish/Southern/Russian etc. accent** *He spoke with a thick German accent.*

9 VOICE not as clear or high as usual because someone is angry, confused etc. about something: *His voice was thick and gruff.* | +**with** *Her voice was thick with emotion.*

10 STUPID INFORMAL not intelligent

11 be (as) thick as thieves if two people are as thick as thieves, they are very friendly with each other and seem to share a lot of secrets

12 get sth through/into your thick head/skull SPOKEN, INFORMAL used to tell someone angrily to understand something that you want them to understand

13 be thick with sb OLD-FASHIONED to be very friendly with someone

[**Origin:** Old English *thicce*] —**thickly** *adv.* → see also **have thick/thin skin** at SKIN[1] (6), THICKNESS, THICK-SKINNED

thick[2] *adv.* **1** if you spread, cut etc. something thick, you spread or cut it in a way that produces a thick layer or piece: *Slice the cheese a little thicker.* **2 pour/lay it on thick** INFORMAL to do or say something in a way that makes something seem better, more amusing, bigger etc. than it really is **3 thick and fast** arriving or happening very frequently, in large amounts or numbers

thick[3] *n.* **1 in the thick of sth** in the busiest, most active, most dangerous etc. part of a situation: *Williams was wounded in the thick of the battle.* **2 through thick and thin** in spite of any difficulties or problems: *Barb has supported me through thick and thin.*

thick·en /ˈθɪkən/ *v.* **1** [I,T] to become thicker or more DENSE, or to make liquid, smoke, mist etc. thicker or more dense: *The fog was beginning to thicken.* | **thicken sth with sth** *You can thicken the soup slightly with flour.* **2** [I] if part of someone's body thickens, it becomes fatter and bigger **3** [I] WRITTEN if someone's voice thickens, it becomes slightly lower, often because of strong emotion → see also **the plot thickens** at PLOT[1] (3)

thick·en·er /ˈθɪkənɚ/ also **thick·en·ing** /ˈθɪkənɪŋ/ *n.* [C,U] a substance used to make a liquid thicker

thick·et /ˈθɪkɪt/ *n.* [C] a group of bushes and small trees

ˌthick-ˈheaded *adj.* INFORMAL extremely stupid

thick·ness /ˈθɪknɪs/ *n.* **1** [C,U] how thick something is: *carpets of different thicknesses* **2** [C] a layer of something

thick·set /ˌθɪkˈsɛt◂/ *adj.* having a wide strong body: *a short thickset man*

ˌthick-ˈskinned *adj.* not easily offended by other people's criticism or insults OPP **thin-skinned**

thief /θif/ *n. plural* **thieves** /θivz/ [C] someone who steals things, especially without using violence: *a car thief* | *The thieves stole over $8,000 worth of electronics.* | ***a gang of jewel thieves*** → see also BURGLAR, ROBBER, **be (as) thick as thieves** at THICK[1] (11)

thiev·er·y /ˈθivəri/ also **thieving** *n.* [U] FORMAL the practice of stealing things

thiev·ing /ˈθivɪŋ/ *adj.* [only before noun] involved in the practice of stealing things from other people: *thieving politicians*

thiev·ish /ˈθivɪʃ/ *adj.* LITERARY like a thief

thigh /θaɪ/ *n.* [C] BIOLOGY **1** the top part of your leg, between your knee and your HIP **2** the top part of a bird's leg, used as food: *chicken thighs*

thigh·bone /ˈθaɪboʊn/ *n.* [C] NOT TECHNICAL the bone in your thigh SYN **femur**

thig·mot·ro·pism /θɪgˈmɑtrəˌpɪzəm/ *n.* [U] BIOLOGY the way a plant moves or grows as a reaction to being touched, for example bending or turning → see also GRAVITROPISM, PHOTOTROPISM, TROPISM

thim·ble /ˈθɪmbəl/ *n.* [C] a small metal or plastic cap used to protect your finger when you are sewing

thim·ble·ful /ˈθɪmbəlfʊl/ *n.* [C + of] INFORMAL a very small quantity of liquid

Thim·pu /ˈθɪmbu/ the capital city of Bhutan

thin[1] /θɪn/ S2 W2 *adj. comparative* **thinner**, *superlative* **thinnest**

1 NOT THICK measuring a small distance or a smaller distance than usual between two opposite sides or surfaces OPP **thick**: *a thin gold chain* | *a thin layer of dust* | *My curtains are too thin to keep the sun out.* | *She had a narrow face and thin lips.* → see also PAPER-THIN

2 NOT FAT having little fat on your body OPP **fat**: *He's tall and thin and wears glasses.* | *I wish my legs were thinner.*

> **THESAURUS**
>
> **slim** and **slender** used about someone who is thin in an attractive way
> **skinny** used about someone who is very thin in a way that is not attractive
> **lean** used about someone who is thin in a healthy way
> **slight** thin and delicate
> **underweight** used, especially by doctors, about someone who is too thin, in a way that is not healthy
> **emaciated** used about someone who is extremely thin and weak because of illness or not eating
> **anorexic** used about someone who is extremely thin because they have a mental illness that makes them stop eating
> **skeletal** used about someone who is so thin that you can see the shape of their bones
> → FAT

3 SMOKE/MIST/FOG smoke, mist, or FOG that is thin is easy to see through OPP **thick**: *The sun quickly burned away the thin fog.*

4 HAIR/FUR ETC. not covering the skin very well because there are spaces between the hairs OPP **thick**: *a thin straggly beard* | *His hair's getting thin on top.* ▸see THESAURUS box at **hair**

5 TREES/BUSHES ETC. not growing very close together, or having only a few leaves, so there is a lot of space in between OPP **thick**: *thin vegetation*

6 LIQUID a thin liquid flows very easily because it has a lot of water in it OPP **thick**: *thin broth*

7 AIR air that is thin is more difficult to breathe than usual because it has less OXYGEN in it: *The air is so thin up here I can hardly breathe.*

8 a thin margin/majority etc. a very small number or amount of something: *They won by a very thin margin.*

9 VOICE/SOUND a thin voice or sound is high and weak, and is not nice to listen to: *a thin frightened voice*

10 SMILE a thin smile does not seem very happy or sincere

11 CONTAINING FEW PEOPLE/THINGS containing only a few people or things: *a thin crowd*

12 EXCUSE/ARGUMENT/EXPLANATION a thin excuse, argument, or explanation is not good or detailed enough to persuade you that it is true

13 INFORMATION/DESCRIPTION a piece of information or a description that is thin is not detailed enough to be useful or effective: **+on** *The report is very thin on material to back up his claims.*

14 disappear/vanish into thin air to disappear or vanish completely in a mysterious way

15 be (skating/walking) on thin ice to be in a situation in which you are likely to upset someone or cause trouble

16 BUSINESS thin trading is a situation in which people are not buying or selling very much at a STOCK EXCHANGE OPP **heavy**

[**Origin:** Old English *thynne*] —**thinness** *n.* [U] → see also **have thick/thin skin** at SKIN[1] (6), THINLY → see Word Choice box at NARROW

thin[2] *v.* **thinned**, **thinning** **1** [I,T] also **thin out** to make a group smaller in number, or to become smaller in number: *The crowd seemed to be thinning.* | *Higher prices have* ***thinned the ranks*** (=reduced the number) *of prospective home owners.* | **thin the herd** (=to kill some animals in a group so that there are not so many of them) **2** [I,T] to make liquid, smoke, mist etc. thinner or less DENSE, or to become thinner or less dense OPP **thicken**: *Add a little oil to thin the mixture.* **3** [I] if someone's hair thins, they gradually lose their hair: *His blond hair was starting to thin.* **4** [T] also **thin out** to cut some of someone's hair so that it is not as full or thick **5** [I,T] ESPECIALLY LITERARY if your mouth or lips thin or you thin them, they form a narrow straight line, usually because you are annoyed **6** [T] also **thin out** to make more room for plants to grow by removing the weaker ones → see also THINNING

thin[3] *adv.* so as to be thin: *Don't cut the bread so thin.*

thine[1] /ðaɪn/ *possessive pron.* OLD USE yours

thine[2] *possessive adj.* OLD USE a word meaning "your," used before a word beginning with a vowel or "h"

thing /θɪŋ/ S1 W1 *n.*

1 IDEA/ACTION/FEELING/FACT [C] anything that you can think of as a single ITEM, for example an idea, an action, a remark, or a fact: *I learned some interesting things about the ocean.* | *A strange thing happened to me this morning.* | *He said some terrible things about her!* | *I have a lot of* ***things to do*** *today.* | *I'm sorry if I seem distracted, I* ***have*** *a few* ***things on*** *my* ***mind*** *right now.* | *That was a really nice* ***thing to say*** (=remark) *to your sister.* | **the strange/funny etc. thing is** *The funny thing is, I really enjoyed being with him.* | **do the right/decent/honorable etc. thing** *He did the decent thing by giving back the money.* | *Christmas is* ***the last thing on my mind*** (=something I am not thinking about at all because I am thinking of other things) *right now.* | *He could tell you* ***a thing or two about*** (=a lot of information about) *farming!*

> **THESAURUS**
>
> **object** ESPECIALLY WRITTEN a thing, especially a hard solid thing: *a sharp metal object*
> **something** a thing, used especially when you do not know its name or what it is: *There's something in my eye.*
> **item** one of the things in a set, group, or list: *Have the children sort the items according to size, color, texture etc.*
> **article** a thing, especially one of a group of things: *an article of clothing*

2 OBJECT [C] an object, especially when you do not know what it is or what it is for: *What does this thing do?* | *There were all kinds of things in the attic.* | *I don't have a thing to wear!*

3 things [plural] life in general and the way it is affecting people: *How are things at work?* | **make things easy/difficult/hard etc. (for sb)** *I think he enjoys making things difficult for me.* | **the way things are/as things stand** *As things stand at the moment, we can't afford a house.*

4 (sb's) things [plural] **a)** what you own or what you are carrying SYN **stuff**: *You can put your things over there for now.* **b)** the equipment and clothes you need for a particular job, sport etc. SYN **stuff**: *my swimming things*

5 among other things used when you are giving one fact, reason, effect etc. but want to suggest that there are many others: *He talked about his days as a senator, among other things.*

6 poor/pretty/funny (little) etc. thing a person or animal that is unlucky, attractive, funny etc.: *Poor thing looks like it hasn't eaten in days.*

T

7 be/become a thing of the past to not exist or happen anymore: *Life-long employment with a single company is a thing of the past.*
8 all things considered having considered all the facts about something: *I think we've done a pretty good job, all things considered.*
9 not a thing nothing at all: *There wasn't a thing to eat.* | **not know/feel/see/say etc. a thing** *It was so dark, I couldn't see a thing.*
10 the (latest) thing INFORMAL the thing that is popular or fashionable at the moment: *Low carb diets were the thing a few years back.*
11 have a thing about sb/sth INFORMAL to have very strong and often unreasonable bad feelings about someone or something: *Judith has a thing about people chewing gum.*
12 have a thing for sb/sth INFORMAL to like someone or a type of person or thing very much: *Claudia has a thing for older men.*
13 make a big thing about/out of sth to make something seem more important than it really is, by getting angry, excited etc.: *Hank didn't want to make a big thing out of his surgery.*
14 be all things to all people used to describe someone or something that tries to please everyone by being exactly what they need: *I finally realized I could not be all things to all people.*
15 in all things in every situation

SPOKEN PHRASES

16 the thing is also **here's the thing** used when explaining a problem or the reason for something: *The thing is, I'm allergic to seafood.*
17 for one thing used to give one reason for something: *We can't invite everyone – for one thing, it would cost too much.*
18 and things (like that) used to mean "and other things," without giving more examples: *We talked about babies and things all afternoon.*
19 be just one of those things used to say that something that has happened is not someone's fault or could not have been avoided
20 it's (just) one thing after another used to say that a lot of bad or unlucky things keep happening to you
21 that/the kind/type/sort of thing used to mean other things of the same type, without giving more examples: *That's the sort of thing that only crazy people do.*
22 sb's thing what someone likes or is good at: *Math was never my thing.*
23 of all things used to show that you are surprised or shocked by something that someone has done or said: *She's started taking karate lessons, of all things.*
24 the thing about sb/sth also **the thing with sb/sth** used to say what the problem with or important feature of someone or something is: *The thing with Josh is that he likes everything planned out first.*
25 just the thing also **the very thing** exactly the thing that you want or that is necessary: *That's just the thing I was looking for.*
26 one thing led to another used when explaining the way in which something happened, without giving many details: *We were drinking and talking and one thing led to another.*
27 it's a boy/girl/man/woman etc. thing used to say that something is liked, understood, or done by only one group of people: *Computer games are mainly a guy thing.*
28 it's one thing to do sth, (but) it's (quite) another thing to sth, used to say that doing one thing is very different from doing another thing: *It's one thing to offer suggestions, but it's another thing to criticize everything.*
29 the...thing used to talk about an activity and everything that is involved with it: **do/try the...thing** *I tried the college thing, but I didn't like it.*

[**Origin:** Old English **meeting, council, thing**] → see also **all (other) things being equal** at EQUAL[1] (6), **first thing** at FIRST[1] (6), **first things first** at FIRST[1] (9), **it's a good thing (that)** at GOOD[1] (31), **all good things must come to an end** at GOOD[1] (32), **too much of a good thing** at GOOD[1] (50), **have a good thing going** at GOOD[1] (58), **the last person/thing etc.** at LAST[1] (5), **be onto a good thing** at ONTO (5), **there's no such thing as sth** at SUCH[1] (5)

thing·a·ma·jig /ˈθɪŋəməˌdʒɪɡ/ also **thing·a·ma·bob** /ˈθɪŋəməˌbɑb/, **thing·y** /ˈθɪŋi/ *n.* [C] SPOKEN used when you cannot remember or do not know the name of the thing you want to mention: *What's this silver thingamajig used for?*

think /θɪŋk/ S1 W1 *v. past tense and past participle* **thought** /θɔt/
1 OPINION/BELIEF [T] to have an opinion or belief about something: **think (that)** *Everyone thought Marilyn was very nice.* | **what sb thinks (of/about sb/sth)** *I couldn't really tell what he thought of my suggestion.*

THESAURUS

believe to think that something is true: *We believe that the risk is small.*
suspect to think that something, especially something bad, is true but not be sure: *She suspected that he was seeing another woman.*
consider to think about something carefully before deciding what to do: *Have you considered changing your job?*
figure INFORMAL used to say what your opinion is: *I figure he's at least 19.*
feel to have a particular opinion, especially one that is based on your feelings, not on facts: *She feels that there is no alternative.*
I guess/I suppose used to say that you think something is true, although you are not sure: *"Is Dan going to be there?" "I guess so."*

2 USE YOUR MIND [I] to use your mind to solve problems, decide something etc.: *Be quiet – I'm thinking.* | **+about** *I've thought a lot about your problem.* | **think hard/carefully/deeply etc.** *She thought hard before she answered.*
3 WORDS/IDEAS IN YOUR MIND [I,T] to have words or ideas in your mind, without telling them to anyone: *"He looks upset," Susan thought.* | **think to yourself** *I don't care what they say, he thought to himself.* | **+of/about** *I was thinking about you earlier.* | *You shouldn't think things like that.*
4 CONSIDER [I,T] to consider someone or something to be a particular thing: **think of sb/sth as sth** *He had always thought of Kate as his friend.* | **think sb/sth (to be) sth** *These coins are thought to be the only two still in existence.*
5 think of/about doing sth to consider the possibility of doing something: *Have you ever thought about starting your own business?*
6 think twice (about/before doing sth) to think very carefully before deciding to do something, because you know about the dangers or problems: *Employers think twice about hiring someone with a criminal record.*
7 think again to think of a new idea or plan because you realize that the first one is wrong: *If you thought running a restaurant was easy, think again.*
8 think nothing of doing sth to do something easily or without complaining, even though other people would find it difficult: *They think nothing of spending $100 on a meal.*
9 not think much of sb/sth to think that someone or something is bad, useless etc.: *We didn't think much of the show.*
10 think better of it to not do something that you had planned to do, because you realize that it is not a good idea: *She felt like slapping him in the face, but thought better of it.*
11 think for yourself to have ideas and thoughts of your own rather than believing what other people say: *I try to encourage my students to think for themselves.*
12 think straight to think clearly and make sensible decisions: *I'm so tired I can't think straight.*
13 think out loud also **think aloud** to say what you are thinking, without talking to anyone in particular: *Oh, sorry – I guess I was thinking out loud.*

14 think a lot of sb/sth also **think highly of sb/sth** to admire or respect someone
15 think little of sb/sth a) to think that someone or something is not very important, impressive, or good **b)** to not think about someone or something very much
16 think big INFORMAL to plan to do things that are difficult, but will be very impressive, make a lot of profit etc.: *To succeed in business, you need to think big.*
17 think on your feet to answer questions or think of ideas quickly, without preparing before: *You have to be able to think on your feet to do this job.*
18 think positively/positive to believe that you are going to be successful or that a situation is going to have a good result
19 think less/badly of sb (for doing sth) to respect someone less than you did before: *Nobody thought less of him for showing his emotions.*
20 think the best/worst of sb to consider someone's actions in a way that makes them seem as good as possible or as bad as possible: *Ellie's the type of person that always thinks the best of people.*
21 think outside the box to think of new, different, or unusual ways of doing something, especially in business
22 think nothing of sth to think something is not important which you later realize is in fact important

SPOKEN PHRASES

23 I think/I don't think (that) used when you are saying that you believe something is or is not true or correct, although you are not sure: *I think you're right.* | *I don't think he likes Penny very much.*
24 I thought/I didn't think (that) used when you are saying what you thought or believed or did not believe was true, although now you are not sure: *I thought the dishwasher was broken – did you get it fixed?*
25 I think so/I don't think so used when answering a question, to say that you believe or do not believe something is true: *"Is she married?" "I think so."* | *"Have we met before?" "I don't think so."*
26 I think I'll do sth used when saying what you will probably do: *I think I'll wait till tomorrow.*
27 do you think (that)...? used to ask someone's opinion: *Do you think it's too late to call her?*
28 do you think (that) you could...? used when you are asking someone politely to do something for you: *Do you think you could give me a ride to work tomorrow?*
29 do you think (that) I/we could...? used when you are politely asking someone for permission to do something: *Do you think we could stay with you for a while?*
30 who/what etc. do you think...? used to ask someone's opinion: *Who do you think should win?* | *How do you think the test went?* | **what do you think of/about sb/sth?** *What do you think of the new teacher?*
31 who/what etc. does sb think...? used when asking someone angrily about something: *Where do you think you're going?* | *Just who does she think she is?*
32 I thought (that) sb could/might do sth used when you are politely suggesting something: *I thought we could go to the lake this weekend.*
33 I would think (that) used when you are saying that you believe something is probably true: *I would think lots of people would be interested.*
34 come to think of it used when you are adding something more to what you have said, because you have just remembered it or realized it: *Come to think of it, I haven't seen him for a few weeks.*
35 who would have thought (that)...? used to say that something is very surprising: *Who would have thought they'd get married?*
36 just think used to ask someone to imagine or consider something: *Just think, in a couple of hours we'll be in Paris.* | **+of** *Just think of what you could buy with a million dollars.*
37 when you think about it used to say that you realize something when you consider a fact or subject: *When you think about it, most of what he says doesn't make sense.*

SPOKEN PHRASES

38 you would think (that) also **you/I would have thought (that)** used to say that you expect something to be true, although it is not: *You would think she might have thanked us.*
39 I wasn't thinking used as a way of saying you are sorry because you have upset someone: *Sorry, I wasn't thinking. Would you like a drink too?*
40 think where/when/how etc. a) to try to remember where, when etc. something happened: *I'm trying to think where we met.* **b)** to produce an idea, suggestion, or explanation about where, when etc. something happened or should happen SYN **imagine**: *I* ***can't think*** *why she would say that.*
41 think the world of sb to like or love someone very much
42 if sb thinks (that)..., they've got another think/thing coming! used to tell someone that if they think something is going to happen, they are wrong: *If they think they're going to win, they've got another think coming!*
43 to think (that)...! used to show that you are very surprised or upset about something: *To think we lived next door to him and never knew what he was doing!*
44 not/never etc. think to do sth to not remember to do something: *Nobody thought to call me.*
45 that's what sb thinks! used to say that you strongly disagree with someone: *"You'll never get into medical school." "That's what you think!"*
46 anyone would think (that) used when you are saying that someone's behavior is making other people think a particular thing, which may not be true: *Why are you complaining? Anyone would think you're jealous.*
47 I think not FORMAL used to strongly say that you believe something is not true or that you disagree with someone
48 I thought as much used to say that you are not surprised by what you have just found out
49 think nothing of it OLD-FASHIONED used when someone has thanked you or said they were sorry for doing something, to say politely that you did not mind

[**Origin:** Old English *thencan*]

think ahead *phr. v.* to think carefully and plan for what might happen or what you might do in the future: **+to** *Rogers was already thinking ahead to the next election.*

think back *phr. v.* to think about things that happened in the past: **+on/to/over** *She thought back on her first conversation with him.*

think of *phr. v.* **1 think of sth** to produce a new idea, name, suggestion etc. by using your mind SYN **think up**: *I can't think of any other way to do this.* | *They're still trying to think of a name for the baby.* **2 think of sth** to remember a name or fact: *Jay couldn't think of the name of that movie either.* **3 think of sb** to behave in a way that shows that you want to treat other people well: *Hannah's always thinking of others.* **4 only think of yourself** to only do what you want or what is good for you **5 I'll/we'll be thinking of you** used when you want to express sympathy for someone who will be in a difficult situation, and to say that you will be thinking about them

think sth ↔ **out** *phr. v.* to think about something carefully, considering all the possible problems, results etc.: *The plan has been carefully thought out.* | *He took a walk to* ***think things out.***

think sth ↔ **over** *phr. v.* to think about something carefully: *Think it over and let me know what you decide.* | *I just need some time to* ***think things over.***

think sth ↔ **through** *phr. v.* to think carefully about the possible results of doing something: *She wants to quit her job, but I don't think she's thought it through.*

think sth ↔ **up** *phr. v.* to produce a new idea, name etc. by using your mind SYN **think of** SYN **come up with**: *Who thinks up the stories for these stupid TV shows?* | *She was trying to think up an excuse.*

think·a·ble /ˈθɪŋkəbəl/ *adj.* [not before noun] able to be thought about or considered SYN **possible** OPP **unthinkable**

think·er /ˈθɪŋkɚ/ *n.* [C] **1** someone who is famous for their important work in a subject such as science or PHILOSOPHY: *great thinkers such as Newton and Darwin* **2 a quick/positive/free etc. thinker** someone who thinks in a particular way

think·ing[1] /ˈθɪŋkɪŋ/ *n.* [U] **1** opinions, ideas, or attitudes about something or about things in general: **+of** *I don't understand the thinking of young people today.* | **the thinking behind sth** *What's the thinking behind the changes?* | **the current thinking on/about sth** (=the opinions that a particular person, group, or society in general have on a particular subject) | ***To my way of thinking*** (=in my opinion), *giving free needles to drug users is morally wrong.* **2** the way you think about things or react to situations: *Jeff's quick thinking had saved her life.* | **positive/negative thinking** *Positive thinking can help fight illness.* **3 do some thinking** to think about something, especially in order to solve a problem or have some new ideas about a situation **4 good thinking** SPOKEN used to tell someone that they have had a good idea **5 put on your thinking cap** INFORMAL to think seriously about a problem, in order to try and solve it → see also WISHFUL THINKING

thinking[2] *adj.* [only before noun] **1** a thinking person is intelligent and tries to think carefully about important subjects **2 the thinking man's/woman's/person's sth** used to say that someone or something is liked by or attractive to intelligent people

ˈthink tank *n.* [C] a committee of people with experience in a particular subject, that an organization or government establishes to produce ideas and give advice

thin·ly /ˈθɪnli/ *adv.* **1** in a way that has a very small distance between two sides or two flat surfaces: *thinly sliced carrots* **2** scattered or spread over a large area, with a lot of space in between: *Sow the radish seeds thinly.* | **thinly populated/settled etc.** *Although the Baltic region is quite a large area, most of it is thinly populated.* **3 thinly disguised/veiled/concealed etc.** easy to see or understand what something really is or who someone really is: *a thinly veiled threat* **4 thinly staffed** a thinly staffed business or office does not have enough people to do all of the work that needs to be done **5** not being bought or sold quickly on the STOCK EXCHANGE: *thinly traded stocks*

thin·ner /ˈθɪnɚ/ *n.* [U] a liquid such as TURPENTINE that you add to paint to make it less thick

thin·ning /ˈθɪnɪŋ/ *adj.* someone with thinning hair is losing their hair, so that in the future they will become BALD

ˌthin-ˈskinned *adj.* too easily offended or upset by criticism

third[1] /θɚd/ *adj.* **1** 3rd; next after the second: *This is her third marriage.* **2 (the) third time's the charm** SPOKEN used when you have failed to do something twice and hope to be successful the third time **3 feel like a third wheel** INFORMAL to feel that the two people you are with do not want you to be there

third[2] *pron.* **the third** the 3rd thing in a series: *Is your birthday on the third* (=the 3rd day of the month)*?*

third[3] *n.* [C] ⅓: one of three equal parts: *Divide the sandwich into thirds.* | **+of** *a third of the population* | **one-third/two-thirds** *Two-thirds of the profits are given to various charities.*

ˌthird ˈbase *n.* [singular] the third place that a player must touch before they can earn a point in baseball

ˌthird ˈclass *n.* [U] **1** a cheap class of mail in the U.S., usually used for sending advertisements → see also FIRST CLASS, SECOND CLASS **2** OLD USE the cheapest and least comfortable part of a train or ship —**third-class** *adj., adv.*: *Send the package third-class.*

ˌthird deˈgree *n.* **give sb the third degree** INFORMAL to ask someone a lot of questionsin order to get information from them

ˈthird-degree *adj.* **1 a third-degree burn** the most serious kind of burn, that goes right through your skin **2 third-degree felony/assault/murder etc.** a crime that is less serious than other crimes or types of the same crime

ˌthird ˈeyelid *n.* [C] a thin transparent layer of skin that is closer to the eye than an EYELID, and that can move across the eyes of birds, REPTILES, and some other animals to protect the eye SYN **nictitating membrane**

ˌthird ˈparty *n.* [C] **1** LAW someone who is not one of the two main people involved in an agreement or legal case, but who is affected by it or involved in some way **2** a political group whose CANDIDATES oppose the main political parties, especially in a country like the U.S. that only has two main political parties —**third-party** *adj.*

ˌthird ˈperson *n.* ENG. LANG. ARTS **1 the third person** a form of a verb or PRONOUN that is used for showing the person, thing, or group that is being mentioned. For example, "he," "she," "it," and "they" are pronouns in the third person, and "is" is the third person singular form of the verb "to be." **2 in the third person** a story in the third person is told as the experience of someone else, using the pronouns "he," "she," or "they" → see also FIRST PERSON, SECOND PERSON

ˌthird ˌperson narˈration *n.* [U] ENG. LANG. ARTS a way of telling a story in which the writer writes about the characters by using their names or using "he," "she," or "they" instead of "I"

ˌthird-ˈrate *adj.* of very bad quality: *a third-rate business school*

ˌThird ˈWorld *n.* **the Third World** the poorer countries of the world that are not industrially developed —**Third World** *adj.*: *Third World economies*

thirst[1] /θɚst/ *n.* **1** [singular] the feeling of wanting or needing a drink: *He downed a bottle of water to* ***quench his thirst*** (=get rid of his thirst). **2** [U] the state of not having enough to drink: *Many of them* ***died of thirst.*** **3 a thirst for knowledge/power/education etc.** LITERARY a strong desire for knowledge, power etc. [**Origin:** Old English *thurst*]

thirst[2] *v.* [I] OLD USE to be thirsty

thirst for/after sth *phr. v.* LITERARY to want something very much

thirst·y /ˈθɚsti/ S3 *adj. comparative* **thirstier**, *superlative* **thirstiest** **1** needing to drink or feeling that you want a drink: *We were hot and thirsty after our walk.* **2 thirsty for knowledge/power etc.** LITERARY having a strong desire for knowledge, power etc. **3** LITERARY or INFORMAL thirsty fields or plants need water → see also BLOOD-THIRSTY —**thirstily** *adv.*

thir·teen /ˌθɚˈtin◂/ *number* 13

thir·teenth[1] /ˌθɚˈtinθ◂/ *adj.* 13th; next after the twelfth: *the thirteenth century*

thirteenth[2] *pron.* **the thirteenth** the 13th thing in a series: *I'll see you on the thirteenth* (=the 13th day of the month).

ˌThirteenth Aˈmendment, the HISTORY a change to the U.S. Constitution in 1865 which made it illegal to have slaves

thir·ti·eth[1] /ˈθɚt̬iɪθ/ *adj.* 30th; next after the twenty-ninth: *our thirtieth anniversary*

thirtieth[2] *pron.* **the thirtieth** the 30th thing in a series: *Let's have dinner on the thirtieth* (=the 30th day of the month).

thir·ty /ˈθɚt̬i/ *number* **1** 30 **2 the thirties** also **the '30s** the years from 1930 to 1939 **3 sb's thirties** the time when someone is 30 to 39 years old: **in your early/mid/late thirties** *She got married in her early thirties.* **4 in the thirties** if the temperature is in the thirties, it is between 30° and 39° FAHRENHEIT: **in the high/low thirties** *The temperature was in the high thirties all week.*

thir·ty·some·thing /ˈθɚṭiˌsʌmθɪŋ/ *adj.* INFORMAL between the ages of 30 and 39 —**thirtysomethings** *n.* [plural]

this[1] /ðɪs/ S1 W1 *determiner plural* **these** /ðiz/ **1** SPOKEN used to talk about someone or something that is close to you, especially when you are looking or pointing at them: *Is this pen yours?* | *This jacket cost about $50.* | *This lady is John's grandmother.* | *Are all of these clothes dirty?* **2** used to talk about the present time, or a time that is close to the present: *Steve's going to Miami this Thursday.* | *The band plans to go on tour this year.* **3** used to talk about a person, thing, idea etc. that has just been mentioned or is already known about: *In this chapter, we consider the country's history.* | *Add this mixture to the sauce.* **4** SPOKEN used in conversation to mean a particular person or thing, especially when you do not know their name: *Then this girl came up and kissed him on the lips.* | *When am I going to meet this boyfriend of yours?* **5** SPOKEN used to talk about something you are going to say, or something that is going to happen: *You'll love this story.* **6 (right) this minute/second** SPOKEN immediately: *You don't have to give me your answer right this minute.* **7 what's (all) this...?** SPOKEN used to ask what is happening, what someone's problem is etc.: *What's all this yelling about?* [**Origin:** Old English *thes, this*] → see also THAT

this[2] S1 W1 *pron.* **1** *plural* **these** /ðiz/ used to talk about a person, thing, idea etc. that has just been mentioned or is already known about: *I've never done this before.* | *This is why it is important to diagnose the condition early.* | *These are all very expensive cities to live in.* **2** *plural* **these** used to talk about someone or something that is close to you, especially when you are looking or pointing at them: *This is where I live.* | *This is a picture of my parents.* **3** the present time: *I thought he would have been back before this.* | *This has been a very good year.* | *Is this a good time to talk?* **4** SPOKEN **a)** used to introduce someone to someone else: *Sam, this is my sister, Liz.* **b)** used to give your name when you are speaking on the telephone: *Hi, Barry – this is Mark.* **5** SPOKEN used to talk about something that you are going to say, or something that is going to happen: *Listen to this.* **6 this is it** SPOKEN said to show that you are excited or nervous because something important is about to happen: *This is it – the moment we've been waiting for.* **7 this, that, and the other** also **this and that** SPOKEN various different things, subjects etc.: *"What have you been doing lately?" "Oh, this, that, and the other."* → see also THAT

this[3] *adv.* [+ adj./adv.] **this big/many etc.** SPOKEN used to say how big or how many, especially because you are showing the size, number etc. with your hand: **this big/tall/wide etc.** *Dana's about this tall and has brown hair.* | **this much/many** *He only opened the door about this much.*

this·tle /ˈθɪsəl/ *n.* [C,U] a wild plant with long pointed leaves and purple or white furry flowers

thith·er /ˈθɪðɚ/ *adj.* OLD USE in that direction

tho' /ðoʊ/ *adv.* a short form of THOUGH

Thom·as, Dy·lan /ˈtɑməs, ˈdɪlən/ (1914–1954) a Welsh poet and writer

Thomas, Saint in the Bible, one of the 12 APOSTLES, who did not believe the news that Jesus was alive again after he had been killed

Thomas à Kem·pis /ˌtɑməs ə ˈkɛmpɪs/ → see KEMPIS, THOMAS À

thong /θɔŋ, θɑŋ/ *n.* **1** [C] a piece of underwear or the bottom half of a BIKINI that has a single string instead of the back part **2 thongs** [plural] a type of shoe that covers the bottom of your foot, with a STRAP that goes between your toes to hold it on your foot as you walk SYN **flip-flops** → see picture at SHOE[1] **3** [C] a long thin piece of leather used to fasten something or as part of a whip

Thor /θɔr/ in Norse MYTHOLOGY, the god of THUNDER and the strongest of the gods

tho·rax /ˈθɔræks/ *n. plural* **thoraxes** or **thoraces** /-rəsiz/ [C] BIOLOGY **1** the part of the body between your neck and your DIAPHRAGM (=area above your stomach) **2** the part of an insect's body between its head and its ABDOMEN —**thoracic** /θɔˈræsɪk/ *adj.*

Tho·reau, Hen·ry Da·vid /θəˈroʊ, ˈhɛnri ˈdeɪvɪd/ (1817–1862) a U.S. writer and PHILOSOPHER best known for his simple life in the countryside, and for his ideas about refusing to obey unfair laws, which influenced Gandhi and Martin Luther King, Jr.

thorn /θɔrn/ *n.* **1** [C] BIOLOGY a sharp point that grows on the stem of a plant such as a rose **2 a thorn in your side** someone or something that annoys you or causes problems for a long period of time

thorn·y /ˈθɔrni/ *adj. comparative* **thornier**, *superlative* **thorniest** **1 a thorny question/problem/point etc.** a question, problem etc. that is complicated and difficult **2** BIOLOGY a thorny bush, plant etc. has thorns —**thorniness** *n.* [U]

thor·ough /ˈθɚoʊ, ˈθʌroʊ/ *adj.* **1** including everything that is possible or necessary: *The report was thorough and detailed.* | **a thorough knowledge/understanding** *Students need to have a thorough understanding of the subject.* | **a thorough investigation/examination/search etc.** *A thorough search of the area was made.* **2** careful to do things correctly, so that you avoid mistakes: *He's extremely thorough in his work.* ▸see THESAURUS box at **careful** **3 a thorough pest/nuisance/mess** used to emphasize the bad qualities of someone or something SYN **complete** → see also THOROUGHLY —**thoroughness** *n.* [U]

thor·ough·bred /ˈθɚəˌbrɛd, ˈθɚoʊ-, ˈθʌr-/ *n.* [C] **1** a horse that has parents of the same very good breed **2** someone or something of an extremely high standard —**thoroughbred** *adj.*

thor·ough·fare /ˈθɚəˌfɛr, ˈθɚoʊ-, ˈθʌr-/ *n.* [C] the main road through a place such as a city or town: *a hotel off the town's main thoroughfare*

thor·ough·go·ing /ˌθʌrəˈgoʊɪŋ◂/ *adj.* **1** very thorough and careful **2** [only before noun] a thoroughgoing action or quality is complete or total

thor·ough·ly /ˈθɚoʊli/ *adv.* **1** completely: *I thoroughly enjoyed the party.* | *I was thoroughly confused.* **2** carefully, so that nothing is forgotten: *All complaints are thoroughly investigated.*

Thorpe, Jim /θɔrp, dʒɪm/ (1888–1953) a U.S. ATHLETE famous for winning GOLD MEDALS in the Olympics in 1912

those /ðoʊz/ *determiner, pron.* the plural of THAT

thou /ðaʊ/ *pron.* OLD USE a word meaning "you," used as the subject of a sentence → see also HOLIER-THAN-THOU

though[1] /ðoʊ/ S1 W1 *conjunction* **1** used to introduce a statement that makes the other main statement seem surprising or unlikely SYN **although**: *Though she's retired, she's still very active.* **2** used to add a fact or opinion that makes what you have just said seem less serious, less important etc. SYN **although** SYN **but**: *The test was difficult, though fair.* | *I enjoyed the movie, though I thought it was too long.* → see also **as if.../as though...** at AS[2] (4), **even though** at EVEN[1] (3)

though[2] S1 W2 *adv.* [sentence adverb] SPOKEN used after a fact, opinion, or question that seems surprising after what you have just said, or that makes what you have just said seem less true or important: *I'm busy today. We could meet tomorrow, though.* | *It sounds like fun. Isn't it dangerous, though?* [**Origin:** 1200–1300 Old Norse *tho*]

thought[1] /θɔt/ *v.* the past tense and past participle of THINK

thought[2] W1 *n.*

1 STH YOU THINK ABOUT [C] something that you think of, remember, or realize SYN **idea**: *News of the crash dominated his thoughts.* | **the thought (that)** *The thought that I might lose my job was upsetting me.* | *Even* ***the thought of*** (=used when a thought produces strong emotions) *flying scares me.* | *I've just* ***had a thought*** (=suddenly thought of something) *– why don't we invite Judith?* | *"You need a new car." "Yeah,* ***the thought had crossed my mind*** (=I had thought about

T

that before)." | **a thought occurs to/strikes sb** *On the way home, a thought occurred to me.* | **can't stand/bear the thought of sth** *I can't stand the thought of writing another essay.* ▸see THESAURUS box at **idea**

2 ACT OF THINKING [U] the act of thinking about something: *Greg seemed* ***deep in thought*** (=thinking so much that he did not notice anything) *when I walked in.* | *the* ***thought processes*** (=way people's minds work) *of children*

3 CAREFUL CONSIDERATION [U] careful and serious consideration: *This idea needs a lot more thought.* | *You should* ***give some thought to*** (=think carefully about) *going to art school.*

4 IDEA/OPION [C usually plural] an idea or opinion about something: **+on** *Do you have any thoughts on how we should spend the money?*

5 CARING ABOUT SB/STH [C,U] a feeling of worrying or caring about someone or something: **+for** *He had no thought for anyone but himself.* | *You are* ***always in my thoughts*** (=used to tell someone that you think about them and care about them a lot).

6 INTENTION [C,U] a plan or hope of doing something: **+of** *I had no thought of gaining any personal advantage.*

7 WAY OF THINKING [U] a way of thinking that is typical of a particular group, period of history etc.: *ancient Greek thought*

8 sb's thoughts wander used to say that someone starts to think about something else without intending to

T

9 sb's thoughts turn to sb/sth used to say that someone starts to think about someone or something

SPOKEN PHRASES

10 that's a thought used to say that someone has made a good suggestion: *"You could always take the class next semester." "That's a thought."*

11 (it's) just a thought used to say that what you have just said is only a suggestion and you have not thought about it very much: *We could sell the car – just a thought.*

12 it's the thought that counts used to say that the size or value of a present is unimportant, because it is the action of giving that shows that you care about someone

13 don't give it another thought used to tell someone politely not to worry after they have told you they are sorry

→ see also **perish the thought** at PERISH (3), **school of thought** at SCHOOL[1] (7), **have second thoughts (about sth)** at SECOND[1] (4), **on second thought** at SECOND[1] (5), **not give sth a second thought** at SECOND[1] (6), **without a second thought** at SECOND[1] (7), **sb's train of thought** at TRAIN[1] (2)

thought·ful /ˈθɔtfəl/ *adj.* **1** always thinking of the things you can do to make people happy or comfortable OPP **thoughtless**: *Paula's such a thoughtful girl.* | **+it's thoughtful (of sb) to do sth** *It was thoughtful of him to call.* ▸see THESAURUS box at **kind**[2] **2** well planned or thought about a lot: *thoughtful analysis* **3** serious and quiet because you are thinking a lot: *a thoughtful expression* —**thoughtfully** *adv.* —**thoughtfulness** *n.* [U]

thought·less /ˈθɔtlɪs/ *adj.* **1** not thinking about the needs or feelings of other people OPP **thoughtful**: *a thoughtless selfish man* | **it is thoughtless (of sb) to do sth** *It was thoughtless of him to remember her birthday.* ▸see THESAURUS box at **mean**[3], **unkind** **2** showing a lack of careful or serious thought: *thoughtless actions* —**thoughtlessly** *adv.* —**thoughtlessness** *n.*

ˌthought-ˈout *adj.* **carefully/well/badly etc. thought-out** planned and organized carefully, well etc.: *a well thought-out argument*

ˈthought-proˌvoking *adj.* making you think a lot: *a thought-provoking article*

thou·sand /ˈθaʊzənd/ *number* **1** 1,000: **two/three/four etc. thousand** *It cost 15 thousand dollars.* | **thousands of sth** *It will cost thousands of dollars.* **2** INFORMAL a large number of people or things: *I have a thousand things to do today.* | **thousands of sth** *There were thousands of messages on my answering machine.* [**Origin:** Old English *thusend*] → see Grammar box at HUNDRED[1]

thou·sandth[1] /ˈθaʊzəndθ/ *adj.* 1,000th

thousandth[2] *pron.* **the thousandth** the 1,000th thing in a series

thousandth[3] *n.* [C] 1/1000; one of one thousand equal parts

thrall /θrɔl/ *n.* **in sb's/sth's thrall** also **in thrall to sb/sth** LITERARY controlled or strongly influenced by someone or something

thrall·dom, thraldom /ˈθrɔldəm/ *n.* [U] LITERARY the state of being a slave SYN **slavery**

thrash[1] /θræʃ/ *v.* **1** [I always + adv./prep., T] to move or make part of your body move from side to side in a violent or uncontrolled way: **+around** *The fish started thrashing around in the net.* | *He thrashed his arms and legs, trying to swim.* **2** [T] INFORMAL to defeat someone very easily in a game **3** [T] to beat someone violently in order to punish them

thrash sth ↔ **out** *phr. v.* to discuss a problem thoroughly with someone until you find an answer: *The board of directors met to thrash out a deal.*

thrash[2] *n.* **1** [singular] a violent movement from side to side **2** [U] INFORMAL a type of ROCK music with very loud fast electric GUITAR playing

thrash·ing /ˈθræʃɪŋ/ *n.* [C] **1 give/get a thrashing** to beat someone or be beaten violently as a punishment **2** an easy defeat in a game

thread[1] /θrɛd/ *n.*

1 FOR SEWING [C,U] a long thin string of cotton, silk etc. used to SEW or weave cloth: *a needle and thread* | ***a spool of white thread***

2 THIN STRING a long thin FIBER, for example one made by an insect: *the threads of a spider's web*

3 CONNECTION [C] an idea or feature that is found in all the different parts of an explanation, story, group of people etc. and connects them with each other: *The* ***common thread*** *among these groups is a hate for government.* | **follow/lose the thread (of sth)** *I found it difficult to follow the thread of his argument.*

4 INTERNET/EMAIL [C] a series of related emails, messages etc. on an Internet discussion group concerning the same subject

5 SMALL AMOUNT [C usually singular] a small amount of a quality: *I tried to hold on to a thread of decency and courage.*

6 LINE LITERARY [C] a long thin line of something such as light, smoke etc.

7 ON A SCREW [C] a continuous raised line of metal that winds around the curved surface of a screw

8 threads [plural] OLD-FASHIONED clothes → see also **hang by a thread** at HANG[1] (10), **pick up the threads (of sth)** at PICK UP (25)

thread[2] *v.* [T]

1 thread a needle to put thread through the EYE (=hole) of a needle

2 thread sth through sth to put a thread or string through a hole: *Thread the chain through the holes.*

3 CONNECT OBJECTS to connect objects by pushing a string through a hole in them: *Thread the beads on a string and make a necklace.*

4 FILM/TAPE to put a film, TAPE etc. correctly through parts of a camera, PROJECTOR, or TAPE RECORDER

5 thread (your way) through/into etc. to move through a place by carefully going around things that are blocking your way: *We threaded our way through the crowd.*

thread·bare /ˈθrɛdbɛr/ *adj.* [no comparative] **1** threadbare clothes, CARPETS etc. are very thin and in bad condition because they have been used a lot **2 a threadbare excuse/argument/joke etc.** an excuse etc. that is not effective anymore because it has been used too much

threat /θrɛt/ W2 *n.* **1** [C,U] a statement that you will cause someone pain, unhappiness, or trouble, especially if they do not do something you want: *Your threats don't scare me!* | **+of** *the threat of legal action* | **a**

threat to do sth *threats to use nuclear weapons* | *He denied* ***making*** *any* ***threats.*** | *Nichols never* ***carried out*** *his* ***threat*** *to resign.* | **a death/bomb etc. threat** *The bank has received several bomb threats this year.* | **an empty/idle threat** (=a threat to do something that you will not really do) | **a veiled threat** (=a threat that is not said directly but can be understood) | *Soldiers were* ***under threat of*** (=threatened with) *death if they did not fight.* **2** [C usually singular] the possibility that something very bad will happen: **+of** *the threat of flooding* | **pose/present a threat (to sb/sth)** *Pollution in the river poses a threat to fish.* ▶see THESAURUS box at **danger** **3** [C usually singular] someone or something that is regarded as a possible danger: *The country is still a military threat.* | **+to** *The virus is not a threat to humans.* | *He obviously* ***sees you as a threat.*** [**Origin:** Old English]

threat·en /ˈθrɛt˺n/ S3 W2 *v.* **1** [T] to say that you will cause someone pain, worry, or trouble if they do not do what you want: *Are you threatening me?* | *The unions are threatening a one-day strike.* | **threaten to do sth** *Carol threatened to resign.* | **threaten sb with sth** *He never threatened me with violence.* | *He said the men had* ***threatened*** *his* ***life.*** **2** [T] to be likely to harm, kill, or destroy someone or something: *Pollution is threatening the marine life in the bay.* | **threaten sb/sth with destruction/extinction/death etc.** *Large areas of the jungle are threatened with destruction.* **3 threaten to do sth** to be likely to cause a bad or unpleasant situation: *The scandal threatens to ruin his election chances.* **4** [I,T] LITERARY if something bad threatens or something else threatens it, it seems likely to happen: *Rain threatened.*

threat·en·ing /ˈθrɛt˺n-ɪŋ/ *adj.* **1** talking or behaving in a way that is intended to threaten someone: *threatening movements* **2** making threats: *threatening telephone calls* —**threateningly** *adv.*

three[1] /θri/ *number* **1** 3 **2** three o'clock: *Let's meet* ***at three*** *by the library.* [**Origin:** Old English *thrie, threo*] → see also THIRD[1]

three[2] *n.* **in threes** in groups or sets of three people or things: *Students were grouped in threes.*

three-ˈcornered *adj.* **1** having three corners **2 a three-cornered contest/fight** a competition that involves three people or groups

three-D, 3-D /ˌθri ˈdi◂/ *adj.* a three-D movie or picture is made so that it appears to be three-dimensional —**three-D, 3-D** *n.* [U] *a film in three-D*

three-diˈmensional *adj.* **1** having or seeming to have length, depth, and height: *a three-dimensional drawing* **2** a three-dimensional character in a book, movie etc., seems like a real person

Three-ˈFifths ˌCompromise, the HISTORY an agreement between the U.S. states in 1787 by which each SLAVE counted as three-fifths of a person when deciding the number of LEGISLATIVE representatives for each state

three·fold /ˈθrifoʊld/ *adj.* three times as much or as many —**threefold** *adv.*

three-leg·ged race /ˌθri lɛgɪd ˈreɪs/ *n.* [C] a race in which two people run together, with one person's right leg tied to the other person's left leg

three-peat /ˈθripit/ *n.* [C] INFORMAL the action of winning a sports competition three times, one after the other

three-piece ˈsuit *n.* [C] a suit that consists of a JACKET, VEST, and pants made from the same material

three-ply *adj.* three-ply wood, YARN, TISSUE etc. consists of three layers or threads

three-ˈpointer, 3-pointer *n.* [C] a SHOT in basketball from outside a particular line, so that if the ball goes in the basket, the team receives three points

three-point ˈturn *n.* [C] a way of turning your car so that it faces the opposite way, by driving forward, backward, and then forward again while turning

three-ˈquarter *adj.* [only before noun] three-quarters of the full size, length etc. of something: *a three-quarter moon* | **three-quarter-length/three-quarter-size etc.** *a three-quarter-size piano*

three-ˈquarters *n.* [plural] an amount equal to three of the four equal parts that make up a whole: **+of** *three-quarters of an hour*

ˌthree-ring ˈcircus *n.* **1** [singular] INFORMAL a place or situation that is confusing because there is too much activity **2** [C usually singular] a CIRCUS that has three areas in which people or animals perform at the same time

three R's /ˌθri ˈɑrz/ *n.* **the three R's** INFORMAL reading, writing, and ARITHMETIC (=working with numbers), considered as the basic things that children must learn

three·score /ˈθriskɔr/ *number* OLD USE 60 → see also SCORE[1] (8)

three·some /ˈθrisəm/ *n.* [C usually singular] INFORMAL a group of three people or things

ˈthree-star *adj.* a three-star hotel, restaurant etc. is officially judged to be of a good standard

three-ˈstrikes *adj.* [only before noun] also **three-ˌstrikes-and-you're-ˈout** a three-strikes law puts people in prison for a long time if they are guilty of three serious crimes, without any chance of getting out of prison early

ˌthree-ˈwheeler *n.* [C] a vehicle that has three wheels, especially a MOTORCYCLE, TRICYCLE, or special WHEELCHAIR

thren·o·dy /ˈθrɛnədi/ *n. plural* **threnodies** [C] ENG. LANG. ARTS a funeral song for someone who has died

thresh /θrɛʃ/ *v.* [I,T] to separate the grain from the rest of corn, wheat etc., by beating it with a special tool or machine —**thresher** *n.* [C]

ˈthreshing maˌchine *n.* [C] a machine used for separating the grain from the rest of corn, wheat etc.

thresh·old /ˈθrɛʃhoʊld, -ʃoʊld/ *n.* [C] **1** the entrance to a room or building, or the area of floor at the entrance **2** the level at which something starts to happen, becomes something, or has an effect: *The machine sets off an alarm if the explosion exceeds a certain threshold.* | **have a high/low pain threshold** (=be able or not be able to suffer a lot of pain before you react) **3 on the threshold of sth** at the beginning of a new and important event or development: *The country is on the threshold of a new era.*

threw /θru/ *v.* the past tense of THROW

thrice /θraɪs/ *adv.* OLD USE three times

thrift /θrɪft/ *n.* [U] OLD-FASHIONED wise and careful use of money, so that none is wasted → see also SPENDTHRIFT

ˈthrift shop *n.* [C] a store that sells used goods, especially clothes, often in order to earn money for a CHARITY

thrift·y /ˈθrɪfti/ *adj. comparative* **thriftier**, *superlative* **thriftiest** using money carefully and not wasting any —**thriftily** *adv.* —**thriftiness** *n.* [U]

thrill[1] /θrɪl/ *n.* **1** [C] a sudden strong feeling of excitement and pleasure, or the thing that makes you feel this: *Winning the gold medal was a thrill.* | **the thrill of (doing) sth** *the thrill of bungee jumping* | *Mr. Samuels still* ***gets a thrill out of*** *teaching.* | *He often stole just* ***for the thrill of it*** (=for excitement and not for any serious reason). **2 the thrill of the hunt/chase** the excitement of trying to find or get someone or something that you want **3 thrills and chills** also **thrills and spills** the excitement and danger involved in an activity, especially a sport → see also **cheap thrill** at CHEAP[1] (10)

thrill[2] S3 *v.* [T] to make someone feel excited and happy: *His music continues to thrill audiences.* [**Origin:** Old English *thyrlian* **to make a hole in**, from *thyrel* **hole**]

thrill to sth *phr. v.* FORMAL to make someone feel excited and happy

thrilled /θrɪld/ *adj.* [not before noun] very excited, happy, and pleased: **+with** *We're thrilled with the results.* | **thrilled that** *They were thrilled that you* came. | **thrilled to do sth** *I'm thrilled to be here.* | **thrilled to pieces/bits** (=very thrilled)

thrill·er /ˈθrɪlɚ/ *n.* [C] a book or movie that tells an exciting story about murder, crime, or spies (SPY)

thrill·ing /ˈθrɪlɪŋ/ *adj.* interesting and exciting: *a thrilling adventure* —**thrillingly** *adv.*

thrive /θraɪv/ *v. past tense* **thrived** or **throve** /θroʊv/, *past participle* **thrived** or **thriven** /ˈθrɪvən/ [I] FORMAL to become very successful or very strong and healthy: *The plant needs direct sunlight to thrive.* | *Business thrived in the freedom of the 1920s.*

thrive on sth *phr. v.* to enjoy or be successful in conditions that other people, businesses etc. find difficult or unfavorable: *Some people thrive on pressure.*

thriv·ing /ˈθraɪvɪŋ/ *adj.* a thriving company, business etc. is very successful

throat /θroʊt/ S2 W3 *n.* [C] **1** BIOLOGY the passage from the back of your mouth to the top of the tubes that go down to your lungs and stomach: *Does your throat hurt?* | *I've got* ***a sore throat.*** **2** BIOLOGY the front of your neck: *The attacker grabbed her by the throat.* **3 force/ram sth down sb's throat** INFORMAL DISAPPROVING to force someone to accept or listen to your ideas and opinions: *I don't like people forcing their politics down my throat.* **4 be at each other's throats** if two people are at each other's throats, they are fighting or arguing **5 slit/cut your own throat** to behave in a way that is certain to harm you, especially because you are too proud or angry [**Origin:** Old English *throte*] → see also **clear your throat** at CLEAR² (11), **have a frog in your throat** at FROG (2), **jump down sb's throat** at JUMP¹ (9), **bring a lump to sb's throat** at LUMP¹ (3), **stick in your throat** at STICK¹ (7)

T

throat·y /ˈθroʊt̬i/ *adj. comparative* **throatier**, *superlative* **throatiest** making a low rough sound when you speak or sing: *a throaty voice* —**throatily** *adv.* —**throatiness** *n.* [C,U]

throb¹ /θrɑb/ *v.* **throbbed, throbbing** [I] **1** if a part of your body throbs, you get a regular feeling of pain in it: *His hand began to* ***throb with pain.*** ►see THESAURUS box at **hurt¹** **2** if music or a machine throbs, it makes a sound with a strong regular beat **3** if your heart throbs, it beats faster or more strongly than usual —**throbbing** *adj.*: *a throbbing headache* —**throbbing** *n.* [singular,U]

throb² *n.* [C] a low strong regular beat or pain → see also HEARTTHROB

throes /θroʊz/ *n.* [plural] **1 in the throes of sth** in the middle of a very difficult situation: *Liberia was still in the throes of a civil war.* **2 in the last/final throes of sth** in the last stages of something, just before it ends → see also DEATH THROES

throm·bo·sis /θrɑmˈboʊsɪs/ *n. plural* **thromboses** /-siz/ [C,U] MEDICINE a serious medical problem caused by a CLOT forming in your blood, especially in your heart

throne /θroʊn/ *n.* **1** [C] a special chair used by a king or queen at important ceremonies **2 the throne** POLITICS the position and power of being a king or queen: *Who was* ***on the throne*** (=ruling as king or queen) *in 1935?* | *The prince is* ***the heir to the throne*** (=the person who will become king next). | **ascend/assume the throne** (=become king or queen) **3 on the throne** HUMOROUS on the toilet

throng¹ /θrɔŋ, θrɑŋ/ *n.* [C] LITERARY a large group of people in one place SYN **crowd**: **+of** *a throng of reporters*

throng² *v.* **1** [I always + adv./prep., T] if people throng to a place, they go there in large numbers: **+to/around/through etc.** *Mourners thronged to his tomb.* **2 be thronged with sb** if a place is thronged with people, it is very crowded with them

throt·tle¹ /ˈθrɑt̬l/ *v.* [T] **1** to hold someone's throat very tightly so that they cannot breathe SYN **strangle** **2** WRITTEN to make it difficult or impossible for something to succeed

throttle back *phr. v.* **throttle sth ↔ back** to reduce the amount of gasoline or oil flowing into an engine, in order to reduce speed

throttle² *n.* [C] TECHNICAL **1** a piece of equipment that controls the amount of gasoline, oil etc. going into a vehicle's engine **2 (at) full throttle a)** if a vehicle or its engine is at full throttle, the throttle is open so the vehicle is traveling as fast as possible **b)** happening or being done with as much speed, energy, or effort as possible

through¹ /θru/ S1 W1 *prep.* **1** into one side or end of something such as an entrance, passage, or hole, and out of the other side or end: *Two men walked through the door.* | *The dog got out through a hole in the fence.* | *The oil comes through this pipe.* **2** from one side of an area or group to the other: *We drove through France to Spain.* | *I pushed my way through the crowd.* **3** if you see or hear someone or something through something such as a window or wall, you are on one side of the window or wall and they are on the other side: *I saw her through an upstairs window.* | *The walls are so thin you can hear everything through them.* **4** passing a place where you are supposed to stop: *The driver went through a red light.* **5** cutting, breaking, or making a hole from one side of something to the other: *Workers had to cut a hole through the ceiling to install the heating system.* | *The bullet passed through his right arm.* **6** during and to the end of a period of time: *We've got enough food to last us through the winter.* **7 half-way through sth** also **a quarter/third etc. of the way through sth** at a particular point during a period or during an event: *We're already half-way through the semester.* **8** used to say that someone or something has experienced or dealt with something difficult or unpleasant: *I don't want to live through another experience like that.* **9** until and including a particular day, month, or year: *The exibit will be here through April.* | **(from) Wednesday through Friday/May through October etc.** *The store is open Monday through Saturday.* **10** from the beginning to the end of a process, step, or event: *The book guides you through the procedure of buying a house.* **11** used to say that someone reads or examines all parts of something carefully: *Let's go through these documents again.* **12** because of something: *Many accidents are caused through carelessness.* **13** by using a particular method, service, person etc. to do something: *She got the job through a friend.* | *They learn math through simple games.* **14 be/get through doing sth** INFORMAL to finish doing something: *Tell me when you're through talking about work.* **15** used to say that something exists in, affects, or starts to affect all of a thing, area, or group SYN **throughout**: *The problem extends through the entire system.* **16** used to say that someone uses a supply of something: *Our family goes through a lot of food in a week.* **17** if a law passes through Congress or another group that makes laws, it is accepted as a law: *the bill's passage through Congress* → see also THRU

through² S1 W1 *adv.* **1** from one side or end of a passage, area, group, surface etc. to the other: *Excuse me, could you let me through?* | *I spilled water on the tablecloth, but it didn't soak through.* | **+to** *Gas isn't flowing through to the engine.* **2** completely, in all parts: *Make sure the food is heated through.* **3 read/think/talk etc. sth through** to read, think etc. about something very carefully from beginning to end: *Take some time to read the contract through.* **4 through and through** if someone is a particular type of person through and through, they are completely that type of person: *She's a politician through and through.* **5 through to sth** all the time until the end of a period of time or an event: *A good breakfast will last you through to lunchtime.*

through³ *adj.* **1 be through** INFORMAL **a)** to have finished doing something, using something etc.: *I need to use the computer when you're through.* | **+with** *I'm through with politics.* **b)** to not be having a romantic relationship with someone anymore: *She told me we're through.* ►see THESAURUS box at **done²** **2 a through train/road/street etc.** a train or road by which you can reach a place, without having to use other trains or roads

through·out[1] /θruˈaʊt/ S3 W1 *prep.* **1** in or to every part of a place or thing: *The disease spread throughout Europe.* | *He uses the same spelling throughout the book.* **2** during all of a particular period, from the beginning to the end: *The museum is open throughout the year.*

throughout[2] *adv.* [usually at the end of a sentence] **1** during all of a particular period, from the beginning to the end: *He remained calm throughout.* **2** in every part of a place or thing: *The house is beautifully decorated throughout.*

through·put /ˈθrupʊt/ *n.* [singular, U] the amount of work, materials etc. that can be dealt with in a particular period of time

through·way /ˈθruweɪ/ *n.* [C] another spelling of THRUWAY

throve /θroʊv/ *v.* OLD-FASHIONED a past tense of THRIVE

throw

throw — throw away

throw[1] /θroʊ/ S1 W1 *v. past tense* **threw** /θru/, *past participle* **thrown** /θroʊn/

1 THROW A BALL/STONE ETC. [I,T] to make an object such as a ball move quickly from your hand through the air by moving your arm quickly and letting go of the object: *She can throw pretty well for a little girl.* | **throw sth at/to/toward etc. sb/sth** *Someone threw a bottle at him.* | **throw sb sth** *Could you throw me an apple?*

THESAURUS

toss to throw something, especially in a careless way: *She tossed her coat onto the bed.*
chuck INFORMAL to throw something, often without taking careful aim: *Kids were chucking snowballs at passing cars.*
hurl to throw something with a lot of force: *They hurled a brick through his window.*
fling to throw something somewhere with a lot of force, often in a careless way: *He flung her keys into the river.*

to throw a ball in a sport
pass to throw, kick, or hit a ball to another member of your team
pitch to throw the ball to the person who is trying to hit the ball in a game of baseball

2 PUT STH CARELESSLY [T always + adv./prep.] to put something somewhere quickly and carelessly: **throw sth on/onto/down etc.** *I quickly threw my clothes into a bag and left.*

3 PUSH ROUGHLY [T always + adv./prep.] to make someone or something move roughly and violently in a particular direction or into a particular position: **throw sb/sth into/from etc. sth** *The force of the blast threw her into the air.* | **throw a door/window open** *James threw the door open and ran into the house.* | *Police* ***threw*** *the attacker* ***to the ground.***

4 MOVE HANDS/HEAD ETC. [T always + adv./prep.] to suddenly and quickly move your body or a part of your body into a new position: **throw sth back/up/around etc.** *He threw his head back and laughed.* | *She threw her arms around his neck.* | **throw yourself at/on/into/down etc.** *He threw himself onto the bench.* | **throw up your hands (in horror/protest/disgust etc.)** (=to put your hands in the air to show you think something is not good)

5 MAKE AN OPPONENT FALL [T] to make your opponent fall to the ground in WRESTLING or JUDO

6 HORSE [T] if a horse throws its rider it makes them fall onto the ground

7 throw sb into prison/jail to suddenly put someone in prison: *Taylor was thrown into prison for attempted murder.*

8 throw sb out of work/office etc. to suddenly take away someone's job or position of authority: *More than 500 employees were thrown out of work.*

9 CONFUSE/SURPRISE [T] to confuse or surprise someone, especially by suddenly saying something: *Mom was* ***completely thrown*** *by news of their engagement.* | *His death* ***threw*** *her* ***for a loop*** (=confused and shocked her). | *The rude suggestion had* ***thrown*** *her* ***off balance.***

10 QUESTION/REMARK ETC. [T] to suddenly or quickly ask questions of someone or say something to them, especially in an angry way: **throw sth at sb** *The questions he was throwing at her surprised her.*

11 throw suspicion/doubt on sth also **throw sth into question** to make people think that someone is probably guilty or that something may not be true: *New evidence has thrown doubt on his innocence.*

12 throw sb a look/glance/smile etc. also **throw a look/glance etc. at sb** to quickly look at someone with a particular expression that shows how you are feeling: *Hanson threw a mean look at her.*

13 throw a party/bash etc. to organize a party and invite people: *Let's throw a party to celebrate.*

14 throw a fit/tantrum to react in a very angry, and often physical, way

15 throw a switch/handle/lever to make a large machine or piece of electrical equipment start or stop working by moving a SWITCH

16 throw your weight around to use your position of authority to tell people what to do in an unreasonable way

17 throw your weight behind sb/sth to use all your power and influence to support someone or something

18 throw light/shadows/rays etc. WRITTEN to make light, shadows etc. fall on a particular place: *The buildings threw long shadows across the courtyard.*

19 throw cold water on sth to say that a plan, suggestion etc. is unlikely to succeed, or to prevent a plan from succeeding

20 throw money down the drain also **throw good money after bad** to waste money by spending it on something that has already failed or that is of bad quality

21 throw sth open (to sb) also **throw open sth (to sb)** **a)** to allow people to go into a place that is usually kept private: *The Center will throw open its doors to the public July 8.* **b)** to allow anyone to take part in a competition or a discussion

22 throw a game/match/fight etc. to deliberately and dishonestly lose a fight or sports game that you could have won

23 throw the baby out with the bath water DISAPPROVING to get rid of the good parts of a system, organization etc. in addition to the bad parts, when you are changing it in order to try and make it better

24 throw sth (back) in sb's face also **throw sth back at sb** **a)** to remind someone of something they have done or said in order to embarrass them **b)** to be unkind to someone after they have been kind to you or helped you

25 throw a punch/a left/a right etc. to try to hit someone with your hand in a fight

26 DICE [T] to roll DICE in a game: *I need to throw a five to win.*

27 throw your voice to make your voice sound as if it is coming from a different place from the place where you are

28 POT [T] to make a clay object such as a bowl, using a POTTER'S WHEEL

[**Origin:** Old English *thrawan* **to cause to twist or turn**]

→ see also **throw/fling/cast caution to the wind(s)**

at CAUTION[1] (3), **throw/toss your hat into the ring** at HAT (3), **shed/throw light on sth** at LIGHT[1] (9)

throw sth ↔ **aside** *phr. v.* to refuse to accept or use something anymore

throw at *phr. v.* **1 throw yourself at sb** INFORMAL to make it very clear to someone that you want to have a sexual relationship with them: *It's embarrassing how she throws herself at me.* **2 throw the book at sb** INFORMAL to punish someone as severely as possible, or to CHARGE someone with as many offenses as possible in a court of law **3 throw money at sb/sth** INFORMAL to try to solve a problem by spending a lot of money, but without really thinking carefully about the problem

throw sth ↔ **away** *phr. v.* **1** to get rid of something that you do not want or need: *If it's broken, go ahead and throw it away.* **2** to waste something good that you have, for example a skill, advantage, or opportunity: *The team threw away a 12-point lead.*

throw sth ↔ **back** *phr. v.* INFORMAL to drink something very quickly: *Ted quickly threw back three shots of whiskey.*

throw sb **back on** sth *phr. v.* FORMAL to force someone to depend on their own skills, knowledge etc.

throw in *phr. v.* **1 throw sth ↔ in** to add something to what you are selling, without increasing the price: *If you buy the bike, I'll throw in the lock.* **2 throw in the towel** INFORMAL to stop doing something because you cannot succeed **3 throw sth ↔ in** if you throw in a remark, you say it suddenly without thinking carefully

throw into *phr. v.* **1 throw yourself into sth** to start doing an activity eagerly and using a lot of time and effort: *After the divorce, she threw herself into her work.* **2 throw sth into confusion/chaos/disarray etc.** to suddenly put a situation or group of people in an unpleasant and confusing state: *The new computer system has thrown the office into chaos.*

throw off *phr. v.*

1 CONFUSE SB throw sb ↔ off to make someone slightly confused or surprised, especially in a way that makes them not sure what to do next: *She didn't let the mix-up throw her off.*

2 GET FREE FROM STH throw sb/sth ↔ off to get free from something that has been limiting your freedom: **throw off the yoke/shackles of sth** *The country has thrown off the yoke of communism.*

3 MAKE SB LEAVE throw sb ↔ off, throw sb off sth to force someone to leave a bus, train, airplane etc.: *They threw him off the bus for making too much noise.*

4 ESCAPE FROM SB/STH throw sb/sth ↔ off to escape from someone or something that is chasing you

5 TAKE OFF CLOTHES throw sth ↔ off to take off a piece of clothing in a quick careless way: *She threw off her jacket as she came in.*

6 throw sb off the scent/trail to stop someone from finding you or finding out the truth: *He attempted to throw police off his trail by dressing as a woman.*

7 PRODUCE HEAT/LIGHT ETC. throw sth ↔ off to produce large amounts of heat, light, RADIATION etc.

8 GET RID OF ILLNESS throw sth ↔ off if you throw off a slight illness such as a COLD, you succeed in getting better fairly quickly

throw sth ↔ **on** *phr. v.* to put on a piece of clothing quickly and carelessly: *Give me a minute to throw some clothes on, and I'll go with you.*

throw out *phr. v.*

1 GET RID OF STH throw sth ↔ out to get rid of something that you do not want or need, especially when you are cleaning a place: *My wife made me throw out my old tennis shoes.*

2 MAKE SB LEAVE throw sb ↔ out to make someone leave a place, school, organization etc. quickly, especially because they have been behaving badly or made you angry: **throw sb out of sth** *He was thrown out of school for selling drugs.*

3 REFUSE TO ACCEPT STH throw sth ↔ out if a committee, a court, Congress etc. throws out a plan, suggestion etc., they refuse to accept it: *Simon's case was thrown out of court.*

4 TAKE AWAY JOB throw sb ↔ out to suddenly take away someone's job or position of authority: *Voters are expected to throw the ruling party out.*

5 throw out an idea to suggest an idea

throw together *phr. v.* **1 throw sth ↔ together** to make something quickly and not very carefully: *Our report was thrown together this morning.* **2 throw sb ↔ together** if a situation throws people together, it makes them meet and know each other when they normally would not: *The war had thrown them together.*

throw up *phr. v.* **1 throw sth ↔ up** to bring food or drink up from your stomach and out through your mouth SYN **vomit**: *The smell almost made me throw up.* **2 throw sth ↔ up** to build something quickly: *Citizens threw up roadblocks.* **3 throw sth ↔ up** if a vehicle throws up dirt, water etc., it makes it go up in the air

throw[2] *n.* [C] **1** an act of throwing something such as a ball, or the distance it is thrown: *a perfect throw to third base* **2** a large piece of cloth that you put over a chair to cover it and make it look attractive **3** the action of making your opponent fall to the ground in a sport such as JUDO or WRESTLING **4** the action or result of throwing something such as a DART or DICE in a game

throw·a·way[1] /ˈθroʊəˌweɪ/ *adj.* [usually before noun] **1 a throwaway line/comment/remark etc.** a short remark etc. that is said quickly and without careful thought **2** cheaply produced and able to be thrown away after being used SYN **disposable** **3 a throwaway society** DISAPPROVING a modern society in which products are not made to last a long time and people throw a lot of things away **4 a throwaway song** a song that is not very good or will only be popular for a short time

throwaway[2] *n.* [C] **1** something that is thrown away after it has been used **2** a song that is not very good or will be popular for only a short time

throw·back /ˈθroʊbæk/ *n.* [C usually singular] something that is similar to or is a result of something that happened in the past: +**to** *The film is a throwback to the best of old-fashioned Hollywood movies.*

throw·down /ˈθroʊdaʊn/ *n.* [C] SLANG a party, especially one with music and dancing

ˈthrow-in *n.* [C] the act of throwing the ball back onto the field in SOCCER, after it has gone over the line at the side of the field

thrown /θroʊn/ *v.* the past participle of THROW

ˈthrow ˌpillow *n.* [C] a small CUSHION that you put on SOFAS, chairs, and beds for decoration

ˈthrow rug *n.* [C] a small RUG (=cloth or wool covering for a floor)

thru /θru/ *prep.* INFORMAL a short way of writing "through": *The store is open Monday thru Saturday.* —**thru** *adj., adv.* → see also DRIVE-THROUGH

thrum /θrʌm/ *v.* **thrummed, thrumming** [I,T] to make a low sound like something beating or shaking

thrush /θrʌʃ/ *n.* **1** [C] BIOLOGY a brown bird with spots on its front **2** [U] MEDICINE a FUNGAL infection that affects the mouth, throat, or female sex organs

thrust[1] /θrʌst/ *v. past tense and past participle* **thrust** [T]

1 PUSH VIOLENTLY to push someone or something somewhere with a sudden or violent movement: **thrust sth into/back/forward etc.** *She thrust a letter into my hand.* ▸see THESAURUS box at **put, shove[1]**

2 have sth thrust upon/on you to be forced to accept something that you did not expect or want: *Fame had been thrust upon him at an early age.*

3 MOVE WITH A WEAPON [I] to make a sudden movement toward someone or something with something such as a sword or knife, or your hand: +**at** *She thrust at him with a knife.*

4 MOVE FORWARD [I,T] WRITTEN to move somewhere by pushing hard and quickly: **thrust (your way) through sth/forward etc.** *He thrust his way through the crowd.*

5 thrust upward/out of sth/into sth etc. WRITTEN to

appear, grow, or be able to be seen above or beyond something

thrust sb **into** sth *phr. v.* to put someone in a difficult or unusual situation very quickly: *Saving the child's life has thrust Collins into the media spotlight.*

thrust² *n.* **1** [C usually singular] the main meaning or most important part of what someone says or does: +**of** *the main thrust of the argument* **2** [C] a sudden strong movement that pushes forward: +**of** *a thrust of his chin* **3** [U] PHYSICS the force of an engine that pushes something such as an airplane forward

thru·way, throughway /ˈθruweɪ/ *n. plural* **thruways** [C] a wide road for fast traffic that you pay to use

Thu. *n.* a written abbreviation of Thursday

thud¹ /θʌd/ *n.* [C] the low sound made by a heavy object hitting something else: *She landed on the floor* ***with a thud.***

thud² *v.* **thudded, thudding** [I] to hit or fall onto something with a low sound | *I heard someone thudding along the hallway.*

thug /θʌg/ *n.* [C] DISAPPROVING a violent man or boy, especially a criminal —**thuggish** *adj.* —**thuggery** *n.* [U]

thumb¹ /θʌm/ *n.* [C] **1** BIOLOGY the part of your hand that is shaped like a thick short finger and helps you to hold things: *She held the coin between her thumb and forefinger.* | *My sister* ***sucked*** *her* ***thumb*** *until she was four.* **2** the part of a GLOVE that fits over your thumb **3 be all thumbs** INFORMAL to be unable to do things neatly and carefully with your hands **4 give sth a/the thumbs up/down** INFORMAL to show that you approve or disapprove of something: *The public has given the movie a big thumbs up.* **5 get a/the thumbs up/down (from sb)** INFORMAL to be approved of or disapproved of by someone **6 under sb's thumb** so strongly influenced by someone that they control you completely: *Meg's really got Darren under her thumb.* → see also **have a green thumb** at GREEN¹ (7), **rule of thumb** at RULE¹ (7), **stick/stand out like a sore thumb** at SORE¹ (4)

thumb² *v.* **1 thumb your nose at sb/sth** to show that you do not respect rules, laws, someone's opinion etc. **2 thumb a ride/lift** INFORMAL to persuade a driver of a passing car to stop and take you somewhere, by putting your hand out with your thumb raised SYN **hitch a ride/lift**

thumb through sth *phr. v.* to look through a book, magazine etc. quickly: *He was thumbing through his guidebook.*

ˈthumb ˌindex *n.* [C] a series of U-shaped cuts in the edge of a large book, usually showing the letters of the alphabet, that help you find the part you want

thumb·nail¹ /ˈθʌmneɪl/ *n.* [C] **1** BIOLOGY the NAIL on your thumb **2** COMPUTERS a small picture on a computer screen that you can CLICK to see a bigger image

thumbnail² *adj.* **a thumbnail sketch/description** a short description giving only the main facts about something

thumb·print /ˈθʌmprɪnt/ *n.* [C] a mark made by the pattern of lines at the end of your thumb → see also FINGERPRINT

thumb·screw /ˈθʌmskru/ *n.* [C] an instrument used in past times to punish or TORTURE people by crushing their thumbs

thumb·tack /ˈθʌmtæk/ *n.* [C] a short pin with a broad flat top, used especially for putting a piece of paper on a wall

thump¹ /θʌmp/ *v.* **1** [I always + adv./prep., T] to make a dull loud sound by falling or hitting against a surface: +**against/on/into** *His feet thumped loudly on the bare floorboards.* **2** [I] if your heart thumps, it beats very quickly because you are frightened or excited **3** [T] INFORMAL to hit someone or something with your closed hand or with your KNUCKLES ►see THESAURUS box at **hit¹** **4** [T] INFORMAL to be defeated in a game: *Last night, the Dodgers were thumped at home by the Boston Redsocks.*

thump² *n.* **1** [C] the dull sound that is made when something hits a surface **2 give sb a thump on the back/head etc.** to hit someone on the back, head etc. with your closed hand or with your KNUCKLES

thump·ing¹ /ˈθʌmpɪŋ/ *n.* [C] INFORMAL the act of defeating someone easily in a game

thumping² *adj.* having a strong regular beat that you can feel → see also **chest-thumping/chest-pounding** at CHEST (4)

thun·der¹ /ˈθʌndɚ/ *n.* **1** [U] EARTH SCIENCE the loud noise that you hear during a storm, usually after a flash of LIGHTNING: *The storm brought strong winds and a lot of* ***thunder and lightning.*** | ***A clap of thunder*** (=one sudden noise of thunder) *boomed overhead.* | *Off in the distance, we heard* ***rolling thunder*** (=a noise of thunder that continues for a short time). **2 the thunder of sth** the loud deep noise of something, for example waves, GUNFIRE, or horses' hooves (HOOF) [**Origin:** Old English *thunor*] → see also **steal sb's thunder** at STEAL¹ (9)

thunder² *v.* **1** EARTH SCIENCE if it thunders, there is a loud noise in the sky, usually after a flash of LIGHTNING: *Did you hear it thunder just now?* **2** [I always + adv./prep.] to move in a way that makes a very loud noise: *Fighter jets thundered across the sky.* **3** [T] WRITTEN to shout loudly and angrily **4** [I,T] LITERARY to make a loud noise

thun·der·bolt /ˈθʌndɚˌboʊlt/ *n.* [C] **1** EARTH SCIENCE a noise of thunder with a flash of LIGHTNING that hits something **2** a sudden event or piece of news that shocks you **3** an imaginary weapon of thunder and LIGHTNING, used by the gods to punish people

thun·der·clap /ˈθʌndɚˌklæp/ *n.* [C] a single loud noise of thunder

thun·der·cloud /ˈθʌndɚˌklaʊd/ *n.* [C] EARTH SCIENCE a large dark cloud that you see before or during a storm

thun·der·head /ˈθʌndɚˌhɛd/ *n.* [C] a thundercloud

thun·der·ous /ˈθʌndərəs/ *adj.* extremely loud: *a thunderous bang* —**thunderously** *adv.*

thun·der·show·er /ˈθʌndɚˌʃaʊɚ/ *n.* [C] a short thunderstorm

thun·der·storm /ˈθʌndɚˌstɔrm/ *n.* [C] EARTH SCIENCE a storm with thunder and LIGHTNING: *a severe thunderstorm* → see picture on page A30

thun·der·struck /ˈθʌndɚˌstrʌk/ *adj.* [not before noun] extremely surprised or shocked SYN **dumbfounded**

thun·der·y /ˈθʌndəri/ *adj.* thundery weather is the type of weather that comes before a thunderstorm

thunk /θʌŋk/ *v.* **1 who'd have thunk it?** NONSTANDARD, HUMOROUS used to say that something is surprising or unexpected **2** [I,T] to make a dull sound by hitting or falling against a surface —**thunk** *n.* [singular]

Thur·ber /ˈθɚbɚ/, **James** (1894–1961) a U.S. humorous writer and CARTOONIST

Thurs·day /ˈθɚzdi, -deɪ/ WRITTEN ABBREVIATION **Thu.**, **Thur.**, or **Thurs.** *n.* [C,U] the fifth day of the week, between Wednesday and Friday: *I tried to call you Thursday.* | *Andy's leaving for Chicago* ***on Thursday.*** | *I wasn't home* ***last Thursday.*** | *I made my dentist appointment for* ***next Thursday.*** | *I'm going to do my laundry* ***this Thursday*** (=the next Thursday that is coming). | *We go jogging together* ***on Thursdays*** (=each Thursday). | *Thanksgiving is always* ***on a Thursday.*** | **Thursday morning/afternoon/night etc.** *Let's go out to dinner Thursday night.* [**Origin:** Old English *Thunresdæg*, from *Thunor* god of the sky + *dæg* day] → see Grammar box at SUNDAY

thus /ðʌs/ W1 *adv.* FORMAL **1** [sentence adverb] as a result of something that you have just mentioned: *She is an expert and thus the best person to ask.*

THESAURUS

so used to give the reason something happens, why someone does something etc.: *The smell of paint can give you a headache, so it's a good idea to keep the windows open.*
as a result being the thing that happens or exists

because of something that happened before: *As a result of the court decision, black children were permitted to attend previously all-white schools.*
therefore as a result of something that has just been mentioned: *Money market accounts are not insured, and are therefore considered more risky than passbook accounts.*
consequently as a result: *There is only one rainy period; consequently the dry period is longer.*
for this reason because of the reason mentioned: *Bacteria may grow in warm food; for this reason, any food left outside in the heat should be discarded.*

2 also **thusly** OLD-FASHIONED in this manner or way: *We have finished the work and have thus kept our promise.* | *She describes him thus: "a pleasant but boring man."* **3 thus far** until now SYN **so far**: *Her performance thus far has been impressive.*

thwack /θwæk/ *v.* [T] to hit someone or something making a short loud sound —**thwack** *n.* [C]

thwart¹ /θwɔrt/ *v.* [T] FORMAL to prevent something from succeeding or prevent someone from doing what they are trying to do: *Efforts to clean up the oil spill have been thwarted by storms.*

thwart² *n.* [C] TECHNICAL a seat fastened across a ROWBOAT

thy /ðaɪ/ *possessive adj.* OLD USE your

T

thyme /taɪm/ *n.* [U] a plant used for giving food a special taste

ˈthy·mus /ˈθaɪməs/ also **ˈthymus gland** *n. plural* **thymi** /maɪ/ or **thymuses** [C] a very small organ at the top of your chest that helps produce T CELLS

thy·roid /ˈθaɪrɔɪd/ also **ˈthyroid gland** *n.* [C] BIOLOGY an organ in your neck that produces HORMONES (=substances) that affect the way you develop and behave

thy·self /ðaɪˈsɛlf/ *pron.* OLD USE yourself

ti /ti/ *n.* [singular] the seventh note in a musical SCALE according to the SOL-FA system

ti·a·ra /tiˈɑrə, tiˈɛrə/ *n.* [C] a piece of jewelry like a small CROWN, that a woman wears on her head on formal occasions

Ti·ber, the /ˈtaɪbɚ/ a river in central Italy that flows south and through the city of Rome to the Mediterranean Sea

Ti·bet /tɪˈbɛt/ a large area of southwest China which has been an independent country for much of its history but which came under Chinese control in 1951 —**Tibetan** *n., adj.*

tib·i·a /ˈtɪbiə/ *n. plural* **tibiae** /-bi-i/ or **tibias** [C] BIOLOGY a bone in the front of your leg → see picture at SKELETON¹

tic /tɪk/ *n.* [C] MEDICINE a sudden uncontrolled movement of a muscle in your face, usually because of a nervous illness

tick¹ /tɪk/ *n.* **1** [C] the short repeated sound that a clock or watch makes every second, or a series of these sounds **2** [C] BIOLOGY a very small creature like an insect that lives on the skin of other animals and sucks their blood **3** [C] a small change in the amount or value of something, especially in the price of STOCK in a company

tick² *v.* **1** [I] if a clock or watch ticks, it makes a short sound every second **2 what makes sb tick** INFORMAL the thoughts, desires, opinions etc. that give someone their character or make them behave in a particular way: *Nobody can figure out what makes him tick.*

tick away/by *phr. v.* **1** also **tick away** if time ticks away or by, it passes, especially when you are waiting for something to happen **2 tick sth ↔ away** if a clock or watch ticks away the hours, minutes etc., it shows them as they pass

tick off *phr. v.* **1 tick sb ↔ off** INFORMAL to annoy someone: *Her attitude is really ticking me off.* **2 tick sth ↔ off** to tell someone a list of things, especially when you touch a different finger as you tell each thing on the list: *He began ticking off points on his fingers.*

ˌticked ˈoff *adj.* [not before noun] angry or annoyed: *Joy was ticked off because I was late.*

tick·er /ˈtɪkɚ/ *n.* [C] **1** a special machine that prints or shows STOCK PRICES as they go up and down **2** INFORMAL your heart

ˈticker tape *n.* [U] long narrow paper on which information is printed by a ticker

ˌticker-tape paˈrade *n.* [C] an occasion when someone important or famous walks or drives through a city and pieces of paper are thrown from high buildings to welcome them or celebrate something they have done

tick·et¹ /ˈtɪkɪt/ S1 W2 *n.* [C]

1 MOVIE/BUS/PLANE ETC. a printed piece of paper that shows that you have paid to do something, for example enter a theater, travel on a bus or airplane etc.: **+to** *tickets to the concert* | *They got* ***round-trip tickets*** (=tickets for travel from one place to another and back again) *to Miami for $297.* | *Isn't it more expensive to buy* ***one-way tickets*** (=tickets for travel in one direction)*?* → see also SEASON TICKET

THESAURUS

Types of tickets
one-way ticket a ticket that lets you go to a place but not back again
round-trip ticket a ticket that lets you go to a place and back again
off-peak ticket a ticket that is cheaper than the usual price because you cannot use it at the busiest times
season ticket a ticket that lets you make the same trip every day for a particular period of time
e-ticket a ticket that you buy over the Internet, which you print from your computer or which you pick up when you arrive at the airport to go on your trip

2 DRIVING OFFENSE an official printed note ordering you to pay money because you have done something illegal, especially while driving or parking your car: *a parking ticket*
3 ELECTION [usually singular] a list of the people supported by a particular political party in an election: *He ran unsuccessfully for governor on the Republican ticket.*
4 IN STORES a piece of paper attached to something in a store that shows its price, size etc. SYN **tag**
5 a ticket to success/happiness/fame etc. a way of becoming successful, happy etc.: *Michael thought an MBA from Stanford would be an instant ticket to success.*
6 be (just) the ticket OLD-FASHIONED to be exactly what is needed
[**Origin:** 1500–1600 Early French *etiquet* **notice attached to something**, from Old French *estiquier* **to attach**]
→ see also MEAL TICKET

ticket² *v.* [T] **1** to give someone a ticket for parking their car in the wrong place, driving too fast etc.: *Sanders was ticketed for speeding.* **2** to choose or mark someone or something for a particular use, purpose, job etc.: **ticket sb/sth for sth** *Three of the army bases have been ticketed for closure.* **3** to attach a small piece of paper onto something to show its price, size etc. SYN **tag**

ˈticket ˌagency *n.* [C] a company that sells tickets for sports events or entertainment such as concerts or plays

ˈticket ˌbooth *n.* [C] a very small building or room where you can buy tickets to sports events or entertainment such as movies or concerts

tick·et·ed /ˈtɪkɪt̬ɪd/ *adj.* **1 a ticketed passenger** someone who already has a ticket for an airplane, train etc. **2** a ticket event is one that you can go to only if you have bought a ticket

tick·et·ing /ˈtɪkɪt̬ɪŋ/ *n.* [U] the process or system of selling or printing tickets for airplanes, trains, concerts etc.: *electronic ticketing*

ticket ˌoffice *n.* [C] an office or place in a building that sells tickets for entertainment, sports events, airplanes etc. → see also BOX OFFICE

ticket ˌwindow *n.* [C] a small window in a building or wall where you can buy tickets to sports events, for entertainment, for a train etc.

tick·ing /ˈtɪkɪŋ/ *n.* [U] a thick strong cotton cloth used for making MATTRESS and PILLOW covers

tick·le¹ /ˈtɪkəl/ S3 *v.* **1** [T] to move your fingers lightly over someone's body in order to make them laugh: *Stop tickling me!* ►see THESAURUS box at **touch¹** **2** [I,T] if something touching your body tickles you, it makes you want to rub your body because it is slightly uncomfortable: *Your beard tickles.* | *The dust* ***tickled my nose*** (=made me want to sneeze). **3** [T] INFORMAL if a situation, remark etc. tickles you, it amuses or pleases you: *Dick will be* ***tickled pink*** (=very pleased) *to see you.* **4 tickle sb's fancy** OLD-FASHIONED if something tickles your fancy, it seems interesting and makes you want to do it **5 tickle the ivories** OLD-FASHIONED to play the piano

tickle² *n.* [C] **1** a feeling in your throat that makes you want to cough **2** an act of tickling someone

tick·lish /ˈtɪklɪʃ/ *adj.* **1** [not before noun] sensitive to being tickled: *I didn't know you were so ticklish.* **2** INFORMAL a ticklish situation or problem must be dealt with very carefully, especially because you may offend or upset people SYN **tricky** —**ticklishness** *n.* [U]

tick-tock /ˈtɪk ˌtɑk, ˌtɪk ˈtɑk/ *interjection* the sound that a large clock makes when it TICKS

tick·y-tack·y /ˈtɪki ˌtæki/ *adj.* INFORMAL ticky-tacky houses, buildings etc. are made of material that is cheap and of low quality —**ticky-tacky** *n.* [U]

tic-tac-toe, tick-tack-toe /ˌtɪk tæk ˈtoʊ/ *n.* [U] a children's game in which two players draw X's or O's in a pattern of nine squares, trying to get three in a row

tid·al /ˈtaɪdl/ *adj.* EARTH SCIENCE relating to the regular rising and falling of the ocean: *tidal currents*

tidal wave *n.* [C] **1** EARTH SCIENCE a TSUNAMI **2** a very large amount of a particular kind of feeling or activity happening at one time: **+of** *a tidal wave of crime*

tid·bit /ˈtɪdˌbɪt/ *n.* [C] **1** a small piece of food that tastes good **2** a small piece of interesting information, news etc.: *tidbits of gossip*

tid·dly·winks /ˈtɪdliwɪŋks/ *n.* [U] a children's game in which you try to make small round pieces of plastic jump into a cup by pressing one edge with a larger piece

tide¹ /taɪd/ *n.* **1 a)** [C,U] EARTH SCIENCE the regular rising and lowering of the level of the ocean that happens twice a day because of the force of the sun and moon on the surface of the water: *The girls were stranded when* ***the tide came in*** (=the level of the ocean rose). | **the tide is in/high** (=the ocean is at a high level) | **the tide is out/low** (=the ocean is at a low level) → see also HIGH TIDE, LOW TIDE **b)** [C] a current of water caused by the tide: *Strong tides make swimming dangerous.* **2** [C usually singular] the way in which events, opinions etc. are developing: *The* ***tide*** *of public opinion has* ***turned against*** *the war* (=people's opinions have changed so that they no longer approve of it). → see also **swim against the tide/current/stream** at SWIM¹ (5) **3** WRITTEN [singular] something, usually something bad, that is increasing: *the* ***rising tide*** *of crime in our cities* | *The government has been unable to* ***stem the tide*** *of violence in the south* (=prevent it from developing and getting worse). **4** [singular] a large number of people or things moving along together

tide²

tide sb **over** *phr. v.* if food, money etc. tides you over, it is enough to last until you are able to get some more: *Can you lend me $50 to tide me over till the end of the month?*

tide pool *n.* [C] EARTH SCIENCE a small area of water left among rocks by the ocean when the tide goes out

tide·wa·ter /ˈtaɪdˌwɔtɚ/ *n.* EARTH SCIENCE **1** [U] water that flows onto the land when the tide rises to a very high level **2** [U] water in the parts of rivers that are affected by tides **3** [C] an area of land at or near the ocean coast

tid·ings /ˈtaɪdɪŋz/ *n.* [plural] OLD USE news: **good/glad tidings** (=good news)

ti·dy¹ /ˈtaɪdi/ *adj. comparative* **tidier**, *superlative* **tidiest** **1** a tidy room, house, desk etc. is neatly arranged with everything in the right place SYN **neat**: *Zola's house is always* ***neat and tidy***. **2 a tidy sum/profit etc.** INFORMAL a large amount of money **3** someone who is tidy keeps their house, clothes etc. neat and clean SYN **neat** [**Origin:** 1700–1800 *tidy* **at an appropriate time** (13–18 centuries), from *tide*] —**tidily** *adv.* —**tidiness** *n.* [U]

tidy² also **tidy up** *v.* **tidies, tidied, tidying** [I,T] to make a place look neat: *I was tidying up my desk when the phone rang.*

tie

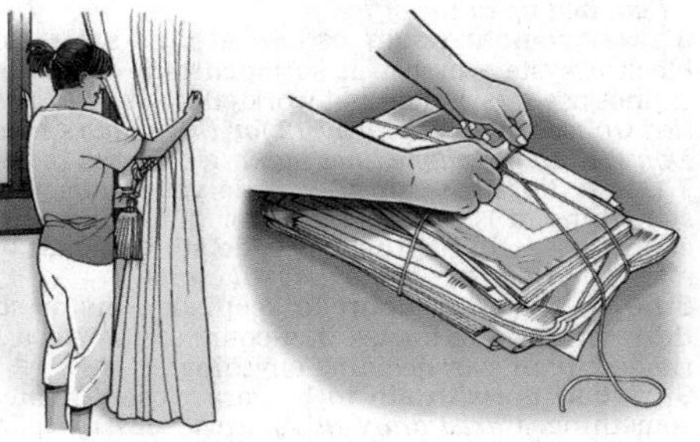

tie¹ /taɪ/ S2 W2 *v.* **ties, tied, tying**

1 STRING/ROPE a) [T] to fasten things together or hold them in a particular position using a piece of string, rope etc.: **tie sth to/behind/onto etc. sth** *A set of keys was tied onto his belt.* | **tie sb to sth** *They tied him to a chair.* | **tie sth together** *We tied the boats together.* | **tie sth with sth** *The flowers were tied with a red ribbon.* | **tie sb's hands/feet** (=tie them together) **b)** [T] to make a knot with a piece or pieces of string, cloth etc., especially to fasten something: *Sheryl tied her sweater around her waist.* | **tie sb's shoes/shoelaces** *Daddy, can you tie my shoe?* | **tie a knot/bow** *I tied a knot in one end of the thread.* **c)** [I] to be fastened using pieces of string, RIBBON etc. in a knot or BOW: *The dress ties at the back.* ►see THESAURUS box at **fasten**

2 GAME/COMPETITION [I] if two players, teams etc. tie in a game or competition, they gain an equal number of points by the end of the competition: **+for** *In the end, three teams tied for third place.* | **+with** *California tied with Louisiana.* → see also **be tied** at TIED

3 CONNECT [T] to connect someone or something closely to someone or something else or form a relationship between them: **tie sb/sth together** *Shared experiences tie people together.* | **+be tied to sth** *At least 20% of their pay was tied to performance.*

4 be tied to sth a) to be unable to leave the situation, place, job etc. that you are in: *I don't want to be tied to one job for the rest of my life.* **b)** to like something that you have very much and not want to lose it or leave it: *Some people are very tied to their pets.*

5 tie the knot INFORMAL to get married

6 tie yourself (up) in knots INFORMAL to become very upset because you are worried, nervous, or confused

7 tie one on INFORMAL to get drunk

[**Origin:** Old English *tigan*] → see also **sb's hands are tied** at HAND¹ (24)

tie sth ↔ **back** *phr. v.* to make your hair stay away from your face by fastening it at the back of your head with a band, RIBBON etc.: *She tied back her hair.*

tie sb **down** *phr. v.* to stop someone from being free to do the things they want to do: **tie sb down to sth** *Ken doesn't want to be tied down to any one woman.*

tie in *phr. v.* **1** if one idea, statement etc. ties in with another, it is similar to it so that they both seem more likely to be true: **+with** *Her description tied in with*

T

that of the other witness. **2 tie sth ↔ in** to be related to something, or to make something have a connection or relationship with something else: **+with** *How does all this tie in with our long term goals?* → see also TIE-IN

tie up *phr. v.*

1 PERSON tie sb ↔ up to tie someone's arms, legs etc. so that they cannot move: *They tied him up so he wouldn't escape.*

2 OBJECT tie sth ↔ up to fasten something together by using string or rope tied in a knot or a BOW: *He tied up all the old newspapers.*

3 BOAT/ANIMAL tie sth ↔ up to tie something such as an animal or a boat to something with a rope or chain so it doesn't go away

4 be tied up SPOKEN to be so busy that you cannot do anything else: *I'm going to be tied up all afternoon.*

5 get tied up SPOKEN to become busy with something so that you cannot leave where you are: *Sorry I'm late – I got tied up at the office.*

6 TRAFFIC/PHONE/COURT OF LAW ETC. tie sth ↔ up to block a system or use it so much that other people cannot use it or it does not work effectively: *Protesters tied up traffic on Highway 12 for three hours today.* | *Don't tie up the phone lines making personal calls.*

7 MONEY tie sth ↔ up if you tie your money up in something, it is all being used for that thing and you cannot use it for anything else: **tie sth up in sth** *We've tied up most of our money in real estate.*

8 tie sb/sth up in court to keep someone or something involved in a CASE in a court of law for a long time without ever deciding anything

9 be tied up with sth to be very closely related to something: *Christianity in Africa is tied up with its colonial past.*

10 tie up (a few/some) loose ends to do the things that are necessary in order to finish a piece of work

11 ARRANGEMENTS tie sth ↔ up to finish arranging all the details of something such as an agreement or a plan

12 BOAT if the passengers of a boat tie up somewhere, they tie their boat to something and stop for a while

tie² S2 W2 *n.* [C]

1 AROUND NECK a long narrow piece of cloth that someone, especially a man, wears around their neck, tied in a special knot in front SYN **necktie**: *Do you know how to* ***tie a tie****?* | **a shirt/suit/jacket and tie** *He was wearing a shirt and tie.* → see also BLACK-TIE, BOW TIE

2 RELATIONSHIP a relationship between two people, groups, or countries: *family ties* | **close/strong etc. ties** *He has strong ties to the business community.* | *She* ***severed*** *her* ***ties with*** *the company six months ago.*

3 RESULT [usually singular] the result of a game, competition, or election in which two or more people get the same number of points, votes etc.: *The game* ***ended in a tie****.* | **a tie for first/second/third etc. (place)** *There was a three-way tie for second place.*

4 FASTENER a piece of string, wire etc. used to fasten or close something such as a bag → see also TWIST TIE

5 RAILROAD a heavy piece of wood or metal supporting a railroad track

'tie-ˌbreaker also **tie·break** /ˈtaɪbreɪk/ *n.* [C] an additional question, point, or game that decides the winner when two people or teams have the same number of points in a competition

'tie clip also **'tie clasp** *n.* [C] a special piece of bent metal used for keeping a man's TIE fastened to his shirt or as a decoration

tied /taɪd/ *adj.* **be tied** two players, teams etc. that are tied in a competition have an equal number of points at some point during the competition: **+for** *Right now, the two teams are tied for first place.* | **+with** *The Saints were tied with Atlanta for the division lead.* → see also TIE¹ (2)

'tie-dye *v.* [T] to color a piece of material with DYE (=colored liquid) after tying string around parts of it in order to make special patterns —**tie-dye**, **tie-dyed** *adj.*: *a tie-dye T-shirt* —**tie-dye** *n.* [U]

'tie-in *n.* [C] a product such as a record, book, or toy that is related to a movie, television show etc. → see also **tie in** at TIE¹

tier /tɪr/ *n.* [C] **1** one of several rows or layers of something, especially seats, that rise one behind another: *the top tier of seats* **2** one of several levels in an organization or system: *the most senior tiers of management* —**tiered** *adj.*

-tier /tɪr/ also **-tiered** /tɪrd/ *suffix* [in adjectives] **two-tier/three-tier etc.** having two, three etc. layers or levels: *a three-tiered wedding cake* | *a two-tier system of government*

ti·er·ra ca·lien·te /tiˌɛrə kɑˈlyenteɪ/ *n.* [U] any area of low land below 2,500 feet in Latin America, for example the Amazon basin. The climate is very hot and tropical crops such as bananas and sugar are grown.

Ti·er·ra del Fue·go /tiˌɛrə dɛl ˈfweɪgoʊ/ a group of islands near the south coast of South America, which belong to Chile and Argentina

ti·er·ra fr·ia /tiˌɛrə ˈfriə/ *n.* [U] any area of high land from 6,000 to 12,000 feet in Latin America, for example the highest parts of Central America. The climate is cold and crops such as potatoes are grown.

ti·er·ra he·la·da /tiˌɛrə hɛˈlɑdə/ *n.* [U] any of the highest areas of land above 12,000 feet in South America, where there is always snow and ice

ti·er·ra tem·pla·da /tiˌɛrə tɛmˈplɑdə/ *n.* [U] any area of land from 2,500 feet to 6,000 feet in Latin America, for example the valleys in the Andes. Most of the population live in these areas, and coffee and wheat are grown.

'tie tack also **'tie pin** *n.* [C] a special pin used for keeping a man's TIE fastened to his shirt or as a decoration

'tie-up *n.* [C] INFORMAL **1** a situation in which traffic is prevented from moving, or in which there is a problem that prevents a system or plan from working: *frustrating traffic tie-ups* **2** an agreement to become business partners: **+with/between** *the company's tie-up with a software firm* → see also **tie up** at TIE¹

tiff /tɪf/ *n.* [C] a slight argument between people who know each other well: *He had a tiff with his wife.*

Tif·fa·ny /ˈtɪfəni/, **Lou·is** /ˈluɪs/ (1848–1933) a U.S. PAINTER and glassmaker, famous for designing glass objects in the ART NOUVEAU style

ti·ger /ˈtaɪgɚ/ *n.* [C] a large strong animal that is orange with black lines on its body and is a member of the cat family → see also PAPER TIGER

tight¹ /taɪt/ S3 W3 *adj.*

1 CLOTHES fitting a part of your body very closely, especially in a way that is uncomfortable OPP **loose**: *a tight skirt* | *This jacket is too tight.* → see also SKIN-TIGHT, TIGHT-FITTING ►see THESAURUS box at **clothes**

2 PULLED/STRETCHED string, wire, cloth etc. that is tight has been pulled or stretched firmly so that it is straight or cannot move OPP **loose**: *If the straps aren't tight enough, the saddle can slip.* | *She tied the rope around the post and* ***pulled it tight****.*

3 a tight hold/grip (on sb/sth) a) a firm hold on something: *His mother had a tight hold on his hand.* **b)** also **a tight rein (on sb/sth)** a situation in which someone controls someone or something very strictly: *The new business manager has a tight hold on the budget.* | *We need to* ***keep a tight rein on*** *costs.*

4 STRICTLY CONTROLLED controlled very strictly and firmly: *tight limits on weapons testing* | *Security at the conference was extremely tight.*

5 FIRMLY ATTACHED/FASTENED something such as a screw or lid that is tight is firmly fastened and is difficult to move: *Make sure the lid is tight enough so that it won't leak.*

6 LITTLE MONEY if money is tight, you do not have enough of it: *Money has been really tight because we had major car problems.*

7 LITTLE TIME if time is tight, it is difficult for you to do everything you need to do in the time available: *My schedule is very tight right now, but I'll try to fit you in.* | *a tight deadline*

8 FEW JOBS/PRODUCTS ETC. a tight market is a situation

in which not many jobs, products etc. are available: *Companies have had to raise salaries in this **tight labor market*** (=one in which few workers are available).
9 run a tight ship to manage a company, organization etc. very effectively by having strict rules
10 LITTLE SPACE if space is tight, there is just barely enough space to fit something into a place: **a tight squeeze/fit** *Three adults in the back seat would be a tight squeeze.*
11 CLOSE RELATIONSHIP a tight group of people, countries etc. have a close relationship with each other and are closely connected with each other SYN **tight-knit**
12 CLOSE TOGETHER placed or standing very close together OPP **loose**: *The planes approached in a tight grouping.*
13 in a tight spot/situation/corner INFORMAL in a difficult situation: *I got into a tight spot but it's okay now.*
14 TURN/BEND a tight turn, bend, corner etc. is very curved and turns very quickly to another direction: *Danny lost control on a tight bend, and the car ran off the road.*
15 SMILE/EXPRESSION/VOICE ETC. showing that you are annoyed or upset: *Her mother gave a tight forced smile.* → see also TIGHT-LIPPED
16 NOT GENEROUS INFORMAL, DISAPPROVING not generous or trying very hard to avoid spending money: *Ken hasn't always been so tight with money.* → see also TIGHT-FISTED
17 CHEST/STOMACH ETC. feeling painful, stiff, or uncomfortable because you are sick or worried: *My chest was tight with tension.*
18 PLAY/PERFORMANCE performed very exactly, with no unnecessary pauses: *a tight, well-rehearsed production*
19 GAME/COMPETITION a tight game, competition etc. is one in which the teams, competitors etc. all play well and it is not easy to win SYN **close**: *They eventually won the tight game in the fourth quarter.*
20 DRUNK [not before noun] OLD-FASHIONED, INFORMAL drunk
[**Origin:** 1400–1500 *thight* **closely packed, solid, thick** (14–19 centuries)] → see also AIRTIGHT, WATERTIGHT
—**tightly** *adj.*: *Cover the pan tightly with foil.*
—**tightness** *n.* [U]

tight² S2 *adv.* very firmly or closely: *Her eyes were shut tight as she screamed.* | ***Hold tight** and don't let go of my hand.* → see also **sit tight** at SIT (5), **sleep tight** at SLEEP¹ (4)

tight·en /ˈtaɪt¬n/ also **tighten up** *v.*
1 CLOSE/FASTEN [T] to close or fasten something firmly by turning it OPP **loosen**: *I need to tighten the screw on my glasses.*
2 ROPE/STRING ETC. [I,T] if you tighten a rope, wire etc., or if it tightens, it is stretched or pulled so that it becomes tight OPP **loosen**: *How do I tighten my seat belt?* | *The rope tightened and Steve was pulled off balance.*
3 BODY to become stiff, or to make a part of your body become stiff OPP **relax**: *Tighten your stomach muscles and hold for three seconds.* | *Judy's lips tightened in a thin smile.*
4 tighten your hold/grip (on sb/sth) **a)** to control a place or situation more strictly: *Rebel forces have tightened their hold on the capital.* **b)** to hold someone or something more firmly: *Sam tightened his grip on my arm.*
5 RULE/LAW ETC. [T] to make a rule, law, or system more strict or effective: *Efforts to tighten the rules have failed.* | **tighten up on sth** *She wants teachers to tighten up on student attendance.*
6 tighten your belt INFORMAL to spend less money than you usually spend: *Businesses are tightening their belts and cutting jobs.* → see also **put/tighten the screws (on sb)** at SCREW¹ (3)

ˈtight end *n.* [C] a football player who begins playing at one of the ends of the front line, and often blocks opposing players or catches the ball

ˌtight-ˈfisted *adj.* INFORMAL not generous with money SYN **stingy** —**tight-fistedness** *n.* [U]

ˌtight-ˈfitting *adj.* fitting very closely or tightly SYN **tight**: *tight-fitting jeans*

tight·ie whit·ies /ˌtaɪt̬i ˈwaɪt̬iz/ *n.* [plural] INFORMAL white JOCKEY SHORTS

ˌtight-ˈknit *adj.* [only before noun] a tight-knit group of people are closely connected with each other: *a tight-knit community*

tight-lipped /ˌtaɪt ˈlɪpt◂ / *adj.* **1** unwilling to talk about something: *Authorities have been extremely tight-lipped about the investigation.* **2** with your lips tightly pressed together because you are angry

ˌtight ˈmoney ˌpolicy *n.* [C,U] ECONOMICS actions taken by a government to reduce the amount of money that exists in a country's economic system at a particular time: *The Thai central bank has employed a tight money policy to fight inflation.*

tight·rope /ˈtaɪt¬roʊp/ *n.* [C] **1** a rope or wire high above the ground that someone walks along in a CIRCUS **2 walk a tightrope** to be in a difficult situation in which you must be careful about what you say or do

tights /taɪts/ *n.* [plural] a piece of clothing that girls, women, dancers, or actors wear, that fits tightly over their legs and feet and goes up to their waist, and that is colored and thick enough that you cannot see through it → see also PANTYHOSE

tight·wad /ˈtaɪt¬wɑd/ *n.* [C] INFORMAL, DISAPPROVING someone who hates to spend or give money

ti·gress /ˈtaɪgrɪs/ *n.* [C] a female tiger

Ti·gris, the /ˈtaɪgrɪs/ a river in southwest Asia that flows through Turkey and Iraq

tike /taɪk/ *n.* [C] another spelling of TYKE

'til /tɪl, ti/ another spelling of TILL

til·de /ˈtɪldə/ *n.* [C] ENG. LANG. ARTS a mark (~) placed over the letter "n" in Spanish to show that it is pronounced /ny/

tile¹ /taɪl/ S3 *n.* **1** [C] a flat square piece of baked clay or other material, used for covering walls, floors etc.: *ceramic tiles* | **a bathroom/kitchen/floor/wall tile** *There were cracks in the floor tiles.* **2** [C] a thin curved piece of baked clay used for covering roofs **3** [C] a RECTANGULAR playing piece in various games such as MAHJONG [**Origin:** Old English *tigele*]

tile² *v.* [T] **1** to cover a floor, wall, roof etc. with tiles **2** TECHNICAL to arrange the WINDOWS on a computer screen side by side so that you can see all of them **3** TECHNICAL to show an image on a computer screen many times in small squares that look like tiles —**tiled** *adj.*: *a tiled floor* —**tiler** *n.* [C]

til·ing /ˈtaɪlɪŋ/ *n.* [U] a set of tiles used to cover a roof, floor etc.

till¹ S1, **'til** /tɪl, tl/ *prep., conjunction* until: *I have to work till 8:00 tonight.* | *Kate didn't walk till she was 18 months old.*

till² /tɪl/ *v.* [T] to prepare land for growing crops, especially by cutting it and turning it over

till³ *n.* [C] **1 have your hand/fingers in the till** also **get caught with your hand/fingers in the till** to be stealing or get caught stealing money from the company or organization that you work for **2 in the till** money in the till is money that a company or organization has **3** OLD-FASHIONED a CASH REGISTER

till·age /ˈtɪlɪdʒ/ *n.* [U] the activity of preparing land for growing crops

til·ler /ˈtɪlɚ/ *n.* [C] **1** a long handle fastened to the RUDDER (=part that controls the direction) of a boat **2** a person or a machine that tills land

tilt¹ /tɪlt/ *v.* **1** [I,T] to move or make something move into a position where one side is higher than the other: *Tilt the pan so that the sauce covers the bottom.* **2** [I,T] if you tilt your head or chin or it tilts, it moves up or to the side: *Carl tilted his head and looked sideways at her.* **3** [I,T] if an opinion or situation tilts or something tilts it, it changes so that people prefer one person, belief etc.: **+toward/away from** *Government tax policy has tilted toward industrial development.* | *This new evidence may **tilt the balance** of opinion in his favor.*

tilt at sb *phr. v.* **1 tilt at windmills** to try to do something that is considered impossible: *Manning admits he was tilting at windmills in trying to change*

T

the nation's prison system. **2** OLD USE to move quickly on a horse toward someone, in order to attack them with a LANCE

tilt² *n.* **1 (at) full tilt** as fast as possible: *Our factories are running at full tilt.* **2** [C] a situation in which someone prefers one person, belief etc., or in which one person, belief etc. has an advantage: *a tilt in the balance of military power* **3** [C,U] a movement or position in which one side of something is higher than the other: *a questioning tilt of the head*

tim·ber¹ /ˈtɪmbɚ/ *n.* **1** [U] trees that are used for producing wood ►see THESAURUS box at **tree** **2** [C] a wooden beam, especially one that forms part of the main structure of a house **3** [U] wood used for building or making things SYN **lumber** → see also HALF-TIMBERED

timber² *interjection* used to warn people that a tree being cut down is about to fall

tim·ber·land /ˈtɪmbɚˌlænd/ *n.* [C,U] an area of land that is covered by trees, especially ones that will be used for wood

tim·ber·line /ˈtɪmbɚˌlaɪn/ *n.* TECHNICAL **1 the timberline** the height above SEA LEVEL above which trees will not grow **2** the northern or southern limit in the world beyond which trees will not grow

tim·bre /ˈtæmbɚ/ *n.* [C,U] the quality of the sound made by a particular instrument or voice

tim·brel /ˈtɪmbrəl/ *n.* [C] OLD USE A TAMBOURINE

Tim·buk·tu /ˌtɪmbʌkˈtu/ *n.* INFORMAL a place that is very far away, or far from any town or anything interesting

T

time¹ /taɪm/ S1 W1 *n.*

1 MINUTES/HOURS ETC. [U] the thing that is measured in minutes, hours, years etc. using clocks: *Drugs can alter our understanding of time and space.* | ***Time passes** slowly when you've got nothing to do.* | *I guess he'll learn as **time goes by**.* | **a period/amount/length of time** *The problem has gone on for a considerable length of time.* | *Friday's meeting was planned **some time*** (=a fairly long period of time) *ago.*

2 ON THE CLOCK [singular, U] a particular point in time shown on a clock in hours and minutes: *Do you know what time it is?* | *What time are we leaving?* | *Susie's just learning to **tell time*** (=know what time it is by looking at the clock). | ***Look at the time*** (=used to say it is later than you thought it was)*! We've got to go!* | **this time tomorrow/yesterday etc.** *This time next week, we'll be in Mexico.*

3 OCCASION [C] an occasion when something happens or someone does something: *That was the only time we disagreed.* | *He's seen the movie at least six times.* | ***How many times** have you been to Hawaii?* | **next/last time** *Tell Bud hello for me next time you see him.* | *I'm not going to help you **this time** – you'll have to do it yourself.* | *I remember **one time*** (=once) *she came dressed in a leather miniskirt.* | *Smoking is not permitted **at any time**.* | **the first/second/last/next etc. time** *Was that the last time you saw him?* | **every/each time** *Every time I see him he's with a different woman.* | **two/three etc. times a day/week etc.** *I usually call Mom two or three times a week.* | **this/next etc. time around** *Who are you going to vote for this time around?*

4 PERIOD OF TIME [singular] a long or short period during which something happens or someone does something: **(for) a long/short time** *We've known each other for a long time.* | **a long/short time ago** *Only a short time ago he was a struggling artist.* | *It **took a long time** for firefighters to control the blaze.* | ***For a time*** (=for a fairly short period of time)*, both countries followed the terms of the treaty.* | *I was thinking about you **the whole time*** (=continuously during the period of time) *I was gone.* | **sb's time in/at/as etc. sth** *I didn't really enjoy my time in Boston.* | *The offer is good for **a limited time** only.*

5 most of the time very often or almost always: *I do the cooking most of the time.*

6 POINT WHEN STH HAPPENS [C,U] a particular point when something happens or should happen: *It's the baby's bath time.* | **it is time to do sth** *Come on. It's time to go.* | **it is time for sth** *Is it time for dinner yet?* | **it is time sb did sth** *It's time Armstrong told the truth about what he knows.* | *The police asked Harry where he was **at the time of** the robbery.* | **at the time (when/that)** *You should make a report at the time the incident happens.* | *Karl and I were hired **at the same time**.* | ***By the time** they got him to the hospital, he was already dead.* | **opening/closing time** (=the time when a store, bar etc. opens or closes) | **an arrival/a departure time** (=the time when a train, airplane etc. arrives or leaves) | **lunch/dinner/break etc. time** *I hate it when the phone rings at dinner time.* | **a time of (the) day/month/year** *The birds start migrating at this time of year.* | **a good/bad time (to do sth)** *I think this is a good time to take a break.* | **the right/wrong time (to do sth)** *Maybe it was the wrong time to tell her.* | *Now is **not the time** to discuss this.*

7 TIME AVAILABLE/NEEDED [U] the amount of time that is available or necessary for you to do something: *How much time do you think they'll need to paint the house?* | *I really don't **have time for** a serious relationship right now.* | **have/get (the) time to do sth** *Most teachers don't have the time to design their own materials.* | *Teenagers seem to **spend** most of their **time** on the phone.* | *Stop **wasting time** – we need to get this finished.* | *Organizing everything first will **save time** in the end.* | ***There's** still **time** if you want to go for a swim.* | **sb's free/spare time** *What do you like to do in your spare time?* | *I never seem to **find time** to go to the gym.* | *We don't want to waste **precious time** training her if she's just going to quit.* | ***Time is running out** in the hostage crisis.* | **have all the time in the world** (=to have as much time as you want in which to do something) | **travel/commute/delivery/response etc. time** *Travel time between the two cities is about two hours.* → see also **make time (for sb/sth)** at MAKE¹ (15)

8 on time arriving or happening at the correct time or the time that was arranged: *Did you get there on time?* | *Mr. Frank ended the meeting **right on time**.*

9 in time a) early or soon enough to do something: **+for** *Will you be back in time for dinner?* | **in time to do sth** *I should be back in time to watch the show.* | *We got to the airport **just in time*** (=with very little extra time). | *We'll be there **in plenty of time** to get things ready.* **b)** after a fairly long period of time, especially after a gradual process of change: *In time I think she'll realize how foolish she's been.*

10 ahead of time before something else happens, or earlier than is expected or necessary: *I'll let you know ahead of time exactly when you should be there.*

11 all the time continuously or very often: *Gabrielle talks about her kids all the time.*

12 one/three/ten etc. at a time separately, or in groups of three, ten etc. together at the same time: *Add the eggs one at a time.* | *I could only read a few pages of the manual at a time.*

13 five/ten/many etc. times... used to say how much bigger, better etc. one thing is than another: *The tower is three **times** taller **than** anything else in the city.* | *He earns about five **times as** much **as** I do.* | **three/four times the size/rate/number etc.** *Some dinosaurs were several times the size of today's elephant.*

14 nine times out of ten/99 times out of 100 etc. used to say that something is almost always true or almost always happens: *Nine times out of ten, stories like that are made up.*

15 from time to time sometimes, but not regularly or very often: *They still get together from time to time.*

16 when the time comes when something that you expect to happen actually happens, or when something becomes necessary: *We'll decide how to tell her when the time comes.*

17 have time on your hands to have a lot of time because you have no work to do: *Since he's retired, he has plenty of time on his hands.*

18 at the/that time at a particular moment or period in the past, especially when the situation is very different now: *It seemed like a good idea at the time.*

19 for the time being now and for a temporary period of time, until the situation changes: *Bob's keeping his car in our garage for the time being.*

20 **take your time** **a)** to do something slowly or carefully without hurrying: *Just take your time and you'll be fine.* **b)** to do something more slowly than seems reasonable: *The bus is certainly taking its time getting here.*
21 **EXPERIENCE** **a)** [singular] a good, bad, enjoyable etc. experience: **have a good/great/fantastic etc. time** *Did you have a good time at the party?* | **have the time of your life** (=have an extremely enjoyable time) **b)** [C] a period of time during which you experience a lot of good, bad etc. things: *I spent some of the happiest times of my life in Germany.* | **a good/bad/hard etc. time** *It was a difficult time for the company.*
22 **HISTORY** [C] a particular period in history: *They were terrible times, and millions of people died.* | **at/during the time of sb/sth** *He wrote at the time of the French Revolution.* | *Global warming is one of the major problems **of our time*** (=of the present period in history). | **Roman/Greek/medieval etc. times** *There was a large villa here in Roman times.*
23 **in no time (at all)** also **in less than no time**, **in next to no time** very quickly or soon, especially in a way that is surprising: *If I leave early, I'll be back in no time.*
24 **IN PART OF THE WORLD** [U] the time in one particular part of the world, or the time used in one particular area: *Eastern Standard Time* | *Welcome to Las Vegas, where **the local time** is 2:30 p.m.*
25 **at times** sometimes but not usually: *At times Jean regretted not having children.*

SPOKEN PHRASES

26 **any time (now)** very soon: *"When's she due back?" "Any time now."*
27 **(it's) about time** said when you are annoyed because you think something should have happened earlier: *"Here's the money I owe you." "About time."*
28 **it's about time sb did sth** used for saying that someone should do something soon: *It's about time you bought a new suit.*
29 **(sb's) time is up** used to say that someone has to stop doing something, because they have done it for long enough: *Time's up! Turn in your tests.*
30 **be out of time** to have no more time left: *It looks like we're out of time, but we'll pick up here tomorrow.*
31 **there's no time like the present** used to say that now is a good time to do something
32 **time flies** used to say that time seems to pass quickly: *He's two already? My, how time flies.*
33 **time flies when you're having fun** used to say that time seems to pass quickly when you are having a good time
34 **there's a first time for everything** used to say that everyone has to do new things sometimes, even though they may seem strange or difficult
35 **time was (when)** INFORMAL used to say that there was a time when something good used to happen that does not happen anymore: *Time was when you could buy a new car for less than $500.*
36 **that time of the month** the time when a woman has her PERIOD

37 **IN A RACE** [C] the amount of time taken by a runner, swimmer etc. in a race: *What's his best time in the 100 meters?*
38 **in time to/with sth** ENG. LANG. ARTS if you do something in time to a piece of music, you do it using the same RHYTHM and speed as the music: *Thousands of young people were moving in time to the music.*
39 **in time (with sb)** if you do something in time with other people, you all do it with the same movements at the same speed
40 **MUSIC** [U] ENG. LANG. ARTS the number of BEATS in each BAR in a piece of music: *Waltzes are usually in three-four time.* | **beat/keep time (with sth)** (=move your hand or play an instrument at the same speed as a piece of music)
41 **do time (for sth)** INFORMAL to spend a period of time in prison: *Hyland **did hard time*** (=spent time in a very strict prison) *for armed robbery.*
42 **at all times** used especially in official notices or announcements to say what always happens or should always happen: *It's best to carry your passport with you at all times.*
43 **time after time** also **time and (time) again** happening often over a long period, especially in a way that is annoying: *I've told him not to do that, time after time.*
44 **at this time** FORMAL at this particular moment: *It would be difficult at this time to explain all the new regulations.*
45 **at one time** at some time in the past but not now: *At one time forests covered about 20% of Lebanon.*
46 **for any length of time** for more than just a short time: *They will not be able to survive in the desert for any length of time.*
47 **for hours/months etc. at a time** for a period that continues for several hours, months etc.: *Because of his work, he's often away for weeks at a time.*
48 **behind the times** people, ideas, or organizations that are behind the times are old-fashioned: *Technologically, they're a little behind the times.*
49 **be (way) ahead of your time** someone who is ahead of their time uses the newest ideas and methods, which are later used by many other people
50 **be (way) ahead of its time** a machine, system, idea etc. that is ahead of its time is more modern or advanced than other similar things
51 **at no time did/should etc. sb do sth** also **at no time was sb do sth** used to say strongly that something never happened or should never happen: *At no time were the prisoners mistreated.*
52 **(only) time will tell** used to say that it will become clear after a period of time whether or not something is true, right etc. at some time in the future: *Only time will tell if this agreement will bring a lasting peace.*
53 **the time is ripe (for sth)** used to say that the conditions are now right or favorable for something to happen: *The time is ripe for educational reform.*
54 **time is money** used to say that wasting time or delaying something costs money
55 **it's (just/only) a matter/question of time** used to say that something will definitely happen at some time in the future, but you do not know when: *It's just a matter of time before he quits or gets fired.*
56 **over time** if something happens over time, it happens gradually during a long period: *Images that people have of themselves change over time.*
57 **there's no time to lose** used to say that you must do something quickly because there is very little time
58 **make good/excellent time** to travel quickly on a trip, especially more quickly than you expected: *Once we got on the freeway, we made good time.*
59 **before sb's time** **a)** before someone was born, before they started working or living somewhere etc.: *"Did you ever see Babe Ruth play?" "No, he was long before my time."* **b)** if you do something before your time, you do it before the time when most people usually do it in their lives: *I don't want to turn into a grumpy old man before my time.*
60 **time heals all wounds** used to say that things you are worried or upset about will gradually disappear as time passes
61 **keep time** if a clock or watch keeps time, it works correctly: **keep good/perfect etc. time** *My watch keeps perfect time.*
62 **on sb's own time** if you work or study on your own time, you do it outside normal work or school hours: *Bob rearranged the office on his own time.*
63 **with time** also **given time** after a period of time, especially after a gradual process of change and development: *I guess things will improve with time.*
64 **not have (much) time for sb/sth** also **have little/no time for sb/sth** INFORMAL to dislike and not want to waste your time on someone or something: *She's always complaining – I don't have time for people like that.*
65 **a time of life** used to talk about someone's age: *At my time of life, you don't take risks like that.*
66 **time is of the essence** FORMAL used to say that it is important that something be done quickly
67 **race/work/battle etc. against time (to do sth)** to try to do something even though you have very little time

T

68 a race/battle against time a situation in which you have very little time in which to do something
69 with time to spare sooner than expected or necessary: *I finished the test with time to spare.*
70 in sb's time during someone's life: *I've met some rude women in my time, but she's the worst.*
71 the best/biggest etc....of all time the best, biggest etc. of a particular kind of person or thing that has ever existed: *the most successful movie of all time*
72 time is on sb's side used to say that someone is in a situation where there is a lot of time left for something good to happen
73 sb's time is up also **sb's time is drawing near** used to say that someone is going to die soon
74 not give sb the time of day to refuse to pay any attention to someone, in an impolite way: *After what she did to you, I wouldn't even give her the time of day!*
75 move/keep up/change with the times to change and become more modern when other things in society, business etc. change: *In the world of today, you have to move with the times.*
76 in sb's own (good) time INFORMAL when someone is ready or when it is convenient for them
77 in ten days'/five years'/a few minutes' etc. time ten days, five years etc. from now in the future
78 since/from time immemorial from a very long time in the past
79 from time out of mind LITERARY for as long as you can remember
[**Origin:** Old English *tima*] → see also **at the best of times** at BEST[3] (13), **bide your time** at BIDE (1), BIG-TIME, **the fullness of time** at FULLNESS (6), FULL-TIME, **all in good time** at GOOD[1] (41), **half the time** at HALF[1] (7), HALFTIME, **it is high time sb did sth** at HIGH[1] (15), **kill time** at KILL[1] (5), **mark time** at MARK[1] (9), **in the nick of time** at NICK[1] (1), **for old times' sake** at OLD (18), **once upon a time** at ONCE[1] (13), PART-TIME, **pass the time of day (with sb)** at PASS[1] (14), **play for time** at PLAY[1] (26), **at the same time** at SAME[1] (3), **be a sign of the times** at SIGN[1] (7), **a stitch in time (saves nine)** at STITCH[1] (10), **have a whale of a time** at WHALE[1] (2)

time[2] S1 W2 *v.* [T] **1** [usually passive] to do something or arrange for something to happen at a particular time: **time sth to do sth** *The bombings were timed to cause as much damage as possible.* | *She **times** her vacations **to coincide with** the school breaks.* | **be perfectly/carefully/brilliantly etc. timed** *The invitation, it seemed to him, was perfectly timed.* **2** to measure how fast someone or something is going, how long it takes to do something etc.: *I'm going to run to the corner and back – time me.* | **time sb/sth at** *Radar guns timed Hershiser's pitches at around 90 miles per hour.* → see also ILL-TIMED, MISTIME, WELL-TIMED
time out *phr. v.* if a computer program times out, it stops working because the computer user has not done any work for a particular period of time

ˌtime and a ˈhalf *n.* [U] one and a half times the normal rate of pay

ˌtime and ˈmotion ˌstudy *n.* [C] a study of working methods to find out how effective they are

ˈtime bomb *n.* [C] **1** a situation that is likely to become a very serious problem: *The rapidly aging population is **a ticking time bomb**.* **2** a bomb that is set to explode at a particular time

ˈtime ˌcapsule *n.* [C] a container that is filled with objects from a particular time, so that people in the future will know what life was like then

ˈtime card *n.* [C] a piece of stiff paper on which the hours you have worked are recorded by a time clock

ˈtime clock *n.* [C] a special clock that records the exact time when someone arrives at and leaves work

ˈtime-conˌsuming *adj.* taking a long time to do: *a time-consuming process*

ˈtime deˌposit *n.* [C] ECONOMICS a bank account that promises to pay a particular amount of interest for a fixed period of time

ˈtime frame *n.* [C] the period of time during which you expect or agree that something will happen or be done.: **+for** *He did not give a time frame for achieving this goal.*

ˈtime-ˌhonored *adj.* a time-honored method, custom etc. is one that has existed for a long time: *time-honored traditions*

time·keep·er /ˈtaɪmˌkipɚ/ *n.* [C] someone who officially records the times taken to do something, especially at a sports event —**timekeeping** *n.* [U]

ˈtime lag also **ˈtime lapse** *n.* [C] the period of time between two related events: **+between** *a long time lag between any proposal and concrete results*

ˈtime-lapse *adj.* time-lapse photography involves taking many pictures of something over a long period of time, and then showing these pictures together so that the changes seem to happen much faster

time·less /ˈtaɪmlɪs/ *adj.* **1** always remaining beautiful, attractive, important etc. and not becoming old-fashioned: *the timeless beauty of Venice* **2** LITERARY continuing forever: *the timeless universe* —**timelessly** *adv.* —**timelessness** *n.* [U]

ˈtime ˌlimit *n.* [C] the longest time that you are allowed to do something in: **+for/on** *You have a 50-minute time limit for the test.*

time·line /ˈtaɪmlaɪn/ *n.* [C] **1** a plan for when things will happen or how much time you expect something to take: **+for** *What's the timeline for the project?* **2** a line next to which you write different events to show the order in which they happened

time·ly /ˈtaɪmli/ *adj.* *comparative* **timelier**, *superlative* **timeliest** done or happening when expected or at exactly the right time: *a piece of timely advice* | **in a timely manner/fashion** *Failure to make payments in a timely manner may lead to penalties.*

ˈtime maˌchine *n.* [C] an imaginary machine in which people can travel backward or forward in time

ˌtime ˈoff *n.* [U] **1** time when you are officially allowed not to be at work or studying: **take/have/get time off** *I need to take some time off and get some rest.* **2 time off for good behavior** time that you do not have to spend in prison because you have behaved well while you are there

ˌtime ˈout *n.* **1 take time out** INFORMAL to rest or do something different from your usual job or activities **2** [C] a short break during a sports game when the teams can rest, get instructions from their COACH etc.: *With 15 seconds left, the coach **called a time out**.* **3** [C] a time when a child must stop what they are doing, sit alone, and be quiet as a punishment for something they have done **4** [C] COMPUTERS an occasion when a computer stops waiting to make a connection with another computer that it is trying to get information from

time·piece /ˈtaɪmpis/ *n.* [C] OLD USE a clock or watch

tim·er /ˈtaɪmɚ/ *n.* [C] **1** an instrument that you use to measure time, when you are doing something such as cooking → see also EGG TIMER **2** a piece of equipment that makes a machine start and stop working at times you have chosen: *Did you **set the timer on** the VCR?* **3 a part-timer/full-timer** someone who works part or all of a normal working week

times /taɪmz/ W2 *prep.* multiplied by: *Two times two equals four* (=2 × 2 = 4).

ˈtime-ˌsaving *adj.* designed to reduce the time usually needed to do something: *time-saving techniques* —**time-saver** *n.* [C]

time·serv·er /ˈtaɪmˌsɚvɚ/ *n.* [C] **1** INFORMAL someone who does the least amount of work possible because they are just waiting until they can get another job or RETIRE **2** someone who changes their behavior or opinions to match everyone else's, especially in order to gain an advantage —**timeserving** *adj.*, *n.* [U]

time·share /ˈtaɪmʃɛr/ *n.* **1** [C] a vacation home that you buy with other people so that you can each spend a period of time there every year **2** [U] the arrangements by which timeshares are bought and sold —**timeshare** *adj.*

ˈtime-ˌsharing *n.* [U] **1** the practice of owning a

timeshare **2** COMPUTERS a situation in which one computer is used by many people at different TERMINALS at the same time —**time-sharing** *adj.*

time sheet *n.* [C] a piece of paper on which the hours you have worked are written or printed

time ˌsignal *n.* [C] a sound on the radio that shows the exact time

time ˌsignature *n.* [C] two numbers at the beginning of a line of music that tell you how many BEATS there are in a MEASURE

times 'table *n.* [C usually plural] INFORMAL a MULTIPLICATION TABLE

time switch *n.* [C] an electronic control that can be set to start or stop a machine at a particular time

time·ta·ble /ˈtaɪmˌteɪbəl/ *n.* [C] **1** a plan of events and activities, with their dates and times [SYN] **schedule**: *Officials have* **set** *no* **timetable for** *deciding on a security plan.* ►see THESAURUS box at **plan**[1] **2** a list of the times at which buses, trains, airplanes etc. arrive and leave [SYN] **schedule**

time trial *n.* [C] a practice race to decide who will take part in an important race and what order they will start in

time warp *n.* [C] **1 be (caught/stuck) in a time warp** to have not changed even though everyone or everything else has: *The sleepy little town seems to be caught in a time warp.* **2** an imaginary situation in which the past or future becomes the present

time-ˌworn *adj.* something time-worn is old and has been used a lot: *time-worn phrases*

time zone *n.* [C] EARTH SCIENCE one of the 24 areas that the world is divided into, each of which has its own time

tim·id /ˈtɪmɪd/ *adj.* not having courage or confidence: *a timid child* —**timidly** *adv.* —**timidity** /təˈmɪdəti/ *n.* [U]

tim·ing /ˈtaɪmɪŋ/ *n.* [U] **1** the skill or luck involved in doing something at exactly the right time: *Good comedy depends on timing.* | **good/bad/perfect etc. timing** *Perfect timing! I was just going to call you.* **2** the time, day etc. when someone does something or something happens, especially when you are considering how appropriate this is: +**of** *the timing of the election* **3** the way in which electricity is sent to the SPARK PLUGS in a car engine

tim·or·ous /ˈtɪmərəs/ *adj.* FORMAL lacking confidence and easily frightened —**timorously** *adv.*

Tim·o·thy /ˈtɪməθi/ **1 Timothy, 2 Timothy** two books in the New Testament of the Christian Bible

tim·pa·ni /ˈtɪmpəni/ *n.* [U] a set of KETTLEDRUMS

tim·pa·nist /ˈtɪmpənɪst/ *n.* [C] someone who plays the TIMPANI

tin[1] /tɪn/ *n.* **1** [U] SYMBOL **Sn** CHEMISTRY a soft white metal that is an ELEMENT and is often used to cover and protect iron and steel: *The container was made of tin.* **2** [C] a metal container with a lid in which food can be stored: *a cookie tin* → see picture at BOX[1] **3** [C] a metal container in which food is cooked [SYN] **pan**: *a muffin tin* **4** [C] BRITISH a CAN in which food, drink, or another substance is sold

tin[2] *adj.* **1** CHEMISTRY made of tin: *a tin cup* **2 have a tin ear** INFORMAL to be unable to hear the difference between musical notes

tin can *n.* [C] a small metal container in which food is sold

tinc·ture /ˈtɪŋktʃɚ/ *n.* [C,U] **1** [+ of] MEDICINE a medical substance mixed with alcohol **2** a substance that is used to DYE (=change the color of) something, or the color it makes

tin·der /ˈtɪndɚ/ *n.* [U] dry material that burns easily and can be used for lighting fires

tin·der·box /ˈtɪndɚˌbɑks/ *n.* **1** [C usually singular] a place or situation that is dangerous and where there could suddenly be a lot of fighting or problems: *The refugee camps are a tinderbox waiting to catch fire.* **2** [C] a box containing things needed to make a fire, used in the past

'tinder-dry *adj.* extremely dry and likely to burn very easily

tine /taɪn/ *n.* [C] a pointed part of something that has several points, for example on a fork → see also PRONG

tin·foil /ˈtɪnfɔɪl/ *n.* [U] thin shiny metal that bends like paper and is used for covering food [SYN] **aluminum foil**

ting /tɪŋ/ *n.* [C] a high clear ringing sound: *the ting of a bell* —**ting** *v.* [I,T]

ting-a-ling /ˌtɪŋ ə ˈlɪŋ/ *n.* [C] INFORMAL the high clear ringing sound that is made by a small bell

tinge[1] /tɪndʒ/ *n.* [C] a very small amount of a color, emotion, or quality: +**of** *She had a tinge of sadness in her voice.*

tinge[2] *v.* [T + with] to give something a small amount of a particular color, emotion, or quality

tinged /tɪndʒd/ *adj.* showing a small amount of a color, emotion, or quality: +**with** *The autumn leaves are tinged with gold.* | **politically/racially/spiritually etc. tinged** *a politically tinged trial* | **lemon-tinged/blue-tinged/jazz-tinged etc.** *gospel-tinged music*

tin·gle /ˈtɪŋgəl/ *v.* [I] if a part of your body tingles, you feel a slight stinging feeling, especially on your skin: +**with** *My skin was tingling with excitement.* —**tingle** *n.* [C] —**tingling** *n.* [C] —**tingly** *adj.*

tin·ker[1] /ˈtɪŋkɚ/ *v.* [I] to make small changes to something in order to repair it or make it work better: +**with** *Congress has spent months tinkering with the new tax legislation.*

tinker[2] *n.* [C] someone who travels from place to place selling things or repairing metal pots, pans etc., especially in the past

tin·kle[1] /ˈtɪŋkəl/ *n.* [C usually singular] **1** a light ringing sound: +**of** *the tinkle of Christmas bells* **2** [U] an expression meaning URINE (=liquid waste from your body), used especially by or to children

tinkle[2] *v.* [I,T] **1** to make light ringing sounds or to make something do this: *Bells tinkled as she opened the door.* **2** a word meaning to URINATE (=pass liquid waste from your body), used especially by and to children

tin·ni·tus /ˈtɪnɪtəs, təˈnaɪtəs/ *n.* [U] MEDICINE an illness in which you hear noises, especially ringing, in your ears

tin·ny /ˈtɪni/ *adj.* *comparative* **tinnier**, *superlative* **tinniest** **1** a tinny sound is high, weak, and not nice to listen to, and sounds like it is coming out of something made of metal **2** a tinny metal object is badly or cheaply made

ˌTin Pan 'Alley *n.* [U] INFORMAL the people who produce popular music and their way of life, used especially about the music business in the early part of the 20th century in the U.S.

tin·plate /ˌtɪnˈpleɪt◂/ *n.* [U] very thin sheets of iron or steel covered with TIN

'tin-pot *adj.* [only before noun] a tin-pot person, organization etc. is not very important, although they think that they are: *a tin-pot dictator*

tin·sel /ˈtɪnsəl/ *n.* [U] **1** thin strings of shiny paper used as decorations, especially at Christmas **2** something that seems attractive but is not valuable or important

Tin·sel·town /ˈtɪnsəlˌtaʊn/ *n.* INFORMAL a name for Hollywood, California, considered as a place where movies are made and MOVIE STARS live

'tin ˌshears *n.* [plural] heavy scissors for cutting metal

tint[1] /tɪnt/ *n.* [C] **1** a light shade or small amount of a particular color ►see THESAURUS box at **color**[1] **2** artificial color, used to slightly change the color of your hair

tint[2] *v.* [T] to give something, especially your hair, a slightly different artificial color

tint·ed /ˈtɪntɪd/ *adj.* [only before noun] tinted glass is colored, rather than completely transparent

T

T-in·ter·sec·tion /'ti ˌɪntɚsɛkʃən/ *n.* [C] a place where two roads meet and form the shape of the letter T

tin·tin·nab·u·la·tion /ˌtɪntəˌnæbyə'leɪʃən/ *n.* [C,U] LITERARY the sound of bells

Tin·to·ret·to /ˌtɪntə'rɛṭoʊ/ (1518–1594) an Italian painter famous for his religious paintings and his PORTRAITS

ti·ny /'taɪni/ S2 W2 *adj. comparative* **tinier**, *superlative* **tiniest** extremely small: *The pay increase is tiny.* | *a **tiny little** baby* [**Origin:** 1500–1600 *tine* **very small** (15–17 centuries)]

-tion /ʃən/ *suffix* [in nouns] another form of the SUFFIX -ION

tip[1] /tɪp/ S2 W3 *n.*
1 END [C] the end of something, especially something pointed: *He held the pen close to its tip.* | **+of** *There was a smudge on the tip of her nose.* → see also FINGERTIP, -TIPPED ►see THESAURUS box at **end[1]**
2 MONEY [C] a small amount of additional money that you give to someone, such as a WAITER or a taxi driver: *a 15% tip* | *I **gave** the taxi driver a big **tip**.* | *Did you **leave a tip**?*
3 ADVICE [C] a helpful piece of advice: **+on** *The book has useful tips on how to find a job.* ►see THESAURUS box at **advice**
4 on the tip of your tongue if a word, name etc. is on the tip of your tongue, you know it but cannot remember it, but you feel as though you are going to remember it very soon
5 SECRET INFORMATION a secret warning or piece of information, especially to police about illegal activities: *Police were acting on a tip when they made the arrest.* | **+about** *The detective got a tip about the stolen vehicle.*
6 the tip of the iceberg a small sign of a problem that is much larger: *These crimes are just the tip of the iceberg.*
7 HORSE RACE [C] INFORMAL special information about which horse will win a race

tip[2] S3 *v.* **tipped**, **tipping**
1 LEAN [I,T] to move into a position where one end or side is higher than the other, or to make something do this: *The canoe tipped and we fell in the water.* | **tip sth forward/back/down/up etc.** *He tipped his chair back.*
2 MONEY [I,T] to give an additional amount of money to someone such as a WAITER or taxi driver: *You're expected to tip in U.S. restaurants.* | **tip sb sth** *I tipped him $5.*
3 tip the balance/scales to give a slight but important advantage to someone or something: *Your support tipped the balance in our favor.*
4 LIKELY TO SUCCEED [T usually passive] to say who you think is most likely to be successful at something: **be tipped to do sth** *He is tipped to become the next prime minister.*
5 tip the scales at 150/180/200 etc. pounds to weigh a particular amount: *Briggs tipped the scales at 227 pounds.*
6 POUR [T] to pour something from one place or container into another: **tip sth out/into/onto etc.** *Ben tipped the contents of the drawer onto the table.*
7 be tipped with sth to have one end covered in something: *The arrows had been tipped with poison.*
8 SECRET INFORMATION to give someone such as the police a secret warning or piece of information, especially about illegal activities: *Investigators were tipped to watch for two men driving a gray van.*
9 tip your hand to allow someone to know your true plans or intentions after keeping them secret, especially when you do not intend to do this
10 tip your hat to sb INFORMAL to show that you think someone is very good, helpful, successful etc.
tip sb ↔ **off** *phr. v.* **1** to give someone such as the police a secret warning or piece of information, especially about illegal activities: **tip sb off to/about sth** *Informants tipped police off to Casey's crimes.* **2** to make you think that something that you did not expect to be true is true: *His behavior should have tipped me off that something was wrong.*
tip over *phr. v.* **tip sb/sth ↔ over** to fall over after leaning backward, forward, or sideways, or to push someone or something so that they fall over: *A bucket had tipped over.* | *A large wave tipped the boat over.*

ti·pi /'tipi/ *n.* [C] another spelling of TEPEE

'tip-off *n.* [C] **1** INFORMAL something that makes you think that something that you did not expect to be true is true: *The fact that he hasn't called should be a tip-off that he's not interested.* **2** the beginning of a basketball game, when the ball is thrown into the air and two players jump up to try to gain control of it **3** INFORMAL a warning that something is going to happen, especially a warning to the police about illegal activities

-tipped /tɪpt/ also **-tip** /tɪp/ *suffix* [in adjectives] **gold-tipped/steel-tipped/rubber-tipped etc.** having a tip that is made of or covered with gold, steel etc.: *felt-tipped pens*

tip·per /'tɪpɚ/ *n.* INFORMAL **a good/bad/big etc. tipper** someone who gives large, small etc. TIPS to WAITERS, taxi drivers etc. for their services

'tipping point *n.* [C] a moment when something happens and changes a situation in such a way that the situation cannot be changed back to what it was before: *Will this bombing be the tipping point of the Iraq war?*

tip·pler /'tɪplɚ/ *n.* [C] INFORMAL someone who drinks alcohol —**tipple** /'tɪpəl/ *v.* [I,T]

tip·py·toes /'tɪpiˌtoʊz/ *n.* [plural] **on (my/your/his/her etc.) tippytoes** a phrase meaning on tiptoe, used especially by children or when speaking to them

tip·ster /'tɪpstɚ/ *n.* [C] **1** someone who gives secret information or warnings to the police or other authorities about something that has happened or is going to happen **2** someone who gives secret information about a crime, about which horse is likely to win a race etc.

tip·sy /'tɪpsi/ *adj. comparative* **tipsier**, *superlative* **tipsiest** INFORMAL slightly drunk —**tipsily** *adv.* —**tipsiness** *n.* [U]

tip·toe[1] /'tɪptoʊ/ *n.* **on tiptoe(s)** if you stand or walk on tiptoe you stand or walk on your toes, in order to make yourself taller or in order to walk very quietly

tiptoe

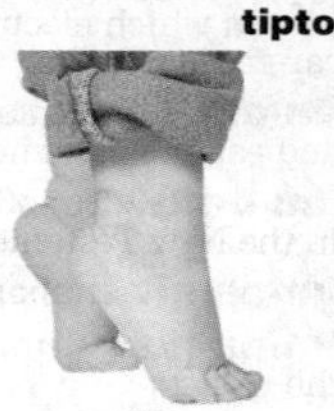

on tiptoe

tiptoe[2] *v.* [I] to walk quietly and carefully on your toes: **+across/down etc.** *Emily tiptoed over to the window and looked outside.* ►see THESAURUS box at **walk[1]**

ˌtip-'top *adj.* INFORMAL excellent: **in tip-top condition/shape** *The car's in tip-top condition.*

ti·rade /'taɪreɪd/ *n.* [C] a long angry speech criticizing someone or something: *a tirade against the government*

Ti·ra·na /tɪ'rɑnə/ the capital and largest city of Albania

tire[1] /taɪɚ/ S2 *n.* [C] a thick round piece of rubber that fits around the wheel of a car, bicycle etc.: *I had **a flat tire** (=all the air went out of it) on the way home.* | *There's **a spare tire** in the trunk.* [**Origin:** Old English *teorian, tyrian*] → see picture at BICYCLE[1] → see picture on page A36

tire[2] *v.* [I,T] to start to feel tired or make someone feel tired: *As I get older, I tire much more easily.*
tire of sb/sth *phr. v.* **1** to become bored with someone or something: *She soon tired of him.* **2 never tire of doing sth** to enjoy doing something again and again, especially in a way that annoys other people: *He never tires of talking about the good old days.*
tire sb ↔ **out** *phr. v.* to make someone very tired: *All that walking really tired me out.*

tired /taɪɚd/ S1 W2 *adj.* **1** feeling that you want to sleep or rest: *I'm too tired to go out tonight.* | *the tired parents of newborns* | *I could see he was **getting tired**.*

THESAURUS

exhausted extremely tired: *I was completely exhausted after the long trip.*
worn out very tired because you have been working or playing hard: *Young children are just worn out by the end of the school day.*
weary WRITTEN very tired, especially because you have been doing something for a long time: *weary travelers*
run-down tired and unhealthy: *If you're tired and run-down all the time, maybe you're trying to do too much.*
beat INFORMAL very tired: *I'm beat.*

2 if a part of your body is tired, it needs to rest because it has been used a lot: *My legs are tired.* **3 tired out** very tired, especially after a lot of hard work, traveling etc. **4 tired of (doing) sth** bored with something because it is not interesting anymore, or has become annoying: *I'm tired of hearing about her new car.* | *I'm getting tired of this hairstyle.* | *We're* **sick and tired** *of covering for him.* **5 a tired (old) subject/joke etc.** a subject, joke etc. that is boring because it is too familiar —**tiredness** *n.* [U] —**tiredly** *adv.* → see also DOG-TIRED

tire·less /ˈtaɪɚlɪs/ *adj.* working very hard in a determined way without stopping for a long period of time: *Lynch's tireless efforts to help the homeless* —**tirelessly** *adv.*

tire·some /ˈtaɪɚsəm/ *adj.* making you feel annoyed, bored, or impatient

tir·ing /ˈtaɪərɪŋ/ *adj.* making you feel that you want to sleep or rest: *Working full time can be extremely tiring.*

'tis /tɪz/ POETIC a short form of "it is"

tis·sue /ˈtɪʃu/ *n.* **1** [C] a piece of soft thin paper, used especially for blowing your nose on SYN **Kleenex®**: *a box of tissues* **2** [U] also **tissue paper** light thin paper used for wrapping, packing etc. **3** [U] BIOLOGY a group of similar cells that together carry out a particular function in an organism: **plant/lung/brain etc. tissue** *The disease destroys brain tissue.* **4 a tissue of lies** a story or account that is completely untrue

ti·tan, Titan /ˈtaɪt̚n/ *n.* [C] a very strong or important person SYN **giant**

ti·tan·ic /taɪˈtænɪk/ *adj.* very big, strong, impressive etc.: *a titanic legal struggle*

ti·ta·ni·um /taɪˈteɪniəm/ *n.* [U] SYMBOL **Ti** CHEMISTRY a strong, light, and very expensive metal that is an ELEMENT

Ti·tans, the /ˈtaɪt̚nz/ in Greek MYTHOLOGY, the first gods who ruled the universe who were thought of as GIANTS

ˌtit for ˈtat *n.* [U] INFORMAL something bad that you do to someone because they have done something bad to you —**tit-for-tat** *adj.* [only before noun] *tit-for-tat insults*

tithe /taɪð/ *n.* [C usually plural] **1** a particular amount, usually 10% of income, that members of some Christian churches are expected to give to the church **2** ECONOMICS a tax paid to the church, in past times —**tithe** *v.* [I]

Ti·tian /ˈtɪʃən/ (1477–1576) an Italian painter admired for his use of color

ti·tian /ˈtɪʃən/ *n.* [C] LITERARY a brownish-orange color —**titian** *adj.*: *titian hair*

Ti·ti·ca·ca, Lake /ˌtɪt̬ɪˈkɑkə/ the largest lake in South America, in the Andes mountains between Bolivia and Peru

tit·il·late /ˈtɪt̬lˌeɪt/ *v.* [T] to make someone feel excited or interested, especially in a sexual way: *The sex scandal is titillating the American public.* —**titillating** *adj.* —**titillation** /ˌtɪt̬lˈeɪʃən/ *n.* [U]

ti·tle¹ /ˈtaɪt̬l/ S2 W2 *n.*

1 NAME OF A BOOK/PAINTING ETC. [C] the name given to a particular book, painting, movie, play etc.: *song titles* | **+of** *The title of her latest novel is "Zoo."*

2 SPECIAL NAME [C] **a)** ENG. LANG. ARTS a name such as "Sir" or "Professor" or abbreviations such as "Mrs." or "Dr." that are used before someone's name to show their rank or profession, whether they are married etc. **b)** a name that describes someone's job or position: *What's your job title?*

3 BOOK/MOVIE ETC. [C] a book, DVD etc. that you can buy: *They publish thousands of titles.*

4 [C] the position of being the winner of an important sports competition: *He was the first American to* **win the title**. → see also TITLIST

5 title to sth LAW the legal right to own something

[**Origin:** 1300–1400 Old French, Latin *titulus*]

title² *v.* [T] to give a title to a book, painting, movie etc. SYN **entitle**

ti·tled /ˈtaɪt̬ld/ *adj.* **1 be titled sth** to have a particular title: *The chapter is titled "Manipulating Public Fear."* **2** having a title such as "lord," "DUKE," "EARL" etc. because of being a member of the NOBILITY → see also SELF-TITLED

ˈtitle deed *n.* [C] LAW a piece of paper giving legal proof that someone owns a particular property

ˈtitle ˌholder *n.* [C] **1** a person or team that is the winner of an important sports competition **2** LAW someone who owns a title deed

ˈtitle page *n.* [C] the page at the front of a book that shows the book's name, writer etc.

ˈtitle role *n.* [C] the main acting part in a play or movie, when it is the same as the name of the play or movie

ˈtitle track *n.* [C] the song on a CD, CASSETTE etc. that has the same name as the whole CD or cassette

ti·tl·ist /ˈtaɪt̬l-ɪst/ *n.* [C] someone who has won a TITLE in an important sports competition

tit·ter /ˈtɪt̬ɚ/ *v.* [I] to laugh quietly in a high voice, especially because you are nervous or embarrassed ▸see THESAURUS box at **laugh¹** —**titter** *n.* [C]

tit·u·lar /ˈtɪtʃələ/ *adj.* [only before noun] **a titular head/leader/monarch etc.** someone who is the official leader or ruler of a country but who does not have real power or authority

Ti·tus /ˈtaɪt̬əs/ a book in the New Testament of the Christian Bible

Ti·Vo /ˈtivoʊ/ *n.* [U] TRADEMARK a system that allows you to record television DIGITALLY —**TiVo** *v.* [T]

Ti·wa /ˈtiwə/ a Native American tribe from the southern area of the U.S.

tiz·zy /ˈtɪzi/ *n.* [singular] INFORMAL **in a tizzy** feeling worried, nervous, and confused

TLC *n.* [U] INFORMAL **tender loving care** kindness and love that you show someone to make them feel better and happier

Tlin·git /ˈtlɪŋgɪt/ a Native American tribe who live in Alaska —**Tlingit** *adj.*

TM¹ a written abbreviation of TRADEMARK

TM² *n.* [U] TRANSCENDENTAL MEDITATION

TN the written abbreviation of Tennessee

T-note /ˈti noʊt/ *n.* [C] ECONOMICS a TREASURY NOTE

TNT *n.* [U] a powerful explosive

to¹ /tə; *before a vowel* tʊ; *strong* tu/ S1 W1 [used before the basic form of a verb, or in place of this verb when it is repeated, to show that it is in the infinitive form] **1** used after some verbs: *I decided to help.* | *The manager finally asked them to leave.* | *You can drive today if you want to.* | *I tried* **not to** *look at him.* **2** used after "how," "where," "who," "whom," "whose," "which," "when," "what," or "whether": *My father still doesn't know how to set the VCR.* | *Melinda is always telling people what to do.* | *Tell me when to stop.* | **how/where etc. not to do sth** *We learned how not to make mistakes.* **3** used after some nouns: *It is his third attempt to climb the mountain.* | *If you get a chance to see the play, you should.* | *I don't see any reason to be nice to her.* **4** used after some adjectives to show what action or experience a feeling, quality, or state relates to: *I'm not ready to start.* | *I'm sorry to bother you.* | *She was surprised to see me.* **5** used after some adjectives when talking about how easy, pleasant etc. making, doing, or dealing with something is: *The cake is easy to make.* | *The game was exciting to watch.* **6** used to show the purpose of an action: *They left early to catch the 7:30 train.* | *To find out more information, call this number.* | *I borrowed money* ***in order to*** *buy my car.* **7** used after "too" and an adjective to say what action or experience is not possible or appropriate: *It's too cold to go out.* | *I've been too lazy to write any letters.* **8** used after an adjective and "enough" or after some nouns to say what action or experience is possible or appropriate: *Are you tall enough to reach that jar for me?* | *He's not old enough yet to chew gum.* | *They think I don't have the guts to sue.* **9** used to describe actions, states, and situations with a verb: *It's nice to feel wanted.* | *Our aim is to cut costs.* | *To lose the game would be a disappointment.* **10** used after SUPERLATIVE adjectives such as "oldest" and "youngest" and after adjectives such as "first" and "last" to say what action is involved: *She's the youngest player to win the championship.* | *They were the last ones to leave.* **11** used to show what needs to be done to something: *Don't you have an essay to write?* **12** used in some fixed phrases to say what your attitude or purpose in saying something is: *To be honest, I didn't enjoy the movie.* | *Dinner was a disaster, to put it bluntly.* **13** used after "there is" and a noun: *There's nothing to do around here.* | *There are some shirts to iron in the bedroom if you're not busy.* **14** used for saying what someone discovers or experiences when they do something: *He arrived home to discover she had left.* **15** FORMAL used after the verb "be" to give an order or to say what order someone has given: *He is to wait here until I return.* | *You are* ***not to*** *talk to strangers.* **16 a)** FORMAL used after the verb "be" in order to state what has been planned or arranged for the future: *They are to be married next month.* **b) a bride/husband/parent etc. to be** someone who will soon be married, soon be a parent etc. **17** used to talk about a particular verb as a part of the English language: *"To look for" is a phrasal verb.* **18** FORMAL used after the verb "be" to say or ask what should or can be done: *He is to be congratulated for his persistence.* **19** LITERARY used after "oh" to express a wish: *Oh, to be young again!*

GRAMMAR

In written English, it is best not to put a word between **to** and the verb that comes after it: *The system allows us to respond to requests more quickly.* Sometimes, however, you can separate **to** from the verb that comes after it in order to emphasize something or because doing so makes the sentence clearer: *To really understand Rice's speech, you need to know a lot about international politics.*

to² S1 W1 *prep.* **1** used to say where someone or something goes: *Where can I catch the bus to the airport?* | *The dog walked right to her.* | *We're going to Egypt next month.* **2** used to say who receives something, or who is told or shown something: *He sent presents to the children.* | *What did he say to you?* | *Who is the letter addressed to?* **3** used to state the event or activity that someone attends or takes part in: *Are you coming to my party?* | *She goes to gymnastics every Friday.* **4** in order to be in a particular situation, or in a particular physical or mental state: *She sang the baby to sleep.* | *They say she starved herself to death.* | *Overnight, the water had turned to ice.* **5** in a particular direction from a person or thing: *a town to the south of Memphis* | *Nathan, you sit here to my right.* **6** as far as a particular level or point: *The temperature dropped to five degrees.* | **down/up to sth** *Jason's hair is down to his shoulders now.* **7** used to show the person or thing that is affected by an action or situation: *Why are you always so mean to me?* | *The pollution is a threat to wildlife.* | *What did you do to the computer?* **8** used to say where something is fastened, attached, or touching: *He tied the rope to a tree.* | *There's some gum stuck to my shoe.* | *She held a finger to her lips.* | *They spent the evening dancing* ***cheek to cheek.*** **9** facing something or in front of it: *He turned his back to me and walked away.* | *Bob and I sat* ***face to face*** *across the table.* **10** starting with one thing, in one place, or at one time and ending with, in, or at another: *A to Z* | *Can you count to ten in Spanish?* | ***From*** *here* ***to*** *the city will take you about 30 minutes.* | *She read the novel* ***from beginning to end.*** **11** used to show that there is a certain amount of time before an event or before a particular time: *It's only two weeks to Christmas.* | *"What time is it?" "Ten to five"* (=ten minutes before 5:00). **12** used to say what something is a part of or is needed for: *Do you have the keys to the house?* | *the answer to the question* **13** used to say who or what there is a relationship or connection with: *She's married to a Canadian.* | *He's an assistant to the manager.* | *The robbery may be linked to other crimes.* **14** used to say who has a particular attitude or opinion, especially after verbs such as "seem," "feel," or "sound": *It seems like a good idea to me.* **15 have sth (all) to yourself** to not have to share something with anyone else: *We had the beach all to ourselves.* **16** according to a particular feeling or attitude: *Jerry's never been married* ***to my knowledge*** (=according to what I know). | ***To*** *Gordon's* ***way of thinking****, cooking was women's work.* | **to sb's liking/taste etc.** *The food was not really to our liking.* **17 to sb's surprise/annoyance/delight etc.** in a way that makes someone feel a particular emotion: *Much to Becky's surprise, she actually liked sushi.* **18** used between the number of points of both teams or players in a game or competition: *The Falcons won the game 27 to nil.* **19** used to show the relationship between two different measurements, quantities etc.: *a ratio of 15 to one* | *The car gets over 40 miles to the gallon.* | *The kids sleep three to a room.* **20** used to say how many people or things form a larger group or thing: *There are 16 ounces to a pound.* | *We should have five people to a team.* **21** used between two numbers when you try to guess an exact number that is between them: *a crowd of 18,000 to 20,000 people* **22** used to say that a particular sound is heard at the same time as something happens: *I enjoy exercising to music.* **23** used when saying what the chances of something happening are or when giving the ODDS for a BET, and usually written with the symbol (–): *I'll bet you 50 to one he doesn't show up.* | *100–1 odds* [**Origin:** Old English]

to³ /tu/ *adv.* if you push a door to, or something moves a door to, it closes: *The wind blew the door to.* → see also COME TO, TO AND FRO¹

toad /toʊd/ *n.* [C] a small animal that looks like a large FROG but is brown and lives mostly on land

toad·stool /ˈtoʊdstul/ *n.* [C] a wild plant like a MUSHROOM, that can be poisonous [**Origin:** 1300–1400 because it looks like a small seat on which a toad could sit]

toad·y¹ /ˈtoʊdi/ *n. plural* **toadies** [C] INFORMAL, DISAPPROVING someone who pretends to like an important person and does whatever that person wants, especially in order to gain an advantage in the future [**Origin:** 1800–1900 *toadeater* helper of a seller of medicines who pretended to eat toads (thought to be poisonous) to prove the value of the medicine (17–19 centuries)]

toady² *v.* **toadies, toadied, toadying**

toady to sb *phr. v.* DISAPPROVING to pretend to like an important person, organization etc., and do whatever that person or organization wants, so that they will help you or like you —**toadying** also **toadyism** *n.* DISAPPROVING

to and fro¹ /ˌtu ən ˈfroʊ/ *adv.* moving in one direction and then back again —**to-and-fro** *adj.* [only before noun]

to and fro² *n.* [U] INFORMAL continuous movement of people or things from place to place

toast¹ /toʊst/ *n.* **1** [U] a piece of bread that has been put near heat so that it turns brown on both sides and is not soft anymore: *a piece of whole wheat toast* | *toast with butter and jam* → see also FRENCH TOAST, MELBA TOAST, TEXAS TOAST **2** [C] the action of drinking wine or other drink in order to thank someone, wish someone luck, or celebrate something: **+to** *A toast to your future success!* | *I'd like to* ***propose a toast*** (=ask people to drink a toast) *to the bride and groom.* **3 be toast** SPOKEN, INFORMAL to be in trouble or a very bad situation, in which you might be punished, be fired, die etc. **4 be**

the toast of Broadway/Hollywood etc. to be very popular and praised by many people for something you have done in a particular field of work

toast² *v.* [T] **1** to drink a glass of wine or other drink in order to thank someone, wish someone luck etc.: *We all toasted Edward's success.* **2** to make bread or other food brown by placing it close to heat: *Lightly toast the nuts.* ►see THESAURUS box at **cook¹** **3** to sit near a fire to make yourself warm

toast·er /ˈtoʊstɚ/ *n.* [C] a machine you use for toasting bread

ˈtoaster ˌoven *n.* [C] a small electric OVEN used for quickly toasting and baking foods

toast·mas·ter /ˈtoʊstˌmæstɚ/ *n.* [C] someone who introduces the speakers at a formal occasion such as a BANQUET (=large formal meal)

toast·mis·tress /ˈtoʊstˌmɪstrɪs/ *n.* [C] a woman who introduces the speakers at a formal occasion such as a BANQUET (=large formal meal)

toast·y /ˈtoʊsti/ also **ˌtoasty ˈwarm** *adj. comparative* **toastier**, *superlative* **toastiest** INFORMAL warm and comfortable

to·bac·co /təˈbækoʊ/ W2 *n.* [U] the dried brown leaves that are smoked in cigarettes, pipes etc., or the plant from which these leaves come: *chewing tobacco* [**Origin:** 1500–1600 Spanish *tabaco*, **tobacco leaves rolled up and smoked**]

to·bac·co·nist /təˈbækənɪst/ *n.* [C] someone who has a special store that sells tobacco, cigarettes etc., or the store itself

To·bit /ˈtoʊbɪt/ a book in the Apocrypha of the Protestant Bible

to·bog·gan¹ /təˈbɑgən/ *n.* [C] a light wooden board with a curved front, used for sliding down hills covered in snow [**Origin:** 1800–1900 Canadian French *tobogan*, from Micmac *tobagun* **sledge made of skin**]

toboggan² *v.* [I] to slide down a hill on a toboggan —**tobogganing** *n.* [U]

toc·ca·ta /təˈkɑtə/ *n.* [C] a piece of music, usually for piano or organ, that is played very quickly

Tocque·ville /ˈtoʊkvɪl/**, A·lex·is de** /əˈlɛksɪs də/ (1805–1859) a French writer and politician who traveled in the U.S. and wrote a book which examined the strengths and weaknesses of the American system of government

toc·sin /ˈtɑksən/ *n.* [C] LITERARY a signal of danger that is made by ringing a bell

to·day¹ /təˈdeɪ/ S1 W1 *adv.* **1** on the day that is happening now: *What did you do today?* | *Today we're going to the beach.* | **a year/two weeks etc. ago today** *I started this job a year ago today.* **2** at the present period of time: *Kids today just don't understand the value of money.* [**Origin:** Old English *todæge*, *todæg*, from *to* **to, at** + *dæg* **day**]

today² *n.* [U] **1** the day that is happening now: *Today is Friday.* | *Have you heard today's news?* | *The forecast for today is rain.* | **a week/month/year etc. from today** *The concert is three weeks from today.* **2** the present period of time: *today's technology* | *the music of today*

tod·dle /ˈtɑdl/ *v.* [I] if a small child toddles, it walks with short unsteady steps

tod·dler /ˈtɑdlɚ/ *n.* [C] a very young child who is just learning to walk

tod·dy /ˈtɑdi/ *n. plural* **toddies** [C] a HOT TODDY

to-do /tə ˈdu/ *n.* [singular] INFORMAL a lot of excitement about something, especially when it is not necessary

to-ˈdo list *n.* [C] a list of things that someone is planning to do

toe¹ /toʊ/ S2 *n.* [C] **1** BIOLOGY one of the five movable parts at the end of your foot: *She wiggled her toes in the water.* | *I hurt my **big toe** (=the largest of your toes) kicking the door.* | *We **stood on our toes** (=stood on the ends of our toes) to get a better view of the parade.* → see also **stub your toe** at STUB² **2** the part of a shoe or sock that covers the front part of your foot → see picture at SHOE¹ **3 keep sb on their toes** to make sure that someone is ready for anything that might happen: *Frequent tests keep students on their toes.* **4 make sb's toes curl** to make someone feel very embarrassed or uncomfortable about something **5 touch your toes** to bend down so that your hands touch your toes **6 put/stick/dip your toe in the water** to try a little of something or try an activity for a short time to see if you like it [**Origin:** Old English *ta*] → see also **from head to toe** at HEAD¹ (7), **step on sb's toes** at STEP² (3), TIPTOE¹, -TOED, TOE-TO-TOE

toe² *v.* [T] **toe the line** to do what other people in a job or organization say you should do, whether you agree with them or not

toe·cap /ˈtoʊkæp/ *n.* [C] a piece of metal or leather that covers the front part of a shoe

-toed /toʊd/ [in adjectives] **1 steel-toed/square-toed/pointy-toed etc.** a steel-toed, square-toed etc. shoe has a toe made of steel, shaped like a square etc. → see also OPEN-TOED **2 three-toed/long-toed/five-toed etc.** having three toes, long toes etc., especially used to describe animals

TOEFL /ˈtoʊfəl/ *n.* [singular] TRADEMARK **Test of English as a Foreign Language** a test that students can take that shows how good their English is, when English is not their first language

toe·hold /ˈtoʊhoʊld/ *n.* **1** [singular] someone's first involvement in a particular activity, from which they can develop and become stronger: **get/gain a toehold** *Local companies are trying to get a toehold in the market.* **2** [C] a small hole, a rock etc. where you can put your foot when you are climbing

TOEIC /ˈtoʊɪk/ *n.* [singular] TRADEMARK **Test of English for International Communication** a test that students can take that shows how good their English is, when English is not their first language

toe·nail /ˈtoʊneɪl/ *n.* [C] the hard part that covers the top of each of your toes

ˌtoe-to-ˈtoe *adv.* **go/stand/fight toe-to-toe (with sb)** to argue or fight with someone in a way that shows you will not stop —**toe-to-toe** *adj.*

tof·fee /ˈtɔfi, ˈtɑfi/ *n.* [C,U] a sticky sweet substance that you can eat, made by boiling sugar, water, and butter together, or a piece of this substance

to·fu /ˈtoʊfu/ *n.* [U] a soft white food like cheese, that is made from SOY BEANS [**Origin:** 1700–1800 Japanese]

tog /tɑg, tɔg/ *n.* **togs** [plural] OLD-FASHIONED, INFORMAL clothes

to·ga /ˈtoʊgə/ *n.* [C] a long loose piece of clothing worn by people in ancient Rome

to·geth·er¹ /təˈgɛðɚ/ S1 W1 *adv.*

1 MAKE ONE THING if you put two or more things together, you join them so that they form a single subject or group OPP **apart**: *I glued the vase back together.* | *Mix the sugar and butter together.* | *Now add the numbers together to get the subtotal.*

2 WITH EACH OTHER if two or more people are together or do something together, they are with each other or do something with each other OPP **separately** OPP **alone**: *We enjoyed working together.* | *Together they went back inside the house.*

3 IN ONE PLACE very near each other, in the same place: *Keep the documents together in one file.* | **close/packed/crowded etc. together** *The trees had been planted too close together.*

4 TOUCHING EACH OTHER if you rub, touch etc. things together, you rub or touch them against each other: *They banged their heads together trying to catch the ball.*

5 AT THE SAME TIME at the same time: *I mailed both packages together.* | ***All together now*** (=used to tell a group of people to do something at the same time)!

6 IN AGREEMENT if people are together, come together etc., they are or become united and work with each other: *Together we can defeat this threat.* | *I hope both countries can **come together** on this issue.*

7 COMBINED used for saying that two or more amounts are combined or added: *Add these numbers together and then divide the total by seven.* | *The paintings are together worth over $1 million.*
8 together with sb/sth in addition to someone or something else, or happening at the same time as something else SYN **along with** SYN **as well as**: *Send the form, together with your payment, to this address.*
9 WITHOUT STOPPING OLD-FASHIONED without interruption: *It rained for four days together.*
[**Origin:** Old English *togædere*, from *to* **to** + *gædere* **together**] → see also **get your act together** at ACT[1] (6)

together[2] *adj.* SPOKEN, APPROVING someone who is together always thinks clearly and does things in a very sensible, organized way: *Jane is such a together person.*

to·geth·er·ness /təˈgɛðənɪs/ *n.* [U] the feeling you have when you are part of a group of people who have a close relationship with each other: *Our family has a strong sense of togetherness.*

tog·gle /ˈtɑgəl/ *n.* [C] **1** COMPUTERS something on a computer that lets you change from one choice to another and back again **2** TECHNICAL also **toggle switch** a small part on a machine that is used to turn electricity on and off by moving it up or down **3** a small piece of wood or plastic that is used as a button on coats, bags etc. → see picture at FASTENER

To·go /ˈtoʊgoʊ/ a country in West Africa between Benin and Ghana —**Togolese** /ˌtoʊgəˈliz◂ / *adj.*

toil[1] /tɔɪl/ *v.* [I always + adv./prep.] **1** also **toil away** to work very hard for a long period of time SYN **labor**: *Workers toiled day and night to make a living.* **2** to move slowly and with great effort SYN **struggle**: **+up/through/against etc.** *They toiled up the long hill in snowshoes.*

toil[2] *n.* [U] FORMAL **1** hard difficult work done over a long time: *a life of toil* **2 the toils of sth** LITERARY bad experiences or feelings, especially in a situation that you cannot escape

toi·let /ˈtɔɪlɪt/ S2 *n.* **1** [C] a large bowl that you sit on to get rid of waste liquid or solid waste from your body: *Someone forgot to* ***flush the toilet*** (=make water go through the toilet to clean it). | *a toilet seat*

THESAURUS

Do not use **toilet** to talk about a room with a toilet in it.
bathroom a room in a house with the toilet in it
restroom, women's/ladies' room, men's room a room in a public place that has one or more toilets in it
lavatory a room with a toilet in it, especially a room in a public building such as a school or on an airplane
latrine an outdoor toilet at a camp or military area
outhouse/privy a small building in which the waste from the toilet goes into a hole below it, used in campgrounds and in the past behind houses

2 go to the toilet to pass waste liquid or solid waste from your body SYN **go to the bathroom** **3** BRITISH a RESTROOM **4** OLD-FASHIONED, FORMAL TOILETTE [**Origin:** 1500–1600 French *toilette* **cloth put around the shoulders while arranging the hair or shaving, toilette, toilet**, from *toile* **net, cloth**]

ˈtoilet ˌpaper *n.* [U] soft thin paper used for cleaning yourself after you have used the toilet

toi·let·ries /ˈtɔɪlətriz/ *n.* [plural] things such as soap and TOOTHPASTE that are used for washing yourself

toi·lette /twɑˈlɛt/ *n.* [U] OLD-FASHIONED, FORMAL the act of washing and dressing yourself

ˈtoilet ˌtraining *n.* [U] the process of teaching a child to use a toilet SYN **potty training** —**toilet-train** *v.* [T] —**toilet-trained** *adj.*

ˈtoilet ˌwater *n.* [U] a type of PERFUME (=pleasant smelling liquid) that does not have a very strong smell

toke[1] /toʊk/ *n.* [C] SLANG **1** the action of taking the smoke of a MARIJUANA cigarette into your lungs **2** a MARIJUANA cigarette SYN **joint**

toke[2] *v.* [I,T] SLANG to smoke a MARIJUANA cigarette

to·ken[1] /ˈtoʊkən/ *n.* [C] **1** a round piece of metal or plastic that you use instead of money in some machines: *a subway token* (=a token used to pay to ride the subway) **2** FORMAL something that represents a feeling, fact, event etc.: **a token of sb's gratitude/respect/appreciation etc.** *Please accept this gift as a small token of our appreciation.* → see also **by the same token** at SAME[1] (5)

token[2] *adj.* [only before noun] **1** a token action, change etc. is small and not very important, and is usually only done so that someone can pretend that they are taking important action: *He faces only token opposition.* | *The aid they're offering is just* ***a token gesture.*** **2 a token black/woman/minority etc.** someone who is included in a group to make people believe that the group is trying to be fair and include all types of people, when this is not really true **3** done as a first sign that an agreement, promise etc. will be kept and that more will be done later: *A token payment will keep the bank happy.*

to·ken·ism /ˈtoʊkəˌnɪzəm/ *n.* [U] actions that are intended to make people think that an organization deals fairly with people or problems when in fact it does not

To·ky·o /ˈtoʊkiˌoʊ/ the capital and largest city of Japan

told /toʊld/ *v.* the past tense and past participle of TELL

tol·er·a·ble /ˈtɑlərəbəl/ *adj.* **1** a tolerable situation is unpleasant, but you are able to accept it or deal with it: *He says the pain is tolerable.* **2** acceptable, but not especially good: *At least the dessert was tolerable.*

tol·er·a·bly /ˈtɑlərəbli/ *adv.* [+ adj./adv.] fairly, but not very much: *The test produces tolerably accurate results.*

tol·er·ance /ˈtɑlərəns/ *n.* **1** [U] willingness to allow people to be, do, say, or believe what they want without criticizing them: *racial tolerance* | **+of/toward/for** *tolerance for people with different views* **2** [C,U] the degree to which someone can accept a bad or difficult situation, even though they do not like it: **+for/of/to** *investors' tolerance for risk* | **a high/low tolerance** *I have a low tolerance for boredom.* **3** [C,U] TECHNICAL the ability of someone's body to deal with a drug or other substance without being affected or becoming sick: **+for/to** *He's built up a tolerance to the drug* | **a high/low tolerance** *Chris has a high tolerance to alcohol.* **4** [C,U] TECHNICAL the amount by which a measurement can be different from what is wanted

tol·er·ant /ˈtɑlərənt/ *adj.* **1** allowing people to do, say, or believe what they want without punishing or criticizing them OPP **intolerant**: *a tolerant community* | **+of** *Officers will be tolerant of peaceful demonstrations.* **2** BIOLOGY not easily affected, harmed, or damaged by particular conditions or substances: *drought-tolerant plants* | **+to** *He has become tolerant to alcohol.*

tol·er·ate /ˈtɑləˌreɪt/ *v.* [T] **1** to allow people to do, say, or believe something without criticizing or punishing them SYN **put up with**: *Such behavior will no longer be tolerated.* | *Mom tolerated Dad's smoking.* **2** to accept something bad or difficult, even though you do not like it SYN **put up with**: *He could not tolerate prison life.*

THESAURUS

accept to agree or deal with a situation you do not like but cannot change: *She found it hard to accept his death.*
put up with sth to accept an annoying situation or someone's annoying behavior, without trying to stop it or change it: *I don't see how you can put up with the constant noise.*
live with sth to accept a bad situation as a permanent part of your life that you cannot change: *Remember, you're going to have to live with the consequences of your decision.*

3 to treat someone you do not like in a polite but

unfriendly way when you have to spend time with them: *The other women tolerated her.* **4** TECHNICAL if you tolerate a particular medicine, it does not have a bad effect on your body; if a person or their body can tolerate a drug or other substance, or a particular environment, it does not make them sick: *The medication is well tolerated by most patients.* **5** TECHNICAL if a plant tolerates particular weather or soil conditions, it can live in them

tol·er·a·tion /ˌtɑləˈreɪʃən/ *n.* [U] willingness to allow people to do, say, or believe what they want without being punished or criticized: *religious toleration*

toll¹ /toʊl/ *n.* [C] **1** [usually singular] the number of people killed or injured in a particular accident, by a particular illness etc.: *The **death toll** of the plane crash has risen to 118.* **2 take a/its toll (on sb/sth)** also **exact a/its toll (on sb/sth)** to have a very bad effect on something or someone over a long period of time: *The extra work is taking a toll on the staff.* **3** the money you have to pay to use a particular road, bridge etc.: *highway tolls* **4 take a heavy/terrible/huge etc. toll (on sb/sth)** to cause many deaths or injuries: *Land mines are taking a heavy toll on children in the region.* **5** the sound of a large bell ringing slowly

toll² *v.* [I,T] if a large bell tolls, or you toll it, it keeps ringing slowly, especially to show that someone has died

toll·booth /ˈtoʊlbuθ/ *n.* [C] a place where you pay to drive on a road, bridge etc.

ˈtoll-bridge *n.* [C] a bridge that you pay to drive across

ˈtoll call *n.* [C] a telephone call that you must pay for → see also TOLL-FREE

ˈtoll-free *adj.* a toll-free telephone number does not cost you anything when you call it —**toll-free** *adv.*

toll·gate /ˈtoʊlgeɪt/ *n.* [C] a gate across a road, at which you have to pay money before you can drive any further

ˈtoll ˌplaza *n.* [C] an area on a HIGHWAY that is wider than the rest, where you stop to pay to use the road

ˈtoll road *n.* [C] a road that you pay to use

toll·way /ˈtoʊlweɪ/ *n. plural* **tollways** a large long road that you pay to use

Tol·stoy /ˈtoʊlstɔɪ/, **Count Leo** /ˈlioʊ/ (1828–1910) a Russian writer of NOVELS

Tol·tec /ˈtoʊltɛk/ one of the tribes who lived in southern Mexico from the 10th century to the 12th century

tom /tɑm/ *n.* [C] INFORMAL a TOMCAT

tom·a·hawk /ˈtɑməˌhɔk/ *n.* [C] a light AX used by Native Americans

to·ma·to /təˈmeɪt̬oʊ/ S2 *n. plural* **tomatoes** [C] BIOLOGY a round soft red fruit eaten raw or cooked as a vegetable: *a salad with fresh sliced tomatoes* | *tomato juice* [**Origin:** 1600–1700 Spanish *tomate*, from Nahuatl *tomatl*]

tomb /tum/ *n.* [C] a grave, especially a large one above the ground: *the tomb of a pharaoh* [**Origin:** 1100–1200 Anglo-French *tumbe*, from Late Latin *tumba* **pile of earth under which a body is buried**]

Tom·bouc·tou /ˌtɑmbukˈtu/ also **Tim·buk·tu** /ˌtɪmbʌkˈtu/ a city in Mali near the River Niger and on the edge of the Sahara Desert

tom·boy /ˈtɑmbɔɪ/ *n.* [C] a girl who likes playing the same games as boys

tomb·stone /ˈtumstoʊn/ *n.* [C] a stone that is put on a grave and shows the dead person's name, dates of birth and death etc. SYN **headstone** SYN **gravestone**

tom·cat /ˈtɑmkæt/ *n.* [C] a male cat

tome /toʊm/ *n.* [C] LITERARY or HUMOROUS a large heavy book

tom·fool /ˌtɑmˈful◂/ *adj.* [only before noun] OLD-FASHIONED very silly or stupid

tom·fool·er·y /ˌtɑmˈfuləri/ *n.* [U] silly behavior

tom·my gun /ˈtɑmi ˌgʌn/ *n.* [C] OLD-FASHIONED, INFORMAL a type of gun that can fire many bullets very quickly

to·mor·row¹ /təˈmɑroʊ, -ˈmɔr-/ S1 W2 *adv.* on or during the day after today: *We're playing tennis tomorrow.* | **tomorrow morning/afternoon/night/evening** *He'll be in town tomorrow afternoon.* [**Origin:** Old English *to morgen*, from *to* **to** + *morgen* **morning**]

tomorrow² *n.* **1** [U] the day after today: *Tomorrow is Thursday.* | *I'll see you at tomorrow's meeting.* | *Are you free **the day after tomorrow**?* | **a week/month from tomorrow** *She starts her new job a week from tomorrow.* **2** [singular, U] the future, especially the near future: *the leaders of tomorrow* | *We all hope for a better tomorrow.* **3 do sth like there's no tomorrow** INFORMAL to do something carelessly and quickly or to an extreme degree, without worrying about the future: *She's spending money like there's no tomorrow.*

ˈtom-tom *n.* [C] a tall narrow drum you play with your hands

ton /tʌn/ S2 W3 *n.* [C] **1** *plural* **tons** or **ton** a unit for measuring weight, equal to 2,000 pounds or 907.2 kilograms in the U.S.: *Each boulder weighs several tons.* **2 a ton** also **tons** INFORMAL a lot of something: *We had a ton left over.* | **+of** *They must be making tons of money.* → see also TONS **3 weigh a ton** INFORMAL to be very heavy: *Your bag weighs a ton!* **4 hit sb like a ton of bricks** INFORMAL to have a strong sudden effect on someone: *The news of her accident hit me like a ton of bricks.* **5 come down on sb like a ton of bricks** INFORMAL to get very angry with someone about something they have done [**Origin:** 1200–1300 *tun* **container, unit of weight** (11–21 centuries), from Old English *tunne*]

to·nal /ˈtoʊnl/ *adj.* [no comparative] ENG. LANG. ARTS **1** relating to tones of color or sound **2** TECHNICAL a tonal language uses different PITCHes of sound to show differences of meaning → see also TONE LANGUAGE **3** TECHNICAL tonal music is based on traditional musical KEYS OPP **atonal**

to·nal·i·ty /toʊˈnæləṭi/ *n. plural* **tonalities** [C,U] TECHNICAL the sound of a piece of music that depends on the KEY of the music and the way in which the tunes and harmonies (=harmony) are combined

tone¹ /toʊn/ S2 W2 *n.*
1 VOICE [C] [plural] the way your voice sounds that shows how you are feeling, or what you mean: *His tone was hesitant.* | *I don't like your **tone of voice**.* | *She spoke **in calm tones**.*
2 FEELING [singular, U] the general feeling or attitude expressed in a piece of writing, an activity etc.: *The meeting had a positive tone.* | **+of** *the urgent tone of the memo* | *The speech was formal **in tone**.* | *Jordan's 25 points in the first quarter **set the tone** (=established the general attitude or feeling) for the game.*
3 SOUND [C,U] the quality of a sound, especially the sound of a musical instrument or someone's voice: *Tony's guitar has a nice tone.* → see also -TONED
4 COLOR [C] one of the many types of a particular color, each slightly darker, lighter, brighter etc. than the next SYN **shade**: *Perhaps a darker tone would be better.* | **+of** *different tones of green* | *an even **skin tone*** → see also TWO-TONE
5 ELECTRONIC SOUND [C] a sound made by electronic equipment, such as a telephone: *Please leave a message after the tone.* → see also DIAL TONE
6 BODY [U] how firm and strong your muscles, skin etc. are: *Swimming improves your **muscle tone**.*
7 VOICE LEVEL [C] TECHNICAL the PITCH of someone's voice as they speak
8 SOCIALLY ACCEPTABLE [U] the degree to which something is considered polite, interesting, socially acceptable etc.: **lower/raise the tone** *That horrible building lowers the whole tone of the neighborhood.*
9 MUSIC [C] ENG. LANG. ARTS the difference in PITCH between two musical notes that are separated by one KEY on the piano SYN **step**
[**Origin:** 1200–1300 Latin *tonus* **tension, tone**, from Greek *tonos*]

tone² *v.* [T] to improve the strength and firmness of your skin, muscles etc.: *It cleanses and tones your skin.*

tone sth ↔ **down** *phr. v.* **1** to reduce the effect of something such as a speech or piece of writing, so that people will not be offended: *She's toned her criticism down a little.* **2** to make a color less bright

tone up *phr. v.* **tone sth ↔ up** to improve the

T

strength and firmness of your muscles, your body, or part of your body: *Aerobics really tones up your muscles.*

toned /toʊnd/ *adj.* toned people, bodies, muscles, or skin are firm and strong

-toned *suffix* [in adjectives] **deep-toned/even-toned/shrill-toned etc.** having a particular tone of voice

ˌtone-ˈdeaf *adj.* unable to hear the difference between musical notes

ˈtone ˌlanguage *n.* [C] ENG. LANG. ARTS a language such as Chinese, in which the way a sound goes up or down affects the meaning of the word

tone·less /ˈtoʊnlɪs/ *adj.* a toneless voice does not express any feelings —**tonelessly** *adv.*

ˈtone ˌpoem *n.* [C] a piece of music written to represent an idea, scene, or story

ton·er /ˈtoʊnɚ/ *n.* [U] **1** a type of ink used in computer PRINTERS, PHOTOCOPIERS etc. **2** a liquid that you put on your face to make your skin feel good

Ton·ga /ˈtɑŋgə/ a country consisting of about 170 small islands in the southwest Pacific Ocean —**Tongan** /ˈtɑŋgən, ˈtɑŋən/ *n., adj.*

tongs /tɑŋz, tɔŋz/ *n.* [plural] a tool that is U- or V-shaped, so that you can press the open ends together to pick things up

tongue¹ /tʌŋ/ S2 W3 *n.*
1 MOUTH [C] BIOLOGY the soft movable part inside your mouth that you use for tasting and speaking: *She moistened her lips with the tip of her tongue.* | *She* ***stuck** her **tongue out*** (=put her tongue outside her mouth as a rude gesture) *at him.* → see picture at DIGESTIVE SYSTEM
2 LANGUAGE [C] LITERARY a language: *a foreign tongue* → see also MOTHER TONGUE, **native tongue** at NATIVE¹ (3) ►see THESAURUS box at **language**
3 SHOE the part of a shoe that lies on top of your foot, under the part where you tie it → see picture at SHOE¹
4 have a silver/smooth tongue if you have a smooth tongue or a silver tongue, you can talk in a way that makes people like you or persuades them that you are right → see also -TONGUED
5 with (your) tongue in (your) cheek if you say something with tongue in cheek, you say it as a joke, not seriously → see also TONGUE-IN-CHEEK
6 roll/trip off sb's tongue if a name, phrase etc. rolls or trips off your tongue, it is easy or pleasant to say: *Their names roll off the tongue very easily.*
7 FOOD [U] the tongue of a cow or sheep, cooked and eaten as food
8 tongues wag INFORMAL if tongues wag, people talk in an unkind way about someone: *They live in a small town and tongues are beginning to wag.*
9 hold your tongue! SPOKEN, OLD-FASHIONED used to tell someone angrily to stop speaking
10 SHAPE [C] LITERARY something that has a long thin shape: +**of** *tongues of flame*
11 get your tongue around sth INFORMAL to be able to say a difficult word or phrase
12 keep a civil tongue in your head SPOKEN, OLD-FASHIONED used when you think someone should speak politely
[**Origin:** Old English *tunge*] → see also **bite your tongue** at BITE¹ (4), **cat got your tongue?** at CAT (7), **find your voice/tongue** at FIND (1), **speak with forked tongue** at FORKED (2), **loosen sb's tongue** at LOOSEN (4), **have a sharp tongue** at SHARP¹ (5), **a slip of the tongue/pen** at SLIP² (3), **speak in tongues** at SPEAK (12), **on the tip of your tongue** at TIP¹ (4), **watch your mouth/language/tongue!** at WATCH¹ (15)

tongue² *v.* **1** [I,T] TECHNICAL to use your tongue to make separate sounds when playing a musical instrument that you blow **2** [T] to touch something with your tongue

ˌtongue and ˈgroove, tongue-and-groove *adj.* [only before noun] tongue and groove boards fit together by pushing a piece that sticks out along the edge of one board into a hollow area along the edge of another board

-tongued /tʌŋd/ *suffix* [in adjectives] **sharp-tongued/silver-tongued etc.** used in adjectives to describe how someone talks

ˈtongue deˌpressor *n.* [C] a little flat piece of wood a doctor uses to hold down your tongue while examining your throat

ˌtongue-in-ˈcheek *adj.* a tongue-in-cheek remark, COMMENT etc. is said or done as a joke, even though it might seem serious —**tongue-in-cheek** *adv.*

ˈtongue-ˌlashing *n.* [C] an occasion when someone criticizes someone else angrily for something they have done wrong

ˈtongue-tied *adj.* unable to speak easily to other people, especially because you feel embarrassed

ˈtongue ˌtwister *n.* [C] a word or phrase that is difficult to say quickly and correctly, for example "she sells sea shells by the sea shore"

ton·ic¹ /ˈtɑnɪk/ *n.* **1** [C,U] also **ˈtonic ˌwater** a clear bitter tasting drink that is mixed with alcoholic drinks: *I'll have a gin and tonic.* **2** [C usually singular] someone or something that makes you feel happy and full of energy: *A weekend on the beach was the perfect tonic.* **3** [C,U] a liquid that you use to make your skin healthier or your hair shinier **4** [C] OLD-FASHIONED a type of liquid medicine, especially one that is designed to give you more energy or strength when you feel tired **5** [C usually singular] ENG. LANG. ARTS the first note in a musical SCALE

tonic² *adj.* [only before noun] **1** FORMAL improving something or making someone feel healthier and stronger **2** TECHNICAL involving the first note in a musical SCALE

to·night¹ /təˈnaɪt/ S1 W2 *adv.* on or during the night of today: *Let's go to a movie tonight.* [**Origin:** Old English *to niht*, from *to* **to, at** + *niht* **night**]

tonight² *n.* [U] the night of today: *Do you have plans for tonight?* | *We hope that tonight's game will be a good one.*

ton·nage /ˈtʌnɪdʒ/ *n.* [C,U] **1** the size of a ship or the amount of goods it can carry, shown in TONS **2** the total number of TONS that something weighs

tons /tʌnz/ *adv.* INFORMAL very much: *Ricky is tons better looking than his brother.* → see also **tons** at TON (2)

ton·sil /ˈtɑnsəl/ *n.* [C] BIOLOGY one of two small round pieces of flesh at the sides of the throat near the back of the tongue: *I have to **have** my **tonsils out*** (=have my tonsils removed by a doctor).

ton·sil·lec·to·my /ˌtɑnsəˈlɛktəmi/ *n. plural* **tonsillectomies** [C] a medical operation in which one or both tonsils are removed

ton·sil·li·tis /ˌtɑnsəˈlaɪt̬ɪs/ *n.* [U] MEDICINE a serious infection of the tonsils

ton·so·ri·al /tɑnˈsɔriəl/ *adj.* HUMOROUS relating to the cutting or styling (STYLE) of hair

ton·sure /ˈtɑnʃɚ/ *n.* [C,U] the act of removing a circle of hair from the top of your head to show that you are a MONK, or the part of your head that has had the hair removed in this way —**tonsured** *adj.*

ton·y /ˈtoʊni/ *adj. comparative* **tonier**, *superlative* **toniest** INFORMAL fashionable, expensive, and having a lot of style: *a tony resort hotel*

too /tu/ S1 W1 *adv.* **1** [+ adj./adv.] more than is needed, wanted, or possible, or more than is reasonable: *The music is too loud.* | *You're walking too slowly.* | **too much/little/many etc. sth** *There's too much salt in the soup.* | **too tall/old etc. for sb/sth** *The hat is too small for me.* | **too young/hot/big etc. to do sth** *It's too cold to go outside.* | **much/far/way etc. too old/expensive/hard etc.** *New York's way too expensive.* **2** [at the end of a sentence or clause, or after the subject of a sentence] also: *Thursday is Vivian's birthday too.* | *I love you, too.* | *You too could be a winner.* | *"I really like him." "**Me too*** (=I like him too)." → see also EITHER **3 not/none too** [+ adj./adv.] used like "not very" for saying that the opposite of something is true: *I wasn't able to get too much sleep last night.* | *It won't be too long before dinnertime.* | *"How are you?" "Not too bad."* | *Her parents were none too pleased.* **4 I am/he is/you are**

etc. too INFORMAL used, especially by children, for saying angrily that something is true when someone else has just said it is not true: *"You're not smart enough to use a computer." "I am too!"* **5 too nice/smart/fast etc. for your own good** used to say that although someone or something seems to have a lot of a good quality, it sometimes causes problems: *Sometimes I think Andy is too smart for his own good.* **6 be too much for sb** to be so difficult, tiring, upsetting etc. that someone cannot do or deal with it: *The shock of his death was too much for her.* **7 all too/only too** used to emphasize that a particular situation exists when you wish it did not exist: *Violent behavior is all too common in our society.* **8 too little, too late** used to say that someone did not do enough to prevent something bad from happening: *The extra money they're offering is too little, too late.* **9** used to emphasize a remark or detail that you are adding: *"Seth finally got a job." "It's about time too."* [**Origin:** Old English *to* **to, too**] → see also **too bad** at BAD¹ (14) → see Word choice box at ALSO

took /tʊk/ *v.* the past tense of TAKE

tool¹ /tul/ S2 W2 *n.* [C] **1** something such as a hammer that you hold in your hand and use to make or repair things: *a mechanic's tools* | *a set of garden tools* **2** something such as a piece of equipment or a skill that is useful for doing your job; something you use to do a particular job or to achieve something, such as a piece of equipment, a computer program, a skill, a plan etc.: *The Internet has been an effective tool for advertising.* | *learning tools* | *Drugs, weapons, and hidden cameras are* ***tools of the trade*** *for undercover agents.* **3** someone who is used unfairly by someone else: +**of** *Many see the senator as a tool of the auto industry.* [**Origin:** Old English *tol*]

tool² *v.* [I] INFORMAL to drive along a street, especially for fun: +**around/along/down** *She tools around town in a yellow convertible.*

tool up *phr. v.* **tool sth ↔ up** to prepare a factory for production by providing the necessary tools and machinery

tool·bar /ˈtulbɑr/ *n.* [C] COMPUTERS a row of small pictures or words at the top of a computer screen that allow you to do particular things in a program

tool·box, tool box /ˈtulbɑks/ *n.* [C] **1** a special box that holds tools **2** COMPUTERS a set of commands or FUNCTIONS that do different things in a computer program

tooled /tuld/ *adj.* tooled leather has been decorated using a special tool that presses designs into the leather

ˈtool kit *n.* [C] a set of various tools

ˈtool shed *n.* [C] a small building outside, where tools are kept

toon /tun/ *n.* [C] INFORMAL a CARTOON

too·nie, twoonie /ˈtuni/ *n.* [C] CANADIAN, INFORMAL a Canadian two-dollar coin

toot¹ /tut/ *v.* [I,T] **1** if you toot a horn, especially a car horn, or if it toots, it makes a short high sound **2 toot your own horn** INFORMAL, DISAPPROVING to tell other people about the good things you have done SYN **brag** SYN **blow your own horn**

toot² *n.* [C] a short high sound, made especially by a car horn

tooth

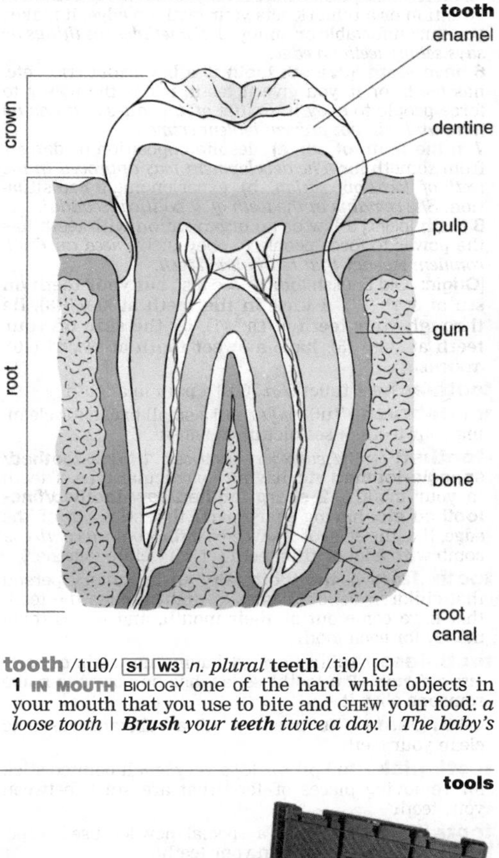

tooth /tuθ/ S1 W3 *n. plural* **teeth** /tiθ/ [C]
1 IN MOUTH BIOLOGY one of the hard white objects in your mouth that you use to bite and CHEW your food: *a loose tooth* | ***Brush your teeth*** *twice a day.* | *The baby's*

T

tools

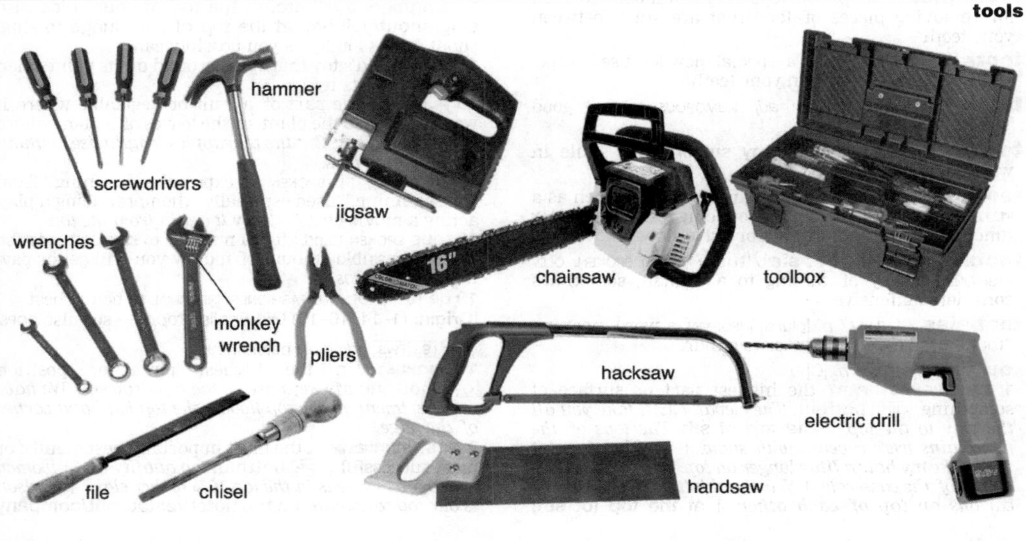

cutting a tooth (=growing a new tooth). | *The dog, a Rottweiler, **sank** its **teeth into*** (=bit into) *the little girl's arm.* | *She went to the dentist to **have a tooth pulled.***
2 ON A TOOL ETC. one of the pointed parts that sticks out from the edge of a comb, SAW, COG etc.
3 fight/battle tooth and nail to try with a lot of effort or determination to do something: *We had to fight tooth and nail to get our money back.*
4 get/sink your teeth into sth INFORMAL to start to do something with eagerness and energy: *It's the kind of project I can really sink my teeth into.*
5 set sb's teeth on edge a) if a sound, taste etc. sets your teeth on edge, it makes you feel physically uncomfortable: *His squeaky voice set my teeth on edge.* **b)** if a situation or a remark sets your teeth on edge, it makes you uncomfortable or annoyed: *Sometimes the things he says set my teeth on edge.*
6 have teeth, give sth teeth if a law, REGULATION etc. has teeth, or if you give it teeth, it has the power to force people to obey it: *Critics of the law say it has no teeth and will not prevent violent crime.*
7 in the teeth of sth a) despite opposition or danger from something: *The development was approved in the teeth of local opposition.* **b)** experiencing a bad situation: *She remains in the teeth of a political scandal.*
8 teeth [plural] a law or an organization with teeth has the power to force people to obey it: *We need an Environment Agency that really **has teeth**.*
[**Origin:** Old English *toth*] → see also **cut your teeth on sth** at CUT[1] (37), **a kick in the teeth** at KICK[2] (3), **lie through your teeth** at LIE[2] (1), **by the skin of your teeth** at SKIN[1] (5), **have a sweet tooth** at SWEET[1] (10), -TOOTHED

T

tooth·ache /ˈtuθeɪk/ *n.* [C,U] a pain in a tooth

tooth·brush /ˈtuθbrʌʃ/ *n.* [C] a small brush for cleaning your teeth → see picture at BRUSH[1]

-toothed /tuθt/ *suffix* [in adjectives] **1 buck-toothed/snaggle-toothed etc.** having a particular type of teeth in your mouth **2 sharp-toothed/saw-toothed/fine-toothed etc.** having sharp parts that stick out of the edge, like the edge of a SAW etc.: *a fine-toothed comb* (=a comb with a lot of thin teeth set very close together)

ˈtooth ˌfairy *n.* **the tooth fairy** an imaginary person that children believe comes at night to take the teeth that have come out of their mouth, and leaves them money for each tooth

tooth·less /ˈtuθlɪs/ *adj.* **1** having no teeth: *a toothless old man* **2** a toothless law has no power to make someone obey it

tooth·paste /ˈtuθpeɪst/ *n.* [U] a substance used to clean your teeth

tooth·pick /ˈtuθˌpɪk/ *n.* [C] a very small pointed stick for removing pieces of food that are stuck between your teeth

ˈtooth ˌpowder *n.* [U] a special powder used, especially in the past, to clean your teeth

tooth·some /ˈtuθsəm/ *adj.* HUMOROUS tasting good SYN **delicious**

tooth·y /ˈtuθi/ *adj.* **a toothy smile/grin** a smile in which you show a lot of teeth

too·tle /ˈtuṭl/ *v.* [I] **1** to play an instrument such as a FLUTE, especially without producing any particular tune **2** OLD-FASHIONED to walk or drive slowly

toots /tʊts/ also **toot·sie** /ˈtʊtsi/ *n.* [C] SPOKEN, OLD-FASHIONED a way of talking to a woman, sometimes considered offensive

toot·sies /ˈtʊtsiz/ *n.* [plural] INFORMAL a word meaning "toes," used especially by or to children

top[1] /tɑp/ S1 W1 *n.* [C]
1 THE HIGHEST PART the highest part or surface of something OPP **bottom**: *The elevator will take you all the way to the top.* | **the top of sth** *The tops of the mountains were covered with snow.* | **on (the) top (of sth)** *I like my hair a little longer on top.* | *Sprinkle cheese on top of the casserole.* | *You shouldn't have put the egg cartons **on top of each other**.* | **at the top (of sth)** *Write the date at the top.* | *Denise stood at the top of the stairs.* | *They had put his shoes at **the very top*** (=the highest part) *of the flag pole.* | **a tree/roof/mountain/hill top etc.** *The moon rose up above the tree tops.* | *My name was at **the very top** of the list.*
2 FURNITURE SURFACE the flat upper surface of a piece of furniture: **a table/dresser/desk/counter top** *stainless steel counter tops*
3 BEST POSITION **the top** the best, most successful, or most important position in an organization, company, group etc. OPP **bottom**: +**of** *His hard work helped him reach the top of his profession.* | *It can be lonely **at the top**.* | **(at) the top of the class/division etc.** *Martin graduated at the top of his class.* | *He is proud of the fact that he **worked** his **way to the top**.* | *She was determined to **make it to the top**.* → see also TOP-OF-THE-LINE
4 COVER something that you put on a pen, bottle etc. to close it, especially something that you push or turn: *Put the top back on the bottle when you're finished.* | *a bottle of wine with a **screw top*** ►see THESAURUS box at cover[2]
5 CLOTHES a piece of clothing that you wear on the upper part of your body: *The skirt comes with a matching top.* | *a bikini top* → see also **halter top** at HALTER (1), TANK TOP
6 on top of sth a) if something bad happens to you on top of something else, it happens when you have other problems: *On top of losing my job, my car broke down.* **b)** in complete control of a job, situation etc.: *Local police have failed to **get on top of** the gang situation.* | *Nathan always stays **on top of things**.*
7 on top of sb if someone or something dangerous or threatening is on top of you, they are very near to you or almost touching you: *FBI agents were on top of them before they could react.*
8 on top in a situation where you are the best or are winning in a game or competition: *Usually the team with the most talent **comes out on top*** (=wins after a difficult struggle or argument).
9 be (at the) top of the list/agenda something that is at the top of the list will be dealt with or discussed first: *Improving education is at the top of the mayor's agenda.*
10 on top of each other INFORMAL if people live, work etc. on top of each other, they are very close to each other in a space that is too small
11 on top of the world INFORMAL extremely happy
12 (from) top to bottom if something is done from top to bottom, it is done very thoroughly: *They've changed the whole system from top to bottom.* | *Police searched his apartment top to bottom.*
13 off the top of your head INFORMAL if you answer a question or provide information off the top of your head, you do it immediately without checking the facts: *"Do you remember her name?" "Not off the top of my head."*
14 sing/shout/yell etc. at the top of your voice also **sing/shout/yell etc. at the top of your lungs** to sing, shout etc. as loudly as you possibly can
15 TOY a child's toy that spins around on its point when the child twists it
16 PLANT [C] the part of a fruit or vegetable where it was attached to the plant, or the leaves of a plant whose root you can eat: *Cut the pineapples lengthwise, without removing the tops.*
17 from the top SPOKEN an expression meaning "from the beginning," used especially when practicing a play, acting a movie etc.: *Let's try it again from the top.*
18 tops SPOKEN used after a number to say that it is the highest possible amount of money you will get or pay: *It'll cost $15 tops.*
19 be (the) top OLD-FASHIONED, INFORMAL to be the best
[**Origin:** (1–14, 16–19) Old English *topp*] → see also TOPS

top[2] S3 W3 *adj.* [only before noun]
1 HIGHEST in the highest place or position OPP **bottom**: *My keys are in the top drawer.* | *We have an apartment on the top floor.* | *the top left-hand corner of the page*
2 MOST SUCCESSFUL the most important, best quality, or most successful OPP **bottom**: *top quality beef* | *women in top jobs* | *Sue is in the top 10% of her class.* | *Carlson is our top salesman.* | **a top hotel/restaurant/company**

etc. *a top New York restaurant.* ►see THESAURUS box at **position¹, rank¹**
3 AMOUNT [only before noun] the greatest or highest that is possible or that happens: *The car has a **top speed** of 140 mph.*
4 the top brass INFORMAL people in positions of high rank, especially in the army, navy etc.
5 top dog INFORMAL the person in the highest or most important position, especially after a struggle or effort

top³ *v.* **topped, topping** [T]
1 BE HIGHER to be higher than a particular amount, especially an unusually large amount: *Their profits have topped $200 million this year.* | *Temperatures regularly topped 120 degrees.*
2 BE ON TOP OF STH [usually passive] if something tops another thing, it is on top of that thing: *A golden cross tops the cathedral.* | **be topped by/with sth** *The fence is topped with razor wire.* → see also TOPPING
3 top the list/charts/agenda etc. to be first in a list or series of things, based on how successful or important they are: *Libraries topped the list of good public services.* → see also CHART-TOPPING
4 BE/DO BETTER a) to be better or greater than something else: *The sale price **topped the record** set last year.* **b)** if you top a good achievement, especially in sports, you do something that is even better or more impressive than that achievement: *They topped their two previous wins with a 31–0 defeat of American Samoa.*
5 top an offer/bid etc. to offer more money than someone else: *Dutton topped their bid and bought the firm for $2.7 billion.*
6 top that SPOKEN used to tell someone to do something better, say something funnier etc. than you have: *Dan got a perfect score – top that!*
7 to top it all (off) SPOKEN in addition to other bad things that have happened to you: *And to top it all off, I wrecked my car.*
8 REACH THE TOP LITERARY if you top a slope, hill, or mountain, you reach the top of it

top sth ↔ **off** *phr. v.* **1** to complete something successfully by doing a last action or adding a last detail: *The team's win topped off a great season.* **2** to fill a partly empty container with liquid: *Let me top off your drink.*

top out *phr. v.* if something such as a price that is increasing tops out, it reaches its highest point and stops rising: *Real estate prices seem to have topped out.*

top sth **with** sth *phr. v.* if you top food with something else, you put a layer of it over the food: *The pie was topped with whipped cream.* → see also TOPPING

Top 40 /ˌtɑp ˈfɔrt̬i/ *n.* **1 the Top 40** the list of 40 most popular songs in the U.S. during a particular week **2** [U] POP MUSIC —**Top-40** *adj.*: *a Top-40 song*

To·pa In·ca /ˈtoʊpə ˌɪŋkə/ an EMPEROR of the Inca people in South America, who lived in the 15th century and greatly increased the size of the Inca EMPIRE

to·paz /ˈtoʊpæz/ *n.* [C,U] EARTH SCIENCE a transparent yellow jewel or the mineral that it is cut from

top-'class *adj.* being the best, most skillful etc.: *a top-class athlete* | *top-class hotels*

top·coat /ˈtɑpkoʊt/ *n.* **1** [C,U] the last layer of paint that is put on a surface **2** [C] OLD-FASHIONED a warm long coat

top-'down *adj.* **1 a top-down business/company/corporation etc.** a top-down business, company etc. is one in which all the ideas and decisions for running the business come from people in the highest positions **2** a top-down plan or way of thinking is one in which you start with a general idea of what you want and then add the details later → BOTTOM-UP

top-'drawer *adj.* OLD-FASHIONED, INFORMAL of the highest quality or social class

top ˌdressing *n.* [C,U] TECHNICAL a layer of FERTILIZER that is spread over land

to·pee, topi /toʊˈpi, ˈtoʊpi/ *n.* [C] a hard hat for protecting your head in tropical SUNSHINE

To·pe·ka /təˈpikə/ the capital city of the U.S. state of Kansas

ˈtop-end *adj.* used to describe the most expensive products in a range of products or a market

ˌtop-ˈflight *adj.* very successful, skillful, or important

ˌtop ˈgear *n.* [U] **1** the highest GEAR of a car, bus etc. **2 move/get into top gear** to begin to be as successful as possible or to work with as much effort as possible

ˈtop-ˌgrossing *adj.* a top-grossing movie earns more money than any other movie at a particular time

ˌtop ˈhat *n.* [C] a man's tall black or gray hat, now worn only on very formal occasions, such as a wedding → see picture at HAT

ˌtop-ˈheavy *adj.* **1** too heavy at the top and therefore likely to fall over **2** a top-heavy organization has too many managers compared to the number of ordinary workers

to·pi /toʊˈpi, ˈtoʊpi/ *n.* [C] another spelling of TOPEE

to·pi·ar·y /ˈtoʊpiˌɛri/ *n. plural* **topiaries** [C,U] trees and bushes cut into the shapes of birds, animals etc., or the art of cutting them in this way

top·ic /ˈtɑpɪk/ Ac S2 W3 *n.* [C] a subject that people talk or write about: *A lot has been written on this topic.* | *a talk on **the topic of** sex discrimination* | **a topic of conversation/debate** *The war was the main topic of conversation all evening.* | **a topic for discussion/conversation etc.** *This is an important topic for future research.* | *Immigration is **a hot topic*** (=a topic people are very interested in now) *at the moment.* [**Origin:** 1400–1500 Latin *Topica* **Topics**, book by the ancient Greek thinker Aristotle, from Greek *Topika*, from *topikos* **of a place, of a useful quotation**]

top·i·cal /ˈtɑpɪkəl/ Ac *adj.* **1** a topical story, subject, problem etc. is interesting because it deals with something that is important at the present time: *topical jokes* **2** TECHNICAL relating to the top part or surface of something: *a topical anesthetic* (=a drug that is put on the skin) —**topically** /-kli/ *adv.* —**topicality** /ˌtɑpɪˈkælət̬i/ *n.* [U]

ˈtopic ˌsentence *n.* [C] the sentence in a PARAGRAPH that states the main idea you are writing about

top·knot /ˈtɑpnɑt/ *n.* [C] hair that is tied together on the top of your head, or feathers that stick up on the top of a bird's head

top·less /ˈtɑplɪs/ *adj.* **1** a woman who is topless is not wearing any clothes on the upper part of her body, so that her breasts are uncovered **2** a topless bar, club etc. is one where the women serving drinks are topless

ˌtop-ˈlevel *adj.* [only before noun] **1** involving or being the most powerful people in a country, organization etc.: *a top-level meeting* **2** involving or being the best people in a sport: *a top-level gymnast*

top·most /ˈtɑpmoʊst/ *adj.* [only before noun] the topmost part of something is its highest part: *the topmost branches of the tree*

ˌtop-ˈnotch *adj.* INFORMAL having the highest quality or standard: *top-notch scientists*

ˌtop-of-the-ˈline *adj.* the best or most expensive of a group of things: *top-of-the-line computers*

to·pog·ra·phy /təˈpɑgrəfi/ *n.* [U] **1** EARTH SCIENCE the shape of an area of land, including its hills, valleys etc.: +**of** *the mountainous topography of the county* **2** EARTH SCIENCE the science of describing an area of land, or making maps of it **3** the state of the different features of a society or country, such as the state of its CULTURE, ECONOMY etc. —**topographer** *n.* [C] —**topographical** /ˌtɑpəˈgræfɪkəl◂/ *adj.*

to·pol·o·gy /təˈpɑlədʒi, tɑ-/ *n. plural* **topologies** [C] COMPUTERS the way in which a computer network is arranged

top·ping /ˈtɑpɪŋ/ *n.* [C,U] something you put on top of food to make it look nicer or taste better: *ice cream with a chocolate topping*

top·ple /ˈtɑpəl/ *v.* **1** [I,T] to become unsteady and then fall over, or to make someone or something do this: *High winds toppled several telephone poles.* | +**over/to/backward etc.** *The magazine rack toppled to the floor.*

T

2 [T] POLITICS to take power away from a leader or government, especially by force [SYN] **overthrow**: *They stopped a plot to topple the government.*

ˌtop-ˈranked *adj.* considered by most people to be the best, especially at a particular sport: *the world's top-ranked golfer*

ˌtop-ˈranking *adj.* most powerful and important within an organization: *top-ranking diplomats*

ˌtop-ˈrated *adj.* INFORMAL considered to be very good by most people: *a top-rated TV show*

ˈtop round *n.* [U] high quality BEEF cut from the upper leg of the cow

tops /tɑps/ *adj.* [not before noun] OLD-FASHIONED someone or something that is tops is the best or most popular

ˌtop-ˈsecret *adj.* top-secret documents or information must be kept completely secret: *top-secret government reports*

top·side /ˈtɑpsaɪd/ *adv.* toward or onto the DECK (=upper surface) of a boat or ship

top·soil /ˈtɑpsɔɪl/ *n.* [U] EARTH SCIENCE the upper level of soil, in which most plants have their roots

top·spin /ˈtɑpˌspɪn/ *n.* [U] the turning movement of a ball that has been hit or thrown in such a way that it spins forward

top·sy-tur·vy /ˌtɑpsi ˈtɚvi◂ / *adj.* INFORMAL **1** in a state of complete disorder or confusion **2** having some very good parts and some very bad parts **3** with the top part on the bottom, and the bottom part on the top [SYN] **upside down**

toque /toʊk/ also **tuque** /tuk/ *n.* [C] CANADIAN a STOCKING CAP

To·rah /ˈtɔrə/ *n.* **the Torah** all the writings and teachings concerned with Judaism, especially the first five books of the Jewish Bible [**Origin:** 1500–1600 a Hebrew word meaning **law, teaching**]

torch¹ /tɔrtʃ/ *n.* [C] **1** a long stick with burning material at one end that produces light: *the Olympic torch* **2** BRITISH a FLASHLIGHT [**Origin:** 1200–1300 Old French *torche* **bunch of twisted straws, torch**, from Vulgar Latin *torca*] → see also **carry a torch for sb** at CARRY¹ (32), **carry the torch of sth** at CARRY¹ (33), **pass the torch to sb** at PASS¹ (23)

torch² *v.* [T] INFORMAL to deliberately make a building start to burn

torch·light /ˈtɔrtʃlaɪt/ *n.* [U] the light produced by burning torches

ˈtorch song *n.* [C] a sad song about love that has ended or about loving someone who does not love you

tore /tɔr/ *v.* the past tense of TEAR²

tor·ment¹ /ˈtɔrmɛnt/ *n.* **1** [U] severe mental or physical suffering, often continuing for a long time: *She lay awake all night **in torment**.* **2** [C] someone or something that makes you suffer

torment² /tɔrˈmɛnt, ˈtɔrmɛnt/ *v.* [T] **1** to make someone suffer a lot, especially so that they feel guilty or very unhappy: *Jealousy tormented Harriet.* **2** to deliberately treat someone cruelly by annoying them or hurting them: *My older sister loved to torment me.* —**tormentor** *n.* [C] —**tormented** *adj.*

torn¹ /tɔrn/ *v.* the past participle of TEAR²

torn² *adj.* [not before noun] **1** unable to decide what to do because you have two different feelings or two different things that you want to do: **+between** *He was torn between loyalty and love.* **2 torn by sth a)** divided and very badly affected by an argument, war etc.: *The nation is still torn by war and riots.* **b)** feeling a negative emotion very strongly and feeling confused and unhappy: *Carl was torn by guilt.*

tor·na·do /tɔrˈneɪdoʊ/ *n. plural* **tornadoes** or **tornados** [C] EARTH SCIENCE an extremely violent storm consisting of air that spins very quickly and causes a lot of damage → see also HURRICANE [**Origin:** 1500–1600 Spanish *tronada* **thunderstorm**] → see picture on page A30

To·ron·to /təˈrɑntoʊ/ the capital and largest city of the Canadian PROVINCE of Ontario

tor·pe·do¹ /tɔrˈpidoʊ/ *n. plural* **torpedoes** [C] a long narrow weapon that is fired under the surface of the ocean and explodes when it hits something [**Origin:** 1700–1800 *torpedo* type of fish that can produce electricity to protect itself (16–21 centuries), from Latin, **stiffness, numbness, torpedo fish**]

torpedo² *v.* [T] **1** to attack or destroy a ship with a torpedo **2** to stop something such as a plan from succeeding: *The CEO torpedoed the deal in its final hours.*

tor·pid /ˈtɔrpɪd/ *adj.* FORMAL lazy or sleepy, and with no energy, activity, or excitement —**torpidly** *adv.*

tor·por /ˈtɔrpɚ/ *n.* [singular, U] FORMAL a state of being lazy or sleepy, and with no energy, activity, or excitement —**torpidity** /tɔrˈpɪdət̬i/ *n.* [U]

torque /tɔrk/ *n.* [U] TECHNICAL the force or power that makes something turn around a central point, especially in an engine

Tor·que·ma·da /ˌtɔrkəˈmɑdə/, **To·más de** /toʊˈmɑs deɪ/ (1420–1498) a Spanish Christian leader who started the Spanish Inquisition, the Catholic organization that punished people whose religious beliefs were considered unacceptable

tor·rent /ˈtɔrənt, ˈtɑr-/ *n.* [C] **1 a torrent of sth** a large number of people or things that all come or happen at the same time: **a torrent of abuse/criticism/protest etc.** *The proposal received a torrent of criticism.* **2** a large amount of water moving very rapidly and strongly in a particular direction: *The river had become **a raging torrent**.*

tor·ren·tial /tɔˈrɛnʃəl, tə-/ *adj.* **torrential rain** very heavy rain

tor·rid /ˈtɔrɪd, ˈtɑr-/ *adj.* **1** involving strong emotions, especially of sexual love: *a torrid love affair* **2** increasing or happening very quickly: *a torrid pace* **3** LITERARY torrid weather is very hot

tor·sion /ˈtɔrʃən/ *n.* [U] TECHNICAL the twisting of a piece of metal

tor·so /ˈtɔrsoʊ/ *n. plural* **torsos** or **torsi** /-saɪ/ [C] **1** BIOLOGY your body, not including your head, arms, or legs **2** ENG. LANG. ARTS a STATUE of a torso [**Origin:** 1700–1800 Italian, Latin *thyrsus* **stalk**]

tort /tɔrt/ *n.* [C] LAW an action that is wrong but not criminal and can be dealt with in a CIVIL court of law

torte /tɔrt/ *n.* [C,U] a type of cake made with a lot of eggs and very little flour

tor·ti·lla /tɔrˈtiyə/ *n.* [C] a piece of thin flat bread made from corn or wheat flour, eaten in Mexican cooking [**Origin:** 1600–1700 American Spanish, Spanish *torta* **cake**, from Late Latin]

torˈtilla chip *n.* [C] a thin CRISP piece of food made from flour, that has been cooked in oil

tor·toise /ˈtɔrt̬əs/ *n.* [C] a slow-moving land animal that can pull its head and legs into the hard round shell that covers its body [**Origin:** 1400–1500 Old French *tortue*, from Vulgar Latin *tartaruca*, from Late Latin *tartaruchus* **of Tartarus**, the land of the dead in ancient stories; because it used to be thought that tortoises and turtles came from hell] → see also TURTLE

tor·toise·shell /ˈtɔrt̬əsˌʃɛl/ *n.* **1** [U] hard shiny brown and white material made from the shell of a tortoise **2** [U] plastic material that looks like tortoiseshell: *tortoiseshell glasses* **3** [C] BIOLOGY a cat that has yellow, brown, and black marks on its fur

tor·tu·ous /ˈtɔrtʃuəs/ *adj.* **1** a tortuous path, stream, road etc. has a lot of bends in it and is therefore difficult to travel along **2** complicated and long and therefore confusing: *six months of tortuous negotiations* —**tortuously** *adv.* —**tortuousness** *n.* [U]

tor·ture¹ /ˈtɔrtʃɚ/ *n.* **1** [U] the act of deliberately hurting someone in order to force them to tell you something, to punish them, or to be cruel: *victims of torture* | *The militias are accused of using torture.* **2** [C,U] severe physical or mental suffering: *High school* *gym class was always torture for me.* [**Origin:** 1500–1600 French, Late Latin *tortura*, from Latin *tortus* **twisted**]

torture² *v.* [T] **1** to deliberately hurt someone to force them to give you information, to punish them, or to be cruel: *Most of the prisoners had been tortured.* **2** if a feeling or knowledge tortures you, it makes you suffer mentally: *Memories of the attack still tortured her.* —**torturer** *n.* [C]

tor·tured /ˈtɔrtʃɚd/ *adj.* **1** full of pain: *a tortured look* **2** too long, difficult, or complicated: *the tortured logic of his argument*

tor·tur·ous /ˈtɔrtʃərəs/ *adj.* **1** very long, slow, and difficult or boring **2** very unpleasant or painful to experience

To·ry /ˈtɔri/ *n. plural* **Tories** [C] **1** HISTORY an American during the Revolutionary War who supported England **2** POLITICS a member of the Progressive Conservative Party in Canada **3** POLITICS a member of the Conservative party in Great Britain [**Origin:** 1700–1800 *Tory* Irish Catholic supporter of King James II (17–18 centuries), from Irish Gaelic *toraidhe* **robber**]

toss¹ /tɔs/ W3 *v.*

1 THROW [T] to throw something, especially something light, without much force SYN **throw**: **toss sth into/down/on etc. sth** *She tossed the ball into the air.* | **toss sth to sb** *He took out a coin and tossed it to Rob.* | **toss sb sth** *Toss me a pillow.* ►see THESAURUS box at **throw¹**

2 THROW AWAY [T] to get rid of something you do not want SYN **toss out**: *I think you can toss those old magazines now.*

3 MOVE [I,T] to move and turn around continuously in a violent or uncontrolled way, or make something do this: *Waves tossed the small boats.* | *I **tossed and turned*** (=kept changing my position in bed because I could not sleep) *all night.*

4 toss your head/hair to move your head back suddenly, often with a shaking movement: *She laughed and tossed her head.*

5 MIX [T] to mix pieces of food and liquid by lifting and turning them together: *Could you toss the salad for me?*

6 A COIN [I,T] to make a coin go up and spin in the air, and then catch it to see which side is on top, used as a way of deciding something SYN **flip**

7 toss your cookies SLANG to VOMIT

toss sth ↔ **back** *phr. v.* INFORMAL to drink something quickly SYN **throw back**: *We tossed back a couple of beers.*

toss sth ↔ **in** *phr. v.* INFORMAL to include something with something else SYN **throw in**

toss off *phr. v.* INFORMAL **1 toss sb ↔ off, toss sb off sth** to make someone leave a place or group, especially because of bad behavior: *They tossed her off the team for missing practice.* **2 toss sth ↔ off** to say or write something quickly without much effort: *She could toss off facts and figures convincingly.*

toss out *phr. v.* INFORMAL **1 toss sth ↔ out** to get rid of something you do not want SYN **throw out**: *Let's toss out the old TV.* **2 toss sth ↔ out** to say something quickly without thinking carefully about it SYN **throw out**: *I tossed out a few suggestions.* **3 toss sb ↔ out** to make someone leave a place, especially because of bad behavior SYN **throw out**: **toss sb out of sth** *They tossed him out of the club for starting a fight.*

toss² *n.* [C] **1** the act of throwing a coin in the air to decide something, especially to make a choice at the beginning of a game or race SYN **coin toss** SYN **flip**: *Who goes first will be decided by **the toss of a coin**.* | **win/lose the toss** *We lost the toss and had to go second.* **2** a sudden backward movement of your head, so that your hair moves: *With **a toss of** her **head**, she walked out of the room.* **3** the act of gently throwing something SYN **throw**

tossed /tɔst/ *adj.* **a tossed salad** a SALAD that is made by mixing together different types of food such as LETTUCE, TOMATOes etc.

ˈtoss-up *n.* [singular] INFORMAL **it's a toss-up** used to say that you do not know which of two things will happen

tot /tɑt/ *n.* [C] INFORMAL a very small child

to·tal¹ /ˈtoʊtl/ S2 W1 *adj.* **1** [only before noun] complete, and affecting or including everything: *a total ban on cigarette advertising* | *The sales campaign was a total disaster.* **2 a total number/amount/cost etc.** the number, amount etc. of all the numbers in a group added together: *a total population of about 100 million* [**Origin:** 1300–1400 Old French, Medieval Latin *totalis*, from Latin *totus* **whole**]

total² *n.* [C] the final number or amount of things, people etc. when everything has been counted: *You had 29 points plus 33 points, so the total is 62.* | **+of** *A total of $950 million was spent on the new system.* | ***In total**, there were about 40 people there.* → see also **grand total** at GRAND¹ (2), SUM TOTAL

total³ *v.* **1** [linking verb] to be a particular total after all the amounts have been added together: *Contributions totaled $28,000.* **2** also **total up** [T] to find the total number or total amount of something by adding: *When you total the costs up, that's a lot of money.* **3** [T] INFORMAL to damage a car so badly that it cannot be repaired: *The truck was totaled, but no one was hurt.*

ˌtotal ˈcost *n.* [C] ECONOMICS the total amount of money it costs a company or business to produce and sell goods or services, including all the FIXED COSTS and all the VARIABLE COSTS

to·tal·i·tar·i·an /toʊˌtæləˈtɛriən/ *adj.* POLITICS based on a political system in which ordinary people have no power and are completely controlled by the government: *a totalitarian regime* —**totalitarianism** *n.* [U]

to·tal·i·ty /toʊˈtæləti/ *n.* [U] FORMAL **1** all of something: *It's essential that we look at the problem **in its totality*** (=as a complete thing). **2** a total amount

to·tal·ly /ˈtoʊtl-i/ S1 W3 *adv.* **1** completely: *I agree totally.* | *The ice had totally melted.* | **totally new/different** *The two cities are totally different.* ►see THESAURUS box at **completely** **2** SLANG used to say that you agree with what someone has said: *"This is such a cool song." "Yeah, totally."*

ˌTotal ˈQuality ˌManagement ABBREVIATION **TQM** *n.* [singular] a system for making sure that each department in an organization works in the most effective way and that the goods or services it produces are of the best quality

ˌtotal ˈrevenue *n.* [U] ECONOMICS all the money a company or business receives from the goods or services it sells

tote¹ /toʊt/ also **tote around** *v.* [T] INFORMAL to carry something, especially regularly ►see THESAURUS box at **carry¹**

tote² also **ˈtote bag** *n.* [C] a large bag for carrying things → see picture at BAG¹

to·tem /ˈtoʊtəm/ *n.* [C] an animal, plant etc. that is believed to have a special SPIRITUAL relationship with a particular TRIBE, especially a tribe of Native Americans, or a figure made to look like one of these animals, plants etc.

ˈtotem ˌpole *n.* [C] **1** a tall wooden pole with one or more totems cut or painted on it, made by the Native Americans of northwest North America **2 the totem pole** used to talk about the system of rank in an organization or business, when saying how high someone's rank is: *At that time I was a **low man on the totem pole**.*

-toting /toʊtɪŋ/ *suffix* [in adjectives] carrying a particular thing: *gun-toting criminals*

toto → see IN TOTO

tot·ter /ˈtɑtɚ/ *v.* [I] **1** to walk or move in an unsteady way from side to side as if you are going to fall over **2** if a political system or organization totters, it becomes less strong and is likely to stop working: **totter on the edge/brink of sth** *Today the country totters on the edge of economic disaster.* **3** if something such as a building totters, it moves and looks as if it is going to fall over —**tottering** *adj.*

tou·can /ˈtukæn, -kɑn/ *n.* [C] BIOLOGY a tropical American bird with bright feathers and a very large beak

T

touch[1] /tʌtʃ/ S1 W2 *v.*

1 FEEL [T] to put your finger, hand etc. on something or someone: *Don't touch that – the paint is still wet.* | *He gently touched her hand and smiled.*

THESAURUS

feel to touch something with your fingers to find out about it: *Feel this material; it's like snake skin.*
stroke to move your hand gently over something: *She stroked the baby's face.*
rub to move your hand or fingers over a surface while pressing it: *He rubbed his elbow where he'd banged it.*
scratch to rub your finger nails on part of your skin: *Try not to scratch those mosquito bites.*
pat to touch someone or something lightly again and again, with your hand flat: *He knelt down to pat the dog.*
pet to touch and move your hand gently over an animal: *Do you want to pet the cat?*
brush to touch someone or something lightly as you pass by: *Her hand brushed mine.*
caress to gently move your hand over a part of someone's body in a loving or sexual way: *Miguel gently caressed her shoulders.*
fondle to gently touch and move your fingers over part of someone's body in a way that shows love or sexual desire: *Tom fondled the dog's soft ears.*
tickle to move your fingers lightly over someone's body in order to make him or her laugh: *Minna tickled the baby's feet and he gurgled.*
grope to touch someone's body in a sexual way when he or she does not want to be touched: *One victim said he groped her.*
handle to touch something or pick it up and hold it in your hands: *Please do not handle the merchandise.*

2 NO SPACE BETWEEN [I,T] if two things touch they come up against each other so that there is no space between them: *Make sure the wires do not touch.* | *Don't let the flag touch the ground.*

3 USE STH [T usually in negatives] to use or handle something, often in a way that changes or spoils it: *Don't let anyone touch my computer while I'm away.*

4 MAKE SB FEEL EMOTIONS [T] to affect someone's emotions, especially by making them feel pity or sympathy: *His concern touched her.* | *The story* ***touched the hearts*** *of millions of our readers.* → see also TOUCHED

5 HAVE AN EFFECT ON SB/STH [T] to have an effect on someone or something, especially by changing or influencing them: *Many people's lives have been touched by the disease.*

6 FOOD/DRINK [T usually in negatives] to eat or drink a particular thing: **barely/hardly touch sth** *You've hardly touched your food.* | *I used to like to drink, but now I* ***never touch the stuff.***

7 not touch sth to not work on something that you should work on, or that needs work to be done on it: *I brought home lots of work, but I haven't touched it yet.*

8 not touch sb to not hit someone or hurt them physically: *Hardin claimed he never touched the man.*

9 touch a nerve to mention a subject that makes someone feel upset or angry: *What you said about his family really touched a nerve.*

10 DEAL WITH STH [T] to deal with or become involved with a particular matter, situation, or problem: *He was the only lawyer who would touch the case.* | **not touch the issue/subject etc.** *Most politicians do not want to touch the abortion issue.*

11 touch base (with sb) to talk for a short time with someone in order to discuss something or give them information: *I just wanted to touch base with you, and see how things were going.*

12 sb wouldn't touch sb/sth with a ten-foot pole SPOKEN used to say that someone thinks someone or something is bad in some way, and does not want to get involved with them

13 touch sth to your lips/mouth/cheek etc. LITERARY to move something so that it comes up against part of your body

14 EXPRESSION [T] LITERARY if an expression such as a smile touches your face, your face has that expression for a short time: *A smile touched her lips.*

15 touch bottom a) to reach the ground at the bottom of the ocean, a river etc. **b)** to reach the lowest level or worst condition: *The housing market has touched bottom.*

16 no one/nothing can touch sb/sth also **there is no one/nothing that can touch sb/sth** used to say that nothing or no one is as good as someone or something

17 RELATE TO [T] to concern or be about a particular subject, situation, or problem

[**Origin:** 1200–1300 Old French *tuchier*, from Vulgar Latin *toccare* **to knock, hit a bell, touch**] → see also TOUCHED, TOUCHING

touch down *phr. v.* if an aircraft or space vehicle touches down, it goes down to the ground

touch sth ↔ **off** *phr. v.* to cause a difficult situation or violent events to begin: *The chairman's statement touched off a controversy.*

touch on/upon sth *phr. v.* to mention or deal with a particular subject for a short period of time when talking or writing: *Many television programs have touched on the subject.*

touch sth ↔ **up** *phr. v.* to improve something by changing it or adding to it slightly: *She quickly touched up her lipstick.*

touch[2] S2 W2 *n.*

1 ACT OF TOUCHING [C usually singular] the action of putting your finger, hand etc. on someone or something, either deliberately or not deliberately: *He felt her touch on his shoulder.*

2 get in touch (with sb) to write or speak to someone on the telephone in order to tell them something: *You can always get in touch with me at the office.*

3 keep/stay in touch (with sb) to continue to talk to someone on the telephone or write to someone regularly even though you do not see them as often as you used to: *We went to different colleges but we still stayed in touch.*

4 be in touch (with sb) to speak to someone, especially on the telephone, or to write to someone about something, especially when you do this regularly: *Are you still in touch with John?*

5 put sb in touch with sb to give someone the name, address, or telephone number of a person or organization they need: *Gary put me in touch with a good lawyer.*

6 with/at the touch of a button used to emphasize that you can do something easily by pressing a button: *With the touch of a button, the satellite dish can be turned.*

7 SENSE [U] the sense that you use to discover what something feels like, by putting your hand or another part of your body on it: *The objects are hard to distinguish* ***by touch.*** | ***The sense of touch*** *is concentrated in the fingertips.*

8 soft/rough/firm etc. to the touch soft, rough, firm etc. when you feel it with your hand, finger etc.: *The silk was beautiful and soft to the touch.*

9 a touch (of sth) a very small amount of something: *All this room needs is a touch of paint.* | *I think I've got a touch of the flu.*

10 in touch with sth a) fully understanding your own feelings or attitudes: *A lot of people just aren't in touch with their own emotions.* **b)** having the latest information, knowledge, and understanding about a subject: *Use the Internet to get in touch with the latest news.*

11 out of touch (with sb/sth) not having the correct information or a good understanding about a subject, group of people, feeling etc.: *The committee was out of touch with residents' wishes.*

12 DETAIL/ADDITION [C] a small detail that improves or completes something: *a decorative touch* | **the final/finishing touch(es)** *Emma put the finishing touches on the cake.*

13 WAY OF DOING STH [singular] a particular way of doing something: *The friendly staff gives the hotel a personal touch.* | **a woman's/man's touch** *This apartment could use a woman's touch.*

14 ABILITY TO DO STH your ability to do something: +**for**

Reid has a good touch for shooting the ball. | *Judging from his latest novel, Goldman hasn't **lost his touch**.* | *She **has the magic touch** when it comes to gardening.*
15 FEEL SB/STH [C usually singular] the way that someone or something feels and the effect they have on your body: *the soft touch of a clean cotton shirt*
16 a touch cold/strange/unfair etc. slightly cold, strange etc. → see also **the common touch** at COMMON¹ (10), **lose touch (with sb/sth)** at LOSE (14), **the midas touch** at MIDAS TOUCH (1), **a soft touch** at SOFT (12)

touch-and-'go *adj.* INFORMAL a touch-and-go situation is one in which there is a serious risk that something bad could happen: ***It was touch-and-go** for a few days after the operation.*

touch·down /ˈtʌtʃdaʊn/ *n.* [C] **1** an act of moving the ball across the opposing team's GOAL LINE in football **2** the moment at which an airplane or SPACECRAFT comes down and touches the ground

tou·ché /tuˈʃeɪ/ *interjection* used when you want to emphasize in a humorous way that someone has made a very good point against you during an argument

touched /tʌtʃt/ *adj.* [not before noun] **1** feeling happy and grateful because of what someone has done for you: **+by** *I was really touched by the invitation.* | **touched that** *Jane was touched that you came to visit her.* | *We were **deeply touched** by their present.* → see also TOUCH¹ (4) **2 be touched with sth** WRITTEN having a small amount of a particular emotion, or quality: *The situation was touched with sadness.* **3** OLD-FASHIONED, INFORMAL slightly strange in your behavior

ˈtouch ˌfootball *n.* [U] a type of football in which you touch the person with the ball instead of tackling (TACKLE) them

touch·ing¹ /ˈtʌtʃɪŋ/ *adj.* affecting your emotions, especially making you feel pity, sympathy, sadness etc.: *a touching moment in the film* ►see THESAURUS box at **emotional** —**touchingly** *adv.* → see also TOUCH¹ (4)

touching² also **ˈtouching on** *prep.* FORMAL concerning: *matters touching the conduct of diplomacy*

touch·line /ˈtʌtʃlaɪn/ *n.* [C] a line along each of the two longer sides of a sports field, especially in SOCCER

ˈtouch screen *n.* [C] COMPUTERS a special computer screen that you touch with your finger or a special electronic pen in order to choose something from the screen that you want the computer to do

touch·stone /ˈtʌtʃstoʊn/ *n.* [C] something used as a test or standard to measure other things by: **+of** *The Alamo is a touchstone of Texan heritage.*

ˈTouch-Tone ˌphone, touch-tone phone *n.* [C] TRADEMARK a telephone that produces different sounds when different numbers are pushed

ˈtouch-type *v.* [I] to be able to use a TYPEWRITER or computer KEYBOARD without having to look at the letters while you are using it

ˈtouch-up *n.* [C] a small improvement you make to something by changing it or adding to it slightly

touch·y /ˈtʌtʃi/ *adj. comparative* **touchier**, *superlative* **touchiest** **1** easily becoming offended or annoyed: **+about** *He's a little touchy about how you pronounce his name.* ►see THESAURUS box at **grumpy** **2 a touchy subject/question etc.** a subject, question etc. that needs to be dealt with very carefully, especially because it may offend people —**touchily** *adv.* —**touchiness** *n.* [U]

ˌtouchy-ˈfeely *adj.* DISAPPROVING too concerned with feelings and emotions, rather than with facts or action: *a touchy-feely drama*

tough¹ /tʌf/ S1 W2 *adj.*
1 DIFFICULT difficult to do or deal with, and needing a lot of effort and determination SYN **hard** SYN **difficult**: *Being the new kid at school is always tough.* | *The reporters were asking a lot of tough questions.* | *It was **a tough call** (=difficult decision), but we had to cancel the event.* ►see THESAURUS box at **difficult**
2 STRONG PERSON very determined and able to deal with or live through difficult or severe conditions: *She's only a kid, but she's tough.* | **a tough cookie/customer** (=someone who is very determined to do what they want) → see also **as tough/hard as nails** at NAIL¹ (4)
3 STRICT very strict or determined: **+on/with** *Mom was always very tough with us kids.* | *Jordan has promised to **get tough on** (=deal with them in a strict way) drugs.* | *The President is **taking a tough line on** (=being very strict about) trade issues.*
4 STRONG THING not easily broken or made weaker: *tough durable plastic* ►see THESAURUS box at **strong**
5 FOOD difficult to cut or eat OPP **tender**: *The meat was tough and stringy.*
6 (that's) tough! also **tough luck!** SPOKEN said when you do not have any sympathy for someone's problems: *Tough luck! You should have gotten here earlier.*
7 UNFORTUNATE SPOKEN used to describe a situation in which something bad or unlucky has happened to someone, especially to show sympathy for them: *"She failed the test." "Oh, that's tough."* | *The accident was **a tough break** for the young dancer.* | *We've **had some tough luck** lately, but that's going to turn around.*
8 VIOLENT PERSON likely to behave violently and having no gentle qualities: *Everyone thinks Jack is **a tough guy**, but he's really very sweet.*
9 VIOLENT AREA a tough part of a town has a lot of crime or violence: *a tough neighborhood*
10 tough on sb causing someone a lot of problems or difficulties: *This past year was really tough on Jim.*
11 a tough nut (to crack) a person or problem that is difficult to understand or deal with
[**Origin:** Old English *toh*] —**toughly** *adv.* —**toughness** *n.* [U]

tough² *v.*
tough sth ↔ **out** *phr. v.* INFORMAL to manage to stay in a difficult situation by being determined: *They were brave and **toughed it out**.*

tough³ *adv.* INFORMAL in a way that shows that you are determined or strong → see also **talk tough** at TALK¹ (25)

tough⁴ *n.* [C] OLD-FASHIONED someone who often behaves in a violent way

tough·en /ˈtʌfən/ also **toughen up** *v.* [I,T] to become tougher, or to make someone or something tougher: *The state is toughening its anti-smoking laws.*

tough·ie /ˈtʌfi/ *n.* [C] SPOKEN **1** a difficult question, problem, situation etc. **2** someone who seems very strict, or not gentle at all

ˌtough ˈlove *n.* [U] a way of helping someone to change their behavior by treating them in a kind but strict way

Tou·louse-Lau·trec /tʊˌluz loʊˈtrɛk/, **Hen·ri de** /ɑnˈri də/ (1864–1901) a French PAINTER famous for his pictures of PROSTITUTES, dancers, actors etc. and his theater POSTERS

tou·pee, toupée /tuˈpeɪ/ [C] a small piece of artificial hair that some men wear over a place on their heads where the hair does not grow anymore → see also WIG

tour¹ /tʊr/ S2 W2 *n.* [C] **1** a trip for pleasure, during which you visit several different towns, areas etc.: *a sightseeing tour* | **+of** *a four-month tour of South America* | *a tour group* → see also PACKAGE TOUR ►see THESAURUS box at **trip¹** **2** a short trip through a place to see it: **+of/through/around** *They took us on a tour of the campus.* | *a **guided tour** of the museum* **3** a planned trip made by musicians, a sports team, a politician etc. in order to perform, play, speak etc. in several places: *a concert tour* | **+of** *The musical is making a year-long tour of the U.S.* | *He is **on tour** promoting his new children's book.* | ***the first leg of** a world **tour*** (=part of a tour) **4** a period during which you go to live somewhere, usually abroad, to do your job, especially military work: *the major's third tour in Afghanistan* → see also TOUR OF DUTY [**Origin:** 1300–1400 Old French *tour, tourn* **circular course, turn**]

tour² *v.* [I,T] to visit somewhere on a tour: *He toured the world with his band.*

tour de force /ˌtʊr də ˈfɔrs/ *n.* [singular] something

that is done very skillfully and successfully, in a way that seems impressive to people

ˈtour guide *n.* [C] someone who leads a tour to different places and tells people about their history, importance etc.

tour·ism /ˈtʊrɪzəm/ *n.* [U] the business of providing things for people to do, places for them to stay etc. while they are on vacation: *Tourism is an important part of Egypt's economy.*

tour·ist /ˈtʊrɪst/ W3 *n.* [C] someone who is traveling or visiting a place for pleasure: *More than three million American tourists visit Britain every year.*

ˈtourist atˌtraction *n.* [C] a place or event that a lot of tourists go to

ˈtourist class *n.* [U] the cheapest standard of traveling conditions on an airplane, ship etc.

ˈtourist ˌoffice also **ˌtourist inforˈmation ˌoffice** *n.* [C] an office that gives information to tourists in an area

ˈtourist ˌtown *n.* [C] a town that many tourists visit

ˈtourist ˌtrap *n.* [C] DISAPPROVING a place that many tourists visit, but where drinks, hotels etc. are very expensive

tour·ist·y /ˈtʊrɪsti/ *adj.* INFORMAL **1** DISAPPROVING a touristy place is full of tourists and the things that attract tourists: *Niagara Falls is too touristy for me.* **2** a touristy activity is typical of the things that tourists do

T

tour·na·ment /ˈtʊrnəmənt, ˈtɚ-/ W3 *n.* [C] **1** a competition in which players compete against each other in a series of games until there is one winner: **a tennis/chess/basketball etc. tournament** *an international golf tournament* ▸see THESAURUS box at **competition** **2** a competition to show courage and fighting skill between soldiers in the Middle Ages [**Origin:** 1100–1200 Old French *torneiement*, from *torneier*, from *tourn* **circular course, turn**]

tour·ney /ˈtʊrni, ˈtɚ-/ *n.* [C] INFORMAL a TOURNAMENT

tour·ni·quet /ˈtʊrnɪkɪt, ˈtɚ-/ *n.* [C] MEDICINE a band of cloth that is twisted tightly around an injured arm or leg to stop it from bleeding

ˌtour of ˈduty *n. plural* **tours of duty** [C] a period of time when you are working in a particular place or job, especially abroad while you are in the military

ˈtour ˌoperator *n.* [C] a company that arranges travel TOURS

tour·ti·ère /ˌtʊrtiˈɛr/ *n.* [C] a type of meat PIE eaten in Canada

tou·sle /ˈtaʊzəl, -səl/ *v.* [T] to make someone's hair look messy

tou·sled /ˈtaʊzəld/ *adj.* tousled hair or a tousled appearance looks messy

tout¹ /taʊt/ *v.* **1** [T] to praise someone or something in order to persuade people that they are important or valuable: *The mayor has been touting his record on fighting crime.* | **be touted as sth** *For years German engineering was touted as the best that money could buy.* **2** [I,T] to try to persuade people to buy goods or services you are offering

tout² *n.* [C] someone who tries to sell goods or services to people passing on the street in a determined or annoying way

tow¹ /toʊ/ *v.* [T] **1** to pull a vehicle or ship along behind another vehicle, using a rope or chain ▸see THESAURUS box at **pull¹** **2** also **tow away** to remove a car by towing it, especially when it has been parked illegally: *If you leave your car there, they'll tow it.*

tow² *n.* **1 in tow** INFORMAL following closely behind: *Hannah arrived with her four kids in tow.* **2** [C] an act of pulling a vehicle behind another vehicle, using a rope or chain **3 under tow** being pulled by another ship or boat **4 take sth in tow** to connect a rope or a chain to a vehicle or ship so that it can be towed

to·ward /tɔrd, təˈwɔrd/ S1 W1 also **towards** *prep.* **1** moving, looking, or pointing in a particular direction: *Two policemen came toward him.* | *I looked toward the door.* | *She was standing with her back toward me.* **2** a feeling, attitude etc. toward someone or something is how you feel or what you think about them: *I was surprised by Carolyn's anger toward her mother.* | *Our responsibilities toward our children.* **3** if you do something toward something, you do it in order to achieve it: *Both sides appear to be working toward an agreement.* | *This meeting is a first step toward finding a solution.* **4** near or just before a particular time: *We left toward the middle of the afternoon.* **5** money put, saved, or given toward something is used to help pay for it: *The money will be put toward repairs.* **6** near a particular place: *We sat toward the front of the plane.*

tow-a-way zone /ˈtoʊəweɪ ˌzoʊn/ *n.* [C] an area where cars are not allowed to park, and from which they can be taken away by the police

tow·boat /ˈtoʊboʊt/ *n.* [C] a TUG

tow·el¹ /ˈtaʊəl/ S2 *n.* [C] a piece of cloth that you use for drying your skin or for drying things such as dishes: *a bath towel* [**Origin:** 1200–1300 Old French *toaille*] → see also PAPER TOWEL, **throw in the towel** at THROW IN (2)

towel² *v.*

towel off *phr. v.* **towel sb/sth ↔ off** to dry yourself or something else using a towel: *Paula climbed out of the pool and toweled off.*

ˈtowel bar *n.* [C] a TOWEL RACK

tow·el·ette /ˌtaʊəˈlɛt/ *n.* [C] a small piece of soft wet paper that you use to clean your hands or face

tow·el·ing /ˈtaʊəlɪŋ/ *n.* [U] **1** thick soft cloth, used especially for making TOWELS or BATHROBES **2** towels considered together

ˈtowel rack *n.* [C] a bar or frame on which TOWELS can be hung, especially in a BATHROOM

tow·er¹ /ˈtaʊɚ/ S3 *n.* [C] **1** a tall narrow building either built on its own or forming part of a castle, church etc.: *a clock tower* **2** a tall structure, often made of metal, used for sending signals, broadcasting etc.: *radio towers* **3** a tall piece of furniture that you use to store things: *a CD tower* **4** a tall box that contains the main part of some computers [**Origin:** 1100–1200 Old French *tor*, *tur*, from Latin *turris*] → see also COOLING TOWER, IVORY TOWER, WATER TOWER

tower² *v.* [I] to be much taller than the people or things around you: **+over/above** *She towers over her husband.*

tower over/above sb/sth *phr. v.* to be much better than any other person or organization that does the same thing as you

tow·er·ing /ˈtaʊərɪŋ/ *adj.* [only before noun] **1** very tall: *towering redwood trees* **2** much better than other people of the same kind: ***a towering figure** in Supreme Court history* **3 in a towering rage** WRITTEN very angry

tow·head /ˈtoʊhɛd/ *n.* [C] someone with very light-colored almost white hair —**towheaded** *adj.*

tow·line /ˈtoʊlaɪn/ *n.* [C] a rope or chain used for pulling vehicles

town /taʊn/ S1 W1 *n.*

1 PLACE [C] an area with houses, stores, offices etc. where people live and work, that is smaller than a city: *He grew up in a small town in Texas.* | *a town of about 35,000 people*

2 WHERE YOU LIVE [U] the town or city where you live: *He has an apartment on the south side of town.* | *I'll be **out of town** for about a week.* | *Let's get together while you're **in town**.* | *We're having some visitors **from out of town*** (=from a different town)? | *The Cubs are **coming to town** Friday.* | *He **left town** without telling anyone.*

3 MAIN CENTER [U] the business or shopping center of a town: *I need to **go into town** to do a little shopping.* → see also DOWNTOWN

4 go to town (on sth) INFORMAL to do something in a very eager or thorough way: *Sandy went to town on the displays.*

5 (out) on the town INFORMAL going to restaurants, bars, theaters etc. for entertainment in the evening: *Frank is taking me out for **a night on the town**.*

6 PEOPLE [singular] all the people who live in a particular town: *Just about the whole town showed up at the funeral.*
7 LOCAL GOVERNMENT [singular] the people who are in charge of the government of a town
[**Origin:** Old English *tun* **yard, buildings inside a wall, village, town**] → see also GHOST TOWN, **paint the town (red)** at PAINT² (7)

ˌtown ˈcenter *n.* [C] the main business area in the center of a town SYN **downtown**

ˌtown ˈclerk *n.* [C] an official who keeps records for a town

ˌtown ˈcouncil *n.* [C] a group of elected officials who are responsible for governing a town and making its laws

ˌtown ˈcrier *n.* [C] someone employed in the past to walk around the streets of a town, shouting news, warnings etc.

ˌtown ˈhall *n.* [C] a public building used for a town's local government

town·house, town house /ˈtaʊnhaʊs/ *n.* [C] **1** also **townhome** a house in a row of houses that share one or more walls ►see THESAURUS box at **house¹** **2** a house in a town or city, especially a fashionable one in a central area

town·ie /ˈtaʊni/ *n.* [C] INFORMAL someone who lives in a town, especially a town that other people often visit

ˌtown ˈmeeting also **ˌtown hall ˈmeeting** *n.* [C] **1** a meeting at which the people who live in a town discuss subjects or problems that affect their town **2** a large discussion in which many different people can express their opinions, especially one using television, radio, or telephones

ˌtown ˈplanning *n.* [U] the study of the way towns work, so that roads, houses, services etc. can be provided as effectively as possible

town·ship /ˈtaʊnʃɪp/ *n.* [C] **1** HISTORY a part of a U.S. or Canadian COUNTY that has some local government **2** a town in South Africa where in the past the government said black people had to live

towns·peo·ple /ˈtaʊnzˌpipəl/ also **towns·folk** /ˈtaʊnzˌfoʊk/ *n.* [plural] all the people who live in a particular town

tow·path /ˈtoʊpæθ/ *n. plural* **towpaths** /-pæðz, -pæθs/ [C] a path along the side of a CANAL or river, used especially in the past by horses pulling boats

ˈtow rope *n.* [C] a TOWLINE

ˈtow truck *n.* [C] a strong truck that is used to pull cars behind it

tox·e·mi·a /tɑkˈsimiə/ *n.* [U] a medical condition in which your blood contains poisons

tox·ic /ˈtɑksɪk/ *adj.* poisonous, or containing poison: *toxic chemicals* [**Origin:** 1600–1700 Late Latin *toxicus*, from Latin *toxicum* **poison**] —**toxicity** /tɑkˈsɪsət̬i/ *n.* [U]

tox·i·col·o·gy /ˌtɑksɪˈkɑlədʒi/ *n.* [U] SCIENCE the science and medical study of poisons and their effects

ˌtoxic ˈshock ˌsyndrome also **ˌtoxic ˈshock** *n.* [U] MEDICINE a serious illness that causes a high temperature and is thought to be related to the use of TAMPONS

ˌtoxic ˈwaste *n.* [C,U] EARTH SCIENCE waste products from industry that are harmful to people, animals, or the environment

tox·in /ˈtɑksɪn/ *n.* [C] BIOLOGY a poisonous substance, especially one that is produced by BACTERIA and causes a particular disease

toy¹ /tɔɪ/ S2 W3 *n. plural* **toys** [C] **1** an object for children to play with: *wooden toys* | *He has lots of* ***toys to play with.*** **2** a machine or piece of equipment that you enjoy using: *The red Porsche is his latest toy.* **3** someone who you treat badly and use so you can have fun SYN **plaything** **4** a toy dog [**Origin:** 1500–1600 *toy* **amusing story or action** (15–18 centuries)]

toy² *v.* **toys, toyed, toying**
toy with *phr. v.* **1 toy with sth** to think about an idea or possibility, usually for a short time and not very seriously: *The new owners briefly* ***toyed with the idea*** *of selling the building.* **2 toy with sb/sth** to treat someone in a careless way that shows you do not really respect or care about them: *Don't toy with my emotions.* **3 toy with sth** to move and touch an object, often while you are thinking about something else: *He toyed with a pen as he spoke.*

toy³ *adj.* [only before noun] **1 a toy boat/car/truck etc.** a model of a boat, car, truck etc. for children to play with **2** a toy dog is a type of dog that is specially bred to be very small

ˈtoy boy *n.* [C] INFORMAL a young man who is having a sexual relationship with an older woman

toy·mak·er /ˈtɔɪˌmeɪkɚ/ *n.* [C] a person or a company that makes toys

TQM *n.* [U] the abbreviation of TOTAL QUALITY MANAGEMENT

trace¹ /treɪs/ Ac *v.*
1 FIND SB/STH [T] to find someone or something that has disappeared by searching for them carefully: *Police are trying to trace relatives of the dead man.* ►see THESAURUS box at **find¹**
2 ORIGINS a) [T usually passive] to find how, when, or where something started: *The origins of the tradition are difficult to trace.* | **trace sth (back) to sth** *She has traced her ancestry to Scotland.* **b)** [I] to have origins in a place, time, or action: **trace (back) to sth** *The trouble in the region traces back to the 15th century.*
3 HISTORY/DEVELOPMENT [T] to study or describe the history, development, or progress of something: *The book traces the dictator's rise to power.*
4 COPY [T] to copy a drawing, map etc. by putting a piece of paper over it and then drawing the lines you can see through it: *"Did you draw this yourself?" "No, I traced it."* ►see THESAURUS box at **draw¹**
5 DRAW [T] to draw real or imaginary lines on the surface of something, usually with your finger or toe: **trace sth on/in/across** *Jen traced her name in the sand.*
6 TELEPHONE [T] to find out where a telephone call is coming from by using special electronic equipment: *Keep him on the line so we can trace the call.*
[**Origin:** 1200–1300 Old French *tracier*, from Vulgar Latin *tractiare* **to pull**] —**traceable** *adj.*

trace² Ac *n.*
1 SMALL AMOUNT [C] a very small amount of a quality, emotion, substance etc. that is difficult to see or notice: +**of** *a trace of poison* | *She speaks English with* ***no trace of*** *an accent.*
2 SIGN OF STH [C,U] a small sign that shows that someone or something was present or existed: *Stewart checked all the hospitals in the area but found* ***no trace of*** *his brother.* | *Cook the chicken until it has lost* ***all trace of*** *pink.* | **disappear/vanish/sink without a trace** (=disappear completely, without leaving any sign of what happened)
3 TELEPHONE [C] TECHNICAL a search to find out where a telephone call came from, using special electronic equipment: *Engineers* ***put a trace on*** *the call.*
4 RECORDED INFORMATION [C] the mark or pattern made on a SCREEN or on paper by a machine that is recording an electrical signal
5 CART/CARRIAGE [C] one of the two pieces of leather, rope etc. by which a CART or carriage is fastened to the animal that is pulling it
6 kick over the traces to stop following the rules of a social group and do what you want

ˈtrace ˌelement *n.* [C] CHEMISTRY **1** a chemical ELEMENT that your body needs a very small amount of to live **2** a chemical ELEMENT that only exists in small amounts on Earth

trac·er /ˈtreɪsɚ/ *n.* [C] a bullet that leaves a line of smoke or flame behind it

trac·er·y /ˈtreɪsəri/ *n. plural* **traceries** [C,U] **1** TECHNICAL the curving and crossing lines of stone in the upper parts of Gothic church windows **2** an attractive pattern of lines that cross each other

tra·che·a /ˈtreɪkiə/ *n. plural* **tracheae** /-ki-i/ or

T

tracheas [C] BIOLOGY the tube down which air goes from the throat to the lungs SYN **windpipe** → see picture at BREATHING

tra·che·ot·o·my /ˌtreɪkiˈɑṭəmi/ *n. plural* **tracheotomies** [C] MEDICINE an operation to cut a hole in someone's throat so that they can breathe

trac·ing /ˈtreɪsɪŋ/ Ac *n.* [C] a copy of a map, drawing etc. made by tracing (TRACE) it

ˈtracing ˌpaper *n.* [U] strong transparent paper used for tracing (TRACE)

track¹ /træk/ S2 W2 *n.*
1 keep track of sb/sth to make sure you always know where someone or something is or what is happening to them: *The computer program helps you keep track of your finances.* OPP **lose track of sb/sth**
2 SERIES OF THOUGHTS/ACTIONS [C] a particular series of thoughts, actions, or developments: *The agreement put relations **on a** more positive **track**.* | **on the right/wrong track** *Is the economy on the right track?*
3 on track a) likely to develop in the best way, or in the way that is expected: **be/get/stay on track** *We want to make sure our relations with Russia stay on track.* | *After the divorce, it took some time to get my life **back on track**.* **b)** dealing with the same subject that was being discussed, without changing to something new: **keep/stay on track** *The talks have stayed on track.*
4 off track a) not developing in the best way, or not developing in the way that was expected: **throw/knock sth off track** *The budget agreement has been thrown off track.* **b)** dealing with a new subject rather than the main one which was being discussed: *That's an interesting point, Katherine, but let's not **get off track**.*
5 FOR RACING [C] a circular road around which runners, cars, horses etc. race, which often has a specially prepared surface ►see THESAURUS box at **sport¹**
6 SPORTS [U] **a)** the sport that involves running on a track: *He **ran track** in high school.* **b)** all the sports that involve running races, jumping, and throwing things: *Are you going to **go out for track** (=join the school's track team) this spring?*
7 MARKS ON GROUND tracks [plural] the marks left on the ground by a moving person, animal, or vehicle, which are usually in a line: *tire tracks* | *dog tracks*
8 MUSIC/SONG [C] ENG. LANG. ARTS one of the songs or pieces of music on a CD, CASSETTE, or record: *There are ten tracks on the CD.* → see also TITLE TRACK ►see THESAURUS box at **music**
9 RAILROAD [C] the two metal lines along which trains travel: *train tracks*
10 SCHOOL [C] a group or set of classes for a particular group of students based on their abilities: *college-track classes* (=classes that prepare you for college)
11 DIRECTION [C] the direction or line taken by something as it moves: +**of** *the track of the asteroid through space*
12 PIECE OF METAL OR PLASTIC [C] a long piece of metal or plastic that something is attached to and moves along: *Spotlights can be fitted to the track.*
13 PATH/ROAD [C] a narrow path or road with a rough uneven surface, especially one made by people or animals frequently moving through the same place: *a dirt track*
14 make tracks (for sth) INFORMAL to leave somewhere quickly, or hurry when going somewhere
15 cover/hide your tracks to be careful not to leave any signs that could let people know where you have been or what you have done, because you want to keep it a secret: *Mozer covered his tracks by changing records of the illegal sales.*
16 be on the track of sb/sth to be hunting or searching for someone or something
17 ON A VEHICLE [C] a metal band over the wheels of a vehicle such as a BULLDOZER or TANK, that allows it to move over uneven ground
18 DRUGS tracks [plural] INFORMAL the marks that are left on the skin of someone who takes drugs such as HEROIN using a needle
19 FOR RECORDING [C] a BAND on a TAPE on which music or information can be recorded: *an eight-track tape*
[**Origin:** 1400–1500 Old French *trac*] → see also **off the beaten track/path** at BEATEN (1), ONE-TRACK MIND, **stop (dead) in your tracks** at STOP¹ (12), **be from the wrong side of the tracks** at WRONG¹ (15)

track² S3 W3 *v.*
1 BEHAVIOR/DEVELOPMENT [T] to record or study the behavior or development of someone or something over time: *The progress of each student is tracked by computer.* | *Customers can track all their stocks from a single Web page.*
2 SEARCH [T] to search for an animal or person by looking for marks, information etc. that show where they have gone: *They hired an expert to track the animal.* | **track sb/sth to sth** *Sniffer dogs tracked them to a remote farm.*
3 FOLLOW STH'S MOVEMENT [T] to follow the movements of something such as an aircraft or ship by using special equipment
4 MARK [T] to leave behind marks of something such as mud or dirt when you walk, especially in a line: *Who tracked mud all over the kitchen floor?*
5 CAMERA [I always + adv./prep.] if a movie or television camera tracks somewhere, it is moved in relation to the thing that is being filmed
6 SCHOOL [T] to put students in groups or classes according to their ability or needs
track sb/sth ↔ **down** *phr. v.* to find someone or something that is difficult to find by searching or asking questions in several different places: *I had to make a few phone calls, but I finally tracked him down.*

ˌtrack and ˈfield *n.* [U] the sports that involve running races, jumping, and throwing things

track·ball /ˈtrækbɔl/ *n.* [C] COMPUTERS a small ball connected to a computer, that you turn in order to move the CURSOR

track·er /ˈtrækɚ/ *n.* [C] **1** someone who follows and finds other people, especially criminals **2** a person or machine that follows the movement of something else **3** a person, computer etc. that records or studies the behavior or development of someone or something

ˈtrack eˌvent *n.* [C] a running race on a track

track·ing /ˈtrækɪŋ/ *n.* [U] **1** the system on a VCR that keeps the picture from a VIDEOTAPE clear on the screen **2** the system of putting students in groups or classes according to their abilities and needs **3** the system that keeps a vehicle's wheels parallel with each other

ˈtracking ˌstation *n.* [C] a place from which objects moving in space, such as SATELLITES and ROCKETS, can be recognized and followed

ˈtrack ˌlighting *n.* [U] a system of LIGHTING in which electric lights are attached in a row to a metal bar on the ceiling or a wall

ˈtrack meet *n.* [C] a sports event consisting of competitions in running, jumping etc.

ˈtrack ˌrecord *n.* [C] **1** the facts that are known about the past successes and failures of a company, product, or person: **a good/proven/successful/impressive etc. track record** *a company with a proven track record in advertising* **2** the fastest time that anyone has completed a race on a particular track

tract /trækt/ *n.* [C] **1 the gastrointestinal/digestive/respiratory etc. tract** a system of connected organs in your body that have one main purpose, such as DIGESTing food etc. **2** a large area of land: +**of** *vast tracts of wild forest land* **3** a short piece of writing, especially about a moral or religious subject: *a religious tract*

trac·ta·ble /ˈtræktəbəl/ *adj.* FORMAL easy to control or deal with OPP **intractable** —**tractability** /ˌtræktəˈbɪləṭi/ *n.* [U]

ˈtract house also **ˈtract home** *n.* [C] a house that is similar in style to the other houses that are built on the same large piece of land —**tract housing** *n.* [U]

trac·tion /ˈtrækʃən/ *n.* [U] **1** PHYSICS the force that prevents something such as a wheel from sliding on a surface: *Rubber soles give the shoes better traction.* **2** MEDICINE the process of treating a broken bone with special medical equipment that pulls it: *He was **in traction** for weeks after the accident.* **3** the action of pulling vehicles or heavy objects **4** support for a plan, person, group etc.

trac·tor /ˈtræktɚ/ *n.* [C] **1** a strong vehicle with large wheels, used for pulling farm machinery **2** a type of big truck that pulls TRAILERS to carry goods [**Origin:** 1700–1800 Modern Latin, Latin *trahere* **to pull**]

tractor-ˌtrailer *n.* [C] a large vehicle consisting of a tractor that pulls one or two TRAILERS (=large boxes on wheels), used for carrying goods

trade¹ /treɪd/ W1 *n.*
1 BUYING/SELLING [U] the activity of buying, selling, or exchanging goods within a country or between countries: *international trade* | +**in** *the trade in precious metals* | +**with** *trade with neighboring countries* | +**between** *Trade between the two countries increased sharply.* | **the arms/drug/slave etc. trade** (=the buying and selling of weapons, drugs etc.) → see also BALANCE OF TRADE, FREE TRADE, SLAVE TRADE ►see THESAURUS box at **business**
2 the hotel/banking/tourist etc. trade the business done by or involving hotels, banks etc.: *The whole town lives off the tourist trade.*
3 JOB [C] a particular job, especially one needing special skill with your hands: *She enrolled in the tech school to* ***learn a trade****.* | *My grandfather was a plumber* ***by trade*** (=that was his job).
4 EXCHANGE [C] an exchange of something you have for something someone else has: *Let's* ***make a trade*** *– my Frisbee for your baseball.*
5 STOCK MARKET [singular] an occasion when a STOCK is bought and sold on a financial market
6 the trade a particular kind of business, and the people who are involved in it: *These companies are known* ***in the trade*** *as "service bureaus."*
7 EXCHANGE IN SPORTS [C] the act of exchanging a player on a sports team for a player on another sports team
[**Origin:** 1300–1400 Middle Low German **course, way, track**] → see also JACK-OF-ALL-TRADES, **ply your trade** at PLY¹ (1), STOCK-IN-TRADE

trade² S2 W1 *v.*
1 BUY/SELL [I,T] ECONOMICS to buy and sell goods, services etc.: +**with** *The U.S. has not traded with the country since the 1980s.*
2 EXCHANGE [I,T] ECONOMICS to exchange something you have for something someone else has: *Your sandwich looks good. Do you want to trade?* | **trade sth (with sb)** *I wouldn't mind trading jobs with her.* | **trade sth for sth** *I'll trade this green car for your red one.* | **trade sb (sth for sth)** *"That dessert looks good." "I'll trade you."* ►see THESAURUS box at **exchange²**
3 STOCK MARKET a) [T usually passive] ECONOMICS to buy or sell something on the STOCK EXCHANGE: *Over a million shares were traded during the day.* **b)** [I] TECHNICAL if STOCKS trade, they are bought and sold on the STOCK EXCHANGE
4 trade insults/blows etc. (with sb) if two people trade insults, blows etc., or if one person trades insults etc. with someone else, the two people insult each other, hit each other etc.
5 SPORTS [T] to exchange a player on a sports team for a player on another team

trade down *phr. v.* **trade sth ↔ down** to sell something such as a car or house in order to buy one that costs less OPP **trade up**

trade sth ↔ **in** *phr. v.* to give something such as a car to the person you are buying a new one from, so that you pay less: **trade sth in for sth** *I'm going to trade my car in for a pickup truck.* → see also TRADE-IN

trade off *phr. v.* **1** if two or more people trade off, they each do something sometimes so that they share the work fairly: *We trade off, so that nobody has to do all the cleaning.* **2 trade sth ↔ off** to balance one situation or quality against another, in order to produce an acceptable result: **trade sth off for/against sth** *They will be trading off economic advantages for political gains.* → see also TRADE-OFF

trade on/upon sth *phr. v.* to use a situation or someone's kindness in order to get an advantage for yourself: *She traded on her father's name to get her job.*

trade up *phr. v.* **trade sth ↔ up** to sell something such as a car or house so you can buy a better car or house OPP **trade down**: +**to** *Computer makers expect people to trade up to faster, more powerful models.*

ˈtrade associˌation also **ˈindustry associˌation** *n.* [C] ECONOMICS a NON-PROFIT organization that supports and protects the rights of a particular industry, for example by trying to persuade the government to make changes to certain laws, so that the industry will develop and be successful

ˈtrade ˌbarrier *n.* [C] ECONOMICS something such as a tax or a law that prevents foreign goods or services from entering a country easily: *negotiations aimed at lowering trade barriers worldwide*

ˈtrade ˌdeficit also **ˈtrade gap** *n.* [C] ECONOMICS the amount by which the value of what a country buys from other countries is more than the value of what it sells to them OPP **trade surplus**

ˈtrade ˌdiscount *n.* [C] a special reduction in the price of goods sold to people who are going to sell the goods in their own store or business

ˈtrade fair *n.* [C] a large event when several companies show their goods or services in one place, to try to sell them

ˈtrade gap *n.* [C] ECONOMICS a TRADE DEFICIT

ˈtrade-in *n.* [C] a used object, often a car, that you give to the seller to reduce the price of the new one that you are buying —**trade-in** *adj.* [only before noun] *the car's trade-in value*

ˈtrade ˌjournal *n.* [C] a magazine that is written for and bought by people in a particular business and not people in general

trade·mark /ˈtreɪdmɑrk/ *n.* [C] **1** a special name, sign, or word that is marked on a product to show that it is made by a particular company **2** a particular way of behaving, dressing etc. by which someone or something can be easily recognized: *Attention to detail is the director's trademark.*

ˈtrade name *n.* [C] a name given to a particular product, that helps you recognize it from other similar products SYN **brand name**

ˈtrade-off *n.* [C] ECONOMICS the act of accepting something that you do not like or giving up an advantage that you have because it allows you to have or achieve something that you want: *Inflation is often a trade-off for healthy economic growth.*

trad·er /ˈtreɪdɚ/ W2 *n.* [C] someone who buys and sells goods

ˈtrade route *n.* [C] a way across land or the ocean often used by traders' vehicles, ships etc.

ˈtrade ˌschool *n.* [C] a school where people go in order to learn a particular job or TRADE that involves skill with their hands

ˌtrade ˈsecret *n.* [C] **1** a piece of secret information about a particular business, that is only known by the people who work there **2** HUMOROUS a piece of information about how to do or make something, that you do not want other people to know

trades·man /ˈtreɪdzmən/ *n. plural* **tradesmen** /-mən/ [C] someone who works at a job or TRADE that involves skill with their hands

trades·peo·ple /ˈtreɪdzˌpipəl/ *n.* [plural] people who work at a job or TRADE that involves skill with their hands

ˌtrade ˈsurplus *n.* [C] ECONOMICS the amount by which the value of the goods that a country sells to other countries is more than the value of what it buys from them OPP **trade deficit**

ˌtrade ˈunion *n.* [C] a LABOR UNION —**trade unionist** *n.* [C]

ˈtrade war *n.* [C] ECONOMICS a situation in which companies or countries compete against each other very strongly, and which usually involves governments putting higher taxes on particular goods brought in from another country: *Japan's automotive trade surplus,*

T

which nearly triggered (=started) *a trade war between the U.S. and Japan last year, has started to decline.*

trade wind /ˈtreɪd wɪnd/ *n.* [C] EARTH SCIENCE a tropical wind that blows continuously toward the EQUATOR from either the northeast or the southeast

trad·ing /ˈtreɪdɪŋ/ *n.* [C] **1** the activity of buying and selling something on the STOCK EXCHANGE: **heavy/light trading** (=a lot of trading or a little trading) **2** the activity of buying and selling goods and services

ˈtrading ˌpartner *n.* [C] a country that buys your goods and sells their goods to you

ˈtrading post *n.* [C] a place where people can buy and exchange goods in an area that is far away from cities or towns, especially in the U.S. or Canada in the past

ˈtrading stamp *n.* [C] a small stamp that a store gives you every time you spend a particular amount of money, which you can collect and use to get other goods, done especially in the past

tra·di·tion /trəˈdɪʃən/ Ac S3 W2 *n.* **1** [C] a belief, custom, or way of doing something that has existed for a long time: *Indian spiritual traditions* | *a family tradition* | +**of** *the tradition of decorating graves with flowers* | *The country has* ***a long tradition of*** *accepting refugees.* ►see THESAURUS box at **habit** **2** [U] a group's or society's beliefs, customs, or ways of doing things in general: *the importance of tradition* | **by/according to tradition** *By tradition, the youngest child reads the questions.* | *The Emperor* ***broke with tradition*** (=stopped doing things the way they had always been done) *and became involved in political affairs.* **3 (be) in the tradition of sb/sth** to have the same features as something that has been made or done in the past: *His latest movie is in the tradition of 1950s horror movies.* **4** [C] a way of thinking about something, especially a religion, or a group of people who think in this way: *They come from very different Christian traditions.* [**Origin:** 1300–1400 Old French, Latin *traditio* **act of handing over**]

tra·di·tion·al /trəˈdɪʃənl/ Ac S3 W2 *adj.* **1** relating to or based on old customs, beliefs, and ways of doing things: *a traditional Thanksgiving dinner* | *the traditional Hindu greeting* | **it is traditional (for sb) to do sth** *It is traditional for the bride to wear a white dress.* **2** following ideas and methods that have existed for a long time rather than doing anything new or different SYN **conventional**: *traditional ideas about education* —**traditionally** *adv.*

traˌditional eˈconomy *n.* [C] an economic system that uses only ideas and methods that have existed for a long time, rather than using new or different ideas or methods SYN **subsistence economy**

tra·di·tion·al·ism /trəˈdɪʃənlˌɪzəm/ *n.* [U] belief in the importance of traditions and customs

tra·di·tion·al·ist /trəˈdɪʃənl-ɪst/ Ac *n.* [C] someone who respects TRADITION and does not like change —**traditionalist** *adj.*

tra·duce /trəˈdus/ *v.* [T] FORMAL to deliberately say things about someone or something that are not true or nice

traf·fic¹ /ˈtræfɪk/ S3 W2 *n.* [U]
1 CARS the vehicles moving along a road or street: *a huge increase in traffic* | *The road is closed to traffic.* | **light/heavy traffic** (=a small or large amount of traffic) | *Sorry I'm late. I* ***got stuck in traffic.*** | *I wanted to avoid the* ***rush-hour traffic.*** | *The car crossed over into* ***oncoming traffic.*** | *a traffic accident*
2 AIRCRAFT/SHIPS ETC. the movement of aircraft, ships, trains etc. from one place to another: *air traffic*
3 BUYING/SELLING the activity of buying and selling illegal goods: +**in** *illegal traffic in chemical weapons*
4 INFORMATION the information that passes through a system such as the Internet: *Internet traffic*
5 PEOPLE/GOODS FORMAL the movement of people or goods by aircraft, ships, or trains: +**of** *the long-distance traffic of heavy goods*
[**Origin:** 1500–1600 Early French *trafique*, from Old Italian *traffico*, from *trafficare* **to trade**]

traffic² *v.* **trafficked, trafficking** [I,T] to buy and sell illegal goods: +**in** *He was arrested for trafficking in drugs.* → see also TRAFFICKER, TRAFFICKING

ˈtraffic ˌcircle *n.* [C] a circular area of road that cars must drive around, where three or more roads join

ˈtraffic ˌcone *n.* [C] a plastic object in the shape of a CONE that is put on the road to show where repairs are being done

ˈtraffic cop *n.* [C] INFORMAL **1** a police officer who stands in the road and directs traffic **2** a police officer who stops drivers who drive in an illegal way

ˈtraffic ˌcourt *n.* [C] a court of law that deals with people who have done something illegal while driving

ˈtraffic ˌisland *n.* [C] a raised area in the middle of the road, that separates the two sides of the road or where people can wait for traffic to pass before crossing

ˈtraffic jam *n.* [C] a long line of vehicles that cannot move along the road, or that can only move very slowly

traf·fick·er /ˈtræfɪkɚ/ *n.* [C] someone who buys and sells illegal goods, especially drugs

traf·fick·ing /ˈtræfɪkɪŋ/ *n.* [U] the activity of buying and selling illegal goods, especially drugs: *drug trafficking*

ˈtraffic ˌlights *n.* [C] a set of lights at a place where roads meet, that control the traffic by means of red, yellow, and green lights

ˈtraffic ˌschool *n.* [C] a class that teaches you about driving laws, that you can go to instead of paying money for something you have done wrong while driving

ˈtraffic ˌsignal *n.* [C] traffic lights

tra·ge·di·an /trəˈdʒidiən/ *n.* [C] FORMAL an actor or writer of tragedy

trag·e·dy /ˈtrædʒədi/ *n. plural* **tragedies** **1** [C,U] a very sad event that shocks people because it involves death: *It was a tragedy in which hundreds of people died.* | ***Tragedy struck*** *the family when their daughter fell to her death.* | **prevent/avert a tragedy** *Could we have prevented this latest tragedy?* **2** [C] INFORMAL something that seems very sad and unnecessary because something will be wasted, lost, or harmed: *It would be a great tragedy if the theater had to close.* **3** ENG. LANG. ARTS **a)** [C] a serious play or book that ends sadly, especially with the death of the main character: *Shakespeare's tragedies* **b)** [U] this style of writing or type of literature in general: *Greek tragedy* [**Origin:** 1300–1400 Old French *tragedie*, from Latin, from Greek *tragoidia*]

tra·gic /ˈtrædʒɪk/ *adj.* **1** a tragic event or situation makes you feel very sad, especially because it involves death: *Both sisters died in a tragic car accident.* | *Her death was* ***a tragic loss*** *for the sports world.* **2** [only before noun] ENG. LANG. ARTS relating to tragedy in books, movies, or plays: *a great tragic actor* | *The movie portrays him as* ***a tragic hero*** (=the main character in a tragedy). → see also COMIC **3 a tragic flaw** a weakness in the character of the main person in a tragedy that causes their own problems and usually death

trag·i·cally /ˈtrædʒɪkli/ *adv.* in a very sad or unfortunate way, especially one involving death: *Her husband died tragically two years ago.*

trag·i·com·e·dy /ˌtrædʒɪˈkɑmədi/ *n. plural* **tragicomedies** [C,U] ENG. LANG. ARTS a play or a story that is both sad and funny —**tragicomic** /ˌtrædʒɪˈkɑmɪk◂/ *adj.*

trail¹ /treɪl/ *v.*
1 BE LOSING [I,T] to be losing in a game, competition, or election: *Nelson is trailing in the polls.* | **trail (sb) by sth** *The Suns trail the Spurs by two games in the playoffs.* | +**behind** *He was trailing behind the other competitors.*
2 PULL BEHIND [I,T] if something trails behind you, or if you trail it behind you, it gets pulled behind you as you move along: +**across/in/through etc.** *Her skirt was trailing along in the mud.* | **trail sth in/on/through sth**

I moved around the kitchen trailing the phone cord behind me.
3 WALK BEHIND SB [I always + adv./prep.] to walk slowly behind someone or go somewhere after them, especially in a slow or bored way: **+along/behind/around** *She trailed lazily behind the others.*
4 TRY TO FOLLOW SB/STH [T] to follow someone or something in order to catch or see them: *Photographers trailed her wherever she went.*
5 LEAVE STH BEHIND YOU [T] to leave a line of a substance or a sign of movement behind you as you move along: *The plane was trailing smoke before it crashed.*
[**Origin:** 1300–1400 Old French *trailler* **to pull after you, tow**, from Latin *tragula* **sledge, net for pulling**] → see also TRAILER
trail away/off *phr. v.* if someone's voice or a sound trails away or off, it becomes gradually quieter and then stops: *Jerry's voice trailed off before he finished the thought.*

trail[2] S3 W3 *n.* [C]
1 PATH a rough path across open country or through a forest: *a hiking trail through the woods* | *We **followed the trail** until we came to a lake.* → see picture on page A31
2 a trail of blood/clues/destruction etc. a series of marks or signs left by someone or something that is moving: *She left a trail of wet footprints across the floor.*
3 be on the trail of sb/sth to be following or looking for someone or something that is difficult to catch or find: *We're always on the trail of new and exciting ideas.* | *Police are **hot on the trail of*** (=trying very hard to catch) *the killer.*
4 MARKS/SMELL ETC. the marks, signs, or smell left by a person or animal, by which they can be hunted or followed: *The dogs followed the trail of the dying animal.*
5 while the trail is still hot if you chase someone while the trail is still hot, you follow them soon after they have left
6 the trail goes cold used to say that someone cannot find any more signs of someone or something and can't follow them anymore
7 a trail of broken hearts/a trail of unpaid bills etc. a series of unhappy people or bad situations all caused by the same person: *As her career advanced, she left behind a trail of damaged friendships.* → see also **blaze a trail** at BLAZE[1] (4)

trail·blaz·er /ˈtreɪlˌbleɪzɚ/ *n.* [C] someone who is the first to do something, or who first discovers or develops new methods of doing something —**trail-blazing** *adj.*

trail·er /ˈtreɪlɚ/ S2 *n.* [C] **1** also **trailer home** a vehicle that can be pulled behind a car, that people live in permanently SYN **mobile home** **2** a vehicle that can be pulled behind a car, used for living and sleeping in during a vacation **3** ENG. LANG. ARTS an advertisement for a new movie or television show, usually consisting of small scenes taken from it **4** an open or closed container with wheels that can be pulled behind another vehicle, used for carrying something heavy **5** a vehicle like a large box on wheels, that is pulled by a truck and is used for carrying goods

ˈtrailer park also **ˈtrailer court** *n.* [C] an area where trailers are parked and used as people's homes

ˈtrailer trash *n.* [U] INFORMAL, OFFENSIVE poor people who live in trailer parks, who are considered to be uneducated and have bad behavior

trail·head /ˈtreɪlhɛd/ *n.* [C] the beginning of a TRAIL

ˌTrail of ˈTears, the the path that the Cherokees traveled in the fall and winter of 1838 to 1839 when the U.S. government forced them to move away from their homes in the southeastern area of the U.S. to RESERVATIONS west of the Mississippi River. The journey was extremely long, cold, and difficult and about 4,000 Cherokees died.

train[1] /treɪn/ S2 W2 *n.* [C]
1 RAILROAD a set of connected railroad cars pulled by an engine along a railroad: *The train was late.* | **+from/to** *an overnight train to Vienna* | *Traveling **by train** is not so convenient in America.* | *She was hurrying to **catch the train**.* | **get on/off a train** *Where do I get off the train?* | *She **boarded the train*** (=got on it) *in Moscow.* | *You can have a meal **on the train**.* | *a train trip*
2 sb's train of thought a related series of thoughts developing in someone's mind: *I'm sorry. I've **lost** my **train of thought*** (=I've forgotten what I was planning to say).
3 PEOPLE/ANIMALS/VEHICLES a long line of moving people, animals, or vehicles: *a wagon train*
4 DRESS a part of a long dress that spreads out over the ground behind the person who is wearing it: *a wedding dress with a long train*
5 a train of sth a series of related events, actions etc.
[**Origin:** 1400–1500 Old French **something that is pulled along behind**, from *trainer*]

train

train[2] S1 W2 *v.*
1 SKILL/JOB a) [T] to teach someone the skills of a particular job or activity: *She trains teachers.* | **train sb in sth** *All personnel will be trained in computer skills.* | **train sb to do sth** *Employees are trained to deal with emergency situations.* **b)** [I] to be taught the skills of a particular job or activity: *Many of the doctors had trained overseas.* | **+as** *He trained as a chef.* | **train to do sth** *Will is training to become a certified counselor.*
2 ANIMALS [T] to teach an animal to do something or to behave correctly: *Hamilton trains and sells horses.* | **train sth to do sth** *The dogs have been trained to attack intruders.*
3 SPORTS a) [I] to prepare for a sports event by exercising and practicing: **+for** *I started training for this race in September.* **b)** [T] to help someone prepare for a sports event by telling them what to do: *I've been training professional athletes for years.* ►see THESAURUS box at **practice**[2]
4 DEVELOP STH [T] to develop and improve a natural ability: *You can train your mind to relax.*
5 POINT STH [T] to aim a gun, camera etc. at someone or something: **train sth on/at sb/sth** *TV stations trained their cameras on the governor.*
6 PLANT [T] to make a plant grow in a particular direction by bending, cutting, or tying it —**trained** *adj.*: *a highly trained professional* —**trainable** *adj.*

train·bear·er /ˈtreɪnˌbɛrɚ/ *n.* [C] someone who holds the train of a dress, especially at a wedding

train·ee /treɪˈni/ *n.* [C] someone who is being trained for a job: *a management trainee*

train·er /ˈtreɪnɚ/ *n.* [C] someone who trains people or animals for sports, work etc.

train·ing /ˈtreɪnɪŋ/ S2 W1 *n.* **1** [singular, U] the process of teaching or being taught skills for a particular job or activity: **+in** *training in different teaching methods* | *I've never had any **formal training** in counseling.* | *a training manual* **2** [U] special physical exercises that you do to stay healthy or prepare for a sporting event: *weight training* | *David's **in training** for the marathon.* → see also SPRING TRAINING

ˈtraining camp *n.* [C] a place where sports teams go to practice playing their sport and live for a short time

train·load /ˈtreɪnloʊd/ *n.* [C] the number or amount of things or people that fill a train

T

'train set *n.* [C] a toy train with railroad tracks

'train ˌstation *n.* [C] the place where trains stop for passengers to get on and off

traipse /treɪps/ *v.* [I always + adv./prep., T] to walk somewhere slowly, without a clear direction: +**up/down/around etc.** *We spent the day traipsing around art galleries.*

trait /treɪt/ *n.* [C] FORMAL **1** a particular quality in someone's character SYN **characteristic**: *Jealousy is a natural human trait.* | **a personality/character trait** *She has a few annoying personality traits.* **2** a particular quality or feature that someone's body has: *physical traits like hair and eye color* **3** BIOLOGY a particular INHERITED quality or feature of an ORGANISM which is different in each individual: *a genetic trait*

trai·tor /'treɪt̬ɚ/ *n.* [C] someone who is not loyal to their country, friends etc.: +**to** *a traitor to the country* [**Origin:** 1200–1300 Old French *traitre*, from Latin *traditor*, from *tradere* **to hand over, deliver, betray**]

trai·tor·ous /'treɪt̬ərəs/ *adj.* LITERARY not loyal to your country, friends etc. —**traitorously** *adv.*

tra·jec·to·ry /trə'dʒɛktəri/ *n. plural* **trajectories** [C] PHYSICS the curved path of an object that is fired or thrown through the air

tram /træm/ also **tram·car** /'træmkɑr/ *n.* [C] **1** a vehicle that hangs from a CABLE, used to take people to the top of mountains SYN **cable car** **2** a vehicle that has several cars connected together to carry a lot of people **3** a vehicle for passengers, that travels along metal tracks in the street SYN **streetcar** [**Origin:** 1800–1900 *tram* **handle of a wheelbarrow**]

tram·mel /'træməl/ *v.* [T] FORMAL to limit or prevent the free movement, activity, or development of someone or something → see also UNTRAMMELED

tram·mels /'træməlz/ *n.* [plural] FORMAL something that limits or prevents free movement, activity, or development

tramp¹ /træmp/ *n.* [C] **1** someone who has no home or job and moves from place to place, often asking for food or money **2 the tramp of feet/boots etc.** the sound of heavy walking **3** a long or difficult walk

tramp² *v.* [I always + adv./prep., T] to walk around or through somewhere with firm or heavy steps: +**across/over/up etc.** *Crowds of tourists tramped across the fields.*

tram·ple /'træmpəl/ *v.* [I always + adv./prep., T] **1** to step heavily on something so that you crush it with your feet: *The kids from next door have trampled the flower beds.* | *Two people were* ***trampled to death*** *in the riot.* **2** to behave in a way that shows that you do not care about someone's rights, hopes, ideas etc.: +**on/over** *Opponents say the law tramples on the right to free speech.*

tram·po·line /ˌtræmpə'lin, 'træmpəˌlin/ *n.* [C] a piece of equipment that you jump up and down on for exercise, made of a sheet of material tightly stretched across a metal frame [**Origin:** 1700–1800 Spanish *trampolín*, from Italian *trampolino*] —**trampoline** *v.* [I] —**trampolining** *n.* [U]

'tramp ˌsteamer *n.* [C] a ship that carries goods from place to place when someone pays for it to do so, but not on a regular basis

trance /træns/ *n.* **1** [C] a state in which you behave as if you were asleep, but you are still able to hear and understand what is said to you: *She was in a hypnotic trance.* **2** [C] a situation in which you are thinking about something so much that you do not notice what is happening around you: *He seemed to be deep* ***in a trance*** *and didn't hear me.* **3** [U] a type of popular electronic dance music with a fast beat and long continuous notes played on a SYNTHESIZER [**Origin:** 1300–1400 Old French *transe*, from *transir* **to pass away, become unconscious**, from Latin *transire*]

tran·quil /'træŋkwəl/ *adj.* pleasantly calm, quiet, and peaceful: *a tranquil pool of water* —**tranquilly** *adv.* —**tranquility** /træŋ'kwɪləti/ *n.* [U]

tran·quil·ize /'træŋkwəˌlaɪz/ *v.* [T] to make a person or animal calm or unconscious by using a drug

tran·qui·liz·er /'træŋkwəˌlaɪzɚ/ *n.* [C] a drug that makes a person or animal calm or unconscious, often used to make someone less nervous or anxious

trans- /træns, trænz/ *prefix* **1** on or to the other side of something SYN **across**: *transatlantic flights* **2** from one place or thing to another: *public transportation* (=that takes you from one place to another) | *We'll transfer the money to your account* (=move it into your account from another one). **3** between or involving two groups: *transracial adoption* (=involving people of different races) **4** used to show that something changes: *a complete transformation* (=change in appearance or character)

trans·act /træn'zækt/ *v.* [I,T] FORMAL to do business: *Most deals are transacted over the phone.*

trans·ac·tion /træn'zækʃən/ *n.* FORMAL **1** [C] a business deal: *real estate transactions* **2 transactions** [plural] business or discussions that take place at a meeting, or a written record of these **3** [U] the process of doing business: *the transaction of business*

trans·at·lan·tic /ˌtrænzət'læntɪk/ *adj.* [only before noun] **1** crossing the Atlantic Ocean: *transatlantic flights* **2** involving countries on both sides of the Atlantic Ocean: *a transatlantic organization* **3** on the other side of the Atlantic Ocean: *a transatlantic ally*

trans·cei·ver /træn'sivɚ/ *n.* [C] a radio that can both send and receive messages

tran·scend /træn'sɛnd/ *v.* [T] FORMAL to go above or beyond the limits of something: *The desire for peace transcended political differences.*

tran·scen·dent /træn'sɛndənt/ *adj.* FORMAL going far beyond ordinary limits —**transcendence** *n.* [U]

tran·scen·den·tal /ˌtrænsɛn'dɛntl/ *adj.* existing above or beyond human knowledge, understanding, and experience: *transcendental harmony*

tran·scen·den·tal·ism /ˌtrænsɛn'dɛntlˌɪzəm/ *n.* [U] **1** the belief, held especially by Kant, that knowledge can be obtained by studying thought and not only by practical experience **2** HISTORY a 19th-century set of beliefs, held especially by Emerson, that emphasized a person's natural ability to know the SPIRITUAL nature of things —**transcendentalist** *n.* [C]

ˌtranscendental medi'tation ABBREVIATION **TM** *n.* [U] a method of becoming calm by repeating special words in your mind

trans·con·ti·nen·tal /ˌtrænskɑntˀn'ɛntl, ˌtrænz-/ *adj.* [only before noun] crossing a CONTINENT: *a transcontinental railroad*

ˌTranscontinental 'Treaty, the HISTORY another name for the ADAMS-ONIS TREATY

tran·scribe /træn'skraɪb/ *v.* [T] FORMAL **1** to write down something exactly as it was said: *The phone conversations were transcribed and sent to the FBI.* **2** to write an exact copy of something: *Secretaries were busy transcribing medical records.* **3** ENG. LANG. ARTS to represent speech sounds with special PHONETIC letters **4** ENG. LANG. ARTS to arrange a piece of music for a different instrument or voice **5 transcribe sth (for sth)** TECHNICAL to copy recorded music, computer information, speech etc. from one system to another, for example from TAPE to CD **6 transcribe sth into sth** TECHNICAL to change a piece of writing into a different writing system or language

tran·script /'trænˌskrɪpt/ S3 *n.* [C] **1** a written or printed copy of a speech, conversation etc.: +**of** *Newspapers printed a full transcript of his testimony.* **2** an official college document that shows a list of a student's classes and the results they received: *a college transcript*

tran·scrip·tion /træn'skrɪpʃən/ *n.* **1** [U] ENG. LANG ARTS the act or process of transcribing something: *transcription of speech sounds* **2** [C] ENG. LANG. ARTS a written or printed copy of a speech, conversation etc. SYN **transcript** **3** [U] BIOLOGY a process in which the

GENETIC information contained in the DNA of living cells is copied onto the chemical substance RNA, and is then carried to new cells

trans·duc·er /trænz'dusɚ/ *n.* [C] TECHNICAL a small piece of electronic equipment that changes one form of energy to another

tran·sect /træn'sɛkt/ *v.* [T] FORMAL to divide something by cutting across it

tran·sept /'trænsɛpt/ *n.* [C] one of the two parts of a large church that are built out from the main area of the church to form a cross shape

trans·fer[1] /'trænsfɚ, træns'fɚ/ Ac S2 W3 *v.* **transferred, transferring**

1 PERSON [I,T] to move from one place, school, job etc. to another, or to make someone do this, especially within the same organization: **+to** *Halfway through the first year, he transferred to Berkeley.* | **transfer sb (from sth) to sth** *Davis is being transferred from New York to Houston next month.*

2 THING/ACTIVITY [T] FORMAL to move something from one place or position to another: **transfer sth (from sth) to sth** *Remove the roast from the oven and transfer it to a platter.*

3 MONEY [T] ECONOMICS to move money from the control of one account or institution to another: *I need to transfer some money from my savings account to my checking account.*

4 SKILL/IDEA/QUALITY [I,T] if a skill, idea, or quality transfers from one situation to another, or if you transfer it, it is used in the new situation: *Ideas that work in one school often don't transfer well to another.*

5 transfer power/responsibility/control to officially give power etc. to another person or organization: **+to** *Republicans want to transfer more power back to the states.*

6 PHONE to connect the telephone call of someone who has called you to someone else's telephone so that that person can speak to them: *Hold one moment while I transfer your call.*

7 PROPERTY [T] ECONOMICS to officially give property or money to someone else: *The assets were transferred into his wife's name.*

8 BUS/AIRPLANE [I] to change from one bus, airplane etc. to another during a trip: *If you take the bus, you'll have to transfer twice.*

9 transfer your affection/loyalty etc. to change from loving or supporting one person to loving or supporting a different one: **+to** *He quickly transferred his loyalty from the old government to the new.*

10 RECORDED INFORMATION [T] to copy recorded information, music etc. from one system to another, for example from TAPE to CD: *Transfer the files onto floppy disk.*

11 PICTURE/PATTERN [I,T] if a pattern, design etc. transfers from one surface to another, or if you transfer it, it appears on the second surface: *The design is transferred to the loom and woven into the carpet.*

[**Origin:** 1300–1400 Latin *transferre*, from *ferre* **to carry**]
—**transferable** *adj.*

trans·fer[2] /'trænsfɚ/ Ac *n.* **1 a)** [C,U] the process by which someone or something moves or is moved from one place, situation, job etc. to another: *a job transfer* | *Most of the bills are paid by electronic transfer.* **b)** [C] someone or something that has been moved in this way **2 transfer of power** a process by which the control of a country is taken from one person or group and given to another: *the smooth transfer of power in Hong Kong* **3** [C] **a)** a ticket that allows a passenger to change from one bus, train etc. to another without paying more money **b)** the action of changing from one bus, airplane etc. to another to continue a trip **4** [C] a drawing, pattern etc. that can be printed onto a surface by pressing it against that surface **5** [C,U] ECONOMICS a way in which advertisers try to persuade someone to buy something by making a connection in people's minds between the product and something attractive or positive

trans·fer·ence /'trænsfərəns, træns'fɚəns/ Ac *n.* [U] **1** TECHNICAL in PSYCHOLOGY, the process by which your feelings or desires concerning one person become connected to another person instead **2** FORMAL a process by which someone or something is moved from one place, position, job etc. to another

'transfer RN,A ABBREVIATION **tRNA** *n.* [C] BIOLOGY MOLECULES of RNA that carry AMINO ACIDS to RIBOSOMES → see also RIBOSOMAL RNA

trans·fig·ure /træns'fɪgyɚ/ *v.* [T] LITERARY to change the way someone or something looks, especially so that they become more beautiful: *The moonlight transfigured the whole landscape.* —**transfiguration** /træns,fɪgyə'reɪʃən/ *n.* [C,U]

trans·fix /træns'fɪks/ *v.* [T] **1** to surprise, interest, or frighten someone so much that they do not move **2** LITERARY to make a hole through someone or something with a sharp pointed weapon

trans·fixed /træns'fɪkst/ *adj.* [not before noun] so surprised, interested, or frightened that you do not move: *The students were completely transfixed during her speech.*

trans·form /træns'fɔrm/ Ac W3 *v.* [I,T] to completely change the appearance, form, or character of something or someone, or to change in this way: *Modern technology has transformed our lives.* | **+into** *In just a few months, she transformed into a beautiful and confident woman.* | **transform sb/sth (from sth) into sth** *At night, the bar is transformed into a disco.* —**transformable** *adj.*

trans·for·ma·tion /,trænsfɚ'meɪʃən/ Ac *n.* [C,U] **1** a complete change in someone or something: **+of** *the transformation of society* | **+in** *a transformation in the way we deal with other countries* | **a transformation from sth to sth** *gradual transformation from teenager to responsible adult* | *The movie industry was* ***undergoing a*** *dramatic* ***transformation***. **2** BIOLOGY a change in a cell that happens when it takes in the DNA from another cell **3** MATH a change in the position, size, or shape of a GEOMETRIC figure → see also DILATION

trans·form·er /træns'fɔrmɚ/ *n.* [C] PHYSICS a piece of equipment for changing electricity from one VOLTAGE to another → see picture at ELECTRICITY

trans·fu·sion /træns'fyuʒən/ *n.* [C,U] **1** MEDICINE the process of putting blood from one person into another person's body: *a blood transfusion* **2** the act of giving something important or necessary such as money to a group or organization that needs it: *a transfusion of funds* —**transfuse** /træns'fyuz/ *v.* [T]

trans·gen·der /trænz'dʒɛndɚ/ also **trans·gendered** /trænz'dʒɛndɚd/ *adj.* a transgender person wants to be or look like a member of the opposite sex, especially by having a medical operation, or has had this operation already SYN **transsexual** —**transgender** *n.* [C] —**transgenderism** *n.* [U]

trans·gen·ic /trænz'dʒɛnɪk/ *adj.* TECHNICAL BIOLOGY having GENES from another ORGANISM of a different type

trans·gress /trænz'grɛs/ *v.* [I,T] FORMAL to do something that is against the rules of social behavior or against a moral principle: *Those who transgress the rules will be punished.* —**transgressor** *n.* [C] —**transgression** /trænz'grɛʃən/ *n.* [C,U]

tran·sient[1] /'trænʒənt/ *adj.* FORMAL **1** working or staying somewhere for only a short time: *The city has a very transient population.* **2** continuing only for a short time: *transient pleasures* —**transience**, **transiency** *n.* [U]

transient[2] *n.* [C] someone who has no home and moves around from place to place

tran·sis·tor /træn'zɪstɚ/ *n.* [C] **1** PHYSICS a small piece of electronic equipment in radios, televisions etc. that controls the flow of electricity **2** a transistor radio

tran·sis·tor·ize /træn'zɪstə,raɪz/ *v.* [T] TECHNICAL to put transistors into something so that it can be made smaller

tran,sistor 'radio *n.* [C] a small radio that has transistors in it instead of VALVES

tran·sit /'trænzɪt/ Ac *n.* **1** [U] the process of moving goods or people from one place to another: *The ship-*

T

*ment was lost **in transit*** (=in the process of being moved). **2** [U] a system for moving people from place to place SYN **transportation**: **public/mass transit** *The museum can be reached using public transit.* | *a transit system* **3** [U] the act of moving through or across a place **4** [C,U] TECHNICAL the movement of a PLANET or moon in front of a larger object in space, such as the sun

ˈtransit ˌcamp *n.* [C] a place where REFUGEES stay before moving to somewhere more permanent

tran·si·tion /trænˈzɪʃən/ Ac S3 W3 *n.* [C,U] **1** FORMAL the act or process of changing from one form or state to another: **+from/to** *a smooth transition from communism to democracy* | *The program helps young people **make the transition** to independent living.* | *a country **in transition*** | *a five-year **transition period*** **2** TECHNICAL a phrase or sentence in a piece of writing or speech that connects two different ideas smoothly: *You need a better transition between the second and third paragraphs.*

tran·si·tion·al /trænˈzɪʃənl/ Ac *adj.* **1** relating to a period during which something is changing from one state, form, or situation to another: **a transitional stage/period/phase etc.** *a transitional year for the company* | **a transitional government/authority** (=a government that is temporary during a period of change) **2 a transitional word/phrase/sentence etc.** a word, phrase etc. that connects two different ideas in a piece of writing or speech —**transitionally** *adv.*

tran·si·tive /ˈtrænsətɪv, -zə-/ *adj.* ENG. LANG. ARTS a transitive verb has an object. For example, in the sentence "I hate bananas," "hate" is transitive. Transitive verbs are marked [T] in this dictionary. → see also INTRANSITIVE —**transitive** *n.* [C] —**transitively** *adv.* —**transitivity** /ˌtrænsəˈtɪvəṭi/ *n.* [U]

ˈtransit ˌlounge *n.* [C] an area in an airport where passengers can wait

tran·si·to·ry /ˈtrænzəˌtɔri/ Ac *adj.* continuing or existing for only a short time: *the transitory nature of teenage love*

ˈtransit ˌvisa *n.* [C] POLITICS a VISA (=special document) that allows someone to pass through one country on their way to another

trans·late /ˈtrænzleɪt, ˌtrænzˈleɪt/ S2 W3 *v.* **1** [I,T] to change speech or writing into another language → see also INTERPRET: *I'll need you to translate for me.* | **translate sth (from sth) into sth** *He translated the article from English into Japanese.* **2** [I always + adv./prep.] if a word, phrase, idea etc. translates in a particular way, it is or can be expressed in another language in that way: *Poetry doesn't usually translate well.* | **+as** *The phrase roughly translates as "I won't be away for long."* **3** [I,T] to be used in a new situation, or to use an idea or method in a new situation: **+to** *Many business ideas translate very well to government.* [**Origin:** 1300–1400 Latin, past participle of *transferre*, from *ferre* **to carry**] —**translatable** *adj.*

translate into *phr. v.* **1 translate into sth**, **translate sth into sth** if one thing translates into another thing or you translate it into another thing, the second thing happens as a result of the first: *Will increased demand translate into more jobs?* | *We need to translate all this enthusiasm into action.* **2 translate into sth** also **translate to sth** to be the same amount as something else: *A 16% raise translates to an extra $700 a month.* **3 translate into sth, translate sth into sth** to change from one form to another form, or to make something do this: *The play should translate well into a ballet.* | *It's often difficult to translate theory into practice.*

trans·la·tion /trænzˈleɪʃən, træns-/ S3 *n.* **1** [C] a book, piece of writing etc. that has been changed into a different language: *An English translation is not available.* | **+of** *a new translation of the Bible* | **+from** *a translation from Arabic* | *She gave me **a rough translation** (=a generally correct one) of the letter.* **2** [U] the process or result of changing speech or writing into another language: *The translation is done by professional translators.* | *Much of the book's humor has been **lost in translation*** (=is no longer effective or understood after being translated). **3 in translation** in a language that is not the original language: *I've only read the book in translation.* **4** [C] a word or phrase that means the same as a word or phrase in a different language: **+of** *the Hebrew translation of the phrase* | *"Outside person" is a **literal translation** of the Japanese word for foreigner.* **5** [C] MATH the movement of a shape when the whole shape moves in the same direction and does not turn **6** [U] FORMAL the process of changing something into a different form, or using it in a new situation: *the translation of beliefs into actions*

transˌlational ˈsymmetry *n.* [U] MATH the quality of a pattern made by taking an image and moving and repeating it one or more times, so that all parts of the pattern look exactly the same → see also POINT SYMMETRY

trans·la·tor /ˈtrænzˌleɪṭɚ/ *n.* [C] **1** someone who changes speech or writing into a different language → see also INTERPRETER **2** a piece of equipment or a computer program that changes one language into another language

trans·lit·er·ate /trænzˈlɪṭəˌreɪt, træns-/ *v.* [T] ENG. LANG. ARTS to write a word, sentence etc. in the alphabet of a different language or writing system —**transliteration** /trænzˌlɪṭəˈreɪʃən/ *n.* [C,U]

trans·lu·cent /trænzˈlusənt/ *adj.* not transparent, but clear enough to allow light to pass through: *translucent paper* —**translucence** *n.* [U] → see also OPAQUE, TRANSPARENT

trans·mi·gra·tion /ˌtrænzmaɪˈgreɪʃən/ *n.* [U] TECHNICAL the time when the soul passes into another body after death, according to some religions —**transmigrate** /trænzˈmaɪgreɪt/ *v.* [I]

trans·mis·si·ble /trænzˈmɪsəbəl/ *adj.* FORMAL able to be passed from one person to another: *a transmissible disease*

trans·mis·sion /trænzˈmɪʃən/ Ac *n.* **1** [U] the process of sending out signals, messages etc. by radio, television, or similar equipment: *electronic transmission of information* **2** [C,U] the part of a vehicle that takes power from the engine to the wheels: *a car with an automatic transmission* **3** [U] FORMAL the process by which a disease is passed from one person to another: *the transmission of HIV* **4** [U] FORMAL the process of passing information, ideas, customs etc. between people: *the transmission of knowledge and culture* **5** [C] FORMAL something that is broadcast on television, radio etc. SYN **broadcast** **6** [U] PHYSICS the process by which energy, electricity, or power is sent from one place to another

trans·mit /trænzˈmɪt/ Ac *v.* **transmitted, transmitting** **1** [I,T] to send out signals, messages etc. by radio, television, or other similar equipment SYN **broadcast**: *The game will be transmitted live via satellite.* **2** [T] FORMAL to spread a disease from one person or animal to another: **transmit sth to sb** *Malaria is transmitted to humans by mosquitoes.* | **transmit sth by/through (doing) sth** *Can the virus be transmitted by kissing?* → see also SEXUALLY TRANSMITTED DISEASE **3** [T] FORMAL to pass knowledge, ideas, customs etc. from one person or group to another: *Cultural values are transmitted from parent to child.* **4** [T] TECHNICAL to send a signal from one nerve in your body to another: *Chemicals transmit nerve impulses.* **5** [T] to send energy, electricity, or power from one place to another **6** [T] PHYSICS if an object or substance transmits sound or light, it allows sound or light to travel through or along it —**transmittal** *n.* [U]

trans·mit·ter /trænzˈmɪṭɚ, ˈtrænzˌmɪṭɚ/ *n.* [C] equipment that sends out radio or television signals

trans·mog·ri·fy /trænzˈmɑgrəfaɪ/ *v.* **transmogrifies, transmogrified, transmogrifying** [T] FORMAL or HUMOROUS to change the shape or character of something completely, as if by magic

trans·mu·ta·tion /ˌtrænzmyuˈteɪʃən/ *n.* [C,U] PHYSICS the change of one chemical ELEMENT into another through a NUCLEAR reaction or series of reactions

trans·mute /trænzˈmyut/ *v.* [I,T] FORMAL to change from one substance or type of thing into another, or to make someone or something do this —**transmutable** *adj.* —**transmutation** /ˌtrænzmyuˈteɪʃən/ *n.* [C,U]

trans·na·tio·nal /trænzˈnæʃənl/ *adj.* involving more than one country, or existing in more than one country

trans·o·ce·an·ic /trænzˌoʊʃiˈænɪk/ *adj.* [only before noun] crossing an ocean, or involving countries on both sides of an ocean: *a transoceanic voyage*

tran·som /ˈtrænsəm/ *n.* [C] **1** a small window over a door or over a larger window **2** a bar of wood above a door, separating the door from a window above it **3** a bar of wood or stone across a window, dividing the window into two parts

trans·par·en·cy /trænsˈpærənsi, -ˈpɛr-/ *n. plural* **transparencies 1** [C] a sheet of plastic through which light can be shone to show a picture or writing on a large screen **2** [U] the quality of glass, plastic etc. that makes it possible for you to see through it **3** [U] the quality of allowing people to see the way you do things so they can see that you are doing things honestly and fairly

trans·par·ent /trænsˈpærənt/ *adj.* **1** something that is transparent allows light to pass through it, so that you can see things through it → see also OPAQUE: *transparent plastic bags* → see also TRANSLUCENT **2** a transparent lie, excuse etc. does not deceive people because it is clearly not true **3** transparent feelings and qualities are easy to see: *His interest in Gayle was transparent.* **4** done in a way that allows people to know what is happening and make sure that things are being done honestly and fairly: *We have to make the election process more transparent.* **5** someone who is transparent has feelings and thoughts that are very easy to see, even if they are trying to hide them **6** FORMAL clear and easy to understand: *a transparent writing style* —**transparently** *adv.*

tran·spi·ra·tion /ˌtrænspəˈreɪʃən/ *n.* [U] **1** the process of transpiring (TRANSPIRE) **2** BIOLOGY the process that happens when a plant loses water through its leaves

tran·spire /trænˈspaɪɚ/ *v.* **1** [T] FORMAL to happen: *I was surprised at what transpired.* **2 it transpires that** FORMAL if it transpires that something is true, people find out that it is true **3** [I,T] BIOLOGY when a plant transpires, it gives off water from its surface

trans·plant¹ /trænsˈplænt/ *v.* [T] **1** BIOLOGY to move a plant from one place and plant it in another: *You need to transplant that cactus.* **2** MEDICINE to move an organ, piece of skin etc. from one person's body to another: *His kidney was transplanted in his daughter.* **3** to move something or someone from one place to another: *They wanted to transplant the business to a new site on the edge of town.* —**transplanted** *adj.* [only before noun] —**transplantation** /ˌtrænsplænˈteɪʃən/ *n.* [U]

trans·plant² /ˈtrænsplænt/ *n.* **1** [C,U] the operation of transplanting an organ, piece of skin etc., or the organ itself: *a liver transplant* **2** [C] INFORMAL someone or something that has moved from one place to another: *a Midwestern transplant to California* → see also IMPLANT

trans·po·lar /trænsˈpoʊlɚ/ *adj.* [only before noun] across the area around the North or South Pole

tran·spond·er /trænˈspɑndɚ/ *n.* [C] TECHNICAL a piece of radio or RADAR equipment that sends out a particular signal when it receives a signal telling it to do this

trans·port¹ /trænsˈpɔrt, ˈtrænspɔrt/ Ac *v.* [T] **1** to take goods, people etc. from one place to another in a vehicle: *The fruit was transported by air.* | **transport sb/sth to sth** *The women were transported to a nearby hospital for treatment.* **2** to move something from one place to another: *Bees transport the pollen.* **3** to make someone imagine that they are in another place or time: *The books transported her into new worlds.* **4 be transported (by/with sth)** LITERARY to feel very strong emotions of pleasure, happiness etc.: *He was transported by the beauty of the music* **5** to send a criminal to a distant country like Australia as a punishment in the past —**transportable** *adj.*

trans·port² /ˈtrænspɔrt/ Ac *n.* **1** [U] the process or business of taking goods, information etc. from one place to another: +**of** *the transport of nuclear waste* **2** [U] TRANSPORTATION **3** [C] a ship or aircraft for carrying soldiers or supplies **4 be in a transport of delight/joy etc.** LITERARY to be feeling very strong emotions of pleasure, happiness etc.

trans·por·ta·tion /ˌtrænspɚˈteɪʃən/ Ac W3 *n.* [U] **1** a system for carrying passengers or goods from one place to another: *I get so tired of taking **public transportation**.* | **a mode/means/method of transportation** *Bicycles were a popular mode of transportation after the war.* **2** the process or business of taking goods from one place to another: +**of** *the transportation of stolen property* **3** the process of traveling from one place to another: *Ticket prices include transportation and lunch.* **4** a vehicle that you can use to go somewhere or carry things in: *You can't really get there without transportation.* **5** the punishment of sending a criminal to a distant country like Australia in the past

trans·port·er /trænsˈpɔrtɚ, ˈtrænsˌpɔrtɚ/ Ac *n.* [C] a large truck, airplane etc. that can carry one or more other vehicles or many people

ˈtransport ˌplane *n.* [C] an airplane that is used especially for carrying military equipment or soldiers

ˈtransport ˌship *n.* [C] a ship used especially for carrying soldiers

trans·pose /trænsˈpoʊz/ *v.* [T] TECHNICAL **1** FORMAL to change the order or position of two or more things: *I had transposed the last two digits of her phone number.* **2** ENG. LANG. ARTS to write or perform a piece of music in a musical KEY that is different from the one that it was first written in —**transposition** /ˌtrænspəˈzɪʃən/ *n.* [C,U]

trans·po·son /trænsˈpoʊzɑn/ *n.* [C] BIOLOGY a piece of DNA that can move to another position on the same or another CHROMOSOME, which can cause MUTATIONS (=changes in the genetic material) SYN **jumping gene**

trans·sex·u·al /trænzˈsɛkʃuəl/ *n.* [C] someone who wants to be or look like a member of the opposite sex, especially by having a medical operation, or who has already had this operation —**transsexual** *adj.* —**transsexualism** *n.* [U]

trans·ship·ment /trænˈʃɪpmənt/ *n.* [C,U] the process or action of moving goods from one ship, airplane, truck etc. to another so that they can be delivered —**transship** *v.* [I,T]

tran·sub·stan·ti·a·tion /ˌtrænsəbˌstænʃiˈeɪʃən/ *n.* [U] TECHNICAL the process by which some Christians believe the bread and wine in the MASS (=a religious ceremony) become the actual body and blood of Jesus Christ → see also CONSUBSTANTIATION

trans·verse /ˌtrænzˈvɚs◂/ *adj.* TECHNICAL lying or placed across something

trans·ves·tite /trænzˈvɛstaɪt/ *n.* [C] someone who enjoys dressing like a person of the opposite sex —**transvestite** *adj.* —**transvestism** *n.* [U]

trap¹ /træp/ *n.* [C]

1 FOR ANIMALS a piece of equipment for catching animals: *Have you **set traps** to catch the squirrels?* → see also MOUSETRAP

2 SMART TRICK a trick that is used to catch someone or to make them do or say something that they did not intend to: *I was sure it was a trap, but I went in anyway.* | **lay/set/spring a trap** *Police laid a trap for the killer.* | **fall/walk into a trap** *She realized too late that she had fallen into their trap.*

3 BAD SITUATION a bad or difficult situation that is difficult to escape from: *It's all too easy to get **caught in the trap of** working too much.*

4 MISTAKE a situation or mistake that you should avoid: *Don't **fall into the trap of** investing all your money in one place.* | *It can be difficult to **avoid the trap of** spending too much.*

T

5 PIPE the part of a pipe from a SINK, toilet etc. that is bent to hold water and stop gases from passing through
6 keep your trap shut SPOKEN to not say anything about things that are secret
7 shut your trap! SPOKEN used to tell someone rudely and angrily to stop talking
8 DOOR a TRAPDOOR
9 GOLF a SAND TRAP
10 PLACE THAT ATTRACTS STH a place where there is often a lot of something because it gets caught there: *The screen is a real dust trap.*
11 SOCCER the act of stopping a moving ball with the bottom of your foot or allowing it to BOUNCE softly off a part of your body other than your hands or arms
12 VEHICLE a light vehicle with two wheels, pulled by a horse
13 DOG RACE a special gate from which a dog is set free at the start of dog race → see also BOOBY TRAP, DEATH TRAP, SPEED TRAP, TRAPSHOOTING

trap² *v.* **trapped, trapping** [T]
1 IN A DANGEROUS PLACE [usually passive] to prevent someone from escaping from a dangerous place: *One hundred and twenty miners were still trapped underground yesterday.*
2 CATCH SB to catch someone by forcing them into a place from which they cannot escape: *Police have the man trapped inside the building.* ▶see THESAURUS box at **catch¹**
3 be/feel trapped to be in a bad situation from which you cannot escape: *Peggy feels trapped in a boring job.*
4 TRICK SB to trick someone so that you make them do or say something that they did not intend to: **trap sb into (doing) sth** *Anthony says she trapped him into marriage before he was ready.*
5 GAS/WATER ETC. to prevent something such as water, dirt, heat etc. from escaping or spreading: *Greenhouse gases trap heat in the Earth's atmosphere.*
6 ANIMAL to catch an animal or bird using a trap
7 SOCCER to stop a moving ball with the bottom of your foot or allow it to BOUNCE softly off a part of your body other than your hands or arms

trap·door, trap door /ˌtræp'dɔr/ *n.* [C] a small door that covers an opening in a roof or floor

tra·peze /træ'piz/ *n.* [C] a short bar hanging from two ropes high above the ground, used by ACROBATS

tra·pe·zi·um /trə'piziəm/ *n. plural* **trapezia** /-ziə/ or **trapeziums** [C] MATH a shape with four sides, none of which are parallel → see picture at SHAPE¹

tra·pe·zi·us /trə'piziəs/ also **tra'pezius ˌmuscle** *n. plural* **trapeziuses** [C] TECHNICAL one of the two large TRIANGLE-shaped muscles in your back

trap·e·zoid /'træpəzɔɪd/ *n.* [C] MATH a flat shape with four sides, of which only two are parallel → see picture at SHAPE¹

trap·per /'træpɚ/ *n.* [C] someone who traps wild animals, especially for their fur

trap·pings /'træpɪŋz/ *n.* [plural] things such as clothes, possessions etc. that show someone's rank, success, or position: +**of** *the trappings of power*

Trap·pist /'træpɪst/ *n.* [C] a member of a Catholic religious society whose members never speak —**Trappist** *adj.*: *Trappist monks*

trap·shoot·ing, trap shooting /'træpˌʃuṭɪŋ/ *n.* [U] the sport of shooting at special clay objects fired into the air

trash¹ /træʃ/ [S2] *n.* [U] **1** waste material that will be thrown away, usually considered together with the container or bag holding it [SYN] **garbage**: *Will you ask one of the kids **take out the trash*** (=take it outside the house)*?* | *Just put it **in the trash**.* ▶see THESAURUS box at **garbage** **2** INFORMAL something that is of very poor quality, especially something such as a newspaper, book, movie, or TV program: *How can you read that trash?* **3 on the trash heap (of sth)** not used or respected anymore [SYN] **on the scrapheap** **4 one man's trash is another man's treasure** used to say that different people like different things or consider things differently [**Origin:** 1300–1400 from a Scandinavian language] → see also **talk trash** at TALK¹ (27), TRAILER TRASH, WHITE TRASH

trash² *v.* [T] INFORMAL **1** to destroy something completely, either deliberately or by using it too much: *Team members trashed their hotel rooms.* **2** to criticize someone or something severely **3** to throw something away → see also TRASHED

'trash bag *n.* [C] a large plastic bag for holding waste material [SYN] **garbage bag**

'trash bin *n.* [C] a large trash can

'trash can *n.* [C] a large container, usually with a lid, used to hold waste material [SYN] **garbage can** → see also WASTEBASKET

'trash comˌpactor *n.* [C] a machine that presses waste material together into a very small mass

trashed /træʃt/ *adj.* INFORMAL **1** very drunk: *We **got so trashed** last night.* **2** completely destroyed: *The place was trashed.*

trash-talk /'træʃ-tɔk/ *n.* [U] INFORMAL unkind things you say about someone else → see also TALK TRASH

trash·y /'træʃi/ *adj. comparative* **trashier**, *superlative* **trashiest** **1** of extremely bad quality, and often about sex: *trashy novels* **2** behaving in a way that is morally unacceptable, especially involving sex —**trashiness** *n.* [U]

trat·to·ri·a /ˌtrætə'riə/ *n.* [C] a restaurant that serves Italian food

trau·ma /'trɔmə, 'traʊmə/ *n.* **1** [C] a very bad and upsetting experience: *major traumas such as death or divorce* **2** [U] a mental state of extreme shock caused by a very frightening or bad experience: ***the emotional trauma of rape*** **3** [C,U] MEDICINE serious physical injury: *a head trauma* [**Origin:** 1600–1700 Greek **wound**]

trau·mat·ic /trə'mæṭɪk, trɔ-/ *adj.* **1** a traumatic experience is so shocking and upsetting that it affects you for a long time: +**for** *My parents' divorce was very traumatic for me.* **2** MEDICINE traumatic injury causes serious damage to the body —**traumatically** /-kli/ *adv.*

trau·ma·tize /'trɔməˌtaɪz, 'traʊ-/ *v.* [T usually passive] to shock someone so badly that they are unable to do things normally: *His war experiences had clearly traumatized him.* —**traumatized** *adj.*

tra·vail /trə'veɪl, 'træveɪl/ *n.* [U] also **travails** [plural] LITERARY a situation that is very difficult and bad or involves very tiring work or effort: +**of** *the travails of old age*

trav·el¹ /'trævəl/ [S2] [W2] *v.*
1 TRIP a) [I] to go from one place to another, or to several places, especially distant ones: *Helena really likes to travel.* | +**to/through/around etc.** *We plan to travel across Europe.* | **travel by train/car etc.** *If you are traveling by car, be sure to leave plenty of time.* | **travel widely/extensively** *They traveled widely to research the book.* | *We always **travel light*** (=without taking many possessions). **b) travel the world/country** to go to most parts of the world or most parts of a particular country

THESAURUS

Ways of traveling
drive or **go by car**
fly or **go by plane**
sail or **go by boat/ship**
take a train/bus/taxi/cab or **go by train/bus etc.**
walk/hike or **go on foot**
bike or **go by bike**

Someone who travels
traveler any person who is traveling
passenger someone who is traveling in a car, bus, train, airplane etc.
tourist someone who is traveling somewhere for a vacation
explorer someone who travels to places that people have not visited before

commuter someone who travels a long distance to work every day
→ AIRPORT, PASSPORT, TRIP

2 NEWS [I] to be passed quickly from one person or place to another: *News travels fast in a small town like this.*
3 DISTANCE [T] to go a particular distance: *We traveled 2,000 miles in 11 days.*
4 SPEED [I] to move at a particular speed: **+at** *The train was traveling at 100 mph.*
5 LIGHT/SOUND [I] to move at a particular speed or in a particular direction: *Light travels faster than sound.*
6 FOR BUSINESS [I] to go from place to place to do your work, especially work buying or selling products: **+for** *Do you have to travel a lot for work?*
7 FOOD/WINE [I] also **travel well** to remain in good condition when taken long distances
8 BASKETBALL [I] to take more than three steps while you are holding the ball in basketball
9 GO FAST [I] INFORMAL to move very quickly
10 EYES [I] LITERARY if your eyes travel over something, you look at different parts of it
[**Origin:** 1300–1400 Old French *travaillier* **to torture, work very hard**] → see also -TRAVELED, TRAVELING

travel² S3 W2 *n.* [U] **1** the act or activity of traveling: *The new job involves a lot of travel.* | **+to/from** *restrictions on travel to Cuba* | **foreign/international travel** *a huge increase in international travel* | **air/rail/road/space etc. travel** *Snow has made road travel difficult.* ►see THESAURUS box at **trip¹** **2 travels** [plural] trips to places that are far away: *Her travels have taken her all over Asia.* | *We met some interesting people **on** our **travels*** (=while traveling).

travel³ *adj.* [only before noun] **1** relating to the act or activity of traveling: *travel plans* **2** designed to be used when you are traveling: *a travel alarm clock*

travel ˌagency *n.* [C] an office or company that makes travel arrangements and organizes vacations for people

travel ˌagent *n.* [C] someone who owns or works in a travel agency

travel ˌbureau *n.* [C] a TRAVEL AGENCY

-traveled /trævəld/ *suffix* [in adjectives] **1 well-traveled/much-traveled** also **widely traveled** having traveled to many different countries: *a well-traveled businesswoman* **2 well-traveled/much-traveled/little-traveled etc.** having been traveled on or through by many or few people: *a well-traveled trade route*

trav·el·er /ˈtrævələ/ W3 *n.* [C] someone who is on a trip, or someone who travels often: **air/rail/space etc. travelers** *The strike will cause problems for air travelers.* | **+to/from** *a frequent traveler to Paris* | *special rates for **business travelers*** | **a seasoned traveler** (=one with a lot of experience traveling)

traveler's check *n.* [C] a special check that you buy, which can be exchanged for that amount of money later

travel exˌpense *n.* [C usually plural] the cost of traveling somewhere for work that is usually paid by your employer

trav·el·ing¹ /ˈtrævəlɪŋ/ *n.* [U] **1** the act or activity of going from one place to another, especially places that are far away: *After retiring, we'll do some traveling.* ►see THESAURUS box at **trip¹** **2** the mistake of taking more than three steps while holding the ball in basketball

traveling² *adj.* [only before noun] **1** relating to the act or activity of going from one place to another: *traveling expenses* | **the traveling public** (=all of the people in a country who travel different places) **2 a traveling musician/show/circus etc.** a musician, show etc. that goes from place to place in order to work or perform

traveling comˌpanion *n.* [C] someone you are on a trip with

traveling ˈsalesman *n.* [C] someone who goes from place to place, selling their company's products

travel inˌsurance *n.* [U] insurance for travelers against illness, accidents, loss of bags etc.

trav·el·ler /ˈtrævələ/ *n.* [C] the British and Canadian spelling of TRAVELER

trav·e·logue, travelog /ˈtrævəˌlɑg, -ˌlɔg/ *n.* [C] a movie, television program, or speech that describes travel in a particular country, or that describes a particular person's travels

tra·verse¹ /trəˈvəs/ *v.* [T] FORMAL to move across, over, or through something

trav·erse² /ˈtrævəs/ *n.* [C] TECHNICAL a sideways movement across a very steep slope, used in mountain climbing

trav·es·ty /ˈtrævəsti/ *n. plural* **travesties** [C] an extremely bad example of something, especially one in which the opposite result should have happened: *It would have been **a travesty of justice** not to punish them.*

trawl¹ /trɔl/ *v.* [I,T] **1** to fish by DRAGging a special wide net behind a boat **2** to search through a lot of documents, lists etc. in order to find out information: **+through** *Investigators trawled through the records.*

trawl² *n.* [C] **1** a wide net that is pulled along the bottom of the ocean to catch fish **2** a TRAWL LINE **3** an act of searching through a lot of documents, lists etc. in order to find something

trawl·er /ˈtrɔlə/ *n.* [C] a fishing boat that trawls

ˈtrawl line *n.* [C] a long fishing line to which many smaller lines are fastened

tray /treɪ/ S3 *n.* [C] **1** a flat piece of plastic, metal, or wood, with raised edges, used for carrying things such as plates, food etc.: *The waiter brought drinks on a tray.* **2** a flat open container with three sides used for holding something [**Origin:** Old English *trig, treg*] → see also ASHTRAY, BAKING TRAY

treach·er·ous /ˈtrɛtʃərəs/ *adj.* **1** someone who is treacherous cannot be trusted because they are not loyal and secretly intend to harm you **2** especially dangerous because you cannot see the dangers very easily: *a treacherous mountain road* —**treacherously** *adv.*

treach·er·y /ˈtrɛtʃəri/ *n. plural* **treacheries** **1** [U] actions that are not loyal to someone who trusts you, especially when these actions help their enemies: *an act of treachery* **2** [C usually plural] a disloyal action against someone who trusts you

trea·cle /ˈtrikəl/ *n.* [U] a way of expressing love and emotions in a way that is too SENTIMENTAL and seems silly or insincere [**Origin:** 1300–1400 Old French *triacle*, from Latin *theriaca*, from Greek *theriake* **cure for a poisonous bite**] —**treacly** *adj.*

tread¹ /trɛd/ *v. past tense* **trod** /trɑd/, *past participle* **trodden** /ˈtrɑdn/ or **trod** **1 tread carefully/warily/cautiously etc.** to be very careful about what you say or do in a difficult situation: *Companies should tread carefully in this area.* **2 tread water a)** to stay floating upright in deep water by moving your legs as if you are riding a bicycle **b)** to make no progress in a particular situation, especially because you are waiting for something to happen **3** [I always + adv./prep.,T] OLD-FASHIONED to walk or step on something SYN **step** **4 tread the boards** INFORMAL to work as an actor → see also **fools rush in (where angels fear to tread)** at FOOL¹ (7)

tread² *n.* **1** [C,U] the pattern of lines on the part of a tire that touches the road **2** [C] the pattern of lines on the bottom of a shoe **3** [C] TECHNICAL the part of a stair that you put your foot on **4** [singular] OLD-FASHIONED the particular sound that someone makes when they walk

tread·le /ˈtrɛdl/ *n.* [C] a flat piece of metal or wood that you move with your foot to turn a wheel in a machine

tread·mill /ˈtrɛdmɪl/ *n.* [C] **1** a piece of exercise equipment that has a large belt around a set of wheels, that moves when you walk or run on it **2** [singular] work or a way of life that seems very boring because you always have to do the same things **3** a MILL worked

T

in the past by prisoners walking on steps attached to a very large wheel

'treadmill test *n.* [C] a medical test in which you walk on a treadmill while electronic machines record how well your heart is working

treas. **1** the written abbreviation of TREASURY **2** the written abbreviation of TREASURER

trea·son /ˈtrizən/ *n.* [U] the crime of being disloyal to your country or its government, especially by helping its enemies or trying to remove the government using violence: **+against** *treason against the U.S. government* → see also HIGH TREASON

trea·son·a·ble /ˈtrizənəbəl/ also **trea·son·ous** /ˈtrizənəs/ *adj.* a treasonable offense can be punished as treason

treas·ure¹ /ˈtrɛʒɚ/ *n.* **1** [U] a collection of valuable things such as gold, silver, jewels etc., especially one that has been hidden somewhere: *The map showed where the treasure was.* | **buried/sunken treasure** (=treasure that is under the ground or in the ocean) **2** [C] a very valuable and important object such as a painting or ancient document: *the treasures of Ancient Egypt* **3** [C] something that you take great care of because it is very valuable or important to you: *The toy was one of my childhood treasures.* **4** [C usually singular] someone who is very useful or important to you → see also **one man's trash is another man's treasure** at TRASH¹ (5)

T

treasure² *v.* [T] to treat something as being very special, important, or valuable: *I treasure our friendship.* —**treasured** *adj.*: *a treasured possession*

'treasure ˌchest *n.* [C] a box that holds treasure

'treasure ˌhunt *n.* [C] a game in which you have to find something that has been hidden by answering questions that are left in different places

treas·ur·er /ˈtrɛʒərɚ/ *n.* [C] someone who is in charge of the money for an organization, club etc.

treasure trove /ˈtrɛʒɚ ˌtroʊv/ *n.* [C] a collection of valuable or interesting things or information

treas·ur·y /ˈtrɛʒəri/ *n. plural* **treasuries** **1 the Treasury (Department)** a government department that controls the money that the country collects and spends **2** [C] a place where money or valuable objects are kept in a castle, church, PALACE etc.

'Treasury ˌbill also **T-bill** *n.* [C] ECONOMICS a BOND sold by the U.S. government, which is worth its full amount in three months to one year. The government does this as a way of borrowing money for a short period of time. → see also TREASURY BOND, TREASURY NOTE

'Treasury bond also **T-bond** *n.* [C] ECONOMICS a BOND sold by the U.S. government, which is worth its full amount after ten years or longer. The government does this as a way of borrowing money for a long period of time. → see also TREASURY BILL, TREASURY NOTE

'Treasury note also **T-note** *n.* [C] ECONOMICS a BOND sold by the U.S. government, which is worth its full amount in one to ten years. The government does this as a way of borrowing money. → see also TREASURY BILL, TREASURY BOND

treat¹ /trit/ S2 W2 *v.* [T]

1 BEHAVE TOWARD SB [always + adv./prep.] to behave toward someone in a particular way: **treat sb like/as sth** *Mom still treats us like children.* | **treat sb badly/well/unfairly etc.** *The prisoners were well treated by their guards.* | **treat sb with respect/contempt/kindness etc.** *He treats all his employees with respect.* | **treat sb like dirt/a dog** (=to treat someone unkindly and without respect) | **treat sb like royalty** (=to treat someone very well)

2 DEAL WITH STH [always + adv./prep.] to deal with, discuss, or consider something in a particular way: **treat sth as sth** *She treats everything I say as a joke.* | **treat sth seriously/carefully/favorably etc.** *School officials are treating this matter very seriously.* | *Threats are never* ***treated lightly*** (=not treated seriously).

3 ILLNESS/INJURY/PATIENT to try to cure someone of an illness or injury by using drugs, hospital care, operations etc.: *The drugs are used to treat arthritis.* | **treat sb/sth with sth** *Many common infections can be treated with antibiotics.* | **treat sb for sth** *Doctors are treating him for cancer.*

4 BUY/DO STH FOR SB to buy something special for someone that you know they will enjoy, or to do something special with someone: **treat sb to sth** *We treated Mom to lunch at the Ritz.* | **treat yourself (to sth)** *Once a year, I treat myself to a ski trip.*

5 PROTECT/CLEAN STH to put a special substance on something or use a chemical process in order to protect, clean, or preserve it: **treat sth with sth** *The water is treated with chemicals.*

[**Origin:** 1200–1300 Old French *traitier*, from Latin *tractare* **to draw out, handle, treat**] → see also TRICK OR TREAT

treat with sb/sth *phr. v.* FORMAL to try to reach an official agreement with someone

treat² S2 *n.* **1** [C] a special food that tastes good, especially one that you do not eat very often: *a tasty treat for kids* **2** [C] something special that you give someone or do for them because you know they will enjoy it: *He took his son to the game as a birthday treat.* **3** [C usually singular] an event that gives you a lot of pleasure, especially if it is unexpected: *Getting your letter was a real treat.* **4 sb's treat** SPOKEN used to say that someone will pay for something such as a meal for someone else: *Let's go out for dinner – my treat.*

treat·a·ble /ˈtriṭəbəl/ *adj.* MEDICINE a treatable illness or injury can be helped with drugs or an operation

trea·tise /ˈtriṭɪs/ *n.* [C] a serious book or article about a particular subject: **+on** *a treatise on medical ethics*

treat·ment /ˈtritˀmənt/ S2 W1 *n.*

1 CURE [C,U] MEDICINE a method or process of trying to cure an injury or illness: *the most effective treatment available* | **+of/for** *advances in the treatment of cancer* | **+with** *Early treatment with antibiotics is vital.* | **get/receive/undergo treatment** *His wife urged him to get treatment for his depression.* | *Michael has* ***responded well to treatment*** (=got better when he was treated).

2 BEHAVIOR TOWARD SB [U] a particular way of behaving toward someone or of dealing with them: **+of** *concerns about the treatment of prisoners* | **special/preferential treatment** (=when one person is treated differently from another)

3 OF A SUBJECT [C,U] a particular way of dealing with or talking about a subject: **+of** *an interesting treatment of the subject of war*

4 CLEANING/PROTECTING [U] a process by which something is cleaned, protected etc.: **+of** *the treatment of radioactive waste* | **water/sewage treatment** *The city needs to improve its sewage treatment.*

5 MOVIE [C] TECHNICAL a description of a movie that someone wants to make

trea·ty /ˈtriṭi/ W3 *n. plural* **treaties** [C] POLITICS a formal written agreement between two or more countries or governments: *The Soviet Union and the U.S.* ***signed*** *a* ***treaty*** *reducing long-range missiles.* | *the* ***peace treaty*** *between Israel and Syria*

Treaty of Brest-Li·tovsk, the /ˌtriṭi əv ˌbrɛst lɪˈtɔfsk/ HISTORY a peace agreement signed on March 3 1918 by Germany and Russia, that ended Russia's involvement in World War I

Treaty of Ghent, the /ˌtriṭi əv ˈgɛnt/ HISTORY an agreement in 1814 which ended the War of 1812 between the U.S. and Great Britain

ˌTreaty of ˈParis, the HISTORY **1** an agreement in 1763 between Great Britain, France, and Spain which ended the Seven Years' War. Each country gave control of some foreign areas and islands to the others, and in particular France gave up control of land in North America and India. **2** an agreement in 1783 in which Great Britain accepted the INDEPENDENCE of the U.S.

Treaty of Ver·sailles, the /ˌtriṭi əv vɚˈsaɪ/ *n.* HISTORY a peace agreement signed on June 28, 1919 by Germany and the ALLIES at the end of World War I. As part of the agreement, Germany had to give the Allies land and money for causing the war.

tre·ble¹ /ˈtrɛbəl/ *adj., adv.* FORMAL **1** three times as big, as much, or as many as something else **2** a boy's treble voice produces high notes when he sings **3** a treble musical instrument produces higher sounds than some other members of its family

treble² *v.* [I,T] to become three times as big in amount, size, or number, or to make something increase in this way SYN **triple**

treble³ *n.* **1** [U] ENG. LANG. ARTS the upper half of the whole range of musical notes → see also BASS **2** [U] the part of a radio or piece of sound equipment that controls the upper half of the whole range of musical notes → see also BASS **3** [C] ENG. LANG. ARTS a boy with a high singing voice, or his voice

ˌtreble ˈclef *n.* [C] ENG. LANG. ARTS a sign (𝄞) at the beginning of a line of written music which shows that the note written on the bottom line of the STAVE is an E above MIDDLE C → see picture at MUSICAL[1]

tree /tri/ S1 W1 *n.* [C] **1** BIOLOGY a very tall plant that has a wooden trunk, branches, and leaves, and lives for many years: *The kids were climbing trees.* | **a maple/pine/peach etc. tree** *We have an apple tree in the backyard.*

THESAURUS

Types of tree
evergreen an evergreen tree does not lose its leaves in winter
deciduous a deciduous tree loses its leaves in winter
conifer a tree such as a pine or fir that has leaves like needles and produces cones containing seeds
fruit tree a tree that produces fruit that can be eaten

Areas of trees
wood/the woods a large area with many trees
woodland land covered with trees
copse a small group of trees
forest a very large area with a lot of trees growing closely together
rain forest a tropical forest with tall trees, in an area where it rains a lot
jungle a tropical forest with trees and large plants

Material from trees
wood the usual word for the hard material that trees are made of
lumber/timber wood used for building and making things
hardwood strong heavy wood from trees such as oak
softwood wood from trees such as pine and fir that is cheap and easy to cut
firewood wood that has been cut or collected in order to be burned in a fire

2 a drawing that shows how several things are related to each other by having lines that connect things **3 up a tree** INFORMAL in a difficult or embarrassing situation [**Origin:** Old English *treow*] → see also CHRISTMAS TREE, FAMILY TREE, **money doesn't grow on trees** at MONEY (20)

ˈtree fern *n.* [C] a large tropical FERN

tree·house /ˈtrihaʊs/ *n.* [C] a wooden structure for children to play in, built in the branches of a tree

ˈtree-ˌhugger *n.* [C] DISAPPROVING, INFORMAL someone who is concerned about the environment in a way that is sometimes not reasonable —**tree-hugging** *adj.* [only before noun] *tree-hugging environmentalists*

tree·less /ˈtrilɪs/ *adj.* a treeless area has no trees in it

ˈtree line *n.* [singular] the TIMBERLINE

ˈtree-lined *adj.* a tree-lined street has trees on both sides

ˈtree ˌsurgery *n.* [U] the treatment of damaged trees, especially by cutting off branches

tree·top /ˈtritɑp/ *n.* [C usually plural] the branches at the top of a tree

ˈtree-trunk *n.* [C] the thick central part of a tree

tre·foil /ˈtrifɔɪl, ˈtrɛ-/ *n.* [C] **1** BIOLOGY a type of small plant that has leaves that divide into three parts **2** a pattern in the shape of these leaves

trek¹ /trɛk/ *v.* **trekked, trekking** [I always + adv./prep.] **1** to make a long and difficult trip, especially on foot: *We had to trek a couple of miles to the nearest store.* **2** to walk a long way, especially in the mountains, as an adventure

trek² *n.* [C] **1** a long and difficult trip, made especially on foot: *a weeklong trek across the mountains* **2** INFORMAL a distance that seems long when you walk it: *It was quite a trek to the grocery store.* [**Origin:** 1800–1900 Afrikaans, Middle Dutch *trecken* **to pull, haul, move to new land**]

trel·lis /ˈtrɛlɪs/ *n.* [C] a frame made of long narrow pieces of wood that cross each other, used to support climbing plants

trem·ble /ˈtrɛmbəl/ *v.* [I] **1** to shake slightly in a way that you cannot control, especially because you are upset or frightened: *My hand trembled as I picked up the phone.* | **tremble with anger/fear/rage etc.** *The young woman trembled with fear.* ►see THESAURUS box at **shake¹** **2** to shake slightly: *The ground beneath them trembled as the trucks rolled past.* **3** if your voice trembles, it sounds nervous and unsteady **4** to be worried or frightened about something: **I tremble to think (that)** *I tremble to think what will happen when she finds out.* —**tremble** *n.* [C] —**trembly** *adj.*

tre·men·dous /trɪˈmɛndəs/ *adj.* **1** excellent: *a tremendous singing voice* **2** very big, fast, powerful, important etc.: *a tremendous explosion* | *The plan could save **a tremendous amount** of money.* | *The kids are under **tremendous pressure** to succeed.*

trem·o·lo /ˈtrɛməloʊ/ *n.* [C] rapidly repeated musical notes

trem·or /ˈtrɛmɚ/ *n.* [C] **1** EARTH SCIENCE a small EARTHQUAKE in which the ground shakes slightly **2** a slight shaking movement that you cannot control, especially because you are sick, weak, or upset **3** a nervous and unsteady sound in your voice **4** a feeling of excitement or fear

trem·u·lous /ˈtrɛmyələs/ *adj.* LITERARY shaking slightly, especially because you are nervous: *a tremulous voice* —**tremulously** *adv.*

trench /trɛntʃ/ *n.* [C] **1** a long narrow hole dug into the surface of the ground: *Workers dug a trench for gas lines.* **2** [C usually plural] a deep trench dug in the ground as a protection for soldiers **3 the trenches** the place or situation where most of the work or action in an activity takes place: *Lane left teaching after 30 years **in the trenches**.* → see also OCEAN TRENCH

tren·chant /ˈtrɛntʃənt/ *adj.* expressed very strongly, effectively, and directly, without worrying about offending people —**trenchantly** *adv.* —**trenchancy** *n.* [U]

ˈtrench coat *n.* [C] a long RAINCOAT with a belt

ˈtrench mouth *n.* [U] an infection of the mouth and throat

ˌtrench ˈwarfare *n.* [U] a method of fighting in which soldiers from opposing armies try to keep safe in TRENCHES across the BATTLEFIELD from each other

trend¹ /trɛnd/ Ac W2 *n.* [C] **1** a general tendency in the way a situation is changing or developing: *social and economic trends* | **+in** *trends in drug use among teenagers* | **+toward** *a worldwide trend toward smaller families* | *Davis is hoping to **reverse the trend*** (=make a trend go in the opposite direction) *of rising taxes.* | **a current/recent/present trend** *If current trends continue, tourism will increase by 10%.* | *There is **a growing trend** in the country toward buying organic foods.* **2** a way of doing something or a way of thinking that is becoming fashionable: **set the trend** to start doing something that other people copy: *fashion trends* | **start/set a trend** *A few small toy companies started the trend a decade ago.* | *Some people don't think for themselves, they just **follow** the latest **trends**.* → see also TRENDSETTER [**Origin:** Old English *trendan* **to turn, go around**]

T

trend² Ac *v.* [I always + adv./prep.] to show a general tendency in the way a situation is changing or developing: +**upward/downward/lower etc.** *Prices of new homes are trending upward.*

trend·set·ter /ˈtrɛndˌsɛt̬ɚ/ *n.* [C] someone who starts a new fashion or makes it popular —**trendsetting** *adj.*

ˈtrend-ˌspotter *n.* [C] someone who notices and reports on new fashions, activities that people are starting to do, or the way a situation is developing

trend·y /ˈtrɛndi/ *adj. comparative* **trendier**, *superlative* **trendiest** influenced by the most fashionable styles and ideas: *a trendy dance club* —**trendily** *adv.* —**trendiness** *n.* [U]

Tren·ton /ˈtrɛntˀn/ the capital city of the U.S. state of New Jersey

tre·pan /trɪˈpæn/ *v.* **trepanned, trepanning** [T] FORMAL to cut a round piece of bone out of your SKULL (=bone in your head) as part of a medical operation

trep·i·da·tion /ˌtrɛpəˈdeɪʃən/ *n.* [U] a feeling of anxiety or fear about something that is going to happen

tres·pass¹ /ˈtrɛspæs/ *v.* [I] **1** LAW to go onto someone's private land without their permission: +**on** *Do not trespass on the property.* ▸see THESAURUS box at **enter** **2** OLD USE to do something wrong SYN **sin** —**trespasser** *n.* [C]

trespass on sth *phr. v.* FORMAL to unfairly use more than you should of someone else's time, help etc. for your own advantage

trespass² *n.* **1** [C,U] LAW the offense of trespassing **2** [C] BIBLICAL something you have done that is morally wrong SYN **sin**

tres·pass·ing /ˈtrɛspæsɪŋ, -pəsɪŋ/ *n.* [U] the offense of going onto someone's land without their permission

tress·es /ˈtrɛsɪz/ *n.* [plural] LITERARY a woman's beautiful long hair

tres·tle /ˈtrɛsəl/ *n.* [C] **1** an A-shaped frame used as one of the supports for a table, shelf, or bridge **2** also **trestle bridge** a bridge with this kind of a frame supporting it

ˈtrestle ˌtable *n.* [C] a table made of a long board supported on trestles

Tre·vi·no /trəˈvinoʊ/, **Lee** /li/ (1939–) a U.S. golfer

trey /treɪ/ *n.* [C] INFORMAL **1** an action of throwing a basketball through the HOOP that is worth three points **2** a playing card or the side of a DIE or DOMINO with three marks on it

tri- /traɪ/ *prefix* three: *trilingual* (=speaking three languages) | *a triangle* (=shape with three sides) → see also BI-, DI-

tri·ad /ˈtraɪæd/ *n.* [C] **1** a group of three people or things that are related or similar to each other **2** a Chinese secret criminal group

tri·age /triˈɑʒ, ˈtriɑʒ/ *n.* [U] TECHNICAL the method of deciding who receives medical treatment first, according to how seriously someone is injured

tri·al /ˈtraɪəl/ S3 W1 *n.*

1 COURT [C,U] LAW a legal process in which a court of law examines a case to decide whether someone is guilty of a crime: *a murder trial* | *Both men* ***are on trial for*** (=are being judged in a court of law concerning) *bank robbery.* | *Warner will* ***stand trial on*** (=be judged in a court of law concerning) *charges of insurance fraud.* | **go/come to trial** (=to begin being judged in a court of law) → see also SHOW TRIAL

2 TEST [C,U] a process of testing to find out whether something works effectively and is safe: *The drug is undergoing* ***clinical trials.***

3 TRY SB/STH [C,U] a short period during which you use something or employ someone to find out whether they are satisfactory for a particular purpose or job: *Call today for your free trial!* | *Smith was hired* ***on a*** *six-month* ***trial basis.*** | *There is* ***a trial period*** *of one month during which you can return the car for a full refund.*

4 by/through trial and error if you do something by trial and error, you test many different methods of doing something in order to find the best: *They learned to farm through trial and error.*

5 DIFFICULTY [C usually plural] someone or something that is difficult to deal with, and that is worrying or annoying: *the* ***trials and tribulations*** *of being a single mother* | **be a trial (to/for sb)** *I was always a real trial to my parents.*

6 SPORTS trials [plural] a special sports competition in which people who want to be on a team are tested, so that the best can be chosen: *the Olympic trials*

7 (a) trial by fire a difficult experience that tests how able someone is to deal with difficult situations

ˈtrial balˌloon *n.* [C] something that you do or say in order to see whether other people will accept something or not: *The senator is* ***floating trial balloons*** *to test public opinion on the bill.*

ˌtrial ˈrun *n.* [C] an occasion when you test a new method or system to see if it works well

triangles

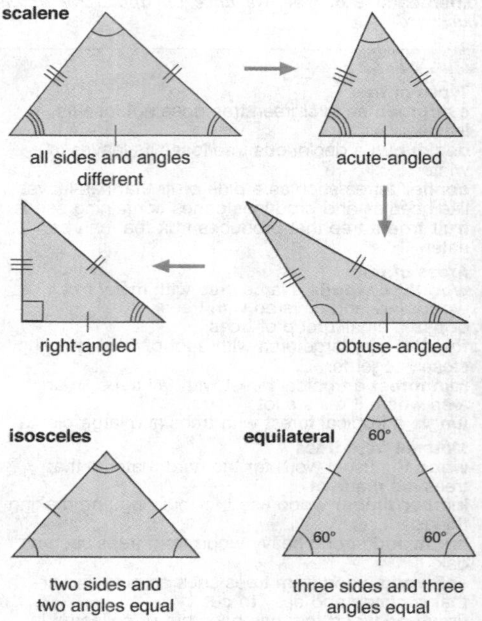

tri·an·gle /ˈtraɪˌæŋgəl/ *n.* [C] **1** MATH a flat shape with three straight sides ▸see THESAURUS box at **shape¹** **2** something that is shaped like a triangle **3** ENG. LANG. ARTS a musical instrument made of metal bent in the shape of a triangle, that you hit to make a ringing sound **4** MATH a flat plastic object with three sides that has one angle of 90° and is used for drawing angles → see also LOVE TRIANGLE

tri·an·gu·lar /traɪˈæŋgyəlɚ/ *adj.* **1** shaped like a triangle ▸see THESAURUS box at **shape¹** **2** involving three people or teams: *a triangular relationship*

triˌangular ˈtrade *n.* [singular] HISTORY a type of trade that happened in the past, in which goods were taken from Europe to Africa, SLAVES were taken from Africa to North, Central, and South America, and substances such as sugar were taken from the Americas to Europe

tri·an·gu·la·tion /traɪˌæŋgyəˈleɪʃən/ *n.* [U] a method of finding your position by measuring the lines and angles of a triangle on a map

tri·ath·lete /traɪˈæθlit/ *n.* [C] someone who takes part in triathlons

tri·ath·lon /traɪˈæθlɑn, -lən/ *n.* [C] a sports competition in which competitors run, swim, and ride a bicycle for long distances

trib·al /ˈtraɪbəl/ *adj.* relating to a tribe or tribes: *tribal leaders* | *tribal warfare*

trib·al·ism /ˈtraɪbəˌlɪzəm/ *n.* [U] **1** the state of being organized into tribes **2** POLITICS behavior and attitudes that are based on strong loyalty to your tribe

tribe /traɪb/ W3 *n.* [C] **1** a social group consisting of related families who have the same beliefs, customs, language etc., and who usually live in one particular area ruled by their leader: *nomadic tribes* ►see THESAURUS box at race[1] **2** HUMOROUS a large family: *The whole tribe turned up.* **3** TECHNICAL a group of related animals or plants [**Origin:** 1200–1300 Latin *tribus* **group within the Roman people, tribe**]

tribes·man /ˈtraɪbzmən/ *n. plural* **tribesmen** /-mən/ [C] a man who is a member of a tribe

tribes·wom·an /ˈtraɪbzˌwʊmən/ *n. plural* **tribeswomen** /-ˌwɪmɪn/ [C] a woman who is a member of a tribe

trib·u·la·tion /ˌtrɪbyəˈleɪʃən/ *n.* [C,U] FORMAL serious trouble or a serious problem: *the tribulations of his personal life* → see also TRIAL

tri·bu·nal /traɪˈbyunl, trɪ-/ *n.* [C] a type of court that is given official authority to deal with a particular situation or problem: *a war-crimes tribunal*

trib·une /ˈtrɪbyun, trɪˈbyun/ *n.* [C] an official in ancient Rome who was elected by the ordinary people to protect their rights

tri·bu·tar·y[1] /ˈtrɪbyəˌtɛri/ *n. plural* **tributaries** [C] EARTH SCIENCE a stream or river that flows into a larger river

tributary[2] *adj.* FORMAL having a duty to pay TRIBUTE: *a tributary state*

trib·ute /ˈtrɪbyut/ *n.* **1** [C,U] something that you say, do, or give in order to express your respect or admiration for someone: **+to** *The song is a tribute to his grandfather.* | *Friends* ***paid tribute to*** (=praised and admired publicly) *the officer's courage.* | *The money was given to the organization* ***in tribute to*** *the soldiers.* | *The event was* ***a fitting tribute*** *to one of the game's greatest players.* **2 be a tribute to sb/sth** to be a clear sign of the good qualities that someone or something has: *It's a tribute to her teaching that so many of her students love school.* **3** [C,U] a payment of goods or money by one ruler or country to a more powerful one [**Origin:** 1300–1400 Latin *tributum*, from *tribuere* **to give out to the tribes, pay**]

trice /traɪs/ *n.* **in a trice** LITERARY very quickly

tri·ceps /ˈtraɪsɛps/ *n. plural* **triceps** [C] BIOLOGY the large muscle at the back of your upper arm

trick[1] /trɪk/ S3 *n.* [C]

1 DECEIVE SB something you do in order to deceive someone: *The story was just a trick to get me to give him money.*

2 JOKE something you do to surprise someone and to make other people laugh: *The girls were always* ***playing tricks on*** *each other.*

3 MAGIC something you do to entertain people, especially something that looks like magic or is very unusual or skillful: *card tricks* | **do/perform a trick** *The dog did a few tricks with a ball.*

4 SMART METHOD a way of doing something that works very well: *I know a trick for remembering names.* | ***The trick is*** *to add the milk to the mix slowly.* | *After 20 years as a lawyer, he knows all* ***the tricks of the trade*** (=methods used in a particular job).

5 STH CONFUSING something that makes things appear to be different from the way they really are: *It must have been a trick of the light.* | *Your imagination can* ***play tricks on*** *you.*

6 do the trick SPOKEN if something does the trick, it solves a problem or provides what is needed to get a good result: *These pills should do the trick.*

7 a dirty/rotten/mean/cheap etc. trick an unkind or unfair thing to do

8 use/try every trick in the book to use or try every method that you know, even dishonest ones, to achieve what you want: *Vicki used every trick in the book to get Patty fired.*

9 be up to your (old) tricks INFORMAL to be doing the same dishonest things that you have often done before

10 sb's bag/arsenal etc. of tricks someone's methods they can use to achieve what they want

11 CARDS [C] the cards played or won in one part of a game of cards

12 have a trick up your sleeve INFORMAL to have a smart plan or idea that you can use if you need to: *If that doesn't work, I have a couple more tricks up my sleeve.*

13 sb can teach/show sb a trick or two INFORMAL used to say that someone knows more than someone else or can do something better than them

14 SEX INFORMAL **a)** someone who pays a PROSTITUTE to have sex **b)** a sex partner that you do not know well or care much about

15 how's tricks? SPOKEN, OLD-FASHIONED used to greet someone in a friendly way

[**Origin:** 1400–1500 Old North French *trique*, from *trikier* **to deceive, cheat**, from Old French *trichier*] → see also CONFIDENCE TRICK, HAT TRICK, **sb doesn't miss a trick** at MISS[1] (14), **you can't teach an old dog new tricks** at TEACH (7)

trick[2] *v.* [T] to deceive someone in order to get something from them or to make them do something: *You tricked me!* | **trick sb into doing sth** *She was tricked into signing the document.* | **trick sb out of sth** *Winston had tricked the elderly couple out of $5,000.* ►see THESAURUS box at cheat[1]

trick sth ↔ out *phr. v.* INFORMAL to decorate or dress someone or something in a special way —**tricked out** *adj.*

trick[3] *adj.* [only before noun] **1** used to describe things that are designed or made to deceive people: *trick photography* | *The trick mirrors make you look fatter than you are.* **2 a trick question** a question that seems easy to answer but has a hidden difficulty **3 a trick knee/ankle/shoulder etc.** a joint that is weak and can suddenly cause you problems

trick·er·y /ˈtrɪkəri/ *n.* [U] the use of tricks to deceive or cheat people

trick·le[1] /ˈtrɪkəl/ *v.* [I always + adv./prep.] **1** if liquid trickles somewhere, it flows slowly in drops or in a thin stream: **+down/into/out** *Blood trickled down the side of her head.* ►see THESAURUS box at flow[1] **2** if people, vehicles, goods etc. trickle somewhere, they move there slowly in small groups or amounts: **+in/into/away** *The first few fans started to trickle into the stadium.*

trickle down *phr. v.* if money, ideas, or advantages trickle down, they move slowly from the richest or most important people to the poorest or least important people

trickle[2] *n.* **1** [C] a thin slow flow of liquid: *A trickle of juice ran down his chin.* **2** [singular] a movement of people, vehicles, goods etc. into a place in very small numbers or amounts

ˈtrickle-down *adj.* [only before noun] relating to the belief that additional wealth gained by the richest people in society will have a good economic effect on the lives of everyone because they will put the money into businesses, INVESTMENTS etc.: *trickle-down economics*

ˌtrick or ˈtreat *interjection* said by children when they go trick-or-treating, in order to say that they will play a trick on someone if they are not given a TREAT (=piece of candy)

ˌtrick-or-ˈtreating *n.* [U] an activity in which children dress in COSTUMES on Halloween and go from house to house saying "trick or treat" in order to get candy

trick·ster /ˈtrɪkstɚ/ *n.* [C] someone who deceives or cheats people

trick·y /ˈtrɪki/ S3 *adj. comparative* **trickier**, *superlative* **trickiest** **1** a tricky situation or job is difficult to deal with or do because it is very complicated and full of problems: *Getting everyone to use the new computer system will be tricky.* | ***The tricky part*** *is keeping the players' enthusiasm up when they lose a lot.* ►see THESAURUS box at difficult **2** a tricky person is likely to deceive you SYN crafty —**trickiness** *n.* [U] —**trickily** *adv.*

T

tri·col·or /ˈtraɪˌkʌlɚ/ *n.* [C] a flag with three equal bands of different colors, especially the national flags of France or Ireland

tri·cus·pid valve /traɪˈkʌspɪd ˌvælv/ *n.* [C] BIOLOGY a part on the right side of your heart that opens and closes to allow blood to flow from the right ATRIUM into the right VENTRICLE and prevent blood from flowing back into the atrium → see picture at HEART

tri·cy·cle /ˈtraɪsɪkəl/ *n.* [C] a bicycle with three wheels, especially one for young children

tri·dent /ˈtraɪdnt/ *n.* [C] **1** a weapon with three points that looks like a large fork **2 Trident** also **Trident missile/submarine** a type of NUCLEAR weapon, or the SUBMARINE that shoots it

tried[1] /traɪd/ *v.* the past tense and past participle of TRY

tried[2] *adj.* **tried and tested** also **tried and true** a tried and tested method has been used successfully many times

tri·en·ni·al /traɪˈɛniəl/ *adj.* happening every three years

tri·fle[1] /ˈtraɪfəl/ *n.* **1 a trifle tired/nervous/sleepy etc.** FORMAL slightly tired, nervous etc. **2** [C] OLD-FASHIONED something unimportant or not valuable **3** [C,U] a cold sweet DESSERT that consists of layers of cake, fruit, JELL-O, CUSTARD, and cream [**Origin:** 1200–1300 Old French *trufe*, *trufle* **deceiving, making fun**]

trifle[2] *v.*
trifle with sb/sth *phr. v.* to treat someone or something without enough respect or seriousness

tri·fling /ˈtraɪflɪŋ/ *adj.* unimportant or of little value: *a trifling matter*

tri·fo·cals /ˈtraɪˌfoʊkəlz/ *n.* [plural] special glasses in which the upper part of the LENS is made for seeing things that are far away, the lower part is made for reading, and the middle part is for seeing things in between → see also BIFOCALS

trig /trɪg/ *n.* [U] SPOKEN TRIGONOMETRY

trig. the written abbreviation of TRIGONOMETRY

trig·ger[1] /ˈtrɪgɚ/ Ac *n.* [C] **1** the part of a gun that you press with your finger to fire it: **pull/squeeze the trigger** *Jackson is convinced Ray pulled the trigger.* **2 be the trigger (for sth)** to be the thing that quickly causes a serious problem: *The hijacking became a trigger for military action.* → see also HAIR-TRIGGER[1], **whatever trips your trigger** at WHATEVER[1] (8)

trigger[2] Ac also **trigger off** *v.* [T] **1** to make something happen very quickly, especially a series of violent events: *The incident could trigger a civil war.* ▸see THESAURUS box at **cause**[2] **2** to suddenly make someone have a particular feeling, memory, or reaction: *Exercise may trigger an asthma attack.* **3** to make something such as a bomb or electrical system start to operate: *The burglars fled after* ***triggering the alarm****.*

ˈtrigger-ˌhappy *adj.* INFORMAL much too willing to shoot at people

ˈtrigger ˌman *n.* [C] the person who shoots someone, especially a criminal who does this

trig·o·nom·e·try /ˌtrɪgəˈnɑmətri/ *n.* [U] MATH the part of mathematics that is concerned with the relationship between the angles and sides of TRIANGLES —**trigonometrical** /ˌtrɪgənəˈmɛtrɪkəl/ *adj.*

trike /traɪk/ *n.* [C] INFORMAL a TRICYCLE

tri·lat·er·al /ˌtraɪˈlæt̬ərəl◂/ *adj.* involving or including three groups or countries: *a trilateral agreement*

tril·by /ˈtrɪlbi/ *n. plural* **trilbies** [C] a man's soft FELT hat [**Origin:** 1800–1900 *Trilby*, female character in the book "Trilby" (1894) by George du Maurier, who in the stage version of the book wore such a hat]

tri·lin·gual /ˌtraɪˈlɪŋgwəl◂/ *adj.* able to speak or use three languages

trill[1] /trɪl/ *v.* [I,T] **1** to sing or play a musical instrument with repeated short high notes **2** to say something in a pleasant high cheerful voice

trill[2] *n.* [C] **1** ENG. LANG. ARTS a musical sound made by quickly going up and down several times between two notes a HALF STEP apart **2** BIOLOGY a sound like a trill, especially one made by a bird **3** ENG. LANG. ARTS a speech sound produced by quickly moving the end of your tongue against the top part of your mouth when you pronounce the sound /r/

tril·lion /ˈtrɪlyən/ *number, quantifier* **1** 1,000,000,000,000 **2** also **trillions** INFORMAL a very large number of something

tri·lo·bite /ˈtraɪləˌbaɪt/ *n.* [C] BIOLOGY a small simple sea creature that lived millions of years ago and is now a FOSSIL

tril·o·gy /ˈtrɪlədʒi/ *n. plural* **trilogies** [C] a group of three related plays, books, movies etc. about the same characters: *the "Lord of the Rings" trilogy*

trim[1] /trɪm/ *v.* **trimmed, trimming** [T] **1** to make something look neater by cutting small pieces off it: *Someone needs to trim the hedge.* | **trim your hair/beard/nails etc.** *I need to trim my mustache.* ▸see THESAURUS box at **cut**[1] **2** to remove parts of a plan in order to reduce its cost: **trim sth from/off sth** *They plan to trim $200 million from the budget.* | **trim sth by 10%/$4 million etc.** *The bill would trim welfare spending by $5 billion.* **3** [usually passive] to decorate something, especially the edges of clothes, by putting something on it: **trim sth with sth** *Her black dress was trimmed with blue ribbon.* | *Three weeks before Christmas we get together and* ***trim the tree*** (=decorate the Christmas tree). **4** to move the sails of a boat into a position that makes the boat go faster
trim sth ↔ **away** *phr. v.* to cut small pieces off something, especially so that it looks neater SYN **trim off**
trim sth ↔ **back** *phr. v.* **1** to reduce a number, amount, or the size of something SYN **cut back**: *Most airlines have trimmed back their operations.* **2** to make something shorter or smaller by cutting it SYN **cut back**
trim down *phr. v.* **1** to lose weight deliberately **2 trim sth ↔ down** to reduce the size, number, or amount of something SYN **cut down**: *The book was trimmed down to just 82 pages.*
trim sth ↔ **off** *phr. v.* to cut small pieces off something, especially so that it looks neater SYN **cut off** SYN **trim away**: *Trim off the excess pastry.*

trim[2] *adj.* **1** thin, attractive, and healthy looking: *Walking to work helps her keep trim.* | *a trim figure* **2** neat and well taken care of: *a trim suburban yard*

trim[3] *n.* **1** [C usually singular] an act of cutting something to make it look neater: *I'm going to the barbershop to get a trim.* **2** [singular, U] decoration on a car, piece of clothing etc., that goes along the length of it: *a blue house with white trim* **3** [U] the degree to which an aircraft is level in relation to the horizon

tri·ma·ran /ˈtraɪməˌræn/ *n.* [C] a sailing boat that has three separate but connected parts that float on the water

tri·mes·ter /ˈtraɪmɛstɚ, traɪˈmɛstɚ/ *n.* [C] **1** BIOLOGY one of the three-month periods of a PREGNANCY **2** one of three periods of equal length that the year is divided into in some schools → see also TERM[1]

trim·mer /ˈtrɪmɚ/ *n.* [C] a machine for cutting the edges of HEDGES, LAWNS etc.

trim·mings /ˈtrɪmɪŋz/ *n.* [plural] **1 all the trimmings** all the other types of food that are traditionally served with the main dish of a meal: *Thanksgiving dinner with all the trimmings* **2** the small pieces that have been cut off something larger: *tree trimmings* **3** pieces of material used to decorate clothes

Trin·i·dad and To·ba·go /ˌtrɪnɪdæd ən təˈbeɪgoʊ/ a country in the south Caribbean Sea, close to the coast of Venezuela, and consisting of the islands of Trinidad and Tobago —**Trinidadian** /ˌtrɪnɪˈdædiən/ *n., adj.*

trin·i·ty /ˈtrɪnət̬i/ *n. plural* **trinities** **1 the Trinity** the union of Father, Son, and Holy Spirit in one God, according to the Christian religion **2** [C] LITERARY a group of three people or things

trin·ket /ˈtrɪŋkɪt/ *n.* [C] a piece of jewelry or a small pretty object that is not worth much money

tri·o /ˈtrioʊ/ *n. plural* **trios** [C] **1** a group of three singers or musicians who perform together: *a jazz trio* **2** a group of three people or three related things: **+of** *an interesting trio of poems* **3** a piece of music for three performers → see also DUET, QUARTET

trip¹ /trɪp/ S1 W1 *n.* [C] **1** an occasion when you travel from one place to another SYN **journey**: *How was your trip?* | **+to** *a trip to New York* | *Let's* ***take a trip*** *to Mexico.* | *They're* ***going on a trip*** *to Canada this summer.* | *He was unable to* ***make the trip*** *to accept the award.* | **a business/school/skiing etc. trip** *a business trip to Japan*

THESAURUS

travel/traveling the general activity of going from one place to another, especially for long distances and long periods of time: *a special ticket for train travel around Europe* | *I haven't really done much traveling.*
journey FORMAL a trip that is long or difficult: *the journey across the plains in a covered wagon*
travels trips to places that are far away, or the act of moving from place to place over a period of time: *her travels in South America*
voyage a trip in which you travel by ship or in a spacecraft, used mainly in stories: *Columbus's voyage across the ocean*
tour a trip for pleasure, during which you visit several different towns, areas etc.: *a tour of Europe*
expedition a long and carefully organized trip, especially to a dangerous or unfamiliar place: *Lewis and Clark's expedition across North America*
excursion a short trip to visit a place, usually by a group of people: *an all-day excursion to Catalina Island*
pilgrimage a trip to a holy place for religious reasons: *a pilgrimage to Lourdes*
commute a trip to or from work that someone does every day: *my daily commute*
crossing a trip by boat from one piece of land to another: *The Atlantic crossing was rough and stormy.*
cruise a trip by boat for pleasure: *a cruise in the Caribbean*
flight a trip in an airplane: *How was your flight?*

2 an occasion when you walk or drive somewhere, for a particular purpose: **+to** *a quick trip to the grocery store* | *We had to* ***make*** *three* ***trips*** *to get everything in the house.* **3** [usually singular] INFORMAL a person or experience that is amusing and very different from normal: *You're a trip.* **4** SLANG the experiences someone has while their mind is affected by a drug such as LSD: *a bad trip* **5** an act of falling as a result of hitting something with your foot → see also ROUND TRIP

trip

trip² S2 *v.* **tripped, tripping**
1 FALL [I] to hit something with your foot while you are walking or running so that you fall or almost fall: *She tripped and hurt her knee.* | **+over/on** *He almost tripped over the dog.* ►see THESAURUS box at **fall¹**
2 MAKE SB FALL [T] to make someone fall by putting your foot in front of them when they are moving: *She put her foot out to trip him as he passed.*
3 TURN ON to accidentally turn on a piece of electrical equipment: *An intruder had tripped the alarm.*
4 WALK/DANCE [I always + adv./prep.] LITERARY to walk or run with quick light steps as if you are dancing: **trip along/over/down etc.** *She watched her two kids tripping down the sidewalk.*
5 be tripping over yourself to do sth also **be tripping over each other to do sth** INFORMAL to be very eager to do something, especially when this seems very surprising: *Suddenly everyone was tripping over each other to praise her.*
6 sb is tripping SLANG used to say that you think someone is not thinking clearly or being reasonable: *Ken's tripping if he thinks I'm going to lend him $500.*
7 be tripping on sb/sth SLANG to enjoy someone or something and think about how unusual they are
8 DRUG [I] SLANG to experience the effects of an illegal drug such as LSD SYN **trip out**
9 trip the light fantastic OLD-FASHIONED to dance
[**Origin:** 1300–1400 Old French *triper*] → see also **roll/trip off sb's tongue** at TONGUE¹ (6), **whatever trips your trigger** at WHATEVER¹ (8)

trip out *phr. v.* SLANG **1** to experience the effects of an illegal drug such as LSD SYN **trip** **2 trip sb ↔ out** SLANG if you trip out or someone or something trips you out, you are surprised by how unusual something is

trip up *phr. v.* **trip sb ↔ up** to trick someone into making a mistake: *The questions are designed to trip you up.*

tri·par·tite /traɪˈpɑrtaɪt/ *adj.* FORMAL **1** POLITICS involving three groups or nations: *a tripartite alliance* **2** having three parts

tripe /traɪp/ *n.* [U] **1** INFORMAL something that has been said or written which is stupid or not true **2** the stomach of a cow or pig used for food

tri·ple¹ /ˈtrɪpəl/ *adj.* [only before noun] **1** having three parts or involving three people or groups: *a triple-layer chocolate cake* | *a triple homicide* | *numbers in the* ***triple digits*** (=at least 100, but less than 1,000) **2** three times more than the usual number or amount, or than a previous number or amount: *a triple shot of espresso* → see also DOUBLE, QUADRUPLE

triple² *v.* [I,T] to become three times as much or as many, or to make something do this: *The population of the valley has tripled in the past 20 years.* | *We hope to triple our profits by next year.* → see also DOUBLE, QUADRUPLE

triple³ *n.* [C] **1** a hit of the ball in BASEBALL that allows the BATTER to reach the third BASE **2** three turns of your body in the same direction in sports such as ICE SKATING, GYMNASTICS etc.

Triple A /ˌtrɪpəl ˈeɪ/ *n.* AAA

ˌTriple Alˈliance HISTORY an agreement made in 1882 by Germany, Austria-Hungary, and Italy in which they promised to give each other military support if any of them were attacked by two or more great powers

ˌTriple Enˈtente HISTORY an agreement made before World War I between France, Russia, and the United Kingdom, in which they agreed to support each other

ˈtriple jump *n.* **the triple jump** a sports event in which you try to jump as far as you can by jumping first with one foot, then onto the other foot, and finally with both feet together

ˈtriple play *n.* [C] the action of making three OUTS at one time in baseball → see also DOUBLE PLAY

tri·plet /ˈtrɪplɪt/ *n.* [C] **1** one of three children born at the same time to the same mother **2** [C] ENG. LANG. ARTS three musical notes or BEATS that are played together or quickly one after the other

trip·lex /ˈtraɪplɛks, ˈtrɪ-/ *n.* [C] **1** a house that has three separate parts that different people live in → see also DUPLEX **2** a movie theater with three separate movie screens

trip·li·cate /ˈtrɪpləkɪt/ *n.* **in triplicate** if a document is written in triplicate, there are three copies of it

tri·pod /ˈtraɪpɑd/ *n.* [C] an object with three legs, used to support a camera, TELESCOPE etc.

tripod

Trip·ol·i /ˈtrɪpəli/ the capital and largest city of Libya

trip·tych /ˈtrɪptɪk/ *n.* [C] ENG. LANG. ARTS a picture, especially a religious one, painted on three pieces of wood that are joined together

trip·wire /ˈtrɪpˌwaɪɚ/ *n.* [C] a wire stretched across the ground as part of a trap

tri·reme /ˈtraɪrim/ *n.* [C] an ancient WARSHIP with three rows of OARS on each side

tri·sect /ˈtraɪsɛkt, traɪˈsɛkt/ *v.* [T] TECHNICAL to divide a line, angle etc. into three equal parts → see also BISECT

tri-state /ˈtraɪsteɪt/ *adj.* relating to a group of three states in the U.S.

trite /traɪt/ *adj.* a trite remark, idea etc. has been used so often that it seems boring and not sincere —**triteness** *n.* [U]

tri·umph[1] /ˈtraɪəmf/ *n.* [C] **1** an important victory or success, especially after a difficult struggle: *Winning the championship is a great personal triumph.* | +**over** *the triumph of science over diseases like smallpox* **2** a feeling of pleasure and satisfaction that you get from victory or success: *a yell of triumph* **3** a very successful example of something: +**of** *The bridge is a triumph of engineering.*

triumph[2] *v.* [I] to gain a victory or success, especially after a difficult struggle: +**over** *Good will triumph over evil.*

tri·um·phal /traɪˈʌmfəl/ *adj.* [only before noun] done or made in order to celebrate a triumph

tri·umph·al·ism /traɪˈʌmfəˌlɪzəm/ *n.* [U] DISAPPROVING the feeling of being too proud about a victory and too pleased about your opponent's defeat —**triumphalist** *adj.*

tri·um·phant /traɪˈʌmfənt/ *adj.* **1** expressing pleasure and pride because of your victory or success: *a triumphant grin* **2** having gained a victory or success: *the triumphant women's gymnastics team* **3** a triumphant event is one in which someone succeeds in something or wins something, or celebrates this success or win: *the army's triumphant return* —**triumphantly** *adv.*

tri·um·vi·rate /traɪˈʌmvərət/ *n.* [C] FORMAL a group of three very powerful people who share control over something

triv·et /ˈtrɪvət/ *n.* [C] **1** an object placed under a hot pot or dish to protect the surface of a table, which is usually made of metal or wood **2** an object for holding a pot over a fire

triv·i·a /ˈtrɪviə/ *n.* [U] **1** detailed facts about past events, famous people, sports etc., often used in games **2** unimportant or useless details: *The news reports tend to focus on trivia.*

triv·i·al /ˈtrɪviəl/ *adj.* unimportant or of little value: *She gets upset over trivial matters.* [**Origin:** 1400–1500 Latin *trivialis* **found everywhere, common**, from *trivium* **place where three roads meet, crossroads**] —**trivially** *adv.*

triv·i·al·i·ty /ˌtrɪviˈæləti/ *n. plural* **trivialities** **1** [U] the fact of being not important or serious at all **2** [C] something that is not important at all

triv·i·al·ize /ˈtrɪviəˌlaɪz/ *v.* [T] to make an important subject seem less important than it really is: *The article trivializes an important issue.* —**trivialization** /ˌtrɪviələˈzeɪʃən/ *n.* [U]

tRNA /ˌti ɑr ɛn ˈeɪ/ *n.* [U] BIOLOGY the abbreviation of TRANSFER RNA

tro·chee /ˈtroʊki/ *n.* [C] ENG. LANG. ARTS a unit in poetry consisting of one strong or long beat followed by one weak or short beat, as in "father"

trod /trɑd/ *v.* the past tense and part participle of TREAD

trod·den /ˈtrɑdn/ *v.* the past participle of TREAD

trog·lo·dyte /ˈtrɑgləˌdaɪt/ *n.* [C] **1** someone living in a CAVE, especially in very ancient times **2** an insulting name for someone who is stupid, badly educated, or old-fashioned in their ideas

troi·ka /ˈtrɔɪkə/ *n.* [C] **1** a group of three people working together, especially in government **2** a Russian carriage pulled by three horses side by side

Tro·jan /ˈtroʊdʒən/ HISTORY one of the people that lived in the ancient city of Troy, whose war with the Greeks is described by the Greek poet Homer

ˌTrojan ˈHorse *n.* [C] **1** something that seems ordinary but that is used to hide someone's real intention **2** COMPUTERS a type of computer VIRUS

troll[1] /troʊl/ *n.* [C] an imaginary creature in ancient Scandinavian stories, like a very large or very small ugly person

troll[2] *v.* [I,T] **1** to try to obtain something by searching, asking people etc.: **troll (sth) for sth** *Stewart spent hours trolling the Web for information.* **2** to try to remove something from a river, ocean etc. by pulling a rope, net etc. through the water

trol·ley /ˈtrɑli/ *n.* [C] **1** also **trolley car** an electric vehicle for carrying passengers which moves along the street on metal tracks **2** a TROLLEYBUS **3** the part of an electric vehicle that connects it to the electric wires above

trol·ley·bus /ˈtrɑliˌbʌs/ *n.* [C] a bus that gets its power from electric wires above the street

trol·lop /ˈtrɑləp/ *n.* [C] OLD-FASHIONED OR HUMOROUS **1** an insulting word for a sexually immoral woman **2** an insulting word for a very messy woman

Trol·lope /ˈtrɑləp/, **An·tho·ny** /ˈænθəni/ (1815–1882) an English writer of NOVELS

trom·bone /trɑmˈboʊn/ *n.* [C] a large musical instrument made of metal that you blow into, and which has a long tube that you slide in and out to change the notes

trom·bon·ist /trɑmˈboʊnɪst/ *n.* [C] a musician who plays a trombone

tromp /trɑmp, trɔmp/ *v.* [I always + adv./prep.] to walk around or through somewhere with firm heavy steps

troop[1] /trup/ W1 *n.* **1 troops** [plural] soldiers, especially in organized groups: *Both countries agreed to* ***deploy troops*** (=send them) *in the region.* | *The President has promised to* ***withdraw the troops*** *soon.* | **troop movements/concentrations/deployment etc.** (=movement, gathering etc. of troops) **2** [C] a group of boy or girl SCOUTS led by an adult **3** [C] a group of soldiers, especially on horses or in TANKS **4** [C] a group of people or wild animals, especially when they are moving [**Origin:** 1500–1600 French, Late Latin *troppus* **group of sheep**] → see also TROUPE

troop[2] *v.* [I always + adv./prep.] to move together in a group: +**into/along/out etc.** *The team trooped out of the clubhouse and onto the field.*

ˈtroop ˌcarrier *n.* [C] a ship, aircraft, or land vehicle used for carrying soldiers

troop·er /ˈtrupɚ/ *n.* **1** [C] the lowest ranking soldier in the part of the army that uses TANKS or horses **2** [C] a member of a state police force in the U.S. SYN **state trooper** **3 sb's a (real) trooper** SPOKEN used to say that someone works hard and keeps trying, even when the situation is difficult **4 swear like a trooper** to swear a lot

troop·ship /ˈtrupˌʃɪp/ *n.* [C] a ship used for carrying a large number of soldiers

trope /troʊp/ *n.* [C] ENG. LANG. ARTS a FIGURE OF SPEECH

tro·phy /ˈtroʊfi/ *n. plural* **trophies** [C] **1** a prize for winning a race or other competition, especially a large metal cup or STATUE: *the NCAA championship trophy* **2** something that you keep to show that you have been successful in something, especially in war or hunting: *hunting trophies*

trophy wife *n. plural* **trophy wives** [C] DISAPPROVING a young beautiful woman who is married to a rich, successful, and usually older man

trop·ic /ˈtrɑpɪk/ *n.* EARTH SCIENCE **1 the tropics** [plural] the hottest part of the world, which is between the Tropic of Cancer and the Tropic of Capricorn **2** [C] one of the two imaginary lines around the world, either the Tropic of Cancer which is 23½° north of the EQUATOR, or the Tropic of Capricorn which is 23½° south of the EQUATOR → see picture at GLOBE

trop·i·cal /ˈtrɑpɪkəl/ *adj.* **1** coming from or existing in the hottest parts of the world: *tropical birds | tropical diseases | a tropical island* **2** EARTH SCIENCE tropical weather is very hot and wet: *a tropical storm* **3 tropical Africa/Asia/America etc.** EARTH SCIENCE used to talk about the parts of Africa, Asia etc. that are within the tropics

tropical ˈcyclone *n.* [C] EARTH SCIENCE a CYCLONE (=very strong wind that moves very fast in a circle) that forms over tropical oceans

tropical ˈstorm *n.* [C] EARTH SCIENCE a storm in a tropical area with a wind speed of more than 39 miles per hour

tropical ˌzone *n.* [C] EARTH SCIENCE parts of the Earth near the TROPICS, where the weather is always hot and the sun shines for most of the year → see also POLAR ZONE

tro·pism /ˈtroʊˌpɪzəm/ *n.* [U] BIOLOGY the ways in which a plant moves or grows as a reaction to things such as light, GRAVITY, or being touched → see also GRAVITROPISM, PHOTOTROPISM, THIGMOTROPISM

tro·po·sphere /ˈtroʊpəˌsfɪr, ˈtrɑ-/ *n.* **the troposphere** the lowest part of the ATMOSPHERE

trot¹ /trɑt/ *v.* **trotted, trotting** **1** [I] if a horse trots, it moves fairly quickly, with each front leg moving at the same time as the opposite back leg **2** [I always + adv./prep.] to run fairly slowly, taking short steps: *She trotted along the path to the river.* **3** [I always + adv./prep.] SPOKEN to walk or go somewhere, especially fairly quickly

trot out *phr. v.* INFORMAL **1 trot sth ↔ out** to give opinions, excuses, reasons etc. that you have used too often to seem sincere: *Steve trotted out the same old excuses.* **2 trot sb/sth ↔ out** to show or present someone or something you want other people to see or notice

trot² *n.* **1** [singular] the movement of a horse at trotting speed **2** [singular] a fairly slow way of running, in which you take short steps **3 the trots** [plural] INFORMAL, HUMOROUS DIARRHEA **4** [C] a ride on a horse at trotting speed

troth /trɑθ, trɔθ, troʊθ/ *n.* OLD USE **1 by my troth** used when expressing an opinion strongly **2 in troth** truly SYN indeed

Trot·sky /ˈtrɑtski/, **Le·on** /ˈliɑn/ (1879–1940) a Russian political leader, born in the Ukraine, who had an important part in the Russian Revolution of 1917

Trot·sky·ite /ˈtrɑtskiˌaɪt/ also **Trot·sky·ist** /ˈtrɑtskiɪst/ *n.* [C] POLITICS someone who believes in the political ideas of Leon Trotsky, especially that the working class should take control of the state —**Trotskyite** *adj.*

trou·ba·dour /ˈtrubəˌdɔr/ *n.* [C] a type of singer and poet who traveled around the PALACES and castles of southern Europe in the 12th and 13th centuries

trou·ble¹ /ˈtrʌbəl/ S1 W1 *n.*

1 PROBLEMS [C,U] problems that make something difficult, make you change your plans, make you worry etc.: *The trouble started when she lost her job. | the country's economic troubles | We found it* ***without any trouble****. | We've been* ***having trouble with*** *our teenage son.* | **have trouble doing sth** *I have trouble staying awake in class. | Our new network software has been* ***causing*** *us a lot of* ***trouble****.*

2 DOING STH WRONG [U] a situation in which someone in authority is angry with you or is likely to punish you: *My brother's* ***in trouble with*** *the police again. | Joseph often* ***got in trouble*** *for not doing his homework.* | **get sb in/into trouble** *I didn't mean to get you in trouble.* | **be in serious/deep/big trouble** *You'll be in big trouble if Dad finds out.*

3 DIFFICULT SITUATION [U] a difficult or dangerous situation: *Their marriage is* ***in trouble****.* | **run/get into trouble** *We ran into trouble installing the water heater.*

4 EFFORT [U] an amount of effort and time that is needed to do something, especially when it is inconvenient for you to do it: *I don't want to* ***put*** *you* ***to*** *any* ***trouble*** (=make someone use a lot of time and effort). | *Only 20% of the people* ***took the trouble to*** *vote* (=made a special effort to do it). | *She* ***went to a lot of trouble*** (=used a lot of time and effort) *organizing the picnic. | Using my credit card* ***saves*** *me* ***the trouble of*** (=makes it unnecessary for me to do something) *going to the bank. | Taking the train is* ***more trouble than it's worth*** (=used to say that something takes too much time and effort to do).

5 MACHINE/SYSTEM [U] something that is wrong with a machine, vehicle, or system: *engine trouble* | **+with** *We're having trouble with our oven.* ▶see THESAURUS box at problem¹

6 HEALTH [U] a problem that you have with your health, especially one that is painful: **+with** *Grandma has had trouble with her heart.* | **heart/stomach/back etc. trouble** *He has a history of heart trouble.*

7 ARGUMENT/VIOLENCE [C,U] a situation in which people argue or fight with each other: *I knew there was going to be trouble. | The troubles are far from over.*

SPOKEN PHRASES

8 the trouble with sb/sth used when explaining what is not satisfactory about someone or something: *The trouble with you is that you don't listen.*

9 the trouble is... used when explaining why something is impossible or difficult: *The trouble is they're all jealous of me.*

10 be asking for trouble to take risks or do something stupid that is likely to cause problems: *Walking around downtown late at night is just asking for trouble.*

11 it's no trouble (at all) used to say that you are very willing to do something because it is not inconvenient for you: *"Thanks for helping me move." "It's no trouble at all."*

12 have trouble with sth to disagree with something, especially because it is against your MORALS or principles: *I have trouble with the idea of casual sex.*

13 sb's (nothing but) trouble used to say that someone often does bad things: *They've been nothing but trouble since they moved here.*

14 sb's no trouble if a child is no trouble, they do not annoy or worry you: *Don't worry – the kids were no trouble.*

15 in trouble OLD-FASHIONED PREGNANT and not married

trouble² *v.* **1** [T] if a problem troubles you, it makes you feel worried: *There is one thing that's been troubling me.* **2 sorry to trouble you** also **may/could I trouble you (for sth)?** SPOKEN, FORMAL used when politely asking someone to do something for you or give you something: *Sorry to trouble you, but could I borrow your pen?* **3** [T] if a medical problem troubles you, it causes you pain or makes you suffer: *Stephen's ear has been troubling him all week.* **4** [T] FORMAL to say something or ask someone to do something that may annoy or upset them: *I didn't want to trouble her with my problems.* **[Origin:** 1200–1300 Old French *troubler*, from Vulgar Latin *turbulare*]

trou·bled /ˈtrʌbəld/ *adj.* **1** feeling worried or anxious: *a troubled expression* **2** having many problems: *a troubled childhood*

ˌtrouble-ˈfree *adj.* causing no difficulty or worry

trou·ble·mak·er /ˈtrʌbəlˌmeɪkɚ/ *n.* [C] someone who deliberately causes problems, especially someone who complains or argues with people

trou·ble·shoot /ˈtrʌbəlˌʃut/ *v.* [I,T] **1** to try to find and fix problems in a machine or piece of electronic equipment **2** to solve serious problems for a company or other organization

trou·ble·shoot·er /ˈtrʌbəlˌʃutɚ/ *n.* [C] **1** a person or computer program that tries to find and fix problems in a machine or piece of electronic equipment **2** someone who is employed by a company to solve difficult or serious problems

trou·ble·shoot·ing /ˈtrʌbəlˌʃutɪŋ/ *n.* [U] **1** the act of trying to find and fix problems in a machine or piece of electronic equipment **2** the act of trying to solve difficult or serious problems

trou·ble·some /ˈtrʌbəlsəm/ *adj.* causing you trouble or worry over a long period of time: *a troublesome back injury*

ˈtrouble ˌspot *n.* [C] a place where trouble often happens, especially war or violence

trough /trɔf/ *n.* [C] **1** a long narrow open container that holds water or food for animals **2** the lowest point on a GRAPH (=drawing with lines showing how sets of measurements are related to each other) containing a series of numbers that represent facts or measurements: *The graph showed peaks and troughs of activity.* **3** the hollow area between two waves in the ocean or between two hills **4** EARTH SCIENCE a long area of fairly low pressure between two areas of high pressure on a weather map **5** ECONOMICS the lowest point in an economic period that has high and low points, when the total value of all goods and services produced in a country will not fall any further: *GDP is now over 10% above the trough of the first quarter in 2000.*

trounce /traʊns/ *v.* [T] to defeat someone by a large amount: *We trounced them 38–6.*

troupe /trup/ *n.* [C] a group of singers, actors, dancers etc. who perform together

troup·er /ˈtrupɚ/ *n.* [C] **1** INFORMAL someone who has a lot of experience of work in the entertainment business **2 sb's a (real) trouper** SPOKEN used to say that someone works hard and keeps trying, even when the situation is difficult

trou·sers /ˈtraʊzɚz/ *n.* [plural] a piece of clothing that covers the lower half of your body and that has a separate part for each leg SYN **pants** —**trouser** *adj.* [only before noun]

trous·seau /ˈtrusoʊ, truˈsoʊ/ *n. plural* **trousseaux** /-soʊz, -ˈsoʊz/ or **trousseaus** [C] OLD-FASHIONED the personal possessions that a woman brings with her when she gets married

trout /traʊt/ *n. plural* **trout** [C,U] BIOLOGY a common river fish or the meat of this fish

trove /troʊv/ *n.* [C] a TREASURE TROVE

trow·el /ˈtraʊəl/ *n.* [C] **1** a garden tool like a very small SHOVEL **2** a small tool with a flat blade, used for spreading CEMENT on bricks etc.

troy ounce /ˌtrɔɪ ˈaʊns/ *n.* [C] a small unit of troy weight that is equal to 31.1 grams

troy weight /ˈtrɔɪ weɪt/ *n.* [U] a system of measuring weight, especially used for weighing gold, silver, GEMS etc.

tru·an·cy /ˈtruənsi/ *n.* [U] the practice of deliberately staying away from school without permission

tru·ant /ˈtruənt/ *adj.* deliberately staying away from school without permission [**Origin:** 1300–1400 Old French **wanderer**] —**truant** *n.* [C]

truce /trus/ *n.* [C] an agreement between enemies to stop fighting or arguing for a short time, or the period for which this is arranged: +**between** *a shaky truce between the two factions* | **call/declare a truce** (=announce a truce) → see also ARMISTICE, CEASE-FIRE

truck¹ /trʌk/ S1 W2 *n.* **1** [C,U] a large road vehicle used by companies to carry goods or pull heavy things: *a garbage truck* | *Most of their package deliveries are made* ***by truck***. **2** [C] a vehicle the size of a car, that has a large open part at the back that is used for carrying things SYN **pick-up**: *You can borrow my truck to go to the store.* **3 have/hold/want no truck with sb/sth** to refuse to become involved with a person or in an activity or to accept an idea **4** [C] a simple piece of equipment consisting of something flat that is attached to wheels, used especially to move heavy things [**Origin:** (1,2,4) 1700–1800 *truck* **small wheel**]

truck² *v.* **1** [T always + adv./prep.] to take something somewhere by truck: **truck sb/sth to/across/into etc. sth** *Food was being trucked into the city.* **2** [I always + adv./prep.] SPOKEN to go, move, or travel quickly **3 get trucking** SPOKEN to leave a place: *I guess it's time to get trucking.* **4 keep on trucking** SPOKEN, OLD-FASHIONED a phrase used to encourage someone to continue what they are doing, used especially in the 1970s

truck sth ↔ **in** *phr. v.* to bring something somewhere by truck, or arrange to have it brought by truck

ˈtruck ˌdriver *n.* [C] someone whose job is to drive a big truck that carries goods

truck·er /ˈtrʌkɚ/ *n.* [C] INFORMAL a truck driver

ˈtruck farm *n.* [C] a small farm for growing vegetables and fruit for sale

truck·ing /ˈtrʌkɪŋ/ *n.* [U] the business of taking goods from place to place by road

truck·load /ˈtrʌkloʊd/ *n.* [C] the amount that fills a truck

ˈtruck stop *n.* [C] a cheap place to eat on a main road, used mainly by TRUCK DRIVERS

truc·u·lent /ˈtrʌkyələnt/ *adj.* FORMAL easily made angry and always willing to argue with people —**truculently** *adv.* —**truculence** *n.* [U]

trudge¹ /trʌdʒ/ *v.* [I always + adv./prep.] to walk with slow heavy steps, especially because you are tired: +**up/along/through etc.** *We trudged to school through the snow.* ►see THESAURUS box at **walk¹**

trudge² *n.* [C usually singular] a long tiring walk

true¹ /tru/ *adj.*

1 NOT FALSE based on facts, and not imagined or invented OPP **false**: *Everything I said is true.* | *a true story* | **be true (that)** *Is it true that you spent time in jail?* | **be true of sb/sth** *The text is poorly written, which is true of many textbooks.* | *Students have to decide whether the statement is* ***true or false***. ►see THESAURUS box at **right¹**

2 the true value/seriousness/nature etc. the real value, seriousness etc. of something rather than what seems at first to be correct: *The house was sold for a fraction of its true value.*

3 sb's true feelings/beliefs/motives etc. your true feelings, beliefs etc. are the ones that you really have and not the ones that you pretend to have: *She tried hard to hide her true feelings.*

4 HAVING TYPICAL QUALITIES OF STH having all the qualities that a particular type of person or thing should have SYN **real** SYN **genuine**: *True courage is facing danger when you are afraid.* | *She's been a true friend to me.*

5 come true if wishes, dreams etc. come true, they happen in the way you hoped they would: *Her dream of owning a home finally came true.* → see also **a dream come true** at DREAM¹ (3)

6 LOYAL faithful and loyal to someone or something, whatever happens: +**to** *Johnson was always true to the Democratic party.* | **be true to your principles/ideals etc.** *If we agree to this deal, then we're not being true to our principles.*

7 ADMITTING STH SPOKEN used to admit that something is correct, even though it seems to be the opposite of another thing you say: *True, my family was wealthy, but my parents taught me to work hard.*

8 true love a) [U] real love that has all the qualities that it is supposed to have: *In the story, she finally finds true love with Henry.* **b)** [C] the person that someone loves the most in a romantic way: *Adrienne was* ***his*** *one* ***true love***.

9 true to form used to say that someone is behaving in the bad way that you expect them to: *True to form, Jimmy did not show up for his court date.*

10 true to sb's word/promise doing exactly what you have promised to do: *True to her word, Susan paid us back the next week.*
11 true mammal/fish/plant etc. having all the qualities of a particular type of animal, plant etc., according to an exact description of it: *Despite its appearance, the whale is a true mammal.*
12 STRAIGHT/LEVEL [not before noun] TECHNICAL built, placed, or formed in a way that is perfectly flat, straight, correct etc.: *The table top isn't completely true.* [**Origin:** Old English *treowe* **faithful**] → see also **be too good to be true** at GOOD¹ (53), **show your true colors** at SHOW¹ (17), TRULY, TRUTH

true² *adv.* **1** in an exact straight line: *The arrow flew straight and true to its target.* **2** OLD USE in a truthful way → see also **not ring true** at RING² (6)

true³ *n.* **out of true** not completely straight, level, or balanced: *The doorway was out of true.*

true-'blue *adj.* completely loyal to a person or idea: *a true-blue friend*

true-ˌbreeding *adj.* BIOLOGY true-breeding plants produce new plants that are exactly the same as the parent

true-'false, true/false *adj.* **1 a true-false question** a statement on a test which you have to decide is true or false **2 a true-false test/exam/quiz etc.** a test that contains true-false questions

true-'life *adj.* [only before noun] based on real facts and not invented: *a true-life horror story* → see also TRUE-TO-LIFE

true 'north *n.* [U] north as it appears on maps, calculated as a line through the center of the Earth rather than by using the MAGNETIC POLE → see also MAGNETIC NORTH

true-to-'life *adj.* a book, play, description etc. that is true-to-life seems real, like something that could happen in real life SYN **realistic** → see also TRUE-LIFE

truf·fle /ˈtrʌfəl/ *n.* [C] **1** a soft creamy candy made with chocolate **2** BIOLOGY a black or light brown FUNGUS that grows under the ground, and is a very expensive food

tru·ism /ˈtruɪzəm/ *n.* [C] a statement that is clearly true, so that there is no need to say it: *His speech was just a collection of clichés and truisms.*

tru·ly /ˈtruli/ S3 W2 *adv.* [+ adj./adv.] **1** used to emphasize that the way you are describing something is really true SYN **really**: *a truly remarkable woman* | *a truly embarrassing moment* **2** in an exact or correct way: *No adult twins are truly identical.* **3** SPOKEN used to emphasize that you really mean what you are saying SYN **really** SYN **sincerely**: *I am truly sorry.* → see also **yours truly** at YOURS (3)

Tru·man /ˈtrumən/, **Har·ry S.** /ˈhæri ɛs/ (1884–1972) the 33rd President of the U.S.

Truman ˌDoctrine, the HISTORY President Truman's POLICY, which he announced in a speech in 1947, of providing support for countries which were threatened by COMMUNISM

Trum·bull /ˈtrʌmbəl/, **John** (1756–1843) a U.S. PAINTER famous for his paintings of scenes from the American Revolutionary War

trump¹ /trʌmp/ *n.* [C] **1** also **trump card** a card from the SUIT (=one of the four types of cards in a pack) that has been chosen to have a higher value than the other suits in a particular game **2** the SUIT chosen to have a higher value than the other suits in a particular game: *Spades are trump.* **3 sb's trump card** something that gives you a big advantage in a particular situation, that you use after keeping it secret for some time: *He decided to* ***play his trump card*** (=use his advantage) *and tell them about the money.*

trump² *v.* [T] **1** to play a trump that beats someone else's card in a game **2** to do something better than someone else, so that you gain an advantage: *They trumped our bid to buy the company.*

trump sth ↔ **up** *phr. v.* to use false information to make someone seem guilty of a crime: *He claims authorities trumped up a sexual assault charge against him.* → see also TRUMPED-UP

'trumped-up *adj.* information that is trumped-up is false and is used to make someone seem guilty of a crime: *He was arrested on trumped-up charges.*

trump·er·y /ˈtrʌmpəri/ *adj.* OLD USE meant to be attractive, but having no value

trum·pet¹ /ˈtrʌmpɪt/ *n.* **1** [C] ENG. LANG. ARTS a musical instrument that you blow into, which consists of a curved metal tube that is wide at the end and three buttons to change the note **2** [singular] the loud noise that an ELEPHANT makes

trumpet² *v.* **1** [T] to tell everyone about something that you are proud of, in an annoying way: *They proudly trumpeted the fact that they created more jobs.* **2** [I] if an ELEPHANT trumpets, it makes a loud noise

trun·cate /ˈtrʌŋkeɪt/ *v.* [T] FORMAL to make something shorter SYN **shorten**: *They decided to truncate the name of the movie.* —**truncation** /trʌŋˈkeɪʃən/ *n.* [U]

trun·cat·ed /ˈtrʌŋˌkeɪṭɪd/ *adj.* made shorter than before, or shorter than usual SYN **shortened**: *a truncated version of the book*

trun·cheon /ˈtrʌnʃən/ *n.* [C] a short thick stick that police officers carry as a weapon SYN **nightstick**

trun·dle /ˈtrʌndl/ *v.* [I always + adv./prep., T] **1** to move slowly and heavily along on wheels, or to make something do this by pushing or pulling it: *Two large army trucks trundled by.* **2** [I always + adv./prep.] to move or walk slowly: *Shoppers trundled from store to store.*

trundle sb ↔ **off to** *phr. v.* to send someone somewhere, even if they do not want to go: *The little kids were trundled off to bed.*

'trundle ˌbed *n.* [C] a low bed on wheels that you can slide under a larger bed

trunk /trʌŋk/ S3 *n.* [C] **1** BIOLOGY the thick central wooden stem of a tree **2** the part at the back of a car where you can put bags, tools etc. **3** BIOLOGY the very long nose of an ELEPHANT **4** BIOLOGY the main part of your body, not including your head, arms, or legs SYN **body** SYN **torso** **5 trunks** [plural] also **swim trunks** short pants that end above the knee, worn by men for swimming **6** a very large box made of wood or metal, in which clothes, books etc. are stored or packed for travel → see picture at BOX¹ [**Origin:** 1400–1500 Old French *tronc* **box, main part of a body**, from Latin *truncus* **tree-trunk, main part of a body**]

truss¹ /trʌs/ *v.* [T] **1** also **truss up** to tie someone's arms, legs etc. very firmly with rope so that they cannot move: *They trussed up their victim and left him to die.* **2** to prepare a chicken, duck etc. for cooking by tying its legs and wings together

truss² *n.* [C] **1** a frame supporting a roof or bridge **2** a special belt worn to support a HERNIA (=medical problem that affects the muscles below your stomach)

trust¹ /trʌst/ W3 *n.*
1 BELIEF [U] a strong belief in the honesty, goodness etc. of someone or something: *Their partnership is based on trust and cooperation.* | *The company has* ***put its trust in*** *Stover to manage the factory.* | *I never thought I would ever* ***betray his trust*** (=do something that shows someone should not have trusted you).
2 FINANCIAL ARRANGEMENT [C,U] ECONOMICS an arrangement by which someone has legal control of your money or property, especially until you are old enough to use it: *The money has been set aside in a trust.* | **hold/put/place sth in trust** *Their inheritance will be held in trust until the children are 18.* → see also TRUST FUND
3 ORGANIZATION [C usually singular] an organization or group that has control over money that will be used to help someone else: *a charitable trust*
4 a position of trust a job or position in which you have been given the responsibility of making important decisions: *McWilliams was in a position of trust as a church leader.*
5 COMPANIES [C] a group of companies that illegally work together to reduce competition and to control prices: *anti-trust laws*

T

6 take sth on trust to believe that something is true without having any proof: *I just had to take it on trust that he would deliver the money.*
[**Origin:** 1100–1200 Old Norse *traust* **confidence, trust**]

trust² S2 W2 *v.* [T]
1 BELIEVE SB IS HONEST to believe that someone is honest and will not harm you, cheat you etc. OPP **distrust**: *I never trusted him.* | **trust sb to do sth** *Managers must trust their employees to get the job done.* | **trust sb completely/implicitly** *His mother is the only person he trusts implicitly.*
2 DEPEND ON STH to believe that something is true or will happen, or to depend on this: *You can trust the quality of the meat they sell.* | **trust sth to do sth** *I wouldn't trust the ladder to support my weight.*
3 trust sb's judgment to think that someone is likely to make the right decisions: *Alfred had trusted Roy's judgment in business matters.*
4 trust sb with sth to believe that someone would be careful with something valuable or dangerous if you gave it to them: *They trusted him with their lives.*
5 trust sth to luck/chance/fate etc. to hope that things will happen in the way that you want, especially because you think there is nothing else you can do: *Organizing a business shouldn't be trusted to chance – get professional advice.*
6 I wouldn't trust sb any farther than I can throw him/her SPOKEN used to say that you do not trust someone very much
7 I trust (that) SPOKEN, FORMAL used to say politely that you hope something is true: *I trust that you will seriously consider my offer.* → see also TRUSTING

trust in sb/sth *phr. v.* FORMAL to believe in someone or something and to depend on them to do something: *The Pilgrims trusted in God to provide food.*

'trust ˌcompany *n.* [C] a TRUST

trust·ee /trʌˈsti/ *n.* [C] ECONOMICS **1** someone who has control of money or property that is in a TRUST for someone else **2** a member of a group that controls the money of a company, college, or other organization: *a trustee of the New York Public Library*

trus·tee·ship /trʌˈstiʃɪp/ *n.* **1** [C,U] ECONOMICS the job of being a trustee **2** [C,U] POLITICS the position of having the authority to govern an area, which is given by the United Nations to a country or countries, or the area that is governed

trust·ful /ˈtrʌstfəl/ *adj.* TRUSTING —**trustfully** *adv.* —**trustfulness** *n.* [U]

'trust fund *n.* [C] ECONOMICS an amount of money belonging to someone, often a child, that is controlled for them by a trustee

trust·ing /ˈtrʌstɪŋ/ *adj.* willing to believe that other people are good and honest: +**of** *You're too trusting of people, even if they're strangers.*

'trust ˌterritory *n.* [C] POLITICS a country or state which is being governed by a country chosen by the United Nations

trust·wor·thy /ˈtrʌstˌwɚði/ *adj.* able to be trusted and depended on: *Most of our employees are very trustworthy.* —**trustworthiness** *n.* [U]

trust·y¹ /ˈtrʌsti/ *adj.* [only before noun] OLD USE OR HUMOROUS a trusty weapon, vehicle, animal etc. is one that you have had for a long time and can depend on: *I quickly started typing on my trusty Macintosh.*

trusty² *n. plural* **trusties** [C] a prisoner who prison officials have given special jobs or rights, because they behave in a way that can be trusted

truth /truθ/ S2 W1 *n.*
1 the truth the actual facts about something, as opposed to what is false, imagined, or guessed OPP **lie** OPP **falsehood**: *I didn't steal the money, and that's the truth.* | +**about** *At first, officials in the local government hid the truth about the accident.* | +**behind** *They never found out the truth behind all the rumors.* | **know/find out/discover/learn etc. the truth** *Later I discovered the truth about my father.* | *We weren't completely sure that he was **telling the truth**.* | *The American public is eager to **get to the truth*** (=find out what really happened) *of the scandal.* | ***The truth is*** (=used to tell someone the truth even if it is unpleasant) *I can't help you, because I don't know what is going to happen.* | *I've never lied to you, and **that's the honest truth*** (=used to emphasize that you are telling the truth).
2 BEING TRUE [U] the state or quality of being true: *The magazine could not prove the **truth of** this statement.* | **there is some/no truth to sth** *There is no truth to the rumors about him being arrested.* | **there is an element/a grain of truth in sth** (=used to say that there is a small amount of truth in something) | *There wasn't **a grain of truth*** (=a small amount of truth) *in Uncle Hal's story.*
3 IMPORTANT IDEAS [C usually plural] FORMAL an important fact or idea that is accepted as being true: +**about** *It was a scary experience, but it taught me a few **basic truths** about what is important in life.*
4 to tell (you) the truth SPOKEN used when giving your personal opinion or admitting something: *I was scared to death, to tell you the truth.*
5 in truth FORMAL used to introduce a statement about what someone or something is really like, or what you really think about a situation SYN **really**: *In truth, the two brothers really did care for each other.*
6 nothing could be further from the truth used to say that something is definitely not true: *They seem like the perfect couple, but nothing could be further from the truth.*
7 (the) truth hurts SPOKEN used to say that it is sometimes difficult or embarrassing to hear someone tell you something that is true
8 (if the) truth be known/told used when telling someone the real facts about a situation, or your real opinion: *Truth be told, I really hate going camping.*
9 the truth will out OLD-FASHIONED used to say that even if you try to stop people from knowing something, they will find out in the end → see also **the gospel truth** at GOSPEL (4), HALF-TRUTH, **the moment of truth** at MOMENT (11), **truth/fact is stranger than fiction** at STRANGE¹ (3)

truth·ful /ˈtruθfəl/ *adj.* **1** someone who is truthful says what is true and does not lie: +**with** *I want you to be truthful with me.* **2** a truthful statement gives the true facts about something: *Give me a truthful answer.* **3** a truthful movie, play, book etc. deals with a subject in an honest way by showing what really happens in a particular situation —**truthfully** *adv.* —**truthfulness** *n.* [U]

ˌTruth in ˈLending Act, the also **ˌTruth in ˈLending Laws** *n.* ECONOMICS a FEDERAL law that makes banks and other organizations follow certain rules when lending money. The law states that when someone asks for a LOAN (=money they want to borrow), the bank must explain clearly how they will calculate the total cost of the loan, including the rate of INTEREST people will have to pay every year.

ˌTruth in ˈSavings Act, the *n.* ECONOMICS a FEDERAL law that says that banks must give people certain information about the different types of DEPOSIT ACCOUNT they offer. Banks must tell people the rate of INTEREST paid on each account and the smallest amount of money needed to open each account. People must also be informed of any charges they will have to pay for taking money out of the account early.

'truth ˌserum *n.* [C,U] a drug that is supposed to make people tell the truth

try¹ /traɪ/ S1 W1 *v.* **tries, tried, trying**
1 ATTEMPT [I,T] to attempt to do or get something: *Tim may not be good at talking about his feelings, but at least he tries.* | **try to do sth** *She tried to forget about what had happened.* | **try and do sth** *You have to try and eat, or you won't get better.* | **try doing sth** *I tried calling him, but he's not answering the phone.* | *I **try and try**, but I can't lose weight.* | *Juanita **tried hard** not to laugh.* | **try your best/hardest (to do sth)** *I'll try my best to finish the work tonight.*

THESAURUS

attempt to try to do something, especially something difficult: *He was attempting to climb Mount Everest without oxygen.*
see if you can do sth SPOKEN to try to do something: *I'll see if I can get you a ticket.*
do your best to try very hard, even if something is difficult and you are not sure you will succeed: *The doctors are doing their best to help him.*
make an effort to do sth to try to do something, especially something difficult: *The teachers make an effort to identify a student's strengths and weaknesses.*
endeavor FORMAL to try very hard to do something: *Herrera had endeavored to keep the peace.*

2 TEST/USE [T] to do or use something to discover if it is effective, appropriate, good, or enjoyable: *Running is really good exercise – you should try it.* | **try doing sth** *Try riding to work instead of driving.* | **try sth on sb/sth** *Scientists are trying the new drugs on rats.* | **try something new/different** (=do or use something that is different from what you usually do or use)
3 DOOR/WINDOW [T] to attempt to open a door, window etc. to see if it is locked, or to attempt to use a machine, piece of equipment etc. to see if it works: *We tried the doors, but they were all locked.* | *I'll go try the phone upstairs.*
4 TRY TO FIND SB/STH [I,T] to go to a place or person, or call them, in order to find something or someone: *She tried six stores before she found the book.*
5 LAW [T usually passive] to examine and judge a legal case, or someone who is thought to be guilty of a crime, in a court of law: **try sb for sth** *Ray was never tried for the murders.* | **try sb on a charge/count** *He was tried on charges of treason.*
6 try as sb might used to say that someone tried as hard as possible to do something but was not successful: *Try as I might, I just couldn't remember her name.*
7 try your hand at sth to try a new activity in order to see whether it interests you or whether you are good at it: *Diane has always wanted to try her hand at acting.*
8 sb couldn't do sth if they tried SPOKEN used to say that someone does not have the skill or ability to do something: *I couldn't make a cake if I tried.*
9 try your luck to try to achieve something or get something you want, usually by taking a risk: *After the war my father went to Canada to try his luck at farming.*
10 try sb's patience/temper/nerves etc. to make someone feel impatient, angry, nervous etc.: *The salesman was beginning to try my patience.*
11 not for want/lack of trying used to say that if someone does not achieve something it is not because they have not tried: *She didn't find a job, but it wasn't for lack of trying.*
[**Origin:** 1200–1300 Old French *trier* **to pick out, sift**]

try for sth *phr. v.* to try and get something you really want such as a job, prize, or a chance to study somewhere: *Why don't you try for the marketing job?* | *We have been **trying for a baby*** (=trying to have a baby) *for three years.*

try sth ↔ **on** *phr. v.* **1** to put on a piece of clothing to see if it fits you or if it looks good on you: *Go try on the sweater, and see if it fits.* **2 try sth on for size a)** to put on a piece of clothing to see if it fits **b)** INFORMAL to consider something to see if it is appropriate for you or your situation: *Ask the committee to try this idea on for size.*

try out *phr. v.* **1 try sth ↔ out** to test something such as a method or a piece of equipment to see if it is effective or works well: *He could hardly wait to try out his new bike.* | **try sth out (on sb/sth)** *I tried out my French on a girl in the coffee shop.* **2** to try to be chosen as a member of a team, for a part in a play etc.: +**for** *I tried out for the basketball team in high school.*

try[2] [S2] *n. plural* **tries** [C] an attempt to do something: *She didn't break the record, but it was a good try.* | **on your first/second etc. try** *I'd never played before, but I hit the ball on my first try.* | *Have you driven a boat before? Take the wheel and **give it a try*** (=try it)*!* | *"Do you think it will help?" "It's **worth a try**."* → see also **give sth the (old) college try** at COLLEGE (5), **nice try** at NICE (6)

try·ing /ˈtraɪ-ɪŋ/ *adj.* annoying or difficult in a way that makes you feel tired, impatient etc.: *My mother's illness has been very trying for us.*

try·out /ˈtraɪ-aʊt/ *n.* [C] **1** a time when people who want to be on a sports team, activity etc. are tested, so that the best can be chosen: *baseball tryouts* **2** a period of time when something is used or tested to see if people like it, if it works, or if it is appropriate for a purpose: *The new comedy show was given a three-month tryout.*

tryst /trɪst/ *n.* [C] **1** a meeting between lovers in a secret place or at a secret time: *secret hotel trysts* **2** a place where lovers meet secretly

tsar /zɑr, tsɑr/ *n.* [C] another spelling of CZAR

tsa·ri·na /zɑˈrinə, tsɑ-/ *n.* [C] another spelling of CZARINA

tsar·ism /ˈzɑrɪzəm, ˈtsɑ-/ *n.* [U] another spelling of CZARISM —**tsarist** *n.* [C] —**tsarist** *adj.*

tset·se fly, tzet·ze fly /ˈtɛtsi ˌflaɪ, ˈtsɛtsi-/ *n.* [C] an African fly that sucks the blood of people and animals and spreads serious diseases

T-shirt [S3], **tee-shirt** /ˈti ʃɚt/ *n.* [C] a soft shirt, usually made of cotton, that has no collar: *She was wearing jeans and a pink T-shirt.* [**Origin:** 1900–2000 because it is shaped like the letter T]

Tsim·shi·an /ˈtʃɪmʃiən, ˈtsɪm-/ a Native American tribe from western Canada and Alaska

tsk tsk *interjection* used in writing to represent a clicking sound that people make with their tongue to show disapproval and sometimes sympathy

tsp. the written abbreviation of TEASPOON: *Add 1 tsp. salt.*

T-square /ˈti skwɛr/ *n.* [C] a large T-shaped piece of wood or plastic used to draw exact plans or pictures

tsu·na·mi /tsʊˈnɑmi/ *n. plural* **tsunami** or **tsunamis** [C] EARTH SCIENCE a very large forceful wave that causes a lot of damage when it hits the land [**Origin:** 1800–1900 a Japanese word meaning **harbor wave**]

Tu. a written abbreviation of TUESDAY

tub /tʌb/ [S3] *n.* [C] **1** a large container in which you sit to wash yourself [SYN] **bathtub**: *I'm going to go get in the tub.* → see also HOT TUB **2** an open container that is usually round, and whose sides are usually shorter than the width of its base: *a tub of popcorn* | *a plastic tub full of dirty dishes* **3** also **tubful** the amount of liquid, food etc. that a tub can contain **4** DISAPPROVING someone who is short and fat **5** INFORMAL an old boat that is in bad condition: *You're not going out in that old tub, are you?* [**Origin:** 1300–1400 Middle Dutch *tubbe*]

tu·ba /ˈtubə/ *n.* [C] a large musical instrument that consists of a curved metal tube with a wide opening that points straight up, that you play by blowing into it, and that produces very low sounds

tub·by /ˈtʌbi/ *adj.* *comparative* **tubbier**, *superlative* **tubbiest** INFORMAL short and fat, with a round stomach ►see THESAURUS box at **fat**[1]

tube[1] /tub/ [S2] *n.*
1 PIPE FOR LIQUID [C] a round pipe made of metal, glass, rubber etc., especially for liquids or gases to go through: *The water leaves the machine through a plastic tube.* → see also INNER TUBE, TEST TUBE → see picture at LABORATORY
2 CONTAINER FOR SOFT SUBSTANCE [C] a narrow container made of plastic or soft metal and closed at one end, that you press between your fingers in order to push out the soft substance that is inside: *a tube of toothpaste* → see picture at CONTAINER
3 CONTAINER FOR ROLLED PAPER [C] a long narrow container shaped like a tube used for storing things like maps and pictures
4 STH SHAPED LIKE A TUBE [C] something that is shaped like a tube: *a toilet paper tube*

T

5 IN YOUR BODY [C] BIOLOGY a tube-shaped part inside your body: *Fallopian tubes*
6 go down the tubes INFORMAL if a situation goes down the tubes, it becomes ruined or spoiled: *All our hard work went down the tubes.*
7 TELEVISION the tube OLD-FASHIONED television
8 ELECTRICAL EQUIPMENT [C] also **picture tube** the part of a television that causes the picture to appear
9 have your tubes tied if a woman has her tubes tied, she has a medical operation on her FALLOPIAN TUBES so that she will not be able to have babies
[**Origin:** 1600–1700 French, Latin *tubus*]

tube² *v.* [I] to float on a river on a large INNER TUBE for fun → see also TUBING

tu·ber /ˈtubɚ/ *n.* [C] BIOLOGY a round swollen part on the stem of some plants, such as the potato, that grows below the ground and from which new plants grow —**tuberous** *adj.*

tu·ber·cu·lo·sis /tʊˌbɚkyəˈloʊsɪs/ *n.* [U] MEDICINE a serious infectious disease that affects many parts of your body, especially your lungs SYN TB —**tubercular** /tʊˈbɚkyəlɚ/ *adj.*

ˈtube sock *n.* [C] a sock, especially a white one, that is long and straight and has no special place for your heel

ˈtube top *n.* [C] a tight piece of women's clothing that goes around your chest and back to cover your breasts, but does not cover your shoulders

tub·ing /ˈtubɪŋ/ *n.* [U] **1** a long piece of round pipe, or a system of tubes connected together: *a piece of rubber tubing* **2** the activity of floating on a river on a large INNER TUBE for fun

Tub·man, Har·ri·et /ˈtʌbmən/, /ˈhæriɪt/ (?1820–1913) an African-American woman who was born a SLAVE, famous for helping many slaves to escape from their owners

Harriet Tubman

ˈtub-ˌthumping *adj.* [only before noun] INFORMAL trying to persuade people about your opinions, especially political opinions, in a loud and forceful way: *He spoke in his usual tub-thumping way.* —**tub-thumping** *n.* [U] —**tub-thumper** *n.* [C]

tu·bu·lar /ˈtubyəlɚ/ *adj.* made of tubes or in the form of a tube: *a tubular steel structure*

tuck¹ /tʌk/ *v.* [T] **1** [always + adv./prep.] to push something, especially the edge of a piece of cloth or paper, into or behind something so that it looks neater or stays in place: **tuck sth in** *Tuck your shirt in!* | **tuck sth into/under/behind sth** *She tucked her hair behind her ear.* **2** [always + adv./prep.] to put something into a small space, especially in order to protect, hide, carry, or hold it: **tuck sth behind/under/into sth** *He tucked the newspaper under his arm.* **3** [always + adv./prep.] to put an arm, leg, or other part of your body into a position where it is not sticking out or sticking up: *She sat on the sofa and tucked her legs under her.* **4** to put a TUCK (=a special fold) in a piece of clothing to make it fit better

tuck sth ↔ **away** *phr. v.* **1 be tucked away** if a place is tucked away, it is in a quiet area: *The hotel is tucked away in a quiet side street.* **2** to put something in a safe or secret place: *I tucked the letter away behind my bed to read later.*

tuck sb/sth ↔ **in** *phr. v.* **1** to make a child comfortable in bed by arranging the sheets around them: *I'll come up and tuck you in.* **2** to move a part of your body in so that it does not stick out so much: *Stand up slowly, keeping your chin tucked in.*

tuck² *n.* [C] **1** a narrow flat fold of cloth sewn into a piece of clothing for decoration or to make it fit closer to the body **2** a small medical operation done to make your face or stomach look flatter and younger: *She has had a face-lift and **a tummy tuck** (=an operation to make her stomach flatter).*

tuck·er /ˈtʌkɚ/ *v.*

tucker sb **out** *phr. v.* INFORMAL to make someone very tired: *The puppy **was all tuckered out** after his run.*

Tuc·son /ˈtusɑn/ a city in the U.S. state of Arizona

ˈtude /tud/ *n.* [C,U] HUMOROUS a style, behavior etc. that shows you have the confidence to do unusual and exciting things without caring what other people think: *They think of themselves as a band with 'tude.*

-tude /tud/ *suffix* [in nouns] the state of having a particular quality: *disquietude* (=anxiety) → see also -ITUDE

Tu·dor /ˈtudɚ/ *adj.* HISTORY relating to the period in British history between 1485 and 1603: **Tudor houses/architecture etc.** (=built in the style used in the Tudor period)

Tues·day /ˈtuzdi, -deɪ/ WRITTEN ABBREVIATION **Tu., Tue.** or **Tues.** *n.* [C,U] the third day of the week, between Monday and Wednesday: *The report is due Tuesday.* | *Do you want to see that new movie with me **on Tuesday**?* | *Rachel had a barbecue **last Tuesday**.* | *We have tickets to the Packers game **next Tuesday**.* | *I'm taking my driving test **this Tuesday*** (=the next Tuesday that is coming). | *I try to clean the house **on Tuesdays*** (=each Tuesday). | *My birthday is **on a Tuesday** this year.* | **Tuesday morning/afternoon/night etc.** *Sam and I went out for lunch Tuesday afternoon.* [**Origin:** Old English *tiwesdæg*, from *Tiw* god of war + *dæg* **day**] → see Grammar box at SUNDAY

tuft /tʌft/ *n.* [C] a mass of hair, feathers, grass etc. growing or held closely together at their base: **+of** *A tuft of red hair poked out from under her scarf.* —**tufty** *adj.*: *We walked across the tufty grass.*

tuft·ed /ˈtʌftɪd/ *adj.* **1** a tufted chair, SOFA etc. has buttons on its surface which are stitched through soft material under the surface **2** BIOLOGY having a tuft or tufts: *The old man's ears were tufted with white hair.*

tug¹ /tʌg/ *v.* **tugged, tugging** [I,T] **1** to pull with one or more short quick pulls: *He tugged the dog's leash.* | **tug on/at sth** *"Come on," Alice said, tugging at his hand.* ►see THESAURUS box at **pull¹** **2 tug at sb's heart/heartstrings** to have a strong effect on your emotions, and make you feel sympathy for someone or something: *a sad story that tugs at your heartstrings*

tug² *n.* [C] **1** also **tugboat** a small strong boat used for pulling or guiding ships into a port, up a river etc. **2** [usually singular] a sudden strong pull: *I grabbed the door handle and gave it a good tug.* **3** something that influences your thoughts or feelings and makes you want to do something, be with someone, or go somewhere: **+of** *Kate felt a tug of jealousy.*

ˌtug-of-ˈwar *n.* **1** [singular, U] a test of strength in which two teams pull opposite ends of a rope against each other **2** [singular] a situation in which two people or groups try very hard to get or keep the same thing: *Divorce creates an emotional tug-of-war for parents and children.*

tu·i·tion /tuˈɪʃən/ *n.* [U] **1** the money you pay for being taught at a school or college: *Tuition is $2,800 per year.* **2** the act of teaching, especially to one person or in small groups: *I had to have private tuition in math.* [**Origin:** 1400–1500 Old French *tuicion*, from Latin, from *tueri* **to look at, look after**]

tu·lip /ˈtulɪp/ *n.* [C] a brightly colored flower that is shaped like a cup and grows from a BULB in the spring [**Origin:** 1500–1600 Modern Latin *tulipa*, from Turkish *tülbend* **turban**; from the shape of the flower]

tulle /tul/ *n.* [U] a thin soft silk or NYLON material like a net

tum·ble¹ /ˈtʌmbəl/ *v.* [I] **1** [always + adv./prep.] to fall down quickly and suddenly, especially with a rolling movement: **+over/backward/down etc.** *She lost her balance and tumbled backward.* | *Huge rocks tumbled down the mountainside.* **2** [always + adv./prep.] to move in an uncontrolled way: **+into/through etc.** *A group of tourists tumbled off the bus.* **3** if prices or numbers tumble, they go down suddenly and by a large amount: *On October 19, 1987, the stock market tumbled 508 points.* **4 come tumbling down a)** if a building or structure comes tumbling down, it falls suddenly to the ground **b)** if an organization, system etc. comes tumbling down, it suddenly stops working completely because of many problems: *Soon her marriage came tumbling down.* **5** [always + adv./prep.] if someone's hair tumbles down, it hangs down, long and thick and often with curls: *Her thick blonde hair tumbled down her back.* **6** [always + adv./prep.] if an amount of water tumbles somewhere, it flows there quickly: *A stream tumbled over the rocks.* **7** to do TUMBLING **8 sth tumbles out** if words tumble out, you say something very quickly without thinking about it first, because you are excited, upset, or surprised: *Suddenly all the words came tumbling out, and she began to cry.*

tumble² *n.* [C] a fall, especially from a high place: *I **took a tumble** and hurt my ankle.* → see also ROUGH-AND-TUMBLE

tum·ble·down /ˈtʌmbəldaʊn/ *adj.* [only before noun] **tumbledown building/house/cottage etc.** a building, house etc. that is old and beginning to fall down: *a tumbledown cabin by the lake*

ˈtumble-dry *v.* **tumble-dries, tumble-dried, tumble-drying** [T] to dry clothes in a DRYER (=machine that uses hot air to dry them after they have been washed)

tum·bler /ˈtʌmblɚ/ *n.* [C] **1** a drinking glass with a flat bottom and no handle **2** OLD-FASHIONED someone who performs special movements such as doing FLIPS (=a jump in which you turn over completely in the air) SYN **acrobat**

tum·ble·weed /ˈtʌmbəlwid/ *n.* [C,U] a plant that grows in the desert areas of North America and is blown from place to place by the wind

tum·bling /ˈtʌmblɪŋ/ *n.* [U] a sport similar to GYMNASTICS but with all the exercises done on the floor

tu·mes·cent /tuˈmɛsənt/ *adj.* BIOLOGY swollen or swelling —**tumescence** *n.* [U]

tum·my /ˈtʌmi/ *n.* *plural* **tummies** [C] a word for STOMACH, used especially by or to children: *Mommy, my tummy hurts.*

tu·mor /ˈtumɚ/ *n.* [C] a mass of diseased cells in your body that have divided and increased too quickly: *a brain tumor* | **a malignant/benign tumor** (=dangerous/harmless tumor) [**Origin:** 1400–1500 Latin *tumere* **to swell**] —**tumorous** *adj.*

tu·mult /ˈtumʌlt/ *n.* [C,U] FORMAL **1** a confused, noisy, and excited situation, often caused by a large crowd: *She could not be heard in the tumult.* **2** a state of mental confusion caused by strong emotions such as anger, sadness etc.: *His voice was shaken by the tumult of his feelings.*

tu·mul·tu·ous /tuˈmʌltʃuəs/ *adj.* **1** full of activity, confusion, or violence SYN **turbulent**: *the tumultuous years of the Civil War* **2** very loud, because people are very excited: *tumultuous applause* —**tumultuously** *adv.*

tu·na /ˈtunə/ *n.* *plural* **tuna** or **tunas** **1** [C] BIOLOGY a large ocean fish caught for food **2** [U] the meat from this fish [**Origin:** 1800–1900 American Spanish, Spanish *atun*, from Arabic *tun*]

tu·na·fish /ˈtunəˌfɪʃ/ *n.* [U] tuna meat, cooked and sold in cans

tun·dra /ˈtʌndrə/ *n.* [C,U] EARTH SCIENCE the large flat areas of land in the north of Russia, Canada etc., where it is very cold and there are no trees

tune¹ /tun/ S3 *n.* **1** ENG. LANG. ARTS **a)** [C] a series of musical notes that are played or sung and are nice to listen to: *an old familiar tune* | *The gospel song is sung **to the tune of** "Danny Boy."* **b)** INFORMAL a song: *That's a great tune.* ►see THESAURUS box at **music** **2 be in tune with sb** to understand or agree with what someone else thinks or wants: *The party leaders should be more in tune with their own members.* **3 be in tune with sth** to match or combine well with something: *The Senator's plan is more in tune with the new economic reality.* **4 in tune** ENG. LANG. ARTS playing or singing the correct musical note: *A trained singer knows when her voice is in tune.* **5 out of tune** ENG. LANG. ARTS playing or singing higher or lower than the correct musical note: *The guitar was badly out of tune.* **6 to the tune of $1,000/$50 million etc.** INFORMAL used to emphasize how large an amount of money is: *I was in debt to the tune of $40,000.* [**Origin:** 1300–1400 *tone*] → see also **carry a tune** at CARRY¹ (28), **sb can't carry a tune in a bucket** at CARRY¹ (29), **change your tune** at CHANGE¹ (12), **dance to sb's tune** at DANCE¹ (6), SHOW TUNE

tune² *v.* [T] **1** to make a radio or television receive broadcasts from a particular place: *The radio was tuned to a classical station.* **2** ENG. LANG. ARTS to make a musical instrument play at the right PITCH: *She was tuning her guitar.* **3** to make small changes to an engine so that it works better: *The engine needs to be tuned.* **4** to develop or train your body or mind so that it has a special skill: *The owl's eyes are **finely tuned** (=extremely well developed) to see the slightest movement.* → see also **stay tuned** at STAY¹ (7)

tune in *phr. v.* **1** to watch or listen to a program on television or the radio: +**to** *Tune in to 97.3 FM for the best music in the city.* **2** also **be tuned in** to realize or understand what is happening or what other people are thinking: +**to** *I suddenly tuned in to what she was trying to say.*

tune out *phr. v.* INFORMAL to ignore or stop listening to someone or something: *A bored child will just tune out in the classroom.* | **tune sb/sth ↔ out** *Liz didn't like what we were talking about, so she tuned us out.*

tune up *phr. v.* **1 tune sth ↔ up** to repair and clean a car's engine → see also TUNE-UP **2** ENG. LANG. ARTS if musicians tune up, they prepare their instruments to play at the same PITCH as each other **3 tune sth ↔ up** ENG. LANG. ARTS to make a musical instrument play at the right PITCH

tune·ful /ˈtunfəl/ *adj.* FORMAL nice to listen to: *tuneful melodies*

tune·less /ˈtunlɪs/ *adj.* tuneless music is unpleasant, because it does not have a nice tune: *His tuneless whistling annoyed me.* —**tunelessly** *adv.*

tun·er /ˈtunɚ/ *n.* [C] **1** the part of a radio or television that you change to receive different stations **2** a PIANO TUNER

tune·smith /ˈtunsmɪθ/ *n.* [C] used in newspapers, television etc. reports to mean someone who writes songs

ˈtune-up *n.* [C] the process of making small changes to an engine so that it works as well as possible: *The engine needs a tune-up.*

tung·sten /ˈtʌŋstən/ *n.* [U] SYMBOL **W** CHEMISTRY a hard metal that is an ELEMENT and is used in LIGHT BULBS and in making steel

tu·nic /ˈtunɪk/ *n.* [C] a long loose shirt

ˈtuning fork *n.* [C] a small U-shaped metal instrument that makes a particular musical note when you hit it

ˈtuning peg *n.* [C] a wooden screw used to make the strings on a VIOLIN, GUITAR etc. tighter

Tu·nis /ˈtunɪs/ the capital and largest city of Tunisia

Tu·ni·sia /tuˈniʒə/ a country in northwest Africa, between Libya and Algeria —**Tunisian** *n., adj.*

tun·nel¹ /ˈtʌnl/ *n.* [C] **1** a passage that has been dug under the ground, through a mountain etc. for people, cars, or trains to go through **2** a passage under the ground that animals have dug to live in [**Origin:** 1400–1500 Old French *tonel* **barrel**, from *tonne*, from Medieval Latin *tunna*]

tunnel² *v.* [I always + adv./prep., T] **1** to dig a long passage under the ground: **tunnel under/through etc. sth** *Rescuers tunneled toward the men trapped in the mine.* **2** if insects or animals tunnel into something, they make holes in it: **tunnel through/into etc. sth** *The grubs tunnel into the wood.*

ˌtunnel ˈvision *n.* [U] **1** the tendency to only think about one part of something, such as a problem or plan, instead of considering all the parts of it: *He has tunnel vision where profits are concerned.* **2** MEDICINE a condition in which someone's eyes are damaged so that they can only see things that are straight ahead

Tun·ney /ˈtʌni/, **Gene** /dʒin/ (1897–1978) a U.S. BOXER who was world CHAMPION in 1926–1928

Tup·per·ware /ˈtʌpɚˌwɛr/ *n.* [U] TRADEMARK a type of plastic container that closes very tightly and is used to store food

ˈTupperware ˌparty *n.* [C] a party at which people, especially women, get together at someone's house to buy TUPPERWARE food containers

tuque /tuk/ *n.* [C] a TOQUE

tur·ban /ˈtɚbən/ *n.* [C] a long piece of cloth that you wind tightly around your head, worn by men in parts of North Africa and southern Asia and sometimes by women as a fashion

tur·bid /ˈtɚbɪd/ *adj.* FORMAL turbid water or liquid is dirty and muddy —**turbidity** /tɚˈbɪdət̬i/ *n.* [U]

tur·bine /ˈtɚbaɪn, -bɪn/ *n.* [C] an engine or motor in which the pressure of a liquid or gas moves a special wheel around → see also GAS TURBINE, WIND TURBINE → see picture at ELECTRICITY

tur·bo /ˈtɚboʊ/ *n. plural* **turbos** [C] **1** a TURBOCHARGER **2** a car with a turbocharger: *an Audi turbo diesel*

tur·bo·charged /ˈtɚboʊˌtʃɑrdʒd/ *adj.* **1** a turbocharged engine or vehicle has a turbocharger: *a turbocharged 2.3-liter five-cylinder engine* **2** INFORMAL or HUMOROUS made much stronger or more powerful: *a turbocharged PC*

tur·bo·charg·er /ˈtɚboʊˌtʃɑrdʒɚ/ *n.* [C] a system that makes a vehicle more powerful by using a turbine to force air and gasoline into the engine under increased pressure

tur·bo·jet /ˈtɚboʊˌdʒɛt/ *n.* [C] **1** a powerful engine that makes something, especially an aircraft, move forward, by forcing out hot air and gases from the back **2** an aircraft that gets power from this type of engine

tur·bo·prop /ˈtɚboʊˌprɑp/ *n.* [C] **1** a TURBINE engine that drives a PROPELLER **2** an aircraft that gets power from this type of engine

tur·bu·lence /ˈtɚbyələns/ *n.* [U] **1** EARTH SCIENCE irregular and violent movements of air or water that are caused by the wind: *The plane encountered severe turbulence during the flight.* **2** a political or emotional situation that is very confused: *Political turbulence is spreading throughout the country.*

tur·bu·lent /ˈtɚbyələnt/ *adj.* **1** a turbulent situation or period of time is one in which there are a lot of sudden changes and often wars or violence: *a turbulent relationship* | *Jason grew up in the South during the turbulent years of the 1960s.* **2** EARTH SCIENCE turbulent air or water moves around a lot because of the wind: *the turbulent white sea* **3** turbulent crowds of people are noisy and violent

tu·reen /tʊˈrin/ *n.* [C] a large dish with a lid, used for serving soup or vegetables

turf /tɚf/ *n.* [U] **1 a)** a thick layer of grass attached to the soil below it by its roots SYN **sod** **b)** an artificial surface made to look like this, especially used on sports fields → see also ASTROTURF **2** INFORMAL an area or part of something that you think of as being your own: *The local companies are trying to defend their turf.* | *I think I can win on my* ***home turf*** (=the place I come from). | **a turf war/battle** (=a fight or argument over the area or things you think belong to you) **3** the track on which horses race → see also ASTROTURF, **surf 'n' turf** at SURF[2] (3)

Tur·ge·nev /tɚˈgeɪnyəf/, **I·van** /ˈaɪvən/ (1818–1883) a Russian writer of NOVELS, short stories, and plays

tur·gid /ˈtɚdʒɪd/ *adj.* FORMAL **1** turgid writing or speech is boring and difficult to understand: *turgid technical articles* **2** LITERARY full and swollen with liquid or air —**turgidly** *adv.* —**turgidity** /tɚˈdʒɪdət̬i/ *n.* [U]

Tur·key /ˈtɚki/ a country which is mainly in west Asia but partly in southeast Europe, between the Mediterranean Sea and the Black Sea —**Turk** *n.* [C] —**Turkish** *adj.*

tur·key /ˈtɚki/ S2 *n. plural* **turkeys** **1** [C] BIOLOGY a bird that looks like a large chicken and is often eaten at Christmas and at Thanksgiving **2** [U] the meat from a turkey: *roast turkey* **3** INFORMAL an unsuccessful movie or play **4** [C] INFORMAL used in a slightly insulting way to talk to someone who is being silly or stupid: *Shut up, you turkey!* [**Origin:** 1500–1600 *Turkey*; because the bird looked like the guinea fowl, which was brought into Europe through Turkey] → see also COLD TURKEY, **talk turkey** at TALK[1] (33)

ˈturkey ˌbaster *n.* [C] a large plastic tube with a hollow rubber part at one end that you use for putting liquid on a large piece of meat while it is cooking

ˈturkey shoot *n.* [C usually singular] a competition or fight in which one person or side is much stronger and defeats the other very easily

ˌTurkish ˈbath *n.* [C] a treatment to help you relax, that involves sitting in a very hot steamy room

ˌTurkish ˈcoffee *n.* [C,U] very strong black coffee that you drink in small cups with sugar

ˌTurkish deˈlight *n.* [U] a type of candy made from GELATIN that is cut into pieces and covered in sugar or chocolate

Turk·men·i·stan /tɚkˈmɛnɪˌstɑn, -ˌstæn/ a country in central Asia between Iran and Uzbekistan, formerly part of the Soviet Union —**Turkmen** /ˈtɚkmɛn, -mən/ *n., adj.*

tur·mer·ic /ˈtɚmərɪk, ˈtu-/ *n.* [U] yellow powder used to give a special color or taste to food

tur·moil /ˈtɚmɔɪl/ *n.* [U, singular] a state of confusion, excitement, and trouble: *His life was* ***in turmoil.*** | **political/economic/religious turmoil** *Most of the country is in political turmoil.*

turn

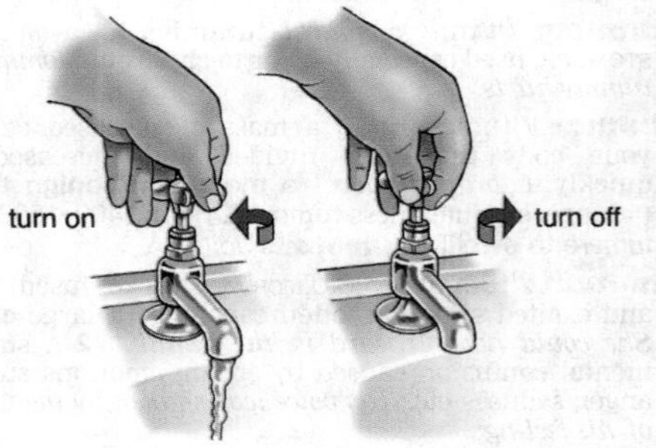

turn[1] /tɚn/ S1 W1 *v.*

1 YOUR BODY [I] to move your body so that you are looking in a different direction: *She turned and looked at me.* | **+around/away/to etc.** *Turn around and show me the back of the dress.* | *She finally turned to Frank and spoke.* | **turn to do sth** *We all turned to watch the kids.* | *Without a word, he* ***turned on his heel*** (=turned away suddenly) *and left the room.*

2 OBJECT [I,T] to move something so that it is pointing or aiming in a different direction: *Turn the plant so it's facing the sun.* | **turn sth around/over etc.** *He turned the computer screen toward me.* | *Come help me turn the mattress over.* | **turn sb/sth to face sb/sth** (=move someone or something so that their front is facing a person or thing) | ***Turn the bottle upside down*** (=so that the top is facing downward) *and shake it gently.* | ***Turn the sweater inside out*** (=so that the outside surface is on the inside) *to wash it.*

3 DIRECTION [I,T] to go in a new direction when you are walking, driving etc., or to make the vehicle you are using do this: **+into/off/left/right etc.** *We turned onto West Glen Road.* | **turn right/left** *Turn left at the next light.* | **turn sth around/into etc.** *The driver didn't have room to turn the bus around.*

4 ROAD/PATH [I] to curve in a particular direction: *The road turns sharply at the top of the hill.*

5 MOVE AROUND CENTRAL POINT [I,T] to move around a central point, or make something move in this way: *The train's wheels started to turn.* | **turn sth** *I knocked and then turned the door knob.*

THESAURUS

twist to turn something using a circular movement: *He twisted the rope around the post.*
spin to turn around and around very quickly: *skaters spinning on the ice*
go around to move in a continuous circular movement: *The clock was open, so that you could see the wheels going around inside.*
revolve to turn around a central point: *People in the past believed that the sun revolved around the Earth.*
rotate to turn around a particular point: *The Earth rotates every 24 hours.*
whirl to turn around and around very quickly or to make something do this: *the noise of the whirling fans*
twirl to turn around and around or to make something do this, especially as part of a dance or performance: *Half a dozen couples were twirling to a waltz.*

6 AGE [linking verb] if someone turns a particular age, they become that age: *Mark will turn 32 in August.*
7 COLOR a) [linking verb] to become a different color: *The sky turned a pale orange as the sun set.* | *I'm only 34, and my hair is already turning gray!* **b)** [T] to make something become a different color: *I got a perm that turned my hair green.* ►see THESAURUS box at **become**
8 SKIN COLOR [linking verb] if a person turns a particular color, their skin looks that color because they feel sick, embarrassed etc.: *I felt myself turn red with embarrassment.*
9 turn a/the corner a) to go around a corner when you are walking, driving etc.: *As Karo turned the corner he saw the girl heading toward him.* **b)** to start to improve after a period of being in a bad condition: *The team has turned a corner and is starting to play better.*
10 turn nasty/sour/violent etc. to change to a worse condition or attitude, especially suddenly: *The protest turned violent by late afternoon.*
11 PAGE [T] if you turn a page in a book, you move it so that you can read the next page → see also **turn to**
12 turn your back (on sb/sth) a) to refuse to help, support, or be involved with someone or something: *He would never turn his back on another veteran.* **b)** to turn so that your back is pointing toward someone or something: *He turned his back on Shauna and walked to the window.*
13 turn the tables (on sb) to change a situation completely so that someone loses an advantage and you gain one: *I was winning by ten points until she turned the tables on me.*
14 turn a profit to make a profit: *The company is not expected to turn a profit for two years.*
15 WEATHER [linking verb] to change, especially becoming cold or worse: *The weather turned cold and it started to rain.*
16 ATTENTION/THOUGHTS ETC. a) [T] to direct your attention, your thoughts, a conversation etc. from one person, thing, or subject to another: *She tried to turn the conversation toward happier subjects.* | **turn your attention/thoughts/efforts etc. to sth** *Many investors have turned their attention to opportunities abroad.* **b)** [I] to be directed in this way: *Joe's thoughts turned to his days on the college football team.*
17 turn upside down a) also **turn sth inside out** to search everywhere for something, in a way that makes a place very messy: *I've turned the house upside down looking for that book!* **b)** also **turn sth on its head** or **turn sth inside out** to do something that makes an organization, a set of rules, a way of understanding something etc. change completely: *Lukens' theories have turned the financial world upside down.*
18 TIME [linking verb] if it has turned a particular time, that time has just passed: *"What time is it?" "It just turned 3:00."*
19 INJURY [T] if you turn your ANKLE, you twist it in a way that injures it
20 turn sb/sth loose to let a person or animal go free from a place: *Someone turned three monkeys loose in the zoo.*
21 an actor-turned-politician/a housewife-turned-author etc. someone who has done one job and then does something so different that it is surprising: *He is a movie star-turned-politician.*
22 turn the tide (of sth) to change the progress or development of something and make it go in the opposite direction: *Their victory turned the tide of the war in North Africa.*
23 turn tail (and run) INFORMAL to run away because you are too frightened to fight or attack: *When they saw us coming with the police, they turned tail and ran.*
24 turn a phrase to say or write something in a clever, interesting, funny etc. way
25 turn (people's) heads if someone or something turns people's heads, people think they are surprising or impressive: *a young artist who is turning heads in New York*
26 turn sb's head OLD-FASHIONED to be attractive in a romantic or sexual way to a particular person: *She's really turned Steve's head.*
27 MAKING BREAD [T always + adv./prep.] also **turn out** to pour DOUGH from a container
28 SOIL [T] to break up land to prepare it for growing crops or for building something
[**Origin:** 1000–1100 partly from Latin *tornare* **to turn on a lathe**; partly from Old French *torner, tourner* **to turn**]
→ see also **turn a blind eye** at BLIND[1] (3), **turn the other cheek** at CHEEK (4), **turn a deaf ear** at DEAF (4), **sb would turn/roll over in their grave** at GRAVE[1] (2), **turn your hand to sth** at HAND[1] (34), **turn your nose up (at sth)** at NOSE[1] (4), **turn sb's stomach** at STOMACH[1] (4) ►see THESAURUS box at **become, open**[1]

turn against *phr. v.* to stop liking someone or supporting a person or idea, usually suddenly, when you have liked or supported them in the past, or to make someone do this: **turn sb against sb/sth** *Brenda even tried to turn my sister against me.* | **turn against sb/sth** *The public was starting to turn against the war.*

turn around *phr. v.* **1** to make something successful again after it has been unsuccessful: *After I met him my whole life turned around.* | **turn sth around** *Jones is trying to turn the company around.* **2 turn around and do sth** SPOKEN to do or say something that is unexpected or seems unfair or unreasonable: *He says he loves me and then turns around and asks me for $500.* **3 every time sb turns around...** SPOKEN very often or all the time: *It seems like every time I turn around my manager is checking up on me.* **4 turn sth around** to consider an idea in a different way, or change the words of something so that it has a different meaning: *You could turn the question around and ask why we shouldn't accept the offer.* **5 turn sth ↔ around** to complete the process of making a product or providing a service: *We can turn around 500 units by next week.*

turn away *phr. v.* **1 turn sb ↔ away** to refuse to let someone into a place such as a theater or restaurant because there is no more space: *The concert is sold out, and they are turning people away.* **2 turn sb ↔ away** to refuse to give someone sympathy, help, or support: *We never turn patients away, even if they don't have money.* | **turn away from sb/sth** *Lots of my friends have turned away from me since I got sick.*

turn back *phr. v.* **1** to go in the opposite direction: *It's getting late – maybe we should turn back.* **2 turn sb ↔ back** to tell someone to go in the opposite direction, often because there is danger ahead: *We got to the gates, and then the police turned us back.* **3** to return to doing something that you did before, or in the way you did it before: *It's too late to turn back now. We have to finish it.* **4 turn back the clock a)** to make a situation like it was at an earlier time, especially when that is worse than the way things are now: *This bill turns back the clock on women's* *rights.* **b)** if you want to turn back the clock, you wish you had the chance to do something again, so you could do it better: *I wish I had the power to turn back the clock and undo the past.*

turn sb/sth ↔ **down** *phr. v.* **1** to make a machine such as an OVEN, radio etc. produce less heat, sound etc. OPP **turn up**: *Could you turn down the air conditioning? It's too cold in here.* **2** to refuse an offer, request, or invitation: *They offered me the job, but I turned it down.*

turn in *phr. v.* **1 turn sth ↔ in** to give back something you have borrowed or rented to a person in authority, or give them something you have found: *We have to turn the bikes in by 6:00.* | **turn sth in to sb** *My wallet was turned in to the police two days after it was stolen.* **2 turn sth ↔ in** to give a piece of work to a teacher, your BOSS etc. SYN **hand in**: *If you don't turn in the assignment, you won't pass.* **3 turn sb ↔ in** to tell the police who or where a criminal is: *Conners drove to the station and turned himself in.* **4 turn in sth** to produce a result, profit etc.: *The 18-year-old* ***turned in*** *a great* ***performance*** *in his first game.* **5** INFORMAL to go to bed: *Well, I think I'll turn in. I've got to get up early.*

turn into sth *phr. v.* **1** to become something different, or make someone or something do this: *These growths could turn into cancer.* | *Winter was turning into spring.* | **turn sb/sth into sth** *Stein turned the garage into an artist's studio.* **2** to change by magic from one thing into another, or make something do this: *At midnight the animals turned into people.* | **turn sb/sth into sth** *With a wave of her hand, the witch turned him into a frog.* **3 days turned into weeks/months turned into years etc.** used to say that time passed slowly while you waited for something to happen: *Weeks turned into months, and still nobody had heard from Joe.*

turn off *phr. v.* **1 turn sth ↔ off** to make a machine or piece of electrical equipment such as a television, car, light etc. stop operating by pushing a button, turning a key etc. OPP **turn on**: *Don't forget to turn off the lights when you leave.* **2 turn sth ↔ off** to stop the supply of water, gas etc. from flowing by turning a handle as far as possible OPP **turn on**: *They turned the gas off for two hours.* **3** to leave one road, especially a large one, and drive along another one: **turn off at/near etc. sth** *Make sure you turn off at the second exit.* | **turn off sth** *We turned off the highway onto a city street.* → see also TURN-OFF **4 turn sb ↔ off** to do something that makes someone decide they do not like someone or something: *Too much mess in the house will turn buyers off.* → see also TURN-OFF **5 turn sb ↔ off** to do something that makes someone feel that they are not attracted to you in a sexual way OPP **turn on**: *He was wearing white socks, which really turns me off.* → see also TURN-OFF

turn on *phr. v.*

1 ELECTRICAL EQUIPMENT **turn sth ↔ on** to make a machine or piece of electrical equipment such as a car, television, light etc. start operating by pushing a button, turning a key etc. OPP **turn off**: *It's so hot – why don't you turn the fan on?*

2 WATER/GAS **turn sth ↔ on** to make the supply of water, gas etc. start flowing from something by turning a handle OPP **turn off**: *He turned on the gas and lit the stove.*

3 ATTACK **turn on sb** to suddenly attack someone or treat them badly, using physical violence or cruel words: *Even dogs that are usually friendly can sometimes turn on people.*

4 DEPEND **turn on sth** if a situation, event, or argument turns on a particular thing or idea, it depends on that thing in order to work: *The trial turned on one key issue: Did Mason know about the plan?*

5 SEXUAL **turn sb on** to make someone feel sexually excited → see also TURN-ON

6 INTEREST **turn sb on** to make someone become interested in a product, idea etc.: **turn sb on to sth** *Reading "Scientific American" really turned me on to biology.*

7 WEAPON **turn sth on sb/sth** to use a weapon, your anger etc. against someone or something: *Cranwell killed six people before turning the gun on himself.*

turn out *phr. v.* **1** to happen in a particular way, or to have a particular result, especially one that you did not expect: *Don't worry – I'm sure it will all turn out fine.* | *The car* ***turned out to be*** *more expensive than we thought.* | ***It turns out that*** *Nancy didn't want to come anyway.* **2 turn sth ↔ out** if you turn out a light, you stop the flow of electricity to it by pushing a button, pulling a string etc. SYN **turn off** OPP **turn on**: *Did you turn out the light in the bathroom?* **3** if people turn out for an event, they gather together to see it happen: **+for** *How many people turned out for the parade?* | **turn out to do sth** *His whole family turned out to welcome him home.* → see also TURNOUT **4 turn sth ↔ out** to produce or make something: *The factory turns out 300 units a day.* **5 turn sb ↔ out** to force someone to leave a place, especially their home: *If the man is found guilty, his family will be turned out on the street.* **6 well/beautifully/badly etc. turned out** to be dressed in good, beautiful etc. clothes: *Tyler is always well turned out.*

turn over *phr. v.* **1 turn sth ↔ over** to give someone the right to own something, or the responsibility for something such as a plan, business, piece of property etc.: **turn sth over to sb** *Local police have turned the case over to the FBI.* **2 turn sb ↔ over** to bring a criminal to the police or other official organization: **turn sb over to sb** *He was so angry that he turned his son over to the authorities.* **3** if an engine turns over, it starts to work **4 turn over sth** if a business turns over a particular amount of money, it makes that amount in a particular period of time **5 turn over a new leaf** to decide to change the way you behave and become a better person **6 turn sth over in your mind** to think about something carefully, considering all the possibilities: *I kept turning the idea over in my mind.*

turn to sb/sth *phr. v.* **1** to try to get help, advice, or sympathy from someone: **turn to sb/sth for sth** *She turned to her mother for advice.* **2** to start to do or use something new, especially when you are in a difficult situation or need to solve a problem: *We may have to turn to solar power to meet our energy needs in the future.* | **turn to drink/drugs/crime etc.** (=start to drink alcohol, take illegal drugs etc. because you are in a difficult situation) **3** to look at a particular page in a book: *Turn to page 655 for more information on this subject.* **4** FORMAL to change to a different form, condition, or attitude, or to make someone or something do this: *The rain has turned to snow in the mountains.* | *My frustration quickly turned to anger.* | **turn sb/sth to sth** *Cooking the mushrooms too long will turn them to mush.* **5** to begin discussing a new subject: *I'd like to turn to the question of immigration control.*

turn up *phr. v.* **1 turn sth ↔ up** to make a machine such as an OVEN, radio etc. produce more heat, sound etc. OPP **turn down**: *If you're cold, I can turn the heat up.* | *Turn up the radio!* **2** to suddenly appear after having been lost or searched for: *Don't worry about the necklace. It'll turn up.* **3** to arrive at a place, especially in a way that is surprising: *Stan's mom turned up in a miniskirt.* **4** if an opportunity or situation turns up, it happens, especially when you are not expecting it: *I'm ready to take any job that turns up.* **5 turn sth ↔ up** to find something by thoroughly searching for it: *The investigation turned up no evidence to support Wood's claims.*

turn upon sb/sth *phr. v.* FORMAL to suddenly attack someone or treat them badly, using physical violence or cruel words SYN **turn on**

turn² S1 W2 *n.*

1 CHANCE TO DO STH the time when it is your chance, duty, or right to do something that a group of people are doing one after another: ***It's your turn.*** *Roll the dice.* | **sb's turn to do sth** *Whose turn is it to wash the dog?*

2 take turns if two or more people take turns doing work or playing a game, they each do it one after the other in order to share work or play fairly: *You'll have to take turns on the swing.* | **take turns doing sth** *We take turns cooking dinner.*
3 in turn a) as a result of something: *Working outside can mean too much sun exposure, which in turn can lead to skin cancer.* **b)** one after the other, especially in a particular order: *The President spoke to each of us at the table in turn.*
4 CHANGE DIRECTION [C] a change in the direction you are moving: **make a left/right turn** *Make a left turn at the light.*
5 ROAD [C] the place where one road goes in a different direction from another: *Take the first turn on your right.*
6 ACT OF TURNING STH [C] the act of turning something completely around a central point: *Tighten the screw another two or three turns.*
7 the turn of the century the time when one century ends and a new one begins: *The population had doubled **at the turn of the century*** (=by 2000, 1900 etc.). → see also TURN-OF-THE-CENTURY
8 take a turn for the worse/better to suddenly become worse or better: *The weather took a turn for the worse.* | ***She took a turn for the worse*** (=her health became worse) *during the night.*
9 turn of events a change in what is happening, especially an unusual one: *We were amazed by the sudden turn of events.*
10 a turn of phrase a) a particular way of saying something: *Calling the palace "small and uninteresting" was a surprising turn of phrase.* **b)** the ability to say things in a clever or funny way: *She has a colorful turn of phrase.*
11 at every turn if something happens at every turn, it happens again and again: *Government officials demanded bribes from us at every turn.*
12 speak/talk out of turn to say something you should not say in a particular situation, especially because you do not have enough authority to say it: *I'm sorry. I was talking out of turn.*
13 by turns LITERARY if someone shows different feelings or qualities by turns, they change from one to another: *She had been by turns confused, angry, and finally jealous.*
14 do sb a good turn OLD-FASHIONED to do something that is helpful for someone
15 turn of mind LITERARY the way that someone usually thinks or feels: *a man with a scientific turn of mind*
16 one good turn deserves another used to say that if someone does something nice for you, you should do something nice for them to thank them
17 give sb a turn OLD-FASHIONED to frighten someone

turn·a·bout /ˈtɚnəˌbaʊt/ *n.* **1 turnabout is fair play** used to say that because someone else has done something to you, you can do it to them too **2** [C usually singular] a complete change in someone's opinions or ideas: *a surprising turnabout in church policy*

turn·a·round /ˈtɚnəˌraʊnd/ *n.* **1** [C usually singular] a complete change from a bad situation to a good one: *Jenkins is confident the company will make a major turnaround this year.* **2** [C,U] the time it takes to receive something, deal with it and send it back, especially on an airplane, ship etc.: *Their products are good, but their **turnaround time** is slow.* → see also **turn around** at TURN[1] **3** [usually singular] a complete change in someone's opinions or ideas: +**in** *a dramatic turnaround in company policy*

turn·coat /ˈtɚnkoʊt/ *n.* [C] someone who stops supporting a political party or group and joins the opposing side SYN **traitor**: *a mafia turncoat*

turn·er /ˈtɚnɚ/ *n.* [C] something, especially a piece of kitchen equipment, used to turn things over: *a pancake turner*

Tur·ner /ˈtɚnɚ/, **J. M. W.** (1775–1851) a British PAINTER

ˈturning ˌcircle *n.* [C] the smallest space in which a vehicle can drive around in a circle

ˈturning point *n.* [C] the time when an important change starts, especially one that improves the situation: *The fall of the Berlin Wall marked a turning point in East-West relations.*

tur·nip /ˈtɚnɪp/ *n.* [C] a large round pale yellow or white vegetable that grows under the ground, or the plant that produces it

turn·key[1] /ˈtɚnki/ *adj.* [only before noun] ready to be used immediately: *The software is a turnkey system that can be simply loaded and run.*

turnkey[2] *n.* [C] OLD USE a prison guard

ˈturn-off *n.* **1** [C] a smaller road that leads off a main road: *I think that was the turn-off for the campground.* **2** [usually singular] INFORMAL something that makes you lose interest in something, especially sex OPP **turn-on**: *Hair on a guy's back is a real turn-off.* **3** [usually singular] INFORMAL something that makes you lose interest in something, because it makes it seem very boring OPP **turn-on**: +**for/to** *The class was mostly about poetry, which was a turn-off for some kids.* → see also **turn off** at TURN[1]

ˌturn-of-the-ˈcentury *adj.* [only before noun] existing or happening around the beginning of a century, especially the beginning of the 20th century: *Turn-of-the-century New Orleans was a fascinating place.*

ˈturn-on *n.* [C usually singular] INFORMAL something that makes you feel excited, especially sexually OPP **turn-off**: *Her voice is a total turn-on.* → see also **turn on** at TURN[1]

turn·out /ˈtɚnaʊt/ *n.* [C] **1** [usually singular] the number of people who go to a party, meeting, or other organized event: **a big/good turnout** *We're expecting a big turnout for tonight's show.* **2** [usually singular] the number of people who vote in an election: **a high/low turnout** *This election had the lowest voter turnout since 1824.* → see also **turn out** at TURN[1] **3** a place at the side of a narrow road where cars can wait to let others pass

turn·o·ver /ˈtɚnˌoʊvɚ/ *n.* **1** [singular, U] the rate at which people leave an organization and are replaced by others: *We're trying to reduce staff turnover.* **2** [singular, U] the rate at which a particular type of goods is sold, or the amount of business done: *Quick turnover is good for cash flow.* **3** [C] a small PIE made with a piece of DOUGH that has been folded over fruit, meat, or vegetables: *an apple turnover* **4** [C] a situation in a football or basketball game in which something happens so that one team loses the ball and the other team gets control of it

turn·pike /ˈtɚnpaɪk/ *n.* [C] a large road for fast traffic that drivers have to pay to use: *the New Jersey Turnpike* [**Origin:** 1700–1800 *turnpike road* (18–20 centuries), from *turnpike* **turning post with sharp points fixed into it, used to control movement past it**]

ˈturn ˌsignal *n.* [C] one of the lights on a car that flash to show which way the car is turning → see picture on page A36

turn·stile /ˈtɚnstaɪl/ *n.* [C] a small gate that spins around and only lets one person at a time go through an entrance

turn·ta·ble /ˈtɚnˌteɪbəl/ *n.* [C] **1** the round flat surface on a RECORD PLAYER that you put records on **2** a round surface that turns around, for example on a table or in a MICROWAVE OVEN **3** a large flat round surface on which railroad engines are turned around

tur·pen·tine /ˈtɚpənˌtaɪn/ *n.* [U] a type of oil used for making paint more liquid or removing it from clothes, brushes etc.

tur·pi·tude /ˈtɚpətud/ *n.* [U] LITERARY evil: *a crime of **moral turpitude***

tur·quoise /ˈtɚkwɔɪz, -kɔɪz/ *n.* [U] **1** EARTH SCIENCE a valuable greenish-blue stone, or a jewel that is made from this **2** a greenish-blue color —**turquoise** *adj.*

tur·ret /ˈtɚɪt, ˈtʌrɪt/ *n.* [C] **1** a small tower on a large building, especially a CASTLE **2** the place on a TANK (=army vehicle) from which guns are fired —**turreted** *adj.*

tur·tle /ˈtɚṭl/ S3 *n.* [C] **1** BIOLOGY an animal that lives in or near water and has a soft body covered by a hard shell. It can pull its head and legs inside the shell to protect itself. **2 turn turtle** if a ship or boat turns turtle, it turns upside down

tur·tle·dove /ˈtɚṭlˌdʌv/ *n.* [C] BIOLOGY a type of bird that makes a pleasant soft sound and is sometimes used to represent love

tur·tle·neck /ˈtɚṭlˌnɛk/ *n.* [C] **1** a type of SWEATER or shirt with a high close-fitting collar that covers most of your neck **2** a high close-fitting collar on a SWEATER or shirt

Tus·ca·ro·ra /ˌtʌskəˈrɔrə/ a Native American tribe from the southeastern area of the U.S.

tush /tʊʃ/ *n.* [C] INFORMAL the part of your body that you sit on

tusk /tʌsk/ *n.* [C] BIOLOGY one of a pair of very long pointed teeth, that stick out of the mouth of animals such as ELEPHANTS

tus·sle¹ /ˈtʌsəl/ *n.* [C] INFORMAL a struggle or fight using a lot of energy: *The two women got into a violent tussle.* | *a tussle for control of the Socialist party*

tussle² *v.* [I + with] INFORMAL to fight or struggle without using any weapons, by pulling or pushing someone rather than hitting them: *He tussled with the doorman when he was not allowed in the club.*

tus·sock /ˈtʌsək/ *n.* [C] LITERARY a small thick mass of grass

T

Tu·tan·kha·men, **Tutankhamon** /ˌtutɑŋˈkɑmən/ (14th century B.C.) an Egyptian PHARAOH (=ruler) whose TOMB and the valuable things in it were discovered in 1922

tu·te·lage /ˈtuṭl-ɪdʒ/ *n.* [U] FORMAL **1** the state or period of being taught or taken care of by someone: *She began her artistic career* ***under the tutelage of*** (=being taught by) *her father.* **2** responsibility for someone's education, actions, or property: *parental tutelage*

tu·tor¹ /ˈtuṭɚ/ *n.* [C] someone who gives private lessons to children in a particular subject: *a math tutor* [**Origin:** 1300–1400 Latin *tutus*, past participle of *tueri* **to look at, guard**] ▸see THESAURUS box at **teacher**

tutor² *v.* [T] to teach someone as a tutor: **tutor sb in sth** *Lydia tutors kids in French during the summer.*

tu·to·ri·al /tuˈtɔriəl/ *n.* [C] **1** COMPUTERS a computer program that is designed to teach you another program without help from someone else **2** a period of teaching and discussion with a tutor: *a psychology tutorial* —**tutorial** *adj.*

tut·ti frut·ti /ˌtuṭi ˈfruṭi/ *n.* [U] a type of ICE CREAM that has very small pieces of fruit and nuts in it

tut-tut¹ /ˌtʌt ˈtʌt/ *interjection* a sound made by touching the top of the mouth with the tongue twice, in order to show disapproval

tut-tut² *v.* [I] to express disapproval, especially by saying "tut-tut"

tu·tu /ˈtutu/ *n.* [C] a short skirt made of many folds of stiff material worn by BALLET dancers

Tu·va·lu /tuˈvɑlu/ a country in the southern Pacific Ocean, east of the Solomon Islands, made up of nine CORAL islands —**Tuvaluan** *n., adj.*

tux·e·do /tʌkˈsidoʊ/ *n. plural* **tuxedos** also **tux** /tʌks/ *plural* **tuxes** [C] **1** a type of man's suit, usually black, that is worn on formal occasions **2** the JACKET that is a part of this suit [**Origin:** 1800–1900 *Tuxedo* Park, town in New York State]

TV S2 W1 *n. plural* **TVs** or **TV's** [C,U] television: *Rob was* ***on TV*** *yesterday, being interviewed on the news.* | **TV show/station/star etc.** *There are several good new TV shows this fall.*

TV-14 /ˌti vi fɔrˈtin/ *adj.* used to show that a television show is not appropriate for children under the age of 14

ˌTV ˈdinner *n.* [C] a meal that is sold already prepared and frozen, so that you just need to heat it before eating

TV-G *adj.* used to show that a television show is appropriate for people of all ages, including children

TV-M *adj.* used to show that a television show is not appropriate for people under the age of 17

TVP *n.* [U] the abbreviation of TEXTURED VEGETABLE PROTEIN

TV-PG *adj.* used to show that a television show may include parts that are not appropriate for young children to see

TV-Y *adj.* used to show that a television show is appropriate for children

TV-Y7 /ˌti vi waɪ ˈsɛvən/ *adj.* used to show that a television show is not appropriate for children under the age of seven

twad·dle /ˈtwɑdl/ *n.* [U] OLD-FASHIONED something that someone has said or written that you think is stupid SYN **nonsense**

twain /tweɪn/ *prep.* **1** OLD USE two **2 (East is East and West is West and) never the twain shall meet** FORMAL or HUMOROUS used to say that two things or people are so different that they can never exist together or agree

Twain /tweɪn/, **Mark** (1835–1910) a U.S. writer famous for his NOVELS. His real name was Samuel Longhorne Clemens.

Mark Twain

twang /twæŋ/ *n.* [C usually singular] **1** a quality in the way someone speaks, produced when the air used to speak passes through their nose as well as their mouth: *a high-pitched Midwestern twang* **2** a quick ringing sound like the one made by pulling a very tight wire and then suddenly letting it go —**twang** *v.* [I,T]

'twas /twəz/ POETIC a short form of "it was": *'Twas the night before Christmas.*

tweak /twik/ *v.* [T] **1** to suddenly pull or twist something: *Matthew tweaked her nose and laughed.* **2** to make small changes to something to improve it: *Maybe you should tweak the last sentence before you send the report.* —**tweak** *n.* [C usually singular]

tweed /twid/ *n.* **1** [U] rough wool cloth woven from threads of different colors, used mostly to make JACKETS, suits, and coats **2 tweeds** [plural] a suit of clothes made from tweed

tweed·y /ˈtwidi/ *adj.* **1** wearing tweed clothes or acting in a way that is thought to be typical of college PROFESSORS, writers etc.: *tweedy academics* **2** made of tweed or like tweed

'tween /twin/ *prep.* POETIC a short form of "between": *'tween heaven and earth*

tweet /twit/ *v.* [I] to make the short high sound of a small bird —**tweet** *n.* [C]

tweet·er /ˈtwiṭɚ/ *n.* [C] a SPEAKER (=piece of equipment) through which the higher sounds from a radio, STEREO etc. come → see also WOOFER

tweez·ers /ˈtwizɚz/ *n.* [plural] a small tool that has two narrow pieces of metal joined at one end, used to pull or move very small objects: *a pair of tweezers*

twelfth¹ /twɛlfθ/ *adj.* 12th; next after the eleventh: *December is the twelfth month.*

twelfth² *pron.* **the twelfth** the 12th thing in a series: *Let's have dinner on the twelfth* (=the 12th day of the month).

twelfth³ *n.* [C] 1/12; one of twelve equal parts

twelve /twɛlv/ *number* **1** 12 **2** 12 o'clock: *We usually eat lunch* ***at about twelve.*** [**Origin:** Old English *twelf*]

ˈTwelve Step, **12-step** *adj.* TRADEMARK **a Twelve Step**

program a method of helping people stop drinking alcohol, using drugs etc., developed by Alcoholics Anonymous

twen·ti·eth¹ /ˈtwɛntiɪθ/ *adj.* 20th; next after the nineteenth: *the twentieth century*

twentieth² *pron.* **the twentieth** the 20th thing in a series: *Let's have dinner on the twentieth* (=the 20th day of the month).

twen·ty¹ /ˈtwɛnti/ *number* **1** 20 **2 the twenties** also **the '20s** the years from 1920 through 1929 **3 sb's twenties** the time when someone is 20 to 29 years old: **be in your early/mid/late twenties** *I'd say he's in his late twenties.* **4 in the twenties** if the temperature is in the twenties, it is between 20° and 29° FAHRENHEIT: **in the high/low twenties** *The temperature was in the low twenties the whole week.* [**Origin:** Old English *twentig*]

twenty² *n. plural* **twenties** [C] a piece of paper money worth $20: *Sorry, I don't have anything smaller than a twenty.*

ˌTwenty-first Aˈmendment, the HISTORY a change to the U.S. Constitution in 1933 which made it legal to buy and drink alcoholic drinks

ˌtwenty-four ˈseven, 24/7 *adv.* INFORMAL 24 hours a day, seven days a week; all the time: *He listens to the radio 24/7.*

ˌTwenty-fourth Aˈmendment, the HISTORY a change to the U.S. Constitution in 1964. Before the change, people were not allowed to vote in FEDERAL elections if they had not paid the Poll Tax. After the change, they had the right to vote whether or not they had paid the tax, which meant that poor people and especially African-Americans could not be prevented from voting.

ˌtwenty-ˈone *n.* [U] a card game, usually played for money SYN **blackjack**

ˌTwenty-sixth Aˈmendment, the HISTORY a change to the U.S. Constitution in 1971 which said that 18 was the age at which people could vote in elections

twen·ty·some·thing /ˈtwɛntiˌsʌmθɪŋ/ *adj.* [only before noun] between the ages of 20 and 29: *a twenty-something lawyer* —**twentysomething** *n.* [C usually plural]

ˌtwenty-ˈtwenty, 20/20 *adj.* **1 20/20 vision** the ability to see things normally, without needing glasses **2 20/20 hindsight** also **hindsight is 20/20** used when saying that it is easy to know what you should have done in a situation after it has happened, but difficult to know as it is happening: *20/20 hindsight says that the team should have chosen a better pitcher.*

ˌtwenty-ˈtwo, .22 *n.* [C] a gun that fires small bullets, used for hunting small animals

twerp /twɚp/ *n.* [C] SPOKEN a small person who you think is stupid or annoying

twice¹ /twaɪs/ W2 *adv.* **1** two times: *I've only met him twice.* | **twice a day/week/year etc** *She goes swimming twice a week.* ►see THESAURUS box at **two** **2** MATH two times more, bigger, better etc. than something else: **twice as many/much (as sb/sth)** *They employ 90 people, twice as many as last year.* | **twice as high/big/large etc. (as sb/sth)** *The image is twice as good as the image on a regular TV.* [**Origin:** Old English *twiga*] → see also **once or twice** at ONCE¹ (14), **once bitten, twice shy** at ONCE¹ (19), **think twice** at THINK (6)

twice² *determiner* two times more, bigger, better etc. than something else: **twice the size/number/rate/amount etc.** *The region is about twice the size of California.*

twid·dle /ˈtwɪdl/ *v.* **1 twiddle your thumbs** INFORMAL **a)** to do nothing while you are waiting for something to happen: *Let's go – I'm not going to sit here twiddling my thumbs forever.* **b)** to join your fingers together and move your thumbs in a circle around each other, because you are bored **2 twiddle (with) sth** to move or turn something around with your fingers many times, especially because you are bored —**twiddle** *n.* [C]

twig /twɪg/ *n.* [C] a small very thin stem of wood that grows from a branch on a tree —**twiggy** *adj.*

twi·light /ˈtwaɪlaɪt/ *n.* [U] **1** the time when day is just starting to become night SYN **dusk**: *We took a walk on the beach **at twilight**.* **2** the small amount of light in the sky as the day ends: *The end of his cigarette glowed **in the twilight**.* | **twilight falls** LITERARY (=twilight begins) **3** the period just before the end of the most active part of someone's life or the end of an important period of time: **+of** *the twilight of the Victorian age* | *She's looking for something to do in her **twilight years*** (=the last years of her life). **4 twilight world** LITERARY a strange situation involving mystery, dishonest activities etc.: *the twilight world of drug smuggling*

twi·lit /ˈtwaɪlɪt/ *adj.* LITERARY lit by twilight

twill /twɪl/ *n.* [U] strong cloth woven to produce parallel sloping lines across its surface: *cotton twill pants*

twin¹ /twɪn/ S3 *n.* [C] one of two children born at the same time to the same mother: *My brother and I are twins.* → see also CONJOINED TWINS, IDENTICAL TWIN, FRATERNAL TWIN, SIAMESE TWIN

twin² *adj.* [only before noun] **1 twin sister/brother/daughters etc.** someone who is a twin: *Did you know George has a twin sister?* | **twin boys/girls** *She gave birth to twin girls.* **2** like something else and considered with it as a pair: *twin towers of the cathedral* **3** used to describe two things that happen at the same time and are related to each other: *the twin problems of poverty and unemployment* | **twin goals/objectives/aims** *How can we reach these twin goals?* [**Origin:** Old English *twinn* **double**]

twin³ *v.* **twinned, twinning** [T usually passive] to form a relationship between two places, people, or ideas, or make people think that this relationship exists: **twin sb/sth with sb/sth** *The Democrat and the Republican were twinned with each other in front of the TV cameras.*

ˌtwin ˈbed *n.* [C] **1** a bed for one person **2** one of a pair of single beds in a hotel room for two people

ˌTwin ˈCities, the the cities of Minneapolis and St. Paul in the U.S. state of Minnesota

twine¹ /twaɪn/ *n.* [U] strong string made by twisting together two or more threads or strings

twine² *v.* [I,T] to wind or twist around something else, or to make something do this: **twine (sth) around sth** *An ivy plant twined around the pole.*

ˌtwin-ˈengine also **ˌtwin-ˈengined** *adj.* a twin-engine aircraft has two engines

twinge /twɪndʒ/ *n.* [C] **1** a sudden feeling of slight pain: *I felt a twinge in my lower back.* | **+of** *a twinge of pain in his knee* **2 a twinge of guilt/fear/jealousy etc.** a sudden slight feeling of guilt, fear etc. SYN **pang**: *For an instant I felt a twinge of sympathy for him.*

twin·kle¹ /ˈtwɪŋkəl/ *v.* [I] **1** if a star or light twinkles, it shines in the dark, quickly changing between being bright and being difficult to see: *Stars twinkled in the sky above.* ►see THESAURUS box at **shine¹** **2** if someone's eyes twinkle, they have a cheerful expression: **twinkle with sth** *Her eyes twinkled with delight as she smiled.*

twinkle² *n.* [C usually singular] **1 a twinkle in your eye** an expression in your eyes that shows you are happy or amused **2** a small bright shining light that becomes brighter, more difficult to see, and then brighter again **3 when you were just a twinkle in your father's eye** before you were born

twin·kling /ˈtwɪŋklɪŋ/ *n.* **1 in the twinkling of an eye** also **in a twinkling** LITERARY very quickly: *In a twinkling he was out of the car and hugging her.* **2** [U] the act of shining with a small light that becomes brighter, more difficult to see, and then brighter again

ˈtwin-size also **ˈtwin-sized** *adj.* relating to a TWIN BED: *twin-size sheets*

ˌTwin ˈTowers → see WORLD TRADE CENTER

twirl /twɚl/ *v.* [I,T] to turn around and around, or make someone or something do this: *The dancers twirled across the stage.* | **twirl sb/sth around** *He lifted the girl* *up and twirled her around.* ►see THESAURUS box at **turn**[1] —**twirl** *n.* [C] —**twirly** *adj.*

twist[1] /twɪst/ S3 *v.*

1 BEND [T] to turn something such as wire, hair, or cloth around itself into a spiral or round shape using your fingers or hands: *Wrap the paper around the candy and twist the ends.* | **twist sth into sth** *She twisted her scarf into a knot.* | **twist sth together** *Twist the two ends of the wire together.*

2 MOVE [I,T] to turn part of your body around, while the rest stays still: *I stopped the car and* ***twisted around*** *in my seat to face her.* | *The fox* ***twisted and turned****, trying to free himself from the trap*

3 TURN [T] to turn something in a circle using your hand or fingers: *She was nervously twisting the ring on her finger.* | **twist sth off** *These bottle caps aren't easy to twist off.* ►see THESAURUS box at **turn**[1]

4 ROAD/RIVER [I] if a road, river etc. twists, it has a lot of curves in it: *The road* ***twisted and turned*** (=curved one way and then the other) *up the side of the mountain.*

5 twist your wrist/ankle/knee etc. to hurt a joint in your body by pulling or turning it too suddenly while you are moving ►see THESAURUS box at **hurt**[1]

6 WORDS [T] to change the true or intended meaning of a statement, especially in order to get some advantage for yourself SYN **distort**: *The magazine completely* ***twisted my words.*** ►see THESAURUS box at **change**[1]

7 SPOIL STH'S SHAPE [T] to spoil the shape of something, especially metal, by bending it in many directions: *The force of the explosion had twisted the truck's body.*

8 WIND [T always + adv./prep.] to wind something around or through an object: **twist sth around/into/through etc. sth** *I twisted my scarf around my neck.*

9 FACE [I,T] if your mouth, lips, face etc. twists, or you twist them, you smile in an unpleasant way or look angry, disapproving etc: *His mouth twisted scornfully.*

10 twist sb's arm a) INFORMAL to persuade someone to do something they do not want to do: *We had to twist her arm to get her to come.* **b)** to bend someone's arm up behind their back in order to hurt them

11 leave sb to twist in the wind to fail to make a definite decision about something important that will affect someone: *I put in my college application months ago, and they're just leaving me to twist in the wind.*

12 DANCE to dance the TWIST

13 twist my arm! SPOKEN, HUMOROUS used to accept an invitation, a drink etc.

[**Origin:** 1300–1400 Old English *twist* **rope**] → see also **twist/wrap sb around your little finger** at FINGER[1] (9), **twist/turn the knife** at KNIFE[1] (6)

twist[2] *n.* [C]

1 UNEXPECTED an unexpected feature or change in a situation or series of events: *This was Sunday afternoon football* ***with a twist*** *– the players were women.* | *It's hard to follow the* ***twists and turns*** *of the movie's plot.* | **a twist of fate/fortune/irony** *By a twist of fate, I was offered a job in Australia where my fiancé was living.*

2 MOVEMENT a twisting action or movement: *The diamond sparkled with each twist of the chain.*

3 BEND a bend in a river or road: *The road was full of* ***twists and turns.***

4 SHAPE a shape made by twisting something, such as paper, rope, or hair: *Lorna wears her hair in a twist.* | **+of** *a twist of lemon*

5 DANCE the twist a popular fast dance from the 1960s, in which you twist the lower part of your body from side to side → see also TWISTY

twist·ed /ˈtwɪstɪd/ *adj.* **1** something twisted has been bent in many directions or turned many times, so that it has lost its original shape: *the twisted wreckage of the plane* ►see THESAURUS box at **bent**[2] **2** seeming to enjoy things that are cruel or shocking, in a way that is not normal, or showing this quality: *Whoever sent those disgusting letters has a twisted mind.* **3** a twisted ANKLE or knee has been injured by being pulled or turned too suddenly while you were moving

twist·er /ˈtwɪstɚ/ *n.* [C] INFORMAL a TORNADO

ˈtwist tie *n.* [C] a small piece of wire covered with paper or plastic that can be twisted around the top of a plastic bag to keep it closed

twist·y /ˈtwɪsti/ *adj.* INFORMAL **1** having a lot of twists or bends: *a twisty road* **2** having a lot of unexpected developments: *a novel with a twisty plot*

twit[1] /twɪt/ *n.* [C] INFORMAL a stupid or silly person

twit[2] *v.* **twitted, twitting** [T] to laugh at someone or try to make them look silly or stupid: *You shouldn't have twitted her about her clothes.*

twitch[1] /twɪtʃ/ *v.* **1** [I,T] if a part of someone's body twitches or if they twitch it, a part of their body makes a small sudden movement: *A muscle in my neck twitched.* | *The cat was twitching her tail.* **2** [T] to move something quickly and suddenly: *Sarah twitched the reins, and the horse started moving.*

twitch[2] *n.* [C] **1** a quick movement of a muscle that you cannot control: *a nervous twitch* **2** a sudden quick movement: *He pulled the curtain back with a twitch of his wrist.*

twitch·y /ˈtwɪtʃi/ *adj. comparative* **twitchier**, *superlative* **twitchiest** **1** behaving in a nervous way because you are anxious about something: *Why are you so twitchy today?* **2** repeatedly making sudden small movements: *twitchy legs*

twit·ter[1] /ˈtwɪtɚ/ *v.* [I] **1** if a bird twitters, it makes a lot of short high sounds very quickly **2** if a woman twitters, she talks very quickly and nervously in a high voice

twitter[2] *n.* **1** [C] the short high fast sounds that birds make **2 be in a twitter** to be excited and nervous → see also ATWITTER

twixt /twɪkst/ *prep.* OLD USE between

two /tu/ *number* **1** 2

THESAURUS

a pair (of sth) two things of the same type that you use together: *a pair of shoes*
a couple (of sth) two things of the same type: *a couple of apples*
a couple two people who are married or have a romantic relationship: *a married couple*
twins two children who were born on the same day to the same mother
double room/bed etc. a room, bed etc. for two people
twice two times: *I phoned her twice yesterday.*
for two for two people: *A table for two, please.*

2 two o'clock: *We're supposed to be there* ***at two.*** **3 a year/a week/a moment/an hour etc. or two** INFORMAL used when you are giving an amount of time that is not exact: *Come and stay with us for a week or two.* **4 in twos** in groups of two people or things SYN **in pairs**: *The students work in twos or threes.* **5 sb's two cents (worth)** INFORMAL someone's opinion or what they want to say about a subject: *We all got a chance to* ***put in our two cents*** *on the topic.* **6 put two and two together** to guess the meaning of something you have heard or seen: *We found the money and the drugs in his room and put two and two together.* | **put two and two together and make five** (=to hear or see something and guess wrongly about what it means) **7 that makes two of us** SPOKEN used to tell someone that you are in the same situation and feel the same way: *"I'd like to live in Hawaii." "Yeah, that makes two of us."* **8 two's company, three's a crowd** used to say that it is better to leave two people alone to spend time with each other **9 two can play at that game** SPOKEN used to say that if someone is going to do something that makes you annoyed or angry, then you will do the same thing to them: *She wasn't talking to me, so I decided, "Well two can play at that game."* **10 for two cents, I'd...** SPOKEN used when you are describing angrily what you would like to do to change a situation: *For two cents, I'd take the kids and leave tomorrow.* **11 two bits** OLD-FASHIONED, INFORMAL 25 CENTS, or a coin that is worth this amount of money [**Origin:** Old English *twa*] → see also **be two of a kind** at KIND[1] (7), **be of two minds about sth** at MIND[1]

(37), **it takes two to tango** at TANGO[2] (2), **no two ways about it** at WAY[1] (67)

two-bit *adj.* [only before noun] INFORMAL not good or important at all: *What do you think I am, some two-bit crook?*

two-by-'four *n.* [C] a long piece of wood that is two inches thick and four inches wide

two-di'mensional *adj.* **1** also **2-D** MATH flat; having length and height, but no depth: *two-dimensional drawings* → see also THREE-DIMENSIONAL **2** ENG. LANG. ARTS a two-dimensional character in a book, play etc. does not seem like a real person

two-'edged *adj.* **a two-edged sword** something that has as many bad results as good ones SYN **double-edged**: *The policy is a two-edged sword – it saves money but angers employees.*

two-'faced *adj.* DISAPPROVING, INFORMAL changing what you say according to who you are talking to, in a way that is insincere and not nice: *You're a two-faced liar!*

two·fer /ˈtufɚ/ *n.* [C] INFORMAL a situation or arrangement in which you receive two things, but you only have to pay for one

two-'fisted *adj.* [only before noun] **1** doing something with a lot of energy and determination, or done in this way: *a two-fisted attack* **2** TWO-HANDED

two·fold /ˈtufoʊld/ *adj.* **1** having two important parts: *The answer to the question is twofold.* **2** [only before noun] two times as much or as many of something: *a twofold increase in the genetic mutations* —**twofold** *adv.*

two-'four *n.* [C] CANADIAN, INFORMAL 24 bottles of beer sold together in a box

two-'handed *adj.* **1** done using both hands: *her powerful two-handed backhand* **2** a two-handed tool is used by two people together

twoo·nie /ˈtuni/ *n.* [C] a TOONIE

two-party ˌsystem *n.* [C] POLITICS a political system in which two political parties compete against each other in elections: *Although the U.S. has many poltical parties, it is still primarily a two-party system of Republicans and Democrats.* → see also MULTIPARTY SYSTEM

two percent 'milk *n.* [U] milk that has had cream removed so that two PERCENT of what remains is fat → see also ONE PERCENT MILK, SKIM MILK, WHOLE MILK

two-piece *adj.* [only before noun] a two-piece suit consists of a matching JACKET and pants → see also THREE-PIECE

two-ply *adj.* consisting of two threads or layers: *two-ply yarn* | *two-ply toilet paper*

two-'seater *n.* [C] a car, aircraft etc. with seats for two people

two-'sided *adj.* **1** having two different parts: *a two-sided issue* **2** having two specially prepared sides: *two-sided adhesive tape* → see also MANY-SIDED, ONE-SIDED

two·some /ˈtusəm/ *n.* [C usually singular] **1** two people who work together or spend a lot of time together: *a well-known comedy twosome* (=two people who work together telling jokes) **2** a game of GOLF for two people

two-step *n.* **1 the two-step** a dance with long sliding steps, or the music for this type of dance **2** a type of quick COUNTRY AND WESTERN dance

two-stroke *adj.* a two-stroke engine is one in which there is a single up-and-down movement of a PISTON

two-time *v.* [T] INFORMAL to have a secret relationship with someone who is not your regular partner: *Ryan was two-timing Jeannie with her best friend.* —**two-timer** *n.* [C]

two-tone *adj.* two-tone furniture, clothes etc. are made of material in two colors: *two-tone shoes*

two-way *adj.* **1** moving or allowing movement in both directions: *Is this a one-way or a two-way street?* | *two-way traffic* → see also ONE-WAY **2** INFORMAL used to describe a situation involving two people or groups, which needs both people or groups to make an effort or to communicate: *Corruption is always a two-way process.* | *Education is **a two-way street*** (=a situation of this type). → see also ONE-WAY **3** able to both send and receive messages OPP **one-way**: *a two-way radio*

ˌtwo-way 'mirror *n.* [C] glass that looks like a mirror from one side, but that you can see through from the other side

TX the written abbreviation of Texas

-ty /ti/ *suffix* [in nouns] the state of having a particular quality, or something that has that quality: *certainty* (=being certain) → see also -ITY

ty·coon /taɪˈkun/ *n.* [C] someone who is successful in business or industry and has a lot of money and power: *a Greek shipping tycoon* [**Origin:** 1800–1900 Japanese *taikun*, from Chinese *taijun*, from *tai* **great** + *jun* **ruler**]

ty·ing /ˈtaɪ-ɪŋ/ *v.* the present participle of TIE

tyke, tike /taɪk/ *n.* [C] INFORMAL a small child

Ty·ler /ˈtaɪlɚ/, **John** (1790–1862) the tenth President of the U.S.

tym·pan·ic mem·brane /tɪmˌpænɪk ˈmɛmbreɪn/ *n.* [C] BIOLOGY the EARDRUM or a similar part in animals or insects

type¹ /taɪp/ S1 W1 *n.* **1** [C] a group of people or things that have similar features or qualities: *We make cosmetics for people of all skin types.* | +**of** *What type of movies do you like?* | *The virus is related to **the type that** has infected 9,000 people in Japan.* | *Accidents **of this type** are extremely common.*

THESAURUS

kind: *What kind of fish is this?*
sort: *I like all sorts of music.*
category a group of people or things that are all of the same type: *The three major categories of rock are: igneous, metamorphic, and sedimentary.*
brand a type of produce made by a particular company: *several different brands of soap*
make a type of product made by a particular company: *"What make of car do you drive?" "A Ford."*
model one particular type or design of a vehicle, machine, weapon etc.: *The new models are much faster.*
genre a type of art, music, literature etc. that has a particular style or feature: *He has written novels in several genres, most notably science fiction.*

2 [C] someone with particular qualities or interests: *The second woman was a grandmotherly type.* | *the artistic type* | **the type to do sth** *He's not the type to complain.* **3 sb's type** the kind of person someone is sexually attracted to: *He wasn't really my type.* **4** [U] printed letters SYN **typeface**: *bold type* **5** [C,U] a small block with a raised letter on it that is used in printing, or a set of these [**Origin:** 1400–1500 Latin *typus* **image**, from Greek *typos* **act of hitting, mark made by hitting, model**] → see also BLOOD TYPE

type² S2 W3 *v.* **1** [I,T] to write something using a computer or TYPEWRITER: *Type your password, and then push "enter."* **2** [T] to print a document on a piece of paper using a TYPEWRITER: *These letters still need to be typed.* **3** [T] TECHNICAL to find out what type a plant, disease etc. is

type sth ↔ **in** *phr. v.* to type information on a computer, so that it appears on the screen: *Type in your name and address.*

type sth ↔ **up** *phr. v.* to type a copy of something that is written by hand, exists in note form, or has been recorded: *I took my notes home and typed them up.*

Type A /ˌtaɪp ˈeɪ◂/ *adj.* relating to the qualities or behavior of the type of people who are often determined, angry, or impatient: **Type A personality/behavior** *People with Type A personalities are at a higher risk for heart attacks.* → see also TYPE B

Type B /ˌtaɪp ˈbi/ *adj.* relating to the qualities or behavior of the type of people who are usually relaxed, friendly, and patient → see also TYPE A

type·cast /ˈtaɪpkæst/ *v.* [T usually passive] to always give an actor the same type of character to play: *I don't want to get typecast as a comedy actress.* —**typecasting** *n.* [U]

type·face /ˈtaɪpfeɪs/ *n.* [C] a group of letters, numbers etc. of the same style and size, used in printing SYN font

type·script /ˈtaɪpˌskrɪpt/ *n.* [C] a copy of a document, made using a TYPEWRITER

type·set·ter /ˈtaɪpˌsɛt̬ɚ/ *n.* [C] a person or machine that arranges the letters, words etc. on a page or screen for printing

type·set·ting /ˈtaɪpˌsɛt̬ɪŋ/ *n.* [U] the job or activity of arranging TYPE for printing —**typeset** *v.* [T]

type·writ·er /ˈtaɪpˌraɪt̬ɚ/ *n.* [C] a machine with keys that you press to print letters of the alphabet onto paper, used before computers

type·writ·ten /ˈtaɪpˌrɪtˀn/ *adj.* written using a TYPEWRITER: *a typewritten letter*

ty·phoid /ˈtaɪfɔɪd/ also **ˌtyphoid ˈfever** *n.* [U] MEDICINE a serious infectious disease that is caused by dirty food or water

ty·phoon /taɪˈfun/ *n.* [C] EARTH SCIENCE a very violent storm in tropical areas in which the wind moves in circles at speeds of over 74 miles per hour [**Origin:** 1800–1900 *touffan* **typhoon** (16–19 centuries), from Arabic *tufan* **hurricane**; influenced by Chinese *daai fong* **great wind**] → see also CYCLONE

T

ty·phus /ˈtaɪfəs/ *n.* [U] MEDICINE a serious infectious disease carried by insects that live on the bodies of people and animals

typ·i·cal /ˈtɪpɪkəl/ S3 W2 *adj.* **1** having the usual features or qualities of a particular group or thing: *Kim's a typical teenager – she doesn't want her parents telling her what to do.* | +**of** *This painting is fairly typical of his early work.* | *The church is* ***a typical example of*** *this style of architecture.* | **your/the typical sth** INFORMAL: *He's not your typical 70-year-old guy. He likes to sky dive.* **2** used about behavior that you expect of someone because it is the way they usually behave SYN **characteristic**: *Bennett accepted the award with typical modesty.* | **it is typical of sb to do sth** *It's typical of Craig not to notice my new dress.* | *Amber was late again?* ***Typical*** (=used when saying you are annoyed by the behavior)!

typ·i·cally /ˈtɪpɪkli/ W3 *adv.* **1** [sentence adverb] usually: *I typically get around 30 emails a day.* **2** [+ adj./adv.] in a way that a person or group is generally believed to behave, or a type of thing is believed to be: *a very nice typically Dutch hotel* | *Lily's gifts were typically generous.*

typ·i·fy /ˈtɪpəˌfaɪ/ *v.* **typifies, typified, typifying** [T not in progressive] **1** to be a typical example of something: *The church typifies the German architecture of the early 1700s.* **2** to be a typical part or feature of something: *These long complicated sentences typify legal documents.*

typ·ing /ˈtaɪpɪŋ/ *n.* [U] the activity of using a computer or TYPEWRITER to write something, or something that is written in this way: *typing skills*

ˈtyping pool *n.* [C] a group of typists in a large office who type letters for other people, especially in past times

typ·ist /ˈtaɪpɪst/ *n.* [C] **1** a secretary whose main job is to TYPE letters **2 a good/bad/fast/slow etc. typist** someone who writes using a computer or TYPEWRITER in a particular way: *I'm not a very good typist.*

ty·po /ˈtaɪpoʊ/ *n.* [C] a small mistake in the way something has been TYPED or printed: *This report is full of typos.*

ty·pog·ra·pher /taɪˈpɑgrəfɚ/ *n.* [C] **1** someone who designs TYPEFACES **2** a COMPOSITOR

ty·po·graph·i·cal /ˌtaɪpəˈgræfɪkəl/ also **ty·po·graph·ic** /ˌtaɪpəˈgræfɪk/ *adj.* relating to typography: *typographical errors* —**typographically** /-kli/ *adv.*

ty·pog·ra·phy /taɪˈpɑgrəfi/ *n.* [U] **1** the work of preparing written material for printing **2** the arrangement, style, and appearance of printed words

ty·pol·o·gy /taɪˈpɑlədʒi/ *n.* [U] the study or system of dividing a large group into smaller groups according to similar features or qualities: *language typology* —**typological** /ˌtaɪpəˈlɑdʒɪkəl/ *adj.*

ty·ran·ni·cal /tɪˈrænɪkəl/ *adj.* **1** behaving in a cruel and unfair way toward someone you have power over: *a tyrannical boss* **2** tyrannical rules, laws etc. are based on a system in which a single ruler uses their power unfairly: *a tyrannical regime*

tyr·an·nize /ˈtɪrəˌnaɪz/ *v.* [T] to use power over someone in a cruel or unfair way: *The household was tyrannized by a brutal father.*

ty·ran·no·saur·us /təˌrænəˈsɔrəs◂/ also **tyrannosaurus rex** /təˌrænəˌsɔrəs ˈrɛks/ *n.* [C] BIOLOGY a very large flesh-eating DINOSAUR

tyr·an·nous /ˈtɪrənəs/ *adj.* OLD-FASHIONED → see TYRANNICAL

tyr·an·ny /ˈtɪrəni/ *n. plural* **tyrannies** **1** [C,U] government by one person or a small group that has gained power unfairly and uses it in a cruel way **2** [U] unfair and strict control over someone that limits someone's freedom, or a single act of this: *parental tyranny* **3 the tyranny of sth** the power that something has to control people's lives, and the way that they behave: *We all live and work by the tyranny of the clock.*

ty·rant /ˈtaɪrənt/ *n.* [C] **1** POLITICS a ruler who has complete power and uses it in a cruel and unfair way: *The Romanian tyrant Ceaucescu was overthrown in 1989.* **2** someone who uses their power or influence over other people unfairly or cruelly: *Little Kyle is an absolute tyrant in the family.* **3** HISTORY a ruler in ancient Greece who took control of a state in a way that the law did not allow, and who had complete power

tyre /taɪɚ/ *n.* [C] the British spelling of TIRE

ty·ro /ˈtaɪroʊ/ *n.* [C] FORMAL someone who is only beginning to learn something

Ty·son /ˈtaɪsən/, **Mike** /maɪk/ (1966–) a U.S. BOXER

tzar /zɑr, tsɑr/ *n.* [C] another spelling of CZAR —**tzarist** *adj.*

tza·ri·na /zɑˈrinə, tsɑ-/ *n.* [C] another spelling of CZARINA

tzar·is·m /ˈzɑˌrɪzəm,ˈtsɑ-/ *n.* [U] another spelling of CZARISM

tze·tze fly /ˈtɛtsi flaɪ, ˈtsɛtsi-/ *n.* [C] another spelling of TSETSE FLY

U,u

U¹, u /yu/ *n. plural* **U's, u's** [C] **1** the 21st letter of the English alphabet **2** a sound represented by this letter

U.², U an abbreviation of UNIVERSITY

UAW **United Automobile, Aerospace, and Agricultural Implement Workers** a UNION in the U.S.

u·biq·ui·tous /yu'bɪkwətəs/ *adj.* FORMAL seeming to be everywhere: *Coffee shops are ubiquitous these days.* —**ubiquitously** *adv.* —**ubiquity** *n.* [U]

U-boat /'yu boʊt/ *n.* [C] a German SUBMARINE, especially one that was used in World War II

ud·der /'ʌdɚ/ *n.* [C] BIOLOGY the part of a female cow, goat etc. where milk comes out

UFO *n.* [C] **Unidentified Flying Object** a strange object in the sky, sometimes thought to be a SPACESHIP from another world

UFW → see UNITED FARM WORKERS

U·gan·da /yu'gændə, -'gɑn-/ a country in central Africa, east of the Democratic Republic of Congo and west of Kenya —**Ugandan** *n., adj.*

ugh /ʌg, ʌk, ʌh/ *interjection* used to show strong dislike: *I saw her haircut. Ugh!*

ug·ly /'ʌgli/ S2 *adj. comparative* **uglier**, *superlative* **ugliest** **1** extremely unattractive, and not nice to look at SYN **unattractive**: *an ugly man* | *the ugliest building in the city* **2** extremely bad or violent, and making you feel frightened or upset: *The situation* ***turned ugly*** (=became bad or violent) *and the police were called.* **3** ugly ideas, feelings, remarks, ways of doing things etc. are unpleasant: *an ugly rumor* | *Jealousy is an ugly emotion.* **4 an ugly duckling** someone who is less attractive, skillful etc. than other people when they are young, but who becomes beautiful or successful later [**Origin:** 1200–1300 Old Norse *uggligr* **frightening**, from *uggr* **fear**] —**ugliness** *n.* [U] → see also **sth rears its ugly head** at REAR³ (4)

uh /ʌ/ *interjection* said when you are thinking about what you are going to say: *Jimmy's from, uh, Texas.*

UHF *n.* [U] **Ultra-High Frequency** a range of radio WAVES between 300 and 3,000 MEGAHERTZ, used also for television → see also VHF

uh huh /n'hn, m'hm, ə'hʌ/ *interjection* INFORMAL a sound that you make to mean "yes" or to show that you understand something OPP **uh-uh**: *"Is that you in the picture?" "Uh huh."*

uh oh /'ˀʌ ˀoʊ/ *interjection* INFORMAL said when you have made a mistake or have realized that something bad has happened: *Uh oh, I think I locked my keys in the car.*

uh-uh /'ʌ ʌ, 'n n/ *interjection* INFORMAL a sound that you make to say "no" OPP **uh huh**: *"You didn't get hurt?" "Uh-uh."*

U-ie /'yui/ *n.* [C] SPOKEN a U-TURN: **do/pull a U-ie** *He pulled a U-ie on Main Street.*

U.K. *n.* the abbreviation of UNITED KINGDOM

U·kraine /yu'kreɪn, yu'kreɪn/ a country in eastern Europe, between Poland and Russia. It was formerly part of the Soviet Union and is now a member of the CIS. —**Ukrainian** /yu'kreɪniən/ *n., adj.*

u·ku·le·le /ˌyukə'leɪli/ *n.* [C] a musical instrument with four strings, like a small GUITAR

U·laan·baa·tar /ˌulɑn'bɑtɑr/ the capital city of Mongolia, formerly called Ulan Bator

-ular /yəlɚ/ *suffix* [in adjectives] relating to something, or shaped like something: *muscular* (=relating to the muscles) | *circular* (=shaped like a circle) → see also -AR

ul·cer /'ʌlsɚ/ *n.* [C] MEDICINE a sore area on your skin or inside your body that may BLEED or produce poisonous substances: *a stomach ulcer* —**ulcerous** *adj.*

ul·cer·ate /'ʌlsəˌreɪt/ *v.* [I,T] MEDICINE to form an ulcer, or become covered with ulcers —**ulcerated** *adj.* —**ulceration** /ˌʌlsə'reɪʃən/ *n.* [U]

-ule /yul, yʊl/ *suffix* [in nouns] TECHNICAL a small type of something: *a granule* (=small grain)

ul·na /'ʌlnə/ *n.* [C] BIOLOGY the inner bone of your lower arm, on the side opposite to your thumb → see picture at SKELETON¹

ul·te·ri·or /ʌl'tɪriɚ/ *adj.* **an ulterior motive/purpose/reason etc.** a reason for doing something that you deliberately hide in order to get an advantage for yourself: *He just being nice. I don't think he* ***has*** *any* ***ulterior motives.***

ul·ti·mate¹ /'ʌltəmɪt/ Ac S3 W3 *adj.* [only before noun] **1** an ultimate aim, purpose etc. is the final and most important one: **sb's ultimate goal/aim/objective etc.** *Our ultimate goal is to own our own farm.* **2** the ultimate result of a long process is what happens at the end of it: *The ultimate outcome of the experiment is, of course, unknown.* **3** better, bigger, worse etc. than all other objects of the same kind: *The Rolling Stones are the ultimate rock and roll band.* **4** an ultimate decision, responsibility etc. is one that you cannot pass on to someone else: *Ultimate responsibility lies with the President.* [**Origin:** 1600–1700 Late Latin *ultimatus* **last**, from *ultimare* **to come to an end, be last**]

ultimate² Ac *n.* **the ultimate in sth** the best or most perfect example of something: *One critic called the fashion designs "the ultimate in bad taste."*

ˌultimate 'frisbee *n.* [U] a sport like football that is played with a FRISBEE rather than a ball

ul·ti·mate·ly /'ʌltəmɪtli/ Ac S3 W3 *adv.* **1** after everything or everyone else has been done or considered: [sentence adverb] *Ultimately, you'll have to decide for yourself.* **2** in the end, after a long series of events: *The proposal was ultimately rejected.* **3** if you are ultimately responsible for something, you are the only one responsible for the important final decisions that have to be made: *On a ship, it is the captain who is ultimately responsible.*

ul·ti·ma·tum /ˌʌltə'meɪt̬əm/ *n.* [C] a threat saying that if someone does not do what you want by a particular time, you will do something to punish them: *After seven years she* ***gave*** *him* ***an ultimatum:*** *either stop drinking or move out.*

ultra- /ʌltrə/ *prefix* **1** TECHNICAL above and beyond something in a range: *ultraviolet* (=beyond the purple end of the range of colors you can see) → see also INFRA- **2** extremely: *ultraconservative* (=having very conservative views)

ˌultra-high 'frequency *n.* [U] UHF

ul·tra·light /'ʌltrəˌlaɪt/ *n.* [C] a very small light aircraft you fly in for fun —**ultralight** *adj.* [only before noun]

ul·tra·ma·rine /ˌʌltrəmə'rin◂/ *n.* [C,U] a very bright blue color —**ultramarine** *adj.*

ul·tra·mod·ern /ˌʌltrə'mɑdɚn◂/ *adj.* extremely modern in style or design: *ultramodern furniture*

ul·tra·na·tion·al·ist /ˌʌltrə'næʃənəlɪst/ *n.* [C] someone who is an extreme supporter of their own country's interests —**ultranationalist** *adj.*

ul·tra·son·ic /ˌʌltrə'sɑnɪk◂/ *adj.* PHYSICS ultrasonic sound waves measure more than 20,000 Hertz, and cannot be heard by humans

ul·tra·sound /'ʌltrəˌsaʊnd/ *n.* **1** [U] PHYSICS sound that is too high for humans to hear, and is often used in medical processes **2** [C] MEDICINE a medical process using this type of sound that produces an image of something inside your body, especially a baby

ul·tra·vi·o·let /ˌʌltrəˈvaɪəlɪt◂/ *adj.* **1** PHYSICS ultraviolet light is beyond the purple end of the range of colors that people can see **2** [only before noun] an ultraviolet lamp, treatment etc. uses this light to treat skin diseases or make your skin darker

ul·u·late /ˈʌlyəˌleɪt/ *v.* [I] to make a long high sound with your voice to show strong emotions —**ululation** /ˌʌlyəˈleɪʃən/ *n.* [C,U]

U·lys·ses /yuˈlɪsiz/ the Roman name for the HERO Odysseus

um /m/ *interjection* SPOKEN used when you are thinking about what to say next: *So, um, I guess I'll be back around 9.*

U·ma·til·la /ˌyuməˈtɪlə/ a Native American tribe from the northwestern area of the U.S.

um·ber /ˈʌmbɚ/ *n.* [C,U] a brown color like earth —**umber** *adj.*

um·bil·i·cal cord /ʌmˈbɪlɪkəl ˌkɔrd/ *n.* [C] BIOLOGY a long narrow tube that joins an unborn baby to its mother

um·bil·i·cus /ʌmˈbɪlɪkəs/ *n.* [C] TECHNICAL **1** the part of an umbilical cord that is left attached to a baby after it is born **2** your NAVEL

um·brage /ˈʌmbrɪdʒ/ *n.* **take umbrage (at sth)** to be offended by something that someone has done or said: *He took umbrage at Campbell's remarks.*

um·brel·la¹ /ʌmˈbrɛlə/ *n.* [C] **1 a)** a circular folding frame covered with cloth or plastic that you hold above your head when it is raining: *It started to rain, so I **put up my umbrella**.* **b)** a similar larger object that is stuck in the ground or on a table to protect you from the sun: *a beach umbrella* **2 under the umbrella of sth** being part of a larger organization, or protected by the larger organization: *The education program was under the umbrella of the State Department.* [**Origin:** 1600–1700 Italian *ombrella*, from Latin *umbella*, from *umbra* **shade, shadow**]

umbrella

umbrella² *adj.* **1 an umbrella organization/group/body etc.** an umbrella organization includes many smaller groups: *an umbrella organization of opposition groups* **2 umbrella term/word** a word which includes many different types of a particular thing: *"Engineering" is an umbrella word that covers a wide range of occupations.*

um·laut /ˈumlaʊt, ˈʊm-/ *n.* [C] ENG. LANG. ARTS a sign written like two periods over a German vowel to show how it is pronounced, for example ä [**Origin:** 1800–1900 German *um-* **around, changing** + *laut* **sound**]

ump /ʌmp/ *n.* [C] SPOKEN an umpire

um·pire¹ /ˈʌmpaɪɚ/ *n.* [C] the person who makes sure that the players obey the rules in sports such as baseball and tennis [**Origin:** 1500–1600 *a numpire*, mistaken for *an umpire*; *numpire* **umpire** from Old French *nonper* **not equal**] ►see THESAURUS box at **referee¹**

umpire² *v.* [I,T] to be the umpire for a game or competition

ump·teenth /ˈʌmptinθ, ˌʌmˈtinθ/ *adj.* INFORMAL a word used when you do not know the specific number of something in a series, but you want to emphasize that the number is very large: *They're showing "The Wizard of Oz" **for the umpteenth time**.* [**Origin:** 1900–2000 *umpty* **many** (a joke word) (1900–2000) + *-teenth* (as in *thirteenth*)] —**umpteen** *quantifier*

U.N., UN *n.* **the U.N. the United Nations** an international organization that tries to find peaceful solutions to world problems: *the U.S. ambassador to the U.N.*

un- /ʌn/ *prefix* **1** [in adjectives and adverbs] used to show an opposite state or a negative SYN **not**: *unfair* | *unhappy* | *unfortunately* **2** [especially in verbs] used to show an opposite action: *undress* (=take your clothes off) | *unpack* (=take your clothes out of your suitcase)

USAGE

Un- is the most frequent negative prefix in English and is used in many common words. It can also be added to adjectives, adverbs, and verbs to make new negative and opposite words. Because of this, there are many more **un-** words than those that appear in this dictionary. The words that are shown here either are very common or have a special meaning besides just the negative or opposite of the meaning of the main part of the word.

un·a·bashed /ˌʌnəˈbæʃt◂/ *adj.* not ashamed or embarrassed, especially when doing something unusual or rude SYN **unashamed**: *She clapped and cheered with unabashed enthusiasm.*

un·a·bat·ed /ˌʌnəˈbeɪt̬ɪd/ *adj.* continuing without becoming any weaker or less violent: *The storm **continued unabated** late into the night.* | *his unabated ambition*

un·a·ble /ʌnˈeɪbəl/ W2 *adj.* [not before noun] not able to do something: **unable to do sth** *Ben was very sick and unable to get out of bed.*

un·a·bridged /ˌʌnəˈbrɪdʒd◂/ *adj.* ENG. LANG. ARTS a piece of writing, speech etc. that is unabridged is in its full form without being made shorter: *an unabridged dictionary*

un·ac·cept·a·ble /ˌʌnəkˈsɛptəbəl/ *adj.* something that is unacceptable is so wrong or bad that you think it should not be allowed: *unacceptable levels of pollution* | **+to** *The proposal was unacceptable to the union.* | **it is unacceptable to do sth** *It was considered politically unacceptable to raise taxes.* —**unacceptably** *adv.*

un·ac·com·pa·nied /ˌʌnəˈkʌmpənid◂/ Ac *adj.* **1** someone who is unaccompanied has no one with them: *Unaccompanied children are not allowed inside.* **2 unaccompanied bags/luggage etc.** bags, SUITCASES etc. that are not with the person who owns them: *Please do not leave your bags unaccompanied in the airport.* **3 unaccompanied by sth** FORMAL without something: *The photo was unaccompanied by any text.* **4** ENG. LANG. ARTS an unaccompanied singer or musician sings or plays alone

un·ac·count·a·ble /ˌʌnəˈkaʊntəbəl/ *adj.* FORMAL **1** very surprising and difficult to explain: *For some unaccountable reason he thought I was rich.* **2** not having to explain your actions or decisions to anyone else: *unaccountable federal agency officials* —**unaccountably** *adv.*

un·ac·count·ed for, unaccounted-for /ˌʌnəˈkaʊntɪd fɔr/ *adj.* something or someone that is unaccounted for cannot be found or their absence cannot be explained: *Fifteen people are still unaccounted for after the fire.*

un·ac·cus·tomed /ˌʌnəˈkʌstəmd◂/ *adj.* FORMAL **1 unaccustomed to (doing) sth** not familiar or comfortable with something because it does not happen often: *I was a boy from the country, unaccustomed to city ways.* **2** [only before noun] not usual, typical, or familiar: *unaccustomed speed and decisiveness*

un·ac·knowl·edged /ˌʌnəkˈnɑlɪdʒd◂/ *adj.* **1** ignored, or not noticed or accepted: *unacknowledged anger* **2** not generally or publicly praised, rewarded, or thanked, even though this is deserved: *Her charity work went unacknowledged for years.*

un·a·dorned /ˌʌnəˈdɔrnd◂/ *adj.* not having any unnecessary or special features or decorations: *an unadorned dress*

un·a·dul·ter·at·ed /ˌʌnəˈdʌltəˌreɪt̬ɪd/ *adj.* **1** [only before noun] complete or total: *What unadulterated nonsense!* **2** not mixed with other less pure substances

un·af·fect·ed /ˌʌnəˈfɛktɪd/ Ac *adj.* **1** not changed or influenced by something: **+by** *Salmon were unaffected by the poison.* **2** APPROVING natural in the way you behave: *He sounds completely unaffected in interviews.* —**unaffectedly** *adv.*

un·aid·ed /ʌnˈeɪdɪd/ Ac *adj.* without help: *Jerry cannot stand up unaided.* | *Venus is easily seen **with the unaided eye*** (=without using special instruments).

un·al·i·en·a·ble /ʌnˈeɪliənəbəl, -lyə-/ *adj.* FORMAL → see INALIENABLE

un·al·loyed /ˌʌnəˈlɔɪd◂ / *adj.* LITERARY complete, pure, or total: *her unalloyed joy*

un·al·ter·a·ble /ʌnˈɔltərəbəl/ Ac *adj.* FORMAL not possible to change: *an unalterable fact* —**unalterably** *adv.*

un·am·big·u·ous /ˌʌnæmˈbɪgyuəs◂ / Ac *adj.* clearly having only one meaning, and therefore easy to understand: *an unambiguous message* —**unambiguously** *adv.*

un-A·mer·i·can /ˌʌn əˈmɛrɪkən◂ / *adj.* **1** DISAPPROVING not loyal to generally accepted American customs and ways of thinking: *This kind of censorship is un-American.* **2 un-American activities** political activity believed to be harmful to the U.S.

u·na·nim·i·ty /ˌyunəˈnɪməṭi/ *n.* [U] FORMAL a state or situation of complete agreement among a group of people: *There is unanimity among scientists on this issue.*

u·nan·i·mous /yuˈnænəməs/ *adj.* if a group is unanimous, or if a decision, vote etc. is unanimous, all the people involved agree on the decision, vote etc.: *Congress gave its unanimous approval of the bill.* | **sb is unanimous in doing sth** *Parents have been unanimous in supporting the after-school program.* —**unanimously** *adv.*

un·an·nounced /ˌʌnəˈnaʊnst◂ / *adj.* happening without anyone expecting or knowing about it: *an unannounced visit*

un·an·swer·a·ble /ʌnˈænsərəbəl/ *adj.* **1** an unanswerable question is one that seems to have no possible answer or solution **2** FORMAL definitely true and therefore impossible to argue against: *unanswerable criminal charges*

un·an·swered /ˌʌnˈænsəd◂ / *adj.* an unanswered question, letter, telephone etc. has not been answered

un·a·pol·o·getic /ˌʌnəˌpɑləˈdʒɛṭɪk◂ / *adj.* not feeling or saying you are sorry for something you have done: **+about/for** *The Mayor remains unapologetic about his remarks.*

un·ap·peal·ing /ˌʌnəˈpilɪŋ◂ / *adj.* not pleasant or attractive: *The book's main character is dull and unappealing.*

un·ap·pe·tiz·ing /ʌnˈæpəˌtaɪzɪŋ/ *adj.* food that is unappetizing has an unattractive appearance that makes you think that it will not taste good: *The fish was an unappetizing shade of gray.*

un·armed /ˌʌnˈɑrmd◂ / *adj.* not carrying any weapons: *Soldiers killed 17 unarmed civilians.*

un·a·shamed /ˌʌnəˈʃeɪmd◂ / *adj.* not feeling embarrassed or ashamed about something that people might disapprove of: *Sue seems completely unashamed about sex.* —**unashamedly** /ˌʌnəˈʃeɪmɪdli/ *adv.*

un·asked /ˌʌnˈæskt◂ / *adj.* an unasked question is not asked, often because people are embarrassed by it

un·as·sail·able /ˌʌnəˈseɪləbəl◂ / *adj.* FORMAL not able to be criticized, attacked, or made weaker: *unassailable logic*

un·as·sist·ed /ˌʌnəˈsɪstɪd◂ / Ac *adj.* without help: *The patient cannot breathe unassisted.*

un·as·sum·ing /ˌʌnəˈsumɪŋ◂ / *adj.* showing no desire to be noticed or given special treatment SYN **modest**: *He was a quiet and unassuming man.*

un·at·tached /ˌʌnəˈtætʃt◂ / Ac *adj.* not involved in a romantic relationship SYN **single**: *Are there any unattached straight men in this city?*

un·at·tain·a·ble /ˌʌnəˈteɪnəbəl◂ / Ac *adj.* impossible to achieve: *an unattainable goal*

un·at·tend·ed /ˌʌnəˈtɛndɪd◂ / *adj.* left alone without anyone being responsible: *unattended luggage* | *The parents **left** the children **unattended** in the playground.*

un·at·trac·tive /ˌʌnəˈtræktɪv◂ / *adj.* **1** not attractive, pretty, or pleasant to look at: *He was physically unattractive.* **2** not good or desirable: **+to** *a career that is unattractive to many people* —**unattractively** *adv.*

un·au·thor·ized /ʌnˈɔθəˌraɪzd/ *adj.* without official approval or permission: *the unauthorized use of federal money*

un·a·vail·a·ble /ˌʌnəˈveɪləbəl/ Ac *adj.* [not before noun] **1** not able to be obtained: **+to** *In the past, these materials were unavailable to researchers.* **2** not able or willing to meet someone: *School officials were **unavailable for comment*** (=not willing to speak to reporters).

un·a·vail·ing /ˌʌnəˈveɪlɪŋ◂ / *adj.* FORMAL not successful or effective: *unavailing efforts*

un·a·void·a·ble /ˌʌnəˈvɔɪdəbəl/ *adj.* impossible to prevent: *The accident was unavoidable.* | *unavoidable delays* —**unavoidably** *adv.*

un·a·ware /ˌʌnəˈwɛr/ Ac *adj.* [not before noun] not noticing or realizing what is happening: **+of** *Mike seems unaware of the trouble he's causing.* | **unaware that** *She was totally unaware that she was being watched.* —**unawareness** *n.* [U]

un·a·wares /ˌʌnəˈwɛrz/ *adv.* **1 take/catch sb unawares** to happen or to do something to someone when they are not expecting it or are not prepared for it: *The question caught me completely unawares.* **2** LITERARY without noticing: *We had walked unawares over the border.*

un·bal·anced /ˌʌnˈbælənst◂ / *adj.* **1** someone who is unbalanced seems slightly crazy: *a neurotic unbalanced woman* **2** an unbalanced report, argument etc. is unfair because it emphasizes one opinion too much SYN **biased**: *unbalanced news reporting* **3 an unbalanced budget** a situation in which a government plans to spend more money than is available **4** an unbalanced situation or relationship is one in which one part, group, or person has more influence, power etc. than the other SYN **unequal** —**unbalance** *v.* [T]

un·bear·a·ble /ʌnˈbɛrəbəl/ *adj.* too bad, painful, or annoying for you to deal with SYN **intolerable**: *The smell in the streets was almost unbearable.* —**unbearably** *adj.*: *an unbearably hot day*

un·beat·a·ble /ʌnˈbiṭəbəl/ *adj.* **1** something that is unbeatable is the best of its kind: *unbeatable prices* **2** an unbeatable team, player etc. cannot be defeated

un·beat·en /ˌʌnˈbitˀn◂ / *adj.* an unbeaten player, team etc. has not been defeated

un·be·com·ing /ˌʌnbɪˈkʌmɪŋ/ *adj.* **1** behavior that is unbecoming is shocking or not appropriate: *Snyder was charged with **conduct unbecoming*** (=behavior that is not appropriate for) *an officer.* **2** OLD-FASHIONED unbecoming clothes do not make you look attractive

un·be·knownst /ˌʌnbɪˈnoʊnst/ also **un·be·known** /ˌʌnbɪˈnoʊn/ [sentence adverb] FORMAL **unbeknownst to sb** without that person knowing about it: *Unbeknownst to his parents, he and his girlfriend had gotten married.*

un·be·lief /ˌʌnbəˈlif/ *n.* [U] FORMAL a lack of belief or a refusal to believe in a religious faith → see also DISBELIEF

un·be·liev·a·ble /ˌʌnbɪˈlivəbəl/ S3 *adj.* **1** very good, successful, or impressive: *He has unbelievable talent.* ►see THESAURUS box at **surprising** **2** very bad or very extreme: *The pain was unbelievable.* **3** very difficult to believe and therefore probably not true: *Her excuse for being late was totally unbelievable.* —**unbelievably** *adv.*: *unbelievably lucky*

un·be·liev·er /ˌʌnbəˈlivə/ *n.* [C] someone who does not believe in a particular religion —**unbelieving** *adj.*

un·bend /ʌnˈbɛnd/ *v.* *past tense and past participle* **unbent** /-ˈbɛnt/ **1** [I,T] to become straight or make something straight **2** [I] to relax and start behaving in a less formal way

un·bend·ing /ʌnˈbɛndɪŋ/ *adj.* not willing to change your opinions, decisions etc.: *an unbending determination*

un·bi·ased /ˌʌnˈbaɪəst/ Ac *adj.* fair and not influenced by someone's opinions: *an unbiased opinion* | *We act as unbiased observers at the election.*

U

un·bid·den /ˌʌnˈbɪdn/ *adj.* LITERARY not having been asked for, expected, or invited

un·blem·ished /ˌʌnˈblɛmɪʃt/ *adj.* **1** not spoiled by any mistake or bad behavior: *an unblemished safety record* **2** not spoiled by any mark: *unblemished skin*

un·blink·ing /ˌʌnˈblɪŋkɪŋ/ *adj.* LITERARY **1** looking at something continuously without BLINKing: *a steady unblinking gaze* **2** considering or showing all the details of something without avoiding the bad parts: *The film offers an unblinking look at life in the prisons.*

un·born /ˌʌnˈbɔrn◂ / *adj.* [only before noun] not yet born: *an unborn child*

un·bound·ed /ˌʌnˈbaʊndɪd/ *adj.* FORMAL extreme or without any limit: *unbounded curiosity*

un·bowed /ʌnˈbaʊd/ *adj.* LITERARY not willing to accept defeat

un·break·a·ble /ˌʌnˈbreɪkəbəl/ *adj.* **1** not able to be broken: *an unbreakable bottle* ►see THESAURUS box at **strong** **2** an unbreakable rule, agreement etc. must be obeyed

un·bridge·a·ble /ˌʌnˈbrɪdʒəbəl/ *adj.* unbridgeable differences between two people, groups, or ideas are too big to be gotten rid of: *There is an unbridgeable gap between the two main parties.*

un·bri·dled /ˌʌnˈbraɪdld/ *adj.* LITERARY not controlled and often too extreme or violent: *unbridled passion*

un·bro·ken /ˌʌnˈbroʊkən/ *adj.* **1** continuing without being broken or interrupted: *an unbroken silence* **2** not broken: *unbroken egg yolks*

U

un·buck·le /ʌnˈbʌkəl/ *v.* [T] to unfasten the BUCKLE on something

un·bur·den /ʌnˈbɚdn/ *v.* [T] **1 unburden yourself (to sb)** to tell someone your problems, secrets etc. so that you feel better: *It felt good to unburdened himself to her.* **2** LITERARY to take a heavy load, a large responsibility etc. away from someone or something

un·but·ton /ʌnˈbʌtˀn/ *v.* [T] to unfasten a piece of clothing that is fastened with buttons: *He unbuttoned his shirt.*

un·called for, **uncalled-for** /ʌnˈkɔld fɔr/ *adj.* INFORMAL behavior or remarks that are uncalled for are unfair or not appropriate: *That comment was totally uncalled for.*

un·can·ny /ʌnˈkæni/ *adj.* *comparative* **uncannier**, *superlative* **uncanniest** very strange and difficult to explain: *He has an uncanny ability to guess what you're thinking.* —**uncannily** *adv.*

un·cared for, **uncared-for** /ʌnˈkɛrd fɔr/ *adj.* not taken care of, or not taken care of in the right way: *The yard was dirty and uncared for.*

un·ceas·ing /ʌnˈsisɪŋ/ *adj.* never stopping: *The verbal abuse was unceasing.* —**unceasingly** *adv.*

un·cer·e·mo·ni·ous·ly /ʌnˌsɛrəˈmoʊniəsli/ *adv.* in a rough or sudden way, without showing any respect or politeness: *My uncle was unceremoniously kicked out of the club.* —**unceremonious** *adj.* —**unceremoniousness** *n.* [U]

un·cer·tain /ʌnˈsɚtˀn/ *adj.* **1** not sure, or feeling doubt: +**about** *I was uncertain about who I should call.* | **uncertain what/who/if etc.** *She was uncertain whether to keep talking or not.* **2** not clear, definite, or decided: *The factory workers face an uncertain future.* **3 in no uncertain terms** if you tell someone something in no uncertain terms, you tell them very clearly without trying to be polite: *They told us in no uncertain terms that we were not welcome.* **4** if someone walks in an uncertain way, they seem as though they might fall: *She took a few uncertain steps forward.* —**uncertainly** *adv.*

un·cer·tain·ty /ʌnˈsɚtˀnti/ *n.* *plural* **uncertainties** **1** [U] a feeling of doubt about what will happen: *a time of political uncertainty* | +**about** *There is a lot of uncertainty about the future of the company.* **2** [C] something that you are not sure about, because you do not know what will happen: *Life is full of uncertainties and problems.*

un·chal·lenged /ʌnˈtʃæləndʒd/ *adj.* **1** accepted and believed by everyone and not doubted: *She couldn't let a crazy statement like that* ***go unchallenged*** (=not be questioned). **2** someone who goes somewhere unchallenged is not stopped and asked who they are or what they are doing: *He was able to walk straight into the airport unchallenged.* **3** not having an opponent in a competition: *an unchallenged candidate for city supervisor*

un·changed /ʌnˈtʃeɪndʒd/ *adj.* not having changed: *Sales have* ***remained unchanged*** *for the past year.*

un·chang·ing /ʌnˈtʃeɪndʒɪŋ/ *adj.* always staying the same: *an unchanging truth*

un·char·ac·ter·is·tic /ʌnˌkærɪktəˈrɪstɪk/ *adj.* not typical of someone or something and therefore surprising: +**of** *It's uncharacteristic of Maggie to get so angry.* —**uncharacteristically** /-kli/ *adv.*

un·char·i·ta·ble /ʌnˈtʃærət̬əbəl/ *adj.* not kind or fair in the way you judge people: *uncharitable thoughts*

un·chart·ed /ˌʌnˈtʃɑrt̬ɪd◂ / Ac *adj.* **1 uncharted waters/territory/terrain** a situation or activity that no one has never experienced or tried before: *We're moving into uncharted territory with the new project.* **2** not marked on any maps: *an uncharted island*

un·checked /ˌʌnˈtʃɛkt◂ / *adj.* an unchecked activity, disease etc. develops and gets worse because it is not controlled or stopped: *These pests can destroy a fruit crop* ***if left unchecked*** (=if they are not controlled).

un·claimed /ˌʌnˈkleɪmd◂ / *adj.* unclaimed money, land, LUGGAGE etc. is money, land etc. that no one has demanded or said belongs to them: *The unclaimed prize money will be given to charity.*

un·cle /ˈʌŋkəl/ S2 *n.* [C] **1** the brother of your mother or father, or the husband of your AUNT: *Uncle Chris* ►see THESAURUS box at **relative**[1] **2** used as a name or title for a man who is a close friend of your parents: *We called him Uncle Dan.* **3 say uncle** SPOKEN used by children to tell someone to admit they have been defeated [**Origin:** 1200–1300 Old French, Latin *avunculus* **mother's brother**] → see also **I'll be a monkey's uncle** at MONKEY[1] (6)

un·clean /ˌʌnˈklin◂ / *adj.* **1** dirty: *unclean drinking water* **2** BIBLICAL morally or SPIRITUALly bad: *an unclean spirit* **3** unclean food, animals etc. are those that must not be eaten, touched etc. in a particular religion

un·clear /ˌʌnˈklɪr◂ / *adj.* **1** difficult to understand or be sure about, so that there is doubt or confusion: *The causes of the disease are unclear.* | **it is unclear whether/who/what etc.** *It is still unclear why he bought the gun in the first place.* **2** not understanding something clearly: +**about** *If you're unclear about the answers, ask more questions.*

Uncle Sam /ˌʌŋkəl ˈsæm/ *n.* [singular] INFORMAL the U.S. government represented by the figure of a man with a white BEARD and tall red, white, and blue hat

Uncle Tom /ˌʌŋkəl ˈtɑm/ *n.* [C] DISAPPROVING an African-American person who is too friendly or respectful to white people

ˌUncle Tom's ˈCabin *n.* a book written in 1852 by Harriet Beecher Stowe, which tells the story of an African-American SLAVE, Uncle Tom, who is treated very badly by his owner. The book strongly criticized the practice of owning slaves and cruel laws such as the FUGITIVE SLAVE ACT.

un·clog /ʌnˈklɑg/ *v.* **unclogged**, **unclogging** [T] to clear a tube, pipe, road etc. that has become blocked, so that it works correctly again

un·clothed /ʌnˈkloʊðd/ *adj.* FORMAL not wearing any clothes SYN **naked**

un·clut·tered /ˌʌnˈklʌt̬ɚd/ *adj.* APPROVING an uncluttered space, room, pattern etc. is not covered or filled with too many things: *an uncluttered house*

un·coil /ʌnˈkɔɪl/ *v.* [I,T] if you uncoil something, or if it uncoils, it stretches out straight, after being wound around in a circle

un·com·fort·a·ble /ʌnˈkʌmftəbəl, ʌnˈkʌmfə̆tabəl/ S2 *adj.* **1** not feeling physically comfortable, or not making you feel comfortable: *uncomfortable shoes* | *You look uncomfortable. Why don't you sit over here?* **2** unable to relax because you are embarrassed or worried: *an uncomfortable silence* | **+with** *Many older people are uncomfortable with computers.* | **+about** *I feel uncomfortable about discussing her when she's not here.* ►see THESAURUS box at **embarrassed** —**uncomfortably** *adv.*

un·com·mit·ted /ˌʌnkəˈmɪt̬ɪd◂ / *adj.* not having decided or promised to support a particular group, political belief etc.: *uncommitted voters*

un·com·mon /ʌnˈkɑmən/ *adj.* rare or unusual: *Violent crimes against the elderly are fortunately very uncommon.* | **it is not uncommon for sb/sth to do sth** *Nowadays, it is not uncommon* (=it is fairly common) *for women in their forties to have babies.*

un·com·mon·ly /ʌnˈkɑmənli/ *adv.* [+ adj./adv.] FORMAL very or especially: *an uncommonly beautiful woman*

un·com·plain·ing /ˌʌnkəmˈpleɪnɪŋ◂ / *adj.* willing to accept a difficult or bad situation without complaining: *an uncomplaining servant* —**uncomplainingly** *adv.*

un·com·pli·cat·ed /ʌnˈkɑmpləˌkeɪt̬ɪd/ *adj.* APPROVING easy to understand without a lot of hidden problems: *an uncomplicated man* | *The instructions were uncomplicated.*

un·com·pre·hend·ing /ˌʌnkɑmprɪˈhɛndɪŋ/ *adj.* not understanding what is happening: *She gave me a helpless uncomprehending look.* —**uncomprehendingly** *adv.*

un·com·pro·mis·ing /ʌnˈkɑmprəˌmaɪzɪŋ/ *adj.* unwilling to change your opinions or intentions: *an uncompromising attitude* —**uncompromisingly** *adv.*

un·con·cern /ˌʌnkənˈsɚn/ *n.* [U] an attitude of not caring about something that other people worry about: *his unconcern for his own safety*

un·con·cerned /ˌʌnkənˈsɚnd◂ / *adj.* **1** not anxious or worried about something: **+about** *The man seemed unconcerned about his wife's health.* **2** not interested in a particular aim or activity: **+with** *The organization is unconcerned with making a profit for now.* —**unconcernedly** /ˌʌnkənˈsɚnɪdli/ *adv.*

un·con·di·tion·al /ˌʌnkənˈdɪʃənl◂ / *adj.* not limited by or depending on any conditions: *My family offers* ***unconditional love*** *and support.* —**unconditionally** *adv.*

un·con·firmed /ˌʌnkənˈfɚmd◂ / *adj.* not yet proved or supported by official information or by definite facts: *There are seven unconfirmed cases of the disease so far.*

un·con·nect·ed /ˌʌnkəˈnɛktɪd◂ / *adj.* not related to or involved with something else: **+to/with** *The question was unconnected to anything they had been discussing.*

un·con·scion·a·ble /ʌnˈkɑnʃənəbəl/ *adj.* FORMAL completely unacceptable or morally wrong: *The war caused an unconscionable amount of suffering.* —**unconscionably** *adv.*

un·con·scious[1] /ˌʌnˈkɑnʃəs◂ / *adj.* **1** unable to see, move, feel etc. in the normal way because you are not conscious: *She lay on the floor, unconscious.* | **knock/beat sb unconscious** *Mike fell off the bike and was knocked unconscious.* **2** relating to or coming from the part of your mind in which there are thoughts and feelings that you do not realize you have: *the unconscious mind* | *unconscious desires* → see also SUBCONSCIOUS **3 unconscious of sth** not realizing the effect of something, especially something you have said or done: *Barb seemed unconscious of the attention her dress was getting.* **4** an action that is unconscious is not deliberate: *His remark was an unconscious insult to women.* —**unconsciously** *adv.* —**unconsciousness** *n.* [U]

unconscious[2] *n.* **the/sb's unconscious** the part of your mind in which there are thoughts and feelings that you do not realize you have SYN **subconscious**

un·con·sti·tu·tion·al /ˌʌnkɑnstəˈtuʃənəl/ Ac *adj.* POLITICS not allowed by the CONSTITUTION (=set of rules or principles by which a country or organization is governed): *Organized prayer in public schools is unconstitutional.* —**unconstitutionality** /ˌʌnkɑnstətuʃəˈnæləti/ *n.* [U]

un·con·test·ed /ˌʌnkənˈtɛstɪd◂ / *adj.* **1** an uncontested action or statement is one which no one opposes or disagrees with **2** an uncontested election is one in which only one person wants to be elected

un·con·trol·la·ble /ˌʌnkənˈtroʊləbəl/ *adj.* **1** uncontrollable emotions, behaviors, or situations are ones that you cannot control or stop: *uncontrollable crying* | *uncontrollable inflation* **2** someone who is uncontrollable behaves badly and will not obey anyone —**uncontrollably** *adv.*

un·con·trolled /ˌʌnkənˈtroʊld◂ / *adj.* **1** uncontrolled emotions or behaviors continue because no one stops or controls them: *uncontrolled laughter* **2** not limited by rules or laws: *uncontrolled violence* **3** an uncontrolled medical condition is not being treated: *uncontrolled diabetes*

un·con·ven·tion·al /ˌʌnkənˈvɛnʃənl◂ / Ac *adj.* very different from the way something is usually done or the way people usually behave, think etc.: *an unconventional way of dressing*

un·con·vinced /ˌʌnkənˈvɪnst/ Ac *adj.* [not before noun] not certain that something is true: **+by** *She was unconvinced by the evidence.*

un·cool /ˌʌnˈkul◂ / *adj.* [not before noun] INFORMAL, DISAPPROVING not fashionable, attractive, or relaxed: *My parents are so uncool!*

un·co·op·er·a·tive /ˌʌnkoʊˈɑprət̬ɪv/ *adj.* not willing to work with or help someone: *Her son was lazy and uncooperative.*

un·co·or·di·nat·ed /ˌʌnkoʊˈɔrdnˌeɪt̬ɪd/ *adj.* **1** someone who is uncoordinated is not good at physical activities, because they cannot control their movements effectively **2** an uncoordinated plan or operation is not well organized, so that the different parts of it do not work together effectively

un·cork /ʌnˈkɔrk/ *v.* [T] to open a bottle by removing its CORK

un·count·a·ble /ˌʌnˈkaʊnt̬əbəl/ *adj.* **1** too many to be counted: *the uncountable galaxies in outer space* **2** ENG. LANG. ARTS an uncountable noun has no plural form and is a word for something that cannot be counted or considered either singular or plural, for example "milk" or "happiness." In this dictionary, uncountable nouns are marked [U]. → see also COUNTABLE

un·count·ed /ˌʌnˈkaʊntɪd◂ / *adj.* **1** not counted: *uncounted votes* **2** very large in number or amount: *uncounted millions of dollars*

un·count noun /ˌʌnkaʊnt˺ ˈnaʊn/ *n.* [C] ENG. LANG. ARTS an uncountable noun → see also COUNT NOUN

un·couth /ʌnˈkuθ/ *adj.* DISAPPROVING behaving and speaking in a way that is impolite or socially unacceptable: *He seemed uncouth and dirty to her.* [**Origin:** Old English *uncuth*, from *un-* + *cuth* **known, familiar**]

un·cov·er /ʌnˈkʌvɚ/ *v.* [T] **1** to discover something that has been kept secret SYN **discover**: *A search of their luggage uncovered two knives.* **2** to remove the cover from something

un·crit·i·cal /ʌnˈkrɪt̬ɪkəl/ *adj.* DISAPPROVING accepting something without questioning it or seeing its faults: *an uncritical attitude toward new technologies* —**uncritically** /-kli/ *adv.*

un·crowned /ˌʌnˈkraʊnd◂ / *adj.* **1 the uncrowned king/queen etc. of sth** the person who is believed to be the best at something, without having an official title: *the uncrowned queen of jazz* **2** not yet officially made king or queen: *the uncrowned King Edward of England*

unc·tu·ous /ˈʌŋktʃuəs/ *adj.* FORMAL **1** DISAPPROVING behaving in a way that is not sincere, by being too friendly or praising other people too much, or showing this behavior: *an unctuous smile* **2** food that is unctu-

U

ous is soft, and tastes very good, because it contains a lot of oil or fat

un·curl /ʌnˈkɚl/ *v.* [I,T] to stretch out straight from a curled position, or to make something do this

un·cut /ˌʌnˈkʌt◂ / *adj.* **1** ENG. LANG. ARTS an uncut movie, book etc. has not been made shorter, for example by having violent or sexual scenes removed: *the uncut version of the interview* **2** not having been cut: *uncut hair* **3** an uncut forest has not had its trees cut down and removed **4** an uncut jewel has not yet been cut into a particular shape: *uncut diamonds*

un·dat·ed /ˌʌnˈdeɪṭɪd◂ / *adj.* an undated letter, article, photograph etc. does not have the date written on it

un·daunt·ed /ˌʌnˈdɔntɪd◂ , -ˈdɑn-/ *adj.* not afraid of continuing to try to do something in spite of difficulties or danger: +**by** *The team was undaunted by its defeat.*

un·de·cid·ed /ˌʌndɪˈsaɪdɪd◂ / *adj.* **1** not having made a decision about something important: *undecided voters* | +**about/on** *We are still undecided about buying a house.* **2** an undecided situation, game, or competition has no clear result or no definite winner —**undecidedly** *adv.*

un·de·clared /ˌʌndɪˈklɛrd◂ / *adj.* not officially announced or called something: *an undeclared war* | *undeclared income* (=money that you earn that you do not tell the tax officials about)

un·de·fined /ˌʌndɪˈfaɪnd◂ / Ac *adj.* **1** not stated in a clear or definite way: *Some of my job duties are still undefined.* **2** not having a clear shape: *undefined shadows in the darkness*

U

un·de·mon·stra·tive /ˌʌndɪˈmɑnstrəṭɪv/ *adj.* not showing your feelings of love or friendliness, especially by not touching or kissing people

un·de·ni·a·ble /ˌʌndɪˈnaɪəbəl◂ / Ac *adj.* definitely true or certain: *Her popularity among teenagers is undeniable.* —**undeniably** *adv.*

un·der[1] /ˈʌndɚ/ S1 W1 *prep.* **1** directly below something, or covered by it SYN **underneath** OPP **over**: *He has a small scar under his nose.* | *I could see something shiny under the water.* | *"Where's the cat?" "She crawled under the couch."*

THESAURUS

underneath under – used to emphasize that something covers, touches, or hides something: *The girls wear shorts underneath their cheerleading skirts.*
beneath OLD-FASHIONED, LITERARY under: *They strolled hand in hand beneath the summer moon.*
below in a lower position than something else, though not always directly under it: *From the cliffs we could barely see the people on the beach below us.*

2 passing beneath something at one side and coming out at the other side OPP **over**: *We sailed under the bridge.* **3** less than a particular number, amount, age, or price OPP **over**: *What can I buy for under ten dollars?* | *toys for kids under age five* **4** controlled by a particular leader, government, system etc.: *Under Schaefer's leadership, the downtown area has been rebuilt.* **5** used for saying that someone or something is having something done to them: **under discussion/consideration/review** *Three sites are under consideration for the new factory.* | *Goodell is* ***under attack*** (=being criticized) *for his recent remarks.* | *The road is still* ***under construction*** (=being built). **6** in a state where you are experiencing something or affected by something: *I've been* ***under*** *a lot of* ***stress*** *lately.* | *She managed to keep her temper* ***under control.*** | **under the influence of alcohol/drugs** *He was arrested for driving under the influence of alcohol.* **7 under sb's control/influence/thumb etc.** controlled or influenced by someone: *Those who came under John's spell did anything he asked.* **8** if you are under someone at your job, you have a lower position than they do, and they help to direct your work OPP **over**: *the soldiers under his command* **9** according to a particular agreement, law etc.: *Is this type of trade illegal under international law?* **10 be under anesthesia/sedation/treatment etc.** to be treated by a doctor using a particular drug or method: *Daniels is under treatment at a psychiatric hospital.* **11** used for saying in which part of a book, list, or system particular information can be found: *The information is filed under the child's last name.* **12** if you write or do something under another name, you do it using a name that is not your real name [**Origin:** Old English] → see also **be under the impression (that)** at IMPRESSION (2)

under[2] S3 *adv.* **1** in or to a place that is below something or covered by it: *He dived into the water and stayed under for a minute.* **2** less in age, number, amount etc. than the age, number etc. mentioned: *Children twelve and under must be accompanied by an adult.* **3** in or into an UNCONSCIOUS condition because a doctor has given you drugs before SURGERY → see also **put sb under** at PUT

under- /ʌndɚ/ *prefix* **1** less of an action or quality than is appropriate, needed, or desired: *underdevelopment* | *undercooked* **2** going under something: *underpass* (=road that goes under another road) **3** inside or beneath other things: *underwear*

un·der·a·chiev·er /ˌʌndərəˈtʃivɚ/ *n.* [C] someone who does not do as well as they could do based on their abilities, especially in education → see also OVERACHIEVER —**underachieve** *v.* [I] —**underachievement** *n.* [U]

un·der·age /ˌʌndɚˈeɪdʒ◂ / *adj.* too young to legally buy alcohol, drive a car, vote etc., or being done by someone who is too young: *underage drinking*

un·der·arm[1] /ˈʌndɚˌɑrm/ *adj.* [only before noun] relating to or used on your ARMPITS: *underarm deodorant*

underarm[2] *n.* [C] your ARMPIT

un·der·bel·ly /ˈʌndɚˌbɛli/ *n. plural* **underbellies** [C] LITERARY **1** the weakest or most easily damaged part of a country, plan etc. **2** the weakest part of a country, plan etc., which someone attacks if they want to destroy it **3** the bottom side of something such as a ship or an airplane **4** the soft stomach or bottom side of an animal

un·der·brush /ˈʌndɚbrʌʃ/ *n.* [U] bushes, small trees etc. growing under and around larger trees in a forest SYN **undergrowth**

un·der·cap·i·tal·ized /ˌʌndɚˈkæpɪṭlˌaɪzd/ *adj.* ECONOMICS if a business is undercapitalized, it does not have enough money to operate effectively —**undercapitalize** *v.* [T usually passive]

un·der·car·riage /ˈʌndɚˌkærɪdʒ/ *n.* [C] the wheels of an aircraft, car etc. and the structure that holds them

und·er·charge /ˌʌndɚˈtʃɑrdʒ/ *v.* [I,T] ECONOMICS to charge too little or less than the correct amount of money for something OPP **overcharge**

un·der·class /ˈʌndɚˌklæs/ *n.* [singular] the lowest social class, consisting of people who are very poor and who are not likely to be able to improve their situation: *an urban underclass* → see also LOWER CLASS, MIDDLE CLASS, UPPER CLASS

un·der·class·man /ˌʌndɚˈklæsmən/ *n.* [C] a student in the first two years of high school or college

un·der·clothes /ˈʌndɚˌkloʊðz, -ˌkloʊz/ also **un·der·clo·thing** /ˈʌndɚˌkloʊðɪŋ/ *n.* [plural] UNDERWEAR

un·der·coat /ˈʌndɚˌkoʊt/ *n.* [C] a layer of paint that you put onto a surface before you put the final layer on

un·der·count /ˈʌndɚˌkaʊnt/ *v.* [T] to make a mistake of counting less than all of a group of people or things, especially in an official situation: *We undercounted the number of people who would need the service.* —**undercount** *n.* [C]

un·der·cov·er /ˌʌndɚˈkʌvɚ◂ / *adj., adv.* working or done secretly, in order to catch criminals or find out information: *an undercover investigation* | *Police* ***went undercover*** (=worked undercover) *to buy the drugs.*

un·der·cur·rent /ˈʌndɚˌkɚənt, -ˌkʌr-/ *n.* [C] **1** a negative feeling, for example anger or sadness, that people do not express openly: **+of** *There's a strong undercurrent of racism in this town.* **2** EARTH SCIENCE a hidden and often dangerous current of water that flows under the surface of the ocean or a river

un·der·cut /ˌʌndɚˈkʌt, ˈʌndɚˌkʌt/ *v.* [T] **1** to make someone's work, plans etc. not be successful or effective: *These rumors greatly undercut his authority at work.* **2** to sell something more cheaply than someone else: *Supermarkets increase their business by undercutting smaller stores.*

un·der·de·vel·oped /ˌʌndɚdɪˈvɛləpt◂/ *adj.* **1 an underdeveloped country/region etc.** a country, REGION etc. that is poor and where there is not much modern industry → see also A DEVELOPING COUNTRY/NATION **2** not having grown or developed as much as is usual or necessary: *The baby had underdeveloped lungs.*

un·der·dog /ˈʌndɚˌdɔg/ *n.* [C] **1** a person or team in a competition that is expected to lose: *We were the underdogs in the tournament.* **2** a person, country etc. that is weak and is always treated badly: *The courts are supposed to protect the underdogs.*

un·der·done /ˌʌndɚˈdʌn◂/ *adj.* meat that is underdone is not completely cooked → see also OVERDONE

un·der·dressed /ˌʌndɚˈdrɛst◂/ *adj.* wearing clothes that are too informal for a particular occasion

un·der·em·ployed /ˌʌndərɪmˈplɔɪd◂/ *adj.* **1** working in a job where you cannot use all your skills or where there is not enough work for you to do **2** ECONOMICS working in a job where you can only work a few hours a day or a few days a week, when you want to work all day or every day

un·der·es·ti·mate[1] /ˌʌndɚˈɛstəˌmeɪt/ Ac *v.* **1** [I,T] to think that something is smaller, cheaper, less important etc. than it really is: *We **underestimated** how difficult it would be.* | **grossly/seriously underestimate** *The city grossly underestimated the cost of the new airport.* **2** [T] to think that someone is not as good, smart, or skillful as they really are: *Don't underestimate her – she's smarter than you think.*

un·der·es·ti·mate[2] /ˌʌndɚˈɛstəmɪt/ Ac *n.* [C] a guessed amount or number that is too low

un·der·ex·pose /ˌʌndərɪkˈspoʊz/ *v.* [T] to not let enough light reach the film when you are taking a photograph OPP **overexpose**

un·der·fed /ˌʌndɚˈfɛd/ *adj.* not given enough food to eat

un·der·foot /ˌʌndɚˈfʊt/ *adv.* **1** under your feet where you are walking: *The sand and rocks crunched underfoot.* **2** if children, animals etc. are underfoot, they are in a position that prevents you from walking or doing things easily

un·der·fund /ˌʌndɚˈfʌnd/ *v.* [T usually passive] to not provide a program, organization etc. with enough money: *The childcare program is seriously underfunded.* —**underfunding** *n.* [U]

un·der·gar·ment /ˈʌndɚˌgɑrmənt/ *n.* [C] OLD-FASHIONED a piece of underwear

un·der·go /ˌʌndɚˈgoʊ/ Ac *v.* **undergoes**, *past tense* **underwent** /-ˈwɛnt/, *past participle* **undergone** /-ˈgɔn/ [T not in passive] if you undergo something, it happens to you or is done to you: *The soldiers **undergo** six weeks of **training**.* | **undergo surgery/treatment/tests etc.** *In March he underwent surgery for the cancer.* | **undergo a change/transformation etc.** *The country has undergone massive changes recently.* | **undergo repairs/refurbishment** *The ship is now undergoing repairs at the dock.*

un·der·grad·u·ate /ˌʌndɚˈgrædʒuɪt◂/ *n.* [C] a student in the first four years of college, who is working for their first degree —**undergraduate** *adj.* [only before noun] *an undergraduate degree* → see also GRADUATE

un·der·ground[1] /ˈʌndɚˌgraʊnd/ *adj.* **1** below the surface of the earth: *The parking garage is underground.* **2** [only before noun] an underground group, organization etc. is secret and illegal: *an underground terrorist organization* **3** underground music, literature, art etc. is not officially approved and usually seems unusual or slightly shocking: *an underground newspaper*

underground[2] *adv.* **1** under the earth's surface: *The insect spends most of its life underground.* **2 go underground** to start doing something secretly, or hide in a secret place: *Denkins went underground to escape police.*

underground[3] *n.* **1 the underground** an illegal group working secretly against the rulers of a country **2** [singular] BRITISH a SUBWAY system

ˌUnderground ˈRailroad, the HISTORY a secret system in the U.S. before the Civil War that helped SLAVES who had escaped to travel to a safe place

un·der·growth /ˈʌndɚˌgroʊθ/ *n.* [U] bushes, small trees, and other plants growing around and under bigger trees: *Something rustled in the undergrowth.*

un·der·hand /ˈʌndɚˌhænd/ *adv.* if you throw a ball underhand, you throw it without moving your arm above your shoulder OPP **overhand**

un·der·hand·ed /ˈʌndɚˌhændɪd/ *adj.* dishonest and done secretly: *The whole deal seemed very underhanded.* —**underhandedly** *adv.* —**underhandedness** *n.* [U]

un·der·lie /ˌʌndɚˈlaɪ/ Ac *v. past tense* **underlay** /-ˈleɪ/, *past participle* **underlain** /-ˈleɪn/ [T] FORMAL **1** to be a very basic part of something, or the real cause of or reason for something: *Lack of communication underlies many of the problems in their marriage.* **2** to exist at a lower level or in a lower layer than something else: *Clay underlies this whole area.*

un·der·line /ˈʌndɚˌlaɪn, ˌʌndɚˈlaɪn/ *v.* [T] **1** to draw a line under a word to show that it is important or because it is the name of a book, movie, play etc. **2** to show that something is important: *The recent shootings underline the need for more security.* ►see THESAURUS box at **emphasize**

un·der·ling /ˈʌndɚlɪŋ/ *n.* [C] an insulting word for someone who has a low rank

un·der·ly·ing /ˈʌndɚˌlaɪ-ɪŋ/ Ac *adj.* [only before noun] very basic or important, but not easily noticed: **an underlying reason/cause/problem etc.** *Stress is the underlying cause of many illnesses.* | **an underlying principle/idea/assumption etc.** *There is an underlying assumption that young people learn faster.*

un·der·manned /ˌʌndɚˈmænd◂/ *adj.* not having enough workers

un·der·mine /ˈʌndɚˌmaɪn, ˌʌndɚˈmaɪn/ *v.* [T] **1** to gradually make someone or something less strong or effective: *Unfair criticism can undermine employees' self-confidence.* | **undermine sb's authority/power/credibility etc.** (=gradually make someone's authority etc. seem weaker by disobeying them, criticizing them etc.) **2** to gradually take away the earth from under something

un·der·neath /ˌʌndɚˈniθ/ S2 *adv., prep.* **1** directly under or below another object, used especially when one thing is covering or hiding another: *He pulled back his shirt to show the scar underneath.* | *a photograph with his name underneath it* ►see THESAURUS box at **under**[1] **2** used for talking about what someone or something is really like, when the appearance is different: *She seems aggressive, but underneath she's pretty shy.* | ***Underneath it all**, he knew Peg really cared about him.* **3** on the lower surface: *The car was pretty rusty underneath.* **4** passing beneath something at one side and coming out at the other side: *The bridge is too low for boats to pass underneath.*

un·der·nour·ished /ˌʌndɚˈnɚɪʃt, -ˈnʌrɪʃt/ *adj.* unhealthy and weak because you have not had enough food: *undernourished children* —**undernourishment** *n.* [U]

un·der·paid /ˌʌndɚˈpeɪd◂/ *adj.* earning less money than you deserve for your work: *underpaid teachers*

un·der·pants /ˈʌndɚˌpænts/ *n.* [plural] a short piece of underwear worn on the lower part of the body

un·der·pass /ˈʌndɚˌpæs/ *n.* [C] a road or path that goes under another road or a railroad

un·der·pay /ˌʌndɚˈpeɪ/ *v. past tense and past participle* **underpaid** /-ˈpeɪd/ **1** [T] to pay someone too little for their work **2** [I,T] to pay less money for something than you should, especially your taxes

un·der·per·form /ˌʌndɚpɚˈfɔrm/ *v.* [I,T] if a business, INVESTMENT etc. underperforms, it earns you less money than expected or than other possible investments would have —**underperformance** *n.* [U]

un·der·pin /ˈʌndɚˌpɪn/ *v.* **underpinned, underpinning** [T] **1** to give strength or support to something and help it succeed: *These laws underpin our society.* **2** to put a solid piece of metal under something such as a wall in order to make it stronger —**underpinning** *n.* [C,U] *the underpinnings of the nation's economy*

un·der·play /ˌʌndɚˈpleɪ/ *v.* **underplays, underplayed, underplaying** [T] to make something seem less important or exciting than it really is OPP **overplay**: *She completely underplays her achievements.*

un·der·priv·i·leged /ˌʌndɚˈprɪvəlɪdʒd◂ / *adj.* very poor, with worse living conditions, educational opportunities etc. than most people in society: *underprivileged youth*

un·der·rat·ed /ˌʌndɚˈreɪt̬ɪd◂ / *adj.* someone or something that is underrated is believed to be less good, important etc. than they really are OPP **overrated**: *the most underrated player on the team* —**underrate** *v.* [T]

un·der·rep·re·sent·ed /ˌʌndɚˌrɛprɪˈzɛntɪd/ *adj.* an underrepresented group of people has fewer members in a particular organization, in a particular job etc. than you would expect there to be, according to the size of the group in general: *Latinos are significantly underrepresented on the campus.* —**underrepresentation** /ˌʌndɚˌrɛprɪzənˈteɪʃən/ *n.* [U]

un·der·score /ˈʌndɚˌskɔr/ *v.* [T] **1** to emphasize something so that people pay attention to it SYN **underline**: *These failures underscore the importance of good planning.* ►see THESAURUS box at **emphasize** **2** to UNDERLINE a word

un·der·sea /ˌʌndɚˈsi◂ / *adj.* [only before noun] happening or existing below the surface of the ocean: *undersea exploration*

un·der·sec·re·tar·y /ˌʌndɚˈsɛkrəˌtɛri/ *n. plural* **undersecretaries** [C] a very important official in a government department who is one position below the SECRETARY

un·der·sell /ˌʌndɚˈsɛl/ *v. past tense and past participle* **undersold** /-ˈsoʊld/ [T] **1** to sell goods at a lower price than someone else: *Foreign companies are underselling us.* **2** to fail to show how good in quality someone or something is: *I think you **undersold yourself*** (=did not show how good you really are) *in the interview.*

un·der·served, under-served /ˌʌndɚˈsɚvd◂ / *adj.* not getting enough care and help, especially from the government: *the underserved areas of the state*

un·der·shirt /ˈʌndɚˌʃɚt/ *n.* [C] a piece of underwear with or without arms, worn under a shirt

un·der·shorts /ˈʌndɚˌʃɔrts/ *n.* [plural] UNDERPANTS for men or boys

un·der·side /ˈʌndɚˌsaɪd/ *n.* **the underside (of sth)** the bottom side or surface of something: *the underside of the bridge*

un·der·signed /ˈʌndɚˌsaɪnd/ *n.* **the undersigned** the person or people who have signed a formal document —**undersigned** *adj.* [only before noun]

un·der·sized /ˌʌndɚˈsaɪzd◂ / also **un·der·size** /-ˈsaɪz◂ / *adj.* smaller than usual, or too small: *undersized clothes*

un·der·staffed /ˌʌndɚˈstæft◂ / *adj.* not having enough workers, or fewer workers than usual OPP **overstaffed**: *The cafeteria is a little understaffed.*

un·der·stand /ˌʌndɚˈstænd/ S1 W1 *v. past tense and past participle* **understood** /-ˈstʊd/ [not in progressive]
1 MEANING [I,T] to know the meaning of what someone is telling you, or the language that they speak: *Unfortunately she doesn't understand English.* | *I still don't understand. Can you say it slower?* | **understand what/whether/where etc.** *I don't understand what you want me to do.* | **be easy/difficult to understand** *The computer manual is written in a way that is easy to understand.* | *Let me see if I **understand** you **correctly**.* | *He was confused and couldn't **make himself understood*** (=explain things in a way that can be understood).

THESAURUS

grasp to completely understand a fact or an idea, especially a complicated one: *I was slow to grasp his meaning.*
comprehend FORMAL to understand something, especially something that is not easy to understand: *Many children can read the words, yet do not comprehend what they read.*
make sense of something to understand something that is not easy to understand, especially by thinking about it: *People are trying to make sense of the news.*
see ESPECIALLY SPOKEN to understand something: *I see what you mean.*
follow to understand something such as an explanation or story as you hear it, read it etc.: *The complicated plot is hard to follow.*

2 FACT/IDEA [I,T] to know how or why a situation, event, process etc. happens or what it is like, especially through learning or experience: *Sandra doesn't understand football at all.* | **understand how/why/where etc.** *Researchers still do not **fully understand** what causes the disease.* | **understand (that)** *I understand that the treatment may not work.*
3 PERSON/FEELINGS [I,T] to know how someone feels, and why they behave the way they do: **understand sb/sth** *I understand her anger.* | *Larry is the only one who really understands me.* | **understand how/what etc.** *I think I understand how you feel.* → see also UNDERSTANDING²
4 FORMAL to believe or think that something is true because you have heard it or read it somewhere: **understand (that)** *I understand you invited Mrs. Struthers.*
5 it is understood (that) FORMAL used in order to say that everyone knows something or has agreed to it and there is no need to discuss it: *It was understood that my parents would choose my husband.*
6 understand sth to be/mean sth to accept something as having a particular meaning, quality etc.: *We understood his lack of response to mean "no."*
7 do you understand (me)? SPOKEN used when you are angry and are telling someone what they should or should not do: *Never talk to me like that again! Do you understand?*
8 [T usually passive] TECHNICAL to recognize that a word or phrase is missing in a sentence and that you have to imagine that it is there: *In the sentence "I was reading," the object "a book" has to be understood.* → see also **give sb to understand/believe that** at GIVE¹ (47)

un·der·stand·a·ble /ˌʌndɚˈstændəbəl/ *adj.* **1** understandable behavior, reactions etc. seem normal and reasonable because of the situation you are in: *an understandable mistake* | **it is understandable (that)** *It is understandable that parents are angry about this.* **2** able to be understood SYN **comprehensible** —**understandably** /-bli/ *adv.*: *They were understandably upset by the news.*

un·der·stand·ing¹ /ˌʌndɚˈstændɪŋ/ *n.* **1** [C usually singular] a private unofficial agreement: *I thought we **had an understanding about** the price.* | *Eventually they **came to an understanding** about Luke's role in the company.* | *We said he could stay with us **on the understanding that** it would just be temporary.* **2** [singular, U] knowledge about something, based on learning or experience: +**of** *an advance in our basic understanding of the brain* | **get/gain/develop etc. an understanding of sth** *How can we gain an understand-*

ing of other cultures? **3** [singular, U] sympathy toward someone's character and behavior: *He thanked us for our understanding.* **4 sb's understanding (of sth)** the way in which someone judges the meaning of something: *My understanding of the memo is that none of us needs to be at the meeting.* **5** [U] the ability to know and learn SYN **intelligence** → see Word Choice box at COMPREHENSION

understanding² *adj.* sympathetic and kind, even when someone behaves badly: *Thank you for being so understanding about the delays.*

un·der·state /ˌʌndɚˈsteɪt/ *v.* [T] to describe something in a way that makes it seem less important than it really is OPP **overstate**: *The media has understated the seriousness of the problem.*

un·der·stat·ed /ˌʌndɚˈsteɪt̬ɪd◂/ *adj.* APPROVING not too strong, colorful, big etc., in a way that is attractive and pleasing: *The design was simple and understated.*

un·der·state·ment /ˈʌndɚˌsteɪtˀmənt/ *n.* **1** [C] a statement that is not strong enough to express how good, bad, impressive etc. something really is: *To say the movie was bad would be an understatement* (=it was an extremely bad movie). **2** [U] the practice of using statements that are not strong enough to express how good, bad, impressive etc. something really is: *"The party wasn't a complete success," she said with typical understatement* (=the party went very badly).

un·der·stood /ˌʌndɚˈstʊd/ *v.* the past tense and past participle of UNDERSTAND

un·der·sto·ry /ˈʌndɚˌstɔri/ *n. plural* **understories** [C] BIOLOGY a layer of small trees, bushes, and plants below the level of the tall trees in a forest, especially a rain forest: *the understory of Malaysian forests*

un·der·stud·y /ˈʌndɚˌstʌdi/ *n. plural* **understudies** [C] an actor who learns a part in a play so that they can perform it if the usual actor cannot —**understudy** *v.* [T]

un·der·take /ˌʌndɚˈteɪk/ Ac *v. past tense* **undertook** /-ˈtʊk/, *past participle* **undertaken** /-ˈteɪkən/ FORMAL **1** [T] to agree to be responsible for a piece of work, and start to do it: *Baker undertook the job of writing the report.* **2 undertake to do sth** to promise or agree to do something

un·der·tak·er /ˈʌndɚˌteɪkɚ/ *n.* [C] OLD-FASHIONED someone whose job is to arrange funerals SYN **funeral director**

un·der·tak·ing /ˈʌndɚˌteɪkɪŋ/ Ac *n.* **1** [C usually singular] an important job, piece of work, or activity, especially a difficult one: *Building the dam will be a major undertaking.* **2** [C] FORMAL a promise to do something **3** [U] the business of an undertaker

un·der·tone /ˈʌndɚˌtoʊn/ *n.* **1** a feeling or quality that is not directly expressed but can still be recognized: **+of** *There was an undertone of sadness in her letter.* **2** [C] a quiet voice or sound → see also OVERTONE

un·der·tow /ˈʌndɚˌtoʊ/ *n.* [singular] EARTH SCIENCE the water current under the surface that pulls back toward the ocean when a wave comes onto the shore

un·der·used /ˌʌndɚˈyuzd◂/ *adj.* something that is underused is not used as much as it could be: *an underused office*

un·der·u·til·i·za·tion /ˌʌndɚˌyutl-əˈzeɪʃən/ *n.* [U] ECONOMICS when the economic system of a company or country fails to use all of the money, skills, property etc. that it has available to use

un·der·u·til·ized /ˌʌndɚˈyut̬lˌaɪzd◂/ *adj.* underused

un·der·val·ue /ˌʌndɚˈvælyu/ *v.* [T] to think that someone or something is less important or valuable than they really are: *She felt that the company undervalued her work.* —**undervalued** *adj.*

un·der·wa·ter /ˌʌndɚˈwɔt̬ɚ◂/ *adj.* [only before noun] below the surface of an area of water, or able to be used there: *underwater equipment* —**underwater** *adv.*

un·der·way, under way /ˌʌndɚˈweɪ/ *adj., adv.* [not before noun] **1** already happening or being done: *The annual Blues Festival* ***gets underway*** (=starts happening) *today.* | *Construction of the new stadium is* ***well underway*** (=has been happening for quite a long time). **2** something such as a boat or train that is underway is moving

un·der·wear /ˈʌndɚˌwɛr/ S3 *n.* [U] clothes that you wear next to your body under your other clothes

un·der·weight /ˌʌndɚˈweɪt◂/ *adj.* weighing less than is expected or usual OPP **overweight**: *a premature underweight baby* ▶see THESAURUS box at **thin¹**

un·der·went /ˌʌndɚˈwɛnt/ Ac *v.* the past tense of UNDERGO

un·der·whelm /ˌʌndɚˈwɛlm/ *v.* [T] HUMOROUS to not seem very impressive to someone OPP **overwhelm** —**underwhelmed** *adj.* —**underwhelming** *adj.*

un·der·wire bra /ˌʌndɚwaɪɚ ˈbrɑ/ *n.* [C] a BRA with wires sewn into it to help support a woman's breasts

un·der·world /ˈʌndɚˌwɚld/ *n.* **1** the criminals in a particular place and the criminal activities they are involved in: *the city's criminal underworld* | *his underworld connections* **2 the underworld** the place where the spirits of the dead are believed to live, especially in ancient Greek stories

un·der·write /ˈʌndɚˌraɪt/ *v. past tense* **underwrote** /-ˌroʊt/, *past participle* **underwritten** /-ˌrɪtˀn/ [T] **1** FORMAL to support an activity, business plan etc. with money, so that you are financially responsible for it: *The state government will underwrite the project.* **2** ECONOMICS if an insurance company underwrites an insurance contract, it agrees to pay for any damage or loss that happens

un·der·writ·er /ˈʌndɚˌraɪt̬ɚ/ *n.* [C] ECONOMICS someone who makes insurance contracts

un·de·served /ˌʌndɪˈzɚvd◂/ *adj.* undeserved criticism, praise etc. is unfair because you do not deserve it: *He has an undeserved reputation as a loser.*

U

un·de·sir·a·ble /ˌʌndɪˈzaɪrəbəl◂/ *adj.* FORMAL something or someone that is undesirable is not welcome or wanted because they may be bad or harmful: *The treatment has some undesirable side effects, such as headaches.*

un·de·sir·a·bles /ˌʌndɪˈzaɪrəbəlz/ *n.* [plural] people who are considered to be immoral, criminal, or socially unacceptable

un·de·tect·a·ble /ˌʌndɪˈtɛktəbəl◂/ *adj.* not large or strong enough to be noticed: *Drugs have reduced the virus to undetectable levels.*

un·de·tect·ed /ˌʌndɪˈtɛktɪd◂/ *adj.* not seen or noticed: *How could the bomb go through the X-ray machine undetected?*

un·de·ter·mined /ˌʌndɪˈtɚmɪnd◂/ *adj.* not known, decided, or calculated: *The cause of the accident is still undetermined.*

un·de·terred /ˌʌndɪˈtɚd/ *adj.* not persuaded to stop doing something even though something bad has happened: **+by** *He continues to play, undeterred by his injuries.*

un·de·vel·oped /ˌʌndɪˈvɛləpt◂/ *adj.* undeveloped land has not been built on or used for a particular purpose → see also UNDERDEVELOPED

un·did /ʌnˈdɪd/ *v.* the past tense of UNDO

un·dies /ˈʌndiz/ *n.* [plural] SPOKEN underwear

un·di·lut·ed /ˌʌndɪˈlut̬ɪd◂/ *adj.* **1** LITERARY an undiluted feeling or quality is very strong and is not mixed with other feelings or qualities: *undiluted hate* **2** an undiluted mixture has not been made weaker by adding water

un·di·min·ished /ˌʌndɪˈmɪnɪʃt◂/ Ac *adj.* not weaker or less important than before: *After more than 20 years, the power of the movie remains undiminished.*

un·dis·ci·plined /ʌnˈdɪsɪplɪnd/ *adj.* not controlled, or not obeying appropriate rules or limits: *undisciplined spending*

un·dis·closed /ˌʌndɪsˈkloʊzd◂/ *adj.* undisclosed information has not been made available to people in general: *They bought the company for an undisclosed sum.*

un·dis·guised /ˌʌndɪsˈgaɪzd◂ / *adj.* clearly shown and not hidden: *He looked at us with undisguised hatred.*

un·dis·put·ed /ˌʌndɪˈspyuṭɪd◂ / *adj.* **1** accepted by everyone: **the undisputed leader/master/champion etc.** *In 1927 Stalin became the undisputed leader of the Soviet Union.* **2** known to be definitely true, and not argued about: *undisputed facts* | **undisputed that** *It is undisputed that they had a romantic relationship.*

un·dis·tin·guished /ˌʌndɪˈstɪŋgwɪʃt◂ / *adj.* not having any special features, qualities, or marks, or not having done anything important or noticeable: *an undistinguished politician*

un·dis·turbed /ˌʌndɪˈstɚbd◂ / *adj.* not interrupted, moved, or changed: *The tomb was left undisturbed for over 800 years.*

un·di·vid·ed /ˌʌndɪˈvaɪdɪd◂ / *adj.* **1 undivided attention/support/loyalty etc.** complete attention, support etc.: *I'll give the matter my undivided attention.* **2** not separated into smaller parts or groups

un·do /ʌnˈdu/ *v. past tense* **undid** /-ˈdɪd/, *past participle* **undone** /-ˈdʌn/, **underdoes** **1** [T] to unfasten something that is tied or wrapped: *She carefully undid the ribbons and opened the scroll.* ▸see THESAURUS box at **fasten**, **open**[2] **2** [T] to try to remove the bad effects of something you have done: *I wish it was possible to undo what I've done.* **3** [I,T] COMPUTERS to remove the effect of your previous action on a computer by giving it an instruction: *Just undo that last deletion.* **4** [T] to make someone fail, not have any hope etc.: *He was eventually undone by his political mistakes.*

U

un·doc·u·ment·ed /ʌnˈdɑkyəˌmɛntɪd/ *adj.* **1 an undocumented alien/worker/immigrant etc.** someone who is living or working in a country without official permission **2** undocumented information, claims etc. have not been officially recorded or shown to be true

un·do·ing /ʌnˈduɪŋ/ *n.* **sth is sb's undoing** used in order to say that something is the cause of someone's failure: *His arrogance was his undoing in the end.*

un·done /ˌʌnˈdʌn◂ / *adj.* [not before noun] **1** not fastened: *One of your buttons is **coming undone**.* **2** not finished or completed: *He decided he couldn't **leave** the job **undone**.* **3** OLD USE destroyed and without hope

un·doubt·ed·ly /ʌnˈdaʊṭɪdli/ *adv.* [sentence adverb] used to emphasize that something is definitely true: *This course of action will undoubtedly lead to war.* —**undoubted** *adj.*: *The movie was an undoubted success.*

un·dreamed of, **undreamed-of** /ʌnˈdrimd ʌv/ *adj.* much more or much better than you could imagine: *These technologies were undreamed of 50 years ago.*

un·dress[1] /ʌnˈdrɛs/ *v.* [I,T] to take your clothes off, or take someone else's clothes off: *She undressed and got into bed.*

undress[2] *n.* [U] FORMAL **in a state of undress** wearing few or no clothes

un·dressed /ʌnˈdrɛst/ *adj.* **1** [not before noun] not wearing any clothes: *She refused to **get undressed*** (=take her clothes off) *in front of the doctor.* ▸see THESAURUS box at **naked** **2** an undressed wound has not been covered to protect it

un·due /ˌʌnˈdu◂ / *adj.* [only before noun] FORMAL more than is reasonable, appropriate, or necessary: *The doctor feels that my job is putting undue stress on me.*

un·du·lat·ing /ˈʌndʒəˌleɪṭɪŋ/ *adj.* [only before noun] FORMAL moving or shaped like waves that are rising and falling: *the undulating motion of a snake* | *undulating hills* —**undulate** *v.* [I] —**undulation** /ˌʌndʒəˈleɪʃən/ *n.* [C,U]

un·du·ly /ʌnˈduli/ *adv.* FORMAL much more than necessary or appropriate, or much too extreme: *The criticism of the child seemed unduly harsh.*

un·dy·ing /ˌʌnˈdaɪ-ɪŋ◂ / *adj.* [only before noun] continuing forever: *undying love*

un·earned /ˌʌnˈɚnd◂ / *adj.* **1 unearned income** money that you receive from something other than working, for example from INVESTMENTS **2** not deserved: *unearned sympathy*

un·earth /ʌnˈɚθ/ *v.* [T] **1** to discover something that was hidden, lost, or kept secret SYN **uncover** SYN **dig up**: *The surprising story was unearthed by reporters at the "Post."* ▸see THESAURUS box at **find**[1] **2** to find something that has been buried in the ground SYN **dig up**: *Farmers still sometimes unearth human bones here.*

un·earth·ly /ʌnˈɚθli/ *adj.* very strange and unnatural: *The cabin was surrounded by an unearthly green light.* —**unearthliness** *n.* [U]

un·ease /ʌnˈiz/ *n.* [U] a feeling of nervousness and anxiety that makes you not able to relax: **+about/with/over** *She felt a sudden **sense of unease** about her father's health.*

un·eas·y /ˌʌnˈizi◂ / *adj. comparative* **uneasier**, *superlative* **uneasiest** **1** nervous, anxious, and unable to relax because you think something bad might happen: **+about/at/over/with** *She **felt** a little **uneasy** about being alone in the room with Todd.* | *When I answered the phone, no one said anything, which **made** me **uneasy**.* **2** an uneasy period of time is one when people have agreed to stop fighting or arguing, but which is not really calm: *Since the agreement, there has been an uneasy calm in the region.* **3** not comfortable, peaceful, or relaxed: *After the speech, there was an uneasy silence.* | *their uneasy relationship* —**uneasily** *adv.* —**uneasiness** *n.* [U]

un·ed·u·cat·ed /ʌnˈɛdʒəˌkeɪṭɪd/ *adj.* not educated to the usual level: *uneducated farmworkers*

un·elect·ed /ˌʌnɪˈlɛktɪd◂ / *adj.* having an important government position although you were not elected: *unelected officials*

un·e·mo·tion·al /ˌʌnɪˈmoʊʃənl◂ / *adj.* not showing your feelings: *a cold unemotional voice*

un·em·ployed /ˌʌnɪmˈplɔɪd◂ / *adj.* **1** without a job: *an unemployed steel worker* | *I've only been unemployed for a few weeks.* **2 the unemployed** [plural] people who have no job: *The government is not doing enough to help the unemployed.*

un·em·ploy·ment /ˌʌnɪmˈplɔɪmənt/ W3 *n.* [U] **1** also **unemployment rate** the number of people in a country who do not have a job: *The national unemployment rate is about 6%.* | **low/high unemployment (rate)** (=a small/large number of people without jobs) | **rising/falling unemployment (rate)** (=increasing/decreasing numbers of people who do not have jobs) **2** the fact of having no job: *500 employees at the factory now face unemployment.* **3** money paid regularly by the government to people who have no job: *He's been **on unemployment** for three months.*

unemˈployment ˌbenefits *n.* [plural] also **unemˈployment compenˌsation** [U] money paid regularly by the government to people who do not have a job

unemˈployment line *n.* [C] **1** also **unemployment lines** [plural] people without jobs, in general: *In February, about 450,000 people **joined the unemployment line*** (=became unemployed). **2** a line that people without jobs must stand in to get their unemployment benefits

un·en·cum·bered /ˌʌnɪnˈkʌmbɚd◂ / *adj.* FORMAL not restricted or slowed down by problems, rules etc.: **+by** *The winning candidate was unencumbered by other political duties.*

un·end·ing /ʌnˈɛndɪŋ/ *adj.* seeming to never stop: *the unending winter snow and cold*

un·en·vi·a·ble /ʌnˈɛnviəbəl/ *adj.* used when describing a job or situation that someone is in that is so bad or difficult that you would not want to be in it: **+of** *Lee had the unenviable task of reorganizing the department.*

un·e·qual /ʌnˈikwəl/ *adj.* **1** unfairly treating different people or groups in different ways OPP **equal**: *unequal educational opportunities* **2** not the same in size, number, value, rank, strength etc. SYN **equal**: **+in** *The two ropes were unequal in length.* | **an unequal**

contest/struggle/fight etc. (=a competition or fight in which one side is much stronger than the other) **3 be unequal to the task/job etc.** FORMAL to not have enough strength, ability etc. to do something —**unequally** *adv.*

un·e·qualed, **unequalled** /ʌn'ikwəld/ *adj.* better than any other: *The scenery is unequaled.*

un·e·quiv·o·cal /ˌʌnɪ'kwɪvəkəl/ *adj.* FORMAL completely clear and without any possibility of doubt: *His answer was an unequivocal "No."* —**unequivocally** /-kli/ *adv.*

un·er·ring /ʌn'ɛrɪŋ, ʌn'ɚɪŋ/ *adj.* always exactly right: *He throws the ball with unerring accuracy.* —**unerringly** *adv.*

UNESCO /yu'nɛskoʊ/ **United Nations Educational, Scientific and Cultural Organization** a part of the U.N., based in Paris, which is concerned especially with providing help for poorer countries with education and science

un·eth·i·cal /ʌn'ɛθɪkəl/ Ac *adj.* not obeying rules of moral behavior, especially those concerning a profession: *It would be unethical for me to discuss what my client told me.* —**unethically** /-kli/ *adv.*

un·e·ven /ʌn'ivən/ *adj.* **1** not smooth, flat, or level: *uneven ground* **2** good in some parts and bad in others SYN **spotty**: *the team's uneven performance* **3** not equal or equally balanced: *an uneven income distribution* **4** not happening or appearing in a regular pattern SYN **irregular**: *His breathing had become uneven.* —**unevenly** *adv.* —**unevenness** *n.* [U]

un·e·vent·ful /ˌʌnɪ'vɛntfəl◂ / *adj.* with nothing exciting or unusual happening: *She led a quiet uneventful life.* —**uneventfully** *adv.*

un·ex·cit·ing /ˌʌnɪk'saɪṭɪŋ◂ / *adj.* ordinary and slightly boring

un·ex·cused /ˌʌnɪk'skuzd◂ / *adj.* **an unexcused absence** an occasion when you are away from school or work without permission

un·ex·pect·ed /ˌʌnɪk'spɛktɪd◂ / *adj.* surprising because of not being expected: *the unexpected results of the experiment* | **completely/totally/entirely etc. unexpected** *Her death was completely unexpected.* —**unexpectedness** *n.* [U]

un·ex·pect·ed·ly /ˌʌnɪk'spɛktɪdli/ *adv.* in a way or at a time that you did not expect: *His father died unexpectedly yesterday.*

un·ex·plained /ˌʌnɪk'spleɪnd◂ / *adj.* not understood or made clear: *There have been three unexplained fires at the school.*

un·ex·pur·gat·ed /ʌn'ɛkspɚˌgeɪṭɪd/ *adj.* an unexpurgated book, play etc. is complete and has not had parts that might offend people removed

un·fail·ing /ʌn'feɪlɪŋ/ *adj.* always there, even in times of difficulty or trouble: *Thank you all for your unfailing support.* —**unfailingly** *adv.*

un·fair /ˌʌn'fɛr◂ / *adj.* not right or fair, especially by not giving an equal opportunity to everyone: +**to** *Do you think I'm being unfair to her?* | **it is unfair (of sb) to do sth** *It's unfair to give money to John and not to me.* | **it is unfair that** *It is unfair that some people have so much while others have nothing.* | *These laws are aimed at preventing* ***unfair competition*** (=in business). —**unfairly** *adv.* —**unfairness** *n.* [U]

un·faith·ful /ʌn'feɪθfəl/ *adj.* **1** someone who is unfaithful has sex with someone who is not their wife, husband, or usual partner: +**to** *He accused me of being unfaithful to him.* **2** not loyal to a principle, person etc. —**unfaithfully** *adv.* —**unfaithfulness** *n.* [U]

un·fal·ter·ing /ʌn'fɔltərɪŋ/ *adj.* FORMAL strong, determined, and not becoming weaker: *unfaltering loyalty* —**unfalteringly** *adv.*

un·fa·mil·iar /ˌʌnfə'mɪlyɚ◂ / *adj.* **1** not known to you: *an unfamiliar name* | +**to** *Everything in my old house seemed unfamiliar to me.* **2 be unfamiliar with sth** to not have any knowledge or experience of something: *We were unfamiliar with the neighborhood.* —**unfamiliarity** /ˌʌnfəmɪli'ærəṭi/ *n.*

un·fash·ion·a·ble /ʌn'fæʃənəbəl/ *adj.* not popular or fashionable at the present time: *unfashionable clothes*

un·fas·ten /ˌʌn'fæsən/ *v.* [T] to disconnect or untie something such as a button, belt, rope etc.: *Do not unfasten your safety belt until the plane has stopped.*

un·fath·om·a·ble /ʌn'fæðəməbəl/ *adj.* LITERARY too strange or mysterious to be understood: *His expression was unfathomable.* —**unfathomably** *adv.*

un·fa·vor·a·ble /ʌn'feɪvərəbəl/ *adj.* **1** unfavorable conditions, situations etc. are not as good as they should be or usually are: *It's unfavorable weather for sailing.* **2** expressing disapproval: *58% of the public have an unfavorable opinion of him.* —**unfavorably** *adv.*

un·fazed /ʌn'feɪzd/ *adj.* not confused or shocked by a difficult situation or something bad that has happened: +**by** *Newton seemed unfazed by the gunfire.*

un·feel·ing /ʌn'filɪŋ/ *adj.* not sympathetic toward other people's feelings

un·fet·tered /ʌn'fɛṭɚd◂ / *adj.* FORMAL not restricted by laws or rules: *an unfettered market economy*

un·filled /ˌʌn'fɪld◂ / *adj.* **1 an unfilled order** a request by a customer for a product that has not been sent **2** an unfilled job, position etc. is available but no one has been found for it yet

un·fin·ished /ˌʌn'fɪnɪʃt◂ / *adj.* **1** not completed SYN **incomplete**: *An unfinished letter lay on her desk.* | *She stopped talking,* ***leaving*** *her sentence* ***unfinished*** (=not finishing it). **2 unfinished business** something that needs to be done or dealt with that you have not yet done

un·fit /ʌn'fɪt/ *adj.* **1** below the accepted quality for a particular use or purpose: +**for** *The land is unfit for farming.* | **unfit to do sth** *The produce is unfit to eat.* | **unfit for human habitation/consumption** (=not good enough for someone to live in or to eat) **2** not having the right qualities to do a particular job or activity: *She's an unfit mother.* | +**for** *Brown is unfit for public office.* **3 unfit for sth** also **unfit to do sth** not able to work, serve in the military etc. as a result of illness or injury: *He was declared unfit for military service.*

U

un·flag·ging /ʌn'flægɪŋ/ *adj.* continuing strongly, and never becoming tired or weak: *her unflagging energy*

un·flap·pa·ble /ʌn'flæpəbəl/ *adj.* INFORMAL having the ability to stay calm and not get upset, even in difficult situations: *A good radio-host must be unflappable.*

un·flat·ter·ing /ʌn'flæṭərɪŋ/ *adj.* making someone look or seem bad or unattractive: *an unflattering article about him in the paper*

un·flinch·ing /ʌn'flɪntʃɪŋ/ *adj.* not changing or becoming weaker, even in a very difficult or dangerous situation: *the family's unflinching loyalty* —**unflinchingly** *adv.*

un·fo·cused, **unfocussed** /ʌn'foʊkəst/ *adj.* **1** not dealing with or paying attention to the important ideas, causes etc.: *The class discussion was becoming unfocused.* **2** if someone's eyes are unfocused, their eyes are open but they are not looking at anything

un·fold /ʌn'foʊld/ *v.* [I,T] **1** if a story, plan etc. unfolds, or the author unfolds it, it becomes clearer as you hear or learn more about it: *As the story unfolds, we learn more about Mark's childhood.* **2** to open something that was folded: *She unfolded the map.*

un·fore·seen /ˌʌnfɔr'sin◂ , -fɚ-/ *adj.* an unforeseen situation is one that you did not expect to happen: *unforseen problems* | *The plan is simple, but it could have unforseen effects.* | **unforseen event/circumstances/changes etc.** *Due to unforseen circumstances, the play has been canceled.*

un·for·get·ta·ble /ˌʌnfɚ'gɛṭəbəl/ *adj.* an unforgettable experience, sight etc. affects you so strongly that you will never forget it, especially because it is particularly good or beautiful: *It was an unforgettable performance.* —**unforgettably** *adv.*

un·for·giv·a·ble /ˌʌnfɚˈgɪvəbəl◂/ *adj.* an unforgivable action is so bad or cruel that you cannot forgive the person who did it: **an unforgivable sin/act/crime** *Refusing to help was, in my opinion, an unforgivable act.* —**unforgivably** *adv.*

un·for·giv·ing /ˌʌnfɚˈgɪvɪŋ◂/ *adj.* someone who is unforgiving does not forgive people easily

un·formed /ˌʌnˈfɔrmd◂/ *adj.* not yet completely developed: *The idea was still unformed in my mind.*

un·for·tu·nate¹ /ʌnˈfɔrtʃənɪt/ *adj.* **1** happening because of bad luck SYN **unlucky**: *an unfortunate accident* **2** someone who is unfortunate has something bad happen to them SYN **unlucky**: *The teacher was yelling at some unfortunate student.* **3** an unfortunate situation, condition, quality etc. is a bad or disappointing one that you wish were different SYN **regrettable**: ***It's unfortunate that** so few people seem willing to help.* **4** FORMAL unfortunate behavior, remarks etc. are not appropriate and make people feel embarrassed or offended: *an unfortunate choice of words*

unfortunate² *n.* [C] LITERARY someone who is in an unpleasant situation, especially someone with no money, home, job etc.: *a poor unfortunate*

un·for·tu·nate·ly /ʌnˈfɔrtʃənɪtli/ S3 W3 *adv.* [sentence adverb] **1** used when you are mentioning a fact that you wish were not true SYN **regrettably**: *Unfortunately, I've already made plans for that weekend.* | **unfortunately for sb** *Unfortunately for me, she told me she did not love me.* **2** FORMAL in a way that is not appropriate and makes people feel slightly embarrassed or offended

un·found·ed /ˌʌnˈfaʊndɪd◂/ Ac *adj.* unfounded statements, feelings, opinions etc. are wrong because they are not based on true facts: **unfounded rumors/claims/allegations etc.** *unfounded allegations against the police* | *We hoped our fears would* ***prove to be unfounded*** (=be shown later to be wrong).

un·friend·ly /ʌnˈfrɛndli/ *adj. comparative* **unfriendlier**, *superlative* **unfriendliest** **1** not kind or friendly: *an unfriendly expression* | **+to/toward** *The villagers were pretty unfriendly toward us.* **2** having a bad or harmful effect on someone: **+to** *We have created cities that are unfriendly to bicycles.* **3** an unfriendly government, power, nation etc. is one that opposes yours

un·ful·filled /ˌʌnfʊlˈfɪld◂/ *adj.* **1** an unfulfilled wish, desire, hope etc. has not been achieved: *politicians' unfulfilled promises* **2** someone who is unfulfilled feels they could be achieving more in their job, relationship etc. and is unhappy because of this: *Nick felt dissatisfied and unfulfilled at work.*

un·fund·ed /ˌʌnˈfʌndɪd◂/ *adj.* **1** an unfunded PROJECT has not been given the money it needs to work **2 an unfunded mandate** something that the U.S. government demands the states do although they do not give them money to do it

un·fun·ny /ʌnˈfʌni/ *adj.* INFORMAL, DISAPPROVING an unfunny joke or action is not amusing, although it is intended to be

un·furl /ʌnˈfɚl/ *v.* [T] to unroll and open a flag, sail etc.

un·fur·nished /ˌʌnˈfɚnɪʃt◂/ *adj.* an unfurnished room, house etc. has no furniture in it

un·gain·ly /ʌnˈgeɪnli/ *adj.* moving in a way that does not look graceful: *I felt fat and ungainly.*

un·glued /ʌnˈglud/ *adj.* **1 come unglued** INFORMAL **a)** if a plan, situation etc. comes unglued, it stops working well: *When his parents got divorced, his whole world came unglued.* **b)** to become extremely upset or angry about something **2** no longer glued together: *The label on the bottle had* ***come unglued*** (=become unglued).

un·god·ly /ʌnˈgɑdli/ *adj.* **1 ungodly hour/time** INFORMAL used when saying that someone is doing something at a time that is too late or too early to be appropriate: *Why did you wake me up at such an ungodly hour?* **2** [only before noun] unreasonable or extreme: *an ungodly noise* **3** LITERARY showing a lack of respect for God

un·gov·ern·a·ble /ʌnˈgʌvɚnəbəl/ *adj.* **1** a country or area that is ungovernable is one in which the people cannot be controlled by the government, the police etc. **2** FORMAL feelings or types of behavior that are ungovernable are impossible to control: *her ungovernable temper*

un·gra·cious /ʌnˈgreɪʃəs/ *adj.* not polite or friendly: *an ungracious loser* —**ungraciously** *adv.*

un·grate·ful /ʌnˈgreɪtfəl/ *adj.* not expressing thanks for something that someone has given to you or done for you: *I don't mean to be ungrateful, but I really don't need any help.* —**ungratefully** *adv.*

un·guard·ed /ˌʌnˈgɑrdɪd◂/ *adj.* **1 an unguarded moment** a time when you are not paying attention to what you are doing or saying: *In an unguarded moment, he admitted taking the file.* **2** not guarded or protected by anyone: *an unguarded part of the Mexican border* **3** an unguarded remark, statement etc. is one that you make carelessly without thinking of the possible effects

un·guent /ˈʌŋgwənt/ *n.* [C] LITERARY an oily substance used on your skin SYN **ointment**

un·hand /ʌnˈhænd/ *v.* [T] OLD USE to stop holding someone you have caught

un·hap·pi·ly /ʌnˈhæpəli/ *adv.* **1** in a way that shows you are not happy: *"I don't know what to do," Bill answered unhappily.* **2** [sentence adverb] OLD-FASHIONED used when you are mentioning a fact that you wish were not true SYN **unfortunately**

un·hap·py /ʌnˈhæpi/ S3 *adj. comparative* **unhappier**, *superlative* **unhappiest** **1** not happy: *I was very unhappy in college.* | *She had a* ***deeply unhappy*** *life.* ►see THESAURUS box at **sad** **2** feeling worried or annoyed because you do not like what is happening in a situation SYN **dissatisfied**: **+with** *The coach was unhappy with the team's performance.* | **+about** *Dennis is unhappy about having to work on a Saturday.* **3** FORMAL not appropriate, lucky, or desirable: *an unhappy situation* —**unhappiness** *n.* [U]

un·harmed /ʌnˈhɑrmd/ *adj.* [not before noun] not hurt or harmed: *The hostages were released unharmed.*

un·health·y /ʌnˈhɛlθi/ *adj. comparative* **unhealthier**, *superlative* **unhealthiest** **1** likely to make you sick: *Junk food is really unhealthy.* | *an unhealthy lifestyle* **2** not normal or natural and likely to be harmful: *an unhealthy relationship* | **an unhealthy interest/obsession/fear etc.** *Ben is showing an unhealthy interest in guns.* **3** not physically healthy: *an unhealthy baby* **4** unhealthy skin, hair etc. shows that you are sick or not healthy: *an unhealthy pale complexion* —**unhealthily** *adv.* —**unhealthiness** *n.* [U]

un·heard /ˌʌnˈhɚd/ *adj.* not heard, or not listened to: *His suggestions* ***went unheard*** (=were not listened to).

un'heard of, **unheard-of** *adj.* something that is unheard of is extremely unusual or has never happened before: *In 1957 $1 million was an unheard of sum of money to be paid.*

un·heed·ed /ʌnˈhidɪd/ *adj.* LITERARY noticed but not listened to, accepted, or believed: *Their appeal for help* ***went unheeded***.

un·help·ful /ʌnˈhɛlpfəl/ *adj.* **1** not willing or able to help someone: *The secretary was rude and unhelpful.* **2** something that is unhelpful is not useful and may make a situation worse: *The arguments during the meeting were unhelpful.* —**unhelpfully** *adv.* —**unhelpfulness** *n.* [U]

un·her·ald·ed /ʌnˈhɛrəldɪd/ *adj.* FORMAL **1** something or someone that is unheralded is not widely known about or praised, even though it deserves attention, praise, or respect: *an unheralded hero in the fight against poverty* **2** if an event is unheralded, there is no warning that it is going to happen: *an unheralded visit from the governor*

un·hinge /ʌnˈhɪndʒ/ *v.* [T] to make someone become very upset or mentally ill: *The terrible experience unhinged him slightly.* —**unhinged** *adj.*

un·hip /ˌʌnˈhɪp◂/ *adj.* SPOKEN, INFORMAL unfashionable

un·ho·ly /ʌn'houli/ *adj.* [no comparative] **1** ESPECIALLY HUMOROUS **an unholy alliance** an unusual agreement between two people or organizations who would not normally work together, usually when each is only interested in gaining something for themselves **2** [only before noun] INFORMAL bad and extreme: *The situation is an unholy mess.* **3** not holy, or not respecting what is holy

un·hook /ʌn'hʊk/ *v.* [T] to unfasten or remove something from a hook: *Can you unhook this necklace for me?*

un·hoped-for /ʌn'houpt fɔr/ *adj.* much better than had been expected: *unhoped-for success*

un·hur·ried /ʌn'hɚid, -'hʌrid/ *adj.* done slowly and calmly: *He liked the unhurried pace of small towns.* —**unhurriedly** *adv.*

un·hurt /ʌn'hɚt/ *adj.* [not before noun] not hurt: *The driver of the car was unhurt.*

uni- /yunɪ/ *prefix* one: *unidirectional* (=going only in one direction)

u·ni·cam·er·al /ˌyunɪ'kæmrəl/ *adj.* [only before noun] a unicameral LEGISLATURE (=law-making organization) consists of only one part → see also BICAMERAL

UNICEF /'yunəˌsɛf/ *n.* **United Nations International Children's Fund** an organization that helps children in the world suffering from disease, HUNGER etc.

u·ni·corn /'yunəˌkɔrn/ *n.* [C] an imaginary animal like a white horse with a long straight horn growing on its head

u·ni·cy·cle /'yunəˌsaɪkəl/ *n.* [C] a vehicle that is like a bicycle but has only one wheel

un·i·den·ti·fied /ˌʌnə'dɛntəˌfaɪd◂, ˌʌnaɪ-/ *adj.* an unidentified person or thing is one that you do not recognize, do not know the name of etc.: *Three of the victims remain unidentified.*

u·ni·fi·ca·tion /ˌyunəfə'keɪʃən/ Ac *n.* [U] the act of combining two or more groups, countries etc. to make a single group or country: *the unification of Germany*

u·ni·form[1] /'yunəˌfɔrm/ Ac S3 W3 *n.* [C,U] **1** a particular type of clothing worn by all the members of a group or organization, such as the police, the army etc.: *The airline employees wore dark blue uniforms.* | *Two soldiers* ***in uniform*** (=wearing one) *came in.* | *She looked different* ***out of uniform*** (=not wearing one). **2 in uniform** someone in uniform is a member of the army, navy etc.: *He spent 33 years in uniform.* **3** the type of clothes that someone usually wears: *the teenager's uniform of jeans and a T-shirt*

uniform[2] Ac *adj.* being the same in all its parts or among all its members: **+in** *The houses are uniform in size and design.* [**Origin:** 1500–1600 French *uniforme*, from Latin *uniformis*, from *uni-* + *-formis* (from *forma* form)] —**uniformly** *adv.*

u·ni·formed /'yunəˌfɔrmd/ *adj.* wearing a uniform: *a uniformed guard*

u·ni·for·mi·ty /ˌyunə'fɔrməṭi/ Ac *n.* [U] the quality of being or looking the same as all other members of a group: *There is a strict uniformity of teaching methods among the schools.*

u·ni·fy /'yunəˌfaɪ/ Ac *v.* **unifies, unified, unifying 1** [I,T] if you unify two or more groups, the parts of a country etc., or they unify, they are combined to make a single unit: *Strong support for the war has unified the nation.* **2** [T] to combine different ideas, styles etc. to make a new idea, style etc.: *His music unifies traditional and modern themes.* —**unified** *adj.*

u·ni·lat·er·al /ˌyunə'læṭərəl/ *adj.* FORMAL a unilateral action or decision is done by only one of the groups involved in a situation: *a unilateral ban on landmines* —**unilateralism** *n.* —**unilaterally** *adv.* → see also BILATERAL, MULTILATERAL

un·i·mag·i·na·ble /ˌʌnɪ'mædʒənəbəl◂/ *adj.* not possible to imagine: *The size of the universe is unimaginable.* —**unimaginably** *adv.*

un·i·mag·i·na·tive /ˌʌnɪ'mædʒənəṭɪv◂/ *adj.* **1** lacking the ability to think of new or unusual ideas: *an unimaginative writer* **2** ordinary and boring, and not involving any new or intelligent ideas: *unimaginative architecture*

un·i·mag·ined /ˌʌnɪ'mædʒɪnd◂/ *adj.* [usually before noun] so good, large, great etc. that it may be difficult to believe: *The invention brought him unimagined wealth.*

un·im·paired /ˌʌnɪm'pɛrd◂/ *adj.* not damaged or made weak: *He cannot speak, but his mind is completely unimpaired.*

un·im·peach·a·ble /ˌʌnɪm'pitʃəbəl◂/ *adj.* FORMAL so good or definite that criticism or doubt is impossible: *unimpeachable evidence*

un·im·ped·ed /ˌʌnɪm'pidɪd◂/ *adj.* happening or moving without being stopped or having difficulty: *unimpeded traffic flow*

un·im·por·tant /ˌʌnɪm'pɔrt¬nt◂/ *adj.* not important, and not worth considering: *unimportant details* | **+to** *Employees' opinions seem to be unimportant to managers.*

THESAURUS

of no/little importance not important, or not very important: *The amount of ice in glaciers is of little importance compared to the Antarctic ice sheet.*
minor small and not very important or serious, especially when compared with other things: *a few minor changes*
trivial not important or serious: *people committing trivial offences*
insignificant too small or unimportant to consider or worry about: *My own problems seemed insignificant in comparison to hers.*
negligible/marginal too slight or small to be important: *The difference is negligible.*
secondary not as important as something else: *All other questions were secondary.*
peripheral FORMAL not as important as other things or people in a particular activity or situation: *peripheral activities*

un·im·pressed /ˌʌnɪm'prɛst/ *adj.* not thinking that someone or something is good, interesting, unusual etc.: **+with/by** *Board members were unimpressed with the plan.*

un·im·pres·sive /ˌʌnɪm'prɛsɪv◂/ *adj.* not as good, large, important, skillful etc. as expected or necessary: *unimpressive test scores*

un·im·proved /ˌʌnɪm'pruvd◂/ *adj.* **1** unimproved land has not been developed for use by being cleared, cultivated, built on etc. **2** not better than before, even though changes have been made or help has been given: *Her health remained unimproved.*

un·in·cor·po·rat·ed /ˌʌnɪŋ'kɔrpəˌreɪṭɪd◂/ *adj.* an unincorporated area of land has not officially become part of a city or town

un·in·formed /ˌʌnɪn'fɔrmd◂/ *adj.* not having enough knowledge or information: *The students were mostly uninformed about politics.*

un·in·hab·it·a·ble /ˌʌnɪn'hæbɪṭəbəl◂/ *adj.* **1** an uninhabitable place is impossible to live in: *an uninhabitable island* **2** an uninhabitable house or apartment is too dirty, cold etc. to live in

un·in·hab·it·ed /ˌʌnɪn'hæbɪṭɪd◂/ *adj.* an uninhabited place does not have anyone living there: *an uninhabited house*

un·in·hib·it·ed /ˌʌnɪn'hɪbɪṭɪd◂/ *adj.* confident or relaxed enough to do or say what you want to: *uninhibited curiosity* —**uninhibitedly** *adv.*

un·in·i·ti·at·ed /ˌʌnɪ'nɪʃiˌeɪṭɪd◂/ *n.* **the uninitiated** [plural] people who do not have special knowledge or experience of something: *The sport can seem scary* ***to the uninitiated.*** —**uninitiated** *adj.*

un·in·spired /ˌʌnɪn'spaɪɚd◂/ *adj.* **1** not showing any imagination: *an uninspired performance* **2** not excited by something: *I was uninspired by the book.*

U

un·in·spir·ing /ˌʌnɪnˈspaɪrɪŋ◂ / *adj.* not interesting or exciting at all: *an uninspiring speaker*

un·in·stall /ˌʌnɪnˈstɔl/ *v.* [T] COMPUTERS to completely remove a piece of SOFTWARE from a computer, often using a special program

un·in·sured /ˌʌnɪnˈʃʊrd◂ / *adj.* not having INSURANCE: *We provide free medical care for uninsured children.* **—the uninsured** *n.* [plural]

un·in·tel·li·gi·ble /ˌʌnɪnˈtɛlədʒəbəl/ *adj.* impossible to understand: *a song with unintelligable lyrics* **—unintelligibly** *adv.*

un·in·tend·ed /ˌʌnɪnˈtɛndɪd◂ / *adj.* FORMAL not planned or expected: *The new law had some unintended results.* | *unintended pregnancies*

un·in·ten·tion·al /ˌʌnɪnˈtɛnʃənl◂ / *adj.* not said or done deliberately: *The jury agreed that the shooting was unintentional.* **—unintentionally** *adv.*

un·in·terest·ed /ʌnˈɪntrɪstɪd, -ˈɪntərɛs-/ *adj.* not interested: **+in** *I was uninterested in traveling when I was young.* → see also DISINTERESTED

un·in·ter·rupt·ed /ˌʌnɪntəˈrʌptɪd◂ / *adj.* **1** continuous, without stopping: *six hours of uninterrupted sleep* **2** [only before noun] an uninterrupted view is not blocked by anything, so you can see a long way

un·in·vit·ed /ˌʌnɪnˈvaɪt̬ɪd◂ / *adj.* not wanted or asked for: *uninvited guests* | *an uninvited opinion*

un·in·vit·ing /ˌʌnɪnˈvaɪt̬ɪŋ◂ / *adj.* an uninviting place seems unattractive or not nice: *The old part of the city is dark and uninviting.*

U

un·ion /ˈyunyən/ S3 W1 *n.* **1** [C] also **labor union** an organization formed by workers to protect their rights: *the National Farmers' Union* | *union members* ▸see THESAURUS box at **organization** **2** [singular, U] FORMAL the act of joining two or more things together, or the state of being joined together: **+with** *Some militants favor independence for Kashmir or union with Pakistan.* | *a mystical union with God* | **+of** *A lecture discussing the union of art and medical science is set for 4 p.m. today.* **3** [singular, U] POLITICS a group of countries or states with the same national government: *Alaska and Hawaii both joined the union* (=the U.S.) *in 1959.* | *the Soviet Union* **4 the Union** HISTORY used to talk about the U.S., or about the northern states of the U.S. during the Civil War: *soldiers who fought for the Union* **5** [C,U] FORMAL marriage **6** [C,U] FORMAL the activity of having sex, or an occasion when this happens [**Origin:** 1400–1500 Old French, Late Latin *unio*, from Latin *unus* **one**]

un·ion·ism /ˈyunyəˌnɪzəm/ *n.* [U] belief in the principles of UNIONS **—unionist** *n.* [C]

un·ion·ize /ˈyunyəˌnaɪz/ *v.* [I,T] if workers unionize or are unionized, they become members of a UNION **—unionization** /ˌyunyənəˈzeɪʃən/ *n.* [U]

ˌUnion ˈJack *n.* **the Union Jack** the national flag of the U.K.

ˈunion ˌlabel *n.* [C] a piece of paper or other material attached to a product which tells you that the product was made by people belonging to a union

ˈunion ˌsteward *n.* [C] a SHOP STEWARD

ˈunion ˌsuit *n.* [C] a piece of underwear that covers the whole body, with long legs and long SLEEVES SYN **long underwear**

u·nique /yuˈnik/ Ac S3 W3 *adj.* **1** unusually good and special: *Joan has a unique talent for languages.* | *a unique business opportunity* **2** [no comparative] being the only one of its kind: *Every person is unique.* **3 unique to sb/sth** existing only in a particular place or in relation to a particular person or people: *Kangaroos are unique to Australia.* [**Origin:** 1600–1700 French, Latin *unicus*, from *unus* **one**] **—uniqueness** *n.* [U]

GRAMMAR

Although you will often hear people say that someone or something is *very unique, more unique, the most unique* etc. to mean that they are, or it is, special or unusual, some teachers consider this usage incorrect.

u·nique·ly /yuˈnikli/ Ac *adv.* **1** used when saying how good, bad etc. something is and saying that very few other things are this good, bad etc.: *They formed a uniquely successful partnership.* **2** in a way that is typical of a particular place or group of people, and that does not exist anywhere else: **uniquely American/French/Japanese etc.** *a uniquely American festival* **3** in a way that is different from anything else: *This aircraft is uniquely equipped.*

u·ni·sex /ˈyunəˌsɛks/ *adj.* intended for both men and women: *unisex clothing*

u·ni·son /ˈyunəsən/ *n.* **1 in unison a)** if people speak or do something in unison, they say the same words at the same time or do the same thing at the same time: *"Good morning!" the students replied in unison.* **b)** if two groups, governments etc. do something in unison, they do it together because they have the same needs or aims: *The countries of the world must* ***work in unison*** *to defeat terrorism.* **2** [C,U] a way of singing, playing music, or dancing in which everyone plays or sings the same tune or dances the same way at the same time

u·nit /ˈyunɪt/ S2 W1 *n.* [C]

1 PART a thing, person, or group that is regarded as one single whole part of something larger: *Sounds are the basic units of language.* | *The family is the basic social unit.*

2 GROUP a group of people working together as part of the structure of a larger group, organization, company etc.: *an elite military unit* | *the hospital's intensive care unit* ▸see THESAURUS box at **hospital**

3 MEASURING an amount or quantity of something used as a standard of measurement: **+of** *The watt is a unit of electrical power.* | *The man was given three units of blood during the operation.*

4 PART OF A BOOK one of the numbered parts into which a TEXTBOOK (=a book used in schools) is divided

5 PRODUCT a single complete product made by a company: *The factory produces 50,000 units a week.* → see also UNIT COST, UNIT PRICE

6 PART OF A MACHINE a piece of equipment which is part of a larger machine: *The cooling unit should be replaced.*

7 APARTMENT one of the parts or areas that a large building is divided into: *a twenty-four-unit apartment building*

8 SCHOOL/COLLEGE the measurement of the amount of work that a student has done to complete their studies: *How many units do you need to graduate?*

9 FURNITURE a piece of furniture, especially one that can be attached to others of the same type: **a kitchen/office/storage etc. unit** (=a piece of furniture designed for the kitchen, office etc.)

10 NUMBER MATH the smallest whole number; the number 1

11 NUMBERS MATH any whole number less than 10

[**Origin:** 1500–1600 *unity*]

U·ni·tar·i·an U·ni·ver·sal·ists /yunəˌtɛriən yunəˈvɚsəlɪsts/ *n.* a member of a religious group that comes from Christianity but that accepts members with many different religious beliefs **—Unitarian Universalist** *adj.*

u·ni·tar·y /ˈyunəˌtɛri/ *adj.* FORMAL existing or working as one single unit

ˌunitary ˈgovernment *n.* [U] POLITICS a system of government in which all of the government's powers belong to a single central government department or organization

ˈunit cost *n.* [C] the amount of money that it costs to produce one of a particular product → see also UNIT PRICE

u·nite /yuˈnaɪt/ *v.* **1** [I,T] to join together with other people, organizations to achieve something, or to make people do this: *The Prime Minister was unable to unite the country.* | **+in/against/behind** *Townspeople have united against the closure of their school.* | **unite to do sth** *In 1960, the regions united to form the Somali Republic.* **2 be united (in marriage/matrimony)** FORMAL if two people are united, they become married in a ceremony

u·nit·ed /yuˈnaɪt̬ɪd/ *adj.* **1** closely connected by having the same ideas, aims, or feelings: *They were united by their love of their country.* | **+in/with/against etc.** *The community is united in its commitment to quality education.* | *Nations of the world must* ***present a united front*** (=show that they are all united) *against terrorists.* **2** [usually before noun] joined together as one country or organization after being separate smaller ones: *a united Europe* **3** [only before noun] involving or done by everyone: *a united effort to reduce pollution*

United Ar·ab Em·ir·ates, the /yuˌnaɪtɪd ˌærəb ˈɛmərɪts/ a country in the Middle East, between Qatar and Oman, consisting of seven small EMIRATES including Abu Dhabi and Dubai

Uˌnited ˈFarm ˌWorkers a UNION in the U.S. for people who work on farms, especially poor MIGRANT workers who pick fruit and vegetables at many different farms

Uˌnited ˈKingdom, the a country in northwest Europe, officially called the United Kingdom of Great Britain and Northern Ireland, consisting of England, Wales, Scotland, and Northern Ireland

Uˌnited ˈNations *n.* **the United Nations** an international organization that tries to find peaceful solutions to world problems SYN U.N.

Uˌnited ˌStates of Aˈmerica, the also **the Uˌnited ˈStates, the U.S., the U.S.A.** a country in North America, made up of 50 states, the District of Columbia, and several territories

Uˌnited ˈWay, the a CHARITY organization in the U.S. which collects money from the public, and then divides this money to give to many different charities

unit ˌprice *n.* [C] the price that is charged for each single thing or quantity that is sold → see also UNIT COST

unit ˌpricing *n.* [U] a method of setting the price of a product based on what it costs to produce it

u·ni·ty /ˈyunət̬i/ *n.* [U] **1** a situation in which a group of people agree, have the same ideas and aims, and work together to achieve something: **+of** *The crisis shattered the unity of the church.* **2** the quality of having different parts that go together well: *His writing often lacks unity.* **3** a situation in which countries or organizations are officially joined together

Univ. *n.* a written abbreviation of UNIVERSITY

u·ni·va·ri·ate /ˌyunɪˈvɛriɪt/ *adj.* MATH having only one VARIABLE (=mathematical quantity that is not fixed and can be any of several amounts): *the univariate analysis of data* → see also BIVARIATE, MULTIVARIATE

u·ni·ver·sal /ˌyunəˈvɚsəl◂ / S3 *adj.* **1** available to everyone in a particular group or society: *universal healthcare* **2** understood by or affecting everyone or every place in the world: *a universal language* **3** true or appropriate in every situation: *a universal truth* —**universally** *adv.* —**universality** /ˌyunəvɚˈsælət̬i/ *n.* [U]

uniˌversal graviˌtational ˈconstant *n.* [singular] PHYSICS a CONSTANT that appears in the EQUATION that describes Newton's law of GRAVITATION. The equation measures the strength of GRAVITY.

ˌuniversal ˈjoint *n.* [C] a part in a machine, at the point where two other parts join together, that can turn in all directions

ˌUniversal ˈProduct Code ABBREVIATION **UPC** *n.* [C] a BAR CODE

ˌuniversal ˈsuffrage *n.* [U] POLITICS a situation in which every adult in a country has the right to vote in public elections

u·ni·verse /ˈyunəˌvɚs/ W3 *n.* [singular] **1 the universe** all space, including all the stars and PLANETS: *When did the universe begin?* **2** [C] a world or area in space that is different from the one we are in: *the possibility of a* ***parallel universe*** (=another universe where similar things are happening at the same time as in our universe) **3 be the center of sb's universe** to be the most important person or thing to someone: *Her grandchildren are the center of her universe.* **4** a person's life, including all of the people, places, and ideas which affect them: *The kitchen was the core of her universe.* [**Origin:** 1300–1400 Latin *universum*, from *universus* **whole**, from *uni-* + *versus* **turned toward**]

u·ni·ver·si·ty /ˌyunəˈvɚsət̬i/ S2 W2 *n. plural* **universities** [C] an educational institution at the highest level, where you can study for a BACHELOR'S DEGREE, a MASTER'S DEGREE, or a DOCTORATE, and where people also do RESEARCH: *the University of Chicago* | *He studied biology* ***at*** *the* ***University*** *of Wisconsin.* → see also COLLEGE

THESAURUS

At a university/college
college a school where you can study and get a bachelor's degree
major a student's main subject of study
minor a student's second subject of study
lecture a long talk on a particular subject, that students listen to
class a set of meetings in which you study a particular subject
seminar a class for a small group of students, in which you study a particular subject
professor a teacher at a college or university
teaching assistant a graduate student at a university who teaches some types of classes
graduate student a student who has a bachelor's degree and is working on a master's degree or Ph.D.
midterm a test that students take in the middle of a semester or quarter
final/final exam a test that students take at the end of a semester or quarter
semester one of the two periods of time into which a year is divided at a college or university, usually about 15 weeks long, during which you would take several classes
quarter one of the three periods of time into which a year is divided at a college or university, usually about ten weeks long, during which you would take several classes
bachelor's degree/B.A. (Bachelor of Arts)/B.S. (Bachelor of Science) the qualification you get when you finish your course of study at a university or college
master's degree/M.A. (Master of Arts)/M.S. (Master of Science) the qualification you get after studying for usually two years longer after receiving your bachelor's degree
doctorate/Ph.D. the highest level of university degree, that you get for studying for several years after your master's degree

UNIX /ˈyunɪks/ *n.* [U] TRADEMARK a type of computer OPERATING SYSTEM used mainly in business, industry, and universities

un·just /ˌʌnˈdʒʌst◂ / *adj.* FORMAL not fair or reasonable: *unjust punishment* —**unjustly** *adv.*

un·jus·ti·fi·a·ble /ʌnˌdʒʌstəˈfaɪəbəl/ *adj.* completely wrong and unacceptable: *unjustifiable delays* —**unjustifiably** *adv.*

un·jus·ti·fied /ʌnˈdʒʌstəˌfaɪd/ Ac *adj.* not having an acceptable explanation or reason: *unjustified federal spending*

un·kempt /ˌʌnˈkɛmpt◂ / *adj.* looking messy because of not being taken care of: *an unkempt beard* | *an unkempt yard* [**Origin:** 1300–1400 *kempt* **combed** (11–21 centuries), from Old English *cemban* **to comb**]

un·kind /ˌʌnˈkaɪnd◂ / *adj.* FORMAL cruel or not nice to someone: *unkind comments* | **+to** *I tried hard not to be unkind to her.* —**unkindly** *adv.* —**unkindness** *n.* [U]

THESAURUS

mean behaving toward other people in a way that is unpleasant or unkind: *My sister was often mean to me.*
spiteful used about someone who is deliberately mean to someone else: *The other women were spiteful, and gave her the hardest tasks.*

malicious deliberately behaving in a way that is likely to upset, hurt, or cause problems for someone: *He was spreading malicious rumors.*
cruel/sadistic making people or animals suffer, often by hurting them: *the guards' cruel treatment of prisoners*
thoughtless/inconsiderate not caring about people's feelings or how your actions will affect them: *He was young and often inconsiderate.*
hard-hearted/heartless not caring about other people's feelings or problems: *He was hard-hearted enough to let his son stay in jail overnight.*
unsympathetic not kind or helpful to someone who is having problems: *Her attitude was completely unsympathetic.*

un·know·ing·ly /ʌn'nouɪŋli/ *adv.* FORMAL without realizing what you are doing or what is happening: *She said she had unknowingly taken the drug.* —**unknowing** *adj.*

un·known[1] /ˌʌn'noun◂/ S3 W3 *adj., adv.* **1** not known about: *The year of Gabor's birth is unknown.* | **+to** *His criminal history was unknown to us.* | ***For some unknown reason****, Fred quit his job and moved to Alaska.* | **unknown to sb** [sentence adverb] *Unknown to his family, Ron was suffering from a brain infection.* **2** not famous: *an unknown artist* **3 an unknown quantity** if someone or something is an unknown quantity, you do not know what their abilities are or how they are likely to behave: *He was an unknown quantity when he started playing professional hockey.*

unknown[2] *n.* **1** [C] someone who is not famous: *Butler was still an unknown when he starred in the movie.* **2** [C] something that is not known: *The long-term effects of the drug are still an unknown.* **3 the unknown** things that you do not know about or have not experienced: *The astronauts began their journey into the unknown.* | *a fear of the unknown*

un·law·ful /ʌn'lɔfəl/ *adj.* FORMAL not legal SYN **illegal**: *unlawful activities* | **unlawful arrest/killing/imprisonment etc.** *The officers were charged with unlawful arrest.* —**unlawfully** *adv.*

un·lead·ed /ˌʌn'lɛdɪd◂/ *adj.* unleaded gasoline does not contain any LEAD —**unleaded** *n.* [U] *Ben's car only takes unleaded.*

un·learn /ʌn'lɚn/ *v.* [T] INFORMAL to deliberately change the way you have learned to think about or do something because the old way was not good or effective: *It's difficult to unlearn bad driving habits.*

un·leash /ʌn'liʃ/ *v.* [T] **1** to do or cause something that has a very powerful or harmful effect: **unleash a storm/torrent/flood/wave etc. of sth** *His comments unleashed a wave of protest in Paris.* **2** to set someone or something free from control: *The dam broke, unleashing 96 million gallons of water.* **3** to let a dog run free after it has been held on a LEASH

un·leav·ened /ˌʌn'lɛvənd◂/ *adj.* **1** unleavened bread is flat because it is not made with YEAST **2 sth is unleavened by sth** LITERARY used when saying that something is boring or difficult when it could have been made more pleasant or easier by adding something: *The long movie is unleavened by wit or style.*

un·less /ən'lɛs, ʌn-/ S1 W2 *conjunction* **1** used when one thing will only happen or be true as long as another thing happens or is true: *Don't call me at the office unless it's absolutely necessary.* | *Unless we raise some extra money, the theater will close.* **2 not unless a)** used as a reply to a question, when you mean "only if": *"Will you go with her?" "Not unless she wants me to."* **b)** used after negative statements to mean "unless": *There were no jobs there either, not unless you had a college degree.* [**Origin:** 1400–1500 *on less than* **on a lower condition than** (1400–1500)]

WORD CHOICE **unless, if... not**
• Use **if... not** about something that did not happen or that you know is not true: *She would have died if the doctors hadn't operated immediately* (=but they did). | *If Troy weren't so stupid* (=but he is stupid) *he would understand.* Do not use **unless** in this way.
• Use **unless** about something that *could* happen if something else does not happen, or if something *could* be true: *Unless the doctors operate immediately, she'll die.* | *She'll die unless the doctors operate immediately* (=the doctors have not operated yet, and may or may not do so). | *Unless he's a complete idiot, he'll understand* (=he may or may not be a complete idiot).
• **Unless** and **if... not** can both be used to say that what you will do depends on something else happening: *Unless Brad comes soon, I'm going without him.* | *If Brad doesn't come soon, I'm going without him.*

un·let·tered /ʌn'lɛt̬ɚd/ *adj.* LITERARY unable to read, or uneducated

un·li·censed /ˌʌn'laɪsənst◂/ Ac *adj.* without a LICENSE (=official document that gives you permission to do or have something): *unlicensed guns* | *unlicensed drivers*

un·like[1] /ˌʌn'laɪk◂/ W2 *prep.* **1** completely different from a particular person or thing: *Ashley was unlike any woman I have ever known.* | *In appearance, John is* ***not unlike*** (=similar to) *his brother.* **2** used when saying how one person or thing is different from another: *Unlike me, she's very intelligent.* **3** not typical of something or someone at all: **it's unlike sb to do sth** *It's unlike Greg to be late.*

unlike[2] *adj.* LITERARY not alike SYN **different**

un·like·ly /ˌʌn'laɪkli◂/ W3 *adj.* **1** not likely to happen: **unlikely to do sth** *The weather is unlikely to improve today.* | ***It's unlikely that*** *we'll be able to get reservations for tonight.* | **very/most/highly/extremely etc. unlikely** *It's highly unlikely that the project will be finished on time.* | **in the unlikely event of sth** also **in the unlikely event (that)** *In the unlikely event of a fire, passengers should move to the top deck.* **2** not likely to be true SYN **improbable**: *an unlikely story* **3** an unlikely place, person, or thing is strange and not what you would expect: *This quiet town is an unlikely setting for such violence.* | **an unlikely pair/couple etc.** (=two people or things that are so different that you would not expect them to like each other, work together well etc.)

un·lim·it·ed /ˌʌn'lɪmɪt̬ɪd◂/ *adj.* without any limit in amount, time, freedom etc.: *We pay $20 a month for unlimited Internet access.* | *an unlimited number of combinations*

un·list·ed /ˌʌn'lɪstɪd◂/ *adj.* **1** not in the list of numbers in the telephone DIRECTORY: *an unlisted phone number* **2** ECONOMICS not shown on an official list, especially the STOCK EXCHANGE list

un·lit /ˌʌn'lɪt◂/ *adj.* **1** dark because there are no lights: *an unlit parking lot* **2** not burning yet: *an unlit cigarette*

unload

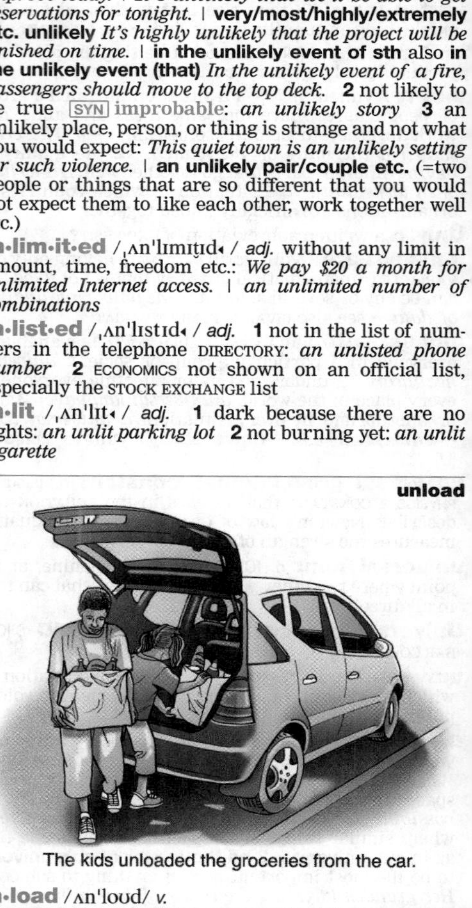

The kids unloaded the groceries from the car.

un·load /ʌn'loud/ *v.*
1 VEHICLE/SHIP a) [T] to remove a load from a vehicle, ship etc.: **unload sth from sth** *We unloaded the sofa*

from the truck. **b)** [I] if a vehicle, ship etc. unloads, the goods that it carries are removed from it: *The ship is unloading at the dock right now.* **c)** [I,T] if a vehicle such as a bus or plane unloads or unloads people, it lets them get off or out of it: *The bus stopped briefly to unload its passengers.*
2 GUN/CAMERA/MACHINE [T] to remove something from a gun, camera, or machine after it has been used, cleaned etc.: *Could you unload the dishwasher?*
3 GET RID OF [T] INFORMAL **a)** to get rid of something illegal or not very good by selling it quickly: *Investors continued to unload technology stocks Thursday.* **b)** to get rid of work or responsibility by giving it to someone else: **unload sth on/onto sb** *Ben has a habit of unloading his work on others.*
4 FEELINGS [I,T] to express strong feelings, especially anger, to someone when you are extremely upset: **unload (sth) on sb** *Green unloaded all his worries on his staff.*

un·lock /ʌnˈlɑk/ *v.* [T] **1** to unfasten the lock on a door, box etc.: *This key unlocks the front door.* ▶see THESAURUS box at open[2] **2 unlock the secrets/mysteries of sth** to discover the most important facts about something: *Scientists finally unlocked the secrets of the cause of polio.*

un·loose /ʌnˈlus/ *v.* [T] LITERARY to untie or unfasten something

un·loved /ˌʌnˈlʌvd◂ / *adj.* not loved by anyone

un·luck·y /ˌʌnˈlʌki/ *adj. comparative* **unluckier**, *superlative* **unluckiest** **1** having bad luck SYN **unfortunate**: **+with** *We were unlucky with the bad weather.* | **unlucky (enough) to do sth** *Chicago was unlucky to lose the game after playing so well.* | *He's been especially* ***unlucky in love*** (=having bad luck in romantic relationships). **2** causing bad luck: *Some people think that black cats are unlucky.* | **it's unlucky to do sth** *They say it's unlucky to walk under ladders.* **3** happening as a result of bad luck: *an unlucky accident* | **it is unlucky (for sb) (that)** *It was unlucky for her that her boss walked in and heard what she said.* —**unluckily** *adv.*

un·made /ˌʌnˈmeɪd◂ / *adj.* an unmade bed is not neat because the sheets, BLANKETS etc. have not been arranged since someone slept in it

un·man·age·a·ble /ʌnˈmænɪdʒəbəl/ *adj.* difficult to control or deal with: *The child's behavior was becoming unmanageable.*

un·man·ly /ʌnˈmænli/ *adj.* not thought to be appropriate for or typical of a man

un·manned /ˌʌnˈmænd◂ / *adj.* a machine, vehicle etc. that is unmanned does not have a person operating or controlling it: *an unmanned spacecraft*

un·marked /ˌʌnˈmɑrkt◂ / *adj.* something that is unmarked has no words or signs on it to show where or what it is: *an unmarked grave*

un·mar·ried /ˌʌnˈmærid◂ / *adj.* not married SYN **single**: *her unmarried son*

un·mask /ʌnˈmæsk/ *v.* [T] to make known the hidden truth about someone: *The CIA finally unmasked the spy who sold military secrets.*

un·matched /ˌʌnˈmætʃt◂ / *adj.* WRITTEN better than any other: *His record of seven wins is unmatched.*

un·me·di·at·ed /ʌnˈmidiˌeɪt̬ɪd/ *adj.* direct, without any other influence in between: *The Internet gives us relatively unmediated access to information.*

un·men·tion·a·ble /ʌnˈmɛnʃənəbəl/ *adj.* too bad or embarrassing to talk about

un·men·tion·a·bles /ʌnˈmɛnʃənəbəlz/ *n.* [plural] OLD-FASHIONED or HUMOROUS underwear

un·met /ˌʌnˈmɛt◂ / *adj.* unmet needs, demands, desires etc. have not been dealt with or achieved: *unmet expectations*

un·mis·tak·a·ble /ˌʌnmɪˈsteɪkəbəl◂ / *adj.* familiar and easy to recognize: *He spoke with an unmistakable Russian accent.* —**unmistakably** *adv.*

un·mit·i·gat·ed /ʌnˈmɪt̬əˌgeɪt̬ɪd/ *adj.* used for emphasizing that something is completely bad or good: *an unmitigated disaster*

un·mo·lest·ed /ˌʌnməˈlɛstɪd◂ / *adj.* FORMAL without being annoyed or interrupted: **do sth unmolested** *People want to be able to walk around unmolested by beggars.*

un·moved /ˌʌnˈmuvd/ *adj.* [not before noun] feeling no pity, sympathy, or sadness, especially in a situation where most people would feel this: *Walter seemed unmoved by the tragedy.*

un·named /ˌʌnˈneɪmd◂ / *adj.* an unnamed person, place, or thing is one whose name is not known publicly: *The newspaper received the information from an unnamed source.*

un·nat·u·ral /ʌnˈnætʃərəl/ *adj.* **1** different from what you normally expect or experience: *It was very cold, which seemed unnatural for late spring.* | **it is unnatural (for sb) to do sth** *It's unnatural for a kid that age to sleep so much.* **2** seeming false, or not real or natural: *Mom's laugh seemed forced and unnatural.* **3** different from normal human behavior in a way that seems morally wrong: *unnatural sexual practices* **4** different from anything produced by nature: *unnatural colors* —**unnaturally** *adv.*

un·nec·es·sar·y /ʌnˈnɛsəˌsɛri/ *adj.* **1** not needed, or more than is needed: *Don't take any unnecessary risks.* | *unnecessary costs* | **it is unnecessary (for sb) to do sth** *It's unnecessary for the police to use that much force.* **2** an unnecessary remark or action is unreasonable or not nice —**unnecessarily** /ˌʌn-nɛsəˈsɛrəli/ *adv.*: *The instructions are unnecessarily complicated.*

un·need·ed /ʌnˈnidɪd/ *adj.* not necessary: *The unneeded power stations are scheduled to be closed.*

un·nerve /ʌnˈnɚv/ *v.* [T] to upset or frighten someone so that they lose their confidence or their ability to think clearly: *He was unnerved by the way she kept staring at him.* —**unnerving** *adj.*: *His strange reaction was slightly unnerving.*

un·no·ticed /ʌnˈnoʊt̬ɪst/ *adj., adv.* without being noticed SYN **unobserved**: *She stood unnoticed at the edge of the crowd.* | **go/pass unnoticed** *His remark went unnoticed by everyone except me.*

un·num·bered /ˌʌnˈnʌmbɚd◂ / *adj.* **1** not having a number: *unnumbered U.S. currency* **2** LITERARY too many to be counted

un·ob·served /ˌʌnəbˈzɚvd/ *adj., adv.* not noticed SYN **unnoticed**: *He was able to enter the building unobserved.*

un·ob·struct·ed /ˌʌnəbˈstrʌktɪd◂ / *adj.* not blocked by anything: *an unobstructed view of the lake*

un·ob·tru·sive /ˌʌnəbˈtrusɪv/ *adj.* not attracting your attention, and not easily noticeable: *The car's antenna is small and unobtrusive.* —**unobtrusively** *adv.*

un·oc·cu·pied /ʌnˈɑkyəˌpaɪd/ *adj.* **1** a seat, house, room etc. that is unoccupied has no one in it **2** an unoccupied country or area is not controlled by the enemy during a war: *The family fled to unoccupied France.*

un·of·fi·cial /ˌʌnəˈfɪʃəl◂ / *adj.* **1** without formal approval and permission from the organization or person in authority: *Unofficial reports claim that eight people were killed.* **2** not done as part of your official job: *The senator's trip to China was called "an unofficial mission."* —**unofficially** *adv.*

un·o·pened /ʌnˈoʊpənd/ *adj.* an unopened package, letter etc. has not been opened yet: *The letter was returned to us unopened.*

un·op·posed /ˌʌnəˈpoʊzd◂ / *adj., adv.* without any opponent or opposition, especially in an election: *Corbin* ***ran unopposed*** *for mayor.*

un·or·gan·ized /ʌnˈɔrgəˌnaɪzd/ *adj.* **1** DISORGANIZED **2** workers who are unorganized do not have an organization, UNION, group etc. to help or support them

un·or·tho·dox /ʌnˈɔrθəˌdɑks/ *adj.* unorthodox beliefs or methods are different from what is usual or accepted by most people: *Her solution to the problem was unorthodox, but it worked.*

un·pack /ʌn'pæk/ *v.* **1** [I,T] to take everything out of a box or SUITCASE: *I just got home. I haven't even unpacked yet.* | *Could you unpack that box?* **2** [T] to make an idea or problem easier to understand by explaining or considering it in separate parts: *Try to unpack some of these sentences in the second paragraph.* **3** [T] COMPUTERS to change information in a computer so that it can be read or used by increasing the size of a FILE to its original size

un·paid /ˌʌn'peɪd◂/ *adj.* **1** an unpaid bill or debt has not been paid **2** done without receiving payment: *an unpaid internship*

un·pal·at·a·ble /ʌn'pælət̬əbəl/ *adj.* FORMAL **1** an unpalatable fact or idea is very bad and difficult to accept: +**to** *The idea of raising taxes was unpalatable to most voters.* **2** unpalatable food tastes bad

un·par·al·leled /ʌn'pærəˌlɛld/ Ac *adj.* FORMAL greater or better than all others: *a time of unparalleled economic prosperity*

un·par·don·a·ble /ʌn'pɑrdn-əbəl/ *adj.* FORMAL unpardonable behavior is completely unacceptable —**unpardonably** *adv.*

un·paved /ˌʌn'peɪvd◂/ *adj.* an unpaved road does not have a hard surface

un·peeled /ˌʌn'pild◂/ *adj.* unpeeled fruits or vegetables still have their skin on them

un·per·turbed /ˌʌnpɚ'tɚbd◂/ *adj.* not worried, annoyed, or upset, even though something bad has happened: *He looked at her, unperturbed, as she yelled.*

un·planned /ˌʌn'plænd◂/ *adj.* not planned or expected: *an unplanned pregnancy*

U

un·pleas·ant /ʌn'plɛzənt/ *adj.* **1** not pleasant or enjoyable: *an unpleasant odor* | *an unpleasant surprise* **2** not nice or friendly: *She said some unpleasant things to me.* —**unpleasantly** *adv.* —**unpleasantness** *n.* [U]

un·plug /ʌn'plʌg/ *v.* **unplugged**, **unplugging** [T] to disconnect a piece of electrical equipment by taking its PLUG out of an OUTLET

un·plugged /ʌn'plʌgd/ *adj., adv.* if a group of musicians performs unplugged, they perform without electric instruments

un·plumbed /ˌʌn'plʌmd◂/ *adj.* **the unplumbed depths of sth** something that is not known about because it has never been examined or EXPLORED

un·pol·ished /ˌʌn'pɑlɪʃt/ *adj.* **1** having a surface that is rough or not shiny because of not being polished **2** not skillful, graceful, or having good MANNERS: *McRae is an unpolished public speaker.*

un·pop·u·lar /ʌn'pɑpyəlɚ/ *adj.* not liked by most people: *a very unpopular leader* | +**with/among** *The decision was extremely unpopular with teachers.* —**unpopularity** /ˌʌnpɑpyə'lærət̬i/ *n.* [U]

un·prec·e·dent·ed /ʌn'prɛsəˌdɛntɪd/ Ac *adj.* never having happened before, or never having happened so much: *an unprecedented demand for tickets* | +**in** *This is an event that is unprecedented in recent history.*

un·pre·dict·a·ble /ˌʌnprɪ'dɪktəbəl◂/ Ac *adj.* **1** something that is unpredictable changes a lot, so that it is impossible to know what will happen: *unpredictable weather* **2** someone who is unpredictable tends to change their behavior or ideas suddenly, so that you never know what they are going to do or think

un·pre·pared /ˌʌnprɪ'pɛrd◂/ *adj.* **1** not ready to deal with something: +**for** *Many high school graduates are unprepared for the workplace.* | **unprepared to do sth** *The ferry was unprepared to handle a disaster.* **2 unprepared to do sth** FORMAL not willing to do something: *I'm am unprepared to lend them any more money.*

un·pre·pos·sess·ing /ˌʌnpripə'zɛsɪŋ/ *adj.* FORMAL not very attractive or noticeable

un·pre·ten·tious /ˌʌnprɪ'tɛnʃəs◂/ *adj.* APPROVING not trying to seem better, more important etc. than you really are: *an unpretentious, well-written comedy*

un·prin·ci·pled /ʌn'prɪnsəpəld/ Ac *adj.* FORMAL not caring about whether what you do is morally right SYN **unscrupulous**

un·print·a·ble /ʌn'prɪnt̬əbəl/ *adj.* words that are unprintable are very offensive or shocking

un·pro·duc·tive /ˌʌnprə'dʌktɪv◂/ *adj.* not producing any good results: *It was a very unproductive meeting.*

un·pro·fes·sion·al /ˌʌnprə'fɛʃənl/ *adj.* DISAPPROVING not following the standards for behavior that are expected in a particular profession or activity: *Johnson was fired for unprofessional conduct.* —**unprofessionally** *adv.*

un·prof·it·a·ble /ʌn'prɑfɪt̬əbəl/ *adj.* **1** making no profit: *unprofitable state-owned enterprises* **2** LITERARY bringing no advantage or gain

un·pro·nounce·a·ble /ˌʌnprə'naʊnsəbəl◂/ *adj.* an unpronounceable word or name is very difficult to say

un·pro·tect·ed /ˌʌnprə'tɛktɪd◂/ *adj.* **1 unprotected sex** sex without a CONDOM, which could allow diseases such as AIDS to be passed on **2** not protected against possible harm or damage: *He had to go into the army, **leaving** his farm **unprotected**.*

un·prov·en /ˌʌn'pruvən◂/ *adj.* not tested, and not shown to be definitely true: *unproven medical treatments*

un·pro·voked /ˌʌnprə'voʊkt◂/ *adj.* unprovoked anger, attacks etc. are directed at someone who has not done anything to deserve them: *unprovoked criticism*

un·pub·lished /ʌn'pʌblɪʃt/ Ac *adj.* an unpublished writing, information etc. has never been published: *an unpublished manuscript*

un·pun·ished /ʌn'pʌnɪʃt/ *adj.* **go unpunished** if someone or someone's bad behavior goes unpunished, they are not punished

un·qual·i·fied /ʌn'kwɑləˌfaɪd/ *adj.* **1** not having the right knowledge, experience, or education to do something: *unqualified teachers* | **be/feel unqualified to do sth** *Marshall is unqualified to manage the department.* **2 unqualified success/praise/disaster etc.** used for emphasizing that a situation or quality is one that is completely good or bad: *The experiment was an unqualified failure.*

un·quench·a·ble /ʌn'kwɛntʃəbəl/ *adj.* FORMAL an unquenchable need, desire, or feeling is strong and impossible to get rid of: *an **unquenchable thirst for*** (=strong unending desire) *knowledge*

un·ques·tion·a·ble /ʌn'kwɛstʃənəbəl/ *adj.* impossible to doubt SYN **certain**: *a man of unquestionable honesty* —**unquestionably** *adv.*

un·ques·tioned /ʌn'kwɛstʃənd/ *adj.* something that is unquestioned is accepted or believed by everyone: *Ogden's authority is unquestioned.*

un·ques·tion·ing /ʌn'kwɛstʃənɪŋ/ *adj.* an unquestioning faith, attitude etc. is very certain and without doubts: *an unquestioning belief in God* —**unquestioningly** *adv.*

un·qui·et /ʌn'kwaɪət/ *adj.* LITERARY tending to make you feel nervous

un·quote /'ʌnkwoʊt/ *adv.* → see **quote... unquote** at QUOTE[1] (4)

un·rat·ed /ʌn'reɪt̬ɪd/ *adj.* an unrated movie or television show has not been given a letter from the system which shows whether or not it is appropriate for children

un·rav·el /ʌn'rævəl/ *v.* **1** [T] to understand or explain something that is very complicated: *Scientists have not yet unraveled every detail of how genes work.* **2** [I] if a plan, agreement, relationship etc. unravels, it fails or stops working well: *After three years, their partnership began to unravel.* **3** [I,T] if something that is twisted or wound around something else unravels or you unravel it, it begins to unwind: *The rope had been cut and was starting to unravel.*

un·read /ˌʌn'rɛd◂/ *adj.* not yet read: *unread emails*

un·read·a·ble /ʌn'ridəbəl/ *adj.* **1** an unreadable book or piece of writing is difficult to read because it is boring or complicated **2** unreadable writing is so messy that you cannot read it SYN **illegible**

un·real /ˌʌnˈrilˌ/ *adj.* **1** not related to real things that happen: *The battle scenes in the movie seemed entirely unreal.* **2** [not before noun] an experience, situation etc. that is unreal seems so strange that you think you must be imagining or dreaming it: *Suddenly we have a baby, and it all seems so unreal to me.* **3** SPOKEN very exciting SYN **excellent** —**unreality** /ˌʌnriˈæləṭi/ *n.* [U]

un·re·al·is·tic /ˌʌnriəˈlɪstɪk/ *adj.* unrealistic ideas, hopes etc. are not based on facts: ***It is unrealistic to*** *expect changes to happen so fast.* | *I think Nick's* ***being unrealistic*** *about how much money he'll make.* —**unrealistically** /-kli/ *adv.*

un·re·al·ized /ʌnˈriəˌlaɪzd/ *adj.* **1** not achieved: *unrealized hopes* **2** TECHNICAL unrealized profits, losses etc. have not been changed into a form that can be used as money

un·rea·son·a·ble /ʌnˈrizənəbəl/ *adj.* **1** not fair or sensible: *I don't want to argue, but I think you're being unreasonable.* | **it is unreasonable to do sth** *It's unreasonable to expect a child to sit still for two hours.* | **unreasonable demands/expectations etc.** *Don't let your boss make unreasonable demands on you.* **2** unreasonable prices, costs etc. are too high —**unreasonably** *adv.*

un·rea·son·ing /ʌnˈrizənɪŋ/ *adj.* FORMAL an unreasoning feeling is one that is not based on fact or reason: *unreasoning anger*

un·rec·og·niz·a·ble /ˌʌnrɛkəgˈnaɪzəbəl/ *adj.* someone or something that is unrecognizable has changed or been damaged so much that you do not recognize them: *I came back to the city 20 years later, and it was unrecognizable.*

un·rec·og·nized /ʌnˈrɛkəgˌnaɪzd/ *adj.* **1** not noticed or not thought to be important: *It is an illness that can* ***go unrecognized*** *for years.* **2** someone who is unrecognized for something they have done has not received the admiration or respect they deserve: *one of the great unrecognized jazz singers of the 1930s* **3** an unrecognized group, meeting, agreement etc. is not considered to be legal or acceptable by someone in authority: *This minority group was unrecognized by the U.N.*

un·re·con·struct·ed /ˌʌnrikənˈstrʌktɪd/ *adj.* not changing your ideas, even though many people think they are not modern or useful anymore

un·re·cord·ed /ˌʌnrɪˈkɔrdɪdˌ/ *adj.* not written down or recorded

un·re·cov·er·a·ble /ˌʌnrɪˈkʌvərəbəl/ *adj.* unrecoverable debts, losses etc. are ones that are impossible to get back

un·reel /ʌnˈril/ *v.* **1** [I,T] to unwind or make something unwind from around an object: *The climber's safety line unreeled behind him.* **2** [I] if a story, movie etc. unreels, it is told or shown to you SYN **unfold**

un·re·fined /ˌʌnrɪˈfaɪndˌ/ *adj.* **1** an unrefined substance is in its natural form OPP **refined**: *unrefined sugar* **2** FORMAL not polite or educated

un·reg·is·tered /ʌnˈrɛdʒɪstɚd/ *adj.* not recorded on an official list, especially when this is illegal or not allowed: *an unregistered gun* | *unregistered voters* (=who cannot vote because they are unregistered)

un·reg·u·lat·ed /ʌnˈrɛgyəˌleɪṭɪd/ Ac *adj.* unregulated businesses, industries etc. are not controlled by the government and are free to do what they want → see also DEREGULATE

un·re·lat·ed /ˌʌnrɪˈleɪṭɪdˌ/ *adj.* **1** two things that are unrelated are not connected to each other in any way: *The police think that the two robberies are unrelated.* | **+to** *His illness is unrelated to the accident.* **2** people who are unrelated are not members of the same family

un·re·lent·ing /ˌʌnrɪˈlɛntɪŋˌ/ *adj.* FORMAL **1** a bad situation that is unrelenting continues for a long time without stopping SYN **relentless**: *unrelenting headaches* **2** continuing to do something in a determined way without thinking about anyone else's feelings SYN **relentless**: *an unrelenting opponent*

un·re·li·a·ble /ˌʌnrɪˈlaɪəbəlˌ/ Ac *adj.* unable to be trusted or depended on: *The local bus service is unreliable.* | *an unreliable witness*

un·re·lieved /ˌʌnrɪˈlivdˌ/ *adj.* a bad situation that is unrelieved continues for a long time because nothing happens to change it: *years of unrelieved poverty*

un·re·mark·a·ble /ˌʌnrɪˈmɑrkəbəlˌ/ *adj.* FORMAL not especially beautiful, interesting, or impressive: *She had a pale and unremarkable face.*

un·re·mit·ting /ˌʌnrɪˈmɪṭɪŋˌ/ *adj.* FORMAL continuing for a long time and unlikely to stop: *the unremitting heat* —**unremittingly** *adv.*

un·re·peat·a·ble /ˌʌnrɪˈpiṭəbəlˌ/ *adj.* **1** too impolite or offensive to repeat: *She called him unrepeatable names.* **2** unable to be done again

un·re·pent·ant /ˌʌnrɪˈpɛntˀntˌ/ *adj.* not feeling ashamed of behavior or beliefs that other people think are wrong: *an unrepentant racist*

un·re·port·ed /ˌʌnrɪˈpɔrṭɪd/ *adj.* not told to the public or to anyone in authority: *Rape is a crime that often* ***goes unreported.***

un·rep·re·sent·a·tive /ˌʌnrɛprɪˈzɛntəṭɪv/ *adj.* not typical of a group: **+of** *These opinions are unrepresentative of the general population.*

un·re·quit·ed /ˌʌnrɪˈkwaɪṭɪdˌ/ *adj.* **unrequited love** romantic love that you feel for someone, but that they do not feel for you

un·re·served /ˌʌnrɪˈzɚvdˌ/ *adj.* complete and without any doubts or limits: *unreserved enthusiasm* —**unreservedly** /ˌʌnrɪˈzɚvɪdli/ *adv.*: *He apologized unreservedly.*

un·re·solved /ˌʌnrɪˈzɑlvdˌ/ Ac *adj.* an unresolved problem or question has not been answered or solved: *unresolved safety issues*

un·re·spon·sive /ˌʌnrɪˈspɑnsɪv/ Ac *adj.* **1** not reacting in the expected or normal way: **+to** *Her infection became totally unresponsive to medication.* **2** not reacting to what people say to you: **+to** *Board members have been very unresponsive to our suggestions.*

un·rest /ʌnˈrɛst/ *n.* [U] a social or political situation in which people protest or behave violently: **social/civil/political etc. unrest** *Due to recent civil unrest, avoid travel in the northwest.*

un·re·strained /ˌʌnrɪˈstreɪndˌ/ Ac *adj.* not controlled or limited: *unrestrained population growth* —**unrestrainedly** /ˌʌnrɪˈstreɪnɪdli/ *adv.*

un·re·strict·ed /ˌʌnrɪˈstrɪktɪdˌ/ Ac *adj.* not limited by anyone or anything: *unrestricted trade between the two countries*

un·ripe /ˌʌnˈraɪp/ also **un·rip·ened** /ʌnˈraɪpənd/ *adj.* unripe fruit, grain etc. is not fully developed or ready to be eaten: *unripe bananas*

un·ri·valed /ʌnˈraɪvəld/ *adj.* FORMAL better than any other: *the unrivaled beauty of the island's white sand beaches*

un·roll /ʌnˈroʊl/ *v.* [I,T] to open something that was curled into the shape of a ball or tube, and make it flat, or to become opened in this way: *He unrolled the carpet.*

un·ruf·fled /ʌnˈrʌfəld/ *adj.* APPROVING calm and not upset by a difficult situation: *After two hours of questioning by the police, he remained unruffled.*

un·ru·ly /ʌnˈruli/ *adj.* **1** difficult to control: *unruly children* **2** unruly hair is difficult to keep neat —**unruliness** *n.* [U]

un·safe /ˌʌnˈseɪfˌ/ *adj.* **1** dangerous, or likely to cause harm or damage: *The water is unsafe to drink.* **2 unsafe sex** sex without a CONDOM, which could allow diseases such as AIDS to be passed on **3** [only before noun] likely to be harmed: *People feel unsafe walking in this area at night.*

un·said /ʌnˈsɛd/ **be left unsaid** if something is left unsaid, you do not say it although you might be thinking it: *Some things are* ***better left unsaid*** (=it is better not to mention them).

U

un·san·i·tar·y /ʌn'sænəˌtɛri/ *adj.* very dirty and likely to cause disease: *unsanitary conditions*

un·sat·is·fac·tory /ʌnˌsæt̬ɪs'fæktəri/ *adj.* not good enough, or not acceptable: *an unsatisfactory explanation*

un·sat·is·fied /ʌn'sæt̬ɪsˌfaɪd/ *adj.* **1** not pleased because you want more of something or you want something to be better SYN **dissatisfied**: *unsatisfied customers* **2** an unsatisfied demand, request etc. has not been dealt with: *an unsatisfied demand for skilled workers* —**unsatisfying** *adj.*: *an unsatisfying explanation*

un·sat·u·rat·ed /ʌn'sætʃəˌreɪt̬ɪd/ *adj.* unsaturated fat, especially vegetable fat, is better for your body than SATURATED fat because it does not make as much CHOLESTEROL

un·sa·vor·y /ʌn'seɪvəri/ *adj.* bad or morally unacceptable: *The train station was full of* ***unsavory characters*** (=dishonest or dangerous people).

un·scathed /ʌn'skeɪðd/ *adj.* [not before noun] not hurt or damaged by a bad or dangerous situation: *Few retailers were* ***left unscathed by*** *the recession.* | **emerge/escape unscathed** *He escaped unscathed from the accident.*

un·sched·uled /ˌʌn'skɛdʒəld◂ / Ac *adj.* not planned or expected: **an unscheduled stop/visit etc.** *Bad weather forced the pilots to make an unscheduled landing.*

un·sci·en·tif·ic /ˌʌnsaɪən'tɪfɪk/ *adj.* DISAPPROVING not following usual scientific methods or systems: *The researchers were criticized for using unscientific methods.*

U

un·scram·ble /ʌn'skræmbəl/ *v.* [T] to change a television SIGNAL or a message that has been sent in CODE so that it can be seen or read

un·screw /ʌn'skru/ *v.* [T] **1** to open or unfasten something by twisting it: *Unscrew the cap on the bottle.* ▸see THESAURUS box at **open**[2] **2** to take the screws out of something

un·script·ed /ˌʌn'skrɪptɪd◂ / *adj.* an unscripted broadcast, speech etc. is not written or planned before it is actually made

un·scru·pu·lous /ʌn'skrupyələs/ *adj.* behaving in an unfair or dishonest way: *unscrupulous lawyers* —**unscrupulously** *adv.* —**unscrupulousness** *n.* [U]

un·seal /ʌn'sil/ *v.* [T] **1** to make something available to be seen or known to everyone, especially legal documents: *The documents were unsealed Friday in the U.S. District Court.* **2** to open a container or envelope that has been tightly closed —**unsealed** *adj.*

un·sea·son·a·bly /ʌn'sizənəbli/ *adj.* **unseasonably warm/cold/dry etc.** unusually warm, cold etc. for the time of year —**unseasonable** *adj.*

un·seat /ʌn'sit/ *v.* [T] **1** to remove someone from a position of power or strength, for example in an election **2** if a horse unseats someone, it throws them off its back

un·se·cured /ˌʌnsɪ'kyʊrd◂ / *adj.* **1** an unsecured LOAN or debt is one which does not make you promise to give the bank something you own if you cannot pay it back **2** not locked, guarded, or safe from attack

ˌU.N. Se'curity ˌCouncil, the POLITICS a part of the UNITED NATIONS which is responsible for making sure that countries behave peacefully toward each other, and for deciding what the United Nations should do if countries go to war. The U.N. Security Council consists of representatives from 15 countries. Five are permanent members (the U.S., the U.K., Russia, France, and China) and ten countries change every year.

un·seed·ed /ˌʌn'sidɪd◂ / *adj.* not chosen as a SEED (=someone with a numbered rank in a competition), especially in a tennis competition

un·see·ing /ˌʌn'siɪŋ◂ / *adj.* LITERARY not noticing anything even though your eyes are open —**unseeingly** *adv.*

un·seem·ly /ʌn'simli/ *adj.* FORMAL unseemly behavior is not polite or appropriate for a particular occasion —**unseemliness** *n.* [U]

un·seen /ˌʌn'sin◂ / *adj.* FORMAL not noticed or seen: *He left the house unseen.* → see also **sight unseen** at SIGHT[1] (11)

un·self·ish /ʌn'sɛlfɪʃ/ *adj.* caring about other people and willing to help them instead of trying to get some advantage for yourself —**unselfishly** *adv.* —**unselfishness** *n.* [U]

Un·ser /'ʌnzɚ/, **Al** /æl/ (1939–) a U.S. race car driver

Unser, Bob·by /'bɑbi/(1934–) a U.S. race car driver

un·set·tle /ʌn'sɛt̬l/ *v.* [T] to make someone feel slightly upset or nervous: *His silence unsettled me.* —**unsettling** *adj.*

un·set·tled /ˌʌn'sɛt̬ld◂ / *adj.*
1 SITUATION making people feel uncertain about what will happen: *unsettled financial markets*
2 ARGUMENT OR DISAGREEMENT still continuing without reaching any agreement: *The issue of pay raises remains unsettled.*
3 LAND an unsettled area of land does not have any people living on it
4 STOMACH making you feel uncomfortable and a little sick: *The bus ride made my stomach feel unsettled.*
5 FEELING slightly worried, upset, or nervous
6 WEATHER changing a lot in a short period of time

un·shak·a·ble, **unshakeable** /ʌn'ʃeɪkəbəl/ *adj.* unshakable faith, beliefs etc. are very strong and cannot be destroyed or changed

un·shav·en /ʌn'ʃeɪvən/ *adj.* a man who is unshaven has short hairs growing on his face because he has not SHAVED

un·sight·ly /ʌn'saɪtli/ *adj.* FORMAL not nice to look at SYN **ugly**: *the unsightly stains on his shirt* —**unsightliness** *n.* [U]

un·signed /ˌʌn'saɪnd◂ / *adj.* **1** an unsigned sports player or musician has not yet signed a contract to play for a sports team or record music for a company **2** an unsigned document or letter has not been signed with someone's name

un·skilled /ˌʌn'skɪld◂ / *adj.* **1** an unskilled worker has not been trained for a particular type of job: *unskilled workers* | *unskilled labor* (=people who have had no special training) **2** unskilled work, jobs etc. do not need people with special skills

un·smil·ing /ʌn'smaɪlɪŋ/ *adj.* LITERARY looking serious and often slightly angry or unhappy: *her unsmiling face*

un·so·cia·ble /ʌn'soʊʃəbəl/ *adj.* not friendly and not liking to be with people or to go to social events

un·sold /ˌʌn'soʊld◂ / *adj.* something that is unsold is for sale and has not yet been sold: *Over 3,000 tickets remain unsold.*

un·so·lic·it·ed /ˌʌnsə'lɪsɪt̬ɪd/ *adj.* unsolicited advice, offers, opinions etc. have not been asked for by the person who receives them and are usually not wanted

un·solved /ˌʌn'sɑlvd◂ / *adj.* a problem, mystery, or crime that is unsolved has never been solved

un·so·phis·ti·cat·ed /ˌʌnsə'fɪstəˌkeɪt̬ɪd/ *adj.* **1** having little knowledge or experience of something, especially modern fashionable things, and showing this by the way you talk or behave: *I felt unsophisticated around my brother's college friends.* **2** unsophisticated tools, methods, processes etc. are simple, without many of the features of more modern ones SYN **crude**: *an unsophisticated pipe bomb*

un·sound /ˌʌn'saʊnd◂ / *adj.* **1** not based on facts or good reasons: *unsound banking practices* **2** bad or incorrect according to a particular point of view: **politically/ideologically/environmentally etc. unsound** *It would be medically unsound to prescribe an untested drug.* **3** an unsound building or structure is in bad condition **4** FORMAL someone with an unsound body or mind is sick or mentally ill

un·spar·ing /ʌn'spɛrɪŋ/ *adj.* expressing strong criticism, even if this hurts someone's feelings: **+in** *He was unsparing in his criticism of the Congress.*

un·speak·a·ble /ʌn'spikəbəl/ *adj.* **1** unspeakable actions or people are extremely bad: *unspeakable crimes* **2** LITERARY unspeakable feelings are so extreme that it is impossible to describe them: *unspeakable loneliness* —**unspeakably** *adv.*

un·spe·ci·fied /ʌn'spɛsəˌfaɪd/ Ac *adj.* not known, or not stated publicly: *The meeting will take place on an unspecified date in the spring.*

un·spoiled /ˌʌn'spɔɪld◂ / *adj.* APPROVING **1** an unspoiled place is beautiful because it has not changed for a long time and does not have a lot of new buildings **2** someone who is unspoiled continues to be a good person, despite the good or bad things that have happened to them: *She remained unspoiled by her success.*

un·spo·ken /ʌn'spoʊkən/ *adj.* **1** an unspoken agreement, rule etc. has not been discussed, but is understood by everyone in a particular group: *We had an unspoken agreement not to ask personal questions.* **2** not said for other people to hear: *unspoken thoughts*

un·sports·man·like /ʌn'spɔrtsmənˌlaɪk/ *adj.* not behaving in a fair, honest, or polite way when competing in sports: **unsportsmanlike conduct/behavior** *Johnson was ejected from the game for unsportsmanlike conduct.*

un·sta·ble /ʌn'steɪbəl/ Ac *adj.* **1** likely to change suddenly and become worse: *an unstable political situation* **2** something that is unstable is likely to move or fall: *That stool is unstable. Don't stand on it.* **3** someone who is unstable changes very suddenly so that you do not know how they will react or behave: *The patient is emotionally unstable.* ►see THESAURUS box at **crazy**[1] **4** CHEMISTRY an unstable chemical substance is likely to separate into simpler substances

un·stat·ed /ʌn'steɪt̬ɪd/ *adj.* not expressed in words: *an unstated threat*

un·stead·y /ʌn'stɛdi/ *adj.* **1** shaking or moving in a way you cannot control: *The baby was a little* ***unsteady on her feet.*** **2** an unsteady situation, relationship etc. could change or end at any time: *an unsteady peace* | *unsteady work* **3** showing that you are nervous or not confident: *I gave her an unsteady smile.*

un·stint·ing /ʌn'stɪnt̬ɪŋ/ *adj.* unstinting support, help, agreement etc. is complete and given willingly, without any limits —**unstintingly** *adv.*

un·stop·pa·ble /ʌn'stɑpəbəl/ *adj.* unable to be stopped: *The team's offense was unstoppable in last night's game.*

un·stressed /ˌʌn'strɛst◂ / Ac *adj.* ENG. LANG. ARTS an unstressed word or part of a word is pronounced with less force than other ones

un·struc·tured /ʌn'strʌktʃɚd/ Ac *adj.* not organized in a detailed way, and allowing people freedom to do what they want: *an unstructured interview* | *Children need time for unstructured play.*

un·stuck /ˌʌn'stʌk◂ / *adj.* **come unstuck** **1** INFORMAL if a person, plan, or system comes unstuck, they fail at what they were trying to achieve **2** if something comes unstuck, it becomes separated from the thing that it was stuck to

un·sub·scribe /ˌʌnsəb'skraɪb/ *v.* [I] to end a SUBSCRIPTION to a magazine, mailing list, email service etc.: *If you would like to unsubscribe, please click here.*

un·sub·stan·ti·at·ed /ˌʌnsəb'stænʃiˌeɪt̬ɪd/ *adj.* not proven or shown to be true: *unsubstantiated reports*

un·suc·cess·ful /ˌʌnsək'sɛsfəl◂ / *adj.* not having a successful result or achieving what was intended: *I regret to inform you that your application was unsuccessful.* | *an* ***unsuccessful attempt*** *to climb Everest* | **unsuccessful in (doing) sth** *We have been unsuccessful in finding a new manager.* —**unsuccessfully** *adv.*: *He tried unsuccessfully to make them change their decision.*

un·suit·a·ble /ʌn'sut̬əbəl/ *adj.* not having the right qualities for a particular person, purpose, or situation: *unsuitable job candidates* | +**for** *The game is unsuitable for children under 12.*

un·sul·lied /ʌn'sʌlid/ *adj.* LITERARY not spoiled or made ugly by anything

un·sung /ˌʌn'sʌŋ◂ / *adj.* not praised or famous, but deserving praise or notice: *Many of the men who died were the* ***unsung heroes*** *of the war.*

un·sure /ˌʌn'ʃʊr◂ / *adj.* **1** not certain about something or about what you have to do: +**of/about** *If you are unsure about anything, just ask for help.* | +**whether/what/who etc.** *He seems unsure what to do next.* **2** **unsure of yourself** not having enough confidence: *Chris seemed nervous and unsure of herself.*

un·sur·passed /ˌʌnsɚ'pæst◂ / *adj.* better or greater than all others of the same type: *his unsurpassed knowledge of American history*

un·sur·pris·ing /ˌʌnsɚ'praɪzɪŋ◂ / *adj.* not making you feel surprised —**unsurprisingly** *adv.* [sentence adverb] *Unsurprisingly, he doesn't want to talk about his private life.*

un·sus·pect·ing /ˌʌnsə'spɛktɪŋ◂ / *adj.* not knowing that something bad is about to happen: *unsuspecting victims*

un·sus·tain·a·ble /ˌʌnsə'steɪnəbəl/ Ac *adj.* **1** unable to continue at the same rate or in the same way: *unsustainable economic growth* **2** unsustainable practices damage the environment by using up things that exist naturally in the environment

un·swayed /ʌn'sweɪd/ *adj.* [not before noun] not changing your opinion, even though someone is trying to make you do so

un·sweet·ened /ˌʌn'swit[¬]nd◂ / *adj.* without sugar added: *unsweetened chocolate*

un·swerv·ing /ʌn'swɚvɪŋ/ *adj.* an unswerving belief, attitude etc. is one that is very strong and never changes: *unswerving loyalty*

un·sym·pa·thet·ic /ˌʌnsɪmpə'θɛt̬ɪk/ *adj.* **1** not kind or helpful to someone who is having problems: *an unsympathetic boss* ►see THESAURUS box at **unkind** **2** not willing to support an idea, aim etc.: +**to/toward** *The book is completely unsympathetic toward men.* **3** an unsympathetic person in a book or play is unpleasant and difficult to like

un·taint·ed /ʌn'teɪntɪd/ *adj.* not affected or influenced by something bad: +**by** *He remains untainted by the corruption in government.*

un·tamed /ˌʌn'teɪmd◂ / *adj.* **1** an untamed animal has not been trained to live or work with people SYN **wild** **2** an untamed area of land is still in its natural state and has not been developed by people

un·tan·gle /ʌn'tæŋgəl/ *v.* [T] **1** to separate pieces of string etc. that are twisted together **2** to make something less complicated: *Let's start by untangling some of the issues.*

un·tapped /ˌʌn'tæpt◂ / *adj.* untapped supplies, markets, TALENT etc. are available but have not yet been used

un·ten·a·ble /ʌn'tɛnəbəl/ *adj.* FORMAL **1** an untenable situation has become so difficult that it is impossible to continue: *The scandal put the President in an untenable position.* **2** an untenable suggestion, argument etc. is impossible to defend against criticism

un·test·ed /ʌn'tɛstɪd/ *adj.* **1** untested ideas, methods, or people have not been used in a particular situation, so you do not know what they are like: *an untested theory* | *untested leadership* **2** untested products, drugs etc. have not been given any scientific tests to see if they work well or are safe to use

un·think·a·ble /ʌn'θɪŋkəbəl/ *adj.* **1** impossible to accept or imagine: ***It is unthinkable that*** *a mistake like this could have happened.* **2** **the unthinkable** [singular] something that is impossible to accept or imagine: *Then the unthinkable happened, and the boat started to sink.*

un·think·ing /ʌn'θɪŋkɪŋ/ *adj.* not thinking about or questioning what you do or say: *unthinking acceptance of the rules* —**unthinkingly** *adv.*

un·ti·dy /ʌn'taɪdi/ *adj.* FORMAL messy

un·tie /ʌn'taɪ/ *v.* [T] to take the knots out of something

U

or undo something that has been tied —**untied** *adj.*: *Your shoelaces are untied.*

un·til /ən'tɪl, ʌn-/ S1 W1 *prep., conjunction* **1** used to say when an action or situation stops: *Stay here until I get back.* | *The meeting went on until 6:30.* | ***Up until** last year, they didn't even own a car.* | **from sth until sth** *The store is open from 10:00 a.m. to 8:00 p.m.* | ***Until recently**, she'd never been on a plane.* **2 not until** used for emphasizing that one thing does not or cannot happen before something else has happened or before a certain time: *You can't watch TV until you've done your homework.* | *She didn't return until the following year.* **3** used for saying how much time there is before something happens: *It's only two weeks until I start college.* | *How long is it until Christmas?* **4** used to show the result of a long or extreme action or event: *I laughed until my stomach hurt.* [**Origin:** 1100–1200 *un-* **unto, until** + *till*]

un·time·ly /ʌn'taɪmli/ *adj.* **1 an untimely death/end etc.** a death, end etc. that is much earlier than usual or expected **2** OLD-FASHIONED not appropriate or good for a particular occasion or time: *an untimely injury* —**untimeliness** *n.* [U]

un·tir·ing /ʌn'taɪərɪŋ/ *adj.* APPROVING never stopping while working hard or trying to do something: *an untiring fighter for democracy* —**untiringly** *adv.*

un·ti·tled /ʌn'taɪtld/ *adj.* an untitled work of art, song etc. has not been given a title

un·to /'ʌntu/ *prep.* OLD USE to: *Thanks be unto God.*

un·told /ˌʌn'toʊld◂ / *adj.* [only before noun] **1** used to emphasize that an amount or quantity is very large: *Untold numbers of innocent people died in the prisons.* **2** used to emphasize how bad something is: *The floods have caused **untold misery** to hundreds of homeowners.*

un·touch·a·ble /ʌn'tʌtʃəbəl/ *adj.* **1** someone who is untouchable is in such a strong position that they cannot be beaten, affected, or punished in any way: *As sheriff of the county, Weber thought he was untouchable.* **2** belonging to the lowest social group, especially in the Hindu CASTE system —**untouchable** *n.* [C]

un·touched /ˌʌn'tʌtʃt◂ / *adj.* **1** not changed, damaged, or affected in any way: *Most residents found their homes untouched by floods.* **2** not touched, moved, eaten etc.: *He walked out of the room, leaving his food untouched.*

un·toward /ˌʌn'tɔrd/ *adj.* FORMAL unexpected, unusual, or not wanted: **nothing untoward/not anything untoward** *Paul went back to work as if nothing untoward had happened.* [**Origin:** 1500–1600 *toward* **obedient** (15–18 centuries)]

un·trained /ˌʌn'treɪnd◂ / *adj.* not trained to do something: *Their army is made up mostly of untrained volunteers.* | ***To the untrained eye*** (=when someone who does not have training looks)*, the two stones look almost the same.*

un·tram·meled /ʌn'træməld/ *adj.* FORMAL without any limits

un·treat·ed /ˌʌn'triṭɪd◂ / *adj.* **1** an untreated illness or injury has not had medical treatment **2** harmful substances that are untreated have not been made safe: *untreated drinking water*

un·tried /ˌʌn'traɪd◂ / *adj.* **1** not yet tested to see whether it is successful: *an untried strategy* **2** not having any experience of doing a particular job: *a young untried movie director*

un·true /ˌʌn'tru◂ / *adj.* **1** a statement that is untrue does not give the right facts SYN **false**: **it is untrue (to say) that** *It is untrue that our company has avoided paying taxes.* ►see THESAURUS box at **wrong**[1] **2 be untrue to sb** LITERARY to deceive someone, especially by not being faithful to them in a relationship

un·trust·wor·thy /ʌn'trʌstˌwɚði/ *adj.* someone who is untrustworthy cannot be trusted, especially because you think they are dishonest

un·truth /ʌn'truθ, 'ʌntruθ/ *n.* [C] FORMAL a word meaning a "lie," used because you want to avoid saying this directly

un·truth·ful /ʌn'truθfəl/ *adj.* dishonest or not true: *an untruthful statement* | *an untruthful politician* —**untruthfully** *adv.*

un·tucked /ʌn'tʌkt/ *adj.* the bottom edge of an untucked shirt is hanging loose, instead of being inside someone's pants

u·num /'unəm/ → see E PLURIBUS UNUM

un·used[1] /ˌʌn'yuzd◂ / *adj.* not being used, or never used: *an unused office* | *unused ammunition*

un·used[2] /ʌn'yust/ *adj.* **unused to (doing) sth** not experienced in dealing with something: *I was unused to the heavy city traffic.*

un·u·su·al /ʌn'yuʒuəl, -ʒəl/ S2 W2 *adj.* **1** different from what is usual or ordinary SYN **strange**: *an unusual flavor* | **highly/very unusual** *a highly unusual situation* | **it is unusual for sb/sth to do sth** *It's unusual for Dave to be late.* | ***It's not unusual to*** (=it is fairly common to) *spend $10,000 fixing up a car.* | **there's nothing unusual about sth** *There was nothing unusual about the man's appearance.* **2** unusual beauty, skill etc. is much better or more impressive than usual: *a land of unusual beauty*

un·u·su·al·ly /ʌn'yuʒuəli, -ʒəli/ *adv.* **1** in a way that is different from what is usual or normal: *The house was unusually quiet.* | **unusually for sb/sth** *Unusually for me, I fell asleep very quickly.* **2** in a way that is much better or more impressive than usual: *an unusually gifted teacher*

un·ut·ter·a·ble /ʌn'ʌṭərəbəl/ *adj.* LITERARY an unutterable feeling is too extreme to be expressed in words —**unutterably** *adv.*

un·var·nished /ˌʌn'vɑrnɪʃt◂ / *adj.* **1** [only before noun] told simply and directly, without any additional descriptions or details: *the unvarnished truth* **2** without any VARNISH (=a transparent substance like paint, used to protect the surface of wood): *unvarnished wood*

un·veil /ʌn'veɪl/ *v.* [T] **1** to show or tell people something that was previously kept secret: *The city unveiled plans for a $1.7 billion airport.* **2** to remove the cover from something such as a work of art, especially as part of a formal ceremony —**unveiling** *n.* [C,U]

un·voiced /ˌʌn'vɔɪst◂ / *adj.* ENG. LANG. ARTS unvoiced CONSONANTS are produced without moving the VOCAL CORDS; for example /d/ and /g/ are VOICED consonants, and /t/ and /k/ are unvoiced

un·want·ed /ˌʌn'wʌntɪd◂ , -'wɑn-, -'wɔn-/ *adj.* not wanted or needed: *an unwanted pregnancy*

un·war·rant·ed /ʌn'wɔrəntɪd, -'wɑr-/ *adj.* unreasonable or unnecessary: *unwarranted criticism*

un·war·y /ʌn'wɛri/ *adj.* not knowing about possible problems or dangers, and therefore easily harmed or deceived

un·washed /ˌʌn'wɑʃt◂ / *adj.* **1** needing to be washed SYN **dirty**: *unwashed dishes* **2 the great unwashed** HUMOROUS poor uneducated people

un·wav·er·ing /ʌn'weɪvərɪŋ/ *adj.* unwavering beliefs, feelings, decisions etc. are strong and do not change: *her unwavering support of the governor*

un·wed /ˌʌn'wɛd◂ / *adj.* FORMAL not married SYN **unmarried**: *an unwed mother*

un·wel·come /ʌn'wɛlkəm/ *adj.* **1** something that is unwelcome is not wanted, especially because it might cause embarrassment or problems: *unwelcome advice* **2** unwelcome guests, visitors etc. are people that you do not want in your home

un·well /ʌn'wɛl/ *adj.* [not before noun] FORMAL sick, especially for a short time

un·wield·y /ʌn'wildi/ *adj.* **1** an unwieldy object is big, heavy, and difficult to carry or use **2** an unwieldy system, argument, or plan is difficult to control or manage because it is too complicated —**unwieldiness** *n.* [U]

un·will·ing /ʌn'wɪlɪŋ/ *adj.* **1** [not before noun] not wanting to do something, and refusing to do it: **unwilling to do sth** *So far the landlord has been unwilling to* lower our rent. **2** [only before noun] not wanting to do something, but doing it: *He was an unwilling participant in the crime.* —**unwillingly** *adv.* —**unwillingness** *n.* [U]

un·wind /ʌnˈwaɪnd/ *v.* past tense and past participle **unwound** /ʌnˈwaʊnd/ **1** [I] to relax and stop feeling anxious: *Reading helps me unwind.* **2** [I,T] to undo something that has been wrapped around something else, or to be undone in this way

un·wise /ˌʌnˈwaɪz◂/ *adj.* not based on good sense and experience: *I think it would be unwise to borrow more money.* —**unwisely** *adv.*

un·wit·ting·ly /ʌnˈwɪt̬ɪŋli/ *adv.* in a way that shows you do not know or realize something: *Laura unwittingly threw away the winning lottery ticket.* —**unwitting** *adj.* [only before noun] *an unwitting victim*

un·world·ly /ʌnˈwɚldli/ *adj.* **1** not interested in money or possessions **2** not having a lot of experience of complicated things in life SYN **naive**

un·wor·thy /ʌnˈwɚði/ *adj.* **1** not good enough to deserve respect, admiration etc.: +**of** *She felt that she was unworthy of his love.* **2** actions or behavior that are unworthy are not acceptable morally: +**of** *behavior that is unworthy of a teacher*

un·wound /ʌnˈwaʊnd/ *v.* the past tense and past participle of UNWIND

un·wrap /ʌnˈræp/ *v.* **unwrapped, unwrapping** [T] to remove the paper, plastic etc. from around something: *Bill unwrapped his present.*

un·writ·ten /ˌʌnˈrɪtˀn◂/ *adj.* known about and understood by everyone but not formally written down: **an unwritten rule/law** *the unwritten rules of social life*

un·yield·ing /ʌnˈyildɪŋ/ *adj.* **1** strict and not willing to change or accept change, even though other people want this **2** LITERARY an object that is unyielding is hard and will not bend **3** LITERARY land that is unyielding does not have many plants growing on it

un·zip /ʌnˈzɪp/ *v.* **unzipped, unzipping** [T] **1** to open the ZIPPER on a piece of clothing, bag etc.: *Unzip your jacket.* ▸see THESAURUS box at **fasten** **2** COMPUTERS to make a computer FILE its normal size again in order to use it, after it has been made to take up less space → see also ZIP FILE

up[1] /ʌp/ S1 W1 *adv.* **1** toward a higher position from the floor, ground, or bottom of something OPP **down**: *He climbed up onto the roof.* | *They both looked up at her.* **2** at or in a high position OPP **down**: *"Where is Alex?" "He's up in his room."* | *The helicopter hovered up above us.* **3** into an upright or raised position OPP **down**: *Everyone stood up for the national anthem.* | *His hair was sticking up.* **4** in or toward the north OPP **down**: *We're driving up to Chicago.* | *My cousins live* ***up north***. **5** toward someone so that you are near, or in the place where they are: *He came right up and asked my name.* | +**to** *I walked up to him and said "hello."* **6** increasing in loudness, strength, level of activity etc.: *Turn up the radio.* | *Violent crime* ***went up*** *by 9% last year.* **7** used with some verbs to mean completely finished or used so that there is nothing left: *Who ate up all the chips?* | *The closet's completely filled up.* **8** used with some verbs to mean in small pieces or divided into equal parts: *We'll split the money up evenly.* | *Why did you tear up the letter?* **9** used with some verbs to mean firmly fastened, covered, or joined: *Can you zip up my coat?* | *Let's cover up the bike in case it rains.* **10** used with some verbs to mean brought or gathered together: *Add up these numbers.* | *I picked up all the beads.* **11** used for saying that something has been built: *Did you put the tent up?* **12** if a surface or part of something is up, it is on top OPP **down**: *Make sure this side of the box is facing up.* | *Put the playing cards* ***right side up*** *on the table.* **13** INFORMAL used for talking about the order in which people will do something, or the order in which things will happen: *First up is a band from Minneapolis.* **14** used with some verbs to mean to receive attention: *Elaine brought up the issue of childcare.* **15** above and including a certain amount or level: *Power was lost* ***from*** *the tenth floor* ***up***. | *The movie is appropriate for children twelve* ***and up***. **16 up and down a)** higher and lower: *We all* ***jumped up and down*** (=jumped repeatedly) *for joy.* **b)** first in one direction, then in the opposite direction, again and again: *Stop running up and down in the hall.* → see also **look sb up and down** at LOOK[1] (20) **17 up to sth a)** up to and including a certain amount or level: *Our car can hold up to five people.* **b)** also **up until sth** if something happens up to a certain time, date etc., it happens until that time: *She continued to care for her father up to the time of his death.*

up[2] S3 W2 *adj.* **1** [not before noun] not in bed: *Are the kids still up?* **2** [not before noun] if a number, level, or amount is up, it is higher than before: +**by** *Interest rates are up by 1%.* | +**on** *Profits are up on last year.* **3** [not before noun] INFORMAL if a period of time is up, it is finished: *I'll give you a signal when the ten minutes are up.* **4 up to sb** depending on someone and what they decide to do: *I'll leave the final decision up to Lloyd.* | *"Which sofa should we get?"* ***"It's up to you."*** **5 up to sth a)** doing something secret or something that you should not be doing: *I have a feeling that Jo's up to something.* | *I think Ken's* ***up to no good*** (=doing something wrong or illegal). **b)** [in negatives and questions] smart, good, or well enough for a particular purpose or in order to do something: *Since the operation, Sue hasn't been up to playing tennis* (=has not felt well enough to play). **c)** if something is up to a particular standard, it is good enough to reach that standard: *This new CD is not up to the group's usual standard.* **6 up for sth** available or intended for a particular purpose: *The house is up for sale.* | *The topic is not up for discussion.* **7 up and running** if a new system or process is up and running, it is working well: *Our new factory is finally up and running.* **8** [not before noun] if a computer system is up, it is working OPP **down** **9 be up against sth/sb** to have to deal with a difficult situation or fight an opponent: *Hugh is up against some stiff competition in the race.* **10** [only before noun] moving or directed to a higher position: *the up escalator* | *Press the up arrow key.* **11 up to your ears/eyes/neck in sth** INFORMAL deeply involved in a difficult or illegal situation: *I'm up to my ears in homework.* **12** INFORMAL used for talking about the order in which people will do something, or the order in which things will happen: **first/next up** *First up is a new band from San Francisco.*

SPOKEN PHRASES

13 be up on sth to know a lot about something: *Conrad's really up on his geography, isn't he?* **14 be up for sth** to be interested in doing something or willing to do something: *Is anybody up for a game of tennis?* **15 bring/get sb up to speed** to tell someone the latest information about something: *Bill, I want you to bring Peter up to speed on the project.* **16 something is up (with sb/sth)** used to say that something bad is happening, for example someone is upset, or something is not working: *You look upset. Is something up?* | *Something's up with the computer.* **17 be up and about** to be well enough to walk around and have a normal life after you have been in bed because of an illness or accident: *It's good to see you up and about again.* **18 What have you been up to (lately)?** used to ask someone what they have been doing since the last time you saw them **19 be up to here (with sb/sth)** to be very upset and angry because of a particular person or situation: *I'm up to here with your lying.*

→ see also **what's up** at WHAT[1] (16), **what's up with sb?** at WHAT[1] (17)

up[3] S1 W1 *prep.* **1** toward or in a higher place: *Go up the stairs and turn right.* | *I dived in, and water went up my nose.* **2** toward or at the top or far end of something: *I'll walk up the road to ask for directions.* **3** if you sail or go up a river, you go toward its SOURCE: *We spent five days sailing up the Mississippi River.*

up[4] *n.* **1 ups and downs** the mixture of good and bad experiences that happen in any situation or relationship: *We had a lot of ups and downs in our marriage.*

U

2 be on the up and up SPOKEN if a person or business is on the up and up, they are honest and do things legally

up[5] *v.* **upped**, **upping** **1** [T] INFORMAL to increase the amount or level of something: *They upped their offer by 5%.* **2 up and...** SPOKEN if you up and do something, you suddenly start to do something different or surprising: *Without saying another word, he* ***up and left***.

up- /ʌp/ *prefix* **1** [in verbs] to make something greater, higher, or better OPP **down-**: *upgrade* (=make a machine, piece of software etc. do more things and work better) **2** [in adverbs and adjectives] at or toward the top or beginning of something OPP **down-**: *uphill* | *upriver* (=nearer to where the river starts) **3** [in verbs] to take something from its place or turn it upside down: *uprooted* (=with the roots pulled out of the ground) **4** [in adjectives and adverbs] at or toward the higher or better part of something OPP **down-**: *upscale* (=attracting richer people)

ˌup-and-ˈcomer *n.* [C] INFORMAL someone or something that is likely to be successful: *an up-and-comer in the computer industry*

ˌup-and-ˈcoming *adj.* [only before noun] likely to be successful or popular: *an up-and-coming Broadway actor*

U·pan·i·shads /uˈpænɪˌʃædz/ *n.* [plural] holy Hindu writings from between the eighth and the third centuries B.C. They help to explain the ideas in the VEDAS (=the oldest collection of holy writings).

up·beat /ˌʌpˈbit◂ / *adj.* happy and confident that good things will happen OPP **downbeat**: *an upbeat person* | *an upbeat report*

up·braid /ʌpˈbreɪd/ *v.* [T] FORMAL to tell someone angrily that they have done something wrong

up·bring·ing /ˈʌpˌbrɪŋɪŋ/ *n.* [singular, U] the care and training that parents give their children when they are growing up: *Our grandmother took charge of our religious upbringing.*

UPC *n.* [C] the abbreviation of UNIVERSAL PRODUCT CODE

up·chuck /ˈʌp-tʃʌk/ *v.* [I] INFORMAL to VOMIT

up·com·ing /ˈʌpˌkʌmɪŋ/ *adj.* [only before noun] happening soon: *my upcoming exams*

up·coun·try /ˌʌpˈkʌntri◂ / *adj.* OLD-FASHIONED from an area of land without many people or towns, especially in the middle of a country

up·date[1] /ˈʌpdeɪt, ˌʌpˈdeɪt/ S3 *v.* **1** [T] to add the most recent information to something: *The information is updated yearly.* **2** [I] if information in a computer updates, the most recent information is added to it: *The page updates every 20 seconds.* **3** [T] to make something more modern in the way it looks or operates: *The company needs to update its image.* **4** [T] INFORMAL to tell someone the most recent information about something: **update sb on sth** *Can you update me on what's been happening?*

up·date[2] /ˈʌpdeɪt/ *n.* [C] the most recent news about something: +**on** *an update on road conditions from the weather station* | *The police are* ***giving*** *the media daily* ***updates*** *on the situation.*

Up·dike /ˈʌpdaɪk/**, John** (1932–) a U.S. writer famous for his NOVELS

up·draft /ˈʌpdræft/ *n.* [C] **1** an UPWARD movement of air OPP **downdraft** **2** a situation in which prices, STOCKS etc. go up, or when business becomes better OPP **downdraft**

up·end /ʌpˈɛnd/ *v.* [T] to push something over, especially so that it is upside down

up·front /ʌpˈfrʌnt/ *adj.* [not before noun] behaving or talking in a direct and honest way: *You need to be upfront with Val about your first marriage.* → see also **up front** at FRONT[1] (10)

up·grade /ˈʌpgreɪd, ˌʌpˈgreɪd/ *v.* **1** [I,T] to improve a machine, system, building etc., by buying new equipment or making the old parts better OPP **downgrade**: *I've just upgraded my computer.* | *The hotel has recently been refurbished and upgraded.* **2** [I,T] to give someone or be given a better seat on an airplane than the one originally paid for, or to get one OPP **downgrade** **3 upgrade your skills** to learn new things about how to do a particular job **4** [T] to change the official description of something to put it at a higher level or rank OPP **downgrade**: **upgrade sb/sth to sth** *The government has upgraded the area to a national park.* —**upgrade** /ˈʌpgreɪd/ *n.* [C]

up·heav·al /ʌpˈhivəl, ˈʌpˌhivəl/ *n.* [C,U] **1** a very big change that often causes problems: *political upheaval* **2** a very strong movement UPWARD, especially of the earth

up·hill[1] /ˌʌpˈhɪl◂ / *adj.* **1** toward the top of a hill OPP **downhill**: *an uphill climb* **2 an uphill battle/struggle/fight etc.** something that is very difficult to do and needs a lot of effort

uphill[2] *adv.* toward the top of a hill OPP **downhill**: *The water had to be pumped uphill.*

up·hold /ʌpˈhoʊld/ *v.* *past tense and past participle* **upheld** /-ˈhɛld/ [T] **1** LAW if a court upholds a decision made by another court, it states that the decision was correct: *The higher court later upheld the decision.* **2** to defend or support a law, system, or principle so that it is not made weaker: *Police officers are responsible for upholding the law.* —**upholder** *n.* [C]

up·hol·ster /əˈpoʊlstɚ, ʌpˈhoʊl-/ *v.* [T] to cover a chair etc. with material —**upholstered** *adj.* —**upholsterer** *n.* [C]

up·hol·ster·y /əˈpoʊlstəri/ *n.* [U] **1** material used to cover chairs etc. **2** the process of covering chairs etc. with material [**Origin:** 1600–1700 *upholster* **dealer in small goods, upholsterer** (15–18 centuries), from *uphold*]

up·keep /ˈʌpkip/ *n.* [U + of] the care needed to keep something in good condition

up·lands /ˈʌpləndz/ *n.* [plural] EARTH SCIENCE the parts of a country that are away from the ocean and are higher than other areas —**upland** *adj.*: *upland forests*

up·lift[1] /ˈʌplɪft/ *n.* [U] a sudden happy feeling

up·lift[2] /ʌpˈlɪft/ *v.* [T] FORMAL **1** to make someone feel happier **2** to make something higher

up·lift·ed /ʌpˈlɪftɪd/ *adj.* **1** feeling happier **2** LITERARY raised up

up·lift·ing /ˌʌpˈlɪftɪŋ/ *adj.* making you feel more cheerful: *an uplifting song*

up·load /ˈʌploʊd/ *v.* [I,T] COMPUTERS if information, a program etc. uploads, or if you upload it, you move it from a computer to a larger computer system that is connected to it → see also DOWNLOAD

up·mar·ket /ˌʌpˈmɑrkət◂ / *adj.* UPSCALE OPP **downmarket**

up·on /əˈpɑn, əˈpɔn/ S2 W1 *prep.* FORMAL on: *A dark cloud descended upon the valley.* | *Her friends look upon her with envy.* [**Origin:** 1100–1200 *up* + *on*] → see also **once upon a time** at ONCE[1] (13), **take it upon yourself to do sth** at TAKE[1] (35)

up·per[1] /ˈʌpɚ/ S2 W3 *adj.* [only before noun] **1** in a higher position than something else OPP **lower**: *His upper arms were huge.* **2** near or at the top of something OPP **lower**: *the upper floors of the building* | *the* ***upper age limit*** (=the top limit) **3 have/gain the upper hand** to have more power than someone else, so that you are able to control a situation: *Police have gained the upper hand over the drug dealers in the area.* **4** more important than other parts or ranks in an organization, system etc. OPP **lower**: *upper-income consumers* | **upper levels/echelons** *the upper levels of society* **5** farther from the ocean or farther north than other parts of an area OPP **lower**: ***the upper reaches*** *of the Mekong River* [**Origin:** 1200–1300 *up*] → see also **keep a stiff upper lip** at STIFF[1] (9)

upper[2] *n.* [C] **1** the top part of a shoe that covers your foot: *leather uppers* → see picture at SHOE[1] **2** INFORMAL an illegal drug that gives you a lot of energy SYN **amphetamine**

ˌupper ˈcase *n.* [U] letters written in capitals (A, B, C) rather than in small form (a, b, c) OPP lower case —**upper-case** *adj.*

ˌupper 'chamber *n.* [C usually singular] UPPER HOUSE

ˌupper 'class *n.* [C] **the upper class** the group of people who belong to the highest social class → see also LOWER CLASS, MIDDLE CLASS, WORKING CLASS —**upper-class** *adj.*

up·per·class·man /ˌʌpɚˈklæsmən/ *n.* [C] a student in the last two years at a school or college → see also UNDERCLASSMAN

ˌupper 'crust *n.* [singular] INFORMAL the group of people who belong to the highest social class —**upper-crust** *adj.*

up·per·cut /ˈʌpɚˌkʌt/ *n.* [C] an act of hitting someone in which you swing your hand up into their chin

ˌupper 'house *n.* [C usually singular] the smaller of two elected groups of government officials that make laws. It is usually less REPRESENTATIVE and made up of more experienced officials than the larger group. → see also LOWER HOUSE

up·per·most /ˈʌpɚˌmoʊst/ *adj.* **1** [usually before noun] higher than anything else: *Place the pizza on the uppermost oven rack.* **2** [usually before noun] more important than anything else: *Succeeding in her career was **uppermost in her mind**.*

Upper Nu·bi·a /ˌʌpɚ ˈnubiə/ HISTORY the southern part of Nubia, in ancient northeast Africa

ˌUpper 'South, the HISTORY an area including the U.S. states of Virginia, North Carolina, Tennessee, and Arkansas. The phrase was used during the Civil War.

up·pi·ty /ˈʌpət̬i/ *adj.* INFORMAL, DISAPPROVING behaving as if you are more important than you really are, and not showing other people enough respect: *Don't get uppity with me, young lady!*

up·raised /ˌʌpˈreɪzd◂ / *adj.* LITERARY raised or lifted up

up·right¹ /ˈʌp-raɪt/ *adv.* **1** with your back straight: **sit/stand (bolt) upright** *Andy sat upright in bed when he heard the noise.* **2** if something is pulled, held etc. upright, it is put into a position in which it is standing straight up: *We struggled to keep the boat upright.*

upright² *adj.* **1** standing straight up **2** always behaving in an honest way: *a brave upright man* —**uprightness** *n.* [U]

upright³ *n.* [C] **1** a long piece of wood or metal that stands straight up and supports something **2** an upright piano

ˌupright pi'ano *n.* [C] a tall piano with strings that are set in an up and down direction → see also GRAND PIANO

up·ris·ing /ˈʌpˌraɪzɪŋ/ *n.* [C] POLITICS an occasion when a group of people use violence to try to change the rules, laws etc. in an institution or country: **+against** *a **popular uprising** (=involving ordinary people) against the monarchy*

up·riv·er /ʌpˈrɪvɚ/ *adv.* toward the place where a river begins OPP downriver

up·roar /ˈʌp-rɔr/ *n.* [singular, U] a lot of noise or angry protest about something: *His speech caused uproar in the hall.* [**Origin:** 1500–1600 Dutch *oproer*, from *op* **up** + *roer* **movement**; influenced by English *roar*]

up·roar·i·ous /ʌpˈrɔriəs/ *adj.* very noisy, because a lot of people are laughing or shouting —**uproariously** *adv.*

up·root /ʌpˈrut/ *v.* [T] **1** to pull a plant and its roots out of the ground **2** to make someone leave their home for a new place, especially when this is difficult or upsetting: *She didn't want to uproot her elderly mother.*

up·scale /ˌʌpˈskeɪl◂ / *adj.* made for or relating to people from a high social class who have a lot of money OPP downscale: *an upscale department store*

up·set¹ /ˌʌpˈsɛt◂ / S1 *adj.* **1** [not before noun] unhappy and worried because something bad or disappointing has happened: *It's OK. Don't **get upset**.* | **+about/over** *She was really upset about the accident.* | **upset that** *Marcy was upset that she wasn't invited.* ►see THESAURUS box at sad **2 an upset stomach** an feeling in your stomach of being sick

up·set² /ʌpˈsɛt/ W3 *v. past tense and past participle* **upset** [T]

1 MAKE UNHAPPY to make someone feel unhappy or worried: *It upsets me when people argue.*

2 upset sb's stomach to make someone feel sick in their stomach: *Spicy food upsets my stomach.*

3 DEFEAT to defeat someone who is expected to win a game or competition: *France upset Brazil in the World Cup final.*

4 CAUSE PROBLEMS to change a plan or situation in a way that causes problems: *I'm sorry if I've upset your plans for this evening.* | *Introduction of new species could **upset** the delicate **balance**.*

5 PUSH STH OVER to push something over without intending to: *She brushed against the table, upsetting two drinks.*

6 upset the apple cart OLD-FASHIONED to completely spoil someone's plans

up·set³ /ˈʌpsɛt/ *n.* **1** [C] an occasion when a person or team that is not expected to win beats a stronger opponent in a competition, election etc.: *We've seen a few upsets in the past week.* **2** [singular, U] the feeling of being upset **3 stomach upset** [U] a feeling in your stomach of being sick

up·set·ting /ʌpˈsɛt̬ɪŋ/ *adj.* making you feel unhappy and worried: *upsetting news*

up·shot /ˈʌpʃɑt/ *n.* **the upshot (of sth)** the final result of a situation or action [**Origin:** 1600–1700 *upshot* **final shot in an archery competition** (16–17 centuries)]

up·side¹ /ˈʌpsaɪd/ *n.* [singular] the positive part of a situation that is generally bad OPP downside: **+of** *The upside of working at home is that I can control my schedule.*

upside² *prep.* **upside the head/face etc.** SPOKEN, NONSTANDARD on the side of someone's head etc.

ˌupside 'down¹ *adv.* with the top at the bottom and the bottom at the top OPP right side up: *You're holding the book upside down.* → see also **turn sth upside down** at TURN¹ (17)

upside down² *adj.* **1** in a position with the top at the bottom and the bottom at the top: *an upside down U shape* **2** messy or not organized

up·stage¹ /ʌpˈsteɪdʒ/ *v.* [T] to do something that takes people's attention away from someone else who is more important: *The young player upstaged several of the experienced team members.*

up·stage² *adv.* toward the back of the stage in a theater —**upstage** *adj.*

up·stairs¹ /ˌʌpˈstɛrz◂ / S2 *adv.* **1** toward or on an upper floor in a building OPP downstairs: *He's upstairs in bed.* | *Come upstairs with me.* **2 sb does not have much upstairs** SPOKEN used to say that someone is not very intelligent **3 the man upstairs** SPOKEN God —**upstairs** *adj.*: *an upstairs bedroom* → see also **kick sb upstairs** at KICK¹ (9)

upstairs² *n.* **the upstairs** one or all of the upper floors in a building

up·stand·ing /ˌʌpˈstændɪŋ/ *adj.* FORMAL honest and responsible: *an upstanding citizen*

up·start /ˈʌpstɑrt/ *n.* [C] someone or an organization that becomes successful very quickly, and is not liked by other people or companies because of their success [**Origin:** 1500–1600 *upstart* **to jump up suddenly** (14–19 centuries)] —**upstart** *adj.*: *a young upstart lawyer*

up·state /ˌʌpˈsteɪt◂ / *adj.* [only before noun] in the northern part of a particular state OPP downstate: *upstate New York* —**upstate** *adv.*

up·stream /ˌʌpˈstrim◂ / *adv.* along a river, in the opposite direction from the way the water is flowing OPP downstream —**upstream** *adj.*

up·surge /ˈʌpsɚdʒ/ *n.* [C] a sudden increase: **+of/in** *an upsurge in the number of cases of flu*

up·swing /ˈʌpswɪŋ/ *n.* [C] an improvement or

U

increase in the level of something OPP **downswing**: +**in** *an upswing in business* | *The airline's earnings are now* ***on the upswing***.

up·take /ˈʌpteɪk/ *n.* **1 be slow/quick on the uptake** INFORMAL to be slow or fast at learning or understanding things **2** [C,U] TECHNICAL the rate at which a substance is taken into a system, machine etc.

up-'tempo *adj.* moving or happening at a fast rate: *up-tempo music* —**up-tempo** *adv.*

up·tick /ˈʌptɪk/ *n.* [C] an UPTURN

up·tight /ˌʌpˈtaɪt◂/ *adj.* **1** nervous and worried, unable to relax, and likely to become angry easily: +**about** *I just try not to get too uptight about anything.* **2** INFORMAL having strict traditional opinions and seeming unable to relax: *Her parents seemed so boring and uptight.*

ˌup-to-'date *adj.* **1** including all the newest information: *up-to-date travel information* | **keep/bring sb up-to-date** (=to give someone all the newest information about something) | **keep/bring sth up-to-date** (=to add all the newest information about something to a list, document etc.) **2** modern or fashionable: *a more up-to-date hairstyle*

ˌup-to-the-'minute *adj.* [only before noun] **1** including all the newest information: *up-to-the-minute financial information* **2** very modern or fashionable

up·town /ˌʌpˈtaʊn◂/ *adv.* in or toward the northern areas of a city, especially away from the city center —**uptown** /ˈʌptaʊn/ *adj.* —**uptown** *n.* [U] → see also DOWNTOWN

up·trend /ˈʌptrɛnd/ *n.* [C] a period of time when business or economic activity increases OPP **downtrend**

up·turn /ˈʌptɚn/ *n.* [C] an increase in the level of something OPP **downturn**: +**in** *an upturn in profits*

up·turned /ˈʌptɚnd, ˌʌpˈtɚnd/ *adj.* **1** curving up at the end: *an upturned nose* **2** turned UPSIDE DOWN: *an upturned flowerpot*

up·ward¹ /ˈʌpwɚd/ also **upwards** *adv.* **1** moving or pointing toward a higher position OPP **downward**: *He pointed upward with his left hand.* | *The road winds upward, away from the river.* **2** increasing to a higher level: *Stock prices have moved upward.* **3** more than a particular amount, time etc.: *The ships can carry a cargo of three hundred tons and upward.* | ***Upward of*** *5,000 workers have lost their jobs.*

upward² *adj.* [only before noun] **1** increasing to a higher level OPP **downward**: *an upward trend in gasoline prices* **2** moving or pointing toward a higher position OPP **downward**: *an upward movement of the hand*

ˌupwardly 'mobile *adj.* moving up through the social classes and becoming richer —**upward mobility** *n.* [U]

U·ral River, the /ˌyʊrəl ˈrɪvɚ/ a river in eastern Europe that flows from the Ural Mountains in Russia through Kazakhstan to the Caspian Sea

U·rals, the /ˈyʊrəlz/ also **the ˌUral 'Mountains** a range of mountains that runs from the north to the south of Russia and is often considered to mark the border between Europe and Asia

u·ra·ni·um /yʊˈreɪniəm/ *n.* [U] SYMBOL **U** CHEMISTRY a heavy white metal that is an ELEMENT, is RADIOACTIVE, and is used to produce NUCLEAR power and weapons [**Origin:** 1700–1800 Modern Latin *Uranus*; because the substance was discovered soon after the planet]

U·ra·nus /yʊˈreɪnəs, ˈyʊrənəs/ **1** PHYSICS the PLANET that is the seventh in order from the sun → see picture at SOLAR SYSTEM **2** in Greek MYTHOLOGY, the god of heaven and the first ruler of the universe

ur·ban /ˈɚbən/ W2 *adj.* [only before noun] relating to a city, or to cities in general OPP **rural**: *Approximately 60% of the population lives in urban areas.* | *urban unemployment* [**Origin:** 1600–1700 Latin *urbanus* **urban, sophisticated**, from *urbs* **city**]

Ur·ban II /ˌɚbən ðə ˈsɛkənd/ (?1042–1099) the POPE who encouraged the First Crusade

ˌurban 'blight *n.* [U] problems that make part of a city ugly and hard to live in

ur·bane /ɚˈbeɪn/ *adj.* behaving in a relaxed and confident way in social situations —**urbanely** *adv.* —**urbanity** /ɚˈbænət̬i/ *n.* [U]

ur·ban·ize /ˈɚbəˌnaɪz/ *v.* [T usually passive] **1** to build houses, cities etc. in the COUNTRYSIDE: *urbanized areas* **2** if a society is urbanized, people move from country areas to live in cities **3** if someone from a country area is urbanized, they become more like people who live in cities —**urbanization** /ˌɚbənəˈzeɪʃən/ *n.* [U]

ˌurban 'legend also **ˌurban 'myth** *n.* [C] something that a lot of people believe although it is not true, especially a story about an unusual or terrible event that is claimed to have happened to an ordinary person

ˌurban re'newal *n.* [U] the process of improving poor city areas by building new houses, stores etc.

ˌurban 'sprawl *n.* [U] the spread of city buildings and houses into an area that was COUNTRYSIDE

ur·chin /ˈɚtʃɪn/ *n.* [C] OLD-FASHIONED a small dirty messy child → see also SEA URCHIN

Ur·du /ˈʊrdu, ˈɚdu/ *n.* [U] the official language of Pakistan, also used in India [**Origin:** 1700–1800 Hindi *urdu-zaban* **camp language**]

-ure /yɚ/ *suffix* [in nouns] used to make nouns that show actions or results: *failure* (=act of failing) | *a closure* (=the act of closing a company)

u·re·ter /yʊˈrit̬ɚ, ˈjʊrət̬ɚ/ *n.* [C] BIOLOGY a tube inside the body for carrying URINE (=the yellow liquid waste produced by the body) from the KIDNEYS to the BLADDER

u·re·thra /yʊˈriθrə/ *n.* [C] BIOLOGY the tube through which URINE flows from the BLADDER, and also through which the SEMEN of males flows

urge¹ /ɚdʒ/ W2 *v.* [T] **1** to strongly suggest that someone do something: **urge sb to do sth** *Katy's family urged her to find another job.* | **urge that** *Graft urged that the city use the money for new playgrounds.* | **urge caution/restraint** *The U.N. urged restraint on both sides.* ►see THESAURUS box at **advise** **2** [always + adv./prep.] LITERARY to make someone or something move by shouting, pushing them etc.: **urge sb into/toward/forward etc.** *Daniel urged the horses forward with a whip.* [**Origin:** 1500–1600 Latin *urgere*]

urge sb ↔ **on** *phr. v.* to encourage a person or animal to work harder, go faster etc.: *Urged on by the crowd, the Italian team scored two more goals.*

urge² *n.* [C] a strong wish or need: *sexual urges* | **an/the urge to do sth** *I resisted the urge to slap his face.*

ur·gent /ˈɚdʒənt/ *adj.* **1** very important and needing to be dealt with immediately: *The letter was marked "urgent."* | *He was* ***in urgent need of*** *medical attention.* **2** FORMAL done or said in a way that shows that you want something to be dealt with immediately: *an urgent whisper* —**urgency** *n.* [U] *a matter of great urgency* —**urgently** *adv.*

u·ric /ˈyʊrɪk/ *adj.* BIOLOGY relating to URINE

u·ri·nal /ˈyʊrənəl/ *n.* [C] a type of toilet for men, that is fastened onto the wall

u·ri·nal·y·sis /ˌyʊrəˈnæləsɪs/ *n.* [C,U] a test of someone's urine to see what substances are in it

u·ri·nar·y /ˈyʊrəˌnɛri/ *adj.* BIOLOGY relating to urine or the parts of your body through which urine passes

u·ri·nate /ˈyʊrəˌneɪt/ *v.* [I] BIOLOGY to make urine flow out of your body —**urination** /ˌyʊrəˈneɪʃən/ *n.* [U]

u·rine /ˈyʊrɪn/ *n.* [U] BIOLOGY the yellow liquid waste that comes out of your body from your BLADDER

URL *n.* [C] COMPUTERS **uniform resource locator** an address for a particular WEBSITE on the Internet

urn /ɚn/ *n.* [C] **1** a decorated container, especially one that is used for holding the ASHES of a dead body **2** a metal container that holds a large amount of tea or coffee

u·rol·o·gist /yʊˈrɑlədʒɪst/ *n.* [C] a doctor who treats conditions relating to the URINARY system and men's sexual organs —**urology** *n.* [U] —**urological** /ˌyʊrəˈlɑdʒɪkəl/ *adj.*

Ur·su·line /ˈɚsəlɪn, -laɪn/ a member of a group of Catholic NUNS

U·ru·guay /ˈyʊrəˌgwaɪ/ a country in South America, between Argentina and Brazil —**Uruguayan** /ˌyʊrəˈgwaɪən/ *n., adj.*

us /əs; strong ʌs/ S1 W1 *pron.* the object form of "we": *Kate told us she was getting a new car.* | *Are you coming with us?* [**Origin:** Old English]

U.S., US *n.* **the U.S.** the United States of America —**U.S.** also **US** *adj.*: *the U.S. Navy*

U.S.A., USA *n.* **the U.S.A.** the United States of America

U.S. of A. /ˌyu ɛs əv ˈeɪ/ *n.* **the (good ol') U.S. of A.** SPOKEN, HUMOROUS the United States of America

us·a·ble /ˈyuzəbəl/ *adj.* in an appropriate condition to be used

USAF the abbreviation of the United States Air Force

us·age /ˈyusɪdʒ/ *n.* **1** [C,U] ENG. LANG. ARTS the way that words are used in a language: *modern English usage* **2** [U] the way in which something is used, or the amount of it that is used: *Water usage is increasing*

USCIS /ˈʌskɪs, ˌyu ɛs si aɪ ˈɛs/ *n.* **U.S. Citizenship and Immigration Services** the part of the Department of Homeland Security that deals with people who come to live in the U.S. from other countries

USDA *n.* [singular] **United States Department of Agriculture** an official government organization that sets standards for food quality and makes sure that places where food is produced or PACKAGEd are clean and the food is safe to eat

use up

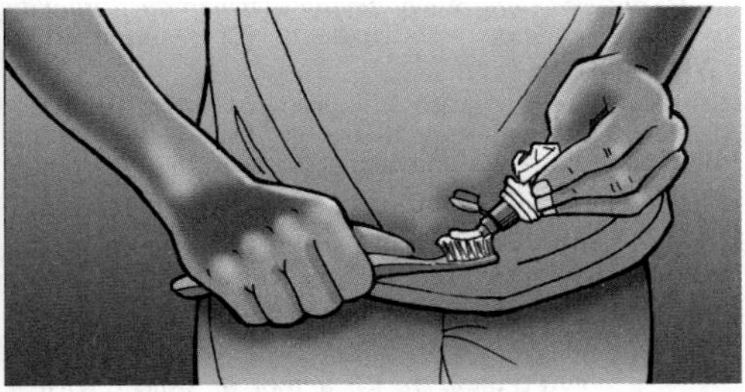

Mark used up all the toothpaste.

use¹ /yuz/ S1 W1 *v.*

1 USE STH [T] to do something with a particular tool, method, service, ability etc., in order to achieve a particular purpose, or do a particular job: *Can I use your phone?* | *Carla often doesn't use good judgment in selecting boyfriends.* | **easy/simple/difficult/hard to use** *The new computer system is easy to use.* | **use sth for (doing) sth** *They use animals for scientific experiments.* | **use sth to do sth** *Use a calculator to check your answers.* | **use sth as sth** *I use the dining-room table as a desk.* | *The officer is accused of **using** excessive **force*** (=using violent methods) *during the arrest.*

2 AMOUNT OF STH [T] to take something from a supply of food, gas, money etc. with the result that there is less left: *Standard washing machines use about 40 gallons of water.*

3 TREAT SB UNFAIRLY to make someone do something for you in order to get something you want: *Can't you see Mike's just using you?* | **use sb to do sth** *They used her to get to her brother.*

4 AN ADVANTAGE [T] to take advantage of a situation: **use sth to do sth** *She used her position as manager to get jobs for her friends.* | *He uses his small size **to** his **advantage**.*

5 sb/sth could use sth SPOKEN used to say that someone or something needs or really wants something: *You look like you could use some sleep.*

6 WORD [T] to say or write a particular word or phrase: *Don't use bad language around the kids.*

7 DRUGS [I,T] to regularly take illegal drugs

8 NAME [T] to call yourself by a name that is not yours in order to keep your real name secret: *Martens uses her stage name when she travels.*

[**Origin:** 1200–1300 Old French *user*, from Latin *usus*, past participle of *uti* **to use**]

use sth ↔ **up** *phr. v.* to use all of something, so there is none left: *Who used up the ketchup?*

use² /yus/ S1 W1 *n.* **1** [C] a purpose for which something can be used: *Robots have many different uses in industry.* | **have/find a use for sth** *The drawer is full of things I never find a use for.* **2** [U] the act of using something, or the amount that is used: *an exit for use in emergencies* | **+of** *Increased use of fertilizers has led to water pollution.* **3 make use of sth** to use something that is available in order to achieve something or get an advantage for yourself: *More students should make use of the language lab.* | *I have to learn to **make better use of** my time.* **4 put sth to (good) use** to use knowledge, skills etc. for a particular purpose: *The job gives me an opportunity to put my language skills to good use.* **5** [U] the ability or right to use something: *Joe's **given** me **the use of** his office till he gets back.* | *He **lost the use of** both legs as a result of the accident.* **6 be (of) no use (to sb)** to be completely useless: *Now that I've quit law school, the books are of no use to me.* **7 be of use** to be useful: *Were my directions of any use?*

SPOKEN PHRASES

8 it's/there's no (use doing sth) used to tell someone not to do something because it will have no effect: *There's no use complaining.* **9 it's no use!** used to say that you are going to stop doing something because you do not think it will be successful: *Oh, it's no use! I can't fix it.* **10 what's the use (of doing sth)?** used to say that something seems to be a waste of time: *What's the use of having a window in your office if you can't open it?* **11 sth has its uses** HUMOROUS used to say that something can sometimes be useful, even though it may not seem that way: *Being stubborn can have its uses.*

12 be in use a machine, place etc. that is in use is being used: *All of the washing machines are in use.* **13 for the use of sb** provided for a particular person or group of people to use: *The board room is for the use of company executives only.* **14 come into use** to start being used: *Tanning beds came into use around 1979.* **15 bring sth into use** to start using something **16 go/be out of use** a machine, place etc. that goes out of use or is out of use, stops being used, or is not being used **17 have no use for sb/sth** to have no respect for someone or something: *My company has no use for workers who aren't motivated.* **18** [C] ENG. LANG. ARTS one of the meanings of a word, or the way that a particular word is used

used¹ /yust/ S2 W2 *adj.* **used to (doing) sth 1** familiar with something through experience so that it does not seem surprising, difficult, strange etc. anymore SYN **accustomed to**: *Zach's not used to such spicy food.* | *I still haven't **gotten used to** working nights.* → see Word Choice box at USED TO **2** if someone is used to doing or having something, they expect it to happen, because this has always happened in the past SYN **accustomed to**: *She's used to having her own way.*

used² /yuzd/ *adj.* [usually before noun] **1** used goods have already had an owner, and are offered for sale again SYN **second hand**: *used cars* | ►see THESAURUS box at **old** **2** dirty or not in good condition anymore, as a result of use: *used tissues* | *a used syringe*

used to /ˈyustə; *final or before a vowel* ˈyustu/ S1 W1 *modal verb* used to say that something happened regularly or all the time in the past, or was true in the past, but does not happen or is not true now: *He used to be in my class.* | *The shop used to do bicycle repairs too.* | *"Do you play golf?" "No, but I used to."* | *I **didn't use** to like butter.* | ***Did** she **use** to be your girlfriend?*

WORD CHOICE used to/be used to/get used to

• We use **used to** before a verb to talk about something that someone did regularly in the past: *Marianne used to play the piano every day, but she hardly ever plays now.*

• Use **be used to** and **get used to** to talk about being or becoming more comfortable with a situation or activity, so that it does not seem strange or difficult anymore: *Tina's used to getting up at 5:30.* | *I can't get used to the climate here.*

use·ful /ˈyusfəl/ S3 W2 *adj.* **1** helping you to do or get what you want: *She gave me some useful advice.* | **+to** *The information would be useful to terrorists.* | **+for** *Do you feel your training was useful for your job?* | *Such techniques might* ***prove useful*** *in detecting breast cancer.* | **it is useful to do sth** *It is useful to have a good first aid kit handy.* **2 make yourself useful** INFORMAL to do something to help someone → see also **come in useful/handy** at COME IN (6) —**usefully** *adv.*

use·ful·ness /ˈyusfəlnɪs/ *n.* [U] the state of being useful: *The test is of limited usefulness.* → see also **outlive your usefulness** at OUTLIVE (3)

use·less /ˈyuslɪs/ *adj.* **1** not useful or effective in any way: *a useless piece of information* | *Without electricity, the radio's completely useless.* | **+for** *These shoes are useless for long walks.* | **it is useless to do sth** *She knew it was useless to complain.* ►see THESAURUS box at **pointless** **2** INFORMAL unable or unwilling to do anything well: *As a secretary, she was useless.* —**uselessly** *adv.* —**uselessness** *n.* [U]

Use·net /ˈyuznɛt/ *n.* [singular] a very large network of NEWSGROUPS and news SERVERS on the Internet, by which users can post messages on specific subjects that are sent to all members

us·er /ˈyuzɚ/ W2 *n.* [C] **1** someone or something that uses a product, service etc.: *library users* | *a computer user* **2** INFORMAL someone who regularly takes illegal drugs **3** DISAPPROVING, INFORMAL someone who uses other people to get advantages for themselves → see also END USER

ˈuser fee *n.* [C] an amount of money that someone must pay for using a particular service: *airport user fees*

ˌuser-ˈfriendly *adj.* easy to use or operate: *user-friendly software* —**user-friendliness** *n.* [U]

ˌuser ˈinterface *n.* [C] COMPUTERS how a computer program looks on screen and how the user enters commands and information into the program

ˈuser name also **ˌuser IˈD** *n.* [C] COMPUTERS a name or special word that proves who you are and allows you to enter a computer system

ush·er¹ /ˈʌʃɚ/ *n.* [C] someone who guides people to their seats at a theater, wedding etc. [**Origin:** 1300–1400 Old French *ussier*, from Vulgar Latin *ustiarius* **door-guard**]

usher² *v.* [T] to help someone to get from one place to another, especially by guiding them: **usher sb into/to etc. sth** *Security guards ushered the man out of the theater.* ►see THESAURUS box at **lead¹**

usher sth ↔ **in** *phr. v.* to be the start of something new: *Global warming is likely to usher in an era of more extreme weather patterns.*

USIA **United States Information Agency** a government department which sends representatives to other countries to provide information about the United States

USMC the abbreviation of the **United States Marine Corps**

USN the abbreviation of the **United States Navy**

USO **United Services Organizations** an organization that helps members of the U.S. military

USP *n.* [C] **unique selling proposition** a feature of a product that makes it different from other similar products, and therefore more attractive to people who might buy it

USS, U.S.S. **United States Ship** used at the beginning of a military ship's name: *the USS Nimitz*

u·su·al¹ /ˈyuʒuəl, -ʒəl/ S3 W2 *adj.* **1** the same as what happens most of the time or in most situations: *I'll meet you at the usual time.* | *The usual adult dose is 600 mg daily.* | **better/more/worse etc. than usual** *The trip home seemed to take longer than usual.* | **the usual way/method/manner** *I cooked the pasta in the usual way.* **2 as usual** in the way that happens or exists most of the time: *Dorothy arrived late as usual.* **3 be your usual self** [usually in negatives] behaving or feeling the way you usually do, and not upset, sick etc.: *Tom wasn't his usual self at all today.* [**Origin:** 1300–1400 Late Latin *usualis*, from Latin *usus* past participle of *uti* **to use**] → see also **business as usual** at BUSINESS (11)

usual² *n.* **1 the usual** SPOKEN **a)** something that usually happens, is usually done etc.: *"So what have you been up to?" "Just the usual."* **b)** the drink or food that you usually have, especially at a bar or restaurant: *I'll have the usual, Frank.* **2 (as) per usual** SPOKEN happening again in the way that it happens most of the time

u·su·al·ly /ˈyuʒuəli, -ʒəli/ S1 W1 *adv.* used when describing what happens on most occasions or in most situations: *Janet usually wears jeans to work.* | *It's not usually this cold in April.* | *Usually, I go home right after class.*

u·su·rer /ˈyuʒərɚ/ *n.* [C] OLD-FASHIONED, FORMAL someone who lends money to people and makes them pay too high a rate of INTEREST

u·su·ri·ous /yuˈʒuriəs/ *adj.* FORMAL a usurious price or rate of INTEREST is unfairly high

u·surp /yuˈsɚp/ *v.* [T] FORMAL to take someone else's power, position, job etc. when you do not have the right to: *He accused Congress of trying to usurp the authority of the President.* —**usurper** *n.* [C] —**usurpation** /ˌyusɚˈpeɪʃən/ *n.* [U]

u·su·ry /ˈyuʒəri/ *n.* [U] OLD-FASHIONED, FORMAL the practice of lending money to people, especially making them pay unfairly high rates of INTEREST

UT the written abbreviation of UTAH

U·tah /ˈyutɑ/ WRITTEN ABBREVIATION **UT** a state in the western U.S.

Ute /yut/ *n.* a Native American tribe from the western region of the U.S.

u·ten·sil /yuˈtɛnsəl/ *n.* [C] a tool or object with a particular use, especially in cooking: *kitchen utensils* [**Origin:** 1300–1400 Old French *utensile*, from Latin *utensilis* **useful**]

u·ter·us /ˈyuṭərəs/ *n. plural* **uteri** /-raɪ/ or **uteruses** [C] BIOLOGY the organ in a woman's or female MAMMAL's body where babies develop —**uterine** /ˈyuṭəraɪn, -rən/ *adj.*

u·til·i·tar·i·an /yuˌtɪləˈtɛriən/ *adj.* **1** FORMAL useful and practical rather than being used for decoration: *utilitarian clothes* **2** TECHNICAL based on a belief in utilitarianism

u·til·i·tar·i·an·ism /yuˌtɪləˈtɛriəˌnɪzəm/ *n.* [U] TECHNICAL the belief that an action is good if it produces the greatest happiness for the greatest number of people, or that the aim of society should be to produce the greatest happiness for the greatest number of people

u·til·i·ty /yuˈtɪləṭi/ Ac W3 *n. plural* **utilities** **1** [usually plural] a service such as gas or electricity provided for people to use, or a company that provides one of these services: *Does your rent include utilities?* **2** [U] FORMAL the amount of usefulness that something has **3** [C] COMPUTERS a piece of computer SOFTWARE that has a particular use → see also SPORT-UTILITY VEHICLE

uˈtility ˌpole *n.* [C] a tall wooden pole that supports telephone and electric wires

uˈtility ˌroom *n.* [C] a room in a house where the washing machine, FREEZER, cleaning equipment etc. are kept

u·til·ize /ˈyutl̩ˌaɪz/ Ac *v.* [T] FORMAL to use something for a particular purpose SYN **use**: *Resources need to be utilized in a more efficient way.* —**utilizable** *adj.* —**utilization** /ˌyuṭl-əˈzeɪʃən/ *n.* [U]

ut·most¹ /ˈʌtˀmoʊst/ *adj.* **the utmost importance/respect/care etc.** the greatest possible importance, respect etc.: *I have the utmost respect for his research.* [**Origin:** Old English *utmæst* **farthest out**, from *ut* **out**]

utmost² *n.* **1 do/try your utmost** to try as hard as you can to achieve something: *Kimball said he would do his utmost to achieve a peaceful solution.* **2 the utmost** the most that can be done: *The state's resources have been stretched **to the utmost**.*

u·to·pi·a /yuˈtoʊpiə/ *n.* [C,U] an imaginary perfect world where everyone is happy [**Origin:** 1500–1600 *Utopia* imaginary perfect country in the book "Utopia" (1516) by Sir Thomas More, from Greek *ou* **not, no** + *topos* **place**] —**utopian** *adj.* → see also DYSTOPIA

ut·ter¹ /ˈʌṭɚ/ *adj.* [only before noun] **utter failure/darkness/nonsense etc.** complete failure, darkness etc.: *All of your talk about quitting school is utter nonsense.* [**Origin:** Old English *utera* **further out, outer**, from *ut* **out**]

utter² *v.* [T] FORMAL **1** to say something: *He never uttered a single word of protest.* **2** to make a sound with your voice, especially with difficulty: *The wounded prisoner uttered a groan.*

ut·ter·ance /ˈʌṭərəns/ *n.* **1** [C] FORMAL something that someone says **2 give utterance to sth** LITERARY to express something in words

ut·ter·ly /ˈʌṭɚli/ *adv.* completely or totally: [+ adj./adv.] *Her comments about men are utterly ridiculous.*

U-turn /ˈyu tɚn/ *n.* [C] **1** a turn that you make in a car, on a bicycle etc., so that you go back in the direction you came from: ***Make a U-turn** at the next intersection.* **2** a complete change of ideas, plans etc.: *The government was forced to **make a** humiliating **U-turn** on the issue.*

UV an abbreviation of ULTRAVIOLET

u·vu·la /ˈyuvyələ/ *n.* [C] BIOLOGY a small soft piece of flesh that hangs down from the top of your mouth at the back

Uz·bek·i·stan /ʊzˈbɛkɪˌstɑn, -ˌstæn/ a country in central Asia between Turkmenistan and Kazakhstan, that was formerly part of the Soviet Union —**Uzbek** /ˈʊzbɛk/ *n., adj.*

U·zi /ˈuzi/ *n.* [C] a type of MACHINE GUN

V,v

V¹, **v** /vi/ *n. plural* **V's, v's** [C] **1 a)** the 22nd letter of the English alphabet **b)** the sound represented by this letter **2** [usually singular] something that has a shape like the letter V: *Ducks flew overhead in a V.*

V² **1** the number five in the system of ROMAN NUMERALS **2** used to show that a television show contains violent scenes

v the written abbreviation of VOLT

v. **1** a written abbreviation of VERSUS, used especially when talking about the names of legal TRIALS: *Roe v. Wade* → see also VS. **2** the written abbreviation of VERB **3** the abbreviation of VERSE

VA the written abbreviation of Virginia

vac /væk/ *n.* [C] a VACUUM CLEANER

va·can·cy /ˈveɪkənsi/ *n. plural* **vacancies** **1** [C,U] a room or building that is not being used and is available for someone to stay in, or the situation in which a room or building like this is available: *The hotel had hung out its "No vacancy" sign.* **2** [C] a job that is available for someone to start doing: *There are still two vacancies on the school board.*

va·cant /ˈveɪkənt/ *adj.* **1** a vacant seat, room etc. is empty and available for someone to use: *Half of the apartments in the building are vacant.* | *There were several* ***vacant lots*** (=empty unused areas of land in a city) *downtown.* **2** FORMAL a vacant job or position in an organization is available for someone to start doing **3 a vacant expression/smile/stare etc.** an expression that shows that someone is not thinking about anything —**vacantly** *adv.*: *Loretta smiled vacantly at the others in the room.*

V

va·cate /ˈveɪkeɪt/ *v.* [T] FORMAL **1** to leave a job or position so that it is available for someone else to do: *Clay will vacate the position on June 19.* **2** to leave a seat, room etc. so that someone else can use it: *Renters have refused to vacate the building.*

va·ca·tion¹ /veɪˈkeɪʃən, və-/ S2 W3 *n.* **1** [C,U] a trip that you take to another place for pleasure: *a family vacation* | *They met* ***on vacation*** *in Thailand.* | *I don't like* ***going on vacation*** *alone.* | *We're* ***taking a*** *two-week* ***vacation*** *to Mexico.* **2** [U] a period of time when you are allowed not to work at your job, while still getting paid: *How much vacation do you get at your new job?* | *Don's* ***on vacation*** *this week.*

> **THESAURUS**
>
> **vacation** time you spend away from school or work: *Are you taking a vacation this summer?* | *We met when we were on vacation in Acapulco.*
> **holiday** a day when no one officially has to go to work or school: *the Thanksgiving holiday*
> **break** a time when you stop working or studying in order to rest, or a short vacation from school: *a ten-minute coffee break* | *Mobs of college kids come to the beaches during spring break.*
> **leave** a time when you are allowed not to work for a special reason: *Angela is on maternity leave.*

3 [C,U] a period of time when a school is closed: **summer/winter/Christmas etc. vacation** *How did you spend your summer vacation?* → see also SPRING BREAK [**Origin:** 1300–1400 Old French, Latin *vacatio* **freedom**]

vacation² *v.* [I always + adv./prep.] to go somewhere for a vacation

va·ca·tion·er /veɪˈkeɪʃənɚ/ *n.* [C] someone who has gone somewhere for a vacation

vac·ci·nate /ˈvæksəˌneɪt/ *v.* [T] MEDICINE to protect someone from a disease by giving them a vaccine: **vaccinate sb against sth** *All children should be vaccinated against measles.* → see also IMMUNIZE, INOCULATE

vac·ci·na·tion /ˌvæksəˈneɪʃən/ *n.* [C,U] MEDICINE the act or practice of INJECTing a vaccine into someone's body to prevent disease: *polio vaccinations*

vac·cine /vækˈsin/ *n.* [C,U] MEDICINE a substance which contains a weak or dead form of the BACTERIUM or VIRUS that causes a disease and is used to protect people from that disease: *a hepatitis vaccine* [**Origin:** 1700–1800 Latin *vaccinus* **of a cow**, from *vacca* **cow**; because the substance was originally obtained from sick cows]

vac·il·late /ˈvæsəˌleɪt/ *v.* [I] to continue to change your opinions, ideas, behavior etc. SYN **waver**: +**between** *She vacillated between anger and self-pity.* —**vacillation** /ˌvæsəˈleɪʃən/ *n.* [C,U]

va·cu·i·ty /væˈkyuəṭi, və-/ *n.* [U] FORMAL a lack of intelligent, interesting, or serious thought

vac·u·ole /ˈvækyuˌoʊl/ *n.* [C] BIOLOGY a small space inside a living cell, used for storing water, food, or waste

vac·u·ous /ˈvækyuəs/ *adj.* FORMAL lacking in serious thought or intelligence: *a vacuous expression* —**vacuously** *adv.* —**vacuousness** *n.* [U]

vac·uum¹ /ˈvækyum/ *n.* **1** [C] a vacuum cleaner **2** [C] PHYSICS a space that is completely empty of all gas, especially one from which all the air has been taken away **3** [singular] a situation in which someone or something is missing or lacking: **a power/political/moral etc. vacuum** *Rice's resignation has left a huge power vacuum at the company.* **4 in a vacuum** completely separately from other people or things and with no connection with them: *These laws were not made in a vacuum.* [**Origin:** 1500–1600 Latin *vacuus* **empty**]

vacuum² *v.* [I,T] to clean a place using a vacuum cleaner ►see THESAURUS box at **clean²**

ˈvacuum ˌcleaner *n.* [C] a machine that cleans floors by sucking up the dirt from them

ˈvacuum-ˌpacked *adj.* vacuum-packed food is in a container from which most of the air has been removed, so that the food will stay fresh for longer

ˈvacuum ˌtube *n.* [C] PHYSICS a closed glass tube, used to control the flow of electricity in old radios, televisions etc.

Va·duz /fɑˈduts/ the capital city of Liechtenstein

vag·a·bond /ˈvægəˌbɑnd/ *n.* [C] LITERARY someone who has no home but travels from place to place → see also VAGRANT

va·ga·ries /ˈveɪgəriz/ *n.* [plural] FORMAL unexpected changes in a situation or in someone's behavior, that you cannot control: +**of** *the vagaries of the stock market*

va·gi·na /vəˈdʒaɪnə/ *n.* [C] BIOLOGY the passage between a woman's outer sexual organs and her UTERUS [**Origin:** 1600–1700 Latin **cover for a blade, vagina**] —**vaginal** /ˈvædʒənl/ *adj.*

va·gran·cy /ˈveɪgrənsi/ *n.* [U] the criminal offense of living on the street and BEGGING from people

va·grant /ˈveɪgrənt/ *n.* [C] FORMAL someone who has no home or work, especially someone who BEGS

vague /veɪg/ *adj.* **1** unclear and lacking detail or explanation: *vague promises of support* | *His answer was very vague.* **2** someone who is vague does not explain something or does not give enough details about something: +**about** *Johann was a little vague about where he was going.* **3 have a vague idea/feeling/recollection etc.** to think that something might be true or that you remember something, although you cannot be sure: *Larry had the vague feeling he'd done something embarrassing the night before.* **4** not having a clear or definite shape or form: *She could see the vague outline of his face in the dark.* | *a vague smile* [**Origin:** 1500–1600 French, Latin *vagus* **wandering, vague**] —**vagueness** *n.* [U]

vague·ly /ˈveɪgli/ *adv.* **1** slightly: *Her face is vaguely familiar.* | *The whole situation was vaguely upsetting.*

2 not clearly: *His statement was very vaguely worded.* **3** if you vaguely remember something, know about something etc., you think you remember or know it but you are not completely sure about it: *I vaguely remembered her from school.* **4** in a way that shows you are not thinking about what you are doing: *Audrey smiled vaguely at the ceiling.*

vain /veɪn/ *adj.* **1** DISAPPROVING someone who is vain is too proud of their good looks, abilities, or position: *He is very vain about his looks.* ►see THESAURUS box at **proud** **2 in vain a)** without success in spite of your efforts: *They tried in vain to stop the mudslide.* **b)** without purpose or without positive results: *He did not die in vain.* **3 a vain attempt/hope/effort etc.** an attempt, hope etc. that fails to achieve the result you wanted: *She made a vain attempt to clean the room.* [**Origin:** 1300–1400 Old French, Latin *vanus* **empty, vain**] —**vainly** *adv.*: *He tried vainly to explain his actions.* → see also **take the name of the Lord in vain** at NAME[1] (13), VANITY

vain·glo·ri·ous /veɪn'glɔriəs/ *adj.* LITERARY too proud of your own abilities, importance etc. —**vainglory** *n.* [U] —**vaingloriously** *adv.*

val·ance /'væləns/ *n.* [C] **1** a narrow piece of cloth above a window, covering the bar that the curtains hang from **2** a narrow piece of cloth that hangs from the edge of a shelf or from the frame of a bed to the floor

vale /veɪl/ *n.* [C] LITERARY **1** a broad low valley **2 this/the vale of tears** an expression used to mean the difficulties of life

val·e·dic·to·ri·an /ˌvælədɪk'tɔriən/ *n.* [C] the student who has received the best grades all the way through high school, and usually makes a speech at the GRADUATION ceremony → see also SALUTATORIAN

val·e·dic·to·ry /ˌvælə'dɪktəri◂/ *n. plural* **valedictories** [C] FORMAL a speech or statement in which you say goodbye when you are leaving a school, job etc., especially on a formal occasion —**valedictory** *adj.*: *a valedictory speech*

va·lence /'veɪləns/ also **va·len·cy** /'veɪlənsi/ *n. plural* **valencies** [C] CHEMISTRY a measure of the ability of atoms to combine together to form compounds

val·en·tine /'vælənˌtaɪn/ *n.* [C] **1** a card you send to someone on Valentine's Day **2** someone you love or think is attractive, that you send a card to on Valentine's Day: *Be my valentine!* [**Origin:** 1400–1500 Saint *Valentine* 3rd-century Italian priest]

Valentine's ˌDay *n.* [C,U] February 14, when people give cards, candy, or flowers to people they love

Va·lé·ry /ˌvælə'ri/, **Paul** (1871–1945) a French poet

val·et /væ'leɪ, 'væleɪ/ *n.* [C] **1** also **valet parker** someone who parks your car for you at a hotel or restaurant **2** a male servant who takes care of a man's clothes, serves his meals etc. **3** someone who cleans the clothes of people staying in a hotel, on a ship etc.

ˈvalet ˌparking also **ˈvalet ˌservice** *n.* [U] the service of having someone else park your car for you at a restaurant, hotel etc.

Val·hal·la /væl'hælə/ in Norse MYTHOLOGY, a place in the Norse heaven, to which the souls of those who died bravely in battle are taken by the VALKYRIES

val·iant /'vælyənt/ *adj.* WRITTEN very brave, especially in a difficult situation: *valiant efforts to save the people in the building*

val·id /'vælɪd/ Ac *adj.* **1** a valid ticket, document, or agreement can be used legally or is officially acceptable, especially until a particular time or according to particular rules OPP **invalid**: *a valid driver's license* | *The tourist visa is valid for three months.* **2** a valid reason, argument, criticism etc. is sensible and should be considered in a serious way: *They had some valid concerns about the safety of the airplane.* **3** done according to the law, and therefore legally acceptable OPP **invalid**: *valid elections* **4** a valid PASSWORD, ID etc. is one that will be accepted by a computer system OPP **invalid** [**Origin:** 1500–1600 French *valide*, from Latin *validus* **strong, effective**]

val·i·date /'væləˌdeɪt/ Ac *v.* **1** [T] FORMAL to show that something is true or correct SYN **confirm** OPP **invalidate**: *The evidence validates her claims.* **2** [T] to make someone feel that their ideas and feelings are respected and considered seriously: *She just wants someone to validate her feelings.* **3** [T] to make a document, claim, agreement etc. officially and legally acceptable OPP **invalidate**: *The form must be validated by a Customs official.* **4** [I,T] if a business validates parking or the piece of paper you receive when you park in a PARKING GARAGE, it puts a special mark on the paper showing that it will pay the parking costs —**validation** /ˌvælə'deɪʃən/ *n.* [C,U]

ˌvalidated 'parking *n.* [U] the system in which a business pays the cost of parking for the people who use their business

va·lid·i·ty /və'lɪdəṭi/ Ac *n.* [U] **1** the state of being real, true, or based on facts: +**of** *Educators question the validity of the tests.* **2** the condition of being legally or officially acceptable

va·lise /və'lis, -'liz/ *n.* [C] OLD-FASHIONED a small SUITCASE

Val·i·um /'væliəm/ *n.* [U] TRADEMARK MEDICINE a drug to make people feel calmer and less anxious

Val·kyr·ie /væl'kɪri/ *n.* in Norse MYTHOLOGY, one of Odin's female servants, who ride their horses into battles and take the souls of dead soldiers to Valhalla

Val·let·ta /və'lɛṭə/ the capital city of Malta

val·ley /'væli/ W3 *n. plural* **valleys** [C] EARTH SCIENCE an area of lower land between two lines of hills or mountains, usually with a river flowing through it: *the Mississippi River valley* [**Origin:** 1200–1300 Old French *valee*, from *val*]

Val·ley Forge /ˌvæli 'fɔrdʒ/ a place in the U.S. state of Pennsylvania where George Washington's soldiers stayed during the winter of 1777–1778 in the American Revolutionary War. Many men died because of the cold and lack of food.

Va·lois /væl'wɑ/ the name of a family of French kings who ruled from 1328 to 1589

val·or /'vælɚ/ *n.* [U] LITERARY great courage, especially in war —**valorous** *adj.* → see also **discretion is the better part of valor** at DISCRETION (4)

val·ua·ble /'vælyəbəl, -yuəbəl/ W3 *adj.* **1** worth a lot of money OPP **worthless**: *valuable antiques*

> **THESAURUS**
>
> **precious** valuable because of being rare or expensive: *precious gems*
> **priceless** so valuable that you cannot calculate a financial value: *a priceless painting by Rembrandt*
> **worth a lot/a fortune** to be worth a very large amount of money: *Some rare baseball cards are worth a fortune.*

2 useful, helpful, and important: *I think we've all learned a valuable lesson today.* | +**in** *The drug is valuable in lowering cholesterol levels.* **3** important because there is only a limited amount available: *I won't waste any more of your valuable time.* → see also INVALUABLE

val·ua·bles /'vælyəbəlz/ *n.* [plural] things that you own that are worth a lot of money, such as jewelry, cameras etc.: *Keep valuables with you at all times.*

val·u·a·tion /ˌvælyu'eɪʃən/ *n.* [C,U] a judgment about how much something is worth, how effective or useful a particular idea or plan will be etc.

val·ue[1] /'vælyu/ S2 W1 *n.*
1 MONEY a) [C,U] the amount of money that something is worth, or the qualities that something has that make it worth the money that it costs: *Real estate values continue to rise.* | +**of** *The exact value of the painting is not known.* | **increase/decrease etc. in value** *The dollar has fallen in value against the yen.* | *The only item* ***of value*** (=worth a lot of money) *was a small bronze statue.* → see also MARKET VALUE, STREET VALUE

→ see Word Choice box at WORTH[2] **b)** [C,U] used to talk about whether something is worth the amount of money that you paid for it: **value for your money/dollars** *Customers are demanding more value for their money.* | **sth is a good/great/poor etc. value (for the money)** *The software is a great value and easy to use.* **c)** [C] used in advertising to mean a price that is lower than usual SYN **bargain**
2 IMPORTANCE [singular, U] the importance or usefulness of something: **+of** *He understands the value of friendship.* | **educational/nutritional value** *Fiber has no calories or nutritional value.* | *The locket has great* ***sentimental value*** (=importance because it was a gift, it reminds you of someone etc.). | **place/put (a) value on sth** *The company places a high value on loyalty.* | *The book will be* ***of value to*** *both students and teachers.* | **of great/little/no value** *His research has been of little practical value.*
3 values [plural] your principles about what is right and wrong, or your ideas about what is important in life: *shared cultural values*
4 shock/curiosity/novelty etc. value a good or interesting quality something has because it is surprising, different, new etc.: *Every once in a while I shave my head for shock value.*
5 MATH [C] MATH a mathematical quantity shown by a letter of the alphabet or sign
6 MUSIC [C] TECHNICAL the length of time that a musical note continues
[**Origin:** 1300–1400 Old French, Vulgar Latin *valuta*, from Latin *valere* **to be worth, be strong**] → see also FACE VALUE, FAMILY VALUES

value² W3 *v.* [T] **1** to think that something is important to you: *He valued Lucille's honesty.* **2** [usually passive] to decide how much money something is worth, by comparing it with similar things: **value sth at sth** *The estate has been valued at $3.7 million.* —**valued** *adj.*: *a valued friend*

ˌvalue-ˈadded *adj.* TECHNICAL relating to the increase in value of a product or service at each stage of its production

ˌvalue-added reˈseller ABBREVIATION **VAR** *n.* [C] TECHNICAL a person or company who sells goods after combining them with other goods or services, especially computers

ˌvalue-added ˈtax ABBREVIATION **VAT** *n.* [C,U] ECONOMICS a tax added to the price of goods and services based on their increase in value at each stage of production

ˈvalue ˌjudgment *n.* a decision or judgment about how good something is, based on opinions not facts

val·ue·less /ˈvælyulɪs/ *adj.* worth no money or very little money SYN **worthless**

valve /vælv/ *n.* [C] **1** a part of a tube or pipe that opens and shuts like a door to control the flow of liquid, gas, air etc. passing through it → see picture at BICYCLE[1] **2** BIOLOGY a part of an ARTERY or VEIN that folds or closes in order to stop blood flowing back where it came from → see picture at HEART **3** ENG. LANG. ARTS the part on a TRUMPET or similar musical instrument that you press to change the sound of the note [**Origin:** 1400–1500 Latin *valva* **part of a door**] → see also BIVALVE, SAFETY VALVE

va·moose /væˈmus, və-/ *v.* [I] SPOKEN, OLD-FASHIONED to leave a place, especially in a hurry

vamp¹ /væmp/ *n.* [C] OLD-FASHIONED a woman who uses her sexual attractiveness to make men do things for her

vamp² *v.* [I] OLD-FASHIONED to behave in a sexy way that you think will make people pay attention to you

vam·pire /ˈvæmpaɪɚ/ *n.* [C] a dead person in stories that sucks people's blood by biting their necks [**Origin:** 1700–1800 French, German *vampir*, from Serbo-Croat]

ˈvampire bat *n.* [C] a South American BAT that sucks the blood of other animals

van /væn/ S2 *n.* [C] **1** a large box-like car that can carry a lot of people **2** a truck for carrying goods with an enclosed back: *a moving van*

Van Bu·ren /væn ˈbyʊrən/, **Mar·tin** /ˈmɑrtˀn/ (1782–1862) the eighth President of the U.S. and Vice President under Andrew Jackson

Van·cou·ver /vænˈkuvɚ/ **1** the third largest city in Canada, which is in the PROVINCE of British Columbia **2** an island near the southwest coast of Canada

Van·dal /ˈvændl/ HISTORY one of the Germanic people related to the Goths that moved from Germany into Gaul, Spain, and North Africa, and attacked Rome, in the fifth century A.D.

van·dal /ˈvændl/ *n.* [C] someone who deliberately damages things, especially public property ►see THESAURUS box at **criminal**[2]

van·dal·ism /ˈvændlˌɪzəm/ *n.* [U] the crime of deliberately damaging things, especially public property

van·dal·ize /ˈvændlˌaɪz/ *v.* [T] to damage or destroy things deliberately, especially public property

Van·der·bilt /ˈvændɚˌbɪlt/, **Cor·ne·li·us** /kɔrˈniliəs/ (1794–1877) a U.S. INDUSTRIALIST who became extremely rich by building steamships and railways in the 19th century

Van Dyck /væn ˈdaɪk/, **Sir An·tho·ny** /ˈænθəni/ (1599–1641) a Flemish PAINTER

vane /veɪn/ *n.* [C] a flat surface or blade that is moved by wind or water to produce power to drive a machine → see also WEATHER VANE

Van Gogh /væn ˈgoʊ/, **Vin·cent** /ˈvɪnsɪnt/ (1853–1890) a Dutch PAINTER famous for his paintings using bright colors and thick lines of paint in circular patterns

van·guard /ˈvæŋgɑrd/ *n.* **the vanguard 1** the most advanced group or position in the development of an idea, a change etc.: **in/at the vanguard (of sth)** *a group in the vanguard of social change* **2** the leading position at the front of an army or group of ships moving into battle, or the soldiers who are in this position [**Origin:** 1400–1500 Old French *avangarde*, from *avant-garde*]

va·nil·la¹ /vəˈnɪlə/ *n.* [U] a substance used to give a special taste to ICE CREAM, cakes etc., made from the beans of a tropical plant [**Origin:** 1600–1700 Spanish *vainilla*, from *vaina* **cover for a blade**, from Latin *vagina*]

vanilla² *adj.* **1** having the taste of vanilla: *vanilla ice cream* **2** also **plain-vanilla** plain, ordinary, or uninteresting

van·ish /ˈvænɪʃ/ *v.* [I] **1** to disappear suddenly, especially in a way that cannot easily be explained: *I left the money on my desk for a second, and now it's vanished.* | *Earhart* ***vanished without a trace*** (=disappeared so that no sign remained) *on July 2, 1937.* → see also **disappear/vanish into thin air** at THIN[1] (14) **2** to stop existing, especially suddenly: *Much of the forest has now vanished.* **3 a vanishing act** INFORMAL a situation in which someone or something disappears suddenly in a way that is not expected or explained [**Origin:** 1300–1400 Old French *evanir*, from Vulgar Latin *exvanire*, from Latin *evanescere* **to disappear**]

ˈvanishing ˌpoint *n.* **the vanishing point 1** TECHNICAL the point in the distance, especially on a picture, where parallel lines seem to meet **2** the level at which something almost does not exist anymore

van·i·ty /ˈvænət̬i/ *n.* [U] **1** too much PRIDE in yourself, so that you are always thinking about yourself and your appearance **2** a DRESSING TABLE **3 the vanity of sth** LITERARY the lack of importance of something compared to other things that are much more important

ˈvanity ˌcase *n.* [C] a small box or bag with a handle used by a woman for carrying MAKEUP, a mirror etc.

ˈvanity ˌplate *n.* [C] a car LICENSE PLATE that has a combination of numbers or letters chosen by the owner, usually so that they spell a word

ˈvanity ˌpress also **ˈvanity ˌpublisher** *n.* [C usually singular] a company that writers pay to print their books

van·quish /ˈvæŋkwɪʃ/ *v.* [T] LITERARY to defeat someone or something completely

van·tage point /ˈvæntɪdʒ ˌpɔɪnt/ also **vantage** *n.* [C] **1** a good position from which you can see something: *From my vantage point on the hill, I could see the whole procession.* **2** a way of thinking about things that comes from your own particular situation or experiences SYN point of view

Van·u·a·tu /ˌvænuˈɑtu, ˌvænwɑˈtu/ a country in the southwest Pacific Ocean, east of Australia, made up of many VOLCANIC islands

vap·id /ˈvæpɪd/ *adj.* FORMAL lacking intelligence, interest, or imagination: *a vapid conversation* —**vapidly** *adv.* —**vapidness** *n.* [U] —**vapidity** /væˈpɪdəti/ *n.* [U]

va·por /ˈveɪpɚ/ *n.* **1** [C,U] CHEMISTRY a lot of very small drops of a substance floating in the air, for example because the substance has been heated: *water vapor* **2 the vapors** OLD USE a condition when you suddenly feel as if you might FAINT —**vaporous** *adj.*

va·por·ize /ˈveɪpəˌraɪz/ *v.* [I,T] SCIENCE to change into a vapor, or to make something do this —**vaporization** /ˌveɪpərəˈzeɪʃən/ *n.* [U]

va·por·izer /ˈveɪpəˌraɪzɚ/ *n.* [C] a machine that heats water to make steam for people to breathe when they are sick

ˈvapor trail *n.* [C] the white line that is left in the sky by an airplane

VAR the abbreviation of VALUE-ADDED RESELLER

var·i·a·ble¹ /ˈvɛriəbəl, ˈvær-/ Ac *adj.* **1** likely to change often: *variable weather conditions* **2** sometimes good and sometimes bad: *His work is very variable.* **3** able to be changed: *variable interest rates* —**variably** *adv.* —**variability** /ˌvɛriəˈbɪləti/ *n.* [U]

variable² /ˈvɛriəbəl, ˈvær-/ Ac *n.* [C] **1** something that may be different in different situations, so that you cannot be sure what will happen: *Many variables can affect the result of the experiment.* **2** MATH a mathematical quantity which can represent any of several different values, usually shown as a letter → see also CONSTANT

ˌvariable ˈcost *n.* [C] ECONOMICS a cost to a company or business that changes when the amount of goods being produced changes → see also FIXED COST

ˌvariable exˈpense *n.* [C] ECONOMICS an amount of money which a business has to pay, and which changes each month. For example, the cost of electricity is a variable expense because it depends on how much is used.

var·i·ance /ˈvɛriəns, ˈvær-/ Ac *n.* **1 be at variance (with sb/sth)** FORMAL if two people or things are at variance with each other, they do not agree or are very different: *Her current statement is at variance with what she said July 10.* **2** [C,U] FORMAL the amount by which two or more things are different or by which they change: *a price variance of 5%* **3** [C] LAW the official permission to do something different from what is normally allowed: *a building variance*

var·i·ant /ˈvɛriənt, ˈvær-/ Ac *n.* [C] something that is slightly different from the usual form of something: *a spelling variant* | +**of** *The game is a variant of baseball.* —**variant** *adj.*: *a variant strain of the disease*

var·i·a·tion /ˌvɛriˈeɪʃən, ˌvær-/ Ac *n.* **1** [C,U] a difference or change from the usual amount, level, or form of something: *temperature variations* | *Unemployment rates show a wide degree of regional variation.* | +**in** *variations in the quality of materials* **2** [C] something that is done in a way that is different from the way it is usually done: +**on/of** *a variation of the usual technique* | *Most of his poems are* ***variations on the theme of*** *love.* **3** [C] ENG. LANG. ARTS one of a set of short pieces of music, each based on the same simple tune

var·i·cose veins /ˌværəkoʊs ˈveɪnz/ *n.* [plural] MEDICINE a medical condition in which the VEINS in your leg become swollen and painful

var·ied /ˈvɛrid, ˈvær-/ Ac *adj.* consisting of or including many different kinds of things or people, especially in a way that seems interesting: *a varied diet*

var·i·e·gat·ed /ˈvɛrɪˌgeɪtɪd, ˈvær-/ *adj.* **1** BIOLOGY a variegated plant, leaf etc. has different colored marks on it: *variegated holly* **2** FORMAL consisting of a lot of different types of people or things

va·ri·e·tal¹ /vəˈraɪətl/ *adj.* TECHNICAL **1** made from or relating to a particular type of GRAPE: *varietal wines* **2** relating to a particular type of plant or animal

varietal² *n.* [C] TECHNICAL **1** a particular type of GRAPE **2** wine made from a particular type of GRAPE

va·ri·e·ty /vəˈraɪəti/ W2 *n. plural* **varieties** **1 a variety of sth** a lot of things of the same type that are different from each other in some way: *For a variety of reasons, our team will not be participating.* | *The T-shirts are available in* ***a wide variety of*** *colors.* **2** [C] BIOLOGY a type of something, such as a plant or animal, that is different from others in the same group: +**of** *The lake has more than 20 varieties of fish.* **3** [U] the differences within a group, set of actions etc. that make it interesting: *I really like the variety the store has to offer.* | ***Add variety to*** *your menu with a vegetable puree.* **4 of the... variety** HUMOROUS of a particular type: *The furniture was mostly of the second-hand variety.* **5 variety is the spice of life** used to say that doing a lot of different things, meeting different people etc. is what makes life interesting [**Origin:** 1500–1600 French *variété*, from Latin *varietas*, from *varius*]

vaˈriety ˌshow *n.* [C] a television or radio program or a performance that consists of many different shorter performances, especially musical and humorous ones

vaˈriety ˌstore *n.* [C] a store that sells many different kinds of goods, often at low prices

var·i·ous /ˈvɛriəs, ˈvær-/ S2 W1 *adj.* [usually before noun] **1** several different: *The jacket is available in various colors.* | *He decided to leave college* ***for various reasons.*** **2 various and sundry** of several different types

var·i·ous·ly /ˈvɛriəsli/ *adv.* in many different ways: **variously described/estimated etc.** *His age has been variously reported as 19 and 22.*

V

var·mint /ˈvɑrmənt/ *n.* [C] SPOKEN, OLD-FASHIONED **1** a small wild animal, such as a rabbit, that causes a lot of trouble **2** an annoying person

var·na /ˈvɑrnə/ *n.* the Hindu word for a large division of society into which a person is born. There are four main divisions in Hindu society. → see also CASTE

var·nish¹ /ˈvɑrnɪʃ/ *n.* [C,U] a clear liquid that is painted onto things, especially things made of wood, to protect them, or the hard shiny surface produced by this [**Origin:** 1300–1400 Old French *vernis*, from Medieval Latin *veronix* type of resin used for making varnish]

varnish² *v.* [T] to cover something with varnish → see also UNVARNISHED

var·si·ty /ˈvɑrsəti/ *n. plural* **varsities** [C,U] the main team that represents a university, college, or school in a sport: *the varsity football team* → see also JV

var·y /ˈvɛri, ˈværi/ Ac W3 *v.* **varies, varied, varying** **1** [I] to be different from others of the same type or in the same situation: *Driving regulations vary from state to state.* | +**in** *Tickets vary in price from $8 to $15.* | **vary greatly/considerably/enormously** *Estimates of the size of the population vary widely.* **2** [I] to change and be different at different times: **vary with/according to sth** *The price of seafood varies according to the season.* | *"How often do you play tennis?" "Oh,* ***it varies.****"* **3** [T] to regularly change what you do or the way that you do it: *Good writers vary the length and structure of their sentences.* → see also VARIED

var·y·ing /ˈvɛriɪŋ, ˈvær-/ *adj.* [only before noun] different from each other in degree, amount, condition etc.: *children of varying ages* | **varying degrees/levels/amounts etc. of sth** *tests with varying levels of difficulty*

vas·cu·lar /ˈvæskyəlɚ/ *adj.* BIOLOGY relating to the tubes through which liquids flow in the bodies of animals or in plants: *vascular disease*

ˌvascular ˈtissue *n.* [U] BIOLOGY material through which water, SAP, and other liquids are carried around a plant

vas def·e·rens /ˌvæs ˈdɛfərənz/ *n. plural* **vasa deferentia** /ˌveɪzə dɛfəˈrɛnʃiə/ [C] BIOLOGY a tube inside a male's body for carrying SPERM from the TESTICLES toward the PENIS

vase /veɪs, veɪz, vɑz/ *n.* [C] a container used to put flowers in or for decoration: *a vase of flowers* [**Origin:** 1500–1600 French, Latin *vas* **container**]

va·sec·to·my /vəˈsɛktəmi/ *n. plural* **vasectomies** [C,U] a medical operation to cut the small tube through which a man's SPERM passes so that he is unable to produce children

Vas·e·line /ˈvæsəˌlin, ˌvæsəˈlin/ *n.* [U] TRADEMARK a soft clear substance used for various medical and other purposes SYN **petroleum jelly**

vas·sal /ˈvæsəl/ *n.* [C] **1** a man in the Middle Ages who was given land to live on by a LORD in return for promising to work or fight for him **2** POLITICS a country that is controlled by another country: *a vassal state*

vast /væst/ W2 *adj.* **1** extremely large: *a vast improvement* | *the vast expanse of the desert* | **a vast number/amount of sth** *We received a vast amount of support.* ►see THESAURUS box at **big** **2 the vast majority (of sth)** used when you want to emphasize that something is true about almost all of a group of people or things: *The vast majority of students are honest.* [**Origin:** 1500–1600 Latin *vastus* **empty, desolate, very large**] —**vastness** *n.* [U]

vast·ly /ˈvæstli/ *adv.* very much: *vastly different opinions*

VAT /ˌvi eɪ ˈti, væt/ *n.* [C,U] ECONOMICS VALUE-ADDED TAX

vat /væt/ *n.* [C] a very large container for storing liquids in

Vat·i·can /ˈvætɪkən/ *n.* **the Vatican 1** the large PALACE in Rome where the Pope lives **2** the government of the Pope: *the Vatican's policies on birth control*

V

ˌVatican ˈCity, the an independent state in Italy, in the city of Rome, which contains the Vatican

vaude·ville /ˈvɔdvɪl, ˈvɑ-/ *n.* [U] a type of theater entertainment, popular from the 1880s to the 1950s, in which there were many short performances of different kinds, including singing, dancing, jokes etc.

Vaughan /vɔn/, **Sa·rah** /ˈsærə/ (1924–1990) a JAZZ singer

Vaughan Williams, Ralph /reɪf/ (1872–1958) a British musician who wrote CLASSICAL music

vault

vault¹ /vɔlt/ *n.* [C] **1** a room with thick walls and a strong door where money, jewels etc. are kept to prevent them from being stolen or damaged: *a bank vault* **2** a room where people from the same family are buried, often under the floor of a church **3** a jump over something → see also POLE VAULT **4** a roof or ceiling that consists of several ARCHes that are joined together, especially in a church

vault² *v.* **1** [I] to move quickly from a lower rank or level to a higher one: **+from/to** *The team vaulted to No. 2 in the rankings.* **2** [T] also **vault over** to jump over something in one movement, using your hands or a pole to help you ►see THESAURUS box at **jump¹** **3 vault sb to prominence/power** to make someone suddenly famous or important SYN **catapult** —**vaulter** *n.* [C]

vault·ed /ˈvɔltɪd/ *adj.* **a vaulted roof/ceiling etc.** a roof, ceiling etc. that consists of several ARCHes which are joined together

vault·ing¹ /ˈvɔltɪŋ/ *n.* [U] **1** ARCHes in a roof **2** the POLE VAULT

vaulting² *adj.* **vaulting ambition** LITERARY the desire to achieve as much as possible

vaunt·ed /ˈvɔntɪd, ˈvɑn-/ *adj.* a vaunted achievement, plan, quality etc. is one that people say is very good, important etc., especially with too much pride

V-chip /ˈvi tʃɪp/ *n.* [C] an electronic CHIP in a television that allows parents to prevent their children from watching programs that are violent or have sex in them

VCR *n.* [C] **video cassette recorder** a machine that is used to record television programs or to play VIDEOTAPES

VD *n.* [U] OLD-FASHIONED **venereal disease** MEDICINE a disease that is passed from one person to another during sex SYN **STD**

VDT *n.* [C] **video display terminal** COMPUTERS a machine like a television that shows the information from a computer SYN **monitor**

've /v, əv/ *v.* the short form of "have": *We've started looking through the report.*

veal /vil/ *n.* [U] meat from a CALF (=a young cow) [**Origin:** 1300–1400 Old French *veel*, from Latin *vitellus* **small calf**]

Veb·len /ˈvɛblən/, **Thor·stein** /ˈθɔrstaɪn/ (1857–1929) a U.S. ECONOMIST who wrote books about the way society is organized

vec·tor /ˈvɛktɚ/ *n.* [C] **1** MATH also **vector quantity** a quantity that has a direction as well as a size, usually represented by an ARROW **2** BIOLOGY an insect or small animal that carries disease from one person or animal to another **3** BIOLOGY a molecule of DNA that carries GENETIC material from one cell to another

Ve·das /ˈveɪdəz/ *n.* [plural] the oldest collection of Hindu holy writings, from between 1500 and 500 B.C.

vee·jay /ˈvidʒeɪ/ *n.* [C] a VJ

veep /vip/ *n.* [C] INFORMAL a VICE PRESIDENT

veer /vɪr/ *v.* [I always + adv./prep.] **1** to change direction suddenly: **+off/away/across etc.** *The truck veered across the road and nearly hit a Pontiac coming the other way.* **2** to change suddenly to a very different belief, opinion, or subject: **+toward/from etc.** *The party has veered to the right.*

veg /vɛdʒ/ also **veg out** *v.* **vegges, vegged, vegging** [I] SPOKEN to relax by doing something that needs very little effort: *We spent the whole evening vegging out in front of the TV.*

Ve·ga /ˈveɪgə/, **Lo·pe de** /ˈloʊpeɪ deɪ/ (1562–1635) a Spanish writer of plays

veg·an /ˈvigən, ˈveɪ-, ˈvɛdʒən/ *n.* [C] someone who does not eat meat, fish, eggs, cheese, or milk —**vegan** *adj.*

vege·ta·ble /ˈvɛdʒtəbəl/ S2 W3 *n.* [C] **1** BIOLOGY a plant such as a bean, CARROT, or potato which is eaten raw or cooked: *fresh fruit and vegetables* | *Make sure to eat plenty of* ***green vegetables.*** → see also FRUIT **2** INFORMAL, OFFENSIVE someone who cannot think or move because their brain has been damaged in an accident [**Origin:** 1300–1400 Medieval Latin *vegetabilis* **growing**, from *vegetare* **to grow**]

veg·e·tar·i·an /ˌvɛdʒəˈtɛriən/ *n.* [C] someone who eats only vegetables, bread, fruit, eggs etc. and does not eat meat or fish —**vegetarian** *adj.*: *a vegetarian restaurant* → see also VEGAN

veg·e·tar·i·an·ism /ˌvɛdʒəˈtɛriəˌnɪzəm/ *n.* [U] the practice of not eating meat or fish

veg·e·tate /ˈvɛdʒəˌteɪt/ *v.* [I] to not do anything and feel bored because there is nothing interesting for you to do

veg·e·ta·tion /ˌvɛdʒəˈteɪʃən/ *n.* [U] plants in general, especially in one particular area: *the island's thick vegetation*

veg·e·ta·tive /ˈvɛdʒəˌteɪt̬ɪv/ *adj.* **1 a vegetative state** a condition in which you cannot think or move because your brain has been damaged in an accident **2** relating to plants

ˌvegetative reproˈduction *n.* [U] BIOLOGY the process by which a plant produces new plants without producing seeds or SPORES SYN **asexual reproduction**

veg·gie¹ /ˈvɛdʒi/ *n.* [C usually plural] INFORMAL a vegetable

veggie² *adj.* INFORMAL **a veggie burger/sandwich/burrito etc.** a HAMBURGER, SANDWICH etc. that is made using vegetables or grain, rather than meat

ve·he·ment /ˈviəmənt/ *adj.* showing very strong feelings or opinions: *vehement protests* —**vehemently** *adv.*: *Hoff vehemently denies the accusations.* —**vehemence** *n.* [U]

ve·hi·cle /ˈviɪkəl/ Ac S3 W2 *n.* [C] FORMAL **1** something such as a car, bus etc. that is used for carrying people or things from one place to another: *a motor vehicle* **2** something that you use in order to achieve something or as a way of spreading your ideas, expressing your opinions etc.: +**for** *Drawing can be a vehicle for exploring your feelings.* **3** a movie, TV show etc. that is made to gain public attention for one of the people in it: +**for** *The movie was a star vehicle for the young actor.* [**Origin:** 1600–1700 French *véhicule*, from Latin *vehiculum*, from *vehere* **to carry**]

ve·hic·u·lar /viˈhɪkyələ/ *adj.* FORMAL relating to road vehicles: *vehicular traffic*

veil¹ /veɪl/ *n.* [C] **1** a thin piece of material worn by women to cover their faces at formal occasions such as weddings, or for religious reasons: *a bridal veil* **2 a veil of secrecy/deceit/silence etc.** something that stops you knowing the full truth about a situation: *A veil of secrecy surrounded the investigation.* **3 a veil of smoke/clouds etc.** a thin layer of smoke, clouds etc. that covers something so that you cannot see it clearly **4 the veil** the system in some Islamic countries under which women must keep their faces covered in public places

veil² *v.* [T] **1** to cover someone or something with a veil or other cloth: *The women were veiled from head to foot.* **2 be veiled in mystery/secrecy** if something is veiled in mystery or secrecy, very little is known about it and it seems mysterious

veiled /veɪld/ *adj.* **a veiled threat/attempt/hint etc.** a threat, attempt etc. that is not said or done directly, and is slightly hidden by more acceptable words or actions: ***thinly veiled** hostility*

vein /veɪn/ *n.* [C] **1** BIOLOGY one of the tubes through which blood flows toward the heart from other parts of the body → see also ARTERY → see picture at HEART **2** BIOLOGY one of the thin tubes on a leaf that allows SAP to move through it **3** BIOLOGY a structure that provides support for the wing of an insect **4** one of the thin lines on a piece of wood, cheese, MARBLE (=type of stone) etc. **5** [C] EARTH SCIENCE a thin layer of a valuable metal or mineral which is contained in rock: *a vein of gold* **6 in a... vein** [singular] in a particular style or way of doing something: **in a serious/similar/philosophical etc. vein** *poems in a more humorous vein* | *She's made a number of speeches **in the same vein**.* **7 a vein of humor/malice/talent etc.** an amount of a particular quality

veined /veɪnd/ *adj.* having a pattern of thin lines on its surface that looks like veins: *blue-veined cheese*

ve·lar /ˈvilə/ *adj.* ENG. LANG. ARTS a velar CONSONANT such as /k/ or /g/ is pronounced with the back of your tongue close to the soft part at the top of your mouth —**velar** *n.* [C]

Ve·las·quez /vəˈlɑskɪs, -ˈlæ-/, **Di·e·go Ro·drig·uez de Sil·va y** /diˈeɪgoʊ rɑˈdrigɛs də ˈsɪlvə i/ (1599–1660) a Spanish PAINTER famous for his pictures of the Spanish royal family

Vel·cro /ˈvɛlkroʊ/ *n.* [U] TRADEMARK a material used for fastening clothes, which is made from two special pieces of cloth with different surfaces that stick to each other —**Velcro** *v.* [I,T] → see picture at FASTENER

veldt, veld /vɛlt/ *n.* **the veldt** the high flat area of land in South Africa that is covered in grass and has few trees

vel·lum /ˈvɛləm/ *n.* [U] a material used for making book covers, and in the past for writing on, made from the skins of young cows, sheep, or goats

ve·loc·i·pede /vəˈlɑsəˌpid/ *n.* [C] a type of bicycle, used in the past

ve·loc·i·ty /vəˈlɑsət̬i/ *n. plural* **velocities** **1** [C,U] PHYSICS the rate at which something moves in a particular direction over a period of time: *NASA scientists have calculated the velocity of the comet.* **2** [U] FORMAL a high speed [**Origin:** 1500–1600 French *vélocité*, from Latin *velocitas*, from *velox* **fast**] → see also SPEED

vel·o·drome /ˈvɛləˌdroʊm/ *n.* [C] a circular track for bicycle racing

ve·lour /vəˈlʊr/ *n.* [U] a type of heavy cloth with a soft surface like velvet

vel·vet /ˈvɛlvɪt/ *n.* [U] a type of cloth with a soft surface on one side that is used for making clothes, curtains etc. [**Origin:** 1300–1400 Old French *veluotte*, from *velu* **hairy**, from Latin *villus* **rough hair**]

vel·vet·een /ˌvɛlvəˈtin◂/ *n.* [U] cheap material that looks like velvet

ˌvelvet revoˈlution, the HISTORY a phrase used to talk about the big social and political changes that took place in some former COMMUNIST countries, especially Czechoslovakia, during the late 1980s and early 1990s. These changes were brought about without using violence.

vel·vet·y /ˈvɛlvɪt̬i/ *adj.* looking, feeling, tasting, or sounding smooth and soft: *a deep velvety voice*

ve·na ca·va /ˌvinə ˈkeɪvə/ *n.* [C] BIOLOGY one of two large tubes that carry blood back to your heart from different parts of your body: **the superior vena cava** (=tube that returns blood to the heart from the head and the upper part of the body) | **the inferior vena cava** (=tube that returns blood to the heart from the lower part of the body) → see picture at HEART

ve·nal /ˈvinl/ *adj.* FORMAL using power in a dishonest or unfair way and accepting money as a reward for doing this —**venality** /viˈnælət̬i/ *n.* [U] → see also VENIAL

vend /vɛnd/ *v.* [T] FORMAL or LAW to sell something

vend·er /ˈvɛndə/ *n.* [C] another spelling of VENDOR

ven·det·ta /vɛnˈdɛt̬ə/ *n.* [C] **1** an effort to harm a person or group because you feel very angry about something that they did to you in the past: +**against** *a political vendetta against the former senator* **2** a serious argument that has continued for a long time between two people or groups, so that they try to harm each other [**Origin:** 1800–1900 Italian **vengeance**, from Latin *vindicta*]

ˈvending maˌchine *n.* [C] a machine that you can get candy, drinks etc. from by putting in a coin

ven·dor, vender /ˈvɛndə/ *n.* [C] **1** someone who sells things, especially on the street: *a hot-dog vendor* | *The sidewalks were crowded with **street vendors**.* **2** a company that sells a particular product or service, especially to or for another company: *a computer vendor*

ve·neer¹ /vəˈnɪr/ *n.* **1** [C,U] a thin layer of good quality wood that covers the outside of a piece of furniture which is made of a cheaper material: *walnut veneer* **2** [singular] FORMAL behavior or a quality that hides someone's real character or feelings or the way something really is: +**of** *a thin veneer of modesty*

veneer² *v.* [T + with/in] to cover something with a veneer

ven·er·a·ble /ˈvɛnərəbəl/ *adj.* **1** FORMAL or HUMOROUS a venerable person or thing is very old and respected because of their age, experience, historical importance etc.: *a venerable financial institution* **2** FORMAL also

V

Venerable considered very holy or important in a particular religion

ven·er·ate /ˈvɛnəˌreɪt/ *v.* [T] FORMAL to treat someone or something with great respect, especially because they are old or connected with the past: *Atatürk is still widely venerated in Turkey.* —**veneration** /ˌvɛnəˈreɪʃən/ *n.* [U]

ve·ne·re·al dis·ease /vəˌnɪriəl dɪˈziz/ *n.* [C,U] MEDICINE VD

Ve·ne·tian /vəˈniʃən/ *adj.* relating to or coming from Venice —**Venetian** *n.* [C]

Veˌnetian ˈblind *n.* [C] a set of long flat bars of wood, plastic, or metal which can be raised or lowered to cover a window

Ven·e·zue·la /ˌvɛnəˈzweɪlə/ a country in the north of South America, east of Colombia and west of Brazil —**Venezuelan** *n., adj.*

venge·ance /ˈvɛndʒəns/ *n.* **1** [U] the act of doing something violent or harmful that you do to someone in order to punish them for harming you, your family etc. SYN revenge: *a strong desire for vengeance against his attackers* **2 with a vengeance** more completely or with more energy than is expected or normal: *She set to work with a vengeance.* → see also AVENGE

venge·ful /ˈvɛndʒfəl/ *adj.* LITERARY very eager to punish someone: *a vengeful God* —**vengefully** *adv.*

ve·ni·al /ˈviniəl/ *adj.* FORMAL a venial fault, mistake etc. is not very serious and can therefore be forgiven: *a venial sin* → see also MORTAL SIN, VENAL

ven·i·son /ˈvɛnəsən/ *n.* [U] the meat of a DEER [**Origin:** 1200–1300 Old French *veneison* **hunting, hunted animals**, from Latin *venatio*, from *venari* **to hunt**]

Venn di·a·gram /ˈvɛn ˌdaɪəgræm/ *n.* [C] MATH a picture that shows the relationship between two sets of things by using circles that OVERLAP each other

ven·om /ˈvɛnəm/ *n.* [U] **1** BIOLOGY a liquid poison that some snakes, insects etc. produce and that they use when biting or stinging another animal or insect **2** extreme anger or hatred: *Suzanne reacted with angry venom.* [**Origin:** 1200–1300 Old French *venim*, from Latin *venenum* **use of magic power, drug, poison**]

ven·om·ous /ˈvɛnəməs/ *adj.* **1** BIOLOGY a venomous snake, insect etc. produces poison to attack its enemies **2** full of extreme hatred or anger: *a venomous attack on her ex-husband* —**venomously** *adv.*

ve·nous /ˈvinəs/ *adj.* BIOLOGY relating to the VEINS (=tubes that carry the blood) in your body

vent[1] /vɛnt/ *n.* [C] **1** a hole or pipe through which gases, smoke, liquid etc. can enter or escape from an enclosed space or a container: *an air vent* **2 give vent to sth** FORMAL to do something to express a strong feeling, especially of anger: *He gave vent to his anger and shouted at them.* **3** TECHNICAL a narrow straight opening at the bottom of a JACKET or coat, at the sides or back **4** EARTH SCIENCE a small hole in the ground through which gases and LAVA can escape from under the ground **5** BIOLOGY the small hole through which small animals, birds, fish, and snakes get rid of waste matter from their bodies

vent[2] *v.* **1** [I,T] INFORMAL to do or say something to express your feelings, especially anger, often in a way that is unfair: *Thanks for letting me vent a little.* | *He called up a friend in Chicago to* ***vent his spleen*** (=express his anger). **2** [T] to allow gases, smoke, liquid etc. to escape from an enclosed space or a container, or to make the container able to do this —**venting** *n.* [U]

ven·ti·late /ˈvɛntlˌeɪt/ *v.* [T] **1** to let fresh air into a room, building etc.: *Ventilate your house when painting.* **2** FORMAL to express your opinions or feelings about something [**Origin:** 1400–1500 Latin, past participle of *ventilare*, from *ventus* **wind**] —**ventilation** /ˌvɛntlˈeɪʃən/ *n.* [U] *a ventilation system*

ven·ti·lat·ed /ˈvɛntlˌeɪtɪd/ *adj.* **1** a ventilated room or space has fresh air passing through it: **well/poorly etc. ventilated** *Make sure the attic is well ventilated.* **2** something that is ventilated has holes cut in it to allow air to pass in and out: *ventilated shoes*

ven·ti·la·tor /ˈvɛntlˌeɪtə/ *n.* [C] **1** a piece of equipment that pumps air into and out of someone's lungs when they cannot breathe without help SYN respirator **2** a thing designed to let fresh air into a room, building etc.

ven·tral /ˈvɛntrəl/ *adj.* [only before noun] BIOLOGY relating to the stomach of an animal or fish → see also DORSAL

ven·tri·cle /ˈvɛntrɪkəl/ *n.* [C] BIOLOGY **1** one of the two spaces in the bottom of your heart from which blood is pumped out into your body → see also AURICLE → see picture at HEART **2** a small hollow place in your brain or in an organ

ven·tril·o·quist /vɛnˈtrɪləˌkwɪst/ *n.* [C] someone who can speak without moving their lips and makes the sound seem to come from a DUMMY (=figure of a person or animal), usually as part of a performance —**ventriloquism** *n.* [U]

ven·ture[1] /ˈvɛntʃə/ W3 *n.* [C] a new business activity that involves taking risks: *his latest business venture* [**Origin:** 1400–1500 *adventure*] → see also JOINT VENTURE

venture[2] *v.* FORMAL **1** [I always + adv./prep.] to risk going somewhere when it could be dangerous: **+out/through/into etc.** *I take my dog with me when I venture out at night.* **2** [T] to risk saying or doing something although you are not sure of it, or are afraid of how someone may react to it: *She ventured a glance in his direction.* | *If I may* ***venture an opinion****, I'd say the plan needs more thought.* | **venture to say/ask/claim etc.** *I couldn't even venture to guess how much money he makes.* **3 nothing ventured, nothing gained** used to say that you cannot achieve anything unless you take a risk **4** [T] to take the risk of losing something SYN gamble

ˈventure ˌcapital ABBREVIATION **VC** *n.* [U] ECONOMICS money that is lent to someone so that they can start a new business —**venture capitalist** *n.* [C]

ven·ture·some /ˈvɛntʃəsəm/ *adj.* LITERARY **1** always ready to take risks: *a venturesome spirit* **2** a venturesome action involves taking risks

ven·ue /ˈvɛnyu/ *n.* [C] a place or a building where people go for an arranged event or activity: *a 2,500-seat concert venue* [**Origin:** 1500–1600 Old French **coming**, from *venir* **to come**, from Latin *venire*]

Ve·nus /ˈvinəs/ *n.* **1** PHYSICS the PLANET that is second in order from the sun → see picture at SOLAR SYSTEM **2** the Roman name for the goddess Aphrodite

Venus fly·trap /ˌvinəs ˈflaɪtræp/ *n.* [C] a plant that catches and eats insects

ve·rac·i·ty /vəˈræsəṭi/ *n.* [U] FORMAL the quality of being true or of telling the truth —**veracious** /vəˈreɪʃəs/ *adj.*

ve·ran·da, verandah /vəˈrændə/ *n.* [C] an open area with a floor and usually a roof but no walls that is built on the side of a house

verb /vəb/ *n.* [C] ENG. LANG. ARTS a word or group of words that is used to describe an action, experience, or state, for example "see," "be," "put on," or "may" [**Origin:** 1300–1400 Old French *verbe*, from Latin *verbum* **word, verb**] → see also AUXILIARY VERB, PHRASAL VERB

ver·bal /ˈvəbəl/ *adj.* **1** spoken, rather than written: *verbal communication* → see also NONVERBAL **2** relating to spoken language and your ability to use it: *verbal skills* **3** using words, rather than actions: *verbal abuse* **4** ENG. LANG. ARTS relating to a verb —**verbally** *adv.*

ver·bal·ize /ˈvəbəˌlaɪz/ *v.* [I,T] FORMAL to express something in words: *Encourage your children to verbalize their feelings.*

ˌverbal ˈnoun *n.* [C] ENG. LANG. ARTS a GERUND

ver·ba·tim /vəˈbeɪṭɪm/ *adj., adv.* repeating the actual words that were spoken or written: *a verbatim quote* | *She recited the speech verbatim.*

ver·bi·age /ˈvəbi-ɪdʒ/ *n.* [U] FORMAL, DISAPPROVING too many unnecessary words in speech or writing

ver·bose /vəˈbous/ *adj.* FORMAL, DISAPPROVING talking

too much, or using or containing too many words —**verbosity** /vɚˈbɑsət̬i/ *n.* [U] → see also VERBAL

ver·bo·ten /vɚˈboʊtˀn, fɚ-/ *adj.* HUMOROUS not allowed SYN **forbidden**: *Smoking in the workplace is now strictly verboten.*

ver·dant /ˈvɚdənt/ *adj.* LITERARY verdant land is covered with freshly growing green grass and plants

Ver·di /ˈvɛrdi/, **Giu·sep·pe** /dʒʊˈsɛpi/ (1813–1901) an Italian musician who wrote OPERAS

ver·dict /ˈvɚdɪkt/ *n.* [C] **1** LAW an official decision made by a JURY in a court of law about whether someone is guilty or not guilty of a crime: *a guilty verdict* | *The jury* ***reached a verdict*** *after four days of deliberation.* | **return/deliver/render a verdict** (=give a verdict) ▸see THESAURUS box at **court**[1] **2** an official decision or opinion made by a person or group that has authority: *The Ethics Committee will deliver its verdict next week.* **3** INFORMAL an opinion or decision about something: +**on** *What's your verdict on the movie?* [**Origin:** 1200–1300 Anglo-French, Old French *ver* **true** + *dit* **saying, judgment**]

ver·di·gris /ˈvɚdə,gri, -,gris/ *n.* [U] a greenish-blue substance that forms a thin layer on COPPER or BRASS when they are kept in wet conditions

ver·dure /ˈvɚdʒɚ, -dyɚ/ *n.* [U] LITERARY the bright green color of grass, plants, trees etc., or the plants themselves

verge[1] /vɚdʒ/ *n.* [C] **be on the verge of (doing) sth** to be about to do something: *I was on the verge of giving up.* | *She looked like she was on the verge of tears.* [**Origin:** 1300–1400 Old French **long pole**, from Latin *virga*; from *within the verge* **within the area controlled by someone who carried a pole as a sign of authority**]

verge[2] *v.*

verge on sth *phr. v.* to be very close to an extreme or harmful state or condition: *His attitude verged on defiance.* | **verge on the impossible/ridiculous etc.** *Sometimes his beliefs verge on the fanatical.*

ver·i·fi·ca·tion /,vɛrəfəˈkeɪʃən/ *n.* [U] **1** the act of checking whether something is real, true, legal, or allowed: +**of** *international verification of the ceasefire* **2** proof that something is real, true, legal, or allowed: +**of** *We need verification of your name and address.*

ver·i·fy /ˈvɛrə,faɪ/ *v.* **verifies, verified, verifying** [T] **1** to find out if a fact, statement etc. is correct or true SYN **check**: *Accountants are working to verify the figures.* | **verify that** *Could you call to verify that our names are still on the list?* **2** to state that something is true SYN **confirm**: *The man's statement was verified by several witnesses.* [**Origin:** 1300–1400 Old French *verifier*, from Medieval Latin *verificare*, from Latin *verus* **true**] —**verifiable** /,vɛrəˈfaɪəbəl/ *adj.*

ver·i·ly /ˈvɛrəli/ *adv.* BIBLICAL truly

ver·i·si·mil·i·tude /,vɛrəsəˈmɪlə,tud/ *n.* [U] FORMAL the quality of a piece of art, a performance etc. that makes it seem like something real

ver·i·ta·ble /ˈvɛrət̬əbəl/ *adj.* FORMAL a word used to emphasize a comparison that you think is correct: *The island is a veritable paradise for walkers.* —**veritably** *adv.*

ver·i·ty /ˈvɛrət̬i/ *n. plural* **verities** [C usually plural] FORMAL an important principle or fact about life, the world etc., that is true in all situations

Ver·laine /vɚˈleɪn, -ˈlɛn/, **Paul** (1844–1896) a French poet

Ver·meer /vɚˈmɪr/, **Jan** /yɑn/ (1632–1675) a Dutch PAINTER famous for his pictures of ordinary scenes from daily life

ver·mi·cel·li /,vɚməˈtʃɛli, -ˈsɛli/ *n.* [U] a type of PASTA that is in the shape of long thin strings

ver·mil·lion /vɚˈmɪlyən/ *n.* [U] a very bright red-orange color —**vermillion** *adj.*

ver·min /ˈvɚmɪn/ *n.* [plural] **1** BIOLOGY small animals or insects that are harmful or difficult to control → see also PEST **2** people who cause strong feelings of DISGUST or hate [**Origin:** 1200–1300 Old French, Latin *vermen* **worm**] —**verminous** *adj.*

Ver·mont /vɚˈmɑnt/ WRITTEN ABBREVIATION **VT** a state in the northeastern U.S.

ver·mouth /vɚˈmuθ/ *n.* [U] an alcoholic drink made from wine that has strong-tasting substances added to it

ver·nac·u·lar /vɚˈnækyəlɚ/ *n.* [C usually singular] ENG. LANG. ARTS the language or form of a language that ordinary people use in a country or area, as opposed to the official language or formal language: *In Anglo-Saxon times, portions of the Bible had been translated from Latin into the vernacular.* [**Origin:** 1600–1700 Latin *vernaculus* **born in a place**, from *verna* **slave born in his or her owner's house**] —**vernacular** *adj.*

ver·nal /ˈvɚnl/ *adj.* [only before noun] LITERARY or TECHNICAL relating to the spring season: *the vernal equinox* → see also AUTUMNAL

Verne /vɚn/, **Jules** /dʒulz/ (1828–1905) a French writer of SCIENCE FICTION

ver·sa /ˈvɚsə/ → see VICE VERSA

ver·sa·tile /ˈvɚsət̬l/ *adj.* APPROVING **1** good at doing a lot of different things and able to learn new skills quickly and easily: *a versatile athlete* **2** having many different uses: *Few foods are as versatile as cheese.* [**Origin:** 1600–1700 French, Latin *versatilis* **turning easily**, from *versare* **to turn**] —**versatility** /,vɚsəˈtɪlət̬i/ *n.* [U]

verse /vɚs/ *n.* ENG. LANG. ARTS **1** [C] a set of lines that forms one part of a song: *Let's sing the last verse again.* → see also CHORUS **2** [U] words arranged in the form of poetry: *The entire play is written* ***in verse.*** → see also BLANK VERSE, FREE VERSE, PROSE **3** [C] a set of lines of poetry that forms one part of a poem, especially when it has a pattern that is repeated in the other parts **4** [C] one of the numbered groups of sentences that make up each CHAPTER of a book of the Bible → see also **give/quote chapter and verse** at CHAPTER (5)

versed /vɚst/ *adj.* **be (well) versed in sth** to know a lot about a subject, or to be skillful at doing something: +**in** *The judges are all highly versed in Islamic law.* → see also WELL-VERSED

ver·si·fi·ca·tion /,vɚsəfəˈkeɪʃən/ *n.* [U] TECHNICAL the particular pattern that a poem is written in

ver·sion /ˈvɚʒən/ Ac S2 W2 *n.* [C] **1** a copy of something that is slightly different from other forms of it: *I prefer the original version.* | +**of** *the latest version of the software* **2** a description of an event given by one person, especially when it is compared with someone else's description of the same thing: +**of** *I'm not sure I believe Bobby's version of the story.* ▸see THESAURUS box at **account**[1] **3** a translation of a book, poem, or other piece of writing: +**of** *the King James Version of the Bible* **4** something that is the typical way that one group of people do, experience, or understand a particular type of thing: +**of** *the male version of the menopause* [**Origin:** 1500–1600 French, Medieval Latin *versio* **turning**, from Latin *versus*]

ver·so /ˈvɚsoʊ/ *n.* [C] TECHNICAL a page on the LEFT-HAND side of a book —**verso** *adj.* → see also RECTO

ver·sus /ˈvɚsəs/ S2 *prep.* **1** used when comparing the advantages of two different things, ideas etc.: *It's a question of speed versus accuracy.* | *the old debate about nature versus nurture* **2** used to say that a situation involves one person or thing competing or fighting against another person or thing SYN **against**: *The movie tells a story of man versus nature.* **3** WRITTEN ABBREVIATION **vs.** or **v.** used to show that two players or teams are competing against each other: *the Broncos versus New England* **4** WRITTEN ABBREVIATION **vs.** or **v.** used to say that two people, groups, or organizations are opposing each other in a court case: *the Supreme Court decision in Brown vs. Board of Education* [**Origin:** 1400–1500 Medieval Latin **toward, against**, from Latin *vertere*]

ver·te·bra /ˈvɚṭəbrə/ *n. plural* **vertebrae** /-breɪ, -bri/ [C] BIOLOGY one of the small hollow bones that together make the BACKBONE —**vertebral** *adj.* → see picture at SKELETON[1]

ver·te·brate /ˈvɚṭəbrət, -ˌbreɪt/ *n.* [C] BIOLOGY an animal that has a BACKBONE —**vertebrate** *adj.* → see also INVERTEBRATE

ver·tex /ˈvɚtɛks/ *n. plural* **vertices** /-təsiz/ or **vertexes** [C + of] **1** the highest point of something **2** MATH the point where two sides of a POLYGON or three or more sides of a POLYHEDRON meet **3** MATH the highest or lowest point on a PARABOLA

ver·ti·cal[1] /ˈvɚṭɪkəl/ *adj.* **1** MATH pointing straight up and down in a line and forming an angle of 90 degrees with the ground or with another straight line: *vertical stripes* | *The ride includes a vertical drop of 180 feet.* **2** having a structure in which there are top, middle, and bottom levels: *a vertical management arrangement* **3** TECHNICAL involving all the different stages of a product or service, from producing it to selling it: *vertical integration of the industry* [**Origin:** 1500–1600 Late Latin *verticalis*, from Latin *vertex*] —**vertically** /-kli/ *adv.* → see also HORIZONTAL

vertical

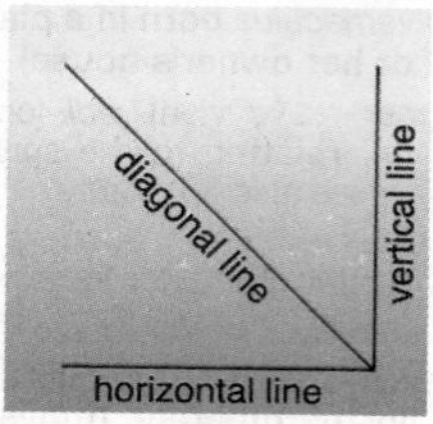

vertical[2] *n.* **1 the vertical** the direction or position of something that is vertical **2** [C] a vertical line, post etc.

ˌvertical ˈclimate *n.* [singular] the weather patterns in an area considered in relation to the different heights of the land above sea level in that area: *a diagram of the vertical climate zones in the Andes*

ˌvertical consoliˈdation *n.* [C,U] ECONOMICS the process in which a company gets control of the companies responsible for all the different stages of making and selling a particular product

ˌvertical inteˈgration *n.* [U] ECONOMICS the process in which a company controls all the different stages in making and selling a particular product

ˌvertical ˈmerger *n.* [C] ECONOMICS a MERGER (=occasion when two or more companies combine to form one larger company) between two or more companies who are involved in producing the same product or service at different stages in the production process

ver·tig·i·nous /vɚˈtɪdʒənəs/ *adj.* FORMAL **1** making you feel DIZZY and sick: *a vertiginous 400-foot drop* **2** feeling DIZZY and sick

ver·ti·go /ˈvɚṭɪˌgoʊ/ *n.* [U] MEDICINE a sick DIZZY feeling, often caused by looking down from a very high place or by too much movement around you

verve /vɚv/ *n.* [U] the quality of being cheerful and excited, which is shown in the way someone does something

ve·ry[1] /ˈvɛri/ S1 W1 *adv.* **1** [+ adj./adv.] used to emphasize an adjective or adverb: *It's very cold outside.* | *She'll be leaving very soon.* | *His accent is very French.* **2** [+ adj.] used to emphasize SUPERLATIVE adjectives and other adjectives that tell specifically which person or thing you are talking about: *Carter went to the very best schools.* | *We finished at the very last minute.* | *The two brothers died on the very same day.* | *Give me your paper by Friday* ***at the very latest.*** **3 not very a)** only slightly: *I'm not very worried about it.* **b)** used before a quality to mean exactly the opposite of that quality: *She's not very smart* (=she's fairly stupid). **4 sb's very own (sth)** used to emphasize the fact that something belongs to one particular person and to no one else: *I finally have my very own bedroom.* **5 very much** a lot, or to a great degree: *I love you very much.* | *I haven't read very much of the book yet.* **6 very few** an extremely small number of people or things: *Very few of us have cars.* **7 very many** [especially in negatives and questions] a large number of people or things: *She doesn't have many friends.* | *It may be many years before something like this happens again.* **8 sb can't very well do sth** SPOKEN used to say that it would not be appropriate or possible for someone to do something: *I already invited them! I can't very well ask them not to come now.* **9 very much so** SPOKEN used to emphasize that you mean "yes" or "to a great degree": *"Were you surprised?" "Very much so."* **10 very well/good** SPOKEN FORMAL said when you understand and accept what someone has said, especially when you are not happy about it

GRAMMAR

Do not use **very** to emphasize adjectives or adverbs that already have strong meanings, such as "starving," "huge," "terrible" etc.: *By the time I got home I was exhausted* (NOT *very exhausted*). Do not use **very** before phrases that begin with "in," "on," "at" etc. In formal English, you can use **very much** instead: *His life is very much in danger* (NOT *very in danger*).

very[2] S2 W2 *adj.* **1 the/this/that very...** used to emphasize that you are talking about one particular thing or person, not about any other thing or person: *He died in this very room.* | *We have to leave* ***this very minute*** (=now). | *Then she went and did* ***the very thing*** *I had asked her not to.* **2 the very top/back/beginning etc.** used to emphasize an extreme point in time or position in space: *We stayed till the very end of the parade.* | *The keys were in the very bottom of my purse.* **3** used to emphasize the great effect of something that seems slight or unimportant: ***The very idea that*** *Dawn could become a famous actress is ridiculous.* | *Abby was disgusted by* ***the very thought of*** (=just thinking about) *touching him.* **4** used to emphasize that something is very important or basic: *The decision changed the very nature of our political system.* **5 (right) before sb's very eyes** used to say that someone directly sees or experiences something important, surprising, or shocking: *His career was being destroyed before his very eyes.* [**Origin:** 1200–1300 Old French *verai*, from Latin *verax* **truthful**, from *verus* **true**]

ˌvery high ˈfrequency *n.* [U] VHF

ˌvery low ˈfrequency *n.* [U] TECHNICAL VLF

ves·pers /ˈvɛspɚz/ *n.* [U] the evening service in some types of Christian churches

Ves·puc·ci /vɛˈsputʃi/, **A·mer·i·go** /əˈmɛrɪˌgoʊ/ (1451–1512) an Italian sailor and EXPLORER who sailed to the Caribbean Sea and South America and discovered the place where the Amazon River flows into the ocean, and after whom America was named

ves·sel /ˈvɛsəl/ *n.* [C] **1** FORMAL a ship or large boat: *a sailing vessel* **2** BIOLOGY a tube that carries blood through your body, such as a VEIN, or that carries liquid through a plant: *a blood vessel* **3** FORMAL a container for holding liquids

vest[1] /vɛst/ *n.* [C] **1** a piece of clothing without SLEEVES that has buttons down the front and is worn over a shirt, often under a JACKET as part of a suit **2** a SWEATER without SLEEVES **3** a piece of special clothing without SLEEVES that is worn to protect your body: *a bulletproof vest* [**Origin:** 1600–1700 French *veste*, from Latin *vestis* **piece of clothing**]

vest[2] *v.* **1** [T usually passive] FORMAL to give someone the official or legal right to use power, property etc.: **vest sb with sth** *The agency has been vested with the authority to regulate work conditions.* **2** [I] TECHNICAL if a right, piece of property, STOCK OPTION etc. vests, it becomes the property of someone and cannot be taken away from them

Ves·ta /ˈvɛstə/ the Roman name for the goddess Hestia

vest·ed /ˈvɛstɪd/ *adj.* **1** vested rights, property etc. belong to you and cannot be taken away: +**in** *The power to grant pardons is vested in the President.* **2** having full rights to use or keep money or property **3** wearing a vest

ˌvested ˈinterest *n.* **1** [C,U] a strong reason for wanting something to happen because you will get an advantage from it: *We all* ***have a vested interest*** *in making this peace process work.* **2 vested interests**

[plural] the groups of people who have a vested interest in something, especially those who will gain financially from it

ves·ti·bule /ˈvɛstəˌbyul/ *n.* [C] FORMAL **1** a wide passage or small room inside the front door of a public building **2** the enclosed passage at each end of a railroad car that connects it with the next car

ves·tige /ˈvɛstɪdʒ/ *n.* [C] FORMAL **1** a small part or amount of something that still remains when most of it does not exist anymore: *The new laws get rid of* ***the last vestiges of*** *royal power.* **2** the smallest possible amount of a quality or feeling: **+of** *He spoke without a vestige of sympathy.*

ves·tig·i·al /vɛˈstɪdʒiəl, -dʒəl/ *adj.* **1** FORMAL remaining as a sign that something existed after most of it has disappeared: *vestigial remnants of colonial rule* **2** BIOLOGY a vestigial body part on an animal has almost disappeared and has no use: *Some snakes have vestigial legs.*

vest·ment /ˈvɛstmənt/ *n.* [C usually plural] a piece of clothing worn by priests during church services

vest-ˈpocket *adj.* [only before noun] **1** using only a small amount of space: *a vest-pocket park* **2** made to fit inside a VEST pocket

ves·try /ˈvɛstri/ *n. plural* **vestries** [C] a small room in a church where the priest and CHOIR change into their vestments and where holy plates, cups etc. are stored

Ve·su·vi·us /vəˈsuviəs/ also **Mount Vesuvius** a VOLCANO in southeast Italy

vet[1] /vɛt/ *n.* [C] INFORMAL **1** a VETERINARIAN **2** a VETERAN: *a Vietnam vet*

vet[2] *v.* **vetted, vetting** [T] **1** to check someone's past activities, relationships etc. in order to make sure they are the right person for a particular job, especially one that involves dealing with secret information: *All applicants are vetted before they are offered a job.* **2** to check a report or speech carefully to make sure it is acceptable

vet·er·an[1] /ˈvɛt̬ərən/ W2 *n.* [C] **1** someone who has been a soldier, sailor etc. in a war: *Gulf War veterans* **2** someone who has had a lot of experience of a particular activity: **+of** *a veteran of the 1960s civil rights battles* [**Origin:** 1500–1600 Latin *veteranus* **old, of long experience**, from *vetus* **old**]

veteran[2] *adj.* [only before noun] having a lot of experience in a particular activity: *a veteran journalist*

Veterans Day *n.* [C,U] a holiday on November 11 to honor people who fought in a war as soldiers, sailors etc.

Veterans of ˌForeign ˈWars → VFW

vet·er·i·nar·i·an /ˌvɛt̬ərəˈnɛriən, ˌvɛtrə-, ˌvɛtˀnˈɛr-/ *n.* [C] someone who is trained to give medical care and treatment to sick animals SYN vet

vet·er·i·nar·y /ˈvɛt̬ərəˌnɛri, ˈvɛtrə-/ *adj.* [only before noun] TECHNICAL relating to the medical care and treatment of sick animals: *veterinary medicine* [**Origin:** 1700–1800 Latin *veterinarius* **of animals used for carrying loads**, from *veterinae* **animals used for carrying loads**]

ve·to[1] /ˈvit̬oʊ/ *v.* **vetoes, vetoed, vetoing** [T] **1** to officially refuse to allow something to happen, especially something that other people or organizations have agreed: *The governor vetoed another version of the bill last fall.* **2** to refuse to accept a particular plan or suggestion: *Jenny wanted to invite all her friends, but I quickly vetoed that idea.*

veto[2] *n. plural* **vetoes** [C,U] POLITICS a refusal to give official permission for something, or the right to refuse to give such permission: *Congress has voted to* ***override*** *the President's* ***veto*** *of the labor bill* (=change his decision to refuse permission for it). [**Origin:** 1600–1700 Latin **I refuse to allow**, from *vetare* **to forbid**]

vex /vɛks/ *v.* [T] OLD-FASHIONED to make someone feel annoyed or worried → see also VEXED, VEXING

vex·a·tion /vɛkˈseɪʃən/ *n.* **1** [U] FORMAL the feeling of being worried or annoyed by something **2** [C] OLD-FASHIONED something that worries or annoys you

vex·a·tious /vɛkˈseɪʃəs/ *adj.* OLD-FASHIONED making you feel annoyed or worried

vexed /vɛkst/ *adj.* **1** OLD-FASHIONED annoyed or worried **2 a vexed question/issue** a complicated problem that has caused a lot of arguments and is difficult to solve

vex·ing /ˈvɛksɪŋ/ *adj.* making you feel annoyed or worried: *a vexing problem*

V-for·ma·tion /ˈvi fɔrˌmeɪʃən/ *n.* [C] if birds or airplanes fly in a V-formation, they form the shape of the letter V as they fly

VFW **Veterans of Foreign Wars** a U.S. organization for former soldiers who have fought in wars abroad

VGA *n.* [singular] COMPUTERS **video graphics array** a standard of GRAPHICS (=pictures and letters) on a computer screen that has many different colors and is of a high quality

VHF *n.* [U] **very high frequency** a range of radio WAVES between 30 and 300 MEGAHERTZ, used also for television → see also UHF

VHS *n.* [U] TRADEMARK the most common type of VIDEOTAPE

vi·a /ˈvaɪə, ˈviə/ Ac W3 *prep.* **1** traveling through a place on the way to another place: *We flew to Bali via Singapore.* **2** using a particular person, machine etc. to send something: *Email is sent via the Internet.* [**Origin:** 1600–1700 Latin **by way of**, from *via* **way**]

vi·a·ble /ˈvaɪəbəl/ *adj.* **1** able to be successful or be done successfully: *a viable presidential candidate* | **a viable alternative/option/solution** *No one has offered a viable alternative to the plan.* | **economically/commercially/politically etc. viable** *a commercially viable business* **2** TECHNICAL able to continue to live or to develop into a living thing: *viable embryos* —**viability** /ˌvaɪəˈbɪlət̬i/ *n.* [U]

vi·a·duct /ˈvaɪəˌdʌkt/ *n.* [C] a long high bridge across a valley that has a road or railroad track on it

Vi·ag·ra /vaɪˈægrə/ *n.* [U] TRADEMARK a drug that helps men have ERECTIONS

vi·al /ˈvaɪəl/ *n.* [C] a small bottle, especially for liquid medicines

vi·ands /ˈvaɪəndz/ *n.* [plural] OLD USE food

vibe /vaɪb/ *n.* INFORMAL **1** [C] the feelings that a particular person, group, or situation seems to produce and that you react to: **a good/bad/strange etc. vibe** *The place has a good vibe.* **2 vibes** INFORMAL a vibraphone

vi·brant /ˈvaɪbrənt/ *adj.* **1** exciting and full of activity and energy: *Hong Kong is a vibrant fascinating city.* **2** a vibrant color or light is bright and strong: *vibrant fall colors* **3** loud and powerful: *a vibrant voice* —**vibrancy** *n.* [U] —**vibrantly** *adv.*

vi·bra·phone /ˈvaɪbrəˌfoʊn/ *n.* [C] a musical instrument that consists of metal bars that you hit to produce a sound —**vibraphonist** *n.* [C]

vi·brate /ˈvaɪbreɪt/ *v.* [I,T] to shake or make something shake continuously with small fast movements: *Strings vibrate more quickly if they are short and thin.* [**Origin:** 1600–1700 Latin, past participle of *vibrare* **to shake**]

vi·bra·tion /vaɪˈbreɪʃən/ *n.* [C,U] **1** a continuous slight shaking movement: *the vibrations of the ship's engine* **2** INFORMAL, OLD-FASHIONED [C usually plural] a VIBE

vib·ra·to /vɪˈbrɑt̬oʊ, vaɪ-/ *n.* [U] a way of singing or playing a musical note so that it goes up and down very slightly in PITCH

vi·bra·tor /ˈvaɪbreɪt̬ɚ/ *n.* [C] a piece of electrical equipment that produces a small shaking movement, used especially in MASSAGE or to get sexual pleasure

vic·ar /ˈvɪkɚ/ *n.* [C] **1** a Catholic priest who represents a BISHOP or the Pope **2** an Episcopal priest who is in charge of a CHAPEL **3** a priest in the official Church of England who is in charge of a church in a particular area [**Origin:** 1300–1400 Latin *vicarius* **deputy**]

vic·ar·age /ˈvɪkərɪdʒ/ *n.* [C] a house where a vicar lives

vi·car·i·ous /vaɪˈkɛriəs/ *adj.* [only before noun] experienced by watching, hearing, or reading about someone else doing something, rather than by doing it yourself: **vicarious pleasure/satisfaction/excitement etc.** *I got a vicarious thrill listening to his stories.* —**vicariously** *adv.*: *Many viewers live vicariously through the show.*

vice¹ /vaɪs/ *adj.* **a vice principal/chairman/mayor etc.** a person next in official rank below someone in a position of authority, who can represent them or act instead of them

vice² *n.* **1** [U] **a)** criminal activities that involve sex, drugs, GAMBLING etc. **b)** the part of the police department that deals with this type of crime **2** [C] a bad habit: *Smoking is his only vice.* **3** [C,U] a bad or immoral quality in someone's character or behavior OPP **virtue** **4** [C] another spelling of VISE [**Origin:** (1–3) 1200–1300 Old French, Latin *vitium* **fault, vice**]

ˌvice ˈadmiral *n.* [C] a high rank in the navy, or someone who has this rank

ˌvice ˈchancellor *n.* [C] someone who is in charge of a particular part of some universities

ˌvice ˈpresident W2 *n.* [C] **1** the person who is next in rank to the president of a country and who is responsible for the president's duties if he or she is unable to do them **2** someone who is responsible for a particular part of a company: *the vice president of marketing*

vice·roy /ˈvaɪsrɔɪ/ *n.* [C] a man who was sent by the king or queen to rule another country in the past

ˈvice squad *n.* [C usually singular] the part of the police force that deals with crimes involving sex, drugs, GAMBLING etc.

vi·ce ver·sa /ˌvaɪs ˈvɚsə, ˌvaɪsə-/ *adv.* used to mean the opposite of a situation you have just described: *There's a bag for you and a box for Tom, or vice versa.*

vi·chys·soise /ˌviʃiˈswɑz/ *n.* [U] a thick potato soup, usually served cold

V

vi·cin·i·ty /vəˈsɪnət̬i/ *n.* FORMAL **1** [U] the area around a particular place: **in the vicinity (of sth)** *There were no schools in the vicinity.* | *Tens of thousands of people live **in the immediate vicinity of** the volcano.* **2 in the vicinity of sth** close to a particular amount or measurement: *We have raised in the vicinity of one million dollars.* [**Origin:** 1500–1600 Latin *vicinitas*, from *vicinus* **near**, from *vicus* **row of houses, village**]

vi·cious /ˈvɪʃəs/ *adj.* **1** violent and dangerous, and likely to hurt someone: *vicious dogs* | *It was a particularly vicious attack.* **2** cruelly and deliberately trying to hurt someone's feelings or make their character seem bad: *John gets pretty vicious when he's drunk.* | **a vicious attack/campaign/rumor etc.** *a vicious attack on his opponent* **3** very strong or severe: *a vicious headache* [**Origin:** 1300–1400 Old French *vicieux*, from Latin *vitiosus* **full of faults**] —**viciously** *adv.*: *The dog growled viciously.* —**viciousness** *n.* [U]

ˌvicious ˈcircle also **ˌvicious ˈcycle** *n.* [singular] a situation in which one problem causes another problem that then causes the first problem again, so that the whole process continues to be repeated

vi·cis·si·tudes /vəˈsɪsəˌtudz/ *n.* [plural] FORMAL the continuous changes and problems that affect a situation or someone's life: +**of** *the vicissitudes of married life*

Vicks·burg /ˈvɪksbɚg/ a city in the U.S. state of Mississippi, where an important battle was fought during the American Civil War

vic·tim /ˈvɪktɪm/ W2 *n.* [C]
1 CRIME someone who has been attacked, robbed, or murdered: *The victim died of head injuries.* | +**of** *victims of crime* | **a crime/rape/murder etc. victim** *Most homicide victims are under 30.*
2 BAD SITUATION/DISEASE someone who suffers because they are affected by a bad situation or by an illness: +**of** *a victim of a tragic accident* | **famine/earthquake/flood etc. victims** *Flood victims spent the night in local shelters.* | **a polio/cholera/AIDS etc. victim** *new treatments for breast cancer victims* | **a victim of circumstance** (=someone who suffers because of something they cannot control)
3 OTHERS' TREATMENT someone who has suffered as a result of the actions or negative attitudes of someone else or of people in general: *I think she likes to think of herself as a victim.* | +**of** *victims of oppression*
4 RUINED something that is badly affected or destroyed by a situation or action: *Many small businesses have **fallen victim to*** (=became a victim of) *the recession.*
5 be a victim of its own success to be badly affected by some unexpected results of being very successful
[**Origin:** 1400–1500 Latin *victima* **person or animal killed as a religious offering**] → see also FASHION VICTIM

vic·tim·ize /ˈvɪktəˌmaɪz/ *v.* [T] to deliberately treat someone unfairly —**victimization** /ˌvɪktəməˈzeɪʃən/ *n.* [U]

vic·tor /ˈvɪktɚ/ *n.* [C] **1** FORMAL the winner of a battle, game, competition etc. **2 to the victor go/belong the spoils** used to say that the person or group that wins a competition, war etc. gets power, valuable things etc.

Vic·to·ri·a /vɪkˈtɔriə/ **1** the capital city of the Canadian PROVINCE of British Columbia **2** a state in southeast Australia **3** the capital city of the Seychelles

Victoria, Lake the largest lake in Africa, which is surrounded by Uganda, Tanzania, and Kenya

Victoria, Queen (1819–1901) the British queen from 1837 until her death, who also had the title "Empress of India"

VicˌtoriaˈFalls a very large WATERFALL on the Zambezi River between Zimbabwe and Zambia in southern Africa

Vic·to·ri·an¹ /vɪkˈtɔriən/ *adj.* **1** HISTORY relating to or coming from the period from 1837 to 1901 when Victoria was Queen of England: *Victorian architecture* **2** old-fashioned and with the strict moral attitudes typical of the society during the Victorian period

Victorian² *n.* [C] **1** a house built in the Victorian style **2** HISTORY an English person living in the period when Queen Victoria ruled

vic·to·ri·ous /vɪkˈtɔriəs/ *adj.* having won a victory: *a victorious candidate* | *We were confident that the team would **emerge victorious*** (=finally win). —**victoriously** *adv.*

vic·to·ry /ˈvɪktəri/ W2 *n. plural* **victories** [C,U] **1** the act of winning a battle, game, competition, or election OPP **defeat**: *Napoleon's military victories* | +**over/against** *the Raiders' 35–17 victory over St. Louis* | *Brock has **won a** major **victory** in court.* | *Clark has **led** the party **to victory**.* | **a clear/decisive/resounding victory** *He won a resounding victory in the country's first democratic elections.* **2 a victory for sb/sth** a situation in which someone's principles or aims become officially accepted: *The decision is a victory for women's rights.* | **a victory for common sense** (=a solution to a problem or argument that is the most sensible or fair one) [**Origin:** 1300–1400 Old French *victorie*, from Latin *victoria*, from *victus*, past participle of *vincere* **to defeat, win**] → see also PYRRHIC VICTORY

vict·uals /ˈvɪt̬lz/ *n.* [plural] OLD USE food and drink

vi·cu·ña, vicuna /vɪˈkunyə, -nə/ *n.* **1** [C] BIOLOGY a large South American animal related to the LLAMA, from which soft wool is obtained **2** [U] the cloth made from this wool

vid·e·o¹ /ˈvɪdioʊ/ S1 W3 *n.* **1** [C] a copy of a movie, television program etc. recorded on VIDEOTAPE: *Let's rent a video tonight.* | *the video store* **2** [U] the FORMAT of recording images on VIDEOTAPE SYN **videotape**: *DVDs give you a lot better quality than video.* | *I have the whole series **on video**.* **3** [C] ENG. LANG. ARTS a short movie or VIDEOTAPE that contains a particular piece of popular music, and is shown as entertainment SYN **music video** **4** [U] ENG. LANG. ARTS the process or result of recording and showing moving images using VIDEOTAPE, film, or DIGITAL FORMATS: *the age of video* → see also AUDIO

video² S2 W3 *adj.* [only before noun] relating to or used in the process of recording and showing moving images using VIDEOTAPE, film, or DIGITAL FORMATS: *video equipment* → see also AUDIO

ˈvideo arˌcade *n.* [C] a public place where there are a lot of VIDEO GAMES that you play by putting money in the machines

ˈvideo ˌcamera *n.* [C] a special camera that can be used to film events using VIDEOTAPE

vid•e•o•cas•sette /ˌvidioʊkəˈsɛt/ *n.* [C] a VIDEOTAPE

ˌvideocasˈsette reˌcorder *n.* [C] a VCR

ˈvideo ˌconferencing *n.* [U] a system that allows people to communicate with each other by sending pictures and sounds electronically

ˌvideo disˈplay ˌterminal *n.* [C] a VDT

ˈvideo ˌgame *n.* [C] a game in which you press electronic controls to move images on a screen

vid•e•og•ra•pher /ˌvɪdiˈɑgrəfɚ/ *n.* [C] FORMAL someone who records events using a VIDEO CAMERA —**videography** *n.* [U]

ˈvideo ˌjockey *n.* [C] a VJ

vid•e•o•phone /ˈvɪdioʊˌfoʊn/ *n.* [C] a type of telephone that allows you to see the person you are talking to on a machine like a television

ˈvideo reˌcorder *n.* [C] a VCR

vid•e•o•tape[1] /ˈvɪdioʊˌteɪp/ *n.* **1** [C,U] a long narrow band of MAGNETIC material in a flat plastic container, on which movies, television programs etc. can be recorded **2** [U] the FORMAT of recording images on VIDEOTAPE: *The robbers were* ***caught on videotape*** (=recorded on videotape).

videotape[2] *v.* [T] **1** to record a television program, movie, event etc. on a videotape **2** to record a real event on videotape using a VIDEO CAMERA

vie /vaɪ/ *v.* **vies, vied, vying** [I] to compete very hard with someone in order to get something: **+for** *The brothers vied for her attention.* | **vie with sb to do sth** *Students are vying with each other to sell the most tickets.* [**Origin:** 1500–1600 Old French *envier* **to invite, challenge**, from Latin *invitare*]

Vi•en•na /viˈɛnə/ the capital and largest city of Austria —**Viennese** /ˌviəˈniz◂ / *n., adj.*

Vien•tiane /ˌvyɛnˈtyɑn/ the capital and largest city of Laos

Viet Cong, the, **Vietcong, the** /ˌvyɛt ˈkɑŋ/ *n. plural* **Viet Cong** [C usually plural] HISTORY a member of a mainly COMMUNIST military group in South Vietnam that fought against its own government in the Vietnam War —**Viet Cong** *adj.*

Viet Minh, the, **Vietminh, the** /ˌvyɛt ˈmɪn/ HISTORY a Vietnamese group led by Ho Chi Minh that fought the Japanese and then the French between 1941 and 1954 to gain INDEPENDENCE for Vietnam —**Viet Minh** *adj.*

Viet•nam /ˌvyɛtˈnɑm, -ˈnæm/ a country in Southeast Asia, south of China and east of Laos and Cambodia —**Vietnamese** /ˌvyɛtnəˈmiz/ *adj.*

Viet•na•mi•za•tion /ˌvyɛtnəməˈzeɪʃən/ *n.* [U] HISTORY a U.S. program during the Vietnam War in which the U.S. tried to make the government and army of South Vietnam responsible for fighting the war, so that U.S. forces could be removed

ˌVietnam ˈWar, the HISTORY a long CIVIL WAR between the Communist forces of North Vietnam and the non-Communist forces of South Vietnam, which began in 1954 and ended when South Vietnam was finally defeated in 1975, and Vietnam was united again as one country. Between 1965 and 1973, U.S. soldiers fought in Vietnam to support the army of South Vietnam.

view[1] /vyu/ S2 W1 *n.*

1 OPINION [C] what you think or believe about something: *Everyone at the meeting had different views.* | **+on/about** *What's your view on the subject?* | ***In my view*** (=I believe), *the President broke the law.* | *Not all her friends* ***share*** *her* ***view.*** | *Another supervisor* ***expressed the view that*** *abortion should be kept legal.* | *We have always* ***taken the view that*** (=had the opinion that) *we should do as much as we can.* → see also POINT OF VIEW ►see THESAURUS box at **opinion**

2 WAY OF CONSIDERING [C usually singular] a way of considering or understanding something: *the liberal view* | **+of** *a romantic view of life* | *Blake's book gives us* ***a clear view of*** (=a definite and specific idea about) *what the war was like.* | *Management* ***takes a dim view of*** (=disapproves of) *union organizing efforts.* | **an inside/insider's view of sth** (=a way of understanding something based on someone's experience in an organization, group etc.)

3 SIGHT [singular, U] what you are able to see from a particular place, or the possibility of seeing it: *Suddenly the pyramids* ***came into view*** (=began to be seen). | *They started fighting* ***in full view of*** *the guests* (=where they could clearly see it happening). | *He left the brandy sitting out* ***in plain view*** (=where it could be easily seen) *on the counter.* | *A big pillar* ***blocked*** *my* ***view*** *of the stage.* | **have a good/bad/wonderful etc. view (of sb/sth)** *We had a great view of the parade from the balcony.* → see also BIRD'S-EYE VIEW

4 SCENERY [C] the whole area, especially a beautiful place, that you can see from somewhere: *a spectacular view across the valley*

5 PICTURE [C] a photograph or picture showing a beautiful or interesting place: **+of** *postcards of 12 different views of the cathedral*

6 on view paintings, photographs etc. that are on view are in a public place where people can go to look at them: *An exhibition of vintage cars is on view at the museum.*

7 in view of sth FORMAL used to introduce the reason for a decision, action, or situation: *In view of all that has happened, he is expected to resign.*

8 with a view to (doing) sth because you are planning to do something in the future: *We bought the house with a view to retiring there.*

[**Origin:** 1400–1500 Old French *veue*, *vue*, from *veeir*, *voir* **to see**, from Latin *videre*]

view[2] W2 *v.* **1** [T always + adv./prep.] to consider someone or something in a particular way: **view sth as sth** *We view this as a serious matter.* | **view sth with caution/enthusiasm/horror etc.** *Townspeople viewed the newcomers with suspicion.* | **view sth from a...standpoint/perspective** *The issue can be viewed from several perspectives.* **2** [T] FORMAL to look at something, especially because it is beautiful or you are interested in it: *Thousands of tourists come every year to view the gardens.* | **view sth from sth** *The public can view the ships from the pier.* **3** [I,T] FORMAL to watch a television show, movie etc. **4 view a house/apartment/property etc.** to go to see the inside of a house, apartment etc. that you are interested in buying

V

view•er /ˈvyuɚ/ W3 *n.* [C] **1** someone who watches television: *The network is trying to attract younger viewers.* → see also LISTENER ►see THESAURUS box at **watch[1]** **2** a small box with a light in it used to look at SLIDES (=color photographs on special film)

view•er•ship /ˈvyuɚˌʃɪp/ *n.* [U] all the people who watch a particular television show, considered together as a group

view•find•er /ˈvyuˌfaɪndɚ/ *n.* [C] the small square of glass on a camera that you look through to see exactly what you are photographing

view•ing /ˈvyuɪŋ/ *n.* **1** [C,U] the activity or act of watching a television program, movie, or play: *The movie is great family viewing.* **2** [C,U] the activity or act of going to look at something, or an occasion when you are able to do this: *The mansion is now open for* ***public viewing.*** | *a* ***private viewing*** *of the paintings* **3** [C] the time before a funeral when friends and relatives meet to remember the dead person and look at the body SYN **wake**

view•point /ˈvyupɔɪnt/ *n.* [C] **1** a particular way of thinking about a problem or subject: ***From*** *his* ***viewpoint,*** *he had done nothing wrong.* | **a different/historical/religious etc. viewpoint** *I'm more tolerant of other cultural viewpoints than I used to be.* **2** a place from which you can see something **3** ENG. LANG. ARTS the opinion or attitude of the person who is writing a story, especially when it has an influence on the story itself

vig·il /ˈvɪdʒəl/ *n.* **1** [C] a silent political protest in which people gather outside, especially during the night: *Demonstrators* ***held a*** *candlelight* ***vigil*** *at the site of the bombing.* **2** [C,U] a period of time, especially during the night, when you stay awake in order to pray or remain with someone who is sick: *Rice has been* ***keeping a*** *bedside* ***vigil*** *since his wife became sick.* **3** [C] an occasion when people stay awake at night to pray or have religious ceremonies, especially before a holy day

vig·i·lance /ˈvɪdʒələns/ *n.* [U] careful attention that you give to what is happening, so that you will notice any danger or illegal activity: ***Constant vigilance*** *against terrorism is necessary to keep the country safe.*

vig·i·lant /ˈvɪdʒələnt/ *adj.* giving careful attention to what is happening, so that you will notice any danger or illegal activity: *Travelers should be vigilant at all times.* [**Origin:** 1400–1500 Latin, present participle of *vigilare* **to stay awake, keep watch**, from *vigil*] —**vigilantly** *adv.*

vig·i·lan·te /ˌvɪdʒəˈlænti/ *n.* [C] someone who illegally catches and punishes criminals, usually because they think the police are ineffective —**vigilantism** *n.* [U]

vi·gnette /vɪˈnyɛt/ *n.* [C] FORMAL ENG. LANG. ARTS **1** a short description in a book or play showing the typical features of a person or situation **2** a small drawing or pattern placed at the beginning of a book or CHAPTER

vig·or /ˈvɪgɚ/ *n.* [U] physical and mental energy and determination: *He began working with renewed vigor.*

vig·or·ous /ˈvɪgərəs/ *adj.* **1** using a lot of energy and strength or determination: *vigorous exercise* | *The question started a vigorous debate.* ►see THESAURUS box at **energetic** **2** strong and very healthy: *At 80, he is still remarkably vigorous.*

vig·or·ous·ly /ˈvɪgərəsli/ *adv.* done with a lot of energy and strength or determination: *Environmentalists vigorously opposed the legislation.*

Vi·king /ˈvaɪkɪŋ/ *n.* [C] HISTORY a member of the group of Scandinavian people in the 8th to 11th centuries who sailed in ships to attack areas along the coasts of northern and western Europe

vile /vaɪl/ *adj.* **1** INFORMAL very bad or disgusting: *a vile smell* **2** evil or immoral: *a vile act of betrayal* [**Origin:** 1200–1300 Old French *vil*, from Latin *vilis* **worthless**] —**vilely** *adv.* —**vileness** *n.* [U]

vil·i·fy /ˈvɪləˌfaɪ/ *v.* **vilifies, vilified, vilifying** [T] FORMAL to say or write bad things about someone or something, especially in a way that is not fair, in order to influence other people against them —**vilification** /ˌvɪləfəˈkeɪʃən/ *n.* [C,U]

vil·la /ˈvɪlə/ *n.* [C] **1** a big country house **2** HISTORY an ancient Roman house or farm with land surrounding it

vil·lage /ˈvɪlɪdʒ/ W2 *n.* [C] **1** a very small town in the country, usually outside the U.S. and Canada: *remote mountain villages* **2 the village** the people who live in a village: *The entire village was invited to the banquet.* **3** an official description of certain small towns or areas in the U.S., used in legal or official documents [**Origin:** 1300–1400 Old French *ville* **farm, village**, from Latin *villa*] —**villager** *n.* [C]

ˌvillage ˈidiot *n.* [C] someone considered to be very stupid by many people in their town, NEIGHBORHOOD etc.

vil·lain /ˈvɪlən/ *n.* [C] **1** ENG. LANG. ARTS the main bad character in a movie, play, or story: *The wicked queen is the villain of the story.* → see also HERO, HEROINE **2 the villain** the person or thing that is blamed for causing all the trouble in a particular situation: *When it comes to obesity, fats and sugars are the real villains.* **3** INFORMAL a bad person or criminal

vil·lain·ous /ˈvɪlənəs/ *adj.* LITERARY evil or criminal

vil·lain·y /ˈvɪləni/ *n.* [U] LITERARY evil or criminal behavior

-ville /vɪl, vəl/ *suffix* **1** used in the names of places to mean "city or town": *Jacksonville, Florida* **2** HUMOROUS used with adjectives or nouns + "s" to show that a person, place, or thing has a particular quality or condition: *This place is dullsville* (=very boring).

vil·lus /ˈvɪləs/ *n. plural* **villi** /-laɪ/ [C] BIOLOGY one of the many very small raised areas on the inside surface of the INTESTINE that improve the way chemicals are taken from food and passed into the blood

Vil·ni·us /ˈvɪlniəs/ the capital and largest city of Lithuania

vim /vɪm/ *n.* [U] OLD-FASHIONED energy: *She was full of* ***vim and vigor.***

vin·ai·grette /ˌvɪnɪˈgrɛt/ *n.* [U] a mixture of oil, VINEGAR, salt, and pepper that you put on a SALAD

Vin·cent de Paul /ˌvɪnsɪnt də ˈpɔl/**, Saint** (?1581–1660) a French priest who started two groups of Catholics that do CHARITY work

vin·di·cate /ˈvɪndəˌkeɪt/ *v.* [T usually passive] FORMAL **1** to prove that someone who was blamed for something is in fact not guilty: *The hospital says it has been vindicated by the verdict.* **2** to prove that someone or something is right or true [**Origin:** 1500–1600 Latin, past participle of *vindicare* **to claim, avenge**, from *vindex* **person who claims, avenger**] —**vindication** /ˌvɪndəˈkeɪʃən/ *n.* [singular, U] *The result was a vindication of his decision to delay the election.*

vin·dic·tive /vɪnˈdɪktɪv/ *adj.* deliberately cruel and unfair toward someone you believe has harmed you, in a way that seems unreasonable to others: *a vindictive ex-wife* —**vindictively** *adv.* —**vindictiveness** *n.* [U]

vine /vaɪn/ *n.* [C] **1** BIOLOGY a plant that grows long thin stems that attach themselves to other plants, trees, buildings etc. **2** BIOLOGY a GRAPEVINE **3 wither/die on the vine** if an idea, process, or business dies or withers on the vine, it fails, especially in the early stage, because of a lack of support

vin·e·gar /ˈvɪnɪgɚ/ *n.* [U] a sour-tasting liquid made from wine that is used to improve the taste of food or to preserve it [**Origin:** 1200–1300 Old French *vinaigre*, from *vin* **wine** + *aigre* **sour**] —**vinegary** *adj.*

vineyard

vine·yard /ˈvɪnyɚd/ *n.* [C] a piece of land where GRAPEVINES are grown in order to produce wine

vi·no /ˈvinoʊ/ *n.* [U] SPOKEN wine

Vin·son /ˈvɪnsən/**, Fred·erick** /ˈfrɛdrɪk/ (1890–1953) a CHIEF JUSTICE on the U.S. Supreme Court

vin·tage[1] /ˈvɪntɪdʒ/ *adj.* [only before noun] **1** vintage wine is good quality wine made in a particular year **2** old, and showing high quality: *vintage cars* ►see THESAURUS box at **old** **3** showing all the best or most typical qualities of something: *The latest film has a vintage Disney charm.* **4 a vintage year a)** a year when a good quality wine was produced **b)** a year when something of very good quality was produced: *This was not a vintage year for new music.*

vintage[2] *n.* **1** [C] all the wine produced somewhere in a particular year, or the year it was produced **2** [C,U] the time when something was produced, built etc. **3 of recent vintage** WRITTEN having happened or started not very long ago: *It was one of his best speeches of recent vintage.* [**Origin:** 1300–1400 Old French *vendenge*, from

Latin *vindemia*, from *vinum* **wine, grapes** + *demere* **to take off**]

vint·ner /ˈvɪntˀnɚ/ *n.* [C] FORMAL someone who buys and sells wines

vi·nyl /ˈvaɪnl/ *n.* [U] **1** a type of strong plastic: *The tablecloth is made of vinyl.* | *a vinyl chair* **2** a word for records that are played on a RECORD PLAYER, used when comparing them to CDs or TAPES

vi·o·la /viˈoʊlə/ *n.* [C] a musical instrument like a VIOLIN but larger and with a lower sound

vi·o·late /ˈvaɪəˌleɪt/ Ac W3 *v.* [T] **1** to do something that disobeys or opposes an official agreement, law, principle etc.: *Such a move would violate the terms of the ceasefire.* ►see THESAURUS box at **disobey** **2** to do something that harms people's feelings, by not respecting their property, privacy, or feelings: *Nearly 80% of those asked feel the media **violates** people's **privacy**.* **3** LITERARY to force a woman to have sex SYN **rape** **4** FORMAL to break open a grave, or force your way into a holy place without showing any respect

vi·o·la·tion /ˌvaɪəˈleɪʃən/ Ac *n.* **1** [C,U] an action that breaks a law, agreement, principle etc.: *human rights violations* | **+of** *The military maneuvers are a clear violation of the treaty.* | *The bar was built **in violation of** city codes.* **2** [C] FORMAL an action that causes harm or damage by treating someone or their possessions without respect: **+of** *All these spy cameras seem like a violation of privacy and freedom.* **3** [C,U] FORMAL the act of forcing someone to have sex SYN **rape**

vi·o·lat·or /ˈvaɪəˌleɪtɚ/ *n.* [C] someone who has done something illegal

vi·o·lence /ˈvaɪələns/ S3 W1 *n.* [U] **1** behavior that is intended to hurt other people physically: *There is too much **sex and violence** on TV.* | *Shea had long been a victim of **domestic violence*** (=violence between family members or people who live together). | *Police suspect Tang's killing was a random **act of violence**.* | ***Violence** between fans **erupted** after the game.* | *Neither side wants to **resort to violence*** (=use violence when nothing else is effective). **2** extreme force: *the tremendous violence of a tornado* **3** LITERARY an angry way of speaking or reacting: *"Leave me alone," she hissed with sudden violence.* **4 do violence to sth** FORMAL to harm or spoil something

vi·o·lent /ˈvaɪələnt/ S3 W3 *adj.*
1 ACTIONS involving actions that are intended to injure or kill people, by hitting them, shooting them etc.: *a rise in violent crime* | *a violent overthrow of the government* | *The campus protests quickly **turned violent*** (=became violent) *on Tuesday.* | *The riots ended in the **violent deaths** of three teenagers.*
2 PEOPLE someone who is violent is likely to attack, hurt, or kill other people: *violent street gangs* | *The man suddenly **turned violent*** (=became violent) *and began smashing chairs.*
3 a violent movie/play/show etc. a movie, play etc. that contains a lot of violence
4 a violent storm/explosion/earthquake etc. a storm, explosion etc. that happens with a lot of force
5 SHOWING ANGER showing very strong emotions or opinions, especially angry ones: *Dad had a violent temper.*
6 PHYSICAL FEELINGS/REACTIONS a violent physical feeling or reaction is severe and often painful: *a violent coughing fit*
7 EMOTIONS a violent emotion is strong and difficult to control: *They took a violent dislike to each other.*
[**Origin:** 1300–1400 Old French, Latin *violentus*]

vi·o·lent·ly /ˈvaɪələntli/ *adv.* **1** in a way that involves violence: *Demonstrators clashed violently with police.* **2** with a lot of force: *The mirror crashed violently to the floor.* **3** severely and in a way that is physically difficult to control: *I was trembling less violently.* | **be violently ill** (=to vomit suddenly and a lot) **4** with a lot of energy or emotion, especially anger: *Mom reacted violently when she found out.*

vi·o·let /ˈvaɪəlɪt/ *n.* **1** [C] BIOLOGY a plant with small dark purple flowers, or sometimes white or yellow ones **2** [U] a bluish-purple color → see also SHRINKING VIOLET —**violet** *adj.*

vi·o·lin /ˌvaɪəˈlɪn/ *n.* [C] the smallest instrument in the group of wooden musical instruments that are played by pulling a BOW (=special stick) across its four strings —**violinist** *n.* [C]

VIP *n.* [C] **very important person** someone who is very famous or powerful and is treated with special care and respect

vi·per /ˈvaɪpɚ/ *n.* [C] **1** BIOLOGY a small poisonous snake **2** LITERARY someone who behaves in a nasty way and harms other people

vi·ra·go /vəˈrɑgoʊ/ *n. plural* **viragoes** or **viragos** [C] LITERARY an angry woman with a loud voice

vi·ral /ˈvaɪrəl/ *adj.* MEDICINE relating to or caused by a VIRUS: *viral pneumonia*

Vir·gil, Vergil /ˈvɚdʒəl/ (70–19 B.C.) an ancient Roman poet

vir·gin¹ /ˈvɚdʒɪn/ *n.* [C] **1** someone who has never had sex, especially a girl or young woman **2 the (Blessed) Virgin** also **the Virgin Mary** a name for Mary, the mother of Jesus Christ, used especially by Catholics **3** SPOKEN, HUMOROUS someone who has never done a particular activity: *a snowboarding virgin*

virgin² *adj.* [only before noun] **1 virgin land/snow/soil etc.** land, snow etc. that is still in its natural state and has not been used or changed by people: *Much of the island is virgin forest.* **2 virgin territory** something new that someone is experiencing for the first time **3** without sexual experience: *a virgin bride* **4** a virgin drink is one that normally contains alcohol, but has been made without any **5** not having done, heard, or seen something before: *He was eager to try out his jokes on a virgin audience.*

vir·gin·al /ˈvɚdʒɪnəl/ *adj.* like a virgin

ˌvirgin ˈbirth *n.* **the virgin birth** the birth of Jesus Christ, which Christians believe was caused by God, not by sex between a man and a woman

Vir·gin·ia /vɚˈdʒɪnyə/ WRITTEN ABBREVIATION **VA** a state on the east coast of the U.S.

Virˌginia ˈcreeper *n.* [C,U] a garden plant that grows up walls and has large leaves that turn deep red in the fall

Virˈginia ˌPlan, the HISTORY an early plan put forward at the 1787 U.S. Federal Constitutional Convention, suggesting a three-part national government. Although all the details of this plan were not accepted by the members of the Convention, the basic idea of three branches of government and two houses of Congress remained.

Vir·gin Is·lands, the /ˌvɚdʒɪn ˈaɪləndz/ a group of about 100 small islands in the east Caribbean Sea, some of which are ruled by the U.S.

vir·gin·i·ty /vɚˈdʒɪnət̬i/ *n.* [U] the condition of never having had sex: *I was 18 when I **lost my virginity*** (=had sex for the first time). → see also CHASTITY

ˌvirgin ˌolive ˈoil *n.* [U] EXTRA VIRGIN OLIVE OIL

Vir·go /ˈvɚgoʊ/ *n.* **1** [U] the sixth sign of the ZODIAC, represented by a young woman, and believed to affect the character and life of people born between August 23 and September 22 **2** [C] someone who was born between August 23 and September 22

vir·ile /ˈvɪrəl/ *adj.* APPROVING having or showing traditionally male qualities such as strength, courage, and sexual attractiveness SYN **manly**

vi·ril·i·ty /vəˈrɪlət̬i/ *n.* [U] **1** APPROVING the typically male quality of being strong, brave, and full of energy, in a way that is sexually attractive SYN **manliness** **2** the ability of a man to have sex or make a woman PREGNANT SYN **potency**

vi·rol·o·gy /vaɪˈrɑlədʒi/ *n.* [U] MEDICINE the scientific study of VIRUSES or of the diseases caused by them

vir·tu·al /ˈvɚtʃuəl/ Ac *adj.* [only before noun] **1** so nearly a particular thing that any difference is unimportant: *The children in the factory were virtual slaves.* | *They drove home in virtual silence.* | *Buying a week's worth of groceries for this family in one trip is* ***a virtual impossibility***. **2** COMPUTERS relating to something that is made, done, seen etc. on a computer, rather than in the real world: *The website allows you to take a virtual tour of the campus.* ►see THESAURUS box at **artificial** [**Origin:** 1300–1400 Medieval Latin *virtualis* **having certain qualities or powers**]

vir·tu·al·ly /ˈvɚtʃuəli, -tʃəli/ Ac W2 *adv.* **1** almost SYN **practically**: *Virtually everyone expects Monica to win.* | *He was virtually unknown before running for office.* **2** COMPUTERS done on a computer, rather than in the real world

ˌvirtual ˈmemory *n.* [U] COMPUTERS memory that a computer appears to produce by saving things from its active memory onto the HARD DRIVE

ˌvirtual reˈality *n.* [U] COMPUTERS an environment produced by a computer that looks and seems real to the person experiencing it

vir·tue /ˈvɚtʃu/ *n.*
1 GOOD QUALITY [C] a particular good quality in someone's character OPP **vice**: *Patience is a virtue.* | *heroic virtues*
2 GOODNESS [U] FORMAL moral goodness of character and behavior OPP **vice**: *men of virtue*
3 ADVANTAGE [C,U] an advantage that makes something better or more useful than something else: +**of** *the virtues of democracy*
4 by virtue of sth FORMAL by means of, or as a result of something: *He was given the award by virtue of his age.*
5 preach/extol/tout etc. the virtues of sth to talk about how good or important something is and try to persuade other people about this
6 make a virtue (out) of necessity to pretend that you are doing something because you want to do it, when actually it is something that you must do
7 NO SEX [U] OLD-FASHIONED the state of not having sex with someone, or not with anyone except your husband or wife
[**Origin:** 1100–1200 Old French *virtu*, from Latin *virtus* **strength, virtue**, from *vir* **man**]

V

vir·tu·os·i·ty /ˌvɚtʃuˈɑsət̬i/ *n.* [U] FORMAL a very high degree of skill in doing something, especially playing music

vir·tu·o·so /ˌvɚtʃuˈoʊsoʊ/ *n. plural* **virtuosos** [C] someone who is a very skillful performer, especially in music —**virtuoso** *adj.* [only before noun] *a virtuoso performance*

vir·tu·ous /ˈvɚtʃuəs/ *adj.* **1** FORMAL behaving in a very honest and moral way: *He led a virtuous life.* **2** OLD-FASHIONED not willing to have sex, at least until you are married —**virtuously** *adv.*

vir·u·lent /ˈvɪrələnt, ˈvɪryə-/ *adj.* **1** MEDICINE a virulent poison, disease etc. is very dangerous and affects people very quickly: *a more virulent strain of HIV* **2** FORMAL, DISAPPROVING full of hatred for something, or expressing this in a strong way: *virulent nationalism* —**virulence** *n.* [U] —**virulently** *adv.*

vi·rus /ˈvaɪrəs/ W3 *n. plural* **viruses** **1** [C] BIOLOGY a very small living thing that causes infectious illnesses. Viruses can only make new viruses when they are inside the cells of another ORGANISM: *the common cold virus* → see also BACTERIA **2** [C] the illness caused by a virus: *She caught a virus that was going around.* **3** [C,U] COMPUTERS a set of instructions secretly put into a computer or computer program, that can destroy information stored there and possibly the equipment itself SYN **computer virus** [**Origin:** 1500–1600 Latin **thick slippery liquid, poison, bad smell**]

vi·sa /ˈvizə/ *n.* [C] LAW an official mark or document put in your PASSPORT by the representative of a foreign country, that gives you permission to enter, pass through, stay in, or leave that country: *You will need to* ***apply for a visa***. | **grant/refuse sb a visa** *Israel had refused him an entry visa.* | **a work/exit/entry etc. visa** *A tourist visa is good for three months.* [**Origin:** 1800–1900 French, Latin, **things seen**, from *visus*]

vis·age /ˈvɪzɪdʒ/ *n.* [C] LITERARY a face

vis-à-vis /ˌvizəˈvi/ *prep.* FORMAL in relation to or in comparison with something or someone: *his position vis-à-vis the President*

vis·cer·a /ˈvɪsərə/ *n.* [plural] BIOLOGY the large organs inside your body, such as your heart, lungs, and stomach

vis·cer·al /ˈvɪsərəl/ *adj.* **1** LITERARY relating to or resulting from strong feelings rather than careful thought: *The images provoke a visceral reaction.* **2** relating to the viscera

vis·cous /ˈvɪskəs/ *adj.* TECHNICAL a viscous liquid is thick and sticky and does not flow easily —**viscosity** /vɪˈskɑsət̬i/ *n.* [U]

vise, vice /vaɪs/ *n.* [C] a tool that holds an object firmly so that you can work on it using both your hands

vise·like /ˈvaɪslaɪk/ *adj.* **a viselike grip** a very firm hold

vis·i·bil·i·ty /ˌvɪzəˈbɪlət̬i/ Ac *n.* [U] **1** the distance it is possible to see, especially when this is affected by weather conditions: **good/poor/low visibility** *The flight was canceled due to poor visibility.* **2** the situation of being noticed by people in general: *As head of the Red Cross, she has* ***high visibility***. **3** the fact of being easy to be seen

vis·i·ble /ˈvɪzəbəl/ Ac W3 *adj.* **1** able to be seen OPP **invisible**: *The stars were barely visible that night.* | *In the distance, the mountains were* ***clearly visible***. | +**from** *The moon's craters are visible from Earth.* | +**to** *Reflectors make bikers more visible to motorists.* **2** a visible change or effect is clear and noticeable SYN **noticeable**: *The results of the housing policy are* ***clearly visible***. | *She showed no* ***visible signs of*** *regret.* **3** someone or something that is visible is in a situation in which many people can notice them: *highly visible politicians*

vis·i·bly /ˈvɪzəbli/ Ac *adv.* in a way that is easy to see or notice: *He was visibly upset by the loss.*

Vis·i·goth /ˈvɪzəˌgɑθ/ HISTORY one of a tribe of Goths that settled in France and Spain in the fourth century A.D.

vi·sion /ˈvɪʒən/ Ac S3 W2 *n.*
1 ABILITY TO SEE [U] your ability to see: *As Martha grew older, her vision began to fail.* | *Tears blurred his vision.* | **good/poor/excellent etc. vision** *drivers with poor vision* | **night vision** (=your ability to see when it is dark) → see also DOUBLE VISION, TUNNEL VISION, **twenty-twenty vision** at TWENTY-TWENTY (1)
2 AREA YOU CAN SEE the area that you are able to see without turning your head: **sb's field/line of vision** *He walked around and stood in my line of vision.*
3 IDEA [C] an idea of what you think something should be like: +**of** *a frightening vision of the future*
4 ABILITY TO PLAN [U] the knowledge and imagination that are needed in planning for the future with a clear purpose: *We need a leader with vision and strong principles*
5 RELIGIOUS EXPERIENCE [C] something that you believe you see as part of a powerful religious experience: +**of** *He had a vision of the Virgin Mary.* | *She says that an angel appeared to her* ***in a vision***.
6 STH YOU IMAGINE [C usually plural] something that you imagine happening, which seems almost real: **have visions of (doing) sth** *He had visions of forgetting his whole speech.*
7 a vision (of beauty/loveliness etc.) LITERARY a woman who is very beautiful

vi·sion·ar·y[1] /ˈvɪʒəˌnɛri/ *adj.* **1** having clear ideas of what the world should be like in the future: *visionary leadership* **2** existing only in someone's mind and unlikely to ever exist in the real world

visionary[2] *n. plural* **visionaries** [C] **1** someone who has clear ideas and strong feelings about the way something should be in the future **2** a holy person who has religious VISIONS

vis·it[1] /ˈvɪzɪt/ S1 W1 *v.*
1 GO SEE SB [I,T] to go to see someone socially and spend some time with them: *Eric went to Seattle to visit his cousins.* | *She doesn't visit very often.* | **+in** *He first met her in a club when she was visiting in Miami.* | *I was really pleased that they **came to visit** me.*

THESAURUS

go to a movie, museum, theater etc.
go to see/go and see a person or place
go sightseeing to visit places of interest in a country
come by/over to visit someone informally in his or her home
drop in/by, **stop by/in** to visit someone in his or her home, especially on your way to another place

2 GO TO A PLACE FOR FUN [T] to go to a place and spend time there, for pleasure or interest: *Thousands of people visit the museum every year.* | *Which cities did you visit in Spain?*
3 GO TO A PLACE FOR WORK [T] to go to a place as part of your official job, especially to examine it: *The inspection team visited the plant twice in October.*
4 INTERNET [T] to look at a WEBSITE on the Internet: *Over 1,000 people visit the site every day.*
5 TALK [I] INFORMAL to talk socially with someone SYN **chat**: *They sat on the porch visiting.* | **+with** *She spends all her time visiting with neighbors.*
6 DOCTOR/LAWYER ETC. [T] FORMAL to go to see a doctor, lawyer etc. in order to get treatment or advice SYN **see**: *You should visit the dentist twice a year.*
[**Origin:** 1100–1200 Old French *visiter*, from Latin *visitare*, from *visere* **to go to see**]
visit sth **on/upon** sb/sth *phr. v.* BIBLICAL or LITERARY to make something bad happen to someone, often as a punishment: *God visited his wrath upon the sinful men.*

visit[2] S3 W2 *n.* [C] **1** an occasion when someone goes to spend time in a place or goes to see a person: **+to** *a visit to London* | **+from** *Liz is expecting a visit from her brother, Frank.* | *Lang will accompany the President **on a visit to** Rome.* | *I decided to **pay** him **a visit** at his office.* **2** INFORMAL an occasion when you talk socially with someone, or the time you spend doing this: *Polly and I had a nice long visit.* **3** an occasion when you see a doctor, lawyer etc. for treatment or advice → see also HOME VISIT

vis·it·a·tion /ˌvɪzəˈteɪʃən/ *n.* **1** [C] FORMAL an official visit to a place or a person, especially to see a dead body after someone has died **2** [C,U] LAW an occasion when a parent is allowed to spend time with their children when the children live with the other parent after a DIVORCE, or the right to do this: *visitation rights* **3** [C] LITERARY an event that is believed to be God's punishment for something: **+of** *visitations of plague, famine, and war* **4** [C] an occasion when God or a spirit is believed to appear to someone on Earth

visiting hours *n.* [plural] the period of time when you can visit people who are in the hospital

visiting proˈfessor *n.* [C] a university teacher who has come from another university to teach for a period of time

vis·i·tor /ˈvɪzətɚ/ W2 *n.* [C] **1** someone who comes to visit a place or a person: *The theme park attracts over two million visitors a year.* | **+to/from** *Rina is a frequent visitor to the city.* | *Doug, I think you **have a visitor**.* **2** someone who looks at a particular WEB SITE **3 the visitors** [plural] in sports, the team that has traveled to their opponent's sportsfield to play against them

vi·sor /ˈvaɪzɚ/ *n.* [C] **1** the curved part of a cap that sticks out in front above your eyes **2** the part of a HELMET (=protective hard hat) that can be lowered to protect your face **3** a flat piece of material above the front window inside a car that can be pulled down to keep the sun out of your eyes **4** a curved piece of stiff cloth, plastic, or other material that you wear on your head so that it sticks out above your eyes and protects them from the sun but does not cover the rest of your head

VISTA /ˈvɪstə/ **Volunteers in Service to America** a U.S. program that sends VOLUNTEERS to help people in poor areas

vis·ta /ˈvɪstə/ *n.* [C] **1** LITERARY a view of a large area of beautiful SCENERY, especially one seen by looking between rows of trees, buildings etc.: *a spectacular mountain vista* **2** the possibility of new experiences, ideas, events etc.: *Exchange programs open up **new vistas** for students.*

vis·u·al /ˈvɪʒuəl, ˈvɪʒəl/ Ac *adj.* [usually before noun] **1** relating to things you can see: *Artists translate their ideas into visual images.* | *dramatic visual effects* **2** relating to sight: *a visual handicap* → see also VISUALLY

ˌvisual ˈaid *n.* [C] something such as a map, picture, film etc. that helps people understand, learn, or remember information

ˌvisual ˈarts *n.* [plural] art such as painting, SCULPTURE, etc. that you look at, as opposed to literature or music that you read or hear

vis·u·al·ize /ˈvɪʒuəˌlaɪz/ Ac *v.* [T] to form a picture of someone or something in your mind SYN **imagine**: *I tried to visualize the house as he described it.* | **visualize sb doing sth** *She visualized him coming home and finding her gone.* | **visualize how/what etc.** *I can't really visualize how the bedroom will look.* —**visualization** /ˌvɪʒuələˈzeɪʃən/ *n.* [U]

vi·su·al·ly /ˈvɪʒuəli, ˈvɪʒəli/ Ac *adv.* **1** in appearance: *a visually exciting Website* **2** in a way that involves sight and the eyes: **visually impaired/handicapped** (=unable to see normally)

vi·tal /ˈvaɪtl/ W3 *adj.* **1** extremely important and necessary for something to succeed or exist: *Schools are a vital part of American neighborhoods.* | **+to** *We view this partnership as vital to achieving our goals.* | **+for** *Regular exercise is vital for your health.* | **it is vital that** *It is vital that you tell her the truth.* | *He **played a vital role in** the team's success.* | *The drug problem is **of vital importance** to both our countries.* ▸see THESAURUS box at **important**, **necessary** **2** full of energy in a way that is exciting and attractive: *a strong vital man* **3** [only before noun] BIOLOGY necessary in order to keep you alive: *the body's vital processes* [**Origin:** 1300–1400 Old French, Latin *vitalis* **of life**, from *vita* **life**]

vi·tal·i·ty /vaɪˈtæləti/ *n.* [U] **1** great energy and cheerfulness **2** the strength of an organization, country etc. and its ability to continue working effectively

vi·tal·ize /ˈvaɪtlˌaɪz/ *v.* [T] to make someone or something have more energy, or to make something become more active and successful

vi·tal·ly /ˈvaɪtl-i/ *adv.* in a very important or necessary way: *It is **vitally important** that you follow the directions exactly.*

ˌvital ˈorgan *n.* [C] a part of your body that is necessary to keep you alive, such as your heart and lungs

ˌvital ˈrecord *n.* [C usually plural] an official record of a birth, marriage, or death

vi·tals /ˈvaɪtlz/ *n.* [plural] **1** vital signs **2** OLD USE your vital organs

ˌvital ˈsigns *n.* [plural] things that you can measure to find out whether a person's health is in danger, such as their breathing, body temperature, and how fast their heart is beating

ˌvital staˈtistics *n.* [plural] **1** figures or facts concerning birth, death, marriage etc., especially within a population **2** important information or facts about someone or something such as height, address, cost etc.

vi·ta·min /ˈvaɪtəmɪn/ S3 *n.* [C] **1** CHEMISTRY a chemical substance that is necessary for good health, and is usually obtained by eating food: **vitamin A/B/C etc.** *Does vitamin C really help prevent colds?* **2** a PILL containing vitamins

vi·ti·ate /ˈvɪʃiˌeɪt/ *v.* [T] FORMAL to make something less effective or spoil it —**vitiation** /ˌvɪʃiˈeɪʃən/ *n.* [U]

V

vit·i·cul·ture /ˈvɪt̬əˌkʌltʃɚ/ *n.* [U] the study or practice of growing GRAPES for making wine

vit·re·ous /ˈvɪtriəs/ *adj.* FORMAL made of or looking like glass

vit·ri·ol /ˈvɪtriəl/ *n.* [U] **1** LITERARY very cruel and angry remarks that are intended to hurt someone's feelings **2** OLD-FASHIONED SULFURIC ACID

vit·ri·ol·ic /ˌvɪtriˈɑlɪk/ *adj.* FORMAL vitriolic language, writing etc. is very cruel and angry and intended to hurt someone's feelings —**vitriolically** /-kli/ *adv.*

vi·tro /ˈvitroʊ/ → see IN VITRO FERTILIZATION

vit·tles /ˈvɪt̬lz/ *n.* [plural] OLD-FASHIONED, INFORMAL food

vi·tu·per·a·tion /vaɪˌtupəˈreɪʃən, vɪ-/ *n.* [U] FORMAL angry and cruel criticism —**vituperative** /vaɪˈtupərət̬ɪv, -ˌreɪt̬ɪv/ *adj.*

vi·va /ˈvivə/ *interjection* used before the name of someone or something to show that you approve of or support them and want them to continue to exist or be successful

vi·va·ce /vɪˈvɑtʃeɪ, -tʃi/ *adj., adv.* ENG. LANG. ARTS played or sung quickly and with energy

vi·va·cious /vɪˈveɪʃəs, vaɪ-/ *adj.* someone, especially a woman or girl, who is vivacious has a lot of energy and a happy attractive manner [**Origin:** 1600–1700 Latin *vivax* **living a long time, vivacious**, from *vivere*] —**vivaciousness** *n.* [U] —**vivacity** /vɪˈvæsət̬i/ *n.* [U]

Vi·val·di /vɪˈvɑldi/**, An·to·ni·o** /ænˈtoʊnioʊ/ (1678–1741) an Italian musician who wrote CLASSICAL music

viv·id /ˈvɪvɪd/ *adj.* **1** vivid memories, dreams, descriptions etc. are so clear that they seem real: *I still have vivid memories of that summer.* | *Add details to make your writing more vivid.* **2 a vivid imagination** an ability to imagine unlikely situations very clearly **3** vivid colors or patterns are very bright: *a vivid red cape* ►see THESAURUS box at **color**[1] —**vividness** *n.* [U]

viv·id·ly /ˈvɪvɪdli/ *adv.* **1** in a way that is so clear that memories, dreams, descriptions etc. seem real: *I recall what he said vividly.* **2** brightly: *a vividly colored gown*

vi·vip·a·rous /vaɪˈvɪpərəs/ *adj.* BIOLOGY **1** MAMMALS and other animals that are viviparous produce living babies which have developed inside the mother's body, rather than inside an egg, before they are born → see also OVOVIVIPAROUS **2** plants that are viviparous produce BULBS or new plants, not seeds

viv·i·sec·tion /ˌvɪvəˈsɛkʃən/ *n.* [U] FORMAL BIOLOGY the practice of cutting open the bodies of living animals in order to do medical or scientific tests on them —**vivisectionist** *n.* [C]

vix·en /ˈvɪksən/ *n.* [C] **1** LITERARY an unkind woman who is often angry **2** BIOLOGY a female FOX —**vixenish** *adj.*

viz. /vɪz/ *adv.* FORMAL used to introduce specific details or a list of examples that make your meaning clearer SYN **namely**

vi·zier /vəˈzɪr/ *n.* [C] HISTORY **1** an important government official in certain Muslim countries in the past **2** the chief government official in ancient Egypt

VJ *n.* [C] **video jockey** someone who introduces music VIDEOS on television

VLF *n.* [U] TECHNICAL **very low frequency** a range of radio waves between 3 and 30 KILOHERTZ

V-neck /ˈvi nɛk/ *n.* [C] **1** an opening for the neck in a piece of clothing shaped like the letter V **2** a SWEATER with a V-neck —**V-necked** *adj.*: *a V-necked sweater*

vo·cab /ˈvoʊkæb/ *n.* [U] INFORMAL VOCABULARY

vo·cab·u·lar·y /voʊˈkæbyəˌlɛri, və-/ S3 *n. plural* **vocabularies** ENG. LANG. ARTS

1 WORDS YOU KNOW [C,U] all the words that someone knows, learns, or uses: *Reading is a good way to improve your vocabulary.* | **a large/small/limited vocabulary** *an educated person with a large vocabulary* | **sb's active/passive vocabulary** (=the words someone can use, or the words they understand)

2 SPECIAL WORDS [C,U] the words that are typically used when talking about a particular subject: *Most technical jobs use a specialized vocabulary.*

3 WORDS IN A LANGUAGE [C] all the words in a particular language: *English has the largest vocabulary of any language.*

4 SKILLS/FEATURES [C,U] the special skills or features that are typical of a particular subject: +**of** *Mingus expanded the vocabulary of jazz.*

5 LIST OF WORDS [C] a list of words with explanations of their meanings, often in a book for learning a language

6 sth is not in sb's vocabulary also **sth is not part of sb's vocabulary** used to say that someone never thinks of accepting a particular idea or possibility: *"Compromise" was not in her vocabulary.*

[**Origin:** 1500–1600 French *vocabulaire*, from Latin *vocabulum* **word, name**]

vo·cal[1] /ˈvoʊkəl/ *adj.* **1** expressing strong opinions publicly, especially about things with which you disagree: *a vocal critic of the government* | +**about** *Mrs. Rider has been very vocal about her concerns.* | +**in** *The administration was vocal in its opposition to the proposal.* **2** [only before noun] ENG. LANG. ARTS relating to the voice or its use: *vocal music* —**vocally** *adv.*

vocal[2] *n.* [C usually plural] the part of a piece of music that is sung rather than played on an instrument: *The album features Jim Boquist* ***on vocals.***

ˈvocal cords, vocal chords *n.* [plural] BIOLOGY thin pieces of muscle in your throat that produce sounds when you speak

vo·cal·ist /ˈvoʊkəlɪst/ *n.* [C] someone who sings popular songs, especially with a band → see also INSTRUMENTALIST

vo·cal·ize /ˈvoʊkəˌlaɪz/ *v.* **1** [T] to express a feeling or opinion by speaking SYN **express**: *Getz vocalized what everyone else at the meeting was thinking.* **2** [I,T] TECHNICAL to make a sound using the vocal cords —**vocalization** /ˌvoʊkələˈzeɪʃən/ *n.* [C,U]

vo·ca·tion /voʊˈkeɪʃən/ *n.* **1** [C] a particular job or type of work, especially one that you feel is right for you or is your purpose in life: *At 17, she* ***found her vocation*** *as a writer.* ►see THESAURUS box at **job** **2** [U] a strong feeling that the purpose of your life is to do a particular type of work, especially to serve God or to help other people SYN **calling**: **a vocation for the priesthood** (=a feeling that God wants you to be a priest) [**Origin:** 1400–1500 Latin *vocatio* **call, summons**, from *vocare* **to call**]

vo·ca·tion·al /voʊˈkeɪʃənl/ *adj.* **vocational training/guidance/education etc.** training, advice etc. relating to the skills you need to do a particular job

voˌcational ˈschool *n.* [C] a school that teaches students the skills that they will need for particular jobs, especially ones in which they will use their hands such as MECHANICS or CARPENTRY

voc·a·tive /ˈvɑkət̬ɪv/ *n.* [C] ENG. LANG. ARTS a particular form of a noun in certain languages, used when speaking or writing to someone. For example, in the sentence, "Sue, have you seen my hat?", the name "Sue" is a vocative —**vocative** *adj.*

vo·cif·er·ous /voʊˈsɪfərəs/ *adj.* FORMAL **1** expressing your opinions loudly and strongly: *a vociferous opponent of the plan* **2** vociferous opinions, wishes etc. are loudly and strongly expressed —**vociferously** *adv.*

vod·ka /ˈvɑdkə/ *n.* [C,U] a strong clear alcoholic drink from Russia or Poland, or a glass of this drink [**Origin:** 1800–1900 Russian *voda* **water**]

vogue /voʊg/ *n.* [C usually singular, U] the fashion or the popular style, activity etc. at a particular time: +**for** *Before the war, there was a vogue for large families.* | *Untanned skin is back* ***in vogue*** *for the first time since the 1920s.* [**Origin:** 1500–1600 French **act of rowing, course, fashion**, from Old Italian *voga*, from *vogare* **to row**]

voice[1] /vɔɪs/ S1 W1 *n.*

1 SPEAKING [C,U] the sounds that you make when you speak, or your ability to make these sounds: *I thought I heard voices outside.* | *He recognized her voice right away.* | *Kent's got a cold and he's* ***lost*** *his* ***voice*** (=he cannot speak). | *Don't you* ***raise*** *your* ***voice*** (=speak louder, especially in an angry way) *at me.* | ***Keep*** *your* ***voice down*** (=speak more quietly) – *we don't want to wake everyone up.* | *I could tell from his* ***tone of voice*** (=the quality of his voice) *that he was annoyed.* | *They were shouting* ***at the top of*** *their* ***voices*** (=as loud as they could). | ***A small voice*** (=a shy and quiet voice) *in the back of the room said "No."* | **lower/drop your voice** (=to speak more quietly) | **a loud/deep/soft/high-pitched etc. voice** *Angie has a really low voice for a woman.* | **angry/excited/worried etc. voice** *From downstairs came angry voices, arguing over whose turn it was to cook dinner.* | **in a normal/loud/surprised etc. voice** *I called out in a loud voice.* | **sb's voice trembles/shakes/cracks/breaks** *As he spoke of the accident, his voice broke and tears came to his eyes.*

2 SINGING **a)** [C,U] the quality of sound you produce when you sing: *He has a beautiful tenor voice.* | *She was* ***in good voice*** (=singing well) *the night of the concert.* **b)** [C] a person singing: *The piece was written for six voices and piano.*

3 OPINION **a)** [singular] the right or ability to express an opinion, to vote, or to influence decisions: *Shouldn't parents* ***have a voice in*** *deciding how their children are educated?* **b)** [C] an opinion or wish that is expressed: *The government needs to listen to the voice of middle-class Americans.* | *You can* ***make your voice heard*** (=express your opinion so that people notice it) *at the meeting tonight.* | *There were several* ***dissenting voices*** (=people expressing disagreement) *among the members.* | *Senator Prior* ***added*** *her* ***voice to*** (=expressed her support for) *calls for electoral reform.* | *The committee* ***spoke with one voice*** *on the issue.*

4 REPRESENTATIVE [singular] a person, organization, newspaper etc. that expresses the opinions or wishes of a group of people: *The magazine quickly became the voice of the computer generation.*

5 the voice of reason/sanity/experience etc. opinions or ideas that are reasonable, sensible, based on experience etc., or someone with these ideas: *Green has been the voice of reason throughout the crisis.*

6 sb's voice changes/breaks when a boy's voice changes or breaks, it becomes deeper as he becomes a man

7 sb likes the sound of their own voice INFORMAL used to say that someone talks too much

8 give voice to sth to express something openly or publicly: *The report gives voice to a number of criticisms.*

9 the active/passive voice ENG. LANG. ARTS the form of a verb that shows whether the subject of a sentence does an action or has an action done to it

[**Origin:** 1200–1300 Old French *vois*, from Latin *vox*]
→ see also **find your voice** at FIND[1] (18), **sb's inner voice** at INNER (5), -VOICED

voice² *v.* [T] **1** to tell people your opinions or feelings about a particular subject: **voice opinions/doubts/complaints etc.** *He voiced several objections to the plan.* **2** TECHNICAL to produce a sound with a movement of the VOCAL CORDS

voice box *n.* [C] BIOLOGY the part of your throat that you use to produce sounds when you speak SYN **larynx**

voiced /vɔɪst/ *adj.* ENG. LANG. ARTS voiced sounds are made using the VOCAL CORDS. For example, /d/ and /g/ are voiced consonants.

-voiced /vɔɪst/ *suffix* [in adjectives] **deep-voiced/squeaky-voiced/husky-voiced etc.** having a voice that is deep, very high etc.

voice·less /ˈvɔɪslɪs/ *adj.* **1** a voiceless group of people do not have any political power, and their opinions are not listened to or respected **2** ENG. LANG. ARTS voiceless sounds are made without using the VOCAL CORDS. For example, /p/ and /k/ are voiceless consonants. SYN **unvoiced**

voice mail *n.* [U] a system in which people can leave recorded messages for someone who does not answer their telephone

voice-over *n.* [C] an explanation or set of remarks that is spoken in a television advertisement or movie by someone who cannot be seen

ˈvoice print *n.* [C] COMPUTERS someone's voice, recorded on a machine, which can be used to check whether that person is allowed to enter a place, use a computer system etc. by matching their voice to the recording

void¹ /vɔɪd/ *n.* [C usually singular] **1** a feeling of great sadness and emptiness that you have when someone you love dies, when something is taken from you etc.: *She ate to* ***fill the void*** (=put something in the place of something she no longer has) *in her life.* **2** a situation in which something important is lacking or in which someone important, good etc. is no longer present or available: *The amusement park will* ***fill a void*** (=give them something they were lacking) *in this town, which has little entertainment for children.* **3** LITERARY a completely empty area of space: *She looked over the cliff into the void.*

void² *adj.* **1** LAW a contract or official agreement that is void is not legal and has no effect SYN **null and void** **2 void of sth** FORMAL completely empty or lacking something SYN **devoid**: *Her eyes were void of all expression.*

void³ *v.* [T] **1** LAW to make a contract or agreement have no legal effect: *The ruling party voided elections in 14 cities.* **2** to pass waste liquid or solid matter from your body

voi·là /vwɑˈlɑ/ *interjection* used when suddenly showing or telling someone something surprising: *You just press this button, and voilà! Instant music!*

voile /vɔɪl/ *n.* [U] a very light almost transparent cloth made of cotton, wool, or silk

vol. the written abbreviation for VOLUME

vol·a·tile /ˈvɑlət̬l/ *adj.* **1** a volatile situation is likely to change suddenly and without much warning: *an increasingly volatile political situation* **2** someone who is volatile can suddenly become angry or violent **3** CHEMISTRY a volatile liquid or substance changes easily into a gas [**Origin:** 1500–1600 French, Latin *volatilis*, from *volare* **to fly**] —**volatility** /ˌvɑləˈtɪlət̬i/ *n.* [U]

vol·can·ic /vɑlˈkænɪk, vɔl-/ *adj.* **1** EARTH SCIENCE relating to or caused by a volcano: *a volcanic eruption* **2** happening or reacting suddenly and violently

vol·ca·no /vɑlˈkeɪnoʊ/ *n. plural* **volcanoes** or **volcanos** [C] EARTH SCIENCE a mountain with an opening at the top through which hot rocks and ASH sometimes rise into the air→ see picture on p 1766

vole /voʊl/ *n.* [C] a small animal like a mouse with a short tail that lives in fields and woods and near rivers

Vol·ga, the /ˈvɑlgə, ˈvoʊlgə/ a river in Russia that flows into the Caspian Sea and is the longest river in Europe

vo·li·tion /vəˈlɪʃən, voʊ-/ *n.* [U] FORMAL **1 do sth of your own volition** to do something because you want to, not because you are forced to do it: *He went to the police of his own volition.* **2** the power to choose or decide something, or the action of doing this

vol·ley¹ /ˈvɑli/ *n. plural* **volleys** [C] **1** a large number of bullets, ARROWS, rocks etc. shot or thrown through the air at the same time, or the action of shooting or throwing them: +**of** *a volley of gunfire* **2** a lot of questions, insults, attacks etc. that are all said or made at the same time: +**of** *a volley of accusations* **3** a hit in TENNIS, a kick in SOCCER etc. when the player hits or kicks the ball before it touches the ground

volley² *v.* **volleys, volleyed, volleying** **1** [I,T] to hit or kick a ball before it touches the ground, especially in TENNIS or SOCCER **2** [I] if a large number of guns volley, they are all fired at the same time

vol·ley·ball /ˈvɑliˌbɔl/ S3 *n.* **1** [U] a game in which two teams use their hands to hit a ball over a high net **2** [C] the ball used in this game

volt /voʊlt/ *n.* [C] TECHNICAL a unit for measuring the force of an electric current

V

Vol·ta /ˈvoʊltə/, **Al·es·san·dro** /ˌælɪˈsændroʊ/ (1745–1827) an Italian scientist who did important work on electricity and invented the first electric BATTERY

Vol·ta, the /ˈvoʊltə/ a river in West Africa that flows south through Ghana to the Atlantic Ocean

volt·age /ˈvoʊltɪdʒ/ *n.* [C,U] TECHNICAL electrical force measured in volts: *low-voltage electrical current* → see also HIGH-VOLTAGE

vol·ta·ic cell /vɑlˌteɪ-ɪk ˈsɛl/ *n.* [C] CHEMISTRY a PRIMARY CELL

Vol·taire /voʊlˈtɛr, vɔl-/ (1694–1778) a French writer and PHILOSOPHER who was one of the leaders of the Enlightenment

volt·me·ter /ˈvoʊltˀˌmitɚ/ *n.* [C] PHYSICS an instrument for measuring voltage

vol·u·ble /ˈvɑlyəbəl/ *adj.* FORMAL **1** talking a lot **2** a voluble speech, explanation etc. uses a lot of words and is spoken quickly —**volubly** *adv.* —**volubility** /ˌvɑlyəˈbɪləti/ *n.* [U]

vol·ume /ˈvɑlyəm, -yum/ Ac S3 W2 *n.*
1 SOUND [U] the amount of sound produced by a television, radio etc.: *He had his car stereo on **at full volume**.* | **turn the volume up/down** *Can you turn the volume up?*
2 AMOUNT [C,U] the total amount of something, especially when it is large or increasing: *sales volume* | **+of** *a large volume of mail* | *The volume of trade between the two regions continues to grow.*
3 BOOK [C] **a)** a book that is part of a set or one into which a very long book is divided: *The encyclopedia was first published in 12 volumes.* **b)** FORMAL any book: *a slim volume of poetry*
4 LIQUID/SUBSTANCE [U] MATH a measure of the amount of a liquid or substance, measured as the amount of space it takes up: *the volume of blood in the body*
5 CONTAINER [C,U] the amount that a container will hold: *What is the volume of the tank?*
[**Origin:** 1300–1400 Old French, Latin *volumen* **roll, scroll**, from *volvere*] → see also **sth speaks volumes** at SPEAK (9)

vo·lu·mi·nous /vəˈlumənəs/ *adj.* FORMAL **1** voluminous books, documents etc. are very long and contain a lot of detail: *a voluminous report* **2** a voluminous piece of clothing is very large and loose: *a voluminous fiesta skirt* **3** a voluminous container is very large and can hold a lot of things

vol·un·ta·rism /ˈvɑləntəˌrɪzəm/ *n.* [U] VOLUNTEERISM

vol·un·tar·y¹ /ˈvɑlənˌtɛri/ Ac *adj.* **1** done willingly, without being forced by another person or by a rule, law etc. OPP **mandatory** OPP **compulsory**: *voluntary cooperation* | *Participation in the program is strictly voluntary.* | *Early retirement is offered **on a voluntary basis*** (=without being forced). **2 a voluntary organization/group/institution etc.** an organization, group etc. that is organized or supported by people who give their money, services etc. because they want to, without expecting payment SYN **volunteer** **3** done by people without being paid, usually because they want to help other people SYN **volunteer**: **voluntary work/service etc.** (=work that someone does without expecting to be paid) **4** TECHNICAL voluntary movements of your body are consciously controlled by you OPP **involuntary** —**voluntarily** /ˌvɑlənˈtɛrəli/ *adv.*: *She wasn't fired – she left voluntarily.*

voluntary² Ac *n.* [C] a piece of music, usually for the ORGAN, written to be played in church

vol·un·teer¹ /ˌvɑlənˈtɪr/ Ac S2 W3 *n.* [C] **1** someone who does something without being paid, or who is willing to offer to help someone: *Most of the relief work was done by volunteers.* | *I need some volunteers to help with the cleaning.* **2** someone who offers to join the army, navy, or air force [**Origin:** 1500–1600 French *volontaire*, from Latin *voluntarius*, from *voluntas* **will**]

volunteer² Ac S2 *v.* **1** [I,T] to offer to do something without expecting any reward, often something that other people do not want to do: *I asked for help, but no one volunteered.* | **volunteer to do sth** *Helen volunteered to have Thanksgiving at her house this year.* | **+for** *Gage has volunteered for guard duty.* **2** [T] to offer something of yours or allow it to be used without expecting anything in return: *Carol has kindly volunteered her office for our meeting.* | **volunteer your services/time/skills etc.** *Private boat owners volunteered their services to the rescue workers.* **3** [T] to tell someone something without being asked: *Michael volunteered the information before I had a chance to ask.* **4** [I] to offer to join the army, navy, or air force: **+for** *Andy volunteered for the navy.* **5** [T] to say that someone else will do a job even though they may not want to: **volunteer sb for sth** *My mother volunteered me for the job of babysitting the twins.*

volunteer³ Ac *adj.* [only before noun] **1** done by volunteers: *a volunteer fire department* | *volunteer efforts to help hurricane victims* | **volunteer work/service etc.** (=work that someone does without expecting to be paid) **2 a volunteer worker/assistant/helper etc.** someone who does work without expecting to be paid **3 a volunteer organization/group/institution etc.** an organization, group etc. that is organized or supported by people who give their money, services etc. because they want to, without expecting payment SYN **volunteer**

volcano

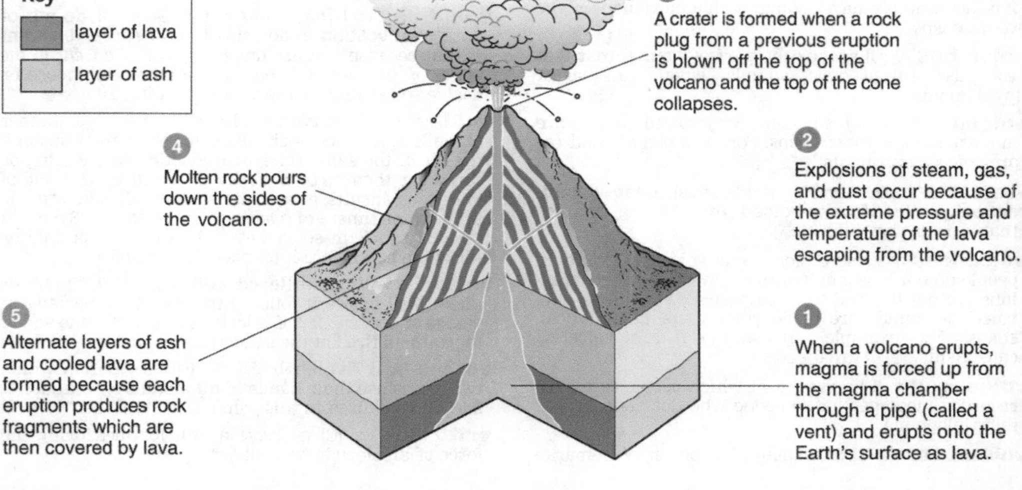
Key
layer of lava
layer of ash
3
A crater is formed when a rock plug from a previous eruption is blown off the top of the volcano and the top of the cone collapses.
4
Molten rock pours down the sides of the volcano.
2
Explosions of steam, gas, and dust occur because of the extreme pressure and temperature of the lava escaping from the volcano.
5
Alternate layers of ash and cooled lava are formed because each eruption produces rock fragments which are then covered by lava.
1
When a volcano erupts, magma is forced up from the magma chamber through a pipe (called a vent) and erupts onto the Earth's surface as lava.

V

vol·un·teer·ism /ˌvɑlənˈtɪrɪzəm/ *n.* [U] the principle of working to support schools, organizations etc. and help other people without expecting payment

vo·lup·tu·ar·y /vəˈlʌptʃuˌɛri/ *n. plural* **voluptuaries** [C] LITERARY someone who enjoys physical, especially sexual, pleasure and owning expensive things

vo·lup·tu·ous /vəˈlʌptʃuəs/ *adj.* **1** a voluptuous woman has large breasts and a soft curved body, and is considered sexually attractive **2** LITERARY something that is voluptuous gives you pleasure because it looks, smells, or tastes good [**Origin:** 1300–1400 Latin *voluptuosus*, from *voluptas* **pleasure**] —**voluptuously** *adv.* —**voluptuousness** *n.* [U]

vom·it¹ /ˈvɑmɪt/ *v.* [I,T] to bring food or drink up from your stomach out through your mouth, because you are sick SYN **throw up**

vomit² *n.* [U] food or other substances that come up from your stomach and through your mouth when you vomit

von Bing·en /fɔn ˈbɪŋən/, **Hil·de·gaard** /ˈhɪldəˌgɑrd/ (1098–1179) a German musician who wrote CLASSICAL music

Von Braun /fɔn ˈbraʊn/, **Wern·her** /ˈvɚnɚ/ (1912–1977) a ROCKET engineer who was born in Germany and developed the V-2 flying bomb for the Nazis. After World War II he went to the U.S. and worked for NASA on the Apollo Program to send a SPACECRAFT to the moon.

voo·doo /ˈvudu/ *n.* [U] magical beliefs and practices used as a form of religion, especially in parts of Africa, Latin America, and the Caribbean —**voodooism** *n.* [U]

voodoo doll *n.* [C] a doll that looks like a particular person that some people believe you can stick pins in, burn etc. in order to hurt that person

vo·ra·cious /vəˈreɪʃəs, vɔ-/ *adj.* [usually before noun] **1** eating or wanting large quantities of food: *Kids can have* ***voracious appetites****.* **2** extremely eager to read books, gain knowledge etc.: *a voracious reader* —**voraciously** *adv.* —**voraciousness** *n.* [U] —**voracity** /vəˈræsət̮i/ *n.* [U]

vor·tex /ˈvɔrtɛks/ *n. plural* **vortexes** or **vortices** /-təsiz/ [C] **1** EARTH SCIENCE a large area of wind or water that spins rapidly and pulls things into its center **2** [usually singular] a situation that has a powerful effect on people's lives and that influences their behavior, even if they did not intend it to: +**of** *He didn't want to be pulled into the vortex of political life.*

vo·ta·ry /ˈvoʊt̮əri/ *n. plural* **votaries** [C] FORMAL someone who is a strong believer of a particular religion, or a strong supporter of a particular leader

vote¹ /voʊt/ S2 W1 *v.*

1 MAKE A CHOICE [I,T] POLITICS to show by marking a paper, raising your hand etc. which person you want to elect or whether you support a particular plan: *Anyone over 18 can vote.* | +**for/in favor of** *Who did you vote for in the last election?* | +**against** *Only Stevens voted against the measure.* | +**on** *If we can't agree, we'll have to vote on it.* | **vote to do sth** *Union members voted to accept management's offer.* | **vote Democrat/Republican/Socialist etc.** *My father always votes Republican.* | *It's not hard to* ***register to vote****.*

2 vote sb into power/office/Congress etc. POLITICS to elect someone to a position of power by voting OPP **vote sb out of power/office/Congress etc.**: *He was first voted into office in 2002.*

3 TITLE/PRIZE [T usually passive] to choose someone or something for a particular title or prize by voting for them: **vote sb/sth sth** *The program was just voted the best show on television.*

4 MONEY [T] to agree to provide money for a particular purpose as a result of voting: *The Board of Supervisors has refused to vote more money for the project.*

5 I vote... SPOKEN said to show that you prefer one choice or possible action: **I vote (that)** *I vote that we go to the movies.* | +**for** *"What do you want to eat?" "I vote for Mexican."*

6 vote with your feet to show that you do not support a decision or action by leaving a place or organization

7 vote with your pocketbook a) also **vote your pocketbook** to vote for someone or something that you think will help you have the most money: *People generally vote their pocketbooks against new taxes.* **b)** also **vote with your dollars** to show your support for someone or something by the way you spend your money

vote sth ↔ **down** *phr. v.* to defeat a plan, law etc. by voting against it: *Various amendments were proposed and voted down.*

vote sb ↔ **in** *phr. v.* POLITICS to elect someone by voting: *A new chairman was voted in last week.*

vote sb ↔ **out** *phr. v.* POLITICS to remove someone from a position of power by voting: *If they don't keep their promises, we'll just vote them out.*

vote² W1 *n.*

1 CHOICE [C] a choice or decision that you make by voting in an election or meeting: *Do you think one vote really makes a difference?* | *All the votes were counted before six o'clock.* | +**for/in favor of/against** *There were 402 votes for Williams, and 372 against.* | *Citizens* ***cast*** *their* ***votes*** *next week.* | *They made a desperate attempt to* ***win votes****.*

2 ELECTION [C usually singular] an act of voting, when a group of people vote in order to decide or choose something: +**on** *a vote on the new immigration bill* | *The three proposals will be* ***put to a vote*** *next week.* | *They* ***took a vote****, and it was unanimous.*

3 RESULT [singular] the result of a vote: *Both sides expect a close vote.* | *The vote was 15 to 4 in favor of the change.* | *The motion was passed* ***by a vote of*** *215 to 84.*

4 the vote a) the total number of votes made in an election or the total number of people who vote: *Davis won the election with 57% of the vote.* | *The party increased its* ***share of the vote*** *by 5%.* | **the African-American/Irish/Jewish etc. vote** (=all the votes of African Americans, Irish people etc.) | **split the vote** (=to cause people to vote for different but similar people or things with the result that something else wins) **b)** the right to vote in political elections: *American women* ***got the vote*** *in 1920.*

5 sb/sth gets my vote SPOKEN used to say that you are ready to support someone or something: *Anything that means a better deal for our children gets my vote.* [**Origin:** 1200–1300 Latin *votum* **promise, wish**, from *vovere* **to promise**]

ˈvote-ˌgetter *n.* [C] INFORMAL someone who is voted for in an election: *Pfeifer was* ***the top vote-getter*** *in last year's election.*

ˌvote of ˈconfidence *n.* [C] **1** POLITICS a formal process in which people vote in order to show that they support someone or something, especially a government **2** something that you do or say that shows you support someone or something: *The new investment is a vote of confidence in the nation's economic future.*

ˌvote of no ˈconfidence, vote of no-confidence *n.* [C] **1** POLITICS a formal process in which people vote in order to show that they do not support someone or something, especially a government **2** something that you do or say that shows that you do not support someone or something

vot·er /ˈvoʊt̮ɚ/ W1 *n.* [C] POLITICS someone who votes or has the right to vote, especially in a political election: *Only 40% of eligible voters participated in the last election.*

ˈvoting booth *n.* [C] an enclosed place where you can vote secretly

ˈvoting maˌchine *n.* [C] POLITICS a machine that records votes as they are made

vo·tive /ˈvoʊt̮ɪv/ *adj.* [only before noun] given or done because of a promise made to God or to a SAINT: *votive offerings*

ˌvotive ˈcandle *n.* [C] a small CANDLE, often used for religious purposes

vouch /vaʊtʃ/ *v.*

vouch for *phr. v.* **1 vouch for sth** to say that you firmly believe that something is true or good because

V

of your experience or knowledge of it: *I can vouch for the quality of his work.* **2 vouch for sb** to say that you know that someone is good and honest, and will behave well, work well, tell the truth etc.: *Don't worry about Andy – I'll vouch for him.*

vouch·er /ˈvaʊtʃɚ/ *n.* [C] **1** a type of ticket that can be used instead of money for a particular purpose: *a gift voucher* **2** an official statement or RECEIPT that is given to someone to prove that their accounts are correct or that money has been paid [**Origin:** 1500–1600 Old French *vocher* **to state, call as a witness**, from Latin *vocare*]

vouch·safe /vaʊtʃˈseɪf/ *v.* [T] to offer, give, or tell someone something in a way that shows you trust them

vow¹ /vaʊ/ *n.* [C] **1** a serious promise: *Jim* ***made a vow that*** *he would find his wife's killer.* | **keep/break a vow** (=to do or not do what you promised) **2** a religious promise that you will do something for God, the church etc.: **a vow of silence/chastity/poverty etc.** (=a promise that you will not speak, have sex etc.) | *She* ***took vows*** (=became a nun) *at the age of 16.* **3 vows** [plural] also **marriage/wedding vows** the promises you make during a wedding ceremony: *Ron and Rhea* ***exchanged vows*** *in front of more than 100 friends on Saturday.* [**Origin:** 1200–1300 Old French *vou*, from Latin *votum* **promise, wish**]

vow² *v.* [T] **1** to make a serious promise to yourself or someone else: **vow to do sth** *He vowed to return.* | **vow (that)** *I vowed that I would never drink again.* ►see THESAURUS box at **promise¹** **2** FORMAL to make a religious promise that you will do something for God, the church etc.

vow·el /ˈvaʊəl/ *n.* [C] ENG. LANG. ARTS **1** one of the speech sounds that you make by letting your breath flow out without closing any part of your mouth or throat **2** a letter of the alphabet used to represent a vowel. In English the vowels are a, e, i, o, u, and sometimes y. [**Origin:** 1300–1400 Old French *vouel*, from Latin *vocalis*, from *vox* **voice**]

V

vox pop·u·li /ˌvɑks ˈpɑpyəlaɪ, -yəli/ *n.* FORMAL **the vox populi** the opinions of ordinary people

voy·age¹ /ˈvɔɪ-ɪdʒ/ *n.* [C] a long trip in a ship or a space vehicle: *The voyage from England to India used to take six months.* ►see THESAURUS box at **trip¹**

voyage² *v.* [I] LITERARY to make a long trip in a ship or a space vehicle

voy·ag·er /ˈvɔɪ-ɪdʒɚ/ *n.* [C] LITERARY someone who makes long and often dangerous trips in a ship

voy·a·geur /ˌvɔɪəˈʒɚ/ *n.* [C] someone who traveled in Canada and North America, buying and selling furs, between the 17th and 19th centuries. Many voyageurs were French, and from Canada.

voy·eur /vɔɪˈɚ/ *n.* [C] **1** someone who gets sexual pleasure from secretly watching other people's sexual activities **2** someone who enjoys watching other people's private behavior or suffering —**voyeurism** *n.* [U] —**voyeuristic** /ˌvɔɪəˈrɪstɪk◂/ *adj.*

VP, V.P. *n.* [C] INFORMAL a VICE PRESIDENT

VR *n.* [U] VIRTUAL REALITY

vs. a written abbreviation of VERSUS, used especially in sports competitions: *UCLA vs. Miami*

V-shaped /ˈvi ʃeɪpt/ *adj.* having a shape like the letter V —**V-shape** *n.* [C]

V-sign /ˈvi saɪn/ *n.* [C] a sign meaning "peace" or "victory" made by holding up the first two fingers of your hand

VT the written abbreviation of VERMONT

Vul·can /ˈvʌlkən/ the Roman name for the god Hephaestus

vul·ca·nize /ˈvʌlkəˌnaɪz/ *v.* [T] CHEMISTRY to make rubber stronger using a special chemical treatment —**vulcanization** /ˌvʌlkənəˈzeɪʃən/ *n.* [U]

vul·gar /ˈvʌlgɚ/ *adj.* **1** DISAPPROVING dealing with or talking about sex and body wastes in a way people think is disgusting and not socially acceptable: *vulgar language* **2** DISAPPROVING not behaving politely in social situations: *Norman was a vulgar ignorant man.* **3** DISAPPROVING not showing good judgment about what is attractive or appropriate SYN **tasteless**: *a vulgar display of wealth* **4** FORMAL relating to ordinary people or the way they speak [**Origin:** 1300–1400 Latin *vulgaris*, from *volgus*, *vulgus* **common people**] —**vulgarly** *adv.*

vul·gar·ism /ˈvʌlgəˌrɪzəm/ *n.* [C] a VULGARITY

vul·gar·i·ty /vʌlˈgærət̬i/ *n. plural* **vulgarities** **1** [U] the state or quality of being vulgar **2** [C usually plural] vulgar remarks, jokes etc.

vul·gar·ize /ˈvʌlgəˌraɪz/ *v.* [T] FORMAL to spoil the quality or lower the standard of something that is good —**vulgarization** /ˌvʌlgərəˈzeɪʃən/ *n.* [U]

Vul·gate /ˈvʌlgeɪt, -gət/ *n.* **the Vulgate** the Latin Bible commonly used in the Catholic Church

vul·ner·a·ble /ˈvʌlnərəbəl/ *adj.* **1** someone who is vulnerable is easily harmed or hurt emotionally, physically, or morally: *I've been feeling very vulnerable since we broke up.* | **+to** *Babies are particularly vulnerable to infections.* **2** a place, thing, or idea that is vulnerable is easy to attack, damage, criticize etc. OPP **invulnerable**: *vulnerable institutions* | **+to** *The country is very vulnerable to attack.* [**Origin:** 1600–1700 Late Latin *vulnerabilis*, from Latin *vulnus* **wound**] —**vulnerably** *adv.* —**vulnerability** /ˌvʌlnərəˈbɪlət̬i/ *n.* [C,U] *the area's vulnerability to flooding*

vul·ture /ˈvʌltʃɚ/ *n.* [C] **1** BIOLOGY a large bird that eats dead animals **2** someone who uses other people's troubles for their own advantage

vul·va /ˈvʌlvə/ *n.* [C] BIOLOGY the outer part of a woman's sexual organs

vy·ing /ˈvaɪ-ɪŋ/ *v.* the present participle of VIE

W,w

W¹, w /ˈdʌbəlyu, / *n. plural* **W's, w's** [C] **a)** the 23rd letter of the English alphabet **b)** a sound represented by this letter

W² **1** also **W.** the written abbreviation of WEST or WESTERN **2** the written abbreviation of WATT

w/ a written abbreviation of "with," used especially when writing notes quickly → see also W/O

WA a written abbreviation of Washington

Wac, WAC /wæk/ *n.* [C] a member of the Women's Army Corps, especially during World War II

wack /wæk/ *adj.* SLANG WHACKED

wack·o, whacko /ˈwækoʊ/ *n. plural* **wackos** [C] INFORMAL someone who is crazy or strange —**wacko** *adj.*

wack·y, whacky /ˈwæki/ *adj. comparative* **wackier**, *superlative* **wackiest** INFORMAL silly in an exciting or amusing way —**wackiness** *n.* [U]

ˈwacky ˌweed *n.* [U] SLANG MARIJUANA

wad¹ /wɑd/ *n.* [C] **1** a thick pile of paper or pieces of thin material: *a wad of dollar bills* **2** a thick soft mass of material that has been pressed together: *a wad of bubble gum* **3 spend/blow your wad (on sth)** INFORMAL to spend all your money on something → see also **shoot your wad** at SHOOT¹ (24), TIGHTWAD

wad² *v.*

wad sth ↔ **up** *phr. v.* to press something such as a piece of paper or cloth into a small tight ball

wad·ding /ˈwɑdɪŋ/ *n.* [U] soft material used for packing or to protect a wound

wad·dle /ˈwɑdl/ *v.* [I] to walk with short steps, swinging from one side to another like a duck: **+up/along/around etc.** *He waddled down the hall to his office.* —**waddle** *n.* [singular]

wade

wade /weɪd/ *v.* [I always + adv./prep.,T] to walk through water that is not deep: **+through/across/into etc.** *One of the bears waded into the river to fish.*

wade through sth *phr. v.* to read or deal with a lot of boring papers or written work: *Employers do not have time to wade through a ten-page resume.*

wad·ers /ˈweɪdɚz/ *n.* [plural] high rubber boots that you wear for walking in water, especially when you are fishing or hunting

wa·di, wady /ˈwɑdi/ *n. plural* **wadis** or **wadies** [C] EARTH SCIENCE a usually dry river bed in a desert, that becomes full of water when there is a lot of rain

ˈwading bird *n.* [C] BIOLOGY a bird that has long legs and a long neck and walks around in water to find its food

ˈwading pool *n.* [C] a small pool filled with water that is not very deep, for small children to play in

wa·fer /ˈweɪfɚ/ *n.* [C] **1** a very thin CRACKER **2** a thin round piece of bread used by some churches in the Christian religious ceremony of COMMUNION

ˈwafer-thin *adj.* extremely thin: *wafer-thin chocolates*

waf·fle¹ /ˈwɑfəl/ *n.* [C] a thin flat cake, marked with a pattern of deep squares, and usually eaten for breakfast

waffle² *v.* [I] INFORMAL to avoid making or stating a clear decision or taking an action: **+on/about/over** *The mayor can't keep waffling on this issue.*

ˈwaffle ˌiron *n.* [C] a piece of kitchen equipment used to cook waffles

waft /wɑft, wæft/ *v.* [I always + adv./prep.] **1** if a smell, wind, or smoke wafts somewhere, it moves gently through the air **2** if music wafts somewhere, you hear it there and it is pleasant and not very loud [**Origin:** 1600–1700 *waft* **to guard a group of ships as they sail along** (16–17 centuries), from Middle Dutch *wachten* **to watch, guard**]

wag

The dog wagged its tail.

wag¹ /wæg/ **wagged, wagging** *v.* **1** [I,T] if a dog wags its tail or if its tail wags, the dog moves its tail repeatedly from one side to the other **2** [T] to shake your finger or head repeatedly, especially to show disapproval: *"No, no," she said,* ***wagging*** *her* ***finger***. → see also **it's (a case of) the tail wagging the dog** at TAIL¹ (12), **tongues wag** at TONGUE¹ (8)

wag² *n.* **1** [C] someone who says amusing things **2** [C usually singular] a wagging movement

wage¹ /weɪdʒ/ W3 *n.* [singular] also **wages** [plural] money you earn that is paid according to the number of hours, days, or weeks that you work: *Steve* ***earns a*** *decent* ***wage***. | *Last year, pilots received* ***a wage increase*** *of 5%.* | **an hourly/daily/weekly wage** *She earns an hourly wage of $12.* | **wage levels/rates** (=fixed amounts of money paid for particular jobs) → see also **a living wage** at LIVING¹ (7), MINIMUM WAGE, SALARY ▶ see THESAURUS box at **pay²**

wage² *v.* [T] to be actively involved in a war, struggle, or fight against someone or something: **wage (a) war on/against** *Rebels have waged a 12-year war against the government.* | **wage a campaign/struggle/fight etc.** *Supporters have been waging a letter-writing campaign for his release from prison.*

ˈwage ˌearner *n.* [C] **1** someone in a family who earns money for the rest of the family **2** someone who works for wages, often someone who works in a factory, builds things etc.

ˈwage freeze *n.* [U] an action taken by a company, government etc. to stop wages from being increased for a period of time

ˌwage-ˈprice ˌspiral *n.* [C] ECONOMICS a continuous economic process in which higher WAGES (=the money people are paid for working) lead to an increase in the cost of producing goods, so that prices rise. Wages then have to rise again, and this then leads to higher and higher prices.

wa·ger¹ /ˈweɪdʒɚ/ *v.* [T] OLD-FASHIONED **1** to agree to risk money on the result of something such as a race or game SYN **bet** **2 I'll wager (that)** SPOKEN used to say that you are very sure that something is true

wager² *n.* [C] an agreement in which you win or lose money according to the result of something such as a race SYN **bet**

wag·gle /ˈwægəl/ *v.* [I,T] to WIGGLE —**waggle** *n.* [C]

Wag·ner /ˈvɑgnɚ/, **Rich·ard** /ˈrɪkɑrt/ (1813–1883) a German musician who is most famous for writing long OPERAS based on German MYTHOLOGY —**Wagnerian** /vɑgˈnɪriən/ *adj.*

wag·on /ˈwægən/ *n.* [C] **1** a small open CART with four wheels and a long handle, often used as a toy for children to play with **2** a strong vehicle with four wheels, used for carrying heavy loads and usually pulled by horses **3** INFORMAL a STATION WAGON **4 be/go**

on the wagon INFORMAL to not drink alcohol anymore, or to stop drinking alcohol **5 fall off the wagon** INFORMAL to start drinking alcohol again after you have decided to stop → see also PADDY WAGON

'wagon train *n.* [C] a long line of wagons and horses used by the people who moved to the West of America in the 19th century

waif /weɪf/ *n.* [C] someone, especially a child, who is pale and thin and looks as if they do not have a home

wail /weɪl/ *v.* **1** [T] to say something in a loud, sad, and complaining way: *"How are we going to pay for this?" Mom wailed.* **2** [I] to cry out with a long, high sound, especially because you are very sad or in pain: *Somewhere behind them a child began to wail.* **3** [I] to make a long, high sound: *Sirens were wailing in the distance.* —**wail** *n.* [C] *the wail of police sirens* —**wailing** *n.* [singular, U]

wain·scot /'weɪnskət, -skoʊt, -skɑt/ also **wain·scot·ing** /'weɪnskət̬ɪŋ/ *n.* [C,U] wood that is put on the bottom part of a wall inside a house or office, as a decoration —**wainscoted** *adj.*

waist /weɪst/ *n.* [C] **1** BIOLOGY the part in the middle of your body, just above the HIPS: *Juliet has a tiny waist.* | **from the waist up/down** *Lota was paralyzed from the waist down.* | *The guy stood there, **stripped to the waist*** (=not wearing any clothes on the top half of his body). **2** the part of a piece of clothing that goes around this part of your body **3** TECHNICAL the middle part of a ship → see also -WAISTED

waist·band /'weɪstbænd/ *n.* [C] the part of a skirt, pair of pants etc. that fastens around your waist

waist·coat /'wɛskət, 'weɪstkoʊt/ *n.* [C] a VEST

,waist-'deep *adj., adv.* deep enough to reach your waist: *The water was waist-deep.*

-waisted /weɪstɪd/ [in adjectives] **slim-waisted/narrow-waisted/thick-waisted etc.** having a thin, thick etc. waist

,waist-'high *adj., adv.* high enough to reach your waist

waist·line /'weɪstlaɪn/ *n.* [C] **1** the area around your waist, especially used to judge how fat or thin you are: *a trim waistline* **2** the part of a piece of clothing that fits around your waist

W

wait[1] /weɪt/ [S1] [W1] *v.*

1 DELAY/NOT START STH [I] to not do something or go somewhere until something else happens, someone arrives etc.: *Hurry up! Everyone's waiting.* | **+for** *Wait for me.* | **wait (for) 3 hours/two weeks etc.** *I've been waiting for 30 minutes.* | **+until/till** *Wait right here until I come back.* | **wait to do sth** *Are you waiting to use the phone?* | **wait for sb/sth to do sth** *She paused, waiting for him to say something.* | *I'm sorry to have **kept you waiting*** (=made you wait, especially because I arrived late or was busy doing something else). | *There were reports of fans **waiting in line** as early as 6 a.m. Saturday.*

THESAURUS

expect to believe that someone or something is going to arrive – used when you do not always change what you are doing because of this: *She's expecting a letter from her boyfriend.* | *I can't talk for very long – I'm expecting guests.*
await FORMAL to wait for something: *The soldiers awaited the order to advance.*

2 EXPECT STH TO HAPPEN [I] to expect something to happen that has not happened yet: *"Have you heard about the job?" "No, I'm still waiting."* | **wait for sth** *I'm still waiting for my test results.* | **wait for sb/sth to do sth** *We're waiting for the prices to go down before we buy a computer.*
3 be waiting (for sb) INFORMAL if something is waiting, it is ready for you to use, get etc.: *The report was waiting on my desk when I got back.* | **be waiting to do sth** *A cab was waiting to take us home.*
4 wait tables to have the job of serving food to people at their table in a restaurant: *I spent the summer waiting tables.*

SPOKEN PHRASES

5 wait a minute/second/moment etc. a) used to stop someone for a short time when they are leaving or starting to do something: *Wait a moment – I've got to get my books.* **b)** used to interrupt someone, especially because you do not agree with what they are saying: *Wait a minute! I've already paid you for that.* **c)** used when you suddenly remember or notice something: *Wait a minute. I think that's her house over there.*
6 sb can't wait also **sb can hardly wait** used to say that someone feels excited and impatient about something that is going to happen soon: *We're going to Australia on Saturday – I can't wait!* | **+for** *I can't wait for my vacation.* | **sb can't wait to do sth** *I can't wait to tell Gloria the good news.* | **sb can't wait for sb/sth to do sth** *John can hardly wait for the football season to start.*
7 I can't wait also **I can hardly wait** HUMOROUS used to say that something seems likely to be very boring: *A lecture on English grammar? I can hardly wait.*
8 sth can/can't wait used to say that something is very urgent or is not urgent: *Go home – the report can wait until tomorrow.*
9 sth will have to wait used to say that something will have to be done or dealt with later because you cannot do it or deal with it now: *Dating will just have to wait until I'm out of graduate school.*
10 wait and see used to say that someone should be patient because they will find out about something later: *"What's for dinner?" "Wait and see."*
11 wait until/till used when you are excited about telling or showing someone something: *Wait till you see Gaby's new house!*
12 sth is (well) worth waiting for used to say that something is very good, even though it takes a long time to come: *Their new album was worth waiting for.*
13 what are you waiting for? used to tell someone to do something immediately: *What are you waiting for? Ask her out on a date.*
14 what are we waiting for? used to say in a cheerful way that you think everyone should start doing something immediately: *What are we waiting for? Let's go eat.*
15 wait your turn (to do sth) used to tell someone to stay calm and wait until it is their turn to do something, instead of trying to move ahead of other people
16 (just) you wait a) used to tell someone that you are sure something will happen: *It'll be a huge success. Just you wait.* **b)** used to threaten someone: *You wait till I tell Mom.*

17 be an accident/a disaster etc. waiting to happen to be someone or something that is likely to cause problems in the future because of the condition they are in or the way they are behaving: *The old building was an accident waiting to happen.*
18 be waiting in the wings to be ready to do something if it is necessary or if an appropriate time comes: *Several talented young players are waiting in the wings.*
19 a/the waiting game a situation in which someone deliberately does nothing and waits to see what other people do, in order to get an advantage for themselves: *She didn't have the patience required to **play a waiting game**.*

wait around *phr. v.* to stay in the same place and do nothing while you are waiting for something to happen, someone to arrive etc.: *I waited around for 20 minutes and she never showed up.*

wait on *phr. v.* **1 wait on sb** to serve food to someone at their table, especially in a restaurant **2 wait on sth** to wait for a particular event, piece of information etc., especially before doing something or making a decision: *I'm waiting on a phone call from our sales rep.* **3 wait on sb hand and foot** to do everything for someone while they do nothing

wait sth ↔ **out** *phr. v.* to wait for an event or period of time, especially a bad one, to finish: *We spent the night at the airport, waiting out the snow storm.*

wait up *phr. v.* **1** to wait for someone to return

before you go to bed: +**for** *Don't wait up for me – I'll be very late.* **2 Wait up!** SPOKEN used to tell someone to stop, so that you can talk to them or go with them [**Origin:** 1100–1200 Old North French *waitier* **to watch**]

wait² S1 *n.* [C] a period of time in which you wait for something to happen, someone to arrive etc.: +**for** *The average wait for an appointment was eight weeks.* → see also **lie in wait (for sb/sth)** at LIE¹ (10)

Waite /weɪt/, **Mor·ri·son** /ˈmɔrəsən/ (1816–1888) a CHIEF JUSTICE on the U.S. Supreme Court

wait·er /ˈweɪt̬ɚ/ *n.* [C] a man who serves food and drinks to the people at the tables in a restaurant

waiting list *n.* [C] a list of people who have asked for something but who must wait before they can have it: *We are second* ***on the waiting list.***

waiting room *n.* [C] a room for people to wait in, for example to see a doctor, take a train etc.

wait-list /ˈweɪtlɪst/ *v.* [T usually passive] to put someone's name on a waiting list

wait·ress /ˈweɪtrɪs/ S3 *n.* [C] a woman who serves food and drink to people at the tables in a restaurant

wait·staff /ˈweɪtstæf/ *n.* [U] all the waiters and waitresses that work at a restaurant

waive /weɪv/ *v.* [T] to state officially that a right, rule etc. can be ignored, because at this time it is not useful or important

waiv·er /ˈweɪvɚ/ *n.* [C] an official written statement saying that a right, claim etc. can be waived

wake¹ /weɪk/ S1 W3 *v.* *past tense* **woke** /woʊk/, *past participle* **woken** /ˈwoʊkən/ [I,T] to stop sleeping, or to make someone stop sleeping SYN **wake up**: *She woke early the next morning.* | *Try not to wake the baby.* | **wake to do sth** *In the morning I woke to find her staring at me.* [**Origin:** Old English *wacan* **to wake up** and *wacian* **to be awake**]

wake up *phr. v.* **1 wake sb ↔ up** to stop sleeping, or to make someone stop sleeping: *I usually wake up at 7:00.* | *I'll wake you up when it's time to leave.* **2** to start to listen or pay attention to something: *Wake up! I'm trying to tell you something important.* **3 wake up and smell the coffee** SPOKEN used to tell someone to recognize the truth or reality of a situation

wake (up) to sth *phr. v.* **1** to start to realize and understand a danger, an idea etc.: *You have to wake up to the fact that alcohol is killing you.* **2** to experience something as you are waking up: *Nancy woke to the sound of birds outside her window.*

wake² *n.* [C] **1 in the wake of sth** if something, especially something bad, happens in the wake of an event, it happens afterward and usually as a result of it: *New laws were passed in the wake of the scandal.* **2 in sb's/sth's wake** behind or after someone or something has moved quickly away: *The tornado left hundreds of damaged homes in its wake.* **3** the track or path made behind a boat, car etc. as it moves along **4** the time before a funeral when friends and relatives meet to remember the dead person

Wake At·oll /ˌweɪk ˈætɔl/ also **ˌWake ˈIsland** a U.S. TERRITORY that is an island in the western Pacific Ocean

wake·ful /ˈweɪkfəl/ *adj.* **1 a)** not sleeping or unable to sleep **b)** a wakeful period of time is one when you cannot sleep **2** FORMAL always watching and ready to do whatever is necessary —**wakefulness** *n.* [U]

wak·en /ˈweɪkən/ *v.* [I,T] FORMAL to wake, or to wake someone: *He wasn't sure if he should waken his mother.*

wake-up ˌcall *n.* [C] **1** a telephone call that someone makes to you, especially at a hotel, to wake you up in the morning **2** an experience or event which shocks you and makes you realize that something bad is happening and that changes must be made

wak·ing /ˈweɪkɪŋ/ *adj.* **sb's waking hours/life/day etc.** all the time when someone is awake: *Children spend almost half their waking day in school.*

Wal·dorf sal·ad /ˌwɔldɔrf ˈsæləd/ *n.* [C] a mixture of small pieces of apples, CELERY, nuts, and MAYONNAISE

Wales /weɪlz/ a country in the United Kingdom, west of England

Wa·le·sa /vəˈlɛnsə/, **Lech** /lɛk/ (1943–) the President of Poland from 1990 to 1995

walk¹ /wɔk/ S1 W1 *v.*

1 MOVE ALONG [I] to move along by putting one foot in front of the other: *"How did you get here?" "We walked."* | *I'll bet we walked at least three miles.* | +**to/along/around etc.** *Turn left and walk up the hill.* | *We spent the day walking around the city.* | **walk back/home** *It's late – are you sure you want to walk back by yourself?* | **walk up/over to sb/sth** *Jane walked over to him and asked the time.*

THESAURUS

march to walk like soldiers, with regular steps
stride to walk with long steps in a determined way
stroll to walk in a relaxed way, especially for pleasure
amble to walk slowly in a relaxed way
wander to walk slowly, often when you are not going to any particular place
tiptoe to walk quietly and carefully on your toes when you do not want to be heard
creep/sneak to walk quietly when you do not want to be seen or heard
hike to take a long walk in the country, mountains etc.
trudge to walk in a tired way or when it is difficult to continue walking
limp to walk with difficulty because one leg is hurt
hobble to walk with difficulty because your legs or feet hurt
wade to walk through water
stagger to walk or move unsteadily, almost falling over, for example because you are drunk
→ RUN, TRAVEL

2 AREA/DISTANCE [T] to walk in order to get somewhere, across a particular area or distance: *I normally walk the six blocks to the office.* ►see THESAURUS box at **travel¹**
3 WALK TO A PLACE WITH SB [T] to walk somewhere with someone, especially to make sure that they are safe: *It's late – I'll walk you home.* | **walk sb to sth** *Will you walk me to my car?*
4 DOG [T] to take a dog outside so that it can walk, run, play etc.: *Karen's out walking the dog.*
5 COURT [I] also **walk free** to leave a court of law without being punished or sent to prison: *If more evidence isn't found, Harris will walk.*
6 walk it SPOKEN to go somewhere by walking: *If the last bus has gone, we'll have to walk it.*
7 BASEBALL [I,T] if a PITCHER walks a BATTER or if the batter walks, the pitcher throws the ball four times outside the area he is aiming at, so that the batter is allowed to go to the first of the four BASES
8 walk on eggshells/eggs to be very careful about how you behave because you do not want to upset someone: *Everyone was walking on eggshells at the office.*
9 HEAVY OBJECT [T] to move a heavy object slowly by moving first one side and then the other: *Let's try walking the refrigerator over to the wall.*
10 walk tall to be proud and confident because you know that you have not done anything wrong
11 be walking on air to feel extremely happy: *On my first pay day, I was walking on air.*
12 walk the walk to do the things that people expect or think are necessary in a particular situation, rather than just talking about them → see also TALK THE TALK
13 walk the streets a) to walk around the streets in a town or city: *It was not safe to walk the streets at night.* **b)** to be free and able to move around as you like: *In three months, he'll be walking the streets again.* **c)** OLD-FASHIONED to be a PROSTITUTE
14 walk a beat if a police officer walks a beat, he or she walks around an area of a town or city in order to make sure no one is doing anything illegal
15 walk the plank to be forced to walk along a board

laid over the side of the ship until you fall off into the ocean, used as a punishment in the past, especially by PIRATES

walk around *phr. v.* to dress or behave in public in a particular way, especially when this makes you look or seem silly: *I can't believe he walks around in those dirty old T-shirts.*

walk away *phr. v.* **1** to leave a situation that you are involved in: **+from** *She walked away from a successful career in pop music to have a family.* **2** to come out of an accident or very bad situation without being harmed: *Amazingly, Darcy walked away without a scratch.*

walk away with sth *phr. v.* to win something easily or in way that surprises everyone: *The lucky winner will walk away with a prize of $10,000.* → see also WALKAWAY

walk in *phr. v.* to enter a building or room, especially in an unexpected way without being invited: *Don't just walk in without knocking first.* | *As soon as I **walked in the door**, she started yelling at me.* | *At the clinic, patients can **walk in off the street*** (=visit someone such as a doctor without having previously arranged to see them).

walk in on sb *phr. v.* to go into a place and interrupt someone who you did not expect to be there: *I walked in on Joe and Susan kissing in his office.*

walk into sth *phr. v.* **1** to hit an object accidentally as you are walking along: **walk straight/right etc. into sth** *He walked straight into the edge of the door.* **2** if you walk into a bad situation, you become involved in it without intending to **3** to make yourself look stupid when you could easily have avoided it if you had been more careful: **walk straight/right into sth** *I guess I walked right into that joke.*

walk off *phr. v.* **1** to leave someone by walking away from them, especially in a rude or angry way: *Don't just walk off when I'm trying to talk to you!* **2 walk sth ↔ off** if you walk off an injury or a bad feeling, you walk for a little while to try to make it go away: *Let's go out – maybe I can walk this headache off.* **3 walk off dinner/a meal etc.** to walk outside for a little while so that your stomach feels less full **4 walk off the/your job** to stop working as a protest: *Without new contracts, mine workers will walk off their jobs Thursday.* **5 walk sb's legs/feet off** SPOKEN to make someone tired by making them walk too far **6 walk your legs/feet off** SPOKEN to walk a lot so that you feel very tired

walk off with sth *phr. v.* **1** to win something easily: *Kayla walked off with the trophy.* **2** to steal something or take something that does not belong to you: *Someone walked off with my jacket.*

walk out *phr. v.* **1** to go outside: **+into** *Jerri and I walked out into the backyard.* **2** to leave a place suddenly, especially because you disapprove of something: **+of** *Several members walked out of the meeting in protest.* **3** to stop working as a protest: *Workers are threatening to walk out if an agreement is not reached.* → see also WALKOUT

walk out on *phr. v.* **1 walk out on sb** to leave your husband, wife etc. suddenly: *When she was three months pregnant, Pete walked out on her.* **2 walk out on sth** to stop doing something you have agreed to do or that you are responsible for: *Several investors have walked out of the project.*

walk over sb *phr. v.* to treat someone badly by always making them do what you want them to do: *Greg lets his older sister **walk all over** him.*

walk through *phr. v.* **1 walk sb through sth** to give someone careful instructions as they do something: *I need someone to walk me through the software installation.* **2 walk sth ↔ through** to practice something: *Let's walk through Scene 2 to see how long it takes.* → see also WALK-THROUGH

walk² S2 W3 *n.*

1 TRIP BY FOOT [C] a trip that you make by walking, especially for exercise or enjoyment: *The beach is only a short walk away.* | *Why don't we **take the kids for a walk**?* | *Let's **go for a walk**.* | *I'm going to **take a walk** at lunchtime.* | **walk to/through/across etc. sth** *The walk across the bridge is wonderful.* | **a five-minute/three-mile etc. walk** *From here to the bus station is a five-minute walk.*

2 ROAD/PATH [C] a particular path or ROUTE that you walk, especially through an attractive or interesting area: *There are some interesting walks round the park.*

3 WALKING GROUP [C] an organized TOUR or group of people walking for pleasure: *a guided walk through the city*

4 EVENT [C] an occasion when a lot of people go for a long walk, especially in order to earn money for a CHARITY SYN **walkathon**: *the annual AIDS walk*

5 WAY OF WALKING [singular, U] the way someone walks SYN **gait**: *He has a funny walk.*

6 SPEED OF WALKING [singular] the speed at which someone or something moves when they are walking: *The horse slowed to a walk.*

7 BASEBALL [C] in baseball, an occasion when a BATTER is allowed to go to the first of the four bases because the PITCHER throws the ball outside the area they are aiming at four times → see also WALK OF LIFE

walk·a·thon /ˈwɔkəˌθɑn/ *n.* [C] an occasion when a lot of people go for a long walk, especially in order to earn money for a CHARITY

walk·a·way /ˈwɔkəweɪ/ *n.* [C] INFORMAL an easy victory → see also WALK AWAY WITH

walk·er /ˈwɔkɚ/ *n.* [C] **1** someone who walks for pleasure or exercise: *The area is popular with walkers and bikers.* **2 a fast/slow etc. walker** someone who walks fast, slowly etc. **3** a metal frame with wheels that old or sick people use to help them walk **4** a frame on wheels that supports a baby so that it can use its legs to move around before it is able to walk

walk·ie-talk·ie /ˌwɔki ˈtɔki/ *n.* [C] a small radio that you can carry and use to speak to other people who have the same type of radio

ˈwalk-in *adj.* [only before noun] big enough for a person to walk inside: *a walk-in closet*

walk·ing¹ /ˈwɔkɪŋ/ *n.* [U] **1** the activity of going for walks: *I like to **go walking** in the woods just to breathe the fresh air.* **2** the sport of walking long distances as fast as you can without actually running

walking² *adj.* [only before noun] **1 walking shoes/boots** shoes or boots that are strong and comfortable, because they are intended for walking long distances **2** HUMOROUS used to describe a person who has the qualities you are mentioning: *Stay away from him – he's a walking time bomb.* | **a walking dictionary/encyclopedia** (=someone who knows a lot, and always has the information that you want) | **a walking disaster (area)** (=someone who always drops things, has accidents, makes mistakes etc.)

ˈwalking ˌpapers *n.* [plural] **give sb their walking papers** to tell someone that they must leave a place or a job

ˈwalking ˌstick *n.* [C] **1** a stick that is used to support someone, especially an old person, while they walk **2** an insect with a long thin body that looks similar to a small stick

ˈwalking ˌtour *n.* [C] a TOUR in which you walk around to see interesting parts of a city, town etc.

Walk·man /ˈwɔkmən/ *n.* [C] TRADEMARK a small TAPE PLAYER or MP3 player with HEADPHONES, that you carry with you so that you can listen to music SYN **personal stereo**

ˌwalk of ˈlife *n.* [C] the position in society someone has, especially the type of job they have: **from every walk of life/from all walks of life** *People from all walks of life took part in the celebration.*

ˈwalk-on *n.* [C] **1** someone who plays for a college sports team without having been given a sports SCHOLARSHIP **2 a)** also **walk-on part** ENG. LANG. ARTS a small acting part with no words to say in a play or movie **b)** an actor who has a part like this

walk·out /ˈwɔk-aʊt/ *n.* [C] an occasion when people stop working or leave somewhere as a protest: *Students* *have **staged** several **walkouts** in protest of tuition increases.* → see also **walk out** at WALK[1]

walk·o·ver /ˈwɔkˌoʊvɚ/ *n.* [C] INFORMAL a very easy victory → see also

walk-through *n.* [C] **1** a short REHEARSAL of a play early in production in which actors read their lines and move as directed **2** a thorough explanation of each step in a process **3** also **walk-through practice** a practice for a sports game such as football in which players go through various plays step by step but do not really play the game **4** the written instructions that give you all the details of how to play a particular computer game successfully

walk-up *n.* [C] INFORMAL **1** a tall apartment building that does not have an ELEVATOR **2** an apartment, office etc. in a building like this

walk·way /ˈwɔk-weɪ/ *n. plural* **walkways** [C] an outside path, sometimes above the ground, built to connect two parts of a building or two buildings

wall[1] /wɔl/ S1 W1 *n.* [C]
1 IN A BUILDING one of the sides of a room or building: *The kitchen walls are white.* | *The walls of the old building were crumbling.* | *I looked at the clock **on the wall**.* | *Johnnie leaned **against the wall** and listened.*
2 AROUND AN AREA an upright structure with flat sides that is made of stone, brick etc., that divides one area from another: *A brick wall surrounds the building.*
3 TUBE/CONTAINER the side of something hollow, such as a pipe or tube: *The embryo implants in the wall of the uterus.*
4 a wall of fire/flames/water etc. a tall mass of something such as fire or water, that prevents anything getting through
5 a wall of silence/secrecy a situation in which no one will tell you what you want to know: *The police investigation was met with a wall of silence.*
6 push/drive/send sb to the wall INFORMAL to put someone into a difficult situation from which they cannot escape unless they do what you want
7 go to the wall INFORMAL if someone goes to the wall for someone or to do something, they do everything that is possible to help someone or to achieve something
8 these four walls SPOKEN the room that you are in, especially considered as a private place: *Please don't repeat this outside these four walls.*
9 if these walls could talk ... SPOKEN used to say that a lot of interesting things have happened in a building or room in the past, which it would be interesting to know more about
10 the walls have ears used to warn people to be careful what they say, because other people, especially enemies, could be listening
11 hit a/the wall INFORMAL if someone hits the wall, they reach the point when they are the most physically tired when doing a sport
[**Origin:** Old English *weall*] → see also **have your back to the wall** at BACK[2] (14), **bang your head against/on a (brick) wall** at BANG[1] (5), **be climbing the walls** at CLIMB[1] (10), **drive sb up the wall** at DRIVE[1] (10), **the handwriting is on the wall** at HANDWRITING (2), **hit a brick wall** at HIT[1] (30), **nail sb to the wall/cross** at NAIL[2] (4), OFF-THE-WALL, **sth is like talking to a brick wall** at TALK[1] (20)

wall[2] *v.*
wall sth ↔ **in** *phr. v.* **1** to surround an open area with walls **2 be walled in (by sth)** if someone or something is walled in, they are surrounded by something, especially so that they cannot move
wall off *phr. v.* **1 wall sth ↔ off** to keep one area or room separate from another, by building a wall: *The back half of the museum was walled off for renovation.* **2 wall sb/sth ↔ off** to completely separate someone or something from someone or something else: *The child began to wall himself off from family and friends.*
wall up *phr. v.* **1 wall sth ↔ up** to fill in a DOORWAY, window etc. with bricks or stone **2 wall sb ↔ up** to keep someone as a prisoner in a room or building

wal·la·by /ˈwɑləbi/ *n. plural* **wallabies** [C] an Australian animal that looks like a small KANGAROO

wall·board /ˈwɔlbɔrd/ *n.* [C] a type of board made of sheets of paper over GYPSUM, that is used to make walls inside a building

wall·chart /ˈwɔltʃɑrt/ *n.* [C] a large piece of paper with information on it that is put on a wall

ˈwall ˌcovering *n.* [C] material such as paper or cloth that is used to cover walls

walled /wɔld/ *adj.* [only before noun] **a walled garden/city/town etc.** a garden, city etc. that has a wall around it

wal·let /ˈwɑlɪt, ˈwɔ-/ S2 *n.* [C] a small flat folding case that you carry in your pocket, for holding paper money etc. → see also PURSE

wall·eye /ˈwɔlaɪ/ also **ˌwalleyed ˈpike** *n.* [C,U] a type of FRESHWATER fish that has large eyes on opposite sides of its head

ˈwall-eyed *adj.* having one or both eyes that seem to point to the side, rather than straight forward

wall·flow·er /ˈwɔlˌflaʊɚ/ *n.* [C] **1** INFORMAL someone at a party, dance etc. who is not asked to dance or take part in the activities **2** BIOLOGY a sweet-smelling garden plant with yellow and red flowers

wal·lop[1] /ˈwɑləp/ *v.* [T] INFORMAL to hit someone or something very hard

wallop[2] *n.* [C] INFORMAL a hard hit, especially with your hand

wal·lop·ing[1] /ˈwɑləpɪŋ/ *n.* SPOKEN **give sb/get a walloping** to hit someone repeatedly as a punishment

walloping[2] *adj.* [only before noun] SPOKEN very big: *walloping steaks*

wal·low[1] /ˈwɑloʊ/ *v.* [I] **1 wallow in self-pity/despair/defeat etc.** DISAPPROVING to seem to enjoy being sad, upset etc., especially because you get sympathy from other people: *Stop wallowing in self-pity, and do something positive.* **2** if an animal wallows, it rolls around in mud, water etc. for pleasure: *Pigs were wallowing in the mud.*

wallow[2] *n.* [C] a place where animals go to wallow, especially in mud

ˈwall ˌpainting *n.* [C] ENG. LANG. ARTS a picture that has been painted directly onto a wall, especially a FRESCO

wall·pa·per[1] /ˈwɔlˌpeɪpɚ/ *n.* [C,U] **1** paper that you stick onto the walls of a room in order to decorate it **2** COMPUTERS the picture on the screen of your computer, behind the FILES you are using

wallpaper[2] *v.* [T] to put wallpaper onto the walls of a room

ˈWall Street *n.* **1** a street in New York City, where the New York STOCK EXCHANGE is **2** ECONOMICS the New York STOCK EXCHANGE, or the people who work there

ˌwall-to-ˈwall *adj.* **1** [only before noun] covering the whole floor: *wall-to-wall carpeting* **2** INFORMAL filling all the space or time available, especially in a way you do not like: *a room of wall-to-wall children*

wal·nut /ˈwɔlnʌt/ *n.* **1** [C] a slightly bitter nut with a large light brown shell: *coffee and walnut cake* → see picture at NUT **2** [C] also **walnut tree** BIOLOGY a tree that produces this type of nut **3** [U] the wood from a walnut tree, often used to make furniture [**Origin:** Old English *wealhhnutu*, from *Wealh* **Welsh person, foreigner** + *hnutu* **nut**; because it was brought into Britain from abroad]

wal·rus /ˈwɔlrəs, ˈwɑl-/ *n.* [C] a large sea animal with two long TUSKS coming out from the sides of its mouth [**Origin:** 1700–1800 Dutch]

waltz[1] /wɔlts/ *n.* [C] ENG. LANG. ARTS **1** a fairly slow dance with RHYTHM consisting of patterns of three beats **2** a piece of music intended for this type of dance [**Origin:** 1700–1800 German *walzer*, from *walzen* **to roll, dance**]

waltz[2] *v.* **1** [I,T] ENG. LANG. ARTS to dance a waltz **2** [I always

W

+ adv./prep.] INFORMAL to walk somewhere calmly and confidently: **waltz in/into etc.** *You can't just waltz in here and start ordering people around.*

waltz off with sth *phr. v.* INFORMAL to take something without permission or without realizing you have done this: *Someone just waltzed off with my pen again.*

waltz through sth *phr. v.* INFORMAL **waltz through a test/game/exam etc.** to pass a test, win a game etc. without any difficulty: *Utah is expected to waltz through the playoffs.*

Wam·pa·no·ag /ˌwɑmpəˈnoʊɑg/ a Native American tribe from the northeastern U.S.

wam·pum /ˈwɑmpəm/ *n.* [U] **1** shells put into strings, belts etc., used in past times as money by Native Americans **2** INFORMAL money

wan /wɑn/ *adj.* LITERARY looking pale, weak, or tired: *Angela looked wan and tired.* —**wanly** *adv.*

wand /wɑnd/ *n.* [C] **1** a thin stick you hold in your hand to do magic tricks → see also MAGIC WAND **2** a tool that looks like a thin stick: *a mascara wand*

wan·der /ˈwɑndɚ/ W3 *v.*

1 WALK WITHOUT PURPOSE [I,T] to move slowly across or around an area, without a clear direction or purpose: **wander in/through/around etc.** *The nightclub closed and people started wandering out to the parking lot.* | *She was* ***wandering aimlessly*** *around the house.* | *The boy was later found* ***wandering the streets.*** ►see THESAURUS box at **walk**[1]

2 WALK AWAY also **wander off** [I] to move away from where you are supposed to stay: *She may have wandered off and become lost.*

3 sb's mind wanders also **sb's thoughts wander a)** if your mind, thoughts etc. wander, you stop paying attention to something and think about something else, especially because you are bored or worried: *I'm sorry, my mind was wandering. What did you say?* | **+to** *I tried to work but my thoughts kept wandering to Sam.* **b)** used to say that someone has become unable to think clearly, especially because they are old

4 TALK ABOUT STH UNRELATED [I] to start to talk about something not related to the main subject that you were talking about before: **+from/off** *Professor Cartmel often wandered from the subject.*

5 ROAD/RIVER [I] if a road or a river wanders somewhere, it does not go straight but in curves: **+through/across/along** *A wooden fence wanders along the edge of the farm.*

6 EYES [I] if your eyes or GAZE wanders, you look around slowly at different things or at all the parts of something SYN **roam** SYN **rove**

[**Origin:** Old English *wandrian*] —**wanderer** *n.* [C]

W

wan·der·ings /ˈwɑndərɪŋz/ *n.* [plural] LITERARY trips to many different places, where you do not stay for very long

wan·der·lust /ˈwɑndɚˌlʌst/ *n.* [singular, U] a strong desire to travel to different places

wane[1] /weɪn/ *v.* [I] **1** if something such as power, influence, or a feeling wanes, it gradually becomes less strong or less important **2** PHYSICS when the moon wanes, you gradually see less of it → see also WAX AND WANE

wane[2] *n.* **on the wane** becoming smaller, weaker, or less important: *His popularity is on the wane.*

wan·gle /ˈwæŋgəl/ *v.* [T] INFORMAL to get something or arrange for something to happen, by persuading or tricking someone: **wangle sth out of sb** *Tanner managed to wangle a pay raise out of him.* | **wangle your way out of sth** (=to get out of a difficult or bad situation) —**wangle** *n.* [singular]

wan·na /ˈwʌnə, ˈwɑnə/ *v.* a short form of "want to" or "want a," used in writing to show how people sound when they speak: *Do you wanna go to a movie tonight?*

wan·na·be /ˈwʌnəbi/ *n.* [C] INFORMAL someone who wants to be like someone famous or have money and power —**wannabe** *adj.* [only before noun] *wannabe rap stars* → see also WOULD-BE

want[1] /wʌnt, wɑnt, wɔnt/ S1 W1 *v.* [T, not usually in progressive]

1 DESIRE STH to have a desire to have something, do something, have someone do something, or have something happen: *I want some coffee.* | **want to do sth** *Most people want to lose weight.* | **want sth for sth** *Ben wants a computer for his birthday.* | **whatever/whenever/wherever you want** *You can order whatever you want.* | **want sb to do sth** *My Mom wants me to be doctor.* | **want sth done** *I want this mess cleaned up right now!* | **want sth from/of sb** *What exactly do you want from me?* | **want nothing more than (to do) sth** (=to want something more than anything else) → see Word Choice box at WISH[1]

2 have sb (just) where you want them INFORMAL to be in a situation in which you have power over another person that helps you get what you want from them

SPOKEN PHRASES

3 do you want (to do) sth? also **want (to do) sth?** INFORMAL used to offer or suggest something: *Do you want another cookie?* | *Do you want to go home?* | *Want to go fishing?*

4 what do you want? used to ask, often in a slightly rude way, what someone wants you to give them, do for them etc.: *What do you want now? I'm busy.*

5 who wants...? a) used when offering something to a group of people: *Who wants ice cream?* **b)** used to say that you do not like something, do not think that it is worth doing etc.: *Who wants to see another stupid horror movie?*

6 if you want used to make a suggestion, give permission, or agree to something that someone else has suggested: *I can go to the store for you if you want.*

7 I don't want to sound/be etc. ..., but... used to be polite when you are going to tell someone something that may upset them: *I don't want to sound rude, but I think you've had too much to drink.*

8 ASK FOR SB to ask for someone to come and talk to you, or to come to a particular place: *He wants you in his office right away.*

9 I want (you to do) sth used to tell someone to do something, especially to show that you are serious or angry: *I want an explanation right now.*

10 SHOULD ought or should: **you (may/might) want to do sth** *You might want to install antivirus software.*

11 what I want used to explain or say exactly what it is that you want: *What I want to know is when we're going to get paid.*

12 all sb wants used to say that someone only wants something simple or small, and you think it is fair to ask for it: *All I want is some peace and quiet around here.*

13 be/have everything sb wants to have all the qualities that someone thinks a particular person or thing should have

14 if you want my advice/opinion,... used when you are going to give someone your honest opinion about something, even though they may not like what you are going to say

15 I (just) wanted to say/know/ask etc. used to politely say something, ask about something etc.: *I just wanted to make sure we're still meeting at 8 p.m.*

16 I want to say/thank etc. used especially in speeches before you politely say something, thank someone etc.: *I want to thank you all for coming.*

17 it's/that's just what I (always) wanted used to say that you like a present you have just been given very much

18 what does sb want with sth? used to say that you cannot understand why someone wants a particular thing: *What does he want with an old car like that?*

19 do you want (me to do) sth? used to threaten to do something unpleasant: *Do you want me to tell your parents?*

20 (do) you want a piece of me? SPOKEN used to ask someone if they want to fight with you

[**Origin:** 1100–1200 Old Norse *vanta*] → see also **waste not, want not** at WASTE² (5)

want for sth *phr. v.* OLD-FASHIONED to not have something that you need: *As kids, we never wanted for anything.*

want in *phr. v.* **1** to want to come into a place: *The dog wants in.* **2** INFORMAL to want to be involved in something: *We definitely want in on the deal.*

want out *phr. v.* **1** to want to go out of a place: +**of** *I want out of this room right now.* **2** INFORMAL to want to stop being involved in something

want² S3 *n.*
1 LACK [C,U] FORMAL something that is needed but is lacking: *The want of accurate maps made travel in the area difficult.*
2 be in want of sth FORMAL to need something, or lack something that is needed: *The building is in want of repair.*
3 wants [plural] things that you want: *For years she had ignored her own* ***wants and needs****.*
4 for want of a better word/term/phrase etc. used to say that there is no exact word to describe what you are talking about, and to give a new word or phrase instead: *For want of a better expression, I'll call these activities "good religion."*
5 not for want of trying/asking etc. used to say that even though something did not happen or succeed, it was not because you did not try hard enough, ask enough etc.
6 for want of anything better (to do) if you do something for want of anything better, you do it only because there is nothing else you want to do
7 for want of sth used to say that the lack of something has caused a particular situation, especially a bad situation: *The gallery might close down for want of funding.*
8 NOT ENOUGH FOOD/MONEY ETC. [U] FORMAL a situation in which people do not have enough food, money, clothes etc.: *People need to have freedom from want.*

want ad *n.* [C] a CLASSIFIED AD

want·ed /ˈwʌntɪd/ *adj.* **1** [usually not before noun] someone who is wanted is being looked for by the police: +**for** *Larson is wanted for bank robbery.* **2** [not before noun] needed or desired OPP **unwanted**: *You're wanted on the phone.* **3** someone, especially a child, who is wanted is loved and cared for OPP **unwanted**: *It's nice to feel wanted.*

want·ing /ˈwʌntɪŋ/ *adj.* [not before noun] FORMAL **1** not as good as or not of as high a standard as you think someone or something should be: *Medical facilities in the country have been* ***found wanting****.* **2** if something is wanting, it is needed but it is not available

wan·ton /ˈwɑntˀn, ˈwɔn-/ *adj.* DISAPPROVING **1** wanton cruelty, destruction etc. deliberately harms someone or damages something for no reason **2** OLD-FASHIONED a wanton woman is considered immoral because she has sex with a lot of men **3** FORMAL uncontrolled —**wantonly** *adv.*

wap·i·ti /ˈwɑpəṭi/ *n. plural* **wapiti** or **wapitis** [C] an ELK

war /wɔr/ S2 W1 *n.* **1** [C,U] fighting between two or more countries or between opposing groups within a country, involving large numbers of soldiers and weapons: *the Spanish-American War* | +**between** *the war between the north and the south* | *Over 250,000 people died* ***in the war****.* | *Congress is not interested in* ***fighting a war*** *with our allies.* | **win/lose a war** *They had no chance of winning the war.* | ***War broke out*** (=war began) *in September of 1939.* | **be at war (with/against sb)** *In 1920, Poland and Russia were still at war.* | *Britain had already* ***declared war on*** (=announced publicly and officially that they were going to fight a war against) *Germany.* | **go to war (with/against sb)** (=start to fight a war with another country) | **wage war (on/against sb)** (=start and continue a war, especially for a long period) | **a nuclear/guerrilla/ground etc. war** (=a war fought with a particular kind of weapon, in a particular kind of way, or in a particular place)

THESAURUS
warfare the activity of fighting in a war – used especially when talking about particular methods of fighting: *guerrilla warfare*
fighting an occasion when people or groups fight each other in a war, in the street etc.: *a peace plan to end the fighting in the region*
conflict fighting or a war: *the conflict in the Middle East*
combat fighting during a war: *the difficult decision to send young soldiers into combat*
action fighting in a war: *He had been killed in action.*
hostilities fighting in a war: *the formal cessation of hostilities*
battle an occasion when two armies, groups of ships, etc. fight each other in one place: *the Battle of Gettysburg*
skirmish a fight between small groups of soldiers, ships etc., especially one that happens away from the main part of a battle: *a skirmish between the soldiers and the Sioux*
clash a short fight between two armies or groups: *border clashes*

2 [C,U] an organized struggle over a long period of time to control something harmful: *the drug war* | +**against/on** *the city's war on hunger* **3** [C] a situation in which people, groups, companies etc. are fighting for power, influence, or control: +**between** *a war between the city's rival gangs* | **a price/trade war** *Gas stations in the city are involved in a price war.* **4 This means war!** SPOKEN, HUMOROUS used to say that you are ready to argue or fight about something [**Origin:** 1100–1200 Old North French *werre*, from Old French *guerre*] → see also CIVIL WAR, COLD WAR, PRICE WAR, PRISONER OF WAR, WAR OF ATTRITION, WAR OF NERVES, WAR OF WORDS, WARRING

ˌWar between the ˈStates, the HISTORY another name for the U.S. CIVIL WAR

war·ble /ˈwɔrbəl/ *v.* [I,T] **1** HUMOROUS to sing **2** to sing with a high continuous but rapidly changing sound, the way a bird does —**warble** *n.* [singular]

war·bler /ˈwɔrblɚ/ *n.* [C] **1** BIOLOGY a bird that can make musical sounds **2** HUMOROUS a singer, especially one who does not sing very well

ˈwar ˌbonnet, warbonnet *n.* [C] a type of Native American hat decorated with feathers

ˈwar bride *n.* [C] a woman who marries a foreign soldier who is in her country because there is a war

ˈwar ˌcabinet *n.* [C] a group of important politicians who meet to make decisions for a government during a war

ˈwar chest *n.* [C] **1** ECONOMICS the money that a group, politician, or business has available to spend on an election, advertising etc. **2** the money that a government has available to spend on war

ˈwar crime *n.* [C] a cruel act done during a war which is illegal under international law —**war criminal** *n.* [C]

ˈwar cry *n. plural* **war cries** [C] a shout used by people fighting in a battle to show their courage and frighten the enemy → see also BATTLE CRY

ward¹ /wɔrd/ *n.* [C] **1** an area in a hospital where people who need medical treatment stay: **the maternity/psychiatric/pediatric etc. ward** (=the ward for women who are having babies, for people who are mentally ill, for children etc.) ►see THESAURUS box at **hospital** **2** LAW someone, especially a child, who is under the legal protection of another person or of a law court: *At the age of five, Jason became a ward of the state.* **3** POLITICS one of the small areas that a city has been divided into for the purpose of local elections

ward² *v.*

ward sth ↔ **off** *phr. v.* to do something to protect

W

yourself from something such as an illness, danger, attack etc.: *He warded off the blows with his arms.*

-ward /wərd/ *suffix* [in adjectives and adverbs] toward a particular direction or place: *a homeward journey* | *Move forward, please.*

Ward /wɔrd/**, A. Mont·gom·ery** /eɪ mənt'gʌmri/ (1844–1913) an American businessman who was the first person to sell goods by MAIL ORDER and started the Montgomery Ward mail order company

'war dance *n.* [C] a dance performed by tribes in preparation for battle or to celebrate a victory

war·den /'wɔrdn/ *n.* [C] **1** the person in charge of a prison **2** an official whose job is to make sure that rules are obeyed → see also GAME WARDEN

'ward ˌheeler *n.* [C] INFORMAL someone who works in a particular area for a POLITICAL MACHINE

war·drobe /'wɔrdroʊb/ *n.* **1** [C] the clothes that someone has: *She bought a whole new wardrobe for the trip.* **2** [C] a piece of furniture like a large cupboard that you hang clothes in **3** [U] also **wardrobe department** ENG. LANG. ARTS a department in a theater, television company etc. that deals with the clothes worn by actors: **a wardrobe master/mistress** (=man or woman who is in charge of this department)

ward·room /'wɔrdrum/ *n.* [C] the space in a ship, especially a WARSHIP, where the officers live and eat, except for the CAPTAIN

-wards /wərdz/ *suffix* [in adverbs] another spelling of -WARD, used only in adverbs: *traveling northwards* | *moving backwards*

-ware /wɛr/ *suffix* [in U nouns] **1** things made of a particular material, especially for use in the home: *glassware* (=glass bowls, glasses etc.) | *silverware* (=silver knives, forks, spoons etc.) **2** things used in a particular place for the preparation or serving of food: *ovenware* (=dishes for use in the OVEN) | *tableware* (=plates, glasses, knives, etc.) **3** things used in operating a computer: *software* (=computer programs) | *hardware* (=computer equipment)

W

'war ˌeffort *n.* [singular] things that all the people in a country do to help when that country is at war

ware·house /'wɛrhaʊs/ *n.* [C] **1** a large building for storing large quantities of goods: *The goods were stored in a warehouse.* **2** a warehouse store

'warehouse ˌstore also **'warehouse ˌclub** *n.* [C] a type of store that sells things in large amounts, so that you can buy them at a lower price than at normal stores

ware·hous·ing /'wɛrˌhaʊzɪŋ/ *n.* [U] the process of storing large quantities of things, especially in a warehouse, so that they can be sold or used at a later time

wares /wɛrz/ *n.* [plural] things that are for sale, usually not in a store: *He traveled to county fairs **selling his wares**.*

war·fare /'wɔrfɛr/ *n.* [U] **1** a word meaning the activity of fighting in a war, used especially when talking about particular methods of fighting: **nuclear/chemical/trench etc. warfare** *Chemical warfare has been banned by the Geneva Convention.* | ***Guerrilla warfare*** (=warfare by small groups of fighters) *continued despite increased American military assistance.* ▸see THESAURUS box at **war** **2** continuous arguing or fighting between groups, countries etc. in which they try to gain an advantage over each other: *gang warfare* | **political/economic/information etc. warfare** (=warfare using politics, economics etc. instead of weapons) → see also **psychological warfare** at PSYCHOLOGICAL (4)

'war game *n.* [C] **1** an activity in which soldiers fight an imaginary battle in order to test military plans **2** a game in which people pretend to fight a war on a computer or with small models

war·head /'wɔrhɛd/ *n.* [C] the explosive part at the front of a MISSILE

War·hol /'wɔrhɔl/**, An·dy** /ændi/ (1926–1987) a U.S. artist who is famous for his pictures in the POP ART style and who also made movies

war·horse /'wɔrhɔs/ *n.* [C] **1** INFORMAL a soldier or politician who has been in their job a long time, and enjoys dealing with all the difficulties involved in it **2** a horse used in battle

war·like /'wɔrlaɪk/ *adj.* **1** liking war and being skillful in it: *a warlike nation* **2** threatening war or attack: *warlike behavior*

war·lock /'wɔrlɑk/ *n.* [C] a man who has magical powers, especially evil powers

war·lord /'wɔrlɔrd/ *n.* [C] the leader of an unofficial military group that is fighting against a government, king, or different group

warm¹ /wɔrm/ [S1] [W2] *adj.*
1 SLIGHTLY HOT slightly hot, especially in a pleasant way: *a warm bath* | *I hope we get some warmer weather soon.* | *I've put your dinner in the oven to **keep it warm*** (=stop it from becoming cold). ▸see THESAURUS box at **hot**
2 FEEL WARM feeling slightly hot, or making you feel this way: *Are you warm enough?* | **keep/stay warm** (=wear enough clothes not to feel cold)
3 CLOTHES/BUILDINGS clothes or buildings that are warm can keep in heat or keep out cold: *a warm jacket*
4 FRIENDLY friendly in a way that makes you feel comfortable: *She's a very warm person.* | *They gave us **a warm welcome.*** ▸see THESAURUS box at **friendly**
5 COLOR warm colors are red, yellow, orange, and similar colors
6 CORRECT used especially in games to say that someone is near to guessing the correct answer or finding a hidden object [OPP] **cold**: *You're getting warmer.*
7 warm (and) fuzzy used to describe something that gives you a good feeling, especially relating to love or caring: *warm and fuzzy campaign commercials*
8 the warm fuzzies INFORMAL good pleasant feelings
9 a warm scent/trail a smell or path that has been made recently, which a hunter can easily follow
10 PLEASANT FEELING a warm feeling is pleasant and you feel happy, relaxed, and satisfied
11 ANGRY/EXCITED OLD-FASHIONED angry or excited
[**Origin:** Old English *wearm*] —**warmness** *n.* [U] → see also WARMTH

warm² [S2] *v.* **1** [I,T] to make someone or something warm or warmer, or to become warm or warmer [SYN] **warm up**: *The water expands as it warms.* | *He was warming his hands on the cup of coffee.* **2 warm sb's heart** to make someone feel happy, relaxed, and comfortable: *The story warmed her heart.*

warm to sb/sth *phr. v.* **1** to begin to like someone you have just met: *He usually doesn't warm to people very fast.* **2** to become more eager, interested, or excited about something: *It took Susan a while to warm to the idea.*

warm up *phr. v.* **1 warm sb/sth ↔ up** to become warm, or to make someone or something warm: *A nice bowl of soup will warm you up.* | *The room should warm up soon.* | **warm yourself up** *Try running around to warm yourself up.* **2 warm sth ↔ up** if you warm up food, especially food that has already been cooked, or it warms up, it becomes hot enough to eat [SYN] **heat up**: *You can warm that up in the microwave.* **3** to do gentle physical exercises to prepare your body for sports, dancing etc.: *Always warm up thoroughly before exercising.* → see also WARM-UP **4** if musicians, singers, or performers warm up, they practice just before a performance: *The orchestra had not had time to warm up.* **5 warm sth ↔ up** if you warm up a machine or engine or it warms up, it becomes ready to work correctly: *It takes a few minutes for the copier to warm up.* **6** if a party, election etc. warms up, it starts to become enjoyable or interesting, especially because more is happening [SYN] **heat up**: *The race for governor is beginning to warm up.* **7 warm sb ↔ up** to become cheerful, eager, and excited, or to make someone feel this way: *He warmed up the audience by telling them a few jokes.*

warm up to sb/sth *phr. v.* to WARM TO someone or something

warm-'blooded *adj.* BIOLOGY a warm-blooded animal has a body temperature that remains fairly high whether the temperature around it is hot or cold → see also COLD-BLOODED

warmed-over *adj.* **1** warmed-over food has been cooked before and then heated again for eating **2** a warmed-over idea or argument has been used before and is not interesting or useful anymore → see also **like death warmed over** at DEATH (11)

war meˌmorial *n.* [C] a MONUMENT put up to remind people of soldiers etc. who were killed in a war

warm 'front *n.* [C] EARTH SCIENCE the front edge of a mass of warm air that is moving toward a place → see also COLD FRONT

warm-'hearted *adj.* friendly, kind, and always willing to help: *a warm-hearted old man* → see also COLD-HEARTED —**warm-heartedly** *adv.* —**warm-heartedness** *n.* [U]

warm·ing /ˈwɔrmɪŋ/ *n.* [singular] **1** an increase in the temperature of something: *a gradual warming of Earth's atmosphere* → see also GLOBAL WARMING **2** a situation in which a relationship becomes more friendly: *a warming in U.S.-Chinese relations*

warming pan *n.* [C] a metal container with a long handle, used in the past to hold hot coals for warming beds

warming trend *n.* [C] a period of time when the weather becomes warmer in a particular area

warm·ly /ˈwɔrmli/ *adv.* **1** in a friendly accepting way: *We were warmly welcomed by the villagers.* **2** in a way that makes something or someone warm: *Make sure the children are **dressed warmly*** (=so they do not become cold).

war·mon·ger /ˈwɔrˌmʌŋgɚ, -ˌmɑŋ-/ *n.* [C] DISAPPROVING someone, especially a politician, who is eager to start a war to achieve an aim —**warmongering** *adj.* —**warmongering** *n.* [U]

warmth /wɔrmθ/ *n.* [U] **1** a feeling of being warm: *the warmth of the fire* **2** friendliness and happiness: *He spoke of his father with great warmth.*

warm-up *n.* [C] **1** a set of gentle exercises you do to prepare your body for sports, dancing, singing etc. → see also **warm up** at WARM² **2** a set of clothes you wear when you are doing these exercises

warm-water 'port *n.* [C] a port where the water never freezes and that can be used all year

warn /wɔrn/ S3 W2 *v.* **1** [I,T] to tell someone that something bad or dangerous may happen, so that they can avoid it or prevent it: **warn sb about sth** *She warned me about the broken chair.* | **warn (sb) of sth** *You were warned of the risks involved.* | **warn sb (not) to do sth** *I warned you not to walk home alone.* | **warn sb (that)** *We warned them that there was a bull in the field.* **2** [I,T] to tell someone about something before it happens so that they are not worried or surprised by it: **warn (sb) that** *He warned me that he might be late.* **3** [T] to tell someone that they will be punished if they do something: *Stop it now – I'm warning you.* | **warn sb about sth** *I've warned you before about staying out late.* **4 be warned** used to tell someone to be careful because something has risks or problems that they may not know about: *Be warned – the paint is difficult to remove from clothes.* [**Origin:** Old English *warnian*]

warn (sb) **against** sth *phr. v.* to advise someone not to do something, because it may have dangerous or bad results: *He warned her against such a risky investment.* | **warn (sb) against doing sth** *Police have warned against approaching the man.*

warn off *phr. v.* **1 warn sb ↔ off** to tell someone that they should not go near something, especially because it might be dangerous: *A sign was posted to warn off trespassers.* **2 warn sb ↔ off, warn sb off sth** to tell someone that they should not do or use something because it might be dangerous

War·ner /ˈwɔrnɚ/, **Har·ry Mor·ris** /ˈhæri ˈmɔrɪs/ (1881–1958) a U.S. movie PRODUCER who started the Warner Brothers movie company with his brothers Albert, Samuel, Louis, and Jack

warn·ing¹ /ˈwɔrnɪŋ/ W3 *n.* **1** [C,U] something, especially a statement, that tells you that something bad, annoying, or dangerous might happen: *the warnings on the back of medicine bottles* | *We were given only three days' warning.* | **+against** *a warning against travel to the region* | **+of** *a warning of traffic delays* | **+to** *Our experience should be a warning to other travelers.* | *The weather service has **issued a** thunder storm **warning**.* | *This type of heart disease kills otherwise healthy people **without warning**.* | **advance/prior warning** *He often toured the factory without prior warning.* | **give fair warning** (=to tell someone about something long enough before it happens that they have time to get ready) **2** [C] a statement telling someone that if they continue to behave in an unsatisfactory way, they will be punished: *This is your last warning – leave or I'll call the police.* | **a verbal/written warning** *She had been given a verbal warning about her work.*

warning² *adj.* [only before noun] a warning action, sign etc. tells you that something bad or dangerous might happen: *Troops fired **warning shots**.* | **a warning sign/signal** *the early warning signs of asthma* | *A **warning light** on the dashboard came on.*

War of 1812, the /ˌwɔr əv ˌeɪṭin ˈtwɛlv/ HISTORY a war between the U.S. and Great Britain from 1812 to 1815, which was mainly caused by problems with trade between the U.S., Britain, and France

ˌwar of at'trition *n.* [C] a struggle in which you harm your opponent in a lot of small ways, so that they gradually become weaker

ˌwar of 'nerves *n.* [C] an attempt to make an enemy worried, and to destroy their courage by threatening them, spreading false information etc.

ˌwar of 'words *n.* [C] a public argument between politicians, countries, organizations etc.

warp¹ /wɔrp/ *v.* **1** [I,T] to become bent or twisted, or to make something do this: *The hot sun had warped the wooden fence.* **2** [T] to have a bad effect on someone so that they think strangely about things → see also WARPED

warp² *n.* **1** [singular] a part of something that is not straight or in the right shape **2 the warp** TECHNICAL the threads used in weaving cloth that go from the top to the bottom → see also TIME WARP, WARP SPEED, WEFT

'war paint *n.* [U] **1** paint that some tribes put on their bodies and faces before going to war **2** HUMOROUS MAKEUP

war·path /ˈwɔrpæθ/ *n.* INFORMAL **on the warpath** angry and looking for someone to argue with or punish

warped /wɔrpt/ *adj.* **1** having ideas or thoughts that most people think are bad or strange: *a warped sense of humor* **2** something that is warped is bent or twisted so that it is not in the correct shape ▸see THESAURUS box at **bent²**

war·plane /ˈwɔrpleɪn/ *n.* [C] an airplane designed to be used in a war

'War ˌPowers ˌAct, the POLITICS a U.S. law passed in 1973 that limits the president's power to involve the country in a war without the approval of Congress

'warp speed *n.* [U] **at warp speed** at an extremely fast speed

war·rant¹ /ˈwɔrənt, ˈwɑ-/ *n.* **1** [C] LAW a legal document signed by a judge, giving the police permission to take a particular action, for example to ARREST someone or to search a building: **+for** *The court **issued a warrant** for his arrest.* | **search/arrest warrant** *The police have got a search warrant signed by a district judge.* → see also DEATH WARRANT, SEARCH WARRANT **2** [U] FORMAL good enough reason for doing something SYN **justification** → see also UNWARRANTED

warrant² *v.* **1** [T] to be a good enough reason for something: *Any plan that could reduce costs warrants serious consideration.* **2** [I,T] OLD-FASHIONED used to say that you are sure about something: *I'll warrant we won't see him again.*

'warrant ˌofficer *n.* [C] a middle rank in the Army,

W

Navy, Air Force, or Marines, or someone who has this rank

war·ran·ty /ˈwɔrənti, ˈwɑ-/ *n. plural* **warranties** [C] a written promise that a company makes to replace or repair a product if it breaks or does not work correctly: *a five-year warranty on all TVs in the store* | *The car is still* ***under warranty*** (=protected by a warranty). → see also GUARANTEE

war·ren /ˈwɔrən, ˈwɑ-/ *n.* [C] **1** BIOLOGY the place under the ground where rabbits live **2** a place with so many streets, rooms etc. that it is difficult to find your way through it

War·ren /ˈwɔrən, ˈwɑr-/, **Earl** /ɚl/ (1891–1974) a CHIEF JUSTICE on the U.S. Supreme Court

Warren, Rob·ert Penn /ˈrɑbɚt pɛn/ (1905–1989) a U.S. poet and writer of NOVELS

ˈWarren Comˌmission, the HISTORY the group that was set up in 1963 to find out the truth about the killing of President Kennedy

war·ring /ˈwɔrɪŋ/ *adj.* [only before noun] at war or fighting each other: **warring factions/countries/sides etc.** (=groups of people fighting each other)

war·ri·or /ˈwɔriɚ, ˈwɑ-/ *n.* [C] a soldier or fighter who is experienced in fighting, especially in the past → see also WEEKEND WARRIOR

War·saw /ˈwɔrsɔ/ the capital and largest city of Poland

ˌWarsaw ˈGhetto, the HISTORY a small area of Warsaw, Poland, in which the Nazis forced the Jews of Warsaw to stay during World War II

ˌWarsaw ˈPact, the HISTORY a military association which was formed by the Soviet Union and seven Eastern European countries in 1955 and which ended in 1991

war·ship /ˈwɔrʃɪp/ *n.* [C] a ship with guns that is used in a war

wart /wɔrt/ *n.* [C] **1** MEDICINE a small hard raised spot on someone's skin, caused by a VIRUS ►see THESAURUS box at **mark**[2] **2 warts and all** INFORMAL including all the faults or bad things —**warty** *adj.*

W

wart·hog /ˈwɔrthɑg, -hɔg/ *n.* [C] an African wild pig with long TUSKS that stick out of the side of its mouth

war·time /ˈwɔrtaɪm/ *n.* [U] a period of time when a nation is fighting a war OPP **peacetime** —**wartime** *adj.*: *the country's wartime economy*

ˈwar-torn *adj.* [only before noun] a war-torn country, city etc. is being destroyed by war, especially war between opposing groups from the same country

ˈwar ˌwidow *n.* [C] a woman whose husband has been killed in a war

war·y /ˈwɛri/ *adj. comparative* **warier**, *superlative* **wariest** careful because you think something might be dangerous or harmful: **be wary of (doing) sth** *He was wary of committing to the project.* —**wariness** *n.* [U] —**warily** *adv.*

ˈwar zone *n.* [C] an area where a war is being fought

was /wəz; *strong* wʌz, wɑz/ *v.* the first and third person singular of the past tense of BE

Wa·satch Range, the /ˈwɔsætʃ ˌreɪndʒ/ a RANGE of mountains in the northwestern U.S. that is part of the Rocky Mountains and runs from the state of Idaho to the state of Utah

Wash. a written abbreviation of WASHINGTON

wash[1] /wɑʃ, wɔʃ/ S1 W3 *v.*

1 CLEAN STH [T] to clean something using water and usually soap: *He washed and ironed a shirt.* | *Can you wash these vegetables?* | *It's your turn to* ***wash the dishes.*** ►see THESAURUS box at **clean**[2]

2 CLEAN BODY [I,T] to clean your body, especially your hands or face, with water and soap: *I just need to wash before dinner.* | *She washed her hands.*

3 FLOW [I always + adv./prep.,T always + adv./prep.] if a liquid or something carried by a liquid washes or is washed somewhere, it flows there: **+against/away etc.** *The waves washed against the shore.* | **wash sth away/against/down etc.** *Floods had washed away the topsoil.* | **wash (sb/sth) ashore/overboard** *Her body washed ashore three weeks later.*

4 sth doesn't/won't wash (with sb) SPOKEN used to say that you do not believe or accept someone's explanation, reason, attitude etc.: *That explanation won't wash with voters.*

5 wash your hands of sb/sth to refuse to be responsible for someone or something anymore: *Dunbar has already washed his hands of the project.*

6 wash well to be easy to clean using soap and water: *Silk doesn't wash well.*

[**Origin:** Old English *wascan*] → see also **wash your dirty laundry/linen in public** at DIRTY[1] (9) → see also WASHED-OUT, WASHOUT

wash sth ↔ **away** *phr. v.* to get rid of feelings or memories, especially bad ones: *His love washed the pain away.*

wash sth ↔ **down** *phr. v.* **1** to drink something to help you swallow food or medicine: **wash sth ↔ down with sth** *I washed down the pills with a glass of water.* **2** to clean something large using a lot of water: *Can you wash down the driveway?*

wash off *phr. v.* **1 wash sth ↔ off, wash sth off sth** to clean dirt, dust etc. from the surface of something with water: *Help me wash this mud off the car.* **2** if a substance washes off, you can remove it from the surface of something by washing: *Don't worry, the paint will wash off.*

wash out *phr. v.* **1 wash sth ↔ out** to wash something quickly to get rid of the dirt in it: *Wash out the cups and leave them in the sink.* **2 wash sth ↔ out** if rain or a storm washes out a road, path etc. or if a road, path etc. is washed out, the water damages or destroys the road, path etc. so that you cannot travel on it **3** if a substance washes out, you can remove it from a material by washing it: *Grass stains don't wash out easily.* **4 be washed out** if an event is washed out, it cannot continue because of rain **5 wash sb's mouth out (with soap)** SPOKEN used to threaten to punish someone for swearing or saying something offensive: *If you say that again, I'm going to wash your mouth out with soap.*

wash over sb *phr. v.* **1** if a feeling washes over you, you suddenly feel it very strongly: *A sense of dread washed over her.* **2** if something washes over you, you do not notice it or it does not affect you: *His words just washed over me.*

wash up *phr. v.* **1** to clean part of your body, especially your hands and face: *I need to wash up before dinner.* **2 wash sth ↔ up** if something washes up or if waves wash it up, it comes in to the shore: *Tons of wreckage have washed up on the shore.* → see also WASHED-UP

GRAMMAR **wash yourself**

Do not use the expression **wash yourself** unless you want to talk about someone's ability to take a shower or bath by themselves: *She got so sick that she couldn't even wash herself.*

wash[2] S3 *n.*

1 CLOTHES [singular, U] clothes that need to be washed, are being washed, or have just been washed: *I have to* ***do the wash*** (=wash dirty clothes) *tonight.* | *Your black pants are* ***in the wash.***

2 ACT OF CLEANING [C] an act of cleaning something using soap and water: *The hair color lasts for six to eight washes.*

3 sth will all come out in the wash SPOKEN used to tell someone not to worry about a problem because it will be solved in the future: *If what you say is true, it'll all come out in the wash.*

4 a/the wash of sth a) the movement or sound made by flowing water, or something that is like this: *I could feel the wash of the surf around my feet.* **b)** a sudden feeling: *A wash of confusion came over me.*

5 sth is a wash SPOKEN used to say that an activity, event, situation etc. has as many bad results as good results, so there is no real effect: *So far, the plan has been a wash in terms of jobs gained or lost.*

6 RIVER also **dry wash** [C] a river in a desert that has no water in it most of the time
7 BOAT/PLANE [singular, U] the movement of water caused by a passing boat or the movement of air caused by an airplane
8 SKIN [C] a liquid used to clean your skin: *an anti-bacterial face wash*
9 COLOR [C] a very thin transparent layer of paint, color, or light
10 AREA OF LAND [singular] an area of land that is sometimes covered by the ocean

wash·a·ble /ˈwɑʃəbəl/ *adj.* **1** something that is washable can be washed without being damaged: *The blouse is **machine washable**.* **2** paint, ink etc. that is washable will come out of cloth when you wash it

ˌwash-and-ˈwear *adj.* wash-and-wear clothes do not need to be IRONED

wash·ba·sin /ˈwɑʃˌbeɪsən/ *n.* [C] a bowl or container that can be filled with water and used for washing your hands and face, used especially in the past

wash·board /ˈwɑʃbɔrd/ *n.* [C] **1** a piece of metal with a slightly rough surface, used in the past for rubbing clothes on when you are washing them **2 a washboard stomach** also **washboard abs** someone's stomach on which you can see all the muscles clearly

wash·bowl /ˈwɑʃboʊl/ *n.* [C] a washbasin

wash·cloth /ˈwɑʃklɔθ/ *n.* [C] a small square cloth used for washing your hands and face

wash·day /ˈwɑʃdeɪ/ *n.* [C,U] OLD-FASHIONED the day each week when you wash your clothes, sheets etc.

ˌwashed-ˈout *adj.* **1** not brightly colored anymore, especially as a result of being washed many times or left in a strong light too long: *The photograph looks kind of washed-out.* **2** feeling weak and looking unhealthy because you are very tired → see also **wash out** at WASH[1]

ˌwashed-ˈup *adj.* a washed-up person or organization will never be successful again: *a washed-up rock band*

wash·er /ˈwɑʃɚ/ *n.* [C] **1** INFORMAL a WASHING MACHINE **2** a thin flat ring of plastic, metal, rubber etc. that is put over a BOLT before the NUT is put on in order to make the bolt fit tighter, or that is put between two pipes to make them fit more tightly together

ˌwasher-ˈdryer also **ˌwasher-ˈdryer ˌunit** *n.* [C] two machines sold as a set, with one that washes clothes and one that dries them

ˈwashing day *n.* [C] WASHDAY

ˈwashing maˌchine *n.* [C] a machine for washing clothes

Wash·ing·ton /ˈwɑʃɪŋtən/ **1** WASHINGTON, D.C. **2** also **Washington State** WRITTEN ABBREVIATION **WA** a state in the northwestern U.S.

Washington, Book·er T. /ˈbʊkɚ ti/ (1856–1915) an African-American teacher who started the Tuskegee Institute, one of the first U.S. colleges for African-Americans

Washington, D.C. /ˌwɑʃɪŋtən di ˈsi/ the capital city of the U.S., which is in the District of Columbia, a special area that governs itself and is not contained in any of the 50 states

Washington, George (1732–1799) the first President of the U.S., who had been commander of the COLONIAL armies during the American Revolutionary War, and the leader of the Constitutional Convention

Washington, Mar·tha /ˈmɑrθə/ (1731–1802) the wife of George Washington, and the FIRST LADY of the U.S. from 1789 to 1797

Washington, Mount a mountain in the northeastern U.S. that is the highest of the White Mountains and is in the state of New Hampshire

Wash·oe /ˈwɑʃoʊ/ a Native American tribe from the western area of the U.S.

wash·out, wash out /ˈwɑʃ-aʊt/ *n.* [C] INFORMAL **1** a failure: *The picnic was a total washout – nobody turned up!* **2** a place where heavy rain has washed away a lot of soil, pieces of a road etc. from a place, or an occasion when this happens → see also **wash out** at WASH[1]

wash·room /ˈwɑʃrum/ *n.* [C] a word meaning a room where you use the toilet, used to avoid saying this directly

wash·stand /ˈwɑʃstænd/ *n.* [C] a table in a BEDROOM used in the past for holding the things needed for washing your face

wash·tub /ˈwɑʃtʌb/ *n.* [C] a large round container, that you wash clothes in

was·n't /ˈwʌzənt, ˈwɑzənt/ *v.* the short form of "was not": *Claire wasn't at school today.*

WASP /wɑsp/ *n.* [C] **White Anglo-Saxon Protestant** an American whose family was originally from northern Europe and who is therefore considered to be part of the most powerful group in society —**WASPy** *adj.*

wasp /wɑsp, wɔsp/ *n.* [C] a thin black and yellow flying insect that can sting you

wasp·ish /ˈwɑspɪʃ/ *adj.* in a bad mood and saying cruel things: *a waspish old woman*

was·sail /ˈwɑseɪl/ *v.* [I] OLD USE to enjoy yourself eating and drinking at Christmas —**wassail** *n.* [U]

wast /wɔst, wɑst/ *v.* **thou wast** OLD USE you were SYN wert

wast·age /ˈweɪstɪdʒ/ *n.* [singular, U] FORMAL the loss or destruction of something, especially in a way that is not useful or reasonable, or the amount that is lost or destroyed

waste¹ /weɪst/ S3 *n.*
1 BAD USE [singular, U] the use of something, for example money or skills, in a way that is not effective, useful, or sensible, or an occasion when you use more of something than you should: *The committee will study the issue of waste in state spending.* | +**of** *Working as a secretary is a waste of your talent.*
2 **be a waste of time/money/effort etc.** to be not worth the time, money etc. that you use because there is little or no result: *We should never have gone – it was a total waste of time.*
3 **go to waste** if something goes to waste, it is not used after it has been prepared or done: *Don't let all this food go to waste.*
4 UNWANTED MATERIALS [U] unwanted materials or substances that are left after you have used something: *It's a good idea to recycle household waste.* | **industrial/chemical/nuclear etc. waste** *the disposal of nuclear waste* ▸see THESAURUS box at **garbage**
5 **sb is a waste of space** SPOKEN used to say that someone has no good qualities
6 LAND [C usually plural] ESPECIALLY LITERARY a large empty or useless area of land: *the icy wastes of Antarctica*
[**Origin:** (1–5) 1200–1300 Old North French *waster*, from Latin *vastare* **to lay waste, destroy**] → see also WASTELAND

waste² S2 W3 *v.*
1 NOT USE STH EFFECTIVELY [T] to not use money, time, energy etc. in a way that is effective, useful, or sensible, or to use more of it than you should: *Leaving lights on all the time wastes electricity.* | **waste sth on sb/sth** *Don't waste your money on that junk!* | *They **wasted** a lot of **time** trying to fix the TV set themselves.*
2 **waste no time (in) doing sth** to do something as quickly as you can because it will help you: *He wasted no time in introducing himself.*
3 **be wasted on sb** if something is wasted on someone, they do not understand it or think it is worth considering: *The irony of the situation was not wasted on me.*
4 **be wasted in sth** if someone is wasted in a job, they are not using all of their abilities: *Her comic talent is wasted in the movie.*
5 **waste not, want not** used to say that if you use what you have carefully, you will always have enough
6 KILL SB [T] SLANG to kill someone or defeat them
7 ILLNESS [T] if an illness wastes someone, they become thinner and weaker → see also **don't waste your breath** at BREATH (4), WASTED, WASTING

waste away *phr. v.* to gradually become thinner and weaker, usually because you are sick

waste³ *adj.* [usually before noun] **1** waste materials, substances etc. are unwanted because the good part of them has been removed **2** used for holding or carrying away materials and substances that are not wanted anymore: *a sewage waste pipe* → see also **lay waste (to sth)** at LAY¹ (8), WASTELAND

waste·bas·ket /ˈweɪstˌbæskɪt/ *n.* [C] a small container, usually indoors, into which you put paper or other things that you want to get rid of → see picture at BASKET

wast·ed /ˈweɪstɪd/ *adj.* **1** [only before noun] not used effectively or successfully, or not producing a useful result: *a wasted opportunity* **2** SLANG very drunk or affected by drugs **3** very tired and weak-looking

ˈwaste disˌposal *n.* [U] the process or system of getting rid of unwanted materials or substances

waste·ful /ˈweɪstfəl/ *adj.* using too much of something or wasting it —**wastefully** *adv.* —**wastefulness** *n.* [U]

waste·land /ˈweɪstlænd/ *n.* [C,U] **1** land that is empty, ugly, and not used for anything: *a barren desert wasteland* **2** DISAPPROVING a situation in which nothing is good or attractive

ˈwaste ˌpaper *n.* [U] paper that has been thrown away, especially because it has already been used

waste·pa·per bas·ket /ˈweɪstˌpeɪpɚ ˌbæskɪt/ *n.* [C] a WASTEBASKET

ˈwaste ˌproduct *n.* [C] something useless, such as GARBAGE or gas, that is produced in a process that produces something useful

wast·er /ˈweɪstɚ/ *n.* [C] **a time-waster/energy-waster/money-waster etc.** someone or something that uses up too much time, energy, money etc.

waste·wa·ter /ˈweɪstˌwɔtɚ/ *n.* [U] water that has been used and contains waste products

wast·ing /ˈweɪstɪŋ/ *n.* [U] the process of losing weight and becoming weaker because of a disease

wast·rel /ˈweɪstrəl/ *n.* [C] LITERARY someone who wastes their time, money etc.

W

wat /wɑt/ *n.* [C] a Buddhist TEMPLE in Cambodia, Thailand, or Laos

watch¹ /wɑtʃ, wɔtʃ/ S1 W1 *v.*

1 LOOK AT [I,T] to look at and pay attention to something that is happening or moving: *Watch carefully – I'll show you.* | *I like to watch the ducks.* | *All she does is sit around and **watch TV**.* | **watch sb/sth do sth** *She watched him drive away.* | **watch sb doing sth** *We watched the children playing.* | **watch what/how/when etc.** *Watch what happens when I add water.*

THESAURUS

People who are watching something
spectator someone who is watching an event or game
viewer someone who is watching a program on television
audience the people who are watching a play or performance
onlooker someone who watches something happening without being involved in it
observer someone who watches an event, activity, or situation, especially in order to make an official report on it
watcher someone who watches a type of animal: *bird watchers*

►see THESAURUS box at **eye²**, **see¹**

2 BE CAREFUL [T] to be careful about something, or about how you use or do something: *Watch your fingers – I'm closing the door.* | **watch what/how/where etc.** *Watch where you're going!* | *I really should be **watching my weight*** (=being careful not to become fat).

3 PAY ATTENTION [T] to pay attention to a person or situation that interests or worries you to see how they develop: *We are watching the situation closely.* | *Of all the players in the tournament, he is the **one to watch**.* | **watch sth with interest/fear/joy etc.** *Supporters are watching the unfolding scandal with shock.*

4 TAKE CARE OF [T] to take care of someone or something so that nothing bad happens to them: *Who can I get to watch the kids tonight?*

5 SECRETLY [T] to secretly watch a person or place: *I feel like I'm being watched.*

6 watch the clock INFORMAL to keep checking what time it is because you are doing something that you do not want to be doing

7 watch your back INFORMAL to be careful and pay attention to what is happening around you so that your opponents cannot attack you or defeat you

8 watch the world go by to spend time looking at what is happening around you, especially in a way that is relaxing

9 watch sb like a hawk to watch someone very carefully, especially to make sure they do not do something bad

10 watch this space INFORMAL used to tell people to wait for more information because things are going to develop further

11 watch yourself a) SPOKEN used to warn someone to be careful not to hurt themselves, get into danger etc. **b)** to be careful not to offend or upset someone: *You really have to watch yourself around Perry.*

SPOKEN PHRASES

12 watch it! a) used to tell someone to be more careful, especially in a dangerous situation: *Hey watch it! You almost hit that truck!* **b)** used to threaten someone: *Watch it or I'll punch you.*

13 watch this! also **just watch!** used to tell someone to watch you while you do something surprising or exciting: *Okay, watch this! I'm going to make the egg disappear.*

14 watch your step a) used to warn someone to be careful, especially about making someone angry: *You'd better watch your step if you want to keep your job.* **b)** used to tell someone to be careful when they are walking

15 watch your mouth/language/tongue! used to tell someone to stop using words that offend you or that could offend other people

16 (you) watch used to tell someone that you know what will happen: *He'll win this time – you watch.*

17 watch the time to make sure you know what time it is to avoid being late

[**Origin:** Old English *wæccan*]

watch for sb/sth *phr. v.* to check for someone or something, so that you are ready to deal with them when they arrive or happen: *Soldiers guarded the camp, watching for any signs of intruders.*

watch out *phr. v.* used to tell someone to be more careful, especially because you notice something dangerous: *Watch out! There's a car coming.*

watch out for sb/sth *phr. v.* **1** to pay attention to and be ready for someone or something that might hurt you or cause problems for you: *Watch out for that branch.* | *Watch out for the guy downstairs – he's a little strange.* **2** to protect someone or something, so that nothing bad happens: *Larry's older sisters watched out for him.*

watch over sb/sth *phr. v.* to guard or take care of someone or something: *The older children watched over the younger ones.*

watch² S1 W3 *n.*

1 CLOCK [C] a small clock that you wear on your wrist or carry in your pocket: *My watch stopped.* | *He kept **looking at his watch**.*

2 keep a (close) watch on sb/sth to check a person, place, or situation carefully so that you always know what is happening and are ready to deal with it: *The government is keeping a close watch on the group's activities.*

3 keep watch (over sb/sth) to continue looking around an area in order to warn people of any danger: *Dan kept watch over the others as they slept.*

4 keep a watch (out) for sb/sth to look carefully in order to try and find someone or something, while you

are doing other things: *We had to keep a watch out for rats.*
5 be on the watch (for sb/sth) to be looking and waiting for something that might happen or someone you might see: *I'm always on the watch for new ideas.*
6 on sb's watch INFORMAL during the time that someone is responsible for a government, organization etc.: *The company had failed on his watch.*
7 GUARDING STH [C,U] a period of the day or night when a group of people must look carefully for any signs of danger or attack: *Who's* ***on watch*** *tonight?*
8 PEOPLE [C] a group of people employed to guard or protect someone or something → see also NEIGHBORHOOD WATCH, SUICIDE WATCH

watch·band /ˈwɑtʃbænd/ *n.* [C] a piece of leather or metal for fastening your watch to your wrist

watch·dog /ˈwɑtʃdɔg/ *n.* [C] **1** a committee or person whose job is to make sure that companies do not do anything illegal or harmful: *a consumer watchdog* **2** a dog used for guarding property

watch·er /ˈwɑtʃɚ/ *n.* **1** [C] someone who watches something, especially an event or TV show: *TV watchers* **2 a market-watcher/trend-watcher/industry-watcher etc.** someone who pays a lot of attention to a particular business, activity, or organization and reports on the changes **3 a bird-watcher/whale-watcher etc.** someone who spends their free time watching birds, WHALES etc. because they find them interesting ▸see THESAURUS box at **watch**[1]

watch·ful /ˈwɑtʃfəl/ *adj.* careful to notice what is happening, in case anything bad happens: *Operators work* ***under the watchful eye of*** *a supervisor.* —**watchfulness** *n.* [U] —**watchfully** *adv.*

watch·mak·er /ˈwɑtʃˌmeɪkɚ/ *n.* [C] someone who makes or repairs watches and clocks

watch·man /ˈwɑtʃmən/ *n.* [C] OLD-FASHIONED someone whose job is to guard a building or place SYN **security guard**: *the building's* ***night watchman***

watch·tow·er /ˈwɑtʃˌtaʊɚ/ *n.* [C] a high tower used for guarding a place, from which you can see things that are happening

watch·word /ˈwɑtʃwɚd/ *n.* [singular] a word or phrase that explains what people should do in a particular situation: *"Service" is our watchword.*

wa·ter[1] /ˈwɔt̬ɚ, ˈwɑ-/ S1 W1 *n.*
1 LIQUID [U] the clear colorless liquid that falls as rain, forms lakes and rivers, and is necessary for life to exist: *a pool of water* | *Could I have a glass of water?* | *Is* ***tap water*** (=from a sink) *OK?* | **bottled/mineral water** *I prefer mineral water.* | *The village has little clean* ***drinking water***. | *She spilled* ***boiling water*** *on her hand.* → see also FRESHWATER, SALTWATER[1]
2 SUPPLY [U] the supply of water that comes to homes, factories etc. through pipes: *The water was cut off for three days after the hurricane.* | *The cabin had no electricity or* ***running water*** (=water that flows out of pipes). | *a water bill* | *The city is facing* ***a serious water shortage*** *because of the drought* (=a situation when there is not much water available).
3 AREA OF WATER [U] **a)** an area of water such as a lake, river etc.: *Come swimming! The water's great!* | *The island has no airport and can be reached only* ***by water*** (=by boat). **b)** the surface of a lake, river etc.: *There's something floating on the water.* | *We were at least 50 feet* ***under water***. → see also UNDERWATER
4 waters [plural] **a)** the water in a particular lake, river etc.: *the icy waters of the Atlantic* **b)** an area of the ocean near or belonging to a particular country: *the coastal waters of Maine* **c)** water containing minerals from a natural spring: *She's gone to a resort in Florida to* ***take the waters*** (=drink the waters because you think it is good for your health).
5 turbulent/murky/uncharted etc. waters a situation that is dangerous and difficult to control: *Troubled waters still lie ahead for the administration.*
6 be water under the bridge SPOKEN to be in the past and not worth worrying about
7 water on the brain/knee etc. liquid that collects around the brain, knee etc. as the result of a disease
8 be (like) water off a duck's back INFORMAL if advice, warnings, or rude remarks are like water off a duck's back to someone, they have no effect on them
9 sb's water breaks when a PREGNANT woman's water breaks, liquid flows out of her body just before the baby is ready to be born
10 high/low water the highest or lowest level of the ocean and some rivers SYN **tide**
11 pass/make water OLD-FASHIONED FORMAL to URINATE
[**Origin:** Old English *wæter*] → see also **in deep water** at DEEP[1] (10), **feel like a fish out of water** at FISH[1] (3), **keep your head above water** at HEAD[1] (8), HEAVY WATER, **not hold water** at HOLD[1] (35), **be in hot water** at HOT (28), **muddy the waters** at MUDDY[2] (2), **pour cold water over/on sth** at POUR (7), **still waters run deep** at STILL[2] (4), **take to something like a duck to water** at TAKE TO (4), **test the waters** at TEST[2] (8), **tread water** at TREAD[1] (2)

water[2] S2 *v.*
1 POUR WATER [T] to pour water on an area of land, a plant etc., especially in order to make things grow: *Could you water my plants while I'm gone?*
2 EYES [I] if your eyes water, TEARS come out of them because of cold weather, pain etc.: *Chopping onions always* ***makes*** *my* ***eyes water***.
3 MOUTH [I] if your mouth waters, liquid comes into it, especially because you have smelled something that you want to eat: *The smell of fresh bread was* ***making her mouth water***. → see also MOUTH-WATERING
4 SUPPLY WITH WATER [T usually passive] EARTH SCIENCE if an area is watered by a river, the river flows through it and provides it with water
5 ANIMAL [T] to give an animal water to drink
water sth **down** *phr. v.* **1** to make a statement, report etc. less forceful by removing parts that may offend people: *The report of the investigation had been watered down.* **2** to add water to a liquid, especially for dishonest reasons SYN **dilute**: *This whiskey's been watered down.* → see also WATERED-DOWN

wa·ter·bed /ˈwɔt̬ɚˌbɛd/ *n.* [C] a bed with a MATTRESS made of rubber that is filled with water

ˈwater bird *n.* [C] BIOLOGY a bird that swims or walks in water

wa·ter·borne /ˈwɔt̬ɚˌbɔrn/ *adj.* waterborne diseases are spread or carried by water

ˈwater ˌbottle *n.* [C] **1** a bottle used for carrying drinking water **2** a HOT-WATER BOTTLE

ˈwater boy *n.* [C] a boy who provides the players on a sports team with water

ˈwater ˌbuffalo *n.* [C] a large black animal like a cow with long horns, used for pulling vehicles and farm equipment in Asia

ˈwater bug *n.* [C] an insect that lives in or on water

ˈwater ˌcannon *n.* [C] a machine that sends out water at high pressure, used by police to control crowds of people

ˈwater ˌchestnut *n.* [C] BIOLOGY a white fruit like a nut from a plant grown in water, used in Chinese cooking

ˈwater ˌcloset *n.* [C] OLD USE a toilet

wa·ter·col·or /ˈwɔt̬ɚˌkʌlɚ/ *n.* **1** [C usually plural, U] paint that you mix with water and use for painting pictures **2** [C] a picture painted with watercolors

ˈwater ˌcooler *n.* [C] **1** a piece of equipment that holds a lot of water for drinking and keeps it cold, used especially in offices **2 the water cooler** used to talk about the place or situation in an office in which workers talk about other people in the office, their lives outside the office etc.: *a hot topic around the water cooler* | *water cooler gossip*

wa·ter·course /ˈwɔt̬ɚˌkɔrs/ *n.* [C] EARTH SCIENCE **1** a passage with water flowing through it, that can be natural or built **2** a flow of water such as a river or UNDERGROUND stream

wa·ter·cress /ˈwɔt̬ɚˌkrɛs/ *n.* [U] a small plant with strong tasting green leaves that grows in water

W

ˈwater ˌcycle *n.* [C] SCIENCE a continuous series of related events, in which water on the ground or in the ocean becomes heated by the sun and changes into very small drops of liquid. These drops rise into the air and then fall back onto the ground or into the ocean as rain.

ˈwatered-down *adj.* **1** a watered-down statement, plan etc. is much weaker and less effective than a previous statement, plan etc.: *a watered-down version of the original* **2** a watered-down drink, especially an alcoholic drink, has had water added to it, especially in order to cheat people → see also WATER DOWN

ˌwatered ˈsilk *n.* [U] a type of silk that looks as if it is covered with shiny waves

wa·ter·fall /ˈwɔt̬ɚˌfɔl/ *n.* [C] EARCH SCIENCE water that falls straight down over a cliff or big rock → see picture on page A31

ˈwater ˌfountain *n.* [C] a DRINKING FOUNTAIN

wa·ter·fowl /ˈwɔt̬ɚˌfaʊl/ *n. plural* **waterfowl** [C,U] a bird that swims in water, such as a duck, GOOSE etc.

wa·ter·front /ˈwɔt̬ɚˌfrʌnt/ *n.* [C usually singular] a part of a town or an area of land that is next to the ocean, a river etc.: *They've opened a new restaurant* ***on the waterfront***. —**waterfront** *adj.* [only before noun] *waterfront property*

Wa·ter·gate /ˈwɔt̬ɚˌgeɪt/ also **ˈWatergate ˌscandal, the** HISTORY events relating to a an attempt to steal information from the Democratic Party HEADQUARTERS in the Watergate Hotel in Washington in 1972. The attempt involved people who were working for the re-election of President Nixon. These events led to Nixon deciding to leave his job in 1974.

ˈwater gun *n.* [C] a WATER PISTOL

ˈwater ˌheater *n.* [C] a piece of equipment in a house that heats and holds water to be used for baths, washing dishes etc.

wa·ter·hole /ˈwɔt̬ɚˌhoʊl/ *n.* [C] a watering hole

ˈwatering ˌcan *n.* [C] a container with a long tube on the front, used for pouring water on garden plants

ˈwatering ˌhole *n.* [C] **1** INFORMAL a bar or other place where people go to drink alcohol **2** a small area of water in a dry country, where wild animals go to drink

ˈwater jump *n.* [C] an area of water that horses or runners have to jump over during a race or competition

ˈwater ˌlily *n. plural* **water lilies** [C] a plant that floats on the surface of water and has large flowers, which are often white or pink

wa·ter·line /ˈwɔt̬ɚˌlaɪn/ *n.* **the waterline a)** the level that water reaches on the side of a ship **b)** the edge or highest level of an area of water, or the mark the water leaves on the ground, a wall etc.

wa·ter·logged /ˈwɔt̬ɚˌlɔgd, -ˌlɑgd/ *adj.* **1** a waterlogged area of land, object etc. is so wet it cannot be used, usually because of a flood **2** a waterlogged boat is full of water and may sink **3** a waterlogged person or animal is so wet they cannot do what they normally do

Wa·ter·loo /ˌwɔt̬ɚˈlu/ *n.* **sb's Waterloo** a situation in which someone who has been very successful, famous etc. fails

ˈwater main *n.* [C] a large pipe under the ground that carries the public supply of water to houses and other buildings

wa·ter·mark /ˈwɔt̬ɚˌmɑrk/ *n.* [C] **1** a design that is put into paper and can only be seen when you hold it up to the light **2** a special mark contained in electronic documents, pictures, music etc. that is used to stop people from copying them **3 the high/low**

water cycle

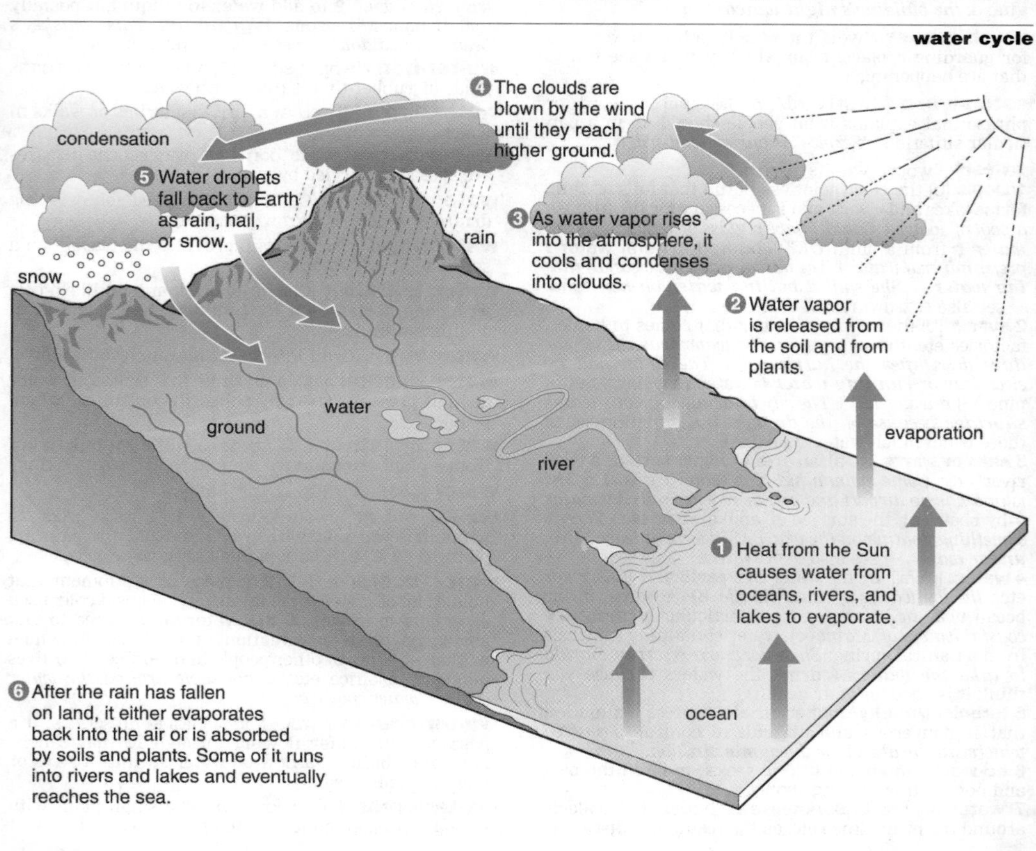

condensation
4 The clouds are blown by the wind until they reach higher ground.
5 Water droplets fall back to Earth as rain, hail, or snow.
rain
3 As water vapor rises into the atmosphere, it cools and condenses into clouds.
snow
2 Water vapor is released from the soil and from plants.
water
ground
evaporation
river
1 Heat from the Sun causes water from oceans, rivers, and lakes to evaporate.
6 After the rain has fallen on land, it either evaporates back into the air or is absorbed by soils and plants. Some of it runs into rivers and lakes and eventually reaches the sea.
ocean

watermark a) a line showing the highest or lowest levels of the ocean or a river **b)** a period of great success or failure: *the high watermark of U.S. power*

wa·ter·mel·on /ˈwɔt̬ɚˌmɛlən/ *n.* [C,U] BIOLOGY a large round fruit with hard green skin, juicy red flesh, and a lot of black seeds → see picture at FRUIT[1]

ˈwater ˌmeter *n.* [C] a piece of equipment that measures how much water passes through a pipe

ˈwater mill *n.* [C] a MILL that has a big wheel that is turned by the flow of water

ˈwater ˌmoccasin *n.* [C] BIOLOGY a poisonous North American snake that lives in water

ˈwater pipe *n.* [C] a pipe used for smoking tobacco, that consists of a long tube and a container of water

ˈwater ˌpistol *n.* [C] a toy gun that shoots water

ˈwater ˌpolo *n.* [U] a game played by two teams of seven swimmers with a ball

ˈwater ˌpower *n.* [U] SCIENCE power obtained from moving water, used to produce electricity or to make a machine work

wa·ter·proof /ˈwɔt̬ɚˌpruf/ *adj.* **1** waterproof clothing or material does not allow water to go through it: *a waterproof tent* **2** substances such as ink, MAKEUP, or SUNSCREEN that are waterproof do not come off or spread when they get wet

ˈwater rat *n.* [C] a small animal like a large mouse that lives in holes near water and can swim

ˈwater-reˌpellent *adj.* water-repellent cloth or clothes are specially treated with chemicals that keeps water from going into them and making them wet —**water repellent** *n.* [C,U]

ˈwater-reˌsistant, water resistant *adj.* something that is water-resistant does not allow water to go through easily, but does not keep all water out: *The watch is water resistant, but not waterproof.*

wa·ter·shed /ˈwɔt̬ɚˌʃɛd/ *n.* [C] **1** an event or period when important changes or improvements happen in history or in someone's life → see also TURNING POINT: +**in** *an important watershed in American history* | **a watershed year/event/moment etc.** *Passage of the law in 1966 was a watershed event.* **2** EARTH SCIENCE the high land separating two river systems

wa·ter·side /ˈwɔt̬ɚˌsaɪd/ *n.* [singular] the edge of a lake, river etc. —**waterside** *adj.*

ˈwater-ˌskiing, water skiing *n.* [U] a sport in which you SKI over water while being pulled by a boat: *Do you want to **go water-skiing**?* —**water-ski** *v.* [I] —**water-skier** *n.* [C] —**water ski** *n.* [C]

ˈwater ˌsoftener *n.* **1** [U] CHEMISTRY a chemical used for removing unwanted minerals from water **2** [C] a piece of equipment used to do this

ˈwater-ˌsoluble *adj.* CHEMISTRY a water-soluble substance becomes part of a liquid when mixed with water

ˈwater sports *n.* [plural] sports played on or in water

wa·ter·spout /ˈwɔt̬ɚˌspaʊt/ *n.* [C] **1** a pipe that lets rain water flow off a building onto the ground **2** EARTH SCIENCE a type of storm over the ocean in which a violent circular wind pulls water into a tall twisting mass → see also TORNADO

ˈwater supˌply *n.* [U] the water provided for a building or area, or the system of lakes, pipes etc. through which it flows

ˈwater ˌtable *n.* [C] EARTH SCIENCE the level below the surface of the ground where there is water

ˈwater ˌtaxi *n.* [C] a boat with a driver that you pay to take you somewhere

wa·ter·tight /ˈwɔt̬ɚˌtaɪt/ *adj.* **1** something that is watertight does not allow water to pass through it: *a watertight compartment* **2 a watertight plan/explanation/argument etc.** a plan, explanation etc. that is so carefully made or done that there is no chance of mistakes or problems → see also AIRTIGHT

ˈwater ˌtower *n.* [C] a very tall structure supporting a large container into which water is pumped in order to supply water to surrounding buildings

ˈwater ˌvapor *n.* [U] water in the form of gas in the air

wa·ter·way /ˈwɔt̬ɚˌweɪ/ *n.* [C] a river or CANAL that boats travel on

ˈwater wheel *n.* [C] a wheel that is turned by water as part of a machine or system

wa·ter·wings /ˈwɔt̬ɚˌwɪŋz/ *n.* [plural] two bags filled with air that you put on your arms when you are learning to swim

wa·ter·works /ˈwɔt̬ɚˌwɚks/ *n.* [plural] **1** the system of pipes and artificial lakes used to clean and store water before it is supplied to a town **2 turn on the waterworks** INFORMAL to start crying in order to get someone's sympathy

wa·ter·y /ˈwɔt̬əri/ *adj.* **1** watery food or drinks contain too much water and have little taste: *a cup of watery coffee* **2** full of water or tears: *a runny nose and watery eyes* **3** weak and difficult to see or hear: *a watery green light* **4 go to a watery grave** LITERARY to DROWN

WATS /wɔts/ also **ˈWATS line** *n.* [C] **wide area telephone service** a telephone service that allows a company or organization to make and receive as many telephone calls, especially long-distance calls, as they want each month for a particular price

Wat·son /ˈwɑtsən/, **James** (1928–) a U.S. scientist who, together with Francis Crick discovered the structure of DNA

watt /wɑt/ *n.* [C] PHYSICS a measure of electrical power: *a 60-watt light bulb*

Watt /wɑt/, **James** (1736–1819) a British engineer who made important improvements to the STEAM engine

watt·age /ˈwɑt̬ɪdʒ/ *n.* [singular, U] PHYSICS the power of a piece of electrical equipment measured in watts

wat·tle /ˈwɑt̬l/ *n.* [U] **1** a piece of loose flesh that grows from the head or neck of some birds such as a TURKEY **2** a material used for making fences consisting of small sticks on a frame of rods

W

wave[1] /weɪv/ S3 W3 *v.*

1 HAND [I,T] to move your hand or arm from side to side in order to greet someone or attract their attention: *Nick was waving from the upstairs window.* | +**to/at** *Who are you waving at?* | **wave goodbye (to sb)** (=to say goodbye to someone by waving to them)

2 MAKE STH MOVE [T] to move your hands, arms, or something that you are holding from side to side: *The fans chanted and waved Brazilian flags.* | **wave sth under/in/at etc. sth** *"Get out of here!" he shouted, waving his gun at us.* | *She **waved** her hands **around** as she talked.*

3 SIGNAL [T always + adv./prep.] to show someone where to go by waving your hand in that direction: **wave sb through/on/away etc.** *The border guards waved us through.*

4 MOVE SMOOTHLY [I] to move smoothly up and down, or from side to side: *The flag waved proudly in the breeze.*

5 HAIR a) [I] if hair waves, it grows in loose curls **b)** [T] to style hair or put chemicals on it, so that it forms loose curls

6 wave goodbye to sth INFORMAL to be forced to accept that something you want will not happen: *Well, we can wave goodbye to first place now.*

7 be like waving a red flag in front of a bull used to say that doing or saying something will definitely make someone angry

wave sth ↔ **aside/away** *phr. v.* to refuse to pay attention to an idea, a question, help etc. because you do not think it is necessary or important, especially by waving your hand: *He waved the suggestion away dismissively.*

wave sb/sth ↔ **down** *phr. v.* to signal to the driver of a car to stop by waving your arm at them

wave off *phr. v.* **1 wave sb ↔ off** to show someone that you want them to go away by waving your hand: *Myrtle closed her eyes and waved us off.* **2 wave sth ↔ off** to refuse to pay attention to an idea, a question, help etc. because you do not think it is necessary or important, especially by waving your hand: *Pamela quickly waved off the criticism.* **3 wave sb ↔ off** to wave goodbye to someone as they leave

wave² S2 W2 *n.*

1 OCEAN [C] EARTH SCIENCE a line of raised water that moves across the surface of the ocean: *Ten-foot waves crashed against the shore.* | *A huge **wave broke*** (=it curled and started to fall) *over me.* → see picture on page A31

2 SUDDEN INCREASE [C] a sudden increase in a particular type of behavior or activity: **+of** *a wave of applause* | ***A crime wave** has been sweeping the city.*

3 GROUP OF PEOPLE/THINGS [C] a large number of people or things arriving somewhere at the same time: **+of** *a new wave of immigrants* | ***Wave after wave of** aircraft passed overhead.* | *Crowds of tourists kept coming **in waves**.*

4 FEELING [C] a sudden strong feeling that spreads over someone or from one person to another: **+of** *A wave of panic spread through the crowd.* | *The pain swept over him **in waves*** (=as a series of sudden strong feelings).

5 HAND MOVEMENT [C usually singular] a movement of your hand or arm from side to side: *She gave a friendly wave.* | *Leona dismissed the servants with a wave of the hand.*

6 SOLDIERS [C] a group of soldiers, aircraft etc. that attack together: **+of** *At 6:00, the first wave of bombers were sent out from the carrier.*

7 LIGHT/SOUND [C] PHYSICS a movement in space or through air, water, etc. which carries energy such as light and sound from one place to another: *Light waves reflect and refract off a surface.* | *radio waves* → see also LONG WAVE, MEDIUM WAVE, SHORTWAVE

8 the wave of the future something modern that is expected to replace something else or an old way of doing something

9 HAIR [C] a part of your hair that curls slightly

10 make waves INFORMAL **a)** to cause problems: *With so many jobs already cut, he didn't want to make waves.* **b)** to do things that make people notice you

11 the waves [plural] LITERARY the ocean

12 the wave a situation in which people in a large group, especially at sports events, stand up and sit down quickly one after another, so that it looks like a wave is moving across the group

[**Origin:** Old English *wafian* **to wave with the hands**]
→ see also HEAT WAVE

wave·band /ˈweɪvbænd/ *n.* [C] a set of sound waves of similar length which are used to broadcast radio programs

wave·length /ˈweɪvleŋkθ/ *n.* [C] **1** someone's opinions, attitudes, and feelings: *We all seemed to be **on the same wavelength*** (=have similar ideas). | *Dad and I are just **on different wavelengths**.* **2** the size of a radio wave used to broadcast a radio signal **3** PHYSICS the distance between the tops of two waves of energy such as sound or light that follow each other

wa·ver /ˈweɪvɚ/ *v.* [I] **1** if someone's support for someone or something wavers, it becomes less certain: *Jessica's faith in her husband never wavered.* **2** if someone's attention, look etc. wavers, they stop looking at or paying attention to something **3** to not make a decision because you have doubts: **+between** *Wallace says he is wavering between the two proposals.* **4** to move in an unsteady way first in one direction then in another

wav·y /ˈweɪvi/ *adj.* *comparative* **wavier**, *superlative* **waviest** **1** wavy hair grows in loose curls ►see THESAURUS box at **bent²**, **hair** **2** a wavy line or edge has smooth curves in it —**waviness** *n.* [U]

wax¹ /wæks/ S3 *n.* [U] **1** a solid material used to make CANDLES, polish etc.: *We put a layer of wax down on the floor.* **2** BIOLOGY a natural sticky substance in your ears **3** CHEMISTRY a substance which is solid at normal temperatures, becomes soft when it is warm, and does not dissolve in water [**Origin:** Old English *weax*] → see also BEESWAX

wax² *v.* **1** [T] to put a thin layer of wax on a floor, table, car etc. in order to polish it **2 wax eloquent/philosophical/poetic etc. (about sb/sth)** HUMOROUS to talk about someone or something in an eager, thoughtful way **3** [T] to put a thin layer of wax on your arms, legs etc. and then pull it off in order to remove hairs **4** [I] PHYSICS when the moon waxes, the part that we see gets bigger each night OPP **wane** **5 wax and wane** LITERARY to increase and then decrease

ˈwax bean *n.* [C] a type of yellowish STRING BEAN

wax·en /ˈwæksən/ *adj.* LITERARY **1** waxen skin looks very pale and unhealthy **2** made of or covered in wax

ˈwax muˌseum also **wax·works** /ˈwækswɚks/ *n.* [C] a place where you pay to see models of famous people made of wax

ˈwax ˌpaper also **ˈwaxed ˌpaper** *n.* [U] paper with a thin layer of WAX on it, used to wrap food

wax·work /ˈwækswɚk/ *n.* [C] a model of a person made of WAX

wax·y /ˈwæksi/ *adj.* *comparative* **waxier**, *superlative* **waxiest** **1** looking or feeling like WAX **2** made of or covered in WAX —**waxiness** *n.* [U]

way¹ /weɪ/ S1 W1 *n.* *plural* **ways**

1 METHOD [C] a method of doing something: *I think my way's better.* | **the way (that) sb/sth does sth** *I like the way you said that.* | **a way of doing sth** *We have no way of knowing whether she got the message.* | **a way to do sth** *What's the best way to lose weight?* | **the right/wrong way** *You're not doing it the right way.* | **in the same/a different way** *You can put the model together in several different ways.* | **this/that way** *This way has always worked best for me.*

2 MANNER [C] a manner in which something happens or is done, especially when there are several possible ones: **the way (that) sb/sth does sth** *Look at the way he's dressed!* | **a good/bad etc. way to do sth** *The argument was a terrible way to end a wonderful week.* | *Emma wondered if he thought of her **in the same way** that she thought of him.* | *The disease affects different people **in different ways**.* | **in a strange/friendly/nasty etc. way** *Marge kept staring at him in a funny way.* | **(in) this/that way** *I didn't know you felt that way.*

3 PATH [C usually singular] a road, path, course of movement etc. that you must follow to get to a particular place: *Which way should we go?* | **+to/from** *What's the quickest way to the station from here?* | *I hope you **know the way** because I don't.* | **find/lose your way** *I was afraid of losing my way in the dark.* | **show/ask/tell sb the way (to sth)** *A teenage boy offered to show us the way to the farm.* | **the right/wrong way** *Are you sure this is the right way?* | **a way in/out/across etc.** *We kept looking for a way down to the beach, but we couldn't find one.*

4 DIRECTION [C] a particular direction from where you are now: *Which way is the wind blowing?* | **this/that way** *Jill's office is that way.* | *A big truck was coming **the other way*** (=the opposite direction). | ***Look both ways** before crossing the street.*

5 FEATURE OF A SITUATION [C] a feature of a situation, idea, plan etc. that you are considering in order to decide how true a statement is: *In what ways are the two cultures similar?* | **in some/many ways** *Life is much easier now, in many ways.* | *Tamara was his equal **in every way**.* | *Gray's comments should **in no way** be considered official policy.*

6 in a way used to say that something is partly true, or to make a statement weaker: *In a way, you're right, I suppose.*

7 DISTANCE [singular] also **ways** INFORMAL a distance, especially a long one: *She slept most of the way home.* | *Ottumwa? That's **quite a ways** from here, isn't it?* | *The dog followed us **a little way**.* | *We still have **a long way** to go.* | *I didn't **come all this way** to listen to you criticize me.* | **all the way down/across/through etc.** *Let's see if we can run all the way back.*

8 CHOICES/POSSIBILITIES [C] used when talking about choices someone could make, or possibilities that could happen, especially when there are two: *I'm not sure*

W

which way he'll decide. | *The doctors haven't given me information* ***one way or the other.***

9 (in) one way or another also **(in) one way or the other** used to say that something will happen somehow, or be done by some means, although you do not know how: *One way or another, we'll get the money.*

10 a way out (of sth) a possible method of solving a problem or difficult situation: *There seems to be no way out of the current economic crisis.* → see also **take the easy way out** at EASY[1] (7)

11 a way around sth a possible method of avoiding dealing with a difficult problem or situation: *There are several ways around this.* → see also **know your way around** at KNOW[1] (12)

12 in the/sb's way a) in between someone and somewhere they want to go or something they want to see so that they cannot go there or see it: *There was a big truck in the way.* **b)** in a place or situation where you are likely to cause a problem for someone, need their attention, be annoying etc.: *Don't come into the kitchen – you'll just be in my way.* | *The kids kept* ***getting in the way*** *so I sent them outside.*

13 stand/get in the way of sth to prevent someone from doing something, or prevent something from happening: *He won't let anything get in the way of spending time with his family.* → see also **stand in sb's way** at STAND[1] (37)

14 go some/a long way toward doing sth to help a little or a lot to make something happen

15 push/grope/inch/elbow etc. your way to/through/along etc. to do something to move to a new place or position, especially in a forceful way: *She elbowed her way to the front of the line.*

16 talk/charm/scam etc. your way into/past/onto etc. sth to do or say something in order get somewhere or achieve something, especially in a dishonest way: *He thinks he can buy his way into the White House.*

17 eat/drink/smoke etc. your way through sth to eat, drink etc. all of a particular amount of something: *He had eaten his way through a whole box of cookies.*

18 go sb's way if an event goes your way, it happens in the way you want: **everything/things/nothing is going sb's way** *Finally things are going my way.*

19 out of the way a) also **out of sb's way** in or to a position that is not blocking a road, someone's path etc.: *We pushed the car out of the way.* | ***Get out of*** *my* ***way.*** **b)** fairly far away from any town or from where other people live: *The house is a little out of the way, but you should be able to find it.* → see also OUT-OF-THE-WAY **c)** also **out of sb's way** somewhere where you are not likely to cause a problem, need attention, be annoying etc.: **keep/stay out of sb's way** *When Mark gets in one of these moods, it's best to keep out of his way.* **d)** also **out of sb's way** not in the same direction that someone else is going: *I live miles out of your way.* **e)** if something is out of the way, especially something difficult or bad, you have dealt with it so that you can do something else: *Good. Now that's out of the way, we can start working.*

20 on the/sb's way while traveling from one place to another: **+to** *I ran out of gas on the way to the airport.* | **on sb's way home/downtown/out etc.** *I've got to pick up some milk on my way home.*

21 be on sb's way to live, exist, or be done in the direction that someone is going [OPP] **be out of sb's way**: *I can pick you up in the morning – you're on my way.*

22 be on the/your way to be moving toward a particular place: *Carla's already on her way here.* | *I'm on my way.* | **+to** *The fleet is on its way to the Coral Sea.*

23 be (well) on the way to (doing) sth to be making progress toward a particular state or aim: *She is now well on the way to recovery.*

24 be on the/your /its way out to be rapidly becoming less popular, important, powerful etc.: *Platform shoes were clearly on the way out.*

25 be on the/your/its way up/down to be becoming richer, more successful etc. or poorer, less successful etc.: *He's on his way up in the company.*

26 sth is on its/the way used to say that something is going to happen soon: *Forecasters say warmer weather is on the way.* → see also **have a baby on the way** at BABY[1] (1)

27 in more ways than one INFORMAL used to say that there are several reasons without mentioning them all: *Trees are important to humans in more ways than one.*

28 BEHAVIOR [C] the particular style of behaving of a person or group of people: *Don't worry if she's quiet – that's just her way.* | *Amelia* ***has a*** *quiet deliberate* ***way about*** *her.* | *She quickly changed the subject as* ***as is*** *her* ***way.*** | **change/mend your ways** (=stop your bad behavior)

29 be born/made that way used to say that someone's character is not likely to change: *I couldn't kill an animal – I guess I'm not made that way.*

30 across/over the way on the opposite side of the street or an area: *They live just over the way from us.*

31 get/have your (own) way to do what you want to, even though someone else wants something different: *Monica's so spoiled – she always gets her own way.*

32 have a way with sb/sth to have a special ability to deal well with someone or something: *He's always had a way with children.* | *Marla really has* ***a way with words*** (=the ability to express ideas and opinions well).

33 have a (long) way to go to need to develop or change a lot in order to reach a particular standard: *We've made some progress, but we still have a long way to go.*

34 that/this way used when telling the results of an action or situation that was just mentioned: *I hope he transfers to another school. That way, I wouldn't have to see him anymore.*

35 in a big/small way a lot or a little: *Things are going to have to change around here in a big way.*

36 by way of sth FORMAL **a)** as a form of something, or instead of something: *"She asked for it," Kyle said by way of explanation.* **b)** if you travel by way of a place, you go through it: *We flew to Europe by way of Iceland.* **c)** using a particular method: *Bacteria communicate by way of chemical messages.*

37 in sb's own way used when you want to say that someone really thinks, feels, or does something, although other people might think that they do not: *I suppose she probably loves me in her own way.*

38 go your (own) way to do what you want to do, make your own decisions etc.

39 to sb's way of thinking used before giving someone's opinion: *To my way of thinking this is not a step forward, but a step back.*

40 TIME [singular] also **ways** [plural] a length of time, especially a long one: **a long way off/ahead/apart etc.** *A peace settlement is still a long way off.* → see also **go back a long way** at GO BACK (2)

41 Way used in the names of roads: *17 Church Way*

42 along the way a) while traveling from one place to another: *I'd like to do a little exploring along the way.* **b)** while developing from one situation or part of your life to another: *Louise has made quite a number of enemies along the way.*

43 be going sb's way to be traveling in the same direction as someone: *I can take you – I'm going your way.*

44 nothing/little/much etc. in the way of sth also **nothing/little/much etc. by way of sth** INFORMAL none of something, little of something, not much of something etc.: *The city doesn't offer much in the way of hotels.*

45 split/divide etc. sth two/three etc. ways to divide something into two, three etc. equal parts: *We'll split the cost between us five ways.*

46 have your way with sb a) OLD-FASHIONED OR HUMOROUS to persuade someone to have sex with you **b)** to easily defeat an enemy

47 ways and means special methods for doing something, especially when this involves deciding how to pay for something

48 way around a particular order or position that something should be in: *Which way around does this skirt go?* | **the right/wrong/other way around** *The batteries go in the other way around.*

49 the way of the world how things always happen or are done, especially when this is not easy to change

SPOKEN PHRASES

50 no way! **a)** used to say that you will definitely not do or allow what someone has asked for: *"Can I borrow your car this weekend?" "No way!"* | *You think I'm going to help you paint your house?* ***No way, José*** (=used to emphasize that you will not do something). **b)** used to say that you do not believe something or are very surprised by it: *"She's 45." "No way!"*

51 way to go! **a)** used to tell someone that they have done something very well, or achieved something special **b)** used, especially as a joke, when someone has done something silly or stupid: *Way to go, Kim! Now we'll have to start all over again.*

52 there's no way (that) used to say that something will definitely not happen: *There's no way I'll ever get married again.*

53 no way is sb doing sth used to say that you definitely will not do or allow something: *No way am I going to take care of all these kids on my own.*

54 the way things are (going) also **the way things stand** used to say that because of the present situation you expect another situation to develop, especially a bad one: *The way things are right now, I don't think we'll be able to afford the trip.*

55 if I had my way used before telling someone how you think something should be done: *If I had my way, we'd leave this place tomorrow.*

56 the way I see it used to give your opinion about something: *The way I see it, it was a fair trade.*

57 have it your way! used to tell someone in an annoyed way that you will allow them to have or do what they want

58 that's (just) the way sth is/goes used to say that a particular situation cannot be changed: *If you want it done right, it's going to cost you. That's the way it is.*

59 isn't it/that always the way? also **isn't it/that just the way?** used to say that something always happens in a particular way that is not good: *The bus left early – isn't that always the way when you're running late?*

60 that's (just) the way sb is used to say that someone has particular qualities that will not change: *Sometimes Tim needs to be alone. That's just the way he is.*

61 not in any way, shape, or form also **in no way, shape, or form** used to emphasize that a statement is not true and could not possibly be true: *I am not responsible for his actions in any way, shape, or form.*

62 the way sb likes sth the particular condition, quality, or situation that someone prefers: *The chicken was nice and crispy – just the way I like it.*

63 have a way of doing sth to usually happen or behave in a particular way: *Don't worry too much. These problems usually have a way of working out.*

64 that's the way used to tell someone that they are doing something correctly or well, especially when you are showing them how

65 be with sb all the way (on sth) to agree with someone completely: *I'm with you all the way on this salary issue.*

66 that's no way to do sth used to tell someone that they should not be doing something in a particular manner: *That's no way to speak to your father!*

67 no two ways about it used to say that something is definitely true, especially something you might want to avoid: *We're just going to have to try to get along. No two ways about it.*

68 there's more than one way to skin a cat used to say that there is more than one possible method of doing something

69 way out! SLANG an expression meaning that something is very good or exciting, used especially in the 1970s

[**Origin:** Old English *weg*] → see also AMERICAN WAY, **you can't have it both ways** at BOTH[1] (2), **by the way** at BY[1] (12), **come sb's way** at COME (24), **either way** at EITHER[2] (3), **see the error of your ways** at ERROR (2), **find your way** at FIND[1] (9), **go the way of all flesh** at FLESH[1] (11), **give way** at GIVE[1] (41), **go out of your way to do sth** at GO[1] (23), HALFWAY, **lead the way** at LEAD[1] (11), **make your way** at MAKE[1] (11), **make way (for sb/sth)** at MAKE[1] (10), ONE-WAY, **pay your way** at PAY[1] (13), RIGHT OF WAY, **see your way (clear) to do sth** at SEE[1] (27), **talk your way out of sth** at TALK[1] (24), TWO-WAY, UNDERWAY, **work your way over/out/back etc.** at WORK[1] (9)

WORD CHOICE **on the way/in the way**

• Use **on the way** to talk about something you do while you are going somewhere, or a place that you will pass as you go there: *I'll get some groceries on the way home.* | *Jenna's house is on the way to the mall.*

• Use **in the way** to say that something is preventing you from getting to the place where you are going: *I can't get my car out of the garage because Dave's motorcycle is in the way.*

way² S1 *adv.* [+ adj./adv.] INFORMAL **1** by a large degree: **way above/below/over etc.** *It is way past your bedtime!* | *Guess again – you're* ***way off*** (=very far from being correct). | *Life was simpler* ***way back when*** (=a long time ago). | **way heavier/smarter/bigger etc.** *Tickets were way more expensive than I thought.* | **way too much/long/early etc.** *The movie was way too long.* **2** by a great distance: **way ahead/behind/out etc.** *She lives way across town.* | *He was way ahead of us.* **3** SLANG very: *I think she's way cool, man.*

way·bill /ˈweɪbɪl/ *n.* [C] TECHNICAL a document sent with goods that says where the goods are to be delivered, how much they are worth, and how much they weigh, used especially with goods being sent by ship, train, airplane etc.

way·far·er /ˈweɪˌfɛrɚ/ *n.* [C] LITERARY a traveler who walks from one place to another —**wayfaring** *adj.* [only before noun]

way·lay /ˈweɪleɪ/ *v.* **waylays, waylaid, waylaying** [T] **1** [usually passive] to delay someone when they are trying to go somewhere or do something **2** to stop someone when they are trying to go some place, especially so that you can talk to them, or so that you can rob or attack them

ˌway of ˈlife *n. plural* **ways of life** [C] **1** the way someone lives, or the way people in a society usually live: *Tribe elders want to protect their traditional way of life.* | **the American/British/Amish etc. way of life** (=the life typical of Americans, British people etc.) **2** a job or interest that is so important that it affects everything you do: *Nursing isn't just a job; it's a whole way of life.*

ˈway-out *adj.* INFORMAL unusual or strange, usually in a modern way

-ways /weɪz/ *suffix* [in adverbs] in a particular direction: *sideways* (=to the side)

way·side /ˈweɪsaɪd/ *n.* [singular] LITERARY the side of a road or path → see also **fall by the wayside** at FALL[1] (20) —**wayside** *adj.* [only before noun] *a wayside inn*

ˈway ˌstation *n.* [C] a place to stop between the main stations on a path, railroad etc.

way·ward /ˈweɪwɚd/ *adj.* behaving in a way that is not considered right or appropriate: *wayward youth*

wa·zoo /wɑˈzu/ *n.* [C] SPOKEN **up/out the wazoo** in a large amount, or to a great degree

WC *n.* [C] OLD-FASHIONED **water closet** a TOILET or BATHROOM

we /wi/ S1 W1 *pron.* [used as the subject of a verb] **1** the person who is speaking and one or more people: *We're looking forward to seeing you on Sunday.* | *We Italians are proud of our history and culture.* | *What should we* (=you and I) *do tonight, Sean?* | *Can we* (=I and the others) *have some cake, Mom?* **2** people in general: *We still know very little about what causes the disease.* | ***We all*** *grew up believing that our parents were perfect.* **3** used by a writer or a speaker to mean you (the reader or listener) and them: *As we saw in Chapter 4, the war had many causes.* **4** used especially to children and people who are sick to mean "you": *We don't hit other people, do we, Tommy?* **5** FORMAL OR OLD USE used by a king or queen in official language to mean "I" [**Origin:** Old English]

weak[1] /wik/ S3 W2 *adj. comparative* **weaker**, *superlative* **weakest**

1 PHYSICALLY not physically strong OPP **strong**: *The weakest members of the herd are attacked first.* | **+with** *We were all weak with hunger.* | **too weak to do sth** *Betty was too weak to get out of bed.* | **weak heart/knees/eyes etc.** (=parts of your body that do not work properly)

THESAURUS

puny small, thin, and weak: *a puny little kid*
feeble very weak: *They had nothing to eat, and were sick and feeble.*
frail weak and thin because you are old or sick: *My grandmother looked small and frail.*
infirm weak or sick for a long time, especially because you are old: *He is elderly and infirm.*
malnourished weak or sick because you have not had enough good food to eat: *Many of the women are too malnourished to feed their babies.*

2 CHARACTER easily influenced by other people because you cannot make decisions by yourself OPP **strong**: *a weak and indecisive man* | *weak management*
3 NOT SKILLED not having much ability or skill in a particular activity or subject OPP **strong**: *Martin is a weak swimmer.* | **+in/at** *I'm kind of weak in algebra.* | *Be honest about your* ***weak points****.*
4 LACKING POWER/INFLUENCE not having much power or influence OPP **strong**: *Recent elections have left the opposition party weak.* | *a weak bargaining position* | **a weak president/leader/ruler/king etc.** *a weak and ineffective president*
5 ARGUMENT/EXPLANATION/STORY ETC. not having the power to persuade or interest people: *a weak excuse* | *The actors are good, but the plot is weak.* | *There are some* ***weak points*** *in her argument.*
6 BUILDINGS/OBJECTS unable to support a lot of weight OPP **strong**: *a weak structure* | **too weak to do sth** *The bridge was too weak to support the weight of the traffic.*

THESAURUS

fragile/delicate easily broken or damaged: *a fragile china figurine*
flimsy used about a house, boat, or structure that is not strong or well-made, so that it is easily damaged: *a flimsy door*
rickety used about a structure or piece of furniture that is in very bad condition and likely to break: *a rickety old bridge*

7 BUSINESS/INDUSTRY ETC. ECONOMICS not successful financially OPP **strong**: *weak sales of men's clothes*
8 MONEY/STOCKS ETC. not valuable when compared to other similar things OPP **strong**: *The dollar was weaker on Monday.*
9 ALCOHOL a weak drink does not contain as much alcohol as you think it should OPP **strong**: *The drinks were all a little weak.*
10 DRINK/LIQUID containing a lot of water or having little taste OPP **strong**: *a weak cup of coffee*
11 LIGHT/SOUND difficult to see or hear OPP **strong**: *a weak radio signal*
12 a weak point/spot a part of something or of someone's character that can easily be attacked or criticized: **+in** *weak spots in Richardson's record*
13 go weak in the knees INFORMAL to suddenly feel weak or strange, especially because you have had a sudden surprise or because you have seen someone you love
14 SMILE a weak smile is slight and not very believable, especially because you are not very happy
15 a weak chin/jaw a weak chin or jaw is not very well developed and people often think it suggests a weak character
16 the weak/weakest link the person or thing in a situation that is not as strong, skillful etc. as the others

17 a weak moment a time when you can be persuaded more easily than usual: ***In a weak moment****, I told him I'd help organize the party.* → see also A MOMENT OF WEAKNESS
18 the weaker sex OLD-FASHIONED an expression meaning "women", now considered offensive
19 VERB ENG. LANG. ARTS a weak verb forms its past tense and past participle in a regular way
20 CONSONANT/SYLLABLE a weak CONSONANT or SYLLABLE is not emphasized when you say the word
[**Origin:** 1200–1300 Old Norse *veikr*]

weak[2] *n.* **the weak** [plural] people or animals who are not strong and who do not have much power compared to others OPP **the strong**

ˌweak ˈacid *n.* [C] CHEMISTRY an acid that does not completely separate into IONS (=atoms with an electric charge) when it is mixed with water → see also STRONG ACID

ˌweak ˈbase *n.* [C] CHEMISTRY a BASE (=substance that combines with an acid to form a salt) that does not completely separate into IONS (=atoms with an electric charge) when it is mixed with water, and has a low PH → see also STRONG BASE

ˌweak eˈlectrolyte *n.* [C] CHEMISTRY a liquid that does not allow electricity to travel through it effectively because it does not contain many IONS (=atoms with an electric charge) → see also STRONG ELECTROLYTE

weak·en /ˈwikən/ *v.* [I,T]
1 POWER/IMPORTANCE to make someone or something less powerful or less important, or to become less powerful or important OPP **strengthen**: *A series of scandals has weakened the government.*
2 BODY to make someone lose their physical strength, or to become physically weak: *Julia had been weakened by a long illness.*
3 STRUCTURE to make a building, structure etc. less strong and less able to support a lot of weight, or to become less strong and less able to support a lot of weight OPP **strengthen**: *The bridge had begun to weaken.*
4 SB'S DETERMINATION to make someone less determined, or to become less determined OPP **strengthen**: **weaken sb's determination/resolve** *These terrorist bombings have not weakened our resolve to remain in the region.*
5 BUSINESS ECONOMICS if a business weakens or is weakened, it becomes less financially successful OPP **strengthen**: *Sales have weakened in recent months.*
6 MONEY ECONOMICS if a particular country's money or a company's STOCK prices weaken or are weakened, their value is reduced OPP **strengthen** —**weakening** *n.* [U]

ˌweak interˈaction also **ˌweak ˈforce** *n.* [singular] PHYSICS one of the basic forces of nature that is related to PARTICLE decay and RADIOACTIVITY → see also STRONG INTERACTION

ˌweak-ˈkneed *adj.* INFORMAL **1** lacking courage and unable to make your own decisions: *a weak-kneed coward* **2** not feeling strong or well, especially because you have had a sudden surprise or because you have seen someone you love → see also **go weak in the knees** at WEAK[1] (13)

weak·ling /ˈwik-lɪŋ/ *n.* [C] someone who is not physically strong

weak·ly /ˈwikli/ *adv.* without much force or energy: *The border is weakly defended.*

weak·ness /ˈwiknɪs/ *n.*
1 BODY [U] the state of being physically weak: *muscle weakness*
2 FAULT [C] a fault in someone's character or in a system, organization, design etc.: *Frank's biggest weakness is his lack of tolerance.* | *The plan has* ***strengths and weaknesses****.* ► see THESAURUS box at **fault**[1]
3 LACK OF POWER [U] lack of power and influence: *the weakness of the country's law-making body*
4 CHARACTER [U] lack of determination shown in someone's behavior: *Compromising might be seen as* ***a sign***

W

of weakness. | ***In a moment of weakness,*** *I agreed to go.*
5 MONEY [U] the condition of not being worth a lot of money: *the weakness of the yen against the dollar*
6 a weakness for sth if you have a weakness for something, you like it very much even though it may not be good for you: *Lisa has a weakness for chocolate.*

ˌweak-ˈwilled *adj.* unable to make decisions easily or do what you intend to do

weal /wil/ *n.* [C] a red swollen mark on the skin where someone has been hit

wealth /wɛlθ/ W2 *n.* **1** [U] a large amount of money and possessions OPP **poverty**: *The country's wealth comes from its oil.* **2** [U] the state of being very rich: *Expensive cars are a sign of wealth.* **3 a wealth of experience/knowledge/resources etc.** a large amount of experience, knowledge etc.: *The report contains a wealth of information.* [**Origin:** 1200–1300 *weal* **good condition of life, prosperity** (11–19 centuries), from Old English *wela*]

wealth·y /ˈwɛlθi/ S3 W3 *adj. comparative* **wealthier**, *superlative* **wealthiest** having a lot of money, possessions etc.: *Joan comes from a wealthy family* —**the wealthy** *n.* [plural]

wean /win/ *v.* **1** [I,T] BIOLOGY to gradually stop feeding a baby or young animal on its mother's milk and start giving it ordinary food **2 be weaned on sth** to be influenced by something from a very early age.

wean sb **from/off** sth *phr. v.* to make someone gradually stop doing something you disapprove of: *She wanted to wean him off junk food.*

weap·on /ˈwɛpən/ W2 *n.* [C] **1** something that you use to fight with, such as a knife, bomb, or gun: *nuclear weapons* | *Police are still looking for* ***the murder weapon.*** | *It is important that we control the spread of* ***weapons of mass destruction*** (=weapons that can kill many people at one time). | *Was he* ***carrying a weapon?*** | **a lethal/deadly weapon** (=a dangerous weapon that could kill someone) **2** a type of behavior, knowledge of a particular subject etc. that you can use against someone or something when you are in a difficult situation: *She was afraid the information would be used as a weapon against her.* [**Origin:** Old English *wæpen*] → see also **secret weapon** at SECRET[1] (2)

weap·on·ry /ˈwɛpənri/ *n.* [U] a word meaning "weapons", used especially when talking about particular types of weapons: *nuclear weaponry*

wear[1] /wɛr/ S1 W1 *v. past tense* **wore** /wɔr/ *past participle* **worn** /wɔrn/
1 ON YOUR BODY [T] to have something such as clothes, shoes, or jewelry on your body: *She was wearing a long black dress.* | *Neither person in the car was* ***wearing a seatbelt.*** | *I* ***wear glasses*** *for reading.* | *She never* ***wears makeup.*** | **wear blue/black/red etc.** *I rarely wear bright colors.* | **wear sth to a party/dance/interview etc.** *What should I wear to the wedding?* ▸see THESAURUS box at **dress[1]**
2 HAIR [T] to have your hair or BEARD in a particular style or shape: *I like it when you wear your hair up.*
3 EXPRESSION [T] to have a particular expression on your face: **wear a frown/grin/scowl etc.** *She wore a polite smile.*
4 BECOME DAMAGED [I] to become thinner, weaker etc. after continuous use: *Her jeans were wearing at the knees.*
5 wear well a) to remain in good condition without becoming broken or damaged after a period of time: *Brass wears as well as steel in most hinges.* **b)** if something wears well, it continues to be interesting even after you have heard or seen it many times: *The group's album from 1991 still wears well.*
6 sth wears thin a) if something wears thin, you are bored with it because it is not interesting anymore, or has become annoying: *His little jokes were starting to wear thin.* **b)** if your patience wears thin, you have very little left: *My patience with Jean is wearing thin.*
7 sb wears sth well a) used to say that someone looks good in a particular piece of clothing **b)** used to say that someone looks good or works effectively in a particular situation: *The twins wore the strain well.*
8 wear your heart on your sleeve INFORMAL to show your true feelings openly
9 wear the pants INFORMAL to be the person in a family who makes the decisions.
[**Origin:** Old English *werian*] —**wearable** *adj.* → see also WORN OUT

wear away *phr. v.* **wear sth ↔ away** to gradually become damaged or thinner or weaker or to disappear completely by being used, rubbed etc., or to make something do this: *Walkers have worn parts of the path away.*

wear down *phr. v.* **1 wear sb ↔ down** to make someone physically weaker or less determined: *Lewis gradually wore down his opponent.* **2** to gradually become smaller or make something smaller, for example by rubbing it or using it a lot: *Mountains are slowly worn down by wind and rain.*

wear sth **in** sth *phr. v.* to make a hole or mark in something such as a piece of clothing or a material, especially by wearing or using it a lot so that it rubs against something again and again: **wear a hole/groove/rut etc.** *He had worn holes in all his socks.*

wear off *phr. v.* if pain or the effect of something wears off, it gradually stops: *The effects of the anesthetic were starting to wear off.*

wear on *phr. v.* **1** if time wears on, it passes very slowly, especially when you are waiting for something to happen: *The weather improved as the day wore on.* **2 wear on sb** to gradually make someone feel tired or annoyed: *The constant travel was beginning to wear on the players.*

wear out *phr. v.* **1 wear sth ↔ out** to become weak, broken, or useless, or to make something do this by using it a lot or for a long time: *After years of running, his knees started to wear out.* | *The kids have worn out the carpet in the living room.* **2 wear sb ↔ out** to make someone feel extremely tired SYN **exhaust**: *Working two jobs can really wear you out.* **3 wear out your welcome** to stay at someone's place longer than they want you to

wear[2] *n.* [U] **1** damage caused by continuous use over a long period: *The carpets are showing signs of wear.* | *You will not be charged for normal* ***wear and tear.*** **2** the amount of use an object, piece of clothing etc. has had, or the use you can expect to get from it: *This type of sofa can take a lot of wear.* | *I've* ***gotten a lot of wear out of*** *these jeans.* **3 casual/evening/children's etc. wear** the clothes worn for a particular occasion or activity, or by a particular group of people: *Men were dressed in formal wear and top hats.* → see also FOOTWEAR, MENSWEAR, SPORTSWEAR, **the worse for (the) wear** at WORSE[2] (3) ▸see THESAURUS box at **clothes**

wear·er /ˈwɛrɚ/ *n.* [C] someone who wears a particular type of clothing, jewelry, etc.: *A bicycle helmet protects the wearer against head injury.*

wear·ing /ˈwɛrɪŋ/ *adj.* **1** making you feel tired or annoyed: *The constant arguments at home are very wearing.* **2** gradually making something weaker or less effective: **+on** *The new process is less wearing on the equipment.*

wea·ri·some /ˈwɪrisəm/ *adj.* FORMAL making you feel bored, tired, or annoyed

wea·ry[1] /ˈwɪri/ *adj. comparative* **wearier**, *superlative* **weariest** **1** very tired: *He gave a weary sigh.* | *She looked weary.* ▸see THESAURUS box at **tired** **2 weary of sth** tired of and impatient about something that has been happening or you have been doing for a long time: *Jo had grown weary of explaining why she was a vegetarian.* **3** very tiring —**wearily** *adv.* —**weariness** *n.* [U]

weary[2] *v.* **wearies, wearied, wearying** [I,T] FORMAL to become very tired, or make someone very tired: *Kerry's constant need for attention wearies me.*

weary of sb/sth *phr. v.* to become tired or bored of and impatient with someone or something

wea·sel[1] /ˈwizəl/ *n.* [C] **1** BIOLOGY a small thin furry animal that kills and eats rats and birds **2** INFORMAL someone who has been disloyal to you or has deceived you

weasel² *v.*

weasel out *phr. v.* INFORMAL to avoid doing something you should do by using dishonest excuses or lies: **+of** *Don't try to weasel out of paying what you owe.*

weasel word *n.* [C usually plural] INFORMAL a word used instead of another word because it is less direct, honest, or clear

weath·er¹ /ˈwɛðɚ/ S2 W2 *n.* **1** [singular, U] EARTH SCIENCE the outdoor conditions such as temperature, clouds, rain, wind etc. in a place: *What's the weather like today?* | **hot/wet/cold etc. weather** *We've had some cold weather lately.* | **good/bad weather** *We're hoping for some good weather this summer.* | *dangerous weather conditions* **2 weather permitting** if the weather is good enough: *I'm playing golf tomorrow, weather permitting.* **3 the weather** INFORMAL the description of what the weather will be like in the near future, on radio, television, in newspapers etc.: *Did you check the weather this morning?* **4 under the weather** INFORMAL slightly sick: *Louise looked a little under the weather when I saw her.* **5 keep a weather eye on sth** OLD-FASHIONED to watch a situation carefully so that you notice anything unusual or bad [**Origin:** Old English *weder*] → see also ALL-WEATHER

weather² *v.* **1** [T] to come through a very difficult situation safely: *The police department has* ***weathered the storm*** *of criticism after the incident.* **2** [I,T usually passive] if rock, wood etc. weathers, or if wind, sun, rain etc. weathers them, they change color or shape over a period of time → see also WEATHERED, WEATHERING

weather balˌloon *n.* [C] a large BALLOON that is sent into the air with special equipment to collect information about the weather

weather-ˌbeaten *adj.* weather-beaten buildings, skin, clothing etc. look old and damaged because they have been outside in bad weather

weather ˌbureau *n.* [C] a place where information about the weather is collected and where reports are produced

weath·er·cock /ˈwɛðɚˌkɑk/ *n.* [C] a WEATHER VANE in the shape of a ROOSTER

weath·ered /ˈwɛðɚd/ *adj.* weathered wood, stone, skin etc. has changed shape or color over a period of time because of the wind, rain, sun etc.

weather ˌforecast *n.* [C] a report saying what the weather is expected to be like in the near future

weather ˌforecaster *n.* [C] someone on television or radio who tells you what the weather will be like

weath·er·ing /ˈwɛðərɪŋ/ *n.* [U] EARTH SCIENCE the effect of the wind, rain etc. on earth and stone over time

weath·er·ize /ˈwɛðəˌraɪz/ *v.* [T] to protect a building against cold weather by putting in INSULATION, making windows fit tightly etc. —**weatherization** /ˌwɛðərəˈzeɪʃən/ *n.* [U]

weath·er·man /ˈwɛðɚˌmæn/ *n.* [C] a male weather forecaster

weather map *n.* [C] a map that shows what the weather is like in a particular place at a particular time

weather ˌpattern *n.* [C] the way the weather usually is or changes over a long period of time in a particular area

weath·er·proof /ˈwɛðɚˌpruf/ *adj.* weatherproof clothing or material can keep out wind and rain —**weatherproof** *v.* [T]

weather reˌport *n.* [C] a report saying what the weather has been like and how it might change

weather ˌstation *n.* [C] a place or building used for studying and recording weather conditions

weather ˌstripping *n.* [U] thin pieces of plastic or other material put along the edge of a door or window to keep out cold air —**weather strip** *v.* [I,T]

ˈweather vane *n.* [C] a metal thing fastened to the top of a building that blows around to show the direction the wind is coming from

weave¹ /wiv/ *v. past tense* **wove** /woʊv/, *past participle* **woven** /ˈwoʊvən/ **1** [I,T] to make threads into cloth by crossing them under and over each other on a LOOM, or to make cloth in this way: *Only a few of the women still weave full time.* | *They wove rugs to sell.* **2** [T] to make something by twisting pieces of something together: *The women weave wicker baskets.* **3** [T] to put many different ideas, subjects, stories etc. together and connect them smoothly: *The book weaves science and mythology together.* **4** *past tense and past participle* **weaved** [I always + adv./prep.,T always + adv./prep.] to move somewhere by turning and changing direction a lot: **+through/across etc.** *The car was weaving in and out of traffic.* | *Miles* ***weaved*** *his* ***way*** *through the crowded room.* —**weaving** *n.* [U]

weave² *n.* [C] **1** the way in which a material is woven, and the pattern formed by this: *a fine weave* **2** INFORMAL a HAIR WEAVE

weav·er /ˈwivɚ/ *n.* [C] someone whose job is to weave cloth

web /wɛb/ W2 *n.* [C] **1 the Web** the system on the Internet that allows you to find and use information that is held on computers all over the world: *I found his address* ***on the Web.*** **2** BIOLOGY a net of thin threads made by a SPIDER to catch insects: *A spider had* ***spun*** *its* ***web*** (=made its web) *across the door.* → see also COBWEB **3 a web of sth** a closely related set of things that can be very complicated: *a web of lies* **4** BIOLOGY a piece of skin that connects the toes of ducks and some other birds, and helps them to swim well [**Origin:** Old English]

webbed /wɛbd/ *adj.* BIOLOGY webbed feet or toes have skin between the toes

web·bing /ˈwɛbɪŋ/ *n.* [U] **1** strong woven material in narrow bands, used for supporting seats, holding things etc. **2** pieces of skin between fingers or toes

web·cam /ˈwɛbkæm/ *n.* [C] a camera that you connect to your computer that lets other people see you on the Internet → see picture at COMPUTER

We·ber /ˈveɪbɚ/, **Max** /mæks/ (1864–1920) a German ACADEMIC and writer whose ideas are important as the beginning of modern SOCIOLOGY

ˈweb-ˌfooted *adj.* BIOLOGY having toes that are connected by pieces of skin

web·log also **web log** /ˈwɛblɔg/ *n.* [C] a BLOG

web·mas·ter /ˈwɛbˌmæstɚ/ *n.* [C] someone who organizes a WEBSITE and keeps it working

ˈweb page, **Web page** *n.* [C] a document or FILE that is part of a WEBSITE and has its own URL (=address)

web·site, **Web site** /ˈwɛbsaɪt/ S2 W2 *n.* [C] a place on the Internet where you can find information about a variety of subjects, including people, products and organizations, that often contains several web pages that are LINKED

Web·ster /ˈwɛbstɚ/, **Dan·iel** /ˈdænyəl/ (1782–1852) a U.S. politician famous for his skill at public speaking

Webster, No·ah /ˈnoʊə/ (1758–1843) a U.S. LEXICOGRAPHER (=someone who writes dictionaries) famous for his American dictionaries and for setting rules for American spelling which were different from British spelling rules

ˈweb-toed *adj.* WEB-FOOTED

Wed. a written abbreviation of Wednesday

we'd /wid/ **1** the short form of "we had" when "had" is an AUXILIARY VERB: *We'd both eaten already.* **2** the short form of "we would": *We'd rather stay.*

wed /wɛd/ *v. past tense and past participle* **wedded** or **wed, wedding** [I,T not in progressive] a word meaning "to marry", used especially in literature or newspapers

wed·ded /ˈwɛdɪd/ *adj.* **1 sb's (lawful/lawfully) wedded husband/wife/spouse** FORMAL someone's legal husband or wife **2 wedded bliss** ESPECIALLY HUMOROUS the happiness that comes when you are married **3 be**

W

wedded to sth to be unable or unwilling to change a particular idea or way of doing things: *We're not wedded to any one solution.*

wed·ding /ˈwɛdɪŋ/ S1 W3 *n.* [C] **1** a ceremony at which two people become married, especially one with a religious service: *They invited over 200 people to the wedding.* | **a wedding present/reception/cake etc.** *We got that silver tray as a wedding present.*

THESAURUS

At a wedding
bride the woman who is getting married
groom/bridegroom the man who is getting married
bridesmaid a girl or woman, usually unmarried, who helps or is with the bride
maid of honor the most important bridesmaid
matron of honor a married woman who helps the bride
best man the man who helps the bridegroom
page a boy who helps or is with the bride
flower girl a girl who carries flowers in the ceremony
(wedding) ceremony the actions by which two people are married
(wedding) service a religious ceremony in which two people are married
reception a large formal meal or party after a wedding
honeymoon a holiday taken by two people who have just gotten married
→ PARTY

2 (hear) wedding bells SPOKEN used to say that you think it is likely that two people will get married

ˈwedding ˌband *n.* [C] a WEDDING RING

ˈwedding ˌchapel *n.* [C] a small building like a church, used for wedding ceremonies

ˈwedding ˌdress also **ˈwedding ˌgown** *n.* [C] a long white dress worn at a traditional wedding

W

ˈwedding ˌparty *n.* [C] all the people who are officially involved in someone's wedding, and who usually wear special clothes

ˈwedding ring *n.* [C] a ring that you wear, usually on your left hand, to show that you are married

ˈwedding ˌvows *n.* [plural] the promises you make during a wedding ceremony

wedge[1] /wɛdʒ/ *n.* [C] **1** a piece of wood, metal etc. that has one thick edge and one pointed edge and is used especially for keeping a door open or for splitting wood **2** a piece of food shaped like this: +**of** *a wedge of cheese* → see also **drive a wedge between sb/sth** at DRIVE[1] (20)

wedge[2] *v.* **1** [T always + adv./prep.] to force something firmly into a narrow space: **wedge sth behind/under/in etc.** *Vicky wedged a book under the table leg.* **2 wedge sth open/shut** to put something under a door, window etc. to make it stay open or shut

wedg·ie /ˈwɛdʒi/ *n.* [C] SLANG the situation of having your underwear pulled too tightly between your BUTTOCKS (=parts of your body you sit on), or the action of pulling someone's underwear into this position as a joke

wed·lock /ˈwɛdlɑk/ *n.* [U] OLD USE the state of being married [**Origin:** Old English *wedlac*, from *wedd* **something given to show that a promise will be kept** + *-lac* **actions, activity**] → see also **be born out of wedlock** at BORN (1)

Wednes·day /ˈwɛnzdi, -deɪ/ WRITTEN ABBREVIATION **Wed.** *n.* [C,U] the fourth day of the week, between Tuesday and Thursday: *Jane comes home Wednesday.* | *The staff meeting is* ***on Wednesday****.* | *I didn't go to work* ***last Wednesday****.* | *I'll be in California* ***next Wednesday****.* | *My yoga class starts* ***this Wednesday*** (=the next Wednesday that is coming). | *We usually go out for lunch* ***on Wednesdays*** (=each Wednesday). | *My birthday is* ***on a Wednesday*** *this year.* | **Wednesday morning/afternoon/night etc.** *She didn't get here till Wednesday afternoon.* → see Grammar box at SUNDAY [**Origin:** Old English *wodnesdæg*, from *Woden* **Odin** + *dæg* **day**]

wee /wi/ *adj.* [usually before noun] **1 the wee (small) hours** the early hours of the morning, just after MIDNIGHT **2 a wee bit** INFORMAL to a small degree: *Don't you think you're being a wee bit harsh?* **3** OLD-FASHIONED very small: *a wee girl* → see also PEEWEE

weed[1] /wid/ S3 *n.* **1** [C] BIOLOGY a wild plant growing where it is not wanted, that prevents crops or garden flowers from growing as they should: *Come help me pull weeds in the garden.* → see also SEAWEED **2** [U] SLANG MARIJUANA **3 spring/sprout up like weeds** to start appearing in large numbers **4 the weed** OLD-FASHIONED cigarettes or tobacco [**Origin:** Old English *weod*] → see also **grow like a weed** at GROW (1)

weed[2] *v.* [I,T] to remove unwanted plants from a garden or other place

weed sb/sth ↔ **out** *phr. v.* to get rid of people or things that are not very good: *Unsuitable recruits were soon weeded out.*

weed·kil·ler /ˈwidˌkɪlɚ/ *n.* [C,U] poison used to kill unwanted plants

ˈweed ˌwhacker, weed wacker *n.* [C] a piece of equipment with a long straight handle and a blade or a piece of strong string that turns around very fast, that is used for cutting weeds and small areas of grass

weed·y /ˈwidi/ *adj. comparative* **weedier**, *superlative* **weediest** INFORMAL **1** full of weeds, or like a weed: *a weedy lawn* **2** tall, thin, and weak: *a weedy young man*

week /wik/ S1 W1 *n.* [C] **1** a period of seven days and nights, beginning Sunday and ending Saturday: *The class meets once a week.* | *Greg just started working here* ***this week****.* | **last/next week** (=the week before or after this one) | **once/twice/three times etc. a week** *I go to the gym three times a week.* **2** any period of seven days and nights: *It would probably take a week to hike that far.* | *I'll see you* ***in a week*** (=seven days after today). | **a week from today/tomorrow/Monday etc.** *Are you free a week from Friday?* **3** the part of the week when you go to work, usually from Monday to Friday SYN **workweek**: *a 40-hour week* | *I don't go out much* ***during the week****.* **4 week after week** also **week in, week out** SPOKEN continuously for many weeks: *We keep practicing the same dance steps week in, week out.* [**Origin:** Old English *wicu*]

week·day /ˈwikdeɪ/ *n. plural* **weekdays** [C] any day of the week except Saturday and Sunday

week·end[1] /ˈwikɛnd/ S1 W2 *n.* [C] **1** Saturday and Sunday (and sometimes also Friday evening), especially when considered as time when you do not work: *What are you planning to do* ***this weekend****?* | ***Over the weekend*** (=during the weekend) *we went to visit my wife's parents.* | *They close at 5:00* ***on weekends****.* | *Rich* ***spent the weekend*** *learning how to use his new computer.* | **last/next weekend** (=the weekend before or after this one) **2 a three-day/four-day weekend** also **a long weekend** three or four days, including Saturday and Sunday, during which you do not have to work **3** a vacation from Friday evening until Sunday evening: *You've won a weekend for two in Chicago!* → see also **a long weekend** at LONG[1] (7)

weekend[2] *v.* [I always + adv./prep.] to spend the weekend somewhere

week·end·er /ˈwikˌɛndɚ/ *n.* [C] someone who spends time in a place only at weekends

ˈweekend ˌwarrior *n.* [C] INFORMAL **1** someone who works during the week, but does activities outside during the weekend that take a lot of energy, such as HIKING, camping etc. **2** someone who is in the National Guard or in the Army, Navy etc. RESERVE

week·long /ˌwikˈlɔŋ◂ / *adj.* [only before noun] continuing for a week: *a weeklong music festival*

week·ly[1] /ˈwikli/ *adj.* **1** happening or done every week: *weekly piano lessons* ▸see THESAURUS box at regular[1] **2** relating to a single week: *weekly hotel rates* —**weekly** *adv.*

weekly[2] *n. plural* **weeklies** [C] a magazine that appears once a week: *a popular news weekly*

week·night /ˈwiknaɪt/ *n.* [C] any night except Saturday or Sunday

wee·nie /ˈwini/ *n.* [C] INFORMAL **1** a type of SAUSAGE SYN wiener **2** a word meaning someone who is weak, afraid, or stupid, used especially by children

weep /wip/ *v. past tense and past participle* **wept** /wɛpt/ **1** [I,T] FORMAL OR LITERARY to cry a lot, especially because you feel very sad: *James broke down and wept.* | *At the trial, she* ***wept bitterly*** (=cried loudly). ▸see THESAURUS box at cry[1] **2** [I] MEDICINE if a wound weeps, liquid comes out of it —**weep** *n.* [singular]

weep·ie /ˈwipi/ *n.* [C] a book or movie that tries to make people cry

weeping ˈwillow *n.* [C] a tree with branches that hang down toward the ground

weep·y /ˈwipi/ *adj. comparative* **weepier**, *superlative* **weepiest** INFORMAL tending to cry a lot, or looking like you will cry: *Her eyes were red and weepy.*

wee·vil /ˈwivəl/ *n.* [C] a small insect that destroys plants, grain etc. by eating them

wee-wee *v.* [I] SPOKEN a word meaning to URINATE (=pass liquid waste from your body) used by or to children —**wee-wee** *n.* [U]

weft /wɛft/ *n.* **the weft** TECHNICAL the threads in a piece of cloth that are woven across the threads that go from top to bottom → see also WARP

weigh /weɪ/ S2 W3 *v.*

1 BE A PARTICULAR WEIGHT [linking verb] to have a particular weight: *How much do you weigh?* | *The birds way just a few ounces.*

2 MEASURE THE WEIGHT [T] to use a machine to find out what someone or something weighs: **weigh yourself** *Have you weighed yourself recently?*

3 weigh a ton to be very heavy: *Your suitcase weighs a ton!*

4 CONSIDER/COMPARE [T] to consider something carefully so that you can make a decision about it: *I haven't had time to weigh all of my options.* | **weigh sth against sth** *We have to weigh the costs of the new system against its benefits.*

5 weigh your words to think very carefully about what you say because you do not want to say the wrong thing

6 INFLUENCE [I always + adv./prep.] FORMAL to influence a result or decision: **+with** *Greg's opinion usually weighs strongly with our supervisor.* | **+in favor of** *The new data weighed in favor of the effectiveness of the drug treatment.* | **+against** *The evidence weighed heavily against him.*

7 weigh anchor to raise an ANCHOR and sail away

[**Origin:** Old English *wegan* **to move, carry, weigh**]

weigh sb/sth ↔ **down** *phr. v.* **1** to make someone or something bend or feel heavy under a load: **+with/by** *Heavy, bulky clothes weigh you down.* **2** to make it difficult for something to progress or improve: **+by/with** *Debt is weighing down the company.* **3** to feel worried about a problem or difficulty: *They let life's problems weigh them down.* | **be weighed down by/with sth** *His conscience was weighed down with guilt.*

weigh in *phr. v.* **1** INFORMAL to add a remark to a discussion or an argument: **+with** *Each member weighed in with their own opinion.* **2** to have your weight tested before taking part in a fight, other sport, or a horse race: **+at** *Williams weighed in at 235 pounds.* → see also WEIGH-IN

weigh on sb/sth *phr. v.* to make someone worried or give them problems: *Boyd's arguments* ***weighed on*** *her* ***mind***. | *The possibility of being laid off* ***weighed heavily*** *on them.*

weigh sth ↔ **out** *phr. v.* to measure an amount of something by weight

weigh-in *n.* [C usually singular] a check on the weight of a BOXER or a JOCKEY before a fight or a horse race → see also **weigh in** at WEIGH

weight[1] /weɪt/ S1 W1 *n.*

1 WHAT SB/STH WEIGHS [C,U] how heavy someone or something is when measured by a particular system: *The average weight of a baby at birth is just over seven pounds.* | **+of** *The cable is strong enough to hold the weight of an elephant.* | *Fruit and vegetables are sold* ***by weight***.

2 HOW FAT [U] how heavy and how fat someone is: *She's always worried about her weight.* | **put on/gain wait** *John's put on a lot of weight recently.* | *Have you* ***lost weight*** (=gotten thinner)? | *Exercise and* ***watch your weight*** (=be careful about what you eat so that you do not get fat). | *For years, Gerry's* ***had a weight problem*** (=been too fat). → see also OVERWEIGHT, UNDERWEIGHT

3 HEAVINESS [U] the fact of being heavy: *Her arm ached from the weight of the suitcase.* | *The roof collapsed* ***under the weight of*** *the snow.*

4 HEAVY THING [C] something that is heavy: *I can't lift heavy weights because of my bad back.*

5 FOR EXERCISE [C] a piece of metal that weighs a certain amount and is lifted by people who want bigger muscles or who are competing in lifting competitions → see also WEIGHTLIFTING

6 WORRY [C] something that causes you a lot of worry because you have to deal with it: **+of** *She felt a great weight of responsibility.*

7 a weight off sb's mind/shoulders something that solves a problem and makes someone feel happier: *Selling the house was a great weight off my mind.*

8 IMPORTANCE [U] the value, influence, or importance that something has when you are forming a judgment or opinion: *The weight of evidence against her led to her conviction.* | *Harry's opinion doesn't* ***carry*** *much* ***weight*** (=have influence) *around here.* | *New findings have* ***added weight to*** *the theory that there is life on other planets.* | *I don't* ***attach*** *too much* ***weight to*** *the rumors* (=I do not think that they are true or important).

9 the weight of sth the large size or amount of something: *The weight of public opinion is behind the teachers.*

10 FOR MEASURING QUANTITIES [C] a piece of metal weighing a particular amount that is used to measure what something else weighs by balancing it in a SCALE

11 SYSTEM [C,U] a system of standard measures of weight: *metric weight* | *weights and measures*

12 SCIENCE [C,U] PHYSICS the amount of force with which an object is pulled down by GRAVITY → see also DEAD WEIGHT, **pull your weight** at PULL[1] (9), **throw your weight around** at THROW[1] (16), **throw your weight behind sb/sth** at THROW[1] (17), -WEIGHT

weight[2] *v.* [T] **1** also **weight down** to add something heavy to something or put a weight on it, especially in order to keep it in place **2** to change something slightly so that you give more importance to particular ideas or people

-weight /weɪt/ [in adjectives] **summer-weight/winter-weight** a piece of clothing that is summer-weight or winter-weight is made of material that is appropriate for summer or winter

weight·ed /ˈweɪtɪd/ *adj.* [not before noun] giving an advantage or disadvantage to one particular group or activity: **+toward/against** *The voting system is weighted against the smaller parties.* | **+in favor of** *His policies are heavily weighted in favor of the rich.*

weight·less /ˈweɪtlɪs/ *adj.* having no weight, especially when you are floating in space or water —**weightlessly** *adv.* —**weightlessness** *n.* [U]

weight·lift·ing /ˈweɪtˌlɪftɪŋ/ *n.* [U] **1** the sport of lifting special WEIGHTS attached to ends of a bar **2** also **weight training** the activity of lifting special weights as a form of exercise —**weightlifter** *n.* [C]

weight·y /ˈweɪṭi/ *adj. comparative* **weightier**, *superlative* **weightiest** **1** important and serious: *We have a weighty matter to discuss.* **2** ESPECIALLY LITERARY heavy

weir /wɪr, wɛr/ *n.* [C] **1** a low structure built across a river or stream to control the flow of water **2** a

W

wooden fence built across a stream to make a pool where you can catch fish

weird /wɪrd/ S1 *adj.* INFORMAL unusual and very strange: *He has some weird ideas.* | *Robin's boyfriend is kind of weird.* [**Origin:** 1800–1900 *weird* **what happens to a person in life, fate, (bad) luck** (11–18 centuries), from Old English *wyrd*] —**weirdly** *adv.* —**weirdness** *n.* [U]

weird·o /ˈwɪrdoʊ/ *n. plural* **weirdos** [C] INFORMAL someone who behaves strangely, wears unusual clothes etc.

welch /wɛltʃ/ *v.* [I] to not do something you have promised to do for someone, such as not paying them money: +**on** *I'll make sure Bill doesn't welch on the bet.*

wel·come¹ /ˈwɛlkəm/ S3 *interjection* **1** an expression of greeting to a guest or someone who has just arrived: +**to** *Welcome to New York!* | ***Welcome home*** (=used when someone has been away and returns home)*!* | ***Welcome back*** (=used when someone has been away and returns to a place) – *it's good to see you again.* **2 welcome to the club** SPOKEN used to make someone feel better when they are in a bad situation, by telling them you are in that situation too

welcome² S1 *adj.* **1** someone who is welcome is gladly accepted in a place: *I don't think I'm welcome there anymore.* | *a welcome guest* | +**at** *You're welcome at my house anytime.* | *They did their best to **make** me **feel welcome*** (=make me feel that they were pleased I had come). **2 you're welcome** SPOKEN a polite way of replying to someone who has just thanked you for something: *"Thank you for your help." "You're welcome."* **3** something that is welcome is pleasant and enjoyable, especially because it is just what you need or want: *The trip to Mexico will be a welcome break from work.* | *welcome news* **4 be welcome to do sth** SPOKEN used to invite someone to do something if they would like to: *You're welcome to borrow my bike.* **5 be welcome to sth** SPOKEN used to say that someone can have something if they want it, often because you do not want it: *If you want to take the job you're welcome to it!*

W

welcome³ *n.* **1** [C] a greeting you give to someone when they arrive: *The team was **given a warm welcome*** (=greeted in a very friendly way) *when they returned to Chicago.* | *Rodney received **a hero's welcome*** (=a very excited friendly welcome to someone who has done something good) *in his hometown.* | *He extended his arms **in welcome**.* **2** [singular] the way in which people react to an idea, and show that they like it or do not like it: *The proposals have received a cautious welcome from members.* **3 overstay/outstay your welcome** FORMAL to stay at someone's house longer than they want you to → see also **wear out your welcome** at WEAR OUT (3)

welcome⁴ W3 *v.* [T] **1** to say hello in a friendly way to someone who has just arrived: *Jill was busy welcoming the guests.* **2** to accept an idea, suggestion etc. happily: *Many of us welcomed his resignation.* | *I **welcome** the challenge **with open arms*** (=very happily). **3 welcome sb with open arms** to be very glad that someone has come [**Origin:** Old English *wilcume*, from *wilcuma* **person you are glad to have as a guest**]

ˈwelcome ˌwagon *n.* [C] **1** actions that are organized to welcome someone who has just arrived in a new place **2 Welcome Wagon** TRADEMARK an organization whose members welcome new people to an area, give them small gifts and information etc.

wel·com·ing /ˈwɛlkəmɪŋ/ *adj.* **1** behaving in a way that shows you are glad to have other people visiting you: *a welcoming smile* ►see THESAURUS box at **friendly** **2** making you feel happy and relaxed: *The room was bright and welcoming.* **3** done or organized to welcome someone somewhere: **a welcoming committee/party** (=a group of people who welcome someone)

weld¹ /wɛld/ *v.* **1** [I,T] to join metals by melting them and pressing them together when they are hot, or to be joined in this way **2** [T always + adv./prep.] to join or unite people into a single, strong group → see also FORGE, SOLDER²

weld² *n.* [C] a joint that is made by welding two pieces of metal

weld·er /ˈwɛldɚ/ *n.* [C] someone whose job is to weld things

wel·fare /ˈwɛlfɛr/ Ac W2 *n.* [U] **1** money paid by the government to people who are very poor, do not have jobs, are sick etc.: *Most of the people in this neighborhood are **on welfare**.* **2** health, comfort, and happiness SYN **well-being**: *Our only concern is the children's welfare.* [**Origin:** 1300–1400 *well fare* **to fare well**] → see also SOCIAL SECURITY

ˌwelfare ˈstate *n.* **1 the welfare state** POLITICS the system by which the government provides money, free medical care etc. for people who are old, do not have jobs, are sick etc. **2** [C] POLITICS a country with such a system

we'll /wɪl; *strong* wil/ the short form of "we will" or "we shall": *We'll leave about eight.*

well¹ /wɛl/ S1 W1 *adv. comparative* **better**, *superlative* **best**

1 SATISFACTORILY in a satisfactory, skillful, or successful way: *Did you sleep well?* | *We didn't win, but at least we played well.* | *The festival was very well organized.* | *Dad doesn't hear **too well*** (=very well) *anymore.* | **fairly/moderately/pretty well** *The condos sold fairly well.* | *I hope that your presentation **goes well*** (=happens in the way you planned or hoped). | *That **went** much **better** than I expected!*

2 be doing well if someone who has been sick or injured is doing well, they are becoming healthy again: *The patient is doing well.*

3 do well (for yourself) to be successful, especially in work or business: *I did very well that first year.*

4 THOROUGHLY in a thorough way: *Before you open it, shake the bottle well.* | *We know the area very well.*

5 as well as in addition to something else: *My son has asthma as well as allergies.* | **as well as doing sth** *As well as being attractive, he's rich.*

6 as well in addition to someone or something else SYN **too**: *Did Joe go as well?* → see Word Choice box at ALSO

7 may/might/could well do sth, may/might/could well be sth used to say that something is likely to happen or is likely to be true: *If he doesn't stop, he could well find himself in jail.* | *What you say may well be true.*

8 may/might/could (just) as well do sth a) INFORMAL used when you do not particularly want to do something but you decide to do it: *I suppose we may as well get started.* **b)** used to mean that another course of action would have an equally good result: *The taxi was so slow we might just as well have taken the bus.*

9 well before/behind/down etc. a long way, a long time, or a large amount before, behind etc.: *It was well after midnight when he got home.* | *The prices are well below the peak of 2004.*

10 be well on the/your way to (doing) sth to have almost finished changing from one state or situation to another, especially a better one: *We are well on the way to reaching our sales targets.*

11 VERY used to emphasize a few specific adjectives: *I'm **well aware** of the potential problems.* | *The museum is **well worth** a visit.*

12 speak/think well of sb to talk about someone in an approving way or to have a favorable opinion of them: *Rick always speaks well of you.*

13 can't very well (do sth) used to say that someone cannot do something because it would be unacceptable: *I can't very well tell him we don't want him to come!*

14 well done!/played! etc. SPOKEN used to praise someone when you think they have done something very well

15 well said! SPOKEN used to say that you agree with what someone has just said, or that you admire them for saying it

16 do well by sb INFORMAL to treat someone generously: *He always did very well by his parents.*

17 as well sb might/may/should FORMAL used to say that there is a good reason for someone's feelings or

reactions: *Marilyn acts very guilty whenever she sees me, as well she should.*
18 well and truly completely
[**Origin:** Old English *wel*] → see also **know full/perfectly etc. well** at KNOW[1] (4), **sb means well** at MEAN[1] (3) → see Word Choice box at GOOD

well[2] S1 W1 *interjection*
1 EMPHASIZING STH used before a statement or question to emphasize it: *Well, I think you should wait for a better offer.* | *"I really like Josh." "**Well then**, call and tell him so."*
2 PAUSING used to pause or give yourself time to think before saying something: *This needs to be copied, and, well, I don't have time to do it.* | *Well, let's see now, I could see you next Thursday.* | ***Well, I mean**, you shouldn't just take things without asking.*
3 ACCEPTING A SITUATION also **oh well** used to show that you accept a situation even though you feel disappointed or annoyed about it: *Well, I suppose this room will be big enough for the meeting.* | *Oh well, at least we have a place to stay tonight.*
4 FINAL REMARK used to show that you are about to finish speaking or stop doing an activity: *Well, that's all for today, I'll see you all tomorrow.*
5 SHOWING SURPRISE also **well, well (,well)** used to express surprise or amusement: *Well, well, look who's here.*
6 SHOWING ANGER used to express anger or disapproval: *Well, he could at least have called and said he'd be late!* | **well honestly/really etc.** *Well really, she didn't have to be so rude.*
7 EXPRESSING DOUBT used to express doubt or the fact that you are not sure about something: *"Are you free Friday evening?" "Well, it depends."*
8 very well FORMAL used to show that you agree with or accept a suggestion, invitation etc.: *Very well, you can go, but be back by 7 p.m.*
9 CONTINUING A STORY used to connect two parts of a story that you are telling people, especially in order to make it seem more interesting: *You remember that article I wrote? Well, they're going to publish it.*
10 CHANGING STH used to slightly change something that you have said: *She looks Italian. Well, southern European, anyway.*
11 Well? used to demand an explanation or answer when you are angry with someone: *Well? What have you got to say for yourself?*

well[3] W3 *adj. comparative* **better**, *superlative* **best**
1 healthy: *Ellen hasn't been very well lately.* | *"How are you?" "Very well, thanks."* | **look/feel well** *What's wrong? Don't you feel well?* | **get well/better** *I hope you get well soon.* ►see THESAURUS box at **healthy** **2 all is well** FORMAL used to say that a situation is satisfactory: *All is not well with their marriage.* **3 all's well that ends well** used to say that a situation has ended in a satisfactory way after some difficulties **4 it is just as well (that)** SPOKEN used to say that things have happened in a way that is fortunate or desirable: *It's just as well I took the train today – I heard the traffic was really bad.* **5 it might/would be just as well to do sth** SPOKEN used to give someone advice or make a helpful suggestion: *It might be just as well to leave him on his own for a few hours.* **6 sth is (all) well and good** SPOKEN used to say that something is good or right, but it is not enough or also has some disadvantages: *Going on vacation is all well and good, but you've got to get back to reality sometime.* → see also **leave well enough alone** at LEAVE[1] (21)

well[4] *n.* [C] **1** EARTH SCIENCE a deep hole in the ground from which people take water: *They help the villagers **dig wells**.* **2** EARTH SCIENCE an OIL WELL **3** an enclosed space in a building which goes straight up and down and surrounds an ELEVATOR, stairs etc. → see also STAIRWELL

well[5] also **well up** *v.* [I usually + adv./prep.] **1** if liquids well or well up, they start to fill something before they flow: *I felt the tears welling up in my eyes.* **2** if someone's eyes well or well up, tears come into them **3** if feelings well or well up, they start to get stronger: *Anger welled up inside him.*

ˌwell-acˈquainted *adj.* knowing someone or something very well

ˌwell-adˈjusted *adj.* emotionally healthy and able to deal well with the problems of life: *a happy well-adjusted child*

ˌwell-adˈvised, **well advised** *adj.* **sb would be well-advised to do sth** used when you are strongly advising someone to do something that will help them avoid trouble: *You would be well-advised to accept his offer.*

ˌwell-apˈpointed *adj.* FORMAL a well-appointed house, hotel etc. has very good furniture and equipment

ˌwell-atˈtended *adj.* if a meeting, event etc. is well-attended, a lot of people go to it

ˌwell-ˈbaby *adj.* [only before noun] relating to or providing medical care and advice for babies who are not sick, to make sure that they stay healthy: *a well-baby check-up*

ˌwell-ˈbalanced *adj.* **1** BIOLOGY a well-balanced meal or DIET contains all the things you need to keep you healthy **2** a well-balanced person is sensible and is not controlled by strong emotions SYN **stable**

ˌwell-beˈhaved *adj.* behaving in a polite or socially acceptable way: *a well-behaved child*

ˈwell-ˌbeing *n.* [U] **1** the state of being happy, healthy, and safe: **physical/emotional etc. well-being** *Divorce has a strong effect on people's psychological well-being.* | *a **sense of well-being*** (=a feeling of being satisfied with your life) **2** a country's well-being is the state of being strong, well-governed, and having a good standard of living

ˌwell-ˈborn *adj.* born into a rich or UPPER CLASS family

ˌwell-ˈbred *adj.* someone who is well-bred is very polite and behaves or speaks as if they come from a family of high social class

ˌwell-brought-ˈup *adj.* a well-brought-up child has been taught to be polite and to behave well

ˌwell-ˈbuilt *adj.* **1** someone who is well-built has a strong attractive body **2** something that is well-built has been made well and is strong and likely to last for a long time: *a well-built car*

ˌwell-ˈchosen *adj.* carefully chosen: *I had a few **well-chosen words*** (=words appropriate for the situation, especially angry or offensive ones) *for the driver who pulled in front of me.*

ˌwell-conˈnected *adj.* knowing or being related to powerful and socially important people

ˌwell-deˈfined *adj.* **1** clearly explained or described: *well-defined roles* **2** very clear and easy to recognize or see: *well-defined muscles*

ˌwell-deˈserved *adj.* earned because of good or bad behavior, work, skill etc.: *well-deserved praise*

ˌwell-deˈveloped *adj.* **1** fully developed or formed and working well: *well-developed muscles* **2** well-developed skills, abilities, systems etc. have reached a high level because someone has worked on them or used them a lot

ˌwell-disˈposed *adj.* FORMAL feeling friendly toward a person or positive about an idea or plan

ˌwell-ˈdocumented *adj.* well-documented events, behavior, information etc. have been written about a lot, and so can be shown to exist or have happened

ˌwell-ˈdone *adj.* food that is well-done, especially meat, has been cooked thoroughly → see also MEDIUM, **well done!/well played! etc.** at WELL[1] (14)

ˌwell-ˈdressed *adj.* wearing attractive, fashionable, and usually expensive clothes

ˌwell-ˈearned *adj.* something that is well-earned is something you deserve because you have worked hard: *The team is taking a well-earned rest.*

ˌwell-ˈeducated *adj.* a well-educated person has had a lot of education and has a lot of knowledge about many different things

ˌwell-enˈdowed *adj.* INFORMAL OR HUMOROUS **1** a woman

W

who is well-endowed has large breasts **2** a man who is well-endowed has a large PENIS (=sex organ)

Welles /wɛlz/, **Or·son** /ˈɔrsən/ (1915–1985) a U.S. actor, movie DIRECTOR, PRODUCER, and writer

ˌwell-esˈtablished *adj.* established for a long time and respected: *a well-established tradition of democratic government*

ˌwell-ˈfed *adj.* regularly eating plenty of good healthy food, especially if this has made you a little fat: *well-fed cattle*

ˌwell-ˈformed *adj.* **1** a well-formed body part has a good shape and size **2** a well-formed sentence, phrase etc. correctly follows all the rules of grammar **3** following all the rules of a formal method of LOGIC: *a well-formed argument*

ˌwell-ˈfounded *adj.* WELL-GROUNDED

ˌwell-ˈgroomed *adj.* having a very neat, clean appearance

ˌwell-ˈgrounded *adj.* **1** a well-grounded belief, feeling etc. is based on facts or good judgment [SYN] **well-founded**: *Their fears were well-grounded.* **2 well-grounded in sth** fully trained in an activity or skill

well·head /ˈwɛlhɛd/ *n.* [C] **1** the top part of an OIL WELL where the oil is pumped out **2 the wellhead price/cost/rate etc.** the WHOLESALE price of oil

ˌwell-ˈheeled *adj.* INFORMAL rich and usually of a high social class

ˌwell-inˈformed *adj.* knowing a lot about a particular subject or about many subjects: **+on/about** *Stacy is well-informed on international politics.*

Wel·ling·ton /ˈwɛlɪŋtən/ the capital city of New Zealand, on the North Island

Wellington, Duke of → see DUKE OF WELLINGTON, THE

ˌwell-inˈtentioned *adj.* trying to be helpful, but failing or actually making things worse: *Even the most well-intentioned doctors can forget to suggest routine tests.*

W

ˌwell-ˈkept *adj.* **1** a well-kept secret is known only to a few people **2** a well-kept building or garden is very well cared for and looks neat and clean

ˌwell-ˈknit *adj.* having several parts or features joined together in a way that works well

ˌwell-ˈknown *adj.* known by a lot of people: *a well-known author* | **+for** *The area is well-known for its lakes.* | **+to** *The problems are well-known to users of the service.* | *It's* ***a well-known fact*** *that smoking can cause lung cancer.* ▸see THESAURUS box at **famous**[1]

ˌwell-ˈmade, **well made** *adj.* **1** well-made furniture, clothes etc. are skillfully made and are of high quality: *a well-made car* **2** a well-made movie, TV program etc. has been skillfully acted, directed, and produced

ˌwell-ˈmannered *adj.* polite and having very good MANNERS [OPP] **ill-mannered** → see also MILD-MANNERED

ˌwell-ˈmeaning *adj.* intending or intended to be helpful, but not succeeding → see also **sb means well** at MEAN[1] (3)

ˌwell-ˈmeant *adj.* something you say or do that is well-meant is intended to be helpful, but does not have the result you intended: *well-meant advice* → see also **sb means well** at MEAN[1] (3)

well·ness /ˈwɛlnɪs/ *n.* [U] the state of being healthy

ˈwell-nigh *adv.* OLD-FASHIONED almost, but not completely

ˌwell-ˈoff *adj.* having more money than many other people, or enough money to have a good standard of living: *Stella's family is well-off.* → see also BADLY-OFF, BAD OFF, BETTER OFF

ˌwell-ˈoiled *adj.* **1 a well-oiled machine/system/organization** an organization or system that works very well **2** covered with a lot of oil, especially enough oil to operate smoothly

ˌwell-ˈordered *adj.* arranged or planned in a very organized or neat way: *a well-ordered household*

ˌwell-ˈpaid *adj.* providing or receiving good pay: *well-paid executives* | *a well-paid job*

ˌwell-ˈplanned *adj.* **1** organized in a way that shows you have thought about something very carefully: *a well-planned event* **2** a well-planned area, building, or room has everything you need and is arranged in a good way

ˌwell-preˈserved *adj.* HUMOROUS someone who is well-preserved still looks fairly young although they are getting old

ˌwell-proˈportioned *adj.* having parts that are the right size relative to each other

ˌwell-ˈqualified *adj.* having a lot of appropriate experience for a particular job: *well-qualified applicants*

well-read /ˌwɛl ˈrɛd◂/ *adj.* having read many books and knowing a lot about different subjects

ˌwell-ˈrounded *adj.* **1** a well-rounded person has a range of interests and skills and a variety of experience: *well-rounded college graduates* **2** well-rounded education or experience is complete and gives you knowledge of a wide variety of subjects **3** including many different styles, parts etc. **4** a woman who is well-rounded has a pleasantly curved figure

ˌwell-ˈrun *adj.* a well-run organization or business is managed well

Wells /wɛlz/, **H.G.** (1866–1946) a British writer of NOVELS and political ESSAYS, known for his SCIENCE FICTION

ˌwell-ˈspoken *adj.* speaking in a clear and polite way, and in a way that is socially approved of

well·spring /ˈwɛlsprɪŋ/ *n.* [C] LITERARY **1** a large amount of something: **+of** *a wellspring of public support* **2** the situation or place from which something begins: **+of** *Poverty and hopelessness are so often the wellspring of crime.*

ˌwell-ˈstocked *adj.* having a large supply and a variety of things: *a well-stocked refrigerator*

ˌwell-ˈsuited *adj.* having the right qualities to do something: **+to** *The plant is well-suited to shady conditions.* | **+for** *He is well-suited for the priesthood.*

ˌwell-ˈthought-of *adj.* liked and admired by other people

ˌwell-thought-ˈout *adj.* carefully and thoroughly planned

ˌwell-ˈthumbed *adj.* a well-thumbed book, magazine etc. has been used a lot

ˌwell-ˈtimed *adj.* said or done at the most appropriate moment: *a well-timed arrival*

ˌwell-to-ˈdo[1] *adj.* rich and with a high social position: *a well-to-do young woman* ▸see THESAURUS box at **rich**

well-to-do[2] *n.* **the well-to-do** [plural] people who are rich

ˌwell-ˈtraveled *adj.* **1** someone who is well-traveled has visited many different countries **2** a well-traveled road, path etc. is one that many people use

ˌwell-ˈturned *adj.* **1** ENG. LANG. ARTS a well-turned phrase or sentence is carefully expressed **2** with an attractive curved shape

ˌwell-turned-ˈout *adj.* wearing fashionable clothes and looking attractive

ˌwell-ˈversed *adj.* [not before noun] knowing a lot about something: **+in/on** *Mr. Chang is well-versed in economic policy.*

ˈwell-ˌwisher *n.* [C] someone who does something to show that they admire someone and want them to succeed, be healthy etc.: *The family has received thousands of letters from well-wishers.*

ˌwell-ˈwoman *adj.* [only before noun] providing medical care and advice for women, to make sure that they stay healthy

ˌwell-ˈworn *adj.* **1** worn or used a lot for a long period of time: *a well-worn pair of slippers* **2** a well-worn argument, phrase etc. has been repeated so often that it is not interesting or effective anymore: *well-worn excuses*

Welsh /wɛlʃ/ *n.* **1** [U] the original language of Wales **2 the Welsh** [plural] people from Wales —**Welsh** *adj.*

welsh /wɛlʃ/ *v.* [I + on] INFORMAL to WELCH

Welsh·man /ˈwɛlʃmən/ *n.* [C] a man from Wales

Welsh·wo·man /ˈwɛlʃˌwʊmən/ *n.* [C] a woman from Wales

welt /wɛlt/ *n.* [C] **1** a raised place on someone's skin where they have been hit or stung **2** a piece of leather around the edge of a shoe, to which the top and bottom of the shoe are stitched

wel·ter /ˈwɛltɚ/ *n.* **a welter of sth** a large and confusing number of different details, emotions etc.: *a welter of tax laws*

wel·ter·weight /ˈwɛltɚˌweɪt/ *n.* [C] a BOXER who is heavier than a LIGHTWEIGHT but lighter than a MIDDLEWEIGHT

Wel·ty, Eu·dor·a /ʊˈdɔrə/ (1909–2001) a U.S. writer of NOVELs and short stories (SHORT STORY)

wench /wɛntʃ/ *n.* [C] OLD USE OR HUMOROUS a girl or young woman, especially a servant

wend /wɛnd/ *v.* **wend your way** LITERARY to move or travel slowly from one place to another: *The train wended its way through the mountain pass.*

went /wɛnt/ *v.* the past tense of GO [**Origin:** 1400–1500 From the old past tense of *wend*]

wept /wɛpt/ *v.* the past tense and past participle of WEEP

we're /wɪr/ the short form of "we are": *We're going to Disneyland!*

were /wɚ/ *v.* a past tense of BE [**Origin:** Old English *wære, wæron, wæren*]

weren't /wɚnt, ˈwɚənt/ the short form of "were not": *Paula and Thea weren't working that night.*

were·wolf /ˈwɛrwʊlf/ *n.* [C] a person in stories who sometimes changes into a WOLF

wert /wɚt/ *v.* **thou wert** OLD USE you were

Wes·ley /ˈwɛsli, ˈwɛz-/, **John** (1703–1791) an English religious leader who started a new type of church in the Christian religion called Methodism

west¹, West /wɛst/ S2 W1 WRITTEN ABBREVIATION **W.** *n.* [singular, U] **1** the direction opposite from that where the sun rises, that is on the left of someone facing north: *Which way is west?* | *The wind was blowing* ***from the west.*** | *We live three miles* ***to the west of*** *the park.* | *The procession moved slowly* ***toward the west.*** **2 the west** the western part of a country, state etc.: *The farmers* ***in the west*** *have been struggling due to the recent drought.* **3 the West a)** the western part of the world and the people that live there, especially Western Europe and North America: *the industrial countries of the West* **b)** the part of the U.S. that is west of the Mississippi River: *Half of U.S. Asians live in the West.* → see also MIDWEST

west² S3 W3 *adj.* **1** WRITTEN ABBREVIATION **W.** in, to, or facing the west: *the west side of the house* **2** EARTH SCIENCE a west wind comes from the west SYN **westerly** [**Origin:** Old English]

west³ *adv.* **1** toward the west: *I packed my bags and headed west.* | *The window faces west.* | +**of** *a spot 70 miles west of Flagstaff* **2 out West** in or to the west of a particular country, state etc., especially the western part of the U.S.: *The family moved out west to Kansas.* → see also BACK EAST

ˈWest Bank *n.* [singular] an area between the Jordan River and the Dead Sea. Israel took control of it after the Arab-Israeli war of 1967, but the Palestinian Arabs consider it to be their land.

west·bound /ˈwɛstbaʊnd/ *adj., adv.* traveling or leading toward the west: *westbound traffic* | *The car was driving westbound on Route 66.*

ˌWest ˈCoast *n.* **the West Coast** the part of the U.S. that is next to the Pacific Ocean

west·er·ly /ˈwɛstɚli/ *adj.* **1** toward or in the west: *The storm is moving in a westerly direction.* **2** a westerly wind comes from the west

west·ern¹, Western /ˈwɛstɚn/ S3 W3 *adj.* **1** from or relating to the west part of a country or area: *the western end of the Bay* **2** relating to ideas or ways of doing things that come from Europe, the Americas, Australia etc.: *Western philosophies*

western² *n.* [C] a movie about life in the 19th century in the American West ▸see THESAURUS box at **movie**

west·ern·er, Westerner /ˈwɛstɚnɚ/ *n.* [C] **1** someone from Europe, the Americas, Australia, or New Zealand, especially as opposed to people from Asia **2** someone who lives in or comes from the western part of the U.S.

ˌWestern ˈEurope *n.* the western part of Europe or the countries in it, especially the ones that did not have COMMUNIST governments, such as France and the Netherlands → see also CENTRAL EUROPE

ˌWestern ˈHemisphere *n.* **the Western Hemisphere** the half of the Earth that includes the Americas and the Caribbean

west·ern·ize /ˈwɛstɚˌnaɪz/ *v.* [T] to bring customs, business methods etc. that are typical of Europe and the U.S. to other countries —**westernization** /ˌwɛstɚnəˈzeɪʃən/ *n.* [U]

west·ern·ized /ˈwɛstɚˌnaɪzd/ *adj.* copying the customs, behavior etc. typical of Europe or the U.S.

ˌwestern ˈmedicine *n.* [U] the type of medical treatment that is standard in the WEST → see also ALTERNATIVE MEDICINE

west·ern·most /ˈwɛstɚnˌmoʊst/ *adj.* furthest west: *the westernmost island of South America*

Western Sa·mo·a /ˌwɛstɚn səˈmoʊə/ a country that consists of a group of islands in the southern Pacific Ocean

West In·dies /wɛst ˈɪndiz/ *n.* **the West Indies** the islands in the Caribbean Sea —**West Indian** *adj.*

West·ing·house /ˈwɛstɪŋˌhaʊs/, **George** (1846–1914) a U.S. engineer who made many improvements to trains and railroads

Wes·ton /ˈwɛstən/, **Ed·ward** /ˈɛdwɚd/ (1886–1958) a U.S. PHOTOGRAPHER

ˌWest ˈPoint the usual name for the United States Military Academy, which is at West Point in New York, and is the oldest military college in the U.S.

West Vir·gin·ia /ˌwɛst vɚˈdʒɪnyə/ WRITTEN ABBREVIATION **WV** a state in the eastern central U.S.

west·ward /ˈwɛstwɚd/ *adv.* also **westwards** toward the west —**westward** *adj.*

wet¹ /wɛt/ S2 W3 *adj. comparative* **wetter**, *superlative* **wettest** **1** covered in or full of water or another liquid: *a wet towel* | *Be careful, the floor is still wet.* | +**with** *His face was wet with sweat.* | *I don't want to* ***get*** *my shoes* ***wet.*** | *Look at your shirt – it's* ***all wet.*** | **soaking/sopping/dripping wet** (=extremely wet)

THESAURUS

damp slightly wet, often in an unpleasant way: *a dark damp apartment*
moist used about something, especially food, that is slightly wet in a pleasant way: *Cooking the meat in this way keeps it moist and tender.*
soggy unpleasantly wet and soft: *My cereal was soggy.*
humid/muggy used about weather that is warm and slightly wet and makes you uncomfortable: *It was mid-July, warm and humid.*
soaked/soaking/drenched very wet or wearing very wet clothes: *His shirt was soaked with blood.* | *I didn't have an umbrella and got drenched.*
saturated extremely wet, so that no more liquid can be taken in: *The ground was saturated with water.*

2 not yet dry: *The paint's still wet.* **3** if the weather is wet, it is raining **4 wet behind the ears** INFORMAL very young and without much life experience **5 sb is all wet** INFORMAL used to say that someone is completely wrong [**Origin:** Old English *wæt*] —**wetness** *n.* [U]

wet² *v. past tense and past participle* **wet** or **wetted** [T] **1** to make something wet: *Wet your hair and apply the shampoo.* **2** to make yourself, your clothes, or your bed wet because you pass liquid waste from your body by accident: *I nearly **wet myself** I was so scared.* | *Sean **wet the bed** again.* **3 wet your whistle** OLD-FASHIONED to have a drink, especially one with alcohol

ˈwet bar *n.* [C] a small bar with a SINK and equipment for making alcoholic drinks, in a house, hotel room etc.

ˌwet ˈblanket *n.* [C] INFORMAL someone who tries to spoil other people's fun

wet·land /ˈwɛtlənd, -lænd/ *n.* [U] also **wetlands** [plural] BIOLOGY an area of land that is usually wet, such as a MARSH OR SWAMP → see also GRASSLAND

ˈwet nurse *n.* [C] a woman who is employed to give her breast milk to another woman's baby, especially in the past

ˈwet suit *n.* [C] a piece of clothing, usually made of rubber, that swimmers, SURFERS etc. wear to keep warm in the ocean, a lake etc.

ˈwetting ˌagent *n.* [C] CHEMISTRY a chemical substance which, when spread on a solid surface, makes it hold liquid

ˈwetting soˌlution *n.* [C,U] a liquid used for storing CONTACT LENSES in, or for making them more comfortable to wear

ˌwet ˈwillie *n.* [C] SLANG the action of putting a wet finger in someone's ear as a joke

we've /wiv/ the short form of "we have" when "have" is an AUXILIARY VERB: *We've tried that already.*

whack¹ /wæk/ *v.* [T] INFORMAL **1** to hit someone or something hard: *Someone whacked the side of my car with their door.* ►see THESAURUS box at **hit¹** **2** to kill someone, especially someone who is involved in crime, as a punishment for something they have done

whack² *n.* [C] SPOKEN **1** the act of hitting something hard or the noise this makes: *She gave my hand a whack with a ruler.* | *Singleton **took a whack at*** (=tried to hit) *Miller's head.* **2 out of whack** if a system, machine etc. is out of whack, the parts are not working together correctly: *The printer is out of whack again.* **3 take a whack at sth** to try to do something **4 in one whack** all on one occasion: *Steve lost $500 in one whack.*

whacked /wækt/ *adj.* [not before noun] INFORMAL **1 whacked out** behaving strangely, especially because of having too much alcohol or drugs **2** also **whack, wack** SLANG a whacked situation is very strange, especially in an unacceptable way **3** also **whacked out** very tired

whac·ko /ˈwækoʊ/ another spelling of WACKO

whac·ky /ˈwæki/ another spelling of WACKY

whale¹ /weɪl/ [W3] *n.* [C] **1** BIOLOGY a very large animal that lives in the ocean, breathes through a hole in the top of its head, and looks like a fish, but is actually a MAMMAL **2 have a whale of a time** OLD-FASHIONED to enjoy yourself very much [**Origin:** Old English *hwæl*]

whale² *v.*

whale on/into sb/sth *phr. v.* to hit someone or something with a lot of force

whale·bone /ˈweɪlboʊn/ *n.* [U] a hard substance taken from the upper jaw of whales, used in the past for making women's clothes stiff

whal·er /ˈweɪlɚ/ *n.* [C] **1** someone who hunts whales **2** a boat used for hunting whales

whal·ing /ˈweɪlɪŋ/ *n.* [U] the activity of hunting whales

wham¹ /wæm/ *interjection* **1** used to describe the sound of something suddenly hitting something else very hard: *Wham! The car hit the wall.* **2** used to express the idea that something very unexpected suddenly happens: *Life is going along nicely and then, wham, you lose your job.*

wham² *n.* [C] the sound made when something is hit very hard —**wham** *v.* [T]

wham·my /ˈwæmi/ *n.* **put the whammy on sb** to use magic powers to make someone have bad luck → see also DOUBLE WHAMMY

wharf /wɔrf/ *n. plural* **wharves** /wɔrvz/ or **wharfs** [C] a structure that is built out into the water so that boats can stop next to it [SYN] **pier**

Whar·ton /ˈwɔrtˀn/, **E·dith** /ˈidɪθ/ (1862–1937) a U.S. writer of NOVELS

whas·sup /ˌwʌsˈʌp/ *interjection* SLANG used to greet people that you know very well and ask them what they are doing → see also WHAT'S UP

what¹ /wət; *strong* wʌt, wɑt/ [S1] [W1] *pron.*

1 used to ask or talk about something that you or someone else is not certain about: *What did you say?* | *"What do you do for a living?" "I'm a doctor."* | *No one knows what happened.* | *I'm not sure **what else** I can do to help you.*

2 used to talk about something specific that you are describing: *I believe what he told me.* | *What he did was wrong.* | *This is what was in the box.* | *Don't tell me what to do.*

SPOKEN PHRASES

3 what? **a)** also **what did you say?, what was that?** used to ask someone to repeat something they have just said because you did not hear it very well: *Could you turn the music down?" "What?"* | *"I went to the store and bought some eggs." "You went to the store and what?"* **b)** also **what is it?** used during conversations when you have heard someone talking to you and want to tell them to continue: *"Mike!" "What?" "Could you help me with something?"* **c)** also **what!** used to show that you are surprised by what someone has said: *"I think the car's out of gas." "What!"* **d)** used to ask someone to complete a name when they have only given you the first part of it: *"His name is David." "David what?"*

4 what about...? **a)** used to make a suggestion: *What about the Czech Republic? I'd like to see Prague.* | **what about doing** *What about going to a movie?* **b)** used to mention someone or something else that you are also interested in or that also needs to be considered: *What about Patrick? What's he doing nowadays?*

5 what (...) for? used to ask why: *"What did you shout at me for?"* | *"I want a new computer." "What for?"*

6 what is sth for? used to ask what purpose something has: *What's this button for?*

7 what's what the real facts about a situation that are important to know: *She's been working here long enough to know what's what.*

8 what on earth/what in the world/what in heaven's name etc. ...? also **what the heck/devil/blazes etc. ...?** used to ask in an extremely angry or surprised way what is happening, what someone is doing etc.: *What on earth are you doing?*

9 what the heck used to say that you have decided to do something despite any possible difficulties: *"Do you want to go dancing tonight?" "Sure, what the heck."*

10 ...or what? **a)** used at the end of a question to show that you are impatient with someone or something: *Are you afraid of him, or what?* **b)** used after a description of someone or something to emphasize it: *Was that stupid or what.*

11 ...or what used after mentioning one or more possibilities to show that you are not certain about something: *I don't know if it was an accident or what.*

12 so what? used to say that you do not care about something or to tell someone angrily that something does not concern them: *"Don't go in there, he's sleeping." "So what?"*

SPOKEN PHRASES

13 what if... **a)** used to make a suggestion: *What if we move the sofa over here?* **b)** used for asking what you should do or what the result will be if something happens, especially something unpleasant: *What if this plan of yours fails?*
14 ... and what have you used at the end of a list of things to mean other things of a similar kind: *The shelves were full of books, documents, and what have you.*
15 have what it takes to have the right qualities or skills in order to succeed: *Elaine has what it takes to make acting her career.*
16 what's up? used to say hello to someone, especially someone you know well → see also WHASSUP: *"Hey Chris, what's up?" "Not much."*
17 what's up with sb/sth? used to ask someone what is wrong or what is happening: +**with** *What's up with Diana?*
18 what's up with that? used to say that you do not understand, or understand the reason for, the thing you have just mentioned: *The college is raising tuition by 20% – what's up with that?*
19 what's with sth? used to ask the reason for something: *What's with the all the sad faces?*
20 what's with sb? used to ask why a person or group of people is behaving strangely: *What's with Nathan? He looks upset.*
21 what of it? used to say that you do not care about something or to tell someone angrily that something does not concern them: *I know he really doesn't love me, but what of it?*
22 EMPHASIS used at the beginning of a statement to emphasize the object of your sentence: *What I need is a nice hot bath.*
23 now what? used to ask what is going to happen next, what you should do etc.
24 what's it to you? used to tell someone angrily that something does not concern them: *"Who's that girl he's with?" "What's it to you?"*
25 (and) what's more used when adding something to what you have already said, especially when it is exciting or interesting: *Natural gas is a very efficient fuel. What's more, it's clean.*
26 what next? used to show surprise that something unusual or strange has happened or exists: *Snow in Florida? What next?*

[**Origin:** Old English *hwæt*] → see also **guess what!** at GUESS¹ (6), **(I'll) tell you what** at TELL (11)

what² *determiner* **1** used to ask or talk about something that you or someone else is not certain about → see also WHICH: *What time is it?* | *Ask him what size shoe he wears.* | *We don't know what color to paint the walls.* | *They're discussing what action to take.* | **what kind/type/sort** *What kind of dog is that?* **2** used to emphasize that you think something or someone is very good, very bad etc.: *What a beautiful day!* | *What a shame he can't be here today.* **3** used to talk about all of an amount of something that you are describing, usually a small amount: *We save what money we can each month.*

what³ S1 W3 *adv.* **1** used especially in questions to ask to what degree or in what way something matters: *We may be a little late, but **what does it matter**?* | ***What do you care*** (=why are you concerned) *if I buy a motorcycle?* **2** SPOKEN used to give yourself time to think before guessing a number or amount: *It'll take us, what, about three hours.* **3 what with sth** SPOKEN used to introduce a list of reasons that have made something happen or have made someone feel a particular way: *They've been under a lot of stress, what with Joe losing his job and all.*

what·cha·ma·call·it /ˈwʌtʃəmə͵kɔlɪt/ *n.* [C] SPOKEN a word you use to talk about something when you cannot remember its name

what·ev·er¹ /wʌṭˈɛvɚ/ S1 W1 *determiner, pron.* **1** any or all of the things that are wanted, needed, or possible: *David will do whatever she asks him.* | *Buy whatever you need.* | *She gathered sticks and **whatever else** could be used as fuel.* **2** used to say that it is not important what happens, what you do etc. because it does not change the situation: *Whatever I do, it's never good enough for him.*

SPOKEN PHRASES

3 used to say that you do not know the exact meaning of something, or the exact name of someone or something: *The doctor says I've got fibromyalgia, whatever that is.* **4 ... or whatever** used after naming things on a list to mean other things of the same kind: *You could put an ad in some magazine, newspaper, or whatever.* **5 whatever you do** used to emphasize that you do not want someone to do something: *Whatever you do, don't tell Judy that I spent so much money.* **6** used as a reply to tell someone that something does not matter, or that you do not care or are not interested when they ask or tell you something: *"It was Monday, not Tuesday." "Whatever."* **7 whatever you say/think/want** used to tell someone that you agree with them or will do what they want, often when you do not really agree or want to do it: *"You need to clean up this stuff." "Whatever you say."* **8 whatever floats your boat/turns you on/trips your trigger** HUMOROUS used to say that what someone else enjoys doing seems strange to you **9** also **what ever** OLD-FASHIONED used to show that you are angry or surprised when making a statement or asking a question: *Whatever do you mean by that?*

whatever² *determiner* **1** of any possible type: *I'll take whatever help I can get.* **2** used to say that it does not matter which thing, or what type of thing, because it does not change the situation: *Whatever choice you make, we'll support you.* **3** of some type that you are not sure about: *Ellen's refusing to come, for whatever reason.*

whatever³ *adv.* used to emphasize a negative statement SYN **whatsoever** SYN **at all**: *She gave no sign whatever of what she was thinking.*

͵what-ˈfor *n.* **give sb what-for** SPOKEN to complain to someone in a loud and angry way

what-ˈif *n.* [C usually plural] INFORMAL something that could happen in the future or could have happened in the past

what·not /ˈwʌt˺nɑt/ *n.* **1 and whatnot** SPOKEN an expression used at the end of a list of things when you do not want to give the names of everything: *Put your bags, suitcases, and whatnot in the back of the car.* **2** [C] a piece of furniture with shelves, used especially in the 19th century to show small pretty objects

what's-her-name, **whatshername** /ˈwʌtsɚ͵neɪm/ also **what's-her-face** /ˈwʌtsɚ͵feɪs/ *pron.* SPOKEN used to talk about a woman or girl when you have forgotten her name: *Have you seen what's-her-name lately?*

what's-his-name, **whatshisname** /ˈwʌtsɪz͵neɪm/ also **what's-his-face** /ˈwʌtsɪz͵feɪs/ *pron.* SPOKEN used to talk about a man or boy when you have forgotten his name: *Is she still dating what's-his-name?*

whats·it /ˈwʌtsɪt/ *n.* [C] SPOKEN a word you use when you cannot think of what something is called

what·so·ev·er /͵wʌtsoʊˈɛvɚ/ *adv.* used to emphasize a negative statement SYN **whatever** SYN **at all**: *I have no reason whatsoever to doubt what he says.* | *There's **nothing whatsoever** to worry about.*

wheat /wit/ S3 *n.* [U] **1** the grain that is used to make flour and such foods as bread **2** the plant that this grain grows on: *a field of wheat* **3 separate/sort/sift the wheat from the chaff** to choose the good and useful things or people and get rid of the others [**Origin:** Old English *hwæte*]

wheat·germ /ˈwitdʒɚm/ *n.* [U] the center of a grain of wheat

whee /wi/ *interjection* used to express happiness or excitement

W

whee·dle /ˈwidl/ *v.* [I,T] to persuade someone to do something by saying pleasant things that you do not really mean: **wheedle sth from/out of sb** *She tried to wheedle the information out of him.*

wheel¹ /wil/ S2 W3 *n.* [C]
1 ON A VEHICLE one of the round things under a car, bus, bicycle etc. that turns and allows it to move: *The rear wheels slipped on the ice.* | *The ball was crushed **under the wheels of** a truck.*
2 FOR TURNING the piece of equipment in the shape of a wheel that you turn to make a car, ship etc. move in a particular direction SYN **steering wheel**: *The driver apparently fell asleep **at the wheel**.* | *Joey wouldn't let her **behind the wheel** (=drive) of his new car.* | *Let me **take the wheel** (=drive instead of someone else).*
3 on wheels with wheels on the bottom: *a table on wheels*
4 EQUIPMENT a piece of equipment or a machine that has a wheel as its main part: *a roulette wheel*
5 IN MACHINE a flat round part in a machine that turns around when the machine operates: *a gear wheel*
6 the wheels of justice/industry/government etc. the way in which a complicated organization, system etc works, with all the different parts working together like a machine
7 wheels also **set of wheels** SPOKEN a car: *Nice wheels!*
8 set the wheels in motion also **start the wheels turning** to make a particular process start
9 a big wheel INFORMAL an important person
[**Origin:** Old English *hweogol, hweol*] → see also WHEELED

wheel² *v.* **1** [T always + adv./prep.] **a)** to move someone or something that is in or on an object with wheels, such as a WHEELCHAIR or a CART: *They then wheeled me into the operating room.* **b)** to push something that has wheels: **wheel sth down/into/across etc. sth** *She slowly wheeled her shopping cart over to the checkout stand.* **2** [I] if birds or airplanes wheel, they fly around in circles **3** [I] to turn around suddenly: **+around** *She wheeled around and started yelling at us.* **4 wheel and deal** to do a lot of complicated and sometimes slightly dishonest deals, especially in politics or business

wheel sb/sth ↔ **out** *phr. v.* INFORMAL to publicly show someone or something: *Then the prosecution wheeled out a surprise witness.*

W

wheel·bar·row /ˈwilˌbæroʊ/ *n.* [C] a small CART that you use outdoors to carry things, that has one wheel in the front and two long handles

wheel·base /ˈwilbeɪs/ *n.* [C] TECHNICAL the distance between the front and back AXLES of a vehicle

wheel·chair /ˈwil-tʃɛr/ *n.* [C] a chair with wheels, used by people who cannot walk → see picture at CHAIR¹

wheeled /wild/ *adj.* having wheels: *a wheeled stretcher* | **three-wheeled/six-wheeled etc.** *four-wheeled vehicles*

ˌwheeler-ˈdealer *n.* [C] someone who does a lot of complicated, often dishonest deals, especially in business or politics

wheel·house /ˈwilhaʊs/ *n.* [C] the place on a ship where the CAPTAIN stands at the WHEEL

wheel·ie /ˈwili/ *n.* [C] **do/pop a wheelie** INFORMAL to balance on the back wheel of a bicycle or MOTORCYCLE that you are riding

ˌwheeling and ˈdealing *n.* [U] the activity of making a lot of complicated and sometimes dishonest deals, especially in business or politics

wheel·wright /ˈwilraɪt/ *n.* [C] someone who made and repaired the wooden wheels of vehicles pulled by horses in the past

wheeze¹ /wiz/ *v.* **1** [I] to breathe with difficulty, making a whistling sound in your throat and chest ▸see THESAURUS box at **breathe** **2** [T] to say something while you are breathing with difficulty, making a noise in your throat and chest **3** [I] to make a high noise that sounds like wheezing

wheeze² *n.* [C] **1** the act or sound of wheezing **2** an old joke that no one thinks is funny anymore

wheez·y /ˈwizi/ *adj. comparative* **wheezier**, *superlative* **wheeziest** wheezing or making a wheezing sound

whelk /wɛlk/ *n.* [C] a small sea animal that has a shell and can be eaten

whelp¹ /wɛlp/ *n.* [C] a young animal, especially a dog or lion

whelp² *v.* [I] OLD-FASHIONED if a dog or lion whelps, it gives birth

when¹ /wɛn/ S1 W1 *adv.* **1** used to ask or talk about a time that you or someone else is not certain about: *When are you going to the store?* | *Do you know when the movie starts?* | *I'm not sure when he's coming.* | **when to do sth** *Tell me when to stop.* **2** used to talk about a specific time you are describing: *We talked about when we were kids.* | **the day/time/afternoon when...** *That's the day when Leigh is coming.* [**Origin:** Old English *hwanne, hwenne*]

THESAURUS

at the time used in order to talk about a particular time in the past, when two things happened at the same time, or when the situation is different now: *He was making $17,000 a year, which at the time was a good salary.*
by the time used in order to say that one thing has or will have already happened when something else happens: *By the time a child is five, he will have watched hundreds of hours of television.*
by that time used in order to mention a particular time when something has already happened: *She called at six, but by that time we had already left.*

when² S1 W1 *conjunction* **1** at or during the time that a situation existed or exists, or something happened or happens: *I hated green beans when I was a little boy.* | *When you come to Baker Street, turn right.* | *The handle broke when he tried to open the door.* **2** every time that something happens SYN **whenever**: *My arm hurts when I play tennis.* | *When she smiles, she looks like her mother.* **3** after something happens, or as soon as something happens or is true SYN **once**: *I'll see you when I get home.* | *When you're ready, I'll show you to your room.* **4** used to say that one thing happens immediately after another thing, or while another thing is happening, usually in a sudden or unexpected way: *I had just walked in when the phone rang.* **5** even though or in spite of the fact that something is true: *Why do you want a new job when you have such a good one already?* **6** used to introduce a second statement that shows that the first statement is not true: *The doctor said Dad was fine, when he was really dying.* **7 when you consider/remember sth** used when mentioning something that helps explain what you have said: *His success isn't surprising when you consider his background.* **8 when all is said and done** used after an explanation or story to give the most important facts about it or to state your opinion about it: *When all is said and done, people will remember him as a great man.* → see also **when you think about it** at THINK (37)

when³ *pron.* **since when** used in questions to mean since what time: *Since when did you smoke cigarettes?*

whence /wɛns/ *adv., pron.* OLD USE also **from whence** from where → see also WHITHER

when·ev·er /wɛnˈɛvɚ, wən-/ S1 W3 *adv., conjunction* **1** every time that a particular thing happens: *Kent always blames me whenever anything goes wrong.* | *Whenever I see her, she's with a different guy.* | ***Whenever possible**, get a receipt.* **2** at any time: *I'd like to see you whenever it's convenient.* **3** SPOKEN used when it does not matter what time something happens, or when you do not know the exact time something happens: *"I can bring you the books this afternoon." "Whenever."* | *Come on Monday or Tuesday **or whenever**.*

where /wɛr/ S1 W1 *adv., pron, conjunction* **1** in, at, or to what place: *Where do you live?* | *I asked Lucy where she was going.* | *Do you know where my glasses are?* | ***Where is she from?*** | **where to do sth** *The mushrooms are easy to find if you know where to look.* **2** used to talk about a specific place that you are describing: *Stay* where you are. | *This is the place where I hid the key.* | *We moved to Boston, where my grandparents lived.* **3** in or to any or every place that you are describing SYN **wherever**: *You can sit where you want.* **4** in, at, or toward what situation, point, or stage in something: *Now where was I? Oh yes, I was telling you about the accident.* | *Where do you want to be in ten years?* | *I don't know where we went wrong.* **5** used to talk about a specific point or stage in something that you are describing: *This is where I disagree with you.* | *The treatment hasn't yet reached the point where the patient begins to feel better.* **6** in any or every situation that you are describing SYN **wherever**: *Where we can, we let the children choose.* **7** used to ask or talk about the origin of something: *I don't know where she gets all her confidence.* | ***Where** did all their money **come from**?* **8** used to say that although something is true for one person, thing, or situation, it is not true for others SYN **whereas**: *Where others would have been satisfied, she wanted more.* [**Origin:** Old English *hwær*]

where·a·bouts¹ /ˈwɛrəˌbaʊts, ˌwɛrəˈbaʊts/ *adv.* SPOKEN used to ask in what general area something or someone is: *Whereabouts did you grow up?*

where·a·bouts² /ˈwɛrəbaʊts/ *n.* [U] the place or area where someone or something is: *None of his friends knew his whereabouts.* | **the whereabouts of sb/sth** *The whereabouts of the painting is still a mystery.*

where·as /ˈwɛrəz; *strong* wɛrˈæz/ Ac S3 *conjunction* **1** used to say that although something is true, a different thing is also true: *The old system was complicated, whereas the new system is very simple.* **2** LAW because of a particular fact

where·at /wɛrˈæt/ *conjunction* OLD USE used when something happens immediately after something else, or as a result of something happening SYN **whereupon**

where·by /wɛrˈbaɪ/ Ac *adv.* FORMAL by means of or according to a particular method, system etc.: *The mall created a plan whereby frequent customers earn discounts.*

where·fore /ˈwɛrfɔr/ *adv., conjunction* OLD USE **1** why **2** for that reason → see also **the why(s) and wherefore(s)** at WHY³

where·in /wɛrˈɪn/ *adv.* FORMAL in which place or part

where·of /wɛrˈʌv/ *adv.* OLD USE of which or about what

where·on /wɛrˈɔn/ *adv.* OLD USE on which

where·so·ev·er /ˈwɛrsoʊˌɛvɚ/ *adv., conjunction* LITERARY WHEREVER

where·to /wɛrˈtu, ˈwɛrtu/ *adv.* OLD USE to which place

where·u·pon /ˌwɛrəˈpɑn, ˈwɛrəˌpɑn/ *conjunction* FORMAL OR LITERARY used when something happens immediately after something else, or as a result of something happening: *Police arrested her, whereupon she asked for a lawyer.*

wher·ev·er /wɛrˈɛvɚ/ S3 *adv., conjunction* **1** in or to any place that you are describing, especially when it is not important to you: *You can sit wherever you want.* | *"Where do you want to eat?" "Wherever – I don't care."* **2** in or to any place that you are describing: *Wherever he goes, he makes friends.* **3** in any or every situation that you are describing: ***Wherever possible**, get the best medical insurance available.* **4** also **where ever** used at the beginning of a question to show surprise: *Wherever did you get that idea?* **5 wherever that is** also **wherever that may be** used to say that you do not know where a place or town is or have never heard of it: *Rita lives in Horwich now, wherever that may be.*

where·with·al /ˈwɛrwɪðˌɔl, -wɪθ-/ *n.* **the wherewithal to do sth** the money you need in order to do something

whet /wɛt/ *v.* [T] **1 whet sb's appetite (for sth)** if an experience whets your appetite for something, it increases your desire for it **2** LITERARY to make the edge of a blade sharp

wheth·er /ˈwɛðɚ/ S1 W1 *conjunction* **1** used when talking about a choice you have to make or about two different possibilities SYN **if**: *He asked me whether I wanted to play golf this afternoon.* | **whether to do sth** *We haven't decided whether to sell the house.* | *She was uncertain **whether** to stay **or** leave.* | *I'm not sure **whether** it's legal **or not**.* **2** used to say that something is true in both of two possible situations: *I'm sure we'll see each other again soon, whether here or in New York.* | ***Whether** you like it **or not**, I'm taking you to the doctor.* [**Origin:** Old English *hwæther, hwether*]

> GRAMMAR **whether, if**
>
> **Whether** and **if** are often used in similar contexts. **Whether** is usually used together in sentences with the word **or**, especially at the beginning of a sentence. People say: *Whether you see Jamie or not, call me later.* | *If you see Jamie, call me.* **If** can usually be used instead of **whether** with clauses following some verbs and adjectives: *Sam wasn't sure if he could come* (NOT *"whether could he come"*). But you use **whether** (NOT **if**) before infinitives: *The question is whether to go or stay.* **Whether** is also used after prepositions: *It depends on whether he's ready or not,* and after nouns: *It's your decision whether you go or stay.*

whet·stone /ˈwɛtstoʊn/ *n.* [C] a stone used to make the blade of cutting tools sharp

whew /hwyu, hwu/ S3 *interjection* used when you are surprised, very hot, or feeling glad that something bad did not happen SYN **phew**: *Whew, that was close.*

whey /weɪ/ *n.* [U] the watery liquid that is left after the solid part has been removed from sour milk, when making cheese

which /wɪtʃ/ S1 W1 *determiner, pron.* **1** used to ask or talk about what person or thing is involved, when there is a limited choice: *Which is the best car for me?* | *Which coat do you like best?* | **which (...) to choose/buy/take etc.** *Both desserts look good – I can't decide which to order.* | **which one/ones** *Which one is the most expensive.* | **+of** *Which of you took my pen?* **2** used to say what specific thing or things you mean: *This is the book which I told you about.* | *The house in which he was born is now a museum.* **3** used in order to add more information about something, or about the first part of a sentence: *This is better than my old apartment, which was always so cold.* | *We got there just in time, which was really lucky.* | **some/many/all etc. of which** *They have two dogs, both of which are black.* | **in which case/at which point/by which time etc.** *They refused to listen to us, at which point we left.* **4 which is which** used to talk about the problem of telling or remembering the difference between two or more similar people or things: *They look so much alike it's difficult to tell which is which.* [**Origin:** Old English *hwilc*]

> USAGE **which, that**
>
> When you are giving more specific information about a particular thing, **that** is used more often than **which** in informal English: *I often visit the farmers' market which/that is held near my house.* In informal or spoken English, you can often leave out **that** or **which.** For example, it is more common to say: *Did you get the things you wanted?* rather than *Did you get the things that/which you wanted?* You would more usually say: *... the club (that) he belonged to.* In relative clauses that add information but do not restrict the meaning of what comes before the clause, you use **which:** *Dave's always really rude, which is why people tend to avoid him.*

which·ev·er /wɪtʃˈɛvɚ/ *determiner, pron.* **1** used to say that it does not matter what thing you choose, what you do etc. because it does not change the situation: *You'll get the same result whichever method you use.* **2** used to talk about a specific thing, method etc.: *I'll use whichever remedy the vet recommends.* | *Come on Monday or Tuesday, whichever is most convenient.*

whiff /wɪf/ *n.* [C] **1** a very slight smell of something: **+of** *a whiff of smoke* | **get/catch a whiff of sth** (=to smell something slightly) **2 a whiff of danger/adventure/freedom etc.** a slight sign that something dangerous, exciting etc. might happen or is happening

W

whif·fle·ball /ˈwɪfəlbɔl/ another spelling of WIFFLE BALL

Whig /wɪg/ *n.* [C] HISTORY **1** a member of the United States Whig Party, a political party formed in 1834 by John Quincy Adams and Henry Clay. The Whig Party lasted until 1860. **2** an American who wanted independence from England around the time of the American Revolutionary War → see also TORY

while¹ /waɪl/ S1 W1 *conjunction* **1** at some point during the time that something is happening: *Someone broke into her house while she was on vacation.* **2** during all the time that something is happening: *He took care of the children while I did the shopping.* **3** used to emphasize the difference between two situations, activities etc. SYN **whereas**: *While her parents are quite short, she's very tall.* **4** used to show that you agree with or accept something before you mention an opposite idea SYN **although**: *While it's true that the city is exciting, it's also dirty.* **5 while you're at it** SPOKEN used to tell someone to do something while they are doing something else, because it would be easier to do both things at the same time: *Mail these letters for me and get me some stamps while you're at it.*

while² S1 W1 *n.* **1 a while** a period of time, especially a short one → see also AWHILE: *Can you wait a while?* | ***For a while,*** *I worked in the Sales Department.* | **a short/little while** *I'm going to the store – I'll be back in a little while.* | *It's been* ***quite a while*** (=a fairly long time) *since I played baseball.* | *Frank left for work* ***a while ago*** (=a fairly long time ago). **2 all the while** during a particular period of time: *All the while I was in college, Joan was traveling.* [**Origin:** Old English *hwil*] → see also **every once in a while** at ONCE¹ (4), **sth is worth your while** at WORTH¹ (3)

while³ *v.* **while away the hours/evening/days etc.** to spend time in a pleasant and lazy way

whim /wɪm/ *n.* [C] a sudden feeling that you would like to do something or have something, especially when there is no particularly important or good reason: *She decided to make the trip* ***on a whim*** (=because of a whim). | *Building permits are issued* ***at the whim of*** *corrupt government officials.* | *Parents shouldn't* ***cater to*** *their child's* ***every whim*** (=they shouldn't give their child everything he or she wants). [**Origin:** 1600–1700 *whim-wham* **decorative object, whim** (16–19 centuries), of unknown origin]

whim·per¹ /ˈwɪmpɚ/ *v.* **1** [I] to make soft weak crying sounds **2** [T] to say something with a voice that sounds like a soft weak crying sound because you are sad, frightened, or in pain

whimper² *n.* [C] **1 with a whimper** if something ends with a whimper, it does not end in an exciting way **2** a low crying sound **3 with nary/hardly/barely a whimper** also **without a whimper** if something happens or ends without a whimper, no one protests about it

whim·si·cal /ˈwɪmzɪkəl/ *adj.* unusual or strange and often amusing —**whimsically** /-kli/ *adv.*

whim·sy /ˈwɪmzi/ *n. plural* **whimsies** **1** [U] an unusual, strange, and often amusing quality **2** [C] a strange idea or desire that does not seem to have any sensible purpose

whine /waɪn/ *v.* [I] **1** to complain in a sad, annoying voice about something: *Stop whining, or you won't get any candy.* | +**about** *I have to listen her whine all day about her boyfriend.* **2** to make a long high sound because you are in pain or unhappy: *The dog's whining for food.* **3** if a machine whines, it makes a continuous high sound [**Origin:** Old English *hwinan* **to move through the air with a loud sound**] —**whine** *n.* [C] *the whine of the plane's engine* —**whiner** *n.* [C]

whin·ny /ˈwɪni/ *v.* **whinnies, whinnied, whinnying** [I] if a horse whinnies, it NEIGHS (=makes the sound that a horse makes) quietly —**whinny** *n.* [C]

whin·y /ˈwaɪni/ *adj. comparative* **whinier**, *superlative* **whiniest** someone who is whiny whines a lot or is whining

whip¹ /wɪp/ *v.* **whipped, whipping**
1 WITH A WHIP [T] to hit a person or an animal with a whip: *The prisoners had been whipped and beaten.*
2 MOVE VIOLENTLY [I always + adv./prep.,T always + adv. prep.] to move quickly and violently, or to make something do this: +**across/around/past etc.** *We stood on the platform as the train whipped past us.* | **whip sth around** *The wind whipped the tree branches around.*
3 REMOVE QUICKLY [T always + adv./prep.] to move or remove something with a quick sudden movement: **whip sth away/off/out etc.** *He whipped out a gun.*
4 LIQUID [T] to mix cream or the clear part of an egg very quickly, until it becomes stiff → see also BEAT, WHISK¹
5 DEFEAT [T] INFORMAL to defeat a team, opponent etc. very badly
6 whip sb/sth into shape INFORMAL to make someone or something better, so that they reach the necessary standard

whip through sth *phr. v.* INFORMAL to finish something such as a job very quickly: *She whipped through the test in less than an hour.*

whip up *phr. v.* **1 whip sth ↔ up** to quickly make something to eat: *I'll whip up some lunch for us.* **2 whip sb/sth ↔ up** to deliberately try to make people feel or react strongly: **whip up support/anger/enthusiasm etc.** *Democrats are trying to whip up public support for the bill.* | *Sanders really knows how to* ***whip up a crowd.***

whip² *n.* [C] **1** a long thin piece of rope or leather with a handle, that you swing and hit with in order to make animals move or punish people **2** POLITICS a member of the U.S. Congress who is responsible for making sure that the members of his or her party attend and vote **3** a long thin piece of LICORICE → see also **crack the whip** at CRACK¹ (19)

whip·cord /ˈwɪpkɔrd/ *n.* [U] **1** a strong type of CORD **2** a strong wool material

whip·lash /ˈwɪplæʃ/ *n.* [C,U] MEDICINE a neck injury caused when your head moves forward and back again suddenly and violently, especially in a car accident

whipped /wɪpt/ *adj.* **1** whipped food has had air mixed into it so it is very light **2** INFORMAL defeated **3** INFORMAL, DISAPPROVING completely controlled by your GIRLFRIEND or wife

ˌwhipped ˈcream *n.* [U] cream that has been beaten until it is thick, eaten on sweet foods such as PIES

whip·per·snap·per /ˈwɪpɚˌsnæpɚ/ *n.* [C] OLD-FASHIONED a young person who is too confident and does not show enough respect to older people

whip·pet /ˈwɪpɪt/ *n.* [C] a small thin racing dog like a GREYHOUND

whip·ping /ˈwɪpɪŋ/ *n.* [C usually singular] a punishment given to someone by whipping them

ˈwhipping boy *n.* [C usually singular] someone or something that is blamed for someone else's mistakes SYN **scapegoat**

ˈwhipping ˌcream *n.* [U] a type of cream that becomes very stiff when you beat it

whip·poor·will /ˈwɪpɚˌwɪl/ *n.* [C] BIOLOGY a small North American bird that makes a noise that sounds like its name

whip·saw¹ /ˈwɪpsɔ/ *v.* **1** [T] if two or more things whipsaw someone or something, they attack or affect them badly at the same time **2** [I,T] INFORMAL if the price of something whipsaws or is whipsawed, it rises and falls repeatedly SYN **fluctuate** **3** [T] to defeat someone in two ways at the same time **4** [I,T] to cut something, especially a tree, with a whipsaw

whipsaw² *n.* [C] a large tool that has a flat blade with a row of sharp points and a handle on each end, used for cutting wood by two people at once

whir /wɚ/ *v.* [I] another spelling of WHIRR

whirl¹ /wɚl/ *v.* **1** [I,T] to spin around very quickly, or to make something do this: *The room began to whirl before my eyes.* | +**around/toward etc.** *Dozens of dancers whirled around the stage.* | **whirl sth around/away etc.** *The wind was whirling the snow around.* ►see

THESAURUS box at turn[1] **2** [I] if your head is whirling or thoughts are whirling in your head, your mind is full of thoughts and ideas, and you feel very confused or excited

whirl² *n.* **1 give sth a whirl** INFORMAL to try something that you are not sure you are going to like or be able to do **2** [singular] a lot of activity **3 be in a whirl** to feel very excited or confused about something **4** [C usually singular] a spinning movement, or the shape of a substance that is spinning: *a whirl of dust*

whirl·i·gig /ˈwɚliˌgɪg/ *n.* [C] a toy that spins

whirling 'dervish *n.* [C] a DERVISH

whirl·pool /ˈwɚlpul/ *n.* [C] **1** a powerful current of water that spins around and can pull things down into it **2** a large bathtub that makes hot water move in strong currents around your body

whirl·wind /ˈwɚlˌwɪnd/ *n.* [C] **1** EARTH SCIENCE an extremely strong wind that moves quickly with a circular movement, causing a lot of damage **2 a whirlwind romance/tour etc.** something that happens much more quickly than usual **3 a whirlwind of activity/emotions etc.** a situation in which you experience a lot of different activities or emotions one after another

whirl·y·bird /ˈwɚliˌbɚd/ *n.* [C] OLD-FASHIONED, INFORMAL a HELICOPTER

whirr /wɚ/ *v.* **whirred, whirring** [I] to make a fairly quiet spinning sound, like the sound of a bird or insect moving its wings very fast: *The hard drive whirred as I copied the files.* —**whirr** *n.* [C usually singular]

whisk¹ /wɪsk/ *v.* **1** [T] to mix liquid or soft things very quickly so that air is mixed in, especially with a fork or a whisk ►see THESAURUS box at cooking[1] → see picture on page A32 **2** [T always + adv./prep.] to take someone or something very quickly from one place to another: **whisk sb/sth away** *He whisked the letter away before I could read it.* | **whisk sb/sth around/across/through etc. sth** *I was whisked across town to the next meeting.* **3** [T] to move something with a short quick movement **4** [I always + adv./prep.] to move somewhere quickly

whisk sb **off** *phr. v.* to take someone quickly away from a place

whisk² *n.* [C] **1** a small kitchen tool made of curved pieces of wire, used for beating eggs, cream etc. **2** [usually singular] a quick light sweeping movement: **+of** *a whisk of the cow's tail*

whisk broom *n.* [C] a small stiff BROOM used especially for brushing clothes

whisk·er /ˈwɪskɚ/ *n.* [C] **1** [usually plural] BIOLOGY one of the long, stiff hairs that grow near the mouth of a cat, mouse etc. **2** [usually plural] BIOLOGY one of the hairs that grow on a man's face **3 win/lose by a whisker** INFORMAL to win or lose by a very small amount **4 come within a whisker of (doing) sth** to almost succeed or fail at doing something [**Origin:** 1600–1700 *whiskers* **mustache** (16–20 centuries), from *whisker* **something that whisks or sweeps** (15–19 centuries), from *whisk*; because the mustache looks like a small brush]

whis·key, whisky /ˈwɪski/ *n. plural* **whiskeys** or **whiskies** [C,U] a strong alcoholic drink made from grain, or a glass of this drink [**Origin:** 1700–1800 Irish Gaelic *uisce beathadh* and Scottish Gaelic *uisge beatha* **water of life**]

whis·per¹ /ˈwɪspɚ/ [W3] *v.* **1** [I,T] to speak or say something very quietly, using your breath rather than your voice: *Those two always sit in the back of the room and whisper.* | **whisper sth to sb** *James leaned over to whisper something to Michael.* | *"I love you," she **whispered in his ear**.* ►see THESAURUS box at say[1], talk[1] **2** [T] to say or suggest something privately or secretly: **whisper that** *Some people were whispering that she was a communist.* [**Origin:** Old English *hwisprian*]

whisper² *n.* [C] **1** the very quiet voice you use when you are whispering: *"Well, that's finally over," I said **in a whisper**.* **2** a piece of news or information that has not been officially announced [SYN] rumor: **+that** *We've been hearing whispers that he might not make the Olympic team.* **3** LITERARY a low soft sound made by wind, snow etc. **4** LITERARY **a whisper of sth** an amount of a quality or substance that is almost too small to notice [SYN] hint [SYN] trace

'whispering camˌpaign *n.* [C] a situation in which someone privately spreads criticism about another person in order to make people have a bad opinion of them

whist /wɪst/ *n.* [U] a card game for four players in two pairs, in which each pair tries to win the most TRICKS

whis·tle¹ /ˈwɪsəl/ [S3] *v.*

1 HIGH SOUND [I,T] to make a high or musical sound by blowing air out through your lips: *Fans yelled and whistled when the band came on stage.* | **whistle at/to sb** *I hate it when men whistle at me!* | **whistle a song/tune** *Tony quietly whistled a tune to himself.*

2 GO/MOVE FAST [I always + adv./prep.] to move quickly with a whistling sound: *A bullet whistled past his left cheek.*

3 STEAM/WIND ETC. [I] to make a high sound when air or steam is forced through a small hole: *The kettle was whistling on the stove.*

4 be whistled for sth if a player is whistled for something during a sports game, the REFEREE blows into a whistle to show they have done something wrong

5 BIRD [I] to make a high, often musical sound

6 be whistling in the dark INFORMAL to be trying to show that you are brave when you are afraid

7 whistle past the graveyard to try to show that you are brave when you are afraid

8 sb's not just whistling Dixie also **sb ain't just whistling Dixie** SPOKEN used to emphasize that what someone says is definitely true

9 be whistling in the wind to be trying to achieve something in a way that will not be successful

whistle² *n.* [C] **1** a small object that produces a high whistling sound when you blow into it: *The lifeguard **blew his whistle**.* **2** a piece of equipment on a train or boat that makes a high noise when air is forced through it: *A **whistle blew** as the train moved off.* **3** a high sound made by blowing a whistle, by blowing air out through your lips, or when air or steam is forced through a small opening → see also WOLF WHISTLE **4** the sound of something moving quickly through the air: *the whistle of jets overhead* [**Origin:** Old English *hwistle*]

'whistle-ˌblower *n.* [C] someone who tells people in authority or the public about dishonest or illegal practices in business, government etc. —**whistle-blowing** *n.* [U] → see also **blow the whistle on sb** at BLOW[1] (11)

Whis·tler /ˈwɪslɚ/, **James Mc·Neill** /dʒeɪmz məkˈnil/ (1834–1903) a U.S. PAINTER famous for his ideas about the COMPOSITION of pictures and the use of color

'whistle-ˌstop *n.* [C] **1 a whistle-stop speech/tour/trip** a short speech that a politician makes while visiting a small town, or a trip during which a politician makes these speeches many times **2** a small town, especially one where, in the past, trains only stopped if there were passengers who wanted to get on or off

whit /wɪt/ *n.* **1 not a/one whit** not at all **2 not a whit of sth** no amount of something

white¹ /waɪt/ [S1] [W1] *adj.*

1 COLOR having the color of milk, salt, or snow: *white daisies* | **pure/snow white** *pure white teeth* ►see THESAURUS box at hair

2 PEOPLE a) belonging to the race of people with pale skin who originally come from Europe **b)** relating to or used by white people: *a white neighborhood*

3 PALE looking pale, because of illness, strong emotion etc.: *Are you OK? You're **white as a sheet*** (=extremely pale).

4 WINE white wine is a pale yellow

5 a white Christmas/Thanksgiving etc. a Christmas, Thanksgiving etc. when there is snow

[**Origin:** Old English *hwit*] —**whiteness** *n.* [U]

white² [S2] [W3] *n.*

1 COLOR [U] the color of milk, salt, or snow: *The children were dressed **in white**.*

2 PEOPLE [C] also **White** someone who belongs to the

W

race of people with pale skin who were originally from Europe: *Whites still make up a majority of the U.S. population.*
3 WINE [C,U] wine that is pale yellow in color: *Californian whites are selling well.*
4 EYE [C] BIOLOGY the white part of your eye
5 EGG [C,U] BIOLOGY the part of an egg that surrounds the YOLK (=yellow part) and becomes white when cooked
6 whites [plural] **a)** white clothes, sheets etc., which are separated from dark colored clothes when they are washed **b)** white clothes that are worn for some sports, such as TENNIS

white³ *v.*
white sth **out** *phr. v.* to cover something written on paper, especially a mistake, with a special white liquid so that it cannot be seen anymore

White /waɪt/, **E.B.** (1899–1985) a U.S. writer famous for his ESSAYS and his books for children

White, Ed·ward /ˈɛdwəd/ (1845–1921) a CHIEF JUSTICE on the U.S. Supreme Court

ˌwhite ˈblood cell *n.* [C] BIOLOGY one of the cells in your blood which fights against infection → see also RED BLOOD CELL

white·board /ˈwaɪtbɔrd/ *n.* [C] a large board with a white smooth surface that you can write on, used in rooms where classes are taught → see also BLACKBOARD → see picture at BOARD¹

ˌwhite ˈbread *n.* [U] bread that is made with white flour

ˈwhite-bread *adj.* INFORMAL relating to white people who have traditional values and who are often considered boring

white·caps /ˈwaɪtkæps/ *n.* [plural] waves in the ocean or on a lake that are white at the top

ˈwhite-ˌcollar *adj.* **1** relating to jobs in offices, banks etc., as opposed to jobs working in factories, building things etc.: *a white-collar worker* **2 white-collar crime** crimes involving white-collar workers, for example when someone secretly steals money from the organization they work for → see also BLUE-COLLAR, PINK-COLLAR

ˌwhite ˈcorpuscle *n.* [C] a WHITE BLOOD CELL

ˌwhite ˈdwarf *n.* [C] PHYSICS a hot star, near the end of its life, that is more solid but less bright than the sun → see also RED GIANT

ˌwhite ˈelephant *n.* [C] something that is completely useless, although it may have cost a lot of money [**Origin:** 1800–1900 from the supposed practice of the King of Siam, who gave to people he did not like a white elephant, which cost a very large amount of money to keep]

white·fish /ˈwaɪtfɪʃ/ *n.* [C,U] BIOLOGY a type of white or silvery fish that lives in lakes or rivers, or the meat of this fish

ˌwhite ˈflag *n.* [C] something that shows that you accept that you have failed or been defeated: **wave/raise/show etc. the white flag** *If things are starting to go well, why raise the white flag?*

ˌwhite ˈflight *n.* [U] the situation in which white people move away from an area or send their children to private schools to avoid being around people who are not white

ˈwhite ˌflour *n.* [U] wheat flour from which the BRAN (=outer layer) and WHEATGERM (=inside seed) have been removed → see also WHOLE WHEAT

white·fly /ˈwaɪtflaɪ/ *n. plural* **whiteflies** [C] a type of insect with long wings that damages plants

white·head /ˈwaɪthɛd/ *n.* [C] a PIMPLE that is white on the surface → see also BLACKHEAD

ˈwhite ˌheat *n.* [U] the very high temperature at which a metal turns white

ˌwhite-ˈhot *adj.* **1** white-hot metal is so hot that it shines white **2** involving a lot of activity or strong feelings: *white-hot anger*

ˈWhite House *n.* **1 the White House** the official home in Washington, D.C., of the president of the U.S. **2** [singular] the president of the U.S. and the people who advise him: *a Democratic White House*

ˌwhite ˈknight *n.* [C] a person or company that puts money into a business in order to save it from being controlled by another company

ˈwhite-ˌknuckle *adj.* making you very worried, nervous, or afraid: *a white-knuckle flight*

ˈwhite-ˌknuckled *adj.* worried, nervous, or afraid

ˈwhite ˌlie *n.* [C] INFORMAL a small lie that you tell someone, especially in order to avoid hurting their feelings

ˌwhite ˈlightning *n.* [U] MOONSHINE (=illegal strong alcohol)

ˌwhite ˈmagic *n.* [U] magic used for good purposes → see also BLACK MAGIC

ˈwhite meat *n.* [U] **1** the pale-colored meat from the breast, wings etc. of a cooked chicken, TURKEY, or other bird → see also DARK MEAT **2** meat such as chicken and TURKEY that is pale in color, not dark like lamb or BEEF → see also RED MEAT

ˈWhite ˌMountains, the a part of the northern Appalachians that is in the U.S. state of New Hampshire

whit·en /ˈwaɪt̚n/ *v.* [I,T] to become more white, or to make something do this: *This stuff is supposed to whiten your teeth.*

whit·en·er /ˈwaɪt̚n-ɚ/ *n.* [C,U] a substance used to make something more white

ˈwhite noise *n.* [U] noise coming from a radio or television which is turned on but not TUNED to any station

white·out /ˈwaɪt̬aʊt/ *n.* [C] weather conditions in which there is so much cloud or snow that you cannot see anything → see also WITE-OUT

ˈwhite ˌpages *n.* **the white pages** also **the White Pages** the white part of a telephone DIRECTORY with the names, addresses, and telephone numbers of people with telephones → see also YELLOW PAGES

ˌwhite ˈpaper *n.* [C] an official report on a particular subject, especially one that is written by a company or government

ˌwhite ˈpepper *n.* [U] a white powder made from the crushed inside of a PEPPERCORN which gives a slightly SPICY taste to food

ˈwhite sale *n.* [C] a period when a store sells sheets, TOWELS etc. for a lower price

ˈwhite sauce *n.* [C,U] a thick white liquid made from flour, milk, and butter which can be eaten with meat and vegetables

ˌwhite ˈslavery *n.* [U] OLD-FASHIONED the practice or business of taking girls to a foreign country and forcing them to be PROSTITUTES

ˌwhite suˈpremacist *n.* [C] someone who believes that white people are better than other races —**white supremacy** *n.* [U]

ˌwhite-tailed ˈdeer *n.* [C] a common North American DEER with a tail that is white on the bottom side

ˈwhite-tie *adj.* a white-tie social occasion is a very formal one at which the men wear white BOW TIES and TAILS → see also BLACK-TIE

ˌwhite ˈtrash *n.* [U] INFORMAL an insulting expression meaning white people who are poor and uneducated

white·wall /ˈwaɪtwɔl/ *n.* [C] a car tire that has a wide white band on its side

white·wash¹ /ˈwaɪt̚wɑʃ/ *v.* [T] **1** to hide the true facts about a serious accident or illegal action: *Investigators are accused of whitewashing the governor's record.* **2** to cover something with whitewash

whitewash² *n.* **1** [C,U] a report or examination of events that hides the true facts about something, so that the person who is responsible will not be punished

2 [U] a white liquid mixture used especially for painting walls

white·wa·ter, white water /ˈwaɪt˺ˌwɔt̬ɚ/ *n.* [U] a part of a river that looks white because the water is running very quickly over rocks: *whitewater rafting*

whith·er /ˈwɪðɚ/ *adv.* **1** FORMAL a word used to ask if something will exist, or how it will develop, in the future: *Whither NATO?* **2** OLD USE to which place SYN where

whit·ing /ˈwaɪt̬ɪŋ/ *n.* [C] BIOLOGY a black and silver fish that lives in the ocean and can be eaten

whit·ish /ˈwaɪt̬ɪʃ/ *adj.* almost white in color

Whit·man /ˈwɪt˺mən/**, Walt** /wɔlt/ (1819–1892) a U.S. writer known for his poetry about the beauty of nature and the value of freedom

Whit·ney /ˈwɪt˺ni/**, E·li** /ˈilaɪ/ (1765–1825) the U.S. inventor of the COTTON GIN → see picture on page A25

Whitney, Mount a mountain in the Sierra Nevada that is the highest mountain in the CONTINENTAL U.S.

Whit·ti·er /ˈwɪt̬iɚ/**, John Green·leaf** /dʒɑn ˈgrinlif/ (1807–1892) a U.S. poet

whit·tle /ˈwɪt̬l/ *v.* [I,T] **1** also **whittle down** to gradually make something smaller by taking parts away: **whittle sth (down) to sth** *The list has been whittled down to just five candidates.* **2** to cut a piece of wood into a particular shape by cutting off small pieces with a small knife

whittle sth ↔ **away** also **whittle away at sth** *phr. v.* to gradually reduce the amount or value of something, especially something that you think should not be reduced

whiz¹ /wɪz/ *v.* **whizzed, whizzing** [I always + adv./prep.] INFORMAL to move very quickly, often making a sound like something rushing through the air: **+by/around/past etc.** *She stood by the side of the road watching the cars whiz by.*

whiz by/past *phr. v.* if time whizzes by or past, it seems to pass very quickly

whiz through sth *phr. v.* to do something very quickly

whiz² *n.* [C] *plural* **whizzes** INFORMAL someone who is very fast, intelligent, or skilled in a particular activity

whiz-bang /ˈwɪzˌbæŋ/ *n.* [C] INFORMAL something that is noticed a lot because it is very good, loud, or fast

whiz kid /ˈwɪzkɪd/ *n.* [C] INFORMAL a young person who is very skilled or successful at something

WHO /ˌdʌbəlyu eɪtʃ ˈoʊ/ → see WORLD HEALTH ORGANIZATION, THE

who /hu/ S1 W1 *pron.* **1** used to ask or talk about which person or people: *Who was that on the phone?* | *Who wants another beer?* | *Someone told them, but I don't know who.* | ***Who else** did you tell?* **2** used especially after a noun to give information about which person or people you are talking about: *The talk was given by a man who used to live in Russia.* | *Oh, now I know who he is!* **3** used to add more information about a specific person or specific people you have already mentioned: *Ron, who usually doesn't drink alcohol, had two beers.* **4** used to ask a question that shows you think something is true of everyone or of no one: *Yeah, we fight. Who doesn't?* **5 who is sb to do sth?** SPOKEN used to say that someone does not have the right or the authority to say or do something: *Who are you to tell me what to do?* **6 who's who** used to talk about the problem of knowing or remembering who each person in a group is: *At parties, I can never remember who's who.* **7 sth is a who's who of sth** used to say that something includes all the important people within a particular organization or group: *The list of musicians she has appeared with reads like a who's who of jazz.*
[**Origin:** Old English *hwa*]

WORD CHOICE who, whom, that

In informal English, you can use **who** as an object, especially in questions: *Who did they end up hiring?* | *Who are you talking about?* In very formal English, it is considered better to use **whom**: *Whom did you see there?* Immediately after a preposition, it is more common to use **whom**, but this still sounds fairly formal: *To whom are you sending that letter?* It is much more natural to say: *Who are you sending that letter to?* In informal or spoken English, it is also very common to use **that** instead of **who** when it is the subject of a relative clause: *I hate people that don't know when to leave.* You can also use **that**, or nothing at all, instead of **whom** when it is the object of a relative clause: *He's the guy that I was talking about.* | *Are you sure she's the one you saw?*

whoa /woʊ, hwoʊ, hoʊ/ *interjection* **1** used to tell someone to become calmer or to do something more slowly: *Whoa! Calm down, dude.* **2** said to show that you are surprised or that you think something is impressive: *Whoa. That's a lot of money.* **3** used to tell a horse to stop

who·dun·it /huˈdʌnɪt/ *n.* [C] INFORMAL a book, movie etc. about a murder, in which you do not find out who killed the person until the end

who·ev·er /huˈɛvɚ/ S2 *pron.* **1** any person: *Give these clothes to whoever needs them.* **2** used to say that it does not matter which person, because the situation will be the same: *Whoever wins the election, taxes will be cut.* **3** used to talk about a specific person or people, although you do not know who they are: *Whoever is responsible for this will be punished.* **4 whoever sb is** used to say that you do not know who someone is: *Your wife is a lucky woman, whoever she is.* **5 or whoever** or some other person: *I'll get the number from Mary or Gloria or whoever.* **6** OLD-FASHIONED also **who ever** used at the beginning of a question to show surprise or anger: *Whoever could be calling at this time of night?*

whole¹ /hoʊl/ S1 W1 *adj.*

1 ALL all of something SYN entire: *It took a whole day to get there.* | *She drank a whole bottle of wine.* | *Ricky just talked about his kids **the whole time**.* | ***The whole thing** (=everything about a situation) really irritates me.* | *I never learned **the whole truth** about what he had done.* | **the whole school/country/town etc.** (=all the people in a school, country etc.)

2 a whole variety/host/range etc. (of sth) used to emphasize that there are a lot of different things of a similar type: *In my job I come into contact with a whole range of people.*

3 a whole lot/bunch INFORMAL **a)** a large amount of something: **+of** *a whole bunch of money* **b)** to a great degree: *I love her a whole lot.*

4 NOT DIVIDED complete and not divided or broken into parts: *Place a whole onion inside the chicken.* | **eat/swallow sth whole** *The snake swallows its prey whole.*

5 the whole point (of sth) an expression used to emphasize that one thing is the reason that something else happens: *The whole point of coming here was to visit the cathedral.*

6 in the whole (wide) world an expression meaning "anywhere" or "at all", used to emphasize a statement: *You're my best friend in the whole wide world!*

7 the whole nine yards SPOKEN including everything that is typical of or possible in an activity, situation, set of things etc.

8 go the whole hog INFORMAL to do something as completely or as well as you can, without any limits

[**Origin:** Old English *hal* **healthy, unhurt, complete**]
→ see also **the whole enchilada** at ENCHILADA (3), **the whole shebang** at SHEBANG, WHOLLY —**wholeness** *n.* [U]

whole² S2 *n.* **1 as a whole** used to say that all the parts of something are being considered together: *The project will benefit the community as a whole.* **2 the whole of sth** all of something, especially something that is not a physical object: *the whole of Latin America* **3 on the whole** used to say that something is generally true: *On the whole, he seems like an intelligent, likable person.* **4** [C usually singular] something that consists of a number of parts, but is considered as a single unit: *Two halves make a whole.*

whole³ *adv.* **1** completely: *a whole new approach* **2 a whole 'nother sth** SPOKEN, NONSTANDARD **a)** used to emphasize that there is another complete thing of the same type as the thing you were talking about: *There's a whole 'nother package in the cupboard.* **b)** used to say that something is completely different from what you have been talking about or from what you are used to: *Texas is like a whole 'nother country for me.* → see also a **whole new ball game** at BALL GAME (2)

'whole food *n.* [C,U] food that is considered healthy because it is in a simple natural form

whole·heart·ed /ˌhoʊlˈhɑrtɪd◂/ *adj.* involving all your feelings, interest etc.: **wholehearted support/approval/effort etc.** *The people have given their wholehearted support to the war effort.* —**wholeheartedly** *adv.*: *The others joined in wholeheartedly.*

'whole milk *n.* [U] milk that has not had any fat removed → see also ONE PERCENT MILK, TWO PERCENT MILK

'whole note *n.* [C] ENG. LANG. ARTS a musical note which continues for as long as two HALF NOTES

ˌwhole 'number *n.* [C] MATH a number such as 0, 1, 2 etc. that is not a FRACTION

whole·sale¹ /ˈhoʊlseɪl/ *n.* [U] the business of selling goods in large quantities to other businesses → see also RETAIL

wholesale² *adj.* **1** relating to the business of selling goods in large quantities to other businesses: *wholesale prices* **2** [only before noun] affecting almost everything or everyone, and often done without any concern for the results: *a wholesale restructuring of the process* —**wholesale** *adv.*: *I can get it for you wholesale.*

whole·sal·er /ˈhoʊlˌseɪlɚ/ *n.* [C] a person or a company that sells goods wholesale

whole·some /ˈhoʊlsəm/ *adj.* **1** likely to make you healthy: *well-balanced wholesome meals* **2** considered to have a good moral effect: *wholesome family life* —**wholesomeness** *n.* [U]

W

'whole wheat *adj.* whole wheat flour or bread is made using every part of the WHEAT grain, including the outer layer

who'll /hul/ the short form of "who will": *You never know who'll show up.*

whol·ly /ˈhoʊli/ *adv.* FORMAL completely: *a wholly satisfactory solution*

whom /hum/ W1 *pron.* the object form of "who", used especially in formal speech or writing: *Whom did you speak to?* | *That's the man about whom I was telling you.* | *I talked to his wife, whom I'd never met before.* → see Word Choice box at WHO

whom·ev·er /huˈmɛvɚ/ *pron.* FORMAL used to say that it does not matter who receives something or has something done to them: *You can invite whomever you want.*

whomp /wɑmp,wɔmp/ *v.* [T] SPOKEN **1** to hit someone very hard with your hand closed **2** to defeat another team easily

whoop /hup, wup/ *v.* [I] **1** to shout loudly and happily **2 whoop it up** INFORMAL to enjoy yourself very much, especially by making a lot of noise in a large group —**whoop** *n.* [C] *excited whoops and cheers*

whoop-de-do¹ /ˌwup di ˈdu, ˌhup-/ *interjection* used to show that you do not think something that someone has told you is as exciting or impressive as they think it is

whoop-de-do² *n.* [C] SPOKEN a noisy party or celebration

whoop·ee¹ /ˈwʊpi, ˈwu-/ *interjection* said when you are very happy about something: *Whoopee! I won!*

whoopee² *n.* **make whoopee** OLD-FASHIONED to have sex

'whoopee ˌcushion *n.* [C] a rubber CUSHION filled with air that makes a noise like air coming out of your bottom when you sit on it

whoop·ing cough /ˈhupɪŋ kɔf, ˈwup-/ *n.* [U] MEDICINE an infectious disease especially affecting children, that makes them cough and have difficulty breathing

whoops /wʊps/ S3 *interjection* **1** said when you have fallen, dropped something, or made a small mistake: *Whoops, sorry. Did I hurt your hand?* **2** also **whoops-a-daisy** said when someone, usually a child, falls down

whoosh /wʊʃ, wuʃ/ *v.* [I always + adv./prep.] to move very fast with a soft rushing sound: *Cars whooshed by.* —**whoosh** *n.* [C usually singular]

whop /wɑp/ *v.* [T] INFORMAL to hit someone or something

whop·per /ˈwɑpɚ/ *n.* [C] INFORMAL **1** a big lie **2** something unusually big

whop·ping /ˈwɑpɪŋ/ *adj.* [only before noun] INFORMAL very large: *a whopping 28% increase*

who're /ˈhuɚ, hʊr/ the short form of "who are": *Who're they?*

whore /hɔr/ *n.* [C] OFFENSIVE a woman who has sex for money SYN **prostitute**

whorl /wɔrl/ *n.* [C] **1** a pattern made of a line that curls out in circles that get bigger and bigger **2** BIOLOGY a circular pattern of leaves or flowers on a stem

who's /huz/ **1** the short form of "who is": *Who's going to take her home?* **2** the short form of "who has", when "has" is an AUXILIARY VERB: *Who's been working here the longest?*

whose /huz/ S3 W1 *possessive adj., possessive pron.* **1** used to ask or talk about which person or people a particular thing belongs to: *Whose is this?* | *She wondered whose car he was driving.* **2** used to give information about someone or something that belongs or relates to someone or something you have just mentioned: *He held a small child whose face I couldn't see.* | *They stayed at the Grand Hotel, whose staff was always welcoming.*

who·so·ev·er /ˌhusoʊˈɛvɚ/ *pron.* OLD USE OR BIBLICAL, WHOEVER

who've /huv/ the short form of "who have": *People who've never had kids wouldn't understand.*

whup /wʌp/ *v.* [T] SPOKEN **1** to defeat someone easily in a sport or fight **2** to hit someone and hurt them very badly, for example by using a belt to hit them

why¹ /waɪ/ S1 W1 *adv.* **1** for what reason: *Why do you want to go to Louisville?* | *I don't understand why I have to type this.* **2** used to give a specific reason for something: *That's why the company collapsed.* | *Let me tell you **the reason why** I disagree.*

SPOKEN PHRASES

3 why not? a) used to ask the reason something does not happen or is not true: *"I just can't do it." "Why not?"* **b)** used to show that you agree with a suggestion or idea: *"Let's go to the beach today." "Yeah, why not."* **4 why doesn't sb do sth?** also **why not do sth?** used to make a suggestion: *Why don't you give me your number, and I'll call you.* | *Why not have the picnic in Glendale?* **5 why sb?** used to ask why something has been done, given etc. to someone and not to a different person: *Why me? Can't someone else drive you?* **6 why do sth?** used to suggest that particular course of action will not bring any good results: *We're not going to win, so why even try?* **7 why should sb (do sth)?** used to rudely refuse to accept that you or someone else should do what someone says: *I'm not going to apologize. Why should I?* **8 why on earth/in the world/in heaven's name etc.?** used to ask in a surprised way why something has happened: *Why on earth would she save all those cards?* **9 why, oh why...?** used to show that you are very sorry about something you did

why² *interjection* OLD-FASHIONED **1** said to show that you are slightly surprised or annoyed: *Why, look who's here!* **2** said when you suddenly realize something: *And I thought to myself, why, I can do that.*

why³ *n.* **the why(s) and wherefore(s)** the reasons or explanations for something

why'd /waɪd/ the short form of "why did": *Why'd you do that?*

WI the written abbreviation of Wisconsin

Wic·ca /ˈwɪkə/ *n.* [U] a religion related to WITCHCRAFT that involves respect for nature —**Wiccan** *adj.* —**Wiccan** *n.* [C]

wick /wɪk/ *n.* [C] **1** the piece of thread in a CANDLE that burns when you light it → see picture at CANDLE **2** a long piece of material in an oil lamp that sucks up oil so that the lamp can burn

wick·ed¹ /ˈwɪkɪd/ *adj.* **1** behaving in a way that is morally wrong SYN **evil**: *a wicked witch* ▸see THESAURUS box at **bad¹** **2** INFORMAL behaving badly in a way that is amusing, attractive, or exciting: *a wicked smile* **3** SLANG very good: *That's a wicked bike!* [**Origin:** 1200–1300 *wick* **wicked** (12–20 centuries)] → see also **no rest for the wicked/weary** at REST¹ (8) —**wickedly** *adv.* —**wickedness** *n.* [U]

wicked² *adv.* [+ adj./adv.] SLANG very

wick·er¹ /ˈwɪkɚ/ *adj.* [only before noun] made from thin dried tree branches woven together: *a wicker chair*

wicker² *n.* [U] thin dried tree branches that are woven together to make furniture, BASKETS etc. → see picture at BASKET

wick·et /ˈwɪkɪt/ *n.* [C] **1** a small window or hole in a wall, especially one at which you can buy tickets **2** a curved wire under which you hit your ball in the game of CROQUET

wide¹ /waɪd/ S2 W1 *adj.*

1 DISTANCE a) measuring a large distance from one side to the other OPP **narrow**: *a wide necktie* | *The river is very wide.* | *Wreckage was spread across a wide area.* **b)** measuring a particular distance from one side to the other: *How wide is the door?* | **five feet/two miles/three inches etc. wide** *The desk is four feet long and two feet wide.*

2 VARIETY including or involving a large variety of different people, things, or situations: *a man with wide experience in business* | **a wide range/variety/selection etc. (of sth)** *A wide range of software is available.* | **a wide circle of friends/acquaintances** (=a large number of friends etc.)

3 IN MANY PLACES [usually before noun] happening among many people or in many places: **wide support/influence** *The plan has attracted wide support.*

4 a wide difference/gap/variation etc. a large and noticeable difference: *He expects to win the election by a **wide margin**.*

5 GENERAL [only before noun, usually in the comparative or superlative] general and not involving just one part or paying too much attention to specific details SYN **broad**: **wider issues/view/context etc.** *We have to consider the student protests in a wider context.* | *The changes will benefit, not only disabled people, but also **the wider community**.*

6 EYES LITERARY wide eyes are fully open, especially when someone is very surprised, excited, or frightened: *Her eyes grew wide in anticipation.*

7 BALL/BULLET ETC. not hitting the point you were aiming at: +**of** *The throw was wide of first base.*

8 give sb/sth a wide berth to avoid someone or something: *Sandie's been giving her a wide berth since the argument.*

9 the (big) wide world SPOKEN places outside the small familiar place where you live → see also **be wide of the mark** at MARK² (6), **in the whole (wide) world** at WHOLE¹ (6), WIDELY, WIDTH

[**Origin:** Old English *wid*]

WORD CHOICE **wide, broad**

- **Wide** is the most usual word to describe something that measures a long distance from one side to another: *a wide road/lake/doorway/entrance/staircase*. You also use **wide** to express how much something measures from side to side: *The gap was only a few inches wide.*
- **Broad** is often used about parts of the body: *broad shoulders/hips* | *a broad nose/forehead.* **Broad** often suggests that something is wide in a good or attractive way: *a broad driveway leading up to the mansion.*

wide² *adv.* **1 wide open/awake/apart** completely open, awake, or apart: *The door was wide open when we got here.* | *It was 3 a.m., but I was wide awake.* → see also WIDE-OPEN **2** opening or spreading as much as possible: **open/spread sth wide** *Spiro spread his arms wide in a welcoming gesture.* **3** not hitting the point you were aiming at: *Wilton hit the ball high and wide.*

-wide /waɪd/ *suffix* [in adjectives] used with nouns that are places or organizations to mean "affecting all the people in that place or organization": *statewide elections* | *a company-wide picnic*

ˌwide-angle ˈlens *n.* [C] a camera LENS that lets you take photographs with a wider view than normal

wide·bod·y /ˈwaɪdˌbɑdi/ *adj.* [only before noun] a wide-body airplane is wider than other airplanes and holds many people —**widebody** *n.* [C]

ˈwide-eyed *adj.* **1** having your eyes wide open, especially because you are surprised or frightened **2** too willing to believe, accept, or admire things because you do not have much experience of life SYN **naive**: *a wide-eyed idealist*

wide·ly /ˈwaɪdli/ W2 *adv.* **1** in a lot of different places or by a lot of people: *Copies of the report have been made widely available.* | **widely accepted/believed/known etc.** *At one time it was widely believed that the sun revolved around the Earth.* | **a widely held view/belief/opinion etc.** *widely held beliefs about God* | *The magazine is **widely read** by teenagers.* **2** by a large degree: **vary/differ widely** *Different brands of tuna can vary widely in price.* | ***widely different** views* **3 widely read** someone who is widely read has read a lot of books

wid·en /ˈwaɪdn/ *v.* **1** [I,T] to become wider, or to make something wider OPP **narrow**: *When are they going to widen the road?* **2** [I,T] to become larger in degree or range, or to make something do this OPP **narrow**: *Maryland widened its lead to 14 points.* **3** [I] if your eyes widen, they open more, especially because you are surprised or frightened OPP **narrow**

ˌwide-ˈopen, wide open *adj.* **1** completely open: **eyes/mouth wide-open** *Kerry stared, her mouth wide-open.* **2** a wide-open area does not have any objects, buildings, etc. in it: *wide-open spaces* **3** a competition, election etc. that is wide open can be won by anyone: *The presidential race is still wide open.* **4 wide open to attack/influence etc.** easily attacked, influenced etc.

ˌwide-ˈranging *adj.* including a wide variety of subjects, things, or people: *a wide-ranging investigation*

ˌwide reˈceiver *n.* [C] a player in football who starts in a position at the end of the line of players, far from the others, and who catches the ball

wide·scale, wide-scale /ˌwaɪdˈskeɪl◂/ *adj.* involving a large number of things, people etc.

wide·spread /ˌwaɪdˈsprɛd◂/ AC *adj.* existing or happening in many places or situations, or among many people: *the widespread use of computers*

widg·et /ˈwɪdʒɪt/ *n.* [C] **1** INFORMAL a word used to represent an imaginary product that a company might produce, used especially in business classes **2** SPOKEN a small piece of equipment that you do not know the name for

wid·ow¹ /ˈwɪdoʊ/ *n.* [C] **1** a woman whose husband has died and who has not married again ▸see THESAURUS box at **married** **2 a football/golf/hunting etc. widow** HUMOROUS a woman whose husband spends all his free time watching football, playing GOLF etc.

widow² *v.* **be widowed** to become a widow or widower: *Carla was widowed very young.* —**widowed** *adj.*

wid·ow·er /ˈwɪdoʊɚ/ *n.* [C] a man whose wife has died and who has not married again

wid·ow·hood /ˈwɪdoʊˌhʊd/ *n.* [U] the time when you are a widow

ˌwidow's ˈpeak *n.* [C] the edge of someone's hair that forms the shape of a "V" at the top of their face

W

width /wɪdθ, wɪtθ/ *n.* **1** [C,U] the distance from one side of something to the other, or the measurement of this: *Paolo saw him across the width of the church.* | *The slits are about 1 mm* ***in width.*** → see also LENGTH, BREADTH (1) **2** [U] the quality or fact of being wide: *I was surprised by the width of his shoulders.* **3** [C] a piece of a material that has been measured and cut

wield /wild/ *v.* [T] **1 wield power/influence/authority etc.** to have a lot of power, influence etc., and be ready to use it **2** to hold a weapon or tool that you are going to use: *The man was wielding a large stick.*

wie·ner /ˈwinɚ, ˈwini/ *n.* [C] **1** a type of SAUSAGE used to make HOT DOGS **2** SPOKEN someone who is silly or stupid **3** SPOKEN a word used by children meaning a PENIS

ˈwiener dog *n.* [C] SPOKEN A DACHSHUND

wie·nie /ˈwini/ another spelling of WEENIE

wife /waɪf/ S1 W1 *n. plural* **wives** /waɪvz/ [C] the woman that a man is married to → see also HUSBAND: *Have you met my wife, Doris?* | **sb's ex-wife/former wife** *My ex-wife is in Connecticut.* [**Origin:** Old English *wif* **woman, wife**]

wife·ly /ˈwaɪfli/ *adj.* OLD-FASHIONED relating to qualities or behavior considered to be typical of a good wife

Wif·fle ball /ˈwɪfəl ˌbɔl/ *n.* [C,U] TRADEMARK a plastic baseball with holes it, or the game that is played with this

Wi-Fi, wi-fi /ˈwaɪ faɪ/ *n.* [U] a system for connecting computers without using wires

wig[1] /wɪg/ *n.* [C] a covering of hair that you wear on your head, either because you have no hair or want to cover your hair: *a blond wig* [**Origin:** 1600–1700 *periwig* type of wig (16–21 centuries), from Old Italian *perrucca* **hair, wig**] → see also TOUPEE

wig[2] *v.*
wig out *phr. v.* **wig sb ↔ out** SLANG to become very anxious, upset, or afraid, or to make someone do this

wig·gle /ˈwɪgəl/ *v.* [I,T] to move with small movements from side to side or up and down, or make something move like this: *Can you wiggle your ears?* —**wiggle** *n.* [C]

ˈwiggle room *n.* [U] INFORMAL the chance to make small changes to a statement, decision, or agreement: *The company has tried to leave itself some wiggle room in the contract.*

wig·gly /ˈwɪgli/ *adj.* INFORMAL a wiggly line is one that has small curves in it SYN **wavy**

wig·wam /ˈwɪgwɑm/ *n.* [C] a structure with a round roof used as a house by some Native American tribes in the past [**Origin:** 1600–1700 Abnaki and Massachusett *wikwam*]

wik·i /ˈwɪki/ *n.* [C,U] a web page, or series of web pages, which can be written or changed by the people who use that website: *Many companies have now replaced their intranets with wikis.*

wild[1] /waɪld/ S2 W2 *adj.*
1 PLANTS/ANIMALS living in a natural state, not changed or controlled by humans OPP **domesticated**: *a wild rose* | *wild horses* ►see THESAURUS box at **natural**[1]
2 LAND not used by people for farming, building etc.: *a wild coastline*
3 EMOTIONS showing strong uncontrolled emotions, especially anger, happiness, or excitement: *wild laughter* | +**with** *His eyes were wild with rage.* | *The crowd* ***went wild*** *as soon as she came on stage.*
4 BEHAVIOR behaving in an uncontrolled, sometimes violent way: *Jed was really wild in high school.*
5 EXCITING SPOKEN exciting, interesting, unusual, or strange: *"It turns out she went to college with my sister." "That's wild."*
6 WITHOUT CAREFUL THOUGHT done or said without much thought or care, or without knowing all the facts: *wild accusations* | *I'm going to take* ***a wild guess*** *and say you're 42.*
7 NOT SENSIBLE wild ideas, plans etc. are not sensible or are not based on fact: *Where do you get these wild ideas?*
8 wild about sb/sth very interested in or excited about someone or something: *I'm not wild about rap music.*
9 THROW/PUNCH not controlled or going where you were aiming: *a wild pitch*
10 beyond sb's wildest dreams beyond anything someone imagined or hoped for: *The business has succeeded beyond our wildest dreams.*
11 not/never in sb's wildest dreams used to say that someone did not expect or imagine that something would happen, especially after it has happened
12 COLORS/PATTERNS bright, unusual, and noticeable: *a wild Hawaiian shirt*
13 WEATHER violent and strong: *wild winds*
14 wild and woolly exciting and dangerous or complicated: *the wild and woolly world of Russian politics*
15 wild horses couldn't drag/stop/keep etc. sb used to emphasize that someone is very determined about something, and will not change their mind
16 CARD GAMES a card that is wild can be used to represent any other card in a game → see also WILD CARD
[**Origin:** Old English *wilde*] —**wildness** *n.* [U] → see also **sow your wild oats** at SOW[1] (3), WILDLY

wild[2] *adv.* **1 run wild** to behave in an uncontrolled way because there are no rules or people to control you: *Pam just lets her kids run wild.* **2 grow wild** if plants grow wild, they are not planted or controlled by people

wild[3] *n.* **1 in the wild** in natural and free conditions, not kept or controlled by humans **2 the wilds of Africa/Alaska/Borneo etc.** areas where there are no towns and not many people live

wild ˈboar *n.* [C] a large wild pig with long hair

wild card *n.* [C] **1** someone or something that may affect a situation, but in a way that you do not know and cannot guess: *China remains a wild card in the negotiations.* **2** a sports team that must win additional games to be allowed to play in an important competition, especially in football and baseball **3** a playing card that can represent any other card **4** COMPUTERS a sign that can represent any letter or set of letters in some computer commands

wild·cat[1] /ˈwaɪldkæt/ *n.* [C] a type of large cat that lives in mountains, forests etc.

wildcat[2] *v.* **wildcatted, wildcatting** [I] to look for oil in a place where no one has found any yet —**wildcatter** *n.* [C]

ˌwildcat ˈstrike *n.* [C] an occasion when people suddenly stop working in an unofficial way in order to protest about something

Wilde /waɪld/, **Os·car** /ˈɑskɚ/ (1854–1900) an Irish writer of poems, stories, and humorous plays, famous for his WIT in conversation

wil·de·beest /ˈwɪldəˌbist/ *n.* [C] a large southern African animal with a tail and curved horns SYN **gnu**

Wild·er /ˈwaɪldɚ/, **Bil·ly** /ˈbɪli/ (1906–2002) a U.S. movie DIRECTOR, who was born in Austria

Wilder, Thorn·ton /ˈθɔrntˀn/ (1897–1975) a U.S. writer of plays and NOVELS

wil·der·ness /ˈwɪldɚnɪs/ *n.* [C usually singular] **1** a large area of land that has never been built on or changed by humans ►see THESAURUS box at **country**[1] **2 the (political) wilderness** a situation away from the center of political power or activity: *the party's return from the political wilderness*

ˈwilderness ˌarea *n.* [C] an area of public land in the U.S. where no buildings or roads are allowed to be built

ˌWilderness ˈRoad, the a way to reach the Ohio River by traveling from Virginia across the Appalachians that was discovered by Daniel Boone in 1775 and used by many people who wanted to settle in the Midwest

ˈWilderness Soˌciety, the an organization that works to protect the environment and wild animals, birds etc.

ˌwild-ˈeyed *adj.* **1** having a crazy look in your eyes

2 extremely determined in a way that is slightly frightening: *a wild-eyed radical*

wild·fire /ˈwaɪldˌfaɪɚ/ *n.* [C,U] a fire that moves quickly and cannot be controlled → see **spread like wildfire** at SPREAD[1] (4)

wild·flow·er /ˈwaɪldˌflaʊɚ/ *n.* [C] a flower that no one has planted, but that grows naturally

wild·fowl /ˈwaɪldfaʊl/ *n.* [plural] wild birds, especially ones that live near water

ˌwild ˈgoose chase *n.* [C] a situation in which you waste a lot of time looking for something that cannot be found: *It looks like we've been **on a wild goose chase**.*

wild·lands /ˈwaɪldlændz/ *n.* [plural] an area of land that has never been developed or farmed —**wildland** *adj.* [only before noun] *wildland fires*

wild·life /ˈwaɪldlaɪf/ *n.* [U] animals and plants living in natural conditions, not kept by people: *The park has an abundance of wildlife.*

wild·ly /ˈwaɪldli/ *adv.* **1** in a way that is not calm or controlled: *The audience cheered wildly.* **2** extremely: *The band is wildly popular in Cuba.*

ˈwild rice *n.* [U] the seed of a type of grass that grows in parts of North America and China that can be cooked and eaten

ˌWild ˈWest *n.* **the Wild West** the western part of the U.S. in the 19th century before the government and laws were strong

wile /waɪl/ *v.* another spelling of WHILE

wiles /waɪlz/ *n.* [plural] things you say or tricks you use to persuade someone to do what you want: *It was impossible to resist her **feminine wiles**.*

Wil·helm I /ˌvɪlhɛlm ðə ˈfɚst/ (1797–1888) the king of Germany when Bismarck joined all the separate German states together to form one country

Wilhelm II /ˌvɪlhɛlm ðə ˈsɛkənd/ also **Kaiser Wilhelm** (1859–1941) the king of Germany during World War I

wi·li·ness /ˈwaɪlinɪs/ *n.* [U] the quality of being WILY

will[1] /wəl, əl; *strong* wɪl/ [S1] [W1] *modal verb* short form **'ll** negative short form **won't** **1** used to talk about the future: *The conference will be held in San Antonio.* | *What time will you get here?* | *I hope they won't be late.* | *I'll call her tonight.* **2** used to show that someone is willing or ready to do something: *Dr. Weir will see you now.* | *The baby won't eat anything.* **3** used to ask someone to do something: *Will you stir the soup while I go downstairs?* **4 sth won't do sth** used to say that you cannot make a machine or other object do the thing that you want it to do: *The window won't open.* **5** used to give the result in CONDITIONAL sentences when the condition is in the present tense: *If Jeff loses his job, we'll have to move.* **6** used like "can" to show what is possible: *This car will seat five people comfortably.* **7** used to say what always happens in a particular situation or what is generally true: *A good doctor will make you feel relaxed.*

SPOKEN PHRASES

8 used to order or tell someone angrily to do something: *Will you two please stop fighting!* **9** used to offer something to someone or to invite them to do something: *Will you have some more tea?* | *Won't you stay for dinner?* **10** used like "must" to show what you think is likely to be true: *That'll be Ron now.* **11** used to describe someone's habits, especially when you find them strange or annoying: *Sometimes she'll even cut her toenails in the office.*

[**Origin:** Old English *wille*, from *wyllan* **to wish for, want, intend to**]

WORD CHOICE will, be going to

Use **will** when you talk about future plans that you make at the time you are speaking: *"Oops. I spilled my juice." "I'll go get a paper towel."* Use **be going to** when you have made the plans earlier: *I'm going to go to the library later. Do you want to come along?*

When you talk about what you think will happen in the future, you can use **will** or **be going to**. However, you usually use **be going to** when something in the present situation makes it very clear what will happen next, and **will** when you are not so sure: *Craig's going to be in big trouble when Mom finds out.* | *Marie will probably show up an hour late again.*

will[2] [W2] *n.*
1 DETERMINATION [C,U] determination to do something that you have decided to do, even if this is difficult: **the will to live/fight/succeed etc.** *It seems that Edith just lost the will to live.* | **a strong/an iron will** *Even as a baby, Joseph had a strong will.* | **a battle/clash/test/contest of wills** (=a situation in which two people who both have strong wills oppose each other) | *There isn't the **political will** for change.* → see also FREE WILL, STRONG-WILLED, WEAK-WILLED
2 LEGAL DOCUMENT [C] LAW a legal document that says who you want your money and property to be given to after you die: *Have you **made a will** yet?* | *Her father left her the entire estate **in his will**.*
3 WHAT SB WANTS [singular] what someone wants to happen in a particular situation: *I guess it's just God's will.* | **+of** *Congress is listening to the will of the people.* | *Anna was forced to marry him **against** her **will**.* | *I don't think the church has the right to **impose** its **will on** the rest of us* (=make us do what it wants).
4 at will whenever you want, and in whatever way you want: *He can't just hire and fire people at will, can he?*
5 where there's a will there's a way SPOKEN used to say that if you really want to do something, you will find a way to succeed
6 sth has a will of its own used to say that a machine or object is doing things that you do not want it to do: *This car **seems to have a will of its own**.*
7 a will of iron an extremely strong and determined character

will[3] *v.* **1** [T] to try to make something happen by thinking about it very hard: **will sb/sth to do sth** *I have willed myself to stop thinking about him.* **2 if you will a)** FORMAL used when choosing a word to describe something, which you think the person listening may not agree with, approve of, believe in etc.: *She possessed all sorts of secret wisdom, or magic, if you will.* **b)** SPOKEN, FORMAL used to ask someone politely to think about something, especially a particular situation: *Imagine, if you will, a frightened seven-year-old child.* **3** [T] LAW to officially give something that you own to someone else after you die: **will sth to sb** *Reid willed all his shares in the company to his wife.* **4 do what you will** FORMAL to do whatever you want: *Students can do what they will with their science education.* **5** [I,T] OLD USE to want something to happen

Wil·lard /ˈwɪlɚd/, **Em·ma** /ˈɛmə/ (1787–1870) a U.S. educator who started the first school in the U.S. that educated women to a level high enough for them to enter college

will ˈcall *n.* [U] the place, especially at a theater, where you can get the tickets you have already ordered

will·ful /ˈwɪlfəl/ *adj.* **1** continuing to do what you want, even after you have been told to stop: *a willful child* **2 willful damage/misconduct/neglect etc.** FORMAL OR LAW deliberate damage, bad behavior etc., when you know that what you are doing is wrong —**willfully** *adv.* —**willfulness** *n.* [U]

Wil·liam I /ˌwɪlyəm ðə ˈfɚst/ also **ˌWilliam the ˈConqueror** (1027–1087) the king of England from 1066 to 1087, who became England's first Norman king after defeating the Saxon King Harold

Wil·liams /ˈwɪlyəmz/, **Hank** /hæŋk/ (1923–1953) a U.S. singer and writer of COUNTRY AND WESTERN music

Williams, Ted /tɛd/ (1918–2002) a U.S. baseball player known for his skill as a BATTER

Williams, Wil·liam Car·los /ˈwɪlyəm ˈkɑrlous/ (1883–1963) a U.S. poet

wil·lies /ˈwɪliz/ *n.* SPOKEN **the willies** a nervous or

W

frightened feeling: *All this talk about dead people is **giving me the willies**.* → see also WET WILLIE

will·ing /ˈwɪlɪŋ/ S2 W2 *adj.* **1** prepared to do something, or having no reason to not want to do it OPP **unwilling**: **willing to do sth** *How much are they willing to pay?* | *I'm **perfectly willing** to wait here.* **2** eager to do something and not needing to be persuaded OPP **unwilling**: *willing participants in the experiment* —**willingness** *n.* [U] → see also **God willing** at GOD (13)

will·ing·ly /ˈwɪlɪŋli/ *adv.* without needing to be forced or persuaded, because you want to do something

ˈwill-o'-the-ˌwisp *n.* [C usually singular] someone that you can never completely depend on, or something that you can never achieve

wil·low /ˈwɪloʊ/ *n.* [C,U] a type of tree that has long thin branches and grows near water, or the wood from this tree

wil·low·y /ˈwɪloʊi/ *adj.* a willowy person, especially a woman, is tall, thin, and graceful

will·pow·er /ˈwɪlˌpaʊɚ/ *n.* [U] the ability to control your mind and body in order to achieve something that you want to do: *Losing weight is largely a matter of willpower.*

Wills (Moo·dy) /wɪlz ˈmudi/**, Hel·en** /ˈhɛlən/ (1905–1998) a U.S. tennis player, famous as the best woman player of the 1920s and 1930s

wil·ly-nil·ly /ˌwɪli ˈnɪli/ *adv.* **1** without planning, clear organization, or control: *Companies were accused of raising prices willy-nilly.* **2** if something happens willy-nilly, it happens whether you want it to or not [**Origin:** 1600–1700 *will I nill I* **(whether) I am willing (or) I am unwilling**; nill **to be unwilling** (11–19 centuries), from Old English *nyllan*]

Wil·son /ˈwɪlsən/**, Au·gust** /ˈɔgəst/ (1945–2005) an African-American writer of plays

Wilson, Ed·mund /ˈɛdmənd/ (1895–1972) a U.S. writer famous especially for his work as a CRITIC of literature

Wilson, Wood·row /ˈwʊdroʊ/ (1856–1924) the 28th President of the U.S.

wilt¹ /wɪlt/ *v.* [I] **1** BIOLOGY if a plant or flower wilts, it bends over because it is too dry or old **2** to feel weak, tired, or upset, especially because you are too hot

wilt² *v.* OLD USE **thou wilt** used to say "you will" when speaking to one person

wil·y /ˈwaɪli/ *adj. comparative* **wilier**, *superlative* **wiliest** good at getting what you want, especially by tricking people in a clever way: *a wily businessman*

wimp¹ /wɪmp/ *n.* [C] INFORMAL **1** someone who has a weak character and is too afraid to do something difficult **2** a man who is thin and physically weak —**wimpy** *adj.* —**wimpish** *adj.*

wimp² *v.*

wimp out *phr. v.* SPOKEN to not do something that you intended to do, because you do not feel brave enough, strong enough etc.

wim·ple /ˈwɪmpəl/ *n.* [C] a piece of cloth that a NUN wears over her head

win¹ /wɪn/ S1 W1 *v. past tense and past participle* **won** /wʌn/ **winning**

1 COMPETITION/RACE [I,T] to be the best or first in a competition, game, election etc.: *Who do you think is going to win?* | **+at** *I never win at tennis.* | **win a game/a race/an election etc.** *The Dodgers really need to win this game.* | **win a war/battle** *We need a military that is able to fight and win wars.* | **win a fight/an argument** *I could never win an argument with my father.* | *Jackson is expected to **win hands down*** (=win very easily). | **win by 10 points/40 votes etc.** *Harris won by 358 votes.*

THESAURUS

come in first to win a competition, game, etc.
be/come in first/second etc. place used to describe someone's position at the end of a race
be in the lead or **be ahead** to be winning at a particular time during the competition
the winning team/horse etc. the one that wins
If you are the **champion** or you **hold the record for something**, you are the person who has beaten all other people in a series of competitions.
→ BEAT

2 PRIZE [T] to earn a prize in a competition or game: *He won an Olympic gold medal.* | *How much money did she win?*

3 GET/ACHIEVE [T] to get or achieve something that you want because of your efforts or abilities: *The company has won a contract to build a new power plant.* | **win sb's approval/trust/love etc.** *Donahue has won the respect of his fellow workers.* | *To succeed, we must **win the hearts and minds of** the people* (=persuade them to support us).

4 MAKE SB GET STH [T] if something, usually something that you do, wins you something, you get it or win it because of that thing: **win sb sth** *That kind of behavior won't win you any friends.*

5 win the day to finally be successful in a discussion, argument, or competition, or to make it possible for someone to do this: *Common sense won the day, and the plans were dropped.*

SPOKEN PHRASES

6 you win used to agree to what someone wants after you have tried to persuade them to do or think something else: *OK, you win – we'll go to the movies.*
7 sb can't win used to say that there is no satisfactory way of dealing with a particular situation: *No matter what I do, I just can't win.*
8 you can't win 'em all also **you win some, you lose some** used to show sympathy when someone has had a disappointing experience

[**Origin:** Old English *winnan* **to work, fight**] → see also **win/capture/steal sb's heart** at HEART (15), WINNABLE, WINNER, WINNING

win sb/sth **↔ back** *phr. v.* to succeed in getting back someone or something that you had before: *How can I win back her trust?*

win out *phr. v.* to finally defeat or be considered more important than everyone or everything else, in spite of problems: **+over** *Style wins out over substance too often in Hollywood movies.*

win sb **↔ over** *phr. v.* to get someone's support or friendship by persuading them or being nice to them: *We'll be working hard to win over undecided voters.* | **win sb over to sth** *She's trying to win him over to her side.*

win² W3 *n.* [C] **1** a success or victory, especially in sports OPP **loss**: *We've had two wins so far this season.* | **+over/against** *Florida's 14–11 win over Cleveland* **2** a prize or amount of money that you win → see also NO-WIN, WIN-WIN

wince /wɪns/ *v.* [I] suddenly change the expression on your face as a reaction to something painful, upsetting, or embarrassing: *When he laughed, he winced with pain.* [**Origin:** 1200–1300 Old North French *wenchier* **to be impatient, move about suddenly**] —**wince** *n.* [singular]

winch¹ /wɪntʃ/ *n.* [C] a machine with a rope or chain for lifting heavy objects

winch² *v.* [T always + adv./prep.] to lift something or someone up using a winch

wind¹ /wɪnd/ S2 W2 *n.*

1 AIR [C,U] the air outside when it moves with a lot of force: *An icy **wind was blowing**.* | *A **gust of wind** rattled the window.* | ***The wind picked up*** (=it began to blow more strongly) *and dust began to swirl.* | *Let's wait till **the wind dies down*** (=it starts blowing less strongly). | **blow/sway/flap etc. in the wind** *She stood on the hill, her hair blowing in the wind.* | **strong/high/**

light/gentle etc. winds *The forecast is for strong winds and heavy rain.* | **a bitter/chill/biting etc. wind** (=a very cold wind) | **an east/a west/a north/a south wind** (=wind coming from the east etc.) → see also HEADWIND

THESAURUS

breeze a light wind
gust a sudden strong movement of wind
gale very strong wind
storm a period of bad weather when there is a lot of wind, rain, snow etc.
hurricane a violent storm with wind that is very strong and fast
tornado/cyclone an extremely violent storm consisting of air that spins very quickly and causes a lot of damage
typhoon a very strong tropical storm
→ RAIN, SNOW, WEATHER

2 get/catch wind of sth INFORMAL to hear or find out about something secret or private: *I hope the press doesn't get wind of this.*
3 take the wind out of sb's sails INFORMAL to make someone lose their confidence, especially by saying or doing something unexpected
4 see which way the wind blows/is blowing to find out what the situation is before you do something or make a decision
5 like the wind LITERARY moving very quickly: *She ran like the wind down the stairs to escape.*
6 sth is in the wind used to say that something is happening or going to happen, but not many people know what it is: *Talk of a merger was in the wind.*
7 the winds of change/freedom/opinion etc. events and changes that have started to happen and will have important effects, and that cannot be stopped
8 [U] also **the wind section, the winds** [plural] the part of an ORCHESTRA that consists of WIND INSTRUMENTS
9 have the wind at your back a) to be walking, moving etc. in the same direction as the wind **b)** to be in a favorable situation that helps you succeed
10 BREATH [U] your ability to breathe without difficulty: **knock the wind out of sb** (=to hit someone in the stomach so that they cannot breathe for a moment)
11 TALK [U] INFORMAL useless talk that does not mean anything
[**Origin:** Old English] → see also **break wind** at BREAK[1] (44), **second wind** at SECOND[1] (12), WINDED, WINDPIPE, WINDY

wind² *v.* [T] to make someone have difficulty breathing, as a result of running or being hit in the stomach → see also WINDED

wind³ /waɪnd/ S2 W2 *v. past tense and past participle* **wound** /waʊnd/ **1** [I always + adv./prep., T always + adv./prep.] to turn or twist something repeatedly around itself or something else, or to move around something in this way: **wind sth around sth** *Delia wound a piece of string around the box to keep it shut.* | **+around** *The snakes wound slowly around her arms.* **2** [T] to turn something such as a handle or part of a machine around and around, especially in order to make something move or start working SYN **wind up**: *I hate watches that you have to wind.* → see also WINDUP[2] **3** [I always + adv./prep., T always + adv./prep.] to move or exist along a course has many smooth bends and is usually very long: **+across/through/around etc.** *Highway 99 winds along the course.* | *The parade* ***wound its way*** *through the narrow streets.* → see also WINDING **4** to make a CASSETTE TAPE or VIDEOTAPE go backward or forward in order to hear or see what is on a different part of it → see also REWIND, UNWIND, WINDUP, WOUND UP
—**wind** *n.* [C]

wind down *phr. v.* **1 wind sth ↔ down** to gradually become slower, less active etc., or to make an activity do this: *The party started winding down after midnight.* **2** to rest and relax after a lot of hard work or excitement SYN **unwind**: *I find it difficult to wind down after a day at work.*

wind up *phr. v.* **1** INFORMAL to do something, go somewhere, become involved in something etc., without intending or wanting to: **+with/in/at etc.** *Patterson eventually wound up in jail.* | **wind up doing sth** *The company could wind up paying $50 million in losses.* | **wind up drunk/dead/sick etc.** *Tucker wound up homeless a year and a half ago.* **2 wind sth ↔ up** to turn part of a machine around several times, in order to make it move or start working: *She wound up the little car and let it go.* **3 wind sth ↔ up** to bring an activity, meeting etc. to an end: *Let's see if we can wind this up by 7.*

wind·bag /ˈwɪndbæg/ *n.* [C] INFORMAL, DISAPPROVING someone who talks too much and says nothing important

wind·blown /ˈwɪndbloʊn/, **wind-blown** *adj.* a windblown place or object is blown by the wind, or has been blown by it: *windblown hair*

wind·break /ˈwɪndbreɪk/ *n.* [C] a fence, line of trees, or wall that is intended to protect a place from the wind

wind break·er /ˈwɪndˌbreɪkɚ/ *n.* [C] a type of coat that is made specially to keep the wind out

wind·burn /ˈwɪndbɚn/ *n.* [C,U] the condition of having sore red skin because you were in the wind too long

wind·chill fac·tor /ˈwɪndtʃɪl ˌfæktɚ/ also **wind-chill** *n.* [U] the combination of cold weather and strong winds that makes the temperature seem colder

wind chime /ˈwɪnd tʃaɪm/ *n.* [C] long thin pieces of metal or glass hanging together in a group that make musical sounds when the wind blows

wind·ed /ˈwɪndɪd/ *adj.* unable to breathe easily, because you have been running or you have been hit in the stomach → see also LONG-WINDED

wind·fall /ˈwɪndfɔl/ *n.* [C] **1** an amount of money that you get unexpectedly: *a $2.2 billion windfall for shareholders* | **a windfall gain/profit etc.** (=a profit that you did not expect to make) **2** a piece of fruit that has fallen off a tree

Wind·hoek /ˈvɪnthʊk/ the capital and largest city of Namibia

wind·ing /ˈwaɪndɪŋ/ *adj.* having a twisting turning shape: *a winding creek* → see also WIND[3]

winding sheet /ˈwaɪndɪŋ ʃit/ *n.* [C] OLD USE a SHROUD

wind in·stru·ment /ˈwɪnd ˌɪnstrəmənt/ *n.* [C] a musical instrument that you play by blowing through it, such as a CLARINET

wind·jam·mer /ˈwɪndˌdʒæmɚ/ *n.* [C] a large sailing ship of the type that was used for trade in the 19th century

wind·lass /ˈwɪndləs/ *n.* [C] a machine for pulling or lifting heavy objects

wind·mill /ˈwɪndˌmɪl/ *n.* [C] a building or structure with parts that turn around in the wind, used for producing electrical power or crushing grain

win·dow /ˈwɪndoʊ/ S1 W1 *n.* [C]
1 BUILDING an opening in the wall of a building, car etc., covered with glass, that lets in light and can usually be opened to let in air: **open/close/shut a window** *Could you open a window?* | *Suddenly a strange face appeared* ***in the window*** (=on the other side of the window). | *I looked* ***out the window*** *and saw her car.* | **the bedroom/kitchen etc. window** *I was leaning out of the bedroom window.*
2 COMPUTER COMPUTERS one of the separate areas on a computer screen where information is shown
3 PERIOD OF TIME a short period of time that is available for a particular activity: *When I see* ***a window of opportunity****, I take advantage of it.*
4 ENVELOPE an area on an envelope with clear plastic in it which lets you see the address written on the letter inside
5 go out the window INFORMAL to disappear completely, or not have any effect anymore: *Any pretense of unity had gone out the window.*
6 throw/toss sth out the window to get rid of some-

W

thing completely or stop considering it so that it no longer has any effect
7 a window on the world a means of seeing and learning about the world
[**Origin:** 1200–1300 Old Norse *vindauga*, from *vindr* **wind** + *auga* **eye**]

'window box *n.* [C] a long narrow box in which you can grow plants outside your window

'window ˌcleaner *n.* **1** [C] a WINDOW WASHER **2** [U] a liquid used to clean windows

'window ˌdresser *n.* [C] someone whose job is to arrange goods attractively in store windows

'window ˌdressing *n.* [U] **1** something that is done to give people a favorable idea about your plans or activities, and to hide the true situation **2** the art of arranging goods in a shop window so that they look attractive to customers

win·dow·pane /'wɪndoʊˌpeɪn/ *n.* [U] a single whole piece of glass in a window

'window ˌseat *n.* [C] **1** a seat next to the window on a bus, airplane etc., as opposed to an AISLE SEAT **2** a seat built directly below a window

'window ˌshade *n.* [C] a SHADE

'window ˌshopping *n.* [U] the activity of looking at goods in store windows without intending to buy them —**window-shop** *v.* [I] —**window shopper** *n.* [C]

win·dow·sill /'wɪndoʊˌsɪl/ *n.* [C] a shelf that is attached to the bottom of a window

'window ˌwasher *n.* [C] someone whose job is to clean windows

wind·pipe /'wɪndpaɪp/ *n.* [C] NOT TECHNICAL the tube through which air passes from your mouth to your lungs SYN **trachea**

wind·screen /'wɪndskrin/ *n.* [C] BRITISH a WINDSHIELD

wind shear /'wɪnd ʃɪr/ *n.* [U] TECHNICAL a sudden change in the direction and speed of wind, which can make airplanes crash to the ground

W

wind·shield /'wɪndʃild/ *n.* [C] the large piece of glass or plastic, that you look through when driving a car, bus, MOTORCYCLE etc. → see picture on page A36

'windshield ˌwiper *n.* [C] a long thin piece of metal with a rubber edge that moves across a windshield to remove rain → see picture on page A36

wind·sock /'wɪndsɑk/ *n.* [C] a tube of material fastened to a pole at airports to show the direction of the wind

Wind·sor /'wɪnzɚ/ the name of the present British royal family

wind·storm /'wɪndstɔrm/ *n.* [C] a period of bad weather when there are strong winds but not much rain

wind·surf·ing /'wɪndˌsɚfɪŋ/ *n.* [U] the sport of sailing across water by standing on a board and holding on to a large sail —**windsurfer** *n.* [C] —**windsurf** *v.* [I]

wind·swept /'wɪndswɛpt/ *adj.* **1** a windswept place is often windy because there are not many trees or buildings to protect it **2** windswept hair, clothes etc. have been blown around by the wind

wind tun·nel /'wɪnd ˌtʌnl/ *n.* [C] a large enclosed passage where models of aircraft, cars etc. are tested by forcing air past them

wind tur·bine /'wɪnd ˌtɚbaɪn, -bɪn/ *n.* [C] a modern WINDMILL for providing electrical power

wind·up¹ /'waɪndʌp/, **wind-up** *n.* [C] **1** a series of actions that are intended to complete a process, meeting etc. **2** a series of movements a baseball PITCHER goes through before throwing the ball

windup², **wind-up** *adj.* [only before noun] a wind-up toy, clock etc. has a small KNOB on it that you twist in order to make it work

wind·ward /'wɪndwɚd/ *adj., adv.* toward the direction from which the wind is blowing OPP **leeward**

Wind·ward Is·lands, the /ˌwɪndwɚd 'aɪləndz/ a group of islands in the Caribbean Sea that includes Martinique, Grenada and St. Lucia

wind-whipped /'wɪnd wɪpt/ *adj.* a wind-whipped place or thing is blown very hard by the wind

wind·y /'wɪndi/ *adj. comparative* **windier**, *superlative* **windiest** **1** with a lot of wind blowing: *It's too cold and windy for hiking.* **2** getting a lot of wind: *a windy street* **3** windy talk is full of words that sound impressive but do not mean much —**windiness** *n.* [U]

wine¹ /waɪn/ S1 W2 *n.* [C,U] **1** an alcoholic drink made from GRAPES, or a particular type of this drink: *a glass of wine* | *a new Australian wine* | **red/white wine** *I'll have a white wine, please.* **2** an alcoholic drink made from another fruit or plant: *elderberry wine* [**Origin:** Old English *win*, from Latin *vinum*]

wine² *v.* [T] **wine and dine sb** to entertain someone well with a meal, wine etc.

'wine bar *n.* [C] a place that serves mainly wine and light meals

'wine ˌcellar *n.* [C] **1** a cool room, usually under the ground, where people keep their wine **2** a collection of wine

'wine ˌcooler *n.* [C] **1** a drink made with wine, fruit juice, and water **2** a special container that you put a bottle of wine into to make it cool

wine·glass /'waɪnglæs/ *n.* [C] a glass for wine with a base, a thin upright part, and a bowl-shaped top

'wine list *n.* [C] a list of wines that you can order in a restaurant

wine·mak·ing /'waɪnˌmeɪkɪŋ/ *n.* [U] the skill or business of making wine —**winemaker** *n.* [C]

win·er·y /'waɪnəri/ *n. plural* **wineries** [C] a place where wine is made and stored

'wine ˌtasting *n.* [C,U] the activity or skill of tasting different types of wine to find out which is good, or an occasion when this happens —**wine taster** *n.* [C]

'wine ˌvinegar *n.* [U] a type of VINEGAR made from sour wine, used in cooking

wing¹ /wɪŋ/ S3 W3 *n.* [C]
1 BIRDS/INSECTS a) BIOLOGY one of the parts of a bird's or insect's body that it uses for flying: *butterfly wings* | **sth flaps/beats its wings** *Two of the swans began flapping their wings and hissing.* | **sth spreads/stretches its wings** *The bug spread its wings and flew off.* **b)** the meat on the wing bone of a chicken, duck etc.: *spicy chicken wings* → see picture at BIRD
2 PLANE one of the large flat parts that stick out from the side of an airplane and help to keep it in the air
3 BUILDING one of the parts of a large building, especially one that sticks out from the main part: *a new children's wing at the hospital*
4 POLITICS a group of people within a political party or other organization who share a particular opinion or aim: *the most conservative wing of the Republican Party* → see also LEFT WING (1), RIGHT WING (1)
5 take sb under your wing to help and protect someone who is younger or less experienced than you are
6 (waiting) in the wings ready to take action or ready to be used when the time is right: *There's no one waiting in the wings who can take over if Gibson resigns.*
7 the wings [plural] the parts at either side of a stage where the actors are hidden from people watching the play
8 on a wing and a prayer without preparation, but still hoping that everything will work out all right
9 take wing LITERARY **a)** if an idea or plan takes wing, it starts developing quickly and successfully **b)** to fly away
10 be on the wing LITERARY if a bird is on the wing, it is flying
11 SPORTS a) the far left or right part of the field or playing area in games like HOCKEY or SOCCER **b)** the position of someone who plays in this area SYN **winger**

12 get your wings to pass the necessary flying examinations and become a pilot → see also **clip sb's wings** at CLIP² (6), **spread your wings** at SPREAD¹ (17)

wing² *v.* **1 wing it** INFORMAL to do something without planning or preparation: *I don't have time to write a speech, so I'm just going to wing it.* **2** [I always + adv./prep., T always + adv./prep.] LITERARY to fly somewhere: *A flock of pelicans was **winging its way** down the coastline.* **3** [T] INFORMAL to wound a person or bird in the arm or wing, especially with a gun shot

'wing chair *n.* [C] a comfortable chair that has a high back and pieces pointing forward on each side where you can rest your head

'wing ˌcollar *n.* [C] a type of shirt collar for men that is worn with very formal clothes

wing·ding /ˈwɪŋdɪŋ/ *n.* [C] OLD-FASHIONED, INFORMAL a party

winged /wɪŋd/ *adj.* having wings: *winged insects*

wing·er /ˈwɪŋɚ/ *n.* [C] **1 a right-winger/left-winger** someone who belongs to the RIGHT WING or LEFT WING of a political group **2** someone who plays on a WING

'wing nut *n.* [C] a NUT for fastening things that has sides that stick out to make it easier to turn

wing·span /ˈwɪŋspæn/ also **wing·spread** /ˈwɪŋsprɛd/ *n.* [C] the distance from the end of one wing of a bird, an airplane etc. to the end of the other

wing·tip /ˈwɪŋtɪp/ *n.* [C] **1** a type of man's shoe with a pattern of small holes on the toe **2** the point at the end of a bird's or an airplane's wing

wink¹ /wɪŋk/ *v.* **1** [I,T] to close and open one eye quickly, usually to communicate amusement or a secret message: **+at** *The woman winked at me and smiled.* **2** [I] to shine with a light that flashes on and off SYN **blink**

wink at sth *phr. v.* to pretend not to notice something bad or illegal, in a way that suggests you approve of it: *Authorities have been winking at the health code violations for years.*

wink² *n.* **1** [C] a quick action of opening and closing of your eye, usually as a signal to someone else: *"How are you girls?" Tom asked with a wink.* **2 not sleep a wink** also **not get a wink of sleep** to not be able to sleep at all → see also **forty winks** at FORTY (5), **quick as a wink** at QUICK³ (2)

win·less /ˈwɪnlɪs/ *adj.* not having won any games

win·na·ble /ˈwɪnəbəl/ *adj.* a winnable game, CONTEST, election etc. can be won

Win·ne·ba·go /ˌwɪnəˈbeɪgoʊ/ a Native American tribe from the Great Lakes area of the U.S.

win·ner /ˈwɪnɚ/ W2 *n.* [C] **1** someone who wins a competition, game, election etc.: *The winner will receive a prize of $500.* | *a Grammy winner* | **+of** *the winner of the tournament* **2** INFORMAL someone or something that is likely to be very successful: *I'm not very good at **picking winners** in the stock market.* **3** the person or group that gains the most advantages in a situation: ***The real winners** in the airline price war are the consumers.*

'winner's ˌcircle *n.* **the winner's circle a)** an area at a RACETRACK where a horse and its rider are taken after winning a race **b)** INFORMAL the state of having won a CONTEST or a race

win·ning /ˈwɪnɪŋ/ *adj.* [only before noun] **1 a winning score/strategy/combination etc.** a SCORE, plan etc. that makes you win something or be successful: *a winning time of 9.86 seconds* **2 a winning team/quarterback/coach etc.** a team, player etc. that wins many games **3 a winning record/season/streak etc.** a period of time during which you win more games, competitions etc. than you lose **4 a winning smile/personality etc.** an attractive smile, way of behaving etc. that makes people like you → see also PRIZE-WINNING

win·ning·est /ˈwɪnɪŋɪst/ *adj.* INFORMAL **the winningest team/pitcher/coach etc. (in sth)** used in sports writing to describe the team, player etc. that has won the most games

win·nings /ˈwɪnɪŋz/ *n.* [plural] money that you win in a game or by GAMBLING: *lottery winnings*

win·now /ˈwɪnoʊ/ *v.* **1** [I,T] also **winnow down** to become smaller, or to make a list, group, or quantity do this, by getting rid of the parts that you do not need or want **2** [I,T] to separate the CHAFF (=outer part) from grain

winnow sth ↔ **out** *phr. v.* to get rid of the parts of something that you do not need or want

win·o /ˈwaɪnoʊ/ *n. plural* **winos** [C] INFORMAL someone who drinks a lot of cheap alcohol and lives on the streets

win·some /ˈwɪnsəm/ *adj.* LITERARY pleasant and attractive, especially in a simple, direct way: *a winsome smile*

win·ter¹ /ˈwɪntɚ/ S2 W2 *n.* [C,U] the season between fall and spring when the weather is coldest: *Does it snow here much **in the winter**?* | *We might go to Mexico **this winter**.* | **last winter/next winter** (=the winter before or after this one) | **a mild/severe/harsh etc. winter** *He missed Arizona's mild winters.* | **winter coat/shoes/gloves etc.** (=clothes that are designed for cold weather) [**Origin:** Old English]

winter² *v.* [I always + adv./prep.] to spend the winter somewhere

win·ter·green /ˈwɪntɚˌgrin/ *n.* [U] an EVERGREEN plant with pleasant smelling leaves, or the oil made from them

ˌwinter 'home *n.* [C] a house you live in only in the winter → see also SUMMER HOME

win·ter·ize /ˈwɪntəˌraɪz/ *v.* [T] to prepare your car, house etc. for winter conditions

ˌwinter 'solstice *n.* [singular] the shortest day of the year, which in the NORTHERN HEMISPHERE (=top half of the earth) is around December 22nd

'winter ˌsports *n.* [plural] sports that take place on snow or ice

win·ter·time /ˈwɪntɚˌtaɪm/ *n.* [U] the time of year when it is winter

win·try /ˈwɪntri/ also **win·ter·y** /ˈwɪntəri/ *adj.* like winter, or typical of winter, especially because it is cold: *a wintry February morning*

ˌwin-'win *adj.* [only before noun] used to describe a situation, agreement etc. that will end well for everyone involved in it: *a win-win situation* → see also NO-WIN

wipe¹ /waɪp/ S2 W3 *v.*

1 CLEAN/RUB [T] also **wipe off a)** to rub a surface with a cloth in order to remove dirt, liquid etc.: *Ask the waitress to wipe off the table.* | **wipe sth with sth** *She wiped her mouth with her sleeve.* | *Bill **wiped his eyes** (=wiped the tears from his face) and apologized.* **b)** to clean something by rubbing it against a surface: *Wipe your feet before you come in.* ▶see THESAURUS box at **clean²**

2 REMOVE DIRT [T always + adv./prep.] to remove liquid, dirt, or marks by wiping: **wipe sth off/from etc.** *Let me wipe that mustard off your cheek.*

3 wipe the slate clean to decide to forget about mistakes or arguments that happened in the past

4 wipe the smile/grin off sb's face INFORMAL to make someone less pleased or satisfied, especially someone who is annoying because they think they are smart

5 PLATES [I,T] to dry plates, cups etc that have been washed: *You wash, I'll wipe.*

6 COMPUTER/TAPE [T] to remove all the information that is stored on a TAPE, VIDEO, or computer DISK

7 wipe the floor with sb INFORMAL to defeat someone completely in a competition or argument

8 wipe sth off the face of the earth also **wipe sth off the map** to destroy something completely so that it does not exist anymore: *Heavy bombing virtually wiped the city off the map.*

9 wipe sth out of your mind/memory also **wipe sth from your mind/memory** to forget an unhappy or upsetting experience

[**Origin:** Old English *wipian*]

W

wipe sth ↔ **away** *phr. v.* to make something stop or go away: *The sound of his voice wiped her smile away.*

wipe sth ↔ **down** *phr. v.* to completely clean a surface using a wet cloth

wipe out *phr. v.* **1 wipe sb/sth ↔ out** to destroy, kill, remove, or get rid of someone or something completely: *Whole villages were wiped out by the floods.* **2 wipe sb ↔ out** INFORMAL to make you feel extremely tired: *Standing on my feet all day really wipes me out.* → see also WIPED OUT **3** SPOKEN to fall or hit another object when driving a car, bicycle etc.: *Scott wiped out on his bike.* **4 wipe sb ↔ out** to make someone lose all of their money

wipe sth ↔ **up** *phr. v.* to remove liquid from a surface using a cloth: *Quick. Get something to wipe up the milk.*

wipe² *n.* [C] **1** a wiping movement with a cloth **2** a special piece of wet material that you use to clean something and then throw away: *antiseptic wipes*

ˌwiped ˈout *adj.* [not before noun] SPOKEN extremely tired SYN **exhausted**

wip·er /ˈwaɪpɚ/ *n.* [C] a WINDSHIELD WIPER

wire¹ /waɪɚ/ S2 W3 *n.*

1 THIN METAL [U] metal in the form of a long thin thread: *The cable is made of many twisted strands of copper wire.*

2 ELECTRICITY/PHONES a) [C] a long thin piece of metal that carries electrical currents or telephone signals: *a telephone wire* **b) by wire** using wires that are connected together: *The signals are sent by wire.*

3 under the wire if something is done under the wire, it is done just before it must be finished: *They got the proposal in just under the wire.*

4 get your wires crossed to become confused about what someone is saying because you think they are talking about something else: *We got our wires crossed and I waited for an hour in the wrong place.*

5 RECORDING EQUIPMENT [C] a piece of electronic recording equipment, usually worn secretly on someone's clothes

6 MESSAGE [C] a TELEGRAM

7 NEWS [U] an electronic system, used by some news organizations, for sending news stories to many different places at once: *wire reports* | *This story just came over the wire.*

[**Origin:** Old English *wir*] → see also CHICKEN WIRE, **go/come/be down to the wire** at DOWN¹ (19), LIVE WIRE, WIRE SERVICE, WIRY

wire² S3 *v.* [T]

1 ELECTRICITY also **wire up** to connect the wires inside a building or a piece of equipment so that electricity can pass through: *The electrician is coming to wire the house tomorrow.* | *Check that the plug has been wired correctly.*

2 ELECTRICAL EQUIPMENT also **wire up** to connect electrical equipment to the electrical system using wires: *The microphone is wired to a loudspeaker.*

3 MONEY to send money electronically: *Could you wire me $50?*

4 FASTEN to fasten two or more things together using wire: *Tracy had to have her jaw wired shut.*

5 RECORDING EQUIPMENT to attach a secret piece of recording equipment to a person or a room

6 MESSAGE to send a TELEGRAM to someone → see also WIRING

ˈwire ˌcutters *n.* [plural] a special tool like very strong scissors, used for cutting wire

wired /waɪɚd/ *adj.* **1** also **wired up** SPOKEN feeling very active, excited, and awake: *I was so wired I couldn't sleep.* **2 be wired for sth** to have the necessary wires and connections for an electrical system to work: *All the rooms are wired for cable TV.* **3** INFORMAL connected to and able to use the Internet → see also HARD-WIRED

ˌwire-ˈhaired *adj.* a wire-haired dog has fur that is stiff not soft

wire·less¹ /ˈwaɪɚlɪs/ *adj.* relating to a system of communication that does not use electrical or telephone wires: *wireless Internet connections*

wireless² *n.* [C,U] OLD-FASHIONED a radio

ˈwire-rimmed also **ˈwire-rim** *adj.* wire-rimmed GLASSES have a thin piece of metal like wire around the part that you look through

ˈwire ˌservice *n.* [C] a business that collects news stories and sends it to newspapers, radio stations etc. electronically

wire·tap /ˈwaɪɚˌtæp/ *n.* [C] an action of secretly listening to other people's telephone conversations, by attaching something to the wires of their telephone —**wiretap** *v.* [T] —**wiretapping** *n.* [U]

ˈwire ˌtransfer *n.* [C] an action of sending money from one bank to another electronically

wir·ing /ˈwaɪərɪŋ/ *n.* [singular] **1** the network of wires that form the electrical system in a building, vehicle, or piece of equipment: *faulty wiring* **2** a length of wire that is used for making a network for electricity: *copper wiring*

wir·y /ˈwaɪəri/ *adj.* **1** thin but with strong muscles **2** wiry hair is stiff and curly ▶see THESAURUS box at **hair**

Wis·con·sin /wɪsˈkɑnsɪn/ WRITTEN ABBREVIATION **WI** a state in the Midwestern area of the U.S.

wis·dom /ˈwɪzdəm/ W3 *n.* [U] **1** good judgment and the ability to make wise decisions: *an old man of great wisdom* → see also WISE **2** all the knowledge that a society or group has, especially gained over a long period of time: **conventional/received/traditional wisdom** *These findings challenge the received wisdom.* | **collective/collected wisdom** *the collected wisdom of many centuries* **3 the wisdom of (doing) sth** how sensible something is: *He was beginning to question the wisdom of contacting Gail.* **4 in sb's (infinite) wisdom** used to say in a joking way that you do not understand why someone, especially someone in authority, has decided to do something: *The board, in its infinite wisdom, has decided to give Waters back his job.* **5 a pearl/word of wisdom** a very wise remark

Wisdom of Sol·o·mon /ˌwɪzdəm əv ˈsɑləmən/ a book in the Apocrypha of the Protestant Bible

ˈwisdom tooth *n.* [C] BIOLOGY one of the four large teeth at the back of your mouth that do not grow until you are an adult

wise¹ /waɪz/ S3 *adj.*

1 DECISION/IDEA ETC. wise decisions and judgments are based on intelligent thinking and experience: **it is wise to do sth** *It's wise to start saving money now for your retirement.* | **be wise to do sth** *She was wise not to accept the job.* | *I don't think leaving school would be a **wise move**.*

2 PERSON someone who is wise makes good decisions, gives good advice etc., especially because they have a lot of experience in life: *a wise old man* | *When you're **older and wiser**, you'll understand.* | *The little girl was **wise beyond** her **years*** (=wiser than most people her age). ▶see THESAURUS box at **intelligent**

3 sb is none the wiser also **no one is the wiser** INFORMAL used to say that someone does not find out about something bad someone else has done: *We replaced the broken vase, and Mom was none the wiser.*

4 wise to sb/sth INFORMAL realizing that someone is doing something bad, especially being dishonest: *I'm wise to all his tricks.*

5 wise in the ways of sth having a lot of knowledge about how something works

[**Origin:** Old English *wis*] —**wisely** *adv.*: *I try to use my time wisely.* → see also STREETWISE, WISDOM

wise² *v.*

wise up *phr. v.* INFORMAL to realize the truth about a bad situation and start behaving differently because of it: **wise up to sth** *Consumers need to wise up to the effect advertising has on them.*

-wise /waɪz/ *suffix* **1 pricewise/timewise etc.** also **price-wise/time-wise etc.** INFORMAL used to talk about how a situation changes or is affected in relation to prices, time etc.: *Security-wise they've made a lot of*

W

improvements. **2 crosswise/lengthwise etc.** in a direction across something, along the length of something etc.: *Cut each tomato crosswise.* → see also CLOCKWISE, COUNTERCLOCKWISE

Wise /waɪz/, **I·saac May·er** /ˈaɪzək ˈmaɪɚ/ (1819–1900) a U.S. religious leader who united Reform Jewish groups in the U.S.

wise·a·cre /ˈwaɪzˌeɪkɚ/ *n.* [C] OLD-FASHIONED someone who says or does annoying things, especially to make themselves seem smarter than other people

wise·crack /ˈwaɪzkræk/ *n.* [C] a clever funny remark or reply ▸see THESAURUS box at **joke**[1] **—wisecrack** *v.* [I] **—wisecracking** *adj.*: *a wisecracking talk show host*

ˈwise guy *n.* [C] INFORMAL **1** someone who says or does annoying things, especially to make themselves seem smarter than other people **2** also **wiseguy** someone who is involved in the MAFIA

wish[1] /wɪʃ/ S1 W2 *v.*

1 HOPE FOR STH [T] to want something to be true, to happen, or to have happened, even though you know this is impossible or very unlikely: **wish (that)** *I wish I didn't have to go to school.* | *Afterward, she wished she hadn't said anything.* | ***I wish I could remember*** (=said when you are trying to remember) *his name.*

2 HAPPINESS/LUCK ETC. [T] to say that you hope someone will have good luck, a happy life etc.: **wish sb sth** *She called to wish me a happy birthday.* | *Wish me luck!* | *They **wished me well*** (=said that they hope that good things will happen to me) *in my new job.*

3 WANT [I,T] FORMAL used in formal situations to say that you want to do something: **wish to do sth** *Do you wish to make a complaint?* | *You may leave now **if you wish**.*

SPOKEN PHRASES

4 I wish sb would do sth used to say that you want someone to do something or stop doing something that annoys you: *I wish you'd hurry!* | *I wish she'd shut up!*

5 I wish! used to say that something is not true, but you wish it was: *"I think he really likes you." "I wish!"*

6 you wish! used to tell someone that something is definitely not true or definitely won't happen, even though they might wish it: *"Mine is better than yours." "You wish!"*

7 wouldn't wish sth on anyone/anybody also **wouldn't wish sth on your worst enemy** used to say that you do not like something you have to do, and you would not want anyone else to have to do it

[**Origin:** Old English *wyscan*]

WORD CHOICE wish, want

In sentences where both can be used, **wish** sounds much more formal than **want.** In a conversation, you might say: *I want to go the store.* In a formal letter, you might write: *I wish to express my dissatisfaction with your service.*

wish sth ↔ **away** *phr. v.* to make something bad or difficult stop just by hoping it will stop: *You can't just wish your problems away, you know!*

wish for sth *phr. v.* **1** to want something to happen or want to have something, especially when it seems unlikely or impossible: *When I was little, I used to wish for an older sister.* **2** to silently ask for something you want and hope that it will happen by magic or good luck **3 be careful what you wish for (it might come true)** used to say that you should think carefully about the changes you want in your life because they might not make you any happier

wish[2] *n.* [C] **1** a feeling that you want to do or have something, or the thing that you want to do or have: **a wish to do sth** *Both sides expressed a wish to reach an agreement.* | *The couple married **against** their families' **wishes*** (=although their families did not want them to). | *It's important to **respect** the patient's **wishes*** (=do what they want). | *Ken finally **got** his **wish** to live in the country.* | **sb's one/only/greatest etc. wish** *His one wish was to see his homeland again.* | **sb's last/dying wish** (=something that you say you want just before you die) | **sb's wish is granted/fulfilled** (=someone gets what they want) **2** a silent request for something to happen as if by magic: *Close your eyes and **make a wish**.* | *The wizard promised to **grant** her **wish**.* | *If you say what it is, your **wish** won't **come true**.* **3 your wish is my command** HUMOROUS used to say that you will do whatever someone asks you to do **4 have no wish to do sth, have no wish for sth** FORMAL used to emphasize that you do not want or intend to do something SYN **desire**: *I have no wish to offend anybody.* → see also **best wishes** at BEST[1] (4)

wish·bone /ˈwɪʃboʊn/ *n.* [C] the breast bone from a cooked chicken or other bird, which two people pull apart to decide whose wish will come true

ˌwishful ˈthinking *n.* [U] the wish to have something or have something happen that is impossible to get or that will not happen

ˈwishing well *n.* [C] a WELL or pool of water that people throw coins into while making a wish

ˈwish list *n.* [C] INFORMAL all the things that you would like to get or have happen

wish·y-wash·y /ˈwɪʃi ˌwɑʃi, -ˌwɔʃi/ *adj.* DISAPPROVING **1** a wishy-washy person does not have firm or clear ideas and seems unable to decide what they want **2** a wishy-washy color is pale, boring, and not bright

wisp /wɪsp/ *n.* [C] **1 a wisp of hair/hay/grass etc.** a thin piece of hair etc. that is separate from the rest **2 a wisp of smoke/steam/incense etc.** a small thin line of smoke, steam etc. that rises up → see also WILL-O'-THE-WISP **—wispy** *adj.*

wis·ter·i·a /wɪˈstɪriə/ *n.* [C,U] a climbing plant with purple or white flowers

wist·ful /ˈwɪstfəl/ *adj.* feeling a little sad, especially because you are thinking of something that you would like but cannot have: *a wistful sigh* [**Origin:** 1600–1700 *wistly* **with close attention** (15–18 centuries)] **—wistfully** *adv.* **—wistfulness** *n.* [U]

wit /wɪt/ *n.* **1** [U] the ability to say things that are clever and amusing: *People love him for his wit and charm.* | *Kelly is known for his **quick wit**.* **2 wits** [plural] your ability to think quickly and make the right decisions: *He had to rely on his wits to survive.* | *A surgeon needs **quick wits** and physical dexterity.* | **keep/have your wits about you** (=be ready to think quickly and do what is necessary in a difficult situation) **3** [C] someone who has the ability to say things that are clever and amusing **4 scare/frighten sb out of their wits** INFORMAL to frighten someone very much **5 be at your wits' end** to be very upset because you have not been able to solve a problem even though you have tried very hard: *I'm at my wits' end trying to fix this computer.* **6 collect/gather your wits** make yourself think about what you are going to do next after you have been surprised by something **7 match wits with/against sb** to use all of your intelligence to try to defeat someone or solve a problem **8 to wit** LITERARY used to give more information that makes it clear exactly what or who you are talking about SYN **namely** → see also **a battle of wits** at BATTLE[1] (6), HALF-WIT, **live by your wits** at LIVE[1] (6), OUTWIT, QUICK-WITTED, WITLESS, WITTY

witch /wɪtʃ/ *n.* [C] **1** a woman in stories who has magic powers, especially an old ugly woman who uses her powers to do bad things → see also WIZARD: *a wicked witch* **2** a woman who people believe has magic powers, especially to do bad things: *She was accused of being a witch.* **3** INFORMAL an insulting word for a woman who is old or not nice → see also BEWITCHED

witch·craft /ˈwɪtʃkræft/ *n.* [U] the use of magic to make things happen

ˈwitch-ˌdoctor *n.* [C] a man who is believed to have magic powers and the ability to cure people of diseases, especially in some parts of Africa

ˈwitch-ˌhazel *n.* [C,U] a substance used for treating small wounds on the skin, or the tree that produces it

ˈwitch-hunt *n.* [C] a deliberate attempt, often based on false information, to find and punish people in a soci-

W

ety or organization whose opinions are considered wrong or dangerous: *a political witch-hunt*

'witching ˌhour *n.* **the witching hour** LITERARY the time in the middle of the night, usually midnight, when strange or magic things are believed to happen

Wite-out /'waɪtaʊt/ *n.* [U] TRADEMARK white liquid that is used to cover mistakes in writing, typing (TYPE) etc.

with /wɪθ, wɪð/ S1 W1 *prep.* **1** together in the same place or at the same time: *She went out to lunch with Jimmy.* | *I always wear these shoes with this dress.* **2** having a particular feature, quality, or possession: *a book with a green cover* | *people with a lot of money* **3** carrying or wearing something: *She came back with a letter in her hand.* | **have/bring/take sth with you** *Did you bring your passport with you?* **4** using something, or by means of something: *Stop eating with your fingers.* | *You can fix it with a screwdriver.* **5** involved in the same activity as someone else: *I used to play chess with him.* | *Discuss the problem with your teacher.* **6** against or opposing someone: *I'm tired of you two arguing with each other.* **7** including something else: *The meal comes with fries and a drink.* **8** used to say what fills or covers something: *Her boots were covered with mud.* | *Fill the bowl with sugar.* **9** used to say what an action or situation is related to: *What's wrong with the radio?* | *Be careful with that glass.* **10** used to say who or what a feeling or attitude relates to: *He's in love with you.* | *We're very pleased with your progress.* **11** because of a particular feeling or physical state: *They were trembling with fear.* | *Mother became seriously ill with pneumonia.* **12** used to give information about the way something happens or is done: *He prepared everything with great care.* | *The rocket exploded with a blinding flash.* **13** used to say what position or state someone or something is in, or what is happening, when someone does something: *She was standing with her back to me.* | *He was sitting in his room with music blaring.* **14** as a result of something, and often at the same time or rate as it: *The wine improves with age.* **15** supporting or liking someone or something: *I agree with what you said.* | *You're either with me or against me.* **16** used to mention one of the things or people involved in a comparison: *Compared with other schools, the salaries here are very low.* **17** in the same direction as someone or something OPP **against**: *It's easier to run with the wind.* **18** used to introduce a particular situation that is happening, and show how it affects something: *With the kids at school, I have more time for my hobbies.* **19** used to say who is taking care of something or someone: *The kids are with my parents this weekend.* **20** employed by someone: *She's been with the company for 17 years.* **21** in spite of something: *With all his faults, I still love him.* **22 be with sb** INFORMAL to understand someone's explanation about something: *Go ahead and continue the story – I'm with you.* **23** used in some expressions to show the idea of separating from something, or of getting rid of something: *I'm reluctant to part with the money.* | *It was a complete break with tradition.* **24 (and) with that** used to say that something happens immediately after something else: *He gave a little wave and with that he was gone.* **25** SPOKEN used in some phrases to show the object of a strong wish or command: *Down with racism!* [**Origin:** Old English **against, from, with**]

with·al /wɪð'ɔl, -wɪθ-/ *adv.* OLD USE in addition to this SYN **besides**

with·draw /wɪθ'drɔ, wɪð-/ W3 *v. past tense* **withdrew** /-'dru/ *past participle* **withdrawn** /-'drɔn/

1 MONEY [T] to take money out of a bank account: **withdraw sth from sth** *I'd like to withdraw $500 from my savings account.*

2 STOP GIVING SUPPORT/MONEY [T] to stop giving money or support to someone or something, especially because of an official decision: *The board is likely to withdraw funding for the project.* | *The U.S. decided to* ***withdraw*** *its* ***support*** *from the rebel government.*

3 FROM ACTIVITY/ORGANIZATION [I,T] to stop taking part in an activity, belonging to an organization etc., or to make someone stop doing this: **+from** *A knee injury forced her to withdraw from the tournament.* | **withdraw sth/sb from sth** *Several parents have withdrawn their children from the school.*

4 OFFER/THREAT ETC. [T] if you withdraw an offer, threat, request etc., you say that you will not now do what you said, or no longer want to do it: *The developers withdrew their request to build on the land.* | **withdraw sth from sth** *Franks has withdrawn his name from consideration for the job.*

5 PRODUCT/SERVICE [T] if a company, organization etc. withdraws a product or service, it no longer offers it for sale or use: *The drug has been* ***withdrawn from the market*** (=stores have stopped selling it) *for further tests.*

6 withdraw a remark/accusation/statement to say that a remark that you made earlier was not correct or true: *Mr. Dryden was asked to withdraw the remark and to apologize.*

7 STOP COMMUNICATING [I] to become quieter, less friendly, and more concerned about your own thoughts: **+from/into** *Ralph has withdrawn from other kids in the class.* → see also WITHDRAWN

8 REMOVE STH [T] FORMAL to remove something from a particular place: **withdraw sth from sth** *He carefully withdrew the letter from the envelope.*

9 LEAVE A PLACE a) [I,T] if an army withdraws or is withdrawn, it leaves a place, especially in order to avoid defeat: **+from/to** *The rebels withdrew to their stronghold in the mountains.* **b)** [I] FORMAL to leave a place, especially in order to be alone or go somewhere quiet

with·draw·al /wɪθ'drɔəl/ *n.*

1 MONEY [C,U] the act of taking money from a bank account, or the amount you take out: *I would like to* ***make a withdrawal*** *from my savings account.*

2 ARMY [C,U] the act of moving an army, weapons etc. away from the area where they were fighting: **+of/from** *The Navy is considering a withdrawal of ships from the area.*

3 OF A SUPPORT/SERVICE ETC. [U] the act of ending or taking away something such as support, an offer, or a service: **+of** *a withdrawal of government aid*

4 ACTIVITY/ORGANIZATION [U] the act of ending your part in an activity or organization: **+from** *the rebels' withdrawal from peace negotiations*

5 DRUGS [U] the period after you have given up a drug that you were dependent on, and the mental and physical effects that this process involves: *the physical effects of withdrawal* | *withdrawal symptoms*

6 STATEMENT [U] the act of saying that something you previously said was not correct or true: **+of** *the withdrawal of all allegations*

7 BEHAVIOR [U] behavior in which someone does not want to talk to or be with other people, which is often a sign of something wrong

with·drawn /wɪθ'drɔn/ *adj.* very shy and quiet, and concerned only about your own thoughts

with·drew /wɪθ'dru/ the past tense of WITHDRAW

with·er /'wɪðɚ/ also **wither away** *v.* [I,T] if a plant withers it becomes drier and smaller and starts to die

with·ered /'wɪðɚd/ *adj.* **1** BIOLOGY a withered plant has become drier and smaller and is dead or dying **2** a withered person looks thin and weak and old **3** MEDICINE a withered arm or leg has not developed correctly and is thin and weak

with·er·ing /'wɪðərɪŋ/ *adj.* **a withering look/remark etc.** a look, remark etc. that makes someone feel stupid, embarrassed, or lose confidence —**witheringly** *adv.*

with·ers /'wɪðɚz/ *n.* [plural] BIOLOGY the highest part of a horse's back, above its shoulders

with·hold /wɪθ'hoʊld, wɪð-/ *v. past tense and past participle* **withheld** /-'hɛld/ [T] to refuse to let someone have something, especially until something else is done: **withhold sth from sb** *Johnson was accused of withholding information from the police.*

with·hold·ing /wɪθ'hoʊldɪŋ, wɪð-/ *n.* [U] ECONOMICS when tax payments are taken away from your salary before you receive it

with'holding ˌtax *n.* [C,U] ECONOMICS money that is taken out of your pay as tax

with·in¹ /wɪð'ɪn, wɪθ-/ S1 W1 *prep.* **1 a)** before a certain period of time has passed: *The job will be finished within a week.* | **within an hour/10 minutes etc. of sth** *Within an hour of our arrival, Caroline was starting to complain.* **b)** during a certain period of time: *Her car has been broken into three times within a month.* | **within the space of a year/month etc.** *Within the space of five days, the fire destroyed over 4,000 acres.* **2** inside a certain area and not beyond it: *Hunting is not permitted within the park.* | *Cigarette advertising is not allowed* ***within*** *1,000 feet* ***of*** (=in an area that is less than 1,000 feet from) *schools.* **3** inside a society, organization, or group of people: *changes within the department* **4** according to particular limits or rules: *We have to operate within the law.* | *Are these expenses within our budget?* | *You can go anywhere you want,* ***within reason.*** **5 within sight/earshot etc.** if someone or something is within sight, earshot etc. you can see or hear them **6 within reach a)** if something you want to achieve is within reach, it is possible to do it: *The dream of owning a house is not within reach for many Americans.* **b)** near enough to be picked up or touched when you stretch out your hand: *I always have my cell phone within reach.* **c)** near, so that people can get there without difficulty: *Lake Tahoe is* ***within easy reach*** *of Bay Area residents.* **7 to within sth** used to emphasize how close in amount, degree, or time one thing is to another: *The clock is accurate to within 1/20th of a second.* **8** FORMAL about someone's body or mind as the place where feelings, thoughts, and personal qualities exist: *She felt a stab of pain deep within her.*

within² *adv.* FORMAL inside a room, building etc.: *The sign read, "Rooms for rent. Enquire within."*

within³ *n.* **from within a)** used to talk about actions and feelings of people who are inside a society, organization, or group: *They want to reform the system from within.* **b)** LITERARY used to talk about someone's mental qualities or character, rather than their appearance or what happens to them

with-it, with it *adj.* **1** feeling full of energy and able to understand things easily **2** fashionable and modern in the way that you dress, think etc.

with·out¹ /wɪð'aʊt, wɪθ-/ S1 W1 *prep.* **1** lacking something, especially something that is basic or necessary: *After the storm, we were without electricity for five days.* | *a book without a cover* **2** not doing, having, or having done something when you do something else or something else happens: *He had gone out without his parents' permission.* | *Without any warning, he started shooting at us.* | *This time Clark finished the race without falling.* | **without doing sth** *For 50 years, she did her job without complaining.* **3 without so much as...** used to talk about something you think someone should have done: *He left without so much as a word of thanks.* **4** not being with someone, or not having them to help you, especially someone you like or need: *I don't know what I would do without Lisa.* **5** not feeling or showing that you feel a particular emotion: *He told his story without anger or bitterness.* **6** OLD USE outside something

without² *adv.* **1** LITERARY outside a room, building, or area **2** not having something, especially something that is basic or necessary: **do/manage/go without** *The stores are closed, so we'll have to do without.*

without³ *n.* **from without a)** from outside a country, area, or group of people **b)** used to talk about things that are done to you by other people, rather than things that you think or feel yourself

with·stand /wɪθ'stænd, wɪð-/ *v. past tense and past participle* **withstood** /-'stʊd/ [T] **1** to be strong enough to remain unharmed by something such as great heat or cold, great pressure etc.: *The bridge can withstand an earthquake of 8.3 magnitude.* **2** to defend yourself successfully against people who attack, criticize, or oppose you: *Owens has withstood many attacks on his leadership.* **3 withstand the test of time** to still be important, effective etc. after a long time

wit·less /'wɪtlɪs/ *adj.* **1 scare sb witless** to make someone very frightened **2** not very intelligent or sensible SYN **silly** —**witlessly** *adv.* —**witlessness** *n.* [U]

wit·ness¹ /'wɪtˀnɪs/ S3 W2 *n.*
1 ACCIDENT/CRIME [C] someone who sees a crime or an accident and can describe what happened: *Witnesses say the smaller plane flew into the larger one.* | **+to** *There appear to have been no witnesses to the killing.*
2 COURT OF LAW [C] LAW someone in a court of law who tells what they saw or what they know about a crime: *At least 17 witnesses have testified in the case.* | *Her brother was* ***called as a witness*** *in the trial.* | **a witness for the prosecution/defense** (=a witness who gives evidence for one side or the other in a court case) ▸see THESAURUS box at **court¹**
3 OFFICIAL DOCUMENT [C] LAW someone who is present when an official document is signed, and who signs it too, to prove that they saw it happen: **+to** *His cousin was a witness to the will.*
4 be witness to sth FORMAL to be present when something happens, and watch it happening: *We have been witness to considerable social change.*
5 CHRISTIAN BELIEFS [C,U] the act of making a public statement of Christian beliefs, or someone who does this
[**Origin:** Old English *witnes* **knowledge, account, witness**] → see also **bear witness to sth** at BEAR¹ (16)

witness² *v.*
1 SEE STH HAPPEN [T] to see something happen, especially a crime or accident: *Several residents claim to have witnessed the attack.* ▸see THESAURUS box at **see¹**
2 EXPERIENCE STH [T] to experience important events or changes: *We have recently witnessed the emergence of several new diseases.*
3 TIME/PLACE [T] if a time or place witnesses an event, the event happens during that time or in that place: *Recent years have witnessed the collapse of the steel industry.*
4 OFFICIAL DOCUMENT [T] LAW to be present when someone signs an official document, and sign it yourself to show this: *Will you witness my signature?*
5 ..., as witnessed by... also **witness...** used to give an example that proves something you have just mentioned: *People are curious about each others' lives. Witness the success of reality TV.*
6 CHRISTIAN BELIEFS [I] to speak publicly about your Christian beliefs

witness to sth *phr. v.* FORMAL to formally state that something is true or happened: *Her principal was called to witness to her good character.*

'witness ˌstand *n.* [C] the place in a court of law where a witness answers questions

Witt·gen·stein /'vɪtgənˌʃtaɪn/, **Lud·wig** /'lʊdvɪg/ (1889–1951) an Austrian PHILOSOPHER who studied the relationship between language and the physical world

wit·ti·cism /'wɪṭəˌsɪzəm/ *n.* [C] a clever amusing remark

wit·ty /'wɪṭi/ *adj. comparative* **wittier**, *superlative* **wittiest** using words in a clever and amusing way: *a witty speaker* | *witty remarks* —**wittily** *adv.* —**wittiness** *n.* [U]

wives /waɪvz/ the plural of WIFE

wiz /wɪz/ *n.* [C] INFORMAL a wizard

wiz·ard /'wɪzɚd/ *n.* [C] **1** a man in stories who has magic powers → see also WITCH **2** someone who is very good at something: **+at/with** *Gail is a wizard with numbers.* | **a computer/guitar/financial etc. wizard** *a 15-year-old computer wizard*

wiz·ard·ry /'wɪzɚdri/ *n.* [U] **1** impressive ability to do something or an impressive achievement: *the movie's technical wizardry* **2** the skill and magic powers of a wizard

wiz·ened /'wɪzənd/ *adj.* a wizened person is small and thin and has skin with a lot of lines and WRINKLES

wk. the written abbreviation of WEEK

W

wkly. the written abbreviation of WEEKLY

w/o the written abbreviation of WITHOUT, especially used when writing notes quickly → see also W/

wob·ble /ˈwɑbəl/ *v.* [I] **1** to move in an unsteady way from side to side ►see THESAURUS box at **shake**[1] **2** [always + adv./prep.] to go in a particular direction, moving in an unsteady way from side to side: +**off/along/across etc.** *The old lady wobbled over to the window.* **3** if your voice wobbles, it goes up and down, usually because you are frightened or not confident, or you are trying not to cry **4** to be unsure whether to do something —**wobble** *n.* [C]

wob·bly /ˈwɑbli/ *adj.* **1** moving in an unsteady way from side to side: *a wobbly chair* **2** INFORMAL feeling weak and unable to keep your balance **3** a wobbly voice is weak and goes up and down in TONE, especially when you feel frightened or upset

woe /woʊ/ *n.* **1 woes** [plural] the problems and troubles affecting someone: *They tend to blame all of Africa's woes on colonialism.* **2** [U] LITERARY great sadness **3 woe is me** OLD USE OR HUMOROUS used to say that you are unhappy or that life is difficult for you **4 woe to/betide sb** LITERARY used to warn someone that there will be trouble if they do something: *Woe to anyone who got in his way.*

woe·be·gone /ˈwoʊbɪˌgɔn, -ˌgɑn/ *adj.* looking very sad or in bad condition

woe·ful /ˈwoʊfəl/ *adj.* **1** used to emphasize that something is very bad: *the woeful state of the economy* **2** LITERARY very sad —**woefully** *adv.*: *woefully inadequate facilities*

wok /wɑk/ *n.* [C] a wide pan shaped like a bowl, used in Chinese cooking

woke /woʊk/ the past tense of WAKE

wo·ken /ˈwoʊkən/ the past participle of WAKE

wolf[1] /wʊlf/ *n. plural* **wolves** /wʊlvz/ [C] **1** BIOLOGY a wild animal that looks like a large dog and lives and hunts in groups: *a pack of wolves* **2 a wolf in sheep's clothing** someone who seems to be friendly but is in fact dishonest, not nice etc. —**wolfish** *adj.*: *a wolfish grin* → see also **cry wolf** at CRY[1] (8), LONE WOLF

wolf[2] also **wolf down** *v.* [T] INFORMAL to eat something very quickly, swallowing it in big pieces

Wolfe /wʊlf/, **Tom** /tɑm/ (1931–) a U.S. JOURNALIST famous for writing about American society and for his NOVELS

wolf·hound /ˈwʊlfhaʊnd/ *n.* [C] BIOLOGY an extremely large dog which used to be trained to hunt wolves

ˈwolf ˌwhistle *n.* [C] a way of whistling that men sometimes use to show that they think a woman is attractive —**wolf-whistle** *v.* [I]

Woll·stone·craft, Mary /ˈwʊlstənˌkræft/ (1759–1797) a British writer who is regarded as one of the first FEMINISTS

wol·ver·ine /ˌwʊlvəˈrin/ *n.* [C] a short strong looking animal with dark fur that is similar to a WEASEL

wolves /wʊlvz/ the plural of WOLF

wom·an /ˈwʊmən/ S1 W1 *n. plural* **women** /ˈwɪmɪn/ **1 FEMALE** [C] an adult female person: *a woman with dark hair* | *married women* | *differences between* ***men and women*** | ***Women and children*** *were rescued first.* | *women's clothes*

THESAURUS

lady a polite word for woman
girl a young female person. This is considered offensive by some people when used about someone over the age of 18.
female FORMAL a woman – used especially by researchers or the police: *Ten males and five females were involved in the study.*
→ MAN

2 ANY WOMAN [singular, U] women in general: *Nowadays, a woman can decide how many children she has.* **3 be your own woman** to make your own decisions and be in charge of your own life, without depending on anyone else **4 the other woman** the woman that a man is having a sexual relationship with, even though he is married to or already in a relationship with someone else **5 another woman** a woman that a man is having a sexual relationship with when he already has a wife or sexual partner: *Her husband ran off with another woman.* **6 WIFE/GIRLFRIEND** [C] INFORMAL someone's wife or GIRLFRIEND **7 WAY OF TALKING TO SB** SPOKEN, OLD-FASHIONED a rude way of talking to a woman when you are annoyed: *Stop talking, woman.*
[**Origin:** Old English *wifman*, from *wif* **woman, wife** + *man* **person**] → see also BUSINESSWOMAN, CAREER WOMAN, CHAIRWOMAN, CONGRESSWOMAN, **make an honest woman (out) of sb** at HONEST (6), SPOKESWOMAN, **a man/woman of the world** at WORLD[1] (24)

wom·an·hood /ˈwʊmənˌhʊd/ *n.* [U] **1** the state of being a woman, not a man or a girl **2** FORMAL women in general → see also MANHOOD

wom·an·ish /ˈwʊmənɪʃ/ *adj.* DISAPPROVING looking or behaving in a way that is typical of women

wom·an·iz·er /ˈwʊməˌnaɪzɚ/ *n.* [C] DISAPPROVING a man who has sexual relationships with many different women —**womanize** *v.* [I] —**womanizing** *n.* [U]

wom·an·kind /ˈwʊmənˌkaɪnd/ *n.* [U] women considered together as a group → see also MANKIND

wom·an·ly /ˈwʊmənli/ *adj.* APPROVING behaving, dressing etc. in a way that is thought to be typical of or appropriate for a woman: *a womanly figure* —**womanliness** *n.* [U]

ˌwoman-to-ˈwoman *adj., adv.* if two women have a woman-to-woman talk or they talk woman-to-woman, they discuss something in an honest open way

womb /wum/ *n.* [C] BIOLOGY the part of a female's body where her baby grows before it is born SYN **uterus**

wom·bat /ˈwɑmbæt/ *n.* [C] an Australian animal like a small bear whose babies live in a pocket of skin on its body

wom·en /ˈwɪmɪn/ the plural of WOMAN

wom·en·folk /ˈwɪmɪnˌfoʊk/ *n.* [plural] OLD-FASHIONED all the women in a particular family or society

ˌwomen's ˈlib also **ˌwomen's libeˈration** *n.* [U] POLITICS the expression, used in the 1960s and 1970s, for all the ideas, actions, and politics related to giving women the same rights and opportunities as men —**women's libber** *n.* [C]

ˈwomen's ˌmovement *n.* **the women's (rights) movement** all the women who are involved in the aim of improving the social, economic, and political position of women and of ending sexual DISCRIMINATION

ˌwomen's ˈrights *n.* [plural] the rights of women to have and do everything that men have and do, especially those rights given by special laws

ˈwomen's room *n.* [C] a public REST ROOM for women SYN **ladies' room**

ˌwomen's ˈshelter *n.* [C] a place where women and their children can go to escape being physically hurt by their husband, partner etc.

won[1] /wʌn/ the past tense and past participle of WIN

won[2] /wɔn/ *n.* [C] the standard unit of money used in Korea

won·der[1] /ˈwʌndɚ/ S1 W1 *v.* [I,T] **1** to think about something that you are not sure about and try to guess what is true, what will happen etc.: **wonder who/what/how etc.** *I wonder where Joe is now.* | **wonder if/whether** *I wonder if it will rain.* | *He's been leaving work early a lot –* ***it makes you wonder****, doesn't it?* **2 I was wondering if/whether** also **we were wondering if/whether** SPOKEN **a)** also **I/we wonder if/whether** used to politely ask someone to help you or give you information: *I was wondering if you could babysit tomorrow night.* **b)** used to ask someone if they would like to do something: *We were wondering if you'd like to* come with us. **3** to have doubts about whether something is good, true, normal etc.: +**about** *Do you ever wonder about his motives?* | **wonder if/whether** *I wonder if this is the right way.* **4** to feel surprised by someone or something, often in an admiring way: +**at** *We wondered at the violent reaction.*

wonder² S3 *n.* **1 a)** [U] a feeling of surprise and admiration for something very beautiful or new to you: *a childlike sense of wonder* | *We listened* ***with wonder*** *to our father's stories.* **b)** [C] something that makes you feel surprise and admiration: *technological wonders* | *the Seven Wonders of the World* **2 (it's) no/small/little wonder (that)** also **is it any wonder (that)?** SPOKEN used to say that you are not surprised by something: *No wonder you have a headache, after the amount you drank last night.* **3 it's a wonder (that)** SPOKEN used to say that something is very surprising: *It's a wonder no one got hurt.* **4 do/work wonders** to be very effective in solving a problem: *This diet is supposed to work wonders.* **5 will wonders never cease?** SPOKEN, HUMOROUS used to show you are surprised and pleased about something **6 sb is a wonder** OLD-FASHIONED used to say that you admire someone because they can do difficult things very well [**Origin:** Old English *wundor*]

wonder³ *adj.* [only before noun] very good and effective: *a new wonder drug*

won·der·ful /ˈwʌndɚfəl/ S1 W2 *adj.* **1** extremely good, impressive, or admirable: *That's wonderful news!* | *He's a wonderful man.* ▸see THESAURUS box at **good¹** **2** extremely enjoyable: *We had a wonderful time in Spain.* ▸see THESAURUS box at **nice** **3** very good at doing something: *a wonderful cook* —**wonderfully** *adv.*

won·der·ing·ly /ˈwʌndərɪŋli/ *adv.* **1** in a way that shows surprise **2** in a way that shows admiration, surprise and pleasure

won·der·land /ˈwʌndɚˌlænd/ *n.* [U] an imaginary place in stories that is full of wonderful things

won·der·ment /ˈwʌndɚmənt/ *n.* [U] LITERARY a feeling of pleasant surprise or admiration

won·drous /ˈwʌndrəs/ *adj.* LITERARY good or impressive in a surprising way

wonk /wɑŋk, wɔŋk/ *n.* [C] INFORMAL someone who works hard and is very serious: ***policy wonks*** (=people interested in details of government)

won't /woʊnt/ *v.* the short form of "will not": *I won't eat my peas.*

wont¹ /wɔnt, woʊnt/ *adj.* LITERARY **be wont to do sth** used to say that someone usually does something: *Tom fell asleep in the movie, as he is wont to do.*

wont² *n.* LITERARY **as is sb's wont** used to say that it is someone's habit to do something

wont·ed /ˈwɔntɪd/ *adj.* [only before noun] LITERARY usual

woo /wu/ *v.* [T] **1** to try to persuade someone to buy something from you, do something for you, work for you etc.: *Women were being wooed back into the workforce.* **2** OLD-FASHIONED to try to persuade a woman to love you and marry you —**wooer** *n.* [C]

wood /wʊd/ S1 W2 *n.* **1** [C,U] the material that trees are made of: *The floor is made of solid wood.* | *a piece of wood* | **cut/chop wood** *He was outside chopping wood for the fire.* | **soft/hard wood** *Pine is a soft wood.* → see also WOODEN **2 the woods** [plural] an area of land covered with trees: *We went for a walk in the woods after lunch.* ▸see THESAURUS box at **tree** **3** [singular] POETIC a small area of land covered with trees **4 not be out of the woods yet** INFORMAL used to say that there are likely to be more difficulties before things improve **5** [C] one of a set of four GOLF CLUBS with wooden heads [**Origin:** Old English *wudu*]

Wood /wʊd/, **Grant** /grænt/ (1892–1942) a U.S. PAINTER

ˈwood ˌalcohol *n.* [U] INFORMAL METHANOL

wood·block /ˈwʊdblɑk/ *n.* [C] **1** a piece of wood with a shape cut on it, used for printing **2** a block of wood used in making a floor

wood·carv·ing /ˈwʊdˌkɑrvɪŋ/ *n.* ENG. LANG. ARTS **1** [U] the process of shaping wood with special tools **2** [C,U] art, or a piece of art, that is produced by shaping wood with special tools

wood·chuck /ˈwʊdtʃʌk/ *n.* [C] a GROUNDHOG

wood·craft /ˈwʊdkræft/ *n.* [U] the practical knowledge of woods and forests

wood·cut /ˈwʊdkʌt/ *n.* [C] **1** ENG. LANG. ARTS a picture that you make by pressing a shaped piece of wood covered with a coloring substance onto paper **2** a WOODBLOCK

wood·cut·ter /ˈwʊdˌkʌtɚ/ *n.* [C] LITERARY someone whose job is to cut down trees in a forest

wood·ed /ˈwʊdɪd/ *adj.* covered with trees: *densely wooded hills*

wood·en /ˈwʊdn/ S3 W3 *adj.* **1** made of wood: *a wooden box* **2** DISAPPROVING not showing any emotion or not looking natural or relaxed, especially when speaking or performing in public —**woodenly** *adv.* —**woodenness** *n.* [U]

ˌwooden-ˈheaded *adj.* INFORMAL stupid and slow to understand things

ˌwooden ˈspoon *n.* [C] a large spoon made of wood that is used in cooking

wood·land /ˈwʊdlənd, -lænd/ *n.* [U] also **woodlands** [plural] land that is covered with trees → see also GRASSLAND, WETLAND

wood·peck·er /ˈwʊdˌpɛkɚ/ *n.* [C] BIOLOGY a bird with a long beak that it uses to make holes in trees

wood·pile /ˈwʊdpaɪl/ *n.* [C] a pile of wood to be burned in a fire

ˈwood pulp *n.* [U] wood crushed into a soft mass, used for making paper

Woods /wʊdz/, **Ti·ger** /ˈtaɪgɚ/ (1975–) a U.S. GOLFER, famous for being one of the youngest and best players in the game

wood·shed /ˈwʊdʃɛd/ *n.* [C] **1** a place for storing wood that is to be used for burning **2 take sb to the woodshed** INFORMAL to severely punish someone for something

woods·man /ˈwʊdzmən/ *n.* *plural* **woodsmen** /-mən/ [C] someone who knows a lot about the woods, especially about living in the woods

woods·y /ˈwʊdzi/ *n.* INFORMAL **1** having a lot of trees: *a woodsy park* **2** relating to the woods: *a woodsy smell*

wood·wind /ˈwʊdˌwɪnd/ *n.* [C,U] ENG. LANG. ARTS **1** [C,U] a musical instrument made of wood or metal that you play by blowing and that usually has finger holes or KEYS, for example the FLUTE or OBOE, or these instruments in general **2 the woodwinds** [plural] also **the woodwind section** [C] the group of woodwind instruments in an ORCHESTRA or band, or the people who play them —**woodwind** *adj.*

wood·work /ˈwʊdwɚk/ *n.* [U] **1** the parts of a house or room that are made of wood: *The woodwork needs to be refinished.* **2 come/crawl out of the woodwork** if someone or something comes out of the woodwork, they suddenly appear where you have not noticed or seen them before, especially in order to take advantage of a situation in an unpleasant way **3 fade/blend into the woodwork** if someone fades or blends into the woodwork, people do not notice them anymore

wood·work·ing /ˈwʊdˌwɚkɪŋ/ *n.* [U] the skill or activity of making wooden objects —**woodworker** *n.* [C]

wood·worm /ˈwʊdwɚm/ *n.* [C] **1** BIOLOGY a small insect that makes holes in wood **2** [U] the damage that is caused to wood by this creature

wood·y /ˈwʊdi/ *adj.* **1** BIOLOGY a woody plant has a stem like wood **2** feeling, smelling, looking etc. like wood

woof¹ /wʊf/ *interjection* a word used for describing the sound a dog makes when it BARKS —**woof** *v.* [I] INFORMAL

woof² /wʊf/ *n.* [C] **1** the sound that a dog makes when it BARKS **2** /wʊf, wuf/ WEFT

W

woof·er /ˈwʊfɚ/ *n.* [C] a LOUDSPEAKER that produces deep sounds → see also TWEETER

wool /wʊl/ *n.* [U] **1** BIOLOGY the soft thick hair that sheep and some goats have on their body **2** material made from wool: *Is this coat wool?* | **a wool jacket/carpet/blanket etc.** *a pure wool skirt* **3** thread made from wool, used for knitting (KNIT) clothes **4 pull the wool over sb's eyes** to deceive someone by not telling the truth → see also DYED-IN-THE-WOOL, STEEL WOOL

wool·en /ˈwʊlən/ *adj.* [usually before noun] made of wool: *woolen mittens*

wool·ens /ˈwʊlənz/ *n.* [plural] clothes made from wool, especially wool that has been knitted (KNIT)

Woolf /wʊlf/, **Vir·gin·ia** /vɚˈdʒɪnyə/ (1882–1941) a British writer

wool·len /ˈwʊlən/ the British and Canadian spelling of WOOLEN

woolly, wooly /ˈwʊli/ *adj.* feeling or looking like wool: *He had gray, woolly hair.* → see also **wild and woolly** at WILD[1] (14)

ˌwoolly-ˈheaded also **ˌwoolly-ˈminded** *adj.* not able to think clearly, or not showing clear thinking: *woolly-headed ideals*

Wool·worth /ˈwʊlwɚθ/, **Frank** (1852–1919) a U.S. businessman who started the F.W. Woolworth Company, opening many stores in the U.S. and other countries and selling goods for five or ten cents

woo·zy /ˈwuzi/ *adj.* INFORMAL feeling weak and unsteady SYN **dizzy**: *When I stood up, I felt a little woozy.*

word[1] /wɚd/ S1 W1 *n.*

1 LANGUAGE [C] the smallest unit of language that people can understand if it is said or written on its own: *Look up any words you don't know in a dictionary.* | *a 500-word essay* | **+for** *"Casa" is the Italian word for "house."* | **the right/wrong word** *Perhaps "lucky" is not exactly the right word.*

2 WHAT SB SAYS/WRITES **sb's words** [plural] the things that someone says or writes: *Those are his words, not mine.* | *Jones was, **in the judge's words**, "an evil man."* | *Tell us **in your own words** what happened.* | **sb's last words** (=the last thing they say before they die)

3 SONG **words** [plural] the words of a song, as opposed to the music → see also LYRICS: **+to** *I don't know all the words to the song.*

4 word for word a) in exactly the same words: *The newspaper printed his speech more or less word for word.* **b)** also **word by word** if you translate a piece of writing from a foreign language word for word, you translate the meaning of each single word rather than the meaning of a whole phrase or sentence

5 NEWS [singular, U] a piece of news or a message: *There's been **no word from** Susan since July.* | ***Word has it that*** (=people are saying that) *Judy's going to be promoted soon.* | *The latest **word is that*** (=people are saying that) *the show will be canceled.* | **word gets out/around** *Word soon got around about our engagement.* | **send/bring word** (=to send or bring a message) | **spread/pass the word** (=to tell other people the news)

6 in other words used to introduce a simpler explanation or description of something you have said: *The tax only affects people on incomes of over $200,000 – in other words, the very rich.*

7 not believe/hear/understand etc. a word (of sth) used to emphasize that you do not believe, cannot hear etc. what someone says or writes: *Don't believe a word he says.* | *I can't hear a word you're saying.*

8 not say a word a) also **not breathe a word** to not tell anyone anything at all about something, because it is very important that no one knows about it: *Don't worry – I won't say a word about what happened.* **b)** also **not say (more than) two words** to not say anything: *He didn't say a word until we got back home.*

9 SHORT CONVERSATION [singular] a short quick talk with someone, especially because you need their advice about something or you want to tell them to do something: *Could I **have a word with** you after the meeting?*

10 a word of advice/warning/thanks etc. also **a few words of advice/warning etc.** something you say to someone for a particular purpose: *I tried to give her a few words of encouragement.*

11 a harsh/kind/cross/angry etc. word something that you say that shows how you feel: *His parents never exchanged an angry word.* | *Thank you for your kind words.*

12 SHORT SPEECH/PIECE OF WRITING [C] a short speech or a short piece of writing about something: **+about/on** *First, a word about why we are here today.* | *I'd like to **say a few words** about the plans.*

13 take sb's word for it SPOKEN used to say that someone should accept what someone else says as true: *Take my word for it – she's really funny.*

14 PROMISE **sb's word** a sincere promise: *I **gave her my word*** (=promised her) *that I wouldn't tell anyone.* | *Can you trust her to **keep** her **word*** (=do what she has promised)? | *Jack's **as good as his word*** (=does exactly what he has promised to do). | *Do I **have your word that** this problem will be corrected?* | **a man of his word/a woman of her word** (=a man or woman who does what they have promised to do)

15 take sb at their word to believe what someone has said, even though it is possible that they do not mean it: *I said, "Come and visit me sometime," and I guess she took me at my word.*

16 the spoken/written word [singular] language in its spoken or written form: *the power of the written word*

17 a man/woman etc. of few words someone who does not talk a lot: *My father was a man of few words.*

18 exchange words (with sb) a) also **have words (with sb)** to argue with someone: *The two of them had words during the party.* **b)** to talk to someone for a short time

19 the last/final word a) the power to decide whether or how to do something: *The final word rests with the board.* | **have the last/final word** *My boss has the final word on hiring staff.* **b)** the last statement or speech in a discussion or argument: **have the last/final word** *I'm not going to let you have the last word this time.*

20 AN ORDER [C usually singular] an order to do something: *On the word "go" I want you to start running.* | **give/say the word** *When I give the word, grab him.*

21 put in a (good) word for sb to praise someone or suggest them for a particular job: *I'll put in a good word for you with management.*

22 get a word in edgewise/edgeways INFORMAL [usually in negatives] to get a chance to speak: *I couldn't get a word in edgewise.*

23 in so/as many words [usually in negatives] in a clear direct way: *"Did he say we got the contract?" "Not in so many words."*

24 in a word used to introduce and emphasize a very simple answer or explanation: *"Did you have a good vacation?" "In a word, no."*

25 not a word used to emphasize that someone has not written, said, or mentioned anything at all: *"Did he say anything to you?" "Not a word."*

26 (right) from the word go INFORMAL from the beginning: *We've been best friends from the word go.*

27 find the words to choose the words that express your feelings or ideas clearly: *She couldn't find the words to describe how she felt.*

28 take the words (right) out of sb's mouth to say exactly what someone else was thinking or going to say

29 put words into sb's mouth to suggest falsely that someone has said a particular thing: *Stop putting words into my mouth – I never said I disliked her.*

30 word of mouth information or news that someone tells you instead of you reading about it or seeing an advertisement: *At first, people learn about the band **by word of mouth**.*

31 the Word (of God) the religious teachings in the Bible

32 without (saying) a word without saying anything when you do something else: *He left without a word.*

33 never have a good word to say about sb/sth to

never praise someone or something, even if they do something well
34 sth is too stupid/funny/ridiculous etc. for words INFORMAL used to say that something is very stupid, funny etc.
35 tired/angry/happy etc. isn't the word for it used to say you are extremely tired, angry etc.
36 words fail me used to say that you are so surprised, angry, or shocked that you do not know what to say
37 my word! OLD-FASHIONED, SPOKEN used to say you are very surprised because something unusual has happened
38 word (up)! SLANG used to say that you understand or agree with what someone has just said
[**Origin:** Old English] → see also **eat your words** at EAT (3), FOUR-LETTER WORD, **be the last word in sth** at LAST[1] (15), **(you) mark my words!** at MARK[1] (10), **not mince words** at MINCE (2), **a play on words** at PLAY[2] (7)

word² *v.* [T] to use words that are carefully chosen in order to express something: *Let me word the question a little differently.*

word·ed /ˈwɚdɪd/ *adj.* **carefully/clearly/strongly etc. worded** using words that express an idea carefully, clearly etc.: *a strongly worded complaint*

word ˌfamily *n.* [C] ENG. LANG. ARTS a group of related words that are all formed from the same base word. For example, the word family of the word 'clever' includes 'cleverly' and 'cleverness'.

word·ing /ˈwɚdɪŋ/ *n.* [U] the words and phrases used to express something: *I'm not happy with the wording of the article.*

word·less /ˈwɚdlɪs/ *adj.* without words SYN **silent**: *wordless amazement* —**wordlessly** *adv.*

word-play *n.* [U] the activity of making jokes by using words in a clever way

word ˌprocessor *n.* [C] COMPUTERS a computer PROGRAM or a small computer that you use for writing letters, reports etc. —**word processing** *n.* [U]

word·smith /ˈwɚdsmɪθ/ *n.* [C] someone who is very skillful at using language —**wordsmith** *v.* [I,T] —**wordsmithing** *n.* [U]

Words·worth /ˈwɚdzwɚθ/, **William** (1770–1850) a British Romantic poet whose poems are mainly about the beauty of nature

word ˌwall *n.* [C] a large area of a CLASSROOM wall where important words are shown to help students with their reading and writing

word·y /ˈwɚdi/ *adj.* DISAPPROVING using too many words, especially long and difficult ones: *a wordy explanation* —**wordily** *adv.* —**wordiness** *n.* [U]

wore /wɔr/ the past tense of WEAR

work¹ /wɚk/ S1 W1 *v.*
1 DO A JOB YOUR ARE PAID FOR a) [I] to do a job that you are paid for: *Where do you work?* | +**at/in** *I've always worked in an office.* | +**for** *I think Linda works for a law firm.* | **work as a secretary/builder etc.** *She works as a management consultant.* | **work in industry/education/publishing etc.** *How long have you worked in advertising?* | **work part-time/full-time** *She works part-time in a library.* **b) work a job** an expression meaning "to have a job", used especially when you are emphasizing something unusual about it: *I had to work two jobs to put food on the table.*
2 DO THINGS AT A JOB [I,T] to do the activities and duties that are part of your job: *We're working as hard as we can.* | +**with** *Jerry will be working with me on the project.* | **work weekends/nights/days etc.** *I get paid more if I work nights.* | *He often has to* ***work late.*** | *I'm* ***working from home*** *tomorrow.*
3 ACTIVITY [I] to do an activity which needs time and effort, especially one that you want to do or that needs to be done: *I've been working in the yard this afternoon.* | **work to do sth** *We had to work non-stop to get the boat ready for the race.* | *You've really* ***worked hard*** *this semester.*
4 TRY TO ACHIEVE STH [I] to try continuously and patiently to achieve a particular thing: +**for** *She spent a lifetime working for equal rights.* | **work to do sth** *The organization is working to preserve the rainforests.* | *They have* ***worked tirelessly*** (=worked hard) *to make living conditions better.*
5 OPERATE CORRECTLY [I] if a machine or piece of equipment works, it does what it is supposed to do: *Does the TV work?* | *The delete key doesn't work.* | *The repairman finally* ***got*** *the heater* ***working*** (=made it work) *again.* | **work fine/well/properly etc.** *We tested the cable and it seems to be working fine.*
6 BE EFFECTIVE/SUCCESSFUL [I] if a method, plan, or system works, it produces the results you want: *Most diets don't work.* | *Surgery usually works well in correcting conditions like this.* | +**for** *You need to find the method that works best for you.* | *You should try this recipe. It* ***works every time.***
7 ART/LITERATURE [I] if a painting, movie, piece of writing etc. works, it is successful because it has the effect on you that the painter, writer etc. intended: *I don't think the scene with the horses really works.*
8 HAVE AN EFFECT [I always + adv./prep.] if something such as a fact, situation, or system works in particular way, it has a particular effect on someone or something: **work in sb's favor/to sb's advantage** *Your experience with this kind of job should work in your favor.* | *Tax laws tend to* ***work against*** (=make things difficult for) *small businesses.*
9 work your way over/out/back etc. a) if you work your way somewhere, you go there slowly and with great effort: *We worked our way carefully across the rocks.* **b)** to use a lot of effort during a long period of time to become successful: *He started in the mailroom and worked his way to the top.*
10 OPERATE MACHINE/EQUIPMENT [T] to make a complicated machine or piece of equipment do what it is supposed to do: *Do you know how to work this copier?*
11 work it/things so that... to make arrangements for something to happen, especially by acting in a clever or skillful way: *We tried to work it so that we could all go together.*
12 (sth) works for sb SPOKEN used to say that something is acceptable to someone: *"Do you want to meet at 8:00?" "Works for me."*
13 MOVE INTO A PLACE/POSITION [I always + adv./prep., T always + adv./prep.] to move into a particular state or position very gradually, or to make something do this, either in a series of small movements or after a long time: *Slowly he worked the screwdriver into the crack.* | *Somehow the bolt had* ***worked its way*** *loose.*
14 AREA [T] to travel around a particular area as part of your job, especially in order to sell something: *I work the northern half of the state.*
15 USE A MATERIAL/SUBSTANCE [I] to use a particular material or substance in order to make something such as a picture, design, jewelry etc.: +**in/with** *I prefer to work in watercolors.*
16 CUT/SHAPE STH [T] if you work a material such as metal, leather, or clay, you cut, sew, or shape it in order to make something
17 work sb (hard) to make someone use a lot of time or effort when doing a job or activity: *The coach has been working us really hard this week.*
18 work the system to understand how a system works so that you can get advantages for yourself, often in a slightly dishonest way
19 PART OF YOUR BODY a) [T] if you work a muscle or part of your body, you do an exercise to make it stronger **b)** [I,T] if a part of your body works or you work it, it moves with a lot of effort: *Robert worked his face into something like a smile.*
20 MIND/BRAIN [I] if your mind or brain is working, you are thinking or trying to solve a problem: *Her mind was working furiously.* | *I could see Brian's brain start to* ***work overtime*** (=think very hard) *as soon as I mentioned the deal.*
21 work it! SLANG used to encourage someone to dance or move with a lot of energy
22 work like magic also **work like a charm/dream** if a plan, method, or trick works like magic or like a charm, it happens in exactly the way you planned it to happen
23 work wonders (on/with sth) to be effective in

W

dealing with a difficult problem or situation in a way that surprises you: *This herbal tea works wonders on headaches.*
24 work under the principle/assumption/basis etc. that also **work on the principle/assumption/basis etc. that** to base ideas, plans etc. on a particular fact that you think is true
25 work your fingers to the bone INFORMAL to work very hard, especially doing something that needs a lot of physical effort
26 work the door to take tickets from people as they enter a theater, club, etc.
27 CALCULATE [T] to calculate the answer to a mathematical problem
28 ENTERTAIN A GROUP [T] if an entertainer or politician works a crowd of people, they entertain them and get their interest or support: *She really knew how to work a crowd.*
29 LAND/SOIL [T] if you work the land or the soil, you do all the work necessary to grow crops on it
30 MINE [T] to remove a substance such as coal, gold etc. from under the ground
[**Origin:** Old English *wyrcan*]

work around sb/sth *phr. v.* to arrange or organize something so that you avoid problems that may stop you from doing something: *John won't be here on the 15th so we'll have to work around that.*

work at sth *phr. v.* to try hard to improve something or achieve something by practicing it over a long period of time and with a lot of effort: *Learning a language isn't easy. You have to work at it.*

work in *phr. v.* **1 work sth ↔ in** to include something you want to say or do while you are doing or saying something else: *Do you think you can work in a mention of our project?* **2 work sb ↔ in** SPOKEN to arrange meet someone even though you are very busy: *Can you work me in some time tomorrow?* **3 work sth ↔ in** to add one substance to another and mix them together in a very thorough way

work sth **into** sth *phr. v.* **1** to include something you want to say or do while you are doing or saying something else so that it becomes part of it **2** to add one substance to another and mix them together in a very thorough way, especially by using your hands: *Slowly work the cream into your skin.* **3 work yourself into a frenzy/rage/panic etc.** to make yourself become very excited, angry etc.

work off *phr. v.* **1 work sth ↔ off** to try to get rid of something such as a feeling or some weight by doing something that involves a lot of physical activity: *Running is a good way of working off stress.* **2 work sth ↔ off** to pay for something you have done wrong, for something you have broken etc. by doing a job for free: *He's working off the window he broke by mowing my lawn.*

work on *phr. v.* **1 work on sth** to spend time making, improving, or repairing something: *As a team, we still need to work on free throws.* | *Every weekend you see him working on his car.* **2 work on sb** INFORMAL to try continuously to influence someone or persuade them to do something: **work on sb to do sth** *She is still working on me to take her to the opera.*

work out *phr. v.*
1 PLAN work sth ↔ out to think carefully about how you are going to do something and plan a good way of doing it: *Have you worked out the schedule for next month?* | **work out what/where/how etc.** *We need to work out how we're going to get there.* | *It sounds like you **have it all worked out*** (=have already planned how you are going to do something).
2 DEAL WITH STH work sth ↔ out to deal with a problem in a satisfactory way: *Have you managed to work out your differences yet?*
3 CALCULATE work sth ↔ out to calculate an answer, amount, price, or value: *I still have to work out a budget for next year.* | **work out how much/many etc.** *We'll have to work out how much food we'll need for the party.*
4 GET BETTER work sth out if a problem or complicated situation works out, or you work it out, it gradually gets better or gets solved: *It's too bad that the deal didn't work out.* | *We can work it out if we just sit down and talk about it.* | *The situation should **work itself out*** (=become better without any help).
5 HAPPEN if a situation works out in a particular way, it happens in that way: *Things didn't work out as we'd planned.* | **work out well/badly** *I hope your new job works out well.*
6 UNDERSTAND work sth ↔ out to think about something and manage to understand it: *I couldn't work her out at all.* | **work sth out for yourself** *I can't tell you what happened – work it out for yourself.*
7 COST if something works out to a particular amount, you calculate that it costs that amount: **+to** *Your total works out to $32.50.* | **work out (to be) expensive/cheap etc.** *It worked out to be cheaper than we thought.*
8 EXERCISE to make your body healthy and strong, especially by doing a program of exercises: *How often do you work out?*
9 be worked out if a mine is worked out, all the coal, gold etc. has been removed from it

work sb **over** *phr. v.* INFORMAL to hit someone hard and repeatedly all over their body

work through sth *phr. v.* **1** to deal with problems or unpleasant feelings until they are gone: *She's got a lot of issues to work through.* **2 work your way through school/college/university** to do a job while you are in college because you need the money to help pay for it: *Galman worked her way through college as a waitress.*

work up *phr. v.* **1 work up enthusiasm/interest/courage etc.** to become excited, interested etc., or to make others feel this way: *I'm trying to work up the courage to visit the dentist.* **2 work up an appetite/thirst/sweat** to become hungry, THIRSTY etc., especially by doing physical exercise: *There's nothing like skiing to work up an appetite.* **3 work sb ↔ up** to make someone very angry, excited, or upset about something: **work yourself up** *You don't have to work yourself up over this.* → see also WORKED UP **4 work sth ↔ up** to develop and improve something such as a piece of writing: *I'd like for you to work up a detailed summary of our meeting.*

work up to sth *phr. v.* to gradually prepare yourself to do something difficult or unpleasant: *I'm working up to running two miles a day.*

work with sb/sth *phr. v.* to do a job that involves a particular group of people or type of thing: *I've always wanted to work with animals.*

work² S1 W1 *n.*
1 JOB [U] a job you are paid to do or an activity that you do regularly to earn money: *How's work these days?* | *There isn't a lot of work at this time of the year.* | *Jean's been **out of work*** (=has not had a job) *for six months.* | *I'm sure you'll **find work** soon.* | *Anne left college a year ago and she's still **looking for work**.* | *In my **line of work*** (=the kind of work I do), *you tend to meet a lot of interesting people.* | **return/go back to work** *I returned to work two months after the accident.* ►see THESAURUS box at **job**
2 TIME AT YOUR JOB [U] the time that you spend working at your job: *We **start work** around here at 9:00.* | **before/after work** *I'll meet you after work.* | **late/early for work** *You're going to be late for work.* | **stop/finish work** *I usually finish work around 6:30.*
3 PLACE [U] a place where you do your job, which is not your home: *Could I ride with you to work tomorrow?* | *I usually leave work around 5 p.m.* | *She's still **at work**. I'll ask her to call you when she gets home.* | *I went out with the guys **from work** last night.*
4 DUTIES [U] the duties and activities that are part of your job: *The work's really interesting, but the pay's lousy.* | *The job involves mostly clerical work.* | *They **stopped work** for a few minutes to consider his offer.* | *I've been doing a lot of **volunteer work*** (=work that you are not paid for).
5 RESULT [U] something that you produce as a result of doing your job or doing an activity: *We're very pleased with the work you've done so far.* | *This report really is an excellent **piece of work**.*

6 PAPERS [U] the papers and other materials you need for doing work: *I left some work in the car.* | *I try not to* ***take work home*** *with me.*
7 USEFUL ACTIVITY [U] the act of doing something that needs to be done or that you want to do, or the time and effort needed to do it: *The yard still needs a lot of work.* | *Dad was* ***hard at work*** *down in the basement.* | *Taking care of children can be* ***hard work***. | *It's time for everyone to* ***get down to work*** (=start doing work).
8 BUILDING/REPAIRING [U] also **works** [plural] activities involved in building or repairing things such as roads, bridges etc.: *Work is expected to last several weeks, with severe delays to traffic.* | **+on** *Work on the bridge is continuing.*
9 STUDY [U] study or RESEARCH, especially for a particular purpose: *Their work could significantly change the way we live today.* | **+on/in** *postgraduate work in sociology*
10 BOOK/PAINTING/MUSIC [C] ENG. LANG. ARTS something such as a book, play, painting, or piece of music produced by a writer, painter, or musician: *The museum is full of Picasso's works.* | **+of** *a great work of literature* | **+on** *a recent work on the Civil War*
11 **at work** having a particular influence or effect: *Other forces may be at work here.*
12 **nice/good work** SPOKEN used to praise someone for doing something well: *Nice work! The project looks good.*
13 **in the works** INFORMAL being planned, developed etc.: *The merger has been in the works for two years.*
14 **the (whole) works** SPOKEN used when you are buying something that has many parts or choices, to choose everything that is available: *The hotel had everything – sauna, swimming pool, the works.*
15 **have your work cut out (for you)** INFORMAL to have to do something very difficult
16 **it's all in a day's work** SPOKEN used to say that you do not mind doing something even though it will give you more work than usual.
17 **iron/gas/cement etc. works** a building or group of buildings where a particular type of goods are produced in large quantities or where an industrial process happens → see also PUBLIC WORKS
18 MACHINE **the works** the moving parts of a machine
19 FORCE [U] PHYSICS force multiplied by distance → see also **do sb's dirty work** at DIRTY[1] (7), **make short work of sth** at SHORT[1] (16), WORKING[2]

work³ *adj.* [only before noun] **1 work clothes/boots etc.** work clothes, boots etc. are designed for people to work in, rather than to look attractive **2 work practices/conditions** the ways of working or the conditions in which people in a particular company work, including safety, health, rights, and duties SYN **working** **3 work hours/time** the time you spend working at your job

work·a·ble /ˈwɚkəbəl/ *adj.* **1** a workable system, idea etc. can be used in a practical and effective way: *a workable solution* **2** a workable substance can be shaped with your hands

work·a·day /ˈwɚkəˌdeɪ/ *adj.* [only before noun] ordinary and not interesting

work·a·hol·ic /ˌwɚkəˈhɔlɪk/ *n.* [C] INFORMAL someone who is always working, and does not have time for anything else

work·bench /ˈwɚkbɛntʃ/ *n.* [C] a strong table with a hard surface for working on things with tools

work·book /ˈwɚkbʊk/ *n.* [C] a school book containing questions and exercises

work·day /ˈwɚkdeɪ/ *n. plural* **workdays** [C] **1** the amount of time that you spend working in a day: *an 8-hour workday* **2** a day when people usually work, especially one that is not a holiday, Saturday, or Sunday

ˌworked ˈup *adj.* [not before noun] INFORMAL very upset or excited about something: **+about/over** *You're getting all worked up over nothing.* → see also **work up** at WORK[1]

work·er /ˈwɚkɚ/ S2 W1 *n.* [C] **1** someone who does a job, especially someone who is below the level of a manager: **a factory/farm/office etc. worker** (=someone who works in a factory, on a farm etc.) | **a skilled/unskilled worker** (=someone who has or does not have special skills) | ***blue-collar workers*** *in the automotive industry* **2** someone who works to achieve a particular purpose, especially one that relates to helping people, improving their health etc.: **a rescue/a civil rights/a healthcare/an aid etc. worker** *Relief workers arrived in the devastated areas.* → see also SOCIAL WORKER **3** used to describe how well, quickly etc. someone works: **a good/hard/quick etc. worker** *Mike's always been a hard worker.* | **a slow/lazy worker** *The company can't afford slow workers.* **4 workers** [plural] people who belong to the WORKING CLASS: *the workers' revolution*

ˌworkers' compenˈsation also **ˌworker's ˈcomp** SPOKEN *n.* [U] money that a company must pay to a worker who is injured or becomes sick as a result of their job

ˈwork ˌethic *n.* [singular] someone's belief about the moral value and importance of hard work

ˈwork exˌperience *n.* the experience you have had of working in a particular type of job

work·fare /ˈwɚkfɛr/ *n.* [U] POLITICS a system that makes it necessary for unemployed people to work before they are given money for food, rent etc. by the government → see also WELFARE

work·force /ˈwɚkfɔrs/ *n.* [singular] all the people who work in a particular country, industry, or factory: *a workforce of 3,500 employees*

ˈwork ˌhazard *n.* [C] something that could be dangerous to people who work in a particular place

work·horse /ˈwɚkhɔrs/ *n.* [C] **1** someone who does most of the work, especially when it is hard or boring **2** a machine or vehicle that can be used to do a lot of work

work·house /ˈwɚkhaʊs/ *n.* [C] HISTORY a building in the past where poor people were sent to live because they could not pay their debts

work·ing¹ /ˈwɚkɪŋ/ *adj.* [only before noun]
1 HAVING A JOB **a)** having a job that you are paid for: *a working mother* **b)** having a job that pays wages, especially one that uses your hands and physical strength, rather than your mind: *an ordinary working man*
2 working practices/conditions the ways of working or the conditions in which people in a particular company work, including safety, health, rights, and duties
3 working day/hours the period of time during the day when you are doing your job: *You can call at any time during working hours.*
4 a working relationship the relationship between people or groups who work together, especially people who work well together: **+between/with** *the working relationship between teacher and student* | **a strong/good/close working relationship** *A company should have a good working relationship with its suppliers.*
5 in (good/perfect) working order working correctly and not broken: *It was an old computer, but still in good working order.*
6 a working knowledge of sth enough knowledge of a system, foreign language etc. to be able to use it, although your knowledge is limited: *You need a working knowledge of Spanish.*
7 a working definition/theory a definition or theory that is not complete in every detail, but is good enough for you to use when you are studying something or starting a job
8 WHILE WORKING done while you continue to work: *The trip to Hawaii is actually a working vacation.* | **a working breakfast/lunch/dinner etc.** (=a breakfast, lunch etc. which is also a business meeting)
9 OPERATING able to be operated or used: *a working fireplace* | **a working model** (=a model that has parts that move and can be used like the real thing) | **working parts** (=the parts of a machine that move and operate the machine)

working² *n.* **1** [singular] also **workings** the way something such as a system, piece of equipment, or organization works: **+of** *The book gives us insight into the*

W

workings of the Pentagon. | **the efficient/smooth/successful etc. working of sth** *Reliable employees are essential to the smooth working of any business.* **2** [C usually plural] a mine or part of a mine where soil has been dug out in order to remove metals or stone

ˈworking ˌcapital *n.* [U] ECONOMICS the money that is available to be used for the costs of a business → see also VENTURE CAPITAL

ˌworking ˈclass *n.* **the working class** the group of people in society who traditionally do physical work and do not have much money or power **—working-class** *adj.*: *a working-class neighborhood* → see also LOWER CLASS, MIDDLE CLASS, UPPER CLASS

ˌworking ˈday *n.* [C] a WORKDAY

ˈworking ˌgirl *n.* [C] OLD-FASHIONED **1** a word for a woman who has sex for money, used when you want to avoid saying this directly **2** a young woman who has a paid job

ˈworking ˌgroup *n.* [C] a committee that is established to examine a particular situation or problem and suggest ways of dealing with it

ˈworking ˌlife *n.* [C] the part of your adult life when you work: *He's been with the company all his working life.*

ˈworking ˌpapers *n.* [plural] official documents that you need in order to get a job if you are young or from a foreign country

ˌworking ˈpoor *n.* **the working poor** [plural] the people who have jobs, but do not earn enough money to live a comfortable life

ˌworking ˈstiff *n.* [C] INFORMAL an ordinary person who works in order to earn enough money to live and usually has a boring job

ˌwork in ˈprogress *n. plural* **works in progress** [C] something such as a work of art, piece of writing etc. that is not yet finished or perfect

work·load /ˈwɚkloʊd/ *n.* [C] the amount of work that a person or machine is expected to do: *Modern technology has failed in some ways to reduce our workload.*

W

work·man /ˈwɚkmən/ *n. plural* **workmen** /-mən/ [C] someone who does physical work such as building, repairing things etc.

work·man·like /ˈwɚkmənˌlaɪk/ *adj.* done or made skillfully, but often in an uninteresting way: *a workmanlike campaign*

work·man·ship /ˈwɚkmənˌʃɪp/ *n.* [U] skill in making things, especially in a way that makes them look good

ˌworkmen's compenˈsation also **ˌworkmen's ˈcomp** SPOKEN *n.* [U] WORKERS' COMPENSATION

ˌwork of ˈart *n. plural* **works of art** [C] **1** ENG. LANG. ARTS a painting, SCULPTURE etc. of very high quality **2** HUMOROUS something that is very attractive and skillfully made: *That cake is a real work of art.*

work·out /ˈwɚk-aʊt/ *n.* [C] a period of physical exercise, especially as training for a sport → see also **work out** at WORK[1]

ˈwork ˌpermit *n.* [C] an official document from a foreign government that gives you permission to work in that country

work·place /ˈwɚkpleɪs/ *n.* [C] **1** the room, building etc. where you work: *a safe workplace* **2 the workplace** people's working life in general: *discrimination **in the workplace***

ˈworkplace ˌdocument *n.* [C] ENG. LANG. ARTS a piece of writing that people use when they are doing their jobs, such as a MEMO or a report → see also CONSUMER DOCUMENT, FUNCTIONAL DOCUMENT, INFORMATIONAL DOCUMENT, PUBLIC DOCUMENT

ˈwork reˌlease *n.* [U] a situation in which a prisoner is allowed to work outside of prison

work·room /ˈwɚkrum/ *n.* [C] a room that you work in, especially where you make things

work·sheet /ˈwɚkʃit/ *n.* [C] a piece of paper with questions, exercises etc. for students

work·shop /ˈwɚkʃɑp/ S2 *n.* [C] **1** a room or building where tools and machines are used for making or repairing things **2** a meeting at which people try to improve their skills by discussing their experiences and doing practical exercises: *a theater workshop for high school students*

work·site /ˈwɚksaɪt/ *n.* [C] a place where people work, especially outside

work·sta·tion /ˈwɚkˌsteɪʃən/ *n.* [C] the part of an office where you work, where your desk, computer etc. are

ˈwork-ˌstudy *n.* [U] work that a student does on a college or university CAMPUS in order to earn money to pay for their education

work·up /ˈwɚkʌp/ *n.* [C] a series of tests used to find out if someone is physically or mentally healthy: *a full medical workup*

work·week /ˈwɚkwik/ *n.* [C] the total amount of time that you spend working during a week: *a 40-hour workweek*

world[1] /wɚld/ S1 W1 *n.*

1 OUR PLANET/ALL PEOPLE the world the PLANET we live on, and all the people, cities, and countries on it SYN **earth**: *the world's tallest building* | *Her death stunned the world.* | *At that time China was the most powerful country **in the world**.* | **all over the world/all around the world/throughout the world** *People from all over the world want to learn English.* | *Malaria is a common disease in some **parts of the world**.* | *Global warming affects **the whole world**.* ►see THESAURUS box at earth

2 SOCIETY [singular] the society that we live in and the kind of life we have: *We thought we could **change the world** when we were young.* | *Parents want **a better world for** their children.* | ***In the real world**, things are never quite so simple.* | **in an ideal/a perfect world** *We don't live in a perfect world.*

3 in the world used to emphasize a statement you are making: *I felt like the luckiest guy in the world.* | ***Nothing in the world can** make up for the loss of a mother.* | **what/who/where/how etc. in the world...?** *What in the world are you talking about?*

4 AREA OF ACTIVITY/WORK [C usually singular] a particular area of activity or work, and the people who are involved in it: *the fast-paced business world* | **+of** *the world of fashion*

5 GROUP OF COUNTRIES [singular] a particular group of countries or part of the world: **the Arab/Western/English-speaking etc. world** *Opinion in the Western world is divided.* | **the industrialized/developing/developed etc. world** *the economies of the industrialized world* → see also THIRD WORLD

6 PERIOD IN HISTORY [singular] a particular period in history and the society and people of that time: **the ancient/medieval/modern etc. world** *The custom was common in the ancient world.* | **+of** *the world of the Anglo-Saxons*

7 the animal/plant/insect world animals, plants etc. considered as a group of living things with their own particular way of living or behaving

8 TYPE OF PLACE/SITUATION [C usually singular] a particular type of place or situation: **+of** *a world of lies and secrecy*

9 SB'S LIFE [C] the life a particular person or group of people lives, especially the things they do and the people they know: *Meeting him changed my world.*

10 sb would give the world to do sth used to say that someone would like to do something very much: *I'd give the world to see her again.*

11 the world over in every country or area of the world SYN **everywhere**: *Hollywood movies are popular the world over.*

12 PLACE LIKE THE EARTH [C] a PLANET in another part of the universe where other things may live: *strange creatures from another world*

13 in a world of your own also **in your own (little) world** INFORMAL in a situation or having a way of thinking in which you do not seem to notice what is happen-

ing around you and are more concerned with your own thoughts: *I tried to talk to Ed about it, but he was off in his own little world.*
14 do sb a world of good INFORMAL to make someone feel much better: *A week by the ocean will do you a world of good.*
15 a world of difference (between sth and sth) a very large difference between two things
16 be worlds apart also **be a world apart** people, opinions, or situations that are worlds apart are so completely different that there is almost nothing about them that is similar: *I realized we were still worlds apart.*
17 be worlds away (from sth) also **be a world away (from sth) a)** to be completely different from something **b)** to be a great distance from something
18 have the world at your feet a) to be very famous, popular, or successful **b)** to be in a position where you have the chance to become very successful
19 give the world sth to produce or invent something that affects many people: *Walton is the man who gave the world linoleum.*
20 out of this world INFORMAL something that is out of this world is so good, enjoyable etc., it is unlike anything else you have ever experienced
21 not for the world if someone would not do a particular thing for the world, they would never do it whatever happened: *I **wouldn't** hurt Amy **for the world**.*
22 think (that) the world revolves around you INFORMAL, DISAPPROVING to think that you are more important than anyone or anything else
23 think (that) the world owes you a living INFORMAL, DISAPPROVING to be unwilling to work in order to get things, and expect them to be provided for you
24 a man/woman of the world someone who has had many experiences, knows how to behave, and is not easily shocked
25 what is the world coming to? used to say that you do not like the way society is changing
26 come into the/this world LITERARY to be born
27 bring sb into the world LITERARY to give birth to a child
28 depart/leave this world LITERARY to die
29 move/go/come up in the world to move to a higher position in society, so that you have a better job, more money etc. OPP **move/go/come down in the world**
30 for all the world like/as if/as though LITERARY exactly like, or exactly as if: *He looked and sounded for all the world like Elvis.*
31 for (all) the world to see also **for the whole world to see** available for everyone to see or know
32 the world is sb's oyster used to tell someone that there is no limit to the opportunities that they have: *If you've got a good education, the world is your oyster.*
33 NOT RELIGIOUS the world the way of life most people live, rather than a SPIRITUAL way of life: *John renounced the world when he became a monk.*
34 workers/women/people etc. of the world used when talking to all workers, women etc. in a speech, book etc.
35 the world to come also **the next world** LITERARY the place where people's souls are believed to go after they die
[**Origin:** Old English *woruld* **human existence, this world, age**] → see also NEW WORLD, OLD WORLD, **think the world of sb** at THINK (41)

world² *adj.* [only before noun] **1** existing in, involving, or affecting the whole world: *a threat to world peace* **2** being the best or most important in the world: *the reigning world champion* | *a meeting of world leaders*

World 'Bank, the *n.* ECONOMICS a bank based in the U.S. that gives financial help to countries that need money for development: *A lot of schemes funded by the World Bank, such as dams, are highly capital-intensive.*

world beat *n.* [U] WORLD MUSIC

world-ˌbeater *n.* [C] someone or something that is the best at a particular activity —**world-beating** *adj.*

world-'class *adj.* among the best in the world: *a world-class orchestra*

ˌworld-'famous *adj.* known about by people all over the world: *a world-famous gymnast*

ˌWorld 'Health Organiˌzation, the an international organization that is part of the U.N. and helps countries to improve their people's health by giving medicines and providing information

world·ly /'wɚldli/ *adj.* [only before noun] **1 sb's worldly goods/possessions** FORMAL OR HUMOROUS the things that someone owns **2** having a lot of experience and knowledge about people and life: *a worldly New Yorker* **3** relating to ordinary daily life, rather than SPIRITUAL or religious ideas: *worldly influences* —**worldliness** *n.* [U]

ˌworldly-'wise *adj.* having a lot of experience and knowledge about life so that you are not easily shocked or deceived

'world ˌmusic *n.* [U] a type of music that combines traditional styles of music from around the world with modern popular styles

ˌworld 'power *n.* [C] a country that has a lot of power and influence in many parts of the world

ˌworld 'record *n.* [C] the fastest speed, longest distance, highest or lowest level etc. that has ever been achieved or reached in the world, especially in sports: *He **holds the world record** in the 400 meters.* —**world-record** *adj.* [only before noun] *a world-record time*

ˌWorld 'Series *n.* **the World Series** the last series of baseball games that is played each year in order to decide the best professional team in the U.S. and Canada

ˌWorld 'Trade ˌCenter a set of seven buildings in New York City, all of which were destroyed on September 11, 2001, when TERRORISTS flew two airplanes into the two tallest buildings → see also AL-QAEDA

ˌWorld 'Trade Organiˌzation, the an international organization that deals with the rules of trade between different nations and encourages them to trade fairly

world·view /ˌwɚld'vyu/, **world view** *n.* [C usually singular] the way in which someone understands the world, which includes their beliefs and attitudes

World War I /ˌwɚld wɔr 'wʌn/ also **the First World War** (1914–1918) HISTORY a war fought in Europe between France, the U.K. and its EMPIRE, Russia, and the U.S. on one side (known together as "the Allies"), and Germany, Austria-Hungary, and Turkey on the other side

World War II /ˌwɚld wɔr 'tu/ also **the Second World War** (1939–1945) HISTORY a war involving almost every major country in the world. On one side were the Allies (including the U.K., France, and Poland, and after 1941 the U.S. and the Soviet Union) and on the other side the Axis (including Germany, Japan, and Italy).

ˌworld-'weary *adj.* feeling that life is not interesting or exciting anymore: *world-weary soldiers*

world·wide /ˌwɚld'waɪd◂/ *adj., adv.* everywhere in the world: *a worldwide economic crisis* | *The credit cards can be used worldwide.*

ˌWorld ˌWide 'Web ABBREVIATION **WWW** *n.* **the World Wide Web** the WEB

worm¹ /wɚm/ *n.* [C] **1** a long thin creature with no bones and no legs, especially one that lives in soil SYN **earthworm** **2** a small thin creature with no legs that is the LARVA (=young form) of an insect **3** COMPUTERS a type of computer VIRUS that keeps copying itself until it fills up the space on a computer **4** INFORMAL someone who you do not like or respect **5 worms** [plural] PARASITES (=small creatures that eat your food or your blood) that live in a person's or animal's body: *The dog **has worms**.* **6 the worm turns** LITERARY used to say that someone who is normally quiet and OBEDIENT has changed and has become strong and active [**Origin:** Old English *wyrm* **snake, worm**] → see also **a (whole) can of worms** at CAN² (5)

W

worm² *v.* [T] **1 worm your way into sb's life/heart/confidence etc.** to gradually make someone love or trust you, especially by being dishonest **2 worm your way into sth** to gradually get yourself into a particular situation, especially using unfair or dishonest methods **3 worm your way out of (doing) sth** to avoid doing something that you have been asked to do by making an excuse that is dishonest **4 worm your way into/through/under etc. sth** to move through a small place or a crowd slowly, carefully, or with difficulty **5** to give an animal medicine in order to remove PARASITES that live inside it

worm sth **out of** sb *phr. v.* to get information from someone who does not want to give it: *We managed to worm the address out of him.*

ˈworm-ˌeaten *adj.* **1** worm-eaten wood or fruit has holes in it because it has been eaten by worms **2** old and damaged

worm·hole /ˈwɚmhoʊl/ *n.* [C] **1** a hole in a piece of wood etc. made by a type of WORM **2** TECHNICAL a HYPOTHETICAL passage through the universe that connects one place or time with another more closely than is normally expected

worm·wood /ˈwɚmwʊd/ *n.* [U] a plant with a bitter taste, used in making some types of alcohol

worm·y /ˈwɚmi/ *adj.* full of worms: *a wormy apple*

worn¹ /wɔrn/ the past participle of WEAR

worn² *adj.* **1** a worn object is old and damaged: *a worn spot on the carpet* **2** someone who looks worn seems tired

ˌworn ˈout, worn-out *adj.* **1** very tired because you have been working hard: *I'm worn out.* ►see THESAURUS box at **tired** **2** too old or damaged to be used: *an old, worn-out pair of pants*

wor·ried /ˈwɚid, ˈwʌrid/ [S1] [W3] *adj.* **1** unhappy because you keep thinking about a problem, or are anxious about something: *What's wrong? You look worried.* | *a worried expression* | **+about** *You shouldn't be so worried about your weight.* | **worried (that)** *Dana's worried that we'll be late again.* | *When you didn't call, I started to* ***get worried.*** | *Where on earth have you been? I was* ***worried sick*** (=extremely worried)*!*

W

THESAURUS

anxious very worried and unable to relax: *She felt anxious and tense, not knowing how he would react.*
concerned worried about a social problem, or about someone's health, safety etc.: *Many scientists are concerned about global warming.*
nervous worried or frightened about something, and unable to relax: *I get really nervous about exams.*
uneasy worried because you think something bad might happen: *I felt uneasy about leaving her home alone.*
stressed (out) so worried that you cannot relax: *I'm getting totally stressed out about work.*
tense feeling nervous and worried because something bad might happen: *All the guys were tense, clutching their rifles.*
apprehensive worried about something you are going to do, or about the future: *The girls were apprehensive before the game, knowing that Illinois was a tough opponent.*

2 you had me worried SPOKEN used to tell someone that they made you feel confused or anxious because you did not correctly understand what they said, or did not realize that it was a joke: *You really had me worried – I thought you didn't like the present.* **—worriedly** *adv.*

wor·ri·er /ˈwɚiɚ/ *n.* [C] someone who often worries about things

wor·ri·some /ˈwɚisəm/ *adj.* FORMAL making you worried and anxious

wor·ry¹ /ˈwɚi, ˈwʌri/ [S1] [W2] *v.* **worries**, *past tense and past participle* **worried, worrying**

1 BE ANXIOUS [I] to be anxious or unhappy because you keep thinking about something bad that has happened or that might happen: *Stop worrying – you'll be fine.* | **+about/over** *Fran worries too much about the way she looks.* | **worry (that)** *I worried that I had offended them.*
2 don't worry SPOKEN **a)** used when you are trying to make someone feel less anxious: *Don't worry. I'll lend you money if you need it.* **b)** used to tell someone that they do not need to do something: **+about** *Don't worry about filing those papers right now.*
3 MAKE SB ANXIOUS [T] to make someone feel anxious about something: *The rise in housing costs worries most young families.* | **worry sb that** *It worries me that Christina hasn't found a job yet.* | *You shouldn't* ***worry yourself*** *so much – everything will be fine.*
4 (there is) nothing to worry about also **sb has nothing to worry about** SPOKEN used to tell someone that something is not as serious or difficult as they think: *Everything is organized, so there's nothing to worry about.*
5 have enough to worry about SPOKEN used to say that someone already has a lot of problems or is very busy: *Don't call her now. She has enough to worry about.*
6 don't worry your (pretty little) head about it SPOKEN used to tell someone not to worry about something in a way that suggests that they are not smart enough to deal with it
7 ANNOY [T] OLD-FASHIONED to annoy someone
[**Origin:** Old English *wyrgan* **to strangle**]

worry² *n. plural* **worries** **1** [C] a problem that you are anxious about or are not sure how to deal with: *financial worries* | **+about** *There are worries about slow economic growth.* | **+for** *Money was always a big worry for us.* | *Not having money for a car was* ***the least of*** *his* ***worries*** (=used to say that he had more important things to worry about). **2** [U] the feeling of being anxious about something: *When she didn't come home, we were* ***sick with worry.***

ˈworry beads *n.* [plural] small stones or wooden balls on a string that you move and turn in order to keep yourself calm

wor·ry·ing /ˈwɚi-ɪŋ/ *adj.* making you feel anxious: *a worrying rise in crime*

wor·ry·wart /ˈwɚiˌwɔrt/ *n.* [C] SPOKEN someone who worries all the time about everything

worse¹ /wɚs/ [S1] [W3] *adj.* [the comparative of "bad"] **1** not as good as, less pleasant than, or more severe than someone or something else [OPP] **better**: *Lying is bad but stealing is worse.* | *The damage was* ***worse than*** *I expected.* | **much/a lot/far worse** *The behavior of some kids is a lot worse.* | *Their relationship has* ***gotten worse*** *recently.* | *It's* ***no worse*** *than having your ears pierced.* | *The second hotel was* ***even worse*** *than the first.* | **make matters/things/it worse** *I tried to help, but I think I made things worse.* **2** sicker than before or in a condition that is not as good as before: *She looks worse today.* | *If the symptoms* ***get worse****, take two of these tablets.* | *My knee feels* ***worse than*** *it did yesterday.*
3 it/things could be worse SPOKEN used to say that a bad situation is not as bad as it could be: *Things could be worse – at least you're not living on the street.*
4 there's nothing worse than (doing) sth SPOKEN used to say that you are very annoyed at something bad that often happens [**Origin:** Old English *wiersa, wyrsa*] → see also **go from bad to worse** at BAD¹ (19)

GRAMMAR **worse, worst**

More and **most** are not used together with **worse** or **worst**: *Math is my worst subject* (NOT *my most worse/most worst subject*). | *The situation is much worse than it was last week* (NOT *much more worse*). Some people think that **worse** should not be used as an adverb meaning "in a worse way". However, many people use it this way in spoken English: *I hope the team doesn't play any worse next week.*

worse² *n.* **1** [U] something that is not as good as something else: *This movie was bad, but I've seen worse.* **2 for the worse** into a worse thing, situation, or person: *The character of the place had changed for the* *worse.* **3 the worse for wear** INFORMAL in poor condition, or very tired **4 all the worse** even worse than it would have been or seemed if the situation had been different: *The accident was all the worse because it happened to a child.* → see also BETTER, **none the worse/better etc.** at NONE² (1), **take a turn for the worse/better** at TURN² (8), **if worse/worst comes to worst** at WORST² (4)

worse³ [W2] *adv.* [comparative of "badly"] **1** in a more severe or serious way than before: *My head hurt* ***worse than ever.*** **2** to a lower standard or quality, or less successfully: *No one sings* ***worse than I do.*** **3** [sentence adverb] used for saying that a particular situation or fact is worse than another bad one that has just been mentioned: *She never went to school and,* ***even worse,*** *never learned to read.* **4 sb can/could do worse than do sth** SPOKEN used to say that you think it is a good idea if someone does a particular thing

wors·en /ˈwɚsən/ *v.* [I,T] to become worse, or to make something worse: *The situation worsened.*

ˌworse ˈoff *adj.* [not before noun] **1** having less money than before or than someone else [SYN] **poorer** [OPP] **better off**: *We're no* ***worse off than*** *a lot of other people.* **2** in a worse situation than before or than someone else: *There's always someone worse off than you.*

wor·ship¹ /ˈwɚʃɪp/ *v.* **worshiped** or **worshipped**, **worshiping** or **worshipping** **1** [I,T] to show respect and love for God or a god, especially by praying in a church, TEMPLE etc. **2** [T] to admire and love someone very much: *Kevin worships his older brother.* **3 worship the ground sb walks on** to admire or love someone so much that you cannot see their faults —**worshiper, worshipper** *n.* [C]

worship² *n.* [U] **1** the activity of praying and singing etc. in order to show respect and love for God or a god: **a house/place of worship** (=a church, temple etc.) **2** USUALLY DISAPPROVING a strong feeling of love or admiration for someone or something, especially so that you cannot see their faults [**Origin:** Old English *weorthscipe* **being worthy, respect**] → see also HERO WORSHIP

wor·ship·ful /ˈwɚʃɪpfəl/ *adj.* LITERARY showing respect or admiration for God, someone, or something

worst¹ /wɚst/ [S2] [W2] *adj.* [the superlative of "bad"] **1** [only before noun] worse than anything else of the same kind or worse than at any time before: *the worst student in the class* | *It was their* ***worst*** *performance* ***ever.*** | *That would be* ***the worst possible*** *result.* | *It's been* ***one of the worst*** *days of my life.* **2 be your own worst enemy** to do things that it harm you or stop you from becoming successful, especially by being stupid **3 sb's worst fears** the thing that someone least wants to happen: *My* ***worst fears were realized*** (=they happened) *when I saw the test questions.* → see Grammar box at WORSE¹

worst² *n.* **1 the worst** the person, thing, situation, state, part etc. that is worse than all others of the same kind or worse than at any time before: *Most of the girls were pretty mean, but Sabrina was the worst.* | **+of** *The worst of the ordeal is over.* | ***The worst of it*** *was that no one believed her.* | **expect/fear the worst** (=to expect the situation to have the worst possible result) **2 at worst** if a situation is as bad as it can be, or in the worst cases: *Her work is at best acceptable and at worst unbelievably bad.* **3 at sb/sth's worst** as bad as someone or something can be: *You haven't seen Tina at her worst.* **4 if worse/worst comes to worst** if the situation develops in the worst possible way: *If worse comes to worst, I can always get my old job back.* **5 get the worst of it** to lose a fight or argument **6 get the worst of sth** to get fewer advantages or more disadvantages from something than someone else gets **7 do your/its worst** used to say that you are not worried by the power of someone or something to harm you: *Do your worst – I don't care.* → see also **bring out the best/worst in sb** at BRING OUT (2)

worst³ *adv.* [the superlative of "badly"] **1** most badly: *It was the worst written book I've ever read.* | *The coastal area was worst affected by the earthquake.* **2 worst of all** used to say what the worst feature of someone or something is: *He was timid, selfish and, worst of all, lazy.*

ˈworst-case *adj.* [only before noun] involving the worst possible situation: ***The worst-case scenario*** *is that I won't make any money.*

worst·ed¹ /ˈwʊstɪd, ˈwɚs-/ *adj.* worsted wool is made from long FIBERS twisted together

worsted² *n.* [U] a type of wool cloth

worth¹ /wɚθ/ [S1] [W2] *prep.*

1 sth is worth sth used to say that something has a particular value in money: *The painting is worth over $1 million.* | *How much is the ring worth?* | *Are these dolls worth anything?* | *Haring's paintings are now* ***worth a fortune*** (=extremely valuable).

2 sb is worth sth used to say what the value of someone's money and possessions is: *She's now worth over $200 million.* | *The family* ***is worth a fortune*** (=extremely rich).

3 STH IS GOOD/USEFUL ETC. used to say that something is good, useful, or enjoyable and as valuable as the time, money, or effort it takes to do: **sth is worth doing/reading/finding etc.** *It's the only TV show worth watching.* | **sth is worth a trip/visit/try etc.** *The exhibition is worth a look.* | **be worth the effort/trouble/time etc.** *The dish is difficult to cook but worth the effort.* | *Taking a computer class would* ***be well worth*** *your* ***while*** (=worth the time it takes). | *It was a lot of hard work, but it* ***was worth it.*** | *Don't start a fight –* ***it's not worth it.*** | **it's worth (doing) sth** *It's worth getting there an hour early if you want a seat.*

4 for what it's worth SPOKEN used to say that you realize that what you are saying may not be important: *For what it's worth, I think you did a fine job.*

5 make it worth sb's while SPOKEN to offer someone money or something if they agree to do something for you, especially something dishonest

6 sth is not worth the paper it's printed on used to say that something printed, especially a contract, has no value

7 worth your salt doing your job well or deserving respect: *A cop worth his salt wouldn't take a bribe.*

8 do sth for all you're worth to do something with as much effort as possible

9 be worth your/its weight in gold to be very useful or valuable: *Efficient systems like these are worth their weight in gold.*

[**Origin:** Old English *weorth* **worthy, of a particular value**]

> WORD CHOICE **worth, value**
> **Worth** as a noun means the same as **value**, but **worth** sounds old-fashioned or literary: *the value of life* (NOT the *worth* of life). In an old story you might read: *a pearl of great worth.*

worth² [S2] [W3] *n.* [U] **1 ten dollars'/15 cents' etc. worth of sth** an amount of something worth ten dollars, 15 cents etc.: *$2,000 worth of computer equipment* **2 ten minutes'/a week's etc. worth of sth** something that takes ten minutes, a week etc. to happen, do, or use: *There's about a week's worth of work left.* **3** how good, useful, or important someone or something is: *These new players have already proved their worth.* **4** the value of something measured in money: *The company's current* ***net worth*** *is $2 million.*

worth·less /ˈwɚθlɪs/ *adj.* **1** having no value, importance, or use: *a completely worthless exercise* **2** a worthless person has no good qualities or useful skills —**worthlessly** *adv.* —**worthlessness** *n.* [U]

worth·while /ˌwɚθˈwaɪl◂/ *adj.* something that is worthwhile deserves the time, effort, or money you give to it: *a worthwhile job*

wor·thy¹ /ˈwɚði/ *adj. comparative* **worthier**, *superlative* **worthiest** **1 be worthy of (sb's) admiration/contempt etc.** to deserve to be thought about or treated in a particular way: **+of** *The proposal is certainly worthy of consideration.* **2** FORMAL deserving the respect, admiration, or effort that people give it: *a worthy opponent* | *The money is being raised for a*

W

worthy cause. **3 worthy of sb** as good or as bad as something that a particular person would do: *That kind of talk is not worthy of you.* **4** having many good qualities, but not very interesting or exciting **5 I'm/We're not worthy!** SPOKEN, HUMOROUS used to say that you consider it a great honor to be with someone because they are much more famous, TALENTED etc. than you are, and you are feeling very strong emotions because of this —**worthiness** *n.* [U]

worthy[2] *n. plural* **worthies** [C usually plural] FORMAL someone who is important and should be respected

Wo·tan /ˈvoʊtɑn/ the German name for the Norse god Odin

would /wəd, əd, d; *strong* wʊd/ S1 W1 *modal verb* short form **'d** negative form **wouldn't** **1** used instead of "will" to report what someone said, asked etc.: *Andy said he would give come later.* **2** used in CONDITIONAL sentences to give the imagined result of something that is expressed in the past tense or SUBJUNCTIVE: *Dad would be really mad if he knew we borrowed his car.* | **would have done sth** *If she'd asked me, I would have said yes.* **3 would you...? a)** used to express a polite request: *Would you shut the window, please?* **b)** used to express a polite offer or invitation: ***Would you like to*** *stay and watch a movie?* **4 sth would not do sth** used to say that you could not make a machine or other object do the thing that you wanted it to do: *The engine wouldn't start.* **5 sb would not do sth** used to say that someone was not willing to do something: *They wouldn't accept my apology.* **6** used to give or ask for advice: ***I would*** *get there early, if you can.* | *What* ***would you*** *do?* **7** used to describe what someone used to do a lot or what used to happen a lot: *We would often go for long walks in the park.* **8** used to express wishes about the present or the future: *I wish the rain would stop.* **9** used with some verbs to say politely that someone wants to do something or wants something: **would like/love/prefer** *My parents would like to meet you.* | *I* ***would rather*** *stay home tonight.* | ***I'd hate*** *to miss anything.* **10 I would think/imagine/say/guess etc.** used when giving your opinion to make it sound less definite: *The total cost, I would guess, might be $100 per person.* **11** WRITTEN used to talk about a time that was in the future at the past time you are talking about, but is now in the past: *I would later realize that this was a mistake.* **12** SPOKEN used to say what you think is likely to be true, when you are not sure: *I guess she'd be about 30 now.* **13** DISAPPROVING used when you are talking about something annoying that someone has done: *You would go and spoil it, you jerk!* **14 would that...** LITERARY used to express a strong wish or desire: *Would that he hadn't died.* [**Origin:** Old English *wolde*]

W

ˈwould-be *adj.* **a would-be actor/thief etc.** someone who hopes to have a particular job or intends to do a particular thing

would·n't /ˈwʊdnt/ *v.* the short form of "would not": *He wouldn't say what was wrong.*

wouldst /wʊdst/ OLD USE **thou wouldst** you would

would've /ˈwʊdəv/ *v.* the short form of "would have": *I would've helped you if I'd known.*

wound[1] /waʊnd/ the past tense and past participle of WIND

wound[2] /wund/ *n.* [C] **1** MEDICINE an injury, especially a cut or hole made in your skin by a weapon such as a knife or a bullet: *gunshot wounds* | *The* ***wound healed*** *fast.* | *Luckily, it was only* ***a flesh wound*** (=slight injury to the skin). ►see THESAURUS box at **injury** **2** a feeling of emotional or mental pain that you get when someone says or does something that is not nice to you: *deep emotional wounds* [**Origin:** Old English *wund*] → see also **lick your wounds** at LICK[1] (5), **open old wounds** at OPEN[2] (21), **rub salt into a wound** at RUB[1] (6)

wound[3] /wund/ *v.* [T usually passive] **1** to injure someone, especially by making a cut or hole in their skin using a knife, gun etc.: *Several people were wounded in the attack.* | **be fatally/mortally wounded** (=to be wounded so badly that you will die) ►see THESAURUS box at **hurt**[1] **2** to make someone feel unhappy or upset

wound·ed /ˈwundɪd/ *adj.* **1** injured by a weapon such as a gun or knife: *a wounded soldier* | **severely/seriously/badly wounded** *a badly wounded animal* **2** very upset because of something that someone has said or done: *wounded pride* —**the wounded** *n.* [plural]

Wound·ed Knee, the Battle of /ˌwundɪd ˈni/ HISTORY the last important battle between the U.S. army and the Native Americans, which took place at Wounded Knee Creek in South Dakota in 1890. U.S. soldiers killed almost 200 Sioux people, including women and children.

wound up /ˌwaʊnd ˈʌp/ *adj.* [not before noun] anxious, worried, or excited

wove /woʊv/ the past tense of WEAVE

wo·ven /ˈwoʊvən/ the past participle of WEAVE

wow[1] /waʊ/ *interjection* INFORMAL used when you think something is impressive or surprising: *Wow! That's a great car!*

wow[2] *v.* [T] INFORMAL to make people admire you very much

WP the abbreviation of WORD PROCESSOR

wpm /ˌdʌbəlyu pi ˈɛm/ the abbreviation of "words per minute"

wrack[1], **rack** /ræk/ *v.* **1 wrack/rack your brain(s)** to think very hard or for a long time: *He wracked his brain for something sensible to say.* **2 be wracked/racked by/with sth a)** to suffer great mental or physical pain: *Lisa was wracked by guilt.* → see also NERVE-RACKING **b)** to suffer with a particular problem: *This region is continually wracked by violence.*

wrack[2] *n.* → see **go to rack/wrack and ruin** at RACK[1] (6)

wraith /reɪθ/ *n.* [C] LITERARY a GHOST, especially of someone who has just died

Wrang·ell, Mount /ˈræŋgəl/ a high mountain that is one of the Wrangell Mountains in southern Alaska

ˈWrangell ˌMountains a RANGE of mountains in southern Alaska

wran·gle[1] /ˈræŋgəl/ *n.* [C] a long and complicated argument

wrangle[2] *v.* **1** [I] to argue with someone angrily for a long time **2** [T] to gather together cows or horses from a large area

wran·gler /ˈræŋglə/ *n.* [C] INFORMAL a COWBOY

wrap

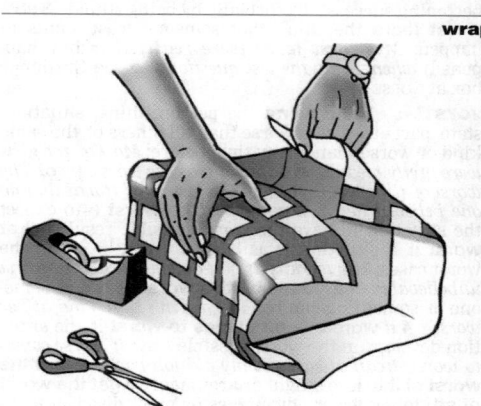

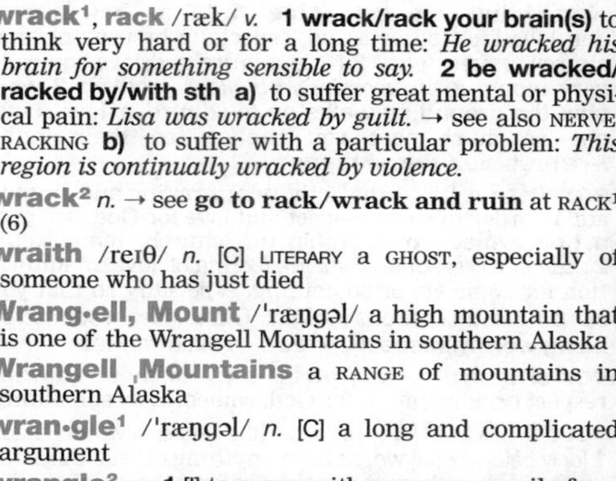

wrap[1] /ræp/ S2 W3 *v.* **wrapped, wrapping** [T] to cover something by folding paper, cloth etc. around it: *Help me to wrap these presents.* | **wrap sb/sth in sth** *Wrap each plate in newspaper.*

wrap sth **around** sb/sth *phr. v.* **1** to wind or fold cloth, paper etc. around something: *Rita wrapped the scarf around her neck.* **2** if you wrap your arms, legs, fingers etc. around something, you use them to hold it: *He wrapped his arms around her waist.* → see also **twist/wrap sb around your little finger** at FINGER[1] (9)

wrap up *phr. v.* **1 wrap sth ↔ up** to cover something by folding paper, cloth etc. around it: *We need to wrap the presents up before the kids see them.* **2 wrap sth ↔ up** to finish or complete a job, meeting etc.: *Both companies hope to wrap up the deal by Friday.* **3** to put on warm clothes: *Wrap up if you're going outside.* **4 be wrapped up in your children/work etc.** to give so much of your attention to your children, your work etc. that you do not have time for anything else

wrap² *n.* **1** [U] thin transparent plastic used to cover food **2** [C] a type of SANDWICH made with thin bread which is rolled around meat, vegetables etc. **3** [C] a piece of cloth that a woman wears around her shoulders to keep her warm **4 keep sth under wraps** to keep something secret **5 it's/that's a wrap** SPOKEN **a)** used to say that you have finished doing something **b)** used to say that filming on a movie has ended **6** [singular] the time when filming ends on a movie

wrap·a·round /ˈræpəˌraʊnd/ *adj.* **1** going around the sides of something, as well as across the front of it: *wraparound sunglasses* | **a wraparound deck/porch** (=one that is built on more than one side of the house) **2 a wraparound skirt/dress** a skirt or dress consisting of a single piece of cloth that you wrap around your body tightly and fasten **3** used to describe a shot, as in HOCKEY, that is made after going behind the GOAL and then turning toward the side or front of the net

wrap·per /ˈræpɚ/ *n.* [C] the piece of paper or plastic that covers something when it is sold: *a candy wrapper*

wrap·ping /ˈræpɪŋ/ *n.* [C,U] cloth, paper, or plastic that is wrapped around something to protect it

wrapping ˌpaper *n.* [U] colored paper that you use for wrapping presents

wrap-up *n.* [C usually singular] INFORMAL a short report at the end of something, giving the main points again

wrath /ræθ/ *n.* [U] FORMAL extreme anger: *He did not want to **incur** the king's **wrath*** (=make him angry). —**wrathful** *adj.* —**wrathfully** *adv.*

wreak /rik/ *v. past tense and past participle* **wreaked** also **wrought** /rɔt/ **1 wreak havoc/devastation/damage etc.** to cause a lot of damage, problems, and suffering **2 wreak vengeance/revenge on sb** to do something unpleasant to someone to punish them for something they have done to you

wreath /riθ/ *n.* [C] **1** a circle of leaves that you hang up on a door or wall as a decoration, for example at Christmas **2** a circle made from flowers or leaves that you put on a grave **3** a circle made from leaves that was given to someone in the past for them to wear on their head as an honor **4 a wreath of sth** LITERARY something in the shape of a circle

wreath

wreathe /rið/ *v.* LITERARY **1 be wreathed in sth** to be surrounded by or covered in something: *Her face was wreathed in curls.* **2 be wreathed in smiles** to look very happy

wreck¹ /rɛk/ *v.* [T] **1** to completely spoil or destroy something such as a plan, relationship, or opportunity: *Alcohol problems wrecked their marriage.* **2** to damage something so badly that it cannot be repaired: *The car was completely wrecked in the accident.* ▸see THESAURUS box at **destroy** **3** [usually passive] if a ship or boat is wrecked, it becomes so badly damaged that it sinks

wreck² *n.* [C] **1** something such as a car, ship, or airplane that has been damaged very badly, especially in an accident: *Investigators are searching the wreck.* → see also SHIPWRECK **2** an accident involving cars or other vehicles SYN **crash**: *Ten people were injured in the wreck.* | **a car/train/plane wreck** *He was killed in a car wreck.* → see also SHIPWRECK ▸see THESAURUS box at **accident** **3** [usually singular] INFORMAL someone who is very nervous, tired, or unhealthy: *He was a complete wreck by the time we got there.* | *I was a **nervous wreck** waiting for you to call.* **4** INFORMAL something, especially a car, that is in a very bad condition: *It's embarrassing to be seen driving that old wreck.* **5** an accident in which a ship sinks

wreck·age /ˈrɛkɪdʒ/ *n.* [U] **1** the parts of something such as an airplane, ship, or building that are left after it has been destroyed in an accident: *Crews are working to clear away the wreckage.* **2** the destruction of someone's relationships, hopes, plans etc.

wreck·er /ˈrɛkɚ/ *n.* [C] **1** a vehicle used to move damaged cars or other vehicles **2** someone who destroys a relationship, plan, opportunity etc.: ***a home wrecker*** (=someone who destroys someone else's marriage)

ˈwrecking ball *n.* [C] a heavy metal ball attached to a chain or CABLE which is used to knock down buildings or other structures

ˈwrecking crew *n.* [C] a group of people whose job is to tear down buildings or other structures

ˈwrecking yard *n.* [C] a place where pieces of destroyed buildings, cars etc. are brought

wren /rɛn/ *n.* [C] BIOLOGY a very small brown bird

Wren /rɛn/, **Christopher** (1632–1723) a British architect

wrench¹ /rɛntʃ/ *n.* **1** [C] **a)** a metal tool with a round end that fits around and turns NUTS and BOLTS **b)** a MONKEY WRENCH **2 throw a (monkey) wrench in sth** to do something that will cause problems or spoil what someone else is planning **3** [singular] a strong feeling of sadness or other strong emotion: *I felt a wrench in my stomach.* **4** [C usually singular] a twisting movement that pulls something violently

wrench² *v.* [T] **1** [always + adv./prep.] to use your strength to pull yourself away from someone or something that is holding you: **wrench yourself away/free etc.** *She managed to wrench herself free.* **2** MEDICINE to injure a part of your body by twisting it suddenly: *Brian wrenched his back trying to carry a heavy box.* **3** [always + adv./prep.] to twist and pull something from its position using force, or to be moved in this way: **wrench sth away/free/off etc.** *I wrenched the package from his grasp.* **4** [always + adv./prep.] LITERARY to move or remove someone or something from one position or state to another with great difficulty or using a lot of determination: *We finally wrenched the kids away from the TV.*

wrench·ing /ˈrɛntʃɪŋ/ *adj.* a wrenching situation, story, movie etc. is extremely difficult to deal with because it makes you feel strong emotions: **gut-wrenching/heart-wrenching** *It was a gut-wrenching decision to leave college.*

wrest /rɛst/ *v.* [T always + adv./prep.] FORMAL **1** to take power or influence away from someone, especially when this is difficult: *Democrats hoped to wrest control of Congress from the Republicans.* **2** to pull something away from someone violently: *He wrested the gun from his assailant.*

wres·tle /ˈrɛsəl/ *v.* [I,T] **1** to fight someone by holding onto them and pulling or pushing them: *The boys wrestled in the dirt.* | +**with** *The men started wrestling with each other.* | *Two officers **wrestled** her **to the ground*** (=pushed her down to the ground and held her). **2** to take part in the sport of wrestling

wrestle with sth *phr. v.* **1** to try to deal with or find a solution to a difficult problem: *The city has been wrestling with the housing issue for years.* **2** to have difficulty controlling or holding something that is very large, heavy, or difficult to use: *She was wrestling with a large box.*

wres·tler /ˈrɛslɚ/ *n.* [C] someone who wrestles as a sport

wres·tling /ˈrɛslɪŋ/ *n.* [U] a sport in which two people fight by holding onto and pushing each other and trying to make each other fall to the ground: *a wrestling match* → see also PROFESSIONAL WRESTLING

wretch /retʃ/ *n.* [C] **1** someone you feel sorry for because their condition is so bad **2** someone you are annoyed or angry with **3** LITERARY an evil person

wretch·ed /ˈretʃɪd/ *adj.* LITERARY **1** extremely bad or unpleasant in a way that makes you feel upset: *wretched living conditions* **2** very unhappy or poor: *a lonely and wretched old man* **3** INFORMAL very bad or of very poor quality: *She's had some wretched luck.* **4** SPOKEN used about something or someone that annoys you: *Where did I put that wretched pen?* **5 wretched excess** behavior that people think is too extreme and immoral, especially because it involves activities such as spending a lot of money, drinking alcohol, having sex etc. —**wretchedly** *adv.* —**wretchedness** *n.* [U]

wrig·gle /ˈrɪgəl/ *v.* **1** [I] to twist from side to side with small quick movements: **+under/through/into etc.** *He wriggled through an open window.* **2** [T] to make part of your body move this way SYN **wiggle**: *She took off her shoes and wriggled her toes.* —**wriggly** *adj.*

wriggle out of sth *phr. v.* to avoid doing something by making excuses: *Once again, he wriggled out of any punishment.*

-wright /raɪt/ *suffix* [in nouns] someone who makes a particular thing: *a playwright* (=someone who writes plays)

Wright /raɪt/, **Frank Lloyd** /fræŋk lɔɪd/ (1869–1959) a U.S. ARCHITECT, generally regarded as one of the most important architects of the 20th century

Wright, Richard (1908–1960) an African-American writer of NOVELS

ˈWright ˌBrothers, the two U.S. brothers, Orville Wright (1871–1948) and Wilbur Wright (1867–1912), who built and flew the world's first plane in 1903 → see picture on page A25

Wrig·ley /ˈrɪgli/, **William** (1861–1932) a U.S. businessman who made CHEWING GUM and started the Wrigley company

W

wring /rɪŋ/ *v. past tense and past participle* **wrung** /rʌŋ/ [T] **1** to tightly twist a wet cloth or wet clothes in order to force out the water SYN **wring out** **2 wring your hands a)** DISAPPROVING to say how worried or upset you are about your situation, instead of doing something to make it better **b)** to rub and twist your hands together because you are worried and upset → see also HAND-WRINGING **3 I'll wring sb's neck** SPOKEN said when you want to punish someone because they did something that has made you angry **4 wring sth's neck** to kill something such as a chicken by twisting its neck

wring sth ↔ **out** *phr. v.* to tightly twist a wet cloth or wet clothes in order to force out the water: *Wring out the cloth first.* → see also WRUNG-OUT

wring sth **out of** sb also **wring sth from sb** *phr. v.* to succeed in getting or achieving something, but only after a lot of effort: *I managed to wring the information out of him.*

wring·er /ˈrɪŋɚ/ *n.* [C] **1 through the wringer** INFORMAL experiencing a difficult, upsetting situation: *His ex-wife is* ***putting him through the wringer***. **2** a machine with two ROLLERS that press the water from washed clothes when you turn a handle, used in the past

ˌwringing ˈwet *adj.* extremely wet

wrin·kle¹ /ˈrɪŋkəl/ *n.* [C] **1** a line on your face or skin that you get when you are old **2** a small messy fold in a piece of clothing or paper SYN **crease**: *My skirt's full of wrinkles.* **3** a small problem: **iron/smooth out the wrinkles (in sth)** (=to solve the small problems in something) **4** a strange and interesting feature or fact that was unexpected or that most people do not know about —**wrinkly** *adj.*

wrinkle² *v.* [I,T] **1** if you wrinkle a piece of clothing, cloth, or paper, or if it wrinkles, it gets small messy folds in it: *My blue jacket wrinkles too easily.* **2** also **wrinkle up** if you wrinkle your nose, face etc., or if it wrinkles, you move it so that there are wrinkles on or around it **3** BIOLOGY if skin wrinkles or something wrinkels it, it develops small folds and lines as you get older or as it becomes damaged

wrin·kled /ˈrɪŋkəld/ also **wrink·ly** /ˈrɪŋkli/ *adj.* wrinkled skin, cloth, or paper has lines or small folds in it

wrist /rɪst/ *n.* [C] **1** BIOLOGY the joint between your hand and the lower part of your arm: *The rope was tied around his wrists.* | **slash/slit your wrists** (=to deliberately cut your wrists to try to kill yourself) **2 it's all in the wrist** SPOKEN, HUMOROUS used as a reply to someone who has praised you for something that you did skillfully with your hands

wrist·band /ˈrɪstbænd/ *n.* [C] **1** the leather, metal, or plastic band that is part of a wristwatch **2** a band worn around your wrist to keep your hand dry, especially when you are playing sports **3** a band worn around your wrist, for example in a hospital → see also BRACELET

wrist·watch /ˈrɪst-wɑtʃ/ *n.* [C] a watch that you wear on your wrist

writ¹ /rɪt/ *n.* [C] LAW a document from a court that orders someone to do or not to do something → see also HOLY WRIT

writ² *adj.* **writ large** [only after noun] FORMAL in a clear noticeable form, or on a large scale

write /raɪt/ S1 W1 *v. past tense* **wrote** /roʊt/ *past participle* **written** /ˈrɪtˀn/ **writing**

1 BOOK/ARTICLE ETC. a) [I,T] to produce a new book, story, poem etc. by putting words together: *She spends the mornings writing.* | *How many books has he written?* | **+about** *We had to write about our summer vacation.* → see also WRITTEN **b)** [I] to be a writer of books, plays, articles etc., especially as a job: *I'd love to write.* | **+on** *LeBrun often writes on women's issues.* | **+for** *He writes for the Washington Post.*

2 LETTER [I,T] to write a letter or message to someone: *Don't forget to write.* | *Chris hasn't written me for a long time.* | *I wrote a few emails before lunch.* | **+to** *I'm going to write to the manager about this.* | **write sth to sb** *I wrote a letter to my former teacher.* | **write sb sth** *I wrote postcards to all my friends.* | **write (sb) that** *Uncle Brian wrote that he'll come visit on the 26th.* | **write to say/ask/express etc. sth** *They wrote to say they were arriving earlier.*

3 PUT WORDS/NUMBERS ON PAPER a) [I,T] to form letters or numbers with a pen or pencil: *Write your name here.* | *He could* ***read and write*** *when he was four.* **b)** [I] if a pen or pencil writes, it works correctly: *Which one of these pens still writes?*

THESAURUS

make a note (of sth) to write down information that you might need later
jot sth down to write something very quickly
scribble sth to write something very quickly and in a messy way
scrawl sth to write something quickly in a big messy way
take/get sth down to write down what someone is saying
fill sth out/in to write information about yourself on a form or other official document
sign sth to write your signature (=name) at the end of a letter, document, etc.
key sth in/type sth in/enter sth to write or record information on a computer
→ READ

4 CHECK/DOCUMENT ETC. [T] to write information on a check, form etc. SYN **write out**: **write sb sth** *Can I write you a check?*

5 SONG/MUSIC [T] to produce a song or piece of music: *She's written songs for several shows.*

6 COMPUTER PROGRAM [T] to produce a computer program: *Engineers at our company wrote the software.*

7 SPELL [T] to spell something or use a specific style or

rule when you write it down: *Katherine's name is written with a K.*
8 sb has sth written all over their face also **sth is written all over sb's face** used to say that it is very clear what someone is feeling or thinking: *He had guilt written all over his face.*
9 sth has sth written all over it used to say that something shows a particular quality or fact very clearly: *The project had "failure" written all over it.*
10 nothing to write home about also **not anything to write home about** INFORMAL not especially good or special: *Their house is nothing to write home about.*
11 sb wrote the book on sth SPOKEN used to say that someone knows a lot about something or is very good at something: *The company wrote the book on quality control.*
12 that's all she wrote SPOKEN used to say that something is completely finished
[**Origin:** Old English *writan* **to scratch, draw, write**]

write away for sth *phr. v.* to write to a company or an organization and ask them for something SYN **write off for** SYN **send off for**: *I wrote away for their free catalog.*

write back *phr. v.* **write sb back** to answer someone's letter by sending them a letter: *I hope she writes back soon.* | *Why didn't you write him back?*

write sth ↔ **down** *phr. v.* to write information, ideas etc. on a piece of paper in order to remember them: *Did you write down his number?*

write in *phr. v.* **1** to write to an organization asking them for information or giving an opinion: *Many viewers wrote in to complain about the show.* **2 write sb ↔ in** to add someone's name to your BALLOT in order to vote for them, when they are not on the official list of CANDIDATES in a particular election → see also WRITE-IN **3 write sth ↔ in** to write information in the space provided for it on a form or document: *Could you write your name in at the top?* **4 write sb/sth ↔ in** to add another part or feature to something that is written, for example a new scene or character to a play or a new condition to a contract

write sth **into** sth *phr. v.* to include something such as a rule or condition in a document, agreement etc. or to add a new part or feature to something that is written, for example a new scene or character to a play or a new condition to a contract: *Time for training was written into the schedule.*

write off *phr. v.* **1 write sb/sth ↔ off** to decide that someone or something is useless, unimportant, or a failure: **write sb/sth off as sth** *Coaches wrote him off as too short to play football.* **2 write sth ↔ off** to officially say that someone does not have to pay a debt, or to accept that money you have paid or lent will not be paid back: *The banks are refusing to write off these loans.* → see also WRITE-OFF **3 write sth ↔ off** to use an amount of money you have spent on something as a way to reduce your taxes → see also WRITE-OFF

write off for sth *phr. v.* to write to a company or an organization and ask them for something SYN **write away for** SYN **send off for**: *I wrote off for some information about the college.*

write out *phr. v.* **1 write sth ↔ out** to write something in its complete form, including all the details: *Could you write out the procedures for ordering new equipment?* **2 write sth ↔ out** to write information on a check or a form: *Write the check out for $235.* **3 write sb ↔ out, write sb out of sth** to remove one of the characters from a regular television or radio program

write up *phr. v.* **1 write sth ↔ up** to write a report, article etc. using notes that you made earlier: *I have to write my report up before the meeting.* **2 be written up** if a person, place, product etc. is written up in a newspaper or magazine, someone has written an article giving their opinion about them: *The diner was written up in the local paper.* → see also WRITE-UP **3 write sb ↔ up** to make an official written report of a crime or something wrong that someone has done: *They wrote me up for being late again.*

'write-in *n.* [C] POLITICS a vote you give to someone by writing their name on your BALLOT

'write-in ˌcandidate *n.* [C] POLITICS someone who is competing in an election but whose name does not appear on the BALLOT (=piece of paper on which you record your vote). Voters choose a write-in candidate by writing down his or her name on the ballot paper.

'write-off *n.* [C] **1** an official agreement that someone does not have to pay a debt **2** ECONOMICS an official reduction from an amount or from the value of something, especially used for calculating how much tax someone owes: *The President proposed a **tax write-off** for tuition expenses.*

writ·er /ˈraɪt̬ɚ/ S2 W1 *n.* [C] **1** ENG. LANG. ARTS someone who writes books, stories etc., especially as a job: *a science-fiction writer* | **+on** *a well-known writer on religion* | **+of** *a writer of romance novels* **2** the person who wrote a particular letter, article etc.: *The writer of the letter was probably a woman.*

ˌwriter's 'block *n.* [U] the problem that a writer sometimes has of not being able to think of new ideas

ˌwriter's 'cramp *n.* [U] a feeling of stiffness in your hand that you get after writing for a long time

'write-up *n.* [C] a written opinion about a new book, play, or product in a newspaper, magazine etc.

writhe /raɪð/ *v.* [I] **1** to twist your body from side to side violently, especially because you are suffering pain: **writhe in pain/agony** *One patient writhed in pain after being given a shot.* **2 writhe with anger/hate/shame etc.** LITERARY to feel anger, hate etc. in a very strong way

writ·ing /ˈraɪt̬ɪŋ/ S2 W2 *n.* **1** [U] words that have been written or printed: *The writing on the label is too small for me to read.* **2 in writing** if you get something in writing, it is official proof of an agreement, promise etc.: **get/put sth in writing** *I want these guarantees put in writing.* **3** [U] books, poems etc. in general, especially those by a particular writer or about a particular subject: *Sherman produced his best writing back in the 1960s.* **4** [U] the activity of writing books, stories etc.: *He later took up writing as a career.* | **creative/business writing** *a course in creative writing* **5** [U] the activity of making words on a page with a pen or pencil: *She's making progress in reading and writing.* **6 writings** [plural] the books, stories etc. that a particular person has written: *Plato's writings* **7** [U] the particular way that someone writes with a pen or pencil SYN **handwriting**: *Your writing is very neat.* **8 the writing is on the wall** also **see/read the writing on the wall** used to say that it seems very likely that something will not exist much longer or someone will fail

'writing desk *n.* [C] a desk with special places for pens, paper etc.

'writing ˌpaper *n.* [U] good quality paper that you use for writing letters

writ·ten¹ /ˈrɪt̚n/ the past participle of WRITE

written² *adj.* **1** [only before noun] in the form of words on paper: *a written agreement* | *There is no written record of the meeting.* **2** [only before noun] involving writing, rather than speaking or listening, especially in relation to language learning: *Her written English is excellent.* | *a written test* **3** used to describe the quality of a piece of writing: **well/poorly/badly written** *The books are very well written.* | **beautifully/clearly/cleverly etc. written** *a beautifully written poem* **4 the written word** FORMAL writing as a way of expressing ideas, emotions etc., as opposed to speaking

wrong¹ /rɔŋ/ S1 W2 *adj.*
1 NOT CORRECT not correct, or based on something that is not correct: *He gave the wrong answer.* | *Your calculations must be wrong.* | *I **got** the first three questions **wrong**.*

W

THESAURUS

incorrect used about facts, answers etc. that are completely wrong: *incorrect spelling*
inaccurate used about information, a number etc. that is not exactly right: *The information the police received was inaccurate.*
misleading used about a statement or piece of information that makes people believe something that is wrong: *He admitted making a false and misleading statement to Congress.* | *misleading advertising*
false/untrue used about facts that are untrue and wrong: *He used false financial statements to defraud investors.*
mistaken FORMAL used about an idea that is wrong, or a person whose opinion about something is wrong: *I must have been mistaken about the time we were to meet.* | *the mistaken belief that the drug is not addictive*
→ RIGHT

2 NOT HAVING THE RIGHT OPINION [not before noun] thinking or believing something that is not correct: *If you think that, then you're wrong.* | **+about** *I think he's French but I might be wrong about that.* | *Doctors said she'd never walk but she* ***proved*** *them all* ***wrong****.* | **be wrong to think/say** *I was wrong to think that I couldn't trust you.*
3 NOT THE RIGHT ONE not the one that you intended or the one that you should use: *She got on the wrong bus.* | *They arrested the wrong man.* | *No, there's no Bruce here – you have* ***the wrong number*** (=used to say that someone has telephoned the wrong person by mistake).
4 PROBLEMS [not before noun] used to talk about situations where there are problems or where someone is unhappy: ***What's wrong****? You look so sad.* | *She could see from his face that* ***something was*** *seriously* ***wrong****.* | ***There is nothing wrong with*** *our marriage.*
5 NOT WORKING CORRECTLY [not before noun] if something is wrong with a vehicle, machine, system, or part of your body, it is not working correctly: *She had lots of X-rays but doctors couldn't find anything wrong.* | ***What's wrong with*** *the washing machine?* | ***There was something wrong with*** *the brakes.* | *You can walk – there's* ***nothing wrong with*** *your legs.* | *Dave* ***has something wrong with*** *his foot.*
6 NOT APPROPRIATE not appropriate for a particular purpose, situation, or person: *These shoes are the wrong size.* | **+for** *We were wrong for each other in many ways.*
7 NOT MORAL not morally right or acceptable OPP right: *Mom always told us that stealing was wrong.* | **it is wrong (of sb) to do sth** *It was wrong of you to lie to Julia.* | **do something/nothing/anything wrong** *I didn't do anything wrong.* | *There's* ***nothing wrong with*** *making lots of money as long as you don't cheat people.* ►see THESAURUS box at bad[1]
8 **what's wrong with (doing) sth?** used to say that you think something is good, fair etc., and you do not understand why other people think it is not: **+with** *What's wrong with wearing blue socks with a black suit?*
9 **get on the wrong side of sb** to do something that gives someone a bad opinion of you, so that they do not like or respect you in the future
10 **get off on the wrong foot** to start a job, relationship etc. badly by making a mistake that annoys people
11 **on the wrong side of the law** having done something illegal and in trouble with the police
12 **take sth the wrong way** to be offended by a remark because you have understood it differently than someone meant it
13 **be in the wrong place at the wrong time** to have something bad happen to you by chance rather than because you did something wrong
14 **be on the wrong track** to have the wrong idea about a situation so that you are unlikely to get the result you want
15 **the wrong side of the tracks** INFORMAL the poor part of a city or a poor part of society
16 **be on the wrong side of 30/40 etc.** HUMOROUS to be older than 30, 40 etc. → see also **get up on the wrong side of the bed** at BED[1] (8), **correct me if I'm wrong** at CORRECT[2] (5)
[**Origin:** 1100–1200 Old Norse *rangr* **not correct or as planned**]

wrong[2] S1 W2 *adv.* **1** not in the correct way: *They spelled my name wrong again.* | *She knew she had done it wrong.* **2 go wrong a)** to stop developing in the way you want: *He felt as though everything was going wrong.* **b)** to do something that makes a plan, relationship etc. fail: *As far the contract was concerned, I don't know where I went wrong.* **3 get sth wrong** to make a mistake in the way you write, judge, or understand something: *You must have gotten the directions wrong.* | **get/have it all wrong** (=understand a situation in completely the wrong way) **4 don't get me wrong** SPOKEN used when you think someone may understand your remarks in the wrong way, or be offended by them: *Don't get me wrong – I like Jenny, but she can be a little bossy.* **5 you can't go wrong (with sth)** SPOKEN used to say that a particular object or plan will always be appropriate, satisfactory, or work well: *You can't go wrong with a dark gray suit.* | *Follow the instructions and you can't go wrong.*

wrong[3] W3 *n.* **1** [U] behavior that is not morally right: *Very young children don't know right from wrong.* | *People who* ***do wrong*** *should be punished.* **2** [C] an action, judgment, or situation that is unfair: *It is time to* ***right*** *society's* ***wrongs*** (=bring justice to an unfair situation). **3 sb can do no wrong** used to say that someone thinks someone else is perfect, especially when you do not agree with this opinion: *As far as Tammy was concerned, Nick could do no wrong.* **4 be in the wrong** FORMAL to make a mistake or deserve the blame for something: *Hardin publicly admitted he had been in the wrong.* **5 do sb wrong** HUMOROUS to treat someone badly and unfairly **6 two wrongs don't make a right** SPOKEN used to say that doing something bad will not make another bad situation right or fair

wrong[4] *v.* [T] FORMAL to treat or judge someone unfairly: *Both athletes felt they had been wronged by the committee's decision.*

wrong·do·er /ˈrɔŋˌduɚ/ *n.* someone who does something bad or illegal —**wrongdoing** *n.* [C,U]

wrong·ful /ˈrɔŋfəl/ *adj.* **1 wrongful arrest/termination/dismissal etc.** a wrongful arrest etc. is unfair or illegal because the person affected by it has done nothing wrong **2 wrongful death** LAW the death of a person caused by someone else doing something illegal —**wrongfully** *adv.*

wrong·head·ed /ˌrɔŋˈhɛdɪd◂/ *adj.* DISAPPROVING based on or influenced by wrong ideas that you are not willing to change —**wrongheadedly** *adv.*

wrong·ly /ˈrɔŋli/ *adv.* **1** not correctly or in a way that is not based on facts: *Perrin had wrongly assumed that he would not get caught.* | *Matthew was wrongly diagnosed as having a brain tumor.* **2** in a way that is unfair or immoral: **wrongly accused/convicted/imprisoned etc.** *Franklin was wrongly accused of murdering a cop.* → see also **rightly or wrongly** at RIGHTLY (2)

wrote /rout/ the past tense of WRITE

wrought /rɔt/ **1** the past tense and past participle of WREAK **2** LITERARY OR OLD USE a past participle of WORK

ˈwrought ˌiron *n.* [U] long thin pieces of iron formed into shapes to make gates, fences etc.

wrung /rʌŋ/ the past tense and past participle of WRING

ˌwrung-ˈout *adj.* INFORMAL feeling very weak and tired

wry /raɪ/ *adj.* [only before noun] showing that you know a situation is bad but that you also think it is slightly amusing: *a wry smile* [**Origin:** 1500–1600 *wry* **to twist** (14–19 centuries), from Old English *wrigian* **to turn**] —**wryly** *adv.*

wt. the written abbreviation of "weight"

W

WTO → see WORLD TRADE ORGANIZATION

Wu·di, Wu Di /ˌwu ˈdi/ HISTORY (156–86 B.C.) the ruler of China from 140 to 86 B.C.

wun·der·kind /ˈvʊndɚˌkɪnt, ˈwʌndɚˌkɪnd/ *n.* [C] a young person who is very successful

wurst /wɚst/ *n.* [U] a type of SAUSAGE

wuss /wʊs/ *n.* [C] SPOKEN someone who you think is weak or lacks courage

WV a written abbreviation of WEST VIRGINIA

W.Va. a written abbreviation of WEST VIRGINIA

WWI the abbreviation of WORLD WAR I

WWII the abbreviation of WORLD WAR II

WWW the written abbreviation of WORLD WIDE WEB

WY a written abbreviation of WYOMING

Wyc·liffe /ˈwɪklɪf/, **John** (?1328–1384) an English religious leader who criticized the power of the Catholic Church, and started the translation of the Bible into English

Wy·eth /ˈwaɪəθ/, **An·drew** /ˈændru/ (1917–) a U.S. PAINTER

Wyo. a written abbreviation of Wyoming

Wy·o·ming /waɪˈoʊmɪŋ/ WRITTEN ABBREVIATION **WY** a state in the western U.S.

WYSIWYG /ˈwɪziˌwɪg/ *n.* [U] **what you see is what you get** COMPUTERS something that appears on a computer screen in exactly the same way as it will look when it is printed

wy·vern /ˈwaɪvɚn/ *n.* [C] an imaginary animal that has two legs and wings and looks like a DRAGON

W

X,x

X[1], x /ɛks/ *n. plural* **X's, x's** **1** [C] **a)** the 24th letter of the English alphabet **b)** a sound represented by this letter **2** [U] MATH used in mathematics to represent an unknown quantity or value that can be calculated: *If 3x=6, then x=2.* **3** [C] a mark used on school work to show that a written answer is wrong **4** [C] POLITICS a mark used to show that you have chosen something on an official piece of paper, for example when voting **5** [C] a mark used instead of a SIGNATURE by someone who cannot write **6** [C,U] used in the past to show that no one under the age of 17 could see a particular movie. It is now used only in an unofficial way for movies that contain a lot of sex. → see also NC-17 **7** used instead of someone or something's real name, because you want to keep it secret, you do not know it, or you are not talking about a specific person or thing: *Let's call the defendant in this case Mr. X.* **8** [C] a mark used to show a kiss, especially at the end of a letter **9 X number of sth** used to say that there are a certain number of people or things, when the exact number is not important: *Everyday I have X number of things to do.* **10 X marks the spot** used in games and on maps in adventure stories to show that something can be found at a particular place **11** [U] SLANG the illegal drug ECSTASY → see also GENERATION X

X[2] the number 10 in the system of ROMAN NUMERALS

X[3] *v.*

X sth ↔ out *phr. v.* SPOKEN to mark or remove a mistake in a piece of writing using an X SYN **cross out**

Xa·vi·er /ˈzeɪviɚ/, **St. Fran·cis** /seɪnt ˈfrænsɪs/ (1506–1552) a Spanish Christian priest who traveled to India, southeast Asia, and Japan as a MISSIONARY and who helped to start the religious ORDER of Jesuits

x-ax·is /ˈɛks ˌæksɪs/ *n.* [singular] MATH the line that goes from left to right on a GRAPH → see also Y-AXIS

X-chro·mo·some /ˈɛks ˌkroʊməˌsoʊm, -zoʊm/ *n.* [C] a type of CHROMOSOME that exists in pairs in female cells, and with a Y-CHROMOSOME in male cells

ˈx-coˌordinate *n.* [C] MATH the position of a point in relation to the x-axis of a GRAPH → see also Y-COORDINATE

xe·non /ˈzinɑn, ˈzɛ-/ *n.* [U] SYMBOL **Xe** CHEMISTRY a rare gas that is one of the chemical ELEMENTS

Xe·noph·a·nes /zɪˈnɑfəˌniz/ (?560–?478 B.C.) a Greek PHILOSOPHER

xen·o·pho·bi·a /ˌzɛnəˈfoʊbiə, ˌzi-/ *n.* [U] extreme fear or hatred of people from other countries [**Origin:** 1900–2000 Greek *xenos* **strange** + *phobos* **fear**] **—xenophobe** /ˈzɛnəˌfoʊb/ *n.* [C] **—xenophobic** /ˌzɛnəˈfoʊbɪk◂/ *adj.*

xe·rog·ra·phy /zɪˈrɑgrəfi/ *n.* [U] TECHNICAL a way of making copies of papers by using an electric machine which makes a special black powder stick onto paper to form words, pictures etc. **—xerographic** /ˌzɪrəˈgræfɪk/ *adj.*

xer·o·phyte /ˈzɪrəfaɪt/ *n.* [C] BIOLOGY a plant such as a CACTUS that can live successfully in a place where there is little water

Xer·ox, xerox /ˈzɪrɑks, ˈzi-/ *n.* [C] TRADEMARK a copy of a piece of paper with writing or printing on it, made using a special machine SYN **photocopy** **—Xerox, xerox** *v.* [I,T] *Can you xerox this report for me?*

x-in·ter·cept /ˈɛks ˌɪntɚˌsɛpt/ *n.* [singular] MATH the point where a line crosses the x-axis of a GRAPH → see also Y-INTERCEPT

XL the written abbreviation of EXTRA large, used especially on clothing

X·mas /ˈkrɪsməs, ˈɛksməs/ *n.* [U] INFORMAL a short way of writing the word CHRISTMAS, which some Christians think is offensive

X-rated /ˈɛks ˌreɪṭɪd/ *adj.* something that is X-rated is not considered appropriate for children and young people because it contains sex, violence, or offensive words: *an X-rated movie*

X-ray[1] /ˈɛks reɪ/ *n. plural* **X-rays** [C] **1** a photograph of part of the inside of the body, which shows the bones and some organs: *This is an X-ray of your left arm.* | *My dentist* ***took*** *two* ***X-rays*** *of my mouth.* **2** a medical examination made using X-rays: *You'd better have an X-ray.* | *a chest X-ray* **3** [usually plural] a beam of RADIATION that can go through solid objects and is often used for photographing the inside of the body [**Origin:** 1800–1900 Translation of German *X-strahl*, X representing **unknown**]

X-ray[2] *v.* **X-rays, X-rayed, X-raying** [T] to photograph the inside of something, especially someone's body, using X-rays: *First, we're going to X-ray your shoulder.*

XS the written abbreviation of EXTRA small, used especially on clothing

XXX *n.* [C,U] used in an unofficial way to show that a movie, magazine etc. contains a lot of sex

xy·lem /ˈzaɪləm/ *n.* [singular, U] BIOLOGY in a plant stem, the woody structure that carries water up from the roots to the other parts of the plant

xylophone

xy·lo·phone /ˈzaɪləˌfoʊn/ *n.* [C] a musical instrument which consists of a set of wooden bars of different lengths that you hit with a special stick

Y,y

Y, y /waɪ/ *n. plural* **Y's, y's** [C] **1 a)** the 25th letter of the English alphabet **b)** a sound represented by this letter **2 the Y** INFORMAL the YMCA or the YWCA

y. **1** a written abbreviation of YEAR **2** a written abbreviation of YARD

-y[1], -ey /i/ *suffix* [in adjectives] **1** full of something, or covered with something: *sugary desserts* (=full of sugar) | *dirty hands* (=covered with dirt) | *a hairy chest* (=covered with hair) **2** having a quality or feeling, or tending to do something: *a messy room* | *a sleepy baby* (=who feels tired) | *curly hair* (=that always curls) **3** like something, or typical of something: *his long, horsey face* (=he looks like a horse) | *a cold wintry day* (=typical of winter) **—-ily** /əli/ *suffix* [in adverbs] **—-iness** *suffix* [in nouns]

-y[2] *suffix* [in nouns] **1** used to make a word or name less formal, and often to show that you care about someone: *Where's little Johnny?* | *my daddy* (=my father) | *What a nice doggy!* → see also -IE **2** used to make nouns from some verbs to show an action: *excessive flattery* (=things you say to someone that are too nice) | *an inquiry* (=the act of asking questions formally or officially)

Y2K /ˌwaɪ tu ˈkeɪ/ *n.* the abbreviation of "Year 2000", used especially when talking about the computer problems that people expected when the date changed to 2000

ya /yʌ/ *pron.* SPOKEN, INFORMAL you: *See ya later.*

yacht /yɑt/ *n.* [C] a large expensive boat, used for racing or traveling for pleasure [**Origin:** 1500–1600 Early modern Dutch *jaght*, from Middle Low German *jachtschiff* **hunting ship**]

yacht·ing /ˈyɑṭɪŋ/ *n.* [U] the activity of traveling or racing in a yacht

yack /yæk/ another spelling of YAK

ya·da ya·da ya·da, yadda yadda yadda /ˌyɑdə ˌyɑdə ˈyɑdə/ SPOKEN said when you do not want to give a lot of detailed information, because it is boring or because the person you are talking to already knows it SYN **blah, blah, blah**

ya·hoo[1] /yɑˈhu/ *interjection* shouted when you are very happy or excited about something

ya·hoo[2] /ˈyɑhu/ *n.* [C] someone who is rough, noisy, and stupid [**Origin:** 1700–1800 From the name of a race of human-like animals in Jonathan Swift's "Gulliver's Travels" (1726)]

Yah·weh /ˈyɑweɪ/ *n.* a Hebrew name for God

yak[1] /yæk/ *n.* [C] an animal of central Asia that looks like a cow with long hair

yak[2], yack *v.* **yakked, yakking** [I + about] INFORMAL to talk continuously about things that are not very serious

y'all /yɔl/ *pron.* SPOKEN a word meaning "you" or "all of you," used mainly in the southeastern U.S.: *See y'all later.* → see also (YOU/THOSE) GUYS

yam /yæm/ *n.* [C] **1** a SWEET POTATO **2** BIOLOGY a tropical plant grown for its large root, which is eaten as a vegetable [**Origin:** 1500–1600 Portuguese *inhame* and Spanish *ñame*, from a West African language]

yam·mer /ˈyæmɚ/ *v.* [I] to talk continuously, in an annoying way

Yam·ous·sou·kro /ˌyɑməˈsukroʊ/ the capital city of the Ivory Coast

yang /yæŋ/ *n.* [U] the male principle in Chinese PHILOSOPHY which is active, light, positive, and which combines with YIN (=the female principle) to influence everything in the world [**Origin:** 1600–1700 a Chinese word meaning **sun, positive**]

Yan·gon /ˌyɑnˈgoʊn/ the capital and largest city of Myanmar

Yang·tze, the /ˌyæŋˈsi/ another name for the Chang river in China

Yank /yæŋk/ *n.* [C] INFORMAL an impolite word meaning an American, used by some British people

yank /yæŋk/ *v.* [I,T] INFORMAL to suddenly pull something quickly and with force: **+on** *Tom grabbed my hair and yanked on it.* | **yank sth out/back/open etc.** *I yanked my arm away from Tom's grip.* **—yank** *n.* [C] *She gave the rope a yank.*

Yan·kee /ˈyæŋki/ *n.* [C] **1** a word meaning someone born in or living in the northern states of the U.S., sometimes used in an insulting way by people from the southern U.S. **2** a word meaning an American, often used in an insulting way by people outside the U.S. **3** someone from New England **4 Yankee ingenuity** the ability that Americans are supposed to have to think of new ideas and interesting ways to solve problems

Ya·oun·dé /ˌyɑunˈdeɪ/ the capital city of Cameroon

yap[1] /yæp/ *v.* **yapped, yapping** [I] **1** if a small dog yaps, it makes short loud sounds in an excited way **2** to talk in a noisy way without saying anything very important or serious: *Some guy was yapping on his cell phone behind us.*

yap[2] *n.* [C] **1** the short loud sound that a small dog makes

Ya·qui /ˈyɑki/ a Native American tribe from northwest Mexico

yard /yɑrd/ S1 W2 *n.* [C] **1** the land around a house, usually covered with grass: *The ball landed in the neighbors' yard.* | **the front/back/side yard** *There's a "for sale" sign in their front yard.* → see also BACKYARD → compare GARDEN[1] (1), LAWN (1) **2** WRITTEN ABBREVIATION **yd.** a unit for measuring length and distance, equal to 3 feet or 0.91 meters **3** an enclosed area next to a building or group of buildings, used for a special purpose, activity, or business: *a prison exercise yard* → see also LUMBERYARD, SCHOOLYARD, SHIPYARD, **the whole nine yards** at WHOLE[1] (7) [**Origin:** (1, 3) Old English *geard* **enclosed area**]

yard·age /ˈyɑrdɪdʒ/ *n.* **1** [U] the number of yards that a team or player moves forward in a game of football **2** [C,U] the size of something measured in yards or square yards: *Calculate the yardage of fabric you need before you go to the store.*

yard·bird /ˈyɑrdbɚd/ *n.* [C] OLD-FASHIONED, SLANG **1** someone who is in prison, especially for a long time **2** someone who has a low rank in the army and has outdoor duties

ˈyard sale *n.* [C] a sale of used clothes and things from someone's house, that takes place in their YARD → see also GARAGE SALE

ˈyard sign *n.* [C] a sign that you put in front of your house before an election to say which person or political party you support

yard·stick /ˈyɑrdˌstɪk/ *n.* [C] **1** something that you compare another thing with, in order to judge how good or successful they are: **+of** *Is profit the only yardstick of success?* **2** a special stick that you use for measuring things, that is exactly one YARD long and is marked in feet and inches

yard·work /ˈyɑrdwɚk/ *n.* [U] work that you do outdoors to make your YARD look nice, such as cutting the grass, removing WEEDS, planting flowers etc.

Yar·en /ˈyɑrɛn/ the capital city of Nauru

yar·mul·ke /ˈyɑməkə, ˈyɑrməlkə/ *n.* [C] a small circular cap worn by some Jewish men

yarn /yɑrn/ *n.* **1** [U] long thick thread made of cotton or wool, which is used to KNIT things **2** [C] ENG. LANG. ARTS a story of adventures, travels etc., usually made more exciting and interesting by adding things that never really happened ▸see THESAURUS box at **story**

Y

yash·mak /ˈyæʃmæk/ *n.* [C] a piece of cloth that Muslim women wear across their faces in public

Ya·va·pai /ˈyɑvɑˌpaɪ/ a Native American tribe from the southwestern area of the U.S.

yaw /yɔ/ *v.* [I] TECHNICAL if a ship, aircraft etc. yaws, it turns away from the correct direction it should be traveling in —**yaw** *n.* [C,U]

yawl /yɔl/ *n.* [C] a type of boat with one main MAST (=pole) and sails, and another small mast and sail close to the back

yawn[1] /yɔn/ *v.* [I] **1** BIOLOGY to open your mouth wide and breathe in deeply, usually because you are tired or bored: *Fred yawned and stretched.* **2** also **yawn open** if a hole in the ground yawns, it is wide open or it suddenly becomes wide open, in a frightening way [**Origin:** Old English *geonian*]

yawn[2] *n.* **1** [C] BIOLOGY an act of yawning: *Kay shook her head and* ***stifled a yawn*** (=tried to stop yawning). **2** also **yawner** [singular] INFORMAL someone or something that is boring

yawn·ing /ˈyɔnɪŋ/ *adj.* **1** [only before noun] **2 a yawning gap/hole/pit etc.** a very large hole or space **3 a yawning gap/gulf/chasm etc.** a very large difference in people's attitudes, opinions etc.: *the yawning gap between the two parties*

y-axis /ˈwaɪ ˌæksɪs/ *n.* [singular] MATH the line that goes from top to bottom on a GRAPH → see also X-AXIS

Y-chro·mo·some /ˈwaɪ ˌkroʊməˌsoʊm, -ˌzoʊm/ *n.* [C] the CHROMOSOME that makes someone a male instead of a female → see also X-CHROMOSOME

ˈy-coˌordinate *n.* [C] MATH the position of a point in relation to the y-axis of a GRAPH → see also X-COORDINATE

yd. a written abbreviation of YARD or yards

ye[1] /yi, yə/ *pron.* BIBLICAL OR OLD USE a word meaning "you"

ye[2] /yi/ *determiner* a word meaning "the," used especially in the names of stores to make them seem old and attractive: *Ye Olde Antique Shoppe*

yea[1] /yeɪ/ *adv.* OLD USE yes OPP **nay**

yea[2] *n.* [C] an answer or vote that means yes OPP **nay**

Yea·ger /ˈyeɪgɚ/, **Charles (Chuck)** /tʃɑrlz, tʃʌk/ (1923–) a U.S. pilot who was the first man to fly faster than the speed of sound

yeah /yɛə/ S1 *adv.* SPOKEN, INFORMAL **1** yes: *"Do you want to come?" "Yeah, okay."* **2 oh, yeah?** used when someone has just told you something surprising or that you do not completely believe: *"He's a doctor." "Oh, yeah? He doesn't act like one."* **3 yeah, right** used to say you do not believe what someone has just told you: *"She's just trying to help you." "Yeah, right."*

year /yɪr/ S1 W1 *n.* [C]
1 12 MONTHS a period of about 365 days or 12 months, measured from any particular time: *I moved here two years ago.* | *Jackie has worked here for several years.* | *a three-year business plan* | **a/per year** *He earns $50,000 a year.* → see also FISCAL YEAR
2 JANUARY THROUGH DECEMBER a period of 365 or 366 days divided into 12 months, beginning on January 1 and ending on December 31 SYN **calendar year**: *The lease expires at the end of the year.* | *the year 2008* | **this/last/next year** *The accident happened on October 20 last year.* | *It's usually a lot colder* ***this time of year***.
3 AGE used in phrases to talk about someone's age: **be five/ten/50 etc. years old** *She could read by the time she was four years old.* | **three-year-old/18-year-old/92-year-old etc. sb/sth** *an eight-year-old child* | **a four-year-old/a six-year-old/a ten-year-old etc.** *You can't expect two-year-olds to know right from wrong.* | *The drug promises to* ***add years to*** *patients' lives.* | **ten/12/39 etc. years of age** *Children under 17 years of age will not be admitted.*
4 A LONG TIME years [plural] a very long period of time: ***It's been years since*** *I heard that joke.* | **in/for years** *I haven't been there for years.* | *It was the first time in years I had seen Kathy smiling.*
5 PERIOD years [plural] a particular period of time in someone's life or in history: **sb's childhood/teenage/retirement etc. years** *They've been friends since their college years.* | **the war/postwar/boom etc. years** *the drought years of the 1930s* | **the Bush/Clinton/Reagan etc. years** (=the period of time when someone was in power) | *They lived in Seattle during* ***the early years of*** *their marriage.* | ***In later years*** (=when he was older) *he turned to writing poetry.* | *My* ***years as*** *a student were among the happiest of my life.*
6 USUAL TIME FOR STH a period of time, about equal to or shorter than a year, that is the usual time for something to happen: **academic/school year** (=the time when schools, colleges etc. normally have classes, usually from September through May or early June in the U.S.) | **the financial/tax/fiscal year** *The company's fiscal year begins on June 1.*
7 all year round during the whole year: *It's warm enough to swim all year round.* → see also YEAR-ROUND
8 year after year also **year in, year out** continuously for many years: *The same birds returned to that tree year after year.*
9 year by year as each year passes: *Year by year, things are getting worse.*
10 SCHOOL/UNIVERSITY LEVEL a particular level that a student stays at for one year: *a first-year law student*
11 EARTH GOING AROUND SUN TECHNICAL a measure of time equal to 365¼ days, which is the amount of time it takes for the Earth to travel once around the sun
12 since the year one INFORMAL OR HUMOROUS for a very long time, or always
[**Origin:** Old English *gear*] → see also **be getting on (in years)** at GET ON (2), **not/never in a million years** at MILLION (4), YEARLY

year·book /ˈyɪrbʊk/ *n.* [C] a book printed once a year, especially by a school or college, with information and pictures about what happened there in the past year

ˈyear-end *n.* [U] the period of time at the end of a year —**year-end** *adj.* [only before noun] *a year-end report*

year·ling /ˈyɪrlɪŋ/ *n.* [C] an animal, especially a young horse, between one and two years old

year·long /ˌyɪrˈlɔŋ◂/ *adj.* [only before noun] continuing for a year, or all through the year: *a yearlong study*

year·ly /ˈyɪrli/ *adj., adv.* happening or appearing every year or once a year: *Investments are reviewed yearly.* | *yearly updates*

yearn /yɚn/ *v.* [I] LITERARY to have a strong desire for something, especially something that is difficult or impossible to get: **+for** *Hannah yearned for a child.* | **yearn to do sth** *Bud had always yearned to be a pilot.*

yearn·ing /ˈyɚnɪŋ/ *n.* [C,U] LITERARY a strong desire or feeling of wanting something: **+for** *a yearning for freedom*

ˈyear-round *adj.* [only before noun] happening or done during the whole year: *year-round schools* —**year-round** *adv.*

yeast /yist/ *n.* [U] a substance that is used and for making bread rise and for producing alcohol in beer and wine [**Origin:** Old English *gist*] —**yeasty** *adj.*

ˈyeast inˌfection *n.* [C] MEDICINE an infectious condition that affects the VAGINA in women

Yeats /yeɪts/, **W.B.** (1865–1939) an Irish writer of poems and plays

yecch /yʌk/ *interjection* SLANG used to say that you think something is very disgusting SYN **yuck** [**Origin:** 1900–2000 From the sound of vomiting]

yell[1] /yɛl/ *v.* **1** also **yell out** [I,T] to shout or say something very loudly, especially because you are frightened, angry, or excited: *Tim counted to three, then yelled "Go!"* | **+at** *Don't yell at me like that!* ►see THESAURUS box at **shout**[1] **2** [I] SPOKEN to ask for help: *If you need me, just yell.*

yell[2] *n.* [C] **1** a loud shout: **let out/give a yell** *He let out a yell and jumped.* **2** words or phrases that students and CHEERLEADERS shout together to show support for their school, college etc.

Y

yel·low¹ /ˈyɛloʊ/ S2 W2 *adj.* **1** having the color of butter or the middle part of an egg **2** also **yellow-bellied** INFORMAL DISAPPROVING not brave SYN cowardly [**Origin:** Old English *geolu*] —**yellow** *n.* [U]

yellow² *v.* [I,T] to become yellow, or make something become yellow: *The paper had yellowed with age.*

yellow ˈcard *n.* [C] a yellow card held up by a SOCCER REFEREE to show that a player has done something wrong

yellow ˌfever *n.* [C] MEDICINE a dangerous tropical disease in which your skin turns slightly yellow

yel·low·ish /ˈyɛloʊɪʃ/ *adj.* having a slight yellow color

yellow ˌjacket, yellowjacket *n.* [C] a type of WASP (=flying insect) with a yellow and black body, that can sting you

yellow ˈjournalism *n.* [U] DISAPPROVING newspaper articles in which shocking or exciting events are written about in an extreme and EXAGGERATED way

yellow ˈpages *n.* **the yellow pages** also **the Yellow Pages** TRADEMARK the name of a book that contains the telephone numbers of businesses and organizations in an area, arranged according to the type of business they do → see also WHITE PAGES

Yellow ˌRiver, the a long river in northern China

Yel·low·stone Na·tion·al Park /ˌyɛloʊstoʊn ˌnæʃənl ˈpɑrk/ a large national park, mostly in the state of Wyoming, known for its HOT SPRINGS and GEYSERS

yelp /yɛlp/ *v.* [I] to make a short sharp high cry because of excitement, pain etc. —**yelp** *n.* [C]

Yelt·sin /ˈyɛltsɪn/, **Bor·is** /ˈbɔrɪs/ (1931–) a Russian politician who was President of Russia from 1991 to 1999

Yem·en /ˈyɛmən/ a country in southwest Asia south of Saudi Arabia —**Yemeni** *n., adj.*

yen /yɛn/ *n. plural* **yen** **1** [C] the standard unit of money in Japan **2** [singular] a strong desire: **+to/for** *He suddenly had a yen to see his old girlfriend.* [**Origin:** (1) 1800–1900 from Japanese *en*, Chinese *yan*]

yeo·man /ˈyoʊmən/ *n. plural* **yeomen** /-mən/ [C] **1** an officer in the U.S. Navy who often works in an office **2** a farmer in Britain and Canada in the past who owned and worked on his own land

yep /yɛp/ S1 *adv.* SPOKEN, INFORMAL yes

yer /yɚ/ *possessive adj.* NONSTANDARD used in writing to show how "your" is pronounced in an informal way

Ye·re·van /ˌyɛrəˈvɑn/ the capital and largest city of Armenia

yes¹ /yɛs/ S1 W1 *adv.* SPOKEN

1 POSITIVE ANSWER used as an answer to say that something is true, that you agree, that you want something, or that you are willing to do something OPP no: *"It was a great show." "Yes, it was."* | *"Is that real gold?" "Yes, it is."* | *Would you like some more coffee?" **"Yes, please."*** | *"Can you give me a hand here?" "Yes, just a second."* | *"Can I have a glass of water?" "Yes, of course."* | *Let's go ask Dad. I'm sure he'll **say yes**.*

2 ANSWER TO NEGATIVE QUESTION used as an answer to a question or statement containing a negative, to say that the opposite is true: *"You didn't remember Dan's birthday did you?" "Yes, I did."* | *"There isn't any bread left." "Yes there is. It's on the table."*

3 yes, but... used to say that you agree with what someone has said but there is another fact to consider: *"He's very rich." "Yes, but money isn't everything."*

4 READY TO LISTEN/TALK used to show that you have heard someone or are ready to speak to them: *"Mike?" "Yes?"* | *Yes, sir, how can I help you?*

5 LISTENING used to show that you are listening to someone and want them to continue talking: *"So, I tried calling him..." "Yes..."*

6 yes and no used to show that there is not one clear answer to a question: *"Were you surprised?" "Well, yes and no."*
[**Origin:** Old English *gese*]

USAGE

In spoken English, **yes** is used mainly in fairly formal situations. In more informal speech, we use many different answers instead of **yes**. Some of these are **yeah**, **yep**, **okay**, **uh-huh**, and **sure**.

yes² *n.* [C] a vote, voter, or reply that agrees with an idea, plan, law etc. → see also AYE

yes³ *interjection* used to show that you are very excited or happy about something: *"Dad says we can go to the movies." "Yes!"*

ye·shi·va, ye·sh·ivah /yəˈʃivə/ *n.* a school for Jewish students, where they can train to become RABBIS (=religious leaders)

ˈyes-man *n. plural* **yes-men** [C] someone who always agrees with and obeys their employer, leader, etc. in order to gain some advantage

ˌyes/ˈno ˌquestion *n.* [C] a question to which you can only answer "yes" or "no"

yes·sir /ˈyɛsɚ/ *interjection* a way of writing how someone says "yes, sir," used to show agreement with a man in authority

yes·ter·day¹ /ˈyɛstɚdi, -ˌdeɪ/ S1 W2 *adv.* on or during the day before today: *What did you do yesterday?* | **yesterday morning/afternoon/evening** *He left yesterday afternoon.* | ***The day before yesterday** was Monday.* [**Origin:** Old English *giestran dæg*, from *giestran* **yesterday** + *dæg* **day**] → see also **I wasn't born yesterday** at BORN (9)

yesterday² *n.* [U] **1** the day before today: *Did you go to yesterday's meeting?* **2** a time in the recent past: *The events of yesterday cannot fully explain the world of today.* **3 yesterday's news** information that is old and not interesting anymore

yes·ter·year /ˈyɛstɚˌyɪr/ *n.* **of yesteryear** LITERARY from a time in the past: *the heroes of yesteryear*

yet¹ /yɛt/ S1 W1 *adv.* **1** [in questions or negatives] **a)** used to ask whether something has happened, or to say that something has not happened, when you are expecting it to happen: *Have they said anything about the money yet?* | *Did Steve call you yet?* | *The potatoes aren't quite ready yet.* → see Grammar box at JUST¹ **b)** used to ask whether something had happened by a particular time in the past, or to say that something had not happened by that time, when it happened later: *At that time we hadn't met yet.* **2 not yet** an expression meaning "not now" or "still not," used especially in the answer to questions: *"Did my package arrive?" "No, not yet."* **3 not (...) yet** used to say that something will not be done until a later time or should not be done until a later time: *I'll tell him soon, but not yet.* | *Don't go yet. I like talking to you.* **4** in addition to what you have already gotten, done etc. SYN still: **yet more/bigger/later etc.** *California could face yet more financial difficulties.* | *This is **yet another** reason to be cautious.* | *The opening has been delayed **yet again*** (=one more time after many others). → see Word Choice box at STILL¹ **5 the biggest/worst/most etc. (sth) yet** used to say that something is the biggest, worst etc. of its kind that has existed up to now: *This could turn out to be our costliest mistake yet.* **6** used to talk about a period of time that starts now and goes into the future: *It won't be light for another hour yet.* **7 as (of) yet** [in questions or negatives] until or before now: *There are no details available as of yet.* **8** FORMAL at some time in the future, in spite of the way that things seem now: *The plan could yet succeed.* **9 sb/sth has yet to do sth** FORMAL used for saying that someone still has not done something: *The bank has yet to respond to a letter we sent in January.* [**Origin:** Old English *giet*]

yet² S1 W1 *conjunction* used to introduce a statement that is surprising after what you have just said

Y

SYN but SYN **nevertheless**: *He was a cruel man, yet many people admired him.* | *a simple yet effective solution* | *Some battered women live in fear of their husbands,* ***and yet*** *are terrified to leave.*

ye·ti /ˈyɛt̬i/ *n.* [C] an ABOMINABLE SNOWMAN

yew /yu/ *n.* [C,U] a tree with dark green leaves and red berries, or the wood of this tree

Yid·dish /ˈyɪdɪʃ/ *n.* [U] a language related to German used by older Jewish people, especially those who are from eastern Europe

yield¹ /yild/ W3 *v.*

1 RESULT [T] to produce a result, answer, or a piece of information: *A search of Mann's home yielded a pair of bloody gloves.*

2 CROPS [T] to produce crops etc.: *Each of these fields could yield billions of barrels of oil.* | *Government securities have traditionally yielded less than stocks.* | **high-yielding/low-yielding** (=producing a large or small amount of something such as crops)

3 AGREE UNWILLINGLY [I,T] to allow yourself to be forced or persuaded to do something or stop having something: *The military has promised to yield power after legislators draw up a new constitution.* | **+to** *Wilson refused to yield to requests to raise salaries.* | **yield to pressure/emotion/temptation etc.** *Further action may be necessary if the leaders do not yield to diplomatic pressure.*

4 TRAFFIC [I] to allow other cars, people etc. to go first: **+to** *Yield to traffic on the right.*

5 MOVE/BEND/BREAK [I] to move, bend, or break because of physical force or pressure: *Ideally, the surface should yield slightly under pressure.*

6 CHANGE [I] if one thing yields to another thing, it is replaced by the new thing: **+to** *Laughter quickly yielded to amazement as the show went on.*

[**Origin:** Old English *gieldan*]

yield sth ↔ **up** *phr. v.* LITERARY to show or give someone something that has been hidden for a long time or is very difficult to obtain: *Darden's detective work yielded up some surprising discoveries.*

yield² W3 *n.* [C] **1** the amount of something that is produced, especially crops **2** ECONOMICS the amount of profit that you receive from a STOCK or BOND: *The 30-year bond yield could rise through 6.25 percent in the next few weeks.*

yield·ing /ˈyildɪŋ/ *adj.* a surface that is yielding is soft and will move or bend when you press it

yikes /yaɪks/ *interjection* said when something frightens you or shocks you

yin /yɪn/ *n.* [U] the female principle in Chinese PHILOSOPHY which is inactive, dark, and negative, and which combines with YANG (=the male principle) to influence everything in the world [**Origin:** 1600–1700 a Chinese word meaning **moon, negative**]

ying yang /ˈyɪŋ yæŋ/ *n.* **have sth up the ying yang** SPOKEN HUMOROUS to have a very large amount or number of something

ˈy-ˌintercept *n.* [C] MATH the point where a line crosses the y-axis of a GRAPH → see also X-INTERCEPT

yip /yɪp/ *v.* **yipped, yipping** [I] if a dog yips, it makes short, high, loud sounds because it is afraid or excited

yip·pee /ˈyɪpi/ *interjection* said when you are very pleased or excited about something

YMCA *n.* **the YMCA** Young Men's Christian Association; an organization in many countries that provides places to stay and sports activities for young people → see also YWCA

yo /yoʊ/ *interjection* SLANG used to greet someone, to get their attention, or as a reply when someone says your name: *Yo, dude! How's it going?*

yo·del /ˈyoʊdl/ *v.* [I,T] to sing while changing between your natural voice and a very high voice, traditionally done in the mountains of countries such as Switzerland and Austria —**yodeler** *n.* [C] —**yodel** *n.* [C] —**yodeling** *n.* [U]

yo·ga /ˈyoʊgə/ *n.* [U] **1** a system of exercises that help you control your mind and body in order to relax **2** a Hindu PHILOSOPHY in which you learn exercises to control your mind and body in order to try to become closer to God [**Origin:** 1700–1800 Sanskrit **union**]

yoga

yo·ghurt /ˈyoʊgɚt/ *n.* [U] another spelling of YOGURT

yo·gi /ˈyoʊgi/ *n.* [C] someone who is very good at yoga and has a lot of knowledge about it, and who often teaches it to other people

yo·gurt /ˈyoʊgɚt/ S3 *n.* [U] a smooth thick food made from milk with a slightly sour taste, often mixed with fruit [**Origin:** 1600–1700 Turkish]

yoke¹ /yoʊk/ *n.* [C] **1** a wooden bar used for keeping two animals, especially cattle, together in order to pull heavy loads **2** a frame that goes across someone's shoulders so that they can carry two equal loads which hang from the frame **3 the yoke of sth** LITERARY something that restricts your freedom, making life difficult: *the yoke of oppression* **4** a part of a skirt or shirt just below the waist or collar, from which the main piece of material hangs in folds

yoke² *v.* [T] **1** to put a yoke on two animals **2** LITERARY to connect two ideas or people together in people's minds: *Beauty is forever yoked to youth in our culture.*

yo·kel /ˈyoʊkəl/ *n.* [C] HUMOROUS someone who comes from the country, seems stupid, and does not know much about modern life, ideas etc.

yolk /yoʊk/ *n.* [C,U] the yellow part in the center of an egg → see also EGG WHITE [**Origin:** Old English *geoloca*, from *geolu* **yellow**] → see picture at EGG¹

Yom Kip·pur /ˌyɑm ˈkɪpɚ, ˌyoʊm kɪˈpʊr/ *n.* [C,U] a Jewish religious holiday on which people do not eat, but pray to be forgiven for the things they have done wrong during the past year SYN **Day of Atonement** [**Origin:** 1800–1900 a Hebrew word meaning **Day of Atonement**]

yon /yɑn/ *determiner* OLD USE YONDER → see also **hither and thither/yon** at HITHER (1)

yon·der¹ /ˈyɑndɚ/ *adv., determiner* OLD USE OR INFORMAL a fairly long distance away: *yonder hills* | *There's some old fellow who lives* ***over yonder***.

yonder² *n.* **the wild blue yonder** LITERARY the sky

yoo-hoo /ˈyu hu/ *interjection* INFORMAL used to attract someone's attention when they are far away

yore /yɔr/ *n.* **of yore** LITERARY happening a long time ago

York·shire ter·ri·er /ˌyɔrkʃɚ ˈtɛriɚ/ *n.* [C] a type of dog that is very small and has long brown hair

Yo·ru·ba /ˈyɔrəbə/ *n.* **1** [C] *plural* **Yoruba** or **Yorubas** a member of a West African people who live mostly in Nigeria, or these people considered as a group **2** [U] the language of the Yoruba people

Yo·sem·i·te Na·tion·al Park /yoʊˌsɛmət̬i ˌnæʃənl ˈpɑrk/ a NATIONAL PARK in the state of California in the southwestern U.S., known for its beautiful lakes, WATERFALLS, and large REDWOOD trees

you /yə, yʊ; *strong* yu/ S1 W1 *pron.* [used as a subject or an object] **1** the person or people someone is speaking or writing to: *I'll see you tomorrow.* | *Hi, Kelly. How are you?* | *I can take all of you in my car.* | *Did Rob give the money to you?* | *I told you this would happen.* **2** people in general: *You have to be over 21 to buy alcohol in this state.* | *You can never be sure what Emily is thinking.* **3** used before nouns or phrases when you are talking to or calling someone: *You boys had better be home by 11:00.* | *You jerk!* | *Hey, you in the blue shirt!* **4 you and yours** LITERARY you and the members of your family: *We* *wish you and yours a very merry Christmas.* [**Origin:** Old English *eow*]

you'd /yəd, yʊd; *strong* yud/ **1** the short form of "you had" when "had" is an AUXILIARY VERB: *If you'd been more careful, this wouldn't have happened.* **2** the short form of "you would": *You'd be better off without him.*

you-know-ˈwhat *pron.* SPOKEN, INFORMAL used to talk about something without mentioning its name, especially so other people will not understand you: *There's some you-know-what in the fridge.*

you-know-ˈwho *pron.* SPOKEN INFORMAL used to talk about someone without mentioning their name, so that other people will not understand you: *Did you see what you-know-who was wearing?*

you'll /yəl, yʊl; *strong* yul/ the short form of "you will": *You'll feel better soon.*

young[1] /yʌŋ/ S1 W1 *adj.*
1 NOT OLD not yet old or not as old as other people OPP **old**: *an ambitious young woman* | *You're too young to get married.* | *At thirty, you're still very young.* | *Sometimes I forget you're younger than I am.* | *My father* ***died young****, from a heart attack.* | **a younger brother/sister** *I have two younger brothers.* | *Here's a photograph of Jeff* ***in his younger days****.*

> **THESAURUS**
> **small/little** very young
> **teenage** between the ages of 13 and 19
> **adolescent** changing from being a child to an adult
> **youthful** typical of young people, or seeming young
> **When you are young**
> **youth** the time when you are young
> **childhood** the time when you are a child
> **adolescence** the time when you are becoming an adult
> → CHILD, OLD

2 CHILD/ANIMAL/PLANT having lived for only a short time and not adult or fully developed OPP **old**: *Very young babies may sleep for most of the day.* | *Dogs should be trained when they're young.*
3 IDEA/ORGANIZATION ETC. not having existed for a long time OPP **old**: *At that time, America was still a young nation.*
4 young lady/man SPOKEN used to speak to a girl or boy when you are angry with them: *Now, you listen to me, young man!*
5 APPEARANCE seeming or looking younger than you are SYN **youthful**: *In just a week, you can have younger, smoother skin.*
6 young blood young people with new ideas: *We need some young blood in this company.*
7 young at heart APPROVING thinking and behaving as if you were young, even though you are old
8 keep sb young to keep someone healthy and active: *Working with children keeps me young.*
9 the night/year/season etc. is still young used to say that there is still a lot of time to do something or have fun because a period of time has just started
10 65/82/97 etc. years young SPOKEN, HUMOROUS used to give the age of an old person who seems or feels much younger
11 FOR YOUNG PEOPLE designed or meant for young people: *Is this dress too young for me?*
12 CONSISTING OF YOUNG PEOPLE consisting of young children or young people: *a young family*
13 the Younger used after the name of a famous person who lived in the past to show that they are the younger of two people with the same name → see also ELDER: *Pliny the Younger*
[**Origin:** Old English *geong*]

young[2] *n.* [plural] **1** BIOLOGY a group of young animals that belong to a particular mother or type of animal: *The lioness fought to protect her young.* **2 the young** young people in general: *Certain drugs have a special appeal to the young.*

Young /yʌŋ/, **Brig·ham** /ˈbrɪgəm/ (1801–1877) a U.S. leader of the Mormon religion, who led 5,000 Mormons to Utah where they built Salt Lake City

Young, Cy /saɪ/ (1867–1955) a U.S. baseball player known for his skill as a PITCHER

young·ster /ˈyʌŋstɚ/ *n.* [C] OLD-FASHIONED a child or young person

your /yɚ; *strong* yɔr/ S1 W1 *possessive adj.* [possessive form of "you"] **1** belonging to or relating to the person or people someone is speaking or writing to: *Could you move your car?* | *That's your problem.* | *Is that your brother over there?* | *Do you have* ***your own*** *computer.* **2** belonging to any person in general: *If you are facing north, east is on your right.* **3** SPOKEN used when mentioning something that is a good example of a particular type of thing or quality: **your average/ordinary/typical etc. sth** *We were just your ordinary American family.*

you're /yɚ; *strong* yɔr/ the short form of "you are": *You're lucky to have such a good job.*

yours /yʊrz, yɔrz/ S1 *possessive pron.* [possessive form of "you"] **1** the thing or things belonging to or relating to the person or people someone is speaking or writing to: *This is our room, and yours* (=your room) *is across the hall.* | *Is Maria a friend* ***of yours****?* **2 be yours for the asking** if something important, desirable etc. is yours for the asking, you can easily get it by just asking someone for it: *If you want the job, it's yours for the asking.* **3 yours truly a)** INFORMAL, HUMOROUS used to mean "I," "me," or "MYSELF": *Members of the judging panel included yours truly.* **b) Yours (truly)** used at the end of a business letter, before the SIGNATURE of the person who wrote it SYN **Sincerely (yours)** → see also, **you and yours** at YOU (4)

your·self /yɚˈsɛlf/ S1 W2 *pron. plural* **yourselves** /-ˈsɛlvz/ **1** [reflexive form of "you"] used to show that the person you are speaking or writing to is affected by his or her own action: *You'll hurt yourself if you're not careful.* | *You can make yourself a cup of coffee.* **2** used instead of "you" after a preposition to talk about the person you are talking or writing to, usually when you have mentioned him or her earlier in the sentence: *May I ask you a few questions about yourself?* **3** the strong form of "you," used to emphasize the subject or object of a sentence: *If you want something done right, you'd better do it yourself.* | *You yourselves signed the papers.* **4** NONSTANDARD used instead of "you" to sound polite, but many teachers think this is incorrect: *This is the perfect suit for a businessman such as yourself, sir.* **5 (all) by yourself a)** alone: *You can't go home by yourself in the dark.* **b)** without help from anyone else: *Do you think you can move the couch by yourself?* ►see THESAURUS box at **alone** **6 not feel/look/seem like yourself** to not feel or behave in the way you usually do because you are nervous, upset, or sick: *Are you sure you're OK? You just don't look like yourself today.* **7 have sth (all) to yourself** if you have something to yourself, you do not have to share it with anyone else: *Would you prefer to have a room to yourself?* → see also DO-IT-YOURSELF, **keep sth to yourself** at KEEP TO (4)

youse /yuz/ *pron.* SPOKEN, NONSTANDARD a word meaning "you," used when talking to more than one person

youth /yuθ/ S3 W2 *n. plural* **youths** /yuθs, yuðz/ **1** [U] the period of time when someone is young, especially the period when someone is a TEENAGER: *memories of our youth and childhood* | ***In his youth****, Tom was a heavy smoker.* ►see THESAURUS box at **young**[1] **2** [C] a TEENAGE boy: *a school for troubled youths* ►see THESAURUS box at **child, man**[1] **3** [plural] young people in general: *the youth of America* **4** [U] the quality or state of being young: *He fell in love with her youth and beauty.* → see also FOUNTAIN OF YOUTH

ˈyouth ˌculture *n.* [U] the interests and activities of young people, especially the popular music, movies etc. which they enjoy

youth·ful /ˈyuθfəl/ *adj.* **1** typical of young people, or seeming young: *youthful idealism* | *a youthful appear-*

Y

ance ►see THESAURUS box at **young¹** **2** young —**youthfully** *adv.* —**youthfulness** *n.* [U]

ˈyouth ˌhostel *n.* [C] an inexpensive hotel for young people

you've /yəv, yʊv; *strong* yuv/ the short form of "you have," used when "have" is an AUXILIARY VERB: *Now you've broken it.*

yow /yaʊ/ *interjection* said when you are surprised or feel sudden pain

yowl /yaʊl/ *v.* [I] if an animal or a person yowls, they make a long loud cry, especially because they are sad or in pain —**yowl** *n.* [C]

yow·za /ˈyaʊzə/ *interjection* said when you think something is surprising or impressive

yo-yo /ˈyoʊyoʊ/ *n. plural* **yo-yos** [C] **1** a toy made of two connected circular parts that go up and down a string that you hold in your hand, as you lift your hand up and down **2** INFORMAL a stupid person [**Origin:** 1900–2000 From a Philippine language]

ˈyo-yo ˌdieting *n.* [U] the habit of losing weight quickly and then gaining it back again over a long period of time

yr. *plural* **yrs.** a written abbreviation of YEAR

yu·an /yʊˈɑn, ˈyuən/ *n. plural* **yuan** [C] the standard unit of money in China [**Origin:** 1900–2000 a Chinese word meaning **round**]

Yu·ca·tán /ˌyukəˈtɑn/ **the Yucatán (Peninsula)** a large PENINSULA in central America, between the Gulf of Mexico and the Caribbean Sea, which consists of Belize, north Guatemala, and part of Mexico

yuc·ca /ˈyʌkə/ *n.* [C] a desert plant with long pointed leaves on a thick straight stem

yuck /yʌk/ *interjection* used to show that you think something tastes bad or is very disgusting: *Oh, yuck! I hate mayonnaise.*

yuck·y /ˈyʌki/ *adj.* INFORMAL extremely disgusting, tasting very bad etc.

Yu·go·sla·vi·a /ˌyugəˈslɑviə/ a former country in southeast Europe, made up of six REPUBLICS: Slovenia, Croatia, Bosnia-Herzegovina, Macedonia, Serbia, and Montenegro. Serbia and Montenegro are now know as the Federal Republic of Yugoslavia and the other republics are all separate independent countries. —**Yugoslav** /ˈyugəˌslɑv/ also **Yugoslavian** /ˌyugəˈslɑviən/ *n., adj.*

yuk¹ /yʌk/ another spelling of YUCK

yuk² *v.* **yukked, yukking yuk it up** HUMOROUS to tell a lot of jokes and behave in a funny way

Yu·kon, the /ˈyukɑn/ **1** a TERRITORY in northwest Canada **2** a river in the northeast of North America, flowing from the Yukon area in Canada, through Alaska, and into the Pacific Ocean

yuks /yʌks/ *n.* [plural] HUMOROUS jokes or laughs, especially in a television program or COMEDY show

Yule /yul/ *n.* OLD USE Christmas

ˈyule log *n.* [C] a long round piece of wood that some people traditionally burn on the evening before Christmas

Yule·tide /ˈyultaɪd/ *n.* [U] LITERARY the time around Christmas

yum /yʌm/ *interjection* INFORMAL said when you think something tastes very good: *Ooh, garlic bread – yum!*

Yu·ma /ˈyumə/ a Native American tribe from the southwestern U.S.

yum·my /ˈyʌmi/ S3 *adj. comparative* **yummier**, *superlative* **yummiest** INFORMAL tasting very good [**Origin:** 1800–1900 *yum*]

yup /yʌp/ *adv.* INFORMAL yes

Yu·pik /ˈyupɪk/ a Native American tribe from western Alaska and Siberia

yup·pie /ˈyʌpi/ *n.* [C] a young adult who only seems to be interested in having a professional job, earning a lot of money, and buying expensive things [**Origin:** 1900–2000 *young urban professional*]

yurt

yup·pi·fy /ˈyʌpəˌfaɪ/ *v.* **yuppifies, yuppified, yuppifying** [T usually passive] to improve an area, its buildings etc. to be more attractive to yuppies —**yuppified** *adj.*: *a yuppified neighborhood*

Yu·rok /ˈyʊrɑk/ a Native American tribe from the southwestern U.S.

yurt /yɚt/ *n.* [C] a round tent, consisting of a wooden frame covered with FELT or animal skins, used by tribes of NOMADS in parts of Asia

YWCA *n.* **the YWCA Young Women's Christian Association** an organization in many countries that provides places to stay and sports activities for young people → see also YMCA

Z,z

Z, z /zi/ *n. plural* **Z's, z's** [C] **1 a)** the 26th and last letter of the English alphabet **b)** the sound represented by this letter **2 catch/get some Z's** INFORMAL to sleep

za·ba·glio·ne /ˌzɑbəlˈyoʊni/ *n.* [U] a thick sweet food made from eggs, sugar, and wine that have been beaten together

zaf·tig /ˈzɑftɪg/ *adj.* HUMOROUS a zaftig woman is slightly fat, with large breasts

Za·greb /ˈzɑgrɛb/ the capital and largest city of Croatia

Zam·be·zi, the /zæmˈbizi/ a large river in south central Africa

Zam·bi·a /ˈzæmbiə/ a country in south central Africa, north of Zimbabwe and south of the Democratic Republic of Congo —**Zambian** *n., adj.*

za·ny /ˈzeɪni/ *adj. comparative* **zanier**, *superlative* **zaniest** crazy or unusual, in a way that is funny and exciting: *a zany new TV comedy* [**Origin:** 1500–1600 Italian *zanni* type of clown, from *Giovanni* **John**]

zap /zæp/ *v.* **zapped, zapping 1** [T] to attack or destroy something quickly, especially using a beam of electricity **2** [T] INFORMAL to cook something in a MICROWAVE OVEN **3** [I,T] to change the CHANNEL on a television by using a REMOTE CONTROL **4** [T] to send information quickly from one computer to another

Za·pa·ta /zɑˈpɑtə/, **E·mi·lia·no** /ˌeɪmɪˈlyɑnoʊ/ (1879–1919) a Mexican military leader, who led an army of native Mexicans against the government in an attempt to get back land that had been taken away from them

zap·per /ˈzæpɚ/ *n.* [C] INFORMAL **1** a piece of electrical equipment that attracts and kills insects **2** a television REMOTE CONTROL

Za·ïre /ˈzaɪ-ɪr/ the former name of the Democratic Republic of Congo

Zaïre, the another name for the Congo river in central Africa

zeal /zil/ *n.* [U] eagerness to do something, especially to achieve a particular religious or political aim: +**for** *the group's zeal for educational reform* [**Origin:** 1300–1400 Late Latin *zelus*, from Greek *zelos*]

zeal·ot /ˈzɛlət/ *n.* [C] DISAPPROVING someone who has extremely strong beliefs, especially religious or political beliefs, and is too eager to make other people share them —**zealotry** *n.* [U]

zeal·ous /ˈzɛləs/ *adj.* extremely interested in and excited about something that you believe in very strongly, and behaving in a way that shows this: *zealous political activists* —**zealously** *adv.* —**zealousness** *n.* [U]

ze·bra /ˈzibrə/ *n.* [C] an animal that looks like a horse, but has black and white lines all over its body [**Origin:** 1600–1700 Italian **wild donkey**]

zebra

ze·bu /ˈzibu/ *n.* [C] an animal from Asia and eastern Africa that looks a little like a cow, but has a large HUMP (=raised part) on its back

Zeb·u·lon /ˈzɛbyələn/ in the Bible, the head of one of the 12 tribes of Israel

Zech·a·ri·ah /ˌzɛkəˈraɪə/ a book in the Old Testament of the Christian Bible

zed /zed/ *n.* [C] a way of writing the letter "Z" to show how it is pronounced in Canadian and British English

zeit·geist /ˈzaɪtgaɪst, ˈtsaɪ-/ *n.* [singular] the general spirit or feeling of a period in history, as shown by people's ideas and beliefs at the time [**Origin:** 1800–1900 German **spirit of the time**]

Zen /zɛn/ also **ˈZen ˌBuddhism** *n.* [U] a type of Buddhism that emphasizes MEDITATION rather than faith or reading religious books [**Origin:** 1700–1800 Japanese, Sanskrit *dhyanam* **watching**]

ze·nith /ˈzinɪθ/ *n.* [C usually singular] **1** the most successful point in the development of something SYN **peak** OPP **nadir**: *The Roman Empire* ***reached its zenith*** *around 100 A.D.* **2** TECHNICAL the highest point that is reached by the sun or the moon in the sky OPP **nadir**

Zeph·a·ni·ah /ˌzɛfəˈnaɪə/ a book in the Old Testament of the Protestant Bible

zeph·yr /ˈzɛfɚ/ *n.* [C] LITERARY a soft gentle wind

zep·pe·lin /ˈzepəlɪn/ *n.* [C] a German AIRSHIP used in World War I

ze·ro¹ /ˈzɪroʊ, ˈziroʊ/ *number plural* **zeros** or **zeroes 1** 0: *Zero times any number is still zero.*

> **THESAURUS**
> **nothing**: *The score was twenty-two to nothing.*
> **O** /oʊ/ used to say the number zero like the letter O: *Their zip code is O two one two five.* (=02125).
> **zip** INFORMAL: *We were behind 3-zip.*

2 the lowest point on a scale for measuring something: *The pressure gauge was almost down to zero.* **3** a temperature of 0° on the Celsius or Fahrenheit scale: **above/below zero** *Temperatures could drop to five degrees below zero* (=-5°) *tonight.* **4** INFORMAL the lowest possible amount or level of something: *Our profits rose from zero to 5.9%.* | *Our* ***chances of*** *winning* ***are*** *virtually zero.* **5 zero growth/inflation/gravity etc.** no growth, INFLATION etc. at all → see also ABSOLUTE ZERO, GROUND ZERO, ZERO TOLERANCE

zero² *v.* **zeroes, zeroed, zeroing**
zero in on sb/sth *phr. v.* **1** to direct all your attention toward a particular person or thing **2** to aim a gun toward something or someone

zero³ *n. plural* **zeros** or **zeroes** [C] INFORMAL someone who is considered stupid or unimportant

ˌzero-ˈcoupon ˌbond *n.* [C] ECONOMICS a type of BOND that does not pay any INTEREST until it is paid back or sold

ˈzero hour *n.* [singular] the time when a military operation or an important event is planned to begin

ˈzero-sum ˌgame *n.* [singular] a situation in which any advantage or success that one person or side gains must be followed by an equal loss by the other person or side

ˌzero ˈtolerance *n.* [U] a way of dealing with crime in which every person who breaks the law, even in a very small way, is punished as severely as possible: *the school's zero-tolerance drug policy*

zest /zɛst/ *n.* **1** [singular, U] eager interest and enjoyment: +**for** *a great zest for life* **2** [singular, U] the quality of being exciting and interesting **3** [U] the outer skin of an orange or LEMON, used in cooking —**zestful** *adj.* —**zestfully** *adv.*

Zeus /zus/ in Greek MYTHOLOGY. the king of the gods, and ruler of the universe

Zhou En·lai /ˌdʒoʊ ɛnˈlaɪ/ (1898–1976) a Chinese politician who was Foreign Minister and Prime Minister of China

zig·gu·rat /ˈzɪgəræt/ *n.* [C] HISTORY a structure with a RECTANGULAR base which has smaller and smaller upper stories and a TEMPLE on top, built in ancient Mesopotamia

zig·zag¹ /ˈzɪgzæg/ *n.* [C] a pattern that looks like a line of z's connected together

zigzag² *v.* **zigzagged**, **zigzagging** [I] to move forward in sharp angles, first to the left and then to the right etc.: *The path zigzagged down the hillside.*

zilch /zɪltʃ/ *n.* [U] INFORMAL nothing at all: *We have gotten absolutely zilch in return.*

zil·lion /ˈzɪlyən/ *n.* [C] INFORMAL an extremely large number of something: +**of** *There were zillions of mosquitoes in the woods.*

Zim·ba·bwe /zɪmˈbɑbweɪ/ a country in south central Africa, south of Zambia and north of South Africa —**Zimbabwean** *n., adj.*

Zim·mer·mann note, the /ˈzɪməmɑn ˌnoʊt/ HISTORY a TELEGRAM sent in 1917 by Germany's foreign secretary to the German AMBASSADOR to Mexico. It said that it was likely that Germany and the U.S. would soon be at war, and that if this happened, the ambassador should encourage Mexico to go to war against the U.S. as well.

zinc /zɪŋk/ *n.* [U] SYMBOL **Zn** CHEMISTRY a bluish-white metal that is an ELEMENT and is used to make BRASS and to cover and protect objects made of iron

zine, 'zine /zin/ *n.* [C] a small magazine, usually about popular CULTURE, that is written and printed by people who are not professional writers

zin·fan·del, Zinfandel /ˈzɪnfənˌdɛl/ *n.* [U] a type of dry red or white wine from California

zing¹ /zɪŋ/ *n.* [U] INFORMAL an exciting or interesting taste or quality: *A little chili pepper will add some zing to the sauce.* —**zingy** *adj.*

zing² *v.* **1** [I always + adv./prep.] INFORMAL to move quickly, making a whistling noise **2** [T] to ask questions, say jokes etc. in a very fast way

zing·er /ˈzɪŋə/ *n.* [C] a short insulting but humorous remark

zin·nia /ˈzɪnyə/ *n.* [C] a garden plant with large brightly colored flowers

Zi·on /ˈzaɪən/ **1** a name given to Israel or to an imagined land where the Jewish people could live in peace, after many centuries of not having a land of their own **2** in the Old Testament of the Bible, another name for Jerusalem

Z

Zi·on·ism /ˈzaɪəˌnɪzəm/ *n.* [U] support for the establishment and development of a nation for the Jews in Israel —**Zionist** *n.* [C] —**Zionist** *adj.*

zip¹ /zɪp/ *n.* INFORMAL **1** [U] an exciting or interesting taste or quality: *A spoonful of mustard will give the dish some zip.* **2** [U] speed or energy: *a car with a lot of zip* **3** [U] zero, or nothing: *The Braves lost, three-zip.* ▶see THESAURUS box at **zero¹** **4** [C usually singular] a ZIP code

zip² *v.* **zipped**, **zipping** **1** [T] to open or close something using a ZIPPER: *Could you zip my dress?* | **zip sth open/closed/shut** *Olsen zipped the bag shut.* **2** [I always + adv./prep.] if a piece of clothing, a bag etc. zips in a particular place or way, it opens or closes in that place or way using a ZIPPER: *The dress zips down the back.* **3** [I always + adv./prep.] to do something or go somewhere very quickly: +**through/past/down etc.** *A few cars zipped by.* **4** TECHNICAL [T] to make a computer document smaller so that it is easier to store or move OPP **unzip** **5 zip your lip** also **zip it** SPOKEN INFORMAL used to tell someone not to say anything about something, or to tell them to be quiet

zip up *phr. v.* **1 zip sth ↔ up** to fasten something such as a piece of clothing using a ZIPPER OPP **unzip** **2 zip sb ↔ up** to close the ZIPPER on a piece of clothing that someone else is wearing **3** to fasten your clothes using a ZIPPER **4** if a piece of clothing zips up in a particular place or way, it fastens in that place or way using a ZIPPER

ZIP code, zip code /ˈzɪp koʊd/ *n.* [C] a number that you write at the end of the address on an envelope to help the post office deliver the mail more quickly [**Origin:** 1900–2000 *zone improvement plan*]

ZIP file /ˈzɪp faɪl/ also **'zipped file** *n.* [C] COMPUTERS a computer FILE that has been made smaller so that it is easier to store and move

'zip gun *n.* [C] a small gun that someone has made himself or herself, used especially by criminals

Zip·loc bag /ˌzɪplɑk ˈbæg/ TRADEMARK also **ˌzip-lock 'bag** *n.* [C] a small transparent plastic bag that you can store food or other small things in, with a part at the top like a zipper that you press to close the bag tightly

zip·per /ˈzɪpə/ *n.* [C] an object with two lines of small metal or plastic pieces that slide together to fasten a piece of clothing, a bag etc. → see picture at FASTENER

zip·po /ˈzɪpoʊ/ *n.* [U] SPOKEN zero SYN **nothing**

zip·py /ˈzɪpi/ *adj.* **1** having a lot of energy or moving quickly: *a zippy little car* **2** having an interesting taste or a exciting quality

zir·co·ni·a /zəˈkoʊniə/ → see CUBIC ZIRCONIA

zit /zɪt/ *n.* [C] INFORMAL a PIMPLE

zith·er /ˈzɪðə/ *n.* [C] a musical instrument from Eastern Europe that you play by pulling its wire strings with your fingers

zlo·ty /ˈzlɑṭi, ˈzlɔ-/ *n. plural* **zlotys** [C] the standard unit of money used in Poland

zo·di·ac /ˈzoʊdiˌæk/ *n.* **the zodiac** an imaginary area through which the sun, moon, and PLANETS appear to travel, which some people believe influences our lives: *Virgo is the sixth* ***sign of the zodiac***. [**Origin:** 1300–1400 French *zodiaque*, from Greek *zoidiakos* **animal figures**] —**zodiacal** /zoʊˈdaɪəkəl/ *adj.* → see also ASTROLOGY

Zo·la /zoʊˈlɑ/, **E·mile** /eɪˈmil/ (1840–1902) a French writer of NOVELS

zom·bie /ˈzɑmbi/ *n.* [C] **1** INFORMAL someone who moves very slowly and does not seem to be thinking about what they are doing, especially because they are very tired **2** a dead person whose body is made to move by magic, according to some African and Caribbean religions [**Origin:** 1800–1900 Kimbundu *nzumbi* **spirit of a dead person**]

zon·al /ˈzoʊnl/ *adj.* [only before noun] TECHNICAL relating to zones, or arranged in zones —**zonally** *adv.*

zone¹ /zoʊn/ *n.* [C] **1** a part of an area that is used for a particular purpose or has a special quality: *This is a no-parking zone.* | *The map shows the average temperatures for each zone.* | **a war/battle/combat etc. zone** *the president's visit to the war zone* ▶see THESAURUS box at **area** **2 in the zone** SLANG playing a sport very well without needing to think about it → see also **a buffer zone** at BUFFER¹ (2), END ZONE, TIME ZONE

zone² *v.* **1** [T usually passive] to officially divide an area into zones for different purposes, or to say officially that a particular area must be used for a particular purpose: *Abrams' land is currently zoned for residential use.* **2** also **zone out** [I] SLANG to stop paying attention and just look in front of you without thinking for a period of time, because you are bored or because you have taken drugs

zoned /zoʊnd/ also **ˌzoned 'out** *adj.* [not before noun] SLANG unable to think clearly and quickly, especially because you are tired or have taken drugs

zon·ing /ˈzoʊnɪŋ/ *n.* [U] an official system of choosing areas to be used for particular purposes, such as building houses or stores

'zoning law *n.* [C] ECONOMICS a law that is used to decide which areas of a city can be used for business or industrial purposes and which areas can be used only as places for people to live in

zonk /zɑŋk/ also **zonk out** *v.* SLANG **1** [I] to fall asleep quickly and completely **2** [I,T] to act strangely or become unconscious by taking drugs, or to make someone do this

zonked /zɑŋkt/ also **ˌzonked 'out** *adj.* [not before noun] SLANG **1** under the influence of illegal drugs **2** extremely tired or completely asleep

zoo /zu/ S3 *n. plural* **zoos** [C] **1** a place, usually in a city, where many kinds of animals are kept so that people can go to look at them **2** INFORMAL a place that is very loud, DISORGANIZED, and full of people: *The grocery store was a real zoo today.* [**Origin:** 1800–1900 *zoological garden*]

ˈzookeeper *n.* [C] someone who takes care of animals in a zoo

ˌzoological ˈgarden *n.* [C] FORMAL a zoo

zo·ol·o·gist /zoʊˈɑlədʒɪst/ *n.* [C] BIOLOGY a scientist who studies animals and their behavior

zo·ol·o·gy /zoʊˈɑlədʒi/ *n.* [U] BIOLOGY the scientific study of animals and their behavior —**zoological** /ˌzoʊəˈlɑdʒɪkəl/ *adj.*

zoom[1] /zum/ *v.* INFORMAL **1** [I always + adv./prep.] to go somewhere quickly, especially in a car or on a MOTORCYCLE making a lot of noise: +**past/through/off etc.** *She jumped into the car and zoomed off.* **2** [I always + adv./prep.] to succeed in doing some work, reading a book etc. very quickly and easily: *I zoomed through the assignment in a half an hour.* **3** [I always + adv./prep.] to increase suddenly and quickly in price, number etc.: +**up/to** *Interest rates zoomed up.* **4** [I,T] to operate the zoom lens on a camera [**Origin:** 1800–1900 From the sound]

zoom in *phr. v.* if a camera or the person using it zooms in, they make the person or thing that they are taking a picture of seem bigger and closer: +**on** *The camera zoomed in on the child's face.*

zoom out *phr. v.* if a camera or the person using it zooms out, they make the person or thing that they are taking a picture of seem smaller and farther away

ˈzoom lens *n.* [C] a camera LENS that can change from a distant to a close view

zo·o·plank·ton /ˌzoʊəˈplæŋktən/ *n.* [U] BIOLOGY the very small animals floating in water that are part of PLANKTON → see also PHYTOPLANKTON

zo·o·spo·ran·gi·um /ˌzoʊəspəˈrændʒiəm/ *n. plural* **zoosporangia** /-dʒiə/ [C] BIOLOGY the place where SPORES (=seeds) are developed in ALGAE and FUNGI before they are released

zoot suit /ˈzut sut/ *n.* [C] a man's suit that consists of wide pants and a long JACKET with wide shoulders, worn especially in the 1940s

Zor·o·as·ter /ˈzɔroʊˌæstɚ/ also **Zar·a·thus·tra** /ˌzærəˈθustrə/ (?628–?553 B.C.) a Persian religious leader who started a new religion called Zoroastrianism

Zor·o·as·tri·an·ism /ˌzɔroʊˈæstriəˌnɪzəm/ *n.* [U] an ancient religion from Persia, which includes a belief in a struggle between good and evil in the universe —**Zoroastrian** *n.* [C] —**Zoroastrian** *adj.*

z-score /ˈzi skɔr/ *n.* [C] MATH a measure of how far a mathematical VALUE is from the average of all the values in a set of data

zuc·chi·ni /zuˈkini/ *n. plural* **zucchini** or **zucchinis** [C] a long green vegetable with dark green skin [**Origin:** 1900–2000 Italian *zucca* **gourd**]

Zu·lu /ˈzulu/ *n. plural* **Zulu** or **Zulus** [C] a member of a large tribe of people who live in South Africa —**Zulu** *adj.*

zwie·back /ˈzwaɪbæk, ˈzwi-/ *n.* [U] a type of hard dry bread, often given to babies

zy·de·co /ˈzaɪdəˌkoʊ/ *n.* [U] a type of Cajun music that is popular in southern Louisiana and combines the styles of French and Caribbean music and the BLUES

zy·gote /ˈzaɪgoʊt/ *n.* [C] BIOLOGY a cell that is formed when a female's egg cell is FERTILIZED

Zzz used in writing, especially in CARTOONS, to show that someone is sleeping

U.S. States, Capitals and Postal Abbreviations

State	Capital	P.A.
Alabama	Montgomery	AL
Alaska	Juneau	AK
Arizona	Phoenix	AZ
Arkansas	Little Rock	AR
California	Sacramento	CA
Colorado	Denver	CO
Connecticut	Hartford	CT
Delaware	Dover	DE
Florida	Tallahassee	FL
Georgia	Atlanta	GA
Hawaii	Honolulu	HI
Idaho	Boise	ID
Illinois	Springfield	IL
Indiana	Indianapolis	IN
Iowa	Des Moines	IA
Kansas	Topeka	KS
Kentucky	Frankfort	KY
Louisiana	Baton Rouge	LA
Maine	Augusta	ME
Maryland	Annapolis	MD
Massachusetts	Boston	MA
Michigan	Lansing	MI
Minnesota	St. Paul	MN
Mississippi	Jackson	MS
Missouri	Jefferson City	MO

State	Capital	P.A.
Montana	Helena	MT
Nebraksa	Lincoln	NE
Nevada	Carson City	NV
New Hampshire	Concord	NH
New Jersey	Trenton	NJ
New Mexico	Santa Fé	NM
New York	Albany	NY
North Carolina	Raleigh	NC
North Dakota	Bismarck	ND
Ohio	Columbus	OH
Oklahoma	Oklahoma City	OK
Oregon	Salem	OR
Pennsylvania	Harrisburg	PA
Rhode Island	Providence	RI
South Carolina	Columbia	SC
South Dakota	Pierre	SD
Tennessee	Nashville	TN
Texas	Austin	TX
Utah	Salt Lake City	UT
Vermont	Montpelier	VT
Virginia	Richmond	VA
Washington	Olympia	WA
West Virginia	Charleston	WV
Wisconsin	Madison	WI
Wyoming	Cheyenne	WY

Capital of the U.S.A.

District of Columbia, Washington DC
(commonly abbreviated: Washington, DC)

How Numbers Are Spoken

Numbers over 20

21 twenty-one
22 twenty-two
32 thirty-two
99 ninety-nine

Numbers over 100

101 a/one hundred (and) one
121 a/one hundred twenty-one
200 two hundred
232 two hundred thirty-two
999 nine hundred ninety-nine

Numbers over 1000

1001 a/one thousand (and) one
1121 one thousand one hundred twenty-one
2000 two thousand
2232 two thousand two hundred thirty-two
9999 nine thousand nine hundred ninety-nine

Ordinal Numbers

20th twentieth
21st twenty-first
25th twenty-fifth
90th ninetieth
99th ninety-ninth
100th hundredth
101st a/one hundred (and) first
225th two hundred twenty-fifth

Years

1624 sixteen twenty-four
1903 nineteen-oh-three
1997 nineteen ninety-seven
2000 two thousand
2004 twenty-oh-four

What Numbers Represent

Numbers are often used on their own to show:

Price *It cost eight seventy-five* (=8 dollars and 75 cents: $8.75).

Time *We left at two twenty-five* (=25 minutes after 2 o'clock).

Age *She's forty-six* (=46 years old). | *He's in his sixties* (=between 60 and 69 years old).

Size *This shirt is a twelve* (=size 12).

Temperature *The temperature fell to minus fourteen* (=–14°). | *The temperature was in the mid-thirties* (=about 34–36°).

The score in a game *The Braves were ahead four to two* (=4–2).

Something marked with the stated number *She played two nines and an eight* (=playing cards marked with these numbers). | *I only have a twenty* (=a piece of paper money worth $20).

A set or group of the stated number *The teacher divided us into fours* (=groups of 4).

Numbers and Grammar

Numbers can be used as:

Determiners *Five people were hurt in the accident.* | *the three largest companies in the U.S.* | *several hundred cars*

Pronouns *We invited a lot of people but only twelve came/only twelve of them came.* | *Do exercise five on page nine.*

Nouns *Six can be divided by two and three.* | *I got a seventy-five on the biology test.*

U.S. Customary System

Units of Length

1 inch = 2.54 cm
12 inches = 1 foot = 0.3048 m
3 feet = 1 yard = 0.9144 m
1,760 yards or 5,280 feet = 1 mile = 1.609 km
2,025 yards or 6,076 feet = 1 nautical mile = 1.852 km

Units of Weight

1 ounce = 28.35 g
16 ounces = 1 pound = 0.4536 kg
2,000 pounds = 1 ton = 907.18 kg
2,240 pounds = 1 long ton = 1,016.0 kg

Units of Volume (liquid)

1 fluid ounce = 29.574 ml
8 fluid ounces = 1 cup = 0.2366 l
16 fluid ounces = 1 pint = 0.4732 l
2 pints = 1 quart = 0.9463 l
4 quarts = 1 gallon = 3.7853 l

Units of Volume (dry measure)

1 peck = 8,809.5 cm^3
4 pecks = 1 bushel = 35,239 cm^3

Units of Area

1 square inch = 645.16 mm^2
144 square inches = 1 square foot = 0.0929 m^2
9 square feet = 1 square yard = 0.8361 m^2
4840 square yards = 1 acre = 4047 m^2
640 acres = 1 square mile = 259 ha

Units of Temperature

degrees Fahrenheit = (°C x 9/5) ÷ 32
degrees Celsius = (°F – 32) x 5/9

Metric System

Units of Length

1 millimeter = 0.03937 inch
10 mm = 1 centimeter = 0.3937 inch
100 cm = 1 meter = 39.37 inches
1,000 m = 1 kilometer = 0.6214 mile

Units of Weight

1 milligram = 0.000035 ounce
1,000 mg = 1 gram = 0.035 ounce
1,000 g = 1 kilogram = 2.205 pounds
1,000 kg = 1 metric ton = 2,205 pounds

Units of Volume

1 milliliter = 0.03 fluid ounce
1,000 ml = 1 liter = 1.06 quarts

Units of Area

1 square centimeter = 0.1550 square inch
10,000 cm^2 = 1 square meter = 1.196 square yards
10,000 m^2 = 1 hectare = 2.471 acres

Verb	Past Tense	Past Participle
abide	abided, abode	abided
alight	alighted, alit	alighted, alit
arise	arose	arisen
awake	awoke	awoken
babysit	babysat	babysat
be	(see dictionary entry)	
bear	bore	borne
beat	beat	beaten
become	became	become
befall	befell	befallen
befit	befitted	befitted
beget	begot, begat	begotten
begin	began	begun
behold	beheld	beheld
bend	bent	bent
beseech	beseeched, besought	beseeched, besought
beset	beset	beset
bespeak	bespoke	bespoken
bestride	bestrode	bestridden
bet	bet	bet
betake	betook	betaken
bethink	bethought	bethought
bid[2]	bid	bid
bind	bound	bound
bite	bit	bitten
bleed	bled	bled
blow	blew	blown
bottle-feed	bottle-fed	bottle-fed
break	broke	broken
breast-feed	breast-fed	breast-fed
breed	bred	bred
bring	brought	brought
broadcast	broadcast	broadcast
browbeat	browbeat	browbeaten
build	built	built
burn	burned, burnt	burned, burnt
burst	burst	burst
buy	bought	bought
can	(see dictionary entry)	
cast	cast	cast
catch	caught	caught
choose	chose	chosen
cleave	cleaved, clove, cleft	cleaved, cloven, cleft
cling	clung	clung
come	came	come
cost[2]	cost	cost
could	(see dictionary entry)	
creep	crept	crept
cut	cut	cut
deal	dealt /dɛlt/	dealt
dig	dug	dug
dive	dived, dove	dived
do	did	done
draw	drew	drawn
dream	dreamed, dreamt	dreamed, dreamt
drink	drank	drunk

Verb	Past Tense	Past Participle
drive	drove	driven
dwell	dwelled, dwelt	dwelled, dwelt
eat	ate	eaten
fall	fell	fallen
feed	fed	fed
feel	felt	felt
fight	fought	fought
find	found	found
fit	fit, fitted	fit, fitted
flee	fled	fled
fling	flung	flung
fly	flew	flown
forbear	forbore	forborne
forbid	forbade, forbid	forbidden
force-feed	force-fed	force-fed
forecast	forecast	forecast
foresee	foresaw	foreseen
foretell	foretold	foretold
forget	forgot	forgotten
forgive	forgave	forgiven
forgo	forwent	forgone
freeze	froze	frozen
gainsay	gainsaid	gainsaid
get	got	gotten
gird	girded, girt	girded, girt
give	gave	given
go	went	gone
grind	ground	ground
grow	grew	grown
hamstring	hamstrung	hamstrung
hang[1]	hung	hung
have	had	had
hear	heard	heard
heave	heaved, hove	heaved, hove
hew	hewed	hewn, hewed
hide	hid	hidden, hid
hit	hit	hit
hold	held	held
hurt	hurt	hurt
input	inputted, input	inputted, input
inset	inset	inset
interbreed	interbred	interbred
interweave	interwove	interwoven
keep	kept	kept
kneel	knelt, kneeled	knelt, kneeled
knit	knit, knitted	knit, knitted
know	knew	known
lay	laid	laid
lead	led	led
leap	leaped, leapt	leaped, leapt
leave	left	left
lend	lent	lent
let	let	let
lie	lay	lain

Verb	Past Tense	Past Participle
light	lit, lighted	lit, lighted
lose	lost	lost
make	made	made
may	(see dictionary entry)	
mean	meant	meant
meet	met	met
might	(see dictionary entry)	
miscast	miscast	miscast
mishear	misheard	misheard
mislay	mislaid	mislaid
mislead	misled	misled
misread	misread /ˌmɪsˈrɛd/	misread /ˌmɪsˈrɛd/
misspend	misspent	misspent
mistake	mistook	mistaken
misunderstand	misunderstood	misunderstood
mow	mowed	mown, mowed
offset	offset	offset
outbid	outbid	outbid
outdo	outdid	outdone
outgrow	outgrew	outgrown
outride	outrode	outridden
outrun	outran	outrun
outsell	outsold	outsold
outshine	outshone	outshone
outshoot	outshot	outshot
outspend	outspent	outspent
overcome	overcame	overcome
overdo	overdid	overdone
overeat	overate	overeaten
overhang	overhung	overhung
overhear	overheard	overheard
overlay	overlaid	overlaid
overpay	overpaid	overpaid
override	overrode	overridden
overrun	overran	overrun
oversee	oversaw	overseen
oversell	oversold	oversold
overshoot	overshot	overshot
oversleep	overslept	overslept
overspend	overspent	overspent
overtake	overtook	overtaken
overthrow	overthrew	overthrown
partake	partook	partaken
pay	paid	paid
plead	pleaded, pled	pleaded, pled
proofread	proofread /ˈprufrɛd/	proofread /ˈprufrɛd/
prove	proved	proved, proven
put	put	put
quit	quit	quit
read	read /rɛd/	read /rɛd/
rebuild	rebuilt	rebuilt
recast	recast	recast
redo	redid	redone
relay[3]	relaid	relaid
remake	remade	remade

Verb	Past Tense	Past Participle
rend	rent	rent
repay	repaid	repaid
resell	resold	resold
reset	reset	reset
retell	retold	retold
rethink	rethought	rethought
rewind	rewound	rewound
rewrite	rewrote	rewritten
rid	rid	rid
ride	rode	ridden
ring	rang	rung
rise	rose	risen
run	ran	run
saw	sawed	sawed, sawn
say	said	said
see	saw	seen
seek	sought	sought
sell	sold	sold
send	sent	sent
set	set	set
sew	sewed	sewn, sewed
shake	shook	shaken
shall	(see dictionary entry)	
shear	sheared	shorn, sheared
shed	shed	shed
shine[1]	shone	shone
shoe	shod	shod
shoot	shot	shot
should	(see dictionary entry)	
show	showed	shown
shrink	shrank, shrunk	shrunk
shut	shut	shut
sight-read	sight-read /ˈsaɪtrɛd/	sight-read /ˈsaɪtrɛd/
simulcast	simulcast	simulcast
sing	sang	sung
sink	sank, sunk	sunk
sit	sat	sat
slay	slew	slain
sleep	slept	slept
slide	slid	slid
sling	slung	slung
slink	slunk	slunk
slit	slit	slit
smite	smote	smitten
sneak	sneaked, snuck	sneaked, snuck
sow	sowed	sowed, sown
speak	spoke	spoken
speed	sped, speeded	sped, speeded
spill	spilled, spilt	spilled, spilt
spin	spun	spun
spit	spit, spat	spit, spat
split	split	split
spoon-feed	spoon-fed	spoon-fed
spotlight	spotlighted, spotlit	spotlighted, spotlit
spread	spread	spread
spring	sprang, sprung	sprung
stand	stood	stood